D1621402

THE TIMES

English Dictionary & Thesaurus

THE TIMES

English Dictionary & Thesaurus

HarperCollins*Publishers* & TIMES BOOKS

First Edition 1993
Second Edition 2000

10 9 8 7 6 5 4 3 2 1

Standard Edition ISBN 0-00-472502-6
Thumb-indexed Edition ISBN 0-00-472503-4
Times Books Edition ISBN 0-00-710857-5

A catalogue record for this book is
available from the British Library.

This edition prepared in conjunction with Market House Books Ltd, Aylesbury, England

Typeset by Market House Books Ltd, Aylesbury, England
Printed and bound in Spain by Mateu Cromo

Corpus Acknowledgments

We would like to thank those authors and publishers who kindly gave permission for copyright material to be used in the Bank of English. We would also like to thank Times Newspapers Ltd for providing valuable data.

General Consultant

J M Sinclair
Formerly Professor, Department of English Language and Literature
University of Birmingham

Special Consultants

AUSTRALIAN ENGLISH
G A Wilkes
Challis Professor of English Literature,
University of Sydney

W A Krebs
Associate Professor in Literature and Communications,
Bond University, Queensland

W S Ramson
Reader in English,
Australian National University

BRITISH REGIONAL ENGLISH, URBAN DIALECTS
Harold Orton
Professor Emeritus, Department of English,
University of Leeds

CANADIAN ENGLISH
R J Gregg
Formerly Professor, Department of Linguistics,
University of British Columbia

Patrick Drysdale
Editor, *A Dictionary of Canadianisms on Historical Principles*

James Arthurs
Professor, Department of Linguistics,
University of Victoria

CARIBBEAN ENGLISH
S R R Allsopp
Coordinator, Caribbean Lexicography Project,
University of the West Indies,
Barbados

EAST AFRICAN ENGLISH
J Kalema
Department of Linguistic Science,
University of Reading

INDIAN ENGLISH
R K Bansal
Professor, Department of Phonetics and Spoken English,
Central Institute of English and Foreign Languages, Hyderabad

IRISH ENGLISH
R J Gregg
Formerly Professor, Department of Linguistics,
University of British Columbia

T de Bhaldraithe
Professor, Department of Irish Dialectology,
University College, Dublin

NEW ZEALAND ENGLISH
Ian A Gordon
Professor Emeritus,
University of Wellington

SCOTTISH ENGLISH
A J Aitken
Department of English Language
University of Edinburgh,
Formerly Editor, *Dictionary of the Older Scottish Tongue*

SOUTH AFRICAN ENGLISH
L W Lanham
Professor, Department of Phonetics and General Linguistics,
University of the Witwatersrand

M V Aldridge
Professor, Department of Phonetics and General Linguistics,
University of the Witwatersrand

Geoffrey Hughes
Professor, Department of English,
University of the Witwatersrand

WEST AFRICAN ENGLISH
J Spencer
Director, Institute of Modern English Language Studies,
University of Leeds

PRONUNCIATION
A C Gimson
Formerly Professor, Department of Phonetics and Linguistics,
University College,
University of London

Specialist Contributors

AERONAUTICS
T C Wooldridge, Angus Boyd
Senior Lecturer in Aerodynamics, The College of Aeronautics, Cranfield

ARCHITECTURE; CIVIL ENGINEERING
Bruce Martin

AUSTRALIAN ENGLISH
Steve Higgs
Melbourne Grammar School

BIOGRAPHIES, PLACES
Market House Books
Aylesbury

BROADCASTING, FILM, ETC.
Patrick Leggatt
Chief Engineer, External Relations, British Broadcasting Corporation

BUSINESS
Alan Isaacs

CHEMISTRY
John Daintith

COMPUTERS
Richard Fryer
Department of Computer Science, University of Strathclyde

CONSTRUCTION
M J Walker
Construction Industry Research and Information Association

EARTH SCIENCES
Peter J Smith
Reader in Earth Sciences, The Open University

ECONOMICS
P Donaldson
Ruskin College, Oxford

EDUCATION
Catherine Playford
Head Teacher of English, Priestnall School

ENGINEERING
J P Quayle
Editor, *Kempe's Engineering Year-Book*

INDUSTRIAL RELATIONS
Professor Angela M Bowey
Strathclyde Business School, University of Strathclyde
Alexander Purdie
Scottish College of Textiles, Galashiels

INFORMATION TECHNOLOGY
Professor Thomas Carbery
Andrew Doswell
Catherine M Young
Department of Information Science, University of Strathclyde

JUDAISM
Ephraim Borowski
Department of Philosophy, University of Glasgow

LANGUAGES & PEOPLES
David Kilby
Formerly, Department of Language and Linguistics, University of Essex

LAW
Richard Latham
Barrister-at-Law
Brian Russell Davis
Barrister-at-Law
Sandra Clarke

LIFE SCIENCES
Miranda Robertson
Life Sciences Editor, *Nature*
Dr W Gratzer
MRC Cell Biophysics Unit

LINGUISTICS
Professor Yorick Wilks
New Mexico State University

LINGUISTICS AND GRAMMAR
Lloyd Humberstone

LOGIC
Ephraim Borowski
Department of Philosophy, University of Glasgow

MALAYSIAN ENGLISH
U Yong-ee

MARKETING
Professor M Christopher
Department of Marketing and Logistics Systems, Cranfield School of Management

METALLURGY
Stanley White

MILITARY
Major S R Elliot
Colonel Andrew Duncan
The International Institute for Strategic Studies

MILITARY AND NAUTICAL TERMS
Cmdr I Johnston RN

PHILOSOPHY
Christopher Sion
Ephraim Borowski
Department of Philosophy, University of Glasgow

PHYSICAL SCIENCES
R Cutler

PHYSICS
J W Warren
Department of Physics, Brunel University

PIDGINS AND CREOLES
Loreto Todd
The School of English, University of Leeds

PLANTS
Sandra Holmes

POP MUSIC
Ingrid von Essen

PRINTING
C H Parsons
Laurence Chizlett

PSYCHOLOGY
Dr Eric Taylor
Professor Stuart Sutherland
Director, Centre for Research on Perception and Cognition, University of Sussex

RAILWAYS
James Barnes

RELIGION
The Rev D Lancashire
University of Essex

RELIGIOUS TERMS
David Bourke
Rev Canon D W Gundry
Chancellor of Leicester Cathedral

SOCIAL WELFARE
Bob Marsden
Harrow Social Services Department

SPORT
Stuart Bathgate
Freelance Journalist

STATISTICS
Ephraim Borowski
Department of Philosophy, University of Glasgow

TOOLS
N J Small
Associate of the Institute of Marine Engineers

Other Contributors

Jane Bartholomew ANIMALS
Jenny Baster COOKERY; CLOTHING AND FASHION; TEXTILES
Denise Bown PLACE NAMES
Ron Brown JAZZ
Daphne Butler CHEMISTRY
Christopher L Clarke HOROLOGY
Brian Dalgleish METALLURGY
Carolyn Eardley ANTIQUES; FURNITURE; TEXTILES
R J Edwards PSYCHOLOGY
Dennis Exton FILMS, TV, AND RADIO
Rosalind Fergusson BIOGRAPHIES
Ian Fuller PSYCHOLOGY
C Gallon PLANTS
Robert Hine BIOGRAPHIES
Amanda Isaacs BIOGRAPHIES
Cherry McDonald-Taylor EDUCATION; LIBRARY SCIENCE
Mary Marshall CARDS; DANCING AND BALLET
David Martin PSYCHOLOGY
Peter Miller SPORTS
Stewart Murray METALLURGY
Serena Penman ART
H G Procter PSYCHOLOGY
Mark Salad PLACE NAMES
David H Shaw ENGINEERING
Brian Street ANTHROPOLOGY
Andrew Treacher PSYCHOLOGY
Ralph Tyler FILMS, TV, AND RADIO; LITERATURE; MYTHOLOGY; THEATRE; BIOGRAPHIES
Jennifer Wearden ARCHAEOLOGY
Irene Wise BIOCHEMISTRY

This dictionary has been compiled by referring to the Bank of English, a unique database of the English language with examples of over 350 million words enabling lexicographers to analyse how English is actually used today and how it is changing. This is the evidence on which the changes in the dictionary are based.

The Bank of English was set up to be a resource for language research and lexicography. It contains a very wide range of material from books, newspapers, radio, TV, magazines, letters, and talks reflecting the whole spectrum of English today. Its size and range make it an unequalled resource and it has purpose-built software for its analysis.

This ensures that the text accurately reflects English as it is used today in a way that is most helpful to the dictionary user as well as including the full range of rarer and historical words and meanings.

Foreword

The **English Dictionary & Thesaurus** is a uniquely useful language reference book, combining as it does dictionary entries and thesaurus entries on the same page. This means that at one look-up you can find not only all the standard dictionary information – pronunciations, meaning, examples, etymologies, but also synonyms for the different meanings, and where applicable, antonyms as well.

The dictionary text includes over 105,000 references, and is a substantial work that provides extensive coverage of all aspects of today's English. It is up to date containing thousands of the most recent new words and terms to have entered the language, reflecting changes and developments in our society. Particular attention is given to the vocabulary of science, technology, and many other special interest subjects with entries based on the latest research and development.

Help is given with difficult or controversial points in the use of English. The dictionary definitions give clear guidance on many aspects of syntax and grammar, and contain thousands of examples of words in use. Particularly problematic words have notes after the main entry in the dictionary text showing the current view on their usage, especially in cases where this usage is changing.

The thesaurus section at the foot of the page provides lists of alternative words for some 16,000 entry words in the dictionary text, the most basic words of the language and therefore those for which an alternative expression is most likely to be needed. Antonyms are included where appropriate. The synonym lists are divided into numbered categories, each relating to the particular meaning of the word in the dictionary text, so that it is easy to identify the synonym that most closely relates to the context required. Italic labels in both the dictionary and the thesaurus text identify words which have a particular area of use; for example, words which are slang or literary, or which are restricted to a particular region of the world.

The book is easy to use, with clear typography, numbered meanings, and every dictionary item which needs a definition given as a main entry in its own right.

The **English Dictionary & Thesaurus** is thus the complete language reference book, providing the fullest, most up-to-date, and helpful range of information available.

Guide to the Text

THESAURUS

Headword — Synonyms

Usage label — Key synonym

Dictionary sense number — Part of speech

"Opposite to"

Idiom or phrase

Antonyms

build up *vb* **2** = **increase**, add to, amplify, augment, develop, enhance, expand, extend, fortify, heighten, improve, intensify, reinforce, strengthen **4** = **hype**, advertise, boost, plug (*inf.*), promote, publicize, spotlight ♦ *n* **build-up 5** = **increase**, accumulation, development, enlargement, escalation, expansion, gain, growth **7** = **hype**, ballyhoo (*inf.*), plug (*inf.*), promotion, publicity, puff

built-in *adj* **2** = **integral**, essential, immanent, implicit, in-built, included, incorporated, inherent, inseparable, part and parcel of

bulbous *adj* **1, 4** = **bulging**, bloated, convex, rounded, swelling, swollen

bulge *n* **1** = **swelling**, bump, hump, lump, projection, protrusion, protuberance **2** = **increase**, boost, intensification, rise, surge ♦ *vb* **3** = **swell out**, bag, dilate, distend, enlarge, expand, project, protrude, puff out, sag, stand out, stick out, swell

Antonyms *n* ≠ **swelling:** bowl, cave, cavity, concavity, crater, dent, depression, hole, hollow, indentation, pit, trough

bulk *n* **1** = **size**, amplitude, bigness, dimensions, immensity, largeness, magnitude, massiveness, substance, volume, weight **2** = **main part**, better part, body, generality, lion's share, majority, major part, mass, most, nearly all, plurality, preponderance ♦ *vb* **7** **bulk large** = **be important**, carry weight, dominate, loom, loom large, preponderate, stand out, threaten

bulky *adj* = **large**, big, colossal, cumbersome, elephantine, enormous, heavy, huge, hulking, immense, mammoth, massive, massy, ponderous, substantial, unmanageable, unwieldy, voluminous, weighty

Antonyms *adj* convenient, handy, manageable, neat, slim, small, wieldy

Guide to the Text

DICTIONARY

build up Ⓣ *vb* (*adv*) **1** (*tr*) to construct gradually, systematically, and in stages. **2** to increase, accumulate, or strengthen, esp. by degrees: *the murmur built up to a roar.* **3** (*tr*) to improve the health or physique of (a person). **4** (*intr*) to prepare for or gradually approach a climax. ◆ *n* **build-up. 5** progressive increase in number, size, etc.: *the build-up of industry.* **6** a gradual approach to a climax. **7** extravagant publicity or praise, esp. in the form of a campaign. **8** *Mil.* the process of attaining the required strength of forces and equipment.

built (bɪlt) *vb* the past tense and past participle of **build**.

built-in Ⓣ *adj* **1** made or incorporated as an integral part: *a built-in cupboard.* **2** essential; inherent. ◆ *n* **3** *Austral.* a built-in cupboard.

built-in obsolescence *n* See **planned obsolescence.**

built-up *adj* **1** having many buildings (esp. in **built-up area**). **2** increased by the addition of parts: *built-up heels.*

bulb Ⓣ (bʌlb) *n* **1** a rounded organ of vegetative reproduction in plants such as the tulip and onion: a flattened stem bearing a central shoot surrounded by fleshy nutritive inner leaves and thin brown outer leaves. **2** a plant, such as a hyacinth or daffodil, that grows from a bulb. **3** See **light bulb. 4** any bulb-shaped thing. [C16: from L *bulbus*, from Gk *bolbos* onion]
▸ **'bulbous** *adj*

bulbil ('bʌlbɪl) *n* **1** a small bulb produced from a parent bulb. **2** a bulblike reproductive organ in a leaf axil of certain plants. **3** any small bulblike structure in an animal. [C19: from NL *bulbillus* BULB]

bulbul ('bʊlbʊl) *n* a songbird of tropical Africa and Asia having brown plumage and, in many species, a distinct crest. [C18: via Persian from Ar.]

Bulgarian (bʌl'gɛərɪən, bʊl-) *adj* **1** of or denoting Bulgaria, a country of SE Europe, on the Balkan Peninsula, its people, or their language. ◆ *n* **2** the official language of Bulgaria. **3** a native or inhabitant of Bulgaria.

bulge Ⓣ (bʌldʒ) *n* **1** a swelling or an outward curve. **2** a sudden increase in number, esp. of population. ◆ *vb* **bulges, bulging, bulged. 3** to swell outwards. [C13: from OF *bouge*, from L *bulga* bag, prob. of Gaulish origin]
▸ **'bulging** *adj* ▸ **'bulgy** *adj*

bulgur ('bʌlgə) *n* cracked wheat that has been hulled, steamed, and roasted so that it requires little or no cooking. [C20: from Ar. *burghul*]

bulimia (bjuː'lɪmɪə) *n* **1** pathologically insatiable hunger. **2** Also called: **bulimia nervosa.** a disorder characterized by compulsive overeating followed by vomiting. [C17: from NL, from Gk *bous* ox + *limos* hunger]

bulk Ⓣ (bʌlk) *n* **1** volume, size, or magnitude, esp. when great. **2** the main part: *the bulk of the work is repetitious.* **3** a large body, esp. of a person. **4** the part of food which passes unabsorbed through the digestive system. **5 in bulk. 5a** in large quantities. **5b** (of a cargo, etc.) unpackaged. ◆ *vb* **6** to cohere or cause to cohere in a mass. **7 bulk large.** to be or seem important or prominent. [C15: from ON *bulki* cargo]

> **USAGE NOTE** The use of a plural noun after *bulk* was formerly considered incorrect, but is now acceptable.

bulk buying *n* the purchase of goods in large amounts, often at reduced prices.

bulkhead ('bʌlk,hɛd) *n* any upright wall-like partition in a ship, aircraft, etc. [C15: prob. from *bulk* projecting framework from ON *bálkr* +HEAD]

bulk modulus *n* a coefficient of elasticity of a substance equal to the ratio of the applied stress to the resulting fractional change in volume.

bulky Ⓣ ('bʌlkɪ) *adj* **bulkier, bulkiest.** very large and massive, esp. so as to be unwieldy.
▸ **'bulkily** *adv* ▸ **'bulkiness** *n*

bull[1] (bʊl) *n* **1** any male bovine animal, esp. one that is sexually mature. Related adj: **taurine. 2** the male of various other animals including the elephant and whale. **3** a very large, strong, or aggressive person. **4** *Stock Exchange.* **4a** a speculator who buys in anticipation of rising prices in order to make a profit on resale. **4b** (*as modifier*): *a bull market.* Cf. **bear**[2] (sense 5). **5** *Chiefly Brit.* short for **bull's-eye** (senses 1, 2). **6** *Sl.* short for **bullshit. 7 a bull in a china shop.** a clumsy person. **8 take the bull by the horns.** to face and tackle a difficulty without shirking. ◆ *adj* **9** male; masculine: *a bull elephant.* **10** large; strong. [OE *bula*]

Headword — Pronunciation — Part of speech — Cross-reference — Sense number — Derived words — Thesaurus symbol — Related adjective — Idiom or phrase

Grammatical information — Subject-field label — Regional label — Etymology — Inflected forms — Example — Usage note — Definition — Usage label

Editorial Staff

EDITORIAL DIRECTOR
Diana Treffry

EDITORIAL CONSULTANT
Alan Isaacs

MANAGING EDITOR
Sheila Ferguson

LEXICOGRAPHERS
Elspeth Summers (Senior Lexicographer)
Ian Brookes **Lorna Gilmour**
Andrew Holmes **Mary O'Neill**

COMPUTER STAFF
Raymond Carrick

USAGE NOTES
John Todd

MARKET HOUSE EDITORS
John Daintith **Elizabeth Martin** **Fran Alexander**
Jonathan Law **Peter Blair**

COMPUTERS
Anne Stibbs

KEYBOARDERS
Jessica Scholes **Sandra McQueen** **Gwynneth Shaw** **Brenda Tomkins**

Guide to the Use of the Dictionary

The Guide that follows sets out the main principles on which the Dictionary is arranged and enables you to make full use of the Dictionary by showing the range of information that it contains.

HEADWORD

All main entries, including place names, biographies, abbreviations, prefixes, and suffixes, are printed in large boldface type and are listed in strict alphabetical order. This applies even if the headword consists of more than one word.

Order of entries

Words that have the same spelling but are derived from different sources (homographs) are entered separately with superscript numbers after the headwords.

> **saw**[1] (sɔː) *n* **1** any of various hand tools ...
> **saw**[2] (sɔː) *vb* the past tense of **see**[1].
> **saw**[3] (sɔː) *n* a wise saying, maxim, or proverb. ...

Abbreviations, acronyms, and symbols

Abbreviations, acronyms, and symbols are entered as headwords in the main alphabetical list. In linewith modern practice, full stops are generally not used but it can be assumed that nearly all abbreviations are equally acceptable with or without stops.

Prefixes, suffixes, and combining forms

Prefixes (e.g. **in-**, **pre-**, **sub-**), suffixes (e.g. **-able**, **-ation**, **-ity**), and combining forms (e.g. **psycho-**, **-iatry**) have been entered as headwords if they are still used freely to produce new words in English.

Variant spellings

Common acceptable variant spellings of English words are given as alternative forms of the headword.

> **capitalize** *or* **capitalise** (ˈkæpɪtəˌlaɪz) *vb* ...

US spellings

Where it is different, the US spelling of a word is also recorded in the headword.

> **centre** *or US* **center** (ˈsɛntə) *n*

PRONUNCIATION

Pronunciations of words in this Dictionary represent those that are common in educated British English speech. They are transcribed in the International Phonetic Alphabet (IPA). A *Pronunciation Key* is printed at the end of this Guide. The pronunciation is normally given in brackets immediately after the headword.

> **abase** (əˈbeɪs) *vb* **abases, abasing, abased.** (*tr*) **1** to humble ...

The stress pattern is marked by the symbols ˈ for primary stress and ˌ for secondary stress. The stress mark precedes the syllable to which it applies.

Variant pronunciations

When a headword has an acceptable variant pronunciation or stress pattern, the variant is given by repeating only the syllable or syllables that change.

> **economic** (ˌiːkəˈnɒmɪk, ˌɛkə-) *adj* **1** of or relating to ...

Pronunciations with different parts of speech

When two or more parts of speech of a word have different pronunciations, the pronunciations are shown in brackets before the relevant group of senses.

> **record** *n* (ˈrɛkɔːd). **1** an account in permanent form, ... ◆ *vb* (rɪˈkɔːd). (*mainly tr*) **18** to set down in some permanent form ...

Pronunciation of individual senses

If one sense of a headword has a different pronunciation from that of the rest, the pronunciation is given in brackets after the sense number.

> **conjure** (ˈkʌndʒə) *vb* **conjures, conjuring, conjured. 1** (*intr*) to practise conjuring. **2** (*intr*) to call upon supposed supernatural forces by spells and incantations. **3** (kənˈdʒʊə). (*tr*) to appeal earnestly to: *I conjure you to help me.* ...

INFLECTED FORMS

Inflected forms are shown for the following:

Nouns and verbs whose inflections involve a change in internal spelling.

> **goose**[1] (guːs) *n, pl* **geese.** ...
> **drive** (draɪv) *vb* **drives, driving, drove, driven.** ...

Nouns, verbs, and adjectives that end in a consonant plus *-y*, where *y* is changed to *i* before inflectional endings.

> **augury** (ˈɔːgjʊrɪ) *n, pl* **auguries.** ...

Nouns having identical singular and plural forms.

> **sheep** (ʃiːp) *n, pl* **sheep.** ...

Nouns that closely resemble others but form their plurals differently.

> **mongoose** (ˈmɒŋˌguːs) *n, pl* **mongooses.** ...

Nouns that end in *-ful*, *-o*, and *-us*.

handful ('hændfʊl) *n, pl* **handfuls.** ...
tomato (tə'mɑːtəʊ) *n, pl* **tomatoes.** ...
prospectus (prə'spɛktəs) *n, pl* **prospectuses.** ...

Nouns whose plurals are not regular English inflections.

basis ('beɪsɪs) *n, pl* **bases** (-siːz) ...

Plural nouns whose singulars are not regular English forms.

bacteria (bæk'tɪərɪə) *pl n, sing* **bacterium.** ...

Nouns whose plurals have regular spellings but involve a change in pronunciation.

house *n* (haʊs), *pl* **houses** ('haʊzɪz). ...

Multiword nouns when it is not obvious which word takes a plural inflection.

attorney-at-law *n, pl* **attorneys-at-law.** ...

Adjectives that change their roots to form comparatives and superlatives.

good (gʊd) *adj* **better, best.** ...

Adjectives and verbs that double their final consonant before adding endings.

fat (fæt) ... ◆ *adj* **fatter, fattest.** ...
control (kən'trəʊl) *vb* **controls, controlling, controlled.** ...

Verbs that are regular and do not (as might be expected) double their final consonant before adding endings.

rivet ('rɪvɪt) ... ◆ *vb* **rivets, riveting, riveted.** ...

Verbs and adjectives that end in a vowel plus *-e*.

canoe (kə'nuː) ... ◆ *vb* **canoes, canoeing, canoed.** ...
free (friː) *adj* **freer, freest.** ... ◆ *vb* **frees, freeing, freed.** ...

Verbs that end in *-e*.

pace[1] (peɪs) ... ◆ *vb* **paces, pacing, paced.** ...

PARTS OF SPEECH

A part-of-speech label in italics precedes the sense or senses relating to that part of speech.

Standard parts of speech

The standard parts of speech, with the abbreviations used, are as follows:

adjective (*adj*), adverb (*adv*), conjunction (*conj*), interjection (*interj*), noun (*n*), preposition (*prep*), pronoun (*pron*), verb (*vb*).

Less traditional parts of speech

Certain other less traditional parts of speech have been used in this Dictionary.

determiner. This denotes such words as *the*, *a*, *some*, *any*, *that*, *this*, as well as the numerals, and possessives such as *my* and *your*. Many determiners can have a pronoun function without change of meaning:

some (sʌm; *unstressed* səm) *determiner* ... **2a** an unknown or unspecified quantity or amount of: *there's some rice on the table; he owns some horses.* **2b** (*as pron; functioning as sing or pl*): *we'll buy some.* ...

sentence connector. This description replaces the traditional classification of certain words, such as *therefore* and *however*, as adverbs or conjunctions. These words link sentences together rather in the manner of conjunctions; however, they are not confined to the first position in a clause as conjunctions are.

sentence substitute. Sentence substitutes are words such as *yes*, *no*, *perhaps*, *definitely*, and *maybe*. They can stand as meaningful utterances by themselves.

Words used as more than one part of speech

If a word can be used as more than one part of speech, the senses of one part of speech are separated from the others by a lozenge (◆).

lure (lʊə) *vb* **lures, luring, lured.** (*tr*) ... **2** *Falconry.* to entice (a hawk or falcon) from the air to the falconer by a lure. ◆ *n* **3** a person or thing that lures. ...

Guide to the Use of the Dictionary

GRAMMATICAL INFORMATION

Grammatical information is provided in brackets and typically in italics to distinguish it from other types of information.

Adjectives and determiners

Some adjectives and determiners are restricted by usage to a particular position relative to the nouns they qualify. This is indicated by the following labels:

postpositive (used predicatively or after the noun, but not before the noun):

ablaze (əˈbleɪz) *adj (postpositive), adv* **1** on fire; burning. ...

immediately postpositive (always used immediately following the noun qualified and never used predicatively):

galore (gəˈlɔː) *determiner (immediately postpositive)* in great numbers or quantity: *there were daffodils galore in the park.* ...

prenominal (used before the noun, and never used predicatively):

chief (tʃiːf) ... ◆ *adj* **4** *(prenominal)* **4a** most important; principal. ...

Intensifiers

Adjectives and adverbs that perform an exclusively intensifying function, with no addition of meaning, are described as (intensifier) without further explanation.

blooming (ˈbluːmɪŋ) *adv, adj Brit. inf.* (intensifier): *a blooming genius; blooming painful.*

Conjunctions

Conjunctions are divided into two classes, marked by the following labels:

coordinating. Coordinating conjunctions connect words, phrases, or clauses that perform an identical function and are not dependent on each other. They include *and, but,* and *or.*

subordinating. Subordinating conjunctions introduce clauses that are dependent on a main clause in a complex sentence. They include *where, until,* and *if.*

Some conjunctions, such as *while* and *whereas,* can function as either coordinating or subordinating conjunctions.

Singular and plural labelling of nouns

Headwords and senses that are apparently plural in form but that take a singular verb, etc., are marked *'functioning as sing'.*

physics (ˈfɪzɪks) *n (functioning as sing)* **1** the branch of science ...

Headwords and senses that appear to be singular, such as collective nouns, but that take a plural verb, etc., are marked *'functioning as pl'.*

cattle (ˈkætᵊl) *n (functioning as pl)* **1** bovid mammals of the tribe *Bovini* ...

Headwords and senses that may take either a singular or a plural verb, etc., are marked *'functioning as sing or pl'.*

bellows (ˈbɛləʊz) *n (functioning as sing or pl)* **1** Also: **pair of bellows.** an instrument consisting of an air chamber ...

Modifiers

A noun that is commonly used as if it were an adjective is labelled *modifier.* If the sense of the modifier can be understood from the sense of the noun, the modifier is shown without further explanation, with an example to illustrate its use. Otherwise its meaning and/or usage is explained separately.

key[1] (kiː) *n* ... **8** *(modifier)* of great importance: *a key issue.*

Verbs

The principal parts given are: 3rd person singular of the present tense; present participle; past tense; past participle if different from the past tense.

Intransitive and transitive verbs

When a sense of a verb (*vb*) is restricted to transitive use, it is labelled (*tr*); if it is intransitive only, it is labelled (*intr*). If all the senses of a verb are transitive or all are intransitive, the appropriate label appears before the first numbered sense and is not repeated.

Absence of a label is significant: it indicates that the sense may be used both transitively and intransitively.

If nearly all the senses of a verb are transitive, the label (*mainly tr*) appears immediately before the first numbered sense. This indicates that, unless otherwise labelled, any given sense of the verb is transitive. Similarly, all the senses of a verb may be labelled (*mainly intr*).

Copulas

A verb that takes a complement is labelled copula.

> **seem** (si:m) *vb (may take an infinitive)* **1** *(copula)* to appear to the mind or eye; look: *the car seems to be running well. ...*

Phrasal verbs

Verbal constructions consisting of a verb and a prepositional or an adverbial particle are given headword status if the meaning of the phrasal verb cannot be deduced from the separate meanings of the verb and the particle.

Phrasal verbs are labelled to show four possible distinctions: a transitive verb with an adverbial particle (*tr, adv*); a transitive verb with a prepositional particle (*tr, prep*); an intransitive verb with an adverbial particle (*intr, adv*); an intransitive verb with a prepositional particle (*intr, prep*):

> **turn on** ... **4** *(tr, adv) Inf.* to produce (charm, tears, etc.) suddenly or automatically.

> **take for** *vb (tr, prep) Inf.* to consider or suppose to be, esp. mistakenly: *the fake coins were taken for genuine; who do you take me for?*

> **break off** ... **3** *(intr, adv)* to stop abruptly: *he broke off in the middle of his speech.*

> **turn on** ... **2** *(intr, prep)* to depend or hinge on: *the success of the party turns on you.*

The absence of a label is significant. If there is no label (*tr*) or (*intr*), the verb may be used either transitively or intransitively. If there is no label (*adv*) or (*prep*), the particle may be either adverbial or prepositional.

Any noun, adjective, or modifier formed from a phrasal verb is entered under the phrasal-verb headword. In some cases, where the noun or adjective is more common than the verb, the phrasal verb is entered after the noun or adjective form:

> **breakaway** ('breɪkə,weɪ) *n* **1a** loss or withdrawal of a group of members from an association, club, etc. **1b** *(as modifier): a breakaway faction. ...* ◆ *vb* **break away.** *(intr, adv)* **3** (often foll. by *from*) to leave hastily or escape. **4** to withdraw or secede.

RESTRICTIVE LABELS

If a particular sense is restricted as to appropriateness, connotation, subject field, etc., an italic label is placed immediately before the relevant definition.

> **hang on** *vb (intr)* ... **5** *(adv) Inf.* to wait: *hang on for a few minutes.*

If a label applies to all senses of one part of speech, it is placed immediately after the part-of-speech label.

> **assured** (ə'ʃʊəd) *adj* ... ◆ *n* **4** *Chiefly Brit.* **4a** the beneficiary under a life assurance policy. **4b** the person whose life is insured. ...

If a label applies to all senses of a headword, it is placed immediately after the pronunciation (or inflections).

> **con**[1] (kɒn) *Inf.* ◆ *n* **1a** short for **confidence trick. 1b** *(as modifier): con man.* ◆ *vb* **cons, conning, conned. 2** *(tr)* to swindle ...

Usage labels

Sl. (*Slang*). Refers to words or senses that are informal and restricted in context, for example, to members of a particular social or cultural group. Slang words are inappropriate in formal speech or writing.

Inf. (*Informal*). Applies to words or senses that may be widely used, especially in conversation, letter-writing, etc., but that are not common in formal writing. Such words are subject to fewer contextual restrictions than slang words.

Taboo. Indicates words that are not acceptable in polite use.

Offens. (*Offensive*). Indicates that a word might be regarded as offensive by the person described or referred to, even if the speaker uses the word without any malicious intention.

Derog. (*Derogatory*). Implies that the connotations of a word are unpleasant with intent on the part of the speaker or writer.

Not standard. Indicates words or senses that are frequently encountered but widely regarded as incorrect.

Arch. (*Archaic*). Denotes a word or sense that is no longer in common use but that may be found in literary works or used to impart a historical colour to contemporary writing.

Obs. (*Obsolete*). Denotes a word or sense that is no longer in use. In specialist or technical fields the label often implies that the term has been superseded.

The word 'formerly' is placed in brackets before a sense when the practice, concept, etc., being described, rather than the word itself, is obsolete or out-of-date.

A number of other usage labels, such as *Ironic*, *Facetious*, and *Euphemistic*, are used where appropriate.

More extended help on usage is provided in usage notes after certain entries.

Subject-field labels

A number of italic labels are used to indicate that a word or sense is used in a particular specialist or technical field.

MEANING

The meaning of each headword in this Dictionary is explained in one or more definitions, together with information about context and typical use.

Order of senses

As a general rule, where a headword has more than one sense, the first sense given is the one most common in current usage.

> **complexion** (kəm'plɛkʃən) *n* **1** the colour and general appearance of a person's skin, esp. of the face. **2** aspect or nature: *the general complexion of a nation's finances.* **3** *Obs.* temperament. ...

Where the lexicographers consider that a current sense is the 'core meaning' in that it illuminates the meaning of other senses, the core meaning may be placed first.

> **competition** (ˌkɒmpɪ'tɪʃən) *n* **1** the act of competing. **2** a contest in which a winner is selected from among two or more entrants. **3** a series of games, sports events, etc. **4** the opposition offered by competitors....

Subsequent senses are arranged so as to give a coherent account of the meaning of a headword. If a word is used as more than one part of speech, all the senses of each part of speech are grouped together in a single block. Within a part-of-speech block, closely related senses are grouped together; technical senses generally follow general senses; archaic and obsolete sense follow technical senses; idioms and fixed phrases are generally placed last.

Scientific and technical definitions

Units, physical quantities, formulas, etc. In accordance with the recommendations of the International Standards Organization, all scientific measurements are expressed in SI units (*Système International d'Unités*). Measurements and quantities in more traditional units are often given as well as SI units. The entries for chemical compounds give the systematic names as well as the more familiar popular names.

CROSS-REFERENCES

Cross-references introduced by the words 'See also' or 'Compare' refer the reader to additional information elsewhere in the Dictionary. If the cross-reference is preceded by a lozenge (◆), it applies to all senses of the headword that have gone before it, unless otherwise stated. If there is no lozenge, the cross-reference applies only to the sense immediately preceding it.

Variant spellings

Variant spellings (e.g. **foetus**...a variant spelling of **fetus**) are generally entered as cross-references if their place in the alphabetical list is more than ten entries distant from the main entry.

Alternative names

Alternative names or terms are printed in boldface type and introduced by the words 'Also' or 'Also called'. If the alternative name or term is preceded by a lozenge, it applies to the entire entry.

RELATED ADJECTIVES

Certain nouns, especially of Germanic origin, have related adjectives that are derived from Latin or French. For example, *mural* (from Latin) is an adjective related in meaning to *wall.* Such adjectives are shown in a number of cases after the sense (or part-of-speech block) to which they are related.

> **wall** (wɔːl) *n* **1a** a vertical construction made of stone, brick, wood, etc. ... Related adj: **mural**. ...

IDIOMS

Fixed noun phrases, such as **dark horse**, and certain other idioms are given full headword status. Other idioms are placed under the key word of the idiom, as a separate sense, generally at the end of the appropriate part-of-speech block.

> **ground**[1] (graʊnd) *n* ... **17 break new ground.** to do something that has not been done before. ...

ETYMOLOGIES

Etymologies are placed in bold square brackets after the definition. They are given for all headwords except those that are derivative forms (consisting of a base word and a suffix or prefix), compound words, inflected forms, and proper names.

Many headwords, such as **enlighten** and **prepossess**, consist of a prefix and a base word and are not accompanied by etymologies since the essential etymological information is shown for the component parts, all of which are entered in the Dictionary as headwords in their own right.

The purpose of the etymologies is to trace briefly the history of the word back from the present day, through its first recorded appearance in English, to its origin, often in some source language other than English. The etymologies show the history of the word both in English (wherever there has been significant change in form or sense) and in its pre-English source languages.

Words printed in SMALL CAPITALS refer to other headwords where relevant or additional information, either in the definition or in the etymology, may be found.

Dating

The etymology records the first known occurrence (a written citation) of a word in English. Words first appearing in the language during the Middle English period or later are dated by century, abbreviated **C**.

> **mantis** (ˈmæntɪs) ... **[**C17: NL, from Gk: prophet, alluding to its praying posture**]**

This indicates that there is a written citation for **mantis** in the seventeenth century. The absence of a New Latin or Greek form in the etymology means that the form of the word was the same in those languages as in English.

Old English

Native words from Old English are not dated, written records of Old English being scarce, but are simply identified as being of Old English origin.

DERIVED WORDS

Words derived from a base word by the addition of suffixes such as *-ly*, *-ness*, etc., are entered in boldface type immediately after the etymology or after the last definition if there is no etymology. They are preceded by an arrow head (▸). The meanings of such words may be deduced from the meanings of the suffix and the headword.

USAGE NOTES

A brief note introduced by the label **USAGE NOTE** has been added at the end of a number of entries in order to comment on matters of usage.

Guide to the Use of the Thesaurus

Entries

Main entry words are alphabetically arranged, with their synonyms also listed alphabetically. When a word has distinctly separate meanings, separate numbered lists are given for the different senses. The sense numbers in the thesaurus correspond to those of the dictionary. Where the listed synonyms can be used as alternatives for more than one dictionary sense, this is indicated, as in the entry for *academic*.

Key synonyms

Key synonyms are shown in bold type and placed first in each list. This feature helps to identify immediately which sense of the word is referred to and also offers the closest alternative to the word being looked up.

Parts of speech

Where it is desirable to distinguish between different parts of speech, labels have been added as follows:

n (noun), *vb* (verb), *adj* (adjective), *adv* (adverb), *pron* (pronoun), *conj* (conjunction), *prep* (preposition), *interj* (interjection). See entries for *living, loaf, loan, local*.

All the synonyms for a particular part of speech are grouped together. Thus, in the entry *catch*, synonyms for all verb senses are given first, followed by synonyms for all the noun senses.

Change of part of speech

When a headword has more than one meaning and can function as more than one part of speech, a new part-of-speech function is shown by a lozenge (◆), as in the entry for *glance* or *grasp*.

Phrases

Commonly used phrases appear as main entries; for instance, *give away* comes after *give*. Expressions such as *a priori* or *en route* are also given as main entries within the alphabetical listing. Short idiomatic phrases are entered under their key word at the end of the appropriate part-of-speech section. Thus, the phrase *take a dim view*, in which *dim* is an adjective, appears immediately after the other adjectival senses of *dim*.

Plurals

Plural forms with a distinct meaning, such as *damages*, are entered at their own alphabetical position, while those with a less distinct difference, such as *features*, are given as a separate sense under the singular form, e.g. *feature…1 plural…*

Antonyms

The antonym lists which follow many entries are also arranged alphabetically. Where there is more than one synonym sense, the corresponding antonym list is introduced with a = sign to indicate the sense to which the antonym list refers.

Labels

A label in brackets applies only to the synonym preceding it, while one which is not bracketed relates to the whole of that particular sense. Labels have been abbreviated when a readily understandable shortened form exists, such as *sl.* (slang), *inf.* (informal), and *arch.* (archaic).

List of Abbreviations Used in the Dictionary

abbrev. abbreviation
Abor. Aboriginal
adj adjective
adv adverb(ial)
Afrik. Afrikaans
Amerind American Indian
Anat. Anatomy
approx. approximate(ly)
Ar. Arabic
Arch. Archaic
Archaeol. Archaeology
Archit. Architecture
Astrol. Astrology
Astron. Astronomy
Austral. Australian

Biol. Biology
Bot. Botany
Brit. Britain; British

C century (e.g. **C14** = 14th century)
°C degrees Celsius
Canad. Canadian
cap. capital
cf. compare
Chem. Chemistry
comp. comparative
conj conjunction

Derog. Derogatory
dim. diminutive
Du. Dutch

E east(ern); (in etymologies) English
Econ. Economics
e.g. for example
esp. especially
est. estimate

F French
fem feminine
foll. followed
ft foot *or* feet

G German
Geog. Geography
Geol. Geology
Geom. Geometry
Gk Greek
Gmc Germanic

Heb. Hebrew

i.e. that is
imit. of imitative origin
in. inch(es)
Inf. Informal
infl. influence(d)
interj interjection
intr intransitive
It. Italian

km kilometre(s)

L Late; Latin
lit. literally
LL Late Latin

m metre(s)
M Middle
masc masculine
Maths Mathematics
Med. Medicine; (in etymologies) Medieval
MHG Middle High German
Mil. Military
Mod. Modern
Myth. Mythology

n noun
N north(ern)
Naut. Nautical
NE northeast(ern)
NL New Latin
no. number
NW northwest(ern)
NZ New Zealand

O Old
Obs. Obsolete
Offens. Offensive
OHG Old High German
ON Old Norse

orig. originally

Photog. Photography
pl plural
pop. population
Port. Portuguese
p.p. past participle
prep preposition(al)
prob. probably
pron pronoun
Psychol. Psychology
pt. point
p.t. past tense

rel. related

S south(ern)
S. African South African
Sansk. Sanskrit
Scand. Scandinavian
Scot. Scottish; Scots
SE southeast(ern)
sing singular
Sl. slang
Sp. Spanish
sq. square
sup. superlative
SW southwest(ern)

Theol. Theology
tr transitive

ult. ultimately
US United States

var. variant
vb verb
vol. volume

W west(ern)
wt. weight

Zool. Zoology

? in etymologies indicates "query"

Pronunciation Key

The symbols used in the pronunciation transcriptions are those of the International Phonetic Alphabet. The following consonant symbols have their usual English values: *b, d, f, h, k, l, m, n, p, r, s, t, v, w, z*. The remaining symbols and their interpretations are listed below.

English Sounds

ɑ: as in *father* ('fɑ:ðə), *alms* (ɑ:mz), *clerk* (klɑ:k), *heart* (hɑ:t), *sergeant* ('sɑ:dʒənt)

æ as in *act* (ækt), *Caedmon* ('kædmən), *plait* (plæt)

aɪ as in *dive* (daɪv), *aisle* (aɪl), *guy* (gaɪ), *might* (maɪt), *rye* (raɪ)

aɪə as in *fire* ('faɪə), *buyer* ('baɪə), *liar* ('laɪə), *tyre* ('taɪə)

aʊ as in *out* (aʊt), *bough* (baʊ), *crowd* (kraʊd), *slouch* (slaʊtʃ)

aʊə as in *flour* ('flaʊə), *cower* ('kaʊə), *flower* ('flaʊə), *sour* ('saʊə)

ɛ as in *bet* (bɛt), *ate* (ɛt), *bury* ('bɛrɪ), *heifer* ('hɛfə), *said* (sɛd), *says* (sɛz)

eɪ as in *paid* (peɪd), *day* (deɪ), *deign* (deɪn), *gauge* (geɪdʒ), *grey* (greɪ), *neigh* (neɪ)

ɛə as in *bear* (bɛə), *dare* (dɛə), *prayer* (prɛə), *stairs* (stɛəz), *where* (wɛə)

g as in *get* (gɛt), *give* (gɪv), *ghoul* (gu:l), *guard* (gɑ:d), *examine* (ɪg'zæmɪn)

ɪ as in *pretty* ('prɪtɪ), *build* (bɪld), *busy* ('bɪzɪ), *nymph* (nɪmf), *pocket* ('pɒkɪt), *sieve* (sɪv), *women* ('wɪmɪn)

i: as in *see* (si:), *aesthete* ('i:sθi:t), *evil* ('i:v^{ə}l), *magazine* (ˌmægə'zi:n), *receive* (rɪ'si:v), *siege* (si:dʒ)

ɪə as in *fear* (fɪə), *beer* (bɪə), *mere* (mɪə), *tier* (tɪə)

j as in *yes* (jɛs), *onion* ('ʌnjən), *vignette* (vɪ'njɛt)

ɒ as in *pot* (pɒt), *botch* (bɒtʃ), *sorry* ('sɒrɪ)

əʊ as in *note* (nəʊt), *beau* (bəʊ), *dough* (dəʊ), *hoe* (həʊ), *slow* (sləʊ), *yeoman* ('jəʊmən)

ɔ: as in *thaw* (θɔ:), *broad* (brɔ:d), *drawer* ('drɔ:ə), *fault* (fɔ:lt), *halt* (hɔ:lt), *organ* ('ɔ:gən)

ɔɪ as in *void* (vɔɪd), *boy* (bɔɪ), *destroy* (dɪ'strɔɪ)

ʊ as in *pull* (pʊl), *good* (gʊd), *should* (ʃʊd), *woman* ('wʊmən)

u: as in *zoo* (zu:), *do* (du:), *queue* (kju:), *shoe* (ʃu:), *spew* (spju:), *true* (tru:), *you* (ju:)

ʊə as in *poor* (pʊə), *skewer* (skjʊə), *sure* (ʃʊə)

ə as in *potter* ('pɒtə), *alone* (ə'ləʊn), *furious* ('fjʊərɪəs), *nation* ('neɪʃən), *the* (ðə)

ɜ: as in *fern* (fɜ:n), *burn* (bɜ:n), *fir* (fɜ:), *learn* (lɜ:n), *term* (tɜ:m), *worm* (wɜ:m)

ʌ as in *cut* (kʌt), *flood* (flʌd), *rough* (rʌf), *son* (sʌn)

ʃ as in *ship* (ʃɪp), *election* (ɪ'lɛkʃən), *machine* (mə'ʃi:n), *mission* ('mɪʃən), *pressure* ('prɛʃə), *schedule* ('ʃɛdju:l), *sugar* ('ʃʊgə)

ʒ as in *treasure* ('trɛʒə), *azure* ('æʒə), *closure* ('kləʊʒə), *evasion* (ɪ'veɪʒən)

tʃ as in *chew* (tʃu:), *nature* ('neɪtʃə)

dʒ as in *jaw* (dʒɔ:), *adjective* ('ædʒɪktɪv), *lodge* (lɒdʒ), *soldier* ('səʊldʒə), *usage* ('ju:sɪdʒ)

θ as in *thin* (θɪn), *strength* (strɛŋθ), *three* (θri:)

ð as in *these* (ði:z), *bathe* (beɪð), *lather* ('lɑ:ðə)

ŋ as in *sing* (sɪŋ), *finger* ('fɪŋgə), *sling* (slɪŋ)

indicates that the following consonant (*l or n*) is syllabic, as in *bundle* ('bʌnd^{ə}l), *button* ('bʌt^{ə}n)

Foreign Sounds

The symbols above are also used to represent foreign sounds where these are similar to English sounds. However, certain common foreign sounds require symbols with markedly different values, as follows:

a *a* in French *ami*, German *Mann*, Italian *pasta*: a sound between English (æ) and (ɑ:), similar to the vowel in Northern English *cat* or London *cut*.

ɑ *a* in French *bas*: a sound made with the tongue position similar to that of English (ɑ:), but shorter.

e *é* in French *été*, *eh* in German *sehr*, *e* in Italian *che*: a sound similar to the first part of the English diphthong (eɪ) in *day* or to the Scottish vowel in *day*.

i *i* in French *il*, German *Idee*, Spanish *filo*, Italian *signor*: a sound made with a tongue position similar to that of English (i:), but shorter.

ɔ *o* in Italian *no*, French *bonne*, German *Sonne*: a vowel resembling English (ɒ), but with a higher tongue position and more rounding of the lips.

o *o* in French *rose*, German *so*, Italian *voce*: a sound between English (ɔ:) and (u:) with closely rounded lips, similar to the Scottish vowel in *so*.

u *ou* in French *genou*, *u* in German *kulant*, Spanish *puna*: a sound made with a tongue position similar to that of English (u:), but shorter.

y *u* in French *tu*, *ü* in German *über* or *fünf*: a sound made with a tongue position similar to that of English (i:), but with closely rounded lips.

ø *eu* in French *deux*, *ö* in German *schön*: a sound made with the tongue position of (e), but with closely rounded lips.

œ *œu* in French *œuf*, *ö* in German *zwölf*: a sound made with a tongue position similar to that of English (ɛ), but with open rounded lips.

~ above a vowel indicates nasalization, as in French *un* (œ̃), *bon* (bɔ̃), *vin* (vɛ̃), *blanc* (blɑ̃).

χ *ch* in Scottish *loch*, German *Buch*, *j* in Spanish *Juan*.

ç *ch* in German *ich*: a (j) sound as in *yes*, said without voice; similar to the first sound in *huge*.

β *b* in Spanish *Habana*: a voiced fricative sound similar to (v), but made by the two lips.

ʎ *ll* in Spanish *llamar*, *gl* in Italian *consiglio*: similar to the (lj) sequence in *million*, but with the tongue tip lowered and the sounds said simultaneously.

ɥ *u* in French *lui*: a short (y).

ɲ *gn* in French *vigne*, Italian *gnocchi*, *ñ* in Spanish *España*: similar to the (nj) sequence in *onion*, but with the tongue tip lowered and the two sounds said simultaneously.

ɣ *g* in Spanish *luego*: a weak (g) made with voiced friction.

Pronunciation Key

Length

The symbol : denotes length and is shown together with certain vowel symbols when the vowels are typically long.

Stress

Three grades of stress are shown in the transcriptions by the presence or absence of marks placed immediately *before* the affected syllable. Primary or strong stress is shown by ', while secondary or weak stress is shown by ˌ. Unstressed syllables are not marked. In *photographic* (ˌfəʊtə'græfɪk), for example, the first syllable carries secondary stress and the third primary stress, while the second and fourth are unstressed.

Notes

(i) Though words like *castle*, *path*, and *fast* are shown as pronounced with an /ɑː/ sound, many speakers use an /æ/. Such variations are acceptable and are to be assumed by the reader.

(ii) The letter "r" in some positions is not sounded in the speech of Southern England and elsewhere. However, many speakers in other areas do sound the "r" in such positions with varying degrees of distinctness. Again such variations are to be assumed, and in such words as *fern*, *fear*, and *arm* the reader will sound or not sound the "r" according to his or her speech habits.

(iii) Though the widely received pronunciation of words like *which* and *why* is with a simple /w/ sound and is so shown in the dictionary, many speakers in Scotland and elsewhere preserve an aspirated sound: /hw/. Once again this variation is to be assumed.

English Dictionary & Thesaurus

Aa

a *or* **A** (eɪ) *n, pl* **a's, A's,** *or* **As. 1** the first letter and first vowel of the English alphabet. **2** any of several speech sounds represented by this letter, as in *take, bag,* or *calm.* **3** Also called: **alpha.** the first in a series, esp. the highest mark. **4 from A to Z.** from start to finish.

a[1] (ə; *emphatic* eɪ) *determiner* (*indefinite article;* used before an initial consonant. Cf. **an**[1]) **1** used preceding a singular countable noun, not previously specified: *a dog; a great pity.* **2** used preceding a noun or determiner of quantity: *a dozen eggs; a great many; to read a lot.* **3** (preceded by *once, twice, several times,* etc.) each or every; per: *once a day.* **4** a certain; one: *a Mr Jones called.* **5** (preceded by *not*) any at all: *not a hope.* ◆ Cf. **the**[1].

a[2] *symbol for:* **1** acceleration. **2** are(s) (metric measure of area). **3** atto-.

A *symbol for:* **1** *Music.* **1a** the sixth note of the scale of C major. **1b** the major or minor key having this note as its tonic. **2** a human blood type of the ABO group, containing the A antigen. **3** (in Britain) a major arterial road. **4** ampere(s). **5** absolute (temperature). **6** area. **7** (*in combination*) atomic: *an A-bomb; an A-plant.* **8a** a person whose job is in top management, or who holds a senior administrative or professional position. **8b** (*as modifier*): *an A worker.* ◆ See also **occupation groupings.**

Å *symbol for* angstrom unit.

a. *abbrev. for:* **1** acre(s). **2** Also: **A.** alto.

A. *abbrev. for:* **1** acre(s). **2** America(n). **3** answer.

a-[1] *or before a vowel* **an-** *prefix* not; without; opposite to: *atonal; asocial.* [from Gk *a-, an-* not, without]

a-[2] *prefix* **1** on; in; towards: *aground; aback.* **2** in the state of: *afloat; asleep.*

A1, A-1, *or* **A-one** ('eɪ'wʌn) *adj* **1** physically fit. **2** *Inf.* first class; excellent. **3** (of a vessel) in first-class condition.

A4 *n* a standard paper size, 297 × 210 mm.

AA *abbrev. for:* **1** Alcoholics Anonymous. **2** anti-aircraft. **3** (in Britain) Automobile Association.

AAA *abbrev. for:* **1** (formerly) *Brit.* Amateur Athletic Association. **2** *US.* Automobile Association of America.

A and E *abbrev. for* Accident and Emergency (in hospitals).

A and R *abbrev. for* artists and repertoire.

AAP *abbrev. for:* **1** Australian Associated Press. **2** (in the US) affirmative action programme.

aardvark ('ɑːdˌvɑːk) *n* a nocturnal burrowing African mammal that has long ears and snout and feeds on termites. Also called: **ant bear.** [C19: from obs. Afrik., from *aarde* earth + *varken* pig]

aardwolf ('ɑːdˌwʊlf) *n, pl* **aardwolves.** a nocturnal mammal of the hyena family that inhabits the plains of southern Africa and feeds on termites and insect larvae. [C19: from Afrik., from *aarde* earth + *wolf* wolf]

Aaron's beard ('ɛərən) *n* another name for **rose of Sharon.**

Aaron's rod *n* a widespread Eurasian plant having tall erect spikes of yellow flowers.

A'asia *abbrev. for* Australasia.

AB *abbrev. for:* **1** Also: **a.b.** able-bodied seaman. **2** Alberta. **3** (in the US) Bachelor of Arts. ◆ **4** *symbol for* a human blood type of the ABO group, containing both the A antigen and the B antigen.

ab-[1] *prefix* away from; opposite to: *abnormal.* [from L *ab* away from]

ab-[2] *prefix* a cgs unit of measurement in the electromagnetic system: *abampere, abwatt, abvolt.* [from ABSOLUTE]

aba ('æbə) *n* **1** a type of cloth from Syria, made of goat or camel hair. **2** a sleeveless outer garment of such cloth. [from Ar.]

abaca ('æbəkə) *n* **1** a Philippine plant, the source of Manila hemp. **2** another name for **Manila hemp.** [via Sp. from Tagalog *abaká*]

aback Ⓣ (ə'bæk) *adv* **taken aback. 1** startled or disconcerted. **2** *Naut.* (of a vessel or sail) having the wind against the forward side so as to prevent forward motion. [OE *on bæc* to the back]

abacus ('æbəkəs) *n, pl* **abaci** (-ˌsaɪ) *or* **abacuses. 1** a counting device that consists of a frame holding rods on which a number of beads are free to move. **2** *Archit.* the flat upper part of the capital of a column. [C16: from L, from Gk *abax* board covered with sand, from Heb. *ābhāq* dust]

abaft (ə'bɑːft) *Naut.* ◆ *adv, adj* (*postpositive*) **1** closer to the stern than to another place on a vessel. ◆ *prep* **2** behind; aft of. [C13: *on baft; baft* from OE *beæftan,* from *be* by + *æftan* behind]

abalone (ˌæbə'ləʊnɪ) *n* an edible marine mollusc having an ear-shaped shell perforated with a row of respiratory holes and lined with mother-of-pearl. Also called: **ear shell.** [C19: from American Sp. *abulón*]

abandon Ⓣ (ə'bændən) *vb* (*tr*) **1** to forsake completely; desert; leave behind. **2** to give up completely: *to abandon hope.* **3** to give up (something begun) before completion: *the game was abandoned.* **4** to surrender (oneself) to emotion without restraint. **5** to give (insured property that has suffered partial loss or damage) to the insurers in order that a claim for a total loss may be made. ◆ *n* **6** freedom from inhibitions, restraint, or worry: *she danced with abandon.* [C14: *abandounen* (vb), from OF, from *a bandon* under one's control, from *a* at, to + *bandon* control]

▸**a'bandonment** *n*

abandoned Ⓣ (ə'bændənd) *adj* **1** deserted: *an abandoned hut.* **2** forsaken: *an abandoned child.* **3** uninhibited.

abase Ⓣ (ə'beɪs) *vb* **abases, abasing, abased.** (*tr*) **1** to humble or belittle (oneself, etc.). **2** to lower or reduce, as in rank. [C15 *abessen,* from OF *abaissier* to make low. See BASE[2]]

▸**a'basement** *n*

abash Ⓣ (ə'bæʃ) *vb* (*tr; usually passive*) to cause to feel ill at ease, embarrassed, or confused. [C14: from OF *esbair* to be astonished, from *es-* out + *bair* to gape]

▸**a'bashed** *adj*

abate Ⓣ (ə'beɪt) *vb* **abates, abating, abated. 1** to make or become less in amount, intensity, degree, etc. **2** (*tr*) *Law.* **2a** to suppress or terminate (a nuisance). **2b** to suspend or extinguish (a claim or action). **2c** to annul (a writ). **3** (*intr*) *Law.* (of a writ, etc.) to become null and void. [C14: from OF *abatre* to beat down]

▸**a'batement** *n*

abatis *or* **abattis** ('æbətɪs) *n* **1** a rampart of felled trees with their branches outwards. **2** a barbed-wire entanglement before a position. [C18: from F, from *abattre* to fell]

abattoir Ⓣ ('æbəˌtwɑː) *n* another name for **slaughterhouse.** [C19: F, from *abattre* to fell]

abbacy ('æbəsɪ) *n, pl* **abbacies.** the office, term of office, or jurisdiction of an abbot or abbess. [C15: from Church L *abbātia,* from *abbāt-* ABBOT]

abbatial (ə'beɪʃəl) *adj* of an abbot, abbess, or abbey. [C17: from Church L *abbātiālis,* from *abbāt-* ABBOT]

abbé ('æbeɪ) *n* **1** a French abbot. **2** a title used in addressing any other French cleric, such as a priest.

abbess ('æbɪs) *n* the female superior of a convent. [C13: from OF, from Church L *abbātissa*]

Abbevillian (æb'vɪlɪən) *Archaeol.* ◆ *n* **1** the period represented by

THESAURUS

aback *adv* **1 taken aback = surprised,** astonished, astounded, bewildered, disconcerted, flabbergasted (*inf.*), floored (*inf.*), nonplussed, staggered, startled, stunned

abandon *vb* **1, 2 = leave,** desert, forsake, jilt, leave behind, leave in the lurch, let (someone) stew in their own juice, strand **1 = evacuate,** quit, vacate, withdraw from **2 = give up,** abdicate, cede, relinquish, renounce, resign, surrender, waive, yield **3 = stop,** desist, discontinue, drop, forgo, kick (*inf.*) ◆ *n* **6 = wildness,** careless freedom, dash, recklessness, unrestraint, wantonness, wild impulse

Antonyms *vb* ≠ **evacuate:** defend, maintain, uphold ≠ **give up:** claim, hold, keep, take ≠ **stop:** continue ◆ *n* ≠ **wildness:** control, moderation, restraint

abandoned *adj* **1, 2 = left,** cast aside, cast away, cast out, derelict, deserted, discarded, ditched, dropped, forlorn, forsaken, jilted, neglected, outcast, out of the window, rejected, relinquished, stranded **1 = unoccupied,** vacant **3 = uninhibited,** uncontrolled, unrestrained, wild

Antonyms *adj* ≠ **unoccupied:** claimed, kept, maintained, occupied ≠ **uninhibited:** conscious, inhibited, restrained

abandonment *n* **1, 2 = leaving,** dereliction, desertion, forsaking, jilting **1 = evacuation,** quitting, withdrawal from **2 = giving up,** abdication, cession, relinquishment, renunciation, resignation, surrender, waiver **3 = stopping,** desistance, discontinuation, dropping

abase *vb* **1, 2 = humble,** belittle, bring low, cast down, debase, degrade, demean, demote, denigrate, depress, disgrace, dishonour, downgrade, humiliate, lower, mortify, put in one's place, reduce

Antonyms *vb* advance, aggrandize, dignify, elevate, exalt, glorify, honour, prefer, promote, raise, upgrade

abasement *n* **1, 2 = humbling,** belittlement, debasement, degradation, demotion, depression, disgrace, dishonour, downgrading, humiliation, lowering, mortification, reduction, shame

abashed *adj* **= embarrassed,** affronted, ashamed, astounded, bewildered, chagrined, confounded, confused, discomfited, discomposed, disconcerted, discountenanced, dismayed, humbled, humiliated, mortified, perturbed, shamefaced, taken aback

Antonyms *adj* at ease, blatant, bold, brazen, composed, confident, unabashed, unashamed, undaunted, undismayed, unperturbed

abate *vb* **1 = decrease,** alleviate, appease, attenuate, decline, diminish, dull, dwindle, ease, ebb, fade, lessen, let up, mitigate, moderate, quell, reduce, relax, relieve, sink, slacken, slake, slow, subside, taper off, wane, weaken

Antonyms *vb* add to, amplify, augment, boost, enhance, escalate, increase, intensify, magnify, multiply, strengthen

abatement *n* **1 = decrease,** alleviation, allowance, attenuation, cessation, decline, diminution, dulling, dwindling, easing, extenuation, fading, lessening, let-up (*inf.*), mitigation, moderation, quelling, reduction, relief, remission, slackening, slaking, slowing, tapering off, waning, weakening

abattoir *n* **= slaughterhouse,** butchery, shambles

DICTIONARY

Lower Palaeolithic European sites containing the earliest hand axes. ◆ *adj* **2** of this period.

abbey Ⓣ (ˈæbɪ) *n* **1** a building inhabited by a community of monks or nuns. **2** a church built in conjunction with such a building. **3** a community of monks or nuns. [C13: via OF *abeie* from Church L *abbātia* ABBACY]

abbot (ˈæbət) *n* the superior of an abbey of monks. [OE *abbod*, from Church L *abbāt-* (stem of *abbas*), ult. from Aramaic *abbā* father] ▸**ˈabbotship** *or* **ˈabbotcy** *n*

abbreviate Ⓣ (əˈbriːvɪˌeɪt) *vb* **abbreviates, abbreviating, abbreviated.** (*tr*) **1** to shorten (a word or phrase) by contraction or omission of some letters or words. **2** to cut short; curtail. [C15: from p.p. of LL *abbreviāre*, from L *brevis* brief]

abbreviation Ⓣ (əˌbriːvɪˈeɪʃən) *n* **1** a shortened or contracted form of a word or phrase. **2** the process or result of abbreviating.

ABC[1] *n* **1** (*pl in US*) the rudiments of a subject. **2** an alphabetical guide. **3** (*often pl in US*) the alphabet.

ABC[2] *abbrev. for:* **1** American Broadcasting Company. **2** Australian Broadcasting Corporation.

abdicate Ⓣ (ˈæbdɪˌkeɪt) *vb* **abdicates, abdicating, abdicated.** to renounce (a throne, rights, etc.), esp. formally. [C16: from L *abdicāre* to disclaim] ▸**ˌabdiˈcation** *n* ▸**ˈabdiˌcator** *n*

abdomen Ⓣ (ˈæbdəmən) *n* **1** the region of the body of a vertebrate that contains the viscera other than the heart and lungs. **2** the front or surface of this region; belly. **3** (in arthropods) the posterior part of the body behind the thorax. [C16: from L; from ?] ▸**abdominal** (æbˈdɒmɪnᵊl) *adj*

abduct Ⓣ (æbˈdʌkt) *vb* (*tr*) **1** to remove (a person) by force or cunning; kidnap. **2** (of certain muscles) to pull (a leg, arm, etc.) away from the median axis of the body. [C19: from L *abdūcere* to lead away] ▸**abˈduction** *n* ▸**abˈductor** *n*

abeam (əˈbiːm) *adv, adj* (*postpositive*) at right angles to the length of a vessel or aircraft. [C19: A-[2] + BEAM]

abed (əˈbɛd) *adv Arch.* in bed.

Aberdeen Angus (ˌæbəˈdiːn ˈæŋgəs) *n* a black hornless breed of beef cattle originating in Scotland.

aberrant Ⓣ (æˈbɛrənt) *adj* **1** deviating from the normal or usual type. **2** behaving in an abnormal or untypical way. **3** deviating from morality. [rare before C19: from L *aberrāre* to wander away] ▸**abˈerrance** *or* **abˈerrancy** *n*

aberration Ⓣ (ˌæbəˈreɪʃən) *n* **1** deviation from what is normal, expected, or usual. **2** departure from truth, morality, etc. **3** a lapse in control of one's mental faculties. **4** *Optics.* a defect in a lens or mirror that causes either a distorted image or one with coloured fringes. **5** *Astron.* the apparent displacement of a celestial body due to the motion of the observer with the earth.

abet Ⓣ (əˈbɛt) *vb* **abets, abetting, abetted.** (*tr*) to assist or encourage, esp. in wrongdoing. [C14: from OF *abeter* to lure on, from *beter* to bait] ▸**aˈbetment** *n* ▸**aˈbetter** *or* (*esp. Law*) **aˈbettor** *n*

abeyance Ⓣ (əˈbeɪəns) *n* **1** (usually preceded by *in* or *into*) a state of being suspended or put aside temporarily. **2** (usually preceded by *in*) *Law.* an indeterminate state of ownership. [C16–17: from Anglo-F, from OF *abeance* expectation, lit. a gaping after]

ABH *abbrev. for* actual bodily harm.

abhor Ⓣ (əbˈhɔː) *vb* **abhors, abhorring, abhorred.** (*tr*) to detest vehemently; find repugnant. [C15: from L *abhorrēre*, from *ab-* away from + *horrēre* to shudder] ▸**abˈhorrer** *n*

abhorrence Ⓣ (əbˈhɒrəns) *n* **1** a feeling of extreme loathing or aversion. **2** a person or thing that is loathsome.

abhorrent Ⓣ (əbˈhɒrənt) *adj* **1** repugnant; loathsome. **2** (when *postpositive*, foll. by *of*) feeling extreme aversion (for): *abhorrent of vulgarity.* **3** (usually *postpositive* and foll. by *to*) conflicting (with): *abhorrent to common sense.*

abide Ⓣ (əˈbaɪd) *vb* **abides, abiding, abode** *or* **abided. 1** (*tr*) to tolerate; put up with. **2** (*tr*) to accept or submit to. **3** (*intr;* foll. by *by*) **3a** to comply (with): *to abide by the decision.* **3b** to remain faithful (to): *to abide by your promise.* **4** (*intr*) to remain or continue. **5** (*intr*) *Arch.* to dwell. **6** (*tr*) *Arch.* to await in expectation. [OE *ābīdan*, from *a-* (intensive) + *bīdan* to wait] ▸**aˈbider** *n*

abiding Ⓣ (əˈbaɪdɪŋ) *adj* permanent; enduring: *an abiding belief.*

ability Ⓣ (əˈbɪlɪtɪ) *n, pl* **abilities. 1** possession of necessary skill, competence, or power. **2** considerable proficiency; natural capability: *a man of ability.* **3** (*pl*) special talents. [C14: from OF from L *habilitās* aptitude, from *habilis* ABLE]

ab initio Ⓣ *Latin.* (æb ɪˈnɪʃɪˌəʊ) from the start.

abiogenesis (ˌeɪbaɪəʊˈdʒɛnɪsɪs) *n* the hypothetical process by which living organisms arise from inanimate matter. Also called: **spontaneous generation.** [C19: NL, from A-[1] + BIO- + GENESIS]

abject Ⓣ (ˈæbdʒɛkt) *adj* **1** utterly wretched or hopeless. **2** forlorn; dejected. **3** submissive: *an abject apology.* **4** contemptible; despicable: *an abject liar.* [C14 (in the sense: rejected, cast out): from L *abjectus* thrown away, from *abjicere*, from *ab-* away + *jacere* to throw] ▸**abˈjection** *n* ▸**ˈabjectly** *adv* ▸**ˈabjectness** *n*

abjure (əbˈdʒʊə) *vb* **abjures, abjuring, abjured.** (*tr*) **1** to renounce or retract, esp. formally or under oath. **2** to abstain from. [C15: from OF *abjurer* or L *abjurāre* to deny on oath] ▸**ˌabjuˈration** *n* ▸**abˈjurer** *n*

ablation (æbˈleɪʃən) *n* **1** the surgical removal of an organ, structure, or part. **2** the melting or wearing away of a part, such as the heat shield of a space re-entry vehicle on passing through the earth's atmo-

THESAURUS

abbey *n* **1, 2** = **monastery**, cloister, convent, friary, nunnery, priory

abbreviate *vb* **1, 2** = **shorten**, abridge, abstract, clip, compress, condense, contract, curtail, cut, digest, epitomize, précis, reduce, summarize, trim, truncate
Antonyms *vb* amplify, draw out, elongate, expand, extend, increase, lengthen, prolong, protract, spin out, stretch out

abbreviated *adj* **1, 2** = **shortened**, abridged, brief, compressed, concise, condensed, cut, potted, pruned, reduced, shorter, summarized, trimmed
Antonyms *adj* amplified, diffuse, drawn out, expanded, increased, prolonged, protracted, unabbreviated, unabridged

abbreviation *n* **1, 2** = **shortening**, abridgment, abstract, clipping, compendium, compression, condensation, conspectus, contraction, curtailment, digest, epitome, précis, reduction, résumé, summary, synopsis, trimming, truncation

abdicate *vb* = **give up**, abandon, abjure, abnegate, cede, forgo, quit, relinquish, renounce, resign, retire, step down (*inf.*), surrender, vacate, waive, yield

abdication *n* = **giving up**, abandonment, abjuration, abnegation, cession, quitting, relinquishment, renunciation, resignation, retiral (*especially Scot.*), retirement, surrender, waiver, yielding

abdomen *n* **2** = **stomach**, belly, breadbasket (*sl.*), corporation (*inf.*), guts (*sl.*), midriff, midsection, paunch, pot, tummy (*inf.*)

abdominal *adj* **1** = **gastric**, intestinal, stomachic, stomachical, visceral

abduct *vb* **1** = **kidnap**, carry off, make off with, run away with, run off with, seize, snatch (*sl.*)

abduction *n* **1** = **kidnapping**, carrying off, seizure

aberrance *n* **1, 2** = **abnormality**, anomaly, deviance, deviation, divergence, eccentricity, irregularity, oddness, peculiarity, variance
Antonyms *n* conformity, consistency, normality, regularity, uniformity

aberrant *adj* **1, 2** = **abnormal**, anomalous, defective, deviant, divergent, eccentric, irregular, odd, outré, peculiar, queer, rambling, straying, untypical, wandering **3** = **wrong**, corrupt, corrupted, degenerate, depraved, deviant, erroneous, perverse, perverted

aberration *n* **1** = **oddity**, aberrancy, abnormality, anomaly, defect, deviation, divergence, eccentricity, irregularity, lapse, peculiarity, quirk, rambling, straying, wandering

abet *vb* = **help**, aid, assist, back, condone, connive at, promote, sanction, second, succour, support, sustain, uphold = **encourage**, egg on, incite, prompt, spur, urge

abetting *n* = **help**, abetment, abettal, aid, assistance, encouragement, facilitation, furtherance, support

abettor *n* = **accomplice**, accessory = **accomplice**, assistant, associate, backer, confederate, conniver, cooperator, helper, henchman, second = **instigator**, encourager, fomenter, inciter = **instigator**, prompter

abeyance *n* **1 in abeyance** = **shelved**, hanging fire, in cold storage (*inf.*), on ice, pending, suspended

abhor *vb* = **hate**, abominate, detest, execrate, loathe, recoil from, regard with repugnance *or* horror, shrink from, shudder at
Antonyms *vb* admire, adore, cherish, covet, delight in, desire, enjoy, like, love, relish

abhorrence *n* **1** = **hatred**, abomination, animosity, aversion, detestation, disgust, distaste, enmity, execration, hate, horror, loathing, odium, repugnance, revulsion

abhorrent *adj* **1** = **hateful**, abominable, detestable, disgusting, distasteful, execrable, hated, heinous, horrible, horrid, loathsome, obnoxious, obscene, odious, offensive, repellent, repugnant, repulsive, revolting, yucky *or* yukky (*sl.*)

abide *vb* **1** = **tolerate**, accept, bear, brook, endure, hack (*sl.*), put up with, stand, stomach, submit to, suffer **3a** = **obey**, acknowledge, agree to, comply with, conform to, follow, observe, submit to, toe the line **3b** = **carry out**, adhere to, discharge, fulfil, hold to, keep to, persist in, stand by **4** = **last**, continue, endure, persist, remain, survive **5** = **stay**, dwell, linger, live, lodge, reside, rest, sojourn, stop, tarry, wait

abiding *adj* = **everlasting**, constant, continuing, durable, enduring, eternal, fast, firm, immortal, immutable, indissoluble, lasting, permanent, persistent, persisting, steadfast, surviving, tenacious, unchanging, unending
Antonyms *adj* brief, ephemeral, evanescent, fleeting, momentary, passing, short, short-lived, temporary, transient, transitory

ability *n* **1-3** = **skill**, adeptness, aptitude, capability, capacity, competence, competency, craft, dexterity, endowment, energy, expertise, expertness, facility, faculty, flair, force, gift, knack, know-how (*inf.*), potentiality, power, proficiency, qualification, talent
Antonyms *n* inability, incapability, incapacity, incompetence, powerlessness, weakness

ab initio *adv* = **from the beginning**, *ab ovo*, from first principles, from scratch (*inf.*), from the first, from the start, initially, originally, to begin *or* start with

abject *adj* **1, 2** = **miserable**, deplorable, forlorn, hopeless, outcast, pitiable, wretched **3, 4** = **servile**, base, contemptible, cringing, debased, degraded, despicable, dishonourable, fawning, grovelling, humiliating, ignoble, ignominious, low, mean, slavish, sordid, submissive, vile, worthless
Antonyms *adj* ≠ **servile:** august, dignified, distinguished, elevated, eminent, exalted, grand, great, high, lofty, noble, patrician, worthy

abjectness *n* **1, 2** = **misery**, destitution, forlornness, hopelessness, pitiableness, pitifulness, squalor, wretchedness **3, 4** = **degradation**, abjection, baseness, contemptibleness, debase-

DICTIONARY

sphere. **3** the wearing away of a rock or glacier. [C15: from LL *ablatiōn-*, from L *auferre* to carry away]
▸**ablate** (æb'leɪt) *vb*

ablative ('æblətɪv) *Grammar.* ◆ *adj* **1** (in certain inflected languages such as Latin) denoting a case of nouns, pronouns, and adjectives indicating the agent, or the instrument, manner, or place of the action. ◆ *n* **2** the ablative case or a speech element in it.

ablaut ('æblaut) *n Linguistics.* vowel gradation, esp. in Indo-European languages. See **gradation** (sense 5). [G, coined 1819 by Jakob Grimm from *ab* off + *Laut* sound]

ablaze 🅣 (ə'bleɪz) *adj* (*postpositive*), *adv* **1** on fire; burning. **2** brightly illuminated. **3** emotionally aroused.

able 🅣 ('eɪbəl) *adj* **1** (*postpositive*) having the necessary power, resources, skill, opportunity, etc., to do something. **2** capable; talented. **3** *Law.* competent or authorized. [C14: ult. from L *habilis* easy to hold, manageable, from *habēre* to have + *-ilis* -ILE]

-able *suffix forming adjectives.* **1** capable of or deserving of (being acted upon as indicated): *enjoyable; washable.* **2** inclined to; able to; causing: *comfortable; variable.* [via OF from L *-ābilis, -ībilis,* forms of *-bilis,* adjectival suffix]
▸**-ably** *suffix forming adverbs.* ▸**-ability** *suffix forming nouns.*

able-bodied 🅣 *adj* physically strong and healthy; robust.

able-bodied seaman *n* a seaman, esp. one in the merchant navy, who has been trained in certain skills. Also: **able seaman.** Abbrev.: **AB, a.b.**

abled ('eɪbəld) *adj* having a range of physical powers as specified (esp. in **less abled, differently abled**).

ableism ('eɪbəlˌɪzəm) *n* discrimination against disabled or handicapped people.

able rating *n* (esp. in the Royal Navy) a rating who is qualified to perform certain duties of seamanship.

abloom (ə'blu:m) *adj* (*postpositive*) in flower; blooming.

ablution 🅣 (ə'blu:ʃən) *n* **1** the ritual washing of a priest's hands or of sacred vessels. **2** (*often pl*) the act of washing: *perform one's ablutions.* **3** (*pl*) *Mil. inf.* a washing place. [C14: ult. from L *ablūere* to wash away]
▸**ab'lutionary** *adj*

ably ('eɪblɪ) *adv* in a competent or skilful manner.

ABM *abbrev. for* antiballistic missile.

abnegate ('æbnɪˌgeɪt) *vb* **abnegates, abnegating, abnegated.** (*tr*) to deny to oneself; renounce. [C17: from L *abnegāre* to deny]
▸ˌ**abne'gation** *n* ▸**'abneˌgator** *n*

abnormal 🅣 (æb'nɔ:məl) *adj* **1** not normal; deviating from the usual or typical. **2** concerned with abnormal behaviour: *abnormal psychology.* **3** *Inf.* odd; strange. [C19: AB-[1] + NORMAL, replacing earlier *anormal* from Med. L *anormalus,* a blend of LL *anōmalus* ANOMALOUS + L *abnormis* departing from a rule]
▸**ab'normally** *adv*

abnormality 🅣 (ˌæbnɔ:'mælɪtɪ) *n, pl* **abnormalities. 1** an abnormal feature, event, etc. **2** a physical malformation. **3** deviation from the usual.

Abo ('æbəu) *n, pl* **Abos.** (*sometimes not cap.*) *Austral. inf., often derog.* short for **Aborigine** (sense 1).

aboard (ə'bɔ:d) *adv, adj* (*postpositive*), *prep* **1** on, in, onto, or into (a ship, train, etc.). **2** *Naut.* alongside. **3 all aboard!** a warning to passengers to board a vehicle, ship, etc.

abode[1] 🅣 (ə'bəud) *n* a place in which one lives; one's home. [C17: n formed from ABIDE]

abode[2] (ə'bəud) *vb* a past tense and past participle of **abide.**

abolish 🅣 (ə'bɒlɪʃ) *vb* (*tr*) to do away with (laws, regulations, customs, etc.). [C15: from OF, ult. from L *abolēre* to destroy]
▸**a'bolishable** *adj* ▸**a'bolisher** *n* ▸**a'bolishment** *n*

abolition 🅣 (ˌæbə'lɪʃən) *n* **1** the act of abolishing or the state of being abolished; annulment. **2** (*often cap.*) (in British territories) the ending of the slave trade (1807) or of slavery (1833). **3** (*often cap.*) (in the US) the emancipation of slaves, by the Emancipation Proclamation (1863, ratified 1865). [C16: from L *abolitio,* from *abolēre* to destroy]
▸ˌ**abo'litionary** *adj* ▸ˌ**abo'litionism** *n* ▸ˌ**abo'litionist** *n, adj*

abomasum (ˌæbə'meɪsəm) *n* the fourth and last compartment of the stomach of ruminants. [C18: NL, from AB-[1] + *omāsum* bullock's tripe]

A-bomb *n* short for **atomic bomb.**

abominable 🅣 (ə'bɒmɪnəbəl) *adj* **1** offensive; loathsome; detestable. **2** *Inf.* very bad or inferior: *abominable workmanship.* [C14: from L, from *abōminārī* to ABOMINATE]
▸**a'bominably** *adv*

abominable snowman *n* a large manlike or apelike creature alleged to inhabit the Himalayas. Also called: **yeti.** [translation of Tibetan *metohkangmi,* from *metoh* foul + *kangmi* snowman]

abominate 🅣 (ə'bɒmɪˌneɪt) *vb* **abominates, abominating, abominated.** (*tr*) to dislike intensely; detest. [C17: from L *abōminārī* to regard as an ill omen, from *ab-* away from + *ōmin-,* from OMEN]
▸**a'bomiˌnator** *n*

abomination 🅣 (əˌbɒmɪ'neɪʃən) *n* **1** a person or thing that is disgusting or loathsome. **2** an action that is vicious, vile, etc. **3** intense loathing or disgust.

aboriginal 🅣 (ˌæbə'rɪdʒɪnəl) *adj* existing in a place from the earliest known period; indigenous.
▸ˌ**abo'riginally** *adv*

Aboriginal (ˌæbə'rɪdʒɪnəl) *adj* **1** of, relating to, or characteristic of the native peoples of Australia. ◆ *n* **2** another word for **Aborigine** (sense 1).
▸ˌ**Aboˌrigiˈnality** *n*

aborigine 🅣 (ˌæbə'rɪdʒɪnɪ) *n* an original inhabitant of a country or region. [C16: back formation from *aborigines,* from L: inhabitants of Latium in pre-Roman times, associated in folk etymology with *ab origine* from the beginning]

Aborigine (ˌæbə'rɪdʒɪnɪ) *n* **1** Also called: **native Australian, Aboriginal.** a member of a dark-skinned hunting and gathering people who were living in Australia when European settlers arrived. **2** any of the languages of this people.

abort 🅣 (ə'bɔ:t) *vb* **1** to undergo or cause (a woman) to undergo the ter-

THESAURUS

ment, dishonour, humbleness, humiliation, ignominy, lowness, meanness, servility, slavishness, sordidness, submissiveness, vileness, worthlessness

ablaze *adj* **1** = **on fire,** afire, aflame, alight, blazing, burning, fiery, flaming, ignited, lighted **2** = **glowing,** aglow, brilliant, flashing, gleaming, illuminated, incandescent, luminous, radiant, sparkling **3** = **furious,** angry, fit to be tied (*sl.*), foaming at the mouth, fuming, incandescent, incensed, on the warpath, raging **3** = **aroused,** enthusiastic, excited, fervent, frenzied, impassioned, passionate, stimulated

able *adj* **1, 2** = **capable,** accomplished, adept, adequate, adroit, clever, competent, effective, efficient, experienced, expert, fit, fitted, gifted, highly endowed, masterful, masterly, powerful, practised, proficient, qualified, skilful, skilled, strong, talented
Antonyms *adj* amateurish, inadequate, incapable, incompetent, ineffective, inefficient, inept, mediocre, no great shakes (*inf.*), unfit, unskilful, weak

able-bodied *adj* = **strong,** firm, fit, hale, hardy, healthy, hearty, lusty, powerful, robust, sound, staunch, stout, strapping, sturdy, vigorous
Antonyms *adj* ailing, debilitated, feeble, fragile, frail, sickly, tender, weak

ablution *n* **2** *often plural* = **washing,** bath, bathing, cleansing, lavation, purification, shower, wash

abnormal *adj* **1, 3** = **unusual,** aberrant, anomalous, atypical, curious, deviant, eccentric, erratic, exceptional, extraordinary, irregular, monstrous, odd, outré, peculiar, queer, singular, strange, uncommon, unexpected, unnatural, untypical, weird
Antonyms *adj* common, conventional, customary, familiar, natural, normal, ordinary, regular, unexceptional, usual

abnormality *n* **1-3** = **oddity,** aberration, anomaly, atypicalness, bizarreness, deformity, deviation, eccentricity, exception, extraordinariness, flaw, irregularity, monstrosity, peculiarity, queerness, singularity, strangeness, uncommonness, unexpectedness, unnaturalness, untypicalness, unusualness, weirdness

abnormally *adv* **1, 3** = **unusually,** atypically, bizarrely, disproportionately, exceptionally, excessively, extraordinarily, extremely, fantastically, freakishly, inordinately, in the extreme, oddly, overly, particularly, peculiarly, prodigiously, singularly, strangely, subnormally, supernormally, uncannily, uncommonly, unnaturally

abode[1] *n* = **home,** domicile, dwelling, dwelling-place, habitat, habitation, house, lodging, pad (*sl.*), quarters, residence

abolish *vb* = **do away with,** abrogate, annihilate, annul, axe (*inf.*), cancel, destroy, eliminate, end, eradicate, expunge, exterminate, extinguish, extirpate, invalidate, nullify, obliterate, overthrow, overturn, put an end to, quash, repeal, repudiate, rescind, revoke, stamp out, subvert, suppress, terminate, vitiate, void, wipe out
Antonyms *vb* authorize, continue, create, establish, found, institute, introduce, legalize, promote, reinstate, reintroduce, restore, revive, sustain

abolition *n* **1** = **ending,** abrogation, annihilation, annulment, cancellation, destruction, elimination, end, eradication, expunction, extermination, extinction, extirpation, invalidation, nullification, obliteration, overthrow, overturning, quashing, repeal, repudiation, rescission, revocation, stamping out, subversion, suppression, termination, vitiation, voiding, wiping out, withdrawal

abominable *adj* **1** = **terrible,** abhorrent, accursed, atrocious, base, contemptible, despicable, detestable, disgusting, execrable, foul, hateful, heinous, hellish, horrible, horrid, loathsome, nauseous, obnoxious, obscene, odious, repellent, reprehensible, repugnant, repulsive, revolting, vile, villainous, wretched
Antonyms *adj* admirable, agreeable, charming, commendable, delightful, desirable, good, laudable, likable *or* likeable, lovable, pleasant, pleasing, wonderful

abominably *adv* **1** = **terribly,** abhorrently, contemptibly, deplorably, despicably, detestably, disgustingly, dreadfully, execrably, foully, heinously, hideously, horribly, horridly, nauseatingly, obnoxiously, odiously, offensively, reprehensibly, repugnantly, repulsively, revoltingly, shamefully, unpalatably, vilely
Antonyms *adv* admirably, commendably, delightfully, excellently, impeccably, perfectly, wonderfully

abominate *vb* = **hate,** abhor, detest, execrate, loathe, recoil from, regard with repugnance, shudder at
Antonyms *vb* admire, adore, cherish, dote on, esteem, idolize, love, revere, treasure, worship

abomination *n* **1** = **evil,** anathema, bête noire, bugbear, curse, disgrace, horror, plague, shame, torment **3** = **hatred,** abhorrence, antipathy, aversion, detestation, disgust, distaste, execration, hate, horror, loathing, odium, repugnance, revulsion

aboriginal *adj* = **native,** ancient, autochthonous, earliest, first, indigenous, original, primary, primeval, primitive, primordial, pristine

aborigine *n* = **native,** aboriginal, autochthon, indigene, original inhabitant

abort *vb* **1, 2, 5** = **terminate** (*a pregnancy*), mis-

DICTIONARY

mination of pregnancy before the fetus is viable. **2** (*tr*) to cause (a fetus) to be expelled from the womb before it is viable. **3** (*intr*) to fail to come to completion. **4** (*tr*) to stop the development of; cause to be abandoned. **5** (*intr*) to give birth to a dead or nonviable fetus. **6** (of a space flight or other undertaking) to fail or terminate prematurely. **7** (*intr*) (of an organism or part of an organism) to fail to develop into the mature form. ◆ *n* **8** the premature termination or failure of (a space flight, etc.). [C16: from L *abortāre,* from *aborīrī* to miscarry, from *ab-* wrongly + *orīrī* to be born]

abortifacient (əˌbɔːtɪˈfeɪʃənt) *adj* **1** causing abortion. ◆ *n* **2** a drug or agent that causes abortion.

abortion **T** (əˈbɔːʃən) *n* **1** an operation or other procedure to terminate pregnancy before the fetus is viable. **2** the premature termination of pregnancy by spontaneous or induced expulsion of a nonviable fetus from the uterus. **3** an aborted fetus. **4** a failure to develop to completion or maturity. **5** a person or thing that is deformed.

abortionist (əˈbɔːʃənɪst) *n* a person who performs abortions, esp. illegally.

abortion pill *n* a drug, such as mifepristone (RU 486), used to terminate a pregnancy in its earliest stage.

abortive **T** (əˈbɔːtɪv) *adj* **1** failing to achieve a purpose; fruitless. **2** (of organisms) imperfectly developed. **3** causing abortion.

ABO system *n* a system for classifying human blood on the basis of the presence or absence of two antigens in the red cells: there are four such blood types (A, B, AB, and O).

aboulia (əˈbuːlɪə, -ˈbjuː-) *n* a variant spelling of **abulia.**

abound **T** (əˈbaʊnd) *vb* (*intr*) **1** to exist or occur in abundance. **2** (foll. by *with* or *in*) to be plentifully supplied (with): *the fields abound in corn.* [C14: via OF from L *abundāre* to overflow, from *undāre* to flow, from *unda* wave]

about **T** (əˈbaʊt) *prep* **1** relating to; concerning. **2** near or close to. **3** carried on: *I haven't any money about me.* **4** on every side of. **5** active in or engaged in. ◆ *adv* **6** near in number, time, degree, etc.: *about 50 years old.* **7** nearby. **8** here and there: *walk about to keep warm.* **9** all around; on every side. **10** in or to the opposite direction. **11** in rotation or revolution: *turn and turn about.* **12** used in informal phrases to indicate understatement: *it's about time you stopped.* **13** *Arch.* around. **14 about to. 14a** on the point of; intending to: *she was about to jump.* **14b** (*with a negative*) determined not to: *nobody is about to miss it.* ◆ *adj* **15** (*predicative*) active; astir after sleep: *up and about.* **16** (*predicative*) in existence, current, or in circulation: *there aren't many about nowadays.* [OE *abūtan, onbūtan,* from ON + *būtan* outside]

about turn **T** *or US* **about face** *sentence substitute.* **1** a military command to a formation of men to reverse the direction in which they are facing. ◆ *n* **about-turn** *or US* **about-face. 2** a complete change of opinion, direction, etc. ◆ *vb* **about-turn** *or US* **about-face. 3** (*intr*) to perform an about-turn.

above **T** (əˈbʌv) *prep* **1** on top of or higher than; over. **2** greater than in quantity or degree: *above average.* **3** superior to or prior to: *to place honour above wealth.* **4** too high-minded for: *above petty gossiping.* **5** too respected for; beyond: *above suspicion.* **6** too difficult to be understood by: *the talk was above me.* **7** louder or higher than (other noise). **8** in preference to. **9** north of. **10** upstream from. **11 above all.** most of all; especially. **12 above and beyond.** in addition to. ◆ *adv* **13** in or to a higher place: *the sky above.* **14a** in a previous place (in something written). **14b** (*in combination*): *the above-mentioned clause.* **15** higher in rank or position. **16** in or concerned with heaven. ◆ *n* **17 the above.** something previously mentioned. ◆ *adj* **18** appearing in a previous place (in something written). [OE *abufan,* from *a-* on + *bufan* above]

above board **T** *adj* (**aboveboard** *when prenominal*), *adv* in the open; without dishonesty, concealment, or fraud.

abracadabra **T** (ˌæbrəkəˈdæbrə) *interj* **1** a spoken formula, used esp. by conjurors. ◆ *n* **2** a word used in incantations, etc., considered to possess magic powers. **3** gibberish. [C17: magical word used in certain Gnostic writings, ? rel. to Gk *Abraxas,* a Gnostic deity]

abrade **T** (əˈbreɪd) *vb* **abrades, abrading, abraded.** (*tr*) to scrape away or wear down by friction. [C17: from L *abrādere,* from AB-[1] + *rādere* to scrape]
▸**aˈbrader** *n*

abranchiate (əˈbræŋkɪɪt, -ˌeɪt) *or* **abranchial** *adj Zool.* having no gills. [C19: A-[1] + BRANCHIATE]

abrasion **T** (əˈbreɪʒən) *n* **1** the process of scraping or wearing down by friction. **2** a scraped area or spot; graze. **3** *Geog.* the effect of mechanical erosion of rock, esp. a river bed, by rock fragments scratching and scraping it. [C17: from Med. L *abrāsiōn-,* from L *abrādere* to ABRADE]

abrasive **T** (əˈbreɪsɪv) *n* **1** a substance or material such as sandpaper, pumice, or emery, used for cleaning, smoothing, or polishing. ◆ *adj* **2** causing abrasion; rough. **3** irritating in manner or personality.

abreaction (ˌæbrɪˈækʃən) *n Psychoanal.* the release and expression of emotional tension associated with repressed ideas by bringing those ideas into consciousness.

abreast **T** (əˈbrɛst) *adj* (*postpositive*) **1** alongside each other and facing in the same direction. **2** (foll. by *of* or *with*) up to date (with).

abridge **T** (əˈbrɪdʒ) *vb* **abridges, abridging, abridged.** (*tr*) **1** to reduce the length of (a written work) by condensing. **2** to curtail. [C14: via OF *abregier* from LL *abbreviāre* to shorten]
▸**aˈbridgable** *or* **aˈbridgeable** *adj* ▸**aˈbridger** *n*

abridgment **T** *or* **abridgement** (əˈbrɪdʒmənt) *n* **1** a shortened version of a written work. **2** the act of abridging or state of being abridged.

abroad **T** (əˈbrɔːd) *adv, adj* (*postpositive*). **1** to or in a foreign country or countries. **2** (of rumours, etc.) in general circulation. **3** out in the open. **4** over a wide area. [C13: from A-[2] + BROAD]

abrogate (ˈæbrəʊˌgeɪt) *vb* **abrogates, abrogating, abrogated.** (*tr*) to cancel or revoke formally or officially. [C16: from L *abrogātus* repealed, from AB-[1] + *rogāre* to propose (a law)]
▸ˌ**abroˈgation** *n* ▸ˈ**abroˌgator** *n*

abrupt **T** (əˈbrʌpt) *adj* **1** sudden; unexpected. **2** brusque or brief in speech, manner, etc. **3** (of a style of writing or speaking) disconnected. **4** precipitous; steep. **5** *Bot.* truncate. **6** *Geol.* (of strata) cropping out suddenly. [C16: from L *abruptus* broken off, from AB-[1] + *rumpere* to break]
▸**abˈruptly** *adv* ▸**abˈruptness** *n*

THESAURUS

carry **3, 4** = **stop**, arrest, axe, call off, check, end, fail, halt, terminate

abortion *n* **1, 2** = **termination**, aborticide, deliberate miscarriage, feticide, miscarriage **4, 5** = **failure**, disappointment, fiasco, misadventure, monstrosity, vain effort

abortive *adj* **1** = **failed**, bootless, failing, fruitless, futile, idle, ineffectual, miscarried, unavailing, unsuccessful, useless, vain **2** = **imperfectly developed**, incomplete, rudimentary, stunted

abound *vb* **1, 2** = **be plentiful**, be jammed with, be packed with, crowd, flourish, increase, infest, luxuriate, overflow, proliferate, superabound, swarm, swell, teem, thrive

about *prep* **1** = **regarding**, anent (*Scot.*), as regards, concerned with, concerning, connected with, dealing with, on, re, referring to, relating to, relative to, respecting, touching, with respect to **2** = **near**, adjacent to, beside, circa (*used with dates*), close to, nearby **4** = **around**, encircling, on all sides, round, surrounding ◆ *adv* **6** = **nearly**, almost, approaching, approximately, around, close to, more or less, nearing, roughly **8** = **here and there**, from place to place, hither and thither, to and fro **14a about to** = **on the point of**, intending to, on the verge *or* brink of, ready to ◆ *adj* **15** = **around**, active, astir, in motion, present, stirring

about-turn *n* **2** = **change of direction**, reversal, reverse, right about (turn), turnabout, turnaround, U-turn, volte-face ◆ *vb* **3** = **change direction**, do *or* perform a U-turn *or* volte-face, face the opposite direction, reverse, turn about *or* around, turn through 180 degrees, volte-face

above *prep* **1** = **over**, atop, beyond, exceeding, higher than, on top of, upon **3** = **superior to**, before, beyond, exceeding, prior to, surpassing ◆ *adv* **13** = **overhead**, aloft, atop, in heaven, on high ◆ *adj* **14** = **preceding**, aforementioned, aforesaid, earlier, foregoing, previous, prior
Antonyms *prep* ≠ **over:** below, beneath, under, underneath ≠ **superior to:** inferior, lesser, less than, lower than, subordinate

above board *adj* **1** = **honest**, candid, fair and square, forthright, frank, guileless, honourable, kosher (*inf.*), legitimate, on the up and up, open, overt, square, straight, straightforward, true, trustworthy, truthful, upfront (*inf.*), upright, veracious ◆ *adv* **1** = **honestly**, candidly, forthrightly, frankly, honourably, openly, overtly, straightforwardly, truly, truthfully, uprightly, veraciously, without guile
Antonyms *adj* ≠ **honest:** clandestine, crooked, deceitful, deceptive, devious, dishonest, fraudulent, furtive, secret, secretive, shady, sly, sneaky, underhand

abracadabra *n* **1, 2** = **spell**, chant, charm, conjuration, hocus-pocus, incantation, invocation, magic, mumbo jumbo, sorcery, voodoo, witchcraft

abrade *vb* = **scrape**, erase, erode, file, grind, rub off, scour, scrape away, scrape out, wear away, wear down, wear off

abrasion *n* **1** = **scraping**, abrading, chafing, erosion, friction, grating, rubbing, scouring, scratching, scuffing, wearing away, wearing down

abrasive *n* **1** = **scourer**, abradant, burnisher, grinder, scarifier ◆ *adj* **2** = **rough**, chafing, erosive, frictional, grating, scraping, scratching, scratchy, scuffing **3** = **unpleasant**, annoying, biting, caustic, cutting, galling, grating, hurtful, irritating, nasty, rough, sharp, vitriolic

abreast *adj* **1** = **alongside**, beside, level, neck and neck, shoulder to shoulder, side by side **2 abreast of** = **informed about**, acquainted with, *au courant* with, *au fait* with, conversant with, familiar with, in the picture about, in touch with, keeping one's finger on the pulse of, knowledgeable about, up to date with, up to speed with

abridge *vb* **1, 2** = **shorten**, abbreviate, abstract, clip, compress, concentrate, condense, contract, curtail, cut, cut down, decrease, digest, diminish, downsize, epitomize, lessen, précis, reduce, summarize, synopsize (*US*), trim
Antonyms *vb* amplify, augment, enlarge, expand, extend, go into detail, lengthen, prolong, protract, spin out, stretch out

abridged *adj* **1, 2** = **shortened**, abbreviated, brief, compressed, concise, condensed, curtailed, cut, diminished, potted (*inf.*), pruned, reduced, shorter, summarized, trimmed
Antonyms *adj* amplified, diffuse, drawn out, expanded, increased, prolonged, protracted, unabbreviated, unabridged

abridgment *n* **1, 2** = **shortening**, abbreviation, abstract, compendium, condensation, conspectus, contraction, curtailment, cutting, decrease, digest, diminishing, diminution, epitome, lessening, limitation, outline, précis, reduction, restraint, restriction, résumé, summary, synopsis

abroad *adv* **1** = **overseas**, beyond the sea, in foreign lands, out of the country **2-4** = **about**, at large, away, circulating, current, elsewhere, extensively, far, far and wide, forth, in circulation, out, out-of-doors, outside, publicly, widely, without

abrupt *adj* **1** = **sudden**, hasty, headlong, hurried, precipitate, quick, surprising, swift, unanticipated, unexpected, unforeseen **2** = **curt**,

ABS brake *n* another name for **antilock brake.** [from G *Antiblockiersystem*]

abscess ❶ ('æbsɛs) *n* **1** a localized collection of pus formed as the product of inflammation. ◆ *vb* **2** (*intr*) to form such a collection of pus. [C16: from L *abscessus,* from *abscēdere* to go away]
▸**'abscessed** *adj*

abscissa (æb'sɪsə) *n, pl* **abscissas** *or* **abscissae** (-'sɪsi:). the horizontal or *x*-coordinate of a point in a two-dimensional system of Cartesian coordinates. It is the distance from the *y*-axis measured parallel to the *x*-axis. Cf. **ordinate.** [C17: NL, orig. *linea abscissa* a cut-off line]

abscission (æb'sɪʒən) *n* **1** the separation of leaves, branches, flowers, and bark from plants. **2** the act of cutting off. [C17: from L, from AB-[1] + *scissiō* a cleaving]

abscond ❶ (əb'skɒnd) *vb* (*intr*) to run away secretly, esp. to avoid prosecution or punishment. [C16: from L *abscondere,* from *abs-* AB-[1] + *condere* to stow]
▸**ab'sconder** *n*

abseil ('æbsaɪl) *Mountaineering.* ◆ *vb* (*intr*) **1** to descend a steep slope or vertical drop by a rope secured from above and coiled around one's body. ◆ *n* **2** an instance or the technique of abseiling. [C20: from G *abseilen,* from *ab-* down + *Seil* rope]

absence ❶ ('æbsəns) *n* **1** the state of being away. **2** the time during which a person or thing is away. **3** the fact of being without something; lack. [C14: via OF from L *absentia,* from *absēns* a being away]

absent ❶ *adj* ('æbsənt). **1** away or not present. **2** lacking. **3** inattentive. ◆ *vb* (æb'sɛnt). **4** (*tr*) to remove (oneself) or keep away. [C14: from L *absent-,* from *abesse* to be away]
▸**ab'senter** *n*

absentee ❶ (ˌæbsən'ti:) *n* **a** a person who is absent. **b** (*as modifier*): *an absentee landlord.*

absenteeism (ˌæbsən'ti:ɪzəm) *n* persistent absence from work, school, etc.

absent-minded ❶ *adj* preoccupied; forgetful.
▸ˌ**absent-'mindedly** *adv* ▸ˌ**absent-'mindedness** *n*

absinthe *or* **absinth** ('æbsɪnθ) *n* **1** a potent green alcoholic drink, originally having high wormwood content. **2** another name for **wormwood** (the plant). [C15: via F and L from Gk *apsinthion* wormwood]

absolute ❶ ('æbsəˌlu:t) *adj* **1** complete; perfect. **2** free from limitations, restrictions, or exceptions. **3** despotic: *an absolute ruler.* **4** undoubted; certain: *the absolute truth.* **5** not dependent on, conditioned by, or relative to anything else; independent: *absolute humidity; absolute units.* **6** pure; unmixed: *absolute alcohol.* **7** (of a grammatical construction) syntactically independent of the main clause, as for example the construction *Joking apart* in the sentence *Joking apart, we'd better leave now.* **8** *Grammar.* (of a transitive verb) used without a direct object, as the verb *intimidate* in the sentence *His intentions are good, but his rough manner tends to intimidate.* **9** *Grammar.* (of an adjective) used as a noun, as for instance *young* and *aged* in the sentence *The young care little for the aged.* ◆ *n* **10** something that is absolute. [C14: from L *absolūtus* unconditional, from *absolvere.* See ABSOLVE]

Absolute ('æbsəˌlu:t) *n* (*sometimes not cap.*) *Philosophy.* **1** the ultimate basis of reality. **2** that which is totally unconditioned, unrestricted, pure, perfect, or complete.

absolutely ❶ (ˌæbsə'lu:tlɪ) *adv* **1** in an absolute manner, esp. completely or perfectly. ◆ *sentence substitute.* **2** yes; certainly.

absolute magnitude *n* the magnitude a given star would have if it were 10 parsecs (32.6 light years) from earth.

absolute majority *n* a number of votes totalling over 50 per cent, such as the total number of votes or seats obtained by a party that beats the combined opposition.

absolute pitch *n* **1** Also called: **perfect pitch.** the ability to identify the pitch of a note, or to sing a given note, without reference to one previously sounded. **2** the exact pitch of a note determined by vibration per second.

absolute temperature *n* another name for **thermodynamic temperature.**

absolute value *n* **1** the positive real number equal to a given real but disregarding its sign: written $|x|$. Where x is positive, $|x| = x = |-x|$. **2** Also called: **modulus.** a measure of the magnitude of a complex number.

absolute zero *n* the lowest temperature theoretically attainable, at which the particles constituting matter would be at rest: equivalent to –273.15°C or –459.67°F.

absolution ❶ (ˌæbsə'lu:ʃən) *n* **1** the act of absolving or the state of being absolved; release from guilt, obligation, or punishment. **2** *Christianity.* **2a** a formal remission of sin pronounced by a priest in the sacrament of penance. **2b** the form of words granting such a remission. [C12: from L *absolūtiōn-* acquittal, from *absolvere* to ABSOLVE]

absolutism ❶ ('æbsəlu:ˌtɪzəm) *n* the principle or practice of a political system in which unrestricted power is vested in a monarch, dictator, etc.; despotism.
▸**abso'lutist** *n, adj*

absolve ❶ (əb'zɒlv) *vb* **absolves, absolving, absolved.** (*tr*) **1** (usually foll. by *from*) to release from blame, sin, obligation, or responsibility. **2** to pronounce not guilty. [C15: from L *absolvere,* from AB-[1] + *solvere* to make loose]
▸**ab'solver** *n*

absorb ❶ (əb'sɔ:b) *vb* (*tr*) **1** to soak or suck up (liquids). **2** to engage or occupy (the interest or time) of (someone). **3** to receive or take in (the energy of an impact). **4** *Physics.* to take in (all or part of incident radiated energy) and retain it. **5** to take in or assimilate; incorporate. **6** to pay for as part of a commercial transaction: *the distributor absorbed the cost of transport.* **7** *Chem.* to cause to undergo a process in which one substance permeates into or is dissolved by a liquid or solid: *porous solids absorb water.* [C15: via OF from L *absorbēre,* from AB-[1] + *sorbēre* to suck]
▸**abˌsorba'bility** *n* ▸**ab'sorbable** *adj*

THESAURUS

blunt, brisk, brusque, clipped, direct, discourteous, gruff, impatient, impolite, monosyllabic, rough, rude, short, snappish, snappy, terse, unceremonious, uncivil, ungracious **3** = **uneven**, broken, disconnected, discontinuous, irregular, jerky **4** = **steep**, precipitous, sharp, sheer, sudden
Antonyms *adj* ≠ **sudden:** easy, leisurely, slow, thoughtful, unhurried ≠ **curt:** civil, courteous, gracious, polite ≠ **steep:** gradual

abruptly *adv* **1** = **suddenly**, all at once, all of a sudden, hastily, hurriedly, precipitately, quickly, sharply, short, unexpectedly **2** = **curtly**, bluntly, briskly, brusquely, gruffly, rudely, sharply, shortly, snappily, tersely
Antonyms *adv* ≠ **suddenly:** bit by bit, gently, gradually, little by little, progressively, slowly, steadily ≠ **curtly:** courteously, politely

abruptness *n* **1** = **suddenness**, precipitateness, unexpectedness **2** = **curtness**, bluntness, briskness, brusqueness, brusquerie, gruffness, sharpness, shortness, terseness
Antonyms *n* ≠ **suddenness:** gradualness, steadiness ≠ **curtness:** courteousness, politeness

abscess *n* **1** = **boil**, bubo, carbuncle, felon, furuncle (*Pathology*), gathering, gumboil, infection, inflammation, parulis (*Pathology*), pustule, whitlow

abscond *vb* = **flee**, bolt, clear out, decamp, disappear, escape, flit (*inf.*), fly, make off, run off, skedaddle (*inf.*), slip away, sneak away, steal away

absence *n* **1** = **nonattendance**, absenteeism, nonappearance, truancy **3** = **lack**, default, defect, deficiency, need, nonexistence, omission, privation, unavailability, want

absent *adj* **1** = **missing**, away, elsewhere, gone, lacking, nonattendant, nonexistent, not present, out, truant, unavailable, wanting **3** = **absent-minded**, absorbed, abstracted, bemused, blank, daydreaming, distracted, dreamy, empty, faraway, heedless, inattentive, musing, oblivious, preoccupied, unaware, unconscious, unheeding, unthinking, vacant, vague ◆ *vb* **4** = **stay away**, abscond, bunk off (*sl.*), depart, keep away, play truant, remove, slope off (*inf.*), truant, withdraw
Antonyms *adj* ≠ **missing:** attendant, in attendance, present ≠ **absent-minded:** alert, attentive, aware, conscious, thoughtful ◆ *vb* ≠ **stay away:** attend, show up (*inf.*)

absentee *n* = **nonattender**, no-show, stay-at-home, stayaway, truant

absent-minded *adj* = **vague**, absent, absorbed, abstracted, bemused, distracted, ditzy *or* ditsy (*sl.*), dreaming, dreamy, engrossed, faraway, forgetful, heedless, inattentive, musing, oblivious, preoccupied, unaware, unconscious, unheeding, unthinking
Antonyms *adj* alert, awake, observant, on one's toes, on the ball, perceptive, quick, vigilant, wary, wide-awake

absent-mindedness *n* = **vagueness**, absence of mind, abstraction, daydreaming, distractedness, forgetfulness, inattention, musing, obliviousness, preoccupation, woolgathering

absolute *adj* **1** = **total**, arrant, complete, consummate, deep-dyed (*usually derogatory*), downright, entire, full-on (*inf.*), out-and-out, outright, perfect, pure, sheer, thorough, unadulterated, unalloyed, unmitigated, unmixed, unqualified, utter **3** = **supreme**, absolutist, arbitrary, autarchical, autocratic, autonomous, despotic, dictatorial, full, peremptory, sovereign, tyrannical, unbounded, unconditional, unlimited, unqualified, unquestionable, unrestrained, unrestricted **4** = **definite**, actual, categorical, certain, conclusive, decided, decisive, exact, genuine, infallible, positive, precise, sure, unambiguous, unequivocal, unquestionable

absolutely *adv* **1** = **totally**, completely, consummately, entirely, every inch, fully, lock, stock and barrel, one hundred per cent, perfectly, purely, thoroughly, to the hilt, unmitigatedly, utterly, wholly **3** = **supremely**, arbitrarily, autocratically, autonomously, despotically, dictatorially, fully, peremptorily, sovereignly, tyrannically, unconditionally, unquestionably, unrestrainedly, without qualification **4** = **definitely**, actually, categorically, certainly, conclusively, decidedly, decisively, exactly, genuinely, infallibly, positively, precisely, surely, truly, unambiguously, unequivocally, unquestionably
Antonyms *adv* ≠ **totally:** fairly, probably, reasonably, somewhat

absolution *n* **1, 2** = **forgiveness**, acquittal, amnesty, deliverance, discharge, dispensation, exculpation, exemption, exoneration, freeing, indulgence, liberation, mercy, pardon, release, remission, setting free, shriving, vindication

absolutism *n* = **dictatorship**, absoluteness, arbitrariness, autarchy, authoritarianism, autocracy, despotism, totalitarianism, tyranny

absolutist *n* = **dictator**, arbiter, authoritarian, autocrat, despot, totalitarian, tyrant

absolve *vb* **1, 2** = **forgive**, acquit, clear, deliver, discharge, exculpate, excuse, exempt, exonerate, free, let off, liberate, loose, pardon, release, remit, set free, shrive, vindicate
Antonyms *vb* blame, censure, charge, condemn, convict, damn, denounce, excoriate, pass sentence on, reprehend, reproach, reprove, sentence, upbraid

absorb *vb* **1, 5** = **soak up**, assimilate, consume, devour, digest, drink in, exhaust, imbibe, incorporate, ingest, osmose, receive, suck up, take in **2** = **preoccupy**, captivate, engage, engross, en-

absorbed Ⓣ (əbˈsɔːbd) *adj* engrossed; deeply interested.
absorbed dose *n* the amount of energy transferred by radiation to a unit mass of absorbing material.
absorbent Ⓣ (əbˈsɔːbənt) *adj* **1** able to absorb. ◆ *n* **2** a substance that absorbs.
▸**abˈsorbency** *n*
absorbing Ⓣ (əbˈsɔːbɪŋ) *adj* occupying one's interest or attention.
▸**abˈsorbingly** *adv*
absorptance (əbˈsɔːptəns) *or* **absorption factor** *n Physics.* the ability of an object to absorb radiation, measured as the ratio of absorbed flux to incident flux. [C20: from ABSORPTION + -ANCE]
absorption Ⓣ (əbˈsɔːpʃən) *n* **1** the process of absorbing or the state of being absorbed. **2** *Physiol.* **2a** normal assimilation by the tissues of the products of digestion. **2b** the process of taking up various fluids, drugs, etc., through the mucous membranes or skin. [C16: from L *absorptiōn-*, from *absorbēre* to ABSORB]
▸**abˈsorptive** *adj*
absorption spectrum *n* the characteristic pattern of dark lines or bands that occurs when electromagnetic radiation is passed through an absorbing medium into a spectroscope. See also **emission spectrum.**
abstain Ⓣ (əbˈsteɪn) *vb* (*intr;* usually foll. by *from*) **1** to choose to refrain. **2** to refrain from voting, esp. in a committee, legislature, etc. [C14: via OF from L *abstinēre,* from *abs-* AB-[1] + *tenēre* to hold]
▸**abˈstainer** *n*
abstemious Ⓣ (əbˈstiːmɪəs) *adj* sparing, esp. in the consumption of alcohol or food. [C17: from L *abstēmius,* from *abs-* AB-[1] + *tēm-,* from *tēmētum* intoxicating drink]
▸**abˈstemiously** *adv* ▸**abˈstemiousness** *n*
abstention Ⓣ (əbˈstɛnʃən) *n* **1** the act of refraining or abstaining. **2** the act of withholding one's vote. [C16: from LL *abstentiōn;* see ABSTAIN]
abstinence Ⓣ (ˈæbstɪnəns) *n* the act or practice of refraining from some action or from the use of something, esp. alcohol. [C13: via OF from L *abstinentia,* from *abstinēre* to ABSTAIN]
▸**ˈabstinent** *adj*
abstract Ⓣ *adj* (ˈæbstrækt). **1** having no reference to material objects or specific examples. **2** not applied or practical; theoretical. **3** hard to understand. **4** denoting art characterized by geometric, formalized, or otherwise nonrepresentational qualities. ◆ *n* (ˈæbstrækt). **5** a condensed version of a piece of writing, speech, etc.; summary. **6** an abstract term or idea. **7** an abstract painting, sculpture, etc. **8 in the abstract.** without reference to specific circumstances. ◆ *vb* (æbˈstrækt). (*tr*) **9** to regard theoretically. **10** to form a general idea of (something) by abstraction. **11** (ˈæbstrækt). (*also intr*) to summarize. **12** to remove or extract. [C14 (in the sense: extracted): from L *abstractus* drawn off, from *abs-* AB-[1] + *trahere* to draw]
abstracted Ⓣ (æbˈstræktɪd) *adj* **1** lost in thought; preoccupied. **2** taken out or separated.
▸**abˈstractedly** *adv*
abstract expressionism *n* a school of painting in the 1940s that combined the spontaneity of expressionism with abstract forms in apparently random compositions.
abstraction Ⓣ (æbˈstrækʃən) *n* **1** preoccupation. **2** the process of formulating generalized concepts by extracting common qualities from specific examples. **3** a concept formulated in this way: *good and evil are abstractions.* **4** an abstract painting, sculpture, etc.
▸**abˈstractive** *adj*
abstract noun *n* a noun that refers to an abstract concept, as for example *peace, joy,* etc.
abstract term *n* in traditional logic, the name of an attribute of many individuals: *humanity is an abstract term.*
abstruse Ⓣ (əbˈstruːs) *adj* not easy to understand. [C16: from L *abstrūsus,* from *abs-* AB-[1] + *trūdere* to thrust]
▸**abˈstrusely** *adv* ▸**abˈstruseness** *n*
absurd Ⓣ (əbˈsɜːd) *adj* **1** at variance with reason; manifestly false. **2** ludicrous; ridiculous. [C16: via F from L *absurdus,* from AB-[1] (intensive) + *surdus* dull-sounding]
▸**abˈsurdity** *or* **abˈsurdness** *n* ▸**abˈsurdly** *adv*
ABTA (ˈæbtə) *n acronym for* Association of British Travel Agents.
abulia *or* **aboulia** (əˈbuːlɪə, -ˈbjuː-) *n Psychiatry.* a pathological inability to take decisions. [C19: NL, from Gk *aboulia* lack of resolution, from A-[1] + *boulē* will]
abundance Ⓣ (əˈbʌndəns) *n* **1** a copious supply; great amount. **2** fullness or benevolence: *from the abundance of my heart.* **3** degree of plentifulness: *the abundance of uranium-235 in natural uranium.* **4** Also: **abondance.** a call in solo whist undertaking to make nine tricks. **5** affluence. [C14: via OF from L, from *abundāre* to ABOUND]
abundant Ⓣ (əˈbʌndənt) *adj* **1** existing in plentiful supply. **2** (*postpositive;* foll. by *in*) having a plentiful supply (of). [C14: from L *abundant-,* p.p. of *abundāre* to ABOUND]
▸**aˈbundantly** *adv*

THESAURUS

wrap, fascinate, fill, fill up, fix, hold, immerse, monopolize, occupy, rivet
absorbed *adj* = **preoccupied**, captivated, concentrating, engaged, engrossed, fascinated, fixed, held, immersed, involved, lost, occupied, rapt, riveted, up to one's ears, wrapped up
absorbency *n* **1** = **permeability**, ability to soak up *or* take in, permeableness, perviousness, porousness, receptiveness, retentiveness, sponginess
Antonyms *n* impermeability, impermeableness, imperviousness
absorbent *adj* **1** = **permeable**, absorptive, assimilative, blotting, imbibing, penetrable, pervious, porous, receptive, spongy
absorbing *adj* = **fascinating**, arresting, captivating, engrossing, gripping, interesting, intriguing, riveting, spellbinding
Antonyms *adj* boring, dreary, dull, humdrum, mind-numbing, monotonous, tedious, tiresome, unexciting
absorption *n* **1** = **soaking up**, assimilation, consumption, digestion, exhaustion, incorporation, osmosis, sucking up **1** = **concentration**, captivation, engagement, fascination, holding, immersion, intentness, involvement, occupation, preoccupation, raptness
abstain *vb* **1** = **refrain**, avoid, cease, decline, deny (oneself), desist, fast, forbear, forgo, give up, keep from, kick (*inf.*), refuse, renounce, shun, stop, withhold
Antonyms *vb* abandon oneself, give in, indulge, partake, yield
abstemious *adj* = **self-denying**, abstinent, ascetic, austere, continent, frugal, moderate, sober, sparing, temperate
Antonyms *adj* edacious (*chiefly humorous*), gluttonous, greedy, immoderate, incontinent, intemperate, self-indulgent
abstemiousness *n* = **self-denial**, abstinence, asceticism, austerity, continence, forbearance, frugality, moderation, restraint, self-restraint, sobriety, temperance
Antonyms *n* dissipation, drunkenness, excess, gluttony, incontinence, self-indulgence
abstention *n* **1** = **refusal**, abstaining, abstinence, avoidance, desistance, eschewal, forbearance, nonindulgence, refraining, self-control, self-denial, self-restraint
abstinence *n* = **self-denial**, abstemiousness, asceticism, avoidance, continence, forbearance, moderation, refraining, self-restraint, soberness, sobriety, teetotalism, temperance
Antonyms *n* abandon, acquisitiveness, covetousness, excess, gluttony, greediness, indulgence, self-indulgence, wantonness
abstinent *adj* = **self-denying**, abstaining, abstemious, continent, forbearing, moderate, self-controlled, self-restraining, sober, temperate
abstract *adj* **1, 2** = **theoretical**, abstruse, arcane, complex, conceptual, deep, general, generalized, hypothetical, indefinite, intellectual, nonconcrete, notional, occult, philosophical, profound, recondite, separate, subtle, theoretic, unpractical, unrealistic ◆ *n* **5** = **summary**, abridgment, compendium, condensation, digest, epitome, essence, outline, précis, recapitulation, résumé, synopsis ◆ *vb* **11** = **summarize**, abbreviate, abridge, condense, digest, epitomize, outline, précis, shorten, synopsize (*US*) **12** = **remove**, detach, dissociate, extract, isolate, separate, steal, take away, take out, withdraw
Antonyms *adj* actual ≠ **theoretical:** concrete, definite, factual, material, real, specific ◆ *n* ≠ **summary:** enlargement, expansion ◆ *vb* ≠ **remove:** add, combine, inject
abstracted *adj* **1** = **preoccupied**, absent, absent-minded, bemused, daydreaming, dreamy, faraway, inattentive, remote, withdrawn, woolgathering
abstraction *n* **1** = **absent-mindedness**, absence, bemusedness, dreaminess, inattention, pensiveness, preoccupation, remoteness, woolgathering **3** = **idea**, concept, formula, generality, generalization, hypothesis, notion, theorem, theory, thought
abstruse *adj* = **obscure**, abstract, arcane, complex, dark, deep, Delphic, enigmatic, esoteric, hidden, incomprehensible, mysterious, mystical, occult, perplexing, profound, puzzling, recondite, subtle, unfathomable, vague
Antonyms *adj* apparent, bold, clear, conspicuous, evident, manifest, open, overt, patent, perceptible, plain, self-evident, transparent, unsubtle
abstruseness *n* = **obscurity**, arcaneness, complexity, deepness, depth, esotericism, incomprehensibility, mysteriousness, occultness, perplexity, profundity, reconditeness, subtlety, vagueness
absurd *adj* **2** = **ridiculous**, crazy (*inf.*), daft (*inf.*), farcical, foolish, idiotic, illogical, inane, incongruous, irrational, laughable, ludicrous, meaningless, nonsensical, preposterous, senseless, silly, stupid, unreasonable
Antonyms *adj* intelligent, logical, prudent, rational, reasonable, sagacious, sensible, smart, wise
absurdity *n* **2** = **ridiculousness**, craziness (*inf.*), daftness (*inf.*), farce, farcicality, farcicalness, folly, foolishness, idiocy, illogicality, illogicalness, incongruity, irrationality, joke, ludicrousness, meaninglessness, nonsense, preposterousness, senselessness, silliness, stupidity, unreasonableness
absurdly *adv* **2** = **ridiculously**, farcically, foolishly, idiotically, illogically, implausibly, inanely, inconceivably, incongruously, incredibly, irrationally, laughably, ludicrously, preposterously, senselessly, unbelievably, unreasonably
abundance *n* **1** = **plenty**, affluence, ampleness, bounty, copiousness, exuberance, fullness, heap (*inf.*), plenitude, plenteousness, profusion
Antonyms *n* ≠ **plenty:** dearth, deficiency, lack, need, paucity, scantiness, scarcity, sparseness
abundant *adj* **1, 2** = **plentiful**, ample, bounteous, bountiful, copious, exuberant, filled, full, lavish, luxuriant, overflowing, plenteous, profuse, rank, rich, teeming, two a penny, well-provided, well-supplied
Antonyms *adj* deficient, few, few and far between, inadequate, in short supply, insufficient, lacking, rare, scant, scanty, scarce, short, sparse
abundantly *adv* **1, 2** = **plentifully**, amply, bounteously, bountifully, copiously, extensively, exuberantly, freely, fully, in abundance, in great *or* large numbers, in plentiful supply, in profusion, lavishly, luxuriantly, plenteously, profusely, richly

abuse ❶ *vb* (əˈbjuːz), **abuses, abusing, abused.** (*tr*) **1** to use incorrectly or improperly; misuse. **2** to maltreat, esp. physically or sexually. **3** to speak insultingly or cruelly to. ◆ *n* (əˈbjuːs). **4** improper, incorrect, or excessive use. **5** maltreatment of a person; injury. **6** insulting or coarse speech. **7** an evil, unjust, or corrupt practice. **8** See **child abuse. 9** *Arch.* a deception. [C14 (vb): via OF from L *abūsus*, p.p. of *abūtī* to misuse, from AB-[1] + *ūtī* to USE]
▸**aˈbuser** *n*

abusive ❶ (əˈbjuːsɪv) *adj* **1** characterized by insulting or coarse language. **2** characterized by maltreatment. **3** incorrectly used.
▸**aˈbusively** *adv* ▸**aˈbusiveness** *n*

abut ❶ (əˈbʌt) *vb* **abuts, abutting, abutted.** (usually foll. by *on, upon,* or *against*) to adjoin, touch, or border on (something) at one end. [C15: from OF *abouter* to join at the ends; infl. by *abuter* to touch at an end]

abutment ❶ (əˈbʌtmənt) *or* **abuttal** *n* **1** the state or process of abutting. **2a** something that abuts. **2b** the thing on which something abuts. **2c** the point of junction between them. **3** a construction that supports the end of a bridge.

abutter (əˈbʌtə) *n Property law.* the owner of adjoining property.

abuzz (əˈbʌz) *adj* (*postpositive*) humming, as with conversation, activity, etc.; buzzing.

abysm (əˈbɪzəm) *n* an archaic word for **abyss.** [C13: via OF from Med. L *abysmus* ABYSS]

abysmal ❶ (əˈbɪzməl) *adj* **1** immeasurable; very great. **2** *Inf.* extremely bad.
▸**aˈbysmally** *adv*

abyss ❶ (əˈbɪs) *n* **1** a very deep gorge or chasm. **2** anything that appears to be endless or immeasurably deep, such as time, despair, or shame. **3** hell. [C16: via LL from Gk *abussos* bottomless, from A-[1] + *bussos* depth]

abyssal (əˈbɪsəl) *adj* **1** of or relating to an abyss. **2** of or belonging to the ocean depths, esp. below 2000 metres (6500 ft): *abyssal zone.*

Ac *the chemical symbol for* actinium.

AC *abbrev. for:* **1** Air Corps. **2** alternating current. Cf. **DC. 3** ante Christum. [L: before Christ] **4** athletic club. **5** Companion of the Order of Australia.

a/c *Book-keeping. abbrev. for:* **1** account. **2** account current.

acacia (əˈkeɪʃə) *n* **1** a tropical or subtropical shrub or tree, having small yellow or white flowers. In Australia, the term is applied esp. to the wattle. **2 false acacia.** another name for **locust** (senses 2, 3). **3 gum acacia.** another name for **gum arabic.** [C16: from L, from Gk *akakia,* ? rel. to *akē* point]

academe (ˈækəˌdiːm) *n Literary.* any place of learning, such as a college or university. [C16: first used by Shakespeare in *Love's Labour's Lost* (1594); see ACADEMY]

academic ❶ (ˌækəˈdɛmɪk) *adj* **1** belonging or relating to a place of learning, esp. a college, university, or academy. **2** of purely theoretical or speculative interest. **3** (esp. of pupils) having an aptitude for study. **4** excessively concerned with intellectual matters. **5** conforming to set rules and traditions: *an academic painter.* **6** relating to studies such as languages and pure science rather than technical, applied, or professional studies. ◆ *n* **7** a member of a college or university.
▸**ˌacaˈdemically** *adv*

academician (əˌkædəˈmɪʃən) *n* a member of an academy (senses 1, 2).

academy ❶ (əˈkædəmɪ) *n, pl* **academies. 1** an institution or society for the advancement of literature, art, or science. **2** a school for training in a particular skill or profession: *a military academy.* **3** a secondary school, esp. in Scotland: now only used as part of a name. [C16: via L from Gk *akadēmeia* the grove where Plato taught, named after the legendary hero *Akadēmos*]
▸**ˌacaˈdemical** *adj*

Academy Award *n* the official name for an **Oscar.**

acanthus (əˈkænθəs) *n, pl* **acanthuses** *or* **acanthi** (-θaɪ). **1** a shrub or herbaceous plant, native to the Mediterranean region but widely cultivated as an ornamental plant, having large spiny leaves and spikes of white or purplish flowers. **2** a carved ornament based on the leaves of the acanthus plant, esp. as used on the capital of a Corinthian column. [C17: NL, from Gk *akanthos,* from *akantha* thorn, spine]

a cappella (ɑː kəˈpɛlə) *adj, adv Music.* without instrumental accompaniment. [It.: lit., according to (the style of the) chapel]

acariasis (ˌækəˈraɪəsɪs) *n* infestation with mites or ticks. [C19: NL: see ACARID, -IASIS]

acarid (ˈækərɪd) *or* **acaridan** (əˈkærɪdᵊn) *n* any of an order of small arachnids that includes the ticks and mites. [C19: from Gk *akari* a small thing, mite]

acarpous (eɪˈkɑːpəs) *adj* (of plants) producing no fruit. [from Gk *akarpos,* from A-[1] + *karpos* fruit]

ACAS *or* **Acas** (ˈeɪkæs) *n* (in Britain) *acronym for* Advisory Conciliation and Arbitration Service.

acc. *abbrev. for:* **1** accompanied. **2** according. **3** *Book-keeping.* account. **4** *Grammar.* accusative.

accede ❶ (ækˈsiːd) *vb* **accedes, acceding, acceded.** (*intr;* usually foll. by *to*) **1** to assent or give one's consent. **2** to enter upon or attain (to an office, right, etc.): *the prince acceded to the throne.* **3** *International law.* to become a party (to an agreement between nations, etc.). [C15: from L *accēdere,* from *ad-* to + *cēdere* to yield]
▸**acˈcedence** *n*

accelerando (ækˌsɛləˈrændəʊ) *adj, adv Music.* (to be performed) with increasing speed. [It.]

accelerate ❶ (ækˈsɛləˌreɪt) *vb* **accelerates, accelerating, accelerated. 1** to go, occur, or cause to go or occur more quickly; speed up. **2** (*tr*) to cause to happen sooner than expected. **3** (*tr*) to increase the velocity of (a body, reaction, etc.). [C16: from L *accelerātus,* from *accelerāre,* from *ad-* (intensive) + *celerāre* to hasten, from *celer* swift]
▸**acˈcelerative** *adj*

acceleration ❶ (ækˌsɛləˈreɪʃən) *n* **1** the act of accelerating or the state of being accelerated. **2** the rate of increase of speed or the rate of change of velocity. **3** the power to accelerate.

acceleration of free fall *n* the acceleration of a body falling freely in a vacuum in the earth's gravitational field. Symbol: *g* Also called: **acceleration due to gravity.**

accelerator (ækˈsɛləˌreɪtə) *n* **1** a device for increasing speed, esp. a pedal for controlling the fuel intake in a motor vehicle; throttle. **2** *Physics.* a machine for increasing the kinetic energy of subatomic particles or atomic nuclei. **3** Also: **accelerant.** *Chem.* a substance that increases the speed of a chemical reaction; catalyst.

accelerometer (ækˌsɛləˈrɒmɪtə) *n* an instrument for measuring acceleration, esp. of an aircraft or rocket.

accent ❶ *n* (ˈæksənt). **1** the characteristic mode of pronunciation of a person or group, esp. one that betrays social or geographical origin. **2** the relative prominence of a spoken or sung syllable, esp. with regard to stress or pitch. **3** a mark (such as ˈ, ˌ, ´, or `) used in writing to indicate the stress or prominence of a syllable. **4** any of various marks or symbols conventionally used in writing certain languages to indicate the quality of a vowel. See **acute** (sense 8), **grave**[2] (sense 5), **circumflex. 5** rhythmic stress in verse or prose. **6** *Music.* **6a** stress placed on certain notes in a piece of music, indicated by a symbol printed over the note concerned. **6b** the rhythmic pulse of a piece or passage, usually represented as the stress on the first beat of each bar. **7** a distinctive characteristic of anything, such as taste, pattern, style, etc. **8** particular attention or emphasis: *an accent on learning.* **9** a strongly contrasting detail. ◆ *vb* (ækˈsɛnt). (*tr*) **10** to mark with an accent in writing, speech, music, etc. **11** to lay particular emphasis or stress on. [C14: via OF from L *accentus,* from *ad-* to + *cantus* chant]

accentor (ækˈsɛntə) *n* a small sparrow-like songbird, which inhabits

THESAURUS

Antonyms *adv* inadequately, in short supply, insufficiently, rarely, scantily, scarcely, sparsely

abuse *vb* **1, 2 = ill-treat,** damage, exploit, harm, hurt, impose upon, injure, maltreat, manhandle, mar, misapply, misuse, oppress, spoil, take advantage of, wrong **3 = insult,** calumniate, castigate, curse, defame, disparage, inveigh against, libel, malign, revile, scold, slander, slate (*inf., chiefly Brit.*), smear, swear at, traduce, upbraid, vilify, vituperate ◆ *n* **4, 5 = ill-treatment,** damage, exploitation, harm, hurt, imposition, injury, maltreatment, manhandling, oppression, spoiling, wrong **4 = misuse,** misapplication **6 = insults,** blame, calumniation, castigation, censure, character assassination, contumely, curses, cursing, defamation, derision, disparagement, invective, libel, opprobrium, reproach, revilement, scolding, slander, swearing, tirade, traducement, upbraiding, vilification, vituperation
Antonyms *vb* ≠ **ill-treat:** care for, protect ≠ **insult:** acclaim, commend, compliment, extol, flatter, praise, respect

abusive *adj* **1 = insulting,** calumniating, castigating, censorious, contumelious, defamatory, derisive, disparaging, invective, libellous, maligning, offensive, opprobrious, reproachful, reviling, rude, scathing, scolding, slanderous, traducing, upbraiding, vilifying, vituperative **2 = harmful,** brutal, cruel, destructive, hurtful, injurious, rough
Antonyms *adj* ≠ **insulting:** approving, complimentary, eulogistic, flattering, laudatory, panegyrical, praising

abusiveness *n* **1 = insults,** calumniation, coarse language, contumely, derisiveness, foul language, invective, offensiveness, philippics, rudeness, traducement, vilification, vitriol, vituperation **2 = ill-treatment,** abuse, brutality, cruelty, exploitation, maltreatment

abut *vb* **= adjoin,** border, impinge, join, meet, touch, verge

abutment *n* **2, 3 = support,** brace, bulwark, buttress, pier, prop, strut

abutting *adj* **= adjoining,** adjacent, bordering, contiguous, joining, meeting, next to, touching, verging

abysmal *adj* **2 = terrible,** appalling, awful, bad, dire, dreadful

abyss *n* **1 = pit,** abysm, bottomless depth, chasm, crevasse, fissure, gorge, gulf, void

academic *adj* **1, 3 = scholarly,** bookish, campus, college, collegiate, erudite, highbrow, learned, lettered, literary, scholastic, school, studious, university **2 = hypothetical,** abstract, conjectural, impractical, notional, speculative, theoretical ◆ *n* **7 = scholar,** academician, don, fellow, lecturer, master, professor, pupil, scholastic, schoolman, student, tutor

academy *n* **2, 3 = college,** centre of learning, institute, institution, school

accede *vb* **1 = agree,** accept, acquiesce, admit, assent, comply, concede, concur, consent, endorse, grant, own, yield **2 = inherit,** assume, attain, come to, enter upon, succeed, succeed to (*as heir*)

accelerate *vb* **1, 2 = speed up,** advance, expedite, forward, further, hasten, hurry, pick up speed, precipitate, quicken, speed, spur, step up (*inf.*), stimulate
Antonyms *vb* decelerate, delay, hinder, impede, obstruct, slow down

acceleration *n* **1 = speeding up,** expedition, hastening, hurrying, quickening, spurring, stepping up (*inf.*), stimulation

accent *n* **1 = pronunciation,** articulation, brogue, enunciation, inflection, intonation, modulation, tone **2, 5, 6 = emphasis,** beat, ca-

mainly mountainous regions of Europe and Asia. See also **hedge sparrow.**

accentual (æk'sentʃuəl) *adj* **1** of, relating to, or having accents; rhythmic. **2** *Prosody.* of or relating to verse based on the number of stresses in a line.
▸**ac'centually** *adv*

accentuate ❶ (æk'sentʃuˌeɪt) *vb* **accentuates, accentuating, accentuated.** (*tr*) to stress or emphasize.
▸**acˌcentu'ation** *n*

accept ❶ (ək'sept) *vb* (*mainly tr*) **1** to take or receive (something offered). **2** to give an affirmative reply to. **3** to take on the responsibilities, duties, etc., of: *he accepted office.* **4** to tolerate. **5** to consider as true or believe in (a philosophy, theory, etc.). **6** (*may take a clause as object*) to be willing to believe: *you must accept that he lied.* **7** to receive with approval or admit, as into a community, group, etc. **8** *Commerce.* to agree to pay (a bill, draft, etc.). **9** to receive as adequate or valid. [C14: from L *acceptāre*, from *ad-* to + *capere* to take]
▸**ac'cepter** *n*

acceptable ❶ (ək'septəbᵊl) *adj* **1** satisfactory; adequate. **2** pleasing; welcome. **3** tolerable.
▸**acˌcepta'bility** *or* **ac'ceptableness** *n* ▸**ac'ceptably** *adv*

acceptance ❶ (ək'septəns) *n* **1** the act of accepting or the state of being accepted or acceptable. **2** favourable reception. **3** (often foll. by *of*) belief (in) or assent (to). **4** *Commerce.* a formal agreement by a debtor to pay a draft, bill, etc. **5** (*pl*) *Austral. & NZ.* a list of horses accepted as starters in a race.

acceptation (ˌæksep'teɪʃən) *n* the accepted meaning, as of a word, phrase, etc.

accepted ❶ (ək'septɪd) *adj* commonly approved or recognized; customary; established.

acceptor (ək'septə) *n* **1** *Commerce.* the person or organization on which a draft or bill of exchange is drawn. **2** *Electronics.* an impurity, such as gallium, added to a semiconductor material to increase its p-type semiconductivity.

access ❶ ('ækses) *n* **1** the act of approaching or entering. **2** the condition of allowing entry, esp. (of a building, etc.) entry by prams, wheelchairs, etc. **3** the right or privilege to approach, enter, or make use of something. **4** a way or means of approach or entry. **5** the opportunity or right to see or approach someone: *my ex-wife sabotages my access to the children.* **6** (*modifier*) designating programmes made by the general public: *access television.* **7** a sudden outburst or attack, as of rage or disease. ◆ *vb* (*tr*) **8** *Computing.* **8a** to obtain or retrieve (information) from a storage device. **8b** to place (information) in a storage device. **9** to gain access to; make accessible or available. [C14: from OF or from L *accessus*, from *accēdere* to ACCEDE]

accessible ❶ (ək'sesəbᵊl) *adj* **1** easy to approach, enter, or use. **2 accessible to.** likely to be affected by. **3** obtainable; available.
▸**acˌcessi'bility** *n*

accession ❶ (ək'seʃən) *n* **1** the act of attaining to an office, right, condition, etc. **2** an increase due to an addition. **3** an addition, as to a collection. **4** *Property law.* an addition to land or property by natural increase or improvement. **5** *International law.* the formal acceptance of a convention or treaty. **6** agreement. ◆ *vb* **7** (*tr*) to make a record of (additions to a collection).
▸**ac'cessional** *adj*

accessory ❶ (ək'sesərɪ) *n, pl* **accessories. 1** a supplementary part or object, as of a car, appliance, etc. **2** (*often pl*) a small accompanying item of dress, esp. of women's dress. **3** (formerly) a person involved in a crime although absent during its commission. ◆ *adj* **4** supplementary; additional. **5** assisting in or having knowledge of an act, esp. a crime. [C17: from LL *accessōrius*: see ACCESS]
▸**accessorial** (ˌækse'sɔːrɪəl) *adj* ▸**ac'cessorily** *adv*

access road *n* a road giving entry to a region or, esp., a motorway.

access time *n Computing.* the time required to retrieve a piece of stored information.

acciaccatura (əˌtʃækə'tʊərə) *n, pl* **acciaccaturas** *or* **acciaccature** (-reɪ). a small grace note melodically adjacent to a principal note and played simultaneously with or immediately before it. [C18: It.: lit., a crushing sound]

accidence ('æksɪdəns) *n* the part of grammar concerned with changes in the form of words for the expression of tense, person, case, number, etc. [C15: from L *accidentia* accidental matters, from *accidere* to happen. See ACCIDENT]

accident ❶ ('æksɪdənt) *n* **1** an unforeseen event or one without an apparent cause. **2** anything that occurs unintentionally or by chance: *I met him by accident.* **3** a misfortune or mishap, esp. one causing injury or death. **4** *Geol.* a surface irregularity in a natural formation. [C14: via OF from L *accident-*, from the p.p. of *accidere* to happen, from *ad-* to + *cadere* to fall]

accidental ❶ (ˌæksɪ'dentᵊl) *adj* **1** occurring by chance, unexpectedly, or unintentionally. **2** nonessential; incidental. **3** *Music.* denoting sharps, flats, or naturals that are not in the key signature of a piece. ◆ *n* **4** an incidental or supplementary circumstance, factor, or attribute. **5** *Music.* a symbol denoting a sharp, flat, or natural that is not a part of the key signature.
▸ˌ**acci'dentally** *adv*

accident-prone *adj* liable to become involved in accidents.

accidie ('æksɪdɪ) *or* **acedia** *n* spiritual sloth; apathy; indifference. [in use C13 to C16 and revived C19: via LL from Gk *akēdia*, from A-[1] + *kēdos* care]

accipiter (æk'sɪpɪtə) *n* any of a genus of hawks having short rounded wings and a long tail. [C19: NL, from L: hawk]
▸**ac'cipitrine** *adj*

acclaim ❶ (ə'kleɪm) *vb* **1** (*tr*) to acknowledge publicly the excellence of (a person, act, etc.). **2** to applaud. **3** (*tr*) to acknowledge publicly: *they acclaimed him king.* ◆ *n* **4** an enthusiastic expression of approval, etc. [C17: from L *acclāmāre*, from *ad-* to + *clamāre* to shout]
▸**ac'claimer** *n*

THESAURUS

dence, force, ictus, pitch, rhythm, stress, timbre, tonality ◆ *vb* **11** = **emphasize**, accentuate, stress, underline, underscore

accentuate *vb* = **emphasize**, accent, draw attention to, foreground, highlight, stress, underline, underscore
Antonyms *vb* gloss over, make light *or* little of, minimize, play down, soft-pedal (*inf.*), underplay

accept *vb* **1** = **receive**, acquire, gain, get, have, obtain, secure, take **3** = **take on**, acknowledge, admit, assume, avow, bear, undertake **4** = **stand**, bear, bow to, brook, defer to, like it or lump it (*inf.*), put up with, submit to, suffer, take, tolerate, yield to **5, 6** = **agree to**, accede, acknowledge, acquiesce, admit, adopt, affirm, approve, believe, concur with, consent to, cooperate with, recognize, swallow (*inf.*), take on board
Antonyms *vb* ≠ **agree to:** decline, deny, disown, rebut, refuse, reject, repudiate, spurn

acceptability *n* **1, 3** = **adequacy**, acceptableness, admissibility, appropriateness, fitness, permissibility, propriety, satisfactoriness, suitability
Antonyms *n* impropriety, inadequacy, inadmissibility, inappropriateness, unacceptability, unsatisfactoriness, unsuitability

acceptable *adj* **1, 3** = **satisfactory**, adequate, admissible, all right, fair, moderate, passable, so-so (*inf.*), standard, suitable, tolerable, up to scratch (*inf.*) **2** = **pleasant**, agreeable, delightful, grateful, gratifying, pleasing, welcome
Antonyms *adj* ≠ **satisfactory:** unacceptable, unsatisfactory, unsuitable

acceptably *adv* **1, 3** = **adequately**, passably, satisfactorily, tolerably **2** = **pleasantly**, agreeably, delightfully, gratifyingly, pleasingly
Antonyms *adv* ≠ **adequately:** unacceptably, unsatisfactorily, unsuitably

acceptance *n* **1** = **accepting**, acquiring, gaining, getting, having, obtaining, receipt, securing, taking **3** = **agreement**, accedence, accession, acknowledgment, acquiescence, admission, adoption, affirmation, approbation, approval, assent, belief, compliance, concession, concurrence, consensus, consent, cooperation, credence, O.K. *or* okay (*inf.*), permission, recognition

accepted *adj* = **agreed**, acceptable, acknowledged, admitted, agreed upon, approved, authorized, common, confirmed, conventional, customary, established, normal, received, recognized, regular, sanctioned, standard, time-honoured, traditional, universal, usual
Antonyms *adj* abnormal, irregular, strange, unconventional, uncustomary, unorthodox, unusual, unwonted

access *n* **1, 4** = **entrance**, admission, admittance, approach, avenue, course, door, entering, entrée, entry, gateway, key, passage, passageway, path, road, way in **7** = **attack**, fit, onset, outburst, paroxysm

accessibility *n* **1** = **approachability**, affability, conversableness, cordiality, friendliness, informality **2** = **openness**, exposedness, susceptibility **3** = **handiness**, approachability, attainability, availability, nearness, obtainability, possibility, readiness

accessible *adj* **1** = **approachable**, affable, available, conversable, cordial, friendly, informal **2** = **open**, exposed, liable, subject, susceptible, vulnerable, wide-open **3** = **handy**, achievable, at hand, at one's fingertips, attainable, available, near, nearby, obtainable, on hand, possible, reachable, ready
Antonyms *adj* ≠ **handy:** far-off, hidden, inaccessible, secreted, unavailable, unobtainable, unreachable

accession *n* **1** = **taking up**, assumption, attaining to, attainment of, entering upon, succession (*to a throne, dignity, or office*), taking on, taking over **2, 3** = **increase**, addition, augmentation, enlargement, extension **6** = **agreement**, accedence, acceptance, acquiescence, assent, concurrence, consent

accessory *n* **1** = **addition**, accent, accompaniment, add-on, adjunct, adornment, aid, appendage, attachment, component, convenience, decoration, extension, extra, frill, help, supplement, trim, trimming **3** = **accomplice**, abettor, assistant, associate (*in crime*), colleague, confederate, helper, partner ◆ *adj* **4, 5** = **additional**, abetting, aiding, ancillary, assisting in, auxiliary, contributory, extra, secondary, subordinate, supplemental, supplementary

accident *n* **1, 2** = **chance**, fate, fluke, fortuity, fortune, hazard, luck **3** = **misfortune**, blow, calamity, casualty, chance, collision, crash, disaster, misadventure, mischance, mishap, pile-up (*inf.*)

accidental *adj* **1, 2** = **unintentional**, adventitious, casual, chance, contingent, fortuitous, haphazard, inadvertent, incidental, inessential, nonessential, random, uncalculated, uncertain, unessential, unexpected, unforeseen, unintended, unlooked-for, unplanned, unpremeditated, unwitting
Antonyms *adj* calculated, designed, expected, foreseen, intended, intentional, planned, prepared

accidentally *adv* **1, 2** = **unintentionally**, adventitiously, by accident, by chance, by mistake, casually, fortuitously, haphazardly, inadvertently, incidentally, randomly, unconsciously, undesignedly, unexpectedly, unwittingly
Antonyms *adv* by design, consciously, deliberately, designedly, on purpose, wilfully

acclaim *vb* **1, 2** = **praise**, applaud, approve, celebrate, cheer, clap, commend, crack up (*inf.*), eulogize, exalt, extol, hail, honour, laud, salute, welcome ◆ *n* **4** = **praise**, acclamation,

DICTIONARY

acclamation Ⓣ (ˌækləˈmeɪʃən) *n* **1** an enthusiastic reception or exhibition of welcome, approval, etc. **2** an expression of approval with shouts or applause. **3** *Canad.* an instance of electing or being elected without opposition.
▸**acclamatory** (əˈklæmətərɪ) *adj*

acclimatize Ⓣ *or* **acclimatise** (əˈklaɪməˌtaɪz) *vb* **acclimatizes, acclimatizing, acclimatized** *or* **acclimatises, acclimatising, acclimatised.** to adapt or become accustomed to a new climate or environment.
▸**acˈclimaˌtizable** *or* **acˈclimaˌtisable** *adj* ▸**acˌclimatiˈzation** *or* **acˌclimatiˈsation** *n*

acclivity (əˈklɪvɪtɪ) *n, pl* **acclivities.** an upward slope, esp. of the ground. Cf. **declivity.** [C17: from L, from *acclīvis* sloping up]
▸**acˈclivitous** *adj*

accolade Ⓣ (ˈækəˌleɪd) *n* **1** strong praise or approval. **2** an award or honour. **3** the ceremonial gesture used to confer knighthood, a touch on the shoulder with a sword. **4** a rare word for **brace** (sense 7). [C17: via F & It. from Vulgar L *accollāre* (unattested) to hug; rel. to L *collum* neck]

accommodate Ⓣ (əˈkɒməˌdeɪt) *vb* **accommodates, accommodating, accommodated.** **1** (*tr*) to supply or provide, esp. with lodging. **2** (*tr*) to oblige or do a favour for. **3** to adapt. **4** (*tr*) to bring into harmony. **5** (*tr*) to allow room for. **6** (*tr*) to lend money to. [C16: from L *accommodāre,* from *ad-* to + *commodus* having the proper measure]

accommodating Ⓣ (əˈkɒməˌdeɪtɪŋ) *adj* willing to help; kind; obliging.

accommodation Ⓣ (əˌkɒməˈdeɪʃən) *n* **1** lodging or board and lodging. **2** adjustment, as of differences or to new circumstances; settlement or reconciliation. **3** something fulfilling a need, want, etc. **4** *Physiol.* the automatic or voluntary adjustment of the thickness of the lens of the eye for far or near vision. **5** willingness to help or oblige. **6** *Commerce.* a loan.

accommodation address *n* an address on letters, etc., to a person or business that does not wish or is not able to receive post at a permanent or actual address.

accommodation ladder *n Naut.* a flight of stairs or a ladder for lowering over the side of a ship for access to and from a small boat, pier, etc.

accompaniment Ⓣ (əˈkʌmpənɪmənt) *n* **1** something that accompanies or is served or used with something else. **2** *Music.* a subordinate or supporting part for an instrument, voices, or an orchestra.

accompanist (əˈkʌmpənɪst) *n* a person who plays a musical accompaniment for another performer.

accompany Ⓣ (əˈkʌmpənɪ) *vb* **accompanies, accompanying, accompanied.** **1** (*tr*) to go along with, so as to be in company with. **2** (*tr;* foll. by *with*) to supplement. **3** (*tr*) to occur or be associated with. **4** to provide a musical accompaniment for (a soloist, etc.). [C15: from OF *accompaignier,* from *compaing* COMPANION[1]]

accomplice Ⓣ (əˈkɒmplɪs, əˈkʌm-) *n* a person who has helped another in committing a crime. [C15: from *a complice,* interpreted as one word, from OF, from LL *complex* partner, from L *complicāre* to COMPLICATE]

accomplish Ⓣ (əˈkɒmplɪʃ, əˈkʌm-) *vb* (*tr*) **1** to manage to do; achieve. **2** to complete. [C14: from OF *acomplir,* ult. from L *complēre* to fill up. See COMPLETE]

accomplished Ⓣ (əˈkɒmplɪʃt, əˈkʌm-) *adj* **1** successfully completed; achieved. **2** expert; proficient.

accomplishment Ⓣ (əˈkɒmplɪʃmənt, əˈkʌm-) *n* **1** the act of achieving. **2** something successfully completed. **3** (*often pl*) skill or talent. **4** (*often pl*) social grace and poise.

accord Ⓣ (əˈkɔːd) *n* **1** agreement; accordance (esp. in **in accord with**). **2** concurrence of opinion. **3 with one accord.** unanimously. **4** pleasing relationship between sounds, colours, etc. **5 of one's own accord.** voluntarily. ◆ *vb* **6** to be or cause to be in harmony or agreement. **7** (*tr*) to grant; bestow. [C12: via OF from L *ad-* to + *cord-,* stem of *cor* heart]

accordance Ⓣ (əˈkɔːdəns) *n* conformity; agreement; accord (esp. in **in accordance with**).

according Ⓣ (əˈkɔːdɪŋ) *adj* **1** (foll. by *to*) in proportion. **2** (foll. by *to*) as stated (by). **3** (foll. by *to*) in conformity (with). **4** (foll. by *as*) depending (on whether).

accordingly Ⓣ (əˈkɔːdɪŋlɪ) *adv* **1** in an appropriate manner; suitably. ◆ *sentence connector.* **2** consequently.

accordion (əˈkɔːdɪən) *n* **1** a portable box-shaped instrument consisting of metallic reeds that are made to vibrate by air from a set of bellows controlled by the player's hands. Notes are produced by means of studlike keys. **2** short for **piano accordion.** [C19: from G, from *Akkord* harmony]
▸**acˈcordionist** *n*

accordion pleats *pl n* tiny knife pleats.

accost Ⓣ (əˈkɒst) *vb* (*tr*) to approach, stop, and speak to (a person), as to ask a question, solicit sexually, etc. [C16: from LL *accostāre,* from L *costa* side, rib]
▸**acˈcostable** *adj*

accouchement *French.* (akuʃmɑ̃) *n* childbirth or the period of confinement. [C19: from *accoucher* to put to bed. See COUCH]

account Ⓣ (əˈkaʊnt) *n* **1** a verbal or written report, description, or narration of some occurrence, event, etc. **2** an explanation of conduct, esp. one made to someone in authority. **3** basis; consideration: *on this account.* **4** importance, consequence, or value: *of little account.* **5** assessment; judgment. **6** profit or advantage: *to good account.* **7** part or be-

THESAURUS

applause, approbation, approval, celebration, cheering, clapping, commendation, eulogizing, exaltation, honour, kudos, laudation, plaudits, welcome
Antonyms *n* ≠ **praise:** bad press, brickbats, censure, criticism, denigration, disparagement, fault-finding, flak (*inf.*), panning (*inf.*), stick (*sl.*), vituperation

acclaimed *adj* **1, 2** = **praised,** acknowledged, admired, celebrated, distinguished, famed, famous, highly esteemed, highly rated, highly thought of, much touted, much vaunted, noted, renowned, well received, well thought of
Antonyms *adj* badly *or* poorly received, criticized, unacclaimed, unacknowledged, undistinguished

acclamation *n* **1, 2** = **praise,** acclaim, adulation, approbation, approval, cheer, cheering, cheers, enthusiasm, kudos, laudation, loud homage, ovation, plaudit, salutation, shouting, tribute

acclimatization *n* = **adaptation,** acclimation, accommodation, acculturation, adjustment, habituation, inurement, naturalization

acclimatize *vb* = **adapt,** accommodate, accustom, adjust, become seasoned to, get used to, habituate, inure, naturalize

acclimatized *adj* = **adapted,** acclimated, accustomed, adjusted, familiarized, inured, orientated, oriented, seasoned, used

accolade *n* **1, 2** = **praise,** acclaim, acclamation, applause, approval, commendation, compliment, congratulation, eulogy, homage, honour, laud (*literary*), laudation (*formal*), ovation, plaudit, recognition, tribute

accommodate *vb* **1** = **house,** billet, board, cater for, entertain, harbour, lodge, put up, quarter, shelter **2** = **help,** afford, aid, assist, furnish, oblige, provide, purvey, serve, supply **3** = **adapt,** accustom, adjust, comply, compose, conform, fit, harmonize, modify, reconcile, settle

accommodating *adj* = **helpful,** complaisant, considerate, cooperative, friendly, hospitable, kind, obliging, polite, unselfish, willing
Antonyms *adj* disobliging, inconsiderate, rude, uncooperative, unhelpful

accommodation *n* **1** = **housing,** board, digs (*Brit. inf.*), harbouring, house, lodging(s), quartering, quarters, shelter, sheltering **2** = **adaptation,** adjustment, compliance, composition, compromise, conformity, fitting, harmony, modification, reconciliation, settlement **5** = **help,** aid, assistance, provision, service, supply

accompaniment *n* **1** = **supplement,** accessory, companion, complement **2** = **backing music,** backing

accompany *vb* **1** = **go with,** attend, chaperon, conduct, convoy, escort, hold (someone's) hand, squire, usher **2, 3** = **occur with,** belong to, coexist with, coincide with, come with, follow, go cheek by jowl, go together with, join with, supplement

accompanying *adj* **1-3** = **additional,** accessory, added, appended, associate, associated, attached, attendant, complementary, concomitant, concurrent, connected, fellow, joint, related, supplemental, supplementary

accomplice *n* = **helper,** abettor, accessory, ally, assistant, associate, coadjutor, collaborator, colleague, confederate, henchman, partner

accomplish *vb* **1, 2** = **do,** achieve, attain, bring about, bring off (*inf.*), carry out, complete, conclude, consummate, effect, effectuate, execute, finish, fulfil, manage, perform, produce, put the tin lid on, realize
Antonyms *vb* fail, fall short, forsake, give up

accomplished *adj* **1** = **done,** achieved, attained, brought about, carried out, completed, concluded, consummated, effected, executed, finished, fulfilled, in the can (*inf.*), managed, performed, produced, realized **2** = **skilled,** adept, consummate, cultivated, expert, gifted, masterly, polished, practised, proficient, skilful, talented
Antonyms *adj* ≠ **skilled:** amateurish, incapable, incompetent, inexpert, unestablished, unproven, unrealized, unskilled, untalented

accomplishment *n* **1** = **completion,** achievement, attainment, bringing about, carrying out, conclusion, consummation, doing, effecting, execution, finishing, fulfilment, management, performance, production, realization **2** = **achievement,** act, attainment, coup, deed, exploit, feat, stroke, triumph **3** *often plural* = **skill,** ability, achievement, art, attainment, capability, craft, gift, proficiency = **skill,** talent

accord *n* **1, 2** = **agreement,** accordance, assent, concert, concurrence, conformity, congruence, correspondence, harmony, rapport, sympathy, unanimity, unison ◆ *vb* **6** = **agree,** assent, be in tune (*inf.*), concur, conform, correspond, fit, harmonize, match, suit, tally **7** = **grant,** allow, bestow, concede, confer, endow, give, present, render, tender, vouchsafe
Antonyms *n* ≠ **agreement:** conflict, contention, disagreement, discord ≠ **agree:** conflict, contrast, differ, disagree, discord ◆ *vb* ≠ **grant:** hold back, refuse, withhold

accordance *n As in* **in accordance with** = **agreement,** accord, assent, concert, concurrence, conformity, congruence, correspondence, harmony, rapport, sympathy, unanimity

according *adj* **1** *foll. by* **to** = **in relation,** commensurate with, in proportion **2** *foll. by* **to** = **as stated by,** as believed by, as maintained by, in the light of, on the authority of, on the report of **3** *foll. by* **to** = **in keeping with,** after, after the manner of, consistent with, in accordance with, in compliance with, in conformity with, in harmony with, in line with, in obedience to, in step with, in the manner of, obedient to

accordingly *adv* **1** = **appropriately,** correspondingly, fitly, properly, suitably ◆ *sentence connector* **2** = **consequently,** as a result, ergo, hence, in consequence, so, therefore, thus

accost *vb* = **approach,** address, buttonhole, confront, greet, hail, halt, salute, solicit (*as a prostitute*), stop

account *n* **1, 2** = **description,** chronicle, detail, explanation, history, narration, narrative, recital, record, relation, report, statement, story, tale, version **3** = **reason,** basis, cause, consider-

half (only in **on one's** *or* **someone's account**). **8** *Finance.* **8a** a business relationship between a bank, department store, etc., and a depositor, customer, or client permitting the latter certain banking or credit services. **8b** the sum of money deposited at a bank. **8c** the amount of credit available to the holder of an account. **8d** a record of these. **9** a statement of monetary transactions with the resulting balance. **10** (formerly, on the London Stock Exchange) the period, ordinarily of a fortnight's duration, at the end of which settlements were made. **11a** a regular client or customer. **11b** an area of business assigned to another: *they transferred their publicity account to a new agent.* **12 call** (*or* **bring**) **to account. 12a** to insist on explanation. **12b** to reprimand. **12c** to hold responsible. **13 give a good** (**bad,** etc.) **account of oneself.** to perform well (badly, etc.). **14 on account. 14a** on credit. **14b** Also: **to account.** as partial payment. **15 on account of.** (*prep*) because of. **16 take account of** *or* **take into account.** to take into consideration; allow for. **17 settle** *or* **square accounts with. 17a** to pay or receive a balance due. **17b** to get revenge on (someone). **18** See **bank account.** ◆ *vb* **19** (*tr*) to consider or reckon: *he accounts himself poor.* [C13: from OF *acont,* from *conter* to COUNT[1]]

accountable Ⓣ (ə'kauntəb^{ə}l) *adj* **1** responsible to someone or for some action. **2** able to be explained.
▸**ac,counta'bility** *n* ▸**ac'countably** *adv*

accountancy (ə'kauntənsı) *n* the profession or business of an accountant.

accountant Ⓣ (ə'kauntənt) *n* a person concerned with the maintenance and audit of business accounts.

account executive *n* an executive in an advertising agency or public relations firm who manages a client's account.

account for Ⓣ *vb* (*intr, prep*) **1** to give reasons for (an event, act, etc.). **2** to make or provide a reckoning of (expenditure, etc.). **3** to be responsible for destroying or putting (people, aircraft, etc.) out of action.

accounting Ⓣ (ə'kauntıŋ) *n* **a** the skill or practice of maintaining and auditing accounts and preparing reports on the assets, liabilities, etc., of a business. **b** (*as modifier*): *an accounting period.*

accoutre *or US* **accouter** (ə'ku:tə) *vb* **accoutres, accoutring, accoutred** *or US* **accouters, accoutering, accoutered.** (*tr; usually passive*) to provide with equipment or dress, esp. military. [C16: from OF *accoustrer,* ult. rel. to L *consuere* to sew together]

accoutrement Ⓣ (ə'ku:trəmənt, ə'ku:tə-) *or US* **accouterment** (ə'ku:tərmənt) *n* **1** equipment worn by soldiers in addition to their clothing and weapons. **2** (*usually pl*) clothing, equipment, etc.; trappings: *the correct accoutrements for any sport.*

accredit Ⓣ (ə'krɛdıt) *vb* (*tr*) **1** to ascribe or attribute. **2** to give official recognition to. **3** to certify as meeting required standards. **4** (often foll. by *at* or *to*) **4a** to send (an envoy, etc.) with official credentials. **4b** to appoint (someone) as an envoy, etc. **5** to believe. **6** *NZ.* to pass (a candidate) for university entrance on school recommendation, without external examination. [C17: from F *accréditer,* from *mettre à crédit* to put to CREDIT]
▸**ac,credi'tation** *n*

accredited Ⓣ (ə'krɛdıtıd) *adj* **1** officially authorized; recognized. **2** (of milk, cattle, etc.) certified as free from disease; meeting certain standards. **3** *NZ.* accepted for university entrance on school recommendation, without external examination.

accrete (ə'kri:t) *vb* **accretes, accreting, accreted. 1** to grow or cause to grow together. **2** to make or become bigger, as by addition. [C18: back formation from ACCRETION]

accretion (ə'kri:ʃən) *n* **1** any gradual increase in size, as through growth or external addition. **2** something added, esp. extraneously, to cause growth or an increase in size. **3** the growing together of normally separate plant or animal parts. [C17: from L *accretiō* increase, from *accrēscere.* See ACCRUE]
▸**ac'cretive** *adj*

accrual (ə'kru:əl) *n* **1** the act of accruing. **2** something that has accrued. **3** *Accounting* a charge incurred in one accounting period that has not been paid by the end of it.

accrue Ⓣ (ə'kru:) *vb* **accrues, accruing, accrued.** (*intr*) **1** to increase by growth or addition, esp. (of capital) to increase by periodic addition of interest. **2** (often foll. by *to*) to fall naturally (to). [C15: from OF *accreue,* ult. from L *accrēscere,* from *ad-* to, in addition + *crēscere* to grow]

acct *Book-keeping. abbrev. for* account.

acculturate (ə'kʌltʃə,reıt) *vb* **acculturates, acculturating, acculturated.** (of a cultural or social group) to assimilate the cultural traits of another group. [C20: from AD- + CULTURE + -ATE[1]]
▸**ac,cultur'ation** *n*

accumulate Ⓣ (ə'kju:mjʊ,leıt) *vb* **accumulates, accumulating, accumulated.** to gather or become gathered together in an increasing quantity; collect. [C16: from L *accumulāre* to heap up, from *cumulus* a heap]
▸**ac'cumulable** *adj* ▸**ac'cumulative** *adj*

accumulation Ⓣ (ə,kju:mjʊ'leıʃən) *n* **1** the act or process of collecting together or becoming collected. **2** something that has been collected, gathered, heaped, etc. **3** *Finance.* the continuous growth of capital by retention of interest or earnings.

accumulator (ə'kju:mjʊ,leıtə) *n* **1** Also called: **battery, storage battery.** a rechargeable device for storing electrical energy in the form of chemical energy. **2** *Horse racing, Brit.* a collective bet on successive races, with both stake and winnings being carried forward to accumulate progressively. **3** a register in a calculator or computer used for holding the results of a computation or data transfer.

accuracy Ⓣ ('ækjʊrəsı) *n, pl* **accuracies.** faithful measurement or representation of the truth; correctness; precision.

accurate Ⓣ ('ækjərıt) *adj* **1** faithfully representing or describing the truth. **2** showing a negligible or permissible deviation from a standard: *an accurate ruler.* **3** without error; precise. **4** *Maths.* (of a number) correctly represented to a specified number of decimal places or significant figures. [C16: from L *accūrāre* to perform with care, from *cūra* care]
▸**'accurately** *adv*

accursed Ⓣ (ə'kɜ:sıd, ə'kɜ:st) *or* **accurst** (ə'kɜ:st) *adj* **1** under or subject to a curse. **2** (*prenominal*) hateful; detestable. [OE *ācursod,* p.p. of *ācursian* to put under a CURSE]
▸**accursedly** (ə'kɜ:sıdlı) *adv* ▸**ac'cursedness** *n*

accusation Ⓣ (,ækjʊ'zeıʃən) *n* **1** an allegation that a person is guilty of some fault or crime. **2** a formal charge brought against a person.

accusative (ə'kju:zətıv) *adj* **1** *Grammar.* denoting a case of nouns, pronouns, and adjectives in inflected languages that is used to identify the direct object of a finite verb, of certain prepositions, and for certain other purposes. **2** another word for **accusatorial.** ◆ *n* **3** *Grammar.* the accusative case or a speech element in it. [C15: from L; in grammar, from *cāsus accūsātīvus* accusative case, a mistaken translation of Gk *ptōsis aitiatikē* the case indicating causation. See ACCUSE]
▸**accusatival** (ə,kju:zə'taıv^{ə}l) *adj* ▸**ac'cusatively** *adv*

accusatorial Ⓣ (ə,kju:zə'tɔ:rıəl) *or* **accusatory** (ə'kju:zətərı) *adj* **1** containing or implying blame or strong criticism. **2** *Law.* denoting a legal system in which the defendant is prosecuted before a judge in public. Cf. **inquisitorial.**

THESAURUS

ation, ground, grounds, interest, motive, regard, sake, score **4** = **importance**, advantage, benefit, consequence, distinction, esteem, honour, import, merit, note, profit, rank, repute, significance, standing, use, value, worth **8, 9** = **statement**, balance, bill, book, books, charge, computation, inventory, invoice, ledger, reckoning, register, score, tally ◆ *vb* **19** = **consider**, appraise, assess, believe, calculate, compute, count, deem, esteem, estimate, explain, gauge, hold, judge, rate, reckon, regard, think, value, weigh

accountability *n* **1** = **responsibility**, answerability, chargeability, culpability, liability

accountable *adj* **1** = **responsible**, amenable, answerable, charged with, liable, obligated, obliged

accountant *n* = **auditor**, bean counter (*inf.*), book-keeper

account for *vb* **1** = **explain**, answer for, clarify, clear up, elucidate, illuminate, justify, rationalize **3** = **put out of action**, destroy, incapacitate, kill, put paid to

accounting *n* = **accountancy**, auditing, book-keeping

accoutrements *pl n* **1, 2** = **equipment**, adornments, appurtenances, array, bells and whistles, clothing, decorations, dress, equipage, fittings, fixtures, furnishings, garb, gear, kit, ornamentation, outfit, paraphernalia, tackle, trappings, trimmings

accredit *vb* **1** = **attribute**, ascribe, assign, credit **2-4** = **authorize**, appoint, certify, commission, depute, empower, endorse, entrust, guarantee, license, recognize, sanction, vouch for

accredited *adj* **1** = **authorized**, appointed, certified, commissioned, deputed, deputized, empowered, endorsed, guaranteed, licensed, official, recognized, sanctioned, vouched for

accrue *vb* **1** = **increase**, accumulate, amass, arise, be added, build up, collect, enlarge, ensue, flow, follow, grow, issue, spring up

accumulate *vb* = **collect**, accrue, amass, build up, cumulate, gather, grow, hoard, increase, pile up, stockpile, store
Antonyms *vb* diffuse, disperse, disseminate, dissipate, distribute, propagate, scatter

accumulation *n* **1, 2** = **collection**, aggregation, augmentation, build-up, conglomeration, gathering, growth, heap, hoard, increase, mass, pile, rick, stack, stock, stockpile, store

accuracy *n* = **exactness**, accurateness, authenticity, carefulness, closeness, correctness, exactitude, faithfulness, faultlessness, fidelity, meticulousness, niceness, nicety, precision, strictness, truth, truthfulness, veracity, verity
Antonyms *n* carelessness, erroneousness, imprecision, inaccuracy, incorrectness, inexactitude, laxity, laxness

accurate *adj* **1, 3** = **exact**, authentic, careful, close, correct, faithful, faultless, just, meticulous, nice, precise, proper, regular, right, scrupulous, spot-on (*Brit. inf.*), strict, true, truthful, unerring, veracious
Antonyms *adj* careless, defective, faulty, imperfect, imprecise, inaccurate, incorrect, inexact, slovenly, wrong

accurately *adv* **1, 3** = **exactly**, authentically, carefully, closely, correctly, faithfully, faultlessly, justly, meticulously, nicely, precisely, properly, regularly, rightly, scrupulously, strictly, to the letter, truly, truthfully, unerringly, veraciously

accursed *adj* **1** = **cursed**, bedevilled, bewitched, condemned, damned, doomed, hopeless, ill-fated, ill-omened, jinxed, luckless, ruined, undone, unfortunate, unlucky, wretched **2** = **hateful**, abominable, despicable, detestable, execrable, hellish, horrible
Antonyms *adj* ≠ **cursed:** blessed, charmed, favoured, fortunate, lucky

accusation *n* **1, 2** = **charge**, allegation, arraignment, attribution, citation, complaint, denunciation, impeachment, imputation, incrimination, indictment, recrimination

accusatorial *adj* **1** = **accusing**, accusative, censorious, condemnatory, critical, denunciatory, imputative, incriminatory, recriminatory, reproachful

accuse ⓣ (əˈkjuːz) *vb* **accuses, accusing, accused.** to charge (a person or persons) with some fault, offence, crime, etc. [C13: via OF from L *accūsāre* to call to account, from *ad-* to + *causa* lawsuit]
▸**acˈcuser** *n* ▸**acˈcusing** *adj* ▸**acˈcusingly** *adv*

accused (əˈkjuːzd) *n* (preceded by *the*) *Law.* the defendant or defendants on a criminal charge.

accustom ⓣ (əˈkʌstəm) *vb* (*tr;* usually foll. by *to*) to make (oneself) familiar (with) or used (to), as by habit or experience. [C15: from OF *acostumer,* from *costume* CUSTOM]

accustomed ⓣ (əˈkʌstəmd) *adj* **1** usual; customary. **2** (*postpositive;* foll. by *to*) used (to). **3** (*postpositive;* foll. by *to*) in the habit (of).

AC/DC *adj Inf.* (of a person) bisexual. [C20: humorous reference to electrical apparatus that is adaptable for ALTERNATING CURRENT and DIRECT CURRENT]

ace ⓣ (eɪs) *n* **1** any die, domino, or any of four playing cards with one spot. **2** a single spot or pip on a playing card, die, etc. **3** *Tennis.* a winning serve that the opponent fails to reach. **4** a fighter pilot accredited with destroying several enemy aircraft. **5** *Inf.* an expert: *an ace at driving.* **6 an ace up one's sleeve.** a hidden and powerful advantage. ◆ *adj* **7** *Inf.* superb; excellent. [C13: via OF from L *as* a unit]

-acea *suffix forming plural proper nouns.* denoting animals belonging to a class or order: *Crustacea* (class); *Cetacea* (order). [NL, from L, neuter pl of *-āceus* -ACEOUS]

-aceae *suffix forming plural proper nouns.* denoting plants belonging to a family: *Liliaceae.* [NL, from L, fem pl of *-āceus* -ACEOUS]

acedia (əˈsiːdɪə) *n* another word for **accidie.**

ACE inhibitor (eɪs) *n* any one of a class of drugs, including captopril and enalapril, that cause the arteries to widen by preventing the synthesis of angiotensin: used to treat high blood pressure and heart failure. [C20: from *a(ngiotensin-)c(onverting) e(nzyme) inhibitor*]

-aceous *suffix forming adjectives.* relating to, having the nature of, or resembling: *herbaceous.* [NL, from L *-āceus* of a certain kind; rel. to *-āc, -āx,* adjectival suffix]

acephalous (əˈsɛfələs) *adj* having no head or one that is reduced and indistinct, as certain insect larvae. [C18: via Med. L from Gk *akephalos.* See A-[1], -CEPHALIC]

acer (ˈeɪsə) *n* any tree or shrub of the genus *Acer,* often cultivated for their brightly coloured foliage. See also **maple.**

acerbate (ˈæsəˌbeɪt) *vb* **acerbates, acerbating, acerbated.** (*tr*) **1** to embitter or exasperate. **2** to make sour or bitter. [C18: from L *acerbāre* to make sour]

acerbic ⓣ (əˈsɜːbɪk) *adj* harsh, bitter, or astringent; sour. [C17: from L *acerbus* sour, bitter]

acerbity (əˈsɜːbɪtɪ) *n, pl* **acerbities. 1** vitriolic or embittered speech, temper, etc. **2** sourness or bitterness of taste.

acetabulum (ˌæsɪˈtæbjʊləm) *n, pl* **acetabula** (-lə). the deep cuplike cavity on the side of the hipbone that receives the head of the thighbone. [L: vinegar cup, hence a cuplike cavity, from *acētum* vinegar + *-abulum,* suffix denoting a container]

acetal (ˈæsɪˌtæl) *n* **1** a type of organic compound formed by addition of an alcohol to an aldehyde or ketone. **2** a colourless pleasant-smelling volatile liquid used in perfumes.

acetaldehyde (ˌæsɪˈtældɪˌhaɪd) *n* a colourless volatile pungent liquid, used in the manufacture of organic compounds and as a solvent. Formula: CH_3CHO. Systematic name: **ethanal.**

acetanilide (ˌæsɪˈtænɪˌlaɪd) *n* a white crystalline powder used in the manufacture of dyes and as an analgesic in medicine.

acetate (ˈæsɪˌteɪt) *n* **1** any salt or ester of acetic acid. Systematic name: **ethanoate. 2** short for **acetate rayon** *or* **cellulose acetate. 3** an audio disc with an acetate lacquer coating: used for demonstration purposes, etc. [C19: from ACETIC + -ATE[1]]

acetate rayon *n* a synthetic textile fibre made from cellulose acetate.

acetic (əˈsiːtɪk) *adj* of, containing, producing, or derived from acetic acid or vinegar. [C19: from L *acētum* vinegar]

acetic acid *n* a colourless pungent liquid widely used in the manufacture of plastics, pharmaceuticals, dyes, etc. Formula: CH_3COOH. Systematic name: **ethanoic acid.** See also **vinegar.**

acetify (əˈsɛtɪˌfaɪ) *vb* **acetifies, acetifying, acetified.** to become or cause to become acetic acid or vinegar.
▸**aˌcetifiˈcation** *n*

aceto- *or before a vowel* **acet-** *combining form.* containing an acetyl group or derived from acetic acid: *acetone.* [from L *acētum* vinegar]

acetone (ˈæsɪˌtəʊn) *n* a colourless volatile pungent liquid used in the manufacture of chemicals and as a solvent for paints, varnishes, and lacquers. Formula: CH_3COCH_3. Systematic name: **propanone.** [C19: from G *Azeton,* from ACETO- + -ONE]

acetous (ˈæsɪtəs) *or* **acetose** (ˈæsɪˌtəʊs) *adj* **1** producing or resembling acetic acid or vinegar. **2** tasting like vinegar. [C18: from LL *acētōsus* vinegary, from *acētum* vinegar]

acetyl (ˈæsɪˌtaɪl, əˈsiːtaɪl) *n* (*modifier*) of or containing the monovalent group CH_3CO-. [C19: from ACET(IC) + -YL]

acetylcholine (ˌæsɪtaɪlˈkəʊliːn, -lɪn) *n* a chemical substance secreted at the ends of many nerve fibres, responsible for the transmission of nervous impulses.

acetylene (əˈsɛtɪˌliːn) *n* **1** a colourless soluble flammable gas used in the manufacture of organic chemicals and in cutting and welding metals. Formula: C_2H_2. Systematic name: **ethyne. 2** another name for **alkyne.**

acetylene series *n* another name for **alkyne series.**

acetylsalicylic acid (ˌæsɪtaɪlˌsælɪˈsɪlɪk) *n* the chemical name for **aspirin.**

Achaean (əˈkiːən) *or* **Achaian** (əˈkaɪən) *n* **1** a member of a principal Greek tribe in the Mycenaean era. ◆ *adj* **2** of or relating to the Achaeans.

Achates (əˈkeɪtiːz) *n* a loyal friend. [from Aeneas' faithful companion in Virgil's *Aeneid*]

ache ⓣ (eɪk) *vb* **aches, aching, ached.** (*intr*) **1** to feel, suffer, or be the source of a continuous dull pain. **2** to suffer mental anguish. ◆ *n* **3** a continuous dull pain. [OE *ācan* (vb), *æce* (n), ME *aken* (vb), *ache* (n)]
▸**ˈaching** *adj*

achene (əˈkiːn) *n* a dry one-seeded indehiscent fruit with the seed distinct from the fruit wall. [C19: from NL *achaenium* that which does not open, from A-[1] + Gk *khainein* to yawn]

Acheulian *or* **Acheulean** (əˈʃuːlɪən) *Archaeol.* ◆ *n* **1** (in Europe) the period in the Lower Palaeolithic following the Abbevillian, represented by the use of soft hammerstones in hand-axe production. **2** (in Africa) the period represented by every stage of hand-axe development. ◆ *adj* **3** of or relating to this period. [C20: after *St Acheul,* town in N France]

achieve ⓣ (əˈtʃiːv) *vb* **achieves, achieving, achieved.** (*tr*) **1** to bring to a successful conclusion. **2** to gain as by hard work or effort: *to achieve success.* [C14: from OF *achever* to bring to an end, from *a chef* to a head]
▸**aˈchievable** *adj* ▸**aˈchiever** *n*

achievement ⓣ (əˈtʃiːvmənt) *n* **1** something that has been accomplished, esp. by hard work, ability, or heroism. **2** successful completion; accomplishment.

achillea (ˌækɪˈliːə) *n* any of several cultivated varieties of yarrow.

Achilles heel (əˈkɪliːz) *n* a small but fatal weakness.

Achilles tendon *n* the fibrous cord that connects the muscles of the calf to the heelbone.

achromat (ˈækrəˌmæt) *or* **achromatic lens** *n* a lens designed to reduce chromatic aberration.

achromatic (ˌækrəˈmætɪk) *adj* **1** without colour. **2** capable of reflecting or refracting light without chromatic aberration. **3** *Music.* involving no sharps or flats.
▸**ˌachroˈmatically** *adv* ▸**achromatism** (əˈkrəʊməˌtɪzəm) *or* **achromaticity** (əˌkrəʊməˈtɪsɪtɪ) *n*

acid ⓣ (ˈæsɪd) *n* **1** any substance that dissociates in water to yield a sour corrosive solution containing hydrogen ions, and turning litmus red. **2** a sour-tasting substance. **3** a slang name for **LSD.** ◆ *adj* **4** *Chem.* **4a** of, derived from, or containing acid. **4b** being or having the properties of an acid. **5** sharp or sour in taste. **6** cutting, sharp, or hurtful in speech, manner, etc. [C17: from F *acide* or L *acidus,* from *acēre* to be sour]
▸**ˈacidly** *adv* ▸**ˈacidness** *n*

THESAURUS

accuse *vb* = **charge**, allege, arraign, attribute, blame, censure, cite, denounce, impeach, impute, incriminate, indict, point a *or* the finger at, recriminate, tax
Antonyms *vb* absolve, answer, defend, deny, exonerate, plead, reply, vindicate

accustom *vb* = **adapt**, acclimatize, acquaint, discipline, exercise, familiarize, habituate, inure, season, train

accustomed *adj* **1** = **usual**, common, conventional, customary, established, everyday, expected, fixed, general, habitual, normal, ordinary, regular, routine, set, traditional, wonted **2, 3** = **used**, acclimatized, acquainted, adapted, disciplined, exercised, familiar, familiarized, given to, habituated, in the habit of, inured, seasoned, trained
Antonyms *adj* ≠ **usual:** abnormal, infrequent, occasional, odd, peculiar, rare, strange, unaccustomed, uncommon, unfamiliar, unusual ≠ **used:** unaccustomed, unfamiliar, unused

ace *n* **1, 2** = **one**, single point **5** *Informal* = **expert**, adept, buff (*inf.*), champion, dab hand (*Brit. inf.*), genius, hotshot (*inf.*), master, maven (*US*), star, virtuoso, whizz (*inf.*), winner, wizard (*inf.*) ◆ *adj* **7** *Informal* = **excellent**, awesome (*sl.*), brilliant, champion, expert, fine, great, masterly, outstanding, superb, virtuoso

acerbic *adj* = **bitter**, acid, acrid, acrimonious, brusque, churlish, harsh, nasty, rancorous, rude, severe, sharp, stern, unfriendly, unkind = **bitter**, acetic, acid, acidulous, acrid, astringent, bitter, harsh, sharp, sour, tart, vinegary

ache *vb* **1** = **hurt**, pain, pound, smart, suffer, throb, twinge **2** = **suffer**, agonize, eat one's heart out, grieve, mourn, sorrow ◆ *n* **3** = **pain**, hurt, pang, pounding, smart, smarting, soreness, suffering, throb, throbbing

achievable *adj* **1, 2** = **attainable**, accessible, accomplishable, acquirable, feasible, obtainable, possible, practicable, reachable, realizable, winnable, within one's grasp

achieve *vb* **1, 2** = **attain**, accomplish, acquire, bring about, carry out, complete, consummate, do, earn, effect, execute, finish, fulfil, gain, get, obtain, perform, procure, put the tin lid on, reach, realize, win

achievement *n* **1** = **accomplishment**, act, deed, effort, exploit, feat, feather in one's cap, stroke **2** = **accomplishment**, accomplishment = **fulfilment**, acquirement, attainment, completion, execution, performance, production, realization

aching *adj* **1** = **painful**, hurting, pounding, smarting, sore, suffering, throbbing, tired

acid *adj* **5** = **sour**, acerb, acerbic, acetic, acidulous, acrid, biting, pungent, sharp, tart, vinegarish, vinegary **6** = **sharp**, acerbic, biting, bitter, caustic, cutting, harsh, hurtful, mordacious, mordant, pungent, stinging, trenchant, vitriolic
Antonyms *adj* ≠ **sour:** alkaline, bland, mild, pleas-

acid-fast *adj* (of bacteria and tissues) resistant to decolorization by mineral acids after staining.
Acid House *or* **Acid** *n* a dance music dominated by beat and bass line, created with synthesizers and digital sampling; popular in the late 1980s. [C20: from ACID (LSD) + HOUSE (MUSIC)]
acidic (ə'sɪdɪk) *adj* another word for **acid.**
acidify (ə'sɪdɪˌfaɪ) *vb* **acidifies, acidifying, acidified.** to convert into or become acid.
▸**a'cidiˌfiable** *adj* ▸**aˌcidifi'cation** *n*
acidity ⓘ (ə'sɪdɪtɪ) *n, pl* **acidities. 1** the quality or state of being acid. **2** the amount of acid present in a solution.
acidosis (ˌæsɪ'dəʊsɪs) *n* a condition characterized by an abnormal increase in the acidity of the blood.
▸**acidotic** (ˌæsɪ'dɒtɪk) *adj*
acid rain *n* rain containing pollutants, chiefly sulphur dioxide and nitrogen oxide, released into the atmosphere by burning coal or oil.
acid rock *n* rock music characterized by bizarre amplified instrumental effects. [C20: from ACID (LSD)]
acid test *n* a rigorous and conclusive test to establish worth or value. [C19: from the testing of gold with nitric acid]
acidulate (ə'sɪdjʊˌleɪt) *vb* **acidulates, acidulating, acidulated.** (*tr*) to make slightly acid or sour. [C18: ACIDULOUS + -ATE[1]]
▸**aˌcidu'lation** *n*
acidulous ⓘ (ə'sɪdjʊləs) *or* **acidulent** *adj* **1** rather sour. **2** sharp or sour in speech, manner, etc.; acid. [C18: from L *acidulus* sourish, dim. of *acidus* sour]
acinus ('æsɪnəs) *n, pl* **acini** (-ˌnaɪ). **1** *Anat.* any of the terminal saclike portions of a compound gland. **2** *Bot.* any of the small drupes that make up the fruit of the raspberry, etc. **3** *Bot., obs.* a collection of berries, such as a bunch of grapes. [C18: NL, from L: grape, berry]
ack-ack ('ækˌæk) *n Mil.* **a** anti-aircraft fire. **b** (*as modifier*): *ack-ack guns.* [C20: British Army World War I phonetic alphabet for AA, abbrev. of *anti-aircraft*]
acknowledge ⓘ (ək'nɒlɪdʒ) *vb* **acknowledges, acknowledging, acknowledged.** (*tr*) **1** (*may take a clause as object*) to recognize or admit the existence, truth, or reality of. **2** to indicate recognition or awareness of, as by a greeting, glance, etc. **3** to express appreciation or thanks for. **4** to make the receipt of known: *to acknowledge a letter.* **5** to recognize, esp. in legal form, the authority, rights, or claims of. [C15: prob. from earlier *knowledge,* on the model of OE *oncnāwan,* ME *aknowen* to confess, recognize]
▸**ac'knowledgeable** *adj*
acknowledgment ⓘ *or* **acknowledgement** (ək'nɒlɪdʒmənt) *n* **1** the act of acknowledging or state of being acknowledged. **2** something done or given as an expression of thanks. **3** (*pl*) an author's statement acknowledging his use of the works of other authors.
aclinic line (ə'klɪnɪk) *n* another name for **magnetic equator.** [C19 *aclinic,* from Gk *aklinēs* not bending, from A-[1] + *klinein* to bend]
acme ⓘ ('ækmɪ) *n* the culminating point, as of achievement or excellence. [C16: from Gk *akmē*]
acne ('æknɪ) *n* a chronic skin disease common in adolescence, characterized by pustules on the face. [C19: NL, from a misreading of Gk *akmē* eruption on the face. See ACME]
acolyte ⓘ ('ækəˌlaɪt) *n* **1** a follower or attendant. **2** *Christianity.* an officer who assists a priest. [C16: via OF & Med. L from Gk *akolouthos* a follower]
aconite ('ækəˌnaɪt) *n* **1** any of a genus of N temperate plants, such as monkshood and wolfsbane, many of which are poisonous. Cf. **winter aconite. 2** the dried poisonous root of many of these plants, sometimes used as a narcotic. [C16: via OF or L from Gk *akoniton* aconite]
▸**aconitic** (ˌækə'nɪtɪk) *adj*
acorn ('eɪkɔːn) *n* the fruit of the oak tree, consisting of a smooth thick-walled nut in a woody scaly cuplike base. [C16: var. (infl. by *corn*) of OE *æcern* the fruit of a tree, acorn]
acoustic (ə'kuːstɪk) *or* **acoustical** *adj* **1** of or related to sound, hearing, or acoustics. **2** designed to respond to or absorb sound: *an acoustic tile.* **3** (of a musical instrument or recording) without electronic amplification: *an acoustic guitar.* [C17: from Gk *akoustikos,* from *akouein* to hear]
▸**a'coustically** *adv*
acoustics (ə'kuːstɪks) *n* **1** (*functioning as sing*) the scientific study of sound and sound waves. **2** (*functioning as pl*) the characteristics of a room, auditorium, etc., that determine the fidelity with which sound can be heard within it.
acquaint ⓘ (ə'kweɪnt) *vb* (*tr*) (foll. by *with* or *of*) to make (a person) familiar (with). [C13: via OF & Med. L from L *accognitus,* from *accognōscere* to know perfectly, from *ad-* (intensive) + *cognōscere* to know]
acquaintance ⓘ (ə'kweɪntəns) *n* **1** a person whom one knows but who is not a close friend. **2** knowledge of a person or thing, esp. when slight. **3 make the acquaintance of.** to come into social contact with. **4** those persons collectively whom one knows.
▸**ac'quaintanceship** *n*
acquainted ⓘ (ə'kweɪntɪd) *adj* (*postpositive*) **1** (sometimes foll. by *with*) on terms of familiarity but not intimacy. **2** (foll. by *with*) familiar (with).
acquiesce ⓘ (ˌækwɪ'ɛs) *vb* **acquiesces, acquiescing, acquiesced.** (*intr;* often foll. by *in* or *to*) to comply (with); assent (to) without protest. [C17: from L *acquiēscere,* from *ad-* at + *quiēscere* to rest, from *quiēs* QUIET]
▸**ˌacqui'escence** *n* ▸**ˌacqui'escent** *adj*

> **USAGE NOTE** The use of *to* after *acquiesce* was formerly regarded as incorrect, but is now acceptable.

acquire ⓘ (ə'kwaɪə) *vb* **acquires, acquiring, acquired.** (*tr*) to get or gain (something, such as an object, trait, or ability). [C15: via OF from L *acquīrere,* from *ad-* in addition + *quaerere* to get, seek]
▸**ac'quirable** *adj* ▸**ac'quirement** *n*
acquired behaviour *n Psychol.* the behaviour of an organism resulting from the effects of the environment.
acquired characteristic *n* a characteristic of an organism resulting from the effects of the environment.
acquired immune deficiency syndrome *or* **acquired immunodeficiency syndrome** *n* the full name for **AIDS.**
acquired immunity *n* the immunity produced by exposure of an organism to antigens, which stimulates the production of antibodies.
acquired taste *n* **1** a liking for something at first considered unpleasant. **2** the thing liked.
acquisition ⓘ (ˌækwɪ'zɪʃən) *n* **1** the act of acquiring or gaining possession. **2** something acquired. **3** a person or thing of special merit added to a group. [C14: from L *acquīsītiōn-,* from *acquīrere* to ACQUIRE]
acquisitive ⓘ (ə'kwɪzɪtɪv) *adj* inclined or eager to acquire things, esp. material possessions.
▸**ac'quisitively** *adv* ▸**ac'quisitiveness** *n*

THESAURUS

ant, sweet ≠ **sharp:** benign, bland, gentle, kindly, mild, pleasant, sweet

acidity *n* **1 = sourness,** acerbity, acidulousness, acridity, acridness, bitterness, pungency, sharpness, tartness, vinegariness, vinegarishness **1 = sharpness,** acerbity, acridity, acridness, bitterness, causticity, causticness, harshness, hurtfulness, mordancy, pungency, trenchancy

acidly *adv* **6 = sharply,** acerbically, acridly, bitingly, bitterly, caustically, cuttingly, harshly, hurtfully, mordantly, pungently, stingingly, tartly, trenchantly
Antonyms *adv* benignly, blandly, gently, kindly, mildly, pleasantly, sweetly

acidulous *adj* **1 = sour,** acerb, acerbic, acetic, acid, bitter, harsh, sharp, tart, vinegarish, vinegary **2 = sharp,** acid, biting, bitter, caustic, cutting, harsh, pungent, sour, vitriolic

acknowledge *vb* **1 = accept,** accede, acquiesce, admit, allow, concede, confess, declare, grant, own, profess, recognize, yield **2 = greet,** address, hail, notice, recognize, salute **4 = reply to,** answer, notice, react to, recognize, respond to, return
Antonyms *vb* ≠ **accept:** contradict, deny, disclaim, discount, reject, renounce, repudiate ≠ **greet:** disdain, disregard, ignore, reject, snub, spurn ≠ **reply to:** deny, disavow, disregard, ignore, rebut

acknowledged *adj* **1 = accepted,** accredited, admitted, answered, approved, conceded, confessed, declared, professed, recognized, returned

acknowledgment *n* **1 = acceptance,** accession, acquiescence, admission, allowing, confession, declaration, profession, realization, yielding **1 = greeting,** addressing, hail, hailing, notice, recognition, salutation, salute **2 = appreciation,** answer, credit, gratitude, reaction, recognition, reply, response, return, thanks

acme *n* **= high point,** apex, climax, crest, crown, culmination, height, optimum, peak, pinnacle, summit, top, vertex, zenith
Antonyms *n* bottom, depths, low point, minimum, nadir, rock bottom, zero

acolyte *n* **1, 2 = attendant,** adherent, admirer, altar boy, assistant, follower, helper

acquaint *vb* **= tell,** advise, announce, apprise, disclose, divulge, enlighten, familiarize, inform, let (someone) know, notify, reveal

acquaintance *n* **1 = associate,** colleague, contact **2 = knowledge,** association, awareness, cognizance, companionship, conversance, conversancy, experience, familiarity, fellowship, intimacy, relationship, social contact, understanding
Antonyms *n* ≠ **associate:** buddy, good friend, intimate ≠ **knowledge:** ignorance, unfamiliarity

acquaintanceship *n* **2 = relationship,** acquaintance, association, companionship, fellowship, knowledge, social contact

acquainted *adj* **2** *foll. by* **with = familiar with,** alive to, apprised of, *au fait* with, aware of, cognizant of, conscious of, conversant with, experienced in, informed of, in on, knowledgeable about, privy to, up to speed with, versed in

acquiesce *vb* **= agree,** accede, accept, allow, approve, assent, bow to, comply, concur, conform, consent, give in, go along with, play ball (*inf.*), submit, yield
Antonyms *vb* balk at, contest, demur, disagree, dissent, fight, object, protest, refuse, resist, veto

acquiescence *n* **= agreement,** acceptance, accession, approval, assent, compliance, concurrence, conformity, consent, giving in, obedience, submission, yielding

acquiescent *adj* **= agreeing,** acceding, accepting, agreeable, approving, assenting, compliant, concurrent, conforming, consenting, obedient, submissive, yielding

acquire *vb* **= get,** achieve, amass, attain, buy, collect, earn, gain, gather, land, obtain, pick up, procure, realize, receive, score (*sl.*), secure, win
Antonyms *vb* be deprived of, forfeit, forgo, give up, lose, relinquish, renounce, surrender, waive

acquirement *n* **= acquisition,** accomplishment, achievement, attainment, gathering, grip

acquisition *n* **1 = acquiring,** achievement, acquirement, attainment, gaining, obtainment, procurement, pursuit **2 = possession,** buy, gain, prize, property, purchase

acquisitive *adj* **= greedy,** avaricious, avid, cov-

acquit ⓣ (ə'kwɪt) *vb* **acquits, acquitting, acquitted.** (*tr*) **1** (foll. by *of*) **1a** to free or release (from a charge of crime). **1b** to pronounce not guilty. **2** (foll. by *of*) to free or relieve (from an obligation, duty, etc.). **3** to repay or settle (a debt or obligation). **4** to conduct (oneself). [C13: from OF *aquiter*, from *quiter* to release, QUIT]
▸**ac'quittal** *n* ▸**ac'quitter** *n*

acquittance (ə'kwɪtəns) *n* **1** a release from or settlement of a debt, etc. **2** a record of this, such as a receipt.

acre ('eɪkə) *n* **1** a unit of area used in certain English-speaking countries, equal to 4840 square yards or 4046.86 square metres. **2** (*pl*) **2a** land, esp. a large area. **2b** *Inf.* a large amount. **3 farm the long acre.** *NZ.* to graze stock on the grass along a highway. [OE *æcer* field, acre]

acreage ('eɪkərɪdʒ) *n* **1** land area in acres. ◆ *adj* **2** *Austral.* of or relating to a large residential block of land, esp. in a rural area.

acrid ⓣ ('ækrɪd) *adj* **1** unpleasantly pungent or sharp to the smell or taste. **2** sharp or caustic, esp. in speech or nature. [C18: from L *ācer* sharp, sour; prob. infl. by ACID]
▸**acridity** (ə'krɪdɪtɪ) *n* ▸**'acridly** *adv*

acridine ('ækrɪˌdiːn) *n* a colourless crystalline solid used in the manufacture of dyes.

acriflavine (ˌækrɪ'fleɪvɪn) *n* a brownish or orange-red powder used in medicine as an antiseptic. [C20: from ACRIDINE + FLAVIN]

acriflavine hydrochloride *n* a red crystalline substance obtained from acriflavine and used as an antiseptic.

Acrilan ('ækrɪˌlæn) *n Trademark.* an acrylic fibre or fabric, characterized by strength and resistance to creasing and used for clothing, carpets, etc.

acrimony ⓣ ('ækrɪmənɪ) *n, pl* **acrimonies.** bitterness or sharpness of manner, speech, temper, etc. [C16: from L *ācrimōnia*, from *ācer* sharp, sour]
▸**acrimonious** (ˌækrɪ'məʊnɪəs) *adj*

acro- *combining form.* **1** denoting something at a height, top, beginning, or end: *acropolis.* **2** denoting an extremity of the human body: *acromegaly.* [from Gk *akros* extreme, topmost]

acrobat ⓣ ('ækrəˌbæt) *n* **1** an entertainer who performs acts that require skill, agility, and coordination, such as swinging from a trapeze or walking a tightrope. **2** a person noted for his frequent and rapid changes of position or allegiance. [C19: via F from Gk *akrobatēs*, one who walks on tiptoe, from ACRO- + *bat-*, from *bainein* to walk]
▸**ˌacro'batic** *adj* ▸**ˌacro'batically** *adv*

acrobatics (ˌækrə'bætɪks) *pl n* **1** the skills or feats of an acrobat. **2** any activity requiring agility and skill: *mental acrobatics.*

acrogen ('ækrədʒən) *n* any flowerless plant, such as a fern or moss, in which growth occurs from the tip of the main stem.
▸**acrogenous** (ə'krɒdʒɪnəs) *adj*

acromegaly (ˌækrəʊ'mɛgəlɪ) *n* a chronic disease characterized by enlargement of the bones of the head, hands, and feet, and swelling and enlargement of soft tissue. It is caused by excessive secretion of growth hormone by the pituitary gland. [C19: from F *acromégalie*, from ACRO- + Gk *megal-*, stem of *megas* big]
▸**acromegalic** (ˌækrəʊmɪ'gælɪk) *adj, n*

acronym ('ækrənɪm) *n* a pronounceable name made from a series of initial letters or parts of a group of words; for example, *UNESCO* for the *United Nations Educational, Scientific, and Cultural Organization.* [C20: from ACRO- + -ONYM]

acrophobia (ˌækrə'fəʊbɪə) *n* abnormal fear or dread of being at a great height. [C19: from ACRO- + -PHOBIA]
▸**ˌacro'phobic** *adj, n*

acropolis (ə'krɒpəlɪs) *n* the citadel of an ancient Greek city. [C17: from Gk, from ACRO- + *polis* city]

across ⓣ (ə'krɒs) *prep* **1** from one side to the other side of. **2** on or at the other side of. **3** so as to transcend the boundaries or barriers of: *across religious divisions.* ◆ *adv* **4** from one side to the other. **5** on or to the other side. [C13 *on croice, acros*, from OF *a croix* crosswise]

across-the-board ⓣ *adj* (**across the board** *when postpositive*) (of salary increases, taxation cuts, etc.) affecting all levels or classes equally.

acrostic (ə'krɒstɪk) *n* a number of lines of writing, such as a poem, certain letters of which form a word, proverb, etc. A **single acrostic** is formed by the initial letters of the lines, a **double acrostic** by the initial and final letters, and a **triple acrostic** by the initial, middle, and final letters. [C16: via F from Gk, from ACRO- + *stikhos* line of verse]

acrylic (ə'krɪlɪk) *adj* **1** of, derived from, or concerned with acrylic acid. ◆ *n* **2** short for **acrylic fibre, acrylic resin.** [C20: from L *ācer* sharp + *olēre* to smell + -IC]

acrylic acid *n* a colourless corrosive pungent liquid, used in the manufacture of acrylic resins. Formula: CH_2: CHCOOH. Systematic name: **propenoic acid.**

acrylic fibre *n* a man-made fibre used in blankets, knitwear, etc.

acrylic resin *n* any of a group of polymers of acrylic acid, its esters, or amides, used as synthetic rubbers, paints, and as plastics such as Perspex.

act ⓣ (ækt) *n* **1** something done or performed. **2** the performance of some physical or mental process; action. **3** (*cap. when part of a name*) the formally codified result of deliberation by a legislative body. **4** (*often pl*) a formal written record of transactions, proceedings, etc., as of a society, committee, or legislative body. **5** a major division of a dramatic work. **6a** a short performance of skill, a comic sketch, dance, etc. **6b** those giving such a performance. **7** an assumed attitude or pose, esp. one intended to impress. **8 get in on the act.** *Inf.* to become involved in a profitable situation in order to share in the benefit. **9 get one's act together.** *Inf.* to organize oneself. ◆ *vb* **10** (*intr*) to do something. **11** (*intr*) to operate; react: *his mind acted quickly.* **12** to perform (a part or role) in a play, etc. **13** (*tr*) to present (a play, etc.) on stage. **14** (*intr;* usually foll. by *for* or *as*) to be a substitute (for). **15** (*intr;* foll. by *as*) to serve the function or purpose (of). **16** (*intr*) to conduct oneself or behave (as if one were): *she usually acts like a lady.* **17** (*intr*) to behave in an unnatural or affected way. **18** (*copula*) to play the part of: *to act the fool.* **19** (*copula*) to behave in a manner appropriate to: *to act one's age.* ◆ See also **act on, act up.** [C14: from L *actus* a doing, & *actum* a thing done, from the p.p. of *agere* to do]
▸**'actable** *adj* ▸**ˌacta'bility** *n*

ACT *abbrev. for:* **1** Australian Capital Territory. **2** advance corporation tax.

ACTH *n* adrenocorticotrophic hormone; a hormone, secreted by the anterior lobe of the pituitary gland, that stimulates growth of the adrenal gland. It is used in treating rheumatoid arthritis, allergic and skin diseases, etc.

acting ⓣ ('æktɪŋ) *adj* (*prenominal*) **1** taking on duties temporarily, esp. as a substitute for another. **2** performing the duties of though not yet holding the rank of: *acting lieutenant.* **3** operating or functioning. **4** intended for stage performance; provided with directions for actors: *an acting version of "Hedda Gabler".* ◆ *n* **5** the art or profession of an actor.

actinia (æk'tɪnɪə) *n, pl* **actiniae** (-'tɪnɪˌiː) *or* **actinias.** a sea anemone common in rock pools. [C18: NL, lit.: things having a radial structure]

actinic (æk'tɪnɪk) *adj* (of radiation) producing a photochemical effect. [C19: from ACTINO- + -IC]
▸**ac'tinically** *adv* ▸**'actinˌism** *n*

actinide series ('æktɪˌnaɪd) *n* a series of 15 radioactive elements with increasing atomic numbers from actinium to lawrencium.

actinium (æk'tɪnɪəm) *n* a radioactive element of the actinide series, occurring as a decay product of uranium. It is used in neutron production. Symbol: Ac; atomic no.: 89; half-life of most stable isotope, ^{227}Ac: 22 years. [C19: NL, from ACTINO- + -IUM]

actino- *or before a vowel* **actin-** *combining form.* **1** indicating a radial

THESAURUS

etous, grabbing, grasping, predatory, rapacious
Antonyms *adj* bounteous, bountiful, generous, lavish, liberal, munificent, open-handed, unselfish, unstinting

acquisitiveness *n* = **greed**, avarice, avidity, avidness, covetousness, graspingness, predatoriness, rapaciousness, rapacity

acquit *vb* **1, 2** = **clear**, absolve, deliver, discharge, exculpate, exonerate, free, fulfil, liberate, release, relieve, vindicate **3** = **pay off**, discharge, pay, repay, satisfy, settle **4** = **behave**, bear, comport, conduct, perform
Antonyms *vb* ≠ **clear**: blame, charge, condemn, convict, damn, find guilty, sentence

acquittal *n* **1, 2** = **clearance**, absolution, deliverance, discharge, exculpation, exoneration, freeing, liberation, release, relief, vindication

acrid *adj* **1** = **pungent**, acerb, acid, astringent, biting, bitter, burning, caustic, harsh, irritating, sharp, stinging, vitriolic **2** = **sharp**, acrimonious, biting, bitter, caustic, cutting, harsh, mordacious, mordant, nasty, sarcastic, trenchant, vitriolic

acrimonious *adj* = **bitter**, acerbic, astringent, biting, caustic, censorious, churlish, crabbed, cutting, irascible, mordacious, mordant, peevish, petulant, pungent, rancorous, sarcastic, severe, sharp, spiteful, splenetic, tart, testy, trenchant, vitriolic
Antonyms *adj* affable, benign, forgiving, good-tempered

acrimony *n* = **bitterness**, acerbity, asperity, astringency, churlishness, harshness, ill will, irascibility, mordancy, peevishness, pungency, rancour, sarcasm, spleen, tartness, trenchancy, virulence
Antonyms *n* amity, friendliness, friendship, good feelings, goodwill, liking, warmth

acrobat *n* **1** = **gymnast**, tumbler

across *prep* **1** = **throughout**, all through, covering, over, over the length and breadth of, straddling **2** = **opposite**, facing **2** = **over**, beyond, on the other *or* far side of, past ◆ *adv* **4** = **from side to side**, athwart, crossways *or* crosswise, transversely **5** = **over**, beyond, past, to the other *or* far side

across-the-board *adj* = **general**, all-embracing, all-encompassing, all-inclusive, blanket, complete, comprehensive, full, indiscriminate, overarching, sweeping, thorough, thoroughgoing, total, universal, wall-to-wall, wholesale, widespread, without exception *or* omission
Antonyms *adj* discriminate, limited, partial, restricted, selective, specific

act *n* **1, 2** = **deed**, accomplishment, achievement, action, blow, doing, execution, exertion, exploit, feat, move, operation, performance, step, stroke, undertaking **3** = **law**, bill, decree, edict, enactment, measure, ordinance, resolution, statute **6a** = **performance**, routine, show, sketch, turn **7** = **pretence**, affectation, attitude, counterfeit, dissimulation, fake, feigning, front, performance, pose, posture, sham, show, stance ◆ *vb* **11, 16** = **do**, acquit, bear, behave, carry, carry out, comport, conduct, enact, execute, exert, function, go about, make, move, operate, perform, react, serve, strike, take effect, undertake, work **12** = **perform**, act out, characterize, enact, impersonate, mime, mimic, personate, personify, play, play *or* take the part of, portray, represent **14** = **stand in for**, cover for, deputize for, fill in for, function in place of, replace, represent, serve, substitute for, take the place of **17** = **pretend**, affect, assume, counterfeit, dissimulate, feign, imitate, perform, pose, posture, put on, seem, sham

acting *adj* **1, 2** = **temporary**, interim, pro tem,

structure: *actinomorphic.* **2** indicating radioactivity or radiation: *actinometer.* [from Gk, from *aktis* ray]

actinobiology (ˌæktɪnəʊbaɪˈɒlədʒɪ) *n* the branch of biology concerned with the effects of radiation on living organisms.

actinoid (ˈæktɪˌnɔɪd) *adj* having a radiate form, as a sea anemone or starfish.

actinometer (ˌæktɪˈnɒmɪtə) *n* an instrument for measuring the intensity of radiation, esp. of the sun's rays.

actinomycin (ˌæktɪnəʊˈmaɪsɪn) *n* any of several toxic antibiotics obtained from soil bacteria, used in treating some cancers.

actinozoan (ˌæktɪnəʊˈzəʊən) *n, adj* another word for **anthozoan.**

action ❶ (ˈækʃən) *n* **1** the state or process of doing something or being active. **2** something done, such as an act or deed. **3** movement or posture during some physical activity. **4** activity, force, or energy: *a man of action.* **5** (*usually pl*) conduct or behaviour. **6** *Law.* a legal proceeding brought by one party against another; lawsuit. **7** the operating mechanism, esp. in a piano, gun, watch, etc. **8** the force applied to a body. **9** the way in which something operates or works. **10 out of action.** not functioning. **11** the events that form the plot of a story, play, or other composition. **12** *Mil.* **12a** a minor engagement. **12b** fighting at sea or on land: *he saw action in the war.* **13** *Inf.* the profits of an enterprise or transaction (esp. in **a piece of the action**). **14** *Sl.* the main activity, esp. social activity. **15** short for **industrial action.** ◆ *vb* (*tr*) **16** to put into effect; take action concerning. ◆ *sentence substitute.* **17** a command given by a film director to indicate that filming is to begin. [C14 *accioun*, ult. from L *āctiōn-*, from *agere* to do]

actionable (ˈækʃənəbᵊl) *adj Law.* affording grounds for legal action.
▸ **ˈactionably** *adv*

action committee *or* **group** *n* a committee or group formed to pursue an end, usually political, using petitions, marches, etc.

action painting *n* a development of abstract expressionism characterized by accidental effects of thrown, smeared, dripped, or spattered paint. Also called: **tachisme.**

action replay *n* the rerunning of a small section of a television film or tape of a match or other sporting contest, often in slow motion.

action stations *pl n* **1** *Mil.* the positions taken up by individuals in preparation for or during a battle. ◆ *sentence substitute.* **2** a command to take up such positions. **3** *Inf.* a warning to get ready for something.

activate ❶ (ˈæktɪˌveɪt) *vb* **activates, activating, activated.** (*tr*) **1** to make active or capable of action. **2** *Physics.* to make radioactive. **3** *Chem.* to increase the rate of (a reaction). **4** to purify (sewage) by aeration. **5** *US mil.* to mobilize or organize (a unit).
▸ **ˌactiˈvation** *n* ▸ **ˈactiˌvator** *n*

activated carbon *n* a highly adsorptive form of carbon used to remove colour or impurities from liquids and gases.

activated sludge *n* a mass of aerated precipitated sewage added to untreated sewage to bring about purification by hastening bacterial decomposition.

active ❶ (ˈæktɪv) *adj* **1** moving, working, or doing something. **2** busy or involved: *an active life.* **3** physically energetic. **4** effective: *an active ingredient.* **5** *Grammar.* denoting a voice of verbs used to indicate that the subject of a sentence is performing the action or causing the event or process described by the verb, as *kicked* in *The boy kicked the football.* **6** being fully engaged in military service. **7** (of a volcano) erupting periodically; not extinct. **8** *Astron.* (of the sun) exhibiting a large number of sunspots, solar flares, etc., and a marked variation in intensity and frequency of radio emission. ◆ *n* **9** *Grammar.* **9a** the active voice. **9b** an active verb. [C14: from L *āctīvus.* See ACT, -IVE]
▸ **ˈactively** *adv* ▸ **ˈactiveness** *n*

active list *n Mil.* a list of officers available for full duty.

activism (ˈæktɪˌvɪzəm) *n* a policy of taking direct and often militant action to achieve an end, esp. a political or social one.
▸ **ˈactivist** *n*

activity ❶ (ækˈtɪvɪtɪ) *n, pl* **activities. 1** the state or quality of being active. **2** lively action or movement. **3** any specific action, pursuit, etc.: *recreational activities.* **4** the number of disintegrations of a radioactive substance in a given unit of time. **5** *Chem.* a measure of the ability of a substance to take part in a chemical reaction.

act of God *n Law.* a sudden and inevitable occurrence caused by natural forces, such as a flood or earthquake.

act on ❶ *or* **upon** *vb* (*intr, prep*) **1** to regulate one's behaviour in accordance with (advice, information, etc.). **2** to have an effect on (illness, a part of the body, etc.).

actor ❶ (ˈæktə) *or* (*fem*) **actress** (ˈæktrɪs) *n* a person who acts in a play, film, broadcast, etc.

actual ❶ (ˈæktʃʊəl) *adj* **1** existing in reality or as a matter of fact. **2** real or genuine. **3** existing at the present time; current. ◆ See also **actuals.** [C14 *actuel* existing, from LL, from L *āctus* ACT]

> **USAGE NOTE** The excessive use of *actual* and *actually* should be avoided. They are unnecessary in sentences such as *in actual fact, he is forty-two,* and *he did actually go to the play but did not enjoy it.*

actual bodily harm *n Criminal law.* injury caused by one person to another that is less serious than grievous bodily harm. Abbrev.: **ABH.**

actuality ❶ (ˌæktʃʊˈælɪtɪ) *n, pl* **actualities. 1** true existence; reality. **2** (*sometimes pl*) a fact or condition that is real.

actualize ❶ *or* **actualise** (ˈæktʃʊəˌlaɪz) *vb* **actualizes, actualizing, actualized** *or* **actualises, actualising, actualised.** (*tr*) **1** to make actual or real. **2** to represent realistically.
▸ **ˌactualiˈzation** *or* **ˌactualiˈsation** *n*

actually ❶ (ˈæktʃʊəlɪ) *adv* **1a** as an actual fact; really. **1b** (*as sentence modifier*): *actually, I haven't seen him.* **2** at present.

actuals (ˈæktʃʊəlz) *pl n Commerce.* commodities that can be purchased and used, as opposed to those bought and sold in a futures market. Also called: **physicals.**

actuarius (ˈæktʃʊˌɛərɪəs) *n S. African history.* an official of the synod of a Dutch Reformed Church. [from L; see ACTUARY]

actuary (ˈæktʃʊərɪ) *n, pl* **actuaries.** a person qualified to calculate commercial risks and probabilities involving uncertain future events, esp. in such contexts as life assurance. [C16 (meaning: registrar): from L *āctuārius* one who keeps accounts, from *actum* public business, & *acta* documents]
▸ **actuarial** (ˌæktʃʊˈɛərɪəl) *adj*

actuate ❶ (ˈæktʃʊˌeɪt) *vb* **actuates, actuating, actuated.** (*tr*) **1** to put into action or mechanical motion. **2** to motivate: *actuated by unworthy desires.* [C16: from Med. L *actuātus*, from *actuāre* to incite to action, from L *āctus* ACT]
▸ **ˌactuˈation** *n* ▸ **ˈactuˌator** *n*

act up ❶ *vb* (*intr, adv*) *Inf.* to behave in a troublesome way: *the engine began to act up.*

acuity (əˈkjuːɪtɪ) *n* keenness or acuteness, esp. in vision or thought. [C15: from OF, from L *acūtus* ACUTE]

aculeus (əˈkjuːlɪəs) *n* **1** a prickle, such as the thorn of a rose. **2** a sting. [C19: from L, dim. of *acus* needle]
▸ **aˈculeate** *adj*

THESAURUS

provisional, substitute, surrogate ◆ *n* **5** = **performance**, characterization, dramatics, enacting, impersonation, performing, playing, portrayal, portraying, stagecraft, theatre

action *n* **1, 2** = **deed**, accomplishment, achievement, act, blow, exercise, exertion, exploit, feat, move, operation, performance, step, stroke, undertaking **4** = **energy**, activity, force, liveliness, spirit, vigour, vim, vitality **4** = **movement**, activity, effect, effort, exertion, force, functioning, influence, motion, operation, power, process, work, working **5** *usually plural* = **behaviour**, bearing, comportment, conduct, demeanour, deportment, manners, ways **6** = **lawsuit**, case, cause, litigation, proceeding, prosecution, suit **12** = **battle**, affray, clash, combat, conflict, contest, encounter, engagement, fight, fighting, fray, skirmish, sortie, warfare

activate *vb* = **start**, actuate, animate, arouse, energize, galvanize, get going, impel, initiate, kick-start (*inf.*), mobilize, motivate, move, prod, prompt, propel, rouse, set going, set in motion, set off, stimulate, stir, switch on, trigger (off), turn on
Antonyms *vb* arrest, check, deactivate, halt, impede, stall, stop, terminate, turn off

activation *n* = **start**, actuation, animation, arousal, initiation, mobilization, setting in motion, switching on, triggering, turning on

active *adj* **1** = **in operation**, acting, astir, at work, doing, effectual, functioning, in action, in business, in force, live, moving, operative, running, stirring, working **2** = **busy**, bustling, engaged, full, hard-working, involved, occupied, on the go (*inf.*), on the move, strenuous **3** = **energetic**, alert, alive and kicking, animated, diligent, industrious, lively, nimble, on the go (*inf.*), quick, spirited, sprightly, spry, vibrant, vigorous, vital, vivacious
Antonyms *adj* dormant, dull, idle, inactive, inoperative, lazy, sedentary, slow, sluggish, torpid, unimaginative, unoccupied

activist *n* = **militant**, organizer, partisan

activity *n* **1, 2** = **action**, activeness, animation, bustle, enterprise, exercise, exertion, hurly-burly, hustle, labour, life, liveliness, motion, movement, stir, work **3** = **pursuit**, act, avocation, deed, endeavour, enterprise, hobby, interest, job, labour, occupation, pastime, project, scheme, task, undertaking, venture, work
Antonyms *n* ≠ **action:** dullness, idleness, immobility, inaction, inactivity, indolence, inertia, lethargy, passivity, sluggishness, torpor

act on *vb* **1** = **obey**, act in accordance with, carry out, comply with, conform to, follow, heed, yield to **2** = **affect**, alter, change, impact, influence, modify, sway, transform

actor *n* = **performer**, dramatic artist, leading man *or* lady, play-actor, player, Thespian, tragedian *or* tragedienne, trouper

actual *adj* **1** = **definite**, absolute, categorical, certain, concrete, corporeal, factual, indisputable, indubitable, physical, positive, real, substantial, tangible, undeniable, unquestionable **2** = **real**, authentic, confirmed, genuine, realistic, true, truthful, verified
Antonyms *adj* fictitious, hypothetical, made-up, probable, supposed, theoretical, unreal, untrue

actuality *n* **1** = **reality**, corporeality, factuality, materiality, realness, substance, substantiality, truth, verity **2** = **fact**, reality, truth, verity

actualize *vb* **1** = **make real**, bring about, bring into being, bring to life, effect, effectuate, give life *or* substance to, incarnate, make concrete, make happen, objectify, put into effect, realize, reify

actually *adv* **1** = **really**, absolutely, as a matter of fact, de facto, essentially, indeed, in fact, in point of fact, in reality, in truth, literally, truly, veritably

actuate *vb* **1, 2** = **motivate**, animate, arouse, cause, dispose, drive, excite, get going, impel, incite, induce, influence, inspire, instigate, move, prompt, quicken, rouse, spur, stimulate, stir, urge

act up *vb* = **misbehave**, be naughty, carry on, cause trouble, give bother, give trouble, horse

acumen Ⓣ ('ækjʊˌmɛn, ə'kjuːmən) *n* the ability to judge well; insight. [C16: from L: sharpness, from *acuere* to sharpen]
►**a'cuminous** *adj*

acuminate *adj* (ə'kjuːmɪnɪt). **1** narrowing to a sharp point, as some types of leaf. ◆ *vb* (ə'kjuːmɪˌneɪt), **acuminates, acuminating, acuminated.** **2** (*tr*) to make pointed or sharp. [C17: from L *acūmināre* to sharpen]
►**aˌcumi'nation** *n*

acupoint ('ækjʊˌpɔɪnt) *n* any of the specific points on the body into which a needle is inserted in acupuncture or onto which pressure is applied in shiatsu. [C19: from ACU(PUNCTURE) + POINT]

acupressure ('ækjʊˌprɛʃə) *n* another name for **shiatsu.** [C19: from ACU(PUNCTURE) + PRESSURE]

acupuncture ('ækjʊˌpʌŋktʃə) *n* the insertion of the tips of needles into the skin at specific points for the purpose of treating various disorders by stimulating nerve impulses. [C17: from L *acus* needle + PUNCTURE]
►**'acuˌpuncturist** *n*

acute Ⓣ (ə'kjuːt) *adj* **1** penetrating in perception or insight. **2** sensitive to details; keen. **3** of extreme importance; crucial. **4** sharp or severe; intense. **5** having a sharp end or point. **6** *Maths.* (of an angle) less than 90°. **7** (of a disease) **7a** arising suddenly and manifesting intense severity. **7b** of relatively short duration. **8** *Phonetics.* of or relating to an accent (ˊ) placed over vowels, denoting that the vowel is pronounced with higher musical pitch (as in ancient Greek) or with certain special quality (as in French). **9** (of a hospital, hospital bed, or ward) intended to accommodate short-term patients. ◆ *n* **10** an acute accent. [C14: from L *acūtus,* p.p. of *acuere* to sharpen, from *acus* needle]
►**a'cutely** *adv* ►**a'cuteness** *n*

acute accent *n* the diacritical mark (ˊ), used in some languages to indicate that the vowel over which it is placed has a special quality (as in French *été*) or that it receives the strongest stress in the word (as in Spanish *hablé*).

acute dose *n* a fatal dose of radiation.

ad (æd) *n Inf.* short for **advertisement.**

A.D. *or* **AD** (indicating years numbered from the supposed year of the birth of Christ) *abbrev. for* anno Domini: *70* A.D. [L: in the year of the Lord]

> **USAGE NOTE** In strict usage, A.D. is only employed with specific years: *he died in 1621* A.D., but *he died in the 17th century* (and not *the 17th century* A.D.). Formerly the practice was to write A.D. preceding the date (A.D. *1621*), and it is also strictly correct to omit *in* when A.D. is used, since this is already contained in the meaning of the Latin *anno Domini* (in the year of Our Lord), but this is no longer general practice. B.C. is used with both specific dates and indications of the period: *Heraclitus was born about 540* B.C.; *the battle took place in the 4th century* B.C.

ad- *prefix* **1** to; towards: *adsorb.* **2** near; next to: *adrenal.* [from L: towards. As a prefix in words of L origin, *ad-* became *ac-, af-, ag-, al-, an-, acq-, ar-, as-,* and *at-* before *c, f, g, l, n, q, r, s,* and *t,* and became *a-* before *gn, sc, sp, st*]

adage Ⓣ ('ædɪdʒ) *n* a traditional saying that is accepted by many as true; proverb. [C16: via OF from L *adagium;* rel. to *āio* I say]

adagio (ə'dɑːdʒɪˌəʊ) *Music.* ◆ *adj, adv* **1** (to be performed) slowly. ◆ *n, pl* **adagios. 2** a movement or piece to be performed slowly. [C18: It., from *ad* at + *agio* ease]

Adam[1] ('ædəm) *n* **1** *Bible.* the first man, created by God (Genesis 2–3). **2** **not know (someone) from Adam.** to have no knowledge of or acquaintance with someone. **3** **Adam's ale** *or* **wine.** water.

Adam[2] ('ædəm) *adj* in the neoclassical style made popular by Robert *Adam* (1728–92), Scottish architect and furniture designer.

adamant Ⓣ ('ædəmənt) *adj* **1** unshakable in determination, purpose, etc.; inflexible. **2** unbreakable; impenetrable. ◆ *n* **3** any extremely hard substance. **4** a legendary stone said to be impenetrable. [OE: from L *adamas,* from Gk, lit.: unconquerable, from A-[1] + *daman* to conquer]
►ˌ**ada'mantine** *adj*

Adam's apple *n* the visible projection of the thyroid cartilage of the larynx at the front of the neck.

adapt Ⓣ (ə'dæpt) *vb* **1** (often foll. by *to*) to adjust (someone or something) to different conditions. **2** (*tr*) to fit, change, or modify to suit a new or different purpose. [C17: from L *adaptāre,* from *ad-* to + *aptāre* to fit]
►**a'daptable** *adj* ►**aˌdapta'bility** *n* ►**a'daptive** *adj*

adaptation Ⓣ (ˌædæp'teɪʃən) *n* **1** the act or process of adapting or the state of being adapted. **2** something that is produced by adapting something else. **3** something that is changed or modified to suit new conditions. **4** *Biol.* a modification in organisms that makes them better suited to survive and reproduce in a particular environment.

adaptor *or* **adapter** (ə'dæptə) *n* **1** a person or thing that adapts. **2** any device for connecting two parts, esp. ones that are of different sizes. **3a** a plug used to connect an electrical device to a mains supply when they have different types of terminals. **3b** a device used to connect several electrical appliances to a single socket.

ADC *abbrev. for:* **1** aide-de-camp. **2** analogue-digital converter.

add Ⓣ (æd) *vb* **1** to combine (two or more numbers or quantities) by addition. **2** (*tr;* foll. by *to*) to increase (a number or quantity) by another number or quantity using addition. **3** (*tr;* often foll. by *to*) to join (something) to something else in order to increase the size, effect, or scope: *to add insult to injury.* **4** (*intr;* foll. by *to*) to have an extra and increased effect (on). **5** (*tr*) to say or write further. **6** (*tr;* foll. by *in*) to include. ◆ See also **add up.** [C14: from L *addere,* from *ad-* to + *-dere,* *dare* to put]

ADD *abbrev. for* attention deficit disorder.

addax ('ædæks) *n* a large light-coloured antelope having ribbed loosely spiralled horns and inhabiting desert regions in N Africa. [C17: L, from an unidentified ancient N African language]

addend ('ædɛnd) *n* any of a set of numbers that is to be added. [C20: short for ADDENDUM]

addendum Ⓣ (ə'dɛndəm) *n, pl* **addenda** (-də). **1** something added; an addition. **2** a supplement or appendix to a book, magazine, etc. [C18: from L, gerundive of *addere* to ADD]

adder ('ædə) *n* **1** Also called: **viper.** a common viper that is widely distributed in Europe, including Britain, and Asia and is dark grey with a black zigzag pattern along the back. **2** any of various similar venomous or nonvenomous snakes. ◆ See also **death adder, puff adder.** [OE *nǣdre* snake; in ME *a naddre* was mistaken for *an addre*]

adder's-tongue *n* any of several ferns that grow in the N hemisphere and have a narrow spore-bearing body that sticks out like a spike from the leaf.

addict Ⓣ *vb* (ə'dɪkt). **1** (*tr; usually passive;* often foll. by *to*) to cause (someone or oneself) to become dependent (on something, esp. a narcotic drug). ◆ *n* ('ædɪkt). **2** a person who is addicted, esp. to narcotic drugs. **3** *Inf.* a person devoted to something: *a jazz addict.* [C16 (as adj and as vb; n use C20): from L *addictus* given over, from *addīcere,* from *ad-* to + *dīcere* to say]
►**ad'diction** *n* ►**ad'dictive** *adj*

Addison's disease ('ædɪsᵊnz) *n* a disease characterized by bronzing of the skin, anaemia, and extreme weakness, caused by underactivity of

THESAURUS

around (*inf.*), malfunction, mess about, play up (*Brit. inf.*), raise Cain

acumen *n* = **judgment**, acuteness, astuteness, cleverness, discernment, ingenuity, insight, intelligence, keenness, penetration, perception, perspicacity, perspicuity, sagacity, sharpness, shrewdness, smartness, wisdom, wit

acute *adj* **1, 2** = **perceptive**, astute, canny, clever, discerning, discriminating, incisive, ingenious, insightful, intuitive, keen, observant, on the ball (*inf.*), penetrating, perspicacious, piercing, sensitive, sharp, smart, subtle **3** = **serious**, critical, crucial, dangerous, decisive, essential, grave, important, severe, sudden, urgent, vital **4** = **sharp**, cutting, distressing, excruciating, exquisite, fierce, harrowing, intense, overpowering, overwhelming, piercing, poignant, powerful, racking, severe, shooting, shrill, stabbing, sudden, violent
Antonyms *adj* ≠ **perceptive:** dense, dim, dim-witted, dull, obtuse, slow, stupid, unintelligent

acuteness *n* **1, 2** = **perceptiveness**, acuity, astuteness, canniness, cleverness, discernment, discrimination, ingenuity, insight, intuition, intuitiveness, keenness, perception, perspicacity, sensitivity, sharpness, smartness, subtleness, subtlety, wit **3** = **seriousness**, criticality, criticalness, cruciality, danger, dangerousness, decisiveness, essentiality, gravity, importance, severity, suddenness, urgency, vitalness **4** = **sharpness**, distressingness, exquisiteness, fierceness, intenseness, intensity, poignancy, powerfulness, severity, shrillness, suddenness, violence

adage *n* = **saying**, aphorism, apophthegm, axiom, by-word, dictum, maxim, motto, precept, proverb, saw

adamant *adj* **1** = **determined**, firm, fixed, immovable, inexorable, inflexible, insistent, intransigent, obdurate, relentless, resolute, rigid, set, stiff, stubborn, unbending, uncompromising, unrelenting, unshakable, unyielding
Antonyms *adj* compliant, compromising, easy-going, flexible, lax, pliant, receptive, responsive, susceptible, tensile, tractable, yielding

adapt *vb* **1, 2** = **adjust**, acclimatize, accommodate, alter, apply, change, comply, conform, convert, customize, familiarize, fashion, fit, habituate, harmonize, make, match, modify, prepare, qualify, remodel, shape, suit, tailor, tweak (*inf.*)

adaptability *n* **1, 2** = **flexibility**, adaptableness, adjustability, alterability, changeability, compliancy, convertibility, malleability, modifiability, plasticity, pliability, pliancy, resilience, variability, versatility

adaptable *adj* **1, 2** = **flexible**, adjustable, alterable, changeable, compliant, conformable, convertible, easy-going, easy-oasy (*sl.*), malleable, modifiable, plastic, pliant, resilient, variable, versatile

adaptation *n* **1** = **conversion**, adjustment, alteration, change, modification, refitting, remodelling, reworking, shift, transformation, variation, version

add *vb* **1** = **count up**, add up, compute, reckon, sum up, total, tot up **3, 6** = **include**, adjoin, affix, amplify, annex, append, attach, augment, enlarge by, increase by, supplement
Antonyms *vb* deduct, diminish, lessen, reduce, remove, subtract, take away, take from

addendum *n* **1, 2** = **addition**, adjunct, affix, appendage, appendix, attachment, augmentation, codicil, extension, extra, postscript, supplement

addict *n* **2** = **junkie** (*inf.*), dope-fiend, fiend (*inf.*), freak (*inf.*), head (*sl.*), pill-popper (*inf.*), user (*inf.*) **3** = **fan**, adherent, buff (*inf.*), devotee, enthusiast, follower, freak (*inf.*), nut (*sl.*)

addicted *adj* **1** = **hooked** (*sl.*), absorbed, accustomed, dedicated, dependent, devoted, disposed, fond, habituated, inclined, obsessed, prone

addiction *n* **1** = **dependence**, craving, enslavement, habit, obsession

addictive *adj* **1** = **habit-forming**, causing addic-

the adrenal glands. [C19: after Thomas *Addison* (1793–1860), E physician who identified it]

addition ➊ (ə'dɪʃən) *n* **1** the act, process, or result of adding. **2** a person or thing that is added or acquired. **3** a mathematical operation in which the sum of two numbers or quantities is calculated. Usually indicated by the symbol + **4** *Obs.* a title. **5 in addition.** (*adv*) also; as well. **6 in addition to.** (*prep*) besides; as well as. [C15: from L *additiōn-*, from *addere* to ADD]
▸**ad'ditional** *adj*

additionality (ə,dɪʃə'nælɪtɪ) *n* (in the European Union) the principle that the EU contributes to the funding of a project in a member country provided that the member country also contributes.

Additional Member System *n* a system of voting in which people vote separately for the candidate and the party of their choice. Parties are allocated extra seats if the number of constituencies they win does not reflect their overall share of the vote. See also **proportional representation.**

additive ➊ ('ædɪtɪv) *adj* **1** characterized or produced by addition. ◆ *n* **2** any substance added to something to improve it, prevent deterioration, etc. **3** short for **food additive.** [C17: from LL *additīvus*, from *addere* to ADD]

addle ➊ ('ædᵊl) *vb* **addles, addling, addled. 1.** to make or become confused or muddled. **2** to make or become rotten. ◆ *adj* **3** (*in combination*) indicating a confused or muddled state: *addle-brained.* [C18 (vb), back formation from *addled,* from C13 *addle* rotten, from OE *adela* filth]

add-on *n* a feature that can be added to a standard model or package to give increased benefits.

address ➊ (ə'drɛs) *n* **1** the conventional form by which the location of a building is described. **2** the written form of this, as on a letter or parcel. **3** the place at which someone lives. **4** a speech or written communication, esp. one of a formal nature. **5** skilfulness or tact. **6** *Arch.* manner of speaking. **7** *Computing.* a number giving the location of a piece of stored information. **8** (*usually pl*) expressions of affection made by a man in courting a woman. ◆ *vb* (*tr*) **9** to mark (a letter, parcel, etc.) with an address. **10** to speak to, refer to in speaking, or deliver a speech to. **11** (used reflexively; foll. by *to*) **11a** to speak or write to. **11b** to apply oneself to: *he addressed himself to the task.* **12** to direct (a message, warning, etc.) to the attention of. **13** to adopt a position facing (the ball in golf, etc.). [C14 (in the sense: to make right, adorn) and C15 (in the modern sense: to direct words): via OF from Vulgar L *addrictiāre* (unattested), from L *ad-* to + *dīrectus* DIRECT]
▸**ad'dresser** *or* **ad'dressor** *n*

addressee (,ædrɛ'siː) *n* a person or organization to whom a letter, etc., is addressed.

adduce (ə'djuːs) *vb* **adduces, adducing, adduced.** (*tr*) to cite (reasons, examples, etc.) as evidence or proof. [C15: from L *addūcere* to lead to]
▸**ad'ducent** *adj* ▸**ad'ducible** *adj* ▸**adduction** (ə'dʌkʃən) *n*

adduct (ə'dʌkt) *vb* (*tr*) **1** (of a muscle) to draw or pull (a leg, arm, etc.) towards the median axis of the body. ◆ *n* **2** *Chem.* a compound formed by direct combination of two or more different compounds or elements. [C19: from L *addūcere;* see ADDUCE]
▸**ad'duction** *n* ▸**ad'ductor** *n*

add up ➊ *vb* (*adv*) **1** to find the sum (of). **2** (*intr*) to result in a correct total. **3** (*intr*) *Inf.* to make sense. **4** (*intr;* foll. by *to*) to amount to.

-ade *suffix forming nouns.* a sweetened drink made of various fruits: *lemonade.* [from F, from L *-āta* made of, fem p.p. of verbs ending in *-āre*]

adenine ('ædənɪn) *n* a purine base present in animal and plant tissues as a constituent of the nucleic acids DNA and RNA.

adeno- *or before a vowel* **aden-** *combining form.* gland or glandular: *adenoid; adenology.* [NL, from Gk *adēn* gland]

adenoidal (,ædɪ'nɔɪdᵊl) *adj* **1** having the nasal tones or impaired breathing of one with enlarged adenoids. **2** of adenoids.

adenoids ('ædɪ,nɔɪdz) *pl n* a mass of lymphoid tissue at the back of the throat behind the uvula: when enlarged it often restricts nasal breathing, esp. in young children. [C19 : from Gk *adenoeidēs.* See ADENO-, -OID]

adenoma (,ædɪ'nəʊmə) *n, pl* **adenomas** *or* **adenomata** (-mətə). **1** a tumour occurring in glandular tissue. **2** a tumour having a glandlike structure.

adenopathy (,ædɪ'nɒpəθɪ) *n Pathol.* **1** enlargement of the lymph nodes. **2** enlargement of a gland.

adenosine (æ'dɛnə,siːn) *n Biochem.* a compound formed by the condensation of adenine and ribose. It is present in all living cells in a combined form. See also **ADP, AMP, ATP.** [C20: a blend of ADENINE + RIBOSE]

adept ➊ *adj* (ə'dɛpt). **1** proficient in something requiring skill or manual dexterity. **2** expert. ◆ *n* ('ædɛpt). **3** a person who is skilled or proficient in something. [C17: from Med. L *adeptus,* from L *adipiscī,* from *ad-* to + *apiscī* to attain]
▸**a'deptness** *n*

adequate ➊ ('ædɪkwɪt) *adj* able to fulfil a need without being abundant, outstanding, etc. [C17: from L *adaequāre,* from *ad-* to + *aequus* EQUAL]
▸**adequacy** ('ædɪkwəsɪ) *n* ▸**'adequately** *adv*

à deux *French.* (a dø) *adj, adv* of or for two persons.

ADFA *abbrev. for* Australian Defence Force Academy.

ADH *abbrev. for* antidiuretic hormone. See **vasopressin.**

adhere ➊ (əd'hɪə) *vb* **adheres, adhering, adhered.** (*intr*) **1** (usually foll. by *to*) to stick or hold fast. **2** (foll. by *to*) to be devoted (to a political party, religion, etc.). **3** (foll. by *to*) to follow exactly. [C16: via Med. L, from L *adhaerēre* to stick to]

adherent ➊ (əd'hɪərənt) *n* **1** (usually foll. by *of*) a supporter or follower. ◆ *adj* **2** sticking, holding fast, or attached.
▸**ad'herence** *n*

> **USAGE NOTE** See at **adhesion.**

adhesion ➊ (əd'hiːʒən) *n* **1** the quality or condition of sticking together or holding fast. **2** ability to make firm contact without slipping. **3** attachment, as to a political party, cause, etc. **4** an attraction or repulsion between the molecules of unlike substances in contact. **5** *Pathol.* abnormal union of structures or parts. [C17: from L *adhaesiōn-* a sticking. See ADHERE]

> **USAGE NOTE** *Adhesion* is the preferred term when talking about sticking or holding fast in a physical sense. *Adherence* is preferred when talking about attachment to a political party, cause, etc.

adhesive ➊ (əd'hiːsɪv) *adj* **1** able or designed to adhere: *adhesive tape.* **2** tenacious or clinging. ◆ *n* **3** a substance used for sticking, such as glue or paste.
▸**ad'hesively** *adv* ▸**ad'hesiveness** *n*

THESAURUS

tion *or* dependency, compelling, moreish *or* morish (*inf.*)

addition *n* **1** = **counting up**, adding up, computation, reckoning, summation, summing up, totalling, totting up **1** = **inclusion**, accession, adding, adjoining, affixing, amplification, annexation, attachment, augmentation, enlargement, extension, increasing **2** = **extra**, addendum, additive, adjunct, affix, appendage, appendix, extension, gain, increase, increment, supplement **5, 6 in addition (to)** = **as well (as)**, additionally, also, besides, into the bargain, moreover, over and above, to boot, too, withal
Antonyms *n* ≠ **inclusion, counting up:** deduction, detachment, diminution, lessening, reduction, removal, subtraction

additional *adj* **2** = **extra**, added, add-on, affixed, appended, fresh, further, increased, more, new, other, over-and-above, spare, supplementary

additive *n* **2, 3** = **added ingredient**, artificial *or* synthetic ingredient, E number, extra, supplement

addle *vb* **1** = **confuse**, befuddle, bewilder, fluster, fuddle, mix up, muddle, perplex, stupefy **2** = **go off** (*Brit. inf.*), go bad, rot, spoil, turn, turn bad

addled *adj* **1** = **confused**, at sea, befuddled, bewildered, flustered, foolish, mixed-up, muddled, perplexed, silly **2** = **off**, bad, gone bad, rancid, rotten, turned

address *n* **2** = **direction**, inscription, superscription **3** = **location**, abode, domicile, dwelling, home, house, lodging, pad (*sl.*), place, residence, situation, whereabouts **4** = **speech**, discourse, disquisition, dissertation, harangue, lecture, oration, sermon, talk ◆ *vb* **10** = **speak to**, accost, apostrophize, approach, greet, hail, invoke, salute, talk to **10** = **give a speech**, discourse, give a talk, harangue, lecture, orate, sermonize, speak, spout, talk **11 address (oneself) to** = **concentrate on**, apply (oneself) to, attend to, devote (oneself) to, engage in, focus on, knuckle down to, look to, take care of, take up, turn to, undertake

add up *vb* **1** = **count up**, add, compute, count, reckon, sum up, total, tot up **3** = **make sense**, be plausible, be reasonable, hold water, ring true, stand to reason **4** = **mean**, amount, come to, imply, indicate, reveal, signify

adept *adj* **1, 2** = **skilful**, able, accomplished, adroit, dexterous, expert, masterful, masterly, practised, proficient, skilled, versed ◆ *n* **3** = **expert**, buff (*inf.*), dab hand (*Brit. inf.*), genius, hotshot (*inf.*), master, maven (*US*), whizz (*inf.*)
Antonyms *adj* ≠ **skilful:** amateurish, awkward, clumsy, inept, unskilled

adeptness *n* **1, 2** = **skill**, ability, adroitness, aptitude, deftness, dexterity, expertise, facility, knack, mastery, proficiency, skilfulness
Antonyms *n* amateurishness, awkwardness, clumsiness, ineptitude, inexpertness

adequacy *n* = **sufficiency**, capability, commensurateness, competence, fairness, requisiteness, satisfactoriness, suitability, tolerability

adequate *adj* = **enough**, capable, commensurate, competent, fair, passable, requisite, satisfactory, sufficient, suitable, tolerable, up to scratch (*inf.*)
Antonyms *adj* deficient, inadequate, insufficient, lacking, meagre, scant, short, unsatisfactory, unsuitable

adhere *vb* **1** = **stick**, attach, cement, cleave, cling, cohere, fasten, fix, glue, glue on, hold fast, paste, stick fast, unite **2, 3** = **support**, abide by, be attached, be constant, be devoted, be faithful, be loyal, be true, cleave to, cling, follow, fulfil, heed, keep, keep to, maintain, mind, obey, observe, respect, stand by

adherent *n* **1** = **supporter**, admirer, advocate, devotee, disciple, fan, follower, hanger-on, henchman, partisan, protagonist, sectary, upholder, votary ◆ *adj* **2** = **sticky**, adhering, adhesive, clinging, gluey, glutinous, gummy, holding, mucilaginous, sticking, tacky, tenacious
Antonyms *n* ≠ **supporter:** adversary, antagonist, disputant, dissentient, enemy, foe, opponent, opposer, opposition, rival

adhesion *n* **1, 2** = **sticking**, adherence, adhesiveness, attachment, coherence, cohesion, grip, holding fast, union **3** = **support**, allegiance, attachment, constancy, devotion, faithfulness, fidelity, fulfilment, heed, loyalty, obedience, observation, respect, troth (*arch.*)

adhesive *adj* **1, 2** = **sticky**, adhering, attaching, clinging, cohesive, gluey, glutinous, gummy, holding, mucilaginous, sticking,

DICTIONARY

ad hoc 🅣 (æd 'hɒk) *adj, adv* for a particular purpose only: *an ad hoc committee.* [L, lit.: to this]

ad hominem *Latin.* (æd 'hɒmɪˌnɛm) *adj, adv* directed against a person rather than his arguments. [lit.: to the man]

adiabatic (ˌædɪə'bætɪk) *adj* **1** (of a thermodynamic process) taking place without loss or gain of heat. ◆ *n* **2** a curve on a graph representing the changes in a system undergoing an adiabatic process. [C19: from Gk, from A-[1] + *diabatos* passable]

adieu 🅣 (ə'dju:) *sentence substitute, n, pl* **adieus** *or* **adieux** (ə'dju:z). goodbye. [C14: from OF, from *a* to + *dieu* God]

ad infinitum 🅣 (æd ˌɪnfɪ'naɪtəm) *adv* without end; endlessly; to infinity. Abbrev.: **ad inf.** [L]

ad interim (æd 'ɪntərɪm) *adj, adv* for the meantime: *ad interim measures.* Abbrev.: **ad int.** [L]

adipocere (ˌædɪpəʊ'sɪə) *n* a waxlike fatty substance sometimes formed during the decomposition of corpses. [C19: from NL *adiposus* fat + F *cire* wax]

adipose ('ædɪˌpəʊs) *adj* **1** of, resembling, or containing fat; fatty. ◆ *n* **2** animal fat. [C18: from NL *adiposus*, from L *adeps* fat]

adit ('ædɪt) *n* an almost horizontal shaft into a mine, for access or drainage. [C17: from L *aditus*, from *adīre*, from *ad-* towards + *īre* to go]

adj. *abbrev. for:* **1** adjective. **2** adjunct. **3** Also: **adjt.** adjutant.

adjacent 🅣 (ə'dʒeɪsᵊnt) *adj* being near or close, esp. having a common boundary; contiguous. [C15: from L *adjacēre*, from *ad-* near + *jacēre* to lie]
▸**ad'jacency** *n* ▸**ad'jacently** *adv*

adjacent angles *pl n* two angles having the same vertex and a side in common.

adjective ('ædʒɪktɪv) *n* **1a** a word imputing a characteristic to a noun or pronoun. **1b** (*as modifier*): *an adjective phrase.* Abbrev.: **adj.** ◆ *adj* **2** additional or dependent. [C14: from LL, from L from *adjicere*, from *ad-* to + *jacere* to throw]
▸**adjectival** (ˌædʒɪk'taɪvᵊl) *adj*

adjoin 🅣 (ə'dʒɔɪn) *vb* **1** to be next to (an area of land, etc.). **2** (*tr;* foll. by *to*) to join; attach. [C14: via OF from L, from *ad-* to + *jungere* to join]
▸**ad'joining** *adj*

adjourn 🅣 (ə'dʒɜ:n) *vb* **1** (*intr*) (of a court, etc.) to close at the end of a session. **2** to postpone or be postponed, esp. temporarily. **3** (*tr*) to put off (a problem, discussion, etc.) for later consideration. **4** (*intr*) *Inf.* to move elsewhere: *let's adjourn to the kitchen.* [C14: from OF *ajourner* to defer to an arranged day, from *a-* to + *jour* day, from LL *diurnum*, from L *diēs* day]
▸**ad'journment** *n*

adjudge 🅣 (ə'dʒʌdʒ) *vb* **adjudges, adjudging, adjudged.** (*tr; usually passive*) **1** to pronounce formally; declare. **2a** to judge. **2b** to decree: *he was adjudged bankrupt.* **2c** to award (costs, damages, etc.). **3** *Arch.* to condemn. [C14: via OF from L *adjūdicāre*. See ADJUDICATE]

adjudicate 🅣 (ə'dʒu:dɪˌkeɪt) *vb* **adjudicates, adjudicating, adjudicated. 1** (when *intr*, usually foll. by *upon*) to give a decision (on), esp. a formal or binding one. **2** (*intr*) to serve as a judge or arbiter, as in a competition. [C18: from L *adjūdicāre*, from *ad-* to + *jūdicāre* to judge, from *jūdex* judge]
▸**adˌjudi'cation** *n* ▸**ad'judiˌcator** *n*

adjunct 🅣 ('ædʒʌŋkt) *n* **1** something incidental or not essential that is added to something else. **2** a person who is subordinate to another. **3** *Grammar.* **3a** part of a sentence other than the subject or the predicate. **3b** a modifier. ◆ *adj* **4** added or connected in a secondary position. [C16: from L *adjunctus*, p.p. of *adjungere* to ADJOIN]
▸**adjunctive** (ə'dʒʌŋktɪv) *adj* ▸**'adjunctly** *adv*

adjure 🅣 (ə'dʒʊə) *vb* **adjures, adjuring, adjured.** (*tr*) **1** to command, often by exacting an oath. **2** to appeal earnestly to. [C14: from L *adjūrāre*, from *ad-* to + *jūrāre* to swear, from *jūs* oath]
▸**adjuration** (ˌædʒʊə'reɪʃən) *n* ▸**ad'juratory** *adj* ▸**ad'jurer** *or* **ad'juror** *n*

adjust 🅣 (ə'dʒʌst) *vb* **1** (*tr*) to alter slightly, esp. to achieve accuracy. **2** to adapt, as to a new environment, etc. **3** (*tr*) to put into order. **4** (*tr*) *Insurance.* to determine the amount payable in settlement of (a claim). [C17: from OF *adjuster*, from *ad-* to + *juste* right, JUST]
▸**ad'justable** *adj* ▸**ad'juster** *n*

adjustment 🅣 (ə'dʒʌstmənt) *n* **1** the act of adjusting or state of being adjusted. **2** a control for regulating.

adjutant ('ædʒətənt) *n* an officer who acts as administrative assistant to a superior officer. [C17: from L *adjūtāre* to AID]
▸**'adjutancy** *n*

adjutant bird *or* **stork** *n* either of two large carrion-eating storks which are similar to the marabou and occur in S and SE Asia. [so called for its supposedly military gait]

adjutant general *n, pl* **adjutants general. 1** *Brit. Army.* a member of the Army Board responsible for personnel and administrative functions. **2** *US Army.* the adjutant of a military unit with general staff.

adjuvant ('ædʒəvənt) *adj* **1** aiding or assisting. ◆ *n* **2** something that aids or assists; auxiliary. [C17: from L *adjuvāre*, from *juvāre* to help]

Adlerian (æd'lɪərɪən) *adj* of or relating to the work of Alfred Adler (1870–1937), Austrian psychiatrist.

ad-lib 🅣 (æd'lɪb) *vb* **ad-libs, ad-libbing, ad-libbed. 1** to improvise and deliver spontaneously (a speech, etc.). ◆ *adj* (**ad lib** *when predicative*) **2** improvised. ◆ *adv* **ad lib. 3** spontaneously; freely. ◆ *n* **4** an improvised performance, often humorous. [C18: short for L *ad libitum*, lit.: according to pleasure]

ad libitum (ˌæd 'lɪbɪtəm) *adv, adj Music.* at the performer's discretion. [L.: see AD-LIB]

Adm. *abbrev. for:* **1** Admiral. **2** Admiralty.

adman ('ædˌmæn) *n, pl* **admen.** *Inf.* a man who works in advertising.

admass ('ædmæs) *n* the section of the public that is susceptible to advertising, etc., and the processes involved in influencing them. [C20: from AD + MASS]

admeasure (æd'mɛʒə) *vb* **admeasures, admeasuring, admeasured.** to measure out (land, etc.) as a share; apportion. [C14 *amesuren*, from OF, from *mesurer* to MEASURE; the modern form derives from AD- + MEASURE]

admin ('ædmɪn) *n Inf.* short for **administration.**

administer 🅣 (əd'mɪnɪstə) *vb* (*mainly tr*) **1** (*also intr*) to direct or control (the affairs of a business, etc.). **2** to dispense: *administer justice.* **3** (when *intr*, foll. by *to*) to give or apply (medicine, etc.). **4** to supervise the taking of (an oath, etc.). **5** to manage (an estate, property, etc.). [C14 *amynistre* via OF from L, from *ad-* to + *ministrāre* to MINISTER]

administrate 🅣 (əd'mɪnɪˌstreɪt) *vb* **administrates, administrating, administrated.** to manage or direct (the affairs of a business, institution, etc.).

administration 🅣 (ədˌmɪnɪ'streɪʃən) *n* **1** management of the affairs of an organization, such as a business or institution. **2** the duties of an administrator. **3** the body of people who administer an organization. **4** the conduct of the affairs of government. **5** term of office: used of governments, etc. **6** the government as a whole. **7** (*often cap.*) *Chiefly US.* the political executive, esp. of the US. **8** *Property law.* **8a** the con-

THESAURUS

tacky, tenacious ◆ *n* **3** = **glue**, cement, gum, mucilage, paste

ad hoc *adj* = **makeshift**, expedient, impromptu, improvised, jury-rigged (*chiefly Nautical*), stopgap ◆ *adv* = **for present purposes**, as the need arises
Antonyms *adj* ≠ **makeshift:** fixed, lasting, permanent, regular, standing (*of a committee*)

adieu *n* = **goodbye**, congé, farewell, leave-taking, parting, valediction

ad infinitum *adv* = **endlessly**, always, boundlessly, eternally, evermore, for all time, for ever (and ever), infinitely, in perpetuity, *in perpetuum*, interminably, limitlessly, perpetually, to infinity, unceasingly, unendingly, without end *or* limit

adjacent *adj* = **next**, abutting, adjoining, alongside, beside, bordering, cheek by jowl, close, contiguous, near, neighbouring, next door, proximate, touching, within sniffing distance (*inf.*)
Antonyms *adj* distant, far away, remote, separated

adjoin *vb* **1, 2** = **connect**, abut, add, affix, annex, append, approximate, attach, border, combine, communicate with, couple, impinge, interconnect, join, link, neighbour, touch, unite, verge

adjoining *adj* **1, 2** = **connecting**, abutting, adjacent, bordering, contiguous, interconnecting, joined, joining, near, neighbouring, next door, touching, verging

adjourn *vb* **1, 2** = **postpone**, defer, delay, discontinue, interrupt, prorogue, put off, put on the back burner (*inf.*), recess, stay, suspend, take a rain check on (*US & Canad. inf.*)
Antonyms *vb* assemble, continue, convene, gather, open, remain, reopen, stay

adjournment *n* **1, 2** = **postponement**, deferment, deferral, delay, discontinuation, interruption, prorogation, putting off, recess, stay, suspension

adjudge *vb* **1, 2** = **judge**, adjudicate, allot, apportion, assign, award, decide, declare, decree, determine, distribute, order, pronounce

adjudicate *vb* **1, 2** = **judge**, adjudge, arbitrate, decide, determine, mediate, referee, settle, umpire

adjudication *n* **1** = **judgment**, adjudgment, arbitration, conclusion, decision, determination, finding, pronouncement, ruling, settlement, verdict

adjudicator *n* **1, 2** = **judge**, arbiter, arbitrator, moderator, referee, umpire

adjunct *n* **1** = **addition**, accessory, addendum, add-on, appendage, appurtenance, auxiliary, complement, supplement

adjure *vb* **1** = **order**, charge, command, direct, enjoin **2** = **beg**, appeal to, beseech, entreat, implore, invoke, pray, supplicate

adjust *vb* **1-3** = **alter**, acclimatize, accommodate, accustom, adapt, arrange, compose, convert, customize, dispose, fit, fix, harmonize, make conform, measure, modify, order, reconcile, rectify, redress, regulate, remodel, set, settle, suit, tune (up), tweak (*inf.*)

adjustable *adj* **1-3** = **alterable**, adaptable, flexible, malleable, modifiable, mouldable, movable, tractable

adjustment *n* **1** = **alteration**, adaptation, arrangement, arranging, fitting, fixing, modification, ordering, rectification, redress, regulation, remodelling, setting, tuning **1** = **acclimatization**, harmonization, orientation, reconciliation, settlement, settling in

ad-lib *vb* **1** = **improvise**, busk, extemporize, make up, speak extemporaneously, speak impromptu, speak off the cuff, vamp, wing it (*inf.*) ◆ *adj* **2** = **improvised**, extemporaneous, extempore, extemporized, impromptu, made up, off-the-cuff (*inf.*), off the top of one's head, unprepared, unrehearsed ◆ *adv* **3 ad lib** = **off the cuff**, extemporaneously, extempore, impromptu, off the top of one's head (*inf.*), spontaneously, without preparation, without rehearsal

administer *vb* **1, 5** = **manage**, conduct, control, direct, govern, handle, oversee, run, superintend, supervise **2, 3** = **give**, apply, contribute, dispense, distribute, execute, impose, mete out, perform, provide

administrate *vb* = **manage**, administer, conduct, control, direct, govern, handle, oversee, run, superintend, supervise

administration *n* **1** = **management**, administering, application, conduct, control, direction, dispensation, distribution, execution, governing, government, overseeing, performance, provision, running, superintendence, supervi-

duct or disposal of the estate of a deceased person. **8b** the management by a trustee of an estate. **9a** the administering of something, such as a sacrament or medical treatment. **9b** the thing that is administered.
▸**ad'ministrative** *adj* ▸**ad'ministratively** *adv*

administration order *n Law.* **1** an order by a court appointing a person to manage a company that is in financial difficulty. **2** an order by a court for the administration of the estate of a debtor who has been ordered by the court to pay money that he owes.

administrator ❶ (əd'mɪnɪˌstreɪtə) *n* **1** a person who administers the affairs of an organization, official body, etc. **2** *Property law.* a person authorized to manage an estate.

admirable ❶ ('ædmərəbᵊl) *adj* deserving or inspiring admiration; excellent.
▸**'admirably** *adv*

admiral ('ædmərəl) *n* **1** the supreme commander of a fleet or navy. **2** Also called: **admiral of the fleet, fleet admiral.** a naval officer of the highest rank. **3** a senior naval officer entitled to fly his own flag. See also **rear admiral, vice admiral. 4** *Chiefly Brit.* the master of a fishing fleet. **5** any of various brightly coloured butterflies, esp. the red admiral or white admiral. [C13 *amyral,* from OF *amiral* emir, & from Med. L *admīrālis* (spelling prob. infl. by *admīrābilis* admirable); both from Ar. *amīr* emir, commander, esp. in *amīr-al* commander of]
▸**'admiralship** *n*

admiralty ('ædmərəltɪ) *n, pl* **admiralties. 1** the office or jurisdiction of an admiral. **2** jurisdiction over naval affairs.

Admiralty Board *n* **the.** a department of the British Ministry of Defence, responsible for the administration of the Royal Navy.

Admiralty House *n* the official residence of the Governor General of Australia, in Sydney.

admiration ❶ (ˌædmə'reɪʃən) *n* **1** pleasurable contemplation or surprise. **2** a person or thing that is admired.

admire ❶ (əd'maɪə) *vb* **admires, admiring, admired.** (*tr*) **1** to regard with esteem, approval, or pleased surprise. **2** *Arch.* to wonder at. [C16: from L *admīrāri,* from *ad-* to, at + *mīrāri* to wonder]
▸**ad'mirer** *n* ▸**ad'miring** *adj* ▸**ad'miringly** *adv*

admissible ❶ (əd'mɪsəbᵊl) *adj* **1** able or deserving to be considered or allowed. **2** deserving to be allowed to enter. **3** *Law.* (esp. of evidence) capable of being admitted in a court of law.
▸**adˌmissi'bility** *n*

admission ❶ (əd'mɪʃən) *n* **1** permission to enter or the right to enter. **2** the price charged for entrance. **3** acceptance for a position, etc. **4** a confession, as of a crime, etc. **5** an acknowledgment of the truth of something. [C15: from L *admissiōn-,* from *admittere* to ADMIT]
▸**ad'missive** *adj*

admit ❶ (əd'mɪt) *vb* **admits, admitting, admitted.** (*mainly tr*) **1** (*may take a clause as object*) to confess or acknowledge (a crime, mistake, etc.). **2** (*may take a clause as object*) to concede (the truth of something). **3** to allow to enter. **4** (foll. by *to*) to allow participation (in) or the right to be part (of). **5** (when *intr,* foll. by *of*) to allow (of). [C14: from L *admittere,* from *ad-* to + *mittere* to send]

admittance ❶ (əd'mɪtᵊns) *n* **1** the right or authority to enter. **2** the act of giving entrance. **3** *Electricity.* the reciprocal of impedance.

admittedly ❶ (əd'mɪtɪdlɪ) *adv* (*sentence modifier*) willingly conceded: *admittedly I am afraid.*

admix (əd'mɪks) *vb* (*tr*) *Rare.* to mix or blend. [C16: back formation from obs. *admixt,* from L *admīscēre* to mix with]

admixture ❶ (əd'mɪkstʃə) *n* **1** a less common word for **mixture. 2** an ingredient.

admonish ❶ (əd'mɒnɪʃ) *vb* (*tr*) **1** to reprove firmly but not harshly. **2** to warn; caution. [C14: via OF from Vulgar L *admonestāre* (unattested), from L *admonēre,* from *monēre* to advise]
▸**admonition** (ˌædmə'nɪʃən) *n* ▸**ad'monitory** *adj*

ad nauseam ❶ (æd 'nɔːzɪˌæm) *adv* to a disgusting extent. [L: to (the point of) nausea]

ado ❶ (ə'duː) *n* bustling activity; fuss; bother; delay (esp. in **without more ado, with much ado**). [C14: from *at do* a to-do, from ON *at* to (marking the infinitive) + DO[1]]

adobe (ə'dəʊbɪ) *n* **1** a sun-dried brick used for building. **2** a building constructed of such bricks. **3** the clayey material from which such bricks are made. [C19: from Sp.]

adolescence ❶ (ˌædə'lɛsəns) *n* the period in human development that occurs between the beginning of puberty and adulthood. [C15: via OF from L, from *adolēscere* to grow up]

adolescent ❶ (ˌædə'lɛsᵊnt) *adj* **1** of or relating to adolescence. **2** *Inf.* behaving in an immature way. ◆ *n* **3** an adolescent person.

Adonis (ə'dəʊnɪs) *n* **1** *Greek myth.* a handsome youth loved by Aphrodite. **2** a handsome young man. [C16: from L via Gk from Phoenician *adōni* my lord; rel. to Heb. *Adonai* Lord]

adopt ❶ (ə'dɒpt) *vb* (*tr*) **1** *Law.* to take (another's child) as one's own child. **2** to choose and follow (a plan, method, etc.). **3** to take over (an idea, etc.) as if it were one's own. **4** to assume: *to adopt a title.* **5** to accept (a report, etc.). [C16: from L *adoptāre,* from *optāre* to choose]
▸**ˌadop'tee** *n* ▸**a'doption** *n*

adopted (ə'dɒptɪd) *adj* having been adopted.

adoptive (ə'dɒptɪv) *adj* **1** acquired or related by adoption: *an adoptive father.* Cf. **adopted. 2** of or relating to adoption.

adorable ❶ (ə'dɔːrəbᵊl) *adj* **1** very attractive; lovable. **2** *Becoming rare.* deserving adoration.
▸**a'dorably** *adv*

adoration ❶ (ˌædə'reɪʃən) *n* **1** deep love or esteem. **2** the act of worshipping.

adore ❶ (ə'dɔː) *vb* **adores, adoring, adored. 1** (*tr*) to love intensely or deeply. **2** to worship (a god) with religious rites. **3** (*tr*) *Inf.* to like very much. [C15: via F from L *adōrāre,* from *ad-* to + *ōrāre* to pray]
▸**a'dorer** *n* ▸**a'doring** *adj* ▸**a'doringly** *adv*

THESAURUS

sion **3, 5, 6** = **government**, executive, governing body, management, ministry, term of office

administrative *adj* **1, 3, 5, 6** = **managerial**, directorial, executive, governmental, gubernatorial (*chiefly US*), management, organizational, regulatory, supervisory

administrator *n* **1** = **manager**, agent, bureaucrat, executive, functionary, mandarin, minister, officer, official, organizer, supervisor

admirable *adj* = **excellent**, choice, commendable, estimable, exquisite, fine, laudable, meritorious, praiseworthy, rare, sterling, superior, valuable, wonderful, worthy
Antonyms *adj* bad, commonplace, deplorable, disappointing, displeasing, mediocre, no great shakes (*inf.*), worthless

admiration *n* **1** = **regard**, adoration, affection, amazement, appreciation, approbation, approval, astonishment, delight, esteem, pleasure, praise, respect, surprise, veneration, wonder, wonderment

admire *vb* **1** = **respect**, adore, appreciate, approve, esteem, idolize, look up to, praise, prize, take one's hat off to, think highly of, value, venerate, worship **2** = **marvel at**, appreciate, delight in, take pleasure in, wonder at
Antonyms *vb* contemn, deride, despise, look down on, look down one's nose at (*inf.*), misprize, scorn, sneer at, spurn, undervalue

admirer *n* **1** = **suitor**, beau, boyfriend, lover, sweetheart, wooer **1** = **fan**, adherent, buff (*inf.*), devotee, disciple, enthusiast, follower, partisan, protagonist, supporter, votary, worshipper

admissible *adj* **1** = **permissible**, acceptable, allowable, allowed, passable, permitted, tolerable, tolerated
Antonyms *adj* disallowed, inadmissible, intolerable, unacceptable

admission *n* **1** = **entrance**, acceptance, access, admittance, entrée, entry, ingress, initiation, introduction **4, 5** = **confession**, acknowledgment, admitting, affirmation, allowance, avowal, concession, declaration, disclosure, divulgence, profession, revelation

admit *vb* **1, 2** = **confess**, acknowledge, affirm, avow, concede, cough (*sl.*), declare, disclose, divulge, own, profess, reveal **3** = **let in**, accept, allow, allow to enter, give access, initiate, introduce, receive, take in **4, 5** = **allow**, agree, grant, let, permit, recognize
Antonyms *vb* ≠ **let in:** exclude, keep out ≠ **allow:** deny, dismiss, forbid, negate, prohibit, reject

admittance *n* **1, 2** = **letting in**, acceptance, access, admitting, allowing, entrance, entry, passage, reception

admittedly *adv* = **it must be admitted**, allowedly, avowedly, certainly, confessedly, it cannot be denied, it must be allowed, it must be confessed, it must be said, to be fair *or* honest, undeniably

admixture *n* **1** = **mixture**, alloy, amalgamation, blend, combination, compound, fusion, intermixture, medley, meld **2** = **ingredient**, component, constituent, element

admonish *vb* **1, 2** = **reprimand**, advise, bawl out (*inf.*), berate, carpet (*inf.*), caution, censure, check, chide, counsel, enjoin, exhort, forewarn, rap over the knuckles, read the riot act, rebuke, reprove, scold, slap on the wrist, tear into (*inf.*), tell off (*inf.*), upbraid, warn
Antonyms *vb* applaud, commend, compliment, congratulate, praise

admonition *n* **1, 2** = **reprimand**, advice, berating, caution, chiding, counsel, rebuke, remonstrance, reproach, reproof, scolding, telling off (*inf.*), upbraiding, warning

admonitory *adj* **1, 2** = **reprimanding**, admonishing, advisory, cautionary, rebuking, reproachful, reproving, scolding, warning

ad nauseam *adv* = **again and again**, ad infinitum, on and on, over and over (again), time after time, time and (time) again, times without number

ado *n* = **fuss**, agitation, bother, bustle, commotion, confusion, delay, disturbance, excitement, flurry, pother, stir, to-do, trouble

adolescence *n* = **youth**, boyhood, girlhood, juvenescence, minority, teens = **youthfulness**, boyishness, childishness, girlishness, immaturity, juvenility, puerility

adolescent *adj* **1, 2** = **young**, boyish, girlish, growing, immature, juvenile, puerile, teenage, youthful ◆ *n* **3** = **youth**, juvenile, minor, teenager, youngster

adopt *vb* **1** = **foster**, take in **2-5** = **choose**, accept, appropriate, approve, assume, embrace, endorse, espouse, follow, maintain, ratify, select, support, take on, take over, take up
Antonyms *vb* ≠ **choose:** abandon, abnegate, cast aside, cast off, disavow, disclaim, disown, forswear, give up, reject, renounce, repudiate, spurn, wash one's hands of

adoption *n* **1** = **fostering**, adopting, fosterage, taking in **2-5** = **choice**, acceptance, approbation, appropriation, approval, assumption, embracing, endorsement, espousal, following, maintenance, ratification, selection, support, taking on, taking over, taking up

adorable *adj* **1** = **lovable**, appealing, attractive, captivating, charming, cute, darling, dear, delightful, fetching, pleasing, precious, sweet
Antonyms *adj* despicable, displeasing, hateful, unlikable *or* unlikeable, unlovable

adoration *n* **1, 2** = **love**, admiration, esteem, estimation, exaltation, glorification, honour, idolatry, idolization, reverence, veneration, worship, worshipping

adore *vb* **1, 2** = **love**, admire, bow to, cherish, dote on, esteem, exalt, glorify, honour, idolize, revere, reverence, venerate, worship
Antonyms *vb* abhor, abominate, despise, detest, execrate, hate, loathe

adorn ❶ (əˈdɔːn) *vb* (*tr*) **1** to decorate. **2** to increase the beauty, distinction, etc., of. [C14: via OF from L *adōrnāre*, from *ōrnāre* to furnish]
▸**aˈdornment** *n*

ADP *n Biochem.* adenosine diphosphate; a substance derived from ATP with the liberation of energy that is then used in the performance of muscular work.

ad rem *Latin.* (æd ˈrɛm) *adj, adv* to the point; without digression.

adrenal (əˈdriːnᵊl) *adj* **1** on or near the kidneys. **2** of or relating to the adrenal glands or their secretions. ◆ *n* **3** an adrenal gland. [C19: from AD- (near) + RENAL]

adrenal gland *n* an endocrine gland at the anterior end of each kidney. It secretes adrenaline. Also called: **suprarenal gland.**

adrenaline *or* **adrenalin** (əˈdrɛnəlɪn) *n* a hormone that is secreted by the adrenal medulla in response to stress and increases heart rate, pulse rate, and blood pressure. It is extracted from animals or synthesized for medical use. US name: **epinephrine.**

adrift ❶ (əˈdrɪft) *adj* (*postpositive*), *adv* **1** floating without steering or mooring; drifting. **2** without purpose; aimless. **3** *Inf.* off course.

adroit ❶ (əˈdrɔɪt) *adj* **1** skilful or dexterous. **2** quick in thought or reaction. [C17: from F *à droit* rightly]
▸**aˈdroitly** *adv* ▸**aˈdroitness** *n*

adsorb (ədˈsɔːb) *vb* to undergo or cause to undergo a process in which a substance, usually a gas, accumulates on the surface of a solid forming a thin film. [C19: AD- + -*sorb* as in ABSORB]
▸**adˈsorbable** *adj* ▸**adˈsorbent** *adj* ▸**adˈsorption** *n*

adsorbate (ədˈsɔːbeɪt) *n* a substance that has been or is to be adsorbed.

ADT (in the US and Canada) *abbrev. for* Atlantic Daylight Time.

adulate ❶ (ˈædjuˌleɪt) *vb* **adulates, adulating, adulated.** (*tr*) to flatter or praise obsequiously. [C17: back formation from C15 *adulation*, from L *adūlārī* to flatter]
▸ˌ**aduˈlation** *n* ▸ˈ**aduˌlator** *n* ▸**adulatory** (ˌædjuˈleɪtərɪ) *adj*

adult ❶ (ˈædʌlt, əˈdʌlt) *adj* **1** having reached maturity; fully developed. **2** of or intended for mature people: *adult education.* **3** suitable only for adults because of being pornographic. ◆ *n* **4** a person who has attained maturity. **5** a mature fully grown animal or plant. **6** *Law.* a person who has attained the age of legal majority. [C16: from L *adultus*, from *adolēscere* to grow up]
▸**aˈdulthood** *n*

adulterant (əˈdʌltərənt) *n* **1** a substance that adulterates. ◆ *adj* **2** adulterating.

adulterate ❶ *vb* (əˈdʌltəˌreɪt), **adulterates, adulterating, adulterated. 1** (*tr*) to debase by adding inferior material: *to adulterate milk with water.* ◆ *adj* (əˈdʌltərɪt). **2** debased or impure. [C16: from L *adulterāre* to corrupt, commit adultery, prob. from *alter* another]
▸**aˌdulterˈation** *n* ▸**aˈdulterˌator** *n*

adulterer ❶ (əˈdʌltərə) *or* (*fem*) **adulteress** *n* a person who has committed adultery. [C16: orig. also *adulter*, from L *adulter*, back formation from *adulterāre* to ADULTERATE]

adulterous ❶ (əˈdʌltərəs) *adj* of, characterized by, or inclined to adultery.
▸**aˈdulterously** *adv*

adultery ❶ (əˈdʌltərɪ) *n, pl* **adulteries.** voluntary sexual intercourse between a married man or woman and a partner other than the legal spouse. [C15 *adulterie*, altered from C14 *avoutrie*, via OF from L *adulterium*, from *adulter*, back formation from *adulterāre*. See ADULTERATE]

adumbrate (ˈædʌmˌbreɪt) *vb* **adumbrates, adumbrating, adumbrated.** (*tr*) **1** to outline; give a faint indication of. **2** to foreshadow. **3** to obscure. [C16: from L *adumbrāre* to cast a shadow on, from *umbra* shadow]
▸ˌ**adumˈbration** *n* ▸**adumbrative** (ædˈʌmbrətɪv) *adj*

adv. *abbrev. for:* **1** adverb. **2** adverbial. **3** adversus. [L: against] **4** advertisement. **5** advocate.

ad valorem (æd vəˈlɔːrəm) *adj, adv* (of taxes) in proportion to the estimated value of the goods taxed. Abbrev.: **ad val., a.v., A/V.** [from L]

advance ❶ (ədˈvɑːns) *vb* **advances, advancing, advanced. 1** to go or bring forward in position. **2** (foll. by *on*) to move (towards) in a threatening manner. **3** (*tr*) to present for consideration. **4** to improve; further. **5** (*tr*) to cause (an event) to occur earlier. **6** (*tr*) to supply (money, goods, etc.) beforehand, either for a loan or as an initial payment. **7** to increase (a price, etc.) or (of a price, etc.) to be increased. **8** (*intr*) to be promoted. ◆ *n* **9** forward movement; progress in time or space. **10** improvement; progress in development. **11** *Commerce.* **11a** the supplying of commodities or funds before receipt of an agreed consideration. **11b** the commodities or funds supplied in this manner. **12** Also called: **advance payment.** a money payment made before it is legally due: *this is an advance on your salary.* **13** a loan of money. **14** an increase in price, etc. **15 in advance. 15a** beforehand: *payment in advance.* **15b** (foll. by *of*) ahead in time or development: *ideas in advance of the time.* **16** (*modifier*) forward in position or time: *advance booking.* ◆ See also **advances.** [C15 *advauncen*, altered from C13 *avauncen*, via OF from L *abante*, from *ab-* away + *ante* before]
▸**adˈvancer** *n*

advance corporation tax *n* a British tax in which a company paying a dividend must deduct the basic rate of income tax from the grossed-up value of the dividend and pay it to the Inland Revenue. Abbrev.: **ACT.**

advanced ❶ (ədˈvɑːnst) *adj* **1** being ahead in development, knowledge, progress, etc. **2** having reached a comparatively late stage: *a man of advanced age.* **3** ahead of the times.

advanced gas-cooled reactor *n* a nuclear reactor using carbon dioxide as the coolant, and ceramic uranium dioxide cased in stainless steel as the fuel. Abbrev.: **AGR.**

advance directive *n* another name for **living will.**

Advanced level *n* a formal name for **A level.**

advancement ❶ (ədˈvɑːnsmənt) *n* **1** promotion in rank, status, etc. **2** a less common word for **advance** (senses 9, 10).

advances ❶ (ədˈvɑːnsɪz) *pl n* (*sometimes sing;* often foll. by *to* or *towards*) overtures made in an attempt to become friendly, etc.

advantage ❶ (ədˈvɑːntɪdʒ) *n* **1** (often foll. by *over* or *of*) a more favourable position; superiority. **2** benefit or profit (esp. in **to one's advantage**). **3** *Tennis.* the point scored after deuce. **4 take advantage of. 4a** to make good use of. **4b** to impose upon the weakness, good nature, etc., of. **4c** to seduce. **5 to advantage.** to good effect. ◆ *vb* **advantages, advantaging, advantaged. 6** (*tr*) to put in a better position; favour. [C14 *avantage* (later altered to *advantage*), from OF *avant* before, from L *abante* from before. See ADVANCE]

THESAURUS

adoring *adj* **1** = **loving**, admiring, adulatory, affectionate, ardent, devoted, doting, enamoured, fond, idolizing, reverent, reverential, venerating, worshipping
Antonyms *adj* abhorring, abominating, despising, detesting, hating, loathing

adorn *vb* **1, 2** = **decorate**, array, beautify, bedeck, deck, embellish, emblazon, engarland, enhance, enrich, festoon, garnish, gild the lily, grace, ornament, trim

adornment *n* **1** = **decoration**, accessory, embellishment, festoon, frill, frippery, ornament, supplement, trimming **2** = **ornamentation**, beautification, decorating, decoration, embellishment, trimming

adrift *adj* **1** = **drifting**, afloat, unanchored, unmoored **2** = **aimless**, directionless, goalless, purposeless ◆ *adv* **3** = **wrong**, amiss, astray, off course

adroit *adj* **1, 2** = **skilful**, able, adept, apt, artful, bright (*inf.*), clever, cunning, deft, dexterous, expert, ingenious, masterful, neat, nimble, proficient, quick-witted, skilled
Antonyms *adj* awkward, blundering, bungling, cack-handed (*inf.*), clumsy, ham-fisted *or* ham-handed (*inf.*), incpt, inexpert, maladroit, uncoordinated, unhandy, unskilful

adroitness *n* **1, 2** = **skill**, ability, ableness, address, adeptness, aptness, artfulness, cleverness, craft, cunning, deftness, dexterity, expertise, ingeniousness, ingenuity, knack, masterfulness, mastery, nimbleness, proficiency, quick-wittedness, skilfulness

adulation *n* = **worship**, blandishment, bootlicking (*inf.*), extravagant flattery, fawning, fulsome praise, servile flattery, sycophancy
Antonyms *n* abuse, calumniation, censure, condemnation, disparagement, revilement, ridicule, vilification, vituperation

adulatory *adj* = **worshipping**, blandishing, bootlicking (*inf.*), fawning, flattering, obsequious, praising, servile, slavish, sycophantic

adult *adj* **1** = **fully grown**, full grown, fully developed, grown-up, mature, of age, ripe ◆ *n* **4, 6** = **grown-up**, grown *or* grown-up person (man *or* woman), person of mature age

adulterate *vb* **1** = **debase**, attenuate, bastardize, contaminate, corrupt, depreciate, deteriorate, devalue, make impure, mix with, thin, vitiate, water down, weaken ◆ *adj* **2** = **debased**, adulterated, attenuated, bastardized, contaminated, corrupt, depreciated, deteriorated, devalued, mixed, thinned, vitiated, watered down, weakened

adulterer *n* = **cheat** (*inf.*), fornicator

adulterous *adj* = **unfaithful**, cheating, extramarital, fornicating, unchaste

adultery *n* = **unfaithfulness**, cheating (*inf.*), extracurricular sex (*inf.*), extramarital congress, extramarital relations, extramarital sex, fornication, having an affair *or* a fling, illicit sex, infidelity, playing away from home (*sl.*), playing the field (*sl.*), unchastity
Antonyms *n* chastity, faithfulness, fidelity

advance *vb* **1** = **progress**, accelerate, come forward, go ahead, go forward, go on, make inroads, move onward, move up, press on, proceed **3** = **suggest**, adduce, allege, cite, offer, present, proffer, put forward, submit **4** = **benefit**, further, grow, improve, multiply, prosper, thrive **5** = **promote**, accelerate, bring forward, bring up, elevate, hasten, send forward, send up, speed, upgrade **6** = **lend**, pay beforehand, supply on credit ◆ *n* **9** = **progress**, advancement, development, forward movement, headway, inroads, onward movement **10** = **improvement**, advancement, amelioration, betterment, breakthrough, furtherance, gain, growth, progress, promotion, step **12-14** = **loan**, credit, deposit, down payment, increase (*in price*), prepayment, retainer, rise (*in price*) ◆ *modifier* **16** = **prior**, beforehand, early, foremost, forward, in front, leading **16 in advance** = **beforehand**, ahead, earlier, in the forefront, in the lead, in the van, previously
Antonyms *vb* ≠ **progress:** decrease, diminish, lessen, move back, regress, retreat, weaken ≠ **suggest:** hide, hold back, suppress, withhold ≠ **promote:** demote, hold back, impede, retard, set back ≠ **lend:** defer payment, withhold payment

advanced *adj* **1, 3** = **foremost**, ahead, avant-garde, extreme, forward, higher, leading, precocious, progressive
Antonyms *adj* backward, behind, late, retarded, underdeveloped, undeveloped

advancement *n* **1** = **promotion**, advance, amelioration, betterment, gain, growth, improvement, preferment, progress, rise **2** = **progress**, advance, forward movement, headway, onward movement

advances *pl n* **advances** = **overtures**, approach, approaches, moves, proposals, proposition

advantage *n* **1, 2** = **benefit**, ace in the hole, ace up one's sleeve, aid, ascendancy, asset, assistance, avail, blessing, boon, convenience, dominance, edge, gain, good, help, inside track, interest, lead, mileage (*inf.*), precedence, preeminence, profit, service, start, superiority, sway, upper hand, use, utility, welfare

advantageous ➊ (ˌædvənˈteɪdʒəs) *adj* producing advantage.
▸ˌ**advan'tageously** *adv*

advection (ədˈvɛkʃən) *n* the transference of heat energy in a horizontal stream of gas, esp. of air. [C20: from L *advectiō*, from *advehere*, from *ad-* to + *vehere* to carry]

advent ➊ (ˈædvɛnt, -vənt) *n* an arrival or coming, esp. one which is awaited. [C12: from L *adventus*, from *advenīre*, from *ad-* to + *venīre* to come]

Advent (ˈædvɛnt) *n* the season including the four Sundays preceding Christmas.

Advent calendar *n* a large card with small numbered doors for children to open on each of the days of Advent, revealing pictures beneath them.

Adventist (ˈædvɛntɪst) *n* a member of a Christian group that holds that the Second Coming of Christ is imminent.

adventitious (ˌædvɛnˈtɪʃəs) *adj* **1** added or appearing accidentally. **2** (of a plant or animal part) developing in an abnormal position. [C17: from L *adventīcius* coming from outside, from *adventus* a coming]
▸ˌ**adven'titiously** *adv*

adventure ➊ (ədˈvɛntʃə) *n* **1** a risky undertaking of unknown outcome. **2** an exciting or unexpected event or course of events. **3** a hazardous financial operation. ◆ *vb* **adventures, adventuring, adventured. 4** to take a risk or put at risk. **5** (*intr*; foll. by *into, on,* or *upon*) to dare to enter (into a place, dangerous activity, etc.). **6** to dare to say (something): *he adventured his opinion.* [C13 *aventure* (later altered to *adventure*), via OF ult. from L *advenīre* to happen to (someone), arrive]

adventure playground *n Brit.* a playground for children that contains building materials, etc., used to build with, climb on, etc.

adventurer ➊ (ədˈvɛntʃərə) *or* (*fem*) **adventuress** *n* **1** a person who seeks adventure, esp. one who seeks success or money through daring exploits. **2** a person who seeks money or power by unscrupulous means. **3** a speculator.

adventurism (ədˈvɛntʃəˌrɪzəm) *n* recklessness, esp. in politics and finance.
▸**ad'venturist** *n*

adventurous ➊ (ədˈvɛntʃərəs) *adj* **1** Also: **adventuresome.** daring or enterprising. **2** dangerous; involving risk.

adverb (ˈædˌvɜːb) *n* **a** a word or group of words that serves to modify a whole sentence, a verb, another adverb, or an adjective; for example, *easily, very,* and *happily* respectively in the sentence *They could easily envy the very happily married couple.* **b** (*as modifier*): *an adverb marker.* Abbrev.: **adv.** [C15–C16: from L *adverbium* adverb, lit.: added word]
▸**ad'verbial** *adj*

adversarial (ˌædvɜːˈsɛərɪəl) *adj* (of political parties) hostile to and opposing each other on party lines; antagonistic.

adversary ➊ (ˈædvəsərɪ) *n, pl* **adversaries. 1** a person or group that is hostile to someone. **2** an opposing contestant in a sport. [C14: from L *adversārius*, from *adversus* against]

adversative (ədˈvɜːsətɪv) *Grammar.* ◆ *adj* **1** (of a word, phrase, or clause) implying opposition. *But* and *although* are adversative conjunctions. ◆ *n* **2** an adversative word or speech element.

adverse ➊ (ˈædvɜːs) *adj* **1** antagonistic; hostile: *adverse criticism.* **2** unfavourable to one's interests: *adverse circumstances.* **3** contrary or opposite: *adverse winds.* [C14: from L *adversus*, from *advertere*, from *ad-* towards + *vertere* to turn]
▸**ad'versely** *adv* ▸**ad'verseness** *n*

adversity ➊ (ədˈvɜːsɪtɪ) *n, pl* **adversities. 1** distress; affliction; hardship. **2** an unfortunate event.

advert[1] ➊ (ədˈvɜːt) *vb* (*intr*; foll. by *to*) to draw attention (to). [C15: from L *advertere* to turn one's attention to]

advert[2] ➊ (ˈædvɜːt) *n Brit. inf.* short for **advertisement.**

advertise ➊ *or US* (*sometimes*) **advertize** (ˈædvəˌtaɪz) *vb* **advertises, advertising, advertised** *or US* (*sometimes*) **advertizes, advertizing, advertized. 1** to present or praise (goods, a service, etc.) to the public, esp. in order to encourage sales. **2** to make (a vacancy, article for sale, etc.) publicly known: *to advertise a job.* **3** (*intr*; foll. by *for*) to make a public request (for): *she advertised for a cook.* [C15: from OF *avertir*, ult. from L *advertere* to turn one's attention to. See ADVERSE]
▸ˈ**adverˌtiser** *or US* (*sometimes*) ˈ**adverˌtizer** *n*

advertisement ➊ *or US* (*sometimes*) **advertizement** (ədˈvɜːtɪsmənt) *n* any public notice, as a printed display in a newspaper, short film on television, etc., designed to sell goods, publicize an event, etc.

advertising *or US* (*sometimes*) **advertizing** (ˈædvəˌtaɪzɪŋ) *n* **1** the promotion of goods or services for sale through impersonal media such as television. **2** the business that specializes in creating such publicity. **3** advertisements collectively.

Advertising Standards Authority *n* (in Britain) an independent body set up by the advertising industry to ensure that all advertisements comply with the British Code of Advertising Practice. Abbrev.: **ASA.**

advertorial (ˌædvɜːˈtɔːrɪəl) *n* **1** advertising presented under the guise of editorial material. ◆ *adj* **2** presented in such a manner. [C20: from blend of ADVERT[2] + EDITORIAL]

advice ➊ (ədˈvaɪs) *n* **1** recommendation as to appropriate choice of action. **2** (*sometimes pl*) formal notification of facts. [C13 *avis* (later *advise*), via OF from Vulgar L, from L *ad* to + *vīsum* view]

advisable ➊ (ədˈvaɪzəbᵊl) *adj* worthy of recommendation; prudent.
▸**ad'visably** *adv* ▸**adˌvisa'bility** *or* **ad'visableness** *n*

advise ➊ (ədˈvaɪz) *vb* **advises, advising, advised.** (*when tr, may take a clause as object or an infinitive*) **1** to offer advice (to a person or persons): *he advised caution.* **2** (*tr*; sometimes foll. by *of*) to inform or notify. **3** (*intr*; foll. by *with*) *Chiefly US, obs. in Britain.* to consult. [C14: via OF from Vulgar L *advīsāre* (unattested), from L *ad-* to + *vidēre* to see]

advised ➊ (ədˈvaɪzd) *adj* resulting from deliberation. See also **ill-advised, well-advised.**
▸**advisedly** (ədˈvaɪzɪdlɪ) *adv*

adviser ➊ *or* **advisor** (ədˈvaɪzə) *n* **1** a person who advises. **2** *Education.* a person responsible for advising students on career guidance, etc. **3** *Brit. education.* a subject specialist who advises on current teaching methods and facilities.

advisory ➊ (ədˈvaɪzərɪ) *adj* **1** empowered to make recommendations: *an advisory body.* ◆ *n, pl* **advisories. 2** a statement issued to give advice, recommendations, or a warning: *a travel advisory.* **3** a person or organization with an advisory function: *the Prime Minister's media advisory.*

advocaat (ˈædvəʊˌkɑː) *n* a liqueur having a raw egg base. [C20: Du.]

advocacy ➊ (ˈædvəkəsɪ) *n, pl* **advocacies.** active support, esp. of a cause.

advocate ➊ *vb* (ˈædvəˌkeɪt), **advocates, advocating, advocated. 1** (*tr*; *may*

THESAURUS

Antonyms *n* curse, difficulty, disadvantage, downside, drawback, handicap, hindrance, inconvenience, snag

advantageous *adj* = **beneficial**, convenient, expedient, helpful, of service, profitable, useful, valuable, worthwhile
Antonyms *adj* detrimental, unfavourable, unfortunate, unhelpful, useless

advent *n* = **coming**, appearance, approach, arrival, entrance, occurrence, onset, visitation

adventure *n* **1-3** = **escapade**, chance, contingency, enterprise, experience, exploit, hazard, incident, occurrence, risk, speculation, undertaking, venture ◆ *vb* **4, 5** = **dare**, endanger, hazard, imperil, jeopardize, risk, venture

adventurer *n* **1** = **hero**, daredevil, heroine, knight-errant, soldier of fortune, swashbuckler, traveller, venturer, voyager, wanderer **2, 3** = **mercenary**, charlatan, fortune-hunter, gambler, opportunist, rogue, speculator

adventurous *adj* **1, 2** = **daring**, adventuresome, audacious, bold, dangerous, daredevil, enterprising, foolhardy, have-a-go (*inf.*), hazardous, headstrong, intrepid, rash, reckless, risky, temerarious (*rare*), venturesome
Antonyms *adj* careful, cautious, chary, circumspect, hesitant, prudent, safe, tentative, timid, timorous, unadventurous, wary

adversary *n* **1, 2** = **opponent**, antagonist, competitor, contestant, enemy, foe, opposer, rival
Antonyms *n* accomplice, ally, associate, collaborator, colleague, confederate, co-worker, friend, helper, partner, supporter

adverse *adj* **1-3** = **unfavourable**, antagonistic, conflicting, contrary, detrimental, disadvantageous, hostile, inexpedient, inimical, injurious, inopportune, negative, opposing, opposite, reluctant, repugnant, unfortunate, unfriendly, unlucky, unpropitious, unwilling
Antonyms *adj* advantageous, auspicious, beneficial, favourable, fortunate, helpful, lucky, opportune, promising, propitious, suitable

adversity *n* **1, 2** = **hardship**, affliction, bad luck, calamity, catastrophe, deep water, disaster, distress, hard times, ill-fortune, ill-luck, misery, misfortune, mishap, reverse, sorrow, suffering, trial, trouble, woe, wretchedness

advert[1] *vb* = **refer**, allude, draw attention (to), mention, notice, observe, regard, remark

advert[2] *n Informal* = **advertisement**, ad (*inf.*), announcement, bill, blurb, circular, commercial, display, notice, placard, plug (*inf.*), poster, promotion, publicity, puff

advertise *vb* **1-3** = **publicize**, advise, announce, apprise, blazon, crack up (*inf.*), declare, display, flaunt, inform, make known, notify, plug (*inf.*), praise, proclaim, promote, promulgate, publish, puff, push (*inf.*), tout

advertisement *n* = **advert** (*Brit. inf.*), ad (*inf.*), announcement, bill, blurb, circular, commercial, display, notice, placard, plug (*inf.*), poster, promotion, publicity, puff

advice *n* **1** = **guidance**, admonition, caution, counsel, help, injunction, opinion, recommendation, suggestion, view **2** = **notification**, information, instruction, intelligence, notice, warning, word

advisability *n* = **wisdom**, appropriateness, aptness, desirability, expediency, fitness, judiciousness, profitability, propriety, prudence, seemliness, soundness, suitability

advisable *adj* = **wise**, appropriate, apt, desirable, expedient, fit, fitting, judicious, politic, profitable, proper, prudent, recommended, seemly, sensible, sound, suggested, suitable
Antonyms *adj* ill-advised, impolitic, improper, imprudent, inappropriate, inexpedient, injudicious, silly, stupid, undesirable, unfitting, unprofitable, unseemly, unsound, unsuitable, unwise

advise *vb* **1** = **recommend**, admonish, caution, commend, counsel, enjoin, prescribe, suggest, urge **2** = **notify**, acquaint, apprise, inform, let (someone) know, make known, report, tell, warn

advisedly *adv* = **deliberately**, after careful consideration, by design, calculatedly, designedly, intentionally, judiciously, on purpose, premeditatedly, prudently, with intent

adviser *n* **1, 2** = **guide**, aide, authority, coach, confidant, consultant, counsel, counsellor, guru, helper, lawyer, mentor, right-hand man, solicitor, teacher, tutor

advisory *adj* **1** = **advising**, consultative, counselling, helping, recommending

advocacy *n* = **recommendation**, advancement, argument for, backing, campaigning for, championing, defence, encouragement, espousal, justification, pleading for, promotion, promulgation, propagation, proposal, spokesmanship, support, upholding, urging

advocate *vb* **1** = **recommend**, advise, argue for, campaign for, champion, commend, countenance, defend, encourage, espouse, favour, justify, plead for, prescribe, press for, promote, propose, speak for, support, uphold,

take a clause as object) to support or recommend publicly. ◆ *n* ('ædvəkɪt). **2** a person who upholds or defends a cause. **3** a person who intercedes on behalf of another. **4** a person who pleads his client's cause in a court of law. **5** *Scots Law.* the usual word for **barrister.** [C14: via OF from L *advocātus* legal witness, from *advocāre,* from *vocāre* to call]

advowson (əd'vauzᵊn) *n English ecclesiastical law.* the right of presentation to a vacant benefice. [C13: via OF from L *advocātiōn-,* from *advocāre* to summon]

advt *abbrev. for* advertisement.

adze *or US* **adz** (ædz) *n* a hand tool with a steel blade attached at right angles to a wooden handle, used for dressing timber. [OE *adesa*]

AEA (in Britain) *abbrev. for* Atomic Energy Authority.

AEC (in the US) *abbrev. for* Atomic Energy Commission.

aedes (eɪ'iːdiːz) *n* a mosquito of tropical and subtropical regions which transmits yellow fever. [C20: NL, from Gk *aēdēs* unpleasant, from A-[1] + *ēdos* pleasant]

aedile *or US (sometimes)* **edile** ('iːdaɪl) *n* a magistrate of ancient Rome in charge of public works, games, buildings, and roads. [C16: from L *aedīlis,* from *aedēs* a building]

AEEU (in Britain) *abbrev. for* Amalgamated Engineering and Electrical Union.

Aegean (iː'dʒiːən) *adj* of or relating to the Aegean Sea or Islands.

aegis **T** *or US (sometimes)* **egis** ('iːdʒɪs) *n* **1** sponsorship or protection (esp. in **under the aegis of**). **2** *Greek myth.* the shield of Zeus. [C18: from L, from Gk *aigis* shield of Zeus]

aegrotat ('aɪgrəʊ,tæt, 'iː-) *n* **1** (in British and certain other universities, and, sometimes, schools) a certificate allowing a candidate to pass an examination although he has missed all or part of it through illness. **2** a degree or other qualification obtained in such circumstances. [C19: L, lit.: he is ill]

-aemia, -haemia, *or US* **-emia, -hemia** *n combining form.* denoting blood, esp. a specified condition of the blood in diseases: *leukaemia.* [NL, from Gk, from *haima* blood]

Aeneid (ɪ'niːɪd) *n* an epic poem in Latin by Virgil relating the experiences of Aeneas after the fall of Troy.

aeolian harp (iː'əʊlɪən) *n* a stringed instrument that produces a musical sound when wind passes over the strings. Also called: **wind harp.**

aeolotropic (,iːələʊ'trɒpɪk) *adj* a less common word for **anisotropic.** [C19: from Gk *aiolos* fickle + -TROPIC]
▸**aeolotropy** (,iːə'lɒtrəpɪ) *n*

aeon *or esp. US* **eon** ('iːən, 'iːɒn) *n* **1** an immeasurably long period of time. **2** *Astron.* a period of one thousand million years. [C17: from Gk *aiōn* an infinitely long time]

aerate ('ɛəreɪt) *vb* **aerates, aerating, aerated.** *(tr)* **1** to charge (a liquid) with a gas, as in the manufacture of effervescent drink. **2** to expose to the action or circulation of the air.
▸**aer'ation** *n* ▸**'aerator** *n*

aeri- *combining form.* a variant of **aero-.**

aerial ('ɛərɪəl) *adj* **1** of or resembling air. **2** existing, moving, or operating in the air: *aerial cable car.* **3** ethereal; light and delicate. **4** imaginary. **5** extending high into the air. **6** of or relating to aircraft: *aerial combat.* ◆ *n* **7** Also called: **antenna.** the part of a radio or television system by means of which radio waves are transmitted or received. [C17: via L from Gk *aērios,* from *aēr* air]

aerialist ('ɛərɪəlɪst) *n* a trapeze artist or tightrope walker.

aerie ('ɛərɪ) *n* a variant spelling (esp. US) of **eyrie.**

aeriform ('ɛərɪ,fɔːm) *adj* **1** having the form of air; gaseous. **2** unsubstantial.

aero ('ɛərəʊ) *n (modifier)* of or relating to aircraft or aeronautics: *an aero engine.*

aero-, aeri-, *or before a vowel* **aer-** *combining form.* **1** denoting air, atmosphere, or gas: *aerodynamics.* **2** denoting aircraft: *aeronautics.* [ult. from Gk *aēr* air]

aerobatics (,ɛərəʊ'bætɪks) *n (functioning as sing or pl)* spectacular or dangerous manoeuvres, such as loops or rolls, performed in an aircraft or glider. [C20: from AERO- + (ACRO)BATICS]

aerobe ('ɛərəʊb) *or* **aerobium** (ɛə'rəʊbɪəm) *n, pl* **aerobes** *or* **aerobia** (-'əʊbɪə). an organism that requires free oxygen or air for respiration. [C19: from AERO- + Gk *bios* life]

aerobic (ɛə'rəʊbɪk) *adj* **1** (of an organism or process) depending on free oxygen or air. **2** of or relating to aerobes. **3** designed for or relating to aerobics: *aerobic shoes; aerobic dances.*

aerobics (ɛə'rəʊbɪks) *n (functioning as sing)* any system of exercises designed to increase the amount of oxygen in the blood.

aerodrome ('ɛərə,drəʊm) *n* a landing area that is smaller than an airport.

aerodynamic braking *n* **1** the use of aerodynamic drag to slow spacecraft re-entering the atmosphere. **2** the use of airbrakes to retard flying vehicles or objects. **3** the use of a parachute or reversed thrust to decelerate an aircraft before landing.

aerodynamics (,ɛərəʊdaɪ'næmɪks) *n (functioning as sing)* the study of the dynamics of gases, esp. of the forces acting on a body passing through air.
▸,**aerody'namic** *adj* ▸,**aerody'namically** *adv* ▸,**aerody'namicist** *n*

aeroembolism (,ɛərəʊ'ɛmbə,lɪzəm) *n* the presence in the blood of nitrogen bubbles, caused by an abrupt reduction in atmospheric pressure. See **decompression sickness.**

aero engine *n* an engine for powering an aircraft.

aerofoil ('ɛərəʊ,fɔɪl) *n* a cross section of a wing, rotor blade, etc.

aerogram *or* **aerogramme** ('ɛərə,græm) *n* an air-mail letter written on a single sheet of lightweight paper that folds and is sealed to form an envelope. Also called: **air letter.**

aerolite ('ɛərə,laɪt) *n* a stony meteorite consisting of silicate minerals.

aerology (ɛə'rɒlədʒɪ) *n* the study of the atmosphere, including its upper layers.
▸**aerological** (,ɛərə'lɒdʒɪkᵊl) *adj* ▸**aer'ologist** *n*

aeromechanics (,ɛərəʊmɪ'kænɪks) *n (functioning as sing)* the mechanics of gases, esp. air.
▸,**aerome'chanical** *adj*

aeronautics (,ɛərə'nɔːtɪks) *n (functioning as sing)* the study or practice of all aspects of flight through the air.
▸,**aero'nautical** *adj*

aeropause ('ɛərə,pɔːz) *n* the region of the upper atmosphere above which aircraft cannot fly.

aeroplane ('ɛərə,pleɪn) *or US* **airplane** ('ɛə,pleɪn) *n* a heavier-than-air powered flying vehicle with fixed wings. [C19: from F *aéroplane,* from AERO- + Gk *-planos* wandering]

aerosol ('ɛərə,sɒl) *n* **1** a colloidal dispersion of solid or liquid particles in a gas. **2** a substance, such as a paint or insecticide, dispensed from a small metal container by a propellant under pressure. **3** Also called: **air spray.** such a substance together with its container. [C20: from AERO- + SOL(UTION)]

aerospace ('ɛərə,speɪs) *n* **1** the atmosphere and space beyond. **2** *(modifier)* of rockets, missiles, space vehicles, etc.: *the aerospace industry.*

aerostat ('ɛərə,stæt) *n* a lighter-than-air craft, such as a balloon. [C18: from F *aérostat,* from AERO- + Gk *-statos* standing]
▸,**aero'static** *adj*

aerostatics (,ɛərə'stætɪks) *n (functioning as sing)* **1** the study of gases in equilibrium and bodies held in equilibrium in gases. Cf. **aerodynamics.** **2** the study of lighter-than-air craft, such as balloons.

aerugo (ɪ'ruːgəʊ) *n* (esp. of old bronze) another name for **verdigris.** [C18: from L, from *aes* copper, bronze]
▸**aeruginous** (ɪ'ruːdʒɪnəs) *adj*

aery ('ɛərɪ) *n, pl* **aeries.** a variant of **eyrie.**

Aeschylean (,iːskə'liːən) *adj* of or relating to the works of Aeschylus, 5th-century B.C. Greek dramatist.

Aesculapian (,iːskju'leɪpɪən) *adj* of or relating to Aesculapius, the Roman god of medicine, or to the art of medicine.

aesthesia *or US* **esthesia** (iːs'θiːzɪə) *n* the normal ability to experience sensation. [C20: back formation from ANAESTHESIA]

aesthete *or US* **esthete** ('iːsθiːt) *n* a person who has or who affects a highly developed appreciation of beauty. [C19: back formation from AESTHETICS]

aesthetic **T** (iːs'θɛtɪk, ɪs-) *or US (sometimes)* **esthetic** *adj also* **aesthetical** *or US (sometimes)* **esthetical.** **1** connected with aesthetics. **2a** relating to pure beauty rather than to other considerations. **2b** artistic: *an aesthetic consideration.* ◆ *n* **3** a principle of taste or style adopted by a particular person, group, or culture: *the Bauhaus aesthetic of functional modernity.* [C19: from Gk *aisthētikos,* from *aisthanesthai* to perceive, feel]
▸**aes'thetically** *or US (sometimes)* **es'thetically** *adv* ▸**aes'theti,cism** *or US (sometimes)* **es'theti,cism** *n*

aesthetics *or US (sometimes)* **esthetics** (iːs'θɛtɪks) *n (functioning as sing)* **1** the branch of philosophy concerned with the study of such concepts as beauty, taste, etc. **2** the study of the rules and principles of art.

aestival *or US* **estival** (iː'staɪvᵊl) *adj Rare.* of or occurring in summer. [C14: from F, from LL *aestīvālis,* from L *aestās* summer]

aestivate *or US* **estivate** ('iːstɪ,veɪt) *vb* **aestivates, aestivating, aestivated** *or US* **estivates, estivating, estivated.** *(intr)* **1** to pass the summer. **2** (of animals) to pass the summer or dry season in a dormant condition. [C17: from L, from *aestīvāre,* from *aestās* summer]
▸,**aesti'vation** *or US* ,**esti'vation** *n*

aet. *or* **aetat.** *abbrev. for* aetatis. [L: at the age of]

aether ('iːθə) *n* a variant spelling of **ether** (senses 3, 4).

aetiology *or* **etiology** (,iːtɪ'ɒlədʒɪ) *n, pl* **aetiologies** *or* **etiologies.** **1** the philosophy or study of causation. **2** the study of the causes of diseases. **3** the cause of a disease. [C16: from LL *aetologia,* from Gk *aitiologia,* from *aitia* cause]
▸,**aetio'logical** *or* ,**etio'logical** *adj* ▸,**aetio'logically** *or* ,**etio'logically** *adv* ▸,**aeti'ologist** *or* ,**eti'ologist** *n*

AEU (in Britain) *abbrev. for* Amalgamated Engineering Union.

a.f. *abbrev. for* audio frequency.

afar (ə'fɑː) *adv* **1** at, from, or to a great distance. ◆ *n* **2** a great distance (esp. in **from afar**). [C14 *a fer,* altered from earlier *on fer* & *of fer;* see A-[2], FAR]

THESAURUS

urge ◆ *n* **2, 3** = **supporter**, apologist, apostle, backer, campaigner, champion, counsellor, defender, pleader, promoter, proponent, proposer, speaker, spokesman, upholder **4, 5** = **lawyer**, attorney, barrister, counsel, solicitor

Antonyms *vb* ≠ **recommend:** contradict, oppose, resist, speak against, take a stand against, take issue with

aegis *n* **1** *As in* **under the aegis of** = **protection**, advocacy, auspices, backing, favour, guardianship, patronage, shelter, sponsorship, support, wing

aesthetic *adj* **2** = **tasteful**, artistic, in good taste, pleasing

DICTIONARY

AFC *abbrev. for:* **1** Air Force Cross. **2** Association Football Club. **3** automatic frequency control.

afeard *or* **afeared** (əˈfɪəd) *adj* (*postpositive*) an archaic or dialect word for **afraid**. [OE *āfǣred*, from *afǣran* to frighten]

affable Ⓣ (ˈæfəbᵊl) *adj* **1** showing warmth and friendliness. **2** easy to converse with; approachable. [C16: from L *affābilis*, from *affārī*, from *ad-* to + *fārī* to speak]
▸ˌ**affaˈbility** *n* ▸ˈ**affably** *adv*

affair Ⓣ (əˈfɛə) *n* **1** a thing to be done or attended to; matter. **2** an event or happening: *a strange affair.* **3** (*qualified by an adjective or descriptive phrase*) something previously specified: *our house is a tumbledown affair.* **4** a sexual relationship between two people who are not married to each other. [C13: from OF, from *à faire* to do]

affairs (əˈfɛəz) *pl n* **1** personal or business interests. **2** matters of public interest: *current affairs.*

affect[1] Ⓣ *vb* (əˈfɛkt). (*tr*) **1** to act upon or influence, esp. in an adverse way. **2** to move or disturb emotionally or mentally. **3** (of pain, disease, etc.) to attack. ◆ *n* (ˈæfɛkt). **4** *Psychol.* the emotion associated with an idea or set of ideas. [C17: from L *affectus*, p.p. of *afficere*, from *ad-* to + *facere* to do]

affect[2] Ⓣ (əˈfɛkt) *vb* (*mainly tr*) **1** to put on an appearance or show of: *to affect ignorance.* **2** to imitate or assume, esp. pretentiously. **3** to have or use by preference. **4** to adopt the character, manner, etc., of. **5** to incline habitually towards. [C15: from L *affectāre* to strive after; rel. to *afficere* to AFFECT[1]]

affectation Ⓣ (ˌæfɛkˈteɪʃən) *n* **1** an assumed manner of speech, dress, or behaviour, esp. one that is intended to impress others. **2** (often foll. by *of*) deliberate pretence. [C16: from L *affectātiōn-*, from *affectāre*; see AFFECT[2]]

affected[1] Ⓣ (əˈfɛktɪd) *adj* (*usually postpositive*) **1** deeply moved, esp. by sorrow or grief. **2** changed, esp. detrimentally. [C17: from AFFECT[1]]

affected[2] Ⓣ (əˈfɛktɪd) *adj* **1** behaving, speaking, etc., in an assumed way, esp. in order to impress others. **2** feigned: *affected indifference.* [C16: from AFFECT[2]]
▸**afˈfectedly** *adv*

affecting Ⓣ (əˈfɛktɪŋ) *adj* evoking feelings of pity; moving.
▸**afˈfectingly** *adv*

affection Ⓣ (əˈfɛkʃən) *n* **1** a feeling of fondness or tenderness for a person or thing. **2** (*often pl*) emotion, feeling, or sentiment: *to play on a person's affections.* **3** *Pathol.* any disease or pathological condition. **4** the act of affecting or the state of being affected. [C13: from L *affectiōn-*, from *afficere* to AFFECT[1]]
▸**afˈfectional** *adj*

affectionate Ⓣ (əˈfɛkʃənɪt) *adj* having or displaying tender feelings, affection, or warmth.
▸**afˈfectionately** *adv*

affective (əˈfɛktɪv) *adj* concerned with the emotions or affection.
▸**affectivity** (ˌæfɛkˈtɪvɪtɪ) *n*

affective disorder *n* any mental disorder, such as depression or mania, that is characterized by abnormal disturbances of mood.

affectless (ˈæfɛktˌlɪs, əˈfɛktlɪs) *adj* **a** showing no emotion or concern for others. **b** not giving rise to any emotion or feeling: *an affectless novel.* [C20: from AFFECT[1] (sense 4) + -LESS]

afferent (ˈæfərənt) *adj* bringing or directing inwards to a part or an organ of the body, esp. towards the brain or spinal cord. [C19: from L *afferre*, from *ad-* to + *ferre* to carry]

affiance Ⓣ (əˈfaɪəns) *vb* **affiances, affiancing, affianced.** (*tr*) to bind (a person or oneself) in a promise of marriage; betroth. [C14: via OF from Med. L *affīdāre* to trust (oneself) to, from *fīdāre* to trust]

affidavit (ˌæfɪˈdeɪvɪt) *n Law.* a declaration in writing made upon oath before a person authorized to administer oaths. [C17: from Med. L, lit.: he declares on oath, from *affīdāre*; see AFFIANCE]

affiliate Ⓣ *vb* (əˈfɪlɪˌeɪt), **affiliates, affiliating, affiliated. 1** (*tr*; foll. by *to* or *with*) to receive into close connection or association (with a larger body, group, organization, etc.). **2** (foll. by *with*) to associate (oneself) or be associated, esp. as a subordinate or subsidiary. ◆ *n* (əˈfɪlɪɪt). **3a** a person or organization that is affiliated with another. **3b** (*as modifier*): *an affiliate member.* [C18: from Med. L *affīliātus* adopted as a son, from *affīliāre*, from L *fīlius* son]
▸**afˌfiliˈation** *n*

affiliation order *n Law.* an order that a man adjudged to be the father of an illegitimate child shall contribute towards the child's maintenance.

affine (ˈæfaɪn) *adj Maths.* denoting transformations which preserve collinearity, esp. those of translation, rotation, and reflection. [C16: from F: see AFFINITY]

affinity Ⓣ (əˈfɪnɪtɪ) *n, pl* **affinities. 1** a natural liking, taste, or inclination for a person or thing. **2** the person or thing so liked. **3** a close similarity in appearance or quality. **4** relationship by marriage. **5** similarity in structure, form, etc., between different animals, plants, or languages. **6** *Chem.* chemical attraction. **7** *Immunol.* a measure of the degree of interaction between an antigen and an antibody. [C14: via OF from L *affīnitāt-*, from *affīnis* bordering on, related]
▸**afˈfinitive** *adj*

affinity card *n* a credit card issued by a bank or credit-card company, which donates a small percentage of the money spent using the card to a specified charity.

affirm Ⓣ (əˈfɜːm) *vb* (*mainly tr*) **1** (*may take a clause as object*) to declare to be true. **2** to uphold, confirm, or ratify. **3** (*intr*) *Law.* to make an affirmation. [C14: via OF from L *affirmāre*, from *ad-* to + *firmāre* to make FIRM[1]]
▸**afˈfirmer** *or* **afˈfirmant** *n*

affirmation Ⓣ (ˌæfəˈmeɪʃən) *n* **1** the act of affirming or the state of being affirmed. **2** a statement of the truth of something; assertion. **3** *Law.* a solemn declaration permitted on grounds of conscientious objection to taking an oath.

affirmative Ⓣ (əˈfɜːmətɪv) *adj* **1** confirming or asserting something as true or valid. **2** indicating agreement or assent. **3** *Logic.* (of a categorical proposition) affirming the satisfaction by the subject of the predicate, as in the proposition *some men are married.* ◆ *n* **4** a positive assertion. **5** a word or phrase stating agreement or assent, such as *yes: to answer in the affirmative.* ◆ *sentence substitute.* **6** *Mil., etc.* a signal codeword used to express assent or confirmation.
▸**afˈfirmatively** *adv*

affix Ⓣ *vb* (əˈfɪks). (*tr*; usually foll. by *to* or *on*) **1** to attach, fasten, join, or stick. **2** to add or append: *to affix a signature to a document.* **3** to attach or attribute (guilt, blame, etc.). ◆ *n* (ˈæfɪks). **4** a linguistic element

THESAURUS

affability *n* **1, 2** = **friendliness**, amiability, amicability, approachability, benevolence, benignity, civility, congeniality, cordiality, courtesy, geniality, good humour, good nature, graciousness, kindliness, mildness, obligingness, pleasantness, sociability, urbanity, warmth

affable *adj* **1, 2** = **friendly**, amiable, amicable, approachable, benevolent, benign, civil, congenial, cordial, courteous, genial, good-humoured, good-natured, gracious, kindly, mild, obliging, pleasant, sociable, urbane, warm
Antonyms *adj* brusque, cold, discourteous, distant, haughty, rude, stand-offish, surly, unapproachable, uncivil, unfriendly, ungracious, unpleasant, unsociable

affair *n* **1, 2** = **event**, activity, business, circumstance, concern, episode, happening, incident, interest, matter, occurrence, proceeding, project, question, subject, transaction, undertaking **4** = **relationship**, amour, intrigue, liaison, romance

affect[1] *vb* **1** = **influence**, act on, alter, bear upon, change, concern, impact, impinge upon, interest, involve, modify, prevail over, regard, relate to, sway, transform **2** = **move**, disturb, impress, overcome, perturb, stir, touch, upset

affect[2] *vb* **1, 2, 4** = **put on**, adopt, aspire to, assume, contrive, counterfeit, feign, imitate, pretend, sham, simulate

affectation *n* **1, 2** = **pretence**, act, affectedness, appearance, artificiality, assumed manners, façade, fakery, false display, insincerity, mannerism, pose, pretension, pretentiousness, sham, show, simulation, unnatural imitation

affected[1] *adj* **1, 2** = **influenced**, afflicted, altered, changed, concerned, damaged, deeply moved, distressed, hurt, impaired, impressed, injured, melted, stimulated, stirred, touched, troubled, upset
Antonyms *adj* cured, unaffected, unconcerned, unharmed, uninjured, unmoved, untouched

affected[2] *adj* **1, 2** = **pretended**, artificial, arty-farty (*inf.*), assumed, camp (*inf.*), conceited, contrived, counterfeit, feigned, insincere, la-di-da (*inf.*), mannered, mincing, phoney *or* phony (*inf.*), pompous, precious, pretentious, put-on, sham, simulated, spurious, stiff, studied, unnatural
Antonyms *adj* genuine, natural, real, unaffected

affecting *adj* = **moving**, pathetic, piteous, pitiable, pitiful, poignant, sad, saddening, touching

affection *n* **1, 2** = **fondness**, amity, attachment, care, desire, feeling, friendliness, goodwill, inclination, kindness, liking, love, passion, propensity, tenderness, warmth

affectionate *adj* = **fond**, attached, caring, devoted, doting, friendly, kind, loving, tender, warm, warm-hearted
Antonyms *adj* cold, cool, glacial, indifferent, stony, uncaring, undemonstrative, unfeeling, unresponsive

affianced *adj* = **engaged**, betrothed, bound, pledged, promised

affiliate *vb* **1, 2** = **join**, ally, amalgamate, annex, associate, band together, combine, confederate, connect, incorporate, link, unite

affiliated *adj* **1, 2** = **connected**, allied, amalgamated, associated, confederated, conjoined, federated, incorporated, joined, linked, united

affiliation *n* **1, 2** = **connection**, alliance, amalgamation, association, banding together, coalition, combination, confederation, incorporation, joining, league, merging, relationship, union

affinity *n* **1** = **attraction**, fondness, inclination, leaning, liking, partiality, rapport, sympathy **3** = **similarity**, alliance, analogy, closeness, compatibility, connection, correspondence, kinship, likeness, relation, relationship, resemblance
Antonyms *n* ≠ **attraction:** abhorrence, animosity, antipathy, aversion, dislike, hatred, hostility, loathing, repugnance, revulsion ≠ **similarity:** difference, disparity, dissimilarity

affirm *vb* **1, 2** = **declare**, assert, asseverate, attest, aver, avouch, avow, certify, confirm, maintain, pronounce, ratify, state, swear, testify
Antonyms *vb* deny, disallow, rebut, refute, reject, renounce, repudiate, rescind, retract

affirmation *n* **1, 2** = **declaration**, assertion, asseveration, attestation, averment, avouchment, avowal, certification, confirmation, oath, pronouncement, ratification, statement, testimony

affirmative *adj* **1, 2** = **agreeing**, approving, assenting, concurring, confirming, consenting, corroborative, favourable, positive
Antonyms *adj* denying, disagreeing, disapproving, dissenting, negating, negative

affix *vb* **1, 2** = **attach**, add, annex, append, bind, fasten, glue, join, paste, put on, stick, subjoin, tack, tag
Antonyms *vb* detach, disconnect, remove, take off, unfasten, unglue

added to a word or root to produce a derived or inflected form, as *-ment* in *establishment*. See also **prefix, suffix, infix. 5** something fastened or attached. [C15: from Med. L *affixāre*, from *ad-* to + *fixāre* to FIX]
▸**affixture** (əˈfɪkstʃə) *n*

afflatus (əˈfleɪtəs) *n* an impulse of creative power or inspiration considered to be of divine origin. [C17: L, from *afflātus*, from *afflāre*, from *flāre* to blow]

afflict ⓣ (əˈflɪkt) *vb* (*tr*) to cause suffering or unhappiness to; distress greatly. [C14: from L *afflictus*, p.p. of *afflīgere* to knock against, from *flīgere* to strike]
▸**afˈflictive** *adj*

affliction ⓣ (əˈflɪkʃən) *n* **1** a condition of great distress or suffering. **2** something responsible for physical or mental suffering.

affluence ⓣ (ˈæfluəns) *n* **1** an abundant supply of money, goods, or property; wealth. **2** *Rare.* abundance or profusion.

affluent ⓣ (ˈæfluənt) *adj* **1** rich; wealthy. **2** abundant; copious. **3** flowing freely. ◆ *n* **4** a tributary stream. [C15: from L *affluent-*, present participle of *affluere*, from *fluere* to flow]

affluent society *n* a society in which the material benefits of prosperity are widely available.

afflux (ˈæflʌks) *n* a flowing towards a point: *an afflux of blood to the head.* [C17: from L *affluxus*, from *fluxus* FLUX]

afford ⓣ (əˈfɔːd) *vb* **1** (preceded by *can, could,* etc.) to be able to do or spare something, esp. without incurring financial difficulties or without risk of undesirable consequences. **2** to give, yield, or supply. [OE *geforthian* to further, promote, from *forth* FORTH]
▸**afˈfordable** *adj* ▸**af,fordaˈbility** *n*

afforest (əˈfɒrɪst) *vb* (*tr*) to plant trees on. [C15: from Med. L *afforestāre*, from *forestis* FOREST]
▸**af,forestˈation** *n*

affranchise (əˈfræntʃaɪz) *vb* **affranchises, affranchising, affranchised.** (*tr*) to release from servitude or an obligation. [C15: from OF *afranchir*]
▸**afˈfranchisement** *n*

affray ⓣ (əˈfreɪ) *n* a fight, noisy quarrel, or disturbance between two or more persons in a public place. [C14: via OF from Vulgar L *exfridāre* (unattested) to break the peace]

affricate (ˈæfrɪkɪt) *n* a composite speech sound consisting of a stop and a fricative articulated at the same point, such as the sound written *ch*, as in *chair.* [C19: from L *affricāre*, from *fricāre* to rub]

affright (əˈfraɪt) *Arch. or poetic.* ◆ *vb* **1** (*tr*) to frighten. ◆ *n* **2** a sudden terror. [OE *āfyrhtan*, from *a-* + *fyrhtan* to FRIGHT]

affront ⓣ (əˈfrʌnt) *n* **1** a deliberate insult. ◆ *vb* (*tr*) **2** to insult, esp. openly. **3** to offend the pride or dignity of. [C14: from OF *afronter* to strike in the face, from L *ad frontem* to the face]

afghan (ˈæfgæn, -gən) *n* **1** a knitted or crocheted wool blanket or shawl, esp. one with a geometric pattern. **2** a sheepskin coat, often embroidered.

Afghan (ˈæfgæn) *or* **Afghani** (æfˈgænɪ) *n* **1** a native, citizen, or inhabitant of Afghanistan. **2** another name for **Pashto** (the language). ◆ *adj* **3** denoting Afghanistan, its people, or their language.

Afghan hound *n* a tall graceful breed of hound with a long silky coat.

aficionado ⓣ (ə,fɪʃjəˈnɑːdəʊ) *n, pl* **aficionados. 1** an ardent supporter or devotee: *a jazz aficionado.* **2** a devotee of bullfighting. [Sp., from *aficionar*, from *afición* AFFECTION]

afield (əˈfiːld) *adv, adj* (*postpositive*) **1** away from one's usual surroundings or home (esp. in **far afield**). **2** off the subject (esp. in **far afield**). **3** in or to the field.

afire ⓣ (əˈfaɪə) *adv, adj* (*postpositive*) **1** on fire. **2** intensely interested or passionate: *he was afire with enthusiasm for the new plan.*

aflame ⓣ (əˈfleɪm) *adv, adj* (*postpositive*) **1** in flames. **2** deeply aroused, as with passion: *he was aflame with desire.*

aflatoxin (,æfləˈtɒksɪn) *n* a toxin produced by a fungus growing on peanuts, maize, etc., causing liver disease (esp. cancer) in man. [C20: from L name of fungus *A*(*spergillus*) *fla*(*vus*) + TOXIN]

afloat ⓣ (əˈfləʊt) *adj* (*postpositive*), *adv* **1** floating. **2** aboard ship; at sea. **3** covered with water. **4** aimlessly drifting. **5** in circulation: *nasty rumours were afloat.* **6** free of debt.

aflutter (əˈflʌtə) *adj* (*postpositive*), *adv* in or into a nervous or excited state.

AFM *abbrev. for* Air Force Medal.

afoot ⓣ (əˈfʊt) *adj* (*postpositive*), *adv* **1** in operation; astir: *mischief was afoot.* **2** on or by foot.

afore (əˈfɔː) *adv, prep, conj* an archaic or dialect word for **before.**

aforementioned (əˈfɔː,mɛnʃənd) *adj* (*usually prenominal*) (chiefly in legal documents) stated or mentioned before.

aforesaid (əˈfɔː,sɛd) *adj* (*usually prenominal*) (chiefly in legal documents) spoken of or referred to previously.

aforethought (əˈfɔː,θɔːt) *adj* (*immediately postpositive*) premeditated (esp. in **malice aforethought**).

a fortiori (ˈeɪ ,fɔːtɪˈɔːraɪ) *adv* for similar but more convincing reasons. [L]

afp *abbrev. for* alpha-fetoprotein.

Afr. *abbrev. for* Africa(n).

afraid ⓣ (əˈfreɪd) *adj* (*postpositive*) **1** (often foll. by *of*) feeling fear or apprehension. **2** reluctant (to do something), as through fear or timidity. **3** (often foll. by *that;* used to lessen the effect of an unpleasant statement) regretful: *I'm afraid that I shall have to tell you to go.* [C14 *affraied*, p.p. of AFFRAY (*obs.*) to frighten]

afreet *or* **afrit** (ˈæfriːt, əˈfriːt) *n Arabian myth.* a powerful evil demon. [C19: from Ar. *ʻifrīt*]

afresh ⓣ (əˈfrɛʃ) *adv* once more; again; anew.

African (ˈæfrɪkən) *adj* **1** denoting or relating to Africa or any of its peoples, languages, nations, etc. ◆ *n* **2** a native or inhabitant of any of the countries of Africa. **3** a member or descendant of any of the peoples of Africa, esp. a Black person.

Africana (,æfrɪˈkɑːnə) *n* objects of cultural or historical interest of southern African origin.

African-American *or* **Afro-American** *n* **1** an American of African descent. ◆ *adj* **2** of or relating to Americans of African descent.

Africander (,æfrɪˈkændə) *n* a breed of hump-backed beef cattle originally raised in southern Africa. [C19: from South African Du., formed on the model of *Hollander*]

African National Congress *n* (in South Africa) a political party, founded in 1912 in South Africa as an African nationalist movement and banned from 1960 until 1990 because of its opposition to apartheid. In 1994 the ANC won South Africa's first multiracial elections. Abbrev.: **ANC.**

African violet *n* a tropical African plant cultivated as a house plant, with violet, white, or pink flowers and hairy leaves.

Afrikaans (,æfrɪˈkɑːns, -ˈkɑːnz) *n* one of the official languages of the Republic of South Africa, closely related to Dutch. Sometimes called: **South African Dutch.** [C20: from Du.: African]

Afrikaner (,æfrɪˈkɑːnə) *n* a White native of the Republic of South Africa whose mother tongue is Afrikaans. See also **Boer.**

afrit (ˈæfriːt, əˈfriːt) *n* a variant spelling of **afreet.**

THESAURUS

afflict *vb* = **torment**, ail, beset, burden, distress, grieve, harass, hurt, oppress, pain, plague, rack, smite, trouble, try, wound

affliction *n* **1, 2** = **suffering**, adversity, calamity, cross, curse, depression, disease, distress, grief, hardship, misery, misfortune, ordeal, pain, plague, scourge, sickness, sorrow, torment, trial, tribulation, trouble, woe, wretchedness

affluence *n* **1** = **wealth**, abundance, big bucks (*inf., chiefly US*), big money, exuberance, fortune, megabucks (*US & Canad. sl.*), opulence, plenty, pretty penny (*inf.*), profusion, prosperity, riches, tidy sum (*inf.*)

affluent *adj* **1** = **wealthy**, loaded (*sl.*), moneyed, opulent, prosperous, rich, rolling in money (*sl.*), well-heeled (*inf.*), well-off, well-to-do **2** = **plentiful**, abundant, copious, exuberant, plenteous
Antonyms *adj* ≠ **wealthy:** broke (*inf.*), destitute, down at heel, hard-up (*inf.*), impecunious, impoverished, indigent, on the breadline, penniless, penurious, poor, poverty-stricken, skint (*Brit. sl.*), stony-broke (*Brit. sl.*)

afford *vb* **1** *As in* **can afford** = **spare**, bear, manage, stand, sustain **2** = **give**, bestow, furnish, grant, impart, offer, produce, provide, render, supply, yield

affordable *adj* **1** = **inexpensive**, cheap, economical, fair, low-cost, low-price, moderate, modest, reasonable
Antonyms *adj* ≠ **inexpensive:** beyond one's means, costly, dear, exorbitant, expensive, prohibitively expensive, unaffordable, uneconomical

affray *n* = **fight**, brawl, contest, disturbance, dogfight, encounter, feud, fracas, free-for-all (*inf.*), mêlée, outbreak, quarrel, scrap, scrimmage, scuffle, set-to (*inf.*), skirmish, tumult

affront *n* **1** = **insult**, abuse, indignity, injury, offence, outrage, provocation, slap in the face (*inf.*), slight, slur, vexation, wrong ◆ *vb* **2, 3** = **offend**, abuse, anger, annoy, displease, insult, outrage, pique, provoke, put *or* get one's back up, slight, vex

affronted *adj* **2, 3** = **offended**, angry, annoyed, cross, displeased, incensed, indignant, insulted, irate, miffed (*inf.*), outraged, peeved (*inf.*), piqued, slighted, stung, upset

aficionado *n* **1** = **fan**, addict, adherent, admirer, buff (*inf.*), connoisseur, devotee, disciple, enthusiast, fanatic, follower, freak (*inf.*), lover, nut (*sl.*), supporter, votary

afire *adj* **1** = **burning**, ablaze, aflame, alight, blazing, fiery, flaming, ignited, lighted, lit, on fire **2** = **passionate**, aglow, aroused, excited, fervent, impassioned, stimulated

aflame *adj* **1** = **burning**, ablaze, afire, alight, blazing, fiery, flaming, ignited, lighted, lit, on fire **2** = **passionate**, afire, aroused, excited, fervent, impassioned, stimulated

afloat *adj* **1** = **floating**, buoyant, keeping one's head above water, on the surface, unsubmerged ◆ *adv* **2** = **at sea**, aboard, on board (ship), on shipboard, sailing, under sail ◆ *adj* **3** = **flooded**, awash, inundated, submerged, swamped, under water **4** = **drifting**, adrift, aweigh, cast off, unanchored, unmoored **5** = **going about** *or* **around**, afoot, current, in circulation, in the air **6** = **solvent**, above water, in business
Antonyms *adj* ≠ **floating:** capsized, immersed, submerged, sunken, under water ≠ **drifting:** anchored, held fast, moored ≠ **solvent:** bankrupt, bust (*inf.*), in receivership, insolvent, out of business

afoot *adj* **1** = **going on**, about, abroad, afloat, astir, brewing, circulating, current, happening, hatching, in preparation, in progress, in the wind, on the go (*inf.*), operating, up (*inf.*)

afraid *adj* **1, 2** = **scared**, alarmed, anxious, apprehensive, cowardly, faint-hearted, fearful, frightened, intimidated, nervous, reluctant, suspicious, timid, timorous **3** = **sorry**, regretful, unhappy
Antonyms *adj* ≠ **scared:** audacious, bold, fearless, inapprehensive, indifferent, unafraid ≠ **sorry:** happy, pleased

afresh *adv* = **again**, anew, newly, once again, once more, over again

Afro (ˈæfrəʊ) *n, pl* **Afros.** a hairstyle in which the hair is shaped into a wide frizzy bush. [C20: independent use of AFRO-]

Afro- *combining form.* indicating Africa or African: *Afro-Asiatic.*

Afro-American *n, adj* another word for **African-American.**

Afro-Caribbean *adj* **1** denoting or relating to Caribbean people of African descent or their culture. ◆ *n* **2** a Caribbean of African descent.

afrormosia (ˌæfrɔːˈməʊzɪə) *n* a hard teaklike wood obtained from a genus of tropical African trees. [C20: from AFRO- + *Ormosia* (genus name)]

aft (ɑːft) *adv, adj Chiefly naut.* towards or at the stern or rear: *the aft deck.* [C17: ? shortened from earlier ABAFT]

after Ⓣ (ˈɑːftə) *prep* **1** following in time; in succession to: *after dinner.* **2** following; behind. **3** in pursuit or search of: *he's only after money.* **4** concerning: *to inquire after his health.* **5** considering: *after what you have done, you shouldn't complain.* **6** next in excellence or importance to. **7** in imitation of; in the manner of. **8** in accordance with or in conformity to: *a man after her own heart.* **9** with a name derived from. **10** *US.* past (the hour of): *twenty after three.* **11 after all. 11a** in spite of everything: *it's only a game after all.* **11b** in spite of expectations, efforts, etc. **12 after you.** please go, enter, etc., before me. ◆ *adv* **13** at a later time; afterwards. **14** coming afterwards. **15** *Naut.* further aft. ◆ *conj* **16** (*subordinating*) at a time later than that at which. ◆ *adj* **17** *Naut.* further aft: *the after cabin.* [OE *æfter*]

afterbirth (ˈɑːftəˌbɜːθ) *n* the placenta and fetal membranes expelled from the uterus after the birth of offspring.

afterburner (ˈɑːftəˌbɜːnə) *n* **1** a device in the exhaust system of an internal-combustion engine for removing dangerous exhaust gases. **2** a device in an aircraft jet engine to produce extra thrust by igniting additional fuel.

aftercare (ˈɑːftəˌkɛə) *n* **1** support services by a welfare agency for a person discharged from a hospital, prison, etc. **2** *Med.* the care of a patient after a serious illness or operation. **3** any system of maintenance or upkeep of an appliance or product: *contact-lens aftercare.*

afterdamp (ˈɑːftəˌdæmp) *n* a poisonous gas, consisting mainly of carbon monoxide, formed after the explosion of firedamp in coal mines.

aftereffect Ⓣ (ˈɑːftərɪˌfɛkt) *n* any result occurring some time after its cause.

afterglow (ˈɑːftəˌgləʊ) *n* **1** the glow left after a light has disappeared, such as that sometimes seen after sunset. **2** the glow of an incandescent metal after the source of heat has been removed.

afterimage (ˈɑːftərˌɪmɪdʒ) *n* a sustained or renewed sensation, esp. visual, after the original stimulus has ceased.

afterlife (ˈɑːftəˌlaɪf) *n* life after death or at a later time in a person's lifetime.

aftermath Ⓣ (ˈɑːftəˌmæθ) *n* **1** signs or results of an event or occurrence considered collectively: *the aftermath of war.* **2** *Agriculture.* a second crop of grass from land that has already yielded one crop earlier in the same year. [C16: AFTER + *math* a mowing, from OE *mæth*]

aftermost (ˈɑːftəˌməʊst) *adj* closer or closest to the rear or (in a vessel) the stern; last.

afternoon (ˌɑːftəˈnuːn) *n* **1a** the period between noon and evening. **1b** (*as modifier*): *afternoon tea.* **2** a later part: *the afternoon of life.*

afternoons (ˌɑːftəˈnuːnz) *adv Inf.* during the afternoon, esp. regularly.

afterpains (ˈɑːftəˌpeɪnz) *pl n* cramplike pains caused by contraction of the uterus after childbirth.

afters (ˈɑːftəz) *n* (*functioning as sing or pl*) *Brit. inf.* dessert; sweet.

aftershave lotion (ˈɑːftəˌʃeɪv) *n* a lotion, usually perfumed, for application to the face after shaving. Often shortened to **aftershave.**

aftertaste (ˈɑːftəˌteɪst) *n* **1** a taste that lingers on after eating or drinking. **2** a lingering impression or sensation.

afterthought (ˈɑːftəˌθɔːt) *n* **1** a comment, reply, etc., that occurs to one after the opportunity to deliver it has passed. **2** an addition to something already completed.

afterwards Ⓣ (ˈɑːftəwədz) *or* **afterward** *adv* after an earlier event or time. [OE *æfterweard, æfteweard,* from AFT + WARD]

Ag *the chemical symbol for* silver. [from L *argentum*]

AG *abbrev. for:* **1** Adjutant General. **2** Attorney General.

aga *or* **agha** (ˈɑːgə) *n* (in the Ottoman Empire) a title of respect, often used with the title of a senior position. [C17: Turkish, lit.: lord]

again Ⓣ (əˈgɛn, əˈgeɪn) *adv* **1** another or a second time: *he had to start again.* **2** once more in a previously experienced state or condition: *he is ill again.* **3** in addition to the original amount, quantity, etc. (esp. in **as much again; half as much again**). **4** (*sentence modifier*) on the other hand. **5** besides; also. **6** *Arch.* in reply; back: *he answered again.* **7 again and again.** continuously; repeatedly. ◆ *sentence connector.* **8** moreover; furthermore. [OE *ongegn* opposite to, from A-^{2} + *gegn* straight]

against Ⓣ (əˈgɛnst, əˈgeɪnst) *prep* **1** opposed to; in conflict or disagreement with. **2** standing or leaning beside: *a ladder against the wall.* **3** coming in contact with. **4** in contrast to: *silhouettes are outlines against a light background.* **5** having an unfavourable effect on: *the system works against small companies.* **6** as a protection from: *a safeguard against contaminated water.* **7** in exchange for or in return for. **8** *Now rare.* in preparation for: *he gave them warm clothing against their journey.* **9 as against.** as opposed to or as compared with. [C12 *ageines,* from *again, ageyn,* etc. AGAIN + *-es,* genitive ending]

Aga Khan (ˈɑːgə ˈkɑːn) *n* the hereditary title of the head of the Ismaili Islamic sect.

agamic (əˈgæmɪk) *adj* asexual; occurring or reproducing without fertilization. [C19: from Gk *agamos* unmarried, from A-^{1} + *gamos* marriage]

agamogenesis (ˌægəməʊˈdʒɛnɪsɪs) *n* asexual reproduction, such as fission or parthenogenesis. [C19: AGAMIC + GENESIS]

agapanthus (ˌægəˈpænθəs) *n* a South African plant with blue funnel-shaped flowers, widely cultivated for ornament. [C19: NL, from Gk *agape* love + *anthos* flower]

agape Ⓣ (əˈgeɪp) *adj* (*postpositive*) **1** (esp. of the mouth) wide open. **2** very surprised, expectant, or eager. [C17: A-^{2} + GAPE]

Agape (ˈægəpɪ) *n* **1** Christian love, esp. as contrasted with erotic love; charity. **2** a communal meal in the early Church in commemoration of the Last Supper. [C17: Gk *agapē* love]

agar (ˈeɪgə) *n* a gelatinous carbohydrate obtained from seaweeds, used as a culture medium for bacteria, as a laxative, a thickening agent (**E406**) in food, etc. Also called: **agar-agar.** [C19: Malay]

agaric (ˈægərɪk) *n* a fungus having gills on the underside of the cap. The group includes the edible mushrooms and poisonous forms such as the fly agaric. [C16: via L from Gk *agarikon*]

agate (ˈægɪt) *n* **1** an impure form of quartz consisting of a variegated, usually banded chalcedony, used as a gemstone and in making pestles and mortars. **2** a playing marble of this quartz or resembling it. [C16: via F from L, from Gk *akhatēs*]

agave (əˈgeɪvɪ) *n* a plant native to tropical America with tall flower stalks rising from thick fleshy leaves. Some species are the source of fibres such as sisal. [C18: NL, from Gk *agauē,* fem. of *agauos* illustrious]

age Ⓣ (eɪdʒ) *n* **1** the period of time that a person, animal, or plant has lived or is expected to live. **2** the period of existence of an object, material, group, etc.: *the age of this table is 200 years.* **3a** a period or state of human life: *he should know better at his age.* **3b** (*as modifier*): *age group.* **4** the latter part of life. **5a** a period of history marked by some feature or characteristic. **5b** (*cap. when part of a name*): *the Middle Ages.* **6** generation: *the Edwardian age.* **7** *Geol., palaeontol.* **7a** a period of the earth's history distinguished by special characteristics: *the age of reptiles.* **7b** a subdivision of an epoch. **8** (*often pl*) *Inf.* a relatively long time: *I've been waiting ages.* **9** *Psychol.* the level in years that a person has reached in any area of development, compared with the normal level for his chronological age. **10 of age.** adult and legally responsible for one's actions (usually at 18 years). ◆ *vb* **ages, ageing** *or* **aging, aged. 11** to become or cause to become old or aged. **12** (*intr*) to begin to seem older: *to have aged a lot in the past year.* **13** *Brewing.* to mature or cause to mature. [C13: via OF from Vulgar L, from L *aetās*]

-age *suffix forming nouns.* **1** indicating a collection, set, or group: *baggage.* **2** indicating a process or action or the result of an action: *breakage.* **3** indicating a state or relationship: *bondage.* **4** indicating a house or place: *orphanage.* **5** indicating a charge or fee: *postage.* **6** indicating a rate: *dosage.* [from OF, from LL *-āticum* belonging to]

aged Ⓣ (ˈeɪdʒɪd) *adj* **1a** advanced in years; old. **1b** (*as collective n; preceded by the*): *the aged.* **2** of, connected with, or characteristic of old age. **3** (eɪdʒd). (*postpositive*) having the age of: *a woman aged twenty.*

ageing Ⓣ *or* **aging** (ˈeɪdʒɪŋ) *n* **1** the process of growing old or developing the appearance of old age. ◆ *adj* **2** becoming or appearing older: *an ageing car.* **3** giving the appearance of elderliness: *that dress is really ageing.*

THESAURUS

after *adv* **13, 14** = **following**, afterwards, behind, below, later, subsequently, succeeding, thereafter

Antonyms *adv* before, earlier, in advance, in front, previously, prior to, sooner

aftereffect *n* = **consequence**, delayed response, hangover (*inf.*), repercussion, spin-off

aftermath *n* **1** = **effects**, aftereffects, consequences, end, end result, outcome, results, sequel, upshot, wake

afterwards *adv* = **later**, after, after that, at a later date *or* time, following that, subsequently, then, thereafter

again *adv* **1** = **once more**, afresh, anew, another time **4** = **on the other hand**, on the contrary **5** = **also**, besides, furthermore, in addition, moreover

against *prep* **1** = **opposed to**, anti, averse to, contra (*inf.*), counter, hostile to, in defiance of, in opposition to, in the face of, opposing, resisting, versus **2, 3** = **beside**, abutting, close up to, facing, fronting, in contact with, on, opposite to, touching, upon **8** = **in preparation for**, in anticipation of, in expectation of, in provision for

agape *adj* **1** = **wide open**, gaping, wide, yawning **2** = **amazed**, agog, astonished, astounded, awe-stricken, dumbfounded, eager, expectant, flabbergasted, gobsmacked (*Brit. sl.*), spellbound, surprised, thunderstruck

age *n* **1, 2** = **time**, date, day(s), duration, epoch, era, generation, lifetime, period, span **4** = **old age**, advancing years, decline (*of life*), majority, maturity, senescence, senility, seniority **8** *often plural Informal* = **a long time** *or* **while**, aeons, a month of Sundays (*inf.*), an age *or* eternity, centuries, coon's age (*US sl.*), donkey's years (*inf.*), for ever (*inf.*), years, yonks (*inf.*) ◆ *vb* **11** = **grow old**, decline, deteriorate, mature, mellow, ripen

Antonyms *n* a flash, a jiffy (*inf.*), a little while, a moment, an instant, a second, a short time, a split second, no time at all, the twinkling *or* wink of an eye, two shakes of a lamb's tail (*inf.*)

aged *adj* **1, 2** = **old**, age-old, ancient, antiquated, antique, cobwebby, elderly, getting on, grey, hoary, past it (*inf.*), senescent, superannuated

Antonyms *adj* adolescent, boyish *or* girlish, childish, immature, juvenile, young, youthful

ageing *n* **1** = **growing old**, decay, decline, degeneration, deterioration, maturation, senescence, senility ◆ *adj* **2** = **growing old** *or* **older**, declining, deteriorating, getting on *or* past it (*inf.*), in decline, long in the tooth, maturing, mellowing, senescent, senile

ageism *or* **agism** ('eɪdʒɪzəm) *n* discrimination against people on the grounds of age.
▸**'ageist** *or* **'agist** *adj*

ageless ❶ ('eɪdʒlɪs) *adj* **1** apparently never growing old. **2** timeless; eternal: *an ageless quality.*

agency ❶ ('eɪdʒənsɪ) *n, pl* **agencies. 1** a business or other organization providing a specific service: *an employment agency.* **2** the place where an agent conducts business. **3** the business, duties, or functions of an agent. **4** action, power, or operation: *the agency of fate.* [C17: from Med. L *agentia,* from L *agere* to do]

agenda ❶ (ə'dʒɛndə) *n* **1** (*functioning as sing*) Also: **agendum.** a schedule or list of items to be attended to. **2** (*functioning as pl*) Also: **agendas, agendums.** matters to be attended to, as at a meeting. [C17: L, lit.: things to be done, from *agere* to do]

agent ❶ ('eɪdʒənt) *n* **1** a person who acts on behalf of another person, business, government, etc. **2** a person or thing that acts or has the power to act. **3** a substance or organism that exerts some force or effect: *a chemical agent.* **4** the means by which something occurs or is achieved. **5** a person representing a business concern, esp. a travelling salesman. [C15: from L *agent-,* noun use of the present participle of *agere* to do]
▸**agential** (eɪ'dʒɛnʃəl) *adj*

agent-general *n, pl* **agents-general.** a representative in London of a Canadian province or an Australian state.

Agent Orange *n* a highly poisonous herbicide used as a spray for defoliation and crop destruction, esp. by US forces during the Vietnam War. [C20: named after the identifying colour stripe on its container]

agent provocateur *French.* (aʒɑ̃ prɔvɔkatœr) *n, pl* ***agents provocateurs*** (aʒɑ̃ prɔvɔkatœr). a secret agent employed to provoke suspected persons to commit illegal acts and so be discredited or liable to punishment.

age of consent *n* **1** the age at which a person, esp. a female, is considered legally competent to consent to marriage or sexual intercourse. **2** the age at which a person can enter into a legally binding contract.

Age of Reason *n* (usually preceded by *the*) the 18th century in W Europe. See also **Enlightenment.**

age-old *or* **age-long** *adj* very old or of long duration; ancient.

ageratum (ˌædʒə'reɪtəm) *n* a tropical American plant with thick clusters of purplish-blue flowers. [C16: NL, via L from Gk *agēraton* that does not age, from A-[1] + *gērat-,* stem of *gēras* old age]

agglomerate *vb* (ə'glɒməˌreɪt), **agglomerates, agglomerating, agglomerated. 1** to form or be formed into a mass or cluster. ◆ *n* (ə'glɒmərɪt, -ˌreɪt). **2** a confused mass. **3** a volcanic rock consisting of angular fragments within a groundmass of lava. ◆ *adj* (ə'glɒmərɪt, -ˌreɪt). **4** formed into a mass. [C17: from L *agglomerāre,* from *glomerāre* to wind into a ball]
▸**agˌglomer'ation** *n* ▸**ag'glomerative** *adj*

agglutinate (ə'glu:tɪˌneɪt) *vb* **agglutinates, agglutinating, agglutinated. 1** to adhere or cause to adhere, as with glue. **2** *Linguistics.* to combine or be combined by agglutination. **3** (*tr*) to cause (bacteria, red blood cells, etc.) to clump together. [C16: from L *agglūtināre* to glue to, from *gluten* glue]
▸**ag'glutinable** *adj* ▸**ag'glutinant** *adj*

agglutination (əˌglu:tɪ'neɪʃən) *n* **1** the act or process of agglutinating. **2** a united mass of parts. **3** *Chem.* the formation of clumps of particles in a suspension. **4** *Immunol.* the formation of a mass of particles, such as red blood cells, by the action of antibodies. **5** *Linguistics.* the building up of words from component morphemes in such a way that these undergo little or no change of form or meaning.

aggrandize ❶ *or* **aggrandise** (ə'grændaɪz) *vb* **aggrandizes, aggrandizing, aggrandized** *or* **aggrandises, aggrandising, aggrandised.** (*tr*) **1** to increase the power, wealth, prestige, scope, etc., of. **2** to cause (something) to seem greater. [C17: from OF *aggrandiss-,* stem of *aggrandir,* from L *grandis* GRAND]
▸**aggrandizement** *or* **aggrandisement** (ə'grændɪzmənt) *n* ▸**'aggranˌdizer** *or* **'aggranˌdiser** *n*

aggravate ❶ ('ægrəˌveɪt) *vb* **aggravates, aggravating, aggravated.** (*tr*) **1** to make (a disease, situation, problem, etc.) worse. **2** *Inf.* to annoy. [C16: from L *aggravāre* to make heavier, from *gravis* heavy]
▸**'aggraˌvating** *adj* ▸**ˌaggra'vation** *n*

aggregate ❶ *adj* ('ægrɪgɪt). **1** formed of separate units collected into a whole. **2** (of fruits and flowers) composed of a dense cluster of florets. ◆ *n* ('ægrɪgɪt, -ˌgeɪt). **3** a sum or assemblage of many separate units. **4** *Geol.* a rock, such as granite, consisting of a mixture of minerals. **5** the sand and stone mixed with cement and water to make concrete. **6 in the aggregate.** taken as a whole. ◆ *vb* ('ægrɪˌgeɪt). **7** to combine or be combined into a body, etc. **8** (*tr*) to amount to (a number). [C16: from L *aggregāre* to add to a flock or herd, from *grex* flock]
▸**ˌaggre'gation** *n* ▸**aggregative** ('ægrɪˌgeɪtɪv) *adj*

aggress ❶ (ə'grɛs) *vb* (*intr*) to attack first or begin a quarrel. [C16: from Med. L *aggressāre,* from L *aggredī* to attack]
▸**aggressor** (ə'grɛsə) *n*

aggression ❶ (ə'grɛʃən) *n* **1** an attack or harmful action, esp. an unprovoked attack by one country against another. **2** any offensive activity, practice, etc. **3** *Psychol.* a hostile or destructive mental attitude. [C17: from L *aggression-,* from *aggrēdi* to attack]

aggressive ❶ (ə'grɛsɪv) *adj* **1** quarrelsome or belligerent. **2** assertive; vigorous.
▸**ag'gressively** *adv* ▸**ag'gressiveness** *n*

aggrieve (ə'gri:v) *vb* **aggrieves, aggrieving, aggrieved.** (*tr*) **1** (*often impersonal or passive*) to grieve; distress; afflict. **2** to injure unjustly, esp. by infringing a person's legal rights. [C14 *agreven,* via OF from L *aggravāre* to AGGRAVATE]
▸**ag'grieved** *adj* ▸**aggrievedly** (ə'gri:vɪdlɪ) *adv*

aggro ('ægrəʊ) *n Brit. sl.* aggressive behaviour. [C20: from AGGRAVATION]

aghast ❶ (ə'gɑ:st) *adj* (*postpositive*) overcome with amazement or horror. [C13 *agast,* from OE *gæstan* to frighten]

agile ❶ ('ædʒaɪl) *adj* **1** quick in movement; nimble. **2** mentally quick or acute. [C15: from L *agilis,* from *agere* to do, act]
▸**'agilely** *adv* ▸**agility** (ə'dʒɪlɪtɪ) *n*

agin (ə'gɪn) *prep Inf. or dialect.* against. [C19: from obs. *again* AGAINST]

Agincourt ('ædʒɪnˌkɔ:t; *French* aʒɛ̃kur) *n* a battle fought in 1415 near the village of Azincourt, N France: a decisive victory for English longbowmen under Henry V over French forces vastly superior in number.

agio ('ædʒɪəʊ) *n, pl* **agios. a** the difference between the nominal and actual values of a currency. **b** the charge payable for conversion of the less valuable currency. [C17: from It., lit.: ease]

agitate ❶ ('ædʒɪˌteɪt) *vb* **agitates, agitating, agitated. 1** (*tr*) to excite, disturb, or trouble (a person, the mind or feelings). **2** (*tr*) to shake, stir, or disturb. **3** (*intr;* often foll. by *for* or *against*) to attempt to stir up public

THESAURUS

ageless *adj* **1, 2** = **eternal**, abiding, deathless, enduring, immortal, perennial, timeless, unchanging, unfading
Antonyms *adj* ephemeral, fleeting, momentary, passing, temporary, transitory

agency *n* **1** = **business**, bureau, department, office, organization **4** = **medium**, action, activity, auspices, efficiency, force, influence, instrumentality, intercession, intervention, means, mechanism, mediation, operation, power, work

agenda *n* **1** = **list**, calendar, diary, plan, programme, schedule, timetable

agent *n* **1, 2, 5** = **representative**, advocate, deputy, emissary, envoy, factor, go-between, negotiator, rep (*inf.*), substitute, surrogate **1, 2** = **worker**, actor, author, doer, executor, mover, officer, operative, operator, performer **4** = **force**, agency, cause, instrument, means, power, vehicle

aggrandize *vb* **1, 2** = **enlarge**, advance, amplify, augment, dignify, elevate, ennoble, enrich, exaggerate, exalt, inflate, intensify, magnify, promote, widen

aggravate *vb* **1** = **make worse**, add insult to injury, exacerbate, exaggerate, fan the flames of, heighten, increase, inflame, intensify, magnify, worsen **2** *Informal* = **annoy**, be on one's back (*sl.*), bother, exasperate, gall, get on one's nerves (*inf.*), get up one's nose (*inf.*), hassle (*inf.*), irk, irritate, nark (*Brit., Austral., & NZ sl.*), needle (*inf.*), nettle, pester, provoke, rub (someone) up the wrong way (*inf.*), tease, vex
Antonyms *vb* ≠ **make worse:** alleviate, assuage, calm, diminish, ease, improve, lessen, mitigate, smooth ≠ **annoy:** assuage, calm, pacify, please

aggravating *adj* **1** = **worsening**, exacerbating, exaggerating, heightening, increasing, inflaming, intensifying, magnifying **2** *Informal* = **annoying**, exasperating, galling, irksome, irritating, provoking, teasing, vexing

aggravation *n* **1** = **worsening**, exacerbation, exaggeration, heightening, increase, inflaming, intensification, magnification **2** *Informal* = **annoyance**, exasperation, gall, grief (*inf.*), hassle (*inf.*), irksomeness, irritation, provocation, teasing, vexation

aggregate *adj* **1** = **total**, accumulated, added, assembled, collected, collective, combined, composite, corporate, cumulative, mixed ◆ *n* **2** = **total**, accumulation, agglomeration, amount, assemblage, body, bulk, collection, combination, heap, lump, mass, mixture, pile, sum, whole ◆ *vb* **7** = **combine**, accumulate, amass, assemble, collect, heap, mix, pile

aggregation *n* **7** = **collection**, accumulation, agglomeration, assemblage, body, bulk, combination, heap, lump, mass, mixture, pile

aggression *n* **1** = **attack**, assault, encroachment, injury, invasion, offence, offensive, onslaught, raid **2** = **hostility**, aggressiveness, antagonism, belligerence, destructiveness, pugnacity

aggressive *adj* **1** = **hostile**, belligerent, destructive, offensive, pugnacious, quarrelsome **2** = **forceful**, assertive, bold, dynamic, energetic, enterprising, in-your-face (*sl.*), militant, pushing, pushy (*inf.*), vigorous, zealous
Antonyms *adj* ≠ **hostile:** friendly, peaceful ≠ **forceful:** mild, quiet, retiring, submissive

aggressor *n* = **attacker**, assailant, assaulter, invader

aggrieved *adj* **1, 2** = **hurt**, afflicted, distressed, disturbed, harmed, ill-used, injured, peeved (*inf.*), saddened, unhappy, woeful, wronged

aghast *adj* = **horrified**, afraid, amazed, appalled, astonished, astounded, awestruck, confounded, frightened, horror-struck, shocked, startled, stunned, thunder-struck

agile *adj* **1** = **nimble**, active, brisk, limber, lissom(e), lithe, lively, quick, sprightly, spry, supple, swift **2** = **acute**, alert, bright (*inf.*), clever, lively, nimble, prompt, quick, quick-witted, sharp
Antonyms *adj* ≠ **nimble:** awkward, clumsy, heavy, lumbering, ponderous, slow, slow-moving, stiff, ungainly, unsupple

agility *n* **1** = **nimbleness**, activity, briskness, litheness, liveliness, quickness, sprightliness, spryness, suppleness, swiftness **2** = **acuteness**, alertness, cleverness, liveliness, promptitude, promptness, quickness, quick-wittedness, sharpness

agitate *vb* **1, 3** = **upset**, alarm, arouse, confuse, disconcert, disquiet, distract, disturb, excite, faze, ferment, fluster, incite, inflame, perturb, rouse, ruffle, stimulate, trouble, unnerve, work up, worry **2** = **stir**, beat, churn, convulse, disturb, rock, rouse, shake, toss

opinion for or against something. [C16: from L *agitātus*, from *agitāre* to set into motion, from *agere* to act]
▸ **'agi,tated** *adj* ▸ **'agi,tatedly** *adv* ▸ **,agi'tation** *n*
agitato (,ædʒɪ'tɑːtəʊ) *adj, adv Music.* (to be performed) in an agitated manner.
agitator ➊ ('ædʒɪ,teɪtə) *n* **1** a person who agitates for or against a cause, etc. **2** a device for mixing or shaking.
agitprop ('ædʒɪt,prɒp) *n* **a** any promotion, as in the arts, of political propaganda, esp. of a Communist nature. **b** (*as modifier*): *agitprop theatre.* [C20: short for Russian *Agitpropbyuro*]
agleam (ə'gliːm) *adj* (*postpositive*) glowing; gleaming.
aglet ('æglɪt) *or* **aiglet** *n* **1** a metal sheath or tag at the end of a shoelace, ribbon, etc. **2** a variant spelling of **aiguillette.** [C15: from OF *aiguillette* a small needle]
agley (ə'gleɪ, ə'gliː, ə'glaɪ) *or* **aglee** (ə'gliː) *adv, adj Scot.* awry; askew. [from *gley* squint]
aglitter (ə'glɪtə) *adj* (*postpositive*) sparkling; glittering.
aglow (ə'gləʊ) *adj* (*postpositive*) glowing.
aglu *or* **agloo** ('ægluː) *n Canad.* a breathing hole made in ice by a seal. [C19: from Eskimo]
AGM *abbrev. for* annual general meeting.
agnail ('æg,neɪl) *n* another name for **hangnail.**
agnate ('ægneɪt) *adj* **1** related by descent from a common male ancestor. **2** related in any way. ◆ *n* **3** a male or female descendant by male links from a common male ancestor. [C16: from L *agnātus* born in addition, from *agnāsci*, from *ad-* in addition + *gnāsci* to be born]
agnostic (æg'nɒstɪk) *n* **1** a person who holds that knowledge of a Supreme Being, ultimate cause, etc., is impossible. Cf. **atheist, theist. 2** a person who claims, with respect to any particular question, that the answer cannot be known with certainty. ◆ *adj* **3** of or relating to agnostics. [C19: coined 1869 by T. H. Huxley from A-[1] + GNOSTIC]
▸ **ag'nosti,cism** *n*
Agnus Dei ('ægnʊs 'deɪɪ) *n* **1** the figure of a lamb bearing a cross or banner, emblematic of Christ. **2** a chant beginning with these words or a translation of them, forming part of the Roman Catholic Mass. [L: Lamb of God]
ago (ə'gəʊ) *adv* in the past: *five years ago; long ago.* [C14 *ago*, from OE *āgān* to pass away]

> **USAGE NOTE** The use of *ago* with *since* (*it's ten years ago since he wrote the novel*) is redundant and should be avoided: *it is ten years since he wrote the novel.*

agog ➊ (ə'gɒg) *adj* (*postpositive*) eager or curious. [C15: ?from OF *en gogues* in merriments]
-agogue *or esp. US* **-agog** *n combining form.* indicating a person or thing that leads or incites to action: *demagogue.* [via LL from Gk *agōgos*, from *agein* to lead]
▸ **-agogic** *adj combining form.* ▸ **-agogy** *n combining form.*
agonic (ə'gɒnɪk) *adj* forming no angle. [C19: from Gk *agōnos*, from A-[1] + *gōnia* angle]
agonic line *n* an imaginary line on the surface of the earth connecting points of zero magnetic declination.
agonize ➊ *or* **agonise** ('ægə,naɪz) *vb* **agonizes, agonizing, agonized** *or* **agonises, agonising, agonised. 1** to suffer or cause to suffer agony. **2** (*intr*) to struggle; strive. [C16: via Med. L from Gk *agōnizesthai* to contend for a prize, from *agōn* contest]
▸ **'ago,nizingly** *or* **'ago,nisingly** *adv*
agony ➊ ('ægənɪ) *n, pl* **agonies. 1** acute physical or mental pain; anguish. **2** the suffering or struggle preceding death. [C14: via LL from Gk *agōnia* struggle, from *agōn* contest]
agony aunt *n* (*sometimes cap.*) a person who replies to readers' letters in an agony column.
agony column *n* **1** a newspaper or magazine feature offering sympathetic advice to readers on their personal problems. **2** *Inf.* a newspaper or magazine column devoted to advertisements relating esp. to personal problems.
agora ('ægərə) *n, pl* **agorae** (-riː, -raɪ) *or* **agoras.** (*often cap.*) **a** the marketplace in Athens, used for popular meetings in ancient Greece. **b** the meeting itself. [from Gk, from *agorein* to gather]
agoraphobia (,ægərə'fəʊbɪə) *n* a pathological fear of being in public spaces.
▸ **,agora'phobic** *adj, n*
agouti (ə'guːtɪ) *n, pl* **agoutis** *or* **agouties.** a rodent of Central and South America and the Caribbean. Agoutis are agile and long-legged, with hooflike claws, and are valued for their meat. [C18: via F & Sp. from Guarani]
AGR *abbrev. for* advanced gas-cooled reactor.
agrarian ➊ (ə'grɛərɪən) *adj* **1** of or relating to land or its cultivation. **2** of or relating to rural or agricultural matters. ◆ *n* **3** a person who favours the redistribution of landed property. [C16: from L *agrārius*, from *ager* field, land]
▸ **a'grarian,ism** *n*
agree ➊ (ə'griː) *vb* **agrees, agreeing, agreed.** (*mainly intr*) **1** (often foll. by *with*) to be of the same opinion. **2** (*also tr;* when *intr*, often foll. by *to;* when *tr, takes a clause as object or an infinitive*) to give assent; consent. **3** (*also tr;* when *intr*, foll. by *on* or *about;* when *tr, may take a clause as object*) to come to terms (about). **4** (foll. by *with*) to be similar or consistent; harmonize. **5** (foll. by *with*) to be agreeable or suitable (to one's health, etc.). **6** (*tr; takes a clause as object*) to concede: *they agreed that the price was too high.* **7** *Grammar.* to undergo agreement. [C14: from OF *agreer*, from *a gre* at will or pleasure]
agreeable ➊ (ə'grɪəbᵊl) *adj* **1** pleasing; pleasant. **2** prepared to consent. **3** (foll. by *to* or *with*) in keeping. **4** (foll. by *to*) to one's liking.
▸ **a'greeableness** *n* ▸ **a'greeably** *adv*
agreed ➊ (ə'griːd) *adj* **1** determined by common consent: *the agreed price.* ◆ *sentence substitute.* **2** an expression of consent or agreement.
agreement ➊ (ə'griːmənt) *n* **1** the act of agreeing. **2** a settlement, esp. one that is legally enforceable. **3** a contract or document containing such a settlement. **4** the state of being of the same opinion. **5** the state of being similar or consistent. **6** *Grammar.* the determination of the inflectional form of one word by some grammatical feature, such as number or gender, of another word. [C14: from OF]
agribusiness ('ægrɪ,bɪznɪs) *n* the various businesses that process and distribute farm products. [C20: from AGRI(CULTURE) + BUSINESS]
agriculture ➊ ('ægrɪ,kʌltʃə) *n* the science or occupation of cultivating land and rearing crops and livestock; farming. [C17: from L *agricultūra*, from *ager* field, land + *cultūra* CULTURE]
▸ **,agri'cultural** *adj* ▸ **,agri'culturist** *or* **,agri'culturalist** *n*
agrimony ('ægrɪmənɪ) *n* **1** any of various plants of the rose family, which have compound leaves, long spikes of small yellow flowers, and bristly burlike fruits. **2** any of several other plants, such as hemp agrimony. [C15: via OF from L, from Gk *argemōnē* poppy]
agro- *combining form.* denoting fields, soil, or agriculture: *agrobiology.* [from Gk *agros* field]

THESAURUS

Antonyms *vb* ≠ **upset:** appease, assuage, calm, calm down, mollify, pacify, placate, quiet, quieten, soothe, still, tranquillize
agitated *adj* **1** = **upset**, alarmed, anxious, discomposed, disconcerted, disquieted, distracted, distressed, disturbed, edgy, excited, fazed, flustered, ill at ease, nervous, on edge, perturbed, rattled (*inf.*), ruffled, shaken, troubled, uneasy, unnerved, unsettled, worked up, worried
Antonyms *adj* at ease, calm, collected, composed, cool, relaxed, sedate, unexcited, unfazed (*inf.*), unperturbed, unruffled, untroubled
agitation *n* **1, 3** = **turmoil**, alarm, arousal, clamour, commotion, confusion, discomposure, disquiet, distraction, disturbance, excitement, ferment, flurry, fluster, incitement, lather (*inf.*), outcry, stimulation, tizzy, tizz *or* tiz-woz (*inf.*), trouble, tumult, upheaval, upset, worry **2** = **turbulence**, churning, convulsion, disturbance, rocking, shake, shaking, stir, stirring, tossing, upheaval
agitator *n* **1** = **troublemaker**, agent provocateur, demagogue, firebrand, inciter, instigator, rabble-rouser, revolutionary, stirrer (*inf.*)
agog *adj* = **eager**, avid, curious, enthralled, enthusiastic, excited, expectant, impatient, in suspense, keen
Antonyms *adj* apathetic, incurious, indifferent, unconcerned, uninterested
agonize *vb* **1, 2** = **suffer**, be distressed, be in agony, be in anguish, go through the mill, labour, strain, strive, struggle, worry, writhe
agonized *adj* **1** = **suffering**, anguished, broken-hearted, distressed, grief-stricken, racked, tormented, tortured, wounded, wretched
agonizing *adj* **1** = **painful**, bitter, distressing, excruciating, grievous, gut-wrenching, harrowing, heartbreaking, heart-rending, hellish, torturous
agony *n* **1, 2** = **suffering**, affliction, anguish, distress, misery, pain, pangs, throes, torment, torture, woe
agrarian *adj* **1, 2** = **agricultural**, agrestic, country, farming, land, rural, rustic
Antonyms *adj* industrial, urban
agree *vb* **1, 2** = **concur**, accede, acquiesce, admit, allow, assent, be of the same mind, be of the same opinion, comply, concede, consent, engage, grant, permit, see eye to eye, settle, shake hands **4** = **get on (together)**, accord, answer, chime, coincide, conform, correspond, fit, harmonize, match, square, suit, tally
Antonyms *vb* ≠ **concur:** contradict, deny, differ, disagree, dispute, dissent, rebut, refute, retract
agreeable *adj* **1** = **pleasant**, acceptable, congenial, delightful, enjoyable, gratifying, likable *or* likeable, pleasing, pleasurable, satisfying, to one's liking, to one's taste **2** = **consenting**, acquiescent, agreeing, amenable, approving, complying, concurring, in accord, onside (*inf.*), responsive, sympathetic, well-disposed, willing
Antonyms *adj* ≠ **pleasant:** disagreeable, displeasing, horrid, offensive, unlikable *or* unlikeable, unpleasant
agreed *adj* **1** = **settled**, arranged, definite, established, firm, fixed, given, guaranteed, predetermined, stipulated ◆ *sentence substitute* **2** = **all right**, done, it's a bargain *or* deal, O.K. *or* okay (*inf.*), settled, you're on (*inf.*)
Antonyms *adj* ≠ **settled:** indefinite, negotiable, to be arranged *or* decided, up in the air, variable
agreement *n* **1, 4** = **concurrence**, agreeing, assent, compliance, concord, consent, harmony, union, unison **2** = **contract**, arrangement, bargain, compact, covenant, deal (*inf.*), pact, settlement, treaty, understanding **5** = **correspondence**, accord, accordance, affinity, agreeing, analogy, compatibility, conformity, congruity, consistency, similarity, suitableness
Antonyms *n* ≠ **concurrence:** altercation, argument, clash, conflict, discord, dispute, dissent, division, falling-out, quarrel, row, squabble, strife, tiff, wrangle ≠ **correspondence:** difference, discrepancy, disparity, dissimilarity, diversity, incompatibility, incongruity
agricultural *adj* = **farming**, agrarian, agrestic, agronomic, agronomical, country, rural, rustic
agriculture *n* = **farming**, agronomics, agronomy, cultivation, culture, husbandry, tillage

agrobiology (ˌægrəʊbaɪˈɒlədʒɪ) *n* the science of plant growth and nutrition in relation to agriculture.

agroforestry (ˌægrəʊˈfɒrɪstrɪ) *n* a method of farming integrating herbaceous and tree crops.

agronomics (ˌægrəˈnɒmɪks) *n* (*functioning as sing*) the branch of economics dealing with the distribution, management, and productivity of land.
▸ **ˌagroˈnomic** *adj*

agronomy (əˈgrɒnəmɪ) *n* the science of cultivation of land, soil management, and crop production.
▸ **aˈgronomist** *n*

agrostemma (ˌægrəʊˈstɛmə) *n* any cultivated variety of corncockle. [NL, from Gk *agros* field + *stemma* wreath]

aground Ⓣ (əˈgraʊnd) *adv, adj* (*postpositive*) on or onto the ground or bottom, as in shallow water.

agterskot (ˈaxtəˌskɒt) *n* (in South Africa) the final payment to a farmer for crops. Cf. **voorskot**. [C20: Afrikaans *agter* after + *skot* shot, payment]

ague (ˈeɪgjuː) *n* **1** malarial fever with successive stages of fever and chills. **2** a fit of shivering. [C14: from OF (*fievre*) *ague* acute fever; see ACUTE]
▸ **ˈaguish** *adj*

ah (ɑː) *interj* an exclamation expressing pleasure, pain, sympathy, etc., according to the intonation of the speaker.

AH (indicating years in the Muslim system of dating, numbered from the Hegira (622 A.D.)) *abbrev. for* anno Hegirae. [L]

aha (ɑːˈhɑː) *interj* an exclamation expressing triumph, surprise, etc., according to the intonation of the speaker.

ahead Ⓣ (əˈhɛd) *adj* **1** (*postpositive*) in front; in advance. ◆ *adv* **2** at or in the front; before. **3** forwards: *go straight ahead*. **4 ahead of. 4a** in front of; at a further advanced position than. **4b** *Stock Exchange*. in anticipation of: *the share price rose ahead of the annual figures*. **5 be ahead.** *Inf.* to have an advantage; be winning. **6 get ahead.** to attain success.

ahem (əˈhɛm) *interj* a clearing of the throat, used to attract attention, express doubt, etc.

ahimsa (ɑːˈhɪmsɑː) *n* (in Hindu, Buddhist, and Jainist philosophy) the law of reverence for, and nonviolence to, every form of life. [Sansk., from *a* without + *himsā* injury]

ahoy (əˈhɔɪ) *interj Naut.* a hail used to call a ship or to attract attention.

Ahriman (ˈɑːrɪmən) *n Zoroastrianism*. the supreme evil spirit and diabolical opponent of Ormazd.

Ahura Mazda (əˈhʊərə ˈmæzdə) *n Zoroastrianism*. another name for **Ormazd**.

ai (ˈɑːɪ) *n, pl* **ais**. another name for **three-toed sloth** (see **sloth** (sense 1)). [C17: from Port., from Tupi]

AI *abbrev. for:* **1** Amnesty International. **2** artificial insemination. **3** artificial intelligence.

aid Ⓣ (eɪd) *vb* **1** to give support to (someone to do something); help or assist. **2** (*tr*) to assist financially. ◆ *n* **3** assistance; help; support. **4** a person, device, etc., that helps or assists. **5** *Mountaineering*. a device such as a piton when used as a direct help in the ascent. **6** (in medieval Europe) a feudal payment made to the king or any lord by his vassals on certain occasions such as the knighting of an eldest son. [C15: via OF *aidier* from L *adjūtāre*, from *juvāre* to help]
▸ **ˈaider** *n*

Aid *or* **-aid** *n combining form*. denoting a charitable organization or function that raises money for a cause: *Band Aid; Ferryaid*.

AID *abbrev. for:* **1** *US*. Agency for International Development. **2** artificial insemination (by) donor: former name for donor insemination (DI).

aide Ⓣ (eɪd) *n* **1** an assistant. **2** short for **aide-de-camp**.

aide-de-camp *or* **aid-de-camp** (ˈeɪd də ˈkɒŋ) *n, pl* **aides-de-camp** *or* **aids-de-camp**. a military officer serving as personal assistant to a senior. Abbrev.: **ADC**. [C17: from F: camp assistant]

aide-mémoire (ˈeɪdmɛmˈwɑː) *n, pl* **aides-mémoire** (ˈeɪdzmɛmˈwɑː). **1** a note serving as a reminder. **2** a summarized diplomatic communication. [F, from *aider* to help + *mémoire* memory]

AIDS *or* **Aids** (eɪdz) *n acronym for* acquired immune (*or* immuno-) deficiency syndrome: a condition, caused by a virus, in which the body loses its ability to resist infection. AIDS is transmitted by sexual intercourse, through infected blood and blood products, and through the placenta.

AIDS-related complex *n* See **ARC**.

AIF (formerly) *abbrev. for* Australian Imperial Force.

aiglet (ˈeɪglɪt) *n* a variant of **aglet**.

aigrette *or* **aigret** (ˈeɪgrɛt) *n* **1** a long plume worn on hats or as a headdress, esp. one of long egret feathers. **2** an ornament in imitation of a plume of feathers. [C17: from F; see EGRET]

aiguille (eɪˈgwiːl) *n* **1** a rock mass or peak shaped like a needle. **2** an instrument for boring holes in rocks or masonry. [C19: F, lit.: needle]

aiguillette (ˌeɪgwɪˈlɛt) *n* **1** an ornamentation worn by certain military officers, consisting of cords with metal tips. **2** a variant of **aglet**. [C19: F; see AGLET]

AIH *abbrev. for* artificial insemination (by) husband.

aikido (aɪˈkiːdəʊ) *n* a Japanese system of self-defence employing similar principles to judo, but including blows from the hands and feet. [from Japanese, from *ai* to join, receive + *ki* spirit, force + *do* way]

ail Ⓣ (eɪl) *vb* **1** (*tr*) to trouble; afflict. **2** (*intr*) to feel unwell. [OE *eglan*, from *egle* painful]

ailanthus (eɪˈlænθəs) *n, pl* **ailanthuses**. an E Asian deciduous tree having pinnate leaves, small greenish flowers, and winged fruits. Also called: **tree of heaven**. [C19: NL, from native name in the Moluccas in the Indian and Pacific Oceans]

aileron (ˈeɪlərɒn) *n* a flap hinged to the trailing edge of an aircraft wing to provide lateral control. [C20: from F, dim. of *aile* wing]

ailing Ⓣ (ˈeɪlɪŋ) *adj* unwell or unsuccessful, esp. over a long period.

ailment Ⓣ (ˈeɪlmənt) *n* a slight but often persistent illness.

aim Ⓣ (eɪm) *vb* **1** to point (a weapon, missile, etc.) or direct (a blow) at a particular person or object. **2** (*tr*) to direct (satire, criticism, etc.) at a person, object, etc. **3** (*intr;* foll. by *at* or an infinitive) to propose or intend. **4** (*intr;* often foll. by *at* or *for*) to direct one's efforts or strive (towards). ◆ *n* **5** the action of directing something at an object. **6** the direction in which something is pointed: *to take aim*. **7** the object at which something is aimed. **8** intention; purpose. [C14: via OF *aesmer* from L *aestimāre* to ESTIMATE]

AIM *abbrev. for* Alternative Investment Market.

aimless Ⓣ (ˈeɪmlɪs) *adj* having no purpose or direction.
▸ **ˈaimlessly** *adv* ▸ **ˈaimlessness** *n*

ain't (eɪnt) *Not standard. contraction of* am not, is not, are not, have not, *or* has not: *I ain't seen it*.

Ainu (ˈaɪnuː) *n* **1** (*pl* **Ainus** *or* **Ainu**) a member of the aboriginal people of Japan. **2** the language of this people, sometimes tentatively associated with Altaic, still spoken in parts of Hokkaido. [Ainu: man]

air Ⓣ (ɛə) *n* **1** the mixture of gases that forms the earth's atmosphere. It consists chiefly of nitrogen, oxygen, argon, and carbon dioxide. **2** the space above and around the earth; sky. Related adj: **aerial**. **3** breeze; slight wind. **4** public expression; utterance. **5** a distinctive quality: *an air of mystery*. **6** a person's distinctive appearance, manner, or bearing. **7** *Music*. a simple tune for either vocal or instrumental performance. **8** transportation in aircraft (esp. in **by air**). **9** an archaic word for **breath** (senses 1–3). **10 in the air. 10a** in circulation; current. **10b** unsettled. **11 into thin air.** leaving no trace behind. **12 on** (*or* **off**) **the air.** (not) in the act of broadcasting or (not) being broadcast on radio or television. **13 take the air.** to go out of doors, as for a short walk. **14 up in the air. 14a** uncertain. **14b** *Inf.* agitated or excited. **15** (*modifier*) *Astrol.* of or relating to a group of three signs of the zodiac, Gemini, Libra, and Aquarius. ◆ *vb* **16** to expose or be exposed to the air so as to cool or freshen. **17** to expose or be exposed to warm or heated air so as to dry: *to air linen*. **18** (*tr*) to make known publicly: *to air one's opinions*. **19** (*intr*) (of a television or radio programme) to be broadcast. ◆ See also **airs**. [C13: via OF & L from Gk *aēr* the lower atmosphere]

air bag *n* a safety device in a car, consisting of a bag that inflates automatically in an accident and prevents the passengers from being thrown forwards.

air base *n* a centre from which military aircraft operate.

air bladder *n* **1** an air-filled sac, lying above the alimentary canal in bony fishes, that regulates buoyancy at different depths by a variation in the pressure of the air. **2** any air-filled sac, such as one in seaweeds.

THESAURUS

aground *adv* = **beached**, ashore, foundered, grounded, high and dry, on the rocks, stranded, stuck

ahead *adv* **2, 3** = **in front**, along, at an advantage, at the head, before, forwards, in advance, in the foreground, in the lead, in the vanguard, leading, on, onwards, to the fore, winning

aid *vb* **1, 2** = **help**, abet, assist, befriend, encourage, favour, give a leg up (*inf.*), promote, relieve, second, serve, subsidize, succour, support, sustain ◆ *n* **3** = **help**, assistance, benefit, encouragement, favour, promotion, relief, service, succour, support **4** = **helper**, abettor, adjutant, aide, aide-de-camp, assistant, second, supporter
Antonyms *vb* ≠ **help:** detract from, harm, hinder, hurt, impede, obstruct, oppose, thwart ◆ *n* ≠ **help:** hindrance

aide *n* **1** = **assistant**, adjutant, attendant, coadjutor (*rare*), deputy, helper, helpmate, henchman, right-hand man, second, supporter

ail *vb* **1** = **trouble**, afflict, annoy, be the matter with, bother, distress, irritate, pain, sicken, upset, worry **2** = **be ill**, be indisposed, be *or* feel off colour, be sick, be unwell, feel unwell

ailing *adj* = **ill**, debilitated, diseased, feeble, indisposed, infirm, invalid, off colour, poorly, sick, sickly, suffering, under the weather (*inf.*), unsound, unwell, weak

ailment *n* = **illness**, affliction, complaint, disease, disorder, infirmity, lurgy (*inf.*), malady, sickness

aim *vb* **1, 3, 4** = **intend**, aspire, attempt, design, direct, draw a bead (on), endeavour, level, mean, plan, point, propose, purpose, resolve, seek, set one's sights on, sight, strive, take aim (at), train, try, want, wish ◆ *n* **7, 8** = **intention**, ambition, aspiration, course, design, desire, direction, end, goal, Holy Grail (*inf.*), intent, mark, object, objective, plan, purpose, scheme, target, wish

aimless *adj* = **purposeless**, chance, directionless, erratic, frivolous, goalless, haphazard, pointless, random, stray, undirected, unguided, unpredictable, vagrant, wayward
Antonyms *adj* decided, deliberate, determined, firm, fixed, positive, purposeful, resolute, resolved, settled, single-minded

air *n* **2** = **atmosphere**, heavens, sky **3** = **wind**, blast, breath, breeze, draught, puff, waft, whiff, zephyr **4** = **circulation**, display, dissemination, exposure, expression, publicity, utterance, vent, ventilation **5** = **manner**, ambience, appearance, atmosphere, aura, bearing, character, demeanour, effect, feeling, flavour, impression, look, mood, quality, style, tone, vibes (*sl.*) **7** = **tune**, aria, lay, melody, song ◆ *vb* **16** = **ventilate**, aerate, expose, freshen **18** = **publicize**, circulate, communicate, declare, disclose, display, disseminate, divulge, exhibit, expose, express,

airborne Ⓣ ('ɛəˌbɔːn) *adj* **1** conveyed by or through the air. **2** (of aircraft) flying; in the air.

air brake *n* **1** a brake operated by compressed air, esp. in heavy vehicles and trains. **2** an articulated flap or small parachute for reducing the speed of an aircraft.

airbrick ('ɛəˌbrɪk) *n Chiefly Brit.* a brick with holes in it, put into the wall of a building for ventilation.

airbrush ('ɛəˌbrʌʃ) *n* **1** an atomizer for spraying paint or varnish by means of compressed air. ◆ *vb (tr)* **2** to paint or varnish (something) by using an airbrush. **3** to improve the image of (a person or thing) by concealing defects beneath a bland exterior: *an airbrushed version of the government's record.*

air chief marshal *n* a senior officer of the Royal Air Force and certain other air forces, of equivalent rank to admiral in the Royal Navy.

air cleaner *n* a filter that prevents dust and other particles from entering the air intake of an internal-combustion engine. Also called: **air filter.**

air commodore *n* a senior officer of the Royal Air Force and certain other air forces, of equivalent rank to brigadier in the Army.

air conditioning *n* a system or process for controlling the temperature and sometimes the humidity of the air in a house, etc.
▸**'air-conˌdition** *vb (tr)* ▸**air conditioner** *n*

air-cool *vb (tr)* to cool (an engine) by a flow of air. Cf. **water-cool.**

aircraft Ⓣ ('ɛəˌkrɑːft) *n, pl* **aircraft.** any machine capable of flying by means of buoyancy or aerodynamic forces, such as a glider, helicopter, or aeroplane.

aircraft carrier *n* a warship with an extensive flat deck for the launch of aircraft.

aircraftman ('ɛəˌkrɑːftmən) *n, pl* **aircraftmen.** a serviceman of the most junior rank in the Royal Air Force.
▸**'aircraftˌwoman** *fem n*

air curtain *n* an air stream across a doorway to exclude draughts, etc.

air cushion *n* **1** an inflatable cushion. **2** the pocket of air that supports a hovercraft.

airdrop ('ɛəˌdrɒp) *n* **1** a delivery of supplies, troops, etc., from an aircraft by parachute. ◆ *vb* **airdrops, airdropping, airdropped.** **2** *(tr)* to deliver (supplies, etc.) by an airdrop.

Airedale ('ɛəˌdeɪl) *n* a large rough-haired tan-coloured breed of terrier with a black saddle-shaped patch covering most of the back. Also called: **Airedale terrier.** [C19: from district in Yorkshire]

air engine *n* **1** an engine that uses the expansion of heated air to drive a piston. **2** a small engine that uses compressed air to drive a piston.

airfield Ⓣ ('ɛəˌfiːld) *n* a landing and taking-off area for aircraft.

air filter *n* another name for **air cleaner.**

airfoil ('ɛəˌfɔɪl) *n* the US and Canad. name for **aerofoil.**

air force *n* **a** the branch of a nation's armed services primarily responsible for air warfare. **b** *(as modifier): an air-force base.*

airframe ('ɛəˌfreɪm) *n* the body of an aircraft, excluding its engines.

air guitar *n* an imaginary guitar played while miming to rock music.

air gun *n* a gun discharged by means of compressed air.

airhead ('ɛəˌhɛd) *n Sl.* a stupid or simple-minded person; idiot. [C20: from AIR + HEAD]

air hole *n* **1** a hole that allows the passage of air, esp. for ventilation. **2** a section of open water in a frozen surface.

air hostess *n* a stewardess on an airliner.

airily Ⓣ ('ɛərɪlɪ) *adv* **1** in a jaunty or high-spirited manner. **2** in a light or delicate manner.

airiness Ⓣ ('ɛərɪnɪs) *n* **1** the quality or condition of being fresh, light, or breezy. **2** gaiety.

airing Ⓣ ('ɛərɪŋ) *n* **1a** exposure to air or warmth, as for drying or ventilation. **1b** *(as modifier): airing cupboard.* **2** an excursion in the open air. **3** exposure to public debate.

airless Ⓣ ('ɛəlɪs) *adj* **1** lacking fresh air; stuffy or sultry. **2** devoid of air.
▸**'airlessness** *n*

air letter *n* another name for **aerogram.**

airlift ('ɛəˌlɪft) *n* **1** the transportation by air of passengers, troops, cargo, etc., esp. when other routes are blocked. ◆ *vb* **2** *(tr)* to transport by an airlift.

airline ('ɛəˌlaɪn) *n* **1a** a system or organization that provides scheduled flights for passengers or cargo. **1b** *(as modifier): an airline pilot.* **2** a hose or tube carrying air under pressure.

airliner ('ɛəˌlaɪnə) *n* a large passenger aircraft.

airlock ('ɛəˌlɒk) *n* **1** a bubble in a pipe causing an obstruction. **2** an airtight chamber with regulated air pressure used to gain access to a space that has air under pressure.

airmail ('ɛəˌmeɪl) *n* **1** the system of conveying mail by aircraft. **2** mail conveyed by aircraft. ◆ *adj* **3** of or for airmail.

airman ('ɛəmən) *n, pl* **airmen.** a man who serves in his country's air force.

air marshal *n* **1** a senior Royal Air Force officer of equivalent rank to a vice admiral in the Royal Navy. **2** a Royal Australian Air Force officer of the highest rank. **3** a Royal New Zealand Air Force officer of the highest rank when chief of defence forces.

air mass *n* a large body of air having characteristics of temperature, moisture, and pressure that are approximately uniform horizontally.

Air Miles *pl n* points awarded by certain companies to purchasers of flight tickets and some other products that may be used to pay for other flights.

air miss *n* a situation in which two aircraft pass very close to one another in the air; near miss.

airplane ('ɛəˌpleɪn) *n* the US and Canad. name for **aeroplane.**

airplay ('ɛəˌpleɪ) *n* (of recorded music) radio exposure.

air pocket *n* a localized region of low air density or a descending air current, causing an aircraft to suffer an abrupt decrease in height.

airport Ⓣ ('ɛəˌpɔːt) *n* a landing and taking-off area for civil aircraft, usually with runways and aircraft maintenance and passenger facilities.

air power *n* the strength of a nation's air force.

air pump *n* a device for pumping air into or out of something.

air raid *n* **a** an attack by hostile aircraft or missiles. **b** *(as modifier): an air-raid shelter.*

air-raid warden *n* a member of a civil defence organization responsible for enforcing regulations, etc., during an air attack.

air rifle *n* a rifle discharged by compressed air.

airs Ⓣ (ɛəz) *pl n* affected manners intended to impress others: *to give oneself airs; put on airs.*

air sac *n* any of the membranous air-filled extensions of the lungs of birds, which increase the efficiency of respiration.

airscrew ('ɛəˌskruː) *n Brit.* an aircraft propeller.

air-sea rescue *n* an air rescue at sea.

air shaft *n* a shaft for ventilation, esp. in a mine or tunnel.

airship ('ɛəˌʃɪp) *n* a lighter-than-air self-propelled craft. Also called: **dirigible.**

airshow ('ɛəˌʃəʊ) *n* an occasion when an air base is open to the public and a flying display and, usually, static exhibitions are held.

airsick ('ɛəˌsɪk) *adj* nauseated from travelling in an aircraft.

airside ('ɛəˌsaɪd) *n* the part of an airport nearest the aircraft, the boundary of which is the security check, customs, passport control, etc. Cf. **landside** (sense 1).

airspace ('ɛəˌspeɪs) *n* the atmosphere above the earth or part of the earth, esp. the atmosphere above a particular country.

airspeed ('ɛəˌspiːd) *n* the speed of an aircraft relative to the air in which it moves.

airstrip ('ɛəˌstrɪp) *n* a cleared area for the landing and taking-off of aircraft; runway. Also called: **landing strip.**

air terminal *n Brit.* a building in a city from which air passengers are taken to an airport.

airtight ('ɛəˌtaɪt) *adj* **1** not permitting the passage of air. **2** having no weak points; rigid or unassailable.

air-to-air *adj* operating between aircraft in flight.

air-traffic control *n* an organization that determines the altitude, speed, and direction at which planes fly in a given area, giving instructions to pilots by radio.
▸**air-traffic controller** *n*

air vice-marshal *n* **1** a senior Royal Air Force officer of equivalent rank to a rear admiral in the Royal Navy. **2** a Royal Australian Air Force officer of the second highest rank. **3** a Royal New Zealand Air Force officer of the highest rank.

airwaves ('ɛəˌweɪvz) *pl n Inf.* radio waves used in radio and television broadcasting.

airway ('ɛəˌweɪ) *n* **1** an air route, esp. one that is fully equipped with navigational aids, etc. **2** a passage for ventilation, esp. in a mine. **3** the passage of air from the nose or mouth to the lungs. **4** *Med.* a tubelike device inserted via the throat to keep open the airway of an unconscious patient.

air waybill *n* a document made out by the consigner of goods by air freight giving details of the goods and the name of the consignee.

airworthy ('ɛəˌwɜːðɪ) *adj* (of an aircraft) safe to fly.

airy Ⓣ ('ɛərɪ) *adj* **airier, airiest.** **1** abounding in fresh air. **2** spacious or uncluttered. **3** nonchalant. **4** visionary; fanciful: *airy promises.* **5** of or relating to air. **6** weightless and insubstantial. **7** light and graceful in movement. **8** high up in the air.

THESAURUS

give vent to, make known, make public, proclaim, reveal, tell, utter, ventilate, voice

airborne *adj* **1, 2** = **flying**, floating, gliding, hovering, in flight, in the air, on the wing, soaring, volitant, wind-borne

aircraft *n* = **plane**, aeroplane, airplane, flying machine, kite (*Brit. sl.*)

airfield *n* = **airport**, aerodrome, airdrome (*US*), air station, airstrip, landing strip

airily *adv* **1** = **light-heartedly**, animatedly, blithely, breezily, buoyantly, gaily, happily, high-spiritedly, jauntily

airiness *n* **1** = **freshness**, breeziness, draughtiness, gustiness, lightness, openness, windiness **2** = **light-heartedness**, animation, blitheness, breeziness, buoyancy, gaiety, happiness, high spirits, jauntiness, lightness of heart

airing *n* **1** = **ventilation**, aeration, drying, freshening **3** = **exposure**, circulation, display, dissemination, expression, publicity, utterance, vent, ventilation

airless *adj* **1, 2** = **stuffy**, breathless, close, heavy, muggy, oppressive, stale, stifling, suffocating, sultry, unventilated
Antonyms *adj* airy, blowy, breezy, draughty, fresh, gusty, light, open, spacious, well- ventilated

airport *n* = **airfield**, aerodrome, airdrome (*US*)

airs *pl n* = **affectation**, affectedness, arrogance, haughtiness, hauteur, pomposity, pretensions, superciliousness, swank (*inf.*)

airy *adj* **1** = **well-ventilated**, blowy, breezy, draughty, fresh, gusty, light, lofty, open, spacious, uncluttered, windy **3** = **light-hearted**, animated, blithe, buoyant, cheerful, cheery, chirpy (*inf.*), debonair, frolicsome, gay, genial, happy, high-spirited, jaunty, light, lively, merry, nonchalant, sprightly, upbeat (*inf.*) **4, 6** = **insubstantial**, aerial, delicate, ethereal, fanciful, flimsy, illusory, imaginary, immaterial, in-

DICTIONARY

aisle (aɪl) *n* **1** a passageway separating seating areas in a theatre, church, etc. **2** a lateral division in a church flanking the nave or chancel. [C14 *ele* (later *aile, aisle,* through confusion with *isle*), via OF from L *āla* wing]
▸**aisled** *adj*

ait (eɪt) *or* **eyot** *n Dialect.* an islet, esp. in a river. [OE *ȳgett* small island, from *ieg* ISLAND]

aitch (eɪtʃ) *n* the letter *h* or the sound represented by it. [C16: a phonetic spelling]

aitchbone ('eɪtʃˌbəʊn) *n* **1** the rump bone in cattle. **2** a cut of beef from or including the rump bone. [C15 *hach-boon,* altered from earlier *nache-bone* (*a nache* mistaken for *an ache, an aitch*); *nache* buttock, via OF from LL *natica,* from L *natis* buttock]

ajar (ə'dʒɑː) *adj* (*postpositive*), *adv* (esp. of a door) slightly open. [C18: altered form of obs. *on char,* lit.: on the turn; from OE *cierran* to turn]

AK-47 *n Trademark.* a type of Kalashnikov.

a.k.a. *or* **AKA** *abbrev. for* also known as.

akene (ə'kiːn) *n* a variant spelling of **achene.**

akimbo (ə'kɪmbəʊ) *adj, adv* (**with**) **arms akimbo.** with hands on hips and elbows out. [C15 *in kenebowe,* lit.: in keen bow, that is, in a sharp curve]

akin (ə'kɪn) *adj* (*postpositive*) **1** related by blood. **2** (often foll. by *to*) having similar characteristics, properties, etc.

Akkadian *or* **Accadian** (ə'kædɪən) *n* **1** a member of an ancient Semitic people who lived in Mesopotamia in the third millennium B.C. **2** the extinct language of this people.

Al *the chemical symbol for* aluminium.

-al[1] *suffix forming adjectives.* of; related to: *functional; sectional; tonal.* [from L *-ālis*]

-al[2] *suffix forming nouns.* the act or process of doing what is indicated by the verb stem: *renewal.* [via OF *-aille, -ail,* from L *-ālia,* neuter pl used as substantive, from *-ālis* -AL[1]]

-al[3] *suffix forming nouns.* **1** (*not used systematically*) indicating any aldehyde: *ethanal.* **2** indicating a pharmaceutical product: *phenobarbital.* [shortened from ALDEHYDE]

ala ('eɪlə) *n, pl* **alae** ('eɪliː). **1** *Zool.* a wing or flat winglike process or structure. **2** *Bot.* a winglike part, such as one of the wings of a sycamore seed. [C18: from L *āla* a wing]

à la (ɑː lɑː) *prep* **1** in the manner or style of. **2** as prepared in (a particular place) or by or for (a particular person). [C17: from F, short for *à la mode de* in the style of]

alabaster ('æləˌbɑːstə) *n* **1** a fine-grained usually white, opaque, or translucent variety of gypsum. **2** a variety of hard semitranslucent calcite. ◆ *adj* **3** of or resembling alabaster. [C14: from OF *alabastre,* from L *alabaster,* from Gk *alabastros*]
▸ˌ**ala'bastrine** *adj*

à la carte (ɑː lɑː 'kɑːt) *adj, adv* (of a menu) having dishes listed separately and individually priced. Cf. **table d'hôte.** [C19: from F, lit.: according to the card]

alack (ə'læk) *or* **alackaday** (ə'lækəˌdeɪ) *interj* an archaic or poetic word for **alas.** [C15: from *a* ah! + *lack* loss, LACK]

alacrity (ə'lækrɪtɪ) *n* liveliness or briskness. [C15: from L, from *alacer* lively]

à la mode (ɑː lɑː 'məʊd) *adj* **1** fashionable in style, design, etc. **2** (of meats) braised with vegetables in wine. [C17: from F: according to the fashion]

Al-Anon ('æləˌnɒn) *n* an association for the families and friends of alcoholics to give mutual support.

alar ('eɪlə) *adj* relating to, resembling, or having wings or alae. [C19: from L *āla* a wing]

Alar ('eɪlɑː) *n* a chemical sprayed on cultivated apple trees in certain countries to increase fruit set; daminozide.

alarm (ə'lɑːm) *vb* (*tr*) **1** to fill with apprehension, anxiety, or fear. **2** to warn about danger; alert. **3** to fit or activate a burglar alarm on (a house, car, etc.). ◆ *n* **4** fear or terror aroused by awareness of danger. **5** apprehension or uneasiness. **6** a noise, signal, etc., warning of danger. **7** any device that transmits such a warning: *a burglar alarm.* **8a** the device in an alarm clock that triggers off the bell or buzzer. **8b** short for **alarm clock. 9** *Arch.* a call to arms. [C14: from OF *alarme,* from OIt. *all'arme* to arms; see ARM[2]]
▸**a'larming** *adj*

alarm clock *n* a clock with a mechanism that sounds at a set time: used esp. for waking a person up.

alarmist (ə'lɑːmɪst) *n* **1** a person who alarms or attempts to alarm others needlessly. **2** a person who is easily alarmed. ◆ *adj* **3** characteristic of an alarmist.

alarum (ə'lærəm, -'lɑːr-) *n* **1** *Arch.* an alarm, esp. a call to arms. **2** (used as a stage direction, esp. in Elizabethan drama) a loud disturbance or conflict (esp. in **alarums and excursions**). [C15: var. of ALARM]

alas (ə'læs) *sentence connector.* **1** unfortunately; regrettably: *there were, alas, none left.* ◆ *interj* **2** *Arch.* an exclamation of grief or alarm. [C13: from OF *ha las!* oh wretched!; *las* from L *lassus* weary]

alate ('eɪleɪt) *adj* having wings or winglike extensions. [C17: from L, from *āla* wing]

alb (ælb) *n Christianity.* a long white linen vestment with sleeves worn by priests and others. [OE *albe,* from Med. L *alba* (*vestis*) white (clothing)]

albacore ('ælbəˌkɔː) *n* a tunny occurring mainly in warm regions of the Atlantic and Pacific. It has very long pectoral fins and is a valued food fish. [C16: from Port., from Ar.]

Albanian (æl'beɪnɪən) *n* **1** the official language of Albania. **2** a native, citizen, or inhabitant of Albania. ◆ *adj* **3** of or relating to Albania, its people, or their language.

albatross ('ælbəˌtrɒs) *n* **1** a large bird of cool southern oceans, with long narrow wings and a powerful gliding flight. See also **wandering albatross. 2** a constant and inescapable burden or handicap. **3** *Golf.* a score of three strokes under par for a hole. [C17: from Port. *alcatraz* pelican, from Ar., from *al* the + *ghattās* white-tailed sea eagle; infl. by L *albus* white: C20 in sense 2, from Coleridge's poem *The Rime of the Ancient Mariner* (1798)]

albedo (æl'biːdəʊ) *n* the ratio of the intensity of light reflected from an object, such as a planet, to that of the light it receives from the sun. [C19: from Church L: whiteness, from L *albus* white]

albeit (ɔːl'biːɪt) *conj* even though. [C14 *al be it,* that is, although it be (that)]

albert ('ælbət) *n* a kind of watch chain usually attached to a waistcoat.

Albertan (æl'bɜːtən) *adj* **1** of or denoting Alberta, a province of W Canada. ◆ *n* **2** a native or inhabitant of Alberta.

albescent (æl'bes[ə]nt) *adj* shading into or becoming white. [C19: from L *albēscere,* from *albus* white]
▸**al'bescence** *n*

Albigenses (ˌælbɪ'dʒensiːz) *pl n* members of a Manichean sect that flourished in S France from the 11th to the 13th century.

albino (æl'biːnəʊ) *n, pl* **albinos. 1** a person with congenital absence of pigmentation in the skin, eyes, and hair. **2** any animal or plant that is deficient in pigment. [C18: via Port. & Sp. from L *albus* white]
▸**albinism** ('ælbɪˌnɪzəm) *n* ▸**albinotic** (ˌælbɪ'nɒtɪk) *adj*

Albion ('ælbɪən) *n Arch. or poetic.* Britain or England. [C13: from L, of Celtic origin]

albite ('ælbaɪt) *n* a white, bluish-green, or reddish-grey feldspar mineral used in the manufacture of glass and as a gemstone. [C19: from L *albus* white]

album ('ælbəm) *n* **1** a book or binder consisting of blank pages, for keeping photographs, stamps, autographs, etc. **2** one or more long-playing CDs, cassettes, or records released as a single item. **3** a booklike holder containing sleeves for gramophone records. **4** *Chiefly Brit.* an anthology. [C17: from L: blank tablet, from *albus* white]

albumen ('ælbjʊmɪn) *n* **1** the white of an egg; the nutritive substance that surrounds the yolk. **2** a variant spelling of **albumin.** [C16: from L: white of an egg, from *albus* white]

albumin *or* **albumen** ('ælbjʊmɪn) *n* any of a group of simple water-soluble proteins that are found in blood plasma, egg white, etc. [C19: from ALBUMEN + -IN]
▸**al'buminous** *adj*

albuminoid (æl'bjuːmɪˌnɔɪd) *adj* **1** resembling albumin. ◆ *n* **2** another name for **scleroprotein.**

albuminuria (ælˌbjuːmɪ'njʊərɪə) *n* the presence of albumin in the urine. Also called: **proteinuria.**

alburnum (æl'bɜːnəm) *n* a former name for **sapwood.** [C17: from L: sapwood, from *albus* white]

Alcaic (æl'keɪɪk) *adj* **1** of a metre used by the Greek poet Alcaeus (7th

THESAURUS

corporeal, light, vaporous, visionary, weightless, wispy
Antonyms *adj* ≠ **well-ventilated:** airless, close, heavy, muggy, oppressive, stale, stifling, stuffy, suffocating, unventilated ≠ **light-hearted:** cheerless, dismal, gloomy, glum, melancholy, miserable, morose, sad ≠ **insubstantial:** concrete, corporeal, material, real, realistic, substantial, tangible

aisle *n* **1** = **passageway,** alley, corridor, gangway, lane, passage, path

ajar *adj* = **open,** agape, gaping, partly open, unclosed

akin *adj* **1, 2 akin to** = **similar to,** affiliated with, allied with, analogous to, cognate with, comparable to, congenial with, connected with *or* to, consanguineous with, corresponding to, kin to, like, of a piece with, parallel to, related to

alacrity *n* = **eagerness,** alertness, avidity, briskness, cheerfulness, dispatch, enthusiasm, gaiety, hilarity, joyousness, liveliness, promptness, quickness, readiness, speed, sprightliness, willingness, zeal
Antonyms *n* apathy, dullness, inertia, lethargy, reluctance, slowness, sluggishness, unconcern, unwillingness

à la mode *adj* **1** = **fashionable,** all the go (*inf.*), all the rage (*inf.*), chic, in (*inf.*), in fashion, in vogue, latest, modish, popular, stylish, the latest rage (*inf.*), with it (*inf.*)

alarm *vb* **1** = **frighten,** daunt, dismay, distress, give (someone) a turn (*inf.*), make (someone's) hair stand on end, panic, put the wind up (someone) (*inf.*), scare, startle, terrify, unnerve ◆ *n* **4, 5** = **fear,** anxiety, apprehension, consternation, dismay, distress, fright, nervousness, panic, scare, terror, trepidation, unease, uneasiness **6** = **danger signal,** alarm bell, alert, bell, distress signal, hooter, siren, tocsin, warning
Antonyms *vb* ≠ **frighten:** assure, calm, comfort, reassure, relieve, soothe ◆ *n* ≠ **fear:** calm, calmness, composure, sang-froid, serenity

alarmed *adj* **1** = **frightened,** anxious, apprehensive, daunted, dismayed, distressed, disturbed, fearful, in a panic, nervous, scared, shocked, startled, terrified, troubled, uneasy, unnerved
Antonyms *adj* assured, calm, composed, fearless, serene, undaunted, untroubled

alarming *adj* **1** = **frightening,** daunting, dismaying, distressing, disturbing, dreadful, scaring, shocking, startling, terrifying, unnerving

albeit *conj* = **even though,** although, even if, notwithstanding that, tho' (*US. or poetic*), though

album *n* **1** = **book,** collection, scrapbook **2** = **record,** cassette, CD, LP

century B.C.), consisting of a strophe of four lines each with four feet. ◆ *n* **2** (*usually pl*) verse written in the Alcaic form.

alcalde (æl'kældɪ) *or* **alcade** (æl'keɪd) *n* (in Spain and Spanish America) the mayor or chief magistrate in a town. [C17: from Sp., from Ar. *al-qāḍī* the judge]

alcazar (ˌælkə'zɑː; *Spanish* al'kaθar) *n* any of various palaces or fortresses built in Spain by the Moors. [C17: from Sp., from Ar. *al-qasr* the castle]

alchemist ('ælkəmɪst) *n* a person who practises alchemy.

alchemize *or* **alchemise** ('ælkəˌmaɪz) *vb* **alchemizes, alchemizing, alchemized** *or* **alchemises, alchemising, alchemised.** (*tr*) to alter (an element, metal, etc.) by alchemy.

alchemy ❶ ('ælkəmɪ) *n, pl* **alchemies. 1** the pseudoscientific predecessor of chemistry that sought a method of transmuting base metals into gold, and an elixir to prolong life indefinitely. **2** a power like that of alchemy: *her beauty had a potent alchemy.* [C14 *alkamye*, via OF from Med. L, from Ar., from *al* the + *kīmiyā'* transmutation, from LGk *khēmeia* the art of transmutation]
▸**alchemic** (æl'kemɪk) *or* **al'chemical** *adj*

alcheringa (ˌæltʃə'rɪŋgə) *n* another name for **Dreamtime.** [from Abor., lit.: dream time]

ALCM *abbrev. for* air-launched cruise missile: a type of cruise missile that can be launched from an aircraft.

alcohol ❶ ('ælkəˌhɒl) *n* **1** a colourless flammable liquid, the active principle of intoxicating drinks, produced by the fermentation of sugars. Formula: C_2H_5OH. Also called: **ethanol, ethyl alcohol. 2** a drink or drinks containing this substance. **3** *Chem.* any one of a class of organic compounds that contain one or more hydroxyl groups bound to carbon atoms that are not part of an aromatic ring. Cf. **phenol** (sense 2). [C16: via NL from Med. L, from Ar. *al-kuhl* powdered antimony]

alcohol-free *adj* **1** (of beer or wine) containing only a trace of alcohol. Cf. **low-alcohol. 2** (of a period of time) during which no alcoholic drink is consumed: *there should be one or two alcohol-free days per week.*

alcoholic ❶ (ˌælkə'hɒlɪk) *n* **1** a person affected by alcoholism. ◆ *adj* **2** of, relating to, containing, or resulting from alcohol.

Alcoholics Anonymous *n* an association of alcoholics who try, esp. by mutual assistance, to overcome alcoholism.

alcoholism ('ælkəhɒˌlɪzəm) *n* a condition in which dependence on alcohol harms a person's health, family life, etc.

alcoholize *or* **alcoholise** ('ælkəhɒˌlaɪz) *vb* **alcoholizes, alcoholizing, alcoholized** *or* **alcoholises, alcoholising, alcoholised.** (*tr*) to turn into alcoholic drink, as by fermenting or mixing with alcohol.
▸ˌ**alcoˌholi'zation** *or* ˌ**alcoˌholi'sation** *n*

alcopop ('ælkəʊˌpɒp) *n Inf.* an alcoholic drink that tastes like a soft drink. [C20: from ALCO(HOL) + POP[1] (sense 11)]

Alcoran *or* **Alkoran** (ˌælkɒ'rɑːn) *n* another name for the **Koran.**
▸ˌ**Alco'ranic** *or* ˌ**Alko'ranic** *adj*

alcove ❶ ('ælkəʊv) *n* **1** a recess or niche in the wall of a room, as for a bed, books, etc. **2** any recessed usually vaulted area, as in a garden wall. **3** any covered or secluded spot. [C17: from F, from Sp. *alcoba*, from Ar. *al-qubbah* the vault]

aldehyde ('ældɪˌhaɪd) *n* **1** any organic compound containing the group -CHO. Aldehydes are oxidized to carboxylic acids. **2** (*modifier*) consisting of, containing, or concerned with the group -CHO. [C19: from NL *al(cohol) dehyd(rogenātum)* dehydrogenated alcohol]
▸**aldehydic** (ˌældə'hɪdɪk) *adj*

al dente (ˌæl 'dentɪ) *adj* (of pasta) still firm after cooking. [It., lit: to the tooth]

alder ('ɔːldə) *n* **1** a shrub or tree of the birch family, having toothed leaves and conelike fruits. The wood is used for bridges, etc., because it resists underwater rot. **2** any of several similar trees or shrubs. [OE *alor*]

alderman ('ɔːldəmən) *n, pl* **aldermen. 1** (in England and Wales until 1974) one of the senior members of a local council, elected by other councillors. **2** (in the US, Canada, Australia, etc.) a member of the governing body of a municipality. **3** *History.* a variant spelling of **ealdorman.** [OE *aldormann*, from *ealdor* chief (comp. of *eald* OLD) + *mann* MAN]
▸**aldermanic** (ˌɔːldə'mænɪk) *adj*

Alderney ('ɔːldənɪ) *n* any of a breed of dairy cattle originating from Alderney, one of the Channel Islands.

Aldis lamp ('ɔːldɪs) *n* a portable signalling lamp. [C20: after its inventor A.C.W. *Aldis*]

aldrin ('ɔːldrɪn) *n* a poisonous crystalline solid, mostly $C_{12}H_8Cl_6$, used as an insecticide. [C20: after K. *Alder* (1902–58), G chemist]

ale (eɪl) *n* **1** a beer fermented in an open vessel using yeasts that rise to the top of the brew. Compare **beer, lager. 2** (formerly) an alcoholic drink made by fermenting a cereal, esp. barley, but differing from beer by being unflavoured by hops. **3** *Chiefly Brit.* another word for **beer.** [OE *alu, ealu*]

aleatory ('eɪlɪətərɪ) *or* **aleatoric** (ˌeɪlɪə'tɒrɪk) *adj* **1** dependent on chance. **2** (esp. of a musical composition) involving elements chosen at random by the performer. [C17: from L, from *āleātor* gambler, from *ālea* game of chance]

alee (ə'liː) *adv, adj* (*postpositive*) *Naut.* on or towards the lee: *with the helm alee.*

alehouse ('eɪlˌhaʊs) *n* **1** *Arch.* a place where ale was sold; tavern. **2** *Inf.* a pub.

alembic (ə'lembɪk) *n* **1** an obsolete type of retort used for distillation. **2** anything that distils or purifies. [C14: from Med. L, from Ar. *al-anbīq* the still, from Gk *ambix* cup]

aleph ('ɑːlɪf; *Hebrew* 'alef) *n* the first letter in the Hebrew alphabet. [Heb.: ox]

aleph-null *or* **aleph-zero** *n* the smallest infinite cardinal number; the cardinal number of the set of positive integers.

alert ❶ (ə'lɜːt) *adj* (*usually postpositive*) **1** vigilantly attentive: *alert to the problems.* **2** brisk, nimble, or lively. ◆ *n* **3** an alarm or warning. **4** the period during which such a warning remains in effect. **5 on the alert. 5a** on guard against danger, attack, etc. **5b** watchful; ready. ◆ *vb* (*tr*) **6** to warn or signal (troops, police, etc.) to prepare for action. **7** to warn of danger, an attack, etc. [C17: from It. *all'erta* on the watch, from *erta* lookout post]
▸**a'lertly** *adv* ▸**a'lertness** *n*

aleurone (ə'lʊərən) *or* **aleuron** (ə'lʊərɒn) *n* a protein that occurs in the form of storage granules in plant cells, esp. in seeds such as maize. [C19: from Gk *aleuron* flour]

Aleut (æ'luːt) *n* **1** a member of a people inhabiting the Aleutian Islands and SW Alaska, related to the Eskimos. **2** the language of this people, related to Eskimo. [from Russian *aleút*, prob. of native origin]
▸**Aleutian** (ə'luːʃən) *n, adj*

A level *n Brit.* **1a** the advanced level of a subject taken for the General Certificate of Education. **1b** (*as modifier*): *A-level maths.* **2** a pass in a subject at A level: *he has two A levels.*

alewife ('eɪlˌwaɪf) *n, pl* **alewives.** a North American fish similar to the herring. [C19: ?from F *alose* shad]

Alexander technique *n* a technique for developing awareness of one's posture and movement in order to improve it. [C20: named after Frederick Matthias *Alexander* (d. 1955), Australian actor who originated it]

Alexandrine (ˌælɪg'zændraɪn) *n* **1** a line of verse having six iambic feet, usually with a caesura after the third foot. ◆ *adj* **2** of or written in Alexandrines. [C16: from F, from *Alexandre*, 15th-cent. poem in this metre]

alexandrite (ˌælɪg'zændraɪt) *n* a green variety of chrysoberyl used as a gemstone.

alexia (ə'leksɪə) *n* a disorder of the central nervous system characterized by impaired ability to read. [C19: from NL, from A-[1] + Gk *lexis* speech]

alfalfa (æl'fælfə) *n* a leguminous plant of Europe and Asia, widely cultivated for forage. Also called: **lucerne.** [C19: from Sp., from Ar. *al-fasfasah*]

alfresco (æl'freskəʊ) *adj, adv* in the open air. [C18: from It.: in the cool]

alg. *abbrev. for* algebra *or* algebraic.

algae ('ældʒiː) *pl n, sing* **alga** ('ælgə). unicellular or multicellular organisms formerly classified as plants, occurring in water or moist ground, that have chlorophyll but lack true stems, roots, and leaves. [C16: from L, pl of *alga* seaweed, from ?]
▸**algal** ('ælgəl) *or* **algoid** ('ælgɔɪd) *adj*

algebra ('ældʒɪbrə) *n* **1** a branch of mathematics in which arithmetical operations and relationships are generalized by using symbols to represent numbers. **2** any abstract calculus, a formal language in which functions and operations can be defined and their properties studied. [C14: from Med. L, from Ar. *al-jabr* the bone-setting, mathematical reduction]
▸**algebraic** (ˌældʒɪ'breɪɪk) *or* ˌ**alge'braical** *adj* ▸**algebraist** (ˌældʒɪ'breɪɪst) *n*

Algerian (æl'dʒɪərɪən) *adj* **1** of or denoting Algeria, a republic in NW Africa, or its inhabitants, their customs, etc. ◆ *n* **2** a native or inhabitant of Algeria.

-algia *n combining form.* denoting pain in the part specified: *neuralgia; odontalgia.* [from Gk *algos* pain]
▸**-algic** *adj combining form.*

THESAURUS

alchemy *n* **1** = **magic**, sorcery, witchcraft, wizardry

alcohol *n* **1** = **ethanol**, ethyl alcohol **2** = **drink**, booze, Dutch courage (*inf.*), firewater, grog (*inf., chiefly Austral. & NZ*), hooch *or* hootch (*inf., chiefly US & Canad.*), intoxicant, John Barleycorn, juice (*inf.*), liquor, spirits, strong drink, the bottle (*inf.*), the hard stuff (*inf.*)

alcoholic *n* **1** = **drunkard**, bibber, boozer (*inf.*), dipsomaniac, drinker, drunk, hard drinker, inebriate, soak (*sl.*), sot, sponge (*inf.*), tippler, toper, tosspot (*inf.*), wino (*inf.*) ◆ *adj* **2** = **intoxicating**, brewed, distilled, fermented, hard, inebriant, inebriating, spirituous, strong, vinous

alcove *n* **1** = **recess**, bay, bower, compartment, corner, cubbyhole, cubicle, niche, nook

alert *adj* **1** = **watchful**, active, agile, attentive, awake, bright-eyed and bushy-tailed (*inf.*), careful, circumspect, heedful, keeping a weather eye on, lively, observant, on guard, on one's toes, on the ball (*inf.*), on the lookout, on the watch, perceptive, quick, ready, spirited, vigilant, wary, wide-awake ◆ *n* **3** = **warning**, alarm, signal, siren ◆ *vb* **7** = **warn**, alarm, forewarn, inform, notify, signal
Antonyms *adj* ≠ **watchful:** careless, heedless, inactive, languid, lethargic, listless, oblivious, slow, unaware, unconcerned, unwary ◆ *n* ≠ **warning:** all clear ◆ *vb* ≠ **warn:** lull

alertness *n* **1, 2** = **watchfulness**, activeness, agility, attentiveness, briskness, carefulness, circumspection, heedfulness, liveliness, nimbleness, perceptiveness, promptitude, quickness, readiness, spiritedness, sprightliness, vigilance, wariness

algid ('ældʒɪd) *adj Med.* chilly or cold. [C17: from L *algidus*, from *algēre* to be cold]
►**al'gidity** *n*

alginate ('ældʒɪˌneɪt) *n* a salt or ester of alginic acid.

alginic acid (æl'dʒɪnɪk) *n* a white or yellowish powdery substance having hydrophilic properties. Extracted from kelp, it is used mainly in the food and textile industries.

Algol ('ælgɒl) *n* a computer-programming language designed for mathematical and scientific purposes. [C20: *alg(orithmic) o(riented) l(anguage)*]

algolagnia (ˌælgə'lægnɪə) *n* sexual pleasure got from suffering or inflicting pain. [ML, from Gk *algos* pain + *lagneia* lust]

Algonquian (æl'gɒŋkɪən, -kwɪ-) *or* **Algonkian** *n* **1** a widespread family of North American Indian languages. **2** (*pl* **Algonquians** *or* **Algonquian**) a member of any of the North American Indian peoples that speak any of these languages. ◆ *adj* **3** denoting or relating to this linguistic family or its speakers.

Algonquin (æl'gɒŋkɪn, -kwɪn) *or* **Algonkin** (æl'gɒŋkɪn) *n* **1** (*pl* **Algonquins, Algonquin** *or* **Algonkins, Algonkin**) a member of a North American Indian people formerly living along the St Lawrence and Ottawa Rivers in Canada. **2** the language of this people, a dialect of Ojibwa. ◆ *n, adj* **3** a variant of **Algonquian.** [C17: from Canad. F., earlier written as *Algoumequin;* perhaps rel. to Micmac *algoomaking* at the fish-spearing place]

algorism ('ælgəˌrɪzəm) *n* **1** the Arabic or decimal system of counting. **2** the skill of computation. **3** an algorithm. [C13: from OF, from Med. L, from Ar., from the name of abu-Ja'far Mohammed ibn-Mūsa *al-Khuwārizmi*, 9th-cent. Persian mathematician]

algorithm ('ælgəˌrɪðəm) *n* **1** a logical arithmetical or computational procedure that if correctly applied ensures the solution of a problem. **2** *Logic, maths.* a recursive procedure whereby an infinite sequence of terms can be generated. ◆ Also called: **algorism.** [C17: changed from ALGORISM, infl. by Gk *arithmos* number]
►ˌ**algo'rithmic** *adj*

Al Hijrah *or* **Al Hijra** (æl 'hɪdʒrə) *n* an annual Muslim festival marking the beginning of the Muslim year. It commemorates Mohammed's move from Mecca to Medina. See also **Hegira.** [from Ar. *hijrah* emigration or flight]

alias ('eɪlɪəs) *adv* **1** at another time or place known as or named: *Dylan, alias Zimmerman.* ◆ *n, pl* **aliases. 2** an assumed name. [C16: from L *aliās* (adv) otherwise, from *alius* other]

aliasing ('eɪlɪəsɪŋ) *n Radio & TV.* the error in a vision or sound signal arising from limitations in the system that generates or processes the signal.

alibi ('ælɪˌbaɪ) *n, pl* **alibis. 1** *Law.* **1a** a defence by an accused person that he was elsewhere at the time the crime was committed. **1b** the evidence given to prove this. **2** *Inf.* an excuse. ◆ *vb* **alibis, alibiing, alibied. 3** (*tr*) to provide with an alibi. [C18: from L *alibī* elsewhere, from *alius* other + *-bī* as in *ubī* where]

Alice band ('ælɪs) *n* an ornamental band worn across the front of the hair to hold it back from the face.

Alice-in-Wonderland *adj* fantastic; irrational. [C20: alluding to the absurdities of Wonderland in Lewis Carroll's book]

alicyclic (ˌælɪ'saɪklɪk, -'sɪk-) *adj* (of an organic compound) having essentially aliphatic properties, in spite of the presence of a ring of carbon atoms. [C19: from ALI(PHATIC) + CYCLIC]

alidade ('ælɪˌdeɪd) *or* **alidad** ('ælɪˌdæd) *n* **1** a surveying instrument used for drawing lines of sight on a distant object and taking angular measurements. **2** the upper rotatable part of a theodolite. [C15: from F, from Med. L, from Ar. *al-'idāda* the revolving radius of a circle]

alien ('eɪlɪən) *n* **1** a person owing allegiance to a country other than that in which he lives. **2** any being or thing foreign to its environment. **3** (in science fiction) a being from another world. ◆ *adj* **4** unnaturalized; foreign. **5** having foreign allegiance: *alien territory.* **6** unfamiliar: *an alien quality.* **7** (*postpositive;* foll. by *to*) repugnant or opposed (to): *war is alien to his philosophy.* **8** (in science fiction) of or from another world. [C14: from L *aliēnus* foreign, from *alius* other]

alienable ('eɪlɪənəbᵊl) *adj Law.* (of property) transferable to another owner.
►ˌ**aliena'bility** *n*

alienate ('eɪlɪəˌneɪt) *vb* **alienates, alienating, alienated.** (*tr*) **1** to cause (a friend, etc.) to become unfriendly or hostile. **2** to turn away: *to alienate the affections of a person.* **3** *Law.* to transfer the ownership of (property, etc.) to another person.
►ˌ**alien'ation** *n* ►'**alienˌator** *n*

alienee (ˌeɪlɪə'niː) *n Law.* a person to whom a transfer of property is made.

alienist ('eɪlɪənɪst) *n US.* a psychiatrist who specializes in the legal aspects of mental illness.

alienor ('eɪlɪənə) *n Law.* a person who transfers property to another.

aliform ('ælɪˌfɔːm) *adj* wing-shaped. [C19: from NL *āliformis,* from L *āla* a wing]

alight[1] (ə'laɪt) *vb* **alights, alighting, alighted** *or* **alit.** (*intr*) **1** (usually foll. by *from*) to step out (of): *to alight from a taxi.* **2** to come to rest; land: *a thrush alighted on the wall.* [OE *ālīhtan,* from A-[2] + *līhtan* to make less heavy]

alight[2] (ə'laɪt) *adj* (*postpositive*), *adv* **1** burning; on fire. **2** illuminated. [OE, from *ālīhtan* to light up]

align (ə'laɪn) *vb* **1** to place or become placed in a line. **2** to bring (components or parts) into proper coordination or relation. **3** (*tr;* usually foll. by *with*) to bring (a person, country, etc.) into agreement with the policy, etc., of another. [C17: from OF, from *à ligne* into line]

alignment (ə'laɪnmənt) *n* **1** arrangement in a straight line. **2** the line or lines formed in this manner. **3** alliance with a party, cause, etc. **4** proper coordination or relation of components. **5** a ground plan of a railway, road, etc.

alike (ə'laɪk) *adj* (*postpositive*) **1** possessing the same or similar characteristics: *they all look alike.* ◆ *adv* **2** in the same or a similar manner or degree: *they walk alike.* [OE *gelīc*]

aliment ('ælɪmənt) *n* something that nourishes or sustains the body or mind. [C15: from L *alimentum* food, from *alere* to nourish]
►ˌ**ali'mental** *adj*

alimentary (ˌælɪ'mɛntərɪ) *adj* **1** of or relating to nutrition. **2** providing sustenance or nourishment.

alimentary canal *n* the tubular passage extending from the mouth to the anus, through which food is passed and digested.

alimentation (ˌælɪmɛn'teɪʃən) *n* **1** nourishment. **2** sustenance; support.

alimony ('ælɪmənɪ) *n Law.* (formerly) an allowance paid under a court order by one spouse to another when they are separated but not divorced. See also **maintenance.** [C17: from L, from *alere* to nourish]

A-line ('eɪˌlaɪn) *adj* (of garments) flaring out slightly from the waist or shoulders.

aliphatic (ˌælɪ'fætɪk) *adj* (of an organic compound) not aromatic, esp. having an open chain structure. [C19: from Gk *aleiphat-, aleiphar* oil]

aliquant ('ælɪkwənt) *adj Maths.* of or signifying a quantity or number that is not an exact divisor of a given quantity or number: *5 is an aliquant part of 12.* [C17: from NL, from L *aliquantus* somewhat, a certain quantity of]

aliquot ('ælɪˌkwɒt) *adj Maths.* of or signifying an exact divisor of a quantity or number: *3 is an aliquot part of 12.* [C16: from L: several, a few]

A list *n* **a** the most socially desirable category. **b** (*as modifier*): *an A-list event.* ◆ Cf. **B list.**

alit (ə'lɪt) *vb* a rare past tense and past participle of **alight**[1].

aliterate (eɪ'lɪtərɪt) *n* **1** a person who is able to read but disinclined to do so. ◆ *adj* **2** of or relating to aliterates.

alive (ə'laɪv) *adj* (*postpositive*) **1** living; having life. **2** in existence; active: *they kept hope alive.* **3** (*immediately postpositive*) now living: *the happiest woman alive.* **4** full of life; lively. **5** (usually foll. by *with*) animated: *a face alive with emotion.* **6** (foll. by *to*) aware (of); sensitive (to). **7** (foll. by *with*) teeming (with): *the mattress was alive with fleas.* **8** *Electronics.* another word for **live**[2] (sense 10). [OE *on līfe* in LIFE]

THESAURUS

alias *adv* **1** = **also known as**, also called, otherwise, otherwise known as ◆ *n* **2** = **pseudonym**, assumed name, nom de guerre, nom de plume, pen name, stage name

alibi *n* **1, 2** = **excuse**, defence, explanation, justification, plea, pretext, reason

alien *n* **1** = **foreigner**, newcomer, outsider, stranger ◆ *adj* **4, 6, 7** = **strange**, adverse, beyond one's ken, conflicting, contrary, estranged, exotic, foreign, inappropriate, incompatible, incongruous, not native, not naturalized, opposed, outlandish, remote, repugnant, separated, unfamiliar
Antonyms *n* ≠ **foreigner:** citizen, countryman, dweller, inhabitant, national, resident ◆ *adj* ≠ **strange:** affiliated, akin, alike, allied, analogous, cognate, connected, corresponding, kindred, like, parallel, related, similar

alienate *vb* **1, 2** = **set against**, break off, disaffect, divert, divorce, estrange, make unfriendly, separate, turn away, withdraw **3** *Law* = **transfer**, abalienate, convey

alienation *n* **1, 2** = **setting against**, breaking off, disaffection, diversion, divorce, estrangement, indifference, remoteness, rupture, separation, turning away, withdrawal **3** *Law* = **transfer**, abalienation, conveyance

alight[1] *vb* **1** = **get off**, descend, disembark, dismount, get down **2** = **land**, come down, come to rest, descend, light, perch, settle, touch down
Antonyms *vb* ≠ **land:** ascend, climb, float up, fly up, go up, lift off, mount, move up, rise, scale, soar, take off

alight[2] *adj* **1** = **on fire**, ablaze, aflame, blazing, burning, fiery, flaming, flaring, ignited, lighted, lit **2** = **lit up**, bright, brilliant, illuminated, shining

align *vb* **1** = **line up**, arrange in line, coordinate, even, even up, make parallel, order, range, regulate, sequence, straighten **3** = **ally**, affiliate, agree, associate, cooperate, join, side, sympathize

alignment *n* **1** = **lining up**, adjustment, arrangement, coordination, evening, evening up, line, order, ranging, regulating, sequence, straightening up **3** = **alliance**, affiliation, agreement, association, cooperation, sympathy, union

alike *adj* **1** = **similar**, akin, analogous, corresponding, cut from the same cloth, duplicate, equal, equivalent, even, identical, like two peas in a pod, of a piece, parallel, resembling, the same, uniform ◆ *adv* **2** = **similarly**, analogously, correspondingly, equally, evenly, identically, uniformly
Antonyms *adj* ≠ **similar:** different, dissimilar, diverse, separate, unlike ◆ *adv* ≠ **similarly:** differently, distinctly, unequally

alimentary *adj* **1, 2** = **nutritional**, beneficial, nourishing, nutritious, nutritive, sustaining, wholesome

alive *adj* **1** = **living**, animate, breathing, having life, in the land of the living (*inf.*), subsisting **2** = **in existence**, active, existent, existing, extant, functioning, in force, operative, unquenched **4,**

alizarin (əˈlɪzərɪn) *n* a brownish-yellow powder or orange-red crystalline solid used as a dye. [C19: prob. from F, from Ar. *al-ʻasārah* the juice, from *ʻasara* to squeeze]
alkali (ˈælkəˌlaɪ) *n, pl* **alkalis** *or* **alkalies. 1** *Chem.* a soluble base or a solution of a base. **2** a soluble mineral salt that occurs in arid soils. [C14: from Med. L, from Ar. *al-qili* the ashes (of saltwort)]
alkali metal *n* any of the monovalent metals lithium, sodium, potassium, rubidium, caesium, and francium.
alkaline (ˈælkəˌlaɪn) *adj* having the properties of or containing an alkali.
▸**alkalinity** (ˌælkəˈlɪnɪtɪ) *n*
alkaline earth *n* **1** Also called: **alkaline earth metal, alkaline earth element.** any of the divalent electropositive metals beryllium, magnesium, calcium, strontium, barium, and radium. **2** an oxide of one of the alkaline earth metals.
alkalize *or* **alkalise** (ˈælkəˌlaɪz) *vb* **alkalizes, alkalizing, alkalized** *or* **alkalises, alkalising, alkalised.** (*tr*) to make alkaline.
▸**ˈalkaˌlizable** *or* **ˈalkaˌlisable** *adj*
alkaloid (ˈælkəˌlɔɪd) *n* any of a group of nitrogenous compounds found in plants. Many are poisonous and some are used as drugs.
alkane (ˈælkeɪn) *n* any saturated aliphatic hydrocarbon with the general formula C_nH_{2n+2}. Former name: **paraffin.**
alkane series *n* a homologous series of saturated hydrocarbons starting with methane and having the general formula C_nH_{2n+2}. Also called: **methane series.**
alkanet (ˈælkəˌnɛt) *n* **1** a European plant, the roots of which yield a red dye. **2** the dye obtained. [C14: from Sp., from Med. L, from Ar. *al* the + *hinnāʼ* henna]
alkene (ˈælkiːn) *n* any unsaturated aliphatic hydrocarbon with the general formula C_nH_{2n}. Former name: **olefine.**
alkene series *n* a homologous series of unsaturated hydrocarbons starting with ethylene (ethene) and having the general formula C_nH_{2n}. Also called: **ethylene series, ethene series.**
Alkoran *or* **Alcoran** (ˌælkɒˈrɑːn) *n* a less common name for the **Koran.**
alkyd resin (ˈælkɪd) *n* any of several synthetic resins made from a dicarboxylic acid, used in paints and adhesives.
alkyl (ˈælkɪl) *n* (*modifier*) of or containing the monovalent group C_nH_{2n+1}: *alkyl radical.* [C19: from G, from *Alk(ohol)* ALCOHOL + -YL]
alkylating agent (ˈælkɪˌleɪtɪŋ) *n* any cytotoxic drug containing alkyl groups that acts by damaging DNA; widely used in chemotherapy.
alkyne (ˈælkaɪn) *n* any unsaturated aliphatic hydrocarbon with the general formula C_nH_{2n-2}.
alkyne series *n* a homologous series of unsaturated hydrocarbons starting with acetylene (ethyne) and having the general formula C_nH_{2n-2}. Also called: **acetylene series.**
all ❶ (ɔːl) *determiner* **1a** the whole quantity or amount of; everyone of a class: *all the rice; all men are mortal.* **1b** (*as pronoun; functioning as sing or pl*): *all of it is nice; all are welcome.* **1c** (*in combination with a noun used as a modifier*): *an all-night sitting; an all-ticket match.* **2** the greatest possible: *in all earnestness.* **3** any whatever: *beyond all doubt.* **4 all along.** all the time. **5 all but.** nearly: *all but dead.* **6 all of.** no less or smaller than: *she's all of thirteen years.* **7 all over. 7a** finished. **7b** everywhere (in, on, etc.): *all over England.* **7c** *Inf.* typically (in **that's me** (**him,** etc.) **all over**). **7d** unduly effusive towards. **8 all in all. 8a** everything considered: *all in all, it was a great success.* **8b** the object of one's attention: *you are my all in all.* **9 all the.** (foll. by a comp. adj or adv) so much (more or less) than otherwise: *we must work all the faster now.* **10 all too.** definitely but regrettably: *it's all too true.* **11 at all. 11a** (*used with a negative or in a question*) in any way or to any degree: *I didn't know that at all.* **11b** anyway: *I'm surprised you came at all.* **12 be all for.** *Inf.* to be strongly in favour of. **13 for all. 13a** in so far as: *for all anyone knows, he was a baron.* **13b** notwithstanding: *for all my pushing, I still couldn't move it.* **14 for all that.** in spite of that: *he was a nice man for all that.* **15 in all.** altogether: *there were five in all.* ◆ *adv* **16** (in scores of games) apiece; each: *the score was three all.* ◆ *n* **17** (preceded by *my, his,* etc.) (one's) complete effort or interest: *to give your all.* **18** totality or whole. [OE *eall*]
all- *combining form.* a variant of **allo-** before a vowel.
alla breve (ˈælə ˈbreɪvɪ) *Music.* ◆ *adj, adv* **1** with two beats to the bar instead of four, i.e. twice as fast as written. ◆ *n* **2** (formerly) a time of two or four minims to the bar. Symbol: ₵ [C19: It., lit.: according to the breve]
Allah (ˈælə) *n* the name of God in Islam. [C16: from Ar., from *al* the + *Ilāh* god]
all-American *adj US.* **1** representative of the whole of the United States. **2** composed exclusively of American members. **3** (of a person) typically American.
allantois (ˌælənˈtəʊɪs, əˈlæntɔɪs) *n* a membranous sac growing out of the ventral surface of the hind gut of embryonic reptiles, birds, and mammals. [C17: NL, from Gk *allantoeidēs* sausage-shaped]
▸**allantoic** (ˌælənˈtəʊɪk) *adj*
allay ❶ (əˈleɪ) *vb* **1** to relieve (pain, grief, etc.) or be relieved. **2** (*tr*) to reduce (fear, anger, etc.). [OE *ālecgan* to put down]
All Blacks *pl n* **the.** the international Rugby Union football team of New Zealand. [so named because of the players' black strip]
all clear *n* **1** a signal indicating that some danger, such as an air raid, is over. **2** permission to proceed.
all-dayer (ˌɔːlˈdeɪə) *n* an entertainment, such as a pop concert or film screening, that lasts all day.
allegation ❶ (ˌælɪˈgeɪʃən) *n* **1** the act of alleging. **2** an unproved assertion, esp. an accusation.
allege ❶ (əˈlɛdʒ) *vb* **alleges, alleging, alleged.** (*tr; may take a clause as object*) **1** to state without or before proof: *he alleged malpractice.* **2** to put forward (an argument or plea) for or against an accusation, claim, etc. [C14 *aleggen,* ult. from L *allēgāre* to dispatch on a mission, from *lēx* law]
alleged ❶ (əˈlɛdʒd) *adj* (*prenominal*) **1** stated to be such: *the alleged murderer.* **2** dubious: *an alleged miracle.*
▸**allegedly** (əˈlɛdʒɪdlɪ) *adv*
allegiance ❶ (əˈliːdʒəns) *n* **1** loyalty, as of a subject to his sovereign. **2** (in feudal society) the obligations of a vassal to his liege lord. [C14: from OF, from *lige* LIEGE]
allegorical ❶ (ˌælɪˈgɒrɪkᵊl) *or* **allegoric** *adj* used in, containing, or characteristic of allegory.
allegorize *or* **allegorise** (ˈælɪgəˌraɪz) *vb* **allegorizes, allegorizing, allegorized** *or* **allegorises, allegorising, allegorised. 1** to transform (a story, fable, etc.) into or compose in the form of allegory. **2** (*tr*) to interpret allegorically.
▸**ˌallegoriˈzation** *or* **ˌallegoriˈsation** *n*
allegory ❶ (ˈælɪgərɪ) *n, pl* **allegories. 1** a poem, play, picture, etc., in which the apparent meaning of the characters and events is used to symbolize a moral or spiritual meaning. **2** use of such symbolism. **3** anything used as a symbol. [C14: from OF, from L, from Gk, from *allēgorein* to speak figuratively, from *allos* other + *agoreuein* to make a speech in public]
▸**ˈallegorist** *n*
allegretto (ˌælɪˈgrɛtəʊ) *Music.* ◆ *adj, adv* **1** (to be performed) fairly quickly or briskly. ◆ *n, pl* **allegrettos. 2** a piece or passage to be performed in this manner. [C19: dim. of ALLEGRO]
allegro (əˈleɪgrəʊ, -ˈlɛg-) *Music.* ◆ *adj, adv* **1** (to be performed) in a brisk lively manner. ◆ *n, pl* **allegros. 2** a piece or passage to be performed in this manner. [C17: from It.: cheerful, from L *alacer* brisk, lively]
allele (əˈliːl) *n* any of two or more genes that are responsible for alternative characteristics, such as smooth or wrinkled seeds in peas. Also called: **allelomorph** (əˈliːləˌmɔːf). [C20: from G *Allel,* from *Allelomorph,* from Gk *allēl-* one another + *morphē* form]
alleluia (ˌælɪˈluːjə) *interj* praise the Lord! Used in liturgical contexts in place of *hallelujah.* [C14: via Med. L from Heb. *hallelūyāh*]
allemande (ˈælɪmænd) *n* **1** the first movement of the classical suite, composed in a moderate tempo. **2** any of several German dances. **3** a figure in country dancing or square dancing by which couples change position in the set. [C17: from F *danse allemande* German dance]
allergen (ˈæləˌdʒɛn) *n* any substance capable of inducing an allergy.
▸**ˌallerˈgenic** *adj*
allergic ❶ (əˈlɜːdʒɪk) *adj* **1** of, having, or caused by an allergy. **2** (*postpositive;* foll. by *to*) *Inf.* having an aversion (to): *allergic to work.*
allergist (ˈælədʒɪst) *n* a physician skilled in the treatment of allergies.
allergy ❶ (ˈælədʒɪ) *n, pl* **allergies. 1** a hypersensitivity to a substance

THESAURUS

5 = **lively,** active, alert, animated, awake, brisk, cheerful, chirpy (*inf.*), eager, energetic, full of beans (*inf.*), full of life, quick, spirited, sprightly, spry, vigorous, vital, vivacious, zestful **6** *foll. by* **to** = **aware of,** alert to, awake to, cognizant of, eager for, sensible of, sensitive to, susceptible to **7** *foll. by* **with** = **swarming with,** abounding in, bristling with, bustling with, buzzing with, crawling with, hopping with, infested with, jumping with, lousy with (*sl.*), overrun by, packed with, teeming with, thronged with
Antonyms *adj* ≠ **living:** dead, deceased, departed, expired, extinct, gone, inanimate, lifeless ≠ **in existence:** extinct, inactive, inoperative, lost ≠ **lively:** apathetic, dull, inactive, lifeless, spiritless

all *determiner* **1** = **the whole of,** every bit of, the complete, the entire, the sum of, the totality of, the total of **1** = **every,** each, each and every, every one of, every single

allay *vb* **1, 2** = **reduce,** alleviate, appease, assuage, blunt, calm, check, compose, diminish, dull, ease, lessen, mitigate, moderate, mollify, pacify, quell, quiet, relax, relieve, smooth, soften, soothe, subdue

allegation *n* **2** = **claim,** accusation, affirmation, assertion, asseveration, averment, avowal, charge, declaration, deposition, plea, profession, statement

allege *vb* **1, 2** = **claim,** advance, affirm, assert, asseverate, aver, avow, charge, declare, depose, maintain, plead, profess, put forward, state
Antonyms *vb* abjure, contradict, deny, disagree with, disavow, disclaim, gainsay (*arch. or literary*), oppose, refute, renounce, repudiate

alleged *adj* **1** = **stated,** affirmed, asserted, averred, declared, described, designated **2** = **supposed,** doubtful, dubious, ostensible, professed, purported, so-called, suspect, suspicious, unproved

allegedly *adv* **1** = **supposedly,** apparently, by all accounts, purportedly, reportedly, reputedly

allegiance *n* **1** = **loyalty,** adherence, constancy, devotion, duty, faithfulness, fealty, fidelity, homage, obedience, obligation, troth (*arch.*)
Antonyms *n* disloyalty, faithlessness, falseness, inconstancy, infidelity, perfidy, treachery, treason, unfaithfulness

allegorical *adj* = **symbolic,** emblematic, figurative, parabolic, symbolizing

allegory *n* **1** = **symbol,** apologue, emblem, fable, myth, parable, story, symbolism, tale

allergic *adj* **1** = **sensitive,** affected by, hypersensitive, sensitized, susceptible **2** *Informal* = **averse,** antipathetic, disinclined, hostile, loath, opposed

allergy *n* **1** = **sensitivity,** antipathy, hypersensitivity, susceptibility **2** *Informal* = **dislike,** antipa-

that causes the body to react to any contact with it. Hay fever is an allergic reaction to pollen. **2** *Inf.* an aversion. [C20: from G *Allergie* (indicating a changed reaction), from Gk *allos* other + *ergon* activity]

alleviate Ⓣ (əˈliːvɪˌeɪt) *vb* **alleviates, alleviating, alleviated.** (*tr*) to make (pain, sorrow, etc.) easier to bear; lessen. [C15: from LL, from L *levis* light]
▸**alˌleviˈation** *n* ▸**alˈleviˌator** *n*

USAGE NOTE See at **ameliorate.**

alley[1] Ⓣ (ˈælɪ) *n* **1** a narrow passage, esp. one between or behind buildings. **2** See **bowling alley. 3** *Tennis, chiefly US.* the space between the singles and doubles sidelines. **4** a walk in a garden, esp. one lined with trees. **5 up** (*or* **down**) **one's alley.** *Sl.* suited to one's abilities or interests. [C14: from OF, from *aler* to go, ult. from L *ambulāre* to walk]

alley[2] (ˈælɪ) *n* a large playing marble. [C18: shortened and changed from ALABASTER]

alleyway (ˈælɪˌweɪ) *n* a narrow passage; alley.

All Fools' Day *n* another name for **April Fools' Day** (see **April fool**).

all found *adj* (of charges for accommodation) inclusive of meals, heating, etc.

all hail *sentence substitute.* an archaic greeting or salutation. [C14, lit.: all health (to someone)]

Allhallows (ˌɔːlˈhæləʊz) *n* a less common term for **All Saints' Day.**

alliaceous (ˌælɪˈeɪʃəs) *adj* **1** of or relating to a genus of plants that have a strong smell and often have bulbs. The genus occurs in the N hemisphere and includes onion and garlic. **2** tasting or smelling like garlic or onions. [C18: from L *allium* garlic]

alliance Ⓣ (əˈlaɪəns) *n* **1** the act of allying or state of being allied; union. **2** a formal agreement, esp. a military one, between two or more countries. **3** the countries involved. **4** a union between families through marriage. **5** affinity or correspondence in characteristics. **6** *Bot.* a taxonomic category consisting of a group of related families. [C13: from OF, from *alier* to ALLY]

allied Ⓣ (əˈlaɪd, ˈælaɪd) *adj* **1** joined, as by treaty or marriage; united. **2** of the same type or class.

Allied (ˈælaɪd) *adj* of or relating to the Allies.

Allies (ˈælaɪz) *pl n* **1** (in World War I) the powers of the Triple Entente (France, Russia, and Britain) together with the nations allied with them. **2** (in World War II) the countries that fought against the Axis and Japan, esp. Britain and the Commonwealth countries, the US, the Soviet Union, China, Poland, and France.

alligator (ˈælɪˌgeɪtə) *n* **1** a large crocodilian of the southern US, having powerful jaws but differing from the crocodiles in having a shorter and broader snout. **2** a similar but smaller species occurring in China. **3** any of various tools or machines having adjustable toothed jaws. [C17: from Sp. *el lagarto* the lizard, from L *lacerta*]

alligator pear *n* another name for **avocado.**

all-important Ⓣ *adj* crucial; vital.

all in *adj* **1** (*postpositive*) *Inf.* completely exhausted. ◆ *adv, adj* (**all-in** *when prenominal*). **2** with all expenses included: *one hundred pounds a week all in.* **3** (of wrestling) in freestyle.

alliterate (əˈlɪtəˌreɪt) *vb* **alliterates, alliterating, alliterated. 1** to contain or cause to contain alliteration. **2** (*intr*) to speak or write using alliteration.

alliteration (əˌlɪtəˈreɪʃən) *n* the use of the same consonant (**consonantal alliteration**) or of a vowel (**vocalic alliteration**), at the beginning of each word or stressed syllable in a line of verse, as in *around the rock the ragged rascal ran.* [C17: from L *litera* letter]
▸**alˈliterative** *adj*

allium (ˈælɪəm) *n* a genus of liliaceous plants that includes the onion, garlic, shallot, leek, and chive. [C19: from L: garlic]

all-nighter (ˌɔːlˈnaɪtə) *n* an entertainment, such as a pop concert or film screening, that lasts all night.

allo- *or before a vowel* **all-** *combining form.* indicating difference, variation, or opposition: *allopathy; allomorph.* [from Gk *allos* other, different]

allocate Ⓣ (ˈæləˌkeɪt) *vb* **allocates, allocating, allocated.** (*tr*) **1** to assign for a particular purpose. **2** a less common word for **locate** (sense 2). [C17: from Med. L, from L *locus* a place]
▸ˈ**alloˌcatable** *adj* ▸ˌ**alloˈcation** *n*

allocution (ˌæləˈkjuːʃən) *n Rhetoric.* a formal or authoritative speech or address. [C17: from LL *allocūtiō*, from L *alloquī* to address]

allomerism (əˈlɒməˌrɪzəm) *n* similarity of crystalline structure in substances of different chemical composition.
▸**allomeric** (ˌæləˈmɛrɪk) *or* **alˈlomerous** *adj*

allomorph (ˈæləˌmɔːf) *n* **1** *Linguistics.* any of the representations of a single morpheme. For example, the final (s) and (z) sounds of *bets* and *beds* are allomorphs. **2** any of the different crystalline forms of a chemical compound, such as a mineral.
▸ˌ**alloˈmorphic** *adj*

allopath (ˈæləˌpæθ) *or* **allopathist** (əˈlɒpəθɪst) *n* a person who practises or is skilled in allopathy.

allopathy (əˈlɒpəθɪ) *n* the usual method of treating disease, by inducing a condition different from the cause of the disease. Cf. **homeopathy.**
▸**allopathic** (ˌæləˈpæθɪk) *adj*

allophone (ˈæləˌfəʊn) *n* **1** any of several speech sounds regarded as variants of the same phoneme. In English the aspirated initial (p) in *pot* and the unaspirated (p) in *spot* are allophones of the phoneme /p/. **2** *Canad.* a Canadian whose native language is neither French nor English.
▸**allophonic** (ˌæləˈfɒnɪk) *adj*

All-Ordinaries Index *n* an index of share prices on the Australian Stock Exchange giving a weighted arithmetic average of 245 ordinary shares.

allot Ⓣ (əˈlɒt) *vb* **allots, allotting, allotted.** (*tr*) **1** to assign or distribute (shares, etc.). **2** to designate for a particular purpose; apportion: *we allotted two hours to the case.* [C16: from OF, from *lot* portion]

allotment Ⓣ (əˈlɒtmənt) *n* **1** the act of allotting. **2** a portion or amount allotted. **3** *Brit.* a small piece of land rented by an individual for cultivation.

allotrope (ˈæləˌtrəʊp) *n* any of two or more physical forms in which an element can exist.

allotropy (əˈlɒtrəpɪ) *or* **allotropism** *n* the existence of an element in two or more physical forms.
▸**allotropic** (ˌæləˈtrɒpɪk) *adj*

all-out Ⓣ *Inf.* ◆ *adj* **1** using one's maximum powers: *an all-out effort.* ◆ *adv* **all out. 2** to one's maximum capacity: *he went all out.*

allow Ⓣ (əˈlaʊ) *vb* **1** (*tr*) to permit (to do something). **2** (*tr*) to set aside: *five hours were allowed to do the job.* **3** (*tr*) to let enter or stay: *they don't allow dogs.* **4** (*tr*) to acknowledge (a point, claim, etc.). **5** (*tr*) to let have: *he was allowed few visitors.* **6** (*intr;* foll. by *for*) to take into account. **7** (*intr;* often foll. by *of*) to permit: *a question that allows of only one reply.* **8** (*tr; may take a clause as object*) *US dialect.* to assert; maintain. [C14: from OF, from LL *allaudāre* to extol, infl. by Med. L *allocāre* to assign]
▸**alˈlowable** *adj* ▸**alˈlowably** *adv*

allowance Ⓣ (əˈlaʊəns) *n* **1** an amount of something, esp. money or food, given at regular intervals. **2** a discount, as in consideration for something given in part exchange; rebate. **3** (in Britain) an amount of a person's income that is not subject to income tax. **4** a portion set aside to cover special expenses. **5** admission; concession. **6** the act of allowing; toleration. **7 make allowances** (*or* **allowance**). (usually foll. by *for*) **7a** to take mitigating circumstances into account. **7b** to allow (for). ◆ *vb* **allowances, allowancing, allowanced.** (*tr*) **8** to supply (something) in limited amounts.

THESAURUS

thy, aversion, disinclination, hostility, loathing, opposition

alleviate *vb* = **ease**, abate, allay, assuage, blunt, check, diminish, dull, lessen, lighten, mitigate, moderate, mollify, palliate, quell, quench, quiet, reduce, relieve, slacken, slake, smooth, soften, soothe, subdue

alleviation *n* = **easing**, diminution, dulling, lessening, lightening, mitigation, moderation, palliation, quelling, quenching, reduction, relief, slackening, slaking

alley[1] *n* **1** = **passage**, alleyway, backstreet, lane, passageway, pathway, walk

alliance *n* **1, 2, 4** = **union**, affiliation, affinity, agreement, association, coalition, combination, compact, concordat, confederacy, confederation, connection, federation, league, marriage, pact, partnership, treaty
Antonyms *n* alienation, breach, break, disaffection, dissociation, disunion, disunity, division, rupture, separation, severance, split, split-up

allied *adj* **1, 2** = **united**, affiliated, amalgamated, associated, bound, combined, confederate, connected, hand in glove (*inf.*), in cahoots (*US inf.*), in league, joined, joint, kindred, leagued, linked, married, related, unified, wed

all-important *adj* = **essential**, central, consequential, critical, crucial, key, momentous, necessary, pivotal, significant, urgent, vital

allocate *vb* **1** = **assign**, allot, allow, apportion, appropriate, budget, designate, earmark, mete, set aside, share out

allocation *n* **1** = **assignment**, allotment, allowance, apportionment, appropriation, grant, lot, measure, portion, quota, ration, share, stint, stipend

allot *vb* **1, 2** = **assign**, allocate, apportion, appropriate, budget, designate, earmark, mete, set aside, share out

allotment *n* **1, 2** = **assignment**, allocation, allowance, apportionment, appropriation, grant, lot, measure, portion, quota, ration, share, stint, stipend **3** = **plot**, kitchen garden, patch, tract

allotted *vb* **1, 2** = **assigned**, allocated, apportioned, designated, earmarked, given, set aside

all-out *adj* **1** = **total**, complete, determined, exhaustive, full, full-on (*inf.*), full-scale, maximum, optimum, outright, resolute, supreme, thorough, thoroughgoing, undivided, unlimited, unremitting, unrestrained, unstinted, utmost
Antonyms *adj* careless, cursory, half-hearted, negligent, off-hand, perfunctory, unenthusiastic

allow *vb* **1** = **permit**, approve, authorize, bear, brook, enable, endure, give leave, let, put up with (*inf.*), sanction, stand, suffer, tolerate **2** = **give**, allocate, allot, assign, deduct, grant, provide, remit, set aside, spare **4** = **acknowledge**, acquiesce, admit, concede, confess, grant, own **6** *foll. by* **for** = **take into account**, arrange for, consider, foresee, keep in mind, make allowances for, make concessions for, make provision for, plan for, provide for, set (something) aside for, take into consideration
Antonyms *vb* ≠ **permit:** ban, disallow, forbid, prohibit, proscribe, refuse ≠ **give:** deny, forbid, refuse ≠ **acknowledge:** contradict, deny, disagree with, gainsay (*arch. or literary*), oppose

allowable *adj* **1** = **permissible**, acceptable, admissible, all right, appropriate, approved, sanctionable, sufferable, suitable, tolerable

allowance *n* **1** = **portion**, allocation, allotment, amount, annuity, apportionment, grant, lot, measure, pension, quota, ration, remittance, share, stint, stipend, subsidy **2** = **concession**, deduction, discount, rebate, reduction

allowedly (ə'lauɪdlɪ) *adv* (*sentence modifier*) by general admission or agreement; admittedly.

alloy ❶ *n* ('ælɔɪ, ə'lɔɪ). **1** a metallic material, such as steel, consisting of a mixture of two or more metals or of metallic with nonmetallic elements. **2** something that impairs the quality of the thing to which it is added. ◆ *vb* (ə'lɔɪ). (*tr*) **3** to add (one metal or element to another) to obtain a substance with a desired property. **4** to debase (a pure substance) by mixing with an inferior element. **5** to diminish or impair. [C16: from OF *aloi* a mixture, from *aloier* to combine, from L *alligāre*]

all-purpose *adj* useful for many things.

all right ❶ *adj* (*postpositive except in slang use*), *adv* **1** adequate; satisfactory. **2** unharmed; safe. **3 all-right.** *US sl.* acceptable; reliable. ◆ *sentence substitute.* **4** very well: used to express assent. ◆ *adv* **5** satisfactorily: *the car goes all right.* **6** without doubt. ◆ Also **alright.**

USAGE NOTE See at **alright.**

all-round *adj* **1** efficient in all respects, esp. in sport: *an all-round player.* **2** comprehensive; many-sided: *an all-round education.*

all-rounder *n* a versatile person, esp. in a sport.

All Saints' Day *n* a Christian festival celebrated on Nov. 1 to honour all the saints.

all-singing all-dancing *adj* having every desirable feature possible: *an all-singing all-dancing computer.*

All Souls' Day *n RC Church.* a day of prayer (Nov. 2) for the dead in purgatory.

allspice ('ɔːlˌspaɪs) *n* **1** a tropical American tree, having small white flowers and aromatic berries. **2** the seeds of this berry used as a spice, having a flavour said to resemble a mixture of cinnamon, cloves, and nutmeg. ◆ Also called: **pimento.**

all-star *adj* (*prenominal*) consisting of star performers.

all-time *adj* (*prenominal*) *Inf.* unsurpassed.

all told *adv* (*sentence modifier*) in all: *we were seven all told.*

allude ❶ (ə'luːd) *vb* **alludes, alluding, alluded.** (*intr*; foll. by *to*) **1** to refer indirectly. **2** (loosely) to mention. [C16: from L *allūdere,* from *lūdere* to sport, from *lūdus* a game]

USAGE NOTE Avoid confusion with **elude.**

allure ❶ (ə'lʊə) *vb* **allures, alluring, allured. 1** (*tr*) to entice or tempt (someone); attract. ◆ *n* **2** attractiveness; appeal. [C15: from OF *alurer,* from *lure* bait]

▸**al'lurement** *n* ▸**al'luring** *adj*

allusion ❶ (ə'luːʒən) *n* **1** the act of alluding. **2** a passing reference. [C16: from LL *allūsiō,* from L *allūdere* to sport with]

allusive (ə'luːsɪv) *adj* containing or full of allusions.

▸**al'lusiveness** *n*

alluvial (ə'luːvɪəl) *adj* **1** of or relating to alluvium. ◆ *n* **2** another name for **alluvium.**

alluvion (ə'luːvɪən) *n* **1a** the wash of the sea or a river. **1b** a flood. **1c** sediment; alluvium. **2** *Law.* the gradual formation of new land, as by the recession of the sea. [C16: from L *alluviō* an overflowing, from *luere* to wash]

alluvium (ə'luːvɪəm) *n, pl* **alluviums** *or* **alluvia** (-vɪə). a fine-grained fertile soil consisting of mud, silt, and sand deposited by flowing water. [C17: from L; see ALLUVION]

ally ❶ *vb* (ə'laɪ), **allies, allying, allied.** (usually foll. by *to* or *with*) **1** to unite or be united, esp. formally, as by treaty. **2** (*tr; usually passive*) to be related, as through being similar. ◆ *n* ('ælaɪ), *pl* **allies. 3** a country, person, or group allied with another. **4** a plant, animal, etc., closely related to another in characteristics or form. [C14: from OF *alier* to join, from L *ligāre* to bind]

allyl resin ('ælɪl) *n* any of several thermosetting synthetic resins, containing the CH_2:$CHCH_2$– group, used as adhesives. [C19: from L *allium* garlic + -YL]

alma mater ('ælmə 'mɑːtə, 'meɪtə) *n* (*often caps.*) one's school, college, or university. [C17: from L: bountiful mother]

almanac ('ɔːlməˌnæk) *n* a yearly calendar giving statistical information, such as the phases of the moon, tides, anniversaries, etc. Also (archaic): **almanack.** [C14: from Med. L *almanachus,* ?from LGk *almenikhiaka*]

almandine ('ælməndɪn) *n* a deep violet-red garnet. [C17: from F, from Med. L, from *Alabanda,* ancient city of Asia Minor where these stones were cut]

almighty ❶ (ɔːl'maɪtɪ) *adj* **1** omnipotent. **2** *Inf.* (intensifier): *an almighty row.* ◆ *adv* **3** *Inf.* (intensifier): *an almighty loud bang.*

almond ('ɑːmənd) *n* **1** a small widely cultivated rosaceous tree that is native to W Asia and has pink flowers and an edible nutlike seed. **2** the seed, which has a yellowish-brown shell. **3** (*modifier*) made of or containing almonds: *almond cake.* [C13: from OF *almande,* ult. from Gk *amugdalē*]

almond-eyed *adj* having narrow oval eyes.

almoner ('ɑːmənə) *n* **1** *Brit.* a former name for a trained hospital social worker. **2** (formerly) a person who distributes charity on behalf of a household or institution. [C13: from OF, from *almosne* alms, ult. from LL *eleēmosyna*]

almost ❶ ('ɔːlməust) *adv* very nearly.

alms ❶ (ɑːmz) *pl n* charitable donations of money or goods to the poor or needy. [OE *ælmysse,* from LL, from Gk *eleēmosunē* pity]

almshouse ('ɑːmzˌhaus) *n Brit. history.* a privately supported house offering accommodation to the aged or needy.

almucantar *or* **almacantar** (ˌælmə'kæntə) *n* **1** a circle on the celestial sphere parallel to the horizon. **2** an instrument for measuring altitudes. [C14: from F, from Ar. *almukantarāt* sundial]

aloe ('æləu) *n, pl* **aloes. 1** any plant of the genus *Aloe,* chiefly native to southern Africa, with fleshy spiny-toothed leaves. **2 American aloe.** Also called: **century plant.** a tropical American agave which blooms only once in 10 to 30 years. [C14: from L *aloē,* from Gk]

aloes ('æləuz) *n* (*functioning as sing*) a bitter purgative drug made from the leaves of several species of aloe. Also called: **bitter aloes.**

aloe vera ('vɪərə) *n* **1** a plant of the species *Aloe vera,* the leaves of which yield a juice used as an emollient. **2** the juice of this plant, used in skin and hair preparations.

aloft ❶ (ə'lɒft) *adv, adj* (*postpositive*) **1** in or into a high or higher place. **2** *Naut.* in or into the rigging of a vessel. [C12: from ON *ā lopt* in the air]

alone ❶ (ə'ləun) *adj* (*postpositive*), *adv* **1** apart from another or others. **2** without anyone or anything else: *one man alone could lift it.* **3** without equal: *he stands alone in the field of microbiology.* **4** to the exclusion of others: *she alone believed him.* **5 leave** *or* **let alone.** to refrain from annoying or interfering with. **6 leave well alone.** to refrain from interfering with something that is satisfactory. **7 let alone.** not to mention; much less: *he can't afford beer, let alone whisky.* [OE *al one,* lit.: all (entirely) one]

along (ə'lɒŋ) *prep* **1** over or for the length of: *along the road.* ◆ *adv* **2** continuing over the length of some specified thing. **3** together with some specified person or people: *he'd like to come along.* **4** forward: *the horse trotted along.* **5** to a more advanced state: *he got the work moving along.* **6 along with.** together with: *consider the advantages along with the disadvantages.* [OE *andlang,* from *and-* against + *lang* LONG[1]]

USAGE NOTE See at **plus.**

alongshore (əˌlɒŋ'ʃɔː) *adv, adj* (*postpositive*) close to, by, or along a shore.

alongside (ə'lɒŋˌsaɪd) *prep* **1** (often foll. by *of*) close beside: *alongside the quay.* ◆ *adv* **2** near the side of something: *come alongside.*

THESAURUS

alloy *n* **1** = **mixture**, admixture, amalgam, blend, combination, composite, compound, hybrid, meld ◆ *vb* **3** = **mix**, admix, amalgamate, blend, combine, compound, fuse, meld

all right *adj* **1** = **satisfactory**, acceptable, adequate, average, fair, O.K. *or* okay (*inf.*), passable, so-so (*inf.*), standard, unobjectionable, up to scratch (*inf.*) **2** = **well**, hale, healthy, O.K. *or* okay (*inf.*), out of the woods, safe, sound, unharmed, unimpaired, uninjured, whole ◆ *adv* **5** = **satisfactorily**, acceptably, adequately, O.K. *or* okay (*inf.*), passably, unobjectionably, well enough

Antonyms *adj* ≠ **satisfactory:** bad, inadequate, not good enough, not up to scratch (*inf.*), objectionable, poor, unacceptable, unsatisfactory ≠ **well:** ailing, bad, ill, injured, off colour, out of sorts, poorly, sick, sickly, unhealthy, unwell

allude *vb* **1, 2** = **refer**, advert, glance, hint, imply, insinuate, intimate, mention, remark, speak of, suggest, tip the wink, touch upon

allure *vb* **1** = **attract**, beguile, cajole, captivate, charm, coax, decoy, enchant, entice, inveigle, lead on, lure, persuade, seduce, tempt, win over ◆ *n* **2** = **attractiveness**, appeal, attraction, charm, enchantment, enticement, glamour, lure, persuasion, seductiveness, temptation

alluring *adj* **1** = **attractive**, beguiling, bewitching, captivating, come-hither, enchanting, fascinating, fetching, glamorous, intriguing, seductive, sexy, tempting

Antonyms *adj* abhorrent, off-putting (*Brit. inf.*), repellent, repugnant, repulsive, unattractive

allusion *n* **2** = **reference**, casual remark, glance, hint, implication, indirect reference, innuendo, insinuation, intimation, mention, suggestion

ally *vb* **1** = **unite**, affiliate, associate, band together, collaborate, combine, confederate, connect, join, join battle with, join forces, league, marry, unify ◆ *n* **3** = **partner**, abettor, accessory, accomplice, associate, coadjutor, collaborator, colleague, confederate, co-worker, friend, helper

Antonyms *vb* ≠ **unite:** alienate, disaffect, disunite, divide, drive apart, separate, set at odds ◆ *n* ≠ **partner:** adversary, antagonist, competitor, enemy, foe, opponent, rival

almighty *adj* **1** = **all-powerful**, absolute, invincible, omnipotent, supreme, unlimited **2** *Informal* = **great**, awful, desperate, enormous, excessive, intense, loud, severe, terrible

Antonyms *adj* ≠ **all-powerful:** helpless, impotent, powerless, weak ≠ **great:** feeble, insignificant, paltry, poor, slight, tame, weak

almost *adv* = **nearly**, about, all but, approximately, as good as, close to, just about, not far from, not quite, on the brink of, practically, so near (and) yet so far, virtually, well-nigh

alms *pl n* = **donation**, benefaction, bounty, charity, gift, relief

aloft *adv* **1** = **in the air**, above, heavenward, higher, high up, in the sky, on high, overhead, skyward, up, up above, upward

alone *adj* **1, 2** = **by oneself**, abandoned, apart, by itself, deserted, desolate, detached, forlorn, forsaken, isolated, lonely, lonesome, only, on one's tod (*sl.*), out on a limb, separate, single, single-handed, sole, solitary, unaccompanied, unaided, unassisted, unattended, uncombined, unconnected, under one's own steam, unescorted

aloof ❶ (əˈluːf) *adj* distant, unsympathetic, or supercilious in manner. [C16: from A-[1] + *loof*, var. of LUFF] ▸**aˈloofly** *adv* ▸**aˈloofness** *n*

alopecia (ˌæləˈpiːʃɪə) *n* baldness. [C14: from L, from Gk *alōpekia*, orig.: mange in foxes]

aloud ❶ (əˈlaʊd) *adv, adj (postpositive)* **1** in a normal voice. **2** in a spoken voice; not silently.

alp (ælp) *n* **1** (in Switzerland) a mountain pasture. **2** a high mountain. **3** **the Alps**. a high mountain range in S central Europe. [C16: from L *Alpes*]

ALP *abbrev. for* Australian Labor Party.

alpaca (ælˈpækə) *n* **1** a domesticated South American mammal related to the llama, with dark shaggy hair. **2** the cloth made from the wool of this animal. **3** a glossy fabric simulating this. [C18: via Sp. from Aymara *allpaca*]

alpenhorn (ˈælpənˌhɔːn) *n* another name for **alphorn**.

alpenstock (ˈælpənˌstɒk) *n* a stout stick with an iron tip used by hikers, mountain climbers, etc. [C19: from G, from *Alpen* Alps + *Stock* STICK[1]]

alpha (ˈælfə) *n* **1** the first letter in the Greek alphabet (Α, α). **2** *Brit.* the highest grade or mark, as in an examination. **3** *(modifier)* **3a** involving helium nuclei. **3b** denoting an isomeric or allotropic form of a substance. [via L from Gk, of Phoenician origin]

alpha and omega *n* the first and last, a phrase used in Revelation 1:8 to signify God's eternity.

alphabet ❶ (ˈælfəˌbɛt) *n* **1** a set of letters or other signs used in a writing system, each letter or sign being used to represent one or sometimes more than one phoneme in the language being transcribed. **2** any set of characters, esp. one representing sounds of speech. **3** basic principles or rudiments. [C15: from LL, from the first two letters of the Gk alphabet; see ALPHA, BETA]

alphabetical (ˌælfəˈbɛtɪkᵊl) *or* **alphabetic** *adj* **1** in the conventional order of the letters of an alphabet. **2** of or expressed by an alphabet.
▸**ˌalphaˈbetically** *adv*

alphabetize *or* **alphabetise** (ˈælfəbəˌtaɪz) *vb* **alphabetizes, alphabetizing, alphabetized** *or* **alphabetises, alphabetising, alphabetised.** *(tr)* **1** to arrange in conventional alphabetical order. **2** to express by an alphabet.
▸**ˌalphabetiˈzation** *or* **ˌalphabetiˈsation** *n*

alpha-blocker *n* any of a class of drugs that prevent the stimulation of alpha receptors, a type of receptor in the sympathetic nervous system, by adrenaline and that therefore cause widening of blood vessels: used in the treatment of high blood pressure.

alpha decay *n* the radioactive decay process resulting in emission of alpha particles.

alpha-fetoprotein (ˌælfəˌfiːtəʊˈprəʊtiːn) *n* a protein that forms in the liver of the human fetus; excessive quantities in the amniotic fluid may indicate spina bifida in the fetus; low levels may point to Down's syndrome. Abbrev.: **afp**.

alphanumeric (ˌælfənjuːˈmɛrɪk) *or* **alphameric** *adj* (of a character set or file of data) consisting of alphabetical and numerical symbols.

alpha particle *n* a helium nucleus, containing two neutrons and two protons, emitted during some radioactive transformations.

alpha ray *n* ionizing radiation consisting of a stream of alpha particles.

alpha rhythm *or* **wave** *n Physiol.* the normal bursts of electrical activity from the cerebral cortex of a person at rest. See also **brain wave**.

alpha stock *n* any of the most active securities on the London stock exchange of which there are between 100 and 200.

alphorn (ˈælpˌhɔːn) *or* **alpenhorn** *n* a wind instrument used in the Swiss Alps, made from a very long tube of wood. [C19: from G: Alps horn]

alpine (ˈælpaɪn) *adj* **1** of or relating to high mountains. **2** (of plants) growing on mountains above the limit for tree growth. **3** connected with mountaineering. **4** *Skiing.* of racing events on steep prepared slopes, such as the slalom and downhill. Cf. **nordic**. ◆ *n* **5** a plant grown in or native to high altitudes.

alpinist (ˈælpɪnɪst) *n* a mountain climber.

already ❶ (ɔːlˈrɛdɪ) *adv* **1** by or before a stated or implied time: *he is already here.* **2** at a time earlier than expected: *is it ten o'clock already?*

alright (ɔːlˈraɪt) *adv, sentence substitute, adj* a variant spelling of **all right**.

> **USAGE NOTE** The form *alright*, though very common, is still considered by many people to be wrong or less acceptable

Alsatian (ælˈseɪʃən) *n* **1** Also called: **German shepherd (dog)**. a large wolflike breed of dog often used as a guard dog and by the police. **2** a native or inhabitant of Alsace, a region of NE France. ◆ *adj* **3** of or relating to Alsace or its inhabitants.

also ❶ (ˈɔːlsəʊ) *adv* **1** *(sentence modifier)* in addition; as well; too. ◆ *sentence connector.* **2** besides; moreover. [OE *alswā*; see ALL, SO[1]]

also-ran *n* **1** a contestant, horse, etc., failing to finish among the first three. **2** a loser.

alstroemeria (ˌælstrəʊˈmɪərɪə) *n* any of several plants with fleshy roots and brightly coloured flowers in summer, esp. the Peruvian lily. [C18: NL, after Claude *Alstroemer* (1736–96), Swedish naturalist]

alt. *abbrev. for:* **1** alternate. **2** altitude. **3** alto.

Alta. *abbrev. for* Alberta.

Altaic (ælˈteɪɪk) *n* **1** a postulated family of languages of Asia and SE Europe, including the Turkic, Tungusic, and Mongolic subfamilies. See also **Ural-Altaic**. ◆ *adj* **2** denoting or relating to this linguistic family or its speakers.

altar (ˈɔːltə) *n* **1** a raised place or structure where sacrifices are offered and religious rites performed. **2** (in Christian churches) the communion table. **3** a step in the wall of a dry dock. [OE, ult. from L *altus* high]

altar boy *n RC Church, Church of England.* a boy serving as an acolyte.

altarpiece (ˈɔːltəˌpiːs) *n* a work of art set above and behind an altar; a reredos.

altazimuth (ælˈtæzɪməθ) *n* an instrument for measuring the altitude and azimuth of a celestial body. [C19: from ALT(ITUDE) + AZIMUTH]

altazimuth mounting *n* a telescope mounting that allows motion of the telescope about a vertical axis (in altitude) and a horizontal axis (in azimuth).

alter ❶ (ˈɔːltə) *vb* **1** to make or become different in some respect; change. **2** *(tr) Inf., chiefly US.* a euphemistic word for **castrate** or **spay**. [C14: from OF, ult. from L *alter* other]
▸**ˈalterable** *adj*

alteration ❶ (ˌɔːltəˈreɪʃən) *n* **1** a change or modification. **2** the act of altering.

alterative (ˈɔːltərətɪv) *adj* **1** likely or able to produce alteration. **2** (of a drug) able to restore health. ◆ *n* **3** such a drug.

altercate (ˈɔːltəˌkeɪt) *vb* **altercates, altercating, altercated.** *(intr)* to argue, esp. heatedly; dispute. [C16: from L *altercārī* to quarrel with another, from *alter* other]

altercation ❶ (ˌɔːltəˈkeɪʃən) *n* an angry or heated discussion or quarrel; argument.

alter ego (ˈæltər ˈiːgəʊ, ˈɛgəʊ) *n* **1** a second self. **2** a very close friend. [L: other self]

alternate ❶ *vb* (ˈɔːltəˌneɪt), **alternates, alternating, alternated. 1** (often foll. by *with*) to occur or cause to occur by turns: *day and night alternate.* **2** *(intr;* often foll. by *between)* to swing repeatedly from one condition, action, etc., to another. **3** *(tr)* to interchange regularly or in succession. **4** *(intr)* (of an electric current, voltage, etc.) to reverse direction or sign at regular intervals. ◆ *adj* (ɔːlˈtɜːnɪt). **5** occurring by turns: *alternate feelings of love and hate.* **6** every other or second one of a series: *he came on alternate days.* **7** being a second choice; alternative: *alternate director.* **8** *Bot.* (of leaves, flowers, etc.) arranged singly at different heights on either side of the stem. ◆ *n* (ˈɔːltənɪt, ɔːlˈtɜːnɪt). **9** *US & Canad.* a person who substitutes for another; stand-in. [C16: from L *alternāre* to do one thing and then another, ult. from *alter* other]
▸**ˌalterˈnation** *n*

alternate angles *pl n* two angles at opposite ends and on opposite sides of a transversal cutting two lines.

alternately (ɔːlˈtɜːnɪtlɪ) *adv* in an alternating sequence or position.

alternating current *n* an electric current that periodically reverses direction. Abbrev.: **AC**.

alternation of generations *n* the occurrence in the life cycle of many plants and lower animals of alternating sexual and asexual reproductive forms.

alternative ❶ (ɔːlˈtɜːnətɪv) *n* **1** a possibility of choice, esp. between two things. **2** either of such choices: *we took the alternative of walking.* ◆ *adj*

THESAURUS

Antonyms *adj* accompanied, aided, among others, assisted, escorted, helped, joint, together

aloof *adj* = **distant**, chilly, cold, cool, detached, forbidding, formal, haughty, indifferent, remote, reserved, standoffish, supercilious, unapproachable, unfriendly, uninterested, unresponsive, unsociable, unsympathetic
Antonyms *adj* friendly, gregarious, neighbourly, open, sociable, sympathetic, warm

aloud *adv* **1, 2** = **out loud**, audibly, clearly, distinctly, intelligibly, plainly

alphabet *n* **1** = **letters**, script, syllabary, writing system

already *adv* **1** = **before now**, as of now, at present, before, by now, by that time, by then, by this time, even now, heretofore, just now, previously

also *adv* **1** = **too**, additionally, along with, and, as well, as well as, besides, further, furthermore, in addition, including, into the bargain, moreover, on top of that, plus, to boot

alter *vb* **1** = **change**, adapt, adjust, amend, convert, diversify, metamorphose, modify, recast, reform, remodel, reshape, revise, shift, transform, transmute, turn, tweak *(inf.)*, vary

alteration *n* **1, 2** = **change**, adaptation, adjustment, amendment, conversion, difference, diversification, metamorphosis, modification, reformation, remodelling, reshaping, revision, shift, transformation, transmutation, variance, variation

altercation *n* = **argument**, bickering, clash, contention, controversy, disagreement, discord, dispute, dissension, quarrel, row, squabble, wrangle

alternate *vb* **1, 3** = **change**, act reciprocally, alter, fluctuate, follow in turn, follow one another, interchange, intersperse, oscillate, rotate, substitute, take turns ◆ *adj* **5, 6** = **every other**, alternating, every second, interchanging, rotating **7** = **second**, alternative, another, different, substitute

alternating *adj* **1, 3** = **changing**, fluctuating, interchanging, occurring by turns, oscillating, rotating, seesawing, shifting, swinging, vacillating

alternation *n* **1, 3** = **change**, fluctuation, oscillation, rotation, swing, vacillation, variation, vicissitude

alternative *n* **1, 2** = **choice**, option, other (*of two*), preference, recourse, selection, substitute ◆ *adj* **3** = **different**, alternate, another, other, second, substitute

alternatively *adv* **3** = **or**, as an alternative, by

3 presenting a choice, esp. between two possibilities only. **4** (of two things) mutually exclusive. **5** denoting a lifestyle, culture, art form, etc., that is regarded as preferable to that of contemporary society because it is less conventional, materialistic, or institutionalized.
▸**al'ternatively** *adv*

alternative curriculum *n Brit. education.* any course of study offered as an alternative to the National Curriculum.

alternative energy *n* a form of energy derived from a natural source, such as the sun, wind, tides, or waves. Also called: **renewable energy.**

Alternative Investment Market *n* a market on the London Stock Exchange for small companies that want to avoid the expenses of a main-market listing. Abbrev.: **AIM.**

alternative medicine *n* the treatment or alleviation of disease by techniques such as osteopathy and acupuncture, allied with attention to a person's general wellbeing. Also called: **complementary medicine.**

alternative society *n* a group of people who agree in rejecting the traditional values of the society around them.

Alternative Vote *n* (*modifier*) of or relating to a system of voting in which voters list the candidates in order of preference. If no candidate obtains more than 50% of first-preference votes, the votes for the bottom candidate are redistributed according to the voters' next preference. See **proportional representation.**

alternator ('ɔ:ltəˌneɪtə) *n* an electrical machine that generates an alternating current.

althaea *or US* **althea** (æl'θi:ə) *n* any Eurasian plant of the genus *Althaea,* such as the hollyhock, having tall spikes of showy flowers. [C17: from L, from Gk *althaia* marsh mallow]

althorn ('ælt,hɔ:n) *n* a valved brass musical instrument belonging to the saxhorn family.

although ❶ (ɔ:l'ðəʊ) *conj* (*subordinating*) even though: *although she was ill, she worked hard.*

altimeter (æl'tɪmɪtə, 'æltɪˌmi:tə) *n* an instrument that indicates height above sea level, esp. one based on an aneroid barometer and fitted to an aircraft. [C19: from L *altus* high + -METER]

altitude ❶ ('æltɪˌtju:d) *n* **1** the vertical height of an object, esp. above sea level. **2** *Geom.* the perpendicular distance from the vertex to the base of a geometrical figure or solid. **3** Also called: **elevation.** *Astron., navigation.* the angular distance of a celestial body from the horizon. **4** *Surveying.* the angle of elevation of a point above the horizontal plane of the observer. **5** (*often pl*) a high place or region. [C14: from L *altus* high, deep]

alto ('æltəʊ) *n, pl* **altos. 1** (in choral singing) short for **contralto. 2** the highest adult male voice; countertenor. **3** a singer with such a voice. **4** a flute, saxophone, etc., that is the third or fourth highest instrument in its group. ◆ *adj* **5** denoting such an instrument. [C18: from It.: high, from L *altus*]

alto clef *n* the clef that establishes middle C as being on the third line of the staff.

altocumulus (ˌæltəʊ'kju:mjʊləs) *n, pl* **altocumuli** (-laɪ). a globular cloud at an intermediate height of about 2400 to 6000 m (8000 to 20 000 ft).

altogether ❶ (ˌɔ:ltə'geðə, 'ɔ:ltəˌgeðə) *adv* **1** with everything included: *altogether he owed me sixty pounds.* **2** completely; utterly: *altogether mad.* **3** on the whole: *altogether it was very good.* ◆ *n* **4 in the altogether.** *Inf.* naked.

altoist ('æltəʊɪst) *n* a person who plays the alto saxophone.

altostratus (ˌæltəʊ'streɪtəs, -'strɑ:-) *n, pl* **altostrati** (-taɪ). a layer cloud at an intermediate height of about 2400 to 6000 m (8000 to 20 000 ft).

altricial (æl'trɪʃəl) *adj* **1** denoting birds whose young, after hatching, are naked, blind, and dependent on the parents for food. ◆ *n* **2** an altricial bird. ◆ Cf. **precocial.** [C19: from NL, from L *altrix* a nurse]

altruism ❶ ('æltru:ˌɪzəm) *n* unselfish concern for the welfare of others. [C19: from F, from It. *altrui* others, from L]
▸**'altruist** *n* ▸ˌ**altru'istic** *adj* ▸ˌ**altru'istically** *adv*

ALU *Computing. abbrev. for* arithmetical and logical unit.

alum ('æləm) *n* **1** a colourless soluble hydrated double sulphate of aluminium and potassium used in manufacturing and in medicine. Formula: $K_2SO_4.Al_2(SO_4)_3.24H_2O$. **2** any of a group of similar hydrated double sulphates of a monovalent metal or group and a trivalent metal. [C14: from OF, from L *alūmen*]

alumina (ə'lu:mɪnə) *n* another name for **aluminium oxide.** [C18: from NL, pl of L *alūmen* ALUM]

aluminium (ˌælju'mɪnɪəm) *or US & Canad.* **aluminum** (ə'lu:mɪnəm) *n* a light malleable silvery-white metallic element that resists corrosion; the third most abundant element in the earth's crust, occurring as a compound, principally in bauxite. Symbol: Al; atomic no.: 13; atomic wt.: 26.981.

aluminium oxide *n* a powder occurring naturally as corundum and used in the production of aluminium, abrasives, glass, and ceramics. Formula: Al_2O_3. Also called: **alumina.**

aluminize *or* **aluminise** (ə'lu:mɪˌnaɪz) *vb* **aluminizes, aluminizing, aluminized** *or* **aluminises, aluminising, aluminised.** (*tr*) to cover with aluminium or aluminium paint.

aluminous (ə'lu:mɪnəs) *adj* resembling aluminium.

alumnus (ə'lʌmnəs) *or* (*fem*) **alumna** (ə'lʌmnə) *n, pl* **alumni** (-naɪ) *or* **alumnae** (-ni:). *Chiefly US & Canad.* a graduate of a school, college, etc. [C17: from L: nursling, pupil, from *alere* to nourish]

alveolar (æl'vɪələ, ˌælvɪ'əʊlə) *adj* **1** *Anat.* of an alveolus. **2** denoting the part of the jawbone containing the roots of the teeth. **3** (of a consonant) articulated with the tongue in contact with the part of the jawbone immediately behind the upper teeth. ◆ *n* **4** an alveolar consonant, such as *t, d,* and *s* in English.

alveolate (æl'vɪəlɪt, -ˌleɪt) *adj* having many small cavities. [C19: from LL *alveolātus* hollowed, from L: ALVEOLUS]
▸ˌ**alveo'lation** *n*

alveolus (æl'vɪələs) *n, pl* **alveoli** (-ˌlaɪ). any small pit, cavity, or saclike dilation, such as a honeycomb cell, a tooth socket, or the tiny air sacs in the lungs. [C18: from L: a little hollow, dim. of *alveus*]

always ❶ ('ɔ:lweɪz) *adv* **1** without exception; every time: *he always arrives on time.* **2** continually; repeatedly. **3** in any case: *you could always take a day off work.* ◆ Also (archaic): **alway.** [C13 *alles weiss,* from OE *ealne weg,* lit.: all the way]

alyssum ('ælɪsəm) *n* a widely cultivated herbaceous garden plant, having clusters of small yellow or white flowers. [C16: from NL, from Gk *alusson,* from *alussos* (adj) curing rabies]

Alzheimer's disease ('ælts,haɪməz) *n* a disorder of the brain resulting in progressive decline and eventual dementia. Often shortened to **Alzheimer's.** [C20: after A. *Alzheimer* (1864–1915), G physician who first identified it]

am (æm; *unstressed* əm) *vb* (used with *I*) a form of the present tense of **be.** [OE *eam*]

Am *the chemical symbol for* americium.

AM *abbrev. for:* **1** Also: **am.** amplitude modulation. **2** *US.* Master of Arts. **3** Member of the Order of Australia.

Am. *abbrev. for* America(n).

a.m., A.M., am, *or* **AM** (indicating the period from midnight to midday) *abbrev. for* ante meridiem. [L: before noon]

amabokoboko (ama'bɒkɒbɒkɒ) *pl n S. African.* an African name for the **Springbok** rugby team. [C20: from Nguni *ama,* a plural prefix + *bokoboko,* from *bok* a diminutive of SPRINGBOK]

Amadhlozi *or* **Amadlozi** (ˌæmæ'hlɒʒi:) *pl n S. African.* the ancestral spirits. [from Zulu, pl. *amadlozi*]

amadoda (ˌæmæ'dɒdə) *pl n S. African.* grown men. [from Nguni *ama,* a plural prefix + *doda* men]

amadou ('æməˌdu:) *n* a spongy substance got from some fungi, used (formerly) as tinder, a styptic, and by fishermen to dry flies. [C18: from F, from Provençal: lover, from L *amāre* to love (because easily set alight)]

amah ('ɑ:mə) *n* (in the East, esp. formerly) a nurse or maidservant. [C19: from Port. *ama* nurse]

amain (ə'meɪn) *adv Arch. or poetic.* with great strength or haste. [C16: from A-[2] + MAIN[1]]

amalgam ❶ (ə'mælgəm) *n* **1** an alloy of mercury with another metal, esp. silver: *dental amalgam.* **2** a blend or combination. [C15: from Med. L *amalgama,* from ?]

amalgamate ❶ (ə'mælgəˌmeɪt) *vb* **amalgamates, amalgamating, amalgamated. 1** to combine or cause to combine; unite. **2** to alloy (a metal) with mercury.

amalgamation ❶ (əˌmælgə'meɪʃən) *n* **1** the process of amalgamating.

THESAURUS

way of alternative, if not, instead, on the other hand, otherwise

although *conj* = **though**, albeit, despite the fact that, even if, even supposing, even though, notwithstanding, tho' (*US or poetic*), while

altitude *n* **1** = **height**, elevation, loftiness, peak, summit

altogether *adv* **1** = **in total**, all told, everything included, in all, in sum, *in toto,* taken together **2** = **completely**, absolutely, every inch, fully, lock, stock and barrel, perfectly, quite, thoroughly, totally, utterly, wholly **3** = **on the whole**, all in all, all things considered, as a whole, collectively, generally, in general, *in toto*
Antonyms *adv* ≠ **completely:** halfway, incompletely, in part, in some measure, not fully, partially, relatively, slightly, somewhat, to a certain degree *or* extent, up to a certain point

altruism *n* = **selflessness**, beneficence, benevolence, bigheartedness, charitableness, charity, consideration, generosity, goodwill, greatheartedness, humanitarianism, magnanimity, philanthropy, self-sacrifice, unselfishness
Antonyms *n* egoism, egotism, greed, meanness, mercenariness, narrowness, self-absorption, self-centredness, self-interest, selfishness, self-seeking

altruist *n* = **humanitarian**, philanthropist

altruistic *adj* = **selfless**, benevolent, charitable, considerate, generous, humanitarian, philanthropic, public-spirited, self-sacrificing, unselfish
Antonyms *adj* egoistic(al), egotistic(al), greedy, mean, self-centred, self-interested, selfish, self-seeking, ungenerous

always *adv* **1, 2** = **continually**, aye (*Scot.*), consistently, constantly, eternally, ever, everlastingly, evermore, every time, forever, *in perpetuum,* invariably, perpetually, repeatedly, unceasingly, without exception
Antonyms *adv* hardly, hardly ever, infrequently, once in a blue moon, once in a while, only now and then, on rare occasions, rarely, scarcely ever, seldom

amalgam *n* **2** = **combination**, admixture, alloy, amalgamation, blend, composite, compound, fusion, meld, mixture, union

amalgamate *vb* **1** = **combine**, alloy, ally, blend, coalesce, commingle, compound, fuse, incorporate, integrate, intermix, meld, merge, mingle, unite
Antonyms *vb* disunite, divide, part, separate, split, split up

amalgamation *n* **1, 2, 4** = **combination**, ad-

2 the state of being amalgamated. **3** a method of extracting precious metals by treatment with mercury. **4** a merger.

amanuensis (əˌmænjuˈɛnsɪs) *n, pl* **amanuenses** (-siːz). a person employed to take dictation or to copy manuscripts. [C17: from L, from *servus ā manū* slave at hand (that is, handwriting)]

amaranth (ˈæməˌrænθ) *n* **1** *Poetic.* an imaginary flower that never fades. **2** any of numerous plants having tassel-like heads of small green, red, or purple flowers. **3** a synthetic red food colouring (**E123**), used in packet soups, cake mixes, etc. [C17: from L *amarantus,* from Gk, from A-[1] + *marainein* to fade]

amaretto (ˌæməˈretəu) *n* an Italian liqueur with a flavour of almonds. [C20: from It. *amaro* bitter]

amaryllis (ˌæməˈrɪlɪs) *n* **1** a plant native to southern Africa having large lily-like reddish or white flowers. **2** any of several related plants. [C18: from NL, from L: after *Amaryllis,* Gk conventional name for a shepherdess]

amass ❶ (əˈmæs) *vb* **1** (*tr*) to accumulate or collect (esp. riches, etc.). **2** to gather in a heap. [C15: from OF, from *masse* MASS]
▸**aˈmasser** *n*

amateur ❶ (ˈæmətə) *n* **1** a person who engages in an activity, esp. a sport, as a pastime rather than for gain. **2** a person unskilled in a subject or activity. **3** a person who is fond of or admires something. **4** (*modifier*) of or for amateurs: *an amateur event.* ◆ *adj* **5** not professional or expert: *an amateur approach.* [C18: from F, from L *amātor* lover, from *amāre* to love]
▸**ˈamateurism** *n*

amateurish ❶ (ˈæmətərɪʃ) *adj* lacking professional skill or expertise.
▸**ˈamateurishly** *adv*

amative (ˈæmətɪv) *adj* a rare word for **amorous.** [C17: from Med. L, from L *amāre* to love]

amatory (ˈæmətərɪ) *or* **amatorial** (ˌæməˈtɔːrɪəl) *adj* of, relating to, or inciting sexual love or desire. [C16: from L *amātōrius,* from *amāre* to love]

amaurosis (ˌæmɔːˈrəusɪs) *n* blindness, esp. when occurring without observable damage to the eye. [C17: via NL from Gk: darkening, from *amauroun* to dim]
▸**amaurotic** (ˌæmɔːˈrɒtɪk) *adj*

amaze ❶ (əˈmeɪz) *vb* **amazes, amazing, amazed.** (*tr*) **1** to fill with incredulity or surprise; astonish. ◆ *n* **2** an archaic word for **amazement.** [OE *āmasian*]
▸**aˈmazing** *adj*

amazement ❶ (əˈmeɪzmənt) *n* incredulity or great astonishment; complete wonder.

Amazon (ˈæməzən) *n* **1** *Greek myth.* one of a race of women warriors of Scythia. **2** (*often not cap.*) any tall, strong, or aggressive woman. [C14: via L from Gk *Amazōn,* from ?]
▸ **Amazonian** (ˌæməˈzəunɪən) *adj*

ambassador ❶ (æmˈbæsədə) *n* **1** a diplomat of the highest rank, accredited as permanent representative to another country. **2 ambassador extraordinary.** a diplomat of the highest rank sent on a special mission. **3 ambassador plenipotentiary.** a diplomat of the first rank with treaty-signing powers. **4 ambassador-at-large.** *US.* an ambassador with special duties who may be sent to more than one government. **5** an authorized representative or messenger. [C14: from OF, from It., from OProvençal *ambaisador,* from *ambaisa* (unattested) mission, errand]
▸**amˈbassadress** *fem n* ▸**ambassadorial** (æmˌbæsəˈdɔːrɪəl) *adj* ▸**amˈbassadorˌship** *n*

amber (ˈæmbə) *n* **1** a yellow translucent fossil resin derived from extinct coniferous trees and often containing trapped insects. **2a** a brownish-yellow colour. **2b** (*as adj*): *an amber dress.* **3** an amber traffic light used as a warning between red and green. [C14: from Med. L *ambar,* from Ar. *ʻanbar* ambergris]

amber gambler *n Brit. inf.* a driver who races through traffic lights when they are at amber.

ambergris (ˈæmbəˌgriːs, -grɪs) *n* a waxy substance secreted by the intestinal tract of the sperm whale and often found floating in the sea: used in the manufacture of some perfumes. [C15: from OF *ambre gris* grey amber]

amberjack (ˈæmbəˌdʒæk) *n* any of several large fishes occurring in tropical and subtropical Atlantic waters. [C19: from AMBER + JACK]

ambi- *combining form.* indicating both: *ambidextrous; ambivalence.* [from L: round, on both sides, both, from *ambo* both]

ambidextrous (ˌæmbɪˈdɛkstrəs) *adj* **1** equally expert with each hand. **2** *Inf.* skilled or adept. **3** underhanded.
▸**ambidexterity** (ˌæmbɪdɛkˈstɛrɪtɪ) *or* **ˌambiˈdextrousness** *n*

ambience ❶ *or* **ambiance** (ˈæmbɪəns) *n* the atmosphere of a place. [C19: from F, from *ambiant* surrounding]

ambient (ˈæmbɪənt) *adj* **1** surrounding. **2** creating a relaxing atmosphere: *ambient music.* [C16: from L *ambiēns* going round, from AMBI- + *īre* to go]

ambiguity ❶ (ˌæmbɪˈgjuːɪtɪ) *n, pl* **ambiguities. 1** the possibility of interpreting an expression in more than one way. **2** an instance or example of this, as in the sentence *they are cooking apples.* **3** vagueness or uncertainty of meaning.

ambiguous ❶ (æmˈbɪgjuəs) *adj* **1** having more than one possible interpretation. **2** difficult to understand; obscure. [C16: from L *ambiguus* going here and there, uncertain, from *ambigere* to go around]
▸**amˈbiguously** *adv* ▸**amˈbiguousness** *n*

ambisexual (ˌæmbɪˈsɛksjuəl) *or* **ambosexual** *adj Biol.* relating to or affecting both the male and female sexes.

ambit ❶ (ˈæmbɪt) *n* **1** scope or extent. **2** limits or boundary. [C16: from L *ambitus* a going round, from *ambīre* to go round]

ambition ❶ (æmˈbɪʃən) *n* **1** strong desire for success or distinction. **2** something so desired; goal. [C14: from OF, from L *ambitiō* a going round (of candidates), from *ambīre* to go round]

ambitious ❶ (æmˈbɪʃəs) *adj* **1** having a strong desire for success or achievement. **2** necessitating extraordinary effort or ability: *an ambitious project.* **3** (often foll. by *of*) having a great desire (for something or to do something).
▸**amˈbitiousness** *n*

ambivalence ❶ (æmˈbɪvələns) *or* **ambivalency** *n* the coexistence of two opposed and conflicting emotions, etc.
▸**amˈbivalent** *adj*

amble ❶ (ˈæmbəl) *vb* **ambles, ambling, ambled.** (*intr*) **1** to walk at a leisurely relaxed pace. **2** (of a horse) to move, lifting both legs on one side together. **3** to ride a horse at an amble. ◆ *n* **4** a leisurely motion in walking. **5** a leisurely walk. **6** the ambling gait of a horse. [C14: from OF, from L *ambulāre* to walk]

amblyopia (ˌæmblɪˈəupɪə) *n* impaired vision with no discernible damage to the eye or optic nerve. [C18: NL, from Gk *ambluōpia,* from *amblus* dull, dim + *ōps* eye]
▸**amblyopic** (ˌæmblɪˈɒpɪk) *adj*

amboyna *or* **amboina** (æmˈbɔɪnə) *n* the mottled curly-grained wood of an Indonesian tree, used in making furniture.

ambrosia (æmˈbrəuzɪə) *n* **1** *Classical myth.* the food of the gods, said to bestow immortality. Cf. **nectar** (sense 2). **2** anything particularly delightful to taste or smell. **3** another name for **beebread.** [C16: via L from Gk: immortality, from A-[1] + *brotos* mortal]
▸**amˈbrosial** or **amˈbrosian** *adj*

ambry (ˈæmbrɪ) *or* **aumbry** (ˈɔːmbrɪ) *n, pl* **ambries** *or* **aumbries. 1** a recessed cupboard in the wall of a church near the altar, used to store sacred vessels, etc. **2** *Obs.* a small cupboard. [C14: from OF *almarie,* ult. from L *armārium* chest for storage, from *arma* arms]

ambulance (ˈæmbjuləns) *n* a motor vehicle designed to carry sick or

THESAURUS

mixture, alliance, alloy, amalgam, amalgamating, blend, coalition, commingling, composite, compound, fusion, incorporation, integration, joining, meld, merger, mingling, mixing, mixture, union

amass *vb* **1, 2 = collect**, accumulate, aggregate, assemble, compile, garner, gather, heap up, hoard, pile up, rake up, scrape together

amateur *n* **1 = nonprofessional**, dabbler, dilettante, layman

amateurish *adj* **= unprofessional**, amateur, bungling, clumsy, crude, inexpert, unaccomplished, unskilful
Antonyms *adj* experienced, expert, practised, professional, skilled

amaze *vb* **1 = astonish**, alarm, astound, bewilder, boggle the mind, bowl over (*inf.*), confound, daze, dumbfound, electrify, flabbergast, shock, stagger, startle, stun, stupefy, surprise

amazement *n* **= astonishment**, admiration, bewilderment, confusion, marvel, perplexity, shock, stupefaction, surprise, wonder

amazing *adj* **1 = astonishing**, astounding, breathtaking, eye-opening, jaw-dropping, mind-boggling, overwhelming, staggering, startling, stunning, surprising

ambassador *n* **1, 5 = representative**, agent, consul, deputy, diplomat, emissary, envoy, legate, minister, plenipotentiary

ambience *n* **= atmosphere**, air, aura, character, complexion, feel, flavour, impression, milieu, mood, quality, setting, spirit, surroundings, temper, tenor, tone, vibes (*sl.*), vibrations (*sl.*)

ambiguity *n* **3 = vagueness**, doubt, doubtfulness, dubiety, dubiousness, enigma, equivocacy, equivocality, equivocation, inconclusiveness, indefiniteness, indeterminateness, obscurity, puzzle, tergiversation, uncertainty

ambiguous *adj* **1, 2 = unclear**, clear as mud (*inf.*), cryptic, Delphic, doubtful, dubious, enigmatic, enigmatical, equivocal, inconclusive, indefinite, indeterminate, obscure, oracular, puzzling, uncertain, vague
Antonyms *adj* clear, definite, explicit, obvious, plain, simple, specific, unequivocal, unmistakable, unquestionable

ambit *n* **1 = range**, extent, radius, reach, scope, sweep **2 = limit**, border, boundary, circumference, circumscription, compass, confine, edge, extremity, frontier, margin, parameter, perimeter, restraint, restriction, verge

ambition *n* **1 = enterprise**, aspiration, avidity, desire, drive, eagerness, get-up-and-go (*inf.*), hankering, longing, striving, yearning, zeal **2 = goal**, aim, aspiration, desire, dream, end, Holy Grail (*inf.*), hope, intent, objective, purpose, wish

ambitious *adj* **1 = enterprising**, aspiring, avid, desirous, driving, eager, hopeful, intent, purposeful, striving, zealous **2 = demanding**, arduous, bold, challenging, difficult, elaborate, energetic, exacting, formidable, grandiose, hard, impressive, industrious, pretentious, severe, strenuous
Antonyms *adj* ≠ **enterprising:** apathetic, good-for-nothing, lazy, unambitious, unaspiring ≠ **demanding:** easy, modest, simple, unambitious

ambivalence *n* **= indecision**, clash, conflict, contradiction, doubt, equivocation, fluctuation, hesitancy, irresolution, opposition, uncertainty, vacillation, wavering

ambivalent *adj* **= undecided**, clashing, conflicting, contradictory, debatable, doubtful, equivocal, fluctuating, hesitant, inconclusive, in two minds, irresolute, mixed, opposed, uncertain, unresolved, unsure, vacillating, warring, wavering
Antonyms *adj* certain, clear, conclusive, convinced, decided, definite, free from doubt, positive, sure, unwavering

amble *vb* **1 = stroll**, dawdle, meander, mosey (*inf.*), ramble, saunter, walk, wander

injured people. [C19: from F, based on *(hôpital) ambulant* mobile or field (hospital), from L *ambulāre* to walk]

ambulance chaser *n US sl.* a lawyer who seeks to encourage and profit from the lawsuits of accident victims.
▸**ambulance chasing** *n*

ambulance stocks *pl n* high-performance stocks and shares recommended by a broker to a dissatisfied client to improve their relationship.

ambulant ('æmbjʊlənt) *adj* **1** moving about from place to place. **2** *Med.* another word for **ambulatory** (sense 3).

ambulate ('æmbjʊˌleɪt) *vb* **ambulates, ambulating, ambulated.** *(intr)* to wander about or move from place to place. [C17: from L *ambulāre* to walk]
▸ˌ**ambu'lation** *n*

ambulatory ('æmbjʊlətərɪ) *adj* **1** of or designed for walking. **2** changing position; not fixed. **3** Also: **ambulant.** able to walk. ◆ *n, pl* **ambulatories. 4** a place for walking, such as an aisle or a cloister.

ambuscade (ˌæmbə'skeɪd) *n* **1** an ambush. ◆ *vb* **ambuscades, ambuscading, ambuscaded. 2** to ambush or lie in ambush. [C16: from F, from OIt. *imboscata,* prob. of Gmc origin; cf. AMBUSH]

ambush ❶ ('æmbʊʃ) *n* **1** the act of waiting in a concealed position in order to launch a surprise attack. **2** a surprise attack from such a position. **3** the concealed position from which such an attack is launched. **4** the person or persons waiting to launch such an attack. ◆ *vb* **5** to lie in wait (for). **6** *(tr)* to attack suddenly from a concealed position. [C14: from OF *embuschier* to position in ambush, from *em-* IM- + *-buschier,* from *busche* piece of firewood, prob. of Gmc origin]

ameba (ə'miːbə) *n, pl* **amebae** (-biː) *or* **amebas.** the usual US spelling of **amoeba.**
▸**a'mebic** *adj*

ameer (ə'mɪə) *n* a variant spelling of **emir.**

ameliorate ❶ (ə'miːljəˌreɪt) *vb* **ameliorates, ameliorating, ameliorated.** to make or become better. [C18: from F *améliorer* to improve, from OF, from *meillor* better, from L *melior*]
▸**aˌmelio'ration** *n* ▸**a'meliorative** *adj* ▸**a'melioˌrator** *n*

> **USAGE NOTE** *Ameliorate* is often wrongly used where *alleviate* is meant. *Ameliorate* is properly used to mean 'improve', not 'make easier to bear', so one should talk about *alleviating* pain or hardship, not *ameliorating* it.

amen (ˌeɪ'mɛn, ˌɑː'mɛn) *sentence substitute.* **1** so be it!: a term used at the end of a prayer. ◆ *n* **2** the use of the word *amen.* [C13: via LL via Gk from Heb. *āmēn* certainly]

amenable ❶ (ə'miːnəbᵊl) *adj* **1** likely to listen, cooperate, etc. **2** accountable to some authority; answerable. **3** capable of being tested, judged, etc. [C16: from Anglo-F, from OF, from L *mināre* to drive (cattle), from *minārī* to threaten]
▸**aˌmena'bility** *or* **a'menableness** *n* ▸**a'menably** *adv*

amend ❶ (ə'mɛnd) *vb (tr)* **1** to improve; change for the better. **2** to correct. **3** to alter or revise (legislation, etc.) by formal procedure. [C13: from OF, from L *ēmendāre* to EMEND]
▸**a'mendable** *adj* ▸**a'mender** *n*

amendment ❶ (ə'mɛndmənt) *n* **1** correction. **2** an addition or alteration to a document, etc.

amends ❶ (ə'mɛndz) *n (functioning as sing)* recompense or compensation for some injury, insult, etc.: *to make amends.* [C13: from OF, from *amende* compensation, from *amender* to EMEND]

amenity ❶ (ə'miːnɪtɪ) *n, pl* **amenities. 1** *(often pl)* a useful or pleasant facility: *a swimming pool was one of the amenities.* **2** the fact or condition of being agreeable. **3** *(usually pl)* a social courtesy. [C14: from L, from *amoenus* agreeable]

amenorrhoea *or esp. US* **amenorrhea** (æˌmɛnə'rɪə, eɪ-) *n* abnormal absence of menstruation. [C19: from A-[1] + MENO- + -RRHOEA]

ament ('æmənt) *n* another name for **catkin.** Also called: **amentum** (ə'mɛntəm). [C18: from L *āmentum* thong]
▸ˌ**amen'taceous** *adj*

amentia (ə'mɛnʃə) *n* severe mental deficiency, usually congenital. [C14: from L: insanity, from *āmēns* mad, from *mēns* mind]

amerce (ə'mɜːs) *vb* **amerces, amercing, amerced.** *(tr) Obs.* **1** *Law.* to punish by a fine. **2** to punish with any arbitrary penalty. [C14: from Anglo-F, from OF *à merci* at the mercy; see MERCY]
▸**a'mercement** *n*

American ❶ (ə'mɛrɪkən) *adj* **1** of or relating to the United States of America, its inhabitants, or their form of English. **2** of or relating to the American continent. ◆ *n* **3** a native or citizen of the US. **4** a native or inhabitant of any country of North, Central, or South America. **5** the English language as spoken or written in the United States.

Americana (əˌmɛrɪ'kɑːnə) *pl n* objects, such as documents, relics, etc., relating to America.

American aloe *n* See **aloe** (sense 2).

American Civil War *n* see **Civil War** (sense 2).

American Dream *n* **the.** the notion that the American social, economic, and political system makes success possible for every individual.

American football *n* **1** a team game similar to rugby, with 11 players on each side. **2** the oval-shaped inflated ball used in this game.

American Indian *n* **1** Also called: **Indian, Amerindian, Native American.** a member of any of the indigenous peoples of America, typically having straight black hair and a yellow-to-brown skin. ◆ *adj* **2** Also called: **Amerindian.** of or relating to any of these peoples, their languages, or their cultures.

Americanism (ə'mɛrɪkəˌnɪzəm) *n* **1** a custom, linguistic usage, or other feature peculiar to or characteristic of the United States. **2** loyalty to the United States.

Americanize *or* **Americanise** (ə'mɛrɪkəˌnaɪz) *vb* **Americanizes, Americanizing, Americanized** *or* **Americanises, Americanising, Americanised.** to make or become American in outlook, attitudes, etc.
▸**Aˌmericani'zation** *or* **Aˌmericani'sation** *n*

American Revolution *n* the usual US term for War of American Independence.

americium (ˌæmə'rɪsɪəm) *n* a white metallic transuranic element artificially produced from plutonium. It is used as an alpha-particle source. Symbol: Am; atomic no.: 95; half-life of most stable isotope, ^{243}Am: 7.4×10^3 years.

Amerindian (ˌæmə'rɪndɪən) *n also* **Amerind** ('æmərɪnd), *adj* another word for **American Indian.**
▸ˌ**Amer'indic** *adj*

amethyst ('æmɪθɪst) *n* **1** a purple or violet variety of quartz used as a gemstone. **2** a purple variety of sapphire. **3a** the purple colour of amethyst. **3b** *(as adj): amethyst shadow.* [C13: from OF, from L, from Gk *amethustos,* lit.: not drunken, from A-[1] + *methuein* to make drunk; from the belief that the stone could prevent intoxication]
▸**amethystine** (ˌæmɪ'θɪstaɪn) *adj*

Amex ('æmɛks) *n acronym for* **1** *Trademark.* American Express. **2** American Stock Exchange.

AMF *abbrev. for* Australian Military Forces.

Amharic (æm'hærɪk) *n* **1** the official language of Ethiopia. ◆ *adj* **2** denoting this language.

amiable ❶ ('eɪmɪəbᵊl) *adj* having or displaying a pleasant or agreeable nature; friendly. [C14: from OF, from LL *amīcābilis* AMICABLE]
▸ˌ**amia'bility** *or* **'amiableness** *n* ▸**'amiably** *adv*

amianthus (ˌæmɪ'ænθəs) *n* any of the fine silky varieties of asbestos. [C17: from L *amiantus,* from Gk *amiantos* unsullied, from A-[1] + *miainein* to pollute]

amicable ❶ ('æmɪkəbᵊl) *adj* characterized by friendliness: *an amicable agreement.* [C15: from LL *amīcābilis,* from L *amīcus* friend]
▸ˌ**amica'bility** *or* **'amicableness** *n* ▸**'amicably** *adv*

THESAURUS

ambush *n* **1-3** = **trap**, ambuscade, attack, concealment, cover, hiding, hiding place, lying in wait, retreat, shelter, waylaying ◆ *vb* **5, 6** = **trap**, ambuscade, attack, bushwhack (*US*), ensnare, surprise, waylay

ameliorate *vb* = **improve**, advance, allay, alleviate, amend, assuage, benefit, better, ease, elevate, make better, meliorate, mend, mitigate, promote, raise, reform, relieve

amelioration *n* = **improvement**, advance, amendment, betterment, change for the better, correction, enhancement, melioration, recovery, upswing

amenability *n* **1** = **receptiveness**, accessibility, acquiescence, agreeableness, compliance, cooperativeness *or* co-operativeness, impressionability, malleability, open-mindedness, openness, persuadability, perviousness, pliancy *or* pliantness, readiness, responsiveness, suggestibleness, susceptibility, tractability, willingness
Antonyms *n* doggedness, fixedness, headstrongness, imperviousness, obduracy *or* obdurateness, obstinacy, self-willedness, single-mindedness, steadfastness, stubbornness

amenable *adj* **1** = **receptive**, able to be influenced, acquiescent, agreeable, compliant, open, persuadable, responsive, susceptible, tractable
Antonyms *adj* inflexible, intractable, mulish, obdurate, obstinate, pig-headed, recalcitrant, stiff-necked, stubborn, unbending, unyielding

amend *vb* **1-3** = **change**, alter, ameliorate, better, correct, enhance, fix, improve, mend, modify, rectify, reform, remedy, repair, revise, tweak (*inf.*)

amendment *n* **1** = **change**, alteration, amelioration, betterment, correction, emendation, enhancement, improvement, mending, modification, rectification, reform, remedy, repair, revision **2** = **alteration**, addendum, addition, adjunct, attachment, clarification

amends *pl n* = **compensation**, apology, atonement, expiation, indemnity, recompense, redress, reparation, requital, restitution, restoration, satisfaction

amenity *n* **1** = **facility**, advantage, comfort, convenience, service **2** = **courtesy**, affability, agreeableness, amiability, complaisance, mildness, pleasantness, politeness, refinement, suavity
Antonyms *n* ≠ **courtesy**: bad manners, discourtesy, impoliteness, incivility, rudeness, ungraciousness

American *adj* **1** = **Yankee** *or* **Yank**, stateside, U.S. ◆ *n* **3** = **Yankee** *or* **Yank**, Yankee Doodle

amiability *n* = **pleasantness**, affability, agreeableness, amiableness, attractiveness, benignity, charm, cheerfulness, delightfulness, engagingness, friendliness, friendship, geniality, good humour, good nature, kindliness, kindness, lovableness, pleasingness, sociability, sweetness, winsomeness

amiable *adj* = **pleasant**, affable, agreeable, attractive, benign, charming, cheerful, congenial, delightful, engaging, friendly, genial, good-humoured, good-natured, kind, kindly, likable *or* likeable, lovable, obliging, pleasing, sociable, sweet-tempered, winning, winsome
Antonyms *adj* disagreeable, displeasing, hostile, ill-natured, loathsome, repellent, sour, unfriendly, unpleasant

amicability *n* = **friendliness**, amiability, amicableness, amity, brotherliness, civility, cordiality, courtesy, fraternity, friendship, goodwill,

amice ('æmɪs) *n Christianity.* a rectangular piece of white linen worn by priests around the neck and shoulders under the alb or, formerly, on the head. [C15: from OF, from L *amictus* cloak]

amicus curiae (æ'mi:kʊs 'kjʊərɪ,i:) *n, pl* **amici curiae** (æ'mi:kaɪ) *Law.* a person, not directly engaged in a case, who advises the court. [L, lit.: friend of the court]

amid ❶ (ə'mɪd) *or* **amidst** *prep* in the middle of; among. [OE *on middan* in the middle]

amide ('æmaɪd) *n* **1** any organic compound containing the group $-CONR_2$, where R denotes a hydrogen atom or a hydrocarbon group. **2** (*modifier*) containing the group $-CONR_2$: *amide group or radical.* **3** an inorganic compound containing the NH_2^- ion and having the general formula $M(NH_2)_x$, where M is a metal atom. [C19: from AM(MONIA) + -IDE]

amidships (ə'mɪdʃɪps) *adv, adj (postpositive) Naut.* at, near, or towards the centre of a vessel.

amigo (æ'mi:gəʊ, ə-) *n, pl* **amigos.** a friend; comrade. [Sp., from L *amicus*]

amine (ə'mi:n, 'æmɪn) *n* an organic base formed by replacing one or more of the hydrogen atoms of ammonia by hydrocarbon groups. [C19: from AM(MONIUM) + -INE[2]]

amino (ə'mi:nəʊ) *n (modifier)* of or containing the group of atoms $-NH_2$: *amino radical.*

amino acid *n* **1** any of a group of organic compounds containing one or more amino groups, $-NH_2$, and one or more carboxyl groups, $-COOH$. **2** any of a group of organic nitrogenous compounds that form the component molecules of proteins.

amino resin *n* a thermosetting synthetic resin used as an adhesive and coating for paper and textiles.

amir (ə'mɪə) *n* a variant spelling of **emir.** [C19: from Ar., var. of EMIR]
▸**a'mirate** *n*

Amish ('æmɪʃ, 'ɑ:-) *adj* of a US and Canadian Mennonite sect. [C19: from G *Amisch,* after Jakob *Amman,* 17th-cent. Swiss Mennonite bishop]

amiss ❶ (ə'mɪs) *adv* **1** in an incorrect or defective manner. **2 take (something) amiss.** to be annoyed or offended by (something). ◆ *adj* **3** (*postpositive*) wrong or faulty. [C13 *a mis,* from *mis* wrong]

amitosis (,æmɪ'təʊsɪs) *n* a form of cell division in which the nucleus and cytoplasm divide without the formation of chromosomes. [C20: from A-[1] + MITOSIS]
▸**amitotic** (,æmɪ'tɒtɪk) *adj*

amity ❶ ('æmɪtɪ) *n, pl* **amities.** friendship; cordiality. [C15: from OF *amité,* ult. from L *amīcus* friend]

ammeter ('æm,mi:tə) *n* an instrument for measuring an electric current in amperes. [C19: AM(PERE) + -METER]

ammo ('æməʊ) *n Inf.* short for **ammunition.**

ammonia (ə'məʊnɪə) *n* **1** a colourless pungent gas used in the manufacture of fertilizers and as a refrigerant and solvent. Formula: NH_3. **2** a solution of ammonia in water, containing ammonium hydroxide. [C18: from NL, from L (*sal*) *ammōniacus* (sal) AMMONIAC]

ammoniac (ə'məʊnɪ,æk) *n* a gum resin obtained from the stems of an Asian plant and formerly used as a stimulant, perfume, and in porcelain cement. Also called: **gum ammoniac.** [C14: from L, from Gk *ammōniakos* belonging to Ammon (apparently the gum resin was extracted from plants found in Libya near the temple of Ammon)]

ammoniacal (,æmə'naɪək[ə]l) *adj* of, containing, or resembling ammonia.

ammoniate (ə'məʊnɪ,eɪt) *vb* **ammoniates, ammoniating, ammoniated.** to unite or treat with ammonia.
▸**am,moni'ation** *n*

ammonify (ə'mɒnɪ,faɪ) *vb* **ammonifies, ammonifying, ammonified.** to treat or impregnate with ammonia or a compound of ammonia.
▸**am,monifi'cation** *n*

ammonite ('æmə,naɪt) *n* **1** any extinct marine cephalopod mollusc of the order *Ammonoidea,* which were common in Mesozoic times and had a coiled partitioned shell. **2** the shell of any of these animals, commonly occurring as a fossil. [C18: from L *cornū Ammōnis,* lit.: horn of Ammon]

ammonium (ə'məʊnɪəm) *n (modifier)* of or containing the monovalent group NH_4– or the ion NH_4^+: *ammonium compounds.*

ammonium chloride *n* a white soluble crystalline solid used as an electrolyte in dry batteries. Formula: NH_4Cl. Also called: **sal ammoniac.**

ammonium hydroxide *n* a compound existing in solution when ammonia is dissolved in water. Formula: NH_4OH.

ammonium sulphate *n* a white soluble crystalline solid used mainly as a fertilizer and in water purification. Formula: $(NH_4)_2SO_4$.

ammunition ❶ (,æmjʊ'nɪʃən) *n* **1** any projectiles, such as bullets, rockets, etc., that can be discharged from a weapon. **2** bombs, missiles, chemicals, etc., capable of use as weapons. **3** any means of defence or attack, as in an argument. [C17: from obs. F *amunition,* by mistaken division from earlier *la munition;* see MUNITION]

amnesia (æm'ni:zjə, -ʒjə, -zɪə) *n* a defect in memory, esp. one resulting from a pathological cause. [C19: via NL from Gk: forgetfulness, prob. from *amnēstia* oblivion]
▸**amnesiac** (æm'ni:zɪ,æk) *or* **amnesic** (æm'ni:sɪk, -zɪk) *adj, n*

amnesty ❶ ('æmnɪstɪ) *n, pl* **amnesties. 1** a general pardon, esp. for offences against a government. **2** a period during which a law is suspended to allow offenders to admit their crime without fear of prosecution. ◆ *vb* **amnesties, amnestying, amnestied. 3** (*tr*) to overlook or forget (an offence). [C16: from L *amnēstia,* from Gk: oblivion, from A-[1] + *-mnēstos,* from *mnasthai* to remember]

Amnesty International *n* an international organization that works to secure the release of people imprisoned for their beliefs, to ban the use of torture, and to abolish the death penalty. Abbrev.: **AI.**

amniocentesis (,æmnɪəʊsɛn'ti:sɪs) *n, pl* **amniocenteses** (-si:z). removal of amniotic fluid for diagnostic purposes by the insertion into the womb of a hollow needle. [C20: from AMNION + *centesis* from Gk *kentēsis* from *kentein* to prick]

amnion ('æmnɪən) *n, pl* **amnions** *or* **amnia** (-nɪə). the innermost of two membranes enclosing an embryonic reptile, bird, or mammal. [C17: via NL from Gk: a little lamb, from *amnos* a lamb]
▸**amniotic** (,æmnɪ'ɒtɪk) *adj*

amniotic fluid *n* the fluid surrounding the fetus in the womb.

amoeba *or US* **ameba** (ə'mi:bə) *n, pl* **amoebae** (-bi:) *or* **amoebas** *or US* **amebae** *or* **amebas.** any of a phylum of protozoans able to change shape because of the movements of cell processes. They live in fresh water or soil or as parasites in man and animals. [C19: from NL, from Gk, from *ameibein* to change, exchange]
▸**a'moebic** *or US* **a'mebic** *adj*

amok ❶ (ə'mʌk, ə'mɒk) *or* **amuck** (ə'mʌk) *n* **1** a state of murderous frenzy. ◆ *adv* **2 run amok.** to run about as with a frenzied desire to kill. [C17: from Malay *amoq* furious assault]

among ❶ (ə'mʌŋ) *or* **amongst** *prep* **1** in the midst of: *he lived among the Indians.* **2** to each of: *divide the reward among yourselves.* **3** in the group, class, or number of: *among the greatest writers.* **4** taken out of (a group): *he is one among many.* **5** with one another within a group: *decide it among yourselves.* **6** in the general opinion or practice of: *accepted among experts.* [OE *amang,* contracted from *on gemang* in the group of, from ON + *gemang* crowd]

> **USAGE NOTE** See at **between.**

amontillado (ə,mɒntɪ'lɑ:dəʊ) *n* a medium-dry sherry. [C19: from Sp. *vino amontillado* wine of *Montilla,* town in Spain]

amoral ❶ (,eɪ'mɒrəl) *adj* **1** having no moral quality; nonmoral. **2** without moral standards or principles.
▸**amorality** (,eɪmɒ'rælɪtɪ) *n*

> **USAGE NOTE** *Amoral* is often wrongly used where *immoral* is meant. *Immoral* is properly used to talk about the breaking of moral rules, *amoral* about people who have no moral code or about places or situations where moral considerations do not apply.

amorist ('æmərɪst) *n* a lover or a writer about love.

amoroso (,æmə'rəʊsəʊ) *adj, adv* **1** *Music.* (to be played) tenderly. ◆ *n* **2** a rich sweet sherry. [from It. & Sp.: AMOROUS]

amorous ❶ ('æmərəs) *adj* **1** inclined towards or displaying love or de-

THESAURUS

harmony, kindliness, kindness, neighbourliness, peace, peaceableness, peacefulness, politeness, sociability

amicable *adj* = **friendly**, amiable, brotherly, civil, cordial, courteous, fraternal, good-humoured, harmonious, kind, kindly, neighbourly, peaceable, peaceful, polite, sociable
Antonyms *adj* antagonistic, bellicose, belligerent, disagreeable, hostile, ill-disposed, impolite, inimical, pugnacious, quarrelsome, uncivil, unfriendly, unkind, unsociable

amid *prep* = **in the middle of**, among, amongst, in the midst of, in the thick of, surrounded by

amiss *adv* **1** = **wrongly**, erroneously, faultily, improperly, inappropriately, incorrectly, mistakenly, unsuitably **2** *As in* **take (something) amiss** = **as an insult**, as offensive, out of turn, wrongly ◆ *adj* **3** = **wrong**, awry, confused, defective, erroneous, fallacious, false, faulty, improper, inaccurate, inappropriate, incorrect, mistaken, out of order, unsuitable, untoward
Antonyms *adv* ≠ **wrongly**: appropriately, correctly, properly, rightly, suitably, well ◆ *adj* ≠ **wrong**: accurate, appropriate, correct, in order, O.K. *or* okay (*inf.*), perfect, proper, right, suitable, true

amity *n* = **friendship**, accord, amicability, brotherhood, comity, comradeship, concord, cordiality, fellowship, fraternity, friendliness, goodwill, harmony, kindliness, peace, peacefulness, tranquillity, understanding

ammunition *n* **1** = **munitions**, armaments, cartridges, explosives, materiel, powder, rounds, shells, shot, shot and shell

amnesty *n* **1** = **general pardon**, absolution, condonation, dispensation, forgiveness, immunity, oblivion, remission (*of penalty*), reprieve

amok *adv* **2** *As in* **run amok** = **madly**, berserk, destructively, ferociously, frenziedly, in a frenzy, insanely, maniacally, murderously, savagely, uncontrollably, violently, wildly

among *prep* **1** = **in the midst of**, amid, amidst, in association with, in the middle of, in the thick of, midst, surrounded by, together with, with **2** = **to each of**, between **3** = **in the group of**, in the class of, in the company of, in the number of, out of

amoral *adj* **1, 2** = **unethical**, nonmoral, unvirtuous

amorous *adj* **1, 2** = **loving**, affectionate, amatory, ardent, attached, doting, enamoured, erotic, fond, impassioned, in love, lovesick, lustful, passionate, tender

sire. **2** in love. **3** of or relating to love. [C14: from OF, from Med. L, from L *amor* love]
▸ **'amorously** *adv* ▸ **'amorousness** *n*

amorphous ❶ (əˈmɔːfəs) *adj* **1** lacking a definite shape. **2** of no recognizable character or type. **3** (of rocks, etc.) not having a crystalline structure. [C18: from NL, from Gk, from A-[1] + *morphē* shape]
▸ **a'morphism** *n* ▸ **a'morphousness** *n*

amortize *or* **amortise** (əˈmɔːtaɪz) *vb* **amortizes, amortizing, amortized** *or* **amortises, amortising, amortised.** (*tr*) **1** *Finance.* to liquidate (a debt, mortgage, etc.) by payments or by periodic transfers to a sinking fund. **2** to write off (a wasting asset) by transfers to a sinking fund. **3** *Property law.* (formerly) to transfer (lands, etc.) in mortmain. [C14: from Med. L, from OF *amortir* to reduce to the point of death, ult. from L *ad* to + *mors* death]
▸ **a,morti'zation** *or* **a,morti'sation** *n*

amount ❶ (əˈmaʊnt) *n* **1** extent; quantity. **2** the total of two or more quantities. **3** the full value or significance of something. **4** a principal sum plus the interest on it, as in a loan. ◆ *vb* **5** (*intr;* usually foll. by *to*) to be equal or add up. [C13: from OF *amonter* to go up, from *amont* upwards, from *a* to + *mont* mountain (from L *mōns*)]

USAGE NOTE The use of a plural noun after *amount of* (*an amount of bananas; the amount of refugees*) should be avoided: *a quantity of bananas; the number of refugees.*

amount of substance *n* a measure of the number of entities (atoms, molecules, ions, electrons, etc.) present in a substance, expressed in moles.

amour ❶ (əˈmʊə) *n* a love affair, esp. a secret or illicit one. [C13: from OF, from L *amor* love]

amour-propre *French.* (amurprɔprə) *n* self-respect.

amp (æmp) *n* **1** an ampere. **2** *Inf.* an amplifier.

AMP *n Biochem.* adenosine monophosphate; a substance produced by hydrolysis of ATP with the liberation of energy. The cyclic form (**cyclic AMP**) acts as a messenger in many hormone-induced biochemical reactions.

ampelopsis (ˌæmpɪˈlɒpsɪs) *n* any of a genus of woody climbing plants of tropical and subtropical Asia and America. [C19: from NL, from Gk *ampelos* grapevine]

amperage (ˈæmpərɪdʒ) *n* the strength of an electric current measured in amperes.

ampere (ˈæmpɛə) *n* **1** the basic SI unit of electric current; the constant current that, when maintained in two parallel conductors of infinite length and negligible cross section placed 1 metre apart in free space, produces a force of 2×10^{-7} newton per metre between them. **2** a former unit of electric current (**international ampere**); the current that, when passed through a solution of silver nitrate, deposits silver at the rate of 0.001118 gram per second. ◆ Abbrev.: **amp.** Symbol: A

ampere-turn *n* a unit of magnetomotive force; the magnetomotive force produced by a current of 1 ampere passing through one complete turn of a coil.

ampersand (ˈæmpəˌsænd) *n* the character (&), meaning *and: John Brown & Co.* [C19: shortened from *and per se and,* that is, the symbol & by itself (represents) *and*]

amphetamine (æmˈfetəˌmiːn) *n* a synthetic colourless liquid used medicinally as the white crystalline sulphate, mainly for its stimulant action on the central nervous system. [C20: from A(LPHA) + M(ETHYL) + PH(ENYL) + ET(HYL) + AMINE]

amphi- *prefix* **1** on both sides; at both ends; of both kinds: *amphipod; amphibious.* **2** around: *amphibole.* [from Gk]

amphibian (æmˈfɪbɪən) *n* **1** any cold-blooded vertebrate of the class *Amphibia,* typically living on land but breeding in water. The class includes newts, frogs, and toads. **2** an aircraft able to land and take off from both water and land. **3** any vehicle able to travel on both water and land. ◆ *adj* **4** another word for **amphibious. 5** of or belonging to the class *Amphibia.*

amphibious (æmˈfɪbɪəs) *adj* **1** able to live both on land and in the water, as frogs, etc. **2** designed for operation on or from both water and land. **3** relating to military forces and operations launched from the sea against an enemy shore. **4** having a dual or mixed nature. [C17: from Gk *amphibios,* lit.: having a double life, from AMPHI- + *bios* life]
▸ **am'phibiousness** *n*

amphibole (ˈæmfɪˌbəʊl) *n* any of a large group of minerals consisting of the silicates of calcium, iron, magnesium, sodium, and aluminium, which are common constituents of igneous rocks. [C17: from F, from Gk *amphibolos* uncertain; so called from the large number of varieties in the group]

amphibology (ˌæmfɪˈbɒlədʒɪ) *or* **amphiboly** (æmˈfɪbəlɪ) *n, pl* **amphibologies** *or* **amphibolies.** ambiguity of expression, esp. when due to a grammatical construction, as in *save rags and waste paper.* [C14: from LL, ult. from Gk *amphibolos* ambiguous]

amphimixis (ˌæmfɪˈmɪksɪs) *n, pl* **amphimixes** (-ˈmɪksiːz). true sexual reproduction, esp. the fusion of gametes from two organisms. [C19: from AMPHI- + Gk *mixis* a blending]
▸ **amphimictic** (ˌæmfɪˈmɪktɪk) *adj*

amphioxus (ˌæmfɪˈɒksəs) *n, pl* **amphioxi** (-ˈɒksaɪ) *or* **amphioxuses.** another name for the **lancelet.** [C19: from NL, from AMPHI- + Gk *oxus* sharp]

amphipod (ˈæmfɪˌpɒd) *n* **1** any marine or freshwater crustacean of the order *Amphipoda,* such as the sand hoppers, in which the body is laterally compressed. ◆ *adj* **2** of or belonging to the *Amphipoda.*

amphiprostyle (æmˈfɪprəˌstaɪl) *adj* **1** (esp. of a classical temple) having a set of columns at both ends but not at the sides. ◆ *n* **2** a temple of this kind.

amphisbaena (æmfɪsˈbiːnə) *n, pl* **amphisbaenae** (-niː) *or* **amphisbaenas. 1** a genus of wormlike lizards of tropical America. **2** *Classical myth.* a fabulous serpent with a head at each end. [C16: from L, from Gk *amphisbaina,* from *amphis* both ways + *bainein* to go]

amphitheatre *or US* **amphitheater** (ˈæmfɪˌθɪətə) *n* **1** a building, usually circular or oval, in which tiers of seats rise from a central open arena. **2** a place where contests are held. **3** any level circular area of ground surrounded by higher ground. **4** a gallery in a theatre. **5** a lecture room in which seats are tiered away from a central area.

amphora (ˈæmfərə) *n, pl* **amphorae** (-fəˌriː) *or* **amphoras.** a Greek or Roman two-handled narrow-necked jar for oil, etc. [C17: from L, from Gk, from AMPHI- + *phoreus* bearer, from *pherein* to bear]

amphoteric (ˌæmfəˈterɪk) *adj Chem.* able to function as either a base or an acid. [C19: from Gk *amphoteros* each of two (from *amphō* both) + -IC]

ampicillin (ˌæmpɪˈsɪlɪn) *n* a form of penicillin used to treat various infections.

ample ❶ (ˈæmpᵊl) *adj* **1** more than sufficient: *an ample helping.* **2** large: *of ample proportions.* [C15: from OF, from L *amplus* spacious]
▸ **'ampleness** *n*

amplification ❶ (ˌæmplɪfɪˈkeɪʃən) *n* **1** the act or result of amplifying. **2** material added to a statement, story, etc., to expand or clarify it. **3** a statement, story, etc., with such additional material. **4** *Electronics.* the increase in strength of an electrical signal by means of an amplifier.

amplifier (ˈæmplɪˌfaɪə) *n* **1** an electronic device used to increase the strength of the current fed into it, esp. one for the amplification of sound signals in a radio, record player, etc. **2** *Photog.* an additional lens for altering focal length. **3** a person or thing that amplifies.

amplify ❶ (ˈæmplɪˌfaɪ) *vb* **amplifies, amplifying, amplified. 1** (*tr*) to increase in size, extent, effect, etc., as by the addition of extra material. **2** *Electronics.* to produce amplification of (electrical signals). **3** (*intr*) to expand a speech, narrative, etc. [C15: from OF, ult. from L *amplificāre* to enlarge, from *amplus* spacious + *facere* to make]

amplitude ❶ (ˈæmplɪˌtjuːd) *n* **1** greatness of extent; magnitude. **2** abundance. **3** breadth or scope, as of the mind. **4** *Astron.* the angular distance along the horizon measured from true east or west to the point of intersection of the vertical circle passing through a celestial body. **5** *Physics.* the maximum displacement from the zero or mean position of a periodic motion. [C16: from L, from *amplus* spacious]

amplitude modulation *n* one of the principal methods of transmitting information using radio waves, the relevant signal being superimposed onto a radio-frequency carrier wave. The frequency of the carrier wave remains unchanged but its amplitude is varied in accordance with the amplitude of the input signal. Cf. **frequency modulation.**

THESAURUS

Antonyms *adj* aloof, cold, distant, frigid, frosty, indifferent, passionless, stand-offish, undemonstrative, unfeeling, unloving

amorousness *n* **1, 2 = desire,** affection, ardour, concupiscence, fondness, lovingness, lust, passion, the hots (*sl.*)

amorphous *adj* **1, 2 = shapeless,** characterless, formless, inchoate, indeterminate, irregular, nebulous, nondescript, unformed, unshaped, unshapen, unstructured, vague
Antonyms *adj* definite, distinct, regular, shaped, structured

amount *n* **1 = quantity,** bulk, expanse, extent, lot, magnitude, mass, measure, number, supply, volume **2 = total,** addition, aggregate, entirety, extent, lot, sum, sum total, whole **3 = importance,** full effect, full value, import, result, significance ◆ *vb* **5 = add up to,** aggregate, become, come to, develop into, equal, grow, mean, purport, total

amour *n* **= love affair,** affair, *affaire de coeur,* intrigue, liaison, relationship, romance

ample *adj* **1, 2 = plenty,** abounding, abundant, big, bountiful, broad, capacious, commodious, copious, enough and to spare, expansive, extensive, full, generous, great, large, lavish, liberal, plenteous, plentiful, profuse, rich, roomy, spacious, substantial, two a penny, unrestricted, voluminous, wide
Antonyms *adj* inadequate, insufficient, little, meagre, restricted, scant, skimpy, small, sparse, unsatisfactory

amplification *n* **1 = increase,** augmentation, boosting, deepening, dilation, enlargement, expansion, extension, heightening, intensification, lengthening, magnification, raising, strengthening, stretching, widening **2 = explanation,** augmentation, development, elaboration, expansion, expatiation, fleshing out, rounding out, supplementing

amplify *vb* **1 = expand,** augment, boost, deepen, dilate, enlarge, extend, heighten, increase, intensify, lengthen, magnify, raise, strengthen, stretch, widen **3 = go into detail,** augment, develop, elaborate, enlarge, expand, expatiate, explain, flesh out, round out, supplement
Antonyms *vb* ≠ **expand:** boil down, condense, curtail, cut down, decrease, reduce ≠ **go into detail:** abbreviate, abridge, simplify

amplitude *n* **1, 3 = extent,** bigness, breadth, bulk, capaciousness, compass, dimension, expanse, greatness, hugeness, largeness, magnitude, mass, range, reach, scope, size, spaciousness, sweep, vastness, width **2 = fullness,** abundance, ampleness, completeness,

amply ⓣ ('æmplɪ) *adv* fully; generously.

ampoule ('æmpu:l, -pju:l) *or esp. US* **ampule** *n Med.* a small glass vessel in which liquids for injection are hermetically sealed. [C19: from F, from L: see AMPULLA]

ampulla (æm'pʊlə) *n, pl* **ampullae** (-'pʊli:). **1** *Anat.* the dilated end part of certain ducts or canals. **2** *Christianity.* **2a** a vessel for the wine and water used at the Eucharist. **2b** a small flask for consecrated oil. **3** a Roman two-handled bottle for oil, wine, or perfume. [C16: from L, dim. of AMPHORA]

amputate ⓣ ('æmpjʊˌteɪt) *vb* **amputates, amputating, amputated.** *Surgery.* to remove (all or part of a limb). [C17: from L, from *am-* around + *putāre* to trim, prune]
▸ˌ**ampu'tation** *n*

amputee (ˌæmpjʊ'ti:) *n* a person who has had a limb amputated.

amu *abbrev. for* atomic mass unit.

amuck ⓣ (ə'mʌk) *n, adv* a variant spelling of **amok.**

amulet ⓣ ('æmjʊlɪt) *n* a trinket or piece of jewellery worn as a protection against evil; charm. [C17: from L *amulētum,* from ?]

amuse ⓣ (ə'mju:z) *vb* **amuses, amusing, amused.** (*tr*) **1** to entertain; divert. **2** to cause to laugh or smile. [C15: from OF *amuser* to cause to be idle, from *muser* to MUSE[1]]

amusement ⓣ (ə'mju:zmənt) *n* **1** something that amuses, such as a game or pastime. **2** a mechanical device used for entertainment, as at a fair. **3** the act of amusing or the state or quality of being amused.

amusement arcade *n Brit.* a covered area having coin-operated game machines.

amusing ⓣ (ə'mju:zɪŋ) *adj* entertaining; causing a smile or laugh.
▸**a'musingly** *adv*

amygdalin (ə'mɪgdəlɪn) *n* a white soluble bitter-tasting glycoside extracted from bitter almonds. [C17: from Gk: ALMOND + -IN]

amyl ('æmɪl) *n* (*modifier*) (no longer in technical usage) of or containing any of eight isomeric forms of the monovalent group C_5H_{11}–: *amyl group or radical.* [C19: from L: AMYLUM]

amylaceous (ˌæmɪ'leɪʃəs) *adj* of or resembling starch.

amyl alcohol *n* **1** any of eight isomeric alcohols with the general formula $C_5H_{11}OH$. **2** a mixture of these alcohols, used in preparing amyl nitrite.

amylase ('æmɪˌleɪz) *n* any of several enzymes that hydrolyse starch and glycogen to simple sugars, such as glucose.

amyl nitrite *n* an ester of amyl alcohol and nitrous acid used as a vasodilator, esp. to treat angina.

amyloid ('æmɪˌlɔɪd) *n* **1** any substance resembling starch. ◆ *adj* **2** starchlike.

amylopsin (ˌæmɪ'lɒpsɪn) *n* an enzyme of the pancreatic juice that converts starch into sugar; pancreatic amylase. [C19: from AMYL + (PE)PSIN]

amylum ('æmɪləm) *n* another name for **starch** (senses 1,2). [L, from Gk *amulon* fine meal, starch]

amyotrophic lateral sclerosis (ˌæmɪəʊ'trəʊfɪk) *n* a form of motor neurone disease in which degeneration of motor tracts in the spinal cord causes progressive muscular paralysis starting in the limbs. Also called: **Lou Gehrig's disease.**

Amytal ('æmɪˌtæl) *n Trademark.* sodium amytal, used as a sedative and hypnotic.

an[1] (æn; *unstressed* ən) *determiner* (*indefinite article*) a form of **a**[1], used before an initial vowel sound: *an old car; an elf; an hour.* [OE *ān* ONE]

> **USAGE NOTE** *An* was formerly often used before words that begin with *h* and are unstressed on the first syllable: *an hotel; an historic meeting.* Sometimes the initial *h* was not pronounced. This usage is now becoming obsolete.

an[2] *or* **an'** (æn; *unstressed* ən) *conj* (*subordinating*) an obsolete or dialect word for **if.** See **and** (sense 8).

An *the chemical symbol for* actinon.

an. *abbrev. for* anno. [L: in the year]

an- *or before a consonant* **a-** *prefix* not; without: *anaphrodisiac.* [from Gk]

-an, -ean, *or* **-ian** *suffix.* **1** (*forming adjectives and nouns*) belonging to; coming from; typical of; adhering to: *European; Elizabethan; Christian.* **2** (*forming nouns*) a person who specializes or is expert in: *dietitian.* [from L *-ānus,* suffix of adjectives]

ana- *or before a vowel* **an-** *prefix* **1** up; upwards: *anadromous.* **2** again: *anagram.* **3** back; backwards: *anapaest.* [from Gk *ana*]

-ana *or* **-iana** *suffix forming nouns.* denoting a collection of objects or information relating to a particular individual, subject or place: *Victoriana, Americana.* [NL, from L *-āna,* lit.: matters relating to, neuter pl of *-ānus;* see -AN]

Anabaptist (ˌænə'bæptɪst) *n* **1** a member of any of various Protestant movements, esp. of the 16th century, that rejected infant baptism, insisted that adults be rebaptized, and sought to establish Christian communism. ◆ *adj* **2** of these sects or their doctrines. [C16: from Ecclesiastical L, from *anabaptīzāre* to baptize again, from LGk *anabaptizein*]
▸ˌ**Ana'baptism** *n*

anabas ('ænəˌbæs) *n* any of several freshwater fishes, esp. the climbing perch, that can travel on land. [C19: from NL, from Gk *anabainein* to go up]

anabasis (ə'næbəsɪs) *n, pl* **anabases** (-ˌsi:z). **1** the march of Cyrus the Younger from Sardis to Cunaxa in Babylonia in 401 B.C., described by Xenophon in his *Anabasis.* **2** any military expedition, esp. one from the coast to the interior. [C18: from Gk: a going up, from *anabainein* to go up]

anabatic (ˌænə'bætɪk) *adj Meteorol.* (of air currents) rising upwards. [C19: from Gk *anabatikos* relating to ascents, from *anabainein* to go up]

anabiosis (ˌænəbaɪ'əʊsɪs) *n* the ability to return to life after apparent death; suspended animation. [C19: via NL from Gk, from *anabioein* to come back to life]
▸**anabiotic** (ˌænəbaɪ'ɒtɪk) *adj*

anabolic steroid *n* any of a group of synthetic steroid hormones (androgens) used to stimulate muscle and bone growth for athletic or therapeutic purposes.

anabolism (ə'næbəˌlɪzəm) *n* a metabolic process in which complex molecules are synthesized from simpler ones with the storage of energy; constructive metabolism. [C19: from ANA- + (META)BOLISM]
▸**anabolic** (ˌænə'bɒlɪk) *adj*

anachronism (ə'nækrəˌnɪzəm) *n* **1** the representation of an event, person, or thing in a historical context in which it could not have occurred or existed. **2** a person or thing that belongs or seems to belong to another time. [C17: from L, from Gk *anakhronismos* a mistake in chronology, from ANA- + *khronos* time]
▸**aˌnachro'nistic** *adj* ▸**aˌnachro'nistically** *adv*

anacoluthon (ˌænəkə'lu:θɒn) *n, pl* **anacolutha** (-θə). a construction that involves the change from one grammatical sequence to another within a single sentence. [C18: from LL, from Gk, from *anakolouthos* not consistent, from AN- + *akolouthos* following]

anaconda (ˌænə'kɒndə) *n* a very large nonvenomous arboreal and semiaquatic snake of tropical South America, which kills its prey by constriction. [C18: prob. changed from Sinhalese *henakandayā* whip snake; orig. referring to a snake of Sri Lanka]

anacrusis (ˌænə'kru:sɪs) *n, pl* **anacruses** (-si:z). **1** *Prosody.* one or more unstressed syllables at the beginning of a line of verse. **2** *Music.* an unstressed note or group of notes immediately preceding the strong first beat of the first bar. [C19: from Gk, from *anakrouein* to strike up, from ANA- + *krouein* to strike]

anadromous (ə'nædrəməs) *adj* (of fishes such as the salmon) migrating up rivers from the sea in order to breed. [C18: from Gk *anadromos* running upwards]

anaemia *or US* **anemia** (ə'ni:mɪə) *n* a deficiency in the number of red blood cells or in their haemoglobin content, resulting in pallor and lack of energy. [C19: from NL, from Gk *anaimia* lack of blood, from AN- + *haima* blood]

anaemic ⓣ *or US* **anemic** (ə'ni:mɪk) *adj* **1** relating to or suffering from anaemia. **2** pale and sickly looking; lacking vitality.

anaerobe (æ'neərəʊb, 'ænərəʊb) *or* **anaerobium** (ˌæneə'rəʊbɪəm) *n, pl* **anaerobes** *or* **anaerobia** (-'əʊbɪə). an organism that does not require, or requires the absence of, free oxygen or air.
▸ˌ**anaer'obic** *adj*

anaesthesia *or US* **anesthesia** (ˌænɪs'θi:zɪə) *n* **1** loss of bodily sensation, esp. of touch, as the result of nerve damage or other abnormality. **2** loss of sensation, esp. of pain, induced by drugs: called **general anaesthesia** when consciousness is lost and **local anaesthesia** when only a specific area of the body is involved. [C19: from NL, from Gk *anaisthēsia* absence of sensation]

anaesthetic ⓣ *or US* **anesthetic** (ˌænɪs'θɛtɪk) *n* **1** a substance that causes anaesthesia. ◆ *adj* **2** causing or characterized by anaesthesia.

THESAURUS

copiousness, plenitude, plethora, profusion, richness

amply *adv* = **fully**, abundantly, bountifully, capaciously, completely, copiously, extensively, generously, greatly, lavishly, liberally, plenteously, plentifully, profusely, richly, substantially, thoroughly, unstintingly, well, without stinting
Antonyms *adv* inadequately, insufficiently, meagrely, poorly, scantily, skimpily, sparsely, thinly

amputate *vb* = **cut off**, curtail, lop, remove, separate, sever, truncate

amuck *see* **amok**

amulet *n* = **charm**, fetish, juju, periapt (*rare*), talisman

amuse *vb* **1, 2** = **entertain**, beguile, charm, cheer, delight, divert, enliven, gladden, gratify, interest, occupy, please, recreate, regale, tickle
Antonyms *vb* be tedious, bore, jade, pall on, send to sleep, tire, weary

amusement *n* **1** = **pastime**, distraction, diversion, entertainment, game, hobby, joke, lark, prank, recreation, sport **3** = **entertainment**, beguilement, cheer, delight, diversion, enjoyment, fun, gladdening, gratification, hilarity, interest, laughter, merriment, mirth, pleasing, pleasure, recreation, regalement, sport
Antonyms *n* ≠ **entertainment**: boredom, displeasure, monotony, sadness, tedium

amusing *adj* = **funny**, charming, cheerful, cheering, comical, delightful, diverting, droll, enjoyable, entertaining, facetious, gladdening, gratifying, humorous, interesting, jocular, laughable, lively, merry, pleasant, pleasing, rib-tickling, waggish, witty
Antonyms *adj* boring, dead, dull, flat, humdrum, monotonous, stale, tedious, tiresome, unamusing, unexciting, unfunny, uninteresting, wearisome

anaemic *adj* **2** = **pale**, ashen, bloodless, characterless, colourless, dull, enervated, feeble, frail, infirm, like death warmed up (*inf.*), pallid, sickly, wan, weak
Antonyms *adj* blooming, florid, full-blooded, glowing, hearty, radiant, rosy, rosy-cheeked, rubicund, ruddy, sanguine

anaesthetic *n* **1** = **painkiller**, analgesic, ano-

anaesthetics (ˌænɪsˈθɛtɪks) *n (functioning as sing)* the science of anaesthesia and its application. US name: **anesthesiology.**

anaesthetist (əˈniːsθətɪst) *n* **1** *Brit.* a doctor specializing in the administration of anaesthetics. US name: **anesthesiologist. 2** *US.* See **anesthetist.**

anaesthetize, anaesthetise, *or US* **anesthetize** (əˈniːsθəˌtaɪz) *vb* **anaesthetizes, anaesthetizing, anaesthetized** *or* **anaesthetises, anaesthetising, anaesthetised** *or* **anesthetizes, anesthetizing, anesthetized.** *(tr)* to render insensible to pain by administering an anaesthetic.
▸**aˌnaesthetiˈzation, aˌnaesthetiˈsation,** *or US* **aˌnesthetiˈzation** *n*

anaglyph (ˈænəˌglɪf) *n* **1** *Photog.* a stereoscopic picture consisting of two images of the same object, taken from slightly different angles, in two complementary colours. When viewed through coloured spectacles, the images merge to produce a stereoscopic sensation. **2** anything cut to stand in low relief, such as a cameo. [C17: from Gk *anagluphē* carved in low relief, from ANA- + *gluphē* carving, from *gluphein* to carve]
▸**ˌanaˈglyphic** *adj*

Anaglypta (ˌænəˈglɪptə) *n Trademark.* a type of thick embossed wallpaper designed to be painted. [C19: from Gk *anagluptos;* see ANAGLYPH]

anagram (ˈænəˌgræm) *n* a word or phrase the letters of which can be rearranged into another word or phrase. [C16: from NL, from Gk, from *anagrammatizein* to transpose letters, from ANA- + *gramma* a letter]
▸**anagrammatic** (ˌænəgrəˈmætɪk) *or* **ˌanagramˈmatical** *adj*

anagrammatize *or* **anagrammatise** (ˌænəˈgræməˌtaɪz) *vb* **anagrammatizes, anagrammatizing, anagrammatized** *or* **anagrammatises, anagrammatising, anagrammatised.** to arrange into an anagram.

anal (ˈeɪn(ə)l) *adj* **1** of or near the anus. **2** *Psychoanal.* relating to a stage of psychosexual development during which the child's interest is concentrated on the anal region and excremental functions. [C18: from NL *ānālis;* see ANUS]
▸**ˈanally** *adv*

analects (ˈænəˌlɛkts) *or* **analecta** (ˌænəˈlɛktə) *pl n* selected literary passages from one or more works. [C17: via L from Gk, from *analegein* to collect up, from *legein* to gather]

analeptic (ˌæn(ə)ˈlɛptɪk) *adj* **1** (of a drug, etc.) restorative or invigorating. ◆ *n* **2** a restorative remedy or drug. [C17: from NL, from Gk *analēptikos* stimulating, from *analambanein* to take up]

anal fin *n* an unpaired fin between the anus and tail fin in fishes that maintains equilibrium.

analgesia (ˌæn(ə)lˈdʒiːzɪə) *or* **analgia** (ænˈældʒɪə) *n* inability to feel pain. [C18: via NL from Gk: insensibility, from AN- + *algēsis* sense of pain]

analgesic (ˌæn(ə)lˈdʒiːzɪk) *adj* **1** of or causing analgesia. ◆ *n* **2** a substance that produces analgesia.

analog (ˈænəˌlɒg) *n* a variant spelling of **analogue.**

> **USAGE NOTE** The spelling *analog* is a US variant of *analogue* in all its senses, and is also the generally preferred spelling in the computer industry.

analog computer *n* a computer that performs arithmetical operations using a variable physical quantity, such as mechanical movement or voltage, to represent numbers.

analogize *or* **analogise** (əˈnæləˌdʒaɪz) *vb* **analogizes, analogizing, analogized** *or* **analogises, analogising, analogised. 1** *(intr)* to make use of analogy, as in argument. **2** *(tr)* to make analogous or reveal analogy in.

analogous ❶ (əˈnæləgəs) *adj* **1** similar or corresponding in some respect. **2** *Biol.* (of organs and parts) having the same function but different evolutionary origin. **3** *Linguistics.* formed by analogy: *an analogous plural.* [C17: from L, from Gk *analogos* proportionate, from ANA- + *logos* speech, ratio]

> **USAGE NOTE** The use of *with* after *analogous* should be avoided: *swimming has no event that is analogous to* (not *with*) *the 100 metres in athletics.*

analogue *or US (sometimes)* **analog** (ˈæn(ə)ˌlɒg) *n* **1a** a physical object or quantity used to measure or represent another quantity. **1b** *(as modifier): analogue watch; analogue recording.* **2** something analogous to something else. **3** *Biol.* an analogous part or organ.

> **USAGE NOTE** See at **analog.**

analogy ❶ (əˈnælədʒɪ) *n, pl* **analogies. 1** agreement or similarity, esp. in a limited number of features. **2** a comparison made to show such a similarity: *an analogy between an atom and the solar system.* **3** *Biol.* the relationship between analogous organs or parts. **4** *Logic, maths, philosophy.* a form of reasoning in which a similarity between two or more things is inferred from a known similarity between them in other respects. **5** *Linguistics.* imitation of existing models or regular patterns in the formation of words, etc.: *a child may use "sheeps" as the plural of "sheep" by analogy with "cat," "cats," etc.* [C16: from Gk *analogia* correspondence, from *analogos* ANALOGOUS]
▸**analogical** (ˌænəˈlɒdʒɪk(ə)l) *adj*

anal retentive *Psychoanal.* ◆ *n* **1** a person who exhibits anal personality traits, such as orderliness, meanness, stubbornness, etc. ◆ *adj* **anal-retentive. 2** exhibiting anal personality traits, such as orderliness, meanness, stubbornness, etc.

analysand (əˈnælɪˌsænd) *n* any person who is undergoing psychoanalysis. [C20: from ANALYSE + *-and,* on the model of *multiplicand*]

analyse ❶ *or US* **analyze** (ˈæn(ə)ˌlaɪz) *vb* **analyses, analysing, analysed** *or US* **analyzes, analyzing, analyzed.** *(tr)* **1** to examine in detail in order to discover meaning, essential features, etc. **2** to break down into components or essential features. **3** to make a mathematical, chemical, etc., analysis of. **4** another word for **psychoanalyse.** [C17: back formation from ANALYSIS]
▸**ˈanaˌlyser** *or US* **ˈanaˌlyzer** *n*

analysis ❶ (əˈnælɪsɪs) *n, pl* **analyses** (-ˌsiːz). **1** the division of a physical or abstract whole into its constituent parts to examine or determine their relationship. **2** a statement of the results of this. **3** short for **psychoanalysis. 4** *Chem.* **4a** the decomposition of a substance in order to determine the kinds of constituents present (**qualitative analysis**) or the amount of each constituent (**quantitative analysis**). **4b** the result obtained by such a determination. **5** *Linguistics.* the use of word order together with word function to express syntactic relations in a language, as opposed to the use of inflections. **6** *Maths.* the branch of mathematics principally concerned with the properties of functions. **7 in the last, final,** *or* **ultimate analysis.** after everything has been given due consideration. [C16: from NL, from Gk *analusis,* lit.: a dissolving, from ANA- + *luein* to loosen]

analysis of variance *n Statistics.* a technique for analysing the total variation of a set of observations as measured by the variance of the observations multiplied by their number.

analyst (ˈænəlɪst) *n* **1** a person who analyses or is skilled in analysis. **2** short for **psychoanalyst.**

analytic ❶ (ˌænəˈlɪtɪk) *or* **analytical** *adj* **1** relating to analysis. **2** capable of or given to analysing: *an analytic mind.* **3** *Linguistics.* denoting languages characterized by analysis. **4** *Logic.* (of a proposition) true or false by virtue of the meanings of the words alone: *all spinsters are unmarried* is analytically true. [C16: via LL from Gk *analutikos,* from *analuein* to dissolve, break down]
▸**ˌanaˈlytically** *adv* ▸**analyticity** (ˌænəlɪˈtɪsɪtɪ) *n*

analytical geometry *n* the branch of geometry that uses algebraic notation to locate a point; coordinate geometry.

analytic philosophy *n* See **philosophical analysis.**

anandrous (ænˈændrəs) *adj* (of flowers) having no stamens. [C19: from Gk *anandros* lacking males, from AN- + *anēr* man]

anapaest *or* **anapest** (ˈænəpɛst, -piːst) *n Prosody.* a metrical foot of three syllables, the first two short, the last long (⏑⏑–). [C17: via L from Gk *anapaistos* reversed, from *ana-* back + *paiein* to strike]
▸**ˌanaˈpaestic** *or* **ˌanaˈpestic** *adj*

anaphora (əˈnæfərə) *n* **1** *Grammar.* the use of a word such as a pronoun to avoid repetition, as for example *one* in *He offered me a drink but I didn't want one.* **2** *Rhetoric.* the repetition of a word or phrase at the beginning of successive clauses. [C16: via L from Gk: repetition, from ANA- + *pherein* to bear]

anaphrodisiac (ˌænæfrəˈdɪzɪˌæk) *adj* **1** tending to lessen sexual desire. ◆ *n* **2** an anaphrodisiac drug.

anaphylaxis (ˌænəfɪˈlæksɪs) *n* extreme sensitivity to an injected antigen following a previous injection. [C20: from ANA- + (PRO)PHYLAXIS]

anaplasmosis (ˌænəplæzˈməʊsɪs) *n* another name for **gallsickness.**

anaptyxis (ˌænæpˈtɪksɪs) *n, pl* **anaptyxes** (-ˈtɪksiːz). the insertion of a short vowel between consonants in order to make a word more easily pronounceable. [C19: via NL from Gk *anaptuxis,* from *anaptussein* to unfold, from ANA- + *ptussein* to fold]

anarchism (ˈænəˌkɪzəm) *n* **1** *Political theory.* a doctrine advocating the abolition of government. **2** the principles or practice of anarchists.

anarchist ❶ (ˈænəkɪst) *n* **1** a person who advocates a society based on

THESAURUS

dyne, narcotic, opiate, sedative, soporific, stupefacient, stupefactive ◆ *adj* **2** = **pain-killing,** analgesic, anodyne, deadening, dulling, narcotic, numbing, opiate, sedative, sleep-inducing, soporific, stupefacient, stupefactive

analogous *adj* **1** = **similar,** agreeing, akin, alike, comparable, corresponding, equivalent, homologous, like, of a piece, parallel, related, resembling
Antonyms *adj* contrasting, different, discrepant, disparate, dissimilar, diverse, unlike

analogy *n* **1, 2** = **similarity,** agreement, comparison, correlation, correspondence, equivalence, homology, likeness, parallel, relation, resemblance, similitude

analyse *vb* **1** = **examine,** assay, estimate, evaluate, interpret, investigate, judge, research, test, work over **2** = **break down,** anatomize, consider, dissect, dissolve, divide, resolve, separate, study, think through

analysis *n* **1** = **finding,** estimation, evaluation, interpretation, judgment, opinion, reasoning, study **1** = **examination,** anatomization, anatomy, assay, breakdown, dissection, dissolution, division, inquiry, investigation, perusal, resolution, scrutiny, separation, sifting, test

analytic *adj* **1, 2** = **rational,** detailed, diagnostic, discrete, dissecting, explanatory, expository, inquiring, inquisitive, interpretative, interpretive, investigative, logical, organized, problem-solving, questioning, searching, studious, systematic, testing

anarchic *adj* **1-4** = **lawless,** chaotic, confused, disordered, disorganized, misgoverned, misruled, off the rails, rebellious, revolutionary, rioting, riotous, ungoverned
Antonyms *adj* controlled, decorous, disciplined, law-abiding, ordered, peaceable, peaceful, quiet, restrained, well-behaved

anarchist *n* **1, 2** = **revolutionary,** insurgent, nihilist, rebel, terrorist

voluntary cooperation and the abolition of government. **2** a person who causes disorder or upheaval.

anarchy Ⓣ ('ænəkɪ) *n* **1** general lawlessness and disorder, esp. when thought to result from an absence or failure of government. **2** the absence of government. **3** the absence of any guiding or uniting principle; chaos. **4** political anarchism. [C16: from Med. L, from Gk, from *anarkhos* without a ruler, from AN- + *arkh-* leader, from *arkhein* to rule]
▸**anarchic** (æn'ɑːkɪk) *or* **an'archical** *adj*

anastigmat (æ'næstɪgmæt, ˌænə'stɪgmæt) *n* a lens system designed to be free of astigmatism. [C19: from AN- + ASTIGMATIC]
▸**ˌanastig'matic** *adj*

anastomose (ə'næstəˌməʊz) *vb* **anastomoses, anastomosing, anastomosed.** to join (two parts of a blood vessel, etc.) by anastomosis.

anastomosis (əˌnæstə'məʊsɪs) *n, pl* **anastomoses** (-siːz). **1** a natural connection between two tubular structures, such as blood vessels. **2** the union of two hollow parts that are normally separate. [C16: via NL from Gk: opening, from *anastomoun* to equip with a mouth, from *stoma* mouth]

anastrophe (ə'næstrəfɪ) *n Rhetoric.* another term for **inversion** (sense 3). [C16: from Gk, from *anastrephein* to invert]

anathema Ⓣ (ə'næθəmə) *n, pl* **anathemas. 1** a detested person or thing: *he is anathema to me.* **2** a formal ecclesiastical excommunication, or denunciation of a doctrine. **3** the person or thing so cursed. **4** a strong curse. [C16: via Church L from Gk: something accursed, from *anatithenai* to dedicate, from ANA- + *tithenai* to set]

anathematize *or* **anathematise** (ə'næθɪməˌtaɪz) *vb* **anathematizes, anathematizing, anathematized** *or* **anathematises, anathematising, anathematised.** to pronounce an anathema (upon a person, etc.); curse.

anatomical (ˌænə'tɒmɪk°l) *adj* of anatomy.

anatomist (ə'nætəmɪst) *n* an expert in anatomy.

anatomize *or* **anatomise** (ə'nætəˌmaɪz) *vb* **anatomizes, anatomizing, anatomized** *or* **anatomises, anatomising, anatomised.** (*tr*) **1** to dissect (an animal or plant). **2** to examine in minute detail.

anatomy Ⓣ (ə'nætəmɪ) *n, pl* **anatomies. 1** the science concerned with the physical structure of animals and plants. **2** the physical structure of an animal or plant or any of its parts. **3** a book or treatise on this subject. **4** dissection of an animal or plant. **5** any detailed analysis: *the anatomy of a crime.* **6** *Inf.* the human body. [C14: from L, from Gk *anatomē,* from ANA- + *temnein* to cut]

anatto (ə'nætəʊ) *n, pl* **anattos.** a variant spelling of **annatto.**

ANC *abbrev. for* African National Congress.

-ance *or* **-ancy** *suffix forming nouns.* indicating an action, state or condition, or quality: *resemblance; tenancy.* [via OF from L *-antia*]

ancestor Ⓣ ('ænsɛstə) *n* **1** a person from whom another is directly descended; forefather. **2** an early animal or plant from which a later type has evolved. **3** a person or thing regarded as a forerunner: *the ancestor of the modern camera.* [C13: from OF, from LL *antecēssor* one who goes before, from L *antecēdere*]
▸**'ancestress** *fem n*

ancestral Ⓣ (æn'sɛstrəl) *adj* of or inherited from ancestors.

ancestry Ⓣ ('ænsɛstrɪ) *n, pl* **ancestries. 1** lineage or descent, esp. when noble or distinguished. **2** ancestors collectively.

anchor Ⓣ ('æŋkə) *n* **1** a device attached to a vessel by a cable and dropped overboard so as to grip the bottom and restrict movement. **2** an object used to hold something else firmly in place: *the rock provided an anchor for the rope.* **3** a source of stability or security. **4** short for **anchorman** *or* **anchorwoman. 5 cast, come to,** *or* **drop anchor.** to anchor a vessel. **6 ride at anchor.** to be anchored. ◆ *vb* **7** to use an anchor to hold (a vessel) in one place. **8** to fasten or be fastened securely; fix or become fixed firmly. ◆ See also **anchors.** [OE *ancor,* from L, from Gk *ankura*]

anchorage Ⓣ ('æŋkərɪdʒ) *n* **1** the act of anchoring. **2** any place where a vessel is anchored. **3** a place designated for vessels to anchor. **4** a fee imposed for anchoring. **5** anything used as an anchor. **6** a source of security or strength.

anchorite Ⓣ ('æŋkəˌraɪt) *n* a person who lives in seclusion, esp. a religious recluse; hermit. [C15: from Med. L, from LL, from Gk, from *anakhōrein* to retire, from *khōra* a space]
▸**'anchoress** *fem n*

anchorman ('æŋkəmæn) *n, pl* **anchormen. 1** *Sport.* the last person in a team to compete, esp. in a relay race. **2** (in broadcasting) a person in a central studio who links up and maintains contact with various outside camera units, reporters, etc.
▸**'anchorˌwoman** *fem n*

anchors ('æŋkəz) *pl n Sl.* the brakes of a motor vehicle: *he rammed on the anchors.*

anchovy ('æntʃəvɪ) *n, pl* **anchovies** *or* **anchovy.** any of various small marine food fishes which have a salty taste and are often tinned or made into a paste or essence. [C16: from Sp. *anchova,* ? ult. from Gk *aphuē* small fish]

anchusa (æŋ'kjuːsə) *n* any of several Eurasian plants having rough hairy stems and leaves and blue flowers. [C18: from L]

anchylose ('æŋkɪˌləʊz) *vb* a variant spelling of **ankylose.**

ancien régime *French.* (ɑ̃sjɛ̃ reʒim) *n, pl* ***anciens régimes*** (ɑ̃sjɛ̃ reʒim). the political and social system of France before the Revolution of 1789. [lit.: old regime]

ancient Ⓣ ('eɪnʃənt) *adj* **1** dating from very long ago: *ancient ruins.* **2** very old. **3** of the far past, esp. before the collapse of the Western Roman Empire (476 A.D.). ◆ *n* **4** (*often pl*) a member of a civilized nation in the ancient world, esp. a Greek or Roman. **5** (*often pl*) one of the classical authors of Greek or Roman antiquity. **6** *Arch.* an old man. [C14: from OF *ancien,* from Vulgar L *anteanus* (unattested), from L *ante* before]
▸**'ancientness** *n*

ancient lights *n* (*usually functioning as sing*) the legal right to receive, by a particular window or windows, adequate and unobstructed daylight.

anciently ('eɪnʃəntlɪ) *adv* in ancient times.

ancillary Ⓣ (æn'sɪlərɪ) *adj* **1** subsidiary. **2** auxiliary; supplementary: *ancillary services.* ◆ *n, pl* **ancillaries. 3** a subsidiary or auxiliary thing or person. [C17: from L *ancillāris* concerning maidservants, ult. from *ancūla* female servant]

ancon ('æŋkɒn) *or* **ancone** ('æŋkəʊn) *n, pl* **ancones** (æŋ'kəʊniːz). *Architect.* a projecting bracket or console supporting a cornice. [C18: from Gk *ankōn* a bend]

-ancy *suffix forming nouns.* a variant of **-ance,** indicating condition or quality: *poignancy.*

ancylostomiasis (ˌænsɪˌlɒstə'maɪəsɪs) *or* **ankylostomiasis** (ˌæŋkɪˌlɒstə'maɪəsɪs) *n* infestation of the intestine with blood-sucking hookworms; hookworm disease. [from NL, ult. from Gk *ankulos* hooked + *stoma* mouth]

and Ⓣ (ænd; *unstressed* ənd, ən) *conj* (*coordinating*) **1** in addition to: *boys and girls.* **2** as a consequence: *he fell down and cut his knee.* **3** afterwards: *we pay and go through that door.* **4** plus: *two and two equals four.* **5** used to give emphasis or indicate repetition or continuity: *it rained and rained.* **6** used to express a contrast between instances of what is named: *there are jobs and jobs.* **7** *Inf.* used in place of *to* in infinitives after verbs such as *try, go,* and *come: try and see it my way.* **8** an obsolete word for **if:** *and it please you.* [OE *and*]

> **USAGE NOTE** See at **to.**

-and *or* **-end** *suffix forming nouns.* indicating a person or thing that is to be dealt with in a specified way: *dividend; multiplicand.* [from L gerundives ending in *-andus, -endus*]

andante (æn'dæntɪ) *Music.* ◆ *adj, adv* **1** (to be performed) at a moderately slow tempo. ◆ *n* **2** a passage or piece to be performed in this manner. [C18: from It., from *andare* to walk, from L *ambulāre*]

andantino (ˌændæn'tiːnəʊ) *Music.* ◆ *adj, adv* **1** (to be performed) slightly faster or slower than andante. ◆ *n, pl* **andantinos. 2** a passage or piece to be performed in this manner. [C19: dim. of ANDANTE]

AND circuit *or* **gate** (ænd) *n Computing.* a logic circuit that has a high-voltage output signal if and only if all input signals are at a high voltage simultaneously. Cf. **NAND circuit, NOR circuit, OR circuit.** [C20: from similarity of operation of *and* in logical conjunctions]

andiron ('ændˌaɪən) *n* either of a pair of metal stands for supporting logs in a hearth. [C14: from OF *andier,* from ?; infl. by IRON]

and/or *conj* (*coordinating*) used to join terms when either one or the other or both is indicated: *passports and/or other means of identification.*

> **USAGE NOTE** Many people think that *and/or* is only acceptable in legal and commercial contexts. In other contexts, it is better to use *or both: some alcoholics lose their jobs or their driving licences or both* (not *their jobs and/or their driving licences*).

andro- *or before a vowel* **andr-** *combining form.* **1** male; masculine:

THESAURUS

anarchy *n* **1-4** = **lawlessness,** chaos, confusion, disorder, disorganization, misgovernment, misrule, rebellion, revolution, riot
Antonyms *n* control, discipline, government, law, law and order, order, peace, rule

anathema *n* **1** = **abomination,** bane, bête noire, bugbear, enemy, pariah

anatomy *n* **2** = **structure,** build, composition, frame, framework, make-up **4, 5** = **examination,** analysis, dismemberment, dissection, division, inquiry, investigation, study

ancestor *n* **1, 2** = **forefather,** forebear, forerunner, precursor, predecessor, progenitor
Antonyms *n* descendant, inheritor, issue, offspring, progeny, successor

ancestral *adj* = **inherited,** ancestorial, antecedent, forefatherly, genealogical, hereditary, lineal, patriarchal

ancestry *n* **1, 2** = **origin,** ancestors, antecedents, blood, derivation, descent, extraction, family, forebears, forefathers, genealogy, house, line, lineage, parentage, pedigree, progenitors, race, stock

anchor *n* **1** = **mooring,** bower (*Nautical*), drogue, hook (*Nautical*), kedge, sheet anchor ◆ *vb* **5 cast anchor** = **moor,** come to anchor, dock, drop anchor, drop the hook, kedge, kedge off, lay anchor, let go the anchor, tie up **8** = **secure,** attach, bolt, chain, fasten, fix, tie

anchorage *n* **2, 3** = **berth,** dock, dockage, harbour, harbourage, haven, moorage, port, quay

anchorite *n* = **hermit,** eremite, recluse

ancient *adj* **1-3** = **old,** aged, age-old, antediluvian, antiquated, antique, archaic, bygone, cobwebby, early, hoary, obsolete, old as the hills, olden, old-fashioned, outmoded, out-of-date, primeval, primordial, superannuated, timeworn
Antonyms *adj* current, fresh, in vogue, late, modern, modish, new, newfangled, new-fashioned, novel, recent, state-of-the-art, up-to-date, with it (*inf.*), young

ancillary *adj* **1, 2** = **supplementary,** accessory, additional, auxiliary, contributory, extra, secondary, subordinate, subsidiary, supporting
Antonyms *adj* cardinal, chief, main, major, premier, primary, prime, principal

and *conj* **1** = **also,** along with, as well as, further-

androsterone. **2** (in botany) stamen or anther: *androecium.* [from Gk *anēr* (genitive *andros*) man]
androecium (æn'dri:sɪəm) *n, pl* **androecia** (-sɪə). the stamens of a flowering plant collectively. [C19: from NL, from ANDRO- + Gk *oikion* a little house]
androgen ('ændrədʒən) *n* any of several steroids that promote development of male sexual characteristics.
▸**androgenic** (ˌændrə'dʒɛnɪk) *adj*
androgyne ('ændrəˌdʒaɪn) *n* another word for **hermaphrodite.** [C17: from OF, via L from Gk *androgunos,* from *anēr* man + *gunē* woman]
androgynous ❶ (æn'drɒdʒɪnəs) *adj* **1** *Bot.* having male and female flowers in the same inflorescence. **2** having male and female characteristics; hermaphrodite.
▸**an'drogyny** *n*
android ❶ ('ændrɔɪd) *n* **1** (in science fiction) a robot resembling a human being. ◆ *adj* **2** resembling a human being. [C18: from LGk *androeidēs* manlike; see ANDRO-, -OID]
andrology (æn'drɒlədʒɪ) *n* the branch of medicine concerned with diseases in men, esp. of the reproductive organs. [C20: from ANDRO- + -LOGY]
▸**an'drologist** *n*
androsterone (æn'drɒstəˌrəʊn) *n* an androgenic steroid hormone produced in the testes.
-androus *adj combining form.* (in botany) indicating number or type of stamens: *diandrous.* [from NL, from Gk *-andros,* from *anēr* man]
ane (eɪn) *determiner, pron, n* a Scottish word for **one.**
-ane *suffix forming nouns.* indicating a hydrocarbon of the alkane series: *hexane.* [coined to replace *-ene, -ine,* and *-one*]
anecdotage ('ænɪkˌdəʊtɪdʒ) *n Humorous.* garrulous old age. [from ANECDOTE + -AGE, with play on *dotage*]
anecdote ❶ ('ænɪkˌdəʊt) *n* a short usually amusing account of an incident. [C17: from Med. L, from Gk *anekdotos* unpublished, from AN- + *ekdotos* published]
▸ˌ**anec'dotal** *or* ˌ**anec'dotic** *adj* ▸ˌ**anec'dotalist** *or* '**anec**ˌ**dotist** *n*
anechoic (ˌænɪ'kəʊɪk) *adj* having a low degree of reverberation: *an anechoic recording studio.*
anemia (ə'ni:mɪə) *n* the usual US spelling of **anaemia.**
▸**anemic** (ə'ni:mɪk) *adj*
anemo- *combining form.* indicating wind: *anemometer; anemophilous.* [from Gk *anemos* wind]
anemograph (ə'nɛməʊˌgrɑ:f) *n* a self-recording anemometer.
anemometer (ˌænɪ'mɒmɪtə) *n* an instrument for recording the speed and often the direction of winds. Also called: **wind gauge.**
▸ˌ**ane'mometry** *n* ▸**anemometric** (ˌænɪməʊ'mɛtrɪk) *adj*
anemone (ə'nɛmənɪ) *n* any woodland plant of the genus *Anemone* of N temperate regions, such as the white-flowered **wood anemone** or **windflower.** Some cultivated anemones have coloured flowers. [C16: via L from Gk: windflower, from *anemos* wind]
anemophilous (ˌænɪ'mɒfɪləs) *adj* (of flowering plants such as grasses) pollinated by the wind.
▸ˌ**ane'mophily** *n*
anent (ə'nɛnt) *prep Arch. or Scot.* **1** lying against; alongside. **2** concerning; about. [OE *on efen,* lit.: on even (ground)]
aneroid barometer ('ænəˌrɔɪd) *n* a device for measuring atmospheric pressure without the use of fluids. It consists of a partially evacuated chamber, the lid of which is displaced by variations in air pressure. This displacement is magnified by levers and made to operate a pointer. [C19 *aneroid,* from F, from AN- + Gk *nēros* wet + -OID]
anesthesia (ˌænɪs'θi:zɪə) *n* the usual US spelling of **anaesthesia.**
anesthesiologist (ˌænɪsˌθi:zɪ'ɒlədʒɪst) *n* the US name for an **anaesthetist.**
anesthesiology (ˌænɪsˌθi:zɪ'ɒlədʒɪ) *n* the US name for **anaesthetics.**
anesthetic (ˌænɪs'θɛtɪk) *n, adj* the usual US spelling of **anaesthetic.**
anesthetist (ə'nɛsθətɪst) *n* (in the US) a person qualified to administer anaesthesia, often a nurse or someone other than a physician.
aneurysm *or* **aneurism** ('ænjəˌrɪzəm) *n* a sac formed by abnormal dilation of the weakened wall of a blood vessel. [C15: from Gk *aneurusma,* from *aneurunein* to dilate]
anew ❶ (ə'nju:) *adv* **1** once more. **2** in a different way; afresh. [OE *of nīwe;* see OF, NEW]
angary ('æŋgərɪ) *n Law.* the right of a belligerent state to use the property of a neutral state or to destroy it subject to payment of compensation to the owners. [C19: from F, from LL *angaria* enforced service, from Gk *angaros* courier]
angel ❶ ('eɪndʒəl) *n* **1** one of a class of spiritual beings attendant upon God. In medieval angelology they are divided by rank into nine orders. **2** a divine messenger from God. **3** a guardian spirit. **4** a conventional representation of any of these beings, depicted in human form with wings. **5** *Inf.* a person who is kind, pure, or beautiful. **6** *Inf.* an investor, esp. in a theatrical production. **7** Also called: **angel-noble.** a former English gold coin with a representation of the archangel Michael on it. **8** *Inf.* an unexplained signal on a radar screen. [OE, from LL *angelus,* from Gk *angelos* messenger]
angel cake *or esp. US* **angel food cake** *n* a very light sponge cake made without egg yolks.
angel dust *n* a slang name for **PCP.**
angelfish ('eɪndʒəlˌfɪʃ) *n, pl* **angelfish** *or* **angelfishes. 1** any of various small tropical marine fishes which have a deep flattened brightly coloured body. **2** a South American freshwater fish having a compressed body and large dorsal and anal fins: a popular aquarium fish. **3** a shark with flattened pectoral fins.
angelic ❶ (æn'dʒɛlɪk) *adj* **1** of or relating to angels. **2** Also: **angelical.** resembling an angel in beauty, etc.
▸**an'gelically** *adv*
angelica (æn'dʒɛlɪkə) *n* **1** an umbelliferous plant, the aromatic seeds, leaves, and stems of which are used in medicine and cookery. **2** the candied stems of this plant, used for decorating and flavouring sweet dishes. [C16: from Med. L (*herba*) *angelica* angelic (herb)]
Angelus ('ændʒɪləs) *n RC Church.* **1** a series of prayers recited in the morning, at midday, and in the evening. **2** the bell (**Angelus bell**) signalling the times of these prayers. [C17: L, from *Angelus domini nuntiavit Mariae* the angel of the Lord brought tidings to Mary]
anger ❶ ('æŋgə) *n* **1** a feeling of great annoyance or antagonism as the result of some real or supposed grievance; rage; wrath. ◆ *vb* (*tr*) **2** to make angry; enrage. [C12: from ON *angr* grief]
angina (æn'dʒaɪnə) *n* **1** any disease marked by painful attacks of spasmodic choking. **2** Also called: **angina pectoris** ('pɛktərɪs). a sudden intense pain in the chest, caused by momentary lack of adequate blood supply to the heart muscle. [C16: from L: quinsy, from Gk *ankhonē* a strangling]
angio- *or before a vowel* **angi-** *combining form.* indicating a blood or lymph vessel; seed vessel. [from Gk *angeion* vessel]
angioma (ˌændʒɪ'əʊmə) *n, pl* **angiomas** *or* **angiomata** (-mətə). a tumour consisting of a mass of blood vessels or a mass of lymphatic vessels.
angioplasty ('ændʒɪəˌplæstɪ) *n* a surgical technique for restoring normal blood flow through an artery narrowed or blocked by atherosclerosis, either by inserting a balloon into it or by using a laser beam.
angiosperm ('ændʒɪəˌspɜ:m) *n* any seed-bearing plant in which the ovules are enclosed in an ovary which develops into the fruit after fertilization; any flowering plant. Cf. **gymnosperm.**
▸ˌ**angio'spermous** *adj*
angle[1] ❶ ('æŋgᵊl) *n* **1** the space between two straight lines or two planes that extend from a common point. **2** the shape formed by two such lines or planes. **3** the extent to which one such line or plane diverges from the other, measured in degrees or radians. **4** a recess; corner. **5** point of view: *look at the question from another angle.* **6** See **angle iron.** ◆ *vb* **angles, angling, angled. 7** to move in or bend into angles or an angle. **8** (*tr*) to produce (an article, statement, etc.) with a particular point of view. **9** (*tr*) to present or place at an angle. **10** (*intr*) to turn in a different direction. [C14: from F, from OL *angulus* corner]
angle[2] ❶ ('æŋgᵊl) *vb* **angles, angling, angled.** (*intr*) **1** to fish with a hook and line. **2** (often foll. by *for*) to attempt to get: *he angled for a compliment.* ◆ *n* **3** *Obs.* a fish-hook. [OE *angul* fish-hook]
Angle ('æŋgᵊl) *n* a member of a people from N Germany who invaded and settled large parts of E and N England in the 5th and 6th centuries A.D. [from L *Anglus,* of Gmc origin, an inhabitant of *Angul,* a district in Schleswig, a name identical with OE *angul* hook, ANGLE[2], referring to its shape]
▸'**Anglian** *adj, n*
angle iron *n* an iron or a steel structural bar that has an L-shaped cross section. Also called: **angle, angle bar.**
angle of incidence *n* **1** the angle that a line or beam of radiation makes with a line perpendicular to the surface at the point of incidence. **2** the angle between the chord line of an aircraft wing or tailplane and the aircraft's longitudinal axis.
angle of reflection *n* the angle that a beam of reflected radiation makes with the normal to a surface at the point of reflection.
angle of refraction *n* the angle that a refracted beam of radiation

THESAURUS

more, in addition to, including, moreover, plus, together with
androgynous *adj* **2** = **hermaphrodite,** androgyne, bisexual, epicene, hermaphroditic
android *n* **1** = **robot,** automaton, bionic man *or* woman, cyborg, humanoid, mechanical man
anecdote *n* = **story,** reminiscence, short story, sketch, tale, urban legend, urban myth, yarn
anew *adv* **1** = **again,** afresh, another time, from scratch, from the beginning, once again, once more, over again
angel *n* **1-4** = **divine messenger,** archangel, cherub, guardian spirit, seraph, spiritual being **5** *Informal* = **dear,** beauty, darling, dream, gem, ideal, jewel, paragon, saint, treasure
angelic *adj* **1** = **heavenly,** celestial, cherubic, ethereal, seraphic **2** = **pure,** adorable, beatific, beautiful, entrancing, innocent, lovely, saintly, virtuous
Antonyms *adj* ≠ **heavenly:** demonic, devilish, diabolic, diabolical, fiendish, hellish, infernal, satanic
anger *n* **1** = **rage,** annoyance, antagonism, choler, displeasure, exasperation, fury, ill humour, ill temper, indignation, ire, irritability, irritation, outrage, passion, pique, resentment, seeing red, spleen, temper, vexation, wrath ◆ *vb* **2** = **enrage,** affront, aggravate (*inf.*), annoy, antagonize, displease, exasperate, excite, fret, gall, hassle (*inf.*), incense, infuriate, irritate, madden, make one's blood boil, nettle, offend, outrage, pique, provoke, put one's back up, rile, vex
Antonyms *n* ≠ **rage:** acceptance, amiability, approval, calmness, forgiveness, goodwill, gratification, liking, patience, peace, pleasure ◆ *vb* ≠ **enrage:** appease, calm, pacify, placate, please, soothe
angle[1] *n* **1, 2** = **intersection,** bend, corner, crook, crotch, cusp, edge, elbow, knee, nook, point **5** = **point of view,** approach, aspect, outlook, perspective, position, side, slant, standpoint, take (*inf.*), viewpoint
angle[2] *vb* **1** = **fish,** cast **2** = **be after** (*inf.*), aim for, cast about *or* around for, contrive, fish for,

makes with the normal to the surface between two media at the point of refraction.

angle of repose *n* the maximum angle to the horizontal at which rock, soil, etc., will remain without sliding.

angler ❶ ('æŋglə) *n* **1** a person who fishes with a hook and line. **2** Also called: **angler fish.** any of various spiny-finned fishes which live at the bottom of the sea and typically have a long movable dorsal fin with which they lure their prey.

Anglican ('æŋglɪkən) *adj* **1** denoting or relating to the Church of England or one of the churches in communion with it. ◆ *n* **2** a member of the Anglican Church. [C17: from Med. L, from *Anglicus* English, from L *Anglī* the Angles]
▸ **'Anglican,ism** *n*

Anglicism ('æŋglɪ,sɪzəm) *n* **1** a word, or idiom peculiar to the English language, esp. as spoken in England. **2** an English mannerism, custom, etc. **3** the fact of being English.

anglicize *or* **anglicise** ('æŋglɪ,saɪz) *vb* **anglicizes, anglicizing, anglicized** *or* **anglicises, anglicising, anglicised.** (*sometimes cap.*) to make or become English in outlook, form, etc.

angling ❶ ('æŋglɪŋ) *n* the art or sport of catching fish with a baited hook or other lure, such as a fly; fishing.

Anglo ('æŋgləʊ) *n, pl* **Anglos. 1** *US.* a White inhabitant of the US who is not of Latin extraction. **2** *Canad.* an English-speaking Canadian, esp. one of Anglo-Celtic origin; an Anglo-Canadian.

Anglo- *combining form.* denoting English or England: *Anglo-Saxon.* [from Med. L *Angliī*]

Anglo-American *adj* **1** of relations between England and the United States. ◆ *n* **2** *Chiefly US.* an inhabitant of the United States who was or whose ancestors were born in England.

Anglo-Catholic *adj* **1** of or relating to a group within the Anglican Church that emphasizes the Catholic elements in its teaching and practice. ◆ *n* **2** a member of this group.
▸ **,Anglo-Ca'tholi,cism** *n*

Anglo-French *adj* **1** of England and France. **2** of Anglo-French. ◆ *n* **3** the Norman-French language of medieval England.

Anglo-Indian *adj* **1** of England and India. **2** denoting or relating to Anglo-Indians. **3** (of a word) introduced into English from an Indian language. ◆ *n* **4** a person of mixed English and Indian descent. **5** an English person who lives or has lived for a long time in India.

Anglomania (,æŋgləʊ'meɪnɪə) *n* excessive respect for English customs, etc.
▸ **,Anglo'mani,ac** *n*

Anglo-Norman *adj* **1** relating to the Norman conquerors of England, their society, or their language. ◆ *n* **2** a Norman inhabitant of England after 1066. **3** the Anglo-French language.

Anglophile ('æŋgləʊfɪl, -,faɪl) *or* **Anglophil** *n* a person having admiration for England or the English.

Anglophobe ('æŋgləʊ,fəʊb) *n* **1** a person who hates or fears England or its people. **2** *Canad.* a person who hates or fears Canadian Anglophones.

Anglophone ('æŋglə,fəʊn) (*often not cap.*) ◆ *n* **1** a person who speaks English. ◆ *adj* **2** speaking English.

Anglo-Saxon *n* **1** a member of any of the West Germanic tribes that settled in Britain from the 5th century A.D. **2** the language of these tribes. See **Old English. 3** any White person whose native language is English. **4** *Inf.* plain blunt English. ◆ *adj* **5** forming part of the Germanic element in Modern English: *"forget" is an Anglo-Saxon word.* **6** of the Anglo-Saxons or the Old English language. **7** of the White Protestant culture of Britain, Australia, and the US.

angora (æŋ'gɔːrə) *n* (*sometimes cap.*) **1** the long soft hair of the Angora goat or the fur of the Angora rabbit. **2** yarn, cloth, or clothing made from this hair or fur. **3** (*as modifier*): *an angora sweater.* ◆ See also **mohair.** [from *Angora*, former name of Ankara, in Turkey]

Angora goat (æŋ'gɔːrə) *n* a breed of domestic goat with long soft hair.

Angora rabbit *n* a breed of rabbit with long silky fur.

angostura bark (,æŋgə'stjʊərə) *n* the bitter aromatic bark of certain South American trees, formerly used to reduce fever.

angostura bitters *pl n* (*often cap.*) *Trademark.* a bitter aromatic tonic, used as a flavouring in alcoholic drinks.

angry ❶ ('æŋgrɪ) *adj* **angrier, angriest. 1** feeling or expressing annoyance, animosity, or resentment. **2** suggestive of anger: *angry clouds.* **3** severely inflamed: *an angry sore.*
▸ **'angrily** *adv*

USAGE NOTE It was formerly considered incorrect to talk about being *angry at* a person, but this use is now acceptable.

angst ❶ (æŋst) *n* an acute but nonspecific sense of anxiety or remorse. [G]

angstrom ('æŋstrəm) *n* a unit of length equal to 10^{-10} metre, used principally to express the wavelengths of electromagnetic radiations. Symbol: Å or A Also called: **angstrom unit.**

anguine ('æŋgwɪn) *adj* of or similar to a snake. [C17: from L *anguīnus*, from *anguis* snake]

anguish ❶ ('æŋgwɪʃ) *n* **1** extreme pain or misery; mental or physical torture; agony. ◆ *vb* **2** to afflict or be afflicted with anguish. [C13: from OF *angoisse* a strangling, from L, from *angustus* narrow]
▸ **'anguished** *adj*

angular ❶ ('æŋgjʊlə) *adj* **1** lean or bony. **2** awkward or stiff. **3** having an angle or angles. **4** placed at an angle. **5** measured by an angle or by the rate at which an angle changes; *angular momentum; angular velocity.* [C15: from L *angulāris*, from *angulus* ANGLE[1]]

angularity (,æŋgjʊ'lærɪtɪ) *n, pl* **angularities. 1** the condition of being angular. **2** an angular shape.

anhedral (æn'hiːdrəl) *n* the downward inclination of an aircraft wing in relation to the lateral axis.

anhydride (æn'haɪdraɪd) *n* **1** a compound that has been formed from another compound by dehydration. **2** a compound that forms an acid or base when added to water. [C19: from ANHYDR(OUS) + -IDE]

anhydrous (æn'haɪdrəs) *adj* containing no water, esp. no water of crystallization. [C19: from Gk *anudros*; see AN-, HYDRO-]

anil ('ænɪl) *n* a leguminous West Indian shrub which is a source of indigo. Also called: **indigo.** [C16: from Port., from Ar. *an-nīl*, the indigo]

aniline ('ænɪlɪn, -,liːn) *n* a colourless oily poisonous liquid used in the manufacture of dyes, plastics, and explosives. Formula: $C_6H_5NH_2$.

aniline dye *n* any synthetic dye originally made from aniline, obtained from coal tar.

anima ('ænɪmə) *n* (in Jungian psychology) **a** the feminine principle as present in the male unconscious. **b** the inner personality. [L: air, breath, spirit, fem of ANIMUS]

animadversion (,ænɪmæd'vɜːʃən) *n* criticism or censure.

animadvert (,ænɪmæd'vɜːt) *vb* (*intr*) **1** (usually foll. by *on* or *upon*) to comment with strong criticism (upon); make censorious remarks (about). **2** to make an observation or comment. [C16: from L *animadvertere* to notice, from *animus* mind + *advertere* to turn to]

animal ❶ ('ænɪməl) *n* **1** *Zool.* any living organism characterized by voluntary movement, the possession of specialized sense organs enabling rapid response to stimuli, and the ingestion of complex organic substances. **2** any mammal, esp. except man. **3** a brutish person. **4** *Facetious.* a person or thing (esp. in **no such animal**). ◆ *adj* **5** of, relating to, or derived from animals. **6** of or relating to physical needs or desires; carnal; sensual. [C14: from L, from *animālis* (adj) living, breathing; see ANIMA]

animalcule (,ænɪ'mælkjuːl) *n* a microscopic animal such as an amoeba or rotifer. [C16: from NL *animalculum* a small animal]
▸ **,ani'malcular** *adj*

animal husbandry *n* the science of breeding, rearing, and caring for farm animals.

animalism ('ænɪmə,lɪzəm) *n* **1** preoccupation with physical matters; sensuality. **2** the doctrine that man lacks a spiritual nature. **3** a mode of behaviour typical of animals.

animality (,ænɪ'mælɪtɪ) *n* **1** the animal side of man, as opposed to the intellectual or spiritual. **2** the characteristics of an animal.

animalize *or* **animalise** ('ænɪmə,laɪz) *vb* **animalizes, animalizing, animalized** *or* **animalises, animalising, animalised.** (*tr*) to rouse to brutality or sensuality or make brutal or sensual.
▸ **,animali'zation** *or* **,animali'sation** *n*

animal magnetism *n* **1** the quality of being attractive, esp. to members of the opposite sex. **2** *Obs.* hypnotism.

animal rights *pl n* **a** the rights of animals to be protected from exploitation and abuse by humans. **b** (*as modifier*): *the animal-rights lobby.*

animal spirits *pl n* boisterous exuberance. [from a vital force once supposed to be dispatched by the brain to all points of the body]

animate ❶ *vb* ('ænɪ,meɪt), **animates, animating, animated.** (*tr*) **1** to give life to or cause to come alive. **2** to make energetic or lively. **3** to encourage or inspire. **4** to impart motion to. **5** to record on film or video tape so

THESAURUS

hunt, invite, look for, scheme, seek, set one's sights on, solicit, try for

angler *n* **1** = **fisherman**, fisher

angling *n* = **fishing**

angry *adj* **1** = **furious**, annoyed, antagonized, at daggers drawn, choked, choleric, cross, displeased, enraged, exasperated, heated, hot, ill-tempered, incandescent, incensed, indignant, infuriated, in high dudgeon, irascible, irate, ireful, irritable, irritated, mad (*inf.*), nettled, on the warpath, outraged, passionate, piqued, provoked, raging, resentful, riled, splenetic, tumultuous, up in arms, wrathful
Antonyms *adj* agreeable, amiable, calm, congenial, friendly, gratified, happy, loving, mild, peaceful, pleasant, pleased

angst *n* = **anxiety**, agitation, apprehension, care, disquietude, distress, fretfulness, inquietude, malaise, perturbation, torment, unease, vexation, worry
Antonyms *n* calmness, collectedness, composure, contentment, ease, fulfilment, nonchalance, peace of mind, satisfaction

anguish *n* **1** = **suffering**, agony, distress, grief, heartache, heartbreak, misery, pain, pang, sorrow, throe, torment, torture, woe

anguished *adj* **1** = **suffering**, afflicted, agonized, brokenhearted, distressed, grief-stricken, tormented, tortured, wounded, wretched

angular *adj* **1** = **skinny**, bony, gaunt, lank, lanky, lean, rangy, rawboned, scrawny, spare

animal *n* **1, 2** = **creature**, beast, brute **3** = **brute**, barbarian, beast, monster, savage, wild man ◆ *adj* **6** = **physical**, bestial, bodily, brutish, carnal, fleshly, gross, sensual

animate *vb* **1-3** = **enliven**, activate, breathe life into, embolden, encourage, energize, excite, fire, gee up, gladden, impel, incite, inspire, inspirit, instigate, invigorate, kindle, liven up, move, prod, quicken, revive, rouse, spark, spur, stimulate, stir, urge, vitalize, vivify ◆ *adj* **6** = **liv-**

as to give movement to. ◆ *adj* ('ænɪmɪt). **6** having life. **7** spirited, or lively. [C16: from L *animāre* to make alive, from *anima* breath, spirit]
▸'**ani͵matedly** *adv*

animated cartoon *n* a film produced by photographing a series of gradually changing drawings, etc., which give the illusion of movement when the series is projected rapidly.

animation Ⓣ (͵ænɪ'meɪʃən) *n* **1** vivacity. **2** the condition of being alive. **3** the techniques used in the production of animated cartoons.

animato (͵ænɪ'mɑːtəʊ) *adj, adv Music.* lively; animated. [It.]

animatronics (͵ænɪmə'trɒnɪks) *n* (*functioning as sing*) a branch of film and theatre technology that combines traditional puppetry techniques with electronics to create lifelike animated effects. [C20: from ANIMA(TION) + (ELEC)TRONICS]

animé ('ænɪ͵meɪ, -mɪ) *n* any of various resins, esp. that obtained from a tropical American leguminous tree. [F: from ?]

animism ('ænɪ͵mɪzəm) *n* **1** the belief that natural objects have desires and intentions. **2** (in the philosophies of Plato and Pythagoras) the hypothesis that there is an immaterial force that animates the universe. [C19: from L *anima* vital breath, spirit]
▸**animistic** (͵ænɪ'mɪstɪk) *adj*

animosity Ⓣ (͵ænɪ'mɒsɪtɪ) *n, pl* **animosities.** a powerful and active dislike or hostility. [C15: from LL *animōsitās,* from ANIMUS]

animus Ⓣ ('ænɪməs) *n* **1** intense dislike; hatred; animosity. **2** motive or purpose. **3** (in Jungian psychology) the masculine principle present in the female unconscious. [C19: from L: mind, spirit]

anion ('æn͵aɪən) *n* a negatively charged ion; an ion that is attracted to the anode during electrolysis. Cf. **cation.** [C19: from ANA- + ION]
▸**anionic** (͵ænaɪ'ɒnɪk) *adj*

anise ('ænɪs) *n* a Mediterranean umbelliferous plant having clusters of small yellowish-white flowers and liquorice-flavoured seeds. [C13: from OF *anis,* via L from Gk *anison*]

aniseed ('ænɪ͵siːd) *n* the liquorice-flavoured aromatic seeds of the anise plant, used medicinally for expelling intestinal gas and in cookery.

anisette (͵ænɪ'zɛt, -'sɛt) *n* a liquorice-flavoured liqueur made from aniseed. [C19: from F]

anisotropic (æn͵aɪsəʊ'trɒpɪk) *adj* **1** having different physical properties in different directions: *anisotropic crystals.* **2** (of a plant) responding unequally to an external stimulus in different parts.
▸**an͵iso'tropically** *adv* ▸**anisotropy** (͵ænaɪ'sɒtrəpɪ) *n*

ankh (æŋk) *n* a tau cross with a loop on the top, symbolizing eternal life: often appearing in Egyptian personal names, such as Tutankhamen. [from Egyptian *'nh* life, soul]

ankle ('æŋkᵊl) *n* **1** the joint connecting the leg and the foot. **2** the part of the leg just above the foot. [C14: from ON]

ankle biter *n Austral. sl.* a child.

anklebone ('æŋkᵊl͵bəʊn) *n* the nontechnical name for **talus**[1].

anklet ('æŋklɪt) *n* an ornamental chain worn around the ankle.

ankylose *or* **anchylose** ('æŋkɪ͵ləʊz) *vb* **ankyloses, ankylosing, ankylosed** *or* **anchyloses, anchylosing, anchylosed.** (of bones in a joint, etc.) to fuse or stiffen by ankylosis.

ankylosis *or* **anchylosis** (͵æŋkɪ'ləʊsɪs) *n* abnormal adhesion or immobility of the bones in a joint, as by a fibrous growth of tissues within the joint. [C18: from NL, from Gk *ankuloun* to crook]
▸**ankylotic** *or* **anchylotic** (͵æŋkɪ'lɒtɪk) *adj*

anna ('ænə) *n* a former Indian coin, worth one sixteenth of a rupee. [C18: from Hindi *ānā*]

annals Ⓣ ('ænᵊlz) *pl n* **1** yearly records of events. **2** history in general. **3** regular reports of the work of a society, learned body, etc. [C16: from L (*librī*) *annālēs* yearly (books), from *annus* year]
▸'**annalist** *n* ▸͵**annal'istic** *adj*

annates ('æneɪts, -əts) *pl n RC Church.* the first year's revenue of a see, etc., paid to the pope. [C16: from F, from Med. L *annāta,* from L *annus* year]

annatto *or* **anatto** (ə'nætəʊ) *n, pl* **annattos** *or* **anattos. 1** a small tropical American tree having pulpy seeds that yield a dye. **2** the yellowish-red dye obtained from the seeds of this tree, used for colouring fabrics, butter, varnish, etc. [from Carib]

anneal (ə'niːl) *vb* **1** to temper or toughen (something) by heat treatment to remove internal stress, crystal defects, and dislocations. **2** (*tr*) to toughen or strengthen (the will, determination, etc.). ◆ *n* **3** an act of annealing. [OE *onǣlan,* from ON + *ǣlan* to burn, from *āl* fire]
▸**an'nealer** *n*

annelid ('ænəlɪd) *n* **1** a worm in which the body is divided into segments both externally and internally, as the earthworms. ◆ *adj* **2** of such worms. [C19: from NL *Annelida,* from OF, ult. from L *ānulus* ring]
▸**annelidan** (ə'nɛlɪdən) *n, adj*

annex Ⓣ *vb* (æ'nɛks). (*tr*) **1** to join or add, esp. to something larger. **2** to add (territory) by conquest or occupation. **3** to add or append as a condition, etc. **4** to appropriate without permission. ◆ *n* ('ænɛks). **5** a variant spelling (esp. US) of **annexe.** [C14: from Med. L, from L *annectere* to attach to, from *nectere* to join]
▸**an'nexable** *adj* ▸͵**annex'ation** *n*

annexe Ⓣ *or esp. US* **annex** ('ænɛks) *n* **1a** an extension to a main building. **1b** a building used as an addition to a main one nearby. **2** something added, esp. a supplement to a document.

annihilate Ⓣ (ə'naɪə͵leɪt) *vb* **annihilates, annihilating, annihilated.** (*tr*) **1** to destroy completely; extinguish. **2** *Inf.* to defeat totally, as in argument. [C16: from LL, from L *nihil* nothing]
▸**an͵nihi'lation** *n* ▸**an'nihi͵lator** *n*

anniversary (͵ænɪ'vɜːsərɪ) *n, pl* **anniversaries. 1** the date on which an event occurred in some previous year: *a wedding anniversary.* **2** the celebration of this. ◆ *adj* **3** of or relating to an anniversary. [C13: from L *anniversārius* returning every year, from *annus* year + *vertere* to turn]

anno Domini ('ænəʊ 'dɒmɪ͵naɪ, -͵niː) **1** the full form of **A.D.** ◆ *n* **2** *Inf.* advancing old age. [L: in the year of our Lord]

annotate Ⓣ ('ænəʊ͵teɪt, 'ænə͵teɪt) *vb* **annotates, annotating, annotated.** to supply (a written work) with critical or explanatory notes. [C18: from L *annotāre,* from *nota* mark]
▸'**anno͵tative** *adj* ▸'**anno͵tator** *n*

annotation Ⓣ (͵ænəʊ'teɪʃən, ͵ænə'teɪʃən) *n* **1** the act of annotating. **2** a note added in explanation, etc., esp. of some literary work.

announce Ⓣ (ə'naʊns) *vb* **announces, announcing, announced. 1** (*tr; may take a clause as object*) to make known publicly. **2** (*tr*) to declare the arrival of: *to announce a guest.* **3** (*tr; may take a clause as object*) to presage: *the dark clouds announced rain.* **4** (*intr*) to work as an announcer, as on radio or television. [C15: from OF, from L *annuntiāre,* from *nuntius* messenger]
▸**an'nouncement** *n*

announcer Ⓣ (ə'naʊnsə) *n* a person who announces, esp. one who reads the news, etc., on radio or television.

annoy Ⓣ (ə'nɔɪ) *vb* **1** to irritate or displease. **2** to harass with repeated attacks. [C13: from OF, from LL *inodiāre* to make hateful, from L *in odiō* (*esse*) (to be) hated, from *odium* hatred]
▸**an'noyer** *n* ▸**an'noying** *adj* ▸**an'noyingly** *adv*

THESAURUS

ing, alive, alive and kicking, breathing, live, moving
Antonyms *vb* ≠ **enliven:** check, curb, deaden, deter, devitalize, discourage, dull, inhibit, kill, make lifeless, put a damper on, restrain

animated *adj* **1-3** = **lively**, active, airy, alive and kicking, ardent, brisk, buoyant, dynamic, ebullient, elated, energetic, enthusiastic, excited, fervent, full of beans (*inf.*), gay, passionate, quick, sparky, spirited, sprightly, vibrant, vigorous, vital, vivacious, vivid, zealous, zestful
Antonyms *adj* apathetic, boring, dejected, depressed, dull, inactive, lethargic, lifeless, listless, monotonous, passive

animation *n* **1** = **liveliness**, action, activity, airiness, ardour, brio, briskness, buoyancy, dynamism, ebullience, elation, energy, enthusiasm, excitement, exhilaration, fervour, gaiety, high spirits, life, passion, pep, sparkle, spirit, sprightliness, verve, vibrancy, vigour, vitality, vivacity, zeal, zest, zing (*inf.*)

animosity *n* = **hostility**, acrimony, animus, antagonism, antipathy, bad blood, bitterness, enmity, hate, hatred, ill will, malevolence, malice, malignity, rancour, resentment, virulence
Antonyms *n* amity, benevolence, congeniality, friendliness, friendship, goodwill, harmony, kindness, love, rapport, sympathy

animus *n* **1** = **ill will**, acrimony, animosity, antagonism, antipathy, bad blood, bitterness, enmity, hate, hatred, hostility, malevolence, malice, malignity, rancour, resentment, virulence **2** = **animating force**, intention, motive, purpose, will

annals *pl n* **1-3** = **records**, accounts, archives, chronicles, history, journals, memorials, registers

annex *vb* **1** = **join**, add, adjoin, affix, append, attach, connect, fasten, subjoin, tack, unite **2, 4** = **seize**, acquire, appropriate, arrogate, conquer, expropriate, occupy, take over
Antonyms *vb* ≠ **join:** detach, disconnect, disengage, disjoin, disunite, remove, separate, unfasten

annexation *n* **2, 4** = **seizure**, annexing, appropriation, arrogation, conquest, expropriation, occupation, takeover

annexe *n* **1** = **extension**, ell, supplementary building, wing **2** = **addition**, addendum, adjunct, affix, appendix, attachment, supplement

annihilate *vb* **1** = **destroy**, abolish, eradicate, erase, exterminate, extinguish, extirpate, liquidate, nullify, obliterate, root out, wipe from the face of the earth, wipe out

annihilation *n* **1** = **destruction**, abolition, eradication, erasure, extermination, extinction, extinguishing, extirpation, liquidation, nullification, obliteration, rooting out, wiping out

annihilator *n* **1** = **destroyer**, eradicator, expunger, exterminator, extinguisher, extirpator, nullifier, obliterator

annotate *vb* = **make notes**, commentate, comment on, elucidate, explain, footnote, gloss, illustrate, interpret, make observations, note

annotation *n* **2** = **note**, comment, commentary, elucidation, exegesis, explanation, explication, footnote, gloss, illustration, interpretation, observation

announce *vb* **1** = **make known**, advertise, broadcast, declare, disclose, divulge, give out, intimate, proclaim, promulgate, propound, publish, report, reveal, tell **3** = **be a sign of**, augur, betoken, foretell, harbinger, herald, portend, presage, signal, signify
Antonyms *vb* ≠ **make known:** bury, conceal, cover up, hide, hold back, hush (up), keep back, keep quiet, keep secret, suppress, withhold

announcement *n* **1** = **statement**, advertisement, broadcast, bulletin, communiqué, declaration, disclosure, divulgence, intimation, proclamation, promulgation, publication, report, revelation

announcer *n* = **presenter**, anchor man, anchor woman, broadcaster, commentator, master of ceremonies, newscaster, newsreader, reporter

annoy *vb* **1** = **irritate**, aggravate (*inf.*), anger, badger, bedevil, bore, bother, bug, displease, disturb, exasperate, gall, get (*inf.*), get up one's nose (*inf.*), harass, harry, hassle (*inf.*), incom-

annoyance ❶ (ə'nɔɪəns) *n* **1** the feeling of being annoyed. **2** the act of annoying. **3** a person or thing that annoys.

annual ❶ ('ænjʊəl) *adj* **1** occurring, done, etc., once a year or every year; yearly: *an annual income.* **2** lasting for a year: *an annual subscription.* ◆ *n* **3** a plant that completes its life cycle in one year. **4** a book, magazine, etc., published once every year. [C14: from LL, from L *annuus* yearly, from *annus* year]
▸**'annually** *adv*

annual general meeting *n* the statutory meeting of the directors and shareholders of a company or of the members of a society, held once every financial year. Abbrev.: **AGM.**

annualize *or* **annualise** ('ænjʊə,laɪz) *vb* **annualizes, annualizing, annualized** *or* **annualises, annualising, annualised.** (*tr*) to convert (a rate of interest) to an annual rate when it is quoted for a period less than a year: *an annualized percentage rate.*

annual percentage rate *n* the annual equivalent of a rate of interest when the rate is quoted more frequently than annually, usually monthly. Abbrev.: **APR.**

annual ring *n* a ring indicating one year's growth, seen in the transverse section of stems and roots of woody plants. Also called: **tree ring.**

annuitant (ə'njuːɪtənt) *n* a person in receipt of or entitled to an annuity.

annuity (ə'njuːɪtɪ) *n, pl* **annuities.** a fixed sum payable at specified intervals over a period, such as the recipient's life, or in perpetuity, in return for a premium paid either in instalments or in a single payment. [C15: from F, from Med. L *annuitās*, from L *annuus* ANNUAL]

annul ❶ (ə'nʌl) *vb* **annuls, annulling, annulled.** (*tr*) to make (something, esp. a law or marriage) void; abolish. [C14: from OF, from LL *adnullāre* to bring to nothing, from L *nullus* not any]
▸**an'nullable** *adj*

annular ('ænjʊlə) *adj* ring-shaped. [C16: from L *annulāris*, from *annulus*, *ānulus* ring]

annular eclipse *n* an eclipse of the sun in which the moon does not cover the entire disc of the sun, so that a ring of sunlight surrounds the shadow of the moon.

annular ligament *n Anat.* any of various ligaments that encircle a part, such as the wrist.

annulate ('ænjʊlɪt, -,leɪt) *adj* having, composed of, or marked with rings. [C19: from L *ānulātus*, from *ānulus* a ring]
▸**,annu'lation** *n*

annulet ('ænjʊlɪt) *n* **1** *Archit.* a moulding in the form of a ring. **2** *Heraldry.* a ring-shaped device on a shield. **3** a little ring. [C16: from L *ānulus* ring + -ET]

annulment ❶ (ə'nʌlmənt) *n* **1** a formal invalidation, as of a marriage, judicial proceeding, etc. **2** the act of annulling.

annulus ('ænjʊləs) *n, pl* **annuli** (-,laɪ) *or* **annuluses. 1** the area between two concentric circles. **2** a ring-shaped part. [C16: from L, var. of *ānulus* ring]

annunciate (ə'nʌnsɪ,eɪt, -ʃɪ-) *vb* **annunciates, annunciating, annunciated.** (*tr*) a less common word for **announce.** [C16: from Med L from L *annuntiāre*; see ANNOUNCE]

Annunciation (ə,nʌnsɪ'eɪʃən) *n* **1 the.** the announcement of the Incarnation by the angel Gabriel to the Virgin Mary (Luke 1:26–38). **2** Also called: **Annunciation Day.** the festival commemorating this, on March 25 (Lady Day).

annunciator (ə'nʌnsɪ,eɪtə) *n* **1** a device that gives a visual indication as to which of a number of electric circuits has operated, such as an indicator showing in which room a bell has been rung. **2** a device giving an audible signal indicating the position of a train. **3** an announcer.

annus horribilis ('ænʊs hɒ'riːbɪlɪs) *n* a terrible year. [C20: from L, modelled on ANNUS MIRABILIS, first used by Elizabeth II of the year 1992]

annus mirabilis ('ænʊs mɪ'ræbɪlɪs) *n, pl* **anni mirabiles** ('ænaɪ mɪ'ræbɪliːz). a year of wonders, catastrophes, or other notable events. [L: wonderful year]

anoa (ə'nəʊə) *n* the smallest of the cattle tribe, having small straight horns and inhabiting the island of Celebes in Indonesia. [from a native name in Celebes]

anode ('ænəʊd) *n* **1** the positive electrode in an electrolytic cell or in an electronic valve. **2** the negative terminal of a primary cell. Cf. **cathode.** [C19: from Gk *anodos* a way up, from *hodos* a way; alluding to the movement of the current]
▸**anodal** (eɪ'nəʊdᵊl) *or* **anodic** (ə'nɒdɪk) *adj*

anodize *or* **anodise** ('ænə,daɪz) *vb* **anodizes, anodizing, anodized** *or* **anodises, anodising, anodised.** to coat (a metal, such as aluminium) with a protective oxide film by electrolysis.

anodyne ❶ ('ænə,daɪn) *n* **1** a drug that relieves pain. **2** anything that alleviates mental distress. ◆ *adj* **3** capable of relieving pain or distress. [C16: from L, from Gk *anōdunos* painless, from AN- + *odunē* pain]

anoint ❶ (ə'nɔɪnt) *vb* (*tr*) **1** to smear or rub over with oil. **2** to apply oil to as a sign of consecration or sanctification. [C14: from OF, from L *inunguere*, from IN-[2] + *unguere* to smear with oil]
▸**a'nointer** *n* ▸**a'nointment** *n*

anointing of the sick *n RC Church.* a sacrament in which a person who is seriously ill or dying is anointed by a priest with consecrated oil. Former name: **extreme unction.**

anomalistic (ə,nɒmə'lɪstɪk) *adj* **1** *Astron.* **1a** (of a month) measured between successive perigees of the moon. **1b** (of a year) between successive perihelia of the earth. **2** anomalous.

anomalous ❶ (ə'nɒmələs) *adj* deviating from the normal or usual order, type, etc. [C17: from LL, from Gk *anōmalos* uneven, inconsistent, from AN- + *homalos* even, from *homos* one and the same]
▸**a'nomalousness** *n*

anomaly ❶ (ə'nɒməlɪ) *n, pl* **anomalies. 1** something anomalous. **2** deviation from the normal; irregularity. **3** *Astron.* the angle between a planet, the sun, and the previous perihelion of the planet.

anomie *or* **anomy** ('ænəʊmɪ) *n Sociol.* lack of social or moral standards in an individual or society. [from Gk *anomia* lawlessness, from A-[1] + *nomos* law]
▸**anomic** (ə'nɒmɪk) *adj*

anon ❶ (ə'nɒn) *adv Arch. or literary.* **1** soon. **2 ever and anon.** now and then. [OE *on āne*, lit.: in one, that is, immediately]

anon. *abbrev. for* anonymous.

anonym ('ænənɪm) *n* **1** a less common word for **pseudonym. 2** an anonymous person or publication.

anonymize *or* **anonymise** (ə'nɒnɪ,maɪz) *vb* **anonymizes, anonymizing, anonymized** *or* **anonymises, anonymising, anonymised.** (*tr*) to carry out or organize in such a way as to preserve anonymity: *anonymized AIDS screening.*

anonymous ❶ (ə'nɒnɪməs) *adj* **1** from or by a person, author, etc., whose name is unknown or withheld. **2** having no known name. **3** lacking individual characteristics. **4** (*often cap.*) denoting an organization which provides help to applicants who remain anonymous: *Alcoholics Anonymous.* [C17: via LL from Gk *anōnumos*, from AN- + *onoma* name]
▸**anonymity** (,ænə'nɪmɪtɪ) *n*

anopheles (ə'nɒfɪ,liːz) *n, pl* **anopheles.** any of various mosquitoes constituting the genus *Anopheles*, some species of which transmit the malaria parasite to man. [C19: via NL from Gk *anōphelēs* useless, from AN- + *ōphelein* to help]

anorak ('ænə,ræk) *n* **1** a warm waterproof hip-length jacket usually with a hood. **2** *Inf.* a boring or socially inept person. [from Eskimo *ánorâq*]

anorexia (,ænɒ'reksɪə) *n* **1** loss of appetite. **2** Also called: **anorexia nervosa** (nɜː'vəʊsə). a disorder characterized by fear of becoming fat and refusal of food, leading to debility and even death. [C17: via NL from Gk, from AN- + *orexis* appetite]
▸**,ano'rectic** *or* **,ano'rexic** *adj, n*

THESAURUS

mode, irk, madden, make one's blood boil, molest, needle (*inf.*), nettle, peeve, pester, piss one off (*taboo sl.*), plague, provoke, put one's back up, rile, ruffle, tease, trouble, vex
Antonyms *vb* appease, calm, comfort, console, mollify, solace, soothe

annoyance *n* **1, 2** = **irritation**, aggravation, anger, bedevilment, bother, displeasure, disturbance, exasperation, grief (*inf.*), harassment, hassle (*inf.*), nuisance, provocation, trouble, vexation **3** = **nuisance**, bind (*inf.*), bore, bother, drag (*inf.*), gall, pain (*inf.*), pain in the neck (*inf.*), pest, plague, tease

annoyed *adj* **1** = **irritated**, aggravated (*inf.*), bothered, browned off (*inf.*), displeased, exasperated, harassed, harried, hassled (*inf.*), irked, maddened, miffed (*inf.*), nettled, peeved (*inf.*), piqued, pissed off (*taboo sl.*), riled, ruffled, vexed

annoying *adj* **1** = **irritating**, aggravating, bedevilling, boring, bothersome, displeasing, disturbing, exasperating, galling, harassing, irksome, maddening, peeving (*inf.*), provoking, teasing, troublesome, vexatious
Antonyms *adj* agreeable, amusing, charming, delightful, diverting, enjoyable, entertaining, gratifying, pleasant

annual *adj* **1, 2** = **yearly**, once a year, yearlong

annually *adv* **1** = **yearly**, by the year, each year, every year, once a year, per annum, per year, year after year

annul *vb* = **invalidate**, abolish, abrogate, cancel, countermand, declare *or* render null and void, negate, nullify, obviate, recall, repeal, rescind, retract, reverse, revoke, void
Antonyms *vb* bring back, re-enforce, re-establish, reimpose, reinstate, reintroduce, restore

annulment *n* **1, 2** = **invalidation**, abolition, abrogation, cancellation, countermanding, negation, nullification, recall, repeal, rescindment, rescission, retraction, reversal, revocation, voiding

anodyne *n* **1** = **painkiller**, analgesic, narcotic, pain reliever, palliative ◆ *adj* **3** = **pain-killing**, analgesic, deadening, dulling, narcotic, numbing, pain-relieving, palliative

anoint *vb* **1** = **smear**, daub, embrocate, grease, oil, rub, spread over **2** = **consecrate**, anele (*arch.*), bless, hallow, sanctify

anomalous *adj* = **unusual**, aberrant, abnormal, atypical, bizarre, deviating, eccentric, exceptional, incongruous, inconsistent, irregular, odd, outré, peculiar, rare
Antonyms *adj* common, customary, familiar, natural, normal, ordinary, regular, typical, usual

anomaly *n* **1, 2** = **irregularity**, aberration, abnormality, departure, deviation, eccentricity, exception, incongruity, inconsistency, oddity, peculiarity, rarity

anon *adv* **1** *Archaic or literary* = **soon**, before long, betimes (*arch.*), erelong (*arch. or poetic*), forthwith, in a couple of shakes (*inf.*), presently, promptly, shortly

anonymity *n* **1, 2** = **namelessness**, innominateness **3** = **unremarkability** *or* **unremarkableness**, characterlessness, unsingularity

anonymous *adj* **1, 2** = **unnamed**, incognito, innominate, nameless, unacknowledged, unattested, unauthenticated, uncredited, unidentified, unknown, unsigned **3** = **nondescript**, characterless, undistinguished, unexceptional
Antonyms *adj* ≠ **unnamed:** accredited, acknowledged, attested, authenticated, credited, identified, known, named, signed

DICTIONARY

anosmia (ænˈɒzmɪə, -ˈɒs-) *n* loss of the sense of smell. [C19: from NL, from AN- + Gk *osmē* smell]
▸**anosmatic** (ˌænɒzˈmætɪk) *or* **anˈosmic** *adj*

another (əˈnʌðə) *determiner* **1a** one more: *another chance.* **1b** (*as pron*): *help yourself to another.* **2a** a different: *another era from ours.* **2b** (*as pron*): *to try one, then another.* **3a** a different example of the same sort. **3b** (*as pron*): *we got rid of one, but I think this is another.* [C14: orig. *an other*]

A.N. Other *n Brit.* an unnamed person: used in team lists, etc., to indicate a place that remains to be filled.

anoxia (ænˈɒksɪə) *n* lack or deficiency of oxygen. [C20: from AN- + OX(YGEN) + -IA]
▸**anˈoxic** *adj*

Anschluss (ˈænʃlʊs) *n* a political or economic union, esp. the annexation of Austria by Nazi Germany (1938). [G, from *anschliessen* to join]

anserine (ˈænsəˌraɪn) *adj* of or resembling a goose. [C19: from L *anserīnus,* from *anser* goose]

answer Ⓣ (ˈɑːnsə) *n* **1** a reply, either spoken or written, as to a question, request, letter, or article. **2** a reaction or response: *drunkenness was his answer to disappointment.* **3** a solution, esp. of a mathematical problem. ◆ *vb* **4** (*when tr, may take a clause as object*) to reply or respond (to) by word or act: *to answer a question; to answer the door.* **5** (*tr*) to reply correctly to; solve: *I could answer only three questions.* **6** (*intr;* usually foll. by *to*) to respond or react: *the steering answers to the slightest touch.* **7a** (when *intr,* often foll. by *for*) to meet the requirements (of); be satisfactory (for): *this will answer his needs.* **7b** to be responsible (to a person or for a thing). **8** (when *intr,* foll. by *to*) to match or correspond (esp. in **answer** (*or* **answer to**) **the description**). **9** (*tr*) to give a defence or refutation of (a charge) or in (an argument). [OE *andswaru* an answer; see SWEAR]

answerable Ⓣ (ˈɑːnsərəbəl) *adj* **1** (*postpositive;* foll. by *for* or *to*) responsible or accountable: *answerable to one's boss.* **2** able to be answered.

answer back Ⓣ *vb* (*adv*) to reply rudely to (a person, esp. someone in authority) when one is expected to remain silent.

answering machine *n* a device by which a telephone call is answered automatically and the caller leaves a recorded message. In full: **telephone answering machine.** Also called: **answerphone.**

ant (ænt) *n* **1** a small social insect of a widely distributed hymenopterous family, typically living in highly organized colonies of winged males, wingless sterile females (workers), and fertile females (queens). Related adj: **formic. 2 white ant.** another name for a **termite.** [OE *ǣmette*]

-ant *suffix forming adjectives and nouns.* causing or performing an action or existing in a certain condition: *pleasant; deodorant; servant.* [from L *-ant,* ending of present participles of the first conjugation]

antacid (æntˈæsɪd) *n* **1** a substance used to treat acidity, esp. in the stomach. ◆ *adj* **2** having the properties of this substance.

antagonism Ⓣ (ænˈtægəˌnɪzəm) *n* **1** openly expressed and usually mutual opposition. **2** the inhibiting or nullifying action of one substance or organism on another.

antagonist Ⓣ (ænˈtægənɪst) *n* **1** an opponent or adversary. **2** any muscle that opposes the action of another. **3** a drug that counteracts the effects of another drug.
▸**anˌtagoˈnistic** *adj* ▸**anˌtagoˈnistically** *adv*

antagonize Ⓣ *or* **antagonise** (ænˈtægəˌnaɪz) *vb* **antagonizes, antagonizing, antagonized** *or* **antagonises, antagonising, antagonised.** (*tr*) **1** to make hostile; annoy or irritate. **2** to act in opposition to or counteract. [C17: from Gk, from ANTI- + *agōnizesthai* to strive, from *agōn* contest]
▸**anˌtagoniˈzation** *or* **anˌtagoniˈsation** *n*

antalkali (æntˈælkəˌlaɪ) *n, pl* **antalkalis** *or* **antalkalies.** a substance that neutralizes alkalis.

Antarctic (æntˈɑːktɪk) *adj* of or relating to the south polar regions. [C14: via L from Gk *antarktikos;* see ANTI-, ARCTIC]

Antarctic Circle *n* the imaginary circle around the earth, parallel to the equator, at latitude 66° 32′ S.

ant bear *n* another name for **aardvark.**

ante (ˈæntɪ) *n* **1** the gaming stake put up before the deal in poker by the players. **2** *Inf.* a sum of money representing a person's share, as in a syndicate. **3 up the ante.** *Inf.* to increase the costs, risks, or considerations involved in taking an action or reaching a conclusion. ◆ *vb* **antes, anteing, anted** *or* **anteed. 4** to place (one's stake) in poker. **5** (usually foll. by *up*) *Inf.* to pay.

ante- *prefix* before in time or position: *antedate; antechamber.* [from L]

anteater (ˈæntˌiːtə) *n* any of several toothless mammals having a long tubular snout used for eating termites.

antebellum (ˌæntɪˈbɛləm) *adj* of or during the period before a war, esp. the American Civil War. [L *ante bellum,* lit.: before the war]

antecede (ˌæntɪˈsiːd) *vb* **antecedes, anteceding, anteceded.** (*tr*) to go before; precede. [C17: from L *antecēdere,* from *cēdere* to go]

antecedent Ⓣ (ˌæntɪˈsiːdənt) *n* **1** an event, etc., that happens before another. **2** *Grammar.* a word or phrase to which a pronoun refers. In "People who live in glass houses shouldn't throw stones," *people* is the antecedent of *who.* **3** *Logic.* the first hypothetical clause in a conditional statement. ◆ *adj* **4** preceding in time or order; prior.
▸ˌ**anteˈcedence** *n*

antecedents Ⓣ (ˌæntɪˈsiːdənts) *pl n* **1** ancestry. **2** a person's past history.

antechamber (ˈæntɪˌtʃeɪmbə) *n* an anteroom. [C17: from OF, from It. *anticamera;* see ANTE-, CHAMBER]

antedate Ⓣ (ˈæntɪˌdeɪt) *vb* (*tr*) **1** to be or occur at an earlier date than. **2** to affix or assign a date to (a document, event, etc.) that is earlier than the actual date. **3** to cause to occur sooner. ◆ *n* **4** an earlier date.

antediluvian Ⓣ (ˌæntɪdɪˈluːvɪən) *adj* **1** of the ages before the biblical Flood. **2** old-fashioned. ◆ *n* **3** an antediluvian person or thing. [C17: from ANTE- + L *dīluvium* flood]

antelope (ˈæntɪˌləʊp) *n, pl* **antelopes** *or* **antelope.** any of a group of mammals of Africa and Asia. They are typically graceful, having long legs and horns, and include the gazelles, springbok, impala, and dik-diks. [C15: from OF, from Med. L, from LGk *antholops* a legendary beast]

antemeridian (ˌæntɪməˈrɪdɪən) *adj* before noon; in the morning. [C17: from L]

ante meridiem (ˈæntɪ məˈrɪdɪəm) the full form of **a.m.** [L, from ANTE- + *merīdiēs* midday]

antenatal (ˌæntɪˈneɪtəl) *adj* occurring or present before birth; during pregnancy.

antenna (ænˈtɛnə) *n* **1** (*pl* **antennae** (-niː)) one of a pair of mobile appendages on the heads of insects, crustaceans, etc., that often respond to touch and taste but may be specialized for swimming. **2** (*pl* **antennas**) an aerial. [C17: from L: sail yard, from ?]
▸**anˈtennal** *or* **anˈtennary** *adj*

antenuptial contract (ˌæntɪˈnʌpʃəl) *n* (in South Africa) a marriage contract effected prior to the wedding giving each partner control over his or her property.

antependium (ˌæntɪˈpɛndɪəm) *n, pl* **antependia** (-dɪə). a covering hung over the front of an altar. [C17: from Med. L, from L ANTE- + *pendēre* to hang]

antepenult (ˌæntɪpɪˈnʌlt) *n* the third last syllable in a word. [C16: shortened from L (*syllaba*) *antepaenultima;* see ANTE-, PENULT]

antepenultimate (ˌæntɪpɪˈnʌltɪmɪt) *adj* **1** third from last. ◆ *n* **2** anything that is third from last.

ante-post *adj Brit.* (of a bet) placed before the runners in a race are confirmed.

anterior Ⓣ (ænˈtɪərɪə) *adj* **1** at or towards the front. **2** earlier. **3** *Zool.* of or near the head end. **4** *Bot.* (of part of a flower or leaf) farthest away from the main stem. [C17: from L, comp. of *ante* before]

anteroom Ⓣ (ˈæntɪˌruːm, -ˌrʊm) *n* a room giving entrance to a larger room, often used as a waiting room.

anthelion (ænˈθiːlɪən) *n, pl* **anthelia** (-lɪə). **1** a faint halo sometimes seen in high altitude regions around a shadow cast onto fog. **2** a white spot occasionally appearing at the same height as and opposite to the sun.

THESAURUS

answer *n* **1, 2** = **reply,** acknowledgment, comeback, counterattack, defence, explanation, plea, reaction, refutation, rejoinder, report, resolution, response, retort, return, riposte, solution, vindication ◆ *vb* **4-6** = **reply,** acknowledge, explain, react, refute, rejoin, resolve, respond, retort, return, solve **7a** = **do,** conform, correlate, correspond, fill, fit, fulfil, measure up, meet, pass, qualify, satisfy, serve, suffice, suit, work **7b** = **be responsible for,** be accountable for, be answerable for, be chargeable for, be liable for, be to blame for, take the rap for (*sl.*) **8** = **fit,** agree, confirm, correspond, match, meet
Antonyms *n* ≠ **reply:** inquiry, interrogation, query, question ◆ *vb* ≠ **reply:** ask, inquire, interrogate, query, question

answerable *adj* **1** *usually foll. by* **for** *or* **to** = **responsible,** accountable, amenable, chargeable, liable, subject, to blame

answer back *vb* = **be impertinent,** argue, be cheeky, cheek (*inf.*), contradict, disagree, dispute, rebut, retort, talk back

antagonism *n* **1** = **hostility,** antipathy, competition, conflict, contention, discord, dissension, friction, opposition, rivalry
Antonyms *n* accord, agreement, amity, friendship, harmony, love, peacefulness, sympathy

antagonist *n* **1** = **opponent,** adversary, competitor, contender, enemy, foe, opposer, rival

antagonistic *adj* **1** = **hostile,** adverse, antipathetic, at odds, at variance, averse, conflicting, contentious, ill-disposed, incompatible, in dispute, inimical, opposed, unfriendly

antagonization *n* **1** = **annoyance,** aggravation (*inf.*), exacerbation, grief (*inf.*), hassle (*inf.*), infuriation, irritation, offence, provocation **2** = **hostility,** adverseness, antipathy, aversion, competition, conflict, contention, counteraction, enmity, friction, inimicalness or inimicality, opposition, oppugnancy (*rare*), rivalry, variance

antagonize *vb* **1** = **annoy,** aggravate (*inf.*), alienate, anger, disaffect, estrange, gall, hassle (*inf.*), insult, irritate, offend, piss one off (*taboo sl.*), repel, rub (someone) up the wrong way (*inf.*)
Antonyms *vb* appease, calm, conciliate, disarm, mollify, pacify, placate, propitiate, soothe, win over

antecedent *adj* **4** = **preceding,** anterior, earlier, foregoing, former, precursory, preliminary, previous, prior
Antonyms *adj* after, coming, consequent, ensuing, following, later, posterior, subsequent, succeeding, successive

antecedents *pl n* **1** = **ancestors,** ancestry, blood, descent, extraction, family, forebears, forefathers, genealogy, line, progenitors, stock **2** = **past,** background, history

antedate *vb* **1** = **come first** *or* **before,** anticipate, forego, go before, precede, predate

antediluvian *adj* **1** = **prehistoric,** primeval, primitive, primordial **2** = **old-fashioned,** ancient, antiquated, antique, archaic, obsolete, old as the hills, out-of-date, out of the ark (*inf.*), passé

anterior *adj* **1** = **front,** fore, forward, frontward **2** = **earlier,** antecedent, foregoing, former, introductory, preceding, previous, prior

anteroom *n* = **outer room,** antechamber, foyer, lobby, reception room, vestibule, waiting room

[C17: from LGk, from *anthēlios* opposite the sun, from ANTE- + *hēlios* sun]

anthelmintic (ˌænθɛlˈmɪntɪk) *or* **anthelminthic** (ˌænθɛlˈmɪnθɪk) *n Med.* another name for **vermifuge.**

anthem ● (ˈænθəm) *n* **1** a song of loyalty: *a national anthem.* **2** a musical composition for a choir, usually set to words from the Bible. **3** a religious chant sung antiphonally. [OE *antemne,* from LL *antiphōna* ANTIPHON]

anthemis (ænˈθiːmɪs) *n* any of several cultivated varieties of camomile. [NL, from L, from Gk *anthos* flower]

anther (ˈænθə) *n* the terminal part of a stamen consisting of two lobes each containing two sacs in which the pollen matures. [C18: from NL, from L, from Gk *anthēros* flowery, from *anthos* flower]

antheridium (ˌænθəˈrɪdɪəm) *n, pl* **antheridia** (-ɪə). the male sex organ of algae, fungi, mosses, etc. [C19: from NL, dim. of *anthēra* ANTHER]

ant hill *n* a mound of soil, leaves, etc., near the entrance of an ants' or termites' nest, deposited there by the ants or termites while constructing the nest.

anthologize *or* **anthologise** (ænˈθɒləˌdʒaɪz) *vb* **anthologizes, anthologizing, anthologized** *or* **anthologises, anthologising, anthologised.** to compile or put into an anthology.

anthology ● (ænˈθɒlədʒɪ) *n, pl* **anthologies. 1** a collection of literary passages, esp. poems, by various authors. **2** any printed collection of literary pieces, songs, etc. [C17: from Med. L, from Gk, lit.: a flower gathering, from *anthos* flower + *legein* to collect]
▸**anˈthologist** *n*

anthozoan (ˌænθəˈzəʊən) *n* **1** any of the sessile marine coelenterates of the class *Anthozoa,* including corals and sea anemones, in which the body is in the form of a polyp. ◆ *adj* also: **actinozoan. 2** of or relating to these.

anthracene (ˈænθrəˌsiːn) *n* a colourless crystalline solid, used in the manufacture of chemicals and as crystals in scintillation counters. [C19: from ANTHRAX + -ENE]

anthracite (ˈænθrəˌsaɪt) *n* a hard coal that burns slowly with a nonluminous flame giving out intense heat. Also called: **hard coal.** [C19: from L, from Gk *anthrakitēs* coal-like, from *anthrax* coal]
▸**anthracitic** (ˌænθrəˈsɪtɪk) *adj*

anthracosis (ˌænθrəˈkəʊsɪs) *n* a lung disease due to inhalation of coal dust.

anthrax (ˈænθræks) *n, pl* **anthraces** (-θrəˌsiːz). **1** a highly infectious bacterial disease of animals, esp. cattle and sheep, which can be transmitted to man. **2** a pustule caused by this disease. [C19: from LL, from Gk: carbuncle]

anthropic principle *n Astron.* the cosmological theory that the presence of life in the universe limits the ways in which the very early universe could have evolved.

anthropo- *combining form.* indicating man or human: *anthropology.* [from Gk *anthrōpos*]

anthropocentric (ˌænθrəpəʊˈsɛntrɪk) *adj* regarding humans as the central factor in the universe.

anthropogenesis (ˌænθrəpəʊˈdʒɛnɪsɪs) *or* **anthropogeny** (ˌænθrəˈpɒdʒɪnɪ) *n* the study of the origins of humans.

anthropoid (ˈænθrəˌpɔɪd) *adj* **1** resembling humans. **2** resembling an ape; apelike. ◆ *n* **3** any primate of the suborder *Anthropoidea,* including monkeys, apes, and humans.

anthropoid ape *n* any of a group of primates having no tail, elongated arms, and a highly developed brain, including gibbons, orang-utans, chimpanzees, and gorillas.

anthropology (ˌænθrəˈpɒlədʒɪ) *n* the study of human beings, their origins, institutions, religious beliefs, social relationships, etc.
▸ˌ**anthropoˈlogical** *adj* ▸ˌ**anthroˈpologist** *n*

anthropometry (ˌænθrəˈpɒmɪtrɪ) *n* the comparative study of sizes and proportions of the human body.
▸ˌ**anthropoˈmetric** *or* ˌ**anthropoˈmetrical** *adj*

anthropomorphic (ˌænθrəpəˈmɔːfɪk) *adj* **1** of or relating to anthropomorphism. **2** resembling the human form.
▸ˈ**anthropoˌmorph** *n* ▸ˌ**anthropoˈmorphically** *adv*

anthropomorphism (ˌænθrəpəˈmɔːfɪzəm) *n* the attribution of human form or behaviour to a deity, animal, etc.

anthropomorphous (ˌænθrəpəˈmɔːfəs) *adj* **1** shaped like a human being. **2** another word for **anthropomorphic.**

anthropophagi (ˌænθrəˈpɒfəˌgaɪ) *pl n, sing* **anthropophagus** (-gəs). cannibals. [C16: from L, from Gk *anthrōpophagos;* see ANTHROPO-, -PHAGE]

anthroposophy (ˌænθrəˈpɒsəfɪ) *n* the spiritual and mystical teachings of Rudolph Steiner, based on the belief that creative activities are psychologically valuable, esp. for educational and therapeutic purposes.
▸ˌ**anthropoˈsophic** *adj*

anti (ˈæntɪ) *Inf.* ◆ *adj* **1** opposed to a party, policy, attitude, etc. ◆ *n* **2** an opponent.

anti- *prefix* **1** against; opposing: *anticlerical.* **2** opposite to: *anticlimax.* **3** rival; false: *antipope.* **4** counteracting or neutralizing: *antifreeze; antihistamine.* **5** designating the antiparticle of the particle specified: *antineutron.* [from Gk *anti*]

anti-aircraft (ˌæntɪˈɛəkrɑːft) *n* (*modifier*) of or relating to defence against aircraft attack: *anti-aircraft batteries.*

anti-apartheid *adj* opposed to a policy of racial segregation.

antiar (ˈæntɪˌɑː) *n* another name for **upas** (senses 1, 2). [from Javanese]

antiballistic missile (ˌæntɪbəˈlɪstɪk) *n* a ballistic missile designed to destroy another ballistic missile in flight.

antibiosis (ˌæntɪbaɪˈəʊsɪs) *n* an association between two organisms, esp. microorganisms, that is harmful to one of them.

antibiotic (ˌæntɪbaɪˈɒtɪk) *n* **1** any of various chemical substances, such as penicillin, produced by microorganisms, esp. fungi, or made synthetically, and capable of destroying microorganisms, esp. bacteria. ◆ *adj* **2** of or relating to antibiotics.

antibody (ˈæntɪˌbɒdɪ) *n, pl* **antibodies.** any of various proteins produced in the blood in response to an antigen. By becoming attached to antigens on infectious organisms antibodies can render them harmless.

antic (ˈæntɪk) *Arch.* ◆ *n* **1** an actor in a ludicrous or grotesque part; clown. ◆ *adj* **2** fantastic; grotesque. ◆ See also **antics.** [C16: from It. *antico* something grotesque (from its application to fantastic carvings found in ruins of ancient Rome)]

anticathode (ˌæntɪˈkæθəʊd) *n* the target electrode for the stream of electrons in a vacuum tube, esp. an X-ray tube.

Antichrist (ˈæntɪˌkraɪst) *n* **1** *Bible.* the antagonist of Christ, expected by early Christians to appear and reign over the world until overthrown at Christ's Second Coming. **2** (*sometimes not cap.*) an enemy of Christ or Christianity.

anticipant (ænˈtɪsɪpənt) *adj* **1** operating in advance. ◆ *n* **2** a person who anticipates.

anticipate ● (ænˈtɪsɪˌpeɪt) *vb* **anticipates, anticipating, anticipated.** (*mainly tr*) **1** (*may take a clause as object*) to foresee and act in advance of; forestall: *I anticipated his punch.* **2** (*also intr*) to mention (something) before its proper time: *don't anticipate the climax of the story.* **3** (*may take a clause as object*) to regard as likely; expect. **4** to make use of in advance of possession: *he anticipated his salary in buying a leather jacket.* [C16: from L *anticipāre* to take before, from *anti-* ANTE- + *capere* to take]
▸**anˈticiˌpator** *n* ▸**anˈticiˌpatory** *or* **anˈticipative** *adj*

> **USAGE NOTE** The use of *anticipate* to mean *expect* should be avoided.

anticipation ● (ænˌtɪsɪˈpeɪʃən) *n* **1** the act of anticipating; expectation, premonition, or foresight. **2** *Music.* an unstressed, usually short note introduced before a downbeat.

anticlerical (ˌæntɪˈklɛrɪkᵊl) *adj* **1** opposed to the power and influence of the clergy, esp. in politics. ◆ *n* **2** a supporter of an anticlerical party.
▸ˌ**antiˈclericalism** *n*

anticlimax ● (ˌæntɪˈklaɪmæks) *n* **1** a disappointing or ineffective conclusion to a series of events, etc. **2** a sudden change from a serious subject to one that is disappointing or ludicrous.
▸**anticlimactic** (ˌæntɪklaɪˈmæktɪk) *adj*

anticline (ˈæntɪˌklaɪn) *n* a formation of stratified rock raised up, by folding, into a broad arch so that the strata slope down on both sides from a common crest.
▸ˌ**antiˈclinal** *adj*

anticlockwise (ˌæntɪˈklɒkˌwaɪz) *adv, adj* in the opposite direction to the rotation of the hands of a clock. US equivalent: **counterclockwise.**

anticoagulant (ˌæntɪkəʊˈægjʊlənt) *adj* **1** acting to prevent or retard coagulation, esp. of blood. ◆ *n* **2** an agent that prevents or retards coagulation.

anti-Communist *adj* opposed to Communism or its principles.

anticonvulsant (ˌæntɪkənˈvʌlsənt) *n* **1** any of a class of drugs used to relieve convulsions. ◆ *adj* **2** of or relating to such drugs.

antics ● (ˈæntɪks) *pl n* absurd acts or postures.

anticyclone (ˌæntɪˈsaɪkləʊn) *n Meteorol.* a body of moving air of higher pressure than the surrounding air, in which the pressure decreases away from the centre. Also called: **high.**
▸**anticyclonic** (ˌæntɪsaɪˈklɒnɪk) *adj*

antidazzle mirror (ˌæntɪˈdæzᵊl) *n* a rear-view mirror for road vehicles that only partially reflects headlights behind.

antidepressant (ˌæntɪdɪˈprɛsᵊnt) *n* **1** any of a class of drugs used to alleviate depression. ◆ *adj* **2** of this class of drugs.

antidiuretic hormone (ˌæntɪˌdaɪjʊˈrɛtɪk) *n* another name for **vasopressin.** Abbrev.: **ADH.**

antidote ● (ˈæntɪˌdəʊt) *n* **1** *Med.* a drug or agent that counteracts or neutralizes the effects of a poison. **2** anything that counteracts or re-

THESAURUS

anthem *n* **1 = song of praise,** paean **2, 3 = hymn,** canticle, carol, chant, chorale, psalm

anthology *n* **1 = collection,** analects, choice, compendium, compilation, digest, garland, miscellany, selection, treasury

anticipate *vb* **1 = forestall,** antedate, beat (someone) to it (*inf.*), intercept, prevent **1, 3 = expect,** apprehend, await, count upon, forecast, foresee, foretell, hope for, look for, look forward to, predict, prepare for

anticipation *n* **1 = expectation,** apprehension, awaiting, expectancy, foresight, foretaste, forethought, hope, preconception, premonition, prescience, presentiment

anticipatory *adj* **1, 3 = expectant,** apprehensive, forecasting, foreseeing, foretelling, forethoughtful, predicting, provident

anticlimax *n* **1, 2 = disappointment,** bathos, comedown, letdown
Antonyms *n* climax, culmination, height, highlight, high point, peak, summit, top, zenith

antics *pl n* **= clowning,** buffoonery, capers, escapades, foolishness, frolics, horseplay, larks, mischief, monkey tricks, playfulness, pranks, silliness, skylarking, stunts, tomfoolery, tricks

lieves a harmful condition. [C15: from L, from Gk *antidoton* something given as a countermeasure, from ANTI- + *didonai* to give]
▸ **ˌantiˈdotal** *adj*

antiemetic (ˌæntɪˈmɛtɪk) *adj* **1** preventing vomiting. ◆ *n* **2** any antiemetic drug, such as promethazine.

antifreeze (ˈæntɪˌfriːz) *n* a liquid, usually ethylene glycol (ethanediol), added to water to lower its freezing point, esp. for use in an internal-combustion engine.

antifungal (ˌæntɪˈfʌŋɡəl) *adj* **1** inhibiting the growth of fungi. **2** (of a drug) possessing antifungal activity and therefore used to treat fungal infections. ◆ Also: **antimycotic.**

antigen (ˈæntɪdʒən, -ˌdʒɛn) *n* a substance, usually a toxin produced by a bacterium, that stimulates the production of antibodies. [C20: from ANTI(BODY) + -GEN]

antihero (ˈæntɪˌhɪərəʊ) *n, pl* **antiheroes.** a central character in a novel, play, etc., who lacks the traditional heroic virtues.

antihistamine (ˌæntɪˈhɪstəˌmiːn, -mɪn) *n* any drug that neutralizes the effects of histamine, used esp. in the treatment of allergies.

anti-inflammatory *adj* **1** reducing inflammation. ◆ *n, pl* **anti-inflammatories. 2** any anti-inflammatory drug, such as cortisone, aspirin, or ibuprofen.

anti-inflationary *adj* (of an economic policy) designed to reduce or counteract the effects of inflation.

antiknock (ˌæntɪˈnɒk) *n* a compound, such as lead tetraethyl, added to petrol to reduce knocking in the engine.

antilock brake (ˈæntɪˌlɒk) *n* a brake fitted to some road vehicles that prevents skidding and improves control by sensing and compensating for overbraking. Also called: **ABS brake.**

antilogarithm (ˌæntɪˈlɒɡəˌrɪðəm) *n* a number whose logarithm to a given base is a given number: *100 is the antilogarithm of 2 to base 10.* Often shortened to **antilog.**
▸ **ˌantiˌlogaˈrithmic** *adj*

antilogy (ænˈtɪlədʒɪ) *n, pl* **antilogies.** a contradiction in terms. [C17: from Gk *antilogia*]

antimacassar (ˌæntɪməˈkæsə) *n* a cloth covering the back and arms of chairs, etc., to prevent soiling. [C19: from ANTI- + MACASSAR (OIL)]

antimagnetic (ˌæntɪmæɡˈnɛtɪk) *adj* of a material that does not acquire permanent magnetism when exposed to a magnetic field.

antimalarial (ˌæntɪməˈlɛərɪəl) *adj* **1** effective in the treatment of malaria. ◆ *n* **2** an antimalarial drug or agent.

antimasque (ˈæntɪˌmɑːsk) *n* a comic dance, presented between the acts of a masque.

antimatter (ˈæntɪˌmætə) *n* a form of matter composed of antiparticles, such as antihydrogen, consisting of antiprotons and positrons.

antimetabolite (ˌæntɪmɪˈtæbəˌlaɪt) *n* any drug that acts by disrupting the normal growth of a cell. Antimetabolites are used in cancer treatment.

antimissile (ˌæntɪˈmɪsaɪl) *adj* **1** relating to defensive measures against missile attack: *an antimissile system.* ◆ *n* **2** Also called: **antimissile missile.** a defensive missile used to intercept and destroy attacking missiles.

antimony (ˈæntɪmənɪ) *n* a toxic metallic element that exists in two allotropic forms and is added to alloys to increase their strength and hardness. Symbol: Sb; atomic no.: 51; atomic wt.: 121.75. [C15: from Med. L *antimōnium,* from ?]
▸ **antimonial** (ˌæntɪˈməʊnɪəl) *adj*

antimuon (ˌæntɪˈmjuːɒn) *n* the antiparticle of a muon.

antimycotic (ˌæntɪmaɪˈkɒtɪk) *adj* another word for **antifungal.**

anti-Nazi *adj* opposed to Nazism or its principles.

antinoise (ˈæntɪˌnɔɪz) *n* sound generated so that it is out of phase with a noise, such as that made by an engine, in order to reduce the noise level by interference.

antinomian (ˌæntɪˈnəʊmɪən) *adj* **1** relating to the doctrine that by faith a Christian is released from the obligation of adhering to any moral law. ◆ *n* **2** a member of a Christian sect holding such a doctrine.
▸ **ˌantiˈnomianism** *n*

antinomy (ænˈtɪnəmɪ) *n, pl* **antinomies. 1** opposition of one law, principle, or rule to another. **2** *Philosophy.* contradiction existing between two apparently indubitable propositions. [C16: from L, from Gk: conflict between laws, from ANTI- + *nomos* law]
▸ **antinomic** (ˌæntɪˈnɒmɪk) *adj*

antinovel (ˈæntɪˌnɒvəl) *n* a type of prose fiction in which conventional or traditional novelistic elements are rejected.

antinuclear (ˌæntɪˈnjuːklɪə) *adj* opposed to nuclear weapons or nuclear power.

antioxidant (ˌæntɪˈɒksɪdənt) *n* **1** any substance that retards deterioration by oxidation, esp. of fats, oils, foods, or rubber. **2** *Biol.* a substance, such as vitamin C, vitamin E, or beta carotene, that counteracts the damaging effects of oxidation in a living organism.

antiparticle (ˈæntɪˌpɑːtɪkəl) *n* any of a group of elementary particles that have the same mass as their corresponding particle but have a charge of equal magnitude but opposite sign. When a particle collides with its antiparticle mutual annihilation occurs.

antipasto (ˌæntɪˈpɑːstəʊ, -ˈpæs-) *n, pl* **antipastos.** a course of hors d'oeuvres in an Italian meal. [It.: before food]

antipathetic (ænˌtɪpəˈθɛtɪk, ˌæntɪpə-) *or* **antipathetical** *adj* (often foll. by *to*) having or arousing a strong aversion.

antipathy ❶ (ænˈtɪpəθɪ) *n, pl* **antipathies. 1** a feeling of dislike or hostility. **2** the object of such a feeling. [C17: from L, from Gk, from ANTI- + *patheia* feeling]

antipersonnel (ˌæntɪˌpɜːsəˈnɛl) *adj* (of weapons, etc.) designed to cause casualties to personnel rather than to destroy equipment.

antiperspirant (ˌæntɪˈpɜːspərənt) *n* **1** a substance applied to the skin to reduce or prevent perspiration. ◆ *adj* **2** reducing perspiration.

antiphlogistic (ˌæntɪfləˈdʒɪstɪk) *adj* **1** of or relating to the prevention or alleviation of inflammation. ◆ *n* **2** an antiphlogistic drug.

antiphon (ˈæntɪfən) *n* **1** a short passage, usually from the Bible, recited or sung as a response after certain parts of a liturgical service. **2** a psalm, hymn, etc., chanted or sung in alternate parts. **3** any response. [C15: from LL *antiphōna* sung responses, from LGk, pl of *antiphōnon* (something) responsive, from ANTI- + *phōnē* sound]
▸ **antiphonal** (ænˈtɪfənəl) *adj*

antiphonary (ænˈtɪfənərɪ) *n, pl* **antiphonaries.** a bound collection of antiphons.

antiphony (ænˈtɪfənɪ) *n, pl* **antiphonies. 1** antiphonal singing. **2** any musical or other sound effect that answers or echoes another.

antipode (ˈæntɪpəʊd) *n* the exact or direct opposite.
▸ **antipodal** (ænˈtɪpədəl) *adj*

antipodes (ænˈtɪpəˌdiːz) *pl n* **1** either or both of two places that are situated diametrically opposite one another on the earth's surface. **2** the people who live there. **3** (*often cap.*) **the.** Australia and New Zealand. [C16: via LL from Gk, pl of *antipous* having the feet opposite, from ANTI- + *pous* foot]
▸ **antipodean** (ænˌtɪpəˈdiːən) *adj*

antipope (ˈæntɪˌpəʊp) *n* a rival pope elected in opposition to one who has been canonically chosen.

anti-Protestant *adj* opposed to Protestantism.

antipsychotic (ˌæntɪsaɪˈkɒtɪk) *adj* **1** preventing or treating psychosis. ◆ *n* **2** any antipsychotic drug, such as chlorpromazine: used to treat such conditions as schizophrenia.

antipyretic (ˌæntɪpaɪˈrɛtɪk) *adj* **1** preventing or alleviating fever. ◆ *n* **2** an antipyretic remedy or drug.

antiquarian (ˌæntɪˈkwɛərɪən) *adj* **1** concerned with the study of antiquities or antiques. ◆ *n* **2** a less common name for **antiquary.**
▸ **ˌantiˈquarianism** *n*

antiquark (ˈæntɪˌkwɑːk) *n* the antiparticle of a quark.

antiquary (ˈæntɪkwərɪ) *n, pl* **antiquaries.** a person who collects, deals in, or studies antiques or ancient works of art. Also called: **antiquarian.**

antiquate ❶ (ˈæntɪˌkweɪt) *vb* **antiquates, antiquating, antiquated.** (*tr*) to make obsolete or old-fashioned. [C15: from L *antīquāre* to make old, from *antīquus* ancient]
▸ **ˈantiˌquated** *adj*

antique ❶ (ænˈtiːk) *n* **1a** a decorative object, piece of furniture, or other work of art created in an earlier period, that is valued for its beauty, workmanship, and age. **1b** (*as modifier*)*: an antique shop.* **2** any object made in an earlier period. **3 the.** the style of ancient art, esp. Greek or Roman. ◆ *adj* **4** made in or in the style of an earlier period. **5** of or belonging to the distant past, esp. of ancient Greece or Rome. **6** *Inf.* old-fashioned. **7** *Arch.* aged or venerable. ◆ *vb* **antiques, antiquing, antiqued. 8** (*tr*) to give an antique appearance to. [C16: from L *antīquus* ancient, from *ante* before]

antiquities (ænˈtɪkwɪtɪz) *pl n* remains or relics, such as statues, buildings, or coins, that date from ancient times.

antiquity ❶ (ænˈtɪkwɪtɪ) *n, pl* **antiquities. 1** the quality of being ancient: *a vase of great antiquity.* **2** the far distant past, esp. preceding the Middle Ages. **3** the people of ancient times collectively.

antiracism (ˌæntɪˈreɪsɪzəm) *n* the policy of challenging racism and promoting racial tolerance.
▸ **ˌantiˈracist** *n, adj*

anti-riot *adj* designed for or employed in controlling crowds: *anti-riot police.*

anti-roll bar *n* a crosswise rubber-mounted bar in the suspension of a motor vehicle, which counteracts the movement downwards on one side when cornering.

antirrhinum (ˌæntɪˈraɪnəm) *n* any plant of the genus *Antirrhinum,* esp. the snapdragon, which has two-lipped flowers of various colours. [C16: via L from Gk *antirrhinon,* from ANTI- (imitating) + *rhis* nose]

THESAURUS

antidote *n* **1, 2** = **cure,** antitoxin, antivenin, corrective, counteragent, countermeasure, neutralizer, nostrum, preventive, remedy, specific

antipathy *n* **1** = **hostility,** abhorrence, animosity, animus, antagonism, aversion, bad blood, contrariety, disgust, dislike, distaste, enmity, hatred, ill will, incompatibility, loathing, odium, opposition, rancour, repugnance, repulsion

Antonyms *n* affection, affinity, attraction, bond, empathy, fellow-feeling, goodwill, harmony, partiality, rapport, sympathy, tie

antiquated *adj* = **obsolete,** antediluvian, antique, archaic, dated, old-fashioned, old hat, outmoded, out-of-date, outworn, passé, past it (*inf.*), superannuated

Antonyms *adj* ≠ **obsolete:** all-singing, all-dancing, current, fashionable, fresh, modern, modish, new, state-of-the-art, stylish, up-to-date, young

antique *n* **1, 2** = **period piece,** bygone, heirloom, object of virtu, relic ◆ *adj* **4** = **vintage,** antiquarian, classic, olden **6** *Inf.* = **old-fashioned,** archaic, obsolete, outdated

antiquity *n* **1** = **old age,** age, ancientness, elderliness, oldness **2** = **distant past,** ancient times, olden days, time immemorial

antiscorbutic (ˌæntɪskɔːˈbjuːtɪk) *adj* **1** preventing or curing scurvy. ◆ *n* **2** an antiscorbutic agent.

anti-Semite *n* a person who persecutes or discriminates against Jews. ▸ **ˌanti-Seˈmitic** *adj* ▸ **ˌanti-ˈSemitism** *n*

antisepsis (ˌæntɪˈsɛpsɪs) *n* **1** destruction of undesirable microorganisms, such as those that cause disease or putrefaction. **2** the state of being free from such microorganisms.

antiseptic ⓘ (ˌæntɪˈsɛptɪk) *adj* **1** of or producing antisepsis. **2** entirely free from contamination. **3** *Inf.* lacking spirit or excitement. ◆ *n* **4** an antiseptic agent. ▸ **ˌantiˈseptically** *adv*

antiserum (ˌæntɪˈsɪərəm) *n, pl* **antiserums** *or* **antisera** (-rə). blood serum containing antibodies against a specific antigen, used to treat or provide immunity to a disease.

antisocial ⓘ (ˌæntɪˈsəʊʃəl) *adj* **1** avoiding the company of other people; unsociable. **2** contrary or injurious to the interests of society in general.

antispasmodic (ˌæntɪspæzˈmɒdɪk) *adj* **1** preventing or arresting spasms. ◆ *n* **2** an antispasmodic drug.

antistatic (ˌæntɪˈstætɪk) *adj* (of a substance, textile, etc.) retaining sufficient moisture to provide a conducting path, thus avoiding the effects of static electricity.

antistrophe (ænˈtɪstrəfɪ) *n* (in ancient Greek drama) **a** the second of two movements made by a chorus during the performance of a choral ode. **b** the second part of a choral ode sung during this movement. ◆ See **strophe.** [C17: via LL from Gk *antistrophē* an answering turn, from ANTI- + *strophē* a turning] ▸ **antistrophically** (ˌæntɪˈstrɒfɪkəlɪ) *adv*

antitank (ˌæntɪˈtæŋk) *adj* designed to immobilize or destroy armoured vehicles.

antithesis ⓘ (ænˈtɪθɪsɪs) *n, pl* **antitheses** (-ˌsiːz). **1** the exact opposite. **2** contrast or opposition. **3** *Rhetoric.* the juxtaposition of contrasting ideas or words to produce an effect of balance, such as *my words fly up, my thoughts remain below.* [C15: via L from Gk: a setting against, from ANTI- + *tithenai* to place] ▸ **antithetical** (ˌæntɪˈθɛtɪkəl) *adj*

antitoxin (ˌæntɪˈtɒksɪn) *n* **1** an antibody that neutralizes a toxin. **2** blood serum that contains a specific antibody. ▸ **ˌantiˈtoxic** *adj*

antitrades (ˈæntɪˌtreɪdz) *pl n* winds in the upper atmosphere blowing in the opposite direction from and above the trade winds.

antitrust (ˌæntɪˈtrʌst) *n* (*modifier*) *Chiefly US.* regulating or opposing trusts, monopolies, cartels, or similar organizations.

antitussive (ˌæntɪˈtʌsɪv) *n* **1** any of a class of drugs used to suppress or alleviate coughing. ◆ *adj* **2** of or relating to such drugs. [from ANTI- + L *tussis* a cough]

antitype (ˈæntɪˌtaɪp) *n* **1** a person or thing that is foreshadowed or represented by a type or symbol. **2** an opposite type. ▸ **antitypical** (ˌæntɪˈtɪpɪkəl) *adj*

antivenin (ˌæntɪˈvɛnɪn) *or* **antivenene** (ˌæntɪvɪˈniːn) *n* an antitoxin that counteracts a specific venom, esp. snake venom. [C19: from ANTI- + VEN(OM) + -IN]

antiviral (ˌæntɪˈvaɪrəl) *adj* **1** inhibiting the growth of viruses. ◆ *n* **2** any antiviral drug.

antler (ˈæntlə) *n* one of a pair of bony outgrowths on the heads of male deer and some related species of either sex. [C14: from OF *antoillier*] ▸ **ˈantlered** *adj*

antlion (ˈæntˌlaɪən) *n* **1** any of various insects which resemble dragonflies and are most common in tropical regions. **2** the larva of this insect, which buries itself in the sand to await its prey.

antonomasia (ˌæntənəˈmeɪzɪə) *n* **1** the substitution of a title or epithet for a proper name, such as *his highness.* **2** the use of a proper name for an idea: *he is a Daniel come to judgment.* [C16: via L from Gk, from *antonomazein* to name differently, from *onoma* name]

antonym (ˈæntənɪm) *n* a word that means the opposite of another. [C19: from Gk, from ANTI- + *onoma* name] ▸ **antonymous** (ænˈtɒnɪməs) *adj*

antrum (ˈæntrəm) *n, pl* **antra** (-trə). *Anat.* a natural cavity, hollow, or sinus, esp. in a bone. [C14: from L: cave, from Gk *antron*] ▸ **ˈantral** *adj*

ANU *abbrev. for* Australian National University.

anuresis (ˌænjuˈriːsɪs) *n* inability to urinate. [C20: NL, from AN- + Gk *ouresis* urination]

anus (ˈeɪnəs) *n* the excretory opening at the end of the alimentary canal. [C16: from L]

anvil (ˈænvɪl) *n* **1** a heavy iron or steel block on which metals are hammered during forging. **2** any part having a similar shape or function, such as the lower part of a telegraph key. **3** *Anat.* the nontechnical name for **incus.** [OE *anfealt*]

anxiety ⓘ (æŋˈzaɪɪtɪ) *n, pl* **anxieties. 1** a state of uneasiness or tension caused by apprehension of possible misfortune, danger, etc. **2** intense desire; eagerness. **3** *Psychol.* a state of intense apprehension, common in mental illness or after a very distressing experience. [C16: from L *anxietas*]

anxiety disorder *n* any of various mental disorders characterized by extreme anxiety.

anxious ⓘ (ˈæŋkʃəs, ˈæŋʃəs) *adj* **1** worried and tense because of possible misfortune, danger, etc. **2** causing anxiety; worrying; distressing: *an anxious time.* **3** intensely desirous: *anxious for promotion.* [C17: from L *anxius;* rel. to L *angere* to torment] ▸ **ˈanxiously** *adv* ▸ **ˈanxiousness** *n*

any (ˈɛnɪ) *determiner* **1a** one, some, or several, as specified, no matter how much, what kind, etc.: *you may take any clothes you like.* **1b** (*as pron; functioning as sing or pl*): *take any you like.* **2** (*usually used with a negative*) **2a** even the smallest amount or even one: *I can't stand any noise.* **2b** (*as pron; functioning as sing or pl*): *don't give her any.* **3** whatever or whichever: *any dictionary will do.* **4** an indefinite or unlimited (amount or number): *any number of friends.* ◆ *adv* **5** (*usually used with a negative*) (foll. by a comp. adj) to even the smallest extent: *it isn't any worse.* [OE *ǣnig*]

anybody (ˈɛnɪˌbɒdɪ) *pron* **1** any person; anyone. **2** (*usually used with a negative or a question*) a person of any importance: *he isn't anybody.* ◆ *n, pl* **anybodies. 3** (often preceded by *just*) any person at random.

anyhow (ˈɛnɪˌhaʊ) *adv* **1** in any case. **2** by any means whatever. **3** carelessly.

any more *or esp. US* **anymore** (ˌɛnɪˈmɔː) *adv* any longer; still; nowadays.

anyone (ˈɛnɪˌwʌn) *pron* **1** any person; anybody. **2** (*used with a negative or a question*) a person of any importance: *is he anyone?* **3** (often preceded by *just*) any person at random.

anyplace (ˈɛnɪˌpleɪs) *adv US & Canad. inf.* anywhere.

anything (ˈɛnɪˌθɪŋ) *pron* **1** any object, event, action, etc., whatever: *anything might happen.* ◆ *n* **2** a thing of any kind: *have you anything to declare?* ◆ *adv* **3** in any way: *he wasn't anything like his father.* **4 anything but.** not in the least: *she was anything but happy.* **5 like anything.** (intensifier): *he ran like anything.*

anyway (ˈɛnɪˌweɪ) *adv* **1** in any case; at any rate; nevertheless. **2** in a careless manner. **3** Usually **any way.** in any manner.

anywhere (ˈɛnɪˌwɛə) *adv* **1** in, at, or to any place. **2 get anywhere.** to be successful.

anywise (ˈɛnɪˌwaɪz) *adv Chiefly US.* in any way.

ANZAAS (ˈænzəs, -zæs) *n acronym for* Australian and New Zealand Association for the Advancement of Science.

Anzac (ˈænzæk) *n* **1** (in World War I) a soldier serving with the Australian and New Zealand Army Corps. **2** (now) any Australian or New Zealand soldier. **3** the Anzac landing at Gallipoli in 1915.

Anzac Day *n* April 25, a public holiday in Australia and New Zealand commemorating the Anzac landing at Gallipoli in 1915.

ANZUS (ˈænzəs) *n acronym for* Australia, New Zealand, and the United States, with reference to the security alliance between them.

AO *abbrev. for* Officer of the Order of Australia.

A/O *or* **a/o** (accounting, etc.) *abbrev. for* account of.

AOB *or* **a.o.b.** *abbrev. for* any other business.

AOC *abbrev. for* appellation d'origine contrôlée: the highest French wine classification; indicates that the wine meets strict requirements concerning area of production, strength, etc. Cf. **VDQS, vin de pays.**

AONB (in England and Wales) *abbrev. for* area of outstanding natural beauty: an area officially designated as requiring protection to conserve and enhance its natural beauty.

aorist (ˈeɪərɪst, ˈɛərɪst) *n Grammar.* a tense of the verb, esp. in classical Greek, indicating past action without reference to whether the action involved was momentary or continuous. [C16: from Gk *aoristos* not limited, from A-[1] + *horistos,* from *horizein* to define]

aorta (eɪˈɔːtə) *n, pl* **aortas** *or* **aortae** (-tiː). the main vessel in the arterial network, which conveys oxygen-rich blood from the heart. [C16: from NL, from Gk *aortē,* lit.: something lifted, from *aeirein* to raise] ▸ **aˈortic** *or* **aˈortal** *adj*

Aotearoa (ˈæɒˌtɪəˌroːə) *n NZ.* the Maori name for New Zealand. [Maori: the long white cloud]

aoudad (ˈɑːʊˌdæd) *n* a wild mountain sheep of N Africa. Also called: **Barbary sheep.** [from F, from Berber *audad*]

THESAURUS

antiseptic *adj* **2** = **hygienic**, aseptic, clean, germ-free, pure, sanitary, sterile, uncontaminated, unpolluted ◆ *n* **4** = **disinfectant**, bactericide, germicide, purifier
Antonyms *adj* ≠ **hygienic:** contaminated, dirty, impure, infected, insanitary, polluted, septic, unhygienic

antisocial *adj* **1** = **unsociable**, alienated, asocial, misanthropic, reserved, retiring, uncommunicative, unfriendly, withdrawn **2** = **disruptive**, antagonistic, belligerent, disorderly, hostile, menacing, rebellious, uncooperative
Antonyms *adj* ≠ **unsociable:** companionable, friendly, gregarious, philanthropic, sociable, social

antithesis *n* **1** = **opposite**, antipode, contrary, contrast, converse, inverse, reverse **2** = **contrast**, contradiction, contraposition, contrariety, inversion, opposition, reversal

anxiety *n* **1** = **uneasiness**, angst, apprehension, care, concern, disquiet, disquietude, distress, foreboding, fretfulness, misgiving, nervousness, restlessness, solicitude, suspense, tension, trepidation, unease, watchfulness, worry
Antonyms *n* assurance, calmness, confidence, contentment, relief, security, serenity

anxious *adj* **1** = **uneasy**, apprehensive, careful, concerned, disquieted, distressed, disturbed, fearful, fretful, in suspense, nervous, neurotic, on tenterhooks, overwrought, restless, solicitous, taut, tense, troubled, twitchy (*inf.*), unquiet (*chiefly literary*), watchful, worried **3** = **eager**, ardent, avid, desirous, expectant, impatient, intent, itching, keen, yearning
Antonyms *adj* ≠ **uneasy:** assured, calm, certain, collected, composed, confident, cool, nonchalant, unfazed (*inf.*), unperturbed ≠ **eager:** disinclined, hesitant, loath, nonchalant, reluctant

ap (æp) son of: occurring as part of some surnames of Welsh origin: *ap Thomas.* [from Welsh *mab* son]

apace ⓣ (əˈpeɪs) *adv* quickly; rapidly. [C14: prob. from OF *à pas,* at a (good) pace]

apache (əˈpæʃ) *n* a Parisian gangster or ruffian. [from F: APACHE]

Apache (əˈpætʃɪ) *n* **1** (*pl* **Apaches** *or* **Apache**) a member of a North American Indian people inhabiting the southwestern US and N Mexico. **2** the language of this people. [from Mexican Sp.]

apanage (ˈæpənɪdʒ) *n* a variant spelling of **appanage.**

apart ⓣ (əˈpɑːt) *adj* (*postpositive*), *adv* **1** to or in pieces: *he had the television apart.* **2** placed or kept separately or for a particular purpose, etc.; aside (esp. in **set** *or* **put apart**). **3** separate in time, place, or position: *he stood apart from the group.* **4** not being taken into account: *these difficulties apart, the project ran smoothly.* **5** individual; distinct: *a race apart.* **6** separately or independently: *considered apart, his reasoning was faulty.* **7** **apart from.** (*prep*) besides. ◆ See also **take apart, tell apart.** [C14: from OF *a part* at (the) side]

apartheid (əˈpɑːthaɪt, -heɪt) *n* (formerly, in South Africa) the government policy of racial segregation; officially renounced in 1992. [C20: Afrik., from *apart* APART + *-heid* -HOOD]

apartment ⓣ (əˈpɑːtmənt) *n* **1** (*often pl*) any room in a building, usually one of several forming a suite, used as living accommodation, offices, etc. **2a** another name (esp. US and Canad.) for **flat**[2] (sense 1). **2b** (*as modifier*): *apartment house.* [C17: from F *appartement,* from It., from *appartare* to separate]

apathetic ⓣ (ˌæpəˈθetɪk) *adj* having or showing little or no emotion or interest. [C18: from APATHY + PATHETIC]
▸ˌ**apaˈthetically** *adv*

apathy ⓣ (ˈæpəθɪ) *n* **1** absence of interest in or enthusiasm for things generally considered interesting or moving. **2** absence of emotion. [C17: from L, from Gk *apatheia,* from A-[1] + *pathos* feeling]

apatite (ˈæpəˌtaɪt) *n* a common naturally occurring mineral consisting basically of calcium fluorophosphate. It is a source of phosphorus and is used in fertilizers. [C19: from G *Apatit,* from Gk *apatē* deceit; from its misleading similarity to other minerals]

ape ⓣ (eɪp) *n* **1** any of various primates in which the tail is very short or absent. **2** (not in technical use) any monkey. **3** an imitator; mimic. ◆ *vb* **apes, aping, aped. 4** (*tr*) to imitate. [OE *apa*]
▸ˈ**apeˌlike** *adj*

APEC *Canad. abbrev. for* Atlantic Provinces Economic Council.

apeman (ˈeɪpˌmæn) *n, pl* **apemen.** any of various extinct apelike primates thought to have been the forerunners of modern man.

aperçu *French.* (apɛrsy) *n* **1** an outline. **2** an insight. [from *apercevoir* to PERCEIVE]

aperient (əˈpɪərɪənt) *Med.* ◆ *adj* **1** laxative. ◆ *n* **2** a mild laxative. [C17: from L *aperīre* to open]

aperiodic (ˌeɪpɪərɪˈɒdɪk) *adj* **1** not periodic; not occurring at regular intervals. **2** *Physics.* **2a** (of a system or instrument) being damped sufficiently to reach equilibrium without oscillation. **2b** (of an oscillation or vibration) not having a regular period. **2c** (of an electrical circuit) not having a measurable resonant frequency.
▸**aperiodicity** (ˌeɪpɪərɪəˈdɪsɪtɪ) *n*

apéritif (əˌpɛrɪˈtiːf) *n* an alcoholic drink before a meal to whet the appetite. [C19: from F, from Med. L, from L *aperīre* to open]

aperture ⓣ (ˈæpətʃə) *n* **1** a hole; opening. **2** *Physics.* a usually circular and often variable opening in an optical instrument or device that controls the quantity of radiation entering or leaving it. [C15: from LL *apertūra* opening, from *aperīre* to open]

apetalous (eɪˈpetələs) *adj* (of flowering plants such as the wood anemone) having no petals. [C18: from NL; see A-[1], PETAL]

apex ⓣ (ˈeɪpeks) *n, pl* **apexes** *or* **apices. 1** the highest point; vertex. **2** the pointed end or tip of something. **3** a high point, as of a career. [C17: from L: point]

APEX (ˈeɪpeks) *n acronym for:* **1** Advance Purchase Excursion, a reduced airline or long-distance rail fare that must be paid a specified number of days in advance. **2** Association of Professional, Executive, Clerical, and Computer Staff.

Apex Club (ˈeɪpeks) *n* (in Australia) an association of business and professional men to promote community welfare.
▸**Apexian** (eɪˈpeksɪən) *adj, n*

apgar score *or* **rating** (ˈæpgɑː) *n* a system for determining the condition of an infant at birth by allotting a maximum of 2 points to each of the following: heart rate, breathing effort, muscle tone, response to stimulation, and colour. [C20: after V. *Apgar* (1909–74), US anaesthetist]

aphaeresis *or* **apheresis** (əˈfɪərɪsɪs) *n* the omission of a letter or syllable at the beginning of a word. [C17: via LL from Gk, from *aphairein* to remove]

aphasia (əˈfeɪzɪə) *n* a disorder of the central nervous system characterized by loss of the ability to communicate, esp. in speech. [C19: via NL from Gk, from A-[1] + *-phasia,* from *phanai* to speak]

aphelion (æpˈhiːlɪən, əˈfiː-) *n, pl* **aphelia** (-lɪə). the point in its orbit when a planet or comet is at its greatest distance from the sun. [C17: from NL *aphēlium,* from AP(O)- + Gk *hēlios* sun]

aphesis (ˈæfɪsɪs) *n* the gradual disappearance of an unstressed vowel at the beginning of a word, as in *squire* from *esquire.* [C19: from Gk, from *aphienai* to set free]
▸**aphetic** (əˈfetɪk) *adj*

aphid (ˈeɪfɪd) *n* any of the small homopterous insects of the family Aphididae, which feed by sucking the juices from plants. [C19: from *aphides,* pl. of APHIS]

aphis (ˈeɪfɪs) *n, pl* **aphides** (ˈeɪfɪˌdiːz). any of a genus of aphids, such as the blackfly. [C18: from NL (coined by Linnaeus for obscure reasons)]

aphonia (əˈfəʊnɪə) *or* **aphony** (ˈæfənɪ) *n* loss of voice caused by damage to the vocal tract. [C18: NL, from Gk, from A-[1] + *phōnē* sound]

aphorism ⓣ (ˈæfəˌrɪzəm) *n* a short pithy saying expressing a general truth; maxim. [C16: from LL, from Gk *aphorismos,* from *aphorizein* to define]
▸ˈ**aphorist** *n* ▸ˌ**aphoˈristic** *adj*

aphrodisiac ⓣ (ˌæfrəˈdɪzɪæk) *n* **1** a drug, food, etc., that excites sexual desire. ◆ *adj* **2** exciting sexual desire. [C18: from Gk, from *aphrodisios* belonging to *Aphrodite,* goddess of love]

aphyllous (əˈfɪləs) *adj* (of plants) having no leaves. [C19: from NL, from Gk A-[1] + *phullon* leaf]

apian (ˈeɪpɪən) *adj* of, relating to, or resembling bees. [C19: from L *apiānus,* from *apis* bee]

apiarist (ˈeɪpɪərɪst) *n* a person who studies or keeps bees.

apiary (ˈeɪpɪərɪ) *n, pl* **apiaries.** a place where bees are kept. [C17: from L *apiārium,* from *apis* bee]

apical (ˈæpɪk[ə]l, ˈeɪ-) *adj* of, at, or being the apex. [C19: from NL *apicālis*]
▸ˈ**apically** *adv*

apices (ˈæpɪˌsiːz, ˈeɪ-) *n* a plural of **apex.**

apiculture (ˈeɪpɪˌkʌltʃə) *n* the breeding and care of bees. [C19: from L *apis* bee + CULTURE]
▸ˌ**apiˈcultural** *adj* ▸ˌ**apiˈculturist** *n*

apiece ⓣ (əˈpiːs) *adv* (*postpositive*) for, to, or from each one: *they were given two apples apiece.*

apish (ˈeɪpɪʃ) *adj* **1** stupid; foolish. **2** resembling an ape. **3** slavishly imitative.
▸ˈ**apishly** *adv* ▸ˈ**apishness** *n*

aplanatic (ˌæpləˈnætɪk) *adj* (of a lens or mirror) free from spherical aberration. [C18: from Gk *aplanetos* free from error, from A-[1] + *planaein* to wander]

aplenty ⓣ (əˈplentɪ) *adj* (*postpositive*), *adv* in plenty.

aplomb ⓣ (əˈplɒm) *n* equanimity, self-confidence, or self-possession. [C18: from F: uprightness, from *à plomb* according to the plumb line]

apnoea *or US* **apnea** (æpˈnɪə) *n* a temporary inability to breathe. [C18: from NL, from Gk *apnoia,* from A-[1] + *pnein* to breathe]

apo- *or* **ap-** *prefix* **1** away from; off: *apogee.* **2** separation of: *apocarpous.* [from Gk *apo* away, off]

Apoc. *abbrev. for:* **1** Apocalypse. **2** Apocrypha *or* Apocryphal.

THESAURUS

apace *adv* = **quickly,** at full speed, expeditiously, posthaste, rapidly, speedily, swiftly, with dispatch, without delay

apart *adv* **1** = **to pieces,** asunder, in bits, in pieces, into parts, to bits **2** = **separate,** afar, alone, aloof, aside, away, by itself, by oneself, cut off, distant, distinct, divorced, excluded, independent, independently, isolated, out on a limb, piecemeal, separated, separately, singly, to itself, to oneself, to one side **7 apart from** = **except for,** aside from, besides, but, excluding, not counting, other than, save

apartment *n* **1, 2** = **room,** accommodation, chambers, compartment, flat, living quarters, penthouse, quarters, rooms, suite

apathetic *adj* = **uninterested,** cold, cool, emotionless, impassive, indifferent, insensible, listless, passive, phlegmatic, sluggish, stoic, stoical, torpid, unconcerned, unemotional, unfeeling, unmoved, unresponsive
Antonyms *adj* active, anxious, aroused, bothered, caring, committed, concerned, emotional, enthusiastic, excited, interested, moved, passionate, responsive, troubled, worried, zealous

apathy *n* **1, 2** = **lack of interest,** coldness, coolness, emotionlessness, impassibility, impassivity, indifference, inertia, insensibility, listlessness, nonchalance, passiveness, passivity, phlegm, sluggishness, stoicism, torpor, unconcern, unfeelingness, uninterestedness, unresponsiveness
Antonyms *n* anxiety, attention, concern, emotion, enthusiasm, feeling, interest, zeal

ape *vb* **4** = **imitate,** affect, caricature, copy, counterfeit, echo, mimic, mirror, mock, parody, parrot

aperture *n* **1** = **opening,** breach, chink, cleft, crack, eye, eyelet, fissure, gap, hole, interstice, orifice, passage, perforation, rent, rift, slit, slot, space, vent

apex *n* **1-3** = **highest point,** acme, apogee, climax, crest, crown, culmination, height, peak, pinnacle, point, summit, tip, top, vertex, zenith
Antonyms *n* base, bottom, depths, lowest point, nadir, perigee, rock bottom

aphorism *n* = **saying,** adage, apothegm, axiom, dictum, gnome, maxim, precept, proverb, saw

aphrodisiac *n* **1** = **love potion,** philter ◆ *adj* **2** = **erotic** *or* **erotical,** arousing, exciting, stimulating, venereal

apiece *adv* = **each,** for each, from each, individually, respectively, separately, severally, to each
Antonyms *adv* all together, as a group, collectively, en masse, overall, together

aplenty *adj* = **in plenty,** à gogo, galore, in abundance, in profusion, in quantity, to spare ◆ *adv* = **plentifully,** abundantly, copiously, in abundance, in plenty, in quantity, plenteously

aplomb *n* = **self-possession,** balance, calmness, composure, confidence, coolness, equanimity, level-headedness, poise, sang-froid, self-assurance, self-confidence, stability
Antonyms *n* awkwardness, chagrin, confusion, discomfiture, discomposure, embarrassment, self-consciousness

apocalypse ❶ (əˈpɒkəlɪps) *n* **1** a prophetic disclosure or revelation. **2** an event of great importance, violence, etc., like the events described in the Apocalypse. [C13: from LL *apocalypsis*, from Gk, from APO- + *kaluptein* to hide]
▸**a͵pocaˈlyptic** *adj*

Apocalypse (əˈpɒkəlɪps) *n Bible*. another name for the Book of Revelation.

apocarpous (͵æpəˈkɑːpəs) *adj* (of the ovaries of flowering plants) consisting of separate carpels. [C19: from NL, from Gk APO- + *karpos* fruit]

apochromat (͵æpəˈkrəʊmæt) *or* **apochromatic lens** (͵æpəkrəˈmætɪk) *n* a lens system designed to bring trichromatic light to a single focus and reduce chromatic aberration.

apocope (əˈpɒkəpɪ) *n* omission of the final sound or sounds of a word. [C16: via LL from Gk, from *apokoptein* to cut off]

apocrine (ˈæpəkraɪn, -krɪn) *adj* losing cellular tissue in the process of secreting, as in mammary glands. Cf. **eccrine**. [C20: from APO- + *-crine*, from Gk *krinein* to separate]

Apocrypha (əˈpɒkrɪfə) *n* **the**. (*functioning as sing or pl*) the 14 books included as an appendix to the Old Testament in the Septuagint and the Vulgate but not in the Hebrew canon. [C14: via LL *apocrypha* (*scripta*) hidden (writings), from Gk, from *apokruptein* to hide away]

apocryphal ❶ (əˈpɒkrɪfəl) *adj* **1** of questionable authenticity. **2** (*sometimes cap.*) of or like the Apocrypha. **3** untrue; counterfeit.

apodal (ˈæpədᵊl) *or* **apodous** (ˈæpədəs) *adj* without feet; having no pelvic fins. [C18: from Gk A-[1] + *pous* foot]

apodosis (əˈpɒdəsɪs) *n, pl* **apodoses** (-͵siːz). *Logic, grammar*. the consequent of a conditional statement, as *I won't go* in *if it rains I won't go*. [C17: via LL from Gk, from *apodidonai* to give back]

apogee ❶ (ˈæpə͵dʒiː) *n* **1** the point in its orbit around the earth when the moon or an artificial satellite is at its greatest distance from the earth. **2** the highest point. [C17: from NL, from Gk, from *apogaios* away from the earth]
▸͵**apoˈgean** *adj*

apolitical (͵eɪpəˈlɪtɪkᵊl) *adj* politically neutral; without political attitudes, content, or bias.

Apollyon (əˈpɒljən) *n* the destroyer, a name given to the Devil (Revelation 9:11). [C14: via LL from Gk, from *apollunai* to destroy totally]

apologetic ❶ (ə͵pɒləˈdʒɛtɪk) *adj* **1** expressing or anxious to make apology; contrite. **2** defending in speech or writing.
▸**a͵poloˈgetically** *adv*

apologetics (ə͵pɒləˈdʒɛtɪks) *n* (*functioning as sing*) **1** the branch of theology concerned with the rational justification of Christianity. **2** a defensive method of argument.

apologia (͵æpəˈləʊdʒɪə) *n* a formal written defence of a cause or one's beliefs or conduct.

apologist (əˈpɒlədʒɪst) *n* a person who offers a defence by argument.

apologize ❶ *or* **apologise** (əˈpɒlə͵dʒaɪz) *vb* **apologizes, apologizing, apologized** *or* **apologises, apologising, apologised.** (*intr*) **1** to express or make an apology; acknowledge faults. **2** to make a formal defence.

apologue (ˈæpə͵lɒg) *n* an allegory or moral fable. [C17: from L, from Gk *apologos*]

apology ❶ (əˈpɒlədʒɪ) *n, pl* **apologies. 1** a verbal or written expression of regret or contrition for a fault or failing. **2** a poor substitute. **3** another word for **apologia**. [C16: from OF, from LL, from Gk: a verbal defence, from APO- + *logos* speech]

apophthegm *or* **apothegm** (ˈæpə͵θɛm) *n* a short remark containing some general or generally accepted truth; maxim. [C16: from Gk *apophthegma*, from *apophthengesthai* to speak frankly]

apoplectic ❶ (͵æpəˈplɛktɪk) *adj* **1** of apoplexy. **2** *Inf.* furious.
▸͵**apoˈplectically** *adv*

apoplexy ❶ (ˈæpə͵plɛksɪ) *n* sudden loss of consciousness, often followed by paralysis, caused by rupture or occlusion of a blood vessel in the brain. [C14: from OF *apoplexie*, from LL, from Gk, from *apoplēssein* to cripple by a stroke]

aport (əˈpɔːt) *adv, adj* (*postpositive*) *Naut.* on or towards the port side: *with the helm aport*.

apostasy ❶ (əˈpɒstəsɪ) *n, pl* **apostasies.** abandonment of one's religious faith, party, a cause, etc. [C14: from Church L *apostasia*, from Gk *apostasis* desertion]

apostate ❶ (əˈpɒsteɪt, -tɪt) *n* **1** a person who abandons his religion, party, etc. ◆ *adj* **2** guilty of apostasy.
▸**apostatical** (͵æpəˈstætɪkᵊl) *adj*

apostatize *or* **apostatise** (əˈpɒstə͵taɪz) *vb* **apostatizes, apostatizing, apostatized** *or* **apostatises, apostatising, apostatised.** (*intr*) to abandon one's belief, faith, or allegiance.

a posteriori (eɪ pɒs͵tɛrɪˈɔːraɪ, -rɪ; ɑː) *adj Logic.* **1** relating to inductive reasoning from particular facts to a general principle. **2** derived from or requiring evidence for its validation; empirical. [C18: from L, lit.: from the latter]

apostle ❶ (əˈpɒsᵊl) *n* **1** (*often cap.*) one of the 12 disciples chosen by Christ to preach his gospel. **2** any prominent Christian missionary, esp. one who first converts a people. **3** an ardent early supporter of a cause, movement, etc. [OE *apostol*, from Church L, from Gk *apostolos* a messenger]

Apostles' Creed *n* a concise statement of Christian beliefs dating from about 500 A.D., traditionally ascribed to the Apostles.

apostolate (əˈpɒstəlɪt, -͵leɪt) *n* the office, authority, or mission of an apostle.

apostolic (͵æpəˈstɒlɪk) *adj* **1** of or relating to the Apostles or their teachings or practice. **2** of or relating to the pope as successor of the Apostles.
▸͵**aposˈtolical** *adj*

Apostolic See (͵æpəˈstɒlɪk) *n* the see of the pope.

Apostolic succession *n* the doctrine that the authority of Christian bishops derives from the Apostles through an unbroken line of consecration.

apostrophe[1] (əˈpɒstrəfɪ) *n* the punctuation mark ' used to indicate the omission of a letter or number, such as *he's* for *he has* or *he is*, also used in English to form the possessive, as in *John's father*. [C17: from LL, from Gk *apostrophos* mark of elision, from *apostrephein* to turn away]

apostrophe[2] (əˈpɒstrəfɪ) *n Rhetoric.* a digression from a discourse, esp. an address to an imaginary or absent person or a personification. [C16: from L *apostrophē*, from Gk: a turning away]

apostrophize *or* **apostrophise** (əˈpɒstrə͵faɪz) *vb* **apostrophizes, apostrophizing, apostrophized** *or* **apostrophises, apostrophising, apostrophised.** (*tr*) to address an apostrophe to.

apothecaries' measure *n* a system of liquid volume measure used in pharmacy in which 20 fluid ounces equal 1 pint.

apothecaries' weight *n* a system of weights formerly used in pharmacy based on the Troy ounce.

apothecary (əˈpɒθɪkərɪ) *n, pl* **apothecaries. 1** an archaic word for **chemist. 2** *Law.* a chemist licensed by the Society of Apothecaries of London to prescribe, prepare, and sell drugs. [C14: from OF, from LL, from Gk *apothēkē* storehouse]

apothegm (ˈæpə͵θɛm) *n* a variant spelling of **apophthegm.**

apothem (ˈæpə͵θɛm) *n* the perpendicular from the centre of a regular polygon to any of its sides. [C20: from APO- + Gk *thema*, from *tithenai* to place]

apotheosis ❶ (ə͵pɒθɪˈəʊsɪs) *n, pl* **apotheoses** (-siːz). **1** elevation to the rank of a god; deification. **2** glorification of a person or thing. **3** a glorified ideal. [C17: via LL from Gk: deification]

apotheosize *or* **apotheosise** (əˈpɒθɪə͵saɪz) *vb* **apotheosizes, apotheosizing, apotheosized** *or* **apotheosises, apotheosising, apotheosised.** (*tr*) **1** to deify. **2** to glorify or idealize.

app. *abbrev. for:* **1** apparatus. **2** appendix (of a book). **3** applied. **4** appointed. **5** apprentice. **6** approved. **7** approximate.

appal ❶ *or US* **appall** (əˈpɔːl) *vb* **appals, appalling, appalled** *or US* **appalls, appalling, appalled.** (*tr*) to fill with horror; shock or dismay. [C14: from OF *appalir* to turn pale]

appalling ❶ (əˈpɔːlɪŋ) *adj* **1** causing dismay, horror, or revulsion. **2** *Inf.* very bad.
▸**apˈpallingly** *adv*

Appaloosa (͵æpəˈluːsə) *n* a breed of horse, originally from America, having a spotted rump. [C19: ?from *Palouse*, river in Idaho]

appanage *or* **apanage** (ˈæpənɪdʒ) *n* **1** land or other provision granted by a king for the support of esp. a younger son. **2** a customary accompaniment or perquisite, as to a job or position. [C17: from OF, from Med. L, from *appānāre* to provide for, from L *pānis* bread]

THESAURUS

apocalypse *n* **2** = **destruction**, carnage, conflagration, devastation, havoc, holocaust

apocryphal *adj* **1** = **dubious**, doubtful, equivocal, fictitious, legendary, mythical, questionable, spurious, unauthenticated, uncanonical, unsubstantiated, unverified
Antonyms *adj* attested, authentic, authenticated, authorized, canonical, credible, factual, substantiated, true, undisputed, unquestionable, verified

apogee *n* **1, 2** = **highest point**, acme, apex, climax, crest, crown, culmination, height, peak, pinnacle, summit, tip, top, vertex, zenith

apologetic *adj* **1** = **regretful**, contrite, penitent, remorseful, rueful, sorry

apologize *vb* **1** = **say sorry**, ask forgiveness, beg pardon, express regret, say one is sorry

apology *n* **1** = **defence**, acknowledgment, confession, excuse, explanation, extenuation, justification, plea, vindication **2** *As in* **an apology for** = **mockery**, caricature, excuse, imitation, travesty

apoplectic *adj* **2** *Informal* = **furious**, beside oneself, boiling, enraged, frantic, frenzied, fuming, incandescent, incensed, infuriated, livid (*inf.*), mad, raging

apoplexy *n* = **fit**, attack, convulsion, paroxysm, seizure

apostasy *n* = **desertion**, backsliding, defection, disloyalty, faithlessness, falseness, heresy, perfidy, recreance *or* recreancy (*arch.*), treachery, unfaithfulness

apostate *n* **1** = **deserter**, backslider, defector, heretic, recreant (*arch.*), renegade, traitor, turncoat ◆ *adj* **2** = **disloyal**, backsliding, faithless, false, heretical, perfidious, recreant, traitorous, treacherous, unfaithful, untrue

apostle *n* **2** = **evangelist**, herald, messenger, missionary, preacher, proselytizer **3** = **supporter**, advocate, champion, pioneer, propagandist, propagator, proponent

apotheosis *n* **1, 2** = **deification**, elevation, exaltation, glorification, idealization, idolization

appal *vb* = **horrify**, alarm, astound, daunt, dishearten, dismay, frighten, harrow, intimidate, make one's hair stand on end (*inf.*), outrage, petrify, scare, shock, terrify, unnerve

appalled *adj* = **horrified**, alarmed, astounded, daunted, disheartened, dismayed, disquieted, frightened, outraged, petrified, scared, shocked, stunned, terrified, unnerved

appalling *adj* **1** = **horrifying**, alarming, astounding, awful, daunting, dire, disheartening, dismaying, dreadful, fearful, frightening, frightful, from hell (*inf.*), ghastly, grim, harrowing, hideous, horrible, horrid, horrific, intimidating, petrifying, scaring, shocking, terrible, terrifying, unnerving

apparatchik (ˌæpəˈrɑːtʃɪk) *n* **1** a member of a Communist Party organization. **2** a bureaucrat in any organization. [C20: from Russian, from *apparat* apparatus, instrument + *-ckik,* suffix denoting agent]

apparatus Ⓣ (ˌæpəˈreɪtəs, -ˈrɑːtəs) *n, pl* **apparatus** *or* **apparatuses. 1** a collection of equipment used for a particular purpose. **2** a machine having a specific function: *breathing apparatus.* **3** the means by which something operates; organization. **4** *Anat.* any group of organs having a specific function. [C17: from L, from *apparāre* to make ready]

apparel Ⓣ (əˈpærəl) *n* **1** *Arch.* clothing. **2** *Naut.* a vessel's gear and equipment. ◆ *vb* **apparels, apparelling, apparelled** *or US* **apparels, appareling, appareled. 3** (*tr*) *Arch.* to clothe, adorn, etc. [C13: from OF *apareillier* to make ready, from Vulgar L *apparicuīāre* (unattested), from L *parāre* to prepare]

apparent Ⓣ (əˈpærənt) *adj* **1** readily seen or understood; obvious. **2** (*usually prenominal*) seeming, as opposed to real: *his apparent innocence.* **3** *Physics.* as observed but ignoring such factors as the motion of the observer, etc. [C14: from L *appārēns,* from *appārēre* to APPEAR]
▸**apˈparently** *adv*

apparent magnitude *n* See **magnitude** (sense 4).

apparition Ⓣ (ˌæpəˈrɪʃən) *n* **1** an appearance, esp. of a ghost or ghostlike figure. **2** the figure so appearing; spectre. **3** the act of appearing. [C15: from LL *appāritiō,* from L *appārēre* to APPEAR]

appassionato (əˌpæsjəˈnɑːtəʊ) *adj, adv Music.* (to be performed) with passion. [It.]

appeal Ⓣ (əˈpiːl) *n* **1** a request for relief, aid, etc. **2** the power to attract, please, stimulate, or interest. **3** an application or resort to another authority, esp. a higher one, as for a decision. **4** *Law.* **4a** the judicial review by a superior court of the decision of a lower tribunal. **4b** a request for such review. **5** *Cricket.* a request to the umpire to declare a batsman out. ◆ *vb* **6** (*intr*) to make an earnest request. **7** (*intr*) to attract, please, stimulate, or interest. **8** *Law.* to apply to a superior court to review (a case or issue decided by a lower tribunal). **9** (*intr*) to resort (to), as for a decision. **10** (*intr*) *Cricket.* to ask the umpire to declare a batsman out. **11** (*intr*) to challenge the umpire's or referee's decision. [C14: from OF *appeler,* from L *appellāre* to entreat, from *pellere* to drive]
▸**apˈpealable** *adj* ▸**apˈpealer** *n* ▸**apˈpealing** *adj* ▸**apˈpealingly** *adv*

appear Ⓣ (əˈpɪə) *vb* (*intr*) **1** to come into sight. **2** (*copula; may take an infinitive*) to seem: *the evidence appears to support you.* **3** to be plain or clear, as after further evidence, etc.: *it appears you were correct after all.* **4** to develop; occur: *faults appeared during testing.* **5** to be published: *his biography appeared last month.* **6** to perform: *he has appeared in many London productions.* **7** to be present in court before a magistrate or judge: *he appeared on two charges of theft.* [C13: from OF *aparoir,* from L *appārēre* to become visible, attend upon, from *pārēre* to appear]

appearance Ⓣ (əˈpɪərəns) *n* **1** the act or an instance of appearing. **2** the outward aspect of a person or thing. **3** an outward show; pretence: *he gave an appearance of not caring.* **4 keep up appearances.** to maintain the public impression of wellbeing or normality. **5 put in** *or* **make an appearance.** to attend briefly, as out of politeness. **6 to all appearances.** apparently.
▸**apˈpeaser** *n*

appearance money *n* money paid by a promoter of an event to a particular celebrity in order to ensure that the celebrity takes part in the event.

appease Ⓣ (əˈpiːz) *vb* **appeases, appeasing, appeased.** (*tr*) **1** to calm or pacify, esp. by acceding to the demands of. **2** to satisfy or quell (a thirst, etc.). [C16: from OF *apaisier,* from *pais* peace, from L *pax*]

appeasement Ⓣ (əˈpiːzmənt) *n* **1** the policy of acceding to the demands of a potentially hostile nation in the hope of maintaining peace. **2** the act of appeasing.

appellant (əˈpɛlənt) *n* **1** a person who appeals. **2** *Law.* the party who appeals to a higher court from the decision of a lower tribunal. ◆ *adj* **3** *Law.* another word for **appellate.** [C14: from OF; see APPEAL]

appellate (əˈpɛlɪt) *adj Law.* **1** of appeals. **2** (of a tribunal) having jurisdiction to review cases on appeal. [C18: from L *appellātus* summoned, from *appellāre* to APPEAL]

appellation Ⓣ (ˌæpɪˈleɪʃən) *n* **1** a name or title. **2** the act of naming.

appellative (əˈpɛlətɪv) *n* **1** a name or title. **2** *Grammar.* another word for **common noun.** ◆ *adj* **3** of or relating to a name. **4** (of a proper noun) used as a common noun.

append Ⓣ (əˈpɛnd) *vb* (*tr*) **1** to add as a supplement: *to append a footnote.* **2** to attach; hang on. [C15: from LL *appendere* to hang (something) from, from L *pendere* to hang]

appendage Ⓣ (əˈpɛndɪdʒ) *n* an ancillary or secondary part attached to a main part; adjunct, such as an organ that projects from the trunk of an animal.

appendant (əˈpɛndənt) *adj* **1** attached or added. **2** attendant or associated as an accompaniment or result. ◆ *n* **3** a person or thing attached or added.

appendicectomy (əˌpɛndɪˈsɛktəmɪ) *or esp. US & Canad.* **appendectomy** (ˌæpənˈdɛktəmɪ) *n, pl* **appendicectomies** *or* **appendectomies.** surgical removal of any appendage, esp. the vermiform appendix.

appendicitis (əˌpɛndɪˈsaɪtɪs) *n* inflammation of the vermiform appendix.

appendix Ⓣ (əˈpɛndɪks) *n, pl* **appendices** (-dɪˌsiːz) *or* **appendixes. 1** a body of separate additional material at the end of a book, etc. **2** any part that is dependent or supplementary. **3** *Anat.* See **vermiform appendix.** [C16: from L: an appendage, from *appendere* to APPEND]

apperceive (ˌæpəˈsiːv) *vb* **apperceives, apperceiving, apperceived.** (*tr*) **1** to be aware of perceiving. **2** *Psychol.* to comprehend by assimilating (a perception) to ideas already in the mind. [C19: from OF, from L *percipere* to PERCEIVE]

apperception (ˌæpəˈsɛpʃən) *n* **1** *Psychol.* the attainment of full awareness of a sensation or idea. **2** the act of apperceiving.
▸ˌ**apperˈceptive** *adj*

appertain Ⓣ (ˌæpəˈteɪn) *vb* (*intr;* usually foll. by *to*) to belong (to) as a part, function, right, etc.; relate (to) or be connected (with). [C14: from OF *apertenir,* from LL, from L AD- + *pertinēre* to PERTAIN]

appetence (ˈæpɪtəns) *or* **appetency** *n, pl* **appetences** *or* **appetencies. 1** a craving or desire. **2** an attraction or affinity. [C17: from L *appetentia,* from *appetere* to crave]

appetite Ⓣ (ˈæpɪˌtaɪt) *n* **1** a desire for food or drink. **2** a desire to satisfy a bodily craving, as for sexual pleasure. **3** (usually foll. by *for*) a liking

THESAURUS

Antonyms *adj* comforting, consolatory, consoling, encouraging, heartening, reassuring

apparatus *n* **1, 2 = equipment**, appliance, contraption (*inf.*), device, gear, implements, machine, machinery, materials, means, mechanism, outfit, tackle, tools, utensils **3 = organization**, bureaucracy, chain of command, hierarchy, network, setup (*inf.*), structure, system

apparel *n* **1** *Archaic* **= clothing**, accoutrements, array (*poetic*), attire, clothes, costume, dress, equipment, garb, garments, gear (*inf.*), habiliments, habit, outfit, raiment (*arch. or poetic*), robes, threads (*sl.*), trappings, vestments

apparent *adj* **1 = obvious**, blatant, bold, clear, conspicuous, discernible, distinct, evident, indubitable, manifest, marked, open, overt, patent, plain, salient, understandable, unmistakable, visible **2 = seeming**, ostensible, outward, specious, superficial
Antonyms *adj* ≠ **obvious:** ambiguous, doubtful, dubious, hazy, indefinite, indistinct, obscure, uncertain, unclear, vague ≠ **seeming:** actual, authentic, bona fide, genuine, honest, intrinsic, real, sincere, true

apparently *adv* **2 = it appears that**, it seems that, on the face of it, ostensibly, outwardly, seemingly, speciously, superficially

apparition *n* **2 = ghost**, chimera, eidolon, phantom, revenant, shade (*literary*), spectre, spirit, spook (*inf.*), visitant, wraith

appeal *n* **1, 3 = plea**, adjuration, application, entreaty, invocation, petition, prayer, request, solicitation, suit, supplication **2 = attraction**, allure, attractiveness, beauty, charm, engagingness, fascination, interestingness, pleasingness ◆ *vb* **6, 9 = plead**, adjure, apply, ask, beg, beseech, call, call upon, entreat, implore, petition, pray, refer, request, resort to, solicit, sue, supplicate **7 = attract**, allure, charm, engage, entice, fascinate, interest, invite, please, tempt
Antonyms *n* ≠ **plea:** denial, refusal, rejection, repudiation ≠ **attraction:** repulsiveness ◆ *vb* ≠ **plead:** deny, refuse, reject, repudiate, repulse ≠ **attract:** alienate, bore, repulse, revolt

appealing *adj* **2 = attractive**, alluring, charming, desirable, endearing, engaging, inviting, prepossessing, taking, winning, winsome
Antonyms *adj* disgusting, forbidding, loathsome, objectionable, obnoxious, odious, offensive, repellent, repugnant, repulsive, revolting, sickening, unalluring, unappealing, unattractive, undesirable, uninviting, unprepossessing

appear *vb* **1, 4 = come into view**, arise, arrive, attend, be present, come forth, come into sight, come out, come to light, crop up (*inf.*), develop, emerge, issue, loom, materialize, occur, show (*inf.*), show one's face, show up (*inf.*), surface, turn out, turn up **2 = look (like** *or* **as if)**, occur, seem, strike one as **3 = be obvious**, be apparent, be clear, be evident, be manifest, be patent, be plain **5 = come into being**, become available, be created, be developed, be invented, be published, come into existence, come out **6 = perform**, act, be exhibited, come on, come onstage, enter, play, play a part, take part
Antonyms *vb* ≠ **come into view:** disappear, vanish ≠ **be obvious:** be doubtful, be unclear

appearance *n* **1 = arrival**, advent, appearing, coming, debut, emergence, introduction, presence, showing up (*inf.*), turning up **2 = look**, air, aspect, bearing, demeanour, expression, face, figure, form, image, looks, manner, mien (*literary*) **3 = impression**, front, guise, illusion, image, outward show, pretence, semblance

appease *vb* **1 = pacify**, calm, conciliate, mollify, placate, pour oil on troubled waters, quiet, satisfy, soothe **2 = ease**, allay, alleviate, assuage, blunt, calm, compose, diminish, lessen, lull, mitigate, quell, quench, quiet, relieve, satisfy, soothe, subdue, tranquillize
Antonyms *vb* ≠ **pacify:** aggravate (*inf.*), anger, annoy, antagonize, arouse, disturb, enrage, incense, inflame, infuriate, irritate, madden, provoke, rile, upset

appeasement *n* **1 = pacification**, acceding, accommodation, compromise, concession, conciliation, mollification, placation, propitiation **2 = easing**, abatement, alleviation, assuagement, blunting, lessening, lulling, mitigation, quelling, quenching, quieting, relieving, satisfaction, softening, solace, soothing, tranquillization

appellation *n* **1 = name**, address, description, designation, epithet, sobriquet, style, term, title

append *vb* **1, 2 = add**, adjoin, affix, annex, attach, fasten, hang, join, subjoin, tack on, tag on
Antonyms *vb* detach, disconnect, disengage, remove, separate, take off

appendage *n* **= attachment**, accessory, addendum, addition, adjunct, affix, ancillary, annexe, appendix, appurtenance, auxiliary, supplement **= limb**, extremity, member, projection, protuberance

appendix *n* **1 = supplement**, addendum, addition, add-on, adjunct, appendage, codicil, postscript

appertain *vb, foll. by* **to = relate to**, apply to, bear upon, be characteristic of, be connected to, belong to, be part of, be pertinent to, be proper to, be relevant to, have to do with, inhere in, pertain to, refer to, touch upon

appetite *n* **1-3 = desire**, appetence, appetency, craving, demand, hankering, hunger, inclination, liking, longing, passion, proclivity,

or willingness: *a great appetite for work.* [C14: from OF *apetit,* from L, from *appetere* to desire ardently]
▸**appetitive** (əˈpɛtɪtɪv) *adj*

appetizer Ⓣ *or* **appetiser** (ˈæpɪˌtaɪzə) *n* **1** a small amount of food or drink taken to stimulate the appetite. **2** any stimulating foretaste.

appetizing Ⓣ *or* **appetising** (ˈæpɪˌtaɪzɪŋ) *adj* pleasing or stimulating to the appetite; delicious; tasty.

applaud Ⓣ (əˈplɔːd) *vb* **1** to indicate approval of (a person, performance, etc.) by clapping the hands. **2** (*usually tr*) to express approval or praise of: *I applaud your decision.* [C15: from L *applaudere,* from *plaudere* to beat, applaud]

applause Ⓣ (əˈplɔːz) *n* appreciation or praise, esp. as shown by clapping the hands.

apple (ˈæpᵊl) *n* **1** a rosaceous tree, widely cultivated in temperate regions in many varieties. **2** the fruit of this tree, having red, yellow, or green skin and crisp whitish flesh. **3** the wood of this tree. **4** any of several unrelated trees that have fruit similar to the apple. **5 apple of one's eye.** a person or thing that is very much loved. [OE *æppel*]

apple green *n* **a** a bright light green. **b** (*as adj*): *an apple-green carpet.*

apple-pie bed *n Brit.* a bed made with the sheets folded so as to prevent the person from entering it.

apple-pie order *n Inf.* perfect order or condition.

applet (ˈæplɪt) *n Computing.* a computer program that runs within a page on the World Wide Web. [C20: from APP(LICATION) + -LET]

appliance Ⓣ (əˈplaɪəns) *n* **1** a machine or device, esp. an electrical one used domestically. **2** any piece of equipment having a specific function. **3** another name for a **fire engine.**

applicable Ⓣ (ˈæplɪkəbᵊl, əˈplɪkə-) *adj* being appropriate or relevant; able to be applied; fitting.
▸ˌ**applicaˈbility** *n* ▸ˈ**applicably** *adv*

applicant Ⓣ (ˈæplɪkənt) *n* a person who applies, as for a job, grant, support, etc.; candidate. [C15: from L *applicāns,* from *applicāre* to APPLY]

application Ⓣ (ˌæplɪˈkeɪʃən) *n* **1** the act of applying to a particular use. **2** relevance or value: *the practical applications of space technology.* **3** the act of asking for something. **4** a written request, as for a job, etc. **5** diligent effort: *a job requiring application.* **6** something, such as a lotion, that is applied, esp. to the skin.

applicator (ˈæplɪˌkeɪtə) *n* a device, such as a spatula or rod, for applying a medicine, glue, etc.

applicatory (ˈæplɪkətərɪ) *adj* suitable for application.

applied (əˈplaɪd) *adj* put to practical use: *applied mathematics.* Cf. **pure** (sense 5).

appliqué (æˈpliːkeɪ) *n* **1** a decoration of one material sewn or fixed onto another. **2** the practice of decorating in this way. ◆ *vb* **appliqués, appliquéing, appliquéd. 3** (*tr*) to sew or fix (a decoration) on as an appliqué. [C18: from F, lit.: applied]

apply Ⓣ (əˈplaɪ) *vb* **applies, applying, applied. 1** (*tr*) to put to practical use; employ. **2** (*intr*) to be relevant or appropriate. **3** (*tr*) to cause to come into contact with. **4** (*intr; often foll. by for*) to put in an application or request. **5** (*tr; often foll. by to*) to devote (oneself or one's efforts) with diligence. **6** (*tr*) to bring into use: *the police only applied the law to aliens.* [C14: from OF *aplier,* from L *applicāre* to attach to]
▸**apˈplier** *n*

appoggiatura (əˌpɒdʒəˈtʊərə) *n, pl* **appoggiaturas** *or* **appoggiature** (-reɪ). *Music.* an ornament consisting of a nonharmonic note preceding a harmonic one either before or on the stress. [C18: from It., lit.: a propping]

appoint Ⓣ (əˈpɔɪnt) *vb* (*mainly tr*) **1** (*also intr*) to assign officially, as to a position, responsibility, etc. **2** to establish by agreement or decree. **3** to prescribe: *laws appointed by tribunal.* **4** *Property law.* to nominate (a person) to take an interest in property. **5** to equip with usual features; furnish: *a well-appointed hotel.* [C14: from OF *apointer* to put into a good state]
▸**appoinˈtee** *n* ▸**apˈpointer** *n*

appointive (əˈpɔɪntɪv) *adj Chiefly US.* filled by appointment: *an appointive position.*

appointment Ⓣ (əˈpɔɪntmənt) *n* **1** an arrangement to meet a person or be at a place at a certain time. **2** the act of placing in a job or position. **3** the person who receives such a job. **4** the job or position to which such a person is appointed. **5** (*usually pl*) a fixture or fitting.

apportion Ⓣ (əˈpɔːʃən) *vb* (*tr*) to divide, distribute, or assign shares of; allot proportionally.
▸**apˈportionable** *adj* ▸**apˈportionment** *n*

appose (əˈpəʊz) *vb* **apposes, apposing, apposed.** (*tr*) **1** to place side by side. **2** (usually foll. by *to*) to place (something) near or against another thing. [C16: from OF *apposer,* from *poser* to put, from L *pōnere*]
▸**apˈposable** *adj*

apposite Ⓣ (ˈæpəzɪt) *adj* appropriate; apt. [C17: from L *appositus,* from *appōnere,* from *pōnere* to put]
▸ˈ**appositely** *adv* ▸ˈ**appositeness** *n*

apposition (ˌæpəˈzɪʃən) *n* **1** a putting into juxtaposition. **2** a grammatical construction in which a word, esp. a noun, is placed after another to modify its meaning.
▸ˌ**appoˈsitional** *adj*

appositive (əˈpɒzɪtɪv) *Grammar.* ◆ *adj* **1** in, of, or relating to apposition. ◆ *n* **2** an appositive word or phrase.
▸**apˈpositively** *adv*

appraisal Ⓣ (əˈpreɪzᵊl) *or* **appraisement** *n* **1** an assessment of the worth or quality of a person or thing. **2** a valuation.

appraise Ⓣ (əˈpreɪz) *vb* **appraises, appraising, appraised.** (*tr*) **1** to assess the worth, value, or quality of. **2** to make a valuation of, as for taxation. [C15: from OF, from *prisier* to PRIZE[2]]
▸**apˈpraisable** *adj* ▸**apˈpraiser** *n*

> **USAGE NOTE** *Appraise* is sometimes wrongly used where *apprise* is meant: *they had been apprised* (not *appraised*) *of my arrival.*

appreciable Ⓣ (əˈpriːʃəbᵊl) *adj* sufficient to be easily measured or noticed.
▸**apˈpreciably** *adv*

THESAURUS

propensity, relish, stomach, taste, willingness, yearning, zeal, zest
Antonyms *n* abhorrence, aversion, disgust, disinclination, dislike, distaste, loathing, repugnance, repulsion, revulsion

appetizer *n* **1** = **hors d'oeuvre**, antipasto, canapé, titbit **1** = **apéritif**, cocktail

appetizing *adj* = **delicious**, appealing, inviting, mouthwatering, palatable, savoury, scrumptious (*inf.*), succulent, tasty, tempting
Antonyms *adj* distasteful, nauseating, unappetizing, unpalatable, unsavoury

applaud *vb* **1, 2** = **praise**, acclaim, approve, cheer, clap, commend, compliment, crack up (*inf.*), encourage, eulogize, extol, give (someone) a big hand, laud, magnify (*arch.*)
Antonyms *vb* blast, boo, censure, condemn, criticize, decry, deprecate, deride, disparage, excoriate, hiss, lambast(e), pan (*inf.*), put down, ridicule, run down, slag (off) (*sl.*), tear into (*inf.*), vilify

applause *n* = **ovation**, acclaim, acclamation, accolade, approbation, approval, big hand, cheering, cheers, clapping, commendation, eulogizing, hand, hand-clapping, laudation, plaudit, praise

appliance *n* **1, 2** = **device**, apparatus, gadget, implement, instrument, machine, mechanism, tool

applicable *adj* = **appropriate**, apposite, apropos, apt, befitting, fit, fitting, germane, pertinent, relevant, suitable, suited, to the point, to the purpose, useful
Antonyms *adj* inapplicable, inappropriate, irrelevant, unsuitable, wrong

applicant *n* = **candidate**, aspirant, claimant, inquirer, petitioner, postulant, suitor, suppliant

application *n* **2** = **relevance**, appositeness, appropriateness, exercise, function, germaneness, pertinence, practice, purpose, use, value **3, 4** = **request**, appeal, claim, inquiry, petition, requisition, solicitation, suit **5** = **effort**, assiduity, attention, attentiveness, commitment, dedication, diligence, hard work, industry, perseverance, study **6** = **lotion**, balm, cream, dressing, emollient, ointment, poultice, salve, unguent

apply *vb* **1, 6** = **use**, administer, assign, bring into play, bring to bear, carry out, employ, engage, execute, exercise, exert, implement, practise, put to use, utilize **2** = **be relevant**, appertain, be applicable, be appropriate, bear upon, be fitting, fit, pertain, refer, relate, suit **3** = **put on**, anoint, bring into contact with, cover with, lay on, paint, place, smear, spread on, touch to **4** = **request**, appeal, claim, inquire, make application, petition, put in, requisition, solicit, sue **5 apply oneself** = **try**, address oneself, be assiduous, be diligent, be industrious, buckle down (*inf.*), commit oneself, concentrate, dedicate oneself, devote oneself, make an effort, pay attention, persevere, study, work hard

appoint *vb* **1** = **assign**, choose, commission, delegate, elect, install, name, nominate, select **2** = **decide**, allot, arrange, assign, choose, designate, determine, establish, fix, set, settle **5** = **equip**, fit out, furnish, provide, supply
Antonyms *vb* ≠ **assign**: discharge, dismiss, fire, give the sack (*inf.*), sack (*inf.*) ≠ **decide**: cancel ≠ **equip**: dismantle, divest, strip

appointed *adj* **1** = **assigned**, chosen, commissioned, delegated, elected, installed, named, nominated, selected **2** = **decided**, allotted, arranged, assigned, chosen, designated, determined, established, fixed, set, settled **5** = **equipped**, fitted out, furnished, provided, supplied

appointment *n* **1** = **meeting**, arrangement, assignation, consultation, date, engagement, interview, rendezvous, session, tryst (*arch.*) **2** = **selection**, allotment, assignment, choice, choosing, commissioning, delegation, designation, election, installation, naming, nomination **3** = **appointee**, candidate, delegate, nominee, office-holder, representative **4** = **job**, assignment, berth (*inf.*), office, place, position, post, situation, station **5** *usually plural* = **fittings**, accoutrements, appurtenances, equipage, fixtures, furnishings, gear, outfit, paraphernalia, trappings

apportion *vb* = **divide**, allocate, allot, assign, deal, dispense, distribute, dole out, give out, measure out, mete out, parcel out, ration out, share

apportionment *n* = **division**, allocation, allotment, assignment, dealing out, dispensing, distribution, doling out, measuring out, meting out, parcelling out, rationing out, sharing

apposite *adj* = **appropriate**, appertaining, applicable, apropos, apt, befitting, fitting, germane, pertinent, proper, relevant, suitable, suited, to the point, to the purpose
Antonyms *adj* inapplicable, inappropriate, inapt, irrelevant, unsuitable, unsuited

appraisal *n* **1** = **assessment**, estimate, estimation, evaluation, judgment, opinion, recce (*sl.*), sizing up (*inf.*) **2** = **valuation**, assay, pricing, rating, reckoning, survey

appraise *vb* **1** = **assess**, assay, estimate, evaluate, eye up, gauge, inspect, judge, price, rate, recce (*sl.*), review, size up (*inf.*), survey, value

appreciable *adj* = **significant**, ascertainable, clear-cut, considerable, definite, detectable,

appreciate ➊ (əˈpriːʃɪˌeɪt, -sɪ-) *vb* **appreciates, appreciating, appreciated.** (*mainly tr*) **1** to feel thankful or grateful for. **2** (*may take a clause as object*) to take sufficient account of: *to appreciate a problem.* **3** to value highly. **4** (*usually intr*) to increase in value. [C17: from Med. L *appretiāre* to value, from L *pretium* PRICE]
▸**apˈpreciˌator** *n*

appreciation ➊ (əˌpriːʃɪˈeɪʃən, -sɪ-) *n* **1** thanks or gratitude. **2** assessment of the true worth of persons or things. **3** perceptive recognition of qualities, as in art. **4** an increase in value. **5** a review of a book, etc., esp. when favourable.

appreciative ➊ (əˈpriːʃɪətɪv) *or* **appreciatory** *adj* feeling or expressing appreciation.
▸**apˈpreciatively** *adv* ▸**apˈpreciativeness** *n*

apprehend ➊ (ˌæprɪˈhɛnd) *vb* **1** (*tr*) to arrest and escort into custody. **2** to grasp mentally; understand. **3** to await with fear or anxiety. [C14: from L *apprehendere* to lay hold of]

apprehensible (ˌæprɪˈhɛnsɪbᵊl) *adj* capable of being comprehended or grasped mentally.
▸ˌ**appreˌhensiˈbility** *n*

apprehension ➊ (ˌæprɪˈhɛnʃən) *n* **1** anxiety over what may happen. **2** the act of arresting. **3** understanding. **4** a notion or conception.

apprehensive ➊ (ˌæprɪˈhɛnsɪv) *adj* **1** fearful or anxious. **2** (*usually postpositive* and foll. by *of*) *Arch.* intelligent, perceptive.
▸ˌ**appreˈhensively** *adv* ▸ˌ**appreˈhensiveness** *n*

apprentice ➊ (əˈprɛntɪs) *n* **1** someone who works for a skilled or qualified person in order to learn a trade, esp. for a recognized period. **2** any beginner or novice. ◆ *vb* **apprentices, apprenticing, apprenticed. 3** (*tr*) to take, place, or bind as an apprentice. [C14: from OF *aprentis,* from *aprendre* to learn, from L *apprehendere* to APPREHEND]
▸**apˈprenticeship** *n*

apprise ➊ *or* **apprize** (əˈpraɪz) *vb* **apprises, apprising, apprised** *or* **apprizes, apprizing, apprized.** (*tr;* often foll. by *of*) to make aware; inform. [C17: from F *appris,* from *apprendre* to teach; learn]

USAGE NOTE See at **appraise.**

appro (ˈæprəʊ) *n* an informal shortening of **approval:** *on appro.*

approach ➊ (əˈprəʊtʃ) *vb* **1** to come nearer in position, time, quality, character, etc., to (someone or something). **2** (*tr*) to make a proposal or suggestion to. **3** (*tr*) to begin to deal with. ◆ *n* **4** the act of drawing close or closer. **5** a close approximation. **6** the way or means of entering or leaving. **7** (*often pl*) an overture to a person. **8** a means adopted in tackling a problem, job of work, etc. **9** Also called: **approach path.** the course followed by an aircraft preparing for landing. **10** Also called: **approach shot.** *Golf.* a shot made to or towards the green after a tee shot. [C14: from OF *aprochier,* from LL *appropiāre* to draw near, from L *prope* near]
▸**apˈproachable** *adj* ▸**apˌproachaˈbility** *n*

approbation ➊ (ˌæprəˈbeɪʃən) *n* **1** commendation; praise. **2** official recognition.
▸ˈ**approˌbative** *or* ˈ**approˌbatory** *adj*

appropriate ➊ *adj* (əˈprəʊprɪɪt). **1** right or suitable; fitting. ◆ *vb* (əˈprəʊprɪˌeɪt), **appropriates, appropriating, appropriated.** (*tr*) **2** to take for one's own use, esp. illegally. **3** to put aside (funds, etc.) for a particular purpose or person. [C15: from LL *appropriāre* to make one's own, from L *proprius* one's own]
▸**apˈpropriately** *adv* ▸**apˈpropriateness** *n* ▸**apˈpropriˌator** *n*

appropriation ➊ (əˌprəʊprɪˈeɪʃən) *n* **1** the act of setting apart or taking for one's own use. **2** a sum of money set apart for a specific purpose.

THESAURUS

discernible, distinguishable, evident, marked, material, measurable, noticeable, obvious, perceivable, perceptible, pronounced, recognizable, substantial, visible
Antonyms *adj* immaterial, imperceptible, inappreciable, indiscernible, indistinguishable, insignificant, invisible, minor, minute, negligible, small, trivial, undetectable, unnoticeable, unsubstantial

appreciably *adv* = **significantly,** ascertainably, considerably, definitely, detectably, discernibly, distinguishably, evidently, markedly, measurably, noticeably, obviously, palpably, perceivably, perceptively, recognizably, substantially, visibly

appreciate *vb* **1** = **be grateful for,** be appreciative, be indebted, be obliged, be thankful for, give thanks for **2** = **be aware of,** acknowledge, be alive to, be cognizant of, be conscious of, comprehend, estimate, know, perceive, realize, recognize, sympathize with, take account of, understand **3** = **value,** admire, cherish, enjoy, esteem, like, prize, rate highly, regard, relish, respect, savour, treasure **4** = **increase,** enhance, gain, grow, improve, inflate, raise the value of, rise
Antonyms *vb* ≠ **be grateful for:** be ungrateful for ≠ **be aware of:** be unaware of, misunderstand, underrate ≠ **value:** belittle, denigrate, disdain, disparage, scorn ≠ **increase:** deflate, depreciate, devaluate, fall

appreciation *n* **1** = **gratitude,** acknowledgment, gratefulness, indebtedness, obligation, thankfulness, thanks **2, 3** = **awareness,** admiration, appraisal, assessment, cognizance, comprehension, enjoyment, esteem, estimation, knowledge, liking, perception, realization, recognition, regard, relish, respect, responsiveness, sensitivity, sympathy, understanding, valuation **4** = **increase,** enhancement, gain, growth, improvement, inflation, rise **5** = **praise,** acclamation, criticism, critique, notice, recognition, review, tribute
Antonyms *n* ≠ **gratitude:** ingratitude ≠ **awareness:** ignorance, incomprehension ≠ **increase:** decline, depreciation, devaluation, fall

appreciative *adj* = **aware,** admiring, cognizant, conscious, enthusiastic, in the know (*inf.*), knowledgeable, mindful, perceptive, pleased, regardful, respectful, responsive, sensitive, supportive, sympathetic, understanding

apprehend *vb* **1** = **arrest,** bust (*inf.*), capture, catch, collar (*inf.*), feel one's collar (*sl.*), lift (*sl.*), nab (*inf.*), nail (*inf.*), nick (*sl., chiefly Brit.*), pinch (*inf.*), run in (*sl.*), seize, take, take prisoner **2** = **understand,** appreciate, believe, comprehend, conceive, get the message, get the picture, grasp, imagine, know, perceive, realize, recognize, think
Antonyms *vb* ≠ **arrest:** discharge, free, let go, liberate, release ≠ **understand:** be at cross-purposes, be unaware of, be unconscious of, get one's lines crossed, misapprehend, misconceive, miss, misunderstand

apprehension *n* **1** = **anxiety,** alarm, apprehensiveness, concern, disquiet, doubt, dread, fear, foreboding, misgiving, mistrust, pins and needles, premonition, suspicion, trepidation, unease, uneasiness, worry **2** = **arrest,** capture, catching, seizure, taking **3** = **awareness,** comprehension, grasp, intellect, intelligence, ken, knowledge, perception, understanding **4** = **idea,** belief, concept, conception, conjecture, impression, notion, opinion, sentiment, thought, view
Antonyms *n* ≠ **anxiety:** assurance, composure, confidence, nonchalance, serenity, unconcern ≠ **arrest:** discharge, liberation, release ≠ **awareness:** incomprehension

apprehensive *adj* **1** = **anxious,** afraid, alarmed, concerned, disquieted, doubtful, fearful, foreboding, mistrustful, nervous, neurotic, suspicious, twitchy (*inf.*), uneasy, worried
Antonyms *adj* assured, at ease, composed, confident, nonchalant, unafraid

apprehensiveness *n* **1** = **anxiety,** alarm, anxiousness, concern, disquietedness *or* disquietness, disquietude, doubtfulness, fear, fearfulness, foreboding, forebodingness, misgiving, mistrustfulness, nervousness, suspiciousness, trepidation, uneasiness, worry

apprentice *n* **1, 2** = **trainee,** beginner, learner, neophyte, novice, probationer, pupil, student, tyro
Antonyms *n* ace (*inf.*), adept, dab hand (*Brit. inf.*), expert, master, past master, pro

apprenticeship *n* **1, 2** = **traineeship,** novitiate *or* noviciate, probation, studentship

apprise *vb* = **make aware,** acquaint, advise, communicate, enlighten, give notice, inform, make cognizant, notify, tell, warn

approach *vb* **1** = **move towards,** advance, catch up, come close, come near, come to, draw near, gain on, meet, near, push forward, reach **1** = **be like,** approximate, be comparable to, come close to, come near to, compare with, resemble **2** = **make a proposal to,** appeal to, apply to, broach the matter with, make advances to, make overtures to, sound out **3** = **set about,** begin work on, commence, embark on, enter upon, make a start, undertake ◆ *n* **4** = **coming,** advance, advent, arrival, drawing near, nearing **5** = **likeness,** approximation, semblance **6** = **access,** avenue, entrance, passage, road, way **7** *often plural* = **proposal,** advance, appeal, application, invitation, offer, overture, proposition **8** = **way,** attitude, course, manner, means, method, mode, modus operandi, procedure, style, technique

approachability *n* **1** = **accessibility,** attainability, openness **2** = **friendliness,** affability, congeniality, conversableness, cordiality, expansiveness, sociability
Antonyms *n* ≠ **accessibility:** inaccessibility, remoteness ≠ **friendliness:** aloofness, chilliness, coolness, detachment, distance, frigidity, frostiness, remoteness, reservedness, standoffishness, unaffability, uncongeniality, unexpansiveness, unfriendliness, unsociability, withdrawnness

approachable *adj* **1** = **accessible,** attainable, come-at-able (*inf.*), get-at-able (*inf.*), reachable **2** = **friendly,** affable, congenial, cordial, open, sociable
Antonyms *adj* ≠ **accessible:** inaccessible, out of reach, out-of-the-way, remote, unreachable ≠ **friendly:** aloof, chilly, cold as ice, cool, distant, frigid, remote, reserved, standoffish, unfriendly, unsociable, withdrawn

approbation *n* **1, 2** = **approval,** acceptance, acclaim, applause, assent, commendation, congratulation, encouragement, endorsement, favour, laudation, praise, ratification, recognition, sanction, support
Antonyms *n* blame, censure, condemnation, disapprobation, disapproval, disfavour, dislike, displeasure, dissatisfaction, reproof, stricture

approbative *adj* **1** = **approving,** accepting, acclamatory, applauding, commendatory, congratulatory, encouraging, favourable, laudatory, supportive

appropriate *adj* **1** = **suitable,** adapted, applicable, apposite, appurtenant, apropos, apt, becoming, befitting, belonging, congruous, correct, felicitous, fit, fitting, germane, meet (*arch.*), opportune, pertinent, proper, relevant, right, seemly, to the point, to the purpose, well-suited, well-timed ◆ *vb* **2** = **seize,** annex, arrogate, assume, commandeer, confiscate, expropriate, impound, pre-empt, take, take over, take possession of, usurp **2** = **steal,** embezzle, filch, misappropriate, pilfer, pocket **3** = **allocate,** allot, apportion, assign, devote, earmark, set aside
Antonyms *adj* ≠ **suitable:** improper, inappropriate, incompatible, incorrect, inopportune, irrelevant, unfitting, unsuitable, untimely ◆ *vb* ≠ **seize:** cede, donate, give, relinquish ≠ **allocate:** withhold

appropriateness *n* **1** = **suitability,** applicability, appositeness, aptness, becomingness, congruousness, correctness, felicitousness, felicity, fitness, fittingness, germaneness, opportuneness, pertinence, properness, relevance, rightness, seemliness, timeliness, well-suitedness

appropriation *n* **1** = **setting aside,** allocation, allotment, apportionment, assignment, earmarking **1** = **seizure,** annexation, arrogation, assumption, commandeering, confiscation, expropriation, impoundment, pre-emption, takeover, taking, usurpation

approval ❶ (ə'pru:vᵊl) *n* **1** the act of approving. **2** formal agreement. **3** a favourable opinion. **4 on approval.** (of articles for sale) for examination with an option to buy or return.

approve ❶ (ə'pru:v) *vb* **approves, approving, approved. 1** (when *intr,* often foll. by *of*) to consider fair, good, or right. **2** (*tr*) to authorize or sanction. [C14: from OF *aprover,* from L *approbāre* to approve, from *probāre* to test, PROVE]

approved school *n* (in Britain) a former name for **community home.**

approx. *abbrev. for* approximate(ly).

approximate ❶ *adj* (ə'prɒksɪmɪt). **1** almost accurate or exact. **2** inexact; rough; loose. **3** much alike; almost the same. **4** near; close together. ◆ *vb* (ə'prɒksɪ,meɪt), **approximates, approximating, approximated. 5** (usually foll. by *to*) to come or bring near or close; be almost the same (as). **6** *Maths.* to find an expression for (some quantity) accurate to a specified degree. [C15: from LL *approximāre,* from L *proximus* nearest]
▸**ap'proximately** *adv*

approximation ❶ (ə,prɒksɪ'meɪʃən) *n* **1** the process or result of making a rough calculation, estimate, or guess. **2** an imprecise or unreliable record or version. **3** *Maths.* an inexact number, relationship, or theory that is sufficiently accurate for a specific purpose.

appurtenance ❶ (ə'pɜ:tɪnəns) *n* **1** a less significant thing or part. **2** (*pl*) accessories. **3** *Property law.* a minor right, interest, or privilege. [C14: from Anglo-F *apurtenance,* from OF *apartenance,* from *apartenir* to APPERTAIN]

APR *abbrev. for* annual percentage rate.

Apr. *abbrev. for* April.

apraxia (ə'præksɪə) *n* a disorder of the central nervous system characterized by impaired ability to carry out certain purposeful muscular movements. [C19: via NL from Gk: inactivity, from A-[1] + *praxis* action]

après-ski (,æpreɪ'ski:) *n* **a** social activity following a day's skiing. **b** (*as modifier*): *an après-ski outfit.* [F, lit.: after ski]

apricot ('eɪprɪ,kɒt) *n* **1** a tree native to Africa and W Asia, but widely cultivated for its edible fruit. **2** the yellow juicy fruit of this tree, which resembles a small peach. [C16: from Port., from Ar., from LGk, from L *praecox* early-ripening]

April ('eɪprəl) *n* the fourth month of the year, consisting of 30 days. [C14: from L *Aprīlis*]

April fool *n* a victim of a practical joke performed on the first of April (**April Fools' Day** *or* **All Fools' Day**).

a priori ❶ (eɪ praɪ'ɔ:raɪ, ɑ: prɪ'ɔ:rɪ) *adj* **1** *Logic.* relating to or involving deductive reasoning from a general principle to the expected facts or effects. **2** known to be true independently of experience of the subject matter. [C18: from L, lit.: from the previous]
▸**apriority** (,eɪpraɪ'ɒrɪtɪ) *n*

apron ❶ ('eɪprən) *n* **1** a protective or sometimes decorative garment worn over the front of the body and tied around the waist. **2** the part of a stage extending in front of the curtain. **3** a hard-surfaced area in front of an aircraft hangar, terminal building, etc. **4** a continuous conveyor belt composed of metal slats. **5** a protective plate screening the operator of a machine, artillery piece, etc. **6** *Geol.* a sheet of sand, gravel, etc., deposited at the front of a moraine. **7** another name for **skirt** (sense 3). **8 tied to someone's apron strings.** dominated by someone, esp. a mother or wife. ◆ *vb* **9** (*tr*) to protect or provide with an apron. [C16: mistaken division of *a napron,* from OF, from L *mappa* napkin]

apron stage *n* a stage that projects into the auditorium so that the audience sits on three sides of it.

apropos ❶ (,æprə'pəʊ) *adj* **1** appropriate. ◆ *adv* **2** appropriately. **3** by the way; incidentally. **4 apropos of.** (*prep*) in respect of. [C17: from F *à propos* to the purpose]

apse (æps) *n* a domed or vaulted semicircular or polygonal recess, esp. at the east end of a church. Also called: **apsis.** [C19: from L *apsis,* from Gk: a fitting together, from *haptein* to fasten]
▸**'apsidal** *adj*

apsis ('æpsɪs) *n, pl* **apsides** (æp'saɪdi:z). either of two points lying at the extremities of an eccentric orbit of a planet, satellite, etc. Also called: **apse.** [C17: via L from Gk; see APSE]
▸**apsidal** ('æpsɪdᵊl) *adj*

apt ❶ (æpt) *adj* **1** suitable; appropriate. **2** (*postpositive;* foll. by an infinitive) having a tendency (to behave as specified). **3** having the ability to learn and understand easily. [C14: from L *aptus* fitting, from *apere* to fasten]
▸**'aptly** *adv* ▸**'aptness** *n*

APT *abbrev. for* Advanced Passenger Train.

apterous ('æptərəs) *adj* **1** (of insects) without wings, as silverfish. **2** without winglike expansions, as some seeds and fruits. [C18: from Gk, from A-[1] + *pteron* wing]
▸**'apter,ism** *n*

apteryx ('æptərɪks) *n* another name for **kiwi** (the bird). [C19: from NL; see APTEROUS]

aptitude ❶ ('æptɪ,tju:d) *n* **1** inherent or acquired ability. **2** ease in learning or understanding. **3** the quality of being apt. [C15: via OF from LL, from L *aptus* APT]

aqua ('ækwə) *n, pl* **aquae** ('ækwi:) *or* **aquas. 1** water: used in compound names of certain liquid substances or solutions of substances in water. ◆ *n, adj* **2** short for **aquamarine** (the colour). [L: water]

aquaculture ('ækwə,kʌltʃə) *or* **aquiculture** *n* the cultivation of freshwater and marine organisms for human consumption or use.

aquaerobics *or* **aquarobics** (,ækwə'rəʊbɪks) *n* (*functioning as sing*) the practice of exercising to music in a swimming pool. [C20: from L *aqua* water + AEROBICS]

aqua fortis ('fɔ:tɪs) *n* an obsolete name for **nitric acid.** [C17: from L, lit.: strong water]

aqualung ('ækwə,lʌŋ) *n* breathing apparatus used by divers, etc., consisting of a mouthpiece attached to air cylinders strapped to the back.

aquamarine (,ækwəmə'ri:n) *n* **1** a pale greenish-blue transparent variety of beryl used as a gemstone. **2a** a pale blue to greenish-blue colour. **2b** (*as adj*): *an aquamarine dress.* [C19: from NL, from L: sea water (referring to the gem's colour)]

aquanaut ('ækwənɔ:t) *n* a person who works, swims, or dives underwater. [C20: from AQUA + *-naut,* as in ASTRONAUT]

aquaplane ('ækwə,pleɪn) *n* **1** a board on which a person stands and is towed by a motorboat. ◆ *vb* **aquaplanes, aquaplaning, aquaplaned.** (*intr*) **2** to ride on an aquaplane. **3** (of a motor vehicle travelling at high speeds on wet roads) to rise up onto a thin film of water so that contact with the road is lost.

aqua regia ('ri:dʒɪə) *n* a mixture of nitric acid and hydrochloric acid. [C17: from NL: royal water; referring to its use in dissolving gold, the royal metal]

THESAURUS

approval *n* **1, 2** = **consent**, acquiescence, agreement, assent, authorization, blessing, compliance, concurrence, confirmation, countenance, endorsement, imprimatur, leave, licence, mandate, O.K. *or* okay (*inf.*), permission, ratification, recommendation, sanction, the go-ahead (*inf.*), the green light, validation **3** = **favour**, acclaim, admiration, applause, appreciation, approbation, Brownie points, commendation, esteem, good opinion, liking, praise, regard, respect
Antonyms *n* ≠ **favour:** denigration, disapproval, dislike, disparagement, displeasure, dissatisfaction

approve *vb* **1** = **favour**, acclaim, admire, applaud, appreciate, be pleased with, commend, esteem, have a good opinion of, like, praise, regard highly, respect, think highly of **2** = **agree to**, accede to, accept, advocate, allow, assent to, authorize, bless, buy into (*inf.*), concur in, confirm, consent to, countenance, endorse, go along with, mandate, O.K. *or* okay (*inf.*), pass, permit, ratify, recommend, sanction, second, subscribe to, uphold, validate
Antonyms *vb* ≠ **favour:** blame, censure, condemn, deplore, deprecate, disapprove, dislike, find unacceptable, frown on, look down one's nose at (*inf.*), object to, take exception to ≠ **agree to:** disallow, discountenance, veto

approving *adj* **1** = **favourable**, acclamatory, admiring, applauding, appreciative, commendatory, respectful

approximate *adj* **1** = **close**, almost accurate, almost exact, near **2** = **rough**, estimated, inexact, loose **3** = **like**, analogous, close, comparable, near, relative, similar, verging on ◆ *vb* **5** = **come close**, approach, border on, come near, reach, resemble, touch, verge on
Antonyms *adj* ≠ **close, rough:** accurate, correct, definite, exact, precise, specific

approximately *adv* **1, 2** = **almost**, about, around, circa (*used with dates*), close to, generally, in the neighbourhood of, in the region of, in the vicinity of, just about, loosely, more or less, nearly, not far off, relatively, roughly

approximation *n* **1** = **guess**, ballpark estimate (*inf.*), ballpark figure (*inf.*), conjecture, estimate, estimation, guesswork, rough calculation, rough idea

appurtenance *n* **2** *plural* = **accompaniments**, accessories, accoutrements, appendages, equipment, impedimenta, paraphernalia, trappings

a priori *adj* **1** = **deduced**, deductive, from cause to effect, inferential

apron *n* **1** = **pinny** (*inf.*), pinafore

apropos *adj* **1** = **appropriate**, applicable, apposite, apt, befitting, belonging, correct, fit, fitting, germane, meet (*arch.*), opportune, pertinent, proper, related, relevant, right, seemly, suitable, to the point, to the purpose ◆ *adv* **2** = **appropriately**, aptly, opportunely, pertinently, relevantly, suitably, timely, to the point, to the purpose **3** = **incidentally**, by the bye, by the way, in passing, parenthetically, while on the subject **4 apropos of** = **regarding**, in respect of, on the subject of, re, respecting, with reference to, with regard to, with respect to

apt *adj* **1** = **appropriate**, applicable, apposite, apropos, befitting, correct, fit, fitting, germane, meet (*arch.*), pertinent, proper, relevant, seemly, suitable, timely, to the point, to the purpose **2** = **inclined**, disposed, given, liable, likely, of a mind, prone, ready **3** = **gifted**, astute, bright, clever, expert, ingenious, intelligent, prompt, quick, sharp, skilful, smart, talented, teachable
Antonyms *adj* ≠ **appropriate:** ill-fitted, ill-suited, ill-timed, improper, inapplicable, inapposite, inappropriate, infelicitous, inopportune, irrelevant, unsuitable, untimely ≠ **gifted:** awkward, clumsy, dull, gauche, incompetent, inept, inexpert, maladroit, slow, stupid

aptitude *n* **1** = **tendency**, bent, disposition, inclination, leaning, predilection, proclivity, proneness, propensity **2** = **gift**, ability, aptness, capability, capacity, cleverness, faculty, flair, giftedness, intelligence, knack, proficiency, quickness, talent

aptness *n* **1** = **appropriateness**, applicability, appositeness, becomingness, congruousness, correctness, felicitousness, felicity, fitness, fittingness, germaneness, opportuneness, pertinence, properness, relevance, rightness, seemliness, suitability, timeliness, well-suitedness **2** = **tendency**, aptitude, bent, disposition, inclination, leaning, liability, likelihood, likeliness, predilection, proclivity, proneness, propensity, readiness **3** = **gift**, ability, capability, capacity, cleverness, faculty, fitness, flair, giftedness, intelligence, knack, proficiency, quickness, suitability, talent

aquarist (ˈækwərɪst) *n* **1** the curator of an aquarium. **2** a person who studies aquatic life.

aquarium (əˈkwɛərɪəm) *n, pl* **aquariums** *or* **aquaria** (-rɪə). **1** a tank, bowl, or pool in which aquatic animals and plants are kept for pleasure, study, or exhibition. **2** a building housing a collection of aquatic life, as for exhibition. [C19: from L *aquārius* relating to water, on the model of VIVARIUM]

Aquarius (əˈkwɛərɪəs) *n, Latin genitive* **Aquarii** (əˈkwɛərɪˌaɪ). **1** *Astron.* a S constellation. **2** *Astrol.* also called: the **Water Carrier**. the eleventh sign of the zodiac. The sun is in this sign between about Jan. 20 and Feb. 18. [L]

aquatic (əˈkwætɪk) *adj* **1** growing, living, or found in water. **2** *Sport.* performed in or on water. ◆ *n* **3** a marine animal or plant. [C15: from L *aquāticus*, from *aqua* water]

aquatics (əˈkwætɪks) *pl n* sports or pastimes performed in or on the water.

aquatint (ˈækwəˌtɪnt) *n* **1** a technique of etching copper with acid to produce an effect resembling watercolour. **2** an etching made in this way. ◆ *vb* **3** (*tr*) to etch (a block, etc.) in aquatint. [C18: from It. *acqua tinta* dyed water]

aquavit (ˈækwəˌvɪt) *n* a grain- or potato-based spirit flavoured with aromatic seeds. Also called: **akvavit**. [of Scandinavian origin: see AQUA VITAE]

aqua vitae (ˈviːtaɪ, ˈvaɪtiː) *n* an archaic name for **brandy**. [Med. L: water of life]

aqueduct (ˈækwɪˌdʌkt) *n* **1** a conduit used to convey water over a long distance. **2** a structure, often a bridge, that carries such a conduit or a canal across a valley or river. **3** a channel or conduit in the body. [C16: from L *aquaeductus*, from *aqua* water + *dūcere* to convey]

aqueous (ˈeɪkwɪəs) *adj* **1** of, like, or containing water. **2** dissolved in water: *aqueous ammonia*. **3** (of rocks, etc.) formed from material laid down in water. [C17: from Med. L *aqueus*, from L *aqua* water]

aqueous humour *n Physiol.* the watery fluid within the eyeball between the cornea and the lens.

aquiculture (ˈeɪkwɪˌkʌltʃə, ˈækwɪ-) *n* **1** another name for **hydroponics**. **2** a variant of **aquaculture**.
▸ˈ**aquiˌculturist** *n* ▸ˈ**aquiˌcultural** *adj*

aquifer (ˈækwɪfə) *n* a deposit or rock, such as a sandstone, containing water that can be used to supply wells.

aquilegia (ˌækwɪˈliːdʒɪə) *n* another name for **columbine**. [C19: from Med. L, from ?]

aquiline (ˈækwɪˌlaɪn) *adj* **1** (of a nose) having the curved shape of an eagle's beak. **2** of or like an eagle. [C17: from L, from *aquila* eagle]

Ar *the chemical symbol for* argon.

ar. *abbrev. for:* **1** arrival. **2** arrive(s).

Ar. *abbrev. for:* **1** Arabia(n). **2** Also: **Ar** Arabic. **3** Aramaic.

a.r. *abbrev. for* anno regni. [L: in the year of the reign]

-ar *suffix forming adjectives.* of; belonging to; like: *linear; polar.* [via OF *-er* from L *-āris*]

ARA *abbrev. for:* **1** (in Britain) Associate of the Royal Academy. **2** (in New Zealand) Auckland Regional Authority.

Arab (ˈærəb) *n* **1** a member of a Semitic people originally inhabiting Arabia. **2** a small breed of horse, used for riding. **3** (*modifier*) of or relating to the Arabs. [C14: from L, from Gk *Araps*, from Ar. *ʻArab*]

arabesque (ˌærəˈbɛsk) *n* **1** *Ballet.* a classical position in which the dancer has one leg raised behind. **2** *Music.* a piece or movement with a highly ornamented melody. **3** *Arts.* a type of curvilinear decoration in painting, metalwork, etc., with intricate intertwining designs. [C18: from F, from It. *arabesco* in the Arabic style]

Arabian (əˈreɪbɪən) *adj* **1** of or relating to Arabia or the Arabs. ◆ *n* **2** another word for **Arab**.

Arabian camel *n* a domesticated camel with one hump on its back, used as a beast of burden in the deserts of N Africa and SW Asia.

Arabic (ˈærəbɪk) *n* **1** the Semitic language of the Arabs, which has its own alphabet and is spoken in Algeria, Egypt, Iraq, Jordan, Saudi Arabia, Syria, Tunisia, etc. ◆ *adj* **2** denoting or relating to this language, any of the peoples that speak it, or the countries in which it is spoken.

arabica bean (əˈræbɪkə) *n* a high-quality coffee bean, obtained from the tree *Coffea arabica*.

Arabic numeral *n* one of the numbers 0, 1, 2, 3, 4, 5, 6, 7, 8, 9. Cf. **Roman numerals**.

arabis (ˈærəbɪs) *n* any of several trailing plants having pink or white flowers in spring. Also called: **rock cress**. [C16: from Med. L, from Gk *arabis*, ult. from *Arābios* Arabian, prob. from growing in sandy or stony soil]

Arabist (ˈærəbɪst) *n* a student of Arabic culture, language, history, etc.

arable **T** (ˈærəbᵊl) *adj* **1** (of land) being or capable of being tilled for the production of crops. **2** of, relating to, or using such land. [C15: from L *arābilis*, from *arāre* to plough]

Araby (ˈærəbɪ) *n* an archaic or poetic name for Arabia.

arachnid (əˈræknɪd) *n* any of a class of arthropods characterized by simple eyes and four pairs of legs, including the spiders, scorpions, and ticks. [C19: from NL *Arachnida*, from Gk *arakhnē* spider]
▸**aˈrachnidan** *adj, n*

arachnoid (əˈræknɔɪd) *n* **1** the middle one of three membranes that cover the brain and spinal cord. ◆ *adj* **2** of or relating to this membrane. **3** *Bot.* consisting of or covered with soft fine hairs or fibres.

arachnophobia (əˌræknəˈfəʊbɪə) *n* an abnormal fear of spiders. [C20: from Gk *arakhnē* spider + -PHOBIA]

arak (ˈærək) *n* a variant spelling of **arrack**.

Araldite (ˈærəldaɪt) *n Trademark.* an epoxy resin used as a glue for mending glass, plastic, and china.

Aram. *abbrev. for* Aramaic.

Aramaic (ˌærəˈmeɪɪk) *n* **1** an ancient Semitic language of the Middle East, still spoken in parts of Syria and the Lebanon. ◆ *adj* **2** of, relating to, or using this language.

Aran (ˈærən) *adj* **1** of or relating to the Aran Islands, off the W coast of Ireland. **2** made of thick natural wool: *an Aran sweater.*

araucaria (ˌærɔːˈkɛərɪə) *n* any of a group of coniferous trees of South America, Australia, and Polynesia, such as the monkey puzzle. [C19: from NL (*arbor*) *Araucaria* (tree) from *Arauco*, a province in Chile]

arbalest *or* **arbalist** (ˈɑːbəlɪst) *n* a large medieval crossbow, usually cocked by mechanical means. [C11: from OF, from LL *arcuballista*, from L *arcus* bow + BALLISTA]

arbiter **T** (ˈɑːbɪtə) *n* **1** a person empowered to judge in a dispute; referee. **2** a person having control of something. [C15: from L, from ?]
▸ˈ**arbitress** *fem n*

arbitrament (ɑːˈbɪtrəmənt) *n* **1** the decision or award made by an arbitrator upon a disputed matter. **2** another word for **arbitration**.

arbitrary **T** (ˈɑːbɪtrərɪ) *adj* **1** founded on or subject to personal whims, prejudices, etc. **2** not absolute. **3** (of a government, ruler, etc.) despotic or dictatorial. **4** *Law.* (esp. of a penalty) within the court's discretion. [C15: from L *arbitrārius* arranged through arbitration]
▸ˈ**arbitrarily** *adv* ▸ˈ**arbitrariness** *n*

arbitrate **T** (ˈɑːbɪˌtreɪt) *vb* **arbitrates, arbitrating, arbitrated. 1** to achieve a settlement between parties. **2** to submit to or settle by arbitration. [C16: from L *arbitrārī* to give judgment]
▸ˈ**arbiˌtrator** *n*

arbitration **T** (ˌɑːbɪˈtreɪʃən) *n* the hearing and determination of a dispute, esp. an industrial one, by an impartial referee selected or agreed upon by the parties concerned.

arbor[1] (ˈɑːbə) *n* the US spelling of **arbour**.

arbor[2] (ˈɑːbə) *n* **1** a rotating shaft in a machine on which a milling cutter or grinding wheel is fitted. **2** a rotating shaft. [C17: from L: tree]

arboraceous (ˌɑːbəˈreɪʃəs) *adj Literary.* **1** resembling a tree. **2** wooded.

arboreal (ɑːˈbɔːrɪəl) *adj* **1** of or resembling a tree. **2** living in or among trees.

arborescent (ˌɑːbəˈrɛsᵊnt) *adj* having the shape or characteristics of a tree.
▸ˌ**arboˈrescence** *n*

arboretum (ˌɑːbəˈriːtəm) *n, pl* **arboreta** (-tə) *or* **arboretums**. a place where trees or shrubs are cultivated. [C19: from L, from *arbor* tree]

arboriculture (ˈɑːbərɪˌkʌltʃə) *n* the cultivation of trees or shrubs.
▸ˌ**arboriˈculturist** *n*

arbor vitae (ˈɑːbɔː ˈviːtaɪ, ˈvaɪtiː) *n* any of several Asian and North American evergreen coniferous trees having tiny scalelike leaves and egglike cones. [C17: from NL, lit.: tree of life]

arbour (ˈɑːbə) *n* a leafy glade or bower shaded by trees, vines, shrubs, etc. [C14 *erber*, from OF, from L *herba* grass]

arbutus (ɑːˈbjuːtəs) *n, pl* **arbutuses**. any of a genus of shrubs having clusters of white or pinkish flowers, broad evergreen leaves, and strawberry-like berries. [C16: from L; rel. to *arbor* tree]

arc **T** (ɑːk) *n* **1** something curved in shape. **2** part of an unbroken curved line. **3** a luminous discharge that occurs when an electric current flows between two electrodes separated by a small gap. **4** *Maths.* a section of a curve, graph, or geometric figure. ◆ *vb* **arcs, arcing, arced** *or* **arcs, arcking, arcked. 5** (*intr*) to form an arc. ◆ *adj* **6** *Maths.* specifying an inverse trigonometric function: *arcsin, arccos, arctan.* [C14: from OF, from L *arcus* bow, arch]

ARC *abbrev. for* AIDS-related complex: a condition in which a person infected with the AIDS virus suffers from relatively mild symptoms, such as loss of weight, fever, etc.

THESAURUS

arable *adj* **1** = **productive**, cultivable, farmable, fecund, fertile, fruitful, ploughable, tillable

arbiter *n* **1** = **judge**, adjudicator, arbitrator, referee, umpire **2** = **authority**, controller, dictator, expert, governor, lord, master, pundit, ruler

arbitrariness *n* **1** = **randomness**, capriciousness, fancifulness, inconsistency, subjectivity, unreasonableness, whimsicality, wilfulness **3** = **dictatorialness**, absoluteness, despotism, dogmatism, domineeringness, high-handedness, imperiousness, magisterialness, overbearingness, peremptoriness, summariness, tyrannicalness, tyrannousness, tyranny, uncontrolledness, unlimitedness, unrestrainedness

arbitrary *adj* **1** = **random**, capricious, chance, discretionary, erratic, fanciful, inconsistent, optional, personal, subjective, unreasonable, whimsical, wilful **3** = **dictatorial**, absolute, autocratic, despotic, dogmatic, domineering, high-handed, imperious, magisterial, overbearing, peremptory, summary, tyrannical, tyrannous, uncontrolled, unlimited, unrestrained
Antonyms *adj* ≠ **random**: consistent, judicious, logical, objective, rational, reasonable, reasoned, sensible, sound

arbitrate *vb* **1, 2** = **settle**, adjudge, adjudicate, decide, determine, judge, mediate, pass judgment, referee, sit in judgment, umpire

arbitration *n* = **settlement**, adjudication, arbitrament, decision, determination, judgment

arbitrator *n* **1, 2** = **judge**, adjudicator, arbiter, referee, umpire

arc *n* **1, 2** = **curve**, arch, bend, bow, crescent, half-moon

arcade Ⓣ (ɑːˈkeɪd) *n* **1** a set of arches and their supporting columns. **2** a covered and sometimes arched passageway, usually with shops on one or both sides. [C18: from F, from It. *arcata,* from L *arcus* bow, arch]

Arcadian (ɑːˈkeɪdɪən) *adj* **1** of Arcadia, the idealized setting of pastoral poetry. **2** rustic or bucolic. ◆ *n* **3** a person who leads a quiet simple rural life.

arcane Ⓣ (ɑːˈkeɪn) *adj* requiring secret knowledge to be understood; esoteric. [C16: from L *arcānus* secret, from *arcēre* to keep safe]

arcanum (ɑːˈkeɪnəm) *n, pl* **arcana** (-nə). (*sometimes pl*) a secret or mystery. [C16: from L; see ARCANE]

arch[1] Ⓣ (ɑːtʃ) *n* **1** a curved structure that spans an opening. **2** Also called: **archway.** a structure in the form of an arch that serves as a gateway. **3** something curved like an arch. **4** any of various parts or structures of the body having a curved or archlike outline, such as the raised vault formed by the tarsal and metatarsal bones (**arch of the foot**). ◆ *vb* **5** (*tr*) to span (an opening) with an arch. **6** to form or cause to form an arch or a curve resembling that of an arch. **7** (*tr*) to span or extend over. [C14: from OF *arche,* from L *arcus* bow, ARC]

arch[2] Ⓣ (ɑːtʃ) *adj* **1** (*prenominal*) chief; principal; leading. **2** (*prenominal*) expert: *an arch criminal.* **3** knowing or superior; coyly playful: *an arch look.* [C16: independent use of ARCH-]
▸ **ˈarchly** *adv* ▸ **ˈarchness** *n*

arch. *abbrev. for:* **1** archaic. **2** archaism. **3** archipelago. **4** architect. **5** architectural. **6** architecture.

arch- Ⓣ *or* **archi-** *combining form.* **1** chief; principal: *archbishop.* **2** eminent above all others of the same kind: *archenemy.* [ult. from Gk *arkhi-,* from *arkhein* to rule]

-arch *n combining form.* leader; ruler; chief: *patriarch; monarch.* [from Gk *-arkhēs,* from *arkhein* to rule]

Archaean *or esp. US* **Archean** (ɑːˈkiːən) *adj* of the metamorphosed rocks formed in the early Precambrian era.

archaeology *or* **archeology** (ˌɑːkɪˈɒlədʒɪ) *n* the study of man's past by scientific analysis of the material remains of his cultures. [C17: from LL, from Gk *arkhaiologia* study of what is ancient, from *arkhē* beginning]
▸ **archaeological** *or* **archeological** (ˌɑːkɪəˈlɒdʒɪkəl) *adj* ▸ **ˌarchaeˈologist** *or* **ˌarcheˈologist** *n*

archaeopteryx (ˌɑːkɪˈɒptərɪks) *n* any of several extinct primitive birds which occurred in Jurassic times and had teeth, a long tail, and well-developed wings. [C19: from Gk *arkhaios* ancient + *pterux* winged creature]

archaic Ⓣ (ɑːˈkeɪɪk) *adj* **1** belonging to or characteristic of a much earlier period. **2** out of date; antiquated. **3** (of vocabulary, etc.) characteristic of an earlier period of a language. [C19: from F, from Gk *arkhaïkos,* from *arkhaios* ancient, from *arkhē* beginning, from *arkhein* to begin]
▸ **arˈchaically** *adv*

archaism (ˈɑːkeɪˌɪzəm) *n* **1** the adoption or imitation of archaic words or style. **2** an archaic word, style, etc. [C17: from NL, from Gk, from *arkhaizein* to model one's style upon that of ancient writers; see ARCHAIC]
▸ **ˈarchaist** *n* ▸ **ˌarchaˈistic** *adj*

archangel (ˈɑːkˌeɪndʒəl) *n* a principal angel.
▸ **archangelic** (ˌɑːkænˈdʒelɪk) *adj*

archbishop (ˈɑːtʃˈbɪʃəp) *n* a bishop of the highest rank. Abbrev.: **abp, Abp, Arch., Archbp.**

archbishopric (ˈɑːtʃˈbɪʃəprɪk) *n* the rank, office, or jurisdiction of an archbishop.

archdeacon (ˈɑːtʃˈdiːkən) *n* **1** an Anglican clergyman ranking just below a bishop. **2** a clergyman of similar rank in other Churches.
▸ **ˈarchˈdeaconry** *n*

archdiocese (ˌɑːtʃˈdaɪəˌsiːs) *n* the diocese of an archbishop.
▸ **archdiocesan** (ˌɑːtʃdaɪˈɒsɪsən) *adj*

archducal (ˈɑːtʃˈdjuːkəl) *adj* of or relating to an archduke, archduchess, or archduchy.

archduchess (ˈɑːtʃˈdʌtʃɪs) *n* **1** the wife or widow of an archduke. **2** (since 1453) a princess of the Austrian imperial family.

archduchy (ˈɑːtʃˈdʌtʃɪ) *n, pl* **archduchies.** the territory ruled by an archduke or archduchess.

archduke (ˈɑːtʃˈdjuːk) *n* a chief duke, esp. (since 1453) a prince of the Austrian imperial dynasty.

Archean (ɑːˈkiːən) *adj* a variant spelling (esp. US) of **Archaean.**

archegonium (ˌɑːkɪˈɡəʊnɪəm) *n, pl* **archegonia** (-nɪə). a female sex organ, occurring in mosses, ferns, etc. [C19: from NL, from Gk, from *arkhe-* chief, first + *gonos* seed, race]

archenemy (ˈɑːtʃˈenɪmɪ) *n, pl* **archenemies.** **1** a chief enemy. **2** (*often cap.;* preceded by *the*) the devil.

archeology (ˌɑːkɪˈɒlədʒɪ) *n* a variant of **archaeology.**

archer Ⓣ (ˈɑːtʃə) *n* a person skilled in the use of a bow and arrow. [C13: from OF, from LL, from L *arcus* bow]

Archer (ˈɑːtʃə) *n* **the.** the constellation Sagittarius, the ninth sign of the zodiac.

archerfish (ˈɑːtʃəˌfɪʃ) *n, pl* **archerfish** *or* **archerfishes.** a freshwater fish, related to the perch, of SE Asia and Australia, that catches insects by spitting water at them.

archery (ˈɑːtʃərɪ) *n* **1** the art or sport of shooting with bows and arrows. **2** archers or their weapons collectively.

archetype Ⓣ (ˈɑːkɪˌtaɪp) *n* **1** a perfect or typical specimen. **2** an original model; prototype. **3** *Psychoanal.* one of the inherited mental images postulated by Jung. **4** a recurring symbol or motif in literature, etc. [C17: from L *archetypum* an original, from Gk, from *arkhetupos* first-moulded; see ARCH-, -TYPE]
▸ **ˌarcheˈtypal** *adj*

archfiend (ˌɑːtʃˈfiːnd) *n* (*often cap.*) **the.** the devil; Satan.

archidiaconal (ˌɑːkɪdaɪˈækənəl) *adj* of or relating to an archdeacon or his office.
▸ **ˌarchidiˈaconate** *n*

archiepiscopal (ˌɑːkɪɪˈpɪskəpəl) *adj* of or associated with an archbishop.
▸ **ˌarchieˈpiscopate** *n*

archil (ˈɑːtʃɪl) *n* a variant of **orchil.**

archimandrite (ˌɑːkɪˈmændraɪt) *n Greek Orthodox Church.* the head of a monastery. [C16: from LL, from LGk *arkhimandritēs,* from ARCHI- + *mandra* monastery]

Archimedes' principle (ˌɑːkɪˈmiːdiːz) *n* a law of physics stating that the apparent loss in weight of a body immersed in a fluid is equal to the weight of the displaced fluid. [after *Archimedes* (?287–212 BC), Gk mathematician and physicist]

Archimedes' screw *or* **Archimedean screw** (ˌɑːkɪˈmiːdɪən) *n* an ancient water-lifting device using a spiral passage in an inclined cylinder.

archipelago (ˌɑːkɪˈpelɪˌɡəʊ) *n, pl* **archipelagos** *or* **archipelagoes.** **1** a group of islands. **2** a sea studded with islands. [C16 (meaning: the Aegean Sea): from It., from L *pelagus,* from Gk, from ARCH- + *pelagos* sea]
▸ **archipelagic** (ˌɑːkɪpəˈlædʒɪk) *adj*

architect Ⓣ (ˈɑːkɪˌtekt) *n* **1** a person qualified to design buildings and to supervise their erection. **2** a person similarly qualified in another form of construction: *a naval architect.* **3** any planner or creator. [C16: from F, from L, from Gk *arkhitektōn* director of works, from ARCHI- + *tektōn* workman; rel. to *tekhnē* art, skill]

architectonic (ˌɑːkɪtekˈtɒnɪk) *adj* **1** denoting, relating to, or having architectural qualities. **2** *Metaphysics.* of the systematic classification of knowledge. [C16: from LL *architectonicus* concerning architecture; see ARCHITECT]

architectonics (ˌɑːkɪtekˈtɒnɪks) *n* (*functioning as sing*) **1** the science of architecture. **2** *Metaphysics.* the scientific classification of knowledge.

architecture Ⓣ (ˈɑːkɪˌtektʃə) *n* **1** the art and science of designing and superintending the erection of buildings, etc. **2** a style of building or structure. **3** buildings or structures collectively. **4** the structure or design of anything.
▸ **ˌarchiˈtectural** *adj*

architrave (ˈɑːkɪˌtreɪv) *n Archit.* **1** the lowest part of an entablature that bears on the columns. **2** a moulding around a doorway, window opening, etc. [C16: via F from It., from ARCHI- + *trave* beam, from L *trabs*]

archive Ⓣ (ˈɑːkaɪv) *n* (*often pl*) **1** a collection of records of an institution, family, etc. **2** a place where such records are kept. **3** *Computing.* data transferred to a tape or disk for long-term storage rather than frequent use. ◆ *vb* **4** (*tr*) to store (documents, data, etc.) in an archive or other repository. [C17: from LL, from Gk *arkheion* repository of official records, from *arkhē* government]
▸ **arˈchival** *adj*

archivist (ˈɑːkɪvɪst) *n* a person in charge of archives.

archon (ˈɑːkɒn) *n* (in ancient Athens) one of the nine chief magistrates. [C17: from Gk *arkhōn* ruler, from *arkhein* to rule]
▸ **ˈarchonˌship** *n*

THESAURUS

arcade *n* **1, 2** = **gallery,** cloister, colonnade, covered walk, mall, peristyle, portico

arcane *adj* = **mysterious,** cabbalistic, esoteric, hidden, occult, recondite, secret

arch[1] *n* **1, 2** = **archway,** curve, dome, span, vault **3** = **curve,** arc, bend, bow, curvature, hump, semicircle ◆ *vb* **5, 6** = **curve,** arc, bend, bow, bridge, embow, span

arch[2] *adj* **3** = **playful,** frolicsome, mischievous, pert, roguish, saucy, sly, waggish

arch- *adj* **1, 2** = **chief,** accomplished, consummate, expert, finished, first, foremost, greatest, head, highest, lead, leading, main, major, master, pre-eminent, primary, principal, top

archaic *adj* **1** = **old,** ancient, antique, bygone, olden (*arch.*), primitive **2** = **old-fashioned,** antiquated, behind the times, obsolete, old hat, outmoded, out of date, passé, superannuated
Antonyms *adj* ≠ **old:** contemporary, current, modern, new, present, recent ≠ **old-fashioned:** fresh, latest, modern, modish, new, newfangled, novel, state-of-the-art, up-to-date, up-to-the-minute, with it (*inf.*)

arched *adj* **6** = **curved,** domed, embowed, vaulted

archer *n* = **bowman** (*arch.*), toxophilite (*formal*)

archetypal *adj* **1** = **typical,** classic, exemplary, ideal, model, normal, paradigmatic, standard **2** = **original,** prototypal, prototypic *or* prototypical

archetype *n* **1** = **standard,** classic, exemplar, form, ideal, model, norm, paradigm, pattern, prime example **2** = **original,** prototype

architect *n* **1, 2** = **designer,** master builder, planner **3** = **creator,** author, contriver, deviser, engineer, founder, instigator, inventor, maker, originator, planner, prime mover, shaper

architecture *n* **1** = **design,** architectonics, building, construction, planning **2, 4** = **structure,** construction, design, framework, make-up, style

archive *n often plural* **1** = **records,** annals, chronicles, documents, papers, registers, rolls **2** = **record office,** museum, registry, repository

archpriest (ˈɑːtʃˈpriːst) *n* **1** (formerly) a chief assistant to a bishop. **2** a senior priest.

archway (ˈɑːtʃˌweɪ) *n* a passageway or entrance under an arch or arches.

-archy *n combining form.* government; rule: *anarchy; monarchy.* [from Gk *-arkhia;* see -ARCH]

arc light *n* a light source in which an arc between two electrodes produces intense white illumination. Also called: **arc lamp.**

arctic ❶ (ˈɑːktɪk) *adj* **1** of or relating to the Arctic. **2** *Inf.* cold; freezing. ◆ *n* **3** (*modifier*) suitable for conditions of extreme cold: *arctic clothing.* [C14: from L *arcticus,* from Gk *arktikos* northern, lit.: pertaining to (the constellation of) the Bear, from *arktos* bear]

Arctic ❶ (ˈɑːktɪk) *adj* of or relating to the regions north of the Arctic Circle.

Arctic Circle *n* the imaginary circle round the earth, parallel to the equator, at latitude 66° 32′ N.

arctic hare *n* a large hare of the Canadian Arctic whose fur is white in winter.

arctic willow *n* a low-growing shrub of the Canadian tundra.

Arcturus (ɑːkˈtjʊərəs) *n* the brightest star in the constellation Boötes: a red giant. [C14: from L, from Gk *Arktouros,* from *arktos* bear + *ouros* guard, keeper]

arcuate (ˈɑːkjʊɪt) *adj* shaped or bent like an arc or bow. [C17: from L *arcuāre,* from *arcus* ARC]

arc welding *n* a technique in which metal is welded by heat generated by an electric arc.
▸**arc welder** *n*

-ard *or* **-art** *suffix forming nouns.* indicating a person who does something, esp. to excess: *braggart; drunkard.* [via OF, of Gmc origin]

ardent ❶ (ˈɑːdᵊnt) *adj* **1** expressive of or characterized by intense desire or emotion. **2** intensely enthusiastic; eager. **3** glowing or shining: *ardent eyes.* **4 ardent spirits.** alcoholic drinks. [C14: from L *ārdēre* to burn]
▸ˈ**ardency** *n* ▸ˈ**ardently** *adv*

ardour ❶ *or US* **ardor** (ˈɑːdə) *n* **1** feelings of great intensity and warmth. **2** eagerness; zeal. [C14: from OF, from L *ārdor,* from *ārdēre* to burn]

arduous ❶ (ˈɑːdjuːəs) *adj* **1** difficult to accomplish; strenuous. **2** hard to endure; harsh. **3** steep or difficult: *an arduous track.* [C16: from L *arduus* steep, difficult]
▸ˈ**arduously** *adv* ▸ˈ**arduousness** *n*

are[1] (ɑː; *unstressed* ə) *vb* the plural form of the present tense of **be** and the singular form used with *you.* [OE *aron,* second person pl of *bēon* to BE]

are[2] (ɑː) *n* a unit of area equal to 100 square metres. [C19: from F, from L *ārea* piece of ground; see AREA]

area ❶ (ˈɛərɪə) *n* **1** any flat, curved, or irregular expanse of a surface. **2a** the extent of a two-dimensional surface: *the area of a triangle.* **2b** the two-dimensional extent of a plane or surface: *the area of a sphere.* **3** a section or part. **4** region; district. **5a** a geographical division of administrative responsibility. **5b** (*as modifier*): *area manager.* **6** a part or section, as of a building, town, etc., having some specified function: *reception area; commercial area.* **7** the range or scope of anything. **8** a subject field or field of study. **9** Also called: **areaway.** a sunken area, usually enclosed, giving light, air, and sometimes access to a cellar basement. [C16: from L: level ground, threshing-floor; rel. to *ārēre* to be dry]
▸ˈ**areal** *adj*

arena ❶ (əˈriːnə) *n* **1** an enclosure or platform, usually surrounded by seats, in which sports events, entertainments, etc., take place: *a boxing arena.* **2** the central area of an ancient Roman amphitheatre, in which gladiatorial contests were held. **3** a sphere of intense activity: *the political arena.* [C17: from L *harēna* sand, place where sand was strewn for the combats]

arenaceous (ˌærɪˈneɪʃəs) *adj* **1** (of sedimentary rocks) composed of sand. **2** (of plants) growing in a sandy soil. [C17: from L *harēnāceus* sandy, from *harēna* sand]

aren't (ɑːnt) **1** *contraction of* are not. **2** *Inf., chiefly Brit.* (used in interrogative sentences) *contraction of* am not.

areola (əˈrɪələ) *n, pl* **areolae** (-ˌliː) *or* **areolas.** *Anat.* any small circular area, such as the pigmented ring around the human nipple. [C17: from L: dim. of AREA]
▸**aˈreolar** *or* **areolate** (əˈrɪəlɪt, -ˌleɪt) *adj*

areole (ˈærɪəʊl) *n* **1** *Biol.* a space outlined on a surface, such as an area between veins on a leaf. **2** a sunken area on a cactus from which spines, hairs, etc., arise.
▸ˈ**areoˌlate** *adj*

arête (əˈreɪt, əˈrɛt) *n* a sharp ridge that separates glacial valleys. [C19: from F: fishbone, ridge, from L *arista* ear of corn, fishbone]

argal (ˈɑːgəl) *n* another name for **argol.**

argali (ˈɑːgəlɪ) *or* **argal** *n, pl* **argali** *or* **argals.** a wild sheep, with massive horns in the male, inhabiting semidesert regions in central Asia. [C18: from Mongolian]

argent (ˈɑːdʒənt) *n* **a** an archaic or poetic word for **silver. b** (*as adj; often postpositive, esp. in heraldry*): *a bend argent.* [C15: from OF, from L]

argentiferous (ˌɑːdʒənˈtɪfərəs) *adj* containing or bearing silver.

argentine (ˈɑːdʒənˌtaɪn) *adj* **1** of or resembling silver. ◆ *n* **2** a small marine fish characterized by a long silvery body.

Argentine (ˈɑːdʒənˌtiːn, -ˌtaɪn) *or* **Argentinian** (ˌɑːdʒənˈtɪnɪən) *adj* **1** of or relating to Argentina, a republic in South America. ◆ *n* **2** a native or inhabitant of Argentina.

argillaceous (ˌɑːdʒɪˈleɪʃəs) *adj* (of sedimentary rocks) composed of very fine-grained material, such as clay. [C18: from L *argilla* white clay, from Gk, from *argos* white]

Argive (ˈɑːdʒaɪv, -gaɪv) *adj* **1** of or relating to Argos, a city of ancient Greece. **2** a literary word for **Greek.** ◆ *n* **3** an ancient Greek, esp. one from Argos.

argol (ˈɑːgɒl) *or* **argal** (ˈɑːgəl) *n* crude potassium hydrogentartrate. [C14: from Anglo-F *argoil,* from ?]

argon (ˈɑːgɒn) *n* an unreactive colourless odourless element of the rare gas series that forms almost 1 per cent of the atmosphere. It is used in electric lights. Symbol: Ar; atomic no.: 18; atomic wt.: 39.95. [C19: from Gk, from *argos* inactive, from A-[1] + *ergon* work]

argosy (ˈɑːgəsɪ) *n, pl* **argosies.** *Arch. or poetic.* a large abundantly laden merchant ship, or a fleet of such ships. [C16: from It. *Ragusea* (*nave*) (ship) of Ragusa]

argot ❶ (ˈɑːgəʊ) *n* slang or jargon peculiar to a particular group, esp. (formerly) a group of thieves. [C19: from F, from ?]

arguable ❶ (ˈɑːgjʊəbᵊl) *adj* **1** capable of being disputed. **2** plausible; reasonable.
▸ˈ**arguably** *adv*

argue ❶ (ˈɑːgjuː) *vb* **argues, arguing, argued. 1** (*intr*) to quarrel; wrangle. **2** (*intr; often foll. by for or against*) to present supporting or opposing reasons or cases in a dispute. **3** (*tr; may take a clause as object*) to try to prove by presenting reasons. **4** (*tr; often passive*) to debate or discuss. **5** (*tr*) to persuade. **6** (*tr*) to suggest: *her looks argue despair.* [C14: from OF *arguer* to assert, from L *arguere* to make clear, accuse]
▸ˈ**arguer** *n*

argufy (ˈɑːgjʊˌfaɪ) *vb* **argufies, argufying, argufied.** *Facetious or dialect.* to argue or quarrel, esp. over something trivial.

argument ❶ (ˈɑːgjʊmənt) *n* **1** a quarrel; altercation. **2** a discussion in which reasons are put forward; debate. **3** (*sometimes pl*) a point or series of reasons presented to support or oppose a proposition. **4** a summary of the plot or subject of a book, etc. **5** *Logic.* **5a** a process of reasoning in which the conclusion can be shown to be true or false. **5b** the middle term of a syllogism. **6** *Maths.* another name for **independent variable** of a function.

argumentation (ˌɑːgjʊmɛnˈteɪʃən) *n* **1** the process of reasoning methodically. **2** argument; debate.

argumentative ❶ (ˌɑːgjʊˈmɛntətɪv) *adj* **1** given to arguing. **2** characterized by argument; controversial.

Argus (ˈɑːgəs) *n* **1** *Greek myth.* a giant with a hundred eyes who was made guardian of the heifer Io. **2** a vigilant person.

Argus-eyed (ˌɑːgəsˈaɪd) *adj* observant; vigilant.

THESAURUS

arctic *adj* **2** *Informal* = **freezing**, chilly, cold, cold as ice, frigid, frost-bound, frosty, frozen, gelid, glacial, icy

Arctic *adj* = **polar**, far-northern, hyperborean

ardent *adj* **1** = **passionate**, ablaze, amorous, fervent, fervid, fierce, fiery, flaming, hot, hot-blooded, impassioned, intense, lusty, spirited, vehement, warm, warm-blooded **2** = **enthusiastic**, avid, eager, keen, keen as mustard, zealous
Antonyms *adj* ≠ **passionate:** cold, cool, frigid, impassive ≠ **enthusiastic:** apathetic, indifferent, lukewarm, unenthusiastic

ardour *n* **1** = **passion**, devotion, feeling, fervour, fierceness, fire, heat, intensity, spirit, vehemence, warmth **2** = **enthusiasm**, avidity, eagerness, earnestness, keenness, zeal

arduous *adj* **1-3** = **difficult**, backbreaking, burdensome, exhausting, fatiguing, formidable, gruelling, hard, harsh, heavy, laborious, onerous, painful, punishing, rigorous, severe, steep, strenuous, taxing, tiring, toilsome, tough, troublesome, trying
Antonyms *adj* child's play (*inf.*), easy, easy-peasy (*sl.*), effortless, facile, light, no bother, no trouble, painless, simple, undemanding

area *n* **3** = **part**, portion, section, sector **4** = **region**, district, domain, locality, neck of the woods (*inf.*), neighbourhood, patch, plot, realm, sector, sphere, stretch, territory, tract, turf (*US sl.*), zone **7** = **range**, ambit, breadth, compass, expanse, extent, scope, size, width **8** = **field**, arena, department, domain, province, realm, sphere, territory **9** = **sunken space**, yard

arena *n* **1, 2** = **ring**, amphitheatre, bowl, coliseum, enclosure, field, ground, park (*US & Canad.*), stadium, stage **3** = **sphere**, area, domain, field, province, realm, scene, scope, sector, territory, theatre

argot *n* = **jargon**, cant, dialect, idiom, lingo (*inf.*), parlance, patois, patter, slang, vernacular

arguably *adv* **1** = **debatably**, contestably, controversially, controvertibly, deniably, disputably, dubitably, questionably, refutably **2** = **possibly**, conceivably, feasibly, plausibly, potentially

argue *vb* **1** = **quarrel**, altercate, bandy words, bicker, cross swords, disagree, dispute, fall out (*inf.*), feud, fight, fight like cat and dog, have an argument, squabble, wrangle **3, 4** = **discuss**, assert, claim, contend, controvert, debate, dispute, expostulate, hold, maintain, plead, question, reason, remonstrate **5** = **persuade**, convince, prevail upon, talk into, talk round **6** = **suggest**, demonstrate, denote, display, evince, exhibit, imply, indicate, manifest, point to, show

argument *n* **1** = **quarrel**, altercation, barney (*inf.*), bickering, clash, controversy, difference of opinion, disagreement, dispute, falling out (*inf.*), feud, fight, row, squabble, wrangle **2** = **discussion**, assertion, claim, contention, debate, dispute, expostulation, plea, pleading, questioning, remonstrance, remonstration **3** = **reason**, argumentation, case, defence, dialectic, ground(s), line of reasoning, logic, polemic, reasoning
Antonyms *n* ≠ **quarrel:** accord, agreement, concurrence

argumentative *adj* **1** = **quarrelsome**, belligerent, combative, contentious, contrary, disputatious, litigious, opinionated

argy-bargy *or* **argie-bargie** ('ɑːdʒɪ'bɑːdʒɪ) *n, pl* **argy-bargies.** *Brit. inf.* a wrangling argument or verbal dispute. [C19: from Scot., from dialect *argle,* prob. from ARGUE]

aria ('ɑːrɪə) *n* an elaborate accompanied song for solo voice from a cantata, opera, or oratorio. [C18: from It.: tune, AIR]

Arian ('ɛərɪən) *adj* **1** of or relating to Arius, 3rd-century A.D. Greek Christian theologian, or to Arianism. ◆ *n* **2** an adherent of Arianism.

-arian *suffix forming nouns.* indicating a person or thing that advocates, believes, or is associated with something: *vegetarian; librarian.* [from L *-ārius* -ARY + -AN]

Arianism ('ɛərɪə,nɪzəm) *n* the doctrine of Arius, declared heretical, which asserted that Christ was not of one substance with the Father.

arid Ⓣ ('ærɪd) *adj* **1** having little or no rain; dry. **2** devoid of interest. [C17: from L *āridus,* from *ārēre* to be dry]
▸**aridity** (ə'rɪdɪtɪ) *or* '**aridness** *n*

arid zone *n* either of the zones of latitude 15–30° N and S, with low rainfall and desert or semidesert terrain.

Aries ('ɛəriːz) *n, Latin genitive* **Arietis** (ə'raɪɪtɪs). **1** *Astron.* a N constellation. **2** *Astrol.* Also called: the **Ram.** the first sign of the zodiac. The sun is in this sign between about March 21 and April 19. [C14: from L: ram]

aright Ⓣ (ə'raɪt) *adv* correctly; rightly; properly.

aril ('ærɪl) *n* an additional covering formed on certain seeds, such as those of the yew and nutmeg, after fertilization. [C18: from NL, from Med. L *arilli* raisins, pips of grapes]
▸'**aril,late** *adj*

arioso (,ɑːrɪ'əʊzəʊ) *n, pl* **ariosos** *or* **ariosi** (-siː). *Music.* a recitative with the lyrical quality of an aria. [C18: from It., from ARIA]

arise Ⓣ (ə'raɪz) *vb* **arises, arising, arose, arisen** (ə'rɪzᵊn). (*intr*) **1** to come into being; originate. **2** (foll. by *from*) to proceed as a consequence. **3** to get or stand up, as from a sitting or lying position. **4** to come into notice. **5** to ascend. [OE *ārīsan*]

aristo ('ærɪstəʊ, ə'rɪstəʊ) *n, pl* **aristos.** *Inf.* short for **aristocrat.**

aristocracy Ⓣ (,ærɪ'stɒkrəsɪ) *n, pl* **aristocracies. 1** a privileged class of people usually of high birth; the nobility. **2** such a class as the ruling body of a state. **3** government by such a class. **4** a state governed by such a class. **5** a class of people considered to be outstanding in a sphere of activity. [C16: from LL, from Gk *aristokratia* rule by the best-born, from *aristos* best; see -CRACY]

aristocrat Ⓣ ('ærɪstə,kræt) *n* **1** a member of the aristocracy. **2** a person who has the manners or qualities of a member of a privileged class. **3** a supporter of aristocracy as a form of government.

aristocratic Ⓣ (,ærɪstə'krætɪk) *adj* **1** relating to or characteristic of aristocracy or an aristocrat. **2** elegant or stylish in appearance and behaviour.
▸**,aristo'cratically** *adv*

Aristotelian (,ærɪstə'tiːlɪən) *adj* **1** of or relating to Aristotle, 4th-century B.C. Greek philosopher, or to his philosophy. ◆ *n* **2** a follower of Aristotle.

Aristotelian logic *n* **1** traditional logic, esp. relying on the theory of syllogism. **2** the logical method of Aristotle, esp. as developed in the Middle Ages.

arithmetic *n* (ə'rɪθmətɪk). **1** the branch of mathematics concerned with numerical calculations, such as addition, subtraction, multiplication, and division. **2** calculations involving numerical operations. **3** knowledge of or skill in using arithmetic. ◆ *adj* (,ærɪθ'mɛtɪk) *also* **arithmetical. 4** of, relating to, or using arithmetic. [C13: from L, from Gk *arithmētikē,* from *arithmein* to count, from *arithmos* number]
▸**,arith'metically** *adv* ▸**a,rithme'tician** *n*

arithmetic mean *n* the average value of a set of terms or quantities, expressed as their sum divided by their number: *the arithmetic mean of 3, 4, and 8 is 5.* Also called: **average.**

arithmetic progression *n* a sequence, each term of which differs from the succeeding term by a constant amount, such as 3,6,9,12.

-arium *suffix forming nouns.* indicating a place for or associated with something: *aquarium; solarium.* [from L *-ārium,* neuter of *-ārius* -ARY]

ark (ɑːk) *n* **1** the vessel that Noah built which survived the Flood (Genesis 6–9). **2** a place or thing offering shelter or protection. **3** *Dialect.* a box. [OE *arc,* from L *arca* box, chest]

Ark (ɑːk) *n Judaism.* **1** Also called: **Holy Ark.** the cupboard in a synagogue in which the Torah scrolls are kept. **2** Also called: **Ark of the Covenant.** the most sacred symbol of God's presence among the Hebrew people, carried in their journey from Sinai to the Promised Land (Canaan).

arm[1] Ⓣ (ɑːm) *n* **1** (in man) either of the upper limbs from the shoulder to the wrist. Related adj: **brachial. 2** the part of either of the upper limbs from the elbow to the wrist; forearm. **3a** the corresponding limb of any other vertebrate. **3b** an armlike appendage of some invertebrates. **4** an object that covers or supports the human arm, esp. the sleeve of a garment or the side of a chair, etc. **5** anything considered to resemble an arm in appearance, function, etc.: *an arm of the sea; the arm of a record player.* **6** an administrative subdivision of an organization: *an arm of the government.* **7** power; authority: *the arm of the law.* **8 arm in arm.** with arms linked. **9 at arm's length.** at a distance. **10 in the arms of Morpheus.** sleeping. **11 with open arms.** with great warmth and hospitality. [OE]

arm[2] Ⓣ (ɑːm) *vb* **1** to equip with weapons as a preparation for war. **2** (*tr*) to provide (a person or thing) with something that strengthens, protects, or increases efficiency. **3a** (*tr*) to activate (a fuse) so that it will explode at the required time. **3b** to prepare (an explosive device) for use by introducing a detonator, etc. ◆ *n* **4** (*usually pl*) a weapon, esp. a firearm. [C14: from OF *armes,* from L *arma* arms, equipment]

armada Ⓣ (ɑː'mɑːdə) *n* **1** a large number of ships or aircraft. **2** (*cap.*) **the.** Also called: **Spanish Armada.** the great fleet sent by Philip II of Spain against England in 1588. [C16: from Sp., from Med. L *armāta* fleet, armed forces, from L *armāre* to provide with arms]

armadillo (,ɑːmə'dɪləʊ) *n, pl* **armadillos.** a burrowing mammal of Central and South America with a covering of strong horny plates over most of the body. [C16: from Sp., dim. of *armado* armed (man), from L *armātus* armed; cf. ARMADA]

Armageddon (,ɑːmə'gɛdᵊn) *n* **1** *New Testament.* the final battle between good and evil at the end of the world. **2** a catastrophic and extremely destructive conflict. [C19: from LL, from Gk, from Heb. *har megiddōn,* mountain district of *Megiddo* (in N Palestine)]

Armalite ('ɑːməlaɪt) *n Trademark.* a lightweight high-velocity rifle of various calibres, capable of automatic and semiautomatic operation. [C20: from *Armalite* Division, Fairchild Engine and Airplane Company, manufacturers]

armament Ⓣ ('ɑːməmənt) *n* **1** (*often pl*) the weapon equipment of a military vehicle, ship, or aircraft. **2** a military force raised and armed ready for war. **3** preparation for war. [C17: from L *armāmenta* utensils, from *armāre* to equip]

armature ('ɑːmətjʊə) *n* **1** a revolving structure in an electric motor or generator, wound with the coils that carry the current. **2** any part of an electric machine or device that moves under the influence of a magnetic field or within which an electromotive force is induced. **3** Also called: **keeper.** a soft iron or steel bar placed across the poles of a magnet to close the magnetic circuit. **4** *Sculpture.* a framework to support the clay or other material used in modelling. **5** the protective outer covering of an animal or plant. [C15: from L *armātūra* armour, equipment, from *armāre* to furnish with equipment]

armchair ('ɑːm,tʃɛə) *n* **1** a chair, esp. an upholstered one, that has side supports for the arms or elbows. **2** (*modifier*) taking or involving no active part: *an armchair strategist.*

armed[1] Ⓣ (ɑːmd) *adj* **1** equipped with or supported by arms, armour, etc. **2** prepared for conflict or any difficulty. **3** (of an explosive device) prepared for use. **4** (of plants) having the protection of thorns, spines, etc.

armed[2] (ɑːmd) *adj* **a** having an arm or arms. **b** (*in combination*): *long-armed; one-armed.*

THESAURUS

Antonyms *adj* accommodating, amenable, complaisant, compliant, conciliatory, easy-going, obliging

arid *adj* **1** = **dry,** barren, desert, dried up, moistureless, parched, sterile, torrid, waterless **2** = **boring,** as dry as dust, colourless, dreary, dry, dull, flat, jejune, lifeless, spiritless, tedious, tiresome, uninspired, uninteresting, vapid
Antonyms *adj* ≠ **dry:** fertile, fruitful, lush, rich, verdant ≠ **boring:** exciting, interesting, lively, sexy (*inf.*), spirited, stimulating, vivacious

aridity *n* **1** = **dryness,** barrenness, moisturelessness, parchedness, sterility, waterlessness **2** = **boredom,** colourlessness, dreariness, dryness, dullness, flatness, jejuneness, jejunity, lifelessness, spiritlessness, tediousness, tedium, uninspiredness, uninterestingness, vapidity, vapidness

aright *adv* = **correctly,** accurately, appropriately, aptly, duly, exactly, fitly, in due order, justly, properly, rightly, suitably, truly, without error

arise *vb* **1, 2** = **happen,** appear, begin, come into being, come to light, commence, crop up (*inf.*), emanate, emerge, ensue, follow, issue, occur, originate, proceed, result, set in, spring, start, stem **3** = **get up,** get to one's feet, go up, rise, stand up, wake up **5** = **ascend,** climb, lift, mount, move upward, rise, soar, tower

aristocracy *n* **1** = **upper class,** body of nobles, elite, gentry, *haut monde,* nobility, noblesse (*literary*), patricians, patriciate, peerage, ruling class, upper crust (*inf.*)
Antonyms *n* commoners, common people, hoi polloi, lower classes, masses, plebeians, plebs, proles (*derogatory sl., chiefly Brit.*), proletariat, working classes

aristocrat *n* **1** = **noble,** aristo (*inf.*), childe (*arch.*), grandee, lady, lord, nobleman, noblewoman, patrician, peer, peeress

aristocratic *adj* **1** = **upper-class,** blue-blooded, elite, gentle (*arch.*), gentlemanly, highborn, lordly, noble, patrician, titled, well-born **2** = **refined,** courtly, dignified, elegant, fine, haughty, polished, snobbish, stylish, well-bred
Antonyms *adj* ≠ **upper-class:** common, lower-class, plebeian, proletarian, working-class ≠ **refined:** boorish, coarse, common, crass, crude, ill-bred, uncouth, unrefined, vulgar

arm[1] *n* **1-3** = **upper limb,** appendage, limb **6** = **section,** bough, branch, department, detachment, division, extension, offshoot, projection, sector **7** = **power,** authority, command, force, might, potency, strength, sway

arm[2] *vb* **1** = **equip,** accoutre, array, deck out, furnish, issue with, outfit, provide, rig, supply **1** = **mobilize,** muster forces, prepare for war, take up arms **2** = **provide,** brace, equip, forearm, fortify, gird one's loins, guard, make ready, outfit, prepare, prime, protect, strengthen

armada *n* **1** = **fleet,** flotilla, navy, squadron

armaments *pl n* **1** = **weapons,** ammunition, arms, guns, materiel, munitions, ordnance, weaponry

armed[1] *adj* **1-3** = **carrying weapons,** accoutred, arrayed, equipped, fitted out, forearmed, fortified, furnished, girded, guarded, in arms, prepared, primed, protected, provided, ready, rigged out, strengthened, supplied, tooled up (*sl.*), under arms

armed forces *pl n* the military forces of a nation or nations, including the army, navy, air force, marines, etc.

Armenian (ɑːˈmiːnɪən) *n* **1** a native or inhabitant of Armenia, a republic in NW Asia, or of the ancient kingdom of Armenia in W Asia. **2** the Indo-European language of the Armenians. ◆ *adj* **3** of Armenia, its inhabitants, or their language.

armful (ˈɑːmfʊl) *n, pl* **armfuls.** the amount that can be held by one or both arms.

armhole (ˈɑːmˌhəʊl) *n* the opening in an article of clothing through which the arm passes.

armillary sphere (ɑːˈmɪlərɪ) *n* a model of the celestial sphere formerly used in fixing the positions of heavenly bodies.

Arminian (ɑːˈmɪnɪən) *adj* denoting, relating to, or believing in the Protestant doctrines of Jacobus Arminius, 16th-century Dutch theologian, which rejected absolute predestination and stressed free will in man.
▸**Arˈminianˌism** *n*

armistice ➊ (ˈɑːmɪstɪs) *n* an agreement between opposing armies to suspend hostilities; truce. [C18: from NL, from L *arma* arms + *sistere* to stop]

Armistice Day (ˈɑːmɪstɪs) *n* the anniversary of the signing of the armistice that ended World War I, on Nov. 11, 1918. See also **Remembrance Sunday.**

armlet (ˈɑːmlɪt) *n* **1** a small arm, as of a lake. **2** a band or bracelet worn round the arm.

armoire (ɑːmˈwɑː) *n* a large cabinet, originally used for storing weapons. [C16: from F, from OF *armaire,* from L *armārium* chest, closet; see AMBRY]

armorial (ɑːˈmɔːrɪəl) *adj* of or relating to heraldry or heraldic arms.

armour ➊ *or US* **armor** (ˈɑːmə) *n* **1** any defensive covering, esp. that of metal, chain mail, etc., worn by medieval warriors. **2** the protective metal plates on a tank, warship, etc. **3** *Mil.* armoured fighting vehicles in general. **4** any protective covering, such as the shell of certain animals. **5** heraldic insignia; arms. ◆ *vb* **6** (*tr*) to equip or cover with armour. [C13: from OF *armure,* from L *armātūra* armour, equipment]

armoured ➊ *or US* **armored** (ˈɑːməd) *adj* **1** having a protective covering. **2** comprising units making use of armoured vehicles: *an armoured brigade.*

armourer *or US* **armorer** (ˈɑːmərə) *n* **1** a person who makes or mends arms and armour. **2** a person employed in the maintenance of small arms and weapons in a military unit.

armour plate *n* a tough heavy steel often hardened on the surface, used for protecting warships, tanks, etc.

armoury ➊ *or US* **armory** (ˈɑːmərɪ) *n, pl* **armouries** *or* **armories. 1** a secure place for the storage of weapons. **2** armour generally; military supplies. **3** resources, such as arguments, on which to draw: *a few choice terms from her armoury of invective.*

armpit (ˈɑːmˌpɪt) *n* **1** the small depression beneath the arm where it joins the shoulder. Technical name: **axilla. 2** *Sl.* an extremely unpleasant place: *the armpit of the Middle West.*

armrest (ˈɑːmˌrest) *n* the part of a chair, sofa, etc., that supports the arm. Sometimes shortened to **arm.**

arms ➊ (ɑːmz) *pl n* **1** weapons collectively. See also **small arms. 2** military exploits: *prowess in arms.* **3** the official heraldic symbols of a family, state, etc. **4 bear arms. 4a** to carry weapons. **4b** to serve in the armed forces. **4c** to have a coat of arms. **5 in** *or* **under arms.** armed and prepared for war. **6 lay down one's arms.** to stop fighting; surrender. **7 take (up) arms.** to prepare to fight. **8 up in arms.** indignant; prepared to protest strongly. [C13: from OF, from L *arma;* see ARM[2]]

arm wrestling *n* a contest of strength in which two people rest the elbow of one arm on a flat surface, grasp each other's hand, and try to force their opponent's forearm down flat.

army ➊ (ˈɑːmɪ) *n, pl* **armies. 1** the military land forces of a nation. **2** a military unit usually consisting of two or more corps with supporting arms and services. **3** (*modifier*) of or characteristic of an army. **4** any large body of people united for some specific purpose. **5** a large number of people, animals, etc. [C14: from OF, from Med. L *armāta* armed forces]

army ant *n* any of various tropical American predatory ants which travel in vast hordes preying on other animals. Also called: **legionary ant.**

army worm *n* a type of caterpillar which travels in vast hordes and is a serious pest of cereal crops.

arnica (ˈɑːnɪkə) *n* **1** any of a genus of N temperate or arctic plants having yellow flowers. **2** the tincture of the dried flower heads of any of these plants, used in treating bruises. [C18: from NL, from ?]

aroha (ˈɑːrɒhə) *n NZ.* love, compassion, or affectionate regard. [Maori]

aroid (ˈærɔɪd, ˈɛər-) *adj* of or relating to a plant family that includes the arum, calla, and anthurium. [C19: from ARUM + -OID]

aroint thee *or* **ye** (əˈrɔɪnt) *sentence substitute. Arch.* away! begone! [C17: from ?]

aroma ➊ (əˈrəʊmə) *n* **1** a distinctive usually pleasant smell, esp. of spices, wines, and plants. **2** a subtle pervasive quality or atmosphere. [C18: via L from Gk: spice]

aromatherapy (əˌrəʊməˈθɛrəpɪ) *n* the use of fragrant essential oils as a treatment in alternative medicine to relieve tension and cure certain minor ailments.
▸**aˌromaˈtherapist** *n*

aromatic ➊ (ˌærəˈmætɪk) *adj* **1** having a distinctive, usually fragrant smell. **2** (of an organic compound) having an unsaturated ring, esp. containing a benzene ring. Cf. **aliphatic.** ◆ *n* **3** something, such as a plant or drug, giving off a fragrant smell.
▸**ˌaroˈmatically** *adv* ▸**aˌromaˈticity** *n*

aromatize *or* **aromatise** (əˈrəʊməˌtaɪz) *vb* **aromatizes, aromatizing, aromatized** *or* **aromatises, aromatising, aromatised.** (*tr*) to make aromatic.
▸**aˌromatiˈzation** *or* **aˌromatiˈsation** *n*

arose (əˈrəʊz) *vb* the past tense of **arise.**

around ➊ (əˈraʊnd) *prep* **1** situated at various points in: *a lot of shelves around the house.* **2** from place to place in: *driving around Ireland.* **3** somewhere in or near. **4** approximately in: *it happened around 1957.* ◆ *adv* **5** in all directions from a point of reference: *he owns the land for ten miles around.* **6** in the vicinity, esp. restlessly but idly: *to stand around.* **7** in no particular place or direction: *dotted around.* **8** *Inf.* (of people) active and prominent in a particular area or profession. **9** *Inf.* present in some place (the exact location being unknown or unspecified). **10** *Inf.* in circulation; available: *that type of phone has been around for some years now.* **11** *Inf.* to many places, so as to have gained considerable experience, often of a worldly or social nature: *I've been around.* [C17 (rare earlier): from A-[2] + ROUND]

> **USAGE NOTE** In American English, *around* is usually used instead of *round* in adverbial and prepositional senses, except in a few fixed phrases such as *all year round.* The use of *around* in adverbial senses is less common in British English.

arouse ➊ (əˈraʊz) *vb* **arouses, arousing, aroused. 1** (*tr*) to evoke or elicit (a reaction, emotion, or response). **2** to awaken from sleep.
▸**aˈrousal** *n* ▸**aˈrouser** *n*

arpeggio (ɑːˈpedʒɪəʊ) *n, pl* **arpeggios.** a chord whose notes are played or sung in rapid succession rather than simultaneously. [C18: from It., from *arpeggiare* to perform on the harp, from *arpa* HARP]

arquebus (ˈɑːkwɪbəs) *or* **harquebus** *n* a portable long-barrelled gun dating from the 15th century. [C16: via OF from MDu. *hakebusse,* lit.: hook gun, from the shape of the butt, from *hake* hook + *busse* box, gun, from LL *busis* box]

arr. *abbrev. for:* **1** arranged (by). **2** arrival. **3** arrive(d).

arrack *or* **arak** (ˈærək) *n* a coarse spirit distilled in various Eastern countries from grain, rice, sugar cane, etc. [C17: from Ar. *'araq* sweat, sweet juice, liquor]

arraign ➊ (əˈreɪn) *vb* (*tr*) **1** to bring (a prisoner) before a court to answer an indictment. **2** to call to account; accuse. [C14: from OF, from Vulgar L *ratiōnāre* (unattested) to talk, argue, from L *ratiō* a reasoning]
▸**arˈraigner** *n* ▸**arˈraignment** *n*

arrange ➊ (əˈreɪndʒ) *vb* **arranges, arranging, arranged. 1** (*tr*) to put into a proper or systematic order. **2** (*tr; may take a clause as object or an infinitive*) to arrive at an agreement about. **3** (when *intr,* often foll. by *for;*

THESAURUS

armistice *n* = **truce**, ceasefire, peace, suspension of hostilities

armour *n* **1, 4** = **protection**, armour plate, covering, sheathing, shield

armoured *adj* **1** = **protected**, armour-plated, bombproof, bulletproof, ironclad, mailed, steel-plated

armoury *n* **1** = **arsenal**, ammunition dump, arms depot, magazine, ordnance depot

arms *pl n* **1** = **weapons**, armaments, firearms, guns, instruments of war, ordnance, weaponry **3** = **heraldry**, blazonry, crest, escutcheon, insignia

army *n* **1, 2** = **soldiers**, armed force, host (*arch.*), land forces, legions, military, military force, soldiery, troops **5** = **vast number**, array, horde, host, multitude, pack, swarm, throng

aroma *n* **1** = **scent**, bouquet, fragrance, odour, perfume, redolence, savour, smell

aromatic *adj* **1** = **fragrant**, balmy, odoriferous, perfumed, pungent, redolent, savoury, spicy, sweet-scented, sweet-smelling
Antonyms *adj* acrid, bad-smelling, fetid, foul, foul-smelling, malodorous, noisome, offensive, olid, rank, reeking, smelly, stinking

around *prep* **4** = **approximately**, about, circa (*used with dates*), roughly ◆ *adv* **5** = **everywhere**, about, all over, here and there, in all directions, on all sides, throughout, to and fro **6** = **near**, at hand, close, close at hand, close by, nearby, nigh (*arch. or dialect*)

arousal *n* **1** = **stimulation**, agitation, animation, enlivenment, excitement, exhilaration, incitement, inflammation, movement, provocation, reaction, response, stirring up **2** = **awakening**, rousedness

arouse *vb* **1** = **stimulate**, agitate, animate, call forth, enliven, excite, foment, foster, goad, incite, inflame, instigate, kindle, move, prod, provoke, quicken, sharpen, spark, spur, stir up, summon up, warm, whet, whip up **2** = **awaken**, rouse, waken, wake up
Antonyms *vb* ≠ **stimulate:** allay, alleviate, assuage, calm, dampen, dull, end, lull, pacify, quell, quench, still

arraign *vb* **1, 2** = **accuse**, call to account, charge, complain about, denounce, impeach, incriminate, indict, prosecute, take to task

arraignment *n* **1, 2** = **accusation**, charge, complaint, denunciation, impeachment, incrimination, indictment, prosecution

arrange *vb* **1** = **put in order**, align, array, class, classify, dispose, file, form, group, line up, marshal, order, organize, position, range, rank, sequence, set out, sort, sort out (*inf.*), systematize, tidy **2, 5** = **agree**, adjust, come to terms, compromise, determine, settle **3** = **plan**, construct, contrive, devise, fix up, organize, prepare, project, schedule **4** = **adapt**, instrument, orchestrate, score

when *tr, may take a clause as object or an infinitive*) to make plans or preparations in advance (for something): *we arranged for her to be met.* **4** (*tr*) to adapt (a musical composition) for performance in a different way, esp. on different instruments. **5** (*intr; often foll. by with*) to come to an agreement. [C14: from OF *arangier*, from A-[2] + *rangier* to put in a row, RANGE]
►**ar'rangeable** *adj* ►**ar'ranger** *n*

arrangement ❶ (ə'reɪndʒmənt) *n* **1** the act of arranging or being arranged. **2** the form in which things are arranged. **3** a thing composed of various ordered parts: *a flower arrangement.* **4** (*often pl*) a preparation. **5** an understanding. **6** an adaptation of a piece of music for performance in a different way, esp. on different instruments.

arrant ❶ ('ærənt) *adj* utter; out-and-out: *an arrant fool.* [C14: var. of ERRANT (wandering, vagabond)]
►**'arrantly** *adv*

arras ('ærəs) *n* a wall hanging, esp. of tapestry.

array ❶ (ə'reɪ) *n* **1** an impressive display or collection. **2** an orderly arrangement, esp. of troops in battle order. **3** *Poetic.* rich clothing. **4** *Maths.* a set of numbers or symbols arranged in rows and columns, as in a determinant or matrix. **5** *Law.* a panel of jurors. **6** *Computing.* a regular data structure in which elements may be located by reference to index numbers. ◆ *vb* (*tr*) **7** to dress in rich attire. **8** to arrange in order (esp. troops for battle). **9** *Law.* to draw up (a panel of jurors). [C13: from OF, from *arayer* to arrange, of Gmc origin]
►**ar'rayal** *n*

arrears (ə'rɪəz) *n* (*sometimes sing*) **1** Also called: **arrearage.** something outstanding or owed. **2 in arrears** *or* **arrear.** late in paying a debt or meeting an obligation. [C18: from obs. *arrear* (adv) behindhand, from OF, from Med. L *adretrō*, from L *ad* to + *retrō* backwards]

arrest ❶ (ə'rɛst) *vb* (*tr*) **1** to deprive (a person) of liberty by taking him into custody, esp. under lawful authority. **2** to seize (a ship) under lawful authority. **3** to slow or stop the development of (a disease, growth, etc.). **4** to catch and hold (one's attention, etc.). ◆ *n* **5** the act of taking a person into custody, esp. under lawful authority. **6** the act of seizing and holding a ship under lawful authority. **7** the state of being held: *under arrest.* **8** the slowing or stopping of something: *a cardiac arrest.* [C14: from OF, from Vulgar L *arrestāre* (unattested), from L *ad* at, to + *restāre* to stand firm, stop]

arresting ❶ (ə'rɛstɪŋ) *adj* attracting attention; striking.
►**ar'restingly** *adv*

arrhythmia (ə'rɪðmɪə) *n* any variation from the normal rhythm in the heartbeat. [C19: NL, from Gk *arrhuthmia*, from A-[1] + *rhuthmos* RHYTHM]

arrière-pensée *French.* (arjɛrpɑ̃se) *n* an unrevealed thought or intention. [C19: lit.: behind thought]

arris ('ærɪs) *n, pl* **arris** *or* **arrises.** a sharp edge at the meeting of two surfaces at an angle with one another. [C17: from OF *areste* beard of grain, sharp ridge; see ARÊTE]

arrival ❶ (ə'raɪvᵊl) *n* **1** the act or time of arriving. **2** a person or thing that arrives or has arrived.

arrive ❶ (ə'raɪv) *vb* **arrives, arriving, arrived.** (*intr*) **1** to come to a certain place during or after a journey. **2** to reach: *to arrive at a decision.* **3** to occur eventually: *the moment arrived when pretence was useless.* **4** *Inf.* (of a baby) to be born. **5** *Inf.* to attain success. [C13: from OF, from Vulgar L *arrīpāre* (unattested) to land, reach the bank, from L *ad* to + *rīpa* river bank]

arrivederci *Italian.* (arrive'dertʃi) *sentence substitute.* goodbye.

arriviste ❶ (ˌæriː'viːst) *n* a person who is unscrupulously ambitious. [F: see ARRIVE, -IST]

arrogant ❶ ('ærəgənt) *adj* having or showing an exaggerated opinion of one's own importance, merit, ability, etc.: *an arrogant assumption.* [C14: from L *arrogāre* to claim as one's own; see ARROGATE]
►**'arrogance** *n* ►**'arrogantly** *adv*

arrogate ('ærəˌgeɪt) *vb* **arrogates, arrogating, arrogated.** (*tr*) **1** to claim or appropriate for oneself without justification. **2** to attribute or assign to another without justification. [C16: from L *arrogāre*, from *rogāre* to ask]
►ˌ**arro'gation** *n* ►**arrogative** (ə'rɒgətɪv) *adj*

arrondissement (*French* arɔ̃dismɑ̃) *n* (in France) **1** the largest subdivision of a department. **2** a municipal district of large cities, esp. Paris. [C19: from *arrondir* to make round]

arrow ❶ ('ærəʊ) *n* **1** a long slender pointed weapon, usually having feathers fastened at the end as a balance, that is shot from a bow. **2** any of various things that resemble an arrow in shape, function, or speed. [OE *arwe*]

arrowhead ('ærəʊˌhɛd) *n* **1** the pointed tip of an arrow, often removable from the shaft. **2** something that resembles the head of an arrow in shape. **3** an aquatic herbaceous plant having arrow-shaped leaves.

arrowroot ('ærəʊˌruːt) *n* **1** a white-flowered West Indian plant, whose rhizomes yield an easily digestible starch. **2** the starch obtained from this plant.

arroyo (ə'rɔɪəʊ) *n, pl* **arroyos.** *Chiefly southwestern US.* a steep-sided stream bed that is usually dry except after heavy rain. [C19: from Sp.]

arse (ɑːs) *or US & Canad.* **ass** *n Taboo.* **1** the buttocks. **2** the anus. **3** a stupid person; fool. ◆ Also called (for senses 2, 3): **arsehole,** (US & Canad.) **asshole.** [OE]

arsenal ❶ ('ɑːsənᵊl) *n* **1** a store for arms, ammunition, and other military items. **2** a workshop that produces munitions. **3** a store of anything regarded as weapons. [C16: from It. *arsenale* dockyard, from Ar., from *dār* house + *sinā'ah* manufacture]

arsenate ('ɑːsəˌneɪt, -nɪt) *n* a salt or ester of arsenic acid.

arsenic *n* ('ɑːsnɪk). **1** a toxic metalloid element used in transistors, lead-based alloys, and high-temperature brasses. Symbol: As; atomic no.: 33; atomic wt.: 74.92. **2** a nontechnical name for **arsenic trioxide** (As_2O_3), used as rat poison and an insecticide. ◆ *adj* (ɑː'sɛnɪk). **3** of or containing arsenic, esp. in the pentavalent state; designating an arsenic(V) compound. [C14: from L, from Gk *arsenikon* yellow arsenic ore, from Syriac *zarnīg* (infl. by Gk *arsenikos* virile)]

arsenic acid *n* a white poisonous soluble crystalline solid used in the manufacture of insecticides.

arsenical (ɑː'sɛnɪkᵊl) *adj* **1** of or containing arsenic. ◆ *n* **2** a drug or insecticide containing arsenic.

arsenious (ɑː'siːnɪəs) *or* **arsenous** ('ɑːsɪnəs) *adj* of or containing arsenic in the trivalent state; designating an arsenic(III) compound.

arson ('ɑːsᵊn) *n Criminal law.* the act of intentionally or recklessly setting fire to property for some improper reason. [C17: from OF, from Med. L *ārsiō*, from L *ārdēre* to burn]
►**'arsonist** *n*

art[1] ❶ (ɑːt) *n* **1a** the creation of works of beauty or other special significance. **1b** (*as modifier*): *an art movement.* **2** the exercise of human skill (as distinguished from *nature*). **3** imaginative skill as applied to repre-

THESAURUS

Antonyms *vb* ≠ **put in order:** disarrange, disorganize, disturb, mess up, scatter

arrangement *n* **1, 2, 3** = **order,** alignment, array, classification, design, display, disposition, form, grouping, line-up, marshalling, ordering, organization, ranging, rank, setup (*inf.*), structure, system **4** *often plural* = **plan,** construction, devising, organization, planning, preparation, provision, schedule **5** = **agreement,** adjustment, compact, compromise, deal, settlement, terms, understanding **6** = **adaptation,** instrumentation, interpretation, orchestration, score, version

arrant *adj* = **total,** absolute, atrocious, blatant, complete, deep-dyed (*usually derogatory*), downright, egregious, extreme, flagrant, gross, infamous, monstrous, notorious, out-and-out, outright, rank, thorough, thoroughgoing, undisguised, unmitigated, utter, vile

array *n* **1, 2** = **arrangement,** collection, display, disposition, exhibition, formation, line-up, marshalling, muster, order, parade, show, supply **3** *Poetic* = **clothing,** apparel, attire, clothes, dress, finery, garb, garments, raiment (*arch. or poetic*), regalia ◆ *vb* **7** = **dress,** accoutre, adorn, apparel (*arch.*), attire, bedeck, caparison, clothe, deck, decorate, equip, festoon, fit out, garb, get ready, outfit, robe, supply, wrap **8** = **arrange,** align, display, dispose, draw up, exhibit, form up, group, line up, marshal, muster, order, parade, place in order, range, sequence, set in line (*Military*), show

arrest *vb* **1** = **capture,** apprehend, bust, catch, collar (*inf.*), detain, feel one's collar (*sl.*), lay hold of, lift (*sl.*), nab (*inf.*), nail (*inf.*), nick (*sl., chiefly Brit.*), pinch (*inf.*), run in (*sl.*), seize, take, take into custody, take prisoner **3** = **stop,** block, check, delay, end, halt, hinder, hold, inhibit, interrupt, obstruct, restrain, retard, slow, stall, stay, suppress **4** = **grip,** absorb, catch, engage, engross, fascinate, hold, intrigue, occupy ◆ *n* **5** = **capture,** apprehension, bust (*inf.*), cop (*sl.*), detention, seizure **8** = **stopping,** blockage, check, delay, end, halt, hindrance, inhibition, interruption, obstruction, restraint, stalling, stay, suppression
Antonyms *vb* ≠ **capture:** free, let go, release, set free ≠ **stop:** accelerate, encourage, precipitate, promote, quicken, speed up ◆ *n* ≠ **capture:** freeing, release ≠ **stopping:** acceleration, encouragement, precipitation, promotion, quickening

arresting *adj* = **striking,** conspicuous, dramatic, engaging, extraordinary, impressive, jaw-dropping, noticeable, outstanding, remarkable, salient, stunning, surprising
Antonyms *adj* inconspicuous, unimpressive, unnoticeable, unremarkable

arrival *n* **1** = **coming,** advent, appearance, arriving, entrance, happening, occurrence, taking place **2** = **newcomer,** arriver, caller, comer, entrant, incomer, visitant, visitor

arrive *vb* **1, 2** = **come,** appear, attain, befall, enter, get to, happen, occur, reach, show up (*inf.*), take place, turn up **5** *Informal* = **succeed,** achieve recognition, become famous, make good, make it, make one's mark (*inf.*), make the grade (*inf.*), reach the top
Antonyms *vb* ≠ **come:** depart, disappear, exit, go, go away, leave, pack one's bags (*inf.*), retire, take (one's) leave, vanish, withdraw

arriviste *n* = **upstart,** adventurer *or* adventuress, climber, parvenu *or* parvenue, social climber, status seeker, would-be

arrogance *n* = **conceit,** bluster, conceitedness, contemptuousness, disdainfulness, haughtiness, hauteur, high-handedness, hubris, imperiousness, insolence, loftiness, lordliness, overweeningness, pomposity, pompousness, presumption, pretension, pretentiousness, pride, scornfulness, superciliousness, swagger
Antonyms *n* bashfulness, diffidence, humility, meekness, modesty, politeness, shyness

arrogant *adj* = **conceited,** assuming, blustering, contemptuous, disdainful, haughty, high and mighty (*inf.*), high-handed, imperious, insolent, looking down one's nose at, lordly, overbearing, overweening, pompous, presumptuous, pretentious, proud, scornful, supercilious, swaggering
Antonyms *adj* bashful, deferential, diffident, humble, modest, polite, servile, shy, unassuming

arrow *n* **1** = **dart,** bolt, flight, quarrel, reed (*arch.*), shaft (*arch.*)

arsenal *n* **1** = **armoury,** ammunition dump, arms depot, magazine, ordnance depot, stock, stockpile, store, storehouse, supply

art[1] *n* **7** = **skill,** adroitness, aptitude, artifice (*arch.*), artistry, craft, craftsmanship, dexterity, expertise, facility, ingenuity, knack, knowledge, mastery, method, profession, trade, virtuosity **9** = **cunning,** artfulness, artifice, astuteness, craftiness, deceit, duplicity, guile, trickery, wiliness

sentations of the natural world or figments of the imagination. **4a** works of art collectively, esp. of the visual arts. **4b** (*as modifier*): *an art gallery*. **5** any branch of the visual arts, esp. painting. **6a** any field using the techniques of art to display artistic qualities. **6b** (*as modifier*): *art film*. **7** method, facility, or knack: *the art of threading a needle*. **8** skill governing a particular human activity: *the art of government*. **9** cunning. **10 get something down to a fine art.** to become highly proficient at something through practice. ◆ See also **arts**. [C13: from OF, from L *ars* craftsmanship]

art[2] (ɑːt) *vb Arch.* (used with the pronoun *thou*) a singular form of the present tense of **be**. [OE *eart*, part of *bēon* to BE]

art. *abbrev. for:* **1** article. **2** artificial. **3** Also: **arty.** artillery.

-art *suffix forming nouns.* a variant of **-ard**.

Art Deco (ˈdɛkəʊ) *n* a style of interior decoration, architecture, etc., at its height in the 1930s and characterized by geometrical shapes. [C20: from *art décoratif*, after the *Exposition des arts décoratifs* held in Paris in 1925]

art director *n* a person responsible for the sets and costumes in a film.

artefact *or* **artifact** (ˈɑːtɪˌfækt) *n* **1** something made or given shape by man, such as a tool or a work of art, esp. an object of archaeological interest. **2** anything man-made, such as a spurious experimental result. **3** *Cytology.* a structure seen in dead tissue that is not normally present in the living tissue. [C19: from L *arte factum*, from *ars* skill + *facere* to make]

artel (ɑːˈtɛl) *n* (in the former Soviet Union) a cooperative union or organization, esp. of producers, such as peasants. [from Russian *artel'*, from It. *artieri* artisans, from *arte* work, from L *ars* ART[1]]

arterial (ɑːˈtɪərɪəl) *adj* **1** of or affecting an artery or arteries. **2** denoting or relating to the bright red reoxygenated blood that circulates in the arteries. **3** being a major route, esp. one with many minor branches.
▸**arˈterially** *adv*

arterialize *or* **arterialise** (ɑːˈtɪərɪəˌlaɪz) *vb* **arterializes, arterializing, arterialized** *or* **arterialises, arterialising, arterialised.** (*tr*) **1** to change (venous blood) into arterial blood by replenishing the depleted oxygen. **2** to provide with arteries.
▸**arˌterialiˈzation** *or* **arˌterialiˈsation** *n*

arteriole (ɑːˈtɪərɪˌəʊl) *n Anat.* any of the small subdivisions of an artery that form thin-walled vessels ending in capillaries. [C19: from NL, from L *artēria* ARTERY]

arteriosclerosis (ɑːˌtɪərɪəʊsklɪəˈrəʊsɪs) *n, pl* **arterioscleroses** (-siːz). a thickening and loss of elasticity of the walls of the arteries. Nontechnical name: **hardening of the arteries.**
▸**arteriosclerotic** (ɑːˌtɪərɪəʊsklɪəˈrɒtɪk) *adj*

artery (ˈɑːtərɪ) *n, pl* **arteries. 1** any of the tubular thick-walled muscular vessels that convey oxygenated blood from the heart to various parts of the body. Cf. **pulmonary artery, vein. 2** a major road or means of communication. [C14: from L *artēria*, rel. to Gk *aortē* the great artery, AORTA]

artesian well (ɑːˈtiːzɪən) *n* a well sunk through impermeable strata into strata receiving water from an area at a higher altitude than that of the well, so the water is forced to flow upwards. [C19: from F, from OF *Arteis* Artois, old province, where such wells were common]

Artex (ˈɑːtɛks) *n Trademark.* a textured coating for walls and ceilings.

art form *n* **1** an accepted mode of artistic composition, such as the sonnet, symphony, etc. **2** a recognized medium of artistic expression.

artful 🅣 (ˈɑːtfʊl) *adj* **1** cunning or tricky. **2** skilful in achieving a desired end.
▸ˈ**artfully** *adv* ▸ˈ**artfulness** *n*

art house *n* **1** a cinema that specializes in showing films that are not part of the commercial mainstream. ◆ *adj* **2** of or relating to such films or a cinema that specializes in showing them.

arthralgia (ɑːˈθrældʒə) *n Pathol.* pain in a joint.
▸**arˈthralgic** *adj*

arthritis (ɑːˈθraɪtɪs) *n* inflammation of a joint or joints characterized by pain and stiffness of the affected parts. [C16: via L from Gk *arthron* joint + -ITIS]
▸**arthritic** (ɑːˈθrɪtɪk) *adj, n*

arthropod (ˈɑːθrəˌpɒd) *n* an invertebrate having jointed limbs, a segmented body, and an exoskeleton made of chitin, as the crustaceans, insects, arachnids, and centipedes. [C19: from NL, from Gk *arthron* joint + *-podus* footed, from *pous* foot]

artic (ɑːˈtɪk) *n Inf.* short for **articulated lorry.**

artichoke (ˈɑːtɪˌtʃəʊk) *n* **1** Also called: **globe artichoke.** a thistle-like Eurasian plant, cultivated for its large edible flower head. **2** the unopened flower head of this plant, which can be cooked and eaten. **3** See **Jerusalem artichoke.** [C16: from It., from OSp., from Ar. *al-kharshūf*]

article 🅣 (ˈɑːtɪkəl) *n* **1** one of a class of objects; item. **2** an unspecified or previously named thing, esp. a small object. **3** a written composition on a subject, often being one of several found in a magazine, newspaper, etc. **4** *Grammar.* a kind of determiner, occurring in many languages including English, that lacks independent meaning. See also **definite article, indefinite article. 5** a clause or section in a written document. **6** (*often cap.*) *Christianity.* See **Thirty-nine Articles.** ◆ *vb* **articles, articling, articled.** (*tr*) **7** to bind by a written contract, esp. one that governs a period of training: *an articled clerk.* [C13: from OF, from L *articulus* small joint, from *artus* joint]

articular (ɑːˈtɪkjʊlə) *adj* of or relating to joints or to the structural components in a joint. [C15: from L *articulāris* concerning the joints, from *articulus* small joint]

articulate 🅣 *adj* (ɑːˈtɪkjʊlɪt). **1** able to express oneself fluently and coherently. **2** having the power of speech. **3** distinct, clear, or definite: *an articulate document.* **4** *Zool.* (of arthropods and higher vertebrates) possessing joints or jointed segments. ◆ *vb* (ɑːˈtɪkjʊˌleɪt), **articulates, articulating, articulated. 5** to speak or enunciate (words, syllables, etc.) clearly and distinctly. **6** (*tr*) to express coherently in words. **7** (*intr*) *Zool.* to be jointed or form a joint. [C16: from L *articulāre* to divide into joints]
▸**arˈticulately** *adv* ▸**arˈticulateness** *n* ▸**arˈticuˌlator** *n*

articulated lorry *n* a large lorry made in two separate sections, a tractor and a trailer, connected by a pivoted bar.

articulation 🅣 (ɑːˌtɪkjʊˈleɪʃən) *n* **1** the act or process of speaking or expressing in words. **2a** the process of articulating a speech sound. **2b** the sound so produced, esp. a consonant. **3** the act or the state of being jointed together. **4** *Zool.* **4a** a joint such as that between bones or arthropod segments. **4b** the way in which jointed parts are connected. **5** *Bot.* the part of a plant at which natural separation occurs.

artifact (ˈɑːtɪˌfækt) *n* a variant spelling of **artefact.**

artifice 🅣 (ˈɑːtɪfɪs) *n* **1** a clever expedient. **2** crafty or subtle deception. **3** skill; cleverness. **4** a skilfully contrived device. [C16: from OF, from L *artificium* skill, from *artifex* one possessed of a specific skill, from *ars* skill + *-fex*, from *facere* to make]

artificer (ɑːˈtɪfɪsə) *n* **1** a skilled craftsman. **2** a clever or inventive designer. **3** a serviceman trained in mechanics.

artificial 🅣 (ˌɑːtɪˈfɪʃəl) *adj* **1** produced by man; not occurring naturally. **2** made in imitation of a natural product: *artificial cream.* **3** pretended; insincere. **4** lacking in spontaneity; affected: *an artificial laugh.* [C14: from L *artificiālis* belonging to art, from *artificium* skill, ARTIFICE]
▸**artificiality** (ˌɑːtɪˌfɪʃɪˈælɪtɪ) *n* ▸ˌ**artiˈficially** *adv*

artificial daylight *n Physics.* artificial light having approximately the same spectral characteristics as natural daylight.

artificial disintegration *n Physics.* radioactive transformation of a substance by bombardment with high-energy particles, such as alpha particles or neutrons.

artificial insemination *n* introduction of spermatozoa into the vagina or uterus by means other than sexual union.

artificial intelligence *n* the ability of a machine, such as a computer, to imitate intelligent human behaviour.

artificial respiration *n* **1** any of various methods of restarting breathing after it has stopped. **2** any method of maintaining respiration, as by use of an iron lung.

artillery 🅣 (ɑːˈtɪlərɪ) *n* **1** guns, cannon, mortars, etc., of calibre greater than 20mm. **2** troops or military units specializing in using such guns. **3** the science dealing with the use of guns. [C14: from OF, from *artillier* to equip with weapons, from ?]

artiodactyl (ˌɑːtɪəʊˈdæktɪl) *n* an ungulate with an even number of toes, as pigs, camels, deer, cattle, etc. [C19: from Gk *artios* even-numbered + *daktulos* finger]
▸ˌ**artioˈdactylous** *adj*

artisan 🅣 (ˈɑːtɪˌzæn, ˌɑːtɪˈzæn) *n* a skilled workman; craftsman. [C16: from F, from OIt. *artigiano*, from *arte* ART[1]]
▸**artisanal** (ɑːˈtɪzənəl, ˈɑːtɪzənəl) *adj*

THESAURUS

artful *adj* **1 = cunning**, clever, crafty, deceitful, designing, foxy, intriguing, politic, scheming, sharp, shrewd, sly, smart, subtle, tricky, wily **2 = skilful**, adept, adroit, clever, dexterous, ingenious, masterly, proficient, resourceful, smart, subtle
Antonyms *adj* ≠ **cunning:** artless, frank, ingenuous, open, simple, straightforward ≠ **skilful:** artless, clumsy, unadept, unskilled, untalented

article *n* **1 = thing**, commodity, item, object, piece, substance, unit **3 = piece**, composition, discourse, essay, feature, item, paper, story, treatise **5 = clause**, branch, detail, division, head, heading, item, paragraph, part, passage, piece, point, portion, section

articulate *adj* **1 = expressive**, clear, coherent, comprehensible, eloquent, fluent, intelligible, lucid, meaningful, understandable, vocal, well-spoken ◆ *vb* **5 = express**, enounce, enunciate, pronounce, say, speak, state, talk, utter, verbalize, vocalize, voice
Antonyms *adj* ≠ **expressive:** dumb, faltering, halting, hesitant, incoherent, incomprehensible, indistinct, mumbled, mute, poorly-spoken, silent, speechless, stammering, stuttering, tongue-tied, unclear, unintelligible, voiceless

articulation *n* **1 = expression**, delivery, diction, enunciation, pronunciation, saying, speaking, statement, talking, utterance, verbalization, vocalization, voicing **3, 4 = joint**, connection, coupling, hinge, jointing, juncture

artifice *n* **1 = trick**, contrivance, device, dodge, expedient, hoax, machination, manoeuvre, ruse, stratagem, subterfuge, tactic, wile **2 = cunning**, artfulness, chicanery, craft, craftiness, deception, duplicity, guile, scheming, slyness, trickery **3 = cleverness**, adroitness, deftness, facility, finesse, ingenuity, invention, inventiveness, skill

artificial *adj* **1 = synthetic**, man-made, manufactured, non-natural, plastic **2 = fake**, bogus, counterfeit, ersatz, imitation, mock, phoney *or* phony (*inf.*), pseudo (*inf.*), sham, simulated, specious, spurious **3, 4 = insincere**, affected, assumed, contrived, false, feigned, forced, hollow, meretricious, phoney *or* phony (*inf.*), pretended, spurious, unnatural
Antonyms *adj* ≠ **fake:** authentic ≠ **insincere:** frank, genuine, honest, natural, sincere, true, unaffected

artillery *n* **1 = big guns**, battery, cannon, cannonry, gunnery, ordnance

artisan *n* **= craftsman**, artificer, handicraftsman, journeyman, mechanic, skilled workman, technician

artist ⓘ (ˈɑːtɪst) *n* **1** a person who practises or is skilled in an art, esp. painting, drawing, or sculpture. **2** a person who displays in his work qualities required in art, such as sensibility and imagination. **3** a person whose profession requires artistic expertise. **4** a person skilled in some task or occupation. **5** *Sl.* a person devoted to or proficient in something: *a con artist; a booze artist.*
▸**arˈtistic** *adj* ▸**arˈtistically** *adv*

artiste ⓘ (ɑːˈtiːst) *n* **1** an entertainer, such as a singer or dancer. **2** a person who is highly skilled in some occupation: *a hair artiste.* [F]

artistry ⓘ (ˈɑːtɪstrɪ) *n* **1** artistic workmanship, ability, or quality. **2** artistic pursuits. **3** great skill.

artless ⓘ (ˈɑːtlɪs) *adj* **1** free from deceit; ingenuous: *an artless remark.* **2** natural; unpretentious. **3** without art or skill.
▸ˈ**artlessly** *adv*

Art Nouveau (ɑː nuːˈvəʊ; *French* ar nuvo) *n* a style of art and architecture of the 1890s, characterized by sinuous outlines and stylized natural forms. [F, lit.: new art]

art paper *n* a high-quality type of paper having a smooth coating of china clay or similar substance on it.

arts (ɑːts) *pl n* **1a the.** imaginative, creative, and nonscientific branches of knowledge considered collectively, esp. as studied academically. **1b** (*as modifier*): *an arts degree.* **2** See **fine art**. **3** cunning actions or schemes.

Arts and Crafts *pl n* decorative handicraft and design, esp. that of the **Arts and Crafts movement**, in late nineteenth-century Britain, which sought to revive medieval craftsmanship.

art union *n Austral. & NZ.* an officially approved lottery for prizes other than cash (formerly works of art).

arty ⓘ (ˈɑːtɪ) *adj* **artier, artiest.** *Inf.* having an affected interest in artists or art.
▸ˈ**artiness** *n*

arugula (əˈruːgjʊlə) *n* a Mediterranean plant of the mustard family with yellowish-white flowers and pungent leaves that are used as a salad; rocket. See also **rocket**[2] (sense 1). [C20: from N It. dialect]

arum (ˈɛərəm) *n* **1** any of various aroid plants of Europe and the Mediterranean region, having arrow-shaped leaves and a typically white spathe, such as the cuckoopint. **2 arum lily.** another name for **calla** (sense 1). [C16: from L, var. of *aros* wake-robin, from Gk *aron*]

arvo (ˈɑːvəʊ) *n Austral. inf.* afternoon.

-ary *suffix.* **1** (*forming adjectives*) of; related to; belonging to: *cautionary.* **2** (*forming nouns*) a person or thing connected with: *missionary; aviary.* [from L *-ārius, -āria, -ārium*]

Aryan (ˈɛərɪən) *n* **1** (in Nazi ideology) a Caucasian of non-Jewish descent. **2** a member of any of the peoples supposedly descended from the Indo-Europeans. ◆ *adj* **3** of or characteristic of an Aryan or Aryans. ◆ *adj, n* **4** *Arch.* Indo-European. [C19: from Sansk. *ārya* of noble birth]

as[1] ⓘ (æz; *unstressed* əz) *conj* (*subordinating*) **1** (often preceded by *just*) while; when: *he caught me as I was leaving.* **2** in the way that: *dancing as only she can.* **3** that which; what: *I did as I was told.* **4** (of) which fact, event, etc. (referring to the previous statement): *to become wise, as we all know, is not easy.* **5 as it were.** in a way; as if it were really so. **6** since; seeing that. **7** in the same way that: *he died of cancer, as his father had done.* **8** for instance: *capital cities, as London.* ◆ *adv, conj* **9a** used to indicate identity of extent, amount, etc.: *she is as heavy as her sister.* **9b** used with this sense after a noun phrase introduced by *the same*: *the same height as her sister.* ◆ *prep* **10** in the role of; being: *as his friend, I am probably biased.* **11 as for** *or* **to.** with reference to: *as for my past, I'm not telling you anything.* **12 as if** *or* **though.** as it would be if: *he talked as if he knew all about it.* **13 as (it) is.** in the existing state of affairs. **14 as was.** in a previous state. [OE *alswā* likewise]

> **USAGE NOTE** See at **like.**

as[2] (æs) *n* **1** an ancient Roman unit of weight approximately equal to 1 pound troy (373 grams). **2** a copper coin of ancient Rome. [C17: from L *ās* unity]

As *symbol for:* **1** altostratus. **2** *Chem.* arsenic.

AS *abbrev. for:* **1** Also: **A.S.** Anglo-Saxon. **2** antisubmarine.

ASA *abbrev. for:* **1** (in Britain) Amateur Swimming Association. **2** (in Britain) Advertising Standards Authority. **3** (in the US) American Standards Association.

ASA/BS *abbrev.* an obsolete expression of the speed of a photographic film, replaced by the ISO rating. [C20: from *American Standards Association/British Standard*]

asafoetida *or* **asafetida** (ˌæsəˈfɛtɪdə) *n* a bitter resin with an unpleasant onion-like smell, obtained from the roots of some umbelliferous plants: formerly used to treat flatulence, etc. [C14: from Med. L, from *asa* gum (cf. Persian *azā* mastic) + L *foetidus* evil-smelling]

a.s.a.p. *abbrev. for* as soon as possible.

asbestos (æsˈbɛstɒs) *n* **a** any of the fibrous amphibole minerals that are incombustible and resistant to chemicals. It was formerly widely used in the form of fabric or board as a heat-resistant structural material. **b** (*as modifier*): *asbestos matting.* [C14: via L from Gk: from *asbestos* inextinguishable, from A-[1] + *sbennunai* to extinguish]

asbestosis (ˌæsbɛsˈtəʊsɪs) *n* inflammation of the lungs resulting from chronic inhalation of asbestos particles.

ascarid (ˈæskərɪd) *n* a parasitic nematode worm such as the common roundworm of man and pigs. [C14: from NL, from Gk *askarides*, pl. of *askaris*]

ascend ⓘ (əˈsɛnd) *vb* **1** to go or move up (a ladder, hill, slope, etc.). **2** (*intr*) to slope or incline upwards. **3** (*intr*) to rise to a higher point, level, etc. **4** to trace (a genealogy, etc.) back in time. **5** to sing or play (a scale, etc.) from the lower to higher notes. **6 ascend the throne.** to become king or queen. [C14: from L *ascendere*, from *scandere*]

ascendancy ⓘ, **ascendency** (əˈsɛndənsɪ) *or* **ascendance, ascendence** *n* the condition of being dominant.

ascendant ⓘ *or* **ascendent** (əˈsɛndənt) *adj* **1** proceeding upwards; rising. **2** dominant or influential. ◆ *n* **3** a position or condition of dominance. **4** *Astrol.* (*sometimes cap.*) **4a** a point on the ecliptic that rises on the eastern horizon at a particular moment. **4b** the sign of the zodiac containing this point. **5 in the ascendant.** increasing in influence, etc.

ascender (əˈsɛndə) *n* **1** *Printing.* the part of certain lower-case letters, such as *b* or *h*, that extends above the body of the letter. **2** a person or thing that ascends.

ascension ⓘ (əˈsɛnʃən) *n* the act of ascending.
▸**asˈcensional** *adj*

Ascension (əˈsɛnʃən) *n Bible.* the passing of Jesus Christ from earth into heaven (Acts 1:9).

Ascension Day *n* the 40th day after Easter, when the Ascension of Christ into heaven is celebrated.

ascent ⓘ (əˈsɛnt) *n* **1** the act of ascending; upward movement. **2** an upward slope. **3** movement back through time (esp. in **line of ascent**).

ascertain ⓘ (ˌæsəˈteɪn) *vb* (*tr*) **1** to determine definitely. **2** *Arch.* to make certain. [C15: from OF *acertener* to make certain]
▸ˌ**ascerˈtainable** *adj* ▸ˌ**ascerˈtainment** *n*

ascetic ⓘ (əˈsɛtɪk) *n* **1** a person who practises great self-denial and abstains from worldly comforts and pleasures, esp. for religious reasons. ◆ *adj also* **ascetical**. **2** rigidly abstinent or abstemious. **3** of or relating to ascetics or asceticism. [C17: from Gk *askētikos*, from *askētēs*, from *askein* to exercise]
▸**asˈcetically** *adv* ▸**aˈsceti**ˌ**cism** *n*

ascidian (əˈsɪdɪən) *n* any of a class of minute marine invertebrate animals, such as the sea squirt, the adults of which are degenerate and sedentary.

ascidium (əˈsɪdɪəm) *n, pl* **ascidia** (-ˈsɪdɪə). part of a plant that is shaped

THESAURUS

artist *n* **1, 4** = **creator**, artisan (*obs.*), craftsman, maker, master

artiste *n* **1** = **performer**, entertainer

artistic *adj* **1** = **creative**, aesthetic, beautiful, cultivated, cultured, decorative, elegant, exquisite, graceful, imaginative, ornamental, refined, sensitive, sophisticated, stylish, tasteful
Antonyms *adj* inartistic, inelegant, tasteless, unattractive, untalented

artistry *n* **1, 3** = **skill**, accomplishment, art, artistic ability, brilliance, craft, craftsmanship, creativity, finesse, flair, genius, mastery, proficiency, sensibility, style, talent, taste, touch, virtuosity, workmanship

artless *adj* **1** = **straightforward**, candid, direct, fair, frank, genuine, guileless, honest, open, plain, round, sincere, true, undesigning, upfront (*inf.*) **2** = **natural**, humble, plain, pure, simple, unadorned, unaffected, uncontrived, unpretentious **3** = **unskilled**, awkward, bungling, clumsy, crude, incompetent, inept, maladroit, primitive, rude, untalented
Antonyms *adj* ≠ **straightforward**: artful, crafty, cunning, designing, dishonest, false, insincere ≠ **natural**: affected, artificial, unnatural ≠ **unskilled**: aesthetic, artful, artistic, crafty, cunning, sophisticated

arty *adj Informal* = **artistic**, arty-crafty (*inf.*), arty-farty (*derogatory sl.*)

as[1] *conj* **1** = **when**, at the time that, during the time that, just as, while **2** = **in the way that**, in the manner that, like **3** = **what**, that which **5 as it were** = **in a way**, in a manner of speaking, so to say, so to speak **6** = **since**, because, considering that, seeing that **8** = **for instance**, like, such as ◆ *prep* **10** = **being**, in the character of, in the role of, under the name of **11 as for** = **with regard to**, as regards, in reference to, on the subject of, with reference to, with respect to

ascend *vb* **1-3** = **move up**, climb, float up, fly up, go up, lift off, mount, rise, scale, slope upwards, soar, take off, tower
Antonyms *vb* alight, descend, dip, drop, fall, go down, incline, move down, plummet, plunge, sink, slant, slope, subside, tumble

ascendancy *n* = **influence**, authority, command, control, dominance, domination, dominion, hegemony, mastery, power, predominance, pre-eminence, prevalence, reign, rule, sovereignty, superiority, supremacy, sway, upper hand
Antonyms *n* inferiority, servility, subjection, subordination, weakness

ascendant *adj* **2** = **influential**, authoritative, commanding, controlling, dominant, powerful, predominant, pre-eminent, prevailing, ruling, superior, supreme, uppermost ◆ *n* **5 in the ascendant** = **rising**, ascending, climbing, commanding, dominant, dominating, flourishing, growing, increasing, influential, mounting, on the rise, on the way up, powerful, prevailing, supreme, up-and-coming, uppermost, winning

ascension *n* = **rise**, ascending, ascent, climb, mounting, moving upwards, rising

ascent *n* **1** = **rise**, ascending, ascension, clambering, climb, climbing, mounting, rising, scaling, upward movement **2** = **upward slope**, acclivity, gradient, incline, ramp, rise, rising ground

ascertain *vb* **1** = **find out**, confirm, determine, discover, establish, ferret out, fix, identify, learn, make certain, settle, suss (out) (*sl.*), verify

ascetic *n* **1** = **monk**, abstainer, anchorite, hermit, nun, recluse, self-denier ◆ *adj* **2** = **self-denying**, abstemious, abstinent, austere, celibate, frugal, harsh, plain, puritanical, rigorous, self-disciplined, severe, Spartan, stern
Antonyms *n* ≠ **monk**: hedonist, sensualist, voluptuary ◆ *adj* ≠ **self-denying**: abandoned, comfortable, luxurious, self-indulgent, sensuous, voluptuous

like a pitcher, such as the modified leaf of the pitcher plant. [C18: from NL, from Gk *askidion* a little bag, from *askos* bag]

ascomycete (ˌæskəmaɪˈsiːt) *n* any of a phylum of fungi in which the spores (ascospores) are formed inside a club-shaped cell (ascus). The group includes yeast, penicillium, and certain mildews.
▸ˌ**ascomyˈcetous** *adj*

ascorbic acid (əˈskɔːbɪk) *n* a white crystalline vitamin present in plants, esp. citrus fruits, tomatoes, and green vegetables. A deficiency in the diet of man leads to scurvy. Also called: **vitamin C.**

ascribe ❶ (əˈskraɪb) *vb* **ascribes, ascribing, ascribed.** *(tr)* **1** to credit or assign, as to a particular origin or period. **2** to consider as belonging to: *to ascribe beauty to youth.* [C15: from L *ascrībere* to enrol, from *ad* in addition + *scrībere* to write]
▸**asˈcribable** *adj*

USAGE NOTE *Ascribe* is sometimes wrongly used where *subscribe* is meant: *I do not subscribe* (not *ascribe*) *to this view.*

ascription (əˈskrɪpʃən) *n* **1** the act of ascribing. **2** a statement ascribing something to someone. [C16: from L *ascrīptiō*, from *ascrībere* to ASCRIBE]

asdic (ˈæzdɪk) *n* an early form of **sonar.** [C20: from *A(nti-)S(ubmarine) D(etection) I(nvestigation) C(ommittee)*]

-ase *suffix forming nouns.* indicating an enzyme: *oxidase.* [from DIASTASE]

ASEAN (ˈæsɪˌæn) *n acronym for* Association of South-East Asian Nations.

asepsis (əˈsɛpsɪs, eɪ-) *n* **1** the state of being free from living pathogenic organisms. **2** the methods of achieving a germ-free condition.
▸**aˈseptic** *adj*

asexual ❶ (eɪˈsɛksjuəl) *adj* **1** having no apparent sex or sex organs. **2** (of reproduction) not involving the fusion of male and female gametes.
▸ˌ**asexuˈality** *n* ▸**aˈsexually** *adv*

ash[1] (æʃ) *n* **1** the residue formed when matter is burnt. **2** fine particles of lava thrown out by an erupting volcano. **3** a light silvery-grey colour. ◆ See also **ashes.** [OE *æsce*]

ash[2] (æʃ) *n* **1** a tree having compound leaves, clusters of small greenish flowers, and winged seeds. **2** the wood of this tree, used for tool handles, etc. **3** any of several trees resembling the ash, such as the mountain ash. **4** *Austral.* any of various eucalypts. [OE *æsc*]

ash[3] (æʃ) *n* the digraph æ, as in Old English, representing a vowel approximately like that of the *a* in Modern English *hat.*

ASH (æʃ) *n* (in Britain) *acronym for* Action on Smoking and Health.

ashamed ❶ (əˈʃeɪmd) *adj (usually postpositive)* **1** overcome with shame or remorse. **2** (foll. by *of*) suffering from feelings of shame in relation to (a person or deed). **3** (foll. by *to*) unwilling through fear of humiliation, shame, etc. [OE *āscamod*, p.p. of *āscamian* to shame, from *scamu* SHAME]
▸**ashamedly** (əˈʃeɪmɪdlɪ) *adv*

A shares *pl n* ordinary shares in a company which carry restricted voting rights.

ash can *n* a US word for **dustbin.** Also called: **garbage can, ash bin, trash can.**

ashen[1] ❶ (ˈæʃən) *adj* **1** drained of colour. **2** consisting of or resembling ashes. **3** of a pale greyish colour.

ashen[2] (ˈæʃən) *adj* of, relating to, or made from the ash tree or its timber.

ashes (ˈæʃɪz) *pl n* **1** ruins or remains, as after burning. **2** the remains of a human body after cremation.

Ashes (ˈæʃɪz) *pl n* **the.** a cremated cricket stump constituting a trophy competed for by England and Australia in test cricket since 1882. [from a mock obituary of English cricket after a great Australian victory]

Ashkenazi (ˌæʃkəˈnɑːzɪ) *n, pl* **Ashkenazim** (-zɪm). **1** *(modifier)* of or relating to the Jews of Germany and E Europe. **2** a Jew of German or E European descent. Cf. **Sephardi.** [C19: LHeb., from Heb. *Ashkenaz,* the son of Gomer (Genesis 10:3; I Chronicles 1:6)]

ashlar *or* **ashler** (ˈæʃlə) *n* **1** a square block of hewn stone for use in building. **2** a thin dressed stone with straight edges, used to face a wall. **3** masonry made of ashlar. [C14: from OF *aisselier* crossbeam, from *ais* board, from L *axis* axletree]

ashore ❶ (əˈʃɔː) *adv* **1** towards or onto land from the water. ◆ *adj (postpositive), adv* **2** on land: *a day ashore before sailing.*

ashram (ˈæʃrəm) *n* a religious retreat or community where a Hindu holy man lives. [from Sansk. *āśrama,* from *ā-* near + *śrama* religious exertion]

ashtray (ˈæʃˌtreɪ) *n* a receptacle for tobacco ash, cigarette butts, etc.

Ash Wednesday *n* the first day of Lent, named from the Christian custom of sprinkling ashes on penitents' heads.

ashy (ˈæʃɪ) *adj* **ashier, ashiest. 1** of a pale greyish colour; ashen. **2** consisting of, covered with, or resembling ash.

Asian (ˈeɪʃən, ˈeɪʒən) *adj* **1** of or relating to Asia, the largest of the continents, or to any of its people or languages. **2** *Brit.* of or relating to natives of the Indian subcontinent or their descendants, esp. when living in Britain. ◆ *n* **3** a native or inhabitant of Asia or a descendant of one. **4** *Brit.* a native of the Indian subcontinent or a descendant of one.

USAGE NOTE The use of *Asian* or *Asiatic* as a noun can be offensive and should be avoided.

Asian flu *n* a type of influenza caused by a virus which apparently originated in China in 1957.

Asian pear *n* a variety of pear, apple-shaped with crisp juicy flesh.

Asiatic (ˌeɪʃɪˈætɪk, -zɪ-) *n, adj* another word for **Asian.**

USAGE NOTE See at **Asian.**

Asiatic cholera *n* another name for **cholera.**

aside ❶ (əˈsaɪd) *adv* **1** on or to one side. **2** out of hearing; in or into seclusion. **3** away from oneself: *he threw the book aside.* **4** out of mind or consideration: *he put aside all fears.* **5** in or into reserve: *to put aside money for old age.* ◆ *n* **6** something spoken by an actor, intended to be heard by the audience, but not by the others on stage. **7** any confidential statement spoken in undertones. **8** an incidental remark, note, etc.

A-side *n* the side of a gramophone record regarded as more important.

asinine ❶ (ˈæsɪˌnaɪn) *adj* **1** obstinate or stupid. **2** resembling an ass. [C16: from L *asinīnus,* from *asinus* ASS[1]]
▸ˈ**asiˌninely** *adv* ▸**asininity** (ˌæsɪˈnɪnɪtɪ) *n*

ASIO *abbrev. for* Australian Security Intelligence Organization.

ask ❶ (ɑːsk) *vb* **1** (often foll. by *about*) to put a question (to); request an answer (from). **2** *(tr)* to inquire about: *she asked the way.* **3** *(tr)* to direct or put (a question). **4** *(may take a clause as object or an infinitive;* often foll. by *for)* to make a request or demand: *they asked for a deposit.* **5** *(tr)* to demand or expect (esp. in **ask a lot of, ask too much of**). **6** *(tr)* Also: **ask out, ask over.** to request (a person) politely to come or go to a place: *he asked her to the party.* [OE *āscian*]
▸ˈ**asker** *n*

ask after *vb (prep)* to make inquiries about the health of (someone): *he asked after her mother.*

askance ❶ (əˈskæns) *or* **askant** (əˈskænt) *adv* **1** with an oblique glance. **2** with doubt or mistrust. [C16: from ?]

askew ❶ (əˈskjuː) *adv, adj* at an oblique angle; towards one side; awry.

ask for *vb (prep)* **1** to try to obtain by requesting. **2** *(intr) Inf.* to behave in a provocative manner that is regarded as inviting (trouble, etc.): *you're asking for it.*

asking price *n* the price suggested by a seller but usually considered to be subject to bargaining.

aslant ❶ (əˈslɑːnt) *adv* **1** at a slant. ◆ *prep* **2** at a slant across or athwart.

THESAURUS

asceticism *n* **2** = **self-denial**, abstemiousness, abstinence, austerity, celibacy, frugality, harshness, mortification of the flesh, plainness, puritanism, rigorousness, rigour, self-abnegation, self-discipline, self-mortification

ascribe *vb* **1** = **attribute**, assign, charge, credit, impute, put down, refer, set down

asexual *adj* **1** = **sexless**, neuter, neutral

asexuality *n* **1** = **sexlessness**, neutrality

ashamed *adj* **1, 2** = **embarrassed**, abashed, bashful, blushing, chagrined, conscience-stricken, crestfallen, discomfited, distressed, guilty, humbled, humiliated, mortified, prudish, reluctant, remorseful, shamefaced, sheepish, shy, sorry
Antonyms *adj* gratified, honoured, pleased, proud, satisfied, unashamed, vain

ashen[1] *adj* **1, 3** = **pale**, anaemic, ashy, colourless, grey, leaden, like death warmed up *(inf.)*, livid, pallid, pasty, wan, white
Antonyms *adj* blooming, blushing, florid, flushed, glowing, radiant, red, reddish, rosy, rosy-cheeked, rubicund, ruddy

ashore *adv* **1** = **on land**, aground, landwards, on dry land, on the beach, on the shore, shorewards, to the shore

aside *adv* **1** = **to one side**, alone, alongside, apart, away, beside, in isolation, in reserve, on one side, out of mind, out of the way, privately, separately, to the side ◆ *n* **8** = **interpolation**, interposition, parenthesis **8** = **digression**, departure, excursion, excursus, tangent

asinine *adj* **1** = **stupid**, braindead *(inf.)*, brainless, daft *(inf.)*, dunderheaded, fatuous, foolish, goofy *(inf.)*, gormless *(Brit. inf.)*, halfwitted, idiotic, imbecile, imbecilic, inane, moronic, senseless, silly, thickheaded, thick-witted
Antonyms *adj* brainy *(inf.)*, bright, clever, intelligent, quick-witted, sage, sane, sensible, sharp, smart, wise

asininity *n* **1** = **stupidity**, brainlessness, cloddishness, daftness, doltishness, fatuity, fatuousness, foolishness *(inf.)*, goofiness, gormlessness *(Brit. inf.)*, idiocy, imbecility, inanity, moronism, moronity, oafishness, senselessness, silliness, thickheadedness, thick-wittedness
Antonyms *adj* braininess *(inf.)*, brightness, cleverness, intelligence, keenness, quickness, quick-wittedness, sagacity, sageness, saneness, sensibleness, sharpness, sharp-wittedness, smartness, wisdom

ask *vb* **1-3** = **inquire**, interrogate, query, question, quiz **4** = **request**, appeal, apply, beg, beseech, claim, crave, demand, entreat, implore, petition, plead, pray, seek, solicit, sue, supplicate **6** = **invite**, bid, summon
Antonyms *vb* ≠ **inquire:** answer, reply, respond

askance *adv As in* **look askance at 1** = **out of the corner of one's eye**, awry, indirectly, obliquely, sideways, with a side glance **2** = **suspiciously**, disapprovingly, distrustfully, doubtfully, dubiously, mistrustfully, sceptically

askew *adv* = **crookedly**, aslant, awry, obliquely, off-centre, to one side ◆ *adj* = **crooked**, awry, cockeyed *(inf.)*, lopsided, oblique, off-centre, skewwhiff *(Brit. inf.)*
Antonyms *adv* ≠ **crookedly:** aligned, evenly, in line, level, right, squarely, straight, true ◆ *adj* ≠ **crooked:** aligned, even, in line, level, right, square, straight, true

aslant *adv* **1** = **at a slant**, aslope, atilt, slantingly, slopingly ◆ *prep* **2** = **across**, athwart

asleep ➊ (əˈsliːp) *adj* (*postpositive*) **1** in or into a state of sleep. **2** in or into a dormant or inactive state. **3** (of limbs) numb; lacking sensation. **4** *Euphemistic.* dead.

ASLEF (ˈæzlɛf) *n* (in Britain) *acronym for* Associated Society of Locomotive Engineers and Firemen.

AS level *n Brit.* **1a** an advanced level of a subject taken for the General Certificate of Education, with a smaller course content than an A level. **1b** (*as modifier*): *AS-level English.* **2** a pass in a subject at AS level: *I've got three AS levels.*

ASM *abbrev. for:* **1** air-to-surface missile. **2** *Theatre.* assistant stage manager.

asocial (eɪˈsəʊʃəl) *adj* **1** avoiding contact. **2** unconcerned about the welfare of others. **3** hostile to society.

asp (æsp) *n* **1** the venomous snake that caused the death of Cleopatra. **2** Also called: **asp viper.** a viper that occurs in S Europe and is very similar to but smaller than the adder. **3** **horned asp.** another name for **horned viper.** [C15: from L *aspis,* from Gk]

asparagus (əˈspærəgəs) *n* **1** a plant of the lily family, having small scaly or needle-like leaves. **2** the succulent young shoots, which may be cooked and eaten. **3** **asparagus fern.** a fernlike species of asparagus, native to southern Africa. [C15: from L, from Gk *asparagos,* from ?]

aspartame (əˈspɑːˌteɪm) *n* an artificial sweetener produced from a nonessential amino acid. [C20: from *aspart(ic acid)* + *(phenyl)a(lanine) m(ethyl) e(ster)*]

aspect ➊ (ˈæspɛkt) *n* **1** appearance to the eye; visual effect. **2** a distinct feature or element in a problem, situation, etc.; facet. **3** the way in which a problem, idea, etc., may be considered. **4** a facial expression: *a severe aspect.* **5** a position facing a particular direction: *the southern aspect of a house.* **6** a view in a certain direction. **7** *Astrol.* any of several specific angular distances between two planets. **8** *Grammar.* a category of verbal inflections that expresses such features as the continuity, repetition, or completedness of the action described. [C14: from L *aspectus* a sight, from *ad-* to, at + *specere* to look]

aspect ratio *n* **1** the ratio of width to height of a picture on a television or cinema screen. **2** *Aeronautics.* the ratio of the span of a wing to its mean chord.

aspen (ˈæspən) *n* a kind of poplar tree in which the leaves are attached to the stem by long flattened stalks so that they quiver in the wind. [OE *æspe*]

Asperger's syndrome (ˈæspəgəz) *n* a form of autism in which the sufferer has limited but obsessive interests and has difficulty relating to other people. [C20: after Hans *Asperger* (20th cent.), Austrian physician who first described it]

asperity ➊ (æˈspɛrɪtɪ) *n, pl* **asperities. 1** roughness or sharpness of temper. **2** roughness or harshness of a surface, sound, etc. **3** *Physics.* the elongated compressed region of contact between two surfaces caused by the normal force. [C16: from L *asperitās,* from *asper* rough]

asperse (əˈspɜːs) *vb* **asperses, aspersing, aspersed.** (*tr*) to spread false rumours about; defame. [C15: from L *aspersus,* from *aspergere* to sprinkle]
▸**asˈperser** *n* ▸**asˈpersive** *adj*

aspersion ➊ (əˈspɜːʃən) *n* **1** a disparaging or malicious remark (esp. in **cast aspersions (on)**). **2** the act of defaming.

asphalt (ˈæsfælt) *n* **1** any of several black semisolid substances composed of bitumen and inert mineral matter. They occur naturally and as a residue from petroleum distillation. **2** a mixture of this substance with gravel, used in road-surfacing and roofing materials. **3** (*modifier*) containing or surfaced with asphalt. ◆ *vb* **4** (*tr*) to cover with asphalt. [C14: from LL *aspaltus,* from Gk *asphaltos,* prob. from A-[1] + *sphallein* to cause to fall; referring to its use as a binding agent]
▸**asˈphaltic** *adj*

asphodel (ˈæsfəˌdɛl) *n* **1** any of various S European plants of the lily family having clusters of white or yellow flowers. **2** an unidentified flower of Greek legend said to cover the Elysian fields. [C16: from L *asphodelus,* from Gk *asphodelos,* from ?]

asphyxia (æsˈfɪksɪə) *n* lack of oxygen in the blood due to restricted respiration; suffocation. [C18: from NL, from Gk *asphuxia* a stopping of the pulse, from A-[1] + *sphuxis* pulse, from *sphuzein* to throb]
▸**asˈphyxial** *adj* ▸**asˈphyxiant** *adj*

asphyxiate ➊ (æsˈfɪksɪˌeɪt) *vb* **asphyxiates, asphyxiating, asphyxiated.** to cause asphyxia in or undergo asphyxia; smother; suffocate.
▸**asˌphyxiˈation** *n* ▸**asˈphyxiˌator** *n*

aspic (ˈæspɪk) *n* a savoury jelly based on meat or fish stock, used as a relish or as a mould for meat, vegetables, etc. [C18: from F: aspic (jelly), asp]

aspidistra (ˌæspɪˈdɪstrə) *n* a popular house plant of the lily family with long tough evergreen leaves. [C19: from NL, from Gk *aspis* shield, on the model of *Tupistra,* genus of liliaceous plants]

aspirant ➊ (ˈæspɪrənt) *n* **1** a person who aspires, as to a high position. ◆ *adj* **2** aspiring.

aspirate *vb* (ˈæspɪˌreɪt), **aspirates, aspirating, aspirated.** (*tr*) **1** *Phonetics.* **1a** to articulate (a stop) with some force, so that breath escapes audibly. **1b** to pronounce (a word or syllable) with an initial *h.* **2** to remove by inhalation or suction, esp. to suck (air or fluid) from a body cavity. **3** to supply air to (an internal-combustion engine). ◆ *n* (ˈæspɪrɪt). **4** *Phonetics.* **4a** a stop pronounced with an audible release of breath. **4b** the glottal fricative represented in English and several other languages as *h.* ◆ *adj* (ˈæspɪrɪt). **5** *Phonetics.* (of a stop) pronounced with a forceful expulsion of breath.

aspiration ➊ (ˌæspɪˈreɪʃən) *n* **1** strong desire to achieve something, such as success. **2** the aim of such desire. **3** the act of breathing. **4** *Phonetics.* **4a** the pronunciation of an aspirated consonant. **4b** an aspirated consonant. **5** *Med.* **5a** the sucking of fluid or foreign matter into the air passages of the body. **5b** the removal of air or fluid from the body by suction.
▸**ˌaspiˈrational** *adj* ▸**aspiratory** (əˈspaɪrətərɪ) *adj*

aspirator (ˈæspɪˌreɪtə) *n* a device employing suction, such as a jet pump or one for removing fluids from a body cavity.

aspire ➊ (əˈspaɪə) *vb* **aspires, aspiring, aspired.** (*intr*) **1** (usually foll. by *to* or *after*) to yearn (for), desire, or hope (to do or be something): *to aspire to be a great leader.* **2** to rise to a great height. [C15: from L *aspīrāre* to breathe upon, from *spīrāre* to breathe]
▸**asˈpiring** *adj*

aspirin (ˈæsprɪn) *n, pl* **aspirin** *or* **aspirins. 1** a white crystalline compound widely used in the form of tablets to relieve pain, fever, and colds. Chemical name: **acetylsalicylic acid. 2** a tablet of aspirin. [C19: from G, from *A(cetyl)* + *Spir(säure)* spiraeic acid (modern salicylic acid) + -IN]

Aspirin (ˈæsprɪn) *n* (in Canada) a trademark for **aspirin.**

asquint (əˈskwɪnt) *adv, adj* (*postpositive*) with a glance from the corner of the eye, esp. a furtive one. [C13: ?from Du. *schuinte* slant, from ?]

ass[1] ➊ (æs) *n* **1** a mammal related to the horse. It is hardy and sure-footed, having longer ears than the horse. **2** (not in technical use) the donkey. **3** a foolish or ridiculously pompous person. [OE *assa,* prob. from OIrish *asan,* from L *asinus;* rel. to Gk *onos* ass]

ass[2] (æs) *n* the usual US and Canad. word for **arse.** [OE *ærs*]

assagai (ˈæsəˌgaɪ) *n, pl* **assagais.** a variant spelling of **assegai.**

assai (æˈsaɪ) *adv Music.* (usually preceded by a musical direction) very: *allegro assai.* [It.: enough]

assail ➊ (əˈseɪl) *vb* (*tr*) **1** to attack violently; assault. **2** to criticize or ridicule vehemently. **3** to beset or disturb: *his mind was assailed by doubts.* **4** to encounter with the intention of mastering. [C13: from OF *asalir,* from L *assilīre,* from *salīre* to leap]
▸**asˈsailable** *adj* ▸**asˈsailer** *n*

assailant ➊ (əˈseɪlənt) *n* a person who attacks another, either physically or verbally.

assassin ➊ (əˈsæsɪn) *n* a murderer, esp. one who kills a prominent political figure. [C16: from Med. L *assassīnus,* from Ar. *hashshāshīn,* pl. of *hashshāsh* one who eats HASHISH]

assassinate ➊ (əˈsæsɪˌneɪt) *vb* **assassinates, assassinating, assassinated.** (*tr*) **1** to murder (a political figure). **2** to ruin or harm (a person's reputation, etc.) by slander.
▸**asˌsassiˈnation** *n*

assault ➊ (əˈsɔːlt) *n* **1** a violent attack, either physical or verbal. **2** *Law.*

THESAURUS

asleep *adj* **1** = **sleeping**, crashed out, dead to the world (*inf.*), dormant, dozing, fast asleep, napping, out for the count, slumbering, snoozing (*inf.*), sound asleep

aspect *n* **1, 4** = **appearance**, air, attitude, bearing, condition, countenance, demeanour, expression, look, manner, mien (*literary*) **2** = **feature**, angle, facet, side **3, 6** = **position**, bearing, direction, exposure, outlook, point of view, prospect, scene, situation, view

asperity *n* **1** = **sharpness**, acerbity, acrimony, bitterness, churlishness, crabbedness, crossness, harshness, irascibility, irritability, moroseness, peevishness, ruggedness, severity, sourness, sullenness

aspersion *n* **1** *As in* **cast aspersions on** = **slander**, abuse, calumny, censure, character assassination, defamation, denigration, detraction, disparagement, obloquy, reproach, slur, smear, traducement, vilification, vituperation

asphyxiate *vb* = **suffocate**, choke, smother, stifle, strangle, strangulate, throttle

asphyxiation *n* = **suffocation**, strangulation

aspirant *n* **1** = **candidate**, applicant, aspirer, hopeful, postulant, seeker, suitor ◆ *adj* **2** = **hopeful**, ambitious, aspiring, eager, endeavouring, longing, striving, wishful

aspiration *n* **1, 2** = **aim**, ambition, craving, desire, dream, eagerness, endeavour, goal, hankering, Holy Grail (*inf.*), hope, longing, object, objective, wish, yearning

aspire *vb* **1** = **aim**, be ambitious, be eager, crave, desire, dream, hanker, hope, long, pursue, seek, set one's heart on, wish, yearn

aspiring *adj* **1** = **hopeful**, ambitious, aspirant, eager, endeavouring, longing, striving, wannabe (*inf.*), wishful, would-be

ass[1] *n* **2** = **donkey**, jennet, moke (*sl.*) **3** = **fool**, airhead, berk (*Brit. sl.*), blockhead, coot, daftie (*inf.*), dolt, dope (*inf.*), dunce, fathead (*inf.*), geek (*sl.*), halfwit, idiot, jackass, jerk (*sl., chiefly US & Canad.*), nerd *or* nurd (*sl.*), nincompoop, ninny, nitwit (*inf.*), numbskull *or* numskull, oaf, pillock (*Brit. sl.*), prat (*sl.*), simpleton, twerp *or* twirp (*inf.*), twit (*inf., chiefly Brit.*), wally (*sl.*)

assail *vb* **1** = **attack**, assault, belabour, beset, charge, encounter, fall upon, invade, lay into (*inf.*), maltreat, set about, set upon **2** = **criticize**, abuse, berate, blast, go for the jugular, impugn, lambast(e), malign, put down, revile, tear into (*inf.*), vilify

assailant *n* = **attacker**, aggressor, assailer, assaulter, invader

assassin *n* = **murderer**, eliminator (*sl.*), executioner, hatchet man, hit man (*sl.*), killer, liquidator, slayer

assassinate *vb* **1** = **murder**, blow away (*sl., chiefly US*), eliminate (*sl.*), hit (*sl.*), kill, liquidate, slay, take out (*sl.*)

assassination *n* **1** = **murder**, elimination (*sl.*), hit (*sl.*), killing, liquidation, purge, removal (*euphemistic*), slaying

assault *n* **1** = **attack**, aggression, campaign, charge, incursion, inroad, invasion, offensive, onset, onslaught, storm, storming, strike ◆ *vb* **5**

an act that threatens violence to another. **3a** the culmination of a military attack. **3b** (*as modifier*): *assault troops*. **4** rape or attempted rape. ◆ *vb* (*tr*) **5** to make an assault upon. **6** to rape or attempt to rape. [C13: from OF *asaut*, from Vulgar L, from *assalīre* (unattested) to leap upon; see ASSAIL]
▸**as'saultive** *adj*

assault and battery *n Criminal law*. a threat of attack to another person followed by actual attack.

assault course *n* an obstacle course designed to give soldiers practice in negotiating hazards.

assay ❶ *vb* (ə'seɪ). **1** to subject (a substance, such as silver or gold) to chemical analysis, as in the determination of the amount of impurity. **2** (*tr*) to attempt (something or to do something). ◆ *n* (ə'seɪ, 'æseɪ). **3a** an analysis, esp. a determination of the amount of metal in an ore or the amounts of impurities in a precious metal. **3b** (*as modifier*): *an assay office*. **4** a substance undergoing an analysis. **5** a written report on the results of an analysis. **6** a test. [C14: from OF *assai*; see ESSAY]
▸**as'sayer** *n*

assegai *or* **assagai** ('æsəˌgaɪ) *n, pl* **assegais** *or* **assagais. 1** a southern African tree, the wood of which is used for making spears. **2** a sharp light spear. [C17: from Port. *azagaia*, from Ar. *az zaghāyah*, from *al* the + *zaghāyah* assegai, from Berber]

assemblage ❶ (ə'sɛmblɪdʒ) *n* **1** a number of things or persons assembled together. **2** the act of assembling or the state of being assembled. **3** (ˌæsəm'blɑːʒ). a three-dimensional work of art that combines various objects.

assemble ❶ (ə'sɛmbᵊl) *vb* **assembles, assembling, assembled. 1** to come or bring together; collect or congregate. **2** to fit or join together (the parts of something, such as a machine). [C13: from OF *assembler*, from Vulgar L *assimulāre* (unattested) to bring together, from L *simul* together]

assembler (ə'sɛmblə) *n* **1** a person or thing that assembles. **2** a computer program that converts a program written in assembly language into machine code. Cf. **compiler. 3** another name for **assembly language.**

assembly ❶ (ə'sɛmblɪ) *n, pl* **assemblies. 1** a number of people gathered together, esp. for a formal meeting held at regular intervals. **2** the act of assembling or the state of being assembled. **3** the process of putting together a number of parts to make a machine. **4** *Mil*. a signal for personnel to assemble.

Assembly (ə'sɛmblɪ) *n, pl* **Assemblies. 1** the lower chamber in various state legislatures, esp. in Australia and America. See also **House of Assembly, legislative assembly. 2** *NZ*. short for **General Assembly.**

assembly language *n Computing*. a low-level programming language that allows a programmer complete control of the machine code to be generated.

assembly line *n* a sequence of machines, tools, operations, workers, etc., in a factory, arranged so that at each stage a further process is carried out.

assent ❶ (ə'sɛnt) *n* **1** agreement, as to a statement, proposal, etc. **2** compliance. ◆ *vb* (*intr; usually foll. by to*) **3** to agree or express agreement. [C13: from OF *assenter*, from L *assentīrī*, from *sentīre* to think]

assert ❶ (ə'sɜːt) *vb* (*tr*) **1** to insist upon (rights, etc.). **2** (*may take a clause as object*) to state to be true; declare. **3** to put (oneself) forward in an insistent manner. [C17: from L *asserere* to join to oneself, from *serere* to join]
▸**as'serter** *or* **as'sertor** *n*

assertion ❶ (ə'sɜːʃən) *n* **1** a positive statement, usually made without evidence. **2** the act of asserting.

assertion sign *n* a sign 0 used in symbolic logic to introduce the conclusion of a valid argument: often read as "therefore."

assertive ❶ (ə'sɜːtɪv) *adj* **1** confident and direct in dealing with others. **2** given to making assertions; dogmatic or aggressive.
▸**as'sertively** *adv* ▸**as'sertiveness** *n*

assess ❶ (ə'sɛs) *vb* (*tr*) **1** to evaluate. **2** (foll. by *at*) to estimate the value of (income, property, etc.) for taxation purposes. **3** to determine the amount of (a fine, tax, etc.). **4** to impose a tax, fine, etc., on (a person or property). [C15: from OF *assesser*, from L *assidēre* to sit beside, from *sedēre* to sit]
▸**as'sessable** *adj*

assessment ❶ (ə'sɛsmənt) *n* **1** the act of assessing, esp. (in Britain) the evaluation of a student's achievement on a course. **2** an amount determined as payable. **3** a valuation set on taxable property, etc. **4** evaluation.

assessment tests *pl n Brit. education*. nationally standardized tests for pupil assessment based on attainment targets in the National Curriculum. Formal name: **standard assessment tasks, SATs.**

assessor (ə'sɛsə) *n* **1** a person who evaluates the merits of something. **2** a person who values property for taxation. **3** a person who estimates the value of damage to property for insurance purposes. **4** a person with technical expertise called in to advise a court.
▸**assessorial** (ˌæsɛ'sɔːrɪəl) *adj*

asset ❶ ('æsɛt) *n* anything valuable or useful. [C19: back formation from ASSETS]

assets ❶ ('æsɛts) *pl n* **1** *Accounting*. the property and claims against debtors that are shown balanced against liabilities. **2** *Law*. the property available to an executor for settling a deceased person's estate. **3** any property owned by a person or firm. [C16: from OF *asez* enough, from Vulgar L *ad satis* (unattested) from L *ad* up to + *satis* enough]

asset-stripping *n Commerce*. the practice of taking over a failing company at a low price and then selling the assets piecemeal.
▸**'asset-ˌstripper** *n*

asset value *n* the value of a share in a company calculated by dividing the difference between the total of its assets and its liabilities by the number of ordinary shares issued.

asseverate (ə'sɛvəˌreɪt) *vb* **asseverates, asseverating, asseverated.** (*tr*) to declare solemnly. [C18: from L *assevērāre* to do (something) earnestly, from *sevērus* SEVERE]
▸**asˌsever'ation** *n*

assibilate (ə'sɪbɪˌleɪt) *vb* **assibilates, assibilating, assibilated.** (*tr*) *Phonetics*. to pronounce (a speech sound) with or as a sibilant. [C19: from LL *assībilāre* to hiss at, from *sībilāre* to hiss]
▸**asˌsibi'lation** *n*

assiduity (ˌæsɪ'djuːɪtɪ) *n, pl* **assiduities. 1** constant and close application. **2** (*often pl*) devoted attention.

assiduous ❶ (ə'sɪdjʊəs) *adj* **1** hard-working; persevering. **2** undertaken

THESAURUS

= **attack**, assail, belabour, beset, charge, fall upon, invade, lay into (*inf.*), set about, set upon, storm, strike at
Antonyms *n* ≠ **attack:** defence, protection, resistance ◆ *vb* ≠ **attack:** defend, protect, resist

assay *vb* **1** = **analyse**, appraise, assess, evaluate, examine, inspect, investigate, prove, test, try, weigh ◆ *n* **3, 6** = **analysis**, examination, inspection, investigation, test, trial

assemblage *n* **1, 2** = **group**, accumulation, aggregation, assembly, body, collection, company, conclave, congregation, convocation, crowd, flock, gathering, mass, meeting, multitude, rally, throng

assemble *vb* **1** = **gather**, accumulate, amass, bring together, call together, collect, come together, congregate, convene, convoke, flock, foregather, marshal, meet, muster, rally, round up, summon **2** = **put together**, build up, connect, construct, erect, fabricate, fit together, join, make, manufacture, piece together, set up
Antonyms *vb* ≠ **gather:** adjourn, break up (*inf.*), disband, dismiss, disperse, distribute, scatter ≠ **put together:** disassemble, divide, take apart

assembly *n* **1** = **gathering**, accumulation, aggregation, assemblage, body, collection, company, conclave, conference, congregation, congress, convention, convocation, council, crowd, diet, flock, group, house, mass, meeting, multitude, rally, synod, throng **2, 3** = **putting together**, building up, connecting, construction, erection, fabrication, fitting together, joining, manufacture, piecing together, setting up

assent *n* **1, 2** = **agreement**, acceptance, accession, accord, acquiescence, approval, compliance, concurrence, consent, permission, sanction ◆ *vb* **3** = **agree**, accede, accept, acquiesce, allow, approve, comply, concur, consent, fall in with, go along with, grant, permit, sanction, subscribe
Antonyms *n* ≠ **agreement:** denial, disagreement, disapproval, dissension, dissent, objection, refusal ◆ *vb* ≠ **agree:** deny, differ, disagree, dissent, object, protest, rebut, reject, retract

assert *vb* **1** = **insist upon**, claim, defend, press, put forward, stand up for, stress, uphold, vindicate **2** = **state**, affirm, allege, asseverate, attest, aver, avouch (*arch.*), avow, contend, declare, maintain, predicate, profess, pronounce, swear **3** = **be forceful**, exert one's influence, make one's presence felt, put oneself forward, put one's foot down (*inf.*)
Antonyms *vb* ≠ **insist upon, state:** deny, disavow, disclaim, rebut, refute, retract

assertion *n* **1** = **statement**, affirmation, allegation, asseveration, attestation, avowal, claim, contention, declaration, predication, profession, pronouncement **2** = **insistence**, defence, maintenance, stressing, vindication

assertive *adj* **1, 2** = **confident**, aggressive, can-do, decided, decisive, demanding, dogmatic, domineering, emphatic, feisty (*inf., chiefly US & Canad.*), firm, forceful, forward, insistent, in-your-face (*Brit. sl.*), overbearing, positive, pushy (*inf.*), self-assured, strong-willed
Antonyms *adj* backward, bashful, diffident, hesitant, insecure, meek, modest, reserved, retiring, self-conscious, self-effacing, sheepish, shrinking, shy, timid, timorous, unassertive, unobtrusive

assertiveness *n* **1, 2** = **confidence**, aggressiveness, decidedness, decisiveness, dogmatism, domineeringness, firmness, forcefulness, forwardness, insistence, positiveness, pushiness (*inf.*), self-assuredness
Antonyms *n* backwardness, bashfulness, diffidence, hesitancy, insecurity, meekness, modesty, reservedness, self-consciousness, self-effacement, sheepishness, shyness, tentativeness, timidity, timidness, timorousness

assess *vb* **1** = **judge**, appraise, compute, determine, estimate, evaluate, eye up, fix, gauge, rate, size up (*inf.*), value, weigh **2-4** = **evaluate**, demand, fix, impose, levy, rate, tax, value

assessable *adj* **1-4** = **measurable**, appraisable, computable, determinable, estimable (*rare*), gaugeable *or* gageable, judgeable, ratable *or* rateable

assessment *n* **1** = **judgment**, appraisal, computation, determination, estimate, estimation, evaluation, rating, valuation **2-4** = **evaluation**, charge, demand, duty, fee, impost, levy, rate, rating, tariff, tax, taxation, toll, valuation

asset *n* = **benefit**, ace in the hole, ace up one's sleeve, advantage, aid, blessing, boon, feather in one's cap, help, resource, service
Antonyms *n* albatross, burden, disadvantage, drag, drawback, encumbrance, handicap, hindrance, impediment, liability, millstone, minus (*inf.*), nuisance

assets *pl n* **1, 3** = **property**, capital, estate, funds, goods, holdings, means, money, possessions, reserves, resources, valuables, wealth

assiduous *adj* **1** = **diligent**, attentive, constant, hard-working, indefatigable, industrious, labo-

with perseverance and care. [C16: from L, from *assidēre* to sit beside, from *sedēre* to sit]
▸**as'siduousness** *n*

assign ❶ (ə'saɪn) *vb (mainly tr)* **1** to select for and appoint to a post, etc. **2** to give out or allot (a task, problem, etc.). **3** to set apart (a place, person, time, etc.) for a particular function or event: *to assign a day for the meeting.* **4** to attribute to a specified cause, origin, or source. **5** to transfer (one's right, interest, or title to property) to someone else. ◆ *n* **6** *Law.* a person to whom property is assigned; assignee. [C14: from OF, from L *assignāre*, from *signāre* to mark out]
▸**as'signable** *adj* ▸**as'signer** *or* **ˌassign'or** *n*

assignation ❶ (ˌæsɪg'neɪʃən) *n* **1** a secret or forbidden arrangement to meet, esp. one between lovers. **2** the act of assigning; assignment. [C14: from OF, from L *assignātiō* a marking out]

assignee (ˌæsaɪ'niː) *n Law.* a person to whom some right, interest, or property is transferred.

assignment ❶ (ə'saɪnmənt) *n* **1** something that has been assigned, such as a mission or task. **2** a position or post to which a person is assigned. **3** the act of assigning or state of being assigned. **4** *Law.* **4a** the transfer to another of a right, interest, or title to property. **4b** the document effecting such a transfer.

assimilate ❶ (ə'sɪmɪˌleɪt) *vb* **assimilates, assimilating, assimilated. 1** *(tr)* to learn (information, etc.) and understand it thoroughly. **2** *(tr)* to absorb (food). **3** *(intr)* to become absorbed, incorporated, or learned and understood. **4** (usually foll. by *into* or *with*) to adjust or become adjusted: *the new immigrants assimilated easily.* **5** (usually foll. by *to* or *with*) to become or cause to become similar. **6** (usually foll. by *to*) *Phonetics.* to change (a consonant) or (of a consonant) to be changed into another under the influence of one adjacent to it. [C15: from L *assimilāre* to make one thing like another, from *similis* like, SIMILAR]
▸**as'similable** *adj* ▸**asˌsimi'lation** *n* ▸**as'similative** *or* **as'similatory** *adj* ▸**as'simiˌlator** *n*

assist ❶ (ə'sɪst) *vb* **1** to give help or support to (a person, cause, etc.). **2** to work or act as an assistant or subordinate to (another). ◆ *n* **3** *US.* the act of helping. [C15: from F, from L *assistere* to stand by, from *sistere* to cause to stand, from *stāre* to stand]
▸**as'sister** *n*

assistance ❶ (ə'sɪstəns) *n* **1** help; support. **2** the act of assisting. **3** *Brit. inf.* See **national assistance.**

assistant ❶ (ə'sɪstənt) *n* **1a** a person who assists, esp. in a subordinate position. **1b** *(as modifier): assistant manager.* **2** See **shop assistant.**

assistant referee *n Soccer.* the official name for **linesman** (sense 1).

assize (ə'saɪz) *n Scots Law.* **a** a trial by a jury. **b** a jury. [C13: from OF *assise* session, from *asseoir* to seat, from L *assidēre* to sit beside]

assizes (ə'saɪzɪz) *pl n* (formerly in England and Wales) the sessions of the principal court in each county, exercising civil and criminal jurisdiction: replaced in 1971 by crown courts.

assoc. *abbrev. for:* **1** associate(d). **2** association.

associate ❶ *vb* (ə'səʊʃɪˌeɪt, -sɪ-). (usually foll. by *with*) **associates, associating, associated. 1** *(tr)* to link or connect in the mind or imagination. **2** *(intr)* to mix socially: *to associate with writers.* **3** *(intr)* to form or join an association, group, etc. **4** *(tr; usually passive)* to consider in conjunction: *rainfall is associated with humidity.* **5** *(tr)* to bring (a person, esp. oneself) into friendship, partnership, etc. **6** *(tr; often passive)* to express agreement (with): *Bertrand Russell was associated with the CND movement.* ◆ *n* (ə'səʊʃɪɪt, -sɪ-). **7** a person joined with another or others in an enterprise, business, etc. **8** a companion or friend. **9** something that usually accompanies another thing. **10** a person having a subordinate position in or admitted to only partial membership of an institution, association, etc. ◆ *adj* (ə'səʊʃɪɪt, -sɪ-). *(prenominal)* **11** joined with another or others in an enterprise, business, etc.: *an associate director.* **12** having partial rights or subordinate status: *an associate member.* **13** accompanying; concomitant. [C14: from L *associāre* to ally with, from *sociāre* to join, from *socius* an ally]
▸**as'sociable** *adj* ▸**as'sociˌator** *n* ▸**as'sociateˌship** *n*

association ❶ (əˌsəʊsɪ'eɪʃən, -ʃɪ-) *n* **1** a group of people having a common purpose or interest; a society or club. **2** the act of associating or the state of being associated. **3** friendship or companionship: *their association will not last.* **4** a mental connection of ideas, feelings, or sensations. **5** *Chem.* the formation of groups of molecules and ions held together by weak chemical bonds. **6** *Ecology.* a group of similar plants that grow in a uniform environment.

association football *n* a more formal name for **soccer.**

associative (ə'səʊʃɪətɪv, -sɪ-) *adj* **1** of, relating to, or causing association or union. **2** *Maths, logic.* **2a** of an operation, such as multiplication or addition, in which the answer is the same regardless of the way in which the elements are grouped: $(2 \times 3) \times 4 = 2 \times (3 \times 4)$. **2b** referring to this property: *the associative laws of arithmetic.*

assonance ('æsənəns) *n* **1** the use of the same vowel sound with different consonants or the same consonant with different vowels, as in a line of verse. Examples are *time* and *light* or *mystery* and *mastery.* **2** partial correspondence. [C18: from F, from L *assonāre* to sound, from *sonāre* to sound]
▸**'assonant** *adj, n*

assort (ə'sɔːt) *vb* **1** *(tr)* to arrange or distribute into groups of the same type; classify. **2** *(intr;* usually foll. by *with)* to fit or fall into a class or group. **3** *(tr)* to supply with an assortment of merchandise. **4** *(tr)* to put in the same category as others. [C15: from OF *assorter*, from *sorte* SORT]
▸**as'sortative** *adj*

assorted ❶ (ə'sɔːtɪd) *adj* **1** consisting of various kinds mixed together. **2** classified: *assorted categories.* **3** matched (esp. in **well-assorted, ill-assorted**).

assortment ❶ (ə'sɔːtmənt) *n* **1** a collection or group of various things or sorts. **2** the act of assorting.

ASSR (formerly) *abbrev. for* Autonomous Soviet Socialist Republic.

asst *abbrev. for* assistant.

assuage ❶ (ə'sweɪdʒ) *vb* **assuages, assuaging, assuaged.** *(tr)* **1** to soothe, moderate, or relieve (grief, pain, etc.). **2** to give relief to (thirst, etc.). **3** to pacify; calm. [C14: from OF, from Vulgar L *assuāviāre* (unattested) to sweeten, from L *suāvis* pleasant]
▸**as'suagement** *n* ▸**as'suager** *n*

assume ❶ (ə'sjuːm) *vb* **assumes, assuming, assumed.** *(tr)* **1** *(may take a clause as object)* to take for granted; suppose. **2** to undertake or take on or over (a position, responsibility, etc.): *to assume office.* **3** to pretend to; feign: *he assumed indifference.* **4** to take or put on; adopt: *the problem*

THESAURUS

rious, persevering, persistent, sedulous, steady, studious, unflagging, untiring, unwearied
Antonyms *adj* careless, idle, inattentive, indolent, lax, lazy, negligent, slack

assign *vb* **1** = **select**, appoint, choose, delegate, designate, name, nominate **2** = **give**, allocate, allot, apportion, consign, distribute, give out, grant, make over **3** = **fix**, appoint, appropriate, determine, set apart, stipulate **4** = **attribute**, accredit, ascribe, put down

assignation *n* **1** = **secret meeting**, clandestine meeting, illicit meeting, rendezvous, tryst (*arch.*)

assignment *n* **1, 2** = **task**, appointment, charge, commission, duty, job, mission, position, post, responsibility **3** = **selection**, appointment, choice, delegation, designation, nomination

assimilate *vb* **1, 3** = **learn**, absorb, digest, imbibe (*literary*), incorporate, ingest, take in **4, 5** = **adjust**, acclimatize, accommodate, acculturate, accustom, adapt, become like, become similar, blend in, conform, fit, homogenize, intermix, mingle

assist *vb* **1, 2** = **help**, abet, aid, back, benefit, boost, collaborate, cooperate, encourage, expedite, facilitate, further, give a leg up (*inf.*), lend a helping hand, promote, reinforce, relieve, second, serve, succour, support, sustain, work for, work with
Antonyms *vb* frustrate, hamper, handicap, hinder, hold back, hold up, impede, obstruct, resist, thwart, work against

assistance *n* **1** = **help**, abetment, aid, backing, benefit, boost, collaboration, cooperation, encouragement, furtherance, helping hand, promotion, reinforcement, relief, service, succour, support, sustenance
Antonyms *n* hindrance, obstruction, opposition, resistance

assistant *n* **1** = **helper**, abettor, accessory, accomplice, aide, aider, ally, associate, auxiliary, backer, coadjutor, collaborator, colleague, confederate, cooperator, helpmate, henchman, partner, protagonist, right-hand man, second, supporter

associate *vb* **1, 3** = **connect**, affiliate, ally, combine, confederate, conjoin, correlate, couple, identify, join, league, link, lump together, mention in the same breath, mix, pair, relate, think of together, unite, yoke **2** = **mix**, accompany, befriend, be friends, consort, fraternize, hang, hang about, hang out (*inf.*), hobnob, mingle, run around (*inf.*), socialize ◆ *n* **7** = **partner**, collaborator, colleague, confederate, co-worker **8** = **friend**, ally, companion, compeer, comrade, confrère, mate (*inf.*)
Antonyms *vb* ≠ **connect:** detach, disconnect, dissociate, distance, distinguish, divorce, isolate, segregate, separate, set apart ≠ **mix:** avoid, be alienated, be estranged, break off, part company

associated *adj* **1, 3** = **connected**, affiliated, allied, bound, combined, confederated, correlated, involved, joined, leagued, linked, related, syndicated, tied, united, yoked

association *n* **1** = **group**, affiliation, alliance, band, clique, club, coalition, combine, company, confederacy, confederation, cooperative, corporation, federation, fraternity, league, order, organization, partnership, society, syndicate, union **2, 4** = **connection**, blend, bond, combination, concomitance, correlation, identification, joining, juxtaposition, linkage, linking, lumping together, mixing, mixture, pairing, relation, tie, union, yoking **3** = **friendship**, affinity, companionship, comradeship, familiarity, fellowship, fraternization, intimacy, liaison, partnership, relations, relationship

assorted *adj* **1** = **various**, different, diverse, diversified, heterogeneous, manifold, miscellaneous, mixed, motley, sundry, varied, variegated **2** = **grouped**, arranged, arrayed, categorized, classified, disposed, filed, graded, matched, ranged, ranked, sorted, typed
Antonyms *adj* ≠ **various:** alike, homogeneous, identical, like, same, similar, uniform, unvaried

assortment *n* **1** = **variety**, array, choice, collection, diversity, farrago, hotchpotch, jumble, medley, *mélange*, miscellany, mishmash, mixed bag (*inf.*), mixture, pick 'n' mix, potpourri, salmagundi, selection **2** = **sorting**, arrangement, categorizing, classification, disposition, distribution, filing, grading, grouping, ranging, ranking, typing

assuage *vb* **1, 2** = **relieve**, allay, alleviate, calm, ease, lessen, lighten, mitigate, moderate, palliate, quench, soothe, temper **3** = **calm**, appease, lull, mollify, pacify, pour oil on troubled waters, quiet, relax, satisfy, soften, soothe, still, tranquillize
Antonyms *vb* ≠ **relieve:** aggravate, exacerbate, heighten, increase, intensify, worsen ≠ **calm:** aggravate, embitter, enrage, infuriate, madden, provoke

assume *vb* **1** = **take for granted**, accept, believe, expect, fancy, guess (*inf., chiefly US & Canad.*), imagine, infer, presume, presuppose, suppose, surmise, suspect, think **2** = **take on**, accept, ac-

assumed gigantic proportions. **5** to appropriate or usurp (power, control, etc.). [C15: from L *assūmere* to take up, from *sūmere* to take up, from SUB- + *emere* to take]
▸**as'sumable** *adj* ▸**as'sumer** *n*

assumed ❶ (ə'sju:md) *adj* **1** false; fictitious: *an assumed name.* **2** taken for granted. **3** usurped.

assuming (ə'sju:mɪŋ) *adj* **1** expecting too much; presumptuous. ◆ *conj* **2** (often foll. by *that*) if it is assumed or taken for granted.

assumption ❶ (ə'sʌmpʃən) *n* **1** the act of taking something for granted or something that is taken for granted. **2** an assuming of power or possession. **3** presumption. **4** *Logic.* a statement that is used as the premise of a particular argument but may not be otherwise accepted. [C13: from L *assūmptiō* a taking up, from *assūmere* to ASSUME]
▸**as'sumptive** *adj*

Assumption (ə'sʌmpʃən) *n Christianity.* **1** the taking up of the Virgin Mary (body and soul) into heaven when her earthly life was ended. **2** the feast commemorating this.

assurance ❶ (ə'ʃʊərəns) *n* **1** a statement, assertion, etc., intended to inspire confidence. **2** a promise or pledge of support. **3** freedom from doubt; certainty. **4** forwardness; impudence. **5** *Chiefly Brit.* insurance providing for certainties such as death as contrasted with fire.

assure ❶ (ə'ʃʊə) *vb* **assures, assuring, assured.** (*tr; may take a clause as object*) **1** to convince: *to assure a person of one's love.* **2** to promise; guarantee. **3** to state positively. **4** to make (an event) certain. **5** *Chiefly Brit.* to insure against loss, esp. of life. [C14: from OF, from Med. L *assēcūrāre* to secure or make sure, from *sēcūrus* SECURE]
▸**as'surable** *adj* ▸**as'surer** *n*

assured ❶ (ə'ʃʊəd) *adj* **1** sure; guaranteed. **2** self-assured. **3** *Chiefly Brit.* insured. ◆ *n* **4** *Chiefly Brit.* **4a** the beneficiary under a life assurance policy. **4b** the person whose life is insured.
▸**assuredly** (ə'ʃʊərɪdlɪ) *adv*

asswipe ('æs,waɪp) *n US sl.* a despicable or stupid person. [C20: orig.: toilet paper, from ASS[2] + WIPE]

Assyrian (ə'sɪrɪən) *n* **1** an inhabitant of ancient Assyria, a kingdom of Mesopotamia. **2** the extinct Semitic language of the Assyrians. ◆ *adj* **3** of or characteristic of the ancient Assyrians, their language, or culture.

AST *abbrev. for* Atlantic Standard Time.

astatic (æ'stætɪk, eɪ-) *adj* **1** not static; unstable. **2** *Physics.* having no tendency to assume any particular position or orientation. [C19: from Gk *astatos* unsteady]
▸**a'statically** *adv*

astatine ('æstə,ti:n) *n* a radioactive element that occurs naturally in minute amounts and is artificially produced by bombarding bismuth with alpha particles. Symbol: At; atomic no.: 85; half-life of most stable isotope, ^{210}At: 8.1 hours. [C20: from Gk *astatos* unstable]

aster ('æstə) *n* **1** a plant having white, blue, purple, or pink daisy-like flowers. **2 China aster.** a related Chinese plant widely cultivated for its showy brightly coloured flowers. [C18: from NL, from L *aster* star, from Gk]

-aster *suffix forming nouns.* a person or thing that is inferior to what is specified: *poetaster.* [from L]

asterisk ('æstərɪsk) *n* **1** a star-shaped character (*) used in printing or writing to indicate a cross-reference to a footnote, an omission, etc. ◆ *vb* **2** (*tr*) to mark with an asterisk. [C17: from LL *asteriscus* a small star, from Gk, from *astēr* star]

asterism ('æstə,rɪzəm) *n* **1** three asterisks arranged in a triangle (⁎⁎⁎ or ⁂), to draw attention to the text that follows. **2** a cluster of stars or a constellation. [C16: from Gk *asterismos* arrangement of constellations, from *astēr* star]

astern (ə'stɜ:n) *adv, adj* (*postpositive*) *Naut.* **1** at or towards the stern. **2** with the stern first: *full speed astern!* **3** aft of the stern of a vessel.

asteroid ('æstə,rɔɪd) *n* **1** Also called: **minor planet, planetoid.** any of numerous small celestial bodies that move around the sun mainly between the orbits of Mars and Jupiter. **2** a starfish. ◆ *adj also* **,aste'roidal. 3** of a starfish. **4** shaped like a star. [C19: from Gk *asteroeidēs* starlike, from *astēr* a star]

asthenia (æs'θi:nɪə) *n Pathol.* an abnormal loss of strength; debility. [C19: via NL from Gk *astheneia* weakness, from A-[1] + *sthenos* strength]

asthenic (æs'θɛnɪk) *adj* **1** of or having asthenia; weak. **2** referring to a physique characterized by long limbs and a small trunk. ◆ *n* **3** a person with long limbs and a small trunk.

asthma ('æsmə) *n* a respiratory disorder, often of allergic origin, characterized by difficulty in breathing. [C14: from Gk: laborious breathing, from *azein* to breathe hard]

asthmatic (æs'mætɪk) *adj* **1** of or having asthma. ◆ *n* **2** a person who has asthma.
▸**asth'matically** *adv*

astigmatic (,æstɪg'mætɪk) *adj* relating to or affected with astigmatism. [C19: from A-[1] + Gk *stigmat-, stigma* spot, focus]
▸**,astig'matically** *adv*

astigmatism (ə'stɪgmə,tɪzəm) *or* **astigmia** (ə'stɪgmɪə) *n* **1** a defect of a lens resulting in the formation of distorted images, caused by light rays not meeting at a single focal point. **2** faulty vision resulting from defective curvature of the cornea or lens of the eye.

astilbe (ə'stɪlbɪ) *n* any perennial plant of the genus *Astilbe,* cultivated for its spikes of ornamental pink or white flowers. [C19: NL, from Gk A-[1] + *stilbē,* from *stilbein* to glitter; referring to its inconspicuous individual flowers]

astir ❶ (ə'stɜ:) *adj* (*postpositive*) **1** awake and out of bed. **2** in motion; on the move.

astonish ❶ (ə'stɒnɪʃ) *vb* (*tr*) to fill with amazement; surprise greatly. [C15: from earlier *astonyen,* from OF, from Vulgar L *extonāre* (unattested) to strike with thunder, from L *tonāre* to thunder]
▸**a'stonishing** *adj*

astonishment ❶ (ə'stɒnɪʃmənt) *n* **1** extreme surprise; amazement. **2** a cause of amazement.

astound ❶ (ə'staʊnd) *vb* (*tr*) to overwhelm with amazement; bewilder. [C17: from *astoned* amazed, from OF, from *estoner* to ASTONISH]
▸**a'stounding** *adj*

astraddle (ə'strædᵊl) *adj* **1** (*postpositive*) with a leg on either side of something. ◆ *prep* **2** astride.

astragal ('æstrəgᵊl) *n* **1** *Archit.* Also called: **bead.** a small convex moulding, usually with a semicircular cross section. **2** *Anat.* the ankle or anklebone. [C17: from L, from Gk *astragalos* anklebone, hence, small round moulding]

astragalus (æ'strægələs) *n, pl* **astragali** (-,laɪ). *Anat.* another name for **talus**[1]. [C16: via NL from L: ASTRAGAL]

astrakhan (,æstrə'kæn) *n* **1** a fur, usually black or grey, made of the closely curled wool of lambs from Astrakhan, a city in S Russia. **2** a cloth with curled pile resembling this. **3** (*modifier*) made of such fur or cloth.

astral ('æstrəl) *adj* **1** relating to or resembling the stars. **2** *Theosophy.* re-

THESAURUS

quire, attend to, begin, don, embark upon, embrace, enter upon, put on, set about, shoulder, take over, take responsibility for, take up, undertake **3, 4 = put on,** adopt, affect, counterfeit, feign, imitate, impersonate, mimic, pretend to, sham, simulate **5 = take over,** acquire, appropriate, arrogate, commandeer, expropriate, pre-empt, seize, take, usurp
Antonyms *vb* ≠ **take for granted:** know, prove ≠ **take on, take over:** give up, hand over, leave, put aside, relinquish

assumed *adj* **1 = false,** affected, bogus, counterfeit, fake, feigned, fictitious, imitation, made-up, make-believe, phoney *or* phony (*inf.*), pretended, pseudonymous, sham, simulated, spurious **2 = taken for granted,** accepted, expected, hypothetical, presumed, presupposed, supposed, surmised
Antonyms *adj* ≠ **false:** actual, authentic, natural, real ≠ **taken for granted:** known, positive, stated, true

assumption *n* **1 = presumption,** acceptance, belief, conjecture, expectation, fancy, guess, hypothesis, inference, postulate, postulation, premise, premiss, presupposition, supposition, surmise, suspicion, theory **2 = taking on,** acceptance, acquisition, adoption, embracing, entering upon, putting on, shouldering, takeover, taking up, undertaking **2 = taking,** acquisition, appropriation, arrogation, expropriation, pre-empting, seizure, takeover, usurpation **3 = presumptuousness,** arrogance, conceit, imperiousness, pride, self-importance

assurance *n* **1, 2 = assertion,** affirmation, declaration, guarantee, oath, pledge, profession, promise, protestation, statement, vow, word, word of honour **3 = confidence,** assertiveness, assuredness, boldness, certainty, certitude, conviction, coolness, courage, faith, firmness, nerve, poise, positiveness, security, self-confidence, self-reliance, sureness
Antonyms *n* ≠**assertion:** falsehood, lie ≠**confidence:** apprehension, diffidence, distrust, doubt, self-doubt, self-effacement, shyness, timidity, uncertainty

assure *vb* **1 = convince,** comfort, embolden, encourage, hearten, persuade, reassure, soothe **2, 3 = promise,** affirm, attest, certify, confirm, declare confidently, give one's word to, guarantee, pledge, swear, vow **4 = make certain,** clinch, complete, confirm, ensure, guarantee, make sure, seal, secure

assured *adj* **1 = certain,** beyond doubt, clinched, confirmed, dependable, ensured, fixed, guaranteed, indubitable, in the bag (*sl.*), irrefutable, made certain, sealed, secure, settled, sure, unquestionable **2 = confident,** assertive, audacious, bold, brazen, certain, complacent, overconfident, poised, positive, pushy (*inf.*), self-assured, self-confident, self-possessed, sure of oneself
Antonyms *adj* ≠ **certain:** ambiguous, doubtful, indefinite, questionable, uncertain, unconfirmed, unsettled, unsure ≠ **confident:** bashful, diffident, hesitant, retiring, self-conscious, self-effacing, timid

astir *adj* **1 = out of bed,** awake, roused, up and about, up and around **2 = in motion,** active, afoot, on the go (*inf.*), on the move (*inf.*)

astonish *vb* **= amaze,** astound, bewilder, boggle the mind, confound, daze, dumbfound, flabbergast (*inf.*), stagger, stun, stupefy, surprise

astonished *adj* **= amazed,** astounded, bewildered, confounded, dazed, dumbfounded, flabbergasted (*inf.*), gobsmacked (*inf.*), perplexed, staggered, stunned, stupefied, surprised

astonishing *adj* **= amazing,** astounding, bewildering, breathtaking, brilliant, impressive, jaw-dropping, sensational (*inf.*), staggering, striking, stunning, stupefying, surprising, wondrous (*arch. or literary*)

astonishment *n* **1 = amazement,** awe, bewilderment, confusion, consternation, stupefaction, surprise, wonder, wonderment

astound *vb* **= amaze,** astonish, bewilder, boggle the mind, confound, daze, dumbfound, flabbergast (*inf.*), overwhelm, stagger, stun, stupefy, surprise, take one's breath away

astounding *adj* **= amazing,** astonishing, bewildering, breathtaking, brilliant, impressive, jaw-dropping, sensational (*inf.*), staggering, striking, stunning, stupefying, surprising, wondrous (*arch. or literary*)

lating to a supposed supersensible substance taking the form of an aura discernible to certain gifted individuals. [C17: from LL *astrālis*, from L *astrum* star, from Gk *astron*]

astray ⓣ (ə'streɪ) *adj* (*postpositive*), *adv* **1** out of the correct path or direction. **2** out of the right or expected way. [C13: from OF, from *estraier* to STRAY]

astride (ə'straɪd) *adj* (*postpositive*) **1** with a leg on either side. **2** with the legs far apart. ◆ *prep* **3** with a leg on either side of. **4** with a part on both sides of; spanning.

astringent ⓣ (ə'strɪndʒənt) *adj* **1** severe; harsh. **2** sharp or invigorating. **3** causing contraction of body tissues, checking blood flow; styptic. ◆ *n* **4** an astringent drug or lotion. [C16: from L *astringēns* drawing together]
▸**as'tringency** *n* ▸**as'tringently** *adv*

astro- *combining form.* indicating a star or star-shaped structure: *astrology*. [from Gk, from *astron* star]

astrobiology (ˌæstrəʊbaɪ'ɒlədʒɪ) *n* the branch of biology that investigates the possibility of life on other planets.

astrochemistry (ˌæstrəʊ'kɛmɪstrɪ) *n* the study of the chemistry of celestial bodies and space.

astrodome ('æstrəˌdəʊm) *n* a transparent dome on the top of an aircraft, through which observations can be made.

astrol. *abbrev. for:* **1** astrologer. **2** astrological. **3** astrology.

astrolabe ('æstrəˌleɪb) *n* an instrument used by early astronomers to measure the altitude of stars and planets and also as a navigational aid. [C13: via OF & Med. L from Gk, from *astrolabos*, from *astron* star + *lambanein* to take]

astrology (ə'strɒlədʒɪ) *n* **1** the study of the motions and relative positions of the planets, sun, and moon, interpreted in terms of human characteristics and activities. **2** primitive astronomy. [C14: from OF, from L *astrologia*, from Gk, from *astrologos* (orig.: astronomer); see ASTRO-, -LOGY]
▸**as'trologer** *or* **as'trologist** *n* ▸**astrological** (ˌæstrə'lɒdʒɪkᵊl) *adj*

astron. *abbrev. for:* **1** astronomer. **2** astronomical. **3** astronomy.

astronaut ⓣ ('æstrəˌnɔːt) *n* a person trained for travelling in space. See also **cosmonaut**. [C20: from ASTRO- + *-naut*, from Gk *nautēs* sailor, on the model of *aeronaut*]

astronautics (ˌæstrə'nɔːtɪks) *n* (*functioning as sing*) the science and technology of space flight.
▸ˌ**astro'nautical** *adj*

Astronomer Royal *n* an honorary title awarded to an eminent British astronomer: until 1972, the Astronomer Royal was also director of the Royal Greenwich Observatory.

astronomical ⓣ (ˌæstrə'nɒmɪkᵊl) *or* **astronomic** *adj* **1** enormously large. **2** of or relating to astronomy.
▸ˌ**astro'nomically** *adv*

astronomical clock *n* **1** a complex clock showing astronomical phenomena, such as the phases of the moon. **2** any clock showing sidereal time used in observatories.

astronomical unit *n* a unit of distance used in astronomy equal to the mean distance between the earth and the sun. 1 astronomical unit is equivalent to 1.495×10^{11} metres.

astronomy (ə'strɒnəmɪ) *n* the scientific study of the individual celestial bodies (excluding the earth) and of the universe as a whole. [C13: from OF, from L *astronomia*, from Gk; see ASTRO-, -NOMY]
▸**as'tronomer** *n*

astrophysics (ˌæstrəʊ'fɪzɪks) *n* (*functioning as sing*) the branch of physics concerned with the physical and chemical properties of the celestial bodies.
▸ˌ**astro'physicist** *n*

Astroturf ('æstrəʊˌtɜːf) *n Trademark.* a type of grasslike artificial surface used for playing fields and lawns. [C20: from *Astro(dome)* the baseball stadium in Texas where it was first used + *turf*]

astute ⓣ (ə'stjuːt) *adj* having insight or acumen; perceptive; shrewd. [C17: from L *astūtus* cunning, from *astus* (n) cleverness]
▸**as'tutely** *adv* ▸**as'tuteness** *n*

asunder ⓣ (ə'sʌndə) *adv, adj* (*postpositive*) in or into parts or pieces; apart: *to tear asunder*. [OE *on sundran* apart]

asylum ⓣ (ə'saɪləm) *n* **1** shelter; refuge; sanctuary. **2** a safe or inviolable place of refuge, esp. as formerly offered by the Christian Church. **3** *International law.* refuge afforded to a person whose extradition is sought by a foreign government: *political asylum*. **4** an institution for the care or confinement of individuals, esp. (formerly) a mental hospital. [C15: via L from Gk *asulon* refuge, from A-[1] + *sulon* right of seizure]

asymmetric (ˌæsɪ'mɛtrɪk, ˌeɪ-) *or* **asymmetrical** *adj* **1** not symmetrical; lacking symmetry; misproportioned. **2** *Logic, maths.* (of a relation) never holding between a pair of values *x* and *y* when it holds between *y* and *x*, as in *John is the father of David*.
▸ˌ**asym'metrically** *adv*

asymmetric bars *pl n Gymnastics.* **a** (*functioning as pl*) a pair of wooden or fibreglass bars placed parallel to each other but set at different heights, for various exercises. **b** (*functioning as sing*) an event in a gymnastic competition in which competitors exercise on such bars.

asymmetry (æ'sɪmɪtrɪ, eɪ-) *n* lack or absence of symmetry.

asymptomatic (ˌeɪsɪmptə'mætɪk) *adj* not showing any symptoms of disease.

asymptote ('æsɪmˌtəʊt) *n* a straight line that is closely approached by a curve so that the distance between them decreases to zero as the distance from the origin increases to infinity. [C17: from Gk *asumptōtos* not falling together, from A-[1] + SYN- + *ptōtos* inclined to fall, from *piptein* to fall]
▸**asymptotic** (ˌæsɪm'tɒtɪk) *or* ˌ**asymp'totical** *adj*

asystole (ə'sɪstəlɪ) *n Pathol.* the absence of heartbeat; cardiac arrest.
▸**asystolic** (ˌæsɪs'tɒlɪk) *adj*

at (æt) *prep* **1** used to indicate location or position: *are they at the table?* **2** towards; in the direction of: *looking at television.* **3** used to indicate position in time: *come at three o'clock.* **4** engaged in; in a state of (being): *children at play.* **5** (in expressions concerned with habitual activity) during the passing of: *he used to work at night.* **6** for; in exchange for: *it's selling at four pounds.* **7** used to indicate the object of an emotion: *shocked at his behaviour.* **8 where it's at.** *Sl.* the real place of action. [OE *æt*]

At *the chemical symbol for* astatine.

AT *Brit. education. abbrev. for* attainment target.

at. *abbrev. for:* **1** atmosphere (unit of pressure). **2** atomic.

ataractic (ˌætə'ræktɪk) *or* **ataraxic** (ˌætə'ræksɪk) *adj* **1** able to calm or tranquillize. ◆ *n* **2** an ataractic drug.

ataraxia (ˌætə'ræksɪə) *or* **ataraxy** ('ætəˌræksɪ) *n* calmness or peace of mind; emotional tranquillity. [C17: from Gk: serenity, from A-[1] + *tarassein* to trouble]

atavism ('ætəˌvɪzəm) *n* **1** the recurrence in a plant or animal of certain primitive characteristics that were present in an ancestor but have not occurred in intermediate generations. **2** reversion to a former type. [C19: from F, from L *atavus* strictly: great-grandfather's grandfather, prob. from *atta* daddy + *avus* grandfather]
▸ˌ**ata'vistic** *adj*

ataxia (ə'tæksɪə) *or* **ataxy** (ə'tæksɪ) *n Pathol.* lack of muscular coordination. [C17: via NL from Gk: lack of coordination, from A-[1] + *-taxia*, from *tassein* to put in order]
▸**a'taxic** *adj*

ATB *abbrev. for* Advanced Technology Bomber.

ATC *abbrev. for:* **1** air-traffic control. **2** (in Britain) Air Training Corps.

ate (ɛt, eɪt) *vb* the past tense of **eat**.

-ate[1] *suffix.* **1** (*forming adjectives*) having the appearance or characteristics of: *fortunate.* **2** (*forming nouns*) a chemical compound, esp. a salt or ester of an acid: *carbonate.* **3** (*forming nouns*) the product of a process: *condensate.* **4** forming verbs from nouns and adjectives: *hyphenate.* [from L *-ātus*, p.p. ending of verbs ending in *-āre*]

-ate[2] *suffix forming nouns.* denoting office, rank, or a group having a certain function: *episcopate.* [from L *-ātus*, suffix of collective nouns]

atelier ('ætəlˌjeɪ) *n* an artist's studio or workshop. [C17: from OF, from *astele* chip of wood, from L *astula* splinter, from *assis* board]

a tempo (ɑː 'tɛmpəʊ) *Music.* ◆ *adj, adv* **1** to the original tempo. ◆ *n* **2** a passage thus marked. ◆ Also: **tempo primo.** [It.: in (the original) time]

Athanasian Creed (ˌæθə'neɪʃən) *n Christianity.* a profession of faith widely used in the Western Church formerly attributed to Athanasius, 4th-century A.D. patriarch of Alexandria.

Athapascan, Athapaskan (ˌæθə'pæskən) *or* **Athabascan, Athabaskan** (ˌæθə'bæskən) *n* a group of North American Indian languages including Apache and Navaho. [from Cree *athapaskaaw* scattered grass]

atheism ⓣ ('eɪθɪˌɪzəm) *n* rejection of belief in God or gods. [C16: from F, from Gk *atheos* godless, from A-[1] + *theos* god]
▸'**atheist** *n, adj* ▸ˌ**athe'istic** *adj*

athematic (ˌæθɪ'mætɪk) *adj* **1** *Music.* not based on themes. **2** *Linguistics.* (of verbs) having a suffix attached with no intervening vowel.

athenaeum *or US* **atheneum** (ˌæθɪ'niːəm) *n* **1** an institution for the

THESAURUS

astray *adj, adv* **1** = **off the right track**, adrift, afield, amiss, lost, off, off course, off the mark, off the subject **2** = **into sin**, into error, to the bad, wrong

astringent *adj* **1** = **severe**, acerbic, austere, caustic, exacting, grim, hard, harsh, rigid, rigorous, stern, strict, stringent **3** = **contractive**, contractile, styptic

astronaut *n* = **space traveller**, cosmonaut, spaceman, space pilot, spacewoman

astronomical *adj* **1** = **huge**, boundless, colossal, enormous, galactic, Gargantuan, giant, gigantic, great, immeasurable, immense, infinite, massive, monumental, titanic, vast

astute *adj* = **intelligent**, adroit, artful, bright, calculating, canny, clever, crafty, cunning, discerning, foxy, insightful, keen, knowing, on the ball (*inf.*), penetrating, perceptive, politic, sagacious, sharp, shrewd, sly, subtle, wily
Antonyms *adj* dull, ingenuous, naive, slow, straightforward, stupid, unintelligent, unknowing

astuteness *n* = **intelligence**, acumen, adroitness, artfulness, brightness, canniness, cleverness, craftiness, cunning, discernment, foxiness, insight, keenness, knowledge, penetration, perceptiveness, sagacity, sharpness, shrewdness, slyness, subtlety, suss (*sl.*), wiliness

asunder *adv, adj* = **to pieces**, apart, in pieces, into pieces, rent, to bits, torn, to shreds

asylum *n* **1, 2** = **refuge**, harbour, haven, preserve, retreat, safety, sanctuary, shelter **4** = **mental hospital**, funny farm (*facetious*), hospital, institution, laughing academy (*US. sl.*), loony bin (*sl.*), madhouse (*inf.*), nuthouse (*sl.*), psychiatric hospital

atheism *n* = **nonbelief**, disbelief, freethinking, godlessness, heathenism, infidelity, irreligion, paganism, scepticism, unbelief

atheist *n* = **nonbeliever**, disbeliever, freethinker, heathen, infidel, irreligionist, pagan, sceptic, unbeliever

promotion of learning. **2** a building containing a reading room or library. **[**C18: from LL, from Gk *Athēnaion* temple of Athene, frequented by poets and teachers**]**

Athenian (əˈθiːnɪən) *n* **1** a native or inhabitant of Athens, the capital of Greece. ◆ *adj* **2** of or relating to Athens.

atherosclerosis (ˌæθərəʊsklɪəˈrəʊsɪs) *n, pl* **atheroscleroses** (-siːz). a degenerative disease of the arteries characterized by thickening of the arterial walls, caused by deposits of fatty material. **[**C20: from NL, from Gk *athērōma* tumour full of grainy matter + SCLEROSIS**]**
▸**atherosclerotic** (ˌæθərəʊsklɪəˈrɒtɪk) *adj*

athirst (əˈθɜːst) *adj* (*postpositive*) **1** (often foll. by *for*) having an eager desire; longing. **2** *Arch.* thirsty.

athlete Ⓣ (ˈæθliːt) *n* **1** a person trained to compete in sports or exercises. **2** a person who has a natural aptitude for physical activities. **3** *Chiefly Brit.* a competitor in track and field events. **[**C18: from L via Gk, from *athlein* to compete for a prize, from *athlos* a contest**]**

athlete's foot *n* a fungal infection of the skin of the foot, esp. between the toes and on the soles.

athletic Ⓣ (æθˈlɛtɪk) *adj* **1** physically fit or strong. **2** of, relating to, or suitable for an athlete or for athletics.
▸**athˈletically** *adv* ▸**athˈleticism** *n*

athletics Ⓣ (æθˈlɛtɪks) *n* (*functioning as sing or pl*) **1** *Chiefly Brit.* **1a** track and field events. **1b** (*as modifier*): *an athletics meeting.* **2** sports or exercises engaged in by athletes.

athletic support *n* a more formal term for **jockstrap**.

at-home *n* **1** a social gathering in a person's home. **2** another name for **open day**.

-athon *suffix forming nouns.* a variant of **-thon**.

athwart (əˈθwɔːt) *adv* **1** transversely; from one side to another. ◆ *prep* **2** across the path or line of (esp. a ship). **3** in opposition to; against. **[**C15: from A-[2] + THWART**]**

-atic *suffix forming adjectives.* of the nature of the thing specified: *problematic.* **[**from F, from Gk *-atikos***]**

-ation *suffix forming nouns.* indicating an action, process, state, condition, or result: *arbitration; hibernation.* **[**from L *-ātiōn-*, suffix of abstract nouns**]**

-ative *suffix forming adjectives.* of, relating to, or tending to: *authoritative; informative.* **[**from L *-ātīvus***]**

Atlantean (ˌætlænˈtiːən) *adj Literary.* of, relating to, or like Atlas; extremely strong.

Atlantic (ətˈlæntɪk) *n* **1 the.** short for the **Atlantic Ocean**, the world's second largest ocean. ◆ *adj* **2** of, relating to, or bordering the Atlantic Ocean. **3** of or relating to Atlas or the Atlas Mountains. **[**C15: from L, from Gk (*pelagos*) *Atlantikos* (the sea) of Atlas (so called because it lay beyond the Atlas Mountains)**]**

Atlanticism (ətˈlæntɪˌsɪzəm) *n* advocacy of close cooperation in military, political, and economic matters between Western Europe, esp. the UK, and the US.
▸**Atˈlanticist** *n*

Atlantis (ətˈlæntɪs) *n* (in ancient legend) a continent said to have sunk beneath the Atlantic west of Gibraltar.

atlas (ˈætləs) *n* **1** a collection of maps, usually in book form. **2** a book of charts, graphs, etc.: *an anatomical atlas.* **3** *Anat.* the first cervical vertebra, supporting the skull in man. **4** (*pl* **atlantes**) *Archit.* another name for **telamon**.

Atlas (ˈætləs) *n Greek myth.* **1** a Titan compelled to support the sky on his shoulders as punishment for rebelling against Zeus. **2** a US intercontinental ballistic missile, also used in launching spacecraft.

ATM *abbrev. for* automated teller machine.

atm. *abbrev. for:* **1** atmosphere (unit of pressure). **2** atmospheric.

atman (ˈɑːtmən) *n Hinduism.* **1** the personal soul or self. **2** Brahman considered as the Universal Soul. **[**from Sansk. *ātman* breath**]**

atmolysis (ætˈmɒlɪsɪs) *n, pl* **atmolyses** (-ˌsiːz). the separation of gases by differential diffusion through a porous substance.

atmosphere Ⓣ (ˈætməsˌfɪə) *n* **1** the gaseous envelope surrounding the earth or any other celestial body. **2** the air or climate in a particular place. **3** a general pervasive feeling or mood. **4** the prevailing tone or mood of a novel, symphony, painting, etc. **5** any local gaseous environment or medium: *an inert atmosphere.* **6** Abbrev: **at., atm.** a unit of pressure; the pressure that will support a column of mercury 760 mm high at 0°C at sea level.
▸**atmospheric** (ˌætməsˈfɛrɪk) *adj* ▸ˌ**atmosˈpherically** *adv*

atmospheric pressure *n* the pressure exerted by the atmosphere at the earth's surface. It has an average value of 1 atmosphere.

atmospherics (ˌætməsˈfɛrɪks) *pl n* radio interference, heard as crackling or hissing in receivers, caused by electrical disturbance.

at. no. *abbrev. for* atomic number.

atoll (ˈætɒl) *n* a circular coral reef or string of coral islands surrounding a lagoon. **[**C17: from *atollon*, native name in the Maldive Islands**]**

atom Ⓣ (ˈætəm) *n* **1a** the smallest quantity of an element that can take part in a chemical reaction. **1b** this entity as a source of nuclear energy: *the power of the atom.* **2** the hypothetical indivisible particle of matter postulated by certain ancient philosophers. **3** a very small amount or quantity: *to smash something to atoms.* **[**C16: via OF & L, from Gk, from *atomos* (adj) that cannot be divided, from A-[1] + *temnein* to cut**]**

atomic (əˈtɒmɪk) *adj* **1** of, using, or characterized by atomic bombs or atomic energy: *atomic warfare.* **2** of or comprising atoms: *atomic hydrogen.*
▸**aˈtomically** *adv*

atomic bomb *or* **atom bomb** *n* a type of bomb in which the energy is provided by nuclear fission. Also called: **A-bomb, fission bomb.** Cf. **fusion bomb.**

atomic clock *n* an extremely accurate clock in which an electrical oscillator is controlled by the natural vibrations of an atomic or molecular system such as caesium or ammonia.

atomic energy *n* another name for **nuclear energy.**

atomicity (ˌætəˈmɪsɪtɪ) *n* **1** the state of being made up of atoms. **2** the number of atoms in the molecules of an element. **3** a less common name for **valency.**

atomic mass unit *n* a unit of mass used to express atomic and molecular weights that is equal to one-twelfth of the mass of an atom of carbon-12. Abbrev.: **amu.**

atomic number *n* the number of protons in the nucleus of an atom of an element. Abbrev.: **at. no.**

atomic pile *n* the original name for a **nuclear reactor.**

atomic sentence *n Logic.* a sentence consisting of one predicate and a finite number of terms: *"it is raining" is an atomic sentence.*

atomic structure *n* the concept of an atom as a central positively charged nucleus consisting of protons and neutrons surrounded by a number of electrons. The number of electrons is equal to the number of protons: the whole entity is thus electrically neutral.

atomic theory *n* **1** any theory in which matter is regarded as consisting of atoms. **2** the current concept of the atom as an entity with a definite structure. See **atomic structure.**

atomic weight *n* the former name for **relative atomic mass.** Abbrev.: **at. wt.**

atomize *or* **atomise** (ˈætəˌmaɪz) *vb* **atomizes, atomizing, atomized** *or* **atomises, atomising, atomised. 1** to separate or be separated into free atoms. **2** to reduce (a liquid or solid) to fine particles or spray or (of a liquid or solid) to be reduced in this way. **3** (*tr*) to destroy by weapons, esp. nuclear weapons.

atomizer *or* **atomiser** (ˈætəˌmaɪzə) *n* a device for reducing a liquid to a fine spray, such as a bottle with a fine outlet used to spray perfumes.

atom smasher *n Physics.* the nontechnical name for **accelerator** (sense 2).

atomy (ˈætəmɪ) *n, pl* **atomies.** *Arch.* a minute particle or creature. **[**C16: from L *atomi* atoms, used as sing**]**

atonal (eɪˈtəʊnᵊl) *adj Music.* having no established key.

atonality (ˌeɪtəʊˈnælɪtɪ) *n* **1** absence of or disregard for an established musical key in a composition. **2** the principles of composition embodying this.

atone Ⓣ (əˈtəʊn) *vb* **atones, atoning, atoned.** (*intr;* foll. by *for*) to make amends or reparation (for a crime, sin, etc.). **[**C16: back formation from ATONEMENT**]**
▸**aˈtoner** *n*

atonement Ⓣ (əˈtəʊnmənt) *n* **1** satisfaction, reparation, or expiation given for an injury or wrong. **2** (*often cap.*) *Christian theology.* **2a** the reconciliation of man with God through the sacrificial death of Christ. **2b** the sufferings and death of Christ. **[**C16: from ME *at onement* in harmony**]**

atonic (eɪˈtɒnɪk, æ-) *adj* **1** (of a syllable, word, etc.) carrying no stress; unaccented. **2** lacking body or muscle tone. ◆ *n* **3** an unaccented or unstressed syllable, word, etc. **[**C18: from L, from Gk *atonos* lacking tone**]**

atop (əˈtɒp) *adv* **1** on top; at the top. ◆ *prep* **2** on top of; at the top of.

-ator *suffix forming nouns.* a person or thing that performs a certain action: *agitator; radiator.* **[**from L *-ātor***]**

-atory *suffix forming adjectives.* of, relating to, characterized by, or serving to: *circulatory; explanatory.* **[**from L *-ātōrius***]**

ATP *n* adenosine triphosphate; a substance found in all plant and animal cells. It is the major source of energy for cellular reactions.

atrabilious (ˌætrəˈbɪlɪəs) *or* **atrabiliar** *adj Rare.* irritable or gloomy. **[**C17: from L *ātra bīlis* black bile, from *āter* black + *bīlis* BILE[1]**]**
▸ˌ**atraˈbiliousness** *n*

THESAURUS

atheistic *adj* = **nonbelieving**, disbelieving, faithless, freethinking, godless, heathen, infidel, irreligious, nullifidian, paganistic, sceptic, unbelieving

athlete *n* **1, 3** = **sportsperson**, competitor, contender, contestant, games player, gymnast, player, runner, sportsman, sportswoman

athletic *adj* **1** = **fit**, able-bodied, active, brawny, energetic, herculean, husky (*inf.*), lusty, muscular, powerful, robust, sinewy, strapping, strong, sturdy, vigorous, well-proportioned
Antonyms *adj* delicate, feeble, frail, puny, sickly, weedy (*inf.*)

athletics *pl n* **1, 2** = **sports**, contests, exercises, games of strength, gymnastics, races, track and field events

atmosphere *n* **1** = **air**, aerosphere, heavens, sky **2, 3** = **feeling**, air, ambience, aura, character, climate, environment, feel, flavour, mood, quality, spirit, surroundings, tone, vibes (*sl.*)

atom *n* **3** = **particle**, bit, crumb, dot, fragment, grain, iota, jot, mite, molecule, morsel, mote, scintilla (*rare*), scrap, shred, speck, spot, tittle, trace, whit

atone *vb, foll. by* **for** = **make amends**, answer for, compensate, do penance, make redress, make reparation, make up for, pay for, recompense, redress

atonement *n* **1** = **amends**, compensation, expiation, payment, penance, propitiation, recompense, redress, reparation, restitution, satisfaction

atrazine (ˈætrəziːn) *n* a white crystalline compound widely used as a weedkiller. Formula: $C_8H_{14}N_5Cl$. [C20: from A(MINO) *tr(i)azine*]

atrium (ˈeɪtrɪəm, ˈɑː-) *n, pl* **atria** (ˈeɪtrɪə, ˈɑː-). **1** the open main court of a Roman house. **2** a central often glass-roofed hall that extends through several storeys in a building, such as a shopping centre or hotel. **3** a court in front of an early Christian or medieval church. **4** *Anat.* a cavity or chamber in the body, esp. the upper chamber of each half of the heart. [C17: from L; rel. to *āter* black]
▸ **ˈatrial** *adj*

atrocious Ⓣ (əˈtrəʊʃəs) *adj* **1** extremely cruel or wicked: *atrocious deeds.* **2** horrifying or shocking. **3** *Inf.* very bad: *atrocious writing.* [C17: from L *ātrōx* dreadful, from *āter* black]
▸ **aˈtrociousness** *n*

atrocity Ⓣ (əˈtrɒsɪtɪ) *n, pl* **atrocities. 1** behaviour or an action that is wicked or ruthless. **2** the fact or quality of being atrocious. **3** (*usually pl*) acts of extreme cruelty.

atrophy Ⓣ (ˈætrəfɪ) *n, pl* **atrophies. 1** a wasting away of an organ or part, or a failure to grow to normal size. **2** any degeneration or diminution. ◆ *vb* **atrophies, atrophying, atrophied. 3** to waste away or cause to waste away. [C17: from LL, from Gk, from *atrophos* ill-fed, from A-[1] + *-trophos*, from *trephein* to feed]
▸ **atrophic** (əˈtrɒfɪk) *adj*

atropine (ˈætrəˌpiːn) *n* a poisonous alkaloid obtained from the deadly nightshade, used to treat peptic ulcers, biliary and renal colic, etc. [C19: from NL *atropa* deadly nightshade, from Gk *atropos* unchangeable, inflexible]

attach Ⓣ (əˈtætʃ) *vb* (*mainly tr*) **1** to join, fasten, or connect. **2** (*reflexive or passive*) to become associated with or join. **3** (*intr;* foll. by *to*) to be connected (with): *responsibility attaches to the job.* **4** to attribute or ascribe. **5** to include or append: *a proviso is attached to the contract.* **6** (*usually passive*) *Mil.* to place on temporary duty with another unit. **7** to appoint officially. **8** *Law.* to arrest or take (a person, property, etc.) with lawful authority. [C14: from OF *atachier* to fasten, changed from *estachier* to fasten with a stake]
▸ **atˈtachable** *adj* ▸ **atˈtacher** *n*

attaché (əˈtæʃeɪ) *n* a specialist attached to a diplomatic mission: *military attaché.* [C19: from F: someone attached (to a mission)]

attaché case *n* a small flat rectangular briefcase used for carrying documents, papers, etc.

attached Ⓣ (əˈtætʃt) *adj* **1** (foll. by *to*) fond (of). **2** married, engaged, or associated in an exclusive sexual relationship.

attachment Ⓣ (əˈtætʃmənt) *n* **1** a fastening. **2** (often foll. by *to*) affection or regard (for). **3** an object to be attached: *an attachment for an electric drill.* **4** the act of attaching or the state of being attached. **5a** the lawful seizure of property and placing of it under control of a court. **5b** a writ authorizing such seizure.

attack Ⓣ (əˈtæk) *vb* **1** to launch a physical assault (against) with or without weapons. **2** (*intr*) to take the initiative in a game, sport, etc. **3** (*tr*) to criticize or abuse vehemently. **4** (*tr*) to turn one's mind or energies to (a job, problem, etc.). **5** (*tr*) to begin to injure or affect adversely: *rust attacked the metal.* ◆ *n* **6** the act or an instance of attacking. **7** strong criticism or abuse. **8** an offensive move in a game, sport, etc. **9 the attack.** *Ball games.* the players in a team whose main role is to attack the opponents. **10** commencement of a task, etc. **11** any sudden and usually severe manifestation of a disease or disorder: *a heart attack.* **12** *Music.* **12a** decisiveness in beginning a passage, movement, or piece. **12b** (in electronic instruments) the time between the start of a note and its maximum volume. [C16: from F, from OIt. *attaccare* to attack, attach, from *estaccare* to attach]
▸ **atˈtacker** *n*

attain Ⓣ (əˈteɪn) *vb* **1** (*tr*) to achieve or accomplish (a task, aim, etc.). **2** (*tr*) to reach in space or time. **3** (*intr;* often foll. by *to*) to arrive (at) with effort or exertion. [C14: from OF, from L *attingere* to reach, from *tangere* to touch]
▸ **atˈtainable** *adj* ▸ **atˌtainaˈbility** *or* **atˈtainableness** *n*

attainder (əˈteɪndə) *n* (formerly) the extinction of a person's civil rights resulting from a sentence of death or outlawry on conviction for treason or felony. [C15: from Anglo-F *attaindre* to convict, from OF *ateindre* to ATTAIN]

attainment Ⓣ (əˈteɪnmənt) *n* an achievement or the act of achieving; accomplishment.

attainment target *n Brit. education.* a general defined level of ability that a pupil is expected to achieve in every subject at each key stage in the National Curriculum. Abbrev.: **AT.**

attaint (əˈteɪnt) *vb* (*tr*) *Arch.* **1** to pass judgment of death or outlawry upon (a person). **2** (of sickness) to affect or strike (somebody). ◆ *n* **3** a less common word for **attainder.** [C14: from OF *ateint* convicted, from *ateindre* to ATTAIN]

attar (ˈætə), **otto** (ˈɒtəʊ), *or* **ottar** (ˈɒtə) *n* an essential oil from flowers, esp. the damask rose: *attar of roses.* [C18: from Persian, from *ʻitr* perfume, from Ar.]

attempt Ⓣ (əˈtɛmpt) *vb* (*tr*) **1** to make an effort (to do something) or to achieve (something); try. **2** to try to surmount (an obstacle). **3** to try to climb. ◆ *n* **4** an endeavour to achieve something; effort. **5** a result of an attempt or endeavour. **6** an attack, esp. with the intention to kill. [C14: from OF, from L *attemptāre* to strive after, from *tentāre* to try]
▸ **atˈtemptable** *adj*

> **USAGE NOTE** *Attempt* should not be used in the passive when followed by an infinitive: *attempts were made to find a solution* (not *a solution was attempted to be found*).

attend Ⓣ (əˈtɛnd) *vb* **1** to be present at (an event, etc.). **2** (when *intr,* foll. by *to*) to give care (to); minister (to). **3** (when *intr,* foll. by *to*) to pay attention. **4** (*tr; often passive*) to accompany or follow: *a high temperature attended by a severe cough.* **5** (*intr;* foll. by *on* or *upon*) to follow as a consequence (of). **6** (*intr;* foll. by *to*) to apply oneself: *to attend to the garden.* **7** (*tr*) to escort or accompany. **8** (*intr;* foll. by *on* or *upon*) to provide for the needs (of): *to attend on a guest.* [C13: from OF, from L *attendere* to stretch towards, from *tendere* to extend]

THESAURUS

atrocious *adj* **1** = **cruel**, barbaric, brutal, diabolical, fiendish, flagrant, heinous, infamous, infernal, inhuman, monstrous, nefarious, ruthless, savage, vicious, villainous, wicked **2** = **shocking**, appalling, detestable, execrable, grievous, horrible, horrifying, terrible
Antonyms *adj* ≠ **cruel:** civilized, generous, gentle, good, honourable, humane, kind, merciful ≠ **shocking:** admirable, fine, tasteful

atrocity *n* **1, 2** = **cruelty**, atrociousness, barbarity, barbarousness, brutality, enormity, fiendishness, grievousness, heinousness, horror, infamy, inhumanity, monstrousness, nefariousness, ruthlessness, savagery, shockingness, viciousness, villainousness, wickedness **3** = **act of cruelty**, abomination, barbarity, brutality, crime, cruelty, enormity, evil, horror, monstrosity, outrage, villainy

atrophy *n* **1, 2** = **wasting away**, decay, decaying, decline, degeneration, deterioration, diminution, meltdown (*inf.*), shrivelling, wasting, withering ◆ *vb* **3** = **waste away**, decay, decline, degenerate, deteriorate, diminish, dwindle, fade, shrink, shrivel, waste, wilt, wither

attach *vb* **1** = **connect**, add, adhere, affix, annex, append, bind, couple, fasten, fix, join, link, make fast, secure, stick, subjoin, tie, unite **2** = **join**, accompany, affiliate oneself with, associate with, become associated with, combine with, join forces with, latch on to, sign on with, sign up with, unite with **4** = **put**, ascribe, assign, associate, attribute, connect, impute, invest with, lay, place
Antonyms *vb* ≠ **connect:** detach, disconnect, dissociate, loosen, remove, retire, separate, untie, withdraw

attached *adj* **1** *foll. by* **to** = **fond of**, affectionate towards, devoted to, full of regard for **2** = **spoken for**, accompanied, engaged, married, partnered

attachment *n* **1** = **connector**, adaptor *or* adapter, bond, clamp, connection, coupling, fastener, fastening, joint, junction, link, tie **2** = **fondness**, affection, affinity, attraction, bond, devotion, fidelity, friendship, liking, love, loyalty, partiality, possessiveness, predilection, regard, tenderness **3** = **accessory**, accoutrement, adaptor *or* adapter, addition, add-on, adjunct, appendage, appurtenance, auxiliary, extension, extra, fitting, fixture, supplement, supplementary part
Antonyms *n* ≠ **fondness:** animosity, antipathy, aversion, disinclination, distaste, hatred, hostility, loathing

attack *vb* **1** = **assault**, assail, charge, fall upon, invade, lay into (*inf.*), raid, rush, set about, set upon, storm, strike (at) **3** = **criticize**, abuse, berate, bite someone's head off, blame, blast, censure, excoriate, have a go (at) (*inf.*), impugn, lambast(e), malign, put down, revile, snap someone's head off, tear into (*inf.*), vilify ◆ *n* **6** = **assault**, aggression, campaign, charge, foray, incursion, inroad, invasion, offensive, onset, onslaught, raid, rush, strike **7** = **criticism**, abuse, blame, calumny, censure, character assassination, denigration, impugnment, stick (*sl.*), vilification **11** = **bout**, access, convulsion, fit, paroxysm, seizure, spasm, spell, stroke
Antonyms *vb* ≠ **assault:** defend, guard, protect, retreat, support, sustain, withdraw ◆ *n* ≠ **assault:** defence, retreat, support, withdrawal

attacker *n* **1** = **assailant**, aggressor, assaulter, intruder, invader, raider

attain *vb* **1** = **achieve**, accomplish, acquire, arrive at, bring off, complete, earn, effect, fulfil, gain, get, grasp, land, obtain, procure, reach, realize, reap, score (*sl.*), secure, win

attainable *adj* **1** = **achievable**, accessible, accomplishable, at hand, feasible, gettable, graspable, likely, obtainable, possible, potential, practicable, probable, procurable, reachable, realizable, within reach
Antonyms *adj* impossible, impracticable, improbable, inaccessible, out of reach, unattainable, unfeasible, unlikely, unobtainable, unprocurable, unreachable

attainment *n* = **achievement**, accomplishment, acquirement, acquisition, arrival at, completion, feat, fulfilment, gaining, getting, obtaining, procurement, reaching, realization, reaping, winning

attempt *vb* **1** = **try**, endeavour, essay, experiment, have a crack (*inf.*), have a go (*inf.*), have a shot (*inf.*), have a stab (*inf.*), seek, strive, tackle, take on, try one's hand at, undertake, venture ◆ *n* **4** = **try**, assault, attack, bid, crack (*inf.*), effort, endeavour, essay, experiment, go (*inf.*), shot (*inf.*), stab (*inf.*), trial, undertaking, venture

attempted *vb* **1** = **tried**, assayed, endeavoured, undertaken, ventured

attend *vb* **1** = **be present**, appear, be at, be here, be there, frequent, go to, haunt, make one (*arch.*), put in an appearance, show oneself, show up (*inf.*), turn up, visit **2** = **look after**, care for, mind, minister to, nurse, take care of, tend **3** = **pay attention**, follow, hear, hearken (*arch.*), heed, listen, look on, mark, mind, note, notice, observe, pay heed, regard, take to heart, watch **4, 5** = **accompany**, arise from, be associated with, be connected with, be consequent on, follow, go hand in hand with, issue from, occur with, result from **6** = **apply oneself to**, concentrate on, devote oneself to, get to work on, look after, occupy oneself with, see to, take care of **7** = **escort**, accompany, chaperon, companion,

attendance ➊ (əˈtɛndəns) *n* **1** the act or state of attending. **2** the number of persons present.

attendant ➊ (əˈtɛndənt) *n* **1** a person who accompanies or waits upon another. **2** a person employed to assist, guide, or provide a service for others. **3** a person who is present. ◆ *adj* **4** being in attendance. **5** associated: *attendant problems.*

attendee (əˌtɛnˈdiː) *n* a person who is present at a specified event.

attention ➊ (əˈtɛnʃən) *n* **1** concentrated direction of the mind, esp. to a problem or task. **2** consideration, notice, or observation. **3** detailed care or special treatment: *to pay attention to one's appearance.* **4** (*usually pl*) an act of courtesy or gallantry indicating affection or love. **5** the motionless position of formal military alertness, an upright position with legs and heels together. ◆ *sentence substitute.* **6** the order to be alert or to adopt a position of formal military alertness. [C14: from L, from *attendere* to apply the mind to]

attention deficit disorder *n* a disorder, particularly of children, characterized by excessive activity and inability to concentrate on one task for any length of time. Abbrev.: **ADD.**

attentive ➊ (əˈtɛntɪv) *adj* **1** paying attention; listening carefully. **2** (*postpositive;* often foll. by *to*) careful to fulfil the needs or wants (of).
▸**atˈtentively** *adv* ▸**atˈtentiveness** *n*

attenuate ➊ *vb* (əˈtɛnjʊˌeɪt) **attenuates, attenuating, attenuated. 1** to weaken or become weak. **2** to make or become thin or fine; extend. ◆ *adj* (əˈtɛnjʊɪt, -ˌeɪt). **3** weakened or reduced. **4** *Bot.* tapering. [C16: from L *attenuāre* to weaken, from *tenuis* thin]
▸**atˌtenuˈation** *n*

attest ➊ (əˈtɛst) *vb* **1** (*tr*) to affirm the correctness or truth of. **2** (when *intr,* usually foll. by *to*) to witness (an act, event, etc.) or bear witness (to an act, event, etc.). **3** (*tr*) to make evident; demonstrate. **4** (*tr*) to provide evidence for. [C16: from L, from *testārī* to bear witness, from *testis* a witness]
▸**atˈtestable** *adj* ▸**atˈtestant, atˈtester** *or esp. in legal usage* **atˈtestor** *n* ▸**attestation** (ˌætɛˈsteɪʃən) *n*

attested (əˈtɛstɪd) *adj Brit.* (of cattle, etc.) certified to be free from a disease, esp. from tuberculosis.

attic ➊ (ˈætɪk) *n* **1** a space or room within the roof of a house. **2** *Archit.* a storey or low wall above the cornice of a classical façade. [C18: special use of ATTIC, from use of Attic-style pilasters on façade of top storey]

Attic ➊ (ˈætɪk) *adj* **1** of or relating to Attica, the area around Athens, its inhabitants, or the dialect of Greek spoken there. **2** (*often not cap.*) classically elegant, simple, or pure. ◆ *n* **3** the dialect of Ancient Greek spoken and written in Athens.

Atticism (ˈætɪˌsɪzəm) *n* **1** the idiom or character of the Attic dialect of Ancient Greek. **2** an elegant, simple expression.

Attic salt *or* **wit** *n* refined incisive wit.

attire ➊ (əˈtaɪə) *vb* **attires, attiring, attired. 1** (*tr*) to dress, esp. in fine elegant clothes; array. ◆ *n* **2** clothes or garments, esp. if fine or decorative. [C13: from OF *atirier* to put in order, from *tire* row]

attitude ➊ (ˈætɪˌtjuːd) *n* **1** the way a person views something or tends to behave towards it, often in an evaluative way. **2** a theatrical pose created for effect (esp. in **strike an attitude**). **3** a position of the body indicating mood or emotion. **4** *Inf.* a hostile manner: *don't give me attitude, my girl.* **5** the orientation of an aircraft's axes or a spacecraft in relation to some plane or the direction of motion. [C17: from F, from It. *attitudine* disposition, from LL *aptitūdō* fitness, from L *aptus* APT]
▸**ˌattiˈtudinal** *adj*

attitudinize *or* **attitudinise** (ˌætɪˈtjuːdɪˌnaɪz) *vb* **attitudinizes, attitudinizing, attitudinized** *or* **attitudinises, attitudinising, attitudinised.** (*intr*) to adopt a pose or opinion for effect; strike an attitude.

attn *abbrev. for* attention.

atto- *prefix* denoting 10^{-18}: *attotesla.* Symbol: a [from Norwegian & Danish *atten* eighteen]

attorney (əˈtɜːnɪ) *n* **1** a person legally appointed or empowered to act for another. **2** *US.* a lawyer qualified to represent clients in legal proceedings. [C14: from OF, from *atourner* to direct to, from *tourner* to TURN]
▸**atˈtorneyˌship** *n*

attorney-at-law *n, pl* **attorneys-at-law.** *Law, now chiefly US.* a lawyer.

attorney general *n, pl* **attorneys general** *or* **attorney generals.** a chief law officer and senior legal adviser of some national and state governments.

attract ➊ (əˈtrækt) *vb* (*mainly tr*) **1** to draw (notice, a crowd of observers, etc.) to oneself (esp. in **attract attention**). **2** (*also intr*) to exert a force on (a body) that tends to oppose a separation: *the gravitational pull of the earth attracts objects to it.* **3** to possess some property that pulls or draws (something) towards itself. **4** (*also intr*) to exert a pleasing or fascinating influence (upon). [C15: from L *attrahere* to draw towards, from *trahere* to pull]
▸**atˈtractable** *adj* ▸**atˈtractor** *n*

attraction ➊ (əˈtrækʃən) *n* **1** the act or quality of attracting. **2** a person or thing that attracts or is intended to attract. **3** a force by which one object attracts another: *magnetic attraction.*

attractive ➊ (əˈtræktɪv) *adj* **1** appealing to the senses or mind through beauty, form, character, etc. **2** arousing interest: *an attractive opportunity.* **3** possessing the ability to draw or pull: *an attractive force.*
▸**atˈtractively** *adv*

attrib. *abbrev. for:* **1** attribute. **2** attributive.

attribute ➊ *vb* (əˈtrɪbjuːt). **attributes, attributing, attributed. 1** (*tr;* usually foll. by *to*) to regard as belonging (to), produced (by), or resulting (from): *to attribute a painting to Picasso.* ◆ *n* (ˈætrɪˌbjuːt). **2** a property, quality, or feature belonging to or representative of a person or thing. **3** an object accepted as belonging to a particular office or position. **4** *Grammar.* **4a** an adjective or adjectival phrase. **4b** an attributive adjective. **5** *Logic.* the property or feature that is affirmed or denied concerning the subject of a proposition. [C15: from L *attribuere* to associate with, from *tribuere* to give]
▸**atˈtributable** *adj* ▸**attribution** (ˌætrɪˈbjuːʃən) *n*

attributive (əˈtrɪbjʊtɪv) *adj* **1** relating to an attribute. **2** *Grammar.* (of an adjective or adjectival phrase) preceding the noun modified. Cf. **predicative. 3** *Philosophy.* relative to an understood domain, as *small* in *that elephant is small.*

THESAURUS

convoy, guard, squire, usher **8** = **serve**, be in the service of, wait upon, work for
Antonyms *vb* ≠ **be present:** be absent, miss, play truant ≠ **look after, apply oneself to:** neglect ≠ **pay attention:** discount, disregard, ignore, neglect ≠ **accompany:** dissociate

attendance *n* **1** = **presence**, appearance, attending, being there **2** = **turnout**, audience, crowd, gate, house, number present

attendant *n* **1, 2** = **assistant**, aide, auxiliary, chaperon, companion, custodian, escort, flunky, follower, guard, guide, helper, lackey, menial, page, servant, steward, underling, usher, waiter ◆ *adj* **5** = **accompanying**, accessory, associated, concomitant, consequent, related

attention *n* **1** = **concentration**, consideration, contemplation, deliberation, heed, heedfulness, intentness, mind, scrutiny, thinking, thought, thoughtfulness **2** = **notice**, awareness, consciousness, consideration, observation, recognition, regard **3** = **care**, concern, looking after, ministration, treatment **4** *usually plural* = **courtesy**, assiduities, care, civility, compliment, consideration, deference, gallantry, mindfulness, politeness, regard, respect, service
Antonyms *n* ≠ **concentration, notice:** carelessness, disregard, disrespect, distraction, inattention, laxity, laxness, thoughtlessness, unconcern ≠ **care:** negligence ≠ **courtesy:** discourtesy, impoliteness

attentive *adj* **1** = **intent**, alert, awake, careful, concentrating, heedful, listening, mindful, observant, on one's toes, regardful, studious, watchful **2** = **considerate**, accommodating, civil, conscientious, courteous, devoted, gallant, gracious, helpful, kind, obliging, polite, respectful, thoughtful
Antonyms *adj* ≠ **intent:** absent-minded, careless, distracted, dreamy, heedless, inattentive, preoccupied, unheeding, unmindful ≠ **considerate:** neglectful, negligent, remiss, thoughtless

attenuate *vb* **1** = **weaken**, adulterate, contract, decrease, devaluate, dilute, diminish, enervate, enfeeble, lessen, lower, reduce, sap, water down **2** = **stretch out**, draw out, elongate, extend, lengthen, make fine, make slender, rarefy, refine, slim, spin out, thin ◆ *adj* **3** = **weakened**, adulterated, contracted, decreased, devalued, dilute, diluted, diminished, enervated, enfeebled, lessened, lowered, reduced, sapped, watered down

attest *vb* **1-4** = **testify**, adjure, affirm, assert, authenticate, aver, bear out, bear witness, certify, confirm, corroborate, declare, demonstrate, display, evince, exhibit, give evidence, invoke, manifest, prove, ratify, seal, show, substantiate, swear, verify, vouch for, warrant, witness
Antonyms *vb* contradict, controvert, deny, disprove, gainsay (*arch. or literary*), give the lie to, make a nonsense of, prove false, rebut, refute

attic *n* **1** = **loft**, garret

Attic *adj* **2** = **classical**, chaste, correct, elegant, graceful, polished, pure, refined, simple, tasteful

attire *vb* **1** = **dress**, accoutre, apparel, array, clothe, costume, deck out, equip, fit out, garb, get ready, rig out, robe, turn out ◆ *n* **2** = **clothes**, accoutrements, apparel, array (*poetic*), clothing, costume, dress, garb, garments, gear (*inf.*), habiliments, habit, outfit, raiment (*arch. or poetic*), robes, uniform, vestment, wear

attitude *n* **1** = **disposition**, approach, frame of mind, mood, opinion, outlook, perspective, point of view, position, stance, view **2** = **position**, pose, posture, stance **3** = **manner**, air, aspect, bearing, carriage, condition, demeanour, mien (*literary*)

attract *vb* **4** = **appeal to**, allure, bewitch, captivate, catch (someone's) eye, charm, decoy, draw, enchant, endear, engage, entice, fascinate, incline, induce, interest, invite, lure, pull (*inf.*), tempt
Antonyms *vb* disgust, give one the creeps (*inf.*), put one off, repel, repulse, revolt, turn one off (*inf.*)

attraction *n* **1, 3** = **appeal**, allure, attractiveness, bait, captivation, charm, come-on (*inf.*), draw, enchantment, endearment, enticement, fascination, incentive, inducement, interest, invitation, lure, magnetism, pull (*inf.*), temptation, temptingness

attractive *adj* **1, 2** = **appealing**, agreeable, alluring, beautiful, bonny, captivating, charming, comely, cute, engaging, enticing, fair, fascinating, fetching, glamorous, good-looking, gorgeous, handsome, interesting, inviting, likable *or* likeable, lovely, magnetic, pleasant, pleasing, prepossessing, pretty, seductive, tempting, winning, winsome
Antonyms *adj* disagreeable, displeasing, distasteful, offensive, repulsive, ugly, unappealing, unbecoming, uninviting, unlikable *or* unlikeable, unpleasant, unsightly

attributable *adj* **1** = **ascribable**, accountable, applicable, assignable, blamable *or* blameable, explicable, imputable, placeable, referable *or* referrable, traceable

attribute *vb* **1** = **ascribe**, apply, assign, blame, charge, credit, impute, lay at the door of, put down to, refer, set down to, trace to ◆ *n* **2** = **quality**, aspect, character, characteristic, facet, feature, idiosyncrasy, indication, mark, note, peculiarity, point, property, quirk, sign, symbol, trait, virtue

attribution *n* **1** = **ascription**, assignation, as-

attrition ❶ (əˈtrɪʃən) *n* **1** the act of wearing away or the state of being worn away, as by friction. **2** constant wearing down to weaken or destroy (often in **war of attrition**). **3** *Geog.* the grinding down of rock particles by friction. **4** *Theol.* sorrow for sin arising from fear of damnation, esp. as contrasted with contrition. [C14: from LL *attrītiō* a rubbing against something, from L *atterere* to weaken, from *terere* to rub]
attune ❶ (əˈtjuːn) *vb* **attunes, attuning, attuned.** (*tr*) to adjust or accustom (a person or thing); acclimatize.
ATV *abbrev. for* all-terrain vehicle.
at. vol. *abbrev. for* atomic volume.
at. wt. *abbrev. for* atomic weight.
atypical ❶ (eɪˈtɪpɪkᵊl) *adj* not typical; deviating from or not conforming to type.
▸**aˈtypically** *adv*
Au *the chemical symbol for* gold. [from NL *aurum*]
aubade (əʊˈbɑːd) *n* a poem or short musical piece to greet the dawn. [C19: F, from OProvençal *auba* dawn, ult. from L *albus* white]
aubergine (ˈəʊbəˌʒiːn) *n* **1** *Chiefly Brit.* a tropical Old World plant widely cultivated for its egg-shaped typically dark purple fruit. US, Canad., and Austral. name: **eggplant. 2** the fruit of this plant, which is cooked and eaten as a vegetable. **3a** a dark purple colour. **3b** (*as adj*): *an aubergine dress.* [C18: from F, from Catalan *albergínia,* from Ar. *al-bādindjān,* ult. from Sansk. *vatin-ganah,* from ?]
aubrietia, aubrieta, *or* **aubretia** (ɔːˈbriːʃə) *n* a trailing purple-flowered plant native to European mountains but widely planted in rock gardens. [C19: from NL, after Claude *Aubriet,* 18th-cent. F painter of flowers and animals]
auburn ❶ (ˈɔːbᵊn) *n* **a** a moderate reddish-brown colour. **b** (*as adj*): *auburn hair.* [C15 (orig. meaning: blond): from OF *alborne* blond, from Med. L, from L *albus* white]
au courant *French.* (o kurɑ̃) *adj* up-to-date, esp. in knowledge of current affairs. [lit.: in the current]
auction (ˈɔːkʃən) *n* **1** a public sale of goods or property in which prospective purchasers bid until the highest price is reached. **2** the competitive calls made in bridge before play begins. ◆ *vb* **3** (*tr;* often foll. by *off*) to sell by auction. [C16: from L *auctiō* an increasing, from *augēre* to increase]
auction bridge *n* a variety of bridge in which all the tricks made score towards game.
auctioneer (ˌɔːkʃəˈnɪə) *n* **1** a person who conducts an auction. ◆ *vb* **2** (*tr*) to sell by auction.
auctorial (ɔːkˈtɔːrɪəl) *adj* of or relating to an author. [C19: from L *auctor* AUTHOR]
audacious ❶ (ɔːˈdeɪʃəs) *adj* **1** recklessly bold or daring. **2** impudent or presumptuous. [C16: from L *audāx* bold, from *audēre* to dare]
▸**auˈdaciousness** *or* **audacity** (ɔːˈdæsɪtɪ) *n*
audible ❶ (ˈɔːdɪbᵊl) *adj* perceptible to the hearing; loud enough to be heard. [C16: from LL, from L *audīre* to hear]
▸ˌ**audiˈbility** *or* ˈ**audibleness** *n* ▸ˈ**audibly** *adv*
audience ❶ (ˈɔːdɪəns) *n* **1** a group of spectators or listeners, esp. at a concert or play. **2** the people reached by a book, film, or radio or television programme. **3** the devotees or followers of a public entertainer, etc. **4** a formal interview with a monarch or head of state. [C14: from OF, from L *audientia* a hearing, from *audīre* to hear]
audio (ˈɔːdɪəʊ) *n* (*modifier*) **1** of or relating to sound or hearing: *audio frequency.* **2** relating to or employed in the transmission or reproduction of sound. [C20: from L *audīre* to hear]
audio book *n* a reading of a book recorded on tape.
audio frequency *n* a frequency in the range 20 hertz to 20 000 hertz. A sound wave of this frequency would be audible to the human ear.
audiology (ˌɔːdɪˈɒlədʒɪ) *n* the scientific study of hearing, often including the treatment of persons with hearing defects.
▸ˌ**audiˈologist** *n*
audiometer (ˌɔːdɪˈɒmɪtə) *n* an instrument for testing hearing.
▸ˌ**audiˈometrist** *n* ▸ˌ**audiˈometry** *n*
audiophile (ˈɔːdɪəʊˌfaɪl) *n* a person who has a great interest in high-fidelity sound reproduction.
audiotypist (ˈɔːdɪəʊˌtaɪpɪst) *n* a typist trained to type from a dictating machine.
▸ˈ**audioˌtyping** *n*
audiovisual (ˌɔːdɪəʊˈvɪʒʊəl) *adj* (esp. of teaching aids) involving or directed at both hearing and sight.
▸ˌ**audioˈvisually** *adv*
audit ❶ (ˈɔːdɪt) *n* **1a** an inspection, correction, and verification of business accounts, conducted by an independent qualified accountant. **1b** (*as modifier*): *audit report.* **2** *US.* an audited account. **3** any thoroughgoing examination or check. ◆ *vb* **audits, auditing, audited. 4** to inspect, correct, and certify (accounts, etc.). [C15: from L *audītus* a hearing, from *audīre* to hear]
audition (ɔːˈdɪʃən) *n* **1** a test at which a performer or musician is asked to demonstrate his ability for a particular role, etc. **2** the act or power of hearing. ◆ *vb* **3** to judge by means of or be tested in an audition. [C16: from L *audītiō* a hearing, from *audīre* to hear]
auditor (ˈɔːdɪtə) *n* **1** a person qualified to audit accounts. **2** a person who hears or listens. [C14: from OF, from L *audītor* a hearer]
▸ˌ**audiˈtorial** *adj*
Auditor General *n* (in Canada) an officer appointed by the Governor General to audit the accounts of the Federal Government and report to Parliament.
auditorium (ˌɔːdɪˈtɔːrɪəm) *n, pl* **auditoriums** *or* **auditoria** (-ˈtɔːrɪə). **1** the area of a concert hall, theatre, etc., in which the audience sits. **2** *US & Canad.* a building for public meetings. [C17: from L: a judicial examination]
auditory (ˈɔːdɪtərɪ) *adj* of or relating to hearing or the sense of hearing. [C14: from L *audītōrius* relating to hearing, from *audīre* to hear]
au fait ❶ *French.* (o fɛ) *adj* fully informed; in touch or expert. [C18: lit.: to the point]
au fond *French.* (o fɔ̃) *adv* fundamentally; essentially. [lit.: at the bottom]
auf Wiedersehen *German.* (auf ˈviːdərzeːən) *sentence substitute.* goodbye, until we see each other again.
Aug. *abbrev. for* August.
Augean (ɔːˈdʒiːən) *adj* extremely dirty or corrupt. [C16: from *Augeas,* in Gk myth., king whose filthy stables Hercules cleaned in one day]
augend (ˈɔːdʒɛnd, ɔːˈdʒɛnd) *n* a number to which another number, the addend, is added. [from L *augendum,* from *augēre* to increase]
auger (ˈɔːgə) *n* **1** a hand tool with a bit shaped like a corkscrew, for boring holes in wood. **2** a larger tool of the same kind for boring holes in the ground. [C15: *an augur,* mistaken division of *a nauger,* from OE *nafugār* nave (of a wheel) spear, from *nafu* NAVE[2] + *gār* spear]
aught *or* **ought** (ɔːt) (*used with a negative or in conditional or interrogative sentences or clauses*) *Arch. or literary.* ◆ *pron* **1** anything whatever (esp. in **for aught I know**). ◆ *adv* **2** *Dialect.* to any degree. [OE *āwiht,* from *ā* ever, + *wiht* thing]
augment ❶ (ɔːgˈmɛnt) *vb* to make or become greater in number, strength, etc. [C15: from LL, from *augmentum* growth, from L *augēre* to increase]
▸**augˈmentable** *adj* ▸**augˈmenter** *n*
augmentation ❶ (ˌɔːgmɛnˈteɪʃən) *n* **1** the act of augmenting or the state of being augmented. **2** the amount by which something is increased.
augmentative (ɔːgˈmɛntətɪv) *adj* **1** tending or able to augment. **2** *Grammar.* denoting an affix that may be added to a word to convey the meaning *large* or *great*: for example, the suffix *-ote* in Spanish, where *hombre* means man and *hombrote* big man.
augmented (ɔːgˈmɛntɪd) *adj* **1** *Music.* (of an interval) increased from

THESAURUS

signment, attachment, blame, charge, credit, imputation, placement, referral
attrition *n* **1, 2** = **wearing down**, attenuation, debilitation, harassment, harrying, thinning out, weakening
attune *vb* = **accustom**, acclimatize, accord, adapt, adjust, coordinate, familiarize, harmonize, modulate, regulate, set, tune
attuned *adj* = **accustomed**, acclimatized, adjusted, coordinated, familiarized, harmonized, in accord, in harmony, in tune
atypical *adj* = **unusual**, deviant, exceptional, nonconforming, out of keeping, out of the ordinary, singular, uncharacteristic, uncommon, unconforming, unconventional, uncustomary, unique, unorthodox, unrepresentative
Antonyms *adj* archetypal, average, characteristic, classic, conforming, conventional, customary, illustrative, in character, in keeping, model, normal, ordinary, orthodox, representative, standard, stock, true to type, unexceptional, unsingular, usual
auburn *adj* = **reddish-brown**, chestnut-coloured, copper-coloured, henna, nutbrown, russet, rust-coloured, tawny, Titian red
audacious *adj* **1** = **daring**, adventurous, bold, brave, courageous, daredevil, dauntless, death-defying, enterprising, fearless, intrepid, rash, reckless, risky, valiant, venturesome **2** = **cheeky**, assuming, brazen, defiant, disrespectful, forward, fresh (*inf.*), impertinent, impudent, insolent, in-your-face (*Brit. sl.*), pert, presumptuous, rude, sassy (*US inf.*), shameless
Antonyms *adj* ≠ **daring:** careful, cautious, cowardly, frightened, guarded, prudent, timid, unadventurous, unenterprising ≠ **cheeky:** deferential, gracious, tactful, unassuming
audacity *n* **1** = **daring**, adventurousness, audaciousness, boldness, bravery, courage, dauntlessness, enterprise, face (*inf.*), fearlessness, front, guts (*inf.*), intrepidity, nerve, rashness, recklessness, valour, venturesomeness **2** = **cheek**, audaciousness, brass neck (*Brit. inf.*), chutzpah (*US & Canad. inf.*), defiance, disrespectfulness, effrontery, forwardness, gall (*inf.*), impertinence, impudence, insolence, neck (*inf.*), nerve, pertness, presumption, rudeness, sassiness (*US inf.*), shamelessness
audible *adj* = **clear**, detectable, discernible, distinct, hearable, perceptible
Antonyms *adj* faint, imperceptible, inaudible, indistinct, low, out of earshot
audience *n* **1** = **spectators**, assemblage, assembly, congregation, crowd, gallery, gathering, house, listeners, onlookers, turnout, viewers **3** = **public**, devotees, fans, following, market **4** = **interview**, consultation, hearing, meeting, reception
audit *n* **1** = **inspection**, balancing, check, checking, examination, investigation, review, scrutiny, verification ◆ *vb* **4** = **inspect**, balance, check, examine, go over, go through, investigate, review, scrutinize, verify
au fait *adj* = **fully informed**, abreast of, *au courant*, clued-up (*inf.*), conversant, expert, familiar, in the know, in the loop, in touch, knowledgeable, on the ball (*inf.*), up to speed, well-acquainted, well up
augment *vb* = **increase**, add to, amplify, boost, build up, dilate, enhance, enlarge, expand, extend, grow, heighten, inflate, intensify, magnify, multiply, raise, reinforce, strengthen, swell
Antonyms *vb* contract, curtail, cut down, decrease, diminish, lessen, lower, reduce, shrink
augmentation *n* **1, 2** = **increase**, accession, addition, amplification, boost, build-up, dilation, enhancement, enlargement, expansion, extension, growth, heightening, inflation, in-

being perfect or major by the raising of the higher note or the dropping of the lower note by one semitone: *C to G sharp is an augmented fifth.* **2** having been increased, esp. in number: *an augmented orchestra.*

au gratin (*French* o gratẽ) *adj* covered and cooked with browned breadcrumbs and sometimes cheese. [F, lit.: with the grating]

augur ❶ ('ɔːgə) *n* **1** (in ancient Rome) a religious official who observed and interpreted omens and signs. **2** any prophet or soothsayer. ◆ *vb* **3** to predict (some future event), as from signs or omens. **4** (*tr; may take a clause as object*) to be an omen (of). **5** (*intr*) to foreshadow future events: *this augurs well for us.* [C14: from L: a diviner, ?from *augēre* to increase]
▸**augural** ('ɔːgjʊrəl) *adj*

augury ❶ ('ɔːgjʊrɪ) *n, pl* **auguries. 1** the art of or a rite conducted by an augur. **2** a sign or portent; omen.

august ❶ (ɔː'gʌst) *adj* **1** dignified or imposing. **2** of noble birth or high rank: *an august lineage.* [C17: from L *augustus;* rel. to *augēre* to increase]
▸**au'gustness** *n*

August ('ɔːgəst) *n* the eighth month of the year, consisting of 31 days.

Augustan (ɔː'gʌstən) *adj* **1** characteristic of or relating to the Roman emperor Augustus Caesar (63 B.C.–14 A.D.), his period, or the poets writing during his reign. **2** of or characteristic of any literary period noted for refinement and classicism, esp. the 18th century in England. ◆ *n* **3** an author in an Augustan Age.

Augustinian (ˌɔːgə'stɪnɪən) *adj* **1** of Saint Augustine of Hippo (354–430 A.D.), his doctrines, or the Christian religious orders founded on his doctrines. ◆ *n* **2** a member of any of several religious orders that are governed by the rule of Saint Augustine. **3** a person who follows the doctrines of Saint Augustine.

auk (ɔːk) *n* **1** a diving bird of northern oceans having a heavy body, short tail, narrow wings, and a black-and-white plumage. See also **great auk, razorbill. 2 little auk.** a small short-billed auk, abundant in Arctic regions. [C17: from ON *ālka*]

au lait (əʊ 'leɪ) *adj* prepared or served with milk. [F, lit.: with milk]

auld (ɔːld) *adj* a Scottish word for **old.** [OE *āld*]

auld lang syne ('ɔːld læŋ 'saɪn) *n* times past, esp. those remembered with nostalgia. [Scot., lit.: old long since]

aumbry ('ɔːmbrɪ) *n, pl* **aumbries.** a variant of **ambry.**

au naturel *French.* (o natyrɛl) *adj, adv* **1** naked; nude. **2** uncooked or plainly cooked. [lit.: in (a) natural (condition)]

aunt (ɑːnt) *n* (*often cap., esp. as a term of address*) **1** a sister of one's father or mother. **2** the wife of one's uncle. **3** a term of address used by children for a female friend of the parents. **4 my (sainted) aunt!** an exclamation of surprise. [C13: from OF, from L *amita* a father's sister]

auntie *or* **aunty** ('ɑːntɪ) *n, pl* **aunties.** a familiar or diminutive word for **aunt.**

Auntie ('ɑːntɪ) *n Brit. inf.* the BBC.

Aunt Sally ('sælɪ) *n, pl* **Aunt Sallies.** *Brit.* **1** a figure of an old woman used in fairgrounds and fêtes as a target. **2** any person who is a target for insults or criticism.

au pair (əʊ 'pɛə) *n* **a** a young foreigner, usually a girl, who undertakes housework in exchange for board and lodging, esp. in order to learn the language. **b** (*as modifier*): *an au pair girl.* [C20: from F: on an equal footing]

aura ❶ ('ɔːrə) *n, pl* **auras** *or* **aurae** ('ɔːriː). **1** a distinctive air or quality considered to be characteristic of a person or thing. **2** any invisible emanation, esp. surrounding a person or object. **3** *Pathol.* strange sensations, such as noises in the ears or flashes of light, that immediately precede an attack, esp. of epilepsy. [C18: via L from Gk: breeze]

aural ('ɔːrəl) *adj* of or relating to the sense or organs of hearing; auricular. [C19: from L *auris* ear]
▸**'aurally** *adv*

aureate ('ɔːrɪɪt) *adj* **1** covered with gold; gilded. **2** (of a style of writing or speaking) excessively elaborate. [C15: from LL, from L *aureus* golden, from *aurum* gold]

aureole ('ɔːrɪˌəʊl) *or* **aureola** (ɔː'riːələ) *n* **1** a border of light or radiance enveloping the head of a figure represented as holy. **2** a less common word for **halo. 3** another name for **corona** (sense 2). [C13: from OF, from Med. L (*corōna*) *aureola* golden (crown), from L, from *aurum* gold]

au revoir *French.* (o rəvwar) *sentence substitute.* goodbye. [lit.: to the seeing again]

auric ('ɔːrɪk) *adj* of or containing gold, esp. in the trivalent state; designating a gold(III) compound. [C19: from L *aurum* gold]

auricle ('ɔːrɪkᵊl) *n* **1** the upper chamber of the heart; atrium. **2** Also called: **pinna.** *Anat.* the external part of the ear. **3** *Biol.* an ear-shaped part or appendage. [C17: from L *auricula* the external ear, from *auris* ear]
▸**'auricled** *adj*

auricula (ɔː'rɪkjʊlə) *n, pl* **auriculae** (-ˌliː) *or* **auriculas. 1** Also called: **bear's-ear.** a widely cultivated alpine primrose with leaves shaped like a bear's ear. **2** another word for **auricle** (sense 3). [C17: from NL, from L; see AURICLE]

auricular (ɔː'rɪkjʊlə) *adj* **1** of, relating to, or received by the sense or organs of hearing; aural. **2** shaped like an ear. **3** of or relating to an auricle of the heart.

auriferous (ɔː'rɪfərəs) *adj* (of rock) containing gold; gold-bearing. [C18: from L, from *aurum* gold + *ferre* to bear]

Aurignacian (ˌɔːrɪg'neɪʃən) *adj* of or produced during a flint culture of the Upper Palaeolithic type characterized by the use of bone and antler tools, and also by cave art. [C20: after *Aurignac,* France, near the cave where remains were discovered]

aurochs ('ɔːrɒks) *n, pl* **aurochs.** a recently extinct member of the cattle tribe that inhabited forests in N Africa, Europe, and SW Asia. Also called: **urus.** [C18: from G, from OHG *ūrohso,* from *ūro* bison + *ohso* OX]

aurora (ɔː'rɔːrə) *n, pl* **auroras** *or* **aurorae** (-riː). **1** an atmospheric phenomenon consisting of bands, curtains, or streamers of light, that move across the sky. **2** *Poetic.* the dawn. [C14: from L: dawn]
▸**au'roral** *adj*

aurora australis (ɒ'streɪlɪs) *n* (*sometimes cap.*) the aurora seen around the South Pole. Also called: **southern lights.** [NL: southern aurora]

aurora borealis (ˌbɔːrɪ'eɪlɪs) *n* (*sometimes cap.*) the aurora seen around the North Pole. Also called: **northern lights.** [C17: NL: northern aurora]

aurous ('ɔːrəs) *adj* of or containing gold, esp. in the monovalent state; designating a gold(I) compound. [C19: from F *aureux,* LL *aurōsus* gold-coloured, from L *aurum* gold]

auscultation (ˌɔːskəl'teɪʃən) *n* **1** the diagnostic technique in medicine of listening to the various internal sounds made by the body, usually with the aid of a stethoscope. **2** the act of listening. [C19: from L, from *auscultāre* to listen attentively; rel. to L *auris* ear]
▸**'auscul,tate** *vb* ▸**auscultatory** (ɔː'skʌltətərɪ) *adj*

auspice ❶ ('ɔːspɪs) *n* **1** (*usually pl*) patronage (esp. in **under the auspices of**). **2** (*often pl*) an omen, esp. one that is favourable. [C16: from L *auspicium* augury from birds]

auspicious ❶ (ɔː'spɪʃəs) *adj* **1** favourable or propitious. **2** *Arch.* fortunate.
▸**aus'piciously** *adv* ▸**aus'piciousness** *n*

> **USAGE NOTE** The use of *auspicious* to mean 'very special' (as in *this auspicious occasion*) should be avoided.

Aussie ('ɒzɪ) *n, adj Inf.* Australian.

Aust. *abbrev. for:* **1** Australia(n). **2** Austria(n).

austere ❶ (ɒ'stɪə) *adj* **1** stern or severe in attitude or manner. **2** grave, sober, or serious. **3** self-disciplined, abstemious, or ascetic: *an austere life.* **4** severely simple or plain: *an austere design.* [C14: from OF, from L *austērus* sour, from Gk *austēros* astringent; rel. to Gk *hauein* to dry]
▸**aus'terely** *adv*

austerity ❶ (ɒ'stɛrɪtɪ) *n, pl* **austerities. 1** the state or quality of being austere. **2** (*often pl*) an austere habit, practice, or act. **3a** reduced availability of luxuries and consumer goods. **3b** (*as modifier*): *an austerity budget.*

austral[1] ('ɔːstrəl) *adj* of or coming from the south: *austral winds.* [C14: from L *austrālis,* from *auster* the south wind]

austral[2] (aʊ'strɑːl) *n, pl* **australes** (-'strɑːlɛs). a former monetary unit of Argentina. [from Sp.; see AUSTRAL[1]]

Austral. *abbrev. for:* **1** Australasia. **2** Australia(n).

Australasian (ˌɒstrə'leɪzɪən) *adj* **1** of or relating to Australia, New Zealand, and neighbouring islands. **2** (of organizations) having members in Australia and New Zealand.

THESAURUS

tensification, magnification, multiplication, reinforcement, rise, strengthening, swelling

augur *vb* **3-5** = **bode**, be an omen of, bespeak (*arch.*), betoken, foreshadow, harbinger, herald, portend, predict, prefigure, presage, promise, prophesy, signify

augury *n* **1** = **prediction**, divination, prophecy, soothsaying, sortilege **2** = **omen**, auspice, forerunner, forewarning, harbinger, herald, portent, precursor, presage, prognostication, promise, prophecy, sign, token, warning

august *adj* **1, 2** = **noble**, dignified, exalted, glorious, grand, high-ranking, imposing, impressive, kingly, lofty, magnificent, majestic, monumental, regal, solemn, stately, superb

aura *n* **1** = **air**, ambience, aroma, atmosphere, emanation, feel, feeling, mood, odour, quality, scent, suggestion, tone, vibes (*sl.*), vibrations (*sl.*)

auspice *n* **1** *usually plural As in* **under the auspices of** = **support**, advocacy, aegis, authority, backing, care, championship, charge, control, countenance, guidance, influence, patronage, protection, sponsorship, supervision

auspicious *adj* **1** = **favourable**, bright, encouraging, felicitous, fortunate, happy, hopeful, lucky, opportune, promising, propitious, prosperous, rosy, timely
Antonyms *adj* bad, black, discouraging, ill-omened, inauspicious, infelicitous, ominous, unfavourable, unfortunate, unlucky, unpromising, unpropitious

austere *adj* **1, 2** = **stern**, cold, exacting, forbidding, formal, grave, grim, hard, harsh, inflexible, rigorous, serious, severe, solemn, stiff, strict, stringent, unfeeling, unrelenting **3** = **ascetic**, abstemious, abstinent, chaste, continent, economical, exacting, puritanical, rigid, self-denying, self-disciplined, sober, solemn, Spartan, strait-laced, strict, unrelenting **4** = **plain**, bleak, economical, harsh, severe, simple, spare, Spartan, stark, subdued, unadorned, unornamented
Antonyms *adj* ≠ **stern:** affable, cheerful, convivial, flexible, free-and-easy, genial, indulgent, jovial, kindly, permissive, sweet ≠ **ascetic:** abandoned, free-and-easy, immoral, indulgent, loose, permissive ≠ **plain:** comfortable, indulgent, luxurious

austerity *n* **1** = **sternness**, coldness, exactingness, forbiddingness, formality, gravity, grimness, hardness, harshness, inflexibility, rigour, seriousness, severity, solemnity, stiffness, strictness **1** = **asceticism**, abstemiousness, abstinence, chasteness, chastity, continence, economy, exactingness, puritanism, rigidity, self-denial, self-discipline, sobriety, solemnity,

Australian (ɒ'streɪlɪən) *n* **1** a native or inhabitant of Australia, the smallest continent. **2** the form of English spoken in Australia. ◆ *adj* **3** of, relating to, or characteristic of Australia, the Australians, or their form of English.

Australiana (ɒˌstreɪlɪ'ɑːnə) *pl n* objects, books, documents, etc. relating to Australia and its history and culture.

Australian Rules *n* (*functioning as sing*) a game resembling rugby, played in Australia between teams of 18 men each on an oval pitch, with a ball resembling a large rugby ball. Players attempt to kick the ball between posts (without crossbars) at either end of the pitch.

Australoid ('ɒstrəˌlɔɪd) *adj* **1** denoting, relating to, or belonging to a racial group that includes the native Australians and certain other peoples of southern Asia and the Pacific islands. ◆ *n* **2** any member of this racial group.

australopithecine (ˌɒstrələʊ'pɪθɪˌsiːn) *n* any of various extinct apelike primates whose remains have been found in southern and E Africa. Some species are estimated to be over 4.5 million years old. [C20: from NL, from L *austrālis* southern + Gk *pithēkos* ape]

Australorp ('ɒstrəˌlɔːp) *n* a heavy black breed of domestic fowl laying brown eggs. [shortened from *Austral(ian Black) Orp(ington)*]

Austrian ('ɒstrɪən) *adj* **1** of or relating to Austria, a republic in Central Europe. ◆ *n* **2** a native or inhabitant of Austria.

Austrian blind *n* a window blind consisting of rows of vertically gathered fabric that may be drawn up to form a series of ruches.

Austro-[1] ('ɒstrəʊ) *combining form.* southern: *Austro-Asiatic.* [from L *auster* the south wind]

Austro-[2] ('ɒstrəʊ) *combining form.* Austrian: *Austro-Hungarian.*

AUT (in Britain) *abbrev. for* Association of University Teachers.

autarchy ('ɔːtɑːkɪ) *n, pl* **autarchies.** unlimited rule; autocracy. [C17: from Gk *autarkhia,* from *autarkhos* autocratic]
▸**au'tarchic** *or* **au'tarchical** *adj*

autarky ('ɔːtɑːkɪ) *n, pl* **autarkies.** (esp. of a political unit) a system or policy of economic self-sufficiency. [C17: from Gk *autarkeia,* from *autarkēs* self-sufficient, from AUTO- + *arkein* to suffice]
▸**au'tarkic** *adj* ▸**'autarkist** *n*

auteur (ɔː'tɜː) *n* a director whose creative influence on a film is so great as to be considered its author. [F: author]
▸**au'teurism** *n* ▸**au'teurist** *n*

authentic ⓣ (ɔː'θentɪk) *adj* **1** of undisputed origin or authorship; genuine. **2** trustworthy; reliable: *an authentic account.* **3** (of a deed, etc.) duly executed. **4** *Music.* **4a** using period instruments and historically researched scores and playing techniques. **4b** (*in combination*): *an authentic-instrument performance.* **5** *Music.* commencing on the perfect and ending an octave higher. Cf. **plagal.** [C14: from LL *authenticus* coming from the author, from Gk, from *authentēs* one who acts independently, from AUTO- + *hentēs* a doer]
▸**au'thentically** *adv* ▸**authenticity** (ˌɔːθen'tɪsɪtɪ) *n*

authenticate ⓣ (ɔː'θentɪˌkeɪt) *vb* **authenticates, authenticating, authenticated.** (*tr*) **1** to establish as genuine or valid. **2** to give authority or legal validity to.
▸**auˌthenti'cation** *n* ▸**au'thentiˌcator** *n*

author ⓣ ('ɔːθə) *n* **1** a person who composes a book, article, or other written work. Related adj: **auctorial. 2** a person who writes books as a profession; writer. **3** an originator or creator: *the author of this plan.* ◆ *vb* (*tr*) **4** to write or originate. [C14: from OF, from L *auctor* author, from *augēre* to increase]
▸**authorial** (ɔː'θɔːrɪəl) *adj*

authoritarian ⓣ (ɔːˌθɒrɪ'teərɪən) *adj* **1** favouring or characterized by strict obedience to authority. **2** favouring or relating to government by a small elite. **3** dictatorial; domineering. ◆ *n* **4** a person who favours or practises authoritarian policies.

authoritative ⓣ (ɔː'θɒrɪtətɪv) *adj* **1** recognized or accepted as being true or reliable. **2** commanding: *an authoritative manner.* **3** possessing or supported by authority; official.
▸**au'thoritatively** *adv* ▸**au'thoritativeness** *n*

authority ⓣ (ɔː'θɒrɪtɪ) *n, pl* **authorities. 1** the power or right to control, judge, or prohibit the actions of others. **2** (*often pl*) a person or group of people having this power, such as a government, police force, etc. **3** a position that commands such a power or right (often in **in authority**). **4** such a power or right delegated: *she has his authority.* **5** the ability to influence or control others. **6** an expert or an authoritative written work in a particular field. **7** evidence or testimony. **8** confidence resulting from great expertise. **9** (*cap. when part of a name*) a public board or corporation exercising governmental authority: *Advertising Standards Authority.* [C14: from OF, from L, from *auctor* author]

authorize ⓣ *or* **authorise** ('ɔːθəˌraɪz) *vb* **authorizes, authorizing, authorized** *or* **authorises, authorising, authorised.** (*tr*) **1** to confer authority upon (someone to do something). **2** to permit (someone to do or be something) with official sanction.
▸**ˌauthori'zation** *or* **ˌauthori'sation** *n*

Authorized Version *n* **the.** an English translation of the Bible published in 1611 under James I. Also called: **King James Version.**

authorship ('ɔːθəˌʃɪp) *n* **1** the origin or originator of a written work, plan, etc. **2** the profession of writing books.

autism ('ɔːtɪzəm) *n Psychiatry.* abnormal self-absorption, usually affecting children, characterized by lack of response to people and limited ability to communicate. [C20: from Gk *autos* self + -ISM]
▸**au'tistic** *adj*

auto ('ɔːtəʊ) *n, pl* **autos.** *US & Canad. inf.* **a** short for **automobile. b** (*as modifier*): *auto parts.*

auto. *abbrev. for:* **1** automatic. **2** automobile. **3** automotive.

auto- *or sometimes before a vowel* **aut-** *combining form.* **1** self; same; of or by the same one: *autobiography.* **2** self-caused: *autohypnosis.* **3** self-propelling: *automobile.* [from Gk *autos* self]

autobahn ('ɔːtəˌbɑːn) *n* a motorway in German-speaking countries. [C20: from G from *Auto* car + *Bahn* road, track]

autobiography ⓣ (ˌɔːtəʊbaɪ'ɒgrəfɪ) *n, pl* **autobiographies.** an account of a person's life written or otherwise recorded by that person.
▸**ˌautobi'ographer** *n* ▸**autobiographical** (ˌɔːtəˌbaɪə'græfɪk^{ə}l) *adj*

autocephalous (ˌɔːtəʊ'sefələs) *adj* (of an Eastern Christian Church) governed by its own national synods and appointing its own patriarchs or prelates.

autochthon (ɔː'tɒkθən) *n, pl* **autochthons** *or* **autochthones** (-θəˌniːz). **1** (*often pl*) one of the earliest known inhabitants of any country. **2** an animal or plant that is native to a particular region. [C17: from Gk *autokhthōn* from the earth itself, from AUTO- + *khthōn* the earth]
▸**au'tochthonous** *adj*

autoclave ('ɔːtəˌkleɪv) *n* **1** a strong sealed vessel used for chemical reactions at high pressure. **2** an apparatus for sterilizing objects (esp. surgical instruments) by means of steam under pressure. [C19: from F AUTO- + *-clave,* from L *clāvis* key]

autocracy ⓣ (ɔː'tɒkrəsɪ) *n, pl* **autocracies. 1** government by an individual with unrestricted authority. **2** a country, society, etc., ruled by an autocrat.

autocrat ⓣ ('ɔːtəˌkræt) *n* **1** a ruler who possesses absolute and unrestricted authority. **2** a domineering or dictatorial person.
▸**ˌauto'cratic** *adj* ▸**ˌauto'cratically** *adv*

autocross ('ɔːtəʊˌkrɒs) *n* a motor sport in which cars race over a half-mile circuit of rough grass.

THESAURUS

Spartanism, strictness **1** = **plainness**, economy, severity, simplicity, spareness, Spartanism, starkness

authentic *adj* **1, 2** = **genuine**, accurate, actual, authoritative, bona fide, certain, dependable, factual, faithful, legitimate, on the level (*inf.*), original, pure, real, reliable, simon-pure (*rare*), the real McCoy, true, true-to-life, trustworthy, valid, veritable
Antonyms *adj* counterfeit, fake, false, fictitious, fraudulent, hypothetical, imitation, misleading, mock, pseudo (*inf.*), spurious, supposed, synthetic, unfaithful, unreal, untrue

authenticate *vb* **1, 2** = **verify**, attest, authorize, avouch, certify, confirm, endorse, guarantee, validate, vouch for, warrant
Antonyms *vb* annul, invalidate, render null and void

authenticity *n* **1, 2** = **genuineness**, accuracy, actuality, authoritativeness, certainty, dependability, factualness, faithfulness, legitimacy, purity, realness, reliability, trustworthiness, truth, truthfulness, validity, veritableness, verity

author *n* **1, 2** = **writer**, composer, creator **3** = **creator**, architect, designer, doer, fabricator, father, founder, framer, initiator, inventor, maker, mover, originator, parent, planner, prime mover, producer

authoritarian *adj* **1, 3** = **strict**, absolute, autocratic, despotic, dictatorial, disciplinarian, doctrinaire, dogmatic, domineering, harsh, imperious, rigid, severe, tyrannical, unyielding ◆ *n* **4** = **disciplinarian**, absolutist, autocrat, despot, dictator, tyrant
Antonyms *adj* ≠ **strict:** broad-minded, democratic, flexible, indulgent, lenient, liberal, permissive, tolerant

authoritative *adj* **1** = **reliable**, accurate, authentic, definitive, dependable, factual, faithful, learned, scholarly, sound, true, trustworthy, truthful, valid, veritable **2** = **commanding**, assertive, autocratic, confident, decisive, dictatorial, dogmatic, dominating, imperative, imperious, imposing, lordly, masterly, peremptory, self-assured **3** = **official**, approved, authorized, commanding, legitimate, sanctioned, sovereign
Antonyms *adj* ≠ **reliable:** deceptive, undependable, unreliable ≠ **commanding:** humble, subservient, timid, weak ≠ **official:** unauthorized, unofficial, unsanctioned

authority *n* **1** = **power**, ascendancy, charge, command, control, direction, domination, dominion, force, government, influence, jurisdiction, might, prerogative, right, rule, say-so, strength, supremacy, sway, weight **2** *often plural* = **powers that be**, administration, government, management, officialdom, police, the Establishment **4** = **permission**, authorization, justification, licence, permit, sanction, say-so, warrant **6** = **expert**, arbiter, bible, connoisseur, guru, judge, master, professional, scholar, specialist, textbook

authorization *n* **1** = **power**, ability, authority, right, say-so, strength **2** = **permission**, approval, credentials, leave, licence, permit, sanction, say-so, warrant

authorize *vb* **1** = **empower**, accredit, commission, enable, entitle, give authority **2** = **permit**, accredit, allow, approve, confirm, countenance, give authority for, give leave, give the green light for, license, ratify, sanction, vouch for, warrant
Antonyms *vb* ban, debar, disallow, exclude, forbid, outlaw, preclude, prohibit, proscribe, rule out, veto

authorized *adj* **1** = **official**, approved, commissioned, licensed, ratified, signed and sealed **2** = **permitted**, allowed, approved, countenanced, licensed, sanctioned, warranted

autobiography *n* = **life story**, history, memoirs, record, résumé

autocracy *n* **1** = **dictatorship**, absolutism, despotism, tyranny

autocrat *n* **1** = **dictator**, absolutist, despot, tyrant

autocratic *adj* **1** = **dictatorial**, absolute,

Autocue (ˈɔːtəʊˌkjuː) *n Trademark.* an electronic television prompting device whereby a script, unseen by the audience, is displayed for the speaker.

auto-da-fé (ˌɔːtəʊdəˈfeɪ) *n, pl* **autos-da-fé. 1** *History.* a ceremony of the Spanish Inquisition including the pronouncement and execution of sentences passed on sinners or heretics. **2** the burning to death of people condemned as heretics by the Inquisition. [C18: from Port., lit.: act of the faith]

autoeroticism (ˌɔːtəʊɪˈrɒtɪˌsɪzəm) *or* **autoerotism** (ˌɔːtəʊˈɛrəˌtɪzəm) *n Psychol.* the arousal and use of one's own body as a sexual object.
▸ **ˌautoeˈrotic** *adj*

autoexposure (ˌɔːtəʊɪkˈspəʊʒə) *n* another name for **automatic exposure.**

autofocus (ˈɔːtəʊˌfəʊkəs) *n* another name for **automatic focus.**

autogamy (ɔːˈtɒgəmɪ) *n* self-fertilization.
▸ **auˈtogamous** *adj*

autogenic training (ˌɔːtəʊˈdʒɛnɪk) *n* a technique for reducing stress through mental exercises. Also called: **autogenics.**

autogenous (ɔːˈtɒdʒɪnəs) *adj* **1** originating within the body. **2** self-produced. **3** denoting a weld in which the filler metal and the parent metal are of similar composition.
▸ **auˈtogenously** *adv*

autogiro *or* **autogyro** (ˌɔːtəʊˈdʒaɪrəʊ) *n, pl* **autogiros** *or* **autogyros.** a self-propelled aircraft supported in flight mainly by unpowered rotating horizontal blades. [C20: orig. a trademark]

autograph (ˈɔːtəˌgrɑːf) *n* **1a** a handwritten signature, esp. that of a famous person. **1b** (*as modifier*): *an autograph album.* **2** a person's handwriting. **3a** a book, document, etc., handwritten by its author. **3b** (*as modifier*): *an autograph letter.* ◆ *vb* (*tr*) **4** to write one's signature on or in; sign. **5** to write with one's own hand.
▸ **autographic** (ˌɔːtəˈgræfɪk) *adj* ▸ **ˌautoˈgraphically** *adv*

autohypnosis (ˌɔːtəʊhɪpˈnəʊsɪs) *n Psychol.* the process or result of self-induced hypnosis.

autoimmune (ˌɔːtəʊɪˈmjuːn) *adj* (of a disease) caused by the action of antibodies produced against substances normally present in the body.
▸ **ˌautoimˈmunity** *n*

autointoxication (ˌɔːtəʊɪnˌtɒksɪˈkeɪʃən) *n* self-poisoning caused by toxic products originating within the body.

autologous (ɔːˈtɒləgəs) *adj* (of a tissue graft, blood transfusion, etc.) originating from the recipient rather than from a donor.

autolysis (ɔːˈtɒlɪsɪs) *n* the destruction of cells and tissues of an organism by enzymes produced by the cells themselves.
▸ **autolytic** (ˌɔːtəˈlɪtɪk) *adj*

automat (ˈɔːtəˌmæt) *n* another name, esp. US, for **vending machine.**

automate (ˈɔːtəˌmeɪt) *vb* **automates, automating, automated.** to make (a manufacturing process, factory, etc.) automatic, or (of a manufacturing process, etc.) to be made automatic.

automated teller machine *n* a computerized cash dispenser. Abbrev.: **ATM.**

automatic ⓣ (ˌɔːtəˈmætɪk) *adj* **1** performed from force of habit or without conscious thought: *an automatic smile.* **2a** (of a device, mechanism, etc.) able to activate, move, or regulate itself. **2b** (of an act or process) performed by such automatic equipment. **3** (of the action of a muscle, etc.) involuntary or reflex. **4** occurring as a necessary consequence: *promotion is automatic after a year.* **5** (of a firearm) utilizing some of the force of each explosion to eject the empty shell, replace it with a new one, and fire continuously until release of the trigger. ◆ *n* **6** an automatic firearm. **7** a motor vehicle having automatic transmission. **8** a machine that operates automatically. [C18: from Gk *automatos* acting independently]
▸ **ˌautoˈmatically** *adv*

automatic data processing *n* data processing performed by automatic electromechanical devices. Abbrev.: **ADP, A.D.P., a.d.p.**

automatic door *n* a self-opening door.

automatic exposure *n* the automatic adjustment of the lens aperture and shutter speed of a camera by a control mechanism. Also called: **autoexposure.**

automatic focus *n* **a** a system in a camera that automatically adjusts the lens so that the object being photographed is in focus. **b** (*as modifier*): *automatic-focus lens.* Also called: **autofocus.**

automatic gain control *n* a control of a radio receiver which adjusts the magnitude of the input so that the output (or volume) remains approximately constant.

automatic pilot *n* **1** a device that automatically maintains an aircraft on a preset course. **2** *Inf.* a state of mind in which a person performs familiar tasks automatically: *I was on automatic pilot all day.* ◆ Also called: **autopilot.**

automatic transmission *n* a transmission system in a motor vehicle in which the gears change automatically.

automation (ˌɔːtəˈmeɪʃən) *n* **1** the use of methods for controlling industrial processes automatically, esp. by electronically controlled systems. **2** the extent to which a process is so controlled.

automatism (ɔːˈtɒməˌtɪzəm) *n* **1** the state or quality of being automatic; mechanical or involuntary action. **2** *Psychol.* the performance of actions, such as sleepwalking, without conscious knowledge or control.
▸ **auˈtomatist** *n*

automatize *or* **automatise** (ɔːˈtɒməˌtaɪz) *vb* **automatizes, automatizing, automatized** *or* **automatises, automatising, automatised.** to make (a process, etc.) automatic or (of a process, etc.) to be made automatic.
▸ **auˌtomatiˈzation** *or* **auˌtomatiˈsation** *n*

automaton (ɔːˈtɒmətᵊn) *n, pl* **automatons** *or* **automata. 1** a mechanical device operating under its own hidden power. **2** a person who acts mechanically. [C17: from L, from Gk, from *automatos* spontaneous]

automobile (ˈɔːtəməˌbiːl) *n* another word (esp. US) for **car** (sense 1).
▸ **ˌautomoˈbilist** *n*

automobilia (ˌɔːtəməˈbiːlɪə) *pl n* items connected with cars and motoring that are of interest to the collector.

automotive (ˌɔːtəˈməʊtɪv) *adj* **1** relating to motor vehicles. **2** self-propelling.

autonomic (ˌɔːtəˈnɒmɪk) *adj* **1** occurring spontaneously. **2** of or relating to the autonomic nervous system. **3** Also: **autonomous.** (of plant movements) occurring as a result of internal stimuli.
▸ **ˌautoˈnomically** *adv*

autonomic nervous system *n* the section of the nervous system of vertebrates that controls the involuntary actions of the smooth muscles, heart, and glands.

autonomics (ˌɔːtəˈnɒmɪks) *n* (*functioning as sing*) *Electronics.* the study of self-regulating systems for process control.

autonomous ⓣ (ɔːˈtɒnəməs) *adj* **1** (of a community, country, etc.) possessing a large degree of self-government. **2** of or relating to an autonomous community. **3** independent of others. **4** *Biol.* existing as an organism independent of other organisms or parts. [C19: from Gk *autonomos* living under one's own laws, from AUTO- + *nomos* law]
▸ **auˈtonomously** *adv*

autonomy ⓣ (ɔːˈtɒnəmɪ) *n, pl* **autonomies. 1** the right or state of self-government, esp. when limited. **2** a state or individual possessing autonomy. **3** freedom to determine one's own actions, behaviour, etc. **4** *Philosophy.* the doctrine that the individual human will is, or ought to be, governed only by its own principles and laws. [C17: from Gk *autonomia* freedom to live by one's own laws]

autopilot (ˌɔːtəˈpaɪlət) *n* short for **automatic pilot.**

autopsy ⓣ (ˈɔːtəpsɪ, ɔːˈtɒp-) *n, pl* **autopsies. 1** Also called: **postmortem examination.** dissection and examination of a dead body to determine the cause of death. **2** an eyewitness observation. **3** any critical analysis. [C17: from NL, from Gk: seeing with one's own eyes, from AUTO- + *opsis* sight]

autoroute (ˈɔːtəʊˌruːt) *n* a motorway in French-speaking countries. [C20: from F from *auto* car + *route* road]

autostrada (ˈɔːtəʊˌstrɑːdə) *n* a motorway in Italian-speaking countries. [C20: from It. from *auto* car + *strada* road]

autosuggestion (ˌɔːtəʊsəˈdʒɛstʃən) *n* a process of suggestion in which the person unconsciously supplies the means of influencing his own behaviour or beliefs.

autotelic (ˌɔːtəʊˈtɛlɪk) *adj* being or having an end or justification in itself. [C20: from AUTO- + Gk *telos* end]

autotomy (ɔːˈtɒtəmɪ) *n, pl* **autotomies.** the casting off by an animal of a part of its body, to facilitate escape when attacked.
▸ **autotomic** (ˌɔːtəˈtɒmɪk) *adj*

autotrophic (ˌɔːtəˈtrɒfɪk) *adj* (of organisms such as green plants) capable of manufacturing complex organic nutritive compounds from simple inorganic sources.
▸ **ˈautoˌtroph** *n*

autumn (ˈɔːtəm) *n* **1** (*sometimes cap.*) **1a** Also called (esp. US): **fall.** the season of the year between summer and winter, astronomically from the September equinox to the December solstice in the N hemisphere and from the March equinox to the June solstice in the S hemisphere. **1b** (*as modifier*): *autumn leaves.* **2** a period of late maturity, esp. one followed by a decline. [C14: from L *autumnus*]
▸ **autumnal** (ɔːˈtʌmnᵊl) *adj*

autumn crocus *n* a plant of the lily family having pink or purplish autumn flowers, found in Europe and N Africa.

aux. *abbrev. for* auxiliary.

auxanometer (ˌɔːksəˈnɒmɪtə) *n* an instrument that measures the linear growth of plant shoots. [C19: from Gk *auxanein* to increase + -METER]

auxiliaries (ɔːgˈzɪljərɪz, -ˈzɪlə-) *pl n* foreign troops serving another nation; mercenaries.

auxiliary ⓣ (ɔːgˈzɪljərɪ, -ˈzɪlə-) *adj* **1** secondary or supplementary. **2** supporting. ◆ *n, pl* **auxiliaries. 3** a person or thing that supports or supplements. **4** *Naut.* **4a** a sailing vessel with an engine. **4b** the engine of

THESAURUS

all-powerful, despotic, domineering, imperious, tyrannical, tyrannous, unlimited

automatic *adj* **1, 3** = **involuntary**, instinctive, instinctual, mechanical, natural, reflex, spontaneous, unconscious, unwilled **2** = **mechanical**, automated, mechanized, push-button, robot, self-acting, self-activating, self-moving, self-propelling, self-regulating **4** = **inevitable**, assured, certain, inescapable, necessary, routine, unavoidable
Antonyms *adj* ≠ **involuntary:** conscious, deliberate, intentional, voluntary ≠ **mechanical:** done by hand, hand-operated, human, manual, physical

autonomous *adj* **1, 3** = **self-ruling**, free, independent, self-determining, self-governing, sovereign

autonomy *n* **1, 3** = **independence**, freedom, home rule, self-determination, self-government, self-rule, sovereignty
Antonyms *n* dependency, foreign rule, subjection

autopsy *n* **1** = **postmortem**, dissection, necropsy, postmortem examination

auxiliary *adj* **1** = **supplementary**, back-up, emergency, fall-back, reserve, secondary, sub-

such a vessel. [C17: from L, from *auxilium* help, from *augēre* to increase, strengthen]

auxiliary rotor *n* the tail rotor of a helicopter, used for directional and rotary control.

auxiliary verb *n* a verb used to indicate the tense, voice, or mood of another verb where this is not indicated by inflection, such as English *will* in *he will go.*

auxin ('ɔːksɪn) *n* a plant hormone that promotes growth. [C20: from Gk *auxein* to grow]

AV *abbrev. for* Authorized Version (of the Bible).

av. *abbrev. for:* **1** average. **2** avoirdupois.

Av. *or* **av.** *abbrev. for* avenue.

a.v. *or* **A/V** *abbrev. for* ad valorem.

avadavat (ˌævədə'væt) *or* **amadavat** (ˌæmədə'væt) *n* either of two Asian weaverbirds having a red plumage: often kept as cagebirds. [C18: from *Ahmadabad,* Indian city from which these birds were brought to Europe]

avail ⓣ (ə'veɪl) *vb* **1** to be of use, advantage, profit, or assistance (to). **2 avail oneself of.** to make use of to one's advantage. ◆ *n* **3** use or advantage (esp. in **of no avail, to little avail**). [C13 *availen,* from OF *valoir,* from L *valēre* to be strong]

available ⓣ (ə'veɪləbᵊl) *adj* **1** obtainable or accessible; capable of being made use of. **2** *Arch.* advantageous.
▸**aˌvaila'bility** *or* **a'vailableness** *n* ▸**a'vailably** *adv*

avalanche ⓣ ('ævəˌlɑːntʃ) *n* **1a** a fall of large masses of snow and ice down a mountain. **1b** a fall of rocks, sand, etc. **2** a sudden or overwhelming appearance of a large quantity of things. ◆ *vb* **avalanches, avalanching, avalanched. 3** to come down overwhelmingly (upon). [C18: from F, by mistaken division from *la valanche,* from *valanche,* from dialect *lavantse*]

avant- ('ævɒŋ) *prefix* of or belonging to the avant-garde of a specified field.

avant-garde ⓣ (ˌævɒŋ'gɑːd) *n* **1** those artists, writers, musicians, etc., whose techniques and ideas are in advance of those generally accepted. ◆ *adj* **2** of such artists, etc., their ideas, or techniques. [from F: VANGUARD]

avarice ⓣ ('ævərɪs) *n* extreme greed for riches. [C13: from OF, from L, from *avārus* covetous, from *avēre* to crave]
▸**avaricious** (ˌævə'rɪʃəs) *adj*

avast (ə'vɑːst) *sentence substitute. Naut.* stop! cease! [C17: ?from Du. *hou'vast* hold fast]

avatar ('ævəˌtɑː) *n* **1** *Hinduism.* the manifestation of a deity in human or animal form. **2** a visible manifestation of an abstract concept. [C18: from Sansk. *avatāra* a going down, from *ava* down + *tarati* he passes over]

avaunt (ə'vɔːnt) *sentence substitute. Arch.* go away! depart! [C15: from OF *avant!* forward! from LL *ab ante* forward, from L *ab* from + *ante* before]

avdp. *abbrev. for* avoirdupois.

ave ('ɑːvɪ, 'ɑːveɪ) *sentence substitute.* welcome or farewell. [L]

Ave[1] ('ɑːvɪ) *n RC Church.* short for **Ave Maria:** see **Hail Mary.** [C13: from L: hail!]

Ave[2] *or* **ave** *abbrev. for* avenue.

avenge ⓣ (ə'vendʒ) *vb* **avenges, avenging, avenged.** (*usually tr*) to inflict a punishment in retaliation for (harm, injury, etc.) done to (a person or persons): *to avenge a crime; to avenge a murdered friend.* [C14: from OF, from *vengier,* from L *vindicāre;* see VENGEANCE, VINDICATE]
▸**a'venger** *n*

> **USAGE NOTE** The use of *avenge* with a reflexive pronoun was formerly considered incorrect, but is now acceptable: *she avenged herself on the man who killed her daughter.*

avens ('ævɪnz) *n, pl* **avens.** (*functioning as sing*) **1** any of a genus of plants, such as **water avens,** which has a purple calyx and orange-pink flowers. **2 mountain avens.** a trailing evergreen white-flowered shrub that grows on mountains in N temperate regions. [C15: from OF, from Med. L *avencia* variety of clover]

aventurine (ə'ventjʊrɪn) *or* **avanturine** (ə'væntjʊrɪn) *n* **1** a dark-coloured glass, usually green or brown, spangled with fine particles of gold, copper, or some other metal. **2** a variety of quartz containing red or greenish particles of iron oxide or mica. [C19: from F, from It., from *avventura* chance; so named because usually found by accident]

avenue ⓣ ('ævɪnjuː) *n* **1a** a broad street, often lined with trees. **1b** (*cap. as part of a street name*) a road, esp. in a built-up area. **2** a main approach road, as to a country house. **3** a way bordered by two rows of trees. **4** a line of approach: *explore every avenue.* [C17: from F, from *avenir* to come to, from L, from *venīre* to come]

aver (ə'vɜː) *vb* **avers, averring, averred.** (*tr*) **1** to state positively. **2** *Law.* to allege as a fact or prove to be true. [C14: from OF, from Med. L *adverāre,* from L *vērus* true]
▸**a'verment** *n*

average ⓣ ('ævərɪdʒ, 'ævrɪdʒ) *n* **1** the typical or normal amount, quality, degree, etc.: *above average in intelligence.* **2** Also called: **arithmetic mean.** the result obtained by adding the numbers or quantities in a set and dividing the total by the number of members in the set: *the average of 3, 4, and 8 is 5.* **3** a similar mean for continuously variable ratios, such as speed. **4** *Maritime law.* **4a** a loss incurred or damage suffered by a ship or its cargo at sea. **4b** the equitable apportionment of such loss among the interested parties. **5 on (the** *or* **an) average.** usually; typically. ◆ *adj* **6** usual or typical. **7** mediocre or inferior: *his performance was only average.* **8** constituting a numerical average: *an average speed.* **9** approximately typical of a range of values: *the average contents of a matchbox.* ◆ *vb* **averages, averaging, averaged. 10** (*tr*) to obtain or estimate a numerical average of. **11** (*tr*) to assess the general quality of. **12** (*tr*) to perform or receive a typical number of: *to average eight hours' work a day.* **13** (*tr*) to divide up proportionately. **14** to amount to or be on average: *the children averaged 15 years of age.* [C15 *averay* loss arising from damage to ships, from OIt. *avaria,* ult. from Ar. *awār* damage, blemish]
▸**'averagely** *adv*

averse ⓣ (ə'vɜːs) *adj* (*postpositive;* usually foll. by *to*) opposed, disinclined, or loath. [C16: from L, from *āvertere* to turn from, from *vertere* to turn]
▸ **a'versely** *adv* ▸ **a'verseness** *n*

aversion ⓣ (ə'vɜːʃən) *n* **1** (usually foll. by *to* or *for*) extreme dislike or disinclination. **2** a person or thing that arouses this: *he is my pet aversion.*

aversion therapy *n Psychiatry.* a way of suppressing an undesirable habit, such as smoking, by associating an unpleasant effect, such as an electric shock, with the habit.

avert ⓣ (ə'vɜːt) *vb* (*tr*) **1** to turn away or aside: *to avert one's gaze.* **2** to ward off: *to avert danger.* [C15: from OF, from L *āvertere;* see AVERSE]
▸**a'vertible** *or* **a'vertable** *adj*

THESAURUS

sidiary, substitute **2** = **supporting**, accessory, aiding, ancillary, assisting, helping ◆ *n* **3** = **helper**, accessory, accomplice, ally, assistant, associate, companion, confederate, henchman, partner, protagonist, subordinate, supporter **3** = **backup**, reserve
Antonyms *adj* ≠ **supplementary, supporting:** cardinal, chief, essential, first, leading, main, primary, prime, principal

avail *vb* **1** = **benefit**, aid, assist, be effective, be of advantage, be of use, be useful, help, profit, serve, work **2 avail oneself of** = **make use of**, employ, exploit, have recourse to, make the most of, profit from, take advantage of, turn to account, use, utilize ◆ *n* **3** = **benefit**, advantage, aid, assistance, boot (*obs.*), effectiveness, efficacy, good, help, mileage (*inf.*), profit, purpose, service, use, usefulness, utility

availability *n* **1** = **accessibility**, attainability, handiness, obtainability, readiness

available *adj* **1** = **accessible**, applicable, at hand, at one's disposal, at one's fingertips, attainable, convenient, free, handy, obtainable, on hand, on tap, ready, ready for use, to hand, vacant
Antonyms *adj* busy, engaged, inaccessible, in use, occupied, spoken for, taken, unattainable, unavailable, unobtainable

avalanche *n* **1** = **snow-slide**, landslide, landslip, snow-slip **2** = **flood**, barrage, deluge, inundation, torrent

avant-garde *adj* **2** = **progressive**, experimental, far-out (*sl.*), ground-breaking, innovative, innovatory, pioneering, unconventional, way-out (*inf.*)
Antonyms *adj* conservative, conventional, hidebound, reactionary, traditional

avarice *n* = **greed**, acquisitiveness, close-fistedness, covetousness, cupidity, graspingness, greediness, meanness, miserliness, niggardliness, parsimony, penny-pinching, penuriousness, rapacity, stinginess
Antonyms *n* benevolence, bountifulness, extravagance, generosity, largesse *or* largess, liberality, unselfishness

avaricious *adj* = **grasping**, acquisitive, close-fisted, covetous, greedy, mean, miserable, miserly, niggardly, parsimonious, penny-pinching, penurious, rapacious, stingy, tight as a duck's arse (*taboo sl.*)

avenge *vb* = **get revenge for**, even the score for, get even for (*inf.*), get one's own back, hit back, pay (someone) back for, pay (someone) back in his *or* her own coin, punish, repay, requite, retaliate, revenge, take revenge for, take satisfaction for, take vengeance

avenue *n* **1, 2** = **street**, access, alley, approach, boulevard, channel, course, drive, driveway, entrance, entry, pass, passage, path, pathway, road, route, thoroughfare, way

average *n* **1, 2** = **usual**, common run, mean, medium, midpoint, norm, normal, par, rule, run, run of the mill, standard **5 on average** = **usually**, as a rule, for the most part, generally, normally, typically ◆ *adj* **6** = **usual**, common, commonplace, fair, general, normal, ordinary, regular, standard, typical **7** = **mediocre**, banal, bog-standard (*Brit. & Irish sl.*), indifferent, middle-of-the-road, middling, moderate, no great shakes (*inf.*), not bad, passable, run-of- the-mill, so-so (*inf.*), tolerable, undistinguished, unexceptional **8** = **mean**, intermediate, median, medium, middle ◆ *vb* **14** = **make on average**, balance out to, be on average, do on average, even out to
Antonyms *adj* ≠ **usual:** abnormal, awful, bad, different, exceptional, great, memorable, notable, outstanding, remarkable, special, terrible, unusual ≠ **mean:** maximum, minimum

averse *adj* = **opposed**, antipathetic, backward, disinclined, hostile, ill-disposed, indisposed, inimical, loath, reluctant, unfavourable, unwilling
Antonyms *adj* agreeable, amenable, disposed, eager, favourable, inclined, keen, sympathetic, willing

aversion *n* **1** = **hatred**, abhorrence, animosity, antipathy, detestation, disgust, disinclination, dislike, distaste, hate, horror, hostility, indisposition, loathing, odium, opposition, reluctance, repugnance, repulsion, revulsion, unwillingness
Antonyms *n* desire, inclination, liking, love, willingness

avert *vb* **1** = **turn away**, turn, turn aside **2** = **ward**

Avesta (ə'vɛstə) *n* a collection of sacred writings of Zoroastrianism, including the Songs of Zoroaster.

Avestan (ə'vɛstən) *n* **1** the earliest recorded form of the Iranian language, formerly called **Zend**. ◆ *adj* **2** of the Avesta or its language.

avian ('eɪvɪən) *adj* of, relating to, or resembling a bird. [C19: from L *avis* bird]

aviary ('eɪvjərɪ) *n, pl* **aviaries.** a large enclosure in which birds are kept. [C16: from L, from *aviārius* concerning birds, from *avis* bird]

aviation ➊ (ˌeɪvɪ'eɪʃən) *n* **1** the art or science of flying aircraft. **2** the design, production, and maintenance of aircraft. [C19: from F, from L *avis* bird]

aviator ➊ ('eɪvɪˌeɪtə) *n Old-fashioned.* the pilot of an aeroplane or airship; flyer.
▸**'aviˌatrix** *or* **'aviˌatress** *fem n*

avid ➊ ('ævɪd) *adj* **1** very keen; enthusiastic: *an avid reader.* **2** (*postpositive;* often foll. by *for* or *of*) eager (for): *avid for revenge.* [C18: from L, from *avēre* to long for]
▸**avidity** (ə'vɪdɪtɪ) *n* ▸**'avidly** *adv*

avifauna (ˌeɪvɪ'fɔːnə) *n* all the birds in a particular region.
▸**ˌavi'faunal** *adj*

avionics (ˌeɪvɪ'ɒnɪks) *n* **1** (*functioning as sing*) the science and technology of electronics applied to aeronautics. **2** (*functioning as pl*) the electronic circuits and devices of an aerospace vehicle. [C20: from *avi(ation electr)onics*]
▸**ˌavi'onic** *adj*

avitaminosis (æˌvɪtəmɪn'əʊsɪs) *n, pl* **avitaminoses** (-siːz). any disease caused by a vitamin deficiency in the diet.

avocado (ˌævə'kɑːdəʊ) *n, pl* **avocados. 1** a pear-shaped fruit having a leathery green or blackish skin, a large stony seed, and a green-ish-yellow edible pulp. **2** the tropical American tree that bears this fruit. **3a** a dull greenish colour. **3b** (*as adj*): *an avocado bathroom suite.* ◆ Also called (for senses 1 & 2): **avocado pear, alligator pear.** [C17: from Sp. *aguacate,* from Nahuatl *ahuacatl* testicle, alluding to the shape of the fruit]

avocation (ˌævə'keɪʃən) *n* **1** *Formal.* a minor occupation undertaken as a diversion. **2** *Not standard.* a person's regular job. [C17: from L, from *āvocāre* to distract, from *vocāre* to call]

avocet ('ævəˌsɛt) *n* a long-legged shore bird having black-and-white plumage and a long slender upward-curving bill. [C18: from F, from It. *avocetta,* from ?]

Avogadro constant *or* **number** (ˌævə'gɑːdrəʊ) *n* the number of atoms or molecules in a mole of a substance, equal to 6.02252×10^{23} per mole. [C19: after Amedeo *Avogadro* (1776–1856), It. physicist]

Avogadro's law *or* **hypothesis** *n* the principle that equal volumes of all gases contain the same number of molecules at the same temperature and pressure.

avoid ➊ (ə'vɔɪd) *vb* (*tr*) **1** to keep out of the way of. **2** to refrain from doing. **3** to prevent from happening: *to avoid damage to machinery.* **4** *Law.* to invalidate; quash. [C14: from Anglo-F, from OF *esvuidier,* from *vuidier* to empty]
▸**a'voidable** *adj* ▸**a'voidably** *adv* ▸**a'voidance** *n* ▸**a'voider** *n*

avoirdupois *or* **avoirdupois weight** (ˌævwɑːdjuː'pwɑː) *n* a system of weights used in many English-speaking countries. It is based on the pound, which contains 16 ounces or 7000 grains. [C14: from OF *aver de peis* goods of weight]

avouch ➊ (ə'vaʊtʃ) *vb* (*tr*) *Arch.* **1** to vouch for; guarantee. **2** to acknowledge. **3** to assert. [C16: from OF *avochier* to summon, call on, from L *advocāre;* see ADVOCATE]
▸**a'vouchment** *n*

avow ➊ (ə'vaʊ) *vb* (*tr*) **1** to state or affirm. **2** to admit openly. [C13: from OF *avouer* to confess, from L *advocāre* to appeal to, call upon]
▸**a'vowal** *n* ▸**a'vowed** *adj* ▸**avowedly** (ə'vaʊɪdlɪ) *adv* ▸**a'vower** *n*

avuncular (ə'vʌŋkjʊlə) *adj* **1** of or concerned with an uncle. **2** resembling an uncle; friendly. [C19: from L *avunculus* (maternal) uncle, dim. of *avus* grandfather]

AWACS *or* **Awacs** ('eɪwæks) *n acronym for* Airborne Warning and Control System.

await ➊ (ə'weɪt) *vb* **1** (*tr*) to wait for. **2** (*tr*) to be in store for. **3** (*intr*) to wait, esp. with expectation.

awake ➊ (ə'weɪk) *vb* **awakes, awaking, awoke** *or* **awaked, awoken** *or* **awaked. 1** to emerge or rouse from sleep. **2** to become or cause to become alert. **3** (usually foll. by *to*) to become or make aware (of). **4** Also: **awaken.** (*tr*) to arouse (feelings, etc.) or cause to remember (memories, etc.). ◆ *adj* (*postpositive*) **5** not sleeping. **6** (sometimes foll. by *to*) lively or alert. [OE *awacian, awacan*]

USAGE NOTE See at **wake**[1].

award ➊ (ə'wɔːd) *vb* (*tr*) **1** to give (something due), esp. as a reward for merit: *to award prizes.* **2** *Law.* to declare to be entitled, as by decision of a court or an arbitrator. ◆ *n* **3** something awarded, such as a prize or medal. **4** *Austral. & NZ.* the amount of an **award wage** (esp. in **above award**). **5** *Law.* **5a** the decision of an arbitrator. **5b** a grant made by a court of law. [C14: from Anglo-F *awarder,* from OF *eswarder* to decide after investigation, from *es-* EX-[1] + *warder* to observe]
▸**a'warder** *n*

award wage *n* (in Australia and New Zealand) statutory minimum pay for a particular group of workers. Sometimes shortened to **award.**

aware ➊ (ə'wɛə) *adj* **1** (*postpositive;* foll. by *of*) having knowledge: *aware of his error.* **2** informed of current developments: *politically aware.* [OE *gewær*]
▸**a'wareness** *n*

awash ➊ (ə'wɒʃ) *adv, adj* (*postpositive*) *Naut.* **1** level with the surface of the sea. **2** washed over by the waves.

away ➊ (ə'weɪ) *adv* **1** from a particular place: *to swim away.* **2** in or to another, a usual, or a proper place: *to put toys away.* **3** apart; at a distance: *to keep away from strangers.* **4** out of existence: *the music faded away.* **5** indicating motion, displacement, transfer, etc., from a normal or proper place: *to turn one's head away.* **6** indicating activity that is wasteful or designed to get rid of something: *to sleep away the hours.* **7** continuously: *laughing away.* **8 away with.** a command for a person to go or be removed: *away with him to prison!* ◆ *adj* (*usually postpositive*) **9** not present: *away from school.* **10** distant: *he is a good way away.* **11** having started; released: *he was away before sunrise.* **12** (*also prenominal*) *Sport.* played on an opponent's ground. ◆ *n* **13** *Sport.* a game played or

THESAURUS

off, avoid, fend off, forestall, frustrate, preclude, prevent, stave off

aviation *n* **1** = **flying**, aeronautics, flight, powered flight

aviator *n* = **pilot**, aeronaut, airman, flyer

avid *adj* **1** = **enthusiastic**, ardent, devoted, eager, fanatical, fervent, intense, keen, keen as mustard, passionate, zealous
Antonyms *adj* apathetic, impassive, indifferent, lukewarm, unenthusiastic

avidity *n* **1** = **enthusiasm**, ardour, devotion, eagerness, fervour, keenness, zeal

avoid *vb* **1** = **keep away from**, body-swerve (*Scot.*), bypass, circumvent, dodge, elude, escape, evade, give a wide berth to, keep aloof from, shun, sidestep, slip through the net, steer clear of **2** = **refrain from**, dodge, duck (out of) (*inf.*), eschew, fight shy of, shirk **3** = **prevent**, avert
Antonyms *vb* ≠ **keep away from:** approach, confront, contact, face, face up to, find, invite, pursue, seek out, solicit

avoidable *adj* **1** = **escapable**, evadable **3** = **preventable**, avertible *or* avertable, stoppable
Antonyms *adj* ≠ **escapable:** inescapable, inevitable, necessary, unavoidable ≠ **preventable:** unpreventable, unstoppable

avoidance *n* **1** = **evasion**, body swerve (*Scot.*), circumvention, dodging, eluding, escape, keeping away, shunning, steering clear **2** = **refraining**, dodging, eschewal, shirking **3** = **prevention**

avouch *vb* **1-3** = **vouch for**, acknowledge, affirm, allege, assert, asseverate, aver, avow, declare, guarantee, maintain, proclaim, profess, pronounce, state, swear

avow *vb* **1** = **state**, affirm, allege, assert, asseverate, aver, declare, maintain, proclaim, profess, recognize, swear **2** = **confess**, acknowledge, admit, own

avowal *n* **1** = **statement**, affirmation, allegation, assertion, asseveration, averment, declaration, maintenance, oath, proclamation, profession, recognition **2** = **confession**, acknowledgment, admission, owning

avowed *adj* **1** = **declared**, open, professed, self-proclaimed, sworn **2** = **confessed**, acknowledged, admitted

await *vb* **1, 3** = **wait for**, abide, anticipate, expect, look for, look forward to, stay for **2** = **be in store for**, attend, be in readiness for, be prepared for, be ready for, wait for

awake *vb* **1** = **wake up**, awaken, rouse, wake **2, 4** = **alert**, activate, animate, arouse, awaken, breathe life into, call forth, enliven, excite, fan, incite, kick-start (*inf.*), kindle, provoke, revive, stimulate, stir up, vivify ◆ *adj* **5** = **not sleeping**, aroused, awakened, aware, bright-eyed and bushy-tailed, conscious, wakeful, waking, wide-awake **6** = **alert**, alive, attentive, aware, heedful, observant, on guard, on one's toes, on the alert, on the lookout, vigilant, watchful
Antonyms *adj* ≠ **not sleeping:** asleep, crashed out (*sl.*), dead to the world (*inf.*), dormant, dozing, napping, sleeping, unconscious ≠ **alert:** inattentive, unaware

awaken *vb* = **awake**, arouse, revive, rouse, wake = **alert**, activate, animate, breathe life into, call forth, enliven, excite, fan, incite, kick-start (*inf.*), kindle, provoke, stimulate, stir up, vivify

award *vb* **1** = **give**, accord, adjudge, allot, apportion, assign, bestow, confer, decree, distribute, endow, gift, grant, hand out, present, render ◆ *n* **3** = **prize**, decoration, gift, grant, trophy, verdict **3** = **giving**, allotment, bestowal, conferment, conferral, endowment, hand-out, order, presentation, stipend **5** *Law* = **decision**, adjudication, decree

aware *adj* **1** *foll. by* **of** = **knowing about**, acquainted with, alive to, appreciative of, apprised of, attentive to, cognizant of, conscious of, conversant with, familiar with, hip to (*sl.*), mindful of, sensible of, wise to (*sl.*) **2** = **informed**, *au courant,* clued-up (*inf.*), enlightened, in the loop, in the picture, knowledgeable
Antonyms *adj* ignorant, insensible, oblivious, unaware, unfamiliar with, unknowledgeable

awareness *n* **1, 2** = **knowledge**, acquaintance, appreciation, attention, cognizance, consciousness, enlightenment, familiarity, mindfulness, perception, realization, recognition, sensibility, sentience, understanding

awash *adj* **2** = **flooded**, afloat, deluged, drowned, engulfed, immersed, inundated, overburdened, overwhelmed, submerged, submersed, swamped, swept

away *adv* **1** = **off**, abroad, elsewhere, from here, from home, hence **3** = **at a distance**, apart, far, remote **7** = **continuously**, incessantly, interminably, relentlessly, repeatedly, uninterruptedly, unremittingly ◆ *adj* **9** = **not present**, abroad, absent, elsewhere, gone, not at home, not here, not there, out ◆ *sentence substitute* **14** = **go**

won at an opponent's ground. ◆ *sentence substitute.* **14** an expression of dismissal. [OE *on weg* on way]

awayday (əˈweɪˌdeɪ) *n* a day trip taken for pleasure, relaxation, etc.; day excursion. [C20: from *awayday ticket,* name applied to some special-rate railway day returns]

awe ⓣ (ɔː) *n* **1** overwhelming wonder, respect, or dread. **2** *Arch.* power to inspire fear or reverence. ◆ *vb* **awes, awing, awed. 3** (*tr*) to inspire with reverence or dread. [C13: from ON *agi*]

aweigh (əˈweɪ) *adj* (*postpositive*) *Naut.* (of an anchor) no longer hooked into the bottom; hanging by its rope or chain.

awe-inspiring ⓣ *adj* causing or worthy of admiration or respect; amazing or magnificent.

awesome ⓣ (ˈɔːsəm) *adj* **1** inspiring or displaying awe. **2** *Sl.* excellent or outstanding.
▸ˈ**awesomely** *adv* ▸ˈ**awesomeness** *n*

awestruck ⓣ *or* **awe-stricken** *adj* overcome or filled with awe.

awful ⓣ (ˈɔːfʊl) *adj* **1** very bad; unpleasant. **2** *Arch.* inspiring reverence or dread. **3** *Arch.* overcome with awe. ◆ *adv* **4** *Not standard.* (intensifier): *an awful cold day.* [C13: see AWE, -FUL]
▸ˈ**awfulness** *n*

awfully ⓣ (ˈɔːfəlɪ) *adv* **1** in an unpleasant, bad, or reprehensible manner. **2** *Inf.* (intensifier): *I'm awfully keen to come.* **3** *Arch.* so as to express or inspire awe.

awhile ⓣ (əˈwaɪl) *adv* for a brief period.

awkward ⓣ (ˈɔːkwəd) *adj* **1** lacking dexterity, proficiency, or skill; clumsy. **2** ungainly or inelegant in movements or posture. **3** unwieldy; difficult to use. **4** embarrassing: *an awkward moment.* **5** embarrassed: *he felt awkward about leaving.* **6** difficult to deal with; requiring tact: *an awkward customer.* **7** deliberately unhelpful. **8** dangerous or difficult. [C14: *awk,* from ON *öfugr* turned the wrong way round + -WARD]
▸ˈ**awkwardly** *adv* ▸ˈ**awkwardness** *n*

awl (ɔːl) *n* a pointed hand tool with a fluted blade used for piercing wood, leather, etc. [OE *ǣl*]

awn (ɔːn) *n* any of the bristles growing from the flowering parts of certain grasses and cereals. [OE *agen* ear of grain]
▸**awned** *adj*

awning (ˈɔːnɪŋ) *n* a roof of canvas or other material supported by a frame to provide protection from the weather, esp. one placed over a doorway or part of a deck of a ship. [C17: from ?]

awoke (əˈwəʊk) *vb* a past tense and (now rare or dialectal) past participle of **awake.**

AWOL (ˈeɪwɒl) *or* **A.W.O.L.** *adj Mil.* absent without leave but without intending to desert.

awry ⓣ (əˈraɪ) *adv, adj* (*postpositive*) **1** with a slant or twist to one side; askew. **2** away from the appropriate or right course; amiss. [C14 *on wry;* see A-², WRY]

axe ⓣ *or US* **ax** (æks) *n, pl* **axes. 1** a hand tool with one side of its head forged and sharpened to a cutting edge, used for felling trees, splitting timber, etc. **2 an axe to grind. 2a** an ulterior motive. **2b** a grievance. **2c** a pet subject. **3 the axe.** *Inf.* **3a** dismissal, esp. from employment (esp. in **get the axe**). **3b** *Brit.* severe cutting down of expenditure, esp. in a public service. ◆ *vb* **axes, axing, axed.** (*tr*) **4** to chop or trim with an axe. **5** *Inf.* to dismiss (employees), restrict (expenditure or services), or terminate (a project, etc.). [OE *æx*]

axel (ˈæksəl) *n Skating.* a jump of one and a half, two and a half, or three and a half turns, taking off from the forward outside edge of one skate and landing on the backward outside edge of the other. [C20: after *Axel* Paulsen (d. 1938), Norwegian skater]

axeman (ˈæksmən) *n, pl* **axemen. 1** a man who wields an axe, esp. to cut down trees. **2** a person who makes cuts in expenditure or services, esp. on behalf of another: *the chancellor's axeman.*

axes¹ (ˈæksiːz) *n* the plural of **axis**¹.

axes² (ˈæksɪz) *n* the plural of **axe.**

axial (ˈæksɪəl) *adj* **1** forming or characteristic of an axis. **2** situated in, on, or along an axis.
▸ˌ**axiˈality** *n* ▸ˈ**axially** *adv*

axil (ˈæksɪl) *n* the upper angle between a branch or leafstalk and the stem from which it grows. [C18: from L *axilla* armpit]

axilla (ækˈsɪlə) *n, pl* **axillae** (-liː). **1** the technical name for the **armpit. 2** the area under a bird's wing corresponding to the armpit. [C17: from L: armpit]

axillary (ækˈsɪlərɪ) *adj* **1** of, relating to, or near the armpit. **2** *Bot.* growing in or related to the axil. ◆ *n, pl* **axillaries. 3** (*usually pl*) Also called: **axillar** (ækˈsɪlə). one of the feathers growing from the axilla of a bird's wing.

axiom ⓣ (ˈæksɪəm) *n* **1** a generally accepted proposition or principle, sanctioned by experience. **2** a universally established principle or law that is not a necessary truth. **3** a self-evident statement. **4** *Logic, maths.* a statement that is stipulated to be true for the purpose of a chain of reasoning. [C15: from L *axiōma* a principle, from Gk, from *axioun* to consider worthy, from *axios* worthy]

axiomatic ⓣ (ˌæksɪəˈmætɪk) *adj* **1** self-evident. **2** containing maxims; aphoristic.
▸ˌ**axioˈmatically** *adv*

axis¹ ⓣ (ˈæksɪs) *n, pl* **axes. 1** a real or imaginary line about which a body, such as an aircraft, can rotate or about which an object, form, composition, or geometrical construction is symmetrical. **2** one of

THESAURUS

away, beat it (*sl.*), begone, be off, bugger off (*taboo sl.*), get lost, get out, go, on your bike (*sl.*), on your way

awe *n* **1** = **wonder**, admiration, amazement, astonishment, dread, fear, horror, respect, reverence, terror, veneration ◆ *vb* **3** = **impress**, amaze, astonish, cow, daunt, frighten, horrify, intimidate, put the wind up (*inf.*), stun, terrify
Antonyms *n* ≠ **wonder:** arrogance, boldness, contempt, disrespect, fearlessness, irreverence, scorn

awed *adj* **1** = **impressed**, afraid, amazed, astonished, cowed, daunted, dumbfounded, fearful, frightened, horrified, intimidated, shocked, stunned, terrified, wonder-stricken, wonder-struck

awe-inspiring *adj* = **impressive**, amazing, astonishing, awesome, breathtaking, daunting, fearsome, intimidating, jaw-dropping, magnificent, striking, stunning (*inf.*), wonderful, wondrous (*arch. or literary*)
Antonyms *adj* bland, boring, dull, flat, humdrum, insipid, prosaic, tame, tedious, unimpressive, uninspiring, vapid

awesome *adj* **1** = **awe-inspiring**, alarming, amazing, astonishing, awful, breathtaking, daunting, dreadful, fearful, fearsome, formidable, frightening, horrible, horrifying, imposing, impressive, intimidating, jaw-dropping, magnificent, majestic, overwhelming, redoubtable, shocking, solemn, striking, stunning, stupefying, terrible, terrifying, wonderful, wondrous (*arch. or literary*)

awestruck *adj* = **impressed**, afraid, amazed, astonished, awed, awe-inspired, cowed, daunted, dumbfounded, fearful, frightened, horrified, intimidated, shocked, struck dumb, stunned, terrified, wonder-stricken, wonder-struck

awful *adj* **1** = **terrible**, abysmal, alarming, appalling, deplorable, dire, distressing, dreadful, fearful, frightful, from hell (*inf.*), ghastly, harrowing, hideous, horrendous, horrible, horrid, horrific, horrifying, nasty, shocking, tremendous, ugly, unpleasant, unsightly **2** *Archaic* = **awe-inspiring**, amazing, awesome, dread, fearsome, majestic, portentous, solemn
Antonyms *adj* ≠ **terrible:** amazing, brilliant, excellent, fabulous (*inf.*), fantastic, great (*inf.*), magnificent, marvellous, miraculous, sensational (*inf.*), smashing (*inf.*), super (*inf.*), superb, terrific, tremendous, wonderful

awfully *adv* **1** = **badly**, disgracefully, disreputably, dreadfully, inadequately, reprehensibly, shoddily, unforgivably, unpleasantly, wickedly, woefully, wretchedly **2** *Informal* = **very**, badly, dreadfully, exceedingly, exceptionally, excessively, extremely, greatly, immensely, quite, seriously (*inf.*), terribly, very much

awhile *adv* = **for a while**, briefly, for a little while, for a moment, for a short time

awkward *adj* **1, 2** = **clumsy**, all thumbs, artless, blundering, bungling, clownish, coarse, gauche, gawky, graceless, ham-fisted *or* ham-handed (*inf.*), ill-bred, inelegant, inept, inexpert, lumbering, maladroit, oafish, rude, skill-less, stiff, uncoordinated, uncouth, ungainly, ungraceful, unpolished, unrefined, unskilful, unskilled **3** = **inconvenient**, clunky (*inf.*), cumbersome, difficult, troublesome, unhandy, unmanageable, unwieldy **4, 5** = **embarrassing**, compromising, cringe-making (*Brit. inf.*), cringeworthy (*Brit. inf.*), delicate, difficult, embarrassed, ill at ease, inconvenient, inopportune, painful, perplexing, sticky (*inf.*), thorny, ticklish, toe-curling (*sl.*), troublesome, trying, uncomfortable, unpleasant, untimely **6, 7** = **uncooperative**, annoying, bloody-minded (*Brit. inf.*), difficult, disobliging, exasperating, hard to handle, intractable, irritable, perverse, prickly, stubborn, touchy, troublesome, trying, unhelpful, unpredictable, vexatious, vexing **8** = **risky**, chancy (*inf.*), dangerous, difficult, hazardous, perilous
Antonyms *adj* ≠ **clumsy:** adept, adroit, dexterous, graceful, skilful ≠ **inconvenient:** convenient, easy, handy ≠ **embarrassing:** comfortable, pleasant

awkwardness *n* **1, 2** = **clumsiness**, artlessness, clownishness, coarseness, gaucheness, gaucherie, gawkiness, gracelessness, ill-breeding, inelegance, ineptness, inexpertness, maladroitness, oafishness, rudeness, stiffness, uncoordination, uncouthness, ungainliness, unskilfulness, unskilledness **3** = **unwieldiness**, cumbersomeness, difficulty, inconvenience, troublesomeness, unhandiness, unmanageability **4, 5** = **embarrassment**, delicacy, difficulty, discomfort, inconvenience, inopportuneness, painfulness, perplexingness, stickiness (*inf.*), thorniness, ticklishness, unpleasantness, untimeliness **6, 7** = **uncooperativeness**, bloody-mindedness (*Brit. inf.*), difficulty, disobligingness, intractability, irritability, perversity, prickliness, stubbornness, touchiness, unhelpfulness, unpredictability **8** = **difficulty**, chanciness (*inf.*), danger, hazardousness, peril, perilousness, risk, riskiness

awry *adv* **1** = **askew**, cockeyed (*inf.*), crookedly, obliquely, off-centre, off course, out of line, out of true, skew-whiff (*inf.*), to one side, unevenly ◆ *adj* **1** = **askew**, asymmetrical, cockeyed (*inf.*), crooked, misaligned, off-centre, off course, out of line, out of true, skew-whiff (*inf.*), to one side, twisted, uneven ◆ *adv, adj* **2** = **wrong**, amiss

axe *n* **1** = **hatchet**, adze, chopper **2 an axe to grind** = **pet subject**, grievance, personal consideration, private ends, private purpose, ulterior motive **3 the axe** *Informal* = **the sack** (*inf.*), cancellation, cutback, discharge, dismissal, termination, the boot (*sl.*), the chop (*sl.*), the (old) heave-ho (*inf.*) ◆ *vb* **4** = **cut down**, chop, fell, hew **5** *Informal* = **cut back**, cancel, discharge, dismiss, dispense with, eliminate, fire (*inf.*), get rid of, give the push, oust, pull, pull the plug on, relegate, remove, sack (*inf.*), terminate, throw out, turn off (*inf.*)

axiom *n* **1** = **principle**, adage, aphorism, apophthegm, dictum, fundamental, gnome, maxim, postulate, precept, truism

axiomatic *adj* **1** = **self-evident**, absolute, accepted, apodictic *or* apodeictic, assumed, certain, fundamental, given, granted, indubitable, manifest, presupposed, understood, unquestioned **2** = **epigrammatic**, aphoristic, apophthegmatic, gnomic, pithy, terse

axis¹ *n* **1** = **pivot**, axle, centre line, shaft, spindle

two or three reference lines used in coordinate geometry to locate a point in a plane or in space. **3** *Anat.* the second cervical vertebra. **4** *Bot.* the main central part of a plant, typically consisting of the stem and root. **5** an alliance between a number of states to coordinate their foreign policy. **6** Also called: **principal axis.** *Optics.* the line of symmetry of an optical system, such as the line passing through the centre of a lens. [C14: from L: axletree, earth's axis; rel. to Gk *axōn* axis]

axis[2] ('æksɪs) *n, pl* **axises.** a S Asian deer with a reddish-brown white-spotted coat and slender antlers. [C18: from L: Indian wild animal, from ?]

Axis ('æksɪs) *n* **a the.** the alliance (1936) of Nazi Germany and Fascist Italy, later joined by Japan and other countries, and lasting until their defeat in World War II. **b** (*as modifier*): *the Axis powers.*

axle ❶ ('æksəl) *n* a bar or shaft on which a wheel, pair of wheels, or other rotating member revolves. [C17: from ON *öxull*]

axletree ('æksəl,triː) *n* a bar fixed across the underpart of a wagon or carriage that has rounded ends on which the wheels revolve.

Axminster carpet ('æks,mɪnstə) *n* a type of patterned carpet with a cut pile. Often shortened to **Axminster.** [after *Axminster* in Devon]

axolotl (,æksə'lɒtᵊl) *n* an aquatic salamander of N America, such as the **Mexican axolotl,** in which the larval form (including external gills) is retained throughout life under natural conditions. [C18: from Nahuatl, from *atl* water + *xolotl* servant, doll]

axon ('æksɒn) *n* the long threadlike extension of a nerve cell that conducts nerve impulses from the cell body. [C19: via NL from Gk: axis, axle, vertebra]

ay[1] *or* **aye** (eɪ) *adv Arch., poetic* always.

ay[2] (aɪ) *sentence substitute, n* a variant spelling of **aye.**

ayah ('aɪə) *n* (in parts of the former British Empire) a native maidservant or nursemaid. [C18: from Hindi *āyā,* from Port. *aia,* from L *avia* grandmother]

ayatollah (,aɪə'tɒlə) *n* one of a class of Shiite religious leaders in Iran. [via Persian from Ar., from *aya* creation + ALLAH]

aye *or* **ay** (aɪ) *sentence substitute.* **1** yes: archaic or dialectal except in voting by voice. ◆ *n* **2a** a person who votes in the affirmative. **2b** an affirmative vote. ◆ Cf. **nay.** [C16: prob. from pron *I,* expressing assent]

aye-aye ('aɪ,aɪ) *n* a rare nocturnal arboreal primate of Madagascar related to the lemurs. It has long bony fingers and rodent-like incisor teeth. [C18: from F, from Malagasy *aiay,* prob. imit.]

Aymara (,aɪmə'rɑː) *n* **1** (*pl* **-ras** *or* **-ra**) a member of a S American Indian people of Bolivia and Peru. **2** the language of this people. [from Sp. *aimará,* from Amerind]

Ayrshire ('ɛəʃə) *n* any one of a hardy breed of brown-and-white dairy cattle. [from *Ayrshire,* former Scot. county]

azalea (ə'zeɪljə) *n* an ericaceous plant cultivated for its showy pink or purple flowers. [C18: via NL from Gk, from *azaleos* dry; from its supposed preference for a dry situation]

azeotrope (ə'ziːə,trəʊp) *n* a mixture of liquids that boils at a constant temperature, at a given pressure, without change of composition. [C20: from A-[1] + *zeo-,* from Gk *zein* to boil + -TROPE]

▸**azeotropic** (,eɪzɪə'trɒpɪk) *adj*

azerty *or* **AZERTY keyboard** (ə'zɜːtɪ) *n* a common European version of typewriter keyboard layout with the characters a, z, e, r, t, and y positioned at the top left of the keyboard.

azide ('eɪzaɪd) *n* **a** an acyl derivative or salt of hydrazoic acid, used as a coating to enhance electron emission. **b** (*as modifier*): *an azide group or radical.*

Azilian (ə'zɪlɪən) *n* **1** a Palaeolithic culture of Spain and SW France that can be dated to the 10th millennium B.C., characterized by flat bone harpoons and schematically painted pebbles. ◆ *adj* **2** of or relating to this culture. [C19: after Mas d'*Azil,* France, where artefacts were found]

azimuth ('æzɪməθ) *n* **1** *Astron., navigation.* the angular distance usually measured clockwise from the south point of the horizon in astronomy or from the north point in navigation to the intersection with the horizon of the vertical circle passing through a celestial body. **2** *Surveying.* the horizontal angle of a bearing clockwise from north. [C14: from OF *azimut,* from Ar. *as-sumūt,* pl. of *as-samt* the path, from L *semita* path]

▸**azimuthal** (,æzɪ'mʌθəl) *adj*

azine ('eɪziːn) *n* an organic compound having a six-membered ring with at least one nitrogen atom, the other atoms in the ring being carbon atoms.

azo ('eɪzəʊ, 'æ-) *adj* of, consisting of, or containing the divalent group -N:N-: *an azo group or radical.* See also **diazo.** [from F *azote* nitrogen, from Gk *azōos* lifeless]

azoic (ə'zəʊɪk) *adj* without life; characteristic of the ages that have left no evidence of life in the form of organic remains. [C19: from Gk *azōos* lifeless]

AZT *abbrev. for* azidothymidine: another name for **zidovudine.**

Aztec ('æztɛk) *n* **1** a member of a Mexican Indian people who established a great empire, centred on the valley of Mexico, that was overthrown by Cortés in the early 16th century. **2** the language of the Aztecs. See also **Nahuatl.** ◆ *adj also* **Aztecan. 3** of, relating to, or characteristic of the Aztecs, their civilization, or their language. [C18: from Sp., from Nahuatl *Aztecatl,* from *Aztlan,* their traditional place of origin, lit.: near the cranes]

azure ❶ ('æʒə, 'eɪ-) *n* **1** a deep blue similar to the colour of a clear blue sky. **2** *Poetic.* a clear blue sky. ◆ *adj* **3** of the colour azure. **4** (*usually postpositive*) *Heraldry.* of the colour blue. [C14: from OF, from OSp., from Ar. *lāzaward* lapis lazuli, from Persian *lāzhuward*]

azurite ('æʒʊ,raɪt) *n* a deep blue mineral consisting of hydrated basic copper carbonate. It is used as an ore of copper and as a gemstone.

azygous ('æzɪgəs) *adj Biol.* developing or occurring singly. [C17: via NL from Gk *azugos,* from A-[1] + *zugon* YOKE]

THESAURUS

axle *n* = **shaft,** arbor, axis, mandrel, pin, pivot, rod, spindle

azure *adj* **3** = **sky-blue,** blue, cerulean, clear blue, sky-coloured, ultramarine

Bb

b *or* **B** (biː) *n, pl* **b's, B's,** *or* **Bs. 1** the second letter of the English alphabet. **2** a speech sound represented by this letter **3** Also: **beta.** the second in a series, class, or rank.

B *symbol for:* **1** *Music.* **1a** the seventh note of the scale of C major. **1b** the major or minor key having this note as its tonic. **2** the less important of two things. **3** a human blood type of the ABO group, containing the B antigen. **4** (in Britain) a secondary road. **5** *Chem.* boron. **6** magnetic flux density. **7** *Chess.* bishop. **8** (on Brit. pencils, signifying degree of softness of lead) black. **9** Also: **b** *Physics.* bel. **10** *Physics.* baryon number. **11a** a person whose job is in middle management, or who holds an intermediate administrative or professional position. **11b** (*as modifer*): *a B worker.* ◆ See also **occupation groupings.**

b. *abbrev. for:* **1** born. **2** *Cricket.* **2a** bowled. **2b** bye.

b. *or* **B.** *abbrev. for:* **1** *Music.* bass *or* basso. **2** billion. **3** book. **4** breadth.

B. *abbrev. for:* **1** (on maps, etc.) bay. **2** Bible.

B- (of US military aircraft) *abbrev. for* bomber.

Ba the chemical symbol for barium.

BA *abbrev. for:* **1** Bachelor of Arts. **2** British Academy. **3** British Airways. **4** British Association (for the Advancement of Science). **5** British Association screw thread.

baa (bɑː) *vb* **baas, baaing, baaed. 1** (*intr*) to make the cry of a sheep; bleat. ◆ *n* **2** the cry made by sheep.

BAA *abbrev. for* British Airports Authority.

Baader-Meinhof Gang (*German* ˈbaːdər ˈmainhoːf) *n* **the.** a group of West German guerrillas dedicated to the violent overthrow of capitalist society. Also called: **Red Army Faction.** [C20: named after its leading members, Andreas *Baader* (1943–77) and Ulrike *Meinhof* (1934–76).

baas (bɑːs) *n* a South African word for **boss**[1] (sense 1): used by Africans and Coloured people in addressing European managers or overseers. [C17: from Afrik., from MDu. *baes* master]

baaskap *or* **baasskap** (ˈbɑːsˌkap) *n* (*sometimes cap.*) (in South Africa) control by Whites of non-Whites. [from Afrik., from BAAS + *-skap* -SHIP]

baba (ˈbɑːbɑː) *n* a small cake, usually soaked in rum (**rum baba**). [C19: from F, from Polish, lit.: old woman]

babalas (ˈbæbəˌlæs) *n S. African.* a hangover. [from Zulu *ibhabhalasi*]

babbitt (ˈbæbɪt) *vb* (*tr*) to line (a bearing) or face (a surface) with Babbitt metal.

Babbitt (ˈbæbɪt) *n US derog.* a narrow-minded and complacent member of the middle class. [C20: after George *Babbitt,* central character in the novel *Babbitt* (1922) by Sinclair Lewis]
▸ **ˈBabbittry** *n*

Babbitt metal *n* any of a number of alloys originally based on tin, antimony, and copper but now often including lead: used esp. in bearings. [C19: after Isaac *Babbitt* (1799–1862), US inventor]

babble Ⓣ (ˈbæbəl) *vb* **babbles, babbling, babbled. 1** to utter (words, sounds, etc.) in an incoherent jumble. **2** (*intr*) to talk foolishly, incessantly, or irrelevantly. **3** (*tr*) to disclose (secrets, etc.) carelessly. **4** (*intr*) (of streams, birds, etc.) to make a low murmuring sound. ◆ *n* **5** incoherent or foolish speech. **6** a murmuring sound. [C13: prob. imit.]

babbler (ˈbæblə) *n* **1** a person or thing that babbles. **2** any of various birds of the Old World tropics and subtropics having an incessant song.

babe Ⓣ (beɪb) *n* **1** a baby. **2** *Inf.* a naive or gullible person. **3** *Sl.* a girl or young woman, esp. an attractive one.

Babel Ⓣ (ˈbeɪbəl) *n* **1** *Old Testament.* Also called: **Tower of Babel.** a tower presumptuously intended to reach from earth to heaven, the building of which was frustrated when Jehovah confused the language of the builders (Genesis 11:1–10). **2** (*often not cap.*) **2a** a confusion of noises or voices. **2b** a scene of noise and confusion. [from Heb. *Bābhél,* from Akkadian *Bāb-ilu,* lit.: gate of God]

babirusa (ˌbɑːbɪˈruːsə) *n* a wild pig of Indonesia. It has an almost hairless wrinkled skin and enormous curved canine teeth. [C17: from Malay, from *bābī* hog + *rūsa* deer]

Babism (ˈbɑːbɪzəm) *n* a pantheistic Persian religious sect, founded in 1844, forbidding polygamy, concubinage, begging, trading in slaves, and indulgence in alcohol and drugs. [C19: from the *Bab,* title of Mirza Ali Mohammed (1819–50), Persian religious leader]

baboon (bəˈbuːn) *n* any of several medium-sized Old World monkeys. They have an elongated muzzle, large teeth, and a fairly long tail. [C14 *babewyn* gargoyle, later, baboon, from OF]

babu (ˈbɑːbuː) *n* (in India) **1** a form of address more or less equivalent to *Mr.* **2** (formerly) an Indian clerk who could write English. [Hindi, lit.: father]

babushka (bəˈbuːʃkə) *n* **1** a headscarf tied under the chin, worn by Russian peasant women. **2** (in Russia) an old woman. [Russian: grandmother, from *baba* old woman]

baby Ⓣ (ˈbeɪbɪ) *n, pl* **babies. 1a** a newborn child; infant. **1b** (*as modifier*): *baby food.* **2** an unborn child; fetus. **3** the youngest or smallest of a family or group. **4** a newborn or recently born animal. **5** *Usually derog.* an immature person. **6** *Sl.* a young woman or sweetheart. **7** a project of personal concern. **8 be left holding the baby.** to be left with the responsibility. ◆ *adj* **9** (*prenominal*) comparatively small of its type: *a baby car.* ◆ *vb* **babies, babying, babied. 10** (*tr*) to treat with love and attention. **11** to treat (someone) like a baby; pamper or overprotect. [C14: prob. childish reduplication]
▸ **ˈbabyˌhood** *n* ▸ **ˈbabyish** *adj*

baby bonus *n Canad. inf.* Family Allowance.

baby boomer *n* a person born during a **baby boom,** a sharp increase in the birth rate, esp. (in Britain and the US) one born during the years 1945–55.

baby buggy *n* **1** *Brit. Trademark.* a child's pushchair. **2** *US & Canad. inf.* a small pram.

baby carriage *n* the US and Canad. name for **pram**[1].

Babylon (ˈbæbɪlən) *n* **1** *Derog.* (in Protestant polemic) the Roman Catholic Church, regarded as the seat of luxury and corruption. **2** *Derog.* any society or group in a society considered as corrupt or as a place of exile by another society or group, esp. White Britain as viewed by Rastafarians. [via L and Gk from Heb. *Bābhel;* see BABEL]
▸ **Babylonian** (bæbɪˈləunɪən) *adj n*

baby-sit *vb* **baby-sits, baby-sitting, baby-sat.** (*intr*) to act or work as a baby-sitter.
▸ **ˈbaby-ˌsitting** *n, adj*

baby-sitter *n* a person who takes care of a child or children while the parents are out.

baby snatcher *n Inf.* **1** a person who steals a baby from its pram. **2** someone who marries or has an affair with a much younger person.

baby wipe *n* a disposable moistened medicated paper towel used for cleaning babies.

baccalaureate (ˌbækəˈlɔːrɪɪt) *n* the university degree of Bachelor of Arts. [C17: from Med. L *baccalaureātus,* from *baccalaureus* advanced student from *baccalārius* BACHELOR]

baccarat (ˈbækəˌrɑː; ˌbækəˈrɑː) *n* a card game in which two or more punters gamble against the banker. [C19: from F *baccara* from ?]

baccate (ˈbækeɪt) *adj Bot.* **1** like a berry. **2** bearing berries. [C19: from L *bāca* berry]

bacchanal Ⓣ (ˈbækənəl) *n* **1** a follower of Bacchus, Greek god of wine. **2** a drunken and riotous celebration. **3** a participant in such a celebration. ◆ *adj* **4** of or relating to Bacchus. [C16: from L *Bacchānālis*]

bacchanalia (ˌbækəˈneɪlɪə) *pl n* **1** (*often cap.*) orgiastic rites associated with Bacchus. **2** any drunken revelry.
▸ **ˌbacchaˈnalian** *adj, n*

bacchant (ˈbækənt) *or* (*fem*) **bacchante** (bəˈkæntɪ) *n, pl* **bacchants** *or* **bacchantes** (bəˈkæntɪz). **1** a priest, priestess, or votary of Bacchus. **2** a drunken reveller. [C17: from L *bacchāns,* from *bacchārī* to celebrate the BACCHANALIA]

Bacchic (ˈbækɪk) *adj* **1** of or relating to Bacchus, the Greek and Roman god of wine. **2** (*often not cap.*) riotously drunk.

baccy (ˈbækɪ) *n* a Brit. informal name for **tobacco.**

bach (bætʃ) *NZ.* ◆ *n* **1** a seaside, bush, or country cottage. ◆ *vb* **2** a variant spelling of **batch**[2].

bachelor (ˈbætʃələ, ˈbætʃlə) *n* **1a** an unmarried man. **1b** (*as modifier*): *a bachelor flat.* **2** a person who holds the degree of Bachelor of Arts, Bachelor of Education, Bachelor of Science, etc. **3** (in the Middle Ages) a young knight serving a great noble. **4 bachelor seal.** a young male seal that has not yet mated. [C13: from OF *bacheler* youth, squire, from Vulgar L *baccalāris* (unattested) farm worker]
▸ **ˈbachelorˌhood** *n*

bachelor girl *n* a young unmarried woman, esp. one who is self-supporting.

Bachelor of Arts *n* **1** a degree conferred on a person who has successfully completed undergraduate studies in the liberal arts or humanities. **2** a person who holds this degree.

Bachelor of Science *n* **1** a degree conferred on a person who has suc-

THESAURUS

babble *vb* **1** = **gibber,** gurgle **2** = **gabble,** burble, chatter, jabber, prate, prattle, rabbit (on) (*Brit. inf.*), waffle (*inf., chiefly Brit.*) **3** = **blab,** run off at the mouth (*sl.*) ◆ *n* **5** = **gabble,** burble, drivel, gibberish, waffle (*inf., chiefly Brit.*)

babe *n* **1** = **baby,** ankle-biter (*Austral. sl.*), bairn (*Scot.*), child, infant, nursling, rug rat (*sl.*), sprog (*sl.*), suckling **2** *Informal* = **innocent,** babe in arms, ingénue *or (masc.)* ingénu

Babel *n, often not cap.* **2** = **din,** bedlam, clamour, confusion, disorder, hubbub, hullabaloo, hurly-burly, pandemonium, tumult, turmoil, uproar

baby *n* **1** = **infant,** ankle-biter (*Austral. sl.*), babe, babe in arms, bairn (*Scot.*), child, newborn child, rug rat (*sl.*), sprog (*sl.*) ◆ *adj* **9** = **small,** diminutive, dwarf, little, midget, mini, miniature, minute, pygmy *or* pigmy, teensy-weensy, teeny-weeny, tiny, wee ◆ *vb* **11** = **mollycoddle,** coddle, cosset, humour, indulge, overindulge, pamper, pet, spoil, spoon-feed

babyish *adj* **5** = **childish,** foolish, immature, infantile, juvenile, puerile
Antonyms *adj* adult, grown-up, mature, of age

bacchanal *n* **2** = **orgy,** debauch, debauchery, revel, revelry **3** = **reveller,** carouser, debauchee, drunkard, roisterer, winebibber

cessfully completed undergraduate studies in a science. **2** a person who holds this degree.

bachelor's-buttons *n* (*functioning as sing or pl*) any of various plants with button-like flower heads, esp. a double-flowered buttercup.

Bach flower remedy (bɑːx) *n Trademark*. an alternative medicine consisting of a distillation from various flowers, supposed to counteract negative states of mind and restore emotional balance. [C20: after Dr E. *Bach* (1886–1936), homeopath who developed this system]

bacillary (bəˈsɪlərɪ) *or* **bacillar** (bəˈsɪlə) *adj* **1** of, relating to, or caused by bacilli. **2** Also: **bacilliform** (bəˈsɪlɪˌfɔːm). shaped like a short rod.

bacillus (bəˈsɪləs) *n, pl* **bacilli** (-ˈsɪlaɪ). **1** any rod-shaped bacterium. **2** any of various rodlike spore-producing bacteria constituting the family Bacillaceae. [C19: from L, from *baculum* walking stick]

back ❶ (bæk) *n* **1** the posterior part of the human body, from the neck to the pelvis. **2** the corresponding or upper part of an animal. **3** the spinal column. **4** the part or side of an object opposite the front. **5** the part or side of anything less often seen or used. **6** the part or side of anything that is furthest from the front or from a spectator: *the back of the stage.* **7** something that supports, covers, or strengthens the rear of an object. **8** *Ball games.* **8a** a mainly defensive player behind a forward. **8b** the position of such a player. **9** the part of a book to which the pages are glued or that joins the covers. **10 at the back of one's mind.** not in one's conscious thoughts. **11 back of Bourke.** *Austral.* a remote or backward place. **12 behind one's back.** secretly or deceitfully. **13 break one's back.** to overwork or work very hard. **14 break the back of.** to complete the greatest or hardest part of (a task). **15 get off someone's back.** *Inf.* to stop criticizing or pestering someone. **16 put one's back into.** to devote all one's strength to (a task). **17 put** (*or* **get**) **someone's back up.** to annoy someone. **18 the back of beyond.** a very remote place. **19 turn one's back on. 19a** to turn away from in anger or contempt. **19b** to refuse to help; abandon. ◆ *vb* (*mainly tr*) **20** (*also intr*) to move or cause to move backwards. **21 back water.** to reverse the direction of a boat, esp. to push the oars of a rowing boat. **22** to provide support, money, or encouragement for (a person, enterprise, etc.). **23** to bet on the success of: *to back a horse.* **24** to provide with a back, backing, or lining. **25** to provide with a musical accompaniment. **26** to countersign or endorse. **27** (*intr;* foll. by *on* or *onto*) to have the back facing (towards): *the house backs onto a river.* **28** (*intr*) (of the wind) to change direction anticlockwise. Cf. **veer** (sense 3). ◆ *adj* (*prenominal*) **29** situated behind: *a back lane.* **30** of the past: *back issues of a magazine.* **31** owing from an earlier date: *back rent.* **32** remote: *a back road.* **33** *Phonetics.* of or denoting a vowel articulated with the tongue retracted towards the soft palate, as for the vowels in English *hard, fall, hot, full, fool.* ◆ *adv* **34** at, to, or towards the rear; behind. **35** in, to, or towards the original starting point, place, or condition: *to go back home; put the book back.* **36** in or into the past: *to look back on one's childhood.* **37** in reply, repayment, or retaliation: *to hit someone back.* **38** in check: *the dam holds back the water.* **39** in concealment; in reserve: *to keep something back.* **40 back and forth.** to and fro. **41 back to front. 41a** in reverse. **41b** in disorder. ◆ See also **back down, back off, back out, back up.** [OE *bæc*]

backbencher (ˈbækˈbɛntʃə) *n Brit., Austral., NZ., etc.* a Member of Parliament who does not hold office in the government or opposition.

backbite ❶ (ˈbækˌbaɪt) *vb* **backbites, backbiting, backbit; backbitten** *or* **backbit.** to talk spitefully about (an absent person).
▸ **ˈbackˌbiter** *n*

backboard (ˈbækˌbɔːd) *n* **1** a board that is placed behind something to form or support its back. **2** a board worn to straighten or support the back, as after surgery. **3** (in basketball) a flat upright surface supported on a high frame, under which the basket is attached.

back boiler *n* a tank or series of pipes at the back of a fireplace for heating water.

backbone ❶ (ˈbækˌbəʊn) *n* **1** a nontechnical name for **spinal column. 2** something that resembles the spinal column in function, position, or appearance. **3** strength of character; courage.

backbreaking ❶ (ˈbækˌbreɪkɪŋ) *adj* exhausting.

backburn (ˈbækˌbɜːn) *Austral. & NZ.* ◆ *vb* **1** (*tr*) to clear (an area of scrub, bush, etc.) by creating a new fire that burns in the opposite direction to the line of advancing fire. ◆ *n* **2** the act or result of backburning.

back-calculate *vb* **back-calculates, back-calculating, back-calculated.** to estimate (the probable amount of alcohol in a person's blood) at an earlier time than that at which the blood test was taken, based on an average rate at which alcohol leaves the bloodstream: used to determine whether a driver had more than the legal limit of alcohol at the time of an accident.
▸ **ˈback-ˌcalcuˈlation** *n*

back catalogue *n* the recordings that a musician has made in the past, as distinct from his or her current recording: *favourites from his back catalogue.*

backchat ❶ (ˈbækˌtʃæt) *n Inf.* the act of answering back, esp. impudently.

backcloth (ˈbækˌklɒθ) *n* a painted curtain at the back of a stage set. Also called: **backdrop.**

backcomb (ˈbækˌkəʊm) *vb* to comb the under layers of (the hair) towards the roots to give more bulk to a hairstyle. Also: **tease.**

back country *n Austral. & NZ.* land remote from settled areas.

backdate (ˌbækˈdeɪt) *vb* **backdates, backdating, backdated.** (*tr*) to make effective from an earlier date.

back door *n* **1** a door at the rear or side of a building. **2** a means of entry to a job, etc., that is secret or obtained through influence.

back down ❶ *vb* **1** (*intr, adv*) to withdraw an earlier claim. ◆ *n* **backdown. 2** abandonment of an earlier claim.

backed (bækt) *adj* **a** having a back or backing. **b** (*in combination*): *high-backed; black-backed.*

backer ❶ (ˈbækə) *n* **1** a person who gives financial or other support. **2** a person who bets on a competitor or contestant.

backfield (ˈbækˌfiːld) *n American football.* **1** (usually preceded by *the*) the quarterback and running backs in a team. **2** the area behind the line of scrimmage from which the backfield begin each play.

backfill (ˈbækˌfɪl) *vb* (*tr*) to refill an excavated trench, esp. (in archaeology) at the end of an investigation.

backfire ❶ (ˌbækˈfaɪə) *vb* **backfires, backfiring, backfired.** (*intr*) **1** (of an internal-combustion engine) to emit a loud noise as a result of an explosion in the exhaust system. **2** to fail to have the desired effect, and, instead, recoil upon the originator. **3** to start a controlled fire in order to halt an advancing forest or prairie fire by creating a barren area. ◆ *n* **4** (in an internal-combustion engine) an explosion of unburnt gases in the exhaust system. **5** a controlled fire started to create a barren area that will halt an advancing forest or prairie fire.

back formation *n* **1** the invention of a new word on the assumption that a familiar word is derived from it. The verbs *edit* and *burgle* in English were so created from *editor* and *burglar.* **2** a word formed by this process.

backgammon (ˈbækˌɡæmən) *n* **1** a game for two people played on a board with pieces moved according to throws of the dice. **2** the most complete form of win in this game. [C17: BACK + *gammon,* var. of GAME[1]]

background ❶ (ˈbækˌɡraʊnd) *n* **1** the part of a scene furthest from the viewer. **2a** an inconspicuous or unobtrusive position (esp. in **in the background**). **2b** (*as modifier*): *a background influence.* **3** the plane or ground in a picture upon which all other planes or forms appear superimposed. **4** a person's social class, education, or experience. **5a** the circumstances that lead up to or help to explain something. **5b** (*as modifier*): *background information.* **6a** a low level of sound, lighting, etc., whose purpose is to be an unobtrusive accompaniment to something else. **6b** (*as modifier*): *background music.* **7** Also called: **background radiation.** *Physics.* low-intensity radiation from small amounts of radioisotopes in soil, air, etc. **8** *Electronics.* unwanted effects, such as noise, occurring in a measuring instrument, electronic device, etc.

backhand (ˈbækˌhænd) *n* **1** *Tennis, etc.* a stroke made across the body with the back of the hand facing the direction of the stroke. **2** the side on which backhand strokes are made. **3** handwriting slanting to the left. ◆ *adv* **4** with a backhand stroke.

backhanded ❶ (ˌbækˈhændɪd) *adj* **1** (of a blow, shot, etc.) performed with the arm moving across the body. **2** double-edged; equivocal: *a backhanded compliment.* **3** (of handwriting) slanting to the left. ◆ *adv* **4** in a backhanded manner.

THESAURUS

back *n* **1, 2** = **rear**, backside, end, hind part, hindquarters, posterior **4** = **end**, far end, reverse, stern, tail end **12 behind one's back** = **secretly**, covertly, deceitfully, sneakily, surreptitiously ◆ *vb* **22** = **support**, abet, advocate, assist, champion, countenance, encourage, endorse, espouse, favour, finance, promote, sanction, second, side with, sponsor, subsidize, sustain, underwrite ◆ *adj* **29** = **rear**, end, hind, hindmost, posterior, tail **30** = **previous**, earlier, former, past **31** = **overdue**, delayed, elapsed

Antonyms *n* ≠ **rear:** face, fore, front, head ◆ *vb* ≠ **support:** attack, combat, hinder, thwart, undermine, weaken ◆ *adj* ≠ **rear:** advance, fore, front ≠ **previous:** future

backbite *vb* = **slander**, abuse, bad-mouth (*sl., chiefly US & Canad.*), calumniate, defame, denigrate, detract, disparage, knock (*inf.*), libel, malign, revile, rubbish (*inf.*), slag (off) (*sl.*), traduce, vilify, vituperate

backbiting *n* = **slander**, abuse, aspersion, bitchiness (*sl.*), calumniation, calumny, cattiness (*inf.*), defamation, denigration, detraction, disparagement, gossip, malice, maligning, scandalmongering, spite, spitefulness, vilification, vituperation

backbone *n* **1** = **spinal column**, spine, vertebrae, vertebral column **2** = **foundation**, basis, mainstay, support **3** = **strength of character**, bottle (*Brit. sl.*), character, courage, determination, firmness, fortitude, grit, hardihood, mettle, moral fibre, nerve, pluck, resolution, resolve, stamina, steadfastness, tenacity, toughness, will, willpower

backbreaking *adj* = **exhausting**, arduous, crushing, gruelling, hard, killing, laborious, punishing, strenuous, toilsome, wearing, wearying

backchat *n Informal* = **cheek**, answering back, impertinence, impudence, insolence, lip (*sl.*), sass (*US & Canad. inf.*), talking back, verbals (*Brit. sl.*)

back down *vb* **1** = **give in**, accede, admit defeat, back-pedal, cave in (*inf.*), concede, surrender, withdraw, yield

backer *n* **1** = **supporter**, advocate, angel (*inf.*), benefactor, patron, promoter, second, sponsor, subscriber, underwriter, well-wisher

backfire *vb* **2** = **fail**, boomerang, disappoint, flop (*inf.*), miscarry, rebound, recoil

background *n* **4** = **credentials**, breeding, culture, education, environment, experience, grounding, milieu, preparation, qualifications, tradition, upbringing **5** = **history**, circumstances

backhanded *adj* **2** = **ambiguous**, double-edged, equivocal, indirect, ironic, oblique, sarcastic, sardonic, two-edged, with tongue in cheek

backhander ('bæk,hændə) *n* **1** a backhanded stroke or blow. **2** *Inf.* an indirect attack. **3** *Sl.* a bribe.

backing ❶ ('bækɪŋ) *n* **1** support. **2** a body of supporters. **3** something that forms, protects, or strengthens the back of something. **4** musical accompaniment, esp. for a pop singer. **5** *Meteorol.* an anticlockwise change in wind direction.

backing dog *n NZ.* a dog that moves a flock of sheep by jumping on their backs.

backlash ❶ ('bæk,læʃ) *n* **1** a sudden and adverse reaction. **2** a reaction or recoil between interacting worn or badly fitting parts in a mechanism. **3** the excessive play between such parts.

backlog ❶ ('bæk,lɒg) *n* an accumulation of uncompleted work, unsold stock, etc., to be dealt with.

back marker *n* a competitor who is at the back of a field in a race.

back matter *n* the parts of a book, such as the index and appendices, that follow the text.

backmost ('bæk,məʊst) *adj* furthest back.

back number *n* **1** an issue of a newspaper, magazine, etc., that appeared on a previous date. **2** *Inf.* a person or thing considered to be old-fashioned.

back off ❶ *vb* (*adv*) *Inf.* **1** (*intr*) to retreat. **2** (*tr*) to abandon (an intention, objective, etc.).

back out ❶ *vb* (*intr, adv;* often foll. by *of*) to withdraw (from an agreement, etc.).

backpack ('bæk,pæk) *n* **1** a rucksack. **2** a pack carried on the back of an astronaut, containing oxygen cylinders, etc. ◆ *vb* (*intr*) **3** to travel about with a backpack.

back passage *n* the rectum.

back-pedal *vb* **back-pedals, back-pedalling, back-pedalled** *or US* **back-pedals, back-pedaling, back-pedaled.** (*intr*) **1** to turn the pedals of a bicycle backwards. **2** to retract or modify a previous opinion, principle, etc.

back projection *n* a method of projecting pictures onto a translucent screen so that they are viewed from the opposite side, used esp. in films to create the illusion that the actors in the foreground are moving.

back room *n* **a** a place where important and usually secret research or planning is done. **b** (*as modifier*): *back-room boys.*

back seat *n* **1** a seat at the back, esp. of a vehicle. **2** *Inf.* a subordinate or inconspicuous position (esp. in **take a back seat**).

back-seat driver *n Inf.* **1** a passenger in a car who offers unwanted advice to the driver. **2** a person who offers advice on or tries to direct matters that are not his or her concern.

backsheesh ('bækʃiːʃ) *n* a variant spelling of **baksheesh.**

back shift *n Brit.* **1** a group of workers who work a shift from late afternoon to midnight in an industry or occupation where a day or a night shift is also worked. **2** the period worked. ◆ US and Canad. name: **swing shift.**

backside ❶ (,bæk'saɪd) *n Inf.* the buttocks.

backslide ❶ (,bæk'slaɪd) *vb* **backslides, backsliding, backslid.** (*intr*) to relapse into former bad habits.
▸ **,back'slider** *n*

backspace ('bæk,speɪs) *vb* **backspaces, backspacing, backspaced.** to move (a typewriter carriage, etc.) backwards.

backspin ('bæk,spɪn) *n Sport.* a backward spin imparted to a ball to reduce its speed at impact.

backstage (,bæk'steɪdʒ) *adv* **1** behind the part of the theatre in view of the audience. **2** towards the rear of the stage. ◆ *adj* **3** situated backstage. **4** *Inf.* away from public view.

backstairs (,bæk'steəz) *pl n* **1** a secondary staircase in a house, esp. one originally for the use of servants. ◆ *adj also* **backstair. 2** underhand: *backstairs gossip.*

backstay ('bæk,steɪ) *n Naut.* a stay leading aft from the upper mast to the deck or stern.

backstreet ('bæk,striːt) *n* **1** a street in a town remote from the main roads. **2** (*modifier*) denoting illicit activities regarded as likely to take place in such a street: *a backstreet abortion.*

backstroke ('bæk,strəʊk) *n Swimming.* a stroke performed on the back, using backward circular strokes of each arm and flipper movements of the feet. Also called: **back crawl.**

back-to-back *adj* (*usually postpositive*) **1** facing in opposite directions, often with the backs touching. **2** *Chiefly Brit.* (of urban houses) built so that their backs are joined or separated only by a narrow alley.

backtrack ❶ ('bæk,træk) *vb* (*intr*) **1** to return by the same route by which one has come. **2** to retract or reverse one's opinion, policy, etc.

back up ❶ *vb* (*adv*) **1** (*tr*) to support. **2** (*intr*) *Cricket.* (of a nonstriking batsman) to move down the wicket in readiness for a run as a ball is bowled. **3** (of water) to accumulate. **4** (of traffic) to become jammed behind an accident or other obstruction. **5** *Computing.* to make a copy of (a data file), esp. as a security copy. **6** (*intr;* usually foll. by *on*) *Austral.* to repeat an action immediately. ◆ *n* **backup. 7** a support or reinforcement. **8a** a substitute. **8b** (*as modifier*): *a backup copy.* **9** the overflow from a blocked drain or pipe.

backward ❶ ('bækwəd) *adj* **1** (*usually prenominal*) directed towards the rear: *a backward glance.* **2** retarded in physical, material, or intellectual development. **3a** conservative or reactionary. **3b** (*in combination*): *backward-looking.* **4** reluctant or bashful: *a backward lover.* ◆ *adv* **5** a variant of **backwards.**
▸ **'backwardness** *n*

backwardation (,bækwə'deɪʃən) *n* **1** the difference between the spot price for a commodity, including rent and interest, and the forward price. **2** (formerly, on the Stock Exchange) postponement of delivery by a seller of securities until the next settlement period.

backwards ❶ ('bækwədz) *or* **backward** *adv* **1** towards the rear. **2** with the back foremost. **3** in the reverse of usual order or direction. **4** to or towards the past. **5** into a worse state. **6** towards the point of origin. **7 bend, lean,** *or* **fall over backwards.** *Inf.* to make a special effort, esp. in order to please.

backwash ('bæk,wɒʃ) *n* **1** water washed backwards by the motion of oars or other propelling devices. **2** the backward flow of air set up by aircraft engines. **3** a repercussion.

backwater ('bæk,wɔːtə) *n* **1** a body of stagnant water connected to a river. **2** an isolated or backward place or condition.

backwoods ❶ ('bækwʊdz) *pl n* **1** partially cleared, sparsely populated forests. **2** any remote sparsely populated place. **3** (*modifier*) of or like the backwoods. **4** (*modifier*) uncouth; rustic.
▸ **'back,woodsman** *n*

backword ('bæk,wɜːd) *n Dialect.* a failure to keep a promise.

back yard *n* **1** a yard at the back of a house, etc. **2 in one's own back yard. 2a** close at hand. **2b** involving or implicating one.

baclava ('bɑːklə,vɑː) *n* a variant spelling of **baklava.**

bacon ('beɪkən) *n* **1** meat from the back and sides of a pig, dried, salted, and usually smoked. **2 bring home the bacon.** *Inf.* **2a** to achieve success. **2b** to provide material support. **3 save (someone's) bacon.** *Brit. inf.* to help (someone) to escape from danger. [C12: from OF *bacon,* from OHG *bahho*]

Baconian (beɪ'kəʊnɪən) *adj* **1** of or relating to Francis Bacon (1561–1626), English philosopher, or his inductive method of reasoning. ◆ *n* **2** a follower of Bacon's philosophy. **3** one who believes that plays attributed to Shakespeare were written by Bacon.

BACS (bæks) *n acronym for* Bankers Automated Clearing System; a method of making payments direct to a creditor's bank without using a cheque.

bacteria ❶ (bæk'tɪərɪə) *pl n, sing* **bacterium.** a large group of typically unicellular microorganisms, many of which cause disease. [C19: NL, from Gk *baktērion,* from *baktron* rod, staff]
▸ **bac'terial** *adj* ▸ **bac'terially** *adv*

bactericide (bæk'tɪərɪ,saɪd) *n* a substance able to destroy bacteria.
▸ **bac,teri'cidal** *adj*

bacterio-, bacteri-, *or sometimes before a vowel* **bacter-** *combining form.* indicating bacteria or an action or condition relating to bacteria: *bacteriology; bactericide.*

bacteriology (bæk,tɪərɪ'ɒlədʒɪ) *n* the study of bacteria.
▸ **bacteriological** (bæk,tɪərɪə'lɒdʒɪkᵊl) *adj* ▸ **bac,teri'ologist** *n*

THESAURUS

backing *n* **1 = support,** abetment, accompaniment, advocacy, aid, assistance, championing, encouragement, endorsement, espousal, funds, grant, moral support, patronage, promotion, sanction, seconding, sponsorship, subsidy

backlash *n* **1 = reaction,** backfire, boomerang, counteraction, repercussion, resentment, resistance, response, retaliation, retroaction **2 = recoil,** counterblast, kickback, reaction

backlog *n* **= build-up,** accumulation, excess, hoard, reserve, reserves, resources, stock, supply

back off *vb* **1 = move back,** backtrack, go back, regress, retire, retreat, reverse, turn tail, withdraw advance, approach, move forward, progress

back out *vb* **= withdraw,** abandon, cancel, chicken out, cop out (*sl.*), give up, go back on, recant, renege, resign, retreat

backside *n Informal* **= buttocks,** arse (*taboo sl.*), ass (*US & Canad. taboo sl.*), behind (*inf.*), bottom, bum (*Brit. sl.*), buns (*US sl.*), butt (*US & Canad. inf.*), coit (*Austral. sl.*), derrière (*euphemistic*), fanny (*sl., chiefly US & Canad.*), jacksy (*Brit. sl.*), keister *or* keester (*sl., chiefly US*), posterior, rear, rear end, rump, seat, tail (*US*)

backslide *vb* **= relapse,** fall from grace, go astray, go wrong, lapse, regress, renege, retrogress, revert, sin, slip, stray, weaken

backslider *n* **= relapser,** apostate, deserter, recidivist, recreant, renegade, reneger, turncoat

backtrack *vb* **1 = retrace one's steps,** back, back-pedal, go back, move back, retreat, reverse **2 = retract,** draw back, eat one's words, recant, retreat, withdraw

back up *vb* **1 = support,** aid, assist, bolster, confirm, corroborate, reinforce, second, stand by, substantiate ◆ *n* **backup 7 = support,** aid, assistance, backing, help, reinforcement, reserves **8 = substitute,** locum, relief, replacement, reserve, second string, stand-by, stand-in, understudy

backward *adj* **2 = slow,** behind, braindead (*inf.*), dead from the neck up (*inf.*), dense, dozy (*Brit. inf.*), dull, obtuse, retarded, stupid, subnormal, underdeveloped, undeveloped ◆ *adv* **5 = towards the rear,** behind, in reverse, rearward
Antonyms *adv* ≠ **towards the rear:** forward, frontward

backwardness *n* **2 = slowness,** arrested development, denseness, doziness (*inf.*), dullness, learning difficulties, retardation, underdevelopment
Antonyms *n* brightness, precociousness, precocity, quickness, smartness

backwards *adv* **1 = towards the rear,** behind, rearward **3 = in reverse**

backwoods *pl n* **2 = sticks** (*inf.*), back country, backlands (*US*), back of beyond, middle of nowhere, outback

bacteria *pl n* **= microorganisms,** bacilli, bugs (*sl.*), germs, microbes, pathogens, viruses

bad[1] *adj* **1 = inferior,** defective, deficient, duff (*Brit. inf.*), erroneous, fallacious, faulty, imper-

bacteriophage (bæk'tɪərɪə,feɪdʒ) *n* a virus that is parasitic in a bacterium and destroys its host. Often shortened to **phage.**
bacterium (bæk'tɪərɪəm) *n* the singular of **bacteria.**
Bactrian camel ('bæktrɪən) *n* a two-humped camel, used in the cold deserts of central Asia. [from *Bactria,* ancient country of SW Asia]
bad[1] (bæd) *adj* **worse, worst. 1** not good; of poor quality; inadequate. **2** (often foll. by *at*) lacking skill or talent; incompetent. **3** (often foll. by *for*) harmful. **4** immoral; evil. **5** naughty; mischievous. **6** rotten; decayed: *a bad egg.* **7** severe; intense: *a bad headache.* **8** incorrect; faulty: *bad pronunciation.* **9** ill or in pain (esp. in **feel bad**). **10** sorry or upset (esp. in **feel bad about**). **11** unfavourable; distressing: *bad news.* **12** offensive; unpleasant: *bad language; bad temper.* **13** not valid or sound: *a bad cheque.* **14** not recoverable: *a bad debt.* **15** (**badder, baddest**) *Sl.* good, excellent. **16 go bad.** to putrefy; spoil. **17 in a bad way.** *Inf.* **17a** seriously ill. **17b** in trouble. **18 make the best of a bad job.** to manage as well as possible in unfavourable circumstances. **19 not bad** *or* **not so bad.** *Inf.* passable; fairly good. **20 too bad.** *Inf.* (often used dismissively) regrettable. ◆ *n* **21** unfortunate or unpleasant events (often in **take the bad with the good**). **22** an immoral or degenerate state (often in **go to the bad**). **23** the debit side of an account: *£200 to the bad.* **24 go from bad to worse.** to deteriorate even more. ◆ *adv* **25** *Not standard.* badly: *to want something bad.* [C13: prob. from *bæd-,* as the first element of OE *bǣddel* hermaphrodite]
▸'**baddish** *adj* ▸'**badness** *n*

USAGE NOTE See at **good.**

bad[2] (bæd) *vb* a variant spelling of **bade.**
bad blood *n* a feeling of intense hatred or hostility; enmity.
baddie *or* **baddy** ('bædɪ) *n, pl* **baddies.** *Inf.* a bad character in a film, etc., esp. an opponent of the hero.
bade (bæd, beɪd) *or* **bad** *vb* past tense of **bid.**
badge (bædʒ) *n* **1** a distinguishing emblem or mark worn to signify membership, employment, achievement, etc. **2** any revealing feature or mark. [C14: from OF *bage*]
badger ('bædʒə) *n* **1** any of various stocky omnivorous mammals occurring in Europe, Asia, and N America. They are large burrowing animals, with strong claws and a thick coat striped black and white on the head. ◆ *vb* **2** (*tr*) to pester or harass. [C16: var. of *badgeard,* prob. from BADGE (from the white mark on its forehead) + -ARD]
bad hair day *n Inf.* **1** a day on which one's hair is untidy and unmanageable. **2** a day of mishaps and general irritation.
badinage ('bædɪ,nɑːʒ) *n* playful or frivolous repartee or banter. [C17: from F, from *badiner* to jest]
badlands ('bæd,lændz) *pl n* any deeply eroded barren area.
badly ('bædlɪ) *adv* **worse, worst. 1** poorly; defectively; inadequately. **2** unfavourably; unsuccessfully: *our scheme worked out badly.* **3** severely; gravely: *badly hurt.* **4** incorrectly or inaccurately: *to speak German badly.* **5** improperly; wickedly: *to behave badly.* **6** cruelly: *to treat badly.* **7** very much (esp. in **need badly, want badly**). **8** regretfully: *he felt badly about it.* **9 badly off.** poor.
badminton ('bædmɪntən) *n* **1** a game played with rackets and a shuttlecock which is hit back and forth across a high net. **2** Also called: **badminton cup.** a long drink of claret with soda water and sugar. [from *Badminton* House, Glos]
bad-mouth *vb* (*tr*) *Sl., chiefly US & Canad.* to speak unfavourably about.
bad-tempered *adj* angry; irritable.
BAe *abbrev. for* British Aerospace.
Baedeker ('beɪdɪkə) *n* any of a series of travel guidebooks issued by the German publisher Karl Baedeker (1801–59) or his firm.
BAF *abbrev. for* British Athletics Federation.
baffle ('bæfᵊl) *vb* **baffles, baffling, baffled.** (*tr*) **1** to perplex; bewilder; puzzle. **2** to frustrate (plans, efforts, etc.). **3** to check, restrain, or regulate (the flow of a fluid or the emission of sound or light). ◆ *n* **4** Also called: **baffle board, baffle plate.** a plate or mechanical device to restrain or regulate the flow of fluid, light, or sound, esp. in a loudspeaker or microphone. [C16: ?from Scot. dialect *bachlen* to condemn publicly]
▸'**bafflement** *n* ▸'**baffler** *n* ▸'**baffling** *adj* ▸'**bafflingly** *adv*
BAFTA ('bæftə) *n acronym for* British Academy of Film and Television Arts.
bag (bæg) *n* **1** a flexible container with an opening at one end. **2** Also: **bagful.** the contents of or amount contained in such a container. **3** a piece of portable luggage. **4** short for **handbag. 5** anything that sags, or is shaped like a bag, such as a loose fold of skin under the eyes. **6** any pouch or sac forming part of the body of an animal. **7** the quantity of quarry taken in a single hunting trip or by a single hunter. **8** *Derog. sl.* an ugly or bad-tempered woman or girl (often in **old bag**). **9 bag and baggage.** *Inf.* **9a** with all one's belongings. **9b** entirely. **10 bag of bones.** a lean creature. **11 in the bag.** *Sl.* almost assured of succeeding or being obtained. **12 rough as bags.** *Austral. sl.* **12a** uncouth. **12b** shoddy. ◆ *vb* **bags, bagging, bagged. 13** (*tr*) to put into a bag. **14** to bulge or cause to bulge. **15** (*tr*) to capture or kill, as in hunting. **16** (*tr*) to catch, seize, or steal. **17** (*intr*) to hang loosely; sag. **18** (*tr*) *Brit. & Austral. inf.* to secure the right to do or to have: *he bagged the best chair.* **19** (*tr*) to achieve or accomplish: *she bagged seven birdies.* ◆ See also **bags.** [C13: prob. from ON *baggi*]
bagasse (bə'gæs) *n* the dry pulp remaining after the extraction of juice from sugar cane or similar plants: used as fuel, for making fibreboard, etc. [C19: from F, from Sp. *bagazo* dregs]
bagatelle (,bægə'tɛl) *n* **1** something of little value. **2** a board game in which balls are struck into holes, with pins as obstacles. **3** a short light piece of music. [C17: from F, from It. *bagattella,* from (dialect) *bagatta* a little possession]
bagel *or* **beigel** ('beɪgᵊl) *n* a hard ring-shaped bread roll. [C20: from Yiddish *beygel*]
baggage ('bægɪdʒ) *n* **1** suitcases, bags, etc., packed for a journey; luggage. **2** an army's portable equipment. **3** *Inf., old-fashioned.* **3a** a pert young woman. **3b** an immoral woman. **4** *Irish inf.* a cantankerous old woman. **5** *Inf.* previous knowledge and experience that a person may use or be influenced by in new circumstances: *cultural baggage.* [C15: from OF *bagage,* from *bague* a bundle]
baggy ('bægɪ) *adj* **baggier, baggiest.** (of clothes) hanging loosely; puffed out.
▸'**baggily** *adv* ▸'**bagginess** *n*
bag lady *n* a homeless woman who wanders city streets with all her possessions in shopping bags.
bagman ('bægmən) *n, pl* **bagmen. 1** *Brit. inf.* a travelling salesman. **2** *Sl., chiefly US.* a person who collects or distributes money for racketeers. **3** *Austral.* a tramp or swagman, esp. one on horseback. **4** *Inf., chiefly Canad.* a person who solicits money for a political party.
bagnio ('bɑːnjəʊ) *n, pl* **bagnios. 1** a brothel. **2** *Obs.* an oriental prison for slaves. **3** *Obs.* an Italian or Turkish bathhouse. [C16: from It. *bagno,* from L *balneum* bath]
bagpipes ('bæg,paɪps) *pl n* any of a family of musical wind instruments in which sounds are produced in reed pipes by air from a bag inflated either by the player's mouth or by arm-operated bellows.
bags (bægz) *pl n* **1** *Inf.* a lot. **2** *Brit. inf.* trousers. ◆ *interj* **3** Also: **bags I.**

THESAURUS

fect, inadequate, incorrect, low-rent (*inf., chiefly US*), of a sort *or* of sorts, pathetic, poor, poxy (*sl.*), substandard, unsatisfactory **3 = harmful,** damaging, dangerous, deleterious, detrimental, hurtful, injurious, ruinous, unhealthy **4 = wicked,** base, corrupt, criminal, delinquent, evil, immoral, mean, sinful, vile, villainous, wrong **5 = naughty,** disobedient, mischievous, unruly **6 = rotten,** decayed, mouldy, off, putrid, rancid, sour, spoiled **7 = severe,** distressing, grave, painful, serious, terrible **9 = ill,** ailing, diseased, sick, unwell **10 = sorry,** apologetic, conscience-stricken, contrite, guilty, regretful, remorseful, sad, upset **11 = unfavourable,** adverse, discouraging, distressing, gloomy, grim, melancholy, troubling, unfortunate, unpleasant **19 not bad** *Informal* **= O.K.** *or* **okay** (*inf.*), all right, average, fair, fair to middling (*inf.*), moderate, passable, respectable, so-so (*inf.*), tolerable
Antonyms *adj* ≠ **inferior:** adequate, fair, satisfactory ≠ **harmful:** agreeable, beneficial, good, healthful, safe, sound, wholesome ≠ **wicked:** ethical, fine, first-rate, good, moral, righteous, virtuous ≠ **naughty:** biddable, docile, good, obedient, well-behaved

bad blood *n* **= ill feeling,** acrimony, anger, animosity, antagonism, dislike, enmity, feud, hatred, ill will, malevolence, malice, rancour, resentment

baddie *n Informal* **= villain,** antihero, bad guy
Antonyms *n* good guy, goody, hero, heroine

badge *n* **1 = mark,** brand, device, emblem, identification, insignia, sign, stamp, token

badger *vb* **2 = pester,** bend someone's ear (*inf.*), bully, chivvy, goad, harass, harry, hound, importune, nag, plague, torment

badinage *n* **= wordplay,** banter, chaff, mockery, pleasantry, repartee, teasing

badly *adv* **1 = poorly,** carelessly, defectively, erroneously, faultily, imperfectly, inadequately, incorrectly, ineptly, shoddily, wrong, wrongly **2 = unfavourably,** unfortunately, unsuccessfully **3 = severely,** acutely, deeply, desperately, gravely, greatly, intensely, painfully, seriously
Antonyms *adv* ≠ **poorly:** ably, competently, correctly, properly, rightly, satisfactorily, splendidly, well

badness *n* **4 = wickedness,** baseness, corruption, delinquency, evil, foulness, immorality, impropriety, meanness, naughtiness, shamefulness, sin, sinfulness, vileness, villainy, wrong
Antonyms *n* excellence, good, goodness, morality, rectitude, righteousness, uprightness, virtue

bad-tempered *adj* **= irritable,** angry, cantankerous, crabbed, cross, crotchety (*inf.*), grouchy (*inf.*), grumbling, huffy, ill-tempered, irascible, peevish, petulant, querulous, ratty (*Brit. & NZ inf.*), sulky, sullen, surly, testy, tetchy
Antonyms *adj* affable, amiable, cheerful, genial, good-humoured, good-tempered, happy, pleasant, sanguine

baffle *vb* **1 = puzzle,** amaze, astound, bewilder, boggle the mind, confound, confuse, daze, disconcert, dumbfound, flummox, mystify, nonplus, perplex, stump, stun **2 = frustrate,** balk, check, defeat, foil, hinder, thwart, upset
Antonyms *vb* ≠ **puzzle:** clarify, clear up, elucidate, explain, explicate, interpret, make plain, shed *or* throw light upon, spell out

baffling *adj* **1 = puzzling,** bewildering, confusing, difficult, enigmatic, inexplicable, mysterious, mystifying, perplexing, strange, unaccountable, unfathomable, weird
Antonyms *adj* clear, easy, intelligible, obvious, simple, understandable

bag *n* **1 = container,** poke (*Scot.*), receptacle, sac, sack ◆ *vb* **14 = bulge,** balloon, droop, sag, swell **15 = catch,** acquire, capture, gain, get, kill, land, shoot, take, trap

baggage *n* **1 = luggage,** bags, belongings, gear, suitcases, things **2 = equipment,** accoutrements, impedimenta, paraphernalia

baggy *adj* **= loose,** billowing, bulging, droopy, floppy, ill-fitting, oversize, roomy, sagging, seated, slack
Antonyms *adj* close, close-fitting, constricted, cramped, narrow, snug, stretched, taut, tight, tight-fitting

Children's sl., Brit. & Austral. an indication of the desire to do, be, or have something.

baguette *or* **baguet** (bæ'gɛt) *n* **1** a narrow French stick loaf. **2** a small gem cut as a long rectangle. **3** *Archit.* a small moulding having a semicircular cross section. [C18: from F, from It. *bacchetta* a little stick, from *bacchio* rod]

bah (bɑː, bæ) *interj* an expression of contempt or disgust.

Bahá'i (bə'hɑːɪ) *n* **1** an adherent of the Bahá'í Faith. ◆ *adj* **2** of or relating to the Bahá'í Faith. [from Persian *bahā'ī*, lit.: of glory]

Bahá'í Faith *or* **Bahí'í** *n* a religious system founded in 1863, based on Babism and emphasizing the value of all religions and the spiritual unity of mankind.

Bahá'ísm (bə'hɑːˌɪzəm) *n* another name, not in Bahá'í use, for the **Bahá'í Faith.**

bail[1] 🅣 (beɪl) *Law.* ◆ *n* **1** a sum of money by which a person is bound to take responsibility for the appearance in court of another person or himself, forfeited if the person fails to appear. **2** the person or persons so binding themselves; surety. **3** the system permitting release of a person from custody where such security has been taken: *he was released on bail.* **4** **jump bail** *or* (*formal*) **forfeit bail.** to fail to appear in court to answer to a charge. **5** **stand** *or* **go bail.** to act as surety (for someone). ◆ *vb* (*tr*) **6** (often foll. by *out*) to release or obtain the release of (a person) from custody, security having been made. [C14: from OF: custody, from *baillier* to hand over, from L *bāiulāre* to carry burdens]

bail[2] 🅣 *or* **bale** (beɪl) *vb* **bails, bailing, bailed** *or* **bales, baling, baled.** (often foll. by *out*) to remove (water) from (a boat). See also **bail out.** [C13: from OF *baille* bucket, from L *bāiulus* carrier]
▸ **'bailer** *or* **'baler** *n*

bail[3] (beɪl) *n* **1** *Cricket.* either of two small wooden bars across the tops of the stumps. **2** a partition between stalls in a stable or barn. **3** *Austral. & NZ.* a framework in a cowshed used to secure the head of a cow during milking. **4** a movable bar on a typewriter that holds the paper against the platen. ◆ *vb* **5** See **bail up.** [C18: from OF *baile* stake, fortification, prob. from L *baculum* stick]

bail[4] *or* **bale** (beɪl) *n* the semicircular handle of a kettle, bucket, etc. [C15: prob. of Scand. origin]

bailey ('beɪlɪ) *n* the outermost wall or court of a castle. [C13: from OF *baille* enclosed court, from *bailler* to enclose]

Bailey bridge ('beɪlɪ) *n* a temporary bridge made of prefabricated steel parts that can be rapidly assembled. [C20: after Sir Donald Coleman *Bailey* (1901–85), its Brit. designer]

bailie ('beɪlɪ) *n* (in Scotland) a municipal magistrate. [C13: from OF *bailli*, from earlier *baillif* BAILIFF]

bailiff ('beɪlɪf) *n* **1** *Brit.* the agent of a landlord or landowner. **2** a sheriff's officer who serves writs and summonses, makes arrests, and ensures that the sentences of the court are carried out. **3** *Chiefly Brit.* (formerly) a high official having judicial powers. **4** *Chiefly US.* an official having custody of prisoners appearing in court. [C13: from OF *baillif*, from *bail* custody; see BAIL[1]]

bailiwick ('beɪlɪwɪk) *n* **1** *Law.* the area over which a bailiff has jurisdiction. **2** a person's special field of interest. [C15: from BAILIE + WICK[2]]

bail out 🅣 *or* **bale out** *vb* (*adv*) **1** (*intr*) to make an emergency parachute jump from an aircraft. **2** (*tr*) *Inf.* to help (a person, organization, etc.) out of a predicament.

bail up *vb* (*adv*) **1** *Austral. & NZ.* to confine (a cow) or (of a cow) to be confined by the head in a bail. See **bail**[3] (sense 3). **2** (*tr*) *Austral.* (of a bushranger) to hold under guard in order to rob. **3** (*intr*) *Austral.* to submit to robbery without offering resistance. **4** (*tr*) *Austral. inf.* to accost or detain, esp. in conversation.

bain-marie *French.* (bɛ̃mari) *n, pl* **bains-marie** (bɛ̃mari). a vessel for holding hot water, in which sauces and other dishes are gently cooked or kept warm. [C19: from F, from Med. L *balneum Mariae*, lit.: bath of Mary, inaccurate translation of Med. Gk *kaminos Marios*, lit.: furnace of *Miriam*, alleged author of a treatise on alchemy]

Bairam (baɪ'ræm, 'baɪræm) *n* either of two Muslim festivals, one (**Lesser Bairam**) at the end of Ramadan, the other (**Greater Bairam**) at the end of the Islamic year. [from Turkish *bayrām*]

bairn (beən) *n Scot. & N English.* a child. [OE *bearn*]

bait[1] 🅣 (beɪt) *n* **1** something edible fixed to a hook or in a trap to attract fish or animals. **2** an enticement; temptation. **3** a variant spelling of **bate**[3]. **4** *Arch.* a short stop for refreshment during a journey. ◆ *vb* **5** (*tr*) to put a piece of food on or in (a hook or trap). **6** (*tr*) to persecute or tease. **7** (*tr*) to entice; tempt. **8** (*tr*) to set dogs upon (a bear, etc.). **9** (*intr*) *Arch.* to stop for rest and refreshment during a journey. [C13: from ON *beita* to hunt]

> **USAGE NOTE** The phrase *with bated breath* is sometimes wrongly spelled *with baited breath.*

bait[2] (beɪt) *vb* a variant spelling of **bate**[2].

baize (beɪz) *n* a woollen fabric resembling felt, usually green, used mainly for the tops of billiard tables. [C16: from OF *baies*, pl. of *baie* baize, from *bai* reddish brown, BAY[5]]

bake 🅣 (beɪk) *vb* **bakes, baking, baked. 1** (*tr*) to cook by dry heat as in an oven. **2** (*intr*) to cook bread, pastry, etc. **3** to make or become hardened by heat. **4** (*intr*) *Inf.* to be extremely hot. ◆ *n* **5** a batch of things baked at one time. **6** *Caribbean.* a small flat fried cake. [OE *bacan*]

baked Alaska (ə'læskə) *n* a dessert made of cake and ice cream covered with meringue and cooked very quickly.

baked beans *pl n* haricot beans, baked and tinned in tomato sauce.

Bakelite ('beɪkəˌlaɪt) *n Trademark.* any one of a class of thermosetting resins used as electric insulators and for making plastic ware, etc. [C20: after L. H. *Baekeland* (1863–1944), Belgian-born US inventor]

baker ('beɪkə) *n* a person whose business or employment is to make or sell bread, cakes, etc.

baker's dozen *n* thirteen. [C16: from the bakers' former practice of giving thirteen rolls where twelve were requested, to protect themselves against accusations of giving light weight]

bakery ('beɪkərɪ) *n, pl* **bakeries. 1** a room or building equipped for baking. **2** a shop in which bread, cakes, etc., are sold.

baking powder *n* a powdered mixture that contains sodium bicarbonate and one or more acidic compounds, such as cream of tartar: used in baking as a raising agent.

baklava *or* **baclava** ('bɑːkləˌvɑː) *n* a rich cake consisting of thin layers of pastry filled with nuts and honey. [from Turkish]

baksheesh *or* **backsheesh** ('bækʃiːʃ) *n* (in some Eastern countries, esp. formerly) money given as a tip, a present, or alms. [C17: from Persian *bakhshīsh*, from *bakhshīdan* to give]

bal. *Book-keeping. abbrev. for* balance.

Balaclava *or* **Balaclava helmet** (ˌbælə'klɑːvə) *n* (*often not caps.*) a close-fitting woollen hood that covers the ears and neck, as originally worn by soldiers in the Crimean War. [C19: from *Balaklava*, Ukrainian port]

balalaika (ˌbælə'laɪkə) *n* a Russian plucked musical instrument, usually having a triangular body and three strings. [C18: from Russian]

balance 🅣 ('bæləns) *n* **1** a weighing device, generally consisting of a horizontal beam pivoted at its centre, from the ends of which two pans are suspended. The substance to be weighed is placed in one pan and weights are placed in the other until the beam returns to the horizontal. **2** a state of equilibrium. **3** something that brings about such a state. **4** equilibrium of the body; steadiness: *to lose one's balance.* **5** emotional stability. **6** harmony in the parts of a whole. **7** the act of weighing factors, quantities, etc., against each other. **8** the power to influence or control: *the balance of power.* **9** something that remains: *the balance of what you owe.* **10** *Accounting.* **10a** equality of debit and credit totals in an account. **10b** a difference between such totals. **11** **in the balance.** in an uncertain or undecided condition. **12** **on balance.** after weighing up all the factors. **13** **strike a balance.** to make a compromise. ◆ *vb* **balances, balancing, balanced. 14** (*tr*) to weigh in or as if in a balance. **15** (*intr*) to be or come into equilibrium. **16** (*tr*) to bring into or hold in equilibrium. **17** (*tr*) to compare the relative weight, importance, etc., of. **18** (*tr*) to be equal to. **19** (*tr*) to arrange so as to create a state of harmony. **20** (*tr*) *Accounting.* **20a** to compare the credit and debit totals of (an account). **20b** to equalize the credit and debit totals of (an account) by making certain entries. **20c** to settle or adjust (an account) by paying any money due. **21** (*intr*) (of a balance sheet, etc.) to have the debit and credit totals equal. [C13: from OF, from Vulgar L *bilancia* (unattested), from LL *bilanx* having two scales, from BI- + *lanx* scale]
▸ **'balanceable** *adj* ▸ **'balancer** *n*

Balance ('bæləns) *n* **the.** the constellation Libra, the seventh sign of the zodiac.

balance of payments *n* the difference over a given time between total payments to foreign nations and total receipts from foreign nations.

balance of power *n* the distribution of power among countries so that no one nation can seriously threaten another.

balance of trade *n* the difference in value between total exports and total imports of goods.

balance sheet 🅣 *n* a statement that shows the financial position of a business by listing the asset balances and the claims on such assets.

THESAURUS

bail[1] *n Law* **1, 3** = **security**, bond, guarantee, guaranty, pledge, surety, warranty

bail[2] *vb* = **scoop**, dip, drain off, ladle

bail out *vb* **1** = **escape**, quit, retreat **2** *Informal* = **help**, aid, relieve, rescue, save (someone's) bacon (*inf., chiefly Brit.*)

bait[1] *n* **1** = **lure**, decoy **2** = **enticement**, allurement, attraction, bribe, carrot and stick, incentive, inducement, snare, temptation ◆ *vb* **6** = **tease**, aggravate (*inf.*), annoy, be on one's back (*sl.*), bother, gall, get in one's hair (*inf.*), get one's back up, get on one's nerves (*inf.*), get or take a rise out of, harass, hassle (*inf.*), hound, irk, irritate, nark (*Brit., Austral., & NZ sl.*), needle (*inf.*), persecute, provoke, put one's back up, torment, wind up (*Brit. sl.*) **7** = **lure**, allure, beguile, entice, seduce, tempt

baked *adj* **3** = **dry**, arid, desiccated, parched, scorched, seared, sun-baked, torrid

balance *n* **2** = **equilibrium**, equipoise **4** = **stability**, poise, steadiness **5** = **composure**, equanimity, self-control, self-possession **6** = **harmony**, correspondence, equity, equivalence, evenness, parity, symmetry **9** = **remainder**, difference, residue, rest, surplus ◆ *vb* **15, 16** = **stabilize**, level, parallel, poise, steady **17** = **compare**, assess, consider, deliberate, estimate, evaluate, weigh **19** = **equalize**, adjust, compensate for, counteract, counterbalance, counterpoise, equate, make up for, neutralize, offset **20** *Accounting* = **calculate**, compute, settle, square, tally, total
Antonyms *n* ≠ **equilibrium**: disproportion, instability, unbalance ◆ *vb* ≠ **stabilize**: outweigh, overbalance, upset

balanced *adj* **17** = **unbiased**, disinterested, equitable, even-handed, fair, impartial, just, unprejudiced
Antonyms *adj* biased, distorted, jaundiced, lopsided, one-sided, partial, predisposed, prejudiced, slanted, unfair, warped, weighted

balance sheet *n* = **statement**, account, budget, credits and debits, ledger, report

balance wheel *n* a wheel oscillating against the hairspring of a timepiece, regulating its beat.

balata ('bælətə) *n* **1** a tropical American tree, yielding a latex-like sap. **2** a rubber-like gum obtained from this sap: a substitute for gutta-percha. [from American Sp., of Carib origin]

balcony ❶ ('bælkənɪ) *n, pl* **balconies. 1** a platform projecting from a building with a balustrade along its outer edge, often with access from a door or window. **2** a gallery in a theatre, above the dress circle. **3** *US & Canad.* any circle in a theatre. [C17: from It. *balcone,* prob. from OHG *balko* beam]
▸'**balconied** *adj*

bald ❶ (bɔːld) *adj* **1** having no hair or fur, esp. (of a man) having no hair on the scalp. **2** lacking natural growth or covering. **3** plain or blunt: *a bald statement.* **4** bare or unadorned. **5** Also: **baldfaced.** (of birds and animals) having white markings on the head and face. **6** (of a tyre) having a worn tread. [C14 *ballede* (lit.: having a white spot)]
▸'**baldish** *adj* ▸'**baldly** *adv* ▸'**baldness** *n*

baldachin *or* **baldaquin** ('bɔːldəkɪn) *n* **1** a richly ornamented brocade. **2** a canopy over an altar, shrine, or throne or carried in Christian religious processions over an object of veneration. [OE *baldekin,* from It. *baldacchino,* lit.: stuff from Baghdad]

bald eagle *n* a large eagle of North America, having a white head and tail. It is the US national bird.

balderdash ❶ ('bɔːldəˌdæʃ) *n* stupid or illogical talk; senseless rubbish. [C16: from ?]

balding ❶ ('bɔːldɪŋ) *adj* somewhat bald or becoming bald.

baldric ('bɔːldrɪk) *n* a sash or belt worn over the right shoulder to the left hip for carrying a sword, etc. [C13: from OF *baudrei,* of Frankish origin]

baldy ('bɔːldɪ) *Inf.* ◆ *adj* **1** bald. ◆ *n, pl* **baldies. 2** a bald person.

bale[1] (beɪl) *n* **1** a large bundle, package, or carton of goods bound by ropes, wires, etc., for storage or transportation. **2** *US.* 500 pounds of cotton. ◆ *vb* **bales, baling, baled. 3** to make (hay, etc.) or put (goods) into a bale or bales. [C14: prob. from OF *bale,* from OHG *balla* BALL[1]]

bale[2] (beɪl) *n Arch.* **1** evil; injury. **2** woe; suffering; pain. [OE *bealu*]

bale[3] ❶ (beɪl) *vb* a variant spelling of **bail**[2].

bale[4] (beɪl) *n* a variant spelling of **bail**[4].

baleen (bə'liːn) *n* whalebone. [C14: from L *bālaena* whale]

baleen whale *n* another name for **whalebone whale.**

baleful ❶ ('beɪlfʊl) *adj* harmful, menacing, or vindictive.
▸'**balefully** *adv* ▸'**balefulness** *n*

baler ('beɪlə) *n* a machine for making bales of hay, etc. Also called: **baling machine.**

balk ❶ *or* **baulk** (bɔːk, bɔːlk) *vb* **1** (*intr;* usually foll. by *at*) to stop short; jib: *the horse balked at the jump.* **2** (*intr;* foll. by *at*) to recoil: *he balked at the idea of murder.* **3** (*tr*) to thwart, check, or foil: *he was balked in his plans.* ◆ *n* **4** a roughly squared heavy timber beam. **5** a timber tie beam of a roof. **6** an unploughed ridge between furrows. **7** an obstacle; hindrance; disappointment. **8** *Baseball.* an illegal motion by a pitcher. ◆ See also **baulk.** [OE *balca*]

Balkan ('bɔːlkən) *adj* of or denoting a large peninsula in SE Europe, between the Adriatic and Aegean Seas, or its inhabitants, countries, etc.

balky *or* **baulky** ('bɔːkɪ, 'bɔːlkɪ) *adj* **balkier, balkiest** *or* **baulkier, baulkiest.** inclined to stop abruptly and unexpectedly: *a balky horse.*

ball[1] ❶ (bɔːl) *n* **1** a spherical or nearly spherical body or mass. **2** a round or roundish body, of a size and composition suitable for any of various games. **3** a ball propelled in a particular way: *a high ball.* **4** any rudimentary game with a ball: *to play ball.* **5** a single delivery of the ball in cricket and other games. **6a** a solid nonexplosive projectile for a firearm, cannon, etc. **6b** such projectiles collectively. **7** any more or less rounded part: *the ball of the foot.* **8 ball of muscle.** *Austral.* a very strong, fit person. **9 have the ball at one's feet.** to have the chance of doing something. **10 keep the ball rolling.** to maintain the progress of a project, plan, etc. **11 on the ball.** *Inf.* alert; informed. **12 play ball.** *Inf.* to cooperate. **13 set** *or* **start the ball rolling.** to initiate an action, discussion, etc. ◆ *vb* **14** to make, form, wind, gather, etc., into a ball or balls. ◆ See also **balls, balls-up.** [C13: from ON *böllr*]

ball[2] (bɔːl) *n* **1** a social function for dancing, esp. one that is lavish or formal. **2** *Inf.* a very enjoyable time (esp. in **have a ball**). [C17: from F *bal* (n), from OF *baller* (vb), from LL *ballāre* to dance]

ballad ('bæləd) *n* **1** a narrative song with a recurrent refrain. **2** a narrative poem in short stanzas of popular origin. **3** a slow sentimental song, esp. a pop song. [C15: from OF *balade,* from OProvençal *balada* song accompanying a dance]

ballade (bæ'lɑːd) *n* **1** *Prosody.* a verse form consisting of three stanzas and an envoy, all ending with the same line. **2** *Music.* an instrumental composition based on or intended to evoke a narrative.

balladeer (ˌbælə'dɪə) *n* a singer of ballads.

ball-and-socket joint *n Anat.* a joint in which a rounded head fits into a rounded cavity, allowing a wide range of movement.

ballast ❶ ('bæləst) *n* **1** any heavy material used to stabilize a vessel, esp. one that is not carrying cargo. **2** crushed rock, broken stone, etc., used for the foundation of a road or railway track or in making concrete. **3** anything that provides stability or weight. **4** *Electronics.* a device for maintaining the current in a circuit. ◆ *vb* (*tr*) **5** to give stability or weight to. [C16: prob. from Low G]

ball bearing *n* **1** a bearing consisting of steel balls rolling between a metal sleeve fitted over the rotating shaft and an outer sleeve held in the bearing housing, so reducing friction. **2** a metal ball, esp. one used in such a bearing.

ball boy *or* (*fem*) **ball girl** *n* (esp. in tennis) a person who retrieves balls that go out of play.

ballbreaker ('bɔːlˌbreɪkə) *n Sl.* someone, esp. a woman, whose behaviour may be regarded as threatening a man's sense of power. [C20: from BALLS (in the sense: testicles) + BREAKER]

ball cock *n* a device for regulating the flow of a liquid into a tank, cistern, etc., consisting of a floating ball mounted at one end of an arm and a valve on the other end that opens and closes as the ball falls and rises.

ballerina (ˌbælə'riːnə) *n* a female ballet dancer. [C18: from It., fem of *ballerino* dancing master, from *ballare* to dance]

ballet ('bæleɪ, bæ'leɪ) *n* **1** a classical style of expressive dancing based on precise conventional steps. **2** a theatrical representation of a story or theme performed by ballet dancers. **3** a troupe of ballet dancers. **4** music written for a ballet. [C17: from F, from It. *balletto,* lit.: a little dance, from *ballare* to dance]
▸**balletic** (bæ'lɛtɪk) *adj*

balletomane ('bælɪtəʊˌmeɪn) *n* a ballet enthusiast.

balletomania (ˌbælɪtəʊ'meɪnɪə) *n* passionate enthusiasm for ballet.

ball game *n* **1** any game played with a ball. **2** *US & Canad.* a game of baseball. **3** *Inf.* a situation; state of affairs (esp. in **a whole new ball game**).

ballista (bə'lɪstə) *n, pl* **ballistae** (-tiː). an ancient catapult for hurling stones, etc. [C16: from L, ult. from Gk *ballein* to throw]

ballistic (bə'lɪstɪk) *adj* **1** of or relating to ballistics. **2** denoting or relating to the flight of projectiles moving under their own momentum and the force of gravity. **3** (of a measurement or measuring instrument) depending on a brief impulse or current that causes a movement related to the quantity to be measured: *a ballistic pendulum.* **4 go ballistic.** *Inf.* to become enraged or frenziedly violent.
▸**bal'listically** *adv*

ballistic missile *n* a missile that has no wings or fins and that follows a ballistic trajectory when its propulsive power is discontinued.

ballistics (bə'lɪstɪks) *n* (*functioning as sing*) **1** the study of the flight dynamics of projectiles. **2** the study of the effects of firing on firearms and their projectiles.

ball lightning *n Meteorol.* a luminous ball occasionally seen during electrical storms.

ballocks ('bɒləks) *pl n, interj* a variant spelling of **bollocks.**

ball of fire *n Inf.* a very lively person.

balloon ❶ (bə'luːn) *n* **1** an inflatable rubber bag used as a plaything or party decoration. **2** a large bag inflated with a lighter-than-air gas, designed to rise and float in the atmosphere. It may have a basket or gondola for carrying passengers, etc. **3** an outline containing the words or thoughts of a character in a cartoon. **4** a large rounded brandy glass. **5** *Commerce.* **5a** a large sum paid as an irregular instalment of a loan repayment. **5b** (*as modifier*): *a balloon loan.* **6** *Surgery.* **6a** an inflatable plastic tube used for dilating obstructed blood vessels or parts of the alimentary canal. **6b** (*as modifier*): *balloon angioplasty.* **7 go down like a lead balloon.** to prove unsuccessful or unpopular; fail: *the suggestion that the chairman should get a 77% pay rise went down like a lead balloon.* **8 when the balloon goes up.** *Inf.* when the action starts. ◆ *vb* **9** (*intr*) to go up or fly in a balloon. **10** to inflate or be inflated: *the wind ballooned the sails.* **11** (*intr*) to increase or expand significantly and rapidly: *losses ballooned to £278 million.* **12** (*tr*) *Brit.* to propel (a ball) high

THESAURUS

balcony *n* **1 = terrace,** veranda **2 = upper circle,** gallery, gods

bald *adj* **1 = hairless,** baldheaded, baldpated, depilated **2 = barren,** bleak, exposed, naked, stark, treeless, uncovered **3 = blunt,** direct, downright, forthright, outright, straight, straightforward, unvarnished, upfront (*inf.*) **4 = plain,** bare, severe, simple, unadorned

balderdash *n* **= nonsense,** bilge (*inf.*), bosh (*inf.*), bunk (*inf.*), bunkum *or* buncombe (*chiefly US*), claptrap (*inf.*), cobblers (*Brit. taboo sl.*), crap (*sl.*), drivel, garbage (*inf.*), hogwash, hot air (*inf.*), piffle (*inf.*), poppycock (*inf.*), rot, rubbish, tommyrot, tosh (*sl., chiefly Brit.*), trash, tripe (*inf.*), twaddle, waffle

balding *adj* **= losing one's hair,** becoming bald, receding, thin on top

baldness *n* **1 = losing one's hair,** alopecia (*Pathology*), baldheadedness, baldpatedness, hairlessness **2 = barrenness,** bleakness, nakedness, sparseness, starkness, treelessness **4 = plainness,** austerity, bluntness, severity, simplicity

bale[3] *see* **bail**[2]

baleful *adj* **= menacing,** calamitous, deadly, evil, harmful, hurtful, injurious, maleficent, malevolent, malignant, noxious, ominous, pernicious, ruinous, sinister, venomous, vindictive
Antonyms *adj* beneficial, benevolent, benign, friendly, good, healthy, salubrious

balk *vb* **1 = jib,** refuse **2 = recoil,** demur, dodge, evade, flinch, hesitate, resist, shirk, shrink from **3 = foil,** baffle, bar, check, counteract, defeat, disconcert, forestall, frustrate, hinder, obstruct, prevent, thwart
Antonyms *vb* ≠ **recoil:** accede, accept, acquiesce, comply, relent, submit, yield ≠ **foil:** abet, advance, aid, assist, further, help, promote, support, sustain

ball[1] *n* **1 = sphere,** drop, globe, globule, orb, pellet, spheroid **6 = shot,** ammunition, bullet, grapeshot, pellet, slug **12 play ball** *Informal* **= cooperate,** collaborate, go along, play along, reciprocate, respond, show willing

ballast *n* **3 = counterbalance,** balance, counterweight, stabilizer, weight

balloon *vb* **10 = inflate,** belly, billow, puff out,

into the air. [C16 (in the sense: ball, ball game): from It. dialect *ballone*]
▸**bal'loonist** *n* ▸**bal'loon-,like** *adj*

balloon loan *n* a loan in respect of which interest and capital are paid off in instalments at regular intervals.

ballot ⓘ ('bælət) *n* **1** the practice of selecting a representative, course of action, etc., by submitting the options to a vote of all qualified persons. **2** an instance of voting, usually in secret. **3** a list of candidates standing for office. **4** the number of votes cast in an election. ◆ *vb* **ballots, balloting, balloted. 5** to vote or elicit a vote from: *we balloted the members on this issue.* **6** (*tr*; usually foll. by *for*) to vote for or decide on by lot or ballot. [C16: from It. *ballotta*, lit.: a little ball]

ballot box *n* a box into which ballot papers are dropped after voting.

ballotini (,bælə'ti:nɪ) *pl n* small glass beads used in reflective paints. [C20: from Italian *ballotini* small balls]

ballot paper *n* a paper used for voting.

ballpark ('bɔ:l,pɑ:k) *n* **1** *US & Canad.* a stadium used for baseball games. **2** *Inf.* **2a** approximate range: *in the right ballpark.* **2b** (*as modifier*): *a ballpark figure.* **3** *Inf.* a situation; state of affairs: *it's a whole new ballpark.*

ball-peen hammer *n* a hammer with one end of the head rounded for beating metal.

ballpoint *or* **ballpoint pen** ('bɔ:l,pɔɪnt) *n* a pen having a small ball bearing as a writing point.

ballroom ('bɔ:l,ru:m, -,rʊm) *n* a large hall for dancing.

ballroom dancing *n* social dancing, popular since the beginning of the 20th century, to dances in conventional rhythms (**ballroom dances**).

balls (bɔ:lz) *Taboo sl.* ◆ *pl n* **1** the testicles. **2** nonsense; rubbish. **3** courage; determination. ◆ *interj* **4** an exclamation of disagreement, contempt, etc.

balls-up *Taboo sl.* ◆ *n* **1** something botched or muddled. ◆ *vb* **balls up. 2** (*tr, adv*) to muddle or botch.

ballsy ('bɔ:lzɪ) *adj* **ballsier, ballsiest.** *Sl., chiefly US.* showing courage or determination; bold. [C20: from BALLS (sense 3) + -Y[1]]
▸**'ballsiness** *n*

bally ('bælɪ) *adj, adv* (intensifier) *Brit. sl.* a euphemistic word for **bloody** (sense 5).

ballyhoo ⓘ (,bælɪ'hu:) *Inf.* ◆ *n* **1** a noisy, confused, or nonsensical situation. **2** sensational or blatant advertising or publicity. ◆ *vb* **ballyhoos, ballyhooing, ballyhooed. 3** (*tr*) *Chiefly US.* to advertise by sensational or blatant methods. [C19: from ?]

balm ⓘ (bɑ:m) *n* **1** any of various oily aromatic substances obtained from certain tropical trees and used for healing and soothing. See also **balsam** (sense 1). **2** any plant yielding such a substance, esp. the balm of Gilead. **3** something comforting or soothing. **4** Also called: **lemon balm.** an aromatic Eurasian plant, having clusters of small fragrant white flowers. **5** a pleasant odour. [C13: from OF *basme*, from L *balsamum* BALSAM]

balm of Gilead ('gɪlɪ,æd) *n* **1** any of several trees of Africa and W Asia that yield a fragrant oily resin. **2** the resin exuded by these trees. **3** a North American poplar tree. **4** a fragrant resin obtained from the balsam fir.

Balmoral (bæl'mɒrəl) *n* (*sometimes not cap.*) **1** a laced walking shoe. **2** a Scottish brimless hat usually with a cockade and plume. [from *Balmoral* Castle, Scotland]

balmy ⓘ ('bɑ:mɪ) *adj* **balmier, balmiest. 1** (of weather) mild and pleasant. **2** having the qualities of balm; fragrant or soothing. **3** a variant spelling of **barmy.**
▸**'balmily** *adv* ▸**'balminess** *n*

balneology (,bælnɪ'ɒlədʒɪ) *n* the branch of medical science concerned with the therapeutic value of baths, esp. with natural mineral waters. [C19: from L *balneum* bath]
▸**balneological** (,bælnɪə'lɒdʒɪk'l) *adj* ▸**,balne'ologist** *n*

baloney *or* **boloney** (bə'ləʊnɪ) *n Inf.* foolish talk; nonsense. [C20: from *Bologna* (sausage)]

BALPA ('bælpə) *n acronym for* British Airline Pilots' Association.

balsa ('bɔ:lsə) *n* **1** a tree of tropical America. **2** Also called: **balsawood.** the very light wood of this tree, used for making rafts, etc. **3** a light raft. [C18: from Sp.: raft]

balsam ('bɔ:lsəm) *n* **1** any of various fragrant oleoresins, such as balm, obtained from any of several trees and shrubs and used as a base for medicines and perfumes. **2** any of various similar substances used as ointments. **3** any of certain aromatic resinous turpentines. See **Canada balsam. 4** any plant yielding balsam. **5** Also called: **busy Lizzie.** any of several plants of the genus *Impatiens.* **6** anything healing or soothing. [C15: from L *balsamum*, from Gk *balsamon*, from Heb. *bāśām* spice]
▸**balsamic** (bɔ:l'sæmɪk) *adj*

balsam fir *n* a fir tree of NE North America, that yields Canada balsam.

balti ('bɔ:ltɪ, 'bæltɪ) *n* **a** a spicy Indian dish, stewed until most of the liquid has evaporated, and served in a woklike pot. **b** (*as modifier*): *a balti house.* [C20: from ?]

Baltic ('bɔ:ltɪk) *adj* **1** denoting or relating to the Baltic Sea in N Europe or the states bordering it. **2** of or characteristic of Baltic as a group of languages. ◆ *n* **3** a branch of the Indo-European family of languages consisting of Lithuanian, Latvian, and Old Prussian. **4** Also called: **Baltic Exchange.** a former commodity and freight-chartering market in the City of London.

baluster ('bæləstə) *n* any of a set of posts supporting a rail or coping. [C17: from F *balustre*, from It. *balaustro* pillar resembling a pomegranate flower, ult. from Gk *balaustion*]

balustrade ('bælə,streɪd) *n* an ornamental rail or coping with its supporting set of balusters. [C17: from F, from *balustre* BALUSTER]

bambino (bæm'bi:nəʊ) *n, pl* **bambinos** *or* **bambini** (-ni:). *Inf.* a young child, esp. Italian. [C18: from It.]

bamboo (bæm'bu:) *n* **1** a tall treelike tropical or semitropical grass having hollow stems with ringed joints. **2** the stem, used for building, poles, and furniture. [C16: prob. from Malay *bambu*]

bamboozle ⓘ (bæm'bu:z'l) *vb* **bamboozles, bamboozling, bamboozled.** (*tr*) *Inf.* **1** to cheat; mislead. **2** to confuse. [C18: from ?]
▸**bam'boozlement** *n* ▸**bam'boozler** *n*

ban ⓘ (bæn) *vb* **bans, banning, banned. 1** (*tr*) to prohibit, esp. officially, from action, display, entrance, sale, etc.; forbid. ◆ *n* **2** an official prohibition or interdiction. **3** a public proclamation, esp. of outlawry. **4** *Arch.* a curse; imprecation. [OE *bannan* to proclaim]

banal ⓘ (bə'nɑ:l) *adj* lacking force or originality; trite; commonplace. [C18: from OF: relating to compulsory feudal service, hence common to all, commonplace]
▸**banality** (bə'nælɪtɪ) *n* ▸**ba'nally** *adv*

banana (bə'nɑ:nə) *n* **1** any of several tropical and subtropical treelike plants, esp. a widely cultivated species having hanging clusters of edible fruit. **2** the crescent-shaped fruit of any of these plants. [C16: from Sp. or Port., of African origin]

banana republic *n Inf. & derog.* a small country, esp. in Central America, that is politically unstable and has an economy dominated by foreign interest, usually dependent on one export.

banana skin *n* **1** the soft outer covering of a banana. **2** *Inf.* something unforeseen that causes an obvious and embarrassing mistake. [sense 2 from the common slapstick joke of slipping on a banana skin]

band[1] ⓘ (bænd) *n* **1** a company of people having a common purpose; group: *a band of outlaws.* **2** a group of musicians playing either brass and percussion instruments only (**brass band**) or brass, woodwind, and percussion instruments (**concert band** or **military band**). **3** a group of musicians who play popular music, jazz, etc., often for dancing. ◆ *vb* **4** (usually foll. by *together*) to unite; assemble. [C15: from F *bande*, prob. from OProvençal *banda*, of Gmc origin]

band[2] ⓘ (bænd) *n* **1** a thin flat strip of some material, used esp. to encircle objects and hold them together: *a rubber band.* **2a** a strip of fabric or other material used as an ornament or to reinforce clothing. **2b** (*in combination*): *waistband; hatband.* **3** a stripe of contrasting colour or texture. **4** a driving belt in machinery. **5** a range of values that are close or related in number, degree, or quality. **6** *Physics.* a range of frequencies or wavelengths between two limits. **7** short for **energy band. 8** *Computing.* one or more tracks on a magnetic disk or drum. **9** *Anat.* any structure resembling a ribbon or cord that connects, encircles, or binds different parts. **10** *Archit.* a strip of flat panelling, such as a fascia, usually attached to a wall. **11** either of a pair of hanging extensions of the collar, forming part of academic, legal, or (formerly) clerical dress. ◆ *vb* (*tr*) **12** to fasten or mark with a band. [C15: from OF *bende*, of Gmc origin]

bandage ⓘ ('bændɪdʒ) *n* **1** a piece of material used to dress a wound, bind a broken limb, etc. ◆ *vb* **bandages, bandaging, bandaged. 2** to cover or bind with a bandage. [C16: from F, from *bande* strip, BAND[2]]

THESAURUS

swell **11** = **expand**, bloat, blow up, dilate, distend, enlarge, grow rapidly

ballot *n* **1, 2, 4** = **vote**, election, poll, polling, voting

ballyhoo *n Informal* **1** = **fuss**, babble, commotion, hubbub, hue and cry, hullabaloo, noise, racket, to-do **2** = **publicity**, advertising, build-up, hype, PR, promotion, propaganda

balm *n* **1** = **ointment**, balsam, cream, embrocation, emollient, lotion, salve, unguent **3** = **comfort**, anodyne, consolation, curative, palliative, restorative, solace

balmy *adj* **1** = **mild**, clement, pleasant, summery, temperate
Antonyms *adj* harsh, inclement, rough, stormy

bamboozle *vb Informal* **1** = **cheat**, con (*inf.*), deceive, defraud, delude, dupe, fool, hoax, hoodwink, pull a fast one on (*inf.*), skin (*sl.*), swindle, trick **2** = **puzzle**, baffle, befuddle, confound, confuse, mystify, perplex, stump

ban *vb* **1** = **prohibit**, banish, bar, black, blackball, block, boycott, debar, disallow, disqualify, exclude, forbid, interdict, outlaw, proscribe, restrict, suppress ◆ *n* **2** = **prohibition**, block, boycott, censorship, disqualification, embargo, interdict, interdiction, proscription, restriction, stoppage, suppression, taboo
Antonyms *vb* ≠ **prohibit:** allow, approve, authorize, enable, let, permit, sanction ◆ *n* ≠ **prohibition:** allowance, approval, permission, sanction

banal *adj* = **unoriginal**, clichéd, cliché-ridden, commonplace, everyday, hackneyed, humdrum, mundane, old hat, ordinary, pedestrian, platitudinous, stale, stereotyped, stock, threadbare, tired, trite, unimaginative, vanilla (*sl.*), vapid
Antonyms *adj* challenging, distinctive, fresh, ground-breaking, imaginative, interesting, new, novel, original, stimulating, unique, unusual

banality *n* = **unoriginality**, bromide (*inf.*), cliché, commonplace, platitude, triteness, trite phrase, triviality, truism, vapidity

band[1] *n* **1** = **gang**, assembly, association, bevy, body, camp, clique, club, company, coterie, crew, group, horde, party, posse (*inf.*), society, troop **2, 3** = **ensemble**, combo, group, orchestra ◆ *vb* **4** = **unite**, affiliate, ally, consolidate, federate, gather, group, join, merge
Antonyms *vb* ≠ **unite:** cleave, disperse, disunite, divide, part, segregate, separate, split, sunder

band[2] *n* **1, 2** = **strip**, belt, binding, cord, fillet, ligature, ribbon, strap, tie

bandage *n* **1** = **dressing**, compress, gauze, plaster ◆ *vb* **2** = **dress**, bind, cover, swathe

bandanna *or* **bandana** (bæn'dænə) *n* a large silk or cotton handkerchief or neckerchief. [C18: from Hindi *bāndhnū* tie-dyeing]

B & B *abbrev. for* bed and breakfast.

bandbox ('bænd,bɒks) *n* a lightweight usually cylindrical box for small articles, esp. hats.

bandeau ('bændəʊ) *n, pl* **bandeaux** (-dəʊz). a narrow band of ribbon, velvet, etc., worn round the head. [C18: from F, from OF *bandel* a little BAND[2]]

banderole *or* **banderol** ('bændə,rəʊl) *n* **1** a long narrow flag, usually with forked ends, esp. one attached to the mast of a ship. **2** a ribbon-like scroll or sculptured band bearing an inscription. [C16: from OF, from It. *banderuola*, lit.: a little banner]

bandicoot ('bændɪ,ku:t) *n* **1** an agile terrestrial marsupial of Australia and New Guinea with a long pointed muzzle and a long tail. **2 bandicoot rat.** Also called: **mole rat.** any of three burrowing rats of S and SE Asia. [C18: from Telugu *pandikokku*]

banding ('bændɪŋ) *n Brit.* the practice of putting schoolchildren into ability groups to ensure a balanced intake to secondary school.

bandit ❶ ('bændɪt) *n, pl* **bandits** *or* **banditti** (bæn'dɪtɪ). a robber, esp. a member of an armed gang. [C16: from It. *bandito*, from *bandire* to proscribe, from *bando* edict]
▸ **'banditry** *n*

bandmaster ('bænd,mɑ:stə) *n* the conductor of a band.

Band of Hope *n* a society devoted to abstinence from alcohol.

bandolier *or* **bandoleer** (,bændə'lɪə) *n* a soldier's broad shoulder belt having small pockets or loops for cartridges. [C16: from OF *bandouliere*]

band-pass filter *n* **1** *Electronics.* a filter that transmits only currents having frequencies within specified limits. **2** an optical device for transmitting waves of predetermined wavelengths.

band saw *n* a power-operated saw consisting of an endless toothed metal band running over and driven by two wheels.

bandsman ('bændzmən) *n, pl* **bandsmen.** a player in a musical band, esp. a brass or military band.

bandstand ('bænd,stænd) *n* a platform for a band, usually out of doors and roofed.

band theory *n* the theory that electrons in solids have a range of energies falling into allowed bands, between which are forbidden bands.

bandwagon ('bænd,wægən) *n* **1** *US.* a wagon for the band in a parade. **2 jump, climb,** *or* **get on the bandwagon.** to join or support a party or movement that seems assured of success.

bandwidth ('bænd,wɪdθ) *n* the range of frequencies within a given waveband used for a particular radio transmission.

bandy ❶ ('bændɪ) *adj* **bandier, bandiest. 1** Also: **bandy-legged.** having legs curved outwards at the knees. **2** (of legs) curved thus. ◆ *vb* **bandies, bandying, bandied.** (*tr*) **3** to exchange (words) in a heated or hostile manner. **4** to give and receive (blows). **5** (often foll. by *about*) to circulate (a name, rumour, etc.). [C16: prob. from OF *bander* to hit the ball back and forth at tennis]

bane ❶ (beɪn) *n* **1** a person or thing that causes misery or distress (esp. in **bane of one's life**). **2** something that causes death or destruction. **3a** a fatal poison. **3b** (*in combination*): *ratsbane.* **4** *Arch.* ruin or distress. [OE *bana*]
▸ **'baneful** *adj*

baneberry ('beɪnbərɪ) *n, pl* **baneberries. 1** Also called: **herb Christopher** (Brit.). a plant which has small white flowers and red or white poisonous berries. **2** the berry.

bang[1] ❶ (bæŋ) *n* **1** a short loud explosive noise, as of the report of a gun. **2** a hard blow or knock, esp. a noisy one. **3** *Sl.* an injection of heroin or other narcotic. **4** *Taboo sl.* an act of sexual intercourse. **5 with a bang.** successfully: *the party went with a bang.* ◆ *vb* **6** to hit or knock, esp. with a loud noise. **7** to move noisily or clumsily: *to bang about the house.* **8** to close (a door, window, etc.) or (of a door, etc.) be closed noisily; slam. **9** (*tr*) to cause to move by hitting vigorously: *he banged the ball over the fence.* **10** to make or cause to make a loud noise, as of an explosion. **11** *Taboo sl.* to have sexual intercourse (with). **12** (*intr*) *Sl.* to inject heroin, etc. **13 bang one's head against a brick wall.** to try to achieve something impossible. ◆ *adv* **14** with a sudden impact or effect: *the car drove bang into a lamppost.* **15** precisely: *bang in the middle.* **16 go bang.** to burst, shut, etc., with a loud noise. [C16: from ON *bang, banga* hammer]

bang[2] (bæŋ) *n* **1** (*usually pl*) a section of hair cut straight across the forehead. ◆ *vb* (*tr*) **2** to cut (the hair) in such a style. **3** to dock (the tail of a horse, etc.). [C19: prob. short for *bangtail* short tail]

banger ('bæŋə) *n Brit.* **1** *Sl.* a sausage. **2** *Inf.* an old decrepit car. **3** a firework that explodes loudly.

Bangla ('bæŋglə) *n* another name for **Bengali** (sense 2).

bangle ('bæŋgəl) *n* a bracelet, usually without a clasp, often worn round the arm or sometimes round the ankle. [C19: from Hindi *bangrī*]

bang on *adj, adv Brit. inf.* **1** with absolute accuracy. **2** excellent or excellently.

bangtail ('bæŋ,teɪl) *n* **1** a horse's tail cut straight across but not through the bone. **2** a horse with a tail cut in this way. [C19: from *bangtail* short tail]

banian ('bænjən) *n* a variant spelling of **banyan.**

banish ❶ ('bænɪʃ) *vb* (*tr*) **1** to expel from a place, esp. by an official decree as a punishment. **2** to drive away: *to banish gloom.* [C14: from OF *banir*, of Gmc origin]
▸ **'banishment** *n*

banisters ❶ *or* **bannisters** ('bænɪstəz) *pl n* the railing and supporting balusters on a staircase; balustrade. [C17: altered from BALUSTER]

banjo ('bændʒəʊ) *n, pl* **banjos** *or* **banjoes.** a stringed musical instrument with a long neck and a circular drumlike body overlaid with parchment, plucked with the fingers or a plectrum. [C18: var. (US Southern pronunciation) of earlier *bandore*, ult. from Gk *pandora*]
▸ **'banjoist** *n*

bank[1] ❶ (bæŋk) *n* **1** an institution offering certain financial services, such as the safekeeping of money and lending of money at interest. **2** the building used by such an institution. **3** a small container used at home for keeping money. **4** the funds held by a banker or dealer in some gambling games. **5** (in various games) **5a** the stock, as of money, etc., on which players may draw. **5b** the player holding this stock. **6** any supply, store, or reserve: *a data bank.* ◆ *vb* **7** (*tr*) to deposit (cash, cheques, etc.) in a bank. **8** (*intr*) to transact business with a bank. **9** (*intr*) to engage in banking. ◆ See also **bank on.** [C15: prob. from It. *banca* bench, moneychanger's table, of Gmc origin]

bank[2] ❶ (bæŋk) *n* **1** a long raised mass, esp. of earth; ridge. **2** a slope, as of a hill. **3** the sloping side of any hollow in the ground, esp. when bordering a river. **4** the ground beside a river or canal. **5a** an elevated section of the bed of a sea, lake, or river. **5b** (*in combination*): *sandbank.* **6** the face of a body of ore in a mine. **7** the lateral inclination of an aircraft about its longitudinal axis during a turn. **8** a bend on a road, athletics track, etc., having the outside built higher than the inside to reduce the effects of centrifugal force on vehicles, runners, etc., rounding it at speed. Also called: **camber, superelevation.** ◆ *vb* **9** (when *tr*, often foll. by *up*) to form into a bank or mound. **10** (*tr*) to border or enclose (a road, etc.) with a bank. **11** (*tr*; sometimes foll. by *up*) to cover (a fire) with ashes, fresh fuel, etc., so that it will burn slowly. **12** to cause (an aircraft) to tip laterally about its longitudinal axis or (of an aircraft) to tip in this way, esp. while turning. [C12: of Scand. origin]

bank[3] ❶ (bæŋk) *n* **1** an arrangement of similar objects in a row or in tiers: *a bank of dials.* **2** a tier of oars in a galley. ◆ *vb* **3** (*tr*) to arrange in a bank. [C17: from OF *banc* bench, of Gmc origin]

bankable ('bæŋkəbəl) *adj* **1** appropriate for receipt by a bank. **2** dependable or reliable: *a bankable promise.* **3** (esp. of a star) likely to ensure the financial success of a film.
▸ **,banka'bility** *n*

bank account *n* **1** an account created by the deposit of money at a bank by a customer. **2** the amount credited to a depositor at a bank.

bank bill *n* **1** Also called: **bank draft.** a bill of exchange drawn by one bank on another. **2** *US.* a banknote.

bankbook ('bæŋk,bʊk) *n* a book held by depositors at certain banks, in which the bank enters a record of deposits, withdrawals, and earned interest. Also called: **passbook.**

bank card *or* **banker's card** *n* any plastic card issued by a bank, such as a cash card or cheque card.

bank draft *n* a cheque drawn by a bank on itself, which is bought by a person to pay a supplier unwilling to accept a normal cheque. Also called: **banker's cheque.**

banker[1] ('bæŋkə) *n* **1** a person who owns or is an executive in a bank. **2** an official or player in charge of the bank in various games. **3** a result

THESAURUS

bandit *n* = **robber**, brigand, crook, desperado, footpad, freebooter, gangster, gunman, highwayman, hijacker, marauder, outlaw, pirate, racketeer, thief

bandy *adj* **1, 2** = **bow-legged**, bandy-legged, bent, bowed, crooked, curved ◆ *vb* **3, 4** = **exchange**, barter, interchange, swap, throw, toss, trade

bane *n* **1** = **plague**, affliction, bête noire, blight, burden, curse, despair, misery, nuisance, pest, scourge, torment, trial, trouble, woe **2** = **destruction**, calamity, disaster, downfall, ruin
Antonyms *n* ≠ **plague:** blessing, comfort, consolation, joy, pleasure, relief, solace, support

bang[1] *n* **1** = **explosion**, boom, burst, clang, clap, clash, detonation, peal, pop, report, shot, slam, thud, thump **2** = **blow**, belt (*inf.*), box, bump, cuff, hit, knock, punch, smack, stroke, wallop (*inf.*), whack ◆ *vb* **6** = **hit**, bash (*inf.*), beat, belt (*inf.*), bump, clatter, crash, hammer, knock, pound, pummel, rap, slam, strike, thump **10** = **explode**, boom, burst, clang, detonate, drum, echo, peal, resound, thump, thunder ◆ *adv* **14** = **hard**, abruptly, headlong, noisily, suddenly **15** = **straight**, precisely, slap, smack

banish *vb* **1** = **expel**, deport, eject, evict, exclude, excommunicate, exile, expatriate, ostracize, outlaw, shut out, transport **2** = **get rid of**, ban, cast out, discard, dislodge, dismiss, dispel, drive away, eliminate, eradicate, oust, remove, shake off
Antonyms *vb* ≠ **expel:** accept, admit, embrace, hail, invite, offer hospitality to, receive, welcome

banishment *n* **1** = **expulsion**, deportation, exile, expatriation, proscription, transportation

banisters *pl n* = **railing**, balusters, balustrade, handrail, rail

bank[1] *n* **1, 2** = **storehouse**, depository, repository **6** = **store**, accumulation, fund, hoard, reserve, reservoir, savings, stock, stockpile ◆ *vb* **7** = **save**, deposit, keep **8** = **deal with**, transact business with

bank[2] *n* **1** = **mound**, heap, mass, pile, ridge **3** = **embankment**, banking **4** = **side**, brink, edge, margin, shore ◆ *vb* **9** = **pile**, amass, heap, mass, mound, stack **12** = **tilt**, camber, cant, heel, incline, pitch, slant, slope, tip

bank[3] *n* **1** = **row**, arrangement, array, file, group, line, rank, sequence, series, succession, tier, train

that has been forecast identically in a series of entries on a football pool coupon. **4** a person whose performance can be relied on.

banker[2] ('bæŋkə) *n Austral. & NZ inf.* a stream almost overflowing its banks (esp. in **run a banker**).

banker's order *n* another name for **standing order** (sense 1).

bank holiday *n* (in Britain) any of several weekdays on which banks are closed by law and which are observed as national holidays.

banking ('bæŋkɪŋ) *n* the business engaged in by a bank.

bank manager *n* a person who directs the business of a local branch of a bank.

banknote ('bæŋk,nəut) *n* a promissory note, esp. one issued by a central bank, serving as money.

Bank of England ('ɪŋglənd) *n* the central bank of the United Kingdom, which acts as banker to the government and the commercial banks.

bank on Ⓣ *vb* (*intr, prep*) to expect or rely with confidence on: *you can bank on him.*

bankroll ('bæŋk,rəul) *Chiefly US & Canad.* ◆ *n* **1** a roll of currency notes. **2** the financial resources of a person, organization, etc. ◆ *vb* **3** (*tr*) *Sl.* to provide the capital for; finance.

bankrupt Ⓣ ('bæŋkrʌpt, -rəpt) *n* **1** a person adjudged insolvent by a court, his property being administered for the benefit of his creditors. **2** any person unable to discharge all his debts. **3** a person whose resources in a certain field are exhausted: *a spiritual bankrupt.* ◆ *adj* **4** adjudged insolvent. **5** financially ruined. **6** depleted in resources: *spiritually bankrupt.* **7** (foll. by *of*) *Brit.* lacking: *bankrupt of intelligence.* ◆ *vb* **8** (*tr*) to make bankrupt. [C16: from OF *banqueroute,* from OIt. *bancarotta,* from *banca* BANK[1] + *rotta* broken, from L *ruptus*]
▸**'bankruptcy** *n*

banksia ('bæŋksɪə) *n* any shrub or tree of the Australian genus *Banksia,* having dense cylindrical heads of flowers that are often yellowish. [C19: NL, after Sir Joseph *Banks* (1743–1820), E botanist]

bank statement *n* a statement of transactions in a bank account, esp. one of a series sent at regular intervals to the depositor.

banner Ⓣ ('bænə) *n* **1** a long strip of material displaying a slogan, advertisement, etc. **2** a placard carried in a procession or demonstration. **3** something that represents a belief or principle. **4** the flag of a nation, army, etc. **5** Also called: **banner headline.** a large headline in a newspaper, etc., extending across the page. [C13: from OF *baniere,* of Gmc origin]
▸**'bannered** *adj*

bannisters ('bænɪstəz) *pl n* a variant spelling of **banisters.**

bannock ('bænək) *n* a round flat cake originating in Scotland, made from oatmeal or barley and baked on a griddle. [OE *bannuc*]

banns *or* **bans** (bænz) *pl n* **1** the public declaration of an intended marriage, usually on three successive Sundays in the parish churches of the betrothed. **2 forbid the banns.** to raise an objection to a marriage announced in this way. [C14: pl of *bann* proclamation]

banquet Ⓣ ('bæŋkwɪt) *n* **1** a sumptuous meal; feast. **2** a ceremonial meal for many people. ◆ *vb* **banquets, banqueting, banqueted. 3** (*intr*) to hold or take part in a banquet. **4** (*tr*) to entertain (a person) with a banquet. [C15: from OF, from It. *banchetto,* from *banco* a table, of Gmc origin]
▸**'banqueter** *n*

banquette (bæŋ'kɛt) *n* **1** an upholstered bench. **2** (formerly) a raised part behind a parapet. [C17: from F, from Provençal *banqueta,* lit.: a little bench]

banshee ('bænʃi:, bæn'ʃi:) *n* (in Irish folklore) a female spirit whose wailing warns of impending death. [C18: from Irish Gaelic *bean sídhe,* lit.: woman of the fairy mound]

bantam ('bæntəm) *n* **1** any of various very small breeds of domestic fowl. **2** a small but aggressive person. **3** *Boxing.* short for **bantamweight.** [C18: after *Bantam,* village in Java, said to be the original home of this fowl]

bantamweight ('bæntəm,weɪt) *n* **1a** a professional boxer weighing 112–118 pounds (51–53.5 kg). **1b** an amateur boxer weighing 51–54 kg (112–119 pounds). **2** an amateur wrestler weighing usually 52–57 kg (115–126 pounds).

banter Ⓣ ('bæntə) *vb* **1** to speak or tease lightly or jokingly. ◆ *n* **2** teasing or joking language or repartee. [C17: from ?]
▸**'banterer** *n*

Bantu ('bɑ:ntu) *n* **1** a group of languages of Africa, including most of the principal languages spoken from the equator to the Cape of Good Hope. **2** (*pl* **Bantu** *or* **Bantus**) *Derog.* a Black speaker of a Bantu language. ◆ *adj* **3** of or relating to this group of peoples or their languages. [C19: from Bantu *Ba-ntu* people]

Bantustan ('bɑ:ntu,stɑ:n) *n Derog.* (formerly, in South Africa) an area reserved for occupation by a Black African people, with limited self-government; abolished in 1993. Official name: **homeland.** [from BANTU + Hindi *-stan* country of]

banyan *or* **banian** ('bænjən) *n* **1** an Indian tree with aerial roots that grow down into the soil forming additional trunks. **2** a member of the Hindu merchant caste of India. **3** a loose-fitting shirt, or robe, worn originally in India. [C16: from Hindi *baniyā,* from Sansk. *vānija* merchant]

banzai ('bɑ:nzaɪ, bɑ:n'zaɪ) *interj* a patriotic cheer, battle cry, or salutation. [Japanese: lit.: (may you live for) ten thousand years]

baobab ('beɪəu,bæb) *n* a tree native to Africa and N Australia that has a very thick trunk, angular branches, and a gourdlike fruit with an edible pulp. [C17: prob. from a native African word]

BAOR *abbrev. for* British Army of the Rhine.

bap (bæp) *n Brit.* a large soft bread roll. [from ?]

baptism Ⓣ ('bæp,tɪzəm) *n* a Christian religious rite consisting of immersion in or sprinkling with water as a sign that the subject is cleansed from sin and constituted as a member of the Church.
▸**bap'tismal** *adj* ▸**bap'tismally** *adv*

baptism of fire *n* **1** a soldier's first experience of battle. **2** any initiating ordeal.

Baptist ('bæptɪst) *n* **1** a member of any of various Christian sects that affirm the necessity of baptism (usually of adults and by immersion). **2 the Baptist.** John the Baptist, the cousin and forerunner of Jesus, whom he baptized. ◆ *adj* **3** denoting or characteristic of any Christian sect of Baptists.

baptistry *or* **baptistery** ('bæptɪstrɪ) *n, pl* **baptistries** *or* **baptisteries. 1** a part of a Christian church in which baptisms are carried out. **2** a tank in a Baptist church in which baptisms are carried out.

baptize Ⓣ *or* **baptise** (bæp'taɪz) *vb* **baptizes, baptizing, baptized** *or* **baptises, baptising, baptised. 1** *Christianity.* to immerse (a person) in water or sprinkle water on (a person) as part of the rite of baptism. **2** (*tr*) to give a name to; christen. [C13: from LL *baptīzāre,* from Gk, from *baptein* to bathe, dip]

bar[1] Ⓣ (bɑ:) *n* **1** a rigid usually straight length of metal, wood, etc., used esp. as a barrier or as a structural part: *a bar of a gate.* **2** a solid usually rectangular block of any material: *a bar of soap.* **3** anything that obstructs or prevents. **4** an offshore ridge of sand, mud, or shingle across the mouth of a river, bay, or harbour. **5** a counter or room where alcoholic drinks are served. **6** a counter, room, or establishment where a particular range of goods, food, services, etc., are sold: *a coffee bar; a heel bar.* **7** a narrow band or stripe, as of colour or light. **8** a heating element in an electric fire. **9** See **Bar. 10** the place in a court of law where the accused stands during his trial. **11** a particular court of law. **12** *Brit.* (in Parliament) the boundary where nonmembers wishing to address either House appear and where persons are arraigned. **13** a plea showing that a plaintiff has no cause of action. **14** anything referred to as an authority or tribunal: *the bar of decency.* **15** *Music.* a group of beats that is repeated with a consistent rhythm throughout a piece of music. The number of beats in the bar is indicated by the time signature. Also called: **measure. 16a** *Brit.* insignia added to a decoration indicating a second award. **16b** *US.* a strip of metal worn with uniform, esp. to signify rank or as an award for service. **17** *Football, etc.* See **crossbar. 18** *Gymnastics.* See **horizontal bar. 19** *Heraldry.* a narrow horizontal line across a shield. **20 behind bars.** in prison. **21 won't have a bar of.** *Austral. & NZ inf.* cannot tolerate; dislikes. ◆ *vb* **bars, barring, barred.** (*tr*) **22** to secure with a bar: *to bar the door.* **23** to shut in or out with or as if with barriers: *to bar the entrances.* **24** to obstruct: *the fallen tree barred the road.* **25** (usually foll. by *from*) to prohibit; forbid: *to bar a couple from meeting.* **26** (usually foll. by *from*) to keep out; exclude: *to bar a person from membership.* **27** to mark with a bar or bars. **28** *Law.* to prevent or halt (an action) by showing that the plaintiff has no cause. ◆ *prep* **29** except for. **30 bar none.** without exception. [C12: from OF *barre,* from Vulgar L *barra* (unattested) bar, rod, from ?]

bar[2] (bɑ:) *n* a cgs unit of pressure equal to 10^6 dynes per square centimetre. [C20: from Gk *baros* weight]

Bar Ⓣ (bɑ:) *n* **the. 1** (in England and elsewhere) barristers collectively. **2** *US.* the legal profession collectively. **3 be called to the Bar.** *Brit.* to become a barrister. **4 be called within the Bar.** *Brit.* to be appointed as a Queen's Counsel.

bar. *abbrev. for:* **1** barometric. **2** barrel. **3** barrister.

THESAURUS

bank on *vb* = **rely on,** assume, believe in, count on, depend on, lean on, look to, trust

bankrupt *adj* **4, 5** = **insolvent,** beggared, broke (*inf.*), destitute, failed, impoverished, in queer street, in the red, on one's uppers, on the rocks, ruined, wiped out (*inf.*) **6** = **exhausted,** depleted, spent
Antonyms *adj* ≠ **insolvent:** in the money (*inf.*), on the up and up, prosperous, solvent, sound, wealthy

bankruptcy *n* **4, 5** = **insolvency,** crash, disaster, failure, indebtedness, liquidation, ruin **6** = **lack,** exhaustion

banner *n* **1** = **flag,** colours, ensign, pennant, pennon, standard, streamer **2** = **placard**

banquet *n* **1** = **feast,** dinner, meal, repast

banter *vb* **1** = **joke,** chaff, deride, jeer, jest, josh (*sl., chiefly US & Canad.*), kid (*inf.*), make fun of, rib (*inf.*), ridicule, take the mickey (*inf.*), taunt, tease, twit ◆ *n* **2** = **joking,** badinage, chaff, chaffing, derision, jeering, jesting, kidding (*inf.*), mockery, pleasantry, repartee, ribbing (*inf.*), ridicule, teasing

baptism *n* = **christening,** immersion, purification, sprinkling

baptize *vb* **1** *Christianity* = **purify,** besprinkle, cleanse, immerse **2** = **name,** call, christen, dub, title

bar[1] *n* **1** = **rod,** batten, crosspiece, paling, palisade, pole, rail, shaft, stake, stick **3** = **obstacle,** barricade, barrier, block, deterrent, hindrance, impediment, interdict, obstruction, rail, railing, stop **5** = **public house,** boozer (*Brit., Austral., & NZ inf.*), canteen, counter, hostelry (*arch. or facetious*), inn, lounge, pub (*inf., chiefly Brit.*), saloon, taproom, tavern, watering hole (*facetious sl.*) **10, 11** = **dock,** bench, court, courtroom, law court ◆ *vb* **22** = **fasten,** barricade, bolt, latch, lock, secure **24** = **obstruct,** hinder, prevent, restrain **26** = **exclude,** ban, black, blackball, forbid, keep out, prohibit
Antonyms *n* ≠ **obstacle:** aid, benefit, help ◆ *vb* ≠ **exclude:** accept, admit, allow, let, permit, receive

Bar *n* **the Bar 1, 2** = **barristers,** body of lawyers, counsel, court, judgment, tribunal

barathea (ˌbærəˈθɪə) *n* a fabric made of silk and wool or cotton and rayon. [C19: from ?]

barb[1] Ⓣ (bɑːb) *n* **1** a point facing in the opposite direction to the main point of a fish-hook, harpoon, etc., intended to make extraction difficult. **2** any of various pointed parts. **3** a cutting remark. **4** any of the hairlike filaments that form the vane of a feather. **5** a beardlike growth, hair, or projection. ◆ *vb* **6** (*tr*) to provide with a barb or barbs. [C14: from OF *barbe* beard, point, from L *barba* beard]
▸**barbed** *adj*

barb[2] (bɑːb) *n* a breed of horse of North African origin, similar to the Arab but less spirited. [C17: from F *barbe*, from It. *barbero* a Barbary (horse)]

Barbadian (bɑːˈbeɪdɪən) *adj* **1** of Barbados, an island in the Caribbean. ◆ *n* **2** a native or inhabitant of Barbados.

barbarian Ⓣ (bɑːˈbɛərɪən) *n* **1** a member of a primitive or uncivilized people. **2** a coarse or uncultured person. **3** a vicious person. ◆ *adj* **4** of an uncivilized culture. **5** uncultured or brutal. [C16: see BARBAROUS]

barbaric Ⓣ (bɑːˈbærɪk) *adj* **1** of or characteristic of barbarians. **2** primitive; unrestrained. **3** brutal. [C15: from L *barbaricus* outlandish; see BARBAROUS]
▸**barˈbarically** *adv*

barbarism Ⓣ (ˈbɑːbəˌrɪzəm) *n* **1** a brutal, coarse, or ignorant act. **2** the condition of being backward, coarse, or ignorant. **3** a substandard word or expression; solecism. **4** any act or object that offends against accepted taste. [C16: from L *barbarismus* error of speech, from Gk *barbarismos*, from *barbaros* BARBAROUS]

barbarity Ⓣ (bɑːˈbærɪtɪ) *n, pl* **barbarities. 1** the state of being barbaric or barbarous. **2** a vicious act.

barbarize *or* **barbarise** (ˈbɑːbəˌraɪz) *vb* **barbarizes, barbarizing, barbarized** *or* **barbarises, barbarising, barbarised. 1** to make or become barbarous. **2** to use barbarisms in (language).
▸ˌ**barbariˈzation** *or* ˌ**barbariˈsation** *n*

barbarous Ⓣ (ˈbɑːbərəs) *adj* **1** uncivilized; primitive. **2** brutal or cruel. **3** lacking refinement. [C15: via L from Gk *barbaros* barbarian, non-Greek, imit. of incomprehensible speech]
▸ˈ**barbarously** *adv* ▸ˈ**barbarousness** *n*

Barbary ape (ˈbɑːbərɪ) *n* a tailless macaque that inhabits NW Africa and Gibraltar. [from *Barbary*, old name for region in N Africa]

barbate (ˈbɑːbeɪt) *adj Biol.* having tufts of long hairs; bearded. [C19: from L *barba* a beard]

barbecue (ˈbɑːbɪˌkjuː) *n* **1** a meal cooked out of doors over an open fire. **2** a grill or fireplace used in barbecuing. **3** the food so cooked. **4** a party or picnic at which barbecued food is served. ◆ *vb* **barbecues, barbecuing, barbecued.** (*tr*) **5** to cook (meat, fish, etc.) on a grill, usually over charcoal and often with a highly seasoned sauce. [C17: from American Sp. *barbacoa*: frame made of sticks]

barbed wire *n* strong wire with sharply pointed barbs at close intervals.

barbel (ˈbɑːbᵊl) *n* **1** any of several slender tactile spines or bristles that hang from the jaws of certain fishes, such as the carp. **2** any of several European cyprinid fishes that resemble the carp. [C14: from OF, from LL from L *barba* beard]

barbell (ˈbɑːˌbɛl) *n* a long metal rod to which heavy discs are attached at each end for weightlifting.

barber (ˈbɑːbə) *n* **1** a person whose business is cutting men's hair and shaving beards. ◆ *vb* (*tr*) **2** to cut the hair of. [C13: from OF *barbeor*, from *barbe* beard, from L *barba*]

barberry (ˈbɑːbərɪ) *n, pl* **barberries.** any spiny Asian shrub of the genus *Berberis*, having clusters of yellow flowers and orange or red berries. [C15: from OF *berberis*, from Ar. *barbāris*]

barbershop (ˈbɑːbəˌʃɒp) *n* **1** *Now chiefly US.* the premises of a barber. **2** (*modifier*) denoting a type of close four-part harmony for male voices: *a barbershop quartet.*

barber's pole *n* a barber's sign consisting of a pole painted with red-and-white spiral stripes.

barbican (ˈbɑːbɪkən) *n* **1** a walled outwork to protect a gate or drawbridge of a fortification. **2** a watchtower projecting from a fortification. [C13: from OF *barbacane*, from Med. L, from ?]

barbicel (ˈbɑːbɪˌsɛl) *n Ornithol.* any of the minute hooks on the barbules of feathers that interlock with those of adjacent barbules. [C19: from NL *barbicella*, lit.: a small beard]

barbitone (ˈbɑːbɪˌtəʊn) *or US* **barbital** (ˈbɑːbɪˌtæl) *n* a long-acting barbiturate. [C20: from BARBIT(URIC ACID) + -ONE]

barbiturate (bɑːˈbɪtjʊrɪt, -ˌreɪt) *n* a derivative of barbituric acid, such as barbitone, used in medicine as a sedative or hypnotic.

barbituric acid (ˌbɑːbɪˈtjʊərɪk) *n* a white crystalline solid used in the preparation of barbiturate drugs. [C19: partial translation of G *Barbitursäure*]

Barbour jacket *or* **Barbour** (ˈbɑːbə) *n Trademark.* a hard-wearing waterproof waxed jacket.

barbule (ˈbɑːbjuːl) *n Ornithol.* any of the minute hairs that project from a barb and in some feathers interlock. [C19: from L *barbula* a little beard]

barcarole *or* **barcarolle** (ˈbɑːkəˌrəʊl, -ˌrɒl; ˌbɑːkəˈrəʊl) *n* **1** a Venetian boat song. **2** an instrumental composition resembling this. [C18: from F, from It. *barcarola*, from *barcaruolo* boatman, from *barca* boat]

bar chart *n* another term for **bar graph.**

bar code *n Commerce.* a machine-readable arrangement of numbers and parallel lines printed on a package, which can be electronically scanned at a checkout to register the price of the goods and to activate computer stock checking and reordering.

bard[1] Ⓣ (bɑːd) *n* **1a** (formerly) one of an ancient Celtic order of poets. **1b** a poet who wins a verse competition at a Welsh eisteddfod. **2** *Arch. or literary.* any poet. [C14: from Scot. Gaelic]
▸ˈ**bardic** *adj*

bard[2] (bɑːd) *n* **1** a piece of bacon or pork fat placed on meat during roasting to prevent drying out. ◆ *vb* (*tr*) **2** to place a bard on. [C15: from OF *barde*, from OIt. *barda*, from Ar. *barda'ah* packsaddle]

bardie (ˈbɑːdɪ) *n* **1** an edible white wood-boring grub of Australia. **2 starve the bardies!** *Austral.* an exclamation of surprise or protest. [from Abor.]

bare[1] Ⓣ (bɛə) *adj* **1** unclothed: used esp. of a part of the body. **2** without the natural, conventional, or usual covering. **3** lacking appropriate furnishings, etc. **4** unembellished; simple: *the bare facts.* **5** (*prenominal*) just sufficient: *the bare minimum.* **6 with one's bare hands.** without a weapon or tool. ◆ *vb* **bares, baring, bared. 7** (*tr*) to make bare; uncover. [OE *bær*]
▸ ˈ**bareness** *n*

bare[2] (bɛə) *vb Arch.* a past tense of **bear**[1].

bareback (ˈbɛəˌbæk) *or* **barebacked** *adj, adv* (of horse-riding) without a saddle.

barefaced Ⓣ (ˈbɛəˌfeɪst) *adj* unconcealed or shameless: *a barefaced lie.*
▸**barefacedly** (ˈbɛəˌfeɪsɪdlɪ) *adv* ▸ˈ**bareˌfacedness** *n*

barefoot (ˈbɛəˌfʊt) *or* **barefooted** *adj, adv* **1** with the feet uncovered. ◆ *adj* **2** denoting a worker with basic training sent to help people in remote rural areas, esp. of developing countries: *barefoot doctor.*

bareheaded (ˌbɛəˈhɛdɪd) *adj, adv* with the head uncovered.

bare-knuckle *adj* **1** without boxing gloves: *a bare-knuckle fighter.* **2** aggressive; without civilized restraint: *a bare-knuckle confrontation.*

barely Ⓣ (ˈbɛəlɪ) *adv* **1** only just: *barely enough.* **2** *Inf.* not quite: *barely old enough.* **3** scantily: *barely furnished.* **4** *Arch.* openly.

> **USAGE NOTE** See at **hardly.**

barf (bɑːf) *vb* (*intr*) *Sl.* to vomit. [C20: prob. imit.]

bargain Ⓣ (ˈbɑːgɪn) *n* **1** an agreement establishing what each party will give, receive, or perform in a transaction. **2** something acquired or received in such an agreement. **3a** something bought or offered at a low price. **3b** (*as modifier*): *a bargain price.* **4 into the bargain.** in excess; besides. **5 make** *or* **strike a bargain.** to agree on terms. ◆ *vb* **6** (*intr*) to negotiate the terms of an agreement, transaction, etc. **7** (*tr*) to exchange, as

THESAURUS

barb[1] *n* **2 = point**, bristle, prickle, prong, quill, spike, spur, thorn **3 = dig**, affront, cut, gibe, insult, rebuff, sarcasm, scoff, sneer

barbarian *n* **1 = savage**, brute, yahoo **2 = lout**, bigot, boor, hooligan, ignoramus, illiterate, lowbrow, philistine, ruffian, vandal ◆ *adj* **4 = uncivilized**, primitive, wild **5 = uncultured**, boorish, crude, lowbrow, philistine, rough, uncouth, uncultivated, unsophisticated, vulgar
Antonyms *adj* ≠ **uncultured:** civil, civilized, cultured, genteel, highbrow, refined, sophisticated, urbane, well-mannered

barbaric *adj* **1, 2 = uncivilized**, primitive, rude, wild **3 = brutal**, barbarous, cruel, fierce, inhuman, savage
Antonyms *adj* ≠ **uncivilized:** civilized, cultivated, cultured, gentlemanly, gracious, refined, sophisticated, urbane ≠ **brutal:** humane

barbarism *n* **1, 4 = atrocity**, barbarity, enormity, outrage **2 = savagery**, coarseness, crudity, uncivilizedness **3 = misuse**, corruption, misusage, solecism, vulgarism

barbarity *n* **1 = viciousness**, brutality, cruelty, inhumanity, ruthlessness, savagery

barbarous *adj* **1 = uncivilized**, barbarian, brutish, primitive, rough, rude, savage, uncouth, wild **2 = brutal**, barbaric, cruel, ferocious, heartless, inhuman, monstrous, ruthless, vicious **3 = ignorant**, coarse, crude, uncultured, unlettered, unrefined, vulgar

barbed *adj* **2 = spiked**, hooked, jagged, prickly, pronged, spiny, thorny, toothed **3 = cutting**, acid, acrid, catty (*inf.*), critical, hostile, hurtful, nasty, pointed, scathing, unkind

bard[1] *n* **2** *Archaic or literary* **= poet**, minstrel, rhymer, singer, troubadour

bare *adj* **1 = naked**, buck naked (*sl.*), denuded, exposed, in the bare scud (*sl.*), in the raw (*inf.*), naked as the day one was born (*inf.*), nude, peeled, shorn, stripped, unclad, unclothed, uncovered, undressed, without a stitch on (*inf.*) **2 = empty**, barren, open, poor, scanty, scarce, unfurnished, vacant, void, wanting **3 = unadorned**, austere, basic, severe, simple, spare, spartan, unembellished, unfussy, unvarnished **4 = plain**, bald, basic, cold, essential, hard, literal, sheer, simple, stark, unembellished
Antonyms *adj* ≠ **naked:** attired, clad, clothed, concealed, covered, dressed, hidden ≠ **empty:** abundant, full, plentiful, profuse, well-stocked ≠ **unadorned:** adorned

barefaced *adj* **= shameless**, audacious, bald, blatant, bold, brash, brazen, flagrant, glaring, impudent, insolent, manifest, naked, open, palpable, patent, transparent, unconcealed
Antonyms *adj* concealed, covered, hidden, inconspicuous, masked, obscured, secret, tucked away, unseen

barely *adv* **1 = only just**, almost, at a push, by the skin of one's teeth, hardly, just, scarcely
Antonyms *adv* amply, completely, fully, profusely

bargain *n* **1 = agreement**, arrangement, business, compact, contract, convention, engagement, negotiation, pact, pledge, promise, stipulation, transaction, treaty, understanding **3 = good buy**, (cheap) purchase, discount, giveaway, good deal, good value, reduction, snip (*inf.*), steal (*inf.*) ◆ *vb* **6 = negotiate**, agree, con-

in a bargain. **8** to arrive at (an agreement or settlement). [C14: from OF *bargaigne,* from *bargaignier* to trade, of Gmc origin]
▸'**bargainer** *n*

bargain away *vb (tr, adv)* to lose (rights, etc.) in return for something valueless.

bargain for ❶ *vb (intr, prep)* to expect; anticipate: *he got more than he bargained for.*

bargain on ❶ *vb (intr, prep)* to rely or depend on (something): *he bargained on her support.*

barge ❶ (bɑːdʒ) *n* **1** a vessel, usually flat-bottomed and with or without its own power, used for transporting freight, esp. on canals. **2** a vessel, often decorated, used in pageants, etc. **3** *Navy.* a boat allocated to a flag officer, used esp. for ceremonial occasions. ◆ *vb* **barges, barging, barged. 4** *(intr;* foll. by *into) Inf.* to bump (into). **5** *Inf.* to push (someone or one's way) violently. **6** *(intr;* foll. by *into* or *in) Inf.* to interrupt rudely or clumsily: *to barge into a conversation.* [C13: from OF, from Med. L *barga,* prob. from LL *barca* a small boat]

bargeboard ('bɑːdʒˌbɔːd) *n* a board, often decorated, along the gable end of a roof.

bargee (bɑː'dʒiː) *n* a person employed on or in charge of a barge.

bargepole ('bɑːdʒˌpəʊl) *n* **1** a long pole used to propel a barge. **2 not touch with a bargepole.** *Inf.* to refuse to have anything to do with.

bar graph *n* a graph consisting of vertical or horizontal bars whose lengths are proportional to amounts or quantities.

bariatrics (ˌbærɪ'ætrɪks) *n (functioning as sing)* the branch of medicine concerned with the treatment of obese people. [C20: from Gk *barōs* weight + -IATRICS]

barite ('bɛəraɪt) *n* the usual US and Canad. name for **barytes.** [C18: from BAR(IUM) + -ITE[1]]

baritone ('bærɪˌtəʊn) *n* **1** the second lowest adult male voice. **2** a singer with such a voice. **3** the second lowest instrument in the families of the saxophone, horn, oboe, etc. ◆ *adj* **4** relating to or denoting a baritone. [C17: from It., from Gk, from *barus* heavy, low + *tonos* TONE]

barium ('bɛərɪəm) *n* a soft silvery-white metallic element of the alkaline earth group. Symbol: Ba; atomic no.: 56; atomic wt.: 137.34. [C19: from BAR(YTA) + -IUM]

barium meal *n* a preparation of barium sulphate, which is opaque to X-rays, swallowed by a patient before X-ray examination of the upper part of his or her alimentary canal.

bark[1] ❶ (bɑːk) *n* **1** the loud abrupt usually harsh cry of a dog or certain other animals. **2** a similar sound, such as one made by a person, gun, etc. **3 his bark is worse than his bite.** he is bad-tempered but harmless. ◆ *vb* **4** *(intr)* (of a dog, etc.) to make its typical cry. **5** *(intr)* (of a person, gun, etc.) to make a similar loud harsh sound. **6** to say or shout in a brusque or angry tone: *he barked an order.* **7 bark up the wrong tree.** *Inf.* to misdirect one's attention, efforts, etc.; be mistaken. [OE *beorcan*]

bark[2] ❶ (bɑːk) *n* **1** a protective layer of dead corky cells on the outside of the stems of woody plants. **2** any of several varieties of this, used in tanning, dyeing, or in medicine. ◆ *vb (tr)* **3** to scrape or rub off skin, as in an injury. **4** to remove the bark or a circle of bark from (a tree). **5** to tan (leather), principally by the tannins in barks. [C13: from ON *börkr*]

bark[3] (bɑːk) *n* a variant spelling of **barque.**

barkentine ('bɑːkənˌtiːn) *n* the usual US and Canad. spelling of **barquentine.**

barker ('bɑːkə) *n* **1** an animal or person that barks. **2** a person at a fair booth, etc., who loudly addresses passers-by to attract customers.

barking ('bɑːkɪŋ) *Sl.* ◆ *adj* **1** mad; crazy. ◆ *adv* **2** (intensifier): *barking mad.*

barley ('bɑːlɪ) *n* **1** any of various annual temperate grasses that have dense bristly flower spikes and are widely cultivated for grain and forage. **2** the grain of any of these grasses, used in making beer and whisky and for soups, puddings, etc. [OE *bærlīc* (adj); rel. to *bere* barley]

barleycorn ('bɑːlɪˌkɔːn) *n* **1** a grain of barley, or barley itself. **2** an obsolete unit of length equal to one third of an inch.

barley sugar *n* a brittle clear amber-coloured sweet.

barley water *n* a drink made from an infusion of barley.

barm (bɑːm) *n* **1** the yeasty froth on fermenting malt liquors. **2** an archaic or dialect word for **yeast.** [OE *beorm*]

barmaid ('bɑːˌmeɪd) *n* a woman who serves in a pub.

barman ('bɑːmən) *n, pl* **barmen.** a man who serves in a pub.

Barmecide ('bɑːmɪˌsaɪd) *adj* lavish in imagination only; illusory; sham: *a Barmecide feast.* [C18: from a prince in the *Arabian Nights' Entertainment* who served empty plates to beggars, alleging that they held sumptuous food]

Bar Mitzvah (bɑː 'mɪtsvə) *(sometimes not caps.) Judaism.* ◆ *adj* **1** (of a Jewish boy) having assumed full religious obligations, being at least thirteen years old. ◆ *n* **2** the occasion or celebration of this. **3** the boy himself. [Heb.: son of the law]

barmy ❶ ('bɑːmɪ) *adj* **barmier, barmiest.** *Sl.* insane. [C16: orig., full of BARM, hence frothing, excited]

barn[1] (bɑːn) *n* **1** a large farm outbuilding, chiefly for storing grain, etc., but also for livestock. **2** *US & Canad.* a large shed for railroad cars, trucks, etc. **3** any large building, esp. an unattractive one. **4** *(modifier)* relating to a system of poultry farming in which birds are allowed to move freely within a barn: *barn eggs.* [OE *beren,* from *bere* barley + *ærn* room]

barn[2] (bɑːn) *n* a unit of nuclear cross section equal to 10^{-28} square metres. Symbol: b [C20: from BARN[1]; so called because of the relatively large cross section]

barnacle ('bɑːnəkᵊl) *n* **1** any of various marine crustaceans that, as adults, live attached to rocks, ship bottoms, etc. **2** a person or thing that is difficult to get rid of. [C16: from earlier *bernak,* from OF *bernac,* from LL, from ?]
▸'**barnacled** *adj*

barnacle goose *n* a N European goose that has a black-and-white head and body. [C13 *bernekke:* it was formerly believed that the goose developed from a shellfish]

barn dance *n* **1** *Brit.* a progressive round country dance. **2** *Brit.* a disco or party held in a barn. **3** *US & Canad.* a party with hoedown music and square-dancing.

barney ('bɑːnɪ) *Inf.* ◆ *n* **1** a noisy fight or argument. ◆ *vb* **2** *(intr) Chiefly Austral. & NZ.* to argue or quarrel. [C19: from ?]

barn owl *n* an owl with a pale brown and white plumage and a heart-shaped face.

barnstorm ('bɑːnˌstɔːm) *vb (intr)* **1** to tour rural districts putting on shows. **2** *Chiefly US & Canad.* to tour rural districts making speeches in a political campaign.
▸'**barnˌstorming** *n, adj*

barnyard ('bɑːnˌjɑːd) *n* **1** a yard adjoining a barn. **2** *(modifier)* characteristic of a barnyard. **3** *(modifier)* crude or earthy.

baro- *combining form.* indicating weight or pressure: *barometer.* [from Gk *baros* weight]

baroceptor ('bærəʊˌsɛptə) *n* another name for **baroreceptor.**

barogram ('bærəˌgræm) *n Meteorol.* the record of atmospheric pressure traced by a barograph or similar instrument.

barograph ('bærəˌgrɑːf) *n Meteorol.* a self-recording aneroid barometer.
▸**barographic** (ˌbærə'græfɪk) *adj*

barometer (bə'rɒmɪtə) *n* **1** an instrument for measuring atmospheric pressure, usually to determine altitude or weather changes. **2** anything that shows change.
▸**barometric** (ˌbærə'mɛtrɪk) *or* ˌ**baro'metrical** *adj* ▸**ba'rometry** *n*

baron ('bærən) *n* **1** a member of a specific rank of nobility, esp. the lowest rank in the British Isles. **2** (in Europe from the Middle Ages) originally any tenant-in-chief of a king or other overlord. **3** a powerful businessman or financier: *a press baron.* [C12: from OF, of Gmc origin]

baronage ('bærənɪdʒ) *n* **1** barons collectively. **2** the rank or dignity of a baron.

baroness ('bærənɪs) *n* **1** the wife or widow of a baron. **2** a woman holding the rank of baron.

baronet ('bærənɪt, -ˌnɛt) *n* (in Britain) a commoner who holds the lowest hereditary title of honour, ranking below a baron. Abbrev.: **Bart, Bt.**
▸'**baronetage** *n* ▸'**baronetcy** *n*

baronial (bə'rəʊnɪəl) *adj* of, relating to, or befitting a baron or barons.

baron of beef *n* a cut of beef consisting of a double sirloin joined at the backbone.

barony ('bærənɪ) *n, pl* **baronies. 1a** the domain of a baron. **1b** (in Ireland) a division of a county. **1c** (in Scotland) a large estate or manor. **2** the rank or dignity of a baron.

baroque ❶ (bə'rɒk, bə'rəʊk) *n (often cap.)* **1** a style of architecture and decorative art in Europe from the late 16th to the early 18th century, characterized by extensive ornamentation. **2** a 17th-century style of music characterized by extensive use of ornamentation. **3** any ornate or heavily ornamented style. ◆ *adj* **4** denoting, in, or relating to the baroque. **5** (of pearls) irregularly shaped. [C18: from F, from Port. *barroco* a rough or imperfectly shaped pearl]

baroreceptor ('bærəʊrɪˌsɛptə) *or* **baroceptor** *n* a collection of sensory nerve endings, principally in the carotid sinuses and the aortic arch, that monitor blood-pressure changes in the body.

baroscope ('bærəˌskəʊp) *n* any instrument for measuring atmospheric pressure.
▸**baroscopic** (ˌbærə'skɒpɪk) *adj*

barouche (bə'ruːʃ) *n* a four-wheeled horse-drawn carriage, popular in the 19th century, having a retractable hood over the rear half. [C19: from G (dialect) *Barutsche,* from It. *baroccio,* from LL *birotus,* from BI- + *rota* wheel]

barperson ('bɑːˌpɜːsᵊn) *n, pl* **barpersons.** a person who serves in a pub: used esp. in advertisements.

THESAURUS

tract, covenant, cut a deal, promise, stipulate, transact **7** = **exchange**, barter, buy, deal, haggle, sell, trade, traffic

bargain for *vb* = **anticipate**, contemplate, expect, foresee, imagine, look for, plan for

bargain on *vb* = **depend on**, assume, bank on, count on, plan on, rely on

barge *n* **1** = **canal boat**, flatboat, lighter, narrow boat, scow ◆ *vb* **4** *foll. by* **into** *Informal* = **bump into**, cannon into, collide with, hit **5** *Informal* = **push**, shove **6** *foll. by* **into** *or* **in** *Informal* = **interrupt**, break in, burst in, butt in, infringe, intrude, muscle in *(inf.)*

bark[1] *n, vb* **1, 4** = **yap**, bay, growl, howl, snarl, woof, yelp **6** = **shout**, bawl, bawl at, berate, bluster, growl, snap, snarl, yell

bark[2] *n* **1** = **covering**, casing, cortex *(Anatomy, botany)*, crust, husk, rind, skin ◆ *vb* **3** = **scrape**, abrade, flay, rub, shave, skin, strip

barmy *adj Slang* = **insane**, crackpot *(inf.)*, crazy, daft, dippy, doolally *(sl.)*, loony *(sl.)*, loopy *(inf.)*, nuts *(sl.)*, nutty *(sl.)*, odd, off one's rocker *(sl.)*, off one's trolley *(sl.)*, out of one's mind, out to lunch *(inf.)*, round the twist *(Brit. sl.)*, up the pole *(inf.)*
Antonyms *adj* all there *(inf.)*, in one's right mind, of sound mind, rational, reasonable, sane, sensible

baroque *adj* **4** = **ornate**, elaborate, extravagant, flamboyant, florid, overdecorated, rococo

barque (bɑːk) *n* **1** a sailing ship of three or more masts having the foremasts rigged square and the aftermast rigged fore-and-aft. **2** *Poetic.* any boat. [C15: from OF, from OProvençal *barca*]

barquentine *or* **barquantine** (ˈbɑːkənˌtiːn) *n* a sailing ship of three or more masts rigged square on the foremast and fore-and-aft on the others. [C17: from BARQUE + (BRIG)ANTINE]

barrack[1] (ˈbærək) *vb* to house (soldiers, etc.) in barracks.

barrack[2] Ⓣ (ˈbærək) *vb Brit., Austral., & NZ inf.* **1** to criticize loudly or shout against (a team, speaker, etc.); jeer. **2** (*intr;* foll. by *for*) to shout support (for). [C19: from Irish: to boast]

barrack-room lawyer *n* a person who freely offers opinions, esp. in legal matters, that he is unqualified to give.

barracks Ⓣ (ˈbærəks) *pl n* (*sometimes sing; when pl, sometimes functions as sing*) **1** a building or group of buildings used to accommodate military personnel. **2** any large building used for housing people, esp. temporarily. **3** a large and bleak building. [C17: from F *baraque,* from OCatalan *barraca* hut, from ?]

barracouta (ˌbærəˈkuːtə) *n* a large predatory Pacific fish. [C17: var. of BARRACUDA]

barracuda (ˌbærəˈkjuːdə) *n, pl* **barracuda** *or* **barracudas.** a predatory marine mostly tropical fish, which attacks man. [C17: from American Sp., from ?]

barrage Ⓣ (ˈbærɑːʒ) *n* **1** *Mil.* the firing of artillery to saturate an area, either to protect against an attack or to support an advance. **2** an overwhelming and continuous delivery of something, as questions. **3** a construction across a watercourse, esp. one to increase the depth. [C19: from F, from *barrer* to obstruct; see BAR[1]]

barrage balloon *n* one of a number of tethered balloons with cables or net suspended from them, used to deter low-flying air attack.

barramundi (ˌbærəˈmʌndɪ) *n, pl* **barramundis, barramundies, barramundi.** a large edible Australian estuary fish of the perch family. [from Abor.]

barratry *or* **barretry** (ˈbærətrɪ) *n* **1** *Criminal law.* (formerly) the vexatious stirring up of quarrels or bringing of lawsuits. **2** *Maritime law.* a fraudulent practice committed by the master or crew of a ship to the prejudice of the owner. **3** the purchase or sale of public or Church offices. [C15: from OF *baraterie* deception, from *barater* to BARTER]
▸ **ˈbarratrous** *or* **ˈbarretrous** *adj* ▸ **ˈbarrator** *n*

barre *French.* (bar) *n* a rail at hip height used for ballet practice and leg exercises. [lit.: bar]

barrel (ˈbærəl) *n* **1** a cylindrical container usually bulging outwards in the middle and held together by metal hoops. **2** Also called: **barrelful.** the amount that a barrel can hold. **3** a unit of capacity of varying amount in different industries. **4** a thing shaped like a barrel, esp. a tubular part of a machine. **5** the tube through which the projectile of a firearm is discharged. **6** the trunk of a four-legged animal: *the barrel of a horse.* **7 over a barrel.** *Inf.* powerless. **8 scrape the barrel.** *Inf.* to be forced to use one's last and weakest resource. ◆ *vb* **barrels, barrelling, barrelled** *or US* **barrels, barreling, barreled. 9** (*tr*) to put into a barrel or barrels. [C14: from OF *baril,* ?from *barre* BAR[1]]

barrel-chested *adj* having a large rounded chest.

barrel organ *n* an instrument consisting of a cylinder turned by a handle and having pins on it that interrupt the air flow to certain pipes or pluck strings, thereby playing tunes.

barrel roll *n* a flight manoeuvre in which an aircraft rolls about its longitudinal axis while following a spiral course in line with the direction of flight.

barrel vault *n Archit.* a vault in the form of a half cylinder.

barren Ⓣ (ˈbærən) *adj* **1** incapable of producing offspring, seed, or fruit; sterile. **2** unable to support the growth of crops, etc.: *barren land.* **3** lacking in stimulation; dull. **4** not producing worthwhile results; unprofitable: *a barren period.* **5** (foll. by *of*) devoid (of): *barren of wit.* **6** (of rock strata) having no fossils. [C13: from OF *brahain,* from ?]
▸ **ˈbarrenness** *n*

barricade (ˌbærɪˈkeɪd, ˈbærɪˌkeɪd) *n* **1** a barrier for defence, esp. one erected hastily, as during street fighting. ◆ *vb* **barricades, barricading, barricaded.** (*tr*) **2** to erect a barricade across (an entrance, etc.) or at points of access to (a room, district, etc.). [C17: from OF, from *barriquer* to barricade, from *barrique* a barrel, from Sp. *barrica,* from *barril* BARREL]

barrier Ⓣ (ˈbærɪə) *n* **1** anything serving to obstruct passage or to maintain separation, such as a fence or gate. **2** anything that prevents progress. **3** anything that separates or hinders union: *a language barrier.* [C14: from OF *barriere,* from *barre* BAR[1]]

barrier cream *n* a cream used to protect the skin, esp. the hands.

barrier-nurse *vb* (*tr*) to tend (infectious patients) in isolation, to prevent the spread of infection.
▸ **barrier nursing** *n*

barrier reef *n* a long narrow coral reef near the shore, separated from it by deep water.

barring (ˈbɑːrɪŋ) *prep* unless (something) occurs; except for.

barrister (ˈbærɪstə) *n* **1** Also called: **barrister-at-law.** (in England) a lawyer who has been called to the bar and is qualified to plead in the higher courts. Cf. **solicitor. 2** (in Canada) a lawyer who pleads in court **3** *US.* a less common word for **lawyer.** [C16: from BAR[1]]

barrow[1] (ˈbærəʊ) *n* **1** See **wheelbarrow, handbarrow. 2** Also called: **barrowful.** the amount contained in or on a barrow. **3** *Chiefly Brit.* a handcart with a canvas roof, used esp. by street vendors. [OE *bearwe*]

barrow[2] (ˈbærəʊ) *n* a heap of earth placed over one or more prehistoric tombs, often surrounded by ditches. [OE *beorg*]

barrow boy *n Brit.* a man who sells his wares from a barrow; street vendor.

bar sinister *n* **1** (not in heraldic usage) another name for **bend sinister. 2** the condition or stigma of being of illegitimate birth.

Bart. *abbrev. for* Baronet.

bartender (ˈbɑːˌtendə) *n* another name (esp. US and Canad.) for **barman** or **barmaid.**

barter Ⓣ (ˈbɑːtə) *vb* **1** to trade (goods, services, etc.) in exchange for other goods, services, etc., rather than for money. **2** (*intr*) to haggle over such an exchange; bargain. ◆ *n* **3** trade by the exchange of goods. [C15: from OF *barater* to cheat]

bartizan (ˈbɑːtɪzən, ˌbɑːtɪˈzæn) *n* a small turret projecting from a wall, parapet, or tower. [C19: var. of *bertisene,* erroneously for *bretising,* from *bretasce* parapet; see BRATTICE]
▸ **bartizaned** (ˈbɑːtɪzənd, ˌbɑːtɪˈzænd) *adj*

baryon (ˈbærɪˌɒn) *n* any of a class of elementary particles that have a mass greater than or equal to that of the proton. Baryons are either nucleons or hyperons. The **baryon number** is the number of baryons in a system minus the number of antibaryons. [C20: from Gk *barus* heavy + -ON]
▸ **ˌbaryˈonic** *adj*

baryta (bəˈraɪtə) *n* another name for barium oxide or barium hydroxide. [C19: NL, from Gk *barutēs* weight, from *barus* heavy]

barytes (bəˈraɪtiːz) *n* a colourless or white mineral occurring in sedimentary rocks and with sulphide ores: a source of barium. [C18: from Gk *barus* heavy + *-itēs* -ITE[1]]

basal (ˈbeɪsᵊl) *adj* **1** at, of, or constituting a base. **2** of or constituting a basis; fundamental.

basal metabolism *n* the amount of energy required by an individual in the resting state, for such functions as breathing and blood circulation.

basalt (ˈbæsɔːlt) *n* **1** a dark basic igneous rock: the most common volcanic rock. **2** a form of black unglazed pottery resembling basalt. [C18: from LL *basaltēs,* var. of *basanītēs,* from Gk *basanitēs* touchstone]
▸ **baˈsaltic** *adj*

bascule (ˈbæskjuːl) *n* **1** a bridge with a movable section hinged about a horizontal axis and counterbalanced by a weight. **2** a movable roadway forming part of such a bridge. [C17: from F: seesaw, from *bas* low + *cul* rump]

base[1] Ⓣ (beɪs) *n* **1** the bottom or supporting part of anything. **2** the fundamental principle or part. **3a** a centre of operations, organization, or supply. **3b** (*as modifier*): *base camp.* **4** starting point: *the new discovery became the base for further research.* **5** the main ingredient of a mixture: *to use rice as a base in cookery.* **6** a chemical compound that combines with an acid to form a salt and water. A solution of a base in water turns litmus paper blue and produces hydroxyl ions. **7** a medium such as oil or water in which the pigment is dispersed in paints, inks, etc. **8** *Biol.* the point of attachment of an organ or part. **9** the bottommost layer or part of anything. **10** *Archit.* the part of a column between the pedestal and the shaft. **11** the lower side or face of a geometric construction. **12** *Maths.* the number of units in a counting system that is equivalent to one in the next higher counting place: *10 is the base of the decimal system.* **13** *Maths.* the number that when raised to a certain power has a logarithm (based on that number) equal to that power: *the logarithm to the base 10 of 1000 is 3.* **14** *Linguistics.* a root or stem. **15** *Electronics.* the region in a transistor between the emitter and collector. **16** a starting or finishing point in any of various games. ◆ *vb* **bases, basing, based. 17** (*tr;* foll. by *on* or *upon*) to use as a basis (for); found (on). **18** (often foll. by *at* or *in*) to station, post, or place (a person or oneself). [C14: from OF, from L *basis* pedestal; see BASIS]

THESAURUS

barrack[2] *vb Brit., Austral., & N.Z. informal* **1** = **heckle**, abuse, boo, criticize, gibe *or* jibe, jeer, mock, taunt

barracks *pl n* **1** = **camp**, billet, cantonment, encampment, garrison, quarters

barrage *n* **1** *Military* = **bombardment**, battery, cannonade, curtain of fire, fusillade, gunfire, salvo, shelling, volley **2** = **torrent**, assault, attack, burst, deluge, hail, mass, onslaught, plethora, profusion, rain, storm, stream

barren *adj* **1** = **infertile**, childless, infecund, sterile, unprolific **2** = **unproductive**, arid, desert, desolate, dry, empty, unfruitful, waste **3** = **dull**, boring, flat, lacklustre, stale, uninformative, uninspiring, uninstructive, uninteresting, unrewarding, vapid **4** = **unprofitable**, fruitless, unsuccessful, useless
Antonyms *adj* ≠ **unproductive:** fecund, fertile, fruitful, lush, productive, profitable, rich, useful ≠ **dull:** instructive, interesting ≠ **unprofitable:** productive, profitable, useful

barricade *n* **1** = **barrier**, blockade, bulwark, fence, obstruction, palisade, rampart, stockade ◆ *vb* **2** = **bar**, block, blockade, defend, fortify, obstruct, protect, shut in

barrier *n* **1** = **barricade**, bar, block, blockade, boundary, ditch, fence, fortification, obstacle, obstruction, pale, railing, rampart, stop, wall **2** = **hindrance**, check, difficulty, drawback, handicap, hazard, hurdle, impediment, limitation, obstacle, restriction, stumbling block

barter *vb* **1** = **trade**, exchange, sell, swap, traffic **2** = **bargain**, drive a hard bargain, haggle

base[1] *n* **1** = **bottom**, bed, foot, foundation, groundwork, pedestal, rest, stand, support **2** = **basis**, core, essence, essential, fundamental, heart, key, origin, principle, root, source **3a** = **centre**, camp, headquarters, home, post, settlement, starting point, station ◆ *vb* **17** = **found**, build, construct, depend, derive, establish, ground, hinge **18** = **place**, locate, post, station

base[2] ❶ (beɪs) *adj* **1** devoid of honour or morality; contemptible. **2** of inferior quality or value. **3** debased; alloyed; counterfeit: *base currency.* **4** *English history.* (of land tenure) held by villein or other ignoble service. **5** *Arch.* born of humble parents. **6** *Arch.* illegitimate. [C14: from OF *bas,* from LL *bassus* of low height]
▸'**baseness** *n*

baseball ('beɪsˌbɔːl) *n* **1** a team game with nine players on each side, played on a field with four bases connected to form a diamond. The object is to score runs by batting the ball and running round the bases. **2** the hard rawhide-covered ball used in this game.

baseball cap *n* a close-fitting thin cap with a deep peak.

baseborn ('beɪsˌbɔːn) *adj Arch.* **1** born of humble parents. **2** illegitimate.

base hospital *n Austral.* a hospital serving a large rural area.

baseless ❶ ('beɪslɪs) *adj* not based on fact; unfounded.
▸'**baselessness** *n*

baseline ('beɪsˌlaɪn) *n* **1** *Surveying.* a measured line through a survey area from which triangulations are made. **2** a line at each end of a tennis court that marks the limit of play.

basement ('beɪsmənt) *n* **1a** a partly or wholly underground storey of a building, esp. one used for habitation rather than storage. **1b** (*as modifier*): *a basement flat.* **2** the foundation of a wall or building.

base metal *n* any of certain common metals, such as copper and lead, as distinct from precious metals.

basenji (bəˈsendʒɪ) *n* a small African breed of dog that is unable to bark. [C20: from Bantu]

base rate *n* **1** *Brit.* the rate of interest used by individual commercial banks as a basis for their lending rates. **2** *Brit. inf.* the rate at which the Bank of England lends to the discount houses, which effectively controls the interest rates charged throughout the banking system. **3** *Statistics.* the average number of times an event occurs divided by the average number of times on which it might occur.

bases[1] ('beɪsiːz) *n* the plural of **basis.**

bases[2] ('beɪsɪz) *n* the plural of **base.**

base unit *n Physics.* any of the fundamental units in a system of measurement. The base SI units are the metre, kilogram, second, ampere, kelvin, candela, and mole.

bash ❶ (bæʃ) *Inf.* ◆ *vb* **1** (*tr*) to strike violently or crushingly. **2** (*tr;* often foll. by *in, down,* etc.) to smash, break, etc., with a crashing blow. **3** (*intr;* foll. by *into*) to crash (into); collide (with). **4** to dent or be dented. ◆ *n* **5** a heavy blow. **6** a party. **7 have a bash.** *Inf.* to make an attempt. [C17: from ?]

bashful ❶ ('bæʃful) *adj* **1** shy or modest; diffident. **2** indicating or characterized by shyness or modesty. [C16: from *bash,* short for ABASH + -FUL]
▸'**bashfully** *adv* ▸'**bashfulness** *n*

-bashing *n and adj combining form. Inf. or sl.* **a** indicating a malicious attack on members of a particular group: *union-bashing.* **b** indicating any of various other activities: *Bible-bashing.*
▸**-basher** *n combining form.*

basho ('bæʃəʊ) *n, pl* **basho.** a grand tournament in sumo wrestling. [C20: from Japanese, lit.: place]

basic ❶ ('beɪsɪk) *adj* **1** of, relating to, or forming a base or basis; fundamental. **2** elementary or simple: *a few basic facts.* **3** excluding additions or extras: *basic pay.* **4** *Chem.* of, denoting, or containing a base; alkaline. **5** *Metallurgy.* of or made by a process in which the furnace or converter is made of a basic material, such as magnesium oxide. **6** (of such igneous rocks as basalt) containing between 52 and 45 per cent silica. ◆ *n* **7** (*usually pl*) a fundamental principle, fact, etc.
▸'**basically** *adv*

BASIC *or* **Basic** ('beɪsɪk) *n* a computer programming language that uses common English terms. [C20: *b(eginner's) a(ll-purpose) s(ymbolic) i(nstruction) c(ode)*]

Basic Curriculum *n Brit. education.* the National Curriculum plus religious education.

basic English *n* a simplified form of English with a vocabulary of approximately 850 common words, intended as an international language.

basic industry *n* an industry which is highly important in a nation's economy.

basicity (beɪˈsɪsɪtɪ) *n Chem.* **a** the state of being a base. **b** the number of molecules of acid required to neutralize one molecule of a given base.

basic slag *n* a slag produced in steel-making, containing calcium phosphate.

basic wage *n* **1** a person's wage excluding overtime, bonuses, etc. **2** *Austral.* the statutory minimum wage for any worker.

basidiomycete (bæˌsɪdɪəʊmaɪˈsiːt) *n* any of a class of fungi, including puffballs and rusts, which produce spores at the tips of slender projecting stalks. [C19: see BASIS, -MYCETE]
▸**baˌsidiomyˈcetous** *adj*

basil ('bæzᵊl) *n* a Eurasian plant having spikes of small white flowers and aromatic leaves used as herbs for seasoning. Also called: **sweet basil.** [C15: from OF *basile,* from LL, from Gk *basilikos* royal]

basilar ('bæsɪlə) *adj Chiefly anat.* of or at a base. Also: **basilary** ('bæsɪlərɪ, -sɪlrɪ). [C16: from NL *basilaris*]

basilica (bəˈzɪlɪkə) *n* **1** a Roman building, used for public administration, having a large rectangular central nave with an aisle on each side and an apse at the end. **2** a Christian church of similar design. **3** a Roman Catholic church having special ceremonial rights. [C16: from L, from Gk, from *basilikē oikia* the king's house]
▸**baˈsilican** *or* **baˈsilic** *adj*

basilisk ('bæzɪˌlɪsk) *n* **1** (in classical legend) a serpent that could kill by its breath or glance. **2** a small semiaquatic lizard of tropical America. The males have an inflatable head crest, used in display. [C14: from L *basiliscus,* from Gk *basiliskos* royal child]

basin ('beɪsᵊn) *n* **1** a round container open and wide at the top with sides sloping inwards towards the bottom. **2** Also called: **basinful.** the amount a basin will hold. **3** a washbasin or sink. **4** any partially enclosed or sheltered area where vessels may be moored. **5** the catchment area of a particular river and its tributaries. **6** a depression in the earth's surface. **7** *Geol.* a part of the earth's surface consisting of rock strata that slope down to a common centre. [C13: from OF *bacin,* from LL *bacchīnon*]

basis ❶ ('beɪsɪs) *n, pl* **bases** (-siːz). **1** something that underlies, supports, or is essential to something else, esp. an idea. **2** a principle on which something depends or from which something has issued. [C14: via L from Gk: step]

bask ❶ (bɑːsk) *vb* (*intr;* usually foll. by *in*) **1** to lie in or be exposed to pleasant warmth, esp. that of the sun. **2** to flourish or feel secure under some benevolent influence or favourable condition. [C14: from ON *bathask* to BATHE]

basket ('bɑːskɪt) *n* **1** a container made of interwoven strips of pliable materials, such as cane, and often carried by a handle. **2** Also called: **basketful.** the amount a basket will hold. **3** something resembling such a container, such as the structure suspended from a balloon. **4** *Basketball.* **4a** the hoop fixed to the backboard, through which a player must throw the ball to score points. **4b** a point or points scored in this way. **5** a group of similar or related things: *a basket of currencies.* **6** *Inf.* a euphemism for **bastard** (senses 1–3). [C13: prob. from OF *baskot* (unattested), from L *bascauda* wickerwork holder]

basketball ('bɑːskɪtˌbɔːl) *n* **1** a game played by two teams of five men (or six women), usually on an indoor court. Points are scored by throwing the ball through an elevated horizontal hoop. **2** the ball used in this game.

basket case *n Sl.* **1** *Chiefly US & Canad.* a person who has had both arms and both legs amputated. **2** a person who is suffering from extreme nervous strain; nervous wreck. **3a** someone or something that is incapable of functioning effectively. **3b** (*as modifier*): *a basket-case economy.*

basket chair *n* a chair made of wickerwork.

basketry ('bɑːskɪtrɪ) *n* **1** the art or practice of making baskets. **2** baskets collectively.

basket weave *n* a weave of yarns, resembling that of a basket.

THESAURUS

Antonyms *n* ≠ **bottom:** apex, crest, crown, peak, summit, top, vertex

base[2] *adj* **1** = **dishonourable,** abject, contemptible, corrupt, depraved, despicable, disreputable, evil, ignoble, immoral, infamous, scandalous, shameful, sordid, vile, villainous, vulgar, wicked **2** = **inferior,** downtrodden, grovelling, low, lowly, mean, menial, miserable, paltry, pitiful, poor, servile, slavish, sorry, subservient, worthless, wretched **3** = **counterfeit,** adulterated, alloyed, debased, fake, forged, fraudulent, impure, pinchbeck, spurious
Antonyms *adj* ≠ **dishonourable:** admirable, good, honest, honourable, just, moral, noble, pure, rare, righteous, upright, valuable, virtuous ≠ **inferior:** lofty, noble ≠ **counterfeit:** pure, unalloyed

baseless *adj* = **unfounded,** groundless, unconfirmed, uncorroborated, ungrounded, unjustifiable, unjustified, unsubstantiated, unsupported
Antonyms *adj* authenticated, confirmed, corroborated, proven, substantiated, supported, validated, verified, well-founded

baseness *n* **1** = **depravity,** contemptibility, degradation, depravation, despicability, disgrace, ignominy, infamy, notoriety, obloquy, turpitude **2** = **inferiority,** lowliness, meanness, misery, poverty, servility, slavishness, subservience, worthlessness, wretchedness

bash *Informal vb* **1-3** = **hit,** belt, biff (*sl.*), break, chin (*sl.*), crash, crush, deck (*sl.*), punch, slosh (*Brit. sl.*), smash, sock (*sl.*), strike, wallop (*inf.*) ◆ *n* **7** = **attempt,** crack (*inf.*), go (*inf.*), shot (*inf.*), stab (*inf.*), try

bashful *adj* **1, 2** = **shy,** abashed, blushing, confused, constrained, coy, diffident, easily embarrassed, nervous, overmodest, reserved, reticent, retiring, self-conscious, self-effacing, shamefaced, sheepish, shrinking, timid, timorous
Antonyms *adj* aggressive, arrogant, bold, brash, conceited, confident, egoistic, fearless, forward, immodest, impudent, intrepid, pushy (*inf.*), self-assured

bashfulness *n* **1, 2** = **shyness,** constraint, coyness, diffidence, embarrassment, hesitation, modesty, reserve, self-consciousness, sheepishness, timidity, timorousness

basic *adj* **1** = **essential,** bog-standard (*inf.*), central, fundamental, immanent, indispensable, inherent, intrinsic, key, necessary, primary, radical, underlying, vital ◆ *n* **7** *usually plural* = **essentials,** brass tacks (*inf.*), core, facts, funda-m entals, hard facts, necessaries, nitty-gritty (*inf.*), nuts and bolts (*inf.*), practicalities, principles, rudiments
Antonyms *adj* ≠ **essential:** complementary, minor, peripheral, secondary, supplementary, supporting, trivial, unessential

basically *adv* **1** = **essentially,** at bottom, at heart, *au fond,* firstly, fundamentally, inherently, in substance, intrinsically, mostly, primarily, radically

basis *n* **1** = **foundation,** base, bottom, footing, ground, groundwork, support **2** = **principle,** chief ingredient, core, essential, fundamental, heart, premise, principal element, theory

bask *vb* **1** = **lie in,** laze, loll, lounge, relax, sunbathe, swim in, toast oneself, warm oneself **2** = **enjoy,** delight in, indulge oneself, luxuriate, relish, revel, savour, take pleasure, wallow

basketwork ('bɑːskɪtˌwɜːk) *n* another word for **wickerwork.**

basking shark *n* a very large plankton-eating shark, often floating at the sea surface.

basmati rice (bəz'mætɪ) *n* a variety of long-grain rice with slender aromatic grains, used for savoury dishes. [from Hindi, lit.: aromatic]

basophil ('beɪsəfɪl) *or* **basophile** *adj also* **basophilic** (ˌbeɪsə'fɪlɪk). **1** (of cells or cell contents) easily stained by basic dyes. ◆ *n* **2** a basophil cell, esp. a leucocyte. [C19: from Gk; see BASIS, -PHILE]

basque (bæsk) *n* a type of tight-fitting bodice for women. [from F, from BASQUE]

Basque (bæsk, bɑːsk) *n* **1** a member of a people living around the W Pyrenees in France and Spain. **2** the language of this people, of no known relationship with any other language. ◆ *adj* **3** of or relating to this people or their language. [C19: from F, from L *Vascō* a Basque]

bas-relief (ˌbɑːrɪ'liːf, 'bæsrɪˌliːf) *n* sculpture in low relief, in which the forms project slightly from the background. [C17: from F, from It. *basso rilievo* low relief]

bass[1] Ⓣ (beɪs) *n* **1** the lowest adult male voice. **2** a singer with such a voice. **3 the bass.** the lowest part in a piece of harmony. **4** *Inf.* short for **bass guitar, double bass. 5a** the low-frequency component of an electrical audio signal, esp. in a record player or tape recorder. **5b** the knob controlling this. ◆ *adj* **6** relating to or denoting the bass. [C15 *bas* BASE[1]; modern spelling infl. by BASSO]

bass[2] (bæs) *n* **1** any of various sea perches. **2** a European spiny-finned freshwater fish. **3** any of various predatory North American freshwater fishes. [C15: from BASE[2], infl. by It. *basso* low]

bass clef (beɪs) *n* the clef that establishes F a fifth below middle C on the fourth line of the staff.

bass drum (beɪs) *n* a large drum of low pitch.

basset ('bæsɪt) *n* a smooth-haired breed of hound with short legs and long ears. Also: **basset hound.** [C17: from F, from *basset* short, from *bas* low]

basset horn *n* an obsolete woodwind instrument. [C19: prob. from G *Bassetthorn*, from It. *bassetto*, dim. of BASSO + HORN]

bass guitar (beɪs) *n* a guitar that has the same pitch and tuning as a double bass, usually electrically amplified.

bassinet (ˌbæsɪ'nɛt) *n* a wickerwork or wooden cradle or pram, usually hooded. [C19: from F: little basin; associated in folk etymology with F *barcelonnette* a little cradle]

bassist ('beɪsɪst) *n* a player of a double bass or bass guitar.

basso ('bæsəʊ) *n, pl* **bassos** *or* **bassi** (-sɪ). (esp. in operatic or solo singing) a singer with a bass voice. [C19: from It., from LL *bassus* low; see BASE[2]]

bassoon (bə'suːn) *n* **1** a woodwind instrument, the tenor of the oboe family. **2** an orchestral musician who plays a bassoon. [C18: from F *basson*, from It., from *basso* deep]
▸**bas'soonist** *n*

basso rilievo (*Italian* 'basso ri'ljeːvo) *n, pl* **basso rilievos.** Italian name for **bas-relief.**

bass viol (beɪs) *n* **1** another name for **viola da gamba. 2** *US.* a less common name for **double bass** (sense 1).

bast (bæst) *n* **1** *Bot.* another name for **phloem. 2** fibrous material obtained from the phloem of jute, flax, etc., used for making rope, matting, etc. [OE *bæst*]

bastard Ⓣ ('bɑːstəd, 'bæs-) *n* **1** *Inf., offens.* an obnoxious or despicable person. **2** *Inf.* a person, esp. a man: *lucky bastard.* **3** *Inf.* something extremely difficult or unpleasant. **4** *Arch. or offens.* a person born of parents not married to each other. **5** something irregular, abnormal, or inferior. **6** a hybrid, esp. an accidental or inferior one. ◆ *adj* (*prenominal*) **7** *Arch. or offens.* illegitimate by birth. **8** irregular, abnormal, or inferior. **9** resembling a specified thing, but not actually being such: *a bastard cedar.* **10** counterfeit; spurious. **11** hybrid. [C13: from OF *bastart*, ?from *fils de bast* son of the packsaddle]
▸**'bastardy** *n*

bastardize Ⓣ *or* **bastardise** ('bɑːstəˌdaɪz, 'bæs-) *vb* **bastardizes, bastardizing, bastardized** *or* **bastardises, bastardising, bastardised.** (*tr*) **1** to debase. **2** *Arch.* to declare illegitimate.

baste[1] (beɪst) *vb* **bastes, basting, basted.** (*tr*) to sew with loose temporary stitches. [C14: from OF *bastir* to build, of Gmc origin]
▸**'basting** *n*

baste[2] (beɪst) *vb* **bastes, basting, basted.** (*tr*) to moisten (meat) during cooking with hot fat and the juices produced. [C15: from ?]

baste[3] (beɪst) *vb* **bastes, basting, basted.** (*tr*) to beat thoroughly; thrash. [C16: prob. from ON *beysta*]

Bastille (bæ'stiːl) *n* a fortress in Paris: a prison until its destruction in 1789, at the beginning of the French Revolution. [C14: from OF *bastile* fortress, from OProvençal *bastida*, from *bastir* to build]

bastinado (ˌbæstɪ'neɪdəʊ) *n, pl* **bastinadoes. 1** punishment or torture in which the soles of the feet are beaten with a stick. ◆ *vb* **bastinadoes, bastinadoing, bastinadoed. 2** (*tr*) to beat (a person) thus. [C16: from Sp. *bastonada*, from *baston* stick]

bastion Ⓣ ('bæstɪən) *n* **1** a projecting part of a fortification, designed to permit fire to the flanks along the the face of the wall. **2** any fortified place. **3** a thing or person regarded as defending a principle, etc. [C16: from F, from earlier *bastillon* bastion, from *bastille* BASTILLE]

bat[1] Ⓣ (bæt) *n* **1** any of various types of club with a handle, used to hit the ball in certain sports, such as cricket. **2** a flat round club with a short handle used by a man on the ground to guide the pilot of an aircraft when taxiing. **3** *Cricket.* short for **batsman. 4** *Inf.* a blow from a stick. **5** *Sl.* speed; pace: *they went at a fair bat.* **6 carry one's bat.** *Cricket.* (of an opening batsman) to reach the end of an innings without being dismissed. **7 off one's own bat. 7a** of one's own accord. **7b** by one's own unaided efforts. ◆ *vb* **bats, batting, batted. 8** (*tr*) to strike with or as if with a bat. **9** (*intr*) *Cricket, etc.* (of a player or a team) to take a turn at batting. [OE *batt* club, prob. of Celtic origin]

bat[2] (bæt) *n* **1** a nocturnal mouselike animal flying with a pair of membranous wings. **2** *Sl.* an irritating or eccentric woman. **3 blind as a bat.** having extremely poor eyesight. **4 have bats in the** (*or* **one's**) **belfry.** *Inf.* to be mad or eccentric. [C14 *bakke*, prob. of Scand. origin]

bat[3] (bæt) *vb* **bats, batting, batted.** (*tr*) **1** to wink or flutter (one's eyelids). **2 not bat an eye** (*or* **eyelid**). *Inf.* to show no surprise or concern. [C17: prob. var. of BATE[2]]

batch[1] Ⓣ (bætʃ) *n* **1** a group or set of usually similar objects or people, esp. if sent off, handled, or arriving at the same time. **2** the bread, cakes, etc., produced at one baking. **3** the amount of a material needed for an operation. ◆ *vb* **4** to group (items) for efficient processing. **5** to handle by batch processing. [C15 *bache*; rel. to OE *bacan* to BAKE]

batch[2] *or* **bach** (bætʃ) *vb* (*intr*) *Austral. & NZ inf.* (of a man) to do his own cooking and housekeeping.

batch processing *n* a system by which the computer programs of a number of individual users are submitted as a single batch.

bate[1] (beɪt) *vb* **bates, bating, bated. 1** another word for **abate. 2 with bated breath.** in suspense or fear.

bate[2] (beɪt) *vb* **bates, bating, bated.** (*intr*) (of a hawk) to jump violently from a perch or the falconer's fist, often hanging from the leash while struggling to escape. [C13: from OF *batre* to beat]

bate[3] (beɪt) *n Brit. Sl.* a bad temper or rage. [C19: from BAIT[1], alluding to the mood of a person who is being baited]

bateau (bæ'təʊ) *n, pl* **bateaux** (-'təʊz). a light flat-bottomed boat used on rivers in Canada and the northern US. [C18: from F: boat]

bateleur eagle ('bætələː) *n* an African short-tailed bird of prey. [C19: from F *bateleur* juggler]

bath Ⓣ (bɑːθ) *n, pl* **baths** (bɑːðz). **1** a large container used for washing the body. **2** the act or an instance of washing in such a container. **3** the amount of liquid contained in a bath. **4** (*usually pl*) a place having baths or a swimming pool for public use. **5a** a vessel in which something is immersed to maintain it at a constant temperature, to process it photographically, etc., or to lubricate it. **5b** the liquid used in such a vessel. ◆ *vb* **6** *Brit.* to wash in a bath. [OE *bæth*]

Bath bun (bɑːθ) *n Brit.* a sweet bun containing spices and dried fruit. [C19: from *Bath*, city in England where orig. made]

Bath chair *n* a wheelchair for invalids.

bath cube *n* a cube of soluble scented material for use in a bath.

bathe Ⓣ (beɪð) *vb* **bathes, bathing, bathed. 1** (*intr*) to swim in a body of open water, esp. for pleasure. **2** (*tr*) to apply liquid to (skin, a wound, etc.) in order to cleanse or soothe. **3** to immerse or be immersed in a liquid. **4** *Chiefly US & Canad.* to wash in a bath. **5** (*tr; often passive*) to suffuse. ◆ *n* **6** *Brit.* a swim in a body of open water. [OE *bathian*]
▸**'bather** *n*

bathers ('beɪðəz) *pl n Austral.* a swimming costume.

bathhouse ('bɑːθˌhaʊs) *n* a building containing baths, esp. for public use.

bathing cap ('beɪðɪŋ) *n* a tight rubber cap worn by a swimmer to keep the hair dry.

bathing costume Ⓣ ('beɪðɪŋ) *n* another name for **swimming costume.**

bathing machine ('beɪðɪŋ) *n* a small hut, on wheels so that it could be pulled to the sea, used in the 18th and 19th centuries for bathers to change their clothes.

bathing suit ('beɪðɪŋ) *n* a garment worn for bathing, esp. an old-fashioned one that covers much of the body.

batho- *combining form.* a variant of **bathy-.**

batholith (ˌbæθəlɪθ) *or* **batholite** ('bæθəˌlaɪt) *n* a very large irregular-shaped mass of igneous rock, esp. granite, formed from an intrusion of magma at great depth, esp. one exposed after erosion of less resistant overlying rocks.
▸ˌ**batho'lithic** *or* **batholitic** (ˌbæθə'lɪtɪk) *adj*

THESAURUS

bass[1] *adj* **6** = **deep**, deep-toned, grave, low, low-pitched, resonant, sonorous

bastard *n* **1** *Informal, offensive* = **rogue**, blackguard, criminal, evildoer, knave (*arch.*), libertine, malefactor, miscreant, profligate, rapscallion, reprobate, scoundrel, villain, wretch **4** *Archaic or offensive* = **illegitimate child**, by-blow (*arch.*), love child, natural child ◆ *adj* **7** *Archaic or offensive* = **illegitimate**, baseborn, misbegotten **10** = **false**, adulterated, counterfeit, illegitimate, imperfect, impure, inferior, irregular, sham, spurious

bastardize *vb* **1** = **corrupt**, adulterate, cheapen, debase, defile, degrade, demean, devalue, distort, pervert

bastion *n* **1, 2** = **stronghold**, bulwark, citadel, defence, fastness, fortress **3** = **mainstay**, prop, rock, support, tower of strength

bat[1] *vb* **8** = **hit**, bang, punch, rap, smack, strike, swat, thump, wallop (*inf.*), whack

batch[1] *n* **1** = **group**, accumulation, aggregation, amount, assemblage, bunch, collection, crowd, lot, pack, quantity, set

bath *n* **2** = **wash**, ablution, cleansing, douche, douse, scrubbing, shower, soak, soaping, sponging, tub, washing ◆ *vb* **6** = **wash**, bathe, clean, douse, scrub down, shower, soak, soap, sponge, tub

bathe *vb* **1** = **swim 2, 4** = **wash**, cleanse, rinse **3** = **cover**, flood, immerse, steep, suffuse ◆ *n* **6** *Brit.* = **swim**, dip, dook (*Scot.*)

bathing costume *n* = **swimming costume**, bathing suit, bikini, swimsuit, trunks

Bath Oliver ('ɒlɪvə) *n Brit.* a kind of unsweetened biscuit [C19: after William *Oliver* (1695–1764), a physician at Bath]

bathometer (bə'θɒmɪtə) *n* an instrument for measuring the depth of water.
▸**bathometric** (ˌbæθə'mɛtrɪk) *adj* ▸**ba'thometry** *n*

bathos ➊ ('beɪθɒs) *n* **1** a sudden ludicrous descent from exalted to ordinary matters or style in speech or writing. **2** insincere or excessive pathos. [C18: from Gk: depth]
▸**ba'thetic** *adj*

bathrobe ('bɑːθˌrəʊb) *n* **1** a loose-fitting garment of towelling, for wear before or after a bath or swimming. **2** *US & Canad.* a dressing gown.

bathroom ➊ ('bɑːθˌruːm, -ˌrʊm) *n* **1** a room containing a bath or shower and usually a washbasin and lavatory. **2** *US & Canad.* another name for **lavatory.**

bath salts *pl n* soluble scented salts for use in a bath.

bathtub ('bɑːθˌtʌb) *n* a bath, esp. one not permanently fixed.

bathy- *or* **batho-** *combining form.* indicating depth: *bathysphere.* [from Gk *bathus* deep]

bathyscaph ('bæθɪˌskæf), **bathyscaphe** ('bæθɪˌskeɪf, -ˌskæf), *or* **bathyscape** ('bæθɪˌskæp) *n* a submersible vessel with an observation capsule underneath, capable of reaching ocean depths of over 10 000 metres. [C20: from BATHY- + Gk *skaphē* light boat]

bathysphere ('bæθɪˌsfɪə) *n* a strong steel deep-sea diving sphere, lowered by cable.

batik ('bætɪk) *n* **a** a process of printing fabric in which parts not to be dyed are covered by wax. **b** fabric printed in this way. [C19: via Malay from Javanese: painted]

batiste (bæ'tiːst) *n* a fine plain-weave cotton. [C17: from F, prob. after *Baptiste* of Cambrai, 13th-cent. F weaver, its reputed inventor]

batman ('bætmən) *n, pl* **batmen.** an officer's servant in the armed forces. [C18: from OF *bat, bast,* from Med. L *bastum* packsaddle]

baton ➊ ('bætən) *n* **1** a thin stick used by the conductor of an orchestra, choir, etc. **2** *Athletics.* a short bar carried by a competitor in a relay race and transferred to the next runner at the end of each stage. **3** a long stick with a knob on one end, carried, twirled, and thrown up and down by a drum major or majorette, esp. at the head of a parade. **4** a police truncheon (esp. in **baton charge**). **5** a staff or club carried as a symbol of authority. [C16: from F *bâton,* from LL *bastum* rod]

baton round *n* the official name for **plastic bullet.**

batrachian (bə'treɪkɪən) *n* **1** any amphibian, esp. a frog or toad. ◆ *adj* **2** of or relating to the frogs and toads. [C19: from NL *Batrachia,* from Gk *batrakhos* frog]

bats (bæts) *adj Inf.* mad or eccentric.

batsman ('bætsmən) *n, pl* **batsmen. 1** *Cricket, etc.* **1a** a person who bats or whose turn it is to bat. **1b** a player who specializes in batting. **2** a person on the ground who uses bats to guide the pilot of an aircraft when taxiing.

battalion ➊ (bə'tæljən) *n* **1** a military unit comprised of three or more companies or formations of similar size. **2** (*usually pl*) any large array. [C16: from F *bataillon,* from OIt., from *battaglia* company of soldiers, BATTLE]

batten[1] ➊ ('bætᵊn) *n* **1** a sawn strip of wood used in building to cover joints, support lathing, etc. **2** a long narrow board used for flooring. **3** a lath used for holding a tarpaulin along the side of a hatch on a ship. **4** *Theatre.* **4a** a row of lights. **4b** the bar supporting them. ◆ *vb* **5** (*tr*) to furnish or strengthen with battens. **6 batten down the hatches. 6a** to use battens in securing a tarpaulin over a hatch on a ship. **6b** to prepare for action, a crisis, etc. [C15: from F *bâton* stick; see BATON]

batten[2] ➊ ('bætᵊn) *vb* (*intr*) (usually foll. by *on*) to thrive, esp. at the expense of someone else. [C16: prob. from ON *batna* to improve]

batter[1] ➊ ('bætə) *vb* **1** to hit (someone or something) repeatedly using heavy blows, as with a club. **2** (*tr; often passive*) to damage or injure, as by blows, heavy wear, etc. **3** (*tr*) to subject (a person, esp. a close relative) to repeated physical violence. [C14: *bateren,* prob. from *batten* to BAT[1]]
▸**'batterer** *n* ▸**'battering** *n*

batter[2] ('bætə) *n* a mixture of flour, eggs, and milk, used to make cakes, pancakes, etc., and to coat certain foods before frying. [C15 *bater,* prob. from *bateren* to BATTER[1]]

batter[3] ('bætə) *n Baseball, etc.* a player who bats.

batter[4] ('bætə) *n* **1** the slope of the face of a wall that recedes gradually backwards and upwards. ◆ *vb* **2** (*intr*) to have such a slope. [C16 (vb: to incline): from ?]

battered[1] ➊ ('bætəd) *adj* subjected to persistent physical violence, esp. by a close relative living in the house: *a battered baby.*

battered[2] ('bætəd) *adj* coated in batter: *battered cod.*

battering ram *n* (esp. formerly) a large beam used to break down fortifications.

battery ➊ ('bætərɪ) *n, pl* **batteries. 1** two or more primary cells connected, usually in series, to provide a source of electric current. **2** another name for **accumulator** (sense 1). **3** a number of similar things occurring together: *a battery of questions.* **4** *Criminal law.* unlawful beating or wounding of a person or mere touching in a hostile or offensive manner. **5** a fortified structure on which artillery is mounted. **6** a group of guns, missile launchers, etc, operated as a single entity. **7** a small unit of artillery. **8** *Chiefly Brit.* **8a** a large group of cages for intensive rearing of poultry and other farm animals. **8b** (*as modifier*): *battery hens.* **9** *Baseball.* the pitcher and the catcher considered together. [C16: from OF *batterie* beating, from *battre* to beat, from L *battuere*]

batting ('bætɪŋ) *n* **1** cotton or woollen wadding used in quilts, etc. **2** the action of a person or team that hits with a bat.

battle ➊ ('bætᵊl) *n* **1** a fight between large armed forces; military or naval engagement. **2** conflict; struggle. **3 do, give,** *or* **join battle.** to engage in conflict or competition. ◆ *vb* **battles, battling, battled. 4** (when *intr,* often foll. by *against, for,* or *with*) to fight in or as if in military combat; contend (with): *shop stewards battling to improve conditions at work.* **5** to struggle: *he battled through the crowd.* **6** (*intr*) *Austral.* to scrape a living. [C13: from OF *bataile,* from LL *battālia* exercises performed by soldiers, from *battuere* to beat]
▸**'battler** *n*

battle-axe ➊ *n* **1** (formerly) a large broad-headed axe. **2** *Inf.* an argumentative domineering woman.

battle-axe block *n Austral.* a block of land behind another, with access from the street through a narrow drive.

battle cruiser *n* a high-speed warship of battleship size but with lighter armour.

battle cry ➊ *n* **1** a shout uttered by soldiers going into battle. **2** a slogan used to rally the supporters of a campaign, movement, etc.

battledore ('bætᵊlˌdɔː) *n* **1** Also called: **battledore and shuttlecock.** an ancient racket game. **2** a light racket used in this game. **3** (formerly) a wooden utensil used for beating clothes, in baking, etc. [C15 *batyldoure,* ?from OProvençal *batedor* beater, from OF *battre* to beat]

battledress ('bætᵊlˌdrɛs) *n* the ordinary uniform of a soldier.

battle fatigue *n Psychol.* mental disorder, characterized by anxiety and depression, caused by the stress of warfare. Also: **combat fatigue.**

battlefield ➊ ('bætᵊlˌfiːld) *or* **battleground** ('bætᵊlˌgraʊnd) *n* the place where a battle is fought.

battlement ➊ ('bætᵊlmənt) *n* a parapet or wall with indentations or embrasures, originally for shooting through. [C14: from OF *batailles,* pl. of *bataille* BATTLE]
▸**'battlemented** *adj*

battle royal *n* **1** a fight, esp. with fists or cudgels, involving more than two combatants; melee. **2** a long violent argument.

battleship ➊ ('bætᵊlˌʃɪp) *n* a heavily armoured warship of the largest type.

batty ➊ ('bætɪ) *adj* **battier, battiest.** *Sl.* **1** insane; crazy. **2** odd; eccentric. [C20: from BAT[2]]

batwoman ('bætwʊmən) *n, pl* **batwomen.** a female servant in any of the armed forces.

bauble ➊ ('bɔːbᵊl) *n* **1** a trinket of little value. **2** (formerly) a mock staff of office carried by a jester. [C14: from OF *baubel* plaything, from ?]

baud (bɔːd) *n* a unit used to measure the speed of electronic code transmissions. [after J. M. E. *Baudot* (1845-1903), F inventor]

bauera ('baʊərə) *n* a small evergreen Australian shrub with pink or pur-

THESAURUS

bathos *n* = **anticlimax**, letdown **2** = **mawkishness**, false pathos, sentimentality

bathroom *n* **1, 2** = **lavatory**, comfort station (*US*), convenience (*chiefly Brit.*), powder room, rest room, shower, toilet, washroom, water closet, WC

baton *n* **4** = **truncheon**, club **5** = **stick**, crook, mace, rod, sceptre, staff, wand

battalion *n* **1** = **army**, brigade, company, contingent, division, force, legion, regiment, squadron, team, troop **2** = **multitude**, horde, host, throng

batten[1] *vb* **6a batten down** = **fasten**, board up, clamp down, cover up, fasten down, fix, nail down, secure, tighten

batten[2] *vb, usually with* **on** = **thrive**, fatten, flourish, gain, grow, increase, prosper

batter[1] *vb* **1, 3** = **beat**, assault, bash (*inf.*), beat the living daylights out of, belabour, break, buffet, clobber (*sl.*), dash against, lambast(e), lash, pelt, pound, pummel, smash, smite, thrash, wallop (*inf.*) **2** = **damage**, bruise, crush, deface, demolish, destroy, disfigure, hurt, injure, mangle, mar, maul, ruin, shatter, shiver, total (*sl.*), trash (*sl.*)

battered[1] *adj* = **beaten**, beat-up (*inf.*), black-and-blue, bruised, injured

battery *n* **3** = **series**, chain, ring, sequence, set, suite **4** *Criminal law* = **beating**, assault, attack, mayhem, onslaught, physical violence, thumping **6, 7** = **artillery**, cannon, cannonry, guns

battle *n* **1** = **fight**, action, attack, combat, encounter, engagement, fray, hostilities, skirmish, war, warfare **2** = **conflict**, agitation, campaign, clash, contest, controversy, crusade, debate, disagreement, dispute, head-to-head, strife, struggle ◆ *vb* **4** = **struggle**, agitate, argue, clamour, combat, contend, contest, dispute, feud, fight, lock horns, strive, war
Antonyms *n* ≠ **fight, conflict:** accord, agreement, armistice, ceasefire, concord, entente, peace, suspension of hostilities, truce

battle-axe *n* **2** *Informal* = **harridan**, ballbreaker (*sl.*), disciplinarian, fury, scold, shrew, tartar, termagant, virago, vixen

battle cry *n* **1** = **war cry**, war whoop **2** = **slogan**, catchword, motto, watchword

battlefield *n* = **battleground**, combat zone, field, field of battle, front

battlement *n* = **rampart**, barbican, bartizan, bastion, breastwork, bulwark, crenellation, fortification, parapet

battleship *n* = **warship**, capital ship, gunboat, man-of-war, ship of the line

batty *adj* **1** = **crazy**, barmy (*sl.*), bats (*sl.*), bonkers, crackers (*Brit. sl.*), daft (*inf.*), insane, loony (*sl.*), loopy (*inf.*), lunatic, mad, nuts (*sl.*), off one's rocker (*sl.*), off one's trolley (*sl.*), out of one's mind, potty (*Brit. inf.*), round the twist (*Brit. sl.*), touched **2** = **eccentric**, crackpot (*inf.*), cranky (*inf.*), dotty (*sl., chiefly Brit.*), odd, oddball (*inf.*), off the rails, off-the-wall (*sl.*), outré, peculiar, queer (*inf.*)

bauble *n* **1** = **trinket**, bagatelle, gewgaw, gim-

ple flowers. [C19: after Franz & Ferdinand *Bauer,* 19th-cent. Austrian botanical artists]

Bauhaus ('bau,haus) *n* a German school of functionalist architecture and applied arts founded in 1919. [G, lit.: building house]

bauhinia (bɔː'hɪnɪə, bəʊ-) *n* a climbing leguminous plant of tropical and warm regions, cultivated for ornament. [C18: NL, after Jean & Gaspard *Bauhin,* 16th-cent. F herbalists]

baulk (bɔːk; *usually for sense 1* bɔːlk) *n* **1** Also: **balk.** *Billiards.* the space between the baulk line and the bottom cushion. **2** *Archaeol.* a strip of earth left between excavation trenches for the study of the complete stratigraphy of a site. ◆ *vb, n* **3** a variant spelling of **balk.**

baulk line *or* **balk line** *n Billiards.* a straight line across a billiard table behind which the cue balls are placed at the start of a game. Also: **string line.**

baulky ('bɔːkɪ, 'bɔːlkɪ) *adj* a variant of **balky.**

bauxite ('bɔːksaɪt) *n* an amorphous claylike substance consisting of hydrated alumina with iron and other impurities: the chief source of alumina and aluminium and also used as an abrasive and catalyst. [C19: from F, from *(Les) Baux* in southern France, where orig. found]

bawd ➊ (bɔːd) *n Arch.* **1** a person who runs a brothel, esp. a woman. **2** a prostitute. [C14: from OF *baude,* fem. of *baud* merry]

bawdy ➊ ('bɔːdɪ) *adj* **bawdier, bawdiest. 1** (of language, plays, etc.) containing references to sex, esp. to be humorous. ◆ *n* **2** obscenity or eroticism, esp. in writing or drama.
▸ **'bawdily** *adv* ▸ **'bawdiness** *n* ▸ **bawdry** ('bɔːdrɪ) *n*

bawdyhouse ('bɔːdɪ,haus) *n* an archaic word for **brothel.**

bawl ➊ (bɔːl) *vb* **1** (*intr*) to utter long loud cries, as from pain or frustration; wail. **2** to shout loudly, as in anger. ◆ *n* **3** a loud shout or cry. [C15: imit.]
▸ **'bawler** *n* ▸ **'bawling** *n*

bawl out *vb (tr, adv) Inf.* to scold loudly.

bay[1] ➊ (beɪ) *n* **1** a wide semicircular indentation of a shoreline, esp. between two headlands. **2** an extension of lowland into hills that partly surround it. [C14: from OF *baie,* ?from OF *baer* to gape, from Med. L *batāre* to yawn]

bay[2] ➊ (beɪ) *n* **1** an alcove or recess in a wall. **2** any partly enclosed compartment. **3** See **bay window. 4** an area off a road in which vehicles may park or unload. **5** a compartment in an aircraft: *the bomb bay.* **6** *Naut.* a compartment in the forward part of a ship between decks, often used as the ship's hospital. **7** *Brit.* a tracked recess in the platform of a railway station, esp. one forming the terminus of a branch line. [C14: from OF *baee* gap, from *baer* to gape; see BAY[1]]

bay[3] ➊ (beɪ) *n* **1** a deep howl, esp. of a hound on the scent. **2 at bay. 2a** forced to turn and face attackers: *the dogs held the deer at bay.* **2b** at a distance. **3 bring to bay.** to force into a position from which retreat is impossible. ◆ *vb* **4** (*intr*) to howl (at) in deep prolonged tones. **5** (*tr*) to utter in a loud prolonged tone. **6** (*tr*) to hold at bay. [C13: from OF, imit.]

bay[4] (beɪ) *n* **1** a Mediterranean laurel. See **laurel** (sense 1). **2** any of several magnolias. See **sweet bay. 3** any of certain other trees or shrubs, esp. bayberry. **4** (*pl*) a wreath of bay leaves. [C14: from OF *baie* laurel berry, from L *bāca* berry]

bay[5] (beɪ) *n, adj* **1** (of) a reddish-brown colour. ◆ *n* **2** an animal of this colour. [C14: from OF *bai,* from L *badius*]

bayberry ('beɪbərɪ) *or* **bay** *n, pl* **bayberries. 1** any of several North American aromatic shrubs or small trees that bear grey waxy berries. **2** a tropical American tree that yields an oil used in making bay rum. **3** the fruit of any of these plants.

bay leaf *n* a leaf, usually dried, of the Mediterranean laurel, used in cooking to flavour soups and stews.

bayonet ➊ ('beɪənɪt) *n* **1** a blade for stabbing that can be attached to the muzzle of a firearm. **2** a type of fastening in which a cylindrical member is inserted into a socket against spring pressure and turned so that pins on its side engage in slots in the socket. ◆ *vb* **bayonets, bayoneting, bayoneted** *or* **bayonets, bayonetting, bayonetted. 3** (*tr*) to stab or kill with a bayonet. [C17: from F *baïonnette,* from *Bayonne,* a port in SW France, where it originated]

bayou ('baɪjuː) *n* (in the southern US) a sluggish marshy tributary of a lake or river. [C18: from Louisiana F, from Amerind *bayuk*]

bay rum *n* an aromatic liquid, used in medicines and cosmetics, originally obtained by distilling the leaves of the bayberry tree with rum: now also synthesized.

bay window *n* a window projecting from a wall and forming an alcove of a room.

bazaar ➊ *or* **bazar** (bə'zɑː) *n* **1** (esp. in the Orient) a market area, esp. a street of small stalls. **2** a sale in aid of charity, esp. of second-hand or handmade articles. **3** a shop where a variety of goods is sold. [C16: from Persian *bāzār*]

bazooka (bə'zuːkə) *n* a portable tubular rocket-launcher, used by infantrymen as a short-range antitank weapon. [C20: after a comic pipe instrument]

BB *abbrev. for:* **1** Boys' Brigade. **2** (on British pencils, signifying degrees of softness of lead) double black.

BBC *abbrev. for* British Broadcasting Corporation.

bbl. *abbrev. for* barrel (container or measure).

BBQ *abbrev. for* barbecue.

BC *abbrev. for* British Columbia.

B.C. *or* **BC** *abbrev. for* (indicating years numbered back from the supposed year of the birth of Christ) before Christ.

> **USAGE NOTE** See at **A.D.**

BCE *abbrev. for:* **1** Before Common Era (used, esp. by non-Christians, in numbering years B.C.). **2** *Brit.* Board of Customs and Excise.

BCG *abbrev. for* Bacillus Calmette-Guérin (antituberculosis vaccine).

BCNZ *abbrev. for* Broadcasting Corporation of New Zealand.

B complex *n* short for **vitamin B complex.**

BD *abbrev. for* Bachelor of Divinity.

bdellium ('dɛlɪəm) *n* **1** any of several African or W Asian trees that yield a gum resin. **2** the aromatic gum resin produced by any of these trees. [C16: from L, from Gk *bdellion,* ? from Heb. *bĕdhōlah*]

BDS *abbrev. for* Bachelor of Dental Surgery.

be ➊ (biː; *unstressed* bɪ) *vb present sing 1st person* **am;** *2nd person* **are;** *3rd person* **is.** *present pl* **are.** *past sing 1st person* **was;** *2nd person* **were;** *3rd person* **was.** *past pl* **were.** *present participle* **being.** *past participle* **been.** (*intr*) **1** to have presence in perceived reality; exist; live: *I think, therefore I am.* **2** (*used in the perfect tenses only*) to pay a visit; go: *have you been to Spain?* **3** to take place: *my birthday was last Thursday.* **4** (*copula*) used as a linking verb between the subject of a sentence and its noun or adjective complement. In this case *be* expresses relationship of equivalence or identity (*John is a man; John is a musician*) or specifies an attribute (*honey is sweet; Susan is angry*). It is also used with an adverbial complement to indicate a relationship in space or time (*Bill is at the office; the party is on Saturday*). **5** (*takes a present participle*) forms the progressive present tense: *the man is running.* **6** (*takes a past participle*) forms the passive voice of all transitive verbs: *a good film is being shown on television tonight.* **7** (*takes an infinitive*) expresses intention, expectation, or obligation: *the president is to arrive at 9.30.* [OE *bēon*]

Be *the chemical symbol for* beryllium.

BE *abbrev. for:* **1** bill of exchange. **2** Bachelor of Education. **3** Bachelor of Engineering.

be- *prefix forming transitive verbs.* **1** (*from nouns*) to surround or cover: *befog.* **2** (*from nouns*) to affect completely: *bedazzle.* **3** (*from nouns*) to consider as or cause to be: *befriend.* **4** (*from nouns*) to provide or cover with: *bejewel.* **5** (*from verbs*) at, for, against, on, or over: *bewail; berate.* [OE *be-, bi-,* unstressed var. of *bī* BY]

beach ➊ (biːtʃ) *n* **1** an area of sand or shingle sloping down to a sea or lake, esp. the area between the high- and low-water marks on a seacoast. ◆ *vb* **2** to run or haul (a boat) onto a beach. [C16: perhaps rel. to OE *bæce* river]

beachcomber ➊ ('biːtʃ,kəʊmə) *n* **1** a person who searches shore debris for anything of worth. **2** a long high wave rolling onto a beach.

beachhead ('biːtʃ,hɛd) *n Mil.* an area on a beach that has been captured from the enemy and on which troops and equipment are landed.

beacon ➊ ('biːkən) *n* **1** a signal fire or light on a hill, tower, etc., esp. formerly as a warning of invasion. **2** a hill on which such fires were lit. **3** a lighthouse, signalling buoy, etc. **4** short for **radio beacon. 5** a radio or other signal marking a flight course in air navigation. **6** short for **Belisha beacon. 7** a person or thing that serves as a guide, inspiration, or warning. [OE *beacen* sign]

bead ➊ (biːd) *n* **1** a small pierced usually spherical piece of glass, wood, plastic, etc., which may be strung with others to form a necklace, etc. **2 tell one's beads.** to pray with a rosary. **3** a small drop of moisture. **4** a small bubble in or on a liquid. **5** a small metallic knob acting as the sight of a firearm. **6 to draw** *or* **hold a bead on.** to aim a rifle or pistol at. **7** *Archit., furniture.* a small convex moulding having a semicircular cross

THESAURUS

crack, kickshaw, knick-knack, plaything, toy, trifle

bawd *n* **1** = **madam**, brothel-keeper, pimp, procuress **2** = **prostitute**, whore, working girl (*facetious sl.*)

bawdy *adj* **1** = **rude**, blue, coarse, dirty, indecent, indelicate, lewd, libidinous, licentious, near the knuckle (*inf.*), obscene, prurient, ribald, risqué, salacious, smutty, suggestive, vulgar, X-rated (*inf.*)
Antonyms *adj* chaste, clean, decent, good, modest, moral, respectable, seemly, undefiled, upright, virtuous

bawl *vb* **1** = **cry**, blubber, sob, squall, wail, weep **2** = **shout**, bellow, call, clamour, halloo, howl, roar, vociferate, yell

bay[1] *n* **1** = **inlet**, bight, cove, gulf, natural harbour, sound

bay[2], 2 *n* = **recess**, alcove, compartment, embrasure, niche, nook, opening

bay[3] *n* **1** = **howl**, bark, bell, clamour, cry, growl, yelp **2a at bay** = **cornered**, caught, trapped

bayonet *vb* **3** = **stab**, impale, knife, run through, spear, stick, transfix

bazaar *n* **1** = **market**, exchange, marketplace, mart **2** = **fair**, bring-and-buy, fête, sale of work

be *vb* **1** = **exist**, be alive, breathe, inhabit, live **3** = **take place**, befall, come about, come to pass, happen, occur, transpire (*inf.*)

beach *n* **1** = **shore**, coast, lido, littoral, margin, sands, seaboard, seashore, seaside, shingle, strand, water's edge

beachcomber *n* **1** = **scavenger**, forager, loafer, scrounger, tramp, vagabond, vagrant, wanderer

beached *adj* **2** = **stranded**, abandoned, aground, ashore, deserted, grounded, high and dry, marooned, wrecked

beacon *n* **1** = **signal**, beam, bonfire, flare, rocket, sign, signal fire, smoke signal **3** = **lighthouse**, pharos, watchtower

bead *n* **1** = **pellet**, blob, dot, pill, spherule **3** = **drop**, droplet, globule **4** = **bubble**

section. ◆ *vb* **8** (*tr*) to decorate with beads. **9** to form into beads or drops. [OE *bed* prayer]
▸ **'beaded** *adj*

beading ('bi:dɪŋ) *n* **1** another name for **bead** (sense 7). **2** Also called: **beadwork** ('bi:dˌwɜ:k). a narrow strip of some material used for edging or ornamentation.

beadle ('bi:dᵊl) *n* **1** *Brit.* (formerly) a minor parish official who acted as an usher and kept order. **2** *Judaism.* a synagogue attendant. **3** *Scot.* a church official who attends the minister. **4** an official in certain British institutions. [OE *bydel*]
▸ **'beadleship** *n*

beadsman *or* **bedesman** ('bi:dzmən) *n, pl* **beadsmen** *or* **bedesmen.** *Arch.* **1** a person who prays for another's soul, esp. one paid or fed for doing so. **2** a person kept in an almshouse.

beady ❶ ('bi:dɪ) *adj* **beadier, beadiest. 1** small, round, and glittering (esp. in **beady eyes**). **2** resembling or covered with beads.
▸ **'beadiness** *n*

beagle ('bi:gᵊl) *n* **1** a small sturdy breed of hound. **2** *Arch.* a spy. ◆ *vb* **beagles, beagling, beagled. 3** (*intr*) to hunt with beagles. [C15: from ?]

beak[1] ❶ (bi:k) *n* **1** the projecting jaws of a bird, covered with a horny sheath. **2** any beaklike mouthpart in other animals. **3** *Sl.* a person's nose. **4** any projecting part, such as the pouring lip of a bucket. **5** *Naut.* another word for **ram** (sense 5). [C13: from OF *bec,* from L *beccus,* of Gaulish origin]
▸ **beaked** *adj* ▸ **'beaky** *adj*

beak[2] (bi:k) *n* a Brit. slang word for **judge, magistrate, headmaster,** or **schoolmaster.** [C19: orig. thieves' jargon]

beaker ('bi:kə) *n* **1** a cup usually having a wide mouth. **2** a cylindrical flat-bottomed container used in laboratories, usually made of glass and having a pouring lip. [C14: from ON *bikarr*]

Beaker folk ('bi:kə) *n* a prehistoric people inhabiting Europe and Britain during the second millennium B.C. [after beakers found among their remains]

be-all and end-all *n Inf.* the ultimate aim or justification.

beam ❶ (bi:m) *n* **1** a long thick piece of wood, metal, etc., esp. one used as a horizontal structural member. **2** the breadth of a ship or boat taken at its widest part. **3** a ray or column of light, as from a beacon. **4** a broad smile. **5** one of two cylindrical rollers on a loom, which hold the warp threads and the finished work. **6** the main stem of a deer's antler. **7** the central shaft of a plough to which all the main parts are attached. **8** a narrow unidirectional flow of electromagnetic radiation or particles: *an electron beam.* **9** the horizontal centrally pivoted bar in a balance. **10 beam in one's eye.** a fault or grave error greater in oneself than in another person. **11 broad in the beam.** *Inf.* having wide hips. **12 off (the) beam. 12a** not following a radio beam to maintain a course. **12b** *Inf.* mistaken or irrelevant. **13 on the beam. 13a** following a radio beam to maintain a course. **13b** *Inf.* correct, relevant, or appropriate. ◆ *vb* **14** to send out or radiate. **15** (*tr*) to divert or aim (a radio signal, light, etc.) in a certain direction: *to beam a programme to Tokyo.* **16** (*intr*) to smile broadly. [OE]
▸ **'beaming** *adj*

beam-ends *pl n* **1 on her beam-ends.** (of a vessel) heeled over through an angle of 90°. **2 on one's beam-ends.** out of resources; destitute.

bean (bi:n) *n* **1** any of various leguminous plants producing edible seeds in pods. **2** any of various other plants whose seeds are produced in pods or podlike fruits. **3** the seed or pod of any of these plants. **4** any of various beanlike seeds, as coffee. **5** *US & Canad. sl.* another word for **head. 6 full of beans.** *Inf.* full of energy and vitality. **7 not have a bean.** *Sl.* to be without money. [OE *bēan*]

beanbag ('bi:nˌbæg) *n* **1** a small cloth bag filled with dried beans and thrown in games. **2** a very large cushion filled with foam rubber or polystyrene granules and used as a seat.

bean counter *n Inf.* an accountant.

bean curd *n* another name for **tofu.**

beanfeast ('bi:nˌfi:st) *n Brit. inf.* **1** an annual dinner given by employers to employees. **2** any festive or merry occasion.

beano ('bi:nəʊ) *n, pl* **beanos.** *Brit. sl.* a celebration, party, or other enjoyable time.

beanpole ('bi:nˌpəʊl) *n* **1** a tall stick used to support bean plants. **2** *Sl.* a tall thin person.

bean sprout *n* the sprout of a newly germinated mung bean, eaten esp. in Chinese dishes.

beanstalk ('bi:nˌstɔ:k) *n* the stem of a bean plant.

bear[1] ❶ (bɛə) *vb* **bears, bearing, bore, borne.** (*mainly tr*) **1** to support or hold up. **2** to bring: *to bear gifts.* **3** to accept or assume the responsibility of: *to bear an expense.* **4** (**born** in passive use except when followed by *by*) to give birth to: *to bear children.* **5** (*also intr*) to produce as by natural growth: *to bear fruit.* **6** to tolerate or endure. **7** to admit of; sustain: *his story does not bear scrutiny.* **8** to hold in the mind: *to bear a grudge.* **9** to show or be marked with: *he still bears the scars.* **10** to render or supply (esp. in **bear witness**). **11** to conduct (oneself, the body, etc.). **12** to have, be, or stand in (relation or comparison): *his account bears no relation to the facts.* **13** (*intr*) to move or lie in a specified direction. **14 bear a hand.** to give assistance. **15 bring to bear.** to bring into operation or effect. ◆ See also **bear down, bear on,** etc. [OE *beran*]

bear[2] (bɛə) *n, pl* **bears** *or* **bear. 1** a plantigrade mammal typically having a large head, a long shaggy coat, and strong claws. **2** any of various bearlike animals, such as the koala. **3** a clumsy, churlish, or ill-mannered person. **4** a teddy bear. **5** *Stock Exchange.* **5a** a speculator who sells in anticipation of falling prices to make a profit on repurchase. **5b** (*as modifier*): *a bear market.* Cf. **bull**[1] (sense 4). ◆ *vb* **bears, bearing, beared. 6** (*tr*) to lower or attempt to lower the price or prices of (a stock market or a security) by speculative selling. [OE *bera*]

Bear (bɛə) *n* **the. 1** the English name for either Ursa Major (Great Bear) or Ursa Minor (Little Bear). **2** an informal name for Russia.

bearable ❶ ('bɛərəbᵊl) *adj* endurable; tolerable.

bear-baiting *n* (formerly) an entertainment in which dogs attacked a chained bear.

beard ❶ (bɪəd) *n* **1** the hair growing on the lower parts of a man's face. **2** any similar growth in animals. **3** a tuft of long hairs in plants such as barley; awn. **4** a barb, as on a fish-hook. ◆ *vb* (*tr*) **5** to oppose boldly or impertinently. [OE *beard*]
▸ **'bearded** *adj*

beardless ❶ ('bɪədlɪs) *adj* **1** without a beard. **2** too young to grow a beard; immature.

bear down ❶ *vb* (*intr, adv;* often foll. by *on* or *upon*) **1** to press or weigh down. **2** to approach in a determined or threatening manner.

bearer ❶ ('bɛərə) *n* **1** a person or thing that bears, presents, or upholds. **2** a person who presents a note or bill for payment. **3** (in Africa, India, etc., formerly) a native porter or servant. **4** (*modifier*) *Finance.* payable to the person in possession: *bearer bonds.*

bear garden *n* **1** (formerly) a place where bear-baiting took place. **2** a scene of tumult.

bear hug *n* **1** a wrestling hold in which the arms are locked tightly round an opponent's chest and arms. **2** any similar tight embrace. **3** *Commerce.* an approach to the board of one company by another to indicate that an offer is to be made for their shares.

bearing ❶ ('bɛərɪŋ) *n* **1** a support for a rotating or reciprocating mechanical part. **2** (foll. by *on* or *upon*) relevance (to): *it has no bearing on this problem.* **3** a person's general social conduct. **4** the act, period, or capability of producing fruit or young. **5** anything that carries weight or acts as a support. **6** the angular direction of a point or course measured from a known position. **7** (*usually pl*) the position, as of a ship, fixed with reference to two or more known points. **8** (*usually pl*) a sense of one's relative position; orientation (esp. in **lose, get,** *or* **take one's bearings**). **9** *Heraldry.* **9a** a device on a heraldic shield. **9b** another name for **coat of arms.**

bearing rein *n Chiefly Brit.* a rein from the bit to the saddle, designed to keep the horse's head in the desired position.

bearish ❶ ('bɛərɪʃ) *adj* **1** like a bear; rough; clumsy; churlish. **2** *Stock Exchange.* causing, expecting, or characterized by a fall in prices: *a bearish feel to the market.*
▸ **'bearishness** *n*

bear on ❶ *vb* (*intr, prep*) **1** to be relevant to; relate to. **2** to be burdensome to or afflict.

THESAURUS

beady *adj* **1** = **bright,** gleaming, glinting, glittering, sharp, shining

beak[1] *n* **1, 2** = **bill,** mandible, neb (*arch. or dialect*), nib **3** *Slang* = **nose,** proboscis, snout

beam *n* **1** = **rafter,** girder, joist, plank, spar, support, timber **3** = **ray,** bar, emission, gleam, glimmer, glint, glow, radiation, shaft, streak, stream **4** = **smile,** grin ◆ *vb* **14** = **radiate,** emit, glare, gleam, glitter, glow, shine **15** = **send out,** broadcast, emit, transmit **16** = **smile,** grin

beaming *adj* **14** = **radiating,** beautiful, bright, brilliant, flashing, gleaming, glistening, glittering, radiant, scintillating, shining, sparkling **16** = **smiling,** cheerful, grinning, happy, joyful, sunny

bear[1] *vb* **1** = **support,** hold up, shoulder, sustain, uphold **2** = **carry,** bring, convey, hump (*Brit. sl.*), move, take, tote (*inf.*), transport **4, 5** = **produce,** beget, breed, bring forth, develop, engender, generate, give birth to, yield **6** = **tolerate,** abide, admit, allow, brook, endure, hack (*sl.*), permit, put up with (*inf.*), stomach, suffer, undergo **8** = **hold,** cherish, entertain, harbour, have, maintain, possess
Antonyms *vb* ≠ **support:** abandon, cease, desert, discontinue, drop, give up, leave, quit, relinquish ≠ **carry:** drop, put down, shed

bearable *adj* = **tolerable,** admissible, endurable, manageable, passable, sufferable, supportable, sustainable
Antonyms *adj* insufferable, insupportable, intolerable, oppressive, too much (*inf.*), unacceptable, unbearable, unendurable

beard *n* **1** = **whiskers,** bristles, five-o'clock shadow, stubble ◆ *vb* **5** = **confront,** brave, dare, defy, face, oppose, tackle

bearded *adj* **1** = **unshaven,** bewhiskered, bristly, bushy, hairy, hirsute, shaggy, stubbly, whiskered

beardless *adj* **1** = **clean-shaven,** barefaced, hairless, smooth, smooth-faced

bear down *vb* **1** = **press down,** burden, compress, encumber, push, strain, weigh down **2** = **approach,** advance on, attack, close in, converge on, move in

bearer *n* **2** = **payee,** beneficiary, consignee **3** = **carrier,** agent, conveyor, messenger, porter, runner, servant

bearing *n* **2** = **relevance,** application, connection, import, pertinence, reference, relation, significance **3** = **manner,** air, aspect, attitude, behaviour, carriage, demeanour, deportment, mien, posture **6, 7** = **position,** course, direction, point of compass **8** *usually plural* = **position,** aim, course, direction, location, orientation, situation, track, way, whereabouts
Antonyms *n* ≠ **relevance:** inappositeness, inappropriateness, inaptness, inconsequence, irrelevance, irrelevancy, non sequitur

bearish *adj* **1** = **gruff,** churlish, clumsy, rough, sullen, surly **2** *Stock Exchange* = **falling,** declining, slumping

bear on *vb* **1** = **be relevant to,** affect, appertain

bear out Ⓣ *vb* (*tr, adv*) to show to be true or truthful; confirm: *the witness will bear me out.*

bear raid *n* an attempt to force down the price of a security or commodity by sustained selling.

bearskin ('bɛə,skɪn) *n* **1** the pelt of a bear, esp. when used as a rug. **2** a tall helmet of black fur worn by certain British Army regiments.

bear up Ⓣ *vb* (*intr, adv*) to endure cheerfully.

bear with Ⓣ *vb* (*intr, prep*) to be patient with.

beast Ⓣ (bi:st) *n* **1** any animal other than man, esp. a large wild quadruped. **2** savage nature or characteristics: *the beast in man.* **3** a brutal, uncivilized, or filthy person. [C13: from OF *beste,* from L *bestia,* from ?]

beastly Ⓣ ('bi:stlɪ) *adj* **beastlier, beastliest. 1** *Inf.* unpleasant; disagreeable. **2** *Obs.* of or like a beast; bestial. ◆ *adv* **3** *Inf.* (intensifier): *the weather is so beastly hot.*
▸ **'beastliness** *n*

beast of burden *n* an animal, such as a donkey or ox, used for carrying loads.

beast of prey *n* any animal that hunts other animals for food.

beat Ⓣ (bi:t) *vb* **beats, beating, beat; beaten** *or* **beat. 1** (when *intr,* often foll. by *against, on,* etc.) to strike with or as if with a series of violent blows. **2** (*tr*) to punish by striking; flog. **3** to move up and down; flap: *the bird beat its wings heavily.* **4** (*intr*) to throb rhythmically; pulsate. **5** (*tr;* sometimes foll. by *up*) *Cookery.* to stir or whisk vigorously. **6** (*tr;* sometimes foll. by *out*) to shape, thin, or flatten (metal) by repeated blows. **7** (*tr*) *Music.* to indicate (time) by one's hand, baton, etc., or by a metronome. **8** (when *tr,* sometimes foll. by *out*) to produce (a sound or signal) by or as if by striking a drum. **9** to overcome; defeat. **10** (*tr*) to form (a path, track, etc.) by repeatedly walking or riding over it. **11** (*tr*) to arrive, achieve, or finish before (someone or something). **12** (*tr;* often foll. by *back, down, off,* etc.) to drive, push, or thrust. **13** to scour (woodlands or undergrowth) so as to rouse game for shooting. **14** (*tr*) *Sl.* to puzzle or baffle: *it beats me.* **15** (*intr*) *Naut.* to steer a sailing vessel as close as possible to the direction from which the wind is blowing. **16 beat a retreat.** to withdraw in haste. **17 beat it.** *Sl.* (*often imperative*) to go away. **18 beat the bounds.** *Brit.* (formerly) to define the boundaries of a parish by making a procession around them and hitting the ground with rods. **19 can you beat it** *or* **that?** *Sl.* an expression of surprise. ◆ *n* **20** a stroke or blow. **21** the sound made by a stroke or blow. **22** a regular throb. **23a** an assigned or habitual round or route, as of a policeman. **23b** (*as modifier*): *beat police officers.* **24** the basic rhythmic unit in a piece of music. **25a** pop or rock music characterized by a heavy rhythmic beat. **25b** (*as modifier*): *a beat group.* **26** *Physics.* one of the regular pulses produced by combining two sounds or electrical signals that have similar frequencies. **27** *Prosody.* the accent or stress in a metrical foot. **28** (*modifier*) (*often cap.*) of, characterized by, or relating to the Beat Generation. ◆ *adj* **29** (*postpositive*) *Sl.* totally exhausted. ◆ See also **beat down, beat up.** [OE *bēatan*]
▸ **'beatable** *adj*

beatbox ('bi:t,bɒks) *n* another name for **drum machine.**

beat down *vb* (*adv*) **1** (*tr*) *Inf.* to force or persuade (a seller) to accept a lower price. **2** (*intr*) (of the sun) to shine intensely.

beaten Ⓣ ('bi:tᵊn) *adj* **1** defeated or baffled. **2** shaped or made thin by hammering: *beaten gold.* **3** much travelled; well trodden. **4 off the beaten track. 4a** in unfamiliar territory. **4b** out of the ordinary; unusual. **5** (of food) mixed by beating; whipped. **6** tired out; exhausted.

beater ('bi:tə) *n* **1** a person who beats or hammers: *a panel beater.* **2** a device used for beating: *a carpet beater.* **3** a person who rouses wild game.

Beat Generation *n* (*functioning as sing or pl*) **1** members of the generation that came to maturity in the 1950s, whose rejection of the social and political systems of the West was expressed through contempt for regular work, possessions, traditional dress, etc. **2** a group of US writers, notably Jack Kerouac, Allen Ginsberg, and William Burroughs, who emerged in the 1950s.

beatific Ⓣ (,bi:ə'tɪfɪk) *adj* **1** displaying great happiness, calmness, etc. **2** of or conferring a state of celestial happiness. [C17: from LL *beātificus,* from L *beātus,* from *beāre* to bless + *facere* to make]
▸ **,bea'tifically** *adv*

beatify (bɪ'ætɪ,faɪ) *vb* **beatifies, beatifying, beatified.** (*tr*) **1** *RC Church.* (of the pope) to declare formally that (a deceased person) showed a heroic degree of holiness in life and is worthy of veneration: the first step towards canonization. **2** to make extremely happy. [C16: from OF *beatifier;* see BEATIFIC]
▸ **beatification** (bɪ,ætɪfɪ'keɪʃən) *n*

beating Ⓣ ('bi:tɪŋ) *n* **1** a whipping or thrashing. **2** a defeat or setback. **3 take some** *or* **a lot of beating.** to be difficult to improve upon.

beatitude Ⓣ (bɪ'ætɪ,tju:d) *n* **1** supreme blessedness or happiness. **2** an honorific title of the Eastern Christian Church, applied to those of patriarchal rank. [C15: from L *beātitūdō,* from *beātus* blessed; see BEATIFIC]

Beatitude (bɪ'ætɪ,tju:d) *n Christianity.* any of eight sayings of Jesus in the Sermon on the Mount (Matthew 5:3 –11) in which he declares that the poor, the meek, etc., will, in various ways, receive the blessings of heaven.

beatnik ('bi:tnɪk) *n* **1** a member of the Beat Generation (sense 1). **2** *Inf.* any person with long hair and shabby clothes. [C20: from BEAT (n) + -NIK]

beat up Ⓣ *Inf.* ◆ *vb* **1** (*tr, adv*) to strike or kick repeatedly, so as to inflict severe physical damage. ◆ *adj* **beat-up. 2** worn-out; dilapidated.

beau Ⓣ (bəʊ) *n, pl* **beaux** (bəʊ, bəʊz) *or* **beaus** (bəʊz). **1** a man who is greatly concerned with his clothes and appearance; dandy. **2** *Chiefly US.* a boyfriend; sweetheart. [C17: from F, from OF *biau,* from L *bellus* handsome]

Beaufort scale ('bəʊfət) *n Meteorol.* an international scale of wind velocities from 0 (calm) to 12 (hurricane) (0 to 17 in the US). [C19: after Sir Francis *Beaufort* (1774–1857), Brit. admiral and hydrographer who devised it]

beau geste *French.* (bo ʒɛst) *n, pl* ***beaux gestes*** (bo ʒɛst). a noble or gracious gesture or act. [lit.: beautiful gesture]

beaujolais ('bəʊʒə,leɪ) *n* (*sometimes cap.*) a popular fresh-tasting red or white wine from southern Burgundy in France.

beau monde ('bəʊ 'mɒnd) *n* the world of fashion and society. [C18: F, lit.: fine world]

beaut (bju:t) *Sl., chiefly Austral. & NZ.* ◆ *n* **1** an outstanding person or thing. ◆ *adj, interj* **2** excellent.

beauteous ('bju:tɪəs) *adj* a poetic word for **beautiful.**
▸ **'beauteousness** *n*

beautician (bju:'tɪʃən) *n* a person who works in or manages a beauty salon.

beautiful Ⓣ ('bju:tɪfʊl) *adj* **1** possessing beauty; aesthetically pleasing. **2** highly enjoyable; very pleasant.
▸ **'beautifully** *adv*

beautify Ⓣ ('bju:tɪ,faɪ) *vb* **beautifies, beautifying, beautified.** to make or become beautiful.
▸ **beautification** (,bju:tɪfɪ'keɪʃən) *n* ▸ **'beauti,fier** *n*

beauty Ⓣ ('bju:tɪ) *n, pl* **beauties. 1** the combination of all the qualities of a person or thing that delight the senses and mind. **2** a very attractive woman. **3** *Inf.* an outstanding example of its kind. **4** *Inf.* an advanta-

THESAURUS

to, belong to, concern, involve, pertain to, refer to, relate to, touch upon

bear out *vb* = **support**, confirm, corroborate, endorse, justify, prove, substantiate, uphold, vindicate

bear up *vb* = **cope**, bear the brunt, carry on, endure, go through the mill, grin and bear it (*inf.*), keep one's chin up, persevere, suffer, take it on the chin (*inf.*), withstand

bear with *vb* = **be patient with**, make allowances for, put up with (*inf.*), suffer, tolerate, wait for

beast *n* **1** = **animal**, brute, creature **3** = **brute**, barbarian, fiend, ghoul, monster, ogre, sadist, savage, swine

beastly *adj* **1** *Informal* = **unpleasant**, awful, disagreeable, foul, horrid, mean, nasty, rotten, terrible **2** *Obsolete* = **brutal**, animal, barbarous, bestial, brutish, coarse, cruel, depraved, inhuman, monstrous, repulsive, sadistic, savage
Antonyms *adj* ≠ **unpleasant:** agreeable, fine, good, pleasant ≠ **brutal:** humane, sensitive

beat *vb* **1, 2** = **hit**, bang, batter, belt (*inf.*), break, bruise, buffet, cane, chin (*sl.*), clobber (*sl.*), cudgel, deck (*sl.*), drub, flog, knock, lash, pelt, pound, punch, strike, thrash, thwack, whip **3** = **flap**, flutter **4** = **throb**, palpitate, pound, pulsate, pulse, quake, quiver, shake, thump, tremble, vibrate **6** = **shape**, fashion, forge, form, hammer, model, work **9** = **defeat**, best, blow out of the water (*sl.*), clobber (*sl.*), conquer, knock spots off (*inf.*), lick (*inf.*), master, outdo, outstrip, overcome, overwhelm, surpass, vanquish, wipe the floor with (*inf.*) **17 beat it** *Slang* = **go away**, depart, exit, get lost (*inf.*), get on one's bike (*Brit. sl.*), hop it (*sl.*), leave, make tracks, scarper (*Brit. sl.*), scram (*inf.*), sling one's hook (*Brit. sl.*), vamoose (*sl., chiefly US*) ◆ *n* **20** = **blow**, belt (*inf.*), hit, lash, punch, shake, slap, strike, swing, thump **22** = **throb**, palpitation, pulsation, pulse **23a** = **route**, circuit, course, path, rounds, way **27** = **rhythm**, accent, cadence, ictus, measure (*Prosody*), metre, stress ◆ *adj* **29** *Slang* = **exhausted**, clapped out (*Austral. & NZ inf.*), fatigued, on one's last legs, tired, wearied, wiped out (*inf.*), worn out, zonked (*sl.*)

beaten *adj* **1** = **defeated**, baffled, cowed, disappointed, disheartened, frustrated, overcome, overwhelmed, thwarted, vanquished **2** = **shaped**, forged, formed, hammered, stamped, worked **3** = **well-trodden**, much travelled, trampled, trodden, well-used, worn **5** = **stirred**, blended, foamy, frothy, mixed, whipped, whisked

beatific *adj* **1** = **blissful**, blissed out, ecstatic, enraptured, exalted, glorious, joyful, rapt, rapturous, serene, sublime **2** = **divine**, blessed, heavenly

beating *n* **1** = **thrashing**, belting (*inf.*), caning, chastisement, corporal punishment, flogging, pasting (*sl.*), slapping, smacking, whipping **2** = **defeat**, conquest, downfall, overthrow, pasting (*sl.*), rout, ruin

beatitude *n* **1** = **blessedness**, beatification, bliss, ecstasy, exaltation, felicity, happiness, holy joy, saintliness

beat up *Informal vb* **1** = **assault**, attack, batter, clobber (*sl.*), do over (*Brit., Austral., & NZ sl.*), duff up (*Brit. sl.*), knock about *or* around, put the boot in (*sl.*), thrash, work over (*sl.*)

beau *n* **1** = **dandy**, coxcomb, fop, gallant, ladies' man, popinjay, swell (*inf.*) **2** *Chiefly U.S.* = **boyfriend**, admirer, escort, fancy man (*sl.*), fiancé, guy (*inf.*), lover, suitor, swain, sweetheart

beautiful *adj* **1** = **attractive**, alluring, appealing, charming, comely, delightful, drop-dead (*sl.*), exquisite, fair, fine, glamorous, good-looking, gorgeous, graceful, handsome, lovely, pleasing, radiant, ravishing, stunning (*inf.*)
Antonyms *adj* awful, bad, hideous, repulsive, terrible, ugly, unattractive, unpleasant, unsightly

beautify *vb* = **make beautiful**, adorn, array, bedeck, deck, decorate, embellish, enhance, festoon, garnish, gild, glamorize, grace, ornament

beauty *n* **1** = **attractiveness**, allure, bloom, charm, comeliness, elegance, exquisiteness, fairness, glamour, grace, handsomeness, loveliness, pulchritude, seemliness, symmetry **2** = **belle**, charmer, cracker (*sl.*), goddess, good-looker, humdinger (*sl.*), lovely (*sl.*), stunner (*inf.*), Venus **4** *Informal* = **advantage**, asset, at-

geous feature: *one beauty of the job is the short hours.* ◆ *interj* **5** (*NZ* ˈbjuːdɪ). *Austral. & NZ sl.* an expression of approval or agreement. [C13: from OF *biauté*, from *biau* beautiful; see BEAU]

beauty queen *n* an attractive young woman, esp. one who has won a beauty contest.

beauty salon *or* **parlour** *n* an establishment providing services such as hairdressing, facial treatment, and massage.

beauty sleep *n Inf.* sleep, esp. sleep before midnight.

beauty spot *n* **1** a place of outstanding beauty. **2** a mole or other similar natural mark on the skin. **3** (esp. in the 18th century) a small dark-coloured patch or spot worn on a lady's face as an adornment.

beaux (bəʊ, bəʊz) *n* a plural of **beau.**

beaux-arts (bəʊˈzɑː) *pl n* **1** another word for **fine art. 2** (*modifier*) relating to the classical decorative style, esp. that of the École des Beaux-Arts in Paris: *beaux-arts influences.* [F]

beaver[1] Ⓣ (ˈbiːvə) *n* **1** a large amphibious rodent of Europe, Asia, and North America. It has soft brown fur, a broad flat hairless tail, and webbed hind feet, and constructs complex dams and houses (lodges) in rivers. **2** its fur. **3** a tall hat of beaver fur worn during the 19th century. **4** a woollen napped cloth resembling beaver fur. **5** *Obs.* a full beard. **6** a bearded man. **7** (*modifier*) made of beaver fur or similar material. ◆ *vb* **8** (*intr; usually foll. by away*) to work industriously or steadily. [OE *beofor*]

beaver[2] (ˈbiːvə) *n* a movable piece on a medieval helmet used to protect the lower face. [C15: from OF *baviere*, from *baver* to dribble]

bebop (ˈbiːbɒp) *n* the full name for **bop** (sense 1). [C20: imit. of the rhythm]
▸ˈ**bebopper** *n*

becalmed Ⓣ (bɪˈkɑːmd) *adj* (of a sailing boat or ship) motionless through lack of wind.

became (bɪˈkeɪm) *vb* the past tense of **become.**

because Ⓣ (bɪˈkɒz, -ˈkəz) *conj* **1** (*subordinating*) on account of the fact that; since: *because it's so cold we'll go home.* **2 because of.** (*prep*) on account of: *I lost my job because of her.* [C14 *bi cause*, from *bi* BY + CAUSE]

> **USAGE NOTE** See at **reason.**

béchamel sauce (ˌbeɪʃəˈmɛl) *n* a thick white sauce flavoured with onion and seasonings. [C18: after the Marquis of *Béchamel*, its F inventor]

bêche-de-mer (ˌbɛʃdəˈmɛə) *n, pl* **bêches-de-mer** (ˌbɛʃdəˈmɛə) *or* **bêche-de-mer.** another name for **trepang.** [C19: quasi-F, from earlier E *biche de mer*, from Port. *bicho do mar* worm of the sea]

Bechuana (beˈtʃwɑːnə; ˌbɛkjuˈɑːnə) *n, pl* **Bechuana** *or* **Bechuanas.** a former name for a Bantu of Botswana, a republic in southern Africa.

beck[1] (bɛk) *n* **1** a nod, wave, or other gesture. **2 at (someone's) beck and call.** subject to (someone's) slightest whim. [C14: short for *becnen* to BECKON]

beck[2] (bɛk) *n* (in N England) a stream. [OE *becc*]

beckon Ⓣ (ˈbɛkən) *vb* **1** to summon with a gesture of the hand or head. **2** to entice or lure. ◆ *n* **3** a summoning gesture. [OE *bīecnan*, from *bēacen* sign]
▸ˈ**beckoner** *n* ▸ˈ**beckoning** *adj, n*

becloud (bɪˈklaʊd) *vb* (*tr*) **1** to cover or obscure with a cloud. **2** to confuse or muddle.

become Ⓣ (bɪˈkʌm) *vb* **becomes, becoming, became, become.** (*mainly intr*) **1** (*copula*) to come to be; develop or grow into: *he became a monster.* **2** (foll. by *of; usually used in a question*) to happen (to): *what became of him?* **3** (*tr*) to suit: *that dress becomes you.* **4** (*tr*) to be appropriate; to befit: *it ill becomes you to complain.* [OE *becuman* to happen]

becoming Ⓣ (bɪˈkʌmɪŋ) *adj* suitable; appropriate.
▸**beˈcomingly** *adv* ▸**beˈcomingness** *n*

becquerel (ˌbɛkəˈrɛl) *n* the SI unit of activity of a radioactive source. [after A.H. *Becquerel* (1852–1908), F physicist]

bed Ⓣ (bɛd) *n* **1** a piece of furniture on which to sleep. **2** the mattress and bedclothes: *an unmade bed.* **3** sleep or rest: *time for bed.* **4** any place in which a person or animal sleeps or rests. **5** *Med.* a unit of potential occupancy in a hospital or residential institution. **6** *Inf.* sexual intercourse. **7** a plot of ground in which plants are grown. **8** the bottom of a river, lake, or sea. **9** a part of this used for cultivation of a plant or animal: *oyster beds.* **10** any underlying structure or part. **11** a layer of rock, esp. sedimentary rock. **12 go to bed. 12a** (often foll. by *with*) to have sexual intercourse (with). **12b** *Journalism, printing.* (of a newspaper, etc.) to go to press; start printing. **13 in bed with.** *Inf.* cooperating closely with (another person, organization, government, etc.), esp. covertly. **14 put to bed.** *Journalism.* to finalize work on (a newspaper, etc.) so that it is ready to go to press. **15 take to one's bed.** to remain in bed, esp. because of illness. ◆ *vb* **beds, bedding, bedded. 16** (usually foll. by *down*) to go to or put into a place to sleep or rest. **17** (*tr*) to have sexual intercourse with. **18** (*tr*) to place firmly into position; embed. **19** *Geol.* to form or be arranged in a distinct layer; stratify. **20** (*tr; often* foll. by *out*) to plant in a bed of soil. [OE *bedd*]

BEd *abbrev. for* Bachelor of Education.

bed and board *n* sleeping accommodation and meals.

bed and breakfast *n Chiefly Brit.* **1** (in a hotel, boarding house, etc.) overnight accommodation and breakfast. **2** the selling of shares after hours one evening on a stock exchange and buying them back the next morning, in order to establish a loss for capital-gains tax purposes.

bedaub Ⓣ (bɪˈdɔːb) *vb* (*tr*) **1** to smear all over with something thick, sticky, or dirty. **2** to ornament in a gaudy or vulgar fashion.

bedazzle Ⓣ (bɪˈdæzəl) *vb* **bedazzles, bedazzling, bedazzled.** (*tr*) to dazzle or confuse, as with brilliance.
▸**beˈdazzlement** *n*

bed bath *n* another name for **blanket bath.**

bedbug (ˈbɛdˌbʌg) *n* any of several bloodsucking wingless insects of temperate regions, infesting dirty houses.

bedchamber (ˈbɛdˌtʃeɪmbə) *n* an archaic word for **bedroom.**

bedclothes Ⓣ (ˈbɛdˌkləʊðz) *pl n* sheets, blankets, and other coverings for a bed.

beddable (ˈbɛdəbəl) *adj* sexually attractive.

bedding Ⓣ (ˈbɛdɪŋ) *n* **1** bedclothes, sometimes considered with a mattress. **2** litter, such as straw, for animals. **3** a foundation, such as mortar under a brick. **4** the stratification of rocks.

bedding plant *n* an immature plant that may be planted out in a garden bed.

bedeck Ⓣ (bɪˈdɛk) *vb* (*tr*) to cover with decorations; adorn.

bedevil Ⓣ (bɪˈdɛvəl) *vb* **bedevils, bedevilling, bedevilled** *or US* **bedevils, bedeviling, bedeviled.** (*tr*) **1** to harass or torment. **2** to throw into confusion. **3** to possess, as with a devil.
▸**beˈdevilment** *n*

bedew Ⓣ (bɪˈdjuː) *vb* (*tr*) to wet as with dew.

bedfellow (ˈbɛdˌfɛləʊ) *n* **1** a person with whom one shares a bed. **2** a temporary ally or associate.

bedight (bɪˈdaɪt) *Arch.* ◆ *vb* **bedights, bedighting, bedight** *or* **bedighted. 1** (*tr*) to array or adorn. ◆ *adj* **2** (*p.p.*) adorned or bedecked. [C14: from DIGHT]

bedim Ⓣ (bɪˈdɪm) *vb* **bedims, bedimming, bedimmed.** (*tr*) to make dim or obscure.

bedizen (bɪˈdaɪzən, -ˈdɪzən) *vb* (*tr*) *Arch.* to dress or decorate gaudily or tastelessly. [C17: from BE- + obs. *dizen* to dress up, from ?]
▸**beˈdizenment** *n*

bed jacket *n* a woman's short upper garment worn over a nightgown when sitting up in bed.

bedlam Ⓣ (ˈbɛdləm) *n* **1** a noisy confused situation. **2** *Arch.* a madhouse. [C13 *bedlem, bethlem*, from Hospital of St Mary of *Bethlehem* in London]

bed linen *n* sheets, pillowcases, etc., for a bed.

Bedouin *or* **Beduin** (ˈbɛduɪn) *n* **1** (*pl* **Bedouins, Bedouin** *or* **Beduins, Beduin**) a nomadic Arab tribesman of the deserts of Arabia, Jordan, and Syria. **2** a wanderer. ◆ *adj* **3** of or relating to the Bedouins. **4** wandering. [C14: from OF *beduin*, from Ar. *badāwi*, pl. of *badwi*, from *badw* desert]

bedpan (ˈbɛdˌpæn) *n* a vessel used by a bedridden patient to collect faeces and urine.

bedraggle Ⓣ (bɪˈdrægəl) *vb* **bedraggles, bedraggling, bedraggled.** (*tr*) to make (hair, clothing, etc.) limp, untidy, or dirty, as with rain or mud.
▸**beˈdraggled** *adj*

THESAURUS

traction, benefit, blessing, boon, excellence, feature, good thing
Antonyms *n ≠* **attractiveness:** repulsiveness, ugliness, unpleasantness, unseemliness *≠* **advantage:** detraction, disadvantage, flaw

beaver[1] *vb* **8** *usually with* **away** = **work,** exert oneself, graft (*inf.*), hammer away, keep one's nose to the grindstone, peg away, persevere, persist, plug away (*inf.*), slog

becalmed *adj* = **still,** motionless, settled, stranded, stuck

because *conj* **1** = **since,** as, in that **2** = **on account of,** by reason of, owing to, thanks to

beckon *vb* **1** = **gesture,** bid, gesticulate, motion, nod, signal, summon, wave at **2** = **lure,** allure, attract, call, coax, draw, entice, invite, pull, tempt

become *vb* **1** = **come to be,** alter to, be transformed into, change into, develop into, evolve into, grow into, mature into, metamorphose into, ripen into **3** = **suit,** embellish, enhance, fit, flatter, grace, harmonize, ornament, set off

becoming *adj* = **appropriate,** befitting, *comme il faut,* compatible, congruous, decent, decorous, fit, fitting, in keeping, meet (*arch.*), proper, seemly, suitable, worthy
Antonyms *adj* improper, inappropriate, unfit, unsuitable, unworthy

bed *n* **1** = **bedstead,** berth, bunk, cot, couch, divan, pallet **7** = **plot,** area, border, garden, patch, row, strip **10** = **bottom,** base, foundation, groundwork **11** = **substratum** ◆ *vb* **16** *usually foll. by* **down** = **sleep,** hit the hay, lie, retire, settle down, turn in (*inf.*) **18** = **fix,** base, embed, establish, found, implant, insert, settle, set up **20** = **plant**

bedaub *vb* **1** = **smear,** besmear, smirch, soil, spatter, splash, stain

bedazzle *vb* = **dazzle,** amaze, astound, bewilder, blind, captivate, confuse, daze, dumbfound, enchant, overwhelm, stagger, stun, sweep off one's feet

bedclothes *pl n* = **bedding,** bed linen, blankets, coverlets, covers, duvets, eiderdowns, pillowcases, pillows, quilts, sheets

bedding *n* **1** = **bedclothes,** bed linen, linen, sheets

bedeck *vb* = **decorate,** adorn, array, embellish, engarland, festoon, garnish, ornament, trim

bedevil *vb* **1** = **torment,** aggravate (*inf.*), annoy, harass, hassle (*inf.*), irk, irritate, pester, plague, torture, trouble, vex, worry **2** = **confuse,** confound

bedew *vb* = **sprinkle,** besprinkle, dampen, drench, moisten, shower, soak, spray, water, wet

bedim *vb* = **dim,** becloud, cloak, cloud, darken, obscure, overcast, shade, shadow

bedlam *n* **1** = **pandemonium,** chaos, clamour, commotion, confusion, furore, hubbub, hullabaloo, noise, tumult, turmoil, uproar

bedraggled *adj* = **messy,** dirty, dishevelled, disordered, drenched, dripping, muddied, muddy, sodden, soiled, stained, sullied, unkempt, untidy

bedridden 🅣 (ˈbɛdˌrɪdᵊn) *adj* confined to bed because of illness, esp. for a long or indefinite period. [OE *bedreda*]

bedrock 🅣 (ˈbɛdˌrɒk) *n* **1** the solid rock beneath the surface soil, etc. **2** basic principles or facts. **3** the lowest point, level, or layer.

bedroll (ˈbɛdˌrəʊl) *n* a portable roll of bedding.

bedroom (ˈbɛdˌruːm, -ˌrʊm) *n* **1** a room used for sleeping. **2** (*modifier*) containing references to sex: *a bedroom comedy.*

Beds (bɛdz) *abbrev. for* Bedfordshire.

bedside (ˈbɛdˌsaɪd) *n* **a** the space beside a bed, esp. a sickbed. **b** (*as modifier*): *a bedside lamp.*

bedsit (ˈbɛdˌsɪt) *n* a furnished sitting room containing sleeping accommodation. Also called: **bedsitting room, bedsitter.**

bedsore (ˈbɛdˌsɔː) *n* a chronic ulcer on the skin of a bedridden person, caused by prolonged pressure.

bedspread (ˈbɛdˌsprɛd) *n* a top cover on a bed.

bedstead (ˈbɛdˌstɛd) *n* the framework of a bed.

bedstraw (ˈbɛdˌstrɔː) *n* any of numerous plants which have small white or yellow flowers and prickly or hairy fruits: formerly used as straw for beds.

bedtime (ˈbɛdˌtaɪm) *n* **a** the time when one usually goes to bed. **b** (*as modifier*): *a bedtime story.*

bed-wetting *n* the act of urinating in bed.

bee[1] (biː) *n* **1** any of various four-winged insects that collect nectar and pollen and make honey and wax. **2 busy bee.** a person who is industrious or has many things to do. **3 have a bee in one's bonnet.** to be obsessed with an idea. [OE *bīo*]

bee[2] (biː) *n Chiefly US.* a social gathering for a specific purpose, as to carry out a communal task: *quilting bee.* [?from dialect *bean* neighbourly help, from OE *bēn* boon]

Beeb (biːb) *n* **the.** an informal name for the **BBC.**

beebread (ˈbiːˌbrɛd) *n* a mixture of pollen and nectar prepared by worker bees and fed to the larvae. Also called: **ambrosia.**

beech (biːtʃ) *n* **1** a European tree having smooth greyish bark. **2** a similar tree of temperate Australasia and South America. **3** the hard wood of either of these trees. **4** See **copper beech.** [OE *bēce*]
▸ˈ**beechen** *or* ˈ**beechy** *adj*

beechnut (ˈbiːtʃˌnʌt) *n* the small brown triangular edible nut of the beech tree, collectively often termed **beech mast.**

bee-eater *n* any of various insectivorous birds of the Old World tropics and subtropics.

beef 🅣 (biːf) *n* **1** the flesh of various bovine animals, esp. the cow, when killed for eating. **2** (*pl* **beeves**) an adult ox, etc., reared for its meat. **3** *Inf.* human flesh, esp. when muscular. **4** (*pl* **beefs**) *Sl.* a complaint. ◆ *vb* **5** (*intr*) *Sl.* to complain, esp. repeatedly. **6** (*tr;* often foll. by *up*) *Inf.* to strengthen; reinforce. [C13: from OF *boef,* from L *bōs* ox]

beefburger (ˈbiːfˌbɜːɡə) *n* a flat fried cake of minced beef; hamburger.

beefcake (ˈbiːfˌkeɪk) *n Sl.* men displayed for their muscular bodies, esp. in photographs.

beefeater (ˈbiːfˌiːtə) *n* a nickname applied to the Yeomen of the Guard, and the Yeomen Warders at the Tower of London.

beef road *n Austral.* a road used for transporting cattle.

beefsteak (ˈbiːfˌsteɪk) *n* a lean piece of beef that can be grilled, fried, etc.

beef tomato *n* a very large fleshy variety of tomato. Also called: **beefsteak tomato.**

beef tea *n* a drink made by boiling pieces of lean beef.

beefy 🅣 (ˈbiːfɪ) *adj* **beefier, beefiest. 1** like beef. **2** *Inf.* muscular; brawny.
▸ˈ**beefiness** *n*

beehive 🅣 (ˈbiːˌhaɪv) *n* **1** a man-made receptacle used to house a swarm of bees. **2** a dome-shaped structure. **3** a place where busy people are assembled. **4 the Beehive.** the dome-shaped building which houses Parliament in Wellington, New Zealand.

beekeeper (ˈbiːˌkiːpə) *n* a person who keeps bees for their honey.
▸ˈ**bee**ˌ**keeping** *n*

beeline (ˈbiːˌlaɪn) *n* the most direct route between two places (esp. in **make a beeline for**).

Beelzebub (bɪˈɛlzɪˌbʌb) *n* Satan or any devil. [OE *Belzebub,* ult. from Heb. *bá'al zebūb,* lit.: lord of flies]

bee moth *n* any of various moths whose larvae live in the nests of bees or wasps, feeding on nest materials and host larvae.

been (biːn, bɪn) *vb* the past participle of **be.**

beep (biːp) *n* **1** a short high-pitched sound, as made by a car horn or by electronic apparatus. ◆ *vb* **2** to make or cause to make such a noise. [C20: imit.]
▸ˈ**beeper** *n*

beer 🅣 (bɪə) *n* **1** an alcoholic drink brewed from malt, sugar, hops, and water. **2** a slightly fermented drink made from the roots or leaves of certain plants: *ginger beer.* **3** (*modifier*) relating to beer: *beer glass.* **4** (*modifier*) in which beer is drunk, esp. (of licensed premises) having a licence to sell beer but not spirits: *beer house; beer garden.* [OE *beor*]

beer and skittles *n* (*functioning as sing*) *Inf.* enjoyment or pleasure.

beer parlour *n Canad.* a licensed place in which beer is sold to the public.

beery (ˈbɪərɪ) *adj* **beerier, beeriest. 1** smelling or tasting of beer. **2** given to drinking beer.
▸ˈ**beerily** *adv* ▸ˈ**beeriness** *n*

bee's knees *n* **the** (*functioning as sing*) *Inf.* an excellent or ideally suitable person or thing.

beestings, biestings, *or US* **beastings** (ˈbiːstɪŋz) *n* (*functioning as sing*) the first milk secreted by a cow or similar animal after giving birth; colostrum. [OE *bȳsting*]

beeswax (ˈbiːzˌwæks) *n* **1** a wax secreted by honeybees for constructing honeycombs. **2** this wax after refining, used in polishes, etc.

beeswing (ˈbiːzˌwɪŋ) *n* a light filmy crust of tartar that forms in some wines after long keeping in the bottle.

beet (biːt) *n* **1** a plant of a genus widely cultivated in such varieties as the sugar beet, mangelwurzel, and beetroot. **2** the leaves of any of several varieties of this plant, cooked and eaten as a vegetable. **3 red beet.** the US name for **beetroot.** [OE *bēte,* from L *bēta*]

beetle[1] 🅣 (ˈbiːtᵊl) *n* **1** an insect having biting mouthparts and forewings modified to form shell-like protective casings. **2** a game in which the players draw or assemble a beetle-shaped form. ◆ *vb* **beetles, beetling, beetled.** (*intr;* foll. by *along, off,* etc.) **3** *Inf.* to scuttle or scurry; hurry. [OE *bitela*]

beetle[2] (ˈbiːtᵊl) *n* **1** a heavy hand tool for pounding or beating. **2** a machine used to finish cloth by stamping it with wooden hammers. [OE *bīetel,* from *bēatan* to BEAT]

beetle[3] 🅣 (ˈbiːtᵊl) *vb* **beetles, beetling, beetled. 1** (*intr*) to overhang; jut. ◆ *adj* **2** overhanging; prominent. [C14: ? rel. to BEETLE[1]]
▸ˈ**beetling** *adj*

beetle-browed 🅣 *adj* having bushy or overhanging eyebrows.

beetroot (ˈbiːtˌruːt) *n* a variety of the beet plant that has a bulbous dark red root that may be eaten as a vegetable, in salads, or pickled.

beet sugar *n* the sucrose obtained from sugar beet, identical in composition to cane sugar.

beeves (biːvz) *n* the plural of **beef** (sense 2).

BEF *abbrev. for* British Expeditionary Force, the British army that served in France 1939-40.

befall 🅣 (bɪˈfɔːl) *vb* **befalls, befalling, befell, befallen.** *Arch. or literary.* **1** (*intr*) to take place. **2** (*tr*) to happen to. **3** (*intr;* usually foll. by *to*) to be due, as by right. [OE *befeallan;* see BE-, FALL]

befit 🅣 (bɪˈfɪt) *vb* **befits, befitting, befitted.** (*tr*) to be appropriate to or suitable for. [C15: from BE- + FIT[1]]
▸**be**ˈ**fitting** *adj* ▸**be**ˈ**fittingly** *adv*

befog 🅣 (bɪˈfɒɡ) *vb* **befogs, befogging, befogged.** (*tr*) **1** to surround with fog. **2** to make confused.

before 🅣 (bɪˈfɔː) *conj* (*subordinating*) **1** earlier than the time when. **2** rather than: *he'll resign before he agrees to it.* ◆ *prep* **3** preceding in space or time; in front of; ahead of: *standing before the altar.* **4** in the presence of: *to be brought before a judge.* **5** in preference to: *to put friendship before money.* ◆ *adv* **6** at an earlier time; previously. **7** in front. [OE *beforan*]

beforehand 🅣 (bɪˈfɔːˌhænd) *adj* (*postpositive*), *adv* early; in advance; in anticipation.

befoul (bɪˈfaʊl) *vb* (*tr*) to make dirty or foul.

befriend 🅣 (bɪˈfrɛnd) *vb* (*tr*) to be a friend to; assist; favour.

befuddle 🅣 (bɪˈfʌdᵊl) *vb* **befuddles, befuddling, befuddled.** (*tr*) **1** to confuse. **2** to make stupid with drink.
▸**be**ˈ**fuddlement** *n*

THESAURUS

bedridden *adj* = **confined to bed**, confined, flat on one's back, incapacitated, laid up (*inf.*)

bedrock *n* **1** = **bottom**, bed, foundation, rock bottom, substratum, substructure **2** = **basics**, basis, core, essentials, fundamentals, nuts and bolts (*inf.*), roots

beef *n* **3** *Informal* = **flesh**, brawn, heftiness, muscle, physique, robustness, sinew, strength **4** *Slang* = **complaint**, criticism, dispute, grievance, gripe (*inf.*), grouch (*inf.*), grouse, grumble, objection, protest, protestation

beefy *adj* **2** *Informal* = **brawny**, bulky, burly, hulking, muscular, stalwart, stocky, strapping, sturdy, thickset
Antonyms *adj* feeble, frail, puny, scrawny, skinny, weak

beehive *n* **1** = **hive**, apiary, comb, honeycomb

beer *n* **1** = **ale**, amber fluid *or* nectar (*Austral. inf.*), brew, hop juice, swipes (*Brit. sl.*), wallop (*Brit. sl.*)

beetle-browed *adj* = **scowling**, frowning, glowering, lowering, pouting, sullen

beetling *adj* **1** = **overhanging**, hanging over, jutting, leaning over, pendent, projecting, prominent, protruding, sticking out, swelling over

befall *vb Archaic or literary* **1** = **happen**, chance, come to pass, ensue, fall, follow, materialize, occur, supervene, take place, transpire (*inf.*) **2** = **happen to**, betide

befit *vb* = **be appropriate**, become, be fitting, behoove (*US*), behove, be seemly, be suitable, suit

befitting *adj* = **appropriate**, apposite, becoming, fit, fitting, meet (*arch.*), proper, right, seemly, suitable
Antonyms *adj* improper, inappropriate, irrelevant, unbecoming, unfit, unsuitable, wrong

befog *vb* **2** = **make unclear**, blur, confuse, darken, fuzz, make hazy, make indistinct, make vague, muddle, muddy the waters, obfuscate, obscure

before *conj* **1** = **earlier than**, in advance of, prior to ◆ *prep* **3** = **ahead of**, in advance of, in front of **4** = **in the presence of**, in front of ◆ *adv* **6** = **previously**, ahead, earlier, formerly, in advance, sooner **7** = **in front**, ahead
Antonyms *prep* ≠ **ahead of, earlier than:** after, behind, following, succeeding ◆ *adv* ≠ **previously, in front:** after, afterwards, behind, later, subsequently, thereafter

beforehand *adv* = **in advance**, ahead of time, already, before, before now, earlier, early, in anticipation, previously, sooner

befriend *vb* = **help**, advise, aid, assist, back, benefit, encourage, favour, patronize, side with, stand by, support, sustain, uphold

befuddle *vb* **1** = **confuse**, baffle, bewilder, dis-

beg Ⓣ (bɛg) *vb* **begs, begging, begged. 1** (when *intr,* often foll. by *for*) to solicit (for money, food, etc.), esp. in the street. **2** to ask formally, humbly, or earnestly: *I beg forgiveness; I beg to differ.* **3** (*intr*) (of a dog) to sit up with forepaws raised expectantly. **4 beg the question. 4a** to evade the issue. **4b** to put forward an argument that assumes the very point it is supposed to establish or that depends on some other questionable assumption. **4c** to suggest that a question needs to be asked: *the firm's success begs the question: why aren't more companies doing the same?* **5 go begging.** to be unwanted or unused. ◆ See also **beg off. [**C13: prob. from OE *bedecian***]**

> **USAGE NOTE** The use of *beg the question* to mean that a question needs to be asked is considered by some people to be incorrect.

began (bɪ'gæn) *vb* the past tense of **begin.**

beget Ⓣ (bɪ'gɛt) *vb* **begets, begetting, begot** *or* **begat; begotten** *or* **begot.** (*tr*) **1** to father. **2** to cause or create. **[**OE *begietan;* see BE-, GET**]**
▸**be'getter** *n*

beggar Ⓣ ('bɛgə) *n* **1** a person who begs, esp. one who lives by begging. **2** a person who has no money or resources; pauper. **3** *Chiefly Brit.* a fellow: *lucky beggar!* ◆ *vb* (*tr*) **4** to be beyond the resources of (esp. in **beggar description**). **5** to impoverish.
▸**'beggardom** *n*

beggarly Ⓣ ('bɛgəlɪ) *adj* meanly inadequate; very poor.
▸**'beggarliness** *n*

beggar-my-neighbour *n* a card game in which one player tries to win all the cards of the other player.

beggary Ⓣ ('bɛgərɪ) *n* extreme poverty or need.

begin Ⓣ (bɪ'gɪn) *vb* **begins, beginning, began, begun. 1** to start or cause to start (something or to do something). **2** to bring or come into being; arise or originate. **3** to start to say or speak. **4** (*with a negative*) to have the least capacity (to do something): *he couldn't begin to compete.* **5 to begin with.** in the first place. **[**OE *beginnan***]**

beginner Ⓣ (bɪ'gɪnə) *n* a person who has just started to do or learn something; novice.

beginning Ⓣ (bɪ'gɪnɪŋ) *n* **1** a start; commencement. **2** (*often pl*) a first or early part or stage. **3** the place where or time when something starts. **4** an origin; source.

begird (bɪ'gɜːd) *vb* **begirds, begirding, begirt** *or* **begirded.** (*tr*) *Poetic.* **1** to surround; gird around. **2** to bind. **[**OE *begierdan;* see BE-, GIRD[1]**]**

beg off *vb* (*intr, adv*) to ask to be released from an engagement, obligation, etc.

begone (bɪ'gɒn) *sentence substitute.* go away! **[**C14: from BE (imperative) + GONE**]**

begonia (bɪ'gəʊnjə) *n* a plant of warm and tropical regions, having ornamental leaves and waxy flowers. **[**C18: NL, after Michel *Bégon* (1638–1710), F patron of science**]**

begorra (bɪ'gɔːrə) *interj* an emphatic exclamation, regarded as characteristic of Irishmen. **[**C19: from *by God!***]**

begot (bɪ'gɒt) *vb* a past tense and past participle of **beget.**

begotten (bɪ'gɒtᵊn) *vb* a past participle of **beget.**

begrime (bɪ'graɪm) *vb* **begrimes, begriming, begrimed.** (*tr*) to make dirty; soil.

begrudge Ⓣ (bɪ'grʌdʒ) *vb* **begrudges, begrudging, begrudged.** (*tr*) **1** to give, admit, or allow unwillingly or with a bad grace. **2** to envy (someone) the possession of (something).
▸**be'grudgingly** *adv*

beguile Ⓣ (bɪ'gaɪl) *vb* **beguiles, beguiling, beguiled.** (*tr*) **1** to charm; fascinate. **2** to delude; influence by slyness. **3** (often foll. by *of* or *out of*) to cheat (someone) of. **4** to pass pleasantly; while away.
▸**be'guilement** *n* ▸**be'guiler** *n* ▸**be'guiling** *adj* ▸**be'guilingly** *adv*

beguine (bɪ'giːn) *n* **1** a dance of South American origin in bolero rhythm. **2** a piece of music in the rhythm of this dance. **[**C20: from Louisiana F, from F *béguin* flirtation**]**

begum ('beɪgəm) *n* (in certain Muslim countries) a woman of high rank. **[**C18: from Urdu *begam,* from Turkish *begim;* see BEY**]**

begun (bɪ'gʌn) *vb* the past participle of **begin.**

behalf Ⓣ (bɪ'hɑːf) *n* interest, part, benefit, or respect (only in **on (someone's) behalf, on** *or US & Canad.* **in behalf of, in this** (*or* **that**) **behalf**). **[**OE *be halfe,* from *be* by + *halfe* side**]**

behave Ⓣ (bɪ'heɪv) *vb* **behaves, behaving, behaved. 1** (*intr*) to act or function in a specified or usual way. **2** to conduct (oneself) in a specified way: *he behaved badly.* **3** to conduct (oneself) properly or as desired. **[**C15: see BE-, HAVE**]**

behaviour Ⓣ *or US* **behavior** (bɪ'heɪvjə) *n* **1** manner of behaving. **2 on one's best behaviour.** behaving with careful good manners. **3** *Psychol.* the response of an organism to a stimulus. **4** the reaction or functioning of a machine, etc., under normal or specified circumstances. **[**C15: from BEHAVE; infl. by ME *havior,* from OF *havoir,* from L *habēre* to have**]**
▸**be'havioural** *or US* **be'havioral** *adj*

behavioural science *n* the scientific study of the behaviour of organisms.

behaviourism *or US* **behaviorism** (bɪ'heɪvjəˌrɪzəm) *n* a school of psychology that regards objective observation of the behaviour of organisms as the only valid subject for study.
▸**be'haviourist** *or US* **be'haviorist** *adj, n* ▸**beˌhaviour'istic** *or US* **beˌhavior'istic** *adj*

behaviour therapy *n* any of various means of treating psychological disorders, such as aversion therapy, that depend on the patient systematically learning new behaviour.

behead Ⓣ (bɪ'hɛd) *vb* (*tr*) to remove the head from. **[**OE *behēafdian,* from BE- + *heafod* HEAD**]**

beheld (bɪ'hɛld) *vb* the past tense and past participle of **behold.**

behemoth (bɪ'hiːmɒθ) *n* **1** *Bible.* a gigantic beast described in Job 40:15. **2** a huge or monstrous person or thing. **[**C14: from Heb. *bĕhēmōth,* pl. of *bĕhēmāh* beast**]**

behest Ⓣ (bɪ'hɛst) *n* an order or earnest request. **[**OE *behǣs,* from *behātan;* see BE-, HEST**]**

behind Ⓣ (bɪ'haɪnd) *prep* **1** in or to a position further back than. **2** in the past in relation to: *I've got the exams behind me now.* **3** late according to: *running behind schedule.* **4** concerning the circumstances surrounding: *the reasons behind his departure.* **5** supporting: *I'm right behind you in your application.* ◆ *adv* **6** in or to a position further back; following. **7** remaining after someone's departure: *he left his books behind.* **8** in debt;

THESAURUS

orient, muddle, puzzle **2** = **intoxicate**, daze, stupefy
Antonyms *vb* ≠ **confuse:** clarify, clear up, elucidate, explicate, illuminate, interpret, make clear, make plain, resolve, simplify, throw *or* shed light on

befuddled *adj* **1** = **confused**, at sea, dazed, fuddled, groggy (*inf.*), muddled **2** = **intoxicated**, inebriated, woozy (*inf.*)

beg *vb* **1** = **scrounge**, blag (*sl.*), cadge, call for alms, mooch (*sl.*), seek charity, solicit charity, sponge on, touch (someone) for (*sl.*) **2** = **implore**, beseech, crave, desire, entreat, importune, petition, plead, pray, request, solicit, supplicate **4a** *As in* **beg the question** = **dodge**, avoid, duck (*inf.*), equivocate, evade, fend off, flannel (*Brit. inf.*), hedge, shirk, sidestep
Antonyms *vb* ≠ **scrounge:** claim, demand, exact, extort, insist on ≠ **implore:** apportion, award, bestow, commit, confer, contribute, donate, give, grant, impart, present

beget *vb* **1** = **father**, breed, generate, get, procreate, propagate, sire **2** = **cause**, bring, bring about, create, effect, engender, give rise to, occasion, produce, result in

begetter *n* **1** = **father**, genitor, parent, procreator, sire **2** = **creator**, architect, author, founder, inventor, originator

beggar *n* **1** = **scrounger** (*inf.*), cadger, mendicant, sponger (*inf.*), supplicant **2** = **tramp**, bag lady (*chiefly US*), bankrupt, bum (*inf.*), down-and-out, pauper, starveling, vagrant ◆ *vb* **4** *As in* **beggar description** = **defy**, baffle, challenge, surpass

beggarly *adj* = **inadequate**, low, meagre, mean, miserly, niggardly, stingy

beggary *n* = **poverty**, bankruptcy, destitution, indigence, need, pauperism, vagrancy, want, wretchedness

begin *vb* **1** = **start**, commence, embark on, get the show on the road (*inf.*), inaugurate, initiate, instigate, institute, prepare, set about, set on foot **2** = **happen**, appear, arise, be born, come into being, come into existence, commence, crop up (*inf.*), dawn, emerge, originate, spring, start
Antonyms *vb* cease, complete, end, finish, stop, terminate

beginner *n* = **novice**, amateur, apprentice, cub, fledgling, freshman, greenhorn (*inf.*), initiate, learner, neophyte, recruit, starter, student, tenderfoot, trainee, tyro
Antonyms *n* authority, expert, master, old hand, old stager, old-timer, past master *or* past mistress, pro (*inf.*), professional, trouper, veteran

beginning *n* **1, 2** = **start**, birth, commencement, inauguration, inception, initiation, onset, opening, opening move, origin, outset, overture, preface, prelude, rise, rudiments, source, starting point **4** = **seed**, embryo, fount, fountainhead, germ, root
Antonyms *n* ≠ **start:** closing, completion, conclusion, end, ending, finish, termination

begrudge *vb* **1** = **resent**, be reluctant, be stingy, grudge **2** = **envy**, be jealous

begrudgingly *adv* **1** = **resentfully**, grudgingly, hesitantly, reluctantly, stingily, unenthusiastically, unwillingly, with bad grace, without enthusiasm
Antonyms *adv* enthusiastically, freely, generously, gladly, willingly, with good grace

beguile *vb* **1** = **charm**, amuse, cheer, delight, distract, divert, engross, entertain, occupy **2** = **fool**, befool, cheat, deceive, delude, dupe, hoodwink, impose on, mislead, take for a ride (*inf.*), trick
Antonyms *vb* ≠ **fool:** alarm, alert, enlighten, put right

beguiling *adj* **1** = **charming**, alluring, attractive, bewitching, captivating, diverting, enchanting, entertaining, enthralling, interesting, intriguing

behalf *n* = **benefit**, account, advantage, defence, good, interest, part, profit, sake, side, support

behave *vb* **1** = **act**, function, operate, perform, run, work **3** = **conduct oneself properly**, act correctly, keep one's nose clean, mind one's manners
Antonyms *vb* ≠ **conduct oneself properly:** act up (*inf.*), be bad, be insubordinate, be naughty, carry on (*inf.*), get up to mischief (*inf.*), misbehave, muck about (*Brit. sl.*)

behaviour *n* **1** = **conduct**, actions, bearing, carriage, comportment, demeanour, deportment, manner, manners, ways **4** = **action**, functioning, operation, performance

behead *vb* = **decapitate**, execute, guillotine, truncate

behest *n* = **command**, bidding, canon, charge, commandment, decree, dictate, direction, injunction, instruction, mandate, order, precept, wish

behind *prep* **1** = **after**, at the back of, at the heels of, at the rear of, following **4** = **causing**, at the bottom of, initiating, instigating, responsi-

in arrears: *to fall behind with payments.* ◆ *adj* **9** (*postpositive*) in a position further back. ◆ *n* **10** *Inf.* the buttocks. **11** *Australian Rules football.* a score of one point made by kicking the ball over the **behind line** between a goalpost and one of the smaller outer posts (**behind posts**). [OE *behindan*]

behindhand ⓣ (bɪˈhaɪndˌhænd) *adj* (*postpositive*), *adv* **1** remiss in fulfilling an obligation. **2** in arrears. **3** backward. **4** late.

behold ⓣ (bɪˈhəʊld) *vb* **beholds, beholding, beheld.** (often imperative) *Arch. or literary.* to look (at); observe. [OE *bihealdan*; see BE-, HOLD[1]]
▸**beˈholder** *n*

beholden ⓣ (bɪˈhəʊldᵊn) *adj* indebted; obliged. [OE *behealden*, p.p. of *behealdan* to BEHOLD]

behoof (bɪˈhuːf) *n, pl* **behooves.** *Rare.* advantage or profit. [OE *behōf*; see BEHOVE]

behove ⓣ (bɪˈhəʊv) *vb* **behoves, behoving, behoved.** (*tr; impersonal*) *Arch.* to be necessary or fitting for: *it behoves me to arrest you.* [OE *behōfian*]

beige ⓣ (beɪʒ) *n* **1a** a very light brown, sometimes with a yellowish tinge. **1b** (*as adj*): *beige gloves.* **2** a fabric made of undyed or unbleached wool. [C19: from OF, from ?]

being ⓣ (ˈbiːɪŋ) *n* **1** the state or fact of existing; existence. **2** essential nature; self. **3** something that exists or is thought to exist: *a being from outer space.* **4** a person; human being.

bejabers (bɪˈdʒeɪbəz) *or* **bejabbers** (bɪˈdʒæbəz) *interj* an exclamation of surprise, emphasis, etc., regarded as characteristic of Irishmen. [C19: from *by Jesus!*]

bejewel (bɪˈdʒuːəl) *vb* **bejewels, bejewelling, bejewelled** *or US* **bejewels, bejeweling, bejeweled.** (*tr*) to decorate as with jewels.

bel (bɛl) *n* a unit for comparing two power levels, equal to the logarithm to the base ten of the ratio of the two powers. [C20: after A. G. *Bell* (1847–1922), US scientist]

belabour ⓣ *or US* **belabor** (bɪˈleɪbə) *vb* (*tr*) **1** to beat severely; thrash. **2** to attack verbally.

Belarussian *or* **Belorussian** (ˌbjɛlɑːˈrʌʃən, ˌbɛləʊˈrʌʃən) *adj* **1** of or relating to Belarus, a country in E Europe. **2** relating to, or characteristic of Belarus, its people, or their language. **3** the official language of Belarus. **4** a native or inhabitant of Belarus. ◆ Also called: **White Russian.**

belated ⓣ (bɪˈleɪtɪd) *adj* late or too late: *belated greetings.*
▸**beˈlatedly** *adv* ▸**beˈlatedness** *n*

belay *vb* (bɪˈleɪ) **belays, belaying, belayed. 1** *Naut.* to secure (a line) to a pin, cleat, or bitt. **2** (*usually imperative*) *Naut.* to stop. **3** (ˈbiːˌleɪ). *Mountaineering.* to secure (a climber) by means of a belay. ◆ *n* (ˈbiːˌleɪ). **4** *Mountaineering.* the attachment of a climber to a mountain by securing a rope round a rock, piton, etc., to safeguard the party in the event of a fall. [OE *belecgan*]

belaying pin *n Naut.* a cylindrical metal or wooden pin used for belaying.

bel canto (ˈbɛl ˈkæntəʊ) *n Music.* a style of singing characterized by beauty of tone rather than dramatic power. [It., lit.: beautiful singing]

belch ⓣ (bɛltʃ) *vb* **1** (*usually intr*) to expel wind from the stomach noisily through the mouth. **2** to expel or be expelled forcefully from inside: *smoke belching from factory chimneys.* ◆ *n* **3** an act of belching. [OE *bialcan*]

beldam *or* **beldame** (ˈbɛldəm) *n Arch.* an old woman. [C15: from *bel-* grand (as in *grandmother*), from OF *bel* beautiful, + *dam* mother]

beleaguer ⓣ (bɪˈliːgə) *vb* (*tr*) **1** to lay siege to. **2** to harass. [C16: from BE- + obs. *leaguer* a siege]

belemnite (ˈbɛləmˌnaɪt) *n* **1** an extinct marine mollusc related to the cuttlefish. **2** its long pointed conical internal shell: a common fossil. [C17: from Gk *belemnon* dart]

belfry (ˈbɛlfrɪ) *n, pl* **belfries. 1** the part of a tower or steeple in which bells are hung. **2** a tower or steeple. [C13: from OF *berfrei*, of Gmc origin]

Belg. *or* **Bel.** *abbrev. for:* **1** Belgian. **2** Belgium.

Belgian (ˈbɛldʒən) *n* **1** a native or inhabitant of Belgium, a kingdom in NW Europe. ◆ *adj* **2** of or relating to Belgium, the Belgians, or their languages.

Belgian hare *n* a large red domestic rabbit.

Belial (ˈbiːlɪəl) *n* the devil or Satan. [C13: from Heb. *bəlīyya'al*, from *bəlīy* without + *ya'al* worth]

belie ⓣ (bɪˈlaɪ) *vb* **belies, belying, belied.** (*tr*) **1** to show to be untrue. **2** to misrepresent; disguise the nature of. **3** to fail to justify; disappoint. [OE *belēogan*; see BE-, LIE[1]]

belief ⓣ (bɪˈliːf) *n* **1** a principle, etc., accepted as true, esp. without proof. **2** opinion; conviction. **3** religious faith. **4** trust or confidence, as in a person's abilities, etc.

believe ⓣ (bɪˈliːv) *vb* **believes, believing, believed. 1** (*tr; may take a clause as object*) to accept (a statement or opinion) as true: *I believe God exists.* **2** (*tr*) to accept the statement or opinion of (a person) as true. **3** (*intr; foll. by in*) to be convinced of the truth or existence (of): *to believe in fairies.* **4** (*intr*) to have religious faith. **5** (when *tr, takes a clause as object*) to think, assume, or suppose. **6** (*tr*) to think that someone is able to do (a particular action): *I wouldn't have believed it of him.* [OE *beliefan*]
▸**beˈlievable** *adj* ▸**beˈliever** *n*

belike (bɪˈlaɪk) *adv Arch.* perhaps; maybe.

Belisha beacon (bəˈliːʃə) *n Brit.* a flashing orange globe on a post, indicating a pedestrian crossing on a road. [C20: after L. Hore-*Belisha* (1893–1957), Brit. politician]

belittle ⓣ (bɪˈlɪtᵊl) *vb* **belittles, belittling, belittled.** (*tr*) **1** to consider or speak of (something) as less important than it really is. **2** to make small; dwarf.
▸**beˈlittlement** *n* ▸**beˈlittler** *n*

bell[1] (bɛl) *n* **1** a hollow, usually metal, cup-shaped instrument that emits a ringing sound when struck. **2** the sound made by such an instrument, as for marking the beginning or end of a period of time. **3** an electrical device that rings or buzzes as a signal. **4** something shaped like a bell, as the tube of certain musical wind instruments, or the corolla of certain flowers. **5** *Naut.* a signal rung on a ship's bell to count the number of half-hour intervals during each of six four-hour watches reckoned from midnight. **6** *Brit. sl.* a telephone call **7 bell, book, and candle. 7a** instruments used formerly in excommunications and other ecclesiastical rites. **7b** *Inf.* the solemn ritual ratification of such acts. **8 ring a bell.** to sound familiar; recall something previously experienced. **9 sound as a bell.** in perfect condition. ◆ *vb* **10** to be or cause to be shaped like a bell. **11** (*tr*) to attach a bell or bells to. [OE *belle*]

bell[2] (bɛl) *n* **1** a bellowing or baying cry, esp. that of a stag in rut. ◆ *vb* **2** to utter (such a cry). [OE *bellan*]

belladonna (ˌbɛləˈdɒnə) *n* **1** either of two alkaloid drugs obtained from the leaves and roots of the deadly nightshade. **2** another name for **deadly nightshade.** [C16: from It., lit.: beautiful lady; supposed to refer to its use as a cosmetic]

bellbird (ˈbɛlˌbɜːd) *n* **1** any of several tropical American birds having a bell-like call. **2** either of two other birds with a bell-like call: an Australian flycatcher (**crested bellbird**) or a New Zealand honeyeater.

bell-bottoms *pl n* trousers that flare from the knee.
▸ˈ**bell-ˌbottomed** *adj*

bellboy (ˈbɛlˌbɔɪ) *n Chiefly US & Canad.* a porter or page in a hotel, club, etc. Also called: **bellhop.**

bell buoy *n* a navigational buoy with a bell which strikes when the waves move the buoy.

THESAURUS

ble for **5** = **supporting**, backing, for, in agreement, on the side of ◆ *adv* **6** = **after**, afterwards, following, in the wake (of), next, subsequently **8** = **overdue**, behindhand, in arrears, in debt ◆ *n* **10** *Informal* = **bottom**, arse (*taboo sl.*), ass (*US & Canad. taboo sl.*), bum (*Brit. sl.*), buns (*US sl.*), butt (*US & Canad. inf.*), buttocks, derrière (*euphemistic*), jacksy (*Brit. sl.*), posterior, rump, seat, tail (*inf.*)
Antonyms *adv* ≠ **after:** earlier than, in advance of, in front of, in the presence of, prior to ≠ **overdue:** ahead, earlier, formerly, in advance, previously, sooner

behindhand *adj* **1** = **late**, dilatory, remiss, slow **4** = **late**, behind time, tardy

behold *vb Archaic or literary* = **look at**, check, check out, consider, contemplate, discern, eye, observe, perceive, recce (*sl.*), regard, scan, survey, view, watch, witness

beholden *adj* = **indebted**, bound, grateful, obligated, obliged, owing, under obligation

behove *vb Archaic* = **be fitting**, be advisable, befit, be incumbent upon, be necessary, benefit, be obligatory, beseem, be wise

beige *n* **1** = **fawn**, biscuit, buff, *café au lait*, camel, cinnamon, coffee, cream, ecru, khaki, mushroom, neutral, oatmeal, sand, tan

being *n* **1** = **existence**, actuality, animation, life, living, reality **2** = **nature**, essence, soul, spirit, substance **3** = **creature**, animal, beast, body, living thing, mortal, thing **4** = **human being**, individual
Antonyms *n* ≠ **existence:** nihility, nonbeing, nonexistence, nothingness, nullity, oblivion

belabour *vb* **1** = **beat**, batter, clobber (*sl.*), flog, thrash, whip **2** = **attack**, berate, blast, castigate, censure, criticize, excoriate, flay, go for the jugular, lay into (*inf.*), put down, tear into (*inf.*)

belated *adj* = **late**, behindhand, behind time, delayed, late in the day, overdue, tardy

belch *vb* **1** = **burp** (*inf.*), eruct, eructate, hiccup **2** = **emit**, discharge, disgorge, erupt, give off, gush, spew forth, vent, vomit

beleaguered *adj* **1** = **besieged**, assailed, beset, blockaded, encompassed, hemmed in, surrounded **2** = **harassed**, aggravated (*inf.*), annoyed, badgered, hassled (*inf.*), persecuted, pestered, plagued, put upon, vexed

belie *vb* **1** = **disprove**, confute, contradict, deny, gainsay (*arch. or literary*), give the lie to, make a nonsense of, negate, rebut, repudiate **2** = **misrepresent**, conceal, deceive, disguise, falsify, gloss over, mislead

belief *n* **2** = **opinion**, assurance, confidence, conviction, feeling, impression, judgment, notion, persuasion, presumption, theory, view **3** = **faith**, credence, credo, creed, doctrine, dogma, ideology, principles, tenet **4** = **trust**, credit, reliance
Antonyms *n* ≠ **trust:** disbelief, distrust, doubt, dubiety, incredulity, mistrust, scepticism

believable *adj* **1, 2** = **credible**, acceptable, authentic, creditable, imaginable, likely, plausible, possible, probable, reliable, trustworthy
Antonyms *adj* cock-and-bull (*inf.*), doubtful, dubious, fabulous, implausible, incredible, questionable, unacceptable, unbelievable

believe *vb* **1, 2** = **accept**, be certain of, be convinced of, buy (*sl.*), count on, credit, depend on, have faith in, hold, place confidence in, presume true, rely on, swallow (*inf.*), swear by, take as gospel, take on board, trust **5** = **think**, assume, conjecture, consider, gather, guess (*inf., chiefly US & Canad.*), imagine, judge, maintain, postulate, presume, reckon, speculate, suppose
Antonyms *vb* ≠ **accept:** disbelieve, distrust, doubt, know, question

believer *n* **4** = **follower**, adherent, convert, devotee, disciple, proselyte, protagonist, supporter, upholder, zealot
Antonyms *n* agnostic, atheist, disbeliever, doubting Thomas, infidel, sceptic, unbeliever

belittle *vb* **1** = **disparage**, decry, denigrate, deprecate, depreciate, deride, derogate, detract, diminish, minimize, scoff at, scorn, sneer at, underestimate, underrate, undervalue

belle 🅣 (bɛl) *n* **1** a beautiful woman. **2** the most attractive woman at a function, etc. (esp. in **belle of the ball**). [C17: from F, fem of BEAU]

belle époque *French.* (bɛl epɔk) *n* the period of comfortable well-established life before World War I. [lit.: fine period]

belles-lettres (*French* bɛllɛtrə) *n* (*functioning as sing*) literary works, esp. essays and poetry, valued for their aesthetic content. [C17: from F: fine letters]
▸**bel'letrist** *n*

bellflower ('bɛlˌflaʊə) *n* another name for **campanula**.

bellfounder ('bɛlˌfaʊndə) *n* a foundry worker who casts bells.

bellicose 🅣 ('bɛlɪˌkəʊs, -ˌkəʊz) *adj* warlike; aggressive; ready to fight. [C15: from L *bellicōsus*, from *bellum* war]
▸**bellicosity** (ˌbɛlɪ'kɒsɪtɪ) *n*

belligerence 🅣 (bɪ'lɪdʒərəns) *n* the act or quality of being belligerent or warlike; aggressiveness.

belligerency (bɪ'lɪdʒərənsɪ) *n* the state of being at war.

belligerent 🅣 (bɪ'lɪdʒərənt) *adj* **1** marked by readiness to fight or argue; aggressive. **2** relating to or engaged in a war. ◆ *n* **3** a person or country engaged in war. [C16: from L *belliger*, from *bellum* war + *gerere* to wage]

bell jar *n* a bell-shaped glass cover to protect flower arrangements, etc., or to cover apparatus in experiments. Also called: **bell glass**.

bellman ('bɛlmən) *n, pl* **bellmen**. a man who rings a bell; (formerly) a town crier.

bell metal *n* an alloy of copper and tin, with some zinc and lead, used in casting bells.

bellow 🅣 ('bɛləʊ) *vb* **1** (*intr*) to make a loud deep cry like that of a bull; roar. **2** to shout (something) unrestrainedly, as in anger or pain. ◆ *n* **3** the characteristic noise of a bull. **4** a loud deep sound, as of pain or anger. [C14: prob. from OE *bylgan*]

bellows ('bɛləʊz) *n* (*functioning as sing or pl*) **1** Also: **pair of bellows**. an instrument consisting of an air chamber with flexible sides that is used to create a stream of air, as for producing a draught for a fire or for sounding organ pipes. **2** a flexible corrugated part, as that connecting the lens system of some cameras to the body. [C16: from pl of OE *belig* BELLY]

bell pull *n* a handle, rope, or cord pulled to operate a doorbell or servant's bell.

bell push *n* a button pressed to operate an electric bell.

bell-ringer *n* a person who rings church bells or musical handbells.
▸**'bell-ˌringing** *n*

bells and whistles *pl n* additional features or accessories which are nonessential but very attractive. [C20: from the bells and whistles which used to decorate fairground organs]

bell tent *n* a cone-shaped tent having a single central supporting pole.

bellwether ('bɛlˌwɛðə) *n* **1** a sheep that leads the herd, often bearing a bell. **2** a leader, esp. one followed blindly.

belly 🅣 ('bɛlɪ) *n, pl* **bellies**. **1** the lower or front part of the body of a vertebrate, containing the intestines and other organs; abdomen. **2** the stomach, esp. when regarded as the seat of gluttony. **3** a part that bulges deeply: *the belly of a sail*. **4** the inside or interior cavity of something. **5** the front, lower, or inner part of something. **6** the surface of a stringed musical instrument over which the strings are stretched. **7** *Austral. & NZ.* the wool from a sheep's belly. **8** *Arch.* the womb. **9 go belly up**. *Inf.* to die, fail, or come to an end. ◆ *vb* **bellies, bellying, bellied**. **10** to swell out or cause to swell out; bulge. [OE *belig*]

bellyache ('bɛlɪˌeɪk) *n* **1** an informal term for **stomachache**. ◆ *vb* **bellyaches, bellyaching, bellyached**. **2** (*intr*) *Sl.* to complain repeatedly.
▸**'bellyˌacher** *n*

bellyband ('bɛlɪˌbænd) *n* a strap around the belly of a draught animal, holding the shafts of a vehicle.

bellybutton ('bɛlɪˌbʌtᵊn) *n* an informal name for the **navel**. Also called: **tummy button**.

belly dance *n* **1** a sensuous dance of Middle Eastern origin, performed by women, with undulating movements of the abdomen. ◆ *vb* **belly-dance, belly-dances, belly-dancing, belly-danced**. **2** (*intr*) to dance thus.
▸**belly dancer** *n*

belly flop *n* **1** a dive into water in which the body lands horizontally. ◆ *vb* **belly-flop, belly-flops, belly-flopping, belly-flopped**. **2** (*intr*) to perform a belly flop.

bellyful 🅣 ('bɛlɪˌfʊl) *n* **1** as much as one wants or can eat. **2** *Sl.* more than one can tolerate.

belly landing *n* the landing of an aircraft on its fuselage without use of its landing gear.

belly laugh *n* a loud deep hearty laugh.

belong 🅣 (bɪ'lɒŋ) *vb* (*intr*) **1** (foll. by *to*) to be the property or possession (of). **2** (foll. by *to*) to be bound (to) by ties of affection, allegiance, etc. **3** (foll. by *to, under, with,* etc.) to be classified (with): *this plant belongs to the daisy family*. **4** (foll. by *to*) to be a part or adjunct (of). **5** to have a proper or usual place. **6** *Inf.* to be acceptable, esp. socially. [C14 *belongen*, from BE- (intensive) + *longen*, from OE *langian* to belong]

belonging 🅣 (bɪ'lɒŋɪŋ) *n* secure relationship; affinity (esp. in **a sense of belonging**).

belongings 🅣 (bɪ'lɒŋɪŋz) *pl n* (*sometimes sing*) the things that a person owns or has with him.

beloved 🅣 (bɪ'lʌvɪd, -'lʌvd) *adj* **1** dearly loved. ◆ *n* **2** a person who is dearly loved.

below 🅣 (bɪ'ləʊ) *prep* **1** at or to a position lower than; under. **2** less than. **3** south of. **4** downstream of. **5** unworthy of; beneath. ◆ *adv* **6** at or to a lower position. **7** at a later place (in something written). **8** *Arch.* on earth or in hell. [C14 *biloogh*e, from *bi* BY + *looghe* LOW[1]]

Bel Paese ('bɛl pɑː'eɪzɪ) *n* a mild creamy Italian cheese. [from It., lit.: beautiful country]

belt 🅣 (bɛlt) *n* **1** a band of cloth, leather, etc., worn, usually around the waist, to support clothing, carry weapons, etc., or as decoration. **2** a belt worn to show rank (as by a knight), to mark expertise (as in judo), or awarded as a prize (as in boxing). **3** a narrow band, circle, or stripe, as of colour. **4** an area where a specific thing is found; zone: *a belt of high pressure*. **5** See **seat belt**. **6** a band of flexible material between rotating shafts or pulleys to transfer motion or transmit goods: *a fan belt; a conveyer belt*. **7** *Inf.* a sharp blow. **8 below the belt**. **8a** *Boxing.* below the waist. **8b** *Inf.* in an unscrupulous or cowardly way. **9 tighten one's belt**. to take measures to reduce expenditure. **10 under one's belt**. **10a** in one's stomach. **10b** as part of one's experience: *he had a degree under his belt*. ◆ *vb* **11** (*tr*) to fasten or attach with or as if with a belt. **12** (*tr*) to hit with a belt. **13** (*tr*) *Sl.* to give a sharp blow; punch. **14** (*intr; often foll. by along*) *Sl.* to move very fast, esp. in a car. **15** (*tr*) *Rare.* to encircle. [OE, from L *balteus*]
▸**'belted** *adj*

belt-and-braces *adj* providing double security, in case one security measure should fail: *a belt-and-braces policy*.

Beltane ('bɛlteɪn, -tən) *n* an ancient Celtic festival with a sacrificial bonfire on May Day. [C15: from Scot. Gaelic *bealltainn*]

belter ('bɛltə) *n Sl.* **1** an event, person, quality, etc., that is admirable, outstanding, or thrilling: *a real belter of a match*. **2a** a rousing or spirited popular song that is sung loudly and enthusiastically. **2b** a person who sings popular songs in a loud and spirited manner.

belting ('bɛltɪŋ) *n* **1** material for belts. **2** belts collectively. **3** *Inf.* a beating.

belt man *n Austral. & NZ.* (formerly) the member of a beach life-saving team who swam out wearing a belt with a line attached.

belt out *vb* (*tr, adv*) *Inf.* to sing or emit sound loudly.

belt up *vb* (*adv*) **1** *Sl.* to stop talking: often imperative. **2** to fasten with a belt.

beluga (bɪ'luːgə) *n* **1** a large white sturgeon of the Black and Caspian Seas: a source of caviar and isinglass. **2** another name for **white whale**. [C18: from Russian *byeluga*, from *byely* white]

belvedere ('bɛlvɪˌdɪə, ˌbɛlvɪ'dɪə) *n* a building, such as a summerhouse, sited to command a fine view. [C16: from It.: beautiful sight]

bemire (bɪ'maɪə) *vb* **bemires, bemiring, bemired**. (*tr*) **1** to soil as with mire. **2** (*usually passive*) to stick fast in mire.

bemoan 🅣 (bɪ'məʊn) *vb* to mourn; lament (esp. in **bemoan one's fate**). [OE *bemǣnan*; see BE-, MOAN]

bemuse 🅣 (bɪ'mjuːz) *vb* **bemuses, bemusing, bemused**. (*tr*) to confuse; bewilder.

THESAURUS

Antonyms *vb* boast about, elevate, exalt, magnify, praise, vaunt

belle *n* **1** = **beauty**, cracker (*inf.*), good-looker, looker (*inf.*), lovely, peach (*inf.*), stunner (*inf.*), Venus

bellicose *adj* = **aggressive**, antagonistic, belligerent, combative, defiant, hawkish, hostile, militaristic, provocative, pugnacious, quarrelsome, warlike, warloving, warmongering

bellicosity *n* = **aggression**, aggressiveness, antagonism, belligerence, combativeness, hostility, pugnacity, truculence, warlike nature

belligerence *n* = **aggressiveness**, animosity, antagonism, combativeness, hostility, pugnacity, unfriendliness

belligerent *adj* **1** = **aggressive**, antagonistic, argumentative, combative, contentious, hostile, pugnacious, quarrelsome, unfriendly **2** = **warring**, bellicose, warlike ◆ *n* **3** = **fighter**, combatant, warring nation

Antonyms *adj* ≠ **aggressive**: amicable, benign, conciliatory, friendly, harmonious, nonviolent, without hostility

bellow *n, vb* = **shout**, bawl, bell, call, clamour, cry, howl, roar, scream, shriek, yell

belly *n* **1** = **abdomen**, gut, insides (*inf.*), vitals **2** = **stomach**, breadbasket, corporation (*inf.*), gut, paunch, potbelly, tummy ◆ *vb* **10** = **swell out**, billow, bulge, fill, spread, swell

bellyful *n* **1, 2** = **surfeit**, enough, excess, glut, plateful, plenty, satiety, superabundance, too much

belong *vb* **1** *foll. by* **to** = **be the property of**, be at the disposal of, be held by, be owned by **2** *foll. by* **to** = **be a member of**, be affiliated to, be allied to, be associated with, be included in **4** *foll. by* **to** = **go with**, attach to, be connected with, be part of, fit, pertain to, relate to

belonging *n* = **relationship**, acceptance, affiliation, affinity, association, attachment, fellowship, inclusion, kinship, loyalty, rapport

belongings *pl n* = **possessions**, accoutrements, chattels, effects, gear, goods, paraphernalia, personal property, stuff, things

beloved *adj* **1** = **dear**, admired, adored, cherished, darling, dearest, loved, pet, precious, prized, revered, sweet, treasured, valued, worshipped

below *prep* **1** = **lesser**, inferior, subject, subordinate **2** = **less than**, lower than **5** = **unworthy of**, beneath ◆ *adv* **6** = **lower**, beneath, down, under, underneath

belt *n* **1** = **waistband**, band, cincture, cummerbund, girdle, girth, sash **4** = **zone**, area, district, layer, region, stretch, strip, tract **8b below the belt** *Informal* = **unfair**, cowardly, foul, not playing the game (*inf.*), unjust, unscrupulous, unsporting, unsportsmanlike

bemoan *vb* = **lament**, bewail, cry over spilt milk, deplore, express sorrow, grieve for, moan over, mourn, regret, rue, weep for

bemuse *vb* = **puzzle**, amaze, bewilder, confuse,

bemused ❶ (bɪ'mju:zd) *adj* preoccupied; lost in thought.
ben[1] (bɛn) *Scot.* ♦ *n* **1** an inner room in a cottage. ♦ *prep, adv* **2** in; within; inside. ♦ Cf. **but**[2]. [OE *binnan*, from BE- + *innan* inside]
ben[2] (bɛn) *n Scot., Irish.* a mountain peak: *Ben Lomond.* [C18: from Gaelic *beinn*, from *beann*]
bench ❶ (bɛntʃ) *n* **1** a long seat for more than one person, usually lacking a back. **2** a plain stout worktable. **3 the bench.** (*sometimes cap.*) **3a** a judge or magistrate sitting in court. **3b** judges or magistrates collectively. **4** a ledge in a mine or quarry from which work is carried out. **5** (in a gymnasium) a low table, which may be inclined, used for various exercises. **6** a platform on which dogs, etc., are exhibited at shows. **7** *NZ.* a hollow formed by sheep on a hillside. ♦ *vb (tr)* **8** to provide with benches. **9** to exhibit (a dog, etc.) at a show. **10** *US & Canad., Sports.* to take (a player) out of a game, often for disciplinary reasons. [OE *benc*]
bencher ('bɛntʃə) *n (often pl) Brit.* **1** a member of the governing body of one of the Inns of Court. **2** See **backbencher.**
benchmark ❶ ('bɛntʃ,mɑ:k) *n* **1** a mark on a stone post or other permanent feature, used as a reference point in surveying. **2** a criterion by which to measure something; reference point.
bench press *n* a weight-training exercise in which a person lies on a bench and pushes a barbell upwards with both hands from chest level until the arms are straight, then lowers it again.
bench test *n* the critical evaluation of a new or repaired component, device, apparatus, etc., prior to installation to ensure that it is in perfect condition.
bench warrant *n* a warrant issued by a judge or court directing that an offender be apprehended.
bend[1] ❶ (bɛnd) *vb* **bends, bending, bent. 1** to form or cause to form a curve. **2** to turn or cause to turn from a particular direction: *the road bends left.* **3** (*intr;* often foll. by *down*, etc.) to incline the body; stoop; bow. **4** to submit or cause to submit: *to bend before superior force.* **5** *(tr)* to turn or direct (one's eyes, steps, attention, etc.). **6** *(tr) Naut.* to attach or fasten, as a sail to a boom. **7 bend (someone's) ear.** to speak at length to an unwilling listener, esp. to voice one's troubles. **8 bend the rules.** *Inf.* to ignore rules or change them to suit one's own convenience. ♦ *n* **9** a curved part. **10** *Naut.* a knot in a line for joining it to another or to an object. **11** the act of bending. **12 round the bend.** *Brit. sl.* mad. [OE *bendan*]
▸ **'bendable** *adj* ▸ **'bendy** *adj*
bend[2] (bɛnd) *n Heraldry.* a diagonal line traversing a shield. [OE *bend* BAND[2]]
bender ('bɛndə) *n Inf.* **1** a drinking bout. **2** a makeshift shelter constructed by placing tarpaulin or plastic sheeting over bent saplings or woven branches.
bends (bɛndz) *pl n (functioning as sing or pl)* **the.** a nontechnical name for **decompression sickness.**
bend sinister *n Heraldry.* a diagonal line bisecting a shield from the top right to the bottom left, typically indicating a bastard line.
beneath ❶ (bɪ'ni:θ) *prep* **1** below, esp. if covered, protected, or obscured by. **2** not as great or good as would be demanded by: *beneath his dignity.* ♦ *adv* **3** below; underneath. [OE *beneothan*, from BE- + *neothan* low]
benedicite (,bɛnɪ'daɪsɪtɪ) *n* (esp. in Christian religious orders) a blessing or grace. [C13: from L, from *benedīcere*, from *bene* well + *dīcere* to speak]
Benedictine *n* **1** (,bɛnɪ'dɪktɪn, -taɪn). a monk or nun who is a member of the order of Saint Benedict, founded about 540 A.D. **2** (,bɛnɪ'dɪkti:n). a greenish-yellow liqueur first made at the Benedictine monastery at Fécamp in France in about 1510. ♦ *adj* (,bɛnɪ'dɪktɪn, -taɪn). **3** of or relating to Saint Benedict or his order.
benediction ❶ (,bɛnɪ'dɪkʃən) *n* **1** an invocation of divine blessing. **2** a Roman Catholic service in which the congregation is blessed with the sacrament. **3** the state of being blessed. [C15: from L *benedictio*, from *benedīcere* to bless; see BENEDICITE]
▸ **,bene'dictory** *adj*
Benedictus (,bɛnɪ'dɪktəs) *n (sometimes not cap.) Christianity.* **1** a canticle beginning *Benedictus qui venit in nomine Domini* in Latin and *Blessed is he that cometh in the name of the Lord* in English. **2** a canticle beginning *Benedictus Dominus Deus Israel* in Latin and *Blessed be the Lord God of Israel* in English.
benefaction ❶ (,bɛnɪ'fækʃən) *n* **1** the act of doing good, esp. by giving a donation to charity. **2** the donation or help given. [C17: from LL *benefactiō*, from L *bene* well + *facere* to do]
benefactor ❶ ('bɛnɪ,fæktə, ,bɛnɪ'fæk-) *n* a person who supports or helps a person, institution, etc., esp. by giving money.
▸ **'bene,factress** *fem n*
benefice ❶ ('bɛnɪfɪs) *n* **1** *Christianity.* an endowed Church office yielding an income to its holder; a Church living. **2** the property or revenue attached to such an office. [C14: from OF, from L *beneficium* benefit, from *bene* well + *facere* to do]
▸ **'beneficed** *adj*
beneficent ❶ (bɪ'nɛfɪsᵊnt) *adj* charitable; generous. [C17: from L *beneficus;* see BENEFICE]
▸ **be'neficence** *n*
beneficial ❶ (,bɛnɪ'fɪʃəl) *adj* **1** (sometimes foll. by *to*) advantageous. **2** *Law.* entitling a person to receive the profits or proceeds of property. [C15: from LL *beneficiālis*, from L *beneficium* kindness]
beneficiary ❶ (,bɛnɪ'fɪʃərɪ) *n, pl* **beneficiaries. 1** a person who gains or benefits. **2** *Law.* a person entitled to receive funds or other property under a trust, will, etc. **3** the holder of a benefice. **4** *NZ.* a person who receives government assistance: *social security beneficiary.* ♦ *adj* **5** of or relating to a benefice.
benefit ❶ ('bɛnɪfɪt) *n* **1** something that improves or promotes. **2** advantage or sake. **3** (*sometimes pl*) a payment or series of payments made by an institution or government to a person who is ill, unemployed, etc. **4** a theatrical performance, sports event, etc., to raise money for a charity. ♦ *vb* **benefits, benefiting, benefited** *or US* **benefits, benefitting, benefitted. 5** to do or receive good; profit. [C14: from Anglo-F *benfet*, from L *benefactum*, from *bene facere* to do well]
benefit in kind *n* a non-pecuniary benefit, such as a company car or medical insurance, given to an employee.
benefit of clergy *n Christianity.* **1** sanction by the church: *marriage without benefit of clergy.* **2** (in the Middle Ages) a privilege that placed the clergy outside the jurisdiction of secular courts.
benefit society *n* a US term for **friendly society.**
benevolence ❶ (bɪ'nɛvələns) *n* **1** inclination to do good; charity. **2** an act of kindness.
benevolent ❶ (bɪ'nɛvələnt) *adj* **1** intending or showing goodwill; kindly; friendly. **2** doing good rather than making profit; charitable: *a benevolent organization.* [C15: from L *benevolēns*, from *bene* well + *velle* to wish]
BEng *abbrev. for* Bachelor of Engineering.
Bengali (bɛn'gɔ:lɪ, bɛŋ-) *n* **1** a member of a people living chiefly in Bangladesh (a republic in S Asia) and in West Bengal (in NE India). **2** Also called: **Bangla.** their language. ♦ *adj* **3** of or relating to Bengal, the Bengalis, or their language.
Bengal light (bɛn'gɔ:l, bɛŋ-) *n* a firework or flare that burns with a bright blue light, formerly used as a signal.
benighted ❶ (bɪ'naɪtɪd) *adj* **1** lacking cultural, moral, or intellectual enlightenment. **2** *Arch.* overtaken by night.
▸ **be'nightedness** *n*
benign ❶ (bɪ'naɪn) *adj* **1** showing kindliness; genial. **2** (of soil, climate, etc.) mild; gentle. **3** favourable; propitious. **4** *Pathol.* (of a tumour,

THESAURUS

daze, flummox, muddle, nonplus, overwhelm, perplex, stun
bemused *adj* = **puzzled,** absent-minded, at sea, bewildered, confused, dazed, engrossed, flummoxed, fuddled, half-drunk, muddled, nonplussed, perplexed, preoccupied, stunned, stupefied, tipsy
bench *n* **1** = **seat,** form, pew, settle, stall **2** = **worktable,** board, counter, table, trestle table, workbench **3 the bench** = **court,** courtroom, judge, judges, judiciary, magistrate, magistrates, tribunal
benchmark *n* **2** = **reference point,** criterion, example, gauge, level, measure, model, norm, par, reference, standard, touchstone, yardstick
bend[1] *vb* **1** = **curve,** arc, arch, bow, buckle, contort, flex, twist, warp **2** = **turn,** deflect, diverge, swerve, veer **3** = **incline,** bow, crouch, lean, stoop **4** = **force,** compel, direct, influence, mould, persuade, shape, subdue, submit, sway, yield ♦ *n* **9** = **curve,** angle, arc, arch, bow, corner, crook, hook, loop, turn, twist, zigzag
beneath *prep* **1** = **under,** below, lower than, underneath **2** = **unworthy of,** below, inferior to, less than, unbefitting ♦ *adv* **3** = **underneath,** below, in a lower place
Antonyms *prep* ≠ **under:** above, atop, higher than, on top of, over, upon
benediction *n* **1** = **blessing,** benison, consecration, invocation, orison, prayer
benefaction *n* **1** = **charity,** beneficence, benevolence, generosity, largesse *or* largess, liberality, munificence, philanthropy **2** = **donation,** alms, bequest, boon, charity, contribution, endowment, gift, grant, gratuity, hand-out, largesse *or* largess, legacy, offering, present, stipend
benefactor *n* = **supporter,** angel (*inf.*), backer, contributor, donor, helper, patron, philanthropist, promoter, sponsor, subscriber, subsidizer, well-wisher
benefice *n* **1** *Christianity* = **office,** Church living, emolument, incumbency, prebend, preferment, sinecure, stipend
beneficence *n* = **generosity,** altruism, benevolence, charity, compassion, goodness, goodwill, helpfulness, kindness, largesse *or* largess, liberality, love, unselfishness, virtue
beneficent *adj* = **generous,** benevolent, benign, bounteous, bountiful, charitable, helpful, kind, liberal, munificent, princely
beneficial *adj* **1** = **helpful,** advantageous, benign, expedient, favourable, gainful, healthful, profitable, salubrious, salutary, serviceable, useful, valuable, wholesome
Antonyms *adj* detrimental, disadvantageous, harmful, pernicious, useless
beneficiary *n* **2** *Law* = **recipient,** assignee, heir, inheritor, legatee, payee, receiver, successor
benefit *n* **1** = **help,** advantage, aid, asset, assistance, avail, betterment, blessing, boon, favour, gain, good, interest, mileage (*inf.*), profit, use, utility ♦ *vb* **5** = **help,** advance, advantage, aid, ameliorate, assist, avail, better, enhance, further, improve, profit, promote, serve
Antonyms *n* ≠ **help:** damage, detriment, disadvantage, downside, harm, impairment, injury, loss ♦ *vb* ≠ **help:** damage, deprive, detract from, harm, impair, injure, worsen
benevolence *n* **1** = **kindness,** altruism, charity, compassion, fellow feeling, generosity, goodness, goodwill, humanity, kind-heartedness, sympathy
Antonyms *n* ill will, malevolence, selfishness, stinginess, unkindness
benevolent *adj* **1** = **kind,** affable, altruistic, beneficent, benign, bounteous, bountiful, caring, charitable, compassionate, considerate, generous, humane, humanitarian, kind-hearted, liberal, philanthropic, tender-hearted, warm-hearted, well-disposed
benighted *adj* **1** = **uncivilized,** backward,

etc.) not malignant. [C14: from OF *benigne,* from L *benignus,* from *bene* well + *gignere* to produce]
▸**be'nignly** *adv*

benignant (bɪ'nɪgnənt) *adj* **1** kind; gracious. **2** a less common word for **benign** (senses 3, 4).
▸**be'nignancy** *n*

benignity (bɪ'nɪgnɪtɪ) *n, pl* **benignities. 1** the quality of being benign. **2** a kind or gracious act.

benison ('bɛnɪzᵊn, -sᵊn) *n Arch.* a blessing. [C13: from OF *beneison,* from L *benedictiō* BENEDICTION]

bent[1] ⓣ (bɛnt) *adj* **1** not straight; curved. **2** (foll. by *on*) resolved (to); determined (to). **3** *Sl.* **3a** dishonest; corrupt. **3b** (of goods) stolen. **3c** crazy. **3d** sexually deviant. ◆ *n* **4** personal inclination or aptitude. **5** capacity of endurance (esp. in **to the top of one's bent**).

bent[2] (bɛnt) *n* **1** short for **bent grass. 2** *Arch.* any stiff grass or sedge. **3** *Arch. or dialect.* heath or moorland. [OE *bionot*]

bent grass *n* a perennial grass which has a spreading panicle of tiny flowers sometimes planted for hay or in lawns.

Benthamism ('bɛnθəmˌɪzəm) *n* the utilitarian philosophy of Jeremy Bentham (1748–1832), English philosopher and jurist, which holds that the ultimate goal of society should be to promote the greatest happiness of the greatest number.
▸**'Benthamˌite** *n, adj*

benthos ('bɛnθɒs) *n* the animals and plants living at the bottom of a sea or lake. [C19: from Gk: depth; rel. to *bathus* deep]
▸**'benthic** *adj*

bentonite ('bɛntəˌnaɪt) *n* a clay that swells as it absorbs water: used as a filler in various industries. [after Fort *Benton,* Montana, USA, where found]

bentwood ('bɛntˌwʊd) *n* **a** wood bent in moulds after being heated by steaming, used mainly for furniture. **b** (*as modifier*): *a bentwood chair.*

benumb ⓣ (bɪ'nʌm) *vb* (*tr*) **1** to make numb or powerless; deaden, as by cold. **2** (*usually passive*) to stupefy (the mind, senses, will, etc.).

Benzedrine ('bɛnzɪˌdriːn, -drɪn) *n* a trademark for **amphetamine.**

benzene ('bɛnziːn) *n* a colourless flammable poisonous liquid used in the manufacture of styrene, phenol, etc., as a solvent for fats, resins, etc., and as an insecticide. Formula: C_6H_6.

benzene ring *n* the hexagonal ring of bonded carbon atoms in the benzene molecule.

benzine ('bɛnziːn, bɛn'ziːn) *or* **benzin** ('bɛnzɪn) *n* a volatile mixture of the lighter hydrocarbon constituents of petroleum.

benzo- *or* **benz-** *combining form.* **1** indicating a fused benzene ring. **2** indicating derivation from benzene or benzoic acid or the presence of phenyl groups. [from BENZOIN]

benzoate ('bɛnzəʊˌeɪt, -ɪt) *n* a salt or ester of benzoic acid.

benzocaine ('bɛnzəʊˌkeɪn) *n* a white crystalline ester used as a local anaesthetic.

benzodiazepine (ˌbɛnzəʊdaɪ'eɪzəˌpiːn) *n* any of a group of chemical compounds that are used as minor tranquillizers, such as diazepam (Valium) and chlordiazepoxide (Librium). [C20: from BENZO- + DI-[1] + AZ(O)- + EP(OXY)- + -INE[2]]

benzoic (bɛn'zəʊɪk) *adj* of, containing, or derived from benzoic acid or benzoin.

benzoic acid *n* a white crystalline solid occurring in many natural resins, used in plasticizers and dyes and as a food preservative (**E210**).

benzoin ('bɛnzɔɪn, -zəʊɪn) *n* a gum resin containing benzoic acid, obtained from various tropical Asian trees and used in ointments, perfume, etc. [C16: from F *benjoin,* from OCatalan *benjui,* from Ar. *lubān jāwī,* lit.: frankincense of Java]

benzol *or* **benzole** ('bɛnzɒl) *n* **1** a crude form of benzene obtained from coal tar or coal gas and used as a fuel. **2** an obsolete name for **benzene.**

bequeath ⓣ (bɪ'kwiːð, -'kwiːθ) *vb* (*tr*) **1** *Law.* to dispose of (property) by will. **2** to hand down; pass on. [OE *becwethan*]
▸**be'queathal** *n*

bequest ⓣ (bɪ'kwɛst) *n* **1** the act of bequeathing. **2** something that is bequeathed. [C14: BE- + OE *-cwiss* degree]

berate ⓣ (bɪ'reɪt) *vb* **berates, berating, berated.** (*tr*) to scold harshly.

Berber ('bɜːbə) *n* **1** a member of a Caucasoid Muslim people of N Africa. **2** the language of this people. ◆ *adj* **3** of or relating to this people or their language.

berberis ('bɜːbərɪs) *n* any of a genus of mainly N temperate shrubs. See **barberry.** [C19: from Med. L, from ?]

berceuse (*French* bɛrsøz) *n* **1** a lullaby. **2** an instrumental piece suggestive of this. [C19: from F: lullaby]

bereave ⓣ (bɪ'riːv) *vb* **bereaves, bereaving, bereaved.** (*tr*) (usually foll. by *of*) to deprive (of) something or someone valued, esp. through death. [OE *bereafian*]
▸**be'reaved** *adj* ▸**be'reavement** *n*

bereft ⓣ (bɪ'rɛft) *adj* (usually foll. by *of*) deprived; parted (from): *bereft of hope.*

beret ('bɛreɪ) *n* a round close-fitting brimless cap. [C19: from F *béret,* from OProvençal *berret*]

berg[1] (bɜːg) *n* short for **iceberg.**

berg[2] (bɜːg) *n* a South African word for **mountain.**

bergamot ('bɜːgəˌmɒt) *n* **1** a small Asian tree having sour pear-shaped fruit. **2 essence of bergamot.** a fragrant essential oil extracted from the fruit rind of this plant, used in perfumery. **3** a Mediterranean mint that yields a similar oil. [C17: from F *bergamote,* from It. *bergamotta,* of Turkic origin]

bergie ('bɜːgiː) *n S. African inf.* a vagabond, esp. one living on the slopes of Table Mountain in SW South Africa. [from Afrik. *berg* mountain]

bergschrund ('bɛrkʃrʊnt) *n* a crevasse at the head of a glacier. [C19: G: mountain crack]

bergwind ('bɜːxvənt) *n* a hot dry wind in South Africa blowing from the plateau down to the coast.

beriberi (ˌbɛrɪ'bɛrɪ) *n* a disease, endemic in E and S Asia, caused by dietary deficiency of thiamine (vitamin B_1). [C19: from Sinhalese, by reduplication from *beri* weakness]

berk *or* **burk** (bɜːk) *n Brit. sl.* a stupid person; fool. [C20: shortened from *Berkeley* or *Berkshire Hunt,* rhyming slang for *cunt*]

berkelium (bɜː'kiːlɪəm, 'bɜːklɪəm) *n* a radioactive transuranic element produced by bombardment of americium. Symbol: Bk; atomic no.: 97; half-life of most stable isotope, ^{247}Bk: 1400 years. [C20: after *Berkeley,* California, where it was discovered]

Berks (bɑːks) *abbrev. for* Berkshire.

berley *or* **burley** ('bɜːlɪ) *Austral.* ◆ *n* **1** bait scattered on water to attract fish. **2** *Sl.* rubbish, nonsense. ◆ *vb* (*tr*) **3** to scatter (bait) on water. **4** to hurry (someone); urge on. [from ?]

berlin (bə'lɪn, 'bɜːlɪn) *n* **1** (*sometimes cap.*) Also called: **berlin wool.** a fine wool yarn used for tapestry work, etc. **2** a four-wheeled two-seated covered carriage, popular in the 18th century. [after *Berlin,* city in N Germany]

berm *or* **berme** (bɜːm) *n* **1** a narrow path or ledge as at the edge of a slope, road, or canal. **2** *Mil.* a man-made ridge of sand or earth, used as an obstacle to tanks. **3** *NZ.* the grass verge of a suburban street, usually kept mown. [C18: from F *berme,* from Du. *berm*]

Bermuda shorts (bə'mjuːdə) *pl n* shorts that come down to the knees. [after the *Bermudas,* islands in the NW Atlantic]

berretta (bɪ'rɛtə) *n* a variant spelling of **biretta.**

berry ('bɛrɪ) *n, pl* **berries. 1** any of various small edible fruits such as the blackberry and strawberry. **2** *Bot.* a fruit with two or more seeds and a fleshy pericarp, such as the grape or gooseberry. **3** any of various seeds or dried kernels, such as a coffee bean. **4** the egg of a lobster, crayfish, or similar animal. ◆ *vb* **berries, berrying, berried.** (*intr*) **5** to bear or produce berries. **6** to gather or look for berries. [OE *berie*]

berserk ⓣ (bə'zɜːk, -'sɜːk) *adj* **1** frenziedly violent or destructive (esp. in **go berserk**). ◆ *n* **2** Also called: **berserker.** one of a class of ancient Norse warriors who fought frenziedly. [C19: Icelandic *berserkr,* from *björn* bear + *serkr* shirt]

berth ⓣ (bɜːθ) *n* **1** a bed or bunk in a vessel or train. **2** *Naut.* a place assigned to a ship at a mooring. **3** *Naut.* sufficient room for a ship to manoeuvre. **4 give a wide berth to.** to keep clear of. **5** *Inf.* a job, esp. as a member of a ship's crew. ◆ *vb* **6** (*tr*) *Naut.* to assign a berth to (a vessel). **7** *Naut.* to dock (a vessel). **8** (*tr*) to provide with a sleeping place. **9** (*intr*) *Naut.* to pick up a mooring in an anchorage. [C17: prob. from BEAR[1] + -TH[1]]

THESAURUS

crude, ignorant, illiterate, primitive, uncultivated, unenlightened

benign *adj* **1 = kindly,** affable, amiable, complaisant, friendly, generous, genial, gracious, kind, liberal, obliging, sympathetic **3 = favourable,** advantageous, auspicious, beneficial, encouraging, good, lucky, propitious, salutary **4** *Pathol.* **= harmless,** curable, limited, remediable, slight, superficial
Antonyms *adj* ≠ **kindly:** bad, disobliging, harsh, hateful, inhumane, malicious, malign, severe, stern, unfavourable, unkind, unpleasant, unsympathetic ≠ **favourable:** bad, unfavourable, unlucky ≠ **harmless:** malignant

bent[1] *adj* **1 = curved,** angled, arched, bowed, crooked, hunched, stooped, twisted **2** *foll. by* **on = curved,** determined to, disposed to, fixed on, inclined to, insistent on, predisposed to, resolved on, set on ◆ *n* **4 = inclination,** ability, aptitude, bag (*sl.*), cup of tea, facility, faculty, flair, forte, knack, leaning, penchant, preference, proclivity, propensity, talent, tendency
Antonyms *adj* ≠ **curved:** aligned, erect, even, horizontal, in line, level, perpendicular, plumb, smooth, square, straight, true, upright, vertical

benumb *vb* **1 = paralyse,** anaesthetize, chill, deaden, freeze, numb **2 = stupefy,** shock, stun

benumbed *adj* **1 = paralysed,** anaesthetized, deadened, frozen, immobilized, insensible, insensitive, numb, unfeeling, unresponsive **2 = stupefied,** dazed, stunned

bequeath *vb* **1, 2 = leave,** bestow, commit, endow, entrust, give, grant, hand down, impart, leave to by will, pass on, transmit, will

bequest *n* **1 = bequeathal,** bestowal, endowment, gift, settlement **2 = legacy,** dower, endowment, estate, gift, heritage, inheritance, settlement, trust

berate *vb* **= scold,** bawl out (*inf.*), blast, castigate, censure, chew out (*US. & Canad. inf.*), chide, criticize, give a rocket (*Brit. & NZ. inf.*), harangue, rail at, rap over the knuckles, read the riot act, rebuke, reprimand, reproach, reprove, revile, slap on the wrist, slate (*inf., chiefly Brit.*), tear into (*inf.*), tear (someone) off a strip (*Brit. inf.*), tell off (*inf.*), upbraid, vituperate
Antonyms *vb* acclaim, admire, applaud, approve, cheer, commend, compliment, congratulate, extol, laud, praise, take one's hat off to

bereavement *n* **= loss,** affliction, death, deprivation, misfortune, tribulation

bereft *adj* **= deprived,** cut off, destitute, devoid, lacking, minus, parted from, robbed of, shorn, wanting

berserk *adj* **1 = crazy,** amok, ape, enraged, frantic, frenzied, insane, mad, maniacal, manic, raging, uncontrollable, violent, wild

berth *n* **1 = bunk,** bed, billet, cot (*Nautical*), hammock **2** *Nautical* **= anchorage,** dock, harbour, haven, pier, port, quay, slip, wharf **5** *Infor-*

bertha (ˈbɜːθə) *n* a wide deep collar, often of lace, usually to cover a low neckline. [C19: from F *berthe*, from *Berthe*, 8th-cent. Frankish queen]

beryl (ˈbɛrɪl) *n* a green, blue, yellow, pink, or white hard mineral consisting of beryllium aluminium silicate in hexagonal crystalline form. Emerald and aquamarine are transparent varieties. [C13: from OF, from L, from Gk *bērullos*]
▸ˈ**beryline** *adj*

beryllium (bɛˈrɪlɪəm) *n* a corrosion-resistant toxic silvery-white metallic element used mainly in X-ray windows and alloys. Symbol: Be; atomic no.: 4; atomic wt.: 9.012. [C19: from L, from Gk *bērullos*]

beseech Ⓣ (bɪˈsiːtʃ) *vb* **beseeches, beseeching, besought** *or* **beseeched.** (*tr*) to ask (someone) earnestly (to do something or for something); beg. [C12: see BE-, SEEK]

beseem (bɪˈsiːm) *vb Arch.* to be suitable for or worthy of; befit.

beset Ⓣ (bɪˈsɛt) *vb* **besets, besetting, beset.** (*tr*) **1** (esp. of dangers or temptations) to trouble or harass constantly. **2** to surround or attack from all sides. **3** *Arch.* to cover with, esp. with jewels.

besetting Ⓣ (bɪˈsɛtɪŋ) *adj* tempting, harassing, or assailing (esp. in **besetting sin**).

beside Ⓣ (bɪˈsaɪd) *prep* **1** next to; at, by, or to the side of. **2** as compared with. **3** away from; wide of. **4** *Arch.* besides. **5 beside oneself.** (*postpositive;* often foll. by *with*) overwhelmed; overwrought: *beside oneself with grief.* ◆ *adv* **6** at, by, to, or along the side of something or someone. [OE *be sīdan;* see BY, SIDE]

besides Ⓣ (bɪˈsaɪdz) *prep* **1** apart from; even considering. ◆ *sentence connector.* **2** anyway; moreover. ◆ *adv* **3** as well.

besiege Ⓣ (bɪˈsiːdʒ) *vb* **besieges, besieging, besieged.** (*tr*) **1** to surround (a fortified area) with military forces to bring about its surrender. **2** to crowd round; hem in. **3** to overwhelm, as with requests.
▸**beˈsieger** *n*

besmear (bɪˈsmɪə) *vb* (*tr*) **1** to smear over; daub. **2** to sully; defile (often in **besmear (a person's) reputation**).

besmirch Ⓣ (bɪˈsmɜːtʃ) *vb* (*tr*) **1** to make dirty; soil. **2** to reduce the brightness of. **3** to sully (often in **besmirch (a person's) name**).

besom[1] (ˈbiːzəm) *n* a broom, esp. one made of a bundle of twigs tied to a handle. [OE *besma*]

besom[2] (ˈbɪzəm) *n Scot. & N English dialect.* a derogatory term for a **woman.** [?from OE *bysen* example; rel. to ON *bysn* wonder]

besotted Ⓣ (bɪˈsɒtɪd) *adj* **1** stupefied with drink. **2** infatuated; doting. **3** foolish; muddled.

besought (bɪˈsɔːt) *vb* a past tense and past participle of **beseech.**

bespangle (bɪˈspæŋɡəl) *vb* **bespangles, bespangling, bespangled.** (*tr*) to cover or adorn with or as if with spangles.

bespatter Ⓣ (bɪˈspætə) *vb* (*tr*) **1** to splash, as with dirty water. **2** to defile; besmirch.

bespeak Ⓣ (bɪˈspiːk) *vb* **bespeaks, bespeaking, bespoke; bespoken** *or* **bespoke.** (*tr*) **1** to engage or ask for in advance. **2** to indicate or suggest: *this act bespeaks kindness.* **3** *Poetic.* to address.

bespectacled (bɪˈspɛktəkəld) *adj* wearing spectacles.

bespoke (bɪˈspəʊk) *adj Chiefly Brit.* **1** (esp. of a suit, jacket, etc.) made to the customer's specifications. **2** making or selling such suits, jackets, etc.: *a bespoke tailor.*

besprinkle (bɪˈsprɪŋkəl) *vb* **besprinkles, besprinkling, besprinkled.** (*tr*) to sprinkle all over with liquid, powder, etc.

Bessemer process (ˈbɛsɪmə) *n* (formerly) a process for producing steel by blowing air through molten pig iron in a **Bessemer converter** (a refractory-lined furnace): impurities are removed and the carbon content is controlled. [C19: after Sir Henry *Bessemer* (1813–98), E engineer]

best Ⓣ (bɛst) *adj* **1** the superlative of **good. 2** most excellent of a particular group, category, etc. **3** most suitable, desirable, etc. **4 the best part of.** most of. ◆ *adv* **5** the superlative of **well**[1]. **6** in a manner surpassing all others; most excellently, attractively, etc. ◆ *n* **7 the best.** the most outstanding or excellent person, thing, or group in a category. **8** the utmost effort. **9** a winning majority. **10** Also: **all the best.** best wishes. **11** a person's smartest outfit of clothing. **12 at best. 12a** in the most favourable interpretation. **12b** under the most favourable conditions. **13 for the best. 13a** for an ultimately good outcome. **13b** with good intentions. **14 get** *or* **have the best of.** to defeat or outwit. **15 give (someone) the best.** to concede (someone's) superiority. **16 make the best of.** to cope as well as possible with. ◆ *vb* **17** (*tr*) to gain the advantage over or defeat. [OE *betst*]

bestead (bɪˈstɛd) *Arch.* ◆ *vb* **besteads, besteading, besteaded; besteaded** *or* **bestead. 1** (*tr*) to help; avail. ◆ *adj also* **bested. 2** placed; situated. [C13: see BE-, STEAD]

bestial Ⓣ (ˈbɛstɪəl) *adj* **1** brutal or savage. **2** sexually depraved. **3** lacking in refinement; brutish. **4** of or relating to a beast. [C14: from LL *bestiālis,* from L *bestia* BEAST]

bestiality Ⓣ (ˌbɛstɪˈælɪtɪ) *n, pl* **bestialities. 1** bestial behaviour. **2** sexual activity between a person and an animal.

bestialize *or* **bestialise** (ˈbɛstɪəˌlaɪz) *vb* **bestializes, bestializing, bestialized** *or* **bestialises, bestialising, bestialised.** (*tr*) to make bestial or brutal.

bestiary (ˈbɛstɪərɪ) *n, pl* **bestiaries.** a moralizing medieval collection of descriptions of real and mythical animals.

bestir Ⓣ (bɪˈstɜː) *vb* **bestirs, bestirring, bestirred.** (*tr*) to cause (oneself) to become active; rouse.

best man *n* the male attendant of the bridegroom at a wedding.

bestow Ⓣ (bɪˈstəʊ) *vb* (*tr*) **1** to present (a gift) or confer (an honour). **2** *Arch.* to apply (energy, resources, etc.). **3** *Arch.* to house (a person) or store (goods).
▸**beˈstowal** *n*

bestrew (bɪˈstruː) *vb* **bestrews, bestrewing, bestrewed; bestrewn** *or* **bestrewed.** (*tr*) to scatter or lie scattered over (a surface).

bestride Ⓣ (bɪˈstraɪd) *vb* **bestrides, bestriding, bestrode** *or* (*Arch.*) **bestrid; bestridden** *or* (*Arch.*) **bestrid.** (*tr*) **1** to have or put a leg on either side of. **2** to extend across; span. **3** to stride over or across.

bestseller Ⓣ (ˌbɛstˈsɛlə) *n* **1** a book or other product that has sold in great numbers. **2** the author of one or more such books, etc.
▸ˌ**bestˈselling** *adj*

bet Ⓣ (bɛt) *n* **1** an agreement between two parties that a sum of money or other stake will be paid by the loser to the party who correctly predicts the outcome of an event. **2** the stake risked. **3** the predicted result in such an agreement. **4** a person, event, etc., considered as likely to succeed or occur. **5** a course of action (esp. in **one's best bet**). **6** *Inf.* an opinion: *my bet is that you've been up to no good.* ◆ *vb* **bets, betting, bet** *or* **betted. 7** (when *intr* foll. by *on* or *against*) to make or place a bet with (a person or persons). **8** (*tr*) to stake (money, etc.) in a bet. **9** (*tr; may take a clause as object*) *Inf.* to predict (a certain outcome). **10 you bet.** *Inf.* of course; naturally. [C16: prob. short for ABET]

THESAURUS

mal = **job**, appointment, employment, living, position, post, situation ◆ *vb* **9** *Nautical* = **anchor**, dock, drop anchor, land, moor, tie up

beseech *vb* = **beg**, adjure, ask, call upon, crave, entreat, implore, importune, petition, plead, pray, solicit, sue, supplicate

beset *vb* **1** = **plague**, badger, bedevil, embarrass, entangle, harass, perplex, pester, trouble **2** = **attack**, assail, besiege, encircle, enclose, encompass, environ, hem in, surround

besetting *adj* = **troublesome**, habitual, harassing, inveterate, persistent, prevalent

beside *prep* **1** = **next to**, abreast of, adjacent to, alongside, at the side of, cheek by jowl, close to, near, nearby, neighbouring, next door to, overlooking **5 beside oneself** = **distraught**, apoplectic, at the end of one's tether, berserk, crazed, delirious, demented, deranged, desperate, frantic, frenzied, insane, mad, out of one's mind, unbalanced, uncontrolled, unhinged

besides *prep* **1** = **apart from**, barring, excepting, excluding, in addition to, other than, over and above, without ◆ *adv* **3** = **too**, also, as well, further, furthermore, in addition, into the bargain, moreover, otherwise, what's more

besiege *vb* **1** = **surround**, beleaguer, beset, blockade, confine, encircle, encompass, environ, hedge in, hem in, invest (*rare*), lay siege to, shut in **3** = **harass**, badger, bend someone's ear (*inf.*), bother, harry, hassle (*inf.*), hound, importune, nag, pester, plague, trouble

besmirch *vb* **1** = **soil**, daub, smear, smirch, stain **2** = **tarnish 3** = **sully**, defame, dishonour, slander, smear

besotted *adj* **1** = **drunk**, befuddled, bevvied (*dialect*), blitzed (*sl.*), blotto (*sl.*), Brahms and Liszt (*sl.*), intoxicated, legless (*inf.*), out of it (*sl.*), out to it (*Austral. & NZ sl.*), paralytic (*inf.*), pissed (*taboo sl.*), smashed (*sl.*), stupefied, wrecked (*sl.*) **2** = **infatuated**, doting, hypnotized, smitten, spellbound **3** = **muddled**, confused, foolish, witless

bespatter *vb* **1** = **splatter**, bedaub, befoul, begrime, besprinkle, muddy, smear, spatter **2** = **defile**, besmirch, dishonour, slander, sully

bespeak *vb* **1** = **order beforehand**, engage, prearrange **2** = **indicate**, betoken, denote, display, evidence, evince, exhibit, imply, proclaim, reveal, show, signify, suggest, testify to

best *adj* **1, 2** = **finest**, chief, first, first-class, first-rate, foremost, highest, leading, most excellent, outstanding, perfect, pre-eminent, principal, superlative, supreme, unsurpassed **3** = **most fitting**, advantageous, apt, correct, golden, most desirable, right ◆ *adv* **5** = **most highly**, extremely, greatly, most deeply, most fully **6** = **excellently**, advantageously, attractively, most fortunately ◆ *n* **7 the best** = **finest**, choice, cream, *crème de la crème*, elite, favourite, first, flower, pick, prime, top **8** = **utmost**, hardest, highest endeavour ◆ *vb* **17** = **defeat**, beat, blow out of the water (*sl.*), conquer, get the better of, lick (*inf.*), master, outclass, outdo, put in the shade (*inf.*), run rings around (*inf.*), surpass, tank (*sl.*), thrash, triumph over, trounce, wipe the floor with (*inf.*)

bestial *adj* **1** = **brutal**, barbaric, barbarous, beastlike, beastly, brutish, inhuman, savage **2** = **depraved**, carnal, degraded, gross, sensual, sordid, vile **4** = **animal**

bestiality *n* **1** = **brutality 2** = **zoophilia**, barbarity, beastliness, brutishness, carnality, cruelty, depravity, inhumanity, savagery

bestir *vb* = **get going**, activate, actuate, animate, awaken, exert, incite, motivate, rouse, set off, stimulate, stir up, trouble

bestow *vb* **1** = **present**, accord, allot, apportion, award, commit, confer, donate, endow, entrust, give, grant, hand out, honour with, impart, lavish, render to
Antonyms *vb* acquire, attain, come by, earn, gain, get, land, make, net, obtain, procure, secure

bestowal *n* **1** = **presentation**, allotment, award, bestowment, conferment, conferral, donation, endowment, gift, grant

bestride *vb* **1** = **straddle**, bestraddle **2** = **span**, bridge, extend across **3** = **step over**

bestseller *n* **1** = **success**, blockbuster, chart-topper (*inf.*), hit (*inf.*), number one, runaway success, smash (*inf.*), smash hit (*inf.*)
Antonyms *n* dud (*inf.*), failure, flop (*inf.*), turkey (*sl., chiefly US & Canad.*)

bestselling *adj* **1** = **successful**, chart-topping (*inf.*), highly successful, hit (*inf.*), number one, smash (*inf.*), smash-hit (*inf.*)

bet *n* **1** = **gamble**, ante, hazard, long shot, pledge, risk, speculation, stake, venture, wager ◆ *vb* **7, 8** = **gamble**, chance, hazard, pledge, punt (*chiefly Brit.*), put money on, risk, speculate, stake, venture, wager

DICTIONARY

beta (ˈbiːtə) *n* **1** the second letter in the Greek alphabet (Β or β). **2** the second in a group or series. [from Gk *bēta*, from Heb.; see BETH]

beta-blocker *n* any of a class of drugs, such as propranolol, that decrease the activity of the heart: used in the treatment of high blood pressure and angina.

betacarotene (ˌbiːtəˈkærəˌtiːn) *n* the most important form of the plant pigment carotene, which occurs in milk, vegetables, and other foods and, when eaten by man and animals, is converted in the body to vitamin A.

beta decay *n* the radioactive change in an atomic nucleus accompanying the emission of an electron.

betake (bɪˈteɪk) *vb* **betakes, betaking, betook, betaken.** (*tr*) **1 betake oneself.** to go; move. **2** *Arch.* to apply (oneself) to.

beta particle *n* a high-speed electron or positron emitted by a nucleus during radioactive decay or nuclear fission.

beta ray *n* a stream of beta particles.

beta rhythm *or* **wave** *n Physiol.* the normal electrical activity of the cerebral cortex.

beta stock *n* any of the second rank of active securities on the London stock exchange, of which there are about 500. Continuous display of prices by market makers is required but not immediate publication of transactions.

betatron (ˈbiːtəˌtrɒn) *n* a type of particle accelerator for producing high-energy beams of electrons by magnetic induction.

betel (ˈbiːtᵊl) *n* an Asian climbing plant, the leaves of which are chewed by the peoples of SE Asia. [C16: from Port., from Malayalam *vettila*]

betel nut *n* the seed of the betel palm, chewed with betel leaves and lime by people in S and SE Asia as a digestive stimulant and narcotic.

betel palm *n* a tropical Asian feather palm.

bête noire **T** *French.* (bɛt nwar) *n, pl* ***bêtes noires*** (bɛt nwar). a person or thing that one particularly dislikes or dreads. [lit.: black beast]

beth (bɛt) *n* the second letter of the Hebrew alphabet. [from Heb. *bēth-, bayith* house]

bethink **T** (bɪˈθɪŋk) *vb* **bethinks, bethinking, bethought.** *Arch. or dialect.* **1** to cause (oneself) to consider or meditate. **2** (*tr;* often foll. by *of*) to remind (oneself).

betide **T** (bɪˈtaɪd) *vb* **betides, betiding, betided.** to happen or happen to (often in **woe betide** (**someone**)). [C13: from BE- + obs. *tide* to happen]

betimes (bɪˈtaɪmz) *adv Arch.* **1** in good time; early. **2** soon. [C14 *bitimes;* see BY, TIME]

betoken **T** (bɪˈtəʊkən) *vb* (*tr*) **1** to indicate; signify. **2** to portend; augur.

betony (ˈbɛtənɪ) *n, pl* **betonies. 1** a Eurasian plant with a spike of red-dish-purple flowers, formerly used in medicine and dyeing. **2** any of several related plants. [C14: from OF, from L]

betray **T** (bɪˈtreɪ) *vb* (*tr*) **1** to hand over or expose (one's nation, friend, etc.) treacherously to an enemy. **2** to disclose (a secret, confidence, etc.) treacherously. **3** to break (a promise) or be disloyal to (a person's trust). **4** to show signs of; indicate. **5** to reveal unintentionally: *his grin betrayed his satisfaction.* [C13: from BE- + *trayen,* from OF, from L *trādere* to hand over]
▸**beˈtrayal** *n* ▸**beˈtrayer** *n*

betroth (bɪˈtrəʊð) *vb* (*tr*) *Arch.* to promise to marry or to give in marriage. [C14 *betreuthen,* from BE- + *treuthe* TROTH, TRUTH]

betrothal **T** (bɪˈtrəʊðəl) *n* **1** engagement to be married. **2** a mutual promise to marry.

betrothed **T** (bɪˈtrəʊðd) *adj* **1** engaged to be married: *he was betrothed to her.* ◆ *n* **2** the person to whom one is engaged; fiancé or fiancée.

better **T** (ˈbɛtə) *adj* **1** the comparative of **good. 2** more excellent than others. **3** more suitable, advantageous, attractive, etc. **4** improved or fully recovered in health. **5 better off.** in more favourable circumstances, esp. financially. **6 the better part of.** a large part of. ◆ *adv* **7** the comparative of **well**[1]. **8** in a more excellent manner; more advantageously, attractively, etc. **9** in or to a greater degree or extent; more. **10 had better.** would be wise, sensible, etc., to: *I had better be off.* **11 think better of. 11a** to change one's mind about (a course of action, etc.) after reconsideration. **11b** to rate more highly. ◆ *n* **12 the better.** something that is the more excellent, useful, etc., of two such things. **13** (*usually pl*) a person who is superior, esp. in social standing or ability. **14 for the better.** by way of improvement. **15 get the better of.** to defeat, outwit, or surpass. ◆ *vb* **16** to make or become better. **17** (*tr*) to improve upon; surpass. [OE *betera*]

better half *n Humorous.* one's spouse.

betterment **T** (ˈbɛtəmənt) *n* **1** a change for the better; improvement. **2** *Property law.* an improvement effected on real property that enhances the value of the property.

betting shop *n* (in Britain) a licensed bookmaker's premises not on a racecourse.

between **T** (bɪˈtwiːn) *prep* **1** at a point or in a region intermediate to two other points in space, times, degrees, etc. **2** in combination; together: *between them, they saved enough money to buy a car.* **3** confined or restricted to: *between you and me.* **4** indicating a reciprocal relation or comparison. **5** indicating two or more alternatives. ◆ *adv also* **in between. 6** between one specified thing and another. [OE *betwēonum;* see TWO, TWAIN]

> **USAGE NOTE** After *distribute* and words with a similar meaning, *among* should be used rather than *between*: *this enterprise issued shares which were distributed among its workers.*

betweentimes (bɪˈtwiːnˌtaɪmz) *or* **betweenwhiles** *adv* between other activities; during intervals.

betwixt (bɪˈtwɪkst) *prep, adv* **1** *Arch.* another word for **between. 2 betwixt and between.** in an intermediate or indecisive position. [OE *betwix*] [Hebrew, literally: married woman]

BeV (in the US) *abbrev. for* gigaelectronvolts (GeV). [C20: from *b(illion) e(lectron) v(olts)*]

bevatron (ˈbɛvəˌtrɒn) *n* a synchrotron used to accelerate protons. [C20: from BEV + -TRON]

bevel **T** (ˈbɛvᵊl) *n* **1** Also called: **cant.** a surface that meets another at an angle other than a right angle. ◆ *vb* **bevels, bevelling, bevelled** *or US* **bevels, beveling, beveled. 2** (*intr*) to be inclined; slope. **3** (*tr*) to cut a bevel on (a piece of timber, etc.). [C16: from OF, from *baer* to gape; see BAY[1]]

bevel gear *n* a gear having teeth cut into a conical surface. Two such gears mesh together to transmit power between two shafts at an angle.

bevel square *n* a tool with an adjustable arm that can be set to mark out an angle.

beverage **T** (ˈbɛvərɪdʒ, ˈbɛvrɪdʒ) *n* any drink, usually other than water. [C13: from OF *bevrage,* from *beivre* to drink, from L *bibere*]

beverage room *n Canad.* another name for **beer parlour.**

bevvy (ˈbɛvɪ) *n, pl* **bevvies.** *Dialect.* **1** a drink, esp. an alcoholic one. **2** a session of drinking. [prob. from OF *bevee, buvee* drinking]

bevy **T** (ˈbɛvɪ) *n, pl* **bevies. 1** a flock of quails. **2** a group, esp. of girls. [C15: from ?]

bewail **T** (bɪˈweɪl) *vb* to express great sorrow over (a person or thing); lament.
▸**beˈwailer** *n*

THESAURUS

bête noire *n French* = **pet hate**, abomination, anathema, aversion, bane, bogey, bugaboo, bugbear, curse, devil, dread, nemesis, nightmare, scourge, thorn in the flesh *or* side

bethink *vb* **1** = **consider**, cogitate, ponder, reconsider, reflect, review, take thought **2** = **remind oneself**, recall, recollect, remember

betide *vb* = **happen**, bechance, befall, chance, come to pass, crop up (*inf.*), ensue, occur, overtake, supervene, take place, transpire (*inf.*)

betoken *vb* **1** = **indicate**, bespeak, declare, denote, evidence, manifest, mark, represent, signify, suggest, typify **2** = **portend**, augur, bode, presage, prognosticate, promise

betray *vb* **1, 3** = **be disloyal**, be treacherous, be unfaithful, break one's promise, double-cross (*inf.*), grass (*Brit. sl.*), grass up (*sl.*), inform on *or* against, sell down the river (*inf.*), sell out (*inf.*), shop (*sl., chiefly Brit.*), stab in the back **2** = **give away**, blurt out, disclose, divulge, evince, expose, lay bare, let slip, manifest, reveal, show, tell, tell on, uncover, unmask

betrayal *n* **1, 3** = **disloyalty**, deception, double-cross (*inf.*), double-dealing, duplicity, falseness, perfidy, sell-out (*inf.*), treachery, treason, trickery, unfaithfulness **2** = **giving away**, blurting out, disclosure, divulgence, revelation, telling
Antonyms *n* ≠ **disloyalty:** allegiance, constancy, devotion, faithfulness, fealty, fidelity, loyalty, steadfastness, trustiness, trustworthiness ≠ **giving away:** guarding, keeping, keeping secret, preserving, safeguarding

betrayer *n* **1** = **traitor**, apostate, conspirator, deceiver, renegade, snake in the grass

betrothal *n* **1, 2** = **engagement**, affiancing, betrothing, marriage compact, plight, promise, troth, vow

betrothed *adj* **1** = **engaged**, affianced, pledged, plighted, promised ◆ *n* **2** = **fiancé** *or* **fiancée**, husband- *or* bride-to-be, future husband *or* wife, intended, prospective spouse

better *adj* **1, 2** = **superior**, bigger, excelling, finer, greater, higher-quality, larger, streets ahead, surpassing, worthier **3** = **more desirable**, fitter, more appropriate, more fitting, more suitable, more useful, more valuable, preferable **4** = **well**, cured, fitter, fully recovered, healthier, improving, less ill, mending, more healthy, on the mend (*inf.*), progressing, recovering, stronger ◆ *adv* **7, 8** = **in a more excellent manner**, in a superior way, more advantageously, more attractively, more competently, more effectively **9** = **to a greater degree**, more completely, more thoroughly **11a think better of** = **change one's mind about**, decide against, go back on, have second thoughts about, reconsider, repent, think again, think twice about ◆ *n* **15 get the better of** = **defeat**, beat, best, get the upper hand, outdo, outsmart (*inf.*), outwit, prevail over, score off, surpass, triumph over, worst ◆ *vb* **16** = **improve**, advance, ameliorate, amend, correct, enhance, forward, further, meliorate, mend, promote, raise, rectify, reform **17** = **beat**, cap (*inf.*), clobber (*sl.*), exceed, excel, improve on *or* upon, knock spots off (*inf.*), lick (*inf.*), outdo, outstrip, put in the shade (*inf.*), run rings around (*inf.*), surpass, top
Antonyms *adj* ≠ **superior:** inferior, lesser, smaller, substandard, worse ≠ **well:** worse ◆ *adv* ≠ **in a more excellent manner:** worse ◆ *vb* ≠ **improve:** depress, devaluate, go downhill, impoverish, lessen, lower, weaken, worsen

betterment *n* **1** = **improvement**, amelioration, edification, melioration

between *prep* **1** = **amidst**, among, betwixt, in the middle of, mid

bevel *n* **1** = **slant**, angle, bezel, cant, chamfer, diagonal, mitre, oblique, slope ◆ *vb* **2** = **cut at an angle**, cant, chamfer, mitre

beverage *n* = **drink**, bevvy (*dialect*), draught, libation (*facetious*), liquid, liquor, potable, potation, refreshment

bevy *n* **1** = **flock**, covey, flight **2** = **group**, band, bunch (*inf.*), collection, company, crowd, gathering, pack, troupe

bewail *vb* = **lament**, bemoan, cry over, express

beware Ⓣ (bɪ'weə) *vb* (*usually used in the imperative or infinitive;* often foll. by *of*) to be cautious or wary (of); be on one's guard (against). [C13 *be war,* from BE (imperative) + *war* WARY]

bewilder Ⓣ (bɪ'wɪldə) *vb* (*tr*) to confuse utterly; puzzle. [C17: see BE-, WILDER]
▸**be'wildering** *adj* ▸**be'wilderingly** *adv* ▸**be'wilderment** *n*

bewitch Ⓣ (bɪ'wɪtʃ) *vb* (*tr*) **1** to attract and fascinate. **2** to cast a spell over. [C13 *bewicchen;* see BE-, WITCH[1]]
▸**be'witching** *adj*

bewray (bɪ'reɪ) *vb* (*tr*) an obsolete word for **betray.** [C13: from BE- + OE *wrēgan* to accuse]

bey (beɪ) *n* **1** (in the Ottoman Empire) a title given to provincial governors. **2** (in modern Turkey) a title of address, corresponding to *Mr.* ◆ Also called: **beg.** [C16: Turkish: lord]

beyond Ⓣ (bɪ'jɒnd) *prep* **1** at or to a point on the other side of; at or to the further side of: *beyond those hills.* **2** outside the limits or scope of. ◆ *adv* **3** at or to the other or far side of something. **4** outside the limits of something. ◆ *n* **5 the beyond.** the unknown, esp. life after death in certain religious beliefs. [OE *begeondan;* see BY, YONDER]

bezel ('bez^{ə}l) *n* **1** the sloping face adjacent to the working edge of a cutting tool. **2** the upper oblique faces of a cut gem. **3** a grooved ring or part holding a gem, watch crystal, etc. **4** a retaining outer rim used in vehicle instruments such as tachometers and speedometers. **5** a small indicator light used in vehicle instrument panels. [C17: prob. from F *biseau*]

bezique (bɪ'ziːk) *n* **1** a card game for two or more players using two packs with nothing below a seven. **2** (in this game) the queen of spades and jack of diamonds declared together. [C19: from F *bésigue,* from ?]

B/F *or* **b/f** *Book-keeping. abbrev. for* brought forward.

BFPO *abbrev. for* British Forces Post Office.

bhaji ('bɑːdʒɪ) *n, pl* **bhaji, bhajis,** *or* **bhajia** ('bɑːdʒɪə). an Indian savoury made of chopped vegetables mixed in a spiced batter and deep-fried. [Hindi *bhājī* fried vegetables]

bhang *or* **bang** (bæŋ) *n* a preparation of the leaves and flower tops of Indian hemp having psychoactive properties: much used in India. [C16: from Hindi *bhāng*]

bhangra ('bæŋgrə) *n* a type of Asian pop music that combines elements of traditional Punjabi music with Western pop. [C20: from Hindi]

bharal *or* **burhel** ('bʌrəl) *n* a wild Himalayan sheep with a bluish-grey coat. [Hindi]

bhindi ('bɪndɪ) *n* the okra as used in Indian cooking. [Hindi]

bhp *abbrev. for* brake horsepower.

BHP *Austral. abbrev. for* Broken Hill Proprietary.

Bi *the chemical symbol for* bismuth.

bi- *or sometimes before a vowel* **bin-** *combining form.* **1** two; having two: *bifocal.* **2** occurring every two; lasting for two: *biennial.* **3** on both sides, directions, etc.: *bilateral.* **4** occurring twice during: *biweekly.* **5a** denoting a compound containing two identical cyclic hydrocarbon systems: *biphenyl.* **5b** (rare in technical usage) indicating an acid salt of a dibasic acid: *sodium bicarbonate.* **5c** (not in technical usage) equivalent of **di-**[1] (sense 2). [from L, from *bis* TWICE]

biannual (baɪ'ænjʊəl) *adj* occurring twice a year. Cf. **biennial.**
▸**bi'annually** *adv*

bias Ⓣ ('baɪəs) *n* **1** mental tendency or inclination, esp. irrational preference or prejudice. **2** a diagonal line or cut across the weave of a fabric. **3** *Electronics.* the voltage applied to an electrode of a transistor or valve to establish suitable working conditions. **4** *Bowls.* **4a** a bulge or weight inside one side of a bowl. **4b** the curved course of such a bowl. **5** *Statistics.* a latent influence that disturbs an analysis. ◆ *adv* **6** obliquely; diagonally. ◆ *vb* **biases, biasing, biased** *or* **biasses, biassing, biassed. 7** (*tr; usually passive*) to cause to have a bias; prejudice; influence. [C16: from OF *biais*]
▸**'biased** *or* **'biassed** *adj*

bias binding *n* a strip of material cut on the bias, used for binding hems or for decoration.

biathlon (baɪ'æθlən, -lɒn) *n Sport.* a contest in which skiers with rifles shoot at four targets along a 20-kilometre (12.5-mile) cross-country course.

biaxial (baɪ'æksɪəl) *adj* (esp. of a crystal) having two axes.

bib (bɪb) *n* **1** a piece of cloth or plastic worn, esp. by babies, to protect their clothes while eating. **2** the upper front part of some aprons, dungarees, etc. **3** Also called: **pout, whiting pout.** a light brown European marine gadoid food fish with a barbel on its lower jaw. **4 stick one's bib in.** *Austral. inf.* to interfere. ◆ *vb* **bibs, bibbing, bibbed. 5** *Arch.* to drink (something). [C14 *bibben* to drink, prob. from L *bibere*]

Bib. *abbrev. for:* **1** Bible. **2** Biblical.

bib and tucker *n Inf.* an outfit of clothes.

bibcock ('bɪbˌkɒk) *or* **bib** *n* a tap with a nozzle bent downwards fed from a horizontal pipe.

bibelot ('bɪbləʊ) *n* an attractive or curious trinket. [C19: from F, from OF *beubelet*]

bibl. *abbrev. for:* **1** bibliographical. **2** bibliography.

Bibl. *abbrev. for* Biblical.

Bible ('baɪb^{ə}l) *n* **1a the.** the sacred writings of the Christian religion, comprising the Old and New Testaments. **1b** (*as modifier*): *a Bible reading.* **2** (*often not cap.*) the sacred writings of a religion. **3** (*usually not cap.*) a book regarded as authoritative. [C13: from OF, from Med. L *biblia* books, from Gk, dim. of *biblos* papyrus]

Bible Belt *n* those states of the S US where Protestant fundamentalism is dominant.

Bible-thumper *n Sl.* an enthusiastic or aggressive exponent of the Bible. Also: **Bible-basher.**
▸**'Bible-ˌthumping** *n, adj*

biblical ('bɪblɪk^{ə}l) *adj* **1** of or referring to the Bible. **2** resembling the Bible in written style.

Biblicist ('bɪblɪsɪst) *or* **Biblist** *n* **1** a biblical scholar. **2** a person who takes the Bible literally.

biblio- *combining form.* indicating book or books: *bibliography.* [from Gk *biblion* book]

bibliography (ˌbɪblɪ'ɒgrəfɪ) *n, pl* **bibliographies. 1** a list of books on a subject or by a particular author. **2** a list of sources used in a book, thesis, etc. **3a** the study of the history, classification, etc., of literary material. **3b** a work on this subject.
▸ˌ**bibli'ographer** *n* ▸**bibliographic** (ˌbɪblɪəʊ'græfɪk) *or* ˌ**biblio'graphical** *adj*

bibliomancy ('bɪblɪəʊˌmænsɪ) *n* prediction of the future by interpreting a passage chosen at random from a book, esp. the Bible.

bibliomania (ˌbɪblɪəʊ'meɪnɪə) *n* extreme fondness for books.
▸ˌ**biblio'maniˌac** *n, adj*

bibliophile ('bɪblɪəˌfaɪl) *or* **bibliophil** ('bɪblɪəfɪl) *n* a person who collects or is fond of books.
▸**bibliophilism** (ˌbɪblɪ'ɒfɪˌlɪzəm) *n* ▸ˌ**bibli'ophily** *n*

bibliopole ('bɪblɪəʊˌpəʊl) *or* **bibliopolist** (ˌbɪblɪ'ɒpəlɪst) *n* a dealer in books, esp. rare or decorative ones. [C18: from L, from Gk, from BIBLIO- + *pōlein* to sell]
▸ˌ**bibli'opoly** *n*

bibulous ('bɪbjʊləs) *adj* addicted to alcohol. [C17: from L *bibulus,* from *bibere* to drink]
▸**'bibulously** *adv* ▸**'bibulousness** *n*

bicameral (baɪ'kæmərəl) *adj* (of a legislature) consisting of two chambers. [C19: from BI- + L *camera* CHAMBER]
▸**bi'cameralˌism** *n*

bicarb ('baɪkɑːb) *n* short for **bicarbonate of soda.**

bicarbonate (baɪ'kɑːbənɪt, -ˌneɪt) *n* a salt of carbonic acid.

bicarbonate of soda *n* sodium bicarbonate, esp. as medicine or a raising agent in baking.

bice (baɪs) *n* **1** Also called: **bice blue.** medium blue. **2** Also called: **bice green.** a yellowish green. [C14: from OF *bis* dark grey, from ?]

bicentenary (ˌbaɪsen'tiːnərɪ) *or US* **bicentennial** (ˌbaɪsen'tenɪəl) *adj* **1** marking a 200th anniversary. **2** occurring every 200 years. **3** lasting 200 years. ◆ *n, pl* **bicentenaries. 4** a 200th anniversary.

bicephalous (baɪ'sefələs) *adj* **1** *Biol.* having two heads. **2** crescent-shaped.

biceps ('baɪseps) *n, pl* **biceps.** *Anat.* any muscle having two heads or origins, esp. the muscle that flexes the forearm. [C17: from L, from BI- + *caput* head]

bichloride (baɪ'klɔːraɪd) *n* another name for **dichloride.**

bichloride of mercury *n* another name for **mercuric chloride.**

bichromate (baɪ'krəʊˌmeɪt, -mɪt) *n* another name for **dichromate.**

bicker Ⓣ ('bɪkə) *vb* (*intr*) **1** to argue over petty matters; squabble. **2** *Po-*

THESAURUS

sorrow, grieve for, keen, moan, mourn, wail, weep over

beware *vb* = **be careful**, avoid, be cautious, be wary, guard against, heed, look out, mind, refrain from, shun, steer clear of, take heed, watch out

bewilder *vb* = **confound**, baffle, befuddle, bemuse, confuse, daze, flummox, mix up, mystify, nonplus, perplex, puzzle, stun, stupefy

bewildered *adj* = **confused**, at a loss, at sea, baffled, bamboozled, disconcerted, flummoxed, mystified, nonplussed, perplexed, puzzled, speechless, startled, stunned, surprised, taken aback

bewildering *adj* = **confusing**, amazing, astonishing, astounding, baffling, mystifying, perplexing, puzzling, staggering, stunning, stupefying, surprising

bewitch *vb* **1** = **fascinate**, absorb, allure, attract, beguile, captivate, charm, enchant, enrapture, entrance, hypnotize, ravish, spellbind **2** = **enchant**, spellbind
Antonyms *vb* ≠ **fascinate:** disgust, give one the creeps (*inf.*), make one sick, offend, repel, repulse, sicken, turn off (*inf.*)

bewitched *adj* **1** = **enchanted**, charmed, entranced, fascinated, mesmerized **2** = **under a spell**, mesmerized, possessed, spellbound

beyond *prep* **1** = **past**, above, apart from, at a distance, away from, outwith (*Scot.*), over **2** = **exceeding**, out of reach of, superior to, surpassing

bias *n* **1** = **prejudice**, bent, bigotry, favouritism, inclination, intolerance, leaning, narrow-mindedness, nepotism, one-sidedness, partiality, penchant, predilection, predisposition, proclivity, proneness, propensity, tendency, turn, unfairness **2** = **slant**, angle, cross, diagonal line ◆ *vb* **7** = **prejudice**, distort, influence, predispose, slant, sway, twist, warp, weight
Antonyms *n* ≠ **prejudice:** equality, equity, fairness, impartiality, neutrality, objectivity, open-mindedness

biased *adj* **1** = **prejudiced**, distorted, embittered, jaundiced, one-sided, partial, predisposed, slanted, swayed, twisted, warped, weighted

bicker *vb* **1** = **quarrel**, argue, disagree, dispute, fight, row (*inf.*), scrap (*inf.*), spar, squabble, wrangle
Antonyms *vb* accord, acquiesce, agree, assent, concur, cooperate, get on, harmonize

etic. **2a** (esp. of a stream) to run quickly. **2b** to flicker; glitter. ◆ *n* **3** a squabble. [C13: from ?]
▸ **'bickerer** *n*

bicolour ('baɪˌkʌlə), **bicoloured** *or US* **bicolor, bicolored** *adj* two-coloured.

biconcave (baɪ'kɒnkeɪv, ˌbaɪkɒn'keɪv) *adj* (of a lens) having concave faces on both sides.

biconditional (ˌbaɪkən'dɪʃənəl) *n* **1** *Logic, maths.* a relation, taken as meaning *if and only if,* between two propositions which are either both true or both false and such that each implies the other. **2** *Logic.* a logical connective between two propositions whose truth table is true only if both propositions are true or both false. ◆ Also called (esp. sense 1): **equivalence.**

biconvex (baɪ'kɒnvɛks, ˌbaɪkɒn'vɛks) *adj* (of a lens) having convex faces on both sides.

bicuspid (baɪ'kʌspɪd) *or* **bicuspidate** (baɪ'kʌspɪˌdeɪt) *adj* **1** having two cusps or points. ◆ *n* **2** a bicuspid tooth; premolar.

bicycle ('baɪsɪkəl) *n* **1** a vehicle with a tubular metal frame mounted on two spoked wheels, one behind the other. The rider sits on a saddle, propels the vehicle by means of pedals, and steers with handlebars on the front wheel. Often shortened to **bike** (inf.), **cycle.** ◆ *vb* **bicycles, bicycling, bicycled. 2** (*intr*) to ride a bicycle.
▸ **'bicyclist** *or* **'bicycler** *n*

bicycle clip *n* one of a pair of clips worn around the ankles by cyclists to keep the trousers tight and out of the chain.

bid Ⓣ (bɪd) *vb* **bids, bidding, bad, bade,** *or* (esp. for senses 1, 2, 5, 6) **bid; bidden** *or* (esp. for senses 1, 2, 5, 6) **bid. 1** (often foll. by *for* or *against*) to offer (an amount) in attempting to buy something. **2** *Commerce.* to respond to an offer by a seller stating (the more favourable terms) on which one is willing to make a purchase. **3** (*tr*) to say (a greeting, etc.): *to bid farewell.* **4** to order; command: *do as you are bid!* **5** (*intr;* usually foll. by *for*) to attempt to attain power, etc. **6** *Bridge, etc.* to declare before play how many tricks one expects to make. **7 bid defiance.** to resist boldly. **8 bid fair.** to seem probable. ◆ *n* **9a** an offer of a specified amount. **9b** the price offered. **10a** the quoting by a seller of a price. **10b** the price quoted. **11** *Commerce.* **11a** a statement by a buyer, in response to an offer by a seller, of the more favourable terms that would be acceptable. **11b** the price or other terms so stated. **12** an attempt, esp. to attain power. **13** *Bridge.* **13a** the number of tricks a player undertakes to make. **13b** a player's turn to make a bid. ◆ See also **bid up.** [OE *biddan*]
▸ **'bidder** *n*

biddable Ⓣ ('bɪdəbəl) *adj* **1** having sufficient value to be bid on, as a hand at bridge. **2** docile; obedient.
▸ **'biddableness** *n*

bidding Ⓣ ('bɪdɪŋ) *n* **1** an order; command. **2** an invitation; summons. **3** bids or the act of making bids.

biddy[1] ('bɪdɪ) *n, pl* **biddies.** a dialect word for **chicken** or **hen.** [C17: ? imit. of calling chickens]

biddy[2] ('bɪdɪ) *n, pl* **biddies.** *Inf.* a woman, esp. an old gossipy one. [C18: from pet form of *Bridget*]

biddy-biddy ('bɪdɪˌbɪdɪ) *n, pl* **biddy-biddies. 1** a low-growing rosaceous plant of New Zealand, having prickly burs. **2** the burs of this plant. ◆ Also: **bidgee-widgee** ('bɪdʒɪˌwɪdʒɪ). [from Maori *piripiri*]

bide (baɪd) *vb* **bides, biding, bided** *or* **bode, bided. 1** (*intr*) *Arch. or dialect.* to continue in a certain place or state; stay. **2** (*tr*) *Arch. or dialect.* to tolerate; endure. **3 bide one's time.** to wait patiently for an opportunity. [OE *bīdan*]

bidentate (baɪ'dɛnˌteɪt) *adj* having two teeth or toothlike parts or processes.

bidet ('bi:deɪ) *n* a small low basin for washing the genital area. [C17: from F: small horse]

bid up *vb* (*adv*) to increase the market price of (a commodity) by making artificial bids.

biennial (baɪ'ɛnɪəl) *adj* **1** occurring every two years. **2** lasting two years. Cf. **biannual.** ◆ *n* **3** a plant that completes its life cycle in two years. **4** an event that takes place every two years.
▸ **bi'ennially** *adv*

bier (bɪə) *n* a platform or stand on which a corpse or a coffin containing a corpse rests before burial. [OE *bǣr;* rel. to *beran* to BEAR[1]]

biestings ('bi:stɪŋz) *n* a variant spelling of **beestings.**

biff (bɪf) *Sl.* ◆ *n* **1** a blow with the fist. ◆ *vb* **2** (*tr*) to give (someone) such a blow. [C20: prob. imit.]

bifid ('baɪfɪd) *adj* divided into two lobes by a median cleft. [C17: from L, from BI- + *-fidus,* from *findere* to split]
▸ **bi'fidity** *n* ▸ **'bifidly** *adv*

bifocal (baɪ'fəʊkəl) *adj* **1** *Optics.* having two different focuses. **2** relating to a compound lens permitting near and distant vision.

bifocals (baɪ'fəʊkəlz) *pl n* a pair of spectacles with bifocal lenses.

BIFU (in Britain) *abbrev. for* Banking, Insurance and Finance Union.

bifurcate *vb* ('baɪfəˌkeɪt), **bifurcates, bifurcating, bifurcated. 1** to fork or divide into two branches. ◆ *adj* ('baɪfəˌkeɪt, -kɪt). **2** forked or divided into two branches. [C17: from Med. L, from L, from BI- + *furca* fork]
▸ **ˌbifur'cation** *n*

big Ⓣ (bɪg) *adj* **bigger, biggest. 1** of great or considerable size, height, weight, number, power, or capacity. **2** having great significance; important. **3** important through having power, influence, wealth, authority, etc. **4** *Inf.* considerable in extent or intensity (esp. in **in a big way**). **5a** elder: *my big brother.* **5b** grown-up. **6a** generous; magnanimous: *that's very big of you.* **6b** (*in combination*): *big-hearted.* **7** extravagant; boastful: *big talk.* **8 too big for one's boots** *or* **breeches.** conceited; unduly self-confident. **9** in an advanced stage of pregnancy (esp. in **big with child**). ◆ *adv Inf.* **10** boastfully; pretentiously (esp. in **talk big**). **11** in an exceptional way; well: *his talk went over big.* **12** on a grand scale (esp. in **think big**). ◆ See also **big up.** [C13: ?from ON]
▸ **'bigness** *n*

bigamy ('bɪgəmɪ) *n, pl* **bigamies.** the crime of making a person while still legally married to someone else. [C13: via F from Med. L; see BI-, -GAMY]
▸ **'bigamist** *n* ▸ **'bigamous** *adj*

Big Apple *n* **the.** *Inf.* New York City. [C20: prob. from US jazzmen's earlier use to mean any big, esp. northern, city; from ?]

Big Bang *n* the reorganization of the London Stock Exchange that took effect in October 1986 when operations became fully computerized, fixed commissions were abolished, and the functions of jobbers and brokers were merged.

big-bang theory *n* a cosmological theory postulating that all the matter of the universe was hurled in all directions by a cataclysmic explosion and that the universe is still expanding. Cf. **steady-state theory.**

Big Brother *n* a person, organization, etc., that exercises total dictatorial control. [C20: from George Orwell's novel *1984* (1949)]

big business *n* large commercial organizations collectively, esp. when considered as exploitative or socially harmful.

Big C *n* **the.** a euphemism for **cancer** (senses 1 and 2).

big deal *interj Sl.* an exclamation of scorn, derision, etc., used esp. to belittle a claim or offer.

big dipper *n* (in amusement parks) a narrow railway with open carriages that run swiftly over a route of sharp curves and steep inclines.

big end *n Brit.* the larger end of a connecting rod in an internal-combustion engine.

big game *n* large animals that are hunted or fished for sport.

big gun *n Inf.* an important person.

bighead Ⓣ ('bɪgˌhɛd) *n Inf.* a conceited person.
▸ **ˌbig'headed** *adj* ▸ **ˌbig'headedness** *n*

bighorn ('bɪgˌhɔ:n) *n, pl* **bighorns** *or* **bighorn.** a large wild sheep inhabiting mountainous regions in North America.

bight (baɪt) *n* **1** a wide indentation of a shoreline, or the body of water bounded by such a curve. **2** the slack middle part or loop in a rope. [OE *byht;* see BOW[2]]

Big Mac (mæk) *n Trademark.* two hamburgers served with salad, dressing, and a pickle on a soft bread roll.

bigmouth ('bɪgˌmaʊθ) *n Sl.* a noisy, indiscreet, or boastful person.
▸ **'big-ˌmouthed** *adj*

big name *n Inf.* **a** a famous person. **b** (*as modifier*): *a big-name performer.*

big noise *n Brit. inf.* an important person.

bignonia (bɪg'nəʊnɪə) *n* a tropical American climbing shrub cultivated for its trumpet-shaped yellow or reddish flowers. [C19: from NL, after the Abbé Jean-Paul *Bignon* (1662–1743)]

big-note *vb* **big-notes, big-noting, big-noted.** (*tr*) *Austral. inf.* to boast about (oneself).

bigot Ⓣ ('bɪgət) *n* a person who is intolerant, esp. regarding religion,

THESAURUS

bid *vb* **1** = **offer,** proffer, propose, submit, tender **3** = **say,** call, greet, tell, wish **4** = **tell,** ask, call, charge, command, desire, direct, enjoin, instruct, invite, order, require, solicit, summon ◆ *n* **9** = **offer,** advance, amount, price, proposal, proposition, submission, sum, tender **12** = **attempt,** crack (*inf.*), effort, endeavour, go (*inf.*), stab (*inf.*), try, venture

biddable *adj* **2** = **obedient,** amenable, complaisant, cooperative, docile, teachable, tractable
Antonyms *adj* awkward, difficult, disobedient, intractable, petulant, querulous, refractory, unruly

bidding *n* **1** = **order,** beck, beck and call, behest, call, charge, command, demand, direction, injunction, instruction **2** = **invitation,** request, summons **3** = **offers,** auction, offer, proposal, tender

big *adj* **1** = **large,** bulky, burly, colossal, considerable, elephantine, enormous, extensive, gigantic, great, huge, hulking, humongous *or* humungous (*US sl.*), immense, mammoth, massive, ponderous, prodigious, sizable *or* sizeable, spacious, substantial, vast, voluminous **2, 3** = **important,** big-time (*inf.*), eminent, influential, leading, main, major league (*inf.*), momentous, paramount, powerful, prime, principal, prominent, serious, significant, valuable, weighty **5b** = **grown-up,** adult, elder, grown, mature **6** = **generous,** altruistic, benevolent, gracious, heroic, magnanimous, noble, princely, unselfish **7** = **boastful,** arrogant, bragging, conceited, haughty, inflated, pompous, pretentious, proud
Antonyms *adj* ≠ **large:** diminutive, insignificant, little, mini, miniature, petite, pint-sized (*inf.*), pocket-sized, pygmy *or* pigmy, small, tiny, wee ≠ **important:** humble, ignoble, insignificant, minor, modest, ordinary, unimportant, unknown ≠ **grown-up:** immature, young

bighead *n Informal* = **boaster,** blowhard (*inf.*), braggadocio, braggart, egotist, know-all (*inf.*)

bigheaded *adj* = **boastful,** arrogant, bumptious, cocky, conceited, egotistic, full of oneself, immodest, overconfident, swollen-headed, too big for one's boots *or* breeches

bigot *n* = **fanatic,** dogmatist, persecutor, racist, sectarian, zealot

bigoted *adj* = **intolerant,** biased, dogmatic, illiberal, narrow-minded, obstinate, opinionated, prejudiced, sectarian, twisted, warped

politics, or race. [C16: from OF: name applied contemptuously to the Normans by the French, from ?]
▸'**bigoted** *adj* ▸'**bigotry** *n*

big shot *n Inf.* an important person.

Big Smoke *n* **the.** *Inf.* a large city, esp. London.

big stick *n Inf.* force or the threat of force.

big time *n Inf.* **a the.** the highest level of a profession, esp. entertainment. **b** (*as modifier*): *a big-time comedian.*
▸'**big-'timer** *n*

big top *n Inf.* **1** the main tent of a circus. **2** the circus itself.

big up *vb* **bigs, bigging, bigged.** (*tr, adv*) *Sl., chiefly Caribbean.* to make important, prominent, or famous: *we'll do our best to big you up.*

bigwig Ⓣ ('bɪgˌwɪg) *n Inf.* an important person.

bijou ('biːʒuː) *n, pl* **bijoux** (-ʒuːz). **1** something small and delicately worked. **2** (*modifier*) *Often ironic.* small but tasteful: *a bijou residence.* [C19: from F, from Breton *bizou* finger ring, from *biz* finger]

bijugate ('baɪdʒʊˌgeɪt, baɪ'dʒuːgeɪt) *or* **bijugous** *adj* (of compound leaves) having two pairs of leaflets.

bike (baɪk) *n* **1** *Inf.* short for **bicycle** or **motorcycle. 2** *Sl.* a promiscuous woman. **3 get off one's bike.** *Austral. & NZ sl.* to lose one's self-control. ◆ *vb* **bikes, biking, biked. 4** (*intr*) *Inf.* to ride a cycle.

biker ('baɪkə) *n* a member of a motorcycle gang. Also called (Austral. and NZ): **bikie.**

biker jacket *n* a short, close-fitting leather jacket with zips and studs, often worn by motorcyclists.

bikini (bɪ'kiːnɪ) *n* a woman's very brief two-piece swimming costume. [C20: after the Pacific atoll of *Bikini*, from a comparison between obvious and powerful effect of the atom-bomb test and the effect (on men) of women wearing bikinis]

bilabial (baɪ'leɪbɪəl) *adj* **1** of or denoting a speech sound articulated using both lips: (*p*) *is a bilabial stop.* ◆ *n* **2** a bilabial speech sound.

bilabiate (baɪ'leɪbɪˌeɪt, -ɪt) *adj Bot.* divided into two lips: *the snapdragon has a bilabiate corolla.*

bilateral (baɪ'lætərəl) *adj* **1** having or involving two sides. **2** affecting or undertaken by two parties; mutual. **3** having identical sides or parts on each side of an axis; symmetrical.

bilateral symmetry *n* symmetry in one plane only. Cf. **radial symmetry.**

bilberry ('bɪlbərɪ) *n, pl* **bilberries. 1** any of several shrubs, such as the whortleberry, having edible blue or blackish berries. **2** the fruit of any of these plants. [C16: prob. of Scand. origin]

bilboes ('bɪlbəʊz) *pl n* a long iron bar with sliding shackles, for the ankles of a prisoner. [C16: ?from *Bilbao*, Spain]

Bildungsroman *German.* ('bɪldʊŋsromaːn) *n* a novel about a person's formative years.

bile Ⓣ (baɪl) *n* **1** a bitter greenish to golden brown alkaline fluid secreted by the liver and stored in the gall bladder. It aids digestion of fats. **2** a health disorder due to faulty secretion of bile. **3** irritability or peevishness. [C17: from F, from L *bīlis*]

bilge (bɪldʒ) *n* **1** *Naut.* the parts of a vessel's hull where the sides curve inwards to form the bottom. **2** (*often pl*) the parts of a vessel between the lowermost floorboards and the bottom. **3** Also called: **bilge water.** the dirty water that collects in a vessel's bilge. **4** *Inf.* silly rubbish; nonsense. **5** the widest part of a cask. ◆ *vb* **bilges, bilging, bilged. 6** (*intr*) *Naut.* (of a vessel) to take in water at the bilge. **7** (*tr*) *Naut.* to damage (a vessel) in the bilge. [C16: prob. var. of BULGE]

bilharzia (bɪl'hɑːtsɪə) *n* **1** another name for a **schistosome. 2** another name for **schistosomiasis.** [C19: NL, after Theodor *Bilharz* (1825–62), G parasitologist who discovered schistosomes]

bilharziasis (ˌbɪlhɑː'tsaɪəsɪs) *or* **bilharziosis** (bɪlˌhɑːtsɪ'əʊsɪs) *n* another name for **schistosomiasis.**

biliary ('bɪlɪərɪ) *adj* of or relating to bile, to the ducts that convey bile, or to the gall bladder.

bilingual (baɪ'lɪŋgwəl) *adj* **1** able to speak two languages, esp. with fluency. **2** expressed in two languages. ◆ *n* **3** a bilingual person.
▸**bi'lingualˌism** *n*

bilious Ⓣ ('bɪlɪəs) *adj* **1** of or relating to bile. **2** affected with or denoting any disorder related to secretion of bile. **3** *Inf.* bad-tempered; irritable. [C16: from L *bīliōsus* full of BILE]
▸'**biliousness** *n*

bilk Ⓣ (bɪlk) *vb* (*tr*) **1** to balk; thwart. **2** (often foll. by *of*) to cheat or deceive, esp. to avoid making payment to. **3** to escape from; elude. ◆ *n* **4** a swindle or cheat. **5** a person who swindles or cheats. [C17: ? var. of BALK]
▸'**bilker** *n*

bill[1] Ⓣ (bɪl) *n* **1** money owed for goods or services supplied. **2** a statement of money owed. **3** *Chiefly Brit.* such an account for food and drink in a restaurant, hotel, etc. **4** any list of items, events, etc., such as a theatre programme. **5** a statute in draft, before it becomes law. **6** a printed notice or advertisement. **7** *US & Canad.* a piece of paper money; note. **8** an obsolete name for **promissory note. 9** See **bill of exchange, bill of fare.** ◆ *vb* (*tr*) **10** to send or present an account for payment to (a person). **11** to enter (items, goods, etc.) on an account or statement. **12** to advertise by posters. **13** to schedule as a future programme. [C14: from Anglo-L *billa*, alteration of LL *bulla* document, BULL[3]]

bill[2] Ⓣ (bɪl) *n* **1** the projecting jaws of a bird, covered with a horny sheath; beak. **2** any beaklike mouthpart in other animals. **3** a narrow promontory. ◆ *vb* (*intr*) (esp. in **bill and coo**). **4** (of birds, esp. doves) to touch bills together. **5** (of lovers) to kiss and whisper amorously. [OE *bile*]

bill[3] (bɪl) *n* **1** a pike or halberd with a narrow hooked blade. **2** short for **billhook.** [OE *bill* sword]

billabong ('bɪləˌbɒŋ) *n Austral.* **1** a backwater channel that forms a lagoon or pool. **2** a branch of a river running to a dead end. [C19: from Abor., from *billa* river + *bong* dead]

billboard ('bɪlˌbɔːd) *n Chiefly US & Canad.* another name for **hoarding.** [C19: from BILL[1] + BOARD]

billet[1] Ⓣ ('bɪlɪt) *n* **1** accommodation, esp. for a soldier, in civilian lodgings. **2** the official requisition for such lodgings. **3** a space or berth in a ship. **4** *Inf.* a job. ◆ *vb* **5** (*tr*) to assign a lodging to (a soldier). **6** to lodge or be lodged. [C15: from OF *billette*, from *bulle* a document; see BULL[3]]

billet[2] ('bɪlɪt) *n* **1** a chunk of wood, esp. for fuel. **2** a small bar of iron or steel. [C15: from OF *billette* a little log, from *bille* log]

billet-doux (ˌbɪlɪ'duː) *n, pl* **billets-doux** (ˌbɪlɪ'duːz). *Old-fashioned or jocular.* a love letter. [C17: from F, lit.: a sweet letter]

billhook ('bɪlˌhʊk) *n* a tool with a curved blade terminating in a hook, used for pruning, chopping, etc. Also called: **bill.**

billiard ('bɪljəd) *n* (*modifier*) of or relating to billiards: *a billiard table; a billiard cue.*

billiards ('bɪljədz) *n* (*functioning as sing*) any of various games in which long cues are used to drive balls on a rectangular table covered with a smooth cloth and having raised cushioned edges. [C16: from OF *billard* curved stick, from *bille* log; see BILLET[2]]

billing ('bɪlɪŋ) *n* **1** *Theatre.* the relative importance of a performer or act as reflected in the prominence given in programmes, advertisements, etc. **2** *Chiefly US & Canad.* public notice or advertising.

billingsgate ('bɪlɪŋzˌgeɪt) *n* obscene or abusive language. [C17: after *Billingsgate*, a London fish market, notorious for such language]

Billings method ('bɪlɪŋz) *n* a natural method of birth control that involves examining the colour and viscosity of the cervical mucus to discover when ovulation is occurring. [C20: after Drs John and Evelyn *Billings*]

billion ('bɪljən) *n, pl* **billions** *or* **billion. 1** one thousand million: written as 1 000 000 000 or 10^9. **2** (formerly, in Britain) one million million: written as 1 000 000 000 000 or 10^{12}. US word: **trillion. 3** (*often pl*) any exceptionally large number. ◆ *determiner* **4** (preceded by *a* or a cardinal number) amounting to a billion. [C17: from F, from BI- + *-llion* as in *million*]
▸'**billionth** *adj, n*

billionaire (ˌbɪljə'nɛə) *n* a person whose wealth exceeds a billion monetary units of his country.

bill of attainder *n* (formerly) a legislative act finding a person guilty without trial of treason or felony and declaring him attainted.

bill of exchange *n* (now chiefly in foreign transactions) a document, usually negotiable, instructing a third party to pay a stated sum at a designated future date or on demand.

bill of fare *n* another name for **menu.**

bill of health *n* **1** a certificate that attests to the health of a ship's company. **2 clean bill of health.** *Inf.* **2a** a good report of one's physical condition. **2b** a favourable account of a person's or a company's financial position.

THESAURUS

Antonyms *adj* broad-minded, equitable, open-minded, tolerant, unbiased, unbigoted, unprejudiced

bigotry *n* = **intolerance**, bias, discrimination, dogmatism, fanaticism, ignorance, injustice, mindlessness, narrow-mindedness, prejudice, provincialism, racialism, racism, sectarianism, sexism, unfairness
Antonyms *n* broad-mindedness, forbearance, open-mindedness, permissiveness, tolerance

bigwig *n Informal* = **important person**, big cheese (*sl., old-fashioned*), big gun (*inf.*), big hitter (*inf.*), big name, big noise (*inf.*), big shot (*inf.*), celeb (*inf.*), celebrity, dignitary, heavy hitter (*inf.*), heavyweight (*inf.*), mogul, notable, panjandrum, personage, somebody, V.I.P.
Antonyms *n* cipher, lightweight (*inf.*), nobody, nonentity, nothing, zero

bile *n* **3** = **bitterness**, anger, churlishness, ill humour, irascibility, irritability, nastiness, peevishness, rancour, spleen

bilious *adj* **2** = **sick**, liverish, nauseated, nauseous, out of sorts, queasy **3** *Informal* = **bad-tempered**, cantankerous, crabby, cross, crotchety, edgy, grouchy (*inf.*), grumpy, ill-humoured, ill-tempered, irritable, like a bear with a sore head, nasty, peevish, ratty (*Brit. & NZ inf.*), short-tempered, testy, tetchy, touchy

bilk *vb* **2** = **cheat**, bamboozle, con (*inf.*), cozen, deceive, defraud, do (*sl.*), fleece, pull a fast one on (*inf.*), rook (*sl.*), sell a pup, skin (*sl.*), stiff (*sl.*), swindle, trick

bill[1] *n* **1** = **charges 2, 3** = **charges**, account, invoice, reckoning, score, statement, tally **4** = **list**, agenda, card, catalogue, inventory, listing, programme, roster, schedule, syllabus **5** = **proposal**, measure, piece of legislation, projected law **6** = **advertisement**, broadsheet, bulletin, circular, handbill, handout, leaflet, notice, placard, playbill, poster ◆ *vb* **10, 11** = **charge**, debit, invoice **12** = **advertise**, announce, give advance notice of, post

bill[2] *n* **1, 2** = **beak**, mandible, neb (*arch. or dialect*), nib

billet[1] *n* **1** = **quarters**, accommodation, barracks, lodging ◆ *vb* **5** = **quarter**, accommodate, berth, station

bill of lading *n* (in foreign trade) a document containing full particulars of goods shipped.
bill of quantities *n* a document drawn up by a quantity surveyor providing details of the prices, dimensions, etc., of the materials required to build a large structure, such as a factory.
Bill of Rights *n* **1** an English statute of 1689 guaranteeing the rights and liberty of the individual subject. **2** the first ten amendments to the US Constitution which guarantee the liberty of the individual. **3** (*usually not caps.*) any charter of basic human rights.
bill of sale *n Law.* a deed transferring personal property.
billow ⓣ (ˈbɪləʊ) *n* **1** a large sea wave. **2** a swelling or surging mass, as of smoke or sound. ◆ *vb* **3** to rise up, swell out, or cause to rise up or swell out. [C16: from ON *bylgja*]
▸ **ˈbillowing** *adj, n* ▸ **ˈbillowy** *adj* ▸ **ˈbillowiness** *n*
billposter (ˈbɪlˌpəʊstə) *or* **billsticker** *n* a person who sticks advertising posters to walls, etc.
▸ **ˈbillˌposting** *or* **ˈbillˌsticking** *n*
billy (ˈbɪlɪ) *or* **billycan** (ˈbɪlɪˌkæn) *n, pl* **billies** *or* **billycans. 1** a metal can or pot for boiling water, etc., over a campfire. **2** *Austral. & NZ.* (*as modifier*): *billy-tea.* **3 boil the billy.** *Austral. & NZ. inf.* to make tea. [C19: from Scot. *billypot* cooking vessel]
billy goat *n* a male goat.
bilobate (baɪˈləʊˌbeɪt) *or* **bilobed** (ˈbaɪˌləʊbd) *adj* divided into or having two lobes.
biltong (ˈbɪlˌtɒŋ) *n S. African.* strips of meat dried and cured in the sun. [C19: Afrik., from Du. *bil* buttock + *tong* TONGUE]
BIM *abbrev. for* British Institute of Management.
bimanous (ˈbɪmənəs, baɪˈmeɪ-) *adj* (of man and the higher primates) having two hands distinct in form and function from the feet. [C19: from NL, from BI- + L *manus* hand]
bimanual (ˌbaɪˈmænjʊəl) *adj* using both hands.
bimbo (ˈbɪmbəʊ) *n, pl* **bimbos.** *Derog. sl.* **1** an attractive but empty-headed young person, esp. a woman. **2** a fellow; a foolish or stupid person. [C20: from It.: little child, perhaps via Polari]
bimetallic (ˌbaɪmɪˈtælɪk) *adj* **1** consisting of two metals. **2** of or based on bimetallism.
bimetallic strip *n* strips of two metals that expand differently welded together for use in a thermostat.
bimetallism (baɪˈmɛtəˌlɪzəm) *n* the use of two metals, esp. gold and silver, in fixed relative values as the standard of value and currency.
▸ **biˈmetallist** *n*
bimonthly (baɪˈmʌnθlɪ) *adj, adv* **1** every two months. **2** twice a month. ◆ *n, pl* **bimonthlies. 3** a periodical published every two months.
bimorph (ˈbaɪmɔːf) *or* **bimorph cell** *n Electron.* two piezoelectric crystals cemented together so that their movement converts electrical signals into mechanical energy or vice versa: used in record-player pick-ups and loudspeakers.
bin (bɪn) *n* **1** a large container for storing something in bulk, such as coal, grain, or bottled wine. **2** Also called: **bread bin.** a small container for bread. **3** Also called: **dustbin, rubbish bin.** a container for rubbish, etc. ◆ *vb* **bins, binning, binned.** (*tr*) **4** to store in a bin. **5** to put in a wastepaper bin. [OE *binne* basket]
binary (ˈbaɪnərɪ) *adj* **1** composed of or involving two; dual. **2** *Maths, computing.* of or expressed in binary notation or binary code. **3** (of a compound or molecule) containing atoms of two different elements. ◆ *n, pl* **binaries. 4** something composed of two parts. **5** *Astron.* See **binary star.** [C16: from LL *bīnārius;* see BI-]
binary code *n Computing.* the representation of each one of a set of numbers, letters, etc., as a unique group of bits.
binary notation *or* **system** *n* a number system having a base of two, numbers being expressed by sequences of the digits 0 and 1: used in computing, as 0 and 1 can be represented electrically as *off* and *on.*
binary number *n* a number expressed in binary notation.
binary star *n* a double star system containing two associated stars revolving around a common centre of gravity in different orbits.
binary weapon *n* a chemical weapon containing two substances separately that mix to produce a lethal agent when the projectile is fired.
binate (ˈbaɪˌneɪt) *adj Bot.* occurring in two parts or in pairs: *binate leaves.* [C19: from NL *bīnātus,* prob. from L *combīnātus* united]
▸ **ˈbiˌnately** *adv*
binaural (baɪˈnɔːrəl, bɪnˈɔːrəl) *adj* **1** relating to, having, or hearing with both ears. **2** employing two separate channels for recording or transmitting sound.
bind ⓣ (baɪnd) *vb* **binds, binding, bound. 1** to make or become fast or secure with or as if with a tie or band. **2** (*tr; often foll. by up*) to encircle or enclose with a band: *to bind the hair.* **3** (*tr*) to place (someone) under obligation; oblige. **4** (*tr*) to impose legal obligations or duties upon (a person). **5** (*tr*) to make (a bargain, agreement, etc.) irrevocable; seal. **6** (*tr*) to restrain or confine with or as if with ties, as of responsibility or loyalty. **7** (*tr*) to place under certain constraints; govern. **8** (*tr; often foll. by up*) to bandage. **9** to cohere or cause to cohere: *egg binds fat and flour.* **10** to make or become compact, stiff, or hard: *frost binds the earth.* **11** (*tr*) to enclose and fasten (the pages of a book) between covers. **12** (*tr*) to provide (a garment, hem, etc.) with a border or edging. **13** (*tr; sometimes foll. by out or over*) to employ as an apprentice; indenture. **14** (*intr*) *Sl.* to complain. ◆ *n* **15** something that binds. **16** *Inf.* a difficult or annoying situation. **17** a situation in which freedom of action is restricted. ◆ See also **bind over.** [OE *bindan*]
binder (ˈbaɪndə) *n* **1** a firm cover or folder for holding loose sheets of paper together. **2** a material used to bind separate particles together. **3** a person who binds books; bookbinder. **4** something used to fasten or tie, such as rope or twine. **5** Also called: **reaper binder.** *Obs.* a machine for cutting grain and binding it into sheaves. **6** an informal agreement giving insurance coverage pending formal issue of a policy.
bindery (ˈbaɪndərɪ) *n, pl* **binderies.** a place in which books are bound.
bindi-eye (ˈbɪndɪˌaɪ) *n Austral.* **1** any of various small weedy Australian herbaceous plants with burlike fruits. **2** any bur or prickle. [C20: ?from Abor.]
binding ⓣ (ˈbaɪndɪŋ) *n* **1** anything that binds or fastens. **2** the covering within which the pages of a book are bound. **3** the tape used for binding hems, etc. ◆ *adj* **4** imposing an obligation or duty. **5** causing hindrance; restrictive.
bind over *vb* (*tr, adv*) to place (a person) under a legal obligation, such as one to keep the peace.
bindweed (ˈbaɪndˌwiːd) *n* any of various plants that twine around a support. See also **convolvulus.**
bine (baɪn) *n* the climbing or twining stem of any of various plants, such as the woodbine. [C19: var. of BIND]
Binet-Simon scale (ˈbiːneɪˈsaɪmən) *n Psychol.* a test used to determine the mental age of subjects. Also called: **Binet scale** *or* **test.** [C20: after Alfred *Binet* (1857–1911) + Théodore *Simon* (1873–1961), F psychologists]
binge ⓣ (bɪndʒ) *Inf.* ◆ *n* **1** a bout of excessive drinking or eating. **2** excessive indulgence in anything. ◆ *vb* **binges, bingeing** *or* **binging, binged. 3** (*intr*) to indulge in a binge. [C19: prob. dial. *binge* to soak]
bingo (ˈbɪŋgəʊ) *n, pl* **bingos.** a gambling game, usually played with several people, in which random numbers are called out and the players cover the numbers on their individual cards. The first to cover a given arrangement of numbers is the winner. [C19: ?from *bing,* imit. of a bell ringing to mark the win]
binman (ˈbɪnˌmæn, ˈbɪnmən) *n, pl* **binmen.** *Inf.* another name for **dustman.**
binnacle (ˈbɪnəkᵊl) *n* a housing for a ship's compass. [C17: changed from C15 *bitakle,* from Port. from LL *habitāculum* dwelling-place, from L *habitāre* to inhabit]
binocular (bɪˈnɒkjʊlə, baɪ-) *adj* involving, relating to, seeing with or intended for both eyes: *binocular vision.* [C18: from BI- + L *oculus* eye]
binoculars (bɪˈnɒkjʊləz, baɪ-) *pl n* an optical instrument for use with both eyes, consisting of two small telescopes joined together.
binomial (baɪˈnəʊmɪəl) *n* **1** a mathematical expression consisting of two terms, such as $3x + 2y$. **2** a two-part taxonomic name for an animal or plant indicating genus and species. ◆ *adj* **3** referring to two names or terms. [C16: from Med. L, from BI- + L *nōmen* name]
▸ **biˈnomially** *adv*
binomial distribution *n* a statistical distribution giving the probability of obtaining a specified number of independent trials of an experiment, with a constant probability of success in each.
binomial theorem *n* a general mathematical formula that expresses any power of a binomial without multiplying out, as in $(x+a)^n=x^n+nx^{n-1}a+[n(n-1)/2]x^{n-2}a^2\ldots+a^n$.
bint (bɪnt) *n Sl.* a derogatory term for **girl** or **woman.** [C19: from Ar., lit.: daughter]
binturong (ˈbɪntjʊˌrɒŋ, bɪnˈtjʊərɒŋ) *n* a long-bodied short-legged arboreal SE Asian mammal having shaggy black hair. [from Malay]
bio- *or before a vowel* **bi-** *combining form.* **1** indicating or involving life or living organisms: *biogenesis.* **2** indicating a human life or career: *biography.* [from Gk *bios* life]
bioassay (ˌbaɪəʊˈæseɪ) *n* **1** a method of determining the concentration or effect of a drug, etc., by comparing its effect on living organisms with that of a standard preparation. ◆ *vb* (*tr*) **2** to subject to a bioassay.
bioastronautics (ˌbaɪəʊˌæstrəˈnɔːtɪks) *n* (*functioning as sing*) the study of the effects of space flight on living organisms.
bioastronomy (ˌbaɪəʊəˈstrɒnəmɪ) *n* the branch of astronomy concerned with the search for life on other planets.
biochemical oxygen demand *n* a measure of the organic pollution of water; the number of milligrams of oxygen per litre of water absorbed in a given period. Abbrev.: **BOD**

THESAURUS

billow *n* **1** = **wave**, breaker, crest, roller, surge, swell, tide **2** = **surge**, cloud, deluge, flood, outpouring, rush, wave ◆ *vb* **3** = **surge**, balloon, belly, puff up, rise up, roll, swell
billowy *adj* **1** = **wavy**, rippling, undulating, waving **2** = **surging**, heaving, rolling, swelling, swirling
bind *vb* **1** = **tie**, attach, fasten, glue, hitch, lash, paste, rope, secure, stick, strap, tie up, truss, wrap **3, 4** = **oblige**, compel, constrain, force, necessitate, obligate, prescribe, require **6, 7** = **restrict**, confine, detain, hamper, hinder, restrain **8** = **bandage**, cover, dress, encase, swathe, wrap **12** = **edge**, border, finish, hem, trim ◆ *n* **16** *Informal* = **nuisance**, bore, difficulty, dilemma, drag (*inf.*), hot water (*inf.*), pain in the arse (*taboo sl.*), pain in the neck (*inf.*), predicament, quandary, spot (*inf.*), tight spot
Antonyms *vb* ≠ **tie:** free, loosen, release, unbind, undo, unfasten, untie
binding *adj* **4** = **compulsory**, conclusive, imperative, indissoluble, irrevocable, mandatory, necessary, obligatory, unalterable
Antonyms *adj* discretionary, free, noncompulsory, optional, uncompelled, unconstrained, unforced, voluntary
binge *n* **1** *Informal* = **bout**, beano, bender (*inf.*), blind (*sl.*), feast, fling, jag (*sl.*), orgy, spree

biochemistry (ˌbaɪəʊˈkɛmɪstrɪ) *n* the study of the chemical compounds, reactions, etc., in living organisms.
▸**biochemical** (ˌbaɪəʊˈkɛmɪkᵊl) *adj* ▸ˌ**bioˈchemist** *n*

biocide (ˈbaɪəˌsaɪd) *n* a chemical capable of killing living organisms.
▸ˌ**bioˈcidal** *adj*

biocoenosis *or US* **biocenosis** (ˌbaɪəʊsɪˈnəʊsɪs) *n* the relationships between animals and plants subsisting together. [C19: NL from BIO- + Gk *koinōsis* sharing]

biodegradable (ˌbaɪəʊdɪˈgreɪdəbᵊl) *adj* (of sewage, packaging, etc.) capable of being decomposed by bacteria or other biological means.
▸**biodegradability** (ˌbaɪəʊdɪˌgreɪdəˈbɪlɪtɪ) *n*

biodiversity (ˌbaɪəʊdaɪˈvɜːsɪtɪ) *n* the existence of a wide variety of plant and animal species in their natural environments, the maintaining of which is the aim of conservationists concerned about the indiscriminate destruction of rainforests and other habitats.

bioengineering (ˌbaɪəʊˌɛndʒɪˈnɪərɪŋ) *n* **1** the design and manufacture of aids, such as artificial limbs, to rectify defective body functions. **2** the design, manufacture, and maintenance of engineering equipment used in biosynthetic processes.
▸ˌ**bioˌengiˈneer** *n*

bioethics (ˌbaɪəʊˈɛθɪks) *n* (*functioning as sing*) the study of ethical problems arising from scientific advances, esp. in biology and medicine.

biofeedback (ˌbaɪəʊˈfiːdˌbæk) *n Physiol., psychol.* the technique of recording and presenting (usually visually) the activity of an autonomic function, such as the rate of heartbeat, in order to teach control of it.

biofuel (ˈbaɪəʊˌfjuəl) *n* a substance of biological origin that is used as a fuel.

biog. *abbrev. for:* **1** biographical. **2** biography.

biogenesis (ˌbaɪəʊˈdʒɛnɪsɪs) *n* the principle that a living organism must originate from a parent organism similar to itself.
▸ˌ**biogeˈnetic** *or* ˌ**biogeˈnetical** *adj*

biogenic (ˌbaɪəʊˈdʒɛnɪk) *adj* produced or originating from a living organism.

biography ❶ (baɪˈɒgrəfɪ) *n, pl* **biographies. 1** an account of a person's life by another. **2** such accounts collectively.
▸**biˈographer** *n* ▸**biographical** (ˌbaɪəˈgræfɪkᵊl) *adj*

biol. *abbrev. for:* **1** biological. **2** biology.

biological (ˌbaɪəˈlɒdʒɪkᵊl) *adj* **1** of or relating to biology. **2** (of a detergent) containing enzymes for removing stains of organic origin from items to be washed. ◆ *n* **3** (*usually pl*) a drug derived from a living organism.

biological clock *n* **1** an inherent periodicity in the physiological processes of living organisms that is independent of external periodicity. **2** the hypothetical mechanism responsible for this. ◆ See also **circadian.**

biological control *n* the control of destructive organisms by nonchemical means, such as introducing the natural enemy of a pest.

biological warfare *n* the use of living organisms or their toxic products to induce death or incapacity in humans.

biology (baɪˈɒlədʒɪ) *n* **1** the study of living organisms. **2** the animal and plant life of a particular region.
▸**biˈologist** *n*

bioluminescence (ˌbaɪəʊˌluːmɪˈnɛsəns) *n* the production of light by living organisms, such as the firefly.
▸ˌ**bioˌlumiˈnescent** *adj*

biomass (ˈbaɪəʊˌmæs) *n* the total number of living organisms in a given area, expressed in terms of living or dry weight per unit area.

biomathematics (ˌbaɪəʊˌmæθəˈmætɪks, -ˌmæθˈmæt-) *n* (*functioning as sing*) the study of the application of mathematics to biology.

biomechanics (ˌbaɪəʊmɪˈkænɪks) *n* (*functioning as sing*) the study of the mechanics of the movement of living organisms.

biomedicine (ˌbaɪəʊˈmɛdɪsɪn) *n* **1** the medical and biological study of the effects of unusual environmental stress, esp. in connection with space travel. **2** the study of herbal remedies.
▸ˌ**bioˈmedical** *adj*

biometry (baɪˈɒmɪtrɪ) *or* **biometrics** (ˌbaɪəˈmɛtrɪks) *n* (*functioning as sing*) the study of biological data by means of statistical analysis.
▸ˌ**bioˈmetric** *adj*

bionic (baɪˈɒnɪk) *adj* **1** of or relating to bionics. **2** (in science fiction) having physiological functions augmented by electronic equipment.

bionics (baɪˈɒnɪks) *n* (*functioning as sing*) **1** the study of certain biological functions that are applicable to the development of electronic equipment designed to operate similarly. **2** the replacement of limbs or body parts by artificial limbs or parts that are electronically or mechanically powered.

bionomics (ˌbaɪəˈnɒmɪks) *n* (*functioning as sing*) a less common name for **ecology.** [C19: from BIO- + *nomics* on pattern of ECONOMICS]
▸ˌ**bioˈnomic** *adj* ▸**bionomist** (baɪˈɒnəmɪst) *n*

biophysics (ˌbaɪəʊˈfɪzɪks) *n* (*functioning as sing*) the physics of biological processes and the application of the methods used in physics to biology.
▸ˌ**bioˈphysical** *adj* ▸ˌ**bioˈphysically** *adv* ▸**biophysicist** (ˌbaɪəʊˈfɪzɪsɪst) *n*

biopic (ˈbaɪəʊˌpɪk) *n Inf.* a film based on the life of a famous person. [C20: from *bio(graphical)* + *pic(ture)*]

biopsy (ˈbaɪɒpsɪ) *n, pl* **biopsies.** examination, esp. under a microscope, of tissue from a living body to determine the cause or extent of a disease. [C20: from BIO- + Gk *opsis* sight]

biorhythm (ˈbaɪəʊˌrɪðəm) *n* a cyclically recurring pattern of physiological states, believed by some to affect a person's physical, emotional, and mental states and behaviour.

bioscope (ˈbaɪəˌskəʊp) *n* **1** a kind of early film projector. **2** a South African word for **cinema.**

bioscopy (baɪˈɒskəpɪ) *n, pl* **bioscopies.** examination of a body to determine whether it is alive.

-biosis *n combining form.* indicating a specified mode of life. [NL, from Gk *biōsis;* see BIO-, -OSIS]
▸**-biotic** *adj combining form.*

biosphere (ˈbaɪəˌsfɪə) *n* the part of the earth's surface and atmosphere inhabited by living things.

biosynthesis (ˌbaɪəʊˈsɪnθɪsɪs) *n* the formation of complex compounds from simple substances by living organisms.
▸**biosynthetic** (ˌbaɪəʊsɪnˈθɛtɪk) *adj* ▸ˌ**biosynˈthetically** *adv*

biotech (ˈbaɪəʊˌtɛk) *n Inf.* short for **biotechnology.**

biotechnology (ˌbaɪəʊtɛkˈnɒlədʒɪ) *n* the use of microorganisms for beneficial effect, as in the processing of waste matter or (using genetic engineering) to produce antibiotics, hormones, vaccines, etc.

biotic (baɪˈɒtɪk) *adj* of or relating to living organisms. [C17: from Gk *biotikos,* from *bios* life]

biotin (ˈbaɪətɪn) *n* a vitamin of the B complex, abundant in egg yolk and liver. [C20: from Gk *biotē* life, way of life + -IN]

bipartisan (ˌbaɪpɑːtɪˈzæn, baɪˈpɑːtɪˌzæn) *adj* consisting of or supported by two political parties.
▸ˌ**bipartiˈsanship** *n*

bipartite (baɪˈpɑːtaɪt) *adj* **1** consisting of or having two parts. **2** affecting or made by two parties. **3** *Bot.* (esp. of some leaves) divided into two parts almost to the base.
▸**biˈpartitely** *adv* ▸**bipartition** (ˌbaɪpɑːˈtɪʃən) *n*

biped (ˈbaɪpɛd) *n* **1** any animal with two feet. ◆ *adj also* **bipedal** (baɪˈpiːdᵊl, -ˈpɛdᵊl). **2** having two feet.

bipinnate (baɪˈpɪneɪt) *adj* (of compound leaves) having both the leaflets and the stems bearing them arranged pinnately.
▸**biˈpinnately** *adv*

biplane (ˈbaɪˌpleɪn) *n* a type of aeroplane having two sets of wings, one above the other.

bipolar (baɪˈpəʊlə) *adj* **1** having two poles: *a bipolar dynamo.* **2** of or relating to the North and South Poles. **3** having or characterized by two opposed opinions, etc. **4** (of a transistor) utilizing both majority and minority charge carriers.
▸ˌ**bipoˈlarity** *n*

biprism (ˈbaɪˌprɪzəm) *n Physics.* a prism that has a highly obtuse angle to facilitate beam splitting.

biquadratic (ˌbaɪkwɒˈdrætɪk) *Maths.* ◆ *adj* **1** of or relating to the fourth power. ◆ *n* **2** a biquadratic equation, such as $x^4 + x + 6 = 0$.

biracial (baɪˈreɪʃəl) *adj* of or for members of two races.
▸**biˈracialism** *n*

birch (bɜːtʃ) *n* **1** any catkin-bearing tree or shrub having thin peeling bark. See also **silver birch. 2** the hard close-grained wood of any of these trees. **3 the birch.** a bundle of birch twigs or a birch rod used, esp. formerly, for flogging offenders. ◆ *adj* **4** consisting or made of birch. ◆ *vb* **5** (*tr*) to flog with a birch. [OE *bierce*]
▸ˈ**birchen** *adj*

bird (bɜːd) *n* **1** any warm-blooded egg-laying vertebrate, characterized by a body covering of feathers and forelimbs modified as wings. **2** *Inf.* a person, as in **rare bird, odd bird, clever bird. 3** *Sl., chiefly Brit.* a girl or young woman. **4** *Sl.* prison or a term in prison (esp. in **do bird**). **5 a bird in the hand.** something definite or certain. **6 birds of a feather.** people with the same characteristics, ideas, interests, etc. **7 get the bird.** *Inf.* **7a** to be fired or dismissed. **7b** (esp. of a public performer) to be hissed at. **8 kill two birds with one stone.** to accomplish two things with one action. **9 (strictly) for the birds.** *Inf.* deserving of disdain or contempt; not important. [OE *bridd,* from ?]

birdbath (ˈbɜːdˌbɑːθ) *n* a small basin or trough for birds to bathe in, usually in a garden.

bird-brained *adj Inf.* silly; stupid.

birdcage (ˈbɜːdˌkeɪdʒ) *n* **1** a wire or wicker cage for captive birds. **2** *Austral. & NZ.* an area on a racecourse where horses parade before a race. **3** *NZ inf.* a second-hand car dealer's yard.

bird call *n* **1** the characteristic call or song of a bird. **2** an imitation of this.

birdie (ˈbɜːdɪ) *n* **1** *Golf.* a score of one stroke under par for a hole. **2** *Inf.* a bird, esp. a small bird. ◆ *vb* **3** (*tr*) *Golf.* to play (a hole) in one stroke under par.

birdlime (ˈbɜːdˌlaɪm) *n* **1** a sticky substance smeared on twigs to catch small birds. ◆ *vb* **birdlimes, birdliming, birdlimed. 2** (*tr*) to smear (twigs) with birdlime to catch (small birds).

bird-nesting *or* **birds'-nesting** *n* searching for birds' nests as a hobby, often to steal the eggs.

bird of paradise *n* **1** any of various songbirds of New Guinea and neighbouring regions, the males having brilliantly coloured plumage. **2 bird-of-paradise flower.** any of various plants native to tropical

THESAURUS

biography *n* **1 = life story,** account, curriculum vitae, CV, life, life history, memoir, memoirs, profile, record

southern Africa and South America that have purple bracts and large orange or yellow flowers resembling birds' heads.

bird of passage *n* **1** a bird that migrates seasonally. **2** a transient person.

bird of prey *n* a bird, such as a hawk or owl, that hunts other animals for food.

birdseed ('bɜːdˌsiːd) *n* a mixture of various kinds of seeds for feeding cagebirds.

bird's-eye *adj* **1a** seen or photographed from high above. **1b** summarizing (esp. in **bird's-eye view**). **2** having markings resembling birds' eyes.

bird's-foot *or* **bird-foot** *n, pl* **bird's-foots** *or* **bird-foots.** any of various plants whose flowers, leaves, or pods resemble a bird's foot or claw.

birdshot ('bɜːdˌʃɒt) *n* small pellets designed for shooting birds.

bird strike *n* a collision of an aircraft with a bird.

bird table *n* a table or platform in the open on which food for birds may be placed.

bird-watcher *n* a person who identifies and studies wild birds in their natural surroundings.
▸**'bird-ˌwatching** *n*

birefringence (ˌbaɪrɪ'frɪndʒəns) *n* another name for **double refraction.**
▸**ˌbire'fringent** *adj*

bireme ('baɪriːm) *n* an ancient galley having two banks of oars. [C17: from L, from BI- + *-rēmus* oar]

biretta *or* **berretta** (bɪ'rɛtə) *n RC Church.* a stiff square clerical cap. [C16: from It. *berretta,* from OProvençal, from LL *birrus* hooded cape]

birl (bɜːl) *vb* **1** *Scot.* to spin; twirl. **2** *US & Canad.* to cause (a floating log) to spin using the feet while standing on it, esp. as a sport among lumberjacks. ◆ *n* **3** a variant spelling of **burl**[2]. [C18: prob. imit. & infl. by WHIRL & HURL]

Biro ('baɪrəʊ) *n, pl* **Biros.** *Trademark, Brit.* a kind of ballpoint. [C20: after Laszlo *Bíró* (1900–85), its Hungarian inventor]

birth Ⓣ (bɜːθ) *n* **1** the process of bearing young; childbirth. **2** the act or fact of being born; nativity. **3** the coming into existence of something; origin. **4** ancestry; lineage: *of high birth.* **5** natural or inherited talent: *an artist by birth.* **6 give birth (to). 6a** to bear (offspring). **6b** to produce or originate (an idea, plan, etc.). ◆ *vb* **7** *(tr) Rare.* to bear or bring forth (a child). [C12: from ON *byrth*]

birth certificate *n* an official form giving details of the time and place of a person's birth.

birth control *n* limitation of child-bearing by means of contraception.

birthday ('bɜːθˌdeɪ) *n* **1a** an anniversary of the day of one's birth. **1b** *(as modifier): birthday present.* **2** the day on which a person was born.

birthing centre ('bɜːθɪŋ) *n NZ.* a private maternity hospital.

birthmark ('bɜːθˌmɑːk) *n* a blemish on the skin formed before birth; naevus.

birth mother *n* the woman who gives birth to a child, regardless of whether she is the genetic mother or subsequently brings up the child.

birthplace ('bɜːθˌpleɪs) *n* the place where someone was born or where something originated.

birth rate *n* the ratio of live births in a specified area, group, etc., to population, usually expressed per 1000 population per year.

birthright ('bɜːθˌraɪt) *n* **1** privileges or possessions that a person has or is believed to be entitled to as soon as he is born. **2** the privileges or possessions of a first-born son. **3** inheritance.

birthstone ('bɜːθˌstəʊn) *n* a precious or semiprecious stone associated with a month or sign of the zodiac and thought to bring luck if worn by a person born in that month or under that sign.

biryani *or* **biriani** (ˌbɪrɪ'ɑːnɪ) *n* an Indian dish made with rice, highly flavoured and coloured, mixed with meat or fish. [from Urdu]

biscuit ('bɪskɪt) *n* **1** *Brit.* a small flat dry sweet or plain cake of many varieties. US and Canad. word: **cookie. 2a** a pale brown or yellowish-grey colour. **2b** *(as adj): biscuit gloves.* **3** Also called: **bisque.** earthenware or porcelain that has been fired but not glazed. **4 take the biscuit.** *Brit.* to be regarded (by the speaker) as most surprising. [C14: from OF, from *(pain) bescuit* twice-cooked (bread), from *bes* twice + *cuire* to cook]

bise (biːz) *n* a cold dry northerly wind in Switzerland and parts of France and Italy. [C14: from OF, of Gmc origin]

bisect Ⓣ (baɪ'sɛkt) *vb* **1** *(tr) Maths.* to divide into two equal parts. **2** to cut or split into two. [C17: BI- + *-sect,* from L *secāre* to cut]
▸**bisection** (baɪ'sɛkʃən) *n*

bisector (baɪ'sɛktə) *n Maths.* a straight line or plane that bisects an angle, etc.

bisexual Ⓣ (baɪ'sɛksjʊəl) *adj* **1** sexually attracted by both men and women. **2** showing characteristics of both sexes. **3** of or relating to both sexes. ◆ *n* **4** a bisexual organism; a hermaphrodite. **5** a bisexual person.
▸**bisexuality** (ˌbaɪsɛksjʊ'ælɪtɪ) *n*

bishop ('bɪʃəp) *n* **1** a clergyman having spiritual and administrative powers over a diocese. See also **suffragan.** Related adj: **episcopal. 2** a chesspiece, capable of moving diagonally. **3** mulled wine, usually port, spiced with oranges, cloves, etc. [OE *biscop,* from LL, from Gk *episkopos,* from EPI- + *skopos* watcher]

bishopric Ⓣ ('bɪʃəprɪk) *n* the see, diocese, or office of a bishop.

bismuth ('bɪzməθ) *n* a brittle pinkish-white crystalline metallic element. It is widely used in alloys; its compounds are used in medicines. Symbol: Bi; atomic no.: 83; atomic wt.: 208.98. [C17: from NL *bisemūtum,* from G *Wismut,* from ?]

bison ('baɪsᵊn) *n, pl* **bison. 1** Also called: **American bison, buffalo.** a member of the cattle tribe, formerly widely distributed over the prairies of W North America, with a massive head, shaggy forequarters, and a humped back. **2** Also called: **wisent, European bison.** a closely related and similar animal formerly widespread in Europe. [C14: from L *bisōn,* of Gmc origin]

bisque[1] (bɪsk) *n* a thick rich soup made from shellfish. [C17: from F]

bisque[2] (bɪsk) *n* **1a** a pink to yellowish tan colour. **1b** *(as adj): a bisque tablecloth.* **2** *Ceramics.* another name for **biscuit** (sense 3). [C20: shortened from BISCUIT]

bisque[3] (bɪsk) *n Tennis, golf, croquet.* an extra point, stroke, or turn allowed to an inferior player, usually taken when desired. [C17: from F, from ?]

bistable (ˌbaɪ'steɪbᵊl) *adj* **1** (of an electrical circuit switch, etc.) having two stable states. ◆ *n* **2** *Computing.* another name for **flip-flop** (sense 2).

bistort ('bɪstɔːt) *n* **1** Also called: **snakeweed.** a Eurasian plant having leaf stipules fused to form a tube around the stem and a spike of small pink flowers. **2** Also called: **snakeroot.** a related plant of W North America, with oval clusters of pink or white flowers. **3** any of several similar plants. [C16: from F, from L *bis* twice + *tortus* from *torquēre* to twist]

bistoury ('bɪstərɪ) *n, pl* **bistouries.** a long narrow-bladed surgical knife. [C15: from OF *bistorie* dagger, from ?]

bistre *or US* **bister** ('bɪstə) *n* **1** a transparent water-soluble brownish-yellow pigment made by boiling the soot of wood. **2a** a yellowish-brown to dark brown colour. **2b** *(as adj): bistre paint.* [C18: from F, from ?]

bistro ('biːstrəʊ) *n, pl* **bistros.** a small restaurant. [F: ?from Russian *bistro* fast]

bisulphate (baɪ'sʌlˌfeɪt) *n* a salt or ester of sulphuric acid containing the monovalent group -HSO_4 or the ion HSO_4^-. Systematic name: **hydrogensulphate.**

bisulphide (baɪ'sʌlfaɪd) *n* another name for **disulphide.**

bit[1] Ⓣ (bɪt) *n* **1** a small piece, portion, or quantity. **2** a short time or distance. **3** *US & Canad. inf.* the value of an eighth of a dollar: spoken of only in units of two: *two bits.* **4** any small coin. **5** short for **bit part. 6 a bit.** rather; somewhat: *a bit dreary.* **7 a bit of. 7a** rather: *a bit of a dope.* **7b** a considerable amount: *it takes quite a bit of time.* **8 bit by bit.** gradually. **9 do one's bit.** to make one's expected contribution. [OE *bite* action of biting; see BITE]

bit[2] Ⓣ (bɪt) *n* **1** a metal mouthpiece on a bridle for controlling a horse. **2** anything that restrains or curbs. **3** a cutting or drilling tool, part, or head in a brace, drill, etc. **4** the part of a key that engages the levers of a lock. **5** the mouthpiece of a smoker's pipe. ◆ *vb* **bits, bitting, bitted.** *(tr)* **6** to put a bit in the mouth of (a horse). **7** to restrain; curb. [OE *bita;* rel. to OE *bītan* to BITE]

bit[3] (bɪt) *vb* the past tense of **bite.**

bit[4] (bɪt) *n Maths, computing.* **1** a single digit of binary notation, represented either by 0 or by 1. **2** the smallest unit of information, indicating the presence or absence of a single feature. [C20: from B(INARY + DIG)IT]

bitch (bɪtʃ) *n* **1** a female dog or other female canine animal, such as a wolf. **2** *Sl., derog.* a malicious, spiteful, or coarse woman. **3** *Inf.* a difficult situation or problem. ◆ *vb Inf.* **4** *(intr)* to complain; grumble. **5** to behave (towards) in a spiteful manner. **6** *(tr; often foll. by up)* to botch; bungle. [OE *bicce*]

bitchin' ('bɪtʃɪn) *or* **bitching** ('bɪtʃɪŋ) *US sl.* ◆ *adj* **1** wonderful or excellent. ◆ *adv* **2** extremely: *bitchin' good.*

bitchy Ⓣ ('bɪtʃɪ) *adj* **bitchier, bitchiest.** *Sl.* of or like a bitch; malicious; snide.
▸**'bitchiness** *n*

bite Ⓣ (baɪt) *vb* **bites, biting, bit, bitten. 1** to grip, cut off, or tear as with the teeth or jaws. **2** (of animals, insects, etc.) to injure by puncturing or tearing (the skin or flesh) with the teeth, fangs, etc. **3** *(tr)* to cut or

THESAURUS

birth *n* **1 = childbirth,** delivery, nativity, parturition **3 = beginning,** emergence, fountainhead, genesis, origin, rise, source **4 = ancestry,** background, blood, breeding, derivation, descent, extraction, forebears, genealogy, line, lineage, nobility, noble extraction, parentage, pedigree, race, stock, strain
Antonyms *n* ≠ **childbirth:** death, demise, end, extinction, passing, passing away *or* on

bisect *vb* **1 = halve,** cut in half **2 = cut in two,** bifurcate, cross, cut across, divide in two, intersect, separate, split, split down the middle

bisexual *adj* **1 = bi** *(sl.)*, AC/DC *(sl.)*, ambidextrous *(sl.)*, swinging both ways *(sl.)* **2 = hermaphrodite,** androgyne, androgynous, epicene, gynandromorphic *or* gynandromorphous *(Entomology)*, gynandrous, hermaphroditic, monoclinous *(Botany)*

bishopric *n* **= diocese,** episcopacy, episcopate, primacy, see

bit[1] *n* **1 = piece,** atom, chip, crumb, fragment, grain, iota, jot, mite, morsel, mouthful, part, remnant, scrap, segment, slice, small piece, speck, tittle, whit **2 = little while,** instant, jiffy *(inf.)*, minute, moment, period, second, spell, tick *(Brit. inf.)*, time

bit[2] *n* **1 = curb,** brake, check, restraint, snaffle

bitchy *adj Slang* **= spiteful,** backbiting, catty *(inf.)*, cruel, malicious, mean, nasty, rancorous, shrewish, snide, venomous, vicious, vindictive, vixenish
Antonyms *adj* charitable, generous, gracious, kindly, magnanimous, nice

bite *vb* **1, 2 = tear,** champ, chew, clamp, crunch, crush, cut, gnaw, grip, hold, masticate, nibble, nip, pierce, pinch, rend, seize, snap, wound **4 =**

penetrate, as with a knife. **4** (of corrosive material such as acid) to eat away or into. **5** to smart or cause to smart; sting. **6** (*intr*) *Angling.* (of a fish) to take or attempt to take the bait or lure. **7** to take firm hold (of) or act effectively (upon). **8** (*tr*) *Sl.* to annoy or worry: *what's biting her?* **9** (*tr;* often foll. by *for*) *Austral.* & *NZ sl.* to ask (for); scrounge from. **10 bite the dust. 10a** to fall down dead. **10b** to be rejected: *another good idea bites the dust.* ◆ *n* **11** the act of biting. **12** a thing or amount bitten off. **13** a wound, bruise, or sting inflicted by biting. **14** *Angling.* an attempt by a fish to take the bait or lure. **15** a light meal; snack. **16** a cutting, stinging, or smarting sensation. **17** *Dentistry.* the angle or manner of contact between the upper and lower teeth. **18 put the bite on.** *Sl.* to cadge or borrow from. [OE *bītan*]
▸**'biter** *n*

biting ❶ ('baɪtɪŋ) *adj* **1** piercing; keen: *a biting wind.* **2** sarcastic; incisive.
▸**'bitingly** *adv*

bitmap ('bɪt,mæp) *Computing.* ◆ *n* **1** a picture created on a visual display unit where each pixel corresponds to one or more bits in memory, the number of bits per pixel determining the number of available colours. ◆ *vb* **bitmaps, bitmapping, bitmapped. 2** (*tr*) to create a bitmap of.

bit part *n* a very small acting role with few lines to speak.

bitt (bɪt) *Naut.* ◆ *n* **1** one of a pair of strong posts on the deck of a ship for securing mooring and other lines. **2** another word for **bollard** (sense 1). ◆ *vb* **3** (*tr*) to secure (a line) by means of a bitt. [C14: prob. from ON]

bitten ('bɪtᵊn) *vb* the past participle of **bite.**

bitter ❶ ('bɪtə) *adj* **1** having or denoting an unpalatable harsh taste, as the peel of an orange. **2** showing or caused by strong unrelenting hostility or resentment. **3** difficult or unpleasant to accept or admit: *a bitter blow.* **4** cutting; sarcastic: *bitter words.* **5** bitingly cold: *a bitter night.* ◆ *adv* **6** very; extremely (esp. in **bitter cold**). ◆ *n* **7** a thing that is bitter. **8** *Brit.* beer with a slightly bitter taste. [OE *biter;* rel. to *bītan* to BITE]
▸**'bitterly** *adv* ▸**'bitterness** *n*

bitter end *n* **1** *Naut.* the end of a line, chain, or cable. **2 to the bitter end. 2a** until the finish of a task, etc., however unpleasant or difficult. **2b** until final defeat or death. [C19: ?from BITT]

bittern ('bɪtən) *n* a wading bird related and similar to the herons but with shorter legs and neck and a booming call. [C14: from OF *butor,* ?from L *būtiō* bittern + *taurus* bull]

bitters ('bɪtəz) *pl n* **1** bitter-tasting spirits of varying alcoholic content flavoured with plant extracts. **2** a similar liquid containing a bitter-tasting substance, used as a tonic.

bittersweet ('bɪtə,swiːt) *n* **1** any of several North American woody climbing plants having orange capsules that open to expose scarlet-coated seeds. **2** another name for **woody nightshade.** ◆ *adj* **3** tasting of or being a mixture of bitterness and sweetness. **4** pleasant but tinged with sadness.

bitty ❶ ('bɪtɪ) *adj* **bittier, bittiest. 1** lacking unity; disjointed. **2** containing bits, sediment, etc.
▸**'bittiness** *n*

bitumen ('bɪtjʊmɪn) *n* **1** any of various viscous or solid impure mixtures of hydrocarbons that occur naturally in asphalt, tar, mineral waxes, etc.: used as a road surfacing and roofing material. **2 the bitumen.** *Austral.* & *NZ inf.* any road with a bitumen surface. [C15: from L *bitūmen*]
▸**bituminous** (bɪ'tjuːmɪnəs) *adj*

bituminize *or* **bituminise** (bɪ'tjuːmɪ,naɪz) *vb* **bituminizes, bituminizing, bituminized** *or* **bituminises, bituminising, bituminised.** (*tr*) to treat with or convert into bitumen.

bituminous coal *n* a soft black coal that burns with a smoky yellow flame.

bivalent (baɪ'veɪlənt, 'bɪvə-) *adj* **1** *Chem.* another word for **divalent. 2** (of homologous chromosomes) associated together in pairs.
▸**bi'valency** *n*

bivalve ('baɪ,vælv) *n* **1** a marine or freshwater mollusc, having a laterally compressed body, a shell consisting of two hinged valves, and gills for respiration. The group includes clams, cockles, oysters, and mussels. ◆ *adj* **2** of or relating to these molluscs. ◆ Also: **lamellibranch.**

bivouac ('bɪvʊ,æk, 'bɪvwæk) *n* **1** a temporary encampment, as used by soldiers, mountaineers, etc. ◆ *vb* **bivouacs, bivouacking, bivouacked. 2** (*intr*) to make such an encampment. [C18: from F *bivuac,* prob. from Swiss G *Beiwacht,* lit.: BY + WATCH]

biweekly (baɪ'wiːklɪ) *adj, adv* **1** every two weeks. **2** twice a week. See **bi-.** ◆ *n, pl* **biweeklies. 3** a periodical published every two weeks.

biyearly (baɪ'jɪəlɪ) *adj, adv* **1** every two years; biennial or biennially. **2** twice a year; biannual or biannually. See **bi-.**

biz (bɪz) *n Inf.* short for **business.**

bizarre ❶ (bɪ'zɑː) *adj* odd or unusual, esp. in an interesting or amusing way. [C17: from F, from It. *bizzarro* capricious, from ?]
▸**bi'zarreness** *n*

bizzy ('bɪzɪ) *n, pl* **bizzies.** *Brit. sl., chiefly Liverpudlian.* a policeman. [C20: from BUSY]

bk *abbrev. for:* **1** bank. **2** book.

Bk *the chemical symbol for* berkelium.

bkg *abbrev. for* banking.

BL *abbrev. for:* **1** Bachelor of Law. **2** Bachelor of Letters. **3** Barrister-at-Law. **4** British Library.

B/L, b/l, *or* **b.l.** *pl* **Bs/L, bs/l,** *or* **bs.l.** *abbrev. for* bill of lading.

blab ❶ (blæb) *vb* **blabs, blabbing, blabbed. 1** to divulge (secrets, etc.) indiscreetly. **2** (*intr*) to chatter thoughtlessly; prattle. ◆ *n* **3** a less common word for **blabber.** [C14: of Gmc origin]

blabber ❶ ('blæbə) *n* **1** a person who blabs. **2** idle chatter. ◆ *vb* **3** (*intr*) to talk without thinking; chatter. [C15 *blabberen,* prob. imit.]

black ❶ (blæk) *adj* **1** of the colour of jet or carbon black, having no hue due to the absorption of all or nearly all incident light. **2** without light; completely dark. **3** without hope of alleviation; gloomy: *the future looked black.* **4** very dirty or soiled. **5** angry or resentful: *black looks.* **6** (of a play or other work) dealing with the unpleasant realities of life, esp. in a cynical or macabre manner: *black comedy.* **7** (of coffee or tea) without milk or cream. **8a** wicked or harmful: *a black lie.* **8b** (*in combination*): *black-hearted.* **9** *Brit.* (of goods, jobs, works, etc.) being subject to boycott by trade unionists. ◆ *n* **10** a black colour. **11** a dye or pigment of or producing this colour. **12** black clothing, worn esp. as a sign of mourning. **13** *Chess, draughts.* a black or dark-coloured piece or square. **14** complete darkness: *the black of the night.* **15 in the black.** in credit or without debt. ◆ *vb* **16** another word for **blacken. 17** (*tr*) to polish (shoes, etc.) with blacking. **18** (*tr*) *Brit., Austral., & NZ.* (of trade unionists) to organize a boycott of (specified goods, jobs, work, etc.). ◆ See also **blackout.** [OE *blæc*]
▸**'blackness** *n*

Black (blæk) *n* **1** *Sometimes derog.* a member of a dark-skinned race, esp. someone of Negroid or Australoid origin. ◆ *adj* **2** of or relating to a Black person or Black people.

blackamoor ('blækə,mʊə, -,mɔː) *n Arch.* a Black person or other person with dark skin. [C16: see BLACK, MOOR]

black-and-blue *adj* **1** (of the skin) discoloured, as from a bruise. **2** feeling pain or soreness, as from a beating.

Black and Tans *pl n* **the.** a specially recruited armed force sent to Ireland in 1921 by the British Government to combat Sinn Féin. [named after the colour of their uniforms]

black-and-white *n* **1a** a photograph, picture, sketch, etc., in black, white, and shades of grey rather than in colour. **1b** (*as modifier*):

THESAURUS

eat into, burn, corrode, eat away, erode, wear away **5** = **eat into**, smart, sting, tingle **10a bite the dust** *Informal* = **die**, drop dead, expire, fall in battle, pass away, perish ◆ *n* **13** = **wound**, itch, nip, pinch, prick, smarting, sting, tooth marks **15** = **snack**, food, light meal, morsel, mouthful, piece, refreshment, taste

biting *adj* **1** = **piercing**, bitter, blighting, cold, cold as ice, cutting, freezing, harsh, nipping, penetrating, sharp **2** = **sarcastic**, caustic, cutting, incisive, mordacious, mordant, scathing, severe, sharp, stinging, trenchant, vitriolic, withering

bitter *adj* **1** = **sour**, acid, acrid, astringent, harsh, sharp, tart, unsweetened, vinegary **2** = **resentful**, acrimonious, begrudging, crabbed, embittered, hostile, morose, rancorous, sore, sour, sullen, with a chip on one's shoulder **3** = **grievous**, calamitous, cruel, dire, distressing, galling, gut-wrenching, harsh, heartbreaking, merciless, painful, poignant, ruthless, savage, vexatious **5** = **freezing**, biting, fierce, intense, severe, stinging
Antonyms *adj* ≠ **sour:** bland, mellow, mild, pleasant, sugary, sweet ≠ **resentful:** appreciative, friendly, gentle, grateful, happy, mellow, mild, pleasant, sweet, thankful ≠ **grievous:** fortunate, happy, pleasant ≠ **freezing:** balmy, gentle, mild, pleasant

bitterly *adv* **1** = **sourly**, acerbically, acidly, acridly, sharply, tartly **2** = **resentfully**, acrimoniously, grudgingly, irascibly, mordantly, sorely, sourly, sullenly, tartly, testily **3** = **grievously**, cruelly, distressingly, harshly, mercilessly, painfully, poignantly, ruthlessly, sadly, savagely, terribly **5** = **intensely**, bitingly, fiercely, severely

bitterness *n* **1** = **sourness**, acerbity, acidity, sharpness, tartness, vinegariness **2** = **resentment**, acrimony, animosity, asperity, chip on one's shoulder, grudge, hostility, pique, rancour, venom, virulence

bitty *adj* **1** = **disjointed**, disconnected, fragmentary, fragmented, incoherent, incomplete, jumbled, patchy, scrappy, sketchy
Antonyms *adj* all-embracing, coherent, complete, comprehensive, unified

bizarre *adj* = **strange**, abnormal, curious, eccentric, extraordinary, fantastic, freakish, grotesque, ludicrous, odd, oddball (*inf.*), off-beat, off-the-wall (*sl.*), outlandish, outré, peculiar, queer, ridiculous, rum (*Brit. sl.*), unusual, way-out (*inf.*), weird, zany
Antonyms *adj* common, customary, normal, ordinary, regular, routine, standard, typical

blab *vb* **1** = **tell**, blow the gaff (*Brit. sl.*), blow wide open (*sl.*), blurt out, disclose, divulge, give away, let slip, let the cat out of the bag, open one's mouth, reveal, spill one's guts (*sl.*), spill the beans (*inf.*), tell all, tell on

blabber *n* **1** = **gossip**, busybody, informer, rumour-monger, scandalmonger, talebearer, tattler, telltale ◆ *vb* **3** = **prattle**, blather, blether, chatter, gab (*inf.*), jabber, run off at the mouth

black *adj* **1, 2** = **dark**, coal-black, dusky, ebony, inky, jet, murky, pitch-black, pitchy, raven, sable, stygian **3** = **gloomy**, atrocious, depressing, dismal, distressing, doleful, foreboding, funereal, hopeless, horrible, lugubrious, mournful, ominous, sad, sombre **4** = **dirty**, dingy, filthy, grimy, grubby, soiled, sooty, stained **5** = **angry**, furious, hostile, menacing, resentful, sullen, threatening **8** = **wicked**, bad, evil, iniquitous, nefarious, villainous ◆ *n* **15 in the black** = **in credit**, in funds, solvent, without debt ◆ *vb* **18** = **boycott**, ban, bar, blacklist
Antonyms *adj* ≠ **dark:** bright, illuminated, light, lighted, lit, moonlit, sunny ≠ **gloomy:** cheerful, happy, warm ≠ **dirty:** clean, pure, white, whitish ≠ **angry:** amicable, cheerful, friendly, happy, pleased, warm ≠ **wicked:** good, honourable, moral, pure

black-and-white film. **2 in black and white. 2a** in print or writing. **2b** in extremes: *he always saw things in black and white.*

black art *n* **the.** another name for **black magic.**

black-backed gull *n* either of two common black-and-white European coastal gulls, **lesser black-backed gull** and **great black-backed gull.**

blackball ('blæk,bɔːl) *n* **1** a negative vote or veto. **2** a black wooden ball used to indicate disapproval or to veto in a vote. ◆ *vb* (*tr*) **3** to vote against. **4** to exclude (someone) from a group, profession, etc.; ostracize. [C18: from *black ball* used to veto]

black bean *n* an Australian leguminous tree: used in furniture manufacture. Also called: **Moreton Bay chestnut.**

black bear *n* **1 American black bear.** a bear inhabiting forests of North America. It is smaller and less ferocious than the brown bear. **2 Asiatic black bear.** a bear of central and E Asia, black with a pale V-shaped mark on the chest.

black belt *n Judo, karate, etc.* **a** a black belt worn by an instructor or expert. **b** a person entitled to wear this.

blackberry ('blækbərɪ) *n, pl* **blackberries. 1** Also called: **bramble.** any of several woody rosaceous plants that have thorny stems and black or purple edible berry-like fruits. **2** the fruit of any of these plants. ◆ *vb* **blackberries, blackberrying, blackberried. 3** (*intr*) to gather blackberries.

blackbird ('blæk,bɜːd) *n* **1** a common European thrush in which the male has black plumage and a yellow bill. **2** any of various American orioles having dark plumage. **3** (formerly) a person, esp. a South Sea Islander, who was kidnapped and sold as a slave, esp. in Australia. ◆ *vb* **4** (*tr*) (formerly) to kidnap and sell into slavery.

blackboard ('blæk,bɔːd) *n* a hard or rigid surface made of a smooth usually dark substance, used for writing or drawing on with chalk, esp. in teaching.

black body *n Physics.* a hypothetical body capable of absorbing all the electromagnetic radiation falling on it. Also called: **full radiator.**

black book *n* **1** a book containing the names of people to be punished, blacklisted, etc. **2 in someone's black books.** *Inf.* out of favour with someone.

black box *n* **1** a self-contained unit in an electronic or computer system whose circuitry need not be known to understand its function. **2** an informal name for **flight recorder.**

blackboy ('blæk,bɔɪ) *n* another name for **grass tree** (sense 1).

blackbuck ('blæk,bʌk) *n* an Indian antelope, the male of which has a dark back.

blackbutt ('blæk,bʌt) *n* any of various Australian eucalyptus trees having rough fibrous bark and hard wood used as timber.

blackcap ('blæk,kæp) *n* a brownish-grey Old World warbler, the male of which has a black crown.

blackcock ('blæk,kɒk) *n* the male of the black grouse.

blackcurrant (,blæk'kʌrənt) *n* **1** a N temperate shrub having red or white flowers and small edible black berries. **2** its fruit.

blackdamp ('blæk,dæmp) *n* air that is low in oxygen content and high in carbon dioxide as a result of an explosion in a mine. Also called: **chokedamp.**

Black Death *n* **the.** a form of bubonic plague pandemic in Europe and Asia during the 14th century. See **bubonic plague.**

black disc *n* a conventional black vinyl gramophone record as opposed to a compact disc.

black earth *n* another name for **chernozem.**

black economy *n* that portion of the income of a nation that remains illegally undeclared.

blacken ('blækən) *vb* **1** to make or become black or dirty. **2** (*tr*) to defame; slander (esp. in **blacken someone's name**).

black eye *n* bruising round the eye.

black-eyed Susan ('suːzᵊn) *n* any of several North American plants having flower heads of orange-yellow rays and brown-black centres.

blackface ('blæk,feɪs) *n* **1** a variety of sheep with a black face. **2** the make-up used by a White performer imitating a Black person.

blackfish ('blæk,fɪʃ) *n, pl* **blackfish** *or* **blackfishes. 1** any of various dark fishes, esp. a common edible Australian estuary fish. **2** a female salmon that has recently spawned. Cf. **redfish** (sense 1).

black flag *n* another name for the **Jolly Roger.**

blackfly ('blæk,flaɪ) *n, pl* **blackflies.** a black aphid that infests beans, sugar beet, and other plants. Also called: **bean aphid.**

Black Friar *n* a Dominican friar.

black grouse *n* **1** a large N European grouse, the male of which has a bluish-black plumage. **2** a related and similar species of W Asia.

blackguard ('blægɑːd, -gəd) *n* **1** an unprincipled contemptible person; scoundrel. ◆ *vb* **2** (*tr*) to ridicule or denounce with abusive language. **3** (*intr*) to behave like a blackguard. [C16: see BLACK, GUARD] ▸'**blackguardism** *n* ▸'**blackguardly** *adj*

blackhead ('blæk,hɛd) *n* **1** a black-tipped plug of fatty matter clogging a pore of the skin. **2** any of various birds with black plumage on the head.

black hole *n* **1a** *Astron.* a hypothetical region of space resulting from the gravitational collapse of a star and surrounded by a gravitational field so high that neither matter nor radiation could escape from it. **1b** a similar but much more massive region of space at the centre of a galaxy. **2** any place regarded as resembling a black hole in that items or information entering it cannot be retrieved.

black ice *n* a thin transparent layer of new ice on a road or similar surface.

blacking ('blækɪŋ) *n* any preparation for giving a black finish to shoes, metals, etc.

blackjack[1] ('blæk,dʒæk) *Chiefly US & Canad.* ◆ *n* **1** a truncheon of leather-covered lead with a flexible shaft. ◆ *vb* (*tr*) **2** to hit as with a blackjack. **3** to compel (a person) by threats. [C19: from BLACK + JACK (implement)]

blackjack[2] ('blæk,dʒæk) *n* pontoon or any similar card game. [C20: from BLACK + JACK (the knave)]

black knight *n Commerce.* a person or firm that makes an unwelcome takeover bid for a company. Cf. **grey knight, white knight.**

black lead (lɛd) *n* another name for **graphite.**

blackleg ('blæk,lɛg) *n* **1** Also called **scab.** *Brit.* a person who acts against the interests of a trade union, as by continuing to work during a strike or taking over a striker's job. ◆ *vb* **blacklegs, blacklegging, blacklegged. 2** (*intr*) *Brit.* to act against the interests of a trade union, esp. by refusing to join a strike.

black light *n* the invisible electromagnetic radiation in the ultraviolet and infrared regions of the spectrum.

blacklist ('blæk,lɪst) *n* **1** a list of persons or organizations under suspicion, or considered untrustworthy, disloyal, etc. ◆ *vb* **2** (*tr*) to put on a blacklist.

black magic *n* magic used for evil purposes.

blackmail ('blæk,meɪl) *n* **1** the act of attempting to obtain money by intimidation, as by threats to disclose discreditable information. **2** the exertion of pressure, esp. unfairly, in an attempt to influence someone. ◆ *vb* (*tr*) **3** to exact or attempt to exact (money or anything of value) from (a person) by threats or intimidation; extort. **4** to attempt to influence (a person), esp. by unfair pressure. [C16: from BLACK + OE *māl* terms] ▸'**black,mailer** *n*

Black Maria (mə'raɪə) *n* a police van for transporting prisoners.

black mark *n* an indication of disapproval, failure, etc.

black market *n* **1** any system in which goods or currencies are sold and bought illegally, esp. in violation of controls or rationing. **2** the place where such a system operates. ◆ *vb* **black-market. 3** to sell (goods) on the black market. ▸**black marketeer** *n*

black mass *n* (*sometimes caps.*) a blasphemous travesty of the Christian Mass, performed by practitioners of black magic.

black money *n* **1** that part of a nation's income that relates to its black economy. **2** any money that a person or organization acquires illegally, as by a means that involves tax evasion. **3** *US.* money to fund a government project that is concealed in the cost of some other project.

Black Muslim *n* (esp. in the US) a member of an Islamic political movement of Black people who seek to establish a new Black nation.

black nightshade *n* a common poisonous weed in cultivated land, having white flowers and black berry-like fruits.

blackout ('blækaʊt) *n* **1** the extinguishing or hiding of all artificial light, esp. in a city visible to an air attack. **2** a momentary loss of consciousness, vision, or memory. **3** a temporary electrical power failure or cut. **4** the suspension of broadcasting, as by a strike or for political reasons. ◆ *vb* **black out.** (*adv*) **5** (*tr*) to obliterate or extinguish (lights). **6** (*tr*) to create a blackout in (a city, etc.). **7** (*intr*) to lose vision, consciousness, or memory temporarily. **8** (*tr*) to stop (news, a television programme, etc.) from being broadcast.

black pepper *n* a pungent condiment made by grinding the dried unripe berries and husks of the pepper plant.

Black Power *n* a social, economic, and political movement of Black people, esp. in the US, to obtain equality with Whites.

THESAURUS

blackball *vb* **4** = **exclude**, ban, bar, blacklist, debar, drum out, expel, ostracize, oust, repudiate, snub

blacken *vb* **1** = **darken**, befoul, begrime, cloud, dirty, grow black, make black, smudge, soil **2** = **discredit**, bad-mouth (*sl., chiefly US & Canad.*), calumniate, decry, defame, denigrate, dishonour, knock (*inf.*), malign, rubbish (*inf.*), slag (off) (*sl.*), slander, smear, smirch, stain, sully, vilify

blackguard *n* **1** = **scoundrel**, bastard (*offens.*), blighter (*Brit. inf.*), bounder (*old-fashioned Brit. sl.*), miscreant, rascal, rogue, scumbag (*sl.*), shit (*taboo sl.*), son-of-a-bitch (*sl., chiefly US & Canad.*), swine, villain, wretch

blacklist *vb* **2** = **exclude**, ban, bar, blackball, boycott, debar, expel, ostracize, preclude, proscribe, reject, repudiate, snub, vote against

black magic *n* = **witchcraft**, black art, diabolism, necromancy, sorcery, voodoo, wizardry

blackmail *n* **1** = **extortion**, exaction, hush money (*sl.*), intimidation, milking, pay-off (*inf.*), protection (*inf.*), ransom, shakedown, threat ◆ *vb* **3** = **extort**, bleed (*inf.*), coerce, compel, demand, exact, force, hold to ransom, intimidate, milk, squeeze, threaten

blackness *n* **1, 2** = **darkness**, duskiness, gloom, inkiness, murkiness, swarthiness
Antonyms *n* brightness, brilliance, effulgence, incandescence, lambency, light, lightness, luminescence, luminosity, phosphorescence, radiance

blackout *n* **2** = **unconsciousness**, coma, faint, loss of consciousness, oblivion, swoon, syncope (*Pathology*) **3** = **power cut**, power failure **4** = **noncommunication**, censorship, radio silence, secrecy, suppression, withholding news ◆ *vb* **black out 5** = **darken**, conceal, cover, eclipse, shade **8** = **pass out**, collapse, faint, flake out, lose consciousness, swoon

black pudding *n* a kind of black sausage made from minced pork fat, pig's blood, and other ingredients. Also called: **blood pudding.**

Black Rod *n* (in Britain) an officer of the House of Lords and of the Order of the Garter, whose main duty is summoning the Commons at the opening and proroguing of Parliament.

black section *n* (in Britain) an unofficial group within the Labour Party in any constituency which represents the interests of local Black people.

black sheep Ⓣ *n* a person who is regarded as a disgrace or failure by his family or peer group.

Blackshirt ('blæk,ʃɜːt) *n* (in Europe) a member of a fascist organization, esp. the Italian Fascist party before and during World War II.

blacksmith ('blæk,smɪθ) *n* an artisan who works iron with a furnace, anvil, hammer, etc. [C14: see BLACK, SMITH]

black snake *n* **1** any of several Old World black venomous snakes, esp. the **Australian black snake. 2** any of various dark nonvenomous snakes.

black spot *n* **1** a place on a road where accidents frequently occur. **2** any dangerous or difficult place. **3** a disease of roses that causes black blotches on the leaves.

black stump *n* **the.** *Austral.* an imaginary marker of the extent of civilization (esp. in **beyond the black stump**).

black tea *n* tea made from fermented tea leaves.

blackthorn ('blæk,θɔːn) *n* a thorny Eurasian shrub with black twigs, white flowers, and small sour plumlike fruits. Also called: **sloe.**

black tie *n* **1** a black bow tie worn with a dinner jacket. **2** (*modifier*) denoting an occasion when a dinner jacket should be worn.

blacktop ('blæk,tɒp) *n Chiefly US & Canad.* a bituminous mixture used for paving.

Black tracker *n Austral.* an Aboriginal tracker working for the police.

black velvet *n* a mixture of stout and champagne in equal proportions.

Black Watch *n* **the.** the Royal Highland Regiment in the British Army.

blackwater fever ('blæk,wɔːtə) *n* a rare and serious complication of malaria, characterized by massive destruction of red blood cells, producing dark red or blackish urine.

black widow *n* an American spider, the female of which is highly venomous, and commonly eats its mate.

Blackwood ('blæk,wʊd) *n Bridge.* a conventional bidding sequence of four and five no-trumps, which are requests to the partner to show aces and kings respectively. [C20: after E. F. *Blackwood,* its US inventor]

bladder ('blædə) *n* **1** *Anat.* a distensible membranous sac, usually containing liquid or gas, esp. the urinary bladder. **2** an inflatable part of something. **3** a hollow saclike part in certain plants, such as the bladderwrack. [OE *blǣdre*]
▸'**bladdery** *adj*

bladderwort ('blædə,wɜːt) *n* an aquatic plant some of whose leaves are modified as small bladders to trap minute aquatic animals.

bladderwrack ('blædə,ræk) *n* any of several seaweeds that grow in the intertidal regions of rocky shores and have branched brown fronds with air bladders.

blade (bleɪd) *n* **1** the part of a sharp weapon, tool, etc., that forms the cutting edge. **2** the thin flattish part of various tools, implements, etc., as of a propeller, turbine, etc. **3** the flattened expanded part of a leaf, sepal, or petal. **4** the long narrow leaf of a grass or related plant. **5** the striking surface of a bat, club, stick, or oar. **6** the metal runner on an ice skate. **7** the upper part of the tongue lying directly behind the tip. **8** *Arch.* a dashing or swaggering young man. **9** short for **shoulder blade. 10** a poetic word for a **sword** or **swordsman.** [OE *blæd*]
▸'**bladed** *adj*

blaeberry ('bleɪbərɪ) *n, pl* **blaeberries.** *Brit.* another name for **whortleberry** (senses 1, 2). [C15: from dialect *blae* bluish + BERRY]

blag (blæg) *Sl.* ◆ *n* **1** a robbery, esp. with violence. ◆ *vb* **blags, blagging, blagged.** (*tr*) **2** to obtain by wheedling or cadging: *she blagged free tickets from her mate.* **3** to snatch (wages, someone's handbag, etc.); steal. **4** to rob (esp. a bank or post office). [C19: from ?]
▸'**blagger** *n*

blah *or* **blah blah** (blɑː) *n Sl.* worthless or silly talk. [C20: imit.]

blain (bleɪn) *n* a blister, blotch, or sore on the skin. [OE *blegen*]

Blairite ('blɛəraɪt) *adj* **1** of or relating to the modernizing policies of Tony Blair, British prime minister from 1997. ◆ *n* **2** a supporter of the modernizing policies of Tony Blair.

blame Ⓣ (bleɪm) *n* **1** responsibility for something that is wrong; culpability. **2** an expression of condemnation. ◆ *vb* **blames, blaming, blamed.** (*tr*) **3** (usually foll. by *for*) to attribute responsibility to: *I blame him for the failure.* **4** (usually foll. by *on*) to ascribe responsibility for (something) to: *I blame the failure on him.* **5** to find fault with. **6 be to blame.** to be at fault. [C12: from OF *blasmer,* ult. from LL *blasphēmāre* to blaspheme]
▸'**blamable** *or* '**blameable** *adj* ▸'**blamably** *or* '**blameably** *adv*

blameful ('bleɪmfʊl) *adj* deserving blame; guilty.
▸'**blamefully** *adv* ▸'**blamefulness** *n*

blameless Ⓣ ('bleɪmlɪs) *adj* free from blame; innocent.
▸'**blamelessness** *n*

blameworthy Ⓣ ('bleɪm,wɜːðɪ) *adj* deserving censure.
▸'**blame,worthiness** *n*

blanch Ⓣ (blɑːntʃ) *vb* (*mainly tr*) **1** to remove colour from; whiten. **2** (*usually intr*) to become or cause to become pale, as with sickness or fear. **3** to prepare (meat, green vegetables, nuts, etc.) by plunging them in boiling water. **4** to cause (celery, chicory, etc.) to grow free of chlorophyll by the exclusion of sunlight. [C14: from OF *blanchir,* from *blanc* white; see BLANK]

blancmange (blə'mɒnʒ) *n* a jelly-like dessert of milk, stiffened usually with cornflour. [C14: from OF *blanc manger,* lit.: white food]

bland Ⓣ (blænd) *adj* **1** devoid of distinctive or stimulating characteristics; uninteresting. **2** gentle and agreeable; suave. **3** mild and soothing. [C15: from L *blandus* flattering]
▸'**blandly** *adv* ▸'**blandness** *n*

blandish ('blændɪʃ) *vb* (*tr*) to seek to persuade or influence by mild flattery; coax. [C14: from OF *blandir,* from L *blandīrī*]

blandishments Ⓣ ('blændɪʃmənts) *pl n* (*rarely sing*) flattery intended to coax or cajole.

blank Ⓣ (blæŋk) *adj* **1** (of a writing surface) bearing no marks; not written on. **2** (of a form, etc.) with spaces left for details to be filled in. **3** without ornament or break. **4** not filled in; empty. **5** exhibiting no interest or expression: *a blank look.* **6** lacking understanding; confused: *he looked blank.* **7** absolute; complete: *blank rejection.* **8** devoid of ideas or inspiration: *his mind went blank.* ◆ *n* **9** an emptiness; void; blank space. **10** an empty space for writing in. **11** a printed form containing such empty spaces. **12** something characterized by incomprehension or confusion: *my mind went a complete blank.* **13** a mark, often a dash, in place of a word, esp. a taboo word. **14** short for **blank cartridge. 15** a piece of material prepared for stamping, punching, forging, or some other operation. **16 draw a blank.** to get no results from something. ◆ *vb* (*tr*) **17** (usually foll. by *out*) to cross out, blot, or obscure. [C15: from OF *blanc* white, of Gmc origin]
▸'**blankness** *n*

blank cartridge *n* a cartridge containing powder but no bullet.

blank cheque *n* **1** a cheque that has been signed but on which the amount payable has not been specified. **2** complete freedom of action.

blanket Ⓣ ('blæŋkɪt) *n* **1** a large piece of thick cloth for use as a bed covering, animal covering, etc. **2** a concealing cover, as of smoke, leaves, or snow. **3** (*modifier*) applying to or covering a wide group or variety of people, conditions, situations, etc.: *blanket insurance against loss, injury, and theft.* **4** (**born**) **on the wrong side of the blanket.** *Inf.* illegitimate. **5 on the blanket.** *Irish.* (of an imprisoned terrorist) wearing only a blanket

THESAURUS

black sheep *n* = **disgrace**, dropout, ne'er-do-well, outcast, prodigal, renegade, reprobate

blamable *adj* **3-5** = **responsible**, answerable, at fault, blameworthy, culpable, deserving of censure, faulty, guilty, in the wrong, liable, reprehensible, reproachable, reprovable

blame *n* **1** = **responsibility**, accountability, accusation, culpability, fault, guilt, incrimination, liability, rap (*sl.*) **2** = **condemnation**, castigation, censure, charge, complaint, criticism, recrimination, reproach, reproof, stick (*sl.*) ◆ *vb* **3, 4** = **hold responsible**, accuse, point a *or* the finger at **5** = **criticize**, admonish, blast, censure, charge, chide, condemn, disapprove, express disapprobation, find fault with, lambast(e), put down, reprehend, reproach, reprove, tax, tear into (*inf.*), upbraid
Antonyms *n* ≠ **responsibility:** absolution, alibi, excuse, exoneration, vindication ≠ **condemnation:** acclaim, Brownie points, commendation, credit, honour, praise, tribute ◆ *vb* ≠ **hold responsible:** absolve, acquit, clear, excuse, exonerate, forgive, vindicate ≠ **criticize:** acclaim, approve of, commend, compliment, praise

blameless *adj* = **innocent**, above suspicion, clean, faultless, guiltless, immaculate, impeccable, in the clear, irreproachable, perfect, squeaky-clean, stainless, unblemished, unimpeachable, unoffending, unspotted, unsullied, untarnished, upright, virtuous
Antonyms *adj* at fault, censurable, culpable, guilty, reprovable, responsible, to blame

blameworthy *adj* = **reprehensible**, discreditable, disreputable, indefensible, inexcusable, iniquitous, reproachable, shameful

blanch *vb* **1** = **whiten**, bleach, fade **2** = **turn pale**, become *or* grow white, become pallid, blench, drain, pale

bland *adj* **1** = **dull**, boring, flat, humdrum, insipid, monotonous, tasteless, tedious, tiresome, undistinctive, unexciting, uninspiring, uninteresting, unstimulating, vanilla (*inf.*), vapid, weak **2** = **smooth**, affable, amiable, congenial, courteous, debonair, friendly, gentle, gracious, suave, unemotional, urbane
Antonyms *adj* ≠ **dull:** distinctive, exciting, inspiring, interesting, rousing, stimulating, turbulent, volatile

blandishments *pl n* = **flattery**, blarney, cajolery, coaxing, compliments, fawning, ingratiation, inveiglement, soft soap (*inf.*), soft words, sweet talk (*inf.*), wheedling

blank *adj* **1, 2, 4** = **unmarked**, bare, clean, clear, empty, plain, spotless, uncompleted, unfilled, void, white **5** = **expressionless**, deadpan, dull, empty, hollow, impassive, inane, lifeless, poker-faced (*inf.*), vacant, vacuous, vague **6** = **puzzled**, at a loss, at sea, bewildered, confounded, confused, disconcerted, dumbfounded, flummoxed, muddled, nonplussed, uncomprehending **7** = **absolute**, complete, out and out, outright, thorough, total, unqualified, utter ◆ *n* **8** = **empty space**, emptiness, gap, nothingness, space, tabula rasa, vacancy, vacuity, vacuum, void
Antonyms *adj* ≠ **unmarked:** completed, filled in, full, marked ≠ **expressionless:** alert, expressive, intelligent, interested, lively, thoughtful

blanket *n* **1** = **cover**, afghan, coverlet, rug **2** = **covering**, carpet, cloak, coat, coating, envelope, film, layer, mantle, sheet, wrapper, wrapping ◆ *modifier* **3** = **comprehensive**, across-the-board, all-inclusive, overall, sweeping, wide-ranging ◆ *vb* **6** = **cover**, cloak, cloud,

instead of prison uniform, as a protest against not being recognized as a political prisoner. ◆ *vb (tr)* **6** to cover as with a blanket; overlie. **7** to cover a wide area; give blanket coverage. **8** (usually foll. by *out*) to obscure or suppress. [C13: from OF *blancquete,* from *blanc;* see BLANK]

blanket bath *n* an all-over wash given to a person confined to bed.

blanket bog *n* a very acid peat bog, low in nutrients, extending widely over a flat terrain, found in cold wet climates.

blanket stitch *n* a strong reinforcing stitch for the edges of blankets and other thick material.

blankety (ˈblæŋkɪtɪ) *adj, adv* a euphemism for any taboo word. [C20: from BLANK]

blank verse *n Prosody.* unrhymed verse, esp. in iambic pentameters.

blare Ⓣ (blɛə) *vb* **blares, blaring, blared. 1** to sound loudly and harshly. **2** to proclaim loudly and sensationally. ◆ *n* **3** a loud harsh noise. [C14: from MDu. *bleren;* imit.]

blarney Ⓣ (ˈblɑːnɪ) *n* **1** flattering talk. ◆ *vb* **2** to cajole with flattery; wheedle. [C19: after the *Blarney* Stone in SW Ireland, said to endow whoever kisses it with skill in flattery]

blasé Ⓣ (ˈblɑːzeɪ) *adj* **1** indifferent to something because of familiarity. **2** lacking enthusiasm; bored. [C19: from F, p.p. of *blaser* to cloy]

blaspheme Ⓣ (blæsˈfiːm) *vb* **blasphemes, blaspheming, blasphemed. 1** *(tr)* to show contempt or disrespect for (God or sacred things), esp. in speech. **2** *(intr)* to utter profanities or curses. [C14: from LL, from Gk, from *blasphēmos* BLASPHEMOUS]

▸**blasˈphemer** *n*

blasphemous Ⓣ (ˈblæsfɪməs) *adj* involving impiousness or gross irreverence towards God or something sacred. [C15: via LL, from Gk *blasphēmos* evil-speaking, from *blapsis* evil + *phēmē* speech]

blasphemy Ⓣ (ˈblæsfɪmɪ) *n, pl* **blasphemies. 1** blasphemous behaviour or language. **2** Also called: **blasphemous libel.** *Law.* the crime committed if a person insults, offends, or vilifies the deity, Christ, or the Christian religion.

blast Ⓣ (blɑːst) *n* **1** an explosion, as of dynamite. **2** the rapid movement of air away from the centre of an explosion; shock wave. **3** the charge used in a single explosion. **4** a sudden strong gust of wind or air. **5** a sudden loud sound, as of a trumpet. **6** a violent verbal outburst, as of criticism. **7** a forcible jet of air, esp. one used to intensify the heating effect of a furnace. **8** any of several diseases of plants and animals. **9** *US sl.* a very enjoyable or thrilling experience: *the party was a blast.* **10** **(at) full blast.** at maximum speed, volume, etc. ◆ *interj* **11** *Sl.* an exclamation of annoyance. ◆ *vb* **12** *(tr)* to destroy or blow up with explosives, shells, etc. **13** to make or cause to make a loud harsh noise. **14** to wither or cause to wither; blight or be blighted. **15** *(tr)* to criticize severely. [OE *blǣst*]

▸ˈ**blaster** *n*

-blast *n combining form.* (in biology) indicating an embryonic cell or formative layer: *mesoblast.* [from Gk *blastos* bud]

blasted Ⓣ (ˈblɑːstɪd) *adj* **1** blighted or withered. ◆ *adj (prenominal), adv* **2** *Sl.* (intensifier): *a blasted idiot.*

blast furnace *n* a vertical cylindrical furnace for smelting into which a blast of preheated air is forced.

blasto- *combining form.* indicating an embryo or bud. [see BLAST]

blastoff Ⓣ (ˈblɑːstˌɒf) *n* **1** the launching of a rocket under its own power. **2** the time at which this occurs. ◆ *vb* **blast off. 3** *(adv; when tr, usually passive)* to be launched.

blastula (ˈblæstjʊlə) *n, pl* **blastulas** *or* **blastulae** (-liː). an early form of an animal embryo that develops a sphere of cells with a central cavity. Also called: **blastosphere.** [C19: NL from Gk, from dim. of *blastos* bud]

▸ˈ**blastular** *adj*

blat (blæt) *n Sl.* a newspaper. [C20: from G *Blatt* leaf, sheet of paper]

blatant Ⓣ (ˈbleɪtᵊnt) *adj* **1** glaringly conspicuous or obvious: *a blatant lie.* **2** offensively noticeable; obtrusive. **3** offensively noisy. [C16: coined by Edmund Spenser (?1552–99), E poet, prob. infl. by L *blatīre* to babble]

▸ˈ**blatancy** *n*

blather (ˈblæðə) *vb, n* a variant of **blether.**

blatherskite (ˈblæðəˌskaɪt) *n* **1** a talkative silly person. **2** foolish talk; nonsense. [C17: from BLATHER + Scot. & N English dialect *skate* fellow]

blaxploitation (ˌblæksplɔɪˈteɪʃən) *n* exploitative use of stereotypical images of Black people in films, books, etc. [C20: from BLACK + EXPLOITATION]

blaze[1] Ⓣ (bleɪz) *n* **1** a strong fire or flame. **2** a very bright light or glare. **3** an outburst (of passion, acclaim, patriotism, etc.). **4** brilliance; brightness. ◆ *vb* **blazes, blazing, blazed.** *(intr)* **5** to burn fiercely. **6** to shine brightly. **7** (often foll. by *up*) to become stirred, as with anger or excitement. **8** (usually foll. by *away*) to shoot continuously. ◆ See also **blazes.** [OE *blæse*]

blaze[2] (bleɪz) *n* **1** a mark, usually indicating a path, made on a tree. **2** a light-coloured marking on the face of a domestic animal. ◆ *vb* **blazes, blazing, blazed.** *(tr)* **3** to mark (a tree, path, etc.) with a blaze. **4** **blaze a trail.** to explore new territories, areas of knowledge, etc., so that others can follow. [C17: prob. from MLow G *bles* white marking]

blaze[3] (bleɪz) *vb* **blazes, blazing, blazed.** *(tr; often foll. by abroad)* to make widely known; proclaim. [C14: from MDu. *blāsen,* from OHG *blāsan*]

blazer (ˈbleɪzə) *n* a fairly lightweight jacket, often in the colours of a sports club, school, etc.

blazes (ˈbleɪzɪz) *pl n* **1** *Sl.* a euphemistic word for **hell. 2** *Inf.* (intensifier): *to run like blazes.*

blazon Ⓣ (ˈbleɪzᵊn) *vb (tr)* **1** (often foll. by *abroad*) to proclaim publicly. **2** *Heraldry.* to describe (heraldic arms) in proper terms. **3** to draw and colour (heraldic arms) conventionally. ◆ *n* **4** *Heraldry.* a conventional description or depiction of heraldic arms. [C13: from OF *blason* coat of arms]

▸ˈ**blazoner** *n*

blazonry (ˈbleɪzənrɪ) *n, pl* **blazonries. 1** the art or process of describing heraldic arms in proper form. **2** heraldic arms collectively. **3** colourful or ostentatious display.

bldg *abbrev. for* building.

bleach Ⓣ (bliːtʃ) *vb* **1** to make or become white or colourless, as by exposure to sunlight, by the action of chemical agents, etc. ◆ *n* **2** a bleaching agent. **3** the act of bleaching. [OE *blǣcan*]

▸ˈ**bleacher** *n*

bleaching powder *n* a white powder consisting of chlorinated calcium hydroxide. Also called: **chloride of lime, chlorinated lime.**

bleak[1] Ⓣ (bliːk) *adj* **1** exposed and barren. **2** cold and raw. **3** offering little hope; dismal: *a bleak future.* [OE *blāc* bright, pale]

▸ˈ**bleakness** *n*

bleak[2] (bliːk) *n* any of various European cyprinid fishes occurring in slow-flowing rivers. [C15: prob. from ON *bleikja* white colour]

blear (blɪə) *Arch.* ◆ *vb* **1** *(tr)* to make (eyes or sight) dim as with tears; blur. ◆ *adj* **2** a less common word for **bleary.** [C13: *blere* to make dim]

bleary Ⓣ (ˈblɪərɪ) *adj* **blearier, bleariest. 1** (of eyes or vision) dimmed or blurred, as by tears or tiredness. **2** indistinct or unclear.

▸ˈ**bleariness** *n*

THESAURUS

coat, eclipse, mask, surround **8** = **suppress**, conceal, hide, obscure

blankness *n* **5** = **indifference**, abstraction, obliviousness **8** = **vacancy**, fatuity, inanity, vacuity

blare *vb* **1** = **sound out**, blast, boom, clamour, clang, honk, hoot, peal, resound, roar, scream, toot, trumpet

blarney *n* **1** = **flattery**, blandishment, cajolery, coaxing, exaggeration, honeyed words, overpraise, soft soap (*inf.*), spiel, sweet talk (*inf.*), wheedling

blasé *adj* **1** = **jaded**, cloyed, glutted, satiated, surfeited **2** = **indifferent**, apathetic, bored, lukewarm, nonchalant, offhand, unconcerned, unexcited, uninterested, unmoved, weary, world-weary
Antonyms *adj* affected, caring, enthusiastic, excited, interested, responsive, stimulated

blaspheme *vb* **1** = **profane**, abuse, desecrate **2** = **swear**, curse, damn, execrate, revile

blasphemous *adj* **1** = **irreverent**, godless, impious, irreligious, profane, sacrilegious, ungodly
Antonyms *adj* devout, God-fearing, godly, pious, religious, respectful, reverent, reverential

blasphemy *n* **1** = **irreverence**, cursing, desecration, execration, impiety, impiousness, profanation, profaneness, profanity, sacrilege, swearing

blast *n* **1** = **explosion**, bang, blow-up, burst, crash, detonation, discharge, eruption, outburst, salvo, volley **4** = **gust**, gale, squall, storm, strong breeze, tempest **5** = **blare**, blow, clang, honk, peal, scream, toot, wail ◆ *vb* **12** = **blow up**, blow sky-high, break up, burst, demolish, destroy, explode, put paid to, ruin, shatter **14** = **blight**, kill, shrivel, wither **15** = **criticize**, attack, castigate, flay, lambast(e), put down, rail at, tear into (*inf.*)

blasted *adj* **1** = **ruined**, blighted, desolated, destroyed, devastated, ravaged, shattered, spoiled, wasted, withered

blastoff *n* **1** = **launch**, discharge, expulsion, firing, launching, liftoff, projection, shot

blatant *adj* **1, 2** = **obvious**, bald, brazen, conspicuous, flagrant, flaunting, glaring, naked, obtrusive, ostentatious, outright, overt, prominent, pronounced, sheer, unmitigated
Antonyms *adj* agreeable, cultured, dignified, hidden, inconspicuous, quiet, refined, soft, subtle, tasteful, unnoticeable, unobtrusive, well-mannered

blaze[1] *n* **1** = **fire**, bonfire, conflagration, flame, flames **2, 4** = **glare**, beam, brilliance, flare, flash, gleam, glitter, glow, light, radiance **3** = **outburst**, blast, burst, eruption, flare-up, fury, outbreak, rush, storm, torrent ◆ *vb* **5** = **burn**, fire, flame **6** = **shine**, beam, flare, flash, glare, gleam, glow **7** = **flare up**, boil, explode, fume, seethe

blazing *adj* **1** = **burning**, ablaze, afire, aflame, alight, fiery, flaming, on fire **2** = **shining**, aglow, brilliant, coruscating, flashing, gleaming, glowing, illuminated, incandescent, luminous, radiant, sparkling **7** = **furious**, angry, excited, fervent, frenzied, fuming, impassioned, incensed, passionate, raging, seething

blazon *vb* **1** = **proclaim**, broadcast, celebrate, flourish, make known, renown, trumpet

bleach *vb* **1** = **whiten**, blanch, etiolate, fade, grow pale, lighten, peroxide, wash out

bleached *adj* **1** = **whiten**, achromatic, etiolated, faded, lightened, peroxided, stonewashed, washed-out

bleak[1] *adj* **1** = **exposed**, bare, barren, desolate, gaunt, open, stark, unsheltered, weatherbeaten, windswept, windy **2** = **cold**, chilly, raw **3** = **dismal**, cheerless, comfortless, depressing, discouraging, disheartening, dreary, gloomy, grim, hopeless, joyless, sombre, unpromising
Antonyms *adj* ≠ **exposed:** protected, sheltered, shielded ≠ **dismal:** cheerful, cosy, encouraging, promising

bleary *adj* **1, 2** = **dim**, blurred, blurry, fogged, foggy, fuzzy, hazy, indistinct, misty

bleary-eyed *or* **blear-eyed** *adj* with eyes blurred, as with old age or after waking.

bleat (bliːt) *vb* **1** (*intr*) (of a sheep, goat, or calf) to utter its characteristic plaintive cry. **2** (*intr*) to speak with any similar sound. **3** to whine; whimper. ◆ *n* **4** the characteristic cry of sheep, goats, and calves. **5** any sound similar to this. **6** a weak complaint or whine. [OE *blǣtan*]
▸ **'bleater** *n* ▸ **'bleating** *n, adj*

bleb (blɛb) *n* **1** a fluid-filled blister on the skin. **2** a small air bubble. [C17: var. of BLOB]

bleed ➊ (bliːd) *vb* **bleeds, bleeding, bled** (blɛd). **1** (*intr*) to lose or emit blood. **2** (*tr*) to remove or draw blood from (a person or animal). **3** (*intr*) to be injured or die, as for a cause. **4** (of plants) to exude (sap or resin), esp. from a cut. **5** (*tr*) *Inf.* to obtain money, etc., from, esp. by extortion. **6** (*tr*) to draw liquid or gas from (a container or enclosed system): *to bleed the hydraulic brakes.* **7** (*intr*) (of dye or paint) to run or become mixed, as when wet. **8** to print or be printed so that text, illustrations, etc., run off the trimmed page. **9 one's heart bleeds.** used to express sympathetic grief, often ironically. [OE *blēdan*]

bleeder ('bliːdə) *n* **1** *Sl.* **1a** *Derog.* a despicable person. **1b** any person. **2** *Pathol.* a nontechnical name for a **haemophiliac.**

bleeding ('bliːdɪŋ) *adj, adv Brit. sl.* (intensifier): *a bleeding fool.*

bleeding heart *n* **1** any of several plants, esp. a widely cultivated Japanese species which has heart-shaped nodding pink flowers. **2** *Inf.* **2a** an excessively softhearted person. **2b** (*as modifier*): *bleeding-heart liberals.*

bleep (bliːp) *n* **1** a single short high-pitched signal made by an electronic apparatus; beep. **2** another word for **bleeper.** ◆ *vb* **3** (*intr*) to make such a noise. **4** (*tr*) to call (somebody) by means of a bleeper. [C20: imit.]

bleeper ('bliːpə) *n* a small portable radio receiver, carried esp. by doctors, that sounds a coded bleeping signal to call the carrier. Also called: **bleep.**

blemish ➊ ('blɛmɪʃ) *n* **1** a defect; flaw; stain. ◆ *vb* **2** (*tr*) to flaw the perfection of; spoil; tarnish. [C14: from OF *blemir* to make pale]

blench ➊ (blɛntʃ) *vb* (*intr*) to shy away, as in fear; quail. [OE *blencan* to deceive]

blend ➊ (blɛnd) *vb* **1** to mix or mingle (components) together thoroughly. **2** (*tr*) to mix (different grades or varieties of tea, whisky, etc.). **3** (*intr*) to look good together; harmonize. **4** (*intr*) (esp. of colours) to shade imperceptibly into each other. ◆ *n* **5** a mixture or type produced by blending. **6** the act of blending. **7** Also called: **portmanteau word.** a word formed by joining together the beginning and the end of two other words: *"brunch" is a blend of "breakfast" and "lunch."* [OE *blandan*]

blende (blɛnd) *n* **1** another name for **sphalerite. 2** any of several sulphide ores. [C17: G, from *blenden* to deceive, BLIND; so called because it is easily mistaken for galena]

blender ('blɛndə) *n* **1** a person or thing that blends. **2** Also called: **liquidizer.** a kitchen appliance with blades used for puréeing vegetables, blending liquids, etc.

blenny ('blɛnɪ) *n, pl* **blennies.** any of various small fishes of coastal waters having a tapering scaleless body, a long dorsal fin, and long raylike pelvic fins. [C18: from L, from Gk *blennos* slime]

blent (blɛnt) *vb Arch. or literary.* a past participle of **blend.**

blepharitis (ˌblɛfə'raɪtɪs) *n* inflammation of the eyelids. [C19: from Gk *blephar(on)* eyelid + -ITIS]

blesbok *or* **blesbuck** ('blɛsˌbʌk) *n, pl* **blesboks, blesbok** *or* **blesbucks, blesbuck.** an antelope of southern Africa. The coat is reddish brown with a white blaze between the eyes; the horns are lyre-shaped. [C19: Afrik., from Du. *bles* BLAZE[2] + *bok* BUCK[1]]

bless ➊ (blɛs) *vb* **blesses, blessing, blessed** *or* **blest.** (*tr*) **1** to consecrate or render holy by means of a religious rite. **2** to give honour or glory to (a person or thing) as holy. **3** to call upon God to protect; give a benediction to. **4** to worship or adore (God). **5** (*often passive*) to grant happiness, health, or prosperity to. **6** (*usually passive*) to endow with a talent, beauty, etc. **7** *Rare.* to protect against evil or harm. **8 bless you!** (*interj*) **8a** a traditional phrase said to a person who has just sneezed. **8b** an exclamation of well-wishing or surprise. **9 bless me!** *or* **(God) bless my soul!** (*interj*) an exclamation of surprise. [OE *blǣdsian* to sprinkle with sacrificial blood]

blessed ➊ ('blɛsɪd, blɛst) *adj* **1** made holy; consecrated. **2** worthy of deep reverence or respect. **3** *RC Church.* (of a person) beatified by the pope. **4** characterized by happiness or good fortune. **5** bringing great happiness or good fortune. **6** a euphemistic word for **damned,** used in mild oaths: *I'm blessed if I know.*
▸ **'blessedly** *adv* ▸ **'blessedness** *n*

Blessed Sacrament *n Chiefly RC Church.* the consecrated elements of the Eucharist.

blessing ➊ ('blɛsɪŋ) *n* **1** the act of invoking divine protection or aid. **2** the words or ceremony used for this. **3** a short prayer before or after a meal; grace. **4** approval; good wishes. **5** the bestowal of a divine gift or favour. **6** a happy event.

blest (blɛst) *vb* a past tense and past participle of **bless.**

blether ➊ ('blɛðə) *Scot.* ◆ *vb* **1** (*intr*) to speak foolishly. ◆ *n* **2** foolish talk; nonsense. [C16: from ON *blathr* nonsense]

blew (bluː) *vb* the past tense of **blow**[1] and **blow**[3].

blight ➊ (blaɪt) *n* **1** any plant disease characterized by withering and shrivelling without rotting. **2** any factor that causes the symptoms of blight in plants. **3** a person or thing that mars or prevents growth. **4** an ugly urban district. ◆ *vb* **5** to cause or suffer a blight. **6** (*tr*) to frustrate or disappoint. **7** (*tr*) to spoil; destroy. [C17: ? rel. to OE *blǣce* rash]

blighter ('blaɪtə) *n Brit. inf.* **1** a fellow. **2** a despicable or irritating person or thing.

Blighty ('blaɪtɪ) *n* (*sometimes not cap.*) *Brit. sl.* (used esp. by troops serving abroad) **1** England; home. **2** (*pl* **Blighties**) Also called: **a blighty one.** (esp. in World War I) a wound that causes the recipient to be sent home to England. [C20: from Hindi *bilāyatī* foreign land, England, from Ar. *wilāyat* country]

blimey ('blaɪmɪ) *interj Brit. sl.* an exclamation of surprise or annoyance. [C19: short for *gorblimey* God blind me]

blimp[1] (blɪmp) *n* **1** a small nonrigid airship. **2** *Films.* a soundproof cover fixed over a camera during shooting. [C20: prob. from (*type*) *B-limp*]

blimp[2] (blɪmp) *n* (*often cap.*) *Chiefly Brit.* a person, esp. a military officer, who is stupidly complacent and reactionary. Also called: **Colonel Blimp.** [C20: from a character created by David Low (1891–1963), Brit. cartoonist, born NZ]
▸ **'blimpish** *adj*

blind ➊ (blaɪnd) *adj* **1a** unable to see; sightless. **1b** (*as collective n; preceded by the*): *the blind.* **2** (usually foll. by *to*) unable or unwilling to understand or discern. **3** not determined by reason: *blind hatred.* **4** acting or performed without control or preparation. **5** done without being able to see, relying on instruments for information. **6** hidden from sight: *a blind corner.* **7** closed at one end: *a blind alley.* **8** completely lacking awareness or consciousness: *a blind stupor.* **9** *Inf.* very drunk. **10** having no openings or outlets: *a blind wall.* **11** (intensifier): *not a blind bit of notice.* ◆ *adv* **12** without being able to see ahead or using only instruments: *to drive blind; flying blind.* **13** without adequate knowledge or information; carelessly: *to buy a house blind.* **14 bake blind.** to bake (an empty pastry case) by half filling with dried peas, crusts, etc., to keep it in shape. ◆ *vb* (*mainly tr*) **15** to deprive of sight permanently or temporarily. **16** to deprive of good sense, reason, or judgment. **17** to darken; conceal. **18** (foll. by *with*) to overwhelm by showing detailed knowledge: *to blind somebody with science.* ◆ *n* **19** (*modifier*) for or intended to help the blind: *a blind school.* **20** a shade for a window, usually on a roller. **21** any obstruction or hindrance to

THESAURUS

bleed *vb* **1** = **lose blood,** exude, flow, gush, ooze, run, seep, shed blood, spurt, trickle, weep **2** = **draw** *or* **take blood,** extract, leech, phlebotomize (*Medical*) **5** *Informal* = **extort,** drain, exhaust, fleece, milk, squeeze **6** = **drain,** extract

blemish *n* **1** = **mark,** blot, blotch, blur, defect, demerit, disfigurement, disgrace, dishonour, fault, flaw, imperfection, scar, smirch, smudge, speck, spot, stain, taint ◆ *vb* **2** = **mark,** blot, blotch, blur, damage, deface, disfigure, flaw, impair, injure, mar, smirch, smudge, spoil, spot, stain, sully, taint, tarnish
Antonyms *n* ≠ **mark:** enhancement, improvement, ornament, perfection, purity, refinement ◆ *vb* ≠ **mark:** correct, enhance, improve, perfect, purify, refine, restore

blench *vb* = **recoil,** cower, cringe, falter, flinch, hesitate, quail, quake, quiver, shrink, shudder, shy, start, wince

blend *vb* **1, 2** = **mix,** amalgamate, coalesce, combine, compound, fuse, intermix, meld, merge, mingle, synthesize, unite **3** = **go well,** complement, fit, go with, harmonize, suit ◆ *n* **5, 6** = **mixture,** alloy, amalgam, amalgamation, combination, composite, compound, concoction, fusion, meld, mix, synthesis, union

bless *vb* **1** = **sanctify,** anoint, consecrate, dedicate, exalt, hallow, invoke happiness on, ordain **2** = **praise,** extol, give thanks to, glorify, magnify, thank **6** = **endow,** bestow, favour, give, grace, grant, provide
Antonyms *vb* ≠ **sanctify:** anathematize, curse, damn, excommunicate, execrate, fulminate, imprecate ≠ **endow:** afflict, blight, burden, curse, destroy, doom, plague, scourge, torment, trouble, vex

blessed *adj* **1** = **holy,** adored, beatified, divine, hallowed, revered, sacred, sanctified **4** = **fortunate,** blissful, contented, endowed, favoured, glad, happy, jammy (*Brit. sl.*), joyful, joyous, lucky

blessedness *n* **1, 3** = **sanctity,** beatitude, heavenly joy, state of grace, *summum bonum* **4** = **happiness,** bliss, blissfulness, content, felicity, pleasure

blessing *n* **1-3** = **benediction,** benison, commendation, consecration, dedication, grace, invocation, thanksgiving **4** = **approval,** approbation, backing, concurrence, consent, favour, good wishes, leave, permission, regard, sanction, support **6** = **benefit,** advantage, boon, bounty, favour, gain, gift, godsend, good fortune, help, kindness, profit, service, windfall
Antonyms *n* ≠ **benediction:** condemnation, curse, malediction ≠ **approval:** disapproval, disfavour, objection, reproof ≠ **benefit:** damage, deprivation, disadvantage, drawback, harm, misfortune

blether *Scot.* **2** *n* = **jabbering,** blather, claptrap, drivel, gibberish, gobbledegook, jabber, moonshine, pap, twaddle

blight *n* **1, 2** = **disease,** canker, decay, fungus, infestation, mildew, pest, pestilence, rot **3** = **curse,** affliction, bane, contamination, corruption, evil, plague, pollution, scourge, woe ◆ *vb* **5** = **destroy,** blast, injure, nip in the bud, ruin, shrivel, taint with mildew, wither **6** = **frustrate,** dash, disappoint **7** = **spoil,** annihilate, crush, mar, nullify, put a damper on, ruin, undo, wreck
Antonyms *n* ≠ **curse:** benefaction, blessing, boon, bounty, favour, godsend, help, service

blind *adj* **1** = **sightless,** destitute of vision, eyeless, stone-blind, unseeing, unsighted, visionless **2** = **unaware of,** careless, heedless, ignorant, inattentive, inconsiderate, indifferent, injudicious, insensitive, neglectful, oblivious,

sight, light, or air. **22** a person, action, or thing that serves to deceive or conceal the truth. **23** Also: **blinder.** *Brit. sl.* a drunken binge. [OE *blind*]
▸ 'blindly *adv* ▸ 'blindness *n*

> **USAGE NOTE** See at **disabled.**

blind alley *n* **1** an alley open at one end only; cul-de-sac. **2** *Inf.* a situation in which no further progress can be made.
blind date *n Inf.* a prearranged social meeting between a man and a woman who have not met before.
blinder ('blaɪndə) *n* **1** an outstanding performance in sport. **2** *Brit. sl.* another name for **blind** (sense 23).
blinders ('blaɪndəz) *pl n* the usual US & Canad. word for **blinkers.**
blindfold ('blaɪnd,fəʊld) *vb (tr)* **1** to prevent (a person or animal) from seeing by covering (the eyes). ◆ *n* **2** a piece of cloth, etc., used to cover the eyes. ◆ *adj, adv* **3** having the eyes covered with a cloth or bandage. **4** rash; inconsiderate. [changed (C16) through association with FOLD[1] from OE *blindfellian* to strike blind; see BLIND, FELL[2]]
blinding ❶ ('blaɪndɪŋ) *adj* **1** making one blind or as if blind. **2** most noticeable; brilliant or dazzling.
blind man's buff *n* a game in which a blindfolded person tries to catch and identify the other players. [C16: *buff*, ?from OF *buffe* a blow; see BUFFET[2]]
blind register *n* (in Britain) a list of those who are blind and are therefore entitled to financial and other benefits.
blindsight ('blaɪnd,saɪt) *n* the ability to respond to visual stimuli without having any conscious visual experience; it can occur after some forms of brain damage.
blind spot *n* **1** a small oval-shaped area of the retina, where the optic nerve enters, in which vision is not experienced. **2** a place or area where vision is obscured. **3** a subject about which a person is ignorant or prejudiced.
blind trust *n* a trust fund that manages the financial affairs of a person without informing him or her of any investments made, so that the beneficiary cannot be accused of using public office for private gain.
blindworm ('blaɪnd,wɜːm) *n* another name for **slowworm.**
blink ❶ (blɪŋk) *vb* **1** to close and immediately reopen (the eyes or an eye), usually involuntarily. **2** *(intr)* to look with the eyes partially closed. **3** to shine intermittently or unsteadily. **4** *(tr; foll. by away, from, etc.)* to clear the eyes of (dust, tears, etc.). **5** (when *tr*, usually foll. by *at*) to be surprised or amazed. **6** (when *intr*, foll. by *at*) to pretend not to know or see (a fault, injustice, etc.). ◆ *n* **7** the act or an instance of blinking. **8** a glance; glimpse. **9** short for **iceblink** (sense 1). **10 on the blink.** *Sl.* not working properly. [C14: var. of BLENCH]
blinker[1] ('blɪŋkə) *n* **1** a flashing light for sending messages, as a warning device, etc., such as a direction indicator on a road vehicle. **2** *(often pl)* a slang word for **eye**[1] (sense 1).
blinker[2] ('blɪŋkə) *vb (tr)* **1** to provide (a horse) with blinkers. **2** to obscure or be obscured with or as with blinkers.
▸ 'blinkered *adj*
blinkers ('blɪŋkəz) *pl n (sometimes sing) Chiefly Brit.* leather sidepieces attached to a horse's bridle to prevent sideways vision.
blinking ('blɪŋkɪŋ) *adj, adv Inf.* (intensifier): *a blinking fool; a blinking good film.*
blip (blɪp) *n* **1** a repetitive sound, such as that produced by an electronic device. **2** Also called: **pip.** the spot of light on a radar screen indicating the position of an object. **3** a temporary irregularity recorded in the performance of something. ◆ *vb* **blips, blipping, blipped. 4** *(intr)* to produce a blip. [C20: imit.]
bliss ❶ (blɪs) *n* **1** perfect happiness; serene joy. **2** the ecstatic joy of heaven. [OE *blīths*; rel. to *blīthe* BLITHE]
blissful ❶ ('blɪsfʊl) *adj* **1** serenely joyful or glad. **2 blissful ignorance.** unawareness or inexperience of something unpleasant.
▸ 'blissfully *adv* ▸ 'blissfulness *n*
B list *n* **a** a category considered to be slightly below the most socially desirable. **b** *(as modifier)*: *B-list celebrities.* ◆ Cf. **A list.**
blister ❶ ('blɪstə) *n* **1** a small bubble-like elevation of the skin filled with serum, produced as a reaction to a burn, mechanical irritation, etc. **2** a swelling containing air or liquid, as on a painted surface. **3** *NZ sl.* **3a** a rebuke. **3b** a summons to court. ◆ *vb* **4** to have or cause to have blisters. **5** *(tr)* to attack verbally with great scorn or sarcasm. [C13: from OF *blestre*]
▸ 'blistered *adj*
blister pack *n* a type of pack for small goods, consisting of a transparent dome on a firm backing. Also called: **bubble pack.**
BLit *abbrev. for* Bachelor of Literature.
blithe ❶ (blaɪð) *adj* **1** very happy or cheerful; gay. **2** heedless; casual and indifferent. [OE *blīthe*]
▸ 'blithely *adv* ▸ 'blitheness *n*
blithering ('blɪðərɪŋ) *adj* **1** talking foolishly; jabbering. **2** *Inf.* stupid; foolish: *you blithering idiot.* [C19: var. of BLETHER + -ING[2]]
blithesome ('blaɪðsəm) *adj Literary.* cheery; merry.
BLitt *abbrev. for* Bachelor of Letters. [L *Baccalaureus Litterarum*]
blitz ❶ (blɪts) *n* **1** a violent and sustained attack, esp. with intensive aerial bombardment. **2** any sudden intensive attack or concerted effort. **3** *American football.* a defensive charge on the quarterback. ◆ *vb* **4** *(tr)* to attack suddenly and intensively. [C20: shortened from G *Blitzkrieg* lightning war]
Blitz (blɪts) *n* **the.** the systematic bombing of Britain in 1940–41 by the German Luftwaffe.
blitzkrieg ('blɪts,kriːg) *n* a swift intensive military attack designed to defeat the opposition quickly. [C20: from G: lightning war]
blizzard ❶ ('blɪzəd) *n* a strong cold wind accompanied by widespread heavy snowfall. [C19: from ?]
bloat ❶ (bləʊt) *vb* **1** to swell or cause to swell, as with a liquid or air. **2** to become or cause to be puffed up, as with conceit. **3** *(tr)* to cure (fish, esp. herring) by half drying in smoke. [C17: prob. rel. to ON *blautr* soaked]
▸ 'bloated *adj*
bloater ('bləʊtə) *n* a herring that has been salted in brine, smoked, and cured.
blob ❶ (blɒb) *n* **1** a soft mass or drop. **2** a spot, dab, or blotch of colour, ink, etc. **3** an indistinct or shapeless form or object. [C15: ? imit.]
bloc ❶ (blɒk) *n* a group of people or countries combined by a common interest. [from F: BLOCK]
block ❶ (blɒk) *n* **1** a large solid piece of wood, stone, or other material usually having at least one face fairly flat. **2** such a piece on which particular tasks may be done, as chopping, cutting, or beheading. **3** Also called: **building block.** one of a set of wooden or plastic cubes as a child's toy. **4** a form on which things are shaped: *a wig block.* **5** *Sl.* a person's head. **6 do one's block.** *Austral. & NZ sl.* to become angry. **7** a dull, unemotional, or hardhearted person. **8** a large building of offices, flats, etc. **9a** a group of buildings in a city bounded by intersecting streets on each side. **9b** the area or distance between such intersecting streets. **10** *Austral. & NZ.* an area of land for a house, farm, etc. **11** *NZ.* an area of bush reserved by licence for a trapper or hunter. **12** a piece of wood, metal, or other material having a design in relief, used for printing. **13** *Austral. & NZ.* a log, usually of willow, fastened to a timber base and used in a wood-chopping competition. **14** a cas-

THESAURUS

thoughtless, unconscious of, uncritical, undiscerning, unmindful of, unobservant **3** = **unreasoning,** indiscriminate, prejudiced **4** = **unthinking,** hasty, impetuous, irrational, mindless, rash, reckless, senseless, uncontrollable, uncontrolled, violent, wild **6** = **hidden,** concealed, dim, obscured **7** = **dead-end,** closed, dark, leading nowhere, obstructed, without exit ◆ *n* **21, 22** = **cover,** camouflage, cloak, façade, feint, front, mask, masquerade, screen, smoke screen
Antonyms *adj* ≠ **sightless:** seeing, sighted ≠ **unaware of:** alive to, attentive, aware, concerned, conscious, discerning, heedful, knowledgeable, noticeable, observant ≠ **hidden:** obvious, open
blinding *adj* **2** = **bright,** bedazzling, blurring, brilliant, dazzling, flaming, glaring, intense
blindly *adv* **4** = **thoughtlessly,** aimlessly, carelessly, heedlessly, impulsively, inconsiderately, madly, passionately, purposelessly, recklessly, regardlessly, senselessly, wildly, wilfully
blink *vb* **1** = **wink,** bat, flutter, nictate, nictitate **2** = **peer,** glimpse, squint **3** = **flicker,** flash, gleam, glimmer, scintillate, shine, sparkle, twinkle, wink **6** = **turn a blind eye to,** condone, connive at, disregard, ignore, overlook, pass by ◆ *n* **10 on the blink** *Slang* = **not working (properly),** faulty, malfunctioning, out of action, out of order, playing up
blinkered[2] *adj* **2** = **narrow-minded,** biased, constricted, discriminatory, hidebound, insular, narrow, one-sided, parochial, partial, prejudiced, restrictive, selective
Antonyms *adj* broad-minded, impartial, open-minded, unbiased, unprejudiced
bliss *n* **1** = **joy,** blissfulness, ecstasy, euphoria, felicity, gladness, happiness, rapture **2** = **heaven,** beatitude, blessedness, nirvana, paradise
Antonyms *n* ≠ **joy:** affliction, anguish, distress, grief, heartbreak, misery, mourning, regret, sadness, sorrow, unhappiness, woe, wretchedness
blissful *adj* **1** = **joyful,** cock-a-hoop, delighted, ecstatic, elated, enchanted, enraptured, euphoric, happy, heavenly *(inf.)*, in ecstasies, joyous, over the moon *(inf.)*, rapt, rapturous
blister *n* **1** = **sore,** abscess, blain, bleb, boil, bubble, canker, carbuncle, cyst, pimple, pustule, swelling, ulcer, welt, wen
blithe *adj* **1** = **happy,** animated, buoyant, carefree, cheerful, cheery, chirpy *(inf.)*, debonair, gay, genial, gladsome, jaunty, light-hearted, merry, mirthful, sprightly, sunny, upbeat *(inf.)*, vivacious **2** = **heedless,** careless, casual, indifferent, nonchalant, thoughtless, unconcerned, untroubled
Antonyms *adj* ≠ **happy:** dejected, depressed, gloomy, melancholy, morose, sad, unhappy ≠ **heedless:** concerned, preoccupied, thoughtful
blitz *n* **1, 2** = **attack,** assault, blitzkrieg, bombardment, campaign, offensive, onslaught, raid, strike
blizzard *n* = **snowstorm,** blast, gale, squall, storm, tempest
bloat *vb* **1** = **puff up,** balloon, blow up, dilate, distend, enlarge, expand, inflate, swell
Antonyms *vb* contract, deflate, shrink, shrivel, wither, wrinkle
bloated *adj* **1** = **puffed up,** blown-up, bulging, dilated, distended, enlarged, expanded, inflated, puffy, swollen, tumescent, tumid, turgid
Antonyms *adj* contracted, deflated, flaccid, shrivelled, shrunken, withered, wrinkled
blob *n* **1** = **drop,** ball, bead, bubble, droplet, glob, globule, lump, mass, pearl, pellet, pill **2** = **dab**
bloc *n* = **group,** alliance, axis, cabal, clique, coalition, combine, entente, faction, league, ring, schism, union, wing
block *n* **1** = **piece,** bar, brick, cake, chunk, cube, hunk, ingot, lump, mass, nugget, square **15** = **obstruction,** bar, barrier, blockage, hindrance, impediment, jam, obstacle, occlusion, stoppage ◆ *vb* **21** = **obstruct,** bung up *(inf.)*, choke,

ing housing one or more freely rotating pulleys. See also **block and tackle.** **15** an obstruction or hindrance. **16** *Pathol.* **16a** interference in the normal physiological functioning of an organ or part. **16b** See **heart block. 16c** See **nerve block. 17** *Psychol.* a short interruption of perceptual or thought processes. **18** obstruction of an opponent in a sport. **19a** a quantity handled or considered as a single unit. **19b** (*as modifier*): *a block booking.* **20** *Athletics.* short for **starting block.** ◆ *vb* (*mainly tr*) **21** (often foll. by *up*) to obstruct (a passage, channel, etc.) or prevent or impede the motion or flow of (something or someone) by introducing an obstacle: *to block the traffic; to block up a pipe.* **22** to impede, retard, or prevent (an action, procedure, etc.). **23** to stamp (a title, design, etc.) on (a book cover, etc.) esp. using gold leaf. **24** to shape by use of a block: *to block a hat.* **25** (*also intr*) *Sport.* to obstruct or impede movement by (an opponent). **26** to interrupt a physiological function, as by use of an anaesthetic. **27** (*also intr*) *Cricket.* to play (a ball) defensively. ◆ See also **block in, block out.** [C14: from OF *bloc,* from Du. *blok*]
▸ **'blocker** *n*

blockade ➊ (blɒ'keɪd) *n* **1** *Mil.* the interdiction of a nation's sea lines of communications, esp. of an individual port by the use of sea power. **2** something that prevents access or progress. **3** *Med.* the inhibition of the effect of a hormone or the action of a nerve by a drug. ◆ *vb* **blockades, blockading, blockaded.** (*tr*) **4** to impose a blockade on. **5** to obstruct the way to. [C17: from BLOCK + *-ade,* as in AMBUSCADE]
▸ **block'ader** *n*

blockage ➊ ('blɒkɪdʒ) *n* **1** the act of blocking or state of being blocked. **2** an object causing an obstruction.

block and tackle *n* a hoisting device in which a rope or chain is passed around a pair of blocks containing one or more pulleys.

blockboard ('blɒk,bɔːd) *n* a bonded board in which strips of soft wood are sandwiched between two layers of veneer.

blockbuster ('blɒk,bʌstə) *n Inf.* **1** a large bomb used to demolish extensive areas. **2** a very successful, effective, or forceful person, thing, etc. **3** a lavish film, show, novel, etc., that proves to be an outstanding popular success.

block diagram *n* **1** a diagram showing the interconnections between the parts of an industrial process. **2** *Computing.* a diagram showing the interconnections between electronic components or parts of a program.

blockhead ➊ ('blɒk,hɛd) *n Derog.* a stupid person.
▸ **'block,headed** *adj*

blockhouse ('blɒk,haʊs) *n* **1** (formerly) a wooden fortification with ports for defensive fire, observation, etc. **2** a concrete structure strengthened to give protection against enemy fire, with apertures to allow defensive gunfire. **3** a building constructed of logs or squared timber.

block in *vb* (*tr, adv*) to sketch or outline with little detail.

blockish ('blɒkɪʃ) *adj* lacking vivacity or imagination; stupid.
▸ **'blockishly** *adv*

block letter *n* **1** *Printing.* a less common name for **sans serif. 2** Also called: **block capital.** a plain capital letter.

block out ➊ *vb* (*tr, adv*) **1** to plan or describe (something) in a general fashion. **2** to prevent the entry or consideration of (something).

block release *n Brit.* the release of industrial trainees from work for study at a college for several weeks.

block vote *n Brit.* (at a trade-union conference) the system whereby each delegate's vote has a value in proportion to the number of people he represents.

bloke ➊ (bləʊk) *n Brit. & Austral.* an informal word for **man.** [C19: from Shelta]

blokeish *or* **blokish** ('bləʊkɪʃ) *adj Brit. inf., sometimes derog.* denoting or exhibiting the characteristics believed typical of an ordinary man. Also: **blokey** ('bləʊkɪ).
▸ **'blokeishness** *or* **'blokishness** *n*

blonde ➊ *or* (*masc*) **blond** (blɒnd) *adj* **1** (of hair) of a light colour; fair. **2** (of people or a race) having fair hair, a light complexion, and, typically, blue or grey eyes. ◆ *n* **3** a person having light-coloured hair and skin. [C15: from OF *blond* (fem *blonde*), prob. of Gmc origin]
▸ **'blondeness** *or* **'blondness** *n*

blood ➊ (blʌd) *n* **1** a reddish fluid in vertebrates that is pumped by the heart through the arteries and veins. **2** a similar fluid in invertebrates. **3** bloodshed, esp. when resulting in murder. **4** life itself; lifeblood. **5** relationship through being of the same family, race, or kind; kinship. **6 flesh and blood. 6a** near kindred or kinship, esp. that between a parent and child. **6b** human nature (esp. in **it's more than flesh and blood can stand**). **7 in one's blood.** as a natural or inherited characteristic or talent. **8 the blood.** royal or noble descent: *a prince of the blood.* **9** temperament; disposition; temper. **10a** good or pure breeding; pedigree. **10b** (*as modifier*): *blood horses.* **11** people viewed as members of a group, esp. as an invigorating force (**new blood, young blood**). **12** *Chiefly Brit., rare.* a dashing young man. **13 in cold blood.** showing no passion; deliberately; ruthlessly. **14 make one's blood boil.** to cause to be angry or indignant. **15 make one's blood run cold.** to fill with horror. ◆ *vb* (*tr*) **16** *Hunting.* to cause (young hounds) to taste the blood of a freshly killed quarry. **17** to initiate (a person) to war or hunting. [OE *blōd*]

blood-and-thunder *adj* denoting or relating to a melodramatic adventure story.

blood bank *n* a place where whole blood or blood plasma is stored until required in transfusion.

blood bath *n* indiscriminate slaughter; a massacre.

blood brother *n* **1** a brother by birth. **2** a man or boy who has sworn to treat another as his brother, often in a ceremony in which their blood is mingled.

blood count *n* determination of the number of red and white blood corpuscles in a specific sample of blood.

bloodcurdling ➊ ('blʌd,kɜːdlɪŋ) *adj* terrifying; horrifying.
▸ **'blood,curdlingly** *adv*

blood donor *n* a person who gives his blood to be used for transfusion.

blood doping *n* the illegal practice of removing a quantity of blood from an athlete long before a race and reinjecting it shortly before a race, so boosting oxygenation of the blood.

blooded ('blʌdɪd) *adj* **1** (of horses, cattle, etc.) of good breeding. **2** (*in combination*) having blood or temperament as specified: *hot-blooded, cold-blooded, warm-blooded, red-blooded.*

blood group *n* any one of the various groups into which human blood is classified on the basis of its specific agglutinating properties. Also called: **blood type.**

blood heat *n* the normal temperature of the human body, 98.4°F. or 37°C.

bloodhound ('blʌd,haʊnd) *n* a large breed of hound, formerly used in tracking and police work.

bloodless ➊ ('blʌdlɪs) *adj* **1** without blood. **2** conducted without violence (esp. in **bloodless revolution**). **3** anaemic-looking; pale. **4** lacking vitality; lifeless. **5** lacking in emotion; unfeeling.
▸ **'bloodlessly** *adv* ▸ **'bloodlessness** *n*

blood-letting ('blʌd,lɛtɪŋ) *n* **1** the therapeutic removal of blood. See also **phlebotomy. 2** bloodshed, esp. in a feud.

bloodline ('blʌd,laɪn) *n* all the members of a family group over generations, esp. regarding characteristics common to that group; pedigree.

blood money *n* **1** compensation paid to the relatives of a murdered person. **2** money paid to a hired murderer. **3** a reward for information about a criminal, esp. a murderer.

blood orange *n* a variety of orange all or part of the pulp of which is dark red when ripe.

blood poisoning *n* a nontechnical term for **septicaemia.**

blood pressure *n* the pressure exerted by the blood on the inner walls of the arteries, being relative to the elasticity and diameter of the vessels and the force of the heartbeat.

blood pudding *n* another name for **black pudding.**

blood relation *or* **relative** *n* a person related to another by birth, as distinct from one related by marriage.

bloodshed ➊ ('blʌd,ʃɛd) *n* slaughter; killing.

bloodshot ('blʌd,ʃɒt) *adj* (of an eye) inflamed.

blood sport *n* any sport involving the killing of an animal, esp. hunting.

bloodstain ('blʌd,steɪn) *n* a dark discoloration caused by blood, esp. dried blood.
▸ **'blood,stained** *adj*

bloodstock ('blʌd,stɒk) *n* thoroughbred horses.

bloodstone ('blʌd,stəʊn) *n* a dark green variety of chalcedony with red spots: used as a gemstone. Also called: **heliotrope.**

bloodstream ('blʌd,striːm) *n* the flow of blood through the vessels of a living body.

blood substitute *n* a mixture of plasma, albumin, and dextran used to replace lost blood or increase the blood volume.

bloodsucker ('blʌd,sʌkə) *n* **1** an animal that sucks blood, esp. a leech or mosquito. **2** *Inf.* a person or thing that preys upon another person, esp. by extorting money.
▸ **'blood,sucking** *adj*

THESAURUS

clog, close, plug, stem the flow, stop up **22** = **stop,** arrest, bar, check, deter, halt, hinder, hobble, impede, obstruct, put a spoke in someone's wheel, throw a spanner in the works, thwart

Antonyms *vb* ≠ **obstruct:** clear, open, unblock, unclog ≠ **stop:** advance, aid, expedite, facilitate, foster, further, lend support to, promote, push, support

blockade *n* **1** = **barricade,** encirclement, siege **2** = **stoppage,** barrier, block, closure, hindrance, impediment, obstacle, obstruction, restriction

blockage *n* **1, 2** = **obstruction,** block, blocking, impediment, occlusion, stoppage, stopping up

blockhead *n* = **fool,** dimwit (*inf.*), dipstick (*Brit. sl.*), divvy (*Brit. sl.*), dolt, dork (*sl.*), dunce, fathead (*inf.*), idiot, ignoramus, jerk (*sl., chiefly US & Canad.*), nerd *or* nurd (*sl.*), nitwit, numbskull *or* numskull, pillock (*Brit. sl.*), plonker (*sl.*), prat (*sl.*), schmuck (*US sl.*), thickhead, twit (*inf., chiefly Brit.*)

block out *vb* **1** = **outline,** chart, map out, plan, sketch

bloke *n Informal* = **man,** chap, character (*inf.*), customer (*inf.*), fellow, guy (*inf.*), individual, person, punter (*inf.*)

blonde *adj* **1** = **fair,** fair-haired, fair-skinned, flaxen, golden-haired, light, light-coloured, light-complexioned, tow-headed

blood *n* **1** = **lifeblood,** gore, vital fluid **5** = **family,** ancestry, birth, consanguinity, descendants, descent, extraction, kindred, kinship, lineage, noble extraction, relations **9** = **feeling,** disposition, passion, spirit, temper

bloodcurdling *adj* = **terrifying,** appalling, chilling, dreadful, fearful, frightening, hair-raising, horrendous, horrifying, scaring, spine-chilling

bloodless *adj* **3** = **pale,** anaemic, ashen, chalky, colourless, like death warmed up (*inf.*), pallid, pasty, sallow, sickly, wan **4, 5** = **listless,** cold, languid, lifeless, passionless, spiritless, torpid, unemotional, unfeeling

bloodshed *n* = **killing,** blood bath,

blood sugar *n Med.* the glucose circulating in the blood: the normal fasting level is between 3·9 and 5·6 millimoles per litre.

bloodthirsty Ⓣ (ˈblʌd,θɜːstɪ) *adj* **bloodthirstier, bloodthirstiest. 1** murderous; cruel. **2** taking pleasure in bloodshed or violence. **3** describing or depicting killing and violence; gruesome.
▸ **ˈblood,thirstily** *adv* ▸ **ˈblood,thirstiness** *n*

blood type *n* another name for **blood group.**

blood vessel *n* an artery, capillary, or vein.

bloodwood (ˈblʌd,wʊd) *n* any of several species of Australian eucalyptus with red sap.

bloody Ⓣ (ˈblʌdɪ) *adj* **bloodier, bloodiest. 1** covered or stained with blood. **2** resembling or composed of blood. **3** marked by much killing and bloodshed: *a bloody war.* **4** cruel or murderous: *a bloody tyrant.* ◆ *adv, adj* **5** *Sl.* (intensifier): *a bloody fool.* ◆ *vb* **bloodies, bloodying, bloodied. 6** (*tr*) to stain with blood.
▸ **ˈbloodily** *adv* ▸ **ˈbloodiness** *n*

Bloody Mary (ˈmɛərɪ) *n* **1** nickname of Mary I of England. **2** a drink consisting of tomato juice and vodka.

bloody-minded Ⓣ *adj Brit. inf.* deliberately obstructive and unhelpful.

bloom[1] Ⓣ (bluːm) *n* **1** a blossom on a flowering plant; a flower. **2** the state, time, or period when flowers open. **3** open flowers collectively. **4** a healthy, vigorous, or flourishing condition; prime. **5** youthful or healthy rosiness in the cheeks or face; glow. **6** a fine whitish coating on the surface of fruits, leaves, etc. **7** Also called: **chill.** a dull area on the surface of old gloss paint, lacquer, or varnish. **8** *Ecology.* a visible increase in the algal constituent of plankton, which may be due to excessive organic pollution. ◆ *vb* (*intr*) **9** (of flowers) to open; come into flower. **10** to bear flowers; blossom. **11** to flourish or grow. **12** to be in a healthy, glowing, or flourishing condition. [C13: of Gmc origin; cf. ON *blōm* flower]

bloom[2] (bluːm) *n* a rectangular mass of metal obtained by rolling or forging a cast ingot. [OE *blōma* lump of metal]

bloomer[1] (ˈbluːmə) *n* a plant that flowers, esp. in a specified way: *a night bloomer.*

bloomer[2] (ˈbluːmə) *n Brit. inf.* a stupid mistake; blunder. [C20: from BLOOMING]

bloomer[3] (ˈbluːmə) *n Brit.* a medium-sized loaf, glazed and notched on top. [C20: from?]

bloomers (ˈbluːməz) *pl n* **1** *Inf.* women's baggy knickers. **2** (formerly) loose trousers gathered at the knee worn by women for cycling, etc. **3** *History.* loose trousers gathered at the ankle and worn under a shorter skirt. [after Amelia *Bloomer* (1818–94), US social reformer]

blooming (ˈbluːmɪŋ) *adv, adj Brit. inf.* (intensifier): *a blooming genius; blooming painful.* [C19: euphemistic for BLOODY]

blossom Ⓣ (ˈblɒsəm) *n* **1** the flower or flowers of a plant, esp. producing edible fruit. **2** the time or period of flowering. ◆ *vb* (*intr*) **3** (of plants) to come into flower. **4** to develop or come to a promising stage. [OE *blōstm*]
▸ **ˈblossomy** *adj*

blot Ⓣ (blɒt) *n* **1** a stain or spot of ink, paint, dirt, etc. **2** something that spoils. **3** a blemish or stain on one's character or reputation. **4** *Austral. sl.* the anus. ◆ *vb* **blots, blotting, blotted. 5** (of ink, dye, etc.) to form spots or blobs on (a material) or (of a person) to cause such spots or blobs to form on (a material). **6** (*intr*) to stain or become stained or spotted. **7** (*tr*) to cause a blemish in or on; disgrace. **8** to soak up (excess ink, etc.) by using blotting paper. **9** (of blotting paper) to absorb (excess ink, etc.). **10** (*tr;* often foll. by *out*) **10a** to darken or hide completely; obscure; obliterate. **10b** to destroy; annihilate. [C14: prob. of Gmc origin]

blotch Ⓣ (blɒtʃ) *n* **1** an irregular spot or discoloration, esp. a dark and relatively large one. ◆ *vb* **2** to become or cause to become marked by such discoloration. [C17: prob. from BOTCH, infl. by BLOT]
▸ **ˈblotchy** *adj*

blotter (ˈblɒtə) *n* something used to absorb excess ink, esp. a sheet of blotting paper.

blotting paper *n* a soft absorbent unsized paper, used esp. for soaking up surplus ink.

blotto (ˈblɒtəʊ) *adj Sl.* unconscious, esp. through drunkenness. [C20: from BLOT (vb)]

blouse (blaʊz) *n* **1** a woman's shirtlike garment. **2** a waist-length belted jacket worn by soldiers. ◆ *vb* **blouses, blousing, bloused. 3** to hang or make so as to hang in full loose folds. [C19: from F, from ?]

blouson (ˈbluːzɒn) *n* a tight-waisted jacket or top that blouses out. [C20: from F]

blow[1] Ⓣ (bləʊ) *vb* **blows, blowing, blew, blown. 1** (of a current of air, the wind, etc.) to be or cause to be in motion. **2** (*intr*) to move or be carried by or as if by wind. **3** to expel (air, cigarette smoke, etc.) through the mouth or nose. **4** to force or cause (air, dust, etc.) to move (into, in, over, etc.) by using an instrument or by expelling breath. **5** (*intr*) to breathe hard; pant. **6** (sometimes foll. by *up*) to inflate with air or the breath. **7** (*intr*) (of wind, a storm, etc.) to make a roaring sound. **8** to cause (a whistle, siren, etc.) to sound by forcing air into it or (of a whistle, etc.) to sound thus. **9** (*tr*) to force air from the lungs through (the nose) to clear out mucus. **10** (often foll. by *up, down, in,* etc.) to explode, break, or disintegrate completely. **11** *Electronics.* to burn out (a fuse, valve, etc.) because of excessive current or (of a fuse, valve, etc.) to burn out. **12** (*tr*) to wind (a horse) by making it run excessively. **13** to cause (a wind instrument) to sound by forcing one's breath into the mouthpiece or (of such an instrument) to sound in this way. **14** (*intr*) (of flies) to lay eggs (in). **15** to shape (glass, ornaments, etc.) by forcing air or gas through the material when molten. **16** (*tr*) *Sl.* to spend (money) freely. **17** (*tr*) *Sl.* to use (an opportunity) ineffectively. **18** *Sl.* to go suddenly away (from). **19** (*tr*) *Sl.* to expose or betray (a secret). **20** (p.p. **blowed**). *Inf.* another word for **damn. 21 blow hot and cold.** *Inf.* to vacillate. **22 blow one's top.** *Inf.* to lose one's temper. ◆ *n* **23** the act or an instance of blowing. **24** the sound produced by blowing. **25** a blast of air or wind. **26a** *Brit.* a slang name for **cannabis** (sense 2). **26b** *US* a slang name for **cocaine. 27** *Austral. sl.* a brief rest; a breather. ◆ See also **blow away, blow in,** etc. [OE *blāwan*]

blow[2] Ⓣ (bləʊ) *n* **1** a powerful or heavy stroke with the fist, a weapon, etc. **2 at one** *or* **a blow.** by or with only one action. **3** a sudden setback. **4 come to blows. 4a** to fight. **4b** to result in a fight. **5** an attacking action: *a blow for freedom.* **6** *Austral. & NZ.* a stroke of the shears in sheep-shearing. [C15: prob. of Gmc origin]

blow[3] (bləʊ) *vb* **blows, blowing, blew, blown. 1** (*intr*) (of a plant or flower) to blossom or open out. ◆ *n* **2** a mass of blossoms. **3** the state or period of blossoming. [OE *blōwan*]

blow away *vb* (*tr, adv*) *Sl., chiefly US.* **1** to kill (someone) by shooting. **2** to defeat decisively.

blow-by-blow *adj* (*prenominal*) explained in great detail: *a blow-by-blow account.*

blow-dry *vb* **blow-dries, blow-drying, blow-dried. 1** (*tr*) to style (the hair) while drying it with a hand-held hair dryer. ◆ *n* **2** this method of styling hair.

blower (ˈbləʊə) *n* **1** a mechanical device, such as a fan, that blows. **2** a low-pressure compressor, esp. in a furnace or internal-combustion engine. **3** an informal name for **telephone.**

blowfish (ˈbləʊ,fɪʃ) *n, pl* **blowfish** *or* **blowfishes.** a popular name for **puffer** (sense 2).

blowfly (ˈbləʊ,flaɪ) *n, pl* **blowflies.** any of various flies that lay their eggs in rotting meat, dung, carrion, and open wounds. Also called: **bluebottle.**

blowgun (ˈbləʊ,gʌn) *n* the US word for **blowpipe** (sense 1).

blowhard (ˈbləʊ,hɑːd) *Inf.* ◆ *n* **1** a boastful person. ◆ *adj* **2** blustering or boastful.

blowhole (ˈbləʊ,həʊl) *n* **1** the nostril of whales, situated far back on the skull. **2** a hole in ice through which whales, seals, etc., breathe. **3** *Geol.* a hole in a cliff top leading to a sea cave through which air is forced by the action of the sea. **4a** a vent for air or gas. **4b** *NZ.* a hole emitting gas or steam in a volcanic region.

blow in *Inf.* ◆ *vb* **1** (*intr, adv*) to arrive or enter suddenly. ◆ *n* **blow-in. 2** *Austral.* a newcomer.

THESAURUS

blood-letting, butchery, carnage, gore, massacre, murder, slaughter, slaying

bloodthirsty *adj* **1, 2** = **cruel**, barbarous, brutal, cut-throat, ferocious, inhuman, murderous, ruthless, savage, vicious, warlike **3** = **gory**

bloody *adj* **1** = **bloodstained**, bleeding, blood-soaked, blood-spattered, gaping, raw, unstaunched **4** = **cruel**, ferocious, fierce, sanguinary, savage

bloody-minded *adj Brit. informal* = **difficult**, awkward, contrary, cussed (*inf.*), obstructive, perverse, uncooperative, unhelpful, unreasonable
Antonyms *adj* accommodating, cooperative, fair-minded, helpful, open-minded, reasonable

bloom[1] *n* **1** = **flower**, blossom, bud **2** = **blossoming**, efflorescence, opening (*of flowers*) **4** = **prime**, beauty, flourishing, health, heyday, perfection, vigour **5** = **glow**, blush, flush, freshness, lustre, radiance, rosiness ◆ *vb* **9, 10** = **blossom**, blow, bud, burgeon, open, sprout **11** = **flourish**, develop, fare well, grow, prosper, succeed, thrive, wax
Antonyms *n* ≠ **glow**: bloodlessness, paleness, pallor, wanness, whiteness ◆ *vb* ≠ **blossom, flourish**: decay, decline, die, droop, fade, fail, languish, perish, shrink, shrivel, wane, waste, wilt, wither

blossom *n* **1** = **flower**, bloom, bud, floret, flowers ◆ *vb* **3** = **flower**, bloom, burgeon **4** = **grow**, bloom, develop, flourish, mature, progress, prosper, thrive

blot *n* **1** = **spot**, blotch, mark, patch, smear, smudge, speck, splodge **2** = **stain**, blemish, blur, defect, fault, flaw, scar, spot, taint **3** = **disgrace**, blot on one's escutcheon, demerit, smirch ◆ *vb* **5, 6** = **stain**, bespatter, disfigure, mark, smudge, spoil, spot, tarnish **7** = **disgrace**, smirch, sully **8, 9** = **soak up**, absorb, dry, take up **10a** = **erase**, darken, destroy, eclipse, efface, obscure, shadow **10b** cancel, expunge

blotch *n, vb* = **mark**, blemish, blot, patch, scar, smirch, smudge, smutch, splash, splodge, spot, stain

blotchy *adj* = **spotty**, blemished, patchy, reddened, scurvy, uneven

blow[1] *vb* **1, 2** = **carry**, bear, buffet, drive, fling, flutter, move, sweep, waft, whirl, whisk **3** = **exhale**, breathe **5** = **pant**, puff **8** = **play**, blare, mouth, pipe, sound, toot, trumpet, vibrate **22 blow one's top** *Informal* = **lose one's temper**, blow up (*inf.*), do one's nut (*Brit. sl.*), explode, flip one's lid (*sl.*), fly into a temper, fly off the handle (*inf.*), go spare (*Brit. sl.*), have a fit (*inf.*), lose it (*inf.*), lose the plot (*inf.*), see red (*inf.*), throw a tantrum ◆ *n* **25** = **gust**, blast, draught, flurry, gale, puff, strong breeze, tempest, wind

blow[2] *n* **1** = **knock**, bang, bash (*inf.*), belt (*inf.*), buffet, clout (*inf.*), clump (*sl.*), punch, rap, slosh (*Brit. sl.*), smack, sock (*sl.*), stroke, thump, wallop (*inf.*), whack **3** = **setback**, affliction, bolt from the blue, bombshell, bummer (*sl.*), calamity, catastrophe, choker (*inf.*), comedown (*inf.*), disappointment, disaster, jolt, misfortune, re-

blow job *Taboo.* a slang term for **fellatio.**

blowlamp ('bləʊˌlæmp) *n* another name for **blowtorch.**

blown (bləʊn) *vb* the past participle of **blow**[1] and **blow**[3].

blow out Ⓣ *vb (adv)* **1** to extinguish (a flame, candle, etc.) or (of a flame, etc.) to become extinguished. **2** *(intr)* (of a tyre) to puncture suddenly, esp. at high speed. **3** *(intr)* (of a fuse) to melt suddenly. **4** *(tr; often reflexive)* to diminish or use up the energy of: *the storm blew itself out.* **5** *(intr)* (of an oil or gas well) to lose oil or gas in an uncontrolled manner. ◆ *n* **blowout. 6** the sudden melting of an electrical fuse. **7** a sudden burst in a tyre. **8** the uncontrolled escape of oil or gas from an oil or gas well. **9** *Sl.* a large filling meal or lavish entertainment.

blow over Ⓣ *vb (intr, adv)* **1** to cease or be finished: *the storm blew over.* **2** to be forgotten.

blowpipe ('bləʊˌpaɪp) *n* **1** a long tube from which pellets, poisoned darts, etc., are shot by blowing. **2** Also called: **blow tube.** a tube for blowing air or oxygen into a flame to intensify its heat. **3** a long narrow iron pipe used to gather molten glass and blow it into shape.

blowsy Ⓣ *or* **blowzy** ('blaʊzɪ) *adj* **blowsier, blowsiest** *or* **blowzier, blowziest. 1** (esp. of a woman) untidy in appearance; slovenly or sluttish. **2** (of a woman) ruddy in complexion. [C18: from dialect *blowze* beggar girl, from ?]

blow through *vb (intr, adv) Austral. inf.* to leave; make off.

blowtorch ('bləʊˌtɔːtʃ) *n* a small burner that produces a very hot flame, used to remove paint, melt soft metal, etc.

blow up Ⓣ *vb (adv)* **1** to explode or cause to explode. **2** *(tr)* to increase the importance of (something): *they blew the whole affair up.* **3** *(intr)* to arise: *we lived very quietly before this affair blew up.* **4** *(intr)* to come into existence with sudden force: *a storm had blown up.* **5** *(intr) Inf.* to lose one's temper (with a person). **6** *(tr) Inf.* to reprimand. **7** *(tr) Inf.* to enlarge the size of (a photograph). ◆ *n* **blow-up. 8** an explosion. **9** *Inf.* an enlarged photograph or part of a photograph. **10** *Inf.* a fit of temper.

blowy ('bləʊɪ) *adj* **blowier, blowiest.** another word for **windy** (sense 1).

blub (blʌb) *vb* **blubs, blubbing, blubbed.** *Brit.* a slang word for **blubber** (senses 1–3).

blubber ('blʌbə) *vb* **1** to sob without restraint. **2** to utter while sobbing. **3** *(tr)* to make (the face) wet and swollen by crying. ◆ *n* **4** the fatty tissue of aquatic mammals such as the whale. **5** *Inf.* flabby body fat. **6** the act or an instance of weeping without restraint. ◆ *adj* **7** *(often in combination)* swollen or fleshy: *blubber-faced.* [C12: ?from Low G *blubbern* to BUBBLE, imit.]
▸ **'blubberer** *n* ▸ **'blubbery** *adj*

bludge (blʌdʒ) *Austral. & NZ inf.* ◆ *vb* **bludges, bludging, bludged. 1** (when *intr,* often foll. by *on*) to scrounge from (someone). **2** *(intr)* to skive. ◆ *n* **3** a very easy task. [C19: back formation from *bludger* pimp, from BLUDGEON]

bludgeon Ⓣ ('blʌdʒən) *n* **1** a stout heavy club, typically thicker at one end. **2** a person, line of argument, etc., that is effective but unsubtle. ◆ *vb (tr)* **3** to hit as with a bludgeon. **4** (often foll. by *into*) to force; bully; coerce. [C18: from ?]

bludger ('blʌdʒə) *n Austral. & NZ inf.* **1** a person who scrounges. **2** a person who avoids work. **3** a person in authority regarded as ineffectual by those working under him.

blue Ⓣ (bluː) *n* **1** any of a group of colours, such as that of a clear unclouded sky or the deep sea. **2** a dye or pigment of any of these colours. **3** blue cloth or clothing: *dressed in blue.* **4** a sportsman who represents or has represented Oxford or Cambridge University and has the right to wear the university colour. **5** *Brit.* an informal name for **Tory. 6** any of numerous small blue-winged butterflies. **7** a blue substance used in laundering. **8** *Austral. & NZ sl.* an argument or fight: *he had a blue with a taxi driver.* **9** Also: **bluey.** *Austral. & NZ sl.* a court summons. **10** *Austral. & NZ inf.* a mistake; error. **11 out of the blue.** apparently from nowhere; unexpectedly. ◆ *adj* **bluer, bluest. 12** of the colour blue. **13** (of the flesh) having a purple tinge, as from cold or contusion. **14** depressed, moody, or unhappy. **15** indecent, titillating, or pornographic: *blue films.* ◆ *vb* **blues, blueing** *or* **bluing, blued. 16** to make, dye, or become blue. **17** *(tr)* to treat (laundry) with blue. **18** *(tr) Sl.* to spend extravagantly or wastefully; squander. ◆ See also **blues.** [C13: from OF *bleu,* of Gmc origin]
▸ **'blueness** *n*

Blue (bluː) *or* **Bluey** ('bluːɪ) *n Austral. inf.* a person with red hair.

blue baby *n* a baby born with a bluish tinge to the skin because of lack of oxygen in the blood.

Bluebeard ('bluːˌbɪəd) *n* **1** a villain in European folk tales who marries several wives and murders them in turn. **2** a man who has had several wives.

bluebell ('bluːˌbɛl) *n* **1** Also called: **wild** *or* **wood hyacinth.** a European woodland plant having a one-sided cluster of blue bell-shaped flowers. **2** a Scottish name for **harebell. 3** any of various other plants with blue bell-shaped flowers.

blueberry ('bluːbərɪ, -brɪ) *n, pl* **blueberries. 1** Also called: **huckleberry.** any of several North American ericaceous shrubs that have blue-black edible berries with tiny seeds. See also **bilberry. 2** the fruit of any of these plants.

bluebird ('bluːˌbɜːd) *n* **1** a North American songbird of the thrush family having a blue or partly blue plumage. **2** any of various other birds having a blue plumage.

blue blood *n* royal or aristocratic descent. [C19: translation of Sp. *sangre azul*]
▸ **ˌblue-'blooded** *adj*

bluebook ('bluːˌbʊk) *n* **1** (in Britain) a government publication bound in a stiff blue paper cover: usually the report of a royal commission or a committee. **2** (in Canada) an annual statement of government accounts.

bluebottle ('bluːˌbɒtᵊl) *n* **1** another name for the **blowfly. 2** any of various blue-flowered plants, esp. the cornflower. **3** *Brit.* an informal word for a **policeman. 4** *Austral. & NZ.* an informal name for **Portuguese man-of-war.**

blue button *n* a trainee market maker on the London stock exchange. [C20: from the *blue button* badge worn in the lapel]

blue cheese *n* cheese containing a blue mould, esp. Stilton, Roquefort, or Danish Blue.

blue chip *n* **1** a gambling chip with the highest value. **2** *Finance.* a stock considered reliable with respect to both dividend income and capital value. **3** *(modifier)* denoting something considered to be a valuable asset.

blue-collar *adj* of or designating manual industrial workers. Cf. **white-collar.**

blue-eyed boy *n Inf., chiefly Brit.* the favourite or darling of a person or group.

bluefish ('bluːˌfɪʃ) *n, pl* **bluefish** *or* **bluefishes. 1** Also called: **snapper.** a bluish marine food and game fish, related to the horse mackerel. **2** any of various other bluish fishes.

Blue Flag *n* an award given to a seaside resort that meets EU standards of cleanliness of beaches and purity of water in bathing areas.

blue fox *n* **1** a variety of the arctic fox that has a pale grey winter coat. **2** the fur of this animal.

blue funk *n Sl.* a state of great terror.

bluegrass ('bluːˌgrɑːs) *n* **1** any of several North American bluish-green grasses, esp. **Kentucky bluegrass,** grown for forage. **2** a type of folk music originating in Kentucky.

blue-green algae *pl n* the former name for **cyanobacteria.**

blue ground *n Mineralogy.* another name for **kimberlite.**

blue gum *n* a tall fast-growing widely cultivated Australian eucalyptus, having bluish aromatic leaves containing a medicinal oil, bark that peels off in shreds, and hard timber.

blue heeler *n Austral.* a type of dog with dark speckled markings: used for herding cattle.

bluejacket ('bluːˌdʒækɪt) *n* a sailor in the Navy.

blue jay *n* a common North American jay having bright blue plumage.

blue moon Ⓣ *n* **once in a blue moon.** *Inf.* very rarely; almost never.

blue mould *n* any fungus that forms a bluish mass on decaying food, leather, etc. Also called: **green mould.**

blue pencil *n* **1** deletion, alteration, or censorship of the contents of a book or other work. ◆ *vb* **blue-pencil, blue-pencils, blue-pencilling, blue-pencilled** *or US* **blue-pencils, blue-penciling, blue-penciled. 2** *(tr)* to alter or delete parts of (a book, film, etc.), esp. to censor.

blue peter *n* a signal flag of blue with a white square at the centre, displayed by a vessel about to leave port. [C19: from the name *Peter*]

blue pointer *n* a large shark of Australian coastal waters, having a blue back and pointed snout.

blueprint Ⓣ ('bluːˌprɪnt) *n* **1** Also called: **cyanotype.** a photographic

THESAURUS

verse, shock, sucker punch, upset, whammy (*inf., chiefly US*)

blow out *vb* **1** = **put out**, extinguish, snuff **2** = **burst**, erupt, explode, rupture, shatter ◆ *n* **blowout 7** = **burst**, break, flat, flat tyre, leak, puncture, rupture, tear **8** = **explosion**, blast, detonation, eruption **9** *Slang* = **binge** (*inf.*), beano (*Brit. sl.*), carousal, carouse, feast, hooley *or* hoolie (*chiefly Irish & NZ*), party, rave (*Brit. sl.*), rave-up (*Brit. sl.*), spree

blow over *vb* **1** = **finish**, cease, die down, disappear, end, pass, pass away, subside, vanish **2** = **be forgotten**

blowsy *adj* **1** = **slovenly**, bedraggled, dishevelled, frowzy, slatternly, sloppy, sluttish, tousled, unkempt, untidy **2** = **red-faced**, florid, ruddy

blow up *vb* **1** = **explode**, blast, blow sky-high, bomb, burst, detonate, dynamite, go off, rupture, shatter **2** = **exaggerate**, blow out of (all) proportion, enlarge, enlarge on, heighten, magnify, make a mountain out of a molehill, make a production out of, overstate **5** *Informal* = **lose one's temper**, become angry, become enraged, blow a fuse (*sl., chiefly US*), crack up (*inf.*), erupt, flip one's lid (*sl.*), fly off the handle (*inf.*), go ballistic (*sl., chiefly US*), go off the deep end (*inf.*), go up the wall (*sl.*), hit the roof (*inf.*), lose it (*inf.*), rage, see red (*inf.*)

bludgeon *n* **1** = **club**, cosh (*Brit.*), cudgel, shillelagh, truncheon ◆ *vb* **3** = **club**, beat, beat up, cosh (*Brit.*), cudgel, knock down, strike **4** = **bully**, browbeat, bulldoze (*inf.*), coerce, dragoon, force, hector, put the screws on, railroad (*inf.*), steamroller

blue *adj* **1** = **azure**, cerulean, cobalt, cyan, navy, sapphire, sky-coloured, ultramarine **14** = **depressed**, dejected, despondent, dismal, downcast, down-hearted, down in the dumps (*inf.*), down in the mouth, fed up, gloomy, glum, low, melancholy, sad, unhappy **15** = **smutty**, bawdy, dirty, indecent, lewd, naughty, near the knuckle (*inf.*), obscene, risqué, vulgar, X-rated (*inf.*)

Antonyms *adj* ≠ **depressed:** blithe, cheerful, cheery, chirpy (*inf.*), elated, genial, happy, jolly, merry, optimistic, sunny ≠ **smutty:** decent, respectable

blue moon *n* **once in a blue moon** *Informal* = **rarely**, almost never, hardly ever, very seldom

blueprint *n* **2** = **plan**, design, draft, layout, outline, pattern, pilot scheme, project, prototype, scheme, sketch

print of plans, technical drawings, etc., consisting of white lines on a blue background. **2** an original plan or prototype. ◆ *vb* **3** (*tr*) to make a blueprint of (a plan, etc.).

blue ribbon *n* **1** (in Britain) a badge of blue silk worn by members of the Order of the Garter. **2** a badge awarded as the first prize in a competition.

blues Ⓣ (blu:z) *pl n* (*sometimes functioning as sing*) **the. 1** a feeling of depression or deep unhappiness. **2** a type of folk song devised by Black Americans, usually employing a basic 12-bar chorus and frequent minor intervals.

blue-sky *n* (*modifier*) of or denoting theoretical research without regard to any future application of its result: *a blue-sky project.*

bluestocking ('blu:ˌstɒkɪŋ) *n Usually disparaging.* a scholarly or intellectual woman. [from the blue worsted stockings worn by members of an 18th-cent. literary society]

bluestone ('blu:ˌstəʊn) *n* **1** a blue-grey sandstone containing much clay, used for building and paving. **2** the blue crystalline form of copper sulphate.

bluetit ('blu:ˌtɪt) *n* a common European tit having a blue crown, wings, and tail, yellow underparts, and a black-and-grey head.

blue whale *n* the largest mammal: a widely distributed bluish-grey whalebone whale, closely related and similar to the rorquals.

bluey ('blu:ɪ) *n Austral. inf.* **1** a blanket. **2** a swagman's bundle. **3 hump (one's) bluey.** to carry one's bundle; tramp. **4** a variant of **blue** (sense 9). **5** a cattle dog. [(for senses 1, 2, 4) C19: from BLUE (on account of their colour) + -Y[2]]

Bluey ('blu:ɪ) *n* a variant of **Blue.**

bluff[1] Ⓣ (blʌf) *vb* **1** to pretend to be confident about an uncertain issue in order to influence (someone). ◆ *n* **2** deliberate deception intended to create the impression of a stronger position than one actually has. **3 call someone's bluff.** to challenge someone to give proof of his claims. [C19: orig. US poker-playing term, from Du. *bluffen* to boast]
▸**'bluffer** *n*

bluff[2] Ⓣ (blʌf) *n* **1** a steep promontory, bank, or cliff. **2** *Canad.* a clump of trees on the prairie; copse. ◆ *adj* **3** good-naturedly frank and hearty. **4** (of a bank, cliff, etc.) presenting a steep broad face. [C17 (in the sense: nearly perpendicular): ?from MDu. *blaf* broad]
▸**'bluffly** *adv* ▸**'bluffness** *n*

bluish *or* **blueish** ('blu:ɪʃ) *adj* somewhat blue.

blunder Ⓣ ('blʌndə) *n* **1** a stupid or clumsy mistake. **2** a foolish tactless remark. ◆ *vb* (*mainly intr*) **3** to make stupid or clumsy mistakes. **4** to make foolish tactless remarks. **5** (often foll. by *about, into,* etc.) to act clumsily; stumble. **6** (*tr*) to mismanage; botch. [C14: of Scand. origin; cf. ON *blunda* to close one's eyes]
▸**'blunderer** *n* ▸**'blundering** *n, adj*

blunderbuss ('blʌndəˌbʌs) *n* an obsolete short musket with large bore and flared muzzle. [C17: changed (infl. by BLUNDER) from Du. *donderbus;* from *donder* THUNDER + obs. *bus* gun]

blunge (blʌndʒ) *vb* **blunges, blunging, blunged.** (*tr*) to mix (clay or a similar substance) with water in order to form a suspension for use in ceramics. [C19: prob. from BLEND + PLUNGE]
▸**'blunger** *n*

blunt Ⓣ (blʌnt) *adj* **1** (esp. of a knife or blade) lacking sharpness or keenness; dull. **2** not having a sharp edge or point: *a blunt instrument.* **3** (of people, manner of speaking, etc.) straightforward and uncomplicated. ◆ *vb* (*tr*) **4** to make less sharp. **5** to diminish the sensitivity or perception of; make dull. [C12: prob. of Scand. origin]
▸**'bluntly** *adv* ▸**'bluntness** *n*

blur Ⓣ (blɜ:) *vb* **blurs, blurring, blurred. 1** to make or become vague or less distinct. **2** to smear or smudge. **3** (*tr*) to make (the judgment, memory, or perception) less clear; dim. ◆ *n* **4** something vague, hazy, or indistinct. **5** a smear or smudge. [C16: ? var. of BLEAR]
▸**blurred** *adj* ▸**'blurry** *adj*

blurb (blɜ:b) *n* a promotional description, as on the jackets of books. [C20: coined by G. Burgess (1866–1951), US humorist & illustrator]

blurt Ⓣ (blɜ:t) *vb* (*tr;* often foll. by *out*) to utter suddenly and involuntarily. [C16: prob. imit.]

blush Ⓣ (blʌʃ) *vb* **1** (*intr*) to become suddenly red in the face from embarrassment, shame, modesty, or guilt; redden. **2** to make or become reddish or rosy. ◆ *n* **3** a sudden reddening of the face from embarrassment, shame, modesty, or guilt. **4** a rosy glow. **5** a cloudy area on the surface of freshly applied gloss paint. **6** another word for **rosé. 7 at first blush.** when first seen; as a first impression. [OE *blȳscan*]

blusher ('blʌʃə) *n* a cosmetic applied to the cheeks to give a rosy colour.

bluster Ⓣ ('blʌstə) *vb* **1** to speak or say loudly or boastfully. **2** to act in a bullying way. **3** (*tr;* foll. by *into*) to force or attempt to force (a person) into doing something by behaving thus. **4** (*intr*) (of the wind) to be noisy or gusty. ◆ *n* **5** boisterous talk or action; swagger. **6** empty threats or protests. **7** a strong wind; gale. [C15: prob. from MLow G *blüsteren* to storm, blow violently]
▸**'blusterer** *n* ▸**'blustery** *adj*

Blvd *abbrev. for* Boulevard.

BM *abbrev. for:* **1** Bachelor of Medicine. **2** *Surveying.* benchmark. **3** British Museum.

BMA *abbrev. for* British Medical Association.

BMC *abbrev. for* British Medical Council.

B-movie *n* a film originally made (esp. in the 1940s and 50s) as a supporting film, now often considered as a genre in its own right.

BMus *abbrev. for* Bachelor of Music.

BMX **1** *abbrev. for* bicycle motocross: stunt riding over an obstacle course on a bicycle. ◆ *n* **2** a bicycle designed for bicycle motocross.

Bn *abbrev. for:* **1** Baron. **2** Battalion.

BNFL *abbrev. for* British Nuclear Fuels Limited.

bo *or* **boh** (bəʊ) *interj* an exclamation to startle or surprise someone, esp. a child in a game.

BO *abbrev. for:* **1** *Inf.* body odour. **2** box office.

b.o. *abbrev. for:* **1** back order. **2** branch office. **3** broker's order. **4** buyer's option.

boa ('bəʊə) *n* **1** any of various large nonvenomous snakes of Central and South America and the Caribbean. They kill their prey by constriction. **2** a woman's long thin scarf, usually of feathers or fur. [C19: from NL, from L]

boa constrictor *n* a very large snake of tropical America and the Caribbean that kills its prey by constriction.

boar (bɔ:) *n* **1** an uncastrated male pig. **2** See **wild boar.** [OE *bār*]

board Ⓣ (bɔ:d) *n* **1** a long wide flat piece of sawn timber. **2a** a smaller flat piece of rigid material for a specific purpose: *ironing board.* **2b** (*in combination*): *breadboard.* **3** a person's meals, provided regularly for money. **4** *Arch.* a table, esp. when laden with food. **5a** (*sometimes functioning as pl*) a group of people who officially administer a company, trust, etc. **5b** (*as modifier*): *a board meeting.* **6** any other committee or council: *a board of interviewers.* **7** stiff cardboard or similar material, used for the outside covers of a book. **8** a flat thin rectangular sheet of composite material, such as plasterboard or chipboard. **9** *Chiefly US.* **9a** a list of stock-exchange prices. **9b** *Inf.* the stock exchange itself. **10** *Naut.* the side of a ship. **11** *Austral. & NZ.* the part of the floor of a sheep-shearing shed where the shearers work. **12** any of various por-

THESAURUS

blues *pl n* **1** = **depression**, dejection, despondency, doldrums, dumps (*inf.*), gloom, gloominess, glumness, low spirits, melancholy, moodiness, the hump (*Brit. inf.*), unhappiness

bluff[1] *vb* **1** = **deceive**, con, defraud, delude, fake, feign, humbug, lie, mislead, pretend, pull the wool over someone's eyes, sham ◆ *n* **2** = **deception**, bluster, boast, braggadocio, bragging, bravado, deceit, fake, feint, fraud, humbug, idle boast, lie, mere show, pretence, sham, show, subterfuge

bluff[2] *n* **1** = **precipice**, bank, cliff, crag, escarpment, headland, peak, promontory, ridge, scarp ◆ *adj* **3** = **hearty**, abrupt, blunt, blustering, downright, frank, genial, good-natured, open, outspoken, plain-spoken **4** = **steep**, abrupt, perpendicular, precipitous, sheer, towering
Antonyms *adj* ≠ **hearty:** delicate, diplomatic, discreet, judicious, sensitive, tactful, thoughtful

blunder *n* **1** = **error**, fault, inaccuracy, mistake, oversight, slip, slip-up (*inf.*) **2** = **mistake**, bloomer, boob (*Brit. sl.*), boo-boo (*inf.*), clanger (*inf.*), faux pas, gaffe, gaucherie, howler (*inf.*), impropriety, indiscretion ◆ *vb* **3** = **make a mistake**, bodge (*inf.*), botch, bungle, err, slip up (*inf.*) **4** = **put one's foot in it** (*inf.*), drop a brick (*Brit. inf.*), drop a clanger (*inf.*) **5** = **stumble**, bumble, confuse, flounder, misjudge
Antonyms *n* ≠ **error:** accuracy, correctness ◆ *vb* ≠ **make a mistake:** be correct, be exact, get it right

blunt *adj* **1, 2** = **dull**, dulled, edgeless, pointless, rounded, unsharpened **3** = **forthright**, bluff, brusque, discourteous, downright, explicit, frank, impolite, outspoken, plain-spoken, rude, straightforward, straight from the shoulder, tactless, trenchant, uncivil, unpolished, upfront (*inf.*) ◆ *vb* **4** = **dull** **5** = **deaden**, dampen, dull, numb, soften, take the edge off, water down, weaken
Antonyms *adj* ≠ **dull:** keen, pointed, sharp ≠ **forthright:** acute, courteous, diplomatic, keen, pointed, sensitive, sharp, subtle, tactful ◆ *vb* ≠ **dull:** sharpen ≠ **deaden:** animate, put an edge on, stimulate, vitalize

bluntness *n* **3** = **forthrightness**, candour, frankness, ingenuousness, openness, outspokenness, plain speaking, truthfulness

blur *vb* **1** = **make indistinct**, becloud, bedim, befog, blear, cloud, darken, dim, fog, make hazy, make vague, mask, obscure, soften **2** = **smudge**, blot, smear, spot, stain ◆ *n* **4** = **indistinctness**, blear, blurredness, cloudiness, confusion, dimness, fog, haze, obscurity **5** = **smudge**, blot, smear, spot, stain

blurred *adj* **1** = **indistinct**, bleary, blurry, dim, faint, foggy, fuzzy, hazy, ill-defined, lacking definition, misty, nebulous, out of focus, unclear, vague

blurt *vb, often foll. by* **out** = **exclaim**, babble, blab, blow the gaff (*Brit. sl.*), disclose, let the cat out of the bag, reveal, spill, spill one's guts (*sl.*), spill the beans (*inf.*), spout (*inf.*), tell all, utter suddenly

blush *vb* **1** = **turn red**, colour, crimson, flush, go red (as a beetroot), redden, turn scarlet ◆ *n* **3** = **flush**, colour, reddening, ruddiness **4** = **glow**, pink tinge, rosiness, rosy tint
Antonyms *vb* ≠ **turn red:** blanch, blench, drain, fade, pale, turn pale, whiten

bluster *vb* **1** = **boast**, blow one's own horn, blow one's own trumpet, brag, swagger, swell, vaunt **2, 3** = **bully**, bulldoze, domineer, hector ◆ *n* **5** = **hot air** (*inf.*), bluff, boasting, boisterousness, bombast, bragging, bravado, crowing, swagger, swaggering

blustery *adj* **4** = **gusty**, blusterous, boisterous, inclement, squally, stormy, tempestuous, violent, wild, windy

board *n* **1** = **plank**, panel, piece of timber, slat, timber **3** = **meals**, daily meals, provisions, victuals **5a** = **directors**, advisers, advisory group, committee, conclave, council, directorate, panel, quango, trustees ◆ *vb* **16** = **get on**, embark, embus, enplane, enter, entrain, mount **19** = **lodge**, feed, room **20** = **accommodate**, house, put up, quarter
Antonyms *vb* ≠ **get on:** alight, arrive, disembark, dismount, get off, go ashore, land

table surfaces specially designed for indoor games such as chess, backgammon, etc. **13 go by the board.** *Inf.* to be in disuse, neglected, or lost: *in these days courtesy goes by the board.* **14 on board.** on or in a ship, boat, aeroplane, or other vehicle. **15 the boards.** the stage. ◆ *vb* **16** to go aboard (a vessel, train, aircraft, or other vehicle). **17** to attack (a ship) by forcing one's way aboard. **18** (*tr; often foll. by up, in*, etc.) to cover or shut with boards. **19** (*intr*) to receive meals or meals and lodging in return for money. **20** (sometimes foll. by *out*) to arrange for (someone, esp. a child) to receive food and lodging away from home. **21** (in ice hockey and box lacrosse) to bodycheck an opponent against the boards. ◆ See also **boards.** [OE *bord*]

boarder ('bɔːdə) *n* **1** a pupil who lives at school during term time. **2** another word for **lodger. 3** a person who boards a ship, esp. in an attack.

boarding ('bɔːdɪŋ) *n* **1** a structure of boards. **2** timber boards collectively. **3a** the act of embarking on an aircraft, train, ship, etc. **3b** (*as modifier*): *a boarding pass.* **4** (in ice hockey and box lacrosse) an act of bodychecking an opponent against the boards.

boarding house *n* a private house in which accommodation and meals are provided for paying guests.

boarding school *n* a school providing living accommodation for some or all of its pupils.

Board of Trade *n* (in Britain) a part of the Department of Trade and Industry responsible for the supervision of commerce and the promotion of export trade.

boardroom ('bɔːdˌruːm, -ˌrʊm) *n* a room where the board of directors of a company meets.

boards (bɔːdz) *pl n* a wooden wall about one metre high forming the enclosure in which ice hockey or box lacrosse is played.

board school *n* (formerly) a school managed by a board of local ratepayers.

boardwalk ('bɔːdˌwɔːk) *n US & Canad.* a promenade, esp. along a beach, usually made of planks.

boast ➊ (bəʊst) *vb* **1** (*intr; sometimes foll. by of or about*) to speak in excessively proud terms of one's possessions, skills, or superior qualities; brag. **2** (*tr*) to possess (something to be proud of): *the city boasts a fine cathedral.* ◆ *n* **3** a bragging statement. **4** a possession, attribute, etc., that is or may be bragged about. [C13: from ?]
▸ **'boaster** *n* ▸ **'boasting** *n, adj*

boastful ➊ ('bəʊstfʊl) *adj* tending to boast; characterized by boasting.
▸ **'boastfully** *adv* ▸ **'boastfulness** *n*

boat ➊ (bəʊt) *n* **1** a small vessel propelled by oars, paddle, sails, or motor. **2** (not in technical use) another word for **ship. 3** a container for gravy, sauce, etc. **4 burn one's boats.** See **burn**[1] (sense 13). **5 in the same boat.** sharing the same problems. **6 miss the boat.** to lose an opportunity. **7 rock the boat.** *Inf.* to cause a disturbance in the existing situation. ◆ *vb* **8** (*intr*) to travel or go in a boat, esp. as a form of recreation. **9** (*tr*) to transport or carry in a boat. [OE *bāt*]

boater ('bəʊtə) *n* a stiff straw hat with a straight brim and flat crown.

boathook ('bəʊtˌhʊk) *n* a pole with a hook at one end, used aboard a vessel for fending off other vessels or for catching a mooring buoy.

boathouse ('bəʊtˌhaʊs) *n* a shelter by the edge of a river, lake, etc., for housing boats.

boatie ('bəʊtɪ) *n Austral. & NZ inf.* a boating enthusiast.

boating ('bəʊtɪŋ) *n* rowing, sailing, or cruising in boats as a form of recreation.

boatload ('bəʊtˌləʊd) *n* the amount of cargo or number of people held by a boat or ship.

boatman ('bəʊtmən) *n, pl* **boatmen.** a man who works on, hires out, or repairs a boat or boats.

boatswain, bosun, *or* **bo's'n** ('bəʊsᵊn) *n* a petty officer or a warrant officer who is responsible for the maintenance of a ship and its equipment. [OE *bātswegen*; see BOAT, SWAIN]

boat train *n* a train scheduled to take passengers to or from a particular ship.

bob[1] ➊ (bɒb) *vb* **bobs, bobbing, bobbed. 1** to move or cause to move up and down repeatedly, as while floating in water. **2** to move or cause to move with a short abrupt movement, as of the head. **3** (*intr; usually foll. by up*) to appear or emerge suddenly. **4** (*intr; usually foll. by for*) to attempt to get hold (of a floating or hanging object, esp. an apple) in the teeth as a game. ◆ *n* **5** a short abrupt movement, as of the head. [C14: from ?]

bob[2] (bɒb) *n* **1** a hairstyle for women and children in which the hair is cut short evenly all round the head. **2** a dangling or hanging object, such as the weight on a pendulum or on a plumb line. **3** short for **bobsleigh. 4** a docked tail, esp. of a horse. ◆ *vb* **bobs, bobbing, bobbed. 5** (*tr*) to cut (the hair) in a bob. **6** (*tr*) to cut short (something, esp. the tail of an animal); dock or crop. **7** (*intr*) to ride on a bobsleigh. [C14 *bobbe* bunch of flowers]

bob[3] (bɒb) *n, pl* **bob.** *Brit.* (formerly) an informal word for a **shilling.** [C19: from ?]

bobbejaan ('bɒbəˌjɑːn) *n S. African.* **1** a baboon. **2** a large black spider. **3** a monkey wrench. [from Afrik., from MDu. *babiaen*]

bobbin ('bɒbɪn) *n* a spool or reel on which thread or yarn is wound. [C16: from OF *bobine*, from ?]

bobble ('bɒbᵊl) *n* **1** a short jerky motion, as of a cork floating on disturbed water; bobbing movement. **2** a tufted ball, usually for ornament, as on a knitted hat. ◆ *vb* **3** (*intr*) *Sport.* (of a ball) to bounce with a rapid, erratic motion due to an uneven playing surface. [C19: from BOB[1] (vb)]

bobby ('bɒbɪ) *n, pl* **bobbies.** *Inf.* a British policeman. [C19: from *Bobby*, after *Robert* Peel (1788–1850), who set up the Metropolitan Police Force in 1828]

bobby calf *n* an unweaned calf culled for slaughter.

bobby-dazzler *n Dialect.* anything outstanding, striking, or showy. [C19: expanded from *dazzler* something striking or attractive]

bobby pin *n US, Canad., Austral., & NZ.* a metal hairpin bent in order to hold the hair in place.

bobby socks *pl n* ankle-length socks worn by teenage girls, esp. in the US in the 1940s.

bobcat ('bɒbˌkæt) *n* a North American feline mammal, closely related to but smaller than the lynx, having reddish-brown fur with dark spots or stripes, tufted ears, and a short tail. Also called: **bay lynx.** [C19: from BOB[2] + CAT[1]]

bobolink ('bɒbəˌlɪŋk) *n* an American songbird, the male of which has a white back and black underparts. [C18: imit.]

bobotie (bʊ'bʊtɪ) *n* a South African dish consisting of curried mincemeat with a topping of beaten egg baked to a crust. [C19: from Afrik., prob. from Malay]

bobsleigh ('bɒbˌsleɪ) *n* **1** a racing sledge for two or more people, with a steering mechanism enabling the driver to direct it down a steeply banked ice-covered run. ◆ *vb* **2** (*intr*) to ride on a bobsleigh. ◆ Also called (esp. US and Canad.): **bobsled** ('bɒbˌslɛd). [C19: BOB[2] + SLEIGH]

bobstay ('bɒbˌsteɪ) *n* a strong stay between a bowsprit and the stem of a vessel for holding down the bowsprit. [C18: ?from BOB[1] + STAY[3]]

bobsy-die ('bɒbzɪˌdaɪ) *n NZ inf.* fuss; confusion (esp. in **kick up bobsy-die**). [from C19 *Bob's a-dying*]

bobtail ('bɒbˌteɪl) *n* **1** a docked or diminutive tail. **2** an animal with such a tail. ◆ *adj also* **bobtailed. 3** having the tail cut short. ◆ *vb* (*tr*) **4** to dock the tail of. **5** to cut short; curtail.

Boche (bɒʃ) *n Derog. sl.* (esp. in World Wars I and II) **1** a German, esp. a German soldier. **2 the.** (*usually functioning as pl*) Germans collectively, esp. German soldiers regarded as the enemy. [C20: from F, prob. shortened from *alboche* German, from *allemand* German + *caboche* pate]

bockedy ('bɒkədɪ) *adj Irish.* (of a structure, piece of furniture, etc.) unsteady. [from Irish Gaelic *bacaideach* limping]

bod (bɒd) *n Inf.* **1** a fellow; chap: *he's a queer bod.* **2** another word for **body** (sense 1). [C18: short for BODY]

BOD *abbrev. for:* biochemical oxygen demand.

bodacious (bəʊ'deɪʃəs) *adj Sl., chiefly US.* impressive or remarkable; excellent. [C19: from E dialect; blend of BOLD and AUDACIOUS]

bode[1] ➊ (bəʊd) *vb* **bodes, boding, boded. 1** to be an omen of (good or ill, esp. of ill); portend; presage. **2** (*tr*) *Arch.* to predict; foretell. [OE *bodian*]
▸ **'bodement** *n*

bode[2] (bəʊd) *vb* a past tense of **bide.**

bodega (bəʊ'diːgə) *n* a shop selling wine and sometimes groceries, esp. in a Spanish-speaking country. [C19: from Sp., ult. from Gk *apothēkē* storehouse]

bodge (bɒdʒ) *vb* **bodges, bodging, bodged.** *Inf.* to make a mess of; botch. [C16: changed from BOTCH]

bodgie ('bɒdʒɪ) *Austral. & NZ sl.* ◆ *n* **1** an unruly or uncouth young man, esp. in the 1950s. ◆ *adj* **2** false, fraudulent. [C20: from BODGE]

Bodhisattva (ˌbəʊdɪ'sætvə, -wə, ˌbɒd-) *n* (in Buddhism) a divine being worthy of nirvana who remains on the human plane to help men to salvation. [Sansk., from *bodhi* enlightenment + *sattva* essence]

bodice ('bɒdɪs) *n* **1** the upper part of a woman's dress, from the shoulder to the waist. **2** a tight-fitting corset worn laced over a blouse, or (formerly) as a woman's undergarment. [C16: orig. Scot. *bodies*, pl. of BODY]

bodice ripper *n Inf.* a romantic novel, usually on a historical theme, that involves some sex and violence.

-bodied *adj* (*in combination*) having a body or bodies as specified: *able-bodied; long-bodied.*

bodiless ('bɒdɪlɪs) *adj* having no body or substance; incorporeal or insubstantial.

THESAURUS

boast *vb* **1 = brag**, blow one's own trumpet, bluster, crow, exaggerate, puff, strut, swagger, talk big (*sl.*), vaunt **2 = possess**, be proud of, congratulate oneself on, exhibit, flatter oneself, pride oneself on, show off ◆ *n* **3 = brag**, avowal, gasconade (*rare*), rodomontade (*literary*), swank (*inf.*), vaunt **4 = source of pride**, gem, joy, pride, pride and joy, treasure
Antonyms *vb* ≠ **brag**: cover up, depreciate, disavow, disclaim ◆ *n* ≠ **brag**: disavowal, disclaimer

boastful *adj* = **bragging**, cocky, conceited, crowing, egotistical, full of oneself, puffed-up, swaggering, swanky (*inf.*), swollen-headed, vainglorious, vaunting
Antonyms *adj* deprecating, humble, modest, self-belittling, self-effacing, unassuming

boat *n* **1, 2 = vessel**, barge, barque, craft, ship **5 in the same boat = alike**, equal, even, on a par, on equal *or* even terms, on the same *or* equal footing, together **6 miss the boat = miss one's chance** *or* **opportunity**, be too late, blow one's chance (*inf.*), let slip, lose out, miss out **7 rock the boat** *Informal* **= cause trouble**, dissent, make waves (*inf.*), throw a spanner in the works, upset the apple cart

bob[1] *vb* **1 = duck**, bounce, hop, jerk, leap, nod, oscillate, quiver, skip, waggle, weave, wobble **3** *usually foll. by* **up = appear**, arise, emerge, materialize, pop up, rise, spring up, surface, turn up

bode[1] *vb* **1 = portend**, augur, be an omen of, betoken, forebode, foreshadow, presage, signify, threaten **2** *Archaic* **= foretell**, forewarn, predict, prophesy

bodily Ⓣ ('bɒdɪlɪ) *adj* **1** relating to or being a part of the human body. ◆ *adv* **2** by taking hold of the body: *he threw him bodily from the platform.* **3** in person; in the flesh.

bodkin ('bɒdkɪn) *n* **1** a blunt large-eyed needle. **2** *Arch.* a dagger. **3** *Arch.* a long ornamental hairpin. [C14: prob. of Celtic origin]

body Ⓣ ('bɒdɪ) *n, pl* **bodies. 1a** the entire physical structure of an animal or human being. Related adj: **corporeal. 1b** (*as modifier*): *body odour.* **2** the trunk or torso. **3** a dead human or animal; corpse. **4** the flesh as opposed to the spirit. **5** the largest or main part of anything: *the body of a vehicle; the body of a plant.* **6** a separate or distinct mass of water or land. **7** a number of individuals regarded as a single entity; group. **8** fullness in the appearance of the hair. **9** the characteristic full quality of certain wines. **10** firmness, esp. of cloth. **11a** the pigment contained in or added to paint, dye, etc. **11b** the opacity of a paint. **11c** (*as modifier*): *body colour.* **12** an informal or dialect word for a **person. 13** another word for **bodysuit** (sense 1). **14 keep body and soul together.** to manage to keep alive; survive. ◆ *vb* **bodies, bodying, bodied.** (*tr*) **15** (usually foll. by *forth*) to give a body or shape to. [OE *bodig*]

body blow *n* **1** *Boxing.* a blow to an opponent's body. **2** a severe disappointment or setback.

body building *n* the practice of exercises to make the muscles of the body conspicuous.

bodycheck ('bɒdɪˌtʃɛk) *Ice hockey, etc.* ◆ *n* **1** obstruction of another player. ◆ *vb* **2** (*tr*) to deliver a bodycheck to (an opponent).

body double *n Films.* a person who substitutes for a star for the filming of a scene that involves shots of the body rather than the face.

bodyguard ('bɒdɪˌgɑːd) *n* a person or group of people who escort and protect someone.

body horror *n* a genre of horror film in which the main feature is the graphically depicted destruction or degeneration of a human body or bodies.

body language *n* the nonverbal imparting of information by means of conscious or subconscious bodily gestures, posture, etc.

body-line *adj Cricket.* denoting or relating to fast bowling aimed at the batsman's body.

body politic *n* **the.** the people of a nation or the nation itself considered as a political entity.

body search *n* **1** a form of search by police, customs officials, etc., that involves examination of a prisoner's or suspect's bodily orifices. ◆ *vb* **body-search. 2** (*tr*) to search (a prisoner or suspect) in this manner.

body shop *n* a repair yard for vehicle bodywork.

body snatcher *n* (formerly) a person who robbed graves and sold the corpses for dissection.

body stocking *n* a one-piece undergarment for women, usually of nylon, covering the torso.

bodysuit ('bɒdɪˌsuːt, -ˌsjuːt) *n* **1** a woman's close-fitting one-piece garment for the torso. Sometimes shortened to **body. 2** a one-piece undergarment for a baby.

body swerve *n* **1** *Sport.* (esp. in football games) the act or an instance of swerving past an opponent. **2** *Scot.* the act or an instance of avoiding (a situation considered unpleasant): *I think I'll give the meeting a body swerve.* ◆ *vb* **body-swerve, body-swerves, body-swerving, body-swerved. 3** *Sport.* (esp. in football games) to pass (an opponent) using a body swerve. **4** *Scot.* to avoid (a situation or person considered unpleasant).

body warmer *n* a sleeveless type of jerkin, usually quilted, worn as an outer garment.

bodywork ('bɒdɪˌwɜːk) *n* the external shell of a motor vehicle.

Boeotian (bɪ'əʊʃɪən) *adj* **1** of Boeotia, a region in ancient Greece. **2** dull or stupid. ◆ *n* **3** a person from Boeotia. **4** a dull or stupid person.

Boer (bʊə) *n* **a** a descendant of any of the Dutch or Huguenot colonists who settled in South Africa. **b** (*as modifier*): *a Boer farmer.* [C19: from Du. *Boer;* see BOOR]

boerbul ('bʊəbəl) *n S. African.* a crossbred mastiff used esp. as a watchdog. [from Afrik. *boerboel,* from *boel* large dog]

boeremusiek ('bʊərəˌmœsɪk) *n S. African.* light music associated with the culture of the Afrikaners. [from Afrik. *boere* country, folk + *musiek* music]

boet (bʊt) *or* **boetie** *n S. African inf.* a friend. [from Afrik.: brother]

boffin ('bɒfɪn) *n Brit. inf.* a scientist, esp. one carrying out military research. [C20: from ?]

boffo ('bɒfəʊ) *adj Sl.* very good; highly successful. [C20: from ?]

Bofors gun ('bəʊfəz) *n* an automatic 40 mm anti-aircraft gun, one or more of which are controlled by a radar-operated computer system mounted on a lightweight vehicle. [C20: after the Swedish armament firm that developed it]

bog Ⓣ (bɒg) *n* **1** wet spongy ground consisting of decomposing vegetation. **2** an area of such ground. **3** a slang word for **lavatory.** [C13: from Gaelic *bogach* swamp, from *bog* soft]
▸'**boggy** *adj* ▸'**bogginess** *n*

bogan ('bəʊgən) *n Canad.* (esp. in the Maritime Provinces) a sluggish side stream. Also called: **logan, pokelogan.** [of Algonquian origin]

bogbean ('bɒgˌbiːn) *n* another name for **buckbean.**

bog down Ⓣ *vb* **bogs, bogging, bogged.** (*adv;* when *tr, often passive*) to impede or be impeded physically or mentally.

bogey Ⓣ *or* **bogy** ('bəʊgɪ) *n* **1** an evil or mischievous spirit. **2** something that worries or annoys. **3** *Golf.* **3a** a score of one stroke over par on a hole. Cf. **par** (sense 5). **3b** *Obs.* a standard score for a hole or course, regarded as one that a good player should make. **4** *Sl.* a piece of dried mucus discharged from the nose. [C19: prob. rel. to obs. *bug* an evil spirit and BOGLE]

bogeyman ('bəʊgɪˌmæn) *n, pl* **bogeymen.** a person, real or imaginary, used as a threat, esp. to children.

boggle Ⓣ ('bɒg^{ə}l) *vb* **boggles, boggling, boggled.** (*intr;* often foll. by *at*) **1** to be surprised, confused, or alarmed (esp. in **the mind boggles**). **2** to hesitate or be evasive when confronted with a problem. [C16: prob. var. of BOGLE]

bogie *or* **bogy** ('bəʊgɪ) *n* **1** an assembly of four or six wheels forming a pivoted support at either end of a railway coach. **2** *Chiefly Brit.* a small railway truck of short wheelbase, used for conveying coal, ores, etc. [C19: from ?]

bogle ('bəʊg^{ə}l, 'bɒg-) *n* a dialect or archaic word for **bogey** (sense 1). [C16: from Scot. *bogill*]

bog myrtle *n* another name for **sweet gale.**

bog oak *n* oak found preserved in peat bogs.

bog off *Brit. sl.* ◆ *interj* **1** go away! ◆ *vb* **bogs, bogging, bogged. 2** (*intr, adv*) to go away.

bogong ('bəʊˌgɒŋ) *or* **bugong** ('buːˌgɒŋ) *n* an edible dark-coloured Australian noctuid moth.

bog-standard *adj Brit. & Irish sl.* completely ordinary; run-of-the-mill.

bogtrotter ('bɒgˌtrɒtə) *n* a derogatory term for an Irishman, esp. an Irish peasant.

bogus Ⓣ ('bəʊgəs) *adj* spurious or counterfeit; not genuine. [C19: from *bogus* apparatus for making counterfeit money]
▸'**bogusly** *adv* ▸'**bogusness** *n*

bogy ('bəʊgɪ) *n, pl* **bogies.** a variant spelling of **bogey** or **bogie.**

bohea (bəʊ'hiː) *n* a black Chinese tea, once regarded as the choicest, but now as an inferior grade. [C18: from Chinese *Wu-i Shan,* range of hills on which this tea was grown]

Bohemian Ⓣ (bəʊ'hiːmɪən) *n* **1** a native or inhabitant of Bohemia, a former kingdom; a Czech. **2** (*often not cap.*) a person, esp. an artist or writer, who lives an unconventional life. **3** the Czech language. ◆ *adj* **4** of, relating to, or characteristic of Bohemia, its people, or their language. **5** unconventional in appearance, behaviour, etc.

Bohemianism (bəʊ'hiːmɪəˌnɪzəm) *n* unconventional behaviour or appearance, esp. of an artist.

bohrium ('bɔːrɪəm) *n* a transuranic element artificially produced in minute quantities by bombarding ^{204}Bi atoms with ^{54}Cr nuclei. Symbol: Bh; atomic no.: 107. Former names: **element 107, unnilheptium.** [C20: after Niels Bohr (1885–1962), Danish physicist]

boil[1] Ⓣ (bɔɪl) *vb* **1** to change or cause to change from a liquid to a vapour so rapidly that bubbles of vapour are formed in the liquid. **2** to reach or cause to reach boiling point. **3** to cook or be cooked by the process of boiling. **4** (*intr*) to bubble and be agitated like something boiling; seethe: *the ocean was boiling.* **5** (*intr*) to be extremely angry or indignant. ◆ *n* **6** the state or action of boiling. ◆ See also **boil away, boil down, boil over.** [C13: from OF, from L, from *bulla* a bubble]

boil[2] Ⓣ (bɔɪl) *n* a red painful swelling with a hard pus-filled core caused by bacterial infection of the skin. Technical name: **furuncle.** [OE *bȳle*]

THESAURUS

bodily *adj* **1 = physical,** actual, carnal, corporal, corporeal, fleshly, material, substantial, tangible

body *n* **1 = physique,** build, figure, form, frame, shape **2 = torso,** trunk **3 = corpse,** cadaver, carcass, dead body, relics, remains, stiff (*sl.*) **5 = main part,** bulk, essence, mass, material, matter, substance **7 = organization,** association, band, bloc, collection, company, confederation, congress, corporation, society **9 = consistency,** density, richness, substance **12 = person,** being, creature, human, human being, individual, mortal

bog *n* **1, 2 = marsh,** fen, marshland, mire, morass, moss (*Scot. & N English dialect*), peat bog, quagmire, slough, swamp, wetlands

bog down *vb* **= hold up,** delay, halt, impede, sink, slow down, slow up, stall, stick

bogey *n* **1 = spirit,** apparition, bogeyman, goblin, hobgoblin, imp, spectre, spook (*inf.*), sprite **2 = bugbear,** bête noire, bugaboo, nightmare

boggle *vb* **1 = be confused,** be alarmed, be surprised, be taken aback, shy, stagger, startle, take fright **2 = hesitate,** demur, dither, doubt, equivocate, falter, hang back, hover, jib, shilly-shally (*inf.*), shrink from, vacillate, waver

boggy *adj* **1 = marshy,** fenny, miry, muddy, oozy, quaggy, soft, spongy, swampy, waterlogged, yielding

bogus *adj* **= fake,** artificial, counterfeit, dummy, ersatz, false, forged, fraudulent, imitation, phoney *or* phony (*inf.*), pseudo (*inf.*), sham, spurious
Antonyms *adj* actual, authentic, genuine, real, true

Bohemian *n* **2** *often not cap.* **= nonconformist,** beatnik, dropout, hippy, iconoclast ◆ *adj* **5** *often not cap.* **= unconventional,** alternative, artistic, arty (*inf.*), avant-garde, eccentric, exotic, left bank, nonconformist, oddball (*inf.*), offbeat, off-the-wall (*sl.*), outré, unorthodox, way-out (*inf.*)
Antonyms *adj* ≠ **unconventional:** bourgeois, conservative, conventional, Pooterish, square (*inf.*), straight (*sl.*), straight-laced, stuffy

boil[1] *vb* **4 = bubble,** agitate, churn, effervesce, fizz, foam, froth, seethe **5 = be furious,** be angry, be indignant, blow a fuse (*sl., chiefly US*), crack up (*inf.*), fly off the handle (*inf.*), foam at the mouth (*inf.*), fulminate, fume, go ballistic (*sl., chiefly US*), go off the deep end (*inf.*), go up the wall (*sl.*), rage, rave, see red (*inf.*), storm, wig out (*sl.*)

boil[2] *n* **= pustule,** blain, blister, carbuncle, gathering, swelling, tumour, ulcer

boil away *vb (adv)* to cause (liquid) to evaporate completely by boiling or (of liquid) to evaporate completely.

boil down ⓣ *vb (adv)* **1** to reduce or be reduced in quantity by boiling. **2 boil down to. 2a** *(intr)* to be the essential element in something. **2b** *(tr)* to summarize; reduce to essentials.

boiled shirt *n Inf.* a dress shirt with a stiff front.

boiler ('bɔɪlə) *n* **1** a closed vessel in which water is heated to supply steam or provide heat. **2** a domestic device to provide hot water, esp. for central heating. **3** a large tub for boiling laundry.

boilermaker ('bɔɪlə,meɪkə) *n* a person who works with metal in heavy industry; plater or welder.

boilerplate ('bɔɪlə,pleɪt) *n* **1** a form of mild-steel plate used in the production of boiler shells. **2** a copy made with the intention of making other copies from it. **3** a set of instructions incorporated in several places in a computer program or a standard form of words used repeatedly in drafting contracts, guarantees, etc. **4** a draft contract that can be modified to cover various types of transaction.

boiler suit *n Brit.* a one-piece overall work garment.

boiling point *n* **1** the temperature at which a liquid boils at sea level. **2** *Inf.* the condition of being angered or highly excited.

boiling-water reactor *n* a nuclear reactor using water as coolant and moderator, steam being produced in the reactor itself. Abbrev.: **BWR.**

boil over *vb (adv)* **1** to overflow or cause to overflow while boiling. **2** *(intr)* to burst out in anger or excitement.

boisterous ⓣ ('bɔɪstərəs, -strəs) *adj* **1** noisy and lively; unruly. **2** (of the wind, sea, etc.) stormy. [C13 *boistuous,* from ?]
▸ **'boisterously** *adv* ▸ **'boisterousness** *n*

bok choy ('bɒk 'tʃɔɪ) *n* a Chinese plant that is related to the cabbage and has edible stalks and leaves. Also called: **Chinese cabbage, Chinese leaf.** [from Chinese dialect, lit.: white vegetable]

bola ('bəʊlə) *or* **bolas** ('bəʊləs) *n, pl* **bolas** *or* **bolases.** a missile used by gauchos and Indians of South America, consisting of heavy balls on a cord. It is hurled at a running quarry, so as to entangle its legs. [Sp.: ball, from L *bulla* knob]

bold ⓣ (bəʊld) *adj* **1** courageous, confident, and fearless; ready to take risks. **2** showing or requiring courage: *a bold plan.* **3** immodest or impudent: *she gave him a bold look.* **4** standing out distinctly; conspicuous: *a figure carved in bold relief.* **5** very steep: *the bold face of the cliff.* **6** imaginative in thought or expression. [OE *beald*]
▸ **'boldly** *adv* ▸ **'boldness** *n*

bold face *Printing.* ◆ *n* **1** a weight of type characterized by thick heavy lines, as the entry words in this dictionary. ◆ *adj* **boldface. 2** (of type) having this weight.

bole (bəʊl) *n* the trunk of a tree. [C14: from ON *bolr*]

bolero (bə'lɛərəʊ) *n, pl* **boleros. 1** a Spanish dance, usually in triple time. **2** a piece of music for or in the rhythm of this dance. **3** *(also* 'bɒlərəʊ). a short open bodice-like jacket not reaching the waist. [C18: from Sp.]

boliviano (bə,lɪvɪ'ɑːnəʊ; *Spanish* boli'βjano) **bolivianos** (-nəʊz; *Spanish* -nos). (until 1963 and from 1987) the standard monetary unit of Bolivia, equal to 100 centavos.

boll (bəʊl) *n* the fruit of such plants as flax and cotton, consisting of a rounded capsule containing the seeds. [C13: from Du. *bolle;* rel. to OE *bolla* BOWL[1]]

bollard ('bɒlɑːd, 'bɒləd) *n* **1** a strong wooden or metal post on a wharf, quay, etc., used for securing mooring lines. **2** *Brit.* a small post placed on a kerb or traffic island to make it conspicuous to motorists. [C14: ?from BOLE + -ARD]

bollocking ('bɒləkɪŋ) *n Sl.* a severe telling-off. [from *bollock* (vb) in the sense "to reprimand"]

bollocks ('bɒləks) *or* **ballocks** *Taboo sl.* ◆ *pl n* **1** another word for **testicles. 2** nonsense; rubbish. ◆ *interj* **3** an exclamation of annoyance, disbelief, etc. [OE *beallucas;* see BALL[1]]

boll weevil *n* a greyish weevil of the southern US and Mexico, whose larvae live in and destroy cotton bolls.

bologna sausage (bə'ləʊnjə) *n Chiefly US & Canad.* a large smoked sausage made of seasoned mixed meats. Also called: **baloney, boloney,** (esp. Brit.) **polony.**

bolometer (bəʊ'lɒmɪtə) *n* a sensitive instrument for measuring radiant energy. [C19: from Gk *bolē* ray of light, from *ballein* to throw + -METER]
▸ **bolometric** (,bəʊlə'mɛtrɪk) *adj*

boloney (bə'ləʊnɪ) *n* **1** a variant of **baloney. 2** another name for **bologna sausage.**

Bolshevik ('bɒlʃɪvɪk) *n, pl* **Bolsheviks** *or* **Bolsheviki** (,bɒlʃɪ'viːkɪ). **1** (formerly) a Russian Communist. Cf. **Menshevik. 2** any Communist. **3** *(often not cap.) Inf. & derog.* any political radical, esp. a revolutionary. [C20: from Russian *Bol'shevik* majority, from *bol'shoi* great]
▸ **'Bolshe,vism** *n* ▸ **'Bolshevist** *adj, n*

bolshie *or* **bolshy** ('bɒlʃɪ) *(sometimes cap.) Brit. inf.* ◆ *adj* **1** difficult to manage; rebellious. **2** politically radical or left-wing. ◆ *n, pl* **bolshies. 3** *Derog.* any political radical. [C20: shortened from BOLSHEVIK]

bolster ⓣ ('bəʊlstə) *vb (tr)* **1** (often foll. by *up*) to support or reinforce; strengthen: *to bolster morale.* **2** to prop up with a pillow or cushion. ◆ *n* **3** a long narrow pillow or cushion. **4** any pad or padded support. **5** a cold chisel used for cutting stone slabs, etc. [OE *bolster*]

bolt[1] ⓣ (bəʊlt) *n* **1** a bar that can be slid into a socket to lock a door, gate, etc. **2** a bar or rod that forms part of a locking mechanism and is moved by a key or a knob. **3** a metal rod or pin that has a head and a screw thread to take a nut. **4** a sliding bar in a breech-loading firearm that ejects the empty cartridge, replaces it with a new one, and closes the breech. **5** a flash of lightning. **6** a sudden start or movement, esp. in order to escape. **7** a roll of something, such as cloth, wallpaper, etc. **8** an arrow, esp. for a crossbow. **9 a bolt from the blue.** a sudden, unexpected, and usually unwelcome event. **10 shoot one's bolt.** to exhaust one's efforts. ◆ *vb* **11** *(tr)* to secure or lock with or as with a bolt. **12** *(tr)* to eat hurriedly. **13** *(intr;* usually foll. by *from* or *out)* to move or jump suddenly: *he bolted from the chair.* **14** *(intr)* (esp. of a horse) to start hurriedly and run away without warning. **15** *(tr)* to roll (cloth, wallpaper, etc.) into bolts. **16** *(intr)* (of cultivated plants) to produce flowers and seeds prematurely. ◆ *adv* **17** stiffly, firmly, or rigidly (archaic except in **bolt upright**). [OE *bolt* arrow]
▸ **'bolter** *n*

bolt[2] *or* **boult** (bəʊlt) *vb (tr)* **1** to pass (a powder, etc.) through a sieve. **2** to examine and separate. [C13: from OF *bulter,* prob. of Gmc origin]
▸ **'bolter** *or* **'boulter** *n*

bolt hole *n* a place of escape from danger.

boltrope ('bəʊlt,rəʊp) *n Naut.* a rope sewn to the foot or luff of a sail to strengthen it.

bolus ('bəʊləs) *n, pl* **boluses. 1** a small round soft mass, esp. of chewed food. **2** a large pill or tablet used in veterinary and clinical medicine. [C17: from NL, from Gk *bōlos* clod, lump]

bomb ⓣ (bɒm) *n* **1a** a hollow projectile containing explosive, incendiary, or other destructive substance. **1b** *(as modifier): bomb disposal; a bomb bay.* **1c** *(in combination): bombproof.* **2** an object in which an explosive device has been planted: *a car bomb; a letter bomb.* **3** a round mass of volcanic rock, solidified from molten lava that has been thrown into the air. **4** *Med.* a container for radioactive material, applied therapeutically to any part of the body: *a cobalt bomb.* **5** *Brit. sl.* a large sum of money. **6** *US & Canad. sl.* a disastrous failure: *the new play was a total bomb.* **7** *Austral. & NZ sl.* an old or dilapidated motorcar. **8** *American football.* a very long high pass. **9 like a bomb.** *Brit. & NZ inf.* with great speed or success; very well. **10 the bomb.** a hydrogen or an atomic bomb considered as the ultimate destructive weapon. ◆ *vb* **11** to attack with or as if with a bomb or bombs; drop bombs (on). **12** *(intr;* often foll. by *off, along,* etc.) *Inf.* to move or drive very quickly. **13** *(intr) US sl.* to fail disastrously. [C17: from F, from It., from L, from Gk *bombos,* imit.]

bombard ⓣ *vb* (bɒm'bɑːd). *(tr)* **1** to attack with concentrated artillery fire or bombs. **2** to attack with vigour and persistence. **3** to attack verbally, esp. with questions. **4** *Physics.* to direct high-energy particles or photons against (atoms, nuclei, etc.). ◆ *n* ('bɒmbɑːd). **5** an ancient type of cannon that threw stone balls. [C15: from OF, from *bombarde* stone-throwing cannon, prob. from L *bombus* booming sound; see BOMB]
▸ **bom'bardment** *n*

bombardier (,bɒmbə'dɪə) *n* **1** the member of a bomber aircrew responsible for aiming and releasing the bombs. **2** *Brit.* a noncommissioned

THESAURUS

boil down *vb* **1** = **reduce**, condense, decrease

boiling[1] *adj* **5** = **furious**, angry, choked, cross, enraged, fit to be tied (*sl.*), foaming at the mouth, fuming, incandescent, incensed, indignant, infuriated, on the warpath

boisterous *adj* **1** = **unruly**, bouncy, clamorous, disorderly, impetuous, loud, noisy, obstreperous, riotous, rollicking, rowdy, rumbustious, unrestrained, uproarious, vociferous, wild **2** = **stormy**, blustery, gusty, raging, rough, squally, tempestuous, tumultuous, turbulent
Antonyms *adj* ≠ **unruly:** calm, controlled, peaceful, quiet, restrained, self-controlled, subdued ≠ **stormy:** calm, peaceful, quiet

bold *adj* **1** = **fearless**, adventurous, audacious, brave, courageous, daring, dauntless, enterprising, gallant, gritty, heroic, intrepid, lion-hearted, valiant, valorous **3** = **impudent**, barefaced, brash, brazen, cheeky, confident, feisty (*inf., chiefly US & Canad.*), forward, fresh (*inf.*), insolent, in-your-face (*Brit. sl.*), pert, pushy (*inf.*), rude, sassy (*US inf.*), saucy, shameless **4** = **conspicuous**, bright, colourful, eye-catching, flashy, forceful, lively, loud, prominent, pronounced, salient, showy, spirited, striking, strong, vivid
Antonyms *adj* ≠ **fearless:** cowardly, faint-hearted, fearful, timid, timorous ≠ **impudent:** conservative, cool, courteous, meek, modest, polite, retiring, shy, tactful ≠ **conspicuous:** dull, ordinary, pale, soft, unimaginative

bolster *vb* **1** = **support**, aid, assist, augment, boost, brace, buoy up, buttress, give a leg up (*inf.*), help, hold up, maintain, reinforce, shore up, stay, strengthen **2** = **prop up**, cushion, pillow

bolt[1] *n* **1, 2** = **bar**, catch, fastener, latch, lock, sliding bar **3** = **pin**, peg, rivet, rod **6** = **dash**, bound, dart, escape, flight, rush, spring, sprint **8** = **arrow**, dart, missile, projectile, shaft, thunderbolt ◆ *vb* **11** = **lock**, bar, fasten, latch, secure **12** = **gobble**, cram, devour, gorge, gulp, guzzle, stuff, swallow whole, wolf **13** = **spring**, bound, jump, leap **14** = **run away**, abscond, dash, decamp, do a runner, escape, flee, fly, fly the coop (*US & Canad. inf.*), hurtle, make a break (for it), run, run for it, rush, skedaddle (*inf.*), sprint

bomb *n* **1** = **explosive**, bombshell, charge, device, grenade, mine, missile, projectile, rocket, shell, torpedo ◆ *vb* **11** = **blow up**, attack, blow sky-high, bombard, destroy, shell, strafe, torpedo

bombard *vb* **1** = **bomb**, assault, blast, blitz, cannonade, fire upon, open fire, pound, shell, strafe **2, 3** = **attack**, assail, barrage, batter, beset, besiege, harass, hound, pester

bombardment *n* **1** = **bombing**, assault, attack,

rank, below the rank of sergeant, in the Royal Artillery. [C16: from OF; see BOMBARD]

Bombardier (ˌbɒmbəˈdɪə) *n Canad. trademark.* a snow tractor, usually having caterpillar tracks at the rear and skis at the front. [C20: after J. A. *Bombardier*, Canadian inventor and manufacturer]

bombast Ⓣ (ˈbɒmbæst) *n* pompous and grandiloquent language. [C16: from OF, from Med. L *bombāx* cotton]
▸**bomˈbastic** *adj* ▸**bomˈbastically** *adv*

Bombay duck (bɒmˈbeɪ) *n* a fish that is eaten dried with curry dishes as a savoury. Also called: **bummalo.** [C19: changed from *bombil* through association with *Bombay*, port in W India]

bombazine *or* **bombasine** (ˌbɒmbəˈziːn, ˈbɒmbəˌziːn) *n* a twilled fabric, esp. one of silk and worsted, formerly worn dyed black for mourning. [C16: from OF, from L, from *bombyx* silk]

bomber (ˈbɒmə) *n* **1** a military aircraft designed to carry out bombing missions. **2** a person who plants bombs.

bomber jacket *n* a short jacket finishing at the waist with an elasticated band, usually having a zip front.

bombora (bɒmˈbɔːrə) *n Austral.* **1** a submerged reef. **2** a turbulent area of sea over such a reef. [from Abor.]

bombshell (ˈbɒmˌʃɛl) *n* **1** (esp. formerly) a bomb or artillery shell. **2** a shocking or unwelcome surprise.

bombsight (ˈbɒmˌsaɪt) *n* a mechanical or electronic device in an aircraft for aiming bombs.

bona fide Ⓣ (ˈbəʊnə ˈfaɪdɪ) *adj* **1** real or genuine: *a bona fide manuscript.* **2** undertaken in good faith: *a bona fide agreement.* [C16: from L]

bona fides (ˈbəʊnə ˈfaɪdiːz) *n Law.* good faith; honest intention. [L]

bonanza (bəˈnænzə) *n* **1** a source, usually sudden and unexpected, of luck or wealth. **2** *US & Canad.* a mine or vein rich in ore. [C19: from Sp., lit.: calm sea, hence, good luck, from Med. L, from L *bonus* good + *malacia* calm, from Gk *malakia* softness]

bonbon (ˈbɒnbɒn) *n* a sweet. [C19: from F, orig. a children's word from *bon* good]

bonce (bɒns) *n Brit. sl.* the head. [C19 (orig.: a large playing marble): from ?]

bond Ⓣ (bɒnd) *n* **1** something that binds, fastens, or holds together. **2** (*often pl*) something that brings or holds people together; tie: *a bond of friendship.* **3** (*pl*) something that restrains or imprisons; captivity or imprisonment. **4** a written or spoken agreement, esp. a promise. **5** *Finance.* a certificate of debt issued in order to raise funds. It is repayable with or without security at a specified future date. **6** *Law.* a written acknowledgment of an obligation to pay a sum or to perform a contract. **7** any of various arrangements of bricks or stones in a wall in which they overlap so as to provide strength. **8 chemical bond.** a mutual attraction between two atoms resulting from a redistribution of their outer electrons, determining chemical properties; shown in some formulae by a dot (.) or score (—). **9** See **bond paper. 10 in bond.** *Commerce.* deposited in a bonded warehouse. ◆ *vb* (*mainly tr*) **11** (*also intr*) to hold or be held together, as by a rope or an adhesive; bind; connect. **12** (*intr*) to become emotionally attached. **13** to put or hold (goods) in bond. **14** *Law.* to place under bond. **15** *Finance.* to issue bonds on; mortgage. [C13: from ON *band;* see BAND[2]]

bondage Ⓣ (ˈbɒndɪdʒ) *n* **1** slavery or serfdom; servitude. **2** subjection to some influence or duty. **3** a sexual practice in which one participant is physically bound.

bonded (ˈbɒndɪd) *adj* **1** *Finance.* consisting of, secured by, or operating under a bond or bonds. **2** *Commerce.* deposited in a bonded warehouse.

bonded warehouse *n* a warehouse in which goods are deposited until duty is paid.

bondholder (ˈbɒndˌhəʊldə) *n* an owner of bonds issued by a company or other institution.

bonding (ˈbɒndɪŋ) *n* the process by which individuals become emotionally attached to one another.

bondmaid (ˈbɒndˌmeɪd) *n* an unmarried female serf or slave.

bond paper *n* a superior quality of strong white paper, used esp. for writing and typing.

bondservant (ˈbɒndˌsɜːvənt) *n* a serf or slave.

bondsman (ˈbɒndzmən) *n, pl* **bondsmen. 1** *Law.* a person bound by bond to act as surety for another. **2** another word for **bondservant.**

bond washing *n* a series of illegal deals in bonds made with the intention of avoiding taxation.

bone (bəʊn) *n* **1** any of the various structures that make up the skeleton in most vertebrates. **2** the porous rigid tissue of which these parts are made. **3** something consisting of bone or a bonelike substance. **4** (*pl*) the human skeleton or body. **5** a thin strip of whalebone, plastic, etc., used to stiffen corsets and brassieres. **6** (*pl*) the essentials (esp. in **the bare bones**). **7** (*pl*) dice. **8 close** *or* **near to the bone. 8a** risqué or indecent. **8b** in poverty; destitute. **9 feel in one's bones.** to have an intuition of. **10 have a bone to pick.** to have grounds for a quarrel. **11 make no bones about. 11a** to be direct and candid about. **11b** to have no scruples about. **12 point the bone.** (often foll. by *at*) *Austral.* **12a** to wish bad luck (on). **12b** to cast a spell (on) in order to kill. ◆ *vb* **bones, boning, boned.** (*mainly tr*) **13** to remove the bones from (meat for cooking, etc.). **14** to stiffen (a corset, etc.) by inserting bones. **15** *Brit.* a slang word for **steal.** ◆ See also **bone up.** [OE *bān*]
▸ˈ**boneless** *adj*

bone ash *n* ash obtained when bones are burnt in air, consisting mainly of calcium phosphate.

bone china *n* porcelain containing bone ash.

bone-dry *adj Inf.* **a** completely dry: *a bone-dry well.* **b** (*postpositive*): *the well was bone dry.*

bonehead (ˈbəʊnˌhɛd) *n Sl.* a stupid or obstinate person.
▸ˈ**boneˌheaded** *adj*

bone idle *adj* very idle; extremely lazy.

bone marrow *n* See **marrow** (sense 1).

bone meal *n* dried and ground animal bones, used as a fertilizer or in stock feeds.

boner (ˈbəʊnə) *n Sl.* a blunder.

bonesetter (ˈbəʊnˌsɛtə) *n* a person who sets broken or dislocated bones, esp. one who has no formal medical qualifications.

boneshaker (ˈbəʊnˌʃeɪkə) *n* **1** an early type of bicycle having solid tyres and no springs. **2** *Sl.* any decrepit or rickety vehicle.

bone up *vb* (*adv;* when *intr*, usually foll. by *on*) *Inf.* to study intensively.

bonfire (ˈbɒnˌfaɪə) *n* a large outdoor fire. [C15: alteration (infl. by F *bon* good) of *bone-fire;* from the use of bones as fuel]

bong (bɒŋ) *n* **1** a deep reverberating sound, as of a large bell. ◆ *vb* **2** to make a deep reverberating sound. [C20: imit.]

bongo[1] (ˈbɒŋgəʊ) *n, pl* **bongo** *or* **bongos.** a rare spiral-horned antelope inhabiting forests of central Africa. The coat is bright red-brown with narrow vertical stripes. [of African origin]

bongo[2] (ˈbɒŋgəʊ) *n, pl* **bongos** *or* **bongoes.** a small bucket-shaped drum, usually one of a pair, played by beating with the fingers. [American Sp., prob. imit.]

bonhomie (ˈbɒnəmiː) *n* exuberant friendliness. [C18: from F, from *bon* good + *homme* man]

bonito (bəˈniːtəʊ) *n, pl* **bonitos.** any of various small tunny-like marine food fishes of warm Atlantic and Pacific waters. [C16: from Sp., from L *bonus* good]

bonk (bɒŋk) *vb Inf.* **1** (*tr*) to hit. **2** to have sexual intercourse (with). [C20: prob. imit.]
▸ˈ**bonking** *n*

bonkbuster (ˈbɒŋkˌbʌstə) *n Inf.* a novel characterized by graphic descriptions of the heroine's frequent sexual encounters. [C20: from BONK (sense 2) + (BLOCK)BUSTER]

bonkers (ˈbɒŋkəz) *adj Sl., chiefly Brit.* mad; crazy. [C20: from ?]

bon mot (*French* bɔ̃ mo) *n, pl* **bons mots** (bɔ̃ mo). a clever and fitting remark. [F, lit.: good word]

bonnet (ˈbɒnɪt) *n* **1** any of various hats worn, esp. formerly, by women and girls, and tied with ribbons under the chin. **2** (in Scotland) Also: **bunnet. 2a** a soft cloth cap. **2b** (formerly) a flat brimless cap worn by men. **3** the hinged metal part of a motor vehicle body that provides access to the engine. US name: **hood. 4** a cowl on a chimney. **5** *Naut.* a piece of sail laced to the foot of a foresail to give it greater area in light winds. **6** (in the US and Canada) a headdress of feathers worn by some tribes of American Indians. [C14: from OF *bonet,* from ?]

bonny Ⓣ (ˈbɒnɪ) *adj* **bonnier, bonniest. 1** *Scot. & N English dialect.* beautiful or handsome: *a bonny lass.* **2** good or fine. **3** (esp. of babies) plump. [C15: from OF *bon* good, from L *bonus*]

bonsai (ˈbɒnsaɪ) *n, pl* **bonsai. 1** the art of growing dwarfed ornamental varieties of trees or shrubs in small shallow pots or trays by selective pruning, etc. **2** a tree or shrub grown by this method. [C20: from Japanese, from *bon* bowl + *sai* to plant]

bontebok (ˈbɒntɪˌbʌk) *n, pl* **bonteboks** *or* **bontebok.** an antelope of southern Africa, having a deep reddish-brown coat with a white blaze, tail, and rump patch. [C18: Afrik. from *bont* pied + *bok* BUCK[1]]

bonus Ⓣ (ˈbəʊnəs) *n* **1** something given, paid, or received above what is due or expected. **2** *Chiefly Brit.* an extra dividend allotted to shareholders out of profits. **3** *Insurance, Brit.* a dividend, esp. a percentage of net profits, distributed to policyholders. [C18: from L *bonus* (adj) good]

bonus issue *n Brit.* a free issue of shares distributed among shareholders pro rata with their holdings.

bon vivant Ⓣ *French.* (bɔ̃ vivɑ̃) *n, pl* ***bons vivants*** (bɔ̃ vivɑ̃). a person who

THESAURUS

barrage, blitz, cannonade, fire, flak, fusillade, shelling, strafe

bombast *n* = **grandiloquence**, bluster, brag, braggadocio, extravagant boasting, grandiosity, hot air (*inf.*), magniloquence, pomposity, rant

bombastic *adj* = **grandiloquent**, declamatory, grandiose, high-flown, histrionic, inflated, magniloquent, pompous, ranting, turgid, verbose, windy, wordy

bona fide *adj* **1** = **genuine**, actual, authentic, honest, kosher (*inf.*), lawful, legal, legitimate, on the level (*inf.*), real, the real McCoy, true
Antonyms *adj* bogus, counterfeit, ersatz, fake, false, imitation, phoney *or* phony (*inf.*), sham

bond *n* **1** = **fastening**, band, binding, chain, cord, fetter, ligature, link, manacle, shackle, tie **2** = **tie**, affiliation, affinity, attachment, connection, link, relation, union **4** = **agreement**, compact, contract, covenant, guarantee, obligation, pledge, promise, word ◆ *vb* **11** = **hold together**, bind, connect, fasten, fix together, fuse, glue, gum, paste

bondage *n* **1** = **slavery**, enslavement, enthralment, serfdom, servitude, subjection, subjugation, thraldom, vassalage, yoke

bonny *adj* **1** *Scot. & N English dialect* = **beautiful**, comely, fair, handsome, lovely, pretty, sweet

bonus *n* **1** = **extra**, benefit, bounty, gift, gratuity, hand-out, icing on the cake, perk (*Brit. inf.*), plus, prize, reward **2** = **dividend**, commission, premium

bon vivant *n* = **gourmet**, bon viveur, epicure, epicurean, foodie, gastronome, hedonist, pleasure-seeker, voluptuary

enjoys luxuries, esp. good food and drink. Also called (but not in French): **bon viveur** (ˌbɒn viːˈvɜː). [lit.: good-living (man)]

bon voyage (*French* bɔ̃ vwajaʒ) *sentence substitute.* a phrase used to wish a traveller a pleasant journey. [F, lit.: good journey]

bony Ⓣ (ˈbəʊnɪ) *adj* **bonier, boniest. 1** resembling or consisting of bone. **2** having many bones. **3** having prominent bones. **4** thin or emaciated.

bony fish *n* any of a class of fishes, including most of the extant species, having a skeleton of bone rather than cartilage.

bonze (bɒnz) *n* a Chinese or Japanese Buddhist priest or monk. [C16: from F, from Port. *bonzo,* from Japanese *bonsō,* from Sanskrit *bon* + *sō* priest or monk]

bonzer (ˈbɒnzə) *adj Austral & NZ sl., arch.* very good; excellent. [C20: ?from BONANZA]

boo (buː) *interj* **1** an exclamation uttered to startle or surprise someone, esp. a child. **2** a shout uttered to express disgust, dissatisfaction, or contempt. ◆ *vb* **boos, booing, booed. 3** to shout "boo" at (someone or something), esp. as an expression of disapproval.

boob (buːb) *Sl.* ◆ *n* **1** an ignorant or foolish person. **2** *Brit.* an embarrassing mistake; blunder. **3** a female breast. ◆ *vb* **4** (*intr*) *Brit.* to make a blunder. [C20: back formation from BOOBY]

boobialla (ˌbuːbɪˈælə) *n Austral.* **1** another name for **golden wattle** (sense 2). **2** any of various trees or shrubs of the genus *Myoporum.*

boo-boo *n, pl* **boo-boos.** an embarrassing mistake; blunder. [C20: ?from nursery talk]

boob tube *n Sl.* **1** a close-fitting strapless top, worn by women. **2** *Chiefly US & Canad.* a television receiver.

booby Ⓣ (ˈbuːbɪ) *n, pl* **boobies. 1** an ignorant or foolish person. **2** *Brit.* the losing player in a game. **3** any of several tropical marine birds related to the gannet. They have a straight stout bill and the plumage is white with darker markings. [C17: from Sp. *bobo,* from L *balbus* stammering]

booby prize *n* a mock prize given to the person having the lowest score.

booby trap *n* **1** a hidden explosive device primed in such a way as to be set off by an unsuspecting victim. **2** a trap for an unsuspecting person, esp. one intended as a practical joke. ◆ *vb* **booby-trap, booby-traps, booby-trapping, booby-trapped. 3** (*tr*) to set a booby trap in or on (a building or object) or for (a person).

boodle (ˈbuːdᵊl) *n Sl.* money or valuables, esp. when stolen, counterfeit, or used as a bribe. [C19: from Du. *boedel* possessions]

boogie (ˈbuːgɪ) *vb* **boogies, boogieing, boogied.** (*intr*) *Sl.* **1** to dance to pop music. **2** to make love. [C20: orig. African-American slang, ?from Bantu *mbugi* devilishly good]

boogie-woogie (ˈbugɪˈwugɪ, ˈbuːgɪˈwuːgɪ) *n* a style of piano jazz using a dotted bass pattern, usually with eight notes in a bar and the harmonies of the 12-bar blues. [C20: ? imit.]

boohai (buːˈhaɪ) *n* **up the boohai.** *NZ inf.* thoroughly lost. [from the remote township of *Puhoi*]

boohoo (ˌbuːˈhuː) *vb* **boohoos, boohooing, boohooed.** (*intr*) **1** to sob or pretend to sob noisily. ◆ *n, pl* **boohoos. 2** (*sometimes pl*) distressed or pretended sobbing. [C20: nursery talk]

book Ⓣ (bʊk) *n* **1** a number of printed or written pages bound together along one edge and usually protected by covers. **2a** a written work or composition, such as a novel, technical manual, or dictionary. **2b** (*as modifier*): *book reviews.* **2c** (*in combination*): *bookseller; bookshop; bookshelf.* **3** a number of blank or ruled sheets of paper bound together, used to record lessons, keep accounts, etc. **4** (*pl*) a record of the transactions of a business or society. **5** the libretto of an opera, musical, etc. **6** a major division of a written composition, as of a long novel or of the Bible. **7** a number of tickets, stamps, etc., fastened together along one edge. **8** a record of betting transactions. **9** (in card games) the number of tricks that must be taken by a side or player before any trick has a scoring value. **10** strict or rigid rules or standards (esp. in **by the book**). **11** a source of knowledge or authority: *the book of life.* **12 a closed book.** a person or subject that is unknown or beyond comprehension: *chemistry is a closed book to him.* **13 an open book.** a person or subject that is thoroughly understood. **14 bring to book.** to reprimand or require (someone) to give an explanation of his conduct. **15 close the books.** *Book-keeping.* to balance accounts in order to prepare a statement or report. **16 in someone's good** (*or* **bad**) **books.** regarded by someone with favour (*or* disfavour). **17 keep the books.** to keep written records of the finances of a business. **18 on the books. 18a** enrolled as a member. **18b** recorded. **19 the book.** (*sometimes cap.*) the Bible. **20 throw the book at. 20a** to charge with every relevant offence. **20b** to inflict the most severe punishment on. ◆ *vb* **21** to reserve (a place, passage, etc.) or engage the services of (a performer, driver, etc.) in advance. **22** (*tr*) to take the name and address of (a person guilty of a minor offence) with a view to bringing a prosecution. **23** (*tr*) (of a football referee) to take the name of (a player) who grossly infringes the rules. **24** (*tr*) *Arch.* to record in a book. ◆ See also **book in.** [OE *bōc;* see BEECH (its bark was used as a writing surface)]

bookbinder (ˈbʊkˌbaɪndə) *n* a person whose business is binding books.
▸ˈ**book**ˌ**binding** *n*

bookbindery (ˈbʊkˌbaɪndərɪ) *n, pl* **bookbinderies.** a place in which books are bound. Often shortened to **bindery.**

bookcase (ˈbʊkˌkeɪs) *n* a piece of furniture containing shelves for books.

book club *n* a club that sells books at low prices to members, usually by mail order.

book end *n* one of a pair of usually ornamental supports for holding a row of books upright.

Booker Prize (ˈbʊkə) *n* an annual prize for a work of British, Commonwealth, or Irish fiction of £20,000, awarded since 1969 by the Booker McConnell engineering company.

bookie (ˈbʊkɪ) *n Inf.* short for **bookmaker.**

book in *vb* (*adv*) **1** to reserve a room at a hotel. **2** *Chiefly Brit.* to register, esp. one's arrival at a hotel.

booking Ⓣ (ˈbʊkɪŋ) *n* **1** *Chiefly Brit.* a reservation, as of a table, room, or seat. **2** *Theatre.* an engagement of an actor or company.

bookish Ⓣ (ˈbʊkɪʃ) *adj* **1** fond of reading; studious. **2** consisting of or forming opinions through reading rather than experience; academic. **3** of or relating to books.
▸ˈ**bookishness** *n*

book-keeping *n* the skill or occupation of systematically recording business transactions.
▸ˈ**book-**ˌ**keeper** *n*

book-learning *n* knowledge gained from books rather than from experience.

booklet Ⓣ (ˈbʊklɪt) *n* a thin book, esp. one having paper covers; pamphlet.

bookmaker (ˈbʊkˌmeɪkə) *n* a person who as an occupation accepts bets, esp. on horseraces, and pays out to winning betters.
▸ˈ**book**ˌ**making** *n*

bookmark (ˈbʊkˌmɑːk) *n* **1** Also called: **bookmarker.** a strip of some material put between the pages of a book to mark a place. **2** *Computing.* an identifier put on a website that enables the user to return to it quickly and easily. ◆ *vb* **3** (*tr*) *Computing.* to identify and store (a website) so that one can return to it quickly and easily.

Book of Common Prayer *n* the official book of church services of the Church of England until 1980, when the Alternative Service Book was sanctioned.

bookplate (ˈbʊkˌpleɪt) *n* a label bearing the owner's name and a design, pasted into a book.

bookstall (ˈbʊkˌstɔːl) *n* a stall or stand where periodicals, newspapers, or books are sold.

book token *n Brit.* a gift token to be exchanged for books.

book value *n* **1** the value of an asset of a business according to its books. **2** the net capital value of an enterprise as shown by the excess of book assets over book liabilities.

bookworm (ˈbʊkˌwɜːm) *n* **1** a person devoted to reading. **2** any of various small insects that feed on the binding paste of books.

Boolean algebra (ˈbuːlɪən) *n* a system of symbolic logic devised to codify nonmathematical logical operations. It is used in computing. [C19: after George *Boole* (1815–64), E mathematician]

boom¹ Ⓣ (buːm) *vb* **1** to make a deep prolonged resonant sound. **2** to prosper or cause to prosper vigorously and rapidly: *business boomed.* ◆ *n* **3** a deep prolonged resonant sound. **4** a period of high economic growth. **5** any similar period of high activity. **6** the activity itself: *a baby boom.* [C15: ?from Du. *bommen,* imit.]

boom² (buːm) *n* **1** *Naut.* a spar to which a sail is fastened to control its position relative to the wind. **2** a pole carrying an overhead microphone and projected over a film or television set. **3** a barrier across a waterway, usually consisting of a chain of logs, to confine free-floating logs, protect a harbour from attack, etc. [C16: from Du. *boom* tree, BEAM]

boomer (ˈbuːmə) *n* **1** *Austral.* a large male kangaroo. **2** *Austral. & NZ inf.* anything exceptionally large.

boomerang Ⓣ (ˈbuːməˌræŋ) *n* **1** a curved flat wooden missile of native Australians, which can be made to return to the thrower. **2** an action or statement that recoils on its originator. ◆ *vb* **3** (*intr*) (of a plan, etc.)

THESAURUS

Antonyms *n* abstainer, ascetic, celibate, self-denier

bony *adj* **3** = **angular**, gangling **4** = **thin**, emaciated, gaunt, lanky, lean, rawboned, scrawny, skin and bone, skinny

booby *n* **1** = **fool**, berk (*Brit. sl.*), blockhead, dimwit, divvy (*Brit. sl.*), dork (*sl.*), duffer, dunce, fathead (*inf.*), idiot, muggins (*Brit. sl.*), numbskull *or* numskull, pillock (*Brit. sl.*), plonker (*sl.*), schmuck (*US sl.*), simpleton, twit (*inf., chiefly Brit.*), wally (*sl.*)

book *n* **1** = **work**, hardback, manual, paperback, publication, roll, scroll, textbook, title, tome, tract, volume **3** = **notebook**, album, diary, exercise book, jotter, pad ◆ *vb* **21** = **reserve**, arrange for, bill, charter, engage, line up, make reservations, organize, programme, schedule **24** *Archaic* = **record**, enter, insert, list, log, mark down, note, put down, register, write down

booking *n* **1** *Chiefly Brit.* = **reservation**, appointment, date **2** *Theatre* = **engagement**, commission, gig (*inf.*)

bookish *adj* **1** = **studious**, academic, donnish, erudite, intellectual, learned, literary, scholarly, well-read

booklet *n* = **brochure**, leaflet, pamphlet

boom¹ *vb* **1** = **bang**, blast, crash, explode, resound, reverberate, roar, roll, rumble, thunder **2** = **flourish**, develop, expand, gain, grow, increase, intensify, prosper, spurt, strengthen, succeed, swell, thrive ◆ *n* **3** = **bang**, blast, burst, clap, crash, explosion, roar, rumble, thunder **4, 5** = **expansion**, advance, boost, development, gain, growth, improvement, increase, jump, push, spurt, upsurge, upswing, upturn
Antonyms *vb* ≠ **flourish:** crash, fail, fall, slump ◆ *n* ≠ **expansion:** bust (*inf.*), collapse, crash, decline, depression, downturn, failure, hard times, recession, slump

boomerang *vb* **3** = **rebound**, backfire, come back, come home to roost, recoil, return, reverse, ricochet

to recoil or return unexpectedly, causing harm to its originator. [C19: from Abor.]

boomslang ('bu:m,slæŋ) *n* a large greenish venomous arboreal snake of southern Africa. [C18: from Afrik., from *boom* tree + *slang* snake]

boon[1] ❶ (bu:n) *n* **1** something extremely useful, helpful, or beneficial; a blessing or benefit. **2** *Arch.* a favour; request. [C12: from ON *bōn* request]

boon[2] ❶ (bu:n) *adj* **1** close, special, or intimate (in **boon companion**). **2** *Arch.* jolly or convivial. [C14: from OF *bon*, from L *bonus* good]

boondocks ('bu:n,dɒks) *pl n* **the.** *US & Canad. sl.* **1** wild, desolate, or uninhabitable country. **2** a remote rural or provincial area. [C20: from Tagalog *bundok* mountain]

boong (bʊŋ) *n Austral. offens.* a Black person. [C20: from Abor.]

boongary (bu:n'geərɪ) *n, pl* **-ries.** a tree kangaroo of NE Queensland. [from Abor.]

boor ❶ (bʊə) *n* an ill-mannered, clumsy, or insensitive person. [OE *gebūr* dweller, farmer; see NEIGHBOUR]
▸ **'boorish** *adj* ▸ **'boorishly** *adv* ▸ **'boorishness** *n*

boost ❶ (bu:st) *n* **1** encouragement, improvement, or help: *a boost to morale.* **2** an upward thrust or push. **3** an increase or rise. **4** the amount by which the induction pressure of a supercharged internal-combustion engine is increased. ◆ *vb (tr)* **5** to encourage, assist, or improve: *to boost morale.* **6** to lift by giving a push from below or behind. **7** to increase or raise: *to boost the voltage in an electrical circuit.* **8** to cause to rise; increase: *to boost sales.* **9** to advertise on a big scale. **10** to increase the induction pressure of (an internal-combustion engine); supercharge. [C19: from ?]

booster ('bu:stə) *n* **1** a person or thing that supports, assists, or increases power. **2** Also called: **launch vehicle.** the first stage of a multistage rocket. **3** a radio-frequency amplifier to strengthen signals. **4** another name for **supercharger. 5** short for **booster shot.**

booster shot *n Inf.* a supplementary injection of a vaccine given to maintain the immunization provided by an earlier dose.

boot[1] ❶ (bu:t) *n* **1** a strong outer covering for the foot; shoe that extends above the ankle, often to the knee. **2** *Brit.* an enclosed compartment of a car for holding luggage, etc., usually at the rear. US and Canad. name: **trunk. 3** an instrument of torture used to crush the foot and lower leg. **4** *Inf.* a kick: *he gave the door a boot.* **5 boots and all.** *Austral. & NZ inf.* making every effort. **6 die with one's boots on.** to die while still active. **7 lick the boots of.** to be servile towards. **8 put the boot in.** *Sl.* **8a** to kick a person, esp. when he is already down. **8b** to harass someone. **8c** to finish off (something) with unnecessary brutality. **9 the boot.** *Sl.* dismissal from employment; the sack. **10 the boot is on the other foot** *or* **leg.** the situation is or has now reversed. ◆ *vb (tr)* **11** to kick. **12** to equip with boots. **13** *Inf.* **13a** (often foll. by *out*) to eject forcibly. **13b** to dismiss from employment. **14** to bootstrap (a computer system). [C14 *bote*, from OF, from ?]

boot[2] (bu:t) *vb (usually impersonal)* **1** *Arch.* to be of advantage or use to (a person): *what boots it to complain?* ◆ *n* **2** *Obs.* an advantage. **3 to boot.** as well; in addition. [OE *bōt* compensation]

bootblack ('bu:t,blæk) *n* (esp. formerly) a person who shines boots and shoes.

boot camp *n* **1** *US sl.* a basic training camp for new recruits to the US Navy or Marine Corps. **2** a centre for juvenile offenders with a strict disciplinary regime, hard physical exercise, and community labour programmes.

bootee ('bu:ti:, bu:'ti:) *n* **1** a soft shoe for a baby, esp. a knitted one. **2** a boot for women and children, esp. an ankle-length one.

Boötes (bəʊ'əʊti:z) *n, Latin genitive* **Boötis** (bəʊ'əʊtɪs). a constellation in the N hemisphere containing the star Arcturus. [C17: via L from Gk: ploughman]

booth (bu:ð, bu:θ) *n, pl* **booths** (bu:ðz). **1** a stall, esp. a temporary one at a fair or market. **2** a small partially enclosed cubicle, such as one for telephoning (**telephone booth**) or for voting (**polling booth**). **3** two high-backed benches with a table between, used esp. in bars and restaurants. **4** (formerly) a temporary structure for shelter, dwelling, storage, etc. [C12: of Scand. origin]

bootjack ('bu:t,dʒæk) *n* a device that grips the heel of a boot to enable the foot to be withdrawn easily.

bootleg ❶ ('bu:t,leg) *vb* **bootlegs, bootlegging, bootlegged. 1** to make, carry, or sell (illicit goods, esp. alcohol). ◆ *n* **2** something made or sold illicitly, such as alcohol. **3** an illegally made copy of a CD, tape, etc. ◆ *adj* **4** produced, distributed, or sold illicitly. [C17: see BOOT[1], LEG; from smugglers carrying bottles of liquor concealed in their boots]
▸ **'boot,legger** *n*

bootless ('bu:tlɪs) *adj* of little or no use; vain; fruitless. [OE *bōtlēas*, from *bōt* compensation]

bootlicker ❶ ('bu:t,lɪkə) *n Inf.* one who seeks favour by servile or ingratiating behaviour towards (someone, esp. in authority); toady.

bootstrap ('bu:t,stræp) *n* **1** a loop on a boot for pulling it on. **2 by one's (own) bootstraps.** by one's own efforts; unaided. **3a** a technique for loading the first few program instructions into a computer main store to enable the rest of the program to be introduced from an input device. **3b** *(as modifier)*: *a bootstrap loader.* **4** *Commerce.* an offer to purchase a controlling interest in a company, esp. with the intention of purchasing the remainder of the equity at a lower price. ◆ *vb* **bootstraps, bootstrapping, bootstrapped.** *(tr)* **5** to initiate (a computer system) by executing a bootstrap; boot.

booty ❶ ('bu:tɪ) *n, pl* **booties.** any valuable article or articles, esp. when obtained as plunder. [C15: from OF, from MLow G *buite* exchange]

booze ❶ (bu:z) *Inf.* ◆ *n* **1** alcoholic drink. **2** a drinking bout. ◆ *vb* **boozes, boozing, boozed. 3** *(usually intr)* to drink (alcohol), esp. in excess. [C13: from MDu. *būsen*]

boozer ❶ ('bu:zə) *n Inf.* **1** a person who is fond of drinking. **2** *Brit., Austral., & NZ.* a bar or pub.

booze-up ❶ *n Brit., Austral., & NZ sl.* a drinking spree.

boozy ('bu:zɪ) *adj* **boozier, booziest.** *Inf.* inclined to or involving excessive drinking of alcohol; drunken: *a boozy lecturer; a boozy party.*

bop (bɒp) *n* **1** a form of jazz originating in the 1940s, characterized by rhythmic and harmonic complexity and instrumental virtuosity. Originally called: **bebop.** ◆ *vb* **bops, bopping, bopped. 2** *(intr) Inf.* to dance to pop music. [C20: shortened from BEBOP]
▸ **'bopper** *n*

bo-peep (,bəʊ'pi:p) *n* a game for very young children, in which one hides (esp. hiding one's face in one's hands) and reappears suddenly.

bora[1] ('bɔ:rə) *n (sometimes cap.)* a violent cold north wind blowing from the Adriatic. [C19: from It. dialect., from L *boreās* the north wind]

bora[2] ('bɔ:rə) *n* an initiation ceremony of native Australians, introducing youths to manhood. [from Abor.]

boracic (bə'ræsɪk) *adj* another word for **boric.**

borage ('bɒrɪdʒ, 'bʌrɪdʒ) *n* a Mediterranean plant with star-shaped blue flowers. The young leaves are sometimes used in salads. [C13: from OF, ?from Ar. *abū 'āraq*, lit.: father of sweat]

borate *n* ('bɔ:reɪt, -ɪt). **1** a salt or ester of boric acid. ◆ *vb* ('bɔ:reɪt), **borates, borating, borated. 2** *(tr)* to treat with borax, boric acid, or borate.

borax ('bɔ:ræks) *n, pl* **boraxes** *or* **boraces** (-rə,si:z). a soluble readily fusible white mineral in monoclinic crystalline form, occurring in alkaline soils and salt deposits. Formula: $Na_2B_4O_7.10H_2O$. [C14: from OF, from Med. L, from Ar., from Persian *būrah*]

borazon ('bɔ:rə,zɒn) *n* an extremely hard form of boron nitride. [C20: from BOR(ON) + AZO + -ON]

borborygmus (,bɔ:bə'rɪgməs) *n, pl* **borborygmi** (-maɪ). rumbling of the stomach. [C18: from Gk]

Bordeaux (bɔ:'dəʊ) *n* any of several red, white, or rosé wines produced around Bordeaux in SW France.

Bordeaux mixture *n Horticulture.* a fungicide consisting of a solution of equal quantities of copper sulphate and quicklime.

THESAURUS

booming *adj* **1** = **loud**, bellowing, deafening, echoing, resonant, resounding, rich, sonorous, stentorian, thundering **2** = **flourishing**, expanding, on the up and up (*Brit.*), prospering, thriving

boon[1] *n* **1** = **benefit**, advantage, blessing, donation, gift, godsend, grant, gratuity, hand-out, manna from heaven, present, windfall

boon[2] *adj* **1** = **intimate**, close, special

boor *n* = **lout**, barbarian, brute, bumpkin, churl, clodhopper (*inf.*), hayseed (*US & Canad. inf.*), hick (*inf., chiefly US & Canad.*), oaf, peasant, philistine, redneck (*US sl.*)

boorish *adj* = **loutish**, awkward, barbaric, bearish, churlish, clownish, coarse, crude, gross, hick (*inf., chiefly US & Canad.*), ill-bred, lubberly, oafish, rude, uncivilized, uncouth, uneducated, unrefined, vulgar
Antonyms *adj* cultured, gallant, genteel, polite, refined, sophisticated, urbane

boost *n* **1** = **help**, encouragement, gee-up, hype, improvement, praise, promotion **2** = **push**, heave, hoist, lift, raise, shove, thrust **3** = **rise**, addition, expansion, improvement, increase, increment, jump ◆ *vb* **6** = **raise**, elevate, heave, hoist, lift, push, shove, thrust **7, 8** = **increase**, add to, amplify, develop, enlarge, expand, heighten, jack up, magnify, raise **9** = **promote**, advance, advertise, assist, crack up (*inf.*), encourage, foster, further, gee up, hype, improve, inspire, plug (*inf.*), praise, support, sustain
Antonyms *n* ≠ **help:** condemnation, criticism, knock (*inf.*) ≠ **rise:** cut-back, decline, decrease, deterioration, fall, reduction ◆ *vb* ≠ **raise:** drop, let down, lower ≠ **increase:** cut, decrease, diminish, drop, lessen, lower, moderate, pare, reduce, scale down ≠ **promote:** condemn, criticize, hinder, hold back, knock (*inf.*)

boot[1] *vb* **11** = **kick**, drive, drop-kick, knock, punt, put the boot in(to) (*sl.*), shove **13a** *Informal often with* **out** = **throw out**, eject, give the bum's rush (*sl.*), kick out, show one the door, throw out on one's ear (*inf.*) **13b** *Informal* = **sack** (*inf.*), dismiss, expel, give (someone) their marching orders, give the boot (*sl.*), give the bullet, give the heave *or* push (*inf.*), kick out, kiss off (*sl., chiefly US & Canad.*), oust, relegate

bootleg *adj* **4** = **illicit**, black-market, contraband, illegal, outlawed, pirate, unauthorized, under-the-counter, under-the-table, unlicensed, unofficial
Antonyms *adj* authorized, legal, licensed, licit, official, on the level (*inf.*)

bootlicker *n Informal* = **toady**, crawler, fawner, flatterer, lackey, spaniel, sycophant, yes man

booty *n* = **plunder**, gains, haul, loot, pillage, prey, spoil, spoils, swag (*sl.*), takings, winnings

booze *Informal n* **1** = **alcohol**, drink, firewater, grog (*inf., chiefly Austral. & NZ*), hooch *or* hootch (*inf., chiefly US & Canad.*), intoxicant, juice (*inf.*), liquor, spirits, strong drink, the bottle (*inf.*), the hard stuff (*inf.*) ◆ *vb* **3** = **drink**, bevvy, carouse, drink like a fish, get drunk, get plastered, get soused, get tanked up (*inf.*), go on a binge *or* bender (*inf.*), hit the booze *or* bottle (*inf.*), imbibe, indulge, tipple, tope

boozer *n Informal* **1** = **drinker**, alcoholic, drunk, drunkard, inebriate, lush (*sl.*), soak (*sl.*), sot, tippler, toper, wino (*inf.*) **2** = **pub** (*inf., chiefly Brit.*), alehouse (*arch.*), bar, hostelry, inn, local (*Brit. inf.*), public house, roadhouse, taproom, tavern, watering hole (*facetious sl.*)

booze-up *n Brit., Austral., & NZ slang* = **drinking**

border ⓣ (ˈbɔːdə) *n* **1** a band or margin around or along the edge of something. **2** the dividing line or frontier between political or geographic regions. **3** a region straddling such a boundary. **4** a design around the edge of something. **5** a long narrow strip of ground planted with flowers, shrubs, etc.: *a herbaceous border.* ◆ *vb* **6** (*tr*) to provide with a border. **7** (when *intr,* foll. by *on* or *upon*) **7a** to be adjacent (to); lie along the boundary (of). **7b** to be nearly the same (as); verge (on): *his stupidity borders on madness.* [C14: from OF, from *bort* side of a ship, of Gmc origin]

borderer (ˈbɔːdərə) *n* a person who lives in a border area.

borderland (ˈbɔːdəˌlænd) *n* **1** land located on or near a frontier or boundary. **2** an indeterminate state or condition.

borderline ⓣ (ˈbɔːdəˌlaɪn) *n* **1** a border; dividing line. **2** an indeterminate position between two conditions: *the borderline between friendship and love.* ◆ *adj* **3** on the edge of one category and verging on another: *a borderline failure in the exam.*

bore[1] ⓣ (bɔː) *vb* **bores, boring, bored. 1** to produce (a hole) in (a material) by use of a drill, auger, or rotary cutting tool. **2** to increase the diameter of (a hole), as by turning. **3** (*tr*) to produce (a hole in the ground, tunnel, mine shaft, etc.) by digging, drilling, etc. **4** (*intr*) *Inf.* (of a horse or athlete in a race) to push other competitors out of the way. ◆ *n* **5** a hole or tunnel in the ground, esp. one drilled in search of minerals, oil, etc. **6** *Austral.* an artesian well. **7a** the hollow part of a tube or cylinder, esp. of a gun barrel. **7b** the diameter of such a hollow part; calibre. [OE *borian*]

bore[2] ⓣ (bɔː) *vb* **bores, boring, bored. 1** (*tr*) to tire or make weary by being dull, repetitious, or uninteresting. ◆ *n* **2** a dull or repetitious person, activity, or state. [C18: from ?]
▸**bored** *adj* ▸ˈ**boring** *adj*

bore[3] (bɔː) *n* a high steep-fronted wave moving up a narrow estuary, caused by the tide. [C17: from ON *bāra* wave, billow]

bore[4] (bɔː) *vb* the past tense of **bear**[1].

boreal (ˈbɔːrɪəl) *adj* of or relating to the north or the north wind. [C15: from L *boreās* the north wind]

Boreal (ˈbɔːrɪəl) *adj* of or denoting the coniferous forests in the north of the N hemisphere.

boredom ⓣ (ˈbɔːdəm) *n* the state of being bored.

boree (ˈbɔːriː) *n Austral.* another name for **myall.** [from Abor.]

borer (ˈbɔːrə) *n* **1** a tool for boring holes. **2** any of various insects, insect larvae, molluscs, or crustaceans, that bore into plant material, esp. wood.

boric (ˈbɔːrɪk) *adj* of or containing boron. Also: **boracic.**

boric acid *n* a white soluble weakly acid crystalline solid used in the manufacture of heat-resistant glass and porcelain enamels, as a fireproofing material, and as a mild antiseptic. Formula: H_3BO_3. Also called: **orthoboric acid.** Systematic name: **trioxoboric(III) acid.**

borlotti bean (bɔːˈlɒtɪ) *n* a variety of kidney bean with a pinkish-brown speckled skin that turns brown when cooked. [from It., plural of *borlotto* kidney bean]

born (bɔːn) *vb* **1** the past participle (in most passive uses) of **bear**[1] (sense 4). **2 not born yesterday.** not gullible or foolish. ◆ *adj* **3** possessing certain qualities from birth: *a born musician.* **4a** being at birth in a particular social status or other condition as specified: *ignobly born.* **4b** (*in combination*): *lowborn.* **5 in all one's born days.** *Inf.* so far in one's life.

> **USAGE NOTE** Care should be taken not to use *born* when *borne* is intended: *he had borne* (not *born*) *his ordeal with great courage; the following points should be borne in mind.*

born-again (ˈbɔːnəˌgɛn) *adj* **1** having experienced conversion, esp. to evangelical Christianity. **2** showing the enthusiasm of one newly converted to any cause: *a born-again monetarist.* ◆ *n* **3** a person who shows fervent enthusiasm for a new-found cause, belief, etc.

borne (bɔːn) *vb* **1** the past participle of **bear**[1] (for all active uses of the verb; also for all passive uses except sense 4 unless foll. by *by*). **2 be borne in on** *or* **upon.** (of a fact, etc.) to be realized by (someone).

boron (ˈbɔːrɒn) *n* a very hard almost colourless crystalline metalloid element that in impure form exists as a brown amorphous powder. It occurs principally in borax and is used in hardening steel. Symbol: B; atomic no.: 5; atomic wt.: 10.81. [C19: from BOR(AX) + (CARB)ON]

boron carbide *n* a black extremely hard inert substance used as an abrasive and in control rods in nuclear reactors. Formula: B_4C.

boronia (bəˈrəʊnɪə) *n* any aromatic shrub of the Australian genus *Boronia.*

boron nitride *n* a white inert crystalline solid, used as a refractory, high-temperature lubricant and insulator, and heat shield.

borosilicate glass (ˌbɔːrəʊˈsɪlɪkɪt, -ˌkeɪt) *n* any of a range of heat- and chemical-resistant glasses, such as Pyrex, prepared by fusing together oxides of boron and silicon and, usually, a metal oxide.

borough (ˈbʌrə) *n* **1** a town, esp. (in Britain) one that forms the constituency of an MP or that was originally incorporated by royal charter. See also **burgh. 2** any of the 32 constituent divisions of Greater London. **3** any of the five constituent divisions of New York City. **4** (in the US) a self-governing incorporated municipality. [OE *burg*]

borrow ⓣ (ˈbɒrəʊ) *vb* **1** to obtain or receive (something, such as money) on loan for temporary use, intending to give it, or something equivalent, back to the lender. **2** to adopt (ideas, words, etc.) from another source; appropriate. **3** *Not standard.* to lend. **4** (*intr*) *Golf.* to putt the ball uphill of the direct path to the hole: *make sure you borrow enough.* [OE *borgian*]
▸ˈ**borrower** *n*

> **USAGE NOTE** The use of *off* after *borrow* was formerly considered incorrect, but is now acceptable in informal contexts.

borscht (bɔːʃt), **borsch** (bɔːʃ), *or* **borshch** (bɔːʃtʃ) *n* a Russian and Polish soup based on beetroot. [from Russian *borshch*]

borscht belt *n Inf., chiefly US.* a resort area of the Catskill Mountains in New York State, popular with Jewish holiday-makers; its hotels and nightclubs (the **borscht circuit**) are regarded as a training ground for entertainers.

borstal (ˈbɔːstəl) *n* **1** (formerly, in Britain) an establishment in which offenders aged 15 to 21 could be detained for corrective training. Since 1982 they have been replaced by **young offender institutions. 2** a similar establishment in Australia and New Zealand. [C20: after *Borstal,* village in Kent where the first institution was founded]

bort, boart (bɔːt), *or* **bortz** (bɔːts) *n* an inferior grade of diamond used for cutting and drilling or, in powdered form, as an industrial abrasive. [OE *gebrot* fragment]

borzoi (ˈbɔːzɔɪ) *n, pl* **borzois.** a tall fast-moving breed of dog with a long coat. Also called: **Russian wolfhound.** [C19: Russian, lit.: swift]

boscage *or* **boskage** (ˈbɒskɪdʒ) *n Literary.* a mass of trees and shrubs; thicket. [C14: from OF *bosc,* prob. of Gmc origin; see BUSH[1], -AGE]

bosh (bɒʃ) *n Inf.* empty or meaningless talk or opinions; nonsense. [C19: from Turkish *boş* empty]

bosk (bɒsk) *n Literary.* a small wood of bushes and small trees. [C13: var. of *busk* BUSH[1]]

bosky (ˈbɒskɪ) *adj* **boskier, boskiest.** *Literary.* containing or consisting of bushes or thickets.

bo's'n (ˈbəʊsᵊn) *n Naut.* a variant spelling of **boatswain.**

bosom ⓣ (ˈbʊzəm) *n* **1** the chest or breast of a person, esp. the female breasts. **2** the part of a woman's dress, coat, etc., that covers the chest. **3** a protective centre or part: *the bosom of the family.* **4** the breast considered as the seat of emotions. **5** (*modifier*) very dear; intimate: *a bosom friend.* ◆ *vb* (*tr*) **6** to embrace. **7** to conceal or carry in the bosom. [OE *bōsm*]

bosomy (ˈbʊzəmɪ) *adj* (of a woman) having large breasts.

boson (ˈbəʊzɒn) *n* any of a group of elementary particles, such as a photon or pion, that has zero or integral spin and does not obey the Pauli exclusion principle. Cf. **fermion.** [C20: after S. N. *Bose* (1894–1974), Indian physicist]

boss[1] ⓣ (bɒs) *Inf.* ◆ *n* **1** a person in charge of or employing others. **2** *Chiefly US.* a professional politician who controls a political organization, often using devious or illegal methods. ◆ *vb* (*tr*) **3** to employ, supervise, or be in charge of. **4** (usually foll. by *around* or *about*) to be domineering or overbearing towards (others). ◆ *adj* **5** *Sl.* excellent; fine: *a boss hand at carpentry; that's boss!* [C19: from Du. *baas* master]

THESAURUS

spree, bevvy (*dialect*), drink, session (*inf.*), wet (*inf.*)

border *n* **1** = **edge**, bound, boundary, bounds, brim, brink, confine, confines, flange, hem, limit, limits, lip, margin, pale, rim, skirt, verge **2** = **frontier**, borderline, boundary, line, march ◆ *vb* **6** = **edge**, bind, decorate, fringe, hem, rim, trim **7a** *foll. by* **on** = **adjoin**, abut, connect, contact, impinge, join, march, neighbour, touch, verge on **7b** *foll. by* **on** = **come close to**, approach, approximate, be like, be similar to, come near, echo, match, parallel, resemble

borderline *adj* **3** = **marginal**, ambivalent, doubtful, equivocal, indecisive, indefinite, indeterminate, inexact, unclassifiable

bore[1] *vb* **1** = **drill**, gouge out, penetrate, perforate, pierce **3** = **tunnel**, burrow, mine, sink ◆ *n* **5** = **hole**, borehole, drill hole, shaft, tunnel

bore[2] *vb* **1** = **tire**, annoy, be tedious, bother, exhaust, fatigue, jade, pall on, pester, send to sleep, trouble, vex, wear out, weary, worry ◆ *n* **2** = **nuisance**, bother, drag (*inf.*), dull person, pain (*inf.*), pain in the neck (*inf.*), pest, tiresome person, yawn (*inf.*)
Antonyms *vb* ≠ **tire:** amuse, divert, engross, excite, fascinate, hold the attention of, interest, stimulate

bored *adj* **1** = **fed up**, listless, tired, uninterested, wearied

boredom *n* = **tedium**, apathy, doldrums, dullness, ennui, flatness, irksomeness, monotony, sameness, tediousness, weariness, world-weariness
Antonyms *n* amusement, entertainment, excitement, interest, stimulation

boring *adj* **1** = **uninteresting**, dead, dull, flat, ho-hum (*inf.*), humdrum, insipid, mind-numbing, monotonous, old, repetitious, routine, stale, tedious, tiresome, tiring, unexciting, unvaried, wearisome

borrow *vb* **1** = **take on loan**, blag (*sl.*), cadge, mooch (*sl.*), scrounge (*inf.*), take and return, touch (someone) for (*sl.*), use temporarily **2** = **steal**, acquire, adopt, appropriate, copy, filch, imitate, obtain, pilfer, pirate, plagiarize, simulate, take, use, usurp
Antonyms *vb* ≠ **take on loan:** advance, give, lend, loan, provide, return, supply

bosom *n* **1** = **breast**, bust, chest **3** = **midst**, centre, circle, core, protection, shelter **4** = **feelings**, affections, emotions, heart, sentiments, soul, spirit, sympathies ◆ *modifier* **5** = **intimate**, boon, cherished, close, confidential, dear, very dear

boss[1] *n* **1** = **head**, administrator, chief, director, employer, executive, foreman, gaffer (*inf., chiefly Brit.*), governor (*inf.*), kingpin, leader, manager, master, overseer, owner, superinten-

boss[2] (bɒs) *n* **1** a knob, stud, or other circular rounded protuberance, esp. an ornamental one on a vault, a ceiling, or a shield. **2** an area of increased thickness, usually cylindrical, that strengthens or provides room for a locating device on a shaft, hub of a wheel, etc. **3** a rounded mass of igneous rock. ◆ *vb (tr)* **4** to ornament with bosses; emboss. [C13: from OF *boce*; rel. to It. *bozza* metal knob, swelling]

bossa nova (ˈbɒsə ˈnəʊvə) *n* **1** a dance similar to the samba, originating in Brazil. **2** a piece of music composed for or in the rhythm of this dance. [C20: from Port., lit.: new voice]

bosset (ˈbɒsɪt) *n* either of the rudimentary antlers found in young deer. [C19: from F *bossette* a small protuberance, from *bosse* BOSS[2]]

bossy (ˈbɒsɪ) *adj* **bossier, bossiest.** *Inf.* domineering, overbearing, or authoritarian.
► **ˈbossily** *adv* ► **ˈbossiness** *n*

bosun (ˈbəʊsən) *n Naut.* a variant spelling of **boatswain.**

bot[1] *or* **bott** (bɒt) *n* **1** the larva of a botfly, which typically develops inside the body of a horse, sheep, or man. **2** any similar larva. [C15: prob. from Low G; rel. to Du. *bot*, from ?]

bot[2] (bɒt) *Austral. inf.* ◆ *vb* **bots, botting, botted. 1** to scrounge or borrow. ◆ *n* **2** a scrounger. **3 on the bot (for).** wanting to scrounge. [C20: ?from BOTFLY, alluding to its bite; see BITE (sense 9)]

bot. *abbrev. for:* **1** botanical. **2** botany. **3** bottle.

botanical (bəˈtænɪkəl) *or* **botanic** *adj* **1** of or relating to botany or plants. ◆ *n* **2** any drug or pesticide that is made from parts of a plant. [C17: from Med. L, from Gk *botanē* plant, pasture]
► **boˈtanically** *adv*

botanize *or* **botanise** (ˈbɒtəˌnaɪz) *vb* **botanizes, botanizing, botanized** *or* **botanises, botanising, botanised. 1** *(intr)* to collect or study plants. **2** *(tr)* to explore and study the plants in (an area or region).

botany (ˈbɒtənɪ) *n, pl* **botanies. 1** the study of plants, including their classification, structure, physiology, ecology, and economic importance. **2** the plant life of a particular region or time. **3** the biological characteristics of a particular group of plants. [C17: from BOTANICAL; cf. ASTRONOMY, ASTRONOMICAL]
► **ˈbotanist** *n*

Botany wool *n* fine wool from merino sheep. [C19: from *Botany* Bay, Australia]

botch (bɒtʃ) *vb (tr; often foll. by up)* **1** to spoil through clumsiness or ineptitude. **2** to repair badly or clumsily. ◆ *n* **3** a badly done piece of work or repair (esp. in **make a botch of**). [C14: from ?]
► **ˈbotcher** *n* ► **ˈbotchy** *adj*

botfly (ˈbɒtˌflaɪ) *n, pl* **botflies.** any of various stout-bodied hairy dipterous flies, the larvae of which are parasites of man, sheep, and horses.

both (bəʊθ) *determiner* **1a** the two; two considered together: *both dogs were dirty.* **1b** *(as pron): both are to blame.* ◆ *conj* **2** *(coordinating)* used preceding words, phrases, or clauses joined by *and: both Ellen and Keith enjoyed the play; both new and exciting.* [C12: from ON *bāthir*]

bother (ˈbɒðə) *vb* **1** *(tr)* to give annoyance, pain, or trouble to. **2** *(tr)* to trouble (a person) by repeatedly disturbing; pester. **3** *(intr)* to take the time or trouble; concern oneself: *don't bother to come with me.* **4** *(tr)* to make (a person) alarmed or confused. ◆ *n* **5** a state of worry, trouble, or confusion. **6** a person or thing that causes fuss, trouble, or annoyance. **7** *Inf.* a disturbance or fight; trouble (esp. in **a spot of bother**). ◆ *interj* **8** *Chiefly Brit.* an exclamation of slight annoyance. [C18: ?from Irish Gaelic *bodhar* deaf, vexed]

botheration (ˌbɒðəˈreɪʃən) *n, interj Inf.* another word for **bother** (senses 5, 8).

bothersome (ˈbɒðəsəm) *adj* causing bother; troublesome.

bothy (ˈbɒθɪ) *n, pl* **bothies.** *Chiefly Scot.* **1** a cottage or hut. **2** a farmworker's summer quarters. [C18: ? rel. to BOOTH]

bo tree (bəʊ) *n* another name for the **peepul.** [C19: from Sinhalese, from Pali *bodhitaru* tree of wisdom]

bott (bɒt) *n* a variant spelling of **bot**[1].

bottle (ˈbɒtəl) *n* **1a** a vessel, often of glass and typically cylindrical with a narrow neck, for containing liquids. **1b** *(as modifier): a bottle rack.* **2** Also called: **bottleful.** the amount such a vessel will hold. **3** *Brit. sl.* courage; nerve; initiative. **4 the bottle.** *Inf.* drinking of alcohol, esp. to excess. ◆ *vb* **bottles, bottling, bottled.** *(tr)* **5** to put or place in a bottle or bottles. **6** to store (gas) in a portable container under pressure. ◆ See also **bottle out, bottle up.** [C14: from OF *botaille*, from Med. L *butticula*, from LL *buttis* cask]

bottle bank *n* a large container into which the public may throw glass bottles for recycling.

bottlebrush (ˈbɒtəlˌbrʌʃ) *n* **1** a cylindrical brush on a thin shaft, used for cleaning bottles. **2** Also called: **callistemon.** any of various Australian shrubs or trees having dense spikes of large red flowers with protruding brushlike stamens.

bottled (*or* **bottle**) **gas** *n* butane or propane liquefied under pressure in portable metal containers for use in camping stoves, blowtorches, etc.

bottle-feed *vb* **bottle-feeds, bottle-feeding, bottle-fed.** to feed (a baby) with milk from a bottle.

bottle glass *n* glass used for making bottles, consisting of a silicate of sodium, calcium, and aluminium.

bottle green *n, adj* (of) a dark green colour.

bottle-jack *n NZ.* a large jack used for heavy lifts.

bottleneck (ˈbɒtəlˌnɛk) *n* **1a** a narrow stretch of road or a junction at which traffic is or may be held up. **1b** the hold-up. **2** something that holds up progress.

bottlenose dolphin (ˈbɒtəlˌnəʊz) *n* a type of dolphin with a bottle-shaped snout.

bottle out *vb (intr, adv) Brit. sl.* to lose one's nerve.

bottle party *n* a party to which guests bring drink.

bottler (ˈbɒtələ) *n Austral. & NZ inf.* an exceptional or outstanding person or thing.

bottle shop *n Austral. & NZ.* a shop selling alcohol in unopened containers for consumption elsewhere. Also called (Austral.): **bottle store.**

bottle tree *n* any of several Australian trees that have a bottle-shaped swollen trunk.

bottle up *vb (tr, adv)* **1** to restrain (powerful emotion). **2** to keep (an army or other force) contained or trapped.

bottom (ˈbɒtəm) *n* **1** the lowest, deepest, or farthest removed part of a thing: *the bottom of a hill.* **2** the least important or successful position: *the bottom of a class.* **3** the ground underneath a sea, lake, or river. **4** the inner depths of a person's true feelings (esp. in **from the bottom of one's heart**). **5** the underneath part of a thing. **6** *Naut.* the parts of a vessel's hull that are under water. **7** (in literary or commercial contexts) a boat or ship. **8** *(often pl) US & Canad.* the low land bordering a river. **9** (esp. of horses) staying power; stamina. **10** *Inf.* the buttocks. **11** importance, seriousness, or influence: *his views have weight and bottom.* **12 at bottom.** in reality; basically. **13 be at the bottom of.** to be the ultimate cause of. **14 get to the bottom of.** to discover the real truth about. ◆ *adj (prenominal)* **15** lowest or last. **16 bet** (*or* **put**) **one's bottom dollar on.** to be absolutely sure of. **17** of, relating to, or situated at the bottom. **18** fundamental; basic. ◆ *vb* **19** *(tr)* to provide (a chair, etc.) with a bottom or seat. **20** *(tr)* to discover the full facts or truth of; fathom. **21** (usually foll. by *on* or *upon*) to base or be founded (on an idea, etc.). [OE *botm*]

bottom drawer *n Brit.* a young woman's collection of linen, cutlery, etc., made in anticipation of marriage. US, Canad., and NZ equivalent: **hope chest.**

bottoming (ˈbɒtəmɪŋ) *n* the lowest level of foundation material for a road or other structure.

bottomless (ˈbɒtəmlɪs) *adj* **1** having no bottom. **2** unlimited; inexhaustible. **3** very deep.

bottom line *n* **1** the last line of a financial statement that shows the net profit or loss of a company or organization. **2** the conclusion or main point of a process, discussion, etc.

bottom out *vb (intr, adv)* to reach the lowest point and level out.

bottomry (ˈbɒtəmrɪ) *n, pl* **bottomries.** *Maritime law.* a contract whereby the owner of a ship borrows money to enable the vessel to complete the voyage and pledges the ship as security for the loan. [C16: from Du. *bodemerij*, from *bodem* BOTTOM (hull of a ship) + *-erij* -RY]

bottom-up processing *n* a processing technique, either in the brain or in a computer, in which incoming information is analysed in successive steps and later-stage processing does not affect processing in earlier stages.

botulism (ˈbɒtjʊˌlɪzəm) *n* severe, often fatal, poisoning resulting from

THESAURUS

dent, supervisor ◆ *vb* **3** = **be in charge**, administrate, call the shots, call the tune, command, control, direct, employ, manage, oversee, run, superintend, supervise, take charge **4** *usually foll. by* **around** *or* **about** = **domineer**, bully, dominate, oppress, order, overbear, push around (*sl.*), put upon, ride roughshod over, tyrannize

boss[2] *n* **1** = **stud**, knob, nub, nubble, point, protuberance, tip

bossy *adj Informal* = **domineering**, arrogant, authoritarian, autocratic, despotic, dictatorial, hectoring, high-handed, imperious, lordly, overbearing, tyrannical

botch *vb* **1** = **spoil**, blunder, bodge (*inf.*), bungle, butcher, cobble, cock up (*Brit. sl.*), make a pig's ear of (*inf.*), mar, mess up, mismanage, muff, screw up (*inf.*) ◆ *n* **3** = **mess**, blunder, bungle, bungling, cock-up (*Brit. sl.*), failure, hash, miscarriage, pig's breakfast (*inf.*), pig's ear (*inf.*)

bother *vb* **1** = **trouble**, annoy, concern, dismay, distress, disturb, gall, inconvenience, irritate, put out, upset, vex, worry **2** = **pester**, bend someone's ear (*inf.*), get on one's nerves (*inf.*), get on one's wick (*Brit. sl.*), harass, hassle (*inf.*), nag, nark (*Brit., Austral., & NZ sl.*), plague ◆ *n* **5** = **trouble**, aggravation, annoyance, difficulty, grief (*inf.*), hassle (*inf.*), inconvenience, irritation, strain, vexation, worry **6** = **nuisance**, pest, problem
Antonyms *vb* ≠ **trouble:** aid, assist, facilitate, further, help, relieve, succour, support ◆ *n* ≠ **trouble:** advantage, aid, benefit, comfort, convenience, help, service, use

bothersome *adj* = **troublesome**, aggravating, annoying, distressing, exasperating, inconvenient, irritating, tiresome, vexatious, vexing
Antonyms *adj* appropriate, beneficial, commodious, convenient, handy, helpful, serviceable, useful

bottleneck *n* = **hold-up**, block, blockage, impediment, jam, obstacle, obstruction

bottle up *vb* **1** = **suppress**, check, contain, curb, keep back, restrict, shut in

bottom *n* **1** = **lowest part**, base, basis, bed, deepest part, depths, floor, foot, foundation, groundwork, pedestal, support **5** = **underside**, lower side, sole, underneath **10** *Informal* = **buttocks**, arse (*taboo sl.*), ass (*US & Canad. taboo sl.*), backside, behind (*inf.*), bum (*Brit. sl.*), buns (*US sl.*), butt (*US & Canad. inf.*), derrière (*euphemistic*), jacksy (*Brit. sl.*), posterior, rear, rear end, rump, seat, tail (*inf.*) ◆ *adj* **15** = **lowest**, last **17** = **undermost**, base, basement, ground
Antonyms *n* ≠ **lowest part:** cover, crown, height, lid, peak, summit, surface, top ◆ *adj* ≠ **undermost:** higher, highest, top, upper

bottomless *adj* **2** = **unlimited**, boundless, fathomless, immeasurable, inexhaustible, infinite, unfathomable

the potent bacterial toxin, **botulin**, produced in imperfectly preserved food, etc. [C19: from G *Botulismus*, lit.: sausage poisoning, from L *botulus* sausage]

bouclé ('buːkleɪ) *n* **1** a curled or looped yarn or fabric giving a thick knobbly effect. ◆ *adj* **2** of or designating such a yarn or fabric. [C19: from F *bouclé* curly, from *boucle* a curl]

boudoir ('buːdwɑː, -dwɔː) *n* a woman's bedroom or private sitting room. [C18: from F, lit.: room for sulking in, from *bouder* to sulk]

bouffant ('buːfɔːŋ) *adj* **1** (of a hairstyle) having extra height and width through backcombing; puffed out. **2** (of sleeves, skirts, etc.) puffed out. [C20: from F, from *bouffer* to puff up]

bougainvillea (ˌbuːgən'vɪlɪə) *n* a tropical woody climbing plant having inconspicuous flowers surrounded by showy red or purple bracts. [C19: NL, after L. A. de *Bougainville* (1729–1811), F navigator]

bough (baʊ) *n* any of the main branches of a tree. [OE *bōg* arm, twig]

bought (bɔːt) *vb* the past tense and past participle of **buy**.

bougie ('buːʒiː, buː'ʒiː) *n Med.* a slender semiflexible instrument for inserting into body passages such as the rectum or urethra to introduce medication, etc. [C18: from F, orig. a wax candle from *Bougie* (Bujiya), Algeria]

bouillabaisse (ˌbuːjə'bɛs) *n* a rich stew or soup of fish and vegetables. [C19: from F, from Provençal *bouiabaisso*, lit.: boil down]

bouillon ('buːjɒn) *n* a plain unclarified broth or stock. [C18: from F, from *bouillir* to BOIL[1]]

boulder ('bəʊldə) *n* a smooth rounded mass of rock that has been shaped by erosion. [C13: prob. from ON; cf. OSwedish *bulder* rumbling + *sten* STONE]

boulder clay *n* an unstratified glacial deposit consisting of fine clay, boulders, and pebbles.

boule ('buːliː) *n* **1** the senate of an ancient Greek city-state. **2** the parliament in modern Greece. [C19: from Gk *boulē* senate]

boules *French.* (bul) *n* (*functioning as sing*) a game, popular in France, in which metal bowls are thrown to land as near as possible to a target ball. [pl. of *boule* BALL[1]: see BOWL[2]]

boulevard ('buːlvɑː, -vɑːd) *n* a wide usually tree-lined road in a city. [C18: from F, from MDu. *bolwerc* BULWARK; so called because orig. often built on the ruins of an old rampart]

boulle, boule, *or* **buhl** (buːl) *adj* **1** denoting or relating to a type of marquetry of patterned inlays of brass and tortoiseshell, etc. ◆ *n* **2** something ornamented with such marquetry. [C18: after A. C. *Boulle* (1642–1732), F cabinet-maker]

boult (bəʊlt) *vb* a variant spelling of **bolt**[2].

bounce ❶ (baʊns) *vb* **bounces, bouncing, bounced. 1** (*intr*) (of a ball, etc.) to rebound from an impact. **2** (*tr*) to cause (a ball, etc.) to hit a solid surface and spring back. **3** to move or cause to move suddenly, excitedly, or violently; spring. **4** *Sl.* (of a bank) to send (a cheque) back or (of a cheque) to be sent back by a bank to a payee unredeemed because of lack of funds in the drawer's account. **5** (*tr*) *Sl.* to force (a person) to leave a place or job; throw out; eject. ◆ *n* **6** the action of rebounding from an impact. **7** a leap; jump; bound. **8** the quality of being able to rebound; springiness. **9** *Inf.* vitality; vigour; resilience. **10** *Brit.* swagger or impudence. [C13: prob. imit.; cf. Low G *bunsen* to beat, Du. *bonken* to thump]

bounce back *vb* (*intr, adv*) to recover one's health, good spirits, confidence, etc., easily.

bouncer ('baʊnsə) *n Sl.* a man employed at a club, disco, etc., to eject drunks or troublemakers.

bouncing ❶ ('baʊnsɪŋ) *adj* (when *postpositive,* foll. by *with*) vigorous and robust (esp. in **a bouncing baby**).

bouncy ❶ ('baʊnsɪ) *adj* **bouncier, bounciest. 1** lively, exuberant, or self-confident. **2** having the capability or quality of bouncing: *a bouncy ball.* **3** responsive to bouncing; springy: *a bouncy bed.*

Bouncy Castle *n Trademark.* a large inflatable model, usually of a castle, on which children may bounce at fairs, etc.

bound[1] ❶ (baʊnd) *vb* **1** the past tense and past participle of **bind.** ◆ *adj* **2** in bonds or chains; tied as with a rope. **3** (*in combination*) restricted; confined: *housebound.* **4** (*postpositive;* foll. by an infinitive) destined; sure; certain: *it's bound to happen.* **5** (*postpositive;* often foll. by *by*) compelled or obliged. **6** *Rare.* constipated. **7** (of a book) secured within a cover or binding. **8** *Logic.* (of a variable) occurring within the scope of a quantifier. Cf. **free** (sense 18). **9 bound up with.** closely or inextricably linked with.

bound[2] ❶ (baʊnd) *vb* **1** to move forwards by leaps or jumps. **2** to bounce; spring away from an impact. ◆ *n* **3** a jump upwards or forwards. **4** a bounce, as of a ball. [C16: from OF *bond* a leap]

bound[3] ❶ (baʊnd) *vb* **1** (*tr*) to place restrictions on; limit. **2** (when *intr,* foll. by *on*) to form a boundary of. ◆ *n* **3** See **bounds.** [C13: from OF *bonde,* from Med. L *bodina*]

bound[4] (baʊnd) *adj* **a** (*postpositive;* often foll. by *for*) going or intending to go towards: *bound for Jamaica; homeward bound.* **b** (*in combination*): *northbound traffic.* [C13: from ON *buinn,* p.p. of *būa* to prepare]

boundary ❶ ('baʊndərɪ, -drɪ) *n, pl* **boundaries. 1** something that indicates the farthest limit, as of an area; border. **2** *Cricket.* **2a** the marked limit of the playing area. **2b** a stroke that hits the ball beyond this limit. **2c** the four or six runs scored with such a stroke.

boundary rider *n Austral.* an employee on a sheep or cattle station whose job is to maintain fences.

bounden ('baʊndən) *adj* morally obligatory (arch. except in **bounden duty**). [arch. p.p. of BIND]

bounder ('baʊndə) *n Old-fashioned Brit. sl.* a morally reprehensible person; cad.

boundless ❶ ('baʊndlɪs) *adj* unlimited; vast: *boundless energy.*
▸ **'boundlessly** *adv*

bounds ❶ (baʊndz) *pl n* **1** (*sometimes sing*) a limit; boundary (esp. in **know no bounds**). **2** something that restrains or confines, esp. the standards of a society: *within the bounds of modesty.* ◆ See also **out of bounds.**

bounteous ('baʊntɪəs) *adj Literary.* **1** giving freely; generous. **2** plentiful; abundant.
▸ **'bounteously** *adv* ▸ **'bounteousness** *n*

bountiful ❶ ('baʊntɪfʊl) *adj* **1** plentiful; ample (esp. in **a bountiful supply**). **2** giving freely; generous.
▸ **'bountifully** *adv*

bounty ❶ ('baʊntɪ) *n, pl* **bounties. 1** generosity; liberality. **2** a generous gift. **3** a payment made by a government, as, formerly, to a sailor on enlisting or to a soldier after a campaign. **4** any reward or premium. [C13 (in the sense: goodness): from OF, from L, from *bonus* good]

bouquet ❶ (buː'keɪ) *n* **1** a bunch of flowers, esp. a large carefully arranged one. **2** the characteristic aroma or fragrance of a wine or liqueur. **3** a compliment or expression of praise. [C18: from F: thicket, from OF *bosc* forest]

bouquet garni ('buːkeɪ gɑː'niː) *n, pl* **bouquets garnis** ('buːkeɪz gɑː'niː). a bunch of herbs tied together and used for flavouring soups, stews, etc. [C19: from F, lit.: garnished bouquet]

bourbon ('bɜːbən) *n* a whiskey distilled, chiefly in the US, from maize, esp. one containing at least 51 per cent maize. [C19: after *Bourbon* county, Kentucky, where it was first made]

bourdon ('bʊədən, 'bɔːdən) *n* **1** a bass organ stop. **2** the drone of a bagpipe. [C14: from OF: drone (of a musical instrument), imit.]

bourgeois ❶ ('bʊəʒwɑː) *Often disparaging.* ◆ *n, pl* **bourgeois. 1** a member of the middle class, esp. one regarded as being conservative and materialistic or capitalistic. **2** a mediocre, unimaginative, or materialistic person. ◆ *adj* **3** characteristic of, relating to, or comprising the middle class. **4** conservative or materialistic in outlook. **5** (in Marxist thought) dominated by capitalists or capitalist interests. [C16: from OF *borjois, burgeis* burgher, citizen; see BURGESS]
▸ **bourgeoise** ('bʊəʒwɑːz, bʊə'ʒwɑːz) *fem n*

bourgeoisie (ˌbʊəʒwɑː'ziː) *n* **the. 1** the middle classes. **2** (in Marxist thought) the capitalist ruling class. The bourgeoisie owns the means of production, through which it exploits the working class.

bourgeon ('bɜːdʒən) *n, vb* a variant spelling of **burgeon.**

bourn[1] *or* **bourne** (bɔːn) *n Arch.* **1** a destination; goal. **2** a boundary. [C16: from OF *borne;* see BOUND[3]]

bourn[2] (bɔːn) *n Chiefly southern Brit.* a stream. [C16: from OF *bodne* limit; see BOUND[3]]

bourrée ('bʊəreɪ) *n* **1** a traditional French dance in fast duple time. **2** a piece of music in the rhythm of this dance. [C18: from F]

THESAURUS

bounce *vb* **1** = **rebound**, bob, bound, bump, jounce, jump, leap, recoil, resile, ricochet, spring, thump **5** *Slang* = **throw out**, boot out (*inf.*), eject, fire (*inf.*), kick out (*inf.*), oust, relegate ◆ *n* **8** = **springiness**, bound, elasticity, give, rebound, recoil, resilience, spring **9** *Informal* = **life**, animation, brio, dynamism, energy, go (*inf.*), liveliness, pep, vigour, vitality, vivacity, zip (*inf.*)

bouncing *adj* = **lively**, alive and kicking, blooming, bonny, fighting fit, fit as a fiddle (*inf.*), healthy, robust, thriving, vigorous

bouncy *adj* **1** = **lively**, bubbly, confident, ebullient, effervescent, enthusiastic, exuberant, full of beans (*inf.*), irrepressible, vivacious, zestful **3** = **springy**, elastic

Antonyms *adj* ≠ **lively**: dull, listless, unenthusiastic ≠ **springy**: flat, inelastic

bound[1] *adj* **2** = **tied**, cased, fastened, fixed, pinioned, secured, tied up **4** = **certain**, destined, doomed, fated, sure **5** = **obliged**, beholden, committed, compelled, constrained, duty-bound, forced, obligated, pledged, required

bound[2] *vb, n* **1, 3** = **leap**, bob, caper, frisk, gambol, hurdle, jump, lope, pounce, prance, skip, spring, vault ◆ *vb, n* **2, 4** = **bounce**

bound[3] *vb* **1, 2** = **limit**, circumscribe, confine, define, delimit, demarcate, encircle, enclose, hem in, restrain, restrict, surround

boundary *n* **1** = **limits**, barrier, border, borderline, bounds, brink, confines, edge, extremity, fringe, frontier, march, margin, pale, precinct, termination, verge

boundless *adj* = **unlimited**, endless, illimitable, immeasurable, immense, incalculable, inexhaustible, infinite, limitless, measureless, unbounded, unconfined, unending, untold, vast

Antonyms *adj* bounded, confined, limited, little, restricted, small

bounds *pl n* **1** = **boundary**, border, confine, edge, extremity, fringe, limit, line, march, margin, pale, periphery, rim, termination, verge

bountiful *adj* **1** = **plentiful**, abundant, ample, bounteous, copious, exuberant, lavish, luxuriant, plenteous, prolific **2** = **generous**, beneficent, bounteous, liberal, magnanimous, munificent, open-handed, princely, prodigal, unstinting

bounty *n* **1** = **generosity**, almsgiving, assistance, beneficence, benevolence, charity, kindness, largesse *or* largess, liberality, openhandedness, philanthropy **2** = **gift**, bonus, donation, grant, gratuity, largesse *or* largess, present **4** = **reward**, meed (*arch.*), premium, recompense

bouquet *n* **1** = **bunch of flowers**, boutonniere, buttonhole, corsage, garland, nosegay, posy, spray, wreath **2** = **aroma**, fragrance, perfume, redolence, savour, scent

bourgeois *adj* **3, 4** = **middle-class**, conven-

Bourse (bʊəs) *n* a stock exchange of continental Europe, esp. Paris. [C19: from F, lit.: purse, from Med. L *bursa,* ult. from Gk: leather]

boustrophedon (ˌbaʊstrəˈfiːdᵊn) *adj* having alternate lines written from right to left and from left to right. [C17: from Gk, lit.: turning as in ploughing with oxen, from *bous* ox + *strephein* to turn]

bout ⓘ (baʊt) *n* **1a** a period of time spent doing something, such as drinking. **1b** a period of illness. **2** a contest or fight, esp. a boxing or wrestling match. [C16: var. of obs. *bought* turn]

boutique (buːˈtiːk) *n* **1** a shop, esp. a small one selling fashionable clothes and other items. **2** (*modifier*) of or denoting a small specialized producer or business: *a boutique operation.* [C18: from F, ult. from Gk *apothēkē* storehouse]

boutonniere (ˌbuːtɒnɪˈɛə) *n* the US name for **buttonhole** (sense 2). [C19: from F: buttonhole]

bouzouki (buːˈzuːkɪ) *n* a Greek long-necked stringed musical instrument related to the mandolin. [C20: from Mod. Gk, ?from Turkish *büjük* large]

bovine ⓘ (ˈbəʊvaɪn) *adj* **1** of or relating to cattle. **2** (of people) dull; sluggish; stolid. [C19: from LL *bovīnus,* from L *bōs* ox, cow]
▸**ˈbovinely** *adv*

bovine somatotrophin *n* the full name for **BST** (sense 1).

bovine spongiform encephalopathy *n* the full name for **BSE**.

Bovril (ˈbɒvrɪl) *n Trademark.* a concentrated beef extract, used for flavouring, as a stock, etc.

bovver (ˈbɒvə) *n Brit. sl.* **a** rowdiness, esp. caused by gangs of teenage youths. **b** (*as modifier*): *a bovver boy.* [C20: sl. pronunciation of BOTHER]

bow[1] ⓘ (baʊ) *vb* **1** to lower (one's head) or bend (one's knee or body) as a sign of respect, greeting, assent, or shame. **2** to bend or cause to bend. **3** (*intr; usually foll. by to or before*) to comply or accept: *bow to the inevitable.* **4** (*tr;* foll. by *in, out, to,* etc.) to usher (someone) in or out with bows and deference. **5** (*tr;* usually foll. by *down*) to bring (a person, nation, etc.) to a state of submission. **6 bow and scrape.** to behave in an excessively deferential or obsequious way. ◆ *n* **7** a lowering or inclination of the head or body as a mark of respect, greeting, or assent. **8 take a bow.** to acknowledge or receive applause or praise. ◆ See also **bow out.** [OE *būgan*]

bow[2] (bəʊ) *n* **1** a weapon for shooting arrows, consisting of an arch of flexible wood, plastic, etc., bent by a string fastened at each end. **2a** a long stick across which are stretched strands of horsehair, used for playing the strings of a violin, viola, cello, etc. **2b** a stroke with such a stick. **3a** a decorative interlacing of ribbon or other fabrics, usually having two loops and two loose ends. **3b** the knot forming such an interlacing. **4** something that is curved, bent, or arched. ◆ *vb* **5** to form or cause to form a curve or curves. **6** to make strokes of a bow across (violin strings). [OE *boga* arch, bow]

bow[3] ⓘ (baʊ) *n* **1** *Chiefly Naut.* **1a** (*often pl*) the forward end or part of a vessel. **1b** (*as modifier*): *the bow mooring line.* **2** *Rowing.* the oarsman at the bow. [C15: prob. from Low G *boog*]

bow compass (bəʊ) *n Geom.* a compass in which the legs are joined by a flexible metal bow-shaped spring rather than a hinge.

bowdlerize ⓘ *or* **bowdlerise** (ˈbaʊdləˌraɪz) *vb* **bowdlerizes, bowdlerizing, bowdlerized** *or* **bowdlerises, bowdlerising, bowdlerised.** (*tr*) to remove passages or words regarded as indecent from (a play, novel, etc.); expurgate. [C19: after Thomas *Bowdler* (1754–1825), E editor who expurgated Shakespeare]
▸**ˌbowdleriˈzation** *or* **ˌbowdleriˈsation** *n* ▸**ˈbowdlerism** *n*

bowel ⓘ (ˈbaʊəl) *n* **1** an intestine, esp. the large intestine in man. **2** (*pl*) innards; entrails. **3** (*pl*) the deep or innermost part (esp. in **the bowels of the earth**). [C13: from OF *bouel,* from L *botellus* a little sausage]

bowel movement *n* **1** the discharge of faeces; defecation. **2** the waste matter discharged; faeces.

bower[1] ⓘ (ˈbaʊə) *n* **1** a shady leafy shelter or recess, as in a wood or garden; arbour. **2** *Literary.* a lady's bedroom or apartments; boudoir. [OE *būr* dwelling]

bower[2] (ˈbaʊə) *n Naut.* a vessel's bow anchor. [C18: from BOW[3] + -ER[1]]

bowerbird (ˈbaʊəˌbɜːd) *n* **1** any of various songbirds of Australia and New Guinea. The males build bower-like display grounds to attract the females. **2** *Inf., chiefly Austral.* a collector of unconsidered trifles. [C17: from Dutch *bouwerij,* from *bouwen* to farm + *erij* -ERY; see BOOR, BOER]

bowfin (ˈbəʊˌfɪn) *n* a primitive North American freshwater bony fish with an elongated body and a very long dorsal fin.

bowhead (ˈbəʊˌhɛd) *n* a large-mouthed arctic right whale. Also called: **Greenland whale.**

bowie knife (ˈbəʊɪ) *n* a stout hunting knife with a short hilt and a guard for the hand. [C19: after Jim *Bowie* (1796–1836), Texan adventurer]

bowl[1] ⓘ (bəʊl) *n* **1** a round container open at the top, used for holding liquid, serving food, etc. **2** Also: **bowlful.** the amount a bowl will hold. **3** the rounded or hollow part of an object, esp. of a spoon or tobacco pipe. **4** any container shaped like a bowl, such as a sink or lavatory. **5** a bowl-shaped building or other structure, such as an amphitheatre. **6** *Chiefly US.* a bowl-shaped depression of the land surface. **7** *Literary.* a drinking cup. [OE *bolla*]

bowl[2] ⓘ (bəʊl) *n* **1** a wooden ball used in the game of bowls, having one flattened side in order to make it run on a curved course. **2** a large heavy ball with holes for gripping, used in tenpin bowling. ◆ *vb* **3** to roll smoothly or cause to roll smoothly along the ground. **4** (*intr; usually foll. by along*) to move easily and rapidly, as in a car. **5** *Cricket.* **5a** to send (a ball) from one's hand towards the batsman. **5b** Also: **bowl out.** to dismiss (a batsman) by delivering a ball that breaks his wicket. **6** (*intr*) to play bowls or tenpin bowling. ◆ See also **bowl over, bowls.** [C15: from F *boule,* ult. from L *bulla* bubble]

bow legs (bəʊ) *pl n* a condition in which the legs curve outwards like a bow between the ankle and the thigh. Also called: **bandy legs.**
▸**bow-legged** (bəʊˈlɛgɪd, bəʊˈlɛgd) *adj*

bowler[1] (ˈbəʊlə) *n* **1** one who bowls in cricket. **2** a player at the game of bowls.

bowler[2] (ˈbəʊlə) *n* a stiff felt hat with a rounded crown and narrow curved brim. US and Canad. name: **derby.** [C19: after John *Bowler,* 19th-cent. London hatter]

bowline (ˈbəʊlɪn) *n Naut.* **1** a line for controlling the weather leech of a square sail when a vessel is close-hauled. **2** a knot used for securing a loop that will not slip at the end of a piece of rope. [C14: prob. from MLow G *bōlīne,* equivalent to BOW[3] + LINE[1]]

bowling (ˈbəʊlɪŋ) *n* **1** any of various games in which a heavy ball is rolled down a special alley at a group of wooden pins. **2** the game of bowls. **3** *Cricket.* the act of delivering the ball to the batsman.

bowling alley *n* **1a** a long narrow wooden lane down which the ball is rolled in tenpin bowling. **1b** a similar lane or alley for playing skittles. **2** a building having lanes for tenpin bowling.

bowling crease *n Cricket.* a line marked at the wicket, over which a bowler must not advance fully before delivering the ball.

bowling green *n* an area of closely mown turf on which the game of bowls is played.

bowl over ⓘ *vb* (*tr, adv*) **1** *Inf.* to surprise (a person) greatly, esp. in a pleasant way; astound; amaze. **2** to knock down.

bowls (bəʊlz) *n* (*functioning as sing*) **1** a game played on a bowling green in which a small bowl (the jack) is pitched from a mark and two opponents take turns to roll biased wooden bowls as near the jack as possible. **2** skittles or tenpin bowling.

bowman (ˈbəʊmən) *n, pl* **bowmen.** *Arch.* an archer.

bow out ⓘ (baʊ) *vb* (*adv; usually tr;* often foll. by *of*) to retire or withdraw gracefully.

bowser (ˈbaʊzə) *n* **1** a tanker containing fuel for aircraft, military vehicles, etc. **2** *Austral. & NZ obs.* a petrol pump at a filling station. [orig. a US proprietary name]

bowshot (ˈbəʊˌʃɒt) *n* the distance an arrow travels from the bow.

bowsprit (ˈbəʊsprɪt) *n Naut.* a spar projecting from the bow of a vessel, esp. a sailing vessel. [C13: from MLow G, from *bōch* BOW[3] + *sprēt* pole]

bowstring (ˈbəʊˌstrɪŋ) *n* the string of an archer's bow.

bow tie (bəʊ) *n* a man's tie tied in a bow, now chiefly in plain black for formal evening wear.

bow window (bəʊ) *n* a bay window in the shape of a curve.

bow-wow (ˈbaʊˌwaʊ, -ˈwaʊ) *n* **1** a child's word for **dog. 2** an imitation of the bark of a dog. ◆ *vb* **3** (*intr*) to bark or imitate a dog's bark.

bowyangs (ˈbəʊjæŋz) *pl n Austral. & NZ sl.* a pair of strings or straps worn around the trouser leg below the knee, orig. esp. by agricultural workers. [C19: from E dialect *bowy-yanks* leggings]

box[1] ⓘ (bɒks) *n* **1** a receptacle or container made of wood, cardboard, etc., usually rectangular and having a removable or hinged lid. **2** Also called: **boxful.** the contents of such a receptacle. **3** (*often in combination*) any of various small cubicles, kiosks, or shelters: *a telephone box; a signal box.* **4** a separate compartment in a public place for a small group of people, as in a theatre. **5** an enclosure within a courtroom: *witness box.* **6** a compartment for a horse in a stable or a vehicle. **7** *Brit.* a small country house occupied by sportsmen when following a field sport, esp. shooting. **8a** a protective housing for machinery or mechanical parts. **8b** (*in combination*): *a gearbox.* **9** a shaped device of light tough material worn by sportsmen to protect the genitals, esp. in cricket. **10**

THESAURUS

tional, hidebound, materialistic, Pooterish, traditional

bout *n* **1** = **period**, course, fit, round, run, session, spell, stint, stretch, term, time, turn **2** = **fight**, battle, boxing match, competition, contest, encounter, engagement, head-to-head, match, set-to, struggle

bovine *adj* **2** = **dull**, dense, dozy (*Brit. inf.*), slow, sluggish, stolid, stupid, thick

bow[1] *vb* **1** = **bend**, bob, droop, genuflect, incline, make obeisance, nod, stoop **3** = **give in**, accept, acquiesce, comply, concede, defer, kowtow, relent, submit, succumb, surrender, yield ◆ *n* **7** = **bending**, bob, genuflexion, inclination, kowtow, nod, obeisance, salaam

bow[3] *n* **1** *Chiefly nautical* = **prow**, beak, fore, head, stem

bowdlerize *vb* = **censor**, blue-pencil, clean up, expurgate, mutilate, sanitize

bowed *adj* **2** = **bent**, crooked, curved, hunched, inclined, lowered, stooped
Antonyms *adj* erect, straight, upright

bowels *pl n* **2** = **guts**, entrails, innards (*inf.*), insides (*inf.*), intestines, viscera, vitals **3** = **depths**, belly, core, deep, hold, inside, interior

bower[1] *n* **1** = **arbour**, alcove, grotto, leafy shelter, shady recess, summerhouse

bowl[1] *n* **1** = **basin**, dish, vessel

bowl[2] *vb* **3** = **roll**, revolve, rotate, spin, trundle, whirl **5a** = **throw**, fling, hurl, pitch

bowl over *vb* **1** *Informal* = **surprise**, amaze, astonish, astound, dumbfound, stagger, startle, stun, sweep off one's feet **2** = **knock down**, bring down, deck (*sl.*), fell, floor, overthrow, overturn

bow out *vb* = **give up**, abandon, back out, call it a day *or* night, cop out (*sl.*), get out, pull out, quit, resign, retire, step down (*inf.*), throw in the sponge, throw in the towel, withdraw

box[1] *n* **1** = **container**, ark (*dialect*), carton, case, casket, chest, pack, package, portmanteau, receptacle, trunk ◆ *vb* **19** = **pack**, package, wrap

a section of printed matter on a page, enclosed by lines, a border, etc. **11** a central agency to which mail is addressed and from which it is collected or redistributed: *a post-office box; a box number in a newspaper advertisement.* **12** short for **penalty box. 13** the raised seat on which the driver sits in a horse-drawn coach. **14** *Austral. & NZ.* an accidental mixing of herds or flocks. **15** *Brit.* (esp. formerly) a present, esp. of money, given at Christmas to tradesmen, etc. **16** *Austral. taboo sl.* the female genitals. **17 out of the box.** *Austral. inf.* outstanding or excellent. **18 the box.** *Brit. inf.* television. ◆ *vb* **19** (*tr*) to put into a box. **20** (*tr; usually foll. by in or up*) to prevent from moving freely; confine. **21** (*tr; foll. by in*) *Printing.* to enclose (text) within a ruled frame. **22** *Austral. & NZ.* to mix (flocks or herds) or (of flocks) to become mixed accidentally. **23 box the compass.** *Naut.* to name the compass points in order. [OE *box*, from L *buxus*, from Gk *puxos* BOX[3]]
▸ **'box,like** *adj*

box[2] ❶ (bɒks) *vb* **1** (*tr*) to fight (an opponent) in a boxing match. **2** (*intr*) to engage in boxing. **3** (*tr*) to hit (a person) with the fist. ◆ *n* **4** a punch with the fist, esp. on the ear. [C14: from ?]

box[3] (bɒks) *n* **1** a slow-growing evergreen tree or shrub with small shiny leaves: used for hedges. **2** the wood of this tree. **3** any of several trees the timber or foliage of which resembles this tree, esp. various eucalyptus trees with rough bark. [OE, from L *buxus*, from Gk *puxus*]

box camera *n* a simple box-shaped camera having an elementary lens, shutter, and viewfinder.

box chronometer *n Naut.* a ship's chronometer, supported on gimbals in a wooden box.

boxer ❶ ('bɒksə) *n* **1** a person who boxes; pugilist. **2** a medium-sized smooth-haired breed of dog with a short nose and a docked tail.

Boxer ('bɒksə) *n* a member of a nationalistic Chinese secret society that led an unsuccessful rebellion in 1900 against foreign interests in China. [C18: rough translation of Chinese *I Ho Ch'üan*, lit.: virtuous harmonious fist]

boxer shorts *pl n* men's underpants shaped like shorts but having a front opening. Also called: **boxers.**

box girder *n* a girder that is hollow and square or rectangular in shape.

boxing ❶ ('bɒksɪŋ) *n* **a** the act, art, or profession of fighting with the fists. **b** (*as modifier*): *a boxing enthusiast.*

Boxing Day *n Brit.* the first day (traditionally and strictly, the first weekday) after Christmas, observed as a holiday. [C19: from the custom of giving Christmas boxes to tradesmen and staff on this day]

boxing glove *n* one of a pair of thickly padded mittens worn for boxing.

box junction *n* (in Britain) a road junction having yellow cross-hatching painted on the road surface. Vehicles may only enter the hatched area when their exit is clear.

box kite *n* a kite with a boxlike frame open at both ends.

box lacrosse *n Canad.* lacrosse played indoors. Also called: **boxla.**

box number *n* **1** the number of an individual pigeonhole at a newspaper to which replies to an advertisement may be addressed. **2** the number of an individual pigeonhole at a post office from which mail may be collected.

box office *n* **1** an office at a theatre, cinema, etc., where tickets are sold. **2a** the public appeal of an actor or production. **2b** (*as modifier*): *a box-office success.*

box pleat *n* a flat double pleat made by folding under the fabric on either side of it.

boxroom ('bɒks,ruːm, -,rʊm) *n* a small room or large cupboard in which boxes, cases, etc., may be stored.

box seat *n* **1** a seat in a theatre box. **2 in the box seat.** *Brit., Austral., & NZ.* in the best position.

box spanner *n* a spanner consisting of a steel cylinder with a hexagonal end that fits over a nut.

box spring *n* a coiled spring contained in a boxlike frame, used for mattresses, chairs, etc.

boxwood ('bɒks,wʊd) *n* **1** the hard close-grained yellow wood of the box tree, used to make tool handles, etc. **2** the box tree.

boxy ('bɒksɪ) *adj* squarish or chunky in style or appearance: *a boxy square-cut jacket.*

boy ❶ (bɔɪ) *n* **1** a male child; lad; youth. **2** a man regarded as immature or inexperienced. **3 the boys.** *Inf.* a group of men, esp. a group of friends. **4** *S. African derog.* a Black male servant. **5 the boy.** *Irish inf.* the right tool for a particular task: *that's the boy to cut it.* ◆ *interj* **6** an exclamation of surprise, pleasure, contempt, etc. [C13 (in the sense: male servant; C14: young male): ?from Anglo-F *abuié* fettered (unattested), from L *boia* fetter]
▸ **'boyish** *adj*

boycott ❶ ('bɔɪkɒt) *vb* **1** (*tr*) to refuse to have dealings with (a person, organization, etc.) or refuse to buy (a product) as a protest or means of coercion. ◆ *n* **2** an instance or the use of boycotting. [C19: after Captain C. C. *Boycott* (1832–97), Irish land agent, a victim of such practices for refusing to reduce rents]

boyfriend ❶ ('bɔɪ,frend) *n* a male friend with whom a person is romantically or sexually involved; sweetheart or lover.

boyhood ('bɔɪhʊd) *n* the state or time of being a boy.

Boyle's law (bɔɪlz) *n* the principle that the pressure of a gas varies inversely with its volume at constant temperature. [C18: after Robert *Boyle* (1627–91), Irish scientist]

boyo ('bɔɪəʊ) *n Brit. inf.* a boy or young man: often used in direct address. [from Irish and Welsh]

boy racer *n Derog. sl.* **a** a young man who drives a car irresponsibly and at high speeds. **b** (*as modifier*): *boy-racer accessories.*

Boys' Brigade *n* (in Britain) an organization for boys, founded in 1883, with the aim of promoting discipline and self-respect.

boy scout *n* See **Scout.**

boysenberry ('bɔɪzᵊnbərɪ) *n, pl* **boysenberries. 1** a type of bramble: a hybrid of the loganberry and various blackberries and raspberries. **2** the large red edible fruit of this plant. [C20: after Rudolph *Boysen*, American botanist]

bp *abbrev. for:* **1** (of alcoholic density) below proof. **2** boiling point. **3** bishop. **4** Also: **B/P.** bills payable.

BP *abbrev. for:* **1** blood pressure. **2** British Pharmacopoeia.

bp. *abbrev. for:* **1** baptized. **2** birthplace.

B/P *or* **bp** *abbrev. for* bills payable.

BPC *abbrev. for* British Pharmaceutical Codex.

BPhil *abbrev. for* Bachelor of Philosophy.

bpi *abbrev. for* bits per inch (used of a computer tape).

bpm *abbrev. for* beats per minute: used in electronic dance music to indicate the tempo of a record.

BPR *abbrev. for* business process re-engineering.

b.pt. *abbrev. for* boiling point.

Bq *Physics. symbol for* becquerel.

br *abbrev. for* brother.

Br 1 *abbrev. for* (in a religious order) Brother. ◆ **2** *the chemical symbol for* bromine.

BR *abbrev. for* British Rail (British Railways).

br. *abbrev. for:* **1** branch. **2** bronze.

Br. *abbrev. for:* **1** Breton. **2** Britain. **3** British.

bra (brɑː) *n* a woman's undergarment for covering and supporting the breasts. [C20: from BRASSIERE]

braai (braɪ) *n* short for **braaivleis.**

braaivleis ('braɪ,fleɪs) *n S. African.* a barbecue. [from Afrik. *braai* grill + *vleis* meat]

brace ❶ (breɪs) *n* **1** a hand tool for drilling holes, with a socket to hold the drill at one end and a cranked handle by which the tool can be turned. See also **brace and bit. 2** something that steadies, binds, or holds up another thing. **3** a structural member, such as a beam or prop, used to stiffen a framework. **4** a pair, esp. of game birds. **5** either of a pair of characters, { }, used for connecting lines of printing or writing. **6** Also called: **accolade.** a line or bracket connecting two or more staves of music. **7** (*often pl*) an appliance of metal bands and wires for correcting uneven alignment of teeth. **8** *Med.* any of various appliances for supporting the trunk or a limb. **9** See **braces.** ◆ *vb* **braces, bracing, braced.** (*mainly tr*) **10** to provide, strengthen, or fit with a brace. **11** to steady or prepare (oneself or something) as before an impact. **12** (*also intr*) to stimulate; freshen; invigorate: *sea air is bracing.* [C14: from OF, from L *bracchia* arms]

brace and bit *n* a hand tool for boring holes, consisting of a cranked handle into which a drilling bit is inserted.

bracelet ('breɪslɪt) *n* an ornamental chain worn around the arm or wrist. [C15: from OF, from L *bracchium* arm]

bracelets ('breɪslɪts) *pl n* a slang name for **handcuffs.**

bracer ('breɪsə) *n* **1** a person or thing that braces. **2** *Inf.* a tonic, esp. an alcoholic drink taken as a tonic.

braces ('breɪsɪz) *pl n Brit.* a pair of straps worn over the shoulders by men for holding up the trousers. US and Canad. word: **suspenders.**

brachial ('breɪkɪəl, 'bræk-) *adj* of or relating to the arm or to an armlike part or structure.

brachiate *adj* ('breɪkɪɪt, -,eɪt, 'bræk-). **1** *Bot.* having widely divergent paired branches. ◆ *vb* ('breɪkɪ,eɪt, 'bræk-), **brachiates, brachiating, brachiated. 2** (*intr*) (of some arboreal apes and monkeys) to swing by the arms from one hold to the next. [C19: from L *bracchiātus* with armlike branches]
▸ **,brachi'ation** *n*

brachio- *or before a vowel* **brachi-** *combining form.* indicating a brachium: *brachiopod.*

brachiopod ('breɪkɪə,pɒd, 'bræk-) *n* any marine invertebrate animal

THESAURUS

20 *usually foll. by* **in** *or* **up** = **confine**, cage, contain, coop up, enclose, hem in, isolate, shut in, surround, trap

box[2] *vb* **1, 2** = **fight**, exchange blows, spar **3** = **punch**, belt (*inf.*), buffet, clout (*inf.*), cuff, deck (*sl.*), hit, lay one on (*sl.*), slap, sock (*sl.*), strike, thwack, wallop (*inf.*), whack ◆ *n* **4** = **punch**, belt (*inf.*), blow, buffet, clout (*inf.*), cuff, slap, stroke, thumping, wallop (*inf.*)

boxer *n* **1** = **fighter**, prizefighter, pugilist, sparrer, sparring partner

boxing *n* = **prizefighting**, fisticuffs, pugilism, sparring, the fight game (*inf.*), the ring

boy *n* **1** = **lad**, fellow, junior, schoolboy, stripling, youngster, youth

boycott *vb* **1** = **embargo**, ban, bar, black, blackball, blacklist, exclude, ostracize, outlaw, prohibit, proscribe, refrain from, refuse, reject, spurn
Antonyms *vb* accept, advocate, back, champion, defend, espouse, help, patronize, promote, support, welcome

boyfriend *n* = **sweetheart**, admirer, beau, date, follower, leman (*arch.*), lover, man, steady, suitor, swain, toy boy, young man

boyish *adj* **1, 2** = **youthful**, adolescent, childish, immature, juvenile, puerile, young

brace *n* **2, 3** = **support**, bolster, bracer, bracket, buttress, prop, reinforcement, stanchion, stay, strut, truss ◆ *vb* **10** = **support**, bandage, bind, bolster, buttress, fasten, fortify, hold up, prop, reinforce, shove, shove up, strap, strengthen, tie, tighten

having a ciliated feeding organ and a shell consisting of dorsal and ventral valves. [C19: from NL *Brachiopoda;* see BRACHIUM, -POD]

brachiosaurus (ˌbreɪkɪəˈsɔːrəs, ˌbræk-) *n* a dinosaur up to 30 metres long: the largest land animal ever known.

brachium (ˈbreɪkɪəm, ˈbræk-) *n, pl* **brachia** (-kɪə). **1** *Anat.* the arm, esp. the upper part. **2** a corresponding part in an animal. **3** *Biol.* a branching or armlike part. [C18: NL, from L *bracchium* arm]

brachy- *combining form.* indicating something short: *brachycephalic.* [from Gk *brakhus* short]

brachycephalic (ˌbrækɪsɪˈfælɪk) *adj* having a head nearly as broad from side to side as from front to back. Also: **brachycephalous** (ˌbrækɪˈsɛfələs).
▸ ˌ**brachyˈcephaly** *n*

bracing ❶ (ˈbreɪsɪŋ) *adj* **1** refreshing; stimulating; invigorating. ◆ *n* **2** a system of braces used to strengthen or support.

bracken (ˈbrækən) *n* **1** Also called: **brake.** any of various large coarse ferns having large fronds with spore cases along the undersides. **2** a clump of any of these ferns. [C14: from ON]

bracket (ˈbrækɪt) *n* **1** an L-shaped or other support fixed to a wall to hold a shelf, etc. **2** one or more wall shelves carried on brackets. **3** *Archit.* a support projecting from the side of a wall or other structure. **4** Also called: **square bracket.** either of a pair of characters, [ ], used to enclose a section of writing or printing. **5** a general name for **parenthesis** (sense 2), **square bracket,** and **brace** (sense 5). **6** a group or category falling within certain defined limits: *the lower income bracket.* **7** the distance between two preliminary shots of artillery fire in range-finding. ◆ *vb* **brackets, bracketing, bracketed.** (*tr*) **8** to fix or support by means of brackets. **9** to put (written or printed matter) in brackets. **10** to couple or join (two lines of text, etc.) with a brace. **11** (often foll. by *with*) to group or class together. **12** to adjust (artillery fire) until the target is hit. [C16: from OF *braguette* codpiece, from OProvençal *braga,* from L *brāca* breeches]

brackish ❶ (ˈbrækɪʃ) *adj* (of water) slightly briny or salty. [C16: from MDu. *brac* salty; see -ISH]
▸ ˈ**brackishness** *n*

bract (brækt) *n* a specialized leaf with a single flower or inflorescence growing in its axil. [C18: from L *bractea* thin metal plate, gold leaf, from ?]
▸ ˈ**bracteal** *adj* ▸ **bracteate** (ˈbræktɪɪt) *adj*

bracteole (ˈbræktɪˌəʊl) *n* a secondary or small bract. Also called: **bractlet.** [C19: from NL *bracteola;* see BRACT]

brad (bræd) *n* a small tapered nail with a small head. [OE *brord* point, prick]

bradawl (ˈbrædˌɔːl) *n* an awl used to pierce wood, leather, etc.

Bradshaw (ˈbrædˌʃɔː) *n* a British railway timetable, published annually from 1839 to 1961. [C19: after its original publisher, George *Bradshaw* (1801–53)]

bradycardia (ˌbrædɪˈkɑːdɪə) *n Pathol.* an abnormally slow heartbeat. [C19: from Gk *bradus* slow + *kardia* heart]

brae (breɪ) *n Scot.* **1** a hill or hillside **2** (*pl*) an upland area. [C14 *bra;* rel to ON *brā* eyelash]

brag ❶ (bræg) *vb* **brags, bragging, bragged. 1** to speak arrogantly and boastfully. ◆ *n* **2** boastful talk or behaviour. **3** something boasted of. **4** a braggart; boaster. **5** a card game: an old form of poker. [C13: from ?]
▸ ˈ**bragger** *n*

braggadocio (ˌbrægəˈdəʊtʃɪˌəʊ) *n, pl* **braggadocios. 1** vain empty boasting. **2** a person who boasts; braggart. [C16: from *Braggadocchio,* a boastful character in Spenser's *Faerie Queene;* prob. from BRAGGART + It. *-occhio* (augmentative suffix)]

braggart ❶ (ˈbrægət) *n* **1** a person who boasts loudly or exaggeratedly; bragger. ◆ *adj* **2** boastful. [C16: see BRAG]

Brahma (ˈbrɑːmə) *n* a Hindu god, the Creator. [from Sansk., from *brahman* praise]

Brahman (ˈbrɑːmən) *n, pl* **Brahmans. 1** (*sometimes not cap.*) Also (esp. formerly): **Brahmin.** a member of the highest or priestly caste in the Hindu caste system. **2** another name for **Brahma.** [C14: from Sansk. *brahman* prayer]
▸ **Brahmanic** (brɑːˈmænɪk) *or* **Brahˈmanical** *adj*

Brahmanism (ˈbrɑːməˌnɪzəm) *or* **Brahminism** *n* (*sometimes not cap.*) the religious and social system of orthodox Hinduism.
▸ ˈ**Brahmanist** *or* ˈ**Brahminist** *n*

Brahmin (ˈbrɑːmɪn) *n, pl* **Brahmin** *or* **Brahmins. 1** the older spelling of **Brahman** (a Hindu priest). **2** *US.* a highly intelligent or socially exclusive person.

braid ❶ (breɪd) *vb* (*tr*) **1** to interweave (hair, thread, etc.); plait. **2** to decorate with an ornamental trim or border. ◆ *n* **3** a length of hair, fabric, etc., that has been braided; plait. **4** narrow ornamental tape of woven silk, wool, etc. [OE *bregdan* to move suddenly, weave together]
▸ ˈ**braider** *n* ▸ ˈ**braiding** *n*

Braille (breɪl) *n* **1** a system of writing for the blind consisting of raised dots interpreted by touch. **2** any writing produced by this method. ◆ *vb* **3** (*tr*) to print or write using this method. [C19: after Louis *Braille* (1809–52), F inventor]

brain ❶ (breɪn) *n* **1** the soft convoluted mass of nervous tissue within the skull of vertebrates that is the controlling and coordinating centre of the nervous system and the seat of thought, memory, and emotion. Related adj: **cerebral. 2** (*often pl*) *Inf.* intellectual ability: *he's got brains.* **3** *Inf.* shrewdness or cunning. **4** *Inf.* an intellectual or intelligent person. **5** (*usually pl; functioning as sing*) *Inf.* a person who plans and organizes. **6** an electronic device, such as a computer, that performs similar functions to those of the human brain. **7 on the brain.** *Inf.* constantly in mind: *I had that song on the brain.* ◆ *vb* (*tr*) **8** to smash the skull of. **9** *Sl.* to hit hard on the head. [OE *brægen*]

brainchild (ˈbreɪnˌtʃaɪld) *n, pl* **brainchildren.** *Inf.* an idea or plan produced by creative thought.

braindead (ˈbreɪnˌdɛd) *adj* **1** having suffered brain death. **2** *Inf.* not using or showing intelligence; stupid.

brain death *n* irreversible cessation of respiration due to irreparable brain damage: widely considered as the criterion of death.

brain drain *n Inf.* the emigration of scientists, technologists, academics, etc.

brain fever *n* inflammation of the brain.

brainless ❶ (ˈbreɪnlɪs) *adj* stupid or foolish.

brainpan (ˈbreɪnˌpæn) *n Inf.* the skull.

brainstem (ˈbreɪnˌstɛm) *n* the part of the brain that controls such reflex actions as breathing and is continuous with the spinal cord.

brainstorm (ˈbreɪnˌstɔːm) *n* **1** a severe outburst of excitement, often as the result of a transitory disturbance of cerebral activity. **2** *Brit. inf.* a sudden mental aberration. **3** *US. & Canad. inf.* another word for **brainwave.**

brainstorming (ˈbreɪnˌstɔːmɪŋ) *n* intensive discussion to solve problems or generate ideas.

brains trust *n* a group of knowledgeable people who discuss topics in public or on radio or television.

brain-teaser *or* **brain-twister** *n Inf.* a difficult problem.

brainwash ❶ (ˈbreɪnˌwɒʃ) *vb* (*tr*) to effect a radical change in the ideas and beliefs of (a person), esp. by methods based on isolation, sleeplessness, etc.
▸ ˈ**brainˌwashing** *n*

brainwave ❶ (ˈbreɪnˌweɪv) *n Inf.* a sudden idea or inspiration.

brain wave *n* any of the fluctuations of electrical potential in the brain.

brainy ❶ (ˈbreɪnɪ) *adj* **brainier, brainiest.** *Inf.* clever; intelligent.
▸ ˈ**braininess** *n*

braise (breɪz) *vb* **braises, braising, braised.** to cook (meat, vegetables, etc.) by lightly browning in fat and then cooking slowly in a closed pan with a small amount of liquid. [C18: from F *braiser,* from OF *brese* live coals]

brak (bræk) *n S. African.* a crossbred dog; mongrel. [from Du. *brak* setter]

brake[1] ❶ (breɪk) *n* **1** (*often pl*) a device for slowing or stopping a vehicle, wheel, shaft, etc., or for keeping it stationary, esp. by means of friction. **2** a machine or tool for crushing or breaking flax or hemp to separate the fibres. **3** Also called: **brake harrow.** a heavy harrow for breaking up clods. **4** short for **shooting brake.** ◆ *vb* **brakes, braking, braked. 5** to slow down or cause to slow down, by or as if by using a brake. **6** (*tr*) to crush or break up using a brake. [C18: from MDu. *braeke;* rel. to *breken* to BREAK]
▸ ˈ**brakeless** *adj*

brake[2] (breɪk) *n* an area of dense undergrowth, shrubs, brushwood, etc.; thicket. [OE *bracu*]

brake[3] (breɪk) *n* another name for **bracken** (sense 1).

brake[4] (breɪk) *vb Arch., chiefly biblical.* a past tense of **break.**

brake-fade *n* a decrease in the efficiency of the braking system of a motor vehicle as a result of overheating of the brakes.

brake horsepower *n* the rate at which an engine does work, expressed in horsepower. It is measured by the resistance of an applied brake. Abbrev.: **bhp.**

THESAURUS

bracing *adj* **1** = **refreshing**, brisk, chilly, cool, crisp, energizing, exhilarating, fortifying, fresh, invigorating, lively, restorative, reviving, rousing, stimulating, tonic, vigorous
Antonyms *adj* debilitating, draining, enervating, exhausting, fatiguing, sapping, soporific, taxing, tiring, weakening

brackish *adj* = **salty**, bitter, briny, saline, salt, undrinkable
Antonyms *adj* clean, clear, fresh, pure, sweet, unpolluted

brag *vb* **1** = **boast**, blow one's own horn (*US & Canad.*), blow one's own trumpet, bluster, crow, swagger, talk big (*sl.*), vaunt

braggart *n* **1** = **boaster**, bigmouth (*sl.*), brag, braggadocio, bragger, show-off (*inf.*), swaggerer

braid *vb* **1** = **interweave**, entwine, interlace, intertwine, lace, plait, ravel, twine, weave

brain 2, 3 *often plural Informal* = **intelligence**, capacity, intellect, mind, nous (*Brit. sl.*), reason, sagacity, savvy (*sl.*), sense, shrewdness, smarts (*sl., chiefly US*), suss (*sl.*), understanding, wit **4** *Informal* = **intellectual**, bluestocking (*usually disparaging*), brainbox, egghead (*inf.*), genius, highbrow, intellect, mastermind, prodigy, pundit, sage, scholar

brainless *adj* = **stupid**, braindead (*inf.*), dead from the neck up (*inf.*), foolish, idiotic, inane, inept, mindless, senseless, thoughtless, unintelligent, witless

brainwashing *n* = **indoctrination**, alteration, conditioning, persuasion, re-education

brainwave *n* = **idea**, bright idea, stroke of genius, thought

brainy *adj Informal* = **intelligent**, bright, brilliant, clever, smart

brake[1] *n* **1** = **control**, check, constraint, curb, rein, restraint ◆ *vb* **5** = **slow**, check, decelerate, halt, moderate, reduce speed, slacken, stop

brake light *n* a red light or lights at the rear of a motor vehicle that light up when the brakes are applied.
brake lining *n* a renewable strip of asbestos riveted to a brake shoe.
brake pad *n* the flat metal casting, together with the attached friction material, in a disc brake.
brake shoe *n* **1** the curved metal casting to which the brake lining is riveted in a drum brake. **2** the curved metal casting together with the attached brake lining. ◆ Sometimes shortened (for both senses) to **shoe.**
brakesman ('breɪksmən) *n, pl* **brakesmen. 1** a pithead winch operator. **2** a brake operator on railway rolling stock.
brake van *n Railways, Brit.* the coach or vehicle from which the guard applies the brakes; guard's van.
bramble ('bræmbᵊl) *n* **1** any of various prickly rosaceous plants or shrubs, esp. the blackberry. **2** any of several similar and related shrubs, such as the dog rose. **3** *Scot. & N English.* a blackberry. [OE *brǣmbel*]
▸**'brambly** *adj*
brambling ('bræmblɪŋ) *n* a Eurasian finch with a speckled head and back and, in the male, a reddish-brown breast.
bran (bræn) *n* **1** husks of cereal grain separated from the flour. **2** food prepared from these husks. [C13: from OF, prob. of Gaulish origin]
branch ❶ (brɑːntʃ) *n* **1** a secondary woody stem arising from the trunk or bough of a tree or the main stem of a shrub. **2** an offshoot or secondary part: *a branch of a deer's antlers.* **3a** a subdivision or subsidiary section of something larger or more complex: *branches of learning; branch of the family.* **3b** *(as modifier): a branch office.* **4** *US.* any small stream. ◆ *vb* **5** *(intr)* (of a tree or other plant) to produce or possess branches. **6** *(intr;* usually foll. by *from)* (of stems, roots, etc.) to grow and diverge (from another part). **7** to divide or be divided into subsidiaries or offshoots. **8** *(intr;* often foll. by *off)* to diverge from the main way, road, topic, etc. [C13: from OF *branche,* from LL *branca* paw, foot]
▸**'branch,like** *adj*
branchia ('bræŋkɪə) *n, pl* **branchiae** (-kɪ,iː). a gill in aquatic animals.
▸**'branchial** *or* **'branchiate** *adj*
branch out ❶ *vb (intr, adv;* often foll. by *into)* to expand or extend one's interests.
brand ❶ (brænd) *n* **1** a particular product or a characteristic that identifies a particular producer. **2** a particular kind or variety. **3** an identifying mark made, usually by burning, on the skin of animals or (formerly) slaves or criminals, esp. as a proof of ownership. **4** an iron heated and used for branding animals, etc. **5** a mark of disgrace or infamy; stigma. **6** a burning or burnt piece of wood, as in a fire. **7** *Arch. or poetic.* **7a** a flaming torch. **7b** a sword. **8** a fungal disease of garden plants characterized by brown spots on the leaves. ◆ *vb (tr)* **9** to label, burn, or mark with or as with a brand. **10** to place indelibly in the memory: *the scene was branded in their minds.* **11** to denounce; stigmatize: *they branded him a traitor.* [OE *brand-;* see BURN[1]]
▸**'brander** *n* ▸**'branding** *n*
brandish ❶ ('brændɪʃ) *vb* **1** *(tr)* to wave or flourish (a weapon, etc.) in a triumphant, threatening, or ostentatious way. ◆ *n* **2** a threatening or defiant flourish. [C14: from OF *brandir,* of Gmc origin]
▸**'brandisher** *n*
brand leader *n* the most widely sold brand of a particular product.
brandling ('brændlɪŋ) *n* a small red earthworm, found in manure and used as bait by anglers. [C17: from BRAND (n) + -LING[1]]
brand name *n* the name used for a particular make of a commodity.
brand-new *adj* absolutely new. [C16: from BRAND (n) + NEW, likened to newly forged iron]
brandy ('brændɪ) *n, pl* **brandies. 1** an alcoholic spirit distilled from grape wine. **2** a distillation of wines made from other fruits: *plum brandy.* [C17: from earlier *brandewine,* from Du. *brandewijn* burnt (or distilled) wine]
brandy butter *n* butter and sugar creamed together with brandy and served with Christmas pudding, etc. Also called: **hard sauce.**
brandy snap *n* a crisp sweet biscuit, rolled into a cylinder and filled with whipped cream.
brant (brænt) *n, pl* **brants** *or* **brant.** another name (esp. US and Canad.) for **brent** (the goose).
bran tub *n Brit.* a tub containing bran in which small wrapped gifts are hidden.
brash[1] ❶ (bræʃ) *adj* **1** tastelessly or offensively loud, showy, or bold. **2** hasty; rash. **3** impudent. [C19: ? infl. by RASH[1]]
▸**'brashly** *adv* ▸**'brashness** *n*
brash[2] (bræʃ) *n* loose rubbish, such as broken rock, hedge clippings, etc. [C18: from ?]
▸**'brashy** *adj*
brasier ('breɪzɪə) *n* a less common spelling of **brazier.**
brass ❶ (brɑːs) *n* **1** an alloy of copper and zinc containing more than 50 per cent of copper. Cf. **bronze** (sense 1). **2** an object, ornament, or utensil made of brass. **3a** the large family of wind instruments including the trumpet, trombone, French horn, etc., made of brass. **3b** *(sometimes functioning as pl)* instruments of this family forming a section in an orchestra. **4** *(functioning as pl) Inf.* important or high-ranking officials, esp. military officers: *the top brass.* See also **brass hat. 5** *N English dialect.* money. **6** *Brit.* an engraved brass memorial tablet or plaque in a church. **7** *Inf.* bold self-confidence; cheek; nerve. **8** *(modifier)* of, consisting of, or relating to brass or brass instruments: *a brass ornament; a brass band.* [OE *bræs*]
brassard ('bræsɑːd) *or* **brassart** ('bræsət) *n* an identifying armband or badge. [C19: from F, from *bras* arm]
brass band *n* See **band**[1] (sense 2).
brasserie ('bræsərɪ) *n* **1** a bar in which drinks and often food are served. **2** a small and usually cheap restaurant. [C19: from F, from *brasser* to stir]
brass hat *n Brit. inf.* a top-ranking official, esp. a military officer. [C20: from the gold decoration on the caps of officers of high rank]
brassica ('bræsɪkə) *n* any plant of the genus *Brassica,* such as cabbage, rape, turnip, and mustard. [C19: from L: cabbage]
brassie *or* **brassy** ('bræsɪ, 'brɑː-) *n, pl* **brassies.** *Golf.* a former name for a club, a No. 2 wood, originally having a brass-plated sole.
brassiere ('bræsɪə, 'bræz-) *n* the full name for **bra.** [C20: from 17th-cent. F: bodice, from OF *braciere* a protector for the arm]
brass rubbing *n* **1** the taking of an impression of an engraved brass tablet or plaque by rubbing a paper placed over it with heelball, chalk, etc. **2** an impression made in this way.
brass tacks *pl n Inf.* basic realities; hard facts (esp. in **get down to brass tacks).**
brassy ❶ ('brɑːsɪ) *adj* **brassier, brassiest. 1** insolent; brazen. **2** flashy; showy. **3** (of sound) harsh and strident. **4** like brass, esp. in colour. **5** decorated with or made of brass.
▸**'brassily** *adv* ▸**'brassiness** *n*
brat ❶ (bræt) *n* a child, esp. one who is ill-mannered or unruly. [C16: ?from earlier *brat* rag, from OE *bratt* cloak]
▸**'bratty** *adj*
bratpack ('bræt,pæk) *n* **1** a group of precocious and successful young actors, writers, etc. **2** a group of ill-mannered young people.
▸**'brat,packer** *n*
brattice ('brætɪs) *n* **1** a partition of wood or treated cloth used to control ventilation in a mine. **2** *Medieval fortifications.* a fixed wooden tower or parapet. [C13: from OF *bretesche* wooden tower]
bravado ❶ (brə'vɑːdəʊ) *n, pl* **bravadoes** *or* **bravados.** vaunted display of courage or self-confidence; swagger. [C16: from Sp. *bravada;* see BRAVE]
brave ❶ (breɪv) *adj* **1a** having or displaying courage, resolution, or daring; not cowardly or timid. **1b** *(as collective n;* preceded by *the): the brave.* **2** fine; splendid: *a brave sight.* ◆ *n* **3** a warrior of a North American Indian tribe. ◆ *vb* **braves, braving, braved.** *(tr)* **4** to dare or defy: *to brave the odds.* **5** to confront with resolution or courage: *to brave the storm.* [C15: from F, from It. *bravo* courageous, wild, ? ult. from L *barbarus* BARBAROUS]
▸**'bravely** *adv* ▸**'braveness** *n* ▸**'bravery** *n*

THESAURUS

branch *n* **1, 2** = **bough,** arm, limb, offshoot, prong, ramification, shoot, spray, sprig **3** = **division,** chapter, department, local office, office, part, section, subdivision, subsection, wing

branch out *vb* = **expand,** add to, develop, diversify, enlarge, extend, increase, multiply, proliferate, ramify, spread out

brand *n* **1** = **label,** emblem, hallmark, logo, mark, marker, sign, stamp, symbol, trademark **2** = **kind,** cast, class, grade, make, quality, sort, species, type, variety **5** = **stigma,** blot, disgrace, infamy, mark, reproach, slur, smirch, stain, taint ◆ *vb* **9** = **mark,** burn, burn in, label, scar, stamp **11** = **stigmatize,** censure, denounce, discredit, disgrace, expose, mark

brandish *vb* **1** = **wave,** display, exhibit, flaunt, flourish, parade, raise, shake, swing, wield

brash[1] *adj* **3** = **bold,** brazen, cocky, forward, impertinent, impudent, insolent, pushy *(inf.),* rude
Antonyms *adj* polite, reserved, respectful, timid, uncertain

brass *n* **7** *Informal* = **nerve** *(inf.),* audacity, brass neck *(Brit. inf.),* cheek, chutzpah *(US & Canad. inf.),* effrontery, face *(inf.),* front, gall, impertinence, impudence, insolence, neck *(inf.),* presumption, rudeness, sassiness *(US inf.)*

brassy *adj* **1** = **brazen,** barefaced, bold, brash, forward, impudent, insolent, loud-mouthed, pert, pushy *(inf.),* saucy **2** = **flashy,** blatant, garish, gaudy, hard, jazzy *(inf.),* loud, obtrusive, showy, vulgar **3** = **strident,** blaring, cacophonous, dissonant, grating, harsh, jangling, jarring, loud, noisy, piercing, raucous, shrill
Antonyms *adj* ≠ **flashy:** discreet, low-key, modest, played down, quiet, restrained, subdued, toned down, understated

brat *n* = **youngster,** cub, guttersnipe, jackanapes, kid *(inf.),* puppy *(inf.),* rascal, spoilt child, urchin, whippersnapper

bravado *n* = **swagger,** bluster, boast, boastfulness, boasting, bombast, brag, braggadocio, swaggering, swashbuckling, vaunting

brave *adj* **1** = **courageous,** bold, daring, dauntless, fearless, gallant, gritty, heroic, intrepid, plucky, resolute, undaunted, valiant, valorous ◆ *vb* **4, 5** = **confront,** bear, beard, challenge, dare, defy, endure, face, face the music, stand up to, suffer, tackle, walk into the lion's den, withstand
Antonyms *adj* ≠ **courageous:** afraid, cowardly, craven, faint-hearted, fearful, frightened, scared, shrinking, timid ◆ *vb* ≠ **confront:** give in to, retreat from, surrender to

bravery *n* **1** = **courage,** balls *(taboo sl.),* ballsiness *(taboo sl.),* boldness, bravura, daring, dauntlessness, doughtiness, fearlessness, fortitude, gallantry, grit, guts *(inf.),* hardihood, hardiness, heroism, indomitability, intrepidity, mettle, pluck, pluckiness, spirit, spunk *(inf.),* valour

DICTIONARY

bravo ❶ *interj* **1** (brɑːˈvəʊ). well done! ◆ *n* **2** (brɑːˈvəʊ) *pl* **bravos.** a cry of "bravo." **3** (ˈbrɑːvəʊ) *pl* **bravoes** *or* **bravos.** a hired killer or assassin. [C18: from It.: splendid! see BRAVE]

bravura ❶ (brəˈvjʊərə, -ˈvʊərə) *n* **1** a display of boldness or daring. **2** *Music.* brilliance of execution. [C18: from It.: spirit, courage; see BRAVE]

braw (brɔː, brɑː) *adj Chiefly Scot.* fine or excellent, esp. in appearance or dress. [C16: Scot. var. of BRAVE]

brawl ❶ (brɔːl) *n* **1** a loud disagreement or fight. **2** *US sl.* an uproarious party. ◆ *vb* (*intr*) **3** to quarrel or fight noisily; squabble. **4** (esp. of water) to flow noisily. [C14: prob. rel. to Du. *brallen* to boast, behave aggressively]
▸ **ˈbrawler** *n*

brawn ❶ (brɔːn) *n* **1** strong well-developed muscles. **2** physical strength, esp. as opposed to intelligence. **3** *Brit.* a seasoned jellied loaf made from the head of a pig or calf. [C14: from OF *braon* slice of meat, of Gmc origin]

brawny ❶ (ˈbrɔːnɪ) *adj* **brawnier, brawniest.** muscular and strong.
▸ **ˈbrawniness** *n*

bray ❶ (breɪ) *vb* **1** (*intr*) (of a donkey) to utter its characteristic loud harsh sound; heehaw. **2** (*intr*) to make a similar sound, as in laughing. **3** (*tr*) to utter with a loud harsh sound. ◆ *n* **4** the loud harsh sound uttered by a donkey. **5** a similar loud cry or uproar. [C13: from OF *braire*, prob. of Celtic origin]

braze[1] (breɪz) *vb* **brazes, brazing, brazed.** (*tr*) **1** to decorate with or make of brass. **2** to make like brass, as in hardness. [OE *bræsen*, from *bræs* BRASS]

braze[2] (breɪz) *vb* **brazes, brazing, brazed.** (*tr*) to make a joint between (two metal surfaces) by fusing a layer of brass or high-melting solder between them. [C16: from OF: to burn, of Gmc origin; see BRAISE]
▸ **ˈbrazer** *n*

brazen ❶ (ˈbreɪzən) *adj* **1** shameless and bold. **2** made of or resembling brass. **3** having a ringing metallic sound. ◆ *vb* (*tr*) **4** (usually foll. by *out* or *through*) to face and overcome boldly or shamelessly. [OE *bræsen*, from *bræs* BRASS]
▸ **ˈbrazenly** *adv* ▸ **ˈbrazenness** *n*

brazier[1] *or* **brasier** (ˈbreɪzɪə) *n* a person engaged in brass-working or brass-founding. [C14: from OE *bræsian* to work in brass + -ER[1]]
▸ **ˈbraziery** *n*

brazier[2] *or* **brasier** (ˈbreɪzɪə) *n* a portable metal receptacle for burning charcoal or coal. [C17: from F *brasier*, from *braise* live coals; see BRAISE]

brazil (brəˈzɪl) *n* **1** Also called: **brazil wood.** the red wood obtained from various tropical trees of America: used for cabinetwork. **2** the red or purple dye extracted from these woods. **3** short for **brazil nut.** [C14: from OSp., from *brasa* glowing coals, of Gmc origin; referring to the redness of the wood]

Brazilian (brəˈzɪlɪən) *adj* **1** of or relating to Brazil, a republic in South America. ◆ *n* **2** a native or inhabitant of Brazil.

brazil nut *n* **1** a tropical South American tree producing large globular capsules, each containing several closely packed triangular nuts. **2** the nut, having an edible oily kernel and a woody shell. ◆ Often shortened to **brazil.**

BRCS *abbrev. for* British Red Cross Society.

breach ❶ (briːtʃ) *n* **1** a crack, break, or rupture. **2** a breaking, infringement, or violation of a promise, obligation, etc. **3** any severance or separation. ◆ *vb* (*tr*) **4** to break through or make an opening, hole, or incursion in. **5** to break a promise, law, etc. [OE *bræc*]

breach of promise *n Law.* (formerly) failure to carry out one's promise to marry.

breach of the peace *n Law.* an offence against public order causing an unnecessary disturbance of the peace.

bread ❶ (brɛd) *n* **1** a food made from a dough of flour or meal mixed with water or milk, usually raised with yeast or baking powder and then baked. **2** necessary food; nourishment. **3** *Sl.* money. **4 cast one's bread upon the waters.** to do good without expectation of advantage or return. **5 know which side one's bread is buttered.** to know what to do in order to keep one's advantages. **6 take the bread out of (someone's) mouth.** to deprive of a livelihood. ◆ *vb* **7** (*tr*) to cover with bread-crumbs before cooking. [OE *brēad*]

bread and butter *Inf.* ◆ *n* **1** a means of support or subsistence; livelihood. ◆ *modifier.* **bread-and-butter. 2a** providing a basic means of subsistence. **2b** expressing gratitude, as for hospitality (esp. in **bread-and-butter letter**).

breadbasket (ˈbrɛdˌbɑːskɪt) *n* **1** a basket for carrying bread or rolls. **2** *Sl.* stomach.

breadboard (ˈbrɛdˌbɔːd) *n* **1** a wooden board on which bread is sliced. **2** an experimental arrangement of electronic circuits.

breadfruit (ˈbrɛdˌfruːt) *n, pl* **breadfruits** *or* **breadfruit. 1** a tree of the Pacific Islands, having edible round, usually seedless, fruit. **2** the fruit, which is eaten baked or roasted and has a texture like bread.

breadline (ˈbrɛdˌlaɪn) *n* **1** a queue of people waiting for free food. **2 on the breadline.** impoverished; living at subsistence level.

breadth ❶ (brɛdθ, brɛtθ) *n* **1** the linear extent or measurement of something from side to side; width. **2** a piece of fabric, etc., having a standard or definite width. **3** distance, extent, size, or dimension. **4** openness and lack of restriction, esp. of viewpoint or interest; liberality. [C16: from obs. *brēde* (from OE *brǣdu*, from *brād* BROAD) + -TH[1]]

breadthways (ˈbrɛdθˌweɪz, ˈbrɛtθ-) *or esp. US* **breadthwise** (ˈbrɛdθˌwaɪz, ˈbrɛtθ-) *adv* from side to side.

breadwinner (ˈbrɛdˌwɪnə) *n* a person supporting a family with his or her earnings.

break ❶ (breɪk) *vb* **breaks, breaking, broke, broken. 1** to separate or become separated into two or more pieces. **2** to damage or become damaged so as to be inoperative: *my radio is broken.* **3** to crack or become cracked without separating. **4** to burst or cut the surface of (skin, etc.). **5** to discontinue or become discontinued: *to break a journey.* **6** to disperse or become dispersed: *the clouds broke.* **7** (*tr*) to fail to observe (an agreement, promise, law, etc.): *to break one's word.* **8** (foll. by *with*) to discontinue an association (with). **9** to disclose or be disclosed: *he broke the news gently.* **10** (*tr*) to fracture (a bone) in (a limb, etc.). **11** (*tr*) to divide (something complete or perfect): *to break a set of books.* **12** to bring or come to an end: *the summer weather broke at last.* **13** (*tr*) to bring to an end as by force: *to break a strike.* **14** (when *intr*, often foll. by *out*) to escape (from): *he broke out of jail.* **15** to weaken or overwhelm or be weakened or overwhelmed, as in spirit. **16** (*tr*) to cut through or penetrate: *a cry broke the silence.* **17** (*tr*) to improve on or surpass: *to break a record.* **18** (*tr;* often foll. by *in*) to accustom (a horse) to the bridle and saddle, to being ridden, etc. **19** (*tr;* often foll. by *of*) to cause (a person) to give up (a habit): *this cure will break you of smoking.* **20** (*tr*) to weaken the impact or force of: *this net will break his fall.* **21** (*tr*) to decipher: *to break a code.* **22** (*tr*) to lose the order of: *to break ranks.* **23** (*tr*) to reduce to poverty or the state of bankruptcy. **24** (when *intr*, foll. by *into*) to obtain, give, or receive smaller units in exchange for; change: *to break a pound note.* **25** (*tr*) *Chiefly mil.* to demote to a lower rank. **26** (*intr;* often foll. by *from* or *out of*) to proceed suddenly. **27** (*intr*) to come into being: *light broke over the mountains.* **28** (*intr;* foll. by *into* or *out into*) **28a** to burst into song, laughter, etc. **28b** to change to a faster pace. **29** (*tr*) to open with explosives: *to break a safe.* **30** (*intr*) (of waves) **30a** (often foll. by *against*) to strike violently. **30b** to collapse into foam or surf. **31** (*intr*) (of prices, esp. stock exchange quotations) to fall sharply. **32** (*intr*) to make a sudden effort, as in running, horse racing, etc. **33** (*intr*) *Cricket.* (of a ball) to change direction on bouncing. **34** (*intr*) *Snooker.* to scatter the balls at the start of a game. **35** (*intr*) *Boxing, wrestling.* (of

THESAURUS

Antonyms *n* cowardice, faint-heartedness, fearfulness, fright, timidity

bravo *n* **3** = **hired killer**, assassin, bandit, brigand, cut-throat, desperado, murderer, villain

bravura *n* **1** = **daring**, audacity, boldness, dash, panache, spirit **2** = **brilliance**, brio, display, élan, virtuosity

brawl *n* **1** = **fight**, affray, altercation, argument, battle, clash, disorder, dispute, donnybrook, fracas, fray, free-for-all (*inf.*), melee *or* mêlée, punch-up (*Brit. inf.*), quarrel, row (*inf.*), ruckus (*inf.*), rumpus, scrap (*inf.*), scrimmage, scuffle, shindig (*inf.*), shindy (*inf.*), skirmish, squabble, tumult, uproar, wrangle ◆ *vb* **3** = **fight**, altercate, argue, battle, dispute, go at it hammer and tongs, quarrel, row (*inf.*), scrap (*inf.*), scuffle, tussle, wrangle, wrestle

brawn *n* **1, 2** = **muscle**, beef (*inf.*), beefiness (*inf.*), brawniness, flesh, might, muscles, muscularity, power, robustness, strength, vigour

brawny *adj* = **muscular**, athletic, beefy (*inf.*), bulky, burly, fleshy, hardy, hefty, herculean, husky (*inf.*), lusty, powerful, robust, sinewy, stalwart, strapping, strong, sturdy, thewy, thickset, vigorous, well-built

Antonyms *adj* frail, scrawny, skinny, thin, undeveloped, weak, weakly, weedy (*inf.*), wimpish *or* wimpy (*inf.*)

bray *vb, n* **1, 4** = **heehaw**, bell, bellow, blare, cry, hoot, roar, screech, trumpet

brazen *adj* **1** = **bold**, audacious, barefaced, brash, brassy (*inf.*), defiant, forward, immodest, impudent, insolent, pert, pushy (*inf.*), saucy, shameless, unabashed, unashamed **2** = **brassy**, brass, bronze, metallic ◆ *vb* **4** *usually foll. by* **out** *or* **through** = **be unashamed**, be impenitent, confront, defy, outface, outstare, persevere

Antonyms *adj* ≠ **bold:** cautious, decorous, diffident, mannerly, modest, reserved, respectful, reticent, secret, shy, stealthy, timid

breach *n* **1** = **crack**, aperture, break, chasm, cleft, fissure, gap, hole, opening, rent, rift, rupture, split **2** = **nonobservance**, contravention, disobedience, infraction, infringement, noncompliance, offence, transgression, trespass, violation **3** = **disagreement**, alienation, difference, disaffection, dissension, division, estrangement, falling-out (*inf.*), parting of the ways, quarrel, schism, separation, severance, variance

Antonyms *n* ≠ **nonobservance:** adherence to, attention, compliance, discharge, fulfilment, heeding, honouring, observation, performance

bread *n* **2** = **food**, aliment, diet, fare, necessities, nourishment, nutriment, provisions, subsistence, sustenance, viands, victuals **3** *Slang* = **money**, brass (*N English dialect*), cash, dibs, dosh (*Brit. & Austral. sl.*), dough (*sl.*), finance, funds, necessary (*inf.*), needful (*inf.*), shekels (*inf.*), silver, spondulicks (*sl.*)

breadth *n* **1** = **width**, beam, broadness, latitude, span, spread, wideness **3** = **extent**, amplitude, area, compass, comprehensiveness, dimension, expanse, extensiveness, magnitude, measure, range, reach, scale, scope, size, space, spread, sweep, vastness **4** = **broadmindedness**, freedom, latitude, liberality, openmindedness, openness, permissiveness

break *vb* **1** = **separate**, disintegrate, divide, fragment, part, rend, sever, shatter, shiver, smash, split, tear **2** = **damage**, demolish, destroy, total (*sl.*), trash (*sl.*) **3** = **crack**, burst, fracture, snap, splinter **7** = **disobey**, breach, contravene, disregard, infract (*Law*), infringe, renege on, transgress, violate **8** *foll. by* **with** = **separate from**, break away from, depart from, ditch, drop (*inf.*), jilt, part company, reject, renounce, repudiate **9** = **reveal**, announce, come out, disclose, divulge, impart, inform, let out, make public, proclaim, tell **12, 13** = **stop**, abandon, cut, discontinue, give up, interrupt, pause, rest, suspend **15** = **weaken**, cow, cripple, demoralize, dispirit, enervate, enfeeble, impair, incapacitate, subdue, tame, undermine **17** = **beat**,

two fighters) to separate from a clinch. **36** (*intr*) (of the male voice) to undergo a change in register, quality, and range at puberty. **37** (*tr*) to open the breech of (certain firearms) by snapping the barrel away from the butt on its hinge. **38** (*tr*) to interrupt the flow of current in (an electrical circuit). **39** *Inf., chiefly US.* to become successful. **40 break camp.** to pack up and leave a camp. **41 break service.** *Tennis.* to win a game in which an opponent is serving. **42 break the bank.** to ruin financially or deplete the resources of a bank (as in gambling). **43 break the mould.** to make a change that breaks an established habit, pattern, etc. ◆ **44** the act or result of breaking; fracture. **45** a crack formed as the result of breaking. **46** a brief respite. **47** a sudden rush, esp. to escape: *to make a break for freedom.* **48** a breach in a relationship. **49** any sudden interruption in a continuous action. **50** *Brit.* a short period between classes at school. **51** *Inf.* a fortunate opportunity, esp. to prove oneself. **52** *Inf.* a piece of good or bad luck. **53** (esp. in a stock exchange) a sudden and substantial decline in prices. **54** *Billiards, snooker.* a series of successful shots during one turn. **55** *Billiards, snooker.* the opening shot that scatters the placed balls. **56** Also called: **service break, break of serve.** *Tennis.* the act or an instance of breaking an opponent's service. **57a** *Jazz.* a short usually improvised solo passage. **57b** an instrumental passage in a pop song. **58** a discontinuity in an electrical circuit. **59** access to a radio channel by a citizens' band radio operator. **60 break of day.** the dawn. ◆ *interj* **61** *Boxing, wrestling.* a command by a referee for two opponents to separate. ◆ See also **breakaway, break down,** etc. [OE *brecan*]

breakable ❶ ('breɪkəbᵊl) *adj* **1** capable of being broken. ◆ *n* **2** (*usually pl*) a fragile easily broken article.

breakage ❶ ('breɪkɪdʒ) *n* **1** the act or result of breaking. **2** the quantity or amount broken. **3** compensation or allowance for goods damaged while in use, transit, etc.

breakaway ❶ ('breɪkəˌweɪ) *n* **1a** loss or withdrawal of a group of members from an association, club, etc. **1b** (*as modifier*): *a breakaway faction.* **2** *Austral.* a stampede of animals, esp. at the smell of water. ◆ *vb* **break away.** (*intr, adv*) **3** (often foll. by *from*) to leave hastily or escape. **4** to withdraw or secede.

break dance *n* **1** an acrobatic dance style of the 1980s. ◆ *vb* **break-dance, break-dances, break-dancing, break-danced.** (*intr*) **2** to perform a break dance.
▸**break dancer** *n* ▸**break dancing** *n*

break down ❶ *vb* (*adv*) **1** (*intr*) to cease to function; become ineffective. **2** to yield or cause to yield, esp. to strong emotion or tears. **3** (*tr*) to crush or destroy. **4** (*intr*) to have a nervous breakdown. **5** to analyse or be subjected to analysis. **6** to separate or cause to separate into simpler chemical elements; decompose. **7 break it down.** *Austral. & NZ inf.* **7a** stop it. **7b** don't expect me to believe that; come off it. ◆ *n* **breakdown. 8** an act or instance of breaking down; collapse. **9** short for **nervous breakdown. 10** an analysis or classification of something into its component parts: *he prepared a breakdown of the report.* **11** a lively American country dance.

breaker ❶ ('breɪkə) *n* **1** a person or thing that breaks something, such as a person or firm that breaks up old cars, etc. **2** a large wave with a white crest on the open sea or one that breaks into foam on the shore. **3** a citizens' band radio operator.

break even *vb* **1** (*intr, adv*) to attain a level of activity, as in commerce, or a point of operation, as in gambling, at which there is neither profit nor loss. ◆ *n* **breakeven. 2** *Accounting.* the level of commercial activity at which the total cost and total revenue of a business enterprise are equal.

breakfast ('brɛkfəst) *n* **1** the first meal of the day. **2** the food at this meal. ◆ *vb* **3** to eat or supply with breakfast. [C15: from BREAK + FAST²]
▸'**breakfaster** *n*

break in ❶ *vb* (*adv*) **1** (sometimes foll. by *on*) to interrupt. **2** (*intr*) to enter a house, etc., illegally, esp. by force. **3** (*tr*) to accustom (a person or animal) to normal duties or practice. **4** (*tr*) to use or wear (shoes, new equipment, etc.) until comfortable or running smoothly. **5** *Austral.* to bring new land under cultivation. ◆ *n* **break-in. 6** the illegal entering of a building, esp. by thieves.

breaking and entering *n* (formerly) the gaining of unauthorized access to a building with intent to commit a crime.

breaking point *n* the point at which something or someone gives way under strain.

breakneck ❶ ('breɪkˌnɛk) *adj* (*prenominal*) (of speed, pace, etc.) excessive and dangerous.

break off ❶ *vb* **1** to sever or detach or be severed or detached. **2** (*adv*) to end (a relationship, association, etc.) or (of a relationship, etc.) to be ended. **3** (*intr, adv*) to stop abruptly: *he broke off in the middle of his speech.*

break out ❶ *vb* (*intr, adv*) **1** to begin or arise suddenly. **2** to make an escape, esp. from prison. **3** (foll. by *in*) (of the skin) to erupt (in a rash, pimples, etc.). ◆ *n* **break-out. 4** an escape, esp. from prison or confinement.

break through ❶ *vb* **1** (*intr*) to penetrate. **2** (*intr, adv*) to achieve success, make a discovery, etc., esp. after lengthy efforts. ◆ *n* **breakthrough. 3** a significant development or discovery, esp. in science. **4** the penetration of an enemy's defensive position.

breakthrough bleeding ('breɪkˌθruː) *n* vaginal bleeding that occurs other than at a menstrual period while a woman is using a low-dose oral contraceptive.

break up ❶ *vb* (*adv*) **1** to separate or cause to separate. **2** to put an end to (a relationship) or (of a relationship) to come to an end. **3** to dissolve or cause to dissolve; disrupt or be disrupted: *the meeting broke up at noon.* **4** (*intr*) *Brit.* (of a school) to close for the holidays. **5** *Inf.* to lose or cause to lose control of the emotions. **6** *Sl.* to be or cause to be overcome with laughter. ◆ *n* **break-up. 7** a separation or disintegration. **8a** in the Canadian north, the breaking up of the ice on a body of water that marks the beginning of spring. **8b** this season.

break-up value *n Commerce.* **1** the value of an organization assuming that it will not continue to trade. **2** the value of a share in a company based only on the value of its assets.

breakwater ❶ ('breɪkˌwɔːtə) *n* **1** Also called: **mole.** a massive wall built out into the sea to protect a shore or harbour from the force of waves. **2** another name for **groyne.**

bream¹ (briːm; *Austral.* brɪm) *or Austral.* **brim** (brɪm) *n, pl* **bream** *or* **brim. 1** any of several Eurasian freshwater cyprinid fishes having a deep compressed body covered with silvery scales. **2** short for **sea bream. 3** *Austral.* any of various marine fishes. [C14: from OF *bresme,* of Gmc origin]

bream² (briːm) *vb Naut.* (formerly) to clean debris from (the bottom of a vessel) by heating to soften the pitch. [C15: prob. from MDu. *bremme* broom; from burning broom as a source of heat]

breast ❶ (brɛst) *n* **1** the front part of the body from the neck to the abdomen; chest. **2** either of the two soft fleshy milk-secreting glands on the chest in sexually mature human females. **3** a similar organ in certain other mammals. **4** anything that resembles a breast in shape or position: *the breast of the hill.* **5** a source of nourishment. **6** the source of human emotions. **7** the part of a garment that covers the breast. **8** a projection from the side of a wall, esp. that formed by a chimney. **9 beat one's breast.** to display guilt and remorse publicly or ostentatiously. **10 make a clean breast of.** to make a confession of. ◆ *vb* (*tr*) **11** to confront boldly; face: *breast the storm.* **12** to oppose with the breast or meet at breast level: *breasting the waves.* **13** to reach the summit of: *breasting the mountain top.* [OE *brēost*]

THESAURUS

better, cap (*inf.*), exceed, excel, go beyond, outdo, outstrip, surpass, top **20** = **reduce**, cushion, diminish, lessen, lighten, moderate, soften, weaken **23** = **ruin**, bankrupt, bust (*inf.*), degrade, demote, discharge, dismiss, humiliate, impoverish, make bankrupt, reduce **27** = **happen**, appear, burst out, come forth suddenly, emerge, erupt, occur **28a** *foll. by* **into** = **begin**, burst into, burst out, commence, give way to, launch into ◆ *n* **44** = **division**, breach, cleft, gap, gash, hole, opening, rent, rift, rupture, split, tear **45** = **crack**, fissure, fracture **46, 49** = **rest**, breather, breathing space, entr'acte, halt, hiatus, interlude, intermission, interruption, interval, let-up (*inf.*), lull, pause, recess, respite, suspension **48** = **breach**, alienation, disaffection, dispute, divergence, estrangement, rift, rupture, schism, separation, split **51** *Informal* = **stroke of luck**, advantage, chance, fortune, opening, opportunity
Antonyms *vb* ≠ **separate:** attach, bind, connect, fasten, join, repair, unite ≠ **disobey:** abide by, adhere to, conform, discharge, follow, obey, observe

breakable *adj* **1** = **fragile**, brittle, crumbly, delicate, flimsy, frail, frangible, friable
Antonyms *adj* durable, indestructible, infrangible, lasting, nonbreakable, resistant, rugged, shatterproof, solid, strong, toughened, unbreakable

breakage *n* **1** = **break**, breach, cleft, crack, cut, fissure, fracture, rent, rift, rupture, tear

breakaway *modifier* **1b** = **dissenting**, heretical, rebel, schismatic, seceding, secessionist ◆ *vb* **break away 3** = **flee**, decamp, escape, fly, hook it (*sl.*), make a break for it, make a run for it (*inf.*), make off, run away **4** = **break with**, detach, part company, secede, separate

break down *vb* **1** = **collapse**, come unstuck, conk out (*inf.*), fail, go kaput (*inf.*), go phut, seize up, stop, stop working **2, 4** = **be overcome**, crack up (*inf.*), go to pieces ◆ *n* **breakdown 8** = **collapse**, crackup (*inf.*), disintegration, disruption, failure, mishap, stoppage **10** = **analysis**, categorization, classification, detailed list, diagnosis, dissection, itemization

breaker *n* **2** = **wave**, billow, comber, roller, whitecap, white horse

break in *vb* **1** = **interrupt**, barge in, burst in, butt in, interfere, interject, interpose, intervene, intrude, put one's oar in, put one's two cents in (*US sl.*) **2** = **burgle**, break and enter, invade, rob **3** = **get used to**, accustom, condition, habituate, initiate, prepare, tame, train ◆ *n* **break-in 6** = **burglary**, breaking and entering, invasion, robbery

breakneck *adj* = **dangerous**, excessive, express, headlong, precipitate, rapid, rash, reckless

break off *vb* **1** = **detach**, divide, part, pull off, separate, sever, snap off, splinter **2, 3** = **stop**, cease, desist, discontinue, end, finish, halt, pause, suspend, terminate

break out *vb* **1** = **begin**, appear, arise, commence, emerge, happen, occur, set in, spring up, start **2** = **escape**, abscond, bolt, break loose, burst out, flee, get free **3** = **erupt**, burst out

break through *vb* **1** = **penetrate**, burst through, emerge, get past **2** = **succeed**, achieve, crack it (*inf.*), cut it, pass, shine forth ◆ *n* **breakthrough 3** = **development**, advance, discovery, find, finding, gain, improvement, invention, leap, progress, quantum leap, step forward

break up *vb* **1** = **separate**, dissolve, divide, divorce, end, part, scatter, sever, split **3** = **stop**, adjourn, disband, disperse, disrupt, end, suspend, terminate ◆ *n* **break-up 7** = **separation**, breakdown, breaking, crackup (*inf.*), disintegration, dispersal, dissolution, divorce, ending, parting, rift, split, splitting, termination, wind-up

breakwater *n* **1, 2** = **sea wall**, groyne, jetty, mole, spur

breast *n* **2, 3** = **bosom**, boob (*sl.*), bust, chest, front, teat, tit (*sl.*), udder **6** = **heart**, being, conscience, core, emotions, feelings, seat of the affections, sentiments, soul, thoughts

breastbone (ˈbrɛstˌbəʊn) *n* the nontechnical name for **sternum.**

breast-feed *vb* **breast-feeds, breast-feeding, breast-fed.** to feed (a baby) with milk from the breast; suckle.

breastpin (ˈbrɛstˌpɪn) *n* a brooch worn on the breast, esp. to close a garment.

breastplate (ˈbrɛstˌpleɪt) *n* a piece of armour covering the chest.

breaststroke (ˈbrɛstˌstrəʊk) *n* a swimming stroke in which the arms are extended in front of the head and swept back on either side while the legs are drawn up beneath the body and thrust back together.

breastwork (ˈbrɛstˌwɜːk) *n Fortifications.* a temporary defensive work, usually breast-high.

breath ❶ (brɛθ) *n* **1** the intake and expulsion of air during respiration. **2** the air inhaled or exhaled during respiration. **3** a single respiration or inhalation of air, etc. **4** the vapour, heat, or odour of exhaled air. **5** a slight gust of air. **6** a short pause or rest. **7** a brief time. **8** a suggestion or slight evidence; suspicion: *a breath of scandal.* **9** a whisper or soft sound. **10** life, energy, or vitality: *the breath of new industry.* **11** *Phonetics.* the exhalation of air without vibration of the vocal cords, as in pronouncing fricatives such as (f) or (h) or stops such as (p) or (k). **12 catch one's breath. 12a** to rest until breathing is normal, esp. after exertion. **12b** to stop breathing momentarily from excitement, fear, etc. **13 in the same breath.** done or said at the same time. **14 out of breath.** gasping for air after exertion. **15 save one's breath.** to refrain from useless talk. **16 take one's breath away.** to overwhelm with surprise, etc. **17 under** *or* **below one's breath.** in a quiet voice or whisper. [OE *brǣth*]

breathable (ˈbriːðəbᵊl) *adj* **1** (of air) fit to be breathed. **2** (of a material) allowing air to pass through so that perspiration can evaporate.

Breathalyser *or* **Breathalyzer** (ˈbrɛθəˌlaɪzə) *n Trademark.* a device for estimating the amount of alcohol in the breath: used in testing people suspected of driving under the influence of alcohol. [C20: BREATH + (AN)ALYSER]
▸ **ˈbreathaˌlyse** *or* **ˈbreathaˌlyze** *vb*

breathe ❶ (briːð) *vb* **breathes, breathing, breathed. 1** to take in oxygen and give out carbon dioxide; respire. **2** (*intr*) to exist; be alive. **3** (*intr*) to rest to regain breath, composure, etc. **4** (*intr*) (esp. of air) to blow lightly. **5** (*intr*) *Machinery.* to take in air, esp. for combustion. **6** (*tr*) *Phonetics.* to articulate (a speech sound) without vibration of the vocal cords. **7** to exhale or emit: *the dragon breathed fire.* **8** (*tr*) to impart; instil: *to breathe confidence into the actors.* **9** (*tr*) to speak softly; whisper. **10** (*tr*) to permit to rest: *to breathe a horse.* **11** (*intr*) (of a material) to allow air to pass through so that perspiration can evaporate. **12 breathe again, freely,** *or* **easily.** to feel relief. **13 breathe one's last.** to die or be finished or defeated. [C13: from BREATH]

breather ❶ (ˈbriːðə) *n* **1** *Inf.* a short pause for rest. **2** a person who breathes in a specified way: *a deep breather.* **3** a vent in a container to equalize internal and external pressure.

breathing (ˈbriːðɪŋ) *n* **1** the passage of air into and out of the lungs to supply the body with oxygen. **2** a single breath: *a breathing between words.* **3** *Phonetics.* **3a** expulsion of breath (**rough breathing**) or absence of such expulsion (**smooth breathing**) preceding the pronunciation of an initial vowel or rho in ancient Greek. **3b** either of two symbols indicating this.

breathless ❶ (ˈbrɛθlɪs) *adj* **1** out of breath; gasping, etc. **2** holding one's breath or having it taken away by excitement, etc. **3** (esp. of the atmosphere) motionless and stifling. **4** *Rare.* lifeless; dead.
▸ **ˈbreathlessly** *adv* ▸ **ˈbreathlessness** *n*

breathtaking ❶ (ˈbrɛθˌteɪkɪŋ) *adj* causing awe or excitement.
▸ **ˈbreathˌtakingly** *adv*

breath test *n Brit.* a chemical test of a driver's breath to determine the amount of alcohol he has consumed.

breathy (ˈbrɛθɪ) *adj* **breathier, breathiest. 1** (of the speaking voice) accompanied by an audible emission of breath. **2** (of the singing voice) lacking resonance.
▸ **ˈbreathily** *adv* ▸ **ˈbreathiness** *n*

breccia (ˈbrɛtʃɪə) *n* a rock consisting of angular fragments embedded in a finer matrix. [C18: from It.]
▸ **ˈbrecciˌated** *adj*

bred (brɛd) *vb* the past tense and past participle of **breed.**

breech ❶ *n* (briːtʃ). **1** the buttocks; rump. **2** the lower part or bottom of something. **3** the part of a firearm behind the barrel or bore. ◆ *vb* (briːtʃ, brɪtʃ). (*tr*) **4** to fit (a gun) with a breech. **5** *Arch.* to clothe in breeches or any other clothing. [OE *brēc*, pl. of *brōc* leg covering]

> **USAGE NOTE** *Breech* is sometimes wrongly used as a verb where *breach* is meant: *the barrier/agreement was breached* (not *breeched*).

breechblock (ˈbriːtʃˌblɒk) *n* a metal block in breech-loading firearms that is withdrawn to insert the cartridge and replaced before firing.

breech delivery *n* birth of a baby with the feet or buttocks appearing first.

breeches (ˈbrɪtʃɪz, ˈbriː-) *pl n* **1** trousers extending to the knee or just below, worn for riding, etc. **2** *Inf. or dialect.* any trousers or pants, esp. extending to the knee.

breeches buoy *n* a ring-shaped life buoy with a support in the form of a pair of short breeches, in which a person is suspended for safe transfer from a ship.

breeching (ˈbrɪtʃɪŋ, ˈbriː-) *n* the strap of a harness that passes behind a horse's haunches.

breech-loader (ˈbriːtʃˌləʊdə) *n* a firearm that is loaded at the breech.
▸ **ˈbreech-ˌloading** *adj*

breed ❶ (briːd) *vb* **breeds, breeding, bred. 1** to bear (offspring). **2** (*tr*) to bring up; raise. **3** to produce or cause to produce by mating; propagate. **4** to produce new or improved strains of (domestic animals and plants). **5** to produce or be produced; generate: *to breed trouble.* ◆ *n* **6** a group of organisms within a species, esp. domestic animals, having clearly defined characteristics. **7** a lineage or race. **8** a kind, sort, or group. [OE *brēdan*, of Gmc origin; rel. to BROOD]

breeder (ˈbriːdə) *n* **1** a person who breeds plants or animals. **2** something that reproduces. **3** an animal kept for breeding purposes. **4** a source or cause: *a breeder of discontent.* **5** short for **breeder reactor.**

breeder reactor *n* a type of nuclear reactor that produces more fissionable material than it consumes.

breeding ❶ (ˈbriːdɪŋ) *n* **1** the process of bearing offspring; reproduction. **2** the process of producing plants or animals by hybridization, inbreeding, or other methods of reproduction. **3** the result of good training, esp. the knowledge of correct social behaviour; refinement.

breeze[1] ❶ (briːz) *n* **1** a gentle or light wind. **2** *Meteorol.* a wind of force two to six (4–31 mph) inclusive on the Beaufort scale. **3** *US & Canad. inf.* an easy task or state of ease. **4** *Inf., chiefly Brit.* a disturbance, esp. a lively quarrel. ◆ *vb* **breezes, breezing, breezed.** (*intr*) **5** to move quickly or casually: *he breezed into the room.* [C16: prob. from OSp. *briza* northeast wind]

breeze[2] (briːz) *n* ashes of coal, coke, or charcoal used to make breeze blocks. [C18: from F *braise* live coals; see BRAISE]

breeze block *n* a light building brick made from the ashes of coal, coke, etc., bonded together by cement.

breezeway (ˈbriːzˌweɪ) *n* a roofed passageway connecting two buildings.

breezy ❶ (ˈbriːzɪ) *adj* **breezier, breeziest. 1** fresh; windy. **2** casual or carefree; lively; light-hearted.
▸ **ˈbreezily** *adv* ▸ **ˈbreeziness** *n*

bremsstrahlung (ˈbrɛmzˌʃtrɑːlʊŋ) *n* the x-radiation produced when an electrically charged particle, such as an electron, is slowed down by the electric field of an atomic nucleus. [G: braking radiation]

Bren gun (brɛn) *n* an air-cooled gas-operated light machine gun: used by the British in World War II. [C20: after *Br(no)*, now in the Czech Republic, where it was first made and *En(field)*, England, where manufacture was continued]

brent goose (brɛnt) *n* a small goose that has a dark grey plumage and short neck and occurs in most northern coastal regions. Also called: **brent,** (esp. US and Canad.) **brant.** [C16: ? of Scand. origin]

THESAURUS

breath *n* **1** = **respiration**, breathing, exhalation, gasp, gulp, inhalation, pant, wheeze **5** = **gust**, faint breeze, flutter, puff, sigh, slight movement, waft, zephyr **6, 7** = **rest**, break, breather, breathing-space, instant, moment, pause, respite, second **8** = **suggestion**, hint, murmur, suspicion, undertone, whisper **10** = **life**, animation, energy, existence, lifeblood, life force, vitality

breathe *vb* **1** = **inhale and exhale**, draw in, gasp, gulp, pant, puff, respire, wheeze **8** = **instil**, imbue, impart, infuse, inject, inspire, transfuse **9** = **whisper**, articulate, express, murmur, say, sigh, utter, voice

breather *n* **1** *Informal* = **rest**, break, breathing space, breath of air, halt, pause, recess, respite

breathless *adj* **1** = **out of breath**, choking, exhausted, gasping, gulping, out of whack (*inf.*), panting, short-winded, spent, wheezing, winded **2** = **excited**, agog, anxious, astounded, avid, eager, flabbergasted (*inf.*), gobsmacked (*Brit. sl.*), on tenterhooks, open-mouthed, thunderstruck, with bated breath

breathtaking *adj* = **amazing**, astonishing, awe-inspiring, awesome, brilliant, dramatic, exciting, heart-stirring, impressive, magnificent, moving, overwhelming, sensational, striking, stunning (*inf.*), thrilling, wondrous (*arch. or literary*)

breech *n* **1** = **buttocks**, arse, ass (*US & Canad. taboo sl.*), backside (*inf.*), behind (*inf.*), bum (*Brit. sl.*), buns (*US sl.*), butt (*US & Canad. inf.*), derrière (*euphemistic*), jacksy (*Brit. sl.*), posterior, rump, seat, tail (*inf.*)

breed *vb* **1** = **reproduce**, bear, beget, bring forth, engender, generate, hatch, multiply, originate, procreate, produce, propagate **2** = **bring up**, cultivate, develop, discipline, educate, foster, instruct, nourish, nurture, raise, rear **5** = **produce**, arouse, bring about, cause, create, generate, give rise to, induce, make, occasion, originate, stir up ◆ *n* **6** = **variety**, pedigree, race, species, stock, strain, type **7** = **lineage**, class, extraction, family, ilk, line, pedigree, race, stock **8** = **kind**, brand, sort, stamp, type, variety

breeding *n* **1** = **reproduction**, nurture, raising, rearing, training, upbringing **2** = **cultivation**, development **3** = **refinement**, civility, conduct, courtesy, cultivation, culture, gentility, manners, polish, sophistication, urbanity

breeze[1] *n* **1** = **light wind**, air, breath of wind, current of air, draught, flurry, gust, puff of air, waft, whiff, zephyr ◆ *vb* **5** = **move briskly**, flit, glide, hurry, pass, sail, sally, sweep, trip

breezy *adj* **1** = **windy**, airy, blowing, blowy, blusterous, blustery, fresh, gusty, squally **2** = **carefree**, airy, animated, blithe, buoyant, casual, cheerful, chirpy (*inf.*), debonair, easy-going, free and easy, full of beans (*inf.*), genial, informal, jaunty, light, light-hearted, lively, sparkling, sparky, spirited, sprightly, sunny, upbeat (*inf.*), vivacious
Antonyms *adj* ≠ **windy:** calm, heavy, oppressive, windless ≠ **carefree:** calm, depressed, dull, heavy, lifeless, mournful, sad, serious

brethren ('brɛðrɪn) *pl n Arch. except when referring to fellow members of a religion, society, etc.* a plural of **brother**.

Breton ('brɛtᵊn) *adj* **1** of, relating to, or characteristic of Brittany, a region of NW France, its people, or their language. ◆ *n* **2** a native or inhabitant of Brittany. **3** the Celtic language of Brittany.

breve (bri:v) *n* **1** an accent, ˘, placed over a vowel to indicate that it is short or is pronounced in a specified way. **2** *Music.* a note, now rarely used, equivalent to two semibreves. **3** *RC Church.* a less common word for **brief** (papal letter). [C13: from Med. L, from L *brevis* short]

brevet ('brɛvɪt) *n* **1** a document entitling a commissioned officer to hold temporarily a higher military rank without the appropriate pay and allowances. ◆ *vb* **brevets, brevetting, brevetted** *or* **brevets, breveting, breveted. 2** (*tr*) to promote by brevet. [C14: from OF, from *brief* letter; see BRIEF]
▸ **'brevetcy** *n*

breviary ('bri:vjərɪ) *n, pl* **breviaries.** *RC Church.* a book of psalms, hymns, prayers, etc., to be recited daily by clerics and certain members of religious orders as part of the divine office. [C16: from L *breviārium* an abridged version, from *brevis* short]

brevity 🅣 ('brɛvɪtɪ) *n, pl* **brevities. 1** conciseness of expression; lack of verbosity. **2** a short duration; brief time. [C16: from L, from *brevis* BRIEF]

brew 🅣 (bru:) *vb* **1** to make (beer, ale, etc.) from malt and other ingredients by steeping, boiling, and fermentation. **2** to prepare (a drink, such as tea) by boiling or infusing. **3** (*tr*) to devise or plan: *to brew a plot.* **4** (*intr*) to be in the process of being brewed. **5** (*intr*) to be impending or forming: *there's a storm brewing.* ◆ *n* **6** a beverage produced by brewing, esp. tea or beer. **7** an instance or time of brewing: *last year's brew.* **8** a mixture. [OE *brēowan*]
▸ **'brewer** *n*

brewery ('bruərɪ) *n, pl* **breweries.** a place where beer, ale, etc., is brewed.

brewing ('bru:ɪŋ) *n* a quantity of a beverage brewed at one time.

briar[1] *or* **brier** ('braɪə) *n* **1** Also called: **tree heath.** a shrub of S Europe, having a hard woody root (briarroot). **2** a tobacco pipe made from the root of this plant. [C19: from F *bruyère* heath]
▸ **'briary** *or* **'briery** *adj*

briar[2] ('braɪə) *n* a variant spelling of **brier**[1].

briarroot *or* **brierroot** ('braɪə,ru:t) *n* the hard woody root of the briar, used for making tobacco pipes. Also called: **briarwood, brierwood.**

bribe 🅣 (braɪb) *vb* **bribes, bribing, bribed. 1** to promise, offer, or give something, often illegally, to (a person) to procure services or gain influence. ◆ *n* **2** a reward, such as money or favour, given or offered for this purpose. **3** any persuasion or lure. [C14: from OF *briber* to beg, from ?]
▸ **'bribery** *n*

bric-a-brac 🅣 ('brɪkə,bræk) *n* miscellaneous small objects, esp. furniture and curios, kept because they are ornamental or rare. [C19: from F]

brick (brɪk) *n* **1a** a rectangular block of clay mixed with sand and fired in a kiln or baked by the sun, used in building construction. **1b** (*as modifier*): *a brick house.* **2** the material used to make such blocks. **3** any rectangular block: *a brick of ice.* **4** bricks collectively. **5** *Inf.* a reliable, trustworthy, or helpful person. **6** *Brit.* a child's building block. **7 drop a brick.** *Brit. inf.* to make a tactless or indiscreet remark. **8 like a ton of bricks.** *Inf.* with great force; severely. ◆ *vb* **9** (*tr; usually foll. by in, up, or over*) to construct, line, pave, fill, or wall up with bricks: *to brick up a window.* [C15: from OF *brique,* from MDu. *bricke*]
▸ **'bricky** *adj*

brickbat ('brɪk,bæt) *n* **1** a piece of brick or similar material, esp. one used as a weapon. **2** blunt criticism. [C16: BRICK + BAT[1]]

brickie ('brɪkɪ) *n Inf.* a bricklayer.

bricklayer ('brɪk,leɪə) *n* a person trained or skilled in laying bricks.
▸ **'brick,laying** *n*

brick red *n, adj* (of) a reddish-brown colour.

brickwork ('brɪk,wɜ:k) *n* **1** a structure built of bricks. **2** construction using bricks.

brickyard ('brɪk,jɑ:d) *n* a place in which bricks are made, stored, or sold.

bricolage ('brɪkə,lɑ:ʒ; *French* brikəlaʒ) *n Archit.* a jumbled effect produced by the close proximity of buildings from different periods or in different styles. [F: odd jobs, do-it-yourself]

bridal 🅣 ('braɪdᵊl) *adj* of or relating to a bride or a wedding; nuptial. [OE *brȳdealu,* lit.: "bride ale", that is, wedding feast]

bride (braɪd) *n* a woman who has just been or is about to be married. [OE *brȳd*]

bridegroom ('braɪd,gru:m, -,grʊm) *n* a man who has just been or is about to be married. [C14: changed (through infl. of GROOM) from OE *brȳdguma,* from *brȳd* BRIDE + *guma* man]

bride price *or* **wealth** *n* (in some societies) money, property, or services given by a bridegroom to the kinsmen of his bride.

bridesmaid ('braɪdz,meɪd) *n* a girl or young unmarried woman who attends a bride at her wedding.

bridge[1] 🅣 (brɪdʒ) *n* **1** a structure that spans and provides a passage over a road, railway, river, or some other obstacle. **2** something that resembles this in shape or function. **3** the hard ridge at the upper part of the nose, formed by the underlying nasal bones. **4** the part of a pair of glasses that rests on the nose. **5** Also called: **bridgework.** a dental plate containing one or more artificial teeth that is secured to the surrounding natural teeth. **6** a platform from which a ship is piloted and navigated. **7** a piece of wood, usually fixed, supporting the strings of a violin, guitar, etc., and transmitting their vibrations to the sounding board. **8** Also called: **bridge passage.** a passage in a musical, literary, or dramatic work linking two or more important sections. **9** Also called: **bridge circuit.** *Electronics.* any of several networks across which a device is connected for measuring resistance, capacitance, etc. **10** *Computing.* a device that connects networks and sends packets between them. **11** *Billiards, snooker.* a support for a cue. **12 cross a bridge when (one) comes to it.** to deal with a problem only when it arises. ◆ *vb* **bridges, bridging, bridged.** (*tr*) **13** to build or provide a bridge over something; span: *to bridge a river.* **14** to connect or reduce the distance between: *let us bridge our differences.* [OE *brycg*]
▸ **'bridgeable** *adj*

bridge[2] (brɪdʒ) *n* a card game for four players, based on whist, in which one hand (the dummy) is exposed and the trump suit decided by bidding between the players. See also **contract bridge, auction bridge.** [C19: from ?]

bridgehead ('brɪdʒ,hɛd) *n* **1** *Mil.* an area of ground secured or to be taken on the enemy's side of an obstacle. **2** *Mil.* a fortified or defensive position at the end of a bridge nearest to the enemy. **3** an advantageous position gained for future expansion.

bridge roll *n* a soft bread roll in a long thin shape. [C20: from BRIDGE[2] or ? BRIDGE[1]]

bridgework ('brɪdʒ,wɜ:k) *n* a partial denture attached to the surrounding teeth.

bridging loan *n* a loan made to cover the period between two transactions, such as the buying of another house before the sale of the first is completed.

bridle 🅣 ('braɪdᵊl) *n* **1** a headgear for a horse, etc., consisting of a series of buckled straps and a metal mouthpiece (bit) by which the animal is controlled through the reins. **2** something that curbs or restrains; check. **3** a Y-shaped cable, rope, or chain, used for holding, towing, etc. ◆ *vb* **bridles, bridling, bridled. 4** (*tr*) to put a bridle on (a horse, mule, etc.). **5** (*tr*) to restrain; curb: *he bridled his rage.* **6** (*intr; often foll. by at*) to show anger, scorn, or indignation. [OE *brigdels*]

bridle path *n* a path suitable for riding or leading horses.

Brie (bri:) *n* a soft creamy white cheese. [C19: F, after *Brie,* region in N France where it originated]

brief 🅣 (bri:f) *adj* **1** short in duration. **2** short in length or extent; scanty: *a brief bikini.* **3** abrupt in manner; brusque: *the professor was brief with me.* **4** terse or concise. ◆ *n* **5** a condensed statement or written synopsis; abstract. **6** *Law.* a document containing all the facts and points of law of a case by which a solicitor instructs a barrister to represent a client. **7** *RC Church.* a letter issuing from the Roman court written in modern characters, as contrasted with a papal bull; papal brief. **8** Also called: **briefing.** instructions. **9 hold a brief for.** to argue for; champion. **10 in brief.** in short; to sum up. ◆ *vb* (*tr*) **11** to prepare or in-

THESAURUS

brevity *n* **1** = **conciseness,** concision, condensation, crispness, curtness, economy, pithiness, succinctness, terseness **2** = **shortness,** briefness, ephemerality, impermanence, transience, transitoriness
Antonyms *n* ≠ **conciseness:** circuity, diffuseness, discursiveness, long-windedness, prolixity, rambling, redundancy, tautology, tediousness, verbiage, verboseness, verbosity, wordiness

brew *vb* **1, 2** = **make** (*beer*), boil, ferment, infuse (*tea*), prepare by fermentation, seethe, soak, steep, stew **3** = **devise,** breed, concoct, contrive, form, hatch, plan, plot, project, scheme, start, stir up **5** = **develop,** foment, gather ◆ *n* **6** = **drink,** beverage, blend, concoction, distillation, fermentation, infusion, liquor, preparation

bribe *vb* **1** = **buy off,** corrupt, get at, grease the palm of (*sl.*), pay off (*inf.*), reward, square, suborn ◆ *n* **2** = **inducement,** backhander, enticement, graft (*inf.*), hush money (*sl.*), incentive, kickback (*US*), pay-off (*inf.*), payola (*inf.*)

bribery *n* **1** = **buying off,** corruption, graft (*inf.*), inducement, palm-greasing (*sl.*), payola (*inf.*), protection, subornation

bric-a-brac *n* = **knick-knacks,** baubles, bibelots, curios, gewgaws, objects of virtu, *objets d'art,* ornaments, trinkets

bridal *adj* = **matrimonial,** bride's, conjugal, connubial, hymeneal, marital, marriage, nuptial, spousal, wedding

bridge[1] *n* **1** = **arch,** flyover, overpass, span, viaduct **2** = **link,** band, bond, connection, tie ◆ *vb* **13** = **connect,** arch over, attach, bind, couple, cross, cross over, extend across, go over, join, link, reach across, span, traverse, unite
Antonyms *vb* ≠ **connect:** cleave, come apart, disjoin, divide, keep apart, separate, sever, split, sunder, widen

bridle *n* **2** = **curb,** check, control, rein, restraint ◆ *vb* **5** = **curb,** check, constrain, control, govern, have in one's pocket, keep a tight rein on, keep in check, keep on a string, master, moderate, rein, repress, restrain, subdue **6** = **get angry,** be indignant, bristle, draw (oneself) up, get one's back up, raise one's hackles, rear up

brief *adj* **1** = **short,** ephemeral, fast, fleeting, hasty, little, momentary, quick, quickie (*inf.*), short-lived, swift, temporary, transitory **3** = **curt,** abrupt, blunt, brusque, sharp, short, surly **4** = **concise,** clipped, compendious, compressed, crisp, curt, laconic, limited, monosyllabic, pithy, short, succinct, terse, thumbnail, to the point ◆ *n* **5** = **summary,** abridgment, abstract, digest, epitome, outline, précis, sketch, synopsis **6** *Law* = **case,** argument, contention, data, defence, demonstration ◆ *vb* **11** = **inform,** advise, clue in, explain, fill in (*inf.*), gen up (*Brit. inf.*), give (someone) a rundown, give (someone) the gen (*Brit. inf.*), instruct, keep posted, prepare, prime, put (someone) in the picture (*inf.*)
Antonyms *adj* ≠ **short:** extensive, lengthy, long, protracted ≠ **concise:** circuitous, detailed, diffuse, lengthy, long, long-drawn-out, long-winded

struct by giving a summary of relevant facts. **12** to make a summary or synopsis of. **13** *English law*. **13a** to instruct (a barrister) by brief. **13b** to retain (a barrister) as counsel. [C14: from OF *bref*, from L *brevis*]
►**'briefly** *adv* ►**'briefness** *n*

briefcase ('bri:f,keɪs) *n* a flat portable case, often of leather, for carrying papers, books, etc.

briefing Ⓣ ('bri:fɪŋ) *n* **1** a meeting at which information and instructions are given. **2** the facts presented at such a meeting.

briefless ('bri:flɪs) *adj* (said of a barrister) without clients.

briefs (bri:fs) *pl n* men's underpants or women's pants without legs.

brier[1] *or* **briar** ('braɪə) *n* any of various thorny shrubs or other plants, such as the sweetbrier. [OE *brēr*, *brǣr*, from ?]
►**'briery** *or* **'briary** *adj*

brier[2] ('braɪə) *n* a variant spelling of **briar**[1].

brierroot ('braɪə,ru:t) *n* a variant spelling of **briarroot**. Also called: **brierwood**.

brig[1] (brɪg) *n* **1** *Naut.* a two-masted square-rigger. **2** *Chiefly US.* a prison, esp. in a navy ship. [C18: shortened from BRIGANTINE]

brig[2] (brɪg) *n* a Scot. and N English word for a **bridge**[1].

Brig. *abbrev. for* Brigadier.

brigade Ⓣ (brɪ'geɪd) *n* **1** a military formation smaller than a division and usually commanded by a brigadier. **2** a group of people organized for a certain task: *a rescue brigade*. ◆ *vb* **brigades, brigading, brigaded.** (*tr*) **3** to organize into a brigade. [C17: from OF, from OIt., from *brigare* to fight; see BRIGAND]

brigadier (,brɪgə'dɪə) *n* **1** an officer of the British Army or Royal Marines junior to a major general but senior to a colonel, usually commanding a brigade. **2** an equivalent rank in other armed forces. [C17: from F, from BRIGADE]

brigalow ('brɪgələʊ) *n Austral.* **a** any of various acacia trees, forming dense scrub. **b** (*as modifier*): *brigalow country*. [C19: from Abor.]

brigand Ⓣ ('brɪgənd) *n* a bandit, esp. a member of a gang operating in mountainous areas. [C14: from OF, from OIt. *brigante* fighter, from *briga* strife]
►**'brigandage** *or* **'brigandry** *n*

brigantine ('brɪgən,ti:n, -,taɪn) *n* a two-masted sailing ship, rigged square on the foremast and fore-and-aft on the mainmast. [C16: from OIt. *brigantino* pirate ship, from *brigante* BRIGAND]

bright Ⓣ (braɪt) *adj* **1** emitting or reflecting much light; shining. **2** (of colours) intense or vivid. **3** full of promise: *a bright future*. **4** full of animation; cheerful: *a bright face*. **5** *Inf.* quick-witted or clever: *a bright child*. **6** magnificent; glorious. **7** polished; glistening. **8** (of a liquid) translucent and clear. **9 bright and early.** very early in the morning. ◆ *adv* **10** brightly: *the fire was burning bright*. [OE *beorht*]
►**'brightly** *adv* ►**'brightness** *n*

brighten Ⓣ ('braɪtᵊn) *vb* **1** to make or become bright or brighter. **2** to make or become cheerful.

brightening agent *n* a compound applied to a textile to increase its brightness by the conversion of ultraviolet radiation to visible (blue) light, used in detergents.

Bright's disease (braɪts) *n* chronic inflammation of the kidneys; chronic nephritis. [C19: after Richard *Bright* (1789–1858), E physician]

brightwork ('braɪt,wɜ:k) *n* shiny metal trimmings or fittings on ships, cars, etc.

brill[1] (brɪl) *n, pl* **brill** *or* **brills.** a European flatfish similar to the turbot. [C15: prob. from Cornish *brȳthel* mackerel, from OCornish *brȳth* speckled]

brill[2] (brɪl) *adj Brit sl.* excellent or wonderful. [C20: shortened form of BRILLIANT]

brilliance Ⓣ ('brɪljəns) *or* **brilliancy** *n* **1** great brightness; radiance. **2** excellence or distinction in physical or mental ability; exceptional talent. **3** splendour; magnificence.

brilliant Ⓣ ('brɪljənt) *adj* **1** shining with light; sparkling. **2** (of a colour) reflecting a considerable amount of light; vivid. **3** outstanding; exceptional: *a brilliant success*. **4** splendid; magnificent: *a brilliant show*. **5** of outstanding intelligence or intellect: *a brilliant mind*. ◆ *n* **6** Also called: **brilliant cut. 6a** a cut for diamonds and other gemstones in the form of two many-faceted pyramids joined at their bases. **6b** a diamond of this cut. [C17: from F *brillant* shining, from It. *brillo* BERYL]
►**'brilliantly** *adv*

brilliantine ('brɪljən,ti:n) *n* a perfumed oil used to make the hair smooth and shiny. [C19: from F, from *brillant* shining]

brim Ⓣ (brɪm) *n* **1** the upper rim of a vessel: *the brim of a cup*. **2** a projecting rim or edge: *the brim of a hat*. **3** the brink or edge of something. ◆ *vb* **brims, brimming, brimmed. 4** to fill or be full to the brim: *eyes brimming with tears*. [C13: from MHG *brem*]
►**'brimless** *adj*

brimful Ⓣ *or* **brimfull** (,brɪm'fʊl) *adj* (*postpositive; foll. by of*) filled up to the brim (with).

brimstone ('brɪm,stəʊn) *n* **1** an obsolete name for **sulphur. 2** a common yellow butterfly of N temperate regions of the Old World. [OE *brynstān*; see BURN[1], STONE]

brindle ('brɪndᵊl) *n* **1** a brindled animal. **2** a brindled colouring. [C17: back formation from BRINDLED]

brindled ('brɪndᵊld) *adj* brown or grey streaked or patched with a darker colour: *a brindled dog*. [C17: changed from C15 *brended*, lit.: branded]

brine Ⓣ (braɪn) *n* **1** a strong solution of salt and water, used for salting and pickling meats, etc. **2** the sea or its water. ◆ *vb* **brines, brining, brined. 3** (*tr*) to soak in or treat with brine. [OE *brīne*]
►**'brinish** *adj*

bring Ⓣ (brɪŋ) *vb* **brings, bringing, brought.** (*tr*) **1** to carry, convey, or take (something or someone) to a designated place or person: *bring that book to me*. **2** to cause to happen or occur to (oneself or another): *to bring disrespect on oneself*. **3** to cause to happen as a consequence: *responsibility brings maturity*. **4** to cause to come to mind: *it brought back memories*. **5** to cause to be in a certain state, position, etc.: *the punch brought him to his knees*. **6** to force, persuade, or make (oneself): *I couldn't bring myself to do it*. **7** to sell for; fetch: *the painting brought 20 pounds*. **8** *Law*. **8a** to institute (proceedings, charges, etc.). **8b** to put (evidence, etc.) before a tribunal. **9 bring forth.** to give birth to. ◆ See also **bring about, bring down,** etc. [OE *bringan*]
►**'bringer** *n*

bring about Ⓣ *vb* (*tr, adv*) **1** to cause to happen. **2** to turn (a ship) around.

bring-and-buy sale *n Brit. & NZ.* an informal sale, often for charity, to

THESAURUS

briefing *n* **1** = **meeting**, conference, preparation **2** = **instructions**, directions, guidance, information, instruction, preamble, rundown

briefly *adv* **1** = **momentarily**, briskly, cursorily, fleetingly, hastily, hurriedly, in passing, precisely, quickly, shortly, temporarily **4** = **concisely**, in a few words, in a nutshell, in brief, in outline

brigade *n* **1, 2** = **group**, band, body, camp, company, contingent, corps, crew, force, organization, outfit, party, squad, team, troop, unit

brigand *n* = **bandit**, desperado, footpad (*arch.*), freebooter, gangster, highwayman, marauder, outlaw, plunderer, robber, ruffian

bright *adj* **1** = **shining**, beaming, blazing, brilliant, dazzling, effulgent, flashing, gleaming, glistening, glittering, glowing, illuminated, intense, lambent, luminous, lustrous, radiant, resplendent, scintillating, shimmering, sparkling, twinkling, vivid **3** = **promising**, auspicious, encouraging, excellent, favourable, golden, good, hopeful, optimistic, palmy, propitious, prosperous, rosy **4** = **cheerful**, chirpy (*inf.*), full of beans (*inf.*), gay, genial, glad, happy, jolly, joyful, joyous, light-hearted, lively, merry, sparky, upbeat (*inf.*), vivacious **5** *Informal* = **intelligent**, acute, astute, aware, brainy, brilliant, clear-headed, clever, ingenious, inventive, keen, quick, quick-witted, sharp, smart, wide-awake
Antonyms *adj* ≠ **intelligent:** dense, dim, dim-witted (*inf.*), dull, dumb (*inf.*), dumb-ass (*sl.*), foolish, idiotic, ignorant, retarded, simple, slow, stupid, thick, unintelligent, witless

brighten *vb* **1** = **light up**, clear up, enliven, gleam, glow, illuminate, lighten, make brighter, shine **2** = **cheer up**, become cheerful, buck up (*inf.*), buoy up, encourage, enliven, gladden, hearten, make happy, perk up
Antonyms *vb* ≠ **light up:** becloud, blacken, cloud over *or* up, dim, dull, obscure, overshadow, shade, shadow ≠ **cheer up:** become angry, become gloomy, blacken, cloud, deject, depress, dispirit, look black, sadden

brightness *n* **1** = **shine**, brilliance, effulgence, glare, incandescence, intensity, light, luminosity, radiance, refulgence, resplendence, sparkle, splendour, vividness **5** = **intelligence**, acuity, alertness, awareness, cleverness, quickness, sharpness, smartness, smarts (*sl., chiefly US.*)
Antonyms *n* ≠ **shine:** dimness, dullness

brilliance *n* **1** = **brightness**, blaze, dazzle, effulgence, gleam, glitter, intensity, luminosity, lustre, radiance, refulgence, resplendence, sheen, sparkle, vividness **2** = **cleverness**, acuity, aptitude, braininess, distinction, excellence, genius, giftedness, greatness, inventiveness, talent, wisdom **3** = **splendour**, éclat, gilt, glamour, gorgeousness, grandeur, illustriousness, magnificence, pizzazz *or* pizazz (*inf.*)
Antonyms *n* ≠ **brightness:** darkness, dimness, dullness, obscurity, paleness ≠ **cleverness:** folly, idiocy, inanity, incompetence, ineptitude, silliness, simple-mindedness, stupidity

brilliant *adj* **1** = **shining**, ablaze, bright, coruscating, dazzling, glittering, glossy, intense, luminous, lustrous, radiant, refulgent, resplendent, scintillating, sparkling **3, 4** = **splendid**, celebrated, eminent, exceptional, famous, glorious, illustrious, magnificent, notable, outstanding, superb **5** = **intelligent**, accomplished, acute, astute, brainy, clever, discerning, expert, gifted, intellectual, inventive, masterly, penetrating, profound, quick, talented
Antonyms *adj* ≠ **shining:** dark, dim, dull, gloomy, obscure ≠ **splendid:** dull, ordinary, run-of-the-mill, unaccomplished, unexceptional, untalented ≠ **intelligent:** dim, simple, slow, stupid

brim *n* **2, 3** = **rim**, border, brink, circumference, edge, flange, lip, margin, skirt, verge ◆ *vb* **4** = **be full**, fill, fill up, hold no more, overflow, run over, spill, well over

brimful *adj* = **full**, brimming, filled, flush, level with, overflowing, overfull, packed, running over

brine *n* **1** = **salt water**, pickling solution, saline solution **2** = **the sea**, sea water

bring *vb* **1** = **take**, accompany, bear, carry, conduct, convey, deliver, escort, fetch, gather, guide, import, lead, transfer, transport, usher **2, 3** = **cause**, contribute to, create, effect, engender, inflict, occasion, produce, result in, wreak **6** = **make**, compel, convince, dispose, force, induce, influence, move, persuade, prevail on *or* upon, prompt, sway **7** = **sell for**, command, earn, fetch, gross, net, produce, return, yield

bring about *vb* **1** = **cause**, accomplish, achieve, bring to pass, compass, create, effect, effectuate, generate, give rise to, make happen, manage, occasion, produce, realize

which people bring items for sale and buy those that others have brought.

bring down Ⓣ *vb* (*tr, adv*) to cause to fall.

bring forward *vb* (*tr, adv*) **1** to present or introduce (a subject) for discussion. **2** *Book-keeping.* to transfer (a sum) to the top of the next page or column.

bring in Ⓣ *vb* (*tr, adv*) **1** to yield (income, profit, or cash). **2** to produce or return (a verdict). **3** to introduce (a legislative bill, etc.).

bring off Ⓣ *vb* (*tr, adv*) to succeed in achieving (something), esp. with difficulty.

bring out *vb* (*tr, adv*) **1** to produce or publish or have published. **2** to expose, reveal, or cause to be seen: *she brought out the best in me.* **3** (foll. by *in*) to cause (a person) to become covered (with spots, a rash, etc.). **4** *Brit.* to introduce (a girl) formally into society as a debutante.

bring over *vb* (*tr, adv*) to cause (a person) to change allegiances.

bring round *or* **around** *vb* (*tr, adv*) **1** to restore (a person) to consciousness, esp. after a faint. **2** to convince (another person, usually an opponent) of an opinion or point of view.

bring to *vb* (*tr, adv*) **1** to restore (a person) to consciousness. **2** to cause (a ship) to turn into the wind and reduce her headway.

bring up Ⓣ *vb* (*tr, adv*) **1** to care for and train (a child); rear. **2** to raise (a subject) for discussion; mention. **3** to vomit (food).

brinjal ('brɪndʒəl) *n* (in India and Africa) another name for the **aubergine.** [C17: from Port. *berinjela,* from Ar.]

brink Ⓣ (brɪŋk) *n* **1** the edge, border, or verge of a steep place. **2** the land at the edge of a body of water. **3** the verge of an event or state: *the brink of disaster.* [C13: from MDu. *brinc,* of Gmc origin]

brinkmanship ('brɪŋkmənˌʃɪp) *n* the art or practice of pressing a dangerous situation, esp. in international affairs, to the limit of safety and peace in order to win an advantage.

briny ('braɪnɪ) *adj* **brinier, briniest. 1** of or resembling brine; salty. ◆ *n* **2** (preceded by *the*) *Inf.* the sea.
▸ **'brininess** *n*

brio Ⓣ ('briːəʊ) *n* liveliness or vigour; spirit. See also **con brio.** [C19: from It., of Celtic origin]

brioche ('briːəʊʃ, -ɒʃ) *n* a soft roll made from a very light yeast dough. [C19: from Norman dialect, from *brier* to knead, of Gmc origin]

briquette *or* **briquet** (brɪ'kɛt) *n* a small brick made of compressed coal dust, sawdust, charcoal, etc., used for fuel. [C19: from F: a little brick, from *brique* BRICK]

brisk Ⓣ (brɪsk) *adj* **1** lively and quick; vigorous: *a brisk walk.* **2** invigorating or sharp: *brisk weather.* ◆ *vb* **3** (often foll. by *up*) to enliven; make or become brisk. [C16: prob. var. of BRUSQUE]
▸ **'briskly** *adv* ▸ **'briskness** *n*

brisket ('brɪskɪt) *n* **1** the breast of a four-legged animal. **2** the meat from this part, esp. of beef. [C14: prob. from ON]

brisling ('brɪslɪŋ) *n* another name for a **sprat.** [C20: from Norwegian; rel. to obs. Danish *bretling*]

bristle Ⓣ ('brɪsᵊl) *n* **1** any short stiff hair of an animal or plant, such as on a pig's back. **2** something resembling these hairs: *toothbrush bristle.* ◆ *vb* **bristles, bristling, bristled. 3** (when *intr,* often foll. by *up*) to stand up or cause to stand up like bristles. **4** (*intr;* sometimes foll. by *up*) to show anger, indignation, etc.: *she bristled at the suggestion.* **5** (*intr*) to be thickly covered or set: *the target bristled with arrows.* [C13 *bristil, brustel,* from earlier *brust,* from OE *byrst*]
▸ **'bristly** *adj*

Bristol board ('brɪstᵊl) *n* a heavy smooth cardboard of fine quality, used for drawing.

Bristol fashion *adv, adj* (*postpositive*) in good order; efficiently arranged.

bristols ('brɪstᵊlz) *pl n Brit. sl.* a woman's breasts. [C20: short for *Bristol Cities,* rhyming slang for *titties*]

Brit (brɪt) *n Inf.* a British person.

Brit. *abbrev. for:* **1** Britain. **2** British.

Britannia (brɪ'tænɪə) *n* **1** a female warrior carrying a trident and wearing a helmet, personifying Great Britain or the British Empire. **2** (in the ancient Roman Empire) the S part of Great Britain. **3** short for **Britannia coin.**

Britannia coin *n* any of four British gold coins introduced in 1987 for investment purposes; their denominations are £100, £50, £25, and £10.

Britannia metal *n* an alloy of tin with antimony and copper: used for decorative purposes and for bearings.

Britannic (brɪ'tænɪk) *adj* of Britain; British (esp. in **His** *or* **Her Britannic Majesty**).

britches ('brɪtʃɪz) *pl n* a variant spelling of **breeches.**

Briticism ('brɪtɪˌsɪzəm) *n* a custom, linguistic usage, or other feature peculiar to Britain or its people. Also: **Britishism.**

British ('brɪtɪʃ) *adj* **1** of or denoting Britain, a country of W Europe, consisting of the island of Great Britain (comprising England, Scotland, and Wales) and part of the island of Ireland (Northern Ireland). **2** relating to, denoting, or characteristic of the inhabitants of Britain. **3** relating to or denoting the English language as spoken and written in Britain. **4** of or relating to the Commonwealth: *British subjects.* ◆ *n* **5 the British.** (*functioning as pl*) the natives or inhabitants of Britain.
▸ **'Britishness** *n*

British Council *n* an organization founded (1934) to extend the influence of British culture and education throughout the world.

Britisher ('brɪtɪʃə) *n* (not used by the British) **1** a native or inhabitant of Great Britain. **2** any British subject.

Britishism ('brɪtɪˌʃɪzəm) *n* a variant of **Briticism.**

British Legion *n Brit.* an organization founded in 1921 to provide services and assistance for former members of the armed forces.

British thermal unit *n* a unit of heat in the fps system equal to the quantity of heat required to raise the temperature of 1 pound of water by 1°F. 1 British thermal unit is equivalent to 1055.06 joules. Abbrev.: **btu, BThU.**

Briton Ⓣ ('brɪtᵊn) *n* **1** a native or inhabitant of Britain. **2** *History.* any of the early Celtic inhabitants of S Britain. [C13: from OF *Breton,* of Celtic origin]

Britpop ('brɪtˌpɒp) *n* the characteristic pop music performed by some British bands of the mid 1990s.

brittle Ⓣ ('brɪtᵊl) *adj* **1** easily cracked, snapped, or broken; fragile. **2** curt or irritable. **3** hard or sharp in quality. ◆ *n* **4** a crunchy sweet made with treacle and nuts: *peanut brittle.* [C14: ult. from OE *brēotan* to break]
▸ **'brittleness** *n*

brittle-star *n* an echinoderm occurring on the sea bottom and having long slender arms radiating from a small central disc.

bro. *abbrev. for* brother.

broach Ⓣ (brəʊtʃ) *vb* (*tr*) **1** to initiate (a topic) for discussion. **2** to tap or pierce (a container) to draw off (a liquid): *to broach a cask.* **3** to open in order to begin to use. ◆ *n* **4** a long tapered toothed cutting tool for enlarging holes. **5** a spit for roasting meat, etc. [C14: from OF *broche,* from L *brochus* projecting]

broad Ⓣ (brɔːd) *adj* **1** having relatively great breadth or width. **2** of vast extent; spacious: *a broad plain.* **3** (*postpositive*) from one side to the other: *four miles broad.* **4** of great scope or potential: *that invention had broad applications.* **5** not detailed; general: *broad plans.* **6** clear and open; full (esp. in **broad daylight**). **7** obvious or plain: *broad hints.* **8** liberal; tolerant: *a broad political stance.* **9** widely spread; extensive: *broad support.* **10** vulgar; coarse; indecent: *a broad joke.* **11** (of a dialect or pronunciation) consisting of a large number of speech sounds characteristic of a particular geographic area: *a broad Yorkshire accent.* **12** *Finance.* denoting an assessment of liquidity as including notes and coin in circulation with the public, banks' till money and balances, most private-sector bank deposits, and sterling bank-deposit certificates: *broad money.* Cf. **narrow** (sense 7). **13** *Phonetics.* the long vowel in English words such as *father, half,* as represented in Received Pronuncia-

THESAURUS

bring down *vb* = **lower**, cut down, drop, fell, floor, lay low, level, pull down, shoot down, upset

bring in *vb* **1** = **produce**, accrue, bear, be worth, fetch, generate, gross, net, profit, realize, return, yield

bring off *vb* = **accomplish**, achieve, bring home the bacon (*inf.*), bring to pass, carry off, carry out, crack it (*inf.*), cut it (*inf.*), discharge, execute, perform, pull off, succeed

bring up *vb* **1** = **rear**, breed, develop, educate, form, nurture, raise, support, teach, train **2** = **mention**, advance, allude to, broach, introduce, move, propose, put forward, raise, submit

brink *n* **1-3** = **edge**, border, boundary, brim, fringe, frontier, limit, lip, margin, point, rim, skirt, threshold, verge

brio *n* = **energy**, animation, dash, élan, enthusiasm, get-up-and-go (*inf.*), gusto, liveliness, panache, pep, spirit, verve, vigour, vivacity, zest, zip (*inf.*)

brisk *adj* **1** = **lively**, active, agile, alert, animated, bustling, busy, energetic, nimble, no-nonsense, quick, sparky, speedy, sprightly, spry, vigorous, vivacious **2** = **invigorating**, biting, bracing, crisp, exhilarating, fresh, keen, nippy, refreshing, sharp, snappy, stimulating
Antonyms *adj* ≠ **lively:** heavy, lazy, lethargic, slow, sluggish, unenergetic ≠ **invigorating:** boring, dull, enervating, tiring, wearisome

briskly *adv* **1** = **quickly**, actively, apace, brusquely, coolly, decisively, efficiently, energetically, firmly, incisively, nimbly, posthaste, promptly, pronto (*inf.*), rapidly, readily, smartly, vigorously

bristle *n* **1** = **hair**, barb, prickle, spine, stubble, thorn, whisker ◆ *vb* **3** = **stand up**, prickle, rise, stand on end **4** = **be angry**, be infuriated, be maddened, bridle, flare up, get one's dander up (*sl.*), go ballistic (*sl., chiefly US*), rage, see red, seethe, spit (*inf.*), wig out (*sl.*) **5** = **be thick**, abound, be alive, crawl, hum, swarm, teem

bristly *adj* **1** = **hairy**, bearded, bewhiskered, prickly, rough, stubbly, unshaven, whiskered

Briton *n* **1** = **Brit** (*inf.*), Anglo-Saxon, Britisher, limey (*US & Canad. sl.*), pommy *or* pom (*Austral. & NZ sl.*)

brittle *adj* **1** = **fragile**, breakable, crisp, crumbling, crumbly, delicate, frail, frangible, friable, shatterable, shivery **2** = **tense**, curt, edgy, irritable, nervous, prim, stiff, stilted, wired (*sl.*)
Antonyms *adj* ≠ **fragile:** durable, elastic, flexible, infrangible, nonbreakable, resistant, rugged, shatterproof, strong, sturdy, toughened

broach *vb* **1** = **bring up**, approach, hint at, introduce, mention, open up, propose, raise the subject, speak of, suggest, talk of, touch on **2, 3** = **open**, crack, draw off, pierce, puncture, start, tap, uncork

broad *adj* **1, 2** = **wide**, ample, beamy (*of a ship*), capacious, expansive, extensive, generous, large, roomy, spacious, vast, voluminous, widespread **4, 5** = **general**, all-embracing, catholic, comprehensive, encyclopedic, far-reaching, global, inclusive, nonspecific, overarching, sweeping, undetailed, universal, unlimited, wide, wide-ranging **6** *As in* **broad daylight** = **clear**, full, obvious, open, plain, straightforward, undisguised **8** = **tolerant**, broad-minded, liberal, open, open-minded, permissive, progressive, unbiased **10** = **vulgar**, blue, coarse,

tion. ◆ *n* **14** the broad part of something. **15** *Sl., chiefly US & Canad.* **15a** a girl or woman. **15b** a prostitute. **16** See **Broads.** [OE *brād*]
▸ **'broadly** *adv*

B-road *n* a secondary road in Britain.

broad arrow *n* **1** a mark shaped like a broad arrowhead designating British government property and formerly used on prison clothing. **2** an arrow with a broad head.

broad bean *n* **1** an erect annual Eurasian bean plant cultivated for its large edible flattened seeds. **2** the seed of this plant.

broadcast Ⓣ ('brɔːdˌkɑːst) *vb* **broadcasts, broadcasting, broadcast** *or* **broadcasted. 1** to transmit (announcements or programmes) on radio or television. **2** (*intr*) to take part in a radio or television programme. **3** (*tr*) to make widely known throughout an area: *to broadcast news.* **4** (*tr*) to scatter (seed, etc.) over an area, esp. by hand. ◆ *n* **5a** a transmission or programme on radio or television. **5b** (*as modifier*): *a broadcast signal.* **6** the act of scattering seeds. ◆ *adj* **7** dispersed over a wide area. ◆ *adv* **8** far and wide.
▸ **'broadˌcaster** *n* ▸ **'broadˌcasting** *n*

Broad Church *n* **1** a party within the Church of England which favours a broad and liberal interpretation of Anglican doctrine. **2** (*usually not caps.*) a group which embraces a wide and varied number of views and opinions. ◆ *adj* **Broad-Church. 3** of or relating to this party in the Church of England.

broadcloth ('brɔːdˌklɒθ) *n* **1** fabric woven on a wide loom. **2** a closely woven fabric of wool, worsted, cotton, or rayon with lustrous finish, used for clothing.

broaden Ⓣ ('brɔːdᵊn) *vb* to make or become broad or broader; widen.

broad gauge *n* **1** a railway track with a greater distance between the lines than the standard gauge of 56½ inches (about 1·44 metres). ◆ *adj* **broad-gauge. 2** of or denoting a railway having this track.

broad-leaved *adj* denoting trees other than conifers; having broad rather than needle-shaped leaves.

broadloom ('brɔːdˌluːm) *n* (*modifier*) of or designating carpets woven on a wide loom.

broad-minded Ⓣ *adj* **1** tolerant of opposing viewpoints; not prejudiced; liberal. **2** not easily shocked by permissive sexual habits, pornography, etc.
▸ **ˌbroad-'mindedly** *adv* ▸ **ˌbroad-'mindedness** *n*

broadsheet ('brɔːdˌʃiːt) *n* **1** a newspaper having a large format, approximately 15 by 24 inches (38 by 61 centimetres). **2** another word for **broadside** (sense 4).

broadside Ⓣ ('brɔːdˌsaɪd) *n* **1** *Naut.* the entire side of a vessel. **2** *Naval.* **2a** all the armament fired from one side of a warship. **2b** the simultaneous discharge of such armament. **3** a strong or abusive verbal or written attack. **4** Also called: **broadside ballad.** a ballad or popular song printed on one side of a sheet of paper, esp. in 16th-century England. ◆ *adv* **5** with a broader side facing an object; sideways.

broad-spectrum *n* (*modifier*) effective against a wide variety of diseases or microorganisms: *a broad-spectrum antibiotic.*

broadsword ('brɔːdˌsɔːd) *n* a broad-bladed sword used for cutting rather than stabbing.

broadtail ('brɔːdˌteɪl) *n* **1** the highly valued black wavy fur obtained from the skins of newly born karakul lambs; caracul. **2** another name for **karakul.**

Broadway('brɔːdˌweɪ) *n* **1** a thoroughfare in New York City: the centre of the commercial theatre in the US. ◆ *adj* **2** of, relating to, or suitable for the commercial theatre, esp. on Broadway.

brocade (brəʊ'keɪd) *n* **1** a rich fabric woven with a raised design, often using gold or silver threads. ◆ *vb* **brocades, brocading, brocaded. 2** (*tr*) to weave with such a design. [C17: from Sp. *brocado,* from It. *broccato* embossed fabric, from L *brochus* projecting]

broccoli ('brɒkəlɪ) *n* **1** a cultivated variety of cabbage having branched greenish flower heads. **2** the flower head, eaten as a vegetable before the buds have opened. [C17: from It., pl of *broccolo* a little sprout, from *brocco* sprout]

broch (brɒk, brɒx) *n* (in Scotland) a prehistoric circular dry-stone tower large enough to serve as a fortified home. [C17: from ON *borg;* rel. to OE *burh* settlement, burgh]

brochette (brɒ'ʃet) *n* a skewer or small spit, used for holding pieces of meat, etc., while roasting or grilling. [C19: from OF *brochete* small pointed tool; see BROACH]

brochure Ⓣ ('brəʊʃjʊə, -ʃə) *n* a pamphlet or booklet, esp. one containing summarized or introductory information or advertising. [C18: from F, from *brocher* to stitch (a book)]

brock (brɒk) *n* a Brit. name for **badger** (sense 1). [OE *broc,* of Celtic origin]

brocket ('brɒkɪt) *n* a small deer of tropical America, having small unbranched antlers. [C15: from Anglo-F *broquet,* from *broque* horn]

broderie anglaise ('brəʊdəriː ɑːŋ'glɛz) *n* open embroidery on white cotton, fine linen, etc. [C19: from F: English embroidery]

Broederbond ('brʊdəˌbɔːnt, 'bruːdəˌbɒnt) *n* (in South Africa) a secret society of Afrikaner Nationalists. [Afrik.: band of brothers]

brogue[1] (brəʊg) *n* a broad gentle-sounding dialectal accent, esp. that used by the Irish in speaking English. [C18: from ?]

brogue[2] (brəʊg) *n* **1** a sturdy walking shoe, often with ornamental perforations. **2** an untanned shoe worn formerly in Ireland and Scotland. [C16: from Irish Gaelic *bróg* shoe]

broil[1] (brɔɪl) *vb* **1** the usual US and Canad. word for **grill** (sense 1). **2** to become or cause to become extremely hot. **3** (*intr*) to be furious. [C14: from OF *bruillir* to burn]

broil[2] (brɔɪl) *Arch.* ◆ *n* **1** a loud quarrel or disturbance; brawl. ◆ *vb* **2** (*intr*) to brawl; quarrel. [C16: from OF *brouiller* to mix]

broiler ('brɔɪlə) *n* **1** a young tender chicken suitable for roasting. **2** a pan, grate, etc., for broiling food. **3** a very hot day.

broke Ⓣ (brəʊk) *vb* **1** the past tense of **break.** ◆ *adj* **2** *Inf.* having no money; bankrupt. **3 go for broke.** *Sl.* to risk everything in a gambling or other venture.

broken Ⓣ ('brəʊkən) *vb* **1** the past participle of **break.** ◆ *adj* **2** fractured, smashed, or splintered: *a broken vase.* **3** interrupted; disturbed; disconnected: *broken sleep.* **4** intermittent or discontinuous: *broken sunshine.* **5** not functioning. **6** spoilt or ruined by divorce (esp. in **broken home, broken marriage**). **7** (of a trust, promise, contract, etc.) violated; infringed. **8** (of the speech of a foreigner) imperfect in grammar, vocabulary, and pronunciation: *broken English.* **9** Also: **broken-in.** made tame or disciplined by training. **10** exhausted or weakened, as through ill-health or misfortune. **11** irregular or rough; uneven: *broken ground.* **12** bankrupt. **13** (of colour) having a multicoloured decorative effect, as by stippling paint onto a surface.
▸ **'brokenly** *adv*

broken chord *n* another term for **arpeggio.**

broken-down Ⓣ *adj* **1** worn out, as by age or long use; dilapidated. **2** not in working order.

brokenhearted Ⓣ (ˌbrəʊkən'hɑːtɪd) *adj* overwhelmed by grief or disappointment.
▸ **ˌbroken'heartedly** *adv*

broken wind (wɪnd) *n Vet. science.* another name for **heaves.**
▸ **ˌbroken'winded** *adj*

broker Ⓣ ('brəʊkə) *n* **1** an agent who, acting on behalf of a principal, buys or sells goods, securities, etc.: *insurance broker.* **2** short for **stockbroker. 3** a person who deals in second-hand goods. [C14: from Anglo-F *brocour* broacher (of casks, hence, one who sells, agent), from OF *broquier* to tap a cask]

brokerage ('brəʊkərɪdʒ) *n* **1** commission charged by a broker. **2** a broker's business or office.

brolga ('brɒlgə) *n* a large grey Australian crane having a red-and-green head and a trumpeting call. Also called: **native companion.** [C19: from Abor.]

THESAURUS

gross, improper, indecent, indelicate, near the knuckle, unrefined
Antonyms *adj* ≠ **wide:** close, confined, constricted, cramped, limited, meagre, narrow, restricted, tight

broadcast *vb* **1** = **transmit,** air, beam, cable, put on the air, radio, relay, show, televise **3** = **make public,** advertise, announce, circulate, disseminate, proclaim, promulgate, publish, report, shout from the rooftops (*inf.*), spread ◆ *n* **5a** = **transmission,** programme, show, telecast

broaden *vb* = **expand,** augment, develop, enlarge, extend, fatten, increase, open up, spread, stretch, supplement, swell, widen
Antonyms *vb* circumscribe, constrain, diminish, narrow, reduce, restrict, simplify, tighten

broadly *adv* **1, 2** = **widely,** expansively, extensively, far and wide, greatly, hugely, vastly **9** = **generally,** commonly, for the most part, in general, in the main, largely, mainly, mostly, on the whole, predominantly, universally, widely
Antonyms *adv* ≠ **widely, generally:** exclusively, narrowly

broad-minded 1 *adj* = **tolerant,** catholic, cosmopolitan, flexible, free-thinking, indulgent, liberal, open-minded, permissive, responsive, unbiased, unbigoted, undogmatic, unprejudiced
Antonyms *adj* biased, bigoted, closed-minded, dogmatic, inflexible, intolerant, narrow-minded, prejudiced, uncharitable

broadside *n* **3** = **attack,** abuse, assault, battering, bombardment, censure, criticism, denunciation, diatribe, stick (*sl.*), swipe

brochure *n* = **booklet,** advertisement, circular, folder, handbill, hand-out, leaflet, mailshot, pamphlet

broke *adj* **2** *Informal* = **penniless,** bankrupt, bust, cleaned out (*sl.*), dirt-poor (*inf.*), down and out, flat broke (*inf.*), impoverished, in queer street, insolvent, in the red, on one's uppers, penurious, ruined, short, skint (*Brit. sl.*), stony-broke (*Brit. sl.*), strapped for cash (*inf.*), without two pennies to rub together (*inf.*)
Antonyms *adj* affluent, comfortable, flush (*inf.*), in the money (*inf.*), prosperous, rich, solvent, wealthy, well-to-do

broken *adj* **2** = **smashed,** burst, demolished, destroyed, fractured, fragmented, rent, ruptured, separated, severed, shattered, shivered **3, 4** = **interrupted,** disconnected, discontinuous, disturbed, erratic, fragmentary, incomplete, intermittent, spasmodic **5** = **not working,** defective, imperfect, kaput (*inf.*), not functioning, on its last legs, on the blink (*sl.*), out of order, ruined **7** = **violated,** dishonoured, disobeyed, disregarded, forgotten, ignored, infringed, not kept, retracted, traduced, transgressed **8** = **imperfect,** disjointed, halting, hesitating, stammering **10** = **defeated,** beaten, browbeaten, crippled, crushed, demoralized, humbled, oppressed, overpowered, subdued, vanquished

broken-down *adj* **1** = **dilapidated,** old, worn out **2** = **not in working order,** collapsed, in disrepair, inoperative, kaput (*inf.*), not functioning, on the blink (*sl.*), out of commission, out of order

brokenhearted *adj* = **heartbroken,** choked, desolate, despairing, devastated, disappointed, disconsolate (*inf.*), grief-stricken, heart-sick, inconsolable, miserable, mournful, prostrated, sorrowful, wretched

broker *n* **1** = **dealer,** agent, factor, go-between, intermediary, middleman, negotiator

brolly ('brɒlɪ) *n, pl* **brollies.** an informal Brit. name for **umbrella** (sense 1).
bromeliad (brəʊ'miːlɪˌæd) *n* any of a family of tropical American plants, typically epiphytes with a rosette of fleshy leaves, such as the pineapple and Spanish moss. [C19: from NL, after Olaf *Bromelius* (1639–1705), Swedish botanist]
bromide ('brəʊmaɪd) *n* **1** any salt of hydrobromic acid. **2** any compound containing a bromine atom. **3** a dose of sodium or potassium bromide given as a sedative. **4a** a platitude. **4b** a boring person.
bromide paper *n* a type of photographic paper coated with an emulsion of silver bromide.
bromine ('brəʊmiːn, -mɪn) *n* a pungent dark red volatile liquid element that occurs in brine and is used in the production of chemicals. Symbol: Br; atomic no.: 35; atomic wt.: 79.91. [C19: from F *brome* bromine, from Gk *brōmos* bad smell, from ?]
bronchi ('brɒŋkaɪ) *n* the plural of **bronchus.**
bronchial ('brɒŋkɪəl) *adj* of or relating to the bronchi or the bronchial tubes.
▸'**bronchially** *adv*
bronchial tubes *pl n* the bronchi or their smaller divisions.
bronchiectasis (ˌbrɒŋkɪ'ɛktəsɪs) *n* chronic dilation and usually infection of the bronchi. [C19: from BRONCHO- + Gk *ektasis* a stretching]
bronchiole ('brɒŋkɪˌəʊl) *n* any of the smallest bronchial tubes. [C19: from NL; see BRONCHUS]
▸ˌ**bronchi'olar** *adj*
bronchitis (brɒŋ'kaɪtɪs) *n* inflammation of the bronchial tubes, characterized by coughing, difficulty in breathing, etc.
▸**bronchitic** (brɒŋ'kɪtɪk) *adj, n*
broncho- *or before a vowel* **bronch-** *combining form.* indicating or relating to the bronchi: *bronchitis.* [from Gk: BRONCHUS]
bronchodilator (ˌbrɒŋkəʊdaɪ'leɪtə, -dɪ-) *n* any drug or other agent that causes dilation of the bronchial tubes by relaxing bronchial muscle: used, esp. in the form of aerosol sprays, for the relief of asthma and chronic bronchitis.
bronchopneumonia (ˌbrɒŋkəʊnjuː'məʊnɪə) *n* inflammation of the lungs, starting in the bronchioles.
bronchoscope ('brɒŋkəˌskəʊp) *n* an instrument for examining and providing access to the interior of the bronchial tubes.
bronchus ('brɒŋkəs) *n, pl* **bronchi.** either of the two main branches of the trachea. [C18: from NL, from Gk *bronkhos* windpipe]
bronco *or* **broncho** ('brɒŋkəʊ) *n, pl* **broncos** *or* **bronchos.** (in the US and Canada) a wild or partially tamed pony or mustang of the western plains. [C19: from Mexican Sp., from Sp.: rough, wild]
brontosaurus (ˌbrɒntə'sɔːrəs) *or* **brontosaur** ('brɒntəˌsɔː) *n* a very large herbivorous quadrupedal dinosaur, common in N America during late Jurassic times, having a long neck and long tail. [C19: from NL, from Gk *brontē* thunder + *sauros* lizard]
Bronx cheer (brɒŋks) *n Chiefly US.* a loud spluttering noise made with the lips and tongue and expressing derision or contempt; raspberry. [C20: from the *Bronx*, a borough of New York City]
bronze 🅣 (brɒnz) *n* **1** any hard water-resistant alloy consisting of copper and smaller proportions of tin and sometimes zinc and lead. **2** a yellowish-brown colour or pigment. **3** a statue, medal, or other object made of bronze. Cf. **bronze** (sense 1). ◆ *adj* **4** made of or resembling bronze. **5** of a yellowish-brown colour. ◆ *vb* **bronzes, bronzing, bronzed. 6** (esp. of the skin) to make or become brown; tan. **7** (*tr*) to give the appearance of bronze to. [C18: from F, from It. *bronzo*]
▸'**bronzy** *adj*
Bronze Age *n* **a** a technological stage between the Stone and Iron Ages, beginning in the Middle East about 4500 B.C. and lasting in Britain from about 2000 to 500 B.C., during which weapons and tools were made of bronze. **b** (*as modifier*): *a Bronze-Age tool.*
bronze medal *n* a medal awarded to a competitor who comes third in a contest or race.
bronzing ('brɒnzɪŋ) *n* **1** blue pigment producing a metallic lustre when ground into paint media at fairly high concentrations. **2** the application of a mixture of powdered metal or pigments of a metallic lustre to a surface.
brooch (brəʊtʃ) *n* an ornament with a hinged pin and catch, worn fastened to clothing. [C13: from OF *broche;* see BROACH]
brood 🅣 (bruːd) *n* **1** a number of young animals, esp. birds, produced at one hatching. **2** all the offspring in one family: often used jokingly or contemptuously. **3** a group of a particular kind; breed. **4** (*modifier*) kept for breeding: *a brood mare.* ◆ *vb* **5** (of a bird) **5a** to sit on or hatch (eggs). **5b** (*tr*) to cover (young birds) protectively with the wings. **6** (when *intr*, often foll. by *on, over,* or *upon*) to ponder morbidly or persistently. [OE *brōd*]
▸'**brooding** *n, adj*
brooder ('bruːdə) *n* **1** a structure, usually heated, used for rearing young chickens or other fowl. **2** a person or thing that broods.
broody ('bruːdɪ) *adj* **broodier, broodiest. 1** moody; introspective. **2** (of poultry) wishing to sit on or hatch eggs. **3** *Inf.* (of a woman) wishing to have a baby.
▸'**broodiness** *n*
brook[1] 🅣 (brʊk) *n* a natural freshwater stream smaller than a river. [OE *brōc*]
brook[2] 🅣 (brʊk) *vb* (*tr*) (*usually used with a negative*) to bear; tolerate. [OE *brūcan*]
brooklet ('brʊklɪt) *n* a small brook.
brooklime ('brʊkˌlaɪm) *n* either of two blue-flowered trailing plants, *Veronica americana* of North America or *V. beccabunga* of Europe and Asia, growing in moist places. See also **speedwell.** [C16: from BROOK[1] + *-lemk*, from OE *hleomoce*]
brook trout *n* a North American trout, valued as a food and game fish.
broom (bruːm, brʊm) *n* **1** an implement for sweeping consisting of a long handle to which is attached either a brush of straw or twigs, bound together, or a solid head into which are set tufts of bristles or fibres. **2** any of various yellow-flowered Eurasian leguminous shrubs. **3 new broom.** a newly appointed official, etc., eager to make changes. ◆ *vb* **4** (*tr*) to sweep with a broom. [OE *brōm*]
broomrape ('bruːmˌreɪp, 'brʊm-) *n* any of a genus of leafless fleshy parasitic plants growing on the roots of other plants, esp. on broom. [C16: adaptation & partial translation of Med. L *rāpum genistae* tuber (hence: root nodule) of Genista (a type of broom plant)]
broomstick ('bruːmˌstɪk, 'brʊm-) *n* the long handle of a broom.
bros. *or* **Bros.** *abbrev. for* brothers.
brose (brəʊz) *n Scot.* a porridge made by adding a boiling liquid to meal, esp. oatmeal. [C13 *broys,* from OF *broez,* from *breu* broth, of Gmc origin]
broth (brɒθ) *n* **1** a soup made by boiling meat, fish, vegetables, etc., in water. **2** another name for **stock** (sense 19). [OE *broth*]
brothel 🅣 ('brɒθəl) *n* **1** a house where men pay to have sexual intercourse with prostitutes. **2** *Austral. inf.* any untidy place. [C16: short for *brothel-house,* from C14 *brothel* useless person, from OE *brēothan* to deteriorate]
brother 🅣 ('brʌðə) *n* **1** a male person having the same parents as another person. **2a** a male person belonging to the same group, profession, nationality, trade union, etc., as another or others; fellow member. **2b** (*as modifier*): *brother workers.* **3** comrade; friend: used as a form of address. **4** *Christianity.* a member of a male religious order. ◆ Related adj: **fraternal.** [OE *brōthor*]
brotherhood 🅣 ('brʌðəˌhʊd) *n* **1** the state of being related as a brother or brothers. **2** an association or fellowship, such as a trade union. **3** all persons engaged in a particular profession, trade, etc. **4** the belief, feeling, or hope that all men should treat one another as brothers.
brother-in-law *n, pl* **brothers-in-law. 1** the brother of one's wife or husband. **2** the husband of one's sister. **3** the husband of the sister of one's husband or wife.
brotherly 🅣 ('brʌðəlɪ) *adj* of, resembling, or suitable to a brother, esp. in showing loyalty and affection; fraternal.
▸'**brotherliness** *n*
brougham ('bruːəm, bruːm) *n* **1** a four-wheeled horse-drawn closed carriage having a raised open driver's seat in front. **2** *Obs.* a large car with an open compartment at the front for the driver. **3** *Obs.* an early electric car. [C19: after Lord *Brougham* (1778–1868)]
brought (brɔːt) *vb* the past tense and past participle of **bring.**
brouhaha ('bruːhɑːhɑː) *n* a loud confused noise; commotion; uproar. [F, imit.]
brow 🅣 (braʊ) *n* **1** the part of the face from the eyes to the hairline; forehead. **2** short for **eyebrow. 3** the expression of the face; countenance: *a troubled brow.* **4** the jutting top of a hill, etc. [OE *brū*]
browbeat 🅣 ('braʊˌbiːt) *vb* **browbeats, browbeating, browbeat, browbeaten.** (*tr*) to discourage or frighten with threats or a domineering manner; intimidate.
brown 🅣 (braʊn) *n* **1** any of various dark colours, such as those of

THESAURUS

bronze *adj* **5** = **reddish-brown**, brownish, chestnut, copper, copper-coloured, metallic brown, reddish-tan, rust, tan, yellowish-brown

bronzed *adj* **6** = **tanned**, brown, sunburnt, suntanned

brood *n* **1** = **offspring**, breed, chicks, children, clutch, family, hatch, infants, issue, litter, progeny, young ◆ *vb* **5a** = **incubate**, cover, hatch, set, sit upon **6** = **think upon**, agonize, dwell upon, eat one's heart out, fret, have a long face, meditate, mope, mull over, muse, obsess, ponder, repine, ruminate

brook[1] *n* = **stream**, beck, burn, gill (*dialect*), rill, rivulet, runnel (*literary*), streamlet, watercourse

brook[2] *vb* = **tolerate**, abide, accept, allow, bear, countenance, endure, hack (*sl.*), put up with, stand, stomach, suffer, support, swallow, thole (*dialect*), withstand

brothel *n* **1** = **whorehouse**, bawdy house (*arch.*), bordello, cathouse (*US sl.*), house of ill fame *or* ill repute, house of prostitution, knocking shop (*sl.*), red-light district

brother *n* **1** = **sibling**, blood brother, kin, kinsman, relation, relative **3** = **comrade**, associate, chum (*inf.*), cock (*Brit. inf.*), colleague, companion, compeer, confrère, fellow member, mate, pal (*inf.*), partner **4** *Christianity* = **monk**, cleric, friar, regular, religious

brotherhood *n* **1** = **fellowship**, brotherliness, camaraderie, companionship, comradeship, friendliness, kinship **2, 3** = **association**, alliance, clan, clique, community, coterie, fraternity, guild, league, order, society, union

brotherly *adj* = **kind**, affectionate, altruistic, amicable, benevolent, cordial, fraternal, friendly, neighbourly, philanthropic, sympathetic

brow *n* **3** = **forehead**, air, appearance, aspect, bearing, countenance, eyebrow, face, front, mien, temple **4** = **top**, brim, brink, crest, crown, edge, peak, rim, summit, tip, verge

browbeat *vb* = **bully**, badger, bulldoze (*inf.*), coerce, cow, domineer, dragoon, hector, intimidate, lord it over, oppress, overawe, overbear, ride roughshod over, threaten, tyrannize
Antonyms *vb* beguile, cajole, coax, entice, flatter, inveigle, lure, manoeuvre, seduce, sweet-talk (*inf.*), tempt, wheedle

brown *adj* **3** = **brunette**, auburn, bay, brick, bronze, bronzed, browned, chestnut, choco-

wood or earth. **2** a dye or pigment producing these colours. ◆ *adj* **3** of the colour brown. **4** (of bread) made from a flour that has not been bleached or bolted, such as wheatmeal or wholemeal flour. **5** deeply tanned or sunburnt. **6 in a brown study.** See **study** (sense 15). ◆ *vb* **7** to make (esp. food as a result of cooking) brown or (esp. of food) to become brown. [OE *brūn*]
▸ **'brownish** *or* **'browny** *adj* ▸ **'brownness** *n*

brown bear *n* a large ferocious brownish bear inhabiting temperate forests of North America, Europe, and Asia.

brown coal *n* another name for **lignite.**

brown dwarf *n* a type of celestial body midway in size between a large planet and a small star, thought to be one possible explanation of dark matter in the universe.

browned-off ❶ *adj Inf.* thoroughly discouraged or disheartened; fed up.

brown fat *n* a dark form of adipose tissue that is readily converted into energy.

Brownian movement ('braʊnɪən) *n* random movement of microscopic particles suspended in a fluid, caused by bombardment of the particles by molecules of the fluid. [C19: after Robert *Brown* (1773–1858), Scot. botanist]

brownie ('braʊnɪ) *n* **1** (in folklore) an elf said to do helpful work at night, esp. household chores. **2** a small square nutty chocolate cake. [C16: dim. of BROWN (that is, a small brown man)]

Brownie Guide *or* **Brownie** ('braʊnɪ) *n* a member of the junior branch of the Guides.

Brownie point *n* a notional mark to one's credit for being seen to do the right thing. [C20: ?from the mistaken notion that Brownie Guides earn points for good deeds]

browning ('braʊnɪŋ) *n Brit.* a substance used to darken soups, gravies, etc.

brown paper *n* a kind of coarse unbleached paper used for wrapping.

brown rice *n* unpolished rice, in which the grains retain the outer yellowish-brown layer (bran).

Brown Shirt *n* **1** (in Nazi Germany) a storm trooper. **2** a member of any fascist party or group.

brownstone ('braʊn,stəʊn) *n US.* a reddish-brown iron-rich sandstone used for building.

brown sugar *n* sugar that is unrefined or only partially refined.

brown trout *n* a common brownish variety of the trout that occurs in the rivers of N Europe.

browse ❶ (braʊz) *vb* **browses, browsing, browsed. 1** to look through (a book, articles for sale in a shop, etc.) in a casual leisurely manner. **2** *Computing.* to read hypertext, esp. on the World Wide Web. **3** (of deer, goats, etc.) to feed upon (vegetation) by continual nibbling. ◆ *n* **4** the act or an instance of browsing. **5** the young twigs, shoots, leaves, etc., on which certain animals feed. [C15: from F *broust, brost* bud, of Gmc origin]

browser ('braʊzə) *n* **1** a person or animal that browses. **2** *Computing.* a software package that enables a user to read hypertext, esp. on the World Wide Web.

BRS *abbrev. for* British Road Services.

Bruce (bru:s) *n Brit.* a jocular name for an Australian man.

brucellosis (,bru:sɪ'ləʊsɪs) *n* an infectious disease of cattle, goats, and pigs, caused by bacteria and transmittable to man. Also called: **undulant fever.** [C20: from NL *Brucella*, after Sir David *Bruce* (1855–1931), Australian bacteriologist & physician]

bruin ('bru:ɪn) *n* a name for a bear, used in children's tales, etc. [C17: from Du. *bruin* brown]

bruise ❶ (bru:z) *vb* **bruises, bruising, bruised.** (*mainly tr*) **1** (*also intr*) to injure (tissues) without breaking the skin, usually with discoloration, or (of tissues) to be injured in this way. **2** to offend or injure (someone's feelings). **3** to damage the surface of (something). **4** to crush (food, etc.) by pounding. ◆ *n* **5** a bodily injury without a break in the skin, usually with discoloration; contusion. [OE *brȳsan*]

bruiser ❶ ('bru:zə) *n Inf.* a strong tough person, esp. a boxer or a bully.

bruit (bru:t) *vb* **1** (*tr; often passive;* usually foll. by *about*) to report; rumour. ◆ *n* **2** *Arch.* **2a** a rumour. **2b** a loud outcry; clamour. [C15: via F from Med. L *brūgītus*, prob. from L *rugīre* to roar]

brumby ('brʌmbɪ) *n, pl* **brumbies.** *Austral.* **1** a wild horse, esp. one descended from runaway stock. **2** *Inf.* a wild or unruly person. [C19: from ?]

brume (bru:m) *n Poetic.* heavy mist or fog. [C19: from F: mist, winter, from L *brūma*, contracted from *brevissima diēs* the shortest day]

brunch (brʌntʃ) *n* a meal eaten late in the morning, combining breakfast with lunch. [C20: from BR(EAKFAST) + (L)UNCH]

brunette (bru:'nɛt) *n* **1** a girl or woman with dark brown hair. ◆ *adj* **2** dark brown: *brunette hair.* [C17: from F, fem of *brunet* dark, brownish, from *brun* brown]

brunt ❶ (brʌnt) *n* the main force or shock of a blow, attack, etc. (esp. in **bear the brunt of**). [C14: from ?]

brush[1] ❶ (brʌʃ) *n* **1** a device made of bristles, hairs, wires, etc., set into a firm back or handle: used to apply paint, clean or polish surfaces, groom the hair, etc. **2** the act or an instance of brushing. **3** a light stroke made in passing; graze. **4** a brief encounter or contact, esp. an unfriendly one; skirmish. **5** the bushy tail of a fox. **6** an electric conductor, esp. one made of carbon, that conveys current between stationary and rotating parts of a generator, motor, etc. ◆ *vb* **7** (*tr*) to clean, polish, scrub, paint, etc., with a brush. **8** (*tr*) to apply or remove with a brush or brushing movement. **9** (*tr*) to touch lightly and briefly. **10** (*intr*) to move so as to graze or touch something lightly. ◆ See also **brush aside, brush off, brush up.** [C14: from OF *broisse*, ?from *broce* BRUSH[2]]
▸ **'brusher** *n*

brush[2] ❶ (brʌʃ) *n* **1** a thick growth of shrubs and small trees; scrub. **2** land covered with scrub. **3** broken or cut branches or twigs; brushwood. **4** wooded sparsely populated country; backwoods. [C16 (dense undergrowth), C14 (cuttings of trees): from OF *broce*, from Vulgar L *bruscia* (unattested) brushwood]
▸ **'brushy** *adj*

brush aside ❶ *or* **away** *vb* (*tr, adv*) to dismiss without consideration; disregard.

brush discharge *n* a slightly luminous brushlike electrical discharge.

brushed (brʌʃt) *adj Textiles.* treated with a brushing process to raise the nap and give a softer and warmer finish: *brushed nylon.*

brushmark ('brʌʃ,mɑ:k) *n* the indented lines sometimes left by the bristles of a brush on a painted surface.

brush off ❶ *Sl.* ◆ *vb* (*tr, adv*) **1** to dismiss and ignore (a person), esp. curtly. ◆ *n* **brushoff. 2** an abrupt dismissal or rejection.

brush turkey *n* any of several gallinaceous flightless birds of New Guinea and Australia, having a black plumage.

brush up ❶ *vb* (*adv*) **1** (*tr;* often foll. by *on*) to refresh one's knowledge, skill, or memory of (a subject). **2** to make (a person or oneself) clean or neat as after a journey. ◆ *n* **brush-up. 3** *Brit.* the act or an instance of tidying one's appearance (esp. in **wash and brush-up**).

brushwood ('brʌʃ,wʊd) *n* **1** cut or broken-off tree branches, twigs, etc. **2** another word for **brush**[2] (sense 1).

brushwork ('brʌʃ,wɜ:k) *n* **1** a characteristic manner of applying paint with a brush: *Rembrandt's brushwork.* **2** work done with a brush.

brusque ❶ (bru:sk, brʊsk) *adj* blunt or curt in manner or speech. [C17: from F, from It. *brusco* sour, rough, from Med. L *bruscus* butcher's broom]
▸ **'brusquely** *adv* ▸ **'brusqueness** *n*

Brussels carpet ('brʌsᵊlz) *n* a worsted carpet with a heavy pile formed by uncut loops of wool on a linen warp.

Brussels lace *n* a fine lace with a raised or appliqué design.

Brussels sprout *n* **1** a variety of cabbage, having a stout stem studded with budlike heads resembling tiny cabbages. **2** the head of this plant, eaten as a vegetable.

brut (bru:t) *adj* (of champagne or sparkling wine) very dry. [F, lit.: dry]

brutal ❶ ('bru:tᵊl) *adj* **1** cruel; vicious; savage. **2** extremely honest or coarse in speech or manner. **3** harsh; severe; extreme: *brutal cold.*
▸ **bru'tality** *n* ▸ **'brutally** *adv*

brutalism ('bru:tə,lɪzəm) *n* an austere style of architecture character-

THESAURUS

late, coffee, dark, donkey brown, dun, dusky, fuscous, ginger, hazel, rust, sunburnt, tan, tanned, tawny, toasted, umber ◆ *vb* **7** = **fry**, cook, grill, sauté, seal, sear

browned-off *adj Informal* = **fed up**, cheesed off (*Brit. sl.*), discontented, discouraged, disgruntled, disheartened, pissed off (*taboo sl.*), sick as a parrot (*inf.*), weary

browse *vb* **1** = **skim**, dip into, examine cursorily, flip through, glance at, leaf through, look round, look through, peruse, scan, survey **3** = **graze**, crop, eat, feed, nibble, pasture

bruise *vb* **1** = **discolour**, blacken, blemish, contuse, deface, injure, mar, mark **2** = **hurt**, displease, grieve, injure, insult, offend, pain, sting, wound **4** = **crush**, pound, pulverize ◆ *n* **5** = **discoloration**, black-and-blue mark, black mark, blemish, contusion, injury, mark, swelling, trauma (*Pathology*)

bruiser *n Informal* = **tough**, bully, bully boy, gorilla (*inf.*), hard man, heavy (*sl.*), hoodlum, rough (*inf.*), roughneck (*sl.*), rowdy, ruffian, thug, tough guy

bruising *n* **5** = **discoloration**, contusion, ecchymosis, marking, swelling

brunt *n* = **full force**, burden, force, impact, pressure, shock, strain, stress, thrust, violence

brush[1] *n* **1** = **broom**, besom, sweeper **4** = **encounter**, clash, conflict, confrontation, fight, fracas, scrap (*inf.*), set-to (*inf.*), skirmish, slight engagement, spot of bother (*inf.*), tussle ◆ *vb* **7** = **clean**, buff, paint, polish, sweep, wash **9** = **touch**, caress, contact, flick, glance, graze, kiss, scrape, stroke, sweep

brush[2] *n* **1, 2** = **shrubs**, brushwood, bushes, copse, scrub, thicket, undergrowth, underwood

brush aside *vb* = **dismiss**, discount, disregard, have no time for, ignore, override, sweep aside

brush off *Slang vb* **1** = **ignore**, blank (*sl.*), cold-shoulder, cut, deny, disdain, dismiss, disown, disregard, put down, rebuff, refuse, reject, repudiate, scorn, send to Coventry, slight, snub, spurn ◆ *n* **brushoff 2** = **snub**, bum's rush (*sl.*), cold shoulder, cut, dismissal, go-by (*sl.*), kick in the teeth (*sl.*), knock-back, rebuff, refusal, rejection, repudiation, repulse, slight, the (old) heave-ho (*inf.*)

brush up *vb* **1** = **revise**, bone up (*inf.*), cram, go over, polish up, read up, refresh one's memory, relearn, study

brusque *adj* = **curt**, abrupt, blunt, discourteous, gruff, hasty, impolite, monosyllabic, sharp, short, surly, tart, terse, unmannerly
Antonyms *adj* accommodating, civil, courteous, gentle, patient, polite, well-mannered

brutal *adj* **1** = **cruel**, barbarous, bloodthirsty, ferocious, heartless, inhuman, merciless, pitiless, remorseless, ruthless, savage, uncivilized, vicious **2** = **harsh**, bearish, callous, gruff, impolite, insensitive, rough, rude, severe, uncivil, unfeeling, unmannerly
Antonyms *adj* ≠ **cruel**: civilized, gentle, humane, kind, merciful, soft-hearted ≠ **harsh**: polite, refined, sensitive

ized by emphasis on such structural materials as undressed concrete and unconcealed service pipes. Also called: **new brutalism.**
▸'**brutalist** *n, adj*

brutalize ⓣ *or* **brutalise** ('bru:tə,laɪz) *vb* **brutalizes, brutalizing, brutalized** *or* **brutalises, brutalising, brutalised. 1** to make or become brutal. **2** (*tr*) to treat brutally.
▸,**brutali'zation** *or* ,**brutali'sation** *n*

brute ⓣ (bru:t) *n* **1a** any animal except man; beast; lower animal. **1b** (*as modifier*): *brute nature.* **2** a brutal person. ◆ *adj* (*prenominal*) **3** wholly instinctive or physical (esp. in **brute strength, brute force**). **4** without reason or intelligence. **5** coarse and grossly sensual. [C15: from L *brūtus* heavy, irrational]

brutish ⓣ ('bru:tɪʃ) *adj* **1** of, relating to, or resembling a brute; animal. **2** coarse; cruel; stupid.
▸'**brutishly** *adv* ▸'**brutishness** *n*

bryology (braɪ'ɒlədʒɪ) *n* the branch of botany concerned with the study of bryophytes.
▸**bryological** (,braɪə'lɒdʒɪk°l) *adj* ▸**bry'ologist** *n*

bryony *or* **briony** ('braɪənɪ) *n, pl* **bryonies** *or* **brionies.** any of several herbaceous climbing plants of Europe and N Africa. [OE *bryōnia,* from L, from Gk *bruōnia*]

bryophyte ('braɪə,faɪt) *n* any plant of the phylum *Bryophyta,* esp. mosses and liverworts. [C19: from Gk *bruon* moss + -PHYTE]
▸**bryophytic** (,braɪə'fɪtɪk) *adj*

bryozoan (,braɪə'zəʊən) *n* any aquatic invertebrate animal forming colonies of polyps each having a ciliated feeding organ. Popular name: **sea mat.** [C19: from Gk *bruon* moss + *zōion* animal]

Brythonic (brɪ'θɒnɪk) *n* **1** the S group of Celtic languages, consisting of Welsh, Cornish, and Breton. ◆ *adj* **2** of or relating to this group of languages. [C19: from Welsh; see BRITON]

bs *abbrev. for:* **1** balance sheet. **2** bill of sale.

BS *abbrev. for* British Standard(s).

BSc *abbrev. for* Bachelor of Science.

BSE *abbrev. for* bovine spongiform encephalopathy: a fatal slow-developing virus disease of cattle, affecting the nervous system. Informal name: **mad cow disease.**

BSI *abbrev. for* British Standards Institution.

B-side *n* the less important side of a gramophone record.

BST *abbrev. for:* **1** bovine somatotrophin: a growth hormone that can be used to increase milk production in dairy cattle. **2** British Summer Time.

Bt *abbrev. for* Baronet.

BT *abbrev. for* British Telecom. [C20: shortened from TELECOMMUNICATIONS]

btu *or* **BThU** *abbrev. for* British thermal unit. US abbrev.: **BTU.**

bu. *abbrev. for* bushel.

bubble ⓣ ('bʌb°l) *n* **1** a thin film of liquid forming a hollow globule around air or a gas: *a soap bubble.* **2** a small globule of air or a gas in a liquid or a solid. **3** the sound made by a bubbling liquid. **4** something lacking substance, stability, or seriousness. **5** an unreliable scheme or enterprise. **6** a dome, esp. a transparent glass or plastic one. ◆ *vb* **bubbles, bubbling, bubbled. 7** to form or cause to form bubbles. **8** (*intr*) to move or flow with a gurgling sound. **9** (*intr;* often foll. by *over*) to overflow (with excitement, anger, etc.). [C14: prob. from ON; imit.]

bubble and squeak *n Brit. & Austral.* a dish of leftover boiled cabbage and potatoes fried together.

bubble bath *n* **1** a powder, liquid, or crystals used to scent, soften, and foam in bath water. **2** a bath to which such a substance has been added.

bubble car *n Brit.* (formerly) a small car with a transparent bubble-shaped top.

bubble chamber *n* a device that enables the tracks of ionizing particles to be photographed as a row of bubbles in a superheated liquid.

bubble gum *n* a type of chewing gum that can be blown into large bubbles.

bubble memory *n Computing.* a method of storing high volumes of data by using minute pockets of magnetism (bubbles) in a semiconducting material.

bubble point *n Chem.* the temperature at which bubbles just start to appear in a heated liquid mixture.

bubble wrap *n* a type of polythene wrapping containing many small air pockets, used as a protective covering when transporting breakable goods.

bubbly ⓣ ('bʌblɪ) *adj* **bubblier, bubbliest. 1** full of or resembling bubbles. **2** lively; animated; excited. ◆ *n* **3** *Inf.* champagne.

bubo ('bju:bəʊ) *n, pl* **buboes.** *Pathol.* inflammation and swelling of a lymph node, esp. in the armpit or groin. [C14: from Med. L *bubō,* from Gk *boubōn* groin]
▸**bubonic** (bju:'bɒnɪk) *adj*

bubonic plague *n* an acute infectious febrile disease characterized by chills, prostration, delirium, and formation of buboes: caused by the bite of an infected rat flea.

buccal ('bʌk°l) *adj* **1** of or relating to the cheek. **2** of or relating to the mouth; oral. [C19: from L *bucca* cheek]

buccaneer ⓣ (,bʌkə'nɪə) *n* **1** a pirate, esp. one who preyed on Spanish shipping in the Caribbean in the 17th and 18th centuries. ◆ *vb* (*intr*) **2** to be or act like a buccaneer. [C17: from *boucan,* dried meat taken on long voyages, from F *boucaner* to smoke meat]

buccinator ('bʌksɪ,neɪtə) *n* either of two flat cheek muscles used in chewing. [C17: from L, from *buccina* a trumpet]

buck[1] ⓣ (bʌk) *n* **1a** the male of various animals including the goat, hare, kangaroo, rabbit, and reindeer. **1b** (*as modifier*): *a buck antelope.* **2** *S. African.* an antelope or deer of either sex. **3** *Arch.* a robust spirited young man. **4** the act of bucking. ◆ *vb* **5** (*intr*) (of a horse or other animal) to jump vertically, with legs stiff and back arched. **6** (*tr*) (of a horse, etc.) to throw (its rider) by bucking. **7** (when *intr,* often foll. by *against* or *at*) *Chiefly US, Canad., & Austral. inf.* to resist or oppose obstinately. **8** (*tr; usually passive*) *Inf.* to cheer or encourage: *I was very bucked at passing the exam.* ◆ See also **buck up.** [OE *bucca* he-goat]
▸'**bucker** *n*

buck[2] (bʌk) *n US, Canad., & Austral. inf.* a dollar. [C19: from ?]

buck[3] (bʌk) *n* **1** *Poker.* a marker in the jackpot to remind the winner of some obligation when his turn comes to deal. **2 pass the buck.** *Inf.* to shift blame or responsibility onto another. [C19: prob. from *buckhorn knife,* placed before a player in poker to indicate that he was the next dealer]

buckbean ('bʌk,bi:n) *n* a marsh plant with white or pink flowers. Also called: **bogbean.**

buckboard ('bʌk,bɔ:d) *n US & Canad.* an open four-wheeled horse-drawn carriage with the seat attached to a flexible board between the front and rear axles.

bucket ('bʌkɪt) *n* **1** an open-topped roughly cylindrical container; pail. **2** Also called: **bucketful.** the amount a bucket will hold. **3** any of various bucket-like parts of a machine, such as the scoop on a mechanical shovel. **4** *Chiefly US.* a turbine rotor blade. **5** *Austral.* a small container for ice cream. **6 kick the bucket.** *Sl.* to die. ◆ *vb* **buckets, bucketing, bucketed. 7** (*tr*) to carry in or put into a bucket. **8** (*intr;* often foll. by *down*) (of rain) to fall very heavily. **9** (*intr;* often foll. by *along*) *Chiefly Brit.* to travel or drive fast. **10** (*tr*) *Austral. sl.* to criticize severely. [C13: from Anglo-F *buket,* from OE *būc*]

bucket seat *n* a seat in a car, etc., having curved sides.

bucket shop *n* **1** an unregistered firm of stockbrokers that engages in fraudulent speculation. **2** *Chiefly Brit.* a firm specializing in cheap airline tickets.

buckeye ('bʌk,aɪ) *n* any of several North American trees of the horse chestnut family having erect clusters of white or red flowers and prickly fruits.

buckhorn ('bʌk,hɔ:n) *n* **a** horn from a buck, used for knife handles, etc. **b** (*as modifier*): *a buckhorn knife.*

buckjumper ('bʌk,dʒʌmpə) *n Austral.* an untamed horse.

buckle ⓣ ('bʌk°l) *n* **1** a clasp for fastening together two loose ends, esp. of a belt or strap, usually consisting of a frame with an attached movable prong. **2** an ornamental representation of a buckle, as on a shoe. **3** a kink, bulge, or other distortion. ◆ *vb* **buckles, buckling, buckled. 4** to fasten or be fastened with a buckle. **5** to bend or cause to bend out of shape. [C14: from OF, from L *buccula* a little cheek, hence, cheek strap of a helmet]

buckle down ⓣ *vb* (*intr, adv*) *Inf.* to apply oneself with determination.

buckler ('bʌklə) *n* **1** a small round shield worn on the forearm. **2** a means of protection; defence. [C13: from OF *bocler,* from *bocle* shield boss]

Buckley's chance ('bʌklɪz) *n Austral. & NZ sl.* no chance at all. Often shortened to **Buckley's.** [C19: from ?]

bucko ('bʌkəʊ) *n, pl* **buckoes.** *Irish.* a lively young fellow: often a term of address.

buckram ('bʌkrəm) *n* **a** cotton or linen cloth stiffened with size, etc.,

THESAURUS

brutality *n* **1** = **cruelty**, atrocity, barbarism, barbarity, bloodthirstiness, brutishness, ferocity, inhumanity, ruthlessness, savageness, savagery, viciousness

brutalize *vb* **1** = **dehumanize**, bestialize, degrade **2** = **terrorize**, barbarize, vandalize

brutally *adv* **1** = **cruelly**, barbarically, barbarously, brutishly, callously, ferociously, fiercely, hardheartedly, heartlessly, in cold blood, inhumanly, meanly, mercilessly, murderously, pitilessly, remorselessly, ruthlessly, savagely, unkindly, viciously

brute *n* **1** = **animal**, beast, creature, wild animal **2** = **savage**, barbarian, beast, devil, fiend, ghoul, monster, ogre, sadist, swine ◆ *adj* **3** = **physical**, bodily, carnal, fleshly **4** = **mindless**, instinctive, senseless, unthinking **5** = **coarse**, animal, bestial, depraved, gross, sensual

brutish *adj* **1** = **coarse**, boorish, crass, crude, gross, loutish, subhuman, swinish, uncouth, vulgar **2** = **stupid**

bubble *n* **1, 2** = **air ball**, bead, blister, blob, drop, droplet, globule, vesicle ◆ *vb* **7** = **foam**, boil, effervesce, fizz, froth, percolate, seethe, sparkle **8** = **gurgle**, babble, burble, murmur, purl, ripple, trickle, trill

bubbly *adj* **1** = **frothy**, carbonated, curly, effervescent, fizzy, foamy, lathery, sparkling, sudsy **2** = **lively**, alive and kicking, animated, bouncy, elated, excited, full of beans, happy, merry, sparky

buccaneer *n* **1** = **pirate**, corsair, freebooter, privateer, sea-rover

buck[1] *n* **3** *Archaic* = **gallant**, beau, blade, blood, coxcomb, dandy, fop, popinjay, spark ◆ *vb* **5** = **jump**, bound, jerk, leap, prance, spring, start, vault **6** = **throw**, dislodge, unseat

buckle *n* **1** = **fastener**, catch, clasp, clip, hasp **3** = **distortion**, bulge, contortion, kink, warp ◆ *vb* **4** = **fasten**, catch, clasp, close, hook, secure **5** = **distort**, bend, bulge, cave in, collapse, contort, crumple, fold, twist, warp

buckle down *vb Informal,* = **apply oneself**,

used in lining clothes, bookbinding, etc. **b** (*as modifier*): *a buckram cover.* [C14: from OF *boquerant*, ult. from *Bukhara*, Uzbekistan, once important for textiles]

Bucks (bʌks) *abbrev. for* Buckinghamshire.

buckshee (ˌbʌkˈʃiː) *adj Brit. sl.* without charge; free. [C20: from BAKSHEESH]

buckshot (ˈbʌkˌʃɒt) *n* lead shot of large size used in shotgun shells, esp. for hunting game.

buckskin (ˈbʌkˌskɪn) *n* **1** the skin of a male deer. **2a** a strong greyish-yellow suede leather, originally made from deerskin but now usually made from sheepskin. **2b** (*as modifier*): *buckskin boots.* **3** a stiffly starched cotton cloth. **4** a strong and heavy satin-woven woollen fabric.

buckthorn (ˈbʌkˌθɔːn) *n* any of several thorny small-flowered shrubs whose berries were formerly used as a purgative. [C16: from BUCK[1] (from the spiny branches resembling antlers) + THORN]

bucktooth (ˈbʌkˌtuːθ) *n, pl* **buckteeth.** *Derog.* a projecting upper front tooth. [C18: from BUCK[1] (deer) + TOOTH]

buck up Ⓣ *vb* (*adv*) *Inf.* **1** to make or cause to make haste. **2** to make or become more cheerful, confident, etc.

buckwheat (ˈbʌkˌwiːt) *n* **1** a cereal plant with fragrant white flowers, cultivated, esp. in the US, for its seeds. **2** the edible seeds of this plant, ground into flour or used as animal fodder. **3** the flour obtained from these seeds. [C16: from MDu. *boecweite*, from *boeke* BEECH + *weite* WHEAT, from the resemblance of the seeds to beechnuts]

buckyball (ˈbʌkɪˌbɔːl) *n Inf.* a ball-like polyhedral carbon molecule, of the type found in buckminsterfullerene and other fullerenes.

bucolic (bjuːˈkɒlɪk) *adj also* **bucolical. 1** of the countryside or country life; rustic. **2** of or relating to shepherds; pastoral. ◆ *n* **3** (*sometimes pl*) a pastoral poem. [C16: from L, from Gk, from *boukolos* cowherd, from *bous* ox]
▸**buˈcolically** *adv*

bud Ⓣ (bʌd) *n* **1** a swelling on a plant stem consisting of overlapping immature leaves or petals. **2a** a partially opened flower. **2b** (*in combination*): *rosebud.* **3** any small budlike outgrowth: *taste buds.* **4** something small or immature. **5** an asexually produced outgrowth in simple organisms such as yeasts that develops into a new individual. **6 nip in the bud.** to put an end to (an idea, movement, etc.) in its initial stages. ◆ *vb* **buds, budding, budded. 7** (*intr*) (of plants and some animals) to produce buds. **8** (*intr*) to begin to develop or grow. **9** (*tr*) *Horticulture.* to graft (a bud) from one plant onto another. [C14 *budde*, of Gmc origin]

Buddha (ˈbʊdə) *n* **the.** ?563–483 B.C., a title applied to Gautama Siddhartha, a religious teacher of N India regarded by his followers as the most recent rediscoverer of the path to enlightenment: the founder of Buddhism.

Buddhism (ˈbʊdɪzəm) *n* a religious teaching propagated by the Buddha and his followers, which declares that by destroying greed, hatred, and delusion, which are the causes of all suffering, man can attain perfect enlightenment.
▸ˈ**Buddhist** *n, adj*

buddleia (ˈbʌdlɪə) *n* an ornamental shrub which has long spikes of mauve flowers. Also called: **butterfly bush.** [C19: after A. *Buddle* (died 1715), Brit. botanist]

buddy (ˈbʌdɪ) *n, pl* **buddies. 1** Also (as a term of address): **bud.** *Chiefly US & Canad.* an informal word for **friend. 2** a volunteer who visits and gives help and support to a person suffering from AIDS. ◆ *vb* **buddies, buddying, buddied. 3** (*intr*) to act as a buddy to a person suffering from AIDS. [C19: prob. baby-talk var. (US) of BROTHER]

buddy-buddy *adj Inf., chiefly US.* on very friendly or intimate terms.

buddy movie *or* **film** *n* a genre of film dealing with the relationship and adventures of two friends.

budge Ⓣ (bʌdʒ) *vb* **budges, budging, budged.** (*usually used with a negative*) **1** to move, however slightly. **2** to change or cause to change opinions, etc. [C16: from OF *bouger*, from L *bullīre* to boil]

budgerigar (ˈbʌdʒərɪˌgɑː) *n* a small green Australian parrot: a popular cagebird bred in many different-coloured varieties. [C19: from Abor., from *budgeri* good + *gar* cockatoo]

budget Ⓣ (ˈbʌdʒɪt) *n* **1** an itemized summary of expected income and expenditure over a specified period. **2** (*modifier*) economical; inexpensive: *budget meals for a family.* **3** the total amount of money allocated for a specific purpose during a specified period. ◆ *vb* **budgets, budgeting, budgeted. 4** (*tr*) to enter or provide for in a budget. **5** to plan the expenditure of (money, time, etc.). **6** (*intr*) to make a budget. [C15 (meaning: leather pouch, wallet): from OF *bougette*, dim. of *bouge*, from L *bulga*]
▸ˈ**budgetary** *adj*

Budget (ˈbʌdʒɪt) *n* **the.** an estimate of British government expenditures and revenues and the financial plans for the ensuing fiscal year presented annually to the House of Commons by the Chancellor of the Exchequer.

budget account *n* **1** an account with a department store, etc., enabling a customer to make monthly payments to cover his past and future purchases. **2** a bank account that allows the holder credit to pay certain bills in return for regular deposits.

budget deficit *n* the amount by which government expenditure exceeds income from taxation, customs duties, etc., in any one fiscal year.

budgie (ˈbʌdʒɪ) *n Inf.* short for **budgerigar.**

buff[1] Ⓣ (bʌf) *n* **1a** a soft thick flexible undyed leather made chiefly from the skins of buffalo, oxen, and elk. **1b** (*as modifier*): *a buff coat.* **2a** a dull yellow or yellowish-brown colour. **2b** (*as adj*): *a buff envelope.* **3** Also called: **buffer. 3a** a cloth or pad of material used for polishing an object. **3b** a disc or wheel impregnated with a fine abrasive for polishing metals, etc. **4** *Inf.* one's bare skin (esp. in **in the buff**). ◆ *vb* **5** to clean or polish (a metal, floor, shoes, etc.) with a buff. **6** to remove the grain surface of (a leather). [C16: from OF, from OIt. *bufalo*, from LL *būfalus* BUFFALO]

buff[2] (bʌf) *n Arch.* a blow or buffet (now only in **blind man's buff**). [C15: back formation from BUFFET[2]]

buff[3] Ⓣ (bʌf) *n Inf.* an expert on or devotee of a given subject. [C20: orig. US: an enthusiastic fire-watcher, from the buff-coloured uniforms worn by volunteer firemen in New York City]

buffalo (ˈbʌfəˌləʊ) *n, pl* **buffaloes** *or* **buffalo. 1** a type of cattle, mostly found in game reserves in southern and eastern Africa and having upward-curving horns. **2** short for **water buffalo. 3** a US & Canad. name for **bison** (sense 1). [C16: from It. *bufalo*, ult. from Gk *bous* ox]

buffalo grass *n* **1** a short grass growing on the dry plains of the central US. **2** *Austral.* a grass, *Stenotaphrum americanum*, introduced from North America.

buffel grass (ˈbʌfᵊl) *n* (in Australia) any of various grasses used for grazing or fodder, originally introduced from Africa.

buffer[1] Ⓣ (ˈbʌfə) *n* **1** one of a pair of spring-loaded steel pads attached at both ends of railway vehicles and at the end of a railway track to reduce shock due to contact. **2** a person or thing that lessens shock or protects from damaging impact, circumstances, etc. **3** *Chem.* **3a** an ionic compound added to a solution to resist changes in its acidity or alkalinity and thus stabilize its pH. **3b** Also called: **buffer solution.** a solution containing such a compound. **4** *Computing.* a memory device for temporarily storing data. ◆ *vb* (*tr*) **5** *Chem.* to add a buffer to (a solution). **6** to insulate against or protect from shock. [C19: from BUFF[2]]

buffer[2] (ˈbʌfə) *n* **1** any device used to shine, polish, etc.; buff. **2** a person who uses such a device.

buffer[3] (ˈbʌfə) *n Brit. inf.* a stupid or bumbling man (esp. in **old buffer**). [C18: ?from ME *buffer* stammerer]

buffer state *n* a small and usually neutral state between two rival powers.

buffer stock *n Commerce.* a stock of a commodity built up by a government or trade organization with the object of using it to stabilize prices.

buffet[1] Ⓣ *n* **1** (ˈbʊfeɪ). a counter where light refreshments are served. **2** (ˈbʊfeɪ). **2a** a meal at which guests help themselves from a number of dishes. **2b** (*as modifier*): *a buffet lunch.* **3** (ˈbʌfɪt, ˈbʊfeɪ). (formerly) a piece of furniture used for displaying plate, etc., and typically comprising cupboards and open shelves. [C18: from F]

buffet[2] Ⓣ (ˈbʌfɪt) *vb* **buffets, buffeting, buffeted. 1** (*tr*) to knock against or about; batter. **2** (*tr*) to hit, esp. with the fist; cuff. **3** to force (one's way), as through a crowd. **4** (*intr*) to struggle; battle. ◆ *n* **5** a blow, esp. with a fist or hand. **6** aerodynamic oscillation of an aircraft structure by separated flows. [C13: from OF *buffet* a light blow]

buffet car (ˈbʊfeɪ) *n Brit.* a railway coach where light refreshments are served.

buffeting (ˈbʌfɪtɪŋ) *n* response of an aircraft structure to buffet, esp. an irregular oscillation of the tail.

bufflehead (ˈbʌfᵊlˌhɛd) *n* a small North American diving duck: the male has black-and-white plumage and a fluffy head. [C17 *buffle*, from obs. *buffle* wild ox, referring to the duck's head]

buffo (ˈbʊfəʊ) *n, pl* **buffi** (-fɪ) *or* **buffos. 1** (in Italian opera of the 18th cen-

THESAURUS

exert oneself, launch into, pitch in, put one's shoulder to the wheel, set to

buck up *vb* **1** *Informal* = **hurry up**, get a move on, hasten, shake a leg, speed up **2** = **cheer up**, brighten, encourage, hearten, inspirit, perk up, rally, take heart

bud *n* **1** = **shoot**, embryo, germ, sprout ◆ *vb* **7** = **develop**, burgeon, burst forth, grow, pullulate, shoot, sprout

budding *adj* **8** = **developing**, beginning, burgeoning, embryonic, fledgling, flowering, germinal, growing, incipient, nascent, potential, promising

budge *vb* **1** = **move**, dislodge, give way, inch, propel, push, remove, roll, shift, slide, stir **2** = **change**, bend, convince, give way, influence, persuade, sway, yield

budget *n* **1** = **fiscal estimate**, finances, financial statement **3** = **allowance**, allocation, cost, funds, means, resources ◆ *vb* **4-6** = **plan**, allocate, apportion, cost, cost out, estimate, ration

buff[1] *adj* **2b** = **yellowish-brown**, sandy, straw, tan, yellowish ◆ *n* **4** *Informal* = **naked**, bare, buck naked (*sl.*), in one's birthday suit (*inf.*), in the altogether (*inf.*), in the bare scud (*sl.*), in the raw (*inf.*), nude, unclad, unclothed, with bare skin, without a stitch on (*inf.*) ◆ *vb* **5** = **polish**, brush, burnish, rub, shine, smooth

buff[3] *n Informal* = **expert**, addict, admirer, aficionado, connoisseur, devotee, enthusiast, fan, fiend (*inf.*), freak (*inf.*), grandmaster, hotshot (*inf.*), maven (*US*), whizz (*inf.*)

buffer[1] *n* **2** = **safeguard**, bulwark, cushion, fender, intermediary, screen, shield, shock absorber

buffet[1] *n* **1** = **snack bar**, brasserie, café, cafeteria, cold table, counter, cupboard, refreshment counter, salad bar, sideboard, smorgasbord

buffet[2] *vb* **1, 2** = **batter**, bang, beat, box, bump, clobber (*sl.*), cuff, flail, knock, lambast(e), pound, pummel, punch, rap, shove, slap, strike, thump, wallop (*inf.*) ◆ *n* **5** = **blow**, bang, box, bump, cuff, jolt, knock, push, rap, shove, slap, smack, thump, wallop (*inf.*)

tury) a comic part, esp. one for a bass. **2** Also called: **buffo bass, basso buffo.** a bass singer who performs such a part. [C18: from It. (adj): comic, from *buffo* (n) BUFFOON]

buffoon Ⓣ (bəˈfuːn) *n* **1** a person who amuses others by ridiculous or odd behaviour, jokes, etc. **2** a foolish person. [C16: from F *bouffon,* from It. *buffone,* from Med. L *būfō,* from L: toad]
▸**bufˈfoonery** *n*

bug Ⓣ (bʌg) *n* **1** an insect having piercing and sucking mouthparts specialized as a beak. **2** *Chiefly US & Canad.* any insect. **3** *Inf.* **3a** a microorganism, esp. a bacterium, that produces disease. **3b** a disease, esp. a stomach infection, caused by a microorganism. **4** *Inf.* an obsessive idea, hobby, etc.; craze. **5** *Inf.* a person having such a craze. **6** (*often pl*) *Inf.* a fault, as in a machine. **7** *Inf.* a concealed microphone used for recording conversations, as in spying. ◆ *vb* **bugs, bugging, bugged.** *Inf.* **8** (*tr*) to irritate; bother. **9** (*tr*) to conceal a microphone in (a room, etc.). **10** (*intr*) *US.* (of eyes) to protrude. [C16: from ?]

bugaboo (ˈbʌgəˌbuː) *n, pl* **bugaboos.** an imaginary source of fear; bugbear; bogey. [C18: prob. of Celtic origin; cf. Cornish *buccaboo* the devil]

bugbear Ⓣ (ˈbʌgˌbɛə) *n* **1** a thing that causes obsessive anxiety. **2** (in English folklore) a goblin in the form of a bear. [C16: from obs. *bug* an evil spirit+ BEAR[2]]

bug-eyed *adj* having protruding eyes.

bugger (ˈbʌgə) *n* **1** a person who practises buggery. **2** *Taboo sl.* a person or thing considered to be contemptible, unpleasant, or difficult. **3** *Sl.* a humorous or affectionate term for a man or child: *a friendly little bugger.* **4 bugger all.** *Sl.* nothing. ◆ *vb* **5** to practise buggery (with). **6** (*tr*) *Sl., chiefly Brit.* to ruin, complicate, or frustrate. **7** (*tr*) *Sl.* to tire; weary. ◆ *interj* **8** *Taboo sl.* an exclamation of annoyance or disappointment. [C16: from OF *bougre,* from Med. L *Bulgarus* Bulgarian; from the condemnation of the Eastern Orthodox Bulgarians as heretics]

bugger about *or* **around** *vb* (*adv*) *Sl.* **1** (*intr*) to fool about and waste time. **2** (*tr*) to create difficulties or complications for (a person).

bugger off *vb* (*intr, adv*) *Taboo sl.* to go away; depart.

buggery (ˈbʌgərɪ) *n* anal intercourse between a man and another man, a woman, or an animal.

buggy[1] (ˈbʌgɪ) *n, pl* **buggies. 1** a light horse-drawn carriage having either four wheels (esp. in the US and Canada) or two wheels (esp. in Britain and India). **2** any small light cart or vehicle, such as a baby buggy. [C18: from ?]

buggy[2] (ˈbʌgɪ) *adj* **buggier, buggiest.** infested with bugs.

bugle[1] (ˈbjuːgᵊl) *n* **1** *Music.* a brass instrument similar to the cornet but usually without valves: used for military fanfares, signal calls, etc. ◆ *vb* **bugles, bugling, bugled. 2** (*intr*) to play or sound (on) a bugle. [C14: short for *bugle horn* ox horn, from OF *bugle,* from L *būculus* young bullock, from *bōs* ox]
▸ˈ**bugler** *n*

bugle[2] (ˈbjuːgᵊl) *n* any of several Eurasian plants having small blue or white flowers. [C13: from LL *bugula,* from ?]

bugle[3] (ˈbjuːgᵊl) *n* a tubular glass or plastic bead sewn onto clothes for decoration. [C16: from ?]

bugloss (ˈbjuːglɒs) *n* any of various hairy Eurasian plants having clusters of blue flowers. [C15: from L, from Gk *buglōssos* ox-tongued]

bugong (ˈbuːgɒŋ) *n* another name for **bogong.**

buhl (buːl) *adj, n* a variant spelling of **boulle.**

build Ⓣ (bɪld) *vb* **builds, building, built. 1** to make, construct, or form by joining parts or materials: *to build a house.* **2** (*tr*) to order the building of: *the government builds most of our hospitals.* **3** (foll. by *on* or *upon*) to base; found: *his theory was not built on facts.* **4** (*tr*) to establish and develop: *it took ten years to build a business.* **5** (*tr*) to make in a particular way or for a particular purpose: *the car was not built for speed.* **6** (*intr;* often foll. by *up*) to increase in intensity. ◆ *n* **7** physical form, figure, or proportions: *a man with an athletic build.* [OE *byldan*]

builder (ˈbɪldə) *n* a person who builds, esp. one who contracts for and supervises the construction or repair of buildings.

building Ⓣ (ˈbɪldɪŋ) *n* **1** something built with a roof and walls. **2** the act, business, occupation, or art of building houses, boats, etc.

building society *n* a cooperative banking enterprise financed by deposits on which interest is paid and from which mortgage loans are advanced on homes and real property; many now offer a range of banking services.

build up Ⓣ *vb* (*adv*) **1** (*tr*) to construct gradually, systematically, and in stages. **2** to increase, accumulate, or strengthen, esp. by degrees: *the murmur built up to a roar.* **3** (*tr*) to improve the health or physique of (a person). **4** (*intr*) to prepare for or gradually approach a climax. ◆ *n* **build-up. 5** progressive increase in number, size, etc.: *the build-up of industry.* **6** a gradual approach to a climax. **7** extravagant publicity or praise, esp. in the form of a campaign. **8** *Mil.* the process of attaining the required strength of forces and equipment.

built (bɪlt) *vb* the past tense and past participle of **build.**

built-in Ⓣ *adj* **1** made or incorporated as an integral part: *a built-in cupboard.* **2** essential; inherent. ◆ *n* **3** *Austral.* a built-in cupboard.

built-in obsolescence *n* See **planned obsolescence.**

built-up *adj* **1** having many buildings (esp. in **built-up area**). **2** increased by the addition of parts: *built-up heels.*

bulb Ⓣ (bʌlb) *n* **1** a rounded organ of vegetative reproduction in plants such as the tulip and onion: a flattened stem bearing a central shoot surrounded by fleshy nutritive inner leaves and thin brown outer leaves. **2** a plant, such as a hyacinth or daffodil, that grows from a bulb. **3** See **light bulb. 4** any bulb-shaped thing. [C16: from L *bulbus,* from Gk *bolbos* onion]
▸ˈ**bulbous** *adj*

bulbil (ˈbʌlbɪl) *n* **1** a small bulb produced from a parent bulb. **2** a bulblike reproductive organ in a leaf axil of certain plants. **3** any small bulblike structure in an animal. [C19: from NL *bulbillus* BULB]

bulbul (ˈbʊlbʊl) *n* a songbird of tropical Africa and Asia having brown plumage and, in many species, a distinct crest. [C18: via Persian from Ar.]

Bulgarian (bʌlˈgɛərɪən, bʊl-) *adj* **1** of or denoting Bulgaria, a country of SE Europe, on the Balkan Peninsula, its people, or their language. ◆ *n* **2** the official language of Bulgaria. **3** a native or inhabitant of Bulgaria.

bulge Ⓣ (bʌldʒ) *n* **1** a swelling or an outward curve. **2** a sudden increase in number, esp. of population. ◆ *vb* **bulges, bulging, bulged. 3** to swell outwards. [C13: from OF *bouge,* from L *bulga* bag, prob. of Gaulish origin]
▸ˈ**bulging** *adj* ▸ˈ**bulgy** *adj*

bulgur (ˈbʌlgə) *n* cracked wheat that has been hulled, steamed, and roasted so that it requires little or no cooking. [C20: from Ar. *burghul*]

bulimia (bjuːˈlɪmɪə) *n* **1** pathologically insatiable hunger. **2** Also called: **bulimia nervosa.** a disorder characterized by compulsive overeating followed by vomiting. [C17: from NL, from Gk *bous* ox + *limos* hunger]

bulk Ⓣ (bʌlk) *n* **1** volume, size, or magnitude, esp. when great. **2** the main part: *the bulk of the work is repetitious.* **3** a large body, esp. of a person. **4** the part of food which passes unabsorbed through the digestive system. **5 in bulk. 5a** in large quantities. **5b** (of a cargo, etc.) unpackaged. ◆ *vb* **6** to cohere or cause to cohere in a mass. **7 bulk large.** to be or seem important or prominent. [C15: from ON *bulki* cargo]

> **USAGE NOTE** The use of a plural noun after *bulk* was formerly considered incorrect, but is now acceptable.

bulk buying *n* the purchase of goods in large amounts, often at reduced prices.

bulkhead (ˈbʌlkˌhɛd) *n* any upright wall-like partition in a ship, aircraft, etc. [C15: prob. from *bulk* projecting framework from ON *bálkr* +HEAD]

bulk modulus *n* a coefficient of elasticity of a substance equal to the ratio of the applied stress to the resulting fractional change in volume.

bulky Ⓣ (ˈbʌlkɪ) *adj* **bulkier, bulkiest.** very large and massive, esp. so as to be unwieldy.
▸ˈ**bulkily** *adv* ▸ˈ**bulkiness** *n*

THESAURUS

buffoon *n* **1 = clown**, comedian, comic, droll, fool, harlequin, jester, joker, wag

buffoonery *n* **1 = clowning**, drollery, jesting, nonsense, tomfoolery, waggishness

bug *n* **3** *Informal* **= illness**, disease, infection, lurgy (*inf.*), virus **4** *Informal* **= mania**, craze, fad, obsession, rage **6 = fault**, blemish, catch, defect, error, failing, flaw, glitch, gremlin, imperfection, snarl-up (*inf., chiefly Brit.*), virus ◆ *vb* **8** *Informal* **= annoy**, aggravate (*inf.*), badger, be on one's back (*sl.*), bother, disturb, gall, get on one's nerves (*inf.*), get under one's skin (*inf.*), harass, hassle (*inf.*), irk, irritate, nark (*Brit., Austral., & NZ sl.*), needle (*inf.*), nettle, pester, piss one off (*taboo sl.*), plague, vex **9 = tap**, eavesdrop, listen in, spy, wiretap

bugbear *n* **1 = pet hate**, anathema, bane, bête noire, bogey, bogeyman, bugaboo, devil, dread, fiend, horror, nightmare

build *vb* **1 = construct**, assemble, erect, fabricate, form, make, put up, raise **4 = establish**, base, begin, constitute, formulate, found, inaugurate, initiate, institute, originate, set up, start **6 = increase**, accelerate, amplify, augment, develop, enlarge, escalate, extend, improve, intensify, strengthen ◆ *n* **7 = physique**, body, figure, form, frame, shape, structure
Antonyms *vb* ≠ **construct:** demolish, dismantle, tear down ≠ **establish:** end, finish, relinquish, suspend ≠ **increase:** contract, debilitate, decline, decrease, dilute, harm, impair, lower, reduce, sap, weaken

building *n* **1 = structure**, domicile, dwelling, edifice, house, pile **2 = construction**, architecture, erection, fabricating, raising

build up *vb* **2 = increase**, add to, amplify, augment, develop, enhance, expand, extend, fortify, heighten, improve, intensify, reinforce, strengthen **4 = hype**, advertise, boost, plug (*inf.*), promote, publicize, spotlight ◆ *n* **build-up 5 = increase**, accumulation, development, enlargement, escalation, expansion, gain, growth **7 = hype**, ballyhoo (*inf.*), plug (*inf.*), promotion, publicity, puff

built-in *adj* **2 = integral**, essential, immanent, implicit, in-built, included, incorporated, inherent, inseparable, part and parcel of

bulbous *adj* **1, 4 = bulging**, bloated, convex, rounded, swelling, swollen

bulge *n* **1 = swelling**, bump, hump, lump, projection, protrusion, protuberance **2 = increase**, boost, intensification, rise, surge ◆ *vb* **3 = swell out**, bag, dilate, distend, enlarge, expand, project, protrude, puff out, sag, stand out, stick out, swell
Antonyms *n* ≠ **swelling:** bowl, cave, cavity, concavity, crater, dent, depression, hole, hollow, indentation, pit, trough

bulk *n* **1 = size**, amplitude, bigness, dimensions, immensity, largeness, magnitude, massiveness, substance, volume, weight **2 = main part**, better part, body, generality, lion's share, majority, major part, mass, most, nearly all, plurality, preponderance ◆ *vb* **7 bulk large = be important**, carry weight, dominate, loom, loom large, preponderate, stand out, threaten

bulky *adj* **= large**, big, colossal, cumbersome, elephantine, enormous, heavy, huge, hulking,

bull[1] (bʊl) *n* **1** any male bovine animal, esp. one that is sexually mature. Related adj: **taurine. 2** the male of various other animals including the elephant and whale. **3** a very large, strong, or aggressive person. **4** *Stock Exchange.* **4a** a speculator who buys in anticipation of rising prices in order to make a profit on resale. **4b** (*as modifier*): *a bull market.* Cf. **bear**[2] (sense 5). **5** *Chiefly Brit.* short for **bull's-eye** (senses 1, 2). **6** *Sl.* short for **bullshit. 7 a bull in a china shop.** a clumsy person. **8 take the bull by the horns.** to face and tackle a difficulty without shirking. ◆ *adj* **9** male; masculine: *a bull elephant.* **10** large; strong. [OE *bula*]

bull[2] (bʊl) *n* a ludicrously self-contradictory or inconsistent statement. [C17: from ?]

bull[3] (bʊl) *n* a formal document issued by the pope. [C13: from Med. L *bulla* seal attached to a bull, from L: round object]

Bull (bʊl) *n* **the.** the constellation Taurus, the second sign of the zodiac.

Bullamakanka (ˌbuːləmə'kæŋkə) *n Austral.* an imaginary very remote place.

bull bars *pl n* a large protective metal grille on the front of some vehicles, esp. four-wheel-drive vehicles.

bulldog ('bʊlˌdɒg) *n* a sturdy thickset breed of dog with an undershot jaw, broad head, and a muscular body.

bulldog clip *n* a clip for holding papers together, consisting of two T-shaped metal clamps held in place by a cylindrical spring.

bulldoze ➊ ('bʊlˌdəʊz) *vb* **bulldozes, bulldozing, bulldozed.** (*tr*) **1** to move, demolish, flatten, etc., with a bulldozer. **2** *Inf.* to force; push. **3** *Inf.* to intimidate or coerce. [C19: prob. from BULL[1] + DOSE]

bulldozer ('bʊlˌdəʊzə) *n* **1** a powerful tractor fitted with caterpillar tracks and a blade at the front, used for moving earth, rocks, etc. **2** *Inf.* a person who bulldozes.

bull dust *n Austral.* **1** fine dust, as on roads in outback Australia. **2** *Sl.* nonsense.

bullet ➊ ('bʊlɪt) *n* **1a** a small metallic missile enclosed in a cartridge, used as the projectile of a gun, rifle, etc. **1b** the entire cartridge. **2** something resembling a bullet, esp. in shape or effect. **3** *Stock Exchange.* a fixed interest security with a single maturity date. **4** *Commerce.* a security that offers a fixed interest and matures on a fixed date. **5** *Commerce.* **5a** the final repayment of a loan that repays the whole of the sum borrowed, as interim payments have been for interest only. **5b** (*as modifier*): *a bullet loan.* [C16: from F *boulette,* dim. of *boule* ball; see BOWL[2]]

bulletin ➊ ('bʊlɪtɪn) *n* **1** an official statement on a matter of public interest. **2** a broadcast summary of the news. **3** a periodical publication of an association, etc. ◆ *vb* **4** (*tr*) to make known by bulletin. [C17: from F, from It., from *bulletta,* dim. of *bulla* papal edict, BULL[3]]

bulletin board *n* **1** the US and Canad. name for **notice board. 2** *Computing.* a facility on a computer network allowing any user to leave messages that can be read by any other user, and to download software and information to the user's own computer.

bulletproof ('bʊlɪtˌpruːf) *adj* **1** not penetrable by bullets. ◆ *vb* **2** (*tr*) to make bulletproof.

bulletwood ('bʊlɪtˌwʊd) *n* the tough durable wood of a tropical American tree, widely used for construction.

bullfight ('bʊlˌfaɪt) *n* a traditional Spanish, Portuguese, and Latin American spectacle in which a matador baits and usually kills a bull in an arena.
▸ **'bullˌfighter** *n* ▸ **'bullˌfighting** *n*

bullfinch ('bʊlˌfɪntʃ) *n* **1** a common European finch: the male has a bright red throat and breast. **2** any of various similar finches. [C14: see BULL[1], FINCH]

bullfrog ('bʊlˌfrɒg) *n* any of various large frogs having a loud deep croak, esp. the **American bullfrog.**

bullhead ('bʊlˌhɛd) *n* any of various small northern mainly marine fishes that have a large head covered with bony plates and spines.

bull-headed ➊ *adj* blindly obstinate; stupid.
▸ **ˌbull-'headedly** *adv* ▸ **ˌbull-'headedness** *n*

bullhorn ('bʊlˌhɔːn) *n* the US and Canad. name for **loud-hailer.**

bullion ('bʊljən) *n* **1** gold or silver in mass. **2** gold or silver in the form of bars and ingots, suitable for further processing. [C14: from Anglo-F: mint, prob. from OF *bouillir* to boil, from L *bullīre*]

bullish ('bʊlɪʃ) *adj* **1** like a bull. **2** *Stock Exchange.* causing, expecting, or characterized by a rise in prices. **3** *Inf.* cheerful and optimistic.
▸ **'bullishness** *n*

bull-necked *adj* having a short thick neck.

bullock ('bʊlək) *n* **1** a gelded bull; steer. ◆ *vb* **2** (*intr*) *Austral. & NZ inf.* to work hard and long. [OE *bulluc;* see BULL[1], -OCK]

bullocky ('bʊləkɪ) *n, pl* **bullockies.** *Austral. & NZ.* a bullock driver; teamster.

bullring ('bʊlˌrɪŋ) *n* an arena for bullfighting.

bullroarer ('bʊlˌrɔːrə) *n* a wooden slat attached to a thong that makes a roaring sound when the thong is whirled: used esp. by native Australians in religious rites.

bull's-eye *n* **1** the small central disc of a target, usually the highest valued area. **2** a shot hitting this. **3** *Inf.* something that exactly achieves its aim. **4** a small circular or oval window or opening. **5** a thick disc of glass set into a ship's deck, etc., to admit light. **6** the glass boss at the centre of a sheet of blown glass. **7a** a small thick plano-convex lens used as a condenser. **7b** a lamp containing such a lens. **8** a peppermint-flavoured boiled sweet.

bullshit ('bʊlˌʃɪt) *Taboo sl.* ◆ *n* **1** exaggerated or foolish talk; nonsense. **2** deceitful or pretentious talk. **3** (in the British Army) exaggerated zeal, esp. for ceremonial drill, cleaning, etc. Usually shortened to **bull.** ◆ *vb* **bullshits, bullshitting, bullshitted** *or* **bullshit. 4** (*intr*) to talk in an exaggerated or foolish manner. **5** (*tr*) to talk bullshit to.

bull terrier *n* a breed of terrier having a muscular body and thick neck, with a short smooth coat. See also **pit bull terrier, Staffordshire bull terrier.**

bully ➊ ('bʊlɪ) *n, pl* **bullies. 1** a person who hurts, persecutes, or intimidates weaker people. **2** a small New Zealand freshwater fish. ◆ *vb* **bullies, bullying, bullied. 3** (when *tr,* often foll. by *into*) to hurt, intimidate, or persecute (a weaker or smaller person), esp. to make him do something. ◆ *adj* **4** dashing; jolly: *my bully boy.* **5** *Inf.* very good; fine. ◆ *interj* **6** Also: **bully for you, him,** etc. *Inf.* well done! bravo! [C16 (in the sense: sweetheart, hence fine fellow, hence swaggering coward): prob. from MDu. *boele* lover, from MHG *buole*]

bully beef *n* canned corned beef. Often shortened to **bully.** [C19 *bully,* anglicized version of F *bouilli,* from *boeuf bouilli* boiled beef]

bully-off *Hockey.* ◆ *n* **1** the method by which a game is restarted after a stoppage. Two opposing players stand with the ball between them and alternately strike their sticks together and against the ground three times before trying to hit the ball. ◆ *vb* **bully off. 2** (*intr, adv*) to restart play with a bully-off. ◆ Often shortened to **bully.** [C19: from ?]

bullyrag ('bʊlɪˌræg) *vb* **bullyrags, bullyragging, bullyragged.** (*tr*) to bully, esp. by means of cruel practical jokes. Also: **ballyrag.** [C18: from ?]

bulrush ('bʊlˌrʌʃ) *n* **1** a popular name for **reed mace. 2** a grasslike marsh plant used for making mats, chair seats, etc. **3** a biblical word for **papyrus** (the plant). [C15 *bulrish, bul-* ?from BULL[1] + *rish* RUSH[2]]

bulwark ➊ ('bʊlwək) *n* **1** a wall or similar structure used as a fortification; rampart. **2** a person or thing acting as a defence. **3** (*often pl*) *Naut.* a solid vertical fencelike structure along the outward sides of a deck. **4** a breakwater or mole. ◆ *vb* **5** (*tr*) to defend or fortify with or as if with a bulwark. [C15: via Du. from MHG *bolwerk,* from *bol* plank, BOLE + *werk* WORK]

bum[1] (bʌm) *n Brit. sl.* the buttocks or anus. [C14: from ?]

bum[2] (bʌm) *Inf.* ◆ *n* **1** a disreputable loafer or idler. **2** a tramp; hobo. ◆ *vb* **bums, bumming, bummed. 3** (*tr*) to get by begging; cadge: *to bum a lift.* **4** (*intr;* often foll. by *around*) to live by begging or as a vagrant or loafer. **5** (*intr;* usually foll. by *around*) to spend time to no good purpose; loaf; idle. **6 bum (someone) off.** *US & Canad. sl.* to disappoint, annoy, or upset (someone). ◆ *adj* **7** (*prenominal*) of poor quality; useless. [C19: prob. shortened from earlier *bummer* a loafer, prob. from G *bummeln* to loaf]

bum bag *n* a small bag worn on a belt, round the waist.

bumbailiff (ˌbʌm'beɪlɪf) *n Brit. derog.* (formerly) an officer employed to collect debts and arrest debtors. [C17: from BUM[1] + *bailiff,* so called because he follows hard behind debtors]

bumble ➊ ('bʌmb°l) *vb* **bumbles, bumbling, bumbled. 1** to speak or do in a clumsy, muddled, or inefficient way. **2** (*intr*) to proceed unsteadily. [C16: ? a blend of BUNGLE + STUMBLE]
▸ **'bumbler** *n* ▸ **'bumbling** *adj, n*

bumblebee ('bʌmb°lˌbiː) *or* **humblebee** *n* any large hairy social bee of temperate regions. [C16: from *bumble* to buzz + BEE[1]]

bumf *or* **bumph** (bʌmf) *n Brit.* **1** *Inf., derog.* official documents, forms, etc. **2** *Sl.* toilet paper. [C19: short for earlier *bumfodder;* see BUM[1]]

bummer ('bʌmə) *n Sl.* a disappointing or unpleasant experience.

bump ➊ (bʌmp) *vb* **1** (when *intr,* usually foll. by *against* or *into*) to knock or strike with a jolt. **2** (*intr;* often foll. by *along*) to travel or proceed in jerks and jolts. **3** (*tr*) to hurt by knocking. **4** *Cricket.* to bowl (a ball) so that it bounces high on pitching or (of a ball) to bounce high when bowled. **5** (*tr*) *Inf.* to exclude (a ticket-holding passenger) from a

THESAURUS

immense, mammoth, massive, massy, ponderous, substantial, unmanageable, unwieldy, voluminous, weighty
Antonyms *adj* convenient, handy, manageable, neat, slim, small, wieldy

bulldoze *vb* **1 = demolish,** flatten, level, raze **2** *Informal* **= push,** drive, force, propel, shove, thrust **3** *Informal* **= force,** browbeat, bully, coerce, cow, dragoon, hector, intimidate, put the screws on, railroad (*inf.*)

bullet *n* **1a = projectile,** ball, missile, pellet, shot, slug

bulletin *n* **1, 2 = announcement,** account, communication, communiqué, dispatch, message, news flash, notification, report, statement

bull-headed *adj* **= stubborn,** headstrong, inflexible, mulish, obstinate, pig-headed, stiff-necked, stupid, tenacious, uncompromising, unyielding, wilful

bully *n* **1 = persecutor,** browbeater, bully boy, coercer, intimidator, oppressor, ruffian, tormentor, tough ◆ *vb* **3 = persecute,** bluster, browbeat, bulldoze (*inf.*), bullyrag, coerce, cow, domineer, hector, intimidate, oppress, overbear, push around (*sl.*), ride roughshod over, swagger, terrorize, tyrannize ◆ *interjection* **6** *Informal* **= well done,** bravo, capital, good, grand, great

bulwark *n* **1 = fortification,** bastion, buttress, defence, embankment, outwork, partition, rampart, redoubt **2 = defence,** buffer, guard, mainstay, safeguard, security, support

bumbler *n* **1 = bungler,** blunderer, duffer (*inf.*), geek (*sl.*), klutz (*US & Canad. sl.*), lummox (*inf.*), muddler

bumbling *adj* **1 = clumsy,** awkward, blundering, botching, bungling, incompetent, inefficient, inept, lumbering, maladroit, muddled
Antonyms *adj* able, brisk, capable, competent, efficient, equal, fit

bump *vb* **1 = knock,** bang, collide (with), crash, hit, slam, smash into, strike **2 = jerk,** bounce, jar, jolt, jostle, jounce, rattle, shake ◆ *n* **6, 7 = knock,** bang, blow, collision, crash, hit, impact, jar, jolt, rap, shock, smash, thud, thump **9 =**

flight as a result of overbooking. ◆ *n* **6** an impact; knock; jolt; collision. **7** a dull thud or other noise from an impact or collision. **8** the shock of a blow or collision. **9** a lump on the body caused by a blow. **10** a protuberance, as on a road surface. **11** any of the natural protuberances of the human skull, said by phrenologists to indicate underlying faculties and character. ◆ See also **bump into, bump off, bump up.** [C16: prob. imit.]

bumper[1] ('bʌmpə) *n* **1** a horizontal usually metal bar attached to the front or rear end of a car, lorry, etc., to protect against damage from impact. **2** *Cricket.* a ball bowled so that it bounces high on pitching; bouncer.

bumper[2] Ⓣ ('bʌmpə) *n* **1** a glass, tankard, etc., filled to the brim, esp. as a toast. **2** an unusually large or fine example of something. ◆ *adj* **3** unusually large, fine, or abundant: *a bumper crop.* [C17 (in the sense: a brimming glass): prob. from *bump* (obs. vb) to bulge; see BUMP]

bumph (bʌmf) *n* a variant spelling of **bumf.**

bump into Ⓣ *vb* (*intr, prep*) *Inf.* to meet by chance; encounter unexpectedly.

bumpkin Ⓣ ('bʌmpkɪn) *n* an awkward simple rustic person (esp. in **country bumpkin**). [C16: ?from Du. *boomken* small tree, or from MDu. *boomekijn* small barrel]

bump off Ⓣ *vb* (*tr, adv*) *Sl.* to murder; kill.

bumptious Ⓣ ('bʌmpʃəs) *adj* offensively self-assertive or conceited. [C19: ?from BUMP + FRACTIOUS]
▸**'bumptiously** *adv* ▸**'bumptiousness** *n*

bump up *vb* (*tr, adv*) *Inf.* to raise or increase.

bumpy Ⓣ ('bʌmpɪ) *adj* **bumpier, bumpiest. 1** having an uneven surface. **2** full of jolts; rough.
▸**'bumpily** *adv* ▸**'bumpiness** *n*

bun (bʌn) *n* **1** a small roll, similar to bread but usually containing sweetening, currants, etc. **2** any of various small round cakes. **3** a hairstyle in which long hair is gathered into a bun shape at the back of the head. [C14: from ?]

bunch Ⓣ (bʌntʃ) *n* **1** a number of things growing, fastened, or grouped together: *a bunch of grapes; a bunch of keys.* **2** a collection; group: *a bunch of queries.* **3** *Inf.* a group or company: *a bunch of boys.* ◆ *vb* **4** (sometimes foll. by *up*) to group or be grouped into a bunch. [C14: from ?]

bunchy ('bʌntʃɪ) *adj* **bunchier, bunchiest. 1** composed of or resembling bunches. **2** bulging.

buncombe ('bʌŋkəm) *n* a variant spelling (esp. US) of **bunkum.**

bundle Ⓣ ('bʌndəl) *n* **1** a number of things or a quantity of material gathered or loosely bound together: *a bundle of sticks.* Related adj: **fascicular. 2** something wrapped or tied for carrying; package. **3** *Sl.* a large sum of money. **4 go a bundle on.** *Sl.* to be extremely fond of. **5** *Biol.* a collection of strands of specialized tissue such as nerve fibres. **6** *Bot.* short for **vascular bundle. 7 drop one's bundle.** *Austral. & NZ sl.* to panic or give up hope. ◆ *vb* **bundles, bundling, bundled. 8** (*tr;* often foll. by *up*) to make into a bundle. **9** (foll. by *out, off, into,* etc.) to go or cause to go, esp. roughly or unceremoniously. **10** (*tr;* usually foll. by *into*) to push or throw, esp. quickly and untidily. **11** (*tr*) to give away (a relatively cheap product) when selling an expensive one to attract business: *software is often bundled with computers.* **12** (*intr*) to sleep or lie in one's clothes on the same bed as one's betrothed: formerly a custom in New England, Wales, and elsewhere. [C14: prob. from MDu. *bundel;* rel. to OE *bindele* bandage; see BIND, BOND]
▸**'bundler** *n*

bundle up Ⓣ *vb* (*adv*) **1** to dress (somebody) warmly and snugly. **2** (*tr*) to make (something) into a bundle or bundles, esp. by tying.

bun fight *n Brit. sl.* **1** a tea party. **2** *Ironic.* an official function.

bung[1] (bʌŋ) *n* **1** a stopper, esp. of cork or rubber, for a cask, etc. **2** short for **bunghole.** ◆ *vb* (*tr*) **3** (often foll. by *up*) *Inf.* to close or seal with or as with a bung. **4** *Brit. sl.* to throw; sling. **5 bung it on.** *Austral. sl.* to behave in a pretentious manner. [C15: from MDu. *bonghe*]

bung[2] (bʌŋ) *adj Austral. & NZ inf.* **1** useless. **2 go bung. 2a** to fail or collapse. **2b** to die. [C19: from Abor.]

bungalow ('bʌŋgəˌləʊ) *n* a one-storey house, sometimes with an attic. [C17: from Hindi *banglā* (house) of the Bengal type]

bungee jumping *or* **bungy jumping** ('bʌndʒɪ) *n* a sport in which a participant jumps from a high bridge, building, etc., secured only by a rubber cord attached to the ankles. [C20: from *bungie,* slang for India rubber, of unknown origin]

bunghole ('bʌŋˌhəʊl) *n* a hole in a cask, barrel, etc., through which liquid can be drained.

bungle Ⓣ ('bʌŋgəl) *vb* **bungles, bungling, bungled. 1** (*tr*) to spoil (an operation) through clumsiness, incompetence, etc. ◆ *n* **2** a clumsy or unsuccessful performance. [C16: ? of Scand. origin]
▸**'bungler** *n* ▸**'bungling** *adj, n*

bunion ('bʌnjən) *n* an inflamed swelling of the first joint of the big toe. [C18: ?from obs. *bunny* a swelling, from ?]

bunk[1] (bʌŋk) *n* **1** a narrow shelflike bed fixed along a wall. **2** short for **bunk bed. 3** *Inf.* any place where one sleeps. ◆ *vb* **4** (*intr;* often foll. by *down*) to prepare to sleep: *he bunked down on the floor.* **5** (*intr*) to occupy a bunk or bed. [C19: prob. short for BUNKER]

bunk[2] (bʌŋk) *n Inf.* short for **bunkum** (sense 1).

bunk[3] Ⓣ (bʌŋk) *n Brit. sl.* a hurried departure, usually under suspicious circumstances (esp. in **do a bunk**). [C19: ?from BUNK[1] (in the sense: to occupy a bunk, hence a hurried departure)]

bunk bed *n* one of a pair of beds constructed one above the other to save space.

bunker ('bʌŋkə) *n* **1** a large storage container or tank, as for coal. **2** Also called (esp. US and Canad.): **sand trap.** an obstacle on a golf course, usually a sand-filled hollow bordered by a ridge. **3** an underground shelter with a bank and embrasures for guns above ground. ◆ *vb* **4** (*tr*) *Golf.* **4a** to drive (the ball) into a bunker. **4b** (*passive*) to have one's ball trapped in a bunker. [C16 (in the sense: chest, box): from Scot. *bonkar,* from ?]

bunkhouse ('bʌŋkˌhaʊs) *n* (in the US and Canada) a building containing the sleeping quarters of workers on a ranch.

bunkum Ⓣ *or* **buncombe** ('bʌŋkəm) *n* **1** empty talk; nonsense. **2** *Chiefly US.* empty or insincere speechmaking by a politician. [C19: after *Buncombe,* a county in North Carolina, alluded to in an inane speech by its Congressional representative Felix Walker (about 1820)]

bunny ('bʌnɪ) *n, pl* **bunnies. 1** Also called: **bunny rabbit.** a child's word for **rabbit** (sense 1). **2** Also called: **bunny girl.** a night-club hostess whose costume includes rabbit-like tail and ears. **3** *Austral. sl.* a mug; dupe. [C17: from Scot. Gaelic *bun* scut of a rabbit]

Bunsen burner ('bʌnsən) *n* a gas burner consisting of a metal tube with an adjustable air valve at the base. [C19: after R. W. *Bunsen* (1811–99), G chemist]

bunting[1] ('bʌntɪŋ) *n* **1** a coarse, loosely woven cotton fabric used for flags, etc. **2** decorative flags, pennants, and streamers. [C18: from ?]

bunting[2] ('bʌntɪŋ) *n* any of numerous seed-eating songbirds of the Old World and North America having short stout bills. [C13: from ?]

buntline ('bʌntlɪn, -ˌlaɪn) *n Naut.* one of several lines fastened to the foot of a square sail for hauling it up to the yard when furling. [C17: from *bunt* centre of a sail + LINE[1] (sense 11)]

bunya ('bʌnjə) *n* a tall dome-shaped Australian coniferous tree having edible cones (**bunya nuts**) and thickish flattened needles. Also called: **bunya-bunya.** [C19: from Abor.]

bunyip ('bʌnjɪp) *n Austral.* a legendary monster said to inhabit swamps and lagoons. [C19: from Abor.]

buoy Ⓣ (bɔɪ; *US* 'buːɪ) *n* **1** a distinctively shaped and coloured float, anchored to the bottom, for designating moorings, navigable channels,

THESAURUS

lump, bulge, contusion, hump, knob, knot, node, nodule, protuberance, swelling

bumper[2] *adj* **3 = exceptional**, abundant, bountiful, excellent, jumbo (*inf.*), massive, mega (*sl.*), prodigal, spanking (*inf.*), teeming, unusual, whacking (*inf., chiefly Brit.*), whopping (*inf.*)

bump into *vb Informal* **= meet**, chance upon, come across, encounter, happen upon, light upon, meet up with, run across, run into

bumpkin *n* **= yokel**, boor, clodhopper, clown, country bumpkin, hayseed (*US & Canad. inf.*), hick (*inf., chiefly US & Canad.*), hillbilly, lout, oaf, peasant, rustic

bump off *vb Slang* **= murder**, assassinate, blow away (*sl., chiefly US*), dispatch, do away with, do in (*sl.*), eliminate, finish off, kill, knock off (*sl.*), liquidate, remove, take out (*sl.*), wipe out (*inf.*)

bumptious *adj* **= cocky**, arrogant, boastful, brash, conceited, egotistic, forward, full of oneself, impudent, overbearing, overconfident, presumptuous, pushy (*inf.*), self-assertive, showy, swaggering, vainglorious, vaunting

bumpy *adj* **1 = uneven**, irregular, knobby, lumpy, pitted, potholed, rough, rutted **2 = rough**, bone-breaking, bouncy, choppy, jarring, jerky, jolting

bunch *n* **1, 2 = number**, assortment, batch, bouquet, bundle, clump, cluster, collection, heap, lot, mass, parcel, pile, quantity, rick, sheaf, spray, stack, tuft **3** *Informal* **= group**, band, bevy, crew (*inf.*), crowd, flock, gang, gathering, knot, mob, multitude, party, posse (*inf.*), swarm, team, troop ◆ *vb* **4 = group**, assemble, bundle, cluster, collect, congregate, cram together, crowd, flock, herd, huddle, mass, pack

bundle *n* **1 = bunch**, accumulation, assortment, batch, collection, group, heap, mass, pile, quantity, rick, stack **2 = package**, bag, bale, box, carton, crate, pack, packet, pallet, parcel, roll ◆ *vb* **8 = package**, bale, bind, fasten, pack, palletize, tie, tie together, tie up, truss, wrap **9, 10** *with* **out, off, into,** etc. **= push**, hurry, hustle, rush, shove, throw, thrust

bundle up *vb* **1 = wrap up**, clothe warmly, muffle up, swathe

bungle *vb* **1 = mess up**, blow (*sl.*), blunder, bodge, botch, butcher, cock up (*Brit. sl.*), drop a brick *or* clanger (*inf.*), foul up, make a mess of, make a nonsense of (*inf.*), make a pig's ear of (*inf.*), mar, miscalculate, mismanage, muff, ruin, screw up (*inf.*), spoil
Antonyms *vb* accomplish, achieve, carry off, effect, fulfil, succeed, triumph

bungler *n* **1 = incompetent**, blunderer, botcher, butcher, butterfingers (*inf.*), duffer (*inf.*), fumbler, lubber, muddler, muff

bungling *adj* **1 = incompetent**, awkward, blundering, botching, cack-handed (*inf.*), clumsy, ham-fisted (*inf.*), ham-handed, inept, maladroit, unskilful

bunk[3] *vb* **do a bunk** *Brit. slang* **= run away**, abscond, beat it (*sl.*), bolt, clear out (*inf.*), cut and run (*inf.*), decamp, do a runner (*sl.*), flee, fly the coop (*US & Canad. inf.*), run for it (*inf.*), scram (*inf.*), skedaddle (*inf.*)

bunkum *n* **1 = nonsense**, balderdash, balls (*taboo sl.*), baloney (*inf.*), bilge (*inf.*), bosh (*inf.*), bullshit (*taboo sl.*), cobblers (*Brit. taboo sl.*), crap (*sl.*), garbage (*inf.*), hogwash, hokum (*sl., chiefly US & Canad.*), hot air (*inf.*), piffle (*inf.*), poppycock (*inf.*), rot, rubbish, shit (*taboo sl.*), stuff and nonsense, tommyrot, tosh (*sl., chiefly Brit.*), trash, tripe (*inf.*), twaddle

buoy *n* **1 = marker**, beacon, float, guide, signal ◆ *vb* **3 buoy up = encourage**, boost, cheer,

or obstructions in a body of water. See also **life buoy.** ◆ *vb* **2** (*tr; usually foll. by up*) to prevent from sinking: *the life belt buoyed him up.* **3** (*tr; usually foll. by up*) to raise the spirits of; hearten. **4** (*tr*) *Naut.* to mark (a channel or obstruction) with a buoy or buoys. **5** (*intr*) to rise to the surface; float. [C13: prob. of Gmc origin]

buoyancy ➊ ('bɔɪənsɪ) *n* **1** the ability to float in a liquid or to rise in liquid, air, or other gas. **2** the tendency of a fluid to keep a body afloat. **3** the ability to recover quickly after setbacks; resilience. **4** cheerfulness.

buoyant ➊ ('bɔɪənt) *adj* **1** able to float in or rise to the surface of a liquid. **2** (of a liquid or gas) able to keep a body afloat. **3** cheerful or resilient. [C16: prob. from Sp. *boyante,* from *boyar* to float]

BUPA ('bu:pə) *n acronym for* The British United Provident Association Limited: a company which provides private medical insurance.

bupivacaine (bju:'pɪvəˌkeɪn) *n* a local anaesthetic of long duration, used for nerve blocks. [C20: ?from BU(TYL) + *pi(pecoloxylidide)* + *-vacaine,* from (NO)VOCAINE]

bur (bɜ:) *n* **1** a seed vessel or flower head having hooks or prickles. **2** any plant that produces burs. **3** a person or thing that clings like a bur. **4** a small surgical or dental drill. ◆ *vb* **burs, burring, burred. 5** (*tr*) to remove burs from. ◆ Also: **burr.** [C14: prob. from ON]

burble ('bɜ:bᵊl) *vb* **burbles, burbling, burbled. 1** to make or utter with a bubbling sound; gurgle. **2** (*intr; often foll. by away or on*) to talk quickly and excitedly. ◆ *n* **3** a bubbling or gurgling sound. **4** a flow of excited speech. [C14: prob. imit.]
▸**'burbler** *n*

burbot ('bɜ:bət) *n, pl* **burbots** *or* **burbot.** a freshwater gadoid food fish that has barbels around its mouth and occurs in Europe, Asia, and North America. [C14: from OF *bourbotte,* from *bourbeter* to wallow in mud, from *bourbe* mud]

burden[1] ➊ ('bɜ:dᵊn) *n* **1** something that is carried; load. **2** something that is exacting, oppressive, or difficult to bear. Related adj: **onerous. 3** *Naut.* **3a** the cargo capacity of a ship. **3b** the weight of a ship's cargo. ◆ *vb* (*tr*) **4** (sometimes foll. by *up*) to put or impose a burden on; load. **5** to weigh down; oppress. [OE *byrthen*]

burden[2] ('bɜ:dᵊn) *n* **1** a line of words recurring at the end of each verse of a song; chorus or refrain. **2** the theme of a speech, book, etc. **3** another word for **bourdon.** [C16: from OF *bourdon* bass horn, droning sound, imit.]

burden of proof *n Law.* the obligation to provide evidence that will convince the court or jury of the truth of one's contention.

burdensome ➊ ('bɜ:dᵊnsəm) *adj* hard to bear.

burdock ('bɜ:ˌdɒk) *n* a coarse weedy Eurasian plant having large heart-shaped leaves, tiny purple flowers surrounded by hooked bristles, and burlike fruits. [C16: from BUR + DOCK[4]]

bureau ➊ ('bjʊərəʊ) *n, pl* **bureaus** *or* **bureaux. 1** *Chiefly Brit.* a writing desk with pigeonholes, drawers, etc., against which the writing surface can be closed when not in use. **2** *US.* a chest of drawers. **3** an office or agency, esp. one providing services for the public. **4** a government department. [C17: from F, orig.: type of cloth used for covering desks, from OF *burel*]

bureaucracy ➊ (bjʊə'rɒkrəsɪ) *n, pl* **bureaucracies. 1** a system of administration based upon organization into bureaus, division of labour, a hierarchy of authority, etc. **2** government by such a system. **3** government or other officials collectively. **4** any administration in which action is impeded by unnecessary official procedures.

bureaucrat ➊ ('bjʊərəˌkræt) *n* **1** an official in a bureaucracy. **2** an official who adheres to bureaucracy, esp. rigidly.
▸**ˌbureau'cratic** *adj* ▸**ˌbureau'cratically** *adv*

bureaucratize *or* **bureaucratise** (bjʊə'rɒkrəˌtaɪz) *vb* **bureaucratizes, bureaucratizing, bureaucratized** *or* **bureaucratises, bureaucratising, bureaucratised.** (*tr*) to administer by or transform into a bureaucracy.
▸**buˌreaucrati'zation** *or* **buˌreaucrati'sation** *n*

bureaux ('bjʊərəʊz) *n* a plural of **bureau.**

burette *or US* **buret** (bjʊ'rɛt) *n* a graduated glass tube with a stopcock on one end for dispensing and transferring known volumes of fluids, esp. liquids. [C15: from F, from OF *buire* ewer]

burg (bɜ:g) *n* **1** *History.* a fortified town. **2** *US inf.* a town or city. [C18 (in the sense: fortress): from OHG *burg*]

burgage ('bɜ:gɪdʒ) *n History.* **1** (in England) tenure of land or tenement in a town or city, which originally involved a fixed money rent. **2** (in Scotland) the tenure of land direct from the crown in Scottish royal burghs in return for watching and warding. [C14: from Med. L *burgāgium,* from OE *burg*]

burgeon *or* **bourgeon** ('bɜ:dʒən) *vb* **1** (often foll. by *forth* or *out*) (of a plant) to sprout (buds). **2** (*intr; often foll. by forth or out*) to develop or grow rapidly; flourish. [C13: from OF *burjon*]

burger ('bɜ:gə) *n Inf.* **a** short for **hamburger. b** (*in combination*): *a cheeseburger.*

burgess ('bɜ:dʒɪs) *n* **1** (in England) a citizen, freeman, or inhabitant of a borough. **2** *English history.* a Member of Parliament from a borough, corporate town, or university. [C13: from OF *burgeis;* see BOROUGH]

burgh ('bʌrə) *n* **1** (in Scotland until 1975) a town, esp. one incorporated by charter, that enjoyed a degree of self-government. **2** an archaic form of **borough.** [C14: Scot. form of BOROUGH]
▸**burghal** ('bɜ:gᵊl) *adj*

burgher ('bɜ:gə) *n* **1** a member of the trading or mercantile class of a medieval city. **2** a respectable citizen; bourgeois. **3** *Arch.* a citizen or inhabitant of a corporate town, esp on the Continent. **4** *S. African history.* a citizen of the Cape Colony or of one of the Transvaal and Free State republics. [C16: from G *Bürger* or Du. *burger* freeman of a BOROUGH]

burglar ➊ ('bɜ:glə) *n* a person who commits burglary; housebreaker. [C15: from Anglo-F, from Med. L *burglātor,* prob. from *burgāre* to thieve]

burglary ➊ ('bɜ:glərɪ) *n, pl* **burglaries.** the crime of entering a building as a trespasser to commit theft or another offence.
▸**burglarious** (bɜ:'glɛərɪəs) *adj*

burgle ('bɜ:gᵊl) *vb* **burgles, burgling, burgled.** to commit burglary upon (a house, etc.).

burgomaster ('bɜ:gəˌmɑ:stə) *n* the chief magistrate of a town in Austria, Belgium, Germany, or the Netherlands; mayor. [C16: partial translation of Du. *burgemeester;* see BOROUGH, MASTER]

Burgundy ('bɜ:gəndɪ) *n, pl* **Burgundies. 1a** any red or white wine produced in the region of Burgundy, around Dijon. **1b** any heavy red table wine. **2** (*often not cap.*) a blackish-purple to purplish-red colour. [OE *byrgels* burial place, tomb; see BURY, -AL[2]]

burial ➊ ('bɛrɪəl) *n* the act of burying, esp. the interment of a dead body. [C17: from *Burgundy,* region of E France]

burial ground ➊ *n* a graveyard or cemetery.

burin ('bjʊərɪn) *n* **1** a chisel of tempered steel used for engraving metal, wood, or marble. **2** *Archaeol.* a prehistoric flint tool. [C17: from F, ?from It. *burino,* of Gmc origin]

burk (bɜ:k) *n* a variant spelling of **berk.**

burl[1] (bɜ:l) *n* **1** a small knot or lump in wool. **2** a roundish warty outgrowth from certain trees. ◆ *vb* **3** (*tr*) to remove the burls from (cloth). [C15: from OF *burle* tuft of wool, prob. ult. from LL *burra* shaggy cloth]

burl[2] *or* **birl** (bɜ:l) *n Inf.* **1** *Scot., Austral., & NZ.* an attempt; try (esp. in **give it a burl**). **2** *Austral, & NZ.* a ride in a car. [C20: ?from BIRL in Scots sense: to spin or turn]

burlap ('bɜ:læp) *n* a coarse fabric woven from jute, hemp, or the like. [C17: from *borel* coarse cloth, from OF *burel* (see BUREAU) + LAP[1]]

burlesque ➊ (bɜ:'lɛsk) *n* **1** an artistic work, esp. literary or dramatic, satirizing a subject by caricaturing it. **2** a ludicrous imitation or caricature. **3** Also: **burlesk.** *US. & Canad. theatre.* a bawdy comedy show of the late 19th and early 20th centuries: the striptease eventually became one of its chief elements. ◆ *adj* **4** of, relating to, or characteristic of a burlesque. ◆ *vb* **burlesques, burlesquing, burlesqued. 5** to represent or imitate (a person or thing) in a ludicrous way; caricature. [C17: from F, from It., from *burla* a jest, piece of nonsense]
▸**bur'lesquer** *n*

burley ('bɜ:lɪ) *n* a variant spelling of **berley.**

THESAURUS

cheer up, gee up, hearten, lift, raise, support, sustain

buoyancy *n* **1** = **lightness**, floatability, weightlessness **4** = **cheerfulness**, animation, bounce, cheeriness, good humour, high spirits, liveliness, pep, spiritedness, sunniness, zing (*inf.*)

buoyant *adj* **1** = **floating**, afloat, floatable, light, weightless **3** = **cheerful**, animated, blithe, bouncy, breezy, bright, carefree, chirpy (*inf.*), debonair, full of beans (*inf.*), genial, happy, jaunty, joyful, light-hearted, lively, peppy (*inf.*), sparky, sunny, upbeat (*inf.*), vivacious
Antonyms *adj* ≠ **cheerful:** cheerless, depressed, despairing, dull, forlorn, gloomy, glum, hopeless, melancholy, moody, morose, pessimistic, sad, sullen, unhappy

burden[1] *n* **1** = **load**, encumbrance, weight **2** = **trouble**, affliction, albatross, anxiety, care, clog, encumbrance, grievance, millstone, obstruction, onus, pigeon (*inf.*), responsibility, sorrow, strain, stress, trial, weight, worry **3** *Nautical* = **tonnage**, cargo, freight, lading ◆ *vb* **5** = **weigh down**, bother, encumber, handicap, load, oppress, overload, overwhelm, saddle with, strain, tax, worry

burdensome *adj* = **troublesome**, crushing, difficult, exacting, heavy, irksome, onerous, oppressive, taxing, trying, weighty

bureau *n* **1** *Chiefly Brit.* = **desk**, writing desk **3, 4** = **office**, agency, branch, department, division, service

bureaucracy *n* **1-3** = **government**, administration, authorities, civil service, corridors of power, directorate, ministry, officialdom, officials, the system **4** = **red tape**, officialdom, regulations

bureaucrat *n* **1** = **official**, apparatchik, civil servant, functionary, mandarin, minister, office-holder, officer, public servant

burglar *n* = **housebreaker**, cat burglar, picklock, robber, sneak thief, thief

burglary *n* = **breaking and entering**, break-in, housebreaking, larceny, robbery, stealing, theft, thieving

burial *n* = **interment**, burying, entombment, funeral, inhumation, obsequies

burial ground *n* = **graveyard**, cemetery, churchyard, necropolis

buried *adj* **1** = **interred**, coffined, consigned to the grave, entombed, laid to rest **3** = **hidden**, cloistered, concealed, private, sequestered, tucked away **5** = **engrossed**, caught up, committed, concentrating, devoted, immersed, intent, lost, occupied, preoccupied, rapt **6** = **forgotten**, covered, hidden, repressed, sunk in oblivion, suppressed

burlesque *n* **1, 2** = **parody**, caricature, mock, mockery, satire, send-up (*Brit. inf.*), spoof (*inf.*), takeoff (*inf.*), travesty ◆ *adj* **4** = **satirical**, caricatural, comic, farcical, ironical, ludicrous, mock, mock-heroic, mocking, parodic, travestying ◆ *vb* **5** = **satirize**, ape, caricature, exaggerate, imitate, lampoon, make a monkey out of, make fun of, mock, parody, ridicule, send up (*Brit. inf.*), spoof (*inf.*), take off (*inf.*), take the piss out of (*taboo sl.*), travesty

burly ⓣ ('bɜːlɪ) *adj* **burlier, burliest.** large and thick of build; sturdy. [C13: of Gmc origin]
▸ **'burliness** *n*

Burmese (bɜː'miːz) *adj also* **Burman. 1** of or denoting Burma (now Myanmar), a country of SE Asia, or its inhabitants, their customs, etc. ◆ *n* **2** (*pl* **Burmese**) a native or inhabitant of Burma (Myanmar). **3** the language of the Burmese.

burn[1] ⓣ (bɜːn) *vb* **burns, burning, burnt** *or* **burned. 1** to undergo or cause to undergo combustion. **2** to destroy or be destroyed by fire. **3** (*tr*) to damage, injure, or mark by heat: *he burnt his hand; she was burnt by the sun.* **4** to die or put to death by fire. **5** (*intr*) to be or feel hot: *my forehead burns.* **6** to smart or cause to smart: *brandy burns one's throat.* **7** (*intr*) to feel strong emotion, esp. anger or passion. **8** (*tr*) to use for the purposes of light, heat, or power: *to burn coal.* **9** (*tr*) to form by or as if by fire: *to burn a hole.* **10** to char or become charred: *the potatoes are burning.* **11** (*tr*) to brand or cauterize. **12** to produce by or subject to heat as part of a process: *to burn charcoal.* **13 burn one's bridges** *or* **boats.** to commit oneself to a particular course of action with no possibility of turning back. **14 burn one's fingers.** to suffer from having meddled or interfered. ◆ *n* **15** an injury caused by exposure to heat, electrical, chemical, or radioactive agents. **16** a mark, e.g. on wood, caused by burning. **17** a controlled use of rocket propellant, esp. for a course correction. **18** a hot painful sensation in a muscle, experienced during vigorous exercise. **19** *Sl.* tobacco or a cigarette. ◆ See also **burn out.** [OE *beornan* (intr), *bærnan* (tr)]

burn[2] (bɜːn) *n Scot. & N English.* a small stream; brook. [OE *burna;* rel. to ON *brunnr* spring]

burner ('bɜːnə) *n* **1** the part of a stove, lamp, etc., that produces flame or heat. **2** an apparatus for burning something, as fuel or refuse.

burnet ('bɜːnɪt) *n* **1** a plant of the rose family which has purple-tinged green flowers and leaves. **2 burnet rose.** a very prickly Eurasian rose with white flowers and purplish-black fruits. **3** a moth with red-spotted dark green wings and antennae with enlarged tips. [C14: from OF *burnete,* var. of *brunete* BRUNETTE]

burning ⓣ ('bɜːnɪŋ) *adj* **1** intense; passionate. **2** urgent; crucial: *a burning problem.*

burning bush *n* **1** any of several shrubs or trees that have bright red fruits or seeds. **2** any of several plants with a bright red autumn foliage. **3** *Bible.* the bush that burned without being consumed, from which God spoke to Moses (Exodus 3:2–4).

burning glass *n* a convex lens for concentrating the sun's rays to produce fire.

burnish ⓣ ('bɜːnɪʃ) *vb* **1** to make or become shiny or smooth by friction; polish. ◆ *n* **2** a shiny finish; lustre. [C14 *burnischen,* from OF *brunir* to make brown, from *brun* BROWN]
▸ **'burnisher** *n*

burnoose, burnous, *or* **burnouse** (bɜː'nuːs, -'nuːz) *n* a long circular cloak with a hood attached, worn esp. by Arabs. [C20: via F *burnous* from Ar. *burnus,* from Gk *birros* cloak]

burn out *vb* (*adv*) **1** to become or cause to become inoperative as a result of heat or friction: *the clutch burnt out.* **2** (*intr*) (of a rocket, jet engine, etc.) to cease functioning as a result of exhaustion of the fuel supply. **3** (*tr; usually passive*) to destroy by fire. **4** to become or cause to become exhausted through overwork or dissipation.

burnt (bɜːnt) *vb* **1** a past tense and past participle of **burn**[1]. ◆ *adj* **2** affected by or as if by burning; charred.

burnt offering *n* a sacrificial offering burnt, usually on an altar, to honour, propitiate, or supplicate a deity.

burnt sienna *n* **1** a reddish-brown pigment obtained by roasting raw sienna. ◆ *n, adj* **2** (of) a reddish-brown colour.

burnt umber *n* **1** a brown pigment obtained by heating umber. ◆ *n, adj* **2** (of) a dark brown colour.

burp (bɜːp) *n* **1** *Inf.* a belch. ◆ *vb* **2** (*intr*) *Inf.* to belch. **3** (*tr*) to cause (a baby) to burp. [C20: imit.]

burr[1] (bɜː) *n* **1** a small power-driven hand-operated rotary file, esp. for removing burrs or for machining recesses. **2** a rough edge left on a workpiece after cutting, drilling, etc. **3** a rough or irregular protuberance, such as a burl on a tree. **4** a variant spelling of **bur.** [C14: var. of BUR]

burr[2] (bɜː) *n* **1** an articulation of (r) characteristic of certain English dialects, esp. the uvular fricative trill of Northumberland or the retroflex *r* of the West of England. **2** a whirring sound. ◆ *vb* **3** to pronounce (words) with a burr. **4** (*intr*) to make a whirring sound. [C18: either special use of BUR (in the sense: rough sound) or imit.]

burrito (bə'riːtəʊ) *n, pl* **burritos.** *Mexican cookery.* a tortilla folded over a filling of minced beef, chicken, cheese, or beans. [C20: from Mexican Sp., from Sp.: literally, a young donkey]

burro ('bʊrəʊ) *n, pl* **burros.** a donkey, esp. one used as a pack animal. [C19: Sp., from Port., from *burrico*]

burrow ⓣ ('bʌrəʊ) *n* **1** a hole dug in the ground by a rabbit or other small animal. **2** a small snug place affording shelter or retreat. ◆ *vb* **3** to dig (a burrow) in, through, or under (ground). **4** (*intr;* often foll. by *through*) to move through by or as by digging. **5** (*intr*) to hide or live in a burrow. **6** (*intr*) to delve deeply: *he burrowed into his pockets.* **7** to hide (oneself). [C13: prob. var. of BOROUGH]
▸ **'burrower** *n*

burry ('bɜːrɪ) *adj* **burrier, burriest. 1** full of or covered in burs. **2** resembling burs; prickly.

bursa ('bɜːsə) *n, pl* **bursae** (-siː) *or* **bursas. 1** *Anat.* a small fluid-filled sac that reduces friction, esp. at joints. **2** *Zool.* any saclike cavity or structure. [C19: from Med. L: bag, pouch, from Gk: skin, hide; see PURSE]
▸ **'bursal** *adj*

bursar ('bɜːsə) *n* **1** a treasurer of a school, college, or university. **2** *Chiefly Scot. & NZ.* a student holding a bursary. [C13: from Med. L *bursārius* keeper of the purse, from *bursa* purse]

bursary ('bɜːsərɪ) *n, pl* **bursaries. 1** Also called: **'bursar,ship.** a scholarship awarded esp. in Scottish and New Zealand schools and universities. **2** *Brit.* the treasury of a college, etc.
▸ **bursarial** (bɜː'sɛərɪəl) *adj*

bursitis (bɜː'saɪtɪs) *n* inflammation of a bursa.

burst ⓣ (bɜːst) *vb* **bursts, bursting, burst. 1** to break or cause to break open or apart suddenly and noisily; explode. **2** (*intr*) to come, go, etc., suddenly and forcibly: *he burst into the room.* **3** (*intr*) to be full to the point of breaking open. **4** (*intr*) to give vent (to) suddenly or loudly: *to burst into song.* **5** (*tr*) to cause or suffer the rupture of: *to burst a blood vessel.* ◆ *n* **6** a sudden breaking open; explosion. **7** a break; breach; rupture. **8** a sudden display or increase of effort; spurt: *a burst of speed.* **9** a sudden and violent emission, occurrence, or outbreak: *a burst of applause.* **10** a volley of fire from a weapon. [OE *berstan*]

burthen ('bɜːðən) *n, vb* an archaic word for **burden**[1].
▸ **'burthensome** *adj*

burton ('bɜːtᵊn) *n* **go for a burton.** *Brit. sl.* **a** to be broken, useless, or lost. **b** to die. [C20: from ?]

bury ⓣ ('berɪ) *vb* **buries, burying, buried.** (*tr*) **1** to place (a corpse) in a grave; inter. **2** to place in the earth and cover with soil. **3** to cover from sight; hide. **4** to embed; sink: *to bury a nail in plaster.* **5** to occupy (oneself) with deep concentration; engross: *to be buried in a book.* **6** to dismiss from the mind; abandon: *to bury old hatreds.* [OE *byrgan*]

bus (bʌs) *n, pl* **buses** *or* **busses. 1** a large motor vehicle designed to carry passengers between stopping places along a regular route. More formal name: **omnibus. 2** (*modifier*) of or relating to a bus or buses: *a bus driver; a bus station.* **3** *Inf.* a car or aircraft, esp. one that is old and shaky. **4** *Electronics, computing.* short for **busbar. 5** *Astronautics.* a platform in a space vehicle used for various experiments and processes. **6 miss the bus.** to miss an opportunity. ◆ *vb* **buses, busing, bused** *or* **busses, bussing, bussed. 7** to travel or transport by bus. **8** *Chiefly US & Canad.* to transport (children) by bus from one area to another in order to create racially integrated schools. [C19: short for OMNIBUS]

bus. *abbrev. for* business.

busbar ('bʌz,bɑː) *n* **1** an electrical conductor usually used to make a common connection between several circuits. **2** a group of such electrical conductors maintained at a low voltage, used for carrying data in binary form between the various parts of a computer or its peripherals.

busby ('bʌzbɪ) *n, pl* **busbies. 1** a tall fur helmet worn by hussars. **2** (not in official usage) another name for **bearskin** (the hat). [C18: ?from a proper name]

bush[1] ⓣ (bʊʃ) *n* **1** a dense woody plant, smaller than a tree, with many branches arising from the lower part of the stem; shrub. **2** a dense cluster of such shrubs; thicket. **3** something resembling a bush, esp.

THESAURUS

burly *adj* = **brawny**, beefy (*inf.*), big, bulky, hefty, hulking, muscular, powerful, stocky, stout, strapping, strong, sturdy, thickset, well-built
Antonyms *adj* lean, puny, scraggy, scrawny, slight, spare, thin, weak, weedy (*inf.*), wimpish *or* wimpy (*inf.*)

burn[1] *vb* **1** = **be on fire**, be ablaze, blaze, flame, flare, flash, flicker, glow, go up in flames, smoke **3** = **set on fire**, brand, char, ignite, incinerate, kindle, light, parch, reduce to ashes, scorch, sear, shrivel, singe, toast, wither **6** = **sting**, bite, hurt, pain, smart, tingle **7** = **be passionate**, be angry, be aroused, be excited, be inflamed, blaze, desire, fume, seethe, simmer, smoulder, yearn

burning *adj* **1** = **intense**, ablaze, afire, all-consuming, ardent, eager, earnest, fervent, fervid, flaming, frantic, frenzied, impassioned, passionate, vehement, zealous **2** = **crucial**, acute, compelling, critical, essential, important, now or never, pressing, significant, urgent, vital
Antonyms *adj* ≠ **intense:** apathetic, calm, cool, faint, indifferent, mild, passive

burnish *vb* **1** = **polish**, brighten, buff, furbish, glaze, rub up, shine, smooth ◆ *n* **2** = **shine**, gloss, lustre, patina, polish, sheen
Antonyms *vb* ≠ **polish:** abrade, graze, scratch, scuff

burrow *n* **1** = **hole**, den, lair, retreat, shelter, tunnel ◆ *vb* **3** = **dig**, delve, excavate, hollow out, scoop out, tunnel

burst *vb* **1** = **explode**, blow up, break, crack, disintegrate, fly open, fragment, puncture, rend asunder, rupture, shatter, shiver, split, tear apart **2** = **rush**, barge, break, break out, erupt, gush forth, run, spout ◆ *n* **6** = **explosion**, bang, blast, blasting, blowout, blow-up, breach, break, crack, discharge, rupture, split **8, 9** = **rush**, eruption, fit, gush, gust, outbreak, outburst, outpouring, spate, spurt, surge, torrent

bury *vb* **1** = **inter**, consign to the grave, entomb, inearth, inhume, lay to rest, sepulchre **3** = **hide**, conceal, cover, cover up, draw a veil over, enshroud, secrete, shroud, stash (*inf.*), stow away **4** = **embed**, drive in, engulf, implant, sink, submerge **5** = **engross**, absorb, engage, immerse, interest, occupy
Antonyms *vb* ≠ **inter, hide:** bring to light, dig up, discover, disinter, dredge up, exhume, expose, find, reveal, turn up, uncover, unearth

bush[1] *n* **1, 2** = **shrub**, hedge, plant, shrubbery, thicket **4** = **the wild**, back country (*US*), backlands, backwoods, brush, scrub, scrubland, woodland

in density: *a bush of hair.* **4** (often preceded by *the*) an uncultivated or sparsely settled area, covered with trees or shrubs, which can vary from open, shrubby country to dense rainforest. **5** a forested area; woodland. **6** *Canad.* Also called: **bush lot, woodlot.** an area on a farm on which timber is grown and cut. **7** (often preceded by *the*) *Inf.* the countryside, as opposed to the city: *out in the bush.* **8** *Obs.* a bunch of ivy hung as a vintner's sign in front of a tavern. **9 beat about the bush.** to avoid the point at issue; prevaricate. ◆ *adj* **10** *Austral. & NZ inf.* rough-and-ready. **11** *US & Canad. inf.* unprofessional, unpolished, or second-rate. **12 go bush.** *Inf.* **12a** *Austral. & NZ.* to abandon city amenities and live rough. **12b** *Austral.* to go into hiding. ◆ *vb* **13** (*intr*) to grow thick and bushy. **14** (*tr*) to cover, decorate, support, etc., with bushes. **15 bush it.** *Austral.* to camp out in the bush. [C13: of Gmc origin]

bush[2] (bʊʃ) *n* **1** a thin metal sleeve or tubular lining serving as a bearing. ◆ *vb* **2** to fit a bush to (a bearing, etc.). [C15: from MDu. *busse* box, bush; rel. to LL *buxis* BOX[1]]

bushbaby ('bʊʃˌbeɪbɪ) *n, pl* **bushbabies.** an agile nocturnal arboreal primate occurring in Africa south of the Sahara. It has large eyes and ears and a long tail. Also called: **galago.**

bushbuck ('bʊʃˌbʌk) *or* **boschbok** ('bɒʃˌbʌk) *n, pl* **bushbucks, bushbuck** *or* **boschboks, boschbok.** a small nocturnal spiral-horned antelope of the bush and tropical forest of Africa.

bush carpenter *n Austral. & NZ sl.* a rough-and-ready unskilled workman.

bushed (bʊʃt) *adj Inf.* **1** (*postpositive*) extremely tired; exhausted. **2** *Canad.* mentally disturbed from living in isolation. **3** *Austral. & NZ.* lost or bewildered, as in the bush.

bushel ('bʊʃəl) *n* **1** a British unit of dry or liquid measure equal to 8 Imperial gallons. 1 Imperial bushel is equivalent to 0.036 37 cubic metres. **2** a US unit of dry measure equal to 64 US pints. 1 US bushel is equivalent to 0.035 24 cubic metres. **3** a container with a capacity equal to either of these quantities. **4** *US inf.* a large amount. **5 hide one's light under a bushel.** to conceal one's abilities or good qualities. [C14: from OF *boissel*]

bushfire ('bʊʃˌfaɪə) *n* an uncontrolled fire in the bush; a scrub or forest fire.

bushfly ('bʊʃˌflaɪ) *n pl* **bushflies.** any of various small black dipterous flies of Australia that breed in faeces and dung.

bush house *n Chiefly Austral.* a shed or hut in the bush or a garden.

Bushido (ˌbuːʃɪ'dəʊ) *n* (*sometimes not cap.*) the feudal code of the Japanese samurai. [C19: from Japanese *bushi* warrior + *dō* way]

bushie ('bʊʃɪ) *n* a variant spelling of **bushy**[2].

bushing ('bʊʃɪŋ) *n* **1** another word for **bush**[2]. **2** an adaptor used to connect pipes of different sizes. **3** a layer of electrical insulation enabling a live conductor to pass through an earthed wall, etc.

bush jacket *or* **shirt** *n* a casual jacket or shirt having four patch pockets and a belt.

bush lawyer *n Austral. & NZ.* **1** a trailing plant with sharp hooks. **2** *Inf.* a person who gives legal opinions but is not qualified to do so.

bush line *n* an airline operating in the bush country of Canada's northern regions.

bushman ('bʊʃmən) *n, pl* **bushmen.** *Austral. & NZ.* a person who lives or travels in the bush, esp. one versed in bush lore.

Bushman ('bʊʃmən) *n, pl* **Bushmen.** a member of a hunting and gathering people of southern Africa. [C18: from Afrik. *boschjesman*]

bushmaster ('bʊʃˌmɑːstə) *n* a large greyish-brown highly venomous snake of tropical America.

bush pilot *n Canad.* a pilot who operates in the bush country.

bushranger ('bʊʃˌreɪndʒə) *n* **1** *Austral.* (formerly) an outlaw living in the bush. **2** *US.* a person who lives away from civilization.

bush tea *n* **1** a leguminous shrub of southern Africa. **2** a beverage prepared from the dried leaves of such a plant.

bush telegraph *n* a means of spreading rumour, gossip, etc.

bushveld ('bʊʃˌfɛlt) *n S. African.* bushy countryside. [from Afrik. *bosveld*]

bushwhack ('bʊʃˌwæk) *vb* **1** (*tr*) *US, Canad., & Austral.* to ambush. **2** (*intr*) *US, Canad., & Austral.* to cut or beat one's way through thick woods. **3** (*intr*) *US, Canad., & Austral.* to range or move around in woods or the bush. **4** (*intr*) *NZ.* to work in the bush. **5** (*intr*) *US & Canad.* to fight as a guerrilla in wild regions.

bushwhacker ('bʊʃˌwækə) *n* **1** *US, Canad., & Austral.* a person who travels around or lives in thinly populated woodlands. **2** *Austral. sl.* an unsophisticated person. **3** *NZ.* a person who works in the bush. **4** a Confederate guerrilla in the American Civil War. **5** *US.* any guerrilla.

bushy[1] Ⓣ ('bʊʃɪ) *adj* **bushier, bushiest. 1** covered or overgrown with bushes. **2** thick and shaggy.
▸ **'bushily** *adv* ▸ **'bushiness** *n*

bushy[2] *or* **bushie** ('bʊʃɪ) *n, pl* **bushies.** *Austral. inf.* **1** a person who lives in the bush. **2** an unsophisticated uncouth person.

business Ⓣ ('bɪznɪs) *n* **1** a trade or profession. **2** the purchase and sale of goods and services. **3** a commercial or industrial establishment. **4** commercial activity; dealings (esp. in **do business**). **5** volume of commercial activity: *business is poor today.* **6** commercial policy: *overcharging is bad business.* **7** proper or rightful concern or responsibility (often in **mind one's own business**). **8** a special task; assignment. **9** an affair; matter. **10** serious work or activity: *get down to business.* **11** a difficult or complicated matter. **12** *Theatre.* an incidental action performed by an actor for dramatic effect. **13 mean business.** to be in earnest. [OE *bisignis* solicitude, from *bisig* BUSY + *-nis* -NESS]

business college *n* a college providing courses in secretarial studies, business management, accounting, commerce, etc.

businesslike Ⓣ ('bɪznɪsˌlaɪk) *adj* efficient and methodical.

businessman Ⓣ ('bɪznɪsˌmæn, -mən) *or* (*fem*) **businesswoman** *n, pl* **businessmen** *or* **businesswomen.** a person engaged in commercial or industrial business, esp. as an owner or executive.

business park *n* an area specially designated and landscaped to accommodate offices, warehouses, etc.

business plan *n* a detailed plan setting out the objectives of a business, the strategy and tactics planned to achieve them, and the expected profits.

business process re-engineering *n* restructuring an organization by means of a reassessment of its core processes and predominant competencies. Abbrev.: **BPR.**

business school *n* an institution that offers courses in aspects of business, such as marketing, finance, and law, designed to train managers in industry and commerce to do their jobs effectively.

busk (bʌsk) *vb* (*intr*) *Brit.* to make money singing, playing an instrument, performing, or dancing in public places. [C20: ?from Sp. *buscar* to look for]
▸ **'busker** *n*

buskin ('bʌskɪn) *n* **1** (formerly) a sandal-like covering for the foot and leg, reaching the calf. **2** a thick-soled laced half-boot worn esp. by actors of ancient Greece. **3** (usually preceded by *the*) *Chiefly literary.* tragic drama. [C16: ?from Sp. *borzeguí*; rel. to OF *bouzequin*]

busman's holiday ('bʌsmənz) *n Inf.* a holiday spent doing the same as one does at work. [C20: from a bus driver having a driving holiday]

buss (bʌs) *n, vb* an archaic or dialect word for **kiss.** [C16: prob. imit.]

bust[1] Ⓣ (bʌst) *n* **1** the chest of a human being, esp. a woman's bosom. **2** a sculpture of the head, shoulders, and upper chest of a person. [C17: from F, from It. *busto* a sculpture, from ?]

bust[2] Ⓣ (bʌst) *Inf.* ◆ *vb* **busts, busting, busted** *or* **bust. 1** to burst or break. **2** to make or become bankrupt. **3** (*tr*) (of the police) to raid, search, or arrest. **4** (*tr*) *US & Canad.* to demote, esp. in military rank. ◆ *n* **5** a raid, search, or arrest by the police. **6** *Chiefly US.* a punch. **7** *US & Canad.* a failure, esp. bankruptcy. **8** a drunken party. ◆ *adj* **9** broken. **10** bankrupt. **11 go bust.** to become bankrupt. [C19: from a dialect pronunciation of BURST]

bustard ('bʌstəd) *n* a large terrestrial bird inhabiting open regions of the Old World. It has long strong legs, a heavy body, a long neck, and speckled plumage. [C15: from OF *bistarde*, from L *avis tarda* slow bird]

bustier ('buːstɪeɪ) *n* a type of close-fitting usually strapless top worn by women.

bustle[1] Ⓣ ('bʌsᵊl) *vb* **bustles, bustling, bustled. 1** (when *intr*, often foll. by *about*) to hurry or cause to hurry with a great show of energy or activity. ◆ *n* **2** energetic and noisy activity. [C16: prob. from obs. *buskle* to make energetic preparation]
▸ **'bustling** *adj*

bustle[2] ('bʌsᵊl) *n* a cushion or framework worn by women in the late 19th century at the back in order to expand the skirt. [C18: from ?]

bust-up *Inf.* ◆ *n* **1** a quarrel, esp. a serious one ending a friendship, etc. **2** *Brit.* a disturbance or brawl. ◆ *vb* **bust up** (*adv*) **3** (*intr*) to quarrel and part. **4** (*tr*) to disrupt (a meeting), esp. violently.

busy Ⓣ ('bɪzɪ) *adj* **busier, busiest. 1** actively or fully engaged; occupied. **2**

THESAURUS

bushy[1] *adj* **2** = **thick**, bristling, bristly, fluffy, fuzzy, luxuriant, rough, shaggy, spreading, stiff, unruly, wiry

busily *adv* **2** = **actively**, assiduously, briskly, carefully, diligently, earnestly, energetically, industriously, intently, purposefully, speedily, strenuously

business *n* **1** = **profession**, calling, career, craft, employment, function, job, line, métier, occupation, pursuit, trade, vocation, work **2** = **trade**, bargaining, commerce, dealings, industry, manufacturing, merchandising, selling, trading, transaction **3** = **establishment**, company, concern, corporation, enterprise, firm, organization, venture **7** = **concern**, assignment, duty, function, pigeon (*inf.*), responsibility, task **9** = **affair**, issue, matter, point, problem, question, subject, topic

businesslike *adj* = **efficient**, correct, matter-of-fact, methodical, orderly, organized, practical, professional, regular, routine, systematic, thorough, well-ordered, workaday
Antonyms *adj* careless, disorderly, disorganized, frivolous, impractical, inefficient, irregular, sloppy, unprofessional, unsystematic, untidy

businessman *n* = **executive**, capitalist, employer, entrepreneur, financier, industrialist, merchant, tradesman, tycoon

bust[1] *n* **1** = **bosom**, breast, chest, front, torso

bust[2] *Informal vb* **1** = **break**, burst, fracture, rupture **3** = **arrest**, catch, collar (*inf.*), cop (*sl.*), feel one's collar (*sl.*), lift (*sl.*), nab (*inf.*), nail (*inf.*), raid, search ◆ *n* **5** = **arrest**, capture, cop (*sl.*), raid, search, seizure ◆ *adj* **10** = **bankrupt**, broken, failed, insolvent, ruined

bustle[1] *vb* **1** = **hurry**, beetle, bestir, dash, flutter, fuss, hasten, rush, scamper, scramble, scurry, scuttle, stir, tear ◆ *n* **2** = **activity**, ado, agitation, commotion, excitement, flurry, fuss, haste, hurly-burly, hurry, pother, stir, to-do, tumult
Antonyms *vb* ≠ **hurry:** be indolent, idle, laze, lie around, loaf, loiter, loll, relax, rest, take it easy ◆ *n* ≠ **activity:** inaction, inactivity, quiet, quietness, stillness, tranquillity

bustling *adj* **1** = **busy**, active, astir, buzzing, crowded, energetic, eventful, full, humming, hustling, lively, rushing, stirring, swarming, teeming, thronged

busy *adj* **1** = **occupied**, active, assiduous, brisk, diligent, employed, engaged, engrossed, hard

crowded with or characterized by activity. **3** *Chiefly US & Canad.* (of a room, telephone line, etc.) in use; engaged. **4** overcrowded with detail: *a busy painting.* **5** meddlesome; inquisitive. ◆ *vb* **busies, busying, busied. 6** (*tr*) to make or keep (someone, esp. oneself) busy. [OE *bisig*] ▸ **'busily** *adv* ▸ **'busyness** *n*

busybody ⓣ ('bɪzɪˌbɒdɪ) *n, pl* **busybodies.** a meddlesome, prying, or officious person.

busy Lizzie ('lɪzɪ) *n* a flowering plant that has pink, red, or white flowers and is often grown as a pot plant.

but[1] ⓣ (bʌt; *unstressed* bət) *conj* (*coordinating*) **1** contrary to expectation: *he cut his knee but didn't cry.* **2** in contrast; on the contrary: *I like opera but my husband doesn't.* **3** (*usually used after a negative*) other than: *we can't do anything but wait.* ◆ *conj* (*subordinating*) **4** (*usually used after a negative*) without it happening: *we never go out but it rains.* **5** (foll. by *that*) except that: *nothing is impossible but that we live forever.* **6** *Arch.* if not; unless. ◆ *prep* **7** except; save: *they saved all but one.* **8 but for.** were it not for: *but for you, we couldn't have managed.* ◆ *adv* **9** just; merely: *he was but a child.* **10** *Dialect & Austral.* though; however: *it's a rainy day; warm, but.* ◆ *n* **11** an objection (esp. in **ifs and buts**). [OE *būtan* without, outside, except, from *be* BY + *ūtan* OUT]

but[2] (bʌt) *n Scot.* the outer room of a two-roomed cottage. Cf. **ben**[1]. [C18: from *but* (adv) outside; see BUT[1]]

butadiene (ˌbju:tə'daɪi:n) *n* a colourless flammable gas used mainly in the manufacture of synthetic rubbers. Formula: CH_2:CHCH:CH_2. Systematic name: **buta-1,3-diene.** [C20: from BUTA(NE) + DI-[1] + -ENE]

butane ('bju:teɪn, bju:'teɪn) *n* a colourless flammable gaseous alkane used mainly in the manufacture of rubber and fuels. Formula: C_4H_{10}. [C20: from BUT(YL) + -ANE]

butanoic acid (ˌbju:tə'nəʊɪk) *n* a carboxylic acid that produces the smell in rancid butter. Formula: $CH_3(CH_2)_2COOH$. Also called: **butyric acid.** [C20: from BUTAN(E) + -OIC]

butanol ('bju:təˌnɒl) *n* a colourless substance existing in four isomeric forms. The three liquid isomers are used as solvents and in the manufacture of organic compounds. Formula: C_4H_9OH. Also called: **butyl alcohol.**

butanone ('bju:təˌnəʊn) *n* a colourless flammable liquid used as a resin solvent, and paint remover, and in lacquers, adhesives, etc. Formula: $CH_3COC_2H_5$.

butch (bʊtʃ) *Sl.* ◆ *adj* **1** (of a woman or man) markedly or aggressively masculine. ◆ *n* **2** a lesbian who is noticeably masculine. **3** a strong rugged man. [C18: back formation from BUTCHER]

butcher ⓣ ('bʊtʃə) *n* **1** a retailer of meat. **2** a person who slaughters or dresses meat. **3** an indiscriminate or brutal murderer. ◆ *vb* (*tr*) **4** to slaughter or dress (animals) for meat. **5** to kill indiscriminately or brutally. **6** to make a mess of; botch. [C13: from OF *bouchier,* from *bouc* he-goat]

butcherbird ('bʊtʃəˌbɜ:d) *n* **1** a shrike, esp. of the genus *Lanius.* **2** any of several Australian magpies that impale their prey on thorns.

butcher's-broom *n* an evergreen shrub with stiff prickle-tipped flattened green stems, formerly used for making brooms.

butchery ⓣ ('bʊtʃərɪ) *n, pl* **butcheries. 1** the business of a butcher. **2** wanton and indiscriminate slaughter. **3** a slaughterhouse.

butler ('bʌtlə) *n* the male servant of a household in charge of the wines, table, etc.: usually the head servant. [C13: from OF, from *bouteille* BOTTLE]

butlery ('bʌtlərɪ) *n, pl* **butleries. 1** a butler's room. **2** another name for **buttery**[2].

butt[1] ⓣ (bʌt) *n* **1** the thicker or blunt end of something, such as the end of the stock of a rifle. **2** the unused end of something, esp. of a cigarette; stub. **3** *Inf., chiefly US & Canad.* the buttocks. **4** *US.* a slang word for **cigarette. 5** *Building.* short for **butt joint.** [C15 (in the sense: thick end of something, buttock): rel. to OE *buttuc* end, ridge]

butt[2] ⓣ (bʌt) *n* **1** a person or thing that is the target of ridicule, wit, etc. **2** *Shooting, archery.* **2a** a mound of earth behind the target that stops bullets or wide shots. **2b** the target itself. **2c** (*pl*) the target range. **3** a low barrier behind which sportsmen shoot game birds, esp. grouse. ◆ *vb* **4** (usually foll. by *on* or *against*) to lie or be placed end on to; abut. [C14 (in the sense: mark for archery practice): from OF *but*]

butt[3] ⓣ (bʌt) *vb* **1** to strike or push (something) with the head or horns. **2** (*intr*) to project; jut. **3** (*intr;* foll. by *in* or *into*) to intrude, esp. into a conversation; interfere. ◆ *n* **4** a blow with the head or horns. [C12: from OF *boter,* of Gmc origin]

butt[4] ⓣ (bʌt) *n* a large cask for storing wine or beer. [C14: from OF *botte,* from LL *buttis* cask]

butte (bju:t) *n US & Canad.* an isolated steep flat-topped hill. [C19: F, from OF *bute* mound behind a target; see BUTT[2]]

butter ('bʌtə) *n* **1** an edible fatty whitish-yellow solid made from cream by churning. **2** any substance with a butter-like consistency, such as peanut butter. **3 look as if butter wouldn't melt in one's mouth.** to look innocent, although probably not so. ◆ *vb* (*tr*) **4** to put butter on or in. **5** to flatter. ◆ See also **butter up.** [OE *butere,* from L, from Gk *bouturon,* from *bous* cow + *turos* cheese]

butter bean *n* a variety of lima bean that has large pale flat edible seeds.

butterbur ('bʌtəˌbɜ:) *n* a plant of the composite family with fragrant whitish or purple flowers, and large leaves formerly used to wrap butter.

buttercup ('bʌtəˌkʌp) *n* any of various yellow-flowered plants of the genus *Ranunculus* of Europe, Asia, and North America.

butterfat ('bʌtəˌfæt) *n* the fatty substance of milk from which butter is made, consisting of a mixture of glycerides.

butterfingers ('bʌtəˌfɪŋgəz) *n* (*functioning as sing*) *Inf.* a person who drops things inadvertently or fails to catch things. ▸ **'butterˌfingered** *adj*

butterfish ('bʌtəˌfɪʃ) *n, pl* **butterfish** *or* **butterfishes.** any of several species of fishes having a slippery skin.

butterflies ('bʌtəˌflaɪz) *pl n Inf.* tremors in the stomach region due to nervousness.

butterfly ('bʌtəˌflaɪ) *n, pl* **butterflies. 1** any diurnal insect that has a slender body with clubbed antennae and typically rests with the wings (often brightly coloured) closed over the back. **2** a person who never settles with one interest or occupation for long. **3** a swimming stroke in which the arms are plunged forward together in large circular movements. **4** *Commerce.* the simultaneous purchase and sale of traded call options, at different exercise prices or with different expiry dates, on a stock exchange or commodity market. [OE *buttorflēoge*]

butterfly collar *n* the Irish name for **wing collar.**

butterfly effect *n* the idea, used in chaos theory, that a very small difference in the initial state of a physical system can make a significant difference to the state at some later time. [C20: from the theory that a butterfly flapping its wings in one part of the world might ultimately cause a hurricane in another part of the world]

butterfly nut *n* another name for **wing nut.**

buttermilk ('bʌtəˌmɪlk) *n* the sourish liquid remaining after the butter has been separated from milk.

butter muslin *n* a fine loosely woven cotton material originally used for wrapping butter.

butternut ('bʌtəˌnʌt) *n* **1** *Austral. & NZ.* a type of small edible pumpkin. **2a** a walnut tree of North America. **2b** its oily edible nut.

butterscotch ('bʌtəˌskɒtʃ) *n* **1** a kind of hard brittle toffee made with butter, brown sugar, etc. **2** a flavouring made from these ingredients. [C19: ? first made in Scotland]

butter up ⓣ *vb* (*tr, adv*) to flatter.

butterwort ('bʌtəˌwɜ:t) *n* a plant that grows in wet places and has violet-blue spurred flowers and fleshy greasy glandular leaves on which insects are trapped and digested.

buttery[1] ('bʌtərɪ) *adj* containing, like, or coated with butter. ▸ **'butteriness** *n*

buttery[2] ('bʌtərɪ) *n, pl* **butteries. 1** a room for storing foods or wines. **2** *Brit.* (in some universities) a room in which food and drink are supplied or sold to students. [C14: from Anglo-F *boterie,* prob. from L *butta* cask, BUTT[4]]

butt joint *n* a joint between two plates, planks, etc., fastened end to end without overlapping or interlocking. Sometimes shortened to **butt.**

buttock ⓣ ('bʌtək) *n* **1** either of the two large fleshy masses of thick muscular tissue that form the human rump. See also **gluteus.** Related adj: **gluteal. 2** the analogous part in some mammals. [C13: ?from OE *buttuc* round slope]

button ('bʌtᵊn) *n* **1** a disc or knob of plastic, wood, etc., attached to a garment, etc., usually for fastening two surfaces together by passing it through a buttonhole or loop. **2** a small round object, such as any of various sweets, decorations, or badges. **3** a small disc that completes an electric circuit when pushed, as one that operates a machine. **4**

THESAURUS

at work, industrious, in harness, on active service, on duty, persevering, rushed off one's feet, slaving, working **2** = **lively**, active, energetic, exacting, full, hectic, hustling, on the go (*inf.*), restless, strenuous, tireless, tiring ◆ *vb* **6** = **occupy**, absorb, employ, engage, engross, immerse, interest

Antonyms *adj* ≠ **occupied, lively:** idle, inactive, indolent, lackadaisical, lazy, off duty, relaxed, shiftless, slothful, unoccupied

busybody *n* = **nosy parker** (*inf.*), eavesdropper, gossip, intriguer, intruder, meddler, pry, scandalmonger, snoop, snooper, stirrer (*inf.*), troublemaker

but[1] *conj* **2** = **however**, further, moreover, nevertheless, on the contrary, on the other hand, still, yet ◆ *prep* **7** = **except**, bar, barring, excepting, excluding, notwithstanding, save, with the exception of ◆ *adv* **9** = **only**, just, merely, simply, singly, solely

butcher *n* **3** = **murderer**, destroyer, killer, slaughterer, slayer ◆ *vb* **4** = **slaughter**, carve, clean, cut, cut up, dress, joint, prepare **5** = **kill**, assassinate, cut down, destroy, exterminate, liquidate, massacre, put to the sword, slaughter, slay **6** = **mess up**, bodge (*inf.*), botch, destroy, mutilate, ruin, spoil, wreck

butchery *n* **2** = **slaughter**, blood bath, blood-letting, bloodshed, carnage, killing, massacre, mass murder, murder

butt[1] *n* **1** = **end**, haft, handle, hilt, shaft, shank, stock **2** = **stub**, base, end, fag end (*inf.*), foot, leftover, tail, tip

butt[2] *n* **1** = **target**, Aunt Sally, dupe, laughing stock, mark, object, point, subject, victim

butt[3] *vb, n* **1, 4** = **knock**, buck, buffet, bump, bunt, jab, poke, prod, punch, push, ram, shove, thrust ◆ *vb* **3** *foll. by* **in** *or* **into** = **interfere**, chip in (*inf.*), cut in, interrupt, intrude, meddle, put one's oar in, put one's two cents in (*US. sl.*), stick one's nose in

butt[4] *n* = **cask**, barrel, pipe

butter up *vb* = **flatter**, blarney, cajole, coax, fawn on *or* upon, kiss (someone's) ass (*US. sl.*), pander to, soft-soap, suck up to (*inf.*), wheedle

buttocks *pl n* **1, 2** = **bottom**, arse (*taboo sl.*), ass

Biol. any rounded knoblike part or organ, such as an unripe mushroom. **5** *Fencing.* the protective knob fixed to the point of a foil. **6** *Brit.* an object of no value (esp. in **not worth a button**). ◆ *vb* **7** to fasten with a button or buttons. **8** (*tr*) to provide with buttons. [C14: from OF *boton*, from *boter* to thrust, butt; see BUTT[3]]
▸ˈ**buttoner** *n* ▸ˈ**buttonless** *adj*

buttonhole ➊ (ˈbʌtᵊnˌhəʊl) *n* **1** a slit in a garment, etc., through which a button is passed to fasten two surfaces together. **2** a flower or small bunch of flowers worn pinned to the lapel or in the buttonhole, esp. at weddings. US name: **boutonniere.** ◆ *vb* **buttonholes, buttonholing, buttonholed.** (*tr*) **3** to detain (a person) in conversation. **4** to make buttonholes in.

buttonhook (ˈbʌtᵊnˌhʊk) *n* a thin tapering hooked instrument formerly used for pulling buttons through the buttonholes of shoes.

button up *vb* (*tr, adv*) **1** to fasten (a garment) with a button or buttons. **2** *Inf.* to conclude (business) satisfactorily. **3 button up one's lip** *or* **mouth.** *Sl.* to be silent.

buttress ➊ (ˈbʌtrɪs) *n* **1** Also called: **pier.** a construction, usually of brick or stone, built to support a wall. **2** any support or prop. **3** something shaped like a buttress, such as a projection from a mountainside. ◆ *vb* (*tr*) **4** to support (a wall) with a buttress. **5** to support or sustain. [C13: from OF *bouterez*, from *bouter* to thrust, BUTT[3]]

butty[1] (ˈbʌtɪ) *n, pl* **butties.** *Chiefly N English dialect.* a sandwich: *a jam butty.* [C19: from *buttered* (bread)]

butty[2] (ˈbʌtɪ) *n, pl* **butties.** *English dialect.* (esp. in mining parlance) a friend or workmate. [C19: ?from obs. *booty* sharing, from BOOT[2]]

butyl (ˈbjuːˌtaɪl, -tɪl) *n* (*modifier*) of or containing any of four isomeric forms of the group C_4H_9–: *butyl rubber.* [C19: from BUT(YRIC ACID) + -YL]

butyl alcohol *n* another name for **butanol.**

butyl rubber *n* a copolymer of isobutene and isoprene, used in tyres and as a waterproofing material.

butyric acid (bjuːˈtɪrɪk) *n* another name for **butanoic acid.** [C19 *butyric*, from L *būtyrum* BUTTER]

buxom ➊ (ˈbʌksəm) *adj* **1** (esp. of a woman) healthily plump, attractive, and vigorous. **2** (of a woman) full-bosomed. [C12: *buhsum* compliant, pliant, from OE *būgan* to bend, BOW[1]]
▸ˈ**buxomness** *n*

buy ➊ (baɪ) *vb* **buys, buying, bought.** (*mainly tr*) **1** to acquire by paying or promising to pay a sum of money; purchase. **2** to be capable of purchasing: *money can't buy love.* **3** to acquire by any exchange or sacrifice: *to buy time by equivocation.* **4** to bribe or corrupt; hire by or as by bribery. **5** *Sl.* to accept as true, practical, etc. **6** (*intr*; foll. by *into*) to purchase shares of (a company). ◆ *n* **7** a purchase (often in **good** or **bad buy**). ◆ See also **buy in, buy into,** etc. [OE *bycgan*]

> **USAGE NOTE** The use of *off* after *buy* as in *I bought this off my neighbour* was formerly considered incorrect, but is now acceptable in informal contexts.

buy-back *n Commerce.* the repurchase by a company of some or all of its shares from an investor, who acquired them by putting venture capital into the company when it was formed.

buyer (ˈbaɪə) *n* **1** a person who buys; customer. **2** a person employed to buy merchandise, materials, etc., as for a shop or factory.

buy in *vb* (*adv*) **1** (*tr*) to buy back for the owner (an item in an auction) at or below the reserve price. **2** (*intr*) to purchase shares in a company. **3** (*tr*) Also: **buy into.** *US inf.* to pay money to secure a position or place for (someone, esp. oneself) in some organization, esp. a business or club. **4** to purchase (goods, etc.) in large quantities. ◆ *n* **buy-in. 5** the purchase of a company by a manager or group who does not work for that company.

buy into *vb* (*intr, prep*) **1** to agree with or accept as valid (an argument, theory, etc.). **2** *Austral. & NZ inf.* to get involved in (an argument, fight, etc.).

buy off *vb* (*tr, adv*) to pay (a person or group) to drop a charge, end opposition, etc.

buy out *vb* (*tr, adv*) **1** to purchase the ownership, controlling interest, shares, etc., of (a company, etc.). **2** to gain the release of (a person) from the armed forces by payment. **3** to pay (a person) to give up ownership of (property, etc.). ◆ *n* **buy-out. 4** the purchase of a company, esp. by its former management or staff. See also **leveraged buyout, management buyout.**

buy up *vb* (*tr, adv*) **1** to purchase all, or all that is available, of (something). **2** to purchase a controlling interest in (a company, etc.).

buzz ➊ (bʌz) *n* **1** a rapidly vibrating humming sound, as of a bee. **2** a low sound, as of many voices in conversation. **3** a rumour; report; gossip. **4** *Inf.* a telephone call. **5** *Inf.* **5a** a pleasant sensation. **5b** a sense of excitement; kick. **6** (*modifier*) fashionable, trendy. ◆ *vb* **7** (*intr*) to make a vibrating sound like that of a prolonged z. **8** (*intr*) to talk or gossip with an air of excitement: *the town buzzed with the news.* **9** (*tr*) to utter or spread (a rumour). **10** (*intr;* often foll. by *about*) to move around quickly and busily. **11** (*tr*) to signal or summon with a buzzer. **12** (*tr*) *Inf.* to call by telephone. **13** (*tr*) *Inf.* to fly an aircraft very low over (an object). **14** (*tr*) (esp. of insects) to make a buzzing sound with (wings, etc.). [C16: imit.]

buzzard (ˈbʌzəd) *n* a diurnal bird of prey of the hawk family, typically having broad wings and tail and a soaring flight. [C13: from OF *buisard*, from L *būteō* hawk]

buzzer (ˈbʌzə) *n* **1** a device that produces a buzzing sound, esp. one similar to an electric bell. **2** *NZ.* a wood-planing machine.

buzz off *vb* (*intr, adv; often imperative*) *Inf., chiefly Brit.* to go away; leave; depart.

buzz word *n Inf.* a word, originally from a particular jargon, which becomes a popular vogue word. [C20: from ?]

BVM *abbrev. for* Beata Virgo Maria. [L: Blessed Virgin Mary]

bwana (ˈbwɑːnə) *n* (in E Africa) a master, often used as a form of address corresponding to *sir.* [Swahili, from Ar. *abūna* our father]

by ➊ (baɪ) *prep* **1** used to indicate the agent after a passive verb: *seeds eaten by the birds.* **2** used to indicate the person responsible for a creative work: *this song is by Schubert.* **3** via; through: *enter by the back door.* **4** foll. by a gerund to indicate a means used: *he frightened her by hiding behind the door.* **5** beside; next to; near: *a tree by the house.* **6** passing the position of; past: *he drove by the old cottage.* **7** not later than; before: *return the books by Tuesday.* **8** used to indicate extent, after a comparative: *it is hotter by five degrees.* **9** (esp. in oaths) invoking the name of: *I swear by all the gods.* **10** multiplied by: *four by three equals twelve.* **11** during the passing of (esp. in **by day, by night**). **12** placed between measurements of the various dimensions of something: *a pane four inches by seven.* ◆ *adv* **13** near: *the house is close by.* **14** away; aside: *he put some money by each week.* **15** passing a point near something; past: *he drove by.* ◆ *n, pl* **byes. 16** a variant spelling of **bye**[1]. [OE *bī*]

by- *or* **bye-** *prefix* **1** near: *bystander.* **2** secondary or incidental: *by-election; by-product.* [from BY]

by and by ➊ *adv* presently or eventually.

by and large *adv* in general; on the whole. [C17: orig. nautical: to the wind and off it]

bye[1] (baɪ) *n* **1** *Sport.* the situation in which a player or team wins a preliminary round by virtue of having no opponent. **2** *Golf.* one or more holes that are left unplayed after the match has been decided. **3** *Cricket.* a run scored off a ball not struck by the batsman. **4** something incidental or secondary. **5 by the bye.** incidentally; by the way. [C16: var. of BY]

bye[2] *or* **bye-bye** *sentence substitute. Brit. inf.* goodbye.

bye-byes *n* (*functioning as sing*) an informal word for **sleep,** used esp. to children (as in **go to bye-byes**).

by-election *or* **bye-election** *n* (in Great Britain and other countries of the Commonwealth) an election held during the life of a parliament to fill a vacant seat.

Byelorussian (ˌbjɛləʊˈrʌʃən) *adj* a variant spelling of **Belarussian.**

bygone ➊ (ˈbaɪˌgɒn) *adj* **1** (*usually prenominal*) past; former. ◆ *n* **2** (*often pl*) a past occurrence. **3** an artefact, implement, etc., of former domestic or industrial use. **4 let bygones be bygones.** to agree to forget past quarrels.

bylaw *or* **bye-law** (ˈbaɪˌlɔː) *n* **1** a rule made by a local authority. **2** a regulation of a company, society, etc. [C13: prob. of Scand. origin; cf. ON *bȳr* dwelling, town]

by-line *n* **1** a line under the title of a newspaper or magazine article giving the author's name. **2** another word for **touchline.**

BYO(G) *n Austral. & NZ.* an unlicensed restaurant at which diners may drink their own wine, etc. [C20: from *bring your own* (*grog*)]

bypass ➊ (ˈbaɪˌpɑːs) *n* **1** a main road built to avoid a city or other congested area. **2** a means of redirecting the flow of a substance around

THESAURUS

(*US. & Canad. taboo sl.*), backside, behind (*inf.*), bum (*Brit. sl.*), buns (*US. sl.*), butt (*US. & Canad. inf.*), derrière (*euphemistic*), gluteus maximus (*Anatomy*), haunches, hindquarters, posterior, rear, rump, seat, tail (*inf.*)

buttonhole *vb* **3 = detain,** accost, bore, catch, grab, importune, persuade importunately, take aside, waylay

buttress *n* **1, 2 = support,** abutment, brace, mainstay, pier, prop, reinforcement, shore, stanchion, stay, strut ◆ *vb* **4, 5 = support,** augment, back up, bolster, brace, prop, prop up, reinforce, shore, shore up, strengthen, sustain, uphold

buxom *adj* **1 = plump,** ample, curvaceous, voluptuous, well-rounded **2 = full-bosomed,** bosomy, busty
Antonyms *adj* ≠ **plump:** delicate, frail, slender, slight, slim, svelte, sylphlike, thin, trim

buy *vb* **1 = purchase,** acquire, get, invest in, obtain, pay for, procure, score (*sl.*), shop for **4 = bribe,** corrupt, fix (*inf.*), grease someone's palm (*sl.*), square, suborn ◆ *n* **6 = purchase,** acquisition, bargain, deal
Antonyms *vb* ≠ **purchase:** auction, barter, retail, sell, vend

buzz *n* **1, 2 = hum,** buzzing, drone, hiss, murmur, purr, ring, ringing, sibilation, whir, whisper **3 = gossip,** dirt (*US sl.*), gen (*Brit. inf.*), hearsay, latest (*inf.*), news, report, rumour, scandal, scuttlebutt (*US sl.*), whisper, word ◆ *vb* **7 = hum,** drone, fizzle, murmur, reverberate, ring, sibilate, whir, whisper, whizz **9 = gossip,** chatter, natter, rumour, tattle

by *prep* **3 = via,** by way of, over **4 = through,** through the agency of, under the aegis of **5 = near,** along, beside, close to, next to, past ◆ *adv* **13 = near,** at hand, close, handy, in reach **14 = past,** aside, away, to one side

by and by *adv* **= presently,** anon, before long, erelong, eventually, in a while, in the course of time, one day, shortly, soon

bygone *adj* **1 = past,** ancient, antiquated, departed, erstwhile, extinct, former, gone by, lost, of old, of yore, olden, one-time, previous
Antonyms *adj* coming, forthcoming, future, prospective, to be, to come

bypass *vb* **5 = go round,** avoid, body-swerve (*Scot.*), circumvent, depart from, detour round, deviate from, get round, give a wide berth to, pass round

an appliance through which it would otherwise pass. **3** *Surgery*. **3a** the redirection of blood flow, either to avoid a diseased blood vessel or in order to perform heart surgery. See **coronary bypass. 3b** (*as modifier*): *bypass surgery*. **4** *Electronics*. an electrical circuit connected in parallel around one or more components, providing an alternative path for certain frequencies. ◆ *vb* (*tr*) **5** to go around or avoid (a city, obstruction, problem, etc.). **6** to cause (traffic, fluid, etc.) to go through a bypass. **7** to proceed without reference to (regulations, a superior, etc.); get round; avoid.

bypass engine *n* a gas turbine in which part of the compressor delivery bypasses the combustion zone, flowing directly into or around the exhaust to provide additional thrust.

bypath ('baɪˌpɑːθ) *n* a little-used path or track.

by-play *n* secondary action or talking carried on apart while the main action proceeds, esp. in a play.

by-product *n* **1** a secondary or incidental product of a manufacturing process. **2** a side effect.

byre ('baɪə) *n Brit.* a shelter for cows. [OE *bȳre;* rel. to *būr* hut, cottage]

byroad ('baɪˌrəʊd) *n* a secondary or side road.

Byronic (baɪ'rɒnɪk) *adj* of, like, or characteristic of Byron, his poetry, or his style. [C19: from Lord *Byron* (1788–1824), E poet]

byssinosis (ˌbɪsɪ'nəʊsɪs) *n* a lung disease caused by prolonged inhalation of fibre dust. [C19: from NL, from Gk *bussinos* of linen + -OSIS]

bystander ⓣ ('baɪˌstændə) *n* a person present but not involved; onlooker; spectator.

byte (baɪt) *n Computing.* **1** a group of bits processed as one unit of data. **2** the storage space allocated to such a group of bits. **3** a subdivision of a word. [C20: prob. a blend of BIT[4] + BITE]

byway ('baɪˌweɪ) *n* **1** a secondary or side road, esp. in the country. **2** an area, field of study, etc., that is very obscure or of secondary importance.

byword ⓣ ('baɪˌwɜːd) *n* **1** a person or thing regarded as a perfect or proverbial example of something: *their name is a byword for good service.* **2** an object of scorn or derision. **3** a common saying; proverb. [OE *bīwyrde;* see BY, WORD]

Byzantine (bɪ'zænˌtaɪn, -ˌtiːn, baɪ-; 'bɪzənˌtiːn, -ˌtaɪn) *adj* **1** of or relating to Byzantium, an ancient Greek city on the Bosphorus. **2** of or relating to the Byzantine Empire, the continuation of the Roman Empire in the East. **3** of, relating to, or characterizing the Orthodox Church. **4** of or relating to the highly coloured stylized form of religious art developed in the Byzantine Empire. **5** of or relating to the style of architecture developed in the Byzantine Empire, characterized by massive domes, rounded arches, spires and minarets, and mosaics. **6** (of attitudes, etc.) inflexible or complicated. ◆ *n* **7** an inhabitant of Byzantium.
▸**Byzantinism** (bɪ'zæntɑɪˌnɪzəm, -tiː-, bɑɪ-; 'bɪzəntiːˌnɪzəm, -tɑɪ-) *n*

Bz *or* **bz.** *abbrev. for* benzene.

THESAURUS

Antonyms *vb* abut, adjoin, come together, connect, converge, cross, intersect, join, link, meet, touch, unite

bystander *n* = **onlooker**, eyewitness, looker-on, observer, passer-by, spectator, viewer, watcher, witness
Antonyms *n* contributor, partaker, participant, party

byword *n* **3** = **saying**, adage, aphorism, apophthegm, dictum, epithet, gnome, maxim, motto, precept, proverb, saw, slogan

Cc

c *or* **C** (siː) *n, pl* **c's, C's,** *or* **Cs. 1** the third letter of the English alphabet. **2** a speech sound represented by this letter, usually either as in *cigar* or as in *case.* **3** the third in a series, esp. the third highest grade in an examination. **4** something shaped like a C.

c *symbol for:* **1** centi-. **2** *Maths.* constant. **3** cubic. **4** cycle. **5** specific heat capacity. **6** the speed of light and other types of electromagnetic radiation in free space.

C *symbol for:* **1** *Music.* **1a** the first degree of a major scale containing no sharps or flats (**C major**). **1b** the major or minor key having this note as its tonic. **1c** a time signature denoting four crotchet beats to the bar. See also **alla breve** (sense 2), **common time. 2** *Chem.* carbon. **3** *Biochem.* cytosine. **4** capacitance. **5** heat capacity. **6** cold (water). **7** *Physics.* compliance. **8** Celsius. **9** centigrade. **10** century: C20. **11** coulomb. **12** *the Roman numeral for* 100. ◆ *n* **13** a type of high-level computer programming language.

c. *abbrev. for:* **1** carat. **2** carbon (paper). **3** *Cricket.* caught. **4** cent(s). **5** century *or* centuries. **6** (*pl* **cc.**) chapter. **7** (used esp. preceding a date) circa: *c. 1800.* [L: about] **8** colt. **9** contralto. **10** copyright. **11** coulomb.

C. *abbrev. for:* **1** (on maps as part of name) Cape. **2** Catholic. **3** Celtic. **4** Conservative. **5** Corps.

c/- (in Australia) *abbrev. for* care for.

C1 (ˈsiːˈwʌn) *n* **a** a person whose job is supervisory or clerical, or who works in junior management. **b** (*as adj*): *a C1 worker.* ◆ See also **occupation groupings.**

C2 (ˈsiːˈtuː) *n* **a** a skilled manual worker, or a manual worker with responsibility for other people. **b** (*as adj*): *a C2 worker.* ◆ See also **occupation groupings.**

Ca *the chemical symbol for* calcium.

CA *abbrev. for:* **1** California. **2** Central America. **3** chartered accountant. **4** Civil Aviation. **5** (in Britain) Consumers' Association.

ca. *abbrev. for* circa. [L: about]

CAA (in Britain) *abbrev. for* Civil Aviation Authority.

Caaba (ˈkɑːbə) *n* a variant spelling of **Kaaba.**

cab 🅣 (kæb) *n* **1a** a taxi. **1b** (*as modifier*): *a cab rank.* **2** the enclosed compartment of a lorry, crane, etc., from which it is driven. **3** (formerly) a horse-drawn vehicle used for public hire. [C19: from CABRIOLET]

cabal 🅣 (kəˈbæl) *n* **1** a small group of intriguers, esp. one formed for political purposes. **2** a secret plot; conspiracy. **3** a clique. ◆ *vb* **cabals, caballing, caballed. 4** (*intr*) to form a cabal; plot. [C17: from F *cabale,* from Med. L *cabala*]

cabala (kəˈbɑːlə) *n* a variant spelling of **cabbala.**

caballero (ˌkæbəˈljɛərəʊ) *n, pl* **caballeros** (-rəʊz). a Spanish gentleman. [C19: from Sp.: gentleman, from LL *caballārius* rider, from *caballus* horse]

cabana (kəˈbɑːnə) *n Chiefly US.* a tent used as a dressing room by the sea. [from Sp. *cabaña:* CABIN]

cabaret (ˈkæbəˌreɪ) *n* **1** a floor show of dancing, singing, etc., at a nightclub or restaurant. **2** *Chiefly US.* a nightclub or restaurant providing such entertainment. [C17: from Norman F: tavern, prob. from LL *camera* an arched roof]

cabbage (ˈkæbɪdʒ) *n* **1** Also called: **cole.** any of various cultivated varieties of a plant of the genus *Brassica* having a short thick stalk and a large head of green or reddish edible leaves. See also **brassica. 2a** the head of a cabbage. **2b** the edible leaf bud of the cabbage palm. **3** *Inf.* a dull or unimaginative person. **4** *Inf.* a person who has no mental faculties and is dependent on others. [C14: from Norman F *caboche* head]

cabbage palm *n* **1** a West Indian palm whose leaf buds are eaten like cabbage. **2** a similar Brazilian palm.

cabbage rose *n* a rose with a round compact full-petalled head.

cabbage tree *n* **1** a tall palmlike ornamental New Zealand tree. **2** a tall palm tree of Eastern Australia.

cabbage white *n* a large white butterfly, the larvae of which feed on the leaves of cabbages and related vegetables.

cabbala, cabala, kabbala, *or* **kabala** 🅣 (kəˈbɑːlə) *n* **1** an ancient Jewish mystical tradition. **2** any secret or occult doctrine. [C16: from Med. L, from Heb. *qabbālāh* tradition, from *qābal* to receive] ▸**cabbalism, cabalism, kabbalism,** *or* **kabalism** (ˈkæbəˌlɪzəm) *n* ▸ˈ**cabbalist,** ˈ**cabalist,** ˈ**kabbalist,** *or* ˈ**kabalist** *n* ▸ˌ**cabbaˈlistic,** ˌ**cabaˈlistic,** ˌ**kabbaˈlistic,** *or* ˌ**kabaˈlistic** *adj*

cabbie *or* **cabby** (ˈkæbɪ) *n, pl* **cabbies.** *Inf.* a cab driver.

caber (ˈkeɪbə) *n Scot.* a heavy section of trimmed tree trunk thrown in competition at Highland games (**tossing the caber**). [C16: from Gaelic *cabar* pole]

Cabernet Sauvignon (ˈkæbəneɪ ˈsəʊvɪnjɒn; *French* kabernɛ soviɲɔ̃) *n* (*sometimes not caps.*) **1** a black grape grown in the Bordeaux area of France, Australia, California, Bulgaria, and elsewhere, used for making wine. **2** any of various red wines made from this grape. [F]

cabin 🅣 (ˈkæbɪn) *n* **1** a small simple dwelling; hut. **2** a simple house providing accommodation for travellers or holiday-makers. **3** a room used as an office or living quarters in a ship. **4** a covered compartment used for shelter in a small boat. **5** *Brit.* another name for **signal box. 6a** the enclosed part of a light aircraft in which the pilot and passengers sit. **6b** the part of an aircraft for passengers or cargo. ◆ *vb* **7** (*tr*) to confine in a small space. [C14: from OF *cabane,* from OProvençal *cabana,* from LL *capanna* hut]

cabin boy *n* a boy who waits on the officers and passengers of a ship.

cabin cruiser *n* a power boat fitted with a cabin for pleasure cruising or racing.

cabinet 🅣 (ˈkæbɪnɪt) *n* **1** a piece of furniture containing shelves, cupboards, or drawers for storage or display. **2** the outer case of a television, radio, etc. **3a** (*often cap.*) the executive and policy-making body of a country, consisting of senior government ministers. **3b** (*sometimes cap.*) an advisory council to a president, governor, etc. **3c** (*as modifier*): *a cabinet reshuffle.* **4a** a standard size of paper, 6 × 4 inches (15 × 10 cm), for mounted photographs. **4b** (*as modifier*): *a cabinet photograph.* **5** *Arch.* a private room. [C16: from OF, dim. of *cabine,* from ?]

cabinet-maker *n* a craftsman specializing in making fine furniture. ▸ˈ**cabinet-ˌmaking** *n*

cabinetwork (ˈkæbɪnɪtˌwɜːk) *n* **1** the making of furniture, esp. of fine quality. **2** an article made by a cabinet-maker.

cabin fever *n Canad.* acute depression resulting from being isolated or sharing cramped quarters in the wilderness.

cable (ˈkeɪbᵊl) *n* **1** a strong thick rope, usually of twisted hemp or steel wire. **2** *Naut.* an anchor chain or rope. **3a** a unit of distance in navigation, equal to one tenth of a sea mile (about 600 ft). **3b** Also called: **cable length, cable's length.** a unit of length in nautical use that has various values, including 100 fathoms (600 ft). **4** a wire or bundle of wires that conducts electricity: *a submarine cable.* **5** Also called: **cablegram.** a telegram sent abroad by submarine cable, telephone line, etc. **6** Also called: **cable stitch.** a knitting pattern resembling a twisted rope. ◆ *vb* **cables, cabling, cabled. 7** to send (a message) to (someone) by cable. **8** (*tr*) to fasten or provide with a cable or cables. **9** (*tr*) to supply (a place) with cable television. [C13: from OF, from LL *capulum* halter]

cable car *n* **1** a cabin suspended from and moved by an overhead cable in a mountain area. **2** the passenger car on a **cable railway,** drawn along by a strong cable operated by a motor.

cable television *n* a television service in which the subscriber's television is connected to the supplier by cable, enabling a much greater choice of channels to be provided.

cabochon (ˈkæbəˌʃɒn) *n* a smooth domed gem, polished but unfaceted. [C16: from OF, from *caboche* head]

caboodle (kəˈbuːdᵊl) *n Inf.* a lot, bunch, or group (esp. in **the whole caboodle**). [C19: prob. contraction of KIT[1] & BOODLE]

caboose (kəˈbuːs) *n* **1** *US inf.* short for **calaboose. 2** *Railways. US & Canad.* a guard's van. **3** *Naut.* **3a** a deckhouse for a galley aboard ship. **3b** *Chiefly Brit.* the galley itself. **4** *Canad.* **4a** a mobile bunkhouse used by lumbermen, etc. **4b** an insulated cabin on runners, equipped with a stove. [C18: from Du. *cabūse,* from ?]

cabotage (ˈkæbəˌtɑːʒ) *n* **1** *Naut.* coastal navigation or shipping. **2** reservation to a country's carriers of its internal traffic, esp. air traffic. [C19: from F, from *caboter* to sail near the coast, apparently from Sp. *cabo* CAPE[2]]

cabriole (ˈkæbrɪˌəʊl) *n* a type of curved furniture leg, popular in the first half of the 18th century. Also called: **cabriole leg.** [C18: from F, from *cabrioler* to caper; from its being based on the leg of a capering animal]

cabriolet (ˌkæbrɪəʊˈleɪ) *n* **1** a small two-wheeled horse-drawn carriage with two seats and a folding hood. **2** a type of motorcar with a folding top. [C18: from F, lit.: a little skip, from L, from *caper* goat; referring to the lightness of movement]

cacao (kəˈkɑːəʊ, -ˈkeɪəʊ) *n* **1** a small tropical American evergreen tree having reddish-brown seed pods from which cocoa and chocolate are prepared. **2 cacao bean.** the seed pod; cocoa bean. **3 cacao butter.** another name for **cocoa butter.** [C16: from Sp., from Nahuatl *cacauatl* cacao beans]

cachalot (ˈkæʃəˌlɒt) *n* another name for **sperm whale.** [C18: from F, from Port. *cachalote,* from ?]

cache 🅣 (kæʃ) *n* **1** a hidden store of provisions, weapons, treasure, etc. **2** the place where such a store is hidden. **3** *Computing.* a small

THESAURUS

cab *n* **1a, 3** = **taxi,** hackney, hackney carriage, minicab, taxicab

cabal *n* **1, 3** = **clique,** camp, caucus, coalition, combination, conclave, confederacy, coterie, faction, junta, league, party, schism, set **2** = **plot,** conspiracy, intrigue, machination, scheme

cabbalistic *adj* **2** = **occult,** cryptic, dark, esoteric, fanciful, mysterious, mystic, mystical, obscure, secret

cabin *n* **1** = **hut,** bothy, chalet, cot, cottage, crib, hovel, lodge, shack, shanty, shed **4** = **room,** berth, compartment, deckhouse, quarters

cabinet *n* **1** = **cupboard,** case, chiffonier, closet, commode, dresser, escritoire, locker **3a** *often cap.* = **council,** administration, assembly, counsellors, ministry

cache *n* **1, 2** = **store,** accumulation, fund, garner, hiding place, hoard, nest egg, repository,

high-speed memory that improves computer performance. ◆ *vb* **caches, caching, cached. 4** (*tr*) to store in a cache. [C19: from F, from *cacher* to hide]

cachepot ('kæʃˌpɒt, kæʃ'pəʊ) *n* an ornamental container for a flowerpot. [F: pot-hider]

cachet ('kæʃeɪ) *n* **1** an official seal on a document, letter, etc. **2** a distinguishing mark. **3** prestige; distinction. **4** *Philately.* a mark stamped by hand on mail for commemorative purposes. **5** a hollow wafer, formerly used for enclosing an unpleasant-tasting medicine. [C17: from OF, from *cacher* to hide]

cachexia (kə'kɛksɪə) *or* **cachexy** *n* a weakened condition of body or mind resulting from any debilitating disease. [C16: from LL, from Gk, from *kakos* bad + *hexis* condition]

cachinnate ('kækɪˌneɪt) *vb* **cachinnates, cachinnating, cachinnated.** (*intr*) to laugh loudly. [C19: from L *cacchināre,* prob. imit.]
▸ **ˌcachin'nation** *n* ▸ **ˌcachin'natory** *adj*

cachou ('kæʃuː, kæ'ʃuː) *n* **1** a lozenge eaten to sweeten the breath. **2** another name for **catechu.** [C18: via F from Port., from Malay *kāchu*]

cacique (kə'siːk) *or* **cazique** (kə'ziːk) *n* **1** an American Indian chief in a Spanish-speaking region. **2** (esp. in Spanish America) a local political boss. [C16: from Sp., of Amerind origin]

cack-handed (ˌkæk'hændɪd) *adj Inf.* **1** left-handed. **2** clumsy. [from dialect *cack* excrement]

cackle ⓣ ('kækᵊl) *vb* **cackles, cackling, cackled. 1** (*intr*) (esp. of a hen) to squawk with shrill broken notes. **2** (*intr*) to laugh or chatter raucously. **3** (*tr*) to utter in a cackling manner. ◆ *n* **4** the noise or act of cackling. **5** noisy chatter. **6 cut the cackle.** *Inf.* to be quiet. [C13: prob. from MLow G *kākelen,* imit.]

caco- *combining form.* bad, unpleasant, or incorrect: *cacophony.* [from Gk *kakos* bad]

cacodyl ('kækəˌdaɪl) *n* an oily poisonous liquid with a strong garlic smell; tetramethyldiarsine. [C19: from Gk, from *kakos* CACO- + *ozein* to smell + -YL]

cacoethes (ˌkækəʊ'iːθiːz) *n* an uncontrollable urge or desire: *a cacoethes for smoking.* [C16: from L *cacoēthes* malignant disease, from Gk, from *kakos* CACO- + *ēthos* character]

cacography (kæ'kɒgrəfɪ) *n* **1** bad handwriting. **2** incorrect spelling.
▸ **cacographic** (ˌkækə'græfɪk) *adj*

cacophony ⓣ (kə'kɒfənɪ) *n, pl* **cacophonies.** harsh discordant sound.
▸ **ca'cophonous** *adj*

cactus ('kæktəs) *n, pl* **cactuses** *or* **cacti** (-taɪ). **1** any of a family of spiny succulent plants of the arid regions of America with swollen tough stems and leaves reduced to spines. **2 cactus dahlia.** a double-flowered variety of dahlia. [C17: from L: prickly plant, from Gk *kaktos* cardoon]
▸ **cactaceous** (kæk'teɪʃəs) *adj*

cacuminal (kæ'kjuːmɪnᵊl) *Phonetics.* ◆ *adj* **1** denoting a consonant articulated with the tip of the tongue turned back towards the hard palate. ◆ *n* **2** a consonant articulated in this manner. [C19: from L *cacūmen* point]

cad ⓣ (kæd) *n Brit. inf. old-fashioned.* a man who does not behave in a gentlemanly manner towards others. [C18: from CADDIE]
▸ **'caddish** *adj*

CAD (kæd) *n acronym for* computer-aided design.

cadaver (kə'deɪvə, -'dɑːv-) *n Med.* a corpse. [C16: from L, from *cadere* to fall]
▸ **cadaveric** (kə'dævərɪk) *adj*

cadaverous ⓣ (kə'dævərəs) *adj* **1** of or like a corpse, esp. in being deathly pale. **2** thin and haggard.
▸ **ca'daverousness** *n*

CADCAM ('kædˌkæm) *n acronym for* computer-aided design and manufacture.

caddie *or* **caddy** ('kædɪ) *Golf.* ◆ *n, pl* **caddies. 1** an attendant who carries clubs, etc., for a player. ◆ *vb* **caddies, caddying, caddied. 2** (*intr*) to act as a caddie. [C17 (C18 (Scot.): an errand-boy): from F CADET]

caddis fly *n* a small mothlike insect having two pairs of hairy wings and aquatic larvae (caddis worms). [C17: from ?]

caddis worm *or* **caddis** ('kædɪs) *n* the aquatic larva of a caddis fly, which constructs a protective case around itself made of silk, sand, stones, etc. Also called: **caseworm, strawworm.**

caddy[1] ('kædɪ) *n, pl* **caddies.** *Chiefly Brit.* a small container, esp. for tea. [C18: from Malay *kati*]

caddy[2] ('kædɪ) *n, pl* **caddies,** *vb* **caddies, caddying, caddied.** a variant spelling of **caddie.**

cadence ⓣ ('keɪdᵊns) *or* **cadency** *n, pl* **cadences** *or* **cadencies. 1** the beat or measure of something rhythmic. **2** a fall in the pitch of the voice, as at the end of a sentence. **3** intonation. **4** rhythm in verse or prose. **5** the close of a musical phrase. [C14: from OF, from OIt. *cadenza,* lit.: a falling, from L *cadere* to fall]

cadenza (kə'dɛnzə) *n* a virtuoso solo passage occurring near the end of a piece of music, formerly improvised by the soloist. [C19: from It.; see CADENCE]

cadet (kə'dɛt) *n* **1** a young person undergoing preliminary training, usually before full entry to the uniformed services, police, etc. **2** (in England and in France before 1789) a gentleman who entered the army to prepare for a commission. **3** a younger son. **4 cadet branch.** the family of a younger son. **5** (in New Zealand, formerly) a person learning sheep farming on a sheep station. [C17: from F, from dialect *capdet* captain, ult. from L *caput* head]
▸ **ca'detship** *n*

cadge ⓣ (kædʒ) *vb* **cadges, cadging, cadged. 1** to get (food, money, etc.) by sponging or begging. ◆ *n* **2** *Brit.* a person who cadges. [C17: from ?]
▸ **'cadger** *n*

cadi *or* **kadi** ('kɑːdɪ, 'keɪdɪ) *n, pl* **cadis** *or* **kadis.** a judge in a Muslim community. [C16: from Ar. *qādī* judge]

Cadmean victory ('kædmɪən) *n* another name for **Pyrrhic victory.** [after *Cadmus,* in Gk myth., who sowed dragon's teeth from which sprang soldiers who fought among themselves]

cadmium ('kædmɪəm) *n* a malleable bluish-white metallic element that occurs in association with zinc ores. It is used in electroplating and alloys. Symbol: Cd; atomic no.: 48; atomic wt.: 112.4. [C19: from NL, from L *cadmīa* zinc ore, CALAMINE: both calamine and cadmium are found in the ore]

cadmium yellow *n* an orange or yellow insoluble solid (cadmium sulphide) used as a pigment in paints, etc.

cadre ('kɑːdə) *n* **1** the nucleus of trained professional servicemen forming the basis for military expansion. **2** a group of activists, esp. in the Communist Party. **3** a basic unit or structure; nucleus. **4** a member of a cadre. [C19: from F, from It. *quadro,* from L *quadrum* square]

caduceus (kə'djuːsɪəs) *n, pl* **caducei** (-sɪˌaɪ). **1** *Classical myth.* a winged staff entwined with two serpents carried by Hermes (Mercury) as messenger of the gods. **2** an insignia resembling this staff used as an emblem of the medical profession. [C16: from L, from Doric Gk *karukeion,* from *karux* herald]

caducous (kə'djuːkəs) *adj Biol.* (of parts of a plant or animal) shed during the life of the organism. [C17: from L, from *cadere* to fall]

caecilian (siː'sɪlɪən) *n* a tropical limbless cylindrical amphibian resembling the earthworm and inhabiting moist soil. [C19: from L, from *caecus* blind]

caecum *or US* **cecum** ('siːkəm) *n, pl* **caeca** *or US* **ceca** (-kə). *Anat.* any structure that ends in a blind sac or pouch, esp. that at the beginning of the large intestine. [C18: short for L *intestinum caecum* blind intestine, translation of Gk *tuphlon enteron*]
▸ **'caecal** *or US* **'cecal** *adj*

Caenozoic (ˌsiːnə'zəʊɪk) *adj* a variant spelling of **Cenozoic.**

Caerphilly (kɛə'fɪlɪ) *n* a creamy white mild-flavoured cheese, orig. made in Caerphilly in SE Wales.

Caesar ('siːzə) **1** any Roman emperor. **2** (*sometimes not cap.*) any emperor, autocrat, or dictator. **3** a title of the Roman emperors from Augustus to Hadrian. [after Gaius Julius *Caesar* (100–44 B.C.), Roman general and statesman]

Caesarean, Caesarian, *or US* **Cesarean, Cesarian** (sɪ'zɛərɪən) *adj* **1** of or relating to any of the Caesars, esp. Julius Caesar. ◆ *n* **2** (*sometimes not cap.*) *Surgery.* **2a** a Caesarean section. **2b** (*as modifier*): *Caesarean operation.*

Caesarean section *n* surgical incision through the abdominal and uterine walls in order to deliver a baby. [C17: from the belief that Julius Caesar was so delivered, the name allegedly being derived from *caedere* to cut]

caesious *or US* **cesious** ('siːzɪəs) *adj Bot.* having a waxy bluish-grey coating. [C19: from L *caesius* bluish grey]

caesium *or US* **cesium** ('siːzɪəm) *n* a ductile silvery-white element of the alkali metal group. It is used in photocells and in an atomic clock (**caesium clock**) that uses the frequency of radiation from changing the spin of electrons. The radioisotope **caesium-137,** with a half-life of 30.2 years, is used in radiotherapy. Symbol: Cs; atomic no.: 55; atomic wt.: 132.905.

caesura (sɪ'zjʊərə) *n, pl* **caesuras** *or* **caesurae** (-riː). **1** (in modern prosody) a pause, esp. for sense, usually near the middle of a verse line. **2** (in classical prosody) a break between words within a metrical foot. [C16: from L, lit.: a cutting, from *caedere* to cut]
▸ **cae'sural** *adj*

café ⓣ ('kæfeɪ, 'kæfɪ) *n* **1** a small or inexpensive restaurant serving light

THESAURUS

reserve, stash (*inf.*), stockpile, storehouse, supply, treasury ◆ *vb* **4** = **store,** bury, conceal, hide, put away, secrete, stash (*inf.*)

cackle *vb* **1, 3** = **squawk,** babble, chatter, cluck, crow, gabble, gibber, jabber, prattle **2** = **laugh,** chuckle, giggle, snicker, snigger, titter

cacophonous *adj* = **discordant,** dissonant, grating, harsh, inharmonious, jarring, raucous, strident

cacophony *n* = **discord,** caterwauling, disharmony, dissonance, stridency

cad *n Old-fashioned, informal* = **scoundrel,** bounder (*old-fashioned Brit. sl.*), churl, cur, dastard (*arch.*), heel (*sl.*), knave, rat (*inf.*), rotter (*sl., chiefly Brit.*), scumbag (*sl.*)

cadaverous *adj* **1, 2** = **deathly,** ashen, blanched, bloodless, corpse-like, deathlike, emaciated, exsanguinous, gaunt, ghastly, haggard, hollow-eyed, like death warmed up (*inf.*), pale, pallid, wan

caddish *adj* = **ungentlemanly,** despicable, ill-bred, low, unmannerly

Antonyms *adj* gentlemanly, honourable, laudable, mannerly, pleasant, praiseworthy

cadence *n* **1** = **rhythm,** beat, lilt, measure (*Prosody*), metre, pulse, swing, tempo, throb **3** = **intonation,** accent, inflection, modulation

cadge *vb* **1** = **scrounge** (*inf.*), beg, freeload (*sl.*), sponge

cadger *n* **1** = **scrounger** (*inf.*), beggar, bloodsucker (*inf.*), freeloader, hanger-on, leech, parasite, sponger

café *n* **1** = **snack bar,** brasserie, cafeteria, coffee

or easily prepared meals and refreshments. **2** *S. African.* a corner shop or grocer. [C19: from F: COFFEE]
café au lait *French.* (kafe o lɛ) *n* **1** coffee with milk. **2a** a light brown colour. **2b** (*as adj*): *café au lait brocade.*
café noir *French.* (kafe nwar) *n* black coffee.
cafeteria (ˌkæfɪˈtɪərɪə) *n* a self-service restaurant. [C20: from American Sp.: coffee shop]
caff (kæf) *n* a slang word for **café.**
caffeine *or* **caffein** (ˈkæfiːn) *n* a white crystalline bitter alkaloid responsible for the stimulant action of tea, coffee, and cocoa. [C19: from G *Kaffein,* from *Kaffee* COFFEE]
caftan (ˈkæfˌtæn, -ˌtɑːn) *n* a variant spelling of **kaftan.**
cage ➊ (keɪdʒ) *n* **1a** an enclosure, usually made with bars or wire, for keeping birds, monkeys, etc. **1b** (*in combination*): *cagebird.* **2** a thing or place that confines. **3** something resembling a cage in function or structure: *the rib cage.* **4** the enclosed platform of a lift, esp. as used in a mine. ◆ *vb* **cages, caging, caged. 5** (*tr*) to confine in or as in a cage. [C13: from OF, from L *cavea* enclosure, from *cavus* hollow]
cagey ➊ *or* **cagy** (ˈkeɪdʒɪ) *adj* **cagier, cagiest.** *Inf.* not frank; wary. [C20: from ?]
▸**ˈcaginess** *n*
cagoule (kəˈguːl) *n* a lightweight usually knee-length type of anorak. [C20: from F]
cahoots (kəˈhuːts) *pl n* (*sometimes sing*) *Inf.* **1** *US.* partnership; league. **2 in cahoots.** in collusion. [C19: from ?]
caiman (ˈkeɪmən) *n, pl* **caimans.** a variant spelling of **cayman.**
Cainozoic (ˌkaɪnəʊˈzəʊɪk, ˌkeɪ-) *adj* a variant spelling of **Cenozoic.**
caïque (kaɪˈiːk) *n* **1** a long rowing skiff used on the Bosporus. **2** a sailing vessel of the E Mediterranean with a square topsail. [C17: from F, from It. *caicco,* from Turkish *kayik*]
cairn (kɛən) *n* **1** a mound of stones erected as a memorial or marker. **2** Also called: **cairn terrier.** a small rough-haired breed of terrier orig. from Scotland. [C15: from Gaelic *carn*]
cairngorm (ˌkɛənˈgɔːm) *n* a smoky yellow or brown variety of quartz, used as a gemstone. Also called: **smoky quartz.** [C18: from *Cairn Gorm* (lit.: blue cairn), mountain in Scotland]
caisson (kəˈsuːn, ˈkeɪsᵊn) *n* **1** a watertight chamber open at the bottom and containing air under pressure, used to carry out construction work under water. **2** a watertight float filled with air, used to raise sunken ships. **3** a watertight structure placed across the entrance of a dry dock, etc., to exclude water. **4a** a box containing explosives formerly used as a mine. **4b** an ammunition chest. [C18: from F, assimilated to *caisse* CASE[2]]
caisson disease *n* another name for **decompression sickness.**
caitiff (ˈkeɪtɪf) *Arch. or poetic.* ◆ *n* **1** a cowardly or base person. ◆ *adj* **2** cowardly. [C13: from OF, from L *captīvus* CAPTIVE]
cajole ➊ (kəˈdʒəʊl) *vb* **cajoles, cajoling, cajoled.** to persuade (someone) by flattery to do what one wants; wheedle; coax. [C17: from F *cajoler* to coax, from ?]
▸**caˈjolement** *n* ▸**caˈjoler** *n* ▸**caˈjolery** *n*
cake ➊ (keɪk) *n* **1** a baked food, usually in loaf or layer form, made from a mixture of flour, sugar, and eggs. **2** a flat thin mass of bread, esp. unleavened bread. **3** a shaped mass of dough or other food: *a fish cake.* **4** a mass, slab, or crust of a solidified substance, as of soap. **5 go** *or* **sell like hot cakes.** *Inf.* to be sold very quickly. **6 have one's cake and eat it.** to enjoy both of two desirable but incompatible alternatives. **7 piece of cake.** *Inf.* something that is easily achieved or obtained. **8 take the cake.** *Inf.* to surpass all others, esp. in stupidity, folly, etc. **9** *Inf.* the whole of something that is to be shared or divided: *a larger slice of the cake.* ◆ *vb* **cakes, caking, caked. 10** (*tr*) to encrust: *the hull was caked with salt.* **11** to form or be formed into a hardened mass. [C13: from ON *kaka*]
cakewalk (ˈkeɪkˌwɔːk) *n* **1** a dance based on a march with intricate steps, orig. performed by African-Americans for the prize of a cake. **2** a piece of music for this dance. **3** *Inf.* an easy task.
CAL (kæl) *acronym for* computer-aided (*or* -assisted) learning.
cal. *abbrev. for:* **1** calendar. **2** calibre. **3** calorie (small).
Cal. *abbrev. for* Calorie (large).
calabash (ˈkæləˌbæʃ) *n* **1** Also called: **calabash tree.** a tropical American evergreen tree that produces large round gourds. **2** the gourd. **3** the dried hollow shell of a gourd used as the bowl of a tobacco pipe, a bottle, etc. **4 calabash nutmeg.** a tropical African shrub whose seeds can be used as nutmegs. [C17: from obs. F *calabasse,* from Sp., ?from Ar., from *qar'ah* gourd + *yābisah* dry]
calaboose (ˈkæləˌbuːs) *n US inf.* a prison. [C18: from Creole F, from Sp. *calabozo* dungeon, from ?]
calabrese (ˌkæləˈbreɪzɪ) *n* a variety of green sprouting broccoli. [C20: from It.: Calabrian]
calamander (ˈkæləˌmændə) *n* the hard black-and-brown striped wood of several trees of India and Sri Lanka, used in making furniture. See also **ebony** (sense 2). [C19: metathetic var. of *Coromandel,* coast in SE India]
calamine (ˈkæləˌmaɪn) *n* a pink powder consisting of zinc oxide and iron(III) oxide, used medicinally in the form of soothing lotions or ointments. [C17: from OF, from Med. L *calamīna,* from L *cadmīa;* see CADMIUM]
calamint (ˈkæləmɪnt) *n* an aromatic Eurasian plant having clusters of purple or pink flowers. [C14: from OF *calament,* from Med. L *calamentum,* from Gk *kalaminthē*]
calamitous ➊ (kəˈlæmɪtəs) *adj* causing, involving, or resulting in a calamity; disastrous.
calamity ➊ (kəˈlæmɪtɪ) *n, pl* **calamities. 1** a disaster or misfortune, esp. one causing distress or misery. **2** a state or feeling of deep distress or misery. [C15: from F *calamité,* from L *calamitās*]
calamus (ˈkæləməs) *n, pl* **calami** (-ˌmaɪ). **1** any of a genus of tropical Asian palms, some of which are a source of rattan and canes. **2** another name for **sweet flag. 3** *Ornithol.* a quill. [C14: from L, from Gk *kalamos* reed, stem]
calandria (kəˈlændrɪə) *n* a cylindrical vessel through which vertical tubes pass, esp. one forming part of a heat exchanger or nuclear reactor. [C20: arbitrarily named, from Sp., lit.: lark]
calash (kəˈlæʃ) *or* **calèche** *n* **1** a horse-drawn carriage with low wheels and a folding top. **2** a woman's folding hooped hood worn in the 18th century. [C17: from F, from G, from Czech *kolesa* wheels]
calcaneus (kælˈkeɪnɪəs) *or* **calcaneum** *n, pl* **calcanei** (-nɪˌaɪ). the largest tarsal bone, forming the heel in man. Nontechnical name: **heel bone.** [C19: from LL: heel, from L *calx* heel]
calcareous (kælˈkɛərɪəs) *adj* of, containing, or resembling calcium carbonate; chalky. [C17: from L *calcārius,* from *calx* lime]
calceolaria (ˌkælsɪəˈlɛərɪə) *n* a tropical American plant cultivated for its speckled slipper-shaped flowers. Also called: **slipperwort.** [C18: from L *calceolus* small shoe, from *calceus*]
calces (ˈkælsiːz) *n* a plural of **calx.**
calci- *or before a vowel* **calc-** *combining form.* indicating lime or calcium: *calcify.* [from L *calx, calc-* limestone]
calciferol (kælˈsɪfərɒl) *n* a fat-soluble steroid, found esp. in fish-liver oils and used in the treatment of rickets. Also called: **vitamin D_2.** [C20: from CALCIF(EROUS + ERGOST)EROL]
calciferous (kælˈsɪfərəs) *adj* producing salts of calcium, esp. calcium carbonate.
calcify (ˈkælsɪˌfaɪ) *vb* **calcifies, calcifying, calcified. 1** to convert or be converted into lime. **2** to harden or become hardened by impregnation with calcium salts.
▸ˌ**calcifiˈcation** *n*
calcine (ˈkælsaɪn, -sɪn) *vb* **calcines, calcining, calcined. 1** (*tr*) to heat (a substance) so that it is oxidized, is reduced, or loses water. **2** (*intr*) to oxidize as a result of heating. [C14: from Med. L *calcināre* to heat, from L *calx* lime]
▸**calcination** (ˌkælsɪˈneɪʃən) *n*
calcite (ˈkælsaɪt) *n* a colourless or white mineral consisting of crystalline calcium carbonate: the transparent variety is Iceland spar. Formula: $CaCO_3$.
calcium (ˈkælsɪəm) *n* a malleable silvery-white metallic element of the alkaline earth group, occurring esp. as forms of calcium carbonate. It is an essential constituent of bones and teeth. Symbol: Ca; atomic no.: 20; atomic wt.: 40.08. [C19: from NL, from L *calx* lime]
calcium antagonist *or* **blocker** *n* any drug that prevents the influx of calcium ions into cardiac and smooth muscle: used to treat high blood pressure and angina.
calcium carbide *n* a grey salt of calcium used in the production of acetylene. Formula: CaC_2. Sometimes shortened to **carbide.**
calcium carbonate *n* a white crystalline salt occurring in limestone, chalk, and pearl: used in the production of lime. Formula: $CaCO_3$.
calcium chloride *n* a white deliquescent salt occurring naturally in seawater and used in the de-icing of roads. Formula: $CaCl_2$.
calcium hydroxide *n* a white crystalline slightly soluble alkali with many uses, esp. in cement, water softening, and the neutralization of acid soils. Formula: $Ca(OH)_2$. Also called: **lime, slaked lime, caustic lime.**
calcium oxide *n* a white crystalline base used in the production of calcium hydroxide and in the manufacture of glass and steel. Formula: CaO. Also called: **lime, quicklime, calx.**
calcium phosphate *n* an insoluble nonacid calcium salt that occurs in bones and is the main constituent of bone ash. Formula: $Ca_3(PO_4)_2$
calcspar (ˈkælkˌspɑː) *n* another name for **calcite.** [C19: from Swedish *kalkspat,* from *kalk* lime (ult. from L *calx*) + *spat* SPAR[3]]

THESAURUS

bar, coffee shop, lunchroom, restaurant, tearoom

cage *n* **1a** = **enclosure**, corral (*US*), pen, pound ◆ *vb* **5** = **shut up**, confine, coop up, fence in, immure, impound, imprison, incarcerate, lock up, mew, pound, restrain

cagey *adj Informal* = **wary**, careful, cautious, chary, discreet, guarded, noncommittal, shrewd, wily
Antonyms *adj* careless, dull, imprudent, indiscreet, reckless, unthinking, unwary

cajole *vb* = **persuade**, beguile, coax, decoy, dupe, entice, entrap, flatter, inveigle, lure, manoeuvre, mislead, seduce, sweet-talk (*inf.*), tempt, wheedle

cake *n* **4** = **block**, bar, cube, loaf, lump, mass, slab ◆ *vb* **11** = **encrust**, bake, cement, coagulate, congeal, consolidate, dry, harden, inspissate (*arch.*), ossify, solidify, thicken

calamitous *adj* = **disastrous**, blighting, cataclysmic, catastrophic, deadly, devastating, dire, fatal, pernicious, ruinous, tragic, woeful
Antonyms *adj* advantageous, beneficial, favourable, fortunate, good, helpful

calamity *n* **1, 2** = **disaster**, adversity, affliction, cataclysm, catastrophe, distress, downfall, hardship, misadventure, mischance, misfortune, mishap, reverse, ruin, scourge, tragedy, trial, tribulation, woe, wretchedness
Antonyms *n* advantage, benefit, blessing, boon, good fortune, good luck, help

calculable Ⓣ ('kælkjʊləbᵊl) *adj* **1** that may be computed or estimated. **2** predictable.
▸ ˌ**calculaˈbility** *n* ▸ ˈ**calculably** *adv*

calculate Ⓣ ('kælkjʊˌleɪt) *vb* **calculates, calculating, calculated. 1** to solve (one or more problems) by a mathematical procedure. **2** (*tr; may take a clause as object*) to determine beforehand by judgment, etc.; estimate. **3** (*tr; usually passive*) to aim: *the car was calculated to appeal to women.* **4** (*intr;* foll. by *on* or *upon*) to rely. **5** (*tr; may take a clause as object*) *US dialect.* to suppose. [C16: from LL *calculāre,* from *calculus* pebble used as a counter]
▸ **calculative** ('kælkjʊlətɪv) *adj*

calculated Ⓣ ('kælkjʊˌleɪtɪd) *adj* (*usually prenominal*) **1** undertaken after considering the likelihood of success or failure. **2** premeditated: *a calculated insult.*

calculating Ⓣ ('kælkjʊˌleɪtɪŋ) *adj* **1** selfishly scheming. **2** shrewd.
▸ ˈ**calcuˌlatingly** *adv*

calculation Ⓣ (ˌkælkjʊ'leɪʃən) *n* **1** the act, process, or result of calculating. **2** a forecast. **3** careful planning, esp. for selfish motives.

calculator ('kælkjʊˌleɪtə) *n* **1** a device for performing mathematical calculations, esp. an electronic device that can be held in the hand. **2** a person or thing that calculates. **3** a set of tables used as an aid to calculations.

calculous ('kælkjʊləs) *adj Pathol.* of or suffering from a calculus.

calculus ('kælkjʊləs) *n, pl* **calculuses. 1** a branch of mathematics, developed independently by Newton and Leibnitz. Both **differential calculus** and **integral calculus** are concerned with the effect on a function of an infinitesimal change in the independent variable. **2** any mathematical system of calculation involving the use of symbols. **3** (*pl* **calculi** (-ˌlaɪ)). *Pathol.* a stonelike concretion of minerals found in organs of the body. [C17: from L: pebble, from *calx* small stone, counter]

caldera (kæl'dɛərə) *n* a large basin-shaped crater at the top of a volcano, formed by the collapse of the cone. [C19: from Sp. *caldera,* lit.: CAULDRON]

caldron ('kɔːldrən) *n* a variant spelling of **cauldron.**

calèche (*French* kalɛʃ) *n* a variant of **calash.**

Caledonia (ˌkælɪ'dəʊnɪə) *n* the Roman name for **Scotland.**

Caledonian (ˌkælɪ'dəʊnɪən) *adj* **1** relating to Scotland. **2** of a period of mountain building in NW Europe in the Palaeozoic era. ◆ *n* **3** *Literary.* a native or inhabitant of Scotland.

calefacient (ˌkælɪ'feɪʃənt) *adj* **1** causing warmth. ◆ *n* **2** *Med.* an agent that warms, such as a mustard plaster. [C17: from L, from *calefacere* to heat]

calendar ('kælɪndə) *n* **1** a system for determining the beginning, length, and order of years and their divisions. **2** a table showing any such arrangement, esp. as applied to one or more successive years. **3** a list or schedule of pending court cases, appointments, etc. ◆ *vb* **calendars, calendaring, calendared. 4** (*tr*) to enter in a calendar; schedule. [C13: via Norman F from Med. L *kalendārium* account book, from *Kalendae* the CALENDS]
▸ **calendrical** (kæ'lɛndrɪkᵊl) *or* **caˈlendric** *adj*

calendar month *n* See **month** (sense 1).

calendar year *n* See **year** (sense 1).

calender ('kælɪndə) *n* **1** a machine in which paper or cloth is smoothed by passing between rollers. ◆ *vb* **2** (*tr*) to subject (material) to such a process. [C17: from F *calandre,* from ?]

calends *or* **kalends** ('kælɪndz) *pl n* the first day of each month in the ancient Roman calendar. [C14: from L *kalendae*]

calendula (kæ'lɛndjʊlə) *n* any of a genus of Eurasian plants, esp. the pot marigold, having orange-and-yellow rayed flowers. [C19: from Med. L, from L *kalendae* CALENDS]

calf[1] (kɑːf) *n, pl* **calves. 1** the young of cattle, esp. domestic cattle. **2** the young of certain other mammals, such as the buffalo and whale. **3** a large piece of ice detached from an iceberg, etc. **4 kill the fatted calf.** to celebrate lavishly, esp. as a welcome. [OE *cealf*]

calf[2] (kɑːf) *n, pl* **calves.** the thick fleshy part of the back of the leg between the ankle and the knee. [C14: from ON *kalfi*]

calf love *n* temporary infatuation of an adolescent for a member of the opposite sex.

calf's-foot jelly *n* a jelly made from the stock of boiled calves' feet and flavourings.

calfskin ('kɑːfˌskɪn) *n* **1** the skin or hide of a calf. **2** Also called: **calf. 2a** fine leather made from this skin. **2b** (*as modifier*): *calfskin boots.*

Calgon ('kælgɒn) *n Trademark.* a chemical compound, sodium hexametaphosphate, with water-softening properties, used in detergents.

calibrate Ⓣ ('kælɪˌbreɪt) *vb* **calibrates, calibrating, calibrated.** (*tr*) **1** to measure the calibre of (a gun, etc.). **2** to mark (the scale of a measuring instrument) so that readings can be made in appropriate units. **3** to determine the accuracy of (a measuring instrument, etc.).
▸ ˌ**caliˈbration** *n* ▸ ˈ**caliˌbrator** *n*

calibre Ⓣ *or US* **caliber** ('kælɪbə) *n* **1** the diameter of a cylindrical body, esp. the internal diameter of a tube or the bore of a firearm. **2** the diameter of a shell or bullet. **3** ability; distinction. **4** personal character: *a man of high calibre.* [C16: from OF, from It. *calibro,* from Ar. *qālib* shoemaker's last]
▸ ˈ**calibred** *or US* ˈ**calibered** *adj*

calices ('kælɪˌsiːz) *n* the plural of **calix.**

calico ('kælɪˌkəʊ) *n, pl* **calicoes** *or* **calicos. 1** a white or unbleached cotton fabric. **2** *Chiefly US.* a coarse printed cotton fabric. [C16: based on *Calicut,* town in India]

calif ('keɪlɪf, 'kæl-) *n* a variant spelling of **caliph.**

California poppy *n* a plant of the poppy family, native to the Pacific coast of North America, having yellow or orange flowers and finely dissected bluish-green leaves. Also called: **eschscholzia** *or* **eschscholtzia.**

californium (ˌkælɪ'fɔːnɪəm) *n* a transuranic element artificially produced from curium. Symbol: Cf; atomic no.: 98; half-life of most stable isotope, ^{251}Cf: 800 years (approx.). [C20: NL; discovered at the University of *California*]

calipash *or* **callipash** ('kælɪˌpæʃ) *n* the greenish glutinous edible part of the turtle found next to the upper shell. [C17: ? changed from Sp. *carapacho* CARAPACE]

calipee ('kælɪˌpiː) *n* the yellow glutinous edible part of the turtle found next to the lower shell. [C17: ? a var. of CALIPASH]

caliper ('kælɪpə) *n* the usual US spelling of **calliper.**

caliph, calif, *or* **khalif** ('keɪlɪf, 'kæl-) *n Islam.* the title of the successors of Mohammed as rulers of the Islamic world. [C14: from OF, from Ar. *khalīfa* successor]

caliphate, califate *or* **khalifate** ('keɪlɪˌfeɪt) *n* the office, jurisdiction, or reign of a caliph.

calisthenics (ˌkælɪs'θɛnɪks) *n* a variant spelling (esp. US) of **callisthenics.**

calix ('keɪlɪks, 'kæ-) *n, pl* **calices.** a cup; chalice. [C18: from L: CHALICE]

calk[1] (kɔːk) *vb* a variant spelling of **caulk.**

calk[2] (kɔːk) *or* **calkin** ('kɔːkɪn, 'kæl-) *n* **1** a metal projection on a horse's shoe to prevent slipping. ◆ *vb* (*tr*) **2** to provide with calks. [C17: from L *calx* heel]

call Ⓣ (kɔːl) *vb* **1** (often foll. by *out*) to speak or utter (words, sounds, etc.) loudly so as to attract attention: *he called out her name.* **2** (*tr*) to ask or order to come: *to call a policeman.* **3** (*intr;* sometimes foll. by *on*) to make a visit (to): *she called on him.* **4** (often foll. by *up*) to telephone (a person). **5** (*tr*) to summon to a specific office, profession, etc. **6** (of animals or birds) to utter (a characteristic sound or cry). **7** (*tr*) to summon (a bird or animal), as by imitating its cry. **8** (*tr*) to name or style: *they called the dog Rover.* **9** (*tr*) to designate: *they called him a coward.* **10** (*tr*) to regard in a specific way: *I call it a foolish waste of time.* **11** (*tr*) to attract (attention). **12** (*tr*) to read (a list, etc.) aloud to check for omissions or absentees. **13** (when *tr,* usually foll. by *for*) to give an order (for): *to call a strike.* **14** (*intr*) to try to predict the result of tossing a coin. **15** (*tr*) to awaken: *I was called early this morning.* **16** (*tr*) to cause to assemble. **17** (*tr*) *Sport.* (of an umpire, etc.) to pass judgment upon (a shot, etc.) with a call. **18** (*tr*) *Austral. & NZ.* to broadcast a commentary on (a horse race, etc.). **19** (*tr*) to demand repayment of (a loan, security, etc.). **20** (*tr*) *Brit.* to award (a student at an Inn of Court) the degree of barrister (esp. in **call to the bar**). **21** (*tr*) *Poker.* to demand that (a player) expose his hand, after equalling his bet. **22** (*intr*) *Bridge.* to make a bid. **23** (in square-dancing) to call out (instructions) to the dancers. **24** (*intr;* foll. by *for*) **24a** to require: *this problem calls for study.* **24b** to come or go (for) in order to fetch. **25** (*intr;* foll. by *on* or *upon*) to make an appeal or request (to): *they called upon him to reply.* **26 call into being.** to create. **27 call**

THESAURUS

calculable *adj* **1** = **computable**, appraisable, assessable, determinable, estimable (*rare*), gaugeable *or* gageable, judgeable, measurable, quantifiable, ratable *or* rateable

calculate *vb* **1, 2** = **work out**, adjust, compute, consider, count, determine, enumerate, estimate, figure, gauge, judge, rate, reckon, value, weigh **3** = **plan**, aim, design, intend

calculated *adj* **1, 2** = **deliberate**, considered, intended, intentional, planned, premeditated, purposeful
Antonyms *adj* haphazard, hasty, heedless, hurried, impetuous, impulsive, rash, spontaneous, unintentional, unplanned, unpremeditated

calculating *adj* **1, 2** = **scheming**, canny, cautious, contriving, crafty, cunning, designing, devious, Machiavellian, manipulative, politic, sharp, shrewd, sly
Antonyms *adj* blunt, direct, downright, frank, guileless, honest, open, outspoken, sincere, undesigning

calculation *n* **1, 2** = **working out**, answer, computation, estimate, estimation, figuring, forecast, judgment, reckoning, result **3** = **planning**, caution, circumspection, contrivance, deliberation, discretion, foresight, forethought, precaution

calibrate *vb* **1-3** = **measure**, gauge

calibre *n* **1** = **diameter**, bore, gauge, measure **3, 4** = **worth**, ability, capacity, distinction, endowment, faculty, force, gifts, merit, parts, quality, scope, stature, strength, talent

call *vb* **1, 15** = **cry**, announce, arouse, awaken, cry out, hail, halloo, proclaim, rouse, shout, waken, yell **3** *sometimes foll. by* **on** = **visit**, drop in on, look in on, look up, see **4** = **phone**, give (someone) a bell (*Brit. sl.*), ring up (*inf., chiefly Brit.*), telephone **8, 9** = **name**, christen, denominate, describe as, designate, dub, entitle, label, style, term **10** = **consider**, estimate, judge, regard, think **16** = **summon**, assemble, bid, collect, contact, convene, convoke, gather, invite, muster, rally **24a** *foll. by* **for** = **require**, demand, entail, involve, necessitate, need, occasion, suggest **24b** *foll. by* **for** = **fetch**, collect, pick up, uplift (*Scot.*) **25** *foll. by* **on** *or* **upon** = **request**, appeal to, ask, bid, call upon, entreat, invite, invoke, summon, supplicate ◆ *n* **29** = **cry**, hail, scream, shout, signal, whoop, yell **32-34** = **summons**, announcement, appeal, command, demand, invitation, notice, order, plea, request, supplication, visit **38, 39** = **need**, cause, claim, excuse, grounds, justification, occasion, reason, right, urge
Antonyms *vb* ≠ **cry**: be quiet, be silent, murmur, mutter, speak softly, whisper ≠ **summon**: call off, cancel, dismiss, disperse, excuse, release ◆ *n* ≠ **cry**: murmur, mutter, whisper ≠ **summons**: dismissal, release

someone's bluff. see **bluff**[1]. **28 call to mind.** to remember or cause to be remembered. ◆ *n* **29** a cry or shout. **30** the characteristic cry of a bird or animal. **31** a device, such as a whistle, intended to imitate the cry of a bird or animal. **32** a summons or invitation. **33** a summons or signal sounded on a horn, bugle, etc. **34** a short visit: *the doctor made six calls this morning.* **35** an inner urge to some task or profession; vocation. **36** allure or fascination, esp. of a place: *the call of the forest.* **37** need, demand, or occasion: *there is no call to shout.* **38** demand or claim (esp. in **the call of duty**). **39** *Theatre.* a notice to actors informing them of times of rehearsals. **40** a conversation or a request for a connection by telephone. **41** *Commerce.* **41a** a demand for repayment of a loan. **41b** (*as modifier*): *call money.* **42** *Finance.* a demand for redeemable bonds or shares to be presented for repayment. **43** *Poker.* a demand for a hand or hands to be exposed. **44** *Bridge.* a bid or a player's turn to bid. **45** *Sport.* a decision of an umpire or referee regarding a shot, pitch, etc. **46** *Austral.* a broadcast commentary on a horse race, etc. **47** Also called: **call option.** *Stock Exchange.* an option to buy a stated amount of securities at a specified price during a specified period. **48 on call. 48a** (of a loan, etc.) repayable on demand. **48b** available to be called for work outside normal working hours. **49 within call.** accessible. ◆ See also **call down, call forth,** etc. [OE *ceallian*]

calla ('kælə) *n* **1** Also called: **calla lily, arum lily.** a southern African plant which has a white funnel-shaped spathe enclosing a yellow spadix. **2** a plant that grows in wet places and has a white spathe and red berries. [C19: from NL, prob. from Gk *kalleia* wattles on a cock, prob. from *kallos* beauty]

Callanetics (ˌkælə'nɛtɪks) *n* (*functioning as sing*) *Trademark.* a system of exercise involving frequent repetition of small muscular movements and squeezes, designed to improve muscle tone. [C20: after *Callan* Pinckney (born 1939), its US inventor]

call bird *n Marketing.* a cheap article displayed in a shop to attract custom, in the hope of selling expensive items.

call box *n* a soundproof enclosure for a public telephone. Also called: **telephone kiosk.**

callboy ('kɔːlˌbɔɪ) *n* a person who notifies actors when it is time to go on stage.

call centre *n* an office where staff carry out an organization's telephone transactions.

call down *vb* (*tr, adv*) to request or invoke: *to call down God's anger.*

caller ('kɔːlə) *n* **1** a person or thing that calls, esp. a person who makes a brief visit. **2** *Austral.* a racing commentator.

call forth *vb* (*tr, adv*) to cause (something) to come into action or existence.

call girl *n* a prostitute with whom appointments are made by telephone.

calligraphy (kə'lɪgrəfɪ) *n* handwriting, esp. beautiful handwriting.
▸**cal'ligrapher** *or* **cal'ligraphist** *n* ▸**calligraphic** (ˌkælɪ'græfɪk) *adj*

call in *vb* (*adv*) **1** (*intr;* often foll. by *on*) to pay a visit, esp. a brief one: *call in if you are in the neighbourhood.* **2** (*tr*) to demand payment of: *to call in a loan.* **3** (*tr*) to take (something) out of circulation, because it is defective. **4** to summon to one's assistance: *to call in a specialist.*

calling ⓣ ('kɔːlɪŋ) *n* **1** a strong inner urge to follow an occupation, etc.; vocation. **2** an occupation, profession, or trade.

calling card *n* the usual US and Canad. term for **visiting card.**

calliope (kə'laɪəpɪ) *n US & Canad.* a steam organ. [after CALLIOPE (lit.: beautiful-voiced)]

calliper *or US* **caliper** ('kælɪpə) *n* **1** (*often pl*) Also called: **calliper compasses.** an instrument for measuring internal or external dimensions, consisting of two steel legs hinged together. **2** Also called: **calliper splint.** *Med.* a metal splint for supporting the leg. ◆ *vb* **3** (*tr*) to measure with callipers. [C16: var. of CALIBRE]

calliper rule *n* a measuring instrument having two parallel jaws, one fixed and the other sliding.

callistemon (kə'lɪstəmən) *n* another name for **bottlebrush** (sense 1).

callisthenics *or* **calisthenics** (ˌkælɪs'θɛnɪks) *n* **1** (*functioning as pl*) light exercises designed to promote general fitness. **2** (*functioning as sing*) the practice of callisthenic exercises. [C19: from Gk *kalli-* beautiful + *sthenos* strength]
▸ˌ**callis'thenic** *or* ˌ**calis'thenic** *adj*

call loan *n* a loan that is repayable on demand. Also called: **demand loan.**

call off *vb* (*tr, adv*) **1** to cancel or abandon: *the game was called off.* **2** to order (an animal or person) to desist: *the man called off his dog.* **3** to stop (something).

callose ('kæləuz, -ləus) *n* a carbohydrate, a polymer of glucose, found in plants.

callosity (kə'lɒsɪtɪ) *n, pl* **callosities. 1** hard-heartedness. **2** a callus.

callous ⓣ ('kæləs) *adj* **1** insensitive. **2** (of skin) hardened and thickened. ◆ *vb* **3** *Pathol.* to make or become callous. [C16: from L *callōsus;* see CALLUS]
▸'**callously** *adv* ▸'**callousness** *n*

call out *vb* (*adv*) **1** to utter aloud, esp. loudly. **2** (*tr*) to summon: *call out the troops.* **3** (*tr*) to order (workers) to strike. **4** (*tr*) to challenge to a duel.

callow ⓣ ('kæləu) *adj* lacking experience of life; immature. [OE *calu*]
▸'**callowness** *n*

call sign *n* a group of letters and numbers identifying a radio transmitting station.

call up *vb* (*tr, adv*) **1** to summon to report for active military service, as in time of war. **2** to recall (something); evoke. **3** to bring or summon (people, etc.) into action. **4** to telephone. ◆ *n* **call-up. 5a** a general order to report for military service. **5b** the number of men so summoned.

callus ('kæləs) *n, pl* **calluses. 1** Also called: **callosity.** an area of skin that is hard or thick, esp. on the sole of the foot. **2** an area of bony tissue formed during the healing of a fractured bone. **3** *Bot.* a mass of hard protective tissue produced in woody plants at the site of an injury. [C16: from L, var. of *callum* hardened skin]

calm ⓣ (kɑːm) *adj* **1** still: *a calm sea.* **2** *Meteorol.* without wind, or with wind of less than 1 mph. **3** not disturbed, agitated, or excited. **4** tranquil; serene: *a calm voice.* ◆ *n* **5** an absence of disturbance or rough motion. **6** absence of wind. **7** tranquillity. ◆ *vb* **8** (often foll. by *down*) to make or become calm. [C14: from OF *calme,* from OIt., from LL *cauma* heat, hence a rest during the heat of the day, from Gk, from *kaiein* to burn]
▸'**calmly** *adv* ▸'**calmness** *n*

calmative ('kælmətɪv, 'kɑːmə-) *adj* (of a remedy or agent) sedative.

caló (kə'ləu; *Spanish* ka'lo) *n* a form of Mexican Spanish incorporating many slang terms and English words: spoken esp. by Mexican Americans in the SW US.

calomel ('kæləˌmɛl, -məl) *n* a colourless tasteless powder consisting chiefly of mercurous chloride, used medicinally, esp. as a cathartic. [C17: ?from NL *calomelas* (unattested), lit.: beautiful black, from Gk *kalos* beautiful + *melas* black]

Calor Gas ('kælə) *n Trademark.* butane gas liquefied under pressure in portable containers for domestic use.

caloric (kə'lɒrɪk) *adj* **1** of or concerned with heat or calories. ◆ *n* **2** *Obs.* a hypothetical elastic fluid, the embodiment of heat.

calorie *or* **calory** ('kælərɪ) *n, pl* **calories.** a unit of heat, equal to 4.1868 joules (**International Table calorie**): formerly defined as the quantity of heat required to raise the temperature of 1 gram of water by 1°C. Abbrev.: **cal.** Also called: **small calorie.** [C19: from F, from L *calor* heat]

Calorie ('kælərɪ) *n* **1** Also called: **kilogram calorie, large calorie.** a unit of heat, equal to one thousand calories. Abbrev.: **Cal. 2** the amount of a specific food capable of producing one thousand calories of energy.

calorific (ˌkælə'rɪfɪk) *adj* of, concerning, or generating heat.
▸ˌ**calo'rifically** *adv*

calorific value *n* the quantity of heat produced by the complete combustion of a given mass of a fuel.

calorimeter (ˌkælə'rɪmɪtə) *n* an apparatus for measuring amounts of heat, esp. to find calorific values, etc.
▸**calorimetric** (ˌkælərɪ'mɛtrɪk) *adj* ▸ˌ**calo'rimetry** *n*

calorize *or* **calorise** ('kæləˌraɪz) *vb* **calorizes, calorizing, calorized** *or* **calorises, calorising, calorised.** (*tr*) to coat (a ferrous metal) by spraying with aluminium powder and then heating.

calque (kælk) *n* another word for **loan translation.** [C20: from F: a tracing, from L *calcāre* to tread]

calumet ('kæljuˌmɛt) *n* the peace pipe. [C18: from Canad. F, from F: straw, from LL *calamellus* a little reed, from L: CALAMUS]

THESAURUS

calling *n* **1, 2** = **profession**, business, career, employment, life's work, line, métier, mission, occupation, province, pursuit, trade, vocation, walk of life, work

callous *adj* **1** = **heartless**, apathetic, case-hardened, cold, hard-bitten, hard-boiled (*inf.*), hardened, hardhearted, harsh, indifferent, indurated (*rare*), insensate, insensible, insensitive, inured, obdurate, soulless, thick-skinned, torpid, uncaring, unfeeling, unresponsive, unsusceptible, unsympathetic
Antonyms *adj* caring, compassionate, considerate, gentle, sensitive, soft, sympathetic, tender, understanding

callously *adv* **1** = **heartlessly**, apathetically, brutally, coldly, hardheartedly, harshly, indifferently, insensately, insensibly, insensitively, obdurately, soullessly, torpidly, unfeelingly

callousness *n* **1** = **heartlessness**, apathy, coldness, hardheartedness, hardness, harshness, indifference, induration (*rare*), insensateness, insensibility, insensibleness, insensitivity, inuredness *or* enuredness, obduracy, obdurateness, soullessness, torpidity, unfeelingness

callow *adj* = **inexperienced**, green, guileless, immature, jejune, juvenile, naive, puerile, raw, unfledged, unsophisticated, untried

callowness *n* = **inexperience**, greenness, guilelessness, immaturity, innocence, jejuneness, jejunity, juvenileness, naïveté *or* naivety, puerility, rawness, unsophisticatedness, unsophistication

calm *adj* **1** = **still**, balmy, halcyon, mild, pacific, peaceful, placid, quiet, restful, serene, smooth, tranquil, windless **3** = **cool**, as cool as a cucumber, collected, composed, dispassionate, equable, impassive, imperturbable, keeping one's cool, relaxed, sedate, self-possessed, undisturbed, unemotional, unexcitable, unexcited, unfazed (*inf.*), unflappable (*inf.*), unmoved, unruffled ◆ *n* **7** = **peacefulness**, calmness, hush, peace, quiet, repose, serenity, stillness ◆ *vb* **8** = **quieten**, hush, mollify, placate, relax, soothe
Antonyms *adj* ≠ **still**: rough, stormy, wild ≠ **cool**: agitated, aroused, discomposed, disturbed, emotional, excited, fierce, frantic, heated, perturbed, shaken, troubled, worried ◆ *n* ≠ **peacefulness**: agitation, disturbance, wildness ◆ *vb* ≠ **quieten**: aggravate, agitate, arouse, disturb, excite, irritate, stir

calmly *adv* **3, 4** = **coolly**, casually, collectedly, composedly, dispassionately, equably, impassively, imperturbably, nonchalantly, placidly, relaxedly, sedately, self-possessedly, serenely, tranquilly, unflappably, unflinchingly

calmness *n* **1** = **peacefulness**, calm, hush, motionlessness, peace, placidity, quiet, repose, restfulness, serenity, smoothness, stillness, tranquillity **3** = **coolness**, composure, cool (*sl.*), dispassion, equanimity, impassivity, imperturbability, poise, sang-froid, self-possession

calumniate (kə'lʌmnɪˌeɪt) *vb* **calumniates, calumniating, calumniated.** (*tr*) to slander.
▸**caˌlumni'ation** *n* ▸**ca'lumniˌator** *n*

calumny ❶ ('kæləmnɪ) *n, pl* **calumnies. 1** the malicious utterance of false charges or misrepresentation. **2** such a false charge or misrepresentation. [C15: from L *calumnia* deception, slander]
▸**calumnious** (kə'lʌmnɪəs) *or* **ca'lumniatory** *adj*

Calvados ('kælvəˌdɒs) *n* an apple brandy distilled from cider in Calvados, a region in Normandy, France.

Calvary ('kælvərɪ) *n* the place just outside the walls of Jerusalem where Jesus was crucified. Also called: **Golgotha.** [from LL *Calvāria,* translation of Gk *kranion* skull, translation of Aramaic *gulgulta* Golgotha]

calve (kɑːv) *vb* **calves, calving, calved. 1** to give birth to (a calf). **2** (of a glacier or iceberg) to release (masses of ice) in breaking up.

calves (kɑːvz) *n* the plural of **calf**[1] and **calf**[2].

Calvin cycle *n Bot.* a series of reactions, occurring during photosynthesis, in which glucose is synthesized from carbon dioxide. [C20: named after M. *Calvin* (1911–97), US chemist who elucidated it]

Calvinism ('kælvɪˌnɪzəm) *n* the theological system of Calvin, 16th-century French theologian, and his followers, characterized by emphasis on predestination and justification by faith.
▸**'Calvinist** *n, adj* ▸**ˌCalvin'istic** *or* **ˌCalvin'istical** *adj*

calx (kælks) *n, pl* **calxes** *or* **calces. 1** the powdery metallic oxide formed when an ore or mineral is roasted. **2** calcium oxide. **3** *Anat.* the heel. [C15: from L: lime, from Gk *khalix* pebble]

calypso (kə'lɪpsəʊ) *n, pl* **calypsos.** a popular type of satirical West Indian ballad, esp. from Trinidad, usually extemporized to a syncopated accompaniment. [C20: from *Calypso,* sea nymph in Gk myth]

calyx ('keɪlɪks, 'kælɪks) *n, pl* **calyxes** *or* **calyces** ('kælɪˌsiːz, 'keɪlɪ-). **1** the sepals of a flower collectively that protect the developing flower bud. **2** any cup-shaped cavity or structure. [C17: from L, from Gk *kalux* shell, from *kaluptein* to cover]

calzone (kæl'tsəʊnɪ) *n* a dish of Italian origin consisting of pizza dough folded over a filling of cheese and tomatoes, herbs, ham, etc. [C20: It., lit.: trouser leg, from *calzoni* trousers]

cam (kæm) *n* a slider or roller attached to a moving shaft to give a particular type of motion to a part in contact with it. [C16: from Du. *kam* comb]

CAM (kæm) *acronym for* computer-aided manufacture.

camaraderie ❶ (ˌkæmə'rɑːdərɪ) *n* a spirit of familiarity and trust existing between friends. [C19: from F, from *camarade* COMRADE]

camarilla (ˌkæmə'rɪlə) *n* a group of confidential advisers, esp. formerly, to the Spanish kings. [C19: from Sp., lit.: a little room]

camber ('kæmbə) *n* **1** a slight upward curve to the centre of the surface of a road, ship's deck, etc. **2** another name for **bank**[2] (sense 8). **3** an outward inclination of the front wheels of a road vehicle so that they are slightly closer together at the bottom. **4** aerofoil curvature expressed by the ratio of the maximum height of the aerofoil mean line to its chord. ◆ *vb* **5** to form or be formed with a surface that curves upwards to its centre. [C17: from OF *cambre* curved, from L *camurus*]

cambium ('kæmbɪəm) *n, pl* **cambiums** *or* **cambia** (-bɪə). *Bot.* a layer of cells that increases the girth of stems and roots. [C17: from Med. L: exchange, from LL *cambiāre* to exchange]
▸**'cambial** *adj*

Cambodian (kæm'bəʊdɪən) *adj* **1** of or relating to Cambodia, in SE Asia, or its people. ◆ *n* **2** a native or inhabitant of Cambodia.

Cambrian ('kæmbrɪən) *adj* **1** of or formed in the first 100 million years of the Palaeozoic era. **2** of or relating to Wales. ◆ *n* **3 the.** the Cambrian period or rock system. **4** a Welshman.

cambric ('keɪmbrɪk) *n* a fine white linen fabric. [C16: from Flemish *Kamerijk* Cambrai, town in N France]

Cambs *abbrev. for* Cambridgeshire.

camcorder ('kæmˌkɔːdə) *n* a video camera and recorder combined in a portable unit.

came (keɪm) *vb* the past tense of **come.**

camel ('kæməl) *n* **1** either of two cud-chewing, humped mammals (see **Arabian camel, Bactrian camel**) that are adapted for surviving long periods without food or water in desert regions. **2** a float attached to a vessel to increase its buoyancy. **3a** a fawn colour. **3b** (*as adj*): *a camel coat.* [OE, from L, from Gk *kamēlos,* of Semitic origin]

cameleer (ˌkæmɪ'lɪə) *n* a camel driver.

camel hair *or* **camel's hair** *n* **1** the hair of the camel, used in rugs, etc. **2a** soft cloth made of or containing this hair or a substitute, usually tan in colour. **2b** (*as modifier*): *a camelhair coat.* **3a** the hair of the squirrel's tail, used for paintbrushes. **3b** (*as modifier*): *a camelhair brush.*

camellia (kə'miːlɪə) *n* any of a genus of ornamental shrubs having glossy evergreen leaves and showy white, pink, or red flowers. Also called: **japonica.** [C18: NL, after Georg Josef *Kamel* (1661–1706), Moravian Jesuit missionary]

camelopard ('kæmɪləˌpɑːd, kə'mɛl-) *n* an obsolete word for **giraffe.** [C14: from Med. L, from Gk, from *kamēlos* CAMEL + *pardalis* LEOPARD, because the giraffe was thought to have a head like a camel's and spots like a leopard's]

Camembert ('kæməmˌbɛə) *n* a soft creamy cheese. [F, from *Camembert,* a village in Normandy]

cameo ('kæmɪˌəʊ) *n, pl* **cameos. 1** a medallion, as on a brooch or ring, with a profile head carved in relief. **2** an engraving upon a gem or other stone so that the background is of a different colour from the raised design. **3** a stone with such an engraving. **4a** a brief dramatic scene played by a well-known actor or actress in a film or television play. **4b** (*as modifier*): *a cameo performance.* **5** a short literary work. [C15: from It. *cammeo,* from ?]

camera ('kæmərə) *n* **1** an optical device consisting of a lens system set in a light-proof construction inside which a light-sensitive film or plate can be positioned. **2** *Television.* the equipment used to convert the optical image of a scene into the corresponding electrical signals. **3** (*pl* **camerae** (-əˌriː)). a judge's private room. **4 in camera. 4a** *Law.* relating to a hearing from which members of the public are excluded. **4b** in private. [C18: from L: vault, from Gk *kamara*]

cameraman ('kæmərəˌmæn) *n, pl* **cameramen.** a person who operates a film or television camera.

camera obscura (ɒb'skjʊərə) *n* a darkened chamber with an aperture, in which images of outside objects are projected onto a flat surface. [NL: dark chamber]

camiknickers ('kæmɪˌnɪkəz) *pl n* women's knickers attached to a camisole top.

camisole ('kæmɪˌsəʊl) *n* **1** a woman's underbodice with shoulder straps, originally designed as a cover for a corset. **2** a woman's short negligee. [C19: from F, from Provençal *camisola,* from *camisa* shirt, from LL *camīsia*]

camomile *or* **chamomile** ('kæməˌmaɪl) *n* **1** any of a genus of aromatic plants whose finely dissected leaves and daisy-like flowers are used medicinally. **2** any plant of a related genus as **German** or **wild camomile. 3 camomile tea.** a herbal beverage made from the fragrant leaves and flowers of any of these plants. [C14: from OF, from Med. L, from Gk *khamaimēlon* lit., earth-apple (referring to the scent of the flowers)]

camouflage ❶ ('kæməˌflɑːʒ) *n* **1** the exploitation of natural surroundings or artificial aids to conceal or disguise the presence of military units, etc. **2** (*modifier*) (of fabric or clothing) having a design of irregular patches, in dull colours (such as browns and greens), as used in military camouflage. **3** the means by which animals escape the notice of predators. **4** a device or expedient designed to conceal or deceive. ◆ *vb* **camouflages, camouflaging, camouflaged. 5** (*tr*) to conceal by camouflage. [C20: from F, from *camoufler,* from It. *camuffare* to disguise, from ?]

camp[1] ❶ (kæmp) *n* **1** a place where tents, cabins, etc., are erected for the use of military troops, etc. **2** tents, cabins, etc., used as temporary lodgings by holiday-makers, Scouts, Gypsies, etc. **3** the group of people living in such lodgings. **4** a group supporting a given doctrine: *the socialist camp.* **5** (*modifier*) suitable for use in temporary quarters, on holiday, etc.: *a camp bed.* **6** *S. African.* a field or pasture. **7** *Austral.* a place where sheep or cattle gather to rest. ◆ *vb* (*intr*) **8** (often foll. by *down*) to establish or set up a camp. **9** (often foll. by *out*) to live temporarily in or as if in a tent. [C16: from OF, ult. from L *campus* field]
▸**'camping** *n*

camp[2] ❶ (kæmp) *Inf.* ◆ *adj* **1** effeminate; affected. **2** homosexual. **3** consciously artificial, vulgar, or mannered. ◆ *vb* **4** (*tr*) to perform or invest with a camp quality. **5 camp it up. 5a** to overact. **5b** to flaunt one's homosexuality. [C20: from ?]
▸**'campy** *adj*

campaign ❶ (kæm'peɪn) *n* **1** a series of coordinated activities, such as public speaking, designed to achieve a social, political, or commercial goal: *a presidential campaign.* **2** *Mil.* a number of operations aimed at achieving a single objective. ◆ *vb* **3** (*intr;* often foll. by *for*) to conduct, serve in, or go on a campaign. [C17: from F *campagne* open country, from It., from LL, from L *campus* field]
▸**cam'paigner** *n*

campanile (ˌkæmpə'niːlɪ) *n* (esp. in Italy) a bell tower, not usually attached to another building. [C17: from It., from *campana* bell]

campanology (ˌkæmpə'nɒlədʒɪ) *n* the art or skill of ringing bells. [C19: from NL, from LL *campāna* bell]
▸**campanological** (ˌkæmpənə'lɒdʒɪkᵊl) *adj* ▸**ˌcampa'nologist** *or* **ˌcampa'nologer** *n*

campanula (kæm'pænjʊlə) *n* any of a genus of N temperate plants having blue or white bell-shaped flowers. Also called: **bellflower.** [C17: from NL: a little bell, from LL *campāna* bell]

camp drafting *n Austral.* a competitive test of horsemen's skill in drafting cattle.

THESAURUS

calumny *n* **1** = **slander**, abuse, aspersion, backbiting, calumniation, defamation, denigration, derogation, detraction, evil-speaking, insult, libel, lying, misrepresentation, obloquy, revilement, smear, stigma, vilification, vituperation

camaraderie *n* = **comradeship**, brotherhood, brotherliness, companionability, companionship, esprit de corps, fellowship, fraternization, good-fellowship, togetherness

camouflage *n* **1, 4** = **disguise**, blind, cloak, concealment, cover, deceptive markings, false appearance, front, guise, mask, masquerade, mimicry, protective colouring, screen, subterfuge ◆ *vb* **5** = **disguise**, cloak, conceal, cover, hide, mask, obfuscate, obscure, screen, veil

Antonyms *vb* ≠ **disguise:** bare, display, exhibit, expose, reveal, show, uncover, unmask, unveil

camp[1] *n* **1** = **camp site**, bivouac, camping ground, cantonment (*Military*), encampment, tents

camp[2] *adj* **1, 3** *Informal* = **effeminate**, affected, artificial, camped up, campy (*inf.*), mannered, ostentatious, poncy (*sl.*), posturing

campaign *n* **1, 2** = **operation**, attack, crusade, drive, expedition, jihad (*rare*), movement, offensive, push

campaigner *n* **1** = **demonstrator**, activist, crusader

camper ('kæmpə) *n* **1** a person who lives or temporarily stays in a tent, cabin, etc. **2** *US & Canad.* a vehicle equipped for camping out.

camp follower *n* **1** any civilian, esp. a prostitute, who unofficially provides services to military personnel. **2** a nonmember who is sympathetic to a particular group, theory, etc.

camphor ('kæmfə) *n* a whitish crystalline aromatic ketone obtained from the wood of an Asian or Australian laurel (**camphor tree**): used in medicine as a liniment. [C15: from OF *camphre,* from Med. L *camphora,* from Ar. *kāfūr,* from Malay *kāpūr* chalk]
▸**camphoric** (kæm'fɒrɪk) *adj*

camphorate ('kæmfəˌreɪt) *vb* **camphorates, camphorating, camphorated.** (*tr*) to apply, treat with, or impregnate with camphor.

camphor ball *n* another name for **mothball** (sense 1).

camphor ice *n* an ointment consisting of camphor, white wax, spermaceti, and castor oil, used to treat skin ailments, esp. chapped skin.

camphor wood *n Austral.* a popular name for any of several trees with pungent smelling wood.

campion ('kæmpɪən) *n* any of various plants related to the pink, having red, pink, or white flowers. [C16: prob. from *campion,* obs. var. of CHAMPION]

camp oven *n Austral. & NZ.* a heavy metal pot or box with a lid, used for baking over an open fire.

camp pie *n Austral.* tinned meat.

camp site *n* an area on which holiday-makers may pitch a tent, etc. Also called: **camping site.**

campus ('kæmpəs) *n, pl* **campuses. 1** the grounds and buildings of a university. **2** *Chiefly US.* the outside area of a college, etc. [C18: from L: field]

campylobacter ('kæmpɪləʊˌbæktə) *n* a rod-shaped bacterium that causes infections in animals and man; a common cause of gastroenteritis. [from Gk *kampulos* bent + BACTER(IUM)]

camshaft ('kæmˌʃɑːft) *n* a shaft having one or more cams attached to it.

can[1] (kæn; *unstressed* kən) *vb, past* **could.** (takes an infinitive without *to* or an implied infinitive) used as an auxiliary: **1** to indicate ability, skill, or fitness to perform a task: *I can run.* **2** to indicate permission or the right to something: *can I have a drink?* **3** to indicate knowledge of how to do something: *he can speak three languages.* **4** to indicate the possibility, opportunity, or likelihood: *my trainer says I can win the race.* [OE *cunnan*]

> **USAGE NOTE** See at **may**[1].

can[2] (kæn) *n* **1** a container, esp. for liquids, usually of thin metal: *a petrol can.* **2** a tin (metal container): *a beer can.* **3** Also: **canful.** the contents of a can or the amount a can will hold. **4** a slang word for **prison. 5** *US & Canad.* a slang word for **toilet. 6** a shallow cylindrical metal container used for storing and handling film. **7 can of worms.** *Inf.* a complicated problem. **8 in the can. 8a** (of a film, piece of music, etc.) having been recorded, edited, etc. **8b** *Inf.* agreed: *the contract is in the can.* ◆ *vb* **cans, canning, canned. 9** to put (food, etc.) into a can or cans. [OE *canne*]
▸**'canner** *n*

Can. *abbrev. for:* **1** Canada. **2** Canadian.

Canaan ('keɪnən) *n* an ancient region between the River Jordan and the Mediterranean: the Promised Land of the Israelites.

Canaanite ('keɪnəˌnaɪt) *n* a member of an ancient Semitic people who occupied the land of Canaan before the Israelite conquest.

Canada balsam *n* **1** a yellow transparent resin obtained from the balsam fir. Because its refractive index is similar to that of glass, it is used as a mounting medium for microscope specimens. **2** another name for **balsam fir.**

Canada Day *n* (in Canada) July 1, the anniversary of the day in 1867 when Canada received dominion status: a public holiday.

Canada goose *n* a large common greyish-brown North American goose with a black neck and head and a white throat patch.

Canada jay *n* a grey crestless jay, notorious in northern parts of N America for its stealing. Also called: **camp robber, whisky-jack.**

Canadian (kə'neɪdɪən) *adj* **1** of or relating to Canada or its people. ◆ *n* **2** a native, citizen, or inhabitant of Canada.

Canadiana (kəˌneɪdɪ'ɑːnə; *Canad.* -'ænə) *n* objects, such as books, furniture, and antiques, relating to Canadian history and culture.

Canadian football *n* a game like American football played on a grass pitch between teams of 12 players.

Canadianism (kə'neɪdɪəˌnɪzəm) *n* **1** the Canadian national character or spirit. **2** a linguistic usage, custom, or other feature peculiar to Canada, its people, or their culture.

Canadianize *or* **Canadianise** (kə'neɪdɪəˌnaɪz) *vb* **Canadianizes, Canadianizing, Canadianized** *or* **Canadianises, Canadianising, Canadianised.** to make or become Canadian by changing customs, ownership, character, content, etc.

Canadian Shield *n* the wide area of Precambrian rock extending over most of E and central Canada: rich in minerals. Also called: **Laurentian Shield.**

Canadien (*French* kanadjẽ; *English* kəˌnædɪ'ɛn) *or* (*fem*) **Canadienne** (*French* kanadjɛn; *English* kəˌnædɪ'ɛn) *n* a French Canadian.

canaille *French.* (kanɑj) *n* the masses; mob; rabble. [C17: from F, from It. *canaglia* pack of dogs]

canakin ('kænɪkɪn) *n* a variant spelling of **cannikin.**

canal ❶ (kə'næl) *n* **1** an artificial waterway constructed for navigation, irrigation, etc. **2** any of various passages or ducts: *the alimentary canal.* **3** any of various intercellular spaces in plants. **4** *Astron.* any of the indistinct surface features of Mars orig. thought to be a network of channels. ◆ *vb* **canals, canalling, canalled** *or US* **canals, canaling, canaled.** (*tr*) **5** to dig a canal through. **6** to provide with a canal or canals. [C15 (in the sense: pipe, tube): from L *canālis* channel, from *canna* reed]

canal boat *n* a long narrow boat used on canals, esp. for carrying freight.

canaliculus (ˌkænə'lɪkjʊləs) *n, pl* **canaliculi** (-ˌlaɪ). a small channel or groove, as in some bones. [C16: from L: a little channel, from *canālis* CANAL]
▸ˌ**cana'licular** *or* ˌ**cana'liculate** *adj*

canalize *or* **canalise** ('kænəˌlaɪz) *vb* **canalizes, canalizing, canalized** *or* **canalises, canalising, canalised.** (*tr*) **1** to provide with or convert into a canal or canals. **2** to give a particular direction to or provide an outlet for.
▸ˌ**canali'zation** *or* ˌ**canali'sation** *n*

canal ray *n Physics.* a stream of positive ions produced in a discharge tube by allowing them to pass through holes in the cathode.

canapé ('kænəpɪ, -ˌpeɪ) *n* a small piece of bread, toast, etc., spread with a savoury topping. [C19: from F: sofa]

canard (kæ'nɑːd) *n* **1** a false report; rumour or hoax. **2** an aircraft in which the tailplane is mounted in front of the wing. [C19: from F: a duck, from OF *caner* to quack, imit.]

canary (kə'nɛərɪ) *n, pl* **canaries. 1** a small finch of the Canary Islands and Azores: a popular cagebird noted for its singing. **2 canary yellow. 2a** a light yellow. **2b** (*as adj*): *a canary-yellow car.* **3** a sweet wine similar to Madeira. **4** *Arch.* a sweet wine from the Canary Islands. [C16: from OSp. *canario* of or from the Canary Islands]

canasta (kə'næstə) *n* **1** a card game for two to six players who seek to amass points by declaring sets of cards. **2** Also called: **meld.** a declared set in this game, containing seven or more like cards. [C20: from Sp.: basket (because two packs of cards are required), from L *canistrum;* see CANISTER]

canaster ('kænəstə) *n* coarsely broken dried tobacco leaves. [C19: (meaning: basket in which tobacco was packed): from Sp.; see CANISTER]

cancan ('kænˌkæn) *n* a high-kicking dance performed by a female chorus, originating in the music halls of 19th-century Paris. [C19: from F, from ?]

cancel ❶ ('kænsᵊl) *vb* **cancels, cancelling, cancelled** *or US* **cancels, canceling, canceled.** (*mainly tr*) **1** to order (something already arranged, such as a meeting or event) to be postponed indefinitely; call off. **2** to revoke or annul: *the order was cancelled.* **3** to delete (writing, numbers, etc.); cross out. **4** to mark (a cheque, stamp, etc.) with an official stamp to prevent further use. **5** (*also intr;* usually foll. by *out*) to counterbalance: *his generosity cancelled out his past unkindness.* **6** *Maths.* to eliminate (numbers or terms) as common factors from both the numerator and denominator of a fraction or as equal terms from opposite sides of an equation. ◆ *n* **7** a new leaf or section of a book replacing one containing errors, or one that has been omitted. **8** a cancellation. **9** *Music.* a US word for **natural** (sense 16). [C14: from OF *canceller,* from Med. L, from LL: to make like a lattice, from L *cancellī* lattice]
▸**'canceller** *or US* **'canceler** *n*

cancellate ('kænsɪˌleɪt) *or* **cancellated** *adj* **1** *Anat.* having a spongy internal structure: *cancellate bones.* **2** *Bot.* forming a network. [C17: from L *cancellāre* to make like a lattice]

cancellation ❶ (ˌkænsɪ'leɪʃən) *n* **1** the fact or an instance of cancelling. **2** something that has been cancelled, such as a theatre ticket: *we have a cancellation in the stalls.* **3** the marks made by cancelling.

cancer ❶ ('kænsə) *n* **1** any type of malignant growth or tumour, caused by abnormal and uncontrolled cell division. **2** the condition resulting from this. **3** an evil influence that spreads dangerously. [C14: from L: crab, a creeping tumour]
▸**'cancerous** *adj*

Cancer ('kænsə) *n, Latin genitive* **Cancri** ('kæŋkriː). **1** *Astron.* Also called: the **Crab.** a small N constellation. **2** *Astrol.* the fourth sign of the zodiac. The sun is in this sign between about June 21 and July 22. **3** **tropic of Cancer.** See **tropic** (sense 1).

cancerophobia (ˌkænsərəʊ'fəʊbɪə) *n* a morbid dread of being afflicted by cancer.

cancroid ('kæŋkrɔɪd) *adj* **1** resembling a cancerous growth. **2** resembling a crab. ◆ *n* **3** a skin cancer.

THESAURUS

canal *n* **1, 2** = **waterway,** channel, conduit, duct, passage, watercourse

cancel *vb* **1-3** = **call off,** abolish, abort, abrogate, annul, blot out, countermand, cross out, delete, do away with, efface, eliminate, erase, expunge, obliterate, obviate, quash, repeal, repudiate, rescind, revoke **5** *usually foll. by* **out** = **make up for,** balance out, compensate for, counterbalance, neutralize, nullify, obviate, offset, redeem

cancellation *n* **1** = **abandonment,** abandoning, abolition, annulment, deletion, elimination, quashing, repeal, revocation

cancer *n* **1-3** = **growth,** blight, canker, carcinoma (*Pathology*), corruption, evil, malignancy, pestilence, rot, sickness, tumour

candela (kæn'diːlə, -'deɪlə) *n* the basic SI unit of luminous intensity; the intensity, in a perpendicular direction, of a surface of 1/600 000 square metre of a black body at the temperature of freezing platinum under a pressure of 101 325 newtons per square metre. Symbol: cd [C20: from L: CANDLE]

candelabrum (ˌkændɪ'lɑːbrəm) *or* **candelabra** *n, pl* **candelabra** (-brə), **candelabrums,** *or* **candelabras.** a large branched candleholder or holder for overhead lights. [C19: from L, from *candēla* CANDLE]

candescent (kæn'desᵊnt) *adj Rare.* glowing or starting to glow with heat. [C19: from L, from *candēre* to be white, shine]
▸**can'descence** *n*

c & f *abbrev. for* cost and freight.

C & G *abbrev. for* City and Guilds.

candid ⊕ ('kændɪd) *adj* **1** frank and outspoken. **2** without partiality; unbiased. **3** unposed or informal: *a candid photograph.* [C17: from L, from *candēre* to be white]
▸**'candidly** *adv* ▸**'candidness** *n*

candida ('kændɪdə) *n* any of a genus of yeastlike parasitic fungi, esp. one that causes thrush (**candidiasis**).

candidate ⊕ ('kændɪˌdeɪt) *n* **1** a person seeking or nominated for election to a position of authority or selection for a job, etc. **2** a person taking an examination or test. **3** a person or thing regarded as suitable or likely for a particular fate or position. [C17: from L *candidātus* clothed in white (because the candidate wore a white toga), from *candidus* white]
▸**candidacy** ('kændɪdəsɪ) *or* **candidature** ('kændɪdətʃə) *n*

candid camera *n* a small camera that may be used to take informal photographs of people.

candied ('kændɪd) *adj* impregnated or encrusted with or as if with sugar: *candied peel.*

candle ('kændᵊl) *n* **1** a cylindrical piece of wax, tallow, or other fatty substance surrounding a wick, which is burned to produce light. **2** *Physics.* another name for **candela. 3 burn the candle at both ends.** to exhaust oneself by doing too much, esp. by being up late and getting up early to work. **4 not hold a candle to.** *Inf.* to be inferior or contemptible in comparison with. **5 not worth the candle.** *Inf.* not worth the price or trouble entailed. ◆ *vb* **candles, candling, candled. 6** (*tr*) to examine (eggs) for freshness or the likelihood of being hatched by viewing them against a bright light. [OE *candel,* from L *candēla,* from *candēre* to glitter]
▸**'candler** *n*

candleberry ('kændᵊlbərɪ) *n, pl* **candleberries.** another name for **wax myrtle.**

candlelight ('kændᵊlˌlaɪt) *n* **1a** the light from a candle or candles. **1b** (*as modifier*): *a candlelight dinner.* **2** dusk; evening.

Candlemas ('kændᵊlməs) *n Christianity.* Feb. 2, the Feast of the Purification of the Virgin Mary and the presentation of Christ in the Temple.

candlenut ('kændᵊlˌnʌt) *n* **1** a tree of tropical Asia and Polynesia. **2** the nut of this tree, which yields an oil used in paints. In their native regions the nuts are burned as candles.

candlepower ('kændᵊlˌpaʊə) *n* the luminous intensity of a source of light in a given direction: now expressed in candelas.

candlestick ('kændᵊlˌstɪk) *or* **candleholder** ('kændᵊlˌhəʊldə) *n* a holder, usually ornamental, with a spike or socket for a candle.

candlewick ('kændᵊlˌwɪk) *n* **1** unbleached cotton or muslin into which loops of yarn are hooked and then cut to give a tufted pattern. **2** (*modifier*) being or made of candlewick fabric.

C & M *abbrev. for* care and maintenance.

can-do *adj* confident and resourceful in the face of challenges: *a can-do attitude.*

candour ⊕ *or US* **candor** ('kændə) *n* **1** the quality of being open and honest; frankness. **2** fairness; impartiality. [C17: from L *candor,* from *candēre* to be white]

C & W *abbrev. for* country and western.

candy ('kændɪ) *n, pl* **candies. 1** *Chiefly US. & Canad.* sweets, chocolate, etc. ◆ *vb* **candies, candying, candied. 2** to cause (sugar, etc.) to become crystalline or (of sugar) to become crystalline. **3** (*tr*) to preserve (fruit peel, ginger, etc.) by boiling in sugar. **4** (*tr*) to cover with any crystalline substance, such as ice or sugar. [C18: from OF *sucre candi* candied sugar, from Ar. *qandi* candied, from *qand* cane sugar]

candyfloss ('kændɪˌflɒs) *n Brit.* a very light fluffy confection made from coloured spun sugar, usually held on a stick. US and Canad. name: **cotton candy.** Austral. name: **fairyfloss.**

candy-striped *adj* (esp. of clothing fabric) having narrow coloured stripes on a white background.
▸**candy stripe** *n*

candytuft ('kændɪˌtʌft) *n* either of two species of *Iberis* having clusters of white, red, or purplish flowers. [C17: *Candy,* obs. var. of *Candia* (former name of city in Crete) + TUFT]

cane (keɪn) *n* **1a** the long jointed pithy or hollow flexible stem of the bamboo, rattan, or any similar plant. **1b** any plant having such a stem. **2a** strips of such stems, woven or interlaced to make wickerwork, etc. **2b** (*as modifier*): *a cane chair.* **3** the woody stem of a reed, blackberry, or loganberry. **4** a flexible rod with which to administer a beating. **5** a slender rod used as a walking stick. **6** See **sugar cane.** ◆ *vb* **canes, caning, caned.** (*tr*) **7** to whip or beat with or as if with a cane. **8** to make or repair with cane. **9** *Inf.* to defeat: *we got well caned in the match.* [C14: from OF, from L *canna,* from Gk *kanna,* of Semitic origin]
▸**'caner** *n*

canebrake ('keɪnˌbreɪk) *n US.* a thicket of canes.

cane sugar *n* **1** the sucrose obtained from sugar cane. **2** another name for **sucrose.**

cangue *or* **cang** (kæŋ) *n* (formerly in China) a large wooden collar worn by petty criminals as a punishment. [C18: from F, from Port. *canga* yoke]

canikin ('kænɪkɪn) *n* a variant spelling of **cannikin.**

canine ('keɪnaɪn, 'kæn-) *adj* **1** of or resembling a dog. **2** of or belonging to the Canidae, a family of mammals, including dogs, wolves, and foxes, typically having a bushy tail, erect ears, and a long muzzle. **3** of or relating to any of the four teeth, two in each jaw, situated between the incisors and the premolars. ◆ *n* **4** any animal of the family Canidae. **5** a canine tooth. [C17: from L *canīnus,* from *canis* dog]

caning ('keɪnɪŋ) *n Inf.* a severe defeat or punishment.

Canis Major ('keɪnɪs) *n, Latin genitive* **Canis Majoris** (mə'dʒɔːrɪs). a S constellation containing Sirius, the brightest star in the sky. Also called: the **Great Dog.** [L: the greater dog]

Canis Minor *n, Latin genitive* **Canis Minoris** (maɪ'nɔːrɪs). a small N constellation. Also called: the **Little Dog.** [L: the lesser dog]

canister ('kænɪstə) *n* **1** a container, usually made of metal, in which dry food, such as tea or coffee, is stored. **2** (formerly) **2a** a type of shrapnel shell for firing from a cannon. **2b** Also called: **canister shot.** the shot or shrapnel packed inside this. [C17: from L *canistrum* basket woven from reeds, from Gk, from *kanna* reed]

canker ⊕ ('kæŋkə) *n* **1** an ulceration, esp. of the lips. **2** *Vet. science.* **2a** a disease of horses in which the horn of the hoofs becomes spongy. **2b** an ulcerative disease of the lining of the external ear, esp. in dogs and cats. **2c** ulceration or abscess of the mouth, eyelids, ears, or cloaca of birds. **3** an open wound in the stem of a tree or shrub. **4** something evil that spreads and corrupts. ◆ *vb* **5** to infect or become infected with or as if with canker. [OE *cancer,* from L *cancer* cancerous sore]
▸**'cankerous** *adj*

cankerworm ('kæŋkəˌwɜːm) *n* the larva of either of two moths, which feed on and destroy fruit and shade trees in North America.

canna ('kænə) *n* any of a genus of tropical plants having broad leaves and red or yellow showy flowers. [C17: from NL CANE]

cannabis ('kænəbɪs) *n* **1** another name for **hemp** (the plant), esp. Indian hemp. **2** the drug obtained from the dried leaves and flowers of the hemp plant, which is smoked or chewed for its psychoactive properties. See also **hashish, marijuana. 3 cannabis resin.** a poisonous resin obtained from the hemp plant. [C18: from L, from Gk *kannabis*]

canned (kænd) *adj* **1** preserved and stored in airtight cans or tins. **2** *Inf.* prepared or recorded in advance: *canned music.* **3** *Sl.* drunk.

cannel coal *or* **cannel** ('kænᵊl) *n* a dull coal burning with a smoky luminous flame. [C16: from N English dialect *cannel* candle]

cannelloni *or* **canneloni** (ˌkænɪ'ləʊnɪ) *pl n* tubular pieces of pasta filled with meat or cheese. [It., pl of *cannellone,* from *cannello* stalk]

cannery ('kænərɪ) *n, pl* **canneries.** a place where foods are canned.

cannibal ('kænɪbᵊl) *n* **1** a person who eats the flesh of other human beings. **2** an animal that feeds on the flesh of others of its kind. [C16: from Sp. *Canibales,* the name used by Columbus to designate the Caribs of Cuba and Haiti]
▸**'cannibaˌlism** *n*

cannibalize *or* **cannibalise** ('kænɪbəˌlaɪz) *vb* **cannibalizes, cannibalizing, cannibalized** *or* **cannibalises, cannibalising, cannibalised.** (*tr*) to use (serviceable parts from one machine or vehicle) to repair another.
▸**ˌcannibali'zation** *or* **ˌcannibali'sation** *n*

cannikin, canakin, *or* **canikin** ('kænɪkɪn) *n* a small can, esp. one used as a drinking vessel. [C16: from MDu. *kanneken;* see CAN², -KIN]

canning ('kænɪŋ) *n* the process or business of sealing food in cans or tins to preserve it.

cannon ⊕ ('kænən) *n, pl* **cannons** *or* **cannon. 1** an automatic aircraft gun. **2** *History.* a heavy artillery piece consisting of a metal tube mounted on a carriage. **3** a heavy tube or drum, esp. one that can rotate freely. **4** See **cannon bone. 5** *Billiards.* a shot in which the cue ball is caused to contact one object ball after another. Usual US and Canad. word:

THESAURUS

candid *adj* **1, 2 = honest,** blunt, downright, fair, forthright, frank, free, guileless, impartial, ingenuous, just, open, outspoken, plain, round, sincere, straightforward, truthful, unbiased, unequivocal, unprejudiced, upfront (*inf.*) **3 = informal,** impromptu, uncontrived, unposed
Antonyms *adj* ≠ **honest:** biased, complimentary, diplomatic, flattering, kind, subtle

candidate *n* **1-3 = contender,** applicant, aspirant, claimant, competitor, contestant, entrant, nominee, possibility, runner, suitor

candour *n* **1, 2 = honesty,** artlessness, directness, fairness, forthrightness, frankness, guilelessness, impartiality, ingenuousness, naïveté, openness, outspokenness, simplicity, sincerity, straightforwardness, truthfulness, unequivocalness
Antonyms *n* bias, cunning, deceit, diplomacy, dishonesty, flattery, insincerity, prejudice, subtlety

canker *n* **1, 3, 4 = disease,** bane, blight, blister, cancer, corrosion, corruption, infection, lesion, rot, scourge, sore, ulcer ◆ *vb* **5 = rot,** blight, consume, corrode, corrupt, embitter, envenom, inflict, poison, pollute, rust, waste away

canniness *n* **1 = shrewdness,** acuteness, artfulness, astuteness, carefulness, cautiousness, circumspection, judiciousness, knowingness, perspicaciousness, perspicacity, prudence, sagacity, sageness, sharpness, subtlety, wariness, wisdom, worldliness

cannon *n* **1, 2 = gun,** artillery piece, big gun, field gun, mortar

carom. ◆ *vb* **6** (*intr*) to rebound; collide (*with* into). **7** (*intr*) *Billiards.* to make a cannon. [C16: from OF *canon,* from It. *cannone* cannon, from *canna* tube]

cannonade (ˌkænəˈneɪd) *n* **1** an intense and continuous artillery bombardment. ◆ *vb* **cannonades, cannonading, cannonaded. 2** to attack (a target) with cannon.

cannonball (ˈkænənˌbɔːl) *n* **1** a projectile fired from a cannon: usually a solid round metal shot. ◆ *vb* (*intr*) **2** (often foll. by *along,* etc.) to rush along. ◆ *adj* **3** very fast or powerful.

cannon bone *n* a bone in the legs of horses and other hoofed animals consisting of greatly elongated fused metatarsals or metacarpals.

cannoneer (ˌkænəˈnɪə) *n* (formerly) a soldier who served and fired a cannon; artilleryman.

cannon fodder *n* men regarded as expendable in war because they are part of a huge army.

cannot (ˈkænɒt, kæˈnɒt) an auxiliary verb expressing incapacity, inability, withholding permission, etc.; can not.

cannula *or* **canula** (ˈkænjʊlə) *n, pl* **cannulas, cannulae** (-ˌliː), *or* **canulas, canulae** (-ˌliː). *Surgery.* a narrow tube for draining fluid from or introducing medication into the body. [C17: from L: a small reed, from *canna* a reed]

canny (ˈkænɪ) *adj* **cannier, canniest. 1** shrewd, esp. in business. **2** *Scot. & NE English dialect.* good or nice: used as a general term of approval. **3** *Scot.* lucky or fortunate. [C16: from CAN[1] (in the sense: to know how) + -Y[1]]
▸ **ˈcannily** *adv* ▸ **ˈcanniness** *n*

canoe (kəˈnuː) *n* **1** a light narrow open boat, propelled by one or more paddles. ◆ *vb* **canoes, canoeing, canoed. 2** to go in or transport by canoe. [C16: from Sp. *canoa,* of Carib origin]
▸ **caˈnoeist** *n*

canon[1] (ˈkænən) *n* **1** *Christianity.* a Church decree enacted to regulate morals or religious practices. **2** (*often pl*) a general rule or standard, as of judgment, morals, etc. **3** (*often pl*) a principle or criterion applied in a branch of learning or art. **4** *RC Church.* the list of the canonized saints. **5** *RC Church.* Also called: **Eucharistic Prayer.** the prayer in the Mass in which the Host is consecrated. **6** a list of writings, esp. sacred writings, recognized as genuine. **7** a piece of music in which an extended melody in one part is imitated successively in one or more other parts. **8** a list of the works of an author that are accepted as authentic. [OE, from L, from Gk *kanōn* rule, rod for measuring]

canon[2] (ˈkænən) *n* **1** one of several priests on the permanent staff of a cathedral, who are responsible for organizing services, maintaining the fabric, etc. **2** *RC Church.* Also called: **canon regular.** a member of either of two religious orders living communally as monks but performing clerical duties. [C13: from Anglo-F, from LL *canonicus* one living under a rule, from CANON[1]]

canonical (kəˈnɒnɪkᵊl) *or* **canonic** *adj* **1** included in a canon of sacred or other officially recognized writings. **2** in conformity with canon law. **3** accepted; authoritative. **4** *Music.* in the form of a canon. **5** of or relating to a cathedral chapter. **6** of a canon (clergyman).
▸ **caˈnonically** *adv*

canonical hour *n* **1** *RC Church.* one of the seven prayer times appointed for each day by canon law. **2** *Church of England.* any time at which marriages may lawfully be celebrated.

canonicals (kəˈnɒnɪkᵊlz) *pl n* the vestments worn by clergy when officiating.

canonicity (ˌkænəˈnɪsɪtɪ) *n* the fact or quality of being canonical.

canonist (ˈkænənɪst) *n* a specialist in canon law.

canonize *or* **canonise** (ˈkænəˌnaɪz) *vb* **canonizes, canonizing, canonized** *or* **canonises, canonising, canonised.** (*tr*) **1** *RC Church.* to declare (a person) to be a saint. **2** to regard as a saint. **3** to sanction by canon law.
▸ **ˌcanoniˈzation** *or* **ˌcanoniˈsation** *n*

canon law *n* the codified body of laws enacted by the supreme authorities of a Christian Church.

canonry (ˈkænənrɪ) *n, pl* **canonries. 1** the office, benefice, or status of a canon. **2** canons collectively. [C15: from CANON[2] + -RY]

canoodle (kəˈnuːdᵊl) *vb* **canoodles, canoodling, canoodled.** (*intr;* often by *with*) *Sl.* to kiss and cuddle. [C19: from ?]

Canopic jar, urn, *or* **vase** (kəˈnəʊpɪk) *n* (in ancient Egypt) one of four containers for holding the entrails of a mummy. [C19: from *Canopus,* a port in ancient Egypt]

canopy (ˈkænəpɪ) *n, pl* **canopies. 1** an ornamental awning above a throne, bed, person, etc. **2** a rooflike covering over an altar, niche, etc. **3** a roofed structure serving as a sheltered passageway. **4** a large or wide covering: *the sky was a grey canopy.* **5** the hemisphere that forms the supporting surface of a parachute. **6** the transparent cover of an aircraft cockpit. **7** the highest level of foliage in a forest, formed by the crowns of the trees. ◆ *vb* **canopies, canopying, canopied. 8** (*tr*) to cover with or as with a canopy. [C14: from Med. L *canōpeum* mosquito net, from L, from Gk *kōnōpeion* bed with protective net]

canst (kænst) *vb Arch.* the form of **can**[1] used with the pronoun *thou* or its relative form.

cant[1] (kænt) *n* **1** insincere talk, esp. concerning religion or morals. **2** phrases that have become meaningless through repetition. **3** specialized vocabulary of a particular group, such as thieves, journalists, or lawyers. ◆ *vb* **4** (*intr*) to speak in or use cant. [C16: prob. via Norman F *canter* to sing, from L *cantāre;* used disparagingly, from the 12th cent., of chanting in religious services]
▸ **ˈcantingly** *adv*

cant[2] (kænt) *n* **1** inclination from a vertical or horizontal plane. **2** a sudden movement that tilts or turns something. **3** the angle or tilt thus caused. **4** a corner or outer angle. **5** an oblique or slanting surface, edge, or line. ◆ *vb* (*tr*) **6** to tip, tilt, or overturn. **7** to set in an oblique position. **8** another word for **bevel** (sense 1). ◆ *adj* **9** oblique; slanting. **10** having flat surfaces. [C14 (in the sense: edge): ?from L *canthus* iron hoop round a wheel, from ?]

can't (kɑːnt) *contraction of* cannot.

Cantab. (kænˈtæb) *abbrev. for* Cantabrigiensis. [L: of Cambridge]

cantabile (kænˈtɑːbɪlɪ) *Music.* ◆ *adj, adv* **1** (to be performed) flowingly and melodiously. ◆ *n* **2** a piece or passage performed in this way. [It., from LL, from L *cantāre* to sing]

Cantabrigian (ˌkæntəˈbrɪdʒɪən) *adj* **1** of or characteristic of Cambridge or Cambridge University. ◆ *n* **2** a member or graduate of Cambridge University. **3** an inhabitant or native of Cambridge. [C17: from Med. L *Cantabrigia*]

cantaloupe *or* **cantaloup** (ˈkæntəˌluːp) *n* **1** a cultivated variety of muskmelon with ribbed warty rind and orange flesh. **2** any of several other muskmelons. [C18: from F, from *Cantaluppi,* near Rome, where first cultivated in Europe]

cantankerous (kænˈtæŋkərəs) *adj* quarrelsome; irascible. [C18: ?from C14 (obs.) *conteckour* a contentious person, from Anglo-F *contek* strife, from ?]
▸ **canˈtankerously** *adv* ▸ **canˈtankerousness** *n*

cantata (kænˈtɑːtə) *n* a musical setting of a text, esp. a religious text, consisting of arias, duets, and choruses. [C18: from It., from *cantare* to sing, from L]

canteen (kænˈtiːn) *n* **1** a restaurant attached to a factory, school, etc., providing meals for large numbers. **2a** a small shop that provides a limited range of items to a military unit. **2b** a recreation centre for military personnel. **3** a temporary or mobile stand at which food is provided. **4a** a box in which a set of cutlery is laid out. **4b** the cutlery itself. **5** a flask for carrying water or other liquids. [C18: from F, from It. *cantina* wine cellar, from *canto* corner, from L *canthus* iron hoop encircling chariot wheel]

canter (ˈkæntə) *n* **1** a gait of horses, etc., between a trot and a gallop in speed. **2 at a canter.** easily; without effort. ◆ *vb* **3** to move or cause to move at a canter. [C18: short for *Canterbury trot,* the supposed pace at which pilgrims rode to Canterbury]

Canterbury bell (ˈkæntəbərɪ) *n* a biennial European plant related to the campanula and widely cultivated for its blue, violet, or white flowers.

cantharides (kænˈθærɪˌdiːz) *pl n, sing* **cantharis** (ˈkænθərɪs). a diuretic and urogenital stimulant prepared from the dried bodies of Spanish fly. Also called: **Spanish fly.** [C15: from L, pl of *cantharis,* from Gk *kantharis* Spanish fly]

cant hook *or* **dog** *n Forestry.* a wooden pole with a blunt steel tip and an adjustable hook at one end, used for handling logs.

canthus (ˈkænθəs) *n, pl* **canthi** (-ˌθaɪ). the inner or outer corner of the eye, formed by the natural junction of the eyelids. [C17: from NL, from L: iron tyre]

canticle (ˈkæntɪkᵊl) *n* a nonmetrical hymn, derived from the Bible and used in the liturgy of certain Christian churches. [C13: from L *canticulum,* dim. of *canticus* a song, from *canere* to sing]

cantilena (ˌkæntɪˈleɪnə) *n* a smooth flowing style in the writing of vocal music. [C18: It.]

cantilever (ˈkæntɪˌliːvə) *n* **1** a beam, girder, or structural framework that is fixed at one end only. **2** a part of a beam or a structure projecting outwards beyond its support. [C17: ?from CANT[2] + LEVER]

cantilever bridge *n* a bridge having spans that are constructed as cantilevers.

cantillate (ˈkæntɪˌleɪt) *vb* **cantillates, cantillating, cantillated. 1** to chant (passages of the Hebrew Scriptures) according to the traditional Jewish melody. **2** to intone or chant. [C19: from LL *cantillāre* to sing softly, from L *cantāre* to sing]
▸ **ˌcantilˈlation** *n*

THESAURUS

canny *adj* **1** = **shrewd,** acute, artful, astute, careful, cautious, circumspect, clever, judicious, knowing, on the ball (*inf.*), perspicacious, prudent, sagacious, sharp, subtle, wise, worldly-wise
Antonyms *adj* bumbling, inept, lumpen (*inf.*), obtuse, unskilled

canon *n* **2, 3** = **rule,** criterion, dictate, formula, precept, principle, regulation, standard, statute, yardstick **8** = **list,** catalogue, roll

canopy *n* **1-4** = **awning,** baldachin, covering, shade, sunshade, tester

cant[1] *n* **1** = **hypocrisy,** affected piety, humbug, insincerity, lip service, pious platitudes, pretence, pretentiousness, sanctimoniousness, sham holiness **3** = **jargon,** argot, lingo, patter, slang, vernacular

cant[2] *vb* **1, 3, 5** = **tilt,** angle, bevel, incline, rise, slant, slope

cantankerous *adj* = **bad-tempered,** captious, choleric, contrary, crabby, cranky (*US, Canad., & Irish informal*), crotchety (*inf.*), crusty, difficult, disagreeable, grouchy (*inf.*), grumpy, ill-humoured, irascible, irritable, liverish, peevish, perverse, quarrelsome, ratty (*Brit. & NZ inf.*), testy, tetchy, waspish
Antonyms *adj* agreeable, amiable, breezy, cheerful, complaisant, congenial, genial, good-natured, happy, kindly, merry, placid, pleasant, vivacious

canter *n* **1** = **jog,** amble, dogtrot, easy gait, lope ◆ *vb* **3** = **jog,** amble, lope

cantle ('kæntəl) *n* **1** the back part of a saddle that slopes upwards. **2** a broken-off piece. [C14: from OF *cantel*, from *cant* corner]

canto ('kæntəu) *n, pl* **cantos.** a main division of a long poem. [C16: from It.: song, from L, from *canere* to sing]

canto fermo ('kæntəu 'fɜ:məu) *or* **cantus firmus** ('kæntəs 'fɜ:məs) *n* **1** a melody that is the basis to which other parts are added in polyphonic music. **2** the traditional Church plainchant as prescribed by use and regulation. [It., from Med L: fixed song]

canton *n* **1** ('kæntɒn, kæn'tɒn). a political division of Switzerland. **2** ('kæntən). *Heraldry.* a small square charge on a shield, usually in the top left corner. ◆ *vb* **3** (kæn'tɒn). (*tr*) to divide into cantons. **4** (kən'tu:n). (esp. formerly) to allocate accommodation to (military personnel, etc.). [C16: from OF: corner, from It., from *canto* corner, from L *canthus* iron rim]
▸ **'cantonal** *adj*

Cantonese (ˌkæntə'ni:z) *n* **1** the Chinese language spoken in the city of Canton, Guangdong and Guanxi provinces, Hong Kong, and elsewhere inside and outside China. **2** (*pl* **Cantonese**) a native or inhabitant of Canton city or Guangdong province. ◆ *adj* **3** of or relating to Canton or Guangdong or the Chinese language spoken there.

cantonment (kən'tu:nmənt) *n Mil.* (esp. formerly) **1** a large training camp. **2** the winter quarters of a campaigning army. **3** *History.* a permanent military camp in British India.

cantor ('kæntɔ:) *n* **1** *Judaism.* a man employed to lead synagogue services. **2** *Christianity.* the leader of the singing in a church choir. [C16: from L: singer, from *canere* to sing]

cantorial (kæn'tɔ:rɪəl) *adj* **1** of a precentor. **2** (of part of a choir) on the same side of a cathedral, etc., as the precentor.

cantoris (kæn'tɔ:rɪs) *adj* (in antiphonal music) to be sung by the cantorial side of a choir. Cf. **decani.** [L: genitive of *cantor* precentor]

Cantuar. ('kæntjuˌɑ:) *abbrev. for* Cantuariensis. [L: (Archbishop) of Canterbury]

Canuck (kə'nʌk) *n, adj US & Canad. inf.* Canadian. [C19: from ?]

canvas ('kænvəs) *n* **1a** a heavy cloth made of cotton, hemp, or jute, used for sails, tents, etc. **1b** (*as modifier*): *a canvas bag.* **2a** a piece of canvas, etc., on which a painting is done, usually in oils. **2b** an oil painting. **3** a tent or tents collectively. **4** *Naut.* the sails of a vessel collectively. **5** any coarse loosely woven cloth on which tapestry, etc., is done. **6** (preceded by *the*) the floor of a boxing or wrestling ring. **7** *Rowing.* the covered part at either end of a racing boat: *to win by a canvas.* **8 under canvas. 8a** in tents. **8b** *Naut.* with sails unfurled. [C14: from Norman F *canevas*, ult. from L *cannabis* hemp]

canvasback ('kænvəsˌbæk) *n, pl* **canvasbacks** *or* **canvasback.** a North American diving duck, the male of which has a reddish-brown head.

canvass Ⓣ ('kænvəs) *vb* **1** to solicit votes, orders, etc., (from). **2** to determine the opinions of (voters before an election, etc.), esp. by conducting a survey. **3** to investigate (something) thoroughly, esp. by discussion. **4** *Chiefly US.* to inspect (votes) to determine their validity. ◆ *n* **5** a solicitation of opinions, votes, etc. [C16: prob. from obs. sense of CANVAS (to toss someone in a canvas sheet, hence, to criticize)]
▸ **'canvasser** *n*

canyon Ⓣ *or* **cañon** ('kænjən) *n* a gorge or ravine, esp. in North America, usually formed by a river. [C19: from Sp., from *caña* tube, from L *canna* cane]

canzonetta (ˌkænzə'nɛtə) *or* **canzonet** (ˌkænzə'nɛt) *n* a short, lively song, typically of the 16th to 18th centuries. [C16: It.: dim. of *canzone*, from L *canere* to sing]

caoutchouc ('kautʃuk) *n* another name for **rubber**[1] (sense 1). [C18: from F, from obs. Sp., from Quechua]

cap Ⓣ (kæp) *n* **1** a covering for the head, esp. a small close-fitting one. **2** such a covering serving to identify the wearer's rank, occupation, etc.: *a nurse's cap.* **3** something that protects or covers: *lens cap.* **4** an uppermost surface or part: *the cap of a wave.* **5a** See **percussion cap. 5b** a small amount of explosive enclosed in paper and used in a toy gun. **6** *Sport, chiefly Brit.* **6a** an emblematic hat or beret given to someone chosen for a representative team. **6b** a player chosen for such a team. **7** any part like a cap in shape. **8** *Bot.* the pileus of a mushroom or toadstool. **9** *Hunting.* money contributed to the funds of a hunt by a follower who is neither a subscriber nor a farmer, in return for a day's hunting. **10** *Anat.* **10a** the natural enamel covering a tooth. **10b** an artificial protective covering for a tooth. **11** Also: **Dutch cap, diaphragm.** a contraceptive membrane placed over the mouth of the cervix. **12** an upper financial limit. **13** a mortarboard worn at an academic ceremony (esp. in **cap and gown**). **14** *Meteorol.* **14a** the cloud covering the peak of a mountain. **14b** the transient top of detached clouds above an increasing cumulus. **15 set one's cap at.** (of a woman) to be determined to win as a husband or lover. **16 cap in hand.** humbly, as when asking a favour. ◆ *vb* **caps, capping, capped.** (*tr*) **17** to cover, as with a cap: *snow capped the mountain tops.* **18** *Inf.* to outdo; excel. **19 cap it all.** to provide the finishing touch. **20** *Sport, Brit.* to select (a player) for a representative team. **21** to seal off (an oil or gas well). **22** to impose an upper limit on the level of increase of (a tax): *charge-cap.* **23** *Chiefly Scot. & NZ.* to award a degree to. [OE *cæppe*, from LL *cappa* hood, ?from L *caput* head]

CAP *abbrev. for:* Common Agricultural Policy: (in the EU) the system for supporting farm incomes by maintaining agricultural prices at agreed levels.

cap. *abbrev. for:* **1** capacity. **2** capital. **3** capitalize. **4** capital letter.

capability Ⓣ (ˌkeɪpə'bɪlɪtɪ) *n, pl* **capabilities. 1** the quality of being capable; ability. **2** the quality of being susceptible to the use or treatment indicated: *the capability of a metal to be fused.* **3** (*usually pl*) potential aptitude.

capable Ⓣ ('keɪpəbəl) *adj* **1** having ability; competent. **2** (*postpositive;* foll. by *of*) able or having the skill (to do something): *she is capable of hard work.* **3** (*postpositive;* foll. by *of*) having the temperament or inclination (to do something): *he seemed capable of murder.* [C16: from F, from LL *capābilis* able to take in, from L *capere* to take]
▸ **'capableness** *n* ▸ **'capably** *adv*

capacious Ⓣ (kə'peɪʃəs) *adj* capable of holding much; roomy. [C17: from L, from *capere* to take]
▸ **ca'paciously** *adv* ▸ **ca'paciousness** *n*

capacitance (kə'pæsɪtəns) *n* **1** the property of a system that enables it to store electric charge. **2** a measure of this, equal to the charge that must be added to such a system to raise its electrical potential by one unit. Former name: **capacity.** [C20: from CAPACIT(Y) + -ANCE]
▸ **ca'pacitive** *adj*

capacitor (kə'pæsɪtə) *n* a device for accumulating electric charge, usually consisting of two conducting surfaces separated by a dielectric. Former name: **condenser.**

capacity Ⓣ (kə'pæsɪtɪ) *n, pl* **capacities. 1** the ability or power to contain, absorb, or hold. **2** the amount that can be contained: *a capacity of six gallons.* **3a** the maximum amount something can contain or absorb (esp. in **filled to capacity**). **3b** (*as modifier*): *a capacity crowd.* **4** the ability to understand or learn: *he has a great capacity for Greek.* **5** the ability to do or produce: *the factory's output was not at capacity.* **6** a specified position or function. **7** a measure of the electrical output of a piece of apparatus such as a generator or accumulator. **8** *Electronics.* a former name for **capacitance. 9** *Computing.* **9a** the number of words or characters that can be stored in a storage device. **9b** the range of numbers that can be processed in a register. **10** legal competence: *the capacity to make a will.* [C15: from OF *capacite*, from L, from *capāx* spacious, from *capere* to take]

cap and bells *n* the traditional garb of a court jester, including a cap with bells.

cap-a-pie (ˌkæpə'pi:) *adv* (dressed, armed, etc.) from head to foot. [C16: from OF]

caparison (kə'pærɪsən) *n* **1** a decorated covering for a horse. **2** rich or elaborate clothing and ornaments. ◆ *vb* **3** (*tr*) to put a caparison on. [C16: via obs. F from OSp. *caparazón* saddlecloth, prob. from *capa* CAPE[1]]

cape[1] (keɪp) *n* a sleeveless garment like a cloak but usually shorter. [C16: from F, from Provençal *capa*, from LL *cappa;* see CAP]

cape[2] Ⓣ (keɪp) *n* a headland or promontory. [C14: from OF *cap*, from OProvençal, from L *caput* head]

Cape Coloured *n* (in South Africa) another name for a **Coloured** (sense 2).

Cape doctor *n S. African inf.* a strong fresh SE wind blowing in the vicinity of Cape Town, esp. in the summer.

Cape Dutch *n* **1** (in South Africa) a distinctive style in furniture or buildings. **2** an obsolete name for **Afrikaans.**

Cape gooseberry *n* another name for **strawberry tomato.**

capelin ('kæpəlɪn) *or* **caplin** ('kæplɪn) *n* a small marine food fish of northern and Arctic seas. [C17: from F *capelan*, from OProvençal, lit.: chaplain]

capellmeister *or* **kapellmeister** (kæ'pɛlˌmaɪstə) *n* a person in charge

THESAURUS

canvass *vb* **1** = **campaign**, electioneer, solicit, solicit votes **2, 3** = **poll**, analyse, examine, fly a kite, inspect, investigate, scan, scrutinize, sift, study, ventilate ◆ *n* **5** = **poll**, examination, investigation, scrutiny, survey, tally

canyon *n* = **gorge**, coulee (*US*), gulch (*US*), gulf, gully, ravine, valley

cap *vb* **18** *Informal* = **beat**, better, clobber (*sl.*), complete, cover, crown, eclipse, exceed, excel, finish, lick (*inf.*), outdo, outstrip, overtop, put in the shade, run rings around (*inf.*), surpass, top, transcend

capability *n* **1** = **ability**, capacity, competence, facility, faculty, means, potential, potentiality, power, proficiency, qualification(s), wherewithal
Antonyms *n* inability, incompetence, inefficiency, ineptitude, powerlessness

capable *adj* **1, 2** = **able**, accomplished, adapted, adept, adequate, apt, clever, competent, efficient, experienced, fitted, gifted, intelligent, masterly, proficient, qualified, skilful, suited, susceptible, talented
Antonyms *adj* incapable, incompetent, ineffective, inept, inexpert, unqualified, unskilled

capacious *adj* = **spacious**, ample, broad, comfortable, commodious, comprehensive, expansive, extended, extensive, generous, liberal, roomy, sizable *or* sizeable, substantial, vast, voluminous, wide
Antonyms *adj* confined, constricted, cramped, enclosed, incommodious, insubstantial, limited, narrow, poky, restricted, small, tight, tiny, uncomfortable, ungenerous

capaciousness *n* = **spaciousness**, ampleness, commodiousness, roominess, sizableness *or* sizeableness

capacity *n* **1** = **size**, amplitude, compass, dimensions, extent, magnitude, range, room, scope, space, volume **4** = **ability**, aptitude, aptness, brains, capability, cleverness, competence, competency, efficiency, facility, faculty, forte, genius, gift, intelligence, power, readiness, strength **6** = **function**, appointment, office, position, post, province, role, service, sphere

cape[2] *n* = **headland**, chersonese (*poetic*), head, ness (*arch.*), peninsula, point, promontory

of an orchestra, esp. in an 18th-century princely household. [from G, from *Kapelle* chapel + *Meister* MASTER]

Cape pigeon *n* a kind of petrel common in S Africa.

caper[1] ● ('keɪpə) *n* **1** a playful skip or leap. **2** a high-spirited escapade. **3 cut a caper** *or* **capers.** to skip, leap, or frolic. **4** *US & Canad. sl.* a crime. ◆ *vb* **5** (*intr*) to leap or dance about in a light-hearted manner. [C16: prob. from CAPRIOLE]

caper[2] ('keɪpə) *n* **1** a spiny trailing Mediterranean shrub with edible flower buds. **2** its pickled flower buds, used in sauces. [C15: from earlier *capers, capres* (assumed to be pl), from L, from Gk *kapparis*]

capercaillie *or* **capercailzie** (ˌkæpə'keɪljɪ) *n* a large European woodland grouse having a black plumage. [C16: from Scot. Gaelic *capull coille* horse of the woods]

Cape sparrow *n* a sparrow very common in southern Africa. Also called (esp. S. African): **mossie.**

capias ('keɪpɪˌæs, 'kæp-) *n Law.* a writ directing a sheriff or other officer to arrest a named person. [C15: from L, lit.: you must take, from *capere*]

capillarity (ˌkæpɪ'lærɪtɪ) *n* a phenomenon caused by surface tension and resulting in the elevation or depression of the surface of a liquid in contact with a solid. Also called: **capillary action.**

capillary (kə'pɪlərɪ) *adj* **1** resembling a hair; slender. **2** (of tubes) having a fine bore. **3** *Anat.* of the delicate thin-walled blood vessels that interconnect between the arterioles and the venules. **4** *Physics.* of or relating to capillarity. ◆ *n, pl* **capillaries. 5** *Anat.* any of the capillary blood vessels. [C17: from L *capillāris,* from *capillus* hair]

capital[1] ● ('kæpɪtᵊl) *n* **1a** the seat of government of a country. **1b** (*as modifier*): *a capital city.* **2** material wealth owned by an individual or business enterprise. **3** wealth available for or capable of use in the production of further wealth, as by industrial investment. **4 make capital (out) of.** to get advantage from. **5** (*sometimes cap.*) the capitalist class or their interests: *capital versus labour.* **6** *Accounting.* **6a** the ownership interests of a business as represented by the excess of assets over liabilities. **6b** the nominal value of the issued shares. **7** any assets or resources. **8a** a capital letter. Abbrev.: **cap. 8b** (*as modifier*): *capital B.* ◆ *adj* **9** (*prenominal*) *Law.* involving or punishable by death: *a capital offence.* **10** very serious: *a capital error.* **11** primary, chief, or principal: *our capital concern.* **12** of, relating to, or designating the large letter used chiefly as the initial letter in personal names and place names and often for abbreviations and acronyms. See also **upper case. 13** *Chiefly Brit.* excellent; first-rate: *a capital idea.* [C13: from L *capitālis* (adj) concerning the head, from *caput* head]

capital[2] ('kæpɪtᵊl) *n* the upper part of a column or pier that supports the entablature. [C14: from OF, from LL *capitellum,* dim. of *caput* head]

capital account *n* **1** *Econ.* that part of a balance of payments composed of movements of capital. **2** *Accounting.* a financial statement showing the net value of a company at a specified date.

capital expenditure *n* expenditure to increase fixed assets.

capital gain *n* the amount by which the selling price of a financial asset exceeds its cost.

capital gains tax *n* a tax on the profit made from sale of an asset.

capital goods *pl n Econ.* goods that are themselves utilized in the production of other goods.

capitalism ● ('kæpɪtəˌlɪzəm) *n* an economic system based on the private ownership of the means of production, distribution, and exchange. Also called: **free enterprise, private enterprise.** Cf. **socialism** (sense 1).

capitalist ('kæpɪtəlɪst) *n* **1** a person who owns capital, esp. capital invested in a business. **2** *Politics.* a supporter of capitalism. ◆ *adj* **3** relating to capital, capitalists, or capitalism.
▸ˌ**capital'istic** *adj*

capitalization *or* **capitalisation** (ˌkæpɪtəlaɪ'zeɪʃən) *n* **1a** the act of capitalizing. **1b** the sum so derived. **2** *Accounting.* the par value of the total share capital issued by a company. **3** the act of estimating the present value of future payments, etc.

capitalize ● *or* **capitalise** ('kæpɪtəˌlaɪz) *vb* **capitalizes, capitalizing, capitalized** *or* **capitalises, capitalising, capitalised.** (*mainly tr*) **1** (*intr;* foll. by *on*) to take advantage (of). **2** to write or print (text) in capital letters. **3** to convert (debt or earnings) into capital stock. **4** to authorize (a business enterprise) to issue a specified amount of capital stock. **5** to provide with capital. **6** *Accounting.* to treat (expenditures) as assets. **7a** to estimate the present value of (a periodical income). **7b** to compute the present value of (a business) from actual or potential earnings.

capitally ('kæpɪtəlɪ) *adv Chiefly Brit.* in an excellent manner; admirably.

capital punishment *n* the punishment of death for a crime; death penalty.

capital ship *n* one of the largest and most heavily armed ships in a naval fleet.

capital stock *n* **1** the par value of the total share capital that a company is authorized to issue. **2** the total physical capital existing in an economy at any moment of time.

capital transfer tax *n* (in Britain) a tax payable from 1974 to 1986 on the cumulative total of gifts of money or property made during the donor's lifetime or after his death. It was replaced by inheritance tax.

capitation (ˌkæpɪ'teɪʃən) *n* **1** a tax levied on the basis of a fixed amount per head. **2 capitation grant.** a grant of money given to every person who qualifies under certain conditions. [C17: from LL, from L *caput* head]

Capitol ('kæpɪtᵊl) *n* **1** the temple on the Capitoline. **2 the.** the main building of the US Congress. [C14: from Latin *Capitōlium,* from *caput* head]

capitulate ● (kə'pɪtjuˌleɪt) *vb* **capitulates, capitulating, capitulated.** (*intr*) to surrender, esp. under agreed conditions. [C16 (meaning: to draw up in order): from Med. L *capitulare* to draw up under heads, from *capitulum* CHAPTER]
▸**ca'pituˌlator** *n*

capitulation ● (kəˌpɪtju'leɪʃən) *n* **1** the act of capitulating. **2** a document containing terms of surrender. **3** a statement summarizing the main divisions of a subject.
▸**ca'pitulatory** *adj*

capitulum (kə'pɪtjuləm) *n, pl* **capitula** (-lə). an inflorescence in the form of a disc, the youngest at the centre. It occurs in the daisy and related plants. [C18: from L, lit.: a little head, from *caput* head]

capo ('kæpəʊ) *n, pl* **capos.** a device fitted across all the strings of a guitar, lute, etc., so as to raise the pitch of each string simultaneously. Also called: **capo tasto** ('tæstəʊ). [from It. *capo tasto* head stop]

capon ('keɪpən) *n* a castrated cock fowl fattened for eating. [OE *capun,* from L *cāpō* capon]
▸'**caponˌize** *or* '**caponˌise** *vb*

capote (kə'pəʊt) *n* a long cloak or soldier's coat, usually with a hood. [C19: from F: cloak, from *cape*]

capping ('kæpɪŋ) *n Scot. & NZ.* **a** the act of conferring an academic degree. **b** (*as modifier*): *Capping Day.*

cappuccino (ˌkæpu'tʃi:nəʊ) *n, pl* **cappuccinos.** coffee with steamed milk, usually sprinkled with powdered chocolate. [It.: CAPUCHIN]

capriccio (kə'prɪtʃɪˌəʊ) *or* **caprice** *n, pl* **capriccios, capricci** (-'pri:tʃɪ), *or* **caprices.** *Music.* a lively piece of irregular musical form. [C17: from It.: CAPRICE]

capriccioso (kəˌprɪtʃɪ'əʊzəʊ) *adv Music.* to be played in a free and lively style. [It.: from *capriccio* CAPRICE]

caprice ● (kə'pri:s) *n* **1** a sudden change of attitude, behaviour, etc. **2** a tendency to such changes. **3** another word for **capriccio.** [C17: from F, from It. *capriccio* a shiver, caprice, from *capo* head + *riccio* lit.: hedgehog]

capricious ● (kə'prɪʃəs) *adj* characterized by or liable to sudden unpredictable changes in attitude or behaviour.
▸**ca'priciously** *adv*

Capricorn ('kæprɪˌkɔ:n) *n* **1** *Astrol.* Also called: the **Goat, Capricornus.** the tenth sign of the zodiac. The sun is in this sign between about Dec. 22 and Jan. 19. **2** *Astron.* a S constellation. **3 tropic of Capricorn.** See **tropic** (sense 1). [C14: from L *Capricornus,* from *caper* goat + *cornū* horn]

caprine ('kæpraɪn) *adj* of or resembling a goat. [C17: from L *caprīnus,* from *caper* goat]

capriole ('kæprɪˌəʊl) *n* **1** *Dressage.* a high upward but not forward leap made by a horse with all four feet off the ground. ◆ *vb* **caprioles, caprioling, caprioled. 2** (*intr*) to perform a capriole. [C16: from F, from OIt., from *capriolo* roebuck, from L *capreolus, caper* goat]

caps. *abbrev. for:* **1** capital letters. **2** capsule.

capsicum ('kæpsɪkəm) *n* **1** any of a genus of tropical American plants related to the potato, having mild or pungent seeds enclosed in a bell-shaped fruit. **2** the fruit of any of these plants, used as a vegetable or ground to produce a condiment. ◆ See also **pepper** (sense 4). [C18: from NL, from L *capsa* box]

capsid[1] ('kæpsɪd) *n* a bug related to the water bug that feeds on plant tissues, causing damage to crops. [C19: from NL *Capsus* (genus)]

capsid[2] ('kæpsɪd) *n* the outer protein coat of a mature virus. [C20: from F *capside,* from L *capsa* box]

THESAURUS

caper[1] *n* **1, 2** = **escapade**, antic, dido (*inf.*), gambol, high jinks, hop, jape, jest, jump, lark (*inf.*), leap, mischief, practical joke, prank, revel, shenanigan (*inf.*), sport, stunt ◆ *vb* **5** = **dance**, bounce, bound, cavort, cut a rug, frisk, frolic, gambol, hop, jump, leap, romp, skip, spring, trip

capital[1] *n* **2,3** = **money**, assets, cash, finance, finances, financing, funds, investment(s), means, principal, property, resources, stock, wealth, wherewithal ◆ *adj* **11** = **principal**, cardinal, central, chief, controlling, essential, foremost, important, leading, main, major, overruling, paramount, pre-eminent, primary, prime, prominent, vital **13** *Old-fashioned* = **first-rate**, excellent, fine, first, prime, splendid, sterling, superb, world-class

capitalism *n* = **private enterprise**, free enterprise, laissez faire *or* laisser faire, private ownership

capitalize *vb* **1** *foll. by* **on** = **take advantage of**, benefit from, cash in on (*inf.*), exploit, gain from, make the most of, profit from

capitulate *vb* = **give in**, cave in (*inf.*), come to terms, give up, relent, submit, succumb, surrender, yield
Antonyms *vb* beat, conquer, crush, defeat, get the better of, lick (*inf.*), overcome, overpower, subdue, subjugate, vanquish

capitulation *n* **1** = **surrender**, accedence, cave-in (*inf.*), submission, yielding

caprice *n* **1, 2** = **whim**, changeableness, fad, fancy, fickleness, fitfulness, freak, humour, impulse, inconstancy, notion, quirk, vagary, whimsy

capricious *adj* = **unpredictable**, changeful, crotchety (*inf.*), erratic, fanciful, fickle, fitful, freakish, impulsive, inconsistent, inconstant, mercurial, odd, queer, quirky, variable, wayward, whimsical
Antonyms *adj* certain, consistent, constant, decisive, determined, firm, immovable, resolute, responsible, stable, unchangeable, unwavering

capsize ⓣ (kæp'saɪz) *vb* **capsizes, capsizing, capsized.** to overturn accidentally; upset. [C18: from ?]
▸**cap'sizal** *n*

capstan ('kæpstən) *n* **1** a machine with a drum equipped with a ratchet, used for hauling in heavy ropes, etc. **2** the rotating shaft in a tape recorder that pulls the tape past the head. [C14: from OProvençal *cabestan,* from L *capistrum* a halter, from *capere* to seize]

capstan lathe *n* a lathe for repetitive work, having a rotatable turret to hold tools for successive operations. Also called: **turret lathe.**

capstone ('kæpˌstəʊn) *n* another word for **copestone** (sense 2).

capsule ⓣ ('kæpsju:l) *n* **1** a soluble case of gelatine enclosing a dose of medicine. **2** a thin metal cap, seal, or cover. **3** *Bot.* **3a** a dry fruit that liberates its seeds by splitting, as in the violet, or through pores, as in the poppy. **3b** the spore-producing organ of mosses and liverworts. **4** *Anat.* a membranous envelope surrounding any of certain organs or parts. **5** See **space capsule. 6** an aeroplane cockpit that can be ejected in a flight emergency, complete with crew, instruments, etc. **7** (*modifier*) in a highly concise form: *a capsule summary.* [C17: from F, from L *capsula,* dim. of *capsa* box]
▸**'capsuˌlate** *adj*

capsulize *or* **capsulise** ('kæpsjuˌlaɪz) *vb* **capsulizes, capsulizing, capsulized** *or* **capsulises, capsulising, capsulised.** (*tr*) **1** to state (information, etc.) in a highly condensed form. **2** to enclose in a capsule.

Capt. *abbrev. for* Captain.

captain ⓣ ('kæptɪn) *n* **1** the person in charge of a vessel. **2** an officer of the navy who holds a rank junior to a rear admiral. **3** an officer of the army, certain air forces, and the marines who holds a rank junior to a major. **4** the officer in command of a civil aircraft. **5** the leader of a team in games. **6** a person in command over a group, organization, etc.: *a captain of industry.* **7** *US.* a policeman in charge of a precinct. **8** *US & Canad.* (formerly) a head waiter. ◆ *vb* **9** (*tr*) to be captain of. [C14: from OF, from LL *capitāneus* chief, from L *caput* head]
▸**'captaincy** *or* **'captainship** *n*

Captain Cooker ('kʊkə) *n NZ.* a wild pig. [from Captain James *Cook* (1728–79), E navigator, who first released pigs in the New Zealand bush]

caption ('kæpʃən) *n* **1** a title, brief explanation, or comment accompanying an illustration. **2** a heading or title of a chapter, article, etc. **3** graphic material used in television presentation. **4** another name for **subtitle** (sense 2). **5** the formal heading of a legal document. ◆ *vb* **6** to provide with a caption or captions. [C14 (meaning: seizure): from L *captiō* a seizing, from *capere* to take]

captious ⓣ ('kæpʃəs) *adj* apt to make trivial criticisms. [C14 (meaning: catching in error): from L *captiōsus,* from *captiō* a seizing]
▸**'captiously** *adv* ▸**'captiousness** *n*

captivate ⓣ ('kæptɪˌveɪt) *vb* **captivates, captivating, captivated.** (*tr*) to hold the attention of by fascinating; enchant. [C16: from LL *captivāre,* from *captīvus* CAPTIVE]
▸**'captiˌvating** *adj* ▸**ˌcapti'vation** *n*

captive ⓣ ('kæptɪv) *n* **1** a person or animal that is confined or restrained. **2** a person whose behaviour is dominated by some emotion: *a captive of love.* ◆ *adj* **3** held as prisoner. **4** held under restriction or control; confined. **5** captivated. **6** unable to avoid speeches, advertisements, etc.: *a captive audience.* [C14: from L *captīvus,* from *capere* to take]

captivity ⓣ (kæp'tɪvɪtɪ) *n, pl* **captivities. 1** imprisonment. **2** the period of imprisonment.

captor ⓣ ('kæptə) *n* a person or animal that holds another captive. [C17: from L, from *capere* to take]

capture ⓣ ('kæptʃə) *vb* **captures, capturing, captured.** (*tr*) **1** to take prisoner or gain control over: *to capture a town.* **2** (in a game) to win possession of: *to capture a pawn in chess.* **3** to succeed in representing (something elusive): *the artist captured her likeness.* **4** *Physics.* (of an atom, etc.) to acquire (an additional particle). **5** to insert or transfer (data) into a computer. ◆ *n* **6** the act of taking by force. **7** the person or thing captured. **8** *Physics.* a process by which an atom, etc., acquires an additional particle. **9** *Geog.* the process by which the headwaters of one river are diverted into another. **10** *Computing.* the collection of data for processing. [C16: from L *captūra* a catching, that which is caught, from *capere* to take]
▸**'capturer** *n*

capuchin ('kæpjʊtʃɪn, -jʊʃɪn) *n* **1** an agile intelligent S American monkey having a cowl of thick hair on the top of the head. **2** a woman's hooded cloak. **3** (*sometimes cap.*) a variety of domestic fancy pigeon. [C16: from F, from It., from *cappuccio* hood]

Capuchin ('kæpjʊtʃɪn, -jʊʃɪn) *n* **1** a friar belonging to a branch of the Franciscan Order founded in 1525. ◆ *adj* **2** of or relating to this order. [C16: from F, from It. *cappuccio* hood]

capybara (ˌkæpɪ'bɑːrə) *n* the largest rodent, resembling a guinea pig and native to Central and South America. [C18: from Port. *capibara,* from Tupi]

car ⓣ (kɑː) *n* **1a** Also called: **motorcar, automobile.** a self-propelled road vehicle designed to carry passengers, that is powered by an internal-combustion engine. **1b** (*as modifier*): *car coat.* **2** a conveyance for passengers, freight, etc., such as a cable car or the carrier of an airship or balloon. **3** *Brit.* a railway vehicle for passengers only. **4** *Chiefly US. & Canad.* a railway carriage or van. **5** a poetic word for **chariot.** [C14: from Anglo-F *carre,* ult. rel. to L *carra, carrum* two-wheeled wagon, prob. of Celtic origin]

CAR *abbrev. for* compound annual return.

carabineer *or* **carabinier** (ˌkærəbɪ'nɪə) *n* variants of **carbineer.**

carabiner (ˌkærə'biːnə) *n* a variant of **karabiner.**

caracal ('kærəˌkæl) *n* **1** a lynxlike feline mammal inhabiting deserts of N Africa and S Asia, having a smooth coat of reddish fur. **2** this fur. [C18: from F, from Turkish *kara kūlāk,* lit.: black ear]

caracara (ˌkɑːrə'kɑːrə) *n* a large carrion-eating bird of prey of Central and South America, having long legs. [C19: from Sp. or Port., from Tupi; imit.]

caracole ('kærəˌkəʊl) *or* **caracol** ('kærəˌkɒl) *Dressage.* ◆ *n* **1** a half turn to the right or left. ◆ *vb* **caracoles, caracoling, caracoled** *or* **caracols, caracoling, caracoled.** (*intr*) **2** to execute a half turn. [C17: from F, from Sp. *caracol* snail, spiral staircase]

caracul ('kærəˌkʌl) *n* **1** Also called: **Persian lamb.** the black loosely curled fur obtained from the skins of newly born lambs of the karakul sheep. **2** a variant spelling of **karakul.**

carafe ⓣ (kə'ræf, -'rɑːf) *n* an open-topped glass container for serving water or wine at table [C18: from F, from It., from Sp., from Ar. *gharrāfah* vessel]

carageen ('kærəˌgiːn) *n* a variant spelling of **carrageen.**

carambola (ˌkærəm'bəʊlə) *n* the yellow edible star-shaped fruit of a Brazilian tree, cultivated in the tropics, esp. SE Asia. Also called: **star fruit.** [Sp., from Port.]

caramel ('kærəməl) *n* **1** burnt sugar, used for colouring and flavouring food. **2** a chewy sweet made from sugar, milk, etc. [C18: from F, from Sp. *caramelo,* from ?]

caramelize *or* **caramelise** ('kærəməˌlaɪz) *vb* **caramelizes, caramelizing, caramelized** *or* **caramelises, caramelising, caramelised.** to convert or be converted into caramel.

carapace ('kærəˌpeɪs) *n* the thick hard shield that covers part of the body of crabs, tortoises, etc. [C19: from F, from Sp. *carapacho,* from ?]

carat ('kærət) *n* **1** a measure of the weight of precious stones, esp. diamonds, now standardized as 0.20 grams. **2** Usual US and Canad. spelling: **karat.** a measure of the gold in an alloy, expressed as the number of parts of gold in 24 parts of the alloy. [C16: from OF, from Med. L, from Ar. *qīrāt* weight of four grains, from Gk, from *keras* horn]

caravan ('kærəˌvæn) *n* **1a** a large enclosed vehicle capable of being pulled by a car and equipped to be lived in. US and Canad. name: **trailer. 1b** (*as modifier*): *a caravan site.* **2** (esp. in some parts of Asia and Africa) a company of traders or other travellers journeying together. **3** a large covered vehicle, esp. a gaily coloured one used by Gypsies, circuses, etc. ◆ *vb* **caravans, caravanning, caravanned. 4** (*intr*) *Brit.* to travel or have a holiday in a caravan. [C16: from It. *caravana,* from Persian *kārwān*]

caravanserai (ˌkærə'vænsəˌraɪ) *or* **caravansary** (ˌkærə'vænsərɪ) *n, pl* **caravanserais** *or* **caravansaries.** (in some Eastern countries) a large inn enclosing a courtyard, providing accommodation for caravans. [C16: from Persian *kārwānsarāī* caravan inn]

caravel ('kærəˌvel) *or* **carvel** *n* a two- or three-masted sailing ship used by the Spanish and Portuguese in the 15th and 16th centuries. [C16: from Port. *caravela,* dim. of *caravo* ship, ult. from Gk *karabos* crab]

caraway ('kærəˌweɪ) *n* **1** an umbelliferous Eurasian plant having finely divided leaves and clusters of small whitish flowers. **2 caraway seed.**

THESAURUS

capsize *vb* = **overturn**, invert, keel over, tip over, turn over, turn turtle, upset

capsule *n* **1** = **pill**, bolus, lozenge, tablet, troche (*Medical*) **3** *Botany* = **pod**, case, pericarp (*Botany*), receptacle, seed case, sheath, shell, vessel

captain *n* **1, 4, 6** = **leader**, boss, chief, chieftain, commander, head, master, number one (*inf.*), officer, (senior) pilot, skipper, torchbearer

captious *adj* = **fault-finding**, carping, cavilling, censorious, critical, deprecating, disparaging, hypercritical, nagging, nit-picking (*inf.*)

captivate *vb* = **charm**, absorb, allure, attract, beguile, bewitch, dazzle, enamour, enchant, enrapture, enslave, ensnare, enthral, entrance, fascinate, hypnotize, infatuate, lure, mesmerize, ravish, seduce, sweep off one's feet, win
Antonyms *vb* alienate, disenchant, disgust, repel, repulse

captivation *n* = **fascination**, absorption, allurement, attraction, beguilement, enchantment, enslavement, ensnarement, enthralment, entrancement, hypnotization *or* hypnotisation, infatuation, mesmerization *or* mesmerisation, ravishment, seduction, tantalization *or* tantalisation

captive *n* **1** = **prisoner**, bondservant, convict, detainee, hostage, internee, prisoner of war, slave ◆ *adj* **3, 4** = **confined**, caged, enslaved, ensnared, imprisoned, incarcerated, locked up, penned, restricted, subjugated

captivity *n* **1** = **confinement**, bondage, custody, detention, durance (*arch.*), duress, enthralment, imprisonment, incarceration, internment, restraint, servitude, slavery, thraldom, vassalage

captor *n* = **capturer**, confiner, custodian, detainer, enslaver, ensnarer, imprisoner, incarcerator, jailer *or* gaoler

capture *vb* **1** = **catch**, apprehend, arrest, bag, collar (*inf.*), feel one's collar (*sl.*), lift (*sl.*), nab (*inf.*), nail (*inf.*), secure, seize, take, take into custody, take prisoner ◆ *n* **6** = **catching**, apprehension, arrest, imprisonment, seizure, taking, taking captive, trapping
Antonyms *vb* ≠ **catch:** free, let go, let out, liberate, release, set free, turn loose

car *n* **1** = **vehicle**, auto (*US*), automobile, jalopy (*inf.*), machine, motor, motorcar, wheels (*inf.*) **4** *US & Canad.* = **(railway) carriage**, buffet car, cable car, coach, dining car, sleeping car, van

carafe *n* = **jug**, decanter, flagon, flask, pitcher

the pungent aromatic fruit of this plant, used in cooking. [C14: prob. from Med. L *carvi*, from Ar. *karawyā*, from Gk *karon*]

carb (kɑːb) *n Inf.* short for **carburettor.**

carbaryl (ˈkɑːbərɪl) *n* an organic compound of the carbamate group: used as an insecticide, esp. to treat head lice.

carbide (ˈkɑːbaɪd) *n* **1** a binary compound of carbon with a metal. **2** See **calcium carbide.**

carbine (ˈkɑːbaɪn) *n* **1** a light automatic or semiautomatic rifle. **2** a light short-barrelled rifle formerly used by cavalry. [C17: from F *carabine*, from OF *carabin* carabineer]

carbineer (ˌkɑːbɪˈnɪə), **carabineer,** *or* **carabinier** (ˌkærəbɪˈnɪə) *n* (formerly) a soldier equipped with a carbine.

carbo- *or before a vowel* **carb-** *combining form.* carbon: *carbohydrate; carbonate.*

carbocyclic (ˌkɑːbəʊˈsaɪklɪk) *adj* (of a chemical compound) containing a closed ring of carbon atoms.

carbohydrate (ˌkɑːbəʊˈhaɪdreɪt) *n* any of a large group of organic compounds, including sugars and starch, that contain carbon, hydrogen, and oxygen, with the general formula $C_m(H_2O)_n$: a source of food and energy for animals.

carbolic acid (kɑːˈbɒlɪk) *n* another name for **phenol,** esp. when used as a disinfectant. [C19: from CARBO- + -OL[1] + -IC]

carbon (ˈkɑːbᵊn) *n* **1a** a nonmetallic element existing in three crystalline forms: graphite, diamond, and buckminsterfullerene: occurring in all organic compounds. The isotope **carbon-12** is the standard for atomic wt.; **carbon-14** is used in radiocarbon dating and as a tracer. Symbol: C; atomic no.: 6; atomic wt.: 12.011 15. **1b** (*as modifier*): *a carbon compound.* **2** short for **carbon paper** or **carbon copy. 3** a carbon electrode used in a carbon-arc light. **4** a rod or plate, made of carbon, used in some types of battery. [C18: from F, from L *carbō* charcoal]

carbon-14 dating *n* another name for **carbon dating.**

carbonaceous (ˌkɑːbəˈneɪʃəs) *adj* of, resembling, or containing carbon.

carbonade (ˌkɑːbəˈneɪd, -ˈnɑːd) *n* beef and onions stewed in beer. [C20: F]

carbonado (ˌkɑːbəˈneɪdəʊ) *n, pl* **carbonados** *or* **carbonadoes.** an inferior variety of diamond used in industry. Also called: **black diamond.** [Port., lit.: carbonated]

carbon arc *n* an electric arc between two carbon electrodes or between a carbon electrode and materials to be welded.

carbonate *n* (ˈkɑːbəˌneɪt, -nɪt). **1** a salt or ester of carbonic acid. ◆ *vb* (ˈkɑːbəˌneɪt), **carbonates, carbonating, carbonated. 2** to turn into a carbonate. **3** (*tr*) to treat with carbon dioxide, as in the manufacture of soft drinks. [C18: from F, from *carbone* CARBON]

carbon black *n* a finely divided form of carbon produced by incomplete combustion of natural gas or petroleum: used in pigments and ink.

carbon brush *n* a small spring-loaded block of carbon used to convey current between the stationary and moving parts of an electric generator, motor, etc.

carbon copy *n* **1** a duplicate copy of writing, typewriting, or drawing obtained by using carbon paper. **2** *Inf.* a person or thing that is identical to another.

carbon dating *n* a technique for determining the age of organic materials, such as wood, based on their content of the radioisotope ^{14}C acquired from the atmosphere when they formed part of a living plant.

carbon dioxide *n* a colourless odourless incombustible gas present in the atmosphere and formed during respiration, etc.: used in fire extinguishers, and as dry ice for refrigeration. Formula: CO_2. Also called: **carbonic-acid gas.**

carbonette (ˌkɑːbəˈnɛt) *n NZ.* a ball of compressed coal dust used as fuel.

carbon fibre *n* a thread of pure carbon used because of its lightness and strength at high temperatures for reinforcing resins, ceramics, and metals, and for fishing rods.

carbonic (kɑːˈbɒnɪk) *adj* (of a compound) containing carbon, esp. tetravalent carbon.

carbonic acid *n* a weak acid formed when carbon dioxide combines with water. Formula: H_2CO_3.

carboniferous (ˌkɑːbəˈnɪfərəs) *adj* yielding coal or carbon.

Carboniferous (ˌkɑːbəˈnɪfərəs) *adj* **1** of, denoting, or formed in the fifth period of the Palaeozoic era during which coal measures were formed. ◆ *n* **2 the.** the Carboniferous period or rock system divided into the **Upper Carboniferous** period and the **Lower Carboniferous** period.

carbonize *or* **carbonise** (ˈkɑːbəˌnaɪz) *vb* **carbonizes, carbonizing, carbonized** *or* **carbonises, carbonising, carbonised. 1** to turn or be turned into carbon as a result of heating, fossilization, chemical treatment, etc. **2** (*tr*) to coat (a substance) with carbon.
▸ˌ**carboniˈzation** *or* ˌ**carboniˈsation** *n*

carbon monoxide *n* a colourless odourless poisonous gas formed when carbon compounds burn in insufficient air. Formula: CO.

carbon paper *n* a thin sheet of paper coated on one side with a dark waxy pigment, often containing carbon, that is transferred by pressure onto the copying surface below.

carbon tax *n* a tax on the emissions caused by the burning of coal, gas, and oil, aimed at reducing the production of greenhouse gases.

carbon tetrachloride *n* a colourless volatile nonflammable liquid made from chlorine and used as a solvent, cleaning fluid, and insecticide. Formula: CCl_4. Systematic name: **tetrachloromethane.**

car-boot sale *n* a sale of goods from car boots in a site hired for the occasion.

Carborundum (ˌkɑːbəˈrʌndəm) *n Trademark.* any of various abrasive materials, esp. one consisting of silicon carbide.

carboxyl group *or* **radical** (kɑːˈbɒksaɪl) *n* the monovalent group -COOH: the functional group in organic acids. [C19 *carboxyl*, from CARBO- + OXY-[2] + -YL]

carboxylic acid (ˌkɑːbɒkˈsɪlɪk) *n* any of a class of organic acids containing the carboxyl group. See also **fatty acid.**

carboy (ˈkɑːˌbɔɪ) *n* a large bottle, usually protected by a basket or box, used for containing corrosive liquids. [C18: from Persian *qarāba*]

carbuncle (ˈkɑːˌbʌŋkᵊl) *n* **1** an extensive skin eruption, similar to a boil, with several openings. **2** a rounded gemstone, esp. a garnet cut without facets. [C13: from L *carbunculus*, dim. of *carbō* coal]
▸**carbuncular** (kɑːˈbʌŋkjʊlə) *adj*

carburation (ˌkɑːbjʊˈreɪʃən) *n* the process of mixing a hydrocarbon fuel with air to make an explosive mixture for an internal-combustion engine.

carburet (ˈkɑːbjʊˌrɛt, ˌkɑːbjʊˈrɛt) *vb* **carburets, carburetting, carburetted** *or US* **carburets, carbureting, carbureted.** (*tr*) to combine or mix (a gas, etc.) with carbon or carbon compounds. [C18: from CARB(ON) + -URET]

carburettor, carburetter (ˌkɑːbəˈrɛtə, ˈkɑːbəˌrɛtə), *or US & Canad.* **carburetor** (ˈkɑːbəˌreɪtə) *n* a device used in some petrol engines for mixing atomized petrol with air, and regulating the intake of the mixture into the engine.

carcajou (ˈkɑːkəˌdʒuː, -kəˌʒuː) *n* a North American name for **wolverine.** [C18: from Canad. F, from Algonquian *karkajou*]

carcass ⓣ *or* **carcase** (ˈkɑːkəs) *n* **1** the dead body of an animal, esp. one that has been slaughtered for food. **2** *Inf., usually facetious or derog.* a person's body. **3** the skeleton or framework of a structure. **4** the remains of anything when its life or vitality is gone. [C14: from OF *carcasse*, from ?]

carcinogen (kɑːˈsɪnədʒən) *n Pathol.* any substance that produces cancer. [C20: from Gk *karkinos* CANCER + -GEN]
▸ˌ**carcinoˈgenic** *adj*

carcinogenesis (ˌkɑːsɪnəʊˈdʒɛnɪsɪs) *n Pathol.* the development of cancerous cells from normal ones.

carcinoma (ˌkɑːsɪˈnəʊmə) *n, pl* **carcinomas** *or* **carcinomata** (-mətə). *Pathol.* any malignant tumour derived from epithelial tissue. [C18: from L, from Gk, from *karkinos* CANCER]

card[1] (kɑːd) *n* **1** a piece of stiff paper or thin cardboard, usually rectangular, with varied uses, as for bearing a written notice for display, etc. **2** such a card used for identification, reference, proof of membership, etc.: *identity card.* **3** such a card used for sending greetings, messages, or invitations: *birthday card.* **4a** one of a set of small pieces of cardboard, marked with figures, symbols, etc., used for playing games or for fortune-telling. See also **playing card. 4b** (*as modifier*): *a card game.* **5** short for **cheque card** or **credit card. 6** *Inf.* a witty or eccentric person. **7** See **compass card. 8** Also called: **racecard.** *Horse racing.* a daily programme of all the races at a meeting. **9 a card up one's sleeve.** a thing or action used in order to gain an advantage, esp. one kept in reserve until needed. ◆ See also **cards.** [C15: from OF *carte*, from L *charta* leaf of papyrus, from Gk *khartēs*, prob. of Egyptian origin]

card[2] (kɑːd) *vb* **1** (*tr*) to comb out and clean (fibres of wool or cotton) before spinning. ◆ *n* **2** (formerly) a machine or comblike tool for carding fabrics or for raising the nap on cloth. [C15: from OF *carde* card, teasel, from L *carduus* thistle]
▸ˈ**carder** *n* ▸ˈ**carding** *n*

cardamom (ˈkɑːdəməm) *or* **cardamon** (ˈkɑːdəmən) *n* **1** a tropical Asian plant that has large hairy leaves. **2** the seeds of this plant, used esp. as a spice or condiment. [C15: from L, from Gk, from *kardamon* cress + *amōmon* an Indian spice]

cardboard (ˈkɑːdˌbɔːd) *n* **1a** a thin stiff board made from paper pulp. **1b** (*as modifier*): *cardboard boxes.* ◆ *adj* **2** (*prenominal*) without substance.

cardboard city *n Inf.* an area of a city in which homeless people sleep rough, often in cardboard boxes.

card-carrying *adj* being an official member of an organization: *a card-carrying Communist.*

cardiac (ˈkɑːdɪˌæk) *adj* **1** of or relating to the heart. **2** of or relating to the portion of the stomach connected to the oesophagus. ◆ *n* **3** a person with a heart disorder. [C17: from L *cardiacus*, from Gk, from *kardia* heart]

cardiac arrest *n* failure of the pumping action of the heart, resulting in loss of consciousness and absence of pulse and breathing: a medical emergency requiring immediate resuscitative treatment.

cardie *or* **cardy** (ˈkɑːdɪ) *n, pl* **cardies.** *Inf.* short for **cardigan.**

cardigan (ˈkɑːdɪgən) *n* a knitted jacket or sweater with buttons up the front. [C19: after 7th Earl of *Cardigan* (1797–1868)]

cardinal ⓣ (ˈkɑːdɪnᵊl) *n* **1** *RC Church.* any of the members of the Sacred College who elect the pope and act as his chief counsellors. **2** Also called: **cardinal red.** a deep red colour. **3** See **cardinal number. 4** Also called (US): **redbird.** a crested North American bunting, the male of which has a bright red plumage. **5** a woman's hooded shoulder cape

THESAURUS

carcass *n* **1-4** = **body,** cadaver (*Medical*), corpse, corse (*arch.*), dead body, framework, hulk, remains, shell, skeleton

cardinal *adj* **6** = **principal,** capital, central, chief, essential, first, foremost, fundamental, greatest, highest, important, key, leading, main, paramount, pre-eminent, primary, prime
Antonyms *adj* dispensable, inessential, least important, lowest, secondary, subordinate

worn in the 17th and 18th centuries. ◆ *adj* **6** (*usually prenominal*) fundamentally important; principal. **7** of a deep red. [C13: from L *cardinālis*, lit.: relating to a hinge, from *cardō* hinge]
▸ **'cardinally** *adv*

cardinalate ('kɑːdɪnᵊˌleɪt) *or* **cardinalship** *n* **1** the rank, office, or term of office of a cardinal. **2** the cardinals collectively.

cardinal flower *n* a lobelia of E North America that has brilliant scarlet flowers.

cardinal number *or* **numeral** *n* a number denoting quantity but not order in a group. Sometimes shortened to **cardinal.** Cf. **ordinal number.**

cardinal points *pl n* the four main points of the compass: north, south, east, and west.

cardinal virtues *pl n* the most important moral qualities, traditionally justice, prudence, temperance, and fortitude.

cardinal vowels *pl n* a set of theoretical vowel sounds, based on the shape of the mouth needed to articulate them, that can be used to classify the vowel sounds of any speaker in any language.

card index *or* **file** *n* **1** an index in which each item is separately listed on systematically arranged cards. ◆ *vb* **card-index** *or* **card-file, card-indexes, card-indexing, card-indexed** *or* **card-files, card-filing, card-filed.** (*tr*) **2** to make such an index of (a book, etc.).

cardio- *or before a vowel* **cardi-** *combining form.* heart: *cardiogram.* [from Gk *kardia* heart]

cardiocentesis (ˌkɑːdɪəʊsɛn'tiːsɪs) *n Med.* surgical puncture of the heart.

cardiogram ('kɑːdɪəʊˌɡræm) *n* short for **electrocardiogram.** See **electrocardiograph.**

cardiograph ('kɑːdɪəʊˌɡrɑːf) *n* **1** an instrument for recording heart movements. **2** short for **electrocardiograph.**
▸ **cardiographer** (ˌkɑːdɪ'ɒɡrəfə) *n* ▸ **ˌcardi'ography** *n*

cardiology (ˌkɑːdɪ'ɒlədʒɪ) *n* the branch of medical science concerned with the heart and its diseases.
▸ **ˌcardi'ologist** *n*

cardioplegia (ˌkɑːdɪəʊ'pliːdʒə) *n Med.* deliberate arrest of the action of the heart, as by hypothermia or the injection of chemicals, to enable complex heart surgery to be carried out.

cardiopulmonary resuscitation (ˌkɑːdɪəʊ'pʌlmənərɪ, -'pʊl-) *n* an emergency measure to revive a patient whose heart has stopped beating, in which compressions applied with the hands to the patient's chest are alternated with mouth-to-mouth respiration. Abbrev.: **CPR.**

cardiovascular (ˌkɑːdɪəʊ'væskjʊlə) *adj* of or relating to the heart and the blood vessels.

cardoon (kɑː'duːn) *n* a thistle-like relative of the artichoke with an edible leafstalk. [C17: from F, from L *carduus* thistle, artichoke]

cardphone ('kɑːdfəʊn) *n* a public telephone operated by the insertion of a phonecard instead of coins.

card punch *n* a device, no longer widely used, controlled by a computer, for transferring information from the central processing unit onto punched cards which can then be read by a **card reader.**

card reader *n* a device, no longer widely used, for reading information on a punched card and transferring it to a computer or storage device.

cards (kɑːdz) *n* **1** (*usually functioning as sing*) **1a** any game played with cards, esp. playing cards. **1b** the playing of such a game. **2** an employee's tax and national insurance documents or information held by the employer. **3 ask for** *or* **get one's cards.** to ask *or* be told to terminate one's employment. **4 on the cards.** possible. **5 play one's cards (right).** to manoeuvre (cleverly). **6 put** *or* **lay one's cards on the table.** to declare one's intentions, etc.

cardsharp ('kɑːdˌʃɑːp) *or* **cardsharper** *n* a professional card player who cheats.

card vote *n Brit.* a vote by delegates, esp. at a trade-union conference, in which each delegate's vote counts as a vote by all his constituents.

care ❶ (kɛə) *vb* **cares, caring, cared. 1** (when *tr, may take a clause as object*) to be troubled or concerned: *he is dying, and she doesn't care.* **2** (*intr;* foll. by *for* or *about*) to have regard or consideration (for): *he cares more for his hobby than his job.* **3** (*intr;* foll. by *for*) to have a desire or taste (for): *would you care for tea?* **4** (*intr;* foll. by *for*) to provide physical needs, help, or comfort (for). **5** (*tr*) to agree or like (to do something): *would you care to sit down?* **6 for all I care** *or* **I couldn't care less.** I am completely indifferent. ◆ *n* **7** careful or serious attention: *he does his work with care.* **8** protective or supervisory control: *in the care of a doctor.* **9** (*often pl*) trouble; worry. **10** an object of or cause for concern. **11** caution: *handle with care.* **12 care of.** at the address of: written on envelopes. Usual abbrev.: **c/o. 13 in** (*or* **into**) **care.** *Brit.* made the legal responsibility of a local authority by order of a court. [OE *cearu* (n), *cearian* (vb), of Gmc origin]
▸ **'carer** *n*

CARE (kɛə) *n acronym for:* **1** Cooperative for American Relief Everywhere. **2** communicated authenticity, regard, empathy: the three qualities believed to be essential in the therapist practising client-centred therapy.

care and maintenance *n Commerce.* the state of a building, ship, machinery, etc., that is not in current use although it is kept in good condition to enable it to be brought into service quickly if there is a demand for it. Abbrev.: **C & M.**

careen (kə'riːn) *vb* **1** to sway or cause to sway over to one side. **2** (*tr*) *Naut.* to cause (a vessel) to keel over to one side, esp. in order to clean its bottom. **3** (*intr*) *Naut.* (of a vessel) to keel over to one side. [C17: from F, from It., from L *carīna* keel]
▸ **ca'reenage** *n*

career ❶ (kə'rɪə) *n* **1** a path through life or history. **2a** a profession or occupation chosen as one's life's work. **2b** (*as modifier*): *a career diplomat.* **3** a course or path, esp. a headlong one. ◆ *vb* **4** (*intr*) to rush in an uncontrolled way. [C16: from F, from LL *carrāria* carriage road, from L *carrus* two-wheeled wagon]

career girl *or* **woman** *n* a woman, often unmarried, who follows a profession.

careerist (kə'rɪərɪst) *n* a person who seeks to advance his career by any possible means.

carefree ❶ ('kɛəˌfriː) *adj* without worry or responsibility.
▸ **'careˌfreeness** *n*

careful ❶ ('kɛəfʊl) *adj* **1** cautious in attitude or action. **2** painstaking in one's work; exact and thorough. **3** (*usually postpositive;* foll. by *of, in,* or *about*) solicitous; protective. **4** *Brit.* mean or miserly.
▸ **'carefully** *adv* ▸ **'carefulness** *n*

careless ❶ ('kɛəlɪs) *adj* **1** done with or acting with insufficient attention. **2** (often foll. by *in, of,* or *about*) unconcerned in attitude or action. **3** (*usually prenominal*) carefree. **4** (*usually prenominal*) unstudied: *careless elegance.*
▸ **'carelessly** *adv* ▸ **'carelessness** *n*

caress ❶ (kə'rɛs) *n* **1** a gentle touch or embrace, esp. one given to show affection. ◆ *vb* **2** (*tr*) to touch or stroke gently with or as with affection. [C17: from F, from It., from L *cārus* dear]

caret ('kærɪt) *n* a symbol (‸) used to indicate the place in written or printed matter at which something is to be inserted. [C17: from L, lit.: there is missing, from *carēre* to lack]

caretaker ❶ ('kɛəˌteɪkə) *n* **1** a person who looks after a place or thing, esp. in the owner's absence. **2** (*modifier*) interim: *a caretaker government.*

careworn ❶ ('kɛəˌwɔːn) *adj* showing signs of care, stress, worry, etc.: *a careworn face.*

cargo ❶ ('kɑːɡəʊ) *n, pl* **cargoes** *or esp. US* **cargos. 1a** goods carried by a ship, aircraft, or other vehicle; freight. **1b** (*as modifier*): *a cargo vessel.* **2** any load: *a cargo of new arrivals.* [C17: from Sp.: from *cargar* to load, from LL, from L *carrus* CAR]

Carib ('kærɪb) *n* **1** (*pl* **Caribs** *or* **Carib**) a member of a group of American Indian peoples of NE South America and the Lesser Antilles. **2** the

THESAURUS

care *vb* **1 = be concerned,** be bothered, be interested, mind **2, 3** *foll. by* **for = like,** be fond of, desire, enjoy, find congenial, love, prize, take to, want **4** *foll. by* **for = look after,** attend, foster, mind, minister to, nurse, protect, provide for, tend, watch over ◆ *n* **7, 11 = caution,** attention, carefulness, circumspection, consideration, direction, forethought, heed, management, meticulousness, pains, prudence, regard, vigilance, watchfulness **8 = protection,** charge, control, custody, guardianship, keeping, management, ministration, supervision, ward **9, 10 = worry,** affliction, anxiety, burden, concern, disquiet, hardship, interest, perplexity, pressure, responsibility, solicitude, stress, tribulation, trouble, vexation, woe
Antonyms *n* ≠ **caution:** abandon, carelessness, heedlessness, inattention, indifference, laxity, laxness, neglect, negligence, unconcern ≠ **worry:** pleasure, relaxation

career *n* **2a = occupation,** calling, employment, life's work, livelihood, pursuit, vocation **3 = progress,** course, passage, path, procedure, race, walk ◆ *vb* **4 = rush,** barrel (along) (*inf., chiefly US & Canad.*), bolt, burn rubber (*inf.*), dash, hurtle, race, speed, tear

carefree *adj* **= untroubled,** airy, blithe, breezy, buoyant, careless, cheerful, cheery, chirpy (*inf.*), easy-going, halcyon, happy, happy-go-lucky, insouciant, jaunty, light-hearted, lightsome (*arch.*), radiant, sunny
Antonyms *adj* blue, careworn, cheerless, dejected, depressed, desolate, despondent, down, down in the dumps (*inf.*), gloomy, low, melancholy, miserable, sad, unhappy, worried

careful *adj* **1 = cautious,** accurate, attentive, chary, circumspect, conscientious, discreet, fastidious, heedful, painstaking, precise, prudent, punctilious, scrupulous, thoughtful, thrifty **2 = thorough,** conscientious, meticulous, painstaking, particular, precise
Antonyms *adj* abandoned, careless, casual, inaccurate, inattentive, inexact, neglectful, negligent, reckless, remiss, slovenly, thoughtless, unconcerned, untroubled

careless *adj* **1 = slapdash,** cavalier, inaccurate, irresponsible, lackadaisical, neglectful, offhand, slipshod, sloppy (*inf.*) **2 = negligent,** absent-minded, cursory, forgetful, hasty, heedless, incautious, inconsiderate, indiscreet, perfunctory, regardless, remiss, thoughtless, unconcerned, unguarded, unmindful, unthinking **4 = nonchalant,** artless, casual, unstudied
Antonyms *adj* ≠ **slapdash:** accurate, careful, neat, orderly, painstaking, tidy ≠ **negligent:** alert, anxious, attentive, careful, cautious, concerned, correct, on the ball (*inf.*), wary, watchful

carelessness *n* **1, 2 = negligence,** inaccuracy, inattention, inconsiderateness, indiscretion, irresponsibility, laxity, laxness, neglect, omission, remissness, slackness, sloppiness (*inf.*), thoughtlessness

caress *n* **1 = stroke,** cuddle, embrace, fondling, hug, kiss, pat ◆ *vb* **2 = stroke,** cuddle, embrace, fondle, hug, kiss, neck (*inf.*), nuzzle, pet

caretaker *n* **1 = warden,** concierge, curator, custodian, janitor, keeper, porter, superintendent, watchman ◆ *modifier* **2 = temporary,** holding, interim, short-term

careworn *adj* **= stressed,** heavy-laden, overburdened

cargo *n* **1a, 2 = load,** baggage, consignment, contents, freight, goods, lading, merchandise, shipment, tonnage, ware

family of languages spoken by these peoples. [C16: from Sp. *Caribe*, from Amerind]

Caribbean (ˌkærɪˈbiːən) *adj* **1** of the Caribbean Sea and its islands. **2** of the Carib or any of their languages. ◆ *n* **3** the Caribbean Sea. **4** a member of any of the peoples inhabiting the islands of the Caribbean Sea, such as a West Indian or a Carib.

caribou (ˈkærɪˌbuː) *n, pl* **caribou** *or* **caribous.** a large North American reindeer. [C18: from Canad. F, of Algonquian origin]

caricature Ⓣ (ˈkærɪkəˌtjʊə) *n* **1** a pictorial, written, or acted representation of a person, which exaggerates his characteristic traits for comic effect. **2** an inadequate or inaccurate imitation. ◆ *vb* **caricatures, caricaturing, caricatured. 3** (*tr*) to represent in caricature or produce a caricature of. [C18: from It. *caricatura* a distortion, from *caricare* to load, exaggerate]
▸ **ˈcaricaˌturist** *n*

CARICOM (ˈkærɪˌkɒm) *n acronym for* Caribbean Community and Common Market.

caries (ˈkɛəriːz) *n, pl* **caries.** progressive decay of a bone or a tooth. [C17: from L: decay]

carillon (kəˈrɪljən) *n Music.* **1** a set of bells usually hung in a tower. **2** a tune played on such bells. **3** a mixture stop on an organ giving the effect of a bell. [C18: from F: set of bells, from OF *quarregnon*, ult. from L *quattuor* four]

carina (kəˈriːnə, -ˈraɪ-) *n, pl* **carinae** (-niː) *or* **carinas.** a keel-like part or ridge, as in the breastbone of birds or the fused lower petals of a leguminous flower. [C18: from L: keel]

carinate (ˈkærɪˌneɪt) *or* **carinated** *adj Biol.* having a keel or ridge. [C17: from L *carīnāre*, from *carīna* keel]

caring Ⓣ (kɛərɪŋ) *adj* **1** showing care and compassion: *a caring attitude*. **2** of or relating to professional social or medical care: *nursing is a caring job*. ◆ *n* **3** the practice of providing care.

carioca (ˌkærɪˈəʊkə) *n* **1** a Brazilian dance similar to the samba. **2** a piece of music for this dance. [C19: from Brazilian Port.]

cariogenic (ˌkɛərɪəʊˈdʒɛnɪk) *adj* (of a substance) producing caries of the teeth.

cariole *or* **carriole** (ˈkærɪˌəʊl) *n* **1** a small open two-wheeled horse-drawn vehicle. **2** a covered cart. [C19: from F, ult. from L *carrus*; see CAR]

carious (ˈkɛərɪəs) *or* **cariose** (ˈkɛərɪˌəʊz) *adj* (of teeth or bone) affected with caries; decayed.

carl *or* **carle** (kɑːl) *n Arch. or Scot.* another word for **churl.** [OE, from ON *karl*]

Carlovingian (ˌkɑːləʊˈvɪndʒɪən) *adj, n History.* a variant of **Carolingian.**

carmagnole (ˌkɑːmənˈjəʊl) *n* **1** a dance and song popular during the French Revolution. **2** the costume worn by many French Revolutionaries. [C18: from F, prob. after *Carmagnola*, Italy]

Carmelite (ˈkɑːməˌlaɪt) *n RC Church.* **1** a member of an order of mendicant friars founded about 1154. **2** a member of a corresponding order of nuns founded in 1452, noted for its austere rule. ◆ *adj* **3** of or relating to either of these orders. [C14: from F, after Mount *Carmel*, in Palestine, where the order was founded]

carminative (ˈkɑːmɪnətɪv) *adj* **1** able to relieve flatulence. ◆ *n* **2** a carminative drug. [C15: from F, from L *carmināre* to card wool]

carmine (ˈkɑːmaɪn) *n* **1a** a vivid red colour. **1b** (*as adj*): *carmine paint*. **2** a pigment of this colour obtained from cochineal. [C18: from Med. L *carmīnus*, from Ar. *qirmiz* KERMES]

carnage Ⓣ (ˈkɑːnɪdʒ) *n* extensive slaughter. [C16: from F, from It., from Med. L, from L *carō* flesh]

carnal Ⓣ (ˈkɑːnᵊl) *adj* relating to the appetites and passions of the body. [C15: from LL, from L *carō* flesh]
▸ **carˈnality** *n* ▸ **ˈcarnally** *adv*

carnal knowledge *n Chiefly law.* sexual intercourse.

carnation (kɑːˈneɪʃən) *n* **1** Also called: **clove pink.** a Eurasian plant cultivated in many varieties for its white, pink, or red flowers, which have a fragrant scent of cloves. **2** the flower of this plant. **3a** a pink or reddish-pink colour. **3b** (*as adj*): *a carnation dress*. [C16: from F: flesh colour, from LL, from L *carō* flesh]

carnauba (kɑːˈnaʊbə) *n* **1** Also called: **wax palm.** a Brazilian fan palm. **2** Also called: **carnauba wax.** the wax obtained from the young leaves of this tree. [from Brazilian Port., prob. of Tupi origin]

carnelian (kɑːˈniːljən) *n* a reddish-yellow translucent variety of chalcedony, used as a gemstone. [C17: var. of *cornelian*, from OF, from ?]

carnet (ˈkɑːneɪ) *n* **1** a customs licence authorizing the temporary importation of a motor vehicle. **2** an official document permitting motorists to cross certain frontiers. [F: notebook, from OF, ult. from L *quaternī* four at a time]

carnival Ⓣ (ˈkɑːnɪvᵊl) *n* **1a** a festive period marked by merrymaking, etc.: esp. in some Roman Catholic countries, the period just before Lent. **1b** (*as modifier*): *a carnival atmosphere*. **2** a travelling fair having sideshows, rides, etc. **3** a show or display arranged as an amusement. **4** *Austral.* a sports meeting. [C16: from It., from OIt. *carnelevare* a removing of meat (referring to the Lenten fast)]

carnivore (ˈkɑːnɪˌvɔː) *n* **1** any of an order of mammals having large pointed canine teeth specialized for eating flesh. The order includes cats, dogs, bears, and weasels. **2** any other animal or any plant that feeds on animals. **3** *Inf.* an aggressively ambitious person. [C19: prob. back formation from CARNIVOROUS]

carnivorous (kɑːˈnɪvərəs) *adj* **1** (esp. of animals) feeding on flesh. **2** (of plants such as the pitcher plant and sundew) able to trap and digest insects. **3** of or relating to the carnivores. **4** *Inf.* aggressively ambitious or reactionary. [C17: from L, from *carō* flesh + *vorāre* to consume]
▸ **carˈnivorousness** *n*

carob (ˈkærəb) *n* **1** an evergreen Mediterranean tree with compound leaves and edible pods. **2** the long blackish sugary pod of this tree, used for animal fodder and sometimes for human food. [C16: from OF, from Med. L *carrūbium*, from Ar. *al kharrūbah*]

carol Ⓣ (ˈkærəl) *n* **1** a joyful hymn or religious song, esp. one (a **Christmas carol**) celebrating the birth of Christ. ◆ *vb* **carols, carolling, carolled** *or US* **carols, caroling, caroled. 2** (*intr*) to sing carols at Christmas. **3** to sing (something) in a joyful manner. [C13: from OF, from ?]

Caroline (ˈkærəˌlaɪn) *or* **Carolean** (ˌkærəˈliːən) *adj* characteristic of or relating to Charles I or Charles II (kings of England, Scotland, and Ireland), the society over which they ruled, or their government. Also called: **Carolinian.**

Carolingian (ˌkærəˈlɪndʒɪən) *adj* **1** of or relating to the Frankish dynasty founded by Pepin the Short which ruled in France from 751–987 A.D. and in Germany until 911 A.D. ◆ *n* **2** a member of the dynasty of the Carolingian Franks. ◆ Also: **Carlovingian, Carolinian.**

Carolinian (ˌkærəˈlɪnɪən) *adj, n* a variant of **Caroline** or **Carolingian.**

carom (ˈkærəm) *n Billiards.* another word (esp. US & Canad.) for **cannon** (sense 5). [C18: from earlier *carambole* (taken as *carom ball*), from Sp. *carambola* a CARAMBOLA]

carotene (ˈkærəˌtiːn) *or* **carotin** (ˈkærətɪn) *n* any of four orange-red isomers of a hydrocarbon present in many plants and converted to vitamin A in the liver. [C19 *carotin*, from L *carōta* CARROT]

carotenoid *or* **carotinoid** (kəˈrɒtɪˌnɔɪd) *n* any of a group of red or yellow pigments, including carotenes, found in plants and certain animal tissues.

carotid (kəˈrɒtɪd) *n* **1** either of the two principal arteries that supply blood to the head and neck. ◆ *adj* **2** of either of these arteries. [C17: from F, from Gk, from *karoun* to stupefy; so named because pressure on them produced unconsciousness]

carousal (kəˈraʊzᵊl) *n* a merry drinking party.

carouse Ⓣ (kəˈraʊz) *vb* **carouses, carousing, caroused. 1** (*intr*) to have a merry drinking spree. ◆ *n* **2** another word for **carousal.** [C16: via F *carrousser* from G (*trinken*) *gar aus* (to drink) right out]
▸ **caˈrouser** *n*

carousel (ˌkærəˈsɛl, -ˈzɛl) *n* **1** a circular tray in which slides for a projector are held in slots from which they can be released in turn. **2** a revolving luggage conveyor, as at an airport. **3** *US and Canad.* a merry-go-round. **4** *History.* a tournament in which horsemen took part in races. [C17: from F, from It. *carosello*, from ?]

carp[1] (kɑːp) *n, pl* **carp** *or* **carps. 1** a freshwater food fish having one long dorsal fin, and two barbels on each side of the mouth. **2** a cyprinid. [C14: from OF *carpe*, of Gmc origin]

carp[2] Ⓣ (kɑːp) *vb* (*intr*; often foll. by *at*) to complain or find fault. [C13: from ON *karpa* to boast]
▸ **ˈcarper** *n* ▸ **ˈcarping** *adj, n*

-carp *n combining form.* (in botany) fruit or a reproductive structure that develops into a particular part of the fruit: *epicarp*. [from NL *-carpium*, from Gk *-karpion*, from *karpos* fruit]

carpal (ˈkɑːpᵊl) *n* **a** any bone of the wrist. **b** (*as modifier*): *carpal bones*. [C18: from NL *carpālis*, from Gk *karpos* wrist]

car park *n* an area or building reserved for parking cars. Usual US and Canad. term: **parking lot.**

carpe diem *Latin.* (ˈkɑːpɪ ˈdiːɛm) *sentence substitute.* enjoy the pleasures of the moment, without concern for the future. [lit.: seize the day!]

carpel (ˈkɑːpᵊl) *n* the female reproductive organ of flowering plants,

THESAURUS

caricature *n* **1** = **parody**, burlesque, cartoon, distortion, farce, lampoon, mimicry, pasquinade, satire, send-up (*Brit. inf.*), takeoff (*inf.*), travesty ◆ *vb* **3** = **parody**, burlesque, distort, lampoon, mimic, mock, ridicule, satirize, send up (*Brit. inf.*), take off (*inf.*)

caring *adj* **1** = **compassionate**, considerate, kindly, loving, receptive, responsive, sensitive, soft, softhearted, sympathetic, tender, tenderhearted, touchy-feely (*inf.*), warm, warmhearted

carnage *n* = **slaughter**, blood bath, bloodshed, butchery, havoc, holocaust, massacre, mass murder, murder, shambles

carnal *adj* = **sexual**, amorous, animal, erotic, fleshly, impure, lascivious, lecherous, lewd, libidinous, licentious, lustful, prurient, randy (*inf., chiefly Brit.*), raunchy (*sl.*), salacious, sensual, sensuous, sexy (*inf.*), steamy (*inf.*), unchaste, voluptuous, wanton

carnality *n* = **lust**, bestiality, corporeality, fleshliness, lechery, lustfulness, prurience, salaciousness, sensuality, voluptuousness, worldliness

carnival *n* **1** = **festival**, celebration, fair, fête, fiesta, gala, holiday, jamboree, jubilee, Mardi Gras, merrymaking, revelry

carol *n* **1** = **song**, canticle, canzonet, chorus, ditty, hymn, lay, noel, strain

carouse *vb* **1** = **drink**, bend the elbow (*inf.*), bevvy (*dialect*), booze (*inf.*), imbibe, make merry, quaff, roister, wassail

carp[2] *vb, often foll. by* **at** = **find fault**, beef (*sl.*), cavil, censure, complain, criticize, knock (*inf.*), nag, pick holes, quibble, reproach

Antonyms *vb* admire, applaud, approve, commend, compliment, extol, laud (*literary*), pay tribute to, praise, sing the praises of, speak highly of

consisting of an ovary, style, and stigma. [C19: from NL *carpellum*, from Gk *karpos* fruit]
▸ **'carpellary** *adj*

carpenter ⓣ ('kɑːpɪntə) *n* **1** a person skilled in woodwork, esp. in buildings, ships, etc. ◆ *vb* **2** (*intr*) to do the work of a carpenter. **3** (*tr*) to make or fit together by or as if by carpentry. [C14: from Anglo-F, from L, from *carpentum* wagon]

carpentry ('kɑːpɪntrɪ) *n* **1** the art or technique of working wood. **2** the work produced by a carpenter; woodwork.

carpet ('kɑːpɪt) *n* **1** a heavy fabric for covering floors. **2** a covering like a carpet: *a carpet of leaves*. **3 on the carpet.** *Inf.* **3a** before authority to be reproved. **3b** under consideration. ◆ *vb* **carpets, carpeting, carpeted.** (*tr*) **4** to cover with or as if with a carpet. **5** *Inf.* to reprimand. [C14: from OF, from OIt., from LL *carpeta*, from L *carpere* to pluck, card]

carpetbag ('kɑːpɪtˌbæg) *n* a travelling bag originally made of carpeting.

carpetbagger ('kɑːpɪtˌbægə) *n* **1** a politician who seeks public office in a locality where he has no real connections. **2** *Brit.* a person who makes a short-term investment in a mutual savings or life-assurance organization in order to benefit from free shares issued following the organization's conversion to a public limited company.

carpet beetle *or US* **carpet bug** *n* any of various beetles, the larvae of which feed on carpets, furnishing fabrics, etc.

carpet bombing *n* systematic intensive bombing of an area.

carpeting ('kɑːpɪtɪŋ) *n* carpet material or carpets in general.

carpet slipper *n* one of a pair of slippers, originally one made with woollen uppers resembling carpeting.

carpet snake *or* **python** *n* a large nonvenomous Australian snake having a carpet-like pattern on its back.

carpet-sweeper *n* a household device with a revolving brush for sweeping carpets.

car phone *n* a telephone that operates by cellular radio for use in a car.

carpo- *combining form.* (in botany) indicating fruit or a seed. [from Gk *karpos* fruit]

carport ('kɑːˌpɔːt) *n* a shelter for a car usually consisting of a roof built out from the side of a building and supported by posts.

-carpous *or* **-carpic** *adj combining form.* (in botany) indicating a certain kind or number of fruit: *apocarpous*. [from NL, from Gk *karpos* fruit]

carpus ('kɑːpəs) *n, pl* **carpi** (-paɪ). **1** the technical name for **wrist. 2** the eight small bones of the human wrist. [C17: NL, from Gk *karpos*]

carrack ('kærək) *n* a galleon sailed in the Mediterranean as a merchantman in the 15th and 16th centuries. [C14: from OF *caraque*, from OSp. *carraca*, from Ar. *qarāqīr* merchant ships]

carrageen, carragheen, *or* **carageen** ('kærəˌgiːn) *n* an edible red seaweed of North America and N Europe. Also called: **Irish moss.** [C19: from *Carragheen*, near Waterford, Ireland]

carrageenan, carragheenan, *or* **carageenan** (ˌkærə'giːnən) *n* a carbohydrate extracted from carrageen, used to make a beverage, medicine, and jelly, and as an emulsifying and gelling agent (**E407**) in various processed desserts and drinks.

carrel *or* **carrell** ('kærəl) *n* a small individual study room or private desk, often in a library. [C20: from obs. *carrel* study area, var. of CAROL]

carriage ⓣ ('kærɪdʒ) *n* **1** *Brit.* a railway coach for passengers. **2** the manner in which a person holds and moves his head and body. **3** a four-wheeled horse-drawn vehicle for persons. **4** the moving part of a machine that bears another part: *a typewriter carriage*. **5** ('kærɪdʒ, 'kærɪɪdʒ). **5a** the act of conveying. **5b** the charge made for conveying (esp. in **carriage forward,** when the charge is to be paid by the receiver, and **carriage paid**). [C14: from OF *cariage*, from *carier* to CARRY]

carriage clock *n* a portable clock, usually in a rectangular case, originally used by travellers.

carriage trade *n* trade from the wealthy part of society.

carriageway ('kærɪdʒˌweɪ) *n Brit.* the part of a road along which traffic passes in a single line moving in one direction only: *a dual carriageway*.

carrier ('kærɪə) *n* **1** a person, thing, or organization employed to carry goods, etc. **2** a mechanism by which something is carried or moved, such as a device for transmitting rotation from the faceplate of a lathe to the workpiece. **3** *Pathol.* another name for **vector** (sense 3). **4** *Pathol.* a person or animal that, without having any symptoms of a disease, is capable of transmitting it to others. **5** Also called: **charge carrier.** *Physics.* an electron or hole that carries the charge in a conductor or semiconductor. **6** short for **carrier wave. 7** *Chem.* **7a** an inert substance used to absorb a dyestuff, transport a sample through a gas chromatography column, contain a radioisotope for radioactive tracing, etc. **7b** a substance used to support a catalyst. **8** See **aircraft carrier.**

carrier bag *n Brit.* a large paper or plastic bag for carrying shopping, etc.

carrier pigeon *n* any homing pigeon, esp. one used for carrying messages.

carrier wave *n Radio.* a wave modulated in amplitude, frequency, or phase in order to carry a signal in radio transmission, etc.

carriole ('kærɪˌəʊl) *n* a variant spelling of **cariole.**

carrion ('kærɪən) *n* **1** dead and rotting flesh. **2** (*modifier*) eating carrion. **3** something rotten. [C13: from Anglo-F *caroine*, ult. from L *carō* flesh]

carrion crow *n* a common predatory and scavenging European crow similar to the rook but having a pure black bill.

carrot ('kærət) *n* **1** an umbelliferous plant with finely divided leaves. **2** the long tapering orange root of this plant, eaten as a vegetable. **3a** something offered as a lure or incentive. **3b carrot and stick.** reward and punishment as methods of persuasion. [C16: from OF *carotte*, from LL *carōta*, from Gk *karōton*]

carroty ('kærətɪ) *adj* **1** of a reddish or yellowish-orange colour. **2** having red hair.

carrousel (ˌkærə'sɛl, -'zɛl) *n* a variant spelling of **carousel.**

carry ⓣ ('kærɪ) *vb* **carries, carrying, carried.** (*mainly tr*) **1** (*also intr*) to take or bear (something) from one place to another. **2** to transfer for consideration: *he carried his complaints to her superior*. **3** to have on one's person: *he carries a watch*. **4** (*also intr*) to be transmitted or serve as a medium for transmitting: *sound carries over water*. **5** to bear or be able to bear the weight, pressure, or responsibility of: *her efforts carry the whole production*. **6** to have as an attribute or result: *this crime carries a heavy penalty*. **7** to bring or communicate: *to carry news*. **8** (*also intr*) to be pregnant with (young). **9** to bear (the head, body, etc.) in a specified manner: *she carried her head high*. **10** to conduct or bear (oneself) in a specified manner: *she carried herself well*. **11** to continue or extend: *the war was carried into enemy territory*. **12** to cause to move or go: *desire for riches carried him to the city*. **13** to influence, esp. by emotional appeal: *his words carried the crowd*. **14** to secure the passage of (a bill, motion, etc.). **15** to win (an election). **16** to obtain victory for (a candidate). **17** *Chiefly US.* to win a majority of votes in (a district, etc.): *the candidate carried 40 states*. **18** to capture: *our troops carried the town*. **19** (of communications media) to include as the content: *this newspaper carries no book reviews*. **20** Also (esp. US): **carry over.** *Book-keeping.* to transfer (an item) to another account, esp. to transfer to the following year's account: *to carry a loss*. **21** *Maths.* to transfer (a number) from one column of figures to the next. **22** (of a shop, trader, etc.) to keep in stock: *to carry confectionery*. **23** to support (a musical part or melody) against the other parts. **24** (*intr*) (of a ball, projectile, etc.) to travel through the air or reach a specified point: *his first drive carried to the green*. **25** *Inf.* to imbibe (alcoholic drink) without showing ill effects. **26** (*intr*) *Sl.* to have drugs on one's person. **27 carry all before (one).** to win unanimous support or approval for (oneself). **28 carry the can (for).** *Inf.* to take responsibility for some misdemeanour, etc. (on behalf of). **29 carry the day.** to be successful. ◆ *n, pl* **carries. 30** the act of carrying. **31** *US & Canad.* a portion of land over which a boat must be portaged. **32** the range of a firearm or its projectile. **33** *Golf.* the distance from where the ball is struck to where it first touches the ground. ◆ See also **carry away, carry forward,** etc. [C14 *carien*, from OF *carier* to move by vehicle, from *car*, from L *carrum* transport wagon]

carryall ('kærɪˌɔːl) *n* the usual US and Canad. name for a **holdall.**

carry away *vb* (*tr, adv*) **1** to remove forcefully. **2** (*usually passive*) to cause (a person) to lose self-control. **3** (*usually passive*) to delight: *he was carried away by the music*.

carrycot ('kærɪˌkɒt) *n* a light cot with handles, similar to but smaller than the body of a pram.

carry forward *vb* (*tr, adv*) **1** *Book-keeping.* to transfer (a balance) to the next column, etc. **2** *Tax accounting.* to apply (a legally permitted credit, esp. an operating loss) to the taxable income of following years. ◆ Also: **carry over.**

carrying-on *n, pl* **carryings-on.** *Inf.* **1** unconventional behaviour. **2** excited or flirtatious behaviour.

carry off *vb* (*tr, adv*) **1** to remove forcefully. **2** to win. **3** to handle (a situation) successfully: *he carried off the introductions well*. **4** to cause to die: *he was carried off by pneumonia*.

carry on ⓣ *vb* (*adv*) **1** (*intr*) to continue or persevere. **2** (*tr*) to conduct: *to carry on a business*. **3** (*intr;* often foll. by *with*) *Inf.* to have an affair. **4** (*intr*) *Inf.* to cause a fuss or commotion. ◆ *n* **carry-on. 5** *Inf., chiefly Brit.* a fuss.

carry out ⓣ *vb* (*tr, adv*) **1** to perform or cause to be implemented: *I wish he could afford to carry out his plan*. **2** to accomplish. ◆ *n* **carry-out.** *Chiefly Scot.* **3** alcohol bought at an off-licence, etc., for consumption elsewhere. **4a** a shop which sells hot cooked food for consumption away from the premises. **4b** (*as modifier*): *a carry-out shop*.

THESAURUS

carpenter *n* **1** = **joiner**, cabinet-maker, woodworker

carping[2] *adj* = **fault-finding**, captious, cavilling, critical, grouchy (*inf.*), hard to please, hypercritical, nagging, nit-picking (*inf.*), on someone's back (*inf.*), picky (*inf.*), reproachful

carriage *n* **1, 3** = **vehicle**, cab, coach, conveyance **2** = **bearing**, air, behaviour, comportment, conduct, demeanour, deportment, gait, manner, mien, posture, presence **5a** = **transportation**, carrying, conveyance, conveying, delivery, freight, transport

carry *vb* **1** = **transport**, bear, bring, conduct, convey, fetch, haul, hump, lift, lug, move, relay, take, tote (*inf.*), transfer, transmit **5** = **support**, bear, bolster, hold up, maintain, shoulder, stand, suffer, sustain, underpin, uphold **7, 19, 22** = **include**, broadcast, communicate, display, disseminate, give, offer, publish, release, stock **14, 15, 18** = **win**, accomplish, capture, effect, gain, secure

carry on *vb* **1** = **continue**, endure, keep going, last, maintain, perpetuate, persevere, persist **2** = **run**, administer, manage, operate **4** *Informal* = **make a fuss**, create (*sl.*), misbehave, raise Cain ◆ *n* **carry-on 5** *Informal, chiefly Brit.* = **fuss**, commotion, disturbance, fracas, hubbub, racket, rumpus, shindy (*inf.*), tumult

carry out *vb* **1, 2** = **perform**, accomplish, achieve, carry through, consummate, discharge, effect, execute, fulfil, implement, realize

carry over *vb (tr, adv)* **1** to postpone or defer. **2** *Book-keeping, tax accounting.* another term for **carry forward.** ◆ *n* **carry-over. 3** something left over for future use, esp. goods to be sold. **4** *Book-keeping.* a sum or balance carried forward.

carry through *vb (tr, adv)* **1** to bring to completion. **2** to enable to endure (hardship, trouble, etc.); support.

carse (kɑːs) *n Scot.* a riverside area of flat fertile alluvium. [C14: from ?]

carsick ('kɑːˌsɪk) *adj* nauseated from riding in a car or other vehicle.
▸**'car,sickness** *n*

cart (kɑːt) *n* **1** a heavy open vehicle, usually having two wheels and drawn by horses. **2** a light open horse-drawn vehicle for business or pleasure. **3** any small vehicle drawn or pushed by hand, such as a trolley. **4 in the cart. 4a** in an awkward situation. **4b** in the lurch. **5 put the cart before the horse.** to reverse the usual order of things. ◆ *vb* **6** *(usually tr)* to use or draw a cart to convey (goods, etc.). **7** *(tr)* to carry with effort: *to cart wood home.* [C13: from ON *kartr*]
▸**'carter** *n*

cartage ('kɑːtɪdʒ) *n* the process or cost of carting.

carte blanche ('kɑːt 'blɑːntʃ) *n, pl* **cartes blanches** ('kɑːts 'blɑːntʃ). complete discretion or authority: *the government gave their negotiator carte blanche.* [C18: from F: blank paper]

cartel (kɑː'tel) *n* **1** Also called: **trust.** a collusive association of independent enterprises formed to monopolize production and distribution of a product or service. **2** *Politics.* an alliance of parties to further common aims. [C20: from G *Kartell*, from F, from It. *cartello* public notice, dim. of *carta* CARD[1]]

Cartesian (kɑː'tiːzɪən) *adj* **1** of or relating to the works of Descartes, 17th-century French philosopher and mathematician. **2** of or used in Descartes' mathematical system.
▸**Car'tesian,ism** *n*

Cartesian coordinates *pl n* a system of coordinates that defines the location of a point in space in terms of its perpendicular distance from each of a set of mutually perpendicular axes.

carthorse ('kɑːtˌhɔːs) *n* a large heavily built horse kept for pulling carts or carriages.

Carthusian (kɑː'θjuːzɪən) *RC Church.* ◆ *n* **1** a member of a monastic order founded by Saint Bruno in 1084 near Grenoble, France. ◆ *adj* **2** of or relating to this order: *a Carthusian monastery.* [C14: from Med. L, from L *Carthusia* Chartreuse, near Grenoble]

cartilage ('kɑːtɪlɪdʒ) *n* a tough elastic tissue composing most of the embryonic skeleton of vertebrates. In the adults of higher vertebrates it is mostly converted into bone. Nontechnical name: **gristle.** [C16: from L *cartilāgō*]
▸**cartilaginous** (ˌkɑːtɪ'lædʒɪnəs) *adj*

cartilaginous fish *n* any of a class of fish including the sharks and rays, having a skeleton composed entirely of cartilage.

cartload ('kɑːtˌləʊd) *n* the amount a cart can hold.

cart off, away, *or* **out** *vb (tr, adv) Inf.* to carry or remove brusquely or by force.

cartogram ('kɑːtəˌgræm) *n* a map showing statistical information in diagrammatic form. [C20: from F *cartogramme*, from *carte* map, CHART]

cartography (kɑː'tɒgrəfɪ) *n* the art, technique, or practice of compiling or drawing maps or charts. [C19: from F *cartographie*, from *carte* map, CHART]
▸**car'tographer** *n* ▸**cartographic** (ˌkɑːtə'græfɪk) *or* **,carto'graphical** *adj*

carton ➊ ('kɑːtᵊn) *n* **1** a cardboard box for containing goods. **2** a container of waxed paper in which liquids, such as milk, are sold. [C19: from F, from It. *cartone* pasteboard, from *carta* CARD[1]]

cartoon ➊ (kɑː'tuːn) *n* **1** a humorous or satirical drawing, esp. one in a newspaper or magazine. **2** Also called: **comic strip.** a sequence of drawings in a newspaper, magazine, etc. **3** See **animated cartoon. 4** a full-size preparatory sketch for a fresco, tapestry, mosaic, etc. [C17: from It. *cartone* pasteboard]
▸**car'toonist** *n*

cartouche *or* **cartouch** (kɑː'tuːʃ) *n* **1** a carved or cast ornamental tablet or panel in the form of a scroll. **2** an oblong figure enclosing characters expressing royal or divine names in Egyptian hieroglyphics. [C17: from F: scroll, cartridge, from It., from *carta* paper]

cartridge ➊ ('kɑːtrɪdʒ) *n* **1** a metal casing containing an explosive charge and often a bullet, for a rifle or other small arms. **2** a stylus unit of a record player, either containing a piezoelectric crystal (**crystal cartridge**) or an induction coil that moves in the field of a permanent magnet (**magnetic cartridge**). **3** an enclosed container of magnetic tape, photographic film, ink, etc., for insertion into a tape deck, camera, pen, etc. **4** *Computing.* a removable unit in a computer, such as an integrated circuit, containing software. [C16: from earlier *cartage*, var. of CARTOUCHE (cartridge)]

cartridge belt *n* a belt with pockets for cartridge clips or loops for cartridges.

cartridge clip *n* a metallic container holding cartridges for an automatic firearm.

cartridge paper *n* **1** an uncoated type of drawing or printing paper. **2** a heavy paper used in making cartridges or as drawing or printing paper.

cartwheel ('kɑːtˌwiːl) *n* **1** the wheel of a cart, usually having wooden spokes. **2** an acrobatic movement in which the body makes a revolution supported on the hands with legs outstretched.

caruncle ('kærəŋkᵊl, kə'rʌŋ-) *n* **1** a fleshy outgrowth on the heads of certain birds, such as a cock's comb. **2** an outgrowth near the hilum on the seeds of some plants. [C17: from obs. F *caruncule*, from L *caruncula* a small piece of flesh, from *carō* flesh]
▸**caruncular** (kə'rʌŋkjʊlə) *or* **ca'runculous** *adj*

carve ➊ (kɑːv) *vb* **carves, carving, carved. 1** *(tr)* to cut or chip in order to form something: *to carve wood.* **2** to form (something) by cutting or chipping: *to carve statues.* **3** to slice (meat) into pieces. ◆ See also **carve out, carve up.** [OE *ceorfan*]

carvel ('kɑːvᵊl) *n* another word for **caravel.**

carvel-built *adj* (of a vessel) having a hull with planks made flush at the seams. Cf. **clinker-built.**

carven ('kɑːvᵊn) *vb* an archaic or literary past participle of **carve.**

carve out *vb (tr, adv) Inf.* to make or create (a career): *he carved out his own future.*

carver ('kɑːvə) *n* **1** a carving knife. **2** *(pl)* a large matched knife and fork for carving meat. **3** *Brit.* a chair having arms that forms part of a set of dining chairs.

carvery ('kɑːvərɪ) *n, pl* **carveries.** an eating establishment at which customers pay a set price for unrestricted helpings from a variety of meats, salads, etc.

carve up *vb (tr, adv)* **1** to cut (something) into pieces. **2** to divide (land, etc.). ◆ *n* **carve-up. 3** *Inf.* an act or instance of dishonestly prearranging the result of a competition. **4** *Sl.* the distribution of something.

carving ➊ ('kɑːvɪŋ) *n* a figure or design produced by carving stone, wood, etc.

carving knife *n* a long-bladed knife for carving cooked meat for serving.

caryatid (ˌkærɪ'ætɪd) *n, pl* **caryatids** *or* **caryatides** (-ɪˌdiːz). a column, used to support an entablature, in the form of a draped female figure. [C16: from L, from Gk *Karuatides* priestesses of Artemis at *Karuai* (Caryae), in Laconia]

Casanova (ˌkæsə'nəʊvə) *n* any man noted for his amorous adventures. [after Giovanni *Casanova*, (1725–98), It. adventurer]

casbah ('kæzbɑː) *n (sometimes cap.)* a variant spelling of **kasbah.**

cascade ➊ (kæs'keɪd) *n* **1** a waterfall or series of waterfalls over rocks. **2** something resembling this, such as folds of lace. **3** a consecutive sequence of chemical or physical processes. **4** a series of stages or devices in which each operates the next in turn. ◆ *vb* **cascades, cascading, cascaded. 5** *(intr)* to flow or fall in or like a cascade. [C17: from F, from It., ult. from L *cadere* to fall]

cascara (kæs'kɑːrə) *n* **1** Also called: **cascara sagrada.** the dried bark of the cascara buckthorn, used as a laxative and stimulant. **2** Also called: **cascara buckthorn.** a shrub or small tree of NW North America. [C19: from Sp.: bark]

case[1] ➊ (keɪs) *n* **1** a single instance or example of something. **2** an instance of disease, injury, etc. **3** a question or matter for discussion. **4** a specific condition or state of affairs; situation. **5** a set of arguments supporting a particular action, cause, etc. **6a** a person attended or served by a doctor, social worker, solicitor, etc. **6b** *(as modifier): a case study.* **7a** an action or suit at law: *he has a good case.* **7b** the evidence offered in court to support a claim. **8** *Grammar.* **8a** a set of grammatical categories of nouns, pronouns, and adjectives indicating the relation of the noun, adjective, or pronoun to other words in the sentence. **8b** any one of these categories: *the dative case.* **9** *Inf.* an eccentric. **10 in any case.** *(adv)* no matter what. **11 in case.** *(adv)* **11a** in order to allow for eventualities. **11b** *(conj)* in order to allow for the possibility that: *take your coat in case it rains.* **12 in case of.** *(prep)* in the event of. **13 in no case.** *(adv)* under no circumstances. [OE *casus* (grammatical) case, associated also with OF *cas* a happening; both from L *cāsus*, a befalling, from *cadere* to fall]

case[2] ➊ (keɪs) *n* **1a** a container, such as a box or chest. **1b** *(in combination): suitcase.* **2** an outer cover, esp. for a watch. **3** a receptacle and its contents: *a case of ammunition.* **4** *Archit.* another word for **casing** (sense 3). **5** a cover ready to be fastened to a book to form its binding. **6** *Printing.* a tray in which a compositor keeps individual metal types of a particular size and style. Cases were originally used in pairs, one (the **upper case**) for capitals, the other (the **lower case**) for small letters.

THESAURUS

carton *n* **1, 2** = **box**, case, container, pack, package, packet

cartoon *n* **1, 2** = **drawing**, caricature, comic strip, lampoon, parody, satire, sketch, takeoff *(inf.)* **3** = **animation**, animated cartoon, animated film

cartridge *n* **1** = **shell**, charge, round **3** = **container**, capsule, case, cassette, cylinder, magazine

carve *vb* **1, 2** = **cut**, chip, chisel, divide, engrave, etch, fashion, form, grave *(arch.)*, hack, hew, incise, indent, inscribe, mould, sculpt, sculpture, slash, slice, whittle

carving *n* = **sculpture**, engraving, etching, inscription

cascade *n* **1** = **waterfall**, avalanche, cataract, deluge, downpour, falls, flood, fountain, outpouring, shower, torrent ◆ *vb* **5** = **flow**, descend, fall, flood, gush, overflow, pitch, plunge, pour, spill, surge, teem, tumble

case[1] *n* **1** = **instance**, example, illustration, occasion, occurrence, specimen **4** = **situation**, circumstance(s), condition, context, contingency, dilemma, event, plight, position, predicament, state **7a** *Law* = **lawsuit**, action, cause, dispute, proceedings, process, suit, trial

case[2] *n* **1** = **container**, box, cabinet, canister, capsule, carton, cartridge, casket, chest, compact, crate, holder, receptacle, suitcase, tray, trunk **2** = **covering**, capsule, casing, cover, enve-

◆ *vb* **cases, casing, cased.** (*tr*) **7** to put into or cover with a case. **8** *Sl.* to inspect carefully (esp. a place to be robbed). [C13: from OF *casse*, from L, from *capere* to take, hold]

casebook ('keɪsˌbʊk) *n* a book in which records of legal or medical cases are kept.

case-harden *vb* (*tr*) **1** *Metallurgy.* to form a hard surface layer of high carbon content on (a steel component). **2** to make callous: *experience case-hardened the judge.*

case history *n* a record of a person's background, medical history, etc.

casein ('keɪsɪɪn, -siːn) *n* a protein, precipitated from milk by the action of rennin, forming the basis of cheese. [C19: from L *cāseus* cheese + -IN]

case law *n* law established by following judicial decisions given in earlier cases. Cf. **statute law.**

caseload ('keɪsˌləʊd) *n* the number of cases constituting the work of a doctor, solicitor, social worker, etc., over a specified period.

casemate ('keɪsˌmeɪt) *n* an armoured compartment in a ship or fortification in which guns are mounted. [C16: from F, from It. *casamatta*, ?from Gk *khasmata* apertures]

casement ('keɪsmənt) *n* **1** a window frame that is hinged on one side. **2** a window containing frames hinged at the side. **3** a poetic word for **window.** [C15: prob. from OF *encassement* frame, from *encasser* to encase, from *casse* framework]

caseous ('keɪsɪəs) *adj* of or like cheese. [C17: from L *cāseus* CHEESE]

casern *or* **caserne** (kə'zɜːn) *n* (formerly) a billet or accommodation for soldiers in a town. [C17: from F *caserne*, from OProvençal *cazerna* group of four men, ult. from L *quattuor* four]

casework ('keɪsˌwɜːk) *n* social work based on close study of the personal histories and circumstances of individuals and families.
▸ **'caseˌworker** *n*

cash[1] ⓣ (kæʃ) *n* **1** banknotes and coins, esp. when readily available. **2** immediate payment for goods or services (esp. in **cash down**). **3** (*modifier*) of, for, or paid by cash: *a cash transaction.* ◆ *vb* **4** (*tr*) to obtain or pay ready money for. ◆ See also **cash in, cash up.** [C16: from OIt. *cassa* money box, from L *capsa* CASE[2]]
▸ **'cashable** *adj*

cash[2] (kæʃ) *n, pl* **cash.** any of various Chinese or Indian coins of low value. [C16: from Port. *caixa*, from Tamil *kāsu*, from Sansk. *karsa* weight of gold]

cash-and-carry *adj, adv* **1** sold or operated on a basis of cash payment for merchandise that is not delivered but removed by the purchaser. ◆ *n, pl* **cash-and-carries. 2** a wholesale store, esp. for groceries, that operates on this basis. **3** an operation on a commodities futures market in which spot goods are purchased for cash and sold at a profit on a futures contract, after paying interest and storage charges.

cash-book *n Book-keeping.* a journal in which all receipts and disbursements are recorded.

cash card *n* a plastic card issued by a bank or building society enabling the holder to obtain cash from a cash dispenser.

cash cow *n* a product, acquisition, etc., that produces a steady flow of cash, esp. one with a well-known brand name commanding a high market share.

cash crop *n* a crop grown for sale rather than for subsistence.

cash desk *n* a counter or till in a shop where purchases are paid for.

cash discount *n* a discount granted to a purchaser who pays before a stipulated date.

cash dispenser *n* a computerized device outside a bank that supplies cash when the user inserts his cash card and keys in his identification number. Also called: **automated teller machine.**

cashew ('kæʃuː, kæ'ʃuː) *n* **1** a tropical American evergreen tree, bearing kidney-shaped nuts. **2** Also called: **cashew nut.** the edible nut of this tree. [C18: from Port. *cajú*, from Tupi *acajú*]

cash flow *n* **1** the movement of money into and out of a business. **2** a document that records or predicts this movement.

cashier[1] ⓣ (kæ'ʃɪə) *n* **1** a person responsible for receiving payments for goods, services, etc., as in a shop. **2** an employee of a bank responsible for receiving deposits, cashing cheques, etc.: bank clerk. **3** any person responsible for handling cash in a business. [C16: from Du. or F, from *casse* money chest]

cashier[2] ⓣ (kæ'ʃɪə) *vb* (*tr*) to dismiss with dishonour, esp. from the armed forces. [C16: from MDu., from OF, from L *quassāre* to QUASH]

cash in *vb* (*adv*) **1** (*tr*) to give (something) in exchange. **2** (*intr*; often foll. by *on*) *Inf.* **2a** to profit (from). **2b** to take advantage (of).

cashmere *or* **kashmir** ('kæʃmɪə) *n* **1** a fine soft wool from goats of the Kashmir area. **2a** cloth or knitted material made from this or similar wool. **2b** (*as modifier*): *a cashmere sweater.*

cash on delivery *n* a service entailing cash payment to the carrier on delivery of merchandise. Abbrev.: **COD.**

cash point *n* **1** any retail outlet at which goods are bought for cash. **2** a cash dispenser.

cash register *n* a till with a keyboard that operates a mechanism for displaying and adding the amounts of cash received in individual sales.

cash up *vb* (*intr, adv*) *Brit.* (of cashiers, shopkeepers, etc.) to add up the money taken, esp. at the end of a working day.

casing ⓣ ('keɪsɪŋ) *n* **1** a protective case or cover. **2** material for a case or cover. **3** Also called: **case.** a frame containing a door or window.

casino (kə'siːnəʊ) *n, pl* **casinos. 1** a public building or room in which gaming takes place. **2** a variant spelling of **cassino.** [C18: from It., dim. of *casa* house, from L]

cask ⓣ (kɑːsk) *n* **1** a strong wooden barrel used mainly to hold alcoholic drink: *a wine cask.* **2** any barrel. **3** the quantity contained in a cask. **4** *Austral.* a lightweight cardboard container used to hold and serve wine. [C15: from Sp. *casco* helmet]

casket ⓣ ('kɑːskɪt) *n* **1** a small box or chest for valuables, esp. jewels. **2** *Chiefly US.* another word for **coffin** (sense 1). [C15: prob. from OF *cassette* little box]

casque (kæsk) *n Zool.* a helmet or a helmet-like structure, as on the bill of most hornbills. [C17: from F, from Sp. *casco*]
▸ **casqued** *adj*

Cassandra (kə'sændrə) *n* **1** *Greek myth.* a daughter of Priam and Hecuba, endowed with the gift of prophecy but fated never to be believed. **2** anyone whose prophecies of doom are unheeded.

cassava (kə'sɑːvə) *n* **1** Also called: **manioc.** any of various tropical plants, esp. the widely cultivated American species (**bitter cassava, sweet cassava**). **2** a starch derived from the root of this plant: a source of tapioca. [C16: from Sp. *cazabe* cassava bread, from Taino *caçábi*]

casserole ('kæsəˌrəʊl) *n* **1** a covered dish of earthenware, glass, etc., in which food is cooked and served. **2** any food cooked and served in such a dish: *chicken casserole.* ◆ *vb* **casseroles, casseroling, casseroled. 3** to cook or be cooked in a casserole. [C18: from F, from OF *casse* ladle, from OProvençal, from LL *cattia* dipper, from Gk *kuathion*, dim. of *kuathos* cup]

cassette (kæ'sɛt) *n* **1a** a plastic container for magnetic tape, inserted into a tape deck to be played or used. **1b** (*as modifier*): *a cassette recorder.* **2** *Photog.* another term for **cartridge** (sense 3). **3** the injection of genes from one species into the fertilized egg of another species. [C18: from F: little box]

cassia ('kæsɪə) *n* **1** any of a genus of tropical plants whose pods yield **cassia pulp,** a mild laxative. See also **senna. 2** a lauraceous tree of tropical Asia. **3 cassia bark.** the cinnamon-like bark of this tree, used as a spice. [OE, from L *casia*, from Gk *kasia*, of Semitic origin]

cassino *or* **casino** (kə'siːnəʊ) *n* a card game for two to four players in which players pair cards with those exposed on the table.

Cassiopeia (ˌkæsɪə'piːə) *n, Latin genitive* **Cassiopeiae** (ˌkæsɪə'piːiː). a very conspicuous W-shaped constellation near the Pole Star.

cassis (kɑː'siːs) *n* a blackcurrant cordial. [C19: from F]

cassiterite (kə'sɪtəˌraɪt) *n* a hard heavy brownish-black mineral, the chief ore of tin. Formula: SnO_2. Also called: **tinstone.** [C19: from Gk *kassiteros* tin]

cassock ('kæsək) *n* an ankle-length garment, usually black, worn by Christian priests. [C16: from OF, from It. *casacca* a long coat, from ?]

cassowary ('kæsəˌwɛərɪ) *n, pl* **cassowaries.** a large flightless bird inhabiting forests in NE Australia, New Guinea, and adjacent islands, having a horny head crest, black plumage, and brightly coloured neck. [C17: from Malay *kĕsuari*]

cast ⓣ (kɑːst) *vb* **casts, casting, cast.** (*mainly tr*) **1** to throw or expel with force. **2** to throw off or away: *she cast her clothes to the ground.* **3** to reject: *he cast the idea from his mind.* **4** to shed or drop: *the horse cast a shoe.* **5** to cause to appear: *to cast a shadow.* **6** to express (doubts, etc.) or cause (them) to be felt. **7** to direct (a glance, etc.): *cast your eye over this.* **8** to place, esp. violently: *he was cast into prison.* **9** (*also intr*) *Angling.* to throw (a line) into the water. **10** to draw or choose (lots). **11** to give or deposit (a vote). **12** to select (actors) to play parts in (a play, etc.). **13a** to shape (molten metal, glass, etc.) by pouring into a mould. **13b** to make (an object) by such a process. **14** (*also intr*; often foll. by *up*) to compute (figures or a total). **15** *Astrol.* to draw on (a horoscope) details concerning the positions of the planets in the signs of the zodiac at a particular time for interpretation. **16** to contrive (esp. in **cast a spell**). **17** to formulate: *he cast his work in the form of a chart.* **18** (*also intr*) to twist or cause to twist. **19** (*intr*) (of birds of prey) to eject from the crop and bill a pellet consisting of the indigestible parts of birds or animals previously eaten. **20** *Printing.* to stereotype or electrotype. **21 be cast.** *NZ.* (of sheep) to have fallen and been unable to rise. ◆ *n* **22** the act of casting or throwing. **23a** Also called: **casting.** something that is shed, dropped, or egested, such as the coil of earth left by an earthworm. **23b** another name for **pellet** (sense 4). **24** the distance an object is or

THESAURUS

lope, folder, integument, jacket, sheath, shell, wrapper, wrapping

cash[1] *n* **1, 2** = **money**, banknotes, brass (*N English dialect*), bread, bullion, change, coin, coinage, currency, dibs (*sl.*), dosh (*Brit. & Austral. sl.*), dough (*sl.*), funds, necessary (*inf.*), needful (*inf.*), notes, payment, ready (*inf.*), ready money, resources, rhino (*Brit. sl.*), shekels (*inf.*), silver, specie, spondulicks (*sl.*), tin (*sl.*), wherewithal

cashier[1] *n* = **1–3 teller**, accountant, bank clerk, banker, bursar, clerk, purser, treasurer

cashier[2] *vb* = **dismiss**, break, cast off, discard, discharge, drum out, expel, give the boot to (*sl.*)

casing *n* **1** = **covering**, cover, integument, shell

cask *n* **2** = **barrel**, cylinder, drum

casket *n* **1** = **box**, ark, case, chest, coffer, coffret, jewel box, kist (*Scot. & Northern English dialect*)

cast *vb* **1** = **throw**, chuck (*inf.*), drive, drop, fling, hurl, impel, launch, lob, pitch, project, shed, shy, sling, thrust, toss **12** = **choose**, allot, appoint, assign, name, pick, select **13** = **form**, found, model, mould, set, shape ◆ *n* **22** = **throw**, fling, lob, thrust, toss **28a** = **actors**, characters, company, dramatis personae, players, troupe **30** = **type**, air, appearance, complexion, demeanour, look, manner, mien, semblance, shade, stamp, style, tinge, tone, turn

may be thrown. **25a** a throw at dice. **25b** the resulting number shown. **26** *Angling.* the act or an instance of casting a line. **27** the wide sweep made by a sheepdog to get behind a flock of sheep or by a hunting dog in search of a scent. **28a** the actors in a play collectively. **28b** (*as modifier*): *a cast list.* **29a** an object made of metal, glass, etc., that has been shaped in a molten state by being poured or pressed into a mould. **29b** the mould used to shape such an object. **30** form or appearance. **31** a sort, kind, or style. **32** a fixed twist or defect, esp. in the eye. **33** a distortion of shape. **34** *Surgery.* a rigid encircling casing, often made of plaster of Paris (**plaster cast**), for immobilizing broken bones while they heal. **35** a slight tinge or trace, as of colour. **36** fortune or stroke of fate. ◆ See also **cast about, castaway,** etc. [C13: from ON *kasta*]

cast about *or* **around** *vb* (*intr, adv*) to make a mental or visual search: *to cast about for a plot.*

castanets (ˌkæstəˈnɛts) *pl n* curved pieces of hollow wood, usually held between the fingers and thumb and made to click together: used esp. by Spanish dancers. [C17 *castanet,* from Sp. *castañeta,* dim. of *castaña* CHESTNUT]

castaway (ˈkɑːstəˌweɪ) *n* **1** a person who has been shipwrecked. ◆ *adj* (*prenominal*) **2** shipwrecked. **3** thrown away or rejected. ◆ *vb* **cast away. 4** (*tr, adv; often passive*) to cause (a ship, person, etc.) to be shipwrecked.

cast back *vb* (*adv*) to turn (the mind) to the past.

cast down **T** *vb* (*tr, adv*) to make (a person) discouraged or dejected.

caste **T** (kɑːst) *n* **1a** any of the four major hereditary classes, namely the **Brahman, Kshatriya, Vaisya,** and **Sudra,** into which Hindu society is divided. **1b** Also called: **caste system.** the system or basis of such classes. **2** any social class or system based on such distinctions as heredity, rank, wealth, etc. **3** the position conferred by such a system. **4 lose caste.** *Inf.* to lose one's social position. **5** *Entomol.* any of various types of individual, such as the worker, in social insects. [C16: from Port. *casta* race, from *casto* pure, chaste, from L *castus*]

castellan (ˈkæstɪlən) *n Rare.* a keeper or governor of a castle. Also called: **chatelain.** [C14: from L *castellānus,* from *castellum* CASTLE]

castellated (ˈkæstɪˌleɪtɪd) *adj* **1** having turrets and battlements, like a castle. **2** having indentations similar to battlements: *a castellated nut.* [C17: from Med. L *castellātus,* from *castellāre* to fortify as a CASTLE]
▸ˌ**castelˈlation** *n*

caster (ˈkɑːstə) *n* **1** a person or thing that casts. **2** a bottle with a perforated top for sprinkling sugar, etc. **3** a small swivelled wheel fixed to a piece of furniture to enable it to be moved easily in any direction. ◆ Also (for senses 2, 3): **castor.**

caster sugar (ˈkɑːstə) *n* finely ground white sugar.

castigate **T** (ˈkæstɪˌgeɪt) *vb* **castigates, castigating, castigated.** (*tr*) to rebuke or criticize in a severe manner. [C17: from L *castīgāre* to correct, from *castum* pure + *agere* to compel (to be)]
▸ˌ**castiˈgation** *n* ▸ˈ**castiˌgator** *n*

Castile soap (kæsˈtiːl) *n* a hard soap made from olive oil and sodium hydroxide.

Castilian (kæˈstɪljən) *n* **1** the Spanish dialect of Castile; the standard form of European Spanish. **2** a native or inhabitant of Castile. ◆ *adj* **3** denoting or of Castile, its inhabitants, or the standard form of European Spanish.

casting (ˈkɑːstɪŋ) *n* **1** an object that has been cast, esp. in metal from a mould. **2** the process of transferring molten steel to a mould. **3** the choosing of actors for a production. **4** *Zool.* another word for **cast** (sense 23) or **pellet** (sense 4).

casting couch *n Inf.* a couch on which a casting director is said to seduce girls seeking a part in a film or play.

casting vote *n* the deciding vote used by the presiding officer of an assembly when votes cast on both sides are equal in number.

cast iron **T** *n* **1** iron containing so much carbon that it cannot be wrought and must be cast into shape. ◆ *adj* **cast-iron. 2** made of cast iron. **3** rigid or unyielding: *a cast-iron decision.*

castle **T** (ˈkɑːsᵊl) *n* **1** a fortified building or set of buildings as in medieval Europe. **2** any fortified place or structure. **3** a large magnificent house, esp. when the present or former home of a nobleman or prince. **4** *Chess.* another name for **rook**[2]. ◆ *vb* **castles, castling, castled. 5** *Chess.* to move (the king) two squares laterally on the first rank and place the nearest rook on the square passed over by the king. [C11: from L *castellum,* dim. of *castrum* fort]

castle in the air *or* **in Spain** *n* a hope or desire unlikely to be realized; daydream.

cast-off **T** *adj* **1** (*prenominal*) abandoned: *cast-off shoes.* ◆ *n* **castoff. 2** a person or thing that has been discarded or abandoned. **3** *Printing.* an estimate of the amount of space that a piece of copy will occupy. ◆ *vb* **cast off.** (*adv*) **4** to remove (mooring lines) that hold (a vessel) to a dock. **5** to knot (a row of stitches, esp. the final row) in finishing off knitted or woven material. **6** *Printing.* to estimate the amount of space that will be taken up by (a book, piece of copy, etc.).

cast on *vb* (*adv*) to form (the first row of stitches) in knitting and weaving.

castor[1] (ˈkɑːstə) *n* **1** the aromatic secretion of a beaver, used in perfumery and medicine. **2** the fur of the beaver. **3** a hat made of beaver or similar fur. [C14: from L, from Gk *kastōr* beaver]

castor[2] (ˈkɑːstə) *n* a variant spelling of **caster** (senses 2, 3).

castor oil *n* an oil obtained from the seeds of the castor-oil plant and used as a lubricant and cathartic.

castor-oil plant *n* a tall Indian plant cultivated for its poisonous seeds, from which castor oil is extracted.

castrate **T** (kæˈstreɪt) *vb* **castrates, castrating, castrated.** (*tr*) **1** to remove the testicles of. **2** to deprive of vigour, masculinity, etc. **3** to remove the ovaries of; spay. [C17: from L *castrāre* to emasculate, geld]
▸**casˈtration** *n*

castrato (kæˈstrɑːtəʊ) *n, pl* **castrati** (-tɪ) *or* **castratos.** (in 17th- and 18th-century opera, etc.) a male singer whose testicles were removed before puberty, allowing the retention of a soprano or alto voice. [C18: from It., from L *castrātus* castrated]

cast steel *n* steel containing varying amounts of carbon, manganese, etc., that is cast into shape rather than wrought.

cast stone *n Building trades.* a building component, such as a block or lintel, made from cast concrete with a facing that resembles natural stone.

casual **T** (ˈkæʒjʊəl) *adj* **1** happening by accident or chance. **2** offhand: *a casual remark.* **3** shallow or superficial: *a casual affair.* **4** being or seeming unconcerned or apathetic: *he assumed a casual attitude.* **5** (esp. of dress) for informal wear: *a casual coat.* **6** occasional or irregular: *a casual labourer.* ◆ *n* **7** (*usually pl*) an informal article of clothing or footwear. **8** an occasional worker. **9** (*usually pl*) a young man dressed in expensive casual clothes who goes to football matches in order to start fights. [C14: from LL *cāsuālis* happening by chance, from L *cāsus* event, from *cadere* to fall]
▸ˈ**casually** *adv* ▸ˈ**casualness** *n*

casualization *or* **casualisation** (ˌkæʒjʊəlaɪˈzeɪʃən) *n* the altering of working practices so that regular workers are re-employed on a casual or short-term basis.

casualty **T** (ˈkæʒjʊəltɪ) *n, pl* **casualties. 1** a serviceman who is killed, wounded, captured, or missing as a result of enemy action. **2** a person who is injured or killed in an accident. **3** the hospital department treating victims of accidents. **4** anything that is lost, damaged, or destroyed as the result of an accident, etc.

casuarina (ˌkæzjʊəˈriːnə) *n* any of a genus of trees of Australia and the East Indies, having jointed leafless branchlets. [C19: from NL, from Malay *kĕsuari* CASSOWARY, referring to the resemblance of the branches to the feathers of the cassowary]

casuist (ˈkæzjʊɪst) *n* **1** a person, esp. a theologian, who attempts to resolve moral dilemmas by the application of general rules and the careful distinction of special cases. **2** a sophist. [C17: from F, from Sp. *casuista,* from L *cāsus* CASE[1]]
▸ˌ**casuˈistic** *or* ˌ**casuˈistical** *adj*

casuistry (ˈkæzjʊɪstrɪ) *n, pl* **casuistries. 1** *Philosophy.* the resolution of particular moral dilemmas, esp. those arising from conflicting general moral rules, by the careful distinction of the cases to which these rules apply. **2** reasoning that is specious or oversubtle.

cat[1] **T** (kæt) *n* **1** Also called: **domestic cat.** a small domesticated feline mammal having thick soft fur and occurring in many breeds in which the colour of the fur varies greatly: kept as a pet or to catch rats and mice. **2** Also called: **big cat.** any of the larger felines, such as a lion or tiger. **3** any wild feline mammal such as the lynx or serval, resembling the domestic cat. **4** *Inf.* a woman who gossips maliciously. **5** *Sl.* a man. **6** *Naut.* a heavy tackle for hoisting an anchor to the cathead. **7** *Austral. sl.* a coward. **8** short for **catboat. 9** *Inf.* short for **caterpillar** (the vehicle). **10** short for **cat-o'-nine-tails. 11 a bag of cats.** *Irish inf.* a

THESAURUS

cast down *vb* = **discourage**, deject, depress, desolate, dishearten, dispirit

caste *n* **2** = **class**, estate, grade, lineage, order, race, rank, social order, species, station, status, stratum

castigate *vb* = **reprimand**, bawl out, beat, berate, blast, cane, carpet (*inf.*), censure, chasten, chastise, correct, criticize, discipline, dress down (*inf.*), excoriate, flail, flay, flog, give a rocket (*Brit. & NZ inf.*), haul over the coals (*inf.*), lambast(e), lash, put down, rap over the knuckles, read the riot act, rebuke, scold, scourge, slap on the wrist, slate (*inf., chiefly Brit.*), tear into (*inf.*), tear (someone) off a strip (*Brit. inf.*), whip

castigation *n* = **reprimand**, bawling-out (*inf.*), beating, blast, caning, censure, chastisement, condemnation, correction, criticism, discipline, dressing down (*inf.*), excoriation, flogging, put-down, whipping

cast iron *adj* **cast-iron 3** = **certain**, copper-bottomed, definite, established, fixed, guaranteed, idiot-proof, settled

castle *n* **2, 3** = **fortress**, chateau, citadel, donjon, fastness, keep, mansion, palace, peel, stronghold, tower

cast-off *adj* **1** = **unwanted**, discarded, rejected, scrapped, surplus to requirements, unneeded, useless ◆ *n* **castoff 2** = **reject**, discard, failure, outcast, second

castrate *vb* **1, 2** = **neuter**, emasculate, geld, unman

casual *adj* **1, 6** = **chance**, accidental, contingent, fortuitous, hit-and-miss *or* hit-or-miss (*inf.*), incidental, irregular, occasional, random, serendipitous, uncertain, unexpected, unforeseen, unintentional, unpremeditated **2, 4** = **careless**, apathetic, blasé, cursory, indifferent, informal, insouciant, lackadaisical, nonchalant, offhand, perfunctory, relaxed, unconcerned **5** = **informal**, non-dressy, sporty

Antonyms *adj* ≠ **chance:** arranged, deliberate, expected, fixed, foreseen, intentional, planned, premeditated ≠ **careless:** committed, concerned, direct, enthusiastic, passionate, serious ≠ **informal:** ceremonial, dressy, formal

casualty *n* **2** = **victim**, death, fatality, loss, sufferer, wounded

cat[1] *n* **1** = **feline**, gib, grimalkin, kitty (*inf.*), moggy (*sl.*), mouser, puss (*inf.*), pussy (*inf.*), tabby

bad-tempered person: *she's a real bag of cats this morning.* **12 fight like Kilkenny cats.** to fight until both parties are destroyed. **13 let the cat out of the bag.** to disclose a secret, often by mistake. **14 like a cat on a hot tin roof** *or* **on hot bricks.** in an uneasy or agitated state. **15 put, set,** etc., **the cat among the pigeons.** to introduce some violently disturbing new element. **16 rain cats and dogs.** to rain very heavily. ◆ *vb* **cats, catting, catted. 17** (*tr*) *Naut.* to hoist (an anchor) to the cathead. **18** (*intr*) *Sl.* to vomit. [OE *catte,* from L *cattus*]
▸**'cat,like** *adj* ▸**'cattish** *adj*

cat[2] (kæt) *adj* short for **catalytic**: *a cat cracker.*

CAT *abbrev. for* computer-assisted trading.

cat. *abbrev. for:* **1** catalogue. **2** catamaran.

cata-, kata-, *before an aspirate* **cath-,** *or before a vowel* **cat-** *prefix* **1** down; downwards; lower in position: *catadromous.* **2** indicating reversal, opposition, degeneration, etc.: *catatonia.* [from Gk *kata-,* from *kata.* In compound words borrowed from Gk *kata-* means: down, away, off, against, according to, and thoroughly]

catabolism *or* **katabolism** (kə'tæbə,lɪzəm) *n* a metabolic process in which complex molecules are broken down into simple ones with the release of energy; destructive metabolism. [C19: from Gk *katabolē* a throwing down, from *kata-* down + *ballein* to throw]
▸**catabolic** *or* **katabolic** (,kætə'bɒlɪk) *adj*

catachresis (,kætə'kriːsɪs) *n* the incorrect use of words, as *luxuriant* for *luxurious.* [C16: from L, from Gk *katakhrēsis* a misusing, from *khrēsthai* to use]
▸**catachrestic** (,kætə'krɛstɪk) *adj*

cataclysm ❶ ('kætə,klɪzəm) *n* **1** a violent upheaval, esp. of a political, military, or social nature. **2** a disastrous flood. [C17: via F from L, from Gk, from *katakluzein* to flood, from *kluzein* to wash]
▸**,cata'clysmic** *or* **,cata'clysmal** *adj* ▸**,cata'clysmically** *adv*

catacomb ❶ ('kætə,kəʊm) *n* **1** (*usually pl*) an underground burial place, esp. in Rome, consisting of tunnels with niches leading off them for tombs. **2** a series of underground tunnels or caves. [OE *catacumbe,* from LL *catacumbas* (sing), name of the cemetery under the Basilica of St Sebastian, near Rome; from ?]

catadioptric (,kætədaɪ'ɒptrɪk) *adj* involving a combination of reflecting and refracting components: *a catadioptric telescope.* [C18: from CATA- + DIOPTRIC(S)]

catadromous (kə'tædrəməs) *adj* (of fishes such as the eel) migrating down rivers to the sea in order to breed. Cf. **anadromous.** [C19: from Gk, from *kata-* down + *dromos,* from *dremein* to run]

catafalque ('kætə,fælk) *n* a temporary raised platform on which a body lies in state before or during a funeral. [C17: from F, from It. *catafalco,* from ?]

Catalan ('kætə,læn) *n* **1** a language of Catalonia, a region of NE Spain, closely related to Spanish and Provençal. **2** a native or inhabitant of Catalonia. ◆ *adj* **3** denoting or characteristic of Catalonia, its inhabitants, or their language.

catalepsy ('kætə,lɛpsɪ) *n* a state of prolonged rigid posture, occurring for example in schizophrenia. [C16: from LL *catalēpsis,* from Gk *katalēpsis,* lit.: a seizing, from *kata-* down + *lambanein* to grasp]
▸**,cata'leptic** *adj*

catalogue ❶ *or US* **catalog** ('kætə,lɒg) *n* **1** a complete, usually alphabetical, list of items. **2** a book, usually illustrated, containing details of items for sale. **3** a list of all the books of a library. **4** *US and Canad.* a publication issued by a university, college, etc., listing courses offered, regulations, services, etc. ◆ *vb* **catalogues, cataloguing, catalogued** *or US* **catalogs, cataloging, cataloged. 5** to compile a catalogue of (a library, etc.). **6** to add (books, items, etc.) to an existing catalogue. [C15: from LL *catalogus,* from Gk, from *katalegein* to list, from *kata-* completely + *legein* to collect]
▸**'cata,loguer** *n*

catalpa (kə'tælpə) *n* any of a genus of trees of North America and Asia, having large leaves, bell-shaped whitish flowers, and long slender pods. [C18: NL, from Carolina Creek *kutuhlpa,* lit.: winged head]

catalyse *or US* **catalyze** ('kætə,laɪz) *vb* **catalyses, catalysing, catalysed** *or US* **catalyzes, catalyzing, catalyzed.** (*tr*) to influence (a chemical reaction) by catalysis.

catalysis (kə'tælɪsɪs) *n, pl* **catalyses** (-,siːz). acceleration of a chemical reaction by the action of a catalyst. [C17: from NL, from Gk, from *kataluein* to dissolve]
▸**catalytic** (,kætə'lɪtɪk) *adj*

catalyst ('kætəlɪst) *n* **1** a substance that increases the rate of a chemical reaction without itself suffering any permanent chemical change. **2** a person or thing that causes a change.

catalytic converter *n* a device using three-way catalysts to reduce the poisonous products of combustion (mainly oxides of nitrogen, carbon monoxide, and unburnt hydrocarbons) from the exhaust of motor vehicles.

catalytic cracker *n* a unit in an oil refinery in which mineral oils with high boiling points are converted to fuels with lower boiling points by a catalytic process.

catamaran (,kætəmə'ræn) *n* **1** a vessel, usually a sailing vessel, with twin hulls held parallel by a rigid framework. **2** a primitive raft made of logs lashed together. **3** *Inf.* a quarrelsome woman. [C17: from Tamil *kattumaram* tied timber]

catamite ('kætə,maɪt) *n* a boy kept for homosexual purposes. [C16: from L *Catamitus,* var. of *Ganymēdēs* Ganymede, cupbearer to the gods in Gk myth]

catamount ('kætə,maʊnt) *or* **catamountain** *n* any of various felines, such as the puma or lynx. [C17: short for *cat of the mountain*]

catananche (kætən'æŋkɪ) *n* any herb of the genus *Catananche,* having blue or yellow flowers. [C18: NL, from L, from Gk *kata* down + *anagkē* compulsion (from its use by ancient Greeks as a philtre)]

cataplexy ('kætə,plɛksɪ) *n* **1** sudden temporary paralysis, brought on by severe shock. **2** a state assumed by animals while shamming death. [C19: from Gk *kataplēxis* amazement, from *kataplēssein,* from *kata-* down + *plēssein* to strike]
▸**,cata'plectic** *adj*

catapult ❶ ('kætə,pʌlt) *n* **1** a Y-shaped implement with a loop of elastic fastened to the ends of the prongs, used mainly by children for shooting stones, etc. US and Canad. name: **slingshot. 2** a war engine used formerly for hurling stones, etc. **3** a device installed in warships to launch aircraft. ◆ *vb* **4** (*tr*) to shoot forth from or as if from a catapult. **5** (foll. by *over, into,* etc.) to move precipitately. [C16: from L, from Gk *katapeltēs,* from *kata-* down + *pallein* to hurl]

cataract ❶ ('kætə,rækt) *n* **1** a large waterfall or rapids. **2** a downpour. **3** *Pathol.* **3a** partial or total opacity of the lens of the eye. **3b** the opaque area. [C15: from L, from Gk, from *katarassein* to dash down, from *arassein* to strike]

catarrh (kə'tɑː) *n* inflammation of a mucous membrane with increased production of mucus, esp. affecting the nose and throat. [C16: via F from LL, from Gk, from *katarrhein* to flow down, from *kata-* down + *rhein* to flow]
▸**ca'tarrhal** *adj*

catarrhine ('kætə,raɪn) *adj* **1** (of apes and Old World monkeys) having the nostrils set close together and opening to the front of the face. ◆ *n* **2** an animal with this characteristic. [C19: ult. from Gk *katarrhin* having a hooked nose, from *kata-* down + *rhis* nose]

catastrophe ❶ (kə'tæstrəfɪ) *n* **1** a sudden, extensive disaster or misfortune. **2** the denouement of a play. **3** a final decisive event, usually causing a disastrous end. [C16: from Gk, from *katastrephein* to overturn, from *strephein* to turn]
▸**catastrophic** (,kætə'strɒfɪk) *adj* ▸**,cata'strophically** *adv*

catastrophism (kə'tæstrə,fɪzəm) *n* **1** a former doctrine that the earth was formed by sudden divine acts rather than by evolutionary processes. **2** a modern doctrine that the evolutionary processes shaping the earth have in the past been supplemented by the effects of huge natural catastrophes.

catatonia (,kætə'təʊnɪə) *n* a form of schizophrenia characterized by stupor, with outbreaks of excitement. [C20: NL, from G *Katatonie,* from CATA- + Gk *tonos* tension]
▸**catatonic** (,kætə'tɒnɪk) *adj, n*

catbird ('kæt,bɜːd) *n* **1** any of several North American songbirds whose call resembles the mewing of a cat. **2** any of several Australian bowerbirds having a catlike call.

catboat ('kæt,bəʊt) *n* a sailing vessel with a single mast, set well forward, and a large sail. Shortened form: **cat.**

cat burglar *n* a burglar who enters buildings by climbing through upper windows, etc.

catcall ❶ ('kæt,kɔːl) *n* **1** a shrill whistle or cry expressing disapproval, as at a public meeting, etc. ◆ *vb* **2** to utter such a call (at).

catch ❶ (kætʃ) *vb* **catches, catching, caught. 1** (*tr*) to take hold of so as to retain or restrain. **2** (*tr*) to take or capture, esp. after pursuit. **3** (*tr*) to ensnare or deceive. **4** (*tr*) to surprise or detect in an act: *he caught the dog rifling the larder.* **5** (*tr*) to reach with a blow: *the stone caught him on the side of the head.* **6** (*tr*) to overtake or reach in time to board. **7** (*tr*) to

THESAURUS

cataclysm *n* **1** = **disaster**, calamity, catastrophe, collapse, convulsion, debacle, upheaval

cataclysmic *adj* **1** = **disastrous**, calamitous, catastrophic, convulsionary

catacomb *n* **1** *usually pl* = **vault**, crypt, ossuary, tomb

catalogue *n* **1** = **list**, directory, gazetteer, index, inventory, record, register, roll, roster, schedule ◆ *vb* **5** = **list**, accession, alphabetize, classify, file, index, inventory, register, tabulate

catapult *n* **1** = **sling**, ballista, slingshot (*US*), trebuchet ◆ *vb* **4** = **shoot**, heave, hurl, hurtle, pitch, plunge, propel, toss

cataract *n* **1, 2** = **waterfall**, cascade, deluge, downpour, falls, Niagara, rapids, torrent **3** *Pathology* = **opacity** (*of the eye*)

catastrophe *n* **1** = **disaster**, adversity, affliction, blow, bummer (*sl.*), calamity, cataclysm, deep water, devastation, failure, fiasco, ill, meltdown (*inf.*), mischance, misfortune, mishap, reverse, tragedy, trial, trouble, whammy (*inf., chiefly US*)

catastrophic *adj* **1** = **disastrous**, calamitous, cataclysmic, devastating, tragic

catcall *n* **1** = **jeer**, boo, gibe, hiss, raspberry, whistle ◆ *vb* **2** = **jeer**, boo, deride, gibe, give the bird to, hiss, whistle

catch *vb* **1** = **seize**, clutch, get, grab, grasp, grip, lay hold of, snatch, take **2** = **capture**, apprehend, arrest, ensnare, entangle, entrap, feel one's collar (*sl.*), lift (*sl.*), nab (*inf.*), nail (*inf.*), snare, trap **4** = **discover**, catch in the act, detect, expose, find out, surprise, take unawares, unmask **8** = **contract**, develop, get, go down with, incur, succumb to, suffer from **12, 13** = **make out**, apprehend, comprehend, discern, feel, follow, get, grasp, hear, perceive, recognize, sense, take in, twig (*Brit. informal*) **14** = **attract**, bewitch, captivate, capture, charm, delight, enchant, enrapture, fascinate ◆ *n* **22** = **fastener**, bolt, clasp, clip, hasp, hook, hook and eye, latch, sneck (*dialect, chiefly Scot. & N. English*), snib (*Scot.*) **27a** *Informal* = **drawback**, disadvan-

see or hear; attend. **8** (*tr*) to be infected with: *to catch a cold.* **9** to hook or entangle or become hooked or entangled. **10** to fasten or be fastened with or as if with a latch or other device. **11** (*tr*) to attract: *she tried to catch his eye.* **12** (*tr*) to comprehend: *I didn't catch his meaning.* **13** (*tr*) to hear accurately: *I didn't catch what you said.* **14** (*tr*) to captivate or charm. **15** (*tr*) to reproduce accurately: *the painter managed to catch his model's beauty.* **16** (*tr*) to hold back or restrain: *he caught his breath in surprise.* **17** (*intr*) to become alight: *the fire won't catch.* **18** (*tr*) *Cricket.* to dismiss (a batsman) by intercepting and holding a ball struck by him before it touches the ground. **19** (*intr;* often foll. by *at*) **19a** to grasp or attempt to grasp. **19b** to take advantage (of): *he caught at the chance.* **20** **catch it.** *Inf.* to be scolded or reprimanded. ◆ *n* **21** the act of catching or grasping. **22** a device that catches and fastens, such as a latch. **23** anything that is caught. **24** the amount or number caught. **25** *Inf.* an eligible matrimonial prospect. **26** a check or break in the voice. **27** *Inf.* **27a** a concealed, unexpected, or unforeseen drawback. **27b** (*as modifier*): *a catch question.* **28** *Cricket.* the catching of a ball struck by a batsman before it touches the ground, resulting in him being out. **29** *Music.* a type of round having a humorous text that is often indecent or bawdy and hard to articulate. ◆ See also **catch on, catch out, catch up.** [C13 *cacchen* to pursue, from OF *cachier,* from L *captāre* to snatch, from *capere* to seize]
▸ **'catchable** *adj*

catch-22 *n* a situation in which a person is frustrated by a set of circumstances that preclude any attempt to escape from them. [C20: from the title of a novel (1961) by J. Heller]

catch-as-catch-can *n* a style of wrestling in which trips, holds below the waist, etc., are allowed.

catchfly ('kætʃ,flaɪ) *n, pl* **catchflies.** any of various plants that have sticky calyxes and stems on which insects are sometimes trapped.

catching Ⓣ ('kætʃɪŋ) *adj* **1** infectious. **2** attractive; captivating.

catching pen *n Austral. & NZ.* a pen adjacent to a shearer's stand containing the sheep ready for shearing.

catchment ('kætʃmənt) *n* **1** the act of catching or collecting water. **2** a structure in which water is collected. **3** the water so collected. **4** *Brit.* the intake of a school from one catchment area.

catchment area *n* **1** the area of land bounded by watersheds draining into a river, basin, or reservoir. **2** the area from which people are allocated to a particular school, hospital, etc.

catch on Ⓣ *vb* (*intr, adv*) *Inf.* **1** to become popular or fashionable. **2** to understand.

catch out *vb* (*tr, adv*) *Inf., chiefly Brit.* to trap (a person), esp. in an error.

catchpenny ('kætʃ,penɪ) *adj* (*prenominal*) designed to have instant appeal, esp. in order to sell quickly: *catchpenny ornaments.*

catch phrase *n* a well-known frequently used phrase, esp. one associated with a particular group, etc.

catch up *vb* (*adv*) **1** (*tr*) to seize and take up (something) quickly. **2** (when *intr,* often foll. by *with*) to reach or pass (someone or something): *he caught him up.* **3** (*intr;* usually foll. by *on* or *with*) to make up for lost ground or deal with a backlog. **4** (*tr; often passive*) to absorb or involve: *she was caught up in her reading.* **5** (*tr*) to raise by or as if by fastening.

catchweight ('kætʃ,weɪt) *adj Wrestling.* of or relating to a contest in which normal weight categories have been waived by agreement.

catchword Ⓣ ('kætʃ,wɜːd) *n* **1** a word or phrase made temporarily popular; slogan. **2** a word printed as a running head in a book. **3** *Theatre.* an actor's cue to speak or enter. **4** the first word of a page repeated at the bottom of the page preceding.

catchy Ⓣ ('kætʃɪ) *adj* **catchier, catchiest.** **1** (of a tune, etc.) pleasant and easily remembered. **2** deceptive: *a catchy question.* **3** irregular: *a catchy breeze.*

cat cracker *n* an informal name for **catalytic cracker.**

catechetical (,kætɪ'ketɪkᵊl) *or* **catechetic** *adj* of or relating to teaching by question and answer.
▸ **,cate'chetically** *adv*

catechism ('kætɪ,kɪzəm) *n* instruction by a series of questions and answers, esp. a book containing such instruction on the religious doctrine of a Christian Church. [C16: from LL, ult. from Gk *katēkhizein* to CATECHIZE]
▸ **,cate'chismal** *adj*

catechize Ⓣ *or* **catechise** ('kætɪ,kaɪz) *vb* **catechizes, catechizing, catechized** *or* **catechises, catechising, catechised.** (*tr*) **1** to teach or examine by means of questions and answers. **2** to give oral instruction in Christianity, esp. by using a catechism. **3** to put questions to (someone). [C15: from LL, from Gk *katēkhizein,* from *katēkhein* to instruct orally, from *kata-* down + *ēkhein* to sound]
▸ **'catechist, 'cate,chizer** *or* **'cate,chiser** *n*

catechu ('kætɪ,tʃuː) *or* **cachou** *n* an astringent resinous substance obtained from certain tropical plants, and used in medicine, tanning, and dyeing. [C17: prob. from Malay *kachu*]

catechumen (,kætɪ'kjuːmɛn) *n Christianity.* a person, esp. in the early Church, undergoing instruction prior to baptism. [C15: via OF, from LL, from Gk *katēkhoumenos* one being instructed verbally]

categorial (,kætɪ'gɔːrɪəl) *adj* **1** of or relating to a category. **2** *Logic.* (of a statement) consisting of a subject, S, and a predicate, P, each of which denote a class, as in: *all S are P.*

categorical Ⓣ (,kætɪ'gɒrɪkᵊl) *or* **categoric** *adj* **1** unqualified; unconditional: *a categorical statement.* **2** relating to or included in a category. **3** another word for **categorial** (sense 2).
▸ **,cate'gorically** *adv*

categorize *or* **categorise** ('kætɪgə,raɪz) *vb* **categorizes, categorizing, categorized** *or* **categorises, categorising, categorised.** (*tr*) to place in a category.
▸ **,categori'zation** *or* **,categori'sation** *n*

category Ⓣ ('kætɪgərɪ) *n, pl* **categories.** **1** a class or group of things, people, etc., possessing some quality or qualities in common. **2** *Metaphysics.* one of the most basic classes into which objects and concepts can be analysed. **3a** (in the philosophy of Aristotle) any one of ten most fundamental modes of being, such as quantity, quality, and substance. **3b** (in the philosophy of Kant) one of twelve concepts required by human beings to interpret the empirical world. [C15: from LL, from Gk *katēgoria,* from *kategorein* to accuse, assert]

catena (kə'tiːnə) *n, pl* **catenae** (-niː). a connected series, esp. of patristic comments on the Bible. [C17: from L: chain]

catenaccio (*Italian* kate'nattʃo) *n Soccer.* an extremely defensive style of play. [C20: from L *catena* chain]

catenary (kə'tiːnərɪ) *n, pl* **catenaries.** **1** the curve formed by a heavy uniform flexible cord hanging freely from two points. **2** the hanging cable between pylons along a railway track, from which the trolley wire is suspended. ◆ *adj* **3** of, resembling, relating to, or constructed using a catenary or suspended chain. [C18: from L *catēnārius* relating to a chain]

catenate ('kætɪ,neɪt) *vb* **catenates, catenating, catenated.** *Biol.* to arrange or be arranged in a series of chains or rings. [C17: from L *catēnāre* to bind with chains]
▸ **,cate'nation** *n*

cater Ⓣ ('keɪtə) *vb* **1** (*intr;* foll. by *for* or *to*) to provide what is required or desired (for). **2** (when *intr,* foll. by *for*) to provide food, services, etc. (for): *we cater for parties.* [C16: from earlier *catour* purchaser, var. of *acatour,* from Anglo-Norman *acater* to buy]
▸ **'catering** *n*

cater-cornered ('kætə,kɔːnəd) *adj, adv US & Canad. inf.* diagonal. Also: **catty-cornered, kitty-cornered.** [C16: from dialect *cater* (adv) diagonally, from obs. *cater* (n) four-spot of dice, from OF *quatre* four, from L *quattuor*]

caterer ('keɪtərə) *n* one who as a profession provides food for large social events, etc.

caterpillar ('kætə,pɪlə) *n* **1** the wormlike larva of butterflies and moths, having numerous pairs of legs and powerful biting jaws. **2** *Trademark.* an endless track, driven by sprockets or wheels, used to propel a heavy vehicle. **3** *Trademark.* a vehicle, such as a tractor, tank, etc., driven by such tracks. [C15 *catyrpel,* prob. from OF *catepelose,* lit.: hairy cat]

caterwaul Ⓣ ('kætə,wɔːl) *vb* (*intr*) **1** to make a yowling noise, as a cat on heat. ◆ *n* **2** a yell made by or sounding like a cat on heat. [C14: imit.]

catfish ('kæt,fɪʃ) *n, pl* **catfish** *or* **catfishes.** **1** any of numerous mainly freshwater fishes having whisker-like barbels around the mouth. **2** another name for **wolffish.**

cat flap *or* **door** *n* a small flap or door in a larger door through which a cat can pass.

catgut ('kæt,gʌt) *n* a strong cord made from the dried intestines of sheep and other animals that is used for stringing certain musical instruments and sports rackets.

Cath. *abbrev. for:* **1** Cathedral. **2** Catholic.

cath- *prefix* a variant of **cata-** before an aspirate: *cathode.*

Cathar ('kæθə) *or* **Catharist** ('kæθərɪst) *n, pl* **Cathars, Cathari** (-ərɪ) *or* **Catharists.** a member of a Christian sect in Provence in the 12th and 13th centuries who believed the material world was evil and only the spiritual was good. [from Med. L, from Gk *katharoi* the pure]
▸ **'Cathar,ism** *n*

catharsis Ⓣ (kə'θɑːsɪs) *n, pl* **catharses** (-siːz). **1** the purging or purification of the emotions through the evocation of pity and fear, as in tragedy. **2** *Psychoanal.* the bringing of repressed ideas or experiences into consciousness, thus relieving tensions. **3** purgation, esp. of

THESAURUS

tage, fly in the ointment, hitch, snag, stumbling block, trap, trick
Antonyms *vb* ≠ **seize:** drop, free, give up, liberate, loose, release ≠ **contract:** avert, avoid, escape, ward off ≠ **attract:** alienate, bore, disenchant, disgust, fail to interest, repel ◆ *n* ≠ **drawback:** advantage, benefit, bonus, boon, reward

catching *adj* **1** = **infectious**, communicable, contagious, infective, transferable, transmittable
Antonyms *adj* incommunicable, non-catching, non-contagious, non-infectious, non-transmittable

catch on *vb* **2** *Informal* = **understand**, comprehend, find out, get the picture, grasp, see, see the light of day, see through, twig (*Brit. inf.*)

catchword *n* **1** = **slogan**, byword, motto, password, refrain, watchword

catchy *adj* **1** = **memorable**, captivating, haunting, popular

catechize *vb* **1, 3** = **question**, cross-examine, drill, examine, grill (*inf.*), interrogate

categorical *adj* **1** = **absolute**, direct, downright, emphatic, explicit, express, positive, unambiguous, unconditional, unequivocal, unqualified, unreserved
Antonyms *adj* conditional, hesitant, indefinite, qualified, questionable, uncertain, vague

category *n* **1** = **class**, classification, department, division, grade, grouping, head, heading, list, order, rank, section, sort, type

cater *vb* **1, 2** = **provide**, furnish, outfit, provision, purvey, supply, victual

caterwaul *vb* **1** = **yowl**, bawl, howl, scream, screech, shriek, squall, wail

catharsis *n* **1, 3** = **release**, abreaction, cleansing, lustration, purgation, purging, purification

the bowels. [C19: NL, from Gk *katharsis,* from *kathairein* to purge, purify]

cathartic (kə'θɑːtɪk) *adj* **1** purgative. **2** effecting catharsis. ◆ *n* **3** a purgative drug or agent.
▸**ca'thartically** *adv*

Cathay (kæ'θeɪ) *n* a literary or archaic name for **China**. [C14: from Med. L *Cataya*]

cathead ('kæt,hɛd) *n* a fitting at the bow of a vessel for securing the anchor when raised.

cathedral (kə'θiːdrəl) *n* **a** the principal church of a diocese, containing the bishop's official throne. **b** (*as modifier*): *a cathedral city*. [C13: from LL (*ecclesia*) *cathedrālis* cathedral (church), from Gk *kathedra* seat]

Catherine wheel (kæθrɪn) *n* **1** a firework which rotates, producing coloured flame. **2** a circular window having ribs radiating from the centre. [C16: after St *Catherine* of Alexandria, martyred on a spiked wheel, 307 A.D.]

catheter ('kæθɪtə) *n Med.* a long slender flexible tube for inserting into a bodily cavity for introducing or withdrawing fluid. [C17: from LL, from Gk *kathetēr,* from *kathienai* to insert]

catheterize *or* **catheterise** ('kæθɪtə,raɪz) *vb* **catheterizes, catheterizing, catheterized** *or* **catheterises, catheterising, catheterised.** (*tr*) to insert a catheter into.

cathexis (kə'θɛksɪs) *n, pl* **cathexes** (-'θɛksiːz). *Psychoanal.* concentration of psychic energy on a single goal. [C20: from NL, from Gk *kathexis,* from *katekhein* to hold fast]

cathode ('kæθəʊd) *n* **1** the negative electrode in an electrolytic cell. **2** the negatively charged electron source in an electronic valve. **3** the positive terminal of a primary cell. ◆ Cf. **anode.** [C19: from Gk *kathodos* a descent, from *kata-* down + *hodos* way]
▸**cathodal** (kæ'θəʊdᵊl) *or* **cathodic** (kæ'θɒdɪk, -'θəʊ-) *adj*

cathode rays *pl n* a stream of electrons emitted from the surface of a cathode in a vacuum tube.

cathode-ray tube *n* a vacuum tube in which a beam of electrons is focused onto a fluorescent screen to give a visible spot of light. The device is used in television receivers, visual display units, etc.

catholic ❶ ('kæθəlɪk, 'kæθlɪk) *adj* **1** universal; relating to all men. **2** broad-minded; liberal. [C14: from L, from Gk *katholikos* universal, from *kata-* according to + *holos* whole]
▸**catholically** *or* **catholicly** (kə'θɒlɪklɪ) *adv*

Catholic ('kæθəlɪk, 'kæθlɪk) *Christianity.* ◆ *adj* **1** denoting or relating to the entire body of Christians, esp. to the Church before separation into the Eastern and Western Churches. **2** denoting or relating to the Latin or Western Church after this separation. **3** denoting or relating to the Roman Catholic Church. ◆ *n* **4** a member of the Roman Catholic Church.

Catholicism (kə'θɒlɪ,sɪzəm) *n* **1** short for **Roman Catholicism. 2** the beliefs, practices, etc., of any Catholic Church.

catholicity (,kæθə'lɪsɪtɪ) *n* **1** a wide range of interests, tastes, etc. **2** comprehensiveness.

catholicize *or* **catholicise** (kə'θɒlɪ,saɪz) *vb* **catholicizes, catholicizing, catholicized** *or* **catholicises, catholicising, catholicised. 1** to make or become catholic. **2** (*often cap.*) to convert to or become converted to Catholicism.

cation ('kætaɪən) *n* a positively charged ion; an ion that is attracted to the cathode during electrolysis. Cf. **anion.** [C19: from CATA- + ION]
▸**cationic** (,kætaɪ'ɒnɪk) *adj*

catkin ('kætkɪn) *n* an inflorescence consisting of a hanging spike of much reduced flowers of either sex: occurs in birch, hazel, etc. [C16: from obs. Du. *katteken* kitten]

cat litter *n* absorbent material used to line a receptacle in which a domestic cat can urinate and defecate.

catmint ('kæt,mɪnt) *n* a Eurasian plant having spikes of purple-spotted white flowers and scented leaves of which cats are fond. Also called: **catnip.**

catnap ❶ ('kæt,næp) *n* **1** a short sleep or doze. ◆ *vb* **catnaps, catnapping, catnapped. 2** (*intr*) to sleep or doze for a short time or intermittently.

cat-o'-nine-tails *n, pl* **cat-o'-nine-tails.** a rope whip consisting of nine knotted thongs, used formerly to flog prisoners. Often shortened to **cat.**

CATS (kæts) *n acronym for* credit accumulation transfer scheme: a scheme enabling school-leavers and others to acquire transferable certificates for relevant work experience and study towards a recognized qualification.

CAT scanner (kæt) *n* former name for **CT scanner.** [C20: from *C*omputerized *A*xial *T*omography]

cat's cradle *n* a game played by making patterns with a loop of string between the fingers.

cat's-eye *n* any of a group of gemstones that reflect a streak of light when cut in a rounded unfaceted shape.

Catseye ('kætsaɪ) *n Trademark, Brit.* a glass reflector set into a small fixture, placed at intervals along roads to indicate traffic lanes at night.

cat's-paw *n* **1** a person used by another as a tool; dupe. **2** a pattern of ripples on the surface of water caused by a light wind. [(sense 1) C18: so called from the tale of the monkey who used a cat's paw to draw chestnuts out of a fire]

catsup ('kætsəp) *n* a variant spelling (esp. US) of **ketchup.**

cat's whisker *n* a pointed wire formerly used to make contact with the crystal in a crystal radio receiver.

cat's whiskers *or* **cat's pyjamas** *n* **the.** *Sl.* a person or thing that is excellent or superior.

cattery ('kætərɪ) *n, pl* **catteries.** a place where cats are bred or looked after.

cattle ❶ ('kætᵊl) *n* (*functioning as pl*) **1** bovid mammals of the tribe *Bovini* (bovines). **2** Also called: **domestic cattle.** any domesticated bovine mammals. [C13: from OF *chatel* CHATTEL]

cattle-cake *n* concentrated food for cattle in the form of cakes.

cattle-grid *n* a grid of metal bars covering a hole dug in a roadway intended to prevent the passage of livestock while allowing vehicles, etc., to pass unhindered.

cattleman ('kætᵊlmən) *n, pl* **cattlemen. 1** a person who breeds, rears, or tends cattle. **2** *Chiefly US & Canad.* a person who rears cattle on a large scale.

cattle market *n* **1** a place in which cattle are bought and sold. **2** *Brit. sl.* a situation or place in which women are on display and judged solely by their appearance.

cattle-stop *n* the New Zealand name for a **cattle-grid.**

catty ❶ ('kætɪ) *or* **cattish** *adj* **cattier, cattiest. 1** *Inf.* spiteful: *a catty remark.* **2** of or resembling a cat.
▸'**cattily** *or* '**cattishly** *adv* ▸'**cattiness** *or* '**cattishness** *n*

CATV *abbrev. for* community antenna television.

catwalk ('kæt,wɔːk) *n* **1** a narrow ramp extending from the stage into the audience in a theatre etc., esp. as used by models in a fashion show. **2** a narrow pathway over the stage of a theatre, along a bridge, etc.

Caucasian (kɔː'keɪzɪən) *adj* **1** another word for **Caucasoid. 2** of or relating to Caucasia or the Caucasus in the SW Soviet Union. ◆ *n* **3** a member of the Caucasoid race; a White person. **4** a native or inhabitant of Caucasia or the Caucasus.

Caucasoid ('kɔːkə,zɔɪd) *adj* **1** denoting or belonging to the light-complexioned racial group of mankind, which includes the peoples indigenous to Europe, N Africa, SW Asia, and the Indian subcontinent. ◆ *n* **2** a member of this racial group.

caucus ❶ ('kɔːkəs) *n, pl* **caucuses. 1** *Chiefly US & Canad.* a closed meeting of the members of one party in a legislative chamber, etc., to coordinate policy, choose candidates, etc. **2** *Chiefly US.* a local meeting of party members. **3** *Brit.* a group or faction within a larger group, esp. a political party, who discuss tactics, choose candidates, etc. **4** *NZ.* a formal meeting of all MPs of one party. **5** *Austral.* a group of MPs from one party who meet to discuss tactics, etc. ◆ *vb* **6** (*intr*) to hold a caucus. [C18: prob. of Algonquian origin]

caudal ('kɔːdᵊl) *adj* **1** *Anat.* of the posterior part of the body. **2** *Zool.* resembling or in the position of the tail. [C17: from NL, from L *cauda* tail]
▸'**caudally** *adv*

caudal fin *n* the tail fin of fishes and some other aquatic vertebrates, used for propulsion.

caudate ('kɔːdeɪt) *or* **caudated** *adj* having a tail or a tail-like appendage. [C17: from NL *caudātus,* from L *cauda* tail]
▸**cau'dation** *n*

caudillo (kɔː'diːljəʊ) *n, pl* **caudillos** (-ljəʊz). (in Spanish-speaking countries) a military or political leader. [Sp., from LL *capitellum,* dim. of L *caput* head]

caudle ('kɔːdᵊl) *n* a hot spiced wine drink made with gruel, formerly used medicinally. [C13: from OF *caudel,* from Med. L, from L *calidus* warm]

caught (kɔːt) *vb* the past tense and past participle of **catch.**

caul (kɔːl) *n Anat.* a portion of the amniotic sac sometimes covering a child's head at birth. [C13: from OF *cale,* back formation from *calotte* close-fitting cap, of Gmc origin]

cauldron *or* **caldron** ('kɔːldrən) *n* a large pot used for boiling, esp. one with handles. [C13: from Anglo-F, from L *caldārium* hot bath, from *calidus* warm]

cauliflower ('kɒlɪ,flaʊə) *n* **1** a variety of cabbage having a large edible head of crowded white flowers on a very short thick stem. **2** the flower head of this plant, used as a vegetable. [C16: from It. *caoli fiori,* lit.: cabbage flowers]

cauliflower ear *n* permanent swelling and distortion of the external ear as the result of ruptures of the blood vessels: usually caused by blows received in boxing.

caulk *or* **calk** (kɔːk) *vb* **1** to stop up (cracks, crevices, etc.) with a filler. **2** *Naut.* to pack (the seams) between the planks of the bottom of (a ves-

THESAURUS

catholic *adj* **1, 2** = **wide**, all-embracing, all-inclusive, broad-minded, charitable, comprehensive, eclectic, ecumenical, general, global, liberal, tolerant, unbigoted, universal, unsectarian, whole, world-wide
Antonyms *adj* bigoted, exclusive, illiberal, limited, narrow-minded, parochial, sectarian

catnap *n* **1** = **doze**, forty winks (*inf.*), kip (*Brit. sl.*), nap, siesta, sleep, snooze ◆ *vb* **2** = **doze**, drowse, kip (*Brit. sl.*), nap, snooze, take forty winks (*inf.*)

cattiness *n* **1** *Informal* = **spitefulness**, bitchiness, ill-naturedness, malevolence, maliciousness, meanness, rancorousness, shrewishness, snideness, venomousness, virulence

cattle *pl n* **2** = **cows**, beasts, bovines, kine (*arch.*), livestock, stock

catty *adj* **1** = **spiteful**, backbiting, bitchy (*inf.*), ill-natured, malevolent, malicious, mean, rancorous, shrewish, snide, venomous
Antonyms *adj* benevolent, charitable, compassionate, considerate, generous, kind, pleasant

caucus *n* **1-5** = **meeting**, assembly, conclave, congress, convention, get-together (*inf.*), parley, session

sel) with waterproof material to prevent leakage. [C15: from OF *cauquer* to press down, from L *calcāre* to trample, from *calx* heel]

causal (ˈkɔːzᵊl) *adj* **1** acting as or being a cause. **2** stating, involving, or implying a cause: *the causal part of the argument.*
▸ **ˈcausally** *adv*

causality (kɔːˈzælɪtɪ) *n, pl* **causalities. 1a** the relationship of cause and effect. **1b** the principle that nothing can happen without being caused. **2** causal agency or quality.

causation (kɔːˈzeɪʃən) *n* **1** the production of an effect by a cause. **2** the relationship of cause and effect.
▸ **cauˈsational** *adj*

causative (ˈkɔːzətɪv) *adj* **1** *Grammar.* relating to a form or class of verbs, such as *persuade,* that express causation. **2** (*often postpositive* and foll. by *of*) producing an effect. ◆ *n* **3** the causative form or class of verbs.
▸ **ˈcausatively** *adv*

cause Ⓣ (kɔːz) *n* **1** a person, thing, event, state, or action that produces an effect. **2** grounds for action; justification: *she had good cause to shout like that.* **3** the ideals, etc., of a group or movement: *the Communist cause.* **4** the welfare or interests of a person or group in a dispute: *they fought for the miners' cause.* **5a** a ground for legal action; matter giving rise to a lawsuit. **5b** the lawsuit itself. **6** *Arch.* a subject of debate or discussion. **7 make common cause with.** to join with (a person, group, etc.) for a common objective. ◆ *vb* **causes, causing, caused. 8** (*tr*) to be the cause of; bring about. [C13: from L *causa* cause, reason, motive]
▸ **ˈcauseless** *adj*

cause célèbre (ˈkɔːz səˈlɛbrə) *n, pl* **causes célèbres** (ˈkɔːz səˈlɛbrəz). a famous lawsuit, trial, or controversy. [C19: from F: famous case]

causerie (ˈkəʊzərɪ) *n* an informal talk or conversational piece of writing. [C19: from F, from *causer* to chat]

causeway (ˈkɔːzˌweɪ) *n* **1** a raised path or road crossing water, marshland, etc. **2** a paved footpath. [C15 *cauciwey* (from *cauci* + WAY); *cauci* paved road, from Med. L, from L *calx* limestone]

caustic Ⓣ (ˈkɔːstɪk) *adj* **1** capable of burning or corroding by chemical action: *caustic soda.* **2** sarcastic; cutting: *a caustic reply.* ◆ *n* **3** Also called: **caustic surface.** a surface that envelops the light rays reflected or refracted by a curved surface. **4** Also called: **caustic curve.** a curve formed by the intersection of a caustic surface with a plane. **5** *Chem.* a caustic substance, esp. an alkali. [C14: from L, from Gk *kaustikos,* from *kaiein* to burn]
▸ **ˈcaustically** *adv* ▸ **causticity** (kɔːˈstɪsɪtɪ) *n*

caustic potash *n* another name for **potassium hydroxide.**

caustic soda *n* another name for **sodium hydroxide.**

cauterize *or* **cauterise** (ˈkɔːtəˌraɪz) *vb* **cauterizes, cauterizing, cauterized** *or* **cauterises, cauterising, cauterised.** (*tr*) (esp. in the treatment of a wound) to burn or sear (body tissue) with a hot iron or caustic agent. [C14: from OF, from LL, from *cautērium* branding iron, from Gk *kautērion,* from *kaiein* to burn]
▸ **ˌcauteriˈzation** *or* **ˌcauteriˈsation** *n*

cautery (ˈkɔːtərɪ) *n, pl* **cauteries. 1** the coagulation of blood or destruction of body tissue by cauterizing. **2** an instrument or agent for cauterizing. [C14: from OF *cautère,* from L *cautērium*]

caution Ⓣ (ˈkɔːʃən) *n* **1** care, forethought, or prudence, esp. in the face of danger. **2** something intended or serving as a warning. **3** *Law, chiefly Brit.* a formal warning given to a person suspected of an offence that his words will be taken down and may be used in evidence. **4** *Inf.* an amusing or surprising person or thing. ◆ *vb* **5** (*tr*) to warn (a person) to be careful. **6** (*tr*) *Law, chiefly Brit.* to give a caution to (a person). **7** (*intr*) to warn, urge, or advise: *he cautioned against optimism.* [C13: from OF, from L *cautiō,* from *cavēre* to beware]

cautionary (ˈkɔːʃənərɪ) *adj* serving as a warning; intended to warn: *a cautionary tale.*

cautious Ⓣ (ˈkɔːʃəs) *adj* showing or having caution.
▸ **ˈcautiously** *adv* ▸ **ˈcautiousness** *n*

cavalcade Ⓣ (ˌkævəlˈkeɪd) *n* **1** a procession of people on horseback, in cars, etc. **2** any procession. [C16: from F, from It., from *cavalcare* to ride on horseback, from LL, from *caballus* horse]

cavalier Ⓣ (ˌkævəˈlɪə) *adj* **1** supercilious; offhand. ◆ *n* **2** a courtly gentleman, esp. one acting as a lady's escort. **3** *Arch.* a horseman, esp. one who is armed. [C16: from It., from OProvençal, from LL *caballārius* rider, from *caballus* horse, from ?]
▸ **ˌcavaˈlierly** *adv*

Cavalier (ˌkævəˈlɪə) *n* a supporter of Charles I during the English Civil War.

cavalry Ⓣ (ˈkævəlrɪ) *n, pl* **cavalries. 1** (esp. formerly) the part of an army composed of mounted troops. **2** the armoured element of a modern army. **3** (*as modifier*): *a cavalry unit.* [C16: from F *cavallerie,* from It., from *cavaliere* horseman]
▸ **ˈcavalryman** *n*

cavatina (ˌkævəˈtiːnə) *n, pl* **cavatine** (-nɪ). **1** a simple solo song. **2** an instrumental composition reminiscent of this. [C19: from It.]

cave[1] Ⓣ (keɪv) *n* **1** an underground hollow with access from the ground surface or from the sea. **2** *Brit. history.* a secession or a group seceding from a political party on some issue. **3** (*modifier*) living in caves. ◆ *vb* **caves, caving, caved. 4** (*tr*) to hollow out. [C13: from OF, from L *cava,* pl. of *cavum* cavity, from *cavus* hollow]

cave[2] (ˈkeɪvɪ) *Brit. school sl.* ◆ *n* **1** lookout: *keep cave.* ◆ *sentence substitute.* **2** watch out! [from L *cavē* beware!]

caveat Ⓣ (ˈkeɪvɪˌæt, ˈkæv-) *n* **1** *Law.* a formal notice requesting the court not to take a certain action without warning the person lodging the caveat. **2** a caution. [C16: from L, lit.: let him beware]

caveat emptor (ˈɛmptɔː) *n* the principle that the buyer must bear the risk for the quality of goods purchased. [L: let the buyer beware]

cave in *vb* (*intr, adv*) **1** to collapse; subside. **2** *Inf.* to yield completely, esp. under pressure. ◆ *n* **cave-in. 3** the sudden collapse of a roof, piece of ground, etc. **4** the site of such a collapse, as at a mine or tunnel.

cavel (ˈkeɪvᵊl) *n NZ.* a drawing of lots among miners for an easy and profitable place at the coalface. [C19: from E dialect *cavel* to cast lots, apportion]

caveman (ˈkeɪvˌmæn) *n, pl* **cavemen. 1** a man of the Palaeolithic age; cave dweller. **2** *Inf.* a man who is primitive or brutal in behaviour, etc.

cavendish (ˈkævəndɪʃ) *n* tobacco that has been sweetened and pressed into moulds to form bars. [C19: ?from the name of the first maker]

cavern Ⓣ (ˈkævᵊn) *n* **1** a cave, esp. when large. ◆ *vb* (*tr*) **2** to shut in or as if in a cavern. **3** to hollow out. [C14: from OF *caverne,* from L *caverna,* from *cavus* hollow]

cavernous Ⓣ (ˈkævənəs) *adj* **1** suggestive of a cavern in vastness, etc.: *cavernous eyes.* **2** filled with small cavities. **3** (of rocks) containing caverns.

caviar *or* **caviare** (ˈkævɪˌɑː, ˌkævɪˈɑː) *n* the salted roe of sturgeon, usually served as an hors d'oeuvre. [C16: from earlier *cavery,* from OIt. *caviari,* pl. of *caviaro* caviar, from Turkish *havyār*]

cavil Ⓣ (ˈkævɪl) *vb* **cavils, cavilling, cavilled** *or US* **cavils, caviling, caviled. 1** (*intr;* foll. by *at* or *about*) to raise annoying petty objections. ◆ *n* **2** a trifling objection. [C16: from OF, from L *cavillārī* to jeer, from *cavilla* raillery]
▸ **ˈcaviller** *n*

caving (ˈkeɪvɪŋ) *n* the sport of climbing in and exploring caves.
▸ **ˈcaver** *n*

cavity Ⓣ (ˈkævɪtɪ) *n, pl* **cavities. 1** a hollow space. **2** *Dentistry.* a decayed area on a tooth. **3** any empty or hollow space within the body. [C16: from F, from LL *cavitās,* from L *cavus* hollow]

cavity wall *n* a wall that consists of two separate walls with an airspace between them.

cavort Ⓣ (kəˈvɔːt) *vb* (*intr*) to prance; caper. [C19: ?from CURVET]
▸ **caˈvorter** *n*

cavy (ˈkeɪvɪ) *n, pl* **cavies.** a small South American rodent having a thickset body and very small tail. See also **guinea pig.** [C18: from NL *Cavia,* from Carib *cabiai*]

caw (kɔː) *n* **1** the cry of a crow, rook, or raven. ◆ *vb* **2** (*intr*) to make this cry. [C16: imit.]

cay (keɪ, kiː) *n* a small low island or bank composed of sand and coral fragments. [C18: from Sp. *cayo,* prob. from OF *quai* QUAY]

cayenne pepper (keɪˈɛn) *n* a very hot red condiment made from the

THESAURUS

cause *n* **1 = origin,** agent, beginning, creator, genesis, mainspring, maker, originator, prime mover, producer, root, source, spring **2 = reason,** account, agency, aim, basis, consideration, end, grounds, incentive, inducement, justification, motivation, motive, object, purpose, the why and wherefore **3 = aim,** attempt, belief, conviction, enterprise, ideal, movement, principle, purpose, undertaking ◆ *vb* **8 = produce,** begin, bring about, compel, create, effect, engender, generate, give rise to, incite, induce, lead to, motivate, occasion, precipitate, provoke, result in
Antonyms *n* ≠ **origin:** consequence, effect, end, outcome, result ◆ *vb* ≠ **produce:** deter, foil, inhibit, prevent, stop

caustic *adj* **1 = burning,** acrid, astringent, biting, corroding, corrosive, keen, mordant, vitriolic **2 = sarcastic,** acrimonious, cutting, mordacious, pungent, scathing, severe, stinging, trenchant, virulent, vitriolic
Antonyms *adj* ≠ **sarcastic:** agreeable, bland, gentle, kind, loving, mild, pleasant, pleasing, soft, soothing, sweet, temperate

caution *n* **1 = care,** alertness, belt and braces, carefulness, circumspection, deliberation, discretion, forethought, heed, heedfulness, prudence, vigilance, watchfulness **2 = warning,** admonition, advice, counsel, injunction ◆ *vb* **5-7 = warn,** admonish, advise, tip off, urge
Antonyms *n* ≠ **care:** carelessness, daring, imprudence, rashness, recklessness ◆ *vb* ≠ **warn:** dare

cautious *adj* **= careful,** alert, belt-and-braces, cagey (*inf.*), chary, circumspect, discreet, guarded, heedful, judicious, keeping a weather eye on, on one's toes, prudent, tentative, vigilant, wary, watchful
Antonyms *adj* adventurous, bold, careless, daring, foolhardy, heedless, impetuous, inattentive, incautious, indiscreet, madcap, rash, reckless, unguarded, unheedful, venturesome, venturous

cautiously *adv* **= carefully,** alertly, cagily (*inf.*), circumspectly, discreetly, guardedly, heedfully, judiciously, mindfully, prudently, tentatively, vigilantly, warily, watchfully

cavalcade *n* **2 = parade,** array, march-past, procession, spectacle, train

cavalier *adj* **1 = haughty,** arrogant, condescending, curt, disdainful, insolent, lofty, lordly, offhand, scornful, supercilious ◆ *n* **2 = gentleman,** beau, blade (*arch.*), escort, gallant **3 = knight,** chevalier, equestrian, horseman

cavalry *n* **1 = horsemen,** horse, mounted troops
Antonyms *n* foot soldiers, infantrymen

cave[1] *n* **1 = hollow,** cavern, cavity, den, grotto

caveat *n* **2 = warning,** admonition, caution

cavern *n* **1 = cave,** hollow, pothole

cavernous *adj* **1 = deep,** concave, hollow, sunken, yawning

cavil *vb* **1 = find fault,** beef (*sl.*), carp, censure, complain, hypercriticize, kvetch (*US sl.*), object, quibble

cavity *n* **1 = hollow,** crater, dent, gap, hole, pit

cavort *vb* **= caper,** caracole, frisk, frolic, gambol, prance, romp, sport

dried seeds of various capsicums. Often shortened to **cayenne.** Also called: **red pepper.** [C18: ult. from Tupi *quiynha*]

cayman *or* **caiman** ('keɪmən) *n, pl* **caymans** *or* **caimans.** a tropical American crocodilian similar to alligators but with a more heavily armoured belly. [C16: from Sp. *caimán,* from Carib *cayman*]

CB *abbrev. for:* **1** Citizens' Band. **2** Companion of the (Order of the) Bath (a Brit. title). **3** County Borough.

CBC *abbrev. for* Canadian Broadcasting Corporation.

CBE *abbrev. for* Commander of the (Order of the) British Empire.

CBI *abbrev. for:* **1** *US.* Central Bureau of Investigation. **2** Confederation of British Industry.

CBT *abbrev. for* computer-based training.

cc *or* **c.c.** *abbrev. for:* **1** carbon copy *or* copies. **2** cubic centimetre(s).

CC *abbrev. for:* **1** City Council. **2** County Council. **3** Cricket Club.

cc. *abbrev. for* chapters.

c.c.c. *abbrev. for* cwmni cyfyngedig cyhoeddus; a public limited company in Wales.

C clef *n Music.* a symbol (𝄡), placed at the beginning of the staff, establishing the position of middle C: see **alto clef, soprano clef, tenor clef.**

CCTV *abbrev. for* closed-circuit television.

CCW *abbrev. for* Curriculum Council for Wales.

cd *symbol for* candela.

Cd *the chemical symbol for* cadmium.

CD *abbrev. for:* **1** compact disc. **2** Civil Defence (Corps). **3** Corps Diplomatique (Diplomatic Corps). **4** Conference on Disarmament: a United Nations standing conference, held in Geneva, to negotiate a global ban on chemical weapons.

CDE *abbrev. for:* compact disc erasable: a compact disc that can be used to record and rerecord. Cf. **CDR.**

CDI *abbrev. for* compact disc interactive.

Cdn *abbrev. for* Canadian.

cDNA *abbrev. for* complementary DNA.

CD player *n* a device for playing compact discs. In full: **compact-disc player.**

Cdr *Mil. abbrev. for* Commander.

CDR *abbrev. for* compact disc recordable: a compact disc that can be used to record only once. Cf. **CDE.**

CD-ROM (ˌsiːdiːˈrɒm) *abbrev. for* compact disc read only memory; a compact disc used for storing written information to be displayed on a visual-display unit.

CDT *abbrev. for:* **1** *US & Canad.* Central Daylight Time. **2** Craft, Design, and Technology: a subject on the GCSE syllabus, related to the National Curriculum.

CDV *abbrev. for* compact disc video.

CD-video *n* a compact-disc player that, when connected to a television and hi-fi, produces high-quality stereo sound and synchronized pictures from a disc resembling a compact audio disc. In full **compact-disc video.**

Ce *the chemical symbol for* cerium.

CE *abbrev. for:* **1** Church of England. **2** civil engineer. **3** Common Era.

cease ➊ (siːs) *vb* **ceases, ceasing, ceased. 1** (when *tr,* may take a gerund or an infinitive as object) to bring or come to an end. ◆ *n* **2 without cease.** without stopping. [C14: from OF, from L *cessāre,* frequentative of *cēdere* to yield]

ceasefire ('siːsˌfaɪə) *Chiefly mil.* ◆ *n* **1** a period of truce, esp. one that is temporary. ◆ *sentence substitute, n* **2** the order to stop firing.

ceaseless ➊ ('siːslɪs) *adj* without stop or pause; incessant.
▸**'ceaselessly** *adv*

cecum ('siːkəm) *n, pl* **ceca** (-kə). *US.* a variant spelling of **caecum.**
▸**'cecal** *adj*

cedar ('siːdə) *n* **1** any of a genus of Old World coniferous trees having needle-like evergreen leaves, and erect barrel-shaped cones. See also **cedar of Lebanon, deodar. 2** any of various other conifers, such as the red cedars and white cedars. **3** the wood of any of these trees. ◆ *adj* **4** made of the wood of a cedar tree. [C13: from OF, from L *cedrus,* from Gk *kedros*]

cedar of Lebanon ('lɛbənən) *n* a cedar of SW Asia with level spreading branches and fragrant wood.

cede ➊ (siːd) *vb* **cedes, ceding, ceded. 1** (when *intr,* often foll. by *to*) to transfer, make over, or surrender (something, esp. territory or legal rights). **2** (*tr*) to allow or concede (a point in an argument, etc.). [C17: from L *cēdere* to yield]
▸**'ceder** *n*

cedilla (sɪ'dɪlə) *n* a character (¸) placed underneath a *c* before *a, o,* or *u,* esp. in French, Portuguese, or Catalan, denoting that it is to be pronounced (s), not (k). [C16: from Sp.: little *z,* from *ceda* zed, from LL *zeta*]

Ceefax ('siːfæks) *n Trademark.* the BBC Teletext service. See **Teletext.**

CEGB (in Britain) *abbrev. for* Central Electricity Generating Board.

ceil (siːl) *vb* (*tr*) **1** to line (a ceiling) with plaster, etc. **2** to provide with a ceiling. [C15 *celen,* ? back formation from CEILING]

ceilidh ('keɪlɪ) *n* (esp. in Scotland and Ireland) an informal social gathering with singing, dancing, and storytelling. [C19: from Gaelic]

ceiling ('siːlɪŋ) *n* **1** the inner upper surface of a room. **2** an upper limit, such as one set by regulation on prices or wages. **3** the upper altitude to which an aircraft can climb measured under specified conditions. **4** *Meteorol.* the highest level in the atmosphere from which the earth's surface is visible at a particular time, usually the base of a cloud layer. [C14: from ?]

celadon ('sɛləˌdɒn) *n* **1** a type of porcelain having a greyish-green glaze: mainly Chinese. **2a** a pale greyish-green colour. **2b** (*as adj*): *a celadon jar.* [C18: from F, from the name of the shepherd hero of *L'Astrée* (1610), a romance by Honoré d'Urfé]

celandine ('sɛlənˌdaɪn) *n* either of two unrelated plants, **greater celandine** or **lesser celandine,** with yellow flowers. [C13: earlier *celydon,* from L, from Gk *khelidōn* swallow; the plant's season was believed to parallel the migration of swallows]

-cele *n combining form.* tumour or hernia: *hydrocele.* [from Gk *kēlē* tumour]

celeb (sɪ'lɛb) *n Inf.* a celebrity.

celebrant ('sɛlɪbrənt) *n* a person participating in a religious ceremony, esp. at the Eucharist.

celebrate ➊ ('sɛlɪˌbreɪt) *vb* **celebrates, celebrating, celebrated. 1** to rejoice in or have special festivities to mark (a happy day, event, etc.). **2** (*tr*) to observe (a birthday, anniversary, etc.). **3** (*tr*) to perform (a solemn or religious ceremony), esp. to officiate at (Mass). **4** (*tr*) to praise publicly; proclaim. [C15: from L, from *celeber* numerous, renowned]
▸ˌ**cele'bration** *n* ▸**'celeˌbrator** *n* ▸**'celeˌbratory** *adj*

celebrated ➊ ('sɛlɪˌbreɪtɪd) *adj* (*usually prenominal*) famous: *a celebrated pianist.*

celebrity ➊ (sɪ'lɛbrɪtɪ) *n, pl* **celebrities. 1** a famous person. **2** fame or notoriety.

celeriac (sɪ'lɛrɪˌæk) *n* a variety of celery with a large turnip-like root, used as a vegetable. [C18: from CELERY + *-ac,* from ?]

celerity (sɪ'lɛrɪtɪ) *n* rapidity; swiftness; speed. [C15: from OF *celerite,* from L *celeritās,* from *celer* swift]

celery ('sɛlərɪ) *n* **1** an umbelliferous Eurasian plant whose blanched leafstalks are used in salads or cooked as a vegetable. **2 wild celery.** a related and similar plant. [C17: from F *céleri,* from It. (Lombardy) dialect *selleri* (pl), from Gk *selinon* parsley]

celesta (sɪ'lɛstə) *or* **celeste** (sɪ'lɛst) *n Music.* a keyboard percussion instrument consisting of a set of steel plates of graduated length that are struck with key-operated hammers. [C19: from F, Latinized var. of *céleste* heavenly]

celestial ➊ (sɪ'lɛstɪəl) *adj* **1** heavenly; divine: *celestial peace.* **2** of or relating to the sky: *celestial bodies.* **3** of or connected with the celestial sphere: *celestial pole.* [C14: from Med. L, from L *caelestis,* from *caelum* heaven]
▸**ce'lestially** *adv*

celestial equator *n* the great circle lying on the celestial sphere the plane of which is perpendicular to the line joining the north and south celestial poles. Also called: **equinoctial, equinoctial circle.**

celestial mechanics *n* the study of the motion of celestial bodies under the influence of gravitational fields.

celestial sphere *n* an imaginary sphere of infinitely large radius enclosing the universe so that all celestial bodies appear to be projected onto its surface.

celiac ('siːlɪˌæk) *adj Anat.* the usual US spelling of **coeliac.**

celibate ➊ ('sɛlɪbɪt) *n* **1** a person who is unmarried, esp. one who has taken a religious vow of chastity. ◆ *adj* **2** abstaining from sexual in-

THESAURUS

cease *vb* **1** = **stop,** break off, bring *or* come to an end, conclude, culminate, desist, die away, discontinue, end, fail, finish, halt, leave off, refrain, stay, terminate
Antonyms *vb* begin, commence, continue, initiate, start

ceaseless *adj* = **continual,** constant, continuous, endless, eternal, everlasting, incessant, indefatigable, interminable, never-ending, nonstop, perennial, perpetual, unending, unremitting, untiring
Antonyms *adj* broken, erratic, intermittent, irregular, occasional, periodic, spasmodic, sporadic

cede *vb* **1, 2** = **surrender,** abandon, abdicate, allow, concede, convey, grant, hand over, make over, relinquish, renounce, resign, step down (*inf.*), transfer, yield

celebrate *vb* **1, 2** = **rejoice,** commemorate, drink to, keep, kill the fatted calf, observe, put the flags out, toast **3** = **perform,** bless, honour, reverence, solemnize **4** = **praise,** commend, crack up (*inf.*), eulogize, exalt, extol, glorify, honour, laud, proclaim, publicize

celebrated *adj* = **well-known,** acclaimed, distinguished, eminent, famed, famous, glorious, illustrious, lionized, notable, outstanding, popular, pre-eminent, prominent, renowned, revered
Antonyms *adj* dishonoured, forgotten, insignificant, obscure, trivial, unacclaimed, undistinguished, unknown, unnotable, unpopular

celebration *n* **1** = **party,** beano (*Brit. sl.*), carousal, -fest (*in combination*), festival, festivity, gala, hooley *or* hoolie (*chiefly Irish & N.Z.*), jollification, jubilee, junketing, merrymaking, rave (*Brit. sl.*), rave-up (*Brit. sl.*), red-letter day, revelry **2, 3** = **performance,** anniversary, commemoration, honouring, observance, remembrance, solemnization

celebrity *n* **1** = **personality,** big name, big shot (*inf.*), bigwig (*inf.*), celeb (*inf.*), dignitary, face (*inf.*), lion, luminary, megastar (*inf.*), name, personage, star, superstar, V.I.P. **2** = **fame,** distinction, éclat, glory, honour, notability, popularity, pre-eminence, prestige, prominence, renown, reputation, repute, stardom
Antonyms *n* ≠ **personality:** has-been, nobody, unknown ≠ **fame:** obscurity

celestial *adj* **1** = **heavenly,** angelic, astral, divine, elysian, empyrean (*poetic*), eternal, ethereal, godlike, immortal, seraphic, spiritual, sublime, supernatural

celibacy *n* **2, 3** = **chastity,** continence, purity, singleness, virginity

tercourse. **3** unmarried. [C17: from L, from *caelebs* unmarried, from ?]
▸**'celibacy** *n*

cell ⓘ (sɛl) *n* **1** a small simple room, as in a prison, convent, etc. **2** any small compartment: *the cells of a honeycomb.* **3** *Biol.* the smallest unit of an organism that is able to function independently. It consists of a nucleus, containing the genetic material, surrounded by the cytoplasm. **4** *Biol.* any small cavity, such as the cavity containing pollen in an anther. **5** a device for converting chemical energy into electrical energy, usually consisting of a container with two electrodes immersed in an electrolyte. See also **dry cell, fuel cell. 6** In full: **electrolytic cell.** a device in which electrolysis occurs. **7** a small religious house dependent upon a larger one. **8** a small group of persons operating as a nucleus of a larger organization: *Communist cell.* **9** the geographical area served by an individual transmitter in a cellular-radio network. [C12: from Med. L *cella* monk's cell, from L: room, storeroom]

cellar ('sɛlə) *n* **1** an underground room, or storey of a building, usually used for storage. **2** a place where wine is stored. **3** a stock of bottled wines. ◆ *vb* **4** *(tr)* to store in a cellar. [C13: from Anglo-F, from L *cellārium* foodstore, from *cella* cell]

cellarage ('sɛlərɪdʒ) *n* **1** an area of a cellar. **2** a charge for storing goods in a cellar, etc.

cellarer ('sɛlərə) *n* a monastic official responsible for food, drink, etc.

cellaret (ˌsɛlə'rɛt) *n* a cabinet or sideboard with compartments for holding wine bottles.

cell line *n Biol.* a cell culture derived from a single cell and thus of invariable genetic make-up.

Cellnet ('sɛlˌnɛt) *n Trademark.* a British Telecom mobile phone.

cello ('tʃɛləʊ) *n, pl* **cellos.** *Music.* a bowed stringed instrument of the violin family. It has four strings, is held between the knees, and has a metal spike at the lower end, which acts as a support. Full name: **violoncello.**
▸**'cellist** *n*

Cellophane ('sɛləˌfeɪn) *n Trademark.* a flexible thin transparent sheeting made from wood pulp and used as a moisture-proof wrapping. [C20: from CELLULOSE + -PHANE]

cellphone ('sɛlˌfəʊn) *n* a portable telephone operated by cellular radio. In full: **cellular telephone.**

cellular ('sɛljʊlə) *adj* **1** of, relating to, or composed of a cell or cells. **2** having cells or small cavities; porous. **3** divided into a network of cells. **4** *Textiles.* woven with an open texture: *a cellular blanket.* **5** designed for or involving cellular radio.

cellular radio *n* radio communication based on a network of transmitters each serving a small area known as a cell: used esp. in car phones in which the receiver switches frequencies automatically as it passes from one cell to another.

cellule ('sɛljuːl) *n* a very small cell. [C17: from L *cellula,* dim. of *cella* CELL]

cellulite ('sɛljʊˌlaɪt) *n* subcutaneous fat alleged to resist dieting.

cellulitis (ˌsɛljʊ'laɪtɪs) *n* inflammation of body tissue, with fever, pain, and swelling. [C19: from L *cellula* CELLULE + -ITIS]

celluloid ('sɛljʊˌlɔɪd) *n* **1** a flammable material consisting of cellulose nitrate and camphor: used in sheets, rods, etc. **2a** a cellulose derivative used for coating film. **2b** cinema film.

cellulose ('sɛljʊˌləʊz, -ˌləʊs) *n* a substance which is the main constituent of plant cell walls and used in making paper, rayon, and film. [C18: from F *cellule* cell (see CELLULE) + -OSE[2]]

cellulose acetate *n* nonflammable material used in the manufacture of film, dopes, lacquers, and artificial fibres.

cellulose nitrate *n* cellulose treated with nitric and sulphuric acids, used in plastics, lacquers, and explosives. See also **guncotton.**

Celsius ('sɛlsɪəs) *adj* denoting a measurement on the Celsius scale. Symbol: C [C18: after Anders *Celsius* (1701–44), Swedish astronomer who invented it]

Celsius scale *n* a scale of temperature in which 0° represents the melting point of ice and 100° represents the boiling point of water. See also **centigrade.** Cf. **Fahrenheit scale.**

celt (sɛlt) *n Archaeol.* a stone or metal axelike instrument. [C18: from LL *celtes* chisel, from ?]

Celt (kɛlt, sɛlt) *or* **Kelt** *n* **1** a person who speaks a Celtic language. **2** a member of an Indo-European people who in pre-Roman times inhabited Britain, Gaul, and Spain.

Celtic ('kɛltɪk, 'sɛl-) *or* **Keltic** *n* **1** a branch of the Indo-European family of languages that includes Gaelic, Welsh, and Breton. Modern Celtic is divided into the Brythonic (southern) and Goidelic (northern) groups. ◆ *adj* **2** of, relating to, or characteristic of the Celts or the Celtic languages.
▸**Celticism** ('kɛltɪˌsɪzəm, 'sɛl-) *or* **'Keltiˌcism** *n*

Celtic cross *n* a Latin cross with a broad ring surrounding the point of intersection.

cembalo ('tʃɛmbələʊ) *n, pl* **cembali** (-lɪ) *or* **cembalos.** another word for **harpsichord.** [C19: from It. *clavicembalo* from Med. L *clāvis* key + *cymbalum* CYMBAL]

cement ⓘ (sɪ'mɛnt) *n* **1** a fine grey powder made of a mixture of limestone and clay, used with water and sand to make mortar, or with water, sand, and aggregate, to make concrete. **2** a binder, glue, or adhesive. **3** something that unites or joins. **4** *Dentistry.* any of various materials used in filling teeth. **5** another word for **cementum.** ◆ *vb (tr)* **6** to join, bind, or glue together with or as if with cement. **7** to coat or cover with cement. [C13: from OF, from L *caementum* stone from the quarry, from *caedere* to hew]

cementum (sɪ'mɛntəm) *n* a thin bonelike tissue that covers the dentine in the root of a tooth. [C19: NL, from L: CEMENT]

cemetery ⓘ ('sɛmɪtrɪ) *n, pl* **cemeteries.** a place where the dead are buried, esp. one not attached to a church. [C14: from LL, from Gk *koimētērion,* from *koiman* to put to sleep]

-cene *n and adj combining form.* denoting a recent geological period. [from Gk *kainos* new]

cenobite ('siːnəʊˌbaɪt) *n* a variant spelling of **coenobite.**

cenotaph ('sɛnəˌtɑːf) *n* a monument honouring a dead person or persons buried elsewhere. [C17: from L, from Gk, from *kenos* empty + *taphos* tomb]

Cenotaph ('sɛnəˌtɑːf) *n* **the.** the monument in Whitehall, London, honouring the dead of both World Wars: designed by Sir Edwin Lutyens: erected in 1920.

Cenozoic, Caenozoic (ˌsiːnəʊ'zəʊɪk), *or* **Cainozoic** *adj* **1** of, denoting, or relating to the most recent geological era characterized by the development and increase of the mammals. ◆ *n* **2 the.** the Cenozoic era. [C19: from Gk *kainos* recent + *zōikos,* from *zōion* animal]

censer ('sɛnsə) *n* a container for burning incense. Also called: **thurible.**

censor ⓘ ('sɛnsə) *n* **1** a person authorized to examine publications, films, letters, etc., in order to suppress in whole or part those considered obscene, politically unacceptable, etc. **2** any person who controls or suppresses the behaviour of others, usually on moral grounds. **3** (in republican Rome) either of two senior magistrates elected to keep the list of citizens up to date, and supervise public morals. **4** *Psychoanal.* the postulated factor responsible for regulating the translation of ideas and desires from the unconscious to the conscious mind. ◆ *vb (tr)* **5** to ban or cut portions of (a film, letter, etc.). **6** to act as a censor of (behaviour, etc.). [C16: from L, from *cēnsēre* to consider]
▸**censorial** (sɛn'sɔːrɪəl) *adj*

censorious ⓘ (sɛn'sɔːrɪəs) *adj* harshly critical; fault-finding.
▸**cen'soriously** *adv*

censorship ⓘ ('sɛnsəˌʃɪp) *n* **1** a policy or programme of censoring. **2** the act or system of censoring.

censure ⓘ ('sɛnʃə) *n* **1** severe disapproval. ◆ *vb* **censures, censuring, censured. 2** to criticize (someone or something) severely. [C14: from L *censūra,* from *cēnsēre*: see CENSOR]
▸**'censurable** *adj*

census ('sɛnsəs) *n, pl* **censuses. 1** an official periodic count of a population including such information as sex, age, occupation, etc. **2** any official count: *a traffic census.* **3** (in ancient Rome) a registration of the population and a property evaluation for taxation. [C17: from L, from *cēnsēre* to assess]

cent (sɛnt) *n* a monetary unit of Australia, Barbados, Canada, Cyprus, Dominica, Estonia, Ethiopia, Fiji, Grenada, Guyana, Jamaica, Kenya, Malaysia, New Zealand, Singapore, South Africa, Tanzania, Trinidad and Tobago, Uganda, the United States, etc. It is worth one hundredth of their respective standard units. [C16: from L *centēsimus* hundredth, from *centum* hundred]

cent. *abbrev. for:* **1** centigrade. **2** central. **3** century.

centaur ('sɛntɔː) *n Greek myth.* one of a race of creatures with the head, arms, and torso of a man, and the lower body and legs of a horse. [C14: from L, from Gk *kentauros,* from ?]

centaurea (sɛntɔː'rɪə, sɛn'tɔːrɪə) *n* any plant of the genus *Centaurea* which includes the cornflower and knapweed. [C19: ult. from Gk *Kentauros* the Centaur; see CENTAURY]

centaury ('sɛntɔːrɪ) *n, pl* **centauries. 1** any of a genus of Eurasian plants having purplish-pink flowers and formerly believed to have medicinal properties. **2** another name for **centaurea.** [C14: ult. from Gk *Kentauros* the Centaur; from the legend that Chiron the Centaur divulged its healing properties]

centavo (sɛn'tɑːvəʊ) *n, pl* **centavos.** a monetary unit of Argentina, Brazil, Colombia, Ecuador, El Salvador, Mexico, Nicaragua, the Phil-

THESAURUS

cell *n* **1** = **room**, cavity, chamber, compartment, cubicle, dungeon, stall **8** = **unit**, caucus, core, coterie, group, nucleus

cement *n* **2** = **mortar**, adhesive, binder, glue, gum, paste, plaster, sealant ◆ *vb* **6** = **stick together**, attach, bind, bond, cohere, combine, glue, gum, join, plaster, seal, solder, unite, weld

cemetery *n* = **graveyard**, burial ground, churchyard, God's acre, necropolis

censor *vb* **5** = **cut**, blue-pencil, bowdlerize, expurgate

censorious *adj* = **critical**, captious, carping, cavilling, condemnatory, disapproving, disparaging, fault-finding, hypercritical, scathing, severe

censorship *n* **2** = **expurgation**, blue pencil, bowdlerization *or* bowdlerisation, purgation, sanitization *or* sanitisation

censure *n* **1** = **disapproval**, blame, castigation, condemnation, criticism, dressing down (*inf.*), obloquy, rebuke, remonstrance, reprehension, reprimand, reproach, reproof, stick (*sl.*), stricture ◆ *vb* **2** = **criticize**, abuse, bawl out (*inf.*), berate, blame, blast, carpet (*inf.*), castigate, chide, condemn, denounce, excoriate, give (someone) a rocket (*Brit. & NZ. inf.*), lambast(e), put down, rap over the knuckles, read the riot act, rebuke, reprehend, reprimand, reproach, reprove, scold, slap on the wrist, slate (*inf., chiefly US.*), tear into (*inf.*), tear (someone) off a strip (*Brit. inf.*), upbraid

Antonyms *n* ≠ **disapproval:** approval, commendation, compliment, encouragement ◆ *vb* ≠ **criticize:** applaud, commend, compliment, laud (*literary*)

ippines, Portugal, etc. It is worth one hundredth of their respective standard units. [Sp.: one hundredth part]

centenarian (ˌsɛntɪˈnɛərɪən) *n* **1** a person who is at least 100 years old. ◆ *adj* **2** being at least 100 years old. **3** of or relating to a centenarian.

centenary (sɛnˈtiːnərɪ) *adj* **1** of or relating to a period of 100 years. **2** occurring once every 100 years. ◆ *n, pl* **centenaries. 3** a 100th anniversary or its celebration. [C17: from L, from *centēnī* a hundred each, from *centum* hundred]

centennial (sɛnˈtɛnɪəl) *adj* **1** relating to or completing a period of 100 years. **2** occurring every 100 years. ◆ *n* **3** *US & Canad.* another name for **centenary.** [C18: from L *centum* hundred, on the model of BIENNIAL]

center (ˈsɛntə) *n, vb* the US spelling of **centre.**

centesimal (sɛnˈtɛsɪməl) *n* **1** hundredth. ◆ *adj* **2** relating to division into hundredths. [C17: from L, from *centum* hundred]
▸**cenˈtesimally** *adv*

centesimo (sɛnˈtɛsɪˌməʊ) *n, pl* **centesimos** *or* **centesimi.** a monetary unit of Italy, Panama, Uruguay, etc. It is worth one hundredth of their respective standard units. [C19: from Sp. & It., from L, from *centum* hundred]

centi- *or before a vowel* **cent-** *prefix* **1** denoting one hundredth: *centimetre.* Symbol: c **2** *Rare.* denoting a hundred: *centipede.* [from F, from L *centum* hundred]

centiare (ˈsɛntɪˌɛə) *or* **centare** (ˈsɛntɛə) *n* a unit of area equal to one square metre. [F, from CENTI- + *are* from L *ārea*]

centigrade (ˈsɛntɪˌgreɪd) *adj* **1** a former name for **Celsius.** ◆ *n* **2** a unit of angle equal to one hundredth of a grade.

> **USAGE NOTE** Although still used in meteorology, *centigrade*, when indicating the Celsius scale of temperature, is now usually avoided because of its possible confusion with the hundredth part of a grade.

centigram *or* **centigramme** (ˈsɛntɪˌgræm) *n* one hundredth of a gram.

centilitre *or US* **centiliter** (ˈsɛntɪˌliːtə) *n* one hundredth of a litre.

centime (ˈsɒnˌtiːm; *French* sɑ̃tim) *n* a monetary unit of Algeria, Belgium, the Central African Republic, France, Guinea, Haiti, Liechtenstein, Luxembourg, Mali, Switzerland, Togo, etc. It is worth one hundredth of their respective standard units. [C18: from F, from OF, from L, from *centum* hundred]

centimetre *or US* **centimeter** (ˈsɛntɪˌmiːtə) *n* one hundredth of a metre.

centimetre-gram-second *n* See **cgs units.**

céntimo (ˈsɛntɪˌməʊ) *n, pl* **céntimos.** a monetary unit of Costa Rica, Peru, Spain, Venezuela, etc. It is worth one hundredth of their respective standard currency units. [from Sp.; see CENTIME]

centipede (ˈsɛntɪˌpiːd) *n* a carnivorous arthropod having a body of between 15 and 190 segments, each bearing one pair of legs.

cento (ˈsɛntəʊ) *n, pl* **centos.** a piece of writing, esp. a poem, composed of quotations from other authors. [C17: from L, lit.: patchwork garment]

CENTO (ˈsɛntəʊ) *n acronym for* Central Treaty Organization; an organization for military and economic cooperation formed in 1959 by the UK, Iran, Pakistan, and Turkey: disbanded 1979.

central ⓘ (ˈsɛntrəl) *adj* **1** in, at, of, from, containing, or forming the centre of something: *the central street in a city.* **2** main, principal, or chief: *the central cause of a problem.*
▸**centrality** (sɛnˈtrælɪtɪ) *n* ▸**ˈcentrally** *adv*

central bank *n* a national bank that does business mainly with a government and with other banks: it regulates the volume of credit.

central heating *n* a system for heating the rooms of a building by means of radiators or air vents connected to a central source of heat.

centralism (ˈsɛntrəˌlɪzəm) *n* the principle or act of bringing something under central control.
▸**ˈcentralist** *n, adj*

centralize ⓘ *or* **centralise** (ˈsɛntrəˌlaɪz) *vb* **centralizes, centralizing, centralized** *or* **centralises, centralising, centralised. 1** to draw or move (something) to or towards a centre. **2** to bring or come under central, esp. governmental, control.
▸**ˌcentraliˈzation** *or* **ˌcentraliˈsation** *n*

central limit theorem *n Statistics.* the fundamental result that the sum of independent identically distributed random variables with finite variance approaches a normally distributed random variable as their number increases.

central locking *n* a system by which all the doors of a motor vehicle can be locked simultaneously.

central nervous system *n* the mass of nerve tissue that controls and coordinates the activities of an animal. In vertebrates it consists of the brain and spinal cord.

central processing unit *n* the part of a computer that performs logical and arithmetical operations on the data. Abbrev.: **CPU.**

central reserve *or* **reservation** *n Brit. & Austral.* the strip, often covered with grass, that separates the two sides of a motorway or dual carriageway.

central tendency *n Statistics.* the tendency of the values of a random variable to cluster around the mean, median, and mode.

centre ⓘ *or US* **center** (ˈsɛntə) *n* **1** *Geom.* **1a** the midpoint of any line or figure, esp. the point within a circle or sphere that is equidistant from any point on the circumference or surface. **1b** the point within a body through which a specified force may be considered to act, such as the centre of gravity. **2** the point, axis, or pivot about which a body rotates. **3** a point, area, or part that is approximately in the middle of a larger area or volume. **4** a place at which some specified activity is concentrated: *a shopping centre.* **5** a person or thing that is a focus of interest. **6** a place of activity or influence: *a centre of power.* **7** a person, group, or thing in the middle. **8** (*usually cap.*) *Politics.* a political party or group favouring moderation. **9** a bar with a conical point upon which a workpiece or part may be turned or ground. **10** *Football, hockey, etc.* **10a** a player who plays in the middle of the forward line. **10b** an instance of passing the ball from a wing to the middle of the field, etc. ◆ *vb* **centres, centring, centred** *or US* **centers, centering, centered. 11** to move towards, mark, put, or be at a centre. **12** (*tr*) to focus or bring together: *to centre one's thoughts.* **13** (*intr;* often foll. by *on*) to have as a main theme: *the novel centred on crime.* **14** (*intr;* foll. by *on* or *round*) to have as a centre. **15** (*tr*) *Football, hockey, etc.* to pass (the ball) into the middle of the field or court. [C14: from L *centrum* the stationary point of a compass, from Gk *kentron* needle, from *kentein* to prick]

centre bit *n* a drilling bit with a central point and two side cutters.

centreboard (ˈsɛntəˌbɔːd) *n* a supplementary keel for a sailing vessel.

centrefold *or US* **centerfold** (ˈsɛntəˌfəʊld) *n* **1** a large coloured illustration folded so that it forms the central spread of a magazine. **2a** a photograph of a nude or nearly nude woman (or man) in a magazine on such a spread. **2b** the subject of such a photograph.

centre forward *n Soccer, hockey, etc.* the central forward in the attack.

centre half *or* **centre back** *n Soccer.* a defender who plays in the middle of the defence.

centre of gravity *n* the point through which the resultant of the gravitational forces on a body always acts.

centre pass *n Hockey.* a push or hit made in any direction to start the game or restart the game after a goal has been scored.

centrepiece ⓘ (ˈsɛntəˌpiːs) *n* an object used as the centre of something, esp. for decoration.

centre spread *n* **1** the pair of two facing pages in the middle of a magazine, newspaper, etc. **2a** a photograph of a nude or nearly nude woman (or man) in a magazine on such pages. **2b** the subject of such a photograph.

centri- *combining form.* a variant of **centro-.**

centric (ˈsɛntrɪk) *or* **centrical** *adj* **1** being central or having a centre. **2** relating to a nerve centre.
▸**centricity** (sɛnˈtrɪsɪtɪ) *n*

-centric *suffix forming adjectives.* having a centre as specified: *heliocentric.* [abstracted from ECCENTRIC, CONCENTRIC, etc.]

centrifugal ⓘ (sɛnˈtrɪfjʊgᵊl, ˈsɛntrɪˌfjuːgᵊl) *adj* **1** acting, moving, or tending to move away from a centre. Cf. **centripetal. 2** of, concerned with, or operated by centrifugal force: *centrifugal pump.* [C18: from NL, from CENTRI- + L *fugere* to flee]
▸**cenˈtrifugally** *adv*

centrifugal force *n* a fictitious force that can be thought of as acting outwards on any body that rotates or moves along a curved path.

centrifuge (ˈsɛntrɪˌfjuːdʒ) *n* **1** any of various rotating machines that separate liquids from solids or other liquids by the action of centrifugal force. **2** any of various rotating devices for subjecting human beings or animals to varying accelerations. ◆ *vb* **centrifuges, centrifuging, centrifuged. 3** (*tr*) to subject to the action of a centrifuge.
▸**centrifugation** (ˌsɛntrɪfjʊˈgeɪʃən) *n*

centring (ˈsɛntrɪŋ) *or US* **centering** (ˈsɛntərɪŋ) *n* a temporary structure, esp. one made of timber, used to support an arch during construction.

centripetal (sɛnˈtrɪpɪtᵊl, ˈsɛntrɪˌpiːtᵊl) *adj* **1** acting, moving, or tending to move towards a centre. Cf. **centrifugal. 2** of, concerned with, or operated by centripetal force. [C17: from NL *centripetus* seeking the centre]
▸**cenˈtripetally** *adv*

centripetal force *n* a force that acts inwards on any body that rotates or moves along a curved path.

centrist (ˈsɛntrɪst) *n* a person holding moderate political views.
▸**ˈcentrism** *n*

centro-, centri-, *or before a vowel* **centr-** *combining form.* denoting a centre: *centrosome; centrist.* [from Gk *kentron* CENTRE]

centrosome (ˈsɛntrəˌsəʊm) *n* a small protoplasmic body found near the cell nucleus.

centuplicate *vb* (sɛnˈtjuːplɪˌkeɪt), **centuplicates, centuplicating, centuplicated. 1** (*tr*) to increase 100 times. ◆ *adj* (sɛnˈtjuːplɪkɪt). **2** increased a hundredfold. ◆ *n* (sɛnˈtjuːplɪkɪt). **3** one hundredfold.

THESAURUS

central *adj* **1** = **middle**, inner, interior, mean, median, mid **2** = **main**, chief, essential, focal, fundamental, key, primary, principal
Antonyms *adj* ≠ **middle:** exterior, outer, outermost ≠ **main:** minor, secondary, subordinate, subsidiary

centralize *vb* **2** = **unify**, amalgamate, compact, concentrate, concentre, condense, converge, incorporate, rationalize, streamline

centre *n* **1-7** = **middle**, bull's-eye, core, crux, focus, heart, hub, kernel, mid (*arch.*), midpoint, nucleus, pivot ◆ *vb* **11, 12** = **focus**, cluster, concentrate, converge, revolve
Antonyms *n* ≠ **middle:** border, boundary, brim, circumference, edge, fringe, limit, lip, margin, perimeter, periphery, rim

centrepiece *n* = **focus**, cynosure, epergne, highlight, hub, star

centrifugal *adj* **1** = **radiating**, diffusive, divergent, diverging, efferent, radial

◆ Also **centuple** ('sɛntjʊpᵊl). [C17: from LL, from *centuplex* hundredfold, from L *centum* hundred + *-plex* -fold]

centurion (sɛn'tjʊərɪən) *n* the officer commanding a Roman century. [C14: from L *centuriō*, from *centuria* CENTURY]

century ('sɛntʃərɪ) *n, pl* **centuries. 1** a period of 100 years. **2** one of the successive periods of 100 years dated before or after an epoch or event, esp. the birth of Christ. **3** a score or grouping of 100: *to score a century in cricket.* **4** (in ancient Rome) a unit of foot soldiers, originally consisting of 100 men. **5** (in ancient Rome) a division of the people for purposes of voting. [C16: from L *centuria*, from *centum* hundred]

cep (sɛp) *n* an edible woodland fungus with a brown shining cap and a rich nutty flavour. [C19: from F, from Gascon dialect *cep*, from L *cippus* stake]

cephalic (sɪ'fælɪk) *adj* **1** of or relating to the head. **2** situated in, on, or near the head.

-cephalic *or* **-cephalous** *adj combining form.* indicating skull or head; -headed: *brachycephalic.* [from Gk *-kephalos*]
▸**-cephaly** *or* **-cephalism** *n combining form*

cephalic index *n* the ratio of the greatest width of the human head to its greatest length, multiplied by 100.

cephalo- *or before a vowel* **cephal-** *combining form.* indicating the head: *cephalopod.* [via L from Gk, from *kephalē* head]

cephalopod ('sɛfələˌpɒd) *n* any of various marine molluscs, characterized by well-developed head and eyes and a ring of sucker-bearing tentacles, including the octopuses, squids, and cuttlefish.
▸ˌ**cepha'lopodan** *adj, n*

cephalothorax (ˌsɛfələʊ'θɔːræks) *n, pl* **cephalothoraxes** *or* **cephalothoraces** (-rəˌsiːz). the anterior part of many crustaceans and some other arthropods consisting of a united head and thorax.

-cephalus *n combining form.* denoting a cephalic abnormality: *hydrocephalus.* [NL *-cephalus*; see -CEPHALIC]

Cepheid variable ('siːfɪɪd) *n Astron.* any of a class of variable stars with regular cycles of variations in luminosity, which are used for measuring distances.

ceramic (sɪ'ræmɪk) *n* **1** a hard brittle material made by firing clay and similar substances. **2** an object made from such a material. ◆ *adj* **3** of or made from a ceramic. **4** of or relating to ceramics: *ceramic arts.* [C19: from Gk, from *keramos* potter's clay]

ceramic hob *n* (on an electric cooker) a flat ceramic cooking surface having heating elements fitted on the underside.

ceramic oxide *n* a compound of oxygen with nonorganic material: recently discovered to act as a high-temperature superconductor.

ceramics (sɪ'ræmɪks) *n* (*functioning as sing*) the art and techniques of producing articles of clay, porcelain, etc.
▸**ceramist** ('sɛrəmɪst) *n*

cere (sɪə) *n* a soft waxy swelling, containing the nostrils, at the base of the upper beak, as in the parrot. [C15: from OF *cire* wax, from L *cēra*]

cereal ('sɪərɪəl) *n* **1** any grass that produces an edible grain, such as oat, wheat, rice, maize, and millet. **2** the grain produced by such a plant. **3** any food made from this grain, esp. breakfast food. **4** (*modifier*) of or relating to any of these plants or their products. [C19: from L *cereālis* concerning agriculture]

cerebellum (ˌsɛrɪ'bɛləm) *n, pl* **cerebellums** *or* **cerebella** (-lə). one of the major divisions of the vertebrate brain whose function is coordination of voluntary movements. [C16: from L, dim. of CEREBRUM]
▸ˌ**cere'bellar** *adj*

cerebral ('sɛrɪbrəl; *US also* sə'riːbrəl) *adj* **1** of or relating to the cerebrum or to the entire brain. **2** involving intelligence rather than emotions or instinct. **3** *Phonetics.* another word for **cacuminal.**
▸'**cerebrally** *adv*

cerebral haemorrhage *n* bleeding from an artery in the brain, which in severe cases causes a stroke.

cerebral palsy *n* a nonprogressive impairment of muscular function and weakness of the limbs, caused by lack of oxygen to the brain immediately after birth, brain injury during birth, or viral infection.

cerebrate ('sɛrɪˌbreɪt) *vb* **cerebrates, cerebrating, cerebrated.** (*intr*) *Usually facetious.* to use the mind; think; ponder; consider.
▸ˌ**cere'bration** *n*

cerebro- *or before a vowel* **cerebr-** *combining form.* indicating the brain: *cerebrospinal.* [from CEREBRUM]

cerebrospinal (ˌsɛrɪbrəʊ'spaɪnᵊl) *adj* of or relating to the brain and spinal cord: *cerebrospinal fluid.*

cerebrovascular (ˌsɛrɪbrəʊ'væskjʊlə) *adj* of or relating to the blood vessels and the blood supply of the brain.

cerebrum ('sɛrɪbrəm) *n, pl* **cerebrums** *or* **cerebra** (-brə). **1** the anterior portion of the brain of vertebrates, consisting of two lateral hemispheres: the dominant part of the brain in man, associated with intellectual function, emotion, and personality. **2** the brain considered as a whole. [C17: from L: the brain]
▸'**cerebric** *adj*

cerecloth ('sɪəˌklɒθ) *n* waxed waterproof cloth of a kind formerly used as a shroud. [C15: from earlier *cered cloth*, from L *cērāre* to wax]

cerement ('sɪəmənt) *n* **1** cerecloth. **2** any burial clothes. [C17: from F, from *cirer* to wax]

ceremonial ❶ (ˌsɛrɪ'məʊnɪəl) *adj* **1** involving or relating to ceremony or ritual. ◆ *n* **2** the observance of formality, esp. in etiquette. **3** a plan for formal observances; ritual. **4** *Christianity.* **4a** the prescribed order of rites and ceremonies. **4b** a book containing this.
▸ˌ**cere'monialism** *n* ▸ˌ**cere'monialist** *n* ▸ˌ**cere'monially** *adv*

ceremonious ❶ (ˌsɛrɪ'məʊnɪəs) *adj* **1** especially or excessively polite or formal. **2** involving formalities.
▸ˌ**cere'moniously** *adv*

ceremony ❶ ('sɛrɪmənɪ) *n, pl* **ceremonies. 1** a formal act or ritual, often set by custom or tradition, performed in observation of an event or anniversary. **2** a religious rite or series of rites. **3** a courteous gesture or act: *the ceremony of toasting the Queen.* **4** ceremonial observances or gestures collectively. **5 stand on ceremony.** to insist on or act with excessive formality. [C14: from Med. L, from L *caerimōnia* what is sacred]

cerise (sə'riːz, -'riːs) *n, adj* (of) a moderate to dark red colour. [C19: from F: CHERRY]

cerium ('sɪərɪəm) *n* a malleable ductile steel-grey element of the lanthanide series of metals, used in lighter flints. Symbol: Ce; atomic no.: 58; atomic wt.: 140.12. [C19: NL, from *Ceres* (the asteroid) + -IUM]

CERN (sɜːn) *n acronym for* Conseil Européen pour la Recherche Nucléaire; an organization of European states with a centre in Geneva, for research in high-energy particle physics, now called the European Laboratory for Particle Physics.

cerography (sɪə'rɒgrəfɪ) *n* the art of engraving on a waxed plate on which a printing surface is created by electrotyping.

ceroplastic (ˌsɪərəʊ'plæstɪk) *adj* **1** relating to wax modelling. **2** modelled in wax.

cert (sɜːt) *n Inf.* something that is a certainty, esp. a horse that is certain to win a race.

cert. *abbrev. for:* **1** certificate. **2** certification. **3** certified.

certain ❶ ('sɜːtᵊn) *adj* **1** (*postpositive*) positive and confident about the truth of something; convinced: *I am certain that he wrote a book.* **2** (*usually postpositive*) definitely known: *it is certain that they were on the bus.* **3** (*usually postpositive*) sure; bound: *he was certain to fail.* **4** fixed: *the date is already certain for the invasion.* **5** reliable: *his judgment is certain.* **6** moderate or minimum: *to a certain extent.* **7 for certain.** without a doubt. ◆ *determiner* **8a** known but not specified or named: *certain people.* **8b** (*as pron; functioning as pl*): *certain of the members have not paid.* **9** named but not known: *he had written to a certain Mrs Smith.* [C13: from OF, from L *certus* sure, from *cernere* to decide]

certainly ❶ ('sɜːtᵊnlɪ) *adv* **1** without doubt: *he certainly rides very well.* ◆ *sentence substitute.* **2** by all means; definitely.

certainty ❶ ('sɜːtᵊntɪ) *n, pl* **certainties. 1** the condition of being certain. **2** something established as inevitable. **3 for a certainty.** without doubt.

CertEd (in Britain) *abbrev. for* Certificate in Education.

certes ('sɜːtɪz) *adv Arch.* with certainty; truly. [C13: from OF, ult. from L *certus* CERTAIN]

certificate ❶ *n* (sə'tɪfɪkɪt). **1** an official document attesting the truth of the facts stated, as of birth, death, completion of an academic course, ownership of shares, etc. ◆ *vb* (sə'tɪfɪˌkeɪt), **certificates, certificating, certificated. 2** (*tr*) to authorize by or present with an official document. [C15: from OF, from *certifier* to CERTIFY]
▸**cer'tificatory** *adj*

Certificate of Secondary Education *n* the full name for **CSE.**

certification (ˌsɜːtɪfɪ'keɪʃən) *n* **1** the act of certifying or state of being certified. **2** *Law.* a document attesting the truth of a fact or statement.

certified ('sɜːtɪˌfaɪd) *adj* **1** holding or guaranteed by a certificate. **2** endorsed or guaranteed: *a certified cheque.* **3** (of a person) declared legally insane.

certified accountant *n* (in Britain) a member of the Chartered Association of Certified Accountants, who is authorized to audit company accounts. Cf. **chartered accountant.**

certify ❶ ('sɜːtɪˌfaɪ) *vb* **certifies, certifying, certified. 1** to confirm or attest (to), usually in writing. **2** (*tr*) to endorse or guarantee that certain re-

THESAURUS

ceremonial *adj* **1** = **ritual**, formal, liturgical, ritualistic, solemn, stately ◆ *n* **3** = **ritual**, ceremony, formality, rite, solemnity
Antonyms *adj* ≠ **ritual:** casual, informal, relaxed, simple

ceremonious *adj* **1** = **formal**, civil, courteous, courtly, deferential, dignified, exact, precise, punctilious, ritual, solemn, starchy (*inf.*), stately, stiff

ceremony *n* **1, 2** = **ritual**, commemoration, function, observance, parade, rite, service, show, solemnities **4** = **formality**, ceremonial, decorum, etiquette, form, formal courtesy, niceties, pomp, propriety, protocol

certain *adj* **1** = **sure**, assured, confident, convinced, positive, satisfied **2** = **known**, ascertained, conclusive, incontrovertible, indubitable, irrefutable, plain, true, undeniable, undoubted, unequivocal, unmistakable, valid **3** = **inevitable**, bound, definite, destined, fated, ineluctable, inescapable, inexorable, sure **4** = **fixed**, decided, definite, established, settled
Antonyms *adj* disputable, doubtful, dubious, equivocal, fallible, indefinite, questionable, uncertain, unconvinced, undecided, unlikely, unreliable, unsettled, unsure

certainly *adv* **1** = **definitely**, absolutely, assuredly, come hell or high water, decidedly, doubtlessly, indisputably, indubitably, irrefutably, positively, surely, truly, undeniably, undoubtedly, unequivocally, unquestionably, without doubt, without question

certainty *n* **1** = **sureness**, assurance, authoritativeness, certitude, confidence, conviction, faith, indubitableness, inevitability, positiveness, trust, validity **2** = **fact**, banker, reality, sure thing (*inf.*), surety, truth
Antonyms *n* ≠ **sureness:** disbelief, doubt, indecision, qualm, scepticism, uncertainty, unsureness

certificate *n* **1** = **document**, authorization, credential(s), diploma, licence, testimonial, voucher, warrant

certify *vb* **1-3** = **confirm**, ascertain, assure, attest, authenticate, aver, avow, corroborate, de-

quired standards have been met. **3** to give reliable information or assurances: *he certified that it was Walter's handwriting.* **4** (*tr*) to declare legally insane. [C14: from OF, from Med. L, from L *certus* CERTAIN + *facere* to make]
▸ **'certi,fiable** *adj*

certiorari (,sɜːtɪɔː'rɛəraɪ) *n Law.* an order of a superior court directing that a record of proceedings in a lower court be sent up for review. [C15: from legal L: to be informed]

certitude ❶ ('sɜːtɪ,tjuːd) *n* confidence; certainty. [C15: from Church L *certitūdō*, from L *certus* CERTAIN]

cerulean (sɪ'ruːlɪən) *n, adj* (of) a deep blue colour. [C17: from L *caeruleus*, prob. from *caelum* sky]

cerumen (sɪ'ruːmɛn) *n* the soft brownish-yellow wax secreted by glands in the external ear. Nontechnical name: **earwax.** [C18: from NL, from L *cēra* wax + ALBUMEN]
▸ **ce'ruminous** *adj*

cervelat ('sɜːvə,læt, -,lɑː) *n* a smoked sausage made from pork and beef. [C17: via obs. F from It. *cervellata*]

cervical (sə'vaɪkᵊl, 'sɜːvɪkᵊl) *adj* of or relating to the neck or cervix. [C17: from NL, from L *cervīx* neck]

cervical smear *n Med.* a smear taken from the neck (cervix) of the uterus for detection of cancer. See also **Pap test** *or* **smear.**

cervine ('sɜːvaɪn) *adj* resembling or relating to a deer. [C19: from L *cervīnus*, from *cervus* a deer]

cervix ('sɜːvɪks) *n, pl* **cervixes** *or* **cervices** (sə'vaɪsiːz). **1** the technical name for **neck. 2** any necklike part, esp. the lower part of the uterus that extends into the vagina. [C18: from L]

cesium ('siːzɪəm) *n* the usual US spelling of **caesium.**

cess[1] (sɛs) *n Brit.* any of several special taxes, such as a land tax in Scotland. [C16: short for ASSESSMENT]

cess[2] (sɛs) *n* an Irish slang word for **luck** (esp. in **bad cess to you!**). [C19: prob. from CESS[1]]

cessation ❶ (sɛ'seɪʃən) *n* a ceasing or stopping; pause: *temporary cessation of hostilities.* [C14: from L, from *cessāre* to be idle, from *cēdere* to yield]

cession ('sɛʃən) *n* **1** the act of ceding. **2** something that is ceded, esp. land or territory. [C14: from L *cessiō*, from *cēdere* to yield]

cessionary ('sɛʃənərɪ) *n, pl* **cessionaries.** *Law.* a person to whom something is transferred.

cesspool ('sɛs,puːl) *or* **cesspit** ('sɛs,pɪt) *n* **1** Also called: **sink, sump.** a covered cistern, etc., for collecting and storing sewage or waste water. **2** a filthy or corrupt place: *a cesspool of iniquity.* [C17: ? changed from earlier *cesperalle*, from OF *souspirail* vent, air, from *soupirer* to sigh]

cestoid ('sɛstɔɪd) *adj* (esp. of tapeworms and similar animals) ribbon-like in form.

cesura (sɪ'zjʊərə) *n, pl* **cesuras** *or* **cesurae** (-riː). *Prosody.* a variant spelling of **caesura.**

cetacean (sɪ'teɪʃən) *adj also* **cetaceous. 1** of or belonging to an order of aquatic placental mammals having no hind limbs and a blowhole for breathing: includes toothed whales (dolphins, porpoises, etc.) and whalebone whales (rorquals, etc.). ◆ *n* **2** a whale. [C19: from NL, ult. from L *cētus* whale, from Gk *kētos*]

cetane ('siːteɪn) *n* a colourless insoluble liquid hydrocarbon used in the determination of the cetane number of diesel fuel. Also called: **hexadecane.** [C19: from L *cētus* whale + -ANE]

cetane number *n* a measure of the quality of a diesel fuel expressed as the percentage of cetane. Also called: **cetane rating.** Cf. **octane number.**

cetrimide ('sɛtrɪ,maɪd) *n* an ammonium compound used as a detergent and, having powerful antiseptic properties, for sterilizing surgical instruments, cleaning wounds, etc.

Cf *the chemical symbol for* californium.

CF *abbrev. for* Canadian Forces.

cf. *abbrev. for:* **1** (in bookbinding, etc.) calfskin. **2** compare. [L: *confer*]

CFB *abbrev. for* Canadian Forces Base.

CFC *abbrev. for* chlorofluorocarbon.

CFL *abbrev. for* Canadian Football League.

CFS *abbrev. for* chronic fatigue syndrome.

cg *abbrev. for* centigram.

CGBR *abbrev. for* Central Government Borrowing Requirement.

cgs units *pl n* a metric system of units based on the centimetre, gram, and second. For scientific and technical purposes these units have been replaced by SI units.

CGT *abbrev. for* Capital Gains Tax.

CH 1 *abbrev. for* Companion of Honour (a Brit. title). **2** *international car registration for* Switzerland. [from F *Confédération Helvétique*]

ch. *abbrev. for:* **1** chain (unit of measure). **2** chapter. **3** *Chess.* check. **4** chief. **5** church.

Chablis ('ʃæblɪ) *n* (*sometimes not cap.*) a dry white wine made around Chablis, France.

cha-cha-cha (,tʃɑːtʃɑː'tʃɑː) *or* **cha-cha** *n* **1** a modern ballroom dance from Latin America with small steps and swaying hip movements. **2** a piece of music composed for this dance. ◆ *vb* (*intr*) **3** to perform this dance. [C20: from American (Cuban) Sp.]

chaconne (ʃə'kɒn) *n* **1** a musical form consisting of a set of continuous variations upon a ground bass. **2** *Arch.* a dance in slow triple time probably originating in Spain. [C17: from F, from Sp. *chacona*]

chafe ❶ (tʃeɪf) *vb* **chafes, chafing, chafed. 1** to make or become sore or worn by rubbing. **2** (*tr*) to warm (the hands, etc.) by rubbing. **3** to irritate or be irritated or impatient. **4** (*intr; often foll. by on, against, etc.*) to rub. ◆ *n* **5** a soreness or irritation caused by friction. [C14: from OF *chaufer* to warm, ult. from L, from *calēre* to be warm + *facere* to make]

chafer ('tʃeɪfə) *n* any of various beetles, such as the cockchafer. [OE *ceafor*]

chaff[1] ❶ (tʃɑːf) *n* **1** the mass of husks, etc., separated from the seeds during threshing. **2** finely cut straw and hay used to feed cattle. **3** something of little worth; rubbish: *to separate the wheat from the chaff.* **4** thin strips of metallic foil released into the earth's atmosphere to deflect radar signals and prevent detection. [OE *ceaf*]
▸ **'chaffy** *adj*

chaff[2] ❶ (tʃɑːf) *n* **1** light-hearted teasing or joking; banter. ◆ *vb* **2** to tease good-naturedly. [C19: prob. slang var. of CHAFE]
▸ **'chaffer** *n*

chaffer ('tʃæfə) *vb* **1** (*intr*) to haggle or bargain. **2** to chatter, talk, or say idly. ◆ *n* **3** haggling or bargaining. [C13 *chaffare*, from *chep* bargain + *fare* journey]
▸ **'chafferer** *n*

chaffinch ('tʃæfɪntʃ) *n* a European finch with black-and-white wings and, in the male, a reddish body and blue-grey head. [OE *ceaffinc*, from *ceaf* CHAFF[1] + *finc* FINCH]

chafing dish *n* a vessel with a heating apparatus beneath it, for cooking or keeping food warm at the table.

chagrin ❶ ('ʃægrɪn) *n* **1** a feeling of annoyance or mortification. ◆ *vb* **2** to embarrass and annoy. [C17: from F *chagrin, chagriner*, from ?]

chain ❶ (tʃeɪn) *n* **1** a flexible length of metal links, used for confining, connecting, etc., or in jewellery. **2** (*usually pl*) anything that confines or restrains: *the chains of poverty.* **3** (*usually pl*) a set of metal links that fit over the tyre of a motor vehicle to reduce skidding on an icy surface. **4** a series of related or connected facts, events, etc. **5a** a number of establishments such as hotels, shops, etc., having the same owner or management. **5b** (*as modifier*): *a chain store.* **6** Also called: **Gunter's chain.** a unit of length equal to 22 yards. **7** Also called: **engineer's chain.** a unit of length equal to 100 feet. **8** Also called: **nautical chain.** a unit of length equal to 15 feet. **9** *Chem.* two or more atoms or groups bonded together so that the resulting molecule, ion, or radical resembles a chain. **10** *Geog.* a series of natural features, esp. mountain ranges. ◆ *vb* **11** (*tr; often foll. by up*) to confine, tie, or make fast with or as if with a chain. [C13: from OF, ult. from L; see CATENA]

chain gang *n US.* a group of convicted prisoners chained together.

chain letter *n* a letter, often with a request for and promise of money, that is sent to many people who add to or recopy it and send it on.

chain mail *n* **a** another term for **mail**[2] (sense 1). **b** (*as modifier*): *a chain-mail hood.*

chain printer *n* a line printer in which the type is on a continuous chain.

chain reaction *n* **1** a process in which a neutron colliding with an atomic nucleus causes fission and the ejection of one or more other neutrons. **2** a chemical reaction in which the product of one step is a reactant in the following step. **3** a series of events, each of which precipitates the next.
▸ **,chain-re'act** *vb* (*intr*)

chain saw *n* a motor-driven saw in which the cutting teeth form links in a continuous chain.

chain-smoke *vb* **chain-smokes, chain-smoking, chain-smoked.** to smoke (cigarettes, etc.) continually, esp. lighting one from the preceding one.
▸ **chain smoker** *n*

chain stitch *n* **1** a looped embroidery stitch resembling the links of a chain. ◆ *vb* **chain-stitch. 2** to sew (something) with this stitch.

chainwheel ('tʃeɪn,wiːl) *n* (esp. on a bicycle) a toothed wheel that transmits drive via the chain.

chair (tʃɛə) *n* **1** a seat with a back on which one person sits, typically

THESAURUS

clare, endorse, guarantee, notify, show, testify, validate, verify, vouch, witness

certitude *n* = **certainty**, assurance, confidence, conviction

cessation *n* = **ceasing**, abeyance, arrest, break, discontinuance, ending, entr'acte, halt, halting, hiatus, intermission, interruption, interval, let-up (*inf.*), pause, recess, remission, respite, rest, standstill, stay, stoppage, suspension, termination, time off

chafe *vb* **1** = **rub**, abrade, rasp, scrape, scratch **3** = **be annoyed**, be angry, be exasperated, be impatient, be incensed, be inflamed, be irritated, be narked (*Brit., Austral., & NZ sl.*), be offended, be ruffled, be vexed, fret, fume, rage, worry

chaff[1] *n* **1, 3** = **waste**, dregs, glumes, hulls, husks, refuse, remains, rubbish, trash

chaff[2] *n* **1** = **teasing**, badinage, banter, joking, josh (*sl., chiefly US & Canad.*), persiflage, raillery ◆ *vb* **2** = **tease**, banter, deride, jeer, josh (*sl., chiefly US & Canad.*), mock, rib (*inf.*), ridicule, scoff, take the piss out of (*taboo sl.*), taunt

chagrin *n* **1** = **annoyance**, discomfiture, discomposure, displeasure, disquiet, dissatisfaction, embarrassment, fretfulness, humiliation, ill-humour, irritation, mortification, peevishness, spleen, vexation ◆ *vb* **2** = **annoy**, discomfit, discompose, displease, disquiet, dissatisfy, embarrass, humiliate, irk, irritate, mortify, peeve, vex

chain *n* **2** *usually plural* = **link**, bond, coupling, fetter, manacle, shackle, union **4** = **series**, concatenation, progression, sequence, set, string, succession, train ◆ *vb* **11** = **bind**, confine, en-

having four legs and often having arms. **2** an official position of authority. **3** the chairman of a debate or meeting: *the speaker addressed the chair.* **4** a professorship. **5** *Railways.* an iron or steel cradle bolted to a sleeper in which the rail is locked. **6** short for **sedan chair. 7 take the chair.** to preside as chairman for a meeting, etc. **8 the chair.** *Inf.* the electric chair. ◆ *vb (tr)* **9** to preside over (a meeting). **10** *Brit.* to carry aloft in a sitting position after a triumph. **11** to provide with a chair of office. **12** to install in a chair. [C13: from OF, from L *cathedra,* from Gk *kathedra,* from *kata-* down + *hedra* seat]

chairlift ('tʃɛəˌlɪft) *n* a series of chairs suspended from a power-driven cable for conveying people, esp. skiers, up a mountain.

chairman ⓘ ('tʃɛəmən) *n, pl* **chairmen.** a person who presides over a company's board of directors, a committee, a debate, etc. Also: **chair, chairperson,** *or (fem)* **chairwoman.**

> **USAGE NOTE** *Chairman* can seem inappropriate when applied to a woman, while *chairwoman* can be offensive. *Chair* and *chairperson* can be applied to either a man or a woman; *chair* is generally preferred to *chairperson.*

chaise (ʃeɪz) *n* **1** a light open horse-drawn carriage, esp. one with two wheels. **2** short for **post chaise** and **chaise longue.** [C18: from F, var. of OF *chaiere* CHAIR]

chaise longue ('ʃeɪz 'lɒŋ) *n, pl* **chaise longues** *or* **chaises longues** ('ʃeɪz 'lɒŋ). a long low chair with a back and single armrest. [C19: from F: long chair]

chakra ('tʃækrə, 'tʃʌkrə) *n* (in yoga) any of the seven major energy centres in the human body. [C19: from Sansk. *cakra* wheel, circle]

chalaza (kə'leɪzə) *n, pl* **chalazas** *or* **chalazae** (-ziː). one of a pair of spiral threads holding the yolk of a bird's egg in position. [C18: NL, from Gk: hailstone]

chalcedony (kæl'sɛdənɪ) *n, pl* **chalcedonies.** a form of quartz with crystals arranged in parallel fibres: a gemstone. [C15: from LL, from Gk *khalkēdōn* a precious stone, ? after *Khalkēdōn* Chalcedon, town in Asia Minor]
▸**chalcedonic** (ˌkælsɪ'dɒnɪk) *adj*

chalcolithic (ˌkælkə'lɪθɪk) *adj Archaeol.* of or relating to the period in which both stone and bronze tools were used. [C19: from Gk *khalkos* copper + *lithos* stone]

chalcopyrite (ˌkælkə'paɪraɪt) *n* a common ore of copper, a crystalline sulphide of copper and iron. Formula: $CuFeS_2$. Also called: **copper pyrites.**

chaldron ('tʃɔːldrən) *n* a unit of capacity equal to 36 bushels. [C17: from OF *chauderon* CAULDRON]

chalet ('ʃæleɪ) *n* **1** a type of wooden house of Swiss origin, with wide projecting eaves. **2** a similar house used as a ski lodge, etc. [C19: from F (Swiss dialect)]

chalice ('tʃælɪs) *n* **1** *Poetic.* a drinking cup; goblet. **2** *Christianity.* a gold or silver cup containing the wine at Mass. **3** a cup-shaped flower. [C13: from OF, from L *calix* cup]

chalk (tʃɔːk) *n* **1** a soft fine-grained white sedimentary rock consisting of nearly pure calcium carbonate, containing minute fossil fragments of marine organisms. **2** a piece of chalk, or substance like chalk, often coloured, used for writing and drawing on blackboards. **3 as alike** (*or* **different**) **as chalk and cheese.** *Inf.* totally different in essentials. **4 by a long chalk.** *Brit. inf.* by far. **5 not by a long chalk.** *Brit. inf.* by no means. **6** (*modifier*) made of chalk. ◆ *vb* **7** to draw or mark (something) with chalk. **8** (*tr*) to mark, rub, or whiten with or as with chalk. [OE *cealc,* from L *calx* limestone, from Gk *khalix* pebble]
▸**'chalk,like** *adj* ▸**'chalky** *adj* ▸**'chalkiness** *n*

chalk out *vb (tr, adv)* to outline (a plan, scheme, etc.); sketch.

chalkpit ('tʃɔːkˌpɪt) *n* a quarry for chalk.

chalk up ⓘ *vb (tr, adv) Inf.* **1** to score or register (something). **2** to credit (money) to an account, etc. (esp. in **chalk it up**).

challenge ⓘ ('tʃælɪndʒ) *vb* **challenges, challenging, challenged.** (*mainly tr*) **1** to invite or summon (someone to do something, esp. to take part in a contest). **2** (*also intr*) to call (something) into question. **3** to make demands on; stimulate: *the job challenges his ingenuity.* **4** to order (a person) to halt and be identified. **5** *Law.* to make formal objection to (a juror or jury). **6** to lay claim to (attention, etc.). **7** to inject (an experimental animal immunized with a test substance) with disease microorganisms to test for immunity to the disease. ◆ *n* **8** a call to engage in a fight, argument, or contest. **9** a questioning of a statement or fact. **10** a demanding or stimulating situation, career, etc. **11** a demand by a sentry, etc., for identification or a password. **12** *Law.* a formal objection to a person selected to serve on a jury or to the whole body of jurors. [C13: from OF *chalenge,* from L *calumnia* CALUMNY]
▸**'challengeable** *adj* ▸**'challenger** *n* ▸**'challenging** *adj*

challis ('ʃælɪ, -lɪs) *or* **challie** ('ʃælɪ) *n* a lightweight fabric of wool, cotton, etc., usually with a printed design. [C19: prob. from a surname]

chalybeate (kə'lɪbɪɪt) *adj* containing or impregnated with iron salts. [C17: from NL *chalybēātus,* ult. from Gk *khalups* iron]

chamber ⓘ ('tʃeɪmbə) *n* **1** a meeting hall, esp. one used for a legislative or judicial assembly. **2** a reception room in an official residence, palace, etc. **3** *Arch. or poetic.* a room in a private house, esp. a bedroom. **4a** a legislative, judicial, or administrative assembly. **4b** any of the houses of a legislature. **5** an enclosed space; compartment; cavity. **6** an enclosure for a cartridge in the cylinder of a revolver or for a shell in the breech of a cannon. **7** short for **chamber pot. 8** (*modifier*) of, relating to, or suitable for chamber music: *a chamber concert.* **9** (*modifier*) on a small, quasi-domestic scale. ◆ See also **chambers.** [C13: from OF, from LL *camera* room, L: vault, from Gk *kamara*]

chamberlain ('tʃeɪmbəlɪn) *n* **1** an officer who manages the household of a king. **2** the steward of a nobleman or landowner. **3** the treasurer of a municipal corporation. [C13: from OF *chamberlayn,* of Frankish origin]

chambermaid ('tʃeɪmbəˌmeɪd) *n* a woman employed to clean bedrooms, esp. in hotels.

chamber music *n* music for performance by a small group of instrumentalists.

chamber of commerce *n* (*sometimes cap.*) an organization composed mainly of local businessmen to promote, regulate, and protect their interests.

chamber orchestra *n* a small orchestra of about 25 players, used for the authentic performance of baroque and early classical music as well as modern music.

chamber pot *n* a vessel for urine, used in bedrooms.

chambers ('tʃeɪmbəz) *pl n* **1** a judge's room for hearing private cases not taken in open court. **2** (in England) the set of rooms occupied by barristers where clients are interviewed.

chambray ('ʃæmbreɪ) *n* a smooth light fabric of cotton, linen, etc., with white weft and a coloured warp. [C19: after *Cambrai;* see CAMBRIC]

chameleon (kə'miːlɪən) *n* **1** a lizard of Africa and Madagascar, having long slender legs, a prehensile tail and tongue, and the ability to change colour. **2** a changeable or fickle person. [C14: from L, from Gk *khamaileōn,* from *khamai* on the ground + *leōn* LION]
▸**chameleonic** (kəˌmiːlɪ'ɒnɪk) *adj*

chamfer ('tʃæmfə) *n* **1** a narrow flat surface at the corner of a beam, post, etc. ◆ *vb (tr)* **2** to cut such a surface on (a beam, etc.). [C16: back formation from *chamfering,* from OF, from *chant* edge (see CANT[2]) + *fraindre* to break, from L *frangere*]

chamois ('ʃæmɪ; *for senses 1 and 4* 'ʃæmwɑː) *n, pl* **chamois. 1** a sure-footed goat antelope of Europe and SW Asia, having vertical horns with backward-pointing tips. **2** a soft suede leather formerly made from this animal, now obtained from the skins of sheep and goats. **3** Also called: **chamois leather, shammy (leather), chammy (leather).** a piece of such leather or similar material used for polishing, etc. **4a** a greyish-yellow colour. **4b** (*as adj*): *a chamois stamp.* ◆ *vb (tr)* **5** to dress (leather or skin) like chamois. **6** to polish with a chamois. [C16: from OF, from LL *camox,* from ?]

chamomile ('kæməˌmaɪl) *n* a variant spelling of **camomile.**

champ[1] (tʃæmp) *vb* **1** to munch (food) noisily like a horse. **2** (when *intr,* often foll. by *on, at,* etc.) to bite (something) nervously or impatiently. **3 champ** (*or* **chafe**) **at the bit.** *Inf.* to be impatient to start work, a journey, etc. ◆ *n* **4** the act or noise of champing. [C16: prob. imit.]

champ[2] (tʃæmp) *n Inf.* short for **champion.**

champagne (ʃæm'peɪn) *n* **1** (*sometimes cap.*) a white sparkling wine produced around Reims and Épernay, France. **2** (loosely) any effervescent white wine. **3a** a pale tawny colour. **3b** (*as adj*): *champagne tights.* **4** (*modifier*) denoting a luxurious lifestyle: *a champagne capitalist.* [from *Champagne,* a region of NE France]

champagne socialist *n* a professed socialist who enjoys an extravagant lifestyle.

champers ('ʃæmpəz) *n* (*functioning as sing*) *Sl.* champagne.

champerty ('tʃæmpətɪ) *n, pl* **champerties.** *Law.* (formerly) an illegal bargain between a party to litigation and an outsider whereby the latter agrees to pay for the action and thereby share in any proceeds recovered. [C14: from Anglo-F *champartie,* from OF *champart* share of produce, from *champ* field + *part* share]

champion ⓘ ('tʃæmpɪən) *n* **1a** a person, plant, or animal that has defeated all others in a competition: *a chess champion.* **1b** (*as modifier*): *a champion team; a champion marrow.* **2** a person who defends a person or cause: *champion of the underprivileged.* **3** (formerly) a knight who did battle for another, esp. a king or queen. ◆ *adj* **4** *N English dialect.* excellent. ◆ *adv* **5** *N English dialect.* very well. ◆ *vb (tr)* **6** to support: *we*

THESAURUS

slave, fetter, gyve (*arch.*), handcuff, manacle, restrain, shackle, tether, trammel, unite

chairman *n* = **director**, chairperson, chairwoman, master of ceremonies, president, presider, speaker, spokesman, toastmaster

chalk up *vb Informal* **1** = **score**, accumulate, achieve, attain, credit, enter, gain, log, mark, record, register, tally, win

challenge *vb* **1-6** = **test**, accost, arouse, beard, brave, call out, call (someone's) bluff, claim, confront, dare, defy, demand, dispute, face off (*sl.*), impugn, investigate, object to, provoke, question, require, stimulate, summon, tackle, tax, throw down the gauntlet, try ◆ *n* **8, 9** = **test**, confrontation, dare, defiance, face-off (*sl.*), interrogation, provocation, question, summons to contest, trial, ultimatum

chamber *n* **1-3, 5** = **room**, apartment, bedroom, cavity, compartment, cubicle, enclosure, hall, hollow **4a** = **council**, assembly, legislative body, legislature

champion *n* **1** = **winner**, challenger, conqueror, hero, nonpareil, title holder, victor, warrior **2** = **defender**, backer, guardian, patron, protector, upholder, vindicator ◆ *vb* **6** = **support**, advocate, back, commend, defend, encourage, espouse, fight for, promote, stick up for (*inf.*), uphold

champion the cause of liberty. [C13: from OF, from LL *campiō*, from L *campus* field]

championship ('tʃæmpɪənˌʃɪp) *n* **1** (*sometimes pl*) any of various contests held to determine a champion. **2** the title of being a champion. **3** support for a cause, person, etc.

champlevé *French.* (ʃɑ̃lve) *adj* **1** of a process of enamelling by which grooves are cut into a metal base and filled with enamel colours. ◆ *n* **2** an object enamelled by this process. [C19: from *champ* field (level surface) + *levé* raised]

Chanc. *abbrev. for:* **1** Chancellor. **2** Chancery.

chance ❶ (tʃɑːns) *n* **1a** the unknown and unpredictable element that causes an event to result in a certain way rather than another, spoken of as a real force. **1b** (*as modifier*): *a chance meeting.* Related adj: **fortuitous. 2** fortune; luck; fate. **3** an opportunity or occasion. **4** a risk; gamble. **5** the extent to which an event is likely to occur; probability. **6** an unpredicted event, esp. a fortunate one. **7 by chance.** accidentally: *he slipped by chance.* **8 on the (off) chance.** acting on the (remote) possibility. ◆ *vb* **chances, chancing, chanced. 9** (*tr*) to risk; hazard. **10** (*intr*) to happen by chance: *I chanced to catch sight of her.* **11 chance on** (*or* **upon**). to come upon by accident. **12 chance one's arm.** to attempt to do something although the chance of success may be slight. [C13: from OF, from *cheoir* to occur, from L *cadere*]
▸**'chanceful** *adj*

chancel ('tʃɑːnsəl) *n* the part of a church containing the altar, sanctuary, and choir. [C14: from OF, from L *cancellī* (pl) lattice]

chancellery *or* **chancellory** ('tʃɑːnsələrɪ) *n, pl* **chancelleries** *or* **chancellories. 1** the building or room occupied by a chancellor's office. **2** the position or office of a chancellor. **3** *US.* the office of an embassy or legation. [C14: from Anglo-F *chancellerie*, from OF *chancelier* CHANCELLOR]

chancellor ('tʃɑːnsələ) *n* **1** the head of the government in several European countries. **2** *US.* the president of a university. **3** *Brit. & Canad.* the honorary head of a university. Cf. **vice chancellor. 4** *Christianity.* a clergyman acting as the law officer of a bishop. [C11: from Anglo-F *chanceler*, from LL *cancellārius* porter, from L *cancellī* lattice]
▸**'chancellorˌship** *n*

Chancellor of the Exchequer *n Brit.* the cabinet minister responsible for finance.

chance-medley *n Law.* a sudden quarrel in which one party kills another. [C15: from Anglo-F *chance medlee* mixed chance]

chancer ('tʃɑːnsə) *n Sl.* an unscrupulous or dishonest opportunist. [C19: from CHANCE + -ER[1]]

chancery ('tʃɑːnsərɪ) *n, pl* **chanceries.** (*usually cap.*) **1** Also called: **Chancery Division.** (in England) the Lord Chancellor's court, now a division of the High Court of Justice. **2** Also called: **court of chancery.** (in the US) a court of equity. **3** *Brit.* the political section or offices of an embassy or legation. **4** another name for **chancellery. 5** a court of public records. **6** *Christianity.* a diocesan office under the supervision of a bishop's chancellor. **7 in chancery. 7a** *Law.* (of a suit) pending in a court of equity. **7b** in an awkward situation. [C14: shortened from CHANCELLERY]

chancre ('ʃæŋkə) *n Pathol.* a small hard growth, which is the first sign of syphilis. [C16: from F, from L: CANCER]
▸**'chancrous** *adj*

chancroid ('ʃæŋkrɔɪd) *n* **1** a soft venereal ulcer, esp. of the male genitals. ◆ *adj* **2** relating to or resembling a chancroid or chancre.

chancy ❶ *or* **chancey** ('tʃɑːnsɪ) *adj* **chancier, chanciest.** *Inf.* uncertain; risky.

chandelier (ˌʃændɪ'lɪə) *n* an ornamental hanging light with branches and holders for several candles or bulbs. [C17: from F: candleholder, from L CANDELABRUM]

chandler ('tʃɑːndlə) *n* **1** a dealer in a specified trade or merchandise: *ship's chandler.* **2** a person who makes or sells candles. [C14: from OF *chandelier* one who makes or deals in candles, from *chandelle* CANDLE]
▸**'chandlery** *n*

Chandrasekhar limit *n Astron.* the upper limit to the mass of a white dwarf, equal to 1.44 solar masses. A star with greater mass will continue to collapse to form a neutron star. [C20: named after S. *Chandrasekhar* (1910–95), US astronomer who calculated it]

change ❶ (tʃeɪndʒ) *vb* **changes, changing, changed. 1** to make or become different; alter. **2** (*tr*) to replace with or exchange for another: *to change one's name.* **3** (sometimes foll. by *to* or *into*) to transform or convert or be transformed or converted. **4** to give and receive (something) in return: *to change places.* **5** (*tr*) to give or receive (money) in exchange for the equivalent sum in a smaller denomination or in a different currency. **6** (*tr*) to remove or replace the coverings of: *to change a baby.* **7** (when *intr*, may be foll. by *into* or *out of*) to put on other clothes. **8** to operate (the gear lever of a motor vehicle): *to change gear.* **9** to alight from (one bus, train, etc.) and board another. ◆ *n* **10** the act or fact of changing or being changed. **11** a variation or modification. **12** the substitution of one thing for another. **13** anything that is or may be substituted for something else. **14** variety or novelty (esp. in **for a change**). **15** a different set, esp. of clothes. **16** money given or received in return for its equivalent in a larger denomination or in a different currency. **17** the balance of money when the amount tendered is larger than the amount due. **18** coins of a small denomination. **19** (*often cap.*) *Arch.* a place where merchants meet to transact business. **20** the act of passing from one state or phase to another. **21** the transition from one phase of the moon to the next. **22** the order in which a peal of bells may be rung. **23 get no change out of (someone).** *Sl.* not to be successful in attempts to exploit (someone). **24 ring the changes.** to vary the manner or performance of an action that is often repeated. ◆ See also **change down, changeover, change up.** [C13: from OF, from L *cambīre* to exchange, barter]
▸**'changeful** *adj* ▸**'changeless** *adj* ▸**'changer** *n*

changeable ❶ ('tʃeɪndʒəbəl) *adj* **1** able to change or be changed: *changeable weather.* **2** varying in colour as when viewed from different angles.
▸**ˌchangea'bility** *n* ▸**'changeably** *adv*

change down *vb* (*intr, adv*) to select a lower gear when driving.

changeling ('tʃeɪndʒlɪŋ) *n* a child believed to have been exchanged by fairies for the parents' true child.

change of life *n* a nontechnical name for **menopause.**

changeover ('tʃeɪndʒˌəʊvə) *n* **1** an alteration or complete reversal from one method, system, or product to another. **2** a reversal of a situation, attitude, etc. **3** *Sport.* the act of transferring to or being relieved by a team-mate in a relay race, as by handing over a baton, etc. ◆ *vb* **change over.** (*adv*) **4** to adopt (a different position or attitude): *the driver and navigator changed over.*

change-ringing *n* the art of bell-ringing in which a set of bells is rung in an established order which is then changed.

change up *vb* (*intr, adv*) to select a higher gear when driving.

channel ❶ ('tʃænəl) *n* **1** a broad strait connecting two areas of sea. **2** the bed or course of a river, stream, or canal. **3** a navigable course through a body of water. **4** (*often pl*) a means or agency of access, communication, etc.: *through official channels.* **5** a course into which something can be directed or moved. **6** *Electronics.* **6a** a band of radio frequencies assigned for a particular purpose, esp. the broadcasting of a television signal. **6b** a path for an electrical signal: *a stereo set has two channels.* **7** a tubular passage for fluids. **8** a groove, as in the shaft of a column. **9** *Computing.* **9a** a path along which data can be transmitted. **9b** one of the lines along the length of a paper tape on which information can be stored in the form of punched holes. ◆ *vb* **channels, channelling, channelled** *or US* **channels, channeling, channeled. 10** to make or cut channels in (something). **11** (*tr*) to guide into or convey through a channel or channels: *information was channelled through to them.* **12** to serve as a medium through whom the spirit of (a person of a former age) allegedly communicates with the living. **13** (*tr*) to form a groove or flute in (a column, etc.). [C13: from OF, from L *canālis* pipe, groove, conduit]

Channel ('tʃænəl) *n* **the.** the English Channel, between England and France.

channel-hop *vb* **channel-hops, channel-hopping, channel-hopped.** (*intr*) to change television channels repeatedly using a remote control device.

chanson de geste *French.* (ʃɑ̃sɔ̃ də ʒɛst) *n* one of a genre of Old French epic poems, the most famous of which is the *Chanson de Roland.* [lit.: song of exploits]

chant ❶ (tʃɑːnt) *n* **1** a simple song. **2** a short simple melody in which

THESAURUS

chance *n* **1a, 2** = **luck**, accident, casualty, coincidence, contingency, destiny, fate, fortuity, fortune, misfortune, peril, providence ◆ *modifier* **1b** = **accidental**, casual, contingent, fortuitous, inadvertent, incidental, random, serendipitous, unforeseeable, unforeseen, unintentional, unlooked-for ◆ *n* **3** = **opportunity**, occasion, opening, scope, time, window **4** = **risk**, gamble, hazard, jeopardy, speculation, uncertainty **5** = **probability**, liability, likelihood, odds, possibility, prospect ◆ *vb* **9** = **risk**, endanger, gamble, go out on a limb, hazard, jeopardize, skate on thin ice, stake, try, venture, wager **10** = **happen**, befall, betide, come about, come to pass, fall out, occur
Antonyms *n* ≠ **probability:** certainty, design, impossibility, improbability, intention, surety, unlikelihood ◆ *modifier* ≠ **accidental:** arranged, deliberate, designed, expected, foreseen, intentional, planned

chancy *adj Informal* = **risky**, dangerous, dicey (*inf., chiefly Brit.*), dodgy (*Brit., Austral., & NZ sl.*), hazardous, perilous, problematical, speculative, uncertain
Antonyms *adj* certain, reliable, safe, secure, sound, stable, sure

change *vb* **1, 3** = **alter**, convert, diversify, fluctuate, metamorphose, moderate, modify, mutate, reform, remodel, reorganize, restyle, shift, transform, transmute, vacillate, vary, veer **2** = **exchange**, alternate, barter, convert, displace, interchange, remove, replace, substitute, swap, trade, transmit ◆ *n* **10** = **alteration**, difference, innovation, metamorphosis, modification, mutation, permutation, revolution, transformation, transition, transmutation, vicissitude **12** = **exchange**, conversion, interchange, substitution, swap, trade **14** = **variety**, break (*inf.*), departure, diversion, novelty, variation, whole new ball game (*inf.*)
Antonyms *vb* ≠ **alter:** hold, keep, remain, stay ◆ *n* ≠ **alteration, variety:** constancy, invariability, monotony, permanence, stability, uniformity

changeable *adj* **1** = **variable**, capricious, changeful, chequered, erratic, fickle, fitful, fluid, inconstant, irregular, kaleidoscopic, mercurial, mobile, mutable, protean, shifting, temperamental, uncertain, uneven, unpredictable, unreliable, unsettled, unstable, unsteady, vacillating, versatile, volatile, wavering, whimsical
Antonyms *adj* constant, invariable, irreversible, regular, reliable, stable, steady, unchangeable

changeless *adj* **10, 11** = **unchanging**, abiding, consistent, constant, eternal, everlasting, fixed, immovable, immutable, permanent, perpetual, regular, reliable, resolute, settled, stationary, steadfast, steady, unalterable, uniform, unvarying

channel *n* **4, 5** = **route**, approach, artery, avenue, course, means, medium, path, way **7, 8** = **passage**, canal, chamber, conduit, duct, fluting, furrow, groove, gutter, main, route, strait ◆ *vb* **11** = **direct**, conduct, convey, guide, transmit

chant *n* **1-3** = **song**, carol, chorus, melody,

several words or syllables are assigned to one note. **3** a psalm or canticle performed by using such a melody. **4** a rhythmic or repetitious slogan, usually spoken or sung, as by sports supporters, etc. ◆ *vb* **5** to sing or recite (a psalm, etc.) as a chant. **6** to intone (a slogan). [C14: from OF *chanter* to sing, from L *cantāre,* frequentative of *canere* to sing]
▸**'chanting** *n, adj*

chanter ('tʃɑːntə) *n* the pipe on a set of bagpipes on which the melody is played.

chanterelle (ˌtʃæntə'rɛl) *n* any of a genus of fungi having an edible yellow funnel-shaped mushroom. [C18: from F, from L *cantharus* drinking vessel, from Gk *kantharos*]

chanteuse (*French* ʃɑ̃tøz) *n* a female singer, esp. in a nightclub or cabaret. [F: singer]

chanticleer (ˌtʃæntɪ'klɪə) *n* a name for a cock, used esp. in fables. [C13: from OF, from *chanter cler* to sing clearly]

chantry ('tʃɑːntrɪ) *n, pl* **chantries.** *Christianity.* **1** an endowment for the singing of Masses for the soul of the founder. **2** a chapel or altar so endowed. [C14: from OF, from *chanter* to sing; see CHANT]

chanty ('ʃæntɪ, 'tʃæn-) *n, pl* **chanties.** a variant of **shanty**[2].

Chanukah *or* **Hanukkah** ('hɑːnəkə, -nʊˌkɑː) *n* the eight-day Jewish festival of lights commemorating the rededication of the temple by Judas Maccabaeus in 165 B.C. Also called: **Feast of Dedication, Feast of Lights.** [from Heb., lit.: a dedication]

chaology (keɪ'ɒlədʒɪ) *n* the study of chaos theory.
▸**cha'ologist** *n*

chaos Ⓣ ('keɪɒs) *n* **1** (*usually cap.*) the disordered formless matter supposed to have existed before the ordered universe. **2** complete disorder; utter confusion. [C15: from L, from Gk *khaos*]
▸**chaotic** (keɪ'ɒtɪk) *adj* ▸**cha'otically** *adv*

chaos theory *n* a theory, applied in various branches of science, that apparently random phenomena have underlying order.

chap[1] (tʃæp) *vb* **chaps, chapping, chapped.** **1** (of the skin) to make or become raw and cracked, esp. by exposure to cold. ◆ *n* **2** (*usually pl*) a cracked patch on the skin. [C14: prob. of Gmc origin]

chap[2] Ⓣ (tʃæp) *n Inf.* a man or boy; fellow. [C16 (in the sense: buyer): shortened from CHAPMAN]

chap[3] (tʃɒp, tʃæp) *n* a less common word for **chop**[3].

chaparejos *or* **chaparajos** (ˌʃæpə'reɪəʊs) *pl n* another name for **chaps.** [from Mexican Sp.]

chaparral (ˌtʃæpə'ræl, ˌʃæp-) *n* (in the southwestern US) a dense growth of shrubs and trees. [C19: from Sp., from *chaparra* evergreen oak]

chapati *or* **chapatti** (tʃə'pætɪ, -'pɑːtɪ) *n, pl* **chapati, chapatis, chapaties** *or* **chapatti, chapattis, chapatties.** (in Indian cookery) a flat unleavened bread resembling a pancake. [from Hindi]

chapbook ('tʃæpˌbʊk) *n* a book of popular ballads, stories, etc., formerly sold by chapmen.

chapel ('tʃæpᵊl) *n* **1** a place of Christian worship, esp. with a separate altar, in a church or cathedral. **2** a similar place of worship in a large house or institution, such as a college. **3** a church subordinate to a parish church. **4** (in Britain) **4a** a Nonconformist place of worship. **4b** Nonconformist religious practices or doctrine. **5a** the members of a trade union in a newspaper office, printing house, etc. **5b** a meeting of these members. [C13: from OF, from LL *cappella,* dim. of *cappa* cloak (see CAP); orig. the sanctuary where the cloak of St Martin was kept]

chaperon Ⓣ *or* **chaperone** ('ʃæpəˌrəʊn) *n* **1** (esp. formerly) an older or married woman who accompanies or supervises a young unmarried woman on social occasions. ◆ *vb* **chaperons, chaperoning, chaperoned** *or* **chaperones, chaperoning, chaperoned.** **2** to act as a chaperon to. [C14: from OF, from *chape* hood; see CAP]
▸**'chaperˌonage** *n*

chapfallen ('tʃæpˌfɔːlən) *or* **chopfallen** *adj* dejected; downhearted. [C16: from CHOPS + FALLEN]

chaplain ('tʃæplɪn) *n* a Christian clergyman attached to a chapel of an institution or ministering to a military body, etc. [C12: from OF, from LL, from *cappella* CHAPEL]
▸**'chaplaincy** *n*

chaplet Ⓣ ('tʃæplɪt) *n* **1** an ornamental wreath of flowers worn on the head. **2** a string of beads. **3** *RC Church.* **3a** a string of prayer beads constituting one third of the rosary. **3b** the prayers counted on this string. **4** a narrow moulding in the form of a string of beads; astragal. [C14: from OF, from *chapel* hat]
▸**'chapleted** *adj*

chapman ('tʃæpmən) *n, pl* **chapmen.** *Arch.* a trader, esp. an itinerant pedlar. [OE *cēapman,* from *cēap* buying and selling]

chappie ('tʃæpɪ) *n Inf.* another word for **chap**[2].

chaps (tʃæps, ʃæps) *pl n* leather overleggings without a seat, worn by cowboys. Also called: **chaparajos, chaparejos.** [C19: shortened from CHAPAREJOS]

chapter Ⓣ ('tʃæptə) *n* **1** a division of a written work. **2** a sequence of events: *a chapter of disasters.* **3** a period in a life, history, etc. **4** a numbered reference to that part of a Parliamentary session which relates to a specified Act of Parliament. **5** a branch of some societies, clubs, etc. **6** the collective body or a meeting of the canons of a cathedral or of the members of a monastic or knightly order. **7 chapter and verse.** exact authority for an action or statement. ◆ *vb* **8** (*tr*) to divide into chapters. [C13: from OF *chapitre,* from L *capitulum,* lit.: little head, hence, section of writing, from *caput* head]

chapterhouse ('tʃæptəˌhaʊs) *n* **1** the building in which a chapter meets. See **chapter** (sense 6). **2** *US.* the meeting place of a college fraternity or sorority.

char[1] Ⓣ (tʃɑː) *vb* **chars, charring, charred.** **1** to burn or be burned partially; scorch. **2** (*tr*) to reduce (wood) to charcoal by partial combustion. [C17: short for CHARCOAL]

char[2] *or* **charr** (tʃɑː) *n, pl* **char, chars** *or* **charr, charrs.** any of various troutlike fishes occurring in cold lakes and northern seas. [C17: from ?]

char[3] (tʃɑː) *n* **1** *Inf.* short for **charwoman.** ◆ *vb* **chars, charring, charred.** **2** (*intr*) *Brit. inf.* to do cleaning as a job. [C18: from OE *cęrran*]

char[4] (tʃɑː) *n Brit.* a slang word for **tea.** [from Chinese *ch'a*]

charabanc ('ʃærəˌbæŋ) *n Brit.* a coach, esp. for sightseeing. [C19: from F: wagon with seats]

character Ⓣ ('kærɪktə) *n* **1** the combination of traits and qualities distinguishing the individual nature of a person or thing. **2** one such distinguishing quality; characteristic. **3** moral force: *a man of character.* **4a** reputation, esp. a good reputation. **4b** (*as modifier*): *character assassination.* **5** a person represented in a play, film, story, etc.; role. **6** an outstanding person: *one of the great characters of the century.* **7** *Inf.* an odd, eccentric, or unusual person: *he's quite a character.* **8** an informal word for **person:** *a shady character.* **9** a symbol used in a writing system, such as a letter of the alphabet. **10** Also called: **sort.** *Printing.* any single letter, numeral, etc., cast as a type. **11** *Computing.* any letter, numeral, etc., which can be represented uniquely by a binary pattern. **12** a style of writing or printing. **13** *Genetics.* any structure, function, attribute, etc., in an organism that is determined by a gene or group of genes. **14** a short prose sketch of a distinctive type of person. **15 in** (*or* **out of**) **character.** typical (*or* not typical) of the apparent character of a person. [C14: from L: distinguishing mark, from Gk *kharaktēr* engraver's tool]
▸**'characterful** *adj* ▸**'characterless** *adj*

character actor *n* an actor who specializes in playing odd or eccentric characters.

character assassination *n* the act of deliberately attempting to destroy a person's reputation by defamatory remarks.

characteristic Ⓣ (ˌkærɪktə'rɪstɪk) *n* **1** a distinguishing quality, attribute, or trait. **2** *Maths.* **2a** the integral part of a common logarithm: *the characteristic of 2.4771 is 2.* **2b** another name for **exponent** (sense 4). ◆ *adj* **3** indicative of a distinctive quality, etc.; typical.
▸**ˌcharacter'istically** *adv*

characterize Ⓣ *or* **characterise** ('kærɪktəˌraɪz) *vb* **characterizes, characterizing, characterized** *or* **characterises, characterising, characterised.** (*tr*) **1** to be a characteristic of. **2** to distinguish or mark as a characteristic. **3** to describe or portray the character of.
▸**ˌcharacteri'zation** *or* **ˌcharacteri'sation** *n*

charade Ⓣ (ʃə'rɑːd) *n* **1** an act in the game of charades. **2** *Chiefly Brit.* an absurd act; travesty.

charades (ʃə'rɑːdz) *n* (*functioning as sing*) a parlour game in which one team acts out each syllable of a word, the other team having to guess the word. [C18: from F, from Provençal *charrado* chat, from *charra* chatter]

charcoal ('tʃɑːˌkəʊl) *n* **1** a black amorphous form of carbon made by heating wood or other organic matter in the absence of air. **2** a stick of this for drawing. **3** a drawing done in charcoal. **4** Also: **charcoal grey.** **4a** a dark grey colour. **4b** (*as adj*): *a charcoal suit.* ◆ *vb* **5** (*tr*) to write, draw, or blacken with charcoal. [C14: from *char* (from ?) + COAL]

THESAURUS

psalm ◆ *vb* **5** = **sing**, carol, chorus, croon, descant, intone, recite, warble

chaos *n* **2** = **disorder**, anarchy, bedlam, confusion, disorganization, entropy, lawlessness, mayhem, pandemonium, tumult
Antonyms *n* neatness, orderliness, organization, tidiness

chaotic *adj* **2** = **disordered**, anarchic, confused, deranged, disorganized, lawless, purposeless, rampageous, riotous, topsy-turvy, tumultuous, uncontrolled

chap[2] *n Informal* = **fellow**, bloke (*Brit. inf.*), character, cove, customer (*inf.*), dude (*US & Canad. inf.*), guy (*inf.*), individual, man, person, sort, type

chaperon *n* **1** = **escort**, companion, duenna, governess ◆ *vb* **2** = **escort**, accompany, attend, protect, safeguard, shepherd, watch over

chaplet *n* **1** = **garland**, bouquet, coronal, wreath

chapter *n* **1, 3** = **section**, clause, division, episode, part, period, phase, stage, topic

char[1] *vb* **1** = **scorch**, carbonize, cauterize, sear, singe

character *n* **1** = **nature**, attributes, bent, calibre, cast, complexion, constitution, disposition, individuality, kidney, make-up, marked traits, personality, quality, temper, temperament, type **3, 4a** = **reputation**, honour, integrity, rectitude, strength, uprightness **5** = **role**, part, persona, portrayal **7** = **eccentric**, card (*inf.*), nut (*sl.*), oddball (*inf.*), odd bod (*inf.*), oddity, original, queer fish (*Brit. inf.*) **8** *Informal* = **person**, fellow, guy (*inf.*), individual, sort, type **9** = **symbol**, cipher, device, emblem, figure, hieroglyph, letter, logo, mark, rune, sign, type

characteristic *n* **1** = **feature**, attribute, faculty, idiosyncrasy, mark, peculiarity, property, quality, quirk, trait ◆ *adj* **3** = **typical**, distinctive, distinguishing, idiosyncratic, individual, peculiar, representative, singular, special, specific, symbolic, symptomatic
Antonyms *adj* ≠ **typical:** rare, uncharacteristic, unrepresentative, unusual

characterize *vb* **1-3** = **identify**, brand, distinguish, indicate, inform, mark, represent, stamp, typify

charade *n* **2** = **pretence**, fake, farce, pantomime, parody, travesty

charge *vb* **3** = **accuse**, arraign, blame, im-

charcuterie (ʃɑːˈkuːtəriː) *n* **1** cooked cold meats. **2** a shop selling cooked cold meats. [F]

chard (tʃɑːd) *n* a variety of beet with large succulent leaves and thick stalks, used as a vegetable. Also called: **Swiss chard.** [C17: prob. from F *carde,* ult. from L *carduus* thistle]

Chardonnay (ˈʃɑːdəˌneɪ) *n* (*sometimes not cap.*) **1** a white grape grown in the Burgundy region of France, Australia, California, New Zealand and elsewhere, used for making wine. **2** any of various white wines made from this grape. [F]

charge ❶ (tʃɑːdʒ) *vb* **charges, charging, charged. 1** to set or demand (a price). **2** (*tr*) to enter a debit against a person or his account. **3** (*tr*) to accuse or impute a fault to (a person, etc.), as formally in a court of law. **4** (*tr*) to command; place a burden upon or assign responsibility to: *I was charged to take the message to headquarters.* **5** to make a rush at or sudden attack upon (a person or thing). **6** (*tr*) to fill (a receptacle) with the proper quantity. **7** (often foll. by *up*) to cause (an accumulator, capacitor, etc.) to take or store electricity or (of an accumulator) to have electricity fed into it. **8** to fill or be filled with matter by dispersion, solution, or absorption: *to charge water with carbon dioxide.* **9** (*tr*) to fill or suffuse with feeling, emotion, etc.: *the atmosphere was charged with excitement.* **10** (*tr*) *Law.* (of a judge) to address (a jury) authoritatively. **11** (*tr*) to load (a firearm). **12** (*tr*) *Heraldry.* to paint (a shield, banner, etc.) with a charge. ◆ *n* **13** a price charged for some article or service; cost. **14** a financial liability, such as a tax. **15** a debt or a book entry recording it. **16** an accusation or allegation, such as a formal accusation of a crime in law. **17a** an onrush, attack, or assault. **17b** the call to such an attack in battle. **18** custody or guardianship. **19** a person or thing committed to someone's care. **20a** a cartridge or shell. **20b** the explosive required to discharge a firearm. **20c** an amount of explosive to be detonated at any one time. **21** the quantity of anything that a receptacle is intended to hold. **22** *Physics.* **22a** the attribute of matter responsible for all electrical phenomena, existing in two forms: *negative charge; positive charge.* **22b** an excess or deficiency of electrons in a system. **22c** a quantity of electricity determined by the product of an electric current and the time for which it flows, measured in coulombs. **22d** the total amount of electricity stored in a capacitor or an accumulator. **23** a load or burden. **24** a duty or responsibility; control. **25** a command, injunction, or order. **26** *Heraldry.* a design depicted on heraldic arms. **27 in charge.** in command. **28 in charge of. 28a** having responsibility for. **28b** *US.* under the care of. [C13: from OF *chargier* to load, from LL *carricāre;* see CARRY]

chargeable (ˈtʃɑːdʒəbᵊl) *adj* **1** liable to be charged. **2** liable to result in a legal charge.

chargeable asset *n* any asset that can give rise to assessment for capital gains tax on its disposal. Exempt assets include principal private residences, cars, investments held in a personal equity plan, and government securities.

charge account *n* another term for **credit account.**

charge-cap (ˈtʃɑːdʒˌkæp) *vb* **charge-caps, charge-capping, charge-capped.** (*tr*) (in Britain) to impose on (a local authority) an upper limit on the community charge it may levy.
▸ˈ**charge-**ˌ**capping** *n*

charge card *n* a card issued by a chain store, shop, or organization, that enables customers to obtain goods and services for which they pay at a later date.

charge carrier *n* an electron, hole, or ion that transports the electric charge in an electric current.

chargé d'affaires (ˈʃɑːʒeɪ dæˈfɛə) *n, pl* **chargés d'affaires** (ˈʃɑːʒeɪ, -ʒeɪz). **1** the temporary head of a diplomatic mission in the absence of the ambassador or minister. **2** the head of a diplomatic mission of the lowest level. [C18: from F: (one) charged with affairs]

charge hand *n Brit.* a workman whose grade of responsibility is just below that of a foreman.

charge nurse *n Brit.* a nurse in charge of a ward in a hospital. Male equivalent of **sister.**

charger[1] (ˈtʃɑːdʒə) *n* **1** a person or thing that charges. **2** a horse formerly ridden into battle. **3** a device for charging an accumulator.

charger[2] (ˈtʃɑːdʒə) *n Antiques.* a large dish. [C14 *chargeour,* from *chargen* to CHARGE]

charge sheet *n Brit.* a document on which a police officer enters details of the charge against a prisoner and the court in which he will appear.

char-grilled *adj* (of food) grilled over charcoal.

charily (ˈtʃɛərɪlɪ) *adv* **1** cautiously; carefully. **2** sparingly.

chariness (ˈtʃɛərɪnɪs) *n* the state of being chary.

chariot (ˈtʃærɪət) *n* **1** a two-wheeled horse-drawn vehicle used in ancient wars, races, etc. **2** a light four-wheeled horse-drawn ceremonial carriage. **3** *Poetic.* any stately vehicle. [C14: from OF, augmentative of *char* CAR]

charioteer (ˌtʃærɪəˈtɪə) *n* the driver of a chariot.

charisma ❶ (kəˈrɪzmə) *or* **charism** (ˈkærɪzəm) *n* **1** a special personal quality or power making an individual capable of influencing or inspiring people. **2** a quality inherent in a thing, such as a particular type of car, which inspires great enthusiasm and devotion. **3** *Christianity.* a divinely bestowed power or talent. [C17: from Church L, from Gk *kharisma,* from *kharis* grace, favour]
▸**charismatic** (ˌkærɪzˈmætɪk) *adj*

charismatic movement *n Christianity.* any of various groups, within existing denominations, emphasizing the charismatic gifts of speaking in tongues, healing, etc.

charitable ❶ (ˈtʃærɪtəbᵊl) *adj* **1** generous in giving to the needy. **2** kind or lenient in one's attitude towards others. **3** of or for charity.
▸ˈ**charitableness** *n* ▸ˈ**charitably** *adv*

charitable trust *n* a trust set up for the benefit of a charity that complies with the regulations of the Charity Commissioners to enable it to be exempt from paying income tax.

charity ❶ (ˈtʃærɪtɪ) *n, pl* **charities. 1a** the giving of help, money, food, etc., to those in need. **1b** (*as modifier*): *a charity show.* **2** an institution or organization set up to provide help, money, etc., to those in need. **3** the help, money, etc., given to the needy; alms. **4** a kindly attitude towards people. **5** love of one's fellow men. [C13: from OF, from L *cāritās* affection, from *cārus* dear]

charivari (ˌʃɑːrɪˈvɑːrɪ), **shivaree,** *or esp. US.* **chivaree** *n* **1** a discordant mock serenade to newlyweds, made with pans, kettles, etc. **2** a confused noise; din. [C17: from F, from LL, from Gk *karēbaria,* from *karē* head + *barus* heavy]

charlady (ˈtʃɑːˌleɪdɪ) *n, pl* **charladies.** another name for **charwoman.**

charlatan ❶ (ˈʃɑːlətᵊn) *n* someone who professes expertise, esp. in medicine, that he does not have; quack. [C17: from F, from It., from *ciarlare* to chatter]
▸ˈ**charlatan**ˌ**ism** *or* ˈ**charlatanry** *n*

Charles's Wain (weɪn) *n* another name for the **Plough.** [OE *Carles wægn,* from *Carl* Charlemagne + *wægn* WAIN]

charleston (ˈtʃɑːlstən) *n* a fast rhythmic dance of the 1920s, characterized by kicking and by twisting of the legs from the knee down. [named after *Charleston,* South Carolina]

charley horse (ˈtʃɑːlɪ) *n US & Canad. inf.* cramp following strenuous athletic exercise. [C19: from ?]

charlie (ˈtʃɑːlɪ) *n Brit. inf.* a silly person; fool.

charlock (ˈtʃɑːlɒk) *n* a weedy Eurasian plant with hairy stems and foliage and yellow flowers. Also called: **wild mustard.** [OE *cerlic,* from ?]

charlotte (ˈʃɑːlət) *n* **1** a dessert made with fruit and layers or a casing of bread or cake crumbs, sponge cake, etc.: *apple charlotte.* **2** short for **charlotte russe.** [C19: from F, from the name *Charlotte*]

charlotte russe (ruːs) *n* a cold dessert made with sponge fingers enclosing a mixture of cream, custard, etc. [F.: Russian charlotte]

charm ❶ (tʃɑːm) *n* **1** the quality of pleasing, fascinating, or attracting people. **2** a pleasing or attractive feature. **3** a small object worn for supposed magical powers; amulet. **4** a trinket worn on a bracelet. **5** a magic spell. **6** a formula used in casting such a spell. **7** *Physics.* a property of certain elementary particles, used to explain some scattering experiments. **8 like a charm.** perfectly; successfully. ◆ *vb* **9** to attract or fascinate; delight greatly. **10** to cast a magic spell on. **11** to protect, influence, or heal, supposedly by magic. **12** (*tr*) to influence or obtain by personal charm. [C13: from OF, from L *carmen* song]
▸ˈ**charmer** *n*

THESAURUS

peach, incriminate, indict, involve **4** *Formal* = **command,** bid, commit, demand, enjoin, entrust, exhort, instruct, order, require **5** = **attack,** assail, assault, rush, stampede, storm **6** = **fill,** instil, lade, load, suffuse ◆ *n* **13** = **price,** amount, cost, damage (*inf.*), expenditure, expense, outlay, payment, rate, toll **16** = **accusation,** allegation, imputation, indictment **17a** = **attack,** assault, onset, onslaught, rush, sortie, stampede **18, 24** = **care,** custody, duty, office, responsibility, safekeeping, trust **19, 23** = **ward,** burden, concern **25** = **instruction,** canon, command, demand, dictate, direction, exhortation, injunction, mandate, order, precept
Antonyms *vb* ≠ **accuse:** absolve, acquit, clear, exonerate, pardon ≠ **attack:** back off, retreat, withdraw ◆ *n* ≠ **accusation:** absolution, acquittal, clearance, exoneration, pardon, reprieve ≠ **attack:** retreat, withdrawal

charisma *n* **1** = **charm,** allure, attraction, lure, magnetism, personality

charismatic *adj* **1** = **charming,** alluring, attractive, enticing, influential, magnetic

charitable *adj* **1** = **generous,** beneficent, benevolent, bountiful, eleemosynary, kind, lavish, liberal, philanthropic **2** = **kind,** broad-minded, considerate, favourable, forgiving, gracious, humane, indulgent, lenient, magnanimous, sympathetic, tolerant, understanding
Antonyms *adj* ≠ **generous:** mean, stingy, ungenerous ≠ **kind:** inconsiderate, mean, strict, uncharitable, unforgiving, unkind, unsympathetic

charity *n* **1** = **donations,** alms-giving, assistance, benefaction, contributions, endowment, fund, gift, hand-out, help, largesse *or* largess, philanthropy, relief **4, 5** = **kindness,** affection, Agape, altruism, benevolence, benignity, bountifulness, bounty, compassion, fellow feeling, generosity, goodness, goodwill, humanity, indulgence, love, pity, tenderheartedness
Antonyms *n* ≠ **donations:** meanness, miserliness, selfishness, stinginess ≠ **kindness:** hatred, ill will, intolerance, malice

charlatan *n* = **fraud,** cheat, con man (*inf.*), fake, fraudster, impostor, mountebank, phoney *or* phony (*inf.*), pretender, quack, sham, swindler

charm *n* **1** = **attraction,** allure, allurement, appeal, desirability, fascination, magnetism **3** = **talisman,** amulet, fetish, good-luck piece, lucky piece, trinket **5** = **spell,** enchantment, magic, sorcery ◆ *vb* **9** = **attract,** absorb, allure, beguile, bewitch, cajole, captivate, delight, enamour, enchant, enrapture, entrance, fascinate, mesmerize, please, ravish, win, win over

charming ❶ ('tʃɑːmɪŋ) *adj* delightful; pleasant; attractive.
▸**'charmingly** *adv*

charm offensive *n* a concentrated attempt to gain favour or respectability by conspicuously cooperative and obliging behaviour.

charnel ('tʃɑːnᵊl) *n* **1** short for **charnel house.** ◆ *adj* **2** ghastly; sepulchral; deathly. [C14: from OF: burial place, from L *carnālis* fleshly, CARNAL]

charnel house *n* (esp. formerly) a building or vault where corpses or bones are deposited.

Charon ('kεərən) *n Greek myth.* the ferryman who brought the dead across the rivers Styx or Acheron to Hades.

chart ❶ (tʃɑːt) *n* **1** a map designed to aid navigation by sea or air. **2** an outline map, esp. one on which weather information is plotted. **3** a sheet giving graphical, tabular, or diagrammatical information. **4 the charts.** *Inf.* the lists produced weekly of the bestselling pop singles and albums or the most popular videos. ◆ *vb* **5** (*tr*) to make a chart of. **6** (*tr*) to plot or outline the course of. **7** (*intr*) (of a record) to appear in the charts. [C16: from L, from Gk *khartēs* papyrus]
▸**'chartless** *adj*

charter ❶ ('tʃɑːtə) *n* **1** a formal document from the sovereign or state incorporating a city, bank, college, etc., and specifying its purposes and rights. **2** (*sometimes cap.*) a formal document granting or demanding certain rights or liberties. **3** a document issued by a society or an organization authorizing the establishment of a local branch or chapter. **4** a special privilege or exemption. **5** (*often cap.*) the fundamental principles of an organization; constitution. **6a** the hire or lease of transportation. **6b** (*as modifier*): *a charter flight.* ◆ *vb* (*tr*) **7** to lease or hire by charter. **8** to hire (a vehicle, etc.). **9** to grant a charter to (a group or person). [C13: from OF, from L *chartula*, dim. of *charta* leaf of papyrus; see CHART]
▸**'charterer** *n*

chartered accountant *n* (in Britain) an accountant who has passed the examinations of the Institute of Chartered Accountants.

chartered bank *n Canad.* a privately owned bank that has been incorporated by Parliament to operate in the commercial banking system.

chartered librarian *n* (in Britain) a librarian who has obtained a qualification from the Library Association in addition to a degree or diploma in librarianship.

chartered surveyor *n* (in Britain) a member of the Royal Institution of Chartered Surveyors.

Chartism ('tʃɑːtɪzəm) *n English history.* a movement (1838-48) to achieve certain political reforms, demand for which was embodied in charters presented to Parliament.
▸**'Chartist** *n, adj*

chartreuse (ʃɑː'trɜːz; *French* ʃartrøz) *n* **1** either of two liqueurs, green or yellow, made from herbs. **2a** a yellowish-green colour. **2b** (*as adj*): *a chartreuse dress.* [C19: from F, after *La Grande Chartreuse*, monastery near Grenoble, where the liqueur is produced]

charwoman ('tʃɑːˌwʊmən) *n, pl* **charwomen.** *Brit.* a woman who is hired to clean a house.

chary ❶ ('tʃεərɪ) *adj* **charier, chariest. 1** wary; careful. **2** choosy; finicky. **3** shy. **4** sparing; mean. [OE *cearig*; rel. to *caru* CARE]

Charybdis (kə'rɪbdɪs) *n* a ship-devouring monster in classical mythology, identified with a whirlpool off the coast of Sicily. Cf. **Scylla.**

chase[1] ❶ (tʃeɪs) *vb* **chases, chasing, chased. 1** to follow or run after (a person, animal, or goal) persistently or quickly. **2** (*tr*; often foll. by *out, away,* or *off*) to force to run (away); drive (out). **3** (*tr*) *Inf.* to court (a member of the opposite sex) in an unsubtle manner. **4** (*tr*; often foll. by *up*) *Inf.* to pursue persistently and energetically in order to obtain results, information, etc. **5** (*intr*) *Inf.* to hurry; rush. ◆ *n* **6** the act of chasing; pursuit. **7** any quarry that is pursued. **8** *Brit.* an unenclosed area of land where wild animals are preserved to be hunted. **9** *Brit.* the right to hunt a particular quarry over the land of others. **10 the chase.** the act or sport of hunting. **11** short for **steeplechase. 12 give chase.** to pursue (a person, animal, or thing) actively. [C13: from OF *chacier*, from Vulgar L *captiāre* (unattested), from L, from *capere* to take; see CATCH]

chase[2] (tʃeɪs) *n* **1** *Letterpress printing.* a rectangular steel frame into which metal type and blocks are locked for printing. **2** the part of a gun barrel from the trunnions to the muzzle. **3** a groove or channel, esp. to take a pipe, cable, etc. ◆ *vb* **chases, chasing, chased.** (*tr*) **4** Also: **chamfer.** to cut a groove, furrow, or flute in (a surface, column, etc.). [C17: prob. from F *châsse* frame, from OF *chas* enclosure, from LL *capsus* pen for animals; both from L *capsa* CASE[2]]

chase[3] (tʃeɪs) *vb* **chases, chasing, chased.** (*tr*) to ornament (metal) by engraving or embossing. Also: **enchase.** [C14: from OF *enchasser* ENCHASE]

chaser ('tʃeɪsə) *n* **1** a person or thing that chases. **2** a drink drunk after another of a different kind, as beer after spirits.

chasm ❶ ('kæzəm) *n* **1** a deep cleft in the ground; abyss. **2** a break in continuity; gap. **3** a wide difference in interests, feelings, etc. [C17: from L, from Gk *khasma*; rel. to *khainein* to gape]
▸**chasmal** ('kæzməl) *or* **'chasmic** *adj*

chasseur (ʃæ'sɜː) *n* **1** *French Army.* a member of a unit specially trained for swift deployment. **2** a uniformed attendant. ◆ *adj* **3** (*often postpositive*) designating or cooked in a sauce consisting of white wine and mushrooms. [C18: from F: huntsman]

Chassid *or* **Hassid** ('hæsɪd) *n pl* **Chassidim** *or* **Hassidim** ('hæsɪˌdiːm, -dɪm). **1** a sect of Jewish mystics founded in Poland about 1750, characterized by religious zeal and a spirit of prayer, joy, and charity. **2** a Jewish sect of the 2nd century B.C., formed to combat Hellenistic influences.
▸**Chassidic** *or* **Hassidic** (hə'sɪdɪk) *adj*

chassis ❶ ('ʃæsɪ) *n, pl* **chassis** (-sɪz). **1** the steel frame, wheels, and mechanical parts of a motor vehicle. **2** *Electronics.* a mounting for the circuit components of an electrical or electronic device, such as a radio or television. **3** the landing gear of an aircraft. **4** the frame on which a cannon carriage moves. [C17 (meaning: window frame): from F *châssis*, from Vulgar L *capsicum* (unattested), ult. from L *capsa* CASE[2]]

chaste ❶ (tʃeɪst) *adj* **1** not having experienced sexual intercourse; virginal. **2** abstaining from unlawful sexual intercourse. **3** abstaining from all sexual intercourse. **4** (of conduct, speech, etc.) pure; decent; modest. **5** (of style) simple; restrained. [C13: from OF, from L *castus* pure]
▸**'chastely** *adv* ▸**'chasteness** *n*

chasten ❶ ('tʃeɪsᵊn) *vb* (*tr*) **1** to bring to submission; subdue. **2** to discipline or correct by punishment. **3** to moderate; restrain. [C16: from OF, from L *castīgāre*; see CASTIGATE]
▸**'chastener** *n*

chastise ❶ (tʃæs'taɪz) *vb* **chastises, chastising, chastised.** (*tr*) **1** to punish, esp. by beating. **2** to scold severely. [C14 *chastisen*, irregularly from *chastien* to CHASTEN]
▸**chastisement** ('tʃæstɪzmənt, tʃæs'taɪz-) *n* ▸**chas'tiser** *n*

chastity ❶ ('tʃæstɪtɪ) *n* **1** the state of being chaste; purity. **2** abstention from sexual intercourse; virginity or celibacy. [C13: from OF, from L, from *castus* CHASTE]

chasuble ('tʃæzjʊbᵊl) *n Christianity.* a long sleeveless outer vestment worn by a priest when celebrating Mass. [C13: from F, from LL *casubla* garment with a hood]

chat ❶ (tʃæt) *n* **1** informal conversation or talk in an easy familiar manner. **2** an Old World songbird of the thrush family, having a harsh chattering cry. **3** any of various North American warblers. **4** any of various Australian wrens. ◆ *vb* **chats, chatting, chatted. 5** (*intr*) to talk in an easy familiar way. ◆ See also **chat up.** [C16: short for CHATTER]

chateau *or* **château** ('ʃætəʊ) *n, pl* **chateaux** (-təʊ, -təʊz), **chateaus** *or* **châteaux, châteaus. 1** a country house or castle, esp. in France. **2** (in the name of a wine) estate or vineyard. [C18: from F, from OF, from L *castellum* CASTLE]

Chateaubriand (*French* ʃɑtobrijɑ̃) *n* a thick steak cut from the fillet of beef. [C19: after F. R. *Chateaubriand* (1768–1848), F writer & statesman]

chatelaine ('ʃætəˌleɪn) *n* **1** (esp. formerly) the mistress of a castle or large household. **2** a chain or clasp worn at the waist by women in the

THESAURUS

Antonyms *n* ≠ **attraction:** repulsiveness, unattractiveness ◆ *vb* ≠ **attract:** alienate, repel, repulse

charming *adj* = **attractive**, appealing, bewitching, captivating, cute, delectable, delightful, engaging, eye-catching, fetching, irresistible, likable *or* likeable, lovely, pleasant, pleasing, seductive, winning, winsome
Antonyms *adj* disgusting, horrid, repulsive, unappealing, unattractive, unlikable *or* unlikeable, unpleasant, unpleasing

chart *n* **1-3** = **table**, blueprint, diagram, graph, map, plan, tabulation ◆ *vb* **5, 6** = **plot**, delineate, draft, graph, map out, outline, shape, sketch

charter *n* **1-4** = **document**, bond, concession, contract, deed, franchise, indenture, licence, permit, prerogative, privilege, right ◆ *vb* **7** = **hire**, commission, employ, lease, rent **9** = **authorize**, sanction

chary *adj* **1** = **wary**, careful, cautious, circumspect, guarded, heedful, leery (*sl.*), prudent, reluctant, scrupulous, slow, suspicious, uneasy **4** = **mean**, careful (*Brit.*), frugal, niggardly, parsimonious, stingy, thrifty

chase *vb* **1** = **pursue**, course, follow, hunt, run after, track **2** *often foll. by* **out, away,** *or* **off** = **drive away**, drive, expel, hound, put to flight ◆ *n* **6** = **pursuit**, hunt, hunting, race

chasm *n* **1-3** = **gulf**, abyss, alienation, breach, cavity, cleft, crack, crater, crevasse, fissure, gap, gorge, hiatus, hollow, opening, ravine, rent, rift, split, void

chassis *n* **1** = **frame**, anatomy, bodywork, framework, fuselage, skeleton, substructure

chaste *adj* **1, 4, 5** = **pure**, austere, decent, decorous, elegant, immaculate, incorrupt, innocent, modest, moral, neat, quiet, refined, restrained, simple, unaffected, uncontaminated, undefiled, unsullied, vestal, virginal, virtuous, wholesome
Antonyms *adj* blemished, corrupt, dirty, dishonourable, immoral, impure, promiscuous, self-indulgent, tainted, unchaste, unclean, unrestrained, wanton

chasten *vb* **1-3** = **subdue**, afflict, castigate, chastise, correct, cow, curb, discipline, humble, humiliate, put in one's place, repress, soften, tame

chastise *vb* **1** *Old-fashioned* = **beat**, flog, lash, lick (*inf.*), punish, scourge, whip **2** = **scold**, berate, castigate, censure, correct, discipline, upbraid
Antonyms *vb* ≠ **beat:** caress, cuddle, embrace, fondle, hug ≠ **scold:** commend, compliment, congratulate, praise, reward

chastity *n* **1, 2** = **purity**, celibacy, continence, innocence, maidenhood, modesty, virginity, virtue
Antonyms *n* debauchery, immorality, lewdness, licentiousness, profligacy, promiscuity, wantonness

chat *n* **1** = **talk**, chatter, chinwag (*Brit. inf.*), confab (*inf.*), conversation, gossip, heart-to-heart, natter, schmooze (*sl.*), tête-à-tête ◆ *vb* **5** = **talk**, chatter, chew the rag *or* fat (*sl.*), gossip, jaw (*sl.*), natter, rabbit (on) (*Brit. inf.*), schmooze (*sl.*), shoot the breeze

16th to the 19th centuries, with handkerchief, keys, etc., attached. [from F, from OF, ult. from L *castellum* CASTLE]

chatline ('tʃæt,laɪn) *n* a telephone service enabling callers to join in general conversation with each other.

chat show *n Brit.* a television or radio show in which guests are interviewed informally.

chattel ('tʃætᵊl) *n* **1** (*often pl*) *Property law.* **1a chattel personal.** an item of movable personal property, such as furniture, etc. **1b chattel real.** an interest in land less than a freehold. **2 goods and chattels.** personal property. [C13: from OF *chatel* personal property, from Med. L *capitāle* wealth]

chatter ⓣ ('tʃætə) *vb* **1** to speak (about unimportant matters) rapidly and incessantly. **2** (*intr*) (of birds, monkeys, etc.) to make rapid repetitive high-pitched noises. **3** (*intr*) (of the teeth) to click together rapidly through cold or fear. **4** (*intr*) to make rapid intermittent contact with a component, as in machining. ◆ *n* **5** idle or foolish talk; gossip. **6** the high-pitched repetitive noise made by a bird, monkey, etc. **7** the rattling of objects, such as parts of a machine. [C13: imit.]
▸'**chatterer** *n*

chatterbox ⓣ ('tʃætə,bɒks) *n Inf.* a person who talks constantly, esp. about trivial matters.

chattering classes *n Inf., often derog.* (usually preceded by *the*) those members of the educated sections of society who enjoy talking about politics, society, culture, etc.

chatty ⓣ ('tʃætɪ) *adj* **chattier, chattiest. 1** full of trivial conversation; talkative. **2** informal and friendly; gossipy.
▸'**chattily** *adv* ▸'**chattiness** *n*

chat up *vb* (*tr, adv*) *Brit. inf.* **1** to talk flirtatiously to (someone) with a view to starting a romantic or sexual relationship. **2** to talk persuasively to (a person), esp. with an ulterior motive.

chauffeur ('ʃəʊfə, ʃəʊ'fɜː) *n* **1** a person employed to drive a car. ◆ *vb* **2** to act as driver for (a person, etc.): *he chauffeured me to the stadium.* [C20: from F, lit.: stoker, from *chauffer* to heat]
▸**chauffeuse** (ʃəʊ'fɜːz) *fem n*

chaunt (tʃɔːnt) *n* a less common variant of **chant.**
▸'**chaunter** *n*

chauvinism ('ʃəʊvɪ,nɪzəm) *n* **1** aggressive or fanatical patriotism; jingoism. **2** enthusiastic devotion to a cause. **3** smug irrational belief in the superiority of one's own race, party, sex, etc.: *male chauvinism.* [C19: from F, after Nicolas *Chauvin,* F soldier under Napoleon, noted for his unthinking patriotism]
▸'**chauvinist** *n, adj* ▸,**chauvin'istic** *adj* ▸,**chauvin'istically** *adv*

cheap ⓣ (tʃiːp) *adj* **1** costing relatively little; inexpensive; of good value. **2** charging low prices: *a cheap hairdresser.* **3** of poor quality; shoddy: *cheap furniture.* **4** worth relatively little: *promises are cheap.* **5** not worthy of respect; vulgar. **6** ashamed; embarrassed: *to feel cheap.* **7** stingy; miserly. **8** *Inf.* mean; despicable: *a cheap liar.* ◆ *n* **9 on the cheap.** *Brit. inf.* at a low cost. ◆ *adv* **10** at very little cost. [OE *ceap* barter, bargain, price, property]
▸'**cheaply** *adv* ▸'**cheapness** *n*

cheapen ⓣ ('tʃiːpᵊn) *vb* **1** to make or become lower in reputation, quality, etc. **2** to make or become cheap or cheaper.
▸'**cheapener** *n*

cheap-jack *Inf.* ◆ *n* **1** a person who sells cheap and shoddy goods. ◆ *adj* **2** shoddy or inferior. [C19: from CHEAP + JACK]

cheapo ('tʃiːpəʊ) *adj Inf.* very cheap and possibly shoddy.

cheapskate ('tʃiːp,skeɪt) *n Inf.* a miserly person.

cheat ⓣ (tʃiːt) *vb* **1** to deceive or practise deceit, esp. for one's own gain; trick or swindle (someone). **2** (*intr*) to obtain unfair advantage by trickery, as in a game of cards. **3** (*tr*) to escape or avoid (something unpleasant) by luck or cunning: *to cheat death.* **4** (when *intr,* usually foll. by *on*) *Inf.* to be sexually unfaithful to (one's wife, husband, or lover). ◆ *n* **5** a person who cheats. **6** a deliberately dishonest transaction, esp. for gain; fraud. **7** *Inf.* sham. **8** *Law.* the obtaining of another's property by fraudulent means. [C14: short for ESCHEAT]
▸'**cheater** *n*

check ⓣ (tʃɛk) *vb* **1** to pause or cause to pause, esp. abruptly. **2** (*tr*) to restrain or control: *to check one's tears.* **3** (*tr*) to slow the growth or progress of; retard. **4** (*tr*) to rebuke or rebuff. **5** (when *intr,* often foll. by *on* or *up on*) to examine, investigate, or make an inquiry into (facts, a product, etc.) for accuracy, quality, or progress. **6** (*tr*) *Chiefly US & Canad.* to mark off so as to indicate approval, correctness, or preference. **7** (*intr;* often foll. by *with*) *Chiefly US & Canad.* to correspond or agree: *this report checks with the other.* **8** (*tr*) *Chiefly US, Canad., & NZ.* to leave in or accept (property) for temporary custody. **9** *Chess.* to place (an opponent's king) in check. **10** (*tr*) to mark with a pattern of squares or crossed lines. **11** to crack or cause to crack. **12** (*tr*) *Ice hockey.* to impede (an opponent). **13** (*intr*) *Hunting.* (of hounds) to pause while relocating a lost scent. ◆ *n* **14** a break in progress; stoppage. **15** a restraint or rebuff. **16** a person or thing that restrains, halts, etc. **17** a control, esp. a rapid or informal one, to ensure accuracy, progress, etc. **18** a means or standard to ensure against fraud or error. **19** the US word for **tick**[1] (senses 3, 6). **20** the US spelling of **cheque. 21** *US & Canad.* the bill in a restaurant. **22** *Chiefly US & Canad.* a tag used to identify property deposited for custody. **23** a pattern of squares or crossed lines. **24** a single square in such a pattern. **25** fabric with a pattern of squares or crossed lines. **26** *Chess.* the state or position of a king under direct attack. **27** a small crack, as one that occurs in timber during drying. **28** a chip or counter used in some card and gambling games. **29** *Hunting.* a pause by the hounds owing to loss of the scent. **30** *Ice hockey.* the act of impeding an opponent with one's body or stick. **31 in check.** under control or restraint. ◆ *sentence substitute.* **32** *Chess.* a call made to an opponent indicating that his king is in check. **33** *Chiefly US & Canad.* an expression of agreement. ◆ See also **check in, check out, checkup.** [C14: from OF *eschec* a check at chess, via Ar. from Persian *shāh* the king]
▸'**checkable** *adj*

checked (tʃɛkt) *adj* having a pattern of squares.

checker[1] ('tʃɛkə) *n, vb* **1** the usual US spelling of **chequer.** ◆ *n* **2** *Textiles.* the US spelling of **chequer** (sense 2). **3** the US and Canad. name for **draughtsman** (sense 3).

checker[2] ('tʃɛkə) *n Chiefly US.* **1** a cashier, esp. in a supermarket. **2** an attendant in a cloakroom, left-luggage office, etc.

checkerboard ('tʃɛkə,bɔːd) *n* the US and Canad. name for a **draughtboard.**

checkers ('tʃɛkəz) *n* (*functioning as sing*) the US and Canad. name for **draughts.**

check in *vb* (*adv*) **1** (*intr*) to record one's arrival, as at a hotel or for work; sign in or report. **2** (*tr*) to register the arrival of (passengers, etc.). ◆ *n* **check-in. 3** the formal registration of arrival, as at an airport or a hotel. **4** the place where one registers arrival at an airport, etc.

check list *n* a list of items, names, etc., to be referred to for identification or verification.

checkmate ('tʃɛk,meɪt) *n* **1** *Chess.* **1a** the winning position in which an opponent's king is under attack and unable to escape. **1b** the move by which this position is achieved. **2** utter defeat. ◆ *vb* **checkmates, checkmating, checkmated.** (*tr*) **3** *Chess.* to place (an opponent's king) in checkmate. **4** to thwart or render powerless. ◆ *sentence substitute.* **5** *Chess.* a call made when placing an opponent's king in checkmate. [C14: from OF, from Ar. *shāh māt* the king is dead; see CHECK]

check out *vb* (*adv*) **1** (*intr*) to pay the bill and depart, esp. from a hotel. **2** (*intr*) to depart from a place; record one's departure from work. **3** (*tr*) to investigate or prove to be in order after investigation: *the police checked out all the statements.* **4** (*tr*) *Inf.* to have a look at; inspect: *check out the wally in the pink shirt.* ◆ *n* **checkout. 5** the latest time for vacating a room in a hotel, etc. **6** a counter, esp. in a supermarket, where customers pay.

THESAURUS

chatter *vb* **1** = **prattle**, babble, blather, chat, gab (*inf.*), gossip, jabber, natter, prate, rabbit (on) (*Brit. inf.*), schmooze (*sl.*), tattle ◆ *n* **5** = **prattle**, babble, blather, chat, gab (*inf.*), gossip, jabber, natter, rabbit (*Brit. informal*), tattle, twaddle

chatterbox *Informal n* = **chatterer**, babbler, blather *or* blether (*Scot.*), gossip, jabberer, natterer, prater, prattler, tattler, tattletale (*Chiefly US & Canad.*), twaddler

chatty *adj* **1, 2** = **talkative**, colloquial, familiar, friendly, gossipy, informal, newsy (*inf.*)
Antonyms *adj* aloof, cold, distant, formal, hostile, quiet, reserved, shy, silent, standoffish, taciturn, timid, unfriendly, unsociable

cheap *adj* **1** = **inexpensive**, bargain, cheapo (*inf.*), cut-price, economical, economy, keen, low-cost, low-priced, reasonable, reduced, sale **3** = **inferior**, bush-league (*Austral. & NZ inf.*), common, crappy (*sl.*), dime-a-dozen (*inf.*), low-rent (*inf., chiefly US*), paltry, piss-poor (*US taboo sl.*), poor, poxy (*sl.*), second-rate, shoddy, tatty, tawdry, two a penny, two-bit (*US & Canad. sl.*), worthless **5, 8** *Informal* = **despicable**, base, contemptible, low, mean, scurvy, sordid, vulgar
Antonyms *adj* ≠ **inexpensive:** costly, dear, expensive, pricey (*inf.*), steep ≠ **inferior:** admirable, decent, elegant, good, high-class, superior, tasteful, valuable ≠ **despicable:** admirable, charitable, decent, generous, good, honourable

cheapen *vb* **1** = **degrade**, belittle, debase, demean, denigrate, depreciate, derogate, devalue, discredit, disparage, lower

cheapness *n* **1** = **inexpensiveness**, affordability, reasonableness **3** = **inferiority**, commonness, crappiness, paltriness, poorness, shoddiness, tattiness, tawdriness, valuelessness, worthlessness

cheat *vb* **1** = **deceive**, bamboozle (*inf.*), beguile, bilk, con (*inf.*), cozen, defraud, diddle (*inf.*), do (*inf.*), double-cross (*inf.*), dupe, finagle (*inf.*), fleece, fool, hoax, hoodwink, kid (*inf.*), mislead, pull a fast one on (*inf.*), rip off (*sl.*), sting (*inf.*), stitch up (*sl.*), swindle, take for a ride (*inf.*), take in (*inf.*), trick ◆ *n* **5** = **deceiver**, charlatan, cheater, chiseller (*inf.*), con man (*inf.*), dodger, double-crosser (*inf.*), fraudster, impostor, knave (*arch.*), rogue, shark, sharper, swindler, trickster **6** = **deception**, artifice, deceit, fraud, imposture, rip-off (*sl.*), scam (*sl.*), sting (*inf.*), swindle, trickery

check *vb* **2, 3** = **stop**, arrest, bar, bridle, control, curb, delay, halt, hinder, hobble, impede, inhibit, limit, nip in the bud, obstruct, pause, put a spoke in someone's wheel, rein, repress, restrain, retard, stem the flow, thwart **5** = **examine**, check out (*inf.*), compare, confirm, inquire into, inspect, investigate, look at, look over, make sure, monitor, note, probe, research, scrutinize, study, test, tick, verify, vet, work over ◆ *n* **14** = **stoppage**, constraint, control, curb, damper, hindrance, impediment, inhibition, limitation, obstacle, obstruction, rein, restraint **15** = **setback**, blow, disappointment, frustration, rejection, reverse, whammy (*inf., chiefly US*) **17** = **examination**, inspection, investigation, once-over (*inf.*), research, scrutiny, test
Antonyms *vb* ≠ **stop:** accelerate, advance, begin, encourage, further, give free rein, help, release, start ≠ **examine:** disregard, ignore, neglect, overlook, pass over, pay no attention to

checkpoint (ˈtʃɛkˌpɔɪnt) *n* a place, as at a frontier, where vehicles or travellers are stopped for official identification, inspection, etc.

checkup (ˈtʃɛkˌʌp) *n* **1** an examination to see if something is in order. **2** *Med.* a medical examination, esp. one taken at regular intervals. ◆ *vb* **check up. 3** (*intr, adv; sometimes foll. by on*) to investigate or make an inquiry into (a person's character, evidence, etc.).

Cheddar (ˈtʃɛdə) *n* (*sometimes not cap.*) any of several types of smooth hard yellow or whitish cheese. [C17: from *Cheddar*, village in Somerset, where it was orig. made]

cheek 🅣 (tʃiːk) *n* **1** either side of the face, esp. that part below the eye. **2** *Inf.* impudence; effrontery. **3** (*often pl*) *Inf.* either side of the buttocks. **4** (*often pl*) a side of a door jamb. **5** one of the jaws of a vice. **6 cheek by jowl.** close together; intimately linked. **7 turn the other cheek.** to be submissive and refuse to retaliate. ◆ *vb* **8** (*tr*) *Inf.* to speak or behave disrespectfully to. [OE *ceace*]

cheekbone (ˈtʃiːkˌbəʊn) *n* the nontechnical name for **zygomatic bone.**

cheeky 🅣 (ˈtʃiːkɪ) *adj* **cheekier, cheekiest.** disrespectful in speech or behaviour; impudent.
▸ˈ**cheekily** *adv* ▸ˈ**cheekiness** *n*

cheep (tʃiːp) *n* **1** the short weak high-pitched cry of a young bird; chirp. ◆ *vb* **2** (*intr*) (of young birds) to utter such sounds.
▸ˈ**cheeper** *n*

cheer 🅣 (tʃɪə) *vb* **1** (usually foll. by *up*) to make or become happy or hopeful; comfort or be comforted. **2** to applaud with shouts. **3** (when *tr*, sometimes foll. by *on*) to encourage (a team, etc.) with shouts. ◆ *n* **4** a shout or cry of approval, encouragement, etc., often using **hurrah! 5 three cheers.** three shouts of hurrah given in unison to honour someone or celebrate something. **6** happiness; good spirits. **7** state of mind; spirits (archaic, except in **be of good cheer, with good cheer**). **8** *Arch.* provisions for a feast; fare. [C13 (in the sense: face, welcoming aspect): from OF *chere*, from LL *cara* face, from Gk *kara* head]

cheerful 🅣 (ˈtʃɪəfʊl) *adj* **1** having a happy disposition; in good spirits. **2** pleasantly bright: *a cheerful room.* **3** ungrudging: *cheerful help.*
▸ˈ**cheerfully** *adv* ▸ˈ**cheerfulness** *n*

cheerio (ˌtʃɪərɪˈəʊ) *Inf.* ◆ *sentence substitute. Chiefly Brit.* **1** a farewell greeting. **2** a drinking toast. ◆ *n, pl* **cheerios. 3** *NZ.* a type of small sausage.

cheerleader (ˈtʃɪəˌliːdə) *n US & Canad.* a person who leads a crowd in cheers, esp. at sports events.

cheerless 🅣 (ˈtʃɪəlɪs) *adj* dreary or gloomy.
▸ˈ**cheerlessly** *adv* ▸ˈ**cheerlessness** *n*

cheers (tʃɪəz) *sentence substitute. Inf., chiefly Brit.* **1** a drinking toast. **2** goodbye! cheerio! **3** thanks!

cheery 🅣 (ˈtʃɪərɪ) *adj* **cheerier, cheeriest.** showing or inspiring cheerfulness.
▸ˈ**cheerily** *adv* ▸ˈ**cheeriness** *n*

cheese (tʃiːz) *n* **1** the curd of milk separated from the whey and variously prepared as a food. **2** a mass or cake of this substance. **3** any of various substances of similar consistency, etc.: *lemon cheese.* **4** *Sl.* an important person (esp. in **big cheese**). [OE *cēse*, from L *cāseus* cheese]

cheeseburger (ˈtʃiːzˌbɜːgə) *n* a hamburger cooked with a slice of cheese on top of it.

cheesecake (ˈtʃiːzˌkeɪk) *n* **1** a rich tart filled with cheese, esp. cream cheese, cream, sugar, etc. **2** *Sl.* women displayed for their sex appeal, as in photographs in magazines or films.

cheesecloth (ˈtʃiːzˌklɒθ) *n* a loosely woven cotton cloth formerly used for wrapping cheese.

cheesed off *adj* (*usually postpositive*) *Brit. sl.* bored, disgusted, or angry. [C20: from ?]

cheeseparing (ˈtʃiːzˌpɛərɪŋ) *adj* **1** penny-pinching. ◆ *n* **2a** a paring of cheese rind. **2b** anything similarly worthless. **3** stinginess.

cheesy (ˈtʃiːzɪ) *adj* **cheesier, cheesiest. 1** like cheese in flavour, smell, or consistency. **2** *Inf.* (of a smile) broad but possibly insincere: *a big cheesy grin.* **3** *Inf.* banal or trite; in poor taste.
▸ˈ**cheesiness** *n*

cheetah *or* **chetah** (ˈtʃiːtə) *n* a large feline of Africa and SW Asia: the swiftest mammal, having very long legs, and a black-spotted coat. [C18: from Hindi *cītā*, from Sansk. *citra* speckled]

chef (ʃɛf) *n* a cook, esp. the principal cook in a restaurant. [C19: from F, from OF *chief* head, CHIEF]

chef-d'œuvre *French.* (ʃɛdœvrə) *n, pl* ***chefs-d'œuvre*** (ʃɛdœvrə). a masterpiece.

chela[1] (ˈkiːlə) *n, pl* **chelae** (-liː). a large pincer-like claw of such arthropods as the crab and scorpion. [C17: NL, from Gk *khēlē* claw]

chela[2] (ˈtʃeɪlə) *n Hinduism.* a disciple of a religious teacher. [C19: from Hindi *celā*, from Sansk. *ceta* servant, slave]

chelate (ˈkiːleɪt) *n* **1** *Chem.* a chemical compound whose molecules contain a closed ring of atoms of which one is a metal atom. ◆ *adj* **2** *Zool.* of or possessing chelae. **3** *Chem.* of a chelate. ◆ *vb* **chelates, chelating, chelated. 4** (*intr*) *Chem.* to form a chelate. [C20: from CHELA[1]]
▸**cheˈlation** *n*

chelicera (kɪˈlɪsərə) *n, pl* **chelicerae** (-əˌriː). one of a pair of appendages on the head of spiders and other arachnids: often modified as food-catching claws. [C19: from NL, from Gk *khēle* claw+ *keras* horn]

cheloid (ˈkiːlɔɪd) *n Pathol.* a variant spelling of **keloid.**
▸**cheˈloidal** *adj*

chelonian (kɪˈləʊnɪən) *n* **1** any reptile of the order *Chelonia*, including the tortoises and turtles, in which most of the body is enclosed in a bony capsule. ◆ *adj* **2** of or belonging to the *Chelonia.* [C19: from NL, from Gk *khelōnē* tortoise]

Chelsea Pensioner (ˈtʃɛlsɪ) *n* an inhabitant of the Chelsea Royal Hospital in SW London, a home for old and infirm soldiers.

chem. *abbrev. for:* **1** chemical. **2** chemist. **3** chemistry.

chem- *combining form.* a variant of **chemo-** before a vowel.

chemical 🅣 (ˈkɛmɪkᵊl) *n* **1** any substance used in or resulting from a reaction involving changes to atoms or molecules. ◆ *adj* **2** of or used in chemistry. **3** of, made from, or using chemicals: *chemical fertilizer.*
▸ˈ**chemically** *adv*

chemical engineering *n* the branch of engineering concerned with the design and manufacture of the plant used in industrial chemical processes.
▸**chemical engineer** *n*

chemical warfare *n* warfare using asphyxiating or nerve gases, poisons, defoliants, etc.

chemiluminescence (ˌkɛmɪˌluːmɪˈnɛsəns) *n* the phenomenon in which a chemical reaction leads to the emission of light without incandescence.
▸ˌ**chemiˌlumiˈnescent** *adj*

chemin de fer (ʃəˈmæn də ˈfɛə) *n* a gambling game, a variation of baccarat. [F: railway, referring to the fast tempo of the game]

chemise (ʃəˈmiːz) *n* **1** an unwaisted loose-fitting dress hanging straight from the shoulders. **2** a loose shirtlike undergarment. ◆ Also called: **shift.** [C14: from OF: shirt, from LL *camisa*]

chemist 🅣 (ˈkɛmɪst) *n* **1** *Brit.* a shop selling medicines, cosmetics, etc. **2** *Brit.* a qualified dispenser of prescribed medicines. **3** a person studying, trained in, or engaged in chemistry. [C16: from earlier *chimist*, from NL, shortened from Med. L *alchimista* ALCHEMIST]

chemistry (ˈkɛmɪstrɪ) *n, pl* **chemistries. 1** the branch of physical science concerned with the composition, properties, and reactions of substances. **2** the composition, properties, and reactions of a particular substance. **3** the nature and effects of any complex phenomenon: *the chemistry of humour.* [C17: from earlier *chimistrie*, from *chimist* CHEMIST]

chemo-, chemi-, *or before a vowel* **chem-** *combining form.* indicating that chemicals or chemical reactions are involved: *chemotherapy.* [NL, from LGk *khēmeia*; see ALCHEMY]

chemoreceptor (ˌkiːməʊrɪˈsɛptə) *or* **chemoceptor** *n* a sensory receptor in a biological cell membrane to which an external molecule binds to generate a smell or taste sensation.

chemosynthesis (ˌkiːməʊˈsɪnθɪsɪs) *n* the formation of organic material by some bacteria using energy from simple chemical reactions.

chemotherapy (ˌkiːməʊˈθɛrəpɪ) *n* treatment of disease, esp. cancer, by means of chemical agents. Cf. **radiotherapy.**
▸ˌ**chemoˈtherapist** *n*

chemurgy (ˈkɛmɜːdʒɪ) *n* the branch of chemistry concerned with the industrial use of organic raw materials, esp. of agricultural origin.
▸**chemˈurgic** *or* **chemˈurgical** *adj*

THESAURUS

cheek *n* **2** *Informal* = **impudence**, audacity, brass neck (*Brit. inf.*), brazenness, chutzpah (*US & Canad. informal*), disrespect, effrontery, face (*inf.*), front, gall (*inf.*), impertinence, insolence, lip (*sl.*), neck (*inf.*), nerve, sassiness (*US inf.*), sauce (*inf.*), temerity

cheeky *adj* = **impudent**, audacious, disrespectful, forward, fresh (*inf.*), impertinent, insolent, insulting, pert, sassy (*US inf.*), saucy
Antonyms *adj* civil, complaisant, courteous, decorous, deferential, mannerly, polite, respectful, well-behaved, well-mannered

cheer *vb* **1** *usually foll. by* **up** = **cheer up**, animate, brighten, buck up (*inf.*), buoy up, comfort, console, elate, elevate, encourage, enliven, exhilarate, gee up, gladden, hearten, incite, inspirit, jolly along (*inf.*), perk up, rally, solace, take heart, uplift, warm **2** = **applaud**, acclaim, clap, hail, hurrah ◆ *n* **4** = **applause**, acclamation, ovation, plaudits **6** = **cheerfulness**, animation, buoyancy, comfort, gaiety, gladness, glee, hopefulness, joy, liveliness, merriment, merry-making, mirth, optimism, solace
Antonyms ≠ **cheer up**: darken, depress, discourage, dishearten, sadden *vb* ≠ **applaud**: blow a raspberry, boo, hiss, jeer, ridicule

cheerful *adj* **1** = **happy**, animated, blithe, bright, buoyant, cheery, chirpy (*inf.*), contented, enlivening, enthusiastic, gay, genial, glad, hearty, jaunty, jolly, joyful, light-hearted, merry, optimistic, pleasant, sparkling, sprightly, sunny, upbeat (*inf.*)
Antonyms *adj* cheerless, dejected, depressed, depressing, despondent, dismal, down, downcast, down in the dumps (*inf.*), dull, gloomy, lifeless, low, melancholy, miserable, morose, pensive, sad, unhappy, unpleasant

cheerfulness *n* **1** = **happiness**, buoyancy, exuberance, gaiety, geniality, gladness, good cheer, good humour, high spirits, jauntiness, joyousness, light-heartedness

cheerless *adj* = **gloomy**, austere, bleak, comfortless, dark, dejected, depressed, desolate, despondent, disconsolate, dismal, dolorous, drab, dreary, dull, forlorn, funereal, grim, joyless, melancholy, miserable, mournful, sad, sombre, sorrowful, sullen, unhappy, woebegone, woeful
Antonyms *adj* cheerful, cheery, elated, happy, jolly, joyful, light-hearted, merry

cheery *adj* = **cheerful**, breezy, carefree, chirpy (*inf.*), full of beans (*inf.*), genial, good-humoured, happy, jovial, lively, pleasant, sunny, upbeat (*inf.*)

chemical *n* **1** = **compound**, drug, potion, substance, synthetic

chemist *n* **2** = **pharmacist**, apothecary, dispenser

chenille (ʃə'ni:l) *n* **1** a thick soft tufty silk or worsted velvet cord or yarn used in embroidery and for trimmings, etc. **2** a fabric of such yarn. **3** a carpet of such fabric. [C18: from F, lit.: hairy caterpillar, from L *canicula,* dim. of *canis* dog]

cheongsam ('tʃɒŋ'sæm) *n* a straight dress with a stand-up collar and a slit in one side of the skirt, worn by Chinese women. [from Chinese *ch'ang shan* long jacket]

cheque *or US* **check** (tʃɛk) *n* **1** a bill of exchange drawn on a bank by the holder of a current account. **2** *Austral. & NZ.* the total sum of money received for contract work or a crop. **3** *Austral. & NZ.* wages. [C18: from CHECK, in the sense: means of verification]

cheque account *n* an account at a bank or a building society upon which cheques can be drawn.

chequebook *or US* **checkbook** ('tʃɛk,bʊk) *n* a book of detachable blank cheques issued by a bank or building society to holders of cheque accounts.

chequebook journalism *n* the practice of securing exclusive rights to material for newspaper stories by paying a high price, regardless of any moral implications.

cheque card *n* a card issued by a bank or building society, guaranteeing payment of a customer's cheques up to a stated value.

chequer *or US* **checker** ('tʃɛkə) *n* **1** any of the marbles, pegs, or other pieces used in the game of Chinese chequers. **2a** a pattern of squares. **2b** one of the squares in such a pattern. ◆ *vb (tr)* **3** to make irregular in colour or character; variegate. **4** to mark off with alternating squares of colour. ◆ See also **chequers**. [C13: chessboard, from Anglo-F *escheker,* from *eschec* CHECK]

chequered *or esp. US* **checkered** ('tʃɛkəd) *adj* marked by fluctuations of fortune (esp. in **a chequered career**).

chequers ('tʃɛkəz) *n (functioning as sing)* another name for **draughts.**

cherish ❶ ('tʃɛrɪʃ) *vb (tr)* **1** to feel or show great tenderness or care for. **2** to cling fondly to (a hope, idea, etc.); nurse: *to cherish ambitions.* [C14: from OF, from *cher* dear, from L *cārus*]

chernozem ('tʃɜ:nəʊ,zɛm) *n* a rich black soil found in temperate semiarid regions, such as the grasslands of Russia. [from Russian *chernaya zemlya* black earth]

Cherokee ('tʃɛrə,ki:) *n* **1** (*pl* **Cherokees** *or* **Cherokee**) a member of a North American Indian people formerly living in the Appalachian Mountains. **2** the Iroquois language of this people.

cheroot (ʃə'ru:t) *n* a cigar with both ends cut off squarely. [C17: from Tamil *curuttu* curl, roll]

cherry ('tʃɛrɪ) *n, pl* **cherries. 1** any of several trees of the genus *Prunus,* having a small fleshy rounded fruit containing a hard stone. **2** the fruit or wood of any of these trees. **3** any of various unrelated plants, such as the ground cherry and Jerusalem cherry. **4a** a bright red colour; cerise. **4b** *(as adj): a cherry coat.* **5** *Taboo sl.* virginity or the hymen as its symbol. [C14: back formation from OE *ciris* (mistakenly thought to be pl), ult. from LL *ceresia,* ?from L *cerasus* cherry tree, from Gk *kerasios*]

cherry tomato *n* a miniature tomato not much bigger than a cherry.

chert (tʃɜ:t) *n* an impure black or grey microcrystalline variety of quartz that resembles flint. [C17: from ?]
▸'**cherty** *adj*

cherub ❶ ('tʃɛrəb) *n, pl* **cherubs** *or (for sense 1)* **cherubim** ('tʃɛrəbɪm, -ʊbɪm). **1** a member of the second order of angels, often represented as a winged child. **2** an innocent or sweet child. [OE, from Heb. *kĕrūbh*]
▸**cherubic** (tʃə'ru:bɪk) *or* **che'rubical** *adj* ▸**che'rubically** *adv*

chervil ('tʃɜ:vɪl) *n* an aromatic umbelliferous Eurasian plant with small white flowers and aniseed-flavoured leaves used as herbs in soups and salads. [OE *cerfelle,* from L, from Gk, from *khairein* to enjoy + *phullon* leaf]

Cheshire cheese *n* a mild-flavoured cheese with a crumbly texture, originally made in Cheshire.

chess (tʃɛs) *n* a game of skill for two players using a chessboard on which chessmen are moved. The object is to checkmate the opponent's king. [C13: from OF *esches,* pl. of *eschec* CHECK]

chessboard ('tʃɛs,bɔ:d) *n* a square board divided into 64 squares of two alternating colours, used for playing chess or draughts.

chessman ('tʃɛs,mæn, -mən) *n, pl* **chessmen.** any of the pieces and pawns used in a game of chess. [C17: from *chessmen,* from ME *chessemeyne* chess company]

chest ❶ (tʃɛst) *n* **1a** the front part of the trunk from the neck to the belly. Related adj: **pectoral. 1b** *(as modifier): a chest cold.* **2 get (something) off one's chest.** *Inf.* to unburden oneself of troubles, worries, etc., by talking about them. **3** a box used for storage or shipping: *a tea chest.* [OE *cest,* from L, from Gk *kistē* box]
▸'**chested** *adj*

chesterfield ('tʃɛstə,fi:ld) *n* **1** a man's overcoat, usually with a velvet collar. **2** a large tightly stuffed sofa, with straight upholstered arms of the same height as the back. [C19: after a 19th-cent. Earl of *Chesterfield*]

chestnut ('tʃɛs,nʌt) *n* **1** a N temperate tree such as the **sweet** or **Spanish chestnut**, which produces flowers in long catkins and nuts in a prickly bur. Cf. **horse chestnut. 2** the edible nut of any of these trees. **3** the hard wood of any of these trees, used in making furniture, etc. **4a** a reddish-brown colour. **4b** *(as adj): chestnut hair.* **5** a horse of a golden-brown colour. **6** *Inf.* an old or stale joke. [C16: from earlier *chesten nut: chesten,* from OF, from L, from Gk *kastanea*]

chest of drawers *n* a piece of furniture consisting of a set of drawers in a frame.

chesty ('tʃɛstɪ) *adj* **chestier, chestiest.** *Inf.* **1** *Brit.* suffering from or symptomatic of chest disease: *a chesty cough.* **2** having a large well-developed chest or bosom.
▸'**chestiness** *n*

cheval glass (ʃə'væl) *n* a full-length mirror mounted so as to swivel within a frame. [C19: from F *cheval* support (lit.: horse)]

chevalier (,ʃɛ'vælɪə) *n* **1** a member of certain orders of merit, such as the French Legion of Honour. **2** the lowest title of rank in the old French nobility. **3** an archaic word for **knight. 4** a chivalrous man; gallant. [C14: from OF, from Med. L *caballārius* horseman, CAVALIER]

Cheviot ('tʃi:vɪət, 'tʃɛv-) *n* **1** a large British breed of sheep reared for its wool. **2** *(often not cap.)* a rough twill-weave woollen suiting fabric. [from *Cheviot* Hills on borders of England and Scotland]

chèvre ('ʃɛvrə) *n* any cheese made from goats' milk. [C20: from F, lit.: goat]

chevron ('ʃɛvrən) *n* **1** *Mil.* a badge or insignia consisting of one or more V-shaped stripes to indicate a noncommissioned rank or length of service. **2** *Heraldry.* an inverted V-shaped charge on a shield. **3** *(usually pl)* a pattern of horizontal black and white V-shapes on a road sign indicating a sharp bend. **4** any V-shaped pattern or device. [C14: from OF, ult. from L *caper* goat; cf. L *capreoli* pair of rafters (lit.: little goats)]

chevrotain ('ʃɛvrə,teɪn, -tɪn) *n* a small timid ruminant mammal of S and SE Asia. Also called: **mouse deer.** [C18: from F, from OF *chevrot* kid, from *chèvre* goat, ult. from L *caper* goat]

chevy ('tʃɛvɪ) *n, vb* a variant spelling of **chivy.**

chew ❶ (tʃu:) *vb* **1** to work the jaws and teeth in order to grind (food); masticate. **2** to bite repeatedly: *she chewed her nails anxiously.* **3** *(intr)* to use chewing tobacco. **4 chew the fat** *or* **rag.** *Sl.* **4a** to argue over a point. **4b** to talk idly; gossip. ◆ *n* **5** the act of chewing. **6** something that is chewed. [OE *ceowan*]
▸'**chewable** *adj* ▸'**chewer** *n*

chewing gum *n* a preparation for chewing, usually made of flavoured and sweetened chicle or such substitutes as polyvinyl acetate.

chew over ❶ *vb (tr, adv)* to consider carefully.

chewy ❶ ('tʃu:ɪ) *adj* **chewier, chewiest.** of a consistency requiring chewing.

chez *French.* (ʃe) *prep* **1** at the home of. **2** with, among, or in the manner of.

chi[1] (kaɪ) *n* the 22nd letter of the Greek alphabet (Χ, χ).

chi[2] *or* **ch'i** *or* **qi** (tʃi:) *n (sometimes cap.)* (in Oriental medicine, martial arts, etc.) vital energy believed to circulate round the body in currents. [Chinese, lit.: energy]

chiack *or* **chyack** ('tʃaɪæk) *Austral inf.* ◆ *vb (tr)* **1** to tease or banter. ◆ *n* **2** good-humoured banter. [C19: from *chi-hike,* a shout of greeting]

chianti (kɪ'æntɪ) *n (sometimes cap.)* a dry red wine produced in Tuscany, Italy.

chiaroscuro (kɪ,ɑ:rə'skʊərəʊ) *n, pl* **chiaroscuros. 1** the artistic distribution of light and dark masses in a picture. **2** monochrome painting using light and dark only. [C17: from It., from *chiaro* CLEAR + *oscuro* OBSCURE]

chiasma (kaɪ'æzmə) *n, pl* **chiasmas, chiasmata** (-mətə) **1** *Cytology.* the cross-shaped connection produced by the crossing over of pairing chromosomes during meiosis. **2** *Anat.* the crossing over of two parts or structures. [C19: from Gk *khiasma,* from *khi* CHI[1]]

chiasmus (kaɪ'æzməs) *n, pl* **chiasmi** (-maɪ). *Rhetoric.* reversal of word order in the second of two parallel phrases: *he came in triumph and in defeat departs.* [NL from Gk: see CHIASMA]
▸**chiastic** (kaɪ'æstɪk) *adj*

chic ❶ (ʃi:k, ʃɪk) *adj* **1** (esp. of fashionable clothes, women, etc.) stylish or elegant. ◆ *n* **2** stylishness, esp. in dress; modishness; fashionable good taste. [C19: from F, from ?]
▸'**chicly** *adv*

chicane (ʃɪ'keɪn) *n* **1** a bridge or whist hand without trumps. **2** *Motor racing.* a short section of sharp narrow bends formed by barriers placed on a motor-racing circuit. **3** a less common word for **chicanery.** ◆ *vb* **chicanes, chicaning, chicaned. 4** *(tr)* to deceive or trick by chicanery. **5** *(intr)* to use tricks or chicanery. [C17: from F *chicaner* to quibble, from ?]
▸**chi'caner** *n*

chicanery ❶ (ʃɪ'keɪnərɪ) *n, pl* **chicaneries. 1** verbal deception or trickery, dishonest or sharp practice. **2** a trick, deception, or quibble.

THESAURUS

cherish *vb* **1** = **care for**, comfort, cosset, hold dear, love, nourish, nurse, shelter, support, treasure **2** = **cling to**, cleave to, encourage, entertain, foster, harbour, hold dear, nurture, prize, sustain, treasure
Antonyms *vb* abandon, desert, despise, disdain, dislike, forsake, hate, neglect

cherubic *adj* **1, 2** = **angelic**, adorable, heavenly, innocent, lovable, seraphic, sweet

chest *n* **3** = **box**, ark (*dialect*), case, casket, coffer, crate, kist (*Scot. & N English dialect*), strongbox, trunk

chew *vb* **1** = **bite**, champ, chomp, crunch, gnaw, grind, masticate, munch

chew over *vb* = **consider**, deliberate upon, meditate, mull (over), muse on, ponder, reflect upon, ruminate, weigh

chewy *adj* = **tough**, as tough as old boots, fibrous, leathery

chic *adj* **1** = **stylish**, elegant, fashionable, modish, sexy, smart, trendy (*Brit. informal*), up-to-date, urbane
Antonyms *adj* dinosaur, inelegant, naff (*Brit. sl.*), old-fashioned, outmoded, out-of-date, passé, shabby, unfashionable

chicanery *n* **1** = **trickery**, artifice, cheating,

chicano (tʃɪ'kɑːnəʊ) *n, pl* **chicanos.** *US.* an American citizen of Mexican origin. [C20: from Sp. *mejicano* Mexican]

chichi ('ʃiːˌʃiː) *adj* **1** affectedly pretty or stylish. ◆ *n* **2** the quality of being affectedly pretty or stylish. [C20: from F]

chick (tʃɪk) *n* **1** the young of a bird, esp. of a domestic fowl. **2** *Sl.* a girl or young woman, esp. an attractive one. **3** a young child: used as a term of endearment. [C14: short for CHICKEN]

chickadee ('tʃɪkəˌdiː) *n* any of various small North American songbirds, typically having grey-and-black plumage. [C19: imit.]

chicken ('tʃɪkɪn) *n* **1** a domestic fowl bred for its flesh or eggs. **2** the flesh of such a bird used for food. **3** any of various similar birds, such as a prairie chicken. **4** *Sl.* a cowardly person. **5** *Sl.* a young inexperienced person. **6** *Inf.* any of various, often dangerous, games or challenges in which the object is to make one's opponent lose his nerve. **7** **count one's chickens before they are hatched.** to be over-optimistic in acting on expectations which are not yet fulfilled. ◆ *adj* **8** *Sl.* easily scared; cowardly; timid. [OE *ciecen*]

chicken feed *n Sl.* a trifling amount of money.

chicken-hearted *or* **chicken-livered** *adj* easily frightened; cowardly.

chicken out *vb* (*intr, adv*) *Inf.* to fail to do something through fear or lack of conviction.

chickenpox ('tʃɪkɪnˌpɒks) *n* a highly communicable viral disease most commonly affecting children, characterized by slight fever and the eruption of a rash.

chicken wire *n* wire netting with a hexagonal mesh.

chickpea ('tʃɪkˌpiː) *n* **1** a bushy leguminous plant, cultivated for its edible pealike seeds. **2** the seed of this plant. [C16 *ciche peasen,* from *ciche* (from F, from L *cicer* chickpea) + *peasen;* see PEA]

chickweed ('tʃɪkˌwiːd) *n* any of various plants of the pink family, esp. a common garden weed with small white flowers.

chicle ('tʃɪkᵊl) *n* a gumlike substance obtained from the sapodilla; the main ingredient of chewing gum. [from Sp., from Nahuatl *chictli*]

chicory ('tʃɪkərɪ) *n, pl* **chicories. 1** a blue-flowered plant, cultivated for its leaves, which are used in salads, and for its roots. **2** the root of this plant, roasted, dried, and used as a coffee substitute. ◆ Cf. **endive.** [C15: from OF, from L *cichorium,* from Gk *kikhōrion*]

chide ➊ (tʃaɪd) *vb* **chides, chiding, chided** *or* **chid** (tʃɪd); **chided, chid** *or* **chidden** ('tʃɪdᵊn). **1** to rebuke or scold. **2** (*tr*) to goad into action. [OE *cīdan*]
▸ **'chider** *n* ▸ **'chidingly** *adv*

chief ➊ (tʃiːf) *n* **1** the head or leader of a group or body of people. **2** *Heraldry.* the upper third of a shield. **3** **in chief.** primarily; especially. ◆ *adj* **4** (*prenominal*) **4a** most important; principal. **4b** highest in rank or authority. ◆ *adv* **5** *Arch.* principally. [C13: from OF, from L *caput* head]

chief executive *n* the person with overall responsibility for the efficient running of a company, organization, etc.

chief justice *n* **1** (in any of several Commonwealth countries) the judge presiding over a supreme court. **2** (in the US) the presiding judge of a court composed of a number of members. ◆ See also **Lord Chief Justice.**

chiefly ➊ ('tʃiːflɪ) *adv* **1** especially or essentially; above all. **2** in general; mainly; mostly. ◆ *adj* **3** of or relating to a chief or chieftain.

Chief of Staff *n* **1** the senior staff officer under the commander of a major military formation or organization. **2** the senior officer of each service of the armed forces.

chief petty officer *n* the senior naval rank for personnel without commissioned or warrant rank.

chieftain ('tʃiːftən, -tɪn) *n* the head or leader of a tribe or clan. [C14: from OF, from LL *capitāneus* commander; see CAPTAIN]
▸ **'chieftaincy** *or* **'chieftainˌship** *n*

chief technician *n* a noncommissioned officer in the Royal Air Force, junior to a flight sergeant.

chiffchaff ('tʃɪfˌtʃæf) *n* a common European warbler with a yellowish-brown plumage. [C18: imit.]

chiffon (ʃɪ'fɒn, 'ʃɪfɒn) *n* **1** a fine almost transparent fabric of silk, nylon, etc. **2** (*often pl*) *Now rare.* feminine finery. ◆ *adj* **3** made of chiffon. **4** (of soufflés, pies, cakes, etc.) having a very light fluffy texture. [C18: from F, from *chiffe* rag]

chiffonier *or* **chiffonnier** (ˌʃɪfə'nɪə) *n* **1** a tall, elegant chest of drawers. **2** a wide low open-fronted cabinet. [C19: from F, from *chiffon* rag]

chigetai (ˌtʃɪgɪ'taɪ) *n* a variety of the Asiatic wild ass of Mongolia. Also spelled: **dziggetai.** [from Mongolian *tchikhitei* long-eared, from *tchikhi* ear]

chigger ('tʃɪgə) *n* **1** *US & Canad.* the parasitic larva of a mite, which causes intense itching. **2** another name for **chigoe.**

chignon ('ʃiːnjɒn) *n* an arrangement of long hair in a roll or knot at the back of the head. [C18: from F, from OF *chaignon* link, from *chaine* CHAIN; infl. also by OF *tignon* coil of hair]

chigoe ('tʃɪgəʊ) *n* **1** a tropical flea, the female of which burrows into the skin of its host, which includes man. **2** another name for **chigger.** [C17: from Carib *chigo*]

Chihuahua (tʃɪ'wɑːwɑː, -wə) *n* a breed of tiny dog originally from Mexico, having short hair and protruding eyes. [after *Chihuahua,* state in Mexico]

chilblain ('tʃɪlˌbleɪn) *n* (*usually pl*) an inflammation of the fingers or toes, caused by exposure to cold. [C16: from CHILL (n) + BLAIN]
▸ **'chilˌblained** *adj*

child ➊ (tʃaɪld) *n, pl* **children. 1a** a boy or girl between birth and puberty. **1b** (*as modifier*): *child labour.* **2** a baby or infant. **3** an unborn baby. **4** **with child.** an old-fashioned term for **pregnant. 5** a human offspring; a son or daughter. Related adj: **filial. 6** a childish or immature person. **7** a member of a family or tribe; descendant: *a child of Israel.* **8** a person or thing regarded as the product of an influence or environment: *a child of nature.* [OE *cild*]
▸ **'childless** *adj* ▸ **'childlessness** *n*

child abuse *n* physical, sexual, or emotional ill-treatment of a child by its parents or other adults responsible for its welfare.

child-bearing *n* **a** the act or process of carrying and giving birth to a child. **b** (*as modifier*): *of child-bearing age.*

childbed ('tʃaɪldˌbɛd) *n* (often preceded by *in*) the condition of giving birth to a child.

child benefit *n* (in Britain and New Zealand) a regular government payment to parents of children up to a certain age.

childbirth ➊ ('tʃaɪldˌbɜːθ) *n* the act of giving birth to a child.

childcare ('tʃaɪldˌkɛə) *n Brit.* **1** care provided for children without homes (or with a seriously disturbed home life) by a local authority. **2** care and supervision of children whose parents are working, provided by a childminder or local authority.

child endowment *n* (in Australia) a social security payment for dependent children.

childhood ➊ ('tʃaɪldhʊd) *n* the condition of being a child; the period of life before puberty.

childish ➊ ('tʃaɪldɪʃ) *adj* **1** in the manner of or suitable to a child. **2** foolish or petty: *childish fears.*
▸ **'childishly** *adv* ▸ **'childishness** *n*

childlike ➊ ('tʃaɪldˌlaɪk) *adj* like or befitting a child, as in being innocent, trustful, etc.

childminder ('tʃaɪldˌmaɪndə) *n* a person who looks after children, esp. those whose parents are working.

children ('tʃɪldrən) *n* the plural of **child.**

Children of Israel *pl n* the Jewish people or nation.

child-resistant *adj* (of packaging etc., esp. of drugs) designed to be difficult for children to open or tamper with. Also: **child-proof.**

child's play *n Inf.* something easy to do.

chile ('tʃɪlɪ) *n* a variant spelling of **chilli.**

Chilean ('tʃɪlɪən) *adj* **1** of or relating to Chile, a republic in South America. ◆ *n* **2** a native or inhabitant of Chile.

Chile pine *n* another name for the **monkey puzzle.**

Chile saltpetre *or* **nitre** *n* a naturally occurring form of sodium nitrate.

chiliad ('kɪlɪˌæd) *n* **1** a group of one thousand. **2** one thousand years. [C16: from Gk, from *khilioi* a thousand]

chill ➊ (tʃɪl) *n* **1** a moderate coldness. **2** a sensation of coldness resulting from a cold or damp environment, or from a sudden emotional reaction. **3** a feverish cold. **4** a check on enthusiasm or joy. ◆ *adj* **5** another word for **chilly.** ◆ *vb* **6** to make or become cold. **7** (*tr*) to cool or freeze (food, drinks, etc.). **8** (*tr*) **8a** to depress (enthusiasm, etc.). **8b** to discourage. **9** (*intr*) *Sl., chiefly US.* to relax; calm oneself. ◆ See also **chill out.** [OE *ciele*]
▸ **'chilling** *adj* ▸ **'chillingly** *adv* ▸ **'chillness** *n*

chiller ('tʃɪlə) *n* **1** short for **spine-chiller. 2** *NZ.* a refrigerated storage area for meat.

THESAURUS

chicane, deception, deviousness, dodge, double-dealing, duplicity, intrigue, sharp practice, skulduggery (*inf.*), sophistry, stratagems, subterfuge, underhandedness, wiles, wire-pulling (*chiefly US*)

chide *vb* **1** = **scold**, admonish, bawl out (*inf.*), berate, blame, blast, carpet (*inf.*), censure, check, criticize, find fault, give (someone) a rocket (*Brit. & NZ inf.*), lambast(e), lecture, put down, rap over the knuckles, read the riot act, rebuke, reprehend, reprimand, reproach, reprove, slap on the wrist, tear into (*inf.*), tear (someone) off a strip (*Brit. inf.*), tell off (*inf.*), tick off (*inf.*), upbraid

chief *n* **1** = **head**, boss (*inf.*), captain, chieftain, commander, director, governor, leader, lord, manager, master, principal, ringleader, ruler, superintendent, superior, suzerain, torchbearer ◆ *adj* **4** = **primary**, big-time (*inf.*), capital, cardinal, central, especial, essential, foremost, grand, highest, key, leading, main, major league (*inf.*), most important, outstanding, paramount, predominant, pre-eminent, premier, prevailing, prime, principal, superior, supreme, uppermost, vital
Antonyms *n* ≠ **head:** follower, subject, subordinate ◆ *adj* ≠ **primary:** least, minor, subordinate, subsidiary

chiefly *adv* **1** = **especially**, above all, essentially, primarily, principally **2** = **mainly**, in general, in the main, largely, mostly, on the whole, predominantly, usually

child *n* **1, 2** = **youngster**, ankle-biter (*Austral. sl.*), babe, babe in arms, baby, bairn (*Scot.*), brat, chit, descendant, infant, issue, juvenile, kid (*inf.*), little one, minor, nipper (*inf.*), nursling, offspring, progeny, rug rat (*sl.*), sprog (*sl.*), suckling, toddler, tot, wean (*Scot.*)

childbirth *n* = **child-bearing**, accouchement, confinement, delivery, labour, lying-in, parturition, travail

childhood *n* = **youth**, boyhood *or* girlhood, immaturity, infancy, minority, schooldays

childish *adj* **1, 2** = **immature**, boyish *or* girlish, foolish, frivolous, infantile, juvenile, puerile, silly, simple, trifling, weak, young
Antonyms *adj* adult, grown-up, manly *or* womanly, mature, sensible, sophisticated

childlike *adj* = **innocent**, artless, credulous, guileless, ingenuous, naive, simple, trustful, trusting, unfeigned

chill *n* **1** = **cold**, bite, coldness, coolness, crispness, frigidity, nip, rawness, sharpness ◆ *vb* **7** =

chilli *or* **chili** (ˈtʃɪlɪ) *n, pl* **chillies** *or* **chilies.** the small red hot-tasting pod of a type of capsicum used for flavouring sauces, etc. [C17: from Sp., from Nahuatl *chilli*]

chilli con carne (ˈtʃɪlɪ kɒn ˈkɑːnɪ) *n* a highly seasoned Mexican dish of meat, onions, beans, and chilli powder. [from Sp.: chilli with meat]

chilli dog *n US.* a frankfurter garnished with chilli con carne, served in a roll.

chilli powder *n* ground chilli blended with other spices.

chilli sauce *n* a highly seasoned sauce made of tomatoes cooked with chilli and other spices.

chill out *Inf.* ◆ *vb* **1** (*intr, adv*) to relax, esp. after energetic dancing at a rave. ◆ *adj* **chill-out. 2** suitable for relaxation after energetic dancing: *a chill-out area; chill-out music.*

chilly 🅣 (ˈtʃɪlɪ) *adj* **chillier, chilliest. 1** causing or feeling cool or moderately cold. **2** without warmth; unfriendly. **3** (of people) sensitive to cold.
▸ **ˈchilliness** *n*

chilly bin *n NZ inf.* a portable insulated container with provision for packing food and drink in ice.

Chiltern Hundreds (ˈtʃɪltən) *pl n* (in Britain) short for **Stewardship of the Chiltern Hundreds;** a nominal office that an MP applies for in order to resign his seat.

chime[1] 🅣 (tʃaɪm) *n* **1** an individual bell or the sound it makes when struck. **2** (*often pl*) the machinery employed to sound a bell in this way. **3** Also called: **bell.** a percussion instrument consisting of a set of vertical metal tubes of graduated length, suspended in a frame and struck with a hammer. **4** agreement; concord. ◆ *vb* **chimes, chiming, chimed. 5a** to sound (a bell) or (of a bell) to be sounded by a clapper or hammer. **5b** to produce (music or sounds) by chiming. **6** (*tr*) to indicate or show (time or the hours) by chiming. **7** (*intr; foll. by with*) to agree or harmonize. [C13: prob. shortened from earlier *chymbe bell,* ult. from L *cymbalum* CYMBAL]
▸ **ˈchimer** *n*

chime[2], **chimb** (tʃaɪm), *or* **chine** *n* the projecting rim of a cask or barrel. [OE *cimb-*]

chime in *vb* (*intr, adv*) *Inf.* **1** to join in or interrupt (a conversation), esp. repeatedly and unwelcomely. **2** to voice agreement.

chimera 🅣 *or* **chimaera** (kaɪˈmɪərə, kɪ-) *n* **1** a wild and unrealistic dream or notion. **2** (*often cap.*) *Greek myth.* a fire-breathing monster with the head of a lion, body of a goat, and tail of a serpent. **3** a fabulous beast made up of parts taken from various animals. **4** *Biol.* an organism consisting of at least two genetically different kinds of tissue as a result of mutation, grafting, etc. [C16: from L, from Gk *khimaira* she-goat]

chimerical (kaɪˈmɛrɪkəl, kɪ-) *or* **chimeric** *adj* **1** wildly fanciful; imaginary. **2** given to or indulging in fantasies.
▸ **chiˈmerically** *adv*

chimney (ˈtʃɪmnɪ) *n* **1** a vertical structure of brick, masonry, or steel that carries smoke or steam away from a fire, engine, etc. **2** another name for **flue** (sense 1). **3** short for **chimney stack. 4** an open-ended glass tube fitting around the flame of an oil or gas lamp in order to exclude draughts. **5** *Brit.* a fireplace, esp. an old and large one. **6** the vent of a volcano. **7** *Mountaineering.* a vertical fissure large enough for a person's body to enter. [C14: from OF *cheminée,* from LL *camīnāta,* from L *camīnus* furnace, from Gk *kaminos* oven]

chimney breast *n* the wall or walls that surround the base of a chimney or fireplace.

chimneypot (ˈtʃɪmnɪˌpɒt) *n* a short pipe on the top of a chimney.

chimney stack *n* the part of a chimney that rises above the roof of a building.

chimney sweep *or* **sweeper** *n* a person who cleans soot from chimneys.

chimp (tʃɪmp) *n Inf.* short for **chimpanzee.**

chimpanzee (ˌtʃɪmpænˈziː) *n* a gregarious and intelligent anthropoid ape, inhabiting forests in central W Africa. [C18: from Central African dialect]

chin (tʃɪn) *n* **1** the protruding part of the lower jaw. **2** the front part of the face below the lips. **3 keep one's chin up.** *Inf.* to keep cheerful under difficult circumstances. **4 take it on the chin.** *Inf.* to face squarely up to a defeat, adversity, etc. ◆ *vb* **chins, chinning, chinned. 5** *Gymnastics.* to raise one's chin to (a horizontal bar, etc.) when hanging by the arms. [OE *cinn*]

Chin. *abbrev. for:* **1** China. **2** Chinese.

china 🅣 (ˈtʃaɪnə) *n* **1** ceramic ware of a type originally from China. **2** any porcelain or similar ware. **3** cups, saucers, etc., collectively. **4** (*modifier*) made of china. [C16 *chiny,* from Persian *chīnī*]

china clay *n* another name for **kaolin.**

Chinagraph (ˈtʃaɪnəˌgrɑːf) *n Trademark.* a coloured pencil used for writing on china, glass, etc.

Chinaman (ˈtʃaɪnəmən) *n, pl* **Chinamen. 1** *Arch. or derog.* a native or inhabitant of China. **2** (*often not cap.*) *Cricket.* a ball bowled by a left-handed bowler to a right-handed batsman that spins from off to leg.

china stone *n* **1** a type of kaolinized granitic rock containing unaltered plagioclase. **2** any of certain limestones having a very fine grain and smooth texture.

Chinatown (ˈtʃaɪnəˌtaʊn) *n* a quarter of any city or town outside China with a predominantly Chinese population.

chinaware (ˈtʃaɪnəˌwɛə) *n* articles made of china, esp. those made for domestic use.

chincherinchee (ˌtʃɪntʃərɪnˈtʃiː, -ˈrɪntʃɪ) *n* a bulbous South African liliaceous plant having long spikes of white or yellow long-lasting flowers. [from ?]

chinchilla (tʃɪnˈtʃɪlə) *n* **1** a small gregarious rodent inhabiting mountainous regions of South America. It is bred in captivity for its soft silvery grey fur. **2** the highly valued fur of this animal. **3** a thick napped woollen cloth used for coats. [C17: from Sp., ?from Aymara]

chin-chin *sentence substitute. Inf.* a greeting or toast. [C18: from Chinese (Peking) *ch'ing-ch'ing,* please-please]

Chindit (ˈtʃɪndɪt) *n* a member of the Allied forces fighting behind the Japanese lines in Burma (1943–45). [C20: from Burmese *chinthé* a fabulous lion]

chine[1] (tʃaɪn) *n* **1** the backbone. **2** the backbone of an animal with adjoining meat, cut for cooking. **3** a ridge or crest of land. ◆ *vb* **chines, chining, chined. 4** (*tr*) to cut (meat) along or across the backbone. [C14: from OF *eschine,* of Gmc origin; see SHIN]

chine[2] (tʃaɪn) *n S English dialect.* a deep fissure in the wall of a cliff. [OE *cīnan* to crack]

Chinese (tʃaɪˈniːz) *adj* **1** of, relating to, or characteristic of China, its people, or their languages. ◆ *n* **2** (*pl* **Chinese**) a native or inhabitant of China or a descendant of one. **3** any of the languages of China.

Chinese cabbage *n* **1** a Chinese plant that is related to the cabbage and has crisp edible leaves growing in a loose cylindrical head. **2** another name for **bok choy.**

Chinese chequers *n* (*functioning as sing*) a board game played with marbles or pegs.

Chinese gooseberry *n* another name for **kiwi fruit.**

Chinese lantern *n* **1** a collapsible lantern made of thin coloured paper. **2** an Asian plant, cultivated for its attractive orange-red inflated calyx.

Chinese leaf *n* another name for **bok choy.**

Chinese puzzle *n* **1** an intricate puzzle, esp. one consisting of boxes within boxes. **2** a complicated problem.

Chinese wall *n* (esp. in financial institutions) a notional barrier between departments in the same company in order to avoid conflicts of interest between them.

chink[1] 🅣 (tʃɪŋk) *n* **1** a small narrow opening, such as a fissure or crack. **2 chink in one's armour.** a small but fatal weakness. [C16: ? var. of earlier *chine,* from OE *cine* crack]

chink[2] (tʃɪŋk) *vb* **1** to make or cause to make a light ringing sound, as by the striking of glasses or coins. ◆ *n* **2** such a sound. [C16: imit.]

chinless wonder (ˈtʃɪnlɪs) *n Brit. inf.* a person, esp. upper-class, lacking strength of character.

chinoiserie (ʃiːnˌwɑːzəˈriː, -ˈwɑːzərɪ) *n* **1** a style of decorative or fine art based on imitations of Chinese motifs. **2** an object or objects in this style. [F, from *chinois* CHINESE; see -ERY]

chinook (tʃɪˈnuːk, -ˈnʊk) *n* **1** a warm dry southwesterly wind blowing down the eastern slopes of the Rocky Mountains. **2** a warm moist wind blowing onto the Washington and Oregon coasts from the sea. [C19: from Amerind]

Chinook (tʃɪˈnuːk, -ˈnʊk) *n* **1** (*pl* **Chinook** *or* **Chinooks**) a North American Indian people of the Pacific coast near the Columbia River. **2** the language of this people.

Chinook Jargon *n* a pidgin language containing elements of North American Indian languages, English, and French: formerly used among fur traders and Indians on the NW coast of North America.

Chinook salmon *n* a Pacific salmon valued as a food fish.

chinos (ˈtʃiːnəʊz) *pl n* trousers made of a durable cotton twill cloth. [C20: from *chino,* the cloth, from ?]

chintz (tʃɪnts) *n* a printed, patterned cotton fabric, with glazed finish. [C17: from Hindi *chīnt,* from Sansk. *citra* gaily-coloured]

chintzy (ˈtʃɪntsɪ) *adj* **chintzier, chintziest. 1** of, resembling, or covered with chintz. **2** *Brit. inf.* typical of the décor associated with the use of chintz soft furnishings.

chinwag (ˈtʃɪnˌwæg) *n Brit. inf.* a chat.

chip 🅣 (tʃɪp) *n* **1** a small piece removed by chopping, cutting, or breaking. **2** a mark left after a small piece has been broken off something. **3** (in some games) a counter used to represent money. **4** a thin strip of potato fried in deep fat. **5** the US, Canad. and Austral. name for **crisp** (sense 10). **6** *Sport.* a shot, kick, etc., lofted into the air, and travelling only a short distance. **7** *Electronics.* Also called: **microchip.** a tiny wafer of semiconductor material, such as silicon, processed to form a type

THESAURUS

cool, congeal, freeze, refrigerate **8 = dishearten,** dampen, deject, depress, discourage, dismay

chilly *adj* **1 = cool,** brisk, cold, crisp, fresh, nippy, parky (*Brit. inf.*), penetrating, sharp, wintry **2 = unfriendly,** aloof, cold as ice, cool, distant, frigid, hostile, stony, ungenial, unresponsive, unsympathetic, unwelcoming
Antonyms *adj* ≠ **cool:** balmy, hot, mild, scorching, sunny, sweltering, warm ≠ **unfriendly:** affable, chummy (*inf.*), congenial, cordial, friendly, responsive, sociable, sympathetic, warm, welcoming

chime *vb* **5a = ring,** boom, clang, dong, jingle, peal, sound, tinkle, toll

chimera *n* **1, 3 = illusion,** bogy, delusion, dream, fantasy, figment, hallucination, ignis fatuus, monster, monstrosity, snare, spectre, will-o'-the-wisp

china *n* **2, 3 = pottery,** ceramics, crockery, porcelain, service, tableware, ware

chink[1] *n* **1 = opening,** aperture, cleft, crack, cranny, crevice, cut, fissure, flaw, gap, rift

chip *n* **1, 2 = scratch,** dent, flake, flaw, fragment, nick, notch, paring, scrap, shard, shav-

of integrated circuit or component such as a transistor. **8** a thin strip of wood or straw used for making woven hats, baskets, etc. **9** *NZ.* a container for soft fruit, made of thin sheets of wood; punnet. **10 chip off the old block.** *Inf.* a person who resembles one of his or her parents in behaviour. **11 have a chip on one's shoulder.** *Inf.* to be aggressive or bear a grudge. **12 have had one's chips.** *Brit. inf.* to be defeated, condemned to die, killed, etc. **13 when the chips are down.** *Inf.* at a time of crisis. ◆ *vb* **chips, chipping, chipped. 14** to break small pieces from or become broken off in small pieces: *will the paint chip?* **15** (*tr*) to break or cut into small pieces: *to chip ice.* **16** (*tr*) to shape by chipping. **17** *Austral.* to dig or weed (a crop) with a hoe. **18** *Sport.* to strike or kick (a ball) in a high arc. [OE *cipp* (n), *cippian* (vb), from ?]

chip-based *adj* using or incorporating microchips in electronic equipment.

chipboard ('tʃɪpˌbɔːd) *n* a thin rigid sheet made of compressed wood chips.

chip heater *n Austral. & NZ.* a domestic water heater that burns chips of wood.

chip in ⓣ *vb* (*adv*) *Inf.* **1** to contribute (money, time, etc.) to a cause or fund. **2** (*intr*) to interpose a remark or interrupt with a remark.

chipmunk ('tʃɪpˌmʌŋk) *n* a burrowing rodent of North America and Asia, typically having black-striped yellowish fur and cheek pouches for storing food. [C19: of Algonquian origin]

chipolata (ˌtʃɪpə'lɑːtə) *n Chiefly Brit.* a small sausage. [via F from It., from *cipolla* onion]

Chippendale ('tʃɪpᵊnˌdeɪl) *adj* (of furniture) designed by, made by, or in the style of Thomas Chippendale (?1718–79), characterized by the use of Chinese and Gothic motifs, cabriole legs, and massive carving.

chipper ('tʃɪpə) *adj Inf.* **1** cheerful; lively. **2** smartly dressed.

chippy[1] ('tʃɪpɪ) *n, pl* **chippies. 1** *Brit. inf.* a fish-and-chip shop. **2** *NZ.* a potato crisp.

chippy[2] ('tʃɪpɪ) *adj* **chippier, chippiest.** *Inf.* resentful or oversensitive about being perceived as inferior: *a chippy miner's son.* [C20: from CHIP (sense 11)]
▸**'chippiness** *n*

chip shot *n Golf.* a short approach shot to the green, esp. one that is lofted.

chiral ('kaɪrəl) *adj* relating to chirality. [C20: from CHIRO- + -AL[1]]

chirality (kaɪ'rælɪtɪ) *n* right- or left-handedness in an asymmetric molecule.

chiro- *or* **cheiro-** *combining form.* of or by means of the hand: *chiromancy; chiropractic.* [via L from Gk *kheir* hand]

chirography (kaɪ'rɒgrəfɪ) *n* another name for **calligraphy.**
▸**chi'rographer** *n* ▸**chirographic** (ˌkaɪrə'græfɪk) *or* **ˌchiro'graphical** *adj*

chiromancy ('kaɪrəˌmænsɪ) *n* another word for **palmistry.**
▸**'chiroˌmancer** *n*

chiropody (kɪ'rɒpədɪ) *n* the treatment of the feet, esp. corns, verrucas, etc.
▸**chi'ropodist** *n*

chiropractic (ˌkaɪrə'præktɪk) *n* a system of treating bodily disorders by manipulation of the spine and other parts. [C20: from CHIRO- + Gk *praktikos* PRACTICAL]
▸**'chiroˌpractor** *n*

chirp ⓣ (tʃɜːp) *vb* (*intr*) **1** (esp. of some birds and insects) to make a short high-pitched sound. **2** to speak in a lively fashion. ◆ *n* **3** a chirping sound. [C15 (as *chirpinge,* gerund): imit.]
▸**'chirper** *n*

chirpy ⓣ ('tʃɜːpɪ) *adj* **chirpier, chirpiest.** *Inf.* cheerful; lively.
▸**'chirpily** *adv* ▸**'chirpiness** *n*

chirr *or* **churr** (tʃɜː) *vb* **1** (*intr*) (esp. of certain insects, such as crickets) to make a shrill trilled sound. ◆ *n* **2** such a sound. [C17: imit.]

chirrup ('tʃɪrəp) *vb* (*intr*) **1** (esp. of some birds) to chirp repeatedly. **2** to make clucking sounds with the lips. ◆ *n* **3** such a sound. [C16: var. of CHIRP]
▸**'chirruper** *n* ▸**'chirrupy** *adj*

chisel ('tʃɪzᵊl) *n* **1a** a hand tool for working wood, consisting of a flat steel blade with a handle. **1b** a similar tool without a handle for working stone or metal. ◆ *vb* **chisels, chiselling, chiselled** *or US* **chisels, chiseling, chiseled. 2** to carve (wood, stone, metal, etc.) or form (an engraving, statue, etc.) with or as with a chisel. **3** *Sl.* to cheat or obtain by cheating. [C14: via OF, from Vulgar L *cīsellus* (unattested), from L *caesus* cut]

chiseller ('tʃɪzᵊlə) *n* **1** a person who uses a chisel. **2** *Inf.* a cheat. **3** *Dublin sl.* a child.

chi-square distribution *n Statistics.* a continuous single-parameter distribution used esp. to measure goodness of fit and to test hypotheses.

chi-square test *n Statistics.* a test derived from the chi-square distribution to compare the goodness of fit of theoretical and observed frequency distributions.

chit[1] (tʃɪt) *n* **1** a voucher for a sum of money owed, esp. for food or drink. **2** Also called: **chitty.** *Chiefly Brit.* **2a** a note or memorandum. **2b** a requisition or receipt. [C18: from earlier *chitty,* from Hindi *cittha* note, from Sansk. *citra* marked]

chit[2] (tʃɪt) *n Facetious or derog.* a pert, impudent, or self-confident girl or child. [C14 (in the sense: young of an animal, kitten): from ?]

chital ('tʃiːtᵊl) *n* another name for **axis**[2] (the deer). [from Hindi]

chitchat ('tʃɪtˌtʃæt) *n* **1** gossip. ◆ *vb* **chitchats, chitchatting, chitchatted. 2** (*intr*) to gossip.

chitin ('kaɪtɪn) *n* a polysaccharide that is the principal component of the exoskeletons of arthropods and of the bodies of fungi. [C19: from F, from Gk *khitōn* CHITON + -IN]
▸**'chitinous** *adj*

chiton ('kaɪtᵊn, -tɒn) *n* **1** (in ancient Greece) a loose woollen tunic worn by men and women. **2** any small primitive marine mollusc having an elongated body covered with eight overlapping shell plates. [C19: from Gk *khitōn* coat of mail]

chitterlings ('tʃɪtəlɪŋz) *or* **chitlings** ('tʃɪtlɪŋz) *pl n* (*sometimes sing*) the intestines of a pig or other animal prepared as a dish. [C13: from ?]

chiv (tʃɪv, ʃɪv) *or* **shiv** (ʃɪv) *Sl.* ◆ *n* **1** a knife. ◆ *vb* **chivs, chivving, chivved** *or* **shivs, shivving, shivved. 2** to stab (someone). [C17: ?from Romany *chiv* blade]

chivalrous ⓣ ('ʃɪvəlrəs) *adj* **1** gallant; courteous. **2** involving chivalry. [C14: from OF, from CHEVALIER]
▸**'chivalrously** *adv* ▸**'chivalrousness** *n*

chivalry ⓣ ('ʃɪvəlrɪ) *n, pl* **chivalries. 1** the combination of qualities expected of an ideal knight, esp. courage, honour, justice, and a readiness to help the weak. **2** courteous behaviour, esp. towards women. **3** the medieval system and principles of knighthood. **4** knights, noblemen, etc., collectively. [C13: from OF *chevalerie,* from CHEVALIER]
▸**'chivalric** *adj*

chive (tʃaɪv) *n* a small Eurasian purple-flowered alliaceous plant, whose long slender hollow leaves are used in cooking. Also called: **chives.** [C14: from OF *cive,* ult. from L *caepa* onion]

chivy ⓣ, **chivvy** ('tʃɪvɪ), *or* **chevy** *Brit.* ◆ *vb* **chivies, chivying, chivied, chivvies, chivvying, chivvied,** *or* **chevies, chevying, chevied. 1** (*tr*) to harass or nag. **2** (*tr*) to hunt. **3** (*intr*) to run about. ◆ *n, pl* **chivies, chivvies,** *or* **chevies. 4** a hunt. **5** *Obs.* a hunting cry. [C19: var. of *chevy,* prob. from *Chevy Chase,* title of a Scottish border ballad]

chlamydia (klə'mɪdɪə) *n* any of a genus of virus-like bacteria responsible for such diseases as trachoma, psittacosis, and some sexually transmitted diseases. [C20: NL, from Gk *khlamus* mantle + -IA]

chloral ('klɔːrəl) *n* **1** a colourless oily liquid with a pungent odour, made from chlorine and acetaldehyde and used in preparing chloral hydrate and DDT. Formula: CCl_3CHO. **2** short for **chloral hydrate.**

chloral hydrate *n* a colourless crystalline soluble solid produced by the reaction of chloral with water and used as a sedative and hypnotic. Formula: $CCl_3C(OH)_3$.

chloramphenicol (ˌklɔːræm'fɛnɪˌkɒl) *n* a broad-spectrum antibiotic used esp. in treating typhoid fever and rickettsial infections. [C20: from CHLORO- + AM(IDE)- + PHE(NO)- + NI(TRO)- + (GLY)COL]

chlorate ('klɔːreɪt, -rɪt) *n* any salt of chloric acid, containing the monovalent ion ClO_3^-.

chlordane ('klɔːdeɪn) *or* **chlordan** *n* a white insoluble toxic solid used as an insecticide. [C20: from CHLORO- + (IN)D(OLE + -ENE) + -ANE]

chlorhexidine (klɔː'hɛksɪdiːn) *n* an antiseptic compound used in skin cleansers, mouthwashes, etc. [C20: from CHLOR(O)- + HEX(ANE) + -I(DE) + (AM)INE]

chloric ('klɔːrɪk) *adj* of or containing chlorine in the pentavalent state.

chloric acid *n* a strong acid with a pungent smell, known only in solution and in the form of chlorate salts. Formula: $HClO_3$.

chloride ('klɔːraɪd) *n* **1** any salt of hydrochloric acid, containing the chloride ion Cl^-. **2** any compound containing a chlorine atom, such as methyl chloride (chloromethane), CH_3Cl.

chloride of lime *or* **chlorinated lime** *n* another name for **bleaching powder.**

chlorinate ('klɔːrɪˌneɪt) *vb* **chlorinates, chlorinating, chlorinated.** (*tr*) **1** to combine or treat (a substance) with chlorine. **2** to disinfect (water) with chlorine.
▸**ˌchlorin'ation** *n* ▸**'chlorinˌator** *n*

chlorine ('klɔːriːn) *or* **chlorin** ('klɔːrɪn) *n* a toxic pungent greenish-yellow gas of the halogen group; occurring only in the combined state, mainly in common salt: used in the manufacture of many organic chemicals, in water purification, and as a disinfectant and bleaching agent. Symbol: Cl; atomic no.: 17; atomic wt.: 35.453. [C19 (coined by Sir Humphrey Davy): from CHLORO- + -INE[2], referring to its colour]

chlorite[1] ('klɔːraɪt) *n* any of a group of green soft secondary minerals

THESAURUS

ing, sliver, wafer ◆ *vb* **14** = **nick**, chisel, damage, gash, whittle

chip in *vb* **1, 2** *Informal* = **contribute**, donate, go Dutch (*inf.*), interpose, interrupt, pay, subscribe

chirp *vb* **1** = **chirrup**, cheep, peep, pipe, tweet, twitter, warble

chirpy *adj Informal* = **cheerful**, animated, blithe, bright, buoyant, enlivening, enthusiastic, full of beans (*inf.*), happy, in high spirits, jaunty, jolly, light-hearted, lively, radiant, sparkling, sprightly, sunny

chivalrous *adj* **1** = **courteous**, bold, brave, courageous, courtly, gallant, gentlemanly, heroic, high-minded, honourable, intrepid, knightly, magnanimous, true, valiant
Antonyms *adj* boorish, cowardly, dishonourable, disloyal, rude, uncourtly, ungallant, unmannerly

chivalry *n* **1-3** = **courtesy**, courage, courtliness, gallantry, gentlemanliness, knight-errantry, knighthood, politeness

chivy *vb Brit.* **1** = **nag**, annoy, badger, bend someone's ear (*inf.*), breathe down someone's neck (*inf.*), bug (*inf.*), harass, hassle (*inf.*), hound, pester, plague, pressure (*inf.*), prod, torment

consisting of the hydrated silicates of aluminium, iron, and magnesium. [C18: from L, from Gk, from *khlōros* greenish yellow]
▸**chloritic** (klɔːˈrɪtɪk) *adj*

chlorite[2] (ˈklɔːraɪt) *n* any salt of chlorous acid.

chloro- *or before a vowel* **chlor-** *combining form*. **1** indicating the colour green: *chlorophyll*. **2** chlorine: *chloroform*.

chlorofluorocarbon (ˌklɔːrəˌfluərəʊˈkɑːbᵊn) *n Chem.* any of various gaseous compounds of carbon, hydrogen, chlorine, and fluorine, used as refrigerants, aerosol propellants, solvents, and in foam: some cause a breakdown of ozone in the earth's atmosphere.

chloroform (ˈklɔːrəˌfɔːm) *n* a heavy volatile liquid with a sweet taste and odour, used as a solvent and cleansing agent and in refrigerants: formerly used as an inhalation anaesthetic. Formula: $CHCl_3$. Systematic name: **trichloromethane.** [C19: from CHLORO- + *formyl* from FORMIC]

Chloromycetin (ˌklɔːrəʊmaɪˈsiːtɪn) *n Trademark*. a brand of **chloramphenicol.**

chlorophyll *or US* **chlorophyl** (ˈklɔːrəfɪl) *n* the green pigment of plants, occurring in chloroplasts, that traps the energy of sunlight for photosynthesis: used as a colouring agent (**E140**) in medicines and food.
▸ˈ**chloroˌphylloid** *adj* ▸ˌ**chloroˈphyllous** *adj*

chloroplast (ˈklɔːrəʊˌplæst) *n* a plastid containing chlorophyll and other pigments, occurring in plants that carry out photosynthesis.

chlorosis (klɔːˈrəʊsɪs) *n* **1** Also called: **greensickness.** *Pathol.* a once-common iron-deficiency disease of adolescent girls, characterized by greenish-yellow skin colour, weakness, and palpitation. **2** *Bot.* a deficiency of chlorophyll in green plants caused by mineral deficiency, lack of light, disease, etc., the leaves appearing uncharacteristically pale. [C17: from CHLORO- + -OSIS]
▸**chlorotic** (klɔːˈrɒtɪk) *adj*

chlorous (ˈklɔːrəs) *adj* **1** of or containing chlorine in the trivalent state. **2** of or containing chlorous acid.

chlorous acid *n* an unstable acid that is a strong oxidizing agent. Formula: $HClO_2$.

chlorpromazine (klɔːˈprɒməˌziːn) *n* a drug used as a sedative and tranquillizer. [C20: from CHLORO- + PRO(PYL + A)M(INE) + AZINE]

chlortetracycline (klɔːˌtetrəˈsaɪkliːn) *n* an antibiotic used in treating many bacterial and rickettsial infections and some viral infections.

chock (tʃɒk) *n* **1** a block or wedge of wood used to prevent the sliding or rolling of a heavy object. **2** *Naut.* **2a** a ringlike device with an opening at the top through which a rope is placed. **2b** a cradle-like support for a boat, barrel, etc. ◆ *vb* (*tr*) **3** (usually foll. by *up*) *Brit.* to cram full. **4** to fit with or secure by a chock. **5** to support (a boat, barrel, etc.) on chocks. ◆ *adv* **6** as closely or tightly as possible: *chock against the wall.* [C17: from ?; ? rel. to OF *çoche* log]

chock-a-block *adj, adv* **1** filled to capacity; in a crammed state. **2** *Naut.* with the blocks brought close together, as when a tackle is pulled as tight as possible.

chocker (ˈtʃɒkə) *adj* **1** *Austral. & NZ inf.* full up; packed. **2** *Brit. sl.* irritated; fed up. [C20: from CHOCK-A-BLOCK]

chock-full *or* **choke-full** *adj* (*postpositive*) completely full. [C17 *choke-full*; see CHOKE, FULL[1]]

choco *or* **chocko** (ˈtʃɒkəʊ) *n, pl* **chocos** *or* **chockos.** *Austral. sl.* a conscript or militiaman. [from *chocolate soldier*]

chocolate (ˈtʃɒkəlɪt, ˈtʃɒklɪt, -lət) *n* **1** a food preparation made from roasted ground cacao seeds, usually sweetened and flavoured. **2** a drink or sweetmeat made from this. **3a** a deep brown colour. **3b** (*as adj*): *a chocolate carpet.* [C17: from Sp., from Aztec *xocolatl*, from *xococ* sour + *atl* water]
▸ˈ**chocolaty** *adj*

chocolate-box *n* (*modifier*) *Inf.* sentimentally pretty or appealing.

Choctaw (ˈtʃɒktɔː) *n* **1** (*pl* **-taws** *or* **-taw**) a member of a N American people originally of Alabama. **2** their language. [C18: from Choctaw *Chahta*]

choice ❶ (tʃɔɪs) *n* **1** the act or an instance of choosing or selecting. **2** the opportunity or power of choosing. **3** a person or thing chosen or that may be chosen: *he was a possible choice.* **4** an alternative action or possibility: *what choice did I have?* **5** a supply from which to select. ◆ *adj* **6** of superior quality; excellent: *choice wine.* **7** carefully chosen, appropriate: *a few choice words will do the trick.* **8** vulgar or rude: *choice language.* [C13: from OF, from *choisir* to CHOOSE]
▸ˈ**choicely** *adv* ▸ˈ**choiceness** *n*

choir (ˈkwaɪə) *n* **1** an organized group of singers, esp. for singing in church services. **2** the part of a cathedral, abbey, or church in front of the altar and used by the choir and clergy. **3** a number of instruments of the same family playing together: *a brass choir.* **4** Also called: **choir organ.** one of the manuals on an organ controlling a set of soft sweet-toned pipes. [C13 *quer*, from OF *cuer*, from L CHORUS]

choirboy (ˈkwaɪəˌbɔɪ) *n* a young boy who sings the treble part in a church choir.

choir school *n* (in Britain) a school attached to a cathedral, college, etc., offering general education to boys whose singing ability is good.

choke ❶ (tʃəʊk) *vb* **chokes, choking, choked.** **1** (*tr*) to hinder or stop the breathing of (a person or animal), esp. by constricting the windpipe or by asphyxiation. **2** (*intr*) to have trouble or fail in breathing, swallowing, or speaking. **3** (*tr*) to block or clog up (a passage, pipe, street, etc.). **4** (*tr*) to retard the growth or action of: *the weeds are choking my plants.* **5** (*tr*) to enrich the petrol-air mixture by reducing the air supply to (a carburettor, petrol engine, etc.). ◆ *n* **6** the act or sound of choking. **7** a device in the carburettor of a petrol engine that enriches the petrol-air mixture by reducing the air supply. **8** any mechanism for reducing the flow of a fluid in a pipe, tube, etc. **9** Also called: **choke coil.** *Electronics.* an inductor having a relatively high impedance, used to prevent the passage of high frequencies or to smooth the output of a rectifier. [OE *ācēocian*]
▸ˈ**choky** *or* ˈ**chokey** *adj*

choke back *or* **down** *vb* (*tr, adv*) to suppress (anger, tears, etc.).

choke chain *n* a collar and lead for a dog so designed that if the dog drags on the lead the collar tightens round its neck.

choked (tʃəʊkt) *adj Brit. inf.* annoyed or disappointed.

choker (ˈtʃəʊkə) *n* **1** a woman's high collar. **2** any neckband or necklace worn tightly around the throat. **3** a high clerical collar; stock. **4** a person who chokes. **5** something that causes a person to choke.

choke up *vb* (*tr, adv*) **1** to block (a drain, pipe, etc.) completely. **2** *Inf.* (*usually passive*) to overcome (a person) with emotion.

chokey *or* **choky** (ˈtʃəʊkɪ) *n Brit. sl.* prison. [C17: from Anglo-Indian, from Hindi *caukī* a lockup]

choko (ˈtʃəʊkəʊ) *n, pl* **chokos.** *Austral. & NZ.* the cucumber-like fruit of a tropical American vine: eaten as a vegetable in the Caribbean, Australia, and New Zealand. [C18: from Brazilian Indian]

cholangiography (kəˌlændʒɪˈɒgrəfɪ) *n* radiographic examination of the bile ducts after the introduction into them of a contrast medium.

chole- *or before a vowel* **chol-** *combining form.* bile or gall: *cholesterol.* [from Gk *kholē*]

choler (ˈkɒlə) *n* **1** anger or ill humour. **2** *Arch.* one of the four bodily humours; yellow bile. [C14: from OF, from Med. L, from L: jaundice, CHOLERA]

cholera (ˈkɒlərə) *n* an acute intestinal infection characterized by severe diarrhoea, cramp, etc.: caused by ingestion of water or food contaminated with the bacterium *Vibrio comma.* [C14: from L, from Gk *kholera* jaundice, from *kholē* bile]
▸**choleraic** (ˌkɒləˈreɪɪk) *adj*

choleric (ˈkɒlərɪk) *adj* **1** bad-tempered. **2** *Obs.* bilious or causing biliousness.
▸ˈ**cholerically** *adv*

cholesterol (kəˈlestəˌrɒl) *or* **cholesterin** (kəˈlestərɪn) *n* a sterol found in all animal tissues, blood, bile, and animal fats. A high level of cholesterol is implicated in some cases of atherosclerosis. [C19: from CHOLE- + Gk *stereos* solid]

choline (ˈkəʊliːn, -ɪn, ˈkɒl-) *n* a colourless viscous soluble alkaline substance present in animal tissues, esp. as a constituent of lecithin. [C19: from CHOLE- + -INE[2]]

chomp (tʃɒmp) *or* **chump** *vb* **1** to chew (food) noisily; champ. ◆ *n* **2** the act or sound of chewing in this manner. [var. of CHAMP[1]]

Chondokyo (ˌtʃɒndəʊˈkjəʊ) *n* an indigenous religion of Korea, incorporating elements of Buddhism, Confucianism, Christianity, and shamanism. Former name: **Tongchak.** [C20: from Korean: Religion of the Heavenly Way]

chondrite (ˈkɒndraɪt) *n* a stony meteorite consisting mainly of silicate minerals in small spherical masses.

choof off (tʃʊf) *vb* (*intr, adv*) *Austral. sl.* to go away; make off.

chook (tʃʊk) *n Inf., chiefly Austral. & NZ.* a hen or chicken. Also called: **chookie.**

choose ❶ (tʃuːz) *vb* **chooses, choosing, chose, chosen.** **1** to select (a person, thing, course of action, etc.) from a number of alternatives. **2** (*tr; takes a clause as object or an infinitive*) to consider it desirable or proper: *I don't choose to read that book.* **3** (*intr*) to like; please: *you may stand if you choose.* [OE *ceosan*]
▸ˈ**chooser** *n*

choosy ❶ (ˈtʃuːzɪ) *adj* **choosier, choosiest.** *Inf.* particular in making a choice; difficult to please.

chop[1] ❶ (tʃɒp) *vb* **chops, chopping, chopped.** **1** (often foll. by *down* or *off*) to cut (something) with a blow from an axe or other sharp tool. **2** (*tr; often foll. by up*) to cut into pieces. **3** (*tr*) *Brit. inf.* to dispense with or reduce. **4** (*intr*) to move quickly or violently. **5** *Tennis, cricket, etc.* to hit (a ball) sharply downwards. **6** *Boxing, karate, etc.* to punch or strike (an opponent) with a short sharp blow. ◆ *n* **7** a cutting blow. **8** the act or an instance of chopping. **9** a piece chopped off. **10** a slice of mutton, lamb, or pork, generally including a rib. **11** *Austral. & NZ sl.* a share (esp. in **get** *or* **hop in for one's chop**). **12** *Austral. & NZ.* a competition of skill and speed in chopping logs. **13** *Sport.* a sharp downward blow or stroke. **14 not much chop.** *Austral. & NZ inf.* not much good; poor. **15 the chop.** *Brit. & Austral. sl.* dismissal from employment. [C16: var. of CHAP[1]]

THESAURUS

choice *n* **1-4** = **option**, alternative, discrimination, election, pick, preference, say **5** = **selection**, range, variety ◆ *adj* **6** = **best**, elect, elite, excellent, exclusive, exquisite, hand-picked, nice, precious, prime, prize, rare, select, special, superior, uncommon, unusual, valuable

choke *vb* **1** = **strangle**, asphyxiate, gag, overpower, smother, stifle, suffocate, suppress, throttle **3** = **block**, bar, bung, clog, close, congest, constrict, dam, obstruct, occlude, stop

choose *vb* **1, 3** = **pick**, adopt, cherry-pick, cull, designate, desire, elect, espouse, fix on, opt for, predestine, prefer, see fit, select, settle upon, single out, take, wish
Antonyms *vb* decline, dismiss, exclude, forgo, leave, refuse, reject, throw aside

choosy *adj Informal* = **fussy**, discriminating, exacting, faddy, fastidious, finicky, particular, picky (*inf.*), selective
Antonyms *adj* easy (*inf.*), easy to please, indiscriminate, undemanding, unselective

chop[1] *vb* **1** = **cut**, axe, cleave, fell, hack, hew, lop, sever, shear, slash, truncate **2** *often foll. by* **up** = **cut up**, cube, dice, divide, fragment, mince

chop[2] (tʃɒp) *vb* **chops, chopping, chopped. 1** (*intr*) to change direction suddenly; vacillate (esp. in **chop and change**). **2 chop logic.** use excessively subtle or involved argument. [OE *ceapian* to barter]

chop[3] (tʃɒp) *n* a design stamped on goods as a trademark, esp. in the Far East. [C17: from Hindi *chhāp*]

chop chop *adv* pidgin English for **quickly.** [C19: from Chinese dialect]

chophouse ('tʃɒp,haʊs) *n* a restaurant specializing in steaks, grills, chops, etc.

chopper ('tʃɒpə) *n* **1** *Chiefly Brit.* a small hand axe. **2** a butcher's cleaver. **3** a person or thing that cuts or chops. **4** an informal name for a **helicopter. 5** a device for periodically interrupting an electric current or beam of radiation to produce a pulsed current or beam. **6** a type of bicycle or motorcycle with very high handlebars. **7** *NZ.* a child's bicycle. **8** *Sl., chiefly US.* a sub-machine-gun.

choppy ❶ ('tʃɒpɪ) *adj* **choppier, choppiest.** (of the sea, weather, etc.) fairly rough.
▸**'choppily** *adv* ▸**'choppiness** *n*

chops (tʃɒps) *pl n* **1** the jaws or cheeks; jowls. **2** the mouth. **3 lick one's chops.** *Inf.* to anticipate with pleasure. [C16: from ?]

chopsticks ('tʃɒpstɪks) *pl n* a pair of thin sticks, of ivory, wood, etc., used for eating Chinese or other East Asian food. [C17: from pidgin E, from *chop* quick, from Chinese dialect + STICK[1]]

chop suey ('su:ɪ) *n* a Chinese-style dish originating in the US, consisting of meat, bean sprouts, etc., served with rice. [C19: from Chinese *tsap sui* odds and ends]

choral ('kɔ:rəl) *adj* relating to, sung by, or designed for a chorus or choir.
▸**'chorally** *adv*

chorale *or* **choral** (kɒ'rɑ:l) *n* **1** a slow stately hymn tune. **2** *Chiefly US.* a choir or chorus. [C19: from G *Choralgesang,* translation of L *cantus chorālis* choral song]

chord[1] (kɔ:d) *n* **1** *Maths.* a straight line connecting two points on a curve or curved surface. **2** *Engineering.* one of the principal members of a truss, esp. one that lies along the top or the bottom. **3** *Anat.* a variant spelling of **cord. 4** an emotional response, esp. one of sympathy: *the story struck the right chord.* [C16: from L, from Gk *khordē* gut, string; see CORD]

chord[2] (kɔ:d) *n* **1** the simultaneous sounding of a group of musical notes, usually three or more in number. ◆ *vb* **2** (*tr*) to provide (a melodic line) with chords. [C15: short for ACCORD; spelling infl. by CHORD[1]]
▸**'chordal** *adj*

chordate ('kɔ:deɪt) *n* **1** an animal with a backbone or notochord. ◆ *adj* **2** of or relating to the chordates. [C19: from Med. L *chordata:* see CHORD[1] & -ATE[1]]

chore ❶ (tʃɔ:) *n* **1** a routine task, esp. a domestic one. **2** a boring task. [C19: from ME *chare,* from OE *cierr* a job]

-chore *n combining form.* (in botany) indicating a plant that is distributed by a certain means: *anemochore.* [from Gk *khōrein* to move]
▸**-chorous** *or* **-choric** *adj combining form.*

chorea (kɒ'rɪə) *n* a disorder of the central nervous system characterized by uncontrollable irregular jerky movements. See **Huntington's disease, Sydenham's chorea.** [C19: from NL, from L: dance, from Gk *khoreia;* see CHORUS]

choreograph ('kɒrɪə,grɑ:f) *vb* (*tr*) to compose the steps and dances for (a ballet, etc.)

choreography (,kɒrɪ'ɒgrəfɪ) *or* **choregraphy** (kɒ'rɛgrəfɪ) *n* **1** the composition of dance steps and sequences for ballet and stage and film dancing. **2** the steps and sequences of a ballet or dance. **3** the notation representing such steps. **4** the art of dancing. [C18: from Gk *khoreia* dance + -GRAPHY]
▸**,chore'ographer** *or* **cho'regrapher** *n* ▸**choreographic** (,kɒrɪə'græfɪk) *or* **choregraphic** (,kɒrə'græfɪk) *adj* ▸**,choreo'graphically** *or* **,chore'graphically** *adv*

choric ('kɒrɪk) *adj* of, like, or for a chorus, esp. of singing, dancing, or the speaking of verse.

chorion ('kɔ:rɪən) *n* the outer membrane surrounding an embryo. [C16: from Gk *khorion* afterbirth]
▸**chorionic** (,kɔ:rɪ'ɒnɪk) *adj*

chorionic gonadotrophin *n* a hormone, secreted by the placenta in mammals, that promotes the secretion of progesterone. See **HCG.**

chorionic villus sampling *n* a method of diagnosing genetic disorders early in pregnancy by the removal by catheter through the cervix of a tiny sample of tissue from the chorionic villi. Abbrev.: **CVS.**

chorister ('kɒrɪstə) *n* a singer in a choir, esp. a choirboy. [C14: from Med. L *chorista*]

choroid ('kɔ:rɔɪd) *or* **chorioid** ('kɔ:rɪ,ɔɪd) *adj* **1** resembling the chorion, esp. in being vascular. ◆ *n* **2** the vascular membrane of the eyeball between the sclera and the retina. [C18: from Gk *khoroeidēs,* erroneously for *khorioeidēs,* from CHORION]

chortle ❶ ('tʃɔ:t[ə]l) *vb* **chortles, chortling, chortled. 1** (*intr*) to chuckle gleefully. ◆ *n* **2** a gleeful chuckle. [C19: coined (1871) by Lewis Carroll; prob. a blend of CHUCKLE + SNORT]
▸**'chortler** *n*

chorus ❶ ('kɔ:rəs) *n, pl* **choruses. 1** a large choir of singers or a piece of music composed for such a choir. **2** a body of singers or dancers who perform together. **3** a section of a song in which a soloist is joined by a group of singers, esp. in a recurring refrain. **4** an intermediate section of a pop song, blues, etc., as distinct from the verse. **5** *Jazz.* any of a series of variations on a theme. **6** (in ancient Greece) **6a** a lyric poem sung by a group of dancers, originally as a religious rite. **6b** an ode or series of odes sung by a group of actors. **6c** the actors who sang the chorus and commented on the action of the play. **7a** (esp. in Elizabethan drama) the actor who spoke the prologue, etc. **7b** the part spoken by this actor. **8** a group of people or animals producing words or sounds simultaneously. **9** any speech, song, or utterance produced by a group of people or animals simultaneously: *the dawn chorus.* **10 in chorus.** in unison. ◆ *vb* **11** to speak, sing, or utter (words, sounds, etc.) in unison. [C16: from L, from Gk *khoros*]

chorus girl *n* a girl who dances or sings in the chorus of a musical comedy, revue, etc.

chose (tʃəʊz) *vb* the past tense of **choose.**

chosen ('tʃəʊz[ə]n) *vb* **1** the past participle of **choose.** ◆ *adj* **2** selected, esp. for some special quality.

chough (tʃʌf) *n* a large black passerine bird of parts of Europe, Asia, and Africa, with a long downward-curving red bill: family Corvidae (crows). [C14: from ?]

choux pastry (ʃu:) *n* a very light pastry made with eggs, used for éclairs, etc. [partial translation of F *pâte choux* cabbage dough]

chow (tʃaʊ) *n* **1** *Inf.* food. **2** short for **chow-chow** (sense 1).

chow-chow *n* **1** a thick-coated breed of dog with a curled tail, originally from China. Often shortened to **chow. 2** a Chinese preserve of ginger, orange peel, etc., in syrup. **3** a mixed vegetable pickle. [C19: from pidgin E, prob. based on Chinese *cha* miscellaneous]

chowder ('tʃaʊdə) *n Chiefly US & Canad.* a thick soup or stew containing clams or fish. [C18: from F *chaudière* kettle, from LL *caldāria;* see CAULDRON]

chow mein (meɪn) *n* a Chinese-American dish, consisting of mushrooms, meat, shrimps, etc., served with fried noodles. [from Chinese *ch'ao mien* fried noodles]

Chr. *abbrev. for:* **1** Christ. **2** Christian.

chrism *or* **chrisom** ('krɪzəm) *n* a mixture of olive oil and balsam used for sacramental anointing in the Greek Orthodox and Roman Catholic Churches. [OE, from Med. L, from Gk, from *khriein* to anoint]
▸**chrismal** ('krɪzməl) *adj*

Christ (kraɪst) *n* **1** Jesus of Nazareth (Jesus Christ), regarded by Christians as fulfilling Old Testament prophecies of the Messiah. **2** the Messiah or anointed one of God as the subject of Old Testament prophecies. **3** an image or picture of Christ. ◆ *interj* **4** *Taboo sl.* an oath expressing anger, etc. ◆ See also **Jesus.** [OE *Crīst,* from L *Chrīstus,* from Gk *khristos* anointed one (from *khriein* to anoint), translating Heb. *māshīah* MESSIAH]
▸ **'Christly** *adj*

Christadelphian (,krɪstə'dɛlfɪən) *n* **1** a member of a Christian millenarian sect founded in the US about 1848, holding that only the just will enter eternal life, and that the ignorant and unconverted will not be raised from the dead. ◆ *adj* **2** of or relating to this body or its beliefs and practices. [C19: from LGk *khristadelphos, khristos* CHRIST + *adelpos* brother]

christen ❶ ('krɪs[ə]n) *vb* (*tr*) **1** to give a Christian name to in baptism as a sign of incorporation into a Christian Church. **2** another word for **baptize. 3** to give a name to anything, esp. with some ceremony. **4** *Inf.* to use for the first time. [OE *cristnian,* from *Crīst* CHRIST]
▸**'christening** *n*

Christendom ('krɪs[ə]ndəm) *n* the collective body of Christians throughout the world.

Christian ('krɪstʃən) *n* **1a** a person who believes in and follows Jesus Christ. **1b** a member of a Christian Church or denomination. **2** *Inf.* a person who possesses Christian virtues. ◆ *adj* **3** of, relating to, or derived from Jesus Christ, his teachings, example, or followers. **4** (*sometimes not cap.*) exhibiting kindness or goodness.
▸**'christianly** *adj, adv*

Christian Democrat *n* a member or supporter of any of various right-of-centre political parties in Europe and Latin America that combine moderate conservatism with historical links to the Christian Church.
▸**Christian Democracy** *n* ▸**Christian Democratic** *adj*

Christian Era *n* the period beginning with the year of Christ's birth.

Christianity (,krɪstɪ'ænɪtɪ) *n* **1** the Christian religion. **2** Christian beliefs or practices. **3** a less common word for **Christendom.**

Christianize *or* **Christianise** ('krɪstʃə,naɪz) *vb* **Christianizes, Christianizing, Christianized** *or* **Christianises, Christianising, Christianised.** (*tr*) **1** to make Christian or convert to Christianity. **2** to imbue with Christian principles, spirit, or outlook.
▸**,Christiani'zation** *or* **,Christiani'sation** *n* ▸**'Christian,izer** *or* **'Christian,iser** *n*

Christian name *n* a personal name formally given to Christians at christening: loosely used to mean any person's first name.

THESAURUS

◆ *n* **15 the chop** *Slang, chiefly Brit.* = **the sack** (*inf.*), dismissal, one's cards, sacking (*inf.*), termination, the axe (*inf.*), the boot (*sl.*), the (old) heave-ho (*inf.*), the order of the boot (*sl.*)

choppy *adj* = **rough**, blustery, broken, ruffled, squally, tempestuous

Antonyms *adj* calm, smooth, windless

chore *n* **1, 2** = **task**, burden, duty, errand, fag (*inf.*), job, no picnic

chortle *vb, n* **1, 2** = **chuckle**, cackle, crow, guffaw

chorus *n* **1** = **choir**, choristers, ensemble, singers, vocalists **3** = **refrain**, burden, response, strain **10** = **unison**, accord, concert, harmony

christen *vb* **2** = **baptize 3** = **name**, call, designate, dub, style, term, title

Christian Science *n* the religious system of the Church of Christ, Scientist, founded by Mary Baker Eddy (1879), emphasizing spiritual regeneration and healing through prayer alone.
▸**Christian Scientist** *n*

Christingle (ˌkrɪsˈtɪŋɡl) *n* (in Britain) a Christian service for children held shortly before Christmas, in which each child is given a decorated fruit with a lighted candle in it. [C20: from CHRIST(MAS) + INGLE]

Christlike (ˈkraɪstˌlaɪk) *adj* resembling the spirit of Jesus Christ.
▸ˈ**Christˌlikeness** *n*

Christmas ⓣ (ˈkrɪsməs) *n* **1a** the annual commemoration by Christians of the birth of Jesus Christ, on Dec. 25. **1b** Also called: **Christmas Day.** Dec. 25, observed as a day of secular celebrations when gifts and greetings are exchanged. **1c** (*as modifier*): *Christmas celebrations.* **2** Also called: **Christmastide.** the season of Christmas extending from Dec. 24 (Christmas Eve) to Jan. 6 (the festival of the Epiphany or Twelfth Night). [OE *Crīstes mæsse* MASS of CHRIST]
▸ˈ**Christmassy** *adj*

Christmas box *n* a tip or present given at Christmas, esp. to postmen, tradesmen, etc.

Christmas Eve *n* the evening or the whole day before Christmas Day.

Christmas pudding *n Brit.* a rich steamed pudding containing suet, dried fruit, spices, etc. Also called: **plum pudding.**

Christmas rose *n* an evergreen plant of S Europe and W Asia with white or pinkish winter-blooming flowers. Also called: **hellebore, winter rose.**

Christmastide (ˈkrɪsməsˌtaɪd) *n* another name for **Christmas** (sense 2).

Christmas tree *n* **1** an evergreen tree or an imitation of one, decorated as part of Christmas celebrations. **2** Also called: **Christmas bush.** *Austral.* any of various trees or shrubs flowering at Christmas and used for decoration. **3** *NZ.* another name for the **pohutukawa.**

Christy *or* **Christie** (ˈkrɪstɪ) *n, pl* **Christies.** *Skiing.* a turn in which the body is swung sharply round with the skis parallel: used for stopping or changing direction quickly. [C20: from *Christiania,* former name of Oslo]

chroma (ˈkrəʊmə) *n* the attribute of a colour that enables an observer to judge how much chromatic colour it contains. See also **saturation** (sense 4). [C19: from Gk *khrōma* colour]

chromate (ˈkrəʊmeɪt) *n* any salt or ester of chromic acid.

chromatic (krəˈmætɪk) *adj* **1** of, relating to, or characterized by a colour or colours. **2** *Music.* **2a** involving the sharpening or flattening of notes or the use of such notes in chords and harmonic progressions. **2b** of or relating to the chromatic scale or an instrument capable of producing it. [C17: from Gk, from *khrōma* colour]
▸**chroˈmatically** *adv* ▸**chroˈmaticism** *n* ▸**chromaticity** (ˌkrəʊməˈtɪsɪtɪ) *n*

chromatic aberration *n* a defect in a lens system in which different wavelengths of light are focused at different distances because they are refracted through different angles. It produces a blurred image with coloured fringes.

chromatics (krəʊˈmætɪks) *n* (*functioning as sing*) the science of colour.

chromatic scale *n* a twelve-note scale including all the semitones of the octave.

chromatin (ˈkrəʊmətɪn) *n* the part of the nucleus that consists of DNA, RNA, and proteins, forms the chromosomes, and stains with basic dyes.

chromato- *or before a vowel* **chromat-** *combining form.* **1** indicating colour or coloured: *chromatophore.* **2** indicating chromatin: *chromatolysis.* [from Gk *khrōma, khrōmat-* colour]

chromatography (ˌkrəʊməˈtɒɡrəfɪ) *n* the technique of separating and analysing the components of a mixture of liquids or gases by selective adsorption.

chrome (krəʊm) *n* **1a** another word for **chromium,** esp. when present in a pigment or dye. **1b** (*as modifier*): *a chrome dye.* **2** anything plated with chromium. **3** a pigment or dye that contains chromium. ◆ *vb* **chromes, chroming, chromed. 4** to plate or be plated with chromium. **5** to treat or be treated with a chromium compound, as in dyeing or tanning. [C19: via F from Gk *khrōma* colour]

-chrome *n and adj combining form.* colour, coloured, or pigment: *monochrome.* [from Gk *khrōma* colour]

chrome dioxide *n* another name for **chromium dioxide.**

chromel (ˈkrəʊmɛl) *n* a nickel-based alloy containing about 10 per cent chromium, used in heating elements. [C20: from CHRO(MIUM) + ME(TA)L]

chrome steel *n* any of various hard rust-resistant steels containing chromium.

chrome yellow *n* any yellow pigment consisting of lead chromate.

chromic (ˈkrəʊmɪk) *adj* **1** of or containing chromium in the trivalent state. **2** of or derived from chromic acid.

chromic acid *n* an unstable dibasic oxidizing acid known only in solution and as chromate salts. Formula: H_2CrO_4.

chromite (ˈkrəʊmaɪt) *n* a brownish-black mineral consisting of a ferrous chromic oxide in crystalline form: the only commercial source of chromium. Formula: $FeCr_2O_4$.

chromium (ˈkrəʊmɪəm) *n* a hard grey metallic element, used in steel alloys and electroplating to increase hardness and corrosion-resistance. Symbol: Cr; atomic no.: 24; atomic wt.: 51.996. [C19: from NL, from F: CHROME]

chromium dioxide *n* a chemical compound used as a magnetic coating on cassette tapes; chromium(IV) oxide. Formula: CrO_2. Also called (*not in technical usage*): **chrome dioxide.**

chromium steel *n* another name for **chrome steel.**

chromo (ˈkrəʊməʊ) *n, pl* **chromos.** short for **chromolithograph.**

chromo- *or before a vowel* **chrom-** *combining form.* **1** indicating colour, coloured, or pigment: *chromogen.* **2** indicating chromium: *chromyl.* [from Gk *khrōma* colour]

chromolithograph (ˌkrəʊməʊˈlɪθəˌɡrɑːf) *n* a picture produced by chromolithography.

chromolithography (ˌkrəʊməʊlɪˈθɒɡrəfɪ) *n* the process of making coloured prints by lithography.
▸ˌ**chromoliˈthographer** *n* ▸**chromolithographic** (ˌkrəʊməʊlɪθəˈɡræfɪk) *adj*

chromosome (ˈkrəʊməˌsəʊm) *n* any of the microscopic rod-shaped structures that appear in a cell nucleus during cell division, consisting of nucleoprotein arranged into units (genes) that are responsible for the transmission of hereditary characteristics.
▸ˌ**chromoˈsomal** *adj*

chromosome map *n* a graphic representation of the positions of genes on chromosomes, obtained by observation of stained chromosomes or by determining the degree of linkage between genes. See also **genetic map.**
▸**chromosome mapping** *n*

chromosphere (ˈkrəʊməˌsfɪə) *n* a gaseous layer of the sun's atmosphere extending from the photosphere to the corona.
▸**chromospheric** (ˌkrəʊməˈsfɛrɪk) *adj*

chromous (ˈkrəʊməs) *adj* of or containing chromium in the divalent state.

chron. *or* **chronol.** *abbrev. for:* **1** chronological. **2** chronology.

Chron. *Bible. abbrev. for* Chronicles.

chronic ⓣ (ˈkrɒnɪk) *adj* **1** continuing for a long time; constantly recurring. **2** (of a disease) developing slowly, or of long duration. Cf. **acute** (sense 7). **3** inveterate; habitual: *a chronic smoker.* **4** *Inf.* **4a** very bad: *the play was chronic.* **4b** very serious: *he left her in a chronic condition.* [C15: from L, from Gk, from *khronos* time]
▸ˈ**chronically** *adv* ▸**chronicity** (krɒˈnɪsɪtɪ) *n*

chronicle ⓣ (ˈkrɒnɪkᵊl) *n* **1** a record or register of events in chronological order. ◆ *vb* **chronicles, chronicling, chronicled. 2** (*tr*) to record in or as if in a chronicle. [C14: from Anglo-F, via L *chronica* (pl), from Gk *khronika* annals; see CHRONIC]
▸ˈ**chronicler** *n*

chrono- *or before a vowel* **chron-** *combining form.* time: *chronology.* [from Gk *khronos* time]

chronograph (ˈkrɒnəˌɡrɑːf, ˈkrəʊnə-) *n* **1** an accurate instrument for recording small intervals of time. **2** any timepiece, esp. a wristwatch designed for maximum accuracy.
▸**chronographic** (ˌkrɒnəˈɡræfɪk) *adj*

chronological ⓣ (ˌkrɒnəˈlɒdʒɪkᵊl, ˌkrəʊ-) *or* **chronologic** *adj* **1** (esp. of a sequence of events) arranged in order of occurrence. **2** relating to or in accordance with chronology.
▸ˌ**chronoˈlogically** *adv*

chronology (krəˈnɒlədʒɪ) *n, pl* **chronologies. 1** the determination of the proper sequence of past events. **2** the arrangement of dates, events, etc., in order of occurrence. **3** a table of events arranged in order of occurrence.
▸**chroˈnologist** *n*

chronometer (krəˈnɒmɪtə) *n* a timepiece designed to be accurate in all conditions of temperature, pressure, etc., used esp. at sea.
▸**chronometric** (ˌkrɒnəˈmɛtrɪk) *or* ˌ**chronoˈmetrical** *adj* ▸ˌ**chronoˈmetrically** *adv*

chronometry (krəˈnɒmɪtrɪ) *n* the science of measuring time with extreme accuracy.

chronon (ˈkrəʊnɒn) *n* a unit of time equal to the time that a photon would take to traverse the diameter of an electron: about 10^{-24} seconds.

chrysalid (ˈkrɪsəlɪd) *n* **1** another name for **chrysalis.** ◆ *adj* **2** of or relating to a chrysalis.

chrysalis (ˈkrɪsəlɪs) *n, pl* **chrysalises** *or* **chrysalides** (krɪˈsælɪˌdiːz). **1** the pupa of a moth or butterfly, in a case or cocoon. **2** anything in the process of developing. [C17: from L, from Gk *khrusallis,* from *khrusos* gold]

chrysanthemum (krɪˈsænθəməm) *n* **1** any of various widely cultivated plants of the composite family, having brightly coloured showy flower heads in autumn. **2** any other plant of the genus *Chrysanthemum,* such as the oxeye daisy. [C16: from L: marigold, from Gk, from *khrusos* gold + *anthemon* flower]

chryselephantine (ˌkrɪsɛlɪˈfæntɪn) *adj* (of ancient Greek statues, etc.)

THESAURUS

Christmas *n* **2** = **festive season**, Noel, Xmas (*inf.*), Yule (*arch.*), Yuletide (*arch.*)

chronic *adj* **3** = **habitual**, confirmed, deep-rooted, deep-seated, incessant, incurable, ineradicable, ingrained, inveterate, persistent **4a** *Informal* = **dreadful**, abysmal, appalling, atrocious, awful
Antonyms *adj* ≠ **habitual**: infrequent, occasional, temporary

chronicle *n* **1** = **record**, account, annals, diary, history, journal, narrative, register, story ◆ *vb* **2** = **record**, enter, narrate, put on record, recount, register, relate, report, set down, tell

chronicler *n* **2** = **recorder**, annalist, diarist, historian, historiographer, narrator, reporter, scribe

chronological *adj* **1** = **in order**, consecutive, historical, in sequence, ordered, progressive, sequential
Antonyms *adj* haphazard, intermittent, irregular, out-of-order, random

made of or overlaid with gold and ivory. [C19: from Gk, from *khrusos* gold + *elephas* ivory]

chrysoberyl ('krɪsəˌbɛrɪl) *n* a rare very hard greenish-yellow mineral consisting of beryllium aluminate: used as a gemstone. Formula: $BeAl_2O_4$. [C17: from L, from Gk, from *khrusos* gold + *bērullos* beryl]

chrysolite ('krɪsəˌlaɪt) *n* a brown or yellowish-green olivine: used as a gemstone. [C14 *crisolite*, from OF, from L, from Gk, from *khrusos* gold + *lithos* stone]

chrysoprase ('krɪsəˌpreɪz) *n* an apple-green variety of chalcedony: used as a gemstone. [C13 *crisopace*, from OF, from L, from Gk, from *khrusos* gold + *prason* leek]

chthonian ('θəʊnɪən) *or* **chthonic** ('θɒnɪk) *adj* of or relating to the underworld. [C19: from Gk *khthonios* in or under the earth, from *khthōn* earth]

chub (tʃʌb) *n, pl* **chub** *or* **chubs. 1** a common European freshwater cyprinid game fish, having a cylindrical dark greenish body. **2** any of various North American fishes, esp. certain whitefishes and minnows. [C15: from ?]

chubby Ⓣ ('tʃʌbɪ) *adj* **chubbier, chubbiest.** (esp. of the human form) plump. [C17: ?from CHUB]
▸**'chubbiness** *n*

chuck[1] Ⓣ (tʃʌk) *vb (mainly tr)* **1** *Inf.* to throw. **2** to pat affectionately, esp. under the chin. **3** *Inf.* (sometimes foll. by *in* or *up*) to give up; reject: *he chucked up his job.* ◆ *n* **4** a throw or toss. **5** a pat under the chin. **6 the chuck.** *Inf.* dismissal. ◆ See also **chuck in, chuck off, chuck out.** [C16: from ?]

chuck[2] (tʃʌk) *n* **1** Also called: **chuck steak.** a cut of beef from the neck to the shoulder blade. **2** a device that holds a workpiece in a lathe or tool in a drill. [C17: var. of CHOCK]

chuck[3] (tʃʌk) *n W Canad.* **1** a large body of water. **2** In full: **saltchuck.** the sea. [C19: from Chinook Jargon, of Amerind origin, from *chauk*]

chuck in *vb (adv)* **1** *(tr) Brit inf.* to abandon or give up: *to chuck in a hopeless attempt.* **2** *(intr) Austral. inf.* to contribute to the cost of something.

chuckle Ⓣ ('tʃʌkᵊl) *vb* **chuckles, chuckling, chuckled.** *(intr)* **1** to laugh softly or to oneself. **2** (of animals, esp. hens) to make a clucking sound. ◆ *n* **3** a partly suppressed laugh. [C16: prob. from *chuck* cluck + *-le*]

chucklehead ('tʃʌkᵊlˌhɛd) *n Inf.* a stupid person; dolt.

chuck off *vb (intr, adv;* often foll. by *at) Austral. & NZ inf.* to abuse or make fun of.

chuck out *vb (tr, adv;* often foll. by *of) Inf.* to eject forcibly (from); throw out (of).

chuff[1] (tʃʌf) *n* **1** a puffing sound as of a steam engine. ◆ *vb* **2** *(intr)* to move while emitting such sounds. [C20: imit.]

chuff[2] (tʃʌf) *vb (tr; usually passive) Brit. sl.* to please or delight: *he was chuffed by his pay rise.* [prob. from *chuff* (adj) pleased, happy]

chug (tʃʌg) *n* **1** a short dull sound, such as that made by an engine. ◆ *vb* **chugs, chugging, chugged. 2** *(intr)* (of an engine, etc.) to operate while making such sounds. [C19: imit.]

chukar (tʃʌ'kɑː) *n* a common Indian partridge having a red bill and black-barred sandy plumage. [from Hindi *cakor*, from Sansk. *cakora*, prob. imit.]

chukka *or US* **chukker** ('tʃʌkə) *n Polo.* a period of continuous play, generally lasting 7½ minutes. [C20: from Hindi *cakkar*, from Sansk. *cakra* wheel]

chukka boot ('tʃʌkə) *or* **chukka** *n* an ankle-high boot worn for playing polo. [C19: from CHUKKA]

chum Ⓣ (tʃʌm) *n* **1** *Inf.* a close friend. ◆ *vb* **chums, chumming, chummed. 2** *(intr;* usually foll. by *up with)* to be or become an intimate friend (of). [C17 (meaning: a person sharing rooms with another): prob. shortened from *chamber fellow*]

chummy Ⓣ ('tʃʌmɪ) *adj* **chummier, chummiest.** *Inf.* friendly.
▸**'chummily** *adv* ▸**'chumminess** *n*

chump (tʃʌmp) *n* **1** *Inf.* a stupid person. **2** a thick heavy block of wood. **3** the thick blunt end of anything, esp. of a piece of meat. **4** *Brit. sl.* the head (esp. in **off one's chump**). [C18: ? a blend of CHUNK + LUMP[1]]

chunder ('tʃʌndə) *Sl., chiefly Austral.* ◆ *vb (intr)* **1** to vomit. ◆ *n* **2** vomit. [C20: from ?]

chunk Ⓣ (tʃʌŋk) *n* **1** a thick solid piece, as of meat, wood, etc. **2** a considerable amount. [C17: var. of CHUCK[2]]

chunky Ⓣ ('tʃʌŋkɪ) *adj* **chunkier, chunkiest. 1** thick and short. **2** containing thick pieces. **3** *Chiefly Brit.* (of clothes, esp. knitwear) made of thick bulky material.
▸**'chunkiness** *n*

Chunnel ('tʃʌnᵊl) *n* an informal name for **Channel Tunnel.** [C20: from CH(ANNEL) + T(UNNEL)]

chunter ('tʃʌntə) *vb (intr;* often foll. by *on) Brit. inf.* to mutter or grumble incessantly in a meaningless fashion. [C16: prob. imit.]

church Ⓣ (tʃɜːtʃ) *n* **1** a building for public worship, esp. Christian worship. **2** an occasion of public worship. **3** the clergy as distinguished from the laity. **4** *(usually cap.)* institutionalized forms of religion as a political or social force: *conflict between Church and State.* **5** *(usually cap.)* the collective body of all Christians. **6** *(often cap.)* a particular Christian denomination or group. **7** *(often cap.)* the Christian religion. ◆ Related adj: **ecclesiastical.** ◆ *vb (tr)* **8** *Church of England.* to bring (someone, esp. a woman after childbirth) to church for special ceremonies. [OE *cirice*, from LGk, from Gk *kuriakon (dōma)* the Lord's (house), from *kurios* master, from *kuros* power]

Church Army *n* a voluntary Anglican organization founded to assist the parish clergy.

Church Commissioners *pl n Brit.* a group of representatives of Church and State that administers the property of the Church of England.

churchgoer ('tʃɜːtʃˌgəʊə) *n* a person who attends church regularly.
▸**'churchˌgoing** *adj, n*

churchly ('tʃɜːtʃlɪ) *adj* appropriate to or associated with the church.
▸**'churchliness** *n*

churchman ('tʃɜːtʃmən) *n, pl* **churchmen. 1** a clergyman. **2** a male member of a church.

Church of Christ, Scientist *n* See **Christian Science.**

Church of England *n* the reformed established state Church in England, with the Sovereign as its temporal head.

Church of Jesus Christ of Latter-Day Saints *n* See **Mormon** (sense 1).

churchwarden (ˌtʃɜːtʃ'wɔːdᵊn) *n* **1** *Church of England, Episcopal Church.* one of two assistants of a parish priest who administer the secular affairs of the church. **2** a long-stemmed tobacco pipe made of clay.

churchwoman ('tʃɜːtʃˌwʊmən) *n, pl* **churchwomen.** a female member of a church.

churchyard ('tʃɜːtʃˌjɑːd) *n* the grounds round a church, used as a graveyard.

churinga (tʃə'rɪŋgə) *n, pl* **churinga** *or* **churingas.** a sacred amulet of the native Australians. [from Abor.]

churl Ⓣ (tʃɜːl) *n* **1** a surly ill-bred person. **2** *Arch.* a farm labourer. **3** *Arch.* a miserly person. [OE *ceorl*]
▸**'churlish** *adj*

churn Ⓣ (tʃɜːn) *n* **1** *Brit.* a large container for milk. **2** a vessel or machine in which cream or whole milk is vigorously agitated to produce butter. ◆ *vb* **3a** to agitate (milk or cream) to make butter. **3b** to make (butter) by this process. **4** (sometimes foll. by *up*) to move or cause to move with agitation. **5** (of a bank, broker, etc.) to encourage an investor or policyholder to change investments, endowment policies, etc., to increase commissions at the client's expense. **6** (of a government) to pay benefits to a wide category of people and claw it back by taxation from the well off. **7** to promote the turnover of existing subscribers leasing, and new subscribers joining, a cable television system. [OE *ciern*]
▸**'churner** *n*

churn out *vb (tr, adv) Inf.* **1** to produce (something) at a rapid rate: *to churn out ideas.* **2** to perform (something) mechanically: *to churn out a song.*

churr (tʃɜː) *vb, n* a variant spelling of **chirr.**

chute[1] Ⓣ (ʃuːt) *n* **1** an inclined channel or vertical passage down which water, parcels, coal, etc., may be dropped. **2** a steep slope, used as a slide as for toboggans. **3** a slide into a swimming pool. **4** a rapid or waterfall. [C19: from OF *cheoite*, fem. p.p. of *cheoir* to fall, from L *cadere*; in some senses, var. spelling of SHOOT]

chute[2] (ʃuːt) *n, vb* **chutes, chuting, chuted.** *Inf.* short for **parachute.**
▸**'chutist** *n*

chutney ('tʃʌtnɪ) *n* a pickle of Indian origin, made from fruit, vinegar, spices, sugar, etc.: *mango chutney.* [C19: from Hindi *catnī*, from ?]

chutzpah ('xʊtspə) *n US & Canad. inf.* shameless audacity; impudence. [C20: from Yiddish]

chyack ('tʃaɪæk) *vb, n* a variant spelling of **chiack.**

chyle (kaɪl) *n* a milky fluid composed of lymph and emulsified fat globules, formed in the small intestine during digestion. [C17: from LL, from Gk *khulos* juice]
▸**chylaceous** (kaɪ'leɪʃəs) *or* **'chylous** *adj*

chyme (kaɪm) *n* the thick fluid mass of partially digested food that leaves the stomach. [C17: from LL, from Gk *khumos* juice]
▸**'chymous** *adj*

THESAURUS

chubby *adj* = **plump**, buxom, flabby, fleshy, podgy, portly, roly-poly, rotund, round, stout, tubby
Antonyms *adj* lean, skinny, slender, slight, slim, sylphlike, thin

chuck[1] *vb* **1** *Informal* = **throw**, cast, discard, fling, heave, hurl, pitch, shy, sling, toss

chuckle *vb* **1** = **laugh**, chortle, crow, exult, giggle, snigger, titter

chum *n* **1** *Informal* = **friend**, cock (*Brit. inf.*), companion, comrade, crony, mate (*inf.*), pal (*inf.*)

chummy *adj Informal* = **friendly**, affectionate, buddy-buddy (*sl., chiefly U.S. & Canad.*), close, intimate, matey *or* maty (*Brit. inf.*), pally (*inf.*), palsy-walsy (*inf.*), thick (*inf.*)

chunk *n* **1, 2** = **piece**, block, dollop (*inf.*), hunk, lump, mass, nugget, portion, slab, wad, wodge (*Brit. inf.*)

chunky *adj* **1** = **thickset**, beefy (*inf.*), dumpy, stocky, stubby

church *n* **1** = **chapel**, basilica, cathedral, house of God, kirk (*Scot.*), minster, place of worship, procathedral, tabernacle, temple

churl *n* **1** = **boor**, lout, oaf **2** *Archaic* = **peasant**, bumpkin, clodhopper (*inf.*), clown, hick (*inf., chiefly US & Canad.*), hillbilly, rustic, yokel

churlish *adj* **1** = **boorish**, brusque, crabbed, harsh, ill-tempered, impolite, loutish, morose, oafish, rude, sullen, surly, uncivil, uncouth, unmannerly, vulgar
Antonyms *adj* agreeable, amiable, civil, courteous, cultivated, good-tempered, mannerly, noble, pleasant, polite, well-bred

churn *vb* **4** *sometimes foll. by* **up** = **stir up**, agitate, beat, boil, convulse, foam, froth, seethe, swirl, toss

chute[1] *n* **1** = **slope**, channel, gutter, incline, ramp, runway, slide, trough

chypre *French.* (ʃiprə) *n* a perfume made from sandalwood. [lit.: Cyprus, ? where it originated]
Ci *symbol for* curie.
CI *abbrev. for* Channel Islands.
CIA *abbrev. for* Central Intelligence Agency; a federal US bureau created in 1947 to coordinate and conduct espionage and intelligence activities.
ciabatta (tʃə'bætə) *n* a type of open-textured bread made with olive oil. [C20: from It., lit.: slipper]
CIB *abbrev. for* Criminal Investigation Branch (of the New Zealand and Australian police).
ciborium (sɪ'bɔːrɪəm) *n, pl* **ciboria** (-rɪə). *Christianity.* **1** a goblet-shaped lidded vessel used to hold consecrated wafers in Holy Communion. **2** a canopy fixed over an altar. [C17: from Med. L, from L, from Gk *kibōrion* cup-shaped seed vessel of the Egyptian lotus]
cicada (sɪ'kɑːdə) *or* **cicala** *n, pl* **cicadas, cicadae** (-diː) *or* **cicale** (-leɪ). any large broad insect, most common in warm regions, having membranous wings: the males produce a high-pitched drone by vibration of a pair of drumlike abdominal organs. [C19: from L]
cicatrix ('sɪkətrɪks) *n, pl* **cicatrices** (ˌsɪkə'traɪsiːz). **1** the tissue that forms in a wound during healing; scar. **2** a scar on a plant indicating the former point of attachment of a part, esp. a leaf. [C17: from L: scar, from ?]
▸**cicatricial** (ˌsɪkə'trɪʃəl) *adj*
cicatrize *or* **cicatrise** ('sɪkəˌtraɪz) *vb* **cicatrizes, cicatrizing, cicatrized** *or* **cicatrises, cicatrising, cicatrised.** (of a wound or defect in tissue) to be closed by scar formation; heal.
▸ˌ**cicatri'zation** *or* ˌ**cicatri'sation** *n*
cicely ('sɪsəlɪ) *n, pl* **cicelies.** short for **sweet cicely.** [C16: from L *seselis*, from Gk, from ?]
cicerone (ˌsɪsə'rəʊnɪ, ˌtʃɪtʃ-) *n, pl* **cicerones** *or* **ciceroni** (-nɪ). a person who conducts and informs sightseers. [C18: from It.: antiquarian scholar, guide, after *Cicero* (106–43 B.C.), Roman orator and writer]
CID (in Britain) *abbrev. for* Criminal Investigation Department; the detective division of a police force.
-cide *n combining form.* **1** indicating a person or thing that kills: *insecticide.* **2** indicating a killing; murder: *homicide.* [from L *-cīda* (agent), *-cīdium* (act), from *caedere* to kill]
▸**-cidal** *adj combining form.*
cider *or* **cyder** ('saɪdə) *n* **1** an alcoholic drink made from the fermented juice of apples. **2** Also called: **sweet cider.** *US & Canad.* an unfermented drink made from apple juice. [C14: from OF, via Med. L, from LGk *sikera* strong drink, from Heb. *shēkhār*]
c.i.f. *or* **CIF** *abbrev. for* cost, insurance, and freight (included in the price quoted).
c.i.f.c.i. *abbrev. for* cost, insurance, freight, commission, and interest (included in the price quoted).
cig (sɪg) *or* **ciggy** ('sɪgɪ) *n, pl* **cigs** *or* **ciggies.** *Inf.* a cigarette.
cigar (sɪ'gɑː) *n* a cylindrical roll of cured tobacco leaves, for smoking. [C18: from Sp. *cigarro*]
cigarette Ⓣ *or US (sometimes)* **cigaret** (ˌsɪgə'rɛt) *n* a short tightly rolled cylinder of tobacco, wrapped in thin paper for smoking. [C19: from F, lit.: a little CIGAR]
cigarette card *n* a small picture card, formerly given away with cigarettes, now collected as a hobby.
cigarillo (ˌsɪgə'rɪləʊ) *n, pl* **cigarillos.** a small cigar, often only slightly larger than a cigarette.
ciliary ('sɪlɪərɪ) *adj* of or relating to cilia.
ciliary body *n* the part of the eye that joins the choroid to the iris.
cilium ('sɪlɪəm) *n, pl* **cilia** ('sɪlɪə). **1** any of the short threads projecting from the surface of a cell, organism, etc., whose rhythmic beating causes movement. **2** the technical name for **eyelash.** [C18: NL, from L: (lower) eyelid, eyelash]
▸**ciliate** ('sɪlɪɪt, -eɪt) *or* '**cili**ˌ**ated** *adj*
C in C *or* **C.-in-C.** *Mil. abbrev. for* Commander in Chief.
cinch (sɪntʃ) *n* **1** *Sl.* an easy task. **2** *Sl.* a certainty. **3** a US and Canad. name for **girth** (sense 2). **4** *US inf.* a firm grip. ◆ *vb* **5** (often foll. by *up*) *US & Canad.* to fasten a girth around (a horse). **6** (*tr*) *Inf.* to make sure of. **7** (*tr*) *Inf., chiefly US.* to get a firm grip on. [C19: from Sp., from L, from *cingere* to encircle]
cinchona (sɪŋ'kəʊnə) *n* **1** any tree or shrub of the South American genus *Cinchona,* having medicinal bark. **2** the dried bark of any of these trees, which yields quinine. **3** any of the drugs derived from cinchona bark. [C18: NL, after the Countess of *Chinchón* (1576–1639), vicereine of Peru]
▸**cinchonic** (sɪŋ'kɒnɪk) *adj*
cincture ('sɪŋktʃə) *n* something that encircles, esp. a belt or girdle. [C16: from L, from *cingere* to gird]
cinder ('sɪndə) *n* **1** a piece of incombustible material left after the combustion of coal, coke, etc.; clinker. **2** a piece of charred material that burns without flames; ember. **3** any solid waste from smelting or refining. **4** (*pl*) fragments of volcanic lava; scoriae. [OE *sinder*]
▸'**cindery** *adj*
Cinderella (ˌsɪndə'rɛlə) *n* **1** a girl who achieves fame after being obscure. **2** a poor, neglected, or unsuccessful person or thing. [C19: after *Cinderella,* the heroine of a fairy tale]
cine- *combining form.* indicating motion picture or cinema: *cine camera; cinephotography.*
cineaste ('sɪnɪˌæst) *n* an enthusiast for films. [C20: F]
cinema Ⓣ ('sɪnɪmə) *n* **1** *Chiefly Brit.* a place designed for the exhibition of films. **2 the cinema. 2a** the art or business of making films. **2b** films collectively. [C19 (earlier spelling: *kinema*): shortened from CINEMATOGRAPH]
▸**cinematic** (ˌsɪnɪ'mætɪk) *adj* ▸ˌ**cine'matically** *adv*
cinematograph (ˌsɪnɪ'mætəˌgrɑːf) *Chiefly Brit.* ◆ *n* **1** a combined camera, printer, and projector. ◆ *vb* **2** to take (pictures) with a film camera. [C19 (earlier spelling: *kinematograph*): from Gk *kinēma* motion + -GRAPH]
▸**cinematographer** (ˌsɪnɪmə'tɒgrəfə) *n* ▸**cinematographic** (ˌsɪnɪˌmætə'græfɪk) *adj* ▸ˌ**cine**ˌ**mato'graphically** *adv* ▸ˌ**cinema'tography** *n*
cinéma vérité (*French* sinema verite) *n* films characterized by subjects, actions, etc., that have the appearance of real life. [F, lit.: truth cinema]
cineraria (ˌsɪnə'rɛərɪə) *n* a plant of the Canary Islands, widely cultivated for its blue, purple, red, or variegated daisy-like flowers. [C16: from NL, from L, from *cinis* ashes; from its downy leaves]
cinerarium (ˌsɪnə'rɛərɪəm) *n, pl* **cineraria** (-'rɛərɪə). a place for keeping the ashes of the dead after cremation. [C19: from L, from *cinerārius* relating to ashes]
▸**cinerary** ('sɪnərərɪ) *adj*
cinerator ('sɪnəˌreɪtə) *n Chiefly US.* a furnace for cremating corpses.
▸ˌ**cine'ration** *n*
cinnabar ('sɪnəˌbɑː) *n* **1** a heavy red mineral consisting of mercury(II) sulphide: the chief ore of mercury. Formula: HgS. **2** the red form of mercury(II) sulphide, esp. when used as a pigment. **3a** a bright red; vermilion. **3b** (*as adj*): *a cinnabar tint.* **4** a large red-and-black European moth. [C15: from OF, from L, from Gk *kinnabari,* of Oriental origin]
cinnamon ('sɪnəmən) *n* **1** a tropical Asian tree, having aromatic yellowish-brown bark. **2** the spice obtained from the bark of this tree, used for flavouring food and drink. **3a** a light yellowish brown. **3b** (*as adj*): *a cinnamon coat.* [C15: from OF, via L & Gk, from Heb. *qinnamown*]
cinque (sɪŋk) *n* the number five in cards, dice, etc. [C14: from OF *cinq* five]
cinquecento (ˌtʃɪŋkwɪ'tʃɛntəʊ) *n* the 16th century, esp. in reference to Italian art, architecture, or literature. [C18: It., shortened from *milcinquecento* 1500]
cinquefoil ('sɪŋkˌfɔɪl) *n* **1** any plant of the N temperate rosaceous genus *Potentilla,* typically having five-lobed compound leaves. **2** an ornamental carving in the form of five arcs arranged in a circle and separated by cusps. [C13 *sink foil,* from OF, from L *quinquefolium* plant with five leaves]
Cinque Ports (sɪŋk) *pl n* an association of ports on the SE coast of England, which from late Anglo-Saxon times until 1685 provided ships for the king's service in return for the profits of justice in their courts.
cipher Ⓣ *or* **cypher** ('saɪfə) *n* **1** a method of secret writing using substitution of letters according to a key. **2** a secret message. **3** the key to a secret message. **4** an obsolete name for **zero** (sense 1). **5** any of the Arabic numerals or the Arabic system of numbering. **6** a person or thing of no importance; nonentity. **7** a design consisting of interwoven letters; monogram. ◆ *vb* **8** to put (a message) into secret writing. **9** *Rare.* to perform (a calculation) arithmetically. [C14: from OF *cifre* zero, from Med. L, from Ar. *sifr* zero]
circa Ⓣ ('sɜːkə) *prep* (used with a date) at the approximate time of: *circa 1182* B.C. Abbrev.: **c, ca.** [L: about]
circadian (sɜː'keɪdɪən) *adj* of or relating to biological processes that occur regularly at 24-hour intervals. See also **biological clock.** [C20: from L *circa* about + *diēs* day]
circle Ⓣ ('sɜːkᵊl) *n* **1** a closed plane curve every point of which is equidistant from a given fixed point, the centre. **2** the figure enclosed by such a curve. **3** *Theatre.* the section of seats above the main level of the auditorium, usually comprising the dress circle and the upper circle. **4** something formed or arranged in the shape of a circle. **5** a group of people sharing an interest, activity, upbringing, etc.; set: *golf circles; a family circle.* **6** a domain or area of activity, interest, or influence. **7** a circuit. **8** a process or chain of events or parts that forms a connected whole; cycle. **9** a parallel of latitude. See also **great circle, small circle. 10** one of a number of Neolithic or Bronze Age rings of standing stones, such as Stonehenge. **11 come full circle.** to arrive back at one's starting point. See also **vicious circle.** ◆ *vb* **circles, circling, circled. 12** to move in

THESAURUS

cigarette *n* = **fag** (*Brit. slang*), cancer stick (*sl.*), ciggy (*inf.*), coffin nail (*sl.*), gasper (*sl.*), smoke
cinema *n* **2 the cinema** = **films,** big screen (*inf.*), flicks (*sl.*), motion pictures, movies, pictures
cipher *n* **1** = **code,** cryptograph **4** *Obsolete* = **zero,** nil, nothing, nought **5** = **symbol,** character, digit, figure, number, numeral **6** = **nobody,** nonentity **7** = **monogram,** device, logo, mark
circa *adv* = **approximately,** about, around, in the region of, roughly
circle *n* **1, 4** = **ring,** band, circumference, coil, cordon, cycle, disc, globe, lap, loop, orb, perimeter, periphery, revolution, round, sphere, turn **5** = **group,** assembly, class, clique, club, company, coterie, crowd, fellowship, fraternity, order, school, set, society **6, 7** = **area,** bounds, circuit, compass, domain, enclosure, field, orbit, province, range, realm, region, scene, sphere ◆ *vb* **12, 13** = **go round,** belt, circumnavigate, circumscribe, coil, compass, curve, encircle, enclose, encompass, envelop, enwreath, gird, hem in, pivot, revolve, ring, rotate, surround, tour, wheel, whirl

a circle (around). **13** (*tr*) to enclose in a circle; encircle. [C14: from L *circulus*, from *circus* ring, circle]
▸'**circler** *n*

circlet ('sɜːklɪt) *n* a small circle or ring, esp. a circular ornament worn on the head. [C15: from OF *cerclet* a little CIRCLE]

circuit Ⓣ ('sɜːkɪt) *n* **1a** a complete route or course, esp. one that is curved or circular or that lies around an object. **1b** the area enclosed within such a route. **2** the act of following such a route: *we made three circuits of the course.* **3a** a complete path through which an electric current can flow. **3b** (*as modifier*): *a circuit diagram.* **4a** a periodical journey around an area, as made by judges, salesmen, etc. **4b** the places visited on such a journey. **4c** the persons making such a journey. **5** an administrative division of the Methodist Church comprising a number of neighbouring churches. **6** a number of theatres, cinemas, etc., under one management. **7** *Sport.* **7a** a series of tournaments in which the same players regularly take part: *the international tennis circuit.* **7b** (usually preceded by *the*) the contestants who take part in such a series. **8** *Chiefly Brit.* a motor-racing track, usually of irregular shape. ◆ *vb* **9** to make or travel in a circuit around (something). [C14: from L *circuitus*, from *circum* around + *īre* to go]
▸'**circuital** *adj*

circuit breaker *n* a device that under abnormal conditions, such as a short circuit, stops the flow of current in an electrical circuit.

circuitous Ⓣ (sə'kjuːɪtəs) *adj* indirect and lengthy; roundabout: *a circuitous route.*
▸**cir'cuitously** *adv* ▸**cir'cuitousness** *n*

circuitry ('sɜːkɪtrɪ) *n* **1** the design of an electrical circuit. **2** the system of circuits used in an electronic device.

circuity (sə'kjuːɪtɪ) *n, pl* **circuities.** (of speech, reasoning, etc.) a roundabout or devious quality.

circular Ⓣ ('sɜːkjʊlə) *adj* **1** of, involving, resembling, or shaped like a circle. **2** circuitous. **3** (of arguments) futile because the truth of the premises cannot be established independently of the conclusion. **4** travelling or occurring in a cycle. **5** (of letters, announcements, etc.) intended for general distribution. ◆ *n* **6** a printed advertisement or notice for mass distribution.
▸**circularity** (ˌsɜːkjʊ'lærɪtɪ) *n* ▸'**circularly** *adv*

circular breathing *n* a technique for sustaining a phrase on a wind instrument, using the cheeks to force air out of the mouth while breathing in through the nose.

circularize *or* **circularise** ('sɜːkjʊləˌraɪz) *vb* **circularizes, circularizing, circularized** *or* **circularises, circularising, circularised.** (*tr*) **1** to distribute circulars to. **2** to canvass or petition (people), as for support, votes, etc., by distributing letters, etc. **3** to make circular.
▸ˌ**circulari'zation** *or* ˌ**circulari'sation** *n*

circular saw *n* a power-driven saw in which a circular disc with a toothed edge is rotated at high speed.

circulate Ⓣ ('sɜːkjʊˌleɪt) *vb* **circulates, circulating, circulated. 1** to send, go, or pass from place to place or person to person: *don't circulate the news.* **2** to distribute or be distributed over a wide area. **3** to move or cause to move through a circuit, system, etc., returning to the starting point: *blood circulates through the body.* **4** to move in a circle. [C15: from L *circulārī*, from *circulus* CIRCLE]
▸'**circulative** *adj* ▸'**circuˌlator** *n* ▸'**circulatory** *adj*

circulating library *n* **1** another word (esp. US) for **lending library. 2** a small library circulated in turn to a group of institutions.

circulation Ⓣ (ˌsɜːkjʊ'leɪʃən) *n* **1** the transport of oxygenated blood through the arteries, and the return of oxygen-depleted blood through the veins to the heart, where the cycle is renewed. **2** the flow of sap through a plant. **3** any movement through a closed circuit. **4** the spreading or transmission of something to a wider group of people or area. **5** (of air and water) free movement within an area or volume. **6a** the distribution of newspapers, magazines, etc. **6b** the number of copies of an issue that are distributed. **7 in circulation. 7a** (of currency) serving as a medium of exchange. **7b** (of people) active in a social or business context.

circulatory system *n Anat., zool.* the system concerned with the transport of blood and lymph, consisting of the heart, blood vessels, lymph vessels, etc.

circum- *prefix* around; surrounding; on all sides: *circumlocution; circumpolar.* [from L *circum* around, from *circus* circle]

circumambient (ˌsɜːkəm'æmbɪənt) *adj* surrounding. [C17: from LL, from L CIRCUM- + *ambīre* to go round]
▸ˌ**circum'ambience** *or* ˌ**circum'ambiency** *n*

circumambulate (ˌsɜːkəm'æmbjʊˌleɪt) *vb* **circumambulates, circumambulating, circumambulated. 1** to walk around (something). **2** (*intr*) to avoid the point. [C17: from LL, from L CIRCUM- + *ambulāre* to walk]
▸ˌ**circumˌambu'lation** *n*

circumcise ('sɜːkəmˌsaɪz) *vb* **circumcises, circumcising, circumcised.** (*tr*) **1** to remove the foreskin of (a male). **2** to incise surgically the skin over the clitoris of (a female). **3** to remove the clitoris of (a female). **4** to perform such an operation as a religious rite on (someone). [C13: from L from CIRCUM- + *caedere* to cut]
▸**circumcision** (ˌsɜːkəm'sɪʒən) *n*

circumference Ⓣ (sə'kʌmfərəns) *n* **1** the boundary of a specific area or figure, esp. of a circle. **2** the length of a closed geometric curve, esp. of a circle. [C14: from OF, from L from CIRCUM- + *ferre* to bear]
▸**circumferential** (səˌkʌmfə'renʃəl) *adj* ▸**cirˌcumfer'entially** *adv*

circumflex ('sɜːkəmˌfleks) *n* **1** a mark (^) placed over a vowel to show that it is pronounced with rising and falling pitch, as in ancient Greek, or as a long vowel, as in French. ◆ *adj* **2** (of nerves, arteries, etc.) bending or curving around. [C16: from L, from CIRCUM- + *flectere* to bend]
▸ˌ**circum'flexion** *n*

circumfuse (ˌsɜːkəm'fjuːz) *vb* **circumfuses, circumfusing, circumfused.** (*tr*) **1** to pour or spread (a liquid, powder, etc.) around. **2** to surround with a substance, such as a liquid. [C16: from L *circumfūsus*, from CIRCUM- + *fundere* to pour]
▸**circumfusion** (ˌsɜːkəm'fjuːʒən) *n*

circumlocution Ⓣ (ˌsɜːkəmlə'kjuːʃən) *n* **1** an indirect way of expressing something. **2** an indirect expression.
▸**circumlocutory** (ˌsɜːkəm'lɒkjətərɪ, -trɪ) *adj*

circumnavigate (ˌsɜːkəm'nævɪˌgeɪt) *vb* **circumnavigates, circumnavigating, circumnavigated.** (*tr*) to sail or fly completely around.
▸ˌ**circumˌnavi'gation** *n* ▸ˌ**circum'naviˌgator** *n*

circumscribe Ⓣ (ˌsɜːkəm'skraɪb, 'sɜːkəmˌskraɪb) *vb* **circumscribes, circumscribing, circumscribed.** (*tr*) **1** to restrict within limits. **2** to mark or set the bounds of. **3** to draw a geometric construction around (another construction) so that the two are in contact but do not intersect. **4** to draw a line round. [C15: from L from CIRCUM- + *scrībere* to write]
▸ˌ**circum'scribable** *adj* ▸ˌ**circum'scriber** *n* ▸**circumscription** (ˌsɜːkəm'skrɪpʃən) *n*

circumspect Ⓣ ('sɜːkəmˌspɛkt) *adj* cautious, prudent, or discreet. [C15: from L, from CIRCUM- + *specere* to look]
▸ˌ**circum'spection** *n* ▸'**circumˌspectly** *adv*

circumstance Ⓣ ('sɜːkəmstəns) *n* **1** (*usually pl*) a condition of time, place, etc., that accompanies or influences an event or condition. **2** an incident or occurrence, esp. a chance one. **3** accessory information or detail. **4** formal display or ceremony (archaic except in **pomp and circumstance**). **5 under** *or* **in no circumstances.** in no case; never. **6 under the circumstances.** because of conditions; this being the case. ◆ *vb* **circumstances, circumstancing, circumstanced.** (*tr*) **7** to place in a particular condition or situation. [C13: from OF, from L *circumstantia*, from CIRCUM- + *stāre* to stand]

circumstantial Ⓣ (ˌsɜːkəm'stænʃəl) *adj* **1** of or dependent on circumstances. **2** fully detailed. **3** incidental.
▸ˌ**circumˌstanti'ality** *n* ▸ˌ**circum'stantially** *adv*

circumstantial evidence *n* indirect evidence that tends to establish a conclusion by inference.

circumstantiate (ˌsɜːkəm'stænʃɪˌeɪt) *vb* **circumstantiates, circumstantiating, circumstantiated.** (*tr*) to support by giving particulars.
▸ˌ**circumˌstanti'ation** *n*

circumvallate (ˌsɜːkəm'væleɪt) *vb* **circumvallates, circumvallating, circumvallated.** (*tr*) to surround with a defensive fortification. [C19: from L, from CIRCUM- + *vallum* rampart]
▸ˌ**circumval'lation** *n*

circumvent Ⓣ (ˌsɜːkəm'vɛnt) *vb* (*tr*) **1** to evade or go around. **2** to out-

THESAURUS

circuit *n* **1** = **range**, area, boundary, bounding line, bounds, circumference, compass, district, journey, lap, limit, orbit, pale, perambulation, region, revolution, round, route, tour, track, tract

circuitous *adj* = **indirect**, ambagious (*arch.*), devious, labyrinthine, meandering, oblique, rambling, roundabout, tortuous, winding
Antonyms *adj* as the crow flies, direct, straight, undeviating, unswerving

circuitousness *n* = **indirectness**, deviousness, obliqueness, rambling, roundaboutness, tortuousness

circular *adj* **1** = **round**, annular, discoid, globelike, orbicular, ring-shaped, rotund, spherical **2** = **orbital**, circuitous, cyclical ◆ *n* **6** = **advertisement**, notice

circulate *vb* **2** = **spread**, broadcast, diffuse, disseminate, distribute, issue, make known, promulgate, propagate, publicize, publish **3** = **flow**, gyrate, radiate, revolve, rotate

circulation *n* **1** = **bloodstream 3** = **flow**, circling, motion, rotation **4** = **distribution**, currency, dissemination, spread, transmission, vogue

circumference *n* **1** = **boundary**, ambit, border, bounds, circuit, edge, extremity, fringe, limits, outline, pale, perimeter, periphery, rim, verge

circumlocution *n* **1** = **indirectness**, beating about the bush (*inf.*), diffuseness, discursiveness, euphemism, periphrasis, prolixity, redundancy, wordiness

circumscribe *vb Formal* **1, 2, 4** = **restrict**, bound, confine, define, delimit, delineate, demarcate, encircle, enclose, encompass, environ, hem in, limit, mark off, restrain, straiten, surround

circumspect *adj* = **cautious**, attentive, canny, careful, deliberate, discreet, discriminating, guarded, heedful, judicious, observant, politic, prudent, sagacious, sage, vigilant, wary, watchful
Antonyms *adj* bold, careless, daring, foolhardy, heedless, imprudent, rash, venturous

circumspection *n* = **caution**, canniness, care, chariness, deliberation, discretion, keeping one's head down, prudence, wariness

circumstance *n* **1, 2** = **event**, accident, condition, contingency, detail, element, fact, factor, happening, incident, item, occurrence, particular, position, respect, situation

circumstantial *adj* **1, 3** = **conjectural**, contingent, founded on circumstances, hearsay, incidental, indirect, inferential, presumptive, provisional **2** = **detailed**, particular, specific

circumvent *vb* **1** = **evade**, bypass, elude, side-

wit. **3** to encircle (an enemy) so as to intercept or capture. [C15: from L, from CIRCUM- + *venīre* to come]
▸ **ˌcircumˈvention** *n*

circus (ˈsɜːkəs) *n, pl* **circuses. 1** a travelling company of entertainers such as acrobats, clowns, trapeze artists, and trained animals. **2** a public performance given by such a company. **3** an arena, usually tented, in which such a performance is held. **4** a travelling group of professional sportsmen: *a cricket circus.* **5** (in ancient Rome) **5a** an open-air stadium, usually oval or oblong, for chariot races or public games. **5b** the games themselves. **6** *Brit.* **6a** an open place, usually circular, where several streets converge. **6b** (*cap. when part of a name*): *Piccadilly Circus.* **7** *Inf.* noisy or rowdy behaviour. **8** *Inf.* a group of people travelling together and putting on a display. [C16: from L, from Gk *kirkos* ring]

ciré (ˈsɪəreɪ) *adj* **1** (of fabric) treated with a heat or wax process to make it smooth. ◆ *n* **2** such a surface on a fabric. **3** a fabric having such a surface. [C20: F, from L *cēra* wax]

cirque (sɜːk) *n* a steep-sided semicircular or crescent-shaped depression found in mountainous regions. [C17: from F, from L *circus* ring]

cirrhosis (sɪˈrəʊsɪs) *n* any of various chronic progressive diseases of the liver, characterized by death of liver cells, irreversible fibrosis, etc. [C19: NL, from Gk *kirrhos* orange-coloured + -OSIS; referring to the appearance of the diseased liver]
▸ **cirrhotic** (sɪˈrɒtɪk) *adj*

cirripede (ˈsɪrɪˌpiːd) *or* **cirriped** (ˈsɪrɪˌpɛd) *n* **1** any marine crustacean of the subclass *Cirripedia,* including the barnacles. ◆ *adj* **2** of, relating to, or belonging to the *Cirripedia.*

cirrocumulus (ˌsɪrəʊˈkjuːmjʊləs) *n, pl* **cirrocumuli** (-ˌlaɪ). a high cloud of ice crystals grouped into small separate globular masses.

cirrostratus (ˌsɪrəʊˈstrɑːtəs) *n, pl* **cirrostrati** (-taɪ). a uniform layer of cloud above about 6000 metres.

cirrus (ˈsɪrəs) *n, pl* **cirri** (-raɪ). **1** a thin wispy fibrous cloud at high altitudes, composed of ice particles. **2** a plant tendril or similar part. **3a** a slender tentacle or filament in barnacles and other marine invertebrates. **3b** any of various hairlike structures in other animals. [C18: from L: curl]

CIS *abbrev. for* Commonwealth of Independent States.

cis- *prefix* on this side of, as in **cismontane** on this side of the mountains. Often retains the original Latin sense of 'side nearest Rome', as in **cispadane** on this (the southern) side of the Po. [from L]

cisalpine (sɪsˈælpaɪn) *adj* on this (the southern) side of the Alps, as viewed from Rome.

cisco (ˈsɪskəʊ) *n, pl* **ciscoes** *or* **ciscos.** any of various whitefish, esp. the lake herring of cold deep lakes of North America. [C19: short for Canad. F *ciscoette,* of Algonquian origin]

cislunar (sɪsˈluːnə) *adj* of or relating to the space between the earth and the moon.

cisplatin (sɪsˈplætɪn) *n* a cytotoxic drug that acts by preventing DNA replication and hence cell divisions, used in the treatment of tumours of the ovary and testis. [C20: from CIS- + PLATIN(UM)]

cissing (ˈsɪsɪŋ) *n Building trades.* the appearance of pinholes, craters, etc., in paintwork due to poor adhesion of the paint to the surface.

cissy (ˈsɪsɪ) *n, pl* **-sies.** a variant spelling of **sissy.**

cist[1] (sɪst) *n* a wooden box for holding ritual objects used in ancient Rome and Greece. [C19: from L *cista* box, from Gk *kistē*]

cist[2] (sɪst) *or* **kist** *n* a box-shaped burial chamber made from stone slabs or a hollowed tree trunk. [C19: from Welsh: chest, from L; see CIST[1]]

Cistercian (sɪˈstɜːʃən) *n* **1** Also called: **White Monk.** a member of a Christian order of monks and nuns founded in 1098, which follows an especially strict form of the Benedictine rule. ◆ *adj* **2** of or relating to this order. [C17: from F, from Med. L, from *Cistercium* (modern *Cîteaux*), original home of the order]

cistern ❶ (ˈsɪstən) *n* **1** a tank for the storage of water, esp. on or within the roof of a house or connected to a WC. **2** an underground reservoir for the storage of a liquid, esp. rainwater. **3** Also called: **cisterna.** *Anat.* a sac or partially enclosed space containing body fluid. [C13: from OF, from L *cisterna* underground tank, from *cista* box]

cistus (ˈsɪstəs) *n* any plant of the genus *Cistus.* See **rockrose.** [C16: NL, from Gk *kistos*]

citadel ❶ (ˈsɪtədᵊl, -ˌdɛl) *n* **1** a stronghold within or close to a city. **2** any strongly fortified building or place of safety; refuge. [C16: from OF, from OIt. *cittadella* a little city, from L *cīvitās*]

citation ❶ (saɪˈteɪʃən) *n* **1** the quoting of a book or author. **2** a passage or source cited. **3a** an official commendation or award, esp. for bravery or outstanding service. **3b** a formal public statement of this. **4** *Law.* **4a** an official summons to appear in court. **4b** the document containing such a summons.
▸ **citatory** (ˈsaɪtətərɪ) *adj*

cite ❶ (saɪt) *vb* **cites, citing, cited.** (*tr*) **1** to quote or refer to (a passage, book, or author). **2** to mention or commend (a soldier, etc.) for outstanding bravery or meritorious action. **3** to summon to appear before a court of law. **4** to enumerate: *he cited the king's virtues.* [C15: from OF *citer* to summon, ult. from L *ciēre* to excite]
▸ **ˈcitable** *or* **ˈciteable** *adj*

cithara (ˈsɪθərə) *or* **kithara** (ˈkɪθərə) *n* a stringed musical instrument of ancient Greece, similar to the lyre. [C18: from Gk *kithara*]

cither (ˈsɪθə) *or* **cithern** (ˈsɪθən) *n* a variant spelling of **cittern.** [C17: from L, from Gk *kithara*]

citified *or* **cityfied** (ˈsɪtɪˌfaɪd) *adj Often derog.* having the customs, manners, or dress of city people.

citizen ❶ (ˈsɪtɪzᵊn) *n* **1** a native registered or naturalized member of a state, nation, or other political community. **2** an inhabitant of a city or town. **3** a civilian, as opposed to a soldier, public official, etc. [C14: from Anglo-F *citesein,* from OF *citeien,* from *cité* CITY]

citizenry (ˈsɪtɪzənrɪ) *n, pl* **citizenries.** citizens collectively.

Citizens' Band *n* a range of radio frequencies assigned officially for use by the public for private communication. Abbrev.: **CB**

Citizens' Charter *n* (in Britain) a government document setting out standards of service for various public and private sector companies.

citizenship (ˈsɪtɪzənʃɪp) *n* **1** the condition or status of a citizen, with its rights and duties. **2** a person's conduct as a citizen.

citrate (ˈsɪtreɪt, -rɪt; ˈsaɪtreɪt) *n* any salt or ester of citric acid. [C18: from CITR(US) + -ATE[1]]

citric (ˈsɪtrɪk) *adj* of or derived from citrus fruits or citric acid.

citric acid *n* a water-soluble weak tribasic acid found in many fruits, esp. citrus fruits, and used in pharmaceuticals and as a flavouring (**E330**). Formula: $CH_2(COOH)C(OH)(COOH)CH_2COOH$.

citrine (ˈsɪtrɪn) *n* **1** a brownish-yellow variety of quartz: a gemstone; false topaz. **2a** the yellow colour of a lemon. **2b** (*as adj*): *citrine hair.*

citron (ˈsɪtrən) *n* **1** a small Asian tree, having lemon-like fruit with a thick aromatic rind. **2** the fruit of this tree. **3** the rind of this fruit candied and used for decoration and flavouring of foods. [C16: from OF, from L *citrus* citrus tree]

citronella (ˌsɪtrəˈnɛlə) *n* **1** a tropical Asian grass with bluish-green lemon-scented leaves. **2** Also called: **citronella oil.** the yellow aromatic oil obtained from this grass, used in insect repellents, soaps, perfumes, etc. [C19: NL, from F, from *citron* lemon]

citrus (ˈsɪtrəs) *n, pl* **citruses. 1** any tree or shrub of the tropical and subtropical genus *Citrus,* which includes the orange, lemon, and lime. ◆ *adj also* **citrous. 2** of or relating to the genus *Citrus* or to the fruits of plants of this genus. [C19: from L: citrus tree]

cittern (ˈsɪtɜːn), **cither,** *or* **cithern** *n* a medieval stringed instrument resembling a lute but having wire strings and a flat back. [C16: ? a blend of CITHER + GITTERN]

city ❶ (ˈsɪtɪ) *n, pl* **cities. 1** any large town or populous place. **2** (in Britain) a town that has received this title from the Crown: usually the seat of a bishop. **3** (in the US) an incorporated urban centre with its own government and administration established by state charter. **4** (in Canada) a similar urban municipality incorporated by the provincial government. **5** the people of a city collectively. **6** (*modifier*) in or characteristic of a city: *city habits.* ◆ Related adjs.: **civic, urban, municipal.** [C13: from OF *cité,* from L *cīvitās* state, from *cīvis* citizen]

City (ˈsɪtɪ) *n* **the. 1** the area in central London in which the United Kingdom's major financial business is transacted. **2** the various financial institutions located in this area.

City and Guilds Institute *n* (in Britain) an examining body for technical and craft skills.

city chambers *n* (*functioning as sing*) (in Scotland) the municipal buildings of a city; town hall.

City Code *n* (in Britain) short for **City Code on Takeovers and Mergers**: a code laid down in 1968 (later modified) to control takeovers and mergers.

city desk *n* the editorial section of a newspaper dealing in Britain with financial news, in the US and Canada with local news.

city editor *n* (on a newspaper) **1** *Brit.* the editor in charge of financial and commercial news. **2** *US & Canad.* the editor in charge of local news.

city father *n* a person who is active or prominent in the public affairs of a city.

cityscape (ˈsɪtɪˌskeɪp) *n* an urban landscape; view of a city.

city-state *n Ancient history.* a state consisting of a sovereign city and its dependencies.

city technology college *n* (in Britain) a type of senior secondary school specializing in technological subjects, set up in inner-city areas with funding from industry as well as the government.

civet (ˈsɪvɪt) *n* **1** a catlike mammal of Africa and S Asia, typically having spotted fur and secreting a powerfully smelling fluid from anal glands. **2** the yellowish fatty secretion of such an animal, used as a fixative in the manufacture of perfumes. **3** the fur of such an animal. [C16: from OF, from It., from Ar. *zabād* civet perfume]

civic ❶ (ˈsɪvɪk) *adj* of or relating to a city, citizens, or citizenship. [C16: from L, from *cīvis* citizen]
▸ **ˈcivically** *adv*

THESAURUS

step, steer clear of **2** = **outwit**, beguile, deceive, dupe, ensnare, entrap, hoodwink, mislead, outflank, outgeneral, overreach, thwart, trick

circumvention *n* **1** = **evasion**, dodging **2** = **trickery**, chicanery, deceit, deception, duplicity, fraud, guile, imposition, imposture, wiles

cistern *n* **1, 2** = **tank**, basin, reservoir, sink, vat

citadel *n* **1** = **fortress**, bastion, fastness, fortification, keep, stronghold, tower

citation *n* **2** = **quotation**, commendation, excerpt, illustration, passage, quote, reference, source **3a** = **commendation**, award, mention

cite *vb* **1** = **quote**, adduce, advance, allude to, enumerate, evidence, extract, mention, name, specify **3** = **summon**, call, subpoena

citizen *n* **2** = **inhabitant**, burgess, burgher, denizen, dweller, freeman, ratepayer, resident, subject, townsman

city *n* **1** = **town**, conurbation, megalopolis, metropolis, municipality ◆ *modifier* **6** = **urban**, civic, metropolitan, municipal

civic *adj* = **public**, borough, communal, community, local, municipal

civic centre *n Brit.* the public buildings of a town, including recreational facilities and offices of local administration.
civics ('sɪvɪks) *n (functioning as sing)* the study of the rights and responsibilities of citizenship.
civies ('sɪvɪz) *pl n Inf.* a variant spelling of **civvies**. See **civvy** (sense 2).
civil Ⓣ ('sɪvəl) *adj* **1** of the ordinary life of citizens as distinguished from military, legal, or ecclesiastical affairs. **2** of or relating to the citizen as an individual: *civil rights.* **3** of or occurring within the state or between citizens: *civil strife.* **4** polite or courteous: *a civil manner.* **5** of or in accordance with Roman law. [C14: from OF, from L *cīvīlis,* from *cīvis* citizen]
▸**'civilly** *adv*
civil defence *n* the organizing of civilians to deal with enemy attacks.
civil disobedience *n* a refusal to obey laws, pay taxes, etc.: a nonviolent means of protesting.
civil engineer *n* a person qualified to design and construct public works, such as roads, bridges, harbours, etc.
▸**civil engineering** *n*
civilian (sɪ'vɪljən) *n* **a** a person whose occupation is civil or nonmilitary. **b** *(as modifier): civilian life.* [C14 (orig.: a practitioner of civil law): from *civile* (from L *jūs cīvīle* civil law) + -IAN]
civility Ⓣ (sɪ'vɪlɪtɪ) *n, pl* **civilities. 1** politeness or courtesy. **2** *(often pl)* an act of politeness.
civilization Ⓣ *or* **civilisation** (ˌsɪvɪlaɪ'zeɪʃən) *n* **1** a human society that has a complex cultural, political, and legal organization; an advanced state in social development. **2** the peoples or nations collectively who have achieved such a state. **3** the total culture and way of life of a particular people, nation, region, or period. **4** the process of bringing or achieving civilization. **5** intellectual, cultural, and moral refinement. **6** cities or populated areas, as contrasted with sparsely inhabited areas, deserts, etc.
civilize Ⓣ *or* **civilise** ('sɪvɪˌlaɪz) *vb* **civilizes, civilizing, civilized** *or* **civilises, civilising, civilised.** *(tr)* **1** to bring out of savagery or barbarism into a state characteristic of civilization. **2** to refine, educate, or enlighten.
▸**'civiˌlizable** *or* **'civiˌlisable** *adj* ▸**'civiˌlized** *or* **'civiˌlised** *adj*
civil law *n* **1** the law of a state relating to private and civilian affairs. **2** the body of law in ancient Rome, esp. as applicable to private citizens. **3** law based on the Roman system as distinguished from common law and canon law.
civil liberty *n* the right of an individual to certain freedoms of speech and action.
civil list *n* (in Britain) the annuities voted by Parliament for the support of the royal household and the royal family.
civil marriage *n Law.* a marriage performed by an official other than a clergyman.
civil rights *pl n* **1** the personal rights of the individual citizen. **2** *(modifier)* of, relating to, or promoting equality in social, economic, and political rights.
civil servant *n* a member of the civil service.
civil service *n* **1** the service responsible for the public administration of the government of a country. It excludes the legislative, judicial, and military branches. **2** the members of the civil service collectively.
civil war *n* war between parties or factions within the same nation.
Civil War *n* **1** *English history.* the conflict between Charles I and the Parliamentarians resulting from disputes over their respective prerogatives. Parliament gained decisive victories at Marston Moor in 1644 and Naseby in 1645, and Charles was executed in 1649. **2** *US history.* the war fought from 1861 to 1865 between the North and the South, sparked off by Lincoln's election as president but with deep-rooted political and economic causes, exacerbated by the slavery issue. The advantages of the North in terms of population, finance, and communications brought about the South's eventual surrender at Appomattox.
civvy ('sɪvɪ) *n, pl* **civvies.** *Sl.* **1** a civilian. **2** *(pl)* Also: **civies.** civilian dress as opposed to uniform. **3 civvy street.** civilian life.
CJ *abbrev. for* Chief Justice.
CJA (in Britain) *abbrev. for* Criminal Justice Act.
CJD *abbrev. for* Creutzfeldt-Jakob disease.
Cl *the chemical symbol for* chlorine.
clachan (*Gaelic* 'klaxən; *English* 'klæ-) *n Scot. & Irish dialect.* a small village; hamlet. [C15: from Scot. Gaelic: prob. from *clach* stone]
clack (klæk) *vb* **1** to make or cause to make a sound like that of two pieces of wood hitting each other. **2** *(intr)* to jabber. ◆ *n* **3** a short sharp sound. **4** chatter. **5** Also called: **clack valve.** a simple nonreturn valve using a hinged flap or a ball. [C13: prob. from ON *klaka* to twitter, imit.]
▸**'clacker** *n*
clad[1] Ⓣ (klæd) *vb* a past tense and past participle of **clothe.** [OE *clāthode* clothed, from *clāthian* to CLOTHE]
clad[2] (klæd) *vb* **clads, cladding, clad.** *(tr)* to bond a metal to (another metal), esp. to form a protective coating. [C14: special use of CLAD[1]]
cladding ('klædɪŋ) *n* **1** the process of protecting one metal by bonding a second metal to its surface. **2** the protective coating so bonded to metal. **3** the material used for the outside facing of a building, etc.
clade (kleɪd) *n Biol.* a group of organisms considered as having evolved from a common ancestor. [C20: from Gk *klados* branch, shoot]
cladistics (klə'dɪstɪks) *n (functioning as sing)* a method of grouping animals by measurable likenesses or homologues. [C20: NL from Gk *klados* branch, shoot]
▸**cladism** ('klædɪzəm) *n* ▸**cladist** ('klædɪst) *n*
claim Ⓣ (kleɪm) *vb (mainly tr)* **1** to demand as being due or as one's property; assert one's title or right to: *he claimed the record.* **2** *(takes a clause as object or an infinitive)* to assert as a fact; maintain against denial: *he claimed to be telling the truth.* **3** to call for or need; deserve: *this problem claims our attention.* **4** to take: *the accident claimed four lives.* ◆ *n* **5** an assertion of a right; a demand for something as due. **6** an assertion of something as true, real, or factual. **7** a right or just title to something; basis for demand: *a claim to fame.* **8** anything that is claimed, such as a piece of land staked out by a miner. **9a** a demand for payment in connection with an insurance policy, etc. **9b** the sum of money demanded. [C13: from OF *claimer* to call, from L *clāmāre* to shout]
▸**'claimable** *adj* ▸**'claimant** *or* **'claimer** *n*
clairvoyance (klɛə'vɔɪəns) *n* **1** the alleged power of perceiving things beyond the natural range of the senses. **2** keen intuitive understanding. [C19: from F: clear-seeing, from *clair* clear + *voyance,* from *voir* to see]
clairvoyant Ⓣ (klɛə'vɔɪənt) *adj* **1** of or possessing clairvoyance. **2** having great insight. ◆ *n* **3** a person claiming to have the power to foretell future events.
▸**clair'voyantly** *adv*
clam (klæm) *n* **1** any of various burrowing bivalve molluscs. **2** the edible flesh of such a mollusc. **3** *Inf.* a reticent person. ◆ *vb* **clams, clamming, clammed. 4** *(intr) Chiefly US.* to gather clams. ◆ See also **clam up.** [C16: from earlier *clamshell,* that is, shell that clamps]
clamant ('kleɪmənt) *adj* **1** noisy. **2** calling urgently. [C17: from L, from *clāmāre* to shout]
clamber Ⓣ ('klæmbə) *vb* **1** (usually foll. by *up, over,* etc.) to climb (something) awkwardly, esp. by using both hands and feet. ◆ *n* **2** a climb performed in this manner. [C15: prob. var. of CLIMB]
▸**'clamberer** *n*
clammy Ⓣ ('klæmɪ) *adj* **clammier, clammiest. 1** unpleasantly sticky; moist. **2** (of the weather) close; humid. [C14: from OE *clǣman* to smear]
▸**'clammily** *adv* ▸**'clamminess** *n*
clamour Ⓣ *or US* **clamor** ('klæmə) *n* **1** a loud persistent outcry. **2** a vehement expression of collective feeling or outrage: *a clamour against higher prices.* **3** a loud and persistent noise: *the clamour of traffic.* ◆ *vb* **4** *(intr;* often foll. by *for* or *against)* to make a loud noise or outcry; make a public demand. **5** *(tr)* to move or force by outcry. [C14: from OF, from L, from *clāmāre* to cry out]
▸**'clamorous** *adj* ▸**'clamorously** *adv* ▸**'clamorousness** *n*
clamp[1] Ⓣ (klæmp) *n* **1** a mechanical device with movable jaws with which an object can be secured to a bench or with which two objects may be secured together. **2** See **wheel clamp.** ◆ *vb (tr)* **3** to fix or fasten with or as if with a clamp **4** to immobilize (a car) by means of a wheel

THESAURUS

civil *adj* **1** = **civic,** domestic, home, interior, municipal, political **4** = **polite,** accommodating, affable, civilized, complaisant, courteous, courtly, obliging, polished, refined, urbane, well-bred, well-mannered
Antonyms *adj* ≠ **civic:** military, religious, state ≠ **polite:** discourteous, ill-mannered, impolite, rude, uncivil, unfriendly, ungracious, unpleasant
civility *n* **1** = **politeness,** affability, amiability, breeding, complaisance, cordiality, courteousness, courtesy, good manners, graciousness, politesse, tact, urbanity
civilization *n* **1** = **society,** community, nation, people, polity **3** = **customs,** mores, way of life **4, 5** = **culture,** advancement, cultivation, development, education, enlightenment, progress, refinement, sophistication
civilize *vb* **2** = **cultivate,** educate, enlighten, humanize, improve, polish, refine, sophisticate, tame
civilized *adj* **2** = **cultured,** educated, enlightened, humane, polite, sophisticated, tolerant, urbane
Antonyms *adj* barbarous, ignorant, naive, primitive, simple, uncivilized, uncultivated, uncultured, undeveloped, uneducated, unenlightened, unsophisticated, untutored, wild
clad[1] *adj* = **dressed,** accoutred, apparelled, arrayed, attired, clothed, covered, decked out, draped, fitted out, invested, rigged out *(inf.)*
claim *vb* **1, 2** = **assert,** allege, challenge, exact, hold, insist, maintain, profess, uphold **3** = **demand,** ask, call for, insist, need, require **4** = **take,** collect, pick up ◆ *n* **5, 6** = **demand,** affirmation, allegation, application, call, petition, pretension, privilege, protestation, request, requirement **7** = **right,** title
claimant *n* **1** = **applicant,** petitioner, pretender, suppliant, supplicant
clairvoyant *adj* **1** = **psychic,** extrasensory, fey, oracular, prescient, prophetic, second-sighted, sibylline, telepathic, vatic, visionary ◆ *n* **3** = **psychic,** augur, diviner, fortune-teller, haruspex, oracle, prophet, prophetess, seer, sibyl, soothsayer, telepath, telepathist, visionary
clamber *vb* **1** = **climb,** claw, scale, scrabble, scramble, shin
clamminess *n* **1, 2** = **moistness,** airlessness, closeness, dampness, dankness, drizzliness, heaviness, humidity, humidness, mugginess, oppressiveness, pastiness, sliminess, stickiness, stuffiness, sultriness, sweatiness, thickness
clammy *adj* **1, 2** = **moist,** close, damp, dank, drizzly, pasty, slimy, sticky, sweating, sweaty
clamorous *adj* **1-3** = **noisy,** blaring, deafening, insistent, loud, lusty, riotous, strident, tumultuous, uproarious, vehement, vociferous
clamour *n* **1** = **noise,** agitation, babel, blare, brouhaha, commotion, din, exclamation, hubbub, hullabaloo, outcry, racket, shout, shouting, uproar, vociferation
clamp[1] *n* **1** = **vice,** bracket, fastener, grip, press

clamp. **5** to inflict or impose forcefully: *they clamped a curfew on the town.* [C14: from Du. or Low G *klamp*]

clamp[2] (klæmp) *n* **1** a mound of a harvested root crop, covered with straw and earth to protect it from winter weather. ◆ *vb* **2** (*tr*) to enclose (a harvested root crop) in a mound. [C16: from MDu. *klamp* heap]

clamp down *vb* (*intr, adv;* often foll. by *on*) **1** to behave repressively; attempt to suppress something regarded as undesirable. ◆ *n* **clampdown. 2** a sudden restrictive measure.

clam up *vb* (*intr, adv*) *Inf.* to keep or become silent or withhold information.

clan ➊ (klæn) *n* **1** a group of people interrelated by ancestry or marriage. **2** a group of families with a common surname and a common ancestor, esp. among the Scots and the Irish. **3** a group of people united by common characteristics, aims, or interests. [C14: from Scot. Gaelic *clann* family, descendants, from L *planta* sprout]

clandestine ➊ (klæn'destɪn) *adj* secret and concealed, often for illicit reasons; furtive. [C16: from L, from *clam* secretly]
▸**clan'destinely** *adv*

clang ➊ (klæŋ) *vb* **1** to make or cause to make a loud resounding noise, as metal when struck. **2** (*intr*) to move or operate making such a sound. ◆ *n* **3** a resounding metallic noise. **4** the harsh cry of certain birds. [C16: from L *clangere*]

clanger ('klæŋə) *n* **1** *Inf.* a conspicuous mistake (esp. in **drop a clanger**). **2** something that clangs or causes a clang. [C20: from CLANG]

clangour *or US* **clangor** ('klæŋgə, 'klæŋə) *n* **1** a loud resonant often-repeated noise. **2** an uproar. ◆ *vb* **3** (*intr*) to make or produce a loud resonant noise.
▸**'clangorous** *adj* ▸**'clangorously** *adv*

clank (klæŋk) *n* **1** an abrupt harsh metallic sound. ◆ *vb* **2** to make or cause to make such a sound. **3** (*intr*) to move or operate making such a sound. [C17: imit.]
▸**'clankingly** *adv*

clannish ➊ ('klænɪʃ) *adj* **1** of or characteristic of a clan. **2** tending to associate closely within a group to the exclusion of outsiders; cliquish.
▸**'clannishly** *adv* ▸**'clannishness** *n*

clansman ('klænzmən) *or* (*fem*) **clanswoman** *n, pl* **clansmen** *or* **clanswomen.** a person belonging to a clan.

clap[1] ➊ (klæp) *vb* **claps, clapping, clapped. 1** to make or cause to make a sharp abrupt sound, as of two nonmetallic objects struck together. **2** to applaud (someone or something) by striking the palms of the hands together sharply. **3** (*tr*) to strike (a person) lightly with an open hand, in greeting, etc. **4** (*tr*) to place or put quickly or forcibly: *they clapped him into jail.* **5** (of certain birds) to flap (the wings) noisily. **6** (*intr;* foll. by *up* or *together*) to contrive or put together hastily. **7 clap eyes on.** *Inf.* to catch sight of. **8 clap hold of.** *Inf.* to grasp suddenly or forcibly. ◆ *n* **9** the sharp abrupt sound produced by striking the hands together. **10** the act of clapping, esp. in applause. **11** a sudden sharp sound, esp. of thunder. **12** a light blow. **13** *Arch.* a sudden action or mishap. [OE *clæppan;* imit.]

clap[2] (klæp) *n* (usually preceded by *the*) a slang word for **gonorrhoea.** [C16: from OF *clapoir* venereal sore, from *clapier* brothel, from ?]

clapboard ('klæpˌbɔːd, 'klæbəd) *n* **1** a long thin timber board, used esp. in the US and Canada in wood-frame construction by lapping each board over the one below. ◆ *vb* **2** (*tr*) to cover with such boards. [C16: partial translation of Low G *klappholt,* from *klappen* to crack + *holt* wood]

clapped out *adj* (**clapped-out** *when prenominal*). *Inf.* **1** *Brit., Austral. & NZ.* worn out; dilapidated. **2** *Austral. & NZ.* extremely tired; exhausted.

clapper ('klæpə) *n* **1** a person or thing that claps. **2** Also called: **tongue.** a small piece of metal suspended within a bell that causes it to sound when made to strike against its side. **3 go (run, move) like the clappers.** *Brit. inf.* to move extremely fast.

clapperboard ('klæpəˌbɔːd) *n* a pair of hinged boards clapped together during film shooting to aid in synchronizing sound and picture prints.

claptrap ➊ ('klæpˌtræp) *n Inf.* **1** contrived but foolish talk. **2** insincere and pretentious talk: *politicians' claptrap.* [C18: from CLAP[1] + TRAP[1]]

claque (klæk) *n* **1** a group of people hired to applaud. **2** a group of fawning admirers. [C19: from F, from *claquer* to clap, imit.]

claret ('klærət) *n* **1** a red wine, esp. one from the Bordeaux district of France. **2a** a purplish-red colour. **2b** (*as adj*): *a claret football strip.* [C14: from OF (*vin*) *claret* clear (wine), from Med. L *clārātum,* from L *clārus* clear]

clarify ➊ ('klærɪˌfaɪ) *vb* **clarifies, clarifying, clarified. 1** to make or become clear or easy to understand. **2** to make or become free of impurities. **3** to make (fat, butter, etc.) clear by heating, etc., or (of fat, etc.) to become clear as a result of such a process. [C14: from OF, from LL, from L *clārus* clear + *facere* to make]
▸ˌ**clarifi'cation** *n* ▸**'clariˌfier** *n*

clarinet (ˌklærɪ'net) *n Music.* **1** a keyed woodwind instrument with a cylindrical bore and a single reed. **2** an orchestral musician who plays the clarinet. [C18: from F, prob. from It., from *clarino* trumpet]
▸ˌ**clari'nettist** *or US sometimes* ˌ**clari'netist** *n*

clarion ('klærɪən) *n* **1** a stop of trumpet quality on an organ. **2** an obsolete, high-pitched, small-bore trumpet. **3** the sound of such an instrument or any similar sound. ◆ *adj* **4** (*prenominal*) clear and ringing; inspiring: *a clarion call to action.* ◆ *vb* **5** to proclaim loudly. [C14: from Med. L *clāriō* trumpet, from L *clārus* clear]

clarity ➊ ('klærɪtɪ) *n* **1** clearness, as of expression. **2** clearness, as of water. [C16: from L *clāritās,* from *clārus* clear]

clarkia ('klɑːkɪə) *n* any North American plant of the genus *Clarkia:* cultivated for their red, purple, or pink flowers. [C19: NL, after William *Clark* (1770–1838), American explorer]

clary ('kleərɪ) *n, pl* **claries.** any of several European plants having aromatic leaves and blue flowers. [C14: from earlier *sclarreye,* from Med. L *sclareia,* from ?]

-clase *n combining form.* (in mineralogy) indicating a particular type of cleavage: *plagioclase.* [via F from Gk *klasis* a breaking]

clash ➊ (klæʃ) *vb* **1** to make or cause to make a loud harsh sound, esp. by striking together. **2** (*intr*) to be incompatible. **3** (*intr*) to engage together in conflict. **4** (*intr*) (of dates or events) to coincide. **5** (*intr*) (of colours) to look inharmonious together. ◆ *n* **6** a loud harsh noise. **7** a collision or conflict. [C16: imit.]
▸**'clasher** *n*

clasp ➊ (klɑːsp) *n* **1** a fastening, such as a catch or hook, for holding things together. **2** a firm grasp or embrace. **3** *Mil.* a bar on a medal ribbon, to indicate either a second award or the battle, campaign, or reason for its award. ◆ *vb* (*tr*) **4** to hold in a firm grasp. **5** to grasp firmly with the hand. **6** to fasten together with or as if with a clasp. [C14: from ?]
▸**'clasper** *n*

claspers ('klɑːspəz) *pl n Zool.* **1** a paired organ of male insects, used to clasp the female during copulation. **2** a paired organ of male sharks and related fish, used to assist the transfer of spermatozoa into the body of the female during copulation.

clasp knife *n* a large knife with one or more blades or other devices folding into the handle.

class ➊ (klɑːs) *n* **1** a collection or division of people or things sharing a common characteristic. **2** a group of persons sharing a similar social and economic position. **3a** the pattern of divisions that exist within a society on the basis of rank, economic status, etc. **3b** (*as modifier*): *the class struggle; class distinctions.* **4a** a group of pupils or students who are taught together. **4b** a meeting of a group of students for tuition. **5** *US.* a group of students who graduated in a specified year: *the class of '53.* **6** (*in combination and as modifier*) *Brit.* a grade of attainment in a university honours degree: *second-class honours.* **7** one of several standards of accommodation in public transport. **8** *Inf.* excellence or elegance, esp. in dress, design, or behaviour. **9** *Biol.* any of the taxonomic groups into which a phylum is divided and which contains one or more orders. **10** *Maths.* another name for **set**[2] (sense 3). **11 in a class of its own** *or* **in a class by oneself.** unequalled; unparalleled. ◆ *vb* **12** to

THESAURUS

◆ *vb* **3** = **fasten**, brace, clinch, fix, impose, make fast, secure

clan *n* **1-3** = **family**, band, brotherhood, clique, coterie, faction, fraternity, gens, group, house, order, race, schism, sect, sept, set, society, sodality, tribe

clandestine *adj* = **secret**, cloak-and-dagger, closet, concealed, covert, fraudulent, furtive, hidden, private, sly, stealthy, surreptitious, underground, underhand, under-the-counter

clang *vb* **1** = **ring**, bong, chime, clank, clash, jangle, resound, reverberate, toll ◆ *n* **3** = **ringing**, clangour, ding-dong, knell, reverberation

clannish *adj* **2** = **cliquish**, exclusive, insular, narrow, sectarian, select, unfriendly

clannishness *n* **2** = **cliquishness**, exclusiveness, exclusivity, insularity, narrowness, sectarianism, selectness, unfriendliness

clap[1] *vb* **1** = **strike**, bang, pat, punch, slap, thrust, thwack, wallop (*inf.*), whack **2** = **applaud**, acclaim, cheer, give (someone) a big hand

Antonyms *vb* ≠ **applaud:** blow a raspberry, boo, catcall, hiss, jeer

claptrap *n Informal* **1, 2** = **nonsense**, affectation, blarney, bombast, bosh (*inf.*), bullshit (*taboo sl.*), bunk (*inf.*), bunkum *or* buncombe (*chiefly US*), cobblers (*Brit. taboo sl.*), crap (*sl.*), drivel, eyewash (*inf.*), flannel (*Brit. inf.*), garbage (*inf.*), guff (*sl.*), hogwash, hot air (*inf.*), humbug, insincerity, moonshine, pap, piffle (*inf.*), poppycock (*inf.*), rot, rubbish, tommyrot, tosh (*sl., chiefly Brit.*), trash, tripe (*inf.*), twaddle

clarification *n* **1** = **explanation**, elucidation, exposition, illumination, interpretation, simplification

clarify *vb* **1** = **explain**, clear the air, clear up, elucidate, explicate, illuminate, interpret, make plain, resolve, simplify, throw *or* shed light on **2** = **refine**, cleanse, purify

clarity *n* **1** = **clearness**, comprehensibility, definition, explicitness, intelligibility, limpidity, lucidity, obviousness, precision, simplicity, transparency

Antonyms *n* cloudiness, complexity, complication, dullness, haziness, imprecision, intricacy, murkiness, obscurity

clash *vb* **1** = **crash**, bang, clang, clank, clatter, jangle, jar, rattle **3** = **conflict**, cross swords, feud, grapple, lock horns, quarrel, war, wrangle ◆ *n* **7** = **conflict**, brush, collision, confrontation, difference of opinion, disagreement, fight, showdown (*inf.*)

clasp *n* **1** = **fastening**, brooch, buckle, catch, clip, fastener, grip, hasp, hook, pin, press stud, snap **2** = **grasp**, embrace, grip, hold, hug ◆ *vb* **4, 5** = **grasp**, attack, clutch, embrace, enfold, grapple, grip, hold, hug, press, seize, squeeze **6** = **fasten**, concatenate, connect

class *n* **1, 2** = **group**, caste, category, classification, collection, denomination, department, division, genre, genus, grade, grouping, kind, league, order, rank, set, sort, species, sphere, stamp, status, type, value ◆ *vb* **12** = **classify**,

have or assign a place within a group, grade, or class. [C17: from L *classis* class, rank, fleet]

class. *abbrev. for:* **1** classic(al). **2** classification. **3** classified.

class-conscious *adj* aware of belonging to a particular social rank.
▸ **,class-'consciousness** *n*

classic Ⓣ ('klæsɪk) *adj* **1** of the highest class, esp. in art or literature. **2** serving as a standard or model of its kind. **3** adhering to an established set of principles in the arts or sciences: *a classic proof.* **4** characterized by simplicity, balance, regularity, and purity of form; classical. **5** of lasting interest or significance. **6** continuously in fashion because of its simple style: *a classic dress.* ◆ *n* **7** an author, artist, or work of art of the highest excellence. **8** a creation or work considered as definitive. **9** *Horse racing.* any of the five principal races for three-year-old horses in Britain, namely the One Thousand Guineas, Two Thousand Guineas, Derby, Oaks, and Saint Leger. [C17: from L *classicus* of the first rank, from *classis* division, rank, class]

classical Ⓣ ('klæsɪkᵊl) *adj* **1** of, relating to, or characteristic of the ancient Greeks and Romans or their civilization. **2** designating, following, or influenced by the art or culture of ancient Greece or Rome: *classical architecture.* **3** *Music.* **3a** of, relating to, or denoting any music or its period of composition marked by stability of form, intellectualism, and restraint. Cf. **romantic** (sense 5). **3b** accepted as a standard: *the classical suite.* **3c** denoting serious art music in general. Cf. **pop**^{2}. **4** denoting or relating to a style in any of the arts characterized by emotional restraint and conservatism: *a classical style of painting.* **5** (of an education) based on the humanities and the study of Latin and Greek. **6** *Physics.* not involving the quantum theory or the theory of relativity: *classical mechanics.*
▸ **,classi'cality** *or* **'classicalness** *n* ▸ **'classically** *adv*

Classical school *n* economic theory based on the works of Adam Smith and David Ricardo, which explains the creation of wealth and advocates free trade.

classic car *n Chiefly Brit.* a car that is more than twenty five years old. Cf. **veteran car, vintage car.**

classicism ('klæsɪ,sɪzəm) *or* **classicalism** ('klæsɪkə,lɪzəm) *n* **1** a style based on the study of Greek and Roman models, characterized by emotional restraint and regularity of form; the antithesis of romanticism. **2** knowledge of the culture of ancient Greece and Rome. **3a** a Greek or Latin expression. **3b** an expression in a modern language that is modelled on a Greek or Latin form.
▸ **'classicist** *n*

classicize *or* **classicise** ('klæsɪ,saɪz) *vb* **classicizes, classicizing, classicized** *or* **classicises, classicising, classicised. 1** (*tr*) to make classic. **2** (*intr*) to imitate classical style.

classics ('klæsɪks) *n* **1 the.** a body of literature regarded as great or lasting, esp. that of ancient Greece or Rome. **2 the.** the ancient Greek and Latin languages. **3** (*functioning as sing*) ancient Greek and Roman culture as a subject for academic study.

classification Ⓣ (,klæsɪfɪ'keɪʃən) *n* **1** systematic placement in categories. **2** one of the divisions in a system of classifying. **3** *Biol.* **3a** the placing of animals and plants in a series of increasingly specialized groups because of similarities in structure, origin, etc., that indicate a common relationship. **3b** the study of the principles and practice of this process; taxonomy. [C18: from F; see CLASS, -IFY, -ATION]
▸ **'classificatory** *adj*

classified ('klæsɪ,faɪd) *adj* **1** arranged according to some system of classification. **2** *Government.* (of information) not available to people outside a restricted group, esp. for reasons of national security. **3** *US & Canad. inf.* (of information) closely concealed or secret. **4** (of advertisements in newspapers, etc.) arranged according to type. **5** *Brit.* (of newspapers) containing sports results. **6** (of British roads) having a number in the national road system.

classify Ⓣ ('klæsɪ,faɪ) *vb* **classifies, classifying, classified.** (*tr*) **1** to arrange or order by classes; categorize. **2** *Government.* to declare (information, documents, etc.) of possible aid to an enemy and therefore not available to people outside a restricted group. [C18: back formation from CLASSIFICATION]
▸ **'classi,fiable** *adj* ▸ **'classi,fier** *n*

class interval *n Statistics.* one of the intervals into which the range of a variable of a distribution is divided, esp. one of the divisions of the base line of a bar chart or histogram.

classless ('klɑːslɪs) *adj* **1** not belonging to a class. **2** characterized by the absence of economic and social distinctions.
▸ **'classlessness** *n*

class list *n* (in Britain) a list categorizing students according to the class of honours they have obtained in their degree examination.

classmate ('klɑːs,meɪt) *n* a friend or contemporary of the same class in a school.

classroom ('klɑːs,ruːm, -,rʊm) *n* a room in which classes are conducted, esp. in a school.

class struggle *n* **the.** *Marxism.* the continual conflict between the capitalist and working classes for economic and political power.

classy Ⓣ ('klɑːsɪ) *adj* **classier, classiest.** *Sl.* elegant; stylish.
▸ **'classiness** *n*

clatter ('klætə) *vb* **1** to make or cause to make a rattling noise, esp. as a result of movement. **2** (*intr*) to chatter. ◆ *n* **3** a rattling sound or noise. **4** a noisy commotion, such as loud chatter. [OE *clatrung* clattering (gerund)]
▸ **'clatterer** *n* ▸ **'clatteringly** *adv*

clause Ⓣ (klɔːz) *n* **1** *Grammar.* a group of words, consisting of a subject and a predicate including a finite verb, that does not necessarily constitute a sentence. Cf. **phrase.** See also **main clause, subordinate clause. 2** a section of a legal document such as a contract, will, or draft statute. [C13: from OF, from Med. L *clausa* a closing (of a rhetorical period), from L, from *claudere* to close]
▸ **'clausal** *adj*

claustrophobia (,klɔːstrə'fəʊbɪə, ,klɒs-) *n* an abnormal fear of being in a confined space. [C19: NL from L *claustrum* CLOISTER + -PHOBIA]
▸ **'claustro,phobe** *n* ▸ **,claustro'phobic** *adj*

clavate ('kleɪveɪt, -vɪt) *or* **claviform** ('klævɪ,fɔːm) *adj Biol.* shaped like a club. [C19: from L *clāva* club]
▸ **'clavately** *adv*

clave^{1} (kleɪv, klɑːv) *n Music.* one of a pair of hardwood sticks struck together to make a hollow sound, esp. to mark the beat in Latin-Ameriian dance music. [C20: from American Sp., from L *clavis* key]

clave^{2} (kleɪv) *vb Arch.* a past tense of **cleave.**

clavichord ('klævɪ,kɔːd) *n* a keyboard instrument consisting of a number of thin wire strings struck from below by brass tangents. [C15: from Med. L, from L *clāvis* key + *chorda* CHORD^{1}]

clavicle ('klævɪkᵊl) *n* **1** either of the two bones connecting the shoulder blades with the upper part of the breastbone. Nontechnical name: **collarbone. 2** the corresponding structure in other vertebrates. [C17: from Med. L *clāvicula,* from L *clāvis* key]
▸ **clavicular** (klə'vɪkjʊlə) *adj*

clavier (klə'vɪə, 'klævɪə) *n* **a** any keyboard instrument. **b** the keyboard itself. [C18: from F: keyboard, from L *clāvis* key]

claw Ⓣ (klɔː) *n* **1** a curved pointed horny process on the end of each digit in birds, some reptiles, and certain mammals. **2** a corresponding structure in some invertebrates, such as the pincer of a crab. **3** a part or member like a claw in function or appearance. ◆ *vb* **4** to scrape, tear, or dig (something or someone) with claws, etc. **5** (*tr*) to create by scratching as with claws: *to claw an opening.* [OE *clawu*]
▸ **'clawer** *n*

claw back *vb* (*tr, adv*) **1** to get back (something) with difficulty. **2** to recover (a sum of money), esp. by taxation or a penalty. ◆ *n* **clawback. 3** the recovery of a sum of money, esp. by taxation or a penalty. **4** the sum so recovered.

claw hammer *n* a hammer with a cleft at one end of the head for extracting nails.

clay (kleɪ) *n* **1** a very fine-grained material that occurs as sedimentary rocks, soils, and other deposits. It becomes plastic when moist but hardens on heating and is used in the manufacture of bricks, ceramics, etc. **2** earth or mud. **3** *Poetic.* the material of the human body. [OE *clǣg*]
▸ **'clayey, 'clayish,** *or* **'clay,like** *adj*

claymore ('kleɪ,mɔː) *n* a large two-edged broadsword used formerly by Scottish Highlanders. [C18: from Gaelic *claidheamh mōr* great sword]

clay pigeon *n* a disc of baked clay hurled into the air from a machine as a target to be shot at.

clay road *n NZ.* an unmetalled road in a rural area.

CLC *abbrev. for* Canadian Labour Congress.

-cle *suffix forming nouns.* indicating smallness: *cubicle; particle.* [via OF from L *-culus.* See -CULE]

clean Ⓣ (kliːn) *adj* **1** without dirt or other impurities; unsoiled. **2** without anything in it or on it: *a clean page.* **3** recently washed; fresh. **4** without extraneous or foreign materials. **5** without defect, difficulties, or problems. **6** (of a nuclear weapon) producing little or no radio-

THESAURUS

brand, categorize, codify, designate, grade, group, label, rank, rate

classic *adj* **1** = **best,** consummate, finest, first-rate, masterly, world-class **2** = **definitive,** archetypal, exemplary, ideal, master, model, paradigmatic, quintessential, standard **3** = **typical,** characteristic, regular, standard, time-honoured, usual **5** = **lasting,** abiding, ageless, deathless, enduring, immortal, undying ◆ *n* **7, 8** = **standard,** exemplar, masterpiece, masterwork, model, paradigm, prototype
Antonyms *adj* ≠ **best:** inferior, modern, poor, second-rate, terrible

classical *adj* **1** = **Greek,** Attic, Augustan, Grecian, Hellenic, Latin, Roman **4** = **pure,** chaste, elegant, harmonious, refined, restrained, symmetrical, understated, well-proportioned

classification *n* **1** = **categorization,** analysis, arrangement, cataloguing, codification, grading, sorting, taxonomy

classify *vb* **1** = **categorize,** arrange, catalogue, codify, dispose, distribute, file, grade, pigeonhole, rank, sort, systematize, tabulate

classy *adj Informal* = **high-class,** elegant, exclusive, high-toned, posh (*inf., chiefly Brit.*), ritzy (*sl.*), select, stylish, superior, swanky (*inf.*), swish (*inf., chiefly Brit.*), top-drawer, up-market, urbane

clause *n* **2** = **section,** article, chapter, condition, heading, item, paragraph, part, passage, point, provision, proviso, rider, specification, stipulation

claw *n* **1, 2** = **nail,** nipper, pincer, talon, tentacle, unguis ◆ *vb* **4** = **scratch,** dig, graze, lacerate, mangle, maul, rip, scrabble, scrape, tear

clean *adj* **1, 3** = **pure,** faultless, flawless, fresh, hygienic, immaculate, impeccable, laundered, sanitary, spotless, squeaky-clean, unblemished, unsoiled, unspotted, unstained, unsullied, washed **1, 4** = **hygienic,** antiseptic, clarified, decontaminated, natural, purified, sterile, sterilized, unadulterated, uncontaminated, unpolluted **8** = **moral,** chaste, decent, exemplary, good, honourable, impeccable, innocent, pure, respectable, undefiled, upright, virtuous **10** = **complete,** conclusive, decisive,

active fallout or contamination. **7** (of a wound, etc.) having no pus or other sign of infection. **8** pure; morally sound. **9** without objectionable language or obscenity. **10** thorough or complete: *a clean break.* **11** dexterous or adroit: *a clean throw.* **12** *Sport.* played fairly and without fouls. **13** simple in design: *a ship's clean lines.* **14** *Aeronautics.* causing little turbulence; streamlined. **15** honourable or respectable. **16** habitually neat. **17** (esp. of a driving licence) showing or having no record of offences. **18** *Sl.* **18a** innocent; not guilty. **18b** not carrying illegal drugs, weapons, etc. ◆ *vb* **19** to make or become free of dirt, filth, etc.: *the stove cleans easily.* **20** (*tr*) to remove in making clean: *to clean marks off the wall.* **21** (*tr*) to prepare (fish, poultry, etc.) for cooking: *to clean a chicken.* ◆ *adv* **22** in a clean way; cleanly. **23** *Not standard.* (intensifier): *clean forgotten.* **24 come clean.** *Inf.* to make a revelation or confession. ◆ *n* **25** the act or an instance of cleaning: *he gave his shoes a clean.* **26 clean sweep.** See **sweep** (sense 28). ◆ See also **clean out, clean up.** [OE *clǣne*]
▸**'cleanable** *adj* ▸**'cleanness** *n*

clean-cut ❶ *adj* **1** clearly outlined; neat: *clean-cut lines of a ship.* **2** definite.

cleaner ('kliːnə) *n* **1** a person, device, chemical agent, etc., that removes dirt, as from clothes or carpets. **2** (*usually pl*) a shop, etc., that provides a dry-cleaning service. **3 take (a person) to the cleaners.** *Inf.* to rob or defraud (a person).

cleanly ❶ ('kliːnlɪ) *adv* **1** in a fair manner. **2** easily or smoothly. ◆ *adj* ('klɛnlɪ), **cleanlier, cleanliest. 3** habitually clean or neat.
▸**cleanlily** ('klɛnlɪlɪ) *adv* ▸**cleanliness** ('klɛnlɪnɪs) *n*

clean out *vb* (*tr, adv*) **1** (foll. by *of* or *from*) to remove (something) (from or away from). **2** *Sl.* to leave (someone) with no money. **3** *Inf.* to exhaust (stocks, goods, etc.) completely.

cleanse ❶ (klɛnz) *vb* **cleanses, cleansing, cleansed.** (*tr*) **1** to remove dirt, filth, etc., from. **2** to remove guilt from. **3** *Arch.* to cure. [OE *clǣnsian;* see CLEAN]

cleanser ❶ ('klɛnzə) *n* a cleansing agent.

clean-shaven *adj* (of men) having the facial hair shaved off.

clean up *vb* (*adv*) **1** to rid (something) of dirt, filth, or other impurities. **2** to make (someone or something) orderly or presentable. **3** (*tr*) to rid (a place) of undesirable people or conditions. **4** *Inf., chiefly US & Canad.* to make (a great profit). ◆ *n* **cleanup. 5** the process of cleaning up. **6** *Inf., chiefly US.* a great profit.

clear ❶ (klɪə) *adj* **1** free from darkness or obscurity; bright. **2** (of weather) free from dullness or clouds. **3** transparent. **4** even and pure in tone or colour. **5** without blemish: *a clear skin.* **6** easy to see or hear; distinct. **7** free from doubt or confusion. **8** (*postpositive*) certain in the mind; sure: *are you clear?* **9** (*in combination*) perceptive, alert: *clear-headed.* **10** evident or obvious: *it is clear that he won't come now.* **11** (of sounds or the voice) not harsh or hoarse. **12** serene; calm. **13** without qualification; complete: *a clear victory.* **14** free of suspicion, guilt, or blame: *a clear conscience.* **15** free of obstruction; open: *a clear passage.* **16** free from debt or obligation. **17** (of money, profits, etc.) without deduction; net. **18** emptied of freight or cargo. **19** *Showjumping.* (of a round) ridden without any points being lost. ◆ *adv* **20** in a clear or distinct manner. **21** completely or utterly. **22** (*postpositive;* often foll. by *of*) not in contact (with); free: *stand clear of the gates.* ◆ *n* **23** a clear space. **24 in the clear. 24a** free of suspicion, guilt, or blame. **24b** *Sport.* able to receive a pass without being tackled. ◆ *vb* **25** to make or become free from darkness, obscurity, etc. **26** (*intr*) **26a** (of the weather) to become free from dullness, fog, rain, etc. **26b** (of mist, fog, etc.) to disappear. **27** (*tr*) to free from impurity or blemish. **28** (*tr*) to free from doubt or confusion. **29** (*tr*) to rid of objects, obstructions, etc. **30** (*tr*) to make or form (a path, way, etc.) by removing obstructions. **31** (*tr*) to free or remove (a person or thing) from something, as of suspicion, blame, or guilt. **32** (*tr*) to move or pass by or over without contact: *he cleared the wall easily.* **33** (*tr*) to rid (the throat) of phlegm. **34** (*tr*) to make or gain (money) as profit. **35** (*tr;* often foll. by *off*) to discharge or settle (a debt). **36** (*tr*) to free (a debtor) from obligation. **37** (*intr*) (of a cheque) to pass through one's bank and be charged against one's account. **38** *Banking.* to settle accounts by exchanging (commercial documents) in a clearing house. **39** to permit (ships, aircraft, cargo, passengers, etc.) to unload, disembark, depart, etc., or (of ships, etc.) to be permitted to unload, etc. **40** to obtain or give (clearance). **41** (*tr*) to obtain clearance from. **42** (*tr*) to permit (a person, company, etc.) to see or handle classified information. **43** (*tr*) *Mil., etc.* to decode (a message, etc.). **44** (*tr*) *Computing.* to remove data from a storage device and revert to zero. **45 clear the air.** to dispel tension, confusion, etc., by settling misunderstandings, etc. ◆ See also **clear away, clear off,** etc. [C13: *clere,* from OF *cler,* from L *clārus* clear]
▸**'clearer** *n* ▸**'clearly** *adv* ▸**'clearness** *n*

clearance ❶ ('klɪərəns) *n* **1a** the process or an instance of clearing: *slum clearance.* **1b** (*as modifier*): *a clearance order.* **2** space between two parts in motion or in relative motion. **3** permission for an aircraft, ship, passengers, etc., to proceed. **4** official permission to have access to secret information, projects, areas, etc. **5** *Banking.* the exchange of commercial documents drawn on the members of a clearing house. **6a** the disposal of merchandise at reduced prices. **6b** (*as modifier*): *a clearance sale.* **7** the act of clearing an area of land by mass eviction: *the Highland Clearances.*

clear away *vb* (*adv*) to remove (objects) from (the table) after a meal.

clear-cut ❶ *adj* (**clear cut** *when postpositive*). **1** definite; not vague: *a clear-cut proposal.* **2** clearly outlined.

clearing ❶ ('klɪərɪŋ) *n* an area with few or no trees or shrubs in wooded or overgrown land.

clearing bank *n* (in Britain) any bank that makes use of the central clearing house in London.

clearing house *n* **1** *Banking.* an institution where cheques and other commercial papers drawn on member banks are cancelled against each other so that only net balances are payable. **2** a central agency for the collection and distribution of information or materials.

clear off *vb* (*intr, adv*) *Inf.* to go away: often used imperatively.

clear out ❶ *vb* (*adv*) **1** (*intr*) *Inf.* to go away: often used imperatively. **2** (*tr*) to remove and sort the contents of (a room, etc.). **3** (*tr*) *Sl.* to leave (someone) with no money. **4** (*tr*) *Sl.* to exhaust (stocks, goods, etc.) completely.

clearstory ('klɪəˌstɔːrɪ) *n* a variant of **clerestory.**

clear up ❶ *vb* (*adv*) **1** (*tr*) to explain or solve (a mystery, misunderstanding, etc.). **2** to put (a place or thing that is disordered) in order. **3** (*intr*) (of the weather) to become brighter.

clearway ('klɪəˌweɪ) *n* **1** *Brit.* a stretch of road on which motorists may stop only in an emergency. **2** an area at the end of a runway over which an aircraft taking off makes its initial climb.

cleat (kliːt) *n* **1** a wedge-shaped block attached to a structure to act as a support. **2** a device consisting of two hornlike prongs projecting horizontally in opposite directions from a central base, used for securing lines on vessels, wharves, etc. ◆ *vb* (*tr*) **3** to supply or support with a cleat or cleats. **4** to secure (a line) on a cleat. [C14: of Gmc origin]

cleavage ('kliːvɪdʒ) *n* **1** *Inf.* the separation between a woman's breasts, esp. as revealed by a low-cut dress. **2** a division or split. **3** (of crystals)

THESAURUS

entire, final, perfect, thorough, total, unimpaired, whole **13** = **neat**, delicate, elegant, graceful, simple, tidy, trim, uncluttered ◆ *vb* **19** = **cleanse**, bath, deodorize, disinfect, do up, dust, launder, lave, mop, purge, purify, rinse, sanitize, scour, scrub, sponge, swab, sweep, vacuum, wash, wipe **24 come clean** *Informal* = **confess**, acknowledge, admit, come out of the closet, cough up (*sl.*), get (something) off one's chest (*inf.*), make a clean breast of, own up, reveal, sing (*sl., chiefly US*), spill one's guts (*sl.*)
Antonyms *adj* ≠ **pure:** dirty, filthy, mucky, scuzzy (*sl., chiefly US*), soiled, sullied, unwashed ≠ **hygienic:** adulterated, contaminated, infected, polluted ≠ **moral:** dishonourable, immoral, impure, indecent, unchaste ≠ **neat:** chaotic, disorderly, disorganized, higgledy-piggledy (*inf.*), shambolic (*inf.*), untidy ◆ *vb* ≠ **cleanse:** adulterate, defile, dirty, infect, mess up, pollute, soil, stain

clean-cut *adj* **1, 2** = **clear**, chiselled, definite, etched, neat, outlined, sharp, trim, well-defined

cleanliness *n* **3** = **cleanness**, asepsis, freshness, immaculacy, immaculateness, neatness, purity, sanitariness, spotlessness, stainlessness, sterility, tidiness, unspottedness, whiteness

cleanse *vb* **1** = **clean**, clear, lustrate, purge, purify, rinse, scour, scrub, wash

cleanser *n* = **detergent**, disinfectant, purifier, scourer, soap, soap powder, solvent

clear *adj* **2** = **bright**, cloudless, fair, fine, halcyon, light, luminous, shining, sunny, unclouded, undimmed **3** = **transparent**, crystalline, glassy, limpid, pellucid, see-through, translucent **6, 7, 10** = **obvious**, apparent, articulate, audible, blatant, bold, coherent, comprehensible, conspicuous, cut-and-dried (*inf.*), definite, distinct, evident, explicit, express, incontrovertible, intelligible, lucid, manifest, palpable, patent, perceptible, plain, pronounced, recognizable, unambiguous, unequivocal, unmistakable, unquestionable **8** = **certain**, convinced, decided, definite, positive, resolved, satisfied, sure **13** = **unobstructed**, empty, free, open, smooth, unhampered, unhindered, unimpeded, unlimited **14** = **unblemished**, clean, guiltless, immaculate, innocent, pure, sinless, stainless, undefiled, untarnished, untroubled ◆ *vb* **26** = **brighten**, break up, clarify, lighten **27** = **clean**, cleanse, erase, purify, refine, sweep away, tidy (up), wipe **29** = **unblock**, disengage, disentangle, extricate, free, loosen, open, rid, unclog, unload, unpack **31** = **absolve**, acquit, excuse, exonerate, justify, vindicate **32** = **pass over**, jump, leap, miss, vault **34** = **gain**, acquire, earn, make, reap, secure
Antonyms *adj* ≠ **bright:** cloudy, dark, dull, foggy, hazy, misty, murky, overcast, stormy ≠ **transparent:** cloudy, muddy, non-translucent, nontransparent, opaque, turbid ≠ **obvious:** ambiguous, confused, doubtful, equivocal, hidden, inarticulate, inaudible, incoherent, indistinct, inexplicit, obscured, unrecognizable ≠ **unobstructed:** barricaded, blocked, closed, engaged, hampered, impeded, obstructed ◆ *vb* ≠ **absolve:** accuse, blame, charge, condemn, convict, find guilty

clearance *n* **2** = **space**, allowance, gap, headroom, margin **3, 4** = **permission**, authorization, blank cheque, consent, endorsement, go-ahead, green light, leave, O.K. *or* okay (*inf.*), sanction **7** = **evacuation**, depopulation, emptying, eviction, removal, unpeopling, withdrawal

clear-cut *adj* **1** = **straightforward**, black-and-white, cut-and-dried (*inf.*), definite, explicit, plain, precise, specific, unambiguous, unequivocal

clearing *n* = **glade**, dell

clearly *adv* **10** = **obviously**, beyond doubt, distinctly, evidently, incontestably, incontrovertibly, markedly, openly, overtly, undeniably, undoubtedly

clearness *n* **1, 3** = **clarity**, audibility, brightness, coherence, distinctness, glassiness, intelligibility, lucidity, luminosity, transparency

clear out *vb* **1** *Informal* = **go away**, beat it (*sl.*), decamp, depart, hook it (*sl.*), leave, make oneself scarce, make tracks, pack one's bags (*inf.*), retire, slope off, take oneself off, withdraw **2** = **get rid of**, empty, exhaust, sort, tidy up

clear up *vb* **1** = **solve**, answer, clarify, elucidate, explain, resolve, straighten out, unravel **2** = **tidy (up)**, order, rearrange

the act of splitting or the tendency to split along definite planes so as to yield smooth surfaces. **4** Also called: **segmentation.** (in animals) the repeated division of a fertilized ovum into a solid ball of cells. **5** the breaking of a chemical bond in a molecule to give smaller molecules or radicals. **6** *Geol.* the natural splitting of certain rocks, such as slates, into thin plates.

cleave[1] Ⓣ (kliːv) *vb* **cleaves, cleaving; cleft, cleaved,** *or* **clove; cleft, cleaved,** *or* **cloven. 1** to split or cause to split, esp. along a natural weakness. **2** (*tr*) to make by or as if by cutting: *to cleave a path.* **3** (when *intr*, foll. by *through*) to penetrate or traverse. [OE *clēofan*]
▸**'cleavable** *adj*

cleave[2] Ⓣ (kliːv) *vb* **cleaves, cleaving, cleaved.** (*intr;* foll. by *to*) to cling or adhere. [OE *cleofian*]

cleaver ('kliːvə) *n* a heavy knife or long-bladed hatchet, esp. one used by butchers.

cleavers ('kliːvəz) *n* (*functioning as sing*) a Eurasian plant, having small white flowers and prickly stems and fruits. Also called: **goosegrass, hairif.** [OE *clīfe;* see CLEAVE[2]]

clef (klɛf) *n* one of several symbols placed on the left-hand side beginning of each stave indicating the pitch of the music written after it. [C16: from F: key, clef, from L *clāvis*]

cleft Ⓣ (klɛft) *vb* **1** a past tense and past participle of **cleave**[1]. ◆ *n* **2** a fissure or crevice. **3** an indentation or split in something, such as the chin, palate, etc. ◆ *adj* **4** split; divided. [OE *geclyft* (n); see CLEAVE[1]]

cleft palate *n* a congenital crack or fissure in the midline of the hard palate, often associated with a harelip.

cleg (klɛg) *n* another name for a **horsefly.** [C15: from ON *kleggi*]

clematis ('klɛmətɪs, klə'meɪtɪs) *n* any N temperate climbing plant of the genus *Clematis.* Many species are cultivated for their large colourful flowers. [C16: from L, from Gk, from *klēma* vine twig]

clemency Ⓣ ('klɛmənsɪ) *n, pl* **clemencies. 1** mercy or leniency. **2** mildness, esp. of the weather. [C15: from L, from *clēmēns* gentle]

clement Ⓣ ('klɛmənt) *adj* **1** merciful. **2** (of the weather) mild. [C15: from L *clēmēns* mild]

clementine ('klɛmənˌtiːn, -ˌtaɪn) *n* a citrus fruit thought to be either a variety of tangerine or a hybrid between a tangerine and sweet orange. [C20: from F *clémentine*]

clench (klɛntʃ) *vb* (*tr*) **1** to close or squeeze together (the teeth, a fist, etc.) tightly. **2** to grasp or grip firmly. ◆ *n* **3** a firm grasp or grip. **4** a device that grasps or grips. ◆ *n, vb* **5** another word for **clinch.** [OE *beclencan*]

Cleopatra's Needle *n* either of two Egyptian obelisks, originally set up at Heliopolis about 1500 B.C.: one was moved to the Thames Embankment, London, in 1878, the other to Central Park, New York, in 1880.

clepsydra ('klɛpsɪdrə) *n, pl* **clepsydras** *or* **clepsydrae** (-ˌdriː). an ancient device for measuring time by the flow of water or mercury through a small aperture. Also called: **water clock.** [C17: from L, from Gk, from *kleptein* to steal + *hudōr* water]

cleptomania (ˌklɛptəʊ'meɪnɪə) *n* a variant spelling of **kleptomania.**

clerestory *or* **clearstory** ('klɪəˌstɔːrɪ) *n, pl* **clerestories** *or* **clearstories. 1** a row of windows in the upper part of the wall of a church that divides the nave from the aisle. **2** the part of the wall in which these windows are set. [C15: from CLEAR + STOREY]
▸**'clereˌstoried** *or* **'clearˌstoried** *adj*

clergy Ⓣ ('klɜːdʒɪ) *n, pl* **clergies.** the collective body of men and women ordained as religious ministers, esp. of the Christian Church. [C13: from OF; see CLERK]

clergyman Ⓣ ('klɜːdʒɪmən) *n, pl* **clergymen.** a member of the clergy.

cleric ('klɛrɪk) *n* a member of the clergy. [C17: from Church L *clēricus* priest, CLERK]

clerical Ⓣ ('klɛrɪkᵊl) *adj* **1** relating to or associated with the clergy: *clerical dress.* **2** of or relating to office clerks or their work: *a clerical error.* **3** supporting or advocating clericalism.
▸**'clerically** *adv*

clerical collar *n* a stiff white collar with no opening at the front that buttons at the back of the neck; the distinctive mark of the clergy in certain Churches. Informal name: **dog collar.**

clericalism ('klɛrɪkᵊˌlɪzəm) *n* **1** a policy of upholding the power of the clergy. **2** the power of the clergy.
▸**'clericalist** *n*

clericals ('klɛrɪkᵊlz) *pl n* the distinctive dress of a clergyman.

clerihew ('klɛrɪˌhjuː) *n* a form of comic or satiric verse, consisting of two couplets of metrically irregular lines, containing the name of a well-known person. [C20: after E. *Clerihew* Bentley (1875–1956), E writer who invented it]

clerk (klɑːk; *US & Canad.* klɜːrk) *n* **1** a worker, esp. in an office, who keeps records, files, etc. **2** an employee of a court, legislature, board, corporation, etc., who keeps records and accounts, etc.: *a town clerk.* **3** Also called: **clerk in holy orders.** a cleric. **4** *US & Canad.* short for **salesclerk. 5** Also called: **desk clerk.** *US & Canad.* a hotel receptionist. **6** *Arch.* a scholar. ◆ *vb* **7** (*intr*) to serve as a clerk. [OE *clerc,* from Church L *clēricus,* from Gk *klērikos* cleric, from *klēros* heritage]
▸**'clerkess** *fem n* (*chiefly Scot.*) ▸**'clerkish** *adj* ▸**'clerkship** *n*

clerk of works *n* an employee who supervises building work in progress.

clever Ⓣ ('klɛvə) *adj* **1** displaying sharp intelligence or mental alertness. **2** adroit or dexterous, esp. with the hands. **3** smart in a superficial way. **4** *Brit. inf.* sly; cunning. [C13 *cliver* (in the sense: quick to seize, adroit), from ?]
▸**'cleverly** *adv* ▸**'cleverness** *n*

clevis ('klɛvɪs) *n* the U-shaped component of a shackle. [C16: rel. to CLEAVE[1]]

clew (kluː) *n* **1** a ball of thread, yarn, or twine. **2** *Naut.* either of the lower corners of a square sail or the after lower corner of a fore-and-aft sail. ◆ *vb* **3** (*tr*) to coil into a ball. [OE *cliewen* (vb)]

clianthus (klɪ'ænθəs) *n* a leguminous plant of Australia and New Zealand with ornamental clusters of slender flowers. [C19: NL, prob. from Gk *klei-, kleos* glory + *anthos* flower]

cliché Ⓣ ('kliːʃeɪ) *n* **1** a word or expression that has lost much of its force through overexposure. **2** an idea, action, or habit that has become trite from overuse. **3** *Printing, chiefly Brit.* a stereotype or electrotype plate. [C19: from F, from *clicher* to stereotype; imit.]
▸**'clichéd** *or* **'cliché'd** *adj*

click Ⓣ (klɪk) *n* **1** a short light often metallic sound. **2** the locking member of a ratchet mechanism, such as a pawl or detent. **3** *Phonetics.* any of various stop consonants that are produced by the suction of air into the mouth. ◆ *vb* **4** to make or cause to make a clicking sound: *to click one's heels.* **5** (usually foll. by *on*) *Computing.* to press and release (a button on a mouse) or to select (a particular function) by pressing and releasing a button on a mouse. **6** (*intr*) *Sl.* to be a great success: *that idea really clicked.* **7** (*intr*) *Inf.* to become suddenly clear: *it finally clicked.* **8** (*intr*) *Sl.* to get on well: *they clicked from their first meeting.* [C17: imit.]
▸**'clicker** *n*

client Ⓣ ('klaɪənt) *n* **1** a person, company, etc., that seeks the advice of a professional man or woman. **2** a customer. **3** a person for whom a social worker, etc., is responsible. **4** *Computing.* a program or work station that requests data or information from a server. [C14: from L *cliēns* retainer, dependent]
▸**cliental** (klaɪ'ɛntᵊl) *adj*

clientele Ⓣ (ˌkliːɒn'tɛl) *or* **clientage** ('klaɪəntɪdʒ) *n* customers or clients collectively. [C16: from L, from *cliēns* CLIENT]

cliff Ⓣ (klɪf) *n* a steep high rock face, esp. one that runs along the seashore. [OE *clif*]
▸**'cliffy** *adj*

cliffhanger ('klɪfˌhæŋə) *n* **1a** a situation of imminent disaster usually occurring at the end of each episode of a serialized film. **1b** the serialized film itself. **2** a situation that is dramatic or uncertain.
▸**'cliffˌhanging** *adj*

climacteric (klaɪ'mæktərɪk, ˌklaɪmæk'tɛrɪk) *n* **1** a critical event or period. **2** another name for **menopause. 3** the period in the life of a man corresponding to the menopause, chiefly characterized by diminished sexual activity. ◆ *adj also* **climacterical** (ˌklaɪmæk'tɛrɪkᵊl). **4** in-

THESAURUS

cleave[1] *vb* **1** = **split**, crack, dissever, disunite, divide, hew, open, part, rend, rive, sever, slice, sunder, tear asunder

cleave[2] *vb* = **stick**, abide by, adhere, agree, attach, be devoted to, be true, cling, cohere, hold, remain, stand by

cleft *n* **2** = **opening**, breach, break, chasm, chink, crack, cranny, crevice, fissure, fracture, gap, rent, rift ◆ *adj* **4** = **split**, cloven, parted, rent, riven, ruptured, separated, sundered, torn

clemency *n* **1** = **mercy**, compassion, forbearance, forgiveness, humanity, indulgence, kindness, leniency, mercifulness, mildness, moderation, pity, quarter, soft-heartedness, tenderness

clement *adj* **1** = **merciful**, compassionate, forbearing, forgiving, gentle, humane, indulgent, kind, kind-hearted, lenient, mild, soft-hearted, tender **2** = **mild**, balmy, calm, fair, fine, temperate

clergy *n* = **priesthood**, churchmen, clergymen, clerics, ecclesiastics, first estate, holy orders, ministry, the cloth

clergyman *n* = **minister**, chaplain, churchman, cleric, curate, divine, father, man of God, man of the cloth, padre, parson, pastor, priest, rabbi, rector, reverend (*inf.*), vicar

clerical *adj* **1** = **ecclesiastical**, pastoral, priestly, sacerdotal **2** = **office**, book-keeping, clerkish, clerkly, secretarial, stenographic

clever *adj* **1-4** = **intelligent**, able, adroit, apt, astute, brainy (*inf.*), bright, canny, capable, cunning, deep, dexterous, discerning, expert, gifted, ingenious, inventive, keen, knowing, knowledgeable, quick, quick-witted, rational, resourceful, sagacious, sensible, shrewd, skilful, smart, talented, witty
Antonyms *adj* awkward, boring, clumsy, dense, dull, dumb (*inf.*), ham-fisted (*inf.*), inept, inexpert, maladroit, slow, stupid, thick, unaccomplished, unimaginative, witless

cleverness *n* **1-4** = **intelligence**, ability, adroitness, astuteness, brains, brightness, canniness, dexterity, flair, gift, gumption (*Brit. inf.*), ingenuity, nous (*Brit. sl.*), quickness, quick wits, resourcefulness, sagacity, sense, sharpness, shrewdness, smartness, suss (*sl.*), talent, wit

cliché *n* **1** = **platitude**, banality, bromide, chestnut (*inf.*), commonplace, hackneyed phrase, old saw, stereotype, truism

click *n, vb* **1, 4** = **snap**, beat, clack, tick **7** *Informal* = **become clear**, come home (to), fall into place, make sense **8** *Slang* = **get on**, be compatible, be on the same wavelength, feel a rapport, get on like a house on fire (*inf.*), go over, hit it off (*inf.*), make a hit, succeed, take to each other

client *n* **1-3** = **customer**, applicant, buyer, consumer, dependant, habitué, patient, patron, protégé, shopper

clientele *n* = **customers**, business, clients, following, market, patronage, regulars, trade

cliff *n* = **rock face**, bluff, crag, escarpment, face, overhang, precipice, scar, scarp

volving a crucial event or period. [C16: from L, from Gk, from *klimakter* rung of a ladder from *klimax* ladder]

climactic ⓣ (klaɪˈmæktɪk) *or* **climactical** *adj* consisting of, involving, or causing a climax.
▸**cliˈmactically** *adv*

> **USAGE NOTE** See at **climate.**

climate ⓣ (ˈklaɪmɪt) *n* **1** the long-term prevalent weather conditions of an area, determined by latitude, altitude, etc. **2** an area having a particular kind of climate. **3** a prevailing trend: *the political climate.* [C14: from LL, from Gk *klima* inclination, region]
▸**climatic** (klaɪˈmætɪk), **cliˈmatical,** *or* **ˈclimatal** *adj* ▸**cliˈmatically** *adv*

> **USAGE NOTE** *Climatic* is sometimes wrongly used where *climactic* is meant. *Climatic* is properly used to talk about things relating to climate; *climactic* is used to describe something which forms a climax.

climatic zone *n* any of the eight principal zones, roughly demarcated by lines of latitude, into which the earth can be divided on the basis of climate.

climatology (ˌklaɪməˈtɒlədʒɪ) *n* the study of climates.
▸**climatologic** (ˌklaɪmətəˈlɒdʒɪk) *or* ˌ**climatoˈlogical** *adj* ▸ˌ**climaˈtologist** *n*

climax ⓣ (ˈklaɪmæks) *n* **1** the most intense or highest point of an experience or of a series of events: *the party was the climax of the week.* **2** a decisive moment in a dramatic or other work. **3** a rhetorical device by which a series of sentences, clauses, or phrases are arranged in order of increasing intensity. **4** *Ecology.* the stage in the development of a community during which it remains stable under the prevailing environmental conditions. **5** another word for **orgasm.** ◆ *vb* **6** to reach or bring to a climax. [C16: from LL, from Gk *klimax* ladder]

climb ⓣ (klaɪm) *vb* (*mainly intr*) **1** (*also tr;* often foll. by *up*) to go up or ascend (stairs, a mountain, etc.). **2** (often foll. by *along*) to progress with difficulty: *to climb along a ledge.* **3** to rise to a higher point or intensity: *the temperature climbed.* **4** to incline or slope upwards: *the road began to climb.* **5** to ascend in social position. **6** (of plants) to grow upwards by twining, using tendrils or suckers, etc. **7** *Inf.* (foll. by *into*) to put (on) or get (into). **8** to be a climber or mountaineer. ◆ *n* **9** the act or an instance of climbing. **10** a place or thing to be climbed, esp. a route in mountaineering. [OE *climban*]
▸**ˈclimbable** *adj*

climb down ⓣ *vb* (*intr, adv*) **1** to descend. **2** (often foll. by *from*) to retreat (from an opinion, position, etc.). ◆ *n* **climb-down. 3** a retreat from an opinion, etc.

climber (ˈklaɪmə) *n* **1** a person or thing that climbs, esp. a mountaineer. **2** a plant that grows upwards by twining or clinging with tendrils and suckers. **3** *Chiefly Brit.* short for **social climber.**

clime (klaɪm) *n Poetic.* a region or its climate. [C16: from LL *clima;* see CLIMATE]

clinch ⓣ (klɪntʃ) *vb* **1** (*tr*) to secure (a driven nail), by bending the protruding point over. **2** (*tr*) to hold together in such a manner. **3** (*tr*) to settle (something, such as an argument, bargain, etc.) in a definite way. **4** (*tr*) *Naut.* to fasten by means of a clinch. **5** (*intr*) to engage in a clinch, as in boxing or wrestling. ◆ *n* **6** the act of clinching. **7a** a nail with its point bent over. **7b** the part of such a nail, etc., that has been bent over. **8** *Boxing, wrestling, etc.* an act or an instance in which one or both competitors hold on to the other to avoid punches, regain wind, etc. **9** *Sl.* a lovers' embrace. **10** *Naut.* a loop or eye formed in a line. ◆ Also (for senses 1, 2, 4, 7, 8, 10): **clench.** [C16: var. of CLENCH]

clincher (ˈklɪntʃə) *n* **1** *Inf.* something decisive, such as fact, score, etc. **2** a person or thing that clinches.

cline (klaɪn) *n* the range of variation of form within a species. [C20: from Gk *klinein* to lean]
▸**ˈclinal** *adj*

-cline *n combining form.* indicating a slope: *anticline.* [back formation from INCLINE]
▸**-clinal** *adj combining form.*

cling ⓣ (klɪŋ) *vb* **clings, clinging, clung.** (*intr*) **1** (often foll. by *to*) to hold fast or adhere closely (to something), as by gripping or sticking. **2** (foll. by *together*) to remain in contact (with each other). **3** to be or remain physically or emotionally close. ◆ *n* **4** short for **clingstone.** [OE *clingan*]
▸**ˈclinging** *adj* ▸**ˈclingingly** *adv* ▸**ˈclingy** *adj* ▸**ˈclinginess** *or* **ˈclingingness** *n*

clingfilm (ˈklɪŋˌfɪlm) *n* a thin polythene material having the power to adhere closely: used for wrapping food.

clingstone (ˈklɪŋˌstəʊn) *n* **a** a fruit, such as certain peaches, in which the flesh adheres to the stone. **b** (*as modifier*)*: a clingstone peach.*

clinic (ˈklɪnɪk) *n* **1** a place in which outpatients are given medical treatment or advice. **2** a similar place staffed by specialist physicians or surgeons: *eye clinic.* **3** *Brit.* a private hospital or nursing home. **4** the teaching of medicine to students at the bedside. **5** *Chiefly US & Canad.* a group or centre that offers advice or instruction. [C17: from L *clīnicus* one on a sickbed, from Gk, from *klinē* bed]

clinical ⓣ (ˈklɪnɪkᵊl) *adj* **1** of or relating to a clinic. **2** of or relating to the observation and treatment of patients directly: *clinical medicine.* **3** scientifically detached; strictly objective: *a clinical attitude to life.* **4** plain, simple, and usually unattractive.
▸**ˈclinically** *adv*

clinical thermometer *n* a thermometer for determining the temperature of the body.

clinician (klɪˈnɪʃən) *n* a physician, psychiatrist, etc., who specializes in clinical work as opposed to one engaged in experimental studies.

clink[1] (klɪŋk) *vb* **1** to make or cause to make a light and sharply ringing sound. ◆ *n* **2** such a sound. [C14: ?from MDu. *klinken*]

clink[2] (klɪŋk) *n* a slang word for **prison.** [C16: after *Clink,* a prison in Southwark, London]

clinker (ˈklɪŋkə) *n* **1** the ash and partially fused residues from a coal-fired furnace or fire. **2** a partially vitrified brick or mass of brick. **3** *Sl., chiefly US.* something of poor quality, such as a film. ◆ *vb* **4** (*intr*) to form clinker. [C17: from Du. *klinker* a type of brick, from *klinken* to CLINK[1]]

clinker-built *or* **clincher-built** *adj* (of a boat or ship) having a hull constructed with each plank overlapping that below. [C18 *clinker* a nailing together, prob. from CLINCH]

clinometer (klaɪˈnɒmɪtə) *n* an instrument used in surveying for measuring an angle of inclination.
▸**clinometric** (ˌklaɪnəˈmetrɪk) *or* ˌ**clinoˈmetrical** *adj* ▸**cliˈnometry** *n*

Clio (ˈklaɪəʊ) *n Greek myth.* the Muse of history. [C19: from L, from Gk *Kleiō,* from *kleein* to celebrate]

clip[1] ⓣ (klɪp) *vb* **clips, clipping, clipped.** (*mainly tr*) **1** (*also intr*) to cut or trim with scissors or shears, esp. in order to shorten or remove a part. **2** *Brit.* to punch (a hole) in something, esp. a ticket. **3** to curtail. **4** to move a short section from (a film, etc.). **5** to shorten (a word). **6** *Inf.* to strike with a sharp, often slanting, blow. **7** *Sl.* to obtain (money) by deception or cheating. ◆ *n* **8** the act or process of clipping. **9** something clipped off. **10** a short extract from a film, etc. **11** *Inf.* a sharp, often slanting, blow. **12** *Inf.* speed: *a rapid clip.* **13** *Austral. & NZ.* the total quantity of wool shorn, as in one season, etc. **14** another word for **clipped form.** [C12: from ON *klippa* to cut]

clip[2] ⓣ (klɪp) *n* **1** any of various small implements used to hold loose articles together or to attach one article to another. **2** an article of jewellery that can be clipped onto a dress, hat, etc. **3** short for **paperclip** or **cartridge clip.** ◆ *vb* **clips, clipping, clipped.** (*tr*) **4** to hold together tightly, as with a clip. [OE *clyppan* to embrace]

clipboard (ˈklɪpˌbɔːd) *n* **1** a portable writing board with a clip at the top for holding paper. **2** *Computing.* a temporary storage area in desktop publishing and other programs where text or graphics are held when cut or copied.

clip joint *n Sl.* a place, such as a nightclub or restaurant, in which customers are overcharged.

clipped (klɪpt) *adj* (of speech or tone of voice) abrupt, terse, and distinct.

clipped form *n* a shortened form of a word.

clipper (ˈklɪpə) *n* **1** any fast sailing ship. **2** a person or thing that cuts or clips.

clippers (ˈklɪpəz) *or* **clips** *pl n* **1** a hand tool for clipping fingernails, veneers, etc. **2** a hairdresser's tool for cutting short hair.

clippie (ˈklɪpɪ) *n Brit. inf.* a bus conductress.

clipping ⓣ (ˈklɪpɪŋ) *n* **1** something cut out, esp. an article from a newspaper; cutting. **2** the distortion of an audio or visual signal in which the tops of peaks with a high amplitude are cut off, caused by, for example, overloading of amplifier circuits.

clique ⓣ (kliːk, klɪk) *n* a small exclusive group of friends or associates. [C18: from F, ?from OF: latch, from *cliquer* to click]
▸**ˈcliquey** *or* **ˈcliquy** *adj* ▸**ˈcliquish** *adj* ▸**ˈcliquishly** *adv* ▸**ˈcliquishness** *n*

clitoridectomy (ˌklɪtərɪˈdektəmɪ) *n* surgical removal of the clitoris: a form of female circumcision, esp. practised as a religious or ethnic rite.

clitoris (ˈklɪtərɪs, ˈklaɪ-) *n* a part of the female genitalia consisting of a

THESAURUS

climactic *adj* = **crucial**, climactical, critical, decisive, paramount, peak

climate *n* **1** = **weather**, clime, country, region, temperature **3** = **trend**, ambience, disposition, feeling, mood, temper, tendency

climax *n* **1** = **culmination**, acme, apogee, crest, head, height, highlight, high point, high spot (*inf.*), *ne plus ultra,* pay-off (*inf.*), peak, summit, top, zenith ◆ *vb* **6** = **culminate**, come to a head, peak

climb *vb* = **ascend**, clamber, mount, rise, scale, shin up, soar, top

climb down *vb* **1** = **descend**, dismount **2** = **back down**, eat crow (*US inf.*), eat one's words, retract, retreat

clinch *vb* **1, 2** = **secure**, bolt, clamp, fasten, fix, make fast, nail, rivet **3** = **settle**, assure, cap, conclude, confirm, decide, determine, seal, secure, set the seal on, sew up (*inf.*), tip the balance, verify

cling *vb* **1** = **stick**, adhere, attach to, be true to, clasp, cleave to, clutch, embrace, fasten, grasp, grip, hug, twine round

clinical *adj* **3** = **unemotional**, analytic, antiseptic, cold, detached, disinterested, dispassionate, emotionless, impersonal, objective, scientific

clip[1] *vb* **1** = **trim**, crop, curtail, cut, cut short, dock, pare, prune, shear, shorten, snip ◆ *n, vb* **6** *Informal* = **smack**, belt (*inf.*), box, clout (*inf.*), cuff, knock, punch, skelp (*dialect*), strike, thump, wallop (*inf.*), whack ◆ *n* **12** *Informal* = **speed**, gallop, lick (*inf.*), rate, velocity

clip[2] *vb* = **attach**, fasten, fix, hold, pin, staple

clipping *n* **1** = **cutting**, excerpt, extract, piece

clique *n* = **group**, cabal, circle, clan, coterie, crew (*inf.*), crowd, faction, gang, mob, pack, posse (*inf.*), schism, set

small elongated highly sensitive erectile organ at the front of the vulva. [C17: from NL, from Gk *kleitoris*]
▸**ˈclitoral** *adj*

Cllr *abbrev. for* Councillor.

cloaca (kləʊˈeɪkə) *n, pl* **cloacae** (-kiː). **1** a cavity in most vertebrates, except higher mammals, and certain invertebrates, into which the alimentary canal and the genital and urinary ducts open. **2** a sewer. [C18: from L: sewer]
▸**cloˈacal** *adj*

cloak Ⓣ (kləʊk) *n* **1** a wraplike outer garment fastened at the throat and falling straight from the shoulders. **2** something that covers or conceals. ◆ *vb (tr)* **3** to cover with or as if with a cloak. **4** to hide or disguise. [C13: from OF *cloque*, from Med. L *clocca* cloak, bell]

cloak-and-dagger *n (modifier)* characteristic of or concerned with intrigue and espionage.

cloakroom (ˈkləʊkˌruːm, -rʊm) *n* **1** a room in which hats, coats, etc., may be temporarily deposited. **2** *Brit.* a euphemistic word for **toilet**.

clobber[1] Ⓣ (ˈklɒbə) *vb (tr) Sl.* **1** to batter. **2** to defeat utterly. **3** to criticize severely. [C20: from ?]

clobber[2] Ⓣ (ˈklɒbə) *n Brit. sl.* personal belongings, such as clothes. [C19: from ?]

clobbering machine *n NZ inf.* pressure to conform with accepted standards.

cloche (klɒʃ) *n* **1** a bell-shaped cover used to protect young plants. **2** a woman's close-fitting hat. [C19: from F: bell, from Med. L *clocca*]

clock[1] (klɒk) *n* **1** a timepiece having mechanically or electrically driven pointers that move constantly over a dial showing the numbers of the hours. Cf. **watch** (sense 7). **2** any clocklike device for recording or measuring, such as a taximeter or pressure gauge. **3** the downy head of a dandelion that has gone to seed. **4** short for **time clock**. **5** (usually preceded by *the*) an informal word for **speedometer** or **mileometer**. **6** *Brit.* a slang word for **face**. **7 around** *or* **round the clock**. all day and all night. ◆ *vb (tr)* **8** *Brit., Austral., & NZ sl.* to strike, esp. on the face or head. **9** to record time as with a stopwatch, esp. in the calculation of speed. **10** *Inf.* to turn back the mileometer on (a car) illegally so that its mileage appears less. [C14: from MDu. *clocke* clock, from Med. L *clocca* bell, ult. of Celtic origin]

clock[2] (klɒk) *n* an ornamental design on the side of a stocking. [C16: see CLOCK[1]]

clock off *or* **out** *vb (intr, adv)* to depart from work, esp. when it involves registering the time of departure on a card.

clock on *or* **in** *vb (intr, adv)* to arrive at work, esp. when it involves registering the time of arrival on a card.

clock up *vb (tr, adv)* to record or register: *this car has clocked up 80 000 miles.*

clock-watcher *n* an employee who frequently checks the time in anticipation of a break or of the end of the working day.

clockwise (ˈklɒkˌwaɪz) *adv, adj* in the direction that the hands of a clock rotate; from top to bottom towards the right when seen from the front.

clockwork (ˈklɒkˌwɜːk) *n* **1** the mechanism of a clock. **2** any similar mechanism, as in a wind-up toy. **3 like clockwork.** with complete regularity and precision; smoothly.

clod Ⓣ (klɒd) *n* **1** a lump of earth or clay. **2** earth, esp. when heavy or in hard lumps. **3** Also called: **clod poll, clodpate.** a dull or stupid person. [OE *clod-* (occurring in compound words) lump]
▸**ˈcloddy** *adj* ▸**ˈcloddish** *adj* ▸**ˈcloddishly** *adv* ▸**ˈcloddishness** *n*

clodhopper Ⓣ (ˈklɒdˌhɒpə) *n Inf.* **1** a clumsy person; lout. **2** (*usually pl*) a large heavy shoe.

clog Ⓣ (klɒg) *vb* **clogs, clogging, clogged. 1** to obstruct or become obstructed with thick or sticky matter. **2** *(tr)* to encumber; hinder; impede. **3** *(intr)* to adhere or stick in a mass. ◆ *n* **4a** any of various wooden or wooden-soled shoes. **4b** *(as modifier)*: *clog dance.* **5** a heavy block, esp. of wood, fastened to the leg of a person or animal to impede motion. **6** something that impedes motion or action; hindrance. [C14 (in the sense: block of wood): from ?]
▸**ˈcloggy** *adj*

cloisonné (klwɑːˈzɒneɪ) *n* **1a** a design made by filling in with coloured enamel an outline of flattened wire. **1b** the method of doing this. ◆ *adj* **2** of or made by cloisonné. [C19: from F, from *cloisonner* to divide into compartments, ult. from L *claudere* to close]

cloister Ⓣ (ˈklɔɪstə) *n* **1** a covered walk, usually around a quadrangle in a religious institution, having an open colonnade on the inside. **2** (*sometimes pl*) a place of religious seclusion, such as a monastery. **3** life in a monastery or convent. ◆ *vb* **4** *(tr)* to confine or seclude in or as if in a monastery. [C13: from OF *cloistre*, from Med. L *claustrum* monastic cell, from L *claudere* to close]
▸**ˈcloistered** *adj* ▸**ˈcloistral** *adj*

clomb (kləʊm) *vb Arch.* a past tense and past participle of **climb**.

clomp (klɒmp) *n, vb* a less common word for **clump** (senses 2, 7).

clone (kləʊn) *n* **1** a group of organisms or cells of the same genetic constitution that are descended from a common ancestor by asexual reproduction, as by cuttings, grafting, etc. **2** Also called: **gene clone.** a segment of DNA that has been isolated and replicated by laboratory manipulation. **3** *Inf.* a person or thing that closely resembles another. **4** *Sl.* **4a** a mobile phone that has been given the electronic identity of an existing mobile phone, so that calls made on it are charged to the owner of that phone. **4b** any similar object, such as a credit card, that has been given the electronic identity of another device, usually in order to commit theft. ◆ *vb* **clones, cloning, cloned. 5** to produce or cause to produce a clone. **6** *Inf.* to produce near copies of (a person or thing). **7** *(tr) Sl.* to give (a mobile phone, etc.) the electronic identity of an existing mobile phone (or other device), so that calls, purchases, etc. made with it are charged to the original owner. [C20: from Gk *klōn* twig, shoot]
▸**ˈcloning** *n*

clonk (klɒŋk) *vb* **1** *(intr)* to make a loud dull thud. **2** *(tr) Inf.* to hit. ◆ *n* **3** a loud thud. [C20: imit.]

clonus (ˈkləʊnəs) *n* a type of convulsion characterized by rapid contraction and relaxation of a muscle. [C19: from NL, from Gk *klonos* turmoil]
▸**clonic** (ˈklɒnɪk) *adj* ▸**clonicity** (klɒˈnɪsɪtɪ) *n*

clop (klɒp) *vb* **clops, clopping, clopped. 1** *(intr)* to make or move along with a sound as of a horse's hooves striking the ground. ◆ *n* **2** a sound of this nature. [C20: imit.]

close[1] Ⓣ (kləʊs) *adj* **1** near in space or time; in proximity. **2** having the parts near together; dense: *a close formation.* **3** near to the surface; short: *a close haircut.* **4** near in relationship: *a close relative.* **5** intimate: *a close friend.* **6** almost equal: *a close contest.* **7** not deviating or varying greatly from a model or standard: *a close resemblance; a close translation.* **8** careful, strict, or searching: *a close study.* **9** confined or enclosed. **10** shut or shut tight. **11** oppressive, heavy, or airless: *a close atmosphere.* **12** strictly guarded: *a close prisoner.* **13** neat or tight in fit. **14** secretive or reticent. **15** miserly; not generous, esp. with money. **16** (of money or credit) hard to obtain. **17** restricted as to public admission or membership. **18** hidden or secluded. **19** Also: **closed.** restricted or prohibited as to the type of game or fish able to be taken. ◆ *adv* **20** closely; tightly. **21** near or in proximity. **22 close to the wind.** *Naut.* sailing as nearly as possible towards the direction from which the wind is blowing. See also **wind**[1] (sense 23). [C13: from OF *clos*, from L *clausus*, from *claudere* to close]
▸**ˈclosely** *adv* ▸**ˈcloseness** *n*

close[2] Ⓣ (kləʊz) *vb* **closes, closing, closed. 1** to put or be put in such a position as to cover an opening; shut: *the door closed behind him.* **2** *(tr)* to bar, obstruct, or fill up (an entrance, a hole, etc.): *to close a road.* **3** to bring the parts or edges of (a wound, etc.) together or (of a wound, etc.) to be brought together. **4** (*intr*; foll. by *on, over*, etc.) to take hold: *his hand closed over the money.* **5** to bring or be brought to an end; terminate. **6** (of agreements, deals, etc.) to complete or be completed successfully. **7** to cease or cause to cease to render service: *the shop closed at six.* **8** *(intr) Stock Exchange.* to have a value at the end of a day's trading, as specified: *steels closed two points down.* **9** *(tr) Arch.* to enclose or shut in. ◆ *n* **10** the act of closing. **11** the end or conclusion: *the close of the day.* **12** (kləʊs). *Brit.* a courtyard or quadrangle enclosed by buildings or an entry leading to such a courtyard. **13** (kləʊs). *Brit.* (*cap. when part of a street name*) a small quiet residential road: *Hillside Close.* **14** (kləʊs). the precincts of a cathedral or similar building. **15** (kləʊs). *Scot.* the entry from the street to a tenement building. ◆ See also

THESAURUS

cloak *n* **1** = **cape**, coat, mantle, wrap **2** = **cover**, blind, front, mask, pretext, shield ◆ *vb* **3, 4** = **cover**, camouflage, conceal, disguise, hide, mask, obscure, screen, veil

clobber[1] *vb* **1** *Informal* = **batter**, assault, bash (*inf.*), beat, beat up (*inf.*), belabour, duff up (*inf.*), lambast(e), lash, pound, pummel, rough up (*inf.*), smash, thrash, wallop (*inf.*)

clobber[2] *n Brit. informal* = **belongings**, accoutrements, effects, gear, possessions

clod *n* **1** = **lump**, block, chunk, clump, hunk, mass, piece

clodhopper *n* **1** *Informal* = **oaf**, booby, boor, bumpkin, clown, galoot, loon (*inf.*), lout, yokel

clog *vb* **1, 2** = **obstruct**, block, bung, burden, congest, dam up, hamper, hinder, impede, jam, occlude, shackle, stop up

cloistered *adj* **4** = **sheltered**, cloistral, confined, hermitic, insulated, protected, reclusive, restricted, secluded, sequestered, shielded, shut off, withdrawn
Antonyms *adj* extrovert, genial, gregarious, outgoing, public, sociable, social

close[1] *adj* **1** = **near**, adjacent, adjoining, approaching, at hand, cheek by jowl, handy, hard by, imminent, impending, just round the corner, nearby, neighbouring, nigh, proximate, upcoming, within sniffing distance, within striking distance (*inf.*) **2** = **compact**, congested, cramped, cropped, crowded, dense, impenetrable, jam-packed, packed, short, solid, thick, tight **5** = **intimate**, attached, confidential, dear, devoted, familiar, inseparable, loving **7** = **accurate**, conscientious, exact, faithful, literal, precise, strict **8** = **careful**, alert, assiduous, attentive, concentrated, detailed, dogged, earnest, fixed, intense, intent, keen, minute, painstaking, rigorous, searching, thorough **11** = **stifling**, airless, confined, frowsty, fuggy, heavy, humid, muggy, oppressive, stale, stuffy, suffocating, sweltering, thick, unventilated **14** = **secretive**, hidden, private, reticent, retired, secluded, secret, taciturn, uncommunicative, unforthcoming **15** = **mean**, illiberal, mingy (*Brit. inf.*), miserly, near, niggardly, parsimonious, penurious, stingy, tight-fisted, ungenerous
Antonyms *adj* ≠ **near:** distant, far, far away, far off, future, outlying, remote ≠ **compact:** dispersed, empty, free, loose, penetrable, porous, uncongested, uncrowded ≠ **intimate:** alienated, aloof, chilly, cold, cool, distant, indifferent, standoffish, unfriendly ≠ **stifling:** airy, fresh, refreshing, roomy, spacious ≠ **mean:** charitable, extravagant, generous, lavish, liberal, magnanimous, unstinting

close[2] *vb* **1, 2** = **shut**, bar, block, bung, choke, clog, confine, cork, fill, lock, obstruct, plug, seal, secure, shut up, stop up **3** = **connect**, come together, couple, fuse, grapple, join, unite **5** =

close down, close in, etc. [C13: from OF *clos,* from L *clausus,* from *claudere* to close]
▸ **'closer** *n*

close company *n* a company that is controlled by its directors or by five or fewer participants.

closed ❶ (kləʊzd) *adj* **1** blocked against entry; shut. **2** restricted; exclusive. **3** not open to question or debate. **4** (of a hunting season, etc.) close. **5** *Maths.* **5a** (of a curve or surface) completely enclosing an area or volume. **5b** (of a set) having members that can be produced by a specific operation on other members of the same set. **6** *Phonetics.* denoting a syllable that ends in a consonant. **7** not open to public entry or membership: *a closed society.*

closed chain *n Chem.* another name for **ring**[1] (sense 17).

closed circuit *n* a complete electrical circuit through which current can flow.

closed-circuit television *n* a television system in which signals are transmitted from the television camera to the receivers by cables or telephone links.

close down (kləʊz) *vb* (*adv*) **1** to cease or cause to cease operations. **2** (*tr*) *Soccer.* to deny (an opposing player) space to run with the ball or to make or receive a pass. ◆ *n* **close-down. 3** a closure or stoppage, esp. in a factory. **4** *Brit. radio, television.* the end of a period of broadcasting, esp. late at night.

closed shop *n* (formerly) an industrial establishment in which there exists a contract between a trade union and the employer permitting the employment of the union's members only.

close-fisted (ˌkləʊs'fɪstɪd) *adj* very careful with money; mean.
▸ **ˌclose-'fistedness** *n*

close harmony (kləʊs) *n* a type of singing in which all the parts except the bass lie close together.

close-hauled (ˌkləʊs'hɔːld) *adj Naut.* with the sails flat, so as to sail as close to the wind as possible.

close in (kləʊz) *vb* (*intr, adv*) **1** (of days) to become shorter with the approach of winter. **2** (foll. by *on* or *upon*) to advance (on) so as to encircle or surround.

close out (kləʊz) *vb* (*adv*) to terminate (a client's or other account) usually by sale of securities to realize cash.

close punctuation (kləʊs) *n* punctuation in which many commas, full stops, etc., are used. Cf. **open punctuation.**

close quarters (kləʊs) *pl n* **1** a narrow cramped space or position. **2 at close quarters. 2a** engaged in hand-to-hand combat. **2b** in close proximity; very near together.

close season (kləʊs) *or* **closed season** *n* **1** the period of the year when it is prohibited to kill certain game or fish. **2** *Sport.* the period of the year when there is no domestic competition.

close shave (kləʊs) *n Inf.* a narrow escape.

closet ❶ ('klɒzɪt) *n* **1** a small cupboard or recess. **2** a small private room. **3** short for **water closet. 4** (*modifier*) private or secret. ◆ *vb* **closets, closeting, closeted. 5** (*tr*) to shut up or confine in a small private room, esp. for conference or meditation. [C14: from OF, from *clos* enclosure; see CLOSE[1]]

close-up ('kləʊsˌʌp) *n* **1** a photograph or film or television shot taken at close range. **2** a detailed or intimate view or examination. ◆ *vb* **close up** (kləʊz). (*adv*) **3** to shut entirely. **4** (*intr*) to draw together: *the ranks closed up.* **5** (*intr*) (of wounds) to heal completely.

close with (kləʊz) *vb* (*intr, prep*) to engage in battle with (an enemy).

closure ❶ ('kləʊʒə) *n* **1** the act of closing or the state of being closed. **2** an end or conclusion. **3** something that closes or shuts, such as a cap or seal for a container. **4** Also called: **gag.** (in a deliberative body) a procedure by which debate may be halted and an immediate vote taken. ◆ *vb* **closures, closuring, closured. 5** (*tr*) (in a deliberative body) to end (debate) by closure. [C14: from OF, from LL, from L *claudere* to close]

clot ❶ (klɒt) *n* **1** a soft thick lump or mass. **2** *Brit. inf.* a stupid person; fool. ◆ *vb* **clots, clotting, clotted. 3** to form or cause to form into a soft thick lump or lumps. [OE *clott,* of Gmc origin]

cloth ❶ (klɒθ) *n, pl* **cloths** (klɒθs, klɒðz). **1a** a fabric formed by weaving, felting or knitting wool, cotton, etc. **1b** (*as modifier*): *a cloth bag.* **2** a piece of such fabric used for a particular purpose, as for a dishcloth. **3** (usually preceded by *the*) the clergy. [OE *clāth*]

clothe ❶ (kləʊð) *vb* **clothes, clothing, clothed** *or* **clad.** (*tr*) **1** to dress or attire (a person). **2** to provide with clothing. **3** to conceal or disguise. **4** to endow or invest. [OE *clāthian,* from *clāth* cloth]

clothes ❶ (kləʊðz) *pl n* **1** articles of dress. **2** *Chiefly Brit.* short for **bedclothes.** [OE *clāthas,* pl. of *clāth* cloth]

clotheshorse ('kləʊðzˌhɔːs) *n* **1** a frame on which to hang laundry for drying or airing. **2** *Inf.* an excessively fashionable person.

clothesline ('kləʊðzˌlaɪn) *n* a piece of rope or wire on which clean washing is hung to dry.

clothes peg *n* a small wooden or plastic clip for attaching washing to a clothesline.

clothes pole *n* a post to which a clothesline is attached. Also called: **clothes post.**

clothes-press *n* a piece of furniture for storing clothes, usually containing wide drawers.

clothes prop *n* a long wooden pole with a forked end used to raise a line of washing to enable it to catch the breeze.

clothier ('kləʊðɪə) *n* a person who makes, sells, or deals in clothes or cloth.

clothing ❶ ('kləʊðɪŋ) *n* **1** garments collectively. **2** something that covers or clothes.

Clotho ('kləʊθəʊ) *n Greek myth.* one of the three Fates, spinner of the thread of life. [L, from Gk *Klōtho,* one who spins, from *klōthein* to spin]

cloth of gold *n* cloth woven from silk threads interspersed with gold.

clotted cream *n Brit.* a thick cream made from scalded milk, esp. in SW England.

clotting factor *n* any one of a group of substances, including factor VIII, the presence of which in the blood is essential for blood clotting to occur. Also called: **coagulation factor.**

cloture ('kləʊtʃə) *n* **1** closure in the US Senate. ◆ *vb* **clotures, cloturing, clotured. 2** (*tr*) to end (debate) by cloture. [C19: from F *clôture,* from OF CLOSURE]

cloud ❶ (klaʊd) *n* **1** a mass of water or ice particles visible in the sky. **2** any collection of particles visible in the air, esp. of smoke or dust. **3** a large number of insects or other small animals in flight. **4** something that darkens, threatens, or carries gloom. **5** *Jewellery.* a cloudlike blemish in a transparent stone. **6 in the clouds.** not in contact with reality. **7 on cloud nine.** *Inf.* elated; very happy. **8 under a cloud. 8a** under reproach or suspicion. **8b** in a state of gloom or bad temper. ◆ *vb* **9** (when *intr,* often foll. by *over* or *up*) to make or become cloudy, overcast, or indistinct. **10** (*tr*) to make obscure; darken. **11** to make or become gloomy or depressed. **12** (*tr*) to place under or render liable to suspicion or disgrace. **13** to render (liquids) milky or dull or (of liquids) to become milky or dull. [C13 (in the sense: a mass of vapour): from OE *clūd* rock, hill]
▸ **'cloudless** *adj* ▸ **'cloudlessly** *adv* ▸ **'cloudlessness** *n*

cloudburst ('klaʊdˌbɜːst) *n* a heavy downpour.

cloud chamber *n Physics.* an apparatus for detecting high-energy particles by observing their tracks through a chamber containing a supersaturated vapour.

cloud-cuckoo-land *n* a realm of fantasy, dreams, or impractical notions.

THESAURUS

end, axe (*inf.*), cease, complete, conclude, culminate, discontinue, finish, mothball, shut down, terminate, wind up ◆ *n* **11** = **end**, cessation, completion, conclusion, culmination, denouement, ending, finale, finish, run-in, termination
Antonyms *vb* ≠ **shut**: clear, free, open, release, unblock, unclog, uncork, unstop, widen ≠ **connect**: disconnect, disjoin, disunite, divide, part, separate, split, uncouple ≠ **end**: begin, commence, initiate, open, start

closed *adj* **1** = **shut**, fastened, locked, out of business, out of service, sealed **2** = **exclusive**, restricted **3** = **finished**, concluded, decided, ended, over, resolved, settled, terminated
Antonyms *adj* ≠ **shut**: ajar, open, unclosed, unfastened, unlocked, unsealed

closeness *n* **1** = **nearness**, adjacency, handiness, imminence, imminentness, impendence, impendency, proximity **2** = **compactness**, crowdedness, denseness, impenetrability, impenetrableness, snugness, solidness, thickness, tightness **5** = **intimacy**, confidentiality, confidentialness, dearness, devotedness, familiarness, inseparability, intimateness, lovingness **7** = **accuracy**, exactness, faithfulness, literality, literalness, preciseness, strictness **8** = **carefulness**, alertness, assiduousness, attentiveness, doggedness, earnestness, fixedness, intensiveness, intentness, keenness, minuteness, painstakingness, rigorousness, searchingness, thoroughness **11** = **stuffiness**, airlessness, confinedness, frowstiness, heaviness, humidity, humidness, mugginess, oppressiveness, staleness, sultriness, thickness **14** = **secretiveness**, reticence, secludedness, taciturnity, uncommunicativeness **15** = **meanness**, illiberality, illiberalness, minginess (*Brit. inf.*), miserliness, niggardliness, parsimony, penuriousness, stinginess

closet *n* **1** = **cupboard**, cabinet, cubbyhole, cubicle, recess ◆ *modifier* **4** = **secret**, concealed, covert, hidden, private

closure *n* **1** = **closing**, cessation, conclusion, end, finish, stoppage **3** = **plug**, bung, cap, lid, seal, stopper **4** = **guillotine**, cloture

clot *n* **1** = **lump**, clotting, coagulation, curdling, embolism, embolus, gob, mass, occlusion, thrombus **2** *Brit. informal* = **idiot**, ass, berk (*Brit. sl.*), buffoon, charlie (*Brit. inf.*), coot, divvy (*Brit. sl.*), dolt, dope (*inf.*), dork (*sl.*), dunderhead, fathead (*inf.*), fool, nincompoop, nit (*inf.*), nitwit (*inf.*), numbskull *or* numskull, pillock (*Brit. sl.*), plank (*Brit. sl.*), plonker (*sl.*), schmuck (*US slang*), wally (*sl.*) ◆ *vb* **3** = **congeal**, coagulate, coalesce, curdle, jell, thicken

cloth *n* **1a** = **fabric**, dry goods, material, stuff, textiles

clothe *vb* **1** = **dress**, accoutre, apparel, array, attire, bedizen (*arch.*), caparison, cover, deck, doll up (*sl.*), drape, endow, enwrap, equip, fit out, garb, get ready, habit, invest, outfit, rig, robe, swathe
Antonyms *vb* disrobe, divest, expose, strip, strip off, unclothe, uncover, undress

clothes *pl n* **1** = **clothing**, apparel, attire, clobber (*Brit. slang*), costume, dress, duds (*inf.*), ensemble, garb, garments, gear (*inf.*), get-up (*inf.*), glad rags (*inf.*), habits, outfit, raiment (*arch. or poetic*), rigout (*inf.*), threads (*sl.*), togs (*inf.*), vestments, vesture, wardrobe, wear

clothing *n* **1** = **clothes**, apparel, attire, clobber (*Brit. slang*), costume, dress, duds (*inf.*), ensemble, garb, garments, gear (*inf.*), get-up (*inf.*), glad rags (*inf.*), habits, outfit, raiment (*arch. or poetic*), rigout (*inf.*), threads (*sl.*), togs (*inf.*), vestments, vesture, wardrobe, wear

cloud *n* **2** = **mist**, billow, darkness, fog, gloom, haze, murk, nebula, nebulosity, obscurity, vapour **3** = **dense mass**, crowd, flock, horde, host, multitude, shower, swarm, throng ◆ *vb* **9** = **obscure**, becloud, darken, dim, eclipse, obfuscate, overcast, overshadow, shade, shadow,

cloudy ⓘ ('klaudɪ) *adj* **cloudier, cloudiest. 1** covered with cloud or clouds. **2** of or like clouds. **3** streaked or mottled like a cloud. **4** opaque or muddy. **5** obscure or unclear. **6** troubled or gloomy.
► **'cloudily** *adv* ► **'cloudiness** *n*

clough (klʌf) *n Dialect.* a ravine. [OE *clōh*]

clout ⓘ (klaut) *n* **1** *Inf.* a blow with the hand or a hard object. **2** power or influence, esp. political. **3** Also called: **clout nail.** a short, flat-headed nail. **4** *Dialect.* **4a** a piece of cloth: *a dish clout.* **4b** a garment. ◆ *vb (tr)* **5** *Inf.* to give a hard blow to, esp. with the hand. [OE *clūt* piece of metal or cloth, *clūtian* to patch (C14: to strike with the hand)]

clove[1] (kləuv) *n* **1** a tropical evergreen tree of the myrtle family. **2** the dried unopened flower buds of this tree, used as a pungent fragrant spice. [C14: from OF, lit.: nail of clove, *clou* from L *clāvus* nail + *girofle* clove tree]

clove[2] (kləuv) *n* any of the segments of a compound bulb that arise from the axils of the scales of a large bulb. [OE *clufu* bulb; see CLEAVE[1]]

clove[3] (kləuv) *vb* a past tense of **cleave**[1].

clove hitch *n* a knot or hitch used for securing a rope to a spar, post, or larger rope.

cloven ⓘ ('kləuvᵊn) *vb* **1** a past participle of **cleave**[1]. ◆ *adj* **2** split; cleft; divided.

cloven hoof *or* **foot** *n* **1** the divided hoof of a pig, goat, cow, deer, or related animal. **2** the mark or symbol of Satan.
► **,cloven-'hoofed** *or* **,cloven-'footed** *adj*

clove oil *n* a volatile pale-yellow aromatic oil obtained from clove flowers, formerly much used in confectionery, dentistry, and microscopy. Also called: **oil of cloves.**

clover ('kləuvə) *n* **1** a leguminous fodder plant having trifoliate leaves and dense flower heads. **2** any of various similar or related plants. **3 in clover.** *Inf.* in a state of ease or luxury. [OE *clāfre*]

cloverleaf ('kləuvə,li:f) *n, pl* **cloverleaves. 1** an arrangement of connecting roads, resembling a four-leaf clover in form, that joins two intersecting main roads. **2** *(modifier)* in the shape or pattern of a leaf of clover.

clown ⓘ (klaun) *n* **1** a comic entertainer, usually grotesquely costumed and made up, appearing in the circus. **2** a person who acts in a comic or buffoon-like manner. **3** a clumsy rude person; boor. **4** *Arch.* a countryman or rustic. ◆ *vb (intr)* **5** to perform as a clown. **6** to play jokes or tricks. **7** to act foolishly. [C16: ?from Low G]
► **'clownery** *n* ► **'clownish** *adj* ► **'clownishly** *adv* ► **'clownishness** *n*

cloy ⓘ (klɔɪ) *vb* to make weary or cause weariness through an excess of something initially pleasurable or sweet. [C14 (orig.: to nail, hence, to obstruct): from earlier *acloyen*, from OF, from Med. L *inclavāre*, from L, from *clāvus* a nail]
► **'cloyingly** *adv*

cloze test (kləuz) *n* a test of the ability to comprehend text in which the reader has to supply the missing words that have been removed from the text. [altered from *close* to complete a pattern (in Gestalt theory)]

club ⓘ (klʌb) *n* **1** a stout stick, usually with one end thicker than the other, esp. one used as a weapon. **2** a stick or bat used to strike the ball in various sports, esp. golf. See **golf club. 3** short for **Indian club. 4** a group or association of people with common aims or interests. **5** the room, building, or facilities used by such a group. **6** a building in which elected, fee-paying members go to meet, dine, read, etc. **7** a commercial establishment in which people can drink and dance; disco. See also **nightclub. 8** *Chiefly Brit.* an organization, esp. in a shop, set up as a means of saving. **9** *Brit.* an informal word for **friendly society. 10a** the black trefoil symbol on a playing card. **10b** a card with one or more of these symbols or *(when pl)* the suit of cards so marked. **11 in the club.** *Brit. sl.* pregnant. ◆ *vb* **clubs, clubbing, clubbed. 12** *(tr)* to beat with or as if with a club. **13** (often foll. by *together*) to gather or become gathered into a group. **14** (often foll. by *together*) to unite or combine (resources, efforts, etc.) for a common purpose. [C13: from ON *klubba*, rel. to CLUMP]
► **'clubbing** *n*

clubbed (klʌbd) *adj* having a thickened end, like a club.

clubber ('klʌbə) *n* a person who regularly frequents nightclubs and similar establishments.

club class *n* **1** a class of air travel that is less luxurious than first class but more luxurious than economy class. ◆ *adj* **club-class. 2** of or relating to this class of travel.

club foot *n* **1** a congenital deformity of the foot, esp. one in which the foot is twisted so that most of the weight rests on the heel. Technical name: **talipes. 2** a foot so deformed.
► **,club-'footed** *adj*

clubhouse ('klʌb,haus) *n* the premises of a sports or other club, esp. a golf club.

clubman ('klʌbmən) *or (fem)* **clubwoman** *n, pl* **clubmen** *or* **clubwomen.** a person who is an enthusiastic member of a club or clubs.

club root *n* a fungal disease of cabbages and related plants, in which the roots become thickened and distorted.

cluck (klʌk) *n* **1** the low clicking sound made by a hen or any similar sound. ◆ *vb* **2** *(intr)* (of a hen) to make a clicking sound. **3** *(tr)* to call or express (a feeling) by making a similar sound. [C17: imit.]

clucky ('klʌkɪ) *adj Austral. inf.* **1** wanting to have a baby. **2** excessively protective towards children.

clue ⓘ (klu:) *n* **1** something that helps to solve a problem or unravel a mystery. **2 not have a clue. 2a** to be completely baffled. **2b** to be ignorant or incompetent. ◆ *vb* **clues, cluing, clued. 3** *(tr;* usually foll. by *in* or *up)* to provide with helpful information. [C15: var. of CLEW]

clued-up *adj Inf.* shrewd; well-informed.

clueless ⓘ ('klu:lɪs) *adj Sl.* helpless; stupid.

clump ⓘ (klʌmp) *n* **1** a cluster, as of trees or plants. **2** a dull heavy tread or any similar sound. **3** an irregular mass. **4** an inactive mass of microorganisms, esp. a mass of bacteria produced as a result of agglutination. **5** an extra sole on a shoe. **6** *Sl.* a blow. ◆ *vb* **7** *(intr)* to walk or tread heavily. **8** to gather or be gathered into clumps, clusters, clots, etc. **9** to cause (bacteria, blood cells, etc.) to collect together or (of bacteria, etc.) to collect together. **10** *(tr) Sl.* to punch (someone). [OE *clympe*]
► **'clumpy** *adj*

clumsy ⓘ ('klʌmzɪ) *adj* **clumsier, clumsiest. 1** lacking in skill or physical coordination. **2** awkwardly constructed or contrived. [C16 (in obs. sense: benumbed with cold; hence, awkward): ?from C13 dialect *clumse* to benumb, prob. of Scand. origin]
► **'clumsily** *adv* ► **'clumsiness** *n*

clung (klʌŋ) *vb* the past tense and past participle of **cling.**

clunk (klʌŋk) *n* **1** a blow or the sound of a blow. **2** a dull metallic sound. ◆ *vb* **3** to make or cause to make such a sound. [C19: imit.]

clunky ('klʌŋkɪ) *adj* **clunkier, clunkiest. 1** making a clunking noise. **2** clumsy or inelegant: *clunky ankle-strap shoes.* **3** awkward or unsophisticated: *then you guffaw at clunky dialogue.*

cluster ⓘ ('klʌstə) *n* **1** a number of things growing, fastened, or occurring close together. **2** a number of persons or things grouped together. ◆ *vb* **3** to gather or be gathered in clusters. [OE *clyster*]
► **'clustered** *adj* ► **'clustery** *adj*

clutch[1] ⓘ (klʌtʃ) *vb* **1** *(tr)* to seize with or as if with hands or claws. **2** *(tr)* to grasp or hold firmly. **3** *(intr;* usually foll. by *at)* to attempt to get hold or possession (of). ◆ *n* **4** a device that enables two revolving shafts to be joined or disconnected, esp. one that transmits the drive from the engine to the gearbox in a vehicle. **5** a device for holding fast. **6** a firm grasp. **7** a hand, claw, or talon in the act of clutching: *in the clutches of a bear.* **8** *(often pl)* power or control: *in the clutches of the Mafia.* [OE *clyccan*]

clutch[2] (klʌtʃ) *n* **1** a hatch of eggs laid by a particular bird or laid in a

THESAURUS

veil **10** = **confuse**, disorient, distort, impair, muddle, muddy the waters

cloudy *adj* **1** = **dull**, dark, dim, dismal, dusky, gloomy, leaden, louring *or* lowering, nebulous, obscure, overcast, sombre, sullen, sunless **4** = **opaque**, emulsified, muddy, murky **5** = **confused**, blurred, hazy, indistinct, unclear
Antonyms *adj* ≠ **dull:** bright, clear, fair, sunny, uncloudy ≠ **confused:** clear, distinct, obvious, plain

clout *Informal n* **2** = **influence**, *Informal n* **2** = **influence**, authority, bottom, power, prestige, pull, standing, weight ◆ *vb* **5** = **hit**, box, chin *(sl.)*, clobber *(sl.)*, cuff, deck *(sl.)*, lay one on *(sl.)*, punch, skelp *(dialect)*, sock *(sl.)*, strike, thump, tonk *(inf.)*, wallop *(inf.)*, wham

cloven *adj* **2** = **split**, bisected, cleft, divided

clown *n* **1** = **comedian**, buffoon, comic, dolt, fool, harlequin, jester, joker, merry-andrew, mountebank, pierrot, prankster, punchinello **3, 4** = **boor**, clodhopper *(inf.)*, hind *(obs.)*, peasant, swain *(arch.)*, yahoo, yokel ◆ *vb* **7** = **play the fool**, act the fool, act the goat, jest, mess about, piss about *or* around *(taboo slang)*, play the goat

clownish *adj* **1** = **comic**, foolish, galumphing *(inf.)*, nonsensical, slapstick, zany **3** = **boorish**, awkward, churlish, clumsy, ill-bred, rough, rude, rustic, uncivil, ungainly, vulgar

cloy *vb* = **sicken**, disgust, glut, gorge, nauseate, sate, satiate, surfeit, weary

club *n* **1** = **stick**, bat, bludgeon, cosh *(Brit.)*, cudgel, truncheon **4** = **association**, circle, clique, company, fraternity, group, guild, lodge, order, set, society, sodality, union ◆ *vb* **12** = **beat**, bash, baste, batter, bludgeon, clobber *(sl.)*, clout *(inf.)*, cosh *(Brit.)*, hammer, pommel *(rare)*, pummel, strike

clue *n* **1** = **indication**, evidence, hint, inkling, intimation, lead, pointer, sign, suggestion, suspicion, tip, tip-off, trace

clueless *adj* = **stupid**, dense, dim, dopey, dozy *(Brit. inf.)*, dull, dumb *(inf.)*, half-witted, moronic, naive, simple, simple-minded, slow, slow on the uptake *(inf.)*, thick, unintelligent, witless

clump *n* **1** = **cluster**, bunch, bundle, group, mass, shock ◆ *vb* **7** = **stomp**, bumble, clomp, lumber, plod, stamp, stump, thud, thump, tramp

clumsiness *n* **1** = **awkwardness**, accident-proneness, gaucheness, gawkiness, gracelessness, heaviness, heavy-handedness, inelegance, inelegancy, ineptitude, ineptness, inexpertness, lumberingness, maladroitness, ponderosity, ponderousness, uncouthness, ungainliness, unskilfulness
Antonyms *n* adeptness, adroitness, agility, deftness, dexterity, dexterousness *or* dextrousness, expertise, finesse, grace, gracefulness, handiness, nimbleness, proficiency, skill

clumsy *adj* **1, 2** = **awkward**, accident-prone, blundering, bumbling, bungling, butterfingered *(inf.)*, cack-handed *(inf.)*, clunky *(inf.)*, gauche, gawky, ham-fisted *(inf.)*, ham-handed *(inf.)*, heavy, ill-shaped, inept, inexpert, klutzy *(US. & Canad. sl.)*, like a bull in a china shop, lumbering, maladroit, ponderous, uncoordinated, uncouth, ungainly, unhandy, unskilful, unwieldy
Antonyms *adj* adept, adroit, competent, deft, dexterous, expert, graceful, handy, proficient, skilful

cluster *n* **1, 2** = **gathering**, assemblage, batch, bunch, clump, collection, group, knot ◆ *vb* **3** = **gather**, assemble, bunch, collect, flock, group

clutch[1] *vb* **1, 2** = **seize**, catch, clasp, cling to, embrace, fasten, grab, grapple, grasp, grip, snatch ◆ *n* **8** *often pl* = **power**, claws, control,

single nest. **2** a brood of chickens. **3** *Inf.* a group or cluster. ◆ *vb* **4** (*tr*) to hatch (chickens). [C17 (N English dialect) *cletch*, from ON *klekja* to hatch]

clutter ⓣ ('klʌtə) *vb* **1** (*usually tr; often foll. by up*) to strew or amass (objects) in a disorderly manner. **2** (*intr*) to move about in a bustling manner. ◆ *n* **3** a disordered heap or mass of objects. **4** a state of disorder. **5** unwanted echoes that confuse the observation of signals on a radar screen. [C15 *clotter*, from *clotteren* to CLOT]

Clydesdale ('klaɪdz,deɪl) *n* a heavy powerful breed of carthorse, originally from Scotland.

clypeus ('klɪpɪəs) *n, pl* **clypei** ('klɪpɪ,aɪ). a cuticular plate on the head of some insects. [C19: from NL, from L *clipeus* round shield]
▸'**clypeal** *adj* ▸**clypeate** ('klɪpɪ,eɪt) *adj*

cm *symbol for* centimetre.

Cm *the chemical symbol for* curium.

Cmdr *Mil. abbrev. for* Commander.

CMEA *abbrev. for* Council for Mutual Economic Assistance. See **Comecon**.

CMG *abbrev. for* Companion of St Michael and St George (a Brit. title).

CMOS ('si:mɒs) *adj Computing. acronym for* complementary metal oxide silicon: *CMOS memory*.

CMV *abbrev. for* cytomegalovirus.

CNAA *abbrev. for* Council for National Academic Awards.

CNAR *abbrev. for* compound net annual rate.

CND *Chiefly Brit. abbrev. for* Campaign for Nuclear Disarmament.

Co *the chemical symbol for* cobalt.

CO *abbrev. for:* **1** Commanding Officer. **2** conscientious objector.

Co. *or* **co.** *abbrev. for:* **1** (esp. in names of business organizations) Company. **2 and co.** (kəʊ) *Inf.* and the rest of them: *Harold and co.*

Co. *abbrev. for* County.

co- *prefix* **1** together; joint or jointly; mutual or mutually: *coproduction*. **2** indicating partnership or equality: *cofounder; copilot*. **3** to the same or a similar degree: *coextend*. **4** (in mathematics and astronomy) of the complement of an angle: *cosecant*. [from L, reduced form of COM-]

c/o *abbrev. for:* **1** care of. **2** *Book-keeping.* carried over.

coach ⓣ (kəʊtʃ) *n* **1** a large vehicle for several passengers, used for transport over long distances, sightseeing, etc. **2** a large four-wheeled enclosed carriage, usually horse-drawn. **3** a railway carriage. **4** a trainer or instructor: *a drama coach*. **5** a tutor who prepares students for examinations. ◆ *vb* **6** to give tuition or instruction to (a pupil). **7** (*tr*) to transport in a bus or coach. [C16: from F *coche*, from Hungarian *kocsi szekér* wagon of Kocs, village in Hungary where coaches were first made]
▸'**coacher** *n*

coach-built *adj* (of a vehicle) having specially built bodywork.
▸'**coach-,builder** *n*

coachman ('kəʊtʃmən) *n, pl* **coachmen**. the driver of a coach or carriage.

coachwork ('kəʊtʃ,wɜ:k) *n* **1** the design and manufacture of car bodies. **2** the body of a car.

coadjutor (kəʊ'ædʒʊtə) *n* **1** a bishop appointed as assistant to a diocesan bishop. **2** *Rare.* an assistant. [C15: via OF from L *co-* together + *adjūtor* helper, from *adjūtāre* to assist]

coagulate ⓣ *vb* (kəʊ'ægjʊ,leɪt), **coagulates, coagulating, coagulated. 1** to cause (a fluid, such as blood) to change into a soft semisolid mass or (of such a fluid) to change into such a mass; clot; curdle. ◆ *n* (kəʊ'ægjʊlɪt, -,leɪt). **2** the solid or semisolid substance produced by coagulation. [C16: from L *coāgulāre*, from *coāgulum* rennet, from *cōgere* to drive together]
▸**co'agulant** *or* **co'agu,lator** *n* ▸**co,agu'lation** *n* ▸**coagulative** (kəʊ'ægjʊlətɪv) *adj*

coagulation factor *n Med.* another name for **clotting factor**.

coal (kəʊl) *n* **1a** a compact black or dark brown carbonaceous rock consisting of layers of partially decomposed vegetation deposited in the Carboniferous period: a fuel and a source of coke, coal gas, and coal tar. **1b** (*as modifier*): *coal cellar; coal mine; coal dust*. **2** one or more lumps of coal. **3** short for **charcoal**. **4 coals to Newcastle**. something supplied where it is already plentiful. ◆ *vb* **5** to take in, provide with, or turn into coal. [OE *col*]
▸'**coaly** *adj*

coaler ('kəʊlə) *n* a ship, train, etc., used to carry or supply coal.

coalesce ⓣ (,kəʊə'lɛs) *vb* **coalesces, coalescing, coalesced.** (*intr*) to unite or come together in one body or mass; merge; fuse; blend. [C16: from L CO- + *alēscere* to increase, from *alere* to nourish]
▸,**coa'lescence** *n* ▸,**coa'lescent** *adj*

coalface ('kəʊl,feɪs) *n* the exposed seam of coal in a mine.

coalfield ('kəʊl,fi:ld) *n* an area rich in deposits of coal.

coalfish ('kəʊl,fɪʃ) *n, pl* **coalfish** *or* **coalfishes**. a dark-coloured gadoid food fish occurring in northern seas. Also called (Brit.): **saithe, coley**.

coal gas *n* a mixture of gases produced by the distillation of bituminous coal and used for heating and lighting.

coalition ⓣ (,kəʊə'lɪʃən) *n* **1a** an alliance between groups or parties, esp. for some temporary and specific reason. **1b** (*as modifier*): *a coalition government*. **2** a fusion or merging into one body or mass. [C17: from Med. L *coalitiō*, from L *coalēscere* to COALESCE]
▸,**coa'litionist** *n*

Coal Measures *pl n* **the.** a series of coal-bearing rocks formed in the upper Carboniferous period.

coal miner's lung *n* an informal name for **anthracosis**.

coal scuttle *n* a container to supply coal to a domestic fire.

coal tar *n* a black tar, produced by the distillation of bituminous coal, that can be further distilled to yield benzene, toluene, etc.

coal tit *n* a small European songbird having a black head with a white patch on the nape.

coaming ('kəʊmɪŋ) *n* a raised frame round a ship's hatchway for keeping out water. [C17: from ?]

coarse ⓣ (kɔ:s) *adj* **1** rough in texture, structure, etc.; not fine: *coarse sand*. **2** lacking refinement or taste; indelicate; vulgar: *coarse jokes*. **3** of inferior quality. **4** (of a metal) not refined. [C14: from ?]
▸'**coarsely** *adv* ▸'**coarseness** *n*

coarse fish *n* a freshwater fish that is not of the salmon family.
▸**coarse fishing** *n*

coarsen ⓣ ('kɔ:sᵊn) *vb* to make or become coarse.

coast ⓣ (kəʊst) *n* **1** the line or zone where the land meets the sea. Related adj: **littoral**. **2** *Brit.* the seaside. **3** *US.* **3a** a slope down which a sledge may slide. **3b** the act or an instance of sliding down a slope. **4 the coast is clear.** *Inf.* the obstacles or dangers are gone. ◆ *vb* **5** to move or cause to move by momentum or force of gravity. **6** (*intr*) to proceed without great effort: *to coast to victory*. **7** to sail along (a coast). [C13: from OF *coste*, from L *costa* side, rib]
▸'**coastal** *adj*

coaster ('kəʊstə) *n* **1** *Brit.* a vessel engaged in coastal commerce. **2** a small tray for holding a decanter, wine bottle, etc. **3** a person or thing that coasts. **4** a protective mat for glasses. **5** *US.* short for **roller coaster**.

Coaster ('kəʊstə) *n NZ.* a person from the West Coast of the South Island, New Zealand.

coastguard ('kəʊst,gɑ:d) *n* **1** a maritime force which aids shipping, saves lives at sea, prevents smuggling, etc. **2** Also called: **coastguardsman**. a member of such a force.

coastline ('kəʊst,laɪn) *n* the outline of a coast.

coat ⓣ (kəʊt) *n* **1** an outdoor garment with sleeves, covering the body from the shoulders to waist, knees, or feet. **2** any similar garment, esp. one forming the top to a suit. **3** a layer that covers or conceals a surface: *a coat of dust*. **4** the hair, wool, or fur of an animal. ◆ *vb* (*tr*) **5** (often foll. by *with*) to cover (with) a layer or covering. **6** to provide with a coat. [C16: from OF *cote*, of Gmc origin]

coat hanger *n* a curved piece of wood, wire, etc., with a hook, used to hang up clothes.

coati (kəʊ'ɑ:tɪ), **coati-mondi,** *or* **coati-mundi** (kəʊ,ɑ:tɪ'mʌndɪ) *n, pl* **coatis, coati-mondis,** *or* **coati-mundis.** an omnivorous mammal of Central and South America, related to but larger than the raccoons, having a long flexible snout and a brindled coat. [C17: from Port., from Tupi, lit.: belt-nosed, from *cua* belt + *tim* nose]

coating ⓣ ('kəʊtɪŋ) *n* **1** a layer or film spread over a surface. **2** fabric suitable for coats.

coat of arms *n* the heraldic bearings of a person, family, or corporation.

coat of mail *n* a protective garment made of linked metal rings or overlapping metal plates.

coat-tail *n* the long tapering tails at the back of a man's tailed coat.

coauthor (kəʊ'ɔ:θə) *n* **1** a person who shares the writing of a book, etc., with another. ◆ *vb* **2** (*tr*) to be the joint author of (a book, etc.).

coax ⓣ (kəʊks) *vb* **1** to seek to manipulate or persuade (someone) by

THESAURUS

custody, grasp, grip, hands, keeping, possession, sway

clutter *vb* **1** *often foll. by* **up** = **litter**, scatter, strew ◆ *n* **4** = **untidiness**, confusion, disarray, disorder, hotchpotch, jumble, litter, mess, muddle
Antonyms *vb* ≠ **litter:** arrange, order, organize, straighten, tidy ◆ *n* ≠ **untidiness:** neatness, order, organization, tidiness

coach *n* **1** = **bus**, car, carriage, charabanc, vehicle **4** = **instructor**, handler, teacher, trainer, tutor ◆ *vb* **6** = **instruct**, cram, drill, exercise, prepare, train, tutor

coagulate *vb* **1** = **congeal**, clot, curdle, jell, thicken

coalesce *vb* = **blend**, amalgamate, cohere, combine, come together, commingle, commix, consolidate, fraternize, fuse, incorporate, integrate, meld, merge, mix, unite

coalition *n* **2** = **alliance**, affiliation, amalgam, amalgamation, association, bloc, combination, compact, confederacy, confederation, conjunction, fusion, integration, league, merger, union

coarse *adj* **1** = **rough**, coarse-grained, crude, homespun, impure, rough-hewn, unfinished, unpolished, unprocessed, unpurified, unrefined **2** = **vulgar**, bawdy, boorish, brutish, coarse-grained, earthy, foul-mouthed, gruff, immodest, impolite, improper, impure, indecent, indelicate, loutish, mean, offensive, raunchy (*sl.*), ribald, rough, rude, smutty, uncivil
Antonyms *adj* ≠ **rough:** fine-grained, polished, purified, refined, smooth, soft ≠ **vulgar:** civilized, cultured, fine, genteel, inoffensive, pleasant, polished, polite, proper, refined, sophisticated, urbane, well-bred, well-mannered

coarsen *vb* = **roughen**, anaesthetize, blunt, callous, deaden, desensitize, dull, harden, indurate

coarseness *n* **1** = **roughness**, crudity, unevenness **3** = **vulgarity**, bawdiness, boorishness, crudity, earthiness, indelicacy, offensiveness, poor taste, ribaldry, roughness, smut, smuttiness, uncouthness

coast *n* **1, 2** = **shore**, beach, border, coastline, littoral, seaboard, seaside, strand ◆ *vb* **5** = **cruise**, drift, freewheel, get by, glide, sail, taxi

coat *n* **3** = **layer**, coating, covering, overlay **4** = **fur**, fleece, hair, hide, pelt, skin, wool ◆ *vb* **5** = **cover**, apply, Artex, plaster, smear, spread

coating *n* **1** = **layer**, blanket, coat, covering, dusting, film, finish, glaze, lamination, membrane, patina, sheet, skin, varnish, veneer

coax *vb* **1** = **persuade**, allure, beguile, cajole, decoy, entice, flatter, inveigle, prevail upon,

tenderness, flattery, pleading, etc. **2** (*tr*) to obtain by persistent coaxing. **3** (*tr*) to work on (something) carefully and patiently so as to make it function as desired: *he coaxed the engine into starting.* [C16: verb formed from obs. noun *cokes* fool, from ?]
▸ **'coaxer** *n* ▸ **'coaxingly** *adv*

coaxial (kəʊ'æksɪəl) *or* **coaxal** (kəʊ'æksᵊl) *adj* **1** having or mounted on a common axis. **2** *Geom.* (of a set of circles) having the same radical axis. **3** *Electronics.* formed from, using, or connected to a coaxial cable.

coaxial cable *n* a cable consisting of an inner insulated core of stranded or solid wire surrounded by an outer insulated flexible wire braid, used esp. as a transmission line for radio-frequency signals. Often shortened to **coax** ('kəʊæks).

cob (kɒb) *n* **1** a male swan. **2** a thickset type of riding and draught horse. **3** short for **corncob** or **cobnut**. **4** *Brit.* another name for **hazel** (sense 1). **5** a small rounded lump or heap of coal, ore, etc. **6** *Brit.* & *NZ.* a building material consisting of a mixture of clay and chopped straw. **7** *Brit.* a round loaf of bread. [C15: from ?]

cobalt ('kəʊbɔːlt) *n* a brittle hard silvery-white element that is a ferromagnetic metal: used in alloys. The radioisotope **cobalt-60** is used in radiotherapy and as a tracer. Symbol: Co; atomic no.: 27; atomic wt.: 58.933. [C17: G *Kobalt,* from MHG *kobolt* goblin; from the miners' belief that goblins placed it in the silver ore]

cobalt blue *n* **1** any greenish-blue pigment containing cobalt aluminate. **2a** a deep blue colour. **2b** (*as adj*): *a cobalt-blue car.*

cobalt bomb *n* **1** a cobalt-60 device used in radiotherapy. **2** a nuclear weapon consisting of a hydrogen bomb encased in cobalt, which releases large quantities of radioactive cobalt-60 into the atmosphere.

cobber ('kɒbə) *n Austral. arch.* & *NZ.* a friend; mate: used as a term of address to males. [C19: from E dialect *cob* to take a liking to someone]

cobble[1] ('kɒbᵊl) *n* **1** short for **cobblestone.** ◆ *vb* **cobbles, cobbling, cobbled. 2** (*tr*) to pave (a road, etc.) with cobblestones. [C15 (in *cobblestone*): from COB]

cobble[2] ❶ ('kɒbᵊl) *vb* **cobbles, cobbling, cobbled.** (*tr*) **1** to make or mend (shoes). **2** to put together clumsily. [C15: back formation from COBBLER[1]]

cobbler[1] ('kɒblə) *n* a person who makes or mends shoes. [C13 (as surname): from ?]

cobbler[2] ('kɒblə) *n* **1** a sweetened iced drink, usually made from fruit and wine. **2** *Chiefly US.* a hot dessert made of fruit covered with a rich cakelike crust. [C19: (for sense 1) ? shortened from *cobbler's punch*]

cobblers ('kɒbləz) *pl n Brit. taboo sl.* **1** another word for **testicles. 2 (a load of old) cobblers.** rubbish; nonsense. [C20: from rhyming sl. *cobblers' awls* balls]

cobblestone ('kɒbᵊl,stəʊn) *n* a rounded stone used for paving. Sometimes shortened to **cobble.**

cobelligerent (,kəʊbɪ'lɪdʒərənt) *n* a country fighting in a war on the side of another country.

cobnut ('kɒb,nʌt) *or* **cob** *n* other names for a **hazelnut.** [C16: from earlier *cobylle nut*]

COBOL *or* **Cobol** ('kəʊ,bɒl) *n* a high-level computer programming language designed for general commercial use. [C20: *co(mmon) b(usiness) o(riented) l(anguage)*]

cobra ('kəʊbrə) *n* any of several highly venomous snakes of tropical Africa and Asia. When alarmed they spread the skin of the neck region into a hood. [C19: from Port. *cobra* (*de capello*) snake (with a hood), from L *colubra* snake]

cobweb ('kɒb,wɛb) *n* **1** a web spun by certain spiders. **2** a single thread of such a web. **3** something like a cobweb, as in its flimsiness or ability to trap. [C14: *cob,* from OE (*ātor*)*coppe* spider]
▸ **'cob,webbed** *adj* ▸ **'cob,webby** *adj*

cobwebs ('kɒb,wɛbz) *pl n* **1** mustiness, confusion, or obscurity. **2** *Inf.* stickiness of the eyelids experienced upon first awakening.

coca ('kəʊkə) *n* either of two shrubs, native to the Andes, the dried leaves of which contain cocaine and are chewed for their stimulating effects. [C17: from Sp., from Quechuan *kúka*]

Coca-Cola (,kəʊkə'kəʊlə) *n* **1** *Trademark.* a carbonated soft drink flavoured with coca leaves, cola nuts, caramel, etc. **2** (*modifier*) denoting the spread of American culture and values to other parts of the world: *Coca-Cola generation.*

cocaine *or* **cocain** (kə'keɪn) *n* an addictive narcotic drug derived from coca leaves or synthesized, used medicinally as a topical anaesthetic. [C19: from COCA + -INE[1]]

coccus ('kɒkəs) *n, pl* **cocci** (-kaɪ, -ksaɪ). any spherical or nearly spherical bacterium, such as a staphylococcus. [C18: from NL, from Gk *kokkos* berry, grain]
▸ **'coccoid** *or* **'coccal** *adj*

coccyx ('kɒksɪks) *n, pl* **coccyges** (kɒk'saɪdʒiːz). a small triangular bone at the end of the spinal column in man and some apes. [C17: from NL, from Gk *kokkux* cuckoo, imit.; from its likeness to a cuckoo's beak]
▸ **coccygeal** (kɒk'sɪdʒɪəl) *adj*

cochineal (,kɒtʃɪ'niːl, 'kɒtʃɪ,niːl) *n* **1** a Mexican insect that feeds on cacti. **2** a crimson substance obtained from the crushed bodies of these insects, used for colouring food and for dyeing. **3** the colour of this dye. [C16: from OSp. *cochinilla,* from L *coccineus* scarlet-coloured, from Gk *kokkos* kermes berry]

cochlea ('kɒklɪə) *n, pl* **cochleae** (-lɪ,iː). the spiral tube that forms part of the internal ear, converting sound vibrations into nerve impulses. [C16: from L: snail, spiral, from Gk *kokhlias*]
▸ **'cochlear** *adj*

cochlear implant ('kɒklɪə) *n* a device that stimulates the acoustic nerve in the inner ear in order to produce some form of hearing in people who are deaf from inner ear disease.

cochleate ('kɒklɪ,eɪt, -lɪɪt) *or* **cochleated** *adj Biol.* shaped like a snail's shell.

cock[1] ❶ (kɒk) *n* **1** the male of the domestic fowl. **2a** any other male bird. **2b** the male of certain other animals, such as the lobster. **2c** (*as modifier*): *a cock sparrow.* **3** short for **stopcock** or **weathercock. 4** a taboo slang word for **penis. 5a** the hammer of a firearm. **5b** its position when the firearm is ready to be discharged. **6** *Brit. inf.* a friend, mate, or fellow. **7** a jaunty or significant tilting upwards: *a cock of the head.* ◆ *vb* **8** (*tr*) to set the firing pin, hammer, or breech block of (a firearm) so that a pull on the trigger will release it and thus fire the weapon. **9** (*tr;* sometimes foll. by *up*) to raise in an alert or jaunty manner. **10** (*intr*) to stick or stand up conspicuously. ◆ See also **cockup.** [OE *cocc,* ult. imit.]

cock[2] (kɒk) *n* **1** a small, cone-shaped heap of hay, straw, etc. ◆ *vb* **2** (*tr*) to stack (hay, etc.) in such heaps. [C14: ? of Scand. origin]

cockabully (,kɒkə'bʊlɪ) *n, pl* **cockabullies.** any of several small freshwater fish of New Zealand. [Maori *kokopu*]

cockade (kɒ'keɪd) *n* a feather or ribbon worn on military headwear. [C18: changed from earlier *cockard,* from F, from *coq* COCK[1]]
▸ **cock'aded** *adj*

cock-a-doodle-doo (,kɒkə,duːdᵊl'duː) *interj* an imitation or representation of a cock crowing.

cock-a-hoop *adj* (*usually postpositive*) **1** in very high spirits. **2** boastful. **3** askew; confused. [C16: ?from *set the cock a hoop*: to put a cock on a *hoop,* a full measure of grain]

cockalorum (,kɒkə'lɔːrəm) *n* **1** a self-important little man. **2** bragging talk. [C18: from COCK[1] + *-alorum,* var. of L genitive pl ending; ? intended to suggest: the cock of all cocks]

cockamamie (,kɒkə'meɪmɪ) *adj Sl., chiefly US.* ridiculous or nonsensical: *a cockamamie story.* [C20: in an earlier sense: a paper transfer, prob. from DECALCOMANIA]

cock-and-bull story *n Inf.* an obviously improbable story, esp. one used as an excuse.

cockatoo (,kɒkə'tuː, 'kɒkə,tuː) *n, pl* **cockatoos. 1** any of a genus of parrots having an erectile crest and light-coloured plumage. **2** *Austral.* & *NZ.* a small farmer or settler. **3** *Austral. inf.* a lookout during some illegal activity. [C17: from Du., from Malay *kakatua*]

cockatrice ('kɒkətrɪs, -,traɪs) *n* **1** a legendary monster, part snake and part cock, that could kill with a glance. **2** another name for **basilisk** (sense 1). [C14: from OF, ult. from L *calcāre* to tread, from *calx* heel]

cockboat ('kɒk,bəʊt) *or* **cockleboat** *n* a ship's small boat. [C15 *cokbote,* ? ult. from LL *caudica* dugout canoe, from L *caudex* tree trunk]

cockchafer ('kɒk,tʃeɪfə) *n* any of various Old World beetles, whose larvae feed on crops and grasses. Also called: **May beetle, May bug.** [C18: from COCK[1] + CHAFER]

cockcrow ('kɒk,krəʊ) *n* daybreak.

cocked hat *n* **1** a hat with brims turned up and caught together in order to give two points (bicorn) or three points (tricorn). **2 knock into a cocked hat.** *Sl.* to outdo or defeat.

cockerel ('kɒkərəl, 'kɒkrəl) *n* a young domestic cock, less than a year old. [C15: dim. of COCK[1]]

cocker spaniel ('kɒkə) *n* a small compact breed of spaniel. [C19: from *cocking* hunting woodcocks]

cockeyed ❶ ('kɒk,aɪd) *adj Inf.* **1** afflicted with strabismus or squint. **2** physically or logically abnormal, absurd, etc.; crooked; askew: *cockeyed ideas.* **3** drunk.

cockfight ('kɒk,faɪt) *n* a fight between two gamecocks fitted with sharp metal spurs.
▸ **'cock,fighting** *n*

cockhorse (,kɒk'hɔːs) *n* another name for **rocking horse** or **hobbyhorse.**

cockieleekie, cockyleeky, *or* **cock-a-leekie** ('kɒkə'liːkɪ) *n Scot.* a soup made from a fowl boiled with leeks.

cockle[1] ('kɒkᵊl) *n* **1** any edible sand-burrowing bivalve mollusc of Europe, typically having a rounded shell with radiating ribs. **2** any of certain similar or related molluscs. **3** short for **cockleshell** (sense 1). **4** a wrinkle or puckering. **5** one's deepest feelings (esp. in **warm the cockles of one's heart**). ◆ *vb* **cockles, cockling, cockled. 6** to contract or cause to contract into wrinkles. [C14: from OF *coquille* shell, from L *conchylium* shellfish, from Gk *konkhule* mussel; see CONCH]

cockle[2] ('kɒkᵊl) *n* any of several plants, esp. the corn cockle, that grow as weeds in cornfields.

cockleshell ('kɒkᵊl,ʃɛl) *n* **1** the shell of the cockle. **2** any of the shells of certain other molluscs. **3** any small light boat.

cockney ('kɒknɪ) (*often cap.*) ◆ *n* **1** a native of London, esp. of the East End, speaking a characteristic dialect of English. Traditionally defined as someone born within the sound of the bells of St Mary-le-Bow church. **2** the urban dialect of London or its East End. ◆ *adj* **3** characteristic of cockneys or their dialect of English. [C14:

THESAURUS

soft-soap (*inf.*), soothe, sweet-talk (*inf.*), talk into, twist (someone's) arm, wheedle
Antonyms *vb* browbeat, bully, coerce, force, harass, intimidate, pressurize, threaten

cobble[2] *vb* **1, 2 = patch,** botch, bungle, clout, mend, tinker

cock1 *n* **1 = cockerel,** chanticleer, rooster ◆ *vb* **9, 10 = raise,** perk up, prick, stand up

cockeyed *adj Informal* **1 = crooked,** askew, asymmetrical, awry, lopsided, skewwhiff (*Brit. inf.*), squint (*inf.*) **2 = absurd,** crazy, ludicrous, nonsensical, preposterous

from *cokeney*, lit.: cock's egg, later applied contemptuously to townsmen, from *cokene*, genitive pl of *cok* COCK[1] + *ey* EGG[1]]
▸ **'cockneyish** *adj* ▸ **'cockney,ism** *n*

cock of the walk *n Inf.* a person who asserts himself in a strutting pompous way.

cockpit ('kɒk,pɪt) *n* **1** the compartment in a small aircraft in which the pilot, crew, and sometimes the passengers sit. Cf. **flight deck** (sense 1). **2** the driver's compartment in a racing car. **3** *Naut.* an enclosed or recessed area towards the stern of a small vessel from which it is steered. **4** the site of numerous battles or campaigns. **5** an enclosure used for cockfights.

cockroach ('kɒk,rəʊtʃ) *n* an insect having an oval flattened body with long antennae and biting mouthparts: a household pest. [C17: from Sp. *cucaracha,* from ?]

cockscomb *or* **coxcomb** ('kɒks,kəʊm) *n* **1** the comb of a domestic cock. **2** a garden plant with yellow, crimson, or purple feathery plumelike flowers in a broad spike resembling the comb of a cock. **3** *Inf.* a conceited dandy.

cockshy ('kɒk,ʃaɪ) *n, pl* **cockshies.** *Brit.* **1** a target aimed at in throwing games. **2** the throw itself. ◆ Often shortened to **shy.** [C18: from shying at a cock, the prize for the person who hit it]

cocksure Ⓣ (,kɒk'ʃʊə, -'ʃɔː) *adj* overconfident; arrogant. [C16: from ?]
▸ **,cock'sureness** *n*

cocktail Ⓣ ('kɒk,teɪl) *n* **1a** any mixed drink with a spirit base. **1b** (*as modifier*): *the cocktail hour.* **2** an appetizer of seafood, mixed fruits, etc. **3** any combination of diverse elements, esp. one considered potent. **4** (*modifier*) appropriate for formal occasions: *a cocktail dress.* [C19: from ?]

cockup ('kɒk,ʌp) *n* **1** *Brit. sl.* something done badly. ◆ *vb* **cock up.** (*tr, adv*) **2** (of an animal) to raise (its ears etc.), esp. in an alert manner. **3** *Brit. sl.* to botch.

cocky[1] Ⓣ ('kɒkɪ) *adj* **cockier, cockiest.** excessively proud of oneself.
▸ **'cockily** *adv* ▸ **'cockiness** *n*

cocky[2] ('kɒkɪ) *n, pl* **cockies.** *Austral. & NZ inf.* short for **cockatoo** (sense 2).

coco ('kəʊkəʊ) *n, pl* **cocos.** short for **coconut** or **coconut palm.** [C16: from Port. *coco* grimace; from the likeness of the three holes of the nut to a face]

cocoa ('kəʊkəʊ) *or* **cacao** *n* **1** a powder made from cocoa beans after they have been roasted and ground. **2** a hot or cold drink made from cocoa and milk or water. **3a** a light to moderate brown colour. **3b** (*as adj*): *cocoa paint.* [C18: altered from CACAO]

cocoa bean *n* the seed of the cacao.

cocoa butter *n* a yellowish-white waxy solid that is obtained from cocoa beans and used for confectionery, soap, etc.

coconut *or* **cocoanut** ('kəʊkə,nʌt) *n* **1** the fruit of the coconut palm, consisting of a thick fibrous oval husk inside which is a thin hard shell enclosing edible white meat. The hollow centre is filled with a milky fluid (**coconut milk**). **2** the meat of the coconut, often shredded and used in cakes, curries, etc. [C18: see COCO]

coconut matting *n* a form of coarse matting made from the fibrous husk of the coconut.

coconut oil *n* the oil obtained from the meat of the coconut and used for making soap, etc.

coconut palm *n* a tall palm tree, widely planted throughout the tropics, having coconuts as fruits. Also called: **coco palm, coconut tree.**

cocoon Ⓣ (kə'kuːn) *n* **1** a silky protective envelope secreted by silkworms and certain other insect larvae, in which the pupae develop. **2** a protective spray covering used as a seal on machinery. **3** a cosy warm covering. ◆ *vb* **4** (*tr*) to wrap in a cocoon. [C17: from F, from Provençal *coucoun* eggshell, from *coco* shell]

cocopan ('kəʊkəʊ,pæn) *n* (in South Africa) a small wagon running on narrow-gauge railway lines used in mines. Also called: **hopper.** [C20: from Zulu *'ngkumbana* short truck]

cocotte (kəʊ'kɒt, kə-) *n* **1** a small fireproof dish in which individual portions of food are cooked and served. **2** a prostitute or promiscuous woman. [C19: from F, from fem of *coq* COCK[1]]

cod[1] (kɒd) *n, pl* **cod** *or* **cods. 1** any of the gadoid food fishes which occur in the North Atlantic and have a long body with three rounded dorsal fins. **2** any of various Australian fishes of fresh or salt water, such as the Murray cod or the red cod. [C13: prob. of Gmc origin]

cod[2] (kɒd) *n* **1** *Brit. & US dialect.* a pod or husk. **2** *Taboo.* an obsolete word for **scrotum.** [OE *codd* husk, bag]

cod[3] (kɒd) *Brit. sl.* ◆ *vb* **cods, codding, codded.** (*tr*) **1** to make fun of; tease. **2** to play a trick on; befool. ◆ *n* **3** a hoax or trick. [C19: ?from earlier *cod* a fool]

COD *abbrev. for:* **1** cash on delivery. **2** (in the US) collect on delivery.

coda ('kəʊdə) *n* **1** *Music.* the final passage of a musical structure. **2** a concluding part of a literary work that rounds off the main work but is independent of it. [C18: from It.: tail, from L *cauda*]

cod-act *vb* (*intr*) *Irish inf.* to play tricks; fool. [from COD[3] + ACT]

coddle Ⓣ ('kɒdᵊl) *vb* **coddles, coddling, coddled.** (*tr*) **1** to treat with indulgence. **2** to cook (something, esp. eggs) in water just below the boiling point. [C16: from ?; ? rel. to CAUDLE]
▸ **'coddler** *n*

code Ⓣ (kəʊd) *n* **1** a system of letters or symbols, by which information can be communicated secretly, briefly, etc.: *binary code; Morse code.* See also **genetic code. 2** a message in code. **3** a symbol used in a code. **4** a conventionalized set of principles or rules: *a code of behaviour.* **5** a system of letters or digits used for identification purposes. ◆ *vb* **codes, coding, coded.** (*tr*) **6** to translate or arrange into a code. [C14: from F, from L *cōdex* book, CODEX]
▸ **'coder** *n*

codeine ('kəʊdiːn) *n* a white crystalline alkaloid prepared mainly from morphine. It is used as an analgesic, a sedative, and to relieve coughing. [C19: from Gk *kōdeia* head of a poppy, from *kōos* hollow place + -INE[2]]

codex ('kəʊdɛks) *n, pl* **codices** ('kəʊdɪ,siːz, 'kɒdɪ-). **1** a volume of manuscripts of an ancient text. **2** *Obs.* a legal code. [C16: from L: tree trunk, wooden block, book]

codfish ('kɒd,fɪʃ) *n, pl* **codfish** *or* **codfishes.** a cod.

codger ('kɒdʒə) *n Inf.* a man, esp. an old or eccentric one: often in **old codger.** [C18: prob. var. of CADGER]

codicil ('kɒdɪsɪl) *n* **1** *Law.* a supplement modifying a will or revoking some provision of it. **2** an additional provision; appendix. [C15: from LL dim. of CODEX]
▸ **,codi'cillary** *adj*

codify Ⓣ ('kəʊdɪ,faɪ, 'kɒ-) *vb* **codifies, codifying, codified.** (*tr*) to organize or collect together (laws, rules, procedures, etc.) into a system or code.
▸ **'codi,fier** *n* ▸ **,codifi'cation** *n*

codling[1] ('kɒdlɪŋ) *or* **codlin** ('kɒdlɪn) *n* **1** any of several varieties of long tapering apples. **2** any unripe apple. [C15 *querdlyng,* from ?]

codling[2] ('kɒdlɪŋ) *n* a codfish, esp. a young one.

cod-liver oil *n* an oil extracted from the livers of cod and related fish, rich in vitamins A and D.

codology (kɒd'ɒlədʒɪ) *n Irish inf.* the art or practice of bluffing or deception.

codpiece ('kɒd,piːs) *n* a bag covering the male genitals, attached to breeches: worn in the 15th and 16th centuries. [C15: from COD[2] + PIECE]

codswallop ('kɒdz,wɒləp) *n Brit. sl.* nonsense. [C20: from ?]

co-ed (,kəʊ'ɛd) *adj* **1** coeducational. ◆ *n* **2** *US.* a female student in a coeducational college or university. **3** *Brit.* a school or college providing coeducation.

coeducation (,kəʊɛdjʊ'keɪʃən) *n* instruction in schools, colleges, etc., attended by both sexes.
▸ **,coedu'cational** *adj* ▸ **,coedu'cationally** *adv*

coefficient (,kəʊɪ'fɪʃənt) *n* **1** *Maths.* a numerical or constant factor in an algebraic term: *the coefficient of the term 3xyz is 3.* **2** *Physics.* a number that is the value of a given substance under specified conditions. [C17: from NL, from L *co-* together + *efficere* to EFFECT]

coefficient of variation *n Statistics.* a measure of the relative variation of distributions independent of the units of measurement; the standard deviation divided by the mean, sometimes expressed as a percentage.

coel- *prefix* indicating a cavity within a body or a hollow organ or part: *coelacanth; coelenterate.* [NL, from Gk *koilos* hollow]

coelacanth ('siːlə,kænθ) *n* a primitive marine bony fish, having fleshy limblike pectoral fins: thought to be extinct until a living specimen was discovered in 1938. [C19: from NL, from COEL- + Gk *akanthos* spine]

coelenterate (sɪ'lɛntə,reɪt, -rɪt) *n* any of various invertebrates having a saclike body with a single opening (mouth), such as jellyfishes, sea anemones, and corals. [C19: from NL *Coelenterata,* hollow-intestined (creatures)]

coeliac *or US* **celiac** ('siːlɪ,æk) *adj* of the abdomen. [C17: from L, from Gk, from *koilia* belly]

coeliac disease *n* an illness, esp. of children, in which the lining of the small intestine is sensitive to gluten in the diet, causing an impairment of food absorption.

coelom *or esp. US* **celom** ('siːləʊm, -ləm) *n* the body cavity of many multicellular animals, containing the digestive tract and other visceral organs. [C19: from Gk, from *koilos* hollow]
▸ **coelomic** *or esp. US* **celomic** (sɪ'lɒmɪk) *adj*

coeno- *or before a vowel* **coen-** *combining form.* common: *coenobite.* [NL, from Gk *koinos*]

coenobite *or* **cenobite** ('siːnəʊ,baɪt) *n* a member of a religious order following a communal rule of life. [C17: from OF or ecclesiastical L, from Gk *koinobion* convent, from *koinos* common + *bios* life]
▸ **coenobitic** (,siːnəʊ'bɪtɪk), **,coeno'bitical** *or* **,ceno'bitic, ,ceno'bitical** *adj*

coenzyme (kəʊ'ɛnzaɪm) *n Biochem.* a nonprotein organic molecule

THESAURUS

cockiness *n* = **overconfidence**, arrogance, bigheadedness, brashness, bumptiousness, cocksureness, conceit, conceitedness, confidence, egotism, lordliness, presumptuousness, self-assurance, vanity

cocksure *adj* = **overconfident**, arrogant, brash, bumptious, cocky, full of oneself, hubristic, presumptuous

cocktail *n* **3** = **mixture**, amalgamation, blend, combination, mix

cocky[1] *adj* = **overconfident**, arrogant, brash, cocksure, conceited, egotistical, full of oneself, lordly, swaggering, swollen-headed, vain
Antonyms *adj* hesitant, lacking confidence, modest, self-effacing, uncertain, unsure

cocoon *vb* **4** = **wrap**, cushion, envelop, insulate, pad, protect, swaddle, swathe

coddle *vb* **1** = **pamper**, baby, cosset, humour, indulge, mollycoddle, nurse, pet, spoil, wet-nurse (*inf.*)

code *n* **1** = **cipher**, cryptograph **4** = **principles**, canon, convention, custom, ethics, etiquette, manners, maxim, regulations, rules, system

codify *vb* = **organize**, catalogue, classify, collect, condense, digest, summarize, systematize, tabulate

that forms a complex with certain enzymes and is essential for their activity.

coequal (kəʊ'iːkwəl) *adj* **1** of the same size, rank, etc. ◆ *n* **2** a person or thing equal with another.
▸**coequality** (ˌkəʊɪ'kwɒlɪtɪ) *n*

coerce ⓣ (kəʊ'ɜːs) *vb* **coerces, coercing, coerced.** (*tr*) to compel or restrain by force or authority without regard to individual wishes or desires. [C17: from L, from *co-* together + *arcēre* to enclose]
▸**co'ercer** *n* ▸**co'ercible** *adj*

coercion ⓣ (kəʊ'ɜːʃən) *n* **1** the act or power of coercing. **2** government by force.
▸**coercive** (kəʊ'ɜːsɪv) *adj* ▸**co'ercively** *adv*

coeval (kəʊ'iːvᵊl) *adj* **1** of or belonging to the same age or generation. ◆ *n* **2** a contemporary. [C17: from LL, from L *co-* + *aevum* age]
▸**coevality** (ˌkəʊɪ'vælɪtɪ) *n* ▸**co'evally** *adv*

coexecutor (ˌkəʊɪg'zɛkjʊtə) *n Law.* a person acting jointly with another or others as executor.

coexist (ˌkəʊɪg'zɪst) *vb* (*intr*) **1** to exist together at the same time or in the same place. **2** to exist together in peace.
▸ˌ**coex'istence** *n* ▸ˌ**coex'istent** *adj*

coextend (ˌkəʊɪk'stɛnd) *vb* to extend or cause to extend equally in space or time.
▸ˌ**coex'tension** *n* ▸ˌ**coex'tensive** *adj*

C of C *abbrev. for* Chamber of Commerce.

C of E *abbrev. for* Church of England.

coffee ('kɒfɪ) *n* **1a** a drink consisting of an infusion of the roasted and ground seeds of the coffee tree. **1b** (*as modifier*): *coffee grounds.* **2** Also called: **coffee beans.** the beanlike seeds of the coffee tree, used to make this beverage. **3** the tree yielding these seeds. **4a** a light brown colour. **4b** (*as adj*): *a coffee carpet.* [C16: from It. *caffè*, from Turkish *kahve*, from Ar. *qahwah* coffee, wine]

coffee bar *n* a café; snack bar.

coffee cup *n* a small cup for serving coffee.

coffee house *n* a place where coffee is served, esp. one that was a fashionable meeting place in 18th-century London.

coffee mill *n* a machine for grinding roasted coffee beans.

coffeepot ('kɒfɪˌpɒt) *n* a pot in which coffee is brewed or served.

coffee shop *n* a shop where coffee is sold or drunk.

coffee table *n* a low table on which coffee may be served.

coffee-table book *n* a book, usually glossily illustrated, designed chiefly to be looked at, rather than read.

coffer ⓣ ('kɒfə) *n* **1** a chest, esp. for storing valuables. **2** (*usually pl*) a store of money. **3** an ornamental sunken panel in a ceiling, dome, etc. **4** a watertight box or chamber. **5** short for **cofferdam.** ◆ *vb* (*tr*) **6** to store, as in a coffer. **7** to decorate (a ceiling, dome, etc.) with coffers. [C13: from OF *coffre*, from L, from Gk *kophinos* basket]

cofferdam ('kɒfəˌdæm) *n* **1** a watertight structure that encloses an area under water, pumped dry to enable construction work to be carried out. **2** (on a ship) a compartment separating two bulkheads, as for insulation or to serve as a barrier against the escape of gas, etc. ◆ Often shortened to **coffer.**

coffin ('kɒfɪn) *n* **1** a box in which a corpse is buried or cremated. **2** the bony part of a horse's foot. ◆ *vb* **3** (*tr*) to place in or as in a coffin. [C14: from OF *cofin*, from L *cophinus* basket]

coffin nail *n* a slang term for **cigarette.**

coffle ('kɒfᵊl) *n* a line of slaves, beasts, etc., fastened together. [C18: from Ar. *qāfilah* caravan]

C of S *abbrev. for* Church of Scotland.

cog[1] (kɒg) *n* **1** any of the teeth or projections on the rim of a gearwheel. **2** a gearwheel, esp. a small one. **3** a person or thing playing a small part in a large organization or process. [C13: of Scand. origin]

cog[2] (kɒg) *n* **1** a tenon that projects from the end of a timber beam for fitting into a mortise. ◆ *vb* **cogs, cogging, cogged. 2** (*tr*) to join (pieces of wood) with cogs. [C19: from ?]

cogent ⓣ ('kəʊdʒənt) *adj* compelling belief or assent; forcefully convincing. [C17: from L *cōgent-*, *cōgēns*, from *co-* together + *agere* to drive]
▸'**cogency** *n* ▸'**cogently** *adv*

cogitate ⓣ ('kɒdʒɪˌteɪt) *vb* **cogitates, cogitating, cogitated.** to think deeply about (a problem, possibility, etc.); ponder. [C16: from L, from *co-* (intensive) + *agitāre* to turn over]
▸ˌ**cogi'tation** *n* ▸'**cogitative** *adj* ▸'**cogiˌtator** *n*

Cognac ('kɒnjæk) *n* (*sometimes not cap.*) a high-quality grape brandy, distilled near Cognac in SW France.

cognate ⓣ ('kɒgneɪt) *adj* **1** akin; related: *cognate languages.* **2** related by blood or descended from a common maternal ancestor. ◆ *n* **3** something that is cognate with something else. [C17: from L, from *co-* same + *gnātus* born, var. of *nātus*, p.p. of *nāscī* to be born]
▸'**cognately** *adv* ▸'**cognateness** *n* ▸**cog'nation** *n*

cognition ⓣ (kɒg'nɪʃən) *n* **1** the mental act or process by which knowledge is acquired, including perception, intuition, and reasoning. **2** the knowledge that results from such an act or process. [C15: from L, from *co-* (intensive) + *nōscere* to learn]
▸**cog'nitional** *adj* ▸'**cognitive** *adj*

cognitive therapy *n Psychol.* a form of psychotherapy in which the patient is encouraged to change the way he sees the world and himself: used particularly to treat depression.

cognizable *or* **cognisable** ('kɒgnɪzəbᵊl, 'kɒnɪ-) *adj* **1** perceptible. **2** *Law.* susceptible to the jurisdiction of a court.

cognizance *or* **cognisance** ('kɒgnɪzəns, 'kɒnɪ-) *n* **1** knowledge; acknowledgment. **2 take cognizance of.** to take notice of; acknowledge, esp. officially. **3** the range or scope of knowledge or perception. **4** *Law.* the right of a court to hear and determine a cause or matter. **5** *Heraldry.* a distinguishing badge or bearing. [C14: from OF, from L *cognōscere* to learn; see COGNITION]

cognizant *or* **cognisant** ('kɒgnɪzənt, 'kɒnɪ-) *adj* (usually foll. by *of*) aware; having knowledge.

cognomen (kɒg'nəʊmɛn) *n, pl* **cognomens** *or* **cognomina** (-'nɒmɪnə, -'nəʊ-). (originally) an ancient Roman's third name or nickname, which later became his family name. [C19: from L: additional name, from *co-* together + *nōmen* name]
▸**cognominal** (kɒg'nɒmɪnᵊl, -'nəʊ-) *adj*

cognoscenti (ˌkɒnjəʊ'ʃɛntɪ, ˌkɒgnəʊ-) *or* **conoscenti** (ˌkɒnəʊ'ʃɛntɪ) *pl n, sing* **cognoscente** *or* **conoscente** (-tiː). (*sometimes sing*) people with informed appreciation of a particular field, esp. in the fine arts; connoisseurs. [C18: from obs. It., from L *cognōscere* to learn]

cogwheel ('kɒgˌwiːl) *n* another name for **gearwheel.**

cohab ('kəʊˌhæb) *n* a sexual partner with whom one lives but to whom one is not married. [C20: a shortened form of *cohabitee*; see COHABIT]

cohabit (kəʊ'hæbɪt) *vb* (*intr*) to live together as husband and wife, esp. without being married. [C16: from L *co-* together + *habitāre* to live]
▸ˌ**cohabi'tee, co'habitant,** *or* **co'habiter** *n*

cohabitation (kəʊˌhæbɪ'teɪʃən) *n* **1** the state or condition of living together as husband and wife without being married. **2** (of political parties) the state or condition of cooperating for specific purposes without forming a coalition.

coheir (kəʊ'ɛə) *n* a person who inherits jointly with others.
▸**co'heiress** *fem n*

cohere ⓣ (kəʊ'hɪə) *vb* **coheres, cohering, cohered.** (*intr*) **1** to hold or stick firmly together. **2** to be connected logically; be consistent. **3** *Physics.* to be held together by the action of molecular forces. [C16: from L *co-* together + *haerēre* to cling]

coherence ⓣ (kəʊ'hɪərəns) *or* **coherency** *n* **1** logical or natural connection or consistency. **2** another word for **cohesion** (sense 1).

coherent ⓣ (kəʊ'hɪərənt) *adj* **1** capable of intelligible speech. **2** logical; consistent and orderly. **3** cohering or sticking together. **4** *Physics.* (of two or more waves) having the same phase or a fixed phase difference: *coherent light.*
▸**co'herently** *adv*

cohesion (kəʊ'hiːʒən) *n* **1** the act or state of cohering; tendency to unite. **2** *Physics.* the force that holds together the atoms or molecules in a solid or liquid, as distinguished from adhesion. **3** *Bot.* the fusion in some plants of flower parts, such as petals, that are usually separate. [C17: from L *cohaesus*, p.p. of *cohaerēre* to COHERE]
▸**co'hesive** *adj*

coho ('kəʊhəʊ) *n, pl* **coho** *or* **cohos.** a Pacific salmon. Also called: **silver salmon.** [from ?]

cohort ⓣ ('kəʊhɔːt) *n* **1** one of the ten units of an ancient Roman Legion. **2** any band of warriors or associates: *the cohorts of Satan.* **3** *Chiefly US.* an associate or follower. [C15: from L *cohors* yard, company of soldiers]

COHSE ('kəʊzɪ) *n* (formerly, in Britain) *acronym for* Confederation of Health Service Employees.

COI (in Britain) *abbrev. for* Central Office of Information.

THESAURUS

coerce *vb* = **force**, browbeat, bulldoze (*inf.*), bully, compel, constrain, dragoon, drive, intimidate, press-gang, pressurize, railroad (*inf.*), twist (someone's) arm (*inf.*)

coercion *n* **1** = **force**, browbeating, bullying, compulsion, constraint, duress, intimidation, pressure, strong-arm tactics (*inf.*), threats

coffer *n* **1** = **chest**, ark (*dialect*), case, casket, kist (*Scot. & N English dialect*), repository, strongbox, treasure chest, treasury **2** *usually plu* = **funds**, assets, capital, finances, means, reserves, treasury, vaults

cogency *n* = **conviction**, force, potency, power, strength

cogent *adj* = **convincing**, compelling, compulsive, conclusive, effective, forceful, forcible, influential, irresistible, potent, powerful, strong, urgent, weighty

cogitate *vb* = **think**, consider, contemplate, deliberate, meditate, mull over, muse, ponder, reflect, ruminate

cogitation *n* = **thought**, consideration, contemplation, deliberation, meditation, reflection, rumination

cognate *adj* **1** = **related**, affiliated, akin, alike, allied, analogous, associated, connected, kindred, similar

cognition *n* **2** = **perception**, apprehension, awareness, comprehension, discernment, insight, intelligence, reasoning, understanding

cohere *vb* **1** = **stick together**, adhere, bind, cling, coalesce, combine, consolidate, fuse, glue, hold, unite **2** = **be consistent**, agree, be connected, be logical, correspond, hang together, harmonize, hold good, hold water, square

coherence *n* **1** = **consistency**, agreement, concordance, congruity, connection, consonance, correspondence, rationality, union, unity

coherent *adj* **1** = **intelligible**, articulate, comprehensible **2** = **consistent**, logical, lucid, meaningful, orderly, organized, rational, reasoned, systematic
Antonyms *adj* ≠ **intelligible**: incomprehensible, unintelligible ≠ **consistent**: confusing, disjointed, illogical, inconsistent, meaningless, rambling, vague

cohort *n* **2** = **company**, band, contingent, legion, regiment, squadron, troop **3** *Chiefly U.S.* =

coif (kɔɪf) *n* **1** a close-fitting cap worn under a veil in the Middle Ages. **2** a leather cap worn under a chain-mail hood. **3** (kwɑːf). a less common word for **coiffure** (sense 1). ◆ *vb* **coifs, coiffing, coiffed.** (*tr*) **4** to cover with or as if with a coif. **5** (kwɑːf). to arrange (the hair). [C14: from OF *coiffe,* from LL *cofea* helmet, cap, from ?]

coiffeur (kwɑːˈfɜː) *n* a hairdresser.
▸**coiffeuse** (kwɑːˈfɜːz) *fem n*

coiffure (kwɑːˈfjʊə) *n* **1** a hairstyle. **2** an obsolete word for **headdress.** ◆ *vb* **coiffures, coiffuring, coiffured. 3** (*tr*) to dress or arrange (the hair).

coign of vantage (kɔɪn) *n* an advantageous position for observation or action.

coil[1] Ⓣ (kɔɪl) *vb* **1** to wind or gather (ropes, hair, etc.) into loops or (of ropes, hair, etc.) to be formed in such loops. **2** (*intr*) to move in a winding course. ◆ *n* **3** something wound in a connected series of loops. **4** a single loop of such a series. **5** an arrangement of pipes in a spiral or loop, as in a condenser. **6** an electrical conductor wound into the form of a spiral, to provide inductance or a magnetic field. **7** an intrauterine contraceptive device in the shape of a coil. **8** the transformer in a petrol engine that supplies the high voltage to the sparking plugs. [C16: from OF *coillir* to collect together; see CULL]

coil[2] (kɔɪl) *n* the troubles of the world (in Shakespeare's phrase **this mortal coil**). [C16: from ?]

coin Ⓣ (kɔɪn) *n* **1** a metal disc or piece used as money. **2** metal currency, as opposed to paper currency, etc. **3** *Archit.* a variant spelling of **quoin. 4 pay (a person) back in (his) own coin.** to treat (a person) in the way that he has treated others. ◆ *vb* (*tr*) **5** to make or stamp (coins). **6** to make into a coin. **7** to fabricate or invent (words, etc.). **8** *Inf.* to make (money) rapidly (esp. in **coin it in**). [C14: from OF: stamping die, from L *cuneus* wedge]

coinage (ˈkɔɪnɪdʒ) *n* **1** coins collectively. **2** the act of striking coins. **3** the currency of a country. **4** the act of inventing something, esp. a word or phrase. **5** a newly invented word, phrase, usage, etc.

coincide Ⓣ (ˌkəʊɪnˈsaɪd) *vb* **coincides, coinciding, coincided.** (*intr*) **1** to occur or exist simultaneously. **2** to be identical in nature, character, etc. **3** to agree. [C18: from Med. L, from L *co-* together + *incidere* to occur, befall, from *cadere* to fall]

coincidence Ⓣ (kəʊˈɪnsɪdəns) *n* **1** a chance occurrence of events remarkable either for being simultaneous or for apparently being connected. **2** the fact, condition, or state of coinciding. **3** (*modifier*) *Electronics.* of or relating to a circuit that produces an output pulse only when both its input terminals receive pulses within a specified interval: *coincidence gate.*

coincident Ⓣ (kəʊˈɪnsɪdənt) *adj* **1** having the same position in space or time. **2** (usually *postpositive* and foll. by *with*) in exact agreement.
▸**coˌinciˈdental** *adj* ▸**coˌinciˈdentally** *adv*

coin-op (ˈkɔɪnˌɒp) *n* a launderette or other installation in which the machines are operated by the insertion of coins.
▸ˈ**coin-ˌoperˌated** *adj*

Cointreau (ˈkwɑːntrəʊ) *n Trademark.* a colourless liqueur with orange flavouring.

coir (ˈkɔɪə) *n* the fibre from the husk of the coconut, used in making rope and matting. [C16: from Malayalam *kāyar* rope, from *kāyaru* to be twisted]

coitus Ⓣ (ˈkəʊɪtəs) *or* **coition** (kəʊˈɪʃən) *n* a technical term for **sexual intercourse.** [C18: from L, from *coīre* to meet, from *īre* to go]
▸ˈ**coital** *adj*

coke[1] (kəʊk) *n* **1** a solid-fuel product produced by distillation of coal to drive off its volatile constituents: used as a fuel. **2** the layer formed in the cylinders of a car engine by incomplete combustion of the fuel. ◆ *vb* **cokes, coking, coked. 3** to become or convert into coke. [C17: prob. var. of C14 N English dialect *colk* core, from ?]

coke[2] (kəʊk) *n Sl.* short for **cocaine.**

Coke (kəʊk) *n Trademark.* short for **Coca-Cola.**

col (kɒl) *n* **1** Also called: **saddle.** the lowest point of a ridge connecting two mountain peaks. **2** *Meteorol.* a low-pressure region between two anticyclones. [C19: from F: neck, col, from L *collum* neck]

Col. *abbrev. for:* **1** Colombia(n). **2** Colonel. **3** *Bible.* Colossians.

Col. *abbrev. for:* **1** Colombia(n). **2** Colonel. **3** *Bible.* Colossians.

col- *prefix* a variant of **com-** before *l: collateral.*

cola *or* **kola** (ˈkəʊlə) *n* **1** either of two trees widely cultivated in tropical regions for their seeds (see **cola nut**). **2** a sweet carbonated drink flavoured with cola nuts. [C18: from *kola,* prob. var. of W African *kolo* nut]

colander (ˈkɒləndə, ˈkʌl-) *or* **cullender** *n* a pan with a perforated bottom for straining or rinsing foods. [C14 *colyndore,* prob. from OProvençal *colador,* from LL, from L *cōlum* sieve]

cola nut *n* any of the seeds of the cola tree, which contain caffeine and theobromine and are used medicinally and in soft drinks.

colchicine (ˈkɒltʃɪˌsiːn, -sɪn, ˈkɒlkɪ-) *n* a pale yellow crystalline alkaloid extracted from seeds or corms of the autumn crocus and used in the treatment of gout. [C19: from COLCHICUM + -INE[2]]

colchicum (ˈkɒltʃɪkəm, ˈkɒlkɪ-) *n* **1** any Eurasian plant of the lily family, such as the autumn crocus. **2** the dried seeds or corms of the autumn crocus. [C16: from L, from Gk, from *kolkhikos* of Colchis, ancient country on the Black Sea]

cold Ⓣ (kəʊld) *adj* **1** having relatively little warmth; of a rather low temperature: *cold weather; cold hands.* **2** without proper warmth: *this meal is cold.* **3** lacking in affection or enthusiasm: *a cold manner.* **4** not affected by emotion: *cold logic.* **5** dead. **6** sexually unresponsive or frigid. **7** lacking in freshness: *a cold scent; cold news.* **8** chilling to the spirit; depressing. **9** (of a colour) having violet, blue, or green predominating; giving no sensation of warmth. **10** *Sl.* unconscious. **11** *Inf.* (of a seeker) far from the object of a search. **12** denoting the contacting of potential customers, voters, etc., without previously approaching them in order to establish their interest: *cold mailing.* **13 cold comfort.** little or no comfort. **14 leave (someone) cold.** *Inf.* to fail to excite: *the performance left me cold.* **15 throw cold water on.** *Inf.* to be unenthusiastic about or discourage. ◆ *n* **16** the absence of heat regarded as a positive force: *the cold took away our breath.* **17** the sensation caused by loss or lack of heat. **18 (out) in the cold.** *Inf.* neglected; ignored. **19** an acute viral infection of the upper respiratory passages characterized by discharge of watery mucus from the nose, sneezing, etc. **20 catch a cold.** *Inf.* to make a financial loss. ◆ *adv* **21** *Inf.* without preparation: *he played his part cold.* [OE *ceald*]
▸ˈ**coldish** *adj* ▸ˈ**coldly** *adv* ▸ˈ**coldness** *n*

cold-blooded Ⓣ *adj* **1** having or showing a lack of feeling or pity. **2** *Inf.* particularly sensitive to cold. **3** (of all animals except birds and mammals) having a body temperature that varies with that of the surroundings. Technical name: **poikilothermic.**
▸ˌ**cold-ˈbloodedly** *adv* ▸ˌ**cold-ˈbloodedness** *n*

cold cathode *n Electronics.* a cathode from which electrons are emitted at an ambient temperature.

cold chisel *n* a toughened steel chisel.

cold cream *n* an emulsion of water and fat used for softening and cleansing the skin.

cold cuts *pl n* cooked meats sliced and served cold.

cold feet *n Inf.* loss or lack of confidence.

cold frame *n* an unheated wooden frame with a glass top, used to protect young plants.

cold front *n Meteorol.* the boundary line between a warm air mass and the cold air pushing it from beneath and behind as it moves.

cold-hearted Ⓣ *adj* lacking in feeling or warmth; unkind.
▸ˌ**cold-ˈheartedly** *adv* ▸ˌ**cold-ˈheartedness** *n*

cold-rolled *adj* (of metal sheets, etc.) having been rolled without heating, producing a smooth surface finish.

cold shoulder *Inf.* ◆ *n* **1** (often preceded by *the*) a show of indifference; a slight. ◆ *vb* **cold-shoulder.** (*tr*) **2** to treat with indifference.

cold sore *n* a cluster of blisters at the margin of the lips: a form of herpes simplex.

cold start *n Computing.* the reloading of a program or operating system.

cold storage *n* **1** the storage of things in an artificially cooled place for preservation. **2** *Inf.* a state of temporary suspension: *to put an idea into cold storage.*

THESAURUS

supporter, accomplice, assistant, associate, comrade, follower, henchman, mate, myrmidon, partner, protagonist, sidekick (*sl.*)

coil[1] *vb* **1, 2 = wind**, convolute, curl, entwine, loop, snake, spiral, twine, twist, wreathe, writhe

coin *n* **2 = money**, cash, change, copper, dosh (*Brit. & Austral. sl.*), silver, specie ◆ *vb* **7 = invent**, conceive, create, fabricate, forge, formulate, frame, make up, mint, mould, originate, think up

coincide *vb* **1 = occur simultaneously**, be concurrent, coexist, synchronize **3 = agree**, accord, concur, correspond, harmonize, match, square, tally
Antonyms *vb* ≠ **agree:** be inconsistent, be unlike, contradict, differ, disagree, diverge, divide, part, separate

coincidence *n* **1 = chance**, accident, eventuality, fluke, fortuity, happy accident, luck, stroke of luck **2 = coinciding**, concomitance, concurrence, conjunction, correlation, correspondence, synchronism

coincident *adj* **1 = coinciding**, concomitant, concurring, consonant, contemporaneous, coordinate, correspondent, synchronous

coincidental *adj* **1 = coinciding**, coincident, concomitant, concurrent, simultaneous, synchronous

coitus *n* **= sexual intercourse**, coition, congress, copulation, coupling, mating, nookie (*sl.*), rumpy-pumpy (*sl.*), the other (*inf.*), union

cold *adj* **1 = chilly**, arctic, biting, bitter, bleak, chilled, cool, freezing, frigid, frosty, frozen, gelid, harsh, icy, inclement, parky (*Brit. inf.*), raw, wintry **3 = unfriendly**, aloof, apathetic, cold-blooded, dead, distant, frigid, glacial, indifferent, inhospitable, lukewarm, passionless, phlegmatic, reserved, spiritless, standoffish, stony, undemonstrative, unfeeling, unmoved, unresponsive, unsympathetic ◆ *n* **16, 17 = coldness**, chill, chilliness, frigidity, frostiness, iciness
Antonyms *adj* ≠ **chilly:** balmy, heated, hot, mild, sunny, warm ≠ **unfriendly:** alive, animated, caring, compassionate, demonstrative, emotional, friendly, loving, open, passionate, responsive, spirited, sympathetic, warm

cold-blooded *adj* **1 = callous**, barbarous, brutal, cruel, dispassionate, heartless, inhuman, merciless, pitiless, ruthless, savage, steely, stony-hearted, unemotional, unfeeling, unmoved
Antonyms *adj* caring, charitable, civilized, concerned, emotional, feeling, friendly, humane, involved, kind, kind-hearted, merciful, open, passionate, sensitive, warm

cold-hearted *adj* **= heartless**, callous, detached, frigid, hardhearted, harsh, indifferent, inhuman, insensitive, stony-hearted, uncaring, unfeeling, unkind, unsympathetic

cold-heartedness *n* **= heartlessness**, callousness, chilliness, coldness, detachment, flintiness, frigidity, frigidness, hardheartedness, harshness, indifference, inhumanity, insensi-

cold sweat *n Inf.* a bodily reaction to fear or nervousness, characterized by chill and moist skin.
cold turkey *n Sl.* **1** a method of curing drug addiction by abrupt withdrawal of all doses. **2** the withdrawal symptoms, esp. nausea and shivering, brought on by this method.
cold war *n* a state of political hostility and military tension between two countries or power blocs, involving propaganda, threats, etc., esp. that between the American and Soviet blocs after World War II (the **Cold War**).
cold wave *n* **1** *Meteorol.* a sudden spell of low temperatures over a wide area. **2** *Hairdressing.* a permanent wave made by chemical agents applied at normal temperatures.
cole (kəʊl) *n* any of various plants such as the cabbage and rape. Also called: **colewort.** [OE *cāl*, from L *caulis* cabbage]
coleopter (ˌkɒlɪ'ɒptə) *n Aeronautics.* an aircraft that has an annular wing with the fuselage and engine on the centre line.
coleopteran (ˌkɒlɪ'ɒptərən) *n also* **coleopteron. 1** any of the order of insects in which the forewings are modified to form shell-like protective elytra. It includes the beetles and weevils. ◆ *adj also* **coleopterous. 2** of, relating to, or belonging to this order. [C18: from NL, from Gk, from *koleon* sheath + *pteron* wing]
coleslaw ('kəʊlˌslɔː) *n* a salad of shredded cabbage, mayonnaise, carrots, onions, etc. [C19: from Du. *koolsla*, from *koolsalade*, lit.: cabbage salad]
colestipol (kə'lɛstɪˌpɒl) *n* a drug that reduces the level of cholesterol in the blood: used to prevent atherosclerosis.
coletit ('kəʊltɪt) *n* another name for **coal tit.**
coleus ('kəʊlɪəs) *n, pl* **coleuses.** any plant of the Old World genus *Coleus:* cultivated for their variegated leaves. [C19: from NL, from Gk, var. of *koleon* sheath]
coley ('kəʊlɪ, 'kɒlɪ) *n Brit.* any of various edible fishes, esp. the coalfish.
colic ('kɒlɪk) *n* a condition characterized by acute spasmodic abdominal pain, esp. that caused by inflammation, distention, etc., of the gastrointestinal tract. [C15: from OF, from LL, from Gk *kōlon*, var. of *kolon* COLON[2]]
▸**'colicky** *adj*
coliform bacteria ('kɒlɪfɔːm) *pl n* a large group of bacteria that inhabit the intestinal tract of man.
coliseum (ˌkɒlɪ'sɪəm) *or* **colosseum** (ˌkɒlə'sɪəm) *n* a large building, such as a stadium, used for entertainments, sports, etc. [C18: from Med. L, var. of *Colosseum*, amphitheatre in Rome]
colitis (kɒ'laɪtɪs) *n* inflammation of the colon.
collaborate 🅣 (kə'læbəˌreɪt) *vb* **collaborates, collaborating, collaborated.** (*intr*) **1** (often foll. by *on, with,* etc.) to work with another or others on a joint project. **2** to cooperate as a traitor, esp. with an enemy occupying one's own country. [C19: from LL, from L *com-* together + *labōrāre* to work]
▸**colˌlabo'ration** *n* ▸**col'laborative** *adj* ▸**col'laboˌrator** *n*
collage (kə'lɑːʒ, kɒ-) *n* **1** an art form in which compositions are made out of pieces of paper, cloth, photographs, etc., pasted on a dry ground. **2** a composition made in this way. **3** any work, such as a piece of music, created by combining unrelated styles. [C20: F, from *colle* glue, from Gk *kolla*]
▸**col'lagist** *n*
collagen ('kɒlədʒən) *n* a fibrous protein of connective tissue and bones that yields gelatine on boiling. [C19: from Gk *kolla* glue + -GEN]
collapsar (kɒ'læpsɑː) *n Astron.* another name for **black hole.**
collapse 🅣 (kə'læps) *vb* **collapses, collapsing, collapsed. 1** (*intr*) to fall down or cave in suddenly: *the whole building collapsed.* **2** (*intr*) to fail completely. **3** (*intr*) to break down or fall down from lack of strength. **4** to fold (furniture, etc.) compactly or (of furniture, etc.) to be designed to fold compactly. ◆ *n* **5** the act or instance of suddenly falling down, caving in, or crumbling. **6** a sudden failure or breakdown. [C18: from L, from *collābī* to fall in ruins, from *lābī* to fall]
▸**col'lapsible** *or* **col'lapsable** *adj* ▸**colˌlapsi'bility** *n*
collar 🅣 ('kɒlə) *n* **1** the part of a garment around the neck and shoulders, often detachable or folded over. **2** any band, necklace, garland, etc., encircling the neck. **3** a band or chain of leather, rope, or metal placed around an animal's neck. **4** *Biol.* a marking resembling a collar, such as that found around the necks of some birds. **5** a section of a shaft or rod having a locally increased diameter to provide a bearing seat or a locating ring. **6** a cut of meat, esp. bacon, taken from around the neck of an animal. ◆ *vb* (*tr*) **7** to put a collar on; furnish with a collar. **8** to seize by the collar. **9** *Inf.* to seize; arrest; detain. [C13: from L *collāre* neckband, from *collum* neck]
collarbone ('kɒləˌbəʊn) *n* the nontechnical name for **clavicle.**
collard ('kɒləd) *n* a variety of the cabbage, having a crown of edible leaves. See also **kale.** [C18: var. of *colewort,* from COLE + WORT]
collate 🅣 (kɒ'leɪt, kə-) *vb* **collates, collating, collated.** (*tr*) **1** to examine and compare (texts, statements, etc.) in order to note points of agreement and disagreement. **2** to check the number and order of (the pages of a book). **3** *Bookbinding.* **3a** to check the sequence of (the sections of a book) after gathering. **3b** a nontechnical word for **gather** (sense 8). **4** (often foll. by *to*) *Christianity.* to appoint (an incumbent) to a benefice. [C16: from L, from *com-* together + *lātus,* p.p. of *ferre* to bring]
▸**col'lator** *n*
collateral 🅣 (kɒ'lætərəl, kə-) *n* **1a** security pledged for the repayment of a loan. **1b** (*as modifier*): *a collateral loan.* **2** a person, animal, or plant descended from the same ancestor as another but through a different line. ◆ *adj* **3** situated or running side by side. **4** descended from a common ancestor but through different lines. **5** serving to support or corroborate. [C14: from Med. L, from L *com-* together + *laterālis* of the side, from *latus* side]
▸**col'laterally** *adv*
collateral damage *n Mil.* unintentional damage to civil property and civilian casualties, caused by military operations.
collation (kɒ'leɪʃən, kə-) *n* **1** the act or process of collating. **2** a description of the technical features of a book. **3** *RC Church.* a light meal permitted on fast days. **4** any light informal meal.
colleague 🅣 ('kɒliːg) *n* a fellow worker or member of a staff, department, profession, etc. [C16: from F, from L *collēga,* from *com-* together + *lēgāre* to choose]
collect[1] 🅣 (kə'lɛkt) *vb* **1** to gather together or be gathered together. **2** to accumulate (stamps, books, etc.) as a hobby or for study. **3** (*tr*) to call for or receive payment of (taxes, dues, etc.). **4** (*tr*) to regain control of (oneself, one's emotions, etc.) as after a shock or surprise: *he collected his wits.* **5** (*tr*) to fetch: *collect your own post.* **6** (*intr;* sometimes foll. by *on*) *Sl.* to receive large sums of money. **7** (*tr*) *Austral. & NZ inf.* to collide with; be hit by. ◆ *adv, adj* **8** *US.* (of telephone calls, etc.) on a reverse-charge basis. [C16: from L, from *com-* together + *legere* to gather]
collect[2] ('kɒlɛkt) *n Christianity.* a short Church prayer in Communion and other services. [C13: from Med. L *collecta* (from *ōrātiō ad collēctam* prayer at the assembly), from L *colligere* to COLLECT[1]]
collectable *or* **collectible** (kə'lɛktəbəl) *adj* **1** (of antiques) of interest to a collector. ◆ *n* **2** (*often pl*) any object regarded as being of interest to a collector.
collected 🅣 (kə'lɛktɪd) *adj* **1** in full control of one's faculties; composed. **2** assembled in totality or brought together into one volume or a set of volumes: *the collected works of Dickens.*
▸**col'lectedly** *adv* ▸**col'lectedness** *n*
collection 🅣 (kə'lɛkʃən) *n* **1** the act or process of collecting. **2** a number of things collected or assembled together. **3** something gathered into a mass or pile; accumulation: *a collection of rubbish.* **4** a sum of money collected or solicited, as in church. **5** removal, esp. regular removal of letters from a postbox. **6** (*often pl*) (at Oxford University) a college examination or an oral report by a tutor.
collective 🅣 (kə'lɛktɪv) *adj* **1** formed or assembled by collection. **2** forming a whole or aggregate. **3** of, done by, or characteristic of individuals acting in cooperation. ◆ *n* **4a** a cooperative enterprise or unit, such as a collective farm. **4b** the members of such a cooperative. **5** short for **collective noun.**
▸**col'lectively** *adv* ▸**col'lectiveness** *n* ▸ˌ**collec'tivity** *n*
collective bargaining *n* negotiation between a trade union and an employer or an employers' organization on the incomes and working conditions of the employees.

THESAURUS

tiveness, insensitivity, mercilessness, pitilessness, steeliness, stony-heartedness, unfeelingness, unkindness, unresponsiveness
collaborate *vb* **1 = work together,** cooperate, coproduce, join forces, participate, play ball (*inf.*), team up **2 = conspire,** collude, cooperate, fraternize
collaboration *n* **1 = teamwork,** alliance, association, concert, cooperation, partnership
collaborator *n* **1 = co-worker,** associate, colleague, confederate, partner, team-mate **2 = traitor,** collaborationist, fraternizer, quisling, turncoat
collapse *vb* **1 = fall down,** cave in, crumple, fall, fall apart at the seams, give way, subside **2 = fail,** come to nothing, fold, founder, go belly-up (*inf.*) **3 = faint,** break down, crack up ◆ *n* **5 = falling down,** cave-in, disintegration, falling apart, ruin, subsidence **6 = failure,** breakdown, downfall, exhaustion, faint, flop, prostration, slump
collar *vb* **9** *Informal* **= seize,** apprehend, appropriate, arrest, capture, catch, catch in the act, grab, lay hands on, nab (*inf.*), nail (*inf.*)
collate *vb* **1 = collect,** adduce, analogize, compare, compose, gather (*Printing*)
collateral *n* **1a = security,** assurance, deposit, guarantee, pledge, surety ◆ *adj* **3 = concurrent,** not lineal, parallel **4 = related 5 = secondary,** ancillary, auxiliary, confirmatory, corroborative, subordinate, supporting
colleague *n* **= fellow worker,** aider, ally, assistant, associate, auxiliary, coadjutor (*rare*), collaborator, companion, comrade, confederate, confrère, helper, partner, team-mate, workmate
collect[1] *vb* **1 = assemble,** cluster, congregate, convene, converge, flock together, rally **2 = gather,** accumulate, aggregate, amass, assemble, heap, hoard, save, stockpile **6 = obtain,** acquire, muster, raise, secure, solicit
Antonyms *vb* ≠ **gather:** disperse, distribute, scatter, spread, strew
collected *adj* **1 = calm,** as cool as a cucumber, composed, confident, cool, keeping one's cool, placid, poised, sedate, self-controlled, self-possessed, serene, together (*sl.*), unfazed (*inf.*), unperturbable, unperturbed, unruffled
Antonyms *adj* agitated, distressed, emotional, excitable, irritable, nervous, perturbed, ruffled, shaky, troubled, twitchy (*inf.*), unpoised, unsteady
collection *n* **2, 3 = accumulation,** anthology, compilation, congeries, heap, hoard, mass, pile, set, stockpile, store **4 = contribution,** alms, offering, offertory
collective *adj* **2, 3 = combined,** aggregate, common, composite, concerted, cooperative, corporate, cumulative, joint, shared, unified, united
Antonyms *adj* divided, individual, piecemeal, split, uncombined, uncooperative

collective noun *n* a noun that is singular in form but that refers to a group of people or things.

> **USAGE NOTE** Collective nouns are usually used with singular verbs: *the family is on holiday; General Motors is mounting a big sales campaign.* In British usage, however, plural verbs are sometimes employed in this context, esp. where reference is being made to a collection of individual objects or people rather than to the group as a unit: *the family are all on holiday.* Care should be taken that the same collective noun is not treated as both singular and plural in the same sentence: *the family is well and sends its best wishes* or *the family are all well and send their best wishes,* but not *the family is well and send their best wishes.*

collective ownership *n* ownership by a group for the benefit of members of that group.
collective unconscious *n* (in Jungian psychological theory) a part of the unconscious mind incorporating patterns of memories, instincts, and experiences common to all mankind.
collectivism (kəˈlɛktɪˌvɪzəm) *n* the principle of ownership of the means of production by the state or the people.
▸**colˈlectivist** *n* ▸**colˌlectivˈistic** *adj*
collectivize *or* **collectivise** (kəˈlɛktɪˌvaɪz) *vb* **collectivizes, collectivizing, collectivized** *or* **collectivises, collectivising, collectivised.** (*tr*) to organize according to the principles of collectivism.
▸**colˌlectiviˈzation** *or* **colˌlectiviˈsation** *n*
collector ⓣ (kəˈlɛktə) *n* **1** a person or thing that collects. **2** a person employed to collect debts, rents, etc. **3** a person who collects objects as a hobby. **4** (in India, formerly) the head of a district administration. **5** *Electronics.* the region in a transistor into which charge carriers flow from the base.
colleen (ˈkɒliːn, kɒˈliːn) *n* an Irish word for **girl.** [C19: from Irish Gaelic *cailīn*]
college (ˈkɒlɪdʒ) *n* **1** an institution of higher education; part of a university. **2** a school or an institution providing specialized courses: *a college of music.* **3** the buildings in which a college is housed. **4** the staff and students of a college. **5** an organized body of persons with specific rights and duties: *an electoral college.* **6** a body organized within a particular profession, concerned with regulating standards. **7** *Brit.* a name given to some secondary schools. [C14: from L, from *collēga;* see COLLEAGUE]
College of Cardinals *n RC Church.* the collective body of cardinals having the function of electing and advising the pope.
college of education *n Brit.* a professional training college for teachers.
collegian (kəˈliːdʒɪən) *n* a member of a college.
collegiate (kəˈliːdʒɪɪt) *adj* **1** Also: **colˈlegial.** of or relating to a college or college students. **2** (of a university) composed of various colleges of equal standing.
collegiate church *n* **1** *RC Church, Church of England.* a church that has an endowed chapter of canons and prebendaries attached to it but that is not a cathedral. **2** *US Protestantism.* one of a group of churches presided over by a body of pastors. **3** *Scot. Protestantism.* a church served by two or more ministers.
col legno (ˈkɒl ˈlɛgnəʊ, ˈleɪnjəʊ) *adv Music.* to be played (on a stringed instrument) with the back of the bow. [It.: with the wood]
Colles' fracture (ˈkɒlɪs) *n* a fracture of the radius just above the wrist with backward and outward displacement of the hand. [C19: after Abraham *Colles* (d. 1843), Irish surgeon]
collet (ˈkɒlɪt) *n* **1** (in a jewellery setting) a band or coronet-shaped claw that holds an individual stone. **2** *Mechanical engineering.* an externally tapered sleeve made in two or more segments and used to grip a shaft passed through its centre. **3** *Horology.* a small metal collar that supports the inner end of the hairspring. [C16: from OF: a little collar, from *col,* from L *collum* neck]
collide ⓣ (kəˈlaɪd) *vb* **collides, colliding, collided.** (*intr*) **1** to crash together with a violent impact. **2** to conflict; clash; disagree. [C17: from L, from *com-* together + *laedere* to strike]
collider (kəˈlaɪdə) *n Physics.* a particle accelerator in which beams of particles are made to collide.
collie (ˈkɒlɪ) *n* any of several silky-coated breeds of dog developed for herding sheep and cattle. [C17: Scot., prob. from earlier *colie* black from *cole* coal]
collier (ˈkɒlɪə) *n Chiefly Brit.* **1** a coal miner. **2a** a ship designed to transport coal. **2b** a member of its crew. [C14: from COAL + -IER]
colliery (ˈkɒljərɪ) *n, pl* **collieries.** *Chiefly Brit.* a coal mine.
collimate (ˈkɒlɪˌmeɪt) *vb* **collimates, collimating, collimated.** (*tr*) **1** to adjust the line of sight of (an optical instrument). **2** to use a collimator on (a beam of radiation). **3** to make parallel or bring into line. [C17: from NL *collimāre,* erroneously for L *collīneāre* to aim, from *com-* (intensive) + *līneāre,* from *līnea* line]
▸**ˌcolliˈmation** *n*
collimator (ˈkɒlɪˌmeɪtə) *n* **1** a small telescope attached to a larger optical instrument as an aid in fixing its line of sight. **2** an optical system of lenses and slits producing a nondivergent beam of light. **3** any device for limiting the size and angle of spread of a beam of radiation or particles.
collinear (kɒˈlɪnɪə) *adj* lying on the same straight line.
▸**collinearity** (ˌkɒlɪnɪˈærɪtɪ) *n*
collins (ˈkɒlɪnz) *n* (*functioning as sing*) an iced drink made with gin, vodka, rum, etc., mixed with fruit juice, soda water, and sugar. [C20: prob. from the name *Collins*]
collision ⓣ (kəˈlɪʒən) *n* **1** a violent impact of moving objects; crash. **2** the conflict of opposed ideas, wishes, attitudes, etc. [C15: from LL, from L *collīdere* to COLLIDE]
collocate (ˈkɒləˌkeɪt) *vb* **collocates, collocating, collocated.** (*tr*) to group or place together in some system or order. [C16: from L, from *com-* together + *locāre* to place]
▸**ˌcolloˈcation** *n*
collocutor (ˈkɒləˌkjuːtə) *n* a person who talks or engages in conversation with another.
collodion (kəˈləʊdɪən) *or* **collodium** (kəˈləʊdɪəm) *n* a syrupy liquid that consists of a solution of pyroxylin in ether and alcohol: used in medicine and in the manufacture of photographic plates, lacquers, etc. [C19: from NL, from Gk *kollōdēs* glutinous, from *kolla* glue]
collogue (kɒˈləʊg) *vb* **collogues, colloguing, collogued.** (*intr;* usually foll. by *with*) to confer confidentially; conspire. [C16: ?from obs. *colleague* (vb) to conspire, infl. by L *colloquī* to talk with]
colloid (ˈkɒlɔɪd) *n* **1** a mixture having particles of one component suspended in a continuous phase of another component. The mixture has properties between those of a solution and a fine suspension. **2** *Physiol.* a gelatinous substance of the thyroid follicles that holds the hormonal secretions of the thyroid gland. [C19: from Gk *kolla* glue + -OID]
▸**colˈloidal** *adj*
collop (ˈkɒləp) *n Dialect.* **1** a slice of meat. **2** a small piece of anything. [C14: of Scand. origin]
colloq. *abbrev. for* colloquial(ly).
colloquial ⓣ (kəˈləʊkwɪəl) *adj* **1** of or relating to conversation. **2** denoting or characterized by informal or conversational idiom or vocabulary.
▸**colˈloquially** *adv* ▸**colˈloquialness** *n*
colloquialism (kəˈləʊkwɪəˌlɪzəm) *n* **1** a word or phrase appropriate to conversation and other informal situations. **2** the use of colloquial words and phrases.
colloquium (kəˈləʊkwɪəm) *n, pl* **colloquiums** *or* **colloquia** (-kwɪə). **1** a gathering for discussion. **2** an academic seminar. [C17: from L: COLLOQUY]
colloquy (ˈkɒləkwɪ) *n, pl* **colloquies. 1** a formal conversation or conference. **2** an informal conference on religious or theological matters. [C16: from L *colloquium,* from *com-* together + *loquī* to speak]
▸**ˈcolloquist** *n*
collotype (ˈkɒləʊˌtaɪp) *n* **1** a method of lithographic printing (usually of high-quality reproductions) from a plate of hardened gelatine. **2** a print so made.
collude ⓣ (kəˈluːd) *vb* **colludes, colluding, colluded.** (*intr*) to conspire together, esp. in planning a fraud. [C16: from L, from *com-* together + *lūdere* to play]
▸**colˈluder** *n*
collusion ⓣ (kəˈluːʒən) *n* **1** secret agreement for a fraudulent purpose; conspiracy. **2** a secret agreement between opponents at law for some improper purpose. [C14: from L, from *collūdere* to COLLUDE]
▸**colˈlusive** *adj*
collywobbles (ˈkɒlɪˌwɒbᵊlz) *pl n* (usually preceded by *the*) *Sl.* **1** an upset stomach. **2** an intense feeling of nervousness. [C19: prob. from NL *cholera morbus,* infl. through folk etymology by COLIC and WOBBLE]
colobus (ˈkɒləbəs) *n* any leaf-eating arboreal Old World monkey of W and central Africa, having long silky fur and reduced or absent thumbs. [C19: NL, from Gk *kolobos* cut short; referring to its thumb]
cologarithm (kəʊˈlɒgəˌrɪðəm) *n* the logarithm of the reciprocal of a number; the negative value of the logarithm: *the cologarithm of 4 is log ¼.* Abbrev.: **colog.**
cologne (kəˈləʊn) *n* a perfumed liquid or solid made of fragrant essential oils and alcohol. Also called: **Cologne water, eau de cologne.** [C18: *Cologne water* from Cologne, where it was first manufactured]
colon[1] (ˈkəʊlən) *n, pl* **colons. 1** the punctuation mark : , usually preceding an explanation or an example, a list, or an extended quotation. **2** this mark used for certain other purposes, such as when a ratio is given in figures, as in *5:3.* [C16: from L, from Gk *kōlon* limb, clause]
colon[2] (ˈkəʊlən) *n, pl* **colons** *or* **cola** (-lə). the part of the large intestine between the caecum and the rectum. [C16: from L: large intestine, from Gk *kolon*]
▸**colonic** (kəˈlɒnɪk) *adj*
colón (kəʊˈləʊn; *Spanish* koˈlon) *n, pl* **colons** *or* **colones** (*Spanish* -ˈlones). **1** the standard monetary unit of Costa Rica, divided into 100 céntimos.

THESAURUS

collector *n* **1** = **gatherer**, acquirer, amasser, hoarder, saver, stockpiler
collide *vb* **1** = **crash**, clash, come into collision, meet head-on **2** = **conflict**, clash
collision *n* **1** = **crash**, accident, bump, impact, pile-up (*inf.*), prang (*inf.*), smash **2** = **conflict**, clash, clashing, confrontation, encounter, opposition, skirmish
colloquial *adj* **2** = **informal**, conversational, demotic, everyday, familiar, idiomatic, vernacular
collude *vb* = **conspire**, abet, be in cahoots (*inf.*), collaborate, complot, connive, contrive, intrigue, machinate, plot, scheme
collusion *n* **1** = **conspiracy**, cahoots (*inf.*), complicity, connivance, craft, deceit, fraudulent artifice, intrigue, secret understanding

2 the standard monetary unit of El Salvador, divided into 100 centavos. [C19: American Sp., from Sp., after Cristóbal *Colón* Christopher Columbus]

colonel (ˈkɜːnᵊl) *n* an officer of land or air forces junior to a brigadier but senior to a lieutenant colonel. [C16: via OF, from OIt. *colonnello* column of soldiers, from *colonna* COLUMN]
▸**ˈcolonelcy** *or* **ˈcolonelship** *n*

colonial (kəˈləʊnɪəl) *adj* **1** of, characteristic of, relating to, possessing, or inhabiting a colony or colonies. **2** (*often cap.*) characteristic of or relating to the 13 British colonies that became the United States of America (1776). **3** (*often cap.*) of or relating to the colonies of the British Empire. **4** denoting or having the style of Neoclassical architecture used in the British colonies in America in the 17th and 18th centuries. **5** of or relating to the period of Australian history before federation (1901). **6** (of animals and plants) having become established in a community in a new environment. ◆ *n* **7** a native of a colony.
▸**coˈlonially** *adv*

colonial goose *n NZ.* an old-fashioned name for stuffed roast mutton.

colonialism (kəˈləʊnɪəˌlɪzəm) *n* the policy and practice of a power in extending control over weaker peoples or areas. Also called: **imperialism.**
▸**coˈlonialist** *n, adj*

Colonies (ˈkɒlənɪz) *pl n* **the. 1** *Brit.* the subject territories formerly in the British Empire. **2** *US history.* the 13 states forming the original United States of America when they declared their independence (1776).

colonist ➊ (ˈkɒlənɪst) *n* **1** a person who settles or colonizes an area. **2** an inhabitant of a colony.

colonize ➊ *or* **colonise** (ˈkɒləˌnaɪz) *vb* **colonizes, colonizing, colonized** *or* **colonises, colonising, colonised. 1** to send colonists to or establish a colony in (an area). **2** to settle in (an area) as colonists. **3** (*tr*) to transform (a community, etc.) into a colony. **4** (of plants and animals) to become established in (a new environment).
▸**ˌcoloniˈzation** *or* **ˌcoloniˈsation** *n* ▸**ˈcoloˌnizer** *or* **ˈcoloˌniser** *n*

colonnade ➊ (ˌkɒləˈneɪd) *n* **1** a set of evenly spaced columns. **2** a row of regularly spaced trees. [C18: from F, from *colonne* COLUMN; on the model of It. *colonnato*]
▸**ˌcolonˈnaded** *adj*

colony ➊ (ˈkɒlənɪ) *n, pl* **colonies. 1** a body of people who settle in a country distant from their homeland but maintain ties with it. **2** the community formed by such settlers. **3** a subject territory occupied by a settlement from the ruling state. **4a** a community of people who form a national, racial, or cultural minority concentrated in a particular place: *an artists' colony.* **4b** the area itself. **5** *Zool.* a group of the same type of animal or plant living or growing together. **6** *Bacteriol.* a group of bacteria, fungi, etc., derived from one or a few spores, esp. when grown on a culture medium. [C16: from L, from *colere* to cultivate, inhabit]

colony-stimulating factor *n Immunol.* any of a number of substances, secreted by the bone marrow, that stimulate the formation of blood cells. Synthetic forms are being tested for their ability to reduce the toxic effects of chemotherapy. Abbrev.: **CSF.**

colophon (ˈkɒləˌfɒn, -fən) *n* **1** a publisher's emblem on a book. **2** (formerly) an inscription at the end of a book showing the title, printer, date, etc. [C17: via LL, from Gk *kolophōn* a finishing stroke]

colophony (kɒˈlɒfənɪ) *n* another name for **rosin** (sense 1). [C14: from L: resin from Colophon, town in Lydia]

color (ˈkʌlə) *n, vb* the US spelling of **colour.**

Colorado beetle (ˌkɒləˈrɑːdəʊ) *n* a black-and-yellow beetle that is a serious pest of potatoes, feeding on the leaves. [from *Colorado*, state of central US]

colorant (ˈkʌlərənt) *n* any substance that imparts colour, such as a pigment, dye, or ink.

coloration *or* **colouration** (ˌkʌləˈreɪʃən) *n* **1** arrangement of colour; colouring. **2** the colouring or markings of insects, birds, etc.

coloratura (ˌkɒlərəˈtʊərə) *n Music.* **1** (in 18th- and 19th-century arias) a florid virtuoso passage. **2** Also called: **coloratura soprano.** a soprano who specializes in such music. [C19: from obs. It., lit.: colouring.]

colorific (ˌkʌləˈrɪfɪk) *adj* producing, imparting, or relating to colour.

colorimeter (ˌkʌləˈrɪmɪtə) *n* apparatus for measuring the quality of a colour by comparison with standard colours or combinations of colours.
▸**colorimetric** (ˌkʌlərɪˈmɛtrɪk) *adj* ▸**ˌcolorˈimetry** *n*

colossal ➊ (kəˈlɒsᵊl) *adj* **1** of immense size; huge; gigantic. **2** (in figure sculpture) approximately twice life-size. **3** *Archit.* of the order of columns that extend more than one storey in a façade.
▸**coˈlossally** *adv*

colossus (kəˈlɒsəs) *n, pl* **colossi** (-saɪ) *or* **colossuses.** something very large, esp. a statue. [C14: from L, from Gk *kolossos*]

Colossus of Rhodes *n* a giant bronze statue of Apollo built on Rhodes in about 292–280 B.C.; destroyed by an earthquake in 225 B.C.; one of the Seven Wonders of the World.

colostomy (kəˈlɒstəmɪ) *n, pl* **colostomies.** the surgical formation of an opening from the colon onto the surface of the body, which functions as an anus.

colostrum (kəˈlɒstrəm) *n* the thin milky secretion from the nipples that precedes and follows true lactation. [C16: from L, from ?]

colotomy (kəˈlɒtəmɪ) *n, pl* **colotomies.** a colonic incision. [C19: COLON[2] + -TOMY]

colour ➊ *or US* **color** (ˈkʌlə) *n* **1a** an attribute of things that results from the light they reflect or emit in so far as this causes a visual sensation that depends on its wavelengths. **1b** the aspect of visual perception by which an observer recognizes this attribute. **1c** the quality of the light producing this visual perception. **2** Also called: **chromatic colour. 2a** a colour, such as red or green, that possesses hue, as opposed to achromatic colours such as white or black. **2b** (*as modifier*): *colour television.* **3** a substance, such as a dye or paint, that imparts colour. **4a** the skin complexion of a person, esp. as determined by his race. **4b** (*as modifier*): *colour prejudice.* **5** the use of all the hues in painting as distinct from composition, form, and light and shade. **6** the quantity and quality of ink used in a printing process. **7** the distinctive tone of a musical sound. **8** vividness or authenticity: *period colour.* **9** semblance or pretext: *under colour of.* **10** *Physics.* one of three characteristics of quarks, designated red, blue, or green, but having only a remote formal relationship with the physical sensation. ◆ *vb* **11** (*tr*) to apply colour to (something). **12** (*tr*) to give a convincing appearance to: *to colour an alibi.* **13** (*tr*) to influence or distort: *anger coloured her judgment.* **14** (*intr;* often foll. by *up*) to become red in the face, esp. when embarrassed or annoyed. ◆ See also **colours.** [C13 from OF *colour* from L *color* tint, hue]

colourable (ˈkʌlərəbᵊl) *adj* **1** capable of being coloured. **2** appearing to be true; plausible. **3** pretended; feigned.

colour bar *n* discrimination against people of a different race, esp. as practised by Whites against Blacks.

colour-blind *adj* of or relating to any defect in the normal ability to distinguish certain colours.
▸**colour blindness** *n*

colour code *n* a system of easily distinguishable colours, as for the identification of electrical wires or resistors.

coloured (ˈkʌləd) *adj* **1** possessing colour. **2** having a strong element of fiction or fantasy; distorted (esp. in **highly coloured**).

Coloured (ˈkʌləd) *n* **1** an individual who is not a White person, esp. a Black person. **2** Also called: **Cape Coloured.** (in South Africa) a person of racially mixed parentage or descent. ◆ *adj* **3a** (in South Africa) designating or relating to a person or people of racially mixed descent. **3b** designating or relating to a person or people who are not White.

> **USAGE NOTE** The use of *Coloured* to refer to people is now generally considered to be offensive.

colourfast (ˈkʌləˌfɑːst) *adj* (of a fabric) having a colour that does not run or change when washed or worn.
▸**ˈcolourˌfastness** *n*

colourful ➊ (ˈkʌləfʊl) *adj* **1** having intense colour or richly varied colours. **2** vivid, rich, or distinctive in character.
▸**ˈcolourfully** *adv*

colour guard *n* a military guard in a parade, ceremony, etc., that carries and escorts the flag.

colouring (ˈkʌlərɪŋ) *n* **1** the process or art of applying colour. **2** anything used to give colour, such as paint. **3** appearance with regard to shade and colour. **4** arrangements of colours, as in the markings of birds. **5** the colour of a person's complexion. **6** a false or misleading appearance.

colourist (ˈkʌlərɪst) *n* a person who uses colour, esp. an artist.

colourize, colourise, *or US* **colorize** (ˈkʌləˌraɪz) *vb* **colourizes, colourizing, colourized** *or* **colourises, colourising, colourised** *or US* **colorizes,**

THESAURUS

colonist *n* **1** = **settler**, colonial, colonizer, frontiersman, homesteader (*US*), immigrant, pioneer, planter

colonize *vb* **1, 2** = **settle**, open up, people, pioneer, populate, put down roots

colonnade *n* **1** = **cloisters**, arcade, covered walk, peristyle, portico

colony *n* **3** = **settlement**, community, dependency, dominion, outpost, possession, province, satellite state, territory

colossal *adj* **1** = **huge**, Brobdingnagian, elephantine, enormous, gargantuan, gigantic, ginormous (*inf.*), herculean, humongous *or* humungous (*US sl.*), immense, mammoth, massive, monstrous, monumental, mountainous, prodigious, stellar (*inf.*), titanic, vast
Antonyms *adj* average, diminutive, little, miniature, minute, ordinary, pygmy *or* pigmy, slight, small, tiny, weak, wee

colour *n* **3** = **hue**, colorant, coloration, complexion, dye, paint, pigment, pigmentation, shade, tincture, tinge, tint **9** = **pretext**, appearance, disguise, excuse, façade, false show, guise, plea, pretence, semblance ◆ *vb* **11** = **paint**, colourwash, dye, stain, tinge, tint **13** = **misrepresent**, disguise, distort, embroider, exaggerate, falsify, garble, gloss over, pervert, prejudice, slant, taint **14** = **blush**, burn, crimson, flush, go as red as a beetroot, go crimson, redden

colourful *adj* **1** = **bright**, brilliant, Day-glo (*Trademark*), intense, jazzy (*inf.*), kaleidoscopic, motley, multicoloured, psychedelic, rich, variegated, vibrant, vivid **2** = **interesting**, characterful, distinctive, graphic, lively, picturesque, rich, stimulating, unusual, vivid
Antonyms *adj* ≠ **bright:** colourless, dark, drab, dreary, dull, faded, pale, washed out ≠ **interesting:** boring, characterless, dull, flat, lifeless, monotonous, unexciting, uninteresting, unvaried

colorizing, colorized. (*tr*) to add colour electronically to (an old black-and-white film).
▸ˌ**colouri'zation,** ˌ**colouri'sation** *or US* ˌ**colori'zation** *n*

colourless ⓘ ('kʌləlɪs) *adj* **1** without colour. **2** lacking in interest: *a colourless individual.* **3** grey or pallid in tone or hue. **4** without prejudice; neutral.
▸**'colourlessly** *adv*

colours ⓘ ('kʌləz) *pl n* **1a** the flag that indicates nationality. **1b** *Mil.* the ceremony of hoisting or lowering the colours. **2** a pair of silk flags borne by a military unit and showing its crest and battle honours. **3** true nature or character (esp. in **show one's colours**). **4** a distinguishing badge or flag. **5** *Sport, Brit.* a badge or other symbol denoting membership of a team, esp. at a school or college. **6 nail one's colours to the mast. 6a** to commit oneself publicly and irrevocably to some party, course of action, etc. **6b** to refuse to admit defeat.

colour sergeant *n* a sergeant who carries the regimental, battalion, or national colours.

colour supplement *n Brit.* an illustrated magazine accompanying a newspaper.

colourway ('kʌləˌweɪ) *n* one of several different combinations of colours in which a given pattern is printed on fabrics or wallpapers, etc.

colposcope ('kɒlpəˌskəʊp) *n* an instrument for examining the cervix. [C20: from Gk *kolpos* womb + -SCOPE]

colt (kəʊlt) *n* **1** a male horse or pony under the age of four. **2** *Sport.* **2a** a young and inexperienced player. **2b** a member of a junior team. [OE *colt* young ass]

colter ('kəʊltə) *n* a variant spelling (esp. US) of **coulter.**

coltish ⓘ ('kəʊltɪʃ) *adj* **1** inexperienced; unruly. **2** playful and lively.
▸**'coltishness** *n*

coltsfoot ('kəʊltsˌfʊt) *n, pl* **coltsfoots.** a European plant with yellow daisy-like flowers and heart-shaped leaves: a common weed.

colubrine ('kɒljʊˌbraɪn) *adj* **1** of or resembling a snake. **2** of or belonging to the Colubrinae, a subfamily of harmless snakes. [C16: from L *colubrīnus,* from *coluber* snake]

columbine ('kɒləmˌbaɪn) *n* any plant of the genus *Aquilegia,* having flowers with five spurred petals. Also called: **aquilegia.** [C13: from Med. L *columbīna herba* dovelike plant]

Columbine ('kɒləmˌbaɪn) *n* the sweetheart of Harlequin in English pantomime.

column ⓘ ('kɒləm) *n* **1** an upright pillar usually having a cylindrical shaft, a base, and a capital. **2a** a form or structure in the shape of a column: *a column of air.* **2b** a monument. **3** a line, as of people in a queue. **4** *Mil.* a narrow formation in which individuals or units follow one behind the other. **5** *Journalism.* **5a** any of two or more vertical sections of type on a printed page, esp. on a newspaper page. **5b** a regular feature in a paper: *the fashion column.* **6** a vertical array of numbers. [C15: from L *columna,* from *columen* top, peak]
▸**columnar** (kə'lʌmnə) *adj* ▸**'columned** *adj*

column inch *n* a unit of measurement for advertising space, one inch deep and one column wide.

columnist ⓘ ('kɒləmnɪst, -əmɪst) *n* a journalist who writes a regular feature in a newspaper.

colure (kə'lʊə, 'kəʊlʊə) *n* either of two great circles on the celestial sphere, one passing through the poles and the equinoxes, the other through the poles and the solstices. [C16: from LL, from Gk *kolourai,* dock-tailed, from *kolos* docked + *oura* tail (because the lower portion is not visible)]

colza ('kɒlzə) *n* another name for **rape**[2]. [C18: via F (Walloon) from Du., from *kool* cabbage, COLE + *zaad* SEED]

COM (kɒm) *n* direct conversion of computer output to microfiche or film. [C20: *C(omputer) O(utput on) M(icrofilm)*]

Com. *abbrev. for:* **1** Commander. **2** Committee. **3** Commodore. **4** Communist.

com- *or* **con-** *prefix* together; with; jointly: *commingle.* [from L *com-;* rel. to *cum* with. In compound words of L origin, *com-* becomes *col-* and *cor-* before *l* and *r, co-* before *gn, h,* and most vowels, and *con-* before consonants other than *b, p,* and *m*]

coma[1] ⓘ ('kəʊmə) *n, pl* **comas.** a state of unconsciousness from which a person cannot be aroused, caused by injury, narcotics, poisons, etc. [C17: from medical L, from Gk *kōma* heavy sleep]

coma[2] ('kəʊmə) *n, pl* **comae** (-miː). **1** *Astron.* the luminous cloud surrounding the nucleus in the head of a comet. **2** *Bot.* **2a** a tuft of hairs attached to the seed coat of some seeds. **2b** the terminal crown of leaves of palms and moss stems. [C17: from L: hair of the head, from Gk *komē*]

comanche (kə'mæntʃɪ) *n* **1** (*pl* **comanches** *or* **comanche**) a member of a North American Indian people formerly inhabiting the W plains of the US. **2** the language of this people.

comatose ⓘ ('kəʊməˌtəʊs) *adj* **1** in a state of coma. **2** torpid; lethargic.

comb ⓘ (kəʊm) *n* **1** a toothed device for disentangling or arranging hair. **2** a tool or machine that cleans and straightens wool, cotton, etc. **3** *Austral. & NZ.* the fixed cutter on a sheep-shearing machine. **4** anything resembling a comb in form or function. **5** the fleshy serrated outgrowth on the heads of certain birds, esp. the domestic fowl. **6** a honeycomb. ◆ *vb* **7** (*tr*) to use a comb on. **8** (when *tr,* often foll. by *through*) to search with great care: *the police combed the woods.* ◆ **See also comb out.** [OE *camb*]

combat ⓘ *n* ('kɒmbæt, -bət, 'kʌm-). **1** a fight, conflict, or struggle. **2a** an action fought between two military forces. **2b** (*as modifier*): *a combat jacket.* **3 single combat.** a duel. ◆ *vb* (kəm'bæt; 'kɒmbæt, 'kʌm-). **-bats, -bating, -bated. 4** (*tr*) to fight. **5** (*intr;* often foll. by *with* or *against*) to struggle or strive (against): *to combat against disease.* [C16: from F, from OF *combattre,* from Vulgar L *combattere* (unattested), from L *com-* with + *battuere* to beat]

combatant ⓘ ('kɒmbətᵊnt, 'kʌm-) *n* **1** a person or group engaged in or prepared for a fight. ◆ *adj* **2** engaged in or ready for combat.

combat fatigue *n* another term for **battle fatigue.**

combative ⓘ ('kɒmbətɪv, 'kʌm-) *adj* eager or ready to fight, argue, etc.
▸**'combativeness** *n*

combe *or* **comb** (kuːm) *n* variant spellings of **coomb.**

comber ('kəʊmə) *n* **1** a person, tool, or machine that combs wool, flax, etc. **2** a long curling wave; roller.

combination ⓘ (ˌkɒmbɪ'neɪʃən) *n* **1** the act of combining or state of being combined. **2** a union of separate parts, qualities, etc. **3** an alliance of people or parties. **4** the set of numbers that opens a combination lock. **5** *Brit.* a motorcycle with a sidecar attached. **6** *Maths.* an arrangement of the numbers, terms, etc., of a set into specified groups without regard to order in the group. **7** the chemical reaction of two or more compounds, usually to form one other compound. **8** *Chess.* a tactical manoeuvre involving a sequence of moves and more than one piece.
▸ˌ**combi'national** *adj*

combination lock *n* a type of lock that can only be opened when a set of dials is turned to show a specific sequence of numbers.

combinations (ˌkɒmbɪ'neɪʃənz) *pl n Brit.* a one-piece undergarment with long sleeves and legs. Often shortened to **combs** or **coms.**

combine ⓘ *vb* (kəm'baɪn), **combines, combining, combined. 1** to join together. **2** to unite or cause to unite to form a chemical compound. ◆ *n* ('kɒmbaɪn). **3** short for **combine harvester. 4** an association of enterprises, esp. in order to gain a monopoly of a market. **5** an association of related bodies, such as business corporations or sports clubs, for a common purpose. [C15: from LL *combīnāre,* from L *com-* together + *bīnī* two by two]
▸**com'binable** *adj* ▸**comˌbina'bility** *n* ▸**combinative** ('kɒmbɪˌneɪtɪv) *or* **combinatory** ('kɒmbɪˌneɪtərɪ) *adj*

combine harvester ('kɒmbaɪn) *n* a machine that simultaneously cuts, threshes, and cleans a standing crop of grain.

combings ('kəʊmɪŋz) *pl n* **1** the loose hair removed by combing. **2** the unwanted fibres removed in combing cotton, etc.

combining form *n* a linguistic element that occurs only as part of a compound word, such as *anthropo-* in *anthropology* and *anthropomorph.*

THESAURUS

colourless *adj* **1, 3 = drab,** achromatic, achromic, anaemic, ashen, bleached, faded, neutral, sickly, wan, washed out **2 = uninteresting,** characterless, dreary, dull, insipid, lacklustre, tame, unmemorable, vacuous, vapid
Antonyms *adj* **≠ drab:** blooming, flushed, glowing, healthy, radiant, robust, ruddy **≠ uninteresting:** animated, bright, colourful, compelling, distinctive, exciting, interesting, unusual

colours *pl n* **1a = flag,** banner, emblem, ensign, standard **3** *As in* **show one's colours = nature,** aspect, breed, character, identity, stamp, strain

coltish *adj* **2 = frisky,** frolicsome, lively, playful, romping, skittish, sportive

column *n* **1 = pillar,** caryatid, obelisk, pilaster, post, shaft, support, upright **3 = line,** cavalcade, file, list, procession, queue, rank, row, string, train

columnist *n* **= journalist,** correspondent, critic, editor, gossip columnist, journo (*sl.*), reporter, reviewer

coma[1] *n* **= unconsciousness,** insensibility, lethargy, oblivion, somnolence, stupor, torpor, trance

comatose *adj* **1, 2 = unconscious,** drugged, insensible, lethargic, somnolent, stupefied, torpid

comb *vb* **7 = untangle,** arrange, curry, dress, groom, tease **8 = search,** forage, go through with a fine-tooth comb, hunt, rake, ransack, rummage, scour, screen, sift, sweep

combat *n* **1 = fight,** action, battle, conflict, contest, encounter, engagement, skirmish, struggle, war, warfare ◆ *vb* **4, 5 = fight,** battle, contend, contest, cope, defy, do battle with, engage, oppose, resist, strive, struggle, withstand
Antonyms *n* **≠ fight:** agreement, armistice, peace, surrender, truce ◆ *vb* **≠ fight:** accept, acquiesce, declare a truce, give up, make peace, support, surrender

combatant *n* **1 = fighter,** adversary, antagonist, belligerent, contender, enemy, fighting man, gladiator, opponent, serviceman, soldier, warrior ◆ *adj* **2 = fighting,** battling, belligerent, combative, conflicting, contending, opposing, warring

combative *adj* **= aggressive,** antagonistic, bellicose, belligerent, contentious, militant, pugnacious, quarrelsome, truculent, warlike
Antonyms *adj* nonaggressive, nonbelligerent, nonviolent, pacific, pacifist, peaceable, peaceful, peace-loving

combination *n* **2 = mixture,** amalgam, amalgamation, blend, coalescence, composite, connection, meld, mix **3 = association,** alliance, cabal, cartel, coalition, combine, compound, confederacy, confederation, consortium, conspiracy, federation, merger, syndicate, unification, union

combine *vb* **1 = join together,** amalgamate, associate, bind, blend, bond, compound, connect, cooperate, fuse, incorporate, integrate, link, marry, meld, merge, mix, pool, put together, synthesize, unify, unite
Antonyms *vb* detach, dissociate, dissolve, disunite, divide, part, separate, sever

combo ('kɒmbəʊ) *n, pl* **combos.** **1** a small group of jazz musicians. **2** *Inf.* any combination.

comb out *vb (tr, adv)* **1** to remove (tangles) from (the hair) with a comb. **2** to examine for a purpose. **3** to examine systematically.

combustible ⓣ (kəm'bʌstɪbᵊl) *adj* **1** capable of igniting and burning. **2** easily annoyed; excitable. ◆ *n* **3** a combustible substance.
▸**com,busti'bility** *or* **com'bustibleness** *n*

combustion (kəm'bʌstʃən) *n* **1** the process of burning. **2** any process in which a substance reacts to produce a significant rise in temperature and the emission of light. **3** a process in which a compound reacts slowly with oxygen to produce little heat and no light. [C15: from OF, from L *combūrere* to burn up]
▸**com'bustive** *n, adj*

combustion chamber *n* an enclosed space in which combustion takes place, such as the space above the piston in the cylinder head of an internal-combustion engine.

combustor (kəm'bʌstə) *n* the combustion system of a jet engine or ramjet.

Comdr *Mil. abbrev. for* Commander.

Comdt *Mil. abbrev. for* Commandant.

come ⓣ (kʌm) *vb* **comes, coming, came, come.** *(mainly intr)* **1** to move towards a specified person or place. **2** to arrive by movement or by making progress. **3** to become perceptible: *light came into the sky.* **4** to occur: *Christmas comes but once a year.* **5** to happen as a result: *no good will come of this.* **6** to be derived: *good may come of evil.* **7** to occur to the mind: *the truth suddenly came to me.* **8** to reach: *she comes up to my shoulder.* **9** to be produced: *that dress comes in red.* **10** to arrive at or be brought into a particular state: *you will soon come to grief.* **11** (foll. by *from*) to be or have been a resident or native (of): *I come from London.* **12** to become: *your wishes will come true.* **13** *(tr; takes an infinitive)* to be given awareness: *I came to realize its value.* **14** *Taboo sl.* to have an orgasm. **15** *(tr) Brit. inf.* to play the part of: *don't come the fine gentleman with me.* **16** *(tr) Brit. inf.* to cause or produce: *don't come that nonsense.* **17** *(subjunctive use): come next August, he will be fifty years old:* when next August arrives. **18 as ... as they come.** the most characteristic example of a type. **19 come again?** *Inf.* what did you say? **20 come good.** to recover and perform well after a setback or poor start. **21 come to light.** to be revealed. **22 come to light with.** *Austral. & NZ inf.* to find or produce. ◆ *interj* **23** an exclamation expressing annoyance, etc.: *come now!* ◆ See also **come about, come across,** etc. [OE *cuman*]

come about ⓣ *vb (intr, adv)* **1** to take place; happen. **2** *Naut.* to change tacks.

come across ⓣ *vb (intr)* **1** *(prep)* to meet or find by accident. **2** *(adv)* to communicate the intended meaning or impression. **3** (often foll. by *with*) to provide what is expected.

come at ⓣ *vb (intr, prep)* **1** to discover (facts, the truth, etc.). **2** to attack: *he came at me with an axe.* **3** *(usually used with a negative) Austral. sl.* to agree to do (something).

comeback ⓣ ('kʌm,bæk) *n Inf.* **1** a return to a former position, status, etc. **2** a response, esp. recriminatory. **3** a quick retort. ◆ *vb* **come back.** *(intr, adv)* **4** to return, esp. to the memory. **5** to become fashionable again. **6 come back to (someone).** (of something forgotten) to return to (someone's) memory.

come between ⓣ *vb (intr, prep)* to cause the estrangement or separation of (two people).

come by ⓣ *vb (intr, prep)* to find or obtain, esp. accidentally: *do you ever come by any old books?*

Comecon ('kɒmɪ,kɒn) *n* (formerly) an association of Soviet-oriented Communist nations, founded in 1949 to coordinate economic development, etc.: disbanded in 1991. [C20: *Co(uncil for) M(utual) Econ(omic Aid)*]

comedian ⓣ (kə'mi:dɪən) *n* **1** an entertainer who specializes in jokes, comic skits, etc. **2** an actor in comedy. **3** an amusing person: sometimes used ironically.

comedienne (kə,mi:dɪ'ɛn) *n* a female comedian.

comedo ('kɒmɪ,dəʊ) *n, pl* **comedos** *or* **comedones** (,kɒmɪ'dəʊni:z). *Pathol.* the technical name for **blackhead.** [C19: from NL, from L: glutton]

comedown ⓣ ('kʌm,daʊn) *n* **1** a decline in status or prosperity. **2** *Inf.* a disappointment. ◆ *vb* **come down.** *(intr, adv)* **3** to come to a place regarded as lower. **4** to lose status, etc. (esp. in **come down in the world**). **5** (of prices) to become lower. **6** to reach a decision: *the report came down in favour of a pay increase.* **7** (often foll. by *to*) to be handed down by tradition or inheritance. **8** *Brit.* to leave university. **9** (foll. by *with*) to succumb (to illness). **10** (foll. by *on*) to rebuke harshly. **11** (foll. by *to*) to amount in essence (to): *it comes down to two choices.*

comedy ⓣ ('kɒmɪdɪ) *n, pl* **comedies.** **1** a dramatic or other work of light and amusing character. **2** the genre of drama represented by works of this type. **3** (in classical literature) a play in which the main characters triumph over adversity. **4** the humorous aspect of life or of events. **5** an amusing event or sequence of events. **6** humour: *the comedy of Chaplin.* [C14: from OF, from L, from Gk *kōmōidia*, from *kōmos* village festival + *aeidein* to sing]
▸**comedic** (kə'mi:dɪk) *adj*

comedy of manners *n* a comedy dealing with the way of life and foibles of a social group.

come forward ⓣ *vb (intr, adv)* **1** to offer one's services; volunteer. **2** to present oneself.

come-hither *adj (usually prenominal) Inf.* alluring; seductive: *a come-hither look.*

come in ⓣ *vb (intr, mainly adv)* **1** to enter. **2** to prove to be: *it came in useful.* **3** to become fashionable or seasonable. **4** *Cricket.* to begin an innings. **5** to finish a race (in a certain position). **6** to be received: *news is coming in of a big fire in Glasgow.* **7** (of money) to be received as income. **8** to play a role: *where do I come in?* **9** (foll. by *for*) to be the object of: *the Chancellor came in for a lot of criticism.*

come into *vb (intr, prep)* **1** to enter. **2** to inherit.

comely ⓣ ('kʌmlɪ) *adj* **comelier, comeliest.** **1** good-looking; attractive. **2** *Arch.* suitable; fitting. [OE *cȳmlīc* beautiful]
▸**'comeliness** *n*

come of *vb (intr, prep)* **1** to be descended from. **2** to result from: *nothing came of it.*

come off ⓣ *vb (intr, mainly adv)* **1** *(also prep)* to fall (from). **2** to become detached. **3** *(prep)* to be removed from (a price, tax, etc.): *will anything come off income tax in the budget?* **4** *(copula)* to emerge from or as if from a contest: *he came off the winner.* **5** *Inf.* to happen. **6** *Inf.* to have the intended effect: *his jokes did not come off.* **7** *Taboo sl.* to have an orgasm.

come on ⓣ *vb (intr, mainly adv)* **1** (of power, water, etc.) to start running or functioning. **2** to progress: *my plants are coming on nicely.* **3** to advance, esp. in battle. **4** to begin: *she felt a cold coming on.* **5** to make an entrance on stage. **6 come on! 6a** hurry up! **6b** cheer up! pull yourself together! **6c** make an effort! **6d** don't exaggerate! stick to the facts! **7** to attempt to give a specified impression: *he came on like a hard man.* **8 come on strong.** to make a forceful or exaggerated impression. **9 come on to.** *Inf.* to make sexual advances to. ◆ *n* **come-on. 10.** anything that serves as a lure or enticement.

come out ⓣ *vb (intr, adv)* **1** to be made public or revealed: *the news of her death came out last week.* **2** to make a debut in society. **3** Also: **come out of the closet. 3a** to declare openly that one is a homosexual. **3b** to reveal or declare any practice or habit formerly concealed. **4** *Chiefly Brit.* to go on strike. **5** to declare oneself: *the government came out in favour of scrapping the project.* **6** to be shown clearly: *you came out very well in the*

THESAURUS

combustible *adj* **1 = flammable**, explosive, incendiary, inflammable

come *vb* **1, 2 = move towards**, advance, appear, approach, arrive, become, draw near, enter, happen, materialize, move, near, occur, originate, show up (*inf.*), turn out, turn up (*inf.*) **3 = arrive**, appear, attain, enter, materialize, reach, show up (*inf.*), turn up (*inf.*) **4 = happen**, fall, occur, take place **6 = result**, arise, emanate, emerge, end up, flow, issue, originate, turn out **8 = reach**, extend **9 = be available**, be made, be offered, be on offer, be produced

come about *vb* **1 = happen**, arise, befall, come to pass, occur, result, take place, transpire (*inf.*)

come across *vb* **1 = find**, bump into (*inf.*), chance upon, discover, encounter, happen upon, hit upon, light upon, meet, notice, stumble upon, unearth

come at *vb* **2 = attack**, assail, assault, charge, fall upon, fly at, go for, light into, rush, rush at

comeback *Informal n* **1 = return**, rally, rebound, recovery, resurgence, revival, triumph **2 = response**, rejoinder, reply, retaliation, retort, riposte ◆ *vb* **come back 4 = return**, reappear, recur, re-enter

come between *vb* **= separate**, alienate, divide, estrange, interfere, meddle, part, set at odds

come by *vb* **= get**, acquire, land, lay hold of, obtain, procure, score (*sl.*), secure, take possession of, win

comedian *n* **1, 3 = comic**, card (*inf.*), clown, funny man, humorist, jester, joker, laugh (*inf.*), wag, wit

comedown *n* **1 = decline**, deflation, demotion, reverse **2** *Informal* **= disappointment**, anticlimax, blow, humiliation, letdown, whammy (*inf., chiefly U.S.*) ◆ *vb* **come down 3 = descend**, go downhill **4 = decline**, degenerate, deteriorate, fall, go to pot (*inf.*), reduce, worsen **6 = decide**, choose, favour, recommend **9** *foll. by* **with = catch**, ail, be stricken with, contract, fall ill, fall victim to, get, sicken, take, take sick **10** *foll. by* **on = reprimand**, bawl out (*inf.*), blast, carpet (*Inf.*), criticize, dress down (*inf.*), jump on (*inf.*), lambast(e), put down, rap over the knuckles, read the riot act, rebuke, tear into (*inf.*), tear (someone) off a strip (*Brit. inf.*) **11** *foll. by* **to = amount to**, boil down to, end up as, result in

comedy *n* **1, 4-6 = humour**, chaffing, drollery, facetiousness, farce, fun, hilarity, jesting, joking, light entertainment, sitcom (*inf.*), slapstick, wisecracking, witticisms
Antonyms *n* high drama, melancholy, melodrama, opera, sadness, seriousness, serious play, soap opera, solemnity, tragedy

come forward *vb* **1, 2 = volunteer**, offer one's services, present *or* proffer oneself

come in *vb* **1 = enter**, appear, arrive, cross the threshold, show up (*inf.*) **5 = finish**, reach **9** *foll. by* **for = receive**, acquire, bear the brunt of, endure, get, suffer

comely *adj* **1** *Old-fashioned* **= good-looking**, attractive, beautiful, becoming, blooming, bonny, buxom, cute, fair, graceful, handsome, lovely, pleasing, pretty, wholesome, winsome **2** *Archaic* **= proper**, decent, decorous, fit, fitting, seemly, suitable
Antonyms *adj* ≠ **good-looking:** disagreeable, distasteful, faded, homely, mumsy, plain, repulsive, ugly, unattractive, unpleasant ≠ **proper:** improper, indecorous, unbecoming, unfitting, unnatural, unseemly

come off *vb* **5** *Informal* **= happen**, go off, occur, succeed, take place, transpire (*inf.*)

come on *vb* **2, 3 = progress**, advance, develop, improve, make headway, proceed **4 = begin**, appear, take place

come out *vb* **1 = be revealed**, appear, be announced, be divulged, be issued, be published, be released, be reported **10** *foll. by* **with = say,**

photos. **7** to yield a satisfactory solution: *these sums just won't come out.* **8** to be published: *the paper comes out on Fridays.* **9** (foll. by *in*) to become covered (with). **10** (foll. by *with*) to declare openly: *you can rely on him to come out with the facts.*

come over *vb (intr, adv)* **1** to communicate the intended meaning or impression: *he came over very well.* **2** to change allegiances. **3** *Inf.* to feel a particular sensation: *I came over funny.*

comer ('kʌmə) *n* **1** *(in combination)* a person who comes: *all-comers; newcomers.* **2** *Inf.* a potential success.

come round ⓣ *vb (intr, adv)* **1** to be restored to consciousness. **2** to modify one's opinion.

comestible (kə'mɛstɪbᵊl) *n (usually pl)* food. [C15: from LL *comestibilis,* from *comedere* to eat up]

comet ('kɒmɪt) *n* a celestial body that travels around the sun, usually in a highly elliptical orbit: thought to consist of a frozen nucleus, part of which vaporizes on approaching the sun to form a long luminous tail. [C13: from OF, from L, from Gk *komētēs* long-haired]
▸'**cometary** *or* **cometic** (kɒ'mɛtɪk) *adj*

come through ⓣ *vb (intr)* **1** *(adv)* to emerge successfully. **2** *(prep)* to survive (an illness, etc.).

come to *vb (intr)* **1** *(adv or prep and reflexive)* to regain consciousness. **2** *(adv) Naut.* to slow a vessel or bring her to a stop. **3** *(prep)* to amount to (a sum of money). **4** *(prep)* to arrive at: *what is the world coming to?*

come up ⓣ *vb (intr, adv)* **1** to come to a place regarded as higher. **2** (of the sun) to rise. **3** to present itself: *that question will come up again.* **4** *Brit.* to begin a term at a university. **5** to appear from out of the ground: *my beans have come up early.* **6** *Inf.* to win: *have your premium bonds ever come up?* **7 come up against.** to come into conflict with. **8 come up to.** to meet a standard. **9 come up with.** to produce.

come upon *vb (intr, prep)* to meet or encounter unexpectedly.

comeuppance ⓣ (,kʌm'ʌpəns) *n Inf.* just retribution. [C19: from *come up* (in the sense): to appear before a court]

comfit ('kʌmfɪt, 'kɒm-) *n* a sugar-coated sweet containing a nut or seed. [C15: from OF, from L *confectum* something prepared]

comfort ⓣ ('kʌmfət) *n* **1** a state of ease or well-being. **2** relief from affliction, grief, etc. **3** a person, thing, or event that brings solace or ease. **4** *(usually pl)* something that affords physical ease and relaxation. ◆ *vb (tr)* **5** to soothe; cheer. **6** to bring physical ease to. [C13: from OF *confort,* from LL *confortāre* to strengthen, from L *con-* (intensive) + *fortis* strong]
▸'**comforting** *adj* ▸'**comfortless** *adj*

comfortable ⓣ ('kʌmftəbᵊl) *adj* **1** giving comfort. **2** at ease. **3** free from affliction or pain. **4** (of a person or situation) relaxing. **5** *Inf.* having adequate income. **6** *Inf.* (of income, etc.) adequate to provide comfort.
▸'**comfortably** *adv*

comforter ('kʌmfətə) *n* **1** a person or thing that comforts. **2** *Chiefly Brit.* a woollen scarf. **3** a baby's dummy. **4** *US.* a quilted bed covering.

Comforter ('kʌmfətə) *n Christianity.* an epithet of the Holy Spirit. [C14: translation of L *consolātor,* representing Gk *paraklētos* advocate]

comfrey ('kʌmfrɪ) *n* a hairy Eurasian plant having blue, purplish-pink, or white flowers. [C15: from OF *cunfirie,* from L *conferva* water plant]

comfy ('kʌmfɪ) *adj* **comfier, comfiest.** *Inf.* short for **comfortable.**

comic ⓣ ('kɒmɪk) *adj* **1** of, characterized by, or characteristic of comedy. **2** *(prenominal)* acting in or composing comedy: *a comic writer.* **3** humorous; funny. ◆ *n* **4** a person who is comic; comedian. **5** a book or magazine containing comic strips. [C16: from L *cōmicus,* from Gk *kōmikos*]

comical ⓣ ('kɒmɪkᵊl) *adj* **1** causing laughter. **2** ludicrous; laughable.
▸'**comically** *adv*

comic opera *n* a play largely set to music, employing comic effects or situations.

comic strip *n* a sequence of drawings in a newspaper, magazine, etc., relating a humorous story or an adventure.

coming ⓣ ('kʌmɪŋ) *adj* **1** *(prenominal)* (of time, events, etc.) approaching or next. **2** promising (esp. in **up and coming**). **3** of future importance: *this is the coming thing.* **4 have it coming to one.** *Inf.* to deserve what one is about to suffer. ◆ *n* **5** arrival or approach.

Comintern *or* **Komintern** ('kɒmɪn,tɜːn) *n* short for **Communist International**; an international Communist organization founded by Lenin in 1919 and dissolved in 1943; it degenerated under Stalin into an instrument of Soviet politics. Also called: **Third International.**

comity ('kɒmɪtɪ) *n, pl* **comities. 1** mutual civility; courtesy. **2** short for **comity of nations.** [C16: from L *cōmitās,* from *cōmis* affable]

comity of nations *n* the friendly recognition accorded by one nation to the laws and usages of another.

comm. *abbrev. for:* **1** commerce. **2** commercial. **3** committee. **4** commonwealth.

comma ('kɒmə) *n* **1** the punctuation mark , indicating a slight pause and used where there is a listing of items or to separate a nonrestrictive clause from a main clause. **2** *Music.* a minute difference in pitch. [C16: from L, from Gk *komma* clause, from *koptein* to cut]

comma bacillus *n* a comma-shaped bacterium that causes cholera in man.

command ⓣ (kə'mɑːnd) *vb* **1** (when *tr,* may take a clause as object or an infinitive) to order or compel. **2** to have or be in control or authority over. **3** *(tr)* to receive as due: *his nature commands respect.* **4** to dominate (a view, etc.) as from a height. ◆ *n* **5** an order. **6** the act of commanding. **7** the right to command. **8** the exercise of the power to command. **9** knowledge; control: *a command of French.* **10** *Chiefly mil.* the jurisdiction of a commander. **11** a military unit or units commanding a specific function, as in the RAF. **12** *Brit.* **12a** an invitation from the monarch. **12b** *(as modifier): a command performance.* **13** *Computing.* a word or phrase that can be selected from a menu or typed after a prompt in order to carry out an action. [C13: from OF *commander,* from L *com-* (intensive) + *mandāre* to enjoin]

commandant ('kɒmən,dænt, -,dɑːnt) *n* an officer commanding a group or establishment.

command economy *n* an economy in which business activities and the allocation of resources are determined by government order rather than market forces. Also called: **planned economy.**

commandeer ⓣ (,kɒmən'dɪə) *vb (tr)* **1** to seize for public or military use. **2** to seize arbitrarily. [C19: from Afrik. *kommandeer,* from F *commander* to COMMAND]

commander ⓣ (kə'mɑːndə) *n* **1** an officer in command of a military formation or operation. **2** a naval commissioned rank junior to captain but senior to lieutenant commander. **3** the second in command of larger British warships. **4** someone who holds authority. **5** a high-ranking member of some knightly orders. **6** an officer responsible for a district of the Metropolitan Police in London.
▸**com'mander,ship** *n*

commander in chief *n, pl* **commanders in chief.** the officer holding supreme command of the forces in an area or operation.

THESAURUS

acknowledge, come clean, declare, disclose, divulge, lay open, own, own up

come round *vb* **1** = **regain consciousness,** come to, rally, recover, revive **2** = **change one's opinion,** accede, acquiesce, allow, concede, grant, mellow, relent, yield

come through *vb* **1** = **accomplish,** achieve, make the grade *(inf.),* prevail, succeed, triumph **2** = **survive,** endure, weather the storm, withstand

come up *vb* **3** = **happen,** arise, crop up, occur, rise, spring up, turn up **8 come up to** = **compare with,** admit of comparison with, approach, equal, match, measure up to, meet, resemble, rival, stand *or* bear comparison with **9 come up with** = **produce,** advance, create, discover, furnish, offer, present, propose, provide, submit, suggest

comeuppance *n Informal* = **punishment,** chastening, deserts, due reward, dues, merit, recompense, requital, retribution

comfort *n* **1** = **luxury,** cosiness, creature comforts, ease, opulence, snugness, wellbeing **2** = **relief,** aid, alleviation, cheer, compensation, consolation, ease, encouragement, enjoyment, help, satisfaction, succour, support ◆ *vb* **5, 6** = **console,** alleviate, assuage, cheer, commiserate with, ease, encourage, enliven, gladden, hearten, inspirit, invigorate, reassure, refresh, relieve, solace, soothe, strengthen
Antonyms *n* ≠ **relief:** aggravation, annoyance, discouragement, displeasure, hassle *(inf.),* inconvenience, irritation ◆ *vb* ≠ **console:** aggravate *(inf.),* agitate, annoy, bother, depress, discomfort, distress, excite, hassle *(inf.),* irk, irritate, rile, ruffle, sadden, trouble

comfortable *adj* **1, 4** = **pleasant,** agreeable, convenient, cosy, delightful, easy, enjoyable, homely, relaxing, restful **2** = **happy,** at ease, at home, contented, gratified, relaxed, serene **5** *Informal* = **well-off,** affluent, in clover *(inf.),* prosperous, well-to-do
Antonyms *adj* ≠ **pleasant:** inadequate, uncomfortable, unpleasant ≠ **happy:** distressed, disturbed, ill at ease, like a fish out of water, miserable, nervous, on tenterhooks, tense, troubled, uncomfortable, uneasy

comforting *adj* **5** = **consoling,** cheering, consolatory, encouraging, heart-warming, inspiriting, reassuring, soothing
Antonyms *adj* alarming, dismaying, disturbing, perplexing, upsetting, worrying

comfortless *adj* **1** = **cheerless,** bleak, cold, desolate, dismal, dreary **2** = **inconsolable,** disconsolate, forlorn, miserable, sick at heart, woebegone, wretched

comic *adj* **3** = **funny,** amusing, comical, droll, facetious, farcical, humorous, jocular, joking, light, rich, waggish, witty ◆ *n* **4** = **comedian,** buffoon, clown, funny man, humorist, jester, joculator *or (fem.)* joculatrix, wag, wit
Antonyms *adj* ≠ **funny:** depressing, melancholy, pathetic, sad, serious, solemn, touching, tragic

comical *adj* **1, 2** = **funny,** absurd, amusing, comic, diverting, droll, entertaining, farcical, hilarious, humorous, laughable, ludicrous, priceless, ridiculous, risible, side-splitting, silly, whimsical, zany

coming *adj* **1** = **approaching,** at hand, due, en route, forthcoming, future, imminent, impending, in store, in the wind, just round the corner, near, next, nigh, on the cards, upcoming **2** = **up-and-coming,** aspiring, future, promising ◆ *n* **5** = **arrival,** accession, advent, approach

command *vb* **1** = **order,** bid, charge, compel, demand, direct, enjoin, require **2** = **have authority over,** administer, call the shots, call the tune, control, dominate, govern, handle, head, lead, manage, reign over, rule, supervise, sway ◆ *n* **5** = **order,** behest, bidding, canon, commandment, decree, demand, direction, directive, edict, fiat, injunction, instruction, mandate, precept, requirement, ultimatum **7, 8** = **authority,** charge, control, direction, domination, dominion, government, grasp, management, mastery, power, rule, supervision, sway, upper hand
Antonyms *vb* ≠ **order:** appeal (to), ask, beg, beseech, plead, request, supplicate ≠ **have authority over:** be inferior, be subordinate, follow

commandeer *vb* **1, 2** = **seize,** appropriate, confiscate, expropriate, hijack, requisition, sequester, sequestrate, usurp

commander *n* **1, 4** = **officer,** boss, captain, chief, C in C, C.O., commander-in-chief, commanding officer, director, head, leader, ruler

commanding ❶ (kəˈmɑːndɪŋ) *adj (usually prenominal)* **1** being in command. **2** having the air of authority: *a commanding voice.* **3** (of a situation) exerting control. **4** (of a viewpoint, etc.) overlooking; advantageous.
▸**comˈmandingly** *adv*

commanding officer *n* an officer in command of a military unit.

command language *n Computing.* the language used to access a computer system.

commandment (kəˈmɑːndmənt) *n* **1** a divine command, esp. one of the Ten Commandments of the Old Testament. **2** *Literary.* any command.

command module *n* the module used as the living quarters in an Apollo spacecraft and functioning as the splashdown vehicle.

commando (kəˈmɑːndəʊ) *n, pl* **commandos** *or* **commandoes. 1a** an amphibious military unit trained for raiding. **1b** a member of such a unit. **2** the basic unit of the Royal Marine Corps. **3** (originally) an armed force raised by Boers during the Boer War. **4** *(modifier)* denoting or relating to commandos: *a commando unit.* [C19: from Afrik. *kommando,* from Du. *commando* command]

command paper *n* (in Britain) a government document that is presented to Parliament, in theory by royal command.

command post *n Mil.* the position from which a commander exercises command.

commedia dell'arte (*Italian* komˈmeːdia delˈlarte) *n* a form of popular improvised comedy in Italy during the 16th to 18th centuries, with stock characters such as Punchinello, Harlequin, and Columbine. [It., lit.: comedy of art]

comme il faut *French.* (kɔm il fo) correct or correctly.

commemorate ❶ (kəˈmɛməˌreɪt) *vb* **commemorates, commemorating, commemorated.** *(tr)* to honour or keep alive the memory of. [C16: from L *commemorāre,* from *com-* (intensive) + *memorāre* to remind]
▸**comˌmemoˈration** *n* ▸**comˈmemorative** *adj* ▸**comˈmemoˌrator** *n*

commence ❶ (kəˈmɛns) *vb* **commences, commencing, commenced.** to begin; come or cause to come into being, operation, etc. [C14: from OF *comencer,* from Vulgar L *cominitiāre* (unattested), from L *com-* (intensive) + *initiāre* to begin]

commencement ❶ (kəˈmɛnsmənt) *n* **1** the beginning; start. **2** *US.* a ceremony for the conferment of academic degrees. **3** *US & Canad.* a ceremony for the presentation of awards at secondary schools.

commend ❶ (kəˈmɛnd) *vb (tr)* **1** to represent as being worthy of regard, confidence, etc.; recommend. **2** to give in charge; entrust. **3** to praise. **4** to give the regards of: *commend me to your aunt.* [C14: from L *commendāre,* from *com-* (intensive) + *mandāre* to entrust]
▸**comˈmendable** *adj* ▸**comˈmendably** *adv* ▸**comˈmendatory** *adj*

commendation ❶ (ˌkɒmɛnˈdeɪʃən) *n* **1** the act of commending; praise. **2** *US.* an award.

commensal (kəˈmɛnsəl) *adj* **1** (of two different species of plant or animal) living in close association without being interdependent. See also **inquiline** (sense 1). **2** *Rare.* of or relating to eating together, esp. at the same table. ◆ *n* **3** a commensal plant or animal. **4** *Rare.* a companion at table. [C14: from Med. L *commensālis,* from L *com-* together + *mensa* table]
▸**comˈmensalism** *n* ▸**commensality** (ˌkɒmɛnˈsælɪtɪ) *n*

commensurable (kəˈmɛnsərəbəl, -ʃə-) *adj* **1** *Maths.* **1a** having a common factor. **1b** having units of the same dimensions and being related by whole numbers. **2** proportionate.
▸**comˌmensuraˈbility** *n* ▸**comˈmensurably** *adv*

commensurate ❶ (kəˈmɛnsərɪt, -ʃə-) *adj* **1** having the same extent or duration. **2** corresponding in degree, amount, or size; proportionate. **3** commensurable. [C17: from LL *commēnsūrātus,* from L *com-* same + *mēnsurāre* to MEASURE]
▸**comˈmensurately** *adv*

comment ❶ (ˈkɒmɛnt) *n* **1** a remark, criticism, or observation. **2** talk or gossip. **3** a note explaining or criticizing a passage in a text. **4** explanatory or critical matter added to a text. ◆ *vb* **5** (when *intr,* often foll. by *on;* when *tr,* takes a clause as object) to remark or express an opinion. **6** *(intr)* to write notes explaining or criticizing a text. [C15: from L *commentum* invention, from *comminiscī* to contrive]
▸**ˈcommenter** *n*

commentary ❶ (ˈkɒməntərɪ) *n, pl* **commentaries. 1** an explanatory series of notes. **2** a spoken accompaniment to a broadcast, film, etc. **3** an explanatory treatise on a text. **4** *(usually pl)* a personal record of events: *the commentaries of Caesar.*

commentate (ˈkɒmənˌteɪt) *vb* **commentates, commentating, commentated. 1** *(intr)* to serve as a commentator. **2** *(tr) US.* to make a commentary on.

> **USAGE NOTE** The verb *commentate,* derived from *commentator,* is sometimes used as a synonym for *comment on* or *provide a commentary for.* It is not yet fully accepted as standard, though widespread in sports reporting and journalism.

commentator ❶ (ˈkɒmənˌteɪtə) *n* **1** a person who provides a spoken commentary for a broadcast, film, etc., esp. of a sporting event. **2** a person who writes notes on a text, etc.

commerce ❶ (ˈkɒmɜːs) *n* **1** the activity embracing all forms of the purchase and sale of goods and services. **2** social relations. **3** *Arch.* sexual intercourse. [C16: from L *commercium,* from *commercārī,* from *mercārī* to trade, from *merx* merchandise]

commercial ❶ (kəˈmɜːʃəl) *adj* **1** of or engaged in commerce. **2** sponsored or paid for by an advertiser: *commercial television.* **3** having profit as the main aim: *commercial music.* **4** (of chemicals, etc.) unrefined and produced in bulk for use in industry. ◆ *n* **5** a commercially sponsored advertisement on radio or television.
▸**commerciality** (kəˌmɜːʃɪˈælɪtɪ) *n* ▸**comˈmercially** *adv*

commercial art *n* graphic art for commercial uses such as advertising, packaging, etc.

commercial bank *n* a bank primarily engaged in making short-term loans from funds deposited in current accounts.

commercial break *n* an interruption in a radio or television programme for the broadcasting of advertisements.

commercialism (kəˈmɜːʃəˌlɪzəm) *n* **1** the spirit, principles, or procedure of commerce. **2** exclusive or inappropriate emphasis on profit.

commercialize *or* **commercialise** (kəˈmɜːʃəˌlaɪz) *vb* **commercializes, commercializing, commercialized** *or* **commercialises, commercialising, commercialised.** *(tr)* **1** to make commercial. **2** to exploit for profit, esp. at the expense of quality.
▸**comˌmercialiˈzation** *or* **comˌmercialiˈsation** *n*

commercial paper *n* a short-term negotiable document, such as a bill of exchange, calling for the transference of a specified sum of money at a designated date.

commercial traveller *n* another name for a **travelling salesman.**

commercial vehicle *n* a vehicle for carrying goods or (less commonly) passengers.

commie *or* **commy** (ˈkɒmɪ) *n, pl* **commies,** *adj Inf. & derog.* short for **communist.**

commination (ˌkɒmɪˈneɪʃən) *n* **1** the act of threatening punishment or vengeance. **2** *Church of England.* a recital of prayers, including a list of God's judgments against sinners, in the office for Ash Wednesday. [C15: from L *comminātiō,* from *com-* (intensive) + *minārī* to threaten]
▸**comminatory** (ˈkɒmɪnətərɪ) *adj*

commingle (kɒˈmɪŋgᵊl) *vb* **commingles, commingling, commingled.** to mix or be mixed.

comminute (ˈkɒmɪˌnjuːt) *vb* **comminutes, comminuting, comminuted. 1** to break (a bone) into small fragments. **2** to divide (property) into small lots. [C17: from L *comminuere,* from *com-* (intensive) + *minuere* to reduce]
▸**ˌcommiˈnution** *n*

commis (ˈkɒmɪs, ˈkɒmɪ) *n, pl* **commis. 1** an agent or deputy. ◆ *adj* **2** (of a

THESAURUS

commanding *adj* **1** = **controlling**, advantageous, decisive, dominant, dominating, superior **2** = **authoritative**, assertive, autocratic, compelling, forceful, imposing, impressive, peremptory
Antonyms *adj* ≠ **authoritative:** retiring, shrinking, shy, submissive, timid, unassertive, unimposing, weak

commemorate *vb* = **remember**, celebrate, honour, immortalize, keep, memorialize, observe, pay tribute to, recognize, salute, solemnize
Antonyms *vb* disregard, forget, ignore, omit, overlook, pass over, take no notice of

commemoration *n* = **remembrance**, ceremony, honouring, memorial service, observance, tribute

commemorative *adj* = **memorial**, celebratory, dedicatory, in honour, in memory, in remembrance

commence *vb* = **begin**, embark on, enter upon, get the show on the road *(inf.)*, inaugurate, initiate, open, originate, start
Antonyms *vb* bring *or* come to an end, cease, complete, conclude, desist, end, finish, halt, stop, terminate, wind up

commencement *n* **1** = **beginning**, birth, dawn, embarkation, inauguration, inception, initiation, launch, onset, opening, origin, outset, square one *(inf.)*, start

commend *vb* **1, 3** = **praise**, acclaim, applaud, approve, compliment, crack up *(inf.)*, eulogize, extol, recommend, speak highly of **2** = **entrust**, commit, confide, consign, deliver, hand over, yield
Antonyms *vb* ≠ **praise:** attack, blast, censure, condemn, criticize, denounce, disapprove, knock *(inf.)*, lambast(e), put down, slam, tear into *(inf.)* ≠ **entrust:** hold back, keep, keep back, retain, withdraw, withhold

commendable *adj* **3** = **praiseworthy**, admirable, creditable, deserving, estimable, exemplary, laudable, meritorious, worthy

commendation *n* **1, 3** = **praise**, acclaim, acclamation, approbation, approval, Brownie points, credit, encomium, encouragement, good opinion, panegyric, recommendation

commensurate *adj* **1, 2** = **proportionate**, adequate, appropriate, coextensive, comparable, compatible, consistent, corresponding, due, equivalent, fit, fitting, in accord, sufficient

comment *n* **1** = **remark**, animadversion, observation, statement **3, 4** = **note**, annotation, commentary, criticism, elucidation, explanation, exposition, illustration ◆ *vb* **5** = **remark**, animadvert, interpose, mention, note, observe, opine, point out, say, utter **6** = **annotate**, criticize, elucidate, explain, interpret

commentary *n* **2** = **narration**, description, voice-over **3** = **notes**, analysis, critique, exegesis, explanation, review, treatise

commentator *n* **1** = **reporter**, commenter, special correspondent, sportscaster **2** = **critic**, annotator, expositor, interpreter, scholiast

commerce *n* **1** = **trade**, business, dealing, exchange, merchandising, traffic **2** *Literary* = **relations**, communication, dealings, intercourse, socializing

commercial *adj* **1** = **mercantile**, business, profit-making, sales, trade, trading

waiter or chef) apprentice. [C16 (meaning: deputy): from F, from *commettre* to employ]

commiserate ❶ (kəˈmɪzəˌreɪt) *vb* **commiserates, commiserating, commiserated.** (when *intr*, usually foll. by *with*) to feel or express sympathy or compassion (for). [C17: from L *commiserārī*, from *com-* together + *miserārī* to bewail]
▸**comˌmiserˈation** *n* ▸**comˈmiserˌator** *n*

commissar (ˈkɒmɪˌsɑː, ˌkɒmɪˈsɑː) *n* (in the former Soviet Union) **1** an official of the Communist Party responsible for political education. **2** (before 1946) the head of a government department. [C20: from Russian *kommissar*]

commissariat (ˌkɒmɪˈsɛərɪət) *n* **1** (in the former Soviet Union) a government department before 1946. **2** a military department in charge of food supplies, etc. [C17: from NL *commissāriātus*, from Med. L *commissārius* COMMISSARY]

commissary (ˈkɒmɪsərɪ) *n, pl* **commissaries. 1** *US.* a shop supplying food or equipment, as in a military camp. **2** *US army.* an officer responsible for supplies. **3** *US.* a restaurant in a film studio. **4** a representative or deputy, esp. of a bishop. [C14: from Med. L *commissārius* official in charge, from L *committere* to COMMIT]
▸**commissarial** (ˌkɒmɪˈsɛərɪəl) *adj*

commission ❶ (kəˈmɪʃən) *n* **1** a duty committed to a person or group to perform. **2** authority to perform certain duties. **3** a document granting such authority. **4** *Mil.* **4a** a document conferring a rank on an officer. **4b** the rank granted. **5** a group charged with certain duties: *a commission of inquiry.* **6** a government board empowered to exercise administrative, judicial, or legislative authority. See also **Royal Commission. 7a** the authority given to a person or organization to act as an agent to a principal in commercial transactions. **7b** the fee allotted to an agent for services rendered. **8** the state of being charged with specific responsibilities. **9** the act of committing a sin, crime, etc. **10** good working condition or (esp. of a ship) active service (esp. in **in commission, out of commission**). ◆ *vb* (*mainly tr*) **11** to grant authority to. **12** *Mil.* to confer a rank on. **13** to equip and test (a ship) for active service. **14** to place an order for (something): *to commission a portrait.* **15** to make or become operative or operable: *the plant is due to commission next year.* [C14: from OF, from L *commissiō* a bringing together, from *committere* to COMMIT]

commissionaire (kəˌmɪʃəˈnɛə) *n Chiefly Brit.* a uniformed doorman at a hotel, theatre, etc. [C18: from F, from COMMISSION]

commissioned officer *n* a military officer holding a commission, such as Second Lieutenant in the British Army, Acting Sub-Lieutenant in the Royal Navy, Pilot Officer in the Royal Air Force, and officers of all ranks senior to these.

commissioner (kəˈmɪʃənə) *n* **1** a person endowed with certain powers. **2** any of several types of civil servant. **3** a member of a commission.
▸**comˈmissionerˌship** *n*

commissioner for oaths *n* a solicitor authorized to authenticate oaths on sworn statements.

commit ❶ (kəˈmɪt) *vb* **commits, committing, committed.** (*tr*) **1** to hand over, as for safekeeping; entrust. **2 commit to memory.** to memorize. **3** to take into custody: *to commit someone to prison.* **4** (*usually passive*) to pledge or align (oneself), as to a particular cause: *a committed radical.* **5** to order (forces) into action. **6** to perform (a crime, error, etc.). **7** to surrender, esp. for destruction: *she committed the letter to the fire.* **8** to refer (a bill, etc.) to a committee. [C14: from L *committere* to join, from *com-* together + *mittere* to send]
▸**comˈmittable** *adj* ▸**comˈmitter** *n*

commitment ❶ (kəˈmɪtmənt) *n* **1** the act of committing or pledging. **2** the state of being committed or pledged. **3** an obligation, promise, etc., that restricts freedom of action. **4** Also called (esp. formerly): **mittimus.** *Law.* a written order of a court directing that a person be imprisoned. **5** a future financial obligation or contingent liability. ◆ Also called (esp. for sense 4): **committal** (kəˈmɪtᵊl).

committee ❶ *n* **1** (kəˈmɪtɪ). a group of people appointed to perform a specified service or function. **2** (ˌkɒmɪˈtiː). (formerly) a person to whom the care of a mentally incompetent person or his property was entrusted by a court. [C15: from *committen* to entrust + -EE]

committeeman (kəˈmɪtɪmən, -ˌmæn) *n, pl* **committeemen.** *Chiefly US.* a member of one or more committees.
▸**comˈmitteeˌwoman** *fem n*

Committee of the Whole House *n* (in Britain) an informal sitting of the House of Commons to discuss and amend a bill.

commode (kəˈməʊd) *n* **1** a piece of furniture, usually highly ornamented, containing drawers or shelves. **2** a bedside table with a cabinet for a chamber pot or washbasin. **3** a chair with a hinged flap concealing a chamber pot. [C17: from F, from L *commodus* COMMODIOUS]

commodious ❶ (kəˈməʊdɪəs) *adj* **1** roomy; spacious. **2** *Arch.* convenient. [C15: from Med. L, from L *commodus* convenient, from *com-* with + *modus* measure]
▸**comˈmodiousness** *n*

commodity (kəˈmɒdɪtɪ) *n, pl* **commodities. 1** an article of commerce. **2** something of use or profit. **3** *Econ.* an exchangeable unit of economic wealth, such as a primary product. [C14: from OF *commodité*, from L *commoditās* suitability; see COMMODIOUS]

commodo (kəˈməʊdəʊ) *adv* a variant spelling of **comodo.**

commodore (ˈkɒməˌdɔː) *n* **1** *Brit.* a naval rank junior to rear admiral and senior to captain. **2** the captain of a shipping line. **3** the officer in command of a merchant convoy. **4** the titular head of a yacht club. [C17: prob. from Du. *commandeur*, from F, from OF *commander* to COMMAND]

common ❶ (ˈkɒmən) *adj* **1** belonging to two or more people: *common property.* **2** belonging to members of one or more communities; public: *a common culture.* **3** of ordinary standard; average. **4** prevailing; widespread: *common opinion.* **5** frequently encountered; ordinary: *a common brand of soap.* **6** notorious: *a common nuisance.* **7** *Derog.* considered by the speaker to be low-class, vulgar, or coarse. **8** (*prenominal*) having no special distinction: *the common man.* **9** *Maths.* having a specified relationship with a group of numbers or quantities: *common denominator.* **10** *Prosody.* (of a syllable) able to be long or short. **11** *Grammar.* (in certain languages) denoting or belonging to a gender of nouns that includes both masculine and feminine referents. **12 common or garden.** *Inf.* ordinary; unexceptional. ◆ *n* **13** a tract of open public land. **14** *Law.* the right to go onto someone else's property and remove natural products, as by pasturing cattle (esp. in **right of common**). **15** *Christianity.* **15a** a form of the proper of the Mass used on festivals that have no special proper of their own. **15b** the ordinary of the Mass. **16 in common.** mutually held or used. ◆ See also **commons.** [C13: from OF *commun*, from L *commūnis* general]
▸**ˈcommonly** *adv* ▸**ˈcommonness** *n*

commonage (ˈkɒmənɪdʒ) *n* **1** *Chiefly law.* **1a** the use of something, esp. a pasture, in common with others. **1b** the right to such use. **2** the state of being held in common. **3** another word for **commonalty** (sense 1).

commonality (ˌkɒməˈnælɪtɪ) *n, pl* **commonalities. 1** the fact of being common. **2** another word for **commonalty** (sense 1).

commonalty (ˈkɒmənəltɪ) *n, pl* **commonalties. 1** the ordinary people as distinct from those with rank or title. **2** the members of an incorporated society. [C13: from OF *comunalte*, from *comunal* communal]

common carrier *n* a person or firm engaged in the business of transporting goods or passengers.

common chord *n Music.* a chord consisting of the keynote, a major or minor third, and a perfect fifth.

common cold *n* a mild viral infection of the upper respiratory tract, characterized by sneezing, coughing, etc.

commoner (ˈkɒmənə) *n* **1** a person who does not belong to the nobility. **2** a person who has a right in or over common land. **3** *Brit.* a student at a university who is not on a scholarship.

common fraction *n* another name for **simple fraction.**

common knowledge *n* something widely or generally known.

common law *n* **1** the body of law based on judicial decisions and custom, as distinct from statute law. **2** (*modifier*) of or denoting a marriage that is deemed to exist after a man and a woman have cohabited for a number of years: *common-law marriage; common-law wife; common-law husband.*

Common Market *n* **the.** an informal name for the European Economic Community (now the **European Union**) and its policies of greater eco-

THESAURUS

commiserate *vb* = **sympathize**, compassionate (*arch.*), condole, console, feel for, pity

commiseration *n* = **sympathy**, compassion, condolence, consolation, fellow feeling, pity

commission *n* **1, 2** = **duty**, appointment, authority, charge, employment, errand, function, mandate, mission, task, trust, warrant **5** = **committee**, board, body of commissioners, commissioners, delegation, deputation, representatives **7b** = **fee**, allowance, brokerage, compensation, cut, percentage, rake-off (*sl.*), royalties ◆ *vb* **11** = **appoint**, authorize, contract, delegate, depute, empower, engage, nominate, order, select, send

commit *vb* **1** = **give**, commend, confide, consign, deliver, deposit, engage, entrust, hand over **3** = **put in custody**, confine, imprison **4** = **pledge**, align, bind, compromise, endanger, make liable, obligate, rank **6** = **do**, carry out, enact, execute, perform, perpetrate
Antonyms *vb* ≠ **give:** receive, withhold ≠ **put in custody:** free, let out, release, set free ≠ **pledge:** disavow, vacillate, waver ≠ **do:** omit

commitment *n* **1** = **pledge**, assurance, guarantee, promise, undertaking, vow, word **2** = **dedication**, adherence, devotion, involvement, loyalty **3** = **responsibility**, duty, engagement, liability, obligation, tie
Antonyms *n* ≠ **dedication:** indecisiveness, vacillation, wavering ≠ **pledge:** disavowal, negation

committee *n* **1** = **group**, commission, delegation, deputation, panel, subcommittee

commodious *adj* **1** = **roomy**, ample, capacious, comfortable, expansive, extensive, large, loose, spacious

common *adj* **1, 2** = **collective**, communal, community, popular, public, social **3, 5** = **average**, a dime a dozen, bog-standard (*Brit. & Irish slang*), commonplace, conventional, customary, daily, everyday, familiar, frequent, general, habitual, humdrum, obscure, ordinary, plain, regular, routine, run-of-the-mill, simple, standard, stock, usual, vanilla (*sl.*), workaday **4** = **popular**, accepted, general, prevailing, prevalent, universal, widespread **7** = **vulgar**, coarse, inferior, low, plebeian, undistinguished
Antonyms *adj* ≠ **average:** abnormal, famous, formal, important, infrequent, noble, outstanding, rare, scarce, sophisticated, strange, superior, uncommon, unknown, unusual ≠ **collective:** personal, private ≠ **vulgar:** cultured, distinguished, gentle, refined, sensitive

commonness *n* **3, 5** = **usualness**, commonplaceness, conventionality, customariness, familiarness, generalness, habitualness, humdrumness, ordinariness, plainness, regularity, simpleness **7** = **vulgarity**, baseness, coarseness, inferiority, lowness
Antonyms *n* ≠ **usualness:** abnormality, extraordinariness, rarity, strangeness, uncommonness, unfamiliarness, uniqueness

nomic cooperation between member states. See also **European Community.**

common noun *n Grammar.* a noun that refers to each member of a whole class sharing the features connoted by the noun, as for example *orange* and *drum.* Cf. **proper noun.**

commonplace ❶ ('kɒmən,pleɪs) *adj* **1** ordinary; everyday. **2** dull; trite: *commonplace prose.* ◆ *n* **3** a platitude; truism. **4** a passage in a book marked for inclusion in a commonplace book, etc. **5** an ordinary thing. [C16: translation of L *locus commūnis* argument of wide application]
▸**'common,placeness** *n*

commonplace book *n* a notebook in which quotations, poems, etc., that catch the owner's attention are entered.

common room *n Chiefly Brit.* a sitting room in schools, colleges, etc.

commons ('kɒmənz) *n* **1** (*functioning as pl*) the lower classes as contrasted with the ruling or noble classes of society. **2** (*functioning as sing*) *Brit.* a hall for dining, recreation, etc., usually attached to a college, etc. **3** (*usually functioning as pl*) *Brit.* food or rations (esp. in **short commons**).

Commons ('kɒmənz) *n* **the.** See **House of Commons.**

common sense ❶ *n* **1** sound practical sense. ◆ *adj* **common-sense;** *also* **common-sensical. 2** inspired by or displaying this.

common time *n Music.* a time signature indicating four crotchet beats to the bar; four-four time. Symbol: **C**

commonweal ('kɒmən,wiːl) *n Arch.* **1** the public good. **2** another name for **commonwealth.**

commonwealth ('kɒmən,wɛlθ) *n* **1** the people of a state or nation viewed politically; body politic. **2** a state in which the people possess sovereignty; republic. **3** a group of persons united by some common interest.

Commonwealth ('kɒmən,wɛlθ) *n* **the. 1** Official name: **the Commonwealth of Nations.** an association of sovereign states, most of which are or at some time were ruled by Britain. **2** the republic that existed in Britain from 1649 to 1660. **3** the official designation of Australia, four states of the US, and Puerto Rico.

Commonwealth Day *n* the anniversary of Queen Victoria's birth, May 24, celebrated (now on the second Monday in March) in many parts of the Commonwealth. Former name: **Empire Day.**

commotion ❶ (kə'məʊʃən) *n* **1** violent disturbance; upheaval. **2** political insurrection. **3** a confused noise; din. [C15: from L *commōtiō,* from *commovēre,* from *com-* (intensive) + *movēre* to MOVE]

communal ❶ ('kɒmjunᵊl) *adj* **1** belonging to a community as a whole. **2** of a commune or a religious community.
▸**communality** (,kɒmju'nælɪtɪ) *n* ▸**'communally** *adv*

communalism ('kɒmjunə,lɪzəm) *n* **1** a system or theory of government in which the state is seen as a loose federation of self-governing communities. **2** the practice or advocacy of communal living or ownership.
▸**'communalist** *n* ▸**,communal'istic** *adj*

communalize *or* **communalise** ('kɒmjunə,laɪz) *vb* **communalizes, communalizing, communalized** *or* **communalises, communalising, communalised.** (*tr*) to render (something) the property of a commune or community.
▸**,communali'zation** *or* **,communali'sation** *n*

communautaire *French.* (kɔmynotɛr) *adj* supporting the principles of the European Union. [lit.: community (as modifier)]

commune[1] *vb* (kə'mjuːn), **communes, communing, communed.** (*intr;* usually foll. by *with*) **1** to talk intimately. **2** to experience strong emotion (for): *to commune with nature.* ◆ *n* ('kɒmjuːn). **3** intimate conversation; communion. [C13: from OF *comuner* to hold in common, from *comun* COMMON]

commune[2] ❶ ('kɒmjuːn) *n* **1** a group of families or individuals living together and sharing possessions and responsibilities. **2** any small group of people having common interests or responsibilities. **3** the smallest administrative unit in Belgium, France, Italy, and Switzerland. **4** a medieval town enjoying a large degree of autonomy. [C18: from F, from Med. L *commūnia,* from L: things held in common]

Commune ('kɒmjuːn) *n French history.* **1** See **Paris Commune. 2** a committee that governed Paris during the French Revolution: suppressed 1794.

communicable ❶ (kə'mjuːnɪkəbᵊl) *adj* **1** capable of being communicated. **2** (of a disease) capable of being passed on readily.
▸**com,munica'bility** *n* ▸**com'municably** *adv*

communicant (kə'mjuːnɪkənt) *n* **1** *Christianity.* a person who receives Communion. **2** a person who communicates or informs.

communicate ❶ (kə'mjuːnɪ,keɪt) *vb* **communicates, communicating, communicated. 1** to impart (knowledge) or exchange (thoughts) by speech, writing, gestures, etc. **2** (*tr;* usually foll. by *to*) to transmit (to): *the dog communicated his fear to the other animals.* **3** (*intr*) to have a sympathetic mutual understanding. **4** (*intr;* usually foll. by *with*) to make or have a connecting passage: *the kitchen communicates with the dining room.* **5** (*tr*) to transmit (a disease). **6** (*intr*) *Christianity.* to receive Communion. [C16: from L *commūnicāre* to share, from *commūnis* COMMON]
▸**com'muni,cator** *n* ▸**com'municatory** *adj*

communication ❶ (kə,mjuːnɪ'keɪʃən) *n* **1** the imparting or exchange of information, ideas, or feelings. **2** something communicated, such as a message. **3** (*usually pl; sometimes functioning as sing*) the study of ways in which human beings communicate. **4** a connecting route or link. **5** (*pl*) *Mil.* the system of routes by which forces, supplies, etc., are moved within an area of operations.

communication cord *n Brit.* a cord or chain in a train which may be pulled by a passenger to stop the train in an emergency.

communications satellite *n* an artificial satellite used to relay radio, television, and telephone signals around the earth's surface, usually in geostationary orbit.

communicative ❶ (kə'mjuːnɪkətɪv) *adj* **1** inclined or able to communicate readily; talkative. **2** of or relating to communication.

communion ❶ (kə'mjuːnjən) *n* **1** an exchange of thoughts, emotions, etc. **2** sharing in common; participation. **3** (foll. by *with*) strong feelings (for): *communion with nature.* **4** a religious group or denomination having common beliefs and practices. **5** spiritual union. [C14: from L *commūniō,* from *commūnis* COMMON]

Communion ❶ (kə'mjuːnjən) *n Christianity.* **1** the act of participating in the Eucharist. **2** the celebration of the Eucharist. **3** the consecrated elements of the Eucharist. ◆ Also called: **Holy Communion.**

communiqué ❶ (kə'mjuːnɪ,keɪ) *n* an official communication or announcement, esp. to the press or public. [C19: from F]

communism ❶ ('kɒmju,nɪzəm) *n* **1** advocacy of a classless society in which private ownership has been abolished and the means of production belong to the community. **2** any movement or doctrine aimed at achieving such a society. **3** (*usually cap.*) a political movement based upon the writings of Marx that considers history in terms of class conflict and revolutionary struggle. **4** (*usually cap.*) a system of government established by a ruling Communist Party, esp. in the former Soviet Union. **5** communal living. [C19: from F *communisme,* from *commun* COMMON]

communist ❶ ('kɒmjunɪst) *n* **1** a supporter of communism. **2** (*often cap.*) a supporter of a Communist movement or state. **3** (*often cap.*) a member of a Communist party. **4** (*often cap.*) *Chiefly US.* any person

THESAURUS

commonplace *adj* **1, 2** = **everyday,** banal, common, customary, dime-a-dozen (*inf.*), humdrum, mundane, obvious, ordinary, pedestrian, run-of-the-mill, stale, threadbare, trite, uninteresting, vanilla (*sl.*), widespread, worn out ◆ *n* **3** = **cliché,** banality, platitude, truism
Antonyms *adj* ≠ **everyday:** exciting, extraordinary, ground-breaking, infrequent, interesting, left-field (*inf.*), new, novel, original, rare, strange, uncommon, unfamiliar, unique, unusual

common sense *n* **1** = **good sense,** gumption (*Brit. inf.*), horse sense, level-headedness, mother wit, native intelligence, nous (*Brit. slang*), practicality, prudence, reasonableness, sound judgment, soundness, wit ◆ *adj* **common-sense 2** = **sensible,** astute, down-to-earth, hard-headed, judicious, level-headed, matter-of-fact, practical, realistic, reasonable, sane, shrewd, sound
Antonyms *adj* airy-fairy (*inf.*), daft (*inf.*), foolish, impractical, irrational, unrealistic, unreasonable, unthinking, unwise

commotion *n* **1** = **disturbance,** ado, agitation, brouhaha, bustle, disorder, excitement, ferment, furore, fuss, hubbub, hue and cry, hullabaloo, hurly-burly, perturbation, racket, riot, rumpus, to-do, tumult, turmoil, upheaval, uproar

communal *adj* **1** = **public,** collective, communistic, community, general, joint, neighbourhood, shared
Antonyms *adj* exclusive, individual, personal, private, single, unshared

commune[2] *n* **1, 2** = **community,** collective, cooperative, kibbutz

commune *vb* **1** *usually foll. by* **with** = **talk to,** communicate with, confer with, confide in, converse with, discourse with, discuss with, parley with

communicable *adj* **2** = **infectious,** catching, contagious, taking, transferable, transmittable

communicate *vb* **1, 2** = **make known,** acquaint, announce, be in contact, be in touch, connect, convey, correspond, declare, disclose, disseminate, divulge, impart, inform, pass on, phone, proclaim, publish, report, reveal, ring up (*inf., chiefly Brit.*), signify, spread, transmit, unfold
Antonyms *vb* conceal, cover up, hold back, hush up, keep back, keep secret, keep under wraps, repress, sit on (*inf.*), suppress, whitewash (*inf.*), withhold

communication *n* **1** = **passing on,** connection, contact, conversation, correspondence, dissemination, intercourse, link, transmission **2** = **message,** announcement, disclosure, dispatch, information, intelligence, news, report, statement, word **3** *usually plu* = **information technology,** media, publicity, public relations, telecommunications **5** *pl* = **transport,** routes, travel

communicative *adj* **1** = **talkative,** candid, chatty, conversable, expansive, forthcoming, frank, informative, loquacious, open, outgoing, unreserved, voluble
Antonyms *adj* quiet, reserved, reticent, secretive, taciturn, uncommunicative, uninformative, untalkative

communion *n* **1-3** = **closeness,** accord, affinity, agreement, communing, concord, consensus, converse, fellowship, harmony, intercourse, participation, rapport, sympathy, togetherness, unity

Communion *n Church* **2** = **Eucharist,** Lord's Supper, Mass, Sacrament

communiqué *n* = **announcement,** bulletin, dispatch, news flash, official communication, report

communism *n, usually cap.* **3, 4** = **socialism,** Bolshevism, collectivism, Eurocommunism, Maoism, Marxism, Marxism-Leninism, Stalinism, state socialism, Titoism, Trotskyism

communist *n, often cap.* **2-4** = **socialist,** Bolshevik, collectivist, Marxist, Red (*inf.*)

holding left-wing views, esp. when considered subversive. **5** a person who practises communal living. ◆ *adj* **6** of, favouring, or relating to communism.
▸ˌ**commuˈnistic** *adj*

community Ⓣ (kəˈmjuːnɪtɪ) *n, pl* **communities. 1a** the people living in one locality. **1b** the locality in which they live. **1c** (*as modifier*): *community spirit.* **2** a group of people having cultural, religious, or other characteristics in common: *the Protestant community.* **3** a group of nations having certain interests in common. **4** the public; society. **5** common ownership. **6** similarity or agreement: *community of interests.* **7** (in Wales and Scotland) the smallest unit of local government. **8** *Ecology.* a group of interdependent plants and animals inhabiting the same region. [C14: from L *commūnitās,* from *commūnis* COMMON]

community centre *n* a building used by a community for social gatherings, etc.

community charge *n* (formerly in Britain) a flat-rate charge paid by each adult in a community to their local authority in place of rates. Also called: **poll tax.**

community chest *n US.* a fund raised by voluntary contribution for local welfare activities.

community council *n* (in Scotland and Wales) an independent voluntary local body set up to attend to local interests and organize community activities.

community education *n* the provision of a wide range of educational and special-interest courses and activities by a local authority.

community home *n* (in Britain) **1** a home provided by a local authority for children who cannot remain with their parents. **2** a boarding school for young offenders.

community medicine *n* the branch of medicine concerned with evaluating and providing for the health needs of populations, esp. through monitoring and preventive measures.

community policing *n* the assigning of the same one or two policemen to a particular area so that they become familiar with the residents and they with them, as a way of reducing crime.

community service *n* work undertaken for the community by an offender without pay, by the order of a court.

communize *or* **communise** (ˈkɒmjʊˌnaɪz) *vb* **communizes, communizing, communized** *or* **communises, communising, communised.** (*tr*) (*sometimes cap.*) **1** to make (property) public; nationalize. **2** to make (a person or country) communist.
▸ˌ**communiˈzation** *or* ˌ**communiˈsation** *n*

commutate (ˈkɒmjʊˌteɪt) *vb* **commutates, commutating, commutated.** (*tr*) **1** to reverse the direction of (an electric current). **2** to convert (an alternating current) into a direct current.

commutation (ˌkɒmjʊˈteɪʃən) *n* **1** a substitution or exchange. **2** the replacement of one method of payment by another. **3** the reduction in severity of a penalty imposed by law. **4** the process of commutating an electric current.

commutative (kəˈmjuːtətɪv, ˈkɒmjʊˌteɪtɪv) *adj* **1** relating to or involving substitution. **2** *Maths, logic.* **2a** giving the same result irrespective of the order of the arguments; thus addition is commutative but subtraction is not. **2b** relating to this property: *the commutative law of addition.*

commutator (ˈkɒmjʊˌteɪtə) *n* **1** a device used to reverse the direction of flow of an electric current. **2** the segmented metal cylinder or disc of an electric motor, generator, etc., used to make electrical contact with the rotating coils.

commute Ⓣ (kəˈmjuːt) *vb* **commutes, commuting, commuted. 1** (*intr*) to travel some distance regularly between one's home and one's place of work. **2** (*tr*) to substitute. **3** (*tr*) *Law.* to reduce (a sentence) to one less severe. **4** to pay (an annuity, etc.) at one time, instead of in instalments. **5** to change: *to commute base metal into gold.* [C17: from L *commūtāre,* from *com-* mutually + *mūtāre* to change]
▸**comˈmutable** *adj* ▸**comˌmutaˈbility** *n*

commuter Ⓣ (kəˈmjuːtə) *n* a person who travels to work over an appreciable distance, usually from the suburbs to the centre of a city.

comodo *or* **commodo** (kəˈməʊdəʊ) *adv Music.* in a convenient tempo. [It.: comfortable, from L *commodus* convenient: see COMMODIOUS]

comose (ˈkəʊməʊs, kəʊˈməʊs) *adj Bot.* having tufts of hair; hairy. Also: **comate.** [C18: from L *comōsus* hairy]

comp (kɒmp) *Inf.* ◆ *n* **1** a compositor. **2** an accompaniment. **3** a competition. ◆ *vb* **4** (*intr*) to work as a compositor in the printing industry. **5** to play an accompaniment (to).

comp. *abbrev. for:* **1** companion. **2** comparative. **3** compare. **4** compiled. **5** composer. **6** composition. **7** compositor. **8** compound. **9** comprehensive. **10** comprising.

compact[1] Ⓣ *adj* (kəmˈpækt). **1** closely packed together. **2** neatly fitted into a restricted space. **3** concise; brief. **4** well constructed; solid; firm. **5** (foll. by *of*) composed (of). ◆ *vb* (kəmˈpækt). (*tr*) **6** to pack closely together; compress. **7** (foll. by *of*) to form by pressing together: *sediment compacted of three types of clay.* **8** *Metallurgy.* to compress (a metal powder) to form a stable product suitable for sintering. ◆ *n* (ˈkɒmpækt). **9** a small flat case containing a mirror, face powder, and powder puff, designed to be carried in a woman's handbag. **10** *US & Canad.* a small and economical car. [C16: from L *compactus,* from *compingere,* from *com-* together + *pangere* to fasten]
▸**comˈpactly** *adv* ▸**comˈpactness** *n*

compact[2] Ⓣ (ˈkɒmpækt) *n* an official contract or agreement. [C16: from L *compactum,* from *compacīscī,* from *com-* together + *pacīscī* to contract]

compact disc (ˈkɒmpækt) *n* a small digital audio disc on which sound is recorded as a series of metallic pits enclosed in PVC and read by an optical laser system. Also called: **compact audio disc.** Abbrev.: **CD, CAD.**

compact video disc *n* a compact laser disc that plays both pictures and sound.

compages (kəmˈpeɪdʒiːz) *n* (*functioning as sing*) a structure or framework. [C17: from L: from *com-* together + *pangĕre* to fasten]

companion[1] Ⓣ (kəmˈpænjən) *n* **1** a person who is an associate of another or others; comrade. **2** (esp. formerly) an employee, usually a woman, who provides company for an employer. **3a** one of a pair. **3b** (*as modifier*): *a companion volume.* **4** a guidebook or handbook. **5** a member of the lowest rank of certain orders of knighthood. **6** *Astron.* the fainter of the two components of a double star. ◆ *vb* **7** (*tr*) to accompany. [C13: from LL *compāniō,* lit.: one who eats bread with another, from L *com-* with + *pānis* bread]
▸**comˈpanionˌship** *n*

companion[2] (kəmˈpænjən) *n Naut.* a raised frame on an upper deck with windows to give light to the deck below. [C18: from Du. *kompanje* quarterdeck, from OF *compagne,* from OIt. *compagna* pantry, ? ult. from L *pānis* bread]

companionable Ⓣ (kəmˈpænjənəbᵊl) *adj* sociable.
▸**comˈpanionableness** *n* ▸**comˈpanionably** *adv*

companionate (kəmˈpænjənɪt) *adj* **1** resembling, appropriate to, or acting as a companion. **2** harmoniously suited.

companionway (kəmˈpænjənˌweɪ) *n* a ladder from one deck to another in a ship.

company Ⓣ (ˈkʌmpənɪ) *n, pl* **companies. 1** a number of people gathered together; assembly. **2** the fact of being with someone; companionship: *I enjoy her company.* **3** a guest or guests. **4** a business enterprise. **5** the members of an enterprise not specifically mentioned in the enterprise's title. Abbrev.: **Co., co. 6** a group of actors. **7** a small unit of troops. **8** the officers and crew of a ship. **9** a unit of Guides. **10** *English history.* a medieval guild. **11 keep company. 11a** to accompany (someone). **11b** (esp. of lovers) to spend time together. ◆ *vb* **companies, companying, companied. 12** *Arch.* to associate (with someone). [C13: from OF *compaignie,* from LL *compāniō;* see COMPANION[1]]

company doctor *n* **1** a businessman or accountant who specializes in turning ailing companies into profitable enterprises. **2** a physician employed by a company to look after its staff and to advise on health matters.

company sergeant major *n Mil.* the senior noncommissioned officer in a company.

company town *n US & Canad.* a town built by a company for its employees.

compar. *abbrev. for* comparative.

comparable Ⓣ (ˈkɒmpərəbᵊl) *adj* **1** worthy of comparison. **2** able to be compared (with).
▸ˌ**comparaˈbility** *or* ˈ**comparableness** *n*

THESAURUS

community *n* **1-4** = **society**, association, body politic, brotherhood, commonwealth, company, district, general public, locality, people, populace, population, public, residents, state

commute *vb* **2** = **substitute**, barter, exchange, interchange, switch, trade **3** *Law* = **reduce**, alleviate, curtail, mitigate, modify, remit, shorten, soften

commuter *n* = **daily traveller**, straphanger (*inf.*), suburbanite

compact[1] *adj* **1** = **closely packed**, compressed, condensed, dense, firm, impenetrable, impermeable, pressed together, solid, thick **3** = **brief**, compendious, concise, epigrammatic, laconic, pithy, pointed, succinct, terse, to the point ◆ *vb* **6** = **pack closely**, compress, condense, cram, stuff, tamp
Antonyms *adj* ≠ **closely packed:** dispersed, large, loose, roomy, scattered, spacious, sprawling ≠ **brief:** circumlocutory, garrulous, lengthy, long-winded, prolix, rambling, verbose, wordy ◆ *vb* ≠ **pack closely:** disperse, loosen, separate

compact[2] *n* = **agreement**, alliance, arrangement, bargain, bond, concordat, contract, covenant, deal, entente, pact, stipulation, treaty, understanding

companion[1] *n* **1** = **friend**, accomplice, ally, associate, buddy (*inf.*), colleague, comrade, confederate, consort, crony, gossip (*arch.*), homeboy (*sl., chiefly US*), mate (*inf.*), partner **2** = **escort**, aide, assistant, attendant, chaperon, duenna, squire **3a** = **mate**, complement, counterpart, fellow, match, twin

companionable *adj* = **friendly**, affable, congenial, conversable, convivial, cordial, familiar, genial, gregarious, neighbourly, outgoing, sociable

companionship *n* **1** = **fellowship**, amity, camaraderie, company, comradeship, conviviality, esprit de corps, fraternity, friendship, rapport, togetherness

company *n* **1** = **group**, assemblage, assembly, band, bevy, body, camp, circle, collection, community, concourse, convention, coterie, crew, crowd, ensemble, gathering, league, party, set, throng, troop, troupe, turnout **2** = **companionship**, fellowship, presence, society **3** = **guests**, callers, party, visitors **4** = **business**, association, concern, corporation, establishment, firm, house, partnership, syndicate

comparable *adj* **1** = **on a par**, a match for, as good as, commensurate, equal, equivalent, in a class with, proportionate, tantamount **2** = **similar**, akin, alike, analogous, cognate, corresponding, cut from the same cloth, of a piece, related

comparative ➊ (kəmˈpærətɪv) *adj* **1** denoting or involving comparison: *comparative literature.* **2** relative: *a comparative loss of prestige.* **3** *Grammar.* denoting the form of an adjective that indicates that the quality denoted is possessed to a greater extent. In English the comparative is marked by the suffix *-er* or the word *more.* ◆ *n* **4** the comparative form of an adjective.
▸**comˈparatively** *adv* ▸**comˈparativeness** *n*

comparative advertising *n* the usual US term for **knocking copy.**

compare ➊ (kəmˈpɛə) *vb* **compares, comparing, compared. 1** (*tr;* foll. by *to*) to regard as similar; liken: *the general has been compared to Napoleon.* **2** (*tr*) to examine in order to observe resemblances or differences: *to compare rum and gin.* **3** (*intr;* usually foll. by *with*) to be the same or similar: *gin compares with rum in alcoholic content.* **4** (*intr*) to bear a specified relation when examined: *this car compares badly with the other.* **5** (*tr*) *Grammar.* to give the positive, comparative, and superlative forms of (an adjective). **6 compare notes.** to exchange opinions. ◆ *n* **7** comparison (esp. in **beyond compare**). [C15: from OF, from L *comparāre,* from *compar,* from *com-* together + *par* equal]

comparison ➊ (kəmˈpærɪsᵊn) *n* **1** the act of comparing. **2** the state of being compared. **3** likeness: *there was no comparison between them.* **4** a rhetorical device involving comparison, such as a simile. **5** Also called: **degrees of comparison.** *Grammar.* the listing of the positive, comparative, and superlative forms of an adjective or adverb. **6 bear** *or* **stand comparison** (**with**). to be sufficiently similar to be compared with (something else), esp. favourably.

compartment ➊ (kəmˈpɑːtmənt) *n* **1** one of the sections into which an area, esp. an enclosed space, is partitioned. **2** any separate section: *a compartment of the mind.* **3** a small storage space. [C16: from F *compartiment,* ult. from LL *compartīrī* to share]
▸**compartmental** (ˌkɒmpɑːtˈmɛntᵊl) *adj* ▸ˌ**compartˈmentally** *adv*

compartmentalize ➊ *or* **compartmentalise** (ˌkɒmpɑːtˈmɛntᵊˌlaɪz) *vb* **compartmentalizes, compartmentalizing, compartmentalized** *or* **compartmentalises, compartmentalising, compartmentalised.** (*usually tr*) to put into categories, etc., esp. to an excessive degree.
▸ˌ**compartˌmentaliˈzation** *or* ˌ**compartˌmentaliˈsation** *n*

compass ➊ (ˈkʌmpəs) *n* **1** Also called: **magnetic compass.** an instrument for finding direction, having a magnetized needle which points to magnetic north. **2** (*often pl*) Also called: **pair of compasses.** an instrument used for drawing circles, measuring distances, etc., that consists of two arms, joined at one end. **3** limits or range: *within the compass of education.* **4** *Music.* the interval between the lowest and highest note attainable. ◆ *vb* (*tr*) **5** to surround; hem in. **6** to grasp mentally. **7** to achieve; accomplish. **8** *Obs.* to plot. [C13: from OF *compas,* from Vulgar L *compassāre* (unattested) to pace out, ult. from L *passus* step]
▸ˈ**compassable** *adj*

compass card *n* a compass in the form of a card that rotates so that "0°" or "North" points to magnetic north.

compassion ➊ (kəmˈpæʃən) *n* a feeling of distress and pity for the suffering or misfortune of another. [C14: from OF, from LL *compassiō,* from L *com-* with + *patī* to suffer]

compassionate ➊ (kəmˈpæʃənɪt) *adj* showing or having compassion.
▸**comˈpassionately** *adv*

compassionate leave *n* leave granted on the grounds of bereavement, family illness, etc.

compassion fatigue *n* the inability to react sympathetically to a crisis, disaster, etc., because of overexposure to previous crises, disasters, etc.

compass rose *n* a circle or decorative device printed on a map or chart showing the points of the compass.

compass saw *n* a hand saw with a narrow tapered blade for making a curved cut.

compatible ➊ (kəmˈpætɪbᵊl) *adj* **1** (usually foll. by *with*) able to exist together harmoniously. **2** (usually foll. by *with*) consistent: *her deeds were not compatible with her ideology.* **3** (of pieces of machinery, etc.) capable of being used together without modification or adaptation. [C15: from Med. L *compatibilis,* from LL *compatī;* see COMPASSION]
▸**comˌpatiˈbility** *n* ▸**comˈpatibly** *adv*

compatriot ➊ (kəmˈpætrɪət) *n* a fellow countryman. [C17: from F *compatriote,* from LL; see PATRIOT]
▸**comˌpatriˈotic** *adj*

compeer (ˈkɒmpɪə) *n* **1** a person of equal rank, status, or ability. **2** a comrade. [C13: from OF *comper,* from Med. L *compater* godfather]

compel ➊ (kəmˈpɛl) *vb* **compels, compelling, compelled.** (*tr*) **1** to cause (someone) by force (to be or do something). **2** to obtain by force; exact: *to compel obedience.* [C14: from L *compellere,* from *com-* together + *pellere* to drive]
▸**comˈpellable** *adj*

compelling ➊ (kəmˈpɛlɪŋ) *adj* **1** arousing or denoting strong interest, esp. admiring interest. **2** (of an argument, evidence, etc.) convincing.

compendious ➊ (kəmˈpɛndɪəs) *adj* stating the essentials of a subject in a concise form.
▸**comˈpendiously** *adv* ▸**comˈpendiousness** *n*

compendium ➊ (kəmˈpɛndɪəm) *n, pl* **compendiums** *or* **compendia** (-dɪə). **1** *Brit.* a book containing a collection of useful hints. **2** *Brit.* a selection, esp. of different games in one container. **3** a summary. [C16: from L: a saving, lit.: something weighed]

compensate ➊ (ˈkɒmpɛnˌseɪt) *vb* **compensates, compensating, compensated. 1** to make amends to (someone), esp. for loss or injury. **2** (*tr*) to serve as compensation or damages for (injury, loss, etc.). **3** to counterbalance the effects of (a force, weight, etc.) so as to produce equilibrium. **4** (*intr*) to attempt to conceal one's shortcomings by the exaggerated exhibition of qualities regarded as desirable. [C17: from L *compēnsāre,* from *pendere* to weigh]
▸**compensatory** (ˈkɒmpɛnˌseɪtərɪ, kəmˈpɛnsətərɪ) *or* **compensative** (ˈkɒmpɛnˌseɪtɪv, kəmˈpɛnsə-) *adj*

compensation ➊ (ˌkɒmpɛnˈseɪʃən) *n* **1** the act of making amends for something. **2** something given as reparation for loss, injury, etc. **3** the attempt to conceal one's shortcomings by the exaggerated exhibition of qualities regarded as desirable.
▸ˌ**compenˈsational** *adj*

comper (ˈkɒmpə) *n Inf.* a person who regularly enters competitions in newspapers, magazines, etc., esp. competitions offering consumer goods as prizes. [C20: COMP(ETITION) + -ER[1]]
▸ˈ**comping** *n*

compere (ˈkɒmpɛə) *Brit.* ◆ *n* **1** a master of ceremonies who introduces cabaret, television acts, etc. ◆ *vb* **comperes, compering, compered. 2** to act as a compere (for). [C20: from F, lit.: godfather]

compete ➊ (kəmˈpiːt) *vb* **competes, competing, competed.** (*intr;* often foll. by *with*) to contend (against) for profit, an award, etc. [C17: from LL *competere,* from L, from *com-* together + *petere* to seek]

competence ➊ (ˈkɒmpɪtəns) *or* **competency** *n* **1** the condition of being capable; ability. **2** a sufficient income to live on. **3** the state of being legally competent or qualified.

THESAURUS

Antonyms *adj* different, dissimilar, incommensurable, incomparable, unequal

comparative *adj* **2** = **relative**, approximate, by comparison, qualified

compare *vb* **1** *foll. by* **to** = **liken to**, correlate to, equate to, identify with, mention in the same breath as, parallel, resemble **2** = **weigh**, balance, collate, contrast, juxtapose, set against **3** *usually with* **with** = **be on a par with**, approach, approximate to, bear comparison, be in the same class as, be the equal of, come up to, compete with, equal, hold a candle to, match, vie

comparison *n* **1** = **contrast**, collation, distinction, juxtaposition **3** = **similarity**, analogy, comparability, correlation, likeness, resemblance

compartment *n* **1, 3** = **section**, alcove, bay, berth, booth, carrel, carriage, cell, chamber, cubbyhole, cubicle, locker, niche, pigeonhole **2** = **category**, area, department, division, section, subdivision

compartmentalize *vb* = **categorize** *or* **categorise**, classify, pigeonhole, sectionalize *or* sectionalise

compass *n* **3** = **range**, area, bound, boundary, circle, circuit, circumference, enclosure, extent, field, limit, reach, realm, round, scope, sphere, stretch, zone ◆ *vb* **5** = **surround**, beset, besiege, blockade, circumscribe, encircle, enclose, encompass, environ, hem in, invest (*rare*)

compassion *n* = **sympathy**, charity, clemency, commiseration, compunction, condolence, fellow feeling, heart, humanity, kindness, mercy, pity, quarter, ruth (*arch.*), soft-heartedness, sorrow, tender-heartedness, tenderness, understanding

Antonyms *n* apathy, cold-heartedness, indifference, mercilessness, unconcern

compassionate *adj* = **sympathetic**, benevolent, charitable, humane, humanitarian, indulgent, kind-hearted, kindly, lenient, merciful, pitying, tender, tender-hearted, understanding

Antonyms *adj* callous, harsh, heartless, inhumane, pitiless, uncaring, unfeeling, unmerciful, unsympathetic

compatibility *n* **1** = **harmony**, affinity, agreement, amity, concord, congeniality, empathy, like-mindedness, rapport, single-mindedness, sympathy

compatible *adj* **1, 2** = **harmonious**, accordant, adaptable, agreeable, congenial, congruent, congruous, consistent, consonant, in harmony, in keeping, like-minded, reconcilable, suitable

Antonyms *adj* contradictory, inappropriate, inapt, incompatible, unfitting, unharmonious, unsuitable

compatriot *n* = **fellow countryman**, countryman, fellow citizen

compel *vb* **1, 2** = **force**, bulldoze (*inf.*), coerce, constrain, dragoon, drive, enforce, exact, hustle (*sl.*), impel, make, necessitate, oblige, railroad (*inf.*), restrain, squeeze, urge

compelling *adj* **1** = **fascinating**, enchanting, enthralling, gripping, hypnotic, irresistible, mesmeric, spellbinding **2** = **convincing**, cogent, conclusive, forceful, irrefutable, powerful, telling, weighty

Antonyms *adj* ≠ **fascinating:** boring, dull, humdrum, monotonous, ordinary, repetitious, tiresome, uneventful, uninteresting, wearisome

compendious *adj* = **concise**, abbreviated, abridged, brief, comprehensive, condensed, contracted, short, succinct, summarized, summary, synoptic

compendium *n* **1** = **collection**, compilation, digest **3** = **summary**, abbreviation, abridgment, abstract, capsule, epitome, outline, précis, synopsis

compensate *vb* **1** = **recompense**, atone, indemnify, make amends, make good, make restitution, refund, reimburse, remunerate, repay, requite, reward, satisfy **2** = **cancel (out)**, balance, counteract, counterbalance, countervail, make up for, offset, redress

compensation *n* **1, 2** = **recompense**, amends, atonement, damages, indemnification, indemnity, meed (*arch.*), offset, payment, reimbursement, remuneration, reparation, requital, restitution, reward, satisfaction

compete *vb* = **contend**, be in the running, challenge, contest, emulate, fight, pit oneself against, rival, strive, struggle, vie

competence *n* **1** = **ability**, adequacy, appropriateness, capability, capacity, competency, craft, expertise, fitness, proficiency, skill, suitability

Antonyms *n* inability, inadequacy, incompetence

competent ❶ (ˈkɒmpɪtənt) *adj* **1** having sufficient skill, knowledge, etc.; capable. **2** suitable or sufficient for the purpose: *a competent answer.* **3** *Law.* (of a witness, etc.) qualified to testify, etc. **[**C14: from L *competēns,* from *competere;* see COMPETE**]**
▸ˈ**competently** *adv*

competition ❶ (ˌkɒmpɪˈtɪʃən) *n* **1** the act of competing. **2** a contest in which a winner is selected from among two or more entrants. **3** a series of games, sports events, etc. **4** the opposition offered by competitors. **5** competitors offering opposition.

competitive ❶ (kəmˈpɛtɪtɪv) *adj* **1** involving rivalry: *competitive sports.* **2** sufficiently low in price or high in quality to be successful against commercial rivals. **3** characterized by an urge to compete: *a competitive personality.*
▸**comˈpetitiveness** *n*

competitor ❶ (kəmˈpɛtɪtə) *n* a person, group, team, firm, etc., that vies or competes; rival.

compile ❶ (kəmˈpaɪl) *vb* **compiles, compiling, compiled.** (*tr*) **1** to make or compose from other sources: *to compile a list of names.* **2** to collect for a book, hobby, etc. **3** *Computing.* to create (a set of machine instructions) from a high-level programming language, using a compiler. **[**C14: from L *compīlāre,* from *com-* together + *pīlāre* to thrust down, pack**]**
▸**compilation** (ˌkɒmpɪˈleɪʃən) *n*

compiler (kəmˈpaɪlə) *n* **1** a person who compiles something. **2** a computer program by which a high-level programming language is converted into machine language that can be acted upon by a computer. Cf. **assembler.**

complacency ❶ (kəmˈpleɪsənsɪ) *or* **complacence** *n* extreme self-satisfaction; smugness.

complacent ❶ (kəmˈpleɪsᵊnt) *adj* extremely self-satisfied. **[**C17: from L *complacēns* very pleasing, from *complacēre,* from *com-* (intensive) + *placēre* to please**]**
▸**comˈplacently** *adv*

complain ❶ (kəmˈpleɪn) *vb* (*intr*) **1** to express resentment, displeasure, etc.; grumble. **2** (foll. by *of*) to state the presence of pain, illness, etc.: *she complained of a headache.* **[**C14: from OF *complaindre,* from Vulgar L *complangere* (unattested), from L *com-* (intensive) + *plangere* to bewail**]**
▸**comˈplainer** *n* ▸**comˈplainingly** *adv*

complainant (kəmˈpleɪnənt) *n Law.* a plaintiff.

complaint ❶ (kəmˈpleɪnt) *n* **1** the act of complaining. **2** a cause for complaining; grievance. **3** a mild ailment.

complaisant ❶ (kəmˈpleɪzᵊnt) *adj* showing a desire to comply or oblige; polite. **[**C17: from F *complaire,* from L *complacēre* to please greatly; cf. COMPLACENT**]**
▸**comˈplaisance** *n*

complement ❶ *n* (ˈkɒmplɪmənt). **1** a person or thing that completes something. **2** a complete amount, number, etc. (often in **full complement**). **3** the officers and crew needed to man a ship. **4** *Grammar.* a word, phrase, or clause that completes the meaning of the predicate, as *an idiot* in *He is an idiot* or *that he would be early* in *I hoped that he would be early.* **5** *Maths.* the angle that when added to a specified angle produces a right angle. **6** *Logic.* the class of all the things that are not members of a given class. **7** *Immunol.* a group of proteins in the blood serum that, when activated by antibodies, destroys alien cells, such as bacteria. ◆ *vb* (ˈkɒmplɪˌmɛnt). **8** (*tr*) to complete or form a complement to. **[**C14: from L *complēmentum,* from *complēre,* from *com-* (intensive) + *plēre* to fill**]**
▸ˌ**complemenˈtation** *n*

> **USAGE NOTE** Avoid confusion with **compliment.**

complementary ❶ (ˌkɒmplɪˈmɛntərɪ) *adj* **1** forming a complement. **2** forming a satisfactory or balanced whole. **3** involving or using the treatments and techniques of alternative (complementary) medicine.
▸ˌ**compleˈmentarily** *adv* ▸ˌ**compleˈmentariness** *n*

complementary angle *n* either of two angles whose sum is 90°. Cf. **supplementary angle.**

complementary colour *n* one of any pair of colours, such as yellow and blue, that give white or grey when mixed in the correct proportions.

complementary DNA *n* a form of DNA artificially synthesized from a messenger RNA template and used in genetic engineering to produce gene clones. Abbrev.: **cDNA.**

complementary medicine *n* another name for **alternative medicine.**

complete ❶ (kəmˈpliːt) *adj* **1** having every necessary part; entire. **2** finished. **3** (*prenominal*) thorough: *he is a complete rogue.* **4** perfect in quality or kind: *he is a complete scholar.* **5** (of a logical system) constituted such that a contradiction or inconsistency arises on the addition of an axiom that cannot be deduced from the axioms of the system. **6** *Arch.* skilled; accomplished. ◆ *vb* **completes, completing, completed.** (*tr*) **7** to make perfect. **8** to finish. **9** (in land law) to pay any outstanding balance on a contract for the conveyance of land in exchange for the title deeds, so that the ownership of the land changes hands. **10** *American football.* (of a quarterback) to make a forward pass successfully. **[**C14: from L *complētus,* p.p. of *complēre* to fill up; see COMPLEMENT**]**
▸**comˈpletely** *adv* ▸**comˈpleteness** *n* ▸**comˈpletion** *n*

completist (kəmˈpliːtɪst) *n* a person who collects objects or memorabilia obsessively.

complex ❶ (ˈkɒmplɛks) *adj* **1** made up of interconnected parts. **2** (of thoughts, writing, etc.) intricate. **3** *Maths.* **3a** of or involving complex numbers. **3b** consisting of a real and an imaginary part, either of which can be zero. ◆ *n* **4** a whole made up of related parts: *a building complex.* **5** *Psychoanal.* a group of emotional impulses that have been banished from the conscious mind but continue to influence a person's behaviour. **6** *Inf.* an obsession: *he's got a complex about cats.* **7** any chemical compound in which one molecule is linked to another by a coordinate bond. **[**C17: from L *complexus,* from *complectī,* from *com-* together + *plectere* to braid**]**
▸ˈ**complexness** *n*

> **USAGE NOTE** *Complex* is sometimes wrongly used where *complicated* is meant. *Complex* is properly used to say only that something consists of several parts. It should not be used to say that, because something consists of many parts, it is difficult to understand or analyse.

THESAURUS

competent *adj* **1, 2** = **able**, adapted, adequate, appropriate, capable, clever, endowed, equal, fit, pertinent, proficient, qualified, sufficient, suitable
Antonyms *adj* cowboy (*inf.*), inadequate, incapable, incompetent, inexperienced, inexpert, undependable, unqualified, unskilled

competition *n* **1** = **rivalry**, contention, contest, emulation, one-upmanship (*inf.*), opposition, strife, struggle **2, 3** = **contest**, championship, event, head-to-head, puzzle, quiz, tournament **5** = **opposition**, challengers, field, rivals

competitive *adj* **1** = **cut-throat**, aggressive, antagonistic, at odds, dog-eat-dog, opposing, rival, vying **3** = **ambitious**, combative

competitor *n* = **contestant**, adversary, antagonist, challenger, competition, emulator, opponent, opposition, rival

compilation *n* **1, 2** = **collection**, accumulation, anthology, assemblage, assortment, treasury

compile *vb* **1** = **put together**, accumulate, amass, anthologize, collect, cull, garner, gather, marshal, organize

complacency *n* = **self-satisfaction**, contentment, gratification, pleasure, satisfaction, smugness

complacent *adj* = **self-satisfied**, contented, gratified, pleased, pleased with oneself, resting on one's laurels, satisfied, self-assured, self-contented, self-righteous, serene, smug, unconcerned
Antonyms *adj* discontent, dissatisfied, insecure, troubled, uneasy, unsatisfied

complain *vb* **1** = **find fault**, beef (*sl.*), bellyache (*sl.*), bemoan, bewail, bleat, carp, deplore, fuss, grieve, gripe (*inf.*), groan, grouch (*inf.*), grouse, growl, grumble, kvetch (*US sl.*), lament, moan, whine, whinge (*inf.*)

complaint *n* **1, 2** = **criticism**, accusation, annoyance, beef (*sl.*), bitch (*sl.*), charge, dissatisfaction, fault-finding, grievance, gripe (*inf.*), grouch (*inf.*), grouse, grumble, lament, moan, plaint, protest, remonstrance, trouble, wail **3** = **illness**, affliction, ailment, disease, disorder, indisposition, malady, sickness, upset

complaisance *n* = **obligingness**, accommodativeness, acquiescence, agreeableness, compliance, deference

complaisant *adj* = **obliging**, accommodating, amiable, compliant, conciliatory, deferential, polite, solicitous

complement *n* **1** = **completion**, companion, consummation, correlative, counterpart, finishing touch, rounding-off, supplement **2** = **total**, aggregate, capacity, entirety, quota, totality, wholeness ◆ *vb* **8** = **complete**, cap (*inf.*), crown, round off, set off

complementary *adj* **1, 2** = **completing**, companion, correlative, corresponding, fellow, interdependent, interrelating, matched, reciprocal
Antonyms *adj* contradictory, different, incompatible, incongruous, uncomplementary

complete *adj* **1** = **entire**, all, faultless, full, intact, integral, plenary, unabridged, unbroken, undivided, unimpaired, whole **2** = **finished**, accomplished, achieved, concluded, ended **3, 4** = **total**, absolute, consummate, deep-dyed (*usually derogatory*), dyed-in-the-wool, outright, perfect, thorough, thoroughgoing, utter ◆ *vb* **8** = **finish**, accomplish, achieve, close, conclude, crown, discharge, do, end, execute, fill in, finalize, fulfil, perfect, perform, put the tin lid on, realize, round off, settle, terminate, wrap up (*inf.*)
Antonyms *adj* ≠ **entire:** deficient, imperfect, incomplete, spoilt ≠ **finished:** inconclusive, unaccomplished, unfinished, unsettled ≠ **total:** partial ◆ *vb* ≠ **finish:** begin, commence, initiate, mar, spoil, start

completely *adv* **3, 4** = **totally**, absolutely, a hundred per cent, altogether, down to the ground, en masse, entirely, every inch, from A to Z, from beginning to end, fully, heart and soul, hook, line and sinker, in full, *in toto,* lock, stock and barrel, one hundred per cent, perfectly, quite, root and branch, solidly, thoroughly, utterly, wholly

completion *n* **2** = **finishing**, accomplishment, attainment, bitter end, close, conclusion, consummation, culmination, end, expiration, finalization, fruition, fulfilment, realization

complex *adj* **1** = **compound**, composite, compounded, heterogeneous, manifold, multifarious, multiple **2** = **complicated**, circuitous, convoluted, Daedalian (*literary*), elaborate, intricate, involved, knotty, labyrinthine, mingled, mixed, tangled, tortuous ◆ *n* **4** = **structure**, aggregate, composite, network, organization, scheme, synthesis, system **6** *Informal* = **obsession**, fixation, fixed idea, *idée fixe,* phobia, preoccupation
Antonyms *adj* ≠ **complicated:** clear, easy,

DICTIONARY

complex fraction *n Maths.* a fraction in which the numerator or denominator or both contain fractions. Also called: **compound fraction.**

complexion Ⓣ (kəm'plɛkʃən) *n* **1** the colour and general appearance of a person's skin, esp. of the face. **2** aspect or nature: *the general complexion of a nation's finances.* **3** *Obs.* temperament. [C14: from L *complexiō* a combination, from *complectī* to embrace; see COMPLEX] ▸**com'plexional** *adj*

complexioned (kəm'plɛkʃənd) *adj* of a specified complexion: *light-complexioned.*

complexity Ⓣ (kəm'plɛksɪtɪ) *n, pl* **complexities. 1** the state or quality of being intricate or complex. **2** something intricate or complex; complication.

complex number *n* any number of the form $a + bi$, where a and b are real numbers and $i = \sqrt{-1}$.

complex sentence *n Grammar.* a sentence containing at least one main clause and one subordinate clause.

compliance Ⓣ (kəm'plaɪəns) *or* **compliancy** *n* **1** acquiescence. **2** a disposition to yield to others. **3** a measure of the ability of a mechanical system to respond to an applied vibrating force.

compliance officer *or* **lawyer** *n* a specialist, usually a lawyer, employed by a financial group operating in a variety of fields and for multiple clients to ensure that no conflict of interest arises and that all obligations and regulations are complied with.

compliant Ⓣ (kəm'plaɪənt) *adj* complying, obliging, or yielding. ▸**com'pliantly** *adv*

complicate Ⓣ *vb* ('kɒmplɪˌkeɪt), **complicates, complicating, complicated. 1** to make or become complex, etc. ◆ *adj* ('kɒmplɪkɪt). **2** *Biol.* folded on itself: *a complicate leaf.* [C17: from L *complicāre* to fold together]

complicated Ⓣ ('kɒmplɪˌkeɪtɪd) *adj* made up of intricate parts or aspects that are difficult to understand or analyse. ▸**'compliˌcatedly** *adv*

complication Ⓣ (ˌkɒmplɪ'keɪʃən) *n* **1** a condition, event, etc., that is complex or confused. **2** the act of complicating. **3** an event or condition that complicates or frustrates: *her coming was a serious complication.* **4** a disease arising as a consequence of another.

complicity Ⓣ (kəm'plɪsɪtɪ) *n, pl* **complicities. 1** the fact of being an accomplice, esp. in a criminal act. **2** a less common word for **complexity.**

compliment Ⓣ *n* ('kɒmplɪmənt). **1** a remark or act expressing respect, admiration, etc. **2** (*usually pl*) a greeting of respect or regard. ◆ *vb* ('kɒmplɪˌmɛnt). (*tr*) **3** to express admiration for; congratulate. **4** to express or show regard for, esp. by a gift. [C17: from F, from It. *complimento,* from Sp. *cumplimiento,* from *cumplir* to complete]

> **USAGE NOTE** Avoid confusion with **complement.**

complimentary Ⓣ (ˌkɒmplɪ'mɛntərɪ) *adj* **1** conveying a compliment. **2** flattering. **3** given free, esp. as a courtesy or for publicity purposes. ▸ˌ**compli'mentarily** *adv*

compline ('kɒmplɪn, -plaɪn) *or* **complin** ('kɒmplɪn) *n RC Church.* the last of the seven canonical hours of the divine office. [C13: from OF *complie,* from Med. L *hōra complēta,* lit.: the completed hour]

comply Ⓣ (kəm'plaɪ) *vb* **complies, complying, complied.** (*intr*) (usually foll. by *with*) to act in accordance with rules, wishes, etc.; be obedient (to). [C17: from It. *complire,* from Sp. *cumplir* to complete]

compo ('kɒmpəʊ) *n, pl* **compos. 1** a mixture of materials, such as mortar, plaster, etc. **2** *Austral. & NZ inf.* compensation, esp. for injury or loss of work. ◆ *adj* **3** *Mil.* intended to last for several days: *a compo pack.* [short for *composition, compensation, composite*]

component Ⓣ (kəm'pəʊnənt) *n* **1** a constituent part or aspect of something more complex. **2** any electrical device that has distinct electrical characteristics and may be connected to other devices to form a circuit. **3** *Maths.* one of a set of two or more vectors whose resultant is a given vector. **4** See **phase rule.** ◆ *adj* **5** forming or functioning as a part or aspect; constituent. [C17: from L *compōnere* to put together] ▸**componential** (ˌkɒmpə'nɛnʃəl) *adj*

comport Ⓣ (kəm'pɔːt) *vb* **1** (*tr*) to conduct or bear (oneself) in a specified way. **2** (*intr;* foll. by *with*) to agree (with). [C16: from L *comportāre* collect, from *com-* together + *portāre* to carry] ▸**com'portment** *n*

compose Ⓣ (kəm'pəʊz) *vb* **composes, composing, composed.** (*mainly tr*) **1** to put together or make up. **2** to be the component elements of. **3** to create (a musical or literary work). **4** (*intr*) to write music. **5** to calm (someone, esp. oneself); make quiet. **6** to adjust or settle (a quarrel, etc.). **7** to order the elements of (a painting, sculpture, etc.); design. **8** *Printing.* to set up (type). [C15: from OF *composer,* from L *compōnere* to put in place]

composed Ⓣ (kəm'pəʊzd) *adj* (of people) calm; tranquil. ▸**composedly** (kəm'pəʊzɪdlɪ) *adv*

composer (kəm'pəʊzə) *n* **1** a person who composes music. **2** a person or machine that composes anything, esp. type for printing.

composite Ⓣ *adj* ('kɒmpəzɪt). **1** composed of separate parts; compound. **2** of or belonging to the plant family Compositae. **3** *Maths.* capable of being factorized: *a composite function.* **4** (*sometimes cap.*) denoting one of the five classical orders of architecture: characterized by a combination of the Ionic and Corinthian styles. ◆ *n* ('kɒmpəzɪt). **5** something composed of separate parts; compound. **6** any plant of the family Compositae, having flower heads composed of many small flowers (e.g. dandelion, daisy). **7** a material, such as reinforced concrete, made of two or more distinct materials. **8** a proposal that has been composited. ◆ *vb* ('kɒmpəˌzaɪt), **composites, compositing, composited.** (*tr*) **9** to merge related motions from local branches (of a political party, trade union, etc.) so as to produce a manageable number of proposals for discussion at national level. [C16: from L *compositus* well arranged, from *compōnere* to arrange] ▸**'compositely** *adv* ▸**'compositeness** *n*

composite school *n E. Canad.* a secondary school offering both academic and nonacademic courses.

composition Ⓣ (ˌkɒmpə'zɪʃən) *n* **1** the act of putting together or making up by combining parts. **2** something formed in this manner; a mixture. **3** the parts of which something is composed; constitution. **4**

THESAURUS

easy-peasy (*sl.*), elementary, obvious, simple, straightforward, uncomplicated

complexion *n* **1 = skin,** colour, colouring, hue, pigmentation, skin tone **2 = nature,** appearance, aspect, cast, character, countenance, disposition, guise, light, look, make-up, stamp

complexity *n* **1 = complication,** convolution, elaboration, entanglement, intricacy, involvement, multiplicity, ramification

compliance *n* **1, 2 = obedience,** acquiescence, agreement, assent, complaisance, concession, concurrence, conformity, consent, deference, observance, passivity, submission, submissiveness, yielding
Antonyms *n* defiance, disobedience, noncompliance, nonconformity, opposition, refusal, resistance, revolt

compliant *adj* **= obedient,** accepting, accommodating, accordant, acquiescent, agreeable, assentient, complaisant, concessive, concurrent, conformable, conformist, consentient, cooperative, deferential, obliging, passive, submissive, willing, yielding

complicate *vb* **1 = make difficult,** confuse, embroil, entangle, interweave, involve, make intricate, muddle, ravel, snarl up
Antonyms *vb* clarify, clear up, disentangle, elucidate, explain, facilitate, simplify, spell out, unsnarl

complicated *adj* **= difficult,** complex, convoluted, elaborate, interlaced, intricate, involved, labyrinthine, perplexing, problematic, puzzling, troublesome
Antonyms *adj* ≠ **difficult:** clear, easy, easy-peasy (*sl.*), simple, straightforward, uncomplicated, undemanding, understandable, uninvolved, user-friendly

complication *n* **1 = complexity,** combination, confusion, entanglement, intricacy, mixture, web **3 = problem,** aggravation, difficulty, drawback, embarrassment, factor, obstacle, snag

complicity *n* **1 = collusion,** abetment, collaboration, concurrence, connivance

compliment *n* **1 = praise,** admiration, bouquet, commendation, congratulations, courtesy, eulogy, favour, flattery, honour, tribute **2** *usually plu* **= greetings,** good wishes, regards, remembrances, respects, salutation ◆ *vb* **3 = praise,** commend, congratulate, crack up (*inf.*), extol, felicitate, flatter, laud, pat on the back, pay tribute to, salute, sing the praises of, speak highly of, wish joy to
Antonyms *n* ≠ **praise:** complaint, condemnation, criticism, disparagement, insult, reproach ◆ *vb* ≠ **praise:** blast, condemn, criticize, decry, disparage, insult, lambast(e), put down, reprehend, reproach, tear into (*inf.*)

complimentary *adj* **2 = flattering,** appreciative, approving, commendatory, congratulatory, eulogistic, laudatory, panegyrical **3 = free,** courtesy, donated, free of charge, gratis, gratuitous, honorary, on the house
Antonyms *adj* ≠ **flattering:** abusive, critical, disparaging, fault-finding, insulting, scathing, uncomplimentary, unflattering

comply *vb* **= obey,** abide by, accede, accord, acquiesce, adhere to, agree to, conform to, consent to, defer, discharge, follow, fulfil, observe, perform, play ball (*inf.*), respect, satisfy, submit, toe the line, yield
Antonyms *vb* break, defy, disobey, disregard, fight, ignore, oppose, refuse to obey, reject, repudiate, resist, spurn, violate

component *n* **1 = part,** constituent, element, ingredient, item, piece, unit ◆ *adj* **5 = constituent,** composing, inherent, intrinsic

comport *vb Formal* **1 = behave,** acquit, act, bear, carry, conduct, demean **2** *foll. by* **with = suit,** accord with, agree with, be appropriate to, coincide with, correspond with, fit, harmonize with, square with, tally with

compose *vb* **1 = put together,** build, compound, comprise, constitute, construct, fashion, form, make, make up **3, 4 = create,** contrive, devise, frame, imagine, indite, invent, produce, write **5 = calm,** appease, assuage, collect, control, pacify, placate, quell, quiet, soothe, still, tranquillize **6 = arrange,** adjust, reconcile, regulate, resolve, settle
Antonyms *vb* ≠ **put together:** bulldoze, demolish, destroy, dismantle, obliterate, raze ≠ **calm:** agitate, disturb, excite, perturb, trouble, unsettle, upset

composed *adj* **= calm,** as cool as a cucumber, at ease, collected, confident, cool, imperturbable, keeping one's cool, laid-back (*inf.*), level-headed, poised, relaxed, sedate, self-controlled, self-possessed, serene, together (*sl.*), tranquil, unfazed (*inf.*), unflappable, unruffled, unworried
Antonyms *adj* agitated, anxious, disturbed, excited, hot and bothered (*inf.*), nervous, ruffled, twitchy (*inf.*), uncontrolled, uneasy, unpoised, upset

composite *adj* **1 = compound,** blended, combined, complex, conglomerate, mixed, synthesized ◆ *n* **5 = compound,** amalgam, blend, conglomerate, fusion, meld, synthesis

composition *n* **1 = creation,** compilation, fashioning, formation, formulation, invention, making, mixture, production, putting together **2 = design,** arrangement, configuration, consti-

a work of music, art, or literature. **5** the harmonious arrangement of the parts of a work of art in relation to each other. **6** a piece of writing undertaken as an academic exercise; an essay. **7** *Printing.* the act or technique of setting up type. **8** a settlement by mutual consent, esp. a legal agreement whereby the creditors agree to accept partial payment of a debt in full settlement. [C14: from OF, from L *compositus;* see COMPOSITE, -ION]

compositor (kəmˈpɒzɪtə) *n Printing.* a person who sets and corrects type.

compos mentis *Latin.* (ˈkɒmpəs ˈmɛntɪs) *adj* (*postpositive*) of sound mind; sane.

compost ➊ (ˈkɒmpɒst) *n* **1** a mixture of organic residues such as decomposed vegetation, manure, etc., used as a fertilizer. **2** a mixture, as of sand, peat, and charcoal, in which plants are grown, esp. in pots. **3** *Rare.* a mixture. ◆ *vb* (*tr*) **4** to make (vegetable matter) into compost. **5** to fertilize with compost. [C14: from OF *compost,* from L *compositus* put together]

composure ➊ (kəmˈpəʊʒə) *n* calmness, esp. of the mind; tranquillity; serenity.

compote (ˈkɒmpəut) *n* a dish of fruit stewed with sugar or in a syrup. [C17: from F *composte,* from L *compositus* put in place]

compound[1] ➊ *n* (ˈkɒmpaʊnd). **1** a substance that contains atoms of two or more chemical elements held together by chemical bonds. **2** any combination of two or more parts, aspects, etc. **3** a word formed from two existing words or combining forms. ◆ *vb* (kəmˈpaʊnd). (*mainly tr*) **4** to combine so as to create a compound. **5** to make by combining parts, aspects, etc.: *to compound a new plastic.* **6** to intensify by an added element: *his anxiety was compounded by her crying.* **7** (*also intr*) to come to an agreement in (a dispute, etc.) or to settle (a debt, etc.) for less than what is owed; compromise. **8** *Law.* to agree not to prosecute in return for a consideration: *to compound a crime.* ◆ *adj* (ˈkɒmpaʊnd). **9** composed of two or more parts, elements, etc. **10** (of a word) consisting of elements that are also words or combining forms. **11** *Grammar.* (of tense, mood, etc.) formed by using an auxiliary verb in addition to the main verb. **12** *Music.* **12a** denoting a time in which the number of beats per bar is a multiple of three: *six-four is an example of compound time.* **12b** (of an interval) greater than an octave. **13** (of a steam engine, etc.) having multiple stages in which the steam or working fluid from one stage is used in a subsequent stage. **14** (of a piston engine) having a supercharger powered by a turbine in the exhaust stream. [C14: from earlier *compounen,* from OF *compondre* to set in order, from L *compōnere*]
▸**comˈpoundable** *adj*

compound[2] (ˈkɒmpaʊnd) *n* **1** (esp. formerly in South Africa) an enclosure, esp. on the mines, containing the living quarters for Black workers. **2** any similar enclosure, such as a camp for prisoners of war. [C17: from Malay *kampong* village]

compound eye *n* the convex eye of insects and some crustaceans, consisting of numerous separate light-sensitive units (ommatidia).

compound fraction *n* another name for **complex fraction.**

compound fracture *n* a fracture in which the broken bone pierces the skin.

compound interest *n* interest calculated on both the principal and its accrued interest.

compound leaf *n* a leaf consisting of two or more leaflets borne on the same leafstalk.

compound number *n* a quantity expressed in two or more different but related units: *3 hours 10 seconds is a compound number.*

compound sentence *n* a sentence containing at least two coordinate clauses.

compound time *n* See **compound**[1] (sense 12).

comprehend ➊ (ˌkɒmprɪˈhɛnd) *vb* **1** to understand. **2** (*tr*) to comprise; include. [C14: from L *comprehendere,* from *prehendere* to seize]

comprehensible ➊ (ˌkɒmprɪˈhɛnsəbᵊl) *adj* capable of being comprehended.
▸ˌ**compreˌhensiˈbility** *n* ▸ˌ**compreˈhensibly** *adv*

comprehension ➊ (ˌkɒmprɪˈhɛnʃən) *n* **1** the act or capacity of understanding. **2** the state of including; comprehensiveness.

comprehensive ➊ (ˌkɒmprɪˈhɛnsɪv) *adj* **1** of broad scope or content. **2** (of a car insurance policy) providing protection against most risks, including third-party liability, fire, theft, and damage. **3** of or being a comprehensive school. ◆ *n* **4** short for **comprehensive school.**
▸ˌ**compreˈhensively** *adv* ▸ˌ**compreˈhensiveness** *n*

comprehensive school *n Chiefly Brit.* a secondary school for children of all abilities from the same district.

compress ➊ *vb* (kəmˈprɛs). **1** (*tr*) to squeeze together; condense. ◆ *n* (ˈkɒmprɛs). **2** a cloth or gauze pad applied firmly to some part of the body to relieve discomfort, reduce fever, etc. [C14: from LL *compressāre,* from L *comprimere,* from *premere* to press]
▸**comˈpressible** *adj* ▸**comˈpressive** *adj*

compressed air *n* air at a higher pressure than atmospheric pressure: used esp. as a source of power for machines.

compressibility (kəmˌprɛsɪˈbɪlɪtɪ) *n* **1** the ability to be compressed. **2** *Physics.* the reciprocal of the bulk modulus; the ratio of volume strain to stress at constant temperature. Symbol: *k*

compression ➊ (kəmˈprɛʃən) *n* **1** the act of compressing or the condition of being compressed. **2** an increase in pressure of the charge in an engine or compressor obtained by reducing its volume.

compressor (kəmˈprɛsə) *n* **1** any device that compresses a gas. **2** the part of a gas turbine that compresses the air before it enters the combustion chambers. **3** any muscle that causes compression. **4** an electronic device for reducing the variation in signal amplitude in a transmission system.

comprise ➊ (kəmˈpraɪz) *vb* **comprises, comprising, comprised.** (*tr*) **1** to be made up of. **2** to constitute the whole of; consist of: *her singing comprised the entertainment.* [C15: from F *compris* included, from *comprendre* to COMPREHEND]
▸**comˈprisable** *adj*

> **USAGE NOTE** The use of *of* after *comprise* should be avoided: *the library comprises* (not *comprises of*) *500,000 books and manuscripts.*

compromise ➊ (ˈkɒmprəˌmaɪz) *n* **1** settlement of a dispute by concessions on both or all sides. **2** the terms of such a settlement. **3** something midway between different things. ◆ *vb* **compromises, compromising, compromised. 4** to settle (a dispute) by making concessions. **5** (*tr*) to expose (oneself or another) to disrepute. [C15: from OF *compromis,* from L, from *comprōmittere,* from *prōmittere* to promise]
▸ˈ**comproˌmiser** *n* ▸ˈ**comproˌmisingly** *adv*

compte rendu *French.* (kɔ̃t rɑ̃dy) *n, pl* ***comptes rendus*** (kɔ̃t rɑ̃dy). **1** a review or notice. **2** an account. [lit.: account rendered]

comptroller (kənˈtrəʊlə) *n* a variant spelling of **controller** (sense 2), esp. as a title of any of various financial executives.

compulsion ➊ (kəmˈpʌlʃən) *n* **1** the act of compelling or the state of being compelled. **2** something that compels. **3** *Psychiatry.* an inner

THESAURUS

tution, form, formation, layout, make-up, organization, structure **5** = **arrangement**, balance, concord, consonance, harmony, placing, proportion, symmetry **6** = **essay**, creation, exercise, literary work, opus, piece, study, treatise, work, writing

compost *n* **1** = **organic fertilizer**, humus, mulch

composure *n* = **calmness**, aplomb, calm, collectedness, cool (*sl.*), coolness, dignity, ease, equanimity, imperturbability, placidity, poise, sang-froid, sedateness, self-assurance, self-possession, serenity, tranquillity
Antonyms *n* agitation, discomposure, excitability, impatience, nervousness, perturbation, uneasiness

compound[1] *n* **2** = **combination**, alloy, amalgam, blend, composite, composition, conglomerate, fusion, medley, meld, mixture, synthesis ◆ *vb* **5** = **combine**, amalgamate, blend, coalesce, concoct, fuse, intermingle, meld, mingle, mix, synthesize, unite **6** = **intensify**, add insult to injury, add to, aggravate, augment, complicate, exacerbate, heighten, magnify, worsen **7** = **settle**, adjust, arrange, compose ◆ *adj* **9** = **complex**, composite, conglomerate, intricate, multiple, not simple
Antonyms *n* ≠ **combination:** element ◆ *vb* ≠ **combine:** divide, part, segregate ≠ **intensify:** decrease, lessen, minimize, moderate, modify ◆ *adj* ≠ **complex:** pure, simple, single, unmixed

comprehend *vb* **1** = **understand**, apprehend, assimilate, conceive, discern, fathom, get the hang of (*inf.*), get the picture, grasp, know, make out, perceive, see, see the light of day, take in **2** = **include**, comprise, contain, embody, embrace, enclose, encompass, involve, take in
Antonyms *vb* ≠ **understand:** be at cross-purposes, get (it) wrong, get one's lines crossed, get the wrong end of the stick, misapprehend, misconceive, misconstrue, misinterpret, miss the point of, mistake, misunderstand, pervert

comprehensibility *n* = **intelligibility**, apprehensibility, clarity, clearness, conceivability, conceivableness, explicitness, intelligibleness, plainness, user-friendliness

comprehensible *adj* = **understandable**, clear, coherent, conceivable, explicit, graspable, intelligible, plain, user-friendly

comprehension *n* **1** = **understanding**, conception, discernment, grasp, intelligence, judgment, knowledge, perception, realization, sense **2** = **inclusion**, compass, domain, field, limits, province, range, reach, scope
Antonyms *n* ≠ **understanding:** incomprehension, misapprehension, misunderstanding, unawareness

comprehensive *adj* **1** = **broad**, all-embracing, all-inclusive, blanket, catholic, complete, encyclopedic, exhaustive, extensive, full, inclusive, overarching, sweeping, thorough, umbrella, wide
Antonyms *adj* incomplete, limited, narrow, restricted, specialized, specific

compress *vb* **1** = **squeeze**, abbreviate, compact, concentrate, condense, constrict, contract, cram, crowd, crush, knit, press, pucker, shorten, squash, summarize, wedge

compression *n* **1** = **squeezing**, condensation, consolidation, constriction, crushing, pressure, wedging

comprise *vb* **1** = **be composed of**, comprehend, consist of, contain, embrace, encompass, include, take in **2** = **make up**, compose, constitute, form

compromise *n* **1** = **give-and-take**, accommodation, accord, adjustment, agreement, concession, half measures, middle ground, settlement, trade-off ◆ *vb* **4** = **meet halfway**, adjust, agree, arbitrate, compose, compound, concede, give and take, go fifty-fifty (*inf.*), settle, strike a balance **5** = **weaken**, discredit, dishonour, embarrass, endanger, expose, hazard, imperil, implicate, jeopardize, prejudice
Antonyms *n* ≠ **give-and-take:** contention, controversy, difference, disagreement, dispute, quarrel ◆ *vb* ≠ **meet halfway:** argue, contest, differ, disagree ≠ **weaken:** assure, boost, enhance, support

compulsion *n* **2** = **force**, coercion, constraint, demand, duress, obligation, pressure, urgency

drive that causes a person to perform actions, often repetitive, against his or her will. See also **obsession.** [C15: from OF, from L *compellere* to COMPEL]

compulsive Ⓣ (kəm'pʌlsɪv) *adj* relating to or involving compulsion.
▸**com'pulsively** *adv*

compulsory Ⓣ (kəm'pʌlsərɪ) *adj* **1** required by regulations or laws; obligatory. **2** involving or employing compulsion; compelling; essential.
▸**com'pulsorily** *adv* ▸**com'pulsoriness** *n*

compulsory purchase *n* purchase of a property by a local authority or government department for public use or development, regardless of whether or not the owner wishes to sell.

compunction Ⓣ (kəm'pʌŋkʃən) *n* a feeling of remorse, guilt, or regret. [C14: from Church L *compunctiō*, from L *compungere* to sting]
▸**com'punctious** *adj* ▸**com'punctiously** *adv*

computation (ˌkɒmpjʊ'teɪʃən) *n* a calculation involving numbers or quantities.
▸ˌ**compu'tational** *adj*

compute Ⓣ (kəm'pju:t) *vb* **computes, computing, computed.** to calculate (an answer, result, etc.), often with the aid of a computer. [C17: from L *computāre*, from *putāre* to think]
▸**com'putable** *adj* ▸**comˌputa'bility** *n*

computed tomography *n Med.* another name (esp. US) for **computerized tomography.**

computer (kəm'pju:tə) *n* **1a** a device, usually electronic, that processes data according to a set of instructions. The **digital computer** stores data in discrete units and performs operations at very high speed. The **analog computer** has no memory and is slower than the digital computer but has a continuous rather than a discrete input. **1b** (*as modifier*): *computer technology*. **2** a person who computes or calculates.

computer-aided design *n* the use of computer techniques in designing products, esp. involving the use of computer graphics. Abbrev.: **CAD.**

computer-aided engineering *n* the use of computers to automate manufacturing processes. Abbrev.: **CAE.**

computer architecture *n* the structure, behaviour, and design of computing.

computerate (kəm'pju:tərɪt) *adj* able to use computing. [C20: COMPUTER + -ATE[1], by analogy with *literate*]

computer dating *n* the use of computers by dating agencies to match their clients.

computer game *n* any of various games, recorded on cassette or disc for use in a home computer, that are played by manipulating a mouse, joystick or the keys on the keyboard of a computer in response to the graphics on the screen.

computer graphics *n* (*functioning as sing*) the use of a computer to produce and manipulate pictorial images on a video screen, as in animation techniques or the production of audiovisual aids.

computerize *or* **computerise** (kəm'pju:təˌraɪz) *vb* **computerizes, computerizing, computerized** *or* **computerises, computerising, computerised. 1** (*tr*) to cause (certain operations) to be performed by a computer, esp. as a replacement for human labour. **2** (*intr*) to install a computer. **3** (*tr*) to control or perform (operations) by means of a computer. **4** (*tr*) to process or store (information) by or in a computer.
▸**comˌputeri'zation** *or* **comˌputeri'sation** *n*

computerized tomography *n Med.* a radiological technique that produces images of cross sections through a patient's body. Also called (esp. US): **computed tomography.** Abbrev.: **CT.** See also **CT scanner.**

computer language *n* another term for **programming language.**

computer science *n* the study of computers and their application.

comrade Ⓣ ('kɒmreɪd, -rɪd) *n* **1** a companion. **2** a fellow member of a political party, esp. a fellow Communist. [C16: from F *camarade*, from Sp. *camarada* group of soldiers sharing a billet, from *cámara* room, from L]
▸**'comradely** *adj* ▸**'comradeˌship** *n*

Comsat ('kɒmsæt) *n Trademark.* short for **communications satellite.**

con[1] Ⓣ (kɒn) *Inf.* ◆ *n* **1a** short for **confidence trick. 1b** (*as modifier*): *con man.* ◆ *vb* **cons, conning, conned. 2** (*tr*) to swindle or defraud. [C19: from CONFIDENCE]

con[2] (kɒn) *n* (*usually pl*) an argument or vote against a proposal, motion, etc. See also **pros and cons.** [from L *contrā* against]

con[3] *or esp. US* **conn** (kɒn) *vb* **cons** *or esp. US* **conns, conning, conned.** (*tr*) *Naut.* to direct the steering of (a vessel). [C17 *cun*, from earlier *condien* to guide, from OF *conduire*, from L *condūcere*; see CONDUCT]

con[4] (kɒn) *vb* **cons, conning, conned.** (*tr*) *Arch.* to study attentively or learn. [C15: var. of CAN[1] in the sense: to come to know]

con[5] (kɒn) *prep Music.* with. [It.]

con. *abbrev. for:* **1** concerto. **2** conclusion. **3** connection. **4** consolidated. **5** continued.

con- *prefix* a variant of **com-.**

con amore (kɒn æ'mɔ:rɪ) *adj, adv Music.* (to be performed) lovingly. [C19: from It.: with love]

con brio (kɒn 'bri:əʊ) *adj, adv Music.* (to be performed) with liveliness or spirit. [It.: with energy]

concatenate (kɒn'kætɪˌneɪt) *vb* **concatenates, concatenating, concatenated.** (*tr*) to link or join together, esp. in a chain or series. [C16: from LL *concatēnāre*, from L *com-* together + *catēna* CHAIN]
▸ˌ**concate'nation** *n*

concave Ⓣ ('kɒnkeɪv, kɒn'keɪv) *adj* **1** curving inwards; having the shape of a section of the interior of a sphere, paraboloid, etc.: *a concave lens.* ◆ *vb* **2** (*tr*) to make concave. [C15: from L *concavus* arched, from *cavus* hollow]
▸**'concavely** *adv* ▸**'concaveness** *n*

concavity (kɒn'kævɪtɪ) *n, pl* **concavities. 1** the state of being concave. **2** a concave surface or thing.

concavo-concave (kɒnˌkeɪvəʊkɒn'keɪv) *adj* (esp. of a lens) having both sides concave.

concavo-convex *adj* **1** having one side concave and the other side convex. **2** (of a lens) having a concave face with greater curvature than the convex face.

conceal Ⓣ (kən'si:l) *vb* (*tr*) **1** to keep from discovery; hide. **2** to keep secret. [C14: from OF *conceler*, from L *concēlāre*, from *com-* (intensive) + *cēlāre* to hide]
▸**con'cealer** *n* ▸**con'cealment** *n*

concede Ⓣ (kən'si:d) *vb* **concedes, conceding, conceded. 1** (when *tr, may take a clause as object*) to admit or acknowledge (something) as true or correct. **2** to yield or allow (something, such as a right). **3** (*tr*) to admit as certain in outcome: *to concede an election.* [C17: from L *concēdere*, from *cēdere* to give way]
▸**con'ceder** *n*

conceit Ⓣ (kən'si:t) *n* **1** a high, often exaggerated, opinion of oneself or one's accomplishments. **2** *Literary.* an elaborate image or far-fetched comparison. **3** *Arch.* **3a** a witty expression. **3b** fancy; imagination. **3c** an idea. ◆ *vb* (*tr*) **4** *Obs.* to think. [C14: from CONCEIVE]

conceited Ⓣ (kən'si:tɪd) *adj* having an exaggerated opinion of oneself or one's accomplishments.
▸**con'ceitedly** *adv* ▸**con'ceitedness** *n*

conceivable Ⓣ (kən'si:vəb[ə]l) *adj* capable of being understood, believed, or imagined; possible.
▸**conˌceiva'bility** *n* ▸**con'ceivably** *adv*

conceive Ⓣ (kən'si:v) *vb* **conceives, conceiving, conceived. 1** (when *intr*, foll. by *of*; when *tr, often takes a clause as object*) to have an idea (of); imagine; think. **2** (*tr; takes a clause as object or an infinitive*) to believe. **3**

THESAURUS

3 = **urge**, drive, necessity, need, obsession, preoccupation

compulsive *adj* = **irresistible**, besetting, compelling, driving, neurotic, obsessive, overwhelming, uncontrollable, urgent

compulsory *adj* **1** = **obligatory**, binding, *de rigueur*, forced, imperative, mandatory, required, requisite
Antonyms *adj* discretionary, elective, non-obligatory, non-requisite, optional, unimperative, unnecessary, voluntary

compunction *n* = **guilt**, contrition, misgiving, penitence, qualm, regret, reluctance, remorse, repentance, sorrow, stab *or* sting of conscience

compute *vb* = **calculate**, add up, cast up, cipher, count, enumerate, estimate, figure, figure out, measure, rate, reckon, sum, tally, total

comrade *n* **1** = **companion**, ally, associate, colleague, compatriot, compeer, confederate, co-worker, crony, fellow, friend, mate (*inf.*), partner

comradely *adj* **1** = **friendly**, associatory, fraternal

comradeship *n* **1** = **fellowship**, alliance, association, camaraderie, companionship, fraternity, membership, partnership, sodality

con *Informal n* **1a** = **swindle**, bluff, canard, deception, fraud, scam, sting (*inf.*), trick ◆ *vb* **2** = **swindle**, bilk, cheat, cozen, deceive, defraud, diddle (*inf.*), double-cross (*inf.*), dupe, gull (*arch.*), hoax, hoodwink, humbug, inveigle, kid (*inf.*), mislead, pull a fast one on (*inf.*), rip off (*sl.*), sting (*inf.*), trick

concave *adj* **1** = **hollow**, cupped, depressed, excavated, hollowed, incurved, indented, scooped, sunken
Antonyms *adj* bulging, convex, curving, protuberant, rounded

conceal *vb* **1, 2** = **hide**, bury, camouflage, cover, disguise, dissemble, draw a veil over, keep dark, keep secret, keep under one's hat, mask, obscure, screen, secrete, shelter, stash (*inf.*)
Antonyms *vb* disclose, display, divulge, expose, lay bare, reveal, show, uncover, unmask, unveil

concealed *adj* **1, 2** = **hidden**, covered, covert, inconspicuous, masked, obscured, screened, secret, secreted, tucked away, under wraps, unseen

concealment *n* **1, 2** = **hiding**, camouflage, cover, disguise, hideaway, hide-out, secrecy
Antonyms *n* disclosure, display, exposure, give-away, leak, revelation, showing, uncovering

concede *vb* **1** = **admit**, accept, acknowledge, allow, confess, grant, own **3** = **give up**, cede, hand over, relinquish, surrender, yield
Antonyms *vb* ≠ **admit:** contest, deny, disclaim, dispute, protest, refute, reject ≠ **give up:** beat, conquer, defeat, fight to the bitter end, make a stand

conceit *n* **1** = **self-importance**, amour-propre, arrogance, complacency, egotism, narcissism, pride, self-love, swagger, vainglory, vanity **3** *Archaic* = **fancy**, belief, fantasy, idea, image, imagination, judgment, notion, opinion, quip, thought, vagary, whim, whimsy

conceited *adj* = **self-important**, arrogant, bigheaded, cocky, egotistical, full of oneself, immodest, narcissistic, overweening, puffed up, stuck up (*inf.*), swollen-headed, too big for one's boots *or* breeches, vain, vainglorious
Antonyms *adj* humble, modest, self-effacing, unassuming

conceivable *adj* = **imaginable**, believable, credible, possible, thinkable
Antonyms *adj* inconceivable, incredible, unbelievable, unimaginable, unthinkable

conceive *vb* **1, 2** = **imagine**, appreciate, apprehend, believe, comprehend, envisage, fancy, get the picture, grasp, realize, suppose, think,

(*tr*) to develop: *she conceived a passion for music.* **4** to become pregnant with (a child). **5** (*tr*) *Rare.* to express in words. [C13: from OF *conceivre,* from L *concipere* to take in, from *capere* to take]

concelebrate (kən'selɪˌbreɪt) *vb* **concelebrates, concelebrating, concelebrated.** *Christianity.* to celebrate (the Eucharist or Mass) jointly with one or more other priests. [C16: from L *concelebrāre*]
▸**conˌcele'bration** *n*

concentrate ❶ ('kɒnsənˌtreɪt) *vb* **concentrates, concentrating, concentrated. 1** to come or cause to come to a single purpose or aim: *to concentrate one's hopes on winning.* **2** to make or become denser or purer by the removal of certain elements. **3** (*intr;* often foll. by *on*) to think intensely (about). ◆ *n* **4** a concentrated material or solution. [C17: back formation from CONCENTRATION, ult. from L *com-* same + *centrum* CENTRE]
▸**'concenˌtrative** *adj* ▸**'concenˌtrator** *n*

concentration ❶ (ˌkɒnsən'treɪʃən) *n* **1** intense mental application. **2** the act of concentrating. **3** something that is concentrated. **4** the strength of a solution, esp. the amount of dissolved substance in a given volume of solvent. **5** *Mil.* **5a** the act of bringing together military forces. **5b** the application of fire from a number of weapons against a target.

concentration camp *n* a guarded prison camp for nonmilitary prisoners, esp. one in Nazi Germany.

concentre *or US* **concenter** (kən'sentə) *vb* **concentres, concentring, concentred** *or US* **concenters, concentering, concentered.** to converge or cause to converge on a common centre; concentrate. [C16: from F *concentrer*]

concentric (kən'sentrɪk) *adj* having a common centre: *concentric circles.* [C14: from Med. L *concentricus,* from L *com-* same + *centrum* CENTRE]
▸**con'centrically** *adv*

concept ❶ ('kɒnsept) *n* **1** an idea, esp. an abstract idea: *the concepts of biology.* **2** *Philosophy.* a general idea that corresponds to some class of entities and consists of the essential features of the class. **3** a new idea; invention. **4** (*modifier*) (of a product, esp. a car) created to demonstrate the technical skills and imagination of the designers, and not for mass production or sale. [C16: from L *conceptum,* from *concipere* to CONCEIVE]

conception ❶ (kən'sepʃən) *n* **1** something conceived; notion, idea, or plan. **2** the description under which someone considers something: *a strange conception of freedom.* **3** the fertilization of an ovum by a sperm in the Fallopian tube followed by implantation in the womb. **4** origin or beginning. [C13: from L *conceptiō,* from *concipere* to CONCEIVE]
▸**con'ceptional** *or* **con'ceptive** *adj*

conceptual (kən'septjʊəl) *adj* of or characterized by concepts.
▸**con'ceptually** *adv*

conceptualize *or* **conceptualise** (kən'septjʊəˌlaɪz) *vb* **conceptualizes, conceptualizing, conceptualized** *or* **conceptualises, conceptualising, conceptualised.** to form (a concept or concepts) out of observations, experience, data, etc.
▸**conˌceptuali'zation** *or* **conˌceptuali'sation** *n*

concern ❶ (kən'sɜːn) *vb* (*tr*) **1** to relate to; affect. **2** (usually foll. by *with* or *in*) to involve or interest (oneself): *he concerns himself with other people's affairs.* ◆ *n* **3** something that affects a person; affair; business. **4** regard or interest: *he felt a strong concern for her.* **5** anxiety or solicitude. **6** important relation: *his news has great concern for us.* **7** a commercial company. **8** *Inf.* a material thing, esp. one of which one has a low opinion. [C15: from LL *concernere,* from L *com-* together + *cernere* to sift]

concerned ❶ (kən'sɜːnd) *adj* **1** (*postpositive*) interested, guilty, or involved: *I shall find the boy concerned and punish him.* **2** worried or solicitous.
▸**concernedly** (kən'sɜːnɪdlɪ) *adv*

concerning ❶ (kən'sɜːnɪŋ) *prep* **1** about; regarding. ◆ *adj* **2** worrying or troublesome.

concernment (kən'sɜːnmənt) *n Rare.* affair or business; concern.

concert ❶ *n* ('kɒnsɜːt). **1a** a performance of music by players or singers that does not involve theatrical staging. **1b** (*as modifier*): *a concert version of an opera.* **2** agreement in design, plan, or action. **3 in concert. 3a** acting with a common purpose. **3b** (of musicians, etc.) performing live. ◆ *vb* (kən'sɜːt). **4** to arrange or contrive (a plan) by mutual agreement. [C16: from F *concerter* to bring into agreement, from It., from LL *concertāre* to work together, from L *certāre* to contend]

concertante (ˌkɒntʃə'tæntɪ) *adj Music.* characterized by contrasting alternating tutti and solo passages. [It.: from *concertare* to perform a CONCERT]

concerted ❶ (kən'sɜːtɪd) *adj* **1** mutually contrived, planned, or arranged; combined: *a concerted effort.* **2** *Music.* arranged in parts for a group of singers or players.

concert grand *n* a grand piano of the largest size.

concertina (ˌkɒnsə'tiːnə) *n* **1** a hexagonal musical instrument similar to the accordion, in which metallic reeds are vibrated by air from a set of bellows operated by the player's hands. ◆ *vb* **concertinas, concertinaing, concertinaed. 2** (*intr*) to collapse or fold up like the bellows of a concertina. [C19: CONCERT + *-ina*]
▸**ˌconcer'tinist** *n*

concertino (ˌkɒntʃə'tiːnəʊ) *n, pl* **concertini** (-nɪ). *Music.* **1** the solo group in a concerto grosso. **2** a short concerto. [It.: a little CONCERTO]

concertmaster ('kɒnsətˌmɑːstə) *n* a US and Canad. word for **leader** (of an orchestra).

concerto (kən'tʃeətəʊ) *n, pl* **concertos** *or* **concerti** (-tɪ). a composition for an orchestra and one or more soloists. [C18: from It.: CONCERT]

concerto grosso ('grɒsəʊ) *n, pl* **concerti grossi** ('grɒsɪ) *or* **concerto grossos.** a composition for an orchestra and a group of soloists. [It., lit.: big concerto]

concert party *n* **1** a musical entertainment popular in the early 20th century, esp. one at a British seaside resort. **2** *Stock Exchange inf.* a group of individuals or companies who secretly agree together to purchase shares separately in a particular company which they plan to amalgamate later into a single holding: a malpractice which is illegal in some countries.

concert pitch *n* **1** the frequency of 440 hertz assigned to the A above middle C. **2** *Inf.* a state of extreme readiness.

concession ❶ (kən'seʃən) *n* **1** the act of yielding or conceding. **2** something conceded. **3** *Brit.* a reduction in the usual price of a ticket granted to a special group of customers: *a student concession.* **4** any grant of rights, land, or property by a government, local authority, corporation, or individual. **5** the right, esp. an exclusive right, to market a particular product in a given area. **6** *Canad.* **6a** a land subdivision in a township survey. **6b** another name for a **concession road.** [C16: from L *concēssiō,* from *concēdere* to CONCEDE]
▸**con'cessible** *adj* ▸**con'cessive** *adj*

concessionaire (kənˌseʃə'neə), **concessioner** (kən'seʃənə), *or* **concessionary** *n* someone who holds or operates a concession.

concessionary (kən'seʃənərɪ) *adj* **1** of, granted, or obtained by a concession. ◆ *n, pl* **concessionaries. 2** another word for **concessionaire.**

concession road *n Canad.* one of a series of roads separating concessions in a township.

conch (kɒŋk, kɒntʃ) *n, pl* **conchs** (kɒŋks) *or* **conches** ('kɒntʃɪz). **1** any of various tropical marine gastropod molluscs characterized by a large brightly coloured spiral shell. **2** the shell of such a mollusc, used as a trumpet. [C16: from L *concha,* from Gk *konkhē* shellfish]

conchie *or* **conchy** ('kɒntʃɪ) *n, pl* **conchies.** *Inf.* short for **conscientious objector.**

conchology (kɒŋ'kɒlədʒɪ) *n* the study of mollusc shells.
▸**con'chologist** *n*

concierge (ˌkɒnsɪ'eəʒ) *n* (esp. in France) a caretaker of a block of flats, hotel, etc., esp. one who lives on the premises. [C17: from F, ult. from L *conservus,* from *servus* slave]

conciliar (kən'sɪlɪə) *adj* of, from, or by means of a council, esp. an ecclesiastical one.

conciliate ❶ (kən'sɪlɪˌeɪt) *vb* **conciliates, conciliating, conciliated.** (*tr*) **1** to overcome the hostility of; win over. **2** to gain (favour, regard, etc.), esp. by making friendly overtures. [C16: from L *conciliāre* to bring together, from *concilium* COUNCIL]
▸**con'ciliable** *adj* ▸**con'ciliˌator** *n*

THESAURUS

understand **3** = **think up**, contrive, create, design, develop, devise, form, formulate, produce, project, purpose **4** = **become pregnant**, become impregnated

concentrate *vb* **1, 3** = **focus one's attention on**, be engrossed in, consider closely, give all one's attention to, put one's mind to, rack one's brains
Antonyms *vb* disregard, let one's mind wander, lose concentration, pay no attention to, pay no heed to

concentration *n* **1** = **single-mindedness**, absorption, application, heed
Antonyms *n* absent-mindedness, disregard, distraction, inattention

concept *n* **1** = **idea**, abstraction, conception, conceptualization, hypothesis, image, impression, notion, theory, view

conception *n* **1** = **idea**, concept, design, image, notion, plan **2** = **understanding**, appreciation, clue, comprehension, impression, inkling, perception, picture **3** = **impregnation**, fertilization, germination, insemination **4** = **origin**, beginning, birth, formation, inception, initiation, invention, launching, outset

concern *vb* **1** = **be relevant to**, affect, apply to, bear on, interest, involve, pertain to, regard, touch ◆ *n* **3** = **business**, affair, charge, department, field, interest, involvement, job, matter, mission, occupation, pigeon (*inf.*), responsibility, task, transaction **5** = **worry**, anxiety, apprehension, attention, burden, care, consideration, disquiet, disquietude, distress, heed, responsibility, solicitude **6** = **importance**, bearing, interest, reference, relation, relevance **7** = **business**, company, corporation, enterprise, establishment, firm, house, organization

concerned *adj* **1** = **involved**, active, implicated, interested, mixed up, privy to **2** = **worried**, anxious, attentive, bothered, caring, distressed, disturbed, exercised, interested, solicitous, troubled, uneasy, upset
Antonyms *adj* aloof, carefree, detached, indifferent, neglectful, unconcerned, uninterested, untroubled, without a care

concerning *prep* **1** = **regarding**, about, apropos of, as regards, as to, in the matter of, on the subject of, re, relating to, respecting, touching, with reference to

concert *n* **2** = **agreement**, accord, concord, concordance, harmony, unanimity, union, unison **3a in concert** = **together**, concertedly, in collaboration, in league, in unison, jointly, shoulder to shoulder, unanimously

concerted *adj* **1** = **coordinated**, agreed upon, collaborative, combined, joint, planned, prearranged, united
Antonyms *adj* disunited, separate, uncontrived, uncooperative, unplanned

concession *n* **1** = **conceding**, acknowledgment, admission, assent, confession, surrender, yielding **2** = **grant**, adjustment, allowance, boon, compromise, indulgence, permit, privilege, sop

conciliate *vb* **1, 2** = **pacify**, appease, clear the

conciliation Ⓣ (kənˌsɪlɪ'eɪʃən) *n* **1** the act or process of conciliating. **2** a method of helping the parties in a dispute to reach agreement, esp. divorcing or separating couples to part amicably.

conciliatory Ⓣ (kən'sɪljətərɪ) *or* **conciliative** (kən'sɪljətɪv) *adj* intended to placate or reconcile.
▸**con'ciliatorily** *adv*

concise Ⓣ (kən'saɪs) *adj* brief and to the point. [C16: from L *concīsus* cut short, from *concīdere,* from *caedere* to cut, strike down]
▸**con'cisely** *adv* ▸**con'ciseness** *or* **concision** (kən'sɪʒən) *n*

conclave Ⓣ ('kɒnkleɪv) *n* **1** a secret meeting. **2** *RC Church.* **2a** the closed apartments where the college of cardinals elects a new pope. **2b** a meeting of the college of cardinals for this purpose. [C14: from Med. L *conclāve,* from L: place that may be locked, from *clāvis* key]

conclude Ⓣ (kən'klu:d) *vb* **concludes, concluding, concluded.** (*mainly tr*) **1** (*also intr*) to come or cause to come to an end. **2** (*takes a clause as object*) to decide by reasoning; deduce: *the judge concluded that the witness had told the truth.* **3** to settle: *to conclude a treaty.* **4** *Obs.* to confine. [C14: from L *conclūdere,* from *claudere* to close]

conclusion Ⓣ (kən'klu:ʒən) *n* **1** end or termination. **2** the last main division of a speech, essay, etc. **3** outcome or result (esp. in **a foregone conclusion**). **4** a final decision or judgment (esp. in **come to a conclusion**). **5** *Logic.* **5a** a statement that purports to follow from another or others (the **premises**) by means of an argument. **5b** a statement that does validly follow from given premises. **6** *Law.* **6a** an admission or statement binding on the party making it; estoppel. **6b** the close of a pleading or of a conveyance. **7 in conclusion.** lastly; to sum up. **8 jump to conclusions.** to come to a conclusion prematurely, without sufficient thought or on incomplete evidence. [C14: via OF from L; see CONCLUDE, -ION]

conclusive Ⓣ (kən'klu:sɪv) *adj* **1** putting an end to doubt; decisive; final. **2** approaching or involving an end.
▸**con'clusively** *adv*

concoct Ⓣ (kən'kɒkt) *vb* (*tr*) **1** to make by combining different ingredients. **2** to invent; make up; contrive. [C16: from L *concoctus* cooked together, from *coquere* to cook]
▸**con'cocter** *or* **con'coctor** *n* ▸**con'coction** *n*

concomitance (kən'kɒmɪtəns) *n* **1** existence together. **2** *Christianity.* the doctrine that the body and blood of Christ are present in the Eucharist.

concomitant (kən'kɒmɪtənt) *adj* **1** existing or occurring together. ◆ *n* **2** a concomitant act, person, etc. [C17: from LL *concomitārī* to accompany, from *com-* with + *comes* companion]

concord Ⓣ ('kɒnkɔ:d) *n* **1** agreement or harmony. **2** a treaty establishing peaceful relations between nations. **3** *Music.* a combination of musical notes, esp. one containing a series of consonant intervals. **4** *Grammar.* another word for **agreement** (sense 6). [C13: from OF *concorde,* from L *concordia,* from *com-* same + *cor* heart]

concordance (kən'kɔ:dᵊns) *n* **1** a state of harmony. **2** a book that indexes the principal words in a literary work, often with the immediate context and an account of the meaning. **3** an index produced by computer or machine.

concordant (kən'kɔ:dᵊnt) *adj* being in agreement; harmonious.
▸**con'cordantly** *adv*

concordat (kɒn'kɔ:dæt) *n* a pact or treaty, esp. one between the Vatican and another state concerning the interests of religion in that state. [C17: via F, from Med. L *concordātum,* from L: something agreed; see CONCORD]

concourse Ⓣ ('kɒnkɔ:s) *n* **1** a crowd; throng. **2** a coming together; confluence. **3** a large open space for the gathering of people in a public place. [C14: from OF *concours,* ult. from L *concurrere* to run together]

concrete Ⓣ ('kɒnkri:t) *n* **1** a construction material made of cement, sand, stone and water that hardens to a stonelike mass. ◆ *adj* **2** relating to a particular instance; specific as opposed to general. **3** relating to things capable of being perceived by the senses, as opposed to abstractions. **4** formed by the coalescence of particles; condensed; solid. ◆ *vb* **concretes, concreting, concreted. 5** (*tr*) to construct in or cover with concrete. **6** (kən'kri:t). to become or cause to become solid; coalesce. [C14: from L *concrētus,* from *concrēscere* to grow together]
▸**'concretely** *adv* ▸**'concreteness** *n*

concrete music *n* music consisting of an electronically modified montage of tape-recorded sounds.

concrete noun *n* a noun that refers to a material object.

concrete poetry *n* poetry in which the visual form of the poem is used to convey meaning.

concretion (kən'kri:ʃən) *n* **1** the act of growing together; coalescence. **2** a solidified mass. **3** something made real, tangible, or specific. **4** a rounded or irregular mineral mass different in composition from the sedimentary rock that surrounds it. **5** *Pathol.* another word for **calculus.**
▸**con'cretionary** *adj*

concretize *or* **concretise** ('kɒnkrɪˌtaɪz) *vb* **concretizes, concretizing, concretized** *or* **concretises, concretising, concretised.** (*tr*) to render concrete; make real or specific.

concubine Ⓣ ('kɒŋkjʊˌbaɪn, 'kɒn-) *n* **1** (in polygamous societies) a secondary wife. **2** a woman who cohabits with a man, esp. (formerly) the mistress of a king, nobleman, etc. [C13: from OF, from L *concubīna,* from *concumbere* to lie together]
▸**concubinage** (kɒn'kju:bɪnɪdʒ) *n* ▸**con'cubinary** *adj*

concupiscence (kən'kju:pɪsəns) *n* strong desire, esp. sexual desire. [C14: from Church L *concupiscentia,* from L *concupiscere* to covet]
▸**con'cupiscent** *adj*

concur Ⓣ (kən'kɜ:) *vb* **concurs, concurring, concurred.** (*intr*) **1** to agree; be in accord. **2** to combine or cooperate. **3** to occur simultaneously; coincide. [C15: from L *concurrere* to run together]

concurrence (kən'kʌrəns) *n* **1** the act of concurring. **2** agreement; accord. **3** cooperation or combination. **4** simultaneous occurrence.

concurrent Ⓣ (kən'kʌrənt) *adj* **1** taking place at the same time or in the same location. **2** cooperating. **3** meeting at, approaching, or having a common point: *concurrent lines.* **4** in agreement; harmonious.
▸**con'currently** *adv*

concurrent engineering *n* a method of designing and marketing new products in which development stages are run in parallel rather than in series, to reduce lead times and costs. Also called: **interactive engineering.**

concuss (kən'kʌs) *vb* (*tr*) **1** to injure (the brain) by a violent blow, fall, etc. **2** to shake violently. [C16: from L *concussus,* from *concutere* to disturb greatly, from *quatere* to shake]

concussion Ⓣ (kən'kʌʃən) *n* **1** a jarring of the brain, caused by a blow or a fall, usually resulting in loss of consciousness. **2** any violent shaking.

condemn Ⓣ (kən'dem) *vb* (*tr*) **1** to express strong disapproval of. **2** to pronounce judicial sentence on. **3** to demonstrate the guilt of: *his secretive behaviour condemned him.* **4** to judge or pronounce unfit for use.

THESAURUS

air, disarm, mediate, mollify, placate, pour oil on troubled waters, propitiate, reconcile, restore harmony, soothe, win over

conciliation *n* **1** = **pacification**, appeasement, disarming, mollification, placation, propitiation, reconciliation, soothing

conciliatory *adj* = **pacifying**, appeasing, disarming, irenic, mollifying, pacific, peaceable, placatory, propitiative

concise *adj* = **brief**, compact, compendious, compressed, condensed, epigrammatic, in a nutshell, laconic, pithy, short, succinct, summary, synoptic, terse, to the point
Antonyms *adj* diffuse, discursive, garrulous, lengthy, long-winded, prolix, rambling, verbose, wordy

conciseness *n* = **brevity**, briefness, compactness, compendiousness, compression, laconicism, pithiness, shortness, succinctness, summariness, synoptic, terseness
Antonyms *n* diffuseness, discursiveness, garrulity, garrulousness, lengthiness, long-windedness, prolixity, verboseness, verbosity, wordiness

conclave *n* **1** = **secret** *or* **private meeting**, assembly, cabinet, conference, congress, council, parley, session

conclude *vb* **1** = **end**, bring down the curtain, cease, close, come to an end, complete, draw to a close, finish, round off, terminate, wind up **2** = **decide**, assume, clinch, deduce, determine, establish, fix, gather, infer, judge, reckon (*inf.*), resolve, settle, sum up, suppose, surmise, work out **3** = **accomplish**, bring about, carry out, effect, pull off
Antonyms *vb* ≠ **end:** begin, commence, extend, initiate, open, protract, start

conclusion *n* **1** = **end**, bitter end, close, completion, ending, finale, finish, result, termination **3** = **outcome**, consequence, culmination, end result, issue, result, sequel, upshot **4** = **decision**, agreement, conviction, deduction, inference, judgment, opinion, resolution, settlement, verdict **7 in conclusion** = **finally**, in closing, lastly, to sum up

conclusive *adj* **1** = **decisive**, clinching, convincing, definite, definitive, final, irrefutable, ultimate, unanswerable, unarguable
Antonyms *adj* contestable, disputable, doubtful, dubious, impeachable, inconclusive, indecisive, indefinite, questionable, refutable, unconvincing, vague

concoct *vb* **1, 2** = **make up**, brew, contrive, cook up, design, devise, fabricate, formulate, hatch, invent, manufacture, mature, plot, prepare, project, think up, trump up

concoction *n* **1, 2** = **mixture**, blend, brew, combination, compound, contrivance, creation, preparation

concord *n* **1** = **harmony**, accord, agreement, amity, concert, consensus, consonance, friendship, good understanding, goodwill, peace, rapport, unanimity, unison **2** = **treaty**, agreement, compact, concordat, convention, entente, protocol

concourse *n* **1, 2** = **crowd**, assemblage, assembly, collection, confluence, convergence, crush, gathering, meeting, multitude, rout (*arch.*), throng **3** = **gathering** *or* **meeting place**, entrance, foyer, hall, lounge, rallying point

concrete *n* **1** = **cement** (*not in technical usage*), concretion ◆ *adj* **2** = **specific**, definite, explicit **3** = **real**, actual, factual, material, sensible, substantial, tangible
Antonyms *adj* ≠ **specific:** indefinite, unspecified, vague ≠ **real:** abstract, immaterial, insubstantial, intangible, notional, theoretical

concubine *n* **2** = **mistress**, courtesan, kept woman, leman (*arch.*), odalisque, paramour

concur *vb* **1-3** = **agree**, accede, accord, acquiesce, approve, assent, buy into (*inf.*), coincide, combine, consent, cooperate, harmonize, join

concurrent *adj* **1** = **simultaneous**, coexisting, coincident, concerted, concomitant, contemporaneous, synchronous **3** = **converging**, confluent, convergent, uniting **4** = **in agreement**, agreeing, at one, compatible, consentient, consistent, cooperating, harmonious, in rapport, like-minded, of the same mind

concussion *n* **1, 2** = **shaking**, clash, collision, crash, impact, jarring, jolt, jolting, shock

condemn *vb* **1** = **disapprove**, blame, censure, criticize, damn, denounce, excoriate, reprehend, reproach, reprobate, reprove, upbraid **2** = **sentence**, convict, damn, doom, pass sentence on, proscribe
Antonyms *vb* ≠ **disapprove:** acclaim, applaud, approve, commend, compliment, condone, praise ≠ **sentence:** acquit, free, liberate

5 to force into a particular state: *his disposition condemned him to boredom.* [C13: from OF *condempner,* from L *condemnāre,* from *damnāre* to condemn]
▸**condemnable** (kən'dɛmnəbᵊl) *adj* ▸**ˌcondem'nation** *n* ▸**condemnatory** (kən'dɛmnətərɪ) *adj*

condensate (kən'dɛnseɪt) *n* a substance formed by condensation.

condensation ⓘ (ˌkɒndɛn'seɪʃən) *n* **1** the act or process of condensing, or the state of being condensed. **2** anything that has condensed from a vapour, esp. on a window. **3** *Chem.* a type of reaction in which two organic molecules combine to form a larger molecule as well as a simple molecule such as water, etc. **4** an abridged version of a book.
▸**ˌconden'sational** *adj*

condensation trail *n* another name for **vapour trail.**

condense ⓘ (kən'dɛns) *vb* **condenses, condensing, condensed. 1** (*tr*) to increase the density of; compress. **2** to reduce or be reduced in volume or size. **3** to change or cause to change from a gaseous to a liquid or solid state. **4** *Chem.* to undergo or cause to undergo condensation. [C15: from L *condēnsāre,* from *dēnsāre* to make thick, from *dēnsus* DENSE]
▸**con'densable** *or* **con'densible** *adj*

condensed matter *n Physics.* **a** crystalline and amorphous solids and liquids, including liquid crystals, glasses, polymers, and gels. **b** (*as modifier*): *condensed-matter physics.*

condensed milk *n* milk reduced by evaporation to a thick concentration, with sugar added.

condenser (kən'dɛnsə) *n* **1a** an apparatus for reducing gases to their liquid or solid form by the abstraction of heat. **1b** a device for abstracting heat, as in a refrigeration unit. **2** a lens that concentrates light. **3** another name for **capacitor. 4** a person or device that condenses.

condescend ⓘ (ˌkɒndɪ'sɛnd) *vb* (*intr*) **1** to act graciously towards another or others regarded as being on a lower level; behave patronizingly. **2** to do something that one regards as below one's dignity. [C14: from Church L *condēscendere,* from L *dēscendere* to DESCEND]
▸**ˌconde'scending** *adj* ▸**ˌconde'scendingly** *adv* ▸**ˌconde'scension** *n*

condign (kən'daɪn) *adj* (esp. of a punishment) fitting; deserved. [C15: from OF *condigne,* from L *condignus,* from *dignus* worthy]
▸**con'dignly** *adv*

condiment ('kɒndɪmənt) *n* any spice or sauce such as salt, pepper, mustard, etc. [C15: from L *condīmentum* seasoning, from *condīre* to pickle]

condition ⓘ (kən'dɪʃən) *n* **1** a particular state of being or existence: *the human condition.* **2** something that limits or restricts; a qualification. **3** (*pl*) circumstances: *conditions were right for a takeover.* **4** state of physical fitness, esp. good health: *out of condition.* **5** an ailment: *a heart condition.* **6** something indispensable: *your happiness is a condition of mine.* **7** something required as part of an agreement; term: *the conditions of the lease are set out.* **8** *Law.* **8a** a provision in a will, contract, etc., that makes some right or liability contingent upon the happening of some event. **8b** the event itself. **9** *Logic.* a statement whose truth is either required for the truth of a given statement (a **necessary condition**) or sufficient to guarantee the truth of the given statement (a **sufficient condition**). **10** rank, status, or position. **11 on condition that.** (*conj*) provided that. ◆ *vb* (*mainly tr*) **12** *Psychol.* **12a** to alter the response of (a person or animal) to a particular stimulus or situation. **12b** to establish a conditioned response in. **13** to put into a fit condition. **14** to improve the condition of (one's hair) by use of special cosmetics. **15** to accustom or inure. **16** to subject to a condition. [C14: from L *conditiō,* from *condīcere* to discuss, from *con-* together + *dīcere* to say]
▸**con'ditioner** *n* ▸**con'ditioning** *n, adj*

conditional ⓘ (kən'dɪʃənᵊl) *adj* **1** depending on other factors. **2** *Grammar.* expressing a condition on which something else is contingent: *"If he comes" is a conditional clause in the sentence "If he comes I shall go"*. **3** *Logic.* Also called: **hypothetical.** (of a proposition) consisting of two component propositions associated by the words *if...then* so that the proposition is false only when the antecedent is true and the consequent false. ◆ *n* **4** a conditional verb form, clause, sentence, etc.
▸**conˌdition'ality** *n* ▸**con'ditionally** *adv*

conditional access *n* the distortion of television programme transmissions so that only authorized subscribers with suitable decoding apparatus may have access to them.

conditioned response *n Psychol.* a response that is transferred from the second to the first of a pair of stimuli. A well-known Pavlovian example is salivation by a dog when it hears a bell ring, because food has always been presented when the bell has been rung previously. Also called (esp. formerly): **conditioned reflex.**

condo ('kɒndəʊ) *n, pl* **condos.** *US & Canad. inf.* a condominium building or apartment.

condole ⓘ (kən'dəʊl) *vb* **condoles, condoling, condoled.** (*intr;* foll. by *with*) to express sympathy with someone in grief, pain, etc. [C16: from Church L *condolēre,* from L *com-* together + *dolēre* to grieve]
▸**con'dolence** *n*

condom ⓘ ('kɒndɒm, 'kɒndəm) *n* a rubber sheath worn on the penis or in the vagina during sexual intercourse to prevent conception or infection. [C18: from ?]

condominium (ˌkɒndə'mɪnɪəm) *n, pl* **condominiums. 1** joint rule or sovereignty. **2** a country ruled by two or more foreign powers. **3** *US & Canad.* **3a** an apartment building in which each apartment is individually owned and the common areas are jointly owned. **3b** an apartment in such a building. Sometimes shortened to **condo.** [C18: from NL, from L *com-* together + *dominium* ownership]

condone ⓘ (kən'dəʊn) *vb* **condones, condoning, condoned.** (*tr*) **1** to overlook or forgive (an offence, etc.). **2** *Law.* (esp. of a spouse) to pardon or overlook (an offence, usually adultery). [C19: from L *condōnāre,* from *com-* (intensive) + *dōnāre* to donate]
▸**condonation** (ˌkɒndəʊ'neɪʃən) *n* ▸**con'doner** *n*

condor ('kɒndɔː) *n* either of two very large rare New World vultures, the **Andean condor,** which has black plumage with white around the neck, and the **California condor,** which is nearly extinct. [C17: from Sp. *cóndor,* from Quechuan *kuntur*]

condottiere (ˌkɒndɒ'tjɛərɪ) *n, pl* **condottieri** (-riː). a commander or soldier in a professional mercenary company in Europe from the 13th to the 16th centuries. [C18: from It., from *condotto* leadership, from *condurre* to lead, from L *condūcere*]

conduce (kən'djuːs) *vb* **conduces, conducing, conduced.** (*intr;* foll. by *to*) to lead or contribute (to a result). [C15: from L *condūcere,* from *com-* together + *dūcere* to lead]

conducive ⓘ (kən'djuːsɪv) *adj* (when *postpositive,* foll. by *to*) contributing, leading, or tending.

conduct ⓘ *n* ('kɒndʌkt). **1** behaviour. **2** the way of managing a business, affair, etc.; handling. **3** *Rare.* the act of leading. ◆ *vb* (kən'dʌkt). **4** (*tr*) to accompany and guide (people, a party, etc.) (esp. in **conducted tour**). **5** (*tr*) to direct (affairs, business, etc.); control. **6** (*tr*) to carry out; organize: *conduct a survey.* **7** (*tr*) to behave (oneself). **8** to control (an orchestra, etc.) by the movements of the hands or a baton. **9** to transmit (heat, electricity, etc.). [C15: from Med. L *conductus* escorted, from L, from *condūcere* to CONDUCE]
▸**con'ductible** *adj* ▸**conˌducti'bility** *n*

conductance (kən'dʌktəns) *n* the ability of a system to conduct electricity, measured by the ratio of the current flowing through the system to the potential difference across it. Symbol: G

THESAURUS

condemnation *n* **1 = disapproval**, blame, censure, denouncement, denunciation, reproach, reprobation, reproof, stricture **2 = sentence**, conviction, damnation, doom, judgment, proscription

condemnatory *adj* **1 = disapproving**, accusatory, accusing, censorious, critical, damnatory, denunciatory, proscriptive, reprobative, scathing

condensation *n* **1 = concentration**, compression, consolidation, crystallization, curtailment, reduction **2 = distillation**, condensate, deliquescence, liquefaction, precipitate, precipitation **4 = abridgment**, contraction, digest, précis, synopsis

condense *vb* **1, 3 = concentrate**, boil down, coagulate, decoct, precipitate (*Chemistry*), reduce, solidify, thicken **2 = abridge**, abbreviate, compact, compress, concentrate, contract, curtail, encapsulate, epitomize, précis, shorten, summarize
Antonyms *vb* ≠ **concentrate:** dilute, make thinner, thin (out), water down, weaken ≠ **abridge:** elaborate, enlarge, expand, expatiate, increase, lengthen, pad out, spin out

condescend *vb* **1 = patronize**, talk down to **2 = lower oneself**, bend, come down off one's high horse (*inf.*), deign, humble *or* demean oneself, see fit, stoop, submit, unbend (*inf.*), vouchsafe

condescending *adj* **1 = patronizing**, disdainful, lofty, lordly, on one's high horse (*inf.*), snobbish, snooty (*inf.*), supercilious, superior, toffee-nosed (*sl., chiefly Brit.*)

condescension *n* **1 = patronizing attitude**, airs, disdain, haughtiness, loftiness, lordliness, superciliousness, superiority

condition *n* **1 = state**, case, circumstances, lie of the land, plight, position, predicament, shape, situation, state of affairs, *status quo* **2 = requirement**, arrangement, article, demand, limitation, modification, prerequisite, provision, proviso, qualification, requisite, restriction, rider, rule, stipulation, terms **3** *pl* **= circumstances**, environment, milieu, situation, surroundings, way of life **4 = health**, fettle, fitness, kilter, order, shape, state of health, trim **5 = ailment**, complaint, infirmity, malady, problem, weakness ◆ *vb* **13, 15 = accustom**, adapt, educate, equip, habituate, inure, make ready, prepare, ready, tone up, train, work out

conditional *adj* **1 = dependent**, contingent, limited, provisional, qualified, subject to, with reservations
Antonyms *adj* absolute, categorical, unconditional, unrestricted

conditioning *n* **13, 15 = accustoming**, familiarization, grooming, hardening, inurement, preparation, readying, reorientation, seasoning, training ◆ *adj* **13 = toning**, astringent

condolence *n* **= sympathy**, commiseration, compassion, consolation, fellow feeling, pity

condom *n* **= sheath**, flunky (*sl.*), French letter (*sl.*), French tickler (*sl.*), rubber (*US sl.*), rubber johnny (*Brit. sl.*), scumbag (*US sl.*)

condone *vb* **1 = overlook**, disregard, excuse, forgive, let pass, look the other way, make allowance for, pardon, turn a blind eye to, wink at
Antonyms *vb* censure, condemn, denounce, disapprove, punish

conducive *adj* **= leading**, calculated to produce, contributive, contributory, favourable, helpful, productive, promotive, tending

conduct *n* **1 = behaviour**, attitude, bearing, carriage, comportment, demeanour, deportment, manners, mien (*literary*), ways **2 = management**, administration, control, direction, guidance, handling, leadership, organization, running, supervision ◆ *vb* **4 = accompany**, attend, chair, convey, escort, guide, lead, pilot, steer, usher **5, 6 = carry out**, administer, control, direct, govern, handle, manage, organize, preside over, regulate, run, supervise **7 = behave**, acquit, act, carry, comport, deport

conducting tissue *n Bot.* another name for **vascular tissue.**

conduction (kən'dʌkʃən) *n* **1** the transfer of energy by a medium without bulk movement of the medium itself. Cf. **convection** (sense 1). **2** the transmission of an impulse along a nerve fibre. **3** the act of conveying or conducting, as through a pipe. **4** *Physics.* another name for **conductivity** (sense 1).
▸**con'ductional** *adj*

conductive (kən'dʌktɪv) *adj* of, denoting, or having the property of conduction.

conductive education *n* an educational system, developed in Hungary, in which teachers (**conductors**) teach children and adults with motor disorders to function independently, by guiding them to attain their own goals in their own way.

conductivity (ˌkɒndʌk'tɪvɪtɪ) *n, pl* **conductivities. 1** the property of transmitting heat, electricity, or sound. **2** a measure of the ability of a substance to conduct electricity. Symbol: κ

conductivity water *n* water that has a conductivity of less than 0.043 $\times 10^{-6}$ S cm^{-1}.

conductor (kən'dʌktə) *n* **1** an official on a bus who collects fares. **2** a person who conducts an orchestra, choir, etc. **3** a person who leads or guides. **4** *US & Canad.* a railway official in charge of a train. **5** a substance, body, or system that conducts electricity, heat, etc. **6** See **lightning conductor.**
▸**con'ductorship** *n* ▸**conductress** (kən'dʌktrɪs) *fem n*

conduit ➊ ('kɒndɪt, -djʊɪt) *n* **1** a pipe or channel for carrying a fluid. **2** a rigid tube for carrying electrical cables. **3** an agency or means of access, communication, etc. [C14: from OF, from Med. L *conductus* channel, from L *condūcere* to lead]

condyle ('kɒndɪl) *n* the rounded projection on the articulating end of a bone. [C17: from L *condylus,* from Gk *kondulos*]
▸**'condylar** *adj*

cone (kəʊn) *n* **1** a geometric solid consisting of a plane base bounded by a closed curve, usually a circle or an ellipse, every point of which is joined to a fixed point lying outside the plane of the base. **2** anything that tapers from a circular section to a point, such as a wafer shell used to contain ice cream. **3a** the reproductive body of conifers and related plants, made up of overlapping scales. **3b** a similar structure in horsetails, club mosses, etc. **4** a small cone used as a temporary traffic marker on roads. **5** any one of the cone-shaped cells in the retina of the eye, sensitive to colour and bright light. ◆ *vb* **cones, coning, coned. 6** *(tr)* to shape like a cone. [C16: from L *cōnus,* from Gk *kōnus* pine cone, geometrical cone]

cone off *vb (tr, adv) Brit.* to close (one carriageway of a motorway) by placing warning cones across it.

coney ('kəʊnɪ) *n* a variant spelling of **cony.**

confab ➊ ('kɒnfæb) *Inf.* ◆ *n* **1** a conversation. ◆ *vb* **confabs, confabbing, confabbed. 2** *(intr)* to converse.

confabulate (kən'fæbjʊˌleɪt) *vb* **confabulates, confabulating, confabulated.** *(intr)* **1** to talk together; chat. **2** *Psychiatry.* to replace the gaps left by a disorder of the memory with imaginary remembered experiences consistently believed to be true. [C17: from L *confābulārī,* from *fābulārī* to talk, from *fābula* a story]
▸**conˌfabu'lation** *n*

confect (kən'fɛkt) *vb (tr)* **1** to prepare by combining ingredients. **2** to make; construct. [C16: from L *confectus* prepared, from *conficere,* from *com-* (intensive) + *facere* to make]

confection (kən'fɛkʃən) *n* **1** the act of compounding or mixing. **2** any sweet preparation, such as a preserve or a sweet. **3** *Old-fashioned.* an elaborate article of clothing, esp. for women. [C14: from OF, from L *confectiō* a preparing, from *conficere;* see CONFECT]

confectioner (kən'fɛkʃənə) *n* a person who makes or sells sweets or confections.

confectionery (kən'fɛkʃənərɪ) *n, pl* **confectioneries. 1** sweets and other confections collectively. **2** the art or business of a confectioner.

confederacy ➊ (kən'fɛdərəsɪ) *n, pl* **confederacies. 1** a union of states, etc.; alliance; league. **2** a combination of groups or individuals for unlawful purposes. [C14: from OF *confederacie,* from LL *confoederātiō* agreement]
▸**con'federal** *adj*

confederate ➊ *n* (kən'fɛdərɪt). **1** a nation, state, or individual that is part of a confederacy. **2** someone who is part of a conspiracy. ◆ *adj* (kən'fɛdərɪt). **3** united; allied. ◆ *vb* (kən'fɛdəˌreɪt), **confederates, confederating, confederated. 4** to form into or become part of a confederacy [C14: from LL *confoederātus,* from *confoederāre* to unite by a league]

Confederate (kən'fɛdərɪt) *adj* **1** of or supporting the Confederate States of America, which seceded from the Union in 1861. ◆ *n* **2** a supporter of the Confederate States.

confederation (kənˌfɛdə'reɪʃən) *n* **1** the act of confederating or the state of being confederated. **2** a loose alliance of political units. **3** (esp. in Canada) another name for a **federation.**
▸**conˌfeder'ationist** *n*

confer ➊ (kən'fɜː) *vb* **confers, conferring, conferred. 1** *(tr;* foll. by *on* or *upon)* to grant or bestow (an honour, gift, etc.). **2** *(intr)* to consult together. [C16: from L *conferre,* from *com-* together + *ferre* to bring]
▸**con'ferment** *or* **con'ferral** *n* ▸**con'ferrable** *adj*

conferee *or* **conferree** (ˌkɒnfɜː'riː) *n* **1** a person who takes part in a conference. **2** a person on whom an honour or gift is conferred.

conference ➊ ('kɒnfərəns) *n* **1** a meeting for consultation or discussion, esp. one with a formal agenda. **2** an assembly of the clergy or of clergy and laity of any of certain Protestant Churches acting as representatives of their denomination. **3** *Sport, US & Canad.* a league or division of clubs or teams. [C16: from Med. L *conferentia,* from L *conferre* to bring together]
▸**conferential** (ˌkɒnfə'rɛnʃəl) *adj*

conference call *n* a special telephone facility by which three or more people using conventional or cellular phones can be linked up to speak to one another.

conferencing ('kɒnfərənsɪŋ) *n* the practice of holding a conference, esp. by means of a telephone service. See **conference call.**

confess ➊ (kən'fɛs) *vb* (when *tr, may take a clause as object*) **1** (when *intr,* often foll. by *to*) to make an admission (of faults, crimes, etc.). **2** *(tr)* to admit to be true; concede. **3** *Christianity.* to declare (one's sins) to God or to a priest as his representative, so as to obtain pardon and absolution. [C14: from OF *confesser,* from LL, from L *confessus* confessed, from *confitērī* to admit]

confessedly (kən'fɛsɪdlɪ) *adv (sentence modifier)* by admission or confession; avowedly.

confession ➊ (kən'fɛʃən) *n* **1** the act of confessing. **2** something confessed. **3** an acknowledgment, esp. of one's faults or crimes. **4** *Christianity.* the act of a penitent accusing himself of his sins. **5 confession of faith.** a formal public avowal of religious beliefs. **6** a religious sect united by common beliefs.
▸**con'fessionary** *adj*

confessional (kən'fɛʃənᵊl) *adj* **1** of or suited to a confession. ◆ *n* **2** *Christianity.* a small stall where a priest hears confessions.

confessor (kən'fɛsə) *n* **1** *Christianity.* a priest who hears confessions and sometimes acts as a spiritual counsellor. **2** *History.* a person who bears witness to his Christian religious faith by the holiness of his life, but does not suffer martyrdom. **3** a person who makes a confession.

confetti (kən'fɛtɪ) *n* small pieces of coloured paper thrown on festive occasions, esp. at weddings. [C19: from It., pl of *confetto,* orig., a bonbon]

confidant ➊ *or (fem)* **confidante** (ˌkɒnfɪ'dænt, 'kɒnfɪˌdænt) *n* a person to whom private matters are confided. [C17: from F *confident,* from It. *confidente,* n. use of adj: trustworthy]

confide ➊ (kən'faɪd) *vb* **confides, confiding, confided. 1** (usually foll. by *in;* when *tr, may take a clause as object*) to disclose (secret or personal matters) in confidence (to). **2** *(intr;* foll. by *in)* to have complete trust. **3** *(tr)* to entrust into another's keeping. [C15: from L *confidere,* from *fidere* to trust]
▸**con'fider** *n*

confidence ➊ ('kɒnfɪdəns) *n* **1** trust in a person or thing. **2** belief in one's own abilities; self-assurance. **3** trust or a trustful relationship: *take me into your confidence.* **4** something confided; secret. **5 in confidence.** as a secret.

confidence trick *or US & Canad.* **confidence game** *n* a swindle involving money in which the victim's trust is won by the swindler.

confident ➊ ('kɒnfɪdənt) *adj* **1** *(postpositive;* foll. by *of)* having or show-

THESAURUS

conduit *n* **1** = **passage,** canal, channel, duct, main, pipe, tube

confab *n* **1** *Informal* = **conversation,** chat, chinwag (*Brit. inf.*), confabulation (*formal*), discussion, gossip, natter, powwow, session, talk

confederacy *n* **1, 2** = **union,** alliance, bund, coalition, compact, confederation, conspiracy, covenant, federation, league

confederate *n* **1, 2** = **associate,** abettor, accessory, accomplice, ally, colleague, partner ◆ *adj* **3** = **allied,** associated, combined, federal, federated, in alliance ◆ *vb* **4** = **unite,** ally, amalgamate, associate, band together, combine, federate, merge

confer *vb* **1** = **grant,** accord, award, bestow, give, hand out, present, vouchsafe **2** = **discuss,** consult, converse, deliberate, discourse, parley, talk

conference *n* **1** = **meeting,** colloquium, congress, consultation, convention, convocation, discussion, forum, seminar, symposium, teach-in

confess *vb* **1, 2** = **admit,** acknowledge, allow, blurt out, come clean (*inf.*), come out of the closet, concede, confide, disclose, divulge, get (something) off one's chest (*inf.*), grant, make a clean breast of, own, own up, recognize, sing (*sl., chiefly U.S.*), spill one's guts (*sl.*)
Antonyms *vb* button one's lips, conceal, cover, deny, hide, hush up, keep mum, keep secret, keep under wraps, repudiate, suppress, withhold

confession *n* **1** = **admission,** acknowledgment, avowal, disclosure, divulgence, exposure, revelation, unbosoming

confidant *n* = **close friend,** alter ego, bosom friend, crony, familiar, intimate

confide *vb* **1** = **tell,** admit, breathe, confess, disclose, divulge, impart, reveal, whisper **3** *Formal* = **entrust,** commend, commit, consign

confidence *n* **1** = **trust,** belief, credence, dependence, faith, reliance **2** = **self-assurance,** aplomb, assurance, boldness, courage, firmness, nerve, self-possession, self-reliance **5 in confidence** = **in secrecy,** between you and me (and the gatepost), confidentially, privately
Antonyms *n* ≠ **trust:** disbelief, distrust, doubt, misgiving, mistrust ≠ **self-assurance:** apprehension, fear, self-doubt, shyness, uncertainty

confident *adj* **1** = **certain,** convinced, counting on, positive, satisfied, secure, sure **2** = **self-assured,** assured, bold, can-do (*inf.*), dauntless, fearless, self-reliant
Antonyms *adj* ≠ **certain:** doubtful, dubious, not sure, tentative, uncertain, unconvinced, unsure ≠ **self-assured:** afraid, hesitant, insecure, jittery,

ing certainty; sure: *confident of success.* **2** sure of oneself. **3** presumptuous. [C16: from L *confidens,* from *confidere* to have complete trust in]
▸**'confidently** *adv*

confidential ⓣ (ˌkɒnfɪ'dɛnʃəl) *adj* **1** spoken or given in confidence; private. **2** entrusted with another's secret affairs: *a confidential secretary.* **3** suggestive of intimacy: *a confidential approach.*
▸**ˌconfiˌdenti'ality** *n* ▸**ˌconfi'dentially** *adv*

confiding (kən'faɪdɪŋ) *adj* unsuspicious; trustful.
▸**con'fidingly** *adv* ▸**con'fidingness** *n*

configuration ⓣ (kənˌfɪgju'reɪʃən) *n* **1** the arrangement of the parts of something. **2** the external form or outline achieved by such an arrangement. **3** *Psychol.* the unit or pattern in perception studied by Gestalt psychologists. [C16: from LL *configūrātiō,* from *configūrāre* to model on something, from *figūrāre* to shape, fashion]
▸**conˌfigu'rational** *or* **con'figurative** *adj*

confine ⓣ *vb* (kən'faɪn), **confines, confining, confined.** (*tr*) **1** to keep within bounds; limit; restrict. **2** to restrict the free movement of: *arthritis confined him to bed.* ◆ *n* ('kɒnfaɪn). **3** (*often pl*) a limit; boundary. [C16: from Med. L *confīnāre,* from L *confīnis* adjacent, from *fīnis* boundary]
▸**con'finer** *n*

confined ⓣ (kən'faɪnd) *adj* **1** enclosed; limited. **2** in childbed; undergoing childbirth.

confinement ⓣ (kən'faɪnmənt) *n* **1** the act of confining or the state of being confined. **2** the period of the birth of a child.

confirm ⓣ (kən'fɜːm) *vb* (*tr*) **1** (*may take a clause as object*) to prove to be true or valid; corroborate. **2** (*may take a clause as object*) to assert for a further time, so as to make more definite: *he confirmed that he would appear in court.* **3** to strengthen: *his story confirmed my doubts.* **4** to make valid by a formal act; ratify. **5** to administer the rite of confirmation to. [C13: from OF *confermer,* from L *confirmāre,* from *firmus* FIRM[1]]
▸**con'firmatory** *or* **con'firmative** *adj*

confirmation ⓣ (ˌkɒnfə'meɪʃən) *n* **1** the act of confirming. **2** something that confirms. **3** a rite in several Christian churches that confirms a baptized person in his faith and admits him to full participation in the church.

confirmed ⓣ (kən'fɜːmd) *adj* **1** (*prenominal*) long-established in a habit, way of life, etc. **2** having received the rite of confirmation.

confiscate ⓣ ('kɒnfɪˌskeɪt) *vb* **confiscates, confiscating, confiscated.** (*tr*) **1** to seize (property), esp. for public use and esp. by way of a penalty. ◆ *adj* **2** confiscated; forfeit. [C16: from L *confiscāre* to seize for the public treasury, from *fiscus* treasury]
▸**ˌconfis'cation** *n* ▸**'confisˌcator** *n* ▸**confiscatory** (kən'fɪskətərɪ) *adj*

Confiteor (kən'fɪtɪˌɔː) *n RC Church.* a prayer consisting of a general confession of sinfulness and an entreaty for forgiveness. [C13: from L: I confess]

conflagration ⓣ (ˌkɒnflə'greɪʃən) *n* a large destructive fire. [C16: from L *conflagrātiō,* from *conflagrāre,* from *com-* (intensive) + *flagrāre* to burn]

conflate (kən'fleɪt) *vb* **conflates, conflating, conflated.** (*tr*) to combine or blend (two things, esp. two versions of a text) so as to form a whole. [C16: from L *conflāre* to blow together, from *flāre* to blow]
▸**con'flation** *n*

conflict ⓣ *n* ('kɒnflɪkt). **1** a struggle between opposing forces; battle. **2** opposition between ideas, interests, etc.; controversy. **3** *Psychol.* opposition between two simultaneous but incompatible wishes or drives, sometimes leading to emotional tension. ◆ *vb* (kən'flɪkt). (*intr*) **4** to come into opposition; clash. **5** to fight. [C15: from L *conflictus,* from *confligere* to combat, from *fligere* to strike]
▸**con'flicting** *adj* ▸**con'flictingly** *adv* ▸**con'fliction** *n*

confluence ('kɒnfluəns) *or* **conflux** ('kɒnflʌks) *n* **1** a flowing together, esp. of rivers. **2** a gathering.
▸**'confluent** *adj*

conform ⓣ (kən'fɔːm) *vb* **1** (*intr;* usually foll. by *to*) to comply in actions, behaviour, etc., with accepted standards. **2** (*intr;* usually foll. by *with*) to be in accordance: *he conforms with my idea of a teacher.* **3** to make or become similar. **4** (*intr*) to comply with the practices of an established church, esp. the Church of England. [C14: from OF *conformer,* from L *confirmāre* to strengthen, from *firmāre* to make firm]
▸**con'former** *n* ▸**con'formist** *n, adj*

conformable (kən'fɔːməbᵊl) *adj* **1** corresponding in character; similar. **2** obedient; submissive. **3** (foll. by *to*) consistent (with). **4** (of rock strata) lying in a parallel arrangement so that their original relative positions have remained undisturbed.
▸**conˌforma'bility** *n* ▸**con'formably** *adv*

conformal (kən'fɔːməl) *adj* (of a map projection) maintaining true shape over a small area and scale in every direction. [C17: from LL *conformālis,* from L *com-* same + *forma* shape]

conformation ⓣ (ˌkɒnfɔː'meɪʃən) *n* **1** the general shape of an object; configuration. **2** the arrangement of the parts of an object. **3** *Chem.* the three-dimensional arrangement of the atoms in a molecule.

conformity ⓣ (kən'fɔːmɪtɪ) *or* **conformance** *n, pl* **conformities** *or* **conformances. 1** compliance in actions, behaviour, etc., with certain accepted standards. **2** likeness; congruity; agreement. **3** compliance with the practices of an established church.

confound ⓣ (kən'faʊnd) *vb* (*tr*) **1** to astound; bewilder. **2** to confuse. **3** to treat mistakenly as similar to or identical with. **4** (kɒn'faʊnd). to curse (usually in **confound it!**). **5** to contradict or refute (an argument, etc.). **6** to rout or defeat (an enemy). [C13: from OF *confondre,* from L *confundere* to mingle, pour together]
▸**con'founder** *n*

confounded (kən'faʊndɪd) *adj* **1** bewildered; confused. **2** (*prenominal*) *Inf.* execrable; damned.
▸**con'foundedly** *adv*

confraternity (ˌkɒnfrə'tɜːnɪtɪ) *n, pl* **confraternities.** a group of men united for some particular purpose, esp. Christian laymen organized for religious or charitable service; brotherhood. [C15: from Med. L *confrāternitās,* ult. from L *frāter* brother]

confrère ('kɒnfrɛə) *n* a fellow member of a profession, etc. [C15: from OF, from Med. L *confrāter*]

confront ⓣ (kən'frʌnt) *vb* (*tr*) **1** (usually foll. by *with*) to present (with something), esp. in order to accuse or criticize. **2** to face boldly; oppose in hostility. **3** to be face to face with. [C16: from Med. L *confrontārī,* from *frons* forehead]
▸**confrontation** (ˌkɒnfrʌn'teɪʃən) *n* ▸**ˌconfron'tational** *adj*

Confucian (kən'fjuːʃən) *adj* **1** of or relating to the doctrines of Confucius (551–479 B.C.), Chinese philosopher. ◆ *n* **2** a follower of Confucius.

Confucianism (kən'fjuːʃəˌnɪzəm) *n* the ethical system of Confucius

THESAURUS

lacking confidence, mousy, nervous, scared, self-doubting, unsure

confidential *adj* **1** = **secret**, classified, hush-hush (*inf.*), intimate, off the record, private, privy **2** = **trusted**, faithful, familiar, trustworthy, trusty

confidentially *adv* **1** = **in secret**, behind closed doors, between ourselves, in camera, in confidence, personally, privately, sub rosa

configuration *n* **1, 2** = **arrangement**, cast, conformation, contour, figure, form, outline, shape

confine *vb* **1** = **restrict**, bind, bound, cage, circumscribe, clip someone's wings, enclose, hem in, hold back, immure, imprison, incarcerate, intern, keep, limit, repress, restrain, shut up, straiten ◆ *n* **3** *often pl* = **limits**, boundaries, bounds, circumference, edge, pale, precincts

confined *adj* **1** = **restricted**, enclosed, limited **2** = **in childbirth**, in childbed, lying-in

confinement *n* **1** = **imprisonment**, custody, detention, incarceration, internment, porridge (*sl.*) **2** = **childbirth**, *accouchement*, childbed, labour, lying-in, parturition, time, travail

confirm *vb* **1** = **prove**, approve, authenticate, bear out, corroborate, endorse, ratify, sanction, substantiate, validate, verify **3** = **strengthen**, assure, buttress, clinch, establish, fix, fortify, reinforce, settle

confirmation *n* **1** = **proof**, authentication, corroboration, evidence, substantiation, testimony, validation, verification **2** = **sanction**, acceptance, agreement, approval, assent, endorsement, ratification
Antonyms *n* ≠ **proof:** contradiction, denial, disavowal, repudiation ≠ **sanction:** annulment, cancellation, disapproval, refusal, rejection

confirmed *adj* **1** = **long-established**, chronic, dyed-in-the-wool, habitual, hardened, ingrained, inured, inveterate, rooted, seasoned

confiscate *vb* **1** = **seize**, appropriate, commandeer, expropriate, impound, sequester, sequestrate
Antonyms *vb* free, give, give back, hand back, release, restore, return

confiscation *n* **1** = **seizure**, appropriation, expropriation, forfeiture, impounding, sequestration, takeover

conflagration *n* = **fire**, blaze, holocaust, inferno, wildfire

conflict *n* **1** = **battle**, clash, collision, combat, contention, contest, encounter, engagement, fight, fracas, head-to-head, set-to (*inf.*), strife, war, warfare **2** = **opposition**, antagonism, bad blood, difference, disagreement, discord, dissension, divided loyalties, friction, hostility, interference, strife, variance ◆ *vb* **4, 5** = **be incompatible**, be at variance, clash, collide, combat, contend, contest, differ, disagree, fight, interfere, strive, struggle
Antonyms *n* ≠ **battle, opposition:** accord, agreement, harmony, peace, treaty, truce ◆ *vb* ≠ **be incompatible:** agree, coincide, harmonize, reconcile

conflicting *adj* **4** = **incompatible**, antagonistic, clashing, contradictory, contrary, discordant, inconsistent, opposed, opposing, paradoxical
Antonyms *adj* accordant, agreeing, compatible, congruous, consistent, harmonious, similar, unopposing

conform *vb* **1** = **comply**, adapt, adjust, fall in with, follow, follow the crowd, obey, run with the pack, toe the line, yield **2, 3** = **agree**, accord, assimilate, correspond, harmonize, match, square, suit, tally

conformation *n* **1, 2** = **shape**, anatomy, arrangement, build, configuration, form, framework, outline, structure

conformist *n* **1** = **traditionalist**, Babbitt (*US.*), conventionalist, stick-in-the-mud (*inf.*), yes man

conformity *n* **1** = **compliance**, allegiance, Babbittry (*US.*), conventionality, observance, orthodoxy, traditionalism **2** = **likeness**, affinity, agreement, conformance, congruity, consonance, correspondence, harmony, resemblance, similarity

confound *vb* **1** = **bewilder**, amaze, astonish, astound, baffle, be all Greek to (*inf.*), boggle the mind, confuse, dumbfound, flabbergast (*inf.*), flummox, mix up, mystify, nonplus, perplex, startle, surprise **5** = **destroy**, annihilate, contradict, demolish, explode, make a nonsense of, overthrow, overwhelm, refute, ruin

confront *vb* **2, 3** = **face**, accost, beard, brave, bring face to face with, call out, challenge, defy, encounter, face off (*sl.*), face the music, face up to, oppose, stand up to, tackle, walk into the lion's den
Antonyms *vb* avoid, body-swerve (*Scot.*), circumvent, dodge, evade, flee, give a wide berth to, keep *or* steer clear of, sidestep

confrontation *n* **2, 3** = **conflict**, contest, crisis, encounter, face-off (*sl.*), fight, head-to-head, set-to (*inf.*), showdown (*inf.*)

emphasizing moral order, the virtue of China's ancient rules, and gentlemanly education.
►**Con'fucianist** *n*

confuse Ⓣ (kən'fju:z) *vb* **confuses, confusing, confused.** (*tr*) **1** to bewilder; perplex. **2** to mix up (things, ideas, etc.). **3** to make unclear: *he confused his talk with irrelevant details.* **4** to mistake (one thing) for another. **5** to disconcert; embarrass. **6** to cause to become disordered: *the enemy ranks were confused by gas.* [C18: back formation from *confused,* from L *confūsus,* from *confundere* to pour together]
►**con'fusable** *adj* ►**confusedly** (kən'fju:zɪdlɪ, -'fju:zd-) *adv* ►**con'fusing** *adj* ►**con'fusingly** *adv*

confusion Ⓣ (kən'fju:ʒən) *n* **1** the act of confusing or the state of being confused. **2** disorder. **3** bewilderment; perplexity. **4** lack of clarity. **5** embarrassment; abashment.

confute (kən'fju:t) *vb* **confutes, confuting, confuted.** (*tr*) to prove (a person or thing) wrong, invalid, or mistaken; disprove. [C16: from L *confūtāre* to check, silence]
►**con'futable** *adj* ►**confutation** (ˌkɒnfju'teɪʃən) *n*

conga ('kɒŋgə) *n* **1** a Latin American dance of three steps and a kick to each bar, performed by a number of people in single file. **2** Also called: **conga drum.** a large tubular bass drum played with the hands. ◆ *vb* **congas, congaing, congaed. 3** (*intr*) to perform this dance. [C20: from American Sp., fem of *congo* belonging to the *Congo*]

congé ('kɒnʒeɪ) *n* **1** permission to depart or dismissal, esp. when formal. **2** a farewell. [C16: from OF *congié,* from L *commeātus* leave of absence, from *meāre* to go]

congeal Ⓣ (kən'dʒi:l) *vb* **1** to change or cause to change from a soft or fluid state to a firm state. **2** to form or cause to form into a coagulated mass; jell. [C14: from OF *congeler,* from L *congelāre,* from *com-* together + *gelāre* to freeze]
►**con'gealable** *adj* ►**con'gealment** *n*

congelation (ˌkɒndʒɪ'leɪʃən) *n* **1** the process of congealing. **2** something formed by this process.

congener (kən'dʒi:nə, 'kɒndʒɪnə) *n* a member of a class, group, or other category, esp. any animal of a specified genus. [C18: from L, from *com-* same + *genus* kind]

congenial Ⓣ (kən'dʒi:njəl) *adj* **1** friendly, pleasant, or agreeable: *a congenial atmosphere to work in.* **2** having a similar disposition, tastes, etc.; compatible. [C17: from CON- (same) + GENIAL[1]]
►**congeniality** (kənˌdʒi:nɪ'ælɪtɪ) *n*

congenital Ⓣ (kən'dʒenɪtᵊl) *adj* **1** denoting any nonhereditary condition, esp. an abnormal condition, existing at birth: *congenital blindness.* **2** *Inf.* complete, as if from birth: *a congenital idiot.* [C18: from L *congenitus,* from *genitus* born, from *gignere* to bear]
►**con'genitally** *adv*

conger ('kɒŋgə) *n* a large marine eel occurring in temperate and tropical coastal waters. [C14: from OF *congre,* from L *conger,* from Gk *gongros*]

congeries (kɒn'dʒɪəri:z) *n* (*functioning as sing or pl*) a collection; mass; heap. [C17: from L, from *congerere* to pile up, from *gerere* to carry]

congest Ⓣ (kən'dʒest) *vb* **1** to crowd or become crowded to excess; overfill. **2** to clog (an organ) with blood or (of an organ) to become clogged with blood. **3** (*tr; usually passive*) to block (the nose) with mucus. [C16: from L *congestus,* from *congerere;* see CONGERIES]
►**con'gestion** *n*

conglomerate Ⓣ *n* (kən'glɒmərɪt). **1** a thing composed of heterogeneous elements. **2** any coarse-grained sedimentary rock consisting of rounded fragments of rock embedded in a finer matrix. **3** a large corporation consisting of a group of companies dealing in widely diversified goods, services, etc. ◆ *vb* (kən'glɒməˌreɪt), **conglomerates, conglomerating, conglomerated. 4** to form into a mass. ◆ *adj* (kən'glɒmərɪt). **5** made up of heterogeneous elements. **6** (of sedimentary rocks) consisting of rounded fragments within a finer matrix. [C16: from L *conglomerāre* to roll up, from *glomerāre* to wind into a ball, from *glomus* ball of thread]
►**conˌglomer'ation** *n*

congrats (kən'græts) *pl n, sentence substitute.* informal shortened form of **congratulations.**

congratulate Ⓣ (kən'grætjuˌleɪt) *vb* **congratulates, congratulating, congratulated.** (*tr*) **1** (usually foll. by *on*) to communicate pleasure, approval, or praise to; compliment. **2** (often foll. by *on*) to consider (oneself) clever or fortunate (as a result of): *she congratulated herself on her tact.* **3** *Obs.* to greet; salute. [C16: from L *congrātulārī,* from *grātulārī* to rejoice, from *grātus* pleasing]
►**conˌgratu'lation** *n* ►**con'gratulatory** *or* **con'gratulative** *adj*

congratulations Ⓣ (kənˌgrætju'leɪʃənz) *pl n, sentence substitute.* expressions of pleasure or joy on another's success, good fortune, etc.

congregate Ⓣ ('kɒŋgrɪˌgeɪt) *vb* **congregates, congregating, congregated.** to collect together in a body or crowd; assemble. [C15: from L *congregāre* to collect into a flock, from *grex* flock]

congregation Ⓣ (ˌkɒŋgrɪ'geɪʃən) *n* **1** a group of persons gathered for worship, prayer, etc., esp. in a church. **2** the act of congregating together. **3** a group collected together; assemblage. **4** the group of persons habitually attending a given church, chapel, etc. **5** *RC Church.* **5a** a society of persons who follow a common rule of life but who are bound only by simple vows. **5b** an administrative subdivision of the papal curia. **6** *Chiefly Brit.* an assembly of senior members of a university.

congregational (ˌkɒŋgrɪ'geɪʃənᵊl) *adj* **1** of or relating to a congregation. **2** (*usually cap.*) of or denoting Congregationalism.

Congregationalism (ˌkɒŋgrɪ'geɪʃənəˌlɪzəm) *n* a system of Christian doctrines and ecclesiastical government in which each congregation is self-governing.
►ˌ**Congre'gationalist** *adj, n*

congress Ⓣ ('kɒŋgres) *n* **1** a meeting or conference, esp. of representatives of sovereign states. **2** a national legislative assembly. **3** a society or association. [C16: from L *congressus,* from *congredī,* from *com-* together + *gradī* to walk]

Congress ('kɒŋgres) *n* **1** the bicameral federal legislature of the US, consisting of the House of Representatives and the Senate. **2** Also called: **Congress Party.** (in India) a major political party.
►**Con'gressional** *adj*

congressional (kən'greʃənᵊl) *adj* of or relating to a congress.
►**con'gressionalist** *n*

Congressman ('kɒŋgresmən) *or* (*fem*) **Congresswoman** *n, pl* **Congressmen** *or* **Congresswomen.** (in the US) a member of Congress, esp. of the House of Representatives.

congruence Ⓣ ('kɒŋgruəns) *or* **congruency** *n* **1** the quality or state of corresponding, agreeing, or being congruent. **2** *Maths.* the relationship between two integers, *x* and *y,* such that their difference, with re-

THESAURUS

confuse *vb* **1** = **bewilder,** baffle, be all Greek to (*inf.*), bemuse, darken, faze, flummox, muddy the waters, mystify, nonplus, obscure, perplex, puzzle **2** = **mix up,** blend, confound, disarrange, disorder, intermingle, involve, jumble, mingle, mistake, muddle, ravel, snarl up (*inf.*), tangle **5** = **disconcert,** abash, addle, demoralize, discomfit, discompose, discountenance, disorient, embarrass, fluster, mortify, nonplus, rattle (*inf.*), shame, throw into disorder, throw off balance, unnerve, upset

confused *adj* **1** = **bewildered,** at a loss, at sea, at sixes and sevens, baffled, dazed, discombobulated (*inf., chiefly US & Canad.*), disorganized, disorientated, flummoxed, muddled, muzzy (*US inf.*), nonplussed, not knowing if one is coming or going, not with it (*inf.*), perplexed, puzzled, taken aback, thrown off balance, upset **2** = **disordered,** at sixes and sevens, chaotic, disarranged, disarrayed, disorderly, disorganized, higgledy-piggledy (*inf.*), hugger-mugger (*arch.*), in disarray, jumbled, mistaken, misunderstood, mixed up, out of order, topsy-turvy, untidy
Antonyms *adj* ≠ **bewildered:** aware, enlightened, informed, on the ball (*inf.*), with it (*inf.*) ≠ **disordered:** arranged, in order, ordered, orderly, organized, tidy

confusing *adj* **1** = **bewildering,** ambiguous, baffling, clear as mud (*inf.*), complicated, contradictory, disconcerting, inconsistent, misleading, muddling, perplexing, puzzling, unclear
Antonyms *adj* clear, definite, explicit, plain, simple, straightforward, uncomplicated, understandable

confusion *n* **1, 3** = **bewilderment,** befuddlement, bemusement, disorientation, mystification, perplexity, puzzlement **2** = **disorder,** bustle, chaos, clutter, commotion, disarrangement, disarray, disorganization, hodgepodge (*US*), hotchpotch, jumble, mess, muddle, pig's breakfast (*inf.*), shambles, state, tangle, turmoil, untidiness, upheaval **5** = **disconcertion,** abashment, chagrin, demoralization, discomfiture, distraction, embarrassment, fluster, mind-fuck (*taboo sl.*), perturbation
Antonyms *n* ≠ **bewilderment:** clarification, enlightenment, explanation, solution ≠ **disorder:** arrangement, neatness, order, organization, tidiness

congeal *vb* **1, 2** = **thicken,** benumb, clot, coagulate, condense, curdle, freeze, gelatinize, harden, jell, set, solidify, stiffen

congenial *adj* **1** = **pleasant,** affable, agreeable, companionable, complaisant, favourable, friendly, genial, kindly, pleasing **2** = **compatible,** adapted, fit, kindred, like-minded, suitable, sympathetic, well-suited

congenital *adj* **1** = **inborn,** constitutional, immanent, inbred, inherent, innate, natural **2** *Informal* = **complete,** deep-dyed (*usually derogatory*), inveterate, thorough, utter

congested *adj* **1** = **overcrowded,** crowded, teeming **2** = **clogged,** blocked-up, crammed, jammed, overfilled, overflowing, packed, stuffed, stuffed-up
Antonyms *adj* ≠ **overcrowded:** empty, half-full, uncrowded ≠ **clogged:** clear, free, uncongested, unhampered, unhindered, unimpeded, unobstructed

congestion *n* **1** = **overcrowding,** crowding **2** = **clogging,** bottleneck, jam, mass, snarl-up (*inf., chiefly Brit.*), surfeit

conglomerate *n* **3** = **corporation,** agglomerate, aggregate, multinational ◆ *vb* **4** = **amass,** accumulate, agglomerate, aggregate, cluster, coalesce, snowball ◆ *adj* **5** = **amassed,** clustered, composite, heterogeneous, massed

conglomeration *n* **4** = **mass,** accumulation, aggregation, assortment, combination, composite, hotchpotch, medley, miscellany, mishmash, potpourri

congratulate *vb* **1** = **compliment,** felicitate, pat on the back, wish joy to

congratulations *pl n, sentence substitute* = **good wishes,** best wishes, compliments, felicitations, greetings, pat on the back

congregate *vb* = **come together,** assemble, collect, concentrate, convene, converge, convoke, flock, forgather, gather, mass, meet, muster, rally, rendezvous, throng
Antonyms *vb* break up, dispel, disperse, dissipate, part, scatter, separate, split up

congregation *n* **1, 3, 4** = **assembly,** brethren, crowd, fellowship, flock, host, laity, multitude, parish, parishioners, throng

congress *n* **1, 2** = **meeting,** assembly, chamber of deputies, conclave, conference, convention, convocation, council, delegates, diet, house, legislative assembly, legislature, parliament, quango, representatives

congruence *n* **1** = **correspondence,** accord,

spect to another integer called the modulus, *n*, is a multiple of the modulus.

congruent ('kɒŋgrʊənt) *adj* **1** agreeing; corresponding. **2** having identical shapes so that all parts correspond: *congruent triangles.* **3** of or concerning two integers related by a congruence. [C15: from L *congruere* to agree]

congruous ('kɒŋgrʊəs) *adj* **1** corresponding or agreeing. **2** appropriate. [C16: from L *congruus;* see CONGRUENT]
▸**congruity** (kən'gru:ɪtɪ) *n*

conic ('kɒnɪk) *adj also* **conical. 1a** having the shape of a cone. **1b** of a cone. ◆ *n* **2** another name for **conic section.**
▸**'conically** *adv*

conics ('kɒnɪks) *n (functioning as sing)* the geometry of the parabola, ellipse, and hyperbola.

conic section *n* one of a group of curves formed by the intersection of a plane and a right circular cone. It is either a circle, ellipse, parabola, or hyperbola.

conidium (kəʊ'nɪdɪəm) *n, pl* **conidia** (-'nɪdɪə). an asexual spore formed at the tip of a specialized hypha in fungi such as *Penicillium.* [C19: from NL, from Gk *konis* dust + -IUM]

conifer ('kəʊnɪfə, 'kɒn-) *n* any tree or shrub of the phylum *Coniferophyta,* typically bearing cones and evergreen leaves. The group includes the pines, spruces, firs, larches, etc. [C19: from L, from *cōnus* CONE + *ferre* to bear]
▸**co'niferous** *adj*

conj. *abbrev. for:* **1** conjugation. **2** conjunction.

conjectural (kən'dʒɛktʃərəl) *adj* involving or inclined to conjecture.
▸**con'jecturally** *adv*

conjecture (kən'dʒɛktʃə) *n* **1** the formation of conclusions from incomplete evidence; guess. **2** the conclusion so formed. ◆ *vb* **conjectures, conjecturing, conjectured. 3** to infer or arrive at (an opinion, conclusion, etc.) from incomplete evidence. [C14: from L *conjectūra,* from *conjicere* to throw together, from *jacere* to throw]
▸**con'jecturable** *adj*

conjoin (kən'dʒɔɪn) *vb* to join or become joined. [C14: from OF *conjoindre,* from L *conjungere,* from *jungere* to JOIN]
▸**con'joiner** *n*

conjoined twins *pl n* the technical name for **Siamese twins.**

conjoint (kən'dʒɔɪnt) *adj* united, joint, or associated.
▸**con'jointly** *adv*

conjugal ('kɒndʒʊgᵊl) *adj* of or relating to marriage or the relationship between husband and wife: *conjugal rights.* [C16: from L *conjugālis,* from *conjunx* wife or husband]
▸**conjugality** (ˌkɒndʒʊ'gælɪtɪ) *n* ▸**'conjugally** *adv*

conjugate *vb* ('kɒndʒʊˌgeɪt), **conjugates, conjugating, conjugated. 1** *(tr) Grammar.* to state or set out the conjugation of (a verb). **2** *(intr)* (of a verb) to undergo inflection according to a specific set of rules. **3** *(intr) Biol.* to undergo conjugation. **4** *(tr) Obs.* to join together, esp. in marriage. ◆ *adj* ('kɒndʒʊgɪt, -ˌgeɪt). **5** joined together in pairs. **6** *Maths.* **6a** (of two angles) having a sum of 360°. **6b** (of two complex numbers) differing only in the sign of the imaginary part as $4 + 3i$ and $4 - 3i$. **7** *Chem.* of the state of equilibrium in which two liquids can exist as separate phases that are both solutions. **8** *Chem.* (of acids and bases) related by loss or gain of a proton. **9** (of a compound leaf) having one pair of leaflets. **10** (of words) cognate; related in origin. ◆ *n* ('kɒndʒʊgɪt). **11** one of a pair or set of conjugate substances, values, quantities, words, etc. [C15: from L *conjugāre,* from *com-* together + *jugāre* to connect, from *jugum* a yoke]
▸**'conjuˌgative** *adj* ▸**'conjuˌgator** *n*

conjugation (ˌkɒndʒʊ'geɪʃən) *n* **1** *Grammar.* **1a** inflection of a verb for person, number, tense, voice, mood, etc. **1b** the complete set of the inflections of a given verb. **2** a joining. **3** a type of sexual reproduction in ciliate protozoans involving the temporary union of two individuals and the subsequent migration and fusion of the gametic nuclei. **4** the union of gametes, as in some fungi. **5** the pairing of chromosomes in the early phase of a meiotic division. **6** *Chem.* the existence of alternating double or triple bonds in a chemical compound, with consequent electron delocalization over part of the molecule.
▸ˌ**conju'gational** *adj*

conjunct ('kɒndʒʌŋkt, kən'dʒʌŋkt) *n Logic.* one of the propositions or formulas in a conjunction.

conjunction (kən'dʒʌŋkʃən) *n* **1** the act of joining together; union. **2** simultaneous occurrence of events; coincidence. **3** any word or group of words, other than a relative pronoun, that connects words, phrases, or clauses; for example *and* and *while.* **4** *Astron.* **4a** the position of a planet when it is in line with the sun as seen from the earth. **4b** the apparent proximity or coincidence of two celestial bodies on the celestial sphere. **5** *Logic.* **5a** the operator that forms a compound sentence from two given sentences, and corresponds to the English *and.* **5b** a sentence so formed: it is true only when both the component sentences are true. **5c** the relation between such sentences.
▸**con'junctional** *adj*

conjunctiva (ˌkɒndʒʌŋk'taɪvə) *n, pl* **conjunctivas** *or* **conjunctivae** (-vi:). the delicate mucous membrane that covers the eyeball and the under surface of the eyelid. [C16: from NL *membrāna conjunctīva* the conjunctive membrane]
▸ˌ**conjunc'tival** *adj*

conjunctive (kən'dʒʌŋktɪv) *adj* **1** joining; connective. **2** joined. **3** of or relating to conjunctions. ◆ *n* **4** a less common word for **conjunction** (sense 3). [C15: from LL *conjunctīvus,* from L *conjungere* to CONJOIN]

conjunctivitis (kənˌdʒʌŋktɪ'vaɪtɪs) *n* inflammation of the conjunctiva.

conjuncture (kən'dʒʌŋktʃə) *n* a combination of events, esp. a critical one.

conjuration (ˌkɒndʒʊ'reɪʃən) *n* **1** a magic spell; incantation. **2** a less common word for **conjuring. 3** *Arch.* supplication; entreaty.

conjure ('kʌndʒə) *vb* **conjures, conjuring, conjured. 1** *(intr)* to practise conjuring. **2** *(intr)* to call upon supposed supernatural forces by spells and incantations. **3** (kən'dʒʊə). *(tr)* to appeal earnestly to: *I conjure you to help me.* **4 a name to conjure with. 4a** a person thought to have great power or influence. **4b** any name that excites the imagination. [C13: from OF *conjurer* to plot, from L *conjūrāre* to swear together]

conjure up *vb (tr, adv)* **1** to present to the mind; evoke or imagine: *he conjured up a picture of his childhood.* **2** to call up or command (a spirit or devil) by an incantation.

conjuring ('kʌndʒərɪŋ) *n* **1** the performance of tricks that appear to defy natural laws. ◆ *adj* **2** denoting or of such tricks or entertainment.

conjuror *or* **conjurer** ('kʌndʒərə) *n* **1** a person who practises conjuring, esp. for people's entertainment. **2** a sorcerer.

conk (kɒŋk) *Sl.* ◆ *vb* **1** to strike (someone) a blow, esp. on the head or nose. ◆ *n* **2** a punch or blow, esp. on the head or nose. **3** the head or nose. [C19: prob. changed from CONCH]

conker ('kɒŋkə) *n* an informal name for the **horse chestnut** (sense 2).

conkers ('kɒŋkəz) *n (functioning as sing) Brit.* a game in which a player swings a horse chestnut (conker), threaded onto a string, against that of another player to try to break it. [C19: from dialect *conker* snail shell, orig. used in the game]

conk out *vb (intr, adv) Inf.* **1** (of machines, cars, etc.) to fail suddenly. **2** to tire suddenly or collapse. [C20: from ?]

con man *n Inf.* a person who swindles another by means of a confidence trick. More formal term: **confidence man.**

con moto (kɒn 'məʊtəʊ) *adj, adv Music.* (to be performed) in a brisk or lively manner. [It., lit.: with movement]

conn (kɒn) *vb, n* a variant spelling (esp. US) of **con**[3].

connate ('kɒneɪt) *adj* **1** existing from birth; congenital or innate. **2** allied in nature or origin. **3** *Biol.* (of similar parts or organs) closely joined or united by growth. **4** *Geol.* (of fluids) produced at the same time as the rocks surrounding them: *connate water.* [C17: from LL *connātus* born at the same time]

connect (kə'nɛkt) *vb* **1** to link or be linked. **2** *(tr)* to associate: *I connect him with my childhood.* **3** *(tr)* to establish telephone communications with or between. **4** *(intr)* to be meaningful or meaningfully related. **5** *(intr)* (of two public vehicles, such as trains or buses) to have the arrival of one timed to occur just before the departure of the other, for the convenient transfer of passengers. **6** *(intr) Inf.* to hit, punch, kick, etc., solidly. [C17: from L *connectere* to bind together, from *nectere* to tie]
▸**con'nectible** *or* **con'nectable** *adj* ▸**con'nector** *or* **con'necter** *n*

connecting rod *n* **1** a rod or bar for transmitting motion, esp. one that connects a rotating part to a reciprocating part. **2** such a rod that connects the piston to the crankshaft in an internal-combustion engine.

connection *or* **connexion** (kə'nɛkʃən) *n* **1** the act of connecting; union. **2** something that connects or relates; link or bond. **3** a relationship or association. **4** logical sequence in thought or expression;

THESAURUS

agreement, coincidence, compatibility, concurrence, conformity, congruity, consistency, harmony, identity

congruent *adj* **1** = **corresponding**, according, agreeing, coinciding, compatible, concurrent, conforming, congruous, consistent, identical

congruous *adj* **1** = **corresponding**, agreeing, compatible, concordant, congruent, consistent, consonant, correspondent **2** = **appropriate**, apt, becoming, fit, meet, seemly, suitable

conic **1a** *adj* = **cone-shaped**, conoid, funnel-shaped, pointed, pyramidal, tapered, tapering

conjectural *adj* = **speculative**, academic, hypothetical, supposed, suppositional, surmised, tentative, theoretical

conjecture *n* **1, 2** = **guess**, assumption, conclusion, fancy, guesstimate (*inf.*), guesswork, hypothesis, inference, notion, presumption, shot in the dark, speculation, supposition, surmise, theorizing, theory ◆ *vb* **3** = **guess**, assume, fancy, hypothesize, imagine, infer, speculate, suppose, surmise, suspect, theorize

conjugal *adj* = **marital**, bridal, connubial, hymeneal, married, matrimonial, nuptial, spousal, wedded

conjunction *n* **1, 2** = **joining**, association, coincidence, combination, concurrence, juxtaposition, union

conjuncture *n* = **crucial point**, combination, concurrence, connection, crisis, crossroads, emergency, exigency, juncture, pass, predicament, stage, turning point

conjure *vb* **1** = **perform tricks**, juggle **2** = **summon up**, bewitch, call upon, cast a spell, charm, enchant, invoke, raise, rouse **3** *Formal* = **appeal to**, adjure, beg, beseech, crave, entreat, implore, importune, pray, supplicate

conjure up *vb* **1** = **bring to mind**, contrive, create, evoke, produce as if by magic, recall, recollect

conjuring *n* **1** = **magic**, juggling, sorcery, thaumaturgy (*rare*), wizardry

conjuror *n* **1, 2** = **magician**, illusionist, miracle-worker, sorcerer, thaumaturge (*rare*), wizard

connect *vb* **1, 2** = **link**, affix, ally, associate, attach, cohere, combine, couple, fasten, join, relate, unite

Antonyms *vb* detach, disconnect, dissociate, divide, part, separate, sever, unfasten

connection *n* **1** = **link**, alliance, association, attachment, coupling, fastening, junction, tie,

coherence. **5** the relation of a word or phrase to its context: *in this connection the word has no political significance.* **6** (*often pl*) an acquaintance, esp. one who is influential. **7** a relative, esp. if distant and related by marriage. **8a** an opportunity to transfer from one train, bus, etc., to another. **8b** the vehicle scheduled to provide such an opportunity. **9** a link, usually a wire or metallic strip, between two components in an electric circuit. **10** a communications link, esp. by telephone. **11** *Sl.* a supplier of illegal drugs, such as heroin. **12** *Rare.* sexual intercourse.
▸**con'nectional** *or* **con'nexional** *adj*

connective (kə'nɛktɪv) *adj* **1** connecting. ◆ *n* **2** a thing that connects. **3** *Grammar, logic.* **3a** any word that connects phrases, clauses, or individual words. **3b** a symbol used in a formal language in the construction of compound sentences, corresponding to terms such as *or, and,* etc., in ordinary speech. **4** *Bot.* the tissue of a stamen that connects the two lobes of the anther.

connective tissue *n* an animal tissue that supports organs, fills the spaces between them, and forms tendons and ligaments.

conning tower ('kɒnɪŋ) *n* **1** a superstructure of a submarine, used as the bridge when the vessel is on the surface. **2** the armoured pilot house of a warship. [C19: see CON³]

connivance (kə'naɪvəns) *n* **1** the act or fact of conniving. **2** *Law.* the tacit encouragement of or assent to another's wrongdoing.

connive (kə'naɪv) *vb* **connives, conniving, connived.** (*intr*) **1** to plot together; conspire. **2** (foll. by *at*) *Law.* to give assent or encouragement (to the commission of a wrong). [C17: from F *conniver,* from L *connīvēre* to blink, hence, leave uncensured]
▸**con'niver** *n*

connoisseur (ˌkɒnɪ'sɜː) *n* a person with special knowledge or appreciation of a field, esp. in the arts. [C18: from F, from OF *conoiseor,* from *connoistre* to know, from L *cognōscere*]
▸ˌ**connois'seurship** *n*

connotation (ˌkɒnə'teɪʃən) *n* **1** an association or idea suggested by a word or phrase. **2** the act of connoting. **3** *Logic.* the characteristic or set of characteristics that determines to which object the common name properly applies. Also, in traditional logic, **intension.**
▸**connotative** ('kɒnəˌteɪtɪv, kə'nəʊtə-) *or* **con'notive** *adj*

connote (kɒ'nəʊt) *vb* **connotes, connoting, connoted.** (*tr; often takes a clause as object*) **1** (of a word, phrase, etc.) to imply or suggest (associations or ideas) other than the literal meaning: *the word "maiden" connotes modesty.* **2** to involve as a consequence or condition. [C17: from Med. L *connotāre,* from L *notāre* to mark, note, from *nota* sign, note]

connubial (kə'njuːbɪəl) *adj* of or relating to marriage: *connubial bliss.* [C17: from L *cōnūbiālis,* from *cōnūbium* marriage]
▸**conˌnubi'ality** *n*

conoid ('kəʊnɔɪd) *n* **1** a cone-shaped object. ◆ *adj also* **conoidal** (kəʊ'nɔɪdᵊl). **2** cone-shaped. [C17: from Gk *kōnoeidēs,* from *kōnos* CONE]
▸**co'noidally** *adv*

conquer ('kɒŋkə) *vb* **1** to overcome (an enemy, army, etc.); defeat. **2** to overcome (an obstacle, desire, etc.); surmount. **3** (*tr*) to gain possession or control of as by force or war; win. [C13: from OF *conquerre,* from Vulgar L *conquērere* (unattested) to obtain, from L *conquīrere* to search for, from *quaerere* to seek]
▸'**conquerable** *adj* ▸'**conquering** *adj* ▸'**conqueror** *n*

Conqueror ('kɒŋkərə) *n* **the.** epithet of William I, duke of Normandy, and king of England (1066–87).

conquest ('kɒnkwest) *n* **1** the act of conquering or the state of having been conquered; victory. **2** a person, thing, etc., that has been conquered. **3** a person, whose compliance, love, etc., has been won. [C13: from OF *conqueste,* from Vulgar L *conquēsta* (unattested), from L *conquīsīta,* fem. p.p. of *conquīrere;* see CONQUER]

Conquest ('kɒnkwɛst) *n* **the.** See **Norman Conquest.**

conquistador (kɒn'kwɪstəˌdɔː) *n, pl* **conquistadors** *or* **conquistadores** (kɒnˌkwɪstə'dɔːres). an adventurer or conqueror, esp. one of the Spanish conquerors of the New World in the 16th century. [C19: from Sp., from *conquistar* to conquer]

cons. *abbrev. for:* **1** consecrated. **2** consigned. **3** consignment. **4** consolidated. **5** consonant. **6** constitutional. **7** construction.

Cons. *abbrev. for* Conservative.

consanguinity (ˌkɒnsæŋ'gwɪnɪtɪ) *n* **1** relationship by blood; kinship. **2** close affinity or connection. [C14: see CON-, SANGUINE]
▸ˌ**consan'guineous** *or* **con'sanguine** *adj*

conscience ('kɒnʃəns) *n* **1** the sense of right and wrong that governs a person's thoughts and actions. **2** conscientiousness; diligence. **3** a feeling of guilt or anxiety: *he has a conscience about his unkind action.* **4** **in (all) conscience. 4a** with regard to truth and justice. **4b** certainly. **5** **on one's conscience.** causing feelings of guilt or remorse. [C13: from OF, from L *conscientia* knowledge, from *conscīre* to know; see CONSCIOUS]

conscience clause *n* a clause in a law or contract exempting persons with moral scruples.

conscience money *n* money paid voluntarily to compensate for dishonesty, esp. for taxes formerly evaded.

conscience-stricken *adj* feeling anxious or guilty. Also: **conscience-smitten.**

conscientious (ˌkɒnʃɪ'ɛnʃəs) *adj* **1** involving or taking great care; painstaking. **2** governed by or done according to conscience.
▸ˌ**consci'entiously** *adv* ▸ˌ**consci'entiousness** *n*

conscientious objector *n* a person who refuses to serve in the armed forces on the grounds of conscience.

conscious ('kɒnʃəs) *adj* **1** alert and awake. **2** aware of one's surroundings, one's own motivations and thoughts, etc. **3a** aware (of) and giving value and emphasis (to a particular fact): *I am conscious of your great kindness to me.* **3b** (*in combination*): *clothes-conscious.* **4** deliberate or intended: *a conscious effort; conscious rudeness.* **5a** denoting a part of the human mind that is aware of a person's self, environment, and mental activity and that to a certain extent determines his choices of action. **5b** (*as n*): *the conscious is only a small part of the mind.* [C17: from L *conscius* sharing knowledge, from *com-* with + *scīre* to know]
▸'**consciously** *adv* ▸'**consciousness** *n*

consciousness raising *n* **a** the process of developing awareness in a person or group of a situation regarded as wrong or unjust, with the aim of producing active participation in changing it. **b** (*as modifier*): *a consciousness-raising group.*

conscript *n* ('kɒnskrɪpt). **1a** a person who is enrolled for compulsory military service. **1b** (*as modifier*): *a conscript army.* ◆ *vb* (kən'skrɪpt). **2** (*tr*) to enrol (youths, civilians, etc.) for compulsory military service. [C15: from L *conscrīptus,* p.p. of *conscrībere* to enrol, from *scrībere* to write]

conscription (kən'skrɪpʃən) *n* compulsory military service.

consecrate ('kɒnsɪˌkreɪt) *vb* **consecrates, consecrating, consecrated.** (*tr*) **1** to make or declare sacred or holy. **2** to dedicate (one's life, time, etc.) to a specific purpose. **3** *Christianity.* to sanctify (bread and wine) for the Eucharist to be received as the body and blood of Christ. **4** to cause to be respected or revered: *time has consecrated this custom.* [C15: from L *consecrāre,* from *com-* (intensive) + *sacrāre* to devote, from *sacer* sacred]
▸ˌ**conse'cration** *n* ▸'**conseˌcrator** *n* ▸'**conseˌcratory** *adj*

Consecration (ˌkɒnsɪ'kreɪʃən) *n RC Church.* the part of the Mass after the sermon during which the bread and wine are believed to change into the Body and Blood of Christ.

consecutive (kən'sɛkjʊtɪv) *adj* **1** (of a narrative, account, etc.) fol-

THESAURUS

union **2** = **association**, affiliation, affinity, bond, commerce, communication, correlation, correspondence, intercourse, interrelation, liaison, link, marriage, nexus, relation, relationship, relevance, tie-in **5** = **context**, frame of reference, reference **6** = **contact**, acquaintance, ally, associate, friend, sponsor **7** = **relative**, kin, kindred, kinsman, kith, relation

connivance *n* **1, 2** = **collusion**, abetment, abetting, complicity, conspiring, tacit consent

connive *vb* **1** = **conspire**, cabal, collude, cook up (*inf.*), intrigue, plot, scheme **2 connive at** = **turn a blind eye to**, abet, aid, be an accessory to, be a party to, be in collusion with, blink at, disregard, lend oneself to, let pass, look the other way, overlook, pass by, shut one's eyes to, wink at

connoisseur *n* = **expert**, aficionado, appreciator, arbiter, authority, buff (*inf.*), cognoscente, devotee, judge, maven (*US*), savant, specialist, whiz (*inf.*)

connotation *n* **1** = **implication**, association, colouring, nuance, significance, suggestion, undertone

connote *vb* **1** = **imply**, betoken, hint at, indicate, intimate, involve, signify, suggest

connubial *adj Formal* = **marital**, conjugal, married, matrimonial, nuptial, wedded

conquer *vb* **1, 2** = **defeat**, beat, bring to their knees, checkmate, clobber (*sl.*), crush, discomfit, get the better of, humble, lick (*inf.*), make mincemeat of (*inf.*), master, overcome, overpower, overthrow, prevail, put in their place, quell, rout, stuff (*sl.*), subdue, subjugate, succeed, surmount, triumph, undo, vanquish **3** = **seize**, acquire, annex, obtain, occupy, overrun, win
Antonyms *vb* ≠ **defeat:** be defeated, capitulate, give in, give up, lose, quit, submit, surrender, throw in the towel, yield

conqueror *n* **1** = **winner**, champion, conquistador, defeater, hero, lord, master, subjugator, vanquisher, victor

conquest *n* **1** = **defeat**, acquisition, annexation, appropriation, coup, discomfiture, invasion, mastery, occupation, overthrow, pasting (*sl.*), rout, subjection, subjugation, takeover, triumph, vanquishment, victory **2, 3** = **catch**, acquisition, adherent, admirer, fan, feather in one's cap, follower, prize, supporter, worshipper

conscience *n* **1** = **principles**, moral sense, scruples, sense of right and wrong, still small voice **4 in all conscience** = **in fairness**, assuredly, certainly, fairly, honestly, in truth, rightly, truly

conscience-stricken *adj* = **guilty**, ashamed, compunctious, contrite, disturbed, penitent, remorseful, repentant, sorry, troubled

conscientious *adj* **1** = **thorough**, careful, diligent, exact, faithful, having one's nose to the grindstone, meticulous, painstaking, particular, punctilious **2** = **honourable**, high-minded, high-principled, honest, incorruptible, just, moral, responsible, scrupulous, straightforward, strict, upright
Antonyms *adj* ≠ **thorough:** careless, irresponsible, negligent, remiss, slack, thoughtless, unconscientious, unreliable, untrustworthy ≠ **honourable:** unprincipled, unscrupulous

conscious *adj* **1** = **aware**, alert, alive to, awake, clued-up (*inf.*), cognizant, percipient, responsive, sensible, sentient, wise to (*sl.*) **4** = **deliberate**, calculated, intentional, knowing, premeditated, rational, reasoning, reflective, responsible, self-conscious, studied, wilful
Antonyms *adj* ≠ **aware:** ignorant, insensible, oblivious, unaware, unconscious ≠ **deliberate:** accidental, uncalculated, unintended, unintentional, unplanned, unpremeditated, unwitting

consciousness *n* **1** = **awareness**, apprehension, knowledge, realization, recognition, sensibility

consecrate *vb* **1, 2** = **sanctify**, dedicate, devote, exalt, hallow, ordain, set apart, venerate

consecutive *adj* **1-3** = **successive**, chronological, following, in sequence, in turn, run-

lowing chronological sequence. **2** following one another without interruption; successive. **3** characterized by logical sequence. **4** *Grammar.* expressing consequence or result: *consecutive clauses.* **5** *Music.* another word for **parallel** (sense 3). [C17: from F *consécutif,* from L *consecūtus,* from *consequī* to pursue]
▸**con'secutively** *adv* ▸**con'secutiveness** *n*

consensual (kən'sɛnsjʊəl) *adj* **1** *Law.* (of a contract, etc.) existing by consent. **2** (of reflex actions of the body) responding to stimulation of another part.
▸**con'sensually** *adv*

consensus (kən'sɛnsəs) *n* general or widespread agreement (esp. in **consensus of opinion**). [C19: from L, from *consentīre;* see CONSENT]

> **USAGE NOTE** Since *consensus* refers to a collective opinion, the words *of opinion* in the phrase *consensus of opinion* are redundant and should therefore be avoided.

consent (kən'sɛnt) *vb* **1** to give assent or permission; agree. ◆ *n* **2** acquiescence to or acceptance of something done or planned by another. **3** harmony in opinion; agreement (esp. in **with one consent**). [C13: from OF *consentir,* from L *consentīre* to agree, from *sentīre* to feel]
▸**con'senting** *adj*

consequence ('kɒnsɪkwəns) *n* **1** a result or effect. **2** an unpleasant result (esp. in **take the consequences**). **3** an inference reached by reasoning; conclusion. **4** significance or importance: *it's of no consequence; a man of consequence.* **5 in consequence.** as a result.

consequent ('kɒnsɪkwənt) *adj* **1** following as an effect. **2** following as a logical conclusion. **3** (of a river) flowing in the direction of the original slope of the land. ◆ *n* **4** something that follows something else, esp. as a result. **5** *Logic.* the resultant clause in a conditional sentence. [C15: from L *consequēns* following closely, from *consequī* to pursue]

> **USAGE NOTE** See at **consequential.**

consequential (ˌkɒnsɪ'kwɛnʃəl) *adj* **1** important or significant. **2** self-important. **3** following as a consequence, esp. indirectly: *consequential loss.*
▸ˌ**conseˌquenti'ality** *n* ▸ˌ**conse'quentially** *adv*

> **USAGE NOTE** Although both *consequential* and *consequent* can refer to something which happens as the result of something else, *consequent* is more common in this sense in modern English: *the new measures were put into effect, and the consequent protest led to the dismissal of those responsible.*

consequently ('kɒnsɪkwəntlɪ) *adv, sentence connector.* as a result or effect; therefore; hence.

conservancy (kən'sɜːvənsɪ) *n, pl* **conservancies. 1** (in Britain) a court or commission with jurisdiction over a river, port, area of countryside, etc. **2** another word for **conservation** (sense 2).

conservation (ˌkɒnsə'veɪʃən) *n* **1** the act of conserving or keeping from change, loss, injury, etc. **2a** protection, preservation, and careful management of natural resources. **2b** (*as modifier*): *a conservation area.* **3** *Physics, etc.* the preservation of a specified aspect or value of a system, as in **conservation of charge, conservation of momentum, conservation of parity.**
▸ˌ**conser'vational** *adj* ▸ˌ**conser'vationist** *n*

conservation of energy *n* the principle that the total energy of any isolated system is constant and independent of any changes occurring within the system.

conservation of mass *n* the principle that the total mass of any isolated system is constant and is independent of any chemical and physical changes taking place within the system.

conservatism (kən'sɜːvəˌtɪzəm) *n* **1** opposition to change and innovation. **2** a political philosophy advocating the preservation of the best of the established order in society.

conservative (kən'sɜːvətɪv) *adj* **1** favouring the preservation of established customs, values, etc., and opposing innovation. **2** of conservatism. **3** moderate or cautious: *a conservative estimate.* **4** conventional in style: *a conservative suit.* **5** *Med.* (of treatment) designed to alleviate symptoms. Cf. **radical** (sense 4). ◆ *n* **6** a person who is reluctant to change or consider new ideas; conformist. **7** a supporter of conservatism.
▸**con'servatively** *adv* ▸**con'servativeness** *n*

Conservative (kən'sɜːvətɪv) ◆ *adj* **1** (in Britain and elsewhere) of, supporting, or relating to a Conservative Party. **2** (in Canada) of, supporting, or relating to the Progressive Conservative Party. **3** of, relating to, or characterizing Conservative Judaism. ◆ *n* **4** a supporter or member of a Conservative Party, or, (in Canada) of the Progressive Conservative Party.

Conservative Judaism *n* a movement rejecting extreme change and advocating moderate relaxations of traditional Jewish law.

Conservative Party *n* **1** (in Britain) the major right-wing party, which developed from the Tories in the 1830s. It encourages property owning and free enterprise. **2** (in Canada) short for Progressive Conservative Party. **3** (in other countries) any of various political parties generally opposing change.

conservatoire (kən'sɜːvəˌtwɑː) *n* an institution or school for instruction in music. Also called: **conservatory.** [C18: from F: CONSERVATORY]

conservator ('kɒnsəˌveɪtə, kən'sɜːvə-) *n* a custodian, guardian, or protector.

conservatorium (kənˌsɜːvə'tɔːrɪəm) *n Austral.* the usual term for **conservatoire.**

conservatory (kən'sɜːvətrɪ) *n, pl* **conservatories. 1** a greenhouse, esp. one attached to a house. **2** another word for **conservatoire.**

conserve *vb* (kən'sɜːv), **conserves, conserving, conserved.** (*tr*) **1** to keep or protect from harm, decay, loss, etc. **2** to preserve (a foodstuff, esp. fruit) with sugar. ◆ *n* ('kɒnsɜːv, kən'sɜːv). **3** a preparation similar to jam but usually containing whole pieces of fruit. [(vb) C14: from L *conservāre* to keep safe, from *servāre* to save; (n) C14: from Med. L *conserva,* from L *conservāre*]

consider (kən'sɪdə) *vb* (*mainly tr*) **1** (*also intr*) to think carefully about (a problem, decision, etc.). **2** (*may take a clause as object*) to judge; deem: *I consider him a fool.* **3** to have regard for: *consider your mother's feelings.* **4** to look at: *he considered her face.* **5** (*may take a clause as object*) to bear in mind: *when buying a car consider this make.* **6** to describe or discuss. [C14: from L *consīderāre* to inspect closely]

considerable (kən'sɪdərəbᵊl) *adj* **1** large enough to reckon with: *a considerable quantity.* **2** a lot of; much: *he had considerable courage.* **3** worthy of respect: *a considerable man in the scientific world.*
▸**con'siderably** *adv*

considerate (kən'sɪdərɪt) *adj* **1** thoughtful towards other people; kind. **2** *Rare.* carefully thought out; considered.
▸**con'siderately** *adv*

consideration (kənˌsɪdə'reɪʃən) *n* **1** deliberation; contemplation. **2 take into consideration.** to bear in mind; consider. **3 under consideration.** being currently discussed. **4** a fact to be taken into account when making a judgment or decision. **5** thoughtfulness for other people; kindness. **6** payment for a service. **7** thought resulting from delibera-

THESAURUS

ning, sequential, seriatim, succeeding, uninterrupted

consensus *n* = **agreement**, assent, common consent, concord, concurrence, general agreement, harmony, unanimity, unity

consent *vb* **1** = **agree**, accede, acquiesce, allow, approve, assent, comply, concede, concur, permit, play ball (*inf.*), yield ◆ *n* **2** = **agreement**, acquiescence, approval, assent, compliance, concession, concurrence, go-ahead (*inf.*), green light, O.K. *or* okay (*inf.*), permission, sanction
Antonyms *vb* ≠ **agree:** decline, demur, disagree, disapprove, dissent, refuse, resist ◆ *n* ≠ **agreement:** disagreement, disapproval, dissent, refusal, unwillingness

consequence *n* **1** = **result**, effect, end, end result, event, issue, outcome, repercussion, sequel, upshot **4** = **importance**, account, concern, distinction, eminence, import, interest, moment, note, portent, rank, significance, standing, status, value, weight **5 in consequence** = **as a result**, because, following

consequent *adj* **1, 2** = **following**, ensuing, resultant, resulting, sequential, subsequent, successive

consequential *adj* **1** = **important**, eventful, far-reaching, grave, momentous, serious, significant, weighty **2** = **arrogant**, bumptious, conceited, inflated, pompous, pretentious, self-important, supercilious, vainglorious **3** = **resultant**, consequent, indirect

consequently *adv* = **as a result**, accordingly, ergo, hence, necessarily, subsequently, therefore, thus

conservation *n* **1** = **protection**, custody, economy, guardianship, husbandry, maintenance, preservation, safeguarding, safekeeping, saving, upkeep

conservative *adj* **1, 3** = **traditional**, cautious, conventional, die-hard, guarded, hidebound, middle-of-the-road, moderate, quiet, reactionary, sober ◆ *n* **6** = **traditionalist**, die-hard, middle-of-the-roader, moderate, reactionary, stick-in-the-mud (*inf.*)
Antonyms *adj* ≠ **traditional:** imaginative, innovative, liberal, progressive, radical ◆ *n* ≠ **traditionalist:** changer, innovator, progressive, radical

Conservative *adj* **1** = **Tory**, right-wing ◆ *n* **4** = **Tory**, right-winger

conservatory *n* **1** = **greenhouse**, glasshouse, hothouse

consider *vb* **1** = **think about**, chew over, cogitate, consult, contemplate, deliberate, discuss, examine, eye up, meditate, mull over, muse, ponder, reflect, revolve, ruminate, study, turn over in one's mind, weigh, work over **2** = **think**, believe, deem, hold to be, judge, rate, regard as **5** = **bear in mind**, care for, keep in view, make allowance for, reckon with, regard, remember, respect, take into account

considerable *adj* **1, 2** = **large**, abundant, ample, appreciable, comfortable, goodly, great, lavish, marked, much, noticeable, plentiful, reasonable, sizable *or* sizeable, substantial, tidy, tolerable **3** = **important**, distinguished, influential, notable, noteworthy, renowned, significant, venerable
Antonyms *adj* ≠ **large:** insignificant, insubstantial, meagre, paltry, small ≠ **important:** insignificant, ordinary, unimportant, unremarkable

considerably *adv* **1, 2** = **greatly**, appreciably, markedly, noticeably, remarkably, seriously (*inf.*), significantly, substantially, very much

considerate *adj* **1** = **thoughtful**, attentive, charitable, circumspect, concerned, discreet, forbearing, kind, kindly, mindful, obliging, patient, tactful, unselfish
Antonyms *adj* heedless, inconsiderate, selfish, thoughtless

consideration *n* **1** = **thought**, analysis, atten-

tion; opinion. **8** *Law.* the promise, object, etc., given by one party to persuade another to enter into a contract. **9** esteem. **10 in consideration of. 10a** because of. **10b** in return for.

considered (kən'sɪdəd) *adj* **1** presented or thought out with care: *a considered opinion.* **2** (*qualified by a preceding adverb*) esteemed: *highly considered.*

considering ➊ (kən'sɪdərɪŋ) *prep* **1** in view of. ◆ *adv* **2** *Inf.* all in all; taking into account the circumstances: *it's not bad considering.* ◆ *conj* **3** (*subordinating*) in view of the fact that.

consign ➊ (kən'saɪn) *vb* (*mainly tr*) **1** to give into the care or charge of; entrust. **2** to commit irrevocably: *he consigned the papers to the flames.* **3** to commit: *to consign someone to jail.* **4** to address or deliver (goods): *it was consigned to his London address.* [C15: from OF *consigner,* from L *consignāre* to put one's seal to, sign, from *signum* mark]
▸**con'signable** *adj* ▸**,consign'ee** *n* ▸**con'signor** *or* **con'signer** *n*

consignment ➊ (kən'saɪnmənt) *n* **1** the act of consigning; commitment. **2** a shipment of goods consigned. **3 on consignment.** for payment by the consignee after sale.

consist ➊ (kən'sɪst) *vb* (*intr*) **1** (foll. by *of* or *in*) to be composed (of). **2** (foll. by *in* or *of*) to have its existence (in): *his religion consists only in going to church.* **3** to be consistent; accord. [C16: from L *consistere* to stand firm, from *sistere* to stand]

consistency ➊ (kən'sɪstənsɪ) *or* **consistence** *n, pl* **consistencies** *or* **consistences. 1** agreement or accordance. **2** degree of viscosity or firmness. **3** the state or quality of holding or sticking together and retaining shape. **4** conformity with previous attitudes, behaviour, practice, etc.

consistent ➊ (kən'sɪstənt) *adj* **1** (usually foll. by *with*) showing consistency or harmony. **2** steady; even: *consistent growth.* **3** *Logic.* (of a logical system) constituted so that the propositions deduced from different axioms of the system do not contradict each other.
▸**con'sistently** *adv*

consistory (kən'sɪstərɪ) *n, pl* **consistories. 1** *Church of England.* the court of a diocese (other than Canterbury) administering ecclesiastical law. **2** *RC Church.* an assembly of the cardinals and the pope. **3** (in certain Reformed Churches) the governing body of a local congregation. **4** *Arch.* a council. [C14: from OF, from Med. L *consistōrium* ecclesiastical tribunal, ult. from L *consistere* to stand still]
▸**consistorial** (ˌkɒnsɪ'stɔːrɪəl) *adj*

consolation ➊ (ˌkɒnsə'leɪʃən) *n* **1** the act of consoling or state of being consoled. **2** a person or thing that is a comfort in a time of grief, disappointment, etc.
▸**consolatory** (kən'sɒlətərɪ) *adj*

consolation prize *n* a prize given to console a loser of a game.

console[1] ➊ (kən'səʊl) *vb* **consoles, consoling, consoled.** to serve as a comfort to (someone) in disappointment, sadness, etc. [C17: from L *consōlārī,* from *sōlārī* to comfort]
▸**con'solable** *adj* ▸**con'soler** *n* ▸**con'solingly** *adv*

console[2] ('kɒnsəʊl) *n* **1** an ornamental bracket used to support a wall fixture, etc. **2** the part of an organ comprising the manuals, pedals, stops, etc. **3** a unit on which the controls of an electronic system are mounted. **4** a cabinet for a television, etc., designed to stand on the floor. **5** See **console table.** [C18: from F, from OF *consolateur* one that provides support; see CONSOLE[1]]

console table *n* a table with one or more curved legs of bracket-like construction, designed to stand against a wall.

consolidate ➊ (kən'sɒlɪˌdeɪt) *vb* **consolidates, consolidating, consolidated. 1** to form or cause to form into a whole. **2** to make or become stronger or more stable. **3** *Mil.* to strengthen one's control over (a situation, area, etc.). [C16: from L *consolidāre* to make firm, from *solidus* strong]
▸**con,soli'dation** *n* ▸**con'soli,dator** *n*

consolidated fund *n Brit.* a fund maintained from tax revenue to meet standing charges, esp. national debt interest.

consols ('kɒnsɒlz, kən'sɒlz) *pl n* irredeemable British government securities carrying annual interest. [short for *consolidated stock*]

consommé (kən'sɒmeɪ) *n* a clear soup made from meat stock. [C19: from F, from *consommer* to use up]

consonance ('kɒnsənəns) *n* **1** agreement, harmony, or accord. **2** *Prosody.* similarity between consonants, but not between vowels, as between the *s* and *t* sounds in *sweet silent thought.* **3** *Music.* a combination of notes which can sound together without harshness.

consonant ('kɒnsənənt) *n* **1** a speech sound or letter of the alphabet other than a vowel. ◆ *adj* **2** (*postpositive;* foll. by *with* or *to*) consistent; in agreement. **3** harmonious. **4** *Music.* characterized by the presence of a consonance. [C14: from L *consonāns,* from *consonāre* to sound at the same time, from *sonāre* to sound]
▸**'consonantly** *adv*

consonantal (ˌkɒnsə'næntᵊl) *adj* relating to, functioning as, or characterized by consonants.

consort ➊ *vb* (kən'sɔːt). (*intr*) **1** (usually foll. by *with*) to keep company (with undesirable people); associate. **2** to harmonize. ◆ *n* ('kɒnsɔːt). **3** (esp. formerly) a small group of instruments, either of the same type (**a whole consort**) or of different types (**a broken consort**). **4** the husband or wife of a reigning monarch. **5** a husband or wife. **6** a ship that escorts another. [C15: from OF, from L *consors* partner, from *sors* lot, portion]

consortium (kən'sɔːtɪəm) *n, pl* **consortia** (-tɪə). **1** an association of financiers, companies, etc., esp. for a particular purpose. **2** *Law.* the right of husband or wife to the company and affection of the other. [C19: from L: partnership; see CONSORT]

conspectus (kən'spɛktəs) *n* **1** an overall view; survey. **2** a summary; résumé. [C19: from L: a viewing, from *conspicere,* from *specere* to look]

conspicuous ➊ (kən'spɪkjʊəs) *adj* **1** clearly visible. **2** attracting attention because of a striking feature: *conspicuous stupidity.* [C16: from L *conspicuus,* from *conspicere* to perceive; see CONSPECTUS]
▸**con'spicuously** *adv* ▸**con'spicuousness** *n*

conspiracy ➊ (kən'spɪrəsɪ) *n, pl* **conspiracies. 1** a secret plan to carry out an illegal or harmful act, esp. with political motivation; plot. **2** the act of making such plans in secret.
▸**con'spirator** *n* ▸**con,spira'torial** *adj*

conspiracy theory *n* the belief that the government or a covert organization is responsible for an unusual or unexplained event.

conspire ➊ (kən'spaɪə) *vb* **conspires, conspiring, conspired.** (when *intr,* sometimes foll. by *against*) **1** to plan (a crime) together in secret. **2** (*intr*) to act together as if by design: *the elements conspired to spoil our picnic.* [C14: from OF, from L *conspīrāre* to plot together, lit.: to breathe together, from *spīrāre* to breathe]

con spirito (kɒn 'spɪrɪtəʊ) *adj, adv Music.* (to be performed) in a spirited or lively manner. [It.: with spirit]

constable ('kʌnstəbᵊl, 'kɒn-) *n* **1** (in Britain, Australia, New Zealand, Canada, etc.) a police officer of the lowest rank. **2** any of various officers of the peace, esp. one who arrests offenders, serves writs, etc. **3** the keeper of a royal castle. **4** (in medieval Europe) the chief military officer and functionary of a royal household. **5** an officer of a hundred in medieval England. [C13: from OF, from LL *comes stabulī* officer in charge of the stable]
▸**'constable,ship** *n*

THESAURUS

tion, cogitation, contemplation, deliberation, discussion, examination, perusal, reflection, regard, review, scrutiny, study **2 take into consideration = bear in mind**, make allowance for, take into account, weigh **4 = factor**, concern, issue, point **5 = thoughtfulness**, concern, considerateness, friendliness, kindliness, kindness, respect, solicitude, tact **6 = payment**, fee, perquisite, recompense, remuneration, reward, tip

considering *prep* **1 = taking into account**, in the light of, in view of ◆ *adv* **2** *Informal* **= all things considered**, all in all

consign *vb* **1 = hand over**, commend to, commit, deposit with, entrust, relegate **4 = deliver**, convey, ship (*cargo*), transfer, transmit

consignment *n* **1 = handing over**, assignment, committal, entrusting, relegation **2 = shipment**, batch, delivery, goods

consist *vb* **1** *foll. by* **of** *or* **in = be made up of**, amount to, be composed of, comprise, contain, embody, include, incorporate, involve **2** *foll. by* *in or* **of = lie in**, be expressed by, be found *or* contained in, inhere in, reside in

consistency *n* **1 = agreement**, accordance, coherence, compatibility, congruity, correspondence, harmony **2 = texture**, compactness, density, firmness, thickness, viscosity **4 = constancy**, evenness, regularity, steadfastness, steadiness, uniformity

consistent *adj* **1 = agreeing**, accordant, all of a piece, coherent, compatible, congruous, consonant, harmonious, logical **2 = unchanging**, constant, dependable, persistent, regular, steady, true to type, undeviating
Antonyms *adj* ≠ **agreeing:** contradictory, contrary, discordant, incompatible, incongruous, inconsistent, inharmonious ≠ **unchanging:** changing, deviating, erratic, inconsistent, irregular

consolation *n* **1 = comfort**, alleviation, assuagement, cheer, ease, easement, encouragement, help, relief, solace, succour, support

console[1] *vb* **= comfort**, assuage, calm, cheer, encourage, express sympathy for, relieve, solace, soothe
Antonyms *vb* aggravate (*inf.*), agitate, annoy, discomfort, distress, hassle (*inf.*), hurt, sadden, torment, trouble, upset

consolidate *vb* **1 = combine**, amalgamate, cement, compact, condense, conjoin, federate, fuse, harden, join, solidify, thicken, unite **2 = strengthen**, fortify, reinforce, secure, stabilize

consolidation *n* **1 = combination**, alliance, amalgamation, association, compression, condensation, federation, fusion **2 = strengthening**, fortification, reinforcement

consort *vb* **1 = associate**, fraternize, go around with, hang about, around *or* out with, hang with (*inf., chiefly US*), keep company, mingle, mix **2 = agree**, accord, be consistent, correspond, harmonize, square, tally ◆ *n* **5 = spouse**, companion, husband, partner, significant other (*US inf.*), wife

conspicuous *adj* **1 = obvious**, apparent, blatant, clear, discernible, easily seen, evident, manifest, noticeable, patent, perceptible, salient, visible **2 = noteworthy**, celebrated, distinguished, eminent, famous, illustrious, notable, outstanding, prominent, remarkable, salient, signal, striking
Antonyms *adj* ≠ **obvious:** concealed, hidden, imperceptible, inconspicuous, indiscernible, invisible, obscure, unnoticeable ≠ **noteworthy:** humble, inconspicuous, insignificant, ordinary, unacclaimed, undistinguished, unmemorable, unnotable

conspiracy *n* **1, 2 = plot**, cabal, collusion, confederacy, frame-up (*sl.*), intrigue, league, machination, scheme, treason

conspirator *n* **1 = plotter**, cabalist, conspirer, intriguer, schemer, traitor

conspire *vb* **1 = plot**, cabal, confederate, contrive, devise, hatch treason, intrigue, machinate, manoeuvre, plan, scheme **2 = work together**, combine, concur, conduce, contribute, cooperate, tend

constabulary (kənˈstæbjʊlərɪ) *Chiefly Brit.* ◆ *n, pl* **constabularies. 1** the police force of a town or district. ◆ *adj* **2** of or relating to constables.

constant Ⓣ (ˈkɒnstənt) *adj* **1** unchanging. **2** incessant: *constant interruptions.* **3** resolute; loyal. ◆ *n* **4** something that is unchanging. **5** a specific quantity that is invariable: *the velocity of light is a constant.* **6a** *Maths.* a symbol representing an unspecified number that remains invariable throughout a particular series of operations. **6b** *Physics.* a quantity or property that is considered invariable throughout a particular series of experiments. [C14: from OF, from L *constāns,* from *constāre* to be steadfast, from *stāre* to stand]
▸ˈ**constancy** *n* ▸ˈ**constantly** *adv*

constellate (ˈkɒnstɪˌleɪt) *vb* **constellates, constellating, constellated.** to form into clusters in or as if in constellations.

constellation (ˌkɒnstɪˈleɪʃən) *n* **1** any of the 88 groups of stars as seen from the earth, many of which were named by the ancient Greeks after animals, objects, or mythological persons. **2** a gathering of brilliant people or things. **3** *Psychoanalysis.* a group of ideas felt to be related. [C14: from LL *constellātiō,* from L *com-* together + *stella* star]
▸**constellatory** (kənˈstɛlətərɪ) *adj*

consternate (ˈkɒnstəˌneɪt) *vb* **consternates, consternating, consternated.** (*tr; usually passive*) to fill with anxiety, dismay, dread, or confusion. [C17: from L *consternāre,* from *sternere* to lay low]

consternation Ⓣ (ˌkɒnstəˈneɪʃən) *n* a feeling of anxiety, dismay, dread, or confusion.

constipate (ˈkɒnstɪˌpeɪt) *vb* **constipates, constipating, constipated.** (*tr*) to cause constipation in. [C16: from L *constīpāre* to press closely together]
▸ˈ**constiˌpated** *adj*

constipation (ˌkɒnstɪˈpeɪʃən) *n* infrequent or difficult evacuation of the bowels.

constituency (kənˈstɪtjʊənsɪ) *n, pl* **constituencies. 1** the whole body of voters who elect one representative to a legislature or all the residents represented by one deputy. **2** a district that sends one representative to a legislature.

constituent Ⓣ (kənˈstɪtjʊənt) *adj* (*prenominal*) **1** forming part of a whole; component. **2** having the power to frame a constitution or to constitute a government: *constituent assembly.* ◆ *n* **3** a component part; ingredient. **4** a resident of a constituency, esp. one entitled to vote. **5** *Chiefly law.* a person who appoints another to act for him. [C17: from L *constituēns,* from *constituere* to establish, CONSTITUTE]
▸**conˈstituently** *adv*

constitute Ⓣ (ˈkɒnstɪˌtjuːt) *vb* **constitutes, constituting, constituted.** (*tr*) **1** to form; compose: *the people who constitute a jury.* **2** to appoint to an office: *a legally constituted officer.* **3** to set up (an institution) formally; found. **4** *Law.* to give legal form to (a court, assembly, etc.). [C15: from L *constituere,* from *com-* (intensive) + *statuere* to place]
▸ˈ**constiˌtutor** *n*

constitution Ⓣ (ˌkɒnstɪˈtjuːʃən) *n* **1** the act of constituting or state of being constituted. **2** physical make-up; structure. **3** the fundamental principles on which a state is governed, esp. when considered as embodying the rights of the subjects. **4** (*often cap.*) (in certain countries, esp. the US and Australia) a statute embodying such principles. **5** a person's state of health. **6** a person's temperament.

constitutional Ⓣ (ˌkɒnstɪˈtjuːʃənᵊl) *adj* **1** of a constitution. **2** authorized by or subject to a constitution: *constitutional monarchy.* **3** inherent in the nature of a person or thing: *a constitutional weakness.* **4** beneficial to one's physical wellbeing. ◆ *n* **5** a regular walk taken for the benefit of one's health.
▸ˌ**constiˌtutionˈality** *n* ▸ˌ**constiˈtutionally** *adv*

constitutionalism (ˌkɒnstɪˈtjuːʃənəˌlɪzəm) *n* **1** the principles or system of government in accord with a constitution. **2** adherence to or advocacy of such a system.
▸ˌ**constiˈtutionalist** *n*

constitutive (ˈkɒnstɪˌtjuːtɪv) *adj* **1** having power to enact or establish. **2** another word for **constituent** (sense 1).
▸ˈ**constiˌtutively** *adv*

constrain Ⓣ (kənˈstreɪn) *vb* (*tr*) **1** to compel, esp. by circumstances, etc. **2** to restrain as by force. [C14: from OF, from L *constringere* to bind together]
▸**conˈstrainer** *n*

constrained Ⓣ (kənˈstreɪnd) *adj* embarrassed, unnatural, or forced: *a constrained smile.*

constraint Ⓣ (kənˈstreɪnt) *n* **1** compulsion or restraint. **2** repression of natural feelings. **3** a forced unnatural manner. **4** something that serves to constrain; restrictive condition.

constrict Ⓣ (kənˈstrɪkt) *vb* (*tr*) **1** to make smaller or narrower, esp. by contracting at one place. **2** to hold in or inhibit; limit. [C18: from L *constrictus,* from *constringere* to tie up together]

constriction Ⓣ (kənˈstrɪkʃən) *n* **1** a feeling of tightness in some part of the body, such as the chest. **2** the act of constricting or condition of being constricted. **3** something that is constricted.
▸**conˈstrictive** *adj*

constrictor (kənˈstrɪktə) *n* **1** any of various nonvenomous snakes, such as the boas, that coil around and squeeze their prey to kill it. **2** any muscle that constricts; sphincter.

construct Ⓣ *vb* (kənˈstrʌkt). (*tr*) **1** to put together substances or parts systematically; build; assemble. **2** to frame mentally (an argument, sentence, etc.). **3** *Geom.* to draw (a line, angle, or figure) so that certain requirements are satisfied. ◆ *n* (ˈkɒnstrʌkt). **4** something formulated or built systematically. **5** a complex idea resulting from a synthesis of simpler ideas. [C17: from L *constructus,* from *construere* to build, from *struere* to arrange, erect]
▸**conˈstructor** *or* **conˈstructer** *n*

construction Ⓣ (kənˈstrʌkʃən) *n* **1** the act of constructing or manner in which a thing is constructed. **2** a structure. **3a** the business or work of building dwellings, offices, etc. **3b** (*as modifier*): *a construction site.* **4** an interpretation: *they put a sympathetic construction on her behaviour.* **5** *Grammar.* a group of words that make up one of the constituents into which a sentence may be analysed; a phrase or clause. **6** an abstract work of art in three dimensions.
▸**conˈstructional** *adj* ▸**conˈstructionally** *adv*

constructive Ⓣ (kənˈstrʌktɪv) *adj* **1** serving to improve; positive: *constructive criticism.* **2** *Law.* deduced by inference; not expressed. **3** another word for **structural.**
▸**conˈstructively** *adv*

constructivism (kənˈstrʌktɪˌvɪzəm) *n* a movement in abstract art evolved after World War I, which explored the use of movement and machine-age materials in sculpture.
▸**conˈstructivist** *adj, n*

construe Ⓣ (kənˈstruː) *vb* **construes, construing, construed.** (*mainly tr*) **1** to interpret the meaning of (something): *you can construe that in different ways.* **2** (*may take a clause as object*) to infer; deduce. **3** to analyse the grammatical structure of; parse (esp. a Latin or Greek text as a prelimi-

THESAURUS

constancy *n* **2 = steadiness**, firmness, fixedness, permanence, perseverance, regularity, stability, steadfastness, tenacity, uniformity **3 = faithfulness**, devotion, fidelity

constant *adj* **1 = unchanging**, continual, even, firm, fixed, habitual, immovable, immutable, invariable, permanent, perpetual, regular, stable, steadfast, steady, unalterable, unbroken, uniform, unvarying **2 = continuous**, ceaseless, continual, endless, eternal, everlasting, incessant, interminable, never-ending, nonstop, perpetual, persistent, relentless, sustained, uninterrupted, unrelenting, unremitting **3 = faithful**, attached, dependable, devoted, loyal, stalwart, staunch, tried-and-true, true, trustworthy, trusty, unfailing
Antonyms *adj* ≠ **unchanging:** changeable, changing, deviating, uneven, unstable, variable ≠ **continuous:** erratic, inconstant, intermittent, irregular, occasional, random, unsustained ≠ **faithful:** disloyal, fickle, irresolute, undependable

constantly *adv* **2 = continuously**, all the time, always, aye (*Scot.*), continually, endlessly, everlastingly, incessantly, interminably, invariably, morning, noon and night, night and day, nonstop, perpetually, persistently, relentlessly
Antonyms *adv* (every) now and then, every so often, from time to time, intermittently, irregularly, now and again, occasionally, off and on, periodically, sometimes

consternation *n* **= dismay**, alarm, amazement, anxiety, awe, bewilderment, confusion, distress, dread, fear, fright, horror, panic, shock, terror, trepidation

constituent *adj* **1 = component**, basic, elemental, essential, integral ◆ *n* **3 = component**, element, essential, factor, ingredient, part, principle, unit **4 = voter**, elector

constitute *vb* **1 = make up**, compose, comprise, create, enact, establish, fix, form, found, make, set up **2 = set up**, appoint, authorize, commission, delegate, depute, empower, name, nominate, ordain

constitution *n* **1 = establishment**, composition, formation, organization **2 = structure**, composition, form, make-up, nature **5, 6 = health**, build, character, disposition, physique, temper, temperament

constitutional *adj* **2 = statutory**, chartered, vested **3 = inherent**, congenital, immanent, inborn, intrinsic, organic ◆ *n* **5 = walk**, airing, stroll, turn

constrain *vb* **1 = force**, bind, coerce, compel, drive, impel, necessitate, oblige, pressure, pressurize, urge **2 = restrict**, chain, check, confine, constrict, curb, hem in, rein, restrain, straiten

constrained *adj* **= forced**, embarrassed, guarded, inhibited, reserved, reticent, subdued, unnatural

constraint *n* **1 = restriction**, check, coercion, compulsion, curb, damper, deterrent, force, hindrance, limitation, necessity, pressure, rein, restraint **2 = repression**, bashfulness, diffidence, embarrassment, inhibition, reservation, restraint, timidity

constrict *vb* **1, 2 = squeeze**, choke, compress, contract, cramp, inhibit, limit, narrow, pinch, restrict, shrink, strangle, strangulate, tighten

constriction *n* **1, 2 = tightness**, blockage, compression, constraint, cramp, impediment, limitation, narrowing, pressure, reduction, restriction, squeezing, stenosis (*Pathology*), stricture

construct *vb* **1 = build**, assemble, compose, create, design, elevate, engineer, erect, establish, fabricate, fashion, form, formulate, found, frame, make, manufacture, organize, put together, put up, raise, set up, shape
Antonyms *vb* bulldoze, demolish, destroy, devastate, dismantle, flatten, knock down, level, pull down, raze, tear down

construction *n* **1 = building**, assembly, composition, creation, edifice, erection, fabrication, formation **2 = structure**, composition, fabric, figure, form, shape **4** *Formal* **= interpretation**, explanation, inference, reading, rendering, take (*inf., chiefly US*)

constructive *adj* **1 = helpful**, positive, practical, productive, useful, valuable
Antonyms *adj* destructive, futile, ineffective, limp-wristed, negative, unhelpful, unproductive, useless, vain, worthless

construe *vb* **1, 2 = interpret**, deduce, explain, expound, read, read between the lines, render,

nary to translation). **4** to combine words syntactically. **5** (*also intr*) *Old-fashioned.* to translate literally, esp. aloud. [C14: from L *construere;* see CONSTRUCT]
▸**con'struable** *adj*

consubstantial (ˌkɒnsəb'stænʃəl) *adj Christian theol.* (esp. of the three persons of the Trinity) regarded as identical in essence though different in aspect. [C15: from Church L, from L *com-* COM- + *substantia* SUBSTANCE]
▸ˌ**consubˌstanti'ality** *n*

consubstantiation (ˌkɒnsəbˌstænʃɪ'eɪʃən) *n Christian theol.* (in the Lutheran branch of Protestantism) the doctrine that after the consecration of the Eucharist the substance of the body and blood of Christ coexists within the substance of the consecrated bread and wine. Cf. **transubstantiation.**

consuetude ('kɒnswɪˌtjuːd) *n* an established custom or usage, esp. one having legal force. [C14: from L *consuētūdō,* from *consuēscere,* from CON- + *suēscere* to be wont]

consul ('kɒns^{ə}l) *n* **1** an official appointed by a sovereign state to protect its commercial interests and aid its citizens in a foreign city. **2** (in ancient Rome) either of two annually elected magistrates who jointly exercised the highest authority in the republic. **3** (in France from 1799 to 1804) any of the three chief magistrates of the First Republic. [C14: from L, from *consulere* to CONSULT]
▸**consular** ('kɒnsjʊlə) *adj* ▸'**consulˌship** *n*

consulate ('kɒnsjʊlɪt) *n* **1** the premises of a consul. **2** government by consuls. **3** the office or period of office of a consul. **4** (*often cap.*) **4a** the government of France by the three consuls from 1799 to 1804. **4b** this period. **5** (*often cap.*) the consular government of the Roman republic.

consul general *n, pl* **consuls general.** a consul of the highest grade, usually stationed in a city of considerable commercial importance.

consult ⓣ (kən'sʌlt) *vb* **1** (when *intr,* often foll. by *with*) to ask advice from (someone). **2** (*tr*) to refer to for information: *to consult a map.* **3** (*tr*) to have regard for (a person's feelings, interests, etc.); consider. [C17: from F, from L *consultāre,* from *consulere* to consult]

consultant ⓣ (kən'sʌlt^{ə}nt) *n* **1a** a specialist physician who is asked to confirm a diagnosis. **1b** a physician or surgeon holding the highest appointment in a particular branch of medicine or surgery in a hospital. **2** a specialist who gives expert advice or information. **3** a person who asks advice in a consultation.
▸**con'sultancy** *n*

consultation ⓣ (ˌkɒns^{ə}l'teɪʃən) *n* **1** the act of consulting. **2** a conference for discussion or the seeking of advice.
▸**consultative** (kən'sʌltətɪv) *adj*

consulting (kən'sʌltɪŋ) *adj* (*prenominal*) acting in an advisory capacity on professional matters: *a consulting engineer.*

consulting room *n* a room in which a doctor sees his patients.

consume ⓣ (kən'sjuːm) *vb* **consumes, consuming, consumed. 1** (*tr*) to eat or drink. **2** (*tr; often passive*) to obsess. **3** (*tr*) to use up; expend. **4** to destroy or be destroyed by: *fire consumed the forest.* **5** (*tr*) to waste. **6** (*passive*) to waste away. [C14: from L *consūmere,* from *com-* (intensive) + *sūmere* to take up]
▸**con'sumable** *adj* ▸**con'suming** *adj*

consumedly (kən'sjuːmɪdlɪ) *adv Old-fashioned.* (intensifier): *consumedly fascinating.*

consumer ⓣ (kən'sjuːmə) *n* **1** a person who purchases goods and services for his own personal needs. Cf. **producer** (sense 6). **2** a person or thing that consumes.

consumer durable *n* a manufactured product that has a relatively long useful life, such as a car or a television.

consumer goods *pl n* goods that satisfy personal needs rather than those required for the production of other goods or services.

consumerism (kən'sjuːməˌrɪzəm) *n* **1** protection of the interests of consumers. **2** advocacy of a high rate of consumption as a basis for a sound economy.
▸**con'sumerist** *n, adj*

consumer terrorism *n* the practice of introducing dangerous substances to foodstuffs or other consumer products, esp. to extort money from the manufacturers.

consummate ⓣ *vb* ('kɒnsəˌmeɪt), **consummates, consummating, consummated.** (*tr*) **1** to bring to completion; fulfil. **2** to complete (a marriage) legally by sexual intercourse. ◆ *adj* (kən'sʌmɪt, 'kɒnsəmɪt). **3** supremely skilled: *a consummate artist.* **4** (*prenominal*) (intensifier): *a consummate fool.* [C15: from L *consummāre* to complete, from *summus* utmost]
▸**con'summately** *adv* ▸ˌ**consum'mation** *n*

consumption ⓣ (kən'sʌmpʃən) *n* **1** the act of consuming or the state of being consumed, esp. by eating, burning, etc. **2** *Econ.* expenditure on goods and services for final personal use. **3** the quantity consumed. **4** a wasting away of the tissues of the body, esp. in tuberculosis of the lungs. [C14: from L *consumptiō,* from *consūmere* to CONSUME]

consumptive (kən'sʌmptɪv) *adj* **1** causing consumption; wasteful; destructive. **2** relating to or affected with tuberculosis of the lungs. ◆ *n* **3** *Pathol.* a person who suffers from consumption.
▸**con'sumptively** *adv* ▸**con'sumptiveness** *n*

cont. *abbrev. for:* **1** contents. **2** continued.

contact ⓣ *n* ('kɒntækt). **1** the act or state of touching. **2** the state or fact of communication (esp. in **in contact, make contact**). **3a** a junction of electrical conductors. **3b** the part of the conductors that makes the junction. **3c** the part of an electrical device to which such connections are made. **4** an acquaintance, esp. one who might be useful in business, etc. **5** any person who has been exposed to a contagious disease. **6** (*modifier*) caused by touching the causative agent: *contact dermatitis.* **7** (*modifier*) denoting a herbicide or insecticide that kills on contact. **8** (*modifier*) of or maintaining contact. **9** (*modifier*) requiring or involving (physical) contact: *a contact sport.* ◆ *vb* ('kɒntækt, kən'tækt). **10** (when *intr,* often foll. by *with*) to put, come, or be in association, touch, or communication. [C17: from L *contactus,* from *contingere* to touch on all sides, from *tangere* to touch]
▸**contactual** (kɒn'tæktjʊəl) *adj*

contact lens *n* a thin convex lens, usually of plastic, which floats on the layer of tears in front of the cornea to correct defects of vision.

contact print *n* a photographic print made by exposing the printing paper through a negative placed directly on to it.

contagion ⓣ (kən'teɪdʒən) *n* **1** the transmission of disease from one person to another by contact. **2** a contagious disease. **3** a corrupting influence that tends to spread. **4** the spreading of an emotional or mental state among a number of people: *the contagion of mirth.* [C14: from L *contāgiō* infection, from *contingere;* see CONTACT]

contagious ⓣ (kən'teɪdʒəs) *adj* **1** (of a disease) capable of being passed on by direct contact with a diseased individual or by handling his clothing, etc. **2** (of an organism) harbouring the causative agent of a transmissible disease. **3** causing or likely to cause the same reaction in several people: *her laughter was contagious.*

contain ⓣ (kən'teɪn) *vb* (*tr*) **1** to hold or be capable of holding: *this contains five pints.* **2** to restrain (feelings, behaviour, etc.). **3** to consist of: *the book contains three sections.* **4** *Mil.* to prevent (enemy forces) from operating beyond a certain area. **5** to be a multiple of, leaving no remainder: *6 contains 2 and 3.* [C13: from OF, from L *continēre,* from *com-* together + *tenēre* to hold]
▸**con'tainable** *adj*

container ⓣ (kən'teɪnə) *n* **1** an object used for or capable of holding, esp. for transport or storage. **2a** a large cargo-carrying standard-sized container that can be loaded from one mode of transport to another. **2b** (*as modifier*): *a container ship.*

containerize *or* **containerise** (kən'teɪnəˌraɪz) *vb* **containerizes, containerizing, containerized** *or* **containerises, containerising, containerised.**

THESAURUS

take **3** = **parse**, analyse **5** *Old-fashioned* = **translate**

consult *vb* **1, 2** = **ask**, ask advice of, commune, compare notes, confer, consider, debate, deliberate, interrogate, pick (someone's) brains, question, refer to, take counsel, turn to **3** = **consider**, have regard for, regard, respect, take account of, take into consideration

consultant *n* **2** = **specialist**, adviser, authority

consultation *n* **2** = **seminar**, appointment, conference, council, deliberation, dialogue, discussion, examination, hearing, interview, meeting, session

consume *vb* **1** = **eat**, devour, eat up, gobble (up), guzzle, polish off (*inf.*), put away, swallow **2** *often passive* = **obsess**, absorb, devour, dominate, eat up, engross, monopolize, preoccupy **3, 5** = **use up**, absorb, deplete, dissipate, drain, eat up, employ, exhaust, expend, finish up, fritter away, lavish, lessen, spend, squander, use, utilize, vanish, waste, wear out **4** = **destroy**, annihilate, decay, demolish, devastate, lay waste, ravage

consumer *n* **1** = **buyer**, customer, purchaser, shopper, user

consuming *adj* **2** = **overwhelming**, absorbing, compelling, devouring, engrossing, excruciating, gripping, immoderate, tormenting

consummate *vb* **1** = **complete**, accomplish, achieve, carry out, compass, conclude, crown, effectuate, end, finish, fulfil, perfect, perform, put the tin lid on ◆ *adj* **3** = **skilled**, accomplished, matchless, perfect, polished, practised, superb, supreme **4** = **complete**, absolute, conspicuous, deep-dyed (*usually derogatory*), extreme, supreme, total, transcendent, ultimate, unqualified, utter
Antonyms *vb* ≠ **complete:** begin, commence, conceive, get under way, inaugurate, initiate, originate, start

consummation *n* **1** = **completion**, achievement, culmination, end, fulfilment, perfection, realization

consumption *n* **1** = **using up**, consuming, decay, decrease, depletion, destruction, diminution, dissipation, drain, exhaustion, expenditure, loss, use, utilization, waste **4** *Old-fashioned* = **tuberculosis**, atrophy, emaciation, phthisis, T.B.

contact *n* **1** = **touch**, approximation, contiguity, junction, juxtaposition, union **2** = **communication**, association, connection **4** = **acquaintance**, connection ◆ *vb* **10** = **get** *or* **be in touch with**, approach, call, communicate with, get hold of, phone, reach, ring (up) (*inf., chiefly Brit.*), speak to, write to

contagion *n* **1, 4** = **spread**, communication, passage, transference, transmittal **2** = **contamination**, corruption, infection, pestilence, plague, pollution, taint

contagious *adj* **1** = **infectious**, catching, communicable, epidemic, epizootic (*Veterinary medicine*), pestiferous, pestilential, spreading, taking (*inf.*), transmissible

contain *vb* **1** = **hold**, accommodate, enclose, have capacity for, incorporate, seat **2** = **restrain**, control, curb, hold back, hold in, keep a tight rein on, repress, stifle **3** = **include**, comprehend, comprise, consist of, embody, embrace, involve

container *n* **1** = **holder**, receptacle, repository, vessel

(*tr*) **1** to convey (cargo) in standard-sized containers. **2** to adapt (a port or transportation system) to the use of standard-sized containers.
►**con,taineri'zation** *or* **con,taineri'sation** *n*

containment (kən'teɪnmənt) *n* the act of containing, esp. of restraining the power of a hostile country or the operations of a hostile military force.

contaminate ❶ (kən'tæmɪ,neɪt) *vb* **contaminates, contaminating, contaminated.** (*tr*) **1** to make impure; pollute. **2** to make radioactive by the addition of radioactive material. **[C15:** from L *contamināre* to defile**]**
►**con'taminable** *adj* ►**con'taminant** *n* ►**con,tami'nation** *n* ►**con'tami,nator** *n*

contango (kən'tæŋgəʊ) *n, pl* **contangos. 1** (formerly, on the London Stock Exchange) postponement of payment for and delivery of stock from one account day to the next. **2** the fee paid for such a postponement. ◆ Also called: **carry-over, continuation.** Cf. **backwardation. [C19:** apparently an arbitrary coinage**]**

conte *French.* (kɔ̃t) *n* a tale or short story.

contemn (kən'tem) *vb* (*tr*) *Formal.* to regard with contempt; scorn. **[C15:** from L *contemnere,* from *temnere* to slight**]**
►**contemner** (kən'tɛmnə, -'tɛmə) *n*

contemplate ❶ ('kɒntɛm,pleɪt) *vb* **contemplates, contemplating, contemplated.** (*mainly tr*) **1** to think about intently and at length. **2** (*intr*) to think intently and at length, esp. for spiritual reasons; meditate. **3** to look at thoughtfully. **4** to have in mind as a possibility. **[C16:** from L *contemplāre,* from *templum* TEMPLE[1]**]**
►**,contem'plation** *n* ►**'contem,plator** *n*

contemplative ❶ ('kɒntɛm,pleɪtɪv, -təm-; kən'tɛmplə-) *adj* **1** denoting, concerned with, or inclined to contemplation; meditative. ◆ *n* **2** a person dedicated to religious contemplation.

contemporaneous (kən,tɛmpə'reɪnɪəs) *adj* existing, beginning, or occurring in the same period of time.
►**contemporaneity** (kən,tɛmpərə'niːɪtɪ) *or* **con,tempo'raneousness** *n*

contemporary ❶ (kən'tɛmprərɪ) *adj* **1** living or occurring in the same period. **2** existing or occurring at the present time. **3** conforming to modern ideas in style, fashion, etc. **4** having approximately the same age as one another. ◆ *n, pl* **contemporaries. 5** a person living at the same time or of approximately the same age as another. **6** something that is contemporary. **[C17:** from Med. L *contemporārius,* from L *com-* together + *temporārius* relating to time, from *tempus* time**]**
►**con'temporarily** *adv* ►**con'temporariness** *n*

> **USAGE NOTE** Since *contemporary* can mean either of the same period or of the present period, it is best to avoid this word where ambiguity might arise, as in *a production of* Othello *in contemporary dress. Modern dress* or *Elizabethan dress* should be used in this example to avoid ambiguity.

contemporize *or* **contemporise** (kən'tɛmpə,raɪz) *vb* **contemporizes, contemporizing, contemporized** *or* **contemporises, contemporising, contemporised.** to be or make contemporary.

contempt ❶ (kən'tɛmpt) *n* **1** the feeling of a person towards a person or thing that he considers despicable; scorn. **2** the state of being scorned; disgrace (esp. in **hold in contempt**). **3** wilful disregard of the authority of a court of law or legislative body: *contempt of court.* **[C14:** from L *contemptus,* from *contemnere* to CONTEMN**]**

contemptible ❶ (kən'tɛmptɪbᵊl) *adj* deserving or worthy of contempt.
►**con,tempti'bility** *or* **con'temptibleness** *n* ►**con'temptibly** *adv*

contemptuous ❶ (kən'tɛmptjʊəs) *adj* (when *predicative,* often foll. by *of*) showing or feeling contempt; disdainful.
►**con'temptuously** *adv*

contend ❶ (kən'tɛnd) *vb* **1** (*intr;* often foll. by *with*) to struggle in rivalry, battle, etc.; vie. **2** to argue earnestly. **3** (*tr; may take a clause as object*) to assert. **[C15:** from L *contendere* to strive, from *com-* with + *tendere* to stretch**]**
►**con'tender** *n*

content[1] ❶ ('kɒntɛnt) *n* **1** (*often pl*) everything inside a container. **2** (*usually pl*) **2a** the chapters or divisions of a book. **2b** a list of these printed at the front of a book. **3** the meaning or significance of a work of art, as distinguished from its style or form. **4** all that is contained or dealt with in a piece of writing, etc.; substance. **5** the capacity or size of a thing. **6** the proportion of a substance contained in an alloy, mixture, etc.: *the lead content of petrol.* **[C15:** from L *contentus* contained, from *continēre* to CONTAIN**]**

content[2] ❶ (kən'tɛnt) *adj* (*postpositive*) **1** satisfied with things as they are. **2** assenting to or willing to accept circumstances, a proposed course of action, etc. ◆ *vb* **3** (*tr*) to make (oneself or another person) satisfied. ◆ *n* **4** peace of mind. **[C14:** from OF, from L *contentus* contented, having restrained desires, from *continēre* to restrain**]**
►**con'tentment** *n*

contented ❶ (kən'tɛntɪd) *adj* accepting one's situation or life with equanimity and satisfaction.
►**con'tentedly** *adv* ►**con'tentedness** *n*

contention ❶ (kən'tɛnʃən) *n* **1** a struggling between opponents; competition. **2** a point of dispute (esp. in **bone of contention**). **3** a point asserted in argument. **[C14:** from L *contentiō,* from *contendere* to CONTEND**]**

contentious ❶ (kən'tɛnʃəs) *adj* **1** tending to quarrel. **2** causing or characterized by dispute; controversial.
►**con'tentiousness** *n*

conterminous (kən'tɜːmɪnəs) *or* **coterminous** (kəʊ'tɜːmɪnəs) *adj* **1** enclosed within a common boundary. **2** without a break or interruption. **[C17:** from L *conterminus,* from CON- + *terminus* boundary**]**

contest ❶ *n* ('kɒntɛst). **1** a formal game or match in which people, teams, etc., compete. **2** a struggle for victory between opposing forces. ◆ *vb* (kən'tɛst). **3** (*tr*) to try to disprove; call in question. **4** (when *intr,* foll. by *with* or *against*) to dispute or contend (with): *to con-*

THESAURUS

contaminate *vb* **1 = pollute**, adulterate, befoul, corrupt, defile, deprave, infect, smirch, soil, stain, sully, taint, tarnish, vitiate
Antonyms *vb* clean, cleanse, decontaminate, deodorize, disinfect, fumigate, purify, sanitize, sterilize

contamination *n* **1 = pollution**, adulteration, contagion, corruption, decay, defilement, dirtying, filth, foulness, impurity, infection, poisoning, rottenness, taint

contemplate *vb* **1 = think about**, brood over, consider, deliberate, meditate, meditate on, mull over, muse over, observe, ponder, reflect upon, revolve *or* turn over in one's mind, ruminate (upon) **3 = look at**, behold, check out (*inf.*), examine, eye, eye up, gaze at, inspect, recce (*sl.*), regard, scrutinize, stare at, study, survey, view, weigh **4 = consider**, aspire to, design, envisage, expect, foresee, have in view *or* in mind, intend, mean, plan, propose, think of

contemplation *n* **1 = thought**, cogitation, consideration, deliberation, meditation, musing, pondering, reflection, reverie, rumination **3 = looking at**, examination, gazing at, inspection, observation, recce (*sl.*), scrutiny, survey, viewing

contemplative *adj* **1 = thoughtful**, deep *or* lost in thought, in a brown study, intent, introspective, meditative, musing, pensive, rapt, reflective, ruminative

contemporary *adj* **1, 2 = coexisting**, coetaneous (*rare*), coeval, coexistent, concurrent, contemporaneous, synchronous **3 = modern**, à la mode, current, happening (*inf.*), in fashion, latest, newfangled, present, present-day, recent, trendy (*Brit. inf.*), ultramodern, up-to-date, up-to-the-minute, with it (*inf.*) ◆ *n* **5 = peer**, compeer, fellow
Antonyms *adj* ≠ **modern:** antecedent, antique, early, obsolete, old, old-fashioned, out-of-date, passé

contempt *n* **1 = scorn**, condescension, contumely, derision, despite (*arch.*), disdain, disregard, disrespect, mockery, neglect, slight
Antonyms *n* admiration, esteem, honour, liking, regard, respect

contemptible *adj* **= despicable**, abject, base, cheap, degenerate, detestable, ignominious, low, low-down (*inf.*), mean, measly, paltry, pitiful, scurvy, shabby, shameful, vile, worthless
Antonyms *adj* admirable, attractive, honourable, laudable, pleasant, praiseworthy

contemptuous *adj* **= scornful**, arrogant, cavalier, condescending, contumelious, derisive, disdainful, haughty, high and mighty, insolent, insulting, on one's high horse (*inf.*), sneering, supercilious, withering
Antonyms *adj* civil, courteous, deferential, gracious, humble, mannerly, obsequious, polite, respectful

contend *vb* **1 = compete**, clash, contest, cope, emulate, fight, grapple, jostle, litigate, skirmish, strive, struggle, vie **3 = argue**, affirm, allege, assert, aver, avow, debate, dispute, hold, maintain

contender *n* **1 = competitor**, contestant, rival, vier

content[1] *n* **1** *often pl* **= constituents**, elements, ingredients, load **2a** *usually pl* **= chapters**, divisions, subject matter, subjects, themes, topics **4 = meaning**, burden, essence, gist, ideas, matter, significance, substance, text, thoughts **5 = amount**, capacity, load, measure, size, volume

content[2] *adj* **1, 2 = satisfied**, agreeable, at ease, comfortable, contented, fulfilled, willing to accept ◆ *vb* **3 = satisfy**, appease, delight, gladden, gratify, humour, indulge, mollify, placate, please, reconcile, sate, suffice ◆ *n* **4 = satisfaction**, comfort, contentment, ease, gratification, peace, peace of mind, pleasure

contented *adj* **= satisfied**, at ease, at peace, cheerful, comfortable, complacent, content, glad, gratified, happy, pleased, serene, thankful
Antonyms *adj* annoyed, discontented, displeased, dissatisfied, pissed off (*taboo sl.*), troubled, uncomfortable, uneasy

contention *n* **1, 2 = dispute**, bone of contention, competition, contest, disagreement, discord, dissension, enmity, feuding, hostility, rivalry, row, strife, struggle, wrangling **3 = assertion**, affirmation, allegation, argument, asseveration, belief, claim, declaration, ground, idea, maintaining, opinion, position, profession, stand, thesis, view

contentious *adj* **1 = argumentative**, bickering, cantankerous, captious, cavilling, combative, cross, disputatious, factious, litigious, peevish, perverse, pugnacious, quarrelsome, querulous, wrangling

contentment *n* **1 = satisfaction**, comfort, complacency, content, contentedness, ease, equanimity, fulfilment, gladness, gratification, happiness, peace, pleasure, repletion, serenity
Antonyms *n* discomfort, discontent, discontentment, displeasure, dissatisfaction, uneasiness, unhappiness

contest *n* **1 = competition**, game, head-to-head, match, tournament, trial **2 = struggle**, affray, altercation, battle, combat, conflict, controversy, debate, discord, dispute, encounter, fight, shock ◆ *vb* **3 = dispute**, argue, call in *or* into question, challenge, debate, doubt, litigate, object to, oppose, question **4 = compete**, contend, fight, fight over, strive, vie

test an election. [C16: from L *contestārī* to introduce a lawsuit, from *testis* witness]
▸**con'testable** *adj* ▸**con'tester** *n*

contestant ❶ (kən'testənt) *n* a person who takes part in a contest; competitor.

context ❶ ('kɒntɛkst) *n* **1** the parts of a piece of writing, speech, etc., that precede and follow a word or passage and contribute to its full meaning: *it is unfair to quote out of context.* **2** the circumstances that are relevant to an event, fact, etc. [C15: from L *contextus* a putting together, from *contexere*, from *com-* together + *texere* to weave]
▸**con'textual** *adj*

contiguous (kən'tɪgjuəs) *adj* **1** touching along the side or boundary; in contact. **2** neighbouring. **3** preceding or following in time. [C17: from L *contiguus*, from *contingere* to touch; see CONTACT]
▸**con'tiguously** *adv*

continent[1] ('kɒntɪnənt) *n* **1** one of the earth's large land masses (Asia, Australia, Africa, Europe, North and South America, and Antarctica). **2** *Obs.* **2a** mainland. **2b** a continuous extent of land. [C16: from the L phrase *terra continens* continuous land]
▸**continental** (,kɒntɪ'nɛntᵊl) *adj* ▸,**conti'nentally** *adv*

continent[2] ❶ ('kɒntɪnənt) *adj* **1** able to control urination and defecation. **2** exercising self-restraint, esp. from sexual activity; chaste. [C14: from L *continēre*; see CONTAIN]
▸**'continence** *n*

Continental (,kɒntɪ'nɛntᵊl) *adj* **1** of or characteristic of Europe, excluding the British Isles. **2** of or relating to the 13 original British North American colonies during the War of American Independence. ◆ *n* **3** (*sometimes not cap.*) an inhabitant of Europe, excluding the British Isles. **4** a regular soldier of the rebel army during the War of American Independence.

continental breakfast *n* a light breakfast of coffee and rolls.

continental climate *n* a climate characterized by hot summers, cold winters, and little rainfall, typical of the interior of a continent.

continental drift *n Geol.* the theory that the earth's continents move gradually over the surface of the planet on a substratum of magma.

continental quilt *n Brit.* a quilt, stuffed with down or a synthetic material, used as a bed cover in place of the top sheet and blankets. Also called: **duvet**, (Austral.) **doona.**

continental shelf *n* the sea bed surrounding a continent at depths of up to about 200 metres (100 fathoms), at the edge of which the **continental slope** drops steeply.

contingency ❶ (kən'tɪndʒənsɪ) *or* **contingence** (kən'tɪndʒəns) *n, pl* **contingencies** *or* **contingences. 1a** a possible but not very likely future event or condition. **1b** (*as modifier*): *a contingency plan.* **2** something dependent on a possible future event. **3** a fact, event, etc., incidental to something else. **4** *Logic.* the state of being contingent. **5** uncertainty. **6** *Statistics.* **6a** the degree of association between theoretical and observed common frequencies of two graded or classified variables. **6b** (*as modifier*): *a contingency table.*

contingent ❶ (kən'tɪndʒənt) *adj* **1** (when *postpositive*, often foll. by *on* or *upon*) dependent on events, conditions, etc., not yet known; conditional. **2** *Logic.* (of a proposition) true under certain conditions, false under others; not logically necessary. **3** happening by chance; accidental. **4** uncertain. ◆ *n* **5** a part of a military force, parade, etc. **6** a group distinguished by common interests, etc., that is part of a larger group. **7** a chance occurrence. [C14: from L *contingere* to touch, befall]

continual ❶ (kən'tɪnjuəl) *adj* **1** recurring frequently, esp. at regular intervals. **2** occurring without interruption; continuous in time. [C14: from OF *continuel*, from L *continuus* uninterrupted, from *continēre* to CONTAIN]
▸**con'tinually** *adv*

> **USAGE NOTE** See at **continuous.**

continuance ❶ (kən'tɪnjuəns) *n* **1** the act of continuing. **2** the duration of an action, etc. **3** *US.* the adjournment of a legal proceeding.

continuant (kən'tɪnjuənt) *Phonetics.* ◆ *n* **1** a speech sound, such as (l), (r), (f), or (s), in which the closure of the vocal tract is incomplete, allowing the continuous passage of the breath. ◆ *adj* **2** relating to or denoting a continuant.

continuation ❶ (kən,tɪnju'eɪʃən) *n* **1** a part or thing added, esp. to a book or play; sequel. **2** a renewal of an interrupted action, process, etc.; resumption. **3** the act of continuing; prolongation. **4** another word for **contango.**

continue ❶ (kən'tɪnju:) *vb* **continues, continuing, continued. 1** (when *tr*, may take an infinitive) to remain or cause to remain in a particular condition or place. **2** (when *tr*, may take an infinitive) to carry on uninterruptedly (a course of action): *he continued running.* **3** (when *tr*, may take an infinitive) to resume after an interruption: *we'll continue after lunch.* **4** to prolong or be prolonged: *continue the chord until it meets the tangent.* **5** (*tr*) *Law, chiefly Scots.* to adjourn (legal proceedings). [C14: from OF *continuer*, from L *continuāre* to join together]

continuity ❶ (,kɒntɪ'nju:ɪtɪ) *n, pl* **continuities. 1** logical sequence. **2** a continuous or connected whole. **3** the comprehensive script or scenario of detail in a film or broadcast. **4** the continuous projection of a film.

continuity girl *or* **man** *n* a woman or man whose job is to ensure continuity and consistency in successive shots of a film.

continuo (kən'tɪnjuəʊ) *n, pl* **continuos. 1** *Music.* **1a** a shortened form of **basso continuo** (see **thorough bass**). **1b** (*as modifier*): *a continuo accompaniment.* **2** the thorough-bass part as played on a keyboard instrument. [It., lit.: continuous]

continuous ❶ (kən'tɪnjuəs) *adj* **1** unceasing: *a continuous noise.* **2** in an unbroken series or pattern. **3** *Statistics.* (of a variable) having a continuum of possible values so that its distribution requires integration rather than summation to determine its cumulative probability. **4** *Grammar.* another word for **progressive** (sense 7). [C17: from L *continuus*, from *continēre* to CONTAIN]
▸**con'tinuously** *adv*

> **USAGE NOTE** Both *continual* and *continuous* can be used to say that something continues without interruption, but only *continual* can correctly be used to say that something keeps happening repeatedly.

continuous assessment *n* the assessment of a pupil's progress throughout a course of study rather than exclusively by examination at the end of it.

continuous creation *n* the theory that matter is created continuously in the universe. See **steady-state theory.**

continuum (kən'tɪnjuəm) *n, pl* **continua** (-'tɪnjuə) *or* **continuums.** a continuous series or whole, no part of which is perceptibly different from the adjacent parts. [C17: from L, neuter of *continuus* CONTINUOUS]

contort ❶ (kən'tɔ:t) *vb* to twist or bend out of place or shape. [C15: from L *contortus* intricate, from *contorquēre* to whirl around, from *torquēre* to twist]
▸**con'tortion** *n* ▸**con'tortive** *adj*

contortionist (kən'tɔ:ʃənɪst) *n* **1** a performer who contorts his body for the entertainment of others. **2** a person who twists or warps meaning.

contour ❶ ('kɒntʊə) *n* **1** the outline of a mass of land, figure, or body; a defining line. **2a** See **contour line. 2b** (*as modifier*): *a contour map.* **3** (*often pl*) the shape of a curving form: *the contours of her body were full and round.* ◆ *vb* (*tr*) **4** to shape so as to form the contour of something. **5** to mark contour lines on. **6** to construct (a road, railway, etc.) to follow the outline of the land. [C17: from F, from It. *contorno*, from *contornare* to sketch, from *tornare* to TURN]

contour line *n* a line on a map or chart joining points of equal height or depth.

THESAURUS

contestant *n* = **competitor**, aspirant, candidate, contender, entrant, participant, player

context *n* **2** = **frame of reference**, ambience, background, conditions, connection, framework, relation, situation

continence *n* **2** = **self-restraint**, abstinence, asceticism, celibacy, chastity, moderation, self-control, temperance

continent[2] *adj* **2** = **self-restrained**, abstemious, abstinent, ascetic, austere, celibate, chaste, sober

contingency *n* **1a** = **possibility**, accident, chance, emergency, event, eventuality, fortuity, happening, incident, juncture, uncertainty

contingent *adj* **1** *often foll. by* **on** *or* **upon** = **dependent on**, conditional on, controlled by, subject to **3, 4** = **chance**, accidental, casual, fortuitous, haphazard, random, uncertain ◆ *n* **6** = **group**, batch, body, bunch, deputation, detachment, mission, quota, section, set

continual *adj* **1, 2** = **constant**, continuous, endless, eternal, everlasting, frequent, incessant, interminable, oft-repeated, perpetual, recurrent, regular, repeated, repetitive, unceasing, uninterrupted, unremitting
Antonyms *adj* broken, ceasing, erratic, fluctuating, fragmentary, infrequent, intermittent, interrupted, irregular, occasional, periodic, spasmodic, sporadic, terminable

continually *adv* **1, 2** = **constantly**, all the time, always, aye (*Scot.*), endlessly, eternally, everlastingly, forever, incessantly, interminably, nonstop, persistently, repeatedly

continuance *n* **1, 2** = **duration**, continuation, period, protraction, term

continuation *n* **1** = **addition**, extension, furtherance, postscript, sequel, supplement **3** = **continuing**, maintenance, perpetuation, prolongation, resumption

continue *vb* **1** = **remain**, abide, carry on, endure, last, live on, persist, rest, stay, stay on, survive **2** = **keep on**, carry on, go on, keep at, keep one's hand in, keep the ball rolling, keep up, maintain, persevere, persist in, prolong, pursue, stick at, stick to, sustain **3** = **resume**, carry on, pick up where one left off, proceed, recommence, return to, take up **4** = **go on**, draw out, extend, lengthen, project, prolong, reach
Antonyms *vb* ≠ **remain:** abdicate, leave, quit, resign, retire, step down ≠ **keep on, resume:** break off, call it a day, cease, discontinue, give up, leave off, pack in (*Brit. informal*), quit, stop

continuing *adj* **2** = **lasting**, enduring, in progress, ongoing, sustained

continuity *n* **1, 2** = **sequence**, cohesion, connection, flow, interrelationship, progression, succession, whole

continuous *adj* **1, 2** = **constant**, connected, continued, extended, prolonged, unbroken, unceasing, undivided, uninterrupted
Antonyms *adj* broken, disconnected, ending, inconstant, intermittent, interrupted, occasional, passing, severed, spasmodic

contort *vb* = **twist**, convolute, deform, distort, gnarl, knot, misshape, warp, wrench, writhe

contortion *n* = **twist**, bend, convolution, deformity, distortion, gnarl, knot, tortuosity, warp

contour ploughing *n* ploughing along the contours of the land to minimize erosion.

Contra ('kɒntrə) *n* a member of a US-backed guerrilla army, founded in 1979, whose aim was to overthrow the Sandinista government in Nicaragua.

contra- *prefix* **1** against; contrary; opposing; contrasting: *contraceptive*. **2** (in music) pitched below: *contrabass*. [from L, from *contrā* against]

contraband ❶ ('kɒntrəˌbænd) *n* **1a** goods that are prohibited by law from being exported or imported. **1b** illegally imported or exported goods. **2** illegal traffic in such goods; smuggling. **3** Also called: **contraband of war.** goods that a neutral country may not supply to a belligerent. ◆ *adj* **4** (of goods) **4a** forbidden by law from being imported or exported. **4b** illegally imported or exported. [C16: from Sp. *contrabanda*, from It., from Med. L, from CONTRA- + *bannum* ban]
▸**'contraˌbandist** *n*

contrabass (ˌkɒntrə'beɪs) *n* **1** another name for **double bass.** ◆ *adj* **2** denoting the instrument of a family that is lower than the bass.

contrabassoon (ˌkɒntrəbə'suːn) *n* the largest instrument in the oboe family, pitched an octave below the bassoon; double bassoon.

contraception (ˌkɒntrə'sɛpʃən) *n* the intentional prevention of conception by artificial or natural means. [C19: from CONTRA- + CONCEPTION]
▸**ˌcontra'ceptive** *adj, n*

contract ❶ *vb* (kən'trækt). **1** to make or become smaller, narrower, shorter, etc. **2** ('kɒntrækt). (when *intr*, sometimes foll. by *for*; when *tr*, may take an infinitive) to enter into an agreement with (a person, company, etc.) to deliver (goods or services) or to do (something) on mutually agreed terms. **3** to draw or be drawn together. **4** (*tr*) to incur or become affected by (a disease, debt, etc.). **5** (*tr*) to shorten (a word or phrase) by the omission of letters or syllables, usually indicated in writing by an apostrophe. **6** (*tr*) to wrinkle (the brow or a muscle). **7** (*tr*) to arrange (a marriage) for; betroth. ◆ *n* ('kɒntrækt). **8** a formal agreement between two or more parties. **9** a document that states the terms of such an agreement. **10** the branch of law treating of contracts. **11** marriage considered as a formal agreement. **12** See **contract bridge. 13** *Bridge.* **13a** the highest bid, which determines trumps and the number of tricks one side must make. **13b** the number and suit of these tricks. **14** *Sl.* **14a** a criminal agreement to kill a particular person in return for an agreed sum of money. **14b** (*as modifier*): *a contract killing*. [C16: from L *contractus* agreement, from *contrahere* to draw together, from *trahere* to draw]
▸**con'tractible** *adj*

contract bridge ('kɒntrækt) *n* the most common variety of bridge, in which the declarer receives points counting towards game and rubber only for tricks he bids as well as makes. Cf. **auction bridge.**

contractile (kən'træktaɪl) *adj* having the power to contract or to cause contraction.

contraction ❶ (kən'trækʃən) *n* **1** an instance of contracting or the state of being contracted. **2** a shortening of a word or group of words, often marked by an apostrophe: *I've come* for *I have come.*
▸**con'tractive** *adj*

contractor (kən'træktə) *n* **1** a person or firm that contracts to supply materials or labour, esp. for building. **2** something that contracts.

contract out ('kɒntrækt) *vb* (*intr, adv*) *Brit.* to agree not to participate in something, esp. the state pension scheme.

contractual (kən'træktjʊəl) *adj* of the nature of or assured by a contract.

contradance ('kɒntrəˌdɑːns) *n* a courtly Continental version of the English country dance.

contradict ❶ (ˌkɒntrə'dɪkt) *vb* **1** (*tr*) to affirm the opposite of (a statement, etc.). **2** (*tr*) to declare (a statement, etc.) to be false or incorrect; deny. **3** (*tr*) to be inconsistent with: *the facts contradicted his theory.* **4** (*intr*) to be at variance; be in contradiction. [C16: from L *contrādīcere*, from CONTRA- + *dīcere* to speak]
▸**ˌcontra'dictable** *adj* ▸**ˌcontra'dictor** *n*

contradiction ❶ (ˌkɒntrə'dɪkʃən) *n* **1** opposition; denial. **2** a declaration of the opposite. **3** a statement that is at variance with itself (often in **a contradiction in terms**). **4** conflict or inconsistency, as between events, qualities, etc. **5** a person or thing containing conflicting qualities. **6** *Logic.* a statement that is false under all circumstances; necessary falsehood.

contradictory ❶ (ˌkɒntrə'dɪktərɪ) *adj* **1** inconsistent; incompatible. **2** given to argument and contention: *a contradictory person.* **3** *Logic.* (of a pair of statements) unable both to be true or both to be false under the same circumstances.
▸**ˌcontra'dictorily** *adv* ▸**ˌcontra'dictoriness** *n*

contradistinction (ˌkɒntrədɪ'stɪŋkʃən) *n* a distinction made by contrasting different qualities.
▸**ˌcontradis'tinctive** *adj*

contraflow ('kɒntrəˌfləʊ) *n Brit.* two-way traffic on one carriageway of a motorway.

contrail ('kɒntreɪl) *n* another name for **vapour trail.** [C20: from CON(DENSATION) + TRAIL]

contralto (kən'træltəʊ) *n, pl* **contraltos** *or* **contralti** (-tɪ). **1** the lowest female voice: in the context of a choir often shortened to **alto. 2** a singer with such a voice. ◆ *adj* **3** of or denoting a contralto: *the contralto part.* [C18: from It.; see CONTRA-, ALTO]

contraposition (ˌkɒntrəpə'zɪʃən) *n* **1** the act of placing opposite or against. **2** *Logic.* the conclusion drawn from a subject-predicate proposition by negating its terms and changing their order.

contraption ❶ (kən'træpʃən) *n Inf., often facetious or derog.* a device or contrivance, esp. one considered strange, unnecessarily intricate, or improvised. [C19: ?from CON(TRIVANCE) + TRAP[1] + (INVEN)TION]

contrapuntal (ˌkɒntrə'pʌntᵊl) *adj Music.* characterized by counterpoint. [C19: from It. *contrappunto*]
▸**ˌcontra'puntally** *adv* ▸**ˌcontra'puntist** *or* **ˌcontra'puntalist** *n*

contrariety (ˌkɒntrə'raɪətɪ) *n, pl* **contrarieties. 1** opposition between one thing and another; disagreement. **2** an instance of such opposition; inconsistency; discrepancy.

contrariwise ('kɒntrərɪˌwaɪz) *adv* **1** from a contrasting point of view. **2** in the reverse way. **3** (kən'trɛərɪˌwaɪz). in a contrary manner.

contrary ❶ ('kɒntrərɪ) *adj* **1** opposed in nature, position, etc.: *contrary ideas.* **2** (kən'trɛərɪ). perverse; obstinate. **3** (esp. of wind) adverse; unfavourable. **4** (of plant parts) situated at right angles to each other. **5** *Logic.* (of a pair of propositions) related so they cannot both be true, although they may both be false. ◆ *n, pl* **contraries. 6** the exact opposite (esp. in **to the contrary**). **7 on the contrary.** quite the reverse. **8** either of two exactly opposite objects, facts, or qualities. ◆ *adv* (usually foll. by *to*) **9** in an opposite or unexpected way: *contrary to usual belief.* **10** in conflict (with): *contrary to nature.* [C14: from L *contrārius* opposite, from *contrā* against]
▸**con'trarily** *adv* ▸**con'trariness** *n*

contrast ❶ *vb* (kən'trɑːst). **1** (often foll. by *with*) to distinguish or be distinguished by comparison of unlike or opposite qualities. ◆ *n* ('kɒntrɑːst). **2** distinction by comparison of opposite or dissimilar things, qualities, etc. (esp. in **by contrast, in contrast to** *or* **with**). **3** a person or thing showing differences when compared with another. **4** the effect of the juxtaposition of different colours, tones, etc. **5** the extent to which adjacent areas of an optical image, esp. on a television screen or in a photograph, differ in brightness. [C16: (n): via F from It., from *contrastare* (vb), from L *contra-* against + *stare* to stand]
▸**con'trasting** *adj* ▸**con'trastive** *adj*

contrast medium *n Med.* a radiopaque substance, such as barium sulphate, used to increase the contrast of an image in radiography.

contravene ❶ (ˌkɒntrə'viːn) *vb* **contravenes, contravening, contravened.** (*tr*) **1** to come into conflict with or infringe (rules, laws, etc.). **2** to dispute or contradict (a statement, proposition, etc.). [C16: from LL *contrāvenīre*, from L CONTRA- + *venīre* to come]
▸**ˌcontra'vener** *n* ▸**contravention** (ˌkɒntrə'vɛnʃən) *n*

THESAURUS

contour *n* **1, 3** = **outline**, curve, figure, form, lines, profile, relief, shape, silhouette

contraband *n* **2** = **smuggling**, black-marketing, bootlegging, moonshine (*US*), rum-running, trafficking ◆ *adj* **4** = **smuggled**, banned, black-market, bootleg, bootlegged, forbidden, hot, illegal, illicit, interdicted, prohibited, unlawful

contract *vb* **1** = **shorten**, abbreviate, abridge, compress, condense, confine, constrict, curtail, diminish, dwindle, epitomize, knit, lessen, narrow, pucker, purse, reduce, shrink, shrivel, tighten, wither, wrinkle **2** = **agree**, arrange, bargain, clinch, close, come to terms, commit oneself, covenant, engage, enter into, negotiate, pledge, shake hands, stipulate **4** = **catch**, acquire, be afflicted with, develop, get, go down with, incur ◆ *n* **8** = **agreement**, arrangement, bargain, bond, commission, commitment, compact, concordat, convention, covenant, deal (*inf.*), engagement, pact, settlement, stipulation, treaty, understanding
Antonyms *vb* ≠ **shorten:** broaden, develop, distend, enlarge, expand, grow, increase, inflate, multiply, spread, stretch, swell, widen ≠ **agree:** decline, disagree, refuse, turn down ≠ **catch:** avert, avoid, escape, ward off

contraction *n* **1** = **shortening**, abbreviation, compression, constriction, diminution, drawing in, elision, narrowing, reduction, shrinkage, shrivelling, tensing, tightening

contradict *vb* **1-4** = **deny**, be at variance with, belie, challenge, contravene, controvert, counter, counteract, dispute, fly in the face of, gainsay (*arch. or literary*), impugn, make a nonsense of, negate, oppose, rebut
Antonyms *vb* affirm, agree, authenticate, confirm, defend, endorse, support, verify

contradiction *n* **4** = **denial**, conflict, confutation, contravention, incongruity, inconsistency, negation, opposite

contradictory *adj* **1** = **inconsistent**, antagonistic, antithetical, conflicting, contrary, discrepant, incompatible, irreconcilable, opposed, opposite, paradoxical, repugnant

contraption *n Informal* = **device**, apparatus, contrivance, gadget, instrument, mechanism, rig, waldo

contrary *adj* **1** = **opposed**, adverse, antagonistic, clashing, contradictory, counter, discordant, hostile, inconsistent, inimical, opposite, paradoxical **2** = **perverse**, awkward, balky, cantankerous, cussed (*inf.*), difficult, disobliging, froward (*arch.*), intractable, obstinate, stroppy (*Brit. sl.*), thrawn (*N English dialect*), unaccommodating, wayward, wilful ◆ *n* **7 on the contrary** = **quite the opposite** *or* **reverse**, conversely, in contrast, not at all, on the other hand **8** = **opposite**, antithesis, converse, reverse
Antonyms *adj* ≠ **opposed:** accordant, congruous, consistent, harmonious, in agreement, parallel, unopposed ≠ **perverse:** accommodating, agreeable, amiable, cooperative, eager to please, helpful, obliging, tractable, willing

contrast *vb* **1** = **differentiate**, compare, differ, distinguish, oppose, set in opposition, set off ◆ *n* **2** = **difference**, comparison, contrariety, differentiation, disparity, dissimilarity, distinction, divergence, foil, opposition

contravene *vb* **1** *Formal* = **break**, disobey, go against, infringe, transgress, violate **2** = **conflict with**, contradict, counteract, cross, go against, hinder, interfere, oppose, refute, thwart

contravention *n* **1** = **breach**, disobedience,

contretemps ('kɒntrəˌtɑːn) *n, pl* **contretemps. 1** an awkward or difficult situation or mishap. **2** a small disagreement that is rather embarrassing. [C17: from F, from *contre* against + *temps* time]

contribute ❶ (kən'trɪbjuːt) *vb* **contributes, contributing, contributed.** (often foll. by *to*) **1** to give (support, money, etc.) for a common purpose or fund. **2** to supply (ideas, opinions, etc.). **3** (*intr*) to be partly responsible (for): *drink contributed to the accident.* **4** to write (articles, etc.) for a publication. [C16: from L *contribuere* to collect, from *tribuere* to grant] ▸**con'tributable** *adj* ▸**con'tributive** *adj* ▸**con'tributor** *n*

contribution ❶ (ˌkɒntrɪ'bjuːʃən) *n* **1** the act of contributing. **2** something contributed, such as money. **3** an article, etc., contributed to a newspaper or other publication. **4** *Arch.* a levy.

contributory (kən'trɪbjutərɪ, -trɪ) *adj* **1** (often foll. by *to*) being partly responsible: *a contributory factor.* **2** giving to a common purpose or fund. **3** of or designating an insurance or pension scheme in which the premiums are paid partly by the employer and partly by the employees who benefit from it. ◆ *n, pl* **contributories. 4** a person or thing that contributes. **5** *Company law.* a member or former member of a company liable to contribute to the assets on the winding-up of the company.

contrite ❶ (kən'traɪt, 'kɒntraɪt) *adj* **1** full of guilt or regret; remorseful. **2** arising from a sense of shame or guilt: *contrite promises.* [C14: from L *contrītus* worn out, from *conterere* to bruise, from *terere* to grind] ▸**con'tritely** *adv* ▸**con'triteness** *or* **contrition** (kən'trɪʃən) *n*

contrivance ❶ (kən'traɪvəns) *n* **1** something contrived, esp. an ingenious device; contraption. **2** inventive skill or ability. **3** an artificial rather than natural arrangement of details, parts, etc. **4** an elaborate or deceitful plan; stratagem.

contrive ❶ (kən'traɪv) *vb* **contrives, contriving, contrived. 1** (*tr*) to manage (something or to do something), esp. by a trick: *he contrived to make them meet.* **2** (*tr*) to think up or adapt ingeniously: *he contrived a new mast for the boat.* **3** to plot or scheme. [C14: from OF *controver,* from LL *contropāre* to represent by figures of speech, compare] ▸**con'triver** *n*

contrived ❶ (kən'traɪvd) *adj* obviously planned; artificial; forced; unnatural.

control ❶ (kən'trəʊl) *vb* **controls, controlling, controlled.** (*tr*) **1** to command, direct, or rule. **2** to check, limit, or restrain: *to control one's emotions.* **3** to regulate or operate (a machine). **4** to verify (a scientific experiment) by conducting a parallel experiment in which the variable being investigated is held constant or is compared with a standard. **5a** to regulate (financial affairs). **5b** to examine (financial accounts). **6** to restrict or regulate the authorized supply of (certain substances, such as drugs). ◆ *n* **7** power to direct: *under control.* **8** a curb; check: *a frontier control.* **9** (*often pl*) a mechanism for operating a car, aircraft, etc. **10a** a standard of comparison used in a statistical analysis, etc. **10b** (*as modifier*): *a control group.* **11a** a device that regulates the operation of a machine. **11b** (*as modifier*): *control room.* [C15: from OF *conteroller* to regulate, from *contrerolle* duplicate register, from *contre-* COUNTER- + *rolle* ROLL] ▸**con'trollable** *adj* ▸**conˌtrolla'bility** *n* ▸**con'trollably** *adv*

control experiment *n* an experiment designed to check or correct the results of another experiment by removing the variable or variables operating in that other experiment.

controller (kən'trəʊlə) *n* **1** a person who directs. **2** Also called: **comptroller.** a business executive or government officer responsible for financial planning, control, etc. **3** the equipment concerned with controlling the operation of an electrical device. ▸**con'trollerˌship** *n*

controlling interest *n* a quantity of shares in a business that is sufficient to ensure control over its direction.

control tower *n* a tower at an airport from which air traffic is controlled.

controversy ❶ ('kɒntrəˌvɜːsɪ, kən'trɒvəsɪ) *n, pl* **controversies.** dispute, argument, or debate, esp. one concerning a matter about which there is strong disagreement and esp. one carried on in public or in the press. [C14: from L *contrōversia,* from *contrōversus,* from CONTRA- + *vertere* to turn] ▸**controversial** (ˌkɒntrə'vɜːʃəl) *adj* ▸**ˌcontro'versialˌism** *n* ▸**ˌcontro'versialist** *n*

controvert ('kɒntrəˌvɜːt, ˌkɒntrə'vɜːt) *vb* (*tr*) **1** to deny, refute, or oppose (argument or opinion). **2** to argue about. [C17: from L *contrōversus;* see CONTROVERSY] ▸**ˌcontro'vertible** *adj*

contumacious (ˌkɒntju'meɪʃəs) *adj* stubbornly resistant to authority. ▸**ˌcontu'maciously** *adv*

contumacy ('kɒntjuməsɪ) *n, pl* **contumacies.** obstinate and wilful resistance to authority, esp. refusal to comply with a court order. [C14: from L *contumācia,* from *contumāx* obstinate]

contumely ('kɒntjumɪlɪ) *n, pl* **contumelies. 1** scornful or insulting language or behaviour. **2** a humiliating insult. [C14: from L *contumēlia,* from *tumēre* to swell, as with wrath] ▸**contumelious** (ˌkɒntju'miːlɪəs) *adj* ▸**ˌcontu'meliously** *adv*

contuse ❶ (kən'tjuːz) *vb* **contuses, contusing, contused.** (*tr*) to injure (the body) without breaking the skin; bruise. [C15: from L *contūsus* bruised, from *contundere* to grind, from *tundere* to beat] ▸**con'tusion** *n*

conundrum ❶ (kə'nʌndrəm) *n* **1** a riddle, esp. one whose answer makes a play on words. **2** a puzzling question or problem. [C16: from ?]

conurbation (ˌkɒnɜː'beɪʃən) *n* a large densely populated urban sprawl formed by the growth and coalescence of individual towns or cities. [C20: from CON- + *-urbation,* from L *urbs* city]

convalesce ❶ (ˌkɒnvə'lɛs) *vb* **convalesces, convalescing, convalesced.** (*intr*) to recover from illness, injury, or the aftereffects of a surgical operation. [C15: from L *convalēscere,* from *com-* (intensive) + *valēscere* to grow strong]

convalescence ❶ (ˌkɒnvə'lɛsəns) *n* **1** gradual return to health after illness, injury, or an operation. **2** the period during which such recovery occurs. ▸**ˌconva'lescent** *n, adj*

convection (kən'vɛkʃən) *n* **1** a process of heat transfer through a gas or liquid by bulk motion of hotter material into a cooler region. Cf. **conduction** (sense 1). **2** *Meteorol.* the process by which masses of relatively warm air are raised into the atmosphere, often cooling and forming clouds, with compensatory downward movements of cooler air. [C19: from LL *convectiō,* from L *convehere* to bring together, from *vehere* to carry] ▸**con'vectional** *adj* ▸**con'vective** *adj*

convector (kən'vɛktə) *n* a space-heating device from which heat is transferred to the surrounding air by convection.

convene ❶ (kən'viːn) *vb* **convenes, convening, convened. 1** to gather, call together or summon, esp. for a formal meeting. **2** (*tr*) to order to appear before a court of law, judge, tribunal, etc. [C15: from L *convenīre* to assemble, from *venīre* to come] ▸**con'venable** *adj*

convener *or* **convenor** (kən'viːnə) *n* **1** a person who convenes or chairs a meeting, committee, etc., esp. one who is specifically elected to do so: *a convener of shop stewards.* **2** the chairman and civic head of certain Scottish councils. Cf. **provost** (sense 2). ▸**con'venership** *or* **con'venorship** *n*

convenience ❶ (kən'viːnɪəns) *n* **1** the quality of being suitable or op-

THESAURUS

infraction, infringement, transgression, trespass, violation **2** = **conflict**, contradiction, counteraction, disputation, hindrance, impugnation, interference, rebuttal, refutation

contribute *vb* **1, 2** = **give**, add, afford, bestow, chip in (*inf.*), donate, furnish, provide, subscribe, supply **3** = **be partly responsible for**, be conducive to, be instrumental in, conduce to, help, lead to, tend to

contribution *n* **2** = **gift**, addition, bestowal, donation, grant, input, offering, stipend, subscription

contributor *n* **1** = **giver**, backer, bestower, conferrer, donor, patron, subscriber, supporter **4** = **writer**, correspondent, freelance, freelancer, journalist, journo, reporter

contrite *adj* **1** = **sorry**, chastened, conscience-stricken, humble, in sackcloth and ashes, penitent, regretful, remorseful, repentant, sorrowful

contriteness *n* **1** = **regret**, compunction, humiliation, penitence, remorse, repentance, self-reproach, sorrow

contrivance *n* **1** = **device**, apparatus, appliance, contraption, equipment, gadget, gear, implement, instrument, invention, machine, mechanism **4** = **plan**, artifice, design, dodge, expedient, fabrication, formation, intrigue, inventiveness, machination, measure, plot, project, ruse, scheme, stratagem, trick

contrive *vb* **1, 3** = **bring about**, arrange, effect, hit upon, manage, manoeuvre, plan, plot, scheme, succeed **2** = **devise**, concoct, construct, create, design, engineer, fabricate, frame, improvise, invent, manufacture, wangle (*inf.*)

contrived *adj* = **forced**, artificial, elaborate, laboured, overdone, planned, recherché, strained, unnatural

Antonyms *adj* genuine, natural, relaxed, spontaneous, unaffected, unconstrained, unfeigned, unforced, unpretentious

control *vb* **1** = **have power over**, administer, boss (*inf.*), call the shots, call the tune, command, conduct, direct, dominate, govern, handle, have charge of, have (someone) in one's pocket, hold the purse strings, keep a tight rein on, keep on a string, lead, manage, manipulate, oversee, pilot, reign over, rule, steer, superintend, supervise **2** = **restrain**, bridle, check, constrain, contain, curb, hold back, limit, master, rein in, repress, subdue ◆ *n* **7** = **power**, authority, charge, command, direction, discipline, government, guidance, jurisdiction, management, mastery, oversight, rule, superintendence, supervision, supremacy **8** = **restraint**, brake, check, curb, limitation, regulation **9** *often pl* = **instruments**, console, control panel, dash, dashboard, dials

controversial *adj* = **disputed**, at issue, contended, contentious, controvertible, debatable, disputable, open to question, polemic, under discussion

controversy *n* = **argument**, altercation, contention, debate, discussion, dispute, dissension, polemic, quarrel, row, squabble, strife, wrangle, wrangling

contusion *n Formal* = **bruise**, discoloration, injury, knock, swelling, trauma (*Pathology*)

conundrum *n* **1, 2** = **puzzle**, brain-teaser, enigma, poser, problem, riddle, teaser

convalesce *vb* = **recover**, improve, rally, recuperate, rehabilitate, rest

convalescence *n* **1** = **recovery**, improvement, recuperation, rehabilitation, return to health

convalescent *adj* **1** = **recovering**, getting better, improving, mending, on the mend, recuperating

convene *vb* **1** = **gather**, assemble, bring together, call, come together, congregate, convoke, meet, muster, rally, summon

convenience *n* **1** = **usefulness**, accessibility, advantage, appropriateness, availability, bene-

portune. **2** a convenient time or situation. **3** **at your convenience.** at a time suitable to you. **4** usefulness, comfort, or facility. **5** an object that is useful, esp. a labour-saving device. **6** *Euphemistic, chiefly Brit.* a lavatory, esp. a public one. **7** **make a convenience of.** to take advantage of; impose upon.

convenience food *n* food that needs little preparation, especially food that has been pre-prepared and preserved for long-term storage.

convenience store *n* a shop that has long opening hours, caters to local tastes, and is conveniently situated.

convenient ❶ (kən'viːnɪənt) *adj* **1** suitable; opportune. **2** easy to use. **3** close by; handy. [C14: from L *conveniēns,* from *convenīre* to be in accord with, from *venīre* to come]
▸**con'veniently** *adv*

convent ❶ ('kɒnvənt) *n* **1** a building inhabited by a religious community, usually of nuns. **2** the religious community inhabiting such a building. **3** Also called: **convent school.** a school in which the teachers are nuns. [C13: from OF, from L *conventus* meeting, from *convenīre;* see CONVENE]

conventicle (kən'ventɪkᵊl) *n* **1** a secret or unauthorized assembly for worship. **2** a small meeting house or chapel, esp. of Dissenters. [C14: from L *conventiculum,* from *conventus;* see CONVENT]

convention ❶ (kən'venʃən) *n* **1** a large formal assembly of a group with common interests, such as a trade union. **2** *US politics.* an assembly of delegates of one party to select candidates for office. **3** an international agreement second only to a treaty in formality. **4** any agreement or contract. **5** the established view of what is thought to be proper behaviour, good taste, etc. **6** an accepted rule, usage, etc.: *a convention used by printers.* **7** *Bridge.* a bid or play not to be taken at its face value, which one's partner can interpret according to a prearranged bidding system. [C15: from L *conventiō* an assembling]

conventional ❶ (kən'venʃənᵊl) *adj* **1** following the accepted customs and proprieties, esp. in a way that lacks originality. **2** established by accepted usage or general agreement. **3** of a convention or assembly. **4** *Visual arts.* conventionalized. **5** (of weapons, warfare, etc.) not nuclear.
▸**con'ventionalism** *n* ▸**con'ventionally** *adv*

conventionality (kən,venʃə'nælɪtɪ) *n, pl* **conventionalities. 1** the quality of being conventional. **2** (*often pl*) something conventional.

conventionalize *or* **conventionalise** (kən'venʃənə,laɪz) *vb* **conventionalizes, conventionalizing, conventionalized** *or* **conventionalises, conventionalising, conventionalised.** (*tr*) **1** to make conventional. **2** to simplify or stylize (a design, decorative device, etc.).
▸**con,ventionali'zation** *or* **con,ventionali'sation** *n*

conventual (kən'ventjʊəl) *adj* **1** of, belonging to, or characteristic of a convent. ◆ *n* **2** a member of a convent.
▸**con'ventually** *adv*

converge ❶ (kən'vɜːdʒ) *vb* **converges, converging, converged. 1** to move or cause to move towards the same point. **2** to meet or join. **3** (*intr*) (of opinions, effects, etc.) to tend towards a common conclusion or result. **4** (*intr*) *Maths.* (of an infinite series) to approach a finite limit as the number of terms increases. **5** (*intr*) (of animals and plants) to undergo convergence. [C17: from LL *convergere,* from L *com-* together + *vergere* to incline]
▸**con'vergent** *adj*

convergence ❶ (kən'vɜːdʒəns) *n* **1** Also: **convergency.** the act, degree, or a point of converging. **2** Also called: **convergent evolution.** the evolutionary development of a superficial resemblance between unrelated animals that occupy a similar environment, as in the evolution of wings in birds and bats.

convergent thinking *n Psychol.* analytical, usually deductive, thinking in which ideas are examined for their logical validity or in which a set of rules is followed, for example in arithmetic.

conversable (kən'vɜːsəbᵊl) *adj* **1** easy or pleasant to talk to. **2** able or inclined to talk.

conversant ❶ (kən'vɜːsᵊnt) *adj* (*usually postpositive* and foll. by *with*) experienced (in), familiar (with), or acquainted (with).
▸**con'versance** *or* **con'versancy** *n* ▸**con'versantly** *adv*

conversation ❶ (,kɒnvə'seɪʃən) *n* the interchange through speech of information, ideas, etc.; spoken communication.

conversational ❶ (,kɒnvə'seɪʃənᵊl) *adj* **1** of, using, or in the manner of conversation. **2** inclined to conversation; conversable.
▸**,conver'sationalist** *n* ▸**,conver'sationally** *adv*

conversation piece *n* **1** something, esp. an unusual object, that provokes conversation. **2** (esp. in 18th-century Britain) a group portrait in a landscape or domestic setting.

converse[1] ❶ *vb* (kən'vɜːs), **converses, conversing, conversed.** (*intr;* often foll. by *with*) **1** to engage in conversation (with). **2** to commune spiritually (with). ◆ *n* ('kɒnvɜːs). **3** conversation (often in **hold converse with**). [C16: from OF *converser,* from L *conversārī* to keep company with, from *conversāre* to turn constantly, from *vertere* to turn]
▸**con'verser** *n*

converse[2] ❶ ('kɒnvɜːs) *adj* **1** (*prenominal*) reversed; opposite; contrary. ◆ *n* **2** something that is opposite or contrary. **3** *Logic.* a categorial proposition obtained from another by the transposition of the subject and predicate, as *no bad man is bald* from *no bald man is bad.* [C16: from L *conversus* turned around; see CONVERSE[1]]
▸**con'versely** *adv*

conversion ❶ (kən'vɜːʃən) *n* **1a** a change or adaptation in form, character, or function. **1b** something changed in one of these respects. **2** a change to another belief, as in a change of religion. **3** alteration to the structure or fittings of a building undergoing a change in function or legal status. **4** *Maths.* a change in the units or form of a number or expression: *the conversion of miles to kilometres.* **5** *Rugby.* a score made after a try by kicking the ball over the crossbar from a place kick. **6** *Physics.* a change of fertile material to fissile material in a reactor. **7** an alteration to a car engine to improve its performance. [C14: from L *conversiō* a turning around; see CONVERT]

conversion disorder *n* a psychological disorder in which severe physical symptoms like blindness or paralysis appear with no apparent physical cause.

convert ❶ *vb* (kən'vɜːt). (*mainly tr*) **1** to change or adapt the form, character, or function of. **2** to cause (someone) to change in opinion, belief, etc. **3** (*intr*) to admit of being changed (into): *the table converts into a tray.* **4** (*also intr*) to change or be changed into another state: *to convert water into ice.* **5** *Law.* to assume unlawful proprietary rights over (personal property). **6** (*also intr*) *Rugby.* to make a conversion after (a try). **7** *Logic.* to transpose the subject and predicate of (a proposition). **8** to change (a value or measurement) from one system of units to another. **9** to exchange (a security or bond) for something of equivalent value. ◆ *n* ('kɒnvɜːt). **10** a person who has been converted to another belief, religion, etc. [C13: from OF, from L *convertere* to turn around, alter, from *vertere* to turn]

converter *or* **convertor** (kən'vɜːtə) *n* **1** a person or thing that converts. **2** *Physics.* **2a** a device for converting alternating current to direct current or vice versa. **2b** a device for converting a signal from one frequency to another. **3** a vessel in which molten metal is refined, using a blast of air or oxygen. **4** *Computing.* a device for converting one form of coded information to another, such as an analogue-to-digital converter.

converter reactor *n* a nuclear reactor for converting one fuel into another, esp. fertile material into fissionable material.

convertible ❶ (kən'vɜːtɪbᵊl) *adj* **1** capable of being converted. **2** (of a car) having a folding or removable roof. **3** *Finance.* **3a** (of a currency) freely exchangeable into other currencies. **3b** (of a paper currency)

THESAURUS

fit, fitness, handiness, opportuneness, serviceability, suitability, utility **2** = **suitable time**, chance, leisure, opportunity, spare moment, spare time **5** = **appliance**, amenity, comfort, facility, help, labour-saving device
Antonyms *n* ≠ **usefulness:** inconvenience, uselessness

convenient *adj* **1** = **useful**, adapted, appropriate, beneficial, commodious, fit, fitted, handy, helpful, labour-saving, opportune, seasonable, serviceable, suitable, suited, timely, well-timed **3** = **nearby**, accessible, at hand, available, close at hand, handy, just round the corner, within reach
Antonyms *adj* ≠ **useful:** awkward, inconvenient, unsuitable, useless ≠ **nearby:** distant, inaccessible, inconvenient, out-of-the-way

convent *n* **1, 2** = **nunnery**, religious community

convention *n* **1** = **assembly**, conference, congress, convocation, council, delegates, meeting, representatives **3, 4** = **agreement**, bargain, compact, concordat, contract, pact, protocol, stipulation, treaty **5** = **custom**, code, etiquette, formality, practice, propriety, protocol, tradition, usage

conventional *adj* **1** = **unoriginal**, banal, bourgeois, commonplace, hackneyed, hidebound, pedestrian, Pooterish, prosaic, routine, run-of-the-mill, stereotyped, vanilla (*sl.*) **2** = **ordinary**, accepted, bog-standard (*Brit. & Irish slang*), common, correct, customary, decorous, expected, formal, habitual, normal, orthodox, prevailing, prevalent, proper, regular, ritual, standard, traditional, usual, wonted
Antonyms *adj* ≠ **ordinary:** abnormal, left-field (*inf.*), off-the-wall (*sl.*), uncommon, unconventional, unorthodox

converge *vb* **1, 2** = **come together**, coincide, combine, concentrate, focus, gather, join, meet, merge, mingle

convergence *n* **1** = **meeting**, approach, blending, coincidence, concentration, concurrence, confluence, conflux, conjunction, junction, merging, mingling

conversant *adj, foll. by* **with** = **experienced in**, acquainted with, *au fait* with, familiar with, knowledgeable about, practised in, proficient in, skilled in, versed in, well-informed about, well up in (*inf.*)

conversation *n* = **talk**, chat, chinwag (*Brit. inf.*), colloquy, communication, communion, confab (*inf.*), confabulation, conference, converse, dialogue, discourse, discussion, exchange, gossip, intercourse, powwow, tête-à-tête

conversational *adj* **1, 2** = **chatty**, colloquial, communicative, informal

converse[1] *vb* **1** = **talk**, chat, commune, confer, discourse, exchange views ◆ *n* **3** = **talk**, chat, communication, conference, conversation, dialogue

converse[2] *adj* **1** = **opposite**, contrary, counter, reverse, reversed, transposed ◆ *n* **2** = **opposite**, antithesis, contrary, obverse, other side of the coin, reverse

conversion *n* **1a** = **change**, metamorphosis, transfiguration, transformation, transmogrification (*jocular*), transmutation **2** = **reformation**, change of heart, proselytization, rebirth, regeneration **3** = **adaptation**, alteration, modification, reconstruction, remodelling, reorganization

convert *vb* **1** = **adapt**, apply, appropriate, customize, modify, remodel, reorganize, restyle, revise **2** = **reform**, baptize, bring to God, convince, proselytize, regenerate, save **3** = **change**, alter, interchange, metamorphose, transform, transmogrify (*jocular*), transmute, transpose, turn ◆ *n* **10** = **neophyte**, catechumen, disciple, proselyte

convertible *adj* **1** = **adaptable**, adjustable, exchangeable, interchangeable

exchangeable on demand for precious metal to an equivalent value. **3c** (of a bond, debenture, etc.) able to be exchanged for a share on a specified date at a specified price. ◆ *n* **4** a car with a folding or removable roof. **5** any convertible document or currency.
▸**con,verti'bility** *n* ▸**con'vertibly** *adv*

convex ⓣ ('kɒnvɛks, kɒn'vɛks) *adj* **1** curving outwards. **2** having one or two surfaces curved or ground in the shape of a section of the exterior of a sphere, ellipsoid, etc.: *a convex lens.* [C16: from L *convexus* vaulted, rounded]
▸**con'vexity** *n* ▸**'convexly** *adv*

convexo-concave (kən,vɛksəʊkɒn'keɪv) *adj* **1** having one side convex and the other side concave. **2** (of a lens) having a convex face with greater curvature than the concave face.

convexo-convex *adj* (esp. of a lens) having both sides convex; biconvex.

convey ⓣ (kən'veɪ) *vb* (*tr*) **1** to take, carry, or transport from one place to another. **2** to communicate (a message, information, etc.). **3** (of a channel, path, etc.) to conduct or transfer. **4** *Law.* to transfer (the title to property). [C13: from OF *conveier,* from Med. L *conviāre* to escort, from L *com-* with + *via* way]
▸**con'veyable** *adj*

conveyance ⓣ (kən'veɪəns) *n* **1** the act of conveying. **2** a means of transport. **3** *Law.* **3a** a transfer of the legal title to property. **3b** the document effecting such a transfer.
▸**con'veyancer** *n* ▸**con'veyancing** *n*

conveyor *or* **conveyer** (kən'veɪə) *n* **1** a person or thing that conveys. **2** short for **conveyor belt.**

conveyor belt *n* a flexible endless strip of fabric or linked plates driven by rollers and used to transport objects, esp. in a factory.

convict ⓣ *vb* (kən'vɪkt). (*tr*) **1** to pronounce (someone) guilty of an offence. ◆ *n* ('kɒnvɪkt). **2** a person found guilty of an offence against the law. **3** a person serving a prison sentence. [C14: from L *convictus* convicted, from *convincere* to prove guilty, CONVINCE]

conviction ⓣ (kən'vɪkʃən) *n* **1** the state of being convinced. **2** a firmly held belief, opinion, etc. **3** the act of convincing. **4** the act of convicting or the state of being convicted. **5 carry conviction.** to be convincing.
▸**con'victional** *adj* ▸**con'victive** *adj*

convince ⓣ (kən'vɪns) *vb* **convinces, convincing, convinced.** (*tr*) (*may take a clause as object*) to make (someone) agree, understand, or realize the truth or validity of something; persuade. [C16: from L *convincere* to demonstrate incontrovertibly, from *com-* (intensive) + *vincere* to overcome]
▸**con'vincer** *n* ▸**con'vincible** *adj* ▸**con'vincing** *adj* ▸**con'vincingly** *adv*

> **USAGE NOTE** The use of *convince* to talk about persuading someone to do something is considered by many British speakers to be wrong or unacceptable.

convivial ⓣ (kən'vɪvɪəl) *adj* sociable; jovial or festive: *a convivial atmosphere.* [C17: from LL *convīviālis,* from L *convīvium,* a living together, banquet, from *vīvere* to live]
▸**con,vivi'ality** *n*

convocation ⓣ (,kɒnvə'keɪʃən) *n* **1** a large formal assembly. **2** the act of convoking or state of being convoked. **3** *Church of England.* either of the synods of the provinces of Canterbury or York. **4** *Episcopal Church.* an assembly of the clergy and part of the laity of a diocese. **5** (*sometimes cap.*) (in some British universities) a legislative assembly. **6** (in Australia and New Zealand) the graduate membership of a university.
▸**,convo'cational** *adj*

convoke ⓣ (kən'vəʊk) *vb* **convokes, convoking, convoked.** (*tr*) to call (a meeting, assembly, etc.) together; summon. [C16: from L *convocāre,* from *vocāre* to call]
▸**con'voker** *n*

convolute ('kɒnvə,luːt) *vb* **convolutes, convoluting, convoluted.** (*tr*) **1** to form into a twisted, coiled, or rolled shape. ◆ *adj* **2** *Bot.* rolled longitudinally upon itself: *a convolute petal.* [C18: from L *convolūtus,* from *convolvere* to roll together, from *volvere* to turn]

convoluted ('kɒnvə,luːtɪd) *adj* **1** (esp. of meaning, style, etc.) difficult to comprehend; involved. **2** coiled.
▸**'convo,lutedly** *adv*

convolution ⓣ (,kɒnvə'luːʃən) *n* **1** a turn, twist, or coil. **2** an intricate or confused matter or condition. **3** any of the numerous convex folds of the surface of the brain.
▸**,convo'lutional** *or* **,convo'lutionary** *adj*

convolve (kən'vɒlv) *vb* **convolves, convolving, convolved.** to wind or roll together; coil; twist. [C16: from L *convolvere;* see CONVOLUTE]

convolvulus (kən'vɒlvjʊləs) *n, pl* **convolvuluses** *or* **convolvuli** (-,laɪ). a twining herbaceous plant having funnel-shaped flowers and triangular leaves. [C16: from L: bindweed; see CONVOLUTE]

convoy ⓣ ('kɒnvɔɪ) *n* **1** a group of merchant ships with an escort of warships. **2** a group of land vehicles assembled to travel together. **3** the act of travelling or escorting by convoy (esp. in **in convoy**). ◆ *vb* **4** (*tr*) to escort while in transit. [C14: from OF *convoier* to CONVEY]

convulse ⓣ (kən'vʌls) *vb* **convulses, convulsing, convulsed. 1** (*tr*) to shake or agitate violently. **2** (*tr*) to cause (muscles) to undergo violent spasms or contractions. **3** (*intr; often foll. by with*) *Inf.* to shake or be overcome (with violent emotion, esp. laughter). **4** (*tr*) to disrupt the normal running of (a country, etc.): *student riots have convulsed India.* [C17: from L *convulsus,* from *convellere,* from *vellere* to pluck, pull]
▸**con'vulsive** *adj* ▸**con'vulsively** *adv*

convulsion ⓣ (kən'vʌlʃən) *n* **1** a violent involuntary muscular contraction. **2** a violent upheaval, esp. a social one. **3** (*usually pl*) *Inf.* uncontrollable laughter: *I was in convulsions.*

cony *or* **coney** ('kəʊnɪ) *n, pl* **conies** *or* **coneys. 1** a rabbit or fur made from the skin of a rabbit. **2** (in the Bible) another name for the **hyrax.** [C13: back formation from *conies,* from OF *conis,* pl. of *conil,* from L *cunīculus* rabbit]

coo (kuː) *vb* **coos, cooing, cooed. 1** (*intr*) (of doves, pigeons, etc.) to make a characteristic soft throaty call. **2** (*tr*) to speak in a soft murmur. **3** (*intr*) to murmur lovingly (esp. in **bill and coo**). ◆ *n* **4** the sound of cooing. ◆ *interj* **5** *Brit. sl.* an exclamation of surprise, awe, etc.
▸**'cooing** *adj, n* ▸**'cooingly** *adv*

cooee *or* **cooey** ('kuːiː) *interj* **1** a call used to attract attention, esp. a long loud high-pitched call on two notes. ◆ *vb* **cooees, cooeeing, cooeed** *or* **cooeys, cooeying, cooeyed. 2** (*intr*) to utter this call. ◆ *n* **3** *Austral. & NZ inf.* calling distance (esp. in **within (a) cooee (of)**). [C19: from Abor.]

cook (kʊk) *vb* **1** to prepare (food) by the action of heat, or (of food) to become ready for eating through such a process. Related adj: **culinary. 2** to subject or be subjected to intense heat: *the town cooked in the sun.* **3** (*tr*) *Sl.* to alter or falsify (figures, accounts, etc.): *to cook the books.* **4** (*tr*) *Sl.* to spoil (something). **5** (*intr*) *Sl.* to happen (esp. in **what's cooking?**). ◆ *n* **6** a person who prepares food for eating. ◆ See also **cook up.** [OE *cōc* (n), from L *coquus* a cook, from *coquere* to cook]
▸**'cookable** *adj*

cook-chill *n* a method of food preparation used by caterers, in which cooked dishes are chilled rapidly and reheated as required.

cooker ('kʊkə) *n* **1** an apparatus heated by gas, electricity, oil, or solid fuel, for cooking food. **2** *Brit.* another name for **cooking apple.**

cookery ('kʊkərɪ) *n* **1** the art, study, or practice of cooking. **2** *US.* a place for cooking.

cookery book *or* **cookbook** ('kʊk,bʊk) *n* a book containing recipes.

cook-general *n, pl* **cooks-general.** *Brit.* (formerly, esp. in the 1920s and 30s) a domestic servant who did cooking and housework.

cookie *or* **cooky** ('kʊkɪ) *n, pl* **cookies. 1** the US and Canad. word for **biscuit. 2** *Inf.* a person: *smart cookie.* **3 that's the way the cookie crumbles.** *Inf.* matters are inevitably so. [C18: from Du. *koekje,* dim. of *koek* cake]

cooking apple *n* any large sour apple used in cooking.

cook shop *n* **1** *Brit.* a shop that sells cookery equipment. **2** *US.* a restaurant.

Cook's tour (kʊks) *n Inf.* a rapid but extensive tour or survey of anything. [C19: after Thomas Cook (1808–92), E travel agent]

cook up ⓣ *vb* (*tr, adv*) **1** *Inf.* to concoct or invent (a story, alibi, etc.). **2** to prepare (a meal), esp. quickly. **3** *Sl.* to prepare (a drug) for use by heating, as by dissolving heroin in a spoon.

THESAURUS

convex *adj* **1** = **rounded**, bulging, gibbous, outcurved, protuberant
Antonyms *adj* concave, cupped, depressed, excavated, hollowed, indented, sunken

convey *vb* **1** = **carry**, bear, bring, conduct, fetch, forward, grant, guide, move, send, support, transmit, transport **2** = **communicate**, disclose, impart, make known, relate, reveal, tell **4** *Law* = **transfer**, bequeath, cede, deliver, demise, devolve, grant, lease, will

conveyance *n* **1** = **transportation**, carriage, movement, transfer, transference, transmission, transport **2** *Old-fashioned* = **vehicle**, transport

convict *vb* **1** = **find guilty**, condemn, imprison, pronounce guilty, sentence ◆ *n* **2, 3** = **prisoner**, con (*sl.*), criminal, culprit, felon, jailbird, lag (*sl.*), malefactor, villain

conviction *n* **1** = **confidence**, assurance, certainty, certitude, earnestness, fervour, firmness, reliance **2** = **belief**, creed, faith, opinion, persuasion, principle, tenet, view

convince *vb* = **persuade**, assure, bring round, gain the confidence of, prevail upon, prove to, satisfy, sway, win over

convincing *adj* = **persuasive**, cogent, conclusive, credible, impressive, incontrovertible, likely, plausible, powerful, probable, telling, verisimilar
Antonyms *adj* beyond belief, cock-and-bull (*inf.*), dubious, far-fetched, implausible, improbable, inconclusive, incredible, unconvincing, unlikely

convivial *adj* = **sociable**, back-slapping, cheerful, festive, friendly, fun-loving, gay, genial, hearty, hilarious, jolly, jovial, lively, merry, mirthful

conviviality *n* = **sociability**, bonhomie, cheer, cordiality, festivity, gaiety, geniality, good fellowship, jollification, jollity, joviality, liveliness, merrymaking, mirth

convocation *n* **1** *Formal* = **meeting**, assemblage, assembly, conclave, concourse, congregation, congress, convention, council, diet, synod

convoke *vb Formal* = **call together**, assemble, collect, convene, gather, muster, summon

convolution *n* **1** = **twist**, coil, coiling, complexity, contortion, curlicue, helix, intricacy, involution, loop, sinuosity, sinuousness, spiral, tortuousness, undulation, winding

convoy *vb* **4** = **escort**, accompany, attend, guard, pilot, protect, shepherd, usher

convulse *vb* **1** = **shake**, agitate, churn up, derange, disorder, disturb, shatter, twist, work

convulsion *n* **1** = **spasm**, contortion, contraction, cramp, fit, paroxysm, seizure, throe (*rare*), tremor **2** = **upheaval**, agitation, commotion, disturbance, furore, shaking, tumult, turbulence

convulsive *adj* **1** = **jerky**, churning, fitful, paroxysmal, spasmodic, sporadic, violent

cook up *vb* **1** *Informal* = **invent**, concoct, con-

cool Ⓣ (kuːl) *adj* **1** moderately cold: *a cool day.* **2** comfortably free of heat: *a cool room.* **3** calm: *a cool head.* **4** lacking in enthusiasm, cordiality, etc.: *a cool welcome.* **5** calmly impudent. **6** *Inf.* (of sums of money, etc.) without exaggeration; actual: *a cool ten thousand.* **7** (of a colour) having violet, blue, or green predominating; cold. **8** (of jazz) economical and rhythmically relaxed. **9** *Inf.* sophisticated or elegant; unruffled. **10** *Inf., chiefly US & Canad.* marvellous. ◆ *n* **11** coolness: *the cool of the evening.* **12** *Sl.* calmness; composure (esp. in **keep** *or* **lose one's cool**). **13** *Sl.* unruffled elegance or sophistication. ◆ *vb* **14** (usually foll. by *down* or *off*) to make or become cooler. **15** (usually foll. by *down* or *off*) to lessen the intensity of (anger or excitement) or (of anger or excitement) to become less intense; calm down. **16 cool it.** (*usually imperative*) *Sl.* to calm down. [OE *cōl*]
▸**'coolly** *adv* ▸**'coolness** *n*

coolant ('kuːlənt) *n* **1** a fluid used to cool a system or to transfer heat from one part of it to another. **2** a liquid used to lubricate and cool the workpiece and cutting tool during machining.

cool bag *or* **box** *n* an insulated container for keeping food cool.

cool-down *n* another name for **warm-down.**

cool drink *n S. African.* a soft drink.

cooler ('kuːlə) *n* **1** a container, vessel, or apparatus for cooling, such as a heat exchanger. **2** a slang word for **prison. 3** a drink consisting of wine, fruit juice, and carbonated water.

coolibah *or* **coolabah** ('kuːləˌbɑː) *n* an Australian eucalyptus that grows along rivers and has smooth bark and long narrow leaves. [from Abor.]

coolie *or* **cooly** ('kuːlɪ) *n, pl* **coolies.** an unskilled Oriental labourer. [C17: from Hindi *kulī*]

cooling-off period *n* **1** a period during which the contending sides to a dispute reconsider their options before taking further action. **2** *Brit.* a period, often 14 days, that begins when a sale contract or life-assurance policy is received by a member of the public, during which the contract or policy can be cancelled without loss.

cooling tower *n* a tall, hollow structure, designed to permit free passage of air, inside which hot water trickles down, becoming cool as it does so: the water is normally reused as part of an industrial process.

coomb, combe, coombe, *or* **comb** (kuːm) *n* **1** *Chiefly southern English.* a short valley or deep hollow. **2** *Chiefly northern English.* another name for a **cirque.** [OE *cumb*]

coon (kuːn) *n* **1** *Inf.* short for **raccoon. 2** *Offens. sl.* a Black or a native Australian. **3** *S. African offens.* a person of mixed race.

coonskin ('kuːnˌskɪn) *n* **1** the pelt of a raccoon. **2** a raccoon cap with the tail hanging at the back. **3** *US.* an overcoat made of raccoon.

coop[1] Ⓣ (kuːp) *n* **1** a cage or small enclosure for poultry or small animals. **2** a small narrow place of confinement, esp. a prison cell. **3** a wicker basket for catching fish. ◆ *vb* **4** (*tr;* often foll. by *up* or *in*) to confine in a restricted area. [C15: prob. from MLow G *kūpe* basket]

coop[2] *or* **co-op** ('kəʊˌɒp) *n* a cooperative society or a shop run by a cooperative society.

cooper ('kuːpə) *n* **1** a person skilled in making and repairing barrels, casks, etc. ◆ *vb* **2** (*tr*) to make or mend (barrels, casks, etc.). [C13: from MDu. *cūper* or MLow G *kūper;* see COOP[1]]

cooperage ('kuːpərɪdʒ) *n* **1** Also called: **coopery.** the craft, place of work, or products of a cooper. **2** the labour fee charged by a cooper.

cooperate Ⓣ *or* **co-operate** (kəʊ'ɒpəˌreɪt) *vb* **cooperates, cooperating, cooperated** *or* **co-operates, co-operating, co-operated.** (*intr*) **1** to work or act together. **2** to be of assistance or be willing to assist. **3** *Econ.* to engage in economic cooperation. [C17: from LL *cooperārī* to combine, from L *operārī* to work]
▸**co'operˌator** *or* **co-'operˌator** *n*

cooperation Ⓣ *or* **co-operation** (kəʊˌɒpə'reɪʃən) *n* **1** joint operation or action. **2** assistance or willingness to assist. **3** *Econ.* the combination of consumers, workers, etc., in activities usually embracing production, distribution, or trade.
▸**coˌoper'ationist** *or* **co-ˌoper'ationist** *n*

cooperative Ⓣ *or* **co-operative** (kəʊ'ɒpərətɪv, -'ɒprə-) *adj* **1** willing to cooperate; helpful. **2** acting in conjunction with others; cooperating. **3a** (of an enterprise, farm, etc.) owned collectively and managed for joint economic benefit. **3b** (of an economy) based on collective ownership and cooperative use of the means of production and distribution. ◆ *n* **4** a cooperative organization, such as a farm.

cooperative society *n* a commercial enterprise owned and managed by and for the benefit of customers or workers.

coopt Ⓣ *or* **co-opt** (kəʊ'ɒpt) *vb* (*tr*) to add (someone) to a committee, board, etc., by the agreement of the existing members. [C17: from L *cooptāre,* from *optāre* to choose]
▸**co'option, co-'option** *or* **ˌcoop'tation, ˌco-op'tation** *n*

coordinate Ⓣ *or* **co-ordinate** *vb* (kəʊ'ɔːdɪˌneɪt), **coordinates, coordinating, coordinated** *or* **co-ordinates, co-ordinating, co-ordinated. 1** (*tr*) to integrate (diverse elements) in a harmonious operation. **2** to place (things) in the same class, or (of things) to be placed in the same class, etc. **3** (*intr*) to work together harmoniously. **4** (*intr*) to take or be in the form of a harmonious order. ◆ *n* (kəʊ'ɔːdɪnɪt). **5** *Maths.* any of a set of numbers that defines the location of a point with reference to a system of axes. **6** a person or thing equal in rank, type, etc. ◆ *adj* (kəʊ'ɔːdɪnɪt). **7** of or involving coordination. **8** of the same rank, type, etc. **9** of or involving the use of coordinates: *coordinate geometry.* **10** *Chem.* denoting a type of covalent bond in which both the shared electrons are provided by one of the atoms.
▸**co'ordinative** *or* **co-'ordinative** *adj* ▸**co'ordiˌnator** *or* **co-'ordiˌnator** *n*

coordinate clause *n* one of two or more clauses in a sentence having the same status and introduced by coordinating conjunctions.

coordinates (kəʊ'ɔːdɪnɪts) *pl n* clothes of matching or harmonious colours and design, suitable for wearing together.

coordinating conjunction *n* a conjunction that introduces coordinate clauses, such as *and, but,* and *or.*

coordination *or* **co-ordination** (kəʊˌɔːdɪ'neɪʃən) *n* balanced and effective interaction of movement, actions, etc. [C17: from LL *coordinātiō,* from L *ordinātiō* an arranging]

coot (kuːt) *n* **1** an aquatic bird of Europe and Asia, having dark plumage, and a white bill with a frontal shield: family Rallidae (rails, etc.). **2** a foolish person, esp. an old man. [C14: prob. from Low G]

cootie ('kuːtɪ) *n US & NZ.* a slang name for the body louse. [C20: from Maori & ? (for US) Malay *kutu* louse]

cop[1] (kɒp) *Sl.* ◆ *n* **1** another name for **policeman. 2** *Brit.* an arrest (esp. in **a fair cop**). ◆ *vb* **cops, copping, copped.** (*tr*) **3** to catch. **4** to steal. **5** to suffer (a punishment): *you'll cop a clout if you do that!* **6 cop it sweet.** *Austral. sl.* **6a** to accept a punishment without complaint. **6b** to have good fortune. **7 cop this!** just look at this! ◆ See also **cop out.** [C18: (vb) ?from obs. *cap* to arrest, from OF *caper* to seize]

cop[2] (kɒp) *n* **1** a conical roll of thread wound on a spindle. **2** *Now chiefly dialect.* the top or crest, as of a hill. [OE *cop, copp* top, summit]

cop[3] (kɒp) *n Brit. sl.* (*usually used with a negative*) value: *not much cop.* [C19: n use of COP[1]]

copal ('kəʊpᵊl, -pæl) *n* a hard aromatic resin obtained from various tropical trees and used in making varnishes and lacquers. [C16: from Sp., from Nahuatl *copalli*]

copartner (kəʊ'pɑːtnə) *n* a partner or associate, esp. an equal partner in business.
▸**co'partnership** *n*

THESAURUS

trive, devise, dream up, fabricate, improvise, manufacture, plot, prepare, scheme, trump up

cool *adj* **1 = cold,** chilled, chilling, chilly, coldish, nippy, refreshing **3 = calm,** collected, composed, deliberate, dispassionate, imperturbable, laid-back (*inf.*), level-headed, placid, quiet, relaxed, sedate, self-controlled, self-possessed, serene, together (*sl.*), unemotional, unexcited, unfazed (*inf.*), unruffled **4 = unfriendly,** aloof, apathetic, distant, frigid, incurious, indifferent, lukewarm, offhand, reserved, standoffish, uncommunicative, unconcerned, unenthusiastic, uninterested, unresponsive, unwelcoming **5 = impudent,** audacious, bold, brazen, cheeky, impertinent, presumptuous, shameless **9** *Informal* **= sophisticated,** cosmopolitan, elegant, urbane ◆ *n* **12** *Slang* **= calmness,** composure, control, poise, self-control, self-discipline, self-possession, temper ◆ *vb* **14 = chill,** cool off, freeze, lose heat, refrigerate **15 = calm (down),** abate, allay, assuage, dampen, lessen, moderate, quiet, temper

Antonyms *adj* ≠ **cold:** lukewarm, moderately hot, sunny, tepid, warm ≠ **calm:** agitated, delirious, excited, impassioned, nervous, overwrought, perturbed, tense, troubled, twitchy (*inf.*) ≠ **unfriendly:** amiable, chummy (*inf.*), cordial, friendly, outgoing, receptive, responsive, sociable, warm ◆ *vb* ≠ **chill:** heat, reheat, take the chill off, thaw, warm (up)

coolness *n* **1 = coldness,** chilliness, freshness, nippiness **3 = calmness,** collectedness, composedness, composure, control, deliberateness, dispassionateness, imperturbability, level-headedness, placidity, placidness, quietness, sedateness, self-control, self-discipline, self-possession **4 = unfriendliness,** aloofness, apathy, distantness, frigidity, frigidness, frostiness, impassiveness, impassivity, incuriosity, incuriousness, indifference, lukewarmness, offhandedness, poise, remoteness, reservedness, standoffishness, uncommunicativeness, unconcernedness, uninterestedness, unresponsiveness **5 = impudence,** audaciousness, audacity, boldness, brazenness, cheekiness, impertinence, insolence, presumptuousness, shamelessness **9** *Informal* **= sophistication,** elegance, urbanity

Antonyms *n* ≠ **coldness:** sunniness, tepidness, warmness ≠ **calmness:** agitation, deliriousness, discomposure, disconcertedness, excitedness, impassionedness, nervousness, perturbation, tenseness, twitchiness (*inf.*) ≠ **unfriendliness:** affability, amiability, amiableness, chumminess (*inf.*), cordiality, friendliness, geniality, receptiveness, receptivity, responsiveness, sociability, sociableness, warmth

coop[1] *n* **1 = pen,** box, cage, corral (*chiefly U.S. & Canad.*), enclosure, hutch, pound ◆ *vb* **4 coop up = confine,** cage, immure, impound, imprison, pen, pound, shut up

cooperate *vb* **1 = work together,** collaborate, combine, concur, conduce, conspire, coordinate, join forces, pool resources, pull together **2 = help,** abet, aid, assist, contribute, go along with, lend a helping hand, pitch in, play ball (*inf.*)

Antonyms *vb* ≠ **work together, help:** conflict, contend with, fight, hamper, hamstring, hinder, impede, obstruct, oppose, prevent, put the mockers on (*inf.*), resist, struggle against, stymie, thwart

cooperation *n* **1 = teamwork,** collaboration, combined effort, concert, concurrence, esprit de corps, give-and-take, unity **2 = help,** assistance, helpfulness, participation, responsiveness

Antonyms *n* ≠ **teamwork, help:** discord, dissension, hindrance, opposition, rivalry

cooperative *adj* **1 = helpful,** accommodating, obliging, onside (*inf.*), responsive, supportive **2 = shared,** coactive, collective, combined, concerted, coordinated, joint, unified, united

coopt *vb* **= appoint,** choose, elect

coordinate *vb* **1 = bring together,** correlate, harmonize, integrate, match, mesh, organize,

cope[1] ➊ (kəʊp) *vb* **copes, coping, coped.** (*intr*) **1** (foll. by *with*) to contend (against). **2** to deal successfully (with); manage: *she coped well with the problem.* [C14: from OF *coper* to strike, cut, from *coup* blow]

cope[2] (kəʊp) *n* **1** a large ceremonial cloak worn at liturgical functions by priests of certain Christian sects. **2** any covering shaped like a cope. ◆ *vb* **copes, coping, coped. 3** (*tr*) to dress (someone) in a cope. [OE *cāp,* from Med. L *cāpa,* from LL *cappa* hooded cloak]

cope[3] (kəʊp) *vb* **copes, coping, coped.** (*tr*) **1** to provide (a wall, etc.) with a coping. ◆ *n* **2** another name for **coping.** [C17: prob. from F *couper* to cut]

copeck (ˈkəʊpɛk) *n* a variant spelling of **kopeck.**

Copenhagen interpretation (ˌkəʊpənˈheɪgən, -ˈhɑː-; ˈkəʊpənˌheɪ-, -ˌhɑː-) *n* an interpretation of quantum mechanics developed by Niels Bohr (1885–1962) and his colleagues at the University of Copenhagen, based on the concept of wave–particle duality and the idea that the observation influences the result of an experiment.

copepod (ˈkəʊpɪˌpɒd) *n* a minute marine or freshwater crustacean, an important constituent of plankton. [C19: from NL *copepoda,* from Gk *kōpē* oar + *pous* foot]

coper (ˈkəʊpə) *n* a horse dealer. [C17 (a dealer): from dialect *cope* to buy, barter, from Low G]

Copernican system (kəˈpɜːnɪkən) *n* the theory published in 1543 by Copernicus (1473–1543), Polish astronomer, which stated that the earth and the planets rotated round the sun.

copestone (ˈkəʊpˌstəʊn) *n* **1** Also called: **coping stone.** a stone used to form a coping. **2** the stone at the top of a building, wall, etc.

copier (ˈkɒpɪə) *n* a person or device that copies.

copilot (ˈkəʊˌpaɪlət) *n* a second or relief pilot of an aircraft.

coping (ˈkəʊpɪŋ) *n* the sloping top course of a wall, usually made of masonry or brick.

coping saw *n* a handsaw with a U-shaped frame used for cutting curves in a material too thick for a fret saw.

copious ➊ (ˈkəʊpɪəs) *adj* **1** abundant; extensive. **2** having an abundant supply. **3** full of words, ideas, etc.; profuse. [C14: from L *cōpiōsus,* from *cōpia* abundance]
▸ˈ**copiously** *adv* ▸ˈ**copiousness** *n*

coplanar (kəʊˈpleɪnə) *adj* lying in the same plane: *coplanar lines.*
▸ˌ**coplaˈnarity** *n*

copolymer (kəʊˈpɒlɪmə) *n* a chemical compound of high molecular weight formed by uniting the molecules of two or more different compounds (monomers).

cop out ➊ *Sl.* ◆ *vb* **1** (*intr, adv*) to fail to assume responsibility or fail to perform. ◆ *n* **cop-out. 2** a way or an instance of avoiding responsibility or commitment. [C20: prob. from COP[1]]

copper[1] (ˈkɒpə) *n* **1** a malleable reddish metallic element occurring as the free metal, copper glance, and copper pyrites: used in such alloys as brass and bronze. Symbol: Cu; atomic no.: 29; atomic wt.: 63.54. Related adjs.: **cupric, cuprous. 2a** the reddish-brown colour of copper. **2b** (*as adj*) *copper hair.* **3** *Inf.* any copper or bronze coin. **4** *Chiefly Brit.* a large vessel, formerly of copper, used for boiling or washing. **5** any of various small widely distributed butterflies having reddish-brown wings. ◆ *vb* **6** (*tr*) to coat or cover with copper. [OE *coper,* from L *Cyprium aes* Cyprian metal, from Gk *Kupris* Cyprus]

copper[2] (ˈkɒpə) *n* a slang word for **policeman.** Often shortened to **cop.** [C19: from COP[1] (vb)]

copperas (ˈkɒpərəs) *n* a less common name for **ferrous sulphate.** [C14 *coperose,* via OF from Med. L *cuperosa,* ? orig. in *aqua cuprosa* copper water]

copper beech *n* a cultivated variety of European beech that has reddish leaves.

copper-bottomed *adj* reliable, esp. financially reliable. [from the practice of coating bottom of ships with copper to prevent the timbers rotting]

copper-fasten *vb* (*tr*) *Irish.* to make (a bargain or agreement) binding.

copperhead (ˈkɒpəˌhɛd) *n* **1** a venomous pit viper of the US, with a reddish-brown head. **2** a venomous marsh snake of Australia, with a reddish band behind the head.

copperplate (ˈkɒpəˌpleɪt) *n* **1** a polished copper plate on which a design has been etched or engraved. **2** a print taken from such a plate. **3** a fine handwriting based upon that used on copperplate engravings.

copper pyrites (ˈpaɪraɪts) *n* (*functioning as sing*) another name for **chalcopyrite.**

coppersmith (ˈkɒpəˌsmɪθ) *n* a person who works in copper.

copper sulphate *n* a copper salt found naturally and made by the action of sulphuric acid on copper oxide: used as a mordant, in electroplating, and in plant sprays. Formula: $CuSO_4$.

coppice (ˈkɒpɪs) *n* **1** a dense growth of small trees or bushes, esp. one regularly trimmed back so that a continual supply of small poles and firewood is obtained. ◆ *vb* **coppices, coppicing, coppiced. 2** (*tr*) to trim back (trees or bushes) to form a coppice. [C14: from OF *copeiz*]
▸ˈ**coppiced** *adj*

copra (ˈkɒprə) *n* the dried, oil-yielding kernel of the coconut. [C16: from Port., from Malayalam *koppara* coconut]

copro- *or before a vowel* **copr-** *combining form.* indicating dung or obscenity, as in **copˈrology** *n* preoccupation with excrement, **copˈrophagous** *adj* feeding on dung. [from Gk *kopros* dung]

copse (kɒps) *n* another word for **coppice** (sense 1). [C16: from COPPICE]

Copt (kɒpt) *n* **1** a member of the Coptic Church. **2** an Egyptian descended from the ancient Egyptians. [C17: from Ar., from Coptic *kyptios* Egyptian, from Gk *Aiguptios,* from *Aiguptos* Egypt]

Coptic (ˈkɒptɪk) *n* **1** an Afro-Asiatic language, written in the Greek alphabet but descended from ancient Egyptian. Extinct as a spoken language, it survives in the Coptic Church. ◆ *adj* **2** of this language. **3** of the Copts.

Coptic Church *n* the ancient Christian Church of Egypt.

copula (ˈkɒpjʊlə) *n, pl* **copulas** *or* **copulae** (-ˌliː). **1** a verb, such as *be, seem,* or *taste,* that is used to identify or link the subject with the complement of a sentence, as in *he became king, sugar tastes sweet.* **2** anything that serves as a link. [C17: from L: bond, from *co-* together + *apere* to fasten]
▸ˈ**copular** *adj*

copulate ➊ (ˈkɒpjʊˌleɪt) *vb* **copulates, copulating, copulated.** (*intr*) to perform sexual intercourse. [C17: from L *copulāre* to join together; see COPULA]
▸ˌ**copuˈlation** *n* ▸ˈ**copulatory** *adj*

copulative (ˈkɒpjʊlətɪv) *adj* **1** serving to join or unite. **2** of copulation. **3** *Grammar.* (of a verb) having the nature of a copula.

copy ➊ (ˈkɒpɪ) *n, pl* **copies. 1** an imitation or reproduction of an original. **2** a single specimen of something that occurs in a multiple edition, such as a book. **3a** matter to be reproduced in print. **3b** written matter or text as distinct from graphic material in books, etc. **4** the words used to present a promotional message in an advertisement. **5** *Journalism, inf.* suitable material for an article: *disasters are always good copy.* **6** *Arch.* a model to be copied, esp. an example of penmanship. ◆ *vb* **copies, copying, copied. 7** (when *tr,* often foll. by *out*) to make a copy (of). **8** (*tr*) to imitate as a model. **9** to imitate unfairly. [C14: from Med. L *cōpia* an imitation, from L: abundance]

copybook (ˈkɒpɪˌbʊk) *n* **1** a book of specimens, esp. of penmanship, for imitation. **2** *Chiefly US.* a book for or containing documents. **3 blot one's copybook.** *Inf.* to spoil one's reputation by a mistake or indiscretion. **4** (*modifier*) trite or unoriginal.

copycat (ˈkɒpɪˌkæt) *n Inf.* **a** a person, esp. a child, who imitates or copies another. **b** (*as modifier*): *copycat murders.*

copyhold (ˈkɒpɪˌhəʊld) *n Law.* (formerly) a tenure less than freehold of land in England evidenced by a copy of the Court roll.

copyist (ˈkɒpɪɪst) *n* **1** a person who makes written copies. **2** a person who imitates.

copyreader (ˈkɒpɪˌriːdə) *n US.* a person who edits and prepares newspaper copy for publication; subeditor.

copyright (ˈkɒpɪˌraɪt) *n* **1** the exclusive right to produce copies and to control an original literary, musical, or artistic work, granted by law for a specified number of years. ◆ *adj* **2** (of a work, etc.) subject to copyright. ◆ *vb* **3** (*tr*) to take out a copyright on.

copy typist *n* a typist whose job is to type from written or typed drafts rather than dictation.

copywriter (ˈkɒpɪˌraɪtə) *n* a person employed to write advertising copy.
▸ˈ**copyˌwriting** *n*

coquet ➊ (kəʊˈkɛt, kɒ-) *vb* **coquets, coquetting, coquetted.** (*intr*) **1** to behave flirtatiously. **2** to dally or trifle. [C17: from F: a gallant, lit.: a little cock, from *coq* cock]
▸ˈ**coquetry** *n*

coquette ➊ (kəʊˈkɛt, kɒ-) *n* **1** a woman who flirts. **2** any hummingbird of the genus *Lophornis.* [C17: from F, fem of COQUET]
▸**coˈquettish** *adj* ▸**coˈquettishness** *n*

THESAURUS

relate, synchronize, systematize ◆ *adj* **8** = **equivalent**, coequal, correlative, correspondent, equal, parallel, tantamount

cope[1] *vb* **1** *foll. by* **with** = **deal with**, contend with, dispatch, encounter, grapple with, handle, struggle with, tangle with, tussle with, weather, wrestle with **2** = **manage**, carry on, get by, hold one's own, make out (*inf.*), make the grade, rise to the occasion, struggle through, survive

copious *adj* **1-3** = **abundant**, ample, bounteous, bountiful, extensive, exuberant, full, generous, lavish, liberal, luxuriant, overflowing, plenteous, plentiful, profuse, rich, superabundant

copiousness *n* **1-3** = **abundance**, amplitude, bountifulness, bounty, cornucopia, exuberance, fullness, horn of plenty, lavishness, luxuriance, plentifulness, plenty, richness, superabundance

cop out *Slang* ◆ **vb 1** = **avoid**, abandon, desert, dodge, quit, renege, renounce, revoke, skip, skive (*Brit. sl.*), withdraw ◆ *n* **cop-out 2** = **dodge**, alibi, fraud, pretence, pretext

copulate *vb* = **have intercourse**, bonk (*inf.*), fuck (*taboo sl.*), have sex, hump (*taboo sl.*), screw (*taboo sl.*), shag (*taboo sl., chiefly Brit.*)

copulation *n* = **sexual intercourse**, carnal knowledge, coition, coitus, congress, coupling, intimacy, legover (*sl.*), love, lovemaking, mating, nookie (*sl.*), rumpy-pumpy (*sl.*), sex, sex act, the other (*inf.*), venery (*arch.*)

copy *n* **1** = **reproduction**, archetype, carbon copy, counterfeit, duplicate, facsimile, fake, fax, forgery, image, imitation, likeness, model, pattern, photocopy, Photostat (*Trademark*), print, replica, replication, representation, transcription, Xerox (*Trademark*) ◆ *vb* **7** = **reproduce**, counterfeit, duplicate, photocopy, Photostat (*Trademark*), replicate, transcribe, Xerox (*Trademark*) **8** = **imitate**, act like, ape, behave like, echo, emulate, follow, follow suit, follow the example of, mimic, mirror, parrot, repeat, simulate
Antonyms *n* ≠ **reproduction:** model, original, pattern, prototype, the real thing ◆ *vb* ≠ **reproduce:** create, originate

coquetry *n* **1, 2** = **flirtation**, dalliance, wantonness

coquettish *adj* **1** = **flirtatious**, amorous, arch,

Cor. *Bible. abbrev. for* Corinthians.
coracle ('kɒrəkᵊl) *n* a small roundish boat made of waterproofed hides stretched over a wicker frame. [C16: from Welsh *corwgl*]
coracoid ('kɒrə,kɔɪd) *n* a paired ventral bone of the pectoral girdle in vertebrates. In mammals it is reduced to a peg (the **coracoid process**) on the scapula. [C18: from NL *coracoīdēs,* from Gk *korakoeidēs* like a raven, from *korax* raven]
coral ('kɒrəl) *n* **1** any of a class of marine colonial coelenterates having a calcareous, horny, or soft skeleton. **2a** the calcareous or horny material forming the skeleton of certain of these animals. **2b** (*as modifier*): *a coral reef.* **3** a rocklike aggregation of certain of these animals or their skeletons, forming an island or reef. **4a** something made of coral. **4b** (*as modifier*): *a coral necklace.* **5a** a yellowish-pink colour. **5b** (*as adj*): *coral lipstick.* **6** the roe of a lobster or crab, which becomes pink when cooked. [C14: from OF, from L *corāllium,* from Gk *korallion,* prob. of Semitic origin]
coral reef *n* a marine reef consisting of coral consolidated into limestone.
coralroot ('kɒrəl,ru:t) *n* a N temperate leafless orchid with branched roots resembling coral.
coral snake *n* **1** a venomous snake of tropical and subtropical America, marked with red, black, yellow, and white transverse bands. **2** any of various other brightly coloured snakes of Africa and SE Asia.
cor anglais ('kɔ:r 'ɑ:ŋgleɪ) *n, pl* **cors anglais** ('kɔ:z 'ɑ:ŋgleɪ). *Music.* a woodwind instrument, the alto of the oboe family. Also called: **English horn.** [C19: from F: English horn]
corbel ('kɔ:bᵊl) *Archit.* ◆ *n* **1** a bracket, usually of stone or brick. ◆ *vb* **corbels, corbelling, corbelled** *or US* **corbels, corbeling, corbeled. 2** (*tr*) to lay (a stone) so that it forms a corbel. [C15: from OF, lit.: a little raven, from Med. L *corvellus,* from L *corvus* raven]
corbie ('kɔ:bɪ) *n* a Scot. name for **raven**[1] (sense 1) or **crow**[1] (sense 1). [C15: from OF *corbin,* from L *corvīnus* CORVINE]
corbie-step *or* **corbel step** *n Archit.* any of a set of steps on the top of a gable. Also called: **crow step.**
cord ⓣ (kɔ:d) *n* **1** string or thin rope made of twisted strands. **2** a length of woven or twisted strands of silk, etc., used as a belt, etc. **3** a ribbed fabric, esp. corduroy. **4** the US and Canad. name for **flex** (sense 1). **5** *Anat.* any part resembling a rope: *the spinal cord.* **6** a unit for measuring cut wood, equal to 128 cubic feet. ◆ *vb* (*tr*) **7** to bind or furnish with a cord or cords. ◆ See also **cords.** [C13: from OF *corde,* from L *chorda,* from Gk *khordē*]
▸ **'cord,like** *adj*
cordage ('kɔ:dɪdʒ) *n* **1** *Naut.* the lines and rigging of a vessel. **2** an amount of wood measured in cords.
cordate ('kɔ:deɪt) *adj* heart-shaped.
corded ('kɔ:dɪd) *adj* **1** bound or fastened with cord. **2** (of a fabric) ribbed. **3** (of muscles) standing out like cords.
cordial ⓣ ('kɔ:dɪəl) *adj* **1** warm and friendly: *a cordial greeting.* **2** stimulating. ◆ *n* **3** a drink with a fruit base: *lime cordial.* **4** another word for **liqueur.** [C14: from Med. L *cordiālis,* from L *cor* heart]
▸ **'cordially** *adv*
cordiality ⓣ (,kɔ:dɪ'ælɪtɪ) *n, pl* **cordialities.** warmth of feeling.
cordillera (,kɔ:dɪl'jɛərə) *n* a series of parallel ranges of mountains, esp. in the northwestern US. [C18: from Sp., from *cordilla,* lit.: a little cord]
cordite ('kɔ:daɪt) *n* any of various explosive materials containing cellulose nitrate, sometimes mixed with nitroglycerine. [C19: from CORD + -ITE[1], from its stringy appearance]
cordless ('kɔ:dlɪs) *adj* (of an electrical device) operated by an internal battery so that no connection to mains supply is needed.
cordless telephone *n* a portable battery-powered telephone with a short-range radio link to a fixed base unit.
cordon ⓣ ('kɔ:dᵊn) *n* **1** a chain of police, soldiers, ships, etc., stationed around an area. **2** a ribbon worn as insignia of honour. **3** a cord or ribbon worn as an ornament. **4** *Archit.* another name for **string course. 5** *Horticulture.* a fruit tree consisting of a single stem bearing fruiting spurs, produced by cutting back all lateral branches. ◆ *vb* **6** (*tr; often foll. by off*) to put or form a cordon (around); close (off). [C16: from OF, lit.: a little cord, from *corde* CORD]
cordon bleu (*French* kɔrdɔ̃ blø) *n* **1** *French history.* the sky-blue ribbon worn by members of the highest order of knighthood under the Bourbon monarchy. **2** any very high distinction. ◆ *adj* **3** of or denoting food prepared to a very high standard. [F, lit.: blue ribbon]
cordon sanitaire *French.* (kɔrdɔ̃ sanitɛr) *n* **1** a guarded line isolating an infected area. **2** a line of buffer states shielding a country. [C19: lit.: sanitary line]
cordovan ('kɔ:dəvᵊn) *n* a fine leather now made mainly from horsehide. [C16: from Sp. *cordobán* of Córdoba, city in Spain]
cords (kɔ:dz) *pl n* trousers made of corduroy.
corduroy ('kɔ:də,rɔɪ, ,kɔ:də'rɔɪ) *n* a heavy cotton pile fabric with lengthways ribs. [C18: ?from the proper name *Corderoy*]
corduroys (,kɔ:də'rɔɪz, 'kɔ:də,rɔɪz) *pl n* trousers or breeches of corduroy.
cordwainer ('kɔ:d,weɪnə) *n Arch.* a shoemaker or worker in leather. [C12: *cordwaner,* from OF, from OSp. *cordovián* CORDOVAN]
cordwood ('kɔ:d,wʊd) *n* wood that has been cut into lengths of four feet so that it can be stacked in cords.
core ⓣ (kɔ:) *n* **1** the central part of certain fleshy fruits, such as the apple, consisting of the seeds. **2** the central or essential part of something: *the core of the argument.* **3** a piece of magnetic material, such as soft iron, inside an electromagnet or transformer. **4** *Geol.* the central part of the earth. **5** a cylindrical sample of rock, soil, etc., obtained by the use of a hollow drill. **6** *Physics.* the region of a nuclear reactor in which the reaction takes place. **7** *Computing.* **7a** a ferrite ring formerly used in a computer memory to store one bit of information. **7b** (*as modifier*): *core memory.* **8** *Archaeol.* a stone or flint from which flakes have been removed. **9** *Physics.* the nucleus together with all complete electron shells of an atom. ◆ *vb* **cores, coring, cored. 10** (*tr*) to remove the core from (fruit). [C14: from ?]
coreligionist (,kəʊrɪ'lɪdʒənɪst) *n* an adherent of the same religion as another.
coreopsis (,kɒrɪ'ɒpsɪs) *n* a plant of America and Africa, with yellow, brown, or yellow-and-red daisy-like flowers. [C18: from NL, from Gk *koris* bedbug + -OPSIS; so called from the appearance of the seed]
co-respondent (,kəʊrɪ'spɒndənt) *n Law.* a person cited in divorce proceedings, alleged to have committed adultery with the respondent.
core subjects *pl n Brit. education.* three foundation subjects (English, mathematics, and science) that are compulsory throughout each key stage in the National Curriculum.
core time *n* See **flexitime.**
corf (kɔ:f) *n, pl* **corves.** *Brit.* a wagon or basket used formerly in mines. [C14: from MDu. *corf* or MLow G *korf,* prob. from L *corbis* basket]
corgi ('kɔ:gɪ) *n* either of two short-legged sturdy breeds of dog, the Cardigan and the Pembroke. [C20: from Welsh, from *cor* dwarf + *ci* dog]
coriander (,kɒrɪ'ændə) *n* a European umbelliferous plant, cultivated for its aromatic seeds and leaves, used in flavouring foods. [C14: from OF *coriandre,* from L *coriandrum,* from Gk *koriannon,* from ?]
Corinthian (kə'rɪnθɪən) *adj* **1** of Corinth, a port in S Greece. **2** denoting one of the five classical orders of architecture: characterized by a bell-shaped capital having carved ornaments based on acanthus leaves. **3** *Obs.* given to luxury; dissolute. ◆ *n* **4** a native or inhabitant of Corinth.
Coriolis force (,kɒrɪ'əʊlɪs) *n* a hypothetical force postulated to explain a deflection in the path of a body moving relative to the earth: it is due to the earth's rotation and is to the left in the S hemisphere and to the right in the N hemisphere. [C19: after Gaspard G. *Coriolis* (1792–1843), F civil engineer]
corium ('kɔ:rɪəm) *n, pl* **coria** (-rɪə). the deep inner layer of the skin, beneath the epidermis, containing connective tissue, blood vessels, and fat. Also called: **derma, dermis.** [C19: from L: rind, skin]
cork (kɔ:k) *n* **1** the thick light porous outer bark of the cork oak. **2** a piece of cork used as a stopper. **3** an angling float. **4** Also called: **phellem.** *Bot.* a protective layer of dead impermeable cells on the outside of the stems and roots of woody plants. Related adj: **suberose.** ◆ *adj* **5** made of cork. ◆ *vb* (*tr*) **6** to stop up (a bottle, etc.) with or as with a cork. **7** (often foll. by *up*) to restrain. **8** to black (the face, hands, etc.) with burnt cork. [C14: prob. from Ar. *qurq,* from L *cortex* bark]
▸ **'cork,like** *adj*
corkage ('kɔ:kɪdʒ) *n* a charge made at a restaurant for serving wine, etc., bought off the premises.
corked (kɔ:kt) *adj* tainted through having a cork containing excess tannin.
corker ('kɔ:kə) *n Old-fashioned sl.* **1** something or somebody striking or outstanding. **2** an irrefutable remark that puts an end to discussion.
cork oak *n* an evergreen Mediterranean oak whose porous bark yields cork.
corkscrew ('kɔ:k,skru:) *n* **1** a device for drawing corks from bottles, typically consisting of a pointed metal spiral attached to a handle or screw mechanism. **2** (*modifier*) resembling a corkscrew in shape. ◆ *vb* **3** to move or cause to move in a spiral or zigzag course.
corm (kɔ:m) *n* an organ of vegetative reproduction in plants such as the crocus, consisting of a globular stem base swollen with food and surrounded by papery scale leaves. [C19: from NL *cormus,* from Gk *kormos* tree trunk from which the branches have been lopped]
cormorant ('kɔ:mərənt) *n* an aquatic bird having a dark plumage, a long neck and body, and a slender hooked beak. [C13: from OF *cormareng,* from *corp* raven + *-mareng* of the sea]
corn[1] (kɔ:n) *n* **1** *Brit.* **1a** any of various cereal plants, esp. the predominant crop of a region, such as wheat in England and oats in Scotland. **1b** the seeds of such plants, esp. after harvesting. **1c** a single seed of such plants; a grain. **2** the usual US, Canad., Austral., and NZ name for **maize. 3** *Sl.* an idea, song, etc., regarded as banal or sentimental. ◆ *vb* (*tr*) **4a** to preserve in brine. **4b** to salt. [OE *corn*]

THESAURUS

come-hither (*inf.*), coy, dallying, flighty, flirty, inviting, teasing
cord *n* **1** = **rope,** line, string, twine
cordial *adj* **1** = **warm,** affable, affectionate, agreeable, cheerful, congenial, earnest, friendly, genial, heartfelt, hearty, sociable, warm-hearted, welcoming, wholehearted
Antonyms *adj* aloof, cold, distant, formal, frigid, reserved, unfriendly, ungracious
cordiality *n* = **warmth,** affability, amiability, friendliness, geniality, heartiness, sincerity, wholeheartedness
cordon *n* **1** = **chain,** barrier, line, ring ◆ *vb* **6** *foll. by* **off** = **surround,** close off, encircle, enclose, fence off, isolate, picket, separate
core *n* **1, 2** = **centre,** crux, essence, gist, heart, kernel, nub, nucleus, pith

corn[2] (kɔːn) *n* **1** a hardening of the skin, esp. of the toes, caused by pressure. **2 tread on (someone's) corns.** *Brit. inf.* to offend or hurt (someone) by touching on a sensitive subject. [C15: from OF *corne* horn, from L *cornū*]

corn borer *n* the larva of a moth native to Europe: in E North America a serious pest of maize.

corn bread *n Chiefly US.* bread made from maize meal. Also called: **Indian bread.**

corn bunting *n* a heavily built European songbird with a streaked brown plumage.

corncob ('kɔːnˌkɒb) *n* the core of an ear of maize, to which kernels are attached.

corncob pipe *n* a pipe with a bowl made from a dried corncob.

corncockle ('kɔːnˌkɒkᵊl) *n* a European plant that has reddish-purple flowers and grows in cornfields and by roadsides.

corncrake ('kɔːnˌkreɪk) *n* a common Eurasian rail with a buff speckled plumage and reddish wings.

corn dolly *n* a decorative figure made by plaiting straw.

cornea ('kɔːnɪə) *n, pl* **corneas** *or* **corneae** (-nɪˌiː). the convex transparent membrane that forms the anterior covering of the eyeball. [C14: from Med. L *cornea tēla* horny web, from L *cornū* HORN]
▸ **'corneal** *adj*

corned (kɔːnd) *adj* (esp. of beef) cooked and then preserved or pickled in salt or brine.

cornel ('kɔːnᵊl) *n* any shrub of the genus *Cornus,* such as the dogwood. [C16: prob. from MLow G *kornelle,* ult. from L *cornus*]

cornelian (kɔːˈniːlɪən) *n* a variant spelling of **carnelian.**

corner Ⓣ ('kɔːnə) *n* **1** the place or angle formed by the meeting of two converging lines or surfaces. **2** a projecting angle of a solid object. **3** the place where two streets meet. **4** any small, secluded, or private place. **5** a dangerous position from which escape is difficult: *a tight corner.* **6** any region, esp. a remote place. **7** something used to protect or mark a corner, as of the hard cover of a book. **8** *Commerce.* a monopoly over the supply of a commodity so that its market price can be controlled. **9** *Soccer, hockey, etc.* a free kick or shot from the corner of the field, taken against a defending team when the ball goes out of play over their goal line after last touching one of their players. **10** either of two opposite angles of a boxing ring in which the opponents take their rests. **11 cut corners.** to take the shortest or easiest way, esp. at the expense of high standards. **12 turn the corner.** to pass the critical point (in an illness, etc.). **13** (*modifier*) on a corner: *a corner shop.* ◆ *vb* **14** (*tr*) to manoeuvre (a person or animal) into a position from which escape is difficult or impossible. **15** (*tr*) **15a** to acquire enough of (a commodity) to attain control of the market. **15b** Also: **engross.** to attain control of (a market) in such a manner. **16** (*intr*) (of vehicles, etc.) to turn a corner. **17** (*intr*) (in soccer, etc.) to take a corner. [C13: from OF *corniere,* from L *cornū* point, HORN]

cornerback ('kɔːnəˌbæk) *n American football.* a defensive back.

cornerstone Ⓣ ('kɔːnəˌstəʊn) *n* **1** a stone at the corner of a wall, uniting two intersecting walls. **2** a stone placed at the corner of a building during a ceremony to mark the start of construction. **3** a person or thing of prime importance: *the cornerstone of the whole argument.*

cornerwise ('kɔːnəˌwaɪz) *or* **cornerways** ('kɔːnəˌweɪz) *adv, adj* with a corner in front; diagonally.

cornet ('kɔːnɪt) *n* **1** a three-valved brass instrument of the trumpet family. **2** a person who plays the cornet. **3** a cone-shaped paper container for sweets, etc. **4** *Brit.* a cone-shaped wafer container for ice cream. **5** (formerly) the lowest rank of commissioned cavalry officer in the British Army. **6** the large white headdress of some nuns. [C14: from OF, from L *cornū* HORN]
▸ **cor'netist** *or* **cor'nettist** *n*

corn exchange *n* a building where corn is bought and sold.

cornfield ('kɔːnˌfiːld) *n* a field planted with cereal crops.

cornflakes ('kɔːnˌfleɪks) *pl n* a breakfast cereal made from toasted maize.

cornflour ('kɔːnˌflaʊə) *n* a fine maize flour, used for thickening sauces. US and Canad. name: **cornstarch.**

cornflower ('kɔːnˌflaʊə) *n* a herbaceous plant, with blue, purple, pink, or white flowers, formerly a common weed in cornfields.

cornice ('kɔːnɪs) *n* **1** *Archit.* **1a** the top projecting mouldings of an entablature. **1b** a continuous horizontal projecting course or moulding at the top of a wall, building, etc. **2** an overhanging ledge of snow. [C16: from OF, from It., ?from L *cornix* crow, but infl. also by L *corōnis* decorative flourish]

corniche ('kɔːnɪʃ) *n* a coastal road, esp. one built into the face of a cliff. [C19: from *corniche road;* see CORNICE]

Cornish ('kɔːnɪʃ) *adj* **1** of Cornwall or its inhabitants. ◆ *n* **2** a former language of Cornwall: extinct by 1800. **3 the.** (*functioning as pl*) the natives or inhabitants of Cornwall.
▸ **'Cornishman** *n*

Cornish pasty ('pæstɪ) *n Cookery.* a pastry case with a filling of meat and vegetables.

corn meal *n* meal made from maize. Also called: **Indian meal.**

corn salad *n* a plant which often grows in cornfields and whose leaves are sometimes used in salads. Also called: **lamb's lettuce.**

cornstarch ('kɔːnˌstɑːtʃ) *n* the US and Canad. name for **cornflour.**

cornucopia (ˌkɔːnjʊˈkəʊpɪə) *n* **1** a representation of a horn in painting, sculpture, etc., overflowing with fruit, vegetables, etc.; horn of plenty. **2** a great abundance. **3** a horn-shaped container. [C16: from LL, from L *cornū cōpiae* horn of plenty]
▸ **ˌcornu'copian** *adj*

corn whisky *n* whisky made from maize.

corny Ⓣ ('kɔːnɪ) *adj* **cornier, corniest.** *Sl.* **1** trite or banal. **2** sentimental or mawkish. **3** abounding in corn. [C16 (C20 in the sense banal): from CORN[1] + -Y[1]]

corolla (kəˈrɒlə) *n* the petals of a flower collectively, forming an inner floral envelope. [C17: dim. of L *corōna* crown]

corollary Ⓣ (kəˈrɒlərɪ) *n, pl* **corollaries. 1** a proposition that follows directly from the proof of another proposition. **2** an obvious deduction. **3** a natural consequence. [C14: from L *corollārium* money paid for a garland, from L *corolla* garland]

corona (kəˈrəʊnə) *n, pl* **coronas** *or* **coronae** (-niː). **1** a circle of light around a luminous body, usually the moon. **2** Also called: **aureole.** the outermost region of the sun's atmosphere, visible as a faint halo during a solar eclipse. **3** *Archit.* the flat vertical face of a cornice. **4** a circular chandelier. **5** *Bot.* **5a** the trumpet-shaped part of the corolla of daffodils and similar plants. **5b** a crown of leafy outgrowths from inside the petals of some flowers. **6** *Anat.* a crownlike structure. **7** a long cigar with blunt ends. **8** *Physics.* an electrical discharge appearing around the surface of a charged conductor. [C16: from L: crown]

coronach ('kɒrənəx) *n Scot. & Irish.* a dirge or lamentation for the dead. [C16: from Scot. Gaelic *corranach*]

coronary ('kɒrənərɪ) *adj* **1** *Anat.* designating blood vessels, nerves, ligaments, etc., that encircle a part or structure. ◆ *n, pl* **coronaries. 2** short for **coronary thrombosis.** [C17: from L *corōnārius* belonging to a wreath or crown]

coronary artery *n* either of the two arteries branching from the aorta and supplying blood to the heart.

coronary bypass *n* the surgical bypass of a narrowed or blocked coronary artery by grafting a section of a healthy blood vessel taken from another part of the patient's body.

coronary heart disease *n* any heart disorder caused by disease of the coronary arteries.

coronary thrombosis *n* a condition of interrupted blood flow to the heart due to a blood clot in a coronary artery.

coronation (ˌkɒrəˈneɪʃən) *n* the act or ceremony of crowning a monarch. [C14: from OF, from *coroner* to crown, from L *corōnāre*]

coroner ('kɒrənə) *n* a public official responsible for the investigation of violent, sudden, or suspicious deaths. [C14: from Anglo-F *corouner,* from OF *corone* CROWN]
▸ **'coronerˌship** *n*

coronet ('kɒrənɪt) *n* **1** any small crown, esp. one worn by princes or peers. **2** a woman's jewelled circlet for the head. **3** the margin between the skin of a horse's pastern and the horn of the hoof. **4** the knob at the base of a deer's antler. [C15: from OF *coronete*]

coroutine ('kəʊruːˌtiːn) *n Computing.* a section of a computer program similar to but differing from a subroutine in that it can be left and re-entered at any point.

corp. *abbrev. for:* **1** corporation. **2** corporal.

corporal[1] Ⓣ ('kɔːpərəl, 'kɔːprəl) *adj* of or relating to the body. [C14: from L *corporālis,* from *corpus* body]
▸ **ˌcorpo'rality** *n* ▸ **'corporally** *adv*

corporal[2] ('kɔːpərəl) *n* **1** a noncommissioned officer junior to a sergeant in the army, air force, or marines. **2** (in the Royal Navy) a petty officer who assists the master-at-arms. [C16: from OF, via It., from L *caput* head; ? also infl. in OF by *corps* body (of men)]

corporal[3] ('kɔːpərəl) *or* **corporale** (ˌkɔːpəˈreɪlɪ) *n* a white linen cloth on which the bread and wine are placed during the Eucharist. [C14: from Med. L *corporāle pallium* eucharistic altar cloth, from L *corporālis,* from *corpus* body (of Christ)]

Corporal of Horse *n* a noncommissioned rank in the British Army, above that of sergeant and below that of staff sergeant.

corporal punishment *n* punishment of a physical nature, such as caning.

corporate Ⓣ ('kɔːpərɪt) *adj* **1** forming a corporation; incorporated. **2** of a corporation or corporations: *corporate finance.* **3** of or belonging to a united group; joint. [C15: from L *corporātus,* from *corpus* body]
▸ **'corporatism** *n*

corporate advertising *n* advertising designed to publicize or create a favourable image of a company rather than a particular product.

THESAURUS

corner *n* **1** = **angle,** bend, crook, joint **4** = **space,** cavity, cranny, hideaway, hide-out, hidey-hole (*inf.*), hole, niche, nook, recess, retreat **5** = **tight spot,** hole (*inf.*), hot water (*inf.*), pickle (*inf.*), predicament, spot (*inf.*) ◆ *vb* **14** = **trap,** bring to bay, run to earth **15** = **monopolize,** dominate, engross, hog

cornerstone *n* **1** = **quoin 3** = **basis,** bedrock, key, premise, starting point

corny *adj Slang* **1, 2** = **unoriginal,** banal, commonplace, dull, feeble, hackneyed, maudlin, mawkish, old-fashioned, old hat, sentimental, stale, stereotyped, trite

corollary *n* **2** = **deduction,** conclusion, induction, inference **3** = **consequence,** result, sequel, upshot

corporal[1] *adj* = **bodily,** anatomical, carnal, corporeal (*arch.*), fleshly, material, physical, somatic

corporate *adj* **3** = **collective,** allied, collaborative, combined, communal, joint, merged, pooled, shared, united

corporate anorexia *n* a malaise of a business organization resulting from making too many creative people redundant in a cost-cutting exercise.

corporate culture *n* the distinctive ethos of an organization that influences the level of formality, loyalty, and general behaviour of its employees.

corporate identity *or* **image** *n* the way an organization is presented to or perceived by its members and the public.

corporate raider *n Finance.* a person or organization that acquires a substantial holding of the shares of a company in order to take it over or to force its management to act in a desired way.

corporate venturing *n Finance.* the provision of venture capital by one company for another in order to obtain information about the company requiring capital or as a step towards acquiring it.

corporation Ⓣ (ˌkɔːpəˈreɪʃən) *n* **1** a group of people authorized by law to act as an individual and having its own powers, duties, and liabilities. **2** Also called: **municipal corporation.** the municipal authorities of a city or town. **3** a group of people acting as one body. **4** See **public corporation. 5** *Inf.* a large paunch.
▸ˈ**corporative** *adj*

corporation tax *n* a British tax on the profits of a company or other incorporated body.

corporeal Ⓣ (kɔːˈpɔːrɪəl) *adj* **1** of the nature of the physical body; not spiritual. **2** of a material nature; physical. [C17: from L *corporeus,* from *corpus* body]
▸**corˌporeˈality** *or* **corporeity** (ˌkɔːpəˈriːɪtɪ) *n* ▸**corˈporeally** *adv*

corps Ⓣ (kɔː) *n, pl* **corps** (kɔːz). **1** a military formation that comprises two or more divisions. **2** a military body with a specific function: *medical corps.* **3** a body of people associated together: *the diplomatic corps.* [C18: from F, from L *corpus* body]

corps de ballet (ˈkɔː də ˈbæleɪ) *n* the members of a ballet company who dance together in a group.

corps diplomatique (ˌdɪpləʊmæˈtiːk) *n* another name for **diplomatic corps.**

corpse Ⓣ (kɔːps) *n* a dead body, esp. of a human being. [C14: from OF *corps,* from L *corpus*]

corpulent Ⓣ (ˈkɔːpjʊlənt) *adj* physically bulky; fat. [C14: from L *corpulentus*]
▸ˈ**corpulence** *n*

cor pulmonale (ˌkɔː ˌpʌlməˈnɑːlɪ) *n* pulmonary heart disease: a serious heart condition in which there is enlargement and failure of the right ventricle resulting from lung disease. [NL]

corpus Ⓣ (ˈkɔːpəs) *n, pl* **corpora** (-pərə). **1** a body of writings, esp. by a single author or on a specific topic: *the corpus of Dickens' works.* **2** the main body or substance of something. **3** *Anat.* **3a** any distinct mass or body. **3b** the main part of an organ or structure. **4** *Obs.* a corpse. [C14: from L: body]

Corpus Christi (ˈkrɪstɪ) *n Chiefly RC Church.* a festival in honour of the Eucharist, observed on the Thursday after Trinity Sunday. [C14: from L: body of Christ]

corpuscle (ˈkɔːpʌsᵊl) *n* **1** any cell or similar minute body that is suspended in a fluid, esp. any of the **red blood corpuscles** (see **erythrocyte**) or **white blood corpuscles** (see **leucocyte**). **2** Also: **corpuscule** (kɔːˈpʌskjuːl). any minute particle. [C17: from L *corpusculum* a little body, from *corpus* body]
▸**corpuscular** (kɔːˈpʌskjʊlə) *adj*

corpuscular theory *n* the theory, originally proposed by Newton, that light consists of a stream of particles. Cf. **wave theory.**

corpus delicti (dɪˈlɪktaɪ) *n Law.* the body of facts that constitute an offence. [NL, lit.: the body of the crime]

corpus juris (ˈdʒʊərɪs) *n* a body of law, esp. of a nation or state. [from LL, lit.: a body of law]

corpus luteum (ˈluːtɪəm) *n, pl* **corpora lutea** (ˈluːtɪə). a mass of tissue that forms in a Graafian follicle following release of an ovum. [NL, lit.: yellow body]

corral Ⓣ (kɒˈrɑːl) *n* **1** *Chiefly US & Canad.* an enclosure for cattle or horses. **2** *Chiefly US.* (formerly) a defensive enclosure formed by a ring of covered wagons. ◆ *vb* **corrals, corralling, corralled.** *(tr) US & Canad.* **3** to drive into a corral. **4** *Inf.* to capture. [C16: from Sp., ult. from L *currere* to run]

corrasion (kəˈreɪʒən) *n* erosion of a rock surface by rock fragments transported over it by water, wind, or ice. [C17: from L *corrādere* to scrape together]

correa (ˈkɒrɪə, kəˈriːə) *n* an Australian evergreen shrub with large showy tubular flowers. [C19: after Jose Francesco *Correa* da Serra (1750-1823), Portuguese botanist]

correct Ⓣ (kəˈrɛkt) *vb (tr)* **1** to make free from errors. **2** to indicate the errors in. **3** to rebuke or punish in order to improve: *to stand corrected.* **4** to rectify (a malfunction, ailment, etc.). **5** to adjust or make conform, esp. to a standard. ◆ *adj* **6** true; accurate: *the correct version.* **7** in conformity with accepted standards: *correct behaviour.* [C14: from L *corrigere* to make straight, from *com-* (intensive) + *regere* to rule]
▸**corˈrectly** *adv* ▸**corˈrectness** *n*

correction Ⓣ (kəˈrɛkʃən) *n* **1** the act of correcting. **2** something substituted for an error; an improvement. **3** a reproof. **4** a quantity added to or subtracted from a scientific calculation or observation to increase its accuracy.
▸**corˈrectional** *adj*

corrective Ⓣ (kəˈrɛktɪv) *adj* **1** tending or intended to correct. ◆ *n* **2** something that tends or is intended to correct.

correlate Ⓣ (ˈkɒrɪˌleɪt) *vb* **correlates, correlating, correlated. 1** to place or be placed in a complementary or reciprocal relationship. **2** *(tr)* to establish or show a correlation between. ◆ *n* **3** either of two things mutually related.

correlation Ⓣ (ˌkɒrɪˈleɪʃən) *n* **1** a mutual relationship between two or more things. **2** the act of correlating or the state of being correlated. **3** *Statistics.* the extent of correspondence between the ordering of two variables. [C16: from Med. L *correlātiō,* from *com-* together + *relātiō* RELATION]
▸ˌ**correˈlational** *adj*

correlation coefficient *n Statistics.* a statistic measuring the degree of correlation between two variables.

correlative (kɒˈrɛlətɪv) *adj* **1** in complementary or reciprocal relationship; corresponding. **2** denoting words, usually conjunctions, occurring together though not adjacently in certain grammatical constructions, as *neither* and *nor.* ◆ *n* **3** either of two things that are correlative. **4** a correlative word.
▸**corˈrelatively** *adv* ▸**corˌrelaˈtivity** *n*

correspond Ⓣ (ˌkɒrɪˈspɒnd) *vb (intr)* **1** (usually foll. by *with* or *to*) to be consistent or compatible (with); tally (with). **2** (usually foll. by *to*) to be similar in character or function. **3** (usually foll. by *with*) to communicate by letter. [C16: from Med. L *corrēspondēre,* from L *rēspondēre* to RESPOND]
▸ˌ**correˈsponding** *adj* ▸ˌ**correˈspondingly** *adv*

USAGE NOTE See at **similar.**

correspondence Ⓣ (ˌkɒrɪˈspɒndəns) *n* **1** the condition of agreeing or corresponding. **2** similarity. **3** agreement or conformity. **4a** communication by letters. **4b** the letters so exchanged.

correspondence school *n* an educational institution that offers tuition (**correspondence courses**) by post.

correspondent Ⓣ (ˌkɒrɪˈspɒndənt) *n* **1** a person who communicates

THESAURUS

corporation *n* **1, 3** = **business**, association, corporate body, society **2** = **town council**, civic authorities, council, municipal authorities **5** *Informal* = **paunch**, beer belly (*inf.*), middle-age spread (*inf.*), pod, pot, potbelly, spare tyre (*Brit. sl.*), spread (*inf.*)

corporeal *adj* **1, 2** = **physical**, bodily, fleshy, human, material, mortal, substantial

corps *n* **1-3** = **team**, band, body, company, contingent, crew, detachment, division, regiment, squad, squadron, troop, unit

corpse *n* = **body**, cadaver, carcass, remains, stiff (*sl.*)

corpulence *n* = **fatness**, beef, blubber, burliness, *embonpoint,* fleshiness, obesity, plumpness, portliness, rotundity, stoutness, tubbiness

corpulent *adj* = **fat**, beefy (*inf.*), bulky, burly, fattish, fleshy, large, lusty, obese, overweight, plump, portly, roly-poly, rotund, stout, tubby, well-padded
Antonyms *adj* anorexic, bony, emaciated, gaunt, scrawny, skin and bones (*inf.*), skinny, slim, thin, thin as a rake, underweight

corpus *n* **1** = **collection**, body, compilation, complete works, entirety, *oeuvre,* whole

corral *U.S. & Canad.* ◆ *n* **1** = **enclosure**, confine, coop, fold, pen, yard ◆ *vb* **3** = **enclose**, cage, confine, coop up, fence in, impound, mew, pen in

correct *vb* **1** = **rectify**, adjust, amend, cure, emend, improve, redress, reform, regulate, remedy, right, set the record straight **3** = **punish**, admonish, chasten, chastise, chide, discipline, rebuke, reprimand, reprove ◆ *adj* **6** = **true**, accurate, equitable, exact, faultless, flawless, just, O.K. *or* okay (*inf.*), on the right lines, precise, regular, right, strict **7** = **proper**, acceptable, appropriate, diplomatic, fitting, kosher (*inf.*), O.K. *or* okay (*inf.*), seemly, standard
Antonyms *vb* ≠ **rectify:** damage, harm, impair, ruin, spoil ≠ **punish:** compliment, excuse, praise ◆ *adj* ≠ **true:** false, inaccurate, incorrect, untrue, wrong ≠ **proper:** improper, inappropriate, unacceptable, unfitting, unsuitable

correction *n* **1, 2** = **rectification**, adjustment, alteration, amendment, emendation, improvement, modification, righting **3** = **punishment**, admonition, castigation, chastisement, discipline, reformation, reproof

corrective *adj* **1** = **disciplinary**, penal, punitive, reformatory

correctly *adv* **6** = **rightly**, accurately, aright, perfectly, precisely, properly, right

correctness *n* **6** = **truth**, accuracy, exactitude, exactness, faultlessness, fidelity, preciseness, precision, regularity **7** = **decorum**, *bon ton,* civility, good breeding, propriety, seemliness

correlate *vb* **1, 2** = **correspond**, associate, compare, connect, coordinate, equate, interact, parallel, tie in

correlation *n* **1** = **correspondence**, alternation, equivalence, interaction, interchange, interdependence, interrelationship, reciprocity

correspond *vb* **1** *usually foll. by* **with** *or* **to** = **be consistent**, accord, agree, be related, coincide, complement, conform, correlate, dovetail, fit, harmonize, match, square, tally **3** = **communicate**, exchange letters, keep in touch, write
Antonyms *vb* ≠ **be consistent:** be at variance, be dissimilar, be inconsistent, belie, be unlike, differ, disagree, diverge, vary

correspondence *n* **1-3** = **relation**, agreement, analogy, coincidence, comparability, comparison, concurrence, conformity, congruity, correlation, fitness, harmony, match, similarity **4** = **letters**, communication, mail, post, writing

correspondent *n* **1** = **letter writer**, pen friend *or* pal **2** = **reporter**, contributor, gazetteer (*arch.*), journalist, journo (*sl.*), special correspondent ◆ *adj* **4** = **corresponding**, analogous,

by letter. **2** a person employed by a newspaper, etc., to report on a special subject or from a foreign country. **3** a person or firm that has regular business relations with another, esp. one abroad. ◆ *adj* **4** similar or analogous.

corrida (ko'rriða) *n* the Spanish word for **bullfight**. [Sp., from *corrida de toros*, lit.: a running of bulls]

corridor ⊤ ('kɒrɪˌdɔː) *n* **1** a passage connecting parts of a building. **2** a strip of land or airspace that affords access, either from a landlocked country to the sea or from a state to an exclave. **3** a passageway connecting the compartments of a railway coach. **4** a flight path that affords safe access for intruding aircraft. **5** the path that a spacecraft must follow when re-entering the atmosphere, above which lift is insufficient and below which heating effects are excessive. **6 corridors of power.** the higher echelons of government, the Civil Service, etc., considered as the location of power and influence. [C16: from OF, from OIt. *corridore*, lit.: place for running]

corrie ('kɒrɪ) *n* **1** (in Scotland) a circular hollow on a hillside. **2** *Geol.* another name for **cirque**. [C18: from Gaelic *coire* cauldron]

corrigendum (ˌkɒrɪ'dʒɛndəm) *n, pl* **corrigenda** (-də). **1** an error to be corrected. **2** (*sometimes pl*) Also called: **erratum.** a slip of paper inserted into a book after printing, listing corrections. [C19: from L: that which is to be corrected]

corrigible ('kɒrɪdʒɪbᵊl) *adj* **1** capable of being corrected. **2** submissive. [C15: from OF, from Med. L *corrigibilis*, from L *corrigere* to CORRECT]

corroborate ⊤ (kə'rɒbəˌreɪt) *vb* **corroborates, corroborating, corroborated.** (*tr*) to confirm or support (facts, opinions, etc.), esp. by providing fresh evidence. [C16: from L *corrōborāre*, from *rōborāre* to make strong, from *rōbur* strength]
▸**corˌrobo'ration** *n* ▸**corroborative** (kə'rɒbərətɪv) *or* **cor'roboratory** *adj*
▸**cor'roboˌrator** *n*

corroboree (kə'rɒbərɪ) *n Austral.* **1** a native assembly of sacred, festive, or warlike character. **2** *Inf.* any noisy gathering. [C19: from Abor.]

corrode ⊤ (kə'rəʊd) *vb* **corrodes, corroding, corroded. 1** to eat away or be eaten away, esp. as in the oxidation or rusting of a metal. **2** (*tr*) to destroy gradually: *his jealousy corroded his happiness.* [C14: from L *corrōdere* to gnaw to pieces, from *rōdere* to gnaw]
▸**cor'rodible** *adj*

corrosion (kə'rəʊʒən) *n* **1** a process in which a solid, esp. a metal, is eaten away and changed by a chemical action, as in the oxidation of iron. **2** slow deterioration by being eaten or worn away. **3** the product of corrosion.

corrosive ⊤ (kə'rəʊsɪv) *adj* **1** tending to eat away or consume. ◆ *n* **2** a corrosive substance, such as a strong acid.
▸**cor'rosively** *adv* ▸**cor'rosiveness** *n*

corrosive sublimate *n* another name for **mercuric chloride**.

corrugate ('kɒrʊˌgeɪt) *vb* **corrugates, corrugating, corrugated.** (*usually tr*) to fold or be folded into alternate furrows and ridges. [C18: from L *corrūgāre*, from *rūga* a wrinkle]
▸**'corruˌgated** *adj* ▸**ˌcorru'gation** *n*

corrugated iron *n* a thin sheet of iron or steel, formed with alternating ridges and troughs.

corrupt ⊤ (kə'rʌpt) *adj* **1** open to or involving bribery or other dishonest practices: *a corrupt official; corrupt practices.* **2** morally depraved. **3** putrid or rotten. **4** (of a text or manuscript) made meaningless or different in meaning by scribal errors or alterations. **5** (of computer programs or data) containing errors. ◆ *vb* **6** to become or cause to become dishonest or disloyal. **7** (*tr*) to deprave. **8** (*tr*) to infect or contaminate. **9** (*tr*) to cause to become rotten. **10** (*tr*) to alter (a text, etc.) from the original. **11** (*tr*) *Computing.* to introduce errors into (data or a program). [C14: from L *corruptus* spoiled, from *corrumpere* to ruin, from *rumpere* to break]
▸**cor'rupter** *or* **cor'ruptor** *n* ▸**cor'ruptly** *adv* ▸**cor'ruptness** *n*

corruptible (kə'rʌptɪbᵊl) *adj* capable of being corrupted.
▸**cor'ruptibly** *adv*

corruption ⊤ (kə'rʌpʃən) *n* **1** the act of corrupting or state of being corrupt. **2** depravity. **3** dishonesty, esp. bribery. **4** decay. **5** alteration, as of a manuscript. **6** an altered form of a word.

corsage (kɔː'sɑːʒ) *n* **1** a small bunch of flowers worn pinned to the lapel, bosom, etc. **2** the bodice of a dress. [C15: from OF, from *cors* body, from L *corpus*]

corsair ('kɔːsɛə) *n* **1** a pirate. **2** a privateer, esp. of the Barbary Coast, the Mediterranean coast of N Africa. [C15: from OF *corsaire*, from Med. L *cursārius*, from L *cursus* a running]

corse (kɔːs) *n* an archaic word for **corpse**.

corselet ('kɔːslɪt) *n* **1** Also spelt: **corslet.** a piece of armour for the top part of the body. **2** a one-piece foundation garment. [C15: from OF, from *cors* bodice, from L *corpus* body]

corset ⊤ ('kɔːsɪt) *n* **1a** a stiffened, elasticated, or laced foundation garment, worn esp. by women. **1b** a similar garment worn because of injury, weakness, etc., by either sex. **2** *Inf.* a restriction or limitation, esp. government control of bank lending. ◆ *vb* **3** (*tr*) to dress or enclose in, or as in, a corset. [C14: from OF, lit.: a little bodice]
▸**corsetière** (ˌkɔːsɛtɪ'ɛə) *n* ▸**'corsetry** *n*

cortege ⊤ *or* **cortège** (kɔː'teɪʒ) *n* **1** a formal procession, esp. a funeral procession. **2** a train of attendants; retinue. [C17: from F, from It. *corteggio*, from *corteggiare* to attend]

cortex ('kɔːtɛks) *n, pl* **cortices** (-tɪˌsiːz). **1** *Anat.* the outer layer of any organ or part, such as the grey matter in the brain that covers the cerebrum (**cerebral cortex**). **2** *Bot.* **2a** the tissue in plant stems and roots between the vascular bundles and the epidermis. **2b** the outer layer of a part such as the bark of a stem. [C17: from L: bark, outer layer]
▸**cortical** ('kɔːtɪkᵊl) *adj*

corticate ('kɔːtɪkɪt, -ˌkeɪt) *or* **corticated** *adj* (of plants, seeds, etc.) having a bark, husk, or rind. [C19: from L *corticātus*]

cortisone ('kɔːtɪˌzəʊn) *n* a steroid hormone, the synthetic form of which has been used in treating rheumatoid arthritis, allergic and skin diseases, leukaemia, etc. [C20: from *corticosterone*, a hormone]

corundum (kə'rʌndəm) *n* a hard mineral consisting of aluminium oxide: used as an abrasive. Precious varieties include ruby and white sapphire. Formula: Al_2O_3. [C18: from Tamil *kuruntam*; rel. to Sansk. *kuruvinda* ruby]

coruscate ('kɒrəˌskeɪt) *vb* **coruscates, coruscating, coruscated.** (*intr*) to emit flashes of light; sparkle. [C18: from L *coruscāre* to flash]
▸**ˌcorus'cation** *n*

corvée ('kɔːveɪ) *n* **1** *European history.* a day's unpaid labour owed by a feudal vassal to his lord. **2** the practice or an instance of forced labour. [C14: from OF, from LL *corrogāta* contribution, from L *corrogāre* to collect, from *rogāre* to ask]

corvette (kɔː'vɛt) *n* a lightly armed escort warship. [C17: from OF, ?from MDu. *corf*]

corvine ('kɔːvaɪn) *adj* **1** of or resembling a crow. **2** of the passerine bird family Corvidae, which includes the crows, ravens, rooks, jackdaws, magpies, and jays. [C17: from L *corvīnus*, from *corvus* a raven]

Corybant ('kɒrɪˌbænt) *n, pl* **Corybants** *or* **Corybantes** (ˌkɒrɪ'bæntiːz). *Classical myth.* a wild attendant of the goddess Cybele. [C14: from L *Corybās*, from Gk *Korubas*]
▸**ˌCory'bantic** *adj*

corymb ('kɒrɪmb, -rɪm) *n* an inflorescence in the form of a flat-topped flower cluster with the oldest flowers at the periphery. [C18: from L *corymbus*, from Gk *korumbos* cluster]

coryza (kə'raɪzə) *n* acute inflammation of the mucous membrane of the nose, with discharge of mucus; a head cold. [C17: from LL: catarrh, from Gk *koruza*]

cos[1] *or* **cos lettuce** (kɒs) *n* a variety of lettuce with a long slender head and crisp leaves. Usual US and Canad. name: **romaine.** [C17: after *Kos*, the Aegean island of its origin]

cos[2] (kɒz) *abbrev. for* cosine.

Cosa Nostra ('kəʊzə 'nɒstrə) *n* the branch of the Mafia that operates in the US. [It.: our thing]

cosec ('kəʊsɛk) *abbrev. for* cosecant.

THESAURUS

comparable, like, of a piece, parallel, reciprocal, similar

corresponding *adj* **2** = **related**, analogous, answering, complementary, correlative, correspondent, equivalent, identical, interrelated, matching, reciprocal, similar, synonymous

corridor *n* **1** = **passage**, aisle, alley, hallway, passageway

corroborate *vb* = **support**, authenticate, back up, bear out, confirm, document, endorse, establish, ratify, substantiate, sustain, validate
Antonyms *vb* contradict, disprove, invalidate, negate, rebut, refute

corroboration *n* = **support**, authentication, certification, circumstantiation, confirmation, documentation, endorsement, establishment, fortification, ratification, substantiation, sustainment, validation

corrode *vb* **1, 2** = **eat away**, canker, consume, corrupt, deteriorate, erode, gnaw, impair, oxidize, rust, waste, wear away

corrosive *adj* **1** = **corroding**, acrid, biting, caustic, consuming, erosive, virulent, vitriolic, wasting, wearing

corrupt *adj* **1** = **dishonest**, bent (*sl.*), bribable, crooked (*inf.*), fraudulent, rotten, shady (*inf.*), unethical, unprincipled, unscrupulous, venal **2** = **depraved**, abandoned, debased, defiled, degenerate, demoralized, dishonoured, dissolute, profligate, vicious **3** = **contaminated**, adulterated, decayed, defiled, infected, polluted, putrescent, putrid, rotten, tainted **4** = **distorted**, altered, doctored, falsified ◆ *vb* **6** = **bribe**, buy off, entice, fix (*inf.*), grease (someone's) palm (*sl.*), lure, square, suborn **7** = **deprave**, debauch, demoralize, pervert, subvert **8, 9** = **contaminate**, adulterate, debase, defile, infect, putrefy, spoil, taint, vitiate **10** = **distort**, doctor, tamper with
Antonyms *adj* ≠ **dishonest, depraved:** ethical, honest, honourable, moral, noble, principled, righteous, scrupulous, straight, upright, virtuous ◆ *vb* ≠ **deprave:** correct, reform ≠ **contaminate:** purify

corrupted *adj* **6, 7** = **depraved**, abandoned, debased, debauched, defiled, degenerate, demoralized, dishonoured, perverted, profligate, reprobate, warped **8, 9** = **contaminated**, adulterated, decayed, defiled, dirtied, infected, polluted, putrefied, rotten, soiled, spoiled, stained, sullied, tainted, tarnished, vitiated **10** = **distorted**, altered, doctored, falsified

corruption *n* **2** = **depravity**, baseness, decadence, degeneration, degradation, evil, immorality, impurity, iniquity, perversion, profligacy, sinfulness, turpitude, vice, viciousness, wickedness **3** = **dishonesty**, breach of trust, bribery, bribing, crookedness (*inf.*), demoralization, extortion, fiddling (*inf.*), fraud, fraudulency, graft (*inf.*), jobbery, profiteering, shadiness, shady dealings (*inf.*), unscrupulousness, venality **4** = **rotting**, adulteration, debasement, decay, defilement, foulness, infection, pollution, putrefaction, putrescence, rot, rottenness **5** = **distortion**, doctoring, falsification

corset *n* **1a** = **girdle**, belt, bodice, corselet, foundation garment, panty girdle, stays (*rare*)

cortege *n* **1, 2** = **procession**, cavalcade, entourage, retinue, suite, train

cosecant (kəʊˈsiːkənt) *n* (of an angle) a trigonometric function that in a right-angled triangle is the ratio of the length of the hypotenuse to that of the opposite side.

coset (ˈkəʊˌsɛt) *n Maths.* a set that produces a specified larger set when added to another set.

cosh[1] (kɒʃ) *Brit.* ◆ *n* **1** a blunt weapon, often made of hard rubber; bludgeon. **2** an attack with such a weapon. ◆ *vb* **3** to hit with such a weapon, esp. on the head. [C19: from Romany *kosh*]

cosh[2] (kɒʃ, kɒsˈeɪtʃ) *n* hyperbolic cosine. [C19: from COS(INE) + H(YPERBOLIC)]

cosignatory (kəʊˈsɪɡnətərɪ, -trɪ) *n, pl* **cosignatories. 1** a person, country, etc., that signs a document jointly with others. ◆ *adj* **2** signing jointly.

cosine (ˈkəʊˌsaɪn) *n* (of an angle) a trigonometric function that in a right-angled triangle is the ratio of the length of the adjacent side to that of the hypotenuse. [C17: from NL *cosinus*; see CO-, SINE[1]]

cosmetic ❶ (kɒzˈmɛtɪk) *n* **1** any preparation applied to the body, esp. the face, with the intention of beautifying it. ◆ *adj* **2** serving or designed to beautify the body, esp. the face. **3** having no other function than to beautify: *cosmetic illustrations in a book.* [C17: from Gk *kosmētikos*, from *kosmein* to arrange, from *kosmos* order]
▸**cosˈmetically** *adv*

cosmic ❶ (ˈkɒzmɪk) *adj* **1** of or relating to the whole universe: *cosmic laws.* **2** occurring or originating in outer space, esp. as opposed to the vicinity of the earth: *cosmic rays.* **3** immeasurably extended; vast.
▸ˈ**cosmically** *adv*

cosmic dust *n* fine particles of solid matter occurring throughout interstellar space and often collecting into clouds of extremely low density.

cosmic rays *pl n* radiation consisting of atomic nuclei, esp. protons, of very high energy, that reach the earth from outer space. Also called: **cosmic radiation.**

cosmic string *n* any of a number of linear defects in space-time postulated in certain theories of cosmology to exist in the universe as a consequence of the big bang.

cosmo- *or before a vowel* **cosm-** *combining form.* indicating the world or universe: *cosmology; cosmonaut.* [from Gk: COSMOS]

cosmogony (kɒzˈmɒɡənɪ) *n, pl* **cosmogonies.** the study of the origin and development of the universe or of a particular system in the universe, such as the solar system. [C17: from Gk *kosmogonia*, from COSMO- + *gonos* creation]
▸**cosmogonic** (ˌkɒzməˈɡɒnɪk) *or* ˌ**cosmoˈgonical** *adj* ▸**cosˈmogonist** *n*

cosmography (kɒzˈmɒɡrəfɪ) *n* **1** a representation of the world or the universe. **2** the science dealing with the whole order of nature.
▸**cosˈmographer** *n* ▸**cosmographic** (ˌkɒzməˈɡræfɪk) *or* ˌ**cosmoˈgraphical** *adj*

cosmological principle *n Astron.* the theory that the universe is uniform, homogenous, and isotropic, and therefore appears the same from any position.

cosmology (kɒzˈmɒlədʒɪ) *n* **1** the study of the origin and nature of the universe. **2** a particular account of the origin or structure of the universe.
▸**cosmological** (ˌkɒzməˈlɒdʒɪkᵊl) *or* ˌ**cosmoˈlogic** *adj* ▸**cosˈmologist** *n*

cosmonaut ❶ (ˈkɒzməˌnɔːt) *n* an astronaut, esp. in the former Soviet Union. [C20: from Russian *kosmonavt*, from COSMO- + Gk *nautēs* sailor]

cosmopolitan ❶ (ˌkɒzməˈpɒlɪtᵊn) *n* **1** a person who has lived and travelled in many countries, esp. one who is free of national prejudices. ◆ *adj* **2** familiar with many parts of the world. **3** sophisticated or urbane. **4** composed of people or elements from all parts of the world or from many different spheres. [C17: from F, ult. from Gk *kosmopolitēs*, from *kosmo-* COSMO- + *politēs* citizen]
▸ˌ**cosmoˈpolitanism** *n*

cosmopolite (kɒzˈmɒpəˌlaɪt) *n* **1** a less common word for **cosmopolitan** (sense 1). **2** an animal or plant that occurs in most parts of the world.
▸**cosˈmopolitˌism** *n*

cosmos ❶ (ˈkɒzmɒs) *n* **1** the universe considered as an ordered system. **2** any ordered system. **3** (*pl* **cosmos** *or* **cosmoses**) any tropical American plant of the genus *Cosmos* cultivated as garden plants for their brightly coloured flowers. [C17: from Gk *kosmos* order]

Cosmos (ˈkɒzmɒs) *n Astronautics.* any of various types of Soviet satellite, including Cosmos 1 (launched 1962) and nearly 2000 subsequent satellites.

Cossack (ˈkɒsæk) *n* **1** (formerly) any of the free warrior-peasants of chiefly East Slavonic descent who served as cavalry under the tsars. ◆ *adj* **2** of, relating to, or characteristic of the Cossacks: *a Cossack dance.* [C16: from Russian *kazak* vagabond, of Turkic origin]

cosset ❶ (ˈkɒsɪt) *vb* **cossets, cosseting, cosseted. 1** (*tr*) to pamper; pet. ◆ *n* **2** any pet animal, esp. a lamb. [C16: from ?]

cost ❶ (kɒst) *n* **1** the price paid or required for acquiring, producing, or maintaining something, measured in money, time, or energy; outlay. **2** suffering or sacrifice: *I know to my cost.* **3a** the amount paid for a commodity by its seller: *to sell at cost.* **3b** (*as modifier*): *the cost price.* **4** (*pl*) *Law.* the expenses of judicial proceedings. **5 at all costs.** regardless of sacrifice involved. **6 at the cost of.** at the expense of losing. ◆ *vb* **costs, costing, cost. 7** (*tr*) to be obtained or obtainable in exchange for: *the ride cost one pound.* **8** to cause or require the loss or sacrifice (of): *the accident cost him dearly.* **9** (*p.t. & p.p.* **costed**) to estimate the cost of (a product, process, etc.) for the purposes of pricing, budgeting, control, etc. [C13: from OF (n), from *coster* to cost, from L *constāre* to stand at, cost, from *stāre* to stand]

costa (ˈkɒstə) *n, pl* **costae** (-tiː). **1** the technical name for **rib**[1] (sense 1). **2** a riblike part. [C19: from L: rib, side]
▸ˈ**costal** *adj*

cost accounting *n* the recording and controlling of all the expenditures of an enterprise in order to facilitate control of separate activities. Also called: **management accounting.**
▸**cost accountant** *n*

cost-benefit *adj* denoting or relating to a method of assessing a project that takes into account its costs and its benefits to society as well as the revenue it generates: *a cost-benefit analysis; the project was assessed on a cost-benefit basis.*

cost-effective *adj* providing adequate financial return in relation to outlay.
▸ˌ**cost-efˈfectiveness** *n*

costermonger (ˈkɒstəˌmʌŋɡə) *or* **coster** *n Brit., rare.* a person who sells fruit, vegetables, etc., from a barrow. [C16: from *costard* a kind of apple + MONGER]

costive (ˈkɒstɪv) *adj* **1** constipated. **2** niggardly. [C14: from OF *costivé*, from L *constipātus*; see CONSTIPATE]
▸ˈ**costiveness** *n*

costly ❶ (ˈkɒstlɪ) *adj* **costlier, costliest. 1** expensive. **2** entailing great loss or sacrifice: *a costly victory.* **3** splendid; lavish.
▸ˈ**costliness** *n*

cost of living *n* **a** the basic cost of the food, clothing, shelter, and fuel necessary to maintain life, esp. at a standard of living regarded as basic. **b** (*as modifier*): *the cost-of-living index.*

cost-plus *n* a method of establishing a selling price in which an agreed percentage is added to the cost price to cover profit.

costume ❶ (ˈkɒstjuːm) *n* **1** a style of dressing, including all the clothes, accessories, etc., worn at one time, as in a particular country or period. **2** *Old-fashioned.* a woman's suit. **3** a set of clothes, esp. unusual or period clothes: *a jester's costume.* **4** short for **swimming costume.** ◆ *vb* **costumes, costuming, costumed.** (*tr*) **5** to furnish the costumes for (a show, film, etc.). **6** to dress (someone) in a costume. [C18: from F, from It.: dress, habit, CUSTOM]

costumier (kɒˈstjuːmɪə) *or* **costumer** *n* a person or firm that makes or supplies theatrical or fancy costumes.

cosy ❶ *or US* **cozy** (ˈkəʊzɪ) *adj* **cosier, cosiest** *or US* **cozier, coziest. 1** warm and snug. **2** intimate; friendly. ◆ *n, pl* **cosies** *or US* **cozies. 3** a cover for keeping things warm: *egg cosy.* [C18: from Scot., from ?]
▸ˈ**cosily** *or US* ˈ**cozily** *adv* ▸ˈ**cosiness** *or US* ˈ**coziness** *n*

cot[1] (kɒt) *n* **1** a child's boxlike bed, usually incorporating vertical bars. **2** a portable bed. **3** a light bedstead. **4** *Naut.* a hammock-like bed. [C17: from Hindi *khāt* bedstead]

cot[2] (kɒt) *n* **1** *Literary or arch.* a small cottage. **2** Also called: **cote. 2a** a small shelter, esp. one for pigeons, sheep, etc. **2b** (*in combination*): *dovecot.* [OE *cot*]

cot[3] (kɒt) *abbrev. for* cotangent.

cotangent (kəʊˈtændʒənt) *n* (of an angle) a trigonometric function that in a right-angled triangle is the ratio of the length of the adjacent side to that of the opposite side.

COTC *abbrev. for* Canadian Officers Training Corps.

cot death *n* the unexplained sudden death of an infant during sleep. Technical name: **sudden infant death syndrome.**

cote (kəʊt) *or* **cot** *n* **1** a small shelter for pigeons, sheep, etc. **2** (*in combination*): *dovecote.* [OE *cote*]

THESAURUS

cosmetic *adj* **3** = **beautifying**, nonessential, superficial, surface, touching-up

cosmic *adj* **1** = **universal**, stellar **3** = **vast**, grandiose, huge, immense, infinite, limitless, measureless

cosmonaut *n* = **astronaut**, spaceman, space pilot

cosmopolitan *n* **1** = **man** *or* **woman of the world**, cosmopolite, jet-setter, sophisticate ◆ *adj* **2, 3** = **sophisticated**, broad-minded, catholic, open-minded, universal, urbane, well-travelled, worldly, worldly-wise
Antonyms *adj* ≠ **sophisticated:** hidebound, illiberal, insular, limited, narrow-minded, parochial, provincial, restricted, rustic, unsophisticated

cosmos *n* **1** = **universe**, creation, macrocosm, world **2** = **order**, harmony, structure

cosset *vb* **1** = **pamper**, baby, coddle, cosher (*Irish*), mollycoddle, pet, wrap up in cotton wool (*inf.*)

cost *n* **1** = **price**, amount, charge, damage (*inf.*), expenditure, expense, figure, outlay, payment, rate, worth **2** = **loss**, damage, deprivation, detriment, expense, harm, hurt, injury, penalty, sacrifice, suffering **5 at all costs** = **no matter what**, at any price, regardless, without fail ◆ *vb* **7** = **sell at**, come to, command a price of, set (someone) back (*inf.*) **8** = **lose**, do disservice to, harm, hurt, injure, necessitate

costly *adj* **1** = **expensive**, dear, excessive, exorbitant, extortionate, highly-priced, steep (*inf.*), stiff, valuable **2** = **damaging**, catastrophic, deleterious, disastrous, harmful, loss-making, ruinous, sacrificial **3** = **splendid**, gorgeous, lavish, luxurious, opulent, precious, priceless, rich, sumptuous
Antonyms *adj* ≠ **expensive:** cheap, cheapo (*inf.*), dirt-cheap, economical, fair, inexpensive, low-priced, reasonable, reduced

costume *n* **1, 3** = **outfit**, apparel, attire, clothing, dress, ensemble, garb, get-up (*inf.*), livery, national dress, robes, uniform

cosy *adj* **1** = **snug**, comfortable, comfy (*inf.*), cuddled up, homely, secure, sheltered, snuggled down, tucked up, warm

coterie ⓣ ('kəʊtərɪ) *n* a small exclusive group of people with common interests; clique. [C18: from F, from OF: association of tenants, from *cotier* (unattested) cottager]

coterminous (kəʊ'tɜːmɪnəs) *or* **conterminous** *adj* **1** having a common boundary. **2** coextensive or coincident in range, time, etc.

coth (kɒθ, 'kɒt'eɪtʃ) *n* hyperbolic cotangent. [C20: from COT(ANGENT) + H(YPERBOLIC)]

cotillion *or* **cotillon** (kə'tɪljən, kəʊ-) *n* **1** a French formation dance of the 18th century. **2** *US.* a quadrille. **3** *US.* a formal ball. [C18: from F *cotillon* dance, from OF: petticoat]

cotinga (kə'tɪŋgə) *n* a tropical American passerine bird having a broad slightly hooked bill.

cotoneaster (kəˌtəʊnɪ'æstə) *n* any Old World shrub of the rosaceous genus *Cotoneaster:* cultivated for their ornamental flowers and red or black berries. [C18: from NL, from L *cotōneum* QUINCE]

cotta ('kɒtə) *n RC Church.* a short form of surplice. [C19: from It.: tunic]

cottage ⓣ ('kɒtɪdʒ) *n* a small simple house, esp. in a rural area. [C14: from COT[2]]

cottage cheese *n* a mild loose soft white cheese made from skimmed milk curds.

cottage hospital *n Brit.* a small rural hospital.

cottage industry *n* an industry in which employees work in their own homes, often using their own equipment.

cottage pie *n Brit.* another term for **shepherd's pie.**

cottager ('kɒtɪdʒə) *n* **1** a person who lives in a cottage. **2** a rural labourer.

cottaging ('kɒtɪdʒɪŋ) *n Brit. sl.* homosexual activity between men in a public lavatory.

cotter[1] ('kɒtə) *n Machinery.* **1** any part, such as a pin, wedge, key, etc., that is used to secure two other parts so that relative motion between them is prevented. **2** short for **cotter pin.** [C14: shortened from *cotterel,* from ?]

cotter[2] ('kɒtə) *n* **1** *English history.* a villein in late Anglo-Saxon and early Norman times occupying a cottage and land in return for labour. **2** Also called: **cottar.** a peasant occupying a cottage and land in the Scottish Highlands. [C14: from Med. L *cotārius,* from ME *cote* COT[2]]

cotter pin *n Machinery.* a split pin secured, after passing through holes in the parts to be attached, by spreading the ends.

cotton ('kɒtᵊn) *n* **1** any of various herbaceous plants and shrubs cultivated in warm climates for the fibre surrounding the seeds and the oil within the seeds. **2** the soft white downy fibre of these plants, used to manufacture textiles. **3** cotton plants collectively, as a cultivated crop. **4** a cloth or thread made from cotton fibres. [C14: from OF *coton,* from Ar. *qutn*]
▸'**cottony** *adj*

cotton bud *n* a small stick with a cotton-wool tip used for cleaning the ears, applying make-up, etc.

cotton grass *n* any of various N temperate and arctic grasslike bog plants whose clusters of long silky hairs resemble cotton tufts.

cotton on *vb* (*intr, adv;* often foll. by *to*) *Inf.* to perceive the meaning (of).

cotton-picking *adj US & Canad. sl.* (intensifier qualifying something undesirable): *you cotton-picking layabout!*

cottonseed ('kɒtᵊnˌsiːd) *n, pl* **cottonseeds** *or* **cottonseed.** the seed of the cotton plant: a source of oil and fodder.

cotton wool *n* **1** *Chiefly Brit.* bleached and sterilized cotton from which the impurities, such as the seeds, have been removed. Usual US term: **absorbent cotton. 2** cotton in the natural state. **3** *Brit. inf.* a state of pampered comfort and protection.

cotyledon (ˌkɒtɪ'liːdᵊn) *n* a simple embryonic leaf in seed-bearing plants, which, in some species, forms the first green leaf after germination. [C16: from L: a plant, navelwort, from Gk *kotulēdōn,* from *kotulē* cup, hollow]
▸ˌ**coty'ledonous** *adj* ▸ˌ**coty'ledonal** *adj*

coucal ('kuːkæl) *n* any ground-living bird of the genus *Centropus* of Africa, S Asia, and Australia. [C19: from F, ?from *couc(ou)* cuckoo + *al(ouette)* lark]

couch ⓣ (kaʊtʃ) *n* **1** a piece of upholstered furniture, usually having a back and armrests, for seating more than one person. **2** a bed, esp. one used in the daytime by the patients of a doctor or a psychoanalyst. ◆ *vb* **3** (*tr*) to express in a particular style of language: *couched in an archaic style.* **4** (when *tr, usually reflexive or passive*) to lie down or cause to lie down for or as for sleep. **5** (*intr*) *Arch.* to crouch. **6** (*intr*) *Arch.* to lie in ambush; lurk. **7** (*tr*) *Surgery.* to remove (a cataract) by downward displacement of the lens of the eye. **8** (*tr*) *Arch.* to lower (a lance) into a horizontal position. [C14: from OF *couche* a bed, lair, from *coucher* to lay down, from L *collocāre* to arrange, from *locāre* to place]

couchant ('kaʊtʃənt) *adj* (*usually postpositive*) *Heraldry.* in a lying position: *a lion couchant.* [C15: from F: lying]

couchette (kuː'ʃɛt) *n* a bed or berth in a railway carriage, esp. one converted from seats. [C20: from F, dim. of *couche* bed]

couch grass (kaʊtʃ, kuːtʃ) *n* a grass with a yellowish-white creeping underground stem by which it spreads quickly: a troublesome weed. Also called: **twitch grass, quitch grass.**

couch potato *n Sl., chiefly US.* a lazy person whose recreation consists chiefly of watching television.

cougar ('kuːgə) *n* another name for **puma.** [C18: from F *couguar,* from Port., from Tupi]

cough ⓣ (kɒf) *vb* **1** (*intr*) to expel air abruptly and explosively through the partially closed vocal chords. **2** (*intr*) to make a sound similar to this. **3** (*tr*) to utter or express with a cough or coughs. ◆ *n* **4** an act or sound of coughing. **5** a condition of the lungs or throat which causes frequent coughing. [OE *cohhetten*]
▸'**cougher** *n*

cough drop *n* a lozenge to relieve a cough.

cough mixture *n* any medicine that relieves coughing.

cough up ⓣ *vb* (*adv*) **1** *Inf.* to surrender (money, information, etc.), esp. reluctantly. **2** (*tr*) to bring into the mouth or eject (phlegm, food, etc.) by coughing.

could (kʊd) *vb* (takes an infinitive without *to* or an implied infinitive) used as an auxiliary: **1** to make the past tense of **can**[1]. **2** to make the subjunctive mood of **can**[1], esp. used in polite requests or in conditional sentences: *could I see you tonight?* **3** to indicate suggestion of a course of action: *you could take the car if it's raining.* **4** (often foll. by *well*) to indicate a possibility: *he could well be a spy.* [OE *cūthe*]

couldn't ('kʊdᵊnt) *contraction of* could not.

couldst (kʊdst) *vb Arch.* the form of **could** used with the pronoun *thou* or its relative form.

coulee ('kuːleɪ, -lɪ) *n* **1a** a flow of molten lava. **1b** such lava when solidified. **2** *Western US & Canad.* a steep-sided ravine. [C19: from Canad. F *coulée* a flow, from F, from *couler* to flow, from L *cōlāre* to sift]

coulis ('kuːliː) *n* a thin purée of vegetables, fruit, etc., usually served as a sauce. [C20: F, lit.: purée]

coulomb ('kuːlɒm) *n* the derived SI unit of electric charge; the quantity of electricity transported in one second by a current of 1 ampere. Symbol: C [C19: after C.A. de *Coulomb* (1736–1806), F physicist]

coulter ('kəʊltə) *n* a blade or sharp-edged disc attached to a plough so that it cuts through the soil vertically in advance of the ploughshare. Also (esp. US): **colter.** [OE *culter,* from L: ploughshare, knife]

coumarin *or* **cumarin** ('kuːmərɪn) *n* a white vanilla-scented crystalline ester, used in perfumes and flavouring. [C19: from F, from *coumarou* tonka-bean tree, from Sp., from Tupi]

council ⓣ ('kaʊnsəl) *n* **1** an assembly of people meeting for discussion, consultation, etc. **2a** a body of people elected or appointed to serve in an administrative, legislative, or advisory capacity: *a student council.* **2b** short for **legislative council. 3** (*sometimes cap.;* often preceded by *the*) *Brit.* the local governing authority of a town, county, etc. **4** *Austral.* an administrative or legislative assembly, esp. the upper house of a state parliament in Australia. **5** a meeting of a council. **6** (*modifier*) of, provided for, or used by a local council: *a council chamber; council offices.* **7** (*modifier*) *Brit.* provided by a local council, esp. (of housing) at a subsidized rent: *a council house; a council estate; a council school.* **8** *Christianity.* an assembly of bishops, etc., convened for regulating matters of doctrine or discipline. [C12: from OF *concile,* from L *concilium* assembly, from *com-* together + *calāre* to call]

USAGE NOTE Avoid confusion with **counsel.**

council area *n* any of the 32 unitary authorities into which Scotland was divided for administrative purposes in 1996.

councillor *or US* **councilor** ('kaʊnsələ) *n* a member of a council.

USAGE NOTE Avoid confusion with **counsellor.**

councilman ('kaʊnsəlmən) *n, pl* **councilmen.** *Chiefly US.* a councillor.

council tax *n* (in Britain) a tax based on the relative value of property levied to fund local council services.

counsel ⓣ ('kaʊnsəl) *n* **1** advice or guidance on conduct, behaviour, etc. **2** discussion; consultation: *to take counsel with a friend.* **3** a person whose advice is sought. **4** a barrister or group of barristers engaged in conducting cases in court and advising on legal matters. **5** *Christianity.* any of the **counsels of perfection,** namely poverty, chastity, and obedience. **6 counsel of perfection.** excellent but unrealizable advice. **7** private opinions (esp. in **keep one's own counsel**). **8** *Arch.* wisdom; prudence. ◆ *vb* **counsels, counselling, counselled** *or US* **counsels, counseling, counseled. 9** (*tr*) to give advice or guidance to. **10** (*tr; often takes a clause as object*) to recommend; urge. **11** (*intr*) *Arch.* to take counsel; consult.

THESAURUS

coterie *n* = **clique,** cabal, camp, circle, gang, group, outfit (*inf.*), posse (*inf.*), set

cottage *n* = **cabin,** but-and-ben (*Scot.*), chalet, cot, hut, lodge, shack

couch *n* **1, 2** = **sofa,** bed, chaise longue, chesterfield, day bed, divan, ottoman, settee ◆ *vb* **3** = **express,** frame, phrase, set forth, utter, word

cough *vb* **1, 2** = **clear one's throat,** bark, hack, hawk, hem ◆ *n* **4** = **frog** *or* **tickle in one's throat,** bark, hack

cough up *vb* **1** *Informal* = **give up,** deliver, fork out, hand over, shell out (*inf.*), surrender

council *n* **1, 2** = **governing body,** assembly, board, cabinet, chamber, committee, conclave, conference, congress, convention, convocation, diet, house, ministry, panel, parliament, quango, synod

counsel *n* **1, 2** = **advice,** admonition, caution, consideration, consultation, deliberation, direction, forethought, guidance, information, recommendation, suggestion, warning **4** = **legal adviser,** advocate, attorney, barrister, lawyer, solicitor ◆ *vb* **9, 10** = **advise,** admonish, advocate, caution, exhort, instruct, prescribe, recommend, urge, warn

[C13: from OF *counseil*, from L *consilium* deliberating body; rel. to CONSULT]

> **USAGE NOTE** Avoid confusion with **council**.

counselling *or US* **counseling** ('kaunsəlɪŋ) *n* systematic guidance offered by social workers, doctors, etc., in which a person's problems are discussed and advice is given.

counsellor *or US* **counselor** ('kaunsələ) *n* **1** a person who gives counsel; adviser. **2** Also called: **counselor-at-law.** *US.* a lawyer, esp. one who conducts cases in court. **3** a senior diplomatic officer.

> **USAGE NOTE** Avoid confusion with **councillor.**

count[1] Ⓣ (kaunt) *vb* **1** to add up or check (each unit in a collection) in order to ascertain the sum: *count your change.* **2** (*tr*) to recite numbers in ascending order up to and including. **3** (*tr;* often foll. by *in*) to take into account or include: *we must count him in.* **4 not counting.** excluding. **5** (*tr*) to consider; deem: *count yourself lucky.* **6** (*intr*) to have importance: *this picture counts as a rarity.* **7** (*intr*) *Music.* to keep time by counting beats. ◆ *n* **8** the act of counting. **9** the number reached by counting; sum: *a blood count.* **10** *Law.* a paragraph in an indictment containing a separate charge. **11 keep** *or* **lose count.** to keep or fail to keep an accurate record of items, events, etc. **12** *Boxing, wrestling.* the act of telling off a number of seconds by the referee, as when a boxer has been knocked down by his opponent. **13 out for the count.** *Boxing.* knocked out and unable to continue after a count of ten by the referee. ◆ See also **count against, countdown,** etc. [C14: from Anglo-F *counter,* from OF *conter,* from L *computāre* to calculate]
▸ **'countable** *adj*

count[2] (kaunt) *n* **1** a nobleman in any of various European countries having a rank corresponding to that of a British earl. **2** any of various officials in the late Roman Empire and in the early Middle Ages. [C16: from OF *conte,* from L *comes* associate, from COM- with + *īre* to go]

count against *vb* (*intr, prep*) to have influence to the disadvantage of.

countdown ('kaunt,daun) *n* **1** the act of counting backwards to time a critical operation exactly, such as the launching of a rocket. ◆ *vb* **count down.** (*intr, adv*) **2** to count thus.

countenance Ⓣ ('kauntɪnəns) *n* **1** the face, esp. when considered as expressing a person's character or mood. **2** support or encouragement; sanction. **3** composure; self-control (esp. in **keep** *or* **lose one's countenance**). ◆ *vb* **countenances, countenancing, countenanced.** (*tr*) **4** to support or encourage; sanction. **5** to tolerate; endure. [C13: from OF *contenance* mien, behaviour, from L *continentia* restraint, control; see CONTAIN]

counter[1] ('kauntə) *n* **1** a horizontal surface, as in a shop or bank, over which business is transacted. **2** (in some cafeterias) a long table on which food is served. **3a** a small flat disc of wood, metal, or plastic, used in various board games. **3b** a similar disc or token used as an imitation coin. **4** a person or thing that may be used or manipulated. **5 under the counter.** (**under-the-counter** *when prenominal*) (of the sale of goods) clandestine or illegal. **6 over the counter.** (**over-the-counter** *when prenominal*) (of security transactions) through a broker rather than on a stock exchange. [C14: from OF *comptouer,* ult. from L *computāre* to COMPUTE]

counter[2] ('kauntə) *n* **1** a person who counts. **2** an apparatus that records the number of occurrences of events. [C14: from OF *conteor,* from L *computātor;* see COUNT[1]]

counter[3] Ⓣ ('kauntə) *adv* **1** in a contrary direction or manner. **2** in a wrong or reverse direction. **3 run counter to.** to have a contrary effect or action to. ◆ *adj* **4** opposing; opposite; contrary. ◆ *n* **5** something that is contrary or opposite to some other thing. **6** an act, effect, or force that opposes another. **7** a return attack, such as a blow in boxing. **8** *Fencing.* a parry in which the foils move in a circular fashion. **9** the portion of the stern of a boat or ship that overhangs the water aft of the rudder. **10** a piece of leather forming the back of a shoe. ◆ *vb* **11** to say or do (something) in retaliation or response. **12** (*tr*) to move, act, or perform in a manner or direction opposite to (a person or thing). **13** to return the attack of (an opponent). [C15: from OF *contre,* from L *contrā* against]

counter- *prefix* **1** against; opposite; contrary: *counterattack.* **2** complementary; corresponding: *counterfoil.* **3** duplicate or substitute: *counterfeit.* [via OF from L *contrā* against, opposite; see CONTRA-]

counteract Ⓣ (,kauntər'ækt) *vb* (*tr*) to oppose or neutralize by contrary action; check.
▸ **,counter'action** *n* ▸ **,counter'active** *adj*

counterattack ('kauntərə,tæk) *n* **1** an attack in response to an attack. ◆ *vb* **2** to make a counterattack (against).

counterbalance Ⓣ *n* ('kauntə,bæləns). **1** a weight or force that balances or offsets another. ◆ *vb* (,kauntə'bæləns), **counterbalances, counterbalancing, counterbalanced.** (*tr*) **2** Also: **counterweigh.** to act as a counterbalance to. ◆ Also: **counterpoise.**

counterblast ('kauntə,blɑ:st) *n* an aggressive response to a verbal attack.

countercheck *n* ('kauntə,tʃɛk). **1** a check or restraint, esp. one that acts in opposition to another. **2** a double check, as for accuracy. ◆ *vb* (,kauntə'tʃɛk). (*tr*) **3** to oppose by counteraction. **4** to double-check.

counterclaim ('kauntə,kleɪm) *Chiefly law.* ◆ *n* **1** a claim set up in opposition to another. ◆ *vb* **2** to set up (a claim) in opposition to another claim.
▸ **,counter'claimant** *n*

counterclockwise (,kauntə'klɒk,waɪz) *adv, adj* the US and Canad. equivalent of **anticlockwise.**

counterculture ('kauntə,kʌltʃə) *n* an alternative culture, deliberately at variance with the social norm.

counterespionage (,kauntər'ɛspɪə,nɑ:ʒ) *n* activities to counteract enemy espionage.

counterfeit Ⓣ ('kauntəfɪt) *adj* **1** made in imitation of something genuine with the intent to deceive or defraud; forged. **2** simulated; sham: *counterfeit affection.* ◆ *n* **3** an imitation designed to deceive or defraud. ◆ *vb* **4** (*tr*) to make a fraudulent imitation of. **5** (*intr*) to make counterfeits. **6** to feign; simulate. [C13: from OF *contrefait,* from *contrefaire* to copy, from *contre-* COUNTER- + *faire* to make]
▸ **'counterfeiter** *n*

counterfoil ('kauntə,fɔɪl) *n Brit.* the part of a cheque, receipt, etc., retained as a record. Also called (esp. in the US and Canada): **stub.**

counterforce ('kauntə,fɔ:s) *n* (*modifier*) denoting military strategy based on retaliation against attacking forces.

counterinsurgency (,kauntərɪn'sɜ:dʒənsɪ) *n* action taken by a government against rebels, guerrillas, etc.

counterintelligence (,kauntərɪn'tɛlɪdʒəns) *n* activities designed to frustrate enemy espionage.

counterintuitive *adj Chiefly US.* (of an idea, proposal, etc.) seemingly contrary to common sense.

counterirritant (,kauntər'ɪrɪtᵊnt) *n* **1** an agent that causes a superficial irritation of the skin and thereby relieves inflammation of deep structures. ◆ *adj* **2** producing a counterirritation.
▸ **,counter,irri'tation** *n*

countermand Ⓣ *vb* (,kauntə'mɑ:nd). (*tr*) **1** to revoke or cancel (a command, order, etc.). **2** to order (forces, etc.) to retreat; recall. ◆ *n* ('kauntə,mɑ:nd). **3** a command revoking another. [C15: from OF *contremander,* from *contre-* COUNTER- + *mander* to command, from L *mandāre*]

countermarch ('kauntə,mɑ:tʃ) *Chiefly mil.* ◆ *vb* **1** to march or cause to march back or in the opposite direction. ◆ *n* **2** the act or an instance of countermarching.

countermeasure ('kauntə,mɛʒə) *n* action taken to oppose, neutralize, or retaliate against some other action.

countermove ('kauntə,mu:v) *n* **1** an opposing move. ◆ *vb* **countermoves, countermoving, countermoved.** **2** to make or do (something) as an opposing move.
▸ **'counter,movement** *n*

counteroffensive ('kauntərə,fɛnsɪv) *n* a series of attacks by a defending force against an attacking enemy.

counteroffer ('kauntər,ɒfə) *n* a response to a bid in which a seller amends his original offer, making it more favourable to the buyer.

counterpane Ⓣ ('kauntə,peɪn) *n* another word for **bedspread.** [C17: from obs. *counterpoint* (infl. by *pane* coverlet), changed from OF *coutepointe* quilt, from Med. L *culcita puncta* quilted mattress]

counterpart Ⓣ ('kauntə,pɑ:t) *n* **1** a person or thing identical to or closely resembling another. **2** one of two parts that complement or

THESAURUS

count[1] *vb* **1** = **add (up)**, calculate, cast up, check, compute, enumerate, estimate, number, reckon, score, tally, tot up **3** = **take into account** *or* **consideration**, include, number among **5** = **consider**, deem, esteem, impute, judge, look upon, rate, regard, think **6** = **matter**, be important, carry weight, cut any ice (*inf.*), enter into consideration, rate, signify, tell, weigh ◆ *n* **8, 9** = **calculation**, computation, enumeration, numbering, poll, reckoning, sum, tally

countenance *n* **1** *Literary* = **face**, appearance, aspect, expression, features, look, mien, physiognomy, visage **2** = **support**, aid, approval, assistance, backing, endorsement, favour, sanction ◆ *vb* **4** = **support**, abet, aid, approve, back, champion, commend, condone, encourage, endorse, help, sanction **5** = **tolerate**, brook, endure, hack (*sl.*), put up with (*inf.*), stand for (*inf.*)

counter[3] *adv* **1** = **opposite to**, against, at variance with, contrarily, contrariwise, conversely, in defiance of, versus ◆ *adj* **4** = **opposing**, adverse, against, conflicting, contradictory, contrary, contrasting, obverse, opposed, opposite ◆ *vb* **11** = **retaliate**, answer, hit back, meet, obviate, offset, oppose, parry, resist, respond, return, ward off
Antonyms *adv* ≠ **opposite to:** in agreement, parallel ◆ *adj* ≠ **opposing:** accordant, parallel, similar ◆ *vb* ≠ **retaliate:** accept, cave in (*inf.*), give in, surrender, take, yield

counteract *vb* = **act against**, annul, check, contravene, counterbalance, countervail, cross, defeat, foil, frustrate, hinder, invalidate, negate, neutralize, obviate, offset, oppose, resist, thwart

counterbalance *vb* **2** = **offset**, balance, compensate, counterpoise, countervail, make up for, set off

counterfeit *adj* **1, 2** = **fake**, bogus, copied, ersatz, false, feigned, forged, fraudulent, imitation, phoney *or* phony (*inf.*), pseud *or* pseudo (*inf.*), sham, simulated, spurious, suppositious ◆ *n* **3** = **fake**, copy, forgery, fraud, imitation, phoney *or* phony (*inf.*), reproduction, sham ◆ *vb* **3-6** = **fake**, copy, fabricate, feign, forge, imitate, impersonate, pretend, sham, simulate
Antonyms *adj* ≠ **fake:** authentic, genuine, good, original, real, the real thing

countermand *vb* **1** = **cancel**, annul, override, repeal, rescind, retract, reverse, revoke

counterpane *n* = **bedspread**, bed cover, cover, coverlet, doona (*Austral.*), quilt

counterpart *n* **2** = **opposite number**, comple-

correspond to each other. **3** a duplicate, esp. of a legal document; copy.

counterparty ('kaʊntəˌpɑːtɪ) *n* a person who is a party to a contract.

counterplot ('kaʊntəˌplɒt) *n* **1** a plot designed to frustrate another plot. ◆ *vb* **counterplots, counterplotting, counterplotted. 2** (*tr*) to oppose with a counterplot.

counterpoint ('kaʊntəˌpɔɪnt) *n* **1** the technique involving the simultaneous sounding of two or more parts or melodies. **2** a melody or part combined with another melody or part. **3** the musical texture resulting from the simultaneous sounding of two or more melodies or parts. ◆ *vb* **4** (*tr*) to set in contrast. ◆ Related adj: **contrapuntal. [**C15: from OF *contrepoint,* from *contre-* COUNTER- + *point* dot, note in musical notation, i.e. an accompaniment set against the notes of a melody**]**

counterpoise ('kaʊntəˌpɔɪz) *n* **1** a force, influence, etc., that counterbalances another. **2** a state of balance; equilibrium. **3** a weight that balances another. ◆ *vb* **counterpoises, counterpoising, counterpoised.** (*tr*) **4** to oppose with something of equal effect, weight, or force; offset. **5** to bring into equilibrium.

counterproductive (ˌkaʊntəprə'dʌktɪv) *adj* tending to hinder the achievement of an aim; having effects contrary to those intended.

counterproposal ('kaʊntəprəˌpəʊzᵊl) *n* a proposal offered as an alternative to a previous proposal.

Counter-Reformation (ˌkaʊntəˌrɛfə'meɪʃən) *n* the reform movement of the Roman Catholic Church in the 16th and early 17th centuries considered as a reaction to the Reformation.

counter-revolution (ˌkaʊntəˌrɛvə'luːʃən) *n* a revolution opposed to a previous revolution.
▶ˌ**counter-ˌrevo'lutionist** *n* ▶**counter-ˌrevo'lutionary** *n, adj*

countershaft ('kaʊntəˌʃɑːft) *n* an intermediate shaft driven by a main shaft, esp. in a gear train.

countersign *vb* ('kaʊntəˌsaɪn, ˌkaʊntə'saɪn). **1** (*tr*) to sign (a document already signed by another). ◆ *n* ('kaʊntəˌsaɪn). **2** Also called: **countersignature.** the signature so written. **3** a secret sign given in response to another sign. **4** *Chiefly mil.* a password.

countersink ('kaʊntəˌsɪŋk) *vb* **countersinks, countersinking, countersank, countersunk.** (*tr*) **1** to enlarge the upper part of (a hole) in timber, metal, etc., so that the head of a bolt or screw can be sunk below the surface. **2** to drive (a screw) or sink (a bolt) into such a hole. ◆ *n* **3** Also called: **countersink bit.** a tool for countersinking. **4** a countersunk hole.

countertenor (ˌkaʊntə'tɛnə) *n* **1** an adult male voice with an alto range. **2** a singer with such a voice.

countervail (ˌkaʊntə'veɪl, 'kaʊntəˌveɪl) *vb* **1** (when *intr,* usually foll. by *against*) to act or act against with equal power or force. **2** (*tr*) to make up for; compensate; offset. **[**C14: from OF *contrevaloir,* from L *contrā valēre,* from *contrā* against + *valēre* to be strong**]**

countervailing duty *n* an extra import duty imposed by a country on certain imports, esp. to prevent dumping or to counteract subsidies in the exporting country.

counterweigh (ˌkaʊntə'weɪ) *vb* another word for **counterbalance** (sense 2).

counterweight ('kaʊntəˌweɪt) *n* a counterbalancing weight, influence, or force.

countess ('kaʊntɪs) *n* **1** the wife or widow of a count or earl. **2** a woman of the rank of count or earl.

counting house *n Rare, chiefly Brit.* a room or building used by the accountants of a business.

countless Ⓣ ('kaʊntlɪs) *adj* innumerable; myriad.

count noun *n* a noun that can be qualified by the indefinite article and may be used in the plural, as *telephone* and *thing* but not *airs and graces* or *bravery*. Cf. **mass noun.**

count on Ⓣ *vb* (*intr, prep*) to rely or depend on.

count out Ⓣ *vb* (*tr, adv*) **1** *Inf.* to leave out; exclude. **2** (of a boxing referee) to judge (a floored boxer) to have failed to recover within the specified time.

count palatine *n, pl* **counts palatine.** *History.* **1** (in the Holy Roman Empire) a count who exercised royal authority in his own domain. **2** (in England and Ireland) the lord of a county palatine.

countrified Ⓣ *or* **countryfied** ('kʌntrɪˌfaɪd) *adj* in the style, manners, etc., of the country; rural.

country Ⓣ ('kʌntrɪ) *n, pl* **countries. 1** a territory distinguished by its people, culture, geography, etc. **2** an area of land distinguished by its political autonomy; state. **3** the people of a territory or state. **4a** the part of the land that is away from cities or industrial areas; rural districts. **4b** (*as modifier*): *country cottage.* Related adjs.: **pastoral, rural. 5** short for **country music. 6 across country.** not keeping to roads, etc. **7 go** *or* **appeal to the country.** *Chiefly Brit.* to dissolve Parliament and hold an election. **8 up country.** away from the coast or the capital. **9** one's native land or nation of citizenship. **[**C13: from OF *contrée,* from Med. L *contrāta,* lit.: that which lies opposite, from L *contrā* opposite**]**

country and western *n* another name for **country music.**

country club *n* a club in the country, having sporting and social facilities.

country dance *n* a type of folk dance in which couples face one another in a line.

country house *n* a large house in the country, esp. belonging to a wealthy family.

countryman Ⓣ ('kʌntrɪmən) *n, pl* **countrymen. 1** a person who lives in the country. **2** a person from a particular country or from one's own country.
▶'**countryˌwoman** *fem n*

country music *n* a type of 20th-century popular music based on White folk music of the southeastern US.

country park *n Brit.* an area of countryside set aside for public recreation.

country seat *n* a large estate or property in the country.

countryside Ⓣ ('kʌntrɪˌsaɪd) *n* a rural area or its population.

county Ⓣ ('kaʊntɪ) *n, pl* **counties. 1a** any of various administrative, political, judicial, or geographic subdivisions of certain English-speaking countries or states. **1b** (*as modifier*): *county cricket.* ◆ *adj* **2** *Brit. inf.* upper class; of or like the landed gentry. **[**C14: from OF *conté* land belonging to a count, from LL *comes* COUNT[2]**]**

county borough *n* **1** (in England from 1888 to 1974 and in Wales from 1888 to 1974 and from 1996) a borough administered independently of any higher tier of local government. **2** (in the Republic of Ireland) a borough governed by an elected council that constitutes an all-purpose authority.

county palatine *n, pl* **counties palatine. 1** the lands of a count palatine. **2** (in England and Ireland) a county in which the earl (or other lord) exercised many royal powers, esp. judicial authority.

county town *n* the town in which a county's affairs are or were administered.

coup Ⓣ (kuː) *n* **1** a brilliant and successful stroke or action. **2** short for **coup d'état. [**C18: from F: blow, from L *colaphus* blow with the fist, from Gk *kolaphos***]**

coup de grâce Ⓣ *French.* (ku də grɑs) *n, pl* **coups de grâce** (ku də grɑs). **1** a mortal or finishing blow, esp. one delivered as an act of mercy to a sufferer. **2** a final or decisive stroke. **[**lit.: blow of mercy**]**

coup d'état Ⓣ ('kuː deɪ'tɑː) *n, pl* **coups d'état** ('kuːz deɪ'tɑː). a sudden violent or illegal seizure of government. **[**F, lit.: stroke of state**]**

coupe (kuːp) *n* **1** a dessert of fruit and ice cream. **2** a dish or stemmed glass bowl designed for this dessert. **[**C19: from F: goblet, CUP**]**

coupé ('kuːpeɪ) *n* **1** a four-seater car with a sloping back, and usually two doors. **2** a four-wheeled horse-drawn carriage with two seats inside and one outside for the driver. **[**C19: from F *carrosse coupé,* lit.: cut-off carriage**]**

couple Ⓣ ('kʌpᵊl) *n* **1** two people who regularly associate with each other or live together: *an engaged couple.* **2** (*functioning as sing or pl*) two people considered as a pair, for or as if for dancing, games, etc. **3** a pair of equal and opposite parallel forces that have a tendency to produce rotation. **4** a connector or link between two members, such as a tie connecting a pair of rafters in a roof. **5 a couple of.** (*functioning as sing or pl*) **5a** a combination of two; a pair of: *a couple of men.* **5b** *Inf.* a small number of; a few: *a couple of days.* ◆ *pron* **6** (usually preceded by *a; functioning as sing or pl*) two; a pair: *give him a couple.* ◆ *vb* **couples, coupling, coupled. 7** (*tr*) to connect (two things) together or to connect (one thing) to (another): *to couple railway carriages.* **8** to form or be formed into a pair or pairs. **9** to associate, put, or connect together. **10**

THESAURUS

ment, correlative, equal, fellow, match, mate, supplement, tally, twin **3 = copy**, duplicate

countless *adj* = **innumerable**, endless, immeasurable, incalculable, infinite, legion, limitless, measureless, multitudinous, myriad, numberless, uncounted, untold
Antonyms *adj* finite, limited, restricted

count on *vb* = **depend on**, bank on, believe (in), lean on, pin one's faith on, reckon on, rely on, take for granted, take on trust, trust

count out *vb Informal* = **leave out**, disregard, except, exclude, leave out of account, pass over

countrified *adj* = **rural**, agrestic, Arcadian, bucolic, cracker-barrel, homespun, idyllic, pastoral, picturesque, provincial, rustic

country *n* **1 = territory**, land, part, region, terrain **2 = nation**, commonwealth, kingdom, people, realm, sovereign state, state **3 = people**, citizenry, citizens, community, electors, grass roots, inhabitants, nation, populace, public, society, voters **4a = countryside**, backlands (*US*), backwoods, farmland, green belt, outback (*Austral. & NZ*), provinces, rural areas, sticks (*inf.*), the back of beyond, wide open spaces (*inf.*) ◆ *modifier* **4b = rural**, agrarian, agrestic, Arcadian, bucolic, georgic (*literary*), landed, pastoral, provincial, rustic ◆ *n* **9 = native land**, fatherland, homeland, motherland, nationality, *patria*
Antonyms *n* ≠ **countryside:** city, metropolis, town ◆ *modifier* ≠ **rural:** city, cosmopolitan, sophisticated, urban, urbane

countryman *n* **1 = yokel**, bumpkin, country dweller, farmer, hayseed (*US & Canad. inf.*), hick (*inf., chiefly US & Canad.*), husbandman, peasant, provincial, rustic, swain **2 = compatriot**, fellow citizen

countryside *n* = **country**, farmland, green belt, outback (*Austral. & NZ*), outdoors, panorama, sticks (*inf.*), view, wide open spaces (*inf.*)

county *n* **1a = province**, shire ◆ *adj* **2** *Informal* = **upper-class**, green-wellie, huntin', shootin', and fishin' (*inf.*), plummy (*inf.*), tweedy, upper-crust (*inf.*)

coup *n* **1 = masterstroke**, accomplishment, action, deed, exploit, feat, manoeuvre, stratagem, stroke, stroke of genius, stunt, *tour de force*

coup de grâce *n* **1 = final blow**, comeuppance (*sl.*), deathblow, kill, knockout blow, mercy stroke, mortal blow, quietus

coup d'état *n* = **overthrow**, coup, palace revolution, putsch, rebellion, seizure of power, takeover

couple *n* **5a = pair**, brace, duo, item, span (*of horses or oxen*), twain (*arch.*), two, twosome ◆ *vb* **7 = link**, buckle, clasp, conjoin, connect, hitch, join, marry, pair, unite, wed, yoke

(*intr*) to have sexual intercourse. [C13: from OF: a pair, from L *cōpula* a bond; see COPULA]

coupledom (ˈkʌpᵊldəm) *n* the state of living as a couple.

coupler (ˈkʌplə) *n Music.* a device on an organ or harpsichord connecting two keys, two manuals, etc., so that both may be played at once.

couplet (ˈkʌplɪt) *n* two successive lines of verse, usually rhymed and of the same metre. [C16: from F, lit.: a little pair; see COUPLE]

coupling (ˈkʌplɪŋ) *n* **1** a mechanical device that connects two things. **2** a device for connecting railway cars or trucks together.

coupon ❶ (ˈkuːpɒn) *n* **1a** a detachable part of a ticket or advertisement entitling the holder to a discount, free gift, etc. **1b** a detachable slip usable as a commercial order form. **1c** a voucher given away with certain goods, a certain number of which are exchangeable for goods offered by the manufacturers. **2** one of a number of detachable certificates attached to a bond, the surrender of which entitles the bearer to receive interest payments. **3** *Brit.* a detachable entry form for any of certain competitions, esp. football pools. [C19: from F, from OF *colpon* piece cut off, from *colper* to cut, var. of *couper*]

courage ❶ (ˈkʌrɪdʒ) *n* **1** the power or quality of dealing with or facing danger, fear, pain, etc. **2 the courage of one's convictions.** the confidence to act in accordance with one's beliefs. [C13: from OF *corage,* from *cuer* heart, from L *cor*]

courageous ❶ (kəˈreɪdʒəs) *adj* possessing or expressing courage.
▸**couˈrageously** *adv* ▸**couˈrageousness** *n*

courante (kuˈrɑːnt) *n Music.* **1** an old dance in quick triple time. **2** a movement of a (mostly) 16th- to 18th-century suite based on this. [C16: from F, lit.: running, from *courir* to run, from L *currere*]

courbaril (ˈkuəbərɪl) *n* a tropical American leguminous tree: its wood is a useful timber and its gum is a source of copal. Also called: **West Indian locust.** [C18: from Amerind]

coureur de bois (*French* kurœr də bwa) *n, pl* **coureurs de bois** (kurœr də bwa). *Canad. history.* a French Canadian woodsman or Métis who traded with Indians for furs. [Canad. F: trapper (lit.: wood-runner)]

courgette (kuəˈʒɛt) *n* a small variety of vegetable marrow. US, Canad., and Austral. name: **zucchini.** [from F, dim. of *courge* marrow, gourd]

courier ❶ (ˈkuərɪə) *n* **1** a special messenger, esp. one carrying diplomatic correspondence. **2** a person employed to collect and deliver parcels, packages, etc. **3** a person who makes arrangements for or accompanies a group of travellers on a journey or tour. ◆ *vb* **4** (*tr*) to send (a parcel, letter, etc.) by courier. [C16: from OF *courrier,* from OIt. *correre* to run, from L *currere*]

course ❶ (kɔːs) *n* **1** a continuous progression in time or space; onward movement. **2** a route or direction followed. **3** the path or channel along which something moves: *the course of a river.* **4** an area or stretch of land or water on which a sport is played or a race is run: *a golf course.* **5** a period of time; duration: *in the course of the next hour.* **6** the usual order of and time required for a sequence of events; regular procedure: *the illness ran its course.* **7** a mode of conduct or action: *if you follow that course, you will fail.* **8** a connected series of events, actions, etc. **9a** a prescribed number of lessons, lectures, etc., in an educational curriculum. **9b** the material covered in such a curriculum. **10** a regimen prescribed for a specific period of time: *a course of treatment.* **11** a part of a meal served at one time. **12** a continuous, usually horizontal, layer of building material, such as a row of bricks, tiles, etc. **13 as a matter of course.** as a natural or normal consequence, mode of action, or event. **14 in course of.** in the process of. **15 in due course.** at some future time, esp. the natural or appropriate time. **16 of course. 16a** (*adv*) as expected; naturally. **16b** (*sentence substitute*) certainly; definitely. **17 the course of nature.** the ordinary course of events. ◆ *vb* **courses, coursing, coursed. 18** (*intr*) to run, race, or flow. **19** to cause (hounds) to hunt by sight rather than scent or (of hounds) to hunt (a quarry) thus. [C13: from OF *cours,* from L *cursus* a running, from *currere* to run]

courser[1] (ˈkɔːsə) *n* **1** a person who courses hounds or dogs, esp. greyhounds. **2** a hound or dog trained for coursing.

courser[2] (ˈkɔːsə) *n Literary.* a swift horse; steed. [C13: from OF *coursier,* from *cours* COURSE]

coursework (ˈkɔːsˌwɜːk) *n* written or oral work completed by a student within a given period, which is assessed as part of an educational course.

coursing (ˈkɔːsɪŋ) *n* **1** hunting with hounds or dogs that follow their quarry by sight. **2** a sport in which hounds are matched against one another in pairs for the hunting of hares by sight.

court ❶ (kɔːt) *n* **1** an area of ground wholly or partly surrounded by walls or buildings. **2** *Brit.* **2a** a block of flats. **2b** a mansion or country house. **2c** a short street, sometimes closed at one end. **3a** the residence, retinues, or household of a sovereign or nobleman. **3b** (*as modifier*): *a court ball.* **4** a sovereign or prince and his retinue, advisers, etc. **5** any formal assembly held by a sovereign or nobleman. **6** homage, flattering attention, or amorous approaches (esp. in **pay court to someone**). **7** *Law.* **7a** a tribunal having power to adjudicate in civil, criminal, military, or ecclesiastical matters. **7b** the regular sitting of such a judicial tribunal. **7c** the room or building in which such a tribunal sits. **8a** a marked outdoor or enclosed area used for any of various ball games, such as tennis, squash, etc. **8b** a marked section of such an area. **9 go to court.** to take legal action. **10 hold court.** to preside over admirers, attendants, etc. **11 out of court.** without a trial or legal case. **12 the ball is in your court.** you are obliged to make the next move. ◆ *vb* **13** to attempt to gain the love of; woo. **14** (*tr*) to pay attention to (someone) in order to gain favour. **15** (*tr*) to try to obtain (fame, honour, etc.). **16** (*tr*) to invite, usually foolishly, as by taking risks. [C12: from OF, from L *cohors* COHORT]

court-bouillon (ˈkuətˈbuːjɒn) *n* a stock made from root vegetables, water, and wine or vinegar, used primarily for poaching fish. [from F, from *court* short, + *bouillon* broth, from *bouillir* to BOIL[1]]

court card *n* (in a pack of playing cards) a king, queen, or jack of any suit. [C17: altered from earlier *coat-card,* from the decorative coats worn by the figures depicted]

court circular *n* a daily report of the activities, engagements, etc., of the sovereign, published in a national newspaper.

Courtelle (kɔːˈtɛl) *n Trademark.* a synthetic acrylic fibre resembling wool.

courteous ❶ (ˈkɜːtɪəs) *adj* polite and considerate in manner. [C13 *corteis,* lit.: with courtly manners, from OF; see COURT]
▸**ˈcourteously** *adv* ▸**ˈcourteousness** *n*

courtesan ❶ *or* **courtezan** (ˌkɔːtɪˈzæn) *n* (esp. formerly) a prostitute, or the mistress of a man of rank. [C16: from OF *courtisane,* from It. *cortigiana* female courtier, from *corte* COURT]

courtesy ❶ (ˈkɜːtɪsɪ) *n, pl* **courtesies. 1** politeness; good manners. **2** a courteous gesture or remark. **3** favour or consent (esp. in **(by) courtesy of**). **4** common consent as opposed to right (esp. in **by courtesy**). [C13 *curteisie,* from OF, from *corteis* COURTEOUS]

courtesy light *n* the interior light in a motor vehicle.

courtesy title *n* any of several titles having no legal significance, such as those borne by the children of peers.

courthouse (ˈkɔːtˌhaus) *n* a public building in which courts of law are held.

courtier ❶ (ˈkɔːtɪə) *n* **1** an attendant at a court. **2** a person who seeks favour in an ingratiating manner. [C13: from Anglo-F *courteour* (unattested), from OF *corteier* to attend at court]

courtly ❶ (ˈkɔːtlɪ) *adj* **courtlier, courtliest. 1** of or suitable for a royal court. **2** refined in manner. **3** ingratiating.
▸**ˈcourtliness** *n*

court martial *n, pl* **court martials** *or* **courts martial. 1** a military court that tries persons subject to military law. ◆ *vb* **court-martial, court-martials,**

THESAURUS

coupon *n* **1** = **slip**, card, certificate, detachable portion, ticket, token, voucher

courage *n* **1** = **bravery**, balls (*taboo sl.*), ballsiness (*taboo sl.*), boldness, bottle (*Brit. sl.*), daring, dauntlessness, fearlessness, firmness, fortitude, gallantry, grit, guts (*inf.*), hardihood, heroism, intrepidity, lion-heartedness, mettle, nerve, pluck, resolution, spunk (*inf.*), valour
Antonyms *n* cowardice, cravenness, faintheartedness, fear, timidity

courageous *adj* = **brave**, audacious, ballsy (*taboo sl.*), bold, daring, dauntless, fearless, gallant, gritty, hardy, heroic, indomitable, intrepid, lion-hearted, plucky, resolute, stalwart, stouthearted, valiant, valorous
Antonyms *adj* chicken (*sl.*), chicken-hearted, cowardly, craven, dastardly, faint-hearted, gutless (*inf.*), lily-livered, pusillanimous, scared, spineless, timid, timorous, yellow (*inf.*)

courier *n* **1, 2** = **messenger**, bearer, carrier, emissary, envoy, herald, pursuivant (*Historical*), runner **3** = **guide**, representative

course *n* **1** = **progression**, advance, advancement, continuity, development, flow, furtherance, march, movement, order, progress, sequence, succession, tenor, unfolding **2** = **route**, channel, direction, line, orbit, passage, path, road, tack, track, trail, trajectory, way **4** = **racecourse**, cinder track, circuit, lap, race, round **5** = **period**, duration, lapse, passage, passing, sweep, term, time **7, 10** = **procedure**, behaviour, conduct, manner, method, mode, plan, policy, programme, regimen **9a** = **classes**, course of study, curriculum, lectures, programme, schedule, studies **15 in due course** = **in time**, eventually, finally, in the course of time, in the end, sooner or later **16 of course** = **naturally**, certainly, definitely, indubitably, needless to say, obviously, undoubtedly, without a doubt ◆ *vb* **18** = **run**, dash, flow, gush, move apace, race, scud, scurry, speed, stream, surge, tumble **19** = **hunt**, chase, follow, pursue

court *n* **1** = **courtyard**, cloister, piazza, plaza, quad (*inf.*), quadrangle, square, yard **3a** = **palace**, hall, manor **4** = **royal household**, attendants, cortege, entourage, retinue, suite, train **7** = **law court**, bar, bench, court of justice, seat of judgment, tribunal ◆ *vb* **13** = **woo**, chase, date, go (out) with, go steady with, keep company with, make love to, pay court to, pay one's addresses to, pursue, run after, serenade, set one's cap at, sue (*arch.*), take out, walk out with **14** = **cultivate**, curry favour with, fawn upon, flatter, pander to, seek, solicit **15, 16** = **invite**, attract, bring about, incite, prompt, provoke, seek

courteous *adj* = **polite**, affable, attentive, ceremonious, civil, courtly, elegant, gallant, gracious, mannerly, polished, refined, respectful, urbane, well-bred, well-mannered
Antonyms *adj* discourteous, disrespectful, ill-mannered, impolite, insolent, rude, uncivil, ungracious, unkind

courtesan *n History* = **mistress**, call girl, demimondaine, *fille de joie,* harlot, hetaera, kept woman, paramour, prostitute, scarlet woman, whore, working girl (*facetious slang*)

courtesy *n* **1** = **politeness**, affability, civility, courteousness, courtliness, elegance, gallantness, gallantry, good breeding, good manners, grace, graciousness, polish, urbanity **3** = **favour**, benevolence, consent, consideration, generosity, indulgence, kindness

courtier *n* **1** = **attendant**, follower, henchman, liegeman, pursuivant (*Historical*), squire, train-bearer

courtliness *n* **2** = **ceremony**, affability, breeding, chivalrousness, correctness, courtesy, decorum, elegance, formality, gallantry, gentility, graciousness, politeness, politesse, propriety, refinement, stateliness, urbanity

courtly *adj* **2** = **ceremonious**, affable, aristocratic, chivalrous, civil, decorous, dignified, ele-

court-martialling, court-martialled *or US* **court-martials, court-martialing, court-martialed. 2** (*tr*) to try by court martial.

Court of Appeal *n* a court that hears appeals from the High Court and from the county and crown courts.

Court of St James's *n* the official name of the royal court of Britain.

court plaster *n* a plaster, composed of isinglass on silk, formerly used to cover superficial wounds. [C18: so called because formerly used by court ladies for beauty spots]

courtroom ('kɔːtˌruːm, -ˌrʊm) *n* a room in which the sittings of a law court are held.

courtship ⓣ ('kɔːtʃɪp) *n* **1** the act, period, or art of seeking the love of someone with intent to marry. **2** the seeking or soliciting of favours.

court shoe *n* a low-cut shoe for women, without any laces or straps.

courtyard ⓣ ('kɔːtˌjɑːd) *n* an open area of ground surrounded by walls or buildings; court.

couscous ('kuːskuːs) *n* a spicy dish, originating in North Africa, consisting of steamed semolina served with a meat stew. [C17: via F from Ar. *kouskous*, from *kaskasa* to pound until fine]

cousin ('kʌzᵊn) *n* **1** Also called: **first cousin, cousin-german, full cousin.** the child of one's aunt or uncle. **2** a relative descended from one of one's common ancestors. **3** a title used by a sovereign when addressing another sovereign or a nobleman. [C13: from OF *cosin*, from L *consōbrīnus*, from *sōbrīnus* cousin on the mother's side]
▸**'cousinˌhood** *or* **'cousinˌship** *n* ▸**'cousinly** *adj, adv*

couture (kuː'tʊə) *n* **a** high-fashion designing and dressmaking. **b** (*as modifier*): *couture clothes.* [from F: sewing, from OF *cousture* seam, from L *consuere* to stitch together]

couturier (kuː'tʊərɪˌeɪ) *n* a person who designs, makes, and sells fashion clothes for women. [from F: dressmaker; see COUTURE]
▸**couturière** (kuːˌtuːrɪ'ɛə) *fem n*

couvade (kuː'vɑːd) *n Anthropol.* the custom in certain cultures of treating the husband of a woman giving birth as if he were bearing the child. [C19: from F, from *couver* to hatch, from L *cubāre* to lie down]

covalency (kəʊ'veɪlənsɪ) *or US* **covalence** *n* **1** the formation and nature of covalent bonds, that is, chemical bonds involving the sharing of electrons between atoms in a molecule. **2** the number of covalent bonds that a particular atom can make with other atoms in forming a molecule.
▸**co'valent** *adj* ▸**co'valently** *adv*

cove[1] ⓣ (kəʊv) *n* **1** a small bay or inlet. **2** a narrow cavern in the side of a cliff, mountain, etc. **3** Also called: **coving.** *Archit.* a concave curved surface between the wall and ceiling of a room. [OE *cofa*]

cove[2] ⓣ (kəʊv) *n Sl., Brit. old-fashioned & Austral.* a fellow; chap. [C16: prob. from Romany *kova* thing, person]

coven ('kʌvᵊn) *n* a meeting of witches. [C16: prob. from OF *covin* group, ult. from L *convenīre* to come together]

covenant ⓣ ('kʌvənənt) *n* **1** a binding agreement; contract. **2** *Law.* an agreement in writing under seal, as to pay a stated annual sum to a charity. **3** *Bible.* God's promise to the Israelites and their commitment to worship him alone. ◆ *vb* **4** to agree to a covenant (concerning). [C13: from OF, from *covenir* to agree, from L *convenīre* to come together, make an agreement; see CONVENE]
▸**covenantal** (ˌkʌvə'næntᵊl) *adj* ▸**'covenantor** *or* **'covenanter** *n*

Covenanter ('kʌvənəntə, ˌkʌvə'næntə) *n Scot. history.* a person upholding either of two 17th-century covenants to establish and defend Presbyterianism.

Coventry ('kɒvəntrɪ) *n* **send to Coventry.** to ostracize or ignore. [after *Coventry*, a city in England, in the W Midlands]

cover ⓣ ('kʌvə) *vb* (*mainly tr*) **1** to place or spread something over so as to protect or conceal. **2** to provide with a covering; clothe. **3** to put a garment, esp. a hat, on (the body or head). **4** to extend over or lie thickly on the surface of: *snow covered the fields.* **5** to bring upon (oneself); invest (oneself) as if with a covering: *covered with shame.* **6** (sometimes foll. by *up*) to act as a screen or concealment for; hide from view. **7** *Mil.* to protect (an individual, formation, or place) by taking up a position from which fire may be returned if those being protected are fired upon. **8** (*also intr*, sometimes foll. by *for*) to assume responsibility for (a person or thing). **9** (*intr*; foll. by *for* or *up for*) to provide an alibi (for). **10** to have as one's territory: *this salesman covers your area.* **11** to travel over. **12** to have or place in the aim and within the range of (a firearm). **13** to include or deal with. **14** (of an asset or income) to be sufficient to meet (a liability or expense). **15a** to insure against loss, risk, etc. **15b** to provide for (loss, risk, etc.) by insurance. **16** to deposit (an equivalent stake) in a bet. **17** to act as reporter or photographer on (a news event, etc.) for a newspaper or magazine: *to cover sports events.* **18** *Music.* to record a cover version of. **19** *Sport.* to guard or protect (an opponent, team-mate, or area). **20** (of a male animal, esp. a horse) to copulate with (a female animal). ◆ *n* **21** anything that covers, spreads over, protects, or conceals. **22a** a blanket used on a bed for warmth. **22b** another word for **bedspread. 23** a pretext, disguise, or false identity: *the thief sold brushes as a cover.* **24** an envelope or package for sending through the post: *under plain cover.* **25a** an individual table setting, esp. in a restaurant. **25b** (*as modifier*): *a cover charge.* **26** Also called: **cover version.** a version by a different artist of a previously recorded musical item. **27** *Cricket.* **27a** (*often pl*) the area more or less at right angles to the pitch on the off side and usually about halfway to the boundary. **27b** (*as modifier*): *a cover drive.* **28** *Philately.* an entire envelope that has been postmarked. **29 break cover.** to come out from a shelter or hiding place. **30 take cover.** to make for a place of safety or shelter. **31 under cover.** protected, concealed, or in secret. ◆ See also **cover-up.** [C13: from OF *covrir*, from L *cooperīre* to cover completely, from *operīre* to cover over]
▸**'coverable** *adj* ▸**'coverer** *n*

coverage ⓣ ('kʌvərɪdʒ) *n* **1** the amount or extent to which something is covered. **2** *Journalism.* the amount and quality of reporting or analysis given to a particular subject or event. **3** the extent of the protection provided by insurance.

cover crop *n* a crop planted between main crops to prevent leaching or soil erosion or to provide green manure.

covered wagon *n US & Canad.* a large horse-drawn wagon with an arched canvas top, used formerly for prairie travel.

cover girl *n* a glamorous girl whose picture appears on the cover of a magazine.

covering letter *n* an accompanying letter sent as an explanation, introduction, or record.

coverlet ('kʌvəlɪt) *n* another word for **bedspread.**

cover note *n Brit.* a certificate issued by an insurance company stating that a policy is operative: used as a temporary measure between the commencement of cover and the issue of the policy.

cover point *n Cricket.* **a** a fielding position in the covers. **b** a fielder in this position.

cover slip *n* a very thin piece of glass placed over a specimen on a glass slide that is to be examined under a microscope.

covert ⓣ ('kʌvət) *adj* **1** concealed or secret. ◆ *n* **2** a shelter or disguise. **3** a thicket or woodland providing shelter for game. **4** short for **covert cloth. 5** *Ornithol.* Also called: **tectrix.** any of the small feathers on the wings and tail of a bird that surround the bases of the larger feathers. [C14: from OF: covered, from *covrir* to COVER]
▸**'covertly** *adv*

covert cloth *n* a twill-weave cotton or worsted suiting fabric.

coverture ('kʌvətjə) *n Rare.* shelter, concealment, or disguise. [C13: from OF, from *covert* covered; see COVERT]

cover-up ⓣ *n* **1** concealment or attempted concealment of a mistake, crime, etc. ◆ *vb* **cover up.** (*adv*) **2** (*tr*) to cover completely. **3** (when *intr*, often foll. by *for*) to attempt to conceal (a mistake or crime).

cover version *n* another name for **cover** (sense 26).

covet ⓣ ('kʌvɪt) *vb* **covets, coveting, coveted.** (*tr*) to wish, long, or crave for (something, esp. the property of another person). [C13: from OF *coveitier*, from *coveitié* eager desire, ult. from L *cupiditās* CUPIDITY]
▸**'covetable** *adj*

covetous ⓣ ('kʌvɪtəs) *adj* (*usually postpositive* and foll. by *of*) jealously

THESAURUS

gant, flattering, formal, gallant, highbred, lordly, obliging, polished, refined, stately, urbane

courtship *n* **1** = **wooing**, courting, engagement, keeping company, pursuit, romance, suit

courtyard *n* = **yard**, area, enclosure, peristyle, playground, quad, quadrangle

cove[1] *n* **1** = **bay**, anchorage, bayou, creek, firth *or* frith (*Scot.*), inlet, sound

cove[2] *n Old-fashioned slang* = **fellow**, bloke (*Brit. inf.*), chap, character, customer, type

covenant *n* **1** = **promise**, agreement, arrangement, bargain, commitment, compact, concordat, contract, convention, pact, pledge, stipulation, treaty, trust **2** *Law* = **deed**, bond ◆ *vb* **4** = **promise**, agree, bargain, contract, engage, pledge, shake hands, stipulate, undertake

cover *vb* **1** = **overlay**, canopy, coat, daub, encase, envelop, layer, mantle, overspread **3** = **clothe**, dress, envelop, invest, put on, wrap **4** = **submerge**, engulf, flood, overrun, wash over **6** = **conceal**, camouflage, cloak, cover up, curtain, disguise, eclipse, enshroud, hide, hood, house, mask, obscure, screen, secrete, shade, shroud, veil **7** = **protect**, defend, guard, reinforce, shelter, shield, watch over **8** *sometimes foll. by* **for** = **stand in for**, double for, fill in for, hold the fort, relieve, substitute, take over, take the rap for (*sl.*) **11** = **travel over**, cross, pass through *or* over, range, traverse **13** = **deal with**, comprehend, comprise, consider, contain, embody, embrace, encompass, examine, include, incorporate, involve, provide for, refer to, survey, take account of **15** = **make up for**, balance, compensate, counterbalance, insure, make good, offset **17** = **report**, describe, detail, investigate, narrate, recount, relate, tell of, write up ◆ *n* **21** = **covering**, awning, binding, canopy, cap, case, clothing, coating, dress, envelope, jacket, lid, sheath, top, wrapper **23** = **disguise**, cloak, cover-up, façade, front, mask, pretence, pretext, screen, smoke screen, veil, window-dressing
Antonyms *vb* ≠ **conceal:** exhibit, expose, reveal, show, unclothe, uncover, unmask, unwrap ≠ **deal with:** exclude, omit ◆ *n* ≠ **covering:** base, bottom

coverage *n* **2** = **reporting**, analysis, description, reportage, treatment

covert *adj* **1** = **secret**, clandestine, concealed, disguised, dissembled, hidden, private, sly, stealthy, surreptitious, underhand, unsuspected, veiled ◆ *n* **3** = **thicket**, brush (*arch.*), bushes, coppice, shrubbery, undergrowth, underwood

cover-up *n* **1** = **concealment**, complicity, conspiracy, front, smoke screen, whitewash (*inf.*) ◆ *vb* **cover up 3** = **conceal**, cover one's tracks, draw a veil over, feign ignorance, hide, hush up, keep dark, keep secret, keep silent about, keep under one's hat (*inf.*), repress, stonewall, suppress, sweep under the carpet, whitewash (*inf.*)

covet *vb* = **long for**, aspire to, begrudge, crave, desire, envy, fancy (*inf.*), hanker after, have one's eye on, lust after, set one's heart on, thirst for, would give one's eyeteeth for, yearn for

covetous *adj* = **envious**, acquisitive, avari-

eager for the possession of something (esp. the property of another person).
▸ 'covetously *adv* ▸ 'covetousness *n*

covey ❶ ('kʌvɪ) *n* **1** a small flock of grouse or partridge. **2** a small group, as of people. [C14: from OF *covee*, from *cover* to sit on, hatch]

cow[1] (kaʊ) *n* **1** the mature female of any species of cattle, esp. domesticated cattle. **2** the mature female of various other mammals, such as the elephant, whale, and seal. **3** (not in technical use) any domestic species of cattle. **4** *Inf.* a disagreeable woman. **5** *Austral. & NZ sl.* something objectionable (esp. in **a fair cow**). [OE *cū*]

cow[2] ❶ (kaʊ) *vb* (*tr*) to frighten or overawe, as with threats. [C17: from ON *kūga* to oppress]

coward ❶ ('kaʊəd) *n* a person who shrinks from or avoids danger, pain, or difficulty. [C13: from OF *cuard*, from *coue* tail, from L *cauda*; ? suggestive of a frightened animal with its tail between its legs]

cowardice ❶ ('kaʊədɪs) *n* lack of courage in facing danger, pain, or difficulty.

cowardly ❶ ('kaʊədlɪ) *adj* of or characteristic of a coward; lacking courage.
▸ 'cowardliness *n*

cowbell ('kaʊˌbel) *n* a bell hung around a cow's neck so that the cow can be easily located.

cowberry ('kaʊbərɪ, -brɪ) *n, pl* **cowberries. 1** a creeping evergreen shrub of N temperate and arctic regions, with pink or red flowers and edible slightly acid berries. **2** the berry of this plant.

cowbird ('kaʊˌbɜːd) *n* any of various American orioles, having dark plumage and a short bill.

cowboy ❶ ('kaʊˌbɔɪ) *n* **1** Also called: **cowhand.** a hired man who herds and tends cattle, usually on horseback, esp. in the western US. **2** a conventional character of Wild West folklore, films, etc., esp. one involved in fighting Indians. **3** *Inf.* an irresponsible or unscrupulous operator in business, etc.
▸ 'cowˌgirl *fem n*

cowcatcher ('kaʊˌkætʃə) *n* a metal frame on the front of a locomotive to clear the track of animals or other obstructions.

cow-cocky *n, pl* **cow-cockies.** *Austral. & NZ.* a one-man dairy farmer.

cower ❶ ('kaʊə) *vb* (*intr*) to crouch or cringe, as in fear. [C13: from MLow G *kūren* to lie in wait; rel. to Swedish *kura*]

cowherd ('kaʊˌhɜːd) *n* a person employed to tend cattle.

cowhide ('kaʊˌhaɪd) *n* **1** the hide of a cow. **2** the leather made from such a hide.

cowl (kaʊl) *n* **1** a hood, esp. a loose one. **2** the hooded habit of a monk. **3** a cover fitted to a chimney to increase ventilation and prevent draughts. **4** the part of a car body that supports the windscreen and the bonnet. ◆ *vb* (*tr*) **5** to cover or provide with a cowl. [OE *cugele*, from LL *cucullа* cowl, from L *cucullus* hood]

cowlick ('kaʊˌlɪk) *n* a tuft of hair over the forehead.

cowling ('kaʊlɪŋ) *n* a streamlined metal covering, esp. around an aircraft engine.

cowman ('kaʊmən) *n, pl* **cowmen. 1** *Brit.* another name for **cowherd. 2** *US & Canad.* a man who owns cattle; rancher.

co-worker *n* a fellow worker; associate.

cow parsley *n* a common Eurasian umbelliferous hedgerow plant having umbrella-shaped clusters of white flowers.

cowpat ('kaʊˌpæt) *n* a single dropping of cow dung.

cowpea ('kaʊˌpiː) *n* **1** a leguminous tropical climbing plant producing pods containing edible pealike seeds. **2** the seed of this plant.

cowpox ('kaʊˌpɒks) *n* a contagious viral disease of cows characterized by vesicles, esp. on the teats and udder. Inoculation of humans with this virus provides temporary immunity to smallpox.

cowpuncher ('kaʊˌpʌntʃə) *or* **cowpoke** ('kaʊˌpəʊk) *n US & Canad.* an informal word for **cowboy.**

cowrie *or* **cowry** ('kaʊrɪ) *n, pl* **cowries. 1** any marine gastropod mollusc of a mostly tropical family having a glossy brightly marked shell. **2** the shell of any of these molluscs, esp. the money cowrie, used as money in parts of Africa and S Asia. [C17: from Hindi *kaurī*, from Sansk. *kaparda*]

cowslip ('kaʊˌslɪp) *n* **1** a primrose native to temperate regions of the Old World, having yellow flowers. **2** *US & Canad.* another name for **marsh marigold.** [OE *cūslyppe*; see COW[1], SLIP[3]]

cox (kɒks) *n* **1** a coxswain. ◆ *vb* **2** to act as coxswain of (a boat).
▸ 'coxless *adj*

coxa ('kɒksə) *n, pl* **coxae** ('kɒksiː). **1** a technical name for the hipbone or hip joint. **2** the basal segment of the leg of an insect. [C18: from L: hip]
▸ 'coxal *adj*

coxalgia (kɒk'sældʒɪə) *n* **1** pain in the hip joint. **2** disease of the hip joint causing pain. [C19: from COXA + -ALGIA]
▸ cox'algic *adj*

coxcomb ('kɒksˌkəʊm) *n* **1** a variant spelling of **cockscomb. 2** *Obs.* the cap, resembling a cock's comb, worn by a jester.
▸ 'coxˌcombry *n*

coxswain ('kɒksən, -ˌsweɪn) *n* **1** (usually shortened to **cox** in competitive rowing) the helmsman of a lifeboat, racing shell, etc. **2** the senior petty officer on a small naval craft. ◆ Also called: **cockswain.** [C15: from *cock* a ship's boat + SWAIN]

coy ❶ (kɔɪ) *adj* **1** affectedly demure, esp. in a playful or provocative manner. **2** shy; modest. **3** evasive, esp. in an annoying way. [C14: from OF *coi* reserved, from L *quiētus* QUIET]
▸ 'coyly *adv* ▸ 'coyness *n*

Coy. *Mil. abbrev. for* company.

coyote ('kɔɪəʊt, kɔɪ'əʊtɪ; *esp. US.* 'kaɪəʊt, kaɪ'əʊtɪ) *n, pl* **coyotes** *or* **coyote.** a predatory canine mammal of the deserts and prairies of North America. Also called: **prairie wolf.** [C19: from Mexican Sp., from Nahuatl *coyotl*]

coypu ('kɔɪpuː) *n, pl* **coypus** *or* **coypu. 1** an aquatic South American rodent, naturalized in Europe. It resembles a small beaver and is bred for its fur. **2** the fur of this animal. ◆ Also called: **nutria.** [C18: from American Sp. *coipú*, from Amerind *kóypu*]

coz (kʌz) *n* an archaic word for **cousin.**

cozen ('kʌz[ə]n) *vb* to cheat or trick (someone). [C16: cant term ? rel. to COUSIN]
▸ 'cozenage *n*

cozy ('kəʊzɪ) *adj, n* the usual US spelling of **cosy.**

CP *abbrev. for:* **1** Canadian Pacific Ltd. **2** Common Prayer. **3** Communist Party.

cp. *abbrev. for* compare.

CPAG *abbrev. for* Child Poverty Action Group.

cpd *abbrev. for* compound.

cpi *abbrev. for* characters per inch.

Cpl *abbrev. for* Corporal.

CPO *abbrev. for* Chief Petty Officer.

CPR *abbrev. for* cardiopulmonary resuscitation.

cps *abbrev. for:* **1** *Physics.* cycles per second. **2** *Computing.* characters per second.

CPS (in England and Wales) *abbrev. for* Crown Prosecution Service.

CPSA *abbrev. for* Civil and Public Services Association.

CPVE (in Britain) *abbrev. for* Certificate of Pre-vocational Education: a certificate awarded for completion of a broad-based course of study offered as a less advanced alternative to traditional school-leaving qualifications.

CQ a symbol transmitted by an amateur radio operator requesting communication with any other amateur radio operator.

Cr 1 *abbrev. for* Councillor. **2** *the chemical symbol for* chromium.

cr. *abbrev. for:* **1** credit. **2** creditor.

crab[1] (kræb) *n* **1** any chiefly marine decapod crustacean having a broad flattened carapace covering the cephalothorax, beneath which is folded the abdomen. The first pair of limbs are pincers. **2** any of various similar or related arthropods. **3** short for **crab louse. 4** a mechanical lifting device, esp. the travelling hoist of a gantry crane. **5 catch a crab.** *Rowing.* to make a stroke in which the oar either misses the water or digs too deeply, causing the rower to fall backwards. ◆ *vb* **crabs, crabbing, crabbed. 6** (*intr*) to hunt or catch crabs. [OE *crabba*]

crab[2] (kræb) *Inf.* ◆ *vb* **crabs, crabbing, crabbed. 1** (*intr*) to find fault; grumble. ◆ *n* **2** an irritable person. [C16: prob. back formation from CRABBED]

crab[3] (kræb) *n* short for **crab apple.** [C15: ? of Scand. origin; cf. Swedish *skrabbe* crab apple]

Crab (kræb) *n* **the.** the constellation Cancer, the fourth sign of the zodiac.

crab apple *n* **1** any of several rosaceous trees that have white, pink, or red flowers and small sour apple-like fruits. **2** the fruit of any of these trees, used to make jam.

crabbed ❶ ('kræbɪd) *adj* **1** surly; irritable; perverse. **2** (esp. of handwrit-

THESAURUS

cious, close-fisted, grasping, greedy, jealous, mercenary, rapacious, yearning

covey *n* = **flock**, bevy, brood, cluster, flight, group, nye *or* nide (*of pheasants*)

cow[2] *vb* = **intimidate**, awe, browbeat, bully, daunt, dishearten, dismay, frighten, overawe, psych out (*inf.*), scare, subdue, terrorize, unnerve

coward *n* = **wimp** (*inf.*), chicken (*sl.*), craven, dastard (*arch.*), faint-heart, poltroon, recreant, renegade, scaredy-cat (*inf.*), yellow-belly (*sl.*)

cowardice *n* = **faint-heartedness**, cravenness, dastardliness, fearfulness, pusillanimity, recreance *or* recreancy (*arch.*), softness, spinelessness, timorousness, weakness

cowardly *adj* = **faint-hearted**, boneless, chicken (*sl.*), chicken-hearted, craven, dastardly, fearful, gutless (*inf.*), lily-livered, pusillanimous, recreant (*arch.*), scared, shrinking, soft, spineless, timorous, weak, weak-kneed (*inf.*), white-livered, yellow (*inf.*)
Antonyms *adj* audacious, bold, brave, courageous, daring, dauntless, doughty, intrepid, plucky, valiant

cowboy *n* **1** = **cowhand**, broncobuster (*US.*), buckaroo (*US.*), cattleman, drover, gaucho (*S. Amer.*), herder, herdsman, rancher, ranchero (*US.*), stockman, wrangler (*US.*)

cower *vb* = **cringe**, crouch, draw back, fawn, flinch, grovel, quail, shrink, skulk, sneak, tremble, truckle

coy *adj* **1-3** = **shy**, arch, backward, bashful, coquettish, demure, evasive, flirtatious, kittenish, modest, overmodest, prudish, reserved, retiring, self-effacing, shrinking, skittish, timid
Antonyms *adj* bold, brash, brass-necked (*Brit. informal*), brassy (*inf.*), brazen, flip (*inf.*), forward, impertinent, impudent, pert, pushy (*inf.*), saucy, shameless

coyness *n* **1-3** = **shyness**, affectation, archness, backwardness, bashfulness, coquettishness, demureness, diffidence, evasiveness, modesty, primness, prissiness (*inf.*), prudery, prudishness, reserve, shrinking, skittishness, timidity

crabbed *adj* **1** = **bad-tempered**, acrid, acrimonious, captious, churlish, cross, cynical, difficult, fretful, harsh, ill-tempered, irritable, morose, perverse, petulant, prickly, ratty (*Brit. & N.Z. in-*

ing) cramped and hard to decipher. **3** *Rare.* abstruse. [C13: prob. from CRAB[1] (from its wayward gait), infl. by CRAB (APPLE) (from its tartness)] ▸'**crabbedly** *adv* ▸'**crabbedness** *n*

crabby Ⓣ ('kræbɪ) *adj* **crabbier, crabbiest.** bad-tempered.

crab louse *n* a parasitic louse that infests the pubic region in man.

crabwise ('kræb,waɪz) *adj, adv* (of motion) sideways; like a crab.

crack Ⓣ (kræk) *vb* **1** to break or cause to break without complete separation of the parts. **2** to break or cause to break with a sudden sharp sound; snap. **3** to make or cause to make a sudden sharp sound: *to crack a whip.* **4** to cause (the voice) to change tone or become harsh or (of the voice) to change tone, esp. to a higher register; break. **5** *Inf.* to fail or cause to fail. **6** to yield or cause to yield. **7** *(tr)* to hit with a forceful or resounding blow. **8** *(tr)* to break into or force open: *to crack a safe.* **9** *(tr)* to solve or decipher (a code, problem, etc.). **10** *(tr) Inf.* to tell (a joke, etc.). **11** to break (a molecule) into smaller molecules or radicals by the action of heat, as in the distillation of petroleum. **12** *(tr)* to open (a bottle) for drinking. **13** *(intr) Scot. & N English dialect.* to chat; gossip. **14** *(tr) Inf.* to achieve (esp. in **crack it**). **15 crack a smile.** *Inf.* to break into a smile. **16 crack hardy** *or* **hearty.** *Austral. & NZ inf.* to disguise one's discomfort, etc.; put on a bold front. ◆ *n* **17** a sudden sharp noise. **18** a break or fracture without complete separation of the two parts. **19** a narrow opening or fissure. **20** *Inf.* a resounding blow. **21** a physical or mental defect; flaw. **22** a moment or specific instant: *the crack of day.* **23** a broken or cracked tone of voice, as a boy's during puberty. **24** (often foll. by *at*) *Inf.* an attempt; opportunity to try. **25** *Sl.* a gibe; wisecrack; joke. **26** *Sl.* a person that excels. **27** *Scot. & N English dialect.* a talk; chat. **28** *Sl.* a concentrated highly addictive form of cocaine made into pellets or powder and smoked. **29** *Inf., chiefly Irish.* fun; informal entertainment. **30 a fair crack of the whip.** *Inf.* a fair chance or opportunity. **31 crack of doom.** doomsday; the end of the world; the Day of Judgment. ◆ *adj* **32** *(prenominal) Sl.* first-class; excellent: *a crack shot.* ◆ See also **crack down, crack up.** [OE *cracian*]

crackbrained Ⓣ ('kræk,breɪnd) *adj* insane, idiotic, or crazy.

crack down Ⓣ *vb (intr, adv;* often foll. by *on)* **1** to take severe measures (against); become stricter (with). ◆ *n* **crackdown. 2** severe or repressive measures.

cracked Ⓣ (krækt) *adj* **1** damaged by cracking. **2** *Inf.* crazy.

cracked wheat *n* whole wheat cracked between rollers so that it will cook more quickly.

cracker ('krækə) *n* **1** a decorated cardboard tube that emits a bang when pulled apart, releasing a toy, a joke, or a paper hat. **2** short for **firecracker. 3** a thin crisp biscuit, usually unsweetened. **4** a person or thing that cracks. **5** *Brit., Austral., & NZ sl.* a thing or person of notable qualities or abilities. **6** See **catalytic cracker.**

crackerjack ('krækə,dʒæk) *Inf.* ◆ *adj* **1** excellent. ◆ *n* **2** a person or thing of exceptional quality or ability. [C20: changed from CRACK (first-class) + JACK (man)]

crackers ('krækəz) *adj (postpositive) Brit.* a slang word for **insane.**

crackhead ('kræk,hɛd) *n Sl.* a person addicted to the drug crack.

cracking ('krækɪŋ) *adj* **1** *(prenominal) Inf.* fast; vigorous (esp. in **a cracking pace**). **2 get cracking.** *Inf.* to start doing something quickly or with increased speed. ◆ *adv, adj* **3** *Brit. inf.* first-class; excellent. ◆ *n* **4** the process in which molecules are cracked, esp. the oil-refining process in which heavy oils are broken down into hydrocarbons of lower molecular weight by heat or catalysis.

crackjaw ('kræk,dʒɔː) *Inf.* ◆ *adj* **1** difficult to pronounce. ◆ *n* **2** a word or phrase that is difficult to pronounce.

crackle ('kræk[ə]l) *vb* **crackles, crackling, crackled. 1** to make or cause to make a series of slight sharp noises, as of paper being crushed. **2** *(tr)* to decorate (porcelain or pottery) by causing fine cracks to appear in the glaze. **3** *(intr)* to abound in vivacity or energy. ◆ *n* **4** the act or sound of crackling. **5** intentional crazing in the glaze of porcelain or pottery. **6** Also called: **crackleware.** porcelain or pottery so decorated. ▸'**crackly** *adj*

crackling ('kræklɪŋ) *n* the crisp browned skin of roast pork.

crackpot ('kræk,pɒt) *Inf.* ◆ *n* **1** an eccentric person; crank. ◆ *adj* **2** eccentric; crazy.

crack up Ⓣ *vb (adv)* **1** *(intr)* to break into pieces. **2** *(intr) Inf.* to undergo a physical or mental breakdown. **3** *(tr) Inf.* to present or report, esp. in glowing terms: *it's not all it's cracked up to be.* **4** *Inf., chiefly US & Canad.* to laugh or cause to laugh uncontrollably. ◆ *n* **crackup. 5** *Inf.* a physical or mental breakdown.

-cracy *n combining form.* indicating a type of government or rule: *plutocracy; mobocracy.* See also **-crat.** [from Gk *-kratia,* from *kratos* power]

cradle Ⓣ ('kreɪd[ə]l) *n* **1** a baby's bed, often with rockers. **2** a place where something originates. **3** a frame, rest, or trolley made to support a piece of equipment, aircraft, ship, etc. **4** a platform or trolley in which workmen are suspended on the side of a building or ship. **5** *Agriculture.* **5a** a framework of several wooden fingers attached to a scythe to gather the grain into bunches as it is cut. **5b** a scythe with such a cradle. **6** Also called: **rocker.** a boxlike apparatus for washing rocks, sand, etc., containing gold or gemstones. **7 rob the cradle.** *Inf.* to take for a lover, husband, or wife a person much younger than oneself. ◆ *vb* **cradles, cradling, cradled.** *(tr)* **8** to rock or place in or as if in a cradle; hold tenderly. **9** to nurture in or bring up from infancy. **10** to wash (soil bearing gold, etc.) in a cradle. [OE *cradol*]

cradle snatcher *n Inf.* another name for **baby snatcher** (sense 2).

cradlesong ('kreɪd[ə]l,sɒŋ) *n* a lullaby.

craft Ⓣ (krɑːft) *n* **1** skill or ability. **2** skill in deception and trickery. **3** an occupation or trade requiring special skill, esp. manual dexterity. **4a** the members of such a trade, regarded collectively. **4b** *(as modifier)*: *a craft union.* **5** a single vessel, aircraft, or spacecraft. **6** *(functioning as pl)* ships, boats, aircraft, or spacecraft collectively. ◆ *vb* **7** *(tr)* to make or fashion with skill, esp. by hand. [OE *cræft* skill, strength]

craftsman Ⓣ ('krɑːftsmən) *n, pl* **craftsmen. 1** a member of a skilled trade; someone who practises a craft; artisan. **2** an artist skilled in an art or craft. ▸'**craftsman,ship** *n*

crafty Ⓣ ('krɑːftɪ) *adj* **craftier, craftiest. 1** skilled in deception; shrewd; cunning. **2** *Arch.* skilful. ▸'**craftily** *adv* ▸'**craftiness** *n*

crag Ⓣ (kræg) *n* a steep rugged rock or peak. [C13: of Celtic origin]

craggy Ⓣ ('krægɪ) *or US* **cragged** ('krægɪd) *adj* **craggier, craggiest. 1** having many crags. **2** (of the face) rugged; rocklike. ▸'**cragginess** *n*

crake (kreɪk) *n Zool.* any of several rails of the Old World, such as the corncrake. [C14: from ON *krāka* crow or *krākr* raven, imit.]

cram Ⓣ (kræm) *vb* **crams, cramming, crammed. 1** *(tr)* to force more (people, material, etc.) into (a room, container, etc.) than it can hold; stuff. **2** to eat or cause to eat more than necessary. **3** *Inf.* to study or cause to study (facts, etc.), esp. for an examination, by hastily memorizing. ◆ *n* **4** the act or condition of cramming. **5** a crush. [OE *crammian*]

crambo ('kræmbəʊ) *n* a word game in which one team says a rhyme or rhyming line for a word or line given by the other team. [C17: from earlier *crambe,* prob. from L *crambē repetīta* cabbage repeated, hence an old story]

THESAURUS

formal), sour, splenetic, surly, tart, testy, tetchy, tough, trying **2** = **unreadable**, awkward, cramped, hieroglyphical, illegible, indecipherable, laboured, squeezed

crabby *adj* = **bad-tempered**, acid, cross, crotchety (*inf.*), grouchy (*inf.*), ill-humoured, irritable, prickly, ratty (*Brit. & NZ inf.*), snappish, snappy, sour, surly, testy, tetchy

crack *vb* **1** = **break**, burst, chip, chop, cleave, crackle, craze, fracture, rive, snap, splinter, split **2** = **snap**, burst, crash, detonate, explode, pop, ring **7** *Informal* = **hit**, buffet, clip (*inf.*), clout (*inf.*), cuff, slap, smack, thump, wallop (*inf.*), whack **9** = **solve**, decipher, fathom, get the answer to, work out ◆ *n* **17** = **snap**, burst, clap, crash, explosion, pop, report **19** = **break**, breach, chink, chip, cleft, cranny, crevice, fissure, fracture, gap, interstice, rift **20** *Informal* = **blow**, buffet, clip (*inf.*), clout (*inf.*), cuff, slap, smack, thump, wallop (*inf.*), whack **24** *Informal* = **attempt**, go (*inf.*), opportunity, shot, stab (*inf.*), try **25** *Informal* = **joke**, dig, funny remark, gag (*inf.*), insult, jibe, quip, smart-alecky remark, wisecrack, witticism ◆ *adj* **32** *Slang* = **first-class**, ace, choice, elite, excellent, first-rate, hand-picked, superior, world-class

crackbrained *adj* = **crazy** (*inf.*), cracked (*sl.*), crackers (*Brit. sl.*), crackpot, idiotic, insane, loopy (*inf.*), lunatic, off one's rocker (*sl.*), off one's trolley (*sl.*), out of one's mind, out to lunch (*inf.*)

crackdown *n* **2** = **suppression**, clampdown, crushing, repression

cracked *adj* **1** = **broken**, chipped, crazed, damaged, defective, faulty, fissured, flawed, imperfect, split **2** *Informal* = **crazy** (*inf.*), batty, crackbrained, crackpot (*inf.*), doolally (*sl.*), eccentric, insane, loony (*sl.*), loopy (*inf.*), nuts (*sl.*), nutty (*sl.*), off one's head *or* nut (*sl.*), off one's trolley (*sl.*), out of one's mind, outré, out to lunch (*inf.*), touched

crack up *vb* **1** *Informal* = **have a breakdown**, break down, collapse, come apart at the seams (*inf.*), flip one's lid (*sl.*), freak out (*inf.*), go crazy (*inf.*), go off one's head (*sl.*), go off the deep end (*inf.*), go out of one's mind, go to pieces, throw a wobbly (*sl.*)

cradle *n* **1** = **crib**, bassinet, cot, Moses basket **2** = **birthplace**, beginning, fount, fountainhead, origin, source, spring, wellspring ◆ *vb* **8** = **hold**, lull, nestle, nurse, rock, support

craft *n* **1** = **skill**, ability, aptitude, art, artistry, cleverness, dexterity, expertise, expertness, ingenuity, knack, know-how (*inf.*), technique, workmanship **2** = **cunning**, artfulness, artifice, contrivance, craftiness, deceit, duplicity, guile, ruse, scheme, shrewdness, stratagem, subterfuge, subtlety, trickery, wiles **3** = **occupation**, business, calling, employment, handicraft, handiwork, line, pursuit, trade, vocation, work **5** = **vessel**, aircraft, barque, boat, plane, ship, spacecraft

craftiness *n* **1** = **cunning**, artfulness, astuteness, canniness, deviousness, duplicity, foxiness, guile, shrewdness, slyness, subtlety, trickiness, wiliness

craftsman *n* **1, 2** = **skilled worker**, artificer, artisan, maker, master, smith, technician, wright

craftsmanship *n* **1** = **workmanship**, artistry, expertise, mastery, technique

crafty *adj* **1** = **cunning**, artful, astute, calculating, canny, deceitful, designing, devious, duplicitous, foxy, fraudulent, guileful, insidious, knowing, scheming, sharp, shrewd, sly, subtle, tricksy, tricky, wily

Antonyms *adj* as green as grass, candid, ethical, frank, honest, ingenuous, innocent, naive, open, simple, wet behind the ears

crag *n* = **rock**, aiguille, bluff, peak, pinnacle, tor

craggy *adj* **1** = **rocky**, broken, cragged, jagged, jaggy (*Scot.*), precipitous, rock-bound, rough, rugged, stony, uneven

cram *vb* **1** = **stuff**, compact, compress, crowd, crush, fill to overflowing, force, jam, overcrowd, overfill, pack, pack in, press, ram, shove, squeeze **2** = **overeat**, glut, gorge, gormandize, guzzle, overfeed, pig out (*sl.*), put *or* pack away, satiate, stuff **3** = **study**, bone up (*inf.*), con, grind, mug up, revise, swot, swot up

crammer ('kræmə) *n* a person or school that prepares pupils for an examination.

cramp[1] (kræmp) *n* **1** a painful involuntary contraction of a muscle, typically caused by overexertion, heat, or chill. **2** temporary partial paralysis of a muscle group: *writer's cramp*. **3** (*usually pl in the US and Canada*) severe abdominal pain. ◆ *vb* **4** (*tr*) to affect with or as if with a cramp. [C14: from OF *crampe*, of Gmc origin]

cramp[2] (kræmp) *n* **1** Also called: **cramp iron.** a strip of metal with its ends bent at right angles, used to bind masonry. **2** a device for holding pieces of wood while they are glued; clamp. **3** something that confines or restricts. ◆ *vb* (*tr*) **4** to hold with a cramp. **5** to confine or restrict. **6 cramp (someone's) style.** *Inf.* to prevent (a person) from using his abilities or acting freely and confidently. [C15: from MDu. *crampe* cramp, hook, of Gmc origin]

cramped (kræmpt) *adj* **1** closed in; restricted. **2** (esp. of handwriting) small and irregular.

crampon ('kræmpən) *or* **crampoon** (kræm'puːn) *n* **1** one of a pair of pivoted steel levers used to lift heavy objects; grappling iron. **2** (*often pl*) one of a pair of frames each with 10 or 12 metal spikes, strapped to boots for climbing or walking on ice or snow. [C15: from F, from MDu. *crampe* hook; see CRAMP[2]]

cran (kræn) *n* a unit of capacity used for fresh herring, equal to 37.5 gallons. [C18: from ?]

cranberry ('krænbərɪ, -brɪ) *n, pl* **cranberries. 1** any of several trailing shrubs that bear sour edible red berries. **2** the berry of this plant. [C17: from Low G *kraanbere*, from *kraan* CRANE + *bere* BERRY]

crane (kreɪn) *n* **1** a large long-necked long-legged wading bird inhabiting marshes and plains in most parts of the world. **2** (not in ornithological use) any similar bird, such as a heron. **3** a device for lifting and moving heavy objects, typically consisting of a pivoted boom rotating about a vertical axis with lifting gear suspended from the end of the boom. ◆ *vb* **cranes, craning, craned. 4** (*tr*) to lift or move (an object) by or as if by a crane. **5** to stretch out (esp. the neck), as to see over other people's heads. [OE *cran*]

crane fly *n* a dipterous fly having long legs, slender wings, and a narrow body. Also called (Brit.): **daddy-longlegs.**

cranesbill ('kreɪnzˌbɪl) *n* any of various plants of the genus *Geranium*, having pink or purple flowers and long slender beaked fruits.

cranial ('kreɪnɪəl) *adj* of or relating to the skull.
► **'cranially** *adv*

cranial index *n* the ratio of the greatest length to the greatest width of the cranium, multiplied by 100.

cranial nerve *n* any of the 12 paired nerves that have their origin in the brain.

craniate ('kreɪnɪɪt, -ˌeɪt) *adj* **1** having a skull or cranium. ◆ *adj, n* **2** another word for **vertebrate.**

cranio- *or before a vowel* **crani-** *combining form.* indicating the cranium or cranial.

craniology (ˌkreɪnɪ'ɒlədʒɪ) *n* the branch of science concerned with the shape and size of the human skull.
► **craniological** (ˌkreɪnɪə'lɒdʒɪkᵊl) *adj* ► **ˌcranio'logically** *adv* ► **ˌcrani'ologist** *n*

craniometry (ˌkreɪnɪ'ɒmɪtrɪ) *n* the study and measurement of skulls.
► **craniometric** (ˌkreɪnɪə'mɛtrɪk) *or* **ˌcranio'metrical** *adj* ► **ˌcranio'metrically** *adv* ► **ˌcrani'ometrist** *n*

craniotomy (ˌkreɪnɪ'ɒtəmɪ) *n, pl* **craniotomies. 1** surgical incision into the skull. **2** surgical crushing of a fetal skull to extract a dead fetus.

cranium ('kreɪnɪəm) *n, pl* **craniums** *or* **crania** (-nɪə). **1** the skull of a vertebrate. **2** the part of the skull that encloses the brain. [C16: from Med. L *crānium* skull, from Gk *kranion*]

crank (kræŋk) *n* **1** a device for communicating or converting motion, consisting of an arm projecting from a shaft, often with a second member attached to it parallel to the shaft. **2** Also called: **crank handle, starting handle.** a handle incorporating a crank, used to start an engine or motor. **3** *Inf.* **3a** an eccentric or odd person. **3b** *US, Canad., Austral., NZ, & Irish.* a bad-tempered person. ◆ *vb* (*tr*) **4** to rotate (a shaft) by means of a crank. **5** to start (an engine, motor, etc.) by means of a crank handle. [OE *cranc*]

crankcase ('kræŋkˌkeɪs) *n* the metal housing that encloses the crankshaft, connecting rods, etc., in an internal-combustion engine.

crankpin ('kræŋkˌpɪn) *n* a short cylindrical surface fitted between two arms of a crank parallel to the main shaft of the crankshaft.

crankshaft ('kræŋkˌʃɑːft) *n* a shaft having one or more cranks, to which the connecting rods are attached.

crank up *vb* (*adv*) *Sl.* **1** (*tr*) to increase (loudness, output, etc.): *he cranked up his pace.* **2** (*tr*) to set in motion or invigorate: *news editors have to crank up tired reporters.* **3** (*intr*) to inject a narcotic drug.

cranky ('kræŋkɪ) *adj* **crankier, crankiest. 1** *Inf.* eccentric. **2** *Inf.* fussy and bad-tempered. **3** shaky; out of order.
► **'crankily** *adv* ► **'crankiness** *n*

crannog ('krænəg) *n* an ancient Celtic lake or bog dwelling. [C19: from Irish Gaelic *crannóg*, from OIrish *crann* tree]

cranny ('krænɪ) *n, pl* **crannies.** a narrow opening, as in a wall or rock face; chink; crevice (esp. in **every nook and cranny**). [C15: from OF *cran* notch, fissure; cf. CRENEL]
► **'crannied** *adj*

crap[1] (kræp) *n* **1** a losing throw in the game of craps. **2** another name for **craps.** [C20: back formation from CRAPS]

crap[2] (kræp) *Sl.* ◆ *n* **1** nonsense. **2** rubbish. **3** a taboo word for **faeces.** ◆ *vb* **craps, crapping, crapped. 4** (*intr*) a taboo word for **defecate.** [C15 *crappe* chaff, from MDu., prob. from *crappen* to break off]

crape (kreɪp) *n* **1** a variant spelling of **crepe. 2** crepe, esp. when used for mourning clothes. **3** a band of black crepe worn in mourning.

crap out *vb* (*intr, adv*) *Sl.* **1** *US.* to make a losing throw in craps. **2** *US.* to fail; withdraw. **3** to fail to attempt something through fear.

craps (kræps) *n* (*usually functioning as sing*) **1** a gambling game using two dice. **2 shoot craps.** to play this game. [C19: prob. from *crabs* lowest throw at dice, pl of CRAB[1]]
► **'crapˌshooter** *n*

crapulent ('kræpjʊlənt) *or* **crapulous** ('kræpjʊləs) *adj* **1** given to or resulting from intemperance. **2** suffering from intemperance; drunken. [C18: from LL *crāpulentus* drunk, from L *crāpula*, from Gk *kraipalē* drunkenness, headache resulting therefrom]
► **'crapulence** *n*

crash[1] (kræʃ) *vb* **1** to make or cause to make a loud noise as of solid objects smashing or clattering. **2** to fall or cause to fall with force, breaking in pieces with a loud noise. **3** (*intr*) to break or smash in pieces with a loud noise. **4** (*intr*) to collapse or fail suddenly. **5** to cause (an aircraft) to land violently resulting in severe damage or (of an aircraft) to land in this way. **6** to cause (a car, etc.) to collide with another car or other object or (of two or more cars) to be involved in a collision. **7** to move or cause to move violently or noisily. **8** (*intr*) (of a computer system or program) to fail suddenly because of a malfunction. **9** *Brit. inf.* short for **gate-crash.** ◆ *n* **10** an act or instance of breaking and falling to pieces. **11** a sudden loud noise. **12** a collision, as between vehicles. **13** a sudden descent of an aircraft as a result of which it hits land or water. **14** the sudden collapse of a business, stock exchange, etc. **15** (*modifier*) requiring or using intensive effort and all possible resources in order to accomplish something quickly: *a crash course.* [C14: prob. from *crasen* to smash, shatter + *dasshen* to strike violently, DASH[1]; see CRAZE]

crash[2] (kræʃ) *n* a coarse cotton or linen cloth. [C19: from Russian *krashenina* coloured linen]

crash barrier *n* a barrier erected along the centre of a motorway, around a racetrack, etc., for safety purposes.

crash dive *n* **1** a sudden steep dive from the surface by a submarine. ◆ *vb* **crash-dive, crash-dives, crash-diving, crash-dived. 2** (*intr*) (usually of an aircraft) to descend steeply and rapidly, before hitting the ground. **3** to perform or cause to perform a crash dive.

crash helmet *n* a padded helmet worn for motorcycling, flying, etc., to protect the head.

crashing ('kræʃɪŋ) *adj* (*prenominal*) *Inf.* (intensifier) (esp. in **a crashing bore**).

crash-land *vb* to land (an aircraft) causing some damage to it or (of an aircraft) to land in this way.
► **'crash-ˌlanding** *n*

crash team *n* a medical team with special equipment able to be mobilized quickly to treat cardiac arrest.

crass (kræs) *adj* **1** stupid; gross. **2** *Rare.* thick or coarse. [C16: from L *crassus* thick, dense, gross]
► **'crassly** *adv* ► **'crassness** *or* **'crassiˌtude** *n*

THESAURUS

cramp[1] *n* **1** = **spasm**, ache, contraction, convulsion, crick, pain, pang, shooting pain, stiffness, stitch, twinge

cramp[2] *vb* **5** = **restrict**, check, circumscribe, clip someone's wings, clog, confine, constrain, encumber, hamper, hamstring, handicap, hinder, impede, inhibit, obstruct, shackle, stymie, thwart

cramped *adj* **1** = **closed in**, awkward, circumscribed, confined, congested, crowded, hemmed in, jammed in, narrow, overcrowded, packed, restricted, squeezed, uncomfortable **2** = **small**, crabbed, indecipherable, irregular
Antonyms *adj* ≠ **closed in:** capacious, commodious, large, open, roomy, sizable *or* sizeable, spacious, uncongested, uncrowded

crank *n* **3a** *Informal* = **eccentric**, case (*inf.*), character (*inf.*), freak (*inf.*), kook (*US & Canad. inf.*), nut (*sl.*), oddball (*inf.*), odd fish (*inf.*), queer fish (*Brit. inf.*), rum customer (*Brit. sl.*), weirdo *or* weirdie (*inf.*)

cranky *adj* **1** *Informal* = **eccentric**, bizarre, capricious, erratic, freaky (*sl.*), funny (*inf.*), idiosyncratic, odd, oddball (*inf.*), off-the-wall (*sl.*), outré, peculiar, queer, quirky, rum (*Brit. sl.*), strange, wacky (*sl.*)

cranny *n* = **crevice**, breach, chink, cleft, crack, fissure, gap, hole, interstice, nook, opening, rift

crash[1] *vb* **2** = **hurtle**, come a cropper (*inf.*), dash, fall, fall headlong, give way, lurch, overbalance, pitch, plunge, precipitate oneself, sprawl, topple **3** = **smash**, break, break up, dash to pieces, disintegrate, fracture, fragment, shatter, shiver, splinter **4** = **collapse**, be ruined, fail, fold, fold up, go belly up (*inf.*), go broke (*inf.*), go bust (*inf.*), go to the wall, go under, smash **5, 6** = **collide**, bang, bump (into), crash-land (*an aircraft*), drive into, have an accident, hit, hurtle into, plough into, run together, wreck ◆ *n* **11** = **smash**, bang, boom, clang, clash, clatter, clattering, din, racket, smashing, thunder **12** = **collision**, accident, bump, jar, jolt, pile-up (*inf.*), prang (*inf.*), smash, smash-up, thud, thump, wreck **14** = **collapse**, bankruptcy, debacle, depression, downfall, failure, ruin, smash ◆ *modifier* **15** = **intensive**, emergency, immediate, round-the-clock, speeded-up, telescoped, urgent

crass *adj* **1** = **insensitive**, asinine, blundering, boorish, bovine, coarse, dense, doltish, gross, indelicate, lumpish, oafish, obtuse, stupid, unrefined, witless
Antonyms *adj* brainy (*inf.*), bright, clever, elegant,

-crat *n combining form.* indicating a person who takes part in or is a member of a form of government or class. [from Gk *-kratēs*, from *-kratia* -CRACY]
▶**-cratic** *or* **-cratical** *adj combining form.*

crate Ⓣ (kreɪt) *n* **1** a fairly large container, usually made of wooden slats or wickerwork, used for packing, storing, or transporting goods. **2** *Sl.* an old car, aeroplane, etc. ◆ *vb* **crates, crating, crated. 3** (*tr*) to pack or place in a crate. [C16: from L *crātis* wickerwork, hurdle]
▶ˈ**crater** *n* ▶ˈ**crateful** *n*

crater Ⓣ (ˈkreɪtə) *n* **1** the bowl-shaped opening in a volcano or a geyser. **2** a similar depression formed by the impact of a meteorite or exploding bomb. **3** any of the roughly circular or polygonal walled formations on the moon and some planets. **4** a large open bowl with two handles, used for mixing wines, esp. in ancient Greece. ◆ *vb* **5** to make or form craters in (a surface, such as the ground). [C17: from L: mixing bowl, crater, from Gk *kratēr*, from *kerannunai* to mix]
▶ˈ**crater-ˌlike** *adj* ▶ˈ**craterous** *adj*

cravat (krəˈvæt) *n* a scarf worn round the neck instead of a tie, esp. by men. [C17: from F *cravate*, from Serbo-Croat *Hrvat* Croat; so called because worn by Croats in the French army during the Thirty Years' War]

crave Ⓣ (kreɪv) *vb* **craves, craving, craved. 1** (when *intr*, foll. by *for* or *after*) to desire intensely; long (for). **2** (*tr*) to need greatly or urgently. **3** (*tr*) to beg or plead for. [OE *crafian*]
▶ˈ**craver** *n* ▶ˈ**craving** *n*

craven Ⓣ (ˈkreɪvᵊn) *adj* **1** cowardly. ◆ *n* **2** a coward. [C13 *cravant*, prob. from OF *crevant* bursting, from *crever* to burst, die, from L *crepāre* to burst, crack]
▶ˈ**cravenly** *adv* ▶ˈ**cravenness** *n*

craw Ⓣ (krɔː) *n* **1** a less common word for **crop** (sense 6). **2** the stomach of an animal. **3 stick in one's craw.** *Inf.* to be difficult, or against one's conscience, for one to accept, utter, etc. [C14: rel. to MHG *krage*, MDu. *crāghe* neck, Icelandic *kragi* collar]

crawfish (ˈkrɔːˌfɪʃ) *n, pl* **crawfish** *or* **crawfishes.** a variant of **crayfish** (esp. sense 2).

crawl[1] Ⓣ (krɔːl) *vb* (*intr*) **1** to move slowly, either by dragging the body along the ground or on the hands and knees. **2** to proceed very slowly or laboriously. **3** to act in a servile manner; fawn. **4** to be or feel as if overrun by something unpleasant, esp. crawling creatures: *the pile of refuse crawled with insects.* **5** (of insects, worms, snakes, etc.) to move with the body close to the ground. **6** to swim the crawl. ◆ *n* **7** a slow creeping pace or motion. **8** *Swimming.* a stroke in which the feet are kicked like paddles while each arm in turn reaches forward and pulls back through the water. [C14: prob. from ON *krafla* to creep]
▶ˈ**crawler** *n* ▶ˈ**crawlingly** *adv*

crawl[2] (krɔːl) *n* an enclosure in shallow, coastal water for fish, lobsters, etc. [C17: from Du. KRAAL]

crawler lane *n* a lane on an uphill section of a motorway reserved for slow vehicles.

crawling (ˈkrɔːlɪŋ) *n* a defect in freshly applied paint or varnish characterized by bare patches and ridging.

crawly (ˈkrɔːlɪ) *adj* **crawlier, crawliest.** *Inf.* feeling or causing a sensation like creatures crawling on one's skin.

crayfish (ˈkreɪˌfɪʃ) *or esp. US* **crawfish** *n, pl* **crayfish** *or* **crayfishes. 1** a freshwater decapod crustacean resembling a small lobster. **2** any of various similar crustaceans, esp. the spiny lobster. [C14: *cray*, by folk etymology, from OF *crevice* crab, from OHG *krebiz* + fish]

crayon (ˈkreɪən, -ɒn) *n* **1** a small stick or pencil of charcoal, wax, clay, or chalk mixed with coloured pigment. **2** a drawing made with crayons. ◆ *vb* **3** to draw or colour with crayons. [C17: from F, from *craie*, from L *crēta* chalk]
▶ˈ**crayonist** *n*

craze Ⓣ (kreɪz) *n* **1** a short-lived fashion. **2** a wild or exaggerated enthusiasm. ◆ *vb* **crazes, crazing, crazed. 3** to make or become mad. **4** *Ceramics, metallurgy.* to develop or cause to develop fine cracks. [C14 (in the sense: to break, shatter): prob. from ON]

crazy Ⓣ (ˈkreɪzɪ) *adj* **crazier, craziest. 1** *Inf.* insane. **2** fantastic; strange; ridiculous. **3** (*postpositive;* foll. by *about* or *over*) *Inf.* extremely fond (of).
▶ˈ**crazily** *adv* ▶ˈ**craziness** *n*

crazy paving *n Brit.* a form of paving, as for a path, made of irregular slabs of stone.

creak Ⓣ (kriːk) *vb* **1** to make or cause to make a harsh squeaking sound. **2** (*intr*) to make such sounds while moving: *the old car creaked along.* ◆ *n* **3** a harsh squeaking sound. [C14: var. of CROAK, imit.]
▶ˈ**creaky** *adj* ▶ˈ**creakily** *adv* ▶ˈ**creakiness** *n* ▶ˈ**creakingly** *adv*

cream Ⓣ (kriːm) *n* **1a** the fatty part of milk, which rises to the top. **1b** (*as modifier*): *cream buns.* **2** anything resembling cream in consistency. **3** the best one or most essential part of something; pick. **4** a soup containing cream or milk: *cream of chicken soup.* **5** any of various foods resembling or containing cream. **6a** a yellowish-white colour. **6b** (*as adj*): *cream wallpaper.* ◆ *vb* (*tr*) **7** to skim or otherwise separate the cream from (milk). **8** to beat (foodstuffs) to a light creamy consistency. **9** to add or apply cream or any creamlike substance to. **10** (sometimes foll. by *off*) to take away the best part of. **11** to prepare or cook (vegetables, chicken, etc.) with cream or milk. [C14: from OF *cresme*, from LL *crāmum* cream, of Celtic origin; infl. by Church L *chrisma* unction, CHRISM]
▶ˈ**creamˌlike** *adj*

cream cheese *n* a smooth soft white cheese made from soured cream or milk.

cream cracker *n Brit.* a crisp unsweetened biscuit, often eaten with cheese.

creamer (ˈkriːmə) *n* **1** a vessel or device for separating cream from milk. **2** a powdered substitute for cream, used in coffee. **3** *Now chiefly US & Canad.* a small jug or pitcher for serving cream.

creamery (ˈkriːmərɪ) *n, pl* **creameries. 1** an establishment where milk and cream are made into butter and cheese. **2** a place where dairy products are sold.

cream of tartar *n* potassium hydrogen tartrate, esp. when used in baking powders.

cream puff *n* a shell of light pastry with a custard or cream filling.

cream soda *n* a soft drink flavoured with vanilla.

cream tea *n* afternoon tea including bread or scones served with clotted cream and jam.

creamy Ⓣ (ˈkriːmɪ) *adj* **creamier, creamiest. 1** resembling cream in colour, taste, or consistency. **2** containing cream.
▶ˈ**creaminess** *n*

crease Ⓣ (kriːs) *n* **1** a line or mark produced by folding, pressing, or wrinkling. **2** a wrinkle or furrow, esp. on the face. **3** *Cricket.* any of four lines near each wicket marking positions for the bowler or batsman. See also **bowling crease, popping crease, return crease.** ◆ *vb* **creases, creas-**

THESAURUS

intelligent, polished, refined, sensitive, sharp, smart

crassness *n* **1** = **insensitivity**, asininity, boorishness, coarseness, denseness, doltishness, grossness, indelicacy, oafishness, stupidity, tactlessness, vulgarity

crate *n* **1** = **container**, box, case, packing case, tea chest ◆ *vb* **3** = **box**, case, encase, enclose, pack, pack up

crater *n* **2** = **hollow**, depression, dip, shell hole

crave *vb* **1, 2** = **long for**, be dying for, cry out for (*inf.*), desire, eat one's heart out over, fancy (*inf.*), hanker after, hope for, hunger after, lust after, need, pant for, pine for, require, set one's heart on, sigh for, thirst for, want, would give one's eyeteeth for, yearn for **3** *Informal* = **beg**, ask, beseech, entreat, implore, petition, plead for, pray for, seek, solicit, supplicate

craven *adj* **1** = **cowardly**, abject, chicken-hearted, dastardly, fearful, lily-livered, mean-spirited, pusillanimous, scared, timorous, weak, yellow (*inf.*) ◆ *n* **2** = **coward**, caitiff (*arch.*), dastard (*arch.*), poltroon, recreant (*arch.*), renegade, yellow-belly (*sl.*)

craving *n* **1** = **longing**, ache, appetite, cacoethes, desire, hankering, hope, hunger, lust, thirst, urge, yearning, yen (*inf.*)

craw *n* **2** = **throat**, crop, gizzard, gullet, maw, stomach

crawl[1] *vb* **1, 2** = **creep**, advance slowly, drag, go on all fours, inch, move at a snail's pace, move on hands and knees, pull *or* drag oneself along, slither, worm one's way, wriggle, writhe **3** = **grovel**, abase oneself, brown-nose, creep, cringe, fawn, kiss ass (*US. & Canad. taboo slang*), lick someone's boots (*sl.*), pander to, suck up to someone (*sl.*), toady, truckle **4** = **be full of**, be alive, be lousy, be overrun (*sl.*), swarm, teem

Antonyms *vb* ≠ **creep:** dart, dash, fly, hasten, hurry, race, run, rush, sprint, step on it (*inf.*), walk

craze *n* **1, 2** = **fad**, enthusiasm, fashion, infatuation, mania, mode, novelty, passion, preoccupation, rage, the latest (*inf.*), thing, trend, vogue ◆ *vb* **3** = **drive mad**, bewilder, confuse, dement, derange, distemper, enrage, infatuate, inflame, madden, make insane, send crazy *or* berserk, unbalance, unhinge, unsettle

crazy *adj* **1** = **insane**, barking (*sl.*), barmy (*sl.*), batty (*sl.*), berserk, bonkers (*sl., chiefly Brit.*), cracked (*sl.*), crazed, cuckoo (*inf.*), daft (*inf.*), delirious, demented, deranged, doolally (*sl.*), idiotic, loopy (*inf.*), lunatic, mad, mad as a hatter, maniacal, mental (*sl.*), not right in the head, not the full shilling (*inf.*), nuts (*sl.*), nutty (*sl.*), off one's head (*sl.*), off one's trolley (*sl.*), of unsound mind, out of one's mind, out to lunch (*inf.*), potty (*Brit. inf.*), touched, unbalanced, unhinged **2** = **ridiculous**, absurd, bird-brained (*inf.*), bizarre, derisory, eccentric, fantastic, fatuous, foolhardy, foolish, half-baked (*inf.*), idiotic, ill-conceived, impracticable, imprudent, inane, inappropriate, irresponsible, ludicrous, nonsensical, odd, oddball, outrageous, peculiar, potty (*Brit. inf.*), preposterous, puerile, quixotic, senseless, short-sighted, silly, strange, unrealistic, unwise, unworkable, weird, wild **3** *foll. by* **about** *or* **over** = **fanatical**, ablaze, ardent, devoted, eager, enamoured, enthusiastic, hysterical, infatuated, into (*inf.*), mad, passionate, smitten, very keen, wild (*inf.*), zealous

Antonyms *adj* ≠ **insane:** all there (*inf.*), *compos mentis*, down-to-earth, in one's right mind, intelligent, mentally sound, practical, prudent, rational, reasonable, sane, sensible, smart, wise ≠ **ridiculous:** appropriate, brilliant, conventional, feasible, orthodox, possible, practicable, prudent, realistic, responsible, sensible, wise, workable ≠ **fanatical:** cool, indifferent, uncaring, unenthusiastic, uninterested

creak *vb* **1** = **squeak**, grate, grind, groan, rasp, scrape, scratch, screech, squeal

creaky *adj* **1** = **squeaky**, creaking, grating, rasping, raspy, rusty, squeaking, unoiled

cream *n* **2** = **lotion**, cosmetic, emulsion, essence, liniment, oil, ointment, paste, salve, unguent **3** = **best**, *crème de la crème*, elite, flower, pick, prime ◆ *adj* **6b** = **off-white**, yellowish-white

creamy *adj* **1** = **smooth**, buttery, creamed, lush, milky, oily, rich, soft, velvety

crease *n* **1** = **line**, bulge, corrugation, fold, groove, overlap, pucker, ridge, ruck, tuck, wrinkle ◆ *vb* **4** = **wrinkle**, corrugate, crimp, crinkle, crumple, double up, fold, pucker, ridge, ruck up, rumple, screw up

ing, creased. **4** to make or become wrinkled or furrowed. **5** (*tr*) to graze with a bullet. [C15: from earlier *crēst;* prob. rel. to OF *cresté* wrinkled] ▸**'creaser** *n* ▸**'creasy** *adj*

create Ⓣ (kriː'eɪt) *vb* **creates, creating, created.** **1** (*tr*) to cause to come into existence. **2** (*tr*) to invest with a new honour, office, or title; appoint. **3** (*tr*) to be the cause of. **4** (*tr*) to act (a role) in the first production of a play. **5** (*intr*) *Brit. sl.* to make a fuss or uproar. [C14 *creat* created, from L *creātus,* from *creāre* to produce, make]

creatine ('kriːəˌtiːn, -tɪn) *n* an important compound involved in many biochemical reactions and present in many types of living cells. [C19: from Gk *kreas* flesh + -INE[2]]

creation Ⓣ (kriː'eɪʃən) *n* **1** the act or process of creating. **2** the fact of being created or produced. **3** something brought into existence or created. **4** the whole universe.

Creation (kriː'eɪʃən) *n Christianity.* **1** (often preceded by *the*) God's act of bringing the universe into being. **2** the universe as thus brought into being by God.

creative Ⓣ (kriː'eɪtɪv) *adj* **1** having the ability to create. **2** characterized by originality of thought; having or showing imagination. **3** designed to or tending to stimulate the imagination. **4** characterized by sophisticated bending of the rules or conventions: *creative accounting.* ▸**cre'atively** *adv* ▸**cre'ativeness** *n* ▸**ˌcrea'tivity** *n*

creator Ⓣ (kriː'eɪtə) *n* a person or thing that creates; originator. ▸**cre'atorship** *n*

Creator (kriː'eɪtə) *n* (usually preceded by *the*) an epithet of God.

creature Ⓣ ('kriːtʃə) *n* **1** a living being, esp. an animal. **2** something that has been created, whether animate or inanimate. **3** a human being; person: used as a term of scorn, pity, or endearment. **4** a person who is dependent upon another; tool. [C13: from Church L *creātūra,* from L *creāre* to create] ▸**'creatural** *or* **'creaturely** *adj*

crèche (krɛʃ, kreɪʃ) *n* **1** *Chiefly Brit.* **1a** a day nursery for very young children. **1b** a supervised play area provided for young children for short periods. **2** a tableau of Christ's Nativity. [C19: from OF: manger, crib, ult. of Gmc origin]

cred (krɛd) *n Sl.* short for **credibility** (esp. in **street cred**).

credence Ⓣ ('kriːdᵊns) *n* **1** acceptance or belief, esp. with regard to the evidence of others. **2** something supporting a claim to belief; credential (esp. in **letters of credence**). **3** short for **credence table.** [C14: from Med. L *crēdentia* trust, credit, from L *crēdere* to believe]

credence table *n Christianity.* a small table on which the Eucharistic bread and wine are placed.

credential Ⓣ (krɪ'dɛnʃəl) *n* **1** something that entitles a person to confidence, authority, etc. **2** (*pl*) a letter or certificate giving evidence of the bearer's identity or competence. [C16: from Med. L *crēdentia* credit, trust; see CREDENCE]

credenza (krɪ'dɛnzə) *n* another name for **credence table.** [It.: see CREDENCE]

credibility gap *n* a disparity between claims or statements made and the evident facts of the situation or circumstances to which they relate.

credible Ⓣ ('krɛdɪbᵊl) *adj* **1** capable of being believed. **2** trustworthy or reliable: *the latest claim is the only one to involve a credible witness.* [C14: from L *crēdibilis,* from L *crēdere* to believe] ▸**'credibleness** *or* **ˌcredi'bility** *n* ▸**'credibly** *adv*

credit Ⓣ ('krɛdɪt) *n* **1** commendation or approval, as for an act or quality. **2** a person or thing serving as a source of good influence, repute, etc. **3** influence or reputation coming from the good opinion of others. **4** belief in the truth, reliability, quality, etc., of someone or something. **5** a sum of money or equivalent purchasing power, available for a person's use. **6a** the positive balance in a person's bank account. **6b** the sum of money that a bank makes available to a client in excess of any deposit. **7a** the practice of permitting a buyer to receive goods or services before payment. **7b** the time permitted for paying for such goods or services. **8** reputation for solvency and probity, inducing confidence among creditors. **9** *Accounting.* **9a** acknowledgment of an income, liability, or capital item by entry on the right-hand side of an account. **9b** the right-hand side of an account. **9c** an entry on this side. **9d** the total of such entries. **9e** (*as modifier*): *credit entries.* **10** *Education.* **10a** a distinction awarded to an examination candidate obtaining good marks. **10b** a section of an examination syllabus satisfactorily completed. **11 on credit.** with payment to be made at a future date. ◆ *vb* **credits, crediting, credited.** (*tr*) **12** (foll. by *with*) to ascribe (to); give credit (for). **13** to accept as true; believe. **14** to do credit to. **15** *Accounting.* **15a** to enter (an item) as a credit in an account. **15b** to acknowledge (a payer) by making such an entry. ◆ See also **credits.** [C16: from OF *crédit,* from It. *credito,* from L *crēditum* loan, from *crēdere* to believe]

creditable Ⓣ ('krɛdɪtəbᵊl) *adj* deserving credit, honour, etc.; praiseworthy. ▸**'creditableness** *or* **ˌcredita'bility** *n* ▸**'creditably** *adv*

credit account *n Brit.* a credit system by means of which customers may obtain goods and services before payment.

credit card *n* a card issued by banks, businesses, etc., enabling the holder to obtain goods and services on credit.

Creditiste (ˌkrɛdɪ'tiːst) *Canad.* ◆ *adj* **1** of, supporting, or relating to the Social Credit Rally of Quebec. ◆ *n* **2** a supporter or member of this organization.

creditor ('krɛdɪtə) *n* a person or commercial enterprise to whom money is owed.

credit rating *n* an evaluation of the creditworthiness of an individual or business.

credits ('krɛdɪts) *pl n* a list of those responsible for the production of a film or a television programme.

credit transfer *n* a method of settling a debt by transferring money through a bank or post office, esp. for those who do not have cheque accounts.

creditworthy ('krɛdɪtˌwɜːðɪ) *adj* (of an individual or business) adjudged as meriting credit on the basis of earning power, previous record of debt repayment, etc. ▸**'creditˌworthiness** *n*

credo ('kriːdəʊ, 'kreɪ-) *n, pl* **credos.** any formal statement of beliefs, principles, or opinions.

Credo ('kriːdəʊ, 'kreɪ-) *n, pl* **Credos.** **1** the Apostles' or Nicene Creed. **2** a musical setting of the Creed. [C12: from L, lit.: I believe; first word of the Apostles' and Nicene Creeds]

credulity Ⓣ (krɪ'djuːlɪtɪ) *n* disposition to believe something on little evidence; gullibility.

credulous Ⓣ ('krɛdjʊləs) *adj* **1** tending to believe something on little evidence. **2** arising from or characterized by credulity: *credulous beliefs.* [C16: from L *crēdulus,* from *crēdere* to believe] ▸**'credulously** *adv* ▸**'credulousness** *n*

Cree (kriː) *n* **1** (*pl* **Cree** *or* **Crees**) a member of a N American Indian people living in Ontario, Saskatchewan, and Manitoba. **2** the language of this people.

creed Ⓣ (kriːd) *n* **1** a concise, formal statement of the essential articles of Christian belief, such as the Apostles' Creed or the Nicene Creed. **2**

THESAURUS

create *vb* **1** = **make**, beget, bring into being *or* existence, coin, compose, concoct, design, develop, devise, dream up (*inf.*), form, formulate, generate, give birth to, give life to, hatch, initiate, invent, originate, produce, spawn **2** = **appoint**, constitute, establish, found, install, invest, set up **3** = **cause**, bring about, lead to, occasion
Antonyms *vb* ≠ **make:** annihilate, demolish, destroy

creation *n* **1** = **making**, conception, constitution, development, establishment, formation, foundation, generation, genesis, inception, institution, laying down, origination, procreation, production, setting up, siring **3** = **invention**, achievement, brainchild (*inf.*), *chef-d'oeuvre,* concept, concoction, handiwork, magnum opus, *pièce de résistance,* production **4** = **universe**, all living things, cosmos, life, living world, natural world, nature, world

creative *adj* **2** = **imaginative**, artistic, clever, fertile, gifted, ingenious, inspired, inventive, original, productive, stimulating, visionary

creativity *n* **2** = **imagination**, cleverness, fecundity, fertility, imaginativeness, ingenuity, inspiration, inventiveness, originality, productivity, talent

creator *n* = **maker**, architect, author, begetter, designer, father, framer, initiator, inventor, originator, prime mover

creature *n* **1** = **living thing**, animal, beast, being, brute, critter (*US dialect*), dumb animal, lower animal, quadruped **3** = **person**, body, character, fellow, human being, individual, man, mortal, soul, wight (*arch.*), woman **4** = **minion**, cohort (*chiefly US*), dependant, hanger-on, hireling, instrument (*inf.*), lackey, puppet, retainer, tool, wretch

credence *n* **1** = **belief**, acceptance, assurance, certainty, confidence, credit, dependence, faith, reliance, trust

credential *n* **2** *pl* = **certification**, attestation, authorization, card, deed, diploma, docket, document, letter of recommendation *or* introduction, letters of credence, licence, missive, papers, passport, recommendation, reference(s), testament, testimonial, title, voucher, warrant

credibility *n* **1, 2** = **believability**, believableness, integrity, plausibility, reliability, tenability, trustworthiness

credible *adj* **1** = **believable**, conceivable, imaginable, likely, plausible, possible, probable, reasonable, supposable, tenable, thinkable, verisimilar **2** = **reliable**, dependable, honest, sincere, trustworthy, trusty
Antonyms *adj* ≠ **believable:** doubtful, implausible, inconceivable, incredible, questionable, unbelievable, unlikely ≠ **reliable:** dishonest, insincere, not dependable, unreliable, untrustworthy

credit *n* **1** = **praise**, acclaim, acknowledgment, approval, Brownie points, commendation, fame, glory, honour, kudos, merit, recognition, thanks, tribute **2** = **source of satisfaction** *or* **pride**, feather in one's cap, honour **3** = **prestige**, character, clout (*inf.*), esteem, estimation, good name, influence, position, regard, reputation, repute, standing, status **4** = **belief**, confidence, credence, faith, reliance, trust **11 on credit** = **on account**, by deferred payment, by instalments, on hire-purchase, on (the) H.P., on the slate (*inf.*), on tick (*inf.*) ◆ *vb* **12** *foll. by* **with** = **attribute to**, accredit to, ascribe to, assign to, chalk up to (*inf.*), impute to, refer to **13** = **believe**, accept, bank on, buy (*sl.*), depend on, fall for, have faith in, rely on, swallow (*inf.*), trust

creditable *adj* = **praiseworthy**, admirable, commendable, deserving, estimable, exemplary, honourable, laudable, meritorious, reputable, respectable, worthy

credulity *n* = **gullibility**, blind faith, credulousness, naïveté, silliness, simplicity, stupidity

credulous *adj* **1** = **gullible**, as green as grass, born yesterday (*inf.*), dupable, green, naive, overtrusting, trustful, uncritical, unsuspecting, unsuspicious, wet behind the ears (*inf.*)
Antonyms *adj* cynical, incredulous, sceptical, suspecting, unbelieving, wary

creed *n* **2** = **belief**, articles of faith, canon, catechism, confession, credo, doctrine, dogma,

any statement or system of beliefs or principles. [OE *crēda*, from L *crēdo* I believe]
▸'**creedal** *or* '**credal** *adj*

creek ➊ (kriːk) *n* **1** *Chiefly Brit.* a narrow inlet or bay, esp. of the sea. **2** *US, Canad., Austral., & NZ.* a small stream or tributary. **3** **up the creek.** *Sl.* in trouble; in a difficult position. [C13: from ON *kriki* nook; rel. to MDu. *krēke* creek, inlet]

Creek (kriːk) *n* **1** (*pl* **Creek** *or* **Creeks**) a member of a confederacy of N American Indian tribes formerly living in Georgia and Alabama. **2** any of their languages.

creel (kriːl) *n* **1** a wickerwork basket, esp. one used to hold fish. **2** a wickerwork trap for catching lobsters, etc. [C15: from Scot., from ?]

creep ➊ (kriːp) *vb* **creeps, creeping, crept.** (*intr*) **1** to crawl with the body near to or touching the ground. **2** to move slowly, quietly, or cautiously. **3** to act in a servile way; fawn; cringe. **4** to move or slip out of place, as from pressure or wear. **5** (of plants) to grow along the ground or over rocks. **6** to develop gradually: *creeping unrest.* **7** to have the sensation of something crawling over the skin. ◆ *n* **8** the act of creeping or a creeping movement. **9** *Sl.* a person considered to be obnoxious or servile. **10** *Geol.* the gradual downward movement of loose rock material, soil, etc., on a slope. [OE *crēopan*]

creeper ➊ ('kriːpə) *n* **1** a person or animal that creeps. **2** a plant, such as the ivy, that grows by creeping. **3** the US and Canad. name for the **tree creeper.** **4** a hooked instrument for dragging deep water. **5** *Inf.* a shoe with a soft sole.

creeps (kriːps) *pl n* (preceded by *the*) *Inf.* a feeling of fear, repulsion, disgust, etc.

creepy ➊ ('kriːpɪ) *adj* **creepiest. 1** *Inf.* having or causing a sensation of repulsion or fear, as of creatures crawling on the skin. **2** creeping; slow-moving.
▸'**creepily** *adv* ▸'**creepiness** *n*

creepy-crawly *Brit. inf.* ◆ *n, pl* **creepy-crawlies. 1** a small crawling creature. ◆ *adj* **2** feeling or causing a sensation as of creatures crawling on one's skin.

cremate (krɪ'meɪt) *vb* **cremates, cremating, cremated.** (*tr*) to burn up (something, esp. a corpse) and reduce to ash. [C19: from L *cremāre*]
▸**cre'mation** *n* ▸**cre'mator** *n* ▸**crematory** ('krɛmətərɪ, -trɪ) *adj*

crematorium (ˌkrɛmə'tɔːrɪəm) *n, pl* **crematoriums** *or* **crematoria** (-rɪə). a building in which corpses are cremated. Also called (esp. US): **crematory.**

crème (krɛm, kriːm, kreɪm; *French* krɛm) *n* **1** cream. **2** any of various sweet liqueurs: *crème de moka.* ◆ *adj* **3** (of a liqueur) rich and sweet.

crème de la crème *French.* (krɛm də la krɛm) *n* the very best. [lit.: cream of the cream]

crème de menthe ('krɛm də 'mɛnθ, 'mɪnt; 'kriːm, 'kreɪm) *n* a liqueur flavoured with peppermint. [F, lit.: cream of mint]

crème fraîche ('krɛm 'frɛʃ) *n* thickened and slightly fermented cream. [F, lit.: fresh cream]

crenate ('kriːneɪt) *or* **crenated** *adj* having a scalloped margin, as certain leaves. [C18: from NL *crēnātus*, from Med. L, prob. from LL *crēna* a notch]
▸'**crenately** *adv* ▸**crenation** (krɪ'neɪʃən) *n*

crenel ('krɛnᵊl) *or* **crenelle** (krɪ'nɛl) *n* any of a set of openings formed in the top of a wall or parapet and having slanting sides, as in a battlement. [C15: from OF, lit.: a little notch, from *cren* notch, from LL *crēna*]

crenellate *or US* **crenelate** ('krɛnɪˌleɪt) *vb* **crenellates, crenellating, crenellated** *or US* **crenelates, crenelating, crenelated.** (*tr*) to supply with battlements. [C19: from OF *creneler*, from CRENEL]
▸'**crenelˌlated** *or US* '**crenelˌated** *adj* ▸ˌ**crenel'lation** *or US* ˌ**crenel'ation** *n*

creole ('kriːəʊl) *n* **1** a language that has its origin in extended contact between two language communities, one of which is European. ◆ *adj* **2** of or relating to creole. **3** (of a sauce or dish) containing or cooked with tomatoes, green peppers, onions, etc. [C17: via F & Sp., prob. from Port. *crioulo* slave born in one's household, prob. from *criar* to bring up, from L *creāre* to CREATE]

Creole ('kriːəʊl) *n* **1** (*sometimes not cap.*) (in the Caribbean and Latin America) **1a** a native-born person of European ancestry. **1b** a native-born person of mixed European and African ancestry who speaks a creole. **2** (in Louisiana and other Gulf States of the US) a native-born person of French ancestry. **3** the French Creole spoken in Louisiana. ◆ *adj* **4** of or relating to any of these peoples.

creosol ('kriːəˌsɒl) *n* a colourless or pale yellow insoluble oily liquid with a smoky odour and a burning taste. [C19: from CREOS(OTE) + -OL[1]]

creosote ('krɪəˌsəʊt) *n* **1** a colourless or pale yellow liquid with a burning taste and penetrating odour distilled from wood tar. It is used as an antiseptic. **2** a thick dark liquid mixture prepared from coal tar: used as a preservative for wood. ◆ *vb* **creosotes, creosoting, creosoted. 3** to treat (wood) with creosote. [C19: from Gk *kreas* flesh + *sōtēr* preserver, from *sōzein* to keep safe]
▸**creosotic** (ˌkrɪə'sɒtɪk) *adj*

crepe *or* **crape** (kreɪp) *n* **1a** a light cotton, silk, or other fabric with a fine ridged or crinkled surface. **1b** (*as modifier*): *a crepe dress.* **2** a black armband originally made of this, worn as a sign of mourning. **3** a very thin pancake, often folded around a filling. **4** short for **crepe paper** or **crepe rubber.** [C19: from F *crêpe*, from L *crispus* curled, uneven, wrinkled]

crepe de Chine (kreɪp də ʃiːn) *n* a very thin crepe of silk or a similar light fabric. [C19: from F: Chinese crepe]

crepe paper *n* thin crinkled coloured paper, resembling crepe and used for decorations.

creperie ('krɛpərɪ, 'kreɪp-) *n* an eating establishment that specializes in pancakes.

crepe rubber *n* a type of rubber in the form of colourless or pale yellow crinkled sheets: used for the soles of shoes.

crêpe suzette (kreɪp suː'zɛt) *n, pl* **crêpes suzettes.** (*sometimes pl*) an orange-flavoured pancake flambéed in a liqueur or brandy.

crepitate ('krɛpɪˌteɪt) *vb* **crepitates, crepitating, crepitated.** (*intr*) to make a rattling or crackling sound. [C17: from L *crepitāre*]
▸'**crepitant** *adj* ▸ˌ**crepi'tation** *n*

crepitus ('krɛpɪtəs) *n* **1** a crackling chest sound heard in pneumonia, etc. **2** the grating sound of two ends of a broken bone rubbing together. ◆ Also called: **crepitation.** [C19: from L, from *crepāre* to crack, creak]

crept (krɛpt) *vb* the past tense and past participle of **creep.**

crepuscular (krɪ'pʌskjʊlə) *adj* **1** of or like twilight; dim. **2** (of certain creatures) active at twilight or just before dawn. [C17: from L *crepusculum* dusk, from *creper* dark]

crepy *or* **crepey** ('kreɪpɪ) *adj* **crepier, crepiest.** (esp. of the skin) having a dry wrinkled appearance.

Cres. *abbrev. for* Crescent.

crescendo (krɪ'ʃɛndəʊ) *n, pl* **crescendos** *or* **crescendi** (-dɪ). **1** *Music.* **1a** a gradual increase in loudness or the musical direction or symbol indicating this. Abbrev.: **cresc.** Symbol: < **1b** (*as modifier*): *a crescendo passage.* **2** any similar gradual increase in loudness. **3** a peak of noise or intensity: *the cheers reached a crescendo.* ◆ *vb* **crescendos, crescendoing, crescendoed. 4** (*intr*) to increase in loudness or force. ◆ *adv* **5** with a crescendo. [C18: from It., lit.: increasing, from *crescere* to grow, from L]

crescent ➊ ('krɛsᵊnt, -zᵊnt) *n* **1** the curved shape of the moon in its first or last quarter. **2** any shape or object resembling this. **3** *Chiefly Brit.* a crescent-shaped street. **4** (*often cap.* and preceded by *the*) **4a** the emblem of Islam or Turkey. **4b** Islamic or Turkish power. ◆ *adj* **5** *Arch. or poetic.* increasing or growing. [C14: from L *crescēns* increasing, from *crescere* to grow]

cresol ('kriːsɒl) *n* an aromatic compound found in coal tar and creosote and used in making synthetic resins and as an antiseptic and disinfectant. Formula: $C_6H_4(CH_3)OH$. Systematic name: **methylphenol.**

cress (krɛs) *n* any of various plants having pungent-tasting leaves often used in salads and as a garnish. [OE *cressa*]

cresset ('krɛsɪt) *n History.* a metal basket mounted on a pole in which oil or pitch was burned for illumination. [C14: from OF *craisset*, from *craisse* GREASE]

crest ➊ (krɛst) *n* **1** a tuft or growth of feathers, fur, or skin along the top of the heads of some birds, reptiles, and other animals. **2** something resembling or suggesting this. **3** the top, highest point, or highest stage of something. **4** an ornamental piece, such as a plume, on top of a helmet. **5** *Heraldry.* a symbol of a family or office, borne in addition to a coat of arms and used in medieval times to decorate the helmet. ◆ *vb* **6** (*intr*) to come or rise to a high point. **7** (*tr*) to lie at the top of; cap. **8** (*tr*) to reach the top of (a hill, wave, etc.). [C14: from OF *creste*, from L *crista*]
▸'**crested** *adj* ▸'**crestless** *adj*

crestfallen ➊ ('krɛstˌfɔːlən) *adj* dejected or disheartened.
▸'**crestˌfallenly** *adv*

cretaceous (krɪ'teɪʃəs) *adj* consisting of or resembling chalk. [C17: from L *crētāceus*, from *crēta*, lit.: Cretan earth, that is, chalk]

THESAURUS

persuasion, principles, profession (*of faith*), tenet

creek *n* **1** = **inlet**, bay, bight, cove, firth *or* frith (*Scot.*) **2** *US, Canad., Austral., & N.Z.* = **stream**, bayou, brook, rivulet, runnel, streamlet, tributary, watercourse

creep *vb* **1** = **crawl**, crawl on all fours, glide, insinuate, slither, squirm, worm, wriggle, writhe **2** = **sneak**, approach unnoticed, crawl, dawdle, edge, inch, proceed at a snail's pace, skulk, slink, steal, tiptoe **3** = **grovel**, bootlick (*inf.*), brown-nose (*taboo sl.*), cower, cringe, fawn, kiss (someone's) ass (*US & Canad. taboo sl.*), kowtow, pander to, scrape, suck up to (*inf.*), toady, truckle ◆ *n* **9** *Slang* = **bootlicker** (*inf.*), ass-kisser (*US & Canad. taboo sl.*), brown-noser (*taboo sl.*), crawler (*sl.*), sneak, sycophant, toady

creeper *n* **2** = **climbing plant**, climber, rambler, runner, trailing plant, vine (*chiefly US*)

creepy *adj* **1** *Informal* = **disturbing**, awful, direful, disgusting, eerie, forbidding, frightening, ghoulish, goose-pimply (*inf.*), gruesome, hair-raising, horrible, macabre, menacing, nightmarish, ominous, scary (*inf.*), sinister, terrifying, threatening, unpleasant, weird

crescent *n* **1** = **meniscus**, half-moon, new moon, old moon, sickle, sickle-shape ◆ *adj* **5** *Archaic* = **waxing**, growing, increasing

crest *n* **1** = **tuft**, aigrette, caruncle (*Zoology*), cockscomb, comb, crown, mane, panache, plume, tassel, topknot **3** = **top**, apex, crown, head, height, highest point, peak, pinnacle, ridge, summit **5** = **emblem**, badge, bearings, charge, device, insignia, symbol

crestfallen *adj* = **disappointed**, chapfallen, choked, dejected, depressed, despondent, disconsolate, discouraged, disheartened, downcast, downhearted, sick as a parrot (*inf.*)
Antonyms *adj* cock-a-hoop, elated, encouraged,

Cretaceous (krɪ'teɪʃəs) *adj* **1** of, denoting, or formed in the last period of the Mesozoic era, during which chalk deposits were formed. ◆ *n* **2** **the.** the Cretaceous period or rock system.

Cretan ('kriːtən) *adj* **1** of or relating to the island of Crete in the W Mediterranean. **2** of the inhabitants of Crete. ◆ *n* **3** a native or inhabitant of Crete.

cretin ('krɛtɪn) *n* **1** a person afflicted with cretinism. **2** a person considered to be extremely stupid. [C18: from F *crétin,* from Swiss F *crestin,* from L *Chrīstiānus* Christian, alluding to the humanity of such people, despite their handicaps]
▸'**cretinous** *adj*

cretinism ('krɛtɪˌnɪzəm) *n* a condition arising from a deficiency of thyroid hormone, present from birth, characterized by dwarfism and mental retardation. See also **myxoedema.**

cretonne (krɛ'tɒn, 'krɛtɒn) *n* a heavy cotton or linen fabric with a printed design, used for furnishing. [C19: from F, from *Creton* Norman village where it originated]

Creutzfeldt-Jakob disease ('krɔɪtsfelt 'jɑːkɒp) *n* a fatal slow-developing disease that affects the central nervous system, characterized by mental deterioration and loss of coordination of the limbs. It is thought to be caused by an abnormal prion protein in the brain. [C20: after Hans G. *Creutzfeldt* (1885–1964) and Alfons *Jakob* (1884–1931), German physicians]

crevasse ❶ (krɪ'væs) *n* **1** a deep crack or fissure, esp. in the ice of a glacier. **2** *US.* a break in a river embankment. ◆ *vb* **crevasses, crevassing, crevassed. 3** (*tr*) *US.* to make a break or fissure in (a dyke, wall, etc.). [C19: from F: CREVICE]

crevice ❶ ('krɛvɪs) *n* a narrow fissure or crack; split; cleft. [C14: from OF *crevace,* from *crever* to burst, from L *crepāre* to crack]

crew[1] ❶ (kruː) *n* (*sometimes functioning as pl*) **1** the men who man a ship, boat, aircraft, etc. **2** *Naut.* a group of people assigned to a particular job or type of work. **3** *Inf.* a gang, company, or crowd. ◆ *vb* **4** to serve on (a ship) as a member of the crew. [C15 *crue* (military) reinforcement, from OF *creue* augmentation, from OF *creistre* to increase, from L *crescere*]

crew[2] (kruː) *vb Arch.* a past tense of **crow**[2].

crew cut *n* a closely cropped haircut for men. [C20: from the style of haircut worn by the boat crews at Harvard and Yale Universities]

crewel ('kruːɪl) *n* a loosely twisted worsted yarn, used in fancy work and embroidery. [C15: from ?]
▸'**crewelist** *n* ▸'**crewel,work** *n*

crew neck *n* a plain round neckline in sweaters.
▸'**crew-ˌneck** *or* '**crew-ˌnecked** *adj*

crib ❶ (krɪb) *n* **1** a child's bed with slatted wooden sides; cot. **2** a cattle stall or pen. **3** a fodder rack or manger. **4** a small crude cottage or room. **5** *NZ.* a weekend cottage: term is South Island usage only. **6** any small confined space. **7** a representation of the manger in which the infant Jesus was laid at birth. **8** *Inf.* a theft, esp. of another's writing or thoughts. **9** *Inf., chiefly Brit.* a translation of a foreign text or a list of answers used by students, often illicitly, as an aid in lessons, examinations, etc. **10** short for **cribbage. 11** *Cribbage.* the discard pile. **12** Also called: **cribwork.** a framework of heavy timbers used in the construction of foundations, mines, etc. ◆ *vb* **cribs, cribbing, cribbed. 13** (*tr*) to put or enclose in or as if in a crib; furnish with a crib. **14** (*tr*) *Inf.* to steal (another's writings or thoughts). **15** (*intr*) *Inf.* to copy either from a crib or from someone else during a lesson or examination. **16** (*intr*) *Inf.* to grumble. [OE *cribb*]
▸'**cribber** *n*

cribbage ('krɪbɪdʒ) *n* a game of cards for two to four, in which players try to win a set number of points before their opponents. [C17: from ?]

cribbage board *n* a board, with pegs and holes, used for scoring at cribbage.

crib-biting *n* a harmful habit of horses in which the animal leans on the manger or seizes it with the teeth and swallows a gulp of air.

crick ❶ (krɪk) *Inf.* ◆ *n* **1** a painful muscle spasm or cramp, esp. in the neck or back. ◆ *vb* **2** (*tr*) to cause a crick in. [C15: from ?]

cricket[1] ('krɪkɪt) *n* an insect having long antennae and, in the males, the ability to produce a chirping sound by rubbing together the leathery forewings. [C14: from OF *criquet,* from *criquer* to creak, imit.]

cricket[2] ('krɪkɪt) *n* **1a** a game played by two teams of eleven players on a field with a wicket at either end of a 22-yard pitch, the object being for one side to score runs by hitting a hard leather-covered ball with a bat while the other side tries to dismiss them by bowling, catching, running them out, etc. **1b** (*as modifier*): *a cricket bat.* **2** **not cricket.** *Inf.* not fair play. ◆ *vb* (*intr*) **3** to play cricket. [C16: from OF *criquet* goalpost, wicket, from ?]
▸'**cricketer** *n*

cricoid ('kraɪkɔɪd) *adj* **1** of or relating to the ring-shaped lowermost cartilage of the larynx. ◆ *n* **2** this cartilage. [C18: from NL *cricoīdes,* from Gk *krikoeidēs* ring-shaped, from *krikos* ring]

cri de coeur (kriː də kɜː) *n, pl* **cris de coeur.** (kriː də kɜː). a heartfelt or impassioned appeal. [C20: altered from F *cri du coeur*]

crier ('kraɪə) *n* **1** a person or animal that cries. **2** (formerly) an official who made public announcements, esp. in a town or court.

crime ❶ (kraɪm) *n* **1** an act or omission prohibited and punished by law. **2** unlawful acts in general. **3** an evil act. **4** *Inf.* something to be regretted. [C14: from OF, from L *crīmen* verdict, accusation, crime]

criminal ❶ ('krɪmɪn°l) *n* **1** a person charged with and convicted of crime. **2** a person who commits crimes for a living. ◆ *adj* **3** of, involving, or guilty of crime. **4** (*prenominal*) of or relating to crime or its punishment. **5** *Inf.* senseless or deplorable. [C15: from LL *crīminālis;* see CRIME, -AL[1]]
▸'**criminally** *adv* ▸ˌ**crimi'nality** *n*

criminal conversation *n* another term for **adultery.**

criminalize *or* **criminalise** ('krɪmɪnəˌlaɪz) *vb* **criminalizes, criminalizing, criminalized** *or* **criminalises, criminalising, criminalised.** (*tr*) to declare (an action or activity) criminal.
▸ˌ**criminali'zation** *or* ˌ**criminali'sation** *n*

criminal law *n* the body of law dealing with offences and offenders.

criminology (ˌkrɪmɪ'nɒlədʒɪ) *n* the scientific study of crime. [C19: from L *crimin-* CRIME, + -LOGY]
▸**criminological** (ˌkrɪmɪnə'lɒdʒɪk°l) *or* ˌ**crimino'logic** *adj* ▸ˌ**crimino'logically** *adv* ▸ˌ**crimi'nologist** *n*

crimp (krɪmp) *vb* (*tr*) **1** to fold or press into ridges. **2** to fold and pinch together (something, such as two pieces of metal). **3** to curl or wave (the hair) tightly, esp. with curling tongs. **4** *Inf., chiefly US.* to hinder. ◆ *n* **5** the act or result of folding or pressing together or into ridges. **6** a tight wave or curl in the hair. [OE *crympan;* rel. to *crump* bent; see CRAMP]
▸'**crimper** *n* ▸'**crimpy** *adj*

Crimplene ('krɪmpliːn) *n Trademark.* a synthetic material similar to Terylene, characterized by its crease-resistance.

crimson ('krɪmzən) *n* **1a** a deep or vivid red colour. **1b** (*as adj*): *a crimson rose.* ◆ *vb* **2** to make or become crimson. **3** (*intr*) to blush. [C14: from OSp. *cremesin,* from Ar. *qirmizi* red of the kermes, from *qirmiz* KERMES]
▸'**crimsonness** *n*

cringe ❶ (krɪndʒ) *vb* **cringes, cringing, cringed.** (*intr*) **1** to shrink or flinch, esp. in fear or servility. **2** to behave in a servile or timid way. **3** *Inf.* to experience a sudden feeling of embarrassment or distaste. ◆ *n* **4** the act of cringing. **5** **the cultural cringe.** *Austral.* subservience to overseas cultural standards. [OE *cringan* to yield in battle]
▸'**cringer** *n*

cringle ('krɪŋg°l) *n* an eyelet at the edge of a sail. [C17: from Low G *Kringel* small ring]

crinkle ❶ ('krɪŋk°l) *vb* **crinkles, crinkling, crinkled. 1** to form or cause to form wrinkles, twists, or folds. **2** to make or cause to make a rustling noise. ◆ *n* **3** a wrinkle, twist, or fold. **4** a rustling noise. [OE *crincan* to bend, give way]

crinkly ❶ ('krɪŋklɪ) *adj* **1** wrinkled; crinkled. ◆ *n, pl* **crinklies. 2** *Sl.* an old person.

crinoid ('kraɪnɔɪd, 'krɪn-) *n* **1** a primitive echinoderm having delicate feathery arms radiating from a central disc. ◆ *adj* **2** of, relating to, or belonging to the *Crinoidea.* **3** shaped like a lily. [C19: from Gk *krinoeidēs* lily-like]
▸**cri'noidal** *adj*

crinoline ('krɪn°lɪn) *n* **1** a stiff fabric, originally of horsehair and linen

THESAURUS

exuberant, happy, in seventh heaven, joyful, on cloud nine (*inf.*), over the moon (*inf.*)

crevasse *n* **1** = **crack,** abyss, bergschrund, chasm, cleft, fissure

crevice *n* = **gap,** chink, cleft, crack, cranny, fissure, fracture, hole, interstice, opening, rent, rift, slit, split

crew[1] *n* **1** = **(ship's) company,** hands, (ship's) complement **2** = **team,** company, corps, gang, party, posse, squad, working party **3** *Informal* = **crowd,** assemblage, band, bunch (*inf.*), camp, company, gang, herd, horde, lot, mob, pack, posse (*inf.*), set, swarm, troop

crib *n* **1** = **cradle,** bassinet, bed, cot **2, 3** = **manger,** bin, box, bunker, rack, stall **9** *Informal* = **translation,** key, trot (*US sl.*) ◆ *vb* **13** = **confine,** box up, cage, coop, coop up, enclose, fence, imprison, limit, pen, rail, restrict, shut in **14, 15** *Informal* = **copy,** cheat, pass off as one's own work, pilfer, pirate, plagiarize, purloin, steal

crick *Informal n* **1** = **spasm,** convulsion, cramp, twinge ◆ *vb* **2** = **rick,** jar, wrench

crime *n* **1** = **offence,** atrocity, fault, felony, job (*inf.*), malfeasance, misdeed, misdemeanour, outrage, transgression, trespass, unlawful act, violation, wrong **3** = **lawbreaking,** corruption, delinquency, guilt, illegality, iniquity, malefaction, misconduct, sin, unrighteousness, vice, villainy, wickedness, wrong, wrongdoing

criminal *n* **1, 2** = **lawbreaker,** con (*sl.*), con man (*inf.*), convict, crook, culprit, delinquent, evildoer, felon, jailbird, lag (*sl.*), malefactor, offender, sinner, transgressor, villain ◆ *adj* **3** = **unlawful,** bent (*sl.*), corrupt, crooked (*inf.*), culpable, felonious, illegal, illicit, immoral, indictable, iniquitous, lawless, nefarious, peccant, under-the-table, unrighteous, vicious, villainous, wicked, wrong **5** *Informal* = **disgraceful,** deplorable, foolish, preposterous, ridiculous, scandalous, senseless

Antonyms *adj* ≠ **unlawful:** commendable, honest, honourable, innocent, law-abiding, lawful, legal, right

criminality *n* **3** = **illegality,** corruption, culpability, delinquency, depravity, guiltiness, sinfulness, turpitude, villainy, wickedness

cringe *vb* **1** = **shrink,** blench, cower, dodge, draw back, duck, flinch, quail, quiver, recoil, shy, start, tremble, wince **2** = **grovel,** bend, bootlick (*inf.*), bow, brown-nose (*taboo sl.*), crawl, creep, crouch, fawn, kiss ass (*US & Canad. taboo sl.*), kneel, kowtow, pander to, sneak, stoop, toady, truckle

crinkle *n, vb* **1** = **crease,** cockle, crimp, crimple, crumple, curl, fold, pucker, ruffle, rumple, scallop, twist, wrinkle **2** = **rustle,** crackle, hiss, swish, whisper

crinkly *adj* **1** = **wrinkled,** buckled, cockled, creased, curly, fluted, frizzy, furrowed, gathered, kinky, knit, puckered, ruffled, scalloped

used in lining garments. **2** a petticoat stiffened with this, worn to distend skirts, esp. in the mid-19th century. **3** a framework of steel hoops worn for the same purpose. [C19: from F, from It. *crinolino,* from *crino* horsehair, from L *crīnis* hair + *lino* flax, from L *līnum*]

cripple Ⓣ ('krɪpᵊl) *n* **1** a person who is lame. **2** a person who is or seems disabled or deficient in some way: *a mental cripple.* ◆ *vb* **cripples, crippling, crippled. 3** (*tr*) to make a cripple of; disable. [OE *crypel;* rel. to *crēopan* to creep]
▸ **'crippler** *n*

crisis Ⓣ ('kraɪsɪs) *n, pl* **crises** (-siːz). **1** a crucial stage or turning point, esp. in a sequence of events or a disease. **2** an unstable period, esp. one of extreme trouble or danger. **3** *Pathol.* a sudden change in the course of a disease. [C15: from L: decision, from Gk *krisis,* from *krinein* to decide]

crisp Ⓣ (krɪsp) *adj* **1** dry and brittle. **2** fresh and firm. **3** invigorating or bracing: *a crisp breeze.* **4** clear; sharp: *crisp reasoning.* **5** lively or stimulating. **6** clean and orderly. **7** concise and pithy. **8** wrinkled or curly: *crisp hair.* ◆ *vb* **9** to make or become crisp. ◆ *n* **10** *Brit.* a very thin slice of potato fried and eaten cold as a snack. **11** something that is crisp. [OE, from L *crispus* curled, uneven, wrinkled]
▸ **'crisply** *adv* ▸ **'crispness** *n*

crispbread ('krɪsp,brɛd) *n* a thin dry biscuit made of wheat or rye.

crisper ('krɪspə) *n* a compartment in a refrigerator for storing salads, vegetables, etc., in order to keep them fresh.

crispy ('krɪspɪ) *adj* **crispier, crispiest. 1** crisp. **2** having waves or curls.
▸ **'crispiness** *n*

crisscross ('krɪs,krɒs) *vb* **1** to move or cause to move in a crosswise pattern. **2** to mark with or consist of a pattern of crossing lines. ◆ *adj* **3** (esp. of lines) crossing one another in different directions. ◆ *n* **4** a pattern made of crossing lines. ◆ *adv* **5** in a crosswise manner or pattern.

crit. *abbrev. for:* **1** *Med.* critical. **2** criticism.

criterion Ⓣ (kraɪ'tɪərɪən) *n, pl* **criteria** (-rɪə) *or* **criterions.** a standard by which something can be judged or decided. [C17: from Gk *kritērion,* from *kritēs* judge, from *krinein* to decide]

> **USAGE NOTE** *Criteria,* the plural of *criterion,* is not acceptable as a singular noun: *this criterion is not valid; these criteria are not valid.*

critic Ⓣ ('krɪtɪk) *n* **1** a person who judges something. **2** a professional judge of art, music, literature, etc. **3** a person who often finds fault and criticizes. [C16: from L *criticus,* from Gk *kritikos* capable of judging, from *kritēs* judge; see CRITERION]

critical Ⓣ ('krɪtɪkᵊl) *adj* **1** containing or making severe or negative judgments. **2** containing analytical evaluations. **3** of a critic or criticism. **4** of or forming a crisis; crucial. **5** urgently needed. **6** *Inf.* so seriously injured or ill as to be in danger of dying. **7** *Physics.* of, denoting, or concerned with a state in which the properties of a system undergo an abrupt change. **8 go critical.** (of a nuclear power station or reactor) to reach a state in which a nuclear-fission chain reaction becomes self-sustaining.
▸ **,criti'cality** *n* ▸ **'critically** *adv* ▸ **'criticalness** *n*

critical mass *n* the minimum mass of fissionable material that can sustain a nuclear chain reaction.

critical path analysis *n* a technique for planning projects with reference to the critical path, which is the sequence of stages requiring the longest time.

critical temperature *n* the temperature of a substance in its critical state. A gas can only be liquefied at temperatures below this.

criticism Ⓣ ('krɪtɪ,sɪzəm) *n* **1** the act or an instance of making an unfavourable or severe judgment, comment, etc. **2** the analysis or evaluation of a work of art, literature, etc. **3** the occupation of a critic. **4** a work that sets out to evaluate or analyse.

criticize Ⓣ *or* **criticise** ('krɪtɪ,saɪz) *vb* **criticizes, criticizing, criticized** *or* **criticises, criticising, criticised. 1** to judge (something) with disapproval; censure. **2** to evaluate or analyse (something).
▸ **'criti,cizable** *or* **'criti,cisable** *adj* ▸ **'criti,cizer** *or* **'criti,ciser** *n*

critique Ⓣ (krɪ'tiːk) *n* **1** a critical essay or commentary. **2** the act or art of criticizing. [C17: from F, from Gk *kritikē,* from *kritikos* able to discern]

croak Ⓣ (krəʊk) *vb* **1** (*intr*) (of frogs, crows, etc.) to make a low, hoarse cry. **2** to utter (something) in this manner. **3** (*intr*) to grumble or be pessimistic. **4** *Sl.* **4a** (*intr*) to die. **4b** (*tr*) to kill. ◆ *n* **5** a low hoarse utterance or sound. [OE *crācettan*]
▸ **'croaky** *adj* ▸ **'croakiness** *n*

croaker ('krəʊkə) *n* **1** an animal, bird, etc., that croaks. **2** a grumbling person.

Croat ('krəʊæt) *n* **1a** a native or inhabitant of Croatia, a country in SE Europe. **1b** a speaker of Croatian. ◆ *n, adj* **2** another word for **Croatian.**

Croatian (krəʊ'eɪʃən) *adj* **1** of or relating to Croatia, its people, or their language. ◆ *n* **2** the official language of Croatia, a dialect of Serbo-Croat. **3a** a native or inhabitant of Croatia. **3b** a speaker of Croatian.

croc (krɒk) *n* short for **crocodile** (senses 1 and 2).

crochet ('krəʊʃeɪ, -ʃɪ) *vb* **crochets, crocheting** (-ʃeɪɪŋ, -ʃɪɪŋ), **crocheted** (-ʃeɪd, -ʃɪd). **1** to make (a piece of needlework, a garment, etc.) by looping and intertwining thread with a hooked needle (**crochet hook**). ◆ *n* **2** work made by crocheting. [C19: from F *crochet,* dim. of *croc* hook, prob. of Scand. origin]
▸ **'crocheter** *n*

crock[1] (krɒk) *n* **1** an earthen pot, jar, etc. **2** a piece of broken earthenware. [OE *crocc* pot]

crock[2] (krɒk) *Sl., chiefly Brit.* ◆ *n* **1** a person or thing that is old or decrepit (esp. in **old crock**). ◆ *vb* **2** to become or cause to become weak or disabled. [C15: orig. Scot.; rel. to Norwegian *krake* unhealthy animal, Du. *kraak* decrepit person or animal]

crockery ('krɒkərɪ) *n* china dishes, earthen vessels, etc., collectively.

crocket ('krɒkɪt) *n* a carved ornament in the form of a curled leaf or cusp, used in Gothic architecture. [C17: from Anglo-F *croket* a little hook, from *croc* hook, of Scand. origin]

crocodile ('krɒkə,daɪl) *n* **1** a large tropical reptile having a broad head, tapering snout, massive jaws, and a thick outer covering of bony plates. **2a** leather made from the skin of any of these animals. **2b** (*as modifier*): *crocodile shoes.* **3** *Brit. inf.* a line of people, esp. schoolchildren walking two by two. [C13: via OF, from L *crocodīlus,* from Gk *krokodeilos* lizard, ult. from *krokē* pebble + *drilos* worm; referring to its basking on shingle]

crocodile clip *n* a clasp with serrated interlocking edges used for making electrical connections, etc.

crocodile tears *pl n* an insincere show of grief; false tears. [from the belief that crocodiles wept over their prey to allure further victims]

crocodilian (,krɒkə'dɪlɪən) *n* **1** any large predatory reptile of the order *Crocodilia,* which includes the crocodiles, alligators, and caymans. ◆ *adj* **2** of, relating to, or belonging to the *Crocodilia.* **3** of, relating to, or resembling a crocodile.

crocus ('krəʊkəs) *n, pl* **crocuses.** any plant of the iridaceous genus *Crocus,* having white, yellow, or purple flowers. [C17: from NL, from L *crocus,* from Gk *krokos* saffron]

Croesus ('kriːsəs) *n* any very rich man. [after *Croesus* (died ?546 BC) the last king of Lydia, noted for his great wealth]

croft (krɒft) *n Brit.* a small enclosed plot of land, adjoining a house, worked by the occupier and his family, esp. in Scotland. [OE *croft*]
▸ **'crofter** *n* ▸ **'crofting** *adj, n*

croissant ('krwʌsɒŋ) *n* a flaky crescent-shaped bread roll. [F, lit.: crescent]

THESAURUS

cripple *vb* **3** = **disable**, debilitate, enfeeble, hamstring, incapacitate, lame, maim, mutilate, paralyse, weaken

crisis *n* **1** = **critical point**, climacteric, climax, confrontation, crunch (*inf.*), crux, culmination, height, moment of truth, point of no return, turning point **2** = **emergency**, catastrophe, critical situation, deep water, dilemma, dire straits, disaster, exigency, extremity, meltdown (*inf.*), mess, panic stations (*inf.*), pass, plight, predicament, quandary, strait, trouble

crisp *adj* **1, 2** = **firm**, brittle, crispy, crumbly, crunchy, fresh, unwilted **3** = **bracing**, brisk, fresh, invigorating, refreshing **4** = **brief**, brusque, clear, incisive, pithy, short, succinct, tart, terse **6** = **clean**, clean-cut, neat, orderly, smart, snappy, spruce, tidy, trig (*arch. or dialect*), trim, well-groomed, well-pressed
Antonyms *adj* ≠ **firm:** drooping, droopy, flaccid, floppy, limp, soft, wilted, withered ≠ **bracing:** balmy, clement, mild, pleasant, warm

criterion *n* = **standard**, bench mark, canon, gauge, measure, norm, par, principle, proof, rule, test, touchstone, yardstick

critic *n* **1, 2** = **judge**, analyst, arbiter, authority, commentator, connoisseur, expert, expositor, pundit, reviewer **3** = **fault-finder**, attacker, carper, caviller, censor, censurer, detractor, knocker (*inf.*), Momus, reviler, vilifier

critical *adj* **1** = **disparaging**, captious, carping, cavilling, censorious, derogatory, disapproving, fault-finding, nagging, niggling, nit-picking (*inf.*), on someone's back (*inf.*), scathing **2** = **analytical**, accurate, diagnostic, discerning, discriminating, fastidious, judicious, penetrating, perceptive, precise **4, 5** = **crucial**, all-important, dangerous, deciding, decisive, grave, hairy (*sl.*), high-priority, momentous, now or never, perilous, pivotal, precarious, pressing, psychological, risky, serious, urgent, vital
Antonyms *adj* ≠ **crucial:** safe, secure, settled, unimportant ≠ **disparaging:** appreciative, approving, complimentary, uncritical ≠ **analytical:** undiscriminating

criticism *n* **1** = **fault-finding**, animadversion, bad press, brickbats (*inf.*), censure, character assassination, critical remarks, denigration, disapproval, disparagement, flak (*inf.*), knocking (*inf.*), panning (*inf.*), slagging (*sl.*), slam (*sl.*), slating (*inf.*), stick (*sl.*), stricture **4** = **analysis**, appraisal, appreciation, assessment, comment, commentary, critique, elucidation, evaluation, judgment, notice, review

criticize *vb* **1** = **find fault with**, animadvert on *or* upon, blast, carp, censure, condemn, disapprove of, disparage, excoriate, give (someone *or* something) a bad press, have a go (at) (*inf.*), knock (*inf.*), lambast(e), nag at, pan (*inf.*), pass strictures upon, pick holes in, pick to pieces, put down, slam (*sl.*), slate (*inf.*), tear into (*inf.*) **2** = **analyse**, appraise, assess, comment upon, evaluate, give an opinion, judge, pass judgment on, review
Antonyms *vb* ≠ **find fault with:** commend, compliment, extol, laud (*literary*), praise

critique *n* **1** = **essay**, analysis, appraisal, assessment, commentary, examination, review, treatise

croak *vb* **2** = **squawk**, caw, gasp, grunt, utter *or* speak harshly, utter *or* speak huskily, utter *or* speak throatily, wheeze **4a** *Slang* = **die**, buy it (*US sl.*), expire, kick it (*sl.*), kick the bucket (*inf.*), pass away, peg it (*inf.*), perish, pop one's clogs (*inf.*)

Croix de Guerre *French.* (krwa də gɛr) *n* a French military decoration awarded for gallantry in battle: established 1915. [lit.: cross of war]

Cro-Magnon man ('krəʊ'mænjɒn, -'mægnɒn) *n* an early type of modern man, *Homo sapiens,* who lived in Europe during late Palaeolithic times. [C19: after the cave (Cro-Magnon), Dordogne, France, where the remains were first found]

cromlech ('krɒmlɛk) *n* **1** a circle of prehistoric standing stones. **2** (no longer in technical usage) a megalithic chamber tomb or dolmen. [C17: from Welsh, from *crom,* fem. of *crwm* bent, arched + *llech* flat stone]

crone Ⓣ (krəʊn) *n* a witchlike old woman. [C14: from OF *carogne* carrion, ult. from L *caro* flesh]

cronk (krɒŋk) *adj Austral. sl.* **1** unfit; unsound. **2** dishonest. [C19: ?from G *krank* ill]

crony Ⓣ ('krəʊnɪ) *n, pl* **cronies.** a friend or companion. [C17: student sl. (Cambridge), from Gk *khronios* of long duration, from *khronos* time]

cronyism ('krəʊnɪˌɪzəm) *n* the practice of appointing friends to high-level posts, esp. political posts, regardless of their suitability.

crook Ⓣ (krʊk) *n* **1** a curved or hooked thing. **2** a staff with a hooked end, such as a bishop's crosier or shepherd's staff. **3** a turn or curve; bend. **4** *Inf.* a dishonest person, esp. a swindler or thief. ◆ *vb* **5** to bend or curve or cause to bend or curve. ◆ *adj* **6** *Austral. & NZ sl.* **6a** ill. **6b** of poor quality. **6c** unpleasant; bad. **7 go (off) crook.** *Austral. & NZ sl.* to lose one's temper. **8 go crook at** *or* **on.** *Austral. & NZ sl.* to rebuke or upbraid. [C12: from ON *krokr* hook]

crooked Ⓣ ('krʊkɪd) *adj* **1** bent, angled or winding. **2** set at an angle; not straight. **3** deformed or contorted. **4** *Inf.* dishonest or illegal. **5 crooked on.** (*also* krʊkt) *Austral. inf.* hostile or averse to.
▸**'crookedly** *adv* ▸**'crookedness** *n*

croon Ⓣ (kru:n) *vb* **1** to sing or speak in a soft low tone. ◆ *n* **2** a soft low singing or humming. [C14: via MDu. *crōnen* to groan]
▸**'crooner** *n*

crop Ⓣ (krɒp) *n* **1** the produce of cultivated plants, esp. cereals, vegetables, and fruit. **2a** the amount of such produce in any particular season. **2b** the yield of some other farm produce: *the lamb crop.* **3** a group of products, thoughts, people, etc., appearing at one time or in one season. **4** the stock of a thonged whip. **5** short for **riding crop. 6** a pouchlike part of the oesophagus of birds, in which food is stored or partially digested before passing on to the gizzard. **7** a short cropped hairstyle. **8** a notch in or a piece cut out of the ear of an animal. **9** the act of cropping. ◆ *vb* **crops, cropping, cropped.** (*mainly tr*) **10** to cut (hair, grass, etc.) very short. **11** to cut and collect (mature produce) from the land or plant on which it has been grown. **12** to clip part of (the ear or ears) of (an animal), esp. as a means of identification. **13** (of herbivorous animals) to graze on (grass or similar vegetation). ◆ See also **crop out, crop up.** [OE *cropp*]

crop-dusting *n* the spreading of fungicide, etc., on crops in the form of dust, often from an aircraft.

crop-eared *adj* having the ears or hair cut short.

crop out *vb* (*intr, adv*) (of a formation of rock strata) to appear or be exposed at the surface.

cropper ('krɒpə) *n* **1** a person who cultivates or harvests a crop. **2 come a cropper.** *Inf.* **2a** to fall heavily. **2b** to fail completely.

crop rotation *n* the system of growing a sequence of different crops on the same ground so as to maintain or increase its fertility.

crop up Ⓣ *vb* (*intr, adv*) *Inf.* to occur or appear, esp. unexpectedly.

croquet ('krəʊkeɪ, -kɪ) *n* a game for two to four players who hit a wooden ball through iron hoops with mallets in order to hit a peg. [C19: ?from F dialect, var. of CROCHET (little hook)]

croquette (krəʊ'kɛt, krɒ-) *n* a savoury cake of minced meat, fish, etc., fried in breadcrumbs. [C18: from F, from *croquer* to crunch, imit.]

crosier *or* **crozier** ('krəʊʒə) *n* a staff surmounted by a crook or cross, carried by bishops as a symbol of pastoral office. [C14: from OF *crossier* staff bearer, from *crosse* pastoral staff]

cross Ⓣ (krɒs) *n* **1** a structure or symbol consisting of two intersecting lines or pieces at right angles to one another. **2** a wooden structure used as a means of execution, consisting of an upright post with a transverse piece to which people were nailed or tied. **3** a representation of the Cross used as an emblem of Christianity or as a reminder of Christ's death. **4** any mark or shape consisting of two intersecting lines, esp. such a symbol (×) used as a signature, error mark, etc. **5** a sign representing the Cross made either by tracing a figure in the air or by touching the forehead, breast, and either shoulder in turn. **6** any variation of the Christian symbol, such as a Maltese or Greek cross. **7** a cruciform emblem awarded to indicate membership of an order or as a decoration for distinguished service. **8** (*sometimes cap.*) Christianity or Christendom, esp. as contrasted with non-Christian religions. **9** the place in a town or village where a cross has been set up. **10** *Biol.* **10a** the process of crossing; hybridization. **10b** an individual produced as a result of this process. **11** a mixture of two qualities or types. **12** an opposition, hindrance, or misfortune; affliction (esp. in **bear one's cross**). **13** *Boxing.* a straight punch delivered from the side, esp. with the right hand. **14** *Football.* the act or an instance of passing the ball from a wing to the middle of the field. ◆ *vb* **15** (sometimes foll. by *over*) to move or go across (something); traverse or intersect. **16a** to meet and pass. **16b** (of each of two letters in the post) to be dispatched before receipt of the other. **17** (*tr; usually foll. by out, off,* or *through*) to cancel with a cross or with lines; delete. **18** (*tr*) to place or put in a form resembling a cross: *to cross one's legs.* **19** (*tr*) to mark with a cross or crosses. **20** (*tr*) *Brit.* to draw two parallel lines across the face of (a cheque) and so make it payable only into a bank account. **21** (*tr*) **21a** to trace the form of the Cross upon (someone or something) in token of blessing. **21b** to make the sign of the Cross upon (oneself). **22** (*intr*) (of telephone lines) to interfere with each other so that several callers are connected together at one time. **23** to cause fertilization between (plants or animals of different breeds, races, varieties, etc.). **24** (*tr*) to oppose the wishes or plans of; thwart. **25** *Football.* to pass (the ball) from a wing to the middle of the field. **26 cross one's fingers.** to fold one finger across another in the hope of bringing good luck. **27 cross one's heart.** to promise or pledge, esp. by making the sign of a cross over one's heart. **28 cross one's mind.** to occur to one briefly or suddenly. **29 cross the path (of).** to meet or thwart (someone). **30 cross swords.** to argue or fight. ◆ *adj* **31** angry; ill-humoured; vexed. **32** lying or placed across; transverse: *a cross timber.* **33** involving interchange; reciprocal. **34** contrary or unfavourable. **35** another word for **crossbred.** [OE *cros,* from OIrish *cross* (unattested), from L *crux;* see CRUX]
▸**'crossly** *adv* ▸**'crossness** *n*

Cross (krɒs) *n* **the. 1** the cross on which Jesus Christ was crucified. **2** the Crucifixion of Jesus.

cross- *combining form.* **1** indicating action from one individual, group, etc., to another: *cross-cultural; cross-fertilize; cross-refer.* **2** indicating movement, position, etc., across something: *crosscurrent; crosstalk.* **3** indicating a crosslike figure or intersection: *crossbones.* [from CROSS (in various senses)]

crossbar ('krɒsˌbɑ:) *n* **1** a horizontal bar, line, stripe, etc. **2** a horizontal beam across a pair of goalposts. **3** the horizontal bar on a man's bicycle.

crossbeam ('krɒsˌbi:m) *n* a beam that spans from one support to another.

THESAURUS

crone *n* = **old woman**, beldam (*arch.*), gammer, hag, old bag (*derogatory slang*), old bat (*sl.*), witch

crony *n* = **friend**, accomplice, ally, associate, buddy (*inf.*), china (*Brit. sl.*), chum (*inf.*), cock, colleague, companion, comrade, gossip (*arch.*), mate (*inf.*), pal (*inf.*), sidekick (*sl.*)

crook *n* **4** *Informal* = **criminal**, cheat, chiseller (*inf.*), fraudster, knave (*arch.*), lag (*sl.*), racketeer, robber, rogue, shark, swindler, thief, villain ◆ *vb* **5** = **bend**, angle, bow, curve, flex, hook

crooked *adj* **1, 3** = **bent**, anfractuous, bowed, crippled, curved, deformed, deviating, disfigured, distorted, hooked, irregular, meandering, misshapen, out of shape, tortuous, twisted, twisting, warped, winding, zigzag **2** = **at an angle**, angled, askew, asymmetric, awry, lopsided, off-centre, skewwhiff (*Brit. inf.*), slanted, slanting, squint, tilted, to one side, uneven, unsymmetrical **4** *Informal* = **dishonest**, bent (*sl.*), corrupt, crafty, criminal, deceitful, dishonourable, dubious, fraudulent, illegal, knavish, nefarious, questionable, shady (*inf.*), shifty, treacherous, underhand, under-the-table, unlawful, unprincipled, unscrupulous
Antonyms *adj* ≠ **bent:** flat, straight ≠ **dishonest:** ethical, fair, honest, honourable, lawful, legal, straight, upright

crookedness *n* **1, 3** = **distortedness**, anfractuosity, contortedness, curvedness, deformedness, deviance, disfigurement, hookedness, irregularity, tortuousness, zigzaggedness **2** = **unevenness**, asymmetry, lopsidedness **4** = **dishonesty**, corruptness, craftiness, criminality, deceitfulness, dishonourableness, dubiousness, fraudulence, fraudulency, illegality, improbity, knavishness, nefariousness, questionability, questionableness, shadiness (*inf.*), shiftiness, treacherousness, underhandedness, unlawfulness, unprincipledness, unscrupulosity, unscrupulousness
Antonyms *n* ≠ **distortedness:** flatness, levelness, straightness ≠ **dishonesty:** ethicality, ethicalness, fairness, honesty, honourableness, lawfulness, legality, straightness, trustworthiness, uprightness

croon *vb* **1** = **sing**, breathe, hum, purr, warble

crop *n* **2a** = **produce**, fruits, gathering, harvest, reaping, season's growth, vintage, yield ◆ *vb* **10** = **cut**, clip, curtail, dock, lop, mow, pare, prune, reduce, shear, shorten, snip, top, trim **11** = **harvest**, bring home, bring in, collect, garner, gather, mow, pick, reap **13** = **graze**, browse, nibble

crop up *vb Informal* = **happen**, appear, arise, emerge, occur, spring up, turn up

cross *n* **3, 4** = **crucifix**, rood **10b** = **crossbreed**, cur, hybrid, mongrel, mutt (*sl.*) **11** = **mixture**, amalgam, blend, combination **12** = **trouble**, affliction, burden, grief, load, misery, misfortune, trial, tribulation, woe, worry ◆ *vb* **15** = **go across**, bridge, crisscross, cut across, extend over, ford, intersect, intertwine, lace, lie athwart of, meet, move across, pass over, ply, span, traverse, zigzag **17** *usually foll. by* **out, off,** *or* **through** = **strike off** *or* **out**, blue-pencil, cancel, delete, eliminate, score off *or* out **23** = **interbreed**, blend, crossbreed, cross-fertilize, cross-pollinate, hybridize, intercross, mix, mongrelize **24** = **oppose**, block, deny, foil, frustrate, hinder, impede, interfere, obstruct, resist, thwart **30 cross swords** = **fight**, argue, come to blows, dispute, spar, wrangle ◆ *adj* **31** = **angry**, annoyed, cantankerous, captious, choked, churlish, crotchety (*inf.*), crusty, disagreeable, fractious, fretful, grouchy (*inf.*), grumpy, hacked (off) (*US sl.*), ill-humoured, ill-tempered, in a bad mood, irascible, irritable, liverish, peeved (*inf.*), peevish, petulant, pissed off (*taboo sl.*), put out, querulous, ratty (*Brit. & NZ inf.*), short, snappish, snappy, splenetic, sullen, surly, testy, tetchy, vexed, waspish **32** = **transverse**, crosswise, diagonal, intersecting, oblique **33** = **reciprocal**, opposite **34** = **opposing**, adverse, contrary, opposed, unfavourable
Antonyms *adj* ≠ **angry:** affable, agreeable, calm, cheerful, civil, congenial, even-tempered, genial, good-humoured, good-natured, nice, placid, pleasant, sweet

cross-bench *n (usually pl) Brit.* a seat in Parliament occupied by a neutral or independent member.
▸'**cross-,bencher** *n*

crossbill ('krɒs,bɪl) *n* any of various widely distributed finches that occur in coniferous woods and have a bill with crossed tips.

crossbones ('krɒs,bəunz) *pl n* See **skull and crossbones.**

crossbow ('krɒs,bəu) *n* a type of medieval bow fixed transversely on a stock grooved to direct a square-headed arrow.
▸'**cross,bowman** *n*

crossbred ('krɒs,brɛd) *adj* **1** (of plants or animals) produced as a result of crossbreeding. ◆ *n* **2** a crossbred plant or animal.

crossbreed ('krɒs,bri:d) *vb* **crossbreeds, crossbreeding, crossbred. 1** Also: **interbreed.** to breed (animals or plants) using parents of different races, varieties, breeds, etc. ◆ *n* **2** the offspring produced by such a breeding.

crosscheck (,krɒs'tʃɛk) *vb* **1** to verify (a fact, report, etc.) by considering conflicting opinions or consulting other sources. ◆ *n* **2** the act or an instance of crosschecking.

cross-country *adj, adv* **1** by way of fields, etc., as opposed to roads. **2** across a country. ◆ *n* **3** a long race held over open ground.

crosscurrent ('krɒs,kʌrənt) *n* **1** a current flowing across another current. **2** a conflicting tendency moving counter to the usual trend.

cross-curricular *adj Brit. education.* denoting or relating to an approach to a topic that includes contributions from several different disciplines and viewpoints.

crosscut ('krɒs,kʌt) *adj* **1** cut at right angles or obliquely to the major axis. ◆ *n* **2** a transverse cut or course. **3** *Mining.* a tunnel through a vein of ore or from the shaft to a vein. ◆ *vb* **crosscuts, crosscutting, crosscut. 4** to cut across.

crosscut saw *n* a saw for cutting timber across the grain.

crosse (krɒs) *n* a light staff with a triangular frame to which a network is attached, used in playing lacrosse. [F, from OF *croce* CROSIER]

cross-examine ❶ *vb* **cross-examines, cross-examining, cross-examined.** (*tr*) **1** *Law.* to examine (a witness for the opposing side), as in attempting to discredit his testimony. **2** to examine closely or relentlessly.
▸'**cross-ex,ami'nation** *n* ▸,**cross-ex'aminer** *n*

cross-eye *n* a turning inwards towards the nose of one or both eyes, caused by abnormal alignment.
▸'**cross-,eyed** *adj*

cross-fertilize *vb* **cross-fertilizes, cross-fertilizing, cross-fertilized. 1** to fertilize by fusion of male and female gametes from different individuals of the same species. **2** a non-technical term for **cross-pollinate.**
▸'**cross-,fertili'zation** *n*

crossfire ('krɒs,faɪə) *n* **1** *Mil., etc.* converging fire from one or more positions. **2** a lively exchange of ideas, opinions, etc.

cross-grained ❶ *adj* **1** (of timber) having the fibres arranged irregularly or across the axis of the piece. **2** perverse, cantankerous, or stubborn.

crosshatch ('krɒs,hætʃ) *vb Drawing.* to shade or hatch with two or more sets of parallel lines that cross one another.

crossing ('krɒsɪŋ) *n* **1** the place where one thing crosses another. **2** a place where a street, railway, etc., may be crossed. **3** the act or an instance of travelling across something, esp. the sea. **4** the act or process of crossbreeding.

crossing over *n Genetics.* the interchange of sections between pairing chromosomes during meiosis that produces variations in inherited characteristics by rearranging genes.

cross-legged ('krɒs'lɛgɪd, -'lɛgd) *adj* standing or sitting with one leg crossed over the other.

cross-match *vb Immunol.* to test the compatibility of (a donor's and recipient's blood) by checking that the red cells of each do not agglutinate in the other's serum.

crossover ('krɒs,əuvə) *n* **1** a place at which a crossing is made. **2** *Railways.* a point of transfer between two main lines. **3** short for **crossover network. 4** *Genetics.* another term for **crossing over. 5** a recording, book, or other product that becomes popular in a genre other than its own. ◆ *adj* **6** (of music, fashion, art, etc.) combining two distinct styles. **7** (of a performer, writer, recording, book, etc.) having become popular in more than one genre.

crossover network *n Electronics.* an arrangement in a loudspeaker system that separates the signal into two or more frequency bands for feeding into different speakers.

crosspatch ❶ ('krɒs,pætʃ) *n Inf.* a bad-tempered person. [C18: from CROSS + obs. *patch* fool]

crosspiece ('krɒs,pi:s) *n* a transverse beam, joist, etc.

cross-ply *adj* (of a motor tyre) having the fabric cords in the outer casing running diagonally to stiffen the sidewalls.

cross-pollinate *vb* **cross-pollinates, cross-pollinating, cross-pollinated.** to transfer pollen from the anthers of one flower to the stigma of another.
▸,**cross-polli'nation** *n*

cross-purpose *n* **1** a contrary aim or purpose. **2 at cross-purposes.** conflicting; opposed; disagreeing.

cross-question *vb* **1** to cross-examine. ◆ *n* **2** a question asked in cross-examination.

cross-refer *vb* to refer from one part of something, esp. a book, to another.

cross-reference *n* **1** a reference within a text to another part of the text. ◆ *vb* **cross-references, cross-referencing, cross-referenced. 2** to cross-refer.

crossroad ('krɒs,rəud) *n US & Canad.* **1** a road that crosses another road. **2** Also called: **crossway.** a road that crosses from one main road to another.

crossroads ('krɒs,rəudz) *n (functioning as sing)* **1** the point at which two or more roads cross each other. **2** the point at which an important choice has to be made (esp. in **at the crossroads**).

crossruff ('krɒs,rʌf) *Bridge, whist.* ◆ *n* **1** the alternate trumping of each other's leads by two partners, or by declarer and dummy. ◆ *vb* **2** (*intr*) to trump alternately in this way.

cross section *n* **1** *Maths.* a plane surface formed by cutting across a solid, esp. perpendicular to its longest axis. **2** a section cut off in this way. **3** the act of cutting anything in this way. **4** a random sample, esp. one regarded as representative.
▸,**cross-'sectional** *adj*

cross-stitch *n* **1** an embroidery stitch made by two stitches forming a cross. **2** embroidery worked with this stitch. ◆ *vb* **3** to embroider (a piece of needlework) with cross-stitch.

crosstalk ('krɒs,tɔ:k) *n* **1** unwanted signals in one channel of a communications system as a result of a transfer of energy from other channels. **2** *Brit.* rapid or witty talk.

cross training *n* training in two or more sports to improve performance, esp. in one's main sport.

crosstree ('krɒs,tri:) *n Naut.* either of a pair of wooden or metal braces on the head of a mast to support the topmast, etc.

crosswise ❶ ('krɒs,waɪz) *or* **crossways** ('krɒs,weɪz) *adj, adv* **1** across; transversely. **2** in the shape of a cross.

crossword puzzle ('krɒs,wɜ:d) *n* a puzzle in which the solver guesses words suggested by numbered clues and writes them into a grid to form a vertical and horizontal pattern.

crotch ❶ (krɒtʃ) *n* **1** Also called (Brit.): **crutch. 1a** the angle formed by the legs where they join the human trunk. **1b** the human genital area. **1c** the corresponding part of a pair of trousers, pants, etc. **2** a forked region formed by the junction of two members. **3** a forked pole or stick. [C16: prob. var. of CRUTCH]
▸**crotched** *adj*

crotchet ('krɒtʃɪt) *n* **1** *Music.* Also called (US and Canad.): **quarter note.** a note having the time value of a quarter of a semibreve. **2** a perverse notion. [C14: from OF *crochet,* lit.: little hook, from *croche* hook; see CROCKET]

crotchety ❶ ('krɒtʃɪtɪ) *adj* **1** *Inf.* irritable; contrary. **2** full of crotchets.
▸'**crotchetiness** *n*

croton ('krəut[ə]n) *n* **1** any shrub or tree of the chiefly tropical genus *Croton,* esp. *C. tiglium,* the seeds of which yield croton oil, formerly used as a purgative. **2** any of various tropical plants of the related genus *Codiaeum.* [C18: from NL, from Gk *krotōn* tick, castor-oil plant (whose berries resemble ticks)]

crouch ❶ (krautʃ) *vb* (*intr*) **1** to bend low with the limbs pulled up close together, esp. (of an animal) in readiness to pounce. **2** to cringe, as in humility or fear. ◆ *n* **3** the act of stooping or bending. [C14: ?from OF *crochir* to become bent like a hook, from *croche* hook]

croup[1] (kru:p) *n* a throat condition, occurring usually in children, characterized by a hoarse cough and laboured breathing, resulting from inflammation of the larynx. [C16 *croup* to cry hoarsely, prob. imit.]
▸'**croupous** *or* '**croupy** *adj*

croup[2] (kru:p) *n* the hindquarters, esp. of a horse. [C13: from OF *croupe;* rel. to G *Kruppe*]

croupier ('kru:pɪə) *n* a person who deals cards, collects bets, etc., at a gaming table. [C18: lit.: one who rides behind another, from F *croupe* CROUP[2]]

crouton ('kru:tɒn) *n* a small piece of fried or toasted bread, usually served in soup. [F: dim. of *croûte* CRUST]

crow[1] (krəu) *n* **1** any large gregarious songbird of the genus *Corvus* of Europe and Asia, such as the raven, rook, and jackdaw. All have a heavy bill, glossy black plumage, and rounded wings. **2** any of various similar birds. **3** *Sl.* an old or ugly woman. **4 as the crow flies.** as directly as possible. **5 eat crow.** *US & Canad. inf.* to be forced to do something humiliating. **6 stone the crows.** (*interj*) *Brit. & Austral. sl.* an expression of surprise, dismay, etc. [OE *crāwa*]

crow[2] ❶ (krəu) *vb* (*intr*) **1** (p.t. **crowed** *or* **crew**) to utter a shrill squawking sound, as a cock. **2** (often foll. by *over*) to boast one's superiority. **3**

THESAURUS

cross-examine *vb* **2** = **question**, catechize, grill (*inf.*), interrogate, pump, quiz

cross-grained *adj* **2** = **difficult**, awkward, cantankerous, crabby, disobliging, ill-natured, morose, peevish, perverse, refractory, shrewish, stubborn, truculent, wayward

crosspatch *n Informal* = **grump** (*inf.*), bear, crank (*US, Canad., & Irish inf.*), curmudgeon, scold, shrew, sourpuss (*inf.*)

crosswise *adv* **1** = **across**, aslant, at an angle, athwart, at right angles, awry, crisscross, diagonally, from side to side, on the bias, over, sideways, transversely

crotch *n* **1a, 1b** = **groin**, crutch

crotchety *adj* **1** *Informal* = **bad-tempered**, awkward, cantankerous, contrary, crabby, cross, crusty, curmudgeonly, difficult, disagreeable, fractious, grumpy, irritable, liverish, obstreperous, peevish, ratty (*Brit. & NZ inf.*), surly, testy, tetchy

crouch *vb* **1** = **bend down**, bow, duck, hunch, kneel, squat, stoop

crow[2] *vb* **2** = **gloat**, blow one's own trumpet,

(esp. of babies) to utter cries of pleasure. ◆ *n* **4** an act or instance of crowing. [OE *crāwan;* rel. to OHG *krāen,* Du. *kraaien*]
▸**'crowingly** *adv*

crowbar ('krəʊ,bɑː) *n* a heavy iron lever with one end forged into a wedge shape.

crowd ⓣ (kraʊd) *n* **1** a large number of things or people gathered or considered together. **2** a particular group of people, esp. considered as a set: *the crowd from the office.* **3** (preceded by *the*) the common people; the masses. ◆ *vb* **4** (*intr*) to gather together in large numbers; throng. **5** (*tr*) to press together into a confined space. **6** (*tr*) to fill to excess; fill by pushing into. **7** (*tr*) *Inf.* to urge or harass by urging. [OE *crūdan*]
▸**'crowded** *adj* ▸**'crowdedness** *n*

crowfoot ('krəʊ,fʊt) *n, pl* **crowfoots.** any of several plants that have yellow or white flowers and divided leaves resembling the foot of a crow.

crown ⓣ (kraʊn) *n* **1** an ornamental headdress denoting sovereignty, usually made of gold embedded with precious stones. **2** a wreath or garland for the head, awarded as a sign of victory, success, honour, etc. **3** (*sometimes cap.*) monarchy or kingship. **4** an award, distinction, or title, given as an honour to reward merit, victory, etc. **5** anything resembling or symbolizing a crown. **6a** a coin worth five shillings (25 pence). **6b** a coin worth £5. **6c** any of several continental coins, such as the krona or krone, with a name meaning *crown.* **7** the top or summit of something: *crown of a hill.* **8** the centre part of a road, esp. when it is cambered. **9** the outstanding quality, achievement, state, etc.: *the crown of his achievements.* **10a** the enamel-covered part of a tooth above the gum. **10b artificial crown.** a substitute crown, usually of gold, porcelain, or acrylic resin, fitted over a decayed or broken tooth. **11** the part of an anchor where the arms are joined to the shank. ◆ *vb* (*tr*) **12** to put a crown on the head of, symbolically vesting with royal title, powers, etc. **13** to place a crown, wreath, garland, etc., on the head of. **14** to place something on or over the head or top of. **15** to confer a title, dignity, or reward upon. **16** to form the summit or topmost part of. **17** to cap or put the finishing touch to (a series of events): *to crown it all it rained, too.* **18** *Draughts.* to promote (a draught) to a king by placing another draught on top of it. **19** to attach a crown to (a tooth). **20** *Sl.* to hit over the head. [C12: from OF *corone,* from L *corōna* wreath, crown, from Gk *korōnē* crown, something curved]

Crown ⓣ (kraʊn) *n* (*sometimes not cap.;* usually preceded by *the*) **1** the sovereignty or realm of a monarch. **2a** the government of a monarchy. **2b** (*as modifier*): *Crown property.*

crown colony *n* a British colony whose administration is controlled by the Crown.

crown court *n English law.* a court of criminal jurisdiction holding sessions in towns throughout England and Wales.

Crown Derby *n* **1** a type of porcelain manufactured at Derby from 1784–1848. **2** *Trademark.* shortened form of Royal Crown Derby.

crown glass *n* **1** another name for **optical crown. 2** an old form of window glass made by blowing a globe and spinning it until it forms a flat disc.

crown green *n* a type of bowling green in which the sides are lower than the middle.

crowning ('kraʊnɪŋ) *n Obstetrics.* the stage of labour at which the infant's head is passing through the vaginal opening.

crown jewels *pl n* the jewellery, including the regalia, used by a sovereign on a state occasion.

Crown Office *n* (in Britain) an administrative office of the Queen's Bench Division of the High Court, where actions are entered for trial.

crown prince *n* the male heir to a sovereign throne.

crown princess *n* **1** the wife of a crown prince. **2** the female heir to a sovereign throne.

Crown Prosecution Service *n* (in England and Wales) an independent prosecuting body, established in 1986, that decides whether cases brought by the police should go to the courts: headed by the Director of Public Prosecutions. Cf. **procurator fiscal.** Abbrev.: **CPS.**

crown wheel *n* **1** *Horology.* a wheel that has one set of teeth at right angles to another. **2** the larger of two wheels in a bevel gear.

crow's-foot *n, pl* **crow's-feet.** (*often pl*) a wrinkle at the outer corner of the eye.

crow's-nest *n* a lookout platform high up on a ship's mast.

crow step *n* another term for **corbie-step.**

crozier ('krəʊʒə) *n* a variant spelling of **crosier.**

CRT *abbrev. for:* **1** cathode-ray tube. **2** (in Britain) composite rate tax: a system of paying interest to savers by which a rate of tax for a period is determined in advance and interest is paid net of tax which is deducted at source.

crucial ⓣ ('kruːʃəl) *adj* **1** involving a final or supremely important decision or event; decisive; critical. **2** *Inf.* very important. **3** *Sl.* very good. [C18: from F, from L *crux* CROSS]
▸**'crucially** *adv*

crucible ('kruːsɪbᵊl) *n* **1** a vessel in which substances are heated to high temperatures. **2** the hearth at the bottom of a metallurgical furnace in which the metal collects. **3** a severe trial or test. [C15 *corusible,* from Med. L *crūcibulum* night lamp, crucible, from ?]

crucifix ('kruːsɪfɪks) *n* a cross or image of a cross with a figure of Christ upon it. [C13: from Church L *crucifixus* the crucified Christ, from *crucifigere* to CRUCIFY]

crucifixion (,kruːsɪ'fɪkʃən) *n* a method of putting to death by nailing or binding to a cross, normally by the hands and feet.

Crucifixion (,kruːsɪ'fɪkʃən) *n* **1** (usually preceded by *the*) the crucifying of Christ. **2** a picture or representation of this.

cruciform ('kruːsɪ,fɔːm) *adj* shaped like a cross. [C17: from L *crux* cross + -FORM]
▸**'cruci,formly** *adv*

crucify ⓣ ('kruːsɪ,faɪ) *vb* **crucifies, crucifying, crucified.** (*tr*) **1** to put to death by crucifixion. **2** *Sl.* to defeat, ridicule, etc., totally. **3** to treat very cruelly; torment. [C13: from OF *crucifier,* from LL *crucifigere* to crucify, to fasten to a cross, from L *crux* cross + *figere* to fasten]
▸**'cruci,fier** *n*

crud (krʌd) *n* **1** *Sl.* a sticky substance, esp. when dirty and encrusted. **2** *Sl.* something or someone that is worthless, disgusting, or contemptible. **3** an undesirable residue, esp. one inside a nuclear reactor. [C14: earlier form of CURD]
▸**'cruddy** *adj*

crude ⓣ (kruːd) *adj* **1** lacking taste, tact, or refinement; vulgar. **2** in a natural or unrefined state. **3** lacking care, knowledge, or skill. **4** (*prenominal*) stark; blunt. ◆ *n* **5** short for **crude oil.** [C14: from L *crūdus* bloody, raw; rel. to L *cruor* blood]
▸**'crudely** *adv* ▸**'crudity** *or* **'crudeness** *n*

crude oil *n* unrefined petroleum.

crudités (,kruːdɪ'teɪ) *pl n* a selection of raw vegetables, served as an hors d'oeuvre. [C20: from F, pl of *crudité,* lit.: rawness]

cruel ⓣ ('kruːəl) *adj* **1** causing or inflicting pain without pity. **2** causing pain or suffering. ◆ *vb* **cruels, cruelling, cruelled** *or US* **cruels, crueling, crueled.** (*tr*) **3 cruel someone's pitch.** *Austral. sl.* to ruin someone's chances. [C13: from OF, from L *crūdēlis,* from *crūdus* raw, bloody]
▸**'cruelly** *adv* ▸**'cruelness** *n*

cruelty ⓣ ('kruːəltɪ) *n, pl* **cruelties. 1** deliberate infliction of pain or suffering. **2** the quality or characteristic of being cruel. **3** a cruel action. **4** *Law.* conduct that causes danger to life or limb or a threat to bodily or mental health.

THESAURUS

bluster, boast, brag, drool, exult, flourish, glory in, strut, swagger, triumph, vaunt

crowd *n* **1** = **multitude**, army, assembly, bevy, company, concourse, flock, herd, horde, host, mass, mob, pack, press, rabble, swarm, throng, troupe **2** = **group**, bunch (*inf.*), circle, clique, lot, set **3** *preceded by* **the** = **masses**, hoi polloi, mob, people, populace, proletariat, public, rabble, rank and file, riffraff, vulgar herd ◆ *vb* **4** = **flock**, cluster, congregate, cram, foregather, gather, huddle, mass, muster, press, push, stream, surge, swarm, throng **5** = **squeeze**, bundle, congest, cram, pack, pile

crowded *adj* **5** = **packed**, busy, congested, cramped, crushed, full, huddled, jam-packed, mobbed, overflowing, populous, swarming, teeming, thronged

crown *n* **1** = **coronet**, chaplet, circlet, coronal (*poetic*), diadem, tiara **2** = **laurel wreath**, bays, distinction, garland, honour, kudos, laurels, prize, trophy, wreath **7** = **high point**, acme, apex, crest, head, perfection, pinnacle, summit, tip, top, ultimate, zenith ◆ *vb* **15** = **honour**, adorn, dignify, festoon, invest, reward **17** = **cap**, be the climax *or* culmination of, complete, consummate, finish, fulfil, perfect, put the finishing touch to, put the tin lid on, round off, surmount, terminate, top **20** *Slang* = **strike**, belt (*inf.*), biff (*sl.*), box, cuff, hit over the head, punch

Crown *n* **1** = **monarch**, emperor *or* empress, king *or* queen, *rex*, ruler, sovereign **2** = **monarchy**, royalty, sovereignty

crucial *adj* **1** = **critical**, central, decisive, pivotal, psychological, searching, testing, trying **2** *Informal* = **vital**, essential, high-priority, important, momentous, now or never, pressing, urgent

crucify *vb* **2** *Slang* = **pan** (*inf.*), lampoon, ridicule, tear to pieces, wipe the floor with (*inf.*) **3** = **torment**, harrow, persecute, rack, torture

crude *adj* **1** = **vulgar**, boorish, coarse, crass, dirty, gross, indecent, lewd, obscene, smutty, tactless, tasteless, uncouth, X-rated (*inf.*) **2** = **unrefined**, natural, raw, unmilled, unpolished, unprepared, unprocessed **3** = **primitive**, clumsy, makeshift, rough, rough-and-ready, rough-hewn, rude, rudimentary, simple, sketchy, undeveloped, unfinished, unformed, unpolished
Antonyms *adj* ≠ **vulgar:** genteel, polished, refined, subtle, tasteful ≠ **unrefined:** fine, fine-grained, polished, prepared, processed, refined

crudely *adv* **1, 4** = **vulgarly**, bluntly, clumsily, coarsely, impolitely, indecently, pulling no punches (*inf.*), roughly, rudely, sketchily, tastelessly

crudity *n* **1** = **vulgarity**, coarseness, crudeness, impropriety, indecency, indelicacy, lewdness, loudness, lowness, obscenity, obtrusiveness, smuttiness **3** = **roughness**, clumsiness, crudeness, primitiveness, rudeness

cruel *adj* **1, 2** = **brutal**, atrocious, barbarous, bitter, bloodthirsty, brutish, callous, cold-blooded, depraved, excruciating, fell (*arch.*), ferocious, fierce, flinty, grim, hard, hard-hearted, harsh, heartless, hellish, implacable, inclement, inexorable, inhuman, inhumane, malevolent, merciless, murderous, painful, pitiless, poignant, ravening, raw, relentless, remorseless, ruthless, sadistic, sanguinary, savage, severe, spiteful, stony-hearted, unfeeling, unkind, unnatural, unrelenting, vengeful, vicious
Antonyms *adj* benevolent, caring, compassionate, gentle, humane, kind, merciful, sympathetic, warm-hearted

cruelly *adv* **1, 2** = **brutally**, barbarously, brutishly, callously, ferociously, fiercely, heartlessly, in cold blood, mercilessly, pitilessly, sadistically, savagely, spitefully, unmercifully, viciously

cruelty *n* **1** = **brutality**, barbarity, bestiality, bloodthirstiness, brutishness, callousness, depravity, ferocity, fiendishness, hardheartedness, harshness, heartlessness, inhumanity, mercilessness, murderousness, ruthlessness, sa-

cruelty-free *adj* (of a cosmetic or other product) developed without being tested on animals.

cruet ('kruːɪt) *n* **1** a small container for holding pepper, salt, vinegar, oil, etc., at table. **2** a set of such containers, esp. on a stand. [C13: from Anglo-F, dim. of OF *crue* flask, of Gmc origin]

cruise Ⓣ (kruːz) *vb* **cruises, cruising, cruised. 1** (*intr*) to make a trip by sea for pleasure, usually calling at a number of ports. **2** to sail or travel over (a body of water) for pleasure. **3** (*intr*) to search for enemy vessels in a warship. **4** (*intr*) (of a vehicle, aircraft, or vessel) to travel at a moderate and efficient speed. ◆ *n* **5** an act or instance of cruising, esp. a trip by sea. [C17: from Du. *kruisen* to cross, from *cruis* CROSS]

cruise control *n* a system in a road vehicle that automatically maintains a selected speed until cancelled.

cruise missile *n* a low-flying subsonic missile that is guided throughout its flight.

cruiser ('kruːzə) *n* **1** a high-speed, long-range warship armed with medium-calibre weapons. **2** Also called: **cabin cruiser.** a pleasure boat, esp. one that is power-driven and has a cabin. **3** any person or thing that cruises.

cruiserweight ('kruːzə,weɪt) *n Boxing.* another term (esp. Brit.) for **light heavyweight.**

crumb Ⓣ (krʌm) *n* **1** a small fragment of bread, cake, or other baked foods. **2** a small piece or bit. **3** the soft inner part of bread. **4** *Sl.* a contemptible person. ◆ *vb* **5** (*tr*) to prepare or cover (food) with breadcrumbs. **6** to break into small fragments. [OE *cruma*]

crumble Ⓣ ('krʌmbᵊl) *vb* **crumbles, crumbling, crumbled. 1** to break or be broken into crumbs or fragments. **2** (*intr*) to fall apart or away. ◆ *n* **3** *Brit., Austral., & NZ.* a baked pudding consisting of a crumbly mixture of flour, fat, and sugar over stewed fruit: *apple crumble.* [C16: var. of *crimble,* of Gmc origin]

crumbly Ⓣ ('krʌmblɪ) *adj* **crumblier, crumbliest. 1** easily crumbled or crumbling. ◆ *n, pl* **crumblies. 2** *Brit. sl.* an older person.
▸**'crumbliness** *n*

crumby ('krʌmɪ) *adj* **crumbier, crumbiest. 1** full of or littered with crumbs. **2** soft, like the inside of bread. **3** a variant spelling of **crummy.**

crummy Ⓣ ('krʌmɪ) *adj* **crummier, crummiest.** *Sl.* **1** of little value; contemptible. **2** unwell or depressed: *to feel crummy.* [C19: var. spelling of CRUMBY]

crumpet ('krʌmpɪt) *n Chiefly Brit.* **1** a light soft yeast cake, eaten toasted and buttered. **2** *Sl.* women collectively. [C17: from ?]

crumple Ⓣ ('krʌmpᵊl) *vb* **crumples, crumpling, crumpled. 1** (when *intr,* often foll. by *up*) to collapse or cause to collapse. **2** (when *tr,* often foll. by *up*) to crush or cause to be crushed so as to form wrinkles or creases. ◆ *n* **3** a loose crease or wrinkle. [C16: from obs. *crump* to bend]
▸**'crumply** *adj*

crumple zones *pl n* parts of a motor vehicle, at the front and the rear, that are designed to crumple in a collision, thereby absorbing part of the energy of the impact.

crunch Ⓣ (krʌntʃ) *vb* **1** to bite or chew with a crushing or crackling sound. **2** to make or cause to make a crisp or brittle sound. ◆ *n* **3** the sound or act of crunching. **4 the crunch.** *Inf.* the critical moment or situation. ◆ *adj* **5** *Inf.* critical; decisive: *crunch time.* [C19: changed (through infl. of MUNCH) from earlier *craunch,* imit.]
▸**'crunchy** *adj* ▸**'crunchily** *adv* ▸**'crunchiness** *n*

crupper ('krʌpə) *n* **1** a strap from the back of a saddle that passes under a horse's tail. **2** the horse's rump. [C13: from OF *crupiere,* from *crupe* CROUP[2]]

crusade Ⓣ (kruː'seɪd) *n* **1** (*often cap.*) any of the military expeditions undertaken in the 11th, 12th, and 13th centuries by the Christian powers of Europe to recapture the Holy Land from the Muslims. **2** (formerly) any holy war. **3** a vigorous and dedicated action or movement in favour of a cause. ◆ *vb* **crusades, crusading, crusaded.** (*intr*) **4** to campaign vigorously for something. **5** to go on a crusade. [C16: from earlier *croisade,* from OF *crois* cross, from L *crux;* infl. also by Sp. *cruzada,* from *cruzar* to take up the cross]
▸**cru'sader** *n*

cruse (kruːz) *n* a small earthenware container used, esp. formerly, for liquids. [OE *crūse*]

crush Ⓣ (krʌʃ) *vb* (*mainly tr*) **1** to press, mash, or squeeze so as to injure, break, crease, etc. **2** to break or grind into small particles. **3** to put down or subdue, esp. by force. **4** to extract (juice, water, etc.) by pressing. **5** to oppress harshly. **6** to hug or clasp tightly. **7** to defeat or humiliate utterly, as in argument or by a cruel remark. **8** (*intr*) to crowd; throng. **9** (*intr*) to become injured, broken, or distorted by pressure. ◆ *n* **10** a dense crowd, esp. at a social occasion. **11** the act of crushing; pressure. **12** a drink or pulp prepared by or as if by crushing fruit: *orange crush.* **13** *Inf.* **13a** an infatuation: *she had a crush on him.* **13b** the person with whom one is infatuated. [C14: from OF *croissir,* of Gmc origin]
▸**'crushable** *adj* ▸**'crusher** *n*

crush barrier *n* a barrier erected to separate sections of large crowds.

crust Ⓣ (krʌst) *n* **1a** the hard outer part of bread. **1b** a piece of bread consisting mainly of this. **2** the baked shell of a pie, tart, etc. **3** any hard or stiff outer covering or surface: *a crust of ice.* **4** the solid outer shell of the earth. **5** the dry covering of a skin sore or lesion; scab. **6** *Sl.* impertinence. **7** *Brit., Austral., & NZ sl.* a living (esp. in **earn a crust**). ◆ *vb* **8** to cover with or acquire a crust. **9** to form or be formed into a crust. [C14: from L *crūsta* hard surface, rind, shell]

crustacean (krʌ'steɪʃən) *n* **1** any arthropod of the mainly aquatic class *Crustacea,* typically having a carapace and including the lobsters, crabs, woodlice, and water fleas. ◆ *adj also* **crustaceous. 2** of, relating to, or belonging to the *Crustacea.* [C19: from NL *crūstāceus* hard-shelled, from L *crūsta* shell]

crustal ('krʌstᵊl) *adj* of or relating to the earth's crust.

crusty Ⓣ ('krʌstɪ) *adj* **crustier, crustiest. 1** having or characterized by a crust. **2** having a rude or harsh character or exterior.
▸**'crustily** *adv* ▸**'crustiness** *n*

crutch (krʌtʃ) *n* **1** a long staff having a rest for the armpit, for supporting the weight of the body. **2** something that supports, helps, or sustains. **3** *Brit.* another word for **crotch** (sense 1). ◆ *vb* **4** (*tr*) to support or sustain (a person or thing) as with a crutch. **5** *Austral. & NZ.* to clip (wool) from the hindquarters of a sheep. [OE *crycc*]

crutchings ('krʌtʃɪŋz) *pl n Austral. & NZ.* wool clipped from a sheep's hindquarters.

crux Ⓣ (krʌks) *n, pl* **cruxes** *or* **cruces** ('kruːsiːz). **1** a vital or decisive stage, point, etc. (often in **the crux of the matter**). **2** a baffling problem or difficulty. [C18: from L: cross]

cruzado (kruː'zeɪdəʊ) *n, pl* **cruzadoes** *or* **cruzados** (-dəʊz). a former standard monetary unit of Brazil. [C16: lit., marked with a cross, from *cruzar* to bear a cross; see CRUSADE]

cruzeiro (kruː'zɛərəʊ) *n, pl* **cruzeiros** (-rəʊz). a former standard monetary unit of Brazil. [Port.: from *cruz* CROSS]

cry Ⓣ (kraɪ) *vb* **cries, crying, cried. 1** (*intr*) to utter inarticulate sounds, esp. when weeping; sob. **2** (*intr*) to shed tears; weep. **3** (*intr;* usually foll. by *out*) to scream or shout in pain, terror, etc. **4** (*tr;* often foll. by *out*) to utter or shout (words of appeal, exclamation, fear, etc.). **5** (*intr;* often foll. by *out*) (of animals, birds, etc.) to utter loud characteristic sounds. **6** (*tr*) to hawk or sell by public announcement: *to cry newspapers.* **7** to announce (something) publicly or in the streets. **8** (*intr;* foll. by *for*) to clamour or beg. **9 cry for the moon.** to desire the unattainable.

THESAURUS

dism, savagery, severity, spite, spitefulness, venom, viciousness

cruise *vb* **1, 2** = **sail**, coast, voyage **4** = **travel along**, coast, drift, keep a steady pace ◆ *n* **5** = **sail**, boat trip, sea trip, voyage

crumb *n* **2** = **bit**, atom, fragment, grain, mite, morsel, particle, scrap, shred, sliver, snippet, *soupçon,* speck

crumble *vb* **1** = **crush**, bruise, crumb, fragment, granulate, grind, pound, powder, pulverize, triturate **2** = **disintegrate**, break down, break up, collapse, come to dust, decay, decompose, degenerate, deteriorate, fall apart, go to pieces, go to wrack and ruin, moulder, perish, tumble down

crumbling *adj* **2** = **disintegrating**, collapsing, decaying, decomposing, deteriorating, eroding, mouldering

crumbly *adj* **1** = **brittle**, brashy, friable, powdery, rotted, short (*of pastry*)

crummy *adj* **1** *Slang* = **second-rate**, bush-league (*Austral. & NZ inf.*), cheap, contemptible, crappy (*sl.*), dime-a-dozen (*inf.*), duff (*Brit. informal*), inferior, lousy (*sl.*), low-rent (*inf., chiefly U.S.*), piss-poor (*taboo sl.*), poor, poxy (*sl.*), rotten (*inf.*), rubbishy, shitty (*taboo sl.*), shoddy, third-rate, tinhorn (*US sl.*), trashy, two-bit (*US & Canad. sl.*), useless, worthless

crumple *vb* **1** = **collapse**, break down, cave in, fall, give way, go to pieces **2** = **crush**, crease, pucker, rumple, screw up, wrinkle

crumpled *adj* **2** = **crushed**, creased, puckered, ruffled, rumpled, shrivelled, wrinkled

crunch *vb* **1** = **chomp**, champ, chew noisily, grind, masticate, munch ◆ *n* **4 the crunch** *Informal* = **critical point**, crisis, crux, emergency, hour of decision, moment of truth, test

crusade *n* **2, 3** = **campaign**, cause, drive, holy war, jihad, movement, push

crusader *n* **4** = **campaigner**, advocate, champion, reformer

crush *vb* **1, 2** = **squash**, break, bruise, comminute, compress, contuse, crease, crumble, crumple, crunch, mash, pound, press, pulverize, rumple, smash, squeeze, wrinkle **3** = **overcome**, conquer, extinguish, overpower, overwhelm, put down, quell, stamp out, subdue, vanquish **6** = **squeeze**, embrace, enfold, hug, press **7** = **humiliate**, abash, browbeat, chagrin, dispose of, mortify, put down (*sl.*), quash, shame ◆ *n* **10** = **crowd**, huddle, jam, party

crust *n* **3** = **layer**, caking, coat, coating, concretion, covering, film, incrustation, outside, scab, shell, skin, surface

crusty *adj* **1** = **crispy**, brittle, crisp, friable, hard, short, well-baked, well-done **2** = **irritable**, brusque, cantankerous, captious, choleric, crabby, cross, curt, gruff, ill-humoured, peevish, prickly, ratty (*Brit. & NZ inf.*), short, short-tempered, snappish, snarling, splenetic, surly, testy, tetchy, touchy

crux *n* **1** = **crucial point**, core, decisive point, essence, heart, nub

cry *vb* **1, 2** = **weep**, bawl, bewail, blubber, boohoo, greet (*Scot. or arch.*), howl one's eyes out, keen, lament, mewl, pule, shed tears, snivel, sob, wail, whimper, whine, whinge (*inf.*), yowl **3** = **shout**, bawl, bell, bellow, call, call out, ejaculate, exclaim, hail, halloo, holler (*inf.*), howl, roar, scream, screech, shriek, sing out, vociferate, whoop, yell **7** = **announce**, advertise, bark (*inf.*), broadcast, bruit, hawk, noise, proclaim, promulgate, publish, shout from the rooftops (*inf.*), trumpet **8** = **beg**, beseech, clamour, entreat, implore, plead, pray ◆ *n* **11** = **weeping**, bawling, blubbering, crying, greet (*Scot. or arch.*), howl, keening, lament, lamentation, plaint (*arch.*), snivel, snivelling, sob, sobbing, sorrowing, wailing, weep **11** = **shout**, bawl, bell, yellow, call, ejaculation, exclamation, holler (*inf.*), hoot, howl, outcry, roar, scream, screech, shriek, squawk, whoop, yell, yelp, yoohoo

Antonyms *vb* ≠ **weep:** chortle, chuckle, giggle, laugh, snicker, snigger, twitter ≠ **shout:** drone, mumble, murmur, mutter, speak in hushed tones, speak softly, utter indistinctly, whisper

10 cry one's eyes *or* **heart out.** to weep bitterly. ◆ *n, pl* **cries. 11** the act or sound of crying; a shout, scream, or wail. **12** the characteristic utterance of an animal or bird. **13** a fit of weeping. **14** *Hunting.* the baying of a pack of hounds hunting their quarry by scent. **15 a far cry. 15a** a long way. **15b** something very different. **16 in full cry.** (esp. of a pack of hounds) in hot pursuit of a quarry. ◆ See also **cry down, cry off,** etc. [C13: from OF *crier,* from L *quirītāre* to call for help]

crybaby ('kraɪ,beɪbɪ) *n, pl* **crybabies.** a person, esp. a child, given to frequent crying or complaint.

cry down ❶ *vb (tr, adv)* to belittle; disparage.

crying ('kraɪɪŋ) *adj (prenominal)* notorious; lamentable (esp. in **crying shame**).

cryo- *combining form.* cold or freezing: *cryogenics.* [from Gk *kruos* icy cold, frost]

cryobiology (,kraɪəubaɪ'ɒlədʒɪ) *n* the biology of the effects of very low temperatures on organisms.
▸**,cryobi'ologist** *n*

cry off ❶ *vb (intr) Inf.* to withdraw from or cancel (an agreement or arrangement).

cryogen ('kraɪədʒən) *n* a substance used to produce low temperatures; a freezing mixture.

cryogenics (,kraɪə'dʒɛnɪks) *n (functioning as sing)* the branch of physics concerned with very low temperatures and the phenomena occurring at these temperatures.
▸**,cryo'genic** *adj*

cryolite ('kraɪə,laɪt) *n* a white or colourless fluoride of sodium and aluminium: used in the production of aluminium, glass, and enamel. Formula: Na_3AlF_6.

cryonics (kraɪ'ɒnɪks) *n (functioning as sing)* the practice of freezing a human corpse in the hope of restoring it to life later.

cryoprecipitate (,kraɪəuprɪ'sɪpɪtɪt) *n* a precipitate obtained by controlled thawing of a previously frozen substance. Factor VIII, for treating haemophilia, is often obtained as a cryoprecipitate from frozen blood.

cryostat ('kraɪə,stæt) *n* an apparatus for maintaining a constant low temperature.

cryosurgery (,kraɪəu'sɜːdʒərɪ) *n* surgery involving quick freezing for therapeutic benefit.

cry out *vb (intr, adv)* **1** to scream or shout aloud, esp. in pain, terror, etc. **2** (often foll. by *for*) *Inf.* to demand in an obvious manner.

crypt ❶ (krɪpt) *n* a vault or underground chamber, esp. beneath a church, often used as a chapel, burial place, etc. [C18: from L *crypta,* from Gk *kruptē* vault, secret place, ult. from *kruptein* to hide]

cryptanalysis (,krɪptə'nælɪsɪs) *n* the study of codes and ciphers; cryptography. [C20: from CRYPTO- + ANALYSIS]
▸**cryptanalytic** (,krɪptænə'lɪtɪk) *adj* ▸**crypt'analyst** *n*

cryptic ❶ ('krɪptɪk) *adj* **1** hidden; secret. **2** esoteric or obscure in meaning. **3** (of coloration) effecting camouflage or concealment. [C17: from LL *crypticus,* from Gk *kruptikos,* from *kruptos* concealed; see CRYPT]
▸**'cryptically** *adv*

crypto- *or before a vowel* **crypt-** *combining form.* secret, hidden, or concealed. [NL, from Gk *kruptos* hidden, from *kruptein* to hide]

cryptocrystalline (,krɪptəu'krɪstəlaɪn) *adj* (of rocks) composed of crystals visible only under a polarizing microscope.

cryptogam ('krɪptəu,gæm) *n* (in former plant classification schemes) any organism that does not produce seeds, including algae, fungi, mosses, and ferns. [C19: from NL *Cryptogamia,* from CRYPTO- + Gk *gamos* marriage]
▸**,crypto'gamic** *or* **cryptogamous** (krɪp'tɒgəməs) *adj*

cryptograph ('krɪptəu,grɑːf) *n* **1** something written in code or cipher. **2** a code using secret symbols (**cryptograms**).

cryptography (krɪp'tɒgrəfɪ) *n* the science or study of analysing and deciphering codes, ciphers, etc. Also called: **cryptanalysis.**
▸**cryp'tographer** *or* **cryp'tographist** *n* ▸**cryptographic** (,krɪptə'græfɪk) *or* **,crypto'graphical** *adj* ▸**,crypto'graphically** *adv*

crystal ('krɪstᵊl) *n* **1** a solid, such as quartz, with a regular shape in which plane faces intersect at definite angles. **2** a single grain of a crystalline substance. **3** anything resembling a crystal, such as a piece of cut glass. **4a** a highly transparent and brilliant type of glass. **4b** (*as modifier*): *a crystal chandelier.* **5** something made of or resembling crystal. **6** crystal glass articles collectively. **7** *Electronics.* **7a** a crystalline element used in certain electronic devices as a detector, oscillator, etc. **7b** (*as modifier*): *crystal pick-up.* **8** a transparent cover for the face of a watch. **9** (*modifier*) of or relating to a crystal or the regular atomic arrangement of crystals: *crystal structure.* ◆ *adj* **10** resembling crystal; transparent: *crystal water.* [OE *cristalla,* from L *crystallum,* from Gk *krustallos* ice, crystal, from *krustainein* to freeze]

crystal ball *n* the glass globe used in crystal gazing.

crystal class *n Crystallography.* any of 32 possible types of crystals, classified according to their rotational symmetry about axes through a point. Also called: **point group.**

crystal detector *n Electronics.* a demodulator, used esp. in early radio receivers, incorporating a semiconductor crystal.

crystal gazing *n* **1** the act of staring into a crystal ball supposedly in order to arouse visual perceptions of the future, etc. **2** the act of trying to foresee or predict.
▸**crystal gazer** *n*

crystal healing *n* (in alternative therapy) the use of the supposed power of crystals to affect the human energy field.

crystal lattice *n* the regular array of points about which the atoms, ions, or molecules composing a crystal are centred.

crystalline ('krɪstə,laɪn) *adj* **1** having the characteristics or structure of crystals. **2** consisting of or containing crystals. **3** made of or like crystal; transparent; clear.

crystalline lens *n* a biconvex transparent elastic lens in the eye.

crystallize ❶ *or* **crystallise** ('krɪstə,laɪz) *vb* **crystallizes, crystallizing, crystallized** *or* **crystallises, crystallising, crystallised. 1** to form or cause to form crystals; assume or cause to assume a crystalline form or structure. **2** to coat or become coated with sugar. **3** to give a definite form or expression to (an idea, argument, etc.) or (of an idea, argument, etc.) to assume a definite form.
▸**'crystal,lizable** *or* **'crystal,lisable** *adj* ▸**,crystalli'zation** *or* **,crystalli'sation** *n*

crystallo- *or before a vowel* **crystall-** *combining form.* crystal: *crystallography.*

crystallography (,krɪstə'lɒgrəfɪ) *n* the science of crystal structure.
▸**,crystal'lographer** *n* ▸**crystallographic** (,krɪstələu'græfɪk) *adj*

crystalloid ('krɪstə,lɔɪd) *adj* **1** resembling or having the properties of a crystal. ◆ *n* **2** a substance that in solution can pass through a semipermeable membrane.

Crystal Palace *n* a building of glass and iron designed by Joseph Paxton to house the Great Exhibition of 1851. Erected in Hyde Park, London, it was moved to Sydenham (1852–53): destroyed by fire in 1936.

crystal set *n* an early form of radio receiver having a crystal detector.

cry up *vb (tr, adv)* to praise highly; extol.

Cs *the chemical symbol for* caesium.

CS *abbrev. for:* **1** Also: **cs.** capital stock. **2** chartered surveyor. **3** Christian Science. **4** Civil Service. **5** Also: **cs.** Court of Session.

CSA (in Britain) *abbrev. for* Child Support Agency.

csc *abbrev. for* cosecant.

CSC *abbrev. for* Civil Service Commission.

CSE (in Britain) *abbrev. for* Certificate of Secondary Education; a former examination the first grade pass of which was an equivalent to a GCE O level.

CSEU *abbrev. for* Confederation of Shipbuilding and Engineering Unions.

CSF *abbrev. for:* **1** cerebrospinal fluid. **2** *Immunol.* colony-stimulating factor.

CS gas *n* a gas causing tears, salivation, and painful breathing, used in civil disturbances. [C20: from the surname initials of its US inventors, Ben Carson and Roger Staughton]

CSIRO (in Australia) *abbrev. for* Commonwealth Scientific and Industrial Research Organization.

CSM (in Britain) *abbrev. for* Company Sergeant-Major.

C-spanner *n* a sickle-shaped spanner having a projection at the end of the curve, used for turning large narrow nuts that have an indentation into which the projection on the spanner fits.

CST (in the US and Canada) *abbrev. for* Central Standard Time.

CSU *abbrev. for* Civil Service Union.

ct *abbrev. for:* **1** carat. **2** cent. **3** court.

CTC (in Britain) *abbrev. for* city technology college.

ctenophore ('tɛnə,fɔː, 'tiːnə-) *n* any marine invertebrate of the phylum *Ctenophora,* whose body bears eight rows of fused cilia, for locomotion. [C19: from NL *ctenophorus,* from Gk *kteno-, kteis* comb + -PHORE]

ctn *abbrev. for* cotangent.

CT scanner *n* computerized tomography scanner: an X-ray machine that can produce multiple cross-sectional images of the soft tissues (**CT scans**). Former name: **CAT scanner.**

CTT *abbrev. for* Capital Transfer Tax.

CTV *abbrev. for* Canadian Television (Network Limited).

Cu *the chemical symbol for* copper. [from LL *cuprum*]

cu. *abbrev. for* cubic.

cub ❶ (kʌb) *n* **1** the young of certain animals, such as the lion, bear, etc. **2** a young or inexperienced person. ◆ *vb* **cubs, cubbing, cubbed. 3** to give birth to (cubs). [C16: ?from ON *kubbi* young seal]
▸**'cubbish** *adj*

Cub (kʌb) *n* short for **Cub Scout.**

Cuban ('kjuːbən) *adj* **1** of or relating to Cuba, a republic and the largest island in the Caribbean. ◆ *n* **2** a native or inhabitant of Cuba.

cubby ('kʌbɪ) *n, pl* **cubbies.** *Austral.* a small room or enclosed area, esp. one used as a child's play area. Also: **cubbyhole, cubby-house.**

THESAURUS

cry down *vb* = **run down**, asperse, bad-mouth (*sl., chiefly U.S. & Canad.*), belittle, decry, denigrate, disparage, knock (*inf.*), rubbish (*inf.*), slag (off) (*sl.*)

cry off *vb Informal* = **back out**, beg off, cop out (*sl.*), excuse oneself, quit, withdraw, withdraw from

crypt *n* = **vault**, catacomb, ossuary, tomb, undercroft

cryptic *adj* **1, 2** = **mysterious**, abstruse, ambiguous, apocryphal, arcane, cabbalistic, coded, dark, Delphic, enigmatic, equivocal, esoteric, hidden, obscure, occult, oracular, perplexing, puzzling, recondite, secret, vague, veiled

crystallize *vb* **1, 3** = **form**, appear, coalesce, harden, materialize, take shape

cub *n* **1** = **young**, offspring, whelp **2** = **youngster**, babe (*inf.*), beginner, fledgling, greenhorn (*inf.*), lad, learner, puppy, recruit, tenderfoot, trainee, whippersnapper

cubbyhole Ⓣ ('kʌbɪˌhəʊl) *n* a small enclosed space or room. [C19: from dialect *cub* cattle pen]

cube (kju:b) *n* **1** a solid having six plane square faces in which the angle between two adjacent sides is a right angle. **2** the product of three equal factors. **3** something in the form of a cube. ◆ *vb* **cubes, cubing, cubed. 4** to raise (a number or quantity) to the third power. **5** (*tr*) to make, shape, or cut (something) into cubes. [C16: from L *cubus* die, cube, from Gk *kubos*]
▸**'cuber** *n*

cubeb ('kju:bɛb) *n* **1** a SE Asian treelike climbing plant. **2** its spicy fruit, dried and used as a stimulant and diuretic and sometimes smoked in cigarettes. [C14: from OF *cubebe*, from Med. L *cubēba*, from Ar. *kubābah*]

cube root *n* the number or quantity whose cube is a given number or quantity: 2 is the cube root of 8 (usually written $\sqrt[3]{8}$ or $8^{1/3}$).

cubic ('kju:bɪk) *adj* **1** having the shape of a cube. **2a** having three dimensions. **2b** denoting or relating to a linear measure that is raised to the third power: *a cubic metre.* **3** *Maths.* of, relating to, or containing a variable to the third power or a term in which the sum of the exponents of the variables is three.
▸**'cubical** *adj*

cubicle ('kju:bɪkᵊl) *n* an enclosed compartment, screened for privacy, as in a dormitory, shower, etc. [C15: from L *cubiculum*, from *cubāre* to lie down]

cubic measure *n* a system of units for the measurement of volumes.

cubiform ('kju:bɪˌfɔ:m) *adj* having the shape of a cube.

cubism ('kju:bɪzəm) *n* (*often cap.*) a French school of art, initiated in 1907 by Picasso and Braque, which amalgamated viewpoints of natural forms into a multifaceted surface of geometrical planes.
▸**'cubist** *adj, n* ▸**cu'bistic** *adj*

cubit ('kju:bɪt) *n* an ancient measure of length based on the length of the forearm. [C14: from L *cubitum* elbow, cubit]

cuboid ('kju:bɔɪd) *adj also* **cuboidal** (kju:'bɔɪdᵊl). **1** shaped like a cube; cubic. **2** of or denoting the cuboid bone. ◆ *n* **3** the cubelike bone of the foot. **4** *Maths.* a geometric solid whose six faces are rectangles.

Cub Scout *or* **Cub** *n* a member of the junior branch of the Scout Association.

cucking stool ('kʌkɪŋ) *n History.* a stool to which suspected witches, scolds, etc., were tied and pelted or ducked into water. [C13 *cucking stol*, lit.: defecating chair, from *cukken* to defecate]

cuckold ('kʌkəld) *n* **1** a man whose wife has committed adultery. ◆ *vb* **2** (*tr*) to make a cuckold of. [C13 *cukeweld*, from OF *cucuault*, from *cucu* CUCKOO; ? an allusion to cuckoos that lay eggs in the nests of other birds]
▸**'cuckoldry** *n*

cuckoo ('kʊku:) *n, pl* **cuckoos. 1** any bird of the family Cuculidae, having pointed wings and a long tail. Many species, including the **European cuckoo,** lay their eggs in the nests of other birds and have a two-note call. **2** *Inf.* an insane or foolish person. ◆ *adj* **3** *Inf.* insane or foolish. ◆ *interj* **4** an imitation or representation of the call of a cuckoo. ◆ *vb* **cuckoos, cuckooing, cuckooed. 5** (*intr*) to make the sound imitated by the word *cuckoo.* [C13: from OF *cucu*, imit.]

cuckoo clock *n* a clock in which a mechanical cuckoo pops out with a sound like a cuckoo's call when the clock strikes.

cuckoopint ('kʊku:ˌpaɪnt, -ˌpɪnt) *n* a European plant with arrow-shaped leaves, a spathe marked with purple, a pale purple spadix, and scarlet berries. Also called: **lords-and-ladies.**

cuckoo spit *n* a white frothy mass on the stems and leaves of many plants, produced by froghopper larvae.

cucumber ('kju:ˌkʌmbə) *n* **1** a creeping plant cultivated in many forms for its edible fruit. **2** the cylindrical fruit of this plant, which has hard thin green rind and white crisp flesh. [C14: from L *cucumis*, from ?]

cucurbit (kju:'kɜ:bɪt) *n* any of a family of creeping flowering plants that includes the pumpkin, cucumber, and gourds. [C14: from OF, from L *cucurbita* gourd, cup]
▸**cuˌcurbi'taceous** *adj*

cud (kʌd) *n* **1** partially digested food regurgitated from the first stomach of ruminants to the mouth for a second chewing. **2 chew the cud.** to reflect or think over something. [OE *cudu*, from *cwidu* what has been chewed]

cuddle Ⓣ ('kʌdᵊl) *vb* **cuddles, cuddling, cuddled. 1** to hold close or (of two people, etc.) to hold each other close, as for affection or warmth; hug. **2** (*intr;* foll. by *up*) to curl or snuggle up into a comfortable or warm position. ◆ *n* **3** a close embrace, esp. when prolonged. [C18: from ?]
▸**'cuddlesome** *adj* ▸**'cuddly** *adj*

cuddy ('kʌdɪ) *n, pl* **cuddies.** a small cabin in a boat. [C17: ?from Du. *kajute*]

cudgel Ⓣ ('kʌdʒəl) *n* **1** a short stout stick used as a weapon. **2 take up the cudgels.** (often foll. by *for* or *on behalf of*) to join in a dispute, esp. to defend oneself or another. ◆ *vb* **cudgels, cudgelling, cudgelled** *or US* **cudgels, cudgeling, cudgeled. 3** (*tr*) to strike with a cudgel. **4 cudgel one's brains.** to think hard. [OE *cycgel*]

cudgerie ('kʌdʒərɪ) *n Austral.* any of various large rainforest trees, such as the pink poplar or blush cudgerie, with pink wood. [from Abor.]

cudweed ('kʌdˌwi:d) *n* any of various temperate woolly plants having clusters of whitish or yellow button-like flowers.

cue[1] Ⓣ (kju:) *n* **1a** (in the theatre, films, music, etc.) anything that serves as a signal to an actor, musician, etc., to follow with specific lines or action. **1b on cue.** at the right moment. **2** a signal or reminder to do something. ◆ *vb* **cues, cueing, cued. 3** (*tr*) to give a cue or cues to (an actor). **4** (usually foll. by *in* or *into*) to signal (to something or somebody) at a specific moment in a musical or dramatic performance. [C16: prob. from name of the letter *q*, used in an actor's script to represent L *quando* when]

cue[2] (kju:) *n* **1** *Billiards, etc.* a long tapered shaft used to drive the balls. **2** hair caught at the back forming a tail or braid. ◆ *vb* **cues, cueing, cued. 3** to drive (a ball) with a cue. [C18: var. of QUEUE]

cue ball *n Billiards, etc.* the ball struck by the cue, as distinguished from the object balls.

cuesta ('kwɛstə) *n* a long low ridge with a steep scarp slope and a gentle back slope. [Sp.: shoulder, from L *costa* side, rib]

cuff[1] Ⓣ (kʌf) *n* **1** the end of a sleeve, sometimes turned back. **2** the part of a glove that extends past the wrist. **3** the US, Canad., and Austral. name for **turn-up** (sense 4). **4 off the cuff.** *Inf.* improvised; extemporary. [C14 *cuffe* glove, from ?]

cuff[2] Ⓣ (kʌf) *vb* **1** (*tr*) to strike with an open hand. ◆ *n* **2** a blow of this kind. [C16: from ?]

cuff link *n* one of a pair of linked buttons, used to join the buttonholes on the cuffs of a shirt.

cui bono *Latin.* (kwi: 'bəʊnəʊ) for whose benefit? for what purpose?

cuirass (kwɪ'ræs) *n* **1** a piece of armour covering the chest and back. ◆ *vb* **2** (*tr*) to equip with a cuirass. [C15: from F *cuirasse*, from LL *coriacea*, from *coriaceus* made of leather]

cuirassier (ˌkwɪərə'sɪə) *n* a mounted soldier, esp. of the 16th century, who wore a cuirass.

Cuisenaire rod (ˌkwɪzə'nɛə) *n Trademark.* one of a set of rods of various colours and lengths representing different numbers, used to teach arithmetic to young children. [C20: after Emil-Georges *Cuisenaire* (?1891–1976), Belgian educationalist]

cuisine (kwɪ'zi:n) *n* **1** a style or manner of cooking: *French cuisine.* **2** the food prepared by a restaurant, household, etc. [C18: from F, lit.: kitchen, from LL *coquīna*, from L *coquere* to cook]

cuisse (kwɪs) *or* **cuish** (kwɪʃ) *n* a piece of armour for the thigh. [C15: back formation from *cuisses* (pl), from OF *cuisseaux*, from *cuisse* thigh]

cul-de-sac Ⓣ ('kʌldəˌsæk, 'kʊl-) *n, pl* **culs-de-sac** *or* **cul-de-sacs. 1** a road with one end blocked off; dead end. **2** an inescapable position. [C18: from F, lit.: bottom of the bag]

-cule *suffix forming nouns.* indicating smallness. [from L *-culus*, dim. suffix]

culex ('kju:lɛks) *n, pl* **culices** (-lɪˌsi:z). any mosquito of the genus *Culex*, such as *C. pipiens*, the common mosquito. [C15: from L: midge, gnat]

culinary ('kʌlɪnərɪ) *adj* of, relating to, or used in the kitchen or in cookery. [C17: from L *culīnārius*, from *culīna* kitchen]
▸**'culinarily** *adv*

cull Ⓣ (kʌl) *vb* (*tr*) **1** to choose or gather the best or required examples of. **2** to take out (an animal, esp. an inferior one) from a herd or group. **3** to reduce the size of (a herd, etc.) by killing a proportion of its members. **4** to gather (flowers, fruit, etc.). ◆ *n* **5** the act or product of culling. **6** an inferior animal taken from a herd or group. [C15: from OF *coillir* to pick, from L *colligere;* see COLLECT[1]]
▸**'culler** *n*

culm[1] (kʌlm) *n Mining.* **1** coal-mine waste. **2** inferior anthracite. [C14: prob. rel. to COAL]

culm[2] (kʌlm) *n* the hollow jointed stem of a grass or sedge. [C17: from L *culmus* stalk; see HAULM]

culminate Ⓣ ('kʌlmɪˌneɪt) *vb* **culminates, culminating, culminated. 1** (when *intr*, usually foll. by *in*) to reach or bring to a final or climactic stage. **2** (*intr*) (of a celestial body) to cross the meridian. [C17: from LL *culmināre* to reach the highest point, from L *culmen* top]
▸**'culminant** *adj*

culmination Ⓣ (ˌkʌlmɪ'neɪʃən) *n* **1** the final or highest point. **2** the act of culminating. **3** *Astron.* the highest or lowest altitude attained by a heavenly body as it crosses the meridian.

THESAURUS

cubbyhole *n* = **compartment**, den, hideaway, hole, niche, pigeonhole, recess, slot, snug

cuddle *vb* **1** = **hug**, bill and coo, canoodle (*sl.*), clasp, cosset, embrace, fondle, nestle, pet, snuggle

cudgel *n* **1** = **club**, bastinado, baton, bludgeon, cosh (*Brit.*), shillelagh, stick, truncheon ◆ *vb* **3** = **beat**, bang, baste, batter, bludgeon, cane, cosh (*Brit.*), drub, maul, pound, pummel, thrash, thump, thwack

cue[1] *n* **1a, 2** = **signal**, catchword, hint, key, nod, prompting, reminder, sign, suggestion

cuff[1] *n* **4 off the cuff** *Informal* = **impromptu**, ad lib, extempore, improvised, offhand, off the top of one's head, on the spur of the moment, spontaneous, spontaneously, unrehearsed

cuff[2] *vb* **1** = **smack**, bat (*inf.*), beat, belt (*inf.*), biff (*sl.*), box, buffet, clap, clobber (*sl.*), clout (*inf.*), hit, knock, lambast(e), pummel, punch, slap, thump, whack ◆ *n* **2** = **smack**, belt (*inf.*), biff (*sl.*), blow, box, buffet, clout (*inf.*), knock, punch, rap, slap, thump, whack

cul-de-sac *n* **1** = **dead end**, blind alley

cull *vb* **1, 3** = **choose**, cherry-pick, pick, pluck, select, sift, thin, thin out, winnow **4** = **gather**, amass, collect, glean, pick up

culminate *vb* **1** = **end up**, climax, close, come to a climax, come to a head, conclude, end, finish, rise to a crescendo, terminate, wind up

culmination *n* **1** = **climax**, acme, apex, apogee, completion, conclusion, consummation, crown, crowning touch, finale, height, *ne plus ultra*, peak, perfection, pinnacle, punch line, summit, top, zenith

DICTIONARY

culottes (kjuː'lɒts) *pl n* women's flared trousers cut to look like a skirt. [C20: from F, lit.: breeches, from *cul* bottom]

culpable 🅣 ('kʌlpəbᵊl) *adj* deserving censure; blameworthy. [C14: from OF *coupable,* from L *culpābilis,* from *culpāre* to blame, from *culpa* fault]
▸ **ˌculpa'bility** *n* ▸ **'culpably** *adv*

culpable homicide *n Scots Law.* manslaughter.

culprit 🅣 ('kʌlprɪt) *n* **1** *Law.* a person awaiting trial. **2** the person responsible for a particular offence, misdeed, etc. [C17: from Anglo-F *cul-,* short for *culpable* guilty + *prit* ready, indicating that the prosecution was ready to prove the guilt of the one charged]

cult 🅣 (kʌlt) *n* **1** a specific system of religious worship. **2** a sect devoted to such a system. **3** a quasi-religious organization using devious psychological techniques to gain and control adherents. **4** intense interest in and devotion to a person, idea, or activity. **5** the person, idea, etc., arousing such devotion. **6** something regarded as fashionable or significant by a particular group; craze. **7** (*modifier*) of, relating to, or characteristic of a cult or cults: *a cult figure; a cult show.* [C17: from L *cultus* cultivation, refinement, from *colere* to till]
▸ **'cultism** *n* ▸ **'cultist** *n*

cultic ('kʌltɪk) *adj* of or relating to a religious cult.

cultish ('kʌltɪʃ) *or* **culty** ('kʌltɪ) *adj* intended to appeal to a small group of fashionable people.

cultivable ('kʌltɪvəbᵊl) *or* **cultivatable** ('kʌltɪˌveɪtəbᵊl) *adj* (of land) capable of being cultivated. [C17: from F, from OF *cultiver* to CULTIVATE]
▸ **ˌcultiva'bility** *n*

cultivar ('kʌltɪˌvɑː) *n* a variety of a plant produced from a natural species and maintained by cultivation. [C20: from CULTI(VATED) + VAR(IETY)]

cultivate 🅣 ('kʌltɪˌveɪt) *vb* **cultivates, cultivating, cultivated.** (*tr*) **1** to prepare (land or soil) for the growth of crops. **2** to plant, tend, harvest, or improve (plants). **3** to break up (land or soil) with a cultivator or hoe. **4** to improve (the mind, body, etc.) as by study, education, or labour. **5** to give special attention to: *to cultivate a friendship.* [C17: from Med. L *cultivāre* to till, from *cultīvus* cultivable, from L *cultus* cultivated, from *colere* to till, toil over]
▸ **'cultiˌvated** *adj*

cultivation 🅣 (ˌkʌltɪ'veɪʃən) *n* **1** *Agriculture.* **1a** the cultivating of crops or plants. **1b** the preparation of ground to promote their growth. **2** development, esp. through education, training, etc. **3** culture or sophistication.

cultivator ('kʌltɪˌveɪtə) *n* **1** a farm implement used to break up soil and remove weeds. **2** a person or thing that cultivates.

cultural 🅣 ('kʌltʃərəl) *adj* **1** of or relating to artistic or social pursuits or events considered valuable or enlightened. **2** of or relating to a culture. **3** obtained by specialized breeding.

culture 🅣 ('kʌltʃə) *n* **1** the total of the inherited ideas, beliefs, values, and knowledge, which constitute the shared bases of social action. **2** the total range of activities and ideas of a people. **3** a particular civilization at a particular period. **4** the artistic and social pursuits, expression, and tastes valued by a society or class. **5** the enlightenment or refinement resulting from these pursuits. **6** the cultivation of plants to improve stock or to produce new ones. **7** the rearing and breeding of animals, esp. with a view to improving the strain. **8** the act or practice of tilling or cultivating the soil. **9** *Biol.* **9a** the experimental growth of microorganisms in a nutrient substance. **9b** a group of microorganisms grown in this way. ◆ *vb* **cultures, culturing, cultured.** (*tr*) **10** to cultivate (plants or animals). **11** to grow (microorganisms) in a culture medium. [C15: from OF, from L *cultūra* a cultivating, from *colere* to till; see CULT]
▸ **'culturist** *n*

cultured 🅣 ('kʌltʃəd) *adj* **1** showing or having good taste, manners, and education. **2** artificially grown or synthesized: *cultured pearls.* **3** treated by a culture of microorganisms.

cultured pearl *n* a pearl induced to grow in the shell of an oyster or clam, by the insertion of a small object.

culture shock *n Sociol.* the feelings of isolation, rejection, etc., experienced when one culture is brought into sudden contact with another.

culture vulture *n Inf.* a person considered to be excessively, and often pretentiously, interested in the arts.

cultus ('kʌltəs) *n, pl* **cultuses** *or* **culti** (-taɪ). another word for **cult** (sense 1). [C17: from L: a toiling over something, refinement, CULT]

culverin ('kʌlvərɪn) *n* **1** a medium-to-heavy cannon used during the 15th, 16th, and 17th centuries. **2** a medieval musket. [C15: from OF *coulevrine,* from *couleuvre,* from L *coluber* serpent]

culvert 🅣 ('kʌlvət) *n* **1** a drain or covered channel that crosses under a road, railway, etc. **2** a channel for an electric cable. [C18: from ?]

cum (kʌm) *prep* used between nouns to designate a combined nature: *a kitchen-cum-dining room.* [L: with, together with]

cumber ('kʌmbə) *vb* (*tr*) **1** to obstruct or hinder. **2** *Obs.* to inconvenience. [C13: prob. from OF *combrer* to impede, prevent, from *combre* barrier; see ENCUMBER]

cumbersome 🅣 ('kʌmbəsəm) *or* **cumbrous** ('kʌmbrəs) *adj* **1** awkward because of size, weight, or shape. **2** difficult because of extent or complexity: *cumbersome accounts.* [C14: *cumber,* short for ENCUMBER + -SOME[1]]
▸ **'cumbersomeness** *or* **'cumbrousness** *n*

cumin *or* **cummin** ('kʌmɪn) *n* **1** an umbelliferous Mediterranean plant with small white or pink flowers. **2** the aromatic seeds (collectively) of this plant, used as a condiment and a flavouring. [C12: from OF, from L *cumīnum,* from Gk *kuminon,* of Semitic origin]

cummerbund ('kʌməˌbʌnd) *n* a wide sash worn round the waist, esp. with a dinner jacket. [C17: from Hindi *kamarband,* from Persian, from *kamar* loins, waist + *band* band]

cum new *adv, adj* (of shares, etc.) with the right to take up any scrip issue or rights issue. Cf. **ex new.**

cumquat ('kʌmkwɒt) *n* a variant spelling of **kumquat.**

cumulate *vb* ('kjuːmjʊˌleɪt), **cumulates, cumulating, cumulated. 1** to accumulate. **2** (*tr*) to combine (two or more sequences) into one. ◆ *adj* ('kjuːmjʊlɪt). **3** heaped up. [C16: from L *cumulāre* from *cumulus* heap]
▸ **ˌcumu'lation** *n*

cumulative 🅣 ('kjuːmjʊlətɪv) *adj* **1** growing in quantity, strength, or effect by successive additions. **2** (of dividends or interest) intended to be accumulated. **3** *Statistics.* **3a** (of a frequency) including all values of a variable either below or above a specified value. **3b** (of error) tending to increase as the sample size is increased.
▸ **'cumulatively** *adv* ▸ **'cumulativeness** *n*

cumulonimbus (ˌkjuːmjʊləʊ'nɪmbəs) *n, pl* **cumulonimbi** (-baɪ) *or* **cumulonimbuses.** *Meteorol.* a cumulus cloud of great vertical extent, the bottom being dark-coloured, indicating rain or hail.

cumulus ('kjuːmjʊləs) *n, pl* **cumuli** (-ˌlaɪ). a bulbous or billowing white or dark grey cloud. [C17: from L: mass]
▸ **'cumulous** *adj*

cuneate ('kjuːnɪɪt, -ˌeɪt) *adj* wedge-shaped. [C19: from L *cuneāre* to make wedge-shaped, from *cuneus* a wedge]
▸ **'cuneately** *adv* ▸ **'cuneal** *adj*

cuneiform ('kjuːnɪˌfɔːm) *adj* **1** Also: **cuneal.** wedge-shaped. **2** of, relating to, or denoting the wedge-shaped characters in several ancient languages of Mesopotamia and Persia. **3** of or relating to a tablet in which this script is employed. ◆ *n* **4** cuneiform characters. [C17: prob. from OF *cunéiforme,* from L *cuneus* wedge]

cunjevoi ('kʌndʒɪˌvɔɪ) *n Austral.* **1** an arum of tropical Asia and Australia, cultivated for its edible rhizome. **2** a sea squirt. Often shortened to **cunjie, cunjy.** [C19: from Abor.]

cunnilingus (ˌkʌnɪ'lɪŋgəs) *or* **cunnilinctus** (ˌkʌnɪ'lɪŋktəs) *n* a sexual activity in which the female genitalia are stimulated by the partner's

THESAURUS

culpability *n* = **blameworthiness**, answerability, blame, fault, guilt, liability, responsibility

culpable *adj* = **blameworthy**, answerable, at fault, blamable, censurable, found wanting, guilty, in the wrong, liable, reprehensible, sinful, to blame, wrong
Antonyms *adj* blameless, clean (*sl.*), guiltless, innocent, in the clear, not guilty, squeaky-clean

culprit *n* **2** = **offender**, criminal, delinquent, evildoer, felon, guilty party, malefactor, miscreant, person responsible, rascal, sinner, transgressor, villain, wrongdoer

cult *n* **1, 2** = **sect**, body, church, clique, denomination, faction, faith, following, party, religion, school **4** = **devotion**, admiration, craze, idolization, reverence, veneration, worship

cultivate *vb* **1, 2** = **farm**, bring under cultivation, fertilize, harvest, plant, plough, prepare, tend, till, work **3** = **develop**, ameliorate, better, bring on, cherish, civilize, discipline, elevate, enrich, foster, improve, polish, promote, refine, train **5** = **encourage**, aid, devote oneself to, forward, foster, further, help, patronize, promote, pursue, support

cultivated *adj* **4** = **well-educated**, accomplished, advanced, civilized, cultured, developed, discerning, discriminating, educated, enlightened, erudite, genteel, polished, refined, sophisticated, urbane, versed, well-bred

cultivation *n* **1** = **farming**, agronomy, gardening, husbandry, planting, ploughing, tillage, tilling, working **2** = **development**, advancement, advocacy, encouragement, enhancement, fostering, furtherance, help, nurture, patronage, promotion, support **3** = **refinement**, breeding, civility, civilization, culture, discernment, discrimination, education, enlightenment, gentility, good taste, learning, letters, manners, polish, sophistication, taste

cultural *adj* **1** = **artistic**, broadening, civilizing, developmental, edifying, educational, educative, elevating, enlightening, enriching, humane, humanizing, liberal, liberalizing

culture *n* **1-4** = **civilization**, customs, lifestyle, mores, society, stage of development, the arts, way of life **5** = **refinement**, accomplishment, breeding, education, elevation, enlightenment, erudition, gentility, good taste, improvement, polish, politeness, sophistication, urbanity **6-8** = **farming**, agriculture, agronomy, cultivation, husbandry

cultured *adj* **1** = **refined**, accomplished, advanced, educated, enlightened, erudite, genteel, highbrow, knowledgeable, polished, scholarly, sophisticated, urbane, versed, well-bred, well-informed, well-read
Antonyms *adj* coarse, common, inelegant, uncultivated, uneducated, unpolished, unrefined, vulgar

culvert *n* **1** = **drain**, channel, conduit, gutter, watercourse

cumbersome *adj* **1** = **awkward**, bulky, burdensome, clumsy, clunky (*inf.*), cumbrous, embarrassing, heavy, hefty (*inf.*), incommodious, inconvenient, oppressive, unmanageable, unwieldy, weighty
Antonyms *adj* compact, convenient, easy to use, handy, manageable, practical, serviceable, wieldy

cumulative *adj* **1** = **collective**, accruing, accumulative, aggregate, amassed, heaped, increasing, snowballing

lips and tongue. Cf. **fellatio.** [C19: from NL, from L *cunnus* vulva + *lingere* to lick]

cunning ❶ ('kʌnɪŋ) *adj* **1** crafty and shrewd, esp. in deception. **2** made with or showing skill; ingenious. ◆ *n* **3** craftiness, esp. in deceiving. **4** skill or ingenuity. [OE *cunnende;* rel. to *cunnan* to know (see CAN[1])]
▸ **'cunningly** *adv* ▸ **'cunningness** *n*

cunt (kʌnt) *n Taboo.* **1** the female genitals. **2** *Offens. sl.* a woman considered sexually. **3** *Offens. sl.* a mean or obnoxious person. [C13: of Gmc origin; rel. to ON *kunta,* MLow G *kunte*]

cup ❶ (kʌp) *n* **1** a small open container, usually having one handle, used for drinking from. **2** the contents of such a container. **3** Also called: **teacup, cupful.** a unit of capacity used in cooking. **4** something resembling a cup. **5** either of two cup-shaped parts of a brassiere. **6** a cup-shaped trophy awarded as a prize. **7** *Brit.* **7a** a sporting contest in which a cup is awarded to the winner. **7b** (*as modifier*): *a cup competition.* **8** a mixed drink with one ingredient as a base: *claret cup.* **9** *Golf.* the hole or metal container in the hole on a green. **10** the chalice or the consecrated wine used in the Eucharist. **11** one's lot in life. **12 in one's cups.** drunk. **13 one's cup of tea.** *Inf.* one's chosen or preferred thing, task, company, etc. ◆ *vb* **cups, cupping, cupped.** (*tr*) **14** to form (something, such as the hands) into the shape of a cup. **15** to put into or as if into a cup. **16** to draw blood to the surface of the body of (a person) by cupping. [OE *cuppe,* from LL *cuppa* cup, alteration of L *cūpa* cask]

cupbearer ('kʌp,bɛərə) *n* an attendant who fills and serves wine cups, as in a royal household.

cupboard ❶ ('kʌbəd) *n* a piece of furniture or a recessed area of a room, with a door concealing storage space.

cupboard love *n* a show of love inspired only by some selfish or greedy motive.

cupcake ('kʌp,keɪk) *n* a small cake baked in a cup-shaped foil or paper case.

cupel ('kju:pᵊl, kju'pɛl) *n* **1** a refractory pot in which gold or silver is refined. **2** a small bowl in which gold and silver are recovered during assaying. ◆ *vb* **cupels, cupelling, cupelled** *or US* **cupels, cupeling, cupeled.** **3** (*tr*) to refine (gold or silver) using a cupel. [C17: from F *coupelle,* dim. of *coupe* CUP]
▸ **,cupel'lation** *n*

Cup Final *n* **1** (often preceded by *the*) the annual final of the FA or Scottish Cup soccer competition. **2** (*often not cap.*) the final of any cup competition.

Cupid ('kju:pɪd) *n* **1** the Roman god of love, represented as a winged boy with a bow and arrow. Greek counterpart: **Eros.** **2** (*not cap.*) any similar figure. [C14: from L *Cupīdō,* from *cupīdō* desire, from *cupidus* desirous; see CUPIDITY]

cupidity (kju:'pɪdɪtɪ) *n* strong desire, esp. for wealth; greed. [C15: from L *cupiditās,* from *cupidus* eagerly desiring, from *cupere* to long for]

cupola ('kju:pələ) *n* **1** a roof or ceiling in the form of a dome. **2** a small structure, usually domed, on the top of a roof or dome. **3** a protective dome for a gun on a warship. **4** a furnace in which iron is remelted. [C16: from It., from LL *cūpula* a small cask, from L *cūpa* tub]
▸ **'cupo,lated** *adj*

cuppa *or* **cupper** ('kʌpə) *n Brit. inf.* a cup of tea.

cupping ('kʌpɪŋ) *n Med.* formerly, the use of an evacuated glass cup to draw blood to the surface of the skin for blood-letting.

cupreous ('kju:prɪəs) *adj* **1** of, containing, or resembling copper. **2** of the colour of copper. [C17: from LL *cupreus,* from *cuprum* COPPER[1]]

cupressus (kə'prɛsəs) *n* any evergreen tree of the genus *Cupressus.*

cupric ('kju:prɪk) *adj* of or containing copper in the divalent state. [C18: from LL *cuprum* copper]

cupriferous (kju:'prɪfərəs) *adj* (of a substance such as an ore) containing or yielding copper.

cupro-, cupri-, *or before a vowel* **cupr-** *combining form.* indicating copper. [from L *cuprum*]

cupronickel (,kju:prəʊ'nɪkᵊl) *n* any copper alloy containing up to 40 per cent nickel: used in coins, condenser tubes, etc.

cuprous ('kju:prəs) *adj* of or containing copper in the monovalent state.

cup tie *n Sport.* an eliminating match or round between two teams in a cup competition.

cupule ('kju:pju:l) *n Biol.* a cup-shaped part or structure. [C19: from LL *cūpula;* see CUPOLA]

cur ❶ (kɜ:) *n* **1** any vicious dog, esp. a mongrel. **2** a despicable or cowardly person. [C13: from *kurdogge;* prob. rel. to ON *kurra* to growl]

curable ('kjʊərəbᵊl) *adj* capable of being cured.
▸ **,cura'bility** *or* **'curableness** *n*

curaçao (,kjʊərə'səʊ) *n* an orange-flavoured liqueur originally made in Curaçao, a Caribbean island.

curacy ('kjʊərəsɪ) *n, pl* **curacies.** the office or position of a curate.

curare *or* **curari** (kjʊ'rɑ:rɪ) *n* **1** black resin obtained from certain tropical South American trees, which causes muscular paralysis: used medicinally as a muscle relaxant and by South American Indians as an arrow poison. **2** any of various trees from which this resin is obtained. [C18: from Port. & Sp., from Carib *kurari*]

curassow ('kjʊərə,səʊ) *n* any of various ground-nesting birds of S North, Central, and South America, having long legs and tail and a crest of curled feathers. [C17: anglicized from *Curaçao,* Caribbean island]

curate ('kjʊərɪt) *n* **1** a clergyman appointed to assist a parish priest. **2** *Irish.* an assistant barman. [C14: from Med. L *cūrātus,* from *cūra* spiritual oversight, CURE]

curate's egg *n* something that has good and bad parts. [C20: derived from a cartoon in *Punch* (Nov., 1895) in which a timid curate, who has been served a bad egg while breakfasting with his bishop, says that parts of the egg are excellent]

curative ❶ ('kjʊərətɪv) *adj* **1** able or tending to cure. ◆ *n* **2** anything able to heal or cure.
▸ **'curatively** *adv* ▸ **'curativeness** *n*

curator (kjʊə'reɪtə) *n* the administrative head of a museum, art gallery, etc. [C14: from L: one who cares, from *cūrāre* to care for, from *cūra* care]
▸ **curatorial** (,kjʊərə'tɔ:rɪəl) *adj* ▸ **cu'rator,ship** *n*

curb ❶ (kɜ:b) *n* **1** something that restrains or holds back. **2** any enclosing framework, such as a wall around the top of a well. **3** Also called: **curb bit.** a horse's bit with an attached chain or strap, which checks the horse. ◆ *vb* (*tr*) **4** to control with or as if with a curb; restrain. ◆ See also **kerb.** [C15: from OF *courbe* curved piece of wood or metal, from L *curvus* curved]

curcuma ('kɜ:kjʊmə) *n* any tropical Asian tuberous plant of the genus *Curcuma,* such as *C. longa,* which is the source of turmeric. [C17: from NL, from Ar. *kurkum* turmeric]

curd (kɜ:d) *n* **1** (*often pl*) a substance formed from the coagulation of milk, used in making cheese or eaten as a food. **2** something similar in consistency. ◆ *vb* **3** to turn into or become curd. [C15: from earlier *crud,* from ?]
▸ **'curdy** *adj*

curdle ❶ ('kɜ:dᵊl) *vb* **curdles, curdling, curdled.** **1** to turn or cause to turn into curd. **2 curdle someone's blood.** to fill someone with fear. [C16 (*crudled,* p.p.): from CURD]

cure ❶ (kjʊə) *vb* **cures, curing, cured.** **1** (*tr*) to get rid of (an ailment or problem); heal. **2** (*tr*) to restore to health or good condition. **3** (*intr*) to bring about a cure. **4** (*tr*) to preserve (meat, fish, etc.) by salting, smoking, etc. **5** (*tr*) **5a** to treat or finish (a substance) by chemical or physical means. **5b** to vulcanize (rubber). **6** (*tr*) to assist the hardening of (concrete, mortar, etc.) by keeping it moist. ◆ *n* **7** a return to health. **8** any course of medical therapy, esp. one proved effective. **9** a means of restoring health or improving a situation, etc. **10** the spiritual and pastoral charge of a parish. **11** a process or method of preserving meat, fish, etc. [(n) C13: from OF, from L *cūra* care; in ecclesiastical sense, from Med. L *cūra* spiritual charge; (vb) C14: from OF *curer,* from L *cūrāre* to attend to, heal, from *cūra* care]
▸ **'cureless** *adj* ▸ **'curer** *n*

curé ('kjʊəreɪ) *n* a parish priest in France. [F, from Med. L *cūrātus;* see CURATE]

cure-all ❶ *n* something reputed to cure all ailments.

curettage (,kjʊərɪ'tɑ:ʒ, kjʊə'rɛtɪdʒ) *or* **curettement** (kjʊə'rɛtmənt) *n* the process of using a curette. See also **D and C.**

curette *or* **curet** (kjʊə'rɛt) *n* **1** a surgical instrument for removing dead tissue, growths, etc., from the walls of body cavities. ◆ *vb* **curettes** *or* **curets, curetting, curetted.** **2** (*tr*) to scrape or clean with such an instrument. [C18: from F *curette,* from *curer* to heal, make clean; see CURE]

curfew ('kɜ:fju:) *n* **1** an official regulation setting restrictions on movement, esp. after a specific time at night. **2** the time set as a deadline by such a regulation. **3** (in medieval Europe) **3a** the ringing of a bell to prompt people to extinguish fires and lights. **3b** the time at which the

THESAURUS

cunning *adj* **1** = **crafty**, artful, astute, canny, devious, foxy, guileful, knowing, Machiavellian, sharp, shifty, shrewd, sly, subtle, tricky, wily **2** = **skilful**, adroit, deft, dexterous, imaginative, ingenious ◆ *n* **3** = **craftiness**, artfulness, astuteness, deceitfulness, deviousness, foxiness, guile, shrewdness, slyness, trickery, wiliness **4** = **skill**, ability, adroitness, art, artifice, cleverness, craft, deftness, dexterity, finesse, ingenuity, subtlety
Antonyms *adj* ≠ **crafty:** artless, dull, ethical, frank, honest, ingenuous ≠ **skilful:** maladroit ◆ *n* ≠ **craftiness:** candour, ingenuousness, sincerity ≠ **skill:** clumsiness

cup *n* **1** = **mug**, beaker, bowl, cannikin, chalice, demitasse, goblet, teacup **6** = **trophy**

cupboard *n* = **cabinet**, ambry, closet, locker, press

cur *n* **1** = **mongrel**, canine, hound, mutt (*sl.*), stray **2** = **scoundrel**, bad egg (*old-fashioned inf.*), bastard, blackguard, coward, good-for-nothing, heel (*sl.*), rat (*inf.*), rotter (*sl., chiefly Brit.*), scumbag (*sl.*), shit (*taboo slang*), son-of-a-bitch (*sl., chiefly U.S. & Canad.*), villain, wretch

curative *adj* **1** = **restorative**, alleviative, corrective, healing, healthful, health-giving, medicinal, remedial, salutary, therapeutic, tonic

curb *n* **1** = **restraint**, brake, bridle, check, control, deterrent, limitation, rein ◆ *vb* **4** = **restrain**, bite back, bridle, check, constrain, contain, control, hinder, impede, inhibit, keep a tight rein on, moderate, muzzle, repress, restrict, retard, stem the flow, subdue, suppress

curdle *vb* **1** = **congeal**, clot, coagulate, condense, curd, solidify, thicken, turn sour
Antonyms *vb* deliquesce, dissolve, liquefy, melt, soften, thaw

cure *vb* **1, 2** = **make better**, alleviate, correct, ease, heal, help, mend, rehabilitate, relieve, remedy, restore, restore to health **4** = **preserve**, dry, kipper, pickle, salt, smoke ◆ *n* **7-9** = **remedy**, alleviation, antidote, corrective, healing, medicine, nostrum, panacea, recovery, restorative, specific, treatment

cure-all *n* = **panacea**, catholicon, elixir, *elixir vitae,* nostrum

curfew bell was rung. **3c** the bell itself. [C13: from OF *cuevrefeu*, lit.: cover the fire]

curia ('kjʊərɪə) *n, pl* **curiae** (-rɪˌiː). **1** (*sometimes cap.*) the papal court and government of the Roman Catholic Church. **2** (in the Middle Ages) a court held in the king's name. [C16: from L, from OL *coviria* (unattested), from CO- + *vir* man]
▸'**curial** *adj*

curie ('kjʊərɪ, -riː) *n* a unit of radioactivity equal to 3.7×10^{10} disintegrations per second. [C20: after Pierre *Curie* (1859–1906), F physicist and chemist]

curio Ⓣ ('kjʊərɪˌəʊ) *n, pl* **curios.** a small article valued as a collector's item, esp. something unusual. [C19: shortened from CURIOSITY]

curiosity Ⓣ (ˌkjʊərɪ'ɒsɪtɪ) *n, pl* **curiosities. 1** an eager desire to know; inquisitiveness. **2** the quality of being curious; strangeness. **3** something strange or fascinating.

curious Ⓣ ('kjʊərɪəs) *adj* **1** eager to learn; inquisitive. **2** overinquisitive; prying. **3** interesting because of oddness or novelty. [C14: from L *cūriōsus* taking pains over something, from *cūra* care]
▸'**curiously** *adv* ▸'**curiousness** *n*

curium ('kjʊərɪəm) *n* a silvery-white metallic transuranic element artificially produced from plutonium. Symbol: Cm; at. no.: 96; half-life of most stable isotope, ^{247}Cm: 1.6×10^{7} years. [C20: NL, after Pierre and Marie *Curie*, F physicists and chemists]

curl Ⓣ (kɜːl) *vb* **1** (*intr*) (esp. of hair) to grow into curves or ringlets. **2** (*tr; sometimes foll. by up*) to twist or roll (esp. hair) into coils or ringlets. **3** (often foll. by *up*) to become or cause to become spiral-shaped or curved. **4** (*intr*) to move in a curving or twisting manner. **5** (*intr*) to play the game of curling. **6 curl one's lip.** to show contempt, as by raising a corner of the lip. ◆ *n* **7** a curve or coil of hair. **8** a curved or spiral shape or mark. **9** the act of curling or state of being curled. ◆ See also **curl up.** [C14: prob. from MDu. *crullen* to curl]

curler ('kɜːlə) *n* **1** any of various pins, clasps, or rollers used to curl or wave hair. **2** a person or thing that curls. **3** a person who plays curling.

curlew ('kɜːljuː) *n* any of certain large shore birds of Europe and Asia. They have a long downward-curving bill and occur in northern and arctic regions. [C14: from OF *corlieu*, ? imit.]

curlicue ('kɜːlɪˌkjuː) *n* an intricate ornamental curl or twist. [C19: from CURLY + CUE[2]]

curling ('kɜːlɪŋ) *n* a game played on ice, esp. in Scotland, in which heavy stones with handles (**curling stones**) are slid towards a target (**tee**).

curling tongs *pl n* a metal scissor-like device that is heated, so that strands of hair may be twined around it in order to form curls. Also called: **curling iron, curling irons, curling pins.**

curl up *vb* (*adv*) **1** (*intr*) to adopt a reclining position with the legs close to the body and the back rounded. **2** to become or cause to become spiral-shaped or curved. **3** (*intr*) to retire to a quiet cosy setting: *to curl up with a good novel.* **4** *Brit. inf.* to be or cause to be embarrassed or disgusted (esp. in **curl up and die**).

curly Ⓣ ('kɜːlɪ) *adj* **curlier, curliest. 1** tending to curl; curling. **2** having curls. **3** (of timber) having waves in the grain.
▸'**curliness** *n*

curmudgeon Ⓣ (kɜː'mʌdʒən) *n* a surly or miserly person. [C16: from ?]
▸**cur'mudgeonly** *adj*

currach *or* **curragh** *Gaelic.* ('kʌrəx, 'kʌrə) *n* a Scottish or Irish name for **coracle.** [C15: from Irish Gaelic *currach;* Cf. CORACLE]

currajong ('kʌrəˌdʒɒŋ) *n* a variant spelling of **kurrajong.**

currant ('kʌrənt) *n* **1** a small dried seedless grape of the Mediterranean region. **2** any of several mainly N temperate shrubs, esp. redcurrant and blackcurrant. **3** the small acid fruit of any of these plants. [C16: shortened from *rayson of Corannte* raisin of Corinth]

currawong ('kʌrəˌwɒŋ) *n* any Australian crowlike songbird of the genus *Strepera*, having black, grey, and white plumage. Also called: **bell-magpie.** [from Abor.]

currency Ⓣ ('kʌrənsɪ) *n, pl* **currencies. 1** a metal or paper medium of exchange in current use in a particular country. **2** general acceptance or circulation; prevalence. **3** the period of time during which something is valid, accepted, or in force. ◆ *adj* **4** *Austral. inf.* native-born as distinct from immigrant: *a currency lad.* [C17: from Med. L *currentia*, lit.: a flowing, from L *currere* to run, flow]

current Ⓣ ('kʌrənt) *adj* **1** of the immediate present; in progress. **2** most recent; up-to-date. **3** commonly known, practised, or accepted. **4** circulating and valid at present: *current coins.* ◆ *n* **5** (esp. of water or air) a steady, usually natural, flow. **6** a mass of air, body of water, etc., that has a steady flow in a particular direction. **7** the rate of flow of such a mass. **8** *Physics.* **8a** a flow of electric charge through a conductor. **8b** the rate of flow of this charge. **9** a general trend or drift: *currents of opinion.* [C13: from OF *corant*, lit.: running, from *corre* to run, from L *currere*]
▸'**currently** *adv* ▸'**currentness** *n*

current account *n* an account at a bank or building society against which cheques may be drawn at any time.

current-cost accounting *n* a method of accounting that values assets at their current replacement cost rather than their original cost. It is often used in times of high inflation. Cf. **historical-cost accounting.**

curricle ('kʌrɪkᵊl) *n* a two-wheeled open carriage drawn by two horses side by side. [C18: from L *curriculum* from *currus* chariot, from *currere* to run]

curriculum (kə'rɪkjʊləm) *n, pl* **curricula** (-lə) *or* **curriculums. 1** a course of study in one subject at a school or college. **2** a list of all the courses of study offered by a school or college. **3** any programme or plan of activities. [C19: from L: course, from *currere* to run]
▸**cur'ricular** *adj*

curriculum vitae (kə'rɪkjʊləm 'viːtaɪ, 'vaɪtiː) *n, pl* **curricula vitae** (kə'rɪkjʊlə). an outline of a person's educational and professional history, usually prepared for job applications. [L, lit.: the course of one's life]

currish ('kɜːrɪʃ) *adj* of or like a cur; rude or bad-tempered.
▸'**currishly** *adv* ▸'**currishness** *n*

curry[1] ('kʌrɪ) *n, pl* **curries. 1** a spicy dish of oriental, esp. Indian, origin that usually consists of meat or fish prepared in a hot piquant sauce. **2** curry seasoning or sauce. **3 give someone curry.** *Austral. sl.* to assault (a person) verbally or physically. ◆ *vb* **curries, currying, curried. 4** (*tr*) to prepare (food) with curry powder or sauce. [C16: from Tamil *kari* sauce, relish]

curry[2] ('kʌrɪ) *vb* **curries, currying, curried. 1** to beat vigorously, as in order to clean. **2** to dress and finish (leather) after it has been tanned. **3** to groom (a horse). **4 curry favour.** to ingratiate oneself, esp. with superiors. [C13: from OF *correer* to make ready]

currycomb ('kʌrɪˌkəʊm) *n* a square comb used for grooming horses.

curry powder *n* a mixture of finely ground pungent spices, such as turmeric, cumin, coriander, ginger, etc., used in making curries.

curse Ⓣ (kɜːs) *n* **1** a profane or obscene expression of anger, disgust, surprise, etc.; oath. **2** an appeal to a supernatural power for harm to come to a specific person, group, etc. **3** harm resulting from an appeal to a supernatural power. **4** something that brings or causes great trouble or harm. **5** (preceded by *the*) *Inf.* menstruation or a menstrual period. ◆ *vb* **curses, cursing, cursed** *or* (*Arch.*) **curst. 6** (*intr*) to utter obscenities or oaths. **7** (*tr*) to abuse (someone) with obscenities or oaths. **8** (*tr*) to invoke supernatural powers to bring harm to (someone or something). **9** (*tr*) to bring harm upon. [OE *cursian* to curse, from *curs* a curse]
▸'**curser** *n*

cursed Ⓣ ('kɜːsɪd, kɜːst) *or* **curst** *adj* **1** under a curse. **2** deserving to be cursed; detestable; hateful.
▸'**cursedly** *adv* ▸'**cursedness** *n*

cursive ('kɜːsɪv) *adj* **1** of or relating to handwriting in which letters are joined in a flowing style. **2** *Printing.* of or relating to typefaces that re-

THESAURUS

curio *n* = **collector's item**, antique, bibelot, bygone, knick-knack, *objet d'art*, trinket

curiosity *n* **1** = **inquisitiveness**, interest, nosiness (*inf.*), prying, snooping (*inf.*) **3** = **oddity**, celebrity, freak, marvel, novelty, phenomenon, rarity, sight, spectacle, wonder

curious *adj* **1** = **inquiring**, inquisitive, interested, puzzled, questioning, searching **2** = **inquisitive**, meddling, nosy (*inf.*), peeping, peering, prying, snoopy (*inf.*) **3** = **unusual**, bizarre, exotic, extraordinary, marvellous, mysterious, novel, odd, peculiar, puzzling, quaint, queer, rare, rum (*Brit. slang*), singular, strange, unconventional, unexpected, unique, unorthodox, wonderful
Antonyms *adj* ≠ **inquiring:** incurious, indifferent, uninquisitive, uninterested ≠ **unusual:** common, everyday, familiar, ordinary

curl *vb* **1-4** = **twirl**, bend, coil, convolute, corkscrew, crimp, crinkle, crisp, curve, entwine, frizz, loop, meander, ripple, spiral, turn, twine, twist, wind, wreathe, writhe ◆ *n* **7, 8** = **twist**, coil, curlicue, kink, ringlet, spiral, whorl

curly *adj* **1, 2** = **curling**, corkscrew, crimped, crimpy, crinkly, crisp, curled, frizzy, fuzzy, kinky, permed, spiralled, waved, wavy, winding

curmudgeon *n* = **grump** (*inf.*), bear, bellyacher (*sl.*), churl, crosspatch (*inf.*), grouch, grouser, grumbler, malcontent, sourpuss (*inf.*)

currency *n* **1** = **money**, bills, coinage, coins, dosh (*Brit. & Austral. sl.*), medium of exchange, notes **2** = **acceptance**, circulation, exposure, popularity, prevalence, publicity, transmission, vogue

current *adj* **1, 3** = **prevalent**, accepted, circulating, common, customary, general, going around, in circulation, in progress, in the air, in the news, ongoing, popular, prevailing, rife, topical, widespread **2** = **present**, contemporary, fashionable, happening (*inf.*), in, in fashion, in vogue, now (*inf.*), present-day, trendy (*Brit. inf.*), up-to-date, up-to-the-minute ◆ *n* **5, 6** = **flow**, course, draught, jet, progression, river, stream, tide, tideway, undertow **9** = **mood**, atmosphere, drift, feeling, inclination, tendency, trend, undercurrent, vibes (*sl.*)
Antonyms *adj* ≠ **present:** archaic, obsolete, old-fashioned, outmoded, out-of-date, passé, past

curse *n* **1** = **oath**, blasphemy, expletive, obscenity, swearing, swearword **2** = **denunciation**, anathema, ban, evil eye, excommunication, execration, hoodoo (*inf.*), imprecation, jinx, malediction, malison (*arch.*) **4** = **affliction**, bane, burden, calamity, cross, disaster, evil, hardship, misfortune, ordeal, plague, scourge, torment, tribulation, trouble, vexation ◆ *vb* **6** = **swear**, be foul-mouthed, blaspheme, cuss (*inf.*), take the Lord's name in vain, turn the air blue (*inf.*), use bad language **8** = **damn**, accurse, anathematize, excommunicate, execrate, fulminate, imprecate **9** = **afflict**, blight, burden, destroy, doom, plague, scourge, torment, trouble, vex

cursed *adj* **1** = **damned**, accursed, bedevilled, blighted, cast out, confounded, doomed, excommunicate, execrable, fey (*Scot.*), foredoomed, ill-fated, star-crossed, unholy, unsanctified, villainous **2** = **hateful**, abominable, damnable, detestable, devilish, fell (*arch.*), fiendish, infamous, infernal, loathsome, odious, pernicious, pestilential, vile

semble handwriting. ◆ *n* **3** a cursive letter or printing type. [C18: from Med. L *cursīvus* running, ult. from L *currere* to run]
▸ **'cursively** *adv*

cursor ('kɜːsə) *n* **1** the sliding part of a measuring instrument, esp. on a slide rule. **2** any of various means, typically a flashing bar or underline, of identifying a particular position on a computer screen.

cursorial (kɜː'sɔːrɪəl) *adj Zool.* adapted for running: *a cursorial skeleton; cursorial birds.*

cursory ➊ ('kɜːsərɪ) *adj* hasty and usually superficial; quick. [C17: from LL *cursōrius* of running, from L *cursus* a course, from *currere* to run]
▸ **'cursorily** *adv* ▸ **'cursoriness** *n*

curst (kɜːst) *vb* **1** *Arch.* a past tense and past participle of **curse**. ◆ *adj* **2** a variant of **cursed**.

curt ➊ (kɜːt) *adj* **1** rudely blunt and brief. **2** short or concise. [C17: from L *curtus* cut short, mutilated]
▸ **'curtly** *adv* ▸ **'curtness** *n*

curtail ➊ (kɜː'teɪl) *vb* (*tr*) to cut short; abridge. [C16: changed (through infl. of TAIL[1]) from obs. *curtal* to dock]
▸ **cur'tailer** *n* ▸ **cur'tailment** *n*

curtain ➊ ('kɜːtᵊn) *n* **1** a piece of material that can be drawn across an opening or window, to shut out light or to provide privacy. **2** a barrier to vision, access, or communication. **3** a hanging cloth or similar barrier for concealing all or part of a theatre stage from the audience. **4** (often preceded by *the*) the end of a scene of a play, opera, etc., marked by the fall or closing of the curtain. **5** the rise or opening of the curtain at the start of a performance. ◆ *vb* **6** (*tr;* sometimes foll. by *off*) to shut off or conceal as with a curtain. **7** (*tr*) to provide (a window, etc.) with curtains. [C13: from OF *courtine,* from LL *cortīna* enclosed place, curtain, prob. from L *cohors* courtyard]

curtain call *n* the appearance of performers at the end of a theatrical performance to acknowledge applause.

curtain lecture *n* a scolding or rebuke given in private, esp. by a wife to her husband. [alluding to the curtained beds where such rebukes were once given]

curtain-raiser *n* **1** *Theatre.* a short dramatic piece presented before the main play. **2** any preliminary event.

curtains ('kɜːtᵊnz) *pl n Inf.* death or ruin: the end.

curtain wall *n* a non-load-bearing external wall attached to a framed structure.

curtsy *or* **curtsey** ('kɜːtsɪ) *n, pl* **curtsies** *or* **curtseys. 1** a formal gesture of greeting and respect made by women, in which the knees are bent and the head slightly bowed. ◆ *vb* **curtsies, curtsying, curtsied** *or* **curtseys, curtseying, curtseyed. 2** (*intr*) to make a curtsy. [C16: var. of COURTESY]

curvaceous ➊ (kɜː'veɪʃəs) *adj Inf.* (of a woman) having a well-rounded body.

curvature ➊ ('kɜːvətʃə) *n* **1** something curved or a curved part of a thing. **2** any curving of a bodily part. **3** the act of curving or the state or degree of being curved or bent.

curve ➊ (kɜːv) *n* **1** a continuously bending line that has no straight parts. **2** something that curves or is curved. **3** the act or extent of curving; curvature. **4** *Maths.* a system of points whose coordinates satisfy a given equation. **5** a line representing data on a graph. ◆ *vb* **curves, curving, curved. 6** to take or cause to take the shape or path of a curve; bend. [C15: from L *curvāre* to bend, from *curvus* crooked]
▸ **'curvedness** *n* ▸ **'curvy** *adj*

curvet (kɜː'vɛt) *n* **1** *Dressage.* a low leap with all four feet off the ground. ◆ *vb* **curvets, curvetting, curvetted** *or* **curvets, curveting, curveted. 2** *Dressage.* to make or cause to make such a leap. **3** (*intr*) to prance or frisk about. [C16: from OIt. *corvetta,* from OF *courbette,* from *courber* to bend, from L *curvāre*]

curvilinear (ˌkɜːvɪ'lɪnɪə) *or* **curvilineal** *adj* consisting of, bounded by, or characterized by a curved line.

cuscus ('kʌskʌs) *n, pl* **cuscuses.** any of several large nocturnal phalangers of N Australia, New Guinea, and adjacent islands, having dense fur, prehensile tails, large eyes, and a yellow nose. [C17: NL, prob. from a native name in New Guinea]

cusec ('kjuːsɛk) *n* a unit of flow equal to 1 cubic foot per second. [C20: from *cu(bic foot per) sec(ond)*]

cushat ('kʌʃət) *n* another name for **wood pigeon.** [OE *cūscote;* ? rel. to *sceōtan* to shoot]

cushion ➊ ('kʊʃən) *n* **1** a bag filled with a yielding substance, used for sitting on, leaning against, etc. **2** something resembling a cushion in function or appearance, esp. one to support or pad or to absorb shock. **3** the resilient felt-covered rim of a billiard table. ◆ *vb* (*tr*) **4** to place on or as on a cushion. **5** to provide with cushions. **6** to protect. **7** to lessen or suppress the effects of. **8** to provide with a means of absorbing shock. [C14: from OF *coussin,* from L *culcita* mattress]
▸ **'cushiony** *adj*

cushion plant *n* a type of low-growing plant having many closely spaced short upright shoots, typical of alpine and arctic habitats.

Cushitic (kʊ'ʃɪtɪk) *n* **1** a group of languages of Somalia, Ethiopia, and adjacent regions. ◆ *adj* **2** of or relating to this group of languages.

cushy ➊ ('kʊʃɪ) *adj* **cushier, cushiest.** *Inf.* easy; comfortable. [C20: from Hindi *khush* pleasant, from Persian *khōsh*]

CUSO ('kjuːsəʊ) *n acronym for* Canadian University Services Overseas; an organization that sends students to work as volunteers in developing countries.

cusp (kʌsp) *n* **1** any of the small elevations on the grinding or chewing surface of a tooth. **2** any of the triangular flaps of a heart valve. **3** a point or pointed end. **4** *Geom.* a point at which two arcs of a curve intersect and at which the two tangents are coincident. **5** *Archit.* a carving at the meeting place of two arcs. **6** *Astron.* either of the points of a crescent moon. **7** *Astrol.* any division between houses or signs of the zodiac. [C16: from L *cuspis* point, pointed end]
▸ **'cuspate** *adj*

cuspid ('kʌspɪd) *n* a tooth having one point; canine tooth.

cuspidate ('kʌspɪˌdeɪt), **cuspidated,** *or* **cuspidal** ('kʌspɪdᵊl) *adj* **1** having a cusp or cusps. **2** (esp. of leaves) narrowing to a point. [C17: from L *cuspidāre* to make pointed, from *cuspis* a point]

cuspidor ('kʌspɪˌdɔː) *n* another name (esp. US) for **spittoon.** [C18: from Port., from *cuspir* to spit, from L *conspuere,* from *spuere* to spit]

cuss (kʌs) *Inf.* ◆ *n* **1** a curse; an oath. **2** a person or animal, esp. an annoying one. ◆ *vb* **3** another word for **curse** (senses 6, 7).

cussed ('kʌsɪd) *adj Inf.* **1** another word for **cursed. 2** obstinate. **3** annoying: *a cussed nuisance.*
▸ **'cussedly** *adv* ▸ **'cussedness** *n*

custard ('kʌstəd) *n* **1** a baked sweetened mixture of eggs and milk. **2** a sauce made of milk and sugar and thickened with cornflour. [C15: alteration of ME *crustade* kind of pie]

custard apple *n* **1** a West Indian tree. **2** its large heart-shaped fruit, which has a fleshy edible pulp.

custard pie *n* **a** a flat, open pie filled with real or artificial custard, as thrown in slapstick comedy. **b** (*as modifier*): *custard-pie humour.*

custodian ➊ (kʌ'stəʊdɪən) *n* **1** a person who has custody, as of a prisoner, ward, etc. **2** a keeper of an art collection, etc.
▸ **cus'todianˌship** *n*

custody ➊ ('kʌstədɪ) *n, pl* **custodies. 1** the act of keeping safe or guarding. **2** the state of being held by the police; arrest. [C15: from L *custōdia,* from *custōs* guard, defender]
▸ **custodial** (kʌ'stəʊdɪəl) *adj*

custom ➊ ('kʌstəm) *n* **1** a usual or habitual practice; typical mode of behaviour. **2** the long-established habits or traditions of a society collectively; convention. **3a** a practice which by long-established usage has come to have the force of law. **3b** such practices collectively (esp. in **custom and practice**). **4** habitual patronage, esp. of a shop or business. **5** the customers of a shop or business collectively. ◆ *adj* **6** made to the specifications of an individual customer. ◆ See also **customs.** [C12: from OF *costume,* from L *consuētūdō,* from *consuēscere* to grow accustomed to]

customary ➊ ('kʌstəmərɪ, -təmrɪ) *adj* **1** in accordance with custom or habitual practice; usual. **2** *Law.* **2a** founded upon long-continued practices and usage. **2b** (of land) held by custom. ◆ *n, pl* **customaries. 3** a statement in writing of customary laws and practices.
▸ **'customarily** *adv* ▸ **'customariness** *n*

custom-built *adj* (of cars, houses, etc.) made according to the specifications of an individual buyer.

THESAURUS

cursory *adj* = **brief**, careless, casual, desultory, hasty, hurried, offhand, passing, perfunctory, rapid, slapdash, slight, summary, superficial

curt *adj* **1, 2** = **short**, abrupt, blunt, brief, brusque, concise, gruff, monosyllabic, offhand, pithy, rude, sharp, snappish, succinct, summary, tart, terse, unceremonious, uncivil, ungracious

curtail *vb* = **cut short**, abbreviate, abridge, contract, cut, cut back, decrease, diminish, dock, lessen, lop, pare down, reduce, retrench, shorten, trim, truncate

curtailment *n* = **cutting short**, abbreviation, abridgment, contraction, cutback, cutting, docking, retrenchment, truncation

curtain *n* **1** = **hanging**, drape (*chiefly US*) ◆ *vb* **6** = **conceal**, drape, hide, screen, shroud, shut off, shutter, veil

curvaceous *adj Informal* = **shapely**, bosomy, buxom, comely, curvy, voluptuous, well-rounded, well-stacked (*Brit. sl.*)

curvature *n* **3** = **curving**, arching, bend, curve, deflection, flexure, incurvation

curve *n* **2** = **bend**, arc, camber, curvature, half-moon, loop, trajectory, turn ◆ *vb* **6** = **bend**, arc, arch, bow, coil, hook, inflect, spiral, swerve, turn, twist, wind

cushion *n* **1** = **pillow**, beanbag, bolster, hassock, headrest, pad, scatter cushion, squab ◆ *vb* **6, 7** = **soften**, bolster, buttress, cradle, dampen, deaden, muffle, pillow, protect, stifle, support, suppress

cushy *adj Informal* = **easy**, comfortable, jammy (*Brit. sl.*), soft, undemanding

custodian *n* **1, 2** = **keeper**, caretaker, curator, guardian, overseer, protector, superintendent, warden, warder, watchdog, watchman

custody *n* **1** = **safekeeping**, aegis, auspices, care, charge, custodianship, guardianship, keeping, observation, preservation, protection, supervision, trusteeship, tutelage, ward, watch **2** = **imprisonment**, arrest, confinement, detention, durance (*arch.*), duress, incarceration

custom *n* **1** = **habit**, habitude (*rare*), manner, matter of course, mode, practice, procedure, routine, way, wont **2** = **tradition**, convention, etiquette, fashion, form, formality, observance, observation, policy, practice, praxis, ritual, rule, style, unwritten law, usage, use **4** = **customers**, patronage, trade

customarily *adv* **1** = **usually**, as a rule, commonly, generally, habitually, in the ordinary way, normally, ordinarily, regularly, traditionally

customary *adj* **1** = **usual**, accepted, accustomed, acknowledged, bog-standard (*Brit. & Irish sl.*), common, confirmed, conventional, established, everyday, familiar, fashionable, general, habitual, normal, ordinary, popular, regular, routine, traditional, wonted
Antonyms *adj* exceptional, infrequent, irregular, occasional, rare, uncommon, unusual

customer ⓣ ('kʌstəmə) *n* **1** a person who buys. **2** *Inf.* a person with whom one has dealings.

custom house *n* a government office, esp. at a port, where customs are collected and ships cleared for entry.

customize *or* **customise** ('kʌstə,maɪz) *vb* **customizes, customizing, customized** *or* **customises, customising, customised.** (*tr*) to make (something) according to a customer's individual requirements.

custom-made *adj* (of suits, dresses, etc.) made according to the specifications of an individual buyer.

customs ⓣ ('kʌstəmz) *n* (*functioning as sing or pl*) **1** duty on imports or exports. **2** the government department responsible for the collection of these duties. **3** the part of a port, airport, etc., where baggage and freight are examined for dutiable goods and contraband.

cut ⓣ (kʌt) *vb* **cuts, cutting, cut. 1** to open up or incise (a person or thing) with a sharp edge or instrument. **2** (of a sharp instrument) to penetrate or incise (a person or thing). **3** to divide or be divided with or as if with a sharp instrument. **4** (*intr*) to use an instrument that cuts. **5** (*tr*) to trim or prune by or as if by clipping. **6** (*tr*) to reap or mow (a crop, grass, etc.). **7** (*tr; sometimes foll. by out*) to make, form, or shape by cutting. **8** (*tr*) to hollow or dig out; excavate. **9** to strike (an object) sharply. **10** *Cricket.* to hit (the ball) to the off side with a roughly horizontal bat. **11** to hurt the feelings of (a person). **12** (*tr*) *Inf.* to refuse to recognize; snub. **13** (*tr*) *Inf.* to absent oneself from, esp. without permission or in haste: *to cut a class.* **14** (*tr*) to abridge or shorten. **15** (*tr; often foll. by down*) to lower, reduce, or curtail. **16** (*tr*) to dilute or weaken: *to cut whisky with water.* **17** (*tr*) to dissolve or break up: *to cut fat.* **18** (when *intr*, foll. by *across* or *through*) to cross or traverse. **19** (*intr*) to make a sharp or sudden change in direction; veer. **20** to grow (teeth) through the gums or (of teeth) to appear through the gums. **21** (*intr*) *Films.* **21a** to call a halt to a shooting sequence. **21b** (foll. by *to*) to move quickly to another scene. **22** *Films.* to edit (film). **23** to switch off (a light, car engine, etc.). **24** (*tr*) to make (a record or tape of a song, performance, etc.). **25** *Cards.* **25a** to divide (the pack) at random into two parts after shuffling. **25b** (*intr*) to pick cards from a spread pack to decide dealer, partners, etc. **26** (*tr*) (of a tool) to bite into (an object). **27 cut a dash.** to make a stylish impression. **28 cut (a person) dead.** *Inf.* to ignore (a person) completely. **29 cut a (good, poor, etc.) figure.** to appear or behave in a specified manner. **30 cut and run.** *Inf.* to make a rapid escape. **31 cut both ways. 31a** to have both good and bad effects. **31b** to affect both sides, as two parties in an argument, etc. **32 cut it fine.** *Inf.* to allow little margin of time, space etc. **33 cut loose.** to free or become freed from restraint, custody, anchorage, etc. **34 cut no ice.** *Inf.* to fail to make an impression. **35 cut one's teeth on.** *Inf.* **35a** to use at an early age or stage. **35b** to practise on. ◆ *adj* **36** detached, divided, or separated by cutting. **37** made, shaped, or fashioned by cutting. **38** reduced or diminished as by cutting: *cut prices.* **39** weakened or diluted. **40** *Brit.* a slang word for **drunk:** *half cut.* **41 cut and dried.** *Inf.* settled or arranged in advance. ◆ *n* **42** the act of cutting. **43** a stroke or incision made by cutting; gash. **44** a piece or part cut off: *a cut of meat.* **45** the edge of anything cut or sliced. **46** a passage, channel, path, etc., cut or hollowed out. **47** an omission or deletion, esp. in a text, film, or play. **48** a reduction in price, salary, etc. **49** a decrease in government finance in a particular department or area. **50** *Inf.* a portion or share. **51** *Inf.* a straw, slip of paper, etc., used in drawing lots. **52** the manner or style in which a thing, esp. a garment, is cut. **53a** *Irish inf.* a person's general appearance: *I didn't like the cut of him.* **53b** *Irish derog.* a dirty or untidy condition: *look at the cut of your shoes.* **54** a direct route; short cut. **55** the US name for **block** (sense 13). **56** *Cricket.* a stroke made with the bat in a roughly horizontal position. **57** *Films.* an immediate transition from one shot to the next. **58** words or an action that hurt another person's feelings. **59** a refusal to recognize an acquaintance; snub. **60** *Brit.* a stretch of water, esp. a canal. **61 a cut above.** *Inf.* superior to; better than. ◆ See also **cut across, cutback,** etc. [C13: prob. from ON]

cut across *vb* (*intr, prep*) **1** to be contrary to ordinary procedure or limitations. **2** to cross or traverse, making a shorter route.

cut and paste *n* a technique used in word processing by which a section of text can be moved within a document.

cutaneous (kju:'teɪnɪəs) *adj* of or relating to the skin. [C16: from NL *cutāneus*, from L *cutis* skin]

cutaway ('kʌtə,weɪ) *n* **1** a man's coat cut diagonally from the front waist to the back of the knees. **2a** a drawing or model of a machine, engine, etc., in which part of the casing is omitted to reveal the workings. **2b** (*as modifier*): *a cutaway model.* **3** *Films, television.* a shot separate from the main action of a scene.

cutback ⓣ ('kʌt,bæk) *n* **1** a decrease or reduction. ◆ *vb* **cut back** (*adv*) **2** (*tr*) to shorten by cutting off the end. **3** (when *intr*, foll. by *on*) to reduce or make a reduction (in).

cut down ⓣ *vb* (*adv*) **1** (*tr*) to fell. **2** (when *intr*, often foll. by *on*) to reduce or make a reduction (in). **3** (*tr*) to remake (an old garment) in order to make a smaller one. **4** (*tr*) to kill. **5 cut (a person) down to size.** to reduce in importance or decrease the conceit of (a person).

cute ⓣ (kju:t) *adj* **1** appealing or attractive, esp. in a pretty way. **2** *Inf.* affecting cleverness or prettiness. **3** clever; shrewd. [C18 (in the sense: clever): shortened from ACUTE]
▸**'cutely** *adv* ▸**'cuteness** *n*

cut glass *n* **1a** glass, esp. bowls, vases, etc., decorated by facet-cutting or grinding. **1b** (*as modifier*): *a cut-glass vase.* **2** (*modifier*) (of an accent) upper-class; refined.

cuticle ('kju:tɪkᵊl) *n* **1** dead skin, esp. round the base of a fingernail or toenail. **2** another name for **epidermis. 3** the protective layer that covers the epidermis of higher plants. **4** the protective layer covering the epidermis of many invertebrates. [C17: from L *cutīcula* dim. of *cutis* skin]
▸**cuticular** (kju:'tɪkjulə) *adj*

cut in ⓣ *vb* (*adv*) **1** (*intr; often foll. by on*) Also: **cut into.** to break in or interrupt. **2** (*intr*) to interrupt a dancing couple to dance with one of them. **3** (*intr*) (of a driver, motor vehicle, etc.) to draw in front of another vehicle leaving too little space. **4** (*tr*) *Inf.* to allow to have a share. **5** (*intr*) to take the place of a person in a card game.

cutis ('kju:tɪs) *n, pl* **cutes** (-ti:z) *or* **cutises.** *Anat.* a technical name for the **skin.** [C17: from L: skin]

cutlass ('kʌtləs) *n* a curved, one-edged sword formerly used by sailors. [C16: from F *coutelas*, from *coutel* knife, ult. from L *culter* knife]

cutler ('kʌtlə) *n* a person who makes or sells cutlery. [C14: from F *coutelier*, ult. from L *culter* knife]

cutlery ('kʌtlərɪ) *n* **1** implements used for eating, such as knives, forks, and spoons. **2** instruments used for cutting. **3** the art or business of a cutler.

cutlet ('kʌtlɪt) *n* **1** a piece of meat taken esp. from the best end of neck of lamb, pork, etc. **2** a flat croquette of minced chicken, lobster, etc. [C18: from OF *costelette*, lit.: a little rib, from *coste* rib, from L *costa*]

cut off ⓣ *vb* (*tr, adv*) **1** to remove by cutting. **2** to intercept or interrupt something, esp. a telephone conversation. **3** to discontinue the supply of. **4** to bring to an end. **5** to deprive of rights; disinherit: *cut off without a penny.* **6** to sever or separate. **7** to occupy a position so as to prevent or obstruct (a retreat or escape). ◆ *n* **cutoff. 8a** the act of cutting off; limit or termination. **8b** (*as modifier*): *the cutoff point.* **9** *Chiefly US.* a short cut. **10** a device to terminate the flow of a fluid in a pipe or duct.

cut out ⓣ *vb* (*adv*) **1** (*tr*) to delete or remove. **2** (*tr*) to shape or form by cutting. **3** (*tr; usually passive*) to suit or equip for: *you're not cut out for this job.* **4** (*intr*) (of an engine, etc.) to cease to operate suddenly. **5** (*intr*) (of an electrical device) to switch off, usually automatically. **6** (*tr*) *Inf.* to oust and supplant (a rival). **7** (*intr*) (of a person) to be excluded from a card game. **8** (*tr*) *Inf.* to cease doing something, esp. something undesirable (esp. in **cut it out**). **9** (*tr*) *Soccer.* to intercept (a pass). **10** (*tr*) to separate (cattle) from a herd. **11** (*intr*) *Austral.* to end or finish: *the road cuts out at the creek.* **12 have one's work cut out.** to have as much work as one can manage. ◆ *n* **cutout. 13** something that has been or is intended to be cut out from something else. **14** a device that switches off or interrupts an electric circuit, esp. as a safety device. **15** *Austral. sl.* the end of shearing.

THESAURUS

customer *n* **1** = **client**, buyer, consumer, habitué, patron, prospect, purchaser, regular (*inf.*), shopper

customs *n* **1** = **duty**, import charges, tariff, tax, toll

cut *vb* **2** = **penetrate**, chop, cleave, divide, gash, incise, lacerate, lance, nick, notch, pierce, score, sever, slash, slice, slit, wound **3** = **divide**, bisect, carve, cleave, cross, dissect, interrupt, intersect, part, segment, sever, slice, split, sunder **5** = **trim**, clip, dock, fell, gather, hack, harvest, hew, lop, mow, pare, prune, reap, saw down, shave, snip **7** = **shape**, carve, chip, chisel, chop, engrave, fashion, form, inscribe, saw, sculpt, sculpture, whittle **11** = **hurt**, grieve, insult, pain, put down, sting, wound **12** *Informal* = **ignore**, avoid, cold-shoulder, freeze (someone) out (*inf.*), look straight through (someone), send to Coventry, slight, snub, spurn, turn one's back on **14** = **abridge**, abbreviate, condense, curtail, delete, edit out, excise, precis, shorten **15** = **reduce**, contract, cut back, decrease, diminish, downsize, ease up on, lower, rationalize, slash, slim (down) ◆ *adj* **41 cut and dried** *Informal* = **prearranged**, automatic, fixed, organized, predetermined, settled, sorted out (*inf.*) ◆ *n* **43** = **incision**, gash, graze, groove, laceration, nick, rent, rip, slash, slit, snip, stroke, wound **48, 49** = **reduction**, cutback, decrease, decrement, diminution, economy, fall, lowering, saving **50** *Informal* = **share**, chop (*sl.*), division, kickback (*chiefly US*), percentage, piece, portion, rake-off (*sl.*), section, slice **52** = **style**, configuration, fashion, form, look, mode, shape **61 a cut above** *Informal* = **superior to**, better than, higher than, more capable than, more competent than, more efficient than, more reliable than, more trustworthy than, more useful than

Antonyms *vb* ≠ **ignore:** accept gladly, embrace, greet, hail, receive, welcome with open arms ≠ **abridge, reduce:** add to, augment, enlarge, expand, extend, fill out, increase

cutback *n* **1** = **reduction**, cut, decrease, economy, lessening, retrenchment ◆ *vb* **cut back 2** = **trim**, prune, shorten **3** = **reduce**, check, curb, decrease, downsize, draw *or* pull in one's horns (*inf.*), economize, lessen, lower, retrench, slash

cut down *vb* **1** = **fell**, hew, level, lop, raze **2** = **reduce**, decrease, lessen, lower **4** = **kill**, blow away (*sl., chiefly US*), dispatch, massacre, mow down, slaughter, slay (*arch.*), take out (*sl.*) **5 cut (a person) down to size** = **make (a person) look small**, abash, humiliate, take the wind out of (a person's) sails

cute *adj* **1** = **appealing**, attractive, charming, delightful, engaging, lovable, sweet, winning, winsome

cut in *vb* **1** = **interrupt**, break in, butt in, interpose, intervene, intrude, move in (*inf.*)

cut off *vb* **2, 3** = **interrupt**, disconnect, intercept, intersect **4** = **halt**, bring to an end, discontinue, obstruct, suspend **5** = **disinherit**, disown, renounce **6** = **separate**, isolate, sever

cut out *vb* **1** = **stop**, cease, delete, extract, give up, kick (*inf.*), refrain from, remove, sever **6** *Informal* = **exclude**, displace, eliminate, oust, supersede, supplant

cut-price ⓣ *or esp. US* **cut-rate** *adj* **1** available at prices or rates below the standard price or rate. **2** (*prenominal*) offering goods or services at prices below the standard price.

cutpurse ⓣ ('kʌt,pɜːs) *n* an archaic word for **pickpocket.**

cutter ('kʌtə) *n* **1** a person or thing that cuts, esp. a person who cuts cloth for clothing. **2** a sailing boat with its mast stepped further aft than that of a sloop. **3** a ship's boat, powered by oars or sail, for carrying passengers or light cargo. **4** a small lightly armed boat, as used in the enforcement of customs regulations.

cut-throat ⓣ ('kʌt,θrəʊt) *n* **1** a person who cuts throats; murderer. **2** Also called: **cut-throat razor, straight razor.** *Brit.* a razor with a long blade that usually folds into the handle. ◆ *adj* **3** bloodthirsty or murderous; cruel. **4** fierce or relentless in competition: *cut-throat prices.* **5** (of some games) played by three people: *cut-throat poker.*

cutting ⓣ ('kʌtɪŋ) *n* **1** a piece cut off from something. **2** *Horticulture.* **2a** a method of propagation in which a part of a plant is induced to form its own roots. **2b** a part separated for this purpose. **3** Also called (esp. US and Canad.): **clipping.** an article, photograph, etc., cut from a publication. **4** the editing process of a film. **5** an excavation in a piece of high land for a road, railway, etc. **6** *Irish inf.* sharp-wittedness: *there is no cutting in him.* ◆ *adj* **7** designed for or adapted to cutting; sharp. **8** keen; piercing. **9** tending to hurt the feelings: *a cutting remark.*
▸**'cuttingly** *adv*

cutting compound *n Engineering.* a mixture, such as oil, water, and soap, used for cooling drills and other cutting tools.

cutting edge *n* the leading position in any field; forefront: *on the cutting edge of space technology.*

cuttlebone ('kʌtᵊl,bəʊn) *n* the internal calcareous shell of the cuttlefish, used as a mineral supplement to the diet of cagebirds and as a polishing agent. [C16: OE *cudele* + BONE]

cuttlefish ('kʌtᵊl,fɪʃ) *n, pl* **cuttlefish** *or* **cuttlefishes.** a cephalopod mollusc which occurs near the bottom of inshore waters and has a broad flattened body. Sometimes shortened to **cuttle.**

cut up ⓣ *vb* (*tr, adv*) **1** to cut into pieces. **2** to inflict injuries on. **3** (*usually passive*) *Inf.* to affect the feelings of deeply. **4** *Inf.* to subject to severe criticism. **5** *Inf.* (of a driver) to overtake or pull in front of (another driver) in a dangerous manner. **6 cut up rough.** *Brit. inf.* to become angry or bad-tempered. ◆ *n* **cut-up. 7** *Inf., chiefly US.* a joker or prankster.

cutwater ('kʌt,wɔːtə) *n* the forward part of the stem of a vessel, which cuts through the water.

cutworm ('kʌt,wɜːm) *n* the caterpillar of various noctuid moths, which is a pest of young crop plants in North America.

cuvée (kuː'veɪ) *n* an individual batch or blend of wine. [C19: from F, lit.: put in a cask, from *cuve* cask]

CV *abbrev. for* curriculum vitae.

CVS *abbrev. for* chorionic villus sampling.

Cwlth *abbrev. for* Commonwealth.

cwm (kuːm) *n* **1** (in Wales) a valley. **2** *Geol.* another name for **cirque.**

c.w.o. *or* **CWO** *abbrev. for* cash with order.

CWS *abbrev. for* Cooperative Wholesale Society.

cwt *abbrev. for* hundredweight. [*c*, from the L numeral *C* one hundred (*centum*)]

CWU (in Britain) *abbrev. for* Communication Workers Union.

-cy *suffix.* **1** indicating state, quality, or condition: *plutocracy; lunacy.* **2** rank or office: *captaincy.* [via OF from L *-cia, -tia,* Gk *-kia, -tia,* abstract noun suffixes]

cyan ('saɪæn, 'saɪən) *n* **1** a green-blue colour. ◆ *adj* **2** of this colour. [C19: from Gk *kuanos* dark blue]

cyanate ('saɪə,neɪt) *n* any salt or ester of cyanic acid.

cyanic (saɪ'ænɪk) *adj* **1** of or containing cyanogen. **2** blue.

cyanic acid *n* a colourless poisonous volatile liquid acid. Formula: HOCN.

cyanide ('saɪə,naɪd) *or* **cyanid** ('saɪənɪd) *n* any salt of hydrocyanic acid. Cyanides are extremely poisonous.
▸**,cyani'dation** *n*

cyanite ('saɪə,naɪt) *n* a grey, green, or blue mineral consisting of aluminium silicate in crystalline form.
▸**cyanitic** (,saɪə'nɪtɪk) *adj*

cyano- *or before a vowel* **cyan-** *combining form.* **1** blue or dark blue. **2** indicating cyanogen. **3** indicating cyanide. [from Gk *kuanos* (adj) dark blue, (n) dark blue enamel, lapis lazuli]

cyanobacteria (,saɪənəʊbæk'tɪərɪə) *pl n, sing* **cyanobacterium** (-rɪəm). a group of bacteria (phylum *Cyanobacteria*) containing a blue photosynthetic pigment and formerly regarded as algae. Former name: **blue-green algae.**

cyanocobalamin (,saɪənəʊkəʊ'bæləmɪn) *n* vitamin B_{12}, a complex crystalline compound of cobalt and cyanide, lack of which leads to pernicious anaemia. [C20: from CYANO- + COBAL(T) + (VIT)AMIN]

cyanogen (saɪ'ænədʒɪn) *n* an extremely poisonous colourless flammable gas. Formula: $(CN)_2$. [C19: from F *cyanogène;* see CYANO-, -GEN; so named because it is one of the constituents of Prussian blue]

cyanosis (,saɪə'nəʊsɪs) *n Pathol.* a bluish-purple discoloration of skin and mucous membranes usually resulting from a deficiency of oxygen in the blood.
▸**cyanotic** (,saɪə'nɒtɪk) *adj*

cyber- *combining form.* indicating computers: *cyberphobia.* [C20: back formation from CYBERNETICS]

cybercafé ('saɪbə,kæfɪ, -,kæfeɪ) *n* a café with computer equipment that gives public access to the Internet.

cybernate ('saɪbə,neɪt) *vb* **cybernates, cybernating, cybernated.** to control with a servomechanism or to be controlled by a servomechanism. [C20: from CYBER(NETICS) + -ATE[1]]
▸**,cyber'nation** *n*

cybernetics (,saɪbə'nɛtɪks) *n* (*functioning as sing*) the branch of science concerned with control systems and comparisons between man-made and biological systems. [C20: from Gk *kubernētēs* steersman, from *kubernan* to steer]
▸**,cyber'netic** *adj* ▸**,cyber'neticist** *n*

cyberpet ('saɪbə,pɛt) *n* an electronic toy that simulates the activities of a pet, requiring the owner to feed, discipline, and entertain it.

cyberphobia (,saɪbə'fəʊbɪə) *n* an irrational fear of computing.
▸**,cyber'phobic** *adj*

cyberpunk ('saɪbə,pʌŋk) *n* **1** a genre of science fiction that features rebellious computer hackers and is set in a society integrated by computer networks. **2** a writer of cyberpunk.

cyberspace ('saɪbə,speɪs) *n* all of the data stored in a large computer or network represented as a three-dimensional model through which a virtual-reality user can move.

cycad ('saɪkæd) *n* a tropical or subtropical plant, having an unbranched stem with fernlike leaves crowded at the top. [C19: from NL *Cycas* name of genus, from Gk *kukas,* scribe's error for *koïkas,* from *koïx* a kind of palm]
▸**,cyca'daceous** *adj*

cyclamate ('saɪklə,meɪt, 'sɪkləmeɪt) *n* any of certain compounds formerly used as food additives and sugar substitutes. [C20: *cycl(ohexyl-sulph)amate*]

cyclamen ('sɪkləmən, -,mɛn) *n* **1** any Old World plant of the genus *Cyclamen,* having white, pink, or red flowers, with reflexed petals. ◆ *adj* **2** of a dark reddish-purple colour. [C16: from Med. L, from L *cyclamīnos,* from Gk *kuklaminos,* prob. from *kuklos* circle, referring to the bulblike roots]

cycle ⓣ ('saɪkᵊl) *n* **1** a recurring period of time in which certain events or phenomena occur and reach completion. **2** a completed series of events that follows or is followed by another series of similar events occurring in the same sequence. **3** the time taken or needed for one such series. **4** a vast period of time; age; aeon. **5** a group of poems or prose narratives about a central figure or event: *the Arthurian cycle.* **6** short for **bicycle, motorcycle,** etc. **7** a recurrent series of events or processes in plants and animals: *a life cycle.* **8** one of a series of repeated changes in the magnitude of a periodically varying quantity, such as current or voltage. ◆ *vb* **cycles, cycling, cycled. 9** (*tr*) to process through a cycle or system. **10** (*intr*) to move in or pass through cycles. **11** to travel by or ride a bicycle or tricycle. [C14: from LL *cyclus,* from Gk *kuklos* cycle, circle, ring, wheel]

cyclic ('saɪklɪk, 'sɪklɪk) *or* **cyclical** *adj* **1** recurring or revolving in cycles. **2** (of an organic compound) containing a closed saturated or unsaturated ring of atoms. **3** *Bot.* **3a** arranged in whorls: *cyclic petals.* **3b** having parts arranged in this way: *cyclic flowers.*
▸**'cyclically** *adv*

cycling shorts *pl n* tight-fitting shorts reaching partway to the knee for cycling, sport, etc.

cyclist ('saɪklɪst) *or US* **cycler** *n* a person who rides or travels by bicycle, motorcycle, etc.

cyclo- *or before a vowel* **cycl-** *combining form.* **1** indicating a circle or ring: *cyclotron.* **2** denoting a cyclic compound: *cyclopropane.* [from Gk *kuklos* CYCLE]

cyclogiro ('saɪkləʊ,dʒaɪrəʊ) *n, pl* **cyclogiros.** *Aeronautics.* an aircraft lifted and propelled by pivoted blades rotating parallel to roughly horizontal transverse axes.

cyclohexanone (,saɪkləʊ'hɛksə,nəʊn) *n* a colourless liquid used as a solvent for cellulose lacquers. Formula: $C_6H_{10}O$.

cycloid ('saɪklɔɪd) *adj* **1** resembling a circle. ◆ *n* **2** *Geom.* the curve described by a point on the circumference of a circle as the circle rolls along a straight line.
▸**cy'cloidal** *adj*

cyclometer (saɪ'klɒmɪtə) *n* a device that records the number of revolutions made by a wheel and hence the distance travelled.

THESAURUS

cut-price *adj* **1, 2** = **cheap**, bargain, cheapo (*inf.*), cut-rate (*chiefly US*), reduced, sale

cutpurse *n* = **pickpocket**, mugger (*inf.*), robber, thief

cut-throat *n* **1** = **murderer**, assassin, bravo, butcher, executioner, heavy (*sl.*), hit man (*sl.*), homicide, killer, liquidator, slayer (*arch.*), thug ◆ *adj* **3** = **murderous**, barbarous, bloodthirsty, bloody, cruel, death-dealing, ferocious, homicidal, savage, thuggish, violent **4** = **competitive**, dog-eat-dog, fierce, relentless, ruthless, unprincipled

cutting *adj* **8** = **piercing**, biting, bitter, chilling, keen, numbing, penetrating, raw, sharp, stinging **9** = **hurtful**, acid, acrimonious, barbed, bitter, caustic, malicious, mordacious, pointed, sarcastic, sardonic, scathing, severe, trenchant, vitriolic, wounding
Antonyms *adj* ≠ **piercing:** balmy, pleasant, soothing ≠ **hurtful:** consoling, flattering, kind, mild

cut up *vb* **1** = **chop**, carve, dice, divide, mince, slice **2** = **slash**, injure, knife, lacerate, wound

cycle *n* **1, 4** = **era**, aeon, age, circle, period, phase, revolution, rotation, round (*of years*)

cyclone Ⓣ ('saɪkləʊn) *n* **1** another name for **depression** (sense 6). **2** a violent tropical storm; hurricane. ◆ *adj* **3** *Austral. & NZ trademark.* (of fencing) made of interlaced wire and metal. [C19: from Gk *kuklōn* a turning around, from *kuklos* wheel]
▸**cyclonic** (saɪ'klɒnɪk) *adj* ▸**cy'clonically** *adv*

Cyclopean (ˌsaɪkləʊ'piːən, saɪ'kləʊpɪən) *adj* **1** of, relating to, or resembling the Cyclops. **2** denoting or having the kind of masonry used in preclassical Greek architecture, characterized by large undressed blocks of stone.

cyclopedia *or* **cyclopaedia** (ˌsaɪkləʊ'piːdɪə) *n* a less common word for **encyclopedia.**

cyclopentadiene (ˌsaɪkləʊˌpɛntə'daɪiːn) *n* a colourless liquid unsaturated cyclic hydrocarbon obtained in the cracking of petroleum hydrocarbons and the distillation of coal tar: used in the manufacture of plastics and insecticides. Formula: C_5H_6.

cyclophosphamide (ˌsaɪkləʊ'fɒsfəˌmaɪd) *n* a cytotoxic drug used in the treatment of leukaemia and lymphoma. [C20: from CYCLO- + PHOSPH(ORUS) + AMIDE]

cyclopropane (ˌsaɪkləʊ'prəʊpeɪn) *n* a colourless gaseous hydrocarbon, used as an anaesthetic. Formula: C_3H_6.

Cyclops ('saɪklɒps) *n, pl* **Cyclopes** (saɪ'kləʊpiːz) *or* **Cyclopses.** *Classical myth.* one of a race of giants having a single eye in the middle of the forehead. [C15: from L *Cyclōps,* from Gk *Kuklōps,* lit.: round eye, from *kuklos* circle + *ōps* eye]

cyclorama (ˌsaɪkləʊ'rɑːmə) *n* **1** a large picture on the interior wall of a cylindrical room, designed to appear in natural perspective to a spectator. **2** *Theatre.* a curtain or wall curving along the back of a stage, usually painted to represent the sky. [C19: CYCLO- + Gk *horama* view, sight, on the model of *panorama*]
▸**cycloramic** (ˌsaɪkləʊ'ræmɪk) *adj*

cyclosporin-A (ˌsaɪkləʊ'spɔːrɪn-) *n* a drug extracted from a fungus and used in transplant surgery to suppress the body's immune mechanisms, and so prevent rejection of an organ.

cyclostome ('saɪkləˌstəʊm, 'sɪk-) *n* any primitive aquatic jawless vertebrate, such as the lamprey, having a round sucking mouth.
▸**cyclostomate** (saɪ'klɒstəmɪt, -ˌmeɪt) *or* **cyclostomatous** (ˌsaɪkləʊ'stɒmətəs, -'stəʊmə-, ˌsɪk-) *adj*

cyclostyle ('saɪkləˌstaɪl) *n* **1** a kind of pen with a small toothed wheel, used for cutting holes in a specially prepared stencil. **2** an office duplicator using such a stencil. ◆ *vb* **cyclostyles, cyclostyling, cyclostyled. 3** (*tr*) to print using such a stencil.
▸**'cycloˌstyled** *adj*

cyclothymia (ˌsaɪkləʊ'θaɪmɪə) *n Psychiatry.* a condition characterized by alternating periods of excitement and depression. [from CYCLO- + Gk *thumos,* cast of mind + -IA]
▸**ˌcyclo'thymic** *adj*

cyclotron ('saɪkləˌtrɒn) *n* a type of particle accelerator in which the particles spiral under the effect of a strong vertical magnetic field.

cyder ('saɪdə) *n* a variant spelling of **cider.**

cygnet ('sɪgnɪt) *n* a young swan. [C15 *sygnett,* from OF *cygne* swan, from L *cygnus,* from Gk *kuknos*]

cylinder ('sɪlɪndə) *n* **1** a solid consisting of two parallel planes bounded by identical closed curves, usually circles, that are interconnected at every point by a set of parallel lines, usually perpendicular to the planes. **2** a surface formed by a line moving round a closed plane curve at a fixed angle to it. **3** any object shaped like a cylinder. **4** the chamber in a reciprocating internal-combustion engine, pump, or compressor within which the piston moves. The cylinders are housed in the metal **cylinder block,** which is topped by the **cylinder head. 5** the rotating mechanism of a revolver, containing cartridge chambers. **6** *Printing.* any of the rotating drums on a printing press. **7** Also called: **cylinder seal.** an ancient cylindrical seal found in the Middle East and Balkans. [C16: from L *cylindrus,* from Gk *kulindros* a roller, from *kulindein* to roll]
▸**'cylinder-ˌlike** *adj*

cylindrical (sɪ'lɪndrɪk^{ə}l) *or* **cylindric** *adj* of, shaped like, or characteristic of a cylinder.
▸**cyˌlindri'cality** *n* ▸**cy'lindrically** *adv*

cymbal ('sɪmb^{ə}l) *n* a percussion instrument consisting of a thin circular piece of brass, which vibrates when clashed together with another cymbal or struck with a stick. [OE *cymbala,* from L *cymbalum,* from Gk *kumbalon,* from *kumbē* something hollow]
▸**'cymbalist** *n*

cyme (saɪm) *n* an inflorescence in which the first flower is the terminal bud of the main stem and subsequent flowers develop as terminal buds of lateral stems. [C18: from L *cȳma* cabbage sprout, from Gk *kuma* anything swollen]
▸**cymiferous** (saɪ'mɪfərəs) *adj* ▸**cymose** ('saɪməʊs, -məʊz, saɪ'məʊs) *adj*

Cymric *or* **Kymric** ('kɪmrɪk) *n* **1** the Welsh language. **2** the Brythonic group of Celtic languages. ◆ *adj* **3** of or relating to the Cymry, any of their languages, Wales, or the Welsh.

Cymry *or* **Kymry** ('kɪmrɪ) *n* **the.** (*functioning as pl*) **1** the Brythonic Celts, comprising the present-day Welsh, Cornish, and Bretons. **2** the Welsh people. [Welsh: the Welsh]

cynic Ⓣ ('sɪnɪk) *n* **1** a person who believes the worst about people or the outcome of events. ◆ *adj* **2** a less common word for **cynical.** [C16: via L from Gk *Kunikos,* from *kuōn* dog]

Cynic ('sɪnɪk) *n* a member of an ancient Greek sect that scorned worldly things.

cynical Ⓣ ('sɪnɪk^{ə}l) *adj* **1** believing the worst of others, esp. that all acts are selfish. **2** sarcastic; mocking. **3** showing contempt for accepted standards, esp. of honesty or morality.
▸**'cynically** *adv* ▸**'cynicalness** *n*

cynicism Ⓣ ('sɪnɪˌsɪzəm) *n* **1** the attitude or beliefs of a cynic. **2** a cynical action, idea, etc.

Cynicism ('sɪnɪˌsɪzəm) *n* the doctrines of the Cynics.

cynosure ('sɪnəˌzjʊə, -ʃʊə) *n* **1** a person or thing that attracts notice. **2** something that serves as a guide. [C16: from L *Cynosūra* the constellation of Ursa Minor, from Gk *Kunosoura,* from *kuōn* dog + *oura* tail]

cypher ('saɪfə) *n, vb* a variant spelling of **cipher.**

cypress ('saɪprəs) *n* **1** any coniferous tree of a N temperate genus having dark green scalelike leaves and rounded cones. **2** any of several similar and related trees. **3** the wood of any of these trees. **4** cypress branches used as a symbol of mourning. [OE *cypresse,* from L *cyparissus,* from Gk *kuparissos;* rel. to L *cupressus*]

cypress pine *n* any coniferous tree of an Australian genus yielding valuable timber.

cyprinid (sɪ'praɪnɪd, 'sɪprɪnɪd) *n* **1** any teleost fish of the mainly freshwater family Cyprinidae, typically having toothless jaws and including the carp, tench, and dace. ◆ *adj* **2** of, relating to, or belonging to the Cyprinidae. **3** resembling a carp; cyprinoid. [C19: from NL *Cyprīnidae,* from L *cyprīnus* carp, from Gk *kuprinos*]

cyprinoid ('sɪprɪˌnɔɪd, sɪ'praɪnɔɪd) *adj* **1** of or relating to the Cyprinoidea, a large suborder of teleost fishes including the cyprinids, electric eels, and loaches. **2** of, relating to, or resembling the carp. ◆ *n* **3** any fish belonging to the Cyprinoidea. [C19: from L *cyprīnus* carp]

Cypriot ('sɪprɪət) *or* **Cypriote** ('sɪprɪˌəʊt) *n* **1** a native or inhabitant of Cyprus, an island in the E Mediterranean. **2** the dialect of Greek spoken in Cyprus. ◆ *adj* **3** denoting or relating to Cyprus, its inhabitants, or dialects.

cypripedium (ˌsɪprɪ'piːdɪəm) *n* any orchid of a genus having large flowers with an inflated pouchlike lip. See also **lady's-slipper.** [C18: from NL, from L *Cypria* the Cyprian, that is, Venus + *pēs* foot (that is, Venus' slipper)]

Cyrenaic (ˌsaɪrə'neɪɪk, ˌsɪrə-) *adj* **1** of or relating to the ancient Greek city of Cyrene in N Africa. **2** of or relating to the philosophical school founded by Aristippus in Cyrene that held pleasure to be the highest good. ◆ *n* **3** a follower of the Cyrenaica school of philosophy.

Cyrillic (sɪ'rɪlɪk) *adj* **1** denoting or relating to the alphabet said to have been devised by Saint Cyril, for Slavonic languages: now used primarily for Russian and Bulgarian. ◆ *n* **2** this alphabet.

cyst Ⓣ (sɪst) *n* **1** *Pathol.* any abnormal membranous sac or blister-like pouch containing fluid or semisolid material. **2** *Anat.* any normal sac in the body. **3** a protective membrane enclosing a cell, larva, or organism. [C18: from NL *cystis,* from Gk *kustis* pouch, bag, bladder]

-cyst *n combining form.* indicating a bladder or sac: *otocyst.* [from Gk *kustis* bladder]

cystectomy (sɪ'stɛktəmɪ) *n, pl* **cystectomies. 1** surgical removal of the gall bladder or part of the urinary bladder. **2** surgical removal of a cyst.

cystic ('sɪstɪk) *adj* **1** of, relating to, or resembling a cyst. **2** having or enclosed within a cyst; encysted. **3** relating to the gall bladder or urinary bladder.

cysticercus (ˌsɪstɪ'sɜːkəs) *n, pl* **cysticerci** (-saɪ). an encysted larval form of many tapeworms, consisting of a head inverted in a fluid-filled bladder. [C19: from NL, from Gk *kustis* pouch, bladder + *kerkos* tail]

cystic fibrosis *n* an inheritable disease of the exocrine glands, controlled by a recessive gene: affected children inherit defective alleles from both parents. It is characterized by chronic infection of the respiratory tract and by pancreatic insufficiency.

cystitis (sɪ'staɪtɪs) *n* inflammation of the urinary bladder.

cysto- *or before a vowel* **cyst-** *combining form.* indicating a cyst or bladder: *cystoscope.*

cystoid ('sɪstɔɪd) *adj* **1** resembling a cyst or bladder. ◆ *n* **2** a tissue mass that resembles a cyst but lacks an outer membrane.

cystoscope ('sɪstəˌskəʊp) *n* a slender tubular medical instrument for examining the interior of the urethra and urinary bladder.
▸**cystoscopic** (ˌsɪstə'skɒpɪk) *adj* ▸**cystoscopy** (sɪs'tɒskəpɪ) *n*

-cyte *n combining form.* indicating a cell. [from NL *-cyta,* from Gk *kutos* vessel]

cyto- *combining form.* indicating a cell: *cytoplasm.* [from Gk *kutos* vessel]

cytogenetics (ˌsaɪtəʊdʒɪ'nɛtɪks) *n* (*functioning as sing*) the branch of ge-

THESAURUS

cyclone *n* **2** = **typhoon,** hurricane, storm, tempest, tornado, twister (*US. inf.*), whirlwind

cynic *n* **1** = **sceptic,** doubter, misanthrope, misanthropist, pessimist, scoffer

cynical *adj* **1-3** = **sceptical,** contemptuous, derisive, distrustful, ironic, misanthropic, misanthropical, mocking, mordacious, pessimistic, sarcastic, sardonic, scoffing, scornful, sneering, unbelieving
Antonyms *adj* credulous, green, gullible, hopeful, optimistic, trustful, trusting, unsceptical, unsuspecting

cynicism *n* **1** = **scepticism,** disbelief, doubt, misanthropy, pessimism, sarcasm, sardonicism

cyst *n* **1-3** = **sac,** bleb, blister, growth, vesicle, wen

netics that correlates the structure of chromosomes with heredity and variation.
▸ **ˌcytoge'netic** *adj*

cytokinin (ˌsaɪtəʊ'kaɪnɪn) *n* any of a group of plant hormones that promote cell division and retard ageing. Also called: **kinin.**

cytology (saɪ'tɒlədʒɪ) *n* **1** the study of plant and animal cells. **2** the detailed structure of a tissue as revealed by microscopic examination.
▸ **cytological** (ˌsaɪtə'lɒdʒɪkᵊl) *adj* ▸ **ˌcyto'logically** *adv* ▸ **cy'tologist** *n*

cytomegalovirus (ˌsaɪtəʊˌmɛgələʊ'vaɪrəs) *n* a virus that may cause serious disease in patients whose immune systems are compromised and the birth of handicapped children to pregnant women infected with it. Abbrev.: **CMV.**

cytoplasm ('saɪtəʊˌplæzəm) *n* the protoplasm of a cell excluding the nucleus.
▸ **ˌcyto'plasmic** *adj*

cytosine ('saɪtəsɪn) *n* a white crystalline base occurring in nucleic acids. [C19: from CYTO- + -OSE² + -INE²]

cytotoxic (ˌsaɪtəʊ'tɒksɪk) *adj* destructive to cells, esp. to cancer cells: *cytotoxic drugs.*
▸ **cytotoxicity** (ˌsaɪtəʊtɒk'sɪsɪtɪ) *n*

cytotoxin (ˌsaɪtəʊ'tɒksɪn) *n* any substance that is poisonous to living cells.

czar (zɑː) *n* a variant spelling (esp. US) of **tsar.**
▸ **'czardom** *n* ▸ **'Czarevitch, cza'revna, cza'rina, 'czarism, 'czarist:** see **ts-** spellings.

czardas ('tʃɑːdæʃ) *n* **1** a Hungarian national dance of alternating slow and fast sections. **2** music for this dance. [from Hungarian *csárdás*]

Czech (tʃɛk) *adj* **1a** of, relating to, or characteristic of the Czech Republic, its people, or their language. **1b** of, relating to, or characteristic of Bohemia and Moravia, their people, or their language. **1c** (loosely) of, relating to, or characteristic of the former Czechoslovakia or its people. ◆ *n* **2** the official languages of the Czech Republic, belonging to the West Slavonic branch of the Indo-European family. Czech is closely related to Slovak; they are mutually intelligible. **3a** a native or inhabitant of the Czech Republic. **3b** a native or inhabitant of Bohemia or Moravia. **3c** (loosely) a native, inhabitant, or citizen of the former Czechoslovakia. [C19: from Polish, from Czech *Čech*]

Czechoslovak (ˌtʃɛkəʊ'sləʊvæk) *or* **Czechoslovakian** (ˌtʃɛkəʊsləʊ'vækɪən) *adj* **1** of or relating to the former Czechoslovakia, its peoples, or languages. ◆ *n* **2** (loosely) either of the two languages of the former Czechoslovakia: Czech or Slovak.

Dd

d *or* **D** (diː) *n, pl* **d's, D's,** *or* **Ds. 1** the fourth letter of the modern English alphabet. **2** a speech sound represented by this letter.

d *symbol for Physics.* density.

D *symbol for:* **1** *Music.* **1a** the second note of the scale of C major. **1b** the major or minor key having this note as its tonic. **2** *Chem.* deuterium. **3a** a semiskilled or unskilled manual worker, or a trainee or apprentice to a skilled worker. **3b** (*as modifier*): *D worker.* ◆ See also **occupation groupings.** ◆ **4.** *the Roman numeral for* 500.

2,4-D *n* a synthetic auxin widely used as a weedkiller; 2,4-dichlorophenoxyacetic acid.

d. *abbrev. for:* **1** date. **2** daughter. **3** degree. **4** delete. **5** *Brit. currency before decimalization.* penny *or* pennies. [L *denarius* or *denarii*] **6** depart(s). **7** diameter. **8** died. **9** dose.

D. *abbrev. for:* **1** *US.* Democrat(ic). **2** Department. **3** Deus. [L: God] **4** *Optics.* dioptre. **5** Director. **6** Dominus. [L: Lord] **7** Dutch.

'd *contraction for* would *or* had: *I'd; you'd.*

DA *abbrev. for:* **1** (in the US) District Attorney. **2** Diploma of Art. **3** duck's arse (hairstyle). **4** drug addict.

dab[1] Ⓣ (dæb) *vb* **dabs, dabbing, dabbed. 1** to touch or pat lightly and quickly. **2** (*tr*) to daub with short tapping strokes: *to dab the wall with paint.* **3** (*tr*) to apply (paint, cream, etc.) with short tapping strokes. ◆ *n* **4** a small amount, esp. of something soft or moist. **5** a light stroke or tap, as with the hand. **6** (*often pl*) *Chiefly Brit.* a slang word for **fingerprint.** [C14: imit.]
▸**'dabber** *n*

dab[2] (dæb) *n* **1** a small common European flatfish covered with rough toothed scales. **2** any of various other small flatfish. [C15: from Anglo-F *dabbe,* from ?]

dabble Ⓣ ('dæbᵊl) *vb* **dabbles, dabbling, dabbled. 1** to dip, move, or splash (the fingers, feet, etc.) in a liquid. **2** (*intr;* usually foll. by *in, with,* or *at*) to deal (with) or work (at) frivolously or superficially. **3** (*tr*) to splash or smear. [C16: prob. from Du. *dabbelen*]
▸**'dabbler** *n*

dabchick ('dæbˌtʃɪk) *n* any of several small grebes. [C16: prob. from OE *dop* to dive + CHICK]

dab hand Ⓣ *n Brit. inf.* a person who is particularly skilled at something: *a dab hand at chess.* [?from DAB[1]]

da capo (dɑː 'kɑːpəʊ) *adj, adv Music.* to be repeated from the beginning. [C18: from It., lit.: from the head]

dace (deɪs) *n, pl* **dace** *or* **daces. 1** a European freshwater fish of the carp family. **2** any of various similar fishes. [C15: from OF *dars* DART]

dacha *or* **datcha** ('dætʃə) *n* a country house or cottage in Russia. [from Russian: a giving, gift]

dachshund ('dæksˌhʊnd, 'dæʃənd) *n* a long-bodied short-legged breed of dog. [C19: from G, from *Dachs* badger + *Hund* dog]

dacoit (də'kɔɪt) *n* (in India and Myanmar) a member of a gang of armed robbers. [C19: from Hindi *dakait,* from *dākā* robbery]

Dacron ('deɪkrɒn, 'dæk-) *n* the US name (trademark) for **Terylene.**

dactyl ('dæktɪl) *n Prosody.* a metrical foot of three syllables, one long followed by two short (–⏑⏑) [C14: via L from Gk *daktulos* finger, comparing the finger's three joints to the three syllables]

dactylic (dæk'tɪlɪk) *adj* **1** of, relating to, or having a dactyl: *dactylic verse.* ◆ *n* **2** a variant of **dactyl.**
▸**dac'tylically** *adv*

dad (dæd) *n* an informal word for **father.** [C16: childish word]

Dada ('dɑːdɑː) *or* **Dadaism** ('dɑːdɑːˌɪzəm) *n* a nihilistic artistic movement of the early 20th century, founded on principles of irrationality, incongruity, and irreverence towards accepted aesthetic criteria. [C20: from F, from children's word for hobbyhorse]
▸**'Dadaist** *n, adj* ▸**ˌDada'istic** *adj*

daddy ('dædɪ) *n, pl* **daddies. 1** an informal word for **father. 2 the daddy.** *Sl., chiefly US, Canad., & Austral.* the supreme or finest example.

daddy-longlegs *n* **1** *Brit., Austral., & NZ.* an informal name for **crane fly. 2** *US, Canad., Austral., & NZ.* an informal name for **harvestman** (sense 2).

dado ('deɪdəʊ) *n, pl* **dadoes** *or* **dados. 1** the lower part of an interior wall that is decorated differently from the upper part. **2** *Archit.* the part of a pedestal between the base and the cornice. ◆ *vb* **3** (*tr*) to provide with a dado. [C17: from It.: die, die-shaped pedestal]

daemon ('diːmən) *or* **daimon** *n* **1** a demigod. **2** the guardian spirit of a place or person. **3** a variant spelling of **demon** (sense 3).
▸**daemonic** (diː'mɒnɪk) *adj*

daff (dæf) *n Inf.* short for **daffodil.**

daffodil ('dæfədɪl) *n* **1** Also called: **Lent lily.** a widely cultivated Eurasian plant, *Narcissus pseudonarcissus,* having spring-blooming yellow nodding flowers. **2** any other plant of the genus *Narcissus.* **3a** a brilliant yellow colour. **3b** (*as adj*): *daffodil paint.* **4** a daffodil as a national emblem of Wales. [C14: from Med. L *affodillus,* var. of L *asphodelus* ASPHODEL]

daffy ('dæfɪ) *adj* **daffier, daffiest.** *Inf.* another word for **daft** (senses 1, 2). [C19: from obs. *daff* fool]

daft Ⓣ (dɑːft) *adj Chiefly Brit.* **1** *Inf.* foolish, simple, or stupid. **2** a slang word for **insane. 3** (*postpositive;* foll. by *about*) *Inf.* extremely fond (of). **4** *Sl.* frivolous; giddy. [OE *gedæfte* gentle, foolish]
▸**'daftness** *n*

daftie ('dɑːftɪ) *n Inf.* a daft person.

dag[1] (dæg) *n* **1** short for **daglock.** ◆ *vb* **dags, dagging, dagged. 2** to cut the daglock away from (a sheep). [C18: from ?]
▸**'dagger** *n*

dag[2] (dæg) *n Austral. & NZ inf.* **1** a character; eccentric. **2** a person who is untidily dressed. **3** a person with a good sense of humour. [back formation from DAGGY]

dagga ('daxə, 'dɑːgə) *n S. African inf.* a local name for marijuana. [C19: from Afrik., from Khoikhoi *dagab*]

dagger Ⓣ ('dægə) *n* **1** a short stabbing weapon with a pointed blade. **2** Also called: **obelisk.** a character (†) used in printing to indicate a cross reference. **3 at daggers drawn.** in a state of open hostility. **4 look daggers.** to glare with hostility; scowl. [C14: from ?]

daggy ('dægɪ) *adj* **daggier, daggiest.** *Austral. & NZ inf.* untidy; dishevelled. [from DAG[1]]

daglock ('dægˌlɒk) *n* a dung-caked lock of wool around the hindquarters of a sheep. [C17: see DAG[1], LOCK[2]]

dago ('deɪgəʊ) *n, pl* **dagos** *or* **dagoes.** *Derog.* a foreigner, esp. a Spaniard or Portuguese. [C19: from *Diego,* a common Sp. name]

daguerreotype (də'gerəʊˌtaɪp) *n* **1** one of the earliest photographic processes, in which the image was produced on iodine-sensitized silver and developed in mercury vapour. **2** a photograph formed by this process. [C19: after L. *Daguerre* (1789–1851), F inventor]
▸**da'guerreoˌtypy** *n*

dahlia ('deɪljə) *n* **1** any herbaceous perennial plant of the Mexican genus *Dahlia,* having showy flowers and tuberous roots. **2** the flower or root of any of these plants. [C19: after Anders *Dahl,* 18th-cent. Swedish botanist]

Dáil Éireann ('dɑːl 'eːrɪn) *or* **Dáil** *n* (in the Republic of Ireland) the lower chamber of parliament. [from Irish *dáil* assembly + *Éireann* of Eire]

daily Ⓣ ('deɪlɪ) *adj* **1** of or occurring every day or every weekday. ◆ *n, pl* **dailies. 2** a daily newspaper. **3** *Brit.* a charwoman. ◆ *adv* **4** every day. **5** constantly; often. [OE *dæglīc*]

daimon ('daɪmɒn) *n* a variant spelling of **daemon** or **demon** (sense 3).
▸**dai'monic** *adj*

daimyo bond ('daɪmjəʊ) *n* a bearer bond issued in Japan and the eurobond market by the World Bank. [from Japanese, from Ancient Chinese]

dainty Ⓣ ('deɪntɪ) *adj* **daintier, daintiest. 1** delicate or elegant. **2** choice; delicious: *a dainty morsel.* **3** excessively genteel; fastidious. ◆ *n, pl* **dainties. 4** a choice piece of food; delicacy. [C13: from OF *deintié,* from L *dignitās* DIGNITY]
▸**'daintily** *adv*

daiquiri ('daɪkɪrɪ, 'dæk-) *n, pl* **daiquiris.** an iced drink containing rum, lime juice, and sugar. [C20: after *Daiquiri,* town in Cuba]

THESAURUS

dab[1] *vb* **1** = **pat**, blot, daub, stipple, swab, tap, touch, wipe ◆ *n* **4** = **spot**, bit, dollop (*inf.*), drop, fleck, pat, smidgen *or* smidgin (*inf., chiefly US & Canad.*), smudge, speck **5** = **pat**, flick, peck, smudge, stroke, tap, touch

dabble *vb* **1** = **splash**, dip, guddle, moisten, paddle, spatter, sprinkle, wet **2** = **play at**, dally, dip into, potter, tinker, trifle (with)

dabbler *n* **2** = **amateur**, dilettante, potterer, tinkerer, trifler

dab hand *n Brit. inf.* = **expert**, ace, adept, buff (*inf.*), dabster (*dialect*), hotshot (*inf.*), maven (*US*), past master, whizz (*inf.*), wizard

daft *adj inf., chiefly Brit.* **1** = **foolish**, absurd, asinine, crackpot (*inf.*), crazy, doolally (*sl.*), dopey, dumb-ass (*sl.*), giddy, goofy (*inf.*), idiotic, inane, loopy (*inf.*), off one's head (*inf.*), off one's trolley (*sl.*), out to lunch (*inf.*), scatty (*Brit. inf.*), silly, simple, stupid, up the pole (*inf.*), witless **2** = **crazy**, barking (*sl.*), barking mad (*sl.*), crackers (*Brit. sl.*), demented, deranged, insane, lunatic, mental (*sl.*), not right in the head, not the full shilling (*inf.*), nuts (*sl.*), nutty (*sl.*), round the bend (*Brit. sl.*), touched, unhinged **3 daft about** = **enthusiastic**, besotted, crazy (*inf.*), doting, dotty (*sl., chiefly Brit.*), infatuated by, mad, nuts (*sl.*), nutty (*inf.*), potty (*Brit. inf.*), sweet on

daftness *n* **1, 2** *inf., chiefly Brit.* = **foolishness**, absurdity, asininity, brainlessness, craziness, dottiness (*sl., chiefly Brit.*), fatuity, fatuousness, folly, foolhardiness, idiocy, inanity, insanity, lunacy, madness, nonsense, scattiness (*Brit. inf.*), senselessness, silliness, stupidity, tomfoolery, witlessness
Antonyms *n* common sense, intelligence, judgment, reason, sanity, sense, wisdom

dagger *n* **1** = **knife**, bayonet, dirk, poniard, skean, stiletto **3 at daggers drawn** = **on bad terms**, at enmity, at loggerheads, at odds, at war, up in arms **4 look daggers** = **glare**, frown, glower, look black, lour *or* lower, scowl

daily *adj* **1** = **everyday**, circadian, diurnal, quotidian ◆ *adv* **3, 4** = **every day**, constantly, day after day, day by day, often, once a day, per diem, regularly

dainty *adj* **1** = **delicate**, charming, elegant, exquisite, fine, graceful, neat, petite, pretty **2** = **delectable**, choice, delicious, palatable, sa-

dairy ('dɛərɪ) *n, pl* **dairies. 1** a company that supplies milk and milk products. **2** a room or building where milk and cream are stored or made into butter and cheese. **3a** (*modifier*) of, relating to, or containing milk and milk products. **3b** (*in combination*): *a dairymaid.* **4a** a general shop, selling provisions, esp. milk and milk products. **4b** *NZ.* a shop that remains open outside normal trading hours. [C13 *daierie,* from OE *dǣge* servant girl, one who kneads bread]

dairying ('dɛərɪɪŋ) *n* the business of producing, processing, and selling dairy products.

dairyman ('dɛərɪmən) *n, pl* **dairymen.** a man who works in a dairy.

dais Ⓣ ('deɪɪs, deɪs) *n* a raised platform, usually at one end of a hall, used by speakers, etc. [C13: from OF *deis,* from L *discus* DISCUS]

daisy ('deɪzɪ) *n, pl* **daisies. 1** a small low-growing European plant having flower heads with a yellow centre and pinkish-white outer rays. **2** any of various other composite plants having conspicuous ray flowers. **3** *Sl.* an excellent person or thing. **4 pushing up the daisies.** dead and buried. [OE *dægesēge* day's eye]
▸'**daisied** *adj*

daisy chain *n* a garland made, esp. by children, by threading daisies together.

daisycutter ('deɪzɪˌkʌtə) *n Cricket.* a ball bowled so that it rolls along the ground.

daisywheel ('deɪzɪˌwiːl) *n Computing.* a component of a computer printer shaped like a wheel with many spokes that prints using a disk with characters around the circumference. Also called: **printwheel.**

daks (dæks) *pl n Austral. inf.* trousers. [C20: from trade name *Daks*]

dal (dɑːl) *n* **1** split grain, a common foodstuff in India; pulse. **2** a variant spelling of **dhal.**

Dalai Lama ('dælaɪ 'lɑːmə) *n* **1** (until 1959) the chief lama and ruler of Tibet. **2** the 14th holder of this office (1940), who fled to India (1959). [from Mongolian *dalai* ocean; see LAMA]

dale Ⓣ (deɪl) *n* an open valley. [OE *dæl*]

Dalek ('dɑːlɛk) *n* a fictional robot-like creation that is aggressive, mobile, and produces rasping staccato speech. [C20: from a children's television series, *Dr Who*]

dalesman ('deɪlzmən) *n, pl* **dalesmen.** a person living in a dale, esp. in the dales of N England.

dalles ('dæləs, dælz) *pl n Canad.* a stretch of river between high rock walls, with rapids and dangerous currents. [from Canad. F.: sink; see DALE]

dalliance Ⓣ ('dælɪəns) *n* waste of time in frivolous action or in dawdling.

dally Ⓣ ('dælɪ) *vb* **dallies, dallying, dallied.** (*intr*) **1** to waste time idly; dawdle. **2** (usually foll. by *with*) to deal frivolously; trifle: *to dally with someone's affections.* [C14: from Anglo-F *dalier* to gossip, from ?]

Dalmatian (dæl'meɪʃən) *n* **1** a large breed of dog having a short smooth white coat with black or brown spots. **2** a native or inhabitant of Dalmatia, a region of W Croatia. ◆ *adj* **3** of Dalmatia or its inhabitants.

dalmatic (dæl'mætɪk) *n* a wide-sleeved tunic-like vestment open at the sides, worn by deacons and bishops, and by a king at his coronation. [C15: from LL *dalmatica* (*vestis*) Dalmatian (robe) (orig. made of Dalmatian wool)]

dal segno ('dæl 'sɛnjəʊ) *adj, adv Music.* to be repeated from the point marked with a sign to the word *fine.* [It., lit.: from the sign]

dalton ('dɔːltən) *n* another name for **atomic mass unit.** [C20: after J. *Dalton* (1766–1844), E scientist]

daltonism ('dɔːltəˌnɪzəm) *n* colour blindness, esp. the confusion of red and green. [C19: from F *daltonisme,* after J. *Dalton*]

Dalton's atomic theory *n Chem.* the theory that matter consists of indivisible particles called atoms and that atoms of a given element are all identical and can neither be created nor destroyed. [C19: after J. *Dalton*]

dam[1] Ⓣ (dæm) *n* **1** a barrier of concrete, earth, etc., built across a river to create a body of water. **2** a reservoir of water created by such a barrier. **3** something that resembles or functions as a dam. ◆ *vb* **dams, damming, dammed. 4** (*tr;* often foll. by *up*) to restrict by a dam. [C12: prob. from MLow G]

dam[2] (dæm) *n* the female parent of an animal, esp. of domestic livestock. [C13: var. of DAME]

damage Ⓣ ('dæmɪdʒ) *n* **1** injury or harm impairing the function or condition of a person or thing. **2** loss of something desirable. **3** *Inf.* cost; expense. ◆ *vb* **damages, damaging, damaged. 4** (*tr*) to cause damage to. **5** (*intr*) to suffer damage. [C14: from OF, from L *damnum* injury, loss]
▸'**damaging** *adj*

damages Ⓣ ('dæmɪdʒɪz) *pl n Law.* money to be paid as compensation for injury, loss, etc.

damascene ('dæməˌsiːn) *vb* **damascenes, damascening, damascened. 1** (*tr*) to ornament (metal, esp. steel) by etching or by inlaying other metals, usually gold or silver. ◆ *n* **2** a design or article produced by this process. ◆ *adj* **3** of or relating to this process. [C14: from L *damascēnus* of Damascus]

Damascene ('dæməˌsiːn) *adj* **1** of Damascus, the capital of Syria. ◆ *n* **2** a native or inhabitant of Damascus.

Damascus steel (də'mɑːskəs, -'mæs-) *or* **damask steel** *n History.* a hard flexible steel with wavy markings, used for sword blades.

damask ('dæməsk) *n* **1a** a reversible fabric, usually silk or linen, with a pattern woven into it. It is used for table linen, curtains, etc. **1b** table linen made from this. **1c** (*as modifier*): *a damask tablecloth.* **2** short for **Damascus steel. 3** the wavy markings on such steel. **4a** the greyish-pink colour of the damask rose. **4b** (*as adj*): *damask wallpaper.* ◆ *vb* **5** (*tr*) another word for **damascene.** [C14: from Med. L *damascus,* from Damascus, where fabric orig. made]

damask rose *n* a rose with fragrant flowers, which are used to make the perfume attar. [C16: from Med. L *rosa damascēna* rose of Damascus]

dame Ⓣ (deɪm) *n* **1** (formerly) a woman of rank or dignity; lady. **2** *Arch., chiefly Brit.* an elderly woman. **3** *Sl., chiefly US & Canad.* a woman. **4** *Brit.* the role of a comic old woman in a pantomime, usually played by a man. [C13: from OF, from L *domina* lady, mistress of household]

Dame (deɪm) *n* (in Britain) **1** the title of a woman who has been awarded the Order of the British Empire or any of certain other orders of chivalry. **2** the title of the wife of a knight or baronet.

dame school *n* (formerly) a small school, offering basic education, usually run by an elderly woman in her own home.

damn Ⓣ (dæm) *interj* **1** *Sl.* an exclamation of annoyance. **2** *Inf.* an exclamation of surprise or pleasure. ◆ *adj* **3** (*prenominal*) *Sl.* deserving damnation. ◆ *adv, adj* (*prenominal*) **4** *Sl.* (intensifier): *a damn good pianist.* ◆ *adv* **5 damn all.** *Sl.* absolutely nothing. ◆ *vb* (*mainly tr*) **6** to condemn as bad, worthless, etc. **7** to curse. **8** to condemn to eternal damnation. **9** (*often passive*) to doom to ruin. **10** (*also intr*) to prove (someone) guilty: *damning evidence.* **11 damn with faint praise.** to praise so unenthusiastically that the effect is condemnation. ◆ *n* **12** *Sl.* something of negligible value (esp. in **not worth a damn**). **13 not give a damn.** *Inf.* not care. [C13: from OF *dampner,* from L *damnāre,* from *damnum* loss, injury]

damnable Ⓣ ('dæmnəbᵊl) *adj* **1** execrable; detestable. **2** liable to or deserving damnation.
▸'**damnableness** *or* ˌ**damna'bility** *n*

damnably Ⓣ ('dæmnəblɪ) *adv* **1** in a detestable manner. **2** (intensifier): *it was damnably unfair.*

damnation Ⓣ (dæm'neɪʃən) *n* **1** the act of damning or state of being damned. ◆ *interj* **2** an exclamation of anger, disappointment, etc.

THESAURUS

voury, tasty, tender, toothsome **3** = **particular**, choosy, fastidious, finical, finicky, fussy, mincing, nice, picky (*inf.*), refined, scrupulous ◆ *n* **4** = **delicacy**, *bonne bouche,* fancy, sweetmeat, titbit
Antonyms *adj* ≠ **delicate:** awkward, clumsy, coarse, gauche, inelegant, maladroit, uncouth, ungainly

dais *n* = **platform**, estrade, podium, rostrum, stage

dale *n* = **valley**, bottom, coomb, dell, dingle, glen, strath (*Scot.*), vale

dalliance *n* = **dawdling**, dabbling, delay, dilly-dallying (*inf.*), frittering, frivolling (*inf.*), idling, loafing, loitering, playing, pottering, procrastination, toying, trifling

dally *vb* **1** *Old-fashioned* = **waste time**, dawdle, delay, dilly-dally (*inf.*), drag one's feet *or* heels, fool (about *or* around), fritter away, hang about, linger, loiter, procrastinate, tarry, while away **2 dally with** = **flirt**, caress, fondle, fool (about *or* around), frivol (*inf.*), lead on, play, play fast and loose (*inf.*), tamper, tease, toy, trifle
Antonyms *vb* ≠ **waste time:** hasten, hurry (up), make haste, push forward *or* on, run, step on it (*inf.*)

dam[1] *n* **1** = **barrier**, barrage, embankment, hindrance, obstruction, wall ◆ *vb* **4** = **block up**, barricade, block, check, choke, confine, hold back, hold in, obstruct, restrict

damage *n* **1** = **harm**, destruction, detriment, devastation, hurt, impairment, injury, loss, mischief, mutilation, suffering **3** *inf.* = **cost**, bill, charge, expense, total ◆ *vb* **4** = **harm**, deface, hurt, impair, incapacitate, injure, mar, mutilate, play (merry) hell with (*inf.*), ruin, spoil, tamper with, undo, weaken, wreck
Antonyms *vb* ≠ **harm:** better, fix, improve, mend, repair ◆ *n* ≠ **harm:** gain, improvement, reparation

damages *pl n Law* = **compensation**, fine, indemnity, reimbursement, reparation, satisfaction

damaging *adj* **4** = **harmful**, deleterious, detrimental, disadvantageous, hurtful, injurious, prejudicial, ruinous
Antonyms *adj* advantageous, favourable, healthful, helpful, profitable, salutary, useful, valuable, wholesome

dame *n* **1** = **noblewoman**, baroness, dowager, *grande dame,* lady, matron (*arch.*), peeress

damn *vb* **6** = **criticize**, blast, castigate, censure, condemn, denounce, denunciate, excoriate, inveigh against, lambast(e), pan (*inf.*), put down, slam (*sl.*), slate (*inf.*), tear into (*inf.*) **7** = **curse**, abuse, anathematize, blaspheme, execrate, imprecate, revile, swear **8** = **sentence**, condemn, doom ◆ *n* **13 not give a damn** *inf.* = **not care**, be indifferent, not care a brass farthing, not care a jot, not care a whit, not give a hoot, not give a tinker's curse *or* damn (*sl.*), not give two hoots, not mind
Antonyms *vb* ≠ **criticize:** acclaim, admire, applaud, approve, cheer, compliment, congratulate, extol, honour, laud, praise, take one's hat off to ≠ **curse:** adore, bless, exalt, glorify, magnify (*arch.*), pay homage to

damnable *adj* **1** = **detestable**, abominable, accursed, atrocious, culpable, cursed, despicable, execrable, hateful, horrible, offensive, wicked
Antonyms *adj* admirable, commendable, creditable, excellent, exemplary, fine, honourable, laudable, meritorious, praiseworthy, worthy

damnably *adv* **1** = **detestably**, abominably, accursedly, atrociously, despicably, disgracefully, execrably, hatefully, horribly, offensively, reprehensibly, wickedly
Antonyms *adv* admirably, commendably, creditably, excellently, honourably, laudably, worthily

damnation *n* **1** *Theology* = **condemnation**, anathema, ban, consigning to perdition,

damnatory (ˈdæmnətərɪ) *adj* threatening or occasioning condemnation.

damned ❶ (dæmd) *adj* **1a** condemned to hell. **1b** (*as collective n*; preceded by *the*): *the damned*. ◆ *adv, adj Sl.* **2** (intensifier): *a damned good try*. **3** used to indicate amazement, disavowal, or refusal (as in **damned if I care**).

damnedest ❶ (ˈdæmdɪst) *n Inf.* utmost; best (esp. in the phrases **do** or **try one's damnedest**).

damnify (ˈdæmnɪˌfaɪ) *vb* **damnifies, damnifying, damnified.** (*tr*) *Law.* to cause loss or damage to (a person); injure. [C16: from OF *damnifier*, ult. from L *damnum* harm, + *facere* to make]
▸ˌ**damnifiˈcation** *n*

damoiselle, damosel, *or* **damozel** (ˌdæməˈzɛl) *n* archaic variants of **damsel.**

damp ❶ (dæmp) *adj* **1** slightly wet. ◆ *n* **2** slight wetness; moisture. **3** rank air or poisonous gas, esp. in a mine. **4** a discouragement; damper. ◆ *vb* (*tr*) **5** to make slightly wet. **6** (often foll. by *down*) to stifle or deaden: *to damp one's ardour*. **7** (often foll. by *down*) to reduce the flow of air to (a fire) to make it burn more slowly. **8** *Physics.* to reduce the amplitude of (an oscillation or wave). **9** *Music.* to muffle (the sound of an instrument). [C14: from MLow G *damp* steam]
▸ˈ**dampness** *n*

dampcourse (ˈdæmpˌkɔːs) *n* a layer of impervious material in a wall, to stop moisture rising. Also called: **damp-proof course.**

dampen ❶ (ˈdæmpən) *vb* **1** to make or become damp. **2** (*tr*) to stifle; deaden.
▸ˈ**dampener** *n*

damper ❶ (ˈdæmpə) *n* **1** a person, event, or circumstance that depresses or discourages. **2 put a damper on.** to produce a depressing or stultifying effect on. **3** a movable plate to regulate the draught in a stove or furnace flue. **4** a device to reduce electronic, mechanical, acoustic, or aerodynamic oscillations in a system. **5** the pad in a piano or harpsichord that deadens the vibration of each string as its key is released. **6** *Chiefly Austral. & NZ.* any of various unleavened loaves and scones, typically cooked on an open fire.

damping off *n* any of various diseases of plants caused by fungi in conditions of excessive moisture.

damp-proof *Building trades.* ◆ *vb* **1** to protect against the incursion of damp by adding a dampcourse or by coating with a moisture-resistant preparation. ◆ *adj* **2** protected against damp or causing protection against damp: *a damp-proof course*.

damsel (ˈdæmzᵊl) *n Arch. or poetic.* a young unmarried woman; maiden. [C13: from OF *damoisele*, from Vulgar L *domnicella* (unattested) young lady, from L *domina* mistress]

damselfly (ˈdæmzᵊlˌflaɪ) *n, pl* **damselflies.** any of various insects similar to dragonflies but usually resting with the wings closed over the back.

damson (ˈdæmzən) *n* **1** a small tree cultivated for its blue-black edible plumlike fruit. **2** the fruit of this tree. [C14: from L *prūnum damascēnum* Damascus plum]

dan (dæn) *n Judo, karate, etc.* **1** any one of the 10 black-belt grades of proficiency. **2** a competitor entitled to dan grading. [Japanese]

Dan. *abbrev. for:* **1** *Bible.* Daniel. **2** Danish.

dance ❶ (dɑːns) *vb* **dances, dancing, danced.** **1** (*intr*) to move the feet and body rhythmically, esp. in time to music. **2** (*tr*) to perform (a particular dance). **3** (*intr*) to skip or leap. **4** to move or cause to move in a rhythmic way. **5 dance attendance on (someone).** to attend (someone) solicitously or obsequiously. ◆ *n* **6** a series of rhythmic steps and movements, usually in time to music. **7** an act of dancing. **8a** a social meeting arranged for dancing. **8b** (*as modifier*): *a dance hall*. **9** a piece of music in the rhythm of a particular dance form. **10** dancelike movements. **11 lead (someone) a dance.** *Brit. inf.* to cause (someone) continued worry and exasperation. [C13: from OF *dancier*]
▸ˈ**danceable** *adj* ▸ˈ**dancer** *n* ▸ˈ**dancing** *n, adj*

dance floor *n* **a** an area of floor in a disco, etc., where patrons may dance. **b** (*as modifier*): *dancefloor music*.

dance of death *n* a medieval representation of a dance in which people are led off to their graves, by a personification of death. Also called (French): **danse macabre.**

D and C *n Med.* dilation (of the cervix) and curettage (of the uterus).

dandelion (ˈdændɪˌlaɪən) *n* **1** a plant native to Europe and Asia and naturalized as a weed in North America, having yellow rayed flowers and deeply notched leaves. **2** any of several similar plants. [C15: from OF *dent de lion*, lit.: tooth of a lion, referring to its leaves]

dander (ˈdændə) *n* **1** small particles of hair or feathers. **2 get one's** (*or* **someone's**) **dander up.** *Inf.* to become (*or* cause to become) annoyed or angry. [C19: from DANDRUFF]

dandify (ˈdændɪˌfaɪ) *vb* **dandifies, dandifying, dandified.** (*tr*) to dress like or cause to resemble a dandy.

dandle ❶ (ˈdændᵊl) *vb* **dandles, dandling, dandled.** (*tr*) **1** to move (a young child) up and down (on the knee or in the arms). **2** to pet; fondle. [C16: from ?]
▸ˈ**dandler** *n*

dandruff (ˈdændrəf) *n* loose scales of dry dead skin shed from the scalp. [C16: *dand-* from ? + *-ruff*, prob. from ME *roufe* scab, from ON *hrūfa*]

dandy ❶ (ˈdændɪ) *n, pl* **dandies.** **1** a man greatly concerned with smartness of dress. ◆ *adj* **dandier, dandiest.** **2** *Inf.* good or fine. [C18: ? short for *jack-a-dandy*]
▸ˈ**dandyish** *adj*

dandy-brush *n* a stiff brush used for grooming a horse.

dandy roll *or* **roller** *n* a roller used in the manufacture of paper to produce watermarks.

Dane (deɪn) *n* **1** a native, citizen, or inhabitant of Denmark. **2** any of the Vikings who invaded England from the late 8th to the 11th century A.D.

Danegeld (ˈdeɪnˌgɛld) *or* **Danegelt** (ˈdeɪnˌgɛlt) *n* the tax levied in Anglo-Saxon England to provide protection money for or to finance forces to oppose Viking invaders. [C11: from *Dan* Dane + *geld* tribute; see YIELD]

Danelaw (ˈdeɪnˌlɔː) *n* the parts of Anglo-Saxon England in which Danish law and custom were observed. [OE *Dena lagu* Danes' law]

danger ❶ (ˈdeɪndʒə) *n* **1** the state of being vulnerable to injury, loss, or evil; risk. **2** a person or thing that may cause injury, pain, etc. **3 in danger of.** liable to. **4 on the danger list.** critically ill in hospital. [C13 *daunger* power, hence power to inflict injury, from OF *dongier* from L *dominium* ownership]
▸ˈ**dangerless** *adj*

danger money *n* extra money paid to compensate for the risks involved in certain dangerous jobs.

dangerous ❶ (ˈdeɪndʒərəs) *adj* causing danger; perilous.
▸ˈ**dangerously** *adv*

dangle ❶ (ˈdæŋgᵊl) *vb* **dangles, dangling, dangled.** **1** to hang or cause to hang freely: *his legs dangled over the wall*. **2** (*tr*) to display as an enticement. [C16: ?from Danish *dangle*, prob. imit.]
▸ˈ**dangler** *n*

Danish (ˈdeɪnɪʃ) *adj* **1** of Denmark, its people, or their language. ◆ *n* **2** the official language of Denmark.

Danish blue *n* a strong-tasting white cheese with blue veins.

Danish pastry *n* a rich puff pastry filled with apple, almond paste, icing, etc.

dank ❶ (dæŋk) *adj* (esp. of cellars, caves, etc.) unpleasantly damp and chilly. [C14: prob. from ON]
▸ˈ**dankly** *adv* ▸ˈ**dankness** *n*

danseur *French.* (dɑ̃sœr) *or* (*fem*) ***danseuse*** (dɑ̃søz) *n* a ballet dancer.

dap (dæp) *vb* **daps, dapping, dapped.** **1** *Angling.* to fly-fish so that the fly bobs on and off the water. **2** (*intr*) to dip lightly into water. **3** to bounce or cause to bounce. [C17: imit.]

daphne (ˈdæfnɪ) *n* any of various Eurasian ornamental shrubs with shiny evergreen leaves and clusters of small bell-shaped flowers. [via L from Gk: laurel]

daphnia (ˈdæfnɪə) *n* any of several waterfleas having a rounded body

THESAURUS

damning, denunciation, doom, excommunication, objurgation, proscription, sending to hell

damned *adj* **1a** = **doomed**, accursed, anathematized, condemned, infernal, lost, reprobate, unhappy

damnedest *n inf.* = **best**, hardest, utmost

damp *adj* **1** = **moist**, clammy, dank, dewy, dripping, drizzly, humid, misty, muggy, sodden, soggy, sopping, vaporous, wet ◆ *n* **2** = **moisture**, clamminess, dampness, dankness, dew, drizzle, fog, humidity, mist, mugginess, vapour ◆ *vb* **5** = **moisten**, dampen, wet **6 damp down** = **curb**, allay, check, chill, cool, dash, deaden, deject, depress, diminish, discourage, dispirit, dull, inhibit, moderate, pour cold water on, reduce, restrain, stifle
Antonyms *adj* ≠ **moist:** arid, dry, watertight ◆ *n* ≠ **moisture:** aridity, dryness ◆ *vb* ≠ **curb:** encourage, gee up, hearten, inspire

dampen *vb* **1** = **reduce**, check, dash, deaden, depress, deter, dishearten, dismay, dull, lessen, moderate, muffle, restrain, smother, stifle **2** = **moisten**, bedew, besprinkle, make damp, spray, wet

damper *n* **2** *As in* **put a damper on** = **discouragement**, chill, cloud, cold water (*inf.*), curb, gloom, hindrance, killjoy, pall, restraint, wet blanket (*inf.*)

dampness *n* **1** = **moistness**, clamminess, damp, dankness, humidity, moisture, mugginess, sogginess, wetness
Antonyms *n* aridity, aridness, dryness

dance *vb* **1** = **prance**, bob up and down, caper, cut a rug (*inf.*), frolic, gambol, hop, jig, rock, skip, spin, sway, swing, trip, whirl ◆ *n* **8a** = **ball**, dancing party, disco, discotheque, hop (*inf.*), knees-up (*Brit. inf.*), social

dancer *n* **1** = **ballerina**, Terpsichorean

dandle *vb* **1, 2** = **rock**, amuse, bounce, caress, cradle, cuddle, dance, fondle, give a knee ride, pet, toss, toy (with)

dandy *n* **1** = **fop**, beau, blade (*arch.*), blood (*rare*), buck (*arch.*), coxcomb, dude (*US & Canad. inf.*), exquisite (*obs.*), macaroni (*obs.*), man about town, peacock, popinjay, swell (*inf.*), toff (*Brit. sl.*) ◆ *adj* **2** *inf.* = **excellent**, capital, fine, first-rate, great, splendid

danger *n* **1** = **peril**, endangerment, hazard, insecurity, jeopardy, menace, pitfall, precariousness, risk, threat, venture, vulnerability

dangerous *adj* = **perilous**, alarming, breakneck, chancy (*inf.*), exposed, hairy, hazardous, insecure, menacing, nasty, parlous (*arch.*), precarious, risky, threatening, treacherous, ugly, unchancy (*Scot.*), unsafe, vulnerable
Antonyms *adj* harmless, innocuous, O.K. *or* okay (*inf.*), out of danger, out of harm's way, protected, safe, safe and sound, secure

dangerously *adv* = **perilously**, alarmingly, carelessly, daringly, desperately, harmfully, hazardously, precariously, recklessly, riskily, unsafely, unsecurely

dangle *vb* **1** = **hang**, depend, flap, hang down, sway, swing, trail **2** = **wave**, brandish, entice, flaunt, flourish, lure, tantalize, tempt

dangling *adj* **1** = **hanging**, disconnected, drooping, loose, swaying, swinging, trailing, unconnected

dank *adj* = **damp**, chilly, clammy, dewy, dripping, moist, slimy, soggy

enclosed in a transparent shell. [C19: prob. from *Daphne*, a nymph in Gk mythology]

dapper Ⓣ (ˈdæpə) *adj* **1** neat in dress and bearing. **2** small and nimble. [C15: from MDu.: active, nimble]
▸ˈ**dapperly** *adv* ▸ˈ**dapperness** *n*

dapple Ⓣ (ˈdæpᵊl) *vb* **dapples, dappling, dappled. 1** to mark or become marked with spots of a different colour; mottle. ◆ *n* **2** mottled or spotted markings. **3** a dappled horse, etc. ◆ *adj* **4** marked with dapples or spots. [C14: from ?]

dapple-grey *n* a horse with a grey coat having spots of darker colour.

darbies (ˈdɑːbɪz) *pl n Brit.* a slang term for **handcuffs.** [C16: ?from *Father Derby's* (or *Darby's*) *bonds,* a rigid agreement between a usurer and his client]

Darby and Joan (ˈdɑːbɪ; dʒəʊn) *n* **1** an ideal elderly married couple living in domestic harmony. **2 Darby and Joan Club.** a club for elderly people. [C18: couple in 18th-cent. English ballad]

dare Ⓣ (dɛə) *vb* **dares, daring, dared. 1** *(tr)* to challenge (a person to do something) as proof of courage. **2** (can take an infinitive with or without *to*) to be courageous enough to try (to do something). **3** *(tr) Rare.* to oppose without fear; defy. **4 I dare say. 4a** (it is) quite possible (that). **4b** probably. ◆ *n* **5** a challenge to do something as proof of courage. **6** something done in response to such a challenge. [OE *durran*]
▸ˈ**darer** *n*

> **USAGE NOTE** When used negatively or interrogatively, *dare* does not usually add *-s: he dare not come; dare she come?* When used negatively in the past tense, however, *dare* usually adds *-d: he dared not come.*

daredevil Ⓣ (ˈdɛəˌdevᵊl) *n* **1** a recklessly bold person. ◆ *adj* **2** reckless; daring; bold.
▸ˈ**dareˌdevilry** *or* ˈ**dareˌdeviltry** *n*

daring Ⓣ (ˈdɛərɪŋ) *adj* **1** bold or adventurous. ◆ *n* **2** courage in taking risks; boldness.

Darjeeling (dɑːˈdʒiːlɪŋ) *n* a high-quality black tea grown in the mountains around Darjeeling, a town in NE India.

dark Ⓣ (dɑːk) *adj* **1** having little or no light. **2** (of a colour) reflecting or transmitting little light: *dark brown.* **3** (of complexion, hair colour, etc.) not fair; swarthy; brunette. **4** gloomy or dismal. **5** sinister; evil: *a dark purpose.* **6** sullen or angry. **7** ignorant or unenlightened: *a dark period in our history.* **8** secret or mysterious. ◆ *n* **9** absence of light; darkness. **10** night or nightfall. **11** a dark place. **12** a state of ignorance (esp. in **in the dark**). [OE *deorc*]
▸ˈ**darkish** *adj* ▸ˈ**darkly** *adv* ▸ˈ**darkness** *n*

Dark Ages *pl n European history.* the period from about the late 5th century A.D. to about 1000 A.D., once considered an unenlightened period.

Dark Continent *n* **the.** a term for Africa when it was relatively unexplored by Europeans.

darken Ⓣ (ˈdɑːkən) *vb* **1** to make or become dark or darker. **2** to make or become gloomy, angry, or sad. **3 darken (someone's) door.** *(usually used with a negative)* to visit someone: *never darken my door again!*
▸ˈ**darkener** *n*

dark horse *n* **1** a competitor in a race or contest about whom little is known. **2** a person who reveals little about himself, esp. one who has unexpected talents. **3** *US politics.* a candidate who is unexpectedly nominated or elected.

dark lantern *n* a lantern having a sliding shutter or panel to dim or hide the light.

darkling (ˈdɑːklɪŋ) *adv, adj Poetic.* in the dark or night. [C15: from DARK + -LING[2]]

dark matter *n Astron.* matter known to make up a substantial part of the mass of the universe, but not detectable by its absorption or emission of electromagnetic radiation.

darkroom (ˈdɑːkˌruːm, -ˌrʊm) *n* a room in which photographs are processed in darkness or safe light.

darksome (ˈdɑːksəm) *adj Literary.* dark or darkish.

dark star *n* an invisible star known to exist only from observation of its radio, infrared, or other spectrum or of its gravitational effect.

darling Ⓣ (ˈdɑːlɪŋ) *n* **1** a person very much loved. **2** a favourite. ◆ *adj (prenominal)* **3** beloved. **4** much admired; pleasing: *a darling hat.* [OE *dēorling*; see DEAR, -LING[1]]

darn[1] Ⓣ (dɑːn) *vb* **1** to mend (a hole or a garment) with a series of crossing or interwoven stitches. ◆ *n* **2** a patch of darned work on a garment. [C16: prob. from F (dialect) *darner*]
▸ˈ**darner** *n*

darn[2] (dɑːn) *interj, adj, adv, n* a euphemistic word for **damn** (senses 1–5, 12, 13).

darnel (ˈdɑːnᵊl) *n* any of several grasses that grow as weeds in grain fields in Europe and Asia. [C14: prob. rel. to F (dialect) *darnelle,* from ?]

darning (ˈdɑːnɪŋ) *n* **1** the act of mending a hole using interwoven stitches. **2** garments needing to be darned.

darning needle *n* a long needle with a large eye used for darning.

dart Ⓣ (dɑːt) *n* **1** a small narrow pointed missile that is thrown or shot, as in the game of darts. **2** a sudden quick movement. **3** *Zool.* a slender pointed structure, as in snails for aiding copulation. **4** a tapered tuck made in dressmaking. ◆ *vb* **5** to move or throw swiftly and suddenly; shoot. [C14: from OF, of Gmc origin]
▸ˈ**darting** *adj*

dartboard (ˈdɑːtˌbɔːd) *n* a circular piece of wood, cork, etc., used as the target in the game of darts.

darter (ˈdɑːtə) *n* **1** Also called: **anhinga, snakebird.** any of various aquatic birds of tropical and subtropical inland waters, having a long slender neck and bill. **2** any of various small brightly coloured North American freshwater fish.

darts (dɑːts) *n (functioning as sing)* any of various competitive games in which darts are thrown at a dartboard.

Darwinian (dɑːˈwɪnɪən) *adj* **1** of or relating to Charles Darwin (1809–92), English naturalist, or his theory of evolution. ◆ *n* **2** a person who accepts, supports, or uses this theory.

Darwinism (ˈdɑːwɪˌnɪzəm) *or* **Darwinian theory** *n* the theory of the origin of animal and plant species by evolution through a process of natural selection.
▸ˈ**Darwinist** *n, adj*

dash[1] Ⓣ (dæʃ) *vb (mainly tr)* **1** to hurl; crash: *he dashed the cup to the floor.* **2** to mix: *white paint dashed with blue.* **3** *(intr)* to move hastily or recklessly; rush. **4** (usually foll. by *off* or *down*) to write (down) or finish (off) hastily. **5** to frustrate: *his hopes were dashed.* **6** to daunt (someone); discourage. ◆ *n* **7** a sudden quick movement. **8** a small admixture:

THESAURUS

dapper *adj* **1** = **neat**, active, brisk, chic, natty (*inf.*), nice, nimble, smart, soigné *or* soignée, spruce, spry, stylish, trig (*arch. or dialect*), trim, well-groomed, well turned out
Antonyms *adj* blowsy, disarrayed, dishevelled, dowdy, frowzy, ill-groomed, rumpled, slobby (*inf.*), sloppy (*inf.*), slovenly, unkempt, untidy

dapple *vb* **1** = **mottle**, bespeckle, dot, fleck, freckle, speckle, spot, stipple

dappled *adj* **1** = **mottled**, brindled, checkered, flecked, freckled, piebald, pied, speckled, spotted, stippled, variegated

dare *vb* **1** = **challenge**, defy, goad, provoke, taunt, throw down the gauntlet **2** = **risk**, brave, endanger, gamble, hazard, make bold, presume, skate on thin ice, stake, venture ◆ *n* **5** = **challenge**, defiance, provocation, taunt

daredevil *n* **1** = **adventurer**, adrenalin junky, desperado, exhibitionist, hot dog (*chiefly US*), madcap, show-off (*inf.*), stunt man ◆ *adj* **2** = **daring**, adventurous, audacious, bold, death-defying, madcap, reckless

daredevilry *n* = **daring**, adventure, adventurousness, boldness, derring-do (*arch.*), fearlessness, foolhardiness, intrepidity, rashness, recklessness, temerity

daring *adj* **1** = **brave**, adventurous, audacious, ballsy (*taboo sl.*), bold, daredevil, fearless, game (*inf.*), have-a-go (*inf.*), impulsive, intrepid, plucky, rash, reckless, valiant, venturesome ◆ *n* **2** = **bravery**, audacity, balls (*taboo sl.*), ballsiness (*taboo sl.*), boldness, bottle (*Brit. sl.*), courage, derring-do (*arch.*), face (*inf.*), fearlessness, grit, guts (*inf.*), intrepidity, nerve (*inf.*), pluck, rashness, spirit, spunk (*inf.*), temerity
Antonyms *adj* ≠ **brave:** anxious, careful, cautious, cowardly, faint-hearted, fearful, timid, uncourageous, wary ◆ *n* ≠ **bravery:** anxiety, caution, cowardice, fear, timidity

dark *adj* **1** = **dim**, cloudy, darksome (*literary*), dingy, indistinct, murky, overcast, pitch-black, pitchy, shadowy, shady, sunless, unlit **3** = **brunette**, black, dark-skinned, dusky, ebony, sable, swarthy **4** = **gloomy**, bleak, cheerless, dismal, doleful, drab, grim, joyless, morbid, morose, mournful, sad, sombre **5** = **evil**, atrocious, damnable, foul, hellish, horrible, infamous, infernal, nefarious, satanic, sinful, sinister, vile, wicked **6** = **angry**, dour, forbidding, frowning, glowering, glum, ominous, scowling, sulky, sullen, threatening **8** = **secret**, abstruse, arcane, concealed, cryptic, deep, Delphic, enigmatic, hidden, mysterious, mystic, obscure, occult, puzzling, recondite ◆ *n* **9** = **darkness**, dimness, dusk, gloom, murk, murkiness, obscurity, semi- darkness **10** = **night**, evening, nightfall, night-time, twilight
Antonyms *adj* ≠ **brunette:** blond, blonde, fair, fair-haired, flaxen-haired, light, light-complexioned, towheaded ≠ **gloomy:** bright, cheerful, clear, genial, glad, hopeful, pleasant, sunny

darken *vb* **1** = **make dark**, becloud, blacken, cloud up *or* over, deepen, dim, eclipse, make darker, make dim, obscure, overshadow, shade, shadow **2** = **become gloomy**, become angry, blacken, cast a pall over, cloud, deject, depress, dispirit, grow troubled, look black, sadden
Antonyms *vb* ≠ **make dark:** brighten, clear up, enliven, gleam, glow, illuminate, lighten, light up, make bright, shine ≠ **become gloomy:** become cheerful, cheer, encourage, gladden, hearten, make happy, perk up

darkness *n* **1** = **dark**, blackness, dimness, dusk, duskiness, gloom, murk, murkiness, nightfall, obscurity, shade, shadiness, shadows **8** = **secrecy**, blindness, concealment, ignorance, mystery, privacy, unawareness

darling *n* **1** = **beloved**, dear, dearest, love, sweetheart, truelove **2** = **favourite**, apple of one's eye, blue-eyed boy, fair-haired boy (*US*), pet, spoilt child ◆ *adj* **3** = **beloved**, adored, cherished, dear, precious, treasured **4** = **adorable**, attractive, captivating, charming, cute, enchanting, lovely, sweet

darn[1] *vb* **1** = **mend**, cobble up, patch, repair, sew up, stitch ◆ *n* **2** = **mend**, invisible repair, patch, reinforcement

dart *vb* **5** = **dash**, bound, flash, flit, fly, race, run, rush, scoot, shoot, spring, sprint, start, tear, whistle, whizz **5** = **throw**, cast, fling, hurl, launch, propel, send, shoot, sling

dash[1] *vb* **1** = **throw**, cast, fling, hurl, slam, sling **1** = **crash**, break, destroy, shatter, shiver, smash, splinter **3** = **rush**, barrel (along) (*inf., chiefly US & Canad.*), bolt, bound, burn rubber (*inf.*), dart, fly, haste, hasten, hurry, race, run, speed, spring, sprint, tear **5** = **frustrate**, blight, foil, ruin, spoil, thwart, undo **6** = **disappoint**, abash, chagrin, confound, dampen, discomfort, dis-

coffee with a dash of cream. **9** a violent stroke or blow. **10** the sound of splashing or smashing. **11** panache; style: *he rides with dash.* **12** Also called: **rule.** the punctuation mark –, used to indicate a sudden change of subject or to enclose a parenthetical remark. **13** the symbol (–) used, in combination with the symbol *dot* (•), in the written representation of Morse and other telegraphic codes. **14** *Athletics.* another word (esp. US and Canad.) for **sprint.** [ME *daschen, dassen,* ?from ON]

dash[2] (dæʃ) *interj Inf.* a euphemistic word for **damn** (senses 1, 2).

dashboard ('dæʃ,bɔːd) *n* **1** Also called (Brit.): **fascia.** the instrument panel in a car, boat, or aircraft. **2** *Obs.* a board at the side of a carriage or boat to protect against splashing.

dasher ('dæʃə) *n* **1** one that dashes. **2** *Canad.* the ledge along the top of the boards of an ice hockey rink.

dashiki (dɑː'ʃiːkɪ) *n* a large loose-fitting upper garment worn esp. by Blacks in the US, Africa, and the Caribbean. [C20: of W African origin]

dashing ❶ ('dæʃɪŋ) *adj* **1** spirited; lively: *a dashing young man.* **2** stylish; showy.

dashlight ('dæʃ,laɪt) *n* a light that illuminates the dashboard of a car, esp. at night.

Dassehra ('dæsεəræ) *n* an annual Hindu festival celebrated on the 10th lunar day of Navaratri; images of the goddess Durga are immersed in water.

dassie ('dæsɪ) *n* another name for a **hyrax,** esp. the rock hyrax. [C19: from Afrik.]

dastardly ❶ ('dæstədlɪ) *adj* mean and cowardly. [C15 *dastard* (in the sense: dullard): prob. from ON *dæstr* exhausted, out of breath]
▸ **'dastardliness** *n*

dasyure ('dæsɪ,jʊə) *n* **1** any of several small carnivorous marsupials of Australia, New Guinea, and adjacent islands. **2** the ursine dasyure. See **Tasmanian devil.** [C19: from NL, from Gk *dasus* shaggy + *oura* tail]

DAT *abbrev. for* digital audio tape.

dat. *abbrev. for* dative.

data ❶ ('deɪtə, 'dɑːtə) *pl n* **1** a series of observations, measurements, or facts; information. **2** Also called: **information.** *Computing.* the information operated on by a computer program. [C17: from L, lit.: (things) given, from *dare* to give]

> **USAGE NOTE** Although now often used as a singular noun, *data* is properly a plural.

database ('deɪtə,beɪs) *n* **1** Also called: **data bank.** a store of a large amount of information, esp. in a form that can be handled by a computer. **2** *Inf.* any large store of information: *a database of knowledge.*

data capture *n* any process for converting information into a form that can be handled by a computer.

data pen *n* a device for reading or scanning magnetically coded data on labels, packets, etc.

data processing *n* **a** a sequence of operations performed on data, esp. by a computer, in order to extract information, reorder files, etc. **b** (*as modifier*): *a data-processing centre.*

data protection *n* (in Britain) safeguards for individuals relating to personal data stored on a computer.

data set *n Computing.* another name for **file**[1] (sense 6).

date[1] ❶ (deɪt) *n* **1** a specified day of the month. **2** the particular day or year of an event. **3** an inscription on a coin, letter, etc., stating when it was made or written. **4a** an appointment for a particular time, esp. with a person of the opposite sex. **4b** the person with whom the appointment is made. **5** the present moment; now (esp. in **to date, up to date**). ◆ *vb* **dates, dating, dated. 6** (*tr*) to mark (a letter, coin, etc.) with the day, month, or year. **7** (*tr*) to assign a date of occurrence or creation to. **8** (*intr; foll. by from* or *back to*) to have originated (at a specified time). **9** (*tr*) to reveal the age of: *that dress dates her.* **10** to make or become old-fashioned: *some good films hardly date at all.* **11** *Inf., chiefly US & Canad.* **11a** to be a boyfriend or girlfriend of (someone of the opposite sex). **11b** to accompany (a member of the opposite sex) on a date. [C14: from OF, from L *dare* to give, as in *epistula data Romae* letter handed over at Rome]
▸ **'datable** *or* **'dateable** *adj*

> **USAGE NOTE** See at **year.**

date[2] (deɪt) *n* **1** the fruit of the date palm, having sweet edible flesh and a single large woody seed. **2** short for **date palm.** [C13: from OF, from L, from Gk *daktulos* finger]

dated ❶ ('deɪtɪd) *adj* **1** unfashionable; outmoded. **2** (of a security) having a fixed date for redemption.

dateless ('deɪtlɪs) *adj* likely to remain fashionable, good, or interesting regardless of age.

dateline ('deɪt,laɪn) *n Journalism.* the date and location of a story, placed at the top of an article.

date line *n* (*often caps.*) short for **International Date Line.**

date palm *n* a tall feather palm grown in tropical regions for its sweet edible fruit.

date rape *n* **1** the act or an instance of a man raping a woman while they are on a date together. **2** an act of sexual intercourse regarded as tantamount to rape, esp. if the woman was encouraged to drink excessively or was subjected to undue pressure.

date stamp *n* **1** an adjustable rubber stamp for recording the date. **2** an inked impression made by this.

dating ('deɪtɪŋ) *n* any of several techniques, such as radioactive dating, dendrochronology, or varve dating, for establishing the age of rocks, palaeontological or archaeological specimens, etc.

dating agency *n* an agency that provides introductions to people seeking a companion with similar interests.

dative ('deɪtɪv) *Grammar.* ◆ *adj* **1** denoting a case of nouns, pronouns, and adjectives used to express the indirect object, to identify the recipients, and for other purposes. ◆ *n* **2a** the dative case. **2b** a word or speech element in this case. [C15: from L *datīvus,* from *dare* to give]
▸ **datival** (deɪ'taɪvᵊl) *adj* ▸ **'datively** *adv*

datum ('deɪtəm, 'dɑːtəm) *n, pl* **data. 1** a single piece of information; fact. **2** a proposition taken as unquestionable, often in order to construct some theoretical framework upon it. See also **sense datum.** [C17: from L: something given; see DATA]

datura (də'tjʊərə) *n* any of various chiefly Indian plants and shrubs with large trumpet-shaped flowers. [C16: from NL, from Hindi]

daub ❶ (dɔːb) *vb* **1** (*tr*) to smear or spread (paint, mud, etc.), esp. carelessly. **2** (*tr*) to cover or coat (with paint, plaster, etc.) carelessly. **3** to paint (a picture) clumsily or badly. ◆ *n* **4** an unskilful or crude painting. **5** something daubed on, esp. as a wall covering. **6** a smear (of paint, mud, etc.). [C14: from OF *dauber* to paint, whitewash, from L *dealbāre,* from *albāre* to whiten]
▸ **'dauber** *n*

daughter ('dɔːtə) *n* **1** a female offspring; a girl or woman in relation to her parents. **2** a female descendant. **3** a female from a certain country, etc., or one closely connected with a certain environment, etc.: *a daughter of the church.* ◆ (*modifier*) **4** *Biol.* denoting a cell or unicellular organism produced by the division of one of its own kind. **5** *Physics.* (of a nuclide) formed from another nuclide by radioactive decay. [OE *dohtor*]
▸ **'daughterhood** *n* ▸ **'daughterless** *adj* ▸ **'daughterly** *adj*

daughter-in-law *n, pl* **daughters-in-law.** the wife of one's son.

daunt ❶ (dɔːnt) *vb* (*tr; often passive*) **1** to intimidate. **2** to dishearten. [C13: from OF *danter,* changed from *donter* to conquer, from L *domitāre* to tame]
▸ **'daunting** *adj* ▸ **'dauntingly** *adv*

dauntless ❶ ('dɔːntlɪs) *adj* bold; fearless; intrepid.
▸ **'dauntlessly** *adv* ▸ **'dauntlessness** *n*

dauphin ('dɔːfɪn; *French* dofɛ̃) *n* (1349–1830) the title of the eldest son of the king of France. [C15: from OF: orig. a family name]

THESAURUS

courage ◆ *n* **7** = **rush**, bolt, dart, haste, onset, race, run, sortie, sprint, spurt **8** = **little**, bit, drop, flavour, hint, pinch, smack, *soupçon*, sprinkling, suggestion, tinge, touch **11** = **style**, brio, élan, flair, flourish, panache, spirit, verve, vigour, vivacity
Antonyms *vb* ≠ **rush:** crawl, dawdle, walk ≠ **frustrate:** enhance, improve ◆ *n* ≠ **little:** lot, much

dashing *adj* **1** = **bold**, daring, debonair, exuberant, gallant, lively, plucky, spirited, swashbuckling **2** = **stylish**, dapper, dazzling, elegant, flamboyant, jaunty, showy, smart, sporty, swish (*inf., chiefly Brit.*), urbane
Antonyms *adj* ≠ **bold:** boring, dreary, dull, lacklustre, stolid, unexciting, uninteresting

dastardly *adj Old-fashioned* = **despicable**, abject, base, caitiff (*arch.*), contemptible, cowardly, craven, faint-hearted, low, mean, niddering (*arch.*), recreant (*arch.*), sneaking, sneaky, spiritless, underhand, vile, weak-kneed (*inf.*)

data *n* **1** = **information**, details, documents, dope (*inf.*), facts, figures, info (*inf.*), input, materials, statistics

date[1] *n* **1, 2** = **day**, time, year **4a** = **appointment**, assignation, engagement, meeting, rendezvous, tryst **4b** = **partner**, escort, friend, steady (*inf.*) ◆ *vb* **7** = **put a date on**, assign a date to, determine the date of, fix the period of **8 date from** *or* date back to = **come from**, bear a date of, belong to, exist from, originate in **10** = **become old-fashioned**, be dated, obsolesce, show one's age

dated *adj* **1** = **old-fashioned**, antiquated, archaic, *démodé*, obsolete, old hat, out, outdated, outmoded, out of date, out of the ark (*inf.*), passé, unfashionable, untrendy (*Brit. inf.*)
Antonyms *adj* à la mode, all the rage, chic, cool (*inf.*), current, hip (*sl.*), in vogue, latest, modern, modish, popular, stylish, trendy (*Brit. inf.*), up-to-date

daub *vb* **1** = **stain**, bedaub, begrime, besmear, blur, deface, dirty, grime, smirch, smudge, spatter, splatter, sully **2** = **smear**, coat, cover, paint, plaster, slap on (*inf.*) ◆ *n* **6** = **smear**, blot, blotch, smirch, splodge, splotch, spot, stain

daunt *vb* **1** = **intimidate**, alarm, appal, cow, dismay, frighten, frighten off, overawe, scare, subdue, terrify **2** = **discourage**, deter, dishearten, dispirit, put off, shake
Antonyms *vb* cheer, comfort, encourage, hearten, inspire, inspirit, reassure, spur, support

daunted *adj* **1, 2** = **intimidated**, alarmed, cowed, demoralized, deterred, discouraged, disillusioned, dismayed, dispirited, downcast, frightened, hesitant, overcome, put off, unnerved

daunting *adj* **1, 2** = **intimidating**, alarming, awesome, demoralizing, disconcerting, discouraging, disheartening, frightening, offputting (*Brit. inf.*), unnerving
Antonyms *adj* cheering, comforting, encouraging, heartening, reassuring

dauntless *adj* = **fearless**, bold, brave, courageous, daring, doughty, gallant, gritty, heroic, indomitable, intrepid, lion-hearted, resolute,

dauphine ('dɔːfiːn; *French* dofin) *or* **dauphiness** ('dɔːfɪnɪs) *n French history.* the wife of a dauphin.

davenport ('dævənˌpɔːt) *n* **1** *Chiefly Brit.* a tall narrow writing desk with drawers. **2** *US & Canad.* a large sofa, esp. one convertible into a bed. [C19: sense 1 supposedly after Captain *Davenport,* who commissioned the first ones]

davit ('dævɪt, 'deɪ-) *n* a cranelike device, usually one of a pair, fitted with a tackle for suspending or lowering equipment, esp. a lifeboat. [C14: from Anglo-F *daviot,* dim. of *Davi* David]

Davy Jones *n* **1** Also called: **Davy Jones's locker.** the ocean's bottom, esp. when regarded as the grave of those lost or buried at sea. **2** the spirit of the sea. [C18: from ?]

Davy lamp *n* See **safety lamp.** [C19: after Sir H. *Davy* (1778–1829), E chemist]

daw (dɔː) *n* an archaic, dialect, or poetic name for a **jackdaw.** [C15: rel. to OHG *taha*]

dawdle ❶ ('dɔːdəl) *vb* **dawdles, dawdling, dawdled. 1** (*intr*) to be slow or lag behind. **2** (when *tr,* often foll. by *away*) to waste (time); trifle. [C17: from ?]
▸**'dawdler** *n*

dawn ❶ (dɔːn) *n* **1** daybreak. Related adj: **auroral. 2** the sky when light first appears in the morning. **3** the beginning of something. ◆ *vb* (*intr*) **4** to begin to grow light after the night. **5** to begin to develop or appear. **6** (usually foll. by *on* or *upon*) to begin to become apparent (to). [OE *dagian* to dawn]
▸**'dawnˌlike** *adj*

dawn chorus *n* the singing of large numbers of birds at dawn.

dawn raid *n Stock Exchange.* an unexpected attempt to acquire a substantial proportion of a company's shares at the start of a day's trading as a preliminary to a takeover bid.

day ❶ (deɪ) *n* **1** Also called: **civil day.** the period of time, the **calendar day,** of 24 hours' duration reckoned from one midnight to the next. **2a** the period of light between sunrise and sunset. **2b** (*as modifier*): *the day shift.* **3** the part of a day occupied with regular activity, esp. work. **4** (*sometimes pl*) a period or point in time: *in days gone by; any day now.* **5** the period of time, the **sidereal day,** during which the earth makes one complete revolution on its axis relative to a particular star. **6** the period of time, the **solar day,** during which the earth makes one complete revolution on its axis relative to the sun. **7** the period of time taken by a specified planet to make one complete rotation on its axis: *the Martian day.* **8** (*often cap.*) a day designated for a special observance: *Christmas Day.* **9** a time of success, recognition, etc.: *his day will come.* **10** a struggle or issue at hand: *the day is lost.* **11 all in a day's work.** part of one's normal activity. **12 at the end of the day.** in the final reckoning. **13 call it a day.** to stop work or other activity. **14 day after day.** without respite; relentlessly. **15 day by day.** gradually or progressively. **16 day in, day out.** every day and all day long. **17 day of rest.** the Sabbath; Sunday. **18 every dog has his day.** one's luck will come. **19 in this day and age.** nowadays. **20 that will be the day. 20a** that is most unlikely to happen. **20b** I look forward to that. ◆ Related adj: **diurnal.** ◆ See also **days.** [OE *dæg*]

Dayak ('daɪæk) *n, pl* **Dayaks** *or* **Dayak.** a variant spelling of **Dyak.**

day bed *n* a narrow bed intended for use as a seat and as a bed.

daybook ('deɪˌbʊk) *n Book-keeping.* a book in which the transactions of each day are recorded as they occur.

dayboy ('deɪˌbɔɪ) *n Brit.* a boy who attends a boarding school daily, but returns home each evening.
▸**'daygirl** *fem n*

daybreak ❶ ('deɪˌbreɪk) *n* the time in the morning when light first appears; dawn; sunrise.

daycare ('deɪˌkɛə) *n Brit. social welfare.* **1** occupation, treatment, or supervision during the working day for people who might be at risk if left on their own. **2** welfare services provided by a local authority, health service, etc., during the day.

daycentre ('deɪˌsɛntə) *or* **day centre** *n Social welfare.* (in Britain) **1** a building used for daycare or other welfare services. **2** the enterprise itself, including staff, users, and organization.

daydream ❶ ('deɪˌdriːm) *n* **1** a pleasant dreamlike fantasy indulged in while awake. **2** a pleasant scheme or wish that is unlikely to be fulfilled. ◆ *vb* **3** (*intr*) to indulge in idle fantasy.
▸**'dayˌdreamer** *n* ▸**'dayˌdreamy** *adj*

Day-Glo *n Trademark.* **a** a brand of fluorescent colouring materials, as of paint. **b** (*as modifier*): *Day-Glo colours.*

day labourer *n* an unskilled worker hired and paid by the day.

daylight ❶ ('deɪˌlaɪt) *n* **1** light from the sun. **2** daytime. **3** daybreak. **4** **see daylight. 4a** to understand something previously obscure. **4b** to realize that the end of a difficult task is approaching.

daylight robbery *n Inf.* blatant overcharging.

daylights ('deɪˌlaɪts) *pl n* consciousness or wits (esp. in **scare, knock,** or **beat the (living) daylights out of someone**).

daylight-saving time *n* time set usually one hour ahead of the local standard time, widely adopted in the summer to provide extra daylight in the evening.

daylong ('deɪˌlɒŋ) *adj, adv* lasting the entire day; all day.

day release *n Brit.* a system whereby workers are released for part-time education without loss of pay.

day return *n* a reduced fare for a journey (by train, etc.) travelling both ways in one day.

day room *n* a communal living room in a residential institution such as a hospital.

days (deɪz) *adv Inf.* during the day, esp. regularly: *he works days.*

day school *n* **1** a private school taking day students only. **2** a school giving instruction during the daytime.

daytime ('deɪˌtaɪm) *n* the time between dawn and dusk.

day-to-day ❶ *adj* routine; everyday.

day trip *n* a journey made to and from a place within one day.
▸**'day-ˌtripper** *n*

daze ❶ (deɪz) *vb* **dazes, dazing, dazed.** (*tr*) **1** to stun, esp. by a blow or shock. **2** to bewilder or amaze. ◆ *n* **3** a state of stunned confusion or shock (esp. in **in a daze**). [C14: from ON *dasa-,* as in *dasast* to grow weary]

dazzle ❶ ('dæzəl) *vb* **dazzles, dazzling, dazzled. 1** (*usually tr*) to blind or be blinded partially and temporarily by sudden excessive light. **2** (*tr*) to amaze, as with brilliance. ◆ *n* **3** bright light that dazzles. **4** bewilderment caused by glamour, brilliance, etc.: *the dazzle of fame.* [C15: from DAZE]
▸**'dazzler** *n* ▸**'dazzling** *adj* ▸**'dazzlingly** *adv*

dazzle gun *n* a weapon consisting of a laser gun used to dazzle enemy pilots.

dB *or* **db** *symbol for* decibel *or* decibels.

DBE *abbrev. for* Dame (Commander of the Order) of the British Empire (a Brit. title).

DBMS *abbrev. for* database management system.

DBS *abbrev. for* direct broadcasting by satellite.

dbx *or* **DBX** *n Trademark. Electronics.* a noise-reduction system that works across the full frequency spectrum.

DC *abbrev. for:* **1** *Music.* da capo. **2** direct current. Cf. **AC. 3** Also: **D.C.** District of Columbia.

DCB *abbrev. for* Dame Commander of the Order of the Bath (a Brit. title).

DCC *abbrev. for* digital compact cassette.

DCM *Brit. mil. abbrev. for* Distinguished Conduct Medal.

DD *abbrev. for:* **1** Doctor of Divinity. **2** Also: **dd.** direct debit.

THESAURUS

stouthearted, undaunted, unflinching, valiant, valorous

dawdle *vb* **1, 2** = **waste time,** dally, delay, dilly-dally (*inf.*), drag one's feet *or* heels, fritter away, hang about, idle, lag, loaf, loiter, potter, trail
Antonyms *vb* fly, get a move on (*inf.*), hasten, hurry, lose no time, make haste, rush, scoot, step on it (*inf.*)

dawdler *n* **1** = **slowcoach** (*Brit. inf.*), laggard, lingerer, loiterer, slowpoke (*US & Canad. inf.*), snail, tortoise

dawn *n* **1** = **daybreak,** aurora (*poetic*), cockcrow, crack of dawn, dawning, daylight, dayspring (*poetic*), morning, sunrise, sunup **3** = **beginning,** advent, birth, dawning, emergence, genesis, inception, onset, origin, outset, rise, start, unfolding ◆ *vb* **4** = **grow light,** break, brighten, gleam, glimmer, lighten **5** = **begin,** appear, develop, emerge, initiate, open, originate, rise, unfold **6 dawn on** *or* **upon** = **hit,** become apparent, come into one's head, come to mind, cross one's mind, flash across one's mind, occur, register (*inf.*), strike

day *n* **1** = **twenty-four hours 2a** = **daytime,** daylight, daylight hours **3** = **working day 4** = **point in time,** date, particular day, set time, time **9** = **time,** age, ascendancy, epoch, era, height, heyday, period, prime, zenith **13 call it a day** *inf.* = **stop,** end, finish, knock off (*inf.*), leave off, pack it in (*sl.*), pack up (*inf.*), shut up shop **14 day after day** = **continually,** monotonously, persistently, regularly, relentlessly **15 day by day** = **gradually,** daily, progressively, steadily

daybreak *n* = **dawn,** break of day, cockcrow, crack of dawn, dayspring (*poetic*), first light, morning, sunrise, sunup

daydream *n* **1, 2** = **fantasy,** castle in the air *or* in Spain, dream, fancy, figment of the imagination, fond hope, imagining, pipe dream, reverie, wish ◆ *vb* **3** = **fantasize,** dream, envision, fancy, hallucinate, imagine, muse, stargaze

daydreamer *n* **1, 2** = **fantasizer,** castle-builder, dreamer, pipe dreamer, visionary, Walter Mitty, wishful thinker, woolgatherer

daylight *n* **1** = **sunlight,** light of day, sunshine **2** = **daytime,** broad day, daylight hours

day-to-day *adj* = **everyday,** accustomed, customary, habitual, quotidian, regular, routine, run-of-the-mill, usual, wonted

daze *vb* **1** = **stun,** benumb, numb, paralyse, shock, stupefy **2** = **confuse,** amaze, astonish, astound, befog, bewilder, blind, dazzle, dumbfound, flabbergast (*inf.*), flummox, nonplus, perplex, stagger, startle, surprise ◆ *n* **3** = **shock,** bewilderment, confusion, distraction, mindfuck (*taboo sl.*), stupor, trance, trancelike state

dazed *adj* **1, 2** = **shocked,** at sea, baffled, bemused, bewildered, confused, disorientated, dizzy, dopey (*sl.*), flabbergasted (*inf.*), flummoxed, fuddled, groggy (*inf.*), light-headed, muddled, nonplussed, numbed, perplexed, punch-drunk, staggered, stunned, stupefied, woozy (*inf.*)

dazzle *vb* **1** = **blind,** bedazzle, blur, confuse, daze **2** = **impress,** amaze, astonish, awe, bowl over (*inf.*), fascinate, hypnotize, overawe, overpower, overwhelm, strike dumb, stupefy, take one's breath away

dazzling *adj* **2** = **splendid,** brilliant, divine, drop-dead (*sl.*), glittering, glorious, radiant, ravishing, scintillating, sensational (*inf.*), shining, sparkling, stunning, sublime, superb, virtuoso
Antonyms *adj* dull, ordinary, tedious, unexceptional, unexciting, uninspiring, uninteresting, unmemorable, unremarkable, vanilla (*sl.*)

dead *adj* **1** = **deceased,** defunct, departed, ex-

D-day *n* the day selected for the start of some operation, esp. of the Allied invasion of Europe on June 6, 1944. [C20: from *D(ay)-day*]

DDR *abbrev. for* Deutsche Demokratische Republik (the former East Germany; GDR).

DDS *or* **DDSc** *abbrev. for* Doctor of Dental Surgery *or* Science.

DDT *n* dichlorodiphenyltrichloroethane; a colourless odourless substance used as an insecticide. It is now banned in the UK.

de- *prefix forming verbs and verbal derivatives.* **1** removal of or from something: *deforest; dethrone.* **2** reversal of something: *decode; desegregate.* **3** departure from: *decamp.* [from L, from *dē* (prep) from, away from, out of, etc. In compound words of Latin origin, *de-* also means away, away from (*decease*); down (*degrade*); reversal (*detect*); removal (*defoliate*); and is used intensively (*devote*) and pejoratively (*detest*)]

deacon ('di:kən) *n Christianity.* **1** (in the Roman Catholic and other episcopal churches) an ordained minister ranking immediately below a priest. **2** (in some other churches) a lay official who assists the minister, esp. in secular affairs. [OE, ult. from Gk *diakonos* servant]
▸**'deaconate** *n* ▸**'deacon,ship** *n*

deaconess ('di:kənɪs) *n Christianity.* (in the early church and in some modern Churches) a female member of the laity with duties similar to those of a deacon.

deactivate (di:'æktɪ,veɪt) *vb* **deactivates, deactivating, deactivated.** **1** (*tr*) to make (a bomb, etc.) harmless or inoperative. **2** (*intr*) to become less radioactive.
▸**de'acti,vator** *n*

dead 🅣 (dɛd) *adj* **1a** no longer alive. **1b** (*as collective n*; preceded by *the*): *the dead.* **2** not endowed with life; inanimate. **3** no longer in use, effective, or relevant: *a dead issue; a dead language.* **4** unresponsive or unaware. **5** lacking in freshness or vitality. **6** devoid of physical sensation; numb. **7** resembling death: *a dead sleep.* **8** no longer burning or hot: *dead coals.* **9** (of flowers or foliage) withered; faded. **10** (*prenominal*) (intensifier): *a dead stop.* **11** *Inf.* very tired. **12** *Electronics.* **12a** drained of electric charge. **12b** not connected to a source of potential difference or electric charge. **13** lacking acoustic reverberation: *a dead sound.* **14** *Sport.* (of a ball, etc.) out of play. **15** accurate; precise (esp. in **a dead shot**). **16** lacking resilience or bounce: *a dead ball.* **17** not yielding a return: *dead capital.* **18** (of colours) not glossy or bright. **19** stagnant: *dead air.* **20** *Mil.* shielded from view, as by a geographic feature. **21 dead from the neck up.** *Inf.* stupid. **22 dead to the world.** *Inf.* unaware of one's surroundings, esp. asleep or drunk. ◆ *n* **23** a period during which coldness, darkness, etc. is at its most intense: *the dead of winter.* ◆ *adv* **24** (intensifier): *dead easy; stop dead.* **25 dead on.** exactly right. [OE *dēad*]
▸**'deadness** *n*

dead-and-alive *adj Brit.* (of a place, activity, or person) dull; uninteresting.

dead-ball line *n Rugby.* a line behind the goal line beyond which the ball is out of play.

deadbeat 🅣 ('dɛd,bi:t) *n* **1** *Inf.* a lazy or socially undesirable person. **2** a high grade escapement used in pendulum clocks. **3** (*modifier*) without recoil.

dead beat *adj Inf.* very tired; exhausted.

dead-cat bounce *n Stock Exchange inf.* a temporary recovery in prices following a substantial fall as a result of speculators buying stocks they have already sold rather than as a result of a genuine reversal of the downward trend.

dead centre *n* **1** the exact top or bottom of the piston stroke in a reciprocating engine or pump. **2** a rod mounted in the tailstock of a lathe to support a workpiece. ◆ Also called: **dead point.**

dead duck *n Sl.* a person or thing doomed to death, failure, etc., esp. because of a mistake.

deaden 🅣 ('dɛdᵊn) *vb* **1** to make or become less sensitive, intense, lively, etc. **2** (*tr*) to make acoustically less resonant.
▸**'deadening** *adj*

dead end *n* **1** a cul-de-sac. **2** a situation in which further progress is impossible.

deadeye ('dɛd,aɪ) *n* **1** *Naut.* either of a pair of disclike wooden blocks, supported by straps in grooves around them, between which a line is rove so as to draw them together to tighten a shroud. **2** *Inf., chiefly US.* an expert marksman.

deadfall ('dɛd,fɔ:l) *n* a trap in which a heavy weight falls to crush the prey.

deadhead ('dɛd,hɛd) *n* **1** a person who uses a free ticket, as for the theatre, etc. **2** a train, etc., travelling empty. **3** *US & Canad.* a dull person. **4** *US & Canad.* a totally or partially submerged log floating in a lake, etc. ◆ *vb* **5** (*intr*) *US & Canad.* to drive an empty bus, train, etc. **6** (*tr*) to remove dead flower heads.

Dead Heart *n* (usually preceded by *the*) *Austral.* the remote interior of Australia. [C20: from *The Dead Heart of Australia* (1906) by J. W. Gregory (1864–1932), British geologist]

dead heat *n* **a** a race or contest in which two or more participants tie for first place. **b** a tie between two or more contestants in any position.

dead leg *n Inf.* temporary loss of sensation in the leg, caused by a blow to a muscle.

dead letter *n* **1** a law or ordinance that is no longer enforced. **2** a letter that cannot be delivered or returned because it lacks adequate directions.

deadlight ('dɛd,laɪt) *n* **1** *Naut.* **1a** a bull's-eye to admit light to a cabin. **1b** a shutter for sealing off a porthole or cabin window. **2** a skylight designed not to be opened.

deadline 🅣 ('dɛd,laɪn) *n* a time limit for any activity.

deadlock 🅣 ('dɛd,lɒk) *n* **1** a state of affairs in which further action between two opposing forces is impossible. **2** a tie between opponents. **3** a lock having a bolt that can be opened only with a key. ◆ *vb* **4** to bring or come to a deadlock.

dead loss *n* **1** a complete loss for which no compensation is paid. **2** *Inf.* a useless person or thing.

deadly 🅣 ('dɛdlɪ) *adj* **deadlier, deadliest.** **1** likely to cause death. **2** *Inf.* extremely boring. ◆ *adv, adj* **3** like death in appearance or certainty.

deadly nightshade *n* a poisonous Eurasian plant having purple bell-shaped flowers and black berries. Also called: **belladonna, dwale.**

deadly sins *pl n* the sins of pride, covetousness, lust, envy, gluttony, anger, and sloth.

dead man's handle *or* **pedal** *n* a safety switch on a piece of machinery that allows operation only while depressed by the operator.

dead march *n* a piece of solemn funeral music played to accompany a procession.

dead-nettle *n* any of several Eurasian plants having leaves resembling nettles but lacking stinging hairs.

deadpan 🅣 ('dɛd,pæn) *adj, adv* with a deliberately emotionless face or manner.

dead reckoning *n* a method of establishing one's position using the distance and direction travelled rather than astronomical observations.

dead set *adv* **1** absolutely: *he is dead set against going to Spain.* ◆ *n* **2** the motionless position of a dog when pointing towards game. ◆ *adj* **3** (of a hunting dog) in this position.

dead soldier *or* **marine** *n Inf.* an empty beer or spirit bottle.

dead time *n Electronics.* the time immediately following a stimulus, during which an electrical device, component, etc. is insensitive to a further stimulus.

dead weight *n* **1** a heavy weight or load. **2** an oppressive burden. **3** the difference between the loaded and the unloaded weights of a ship. **4** the intrinsic invariable weight of a structure, such as a bridge.

deadwood ('dɛd,wʊd) *n* **1** dead trees or branches. **2** *Inf.* a useless person; encumbrance.

deaf 🅣 (dɛf) *adj* **1a** partially or totally unable to hear. **1b** (*as collective n*; preceded by *the*): *the deaf.* **2** refusing to heed. [OE *dēaf*]
▸**'deafness** *n*

USAGE NOTE See at **disabled.**

deaf aid *n* another name for **hearing aid.**

deaf-and-dumb *Offens.* ◆ *adj* **1** unable to hear or speak. ◆ *n* **2** a deaf-mute person.

deafblind ('dɛf,blaɪnd) *adj* **a** unable to hear or ssee. **b** (*as collective n*; preceded by *the*): *the deafblind.*

USAGE NOTE See at **disabled.**

THESAURUS

tinct, gone, late, passed away, perished, pushing up (the) daisies **2** = **inanimate**, lifeless **3** = **not working**, barren, inactive, inoperative, obsolete, stagnant, sterile, still, unemployed, unprofitable, useless **5** = **spiritless**, apathetic, callous, cold, dull, frigid, glassy, glazed, indifferent, lukewarm, torpid, unresponsive, wooden **6** = **numb**, inert, paralysed **10** = **total**, absolute, complete, downright, entire, outright, thorough, unqualified, utter **11** *inf.* = **exhausted**, dead beat (*inf.*), spent, tired, worn out ◆ *n* **23** = **middle**, depth, midst ◆ *adv* **24** *inf.* = **exactly**, absolutely, completely, directly, entirely, totally

Antonyms *adj* ≠ **deceased:** alive, alive and kicking, animate, existing, living ≠ **inanimate:** animated, lively, responsive ≠ **not working:** active, alive, effective, in use, operative, productive, working ≠ **spiritless:** active, alive, alive and kicking, animated, full of beans (*inf.*), lively, vivacious

deadbeat *n* **1** *Inf., chiefly US & Canad.* = **layabout**, bum (*inf.*), cadger, drone, freeloader, good-for-nothing, idler, loafer, lounger, parasite, scrounger (*inf.*), skiver (*Brit. sl.*), slacker (*inf.*), sponge (*inf.*), sponger (*inf.*), waster, wastrel

deaden *vb* **1, 2** = **reduce**, abate, alleviate, anaesthetize, benumb, blunt, check, cushion, damp, dampen, diminish, dull, hush, impair, lessen, muffle, mute, numb, paralyse, quieten, smother, stifle, suppress, weaken

deadline *n* = **time limit**, cutoff point, limit, target date

deadlock *n* **1, 2** = **impasse**, cessation, dead heat, draw, full stop, gridlock, halt, stalemate, standoff, standstill, tie

deadly *adj* **1** = **lethal**, baleful, baneful, dangerous, death-dealing, deathly, destructive, fatal, malignant, mortal, noxious, pernicious, poisonous, venomous **2** *Informal* = **boring**, as dry as dust, dull, ho-hum (*inf.*), mind-numbing, monotonous, tedious, tiresome, uninteresting, wearisome **3** = **deathly**, ashen, deathlike, ghastly, ghostly, pallid, wan, white

deadpan *adj* = **expressionless**, blank, empty, impassive, inexpressive, inscrutable, poker-faced, straight-faced

deaf *adj* **1** = **hard of hearing**, stone deaf, without hearing **2** = **oblivious**, indifferent, unconcerned, unhearing, unmoved

deafen ➊ ('dɛfᵊn) *vb* (*tr*) to make deaf, esp. momentarily, as by a loud noise.
▸ '**deafening** *adj* ▸ '**deafeningly** *adv*

deaf-mute *n* **1** a person who is unable to hear or speak. See also **mute** (sense 7). ◆ *adj* **2** unable to hear or speak. [C19: translation of F *sourd-muet*]

deal[1] ➊ (di:l) *vb* **deals, dealing, dealt. 1** (*intr;* foll. by *in*) to engage in commercially: *to deal in upholstery.* **2** (often foll. by *out*) to apportion or distribute. **3** (*tr*) to give (a blow, etc.) to (someone); inflict. **4** (*intr*) *Sl.* to sell any illegal drug. ◆ *n* **5** *Inf.* a bargain, transaction, or agreement. **6** a particular type of treatment received, esp. as the result of an agreement: *a fair deal.* **7** an indefinite amount (esp. in **good** *or* **great deal**). **8** *Cards.* **8a** the process of distributing the cards. **8b** a player's turn to do this. **8c** a single round in a card game. **9 big deal.** *Sl.* an important person, event, or matter: often used sarcastically. ◆ See also **deal with.** [OE *dǣlan,* from *dǣl* a part; cf. OHG *teil* a part, ON *deild* a share]

deal[2] (di:l) *n* **1** a plank of softwood timber, such as fir or pine, or such planks collectively. **2** the sawn wood of various coniferous trees. ◆ *adj* **3** of fir or pine. [C14: from MLow G *dele* plank]

dealer ➊ ('di:lə) *n* **1** a person or firm engaged in commercial purchase and sale; trader: *a car dealer.* **2** *Cards.* the person who distributes the cards. **3** *Sl.* a person who sells illegal drugs.

dealings ➊ ('di:lɪŋz) *pl n* (*sometimes sing*) transactions or business relations.

dealt (dɛlt) *vb* the past tense and past participle of **deal**[1].

deal with ➊ *vb* (*tr, adv*) **1** to take action on: *to deal with each problem in turn.* **2** to punish: *the headmaster will deal with the culprit.* **3** to treat or be concerned with: *the book deals with architecture.* **4** to conduct onself (towards others), esp. with regard to fairness. **5** to do business with.

dean (di:n) *n* **1** the chief administrative official of a college or university faculty. **2** (at Oxford and Cambridge universities) a college fellow with responsibility for undergraduate discipline. **3** *Chiefly Church of England.* the head of a chapter of canons and administrator of a cathedral or collegiate church. **4** *RC Church.* the cardinal bishop senior by consecration and head of the college of cardinals. Related adj: **decanal.** See also **rural dean.** [C14: from OF *deien,* from LL *decānus* one set over ten persons, from L *decem* ten]

deanery ('di:nərɪ) *n, pl* **deaneries. 1** the office or residence of a dean. **2** the group of parishes presided over by a rural dean.

dear ➊ (dɪə) *adj* **1** beloved; precious. **2** used in conventional forms of address, as in *Dear Sir.* **3** (*postpositive;* foll. by *to*) important; close. **4a** highly priced. **4b** charging high prices. **5** appealing. **6 for dear life.** with extreme vigour or desperation. ◆ *interj* **7** used in exclamations of surprise or dismay, such as *Oh dear!* ◆ *n* **8** Also: **dearest.** (*often used in direct address*) someone regarded with affection and tenderness. ◆ *adv* **9** dearly. [OE *dēore*]
▸ '**dearness** *n*

dearly ➊ ('dɪəlɪ) *adv* **1** very much. **2** affectionately. **3** at a great cost.

dearth ➊ (dɜ:θ) *n* an inadequate amount, esp. of food; scarcity. [C13 *derthe,* from *dēr* DEAR]

deary *or* **dearie** ('dɪərɪ) *n* **1** (*pl* **dearies**) *Inf.* a term of affection: now often sarcastic or facetious. **2 deary** *or* **dearie me!** an exclamation of surprise or dismay.

death ➊ (dɛθ) *n* **1** the permanent end of all functions of life in an organism. **2** an instance of this: *his death ended an era.* **3** a murder or killing. **4** termination or destruction. **5** a state of affairs or an experience considered as terrible as death. **6** a cause or source of death. **7** (*usually cap.*) a personification of death, usually a skeleton or an old man holding a scythe. **8 at death's door.** likely to die soon. **9 catch one's death** (**of cold**). *Inf.* to contract a severe cold. **10 do to death. 10a** to kill. **10b** to overuse. **11 in at the death. 11a** present when a hunted animal is killed. **11b** present at the finish or climax. **12 like death warmed up.** *Inf.* very ill. **13 like grim death.** as if afraid of one's life. **14 put to death.** to kill deliberately or execute. **15 to death. 15a** until dead. **15b** very much. ◆ Related adjs.: **fatal, lethal, mortal.** [OE *dēath*]

death adder *n* a venomous thick-bodied Australian snake.

deathbed ('dɛθˌbɛd) *n* the bed in which a person is about to die.

deathblow ➊ ('dɛθˌbləʊ) *n* a thing or event that destroys life or hope, esp. suddenly.

death camp *n* a concentration camp in which the conditions are so brutal that few prisoners survive, or one to which prisoners are sent for execution.

death cap *or* **angel** *n* a poisonous woodland fungus with white gills and a cuplike structure at the base of the stalk.

death certificate *n* a legal document issued by a qualified medical practitioner certifying the death of a person and stating the cause if known.

death duty *n* a tax on property inheritances, in Britain replaced by capital transfer tax in 1975 and since 1986 by inheritance tax. Also called: **estate duty.**

death futures *pl n* life insurance policies of terminally ill people that are bought speculatively for a lump sum by a company, enabling it to collect the proceeds of the policies when the ill people die.

death knell *or* **bell** *n* **1** something that heralds death or destruction. **2** a bell rung to announce a death.

deathless ➊ ('dɛθlɪs) *adj* immortal, esp. because of greatness; everlasting.
▸ '**deathlessness** *n*

deathly ➊ ('dɛθlɪ) *adj* **1** deadly. **2** resembling death: *a deathly quiet.*

death mask *n* a cast of a dead person's face.

death rate *n* the ratio of deaths in a specified area, group, etc., to the population of that area, group, etc. Also called: **mortality rate.**

death rattle *n* a low-pitched gurgling sound sometimes made by a dying person.

death's-head *n* a human skull or a representation of one.

death's-head moth *n* a European hawk moth having markings resembling a human skull on its upper thorax.

death star *n* a weapon consisting of a flat star-shaped piece of metal with sharpened points that is thrown at an opponent. Also called: **throwing star.**

deathtrap ('dɛθˌtræp) *n* a building, vehicle, etc., that is considered very unsafe.

death warrant *n* **1** the official authorization for carrying out a sentence of death. **2 sign one's** (**own**) **death warrant.** to cause one's own destruction.

deathwatch ('dɛθˌwɒtʃ) *n* **1** a vigil held beside a dying or dead person. **2 deathwatch beetle.** a beetle whose woodboring larvae are a serious pest. The adult produces a tapping sound that was once supposed to presage death.

death wish *n* (in Freudian psychology) the desire for self-annihilation.

deb (dɛb) *n Inf.* short for **debutante.**

debacle ➊ (deɪ'bɑ:kᵊl, dɪ-) *n* **1** a sudden disastrous collapse or defeat; rout. **2** the breaking up of ice in a river, often causing flooding. **3** a violent rush of water carrying along debris. [C19: from F, from OF *desbacler* to unbolt]

debag (di:'bæg) *vb* **debags, debagging, debagged.** (*tr*) *Brit. sl.* to remove the trousers from (someone) by force.

debar ➊ (dɪ'bɑ:) *vb* **debars, debarring, debarred.** (*tr;* usually foll. by *from*) to exclude from a place, a right, etc.; bar.
▸ **de'barment** *n*

USAGE NOTE See at **disbar.**

THESAURUS

deafen *vb* = **make deaf**, din, drown out, split *or* burst the eardrums

deafening *adj* = **ear-piercing**, booming, dinning, ear-splitting, intense, overpowering, piercing, resounding, ringing, thunderous

deal[1] *vb* **1** = **sell**, bargain, buy and sell, do business, negotiate, stock, trade, traffic **2** = **distribute**, allot, apportion, assign, bestow, dispense, divide, dole out, give, mete out, reward, share ◆ *n* **1** *Informal* = **agreement**, arrangement, bargain, contract, pact, transaction, understanding **7** = **amount**, degree, distribution, extent, portion, quantity, share, transaction **8** = **hand**, cut and shuffle, distribution, round, single game

dealer *n* **1** = **trader**, chandler, marketer, merchandiser, merchant, purveyor, supplier, tradesman, wholesaler

dealings *pl n* = **business**, business relations, commerce, trade, traffic, transactions, truck

deal with *vb* **1** = **handle**, attend to, come to grips with, cope with, get to grips with, manage, oversee, see to, take care of, treat **3** = **be concerned with**, consider, treat of **4** = **behave towards**, act towards, conduct oneself towards

dear *adj* **1** = **beloved**, cherished, close, darling, esteemed, familiar, favourite, intimate, precious, prized, respected, treasured **4** = **expensive**, at a premium, costly, high-priced, overpriced, pricey (*inf.*) **6 for dear life** = **desperately**, for all one is worth, intensely, quickly, urgently, vigorously ◆ *n* **8** = **beloved**, angel, darling, loved one, precious, treasure ◆ *adv* **9** = **dearly**, at a heavy cost, at a high price, at great cost
Antonyms *adj* ≠ **beloved:** disliked, hated ≠ **expensive:** cheap, common, inexpensive, worthless

dearly *adv* **1** = **very much**, extremely, greatly, profoundly **3** = **at great cost**, at a heavy cost, at a high price, dear

dearth *n* = **scarcity**, absence, deficiency, exiguousness, famine, inadequacy, insufficiency, lack, need, paucity, poverty, scantiness, shortage, sparsity, want

death *n* **1** = **dying**, bereavement, cessation, curtains (*inf.*), decease, demise, departure, dissolution, end, exit, expiration, loss, passing, quietus, release **4** = **destruction**, annihilation, downfall, ending, eradication, extermination, extinction, finish, grave, obliteration, ruin, ruination, undoing **7** *sometimes capital* = **grim reaper**, Dark Angel
Antonyms *n* ≠ **dying:** birth ≠ **destruction:** beginning, emergence, genesis, growth, origin, rise, source

deathblow *n* = **finishing stroke**, clincher (*inf.*), *coup de grâce*, kill, knockout blow *or* punch, lethal *or* mortal blow, quietus

deathless *adj* = **eternal**, everlasting, immortal, imperishable, incorruptible, timeless, undying
Antonyms *adj* corporeal, earthly, ephemeral, human, mortal, passing, temporal, transient, transitory

deathly *adj* **1** = **fatal**, deadly, extreme, intense, mortal, terrible **2** = **deathlike**, cadaverous, gaunt, ghastly, grim, haggard, like death warmed up (*inf.*), pale, pallid, wan

debacle *n* **1** = **disaster**, catastrophe, collapse, defeat, devastation, downfall, fiasco, havoc, overthrow, reversal, rout, ruin, ruination

debar *vb* = **bar**, black, blackball, deny, exclude, hinder, interdict, keep out, obstruct, preclude, prevent, prohibit, refuse admission to, restrain, segregate, shut out, stop

debark[1] (dɪˈbɑːk) *vb* another word for **disembark.** [C17: from F *débarquer,* from *dé-* DIS-[1] + *barque* BARQUE]
▸**debarkation** (ˌdiːbɑːˈkeɪʃən) *n*

debark[2] (diːˈbɑːk) *vb* (*tr*) to remove the bark from (a tree). [C18: from DE-+ BARK[2]]

debase ➊ (dɪˈbeɪs) *vb* **debases, debasing, debased.** (*tr*) to lower in quality, character, or value; adulterate. [C16: see DE-, BASE[2]]
▸**deˈbasement** *n* ▸**deˈbaser** *n*

debate ➊ (dɪˈbeɪt) *n* **1** a formal discussion, as in a legislative body, in which opposing arguments are put forward. **2** discussion or dispute. **3** the formal presentation and opposition of a specific motion, followed by a vote. ◆ *vb* **debates, debating, debated. 4** to discuss (a motion, etc.), esp. in a formal assembly. **5** to deliberate upon (something). [C13: from OF *debatre* to discuss, argue, from L *battuere*]
▸**deˈbatable** *adj* ▸**deˈbater** *n*

debauch ➊ (dɪˈbɔːtʃ) *vb* **1** (when *tr, usually passive*) to lead into a life of depraved self-indulgence. **2** (*tr*) to seduce (a woman). ◆ *n* **3** an instance or period of extreme dissipation. [C16: from OF *desbaucher* to corrupt, lit.: to shape (timber) roughly, from *bauch* beam, of Gmc origin]
▸**deˈbaucher** *n* ▸**deˈbauchery** *n*

debauchee (ˌdɛbɔːˈtʃiː) *n* a man who leads a life of promiscuity and self-indulgence.

debenture (dɪˈbɛntʃə) *n* **1** a long-term bond, bearing fixed interest and usually unsecured, issued by a company or governmental agency. **2** a certificate acknowledging a debt. **3** a customs certificate providing for a refund of excise or import duty. [C15: from L *dēbentur mihi* there are owed to me, from *dēbēre*]
▸**deˈbentured** *adj*

debenture stock *n* shares issued by a company, which guarantee a fixed return at regular intervals.

debilitate ➊ (dɪˈbɪlɪˌteɪt) *vb* **debilitates, debilitating, debilitated.** (*tr*) to make feeble; weaken. [C16: from L, from *dēbilis* weak]
▸**deˌbiliˈtation** *n* ▸**deˈbilitative** *adj*

debility ➊ (dɪˈbɪlɪtɪ) *n, pl* **debilities.** weakness or infirmity.

debit (ˈdɛbɪt) *n* **1a** acknowledgment of a sum owing by entry on the left side of an account. **1b** the left side of an account. **1c** an entry on this side. **1d** the total of such entries. **1e** (*as modifier*): *a debit balance.* ◆ *vb* **debits, debiting, debited. 2** (*tr*) **2a** to record (an item) as a debit in an account. **2b** to charge (a person or his account) with a debt. [C15: from L *dēbitum* DEBT]

debit card *n* a card issued by a bank or building society enabling customers to pay for goods or services by inserting it into a computer-controlled device at the place of sale, which is connected through the telephone network to the bank or building society.

debonair ➊ *or* **debonnaire** (ˌdɛbəˈnɛə) *adj* **1** suave and refined. **2** carefree; light-hearted. **3** courteous and cheerful. [C13: from OF, from *de bon aire* having a good disposition]
▸ˌ**deboˈnairly** *adv* ▸ˌ**deboˈnairness** *n*

debouch (dɪˈbaʊtʃ) *vb* (*intr*) **1** (esp. of troops) to move into a more open space. **2** (of a river, glacier, etc.) to flow into a larger area or body. [C18: from F *déboucher,* from *dé-* DIS-[1] + *bouche* mouth]
▸**deˈbouchment** *n*

Debrett (dəˈbrɛt) *n* a list, considered exclusive, of the British aristocracy. In full: **Debrett's Peerage.** [C19: after J. *Debrett* (c 1750-1822), London publisher who first issued it]

debrief ➊ (diːˈbriːf) *vb* (*tr*) to elicit a report from (a soldier, diplomat, etc.) after a mission or event.
▸**deˈbriefing** *n*

debris ➊ *or* **débris** (ˈdeɪbrɪ, ˈdɛbrɪ) *n* **1** fragments of something destroyed or broken; rubble. **2** a collection of loose material derived from rocks, or an accumulation of animal or vegetable matter. [C18: from F, from obs. *debrisier* to break into pieces, of Celtic origin]

debt ➊ (dɛt) *n* **1** something owed, such as money, goods, or services. **2 bad debt.** a debt that has little prospect of being paid. **3** an obligation to pay or perform something. **4** the state of owing something, or of being under an obligation (esp. in **in debt, in (someone's) debt**). [C13: from OF *dette,* from L *dēbitum,* from *dēbēre* to owe, from DE- + *habēre* to have]

debt collector *n* a person employed to collect debts for creditors.

debt of honour *n* a debt that is morally but not legally binding.

debtor ➊ (ˈdɛtə) *n* a person or commercial enterprise that owes a financial obligation.

debt swap *n* See **swap** (sense 4).

debud (diːˈbʌd) *vb* **debuds, debudding, debudded.** another word for **disbud.**

debug (diːˈbʌg) *vb* **debugs, debugging, debugged.** (*tr*) *Inf.* **1** to locate and remove concealed microphones from (a room, etc.). **2** to locate and remove defects in (a device, system, plan, etc.). **3** to remove insects from. [C20: from DE- + BUG]

debunk ➊ (diːˈbʌŋk) *vb* (*tr*) *Inf.* to expose the pretensions or falseness of, esp. by ridicule. [C20: from DE- + BUNK[2]]
▸**deˈbunker** *n*

debus (diːˈbʌs) *vb* **debuses, debusing, debused** *or* **debusses, debussing, debussed.** to unload (goods, etc.) or (esp. of troops) to alight from a bus.

debut ➊ (ˈdeɪbjuː, ˈdɛbjuː) *n* **1a** the first public appearance of an actor, musician, etc. **1b** (*as modifier*): *debut album.* **2** the presentation of a debutante. [C18: from F, from OF *desbuter* to play first, from *des-* DE- + *but* goal, target]

debutante (ˈdɛbjʊˌtɑːnt, -ˌtænt) *n* **1** a young upper-class woman who is formally presented to society. **2** a young woman regarded as being upper-class, wealthy, and frivolous. [C19: from F, from *débuter* to lead off in a game, make one's first appearance; see DEBUT]

dec. *abbrev. for:* **1** deceased. **2** decimal. **3** decimetre. **4** declaration. **5** declension. **6** declination. **7** decrease. **8** *Music.* decrescendo.

Dec. *abbrev. for* December.

deca-, deka- *or before a vowel* **dec-, dek-** *prefix* denoting ten: *decagon.* In conjunction with scientific units the symbol **da** is used. [from Gk *deka*]

decade (ˈdɛkeɪd, dɪˈkeɪd) *n* **1** a period of ten years. **2** a group of ten. [C15: from OF, from LL, from Gk, from *deka* ten]
▸**deˈcadal** *adj*

decadence ➊ (ˈdɛkədəns) *or* **decadency** *n* **1** deterioration, esp. of morality or culture. **2** the state reached through such a process. **3** (*often cap.*) the period or style associated with the 19th-century decadents. [C16: from F, from Med. L *dēcadentia,* lit.: a falling away; see DECAY]

decadent ➊ (ˈdɛkədənt) *adj* **1** characterized by decline, as in being self-indulgent or morally corrupt. **2** belonging to a period of decline in artistic standards. ◆ *n* **3** a decadent person. **4** (*often cap.*) one of a group of French and English writers of the late 19th century whose works were characterized by refinement of style and a tendency toward the artificial and abnormal.

decaf (ˈdiːkæf) *Inf.* ◆ *n* **1** decaffeinated coffee. ◆ *adj* **2** decaffeinated.

decaffeinate (dɪˈkæfɪˌneɪt) *vb* **decaffeinates, decaffeinating, decaffeinated.** (*tr*) to remove all or part of the caffeine from (coffee, tea, etc.).

decagon (ˈdɛkəˌgɒn) *n* a polygon having ten sides.
▸**decagonal** (dɪˈkægənˡl) *adj*

THESAURUS

debase *vb* = **degrade**, abase, cheapen, demean, devalue, disgrace, dishonour, drag down, humble, humiliate, lower, reduce, shame = **contaminate**, adulterate, bastardize, corrupt, defile, depreciate, impair, pollute, taint, vitiate
Antonyms *vb* ≠ **degrade:** elevate, enhance, exalt, improve, uplift ≠ **contaminate:** purify

debased *adj* = **degraded**, abandoned, base, corrupt, debauched, depraved, devalued, fallen, low, perverted, sordid, vile = **contaminated**, adulterated, depreciated, impure, lowered, mixed, polluted, reduced
Antonyms *adj* ≠ **degraded:** chaste, decent, ethical, good, honourable, incorruptible, innocent, moral, pure, upright, virtuous ≠ **contaminated:** pure

debasement *n* **1** = **degradation**, abasement, baseness, corruption, depravation, devaluation, perversion **1** = **contamination**, adulteration, depreciation, pollution, reduction

debatable *adj* **4, 5** = **doubtful**, arguable, borderline, controversial, disputable, dubious, iffy (*inf.*), in dispute, moot, open to question, problematical, questionable, uncertain, undecided, unsettled

debate *n* **1** = **consideration**, cogitation, deliberation, meditation, reflection **2** = **discussion**, altercation, argument, contention, controversy, disputation, dispute, polemic, row ◆ *vb* **4** = **discuss**, argue, contend, contest, controvert, dispute, question, wrangle **5** = **consider**, cogitate, deliberate, meditate upon, mull over, ponder, reflect, revolve, ruminate, weigh

debauched *adj* **1** = **corrupt**, abandoned, debased, degenerate, degraded, depraved, dissipated, dissolute, immoral, licentious, perverted, profligate, sleazy, wanton

debauchery *n* **3** = **depravity**, carousal, dissipation, dissoluteness, excess, gluttony, incontinence, indulgence, intemperance, lewdness, licentiousness, lust, orgy, overindulgence, revel

debilitate *vb* = **weaken**, devitalize, enervate, enfeeble, exhaust, incapacitate, prostrate, relax, sap, undermine, wear out
Antonyms *vb* animate, brighten, energize, enliven, excite, fire, invigorate, pep up, perk up, rouse, stimulate, vitalize, wake up

debilitating *adj* = **weakening**, devitalizing, draining, enervating, enfeebling, exhausting, fatiguing, incapacitating, sapping, tiring, wearing, wearisome
Antonyms *adj* animating, energizing, enlivening, exciting, invigorating, rousing, stimulating, vitalizing

debility *n* = **weakness**, decrepitude, enervation, enfeeblement, exhaustion, faintness, feebleness, frailty, incapacity, infirmity, languor, malaise, sickliness

debonair *adj* **1-3** = **elegant**, affable, buoyant, charming, cheerful, courteous, dashing, jaunty, light-hearted, refined, smooth, sprightly, suave, urbane, well-bred

debrief *vb* = **interrogate**, cross-examine, examine, probe, question, quiz

debris *n* **1, 2** = **remains**, bits, brash, detritus, dross, fragments, litter, pieces, rubbish, rubble, ruins, waste, wreck, wreckage

debt *n* **1** = **debit**, arrears, bill, claim, commitment, due, duty, liability, obligation, score **4 in debt** = **owing**, accountable, beholden, in arrears, in hock (*inf., chiefly US*), in the red (*inf.*), liable, responsible

debtor *n* = **borrower**, defaulter, insolvent, mortgagor

debunk *vb Informal* = **expose**, cut down to size, deflate, disparage, lampoon, mock, puncture, ridicule, show up

debut *n* **1a** = **introduction**, beginning, bow, coming out, entrance, first appearance, inauguration, initiation, launching, presentation

decadence *n* **1, 2** = **degeneration**, corruption, debasement, decay, decline, deterioration, dissipation, dissolution, fall, perversion, retrogression

decadent *adj* **1** = **degenerate**, abandoned, corrupt, debased, debauched, decaying, declining, degraded, depraved, dissolute, immoral, self-indulgent
Antonyms *adj* decent, ethical, good, high-minded, honourable, incorruptible, moral, principled, proper, upright, upstanding, virtuous

decahedron (ˌdɛkəˈhiːdrən) *n* a solid figure having ten plane faces. ▸ˌ**decaˈhedral** *adj*

decal (dɪˈkæl, ˈdiːkæl) *n* **1** short for **decalcomania.** ◆ *vb* **decals, decalling, decalled** *or US* **decals, decaling, decaled. 2** to transfer (a design, etc.) by decalcomania.

decalcify (diːˈkælsɪˌfaɪ) *vb* **decalcifies, decalcifying, decalcified.** (*tr*) to remove calcium or lime from (bones, etc.). ▸**deˈcalciˌfier** *n*

decalcomania (dɪˌkælkəˈmeɪnɪə) *n* **1** the process of transferring a design from prepared paper onto another surface, such as glass or paper. **2** a design so transferred. [C19: from F, from *décalquer,* from *de-* DE- + *calquer* to trace + *-manie* -MANIA]

decalitre *or US* **decaliter** (ˈdɛkəˌliːtə) *n* a metric measure of volume equivalent to 10 litres.

Decalogue (ˈdɛkəˌlɒg) *n* another name for the **Ten Commandments.** [C14: from Church L *decalogus,* from Gk, from *deka* ten + *logos* word]

decametre *or US* **decameter** (ˈdɛkəˌmiːtə) *n* a metric measure of length equivalent to 10 metres.

decamp ⓣ (dɪˈkæmp) *vb* (*intr*) **1** to leave a camp; break camp. **2** to depart secretly or suddenly; abscond. ▸**deˈcampment** *n*

decanal (dɪˈkeɪnᵊl) *adj* **1** of a dean or deanery. **2** on the same side of a cathedral, etc., as the dean; on the S side of the choir. [C18: from Med. L *decānālis, decānus* DEAN]

decani (dɪˈkeɪnaɪ) *adj, adv Music.* to be sung by the decanal side of a choir. Cf. **cantoris.** [L: genitive of *decānus*]

decant ⓣ (dɪˈkænt) *vb* **1** to pour (a liquid, such as wine) from one container to another, esp. without disturbing any sediment. **2** (*tr*) to rehouse (people) while their homes are being rebuilt or refurbished. [C17: from Med. L *dēcanthāre,* from *canthus* spout, rim]

decanter (dɪˈkæntə) *n* a stoppered bottle, into which a drink is poured for serving.

decapitate ⓣ (dɪˈkæpɪˌteɪt) *vb* **decapitates, decapitating, decapitated.** (*tr*) to behead. [C17: from LL *dēcapitāre,* from L DE- + *caput* head] ▸**deˌcapiˈtation** *n* ▸**deˈcapiˌtator** *n*

decapod (ˈdɛkəˌpɒd) *n* **1** any crustacean having five pairs of walking limbs, as a crab, lobster, shrimp, etc. **2** any cephalopod mollusc having eight short tentacles and two longer ones, as a squid or cuttlefish. ▸**decapodal** (dɪˈkæpədᵊl), **deˈcapodan,** *or* **deˈcapodous** *adj*

decarbonate (diːˈkɑːbəˌneɪt) *vb* **decarbonates, decarbonating, decarbonated.** (*tr*) to remove carbon dioxide from. ▸**deˌcarbonˈation** *n* ▸**deˈcarbonˌator** *n*

decarbonize *or* **decarbonise** (diːˈkɑːbəˌnaɪz) *vb* **decarbonizes, decarbonizing, decarbonized** *or* **decarbonises, decarbonising, decarbonised.** (*tr*) to remove carbon from (an internal-combustion engine, etc.). Also: **decoke, decarburize.** ▸**deˌcarboniˈzation** *or* **deˌcarboniˈsation** *n* ▸**deˈcarbonˌizer** *or* **deˈcarbonˌiser** *n*

decarboxylase (ˌdiːkɑːˈbɒksɪˌleɪz) *n* an enzyme that catalyses the removal of carbon dioxide from a compound.

decastyle (ˈdɛkəˌstaɪl) *n Archit.* a portico consisting of ten columns.

decasyllable (ˈdɛkəˌsɪləbᵊl) *n* a word or line of verse consisting of ten syllables. ▸**decasyllabic** (ˌdɛkəsɪˈlæbɪk) *adj*

decathlon (dɪˈkæθlɒn) *n* an athletic contest in which each athlete competes in ten different events. [C20: from DECA- + Gk *athlon* contest, prize; see ATHLETE] ▸**deˈcathlete** *n*

decay ⓣ (dɪˈkeɪ) *vb* **1** to decline or cause to decline gradually in health, prosperity, excellence, etc.; deteriorate. **2** to rot or cause to rot; decompose. **3** (*intr*) Also: **disintegrate.** *Physics.* **3a** (of an atomic nucleus) to undergo radioactive disintegration. **3b** (of an elementary particle) to transform into two or more different elementary particles. **4** (*intr*) *Physics.* (of a stored charge, magnetic flux, etc.) to decrease gradually when the source of energy has been removed. ◆ *n* **5** the process of decline, as in health, mentality, etc. **6** the state brought about by this process. **7** decomposition. **8** rotten or decayed matter. **9** *Physics.* **9a** See **radioactive decay. 9b** a spontaneous transformation of an elementary particle into two or more different particles. **10** *Physics.* a gradual decrease of a stored charge, current, etc., when the source of energy has been removed. [C15: from OF *decaïr,* from LL *dēcadere,* lit.: to fall away, from L *cadere* to fall] ▸**deˈcayable** *adj*

decease ⓣ (dɪˈsiːs) *n* **1** a more formal word for **death.** ◆ *vb* **deceases, deceasing, deceased. 2** (*intr*) a more formal word for **die**[1]. [C14 (n): from OF, from L *dēcēdere* to depart]

deceased ⓣ (dɪˈsiːst) *adj* **a** a more formal word for **dead** (sense 1). **b** (*as n; preceded by the*): *the deceased.*

deceit ⓣ (dɪˈsiːt) *n* **1** the act or practice of deceiving. **2** a statement, act, or device intended to mislead; fraud; trick. **3** a tendency to deceive. [C13: from OF, from *deceivre* to DECEIVE]

deceitful ⓣ (dɪˈsiːtful) *adj* full of deceit.

deceive ⓣ (dɪˈsiːv) *vb* **deceives, deceiving, deceived.** (*tr*) **1** to mislead by deliberate misrepresentation or lies. **2** to delude (oneself). **3** to be unfaithful to (one's sexual partner). **4** *Arch.* to disappoint. [C13: from OF *deceivre,* from L *dēcipere* to ensnare, cheat, from *capere* to take] ▸**deˈceivable** *adj* ▸**deˈceiver** *n*

decelerate ⓣ (diːˈsɛləˌreɪt) *vb* **decelerates, decelerating, decelerated.** to slow down or cause to slow down. [C19: from DE- + (AC)CELERATE] ▸**deˌcelerˈation** *n* ▸**deˈcelerˌator** *n*

December (dɪˈsɛmbə) *n* the twelfth month of the year, consisting of 31 days. [C13: from OF, from L: the tenth month (the Roman year orig. began with March), from *decem* ten]

decencies (ˈdiːsᵊnsɪz) *pl n* **1 the.** those things that are considered necessary for a decent life. **2** another word for **proprieties,** see **propriety** (sense 3).

decency ⓣ (ˈdiːsᵊnsɪ) *n, pl* **decencies. 1** conformity to the prevailing standards of propriety, morality, modesty, etc. **2** the quality of being decent.

decennial (dɪˈsɛnɪəl) *adj* **1** lasting for ten years. **2** occurring every ten years. ◆ *n* **3** a tenth anniversary. ▸**deˈcennially** *adv*

decent ⓣ (ˈdiːsᵊnt) *adj* **1** polite or respectable. **2** proper and suitable; fitting. **3** conforming to conventions of sexual behaviour; not indecent. **4** free of oaths, blasphemy, etc. **5** good or adequate: *a decent wage.* **6** *Inf.* kind; generous. **7** *Inf.* sufficiently clothed to be seen by other people: *are you decent?* [C16: from L *decēns* suitable, from *decēre* to be fitting] ▸ˈ**decently** *adv*

decentralize *or* **decentralise** (diːˈsɛntrəˌlaɪz) *vb* **decentralizes, decentralizing, decentralized** *or* **decentralises, decentralising, decentralised. 1** to reorganize into smaller more autonomous units. **2** to disperse (a concentration, as of industry or population). ▸**deˈcentralist** *n, adj* ▸**deˌcentraliˈzation** *or* **deˌcentraliˈsation** *n*

deception ⓣ (dɪˈsɛpʃən) *n* **1** the act of deceiving or the state of being deceived. **2** something that deceives; trick.

THESAURUS

decamp *vb* **1** *Military* = **strike camp,** break up camp, evacuate, march off, move off, vacate **2** = **make off,** abscond, bolt, desert, do a bunk (*Brit. sl.*), do a runner (*sl.*), escape, flee, flit (*inf.*), fly, fly the coop (*US & Canad. inf.*), hightail (*inf., chiefly US*), hook it (*sl.*), run away, scarper (*Brit. sl.*), skedaddle (*inf.*), sneak off, steal away, take a powder (*US & Canad. sl.*), take it on the lam (*US & Canad. sl.*)

decant *vb* **1** = **pour out,** drain, draw off, tap

decapitate *vb* = **behead,** execute, guillotine

decay *vb* **1** = **decline,** atrophy, break down, crumble, degenerate, deteriorate, disintegrate, dissolve, dwindle, moulder, shrivel, sink, spoil, wane, waste away, wear away, wither **2** = **rot,** corrode, decompose, mortify, perish, putrefy ◆ *n* **5** = **decline,** atrophy, collapse, decadence, degeneracy, degeneration, deterioration, dying, fading, failing, wasting, withering **7** = **rot,** caries, cariosity, decomposition, gangrene, mortification, perishing, putrefaction, putrescence, putridity, rotting
Antonyms *vb* ≠ **decline:** expand, flourish, flower, grow, increase ◆ *n* ≠ **decline:** growth

decayed *adj* **1, 2** = **rotten,** bad, carious, carrion, corroded, decomposed, perished, putrefied, putrid, rank, spoiled, wasted, withered

decaying 1, 2 *adj* = **rotting,** crumbling, deteriorating, disintegrating, gangrenous, perishing, putrefacient, wasting away, wearing away

decease *n Formal* **1** = **death,** demise, departure, dissolution, dying, release

deceased *adj* **a** = **dead,** defunct, departed, expired, finished, former, gone, late, lifeless, lost, pushing up daisies

deceit *n* **1** = **dishonesty,** artifice, cheating, chicanery, craftiness, cunning, deceitfulness, deception, dissimulation, double-dealing, duplicity, fraud, fraudulence, guile, hypocrisy, imposition, lying, pretence, slyness, treachery, trickery, underhandedness **2** = **lie,** artifice, blind, cheat, chicanery, deception, duplicity, fake, feint, fraud, imposture, misrepresentation, pretence, ruse, scam (*sl.*), sham, shift, sting (*inf.*), stratagem, subterfuge, swindle, trick, wile
Antonyms *n* ≠ **dishonesty:** candour, frankness, honesty, openness, sincerity, truthfulness

deceitful *adj* = **dishonest,** counterfeit, crafty, deceiving, deceptive, designing, disingenuous, double-dealing, duplicitous, fallacious, false, fraudulent, guileful, hypocritical, illusory, insincere, knavish (*arch.*), sneaky, treacherous, tricky, two-faced, underhand, untrustworthy

deceive *vb* **1** = **take in** (*inf.*), bamboozle (*inf.*), beguile, betray, cheat, con, cozen, delude, disappoint, double-cross (*inf.*), dupe, ensnare, entrap, fool, hoax, hoodwink, impose upon, kid (*inf.*), lead (someone) on (*inf.*), mislead, outwit, pull a fast one (*sl.*), pull the wool over (someone's) eyes, stiff (*sl.*), sting (*inf.*), swindle, take for a ride (*inf.*), trick

deceiver *n* **1** = **liar,** betrayer, charlatan, cheat, chiseller (*inf.*), con man (*inf.*), cozener, crook (*inf.*), deluder, dissembler, double-dealer, fake, fraud, fraudster, hypocrite, impostor, inveigler, mountebank, pretender, sharper, snake in the grass, swindler, trickster

decelerate *vb* = **slow down** *or* **up,** brake, check, put the brakes on, reduce speed, slow
Antonyms *vb* accelerate, pick up speed, quicken, speed up

decency *n* **1, 2** = **respectability,** appropriateness, civility, correctness, courtesy, decorum, etiquette, fitness, good form, good manners, modesty, propriety, seemliness

decent *adj* **2** = **proper,** appropriate, becoming, befitting, comely, *comme il faut,* fit, fitting, seemly, suitable **3** = **respectable,** chaste, decorous, delicate, modest, nice, polite, presentable, proper, pure **5** = **satisfactory,** acceptable, adequate, ample, average, competent, fair, passable, reasonable, sufficient, tolerable **6** *Informal* = **kind,** accommodating, courteous, friendly, generous, gracious, helpful, obliging, thoughtful
Antonyms *adj* ≠ **satisfactory:** clumsy, inept, unsatisfactory ≠ **proper:** awkward, immodest, improper, incorrect, indecent, unseemly, unsuitable ≠ **kind:** awkward, discourteous

deception *n* **1** = **trickery,** craftiness, cunning,

deceptive ⓣ (dɪˈsɛptɪv) *adj* likely or designed to deceive; misleading. ▸**deˈceptively** *adv* ▸**deˈceptiveness** *n*

deci- *prefix* denoting one tenth: *decimetre*. Symbol: d [from F *déci-*, from L *decimus* tenth]

decibel (ˈdɛsɪˌbɛl) *n* **1** a unit for comparing two currents, voltages, or power levels, equal to one tenth of a bel. **2** a similar unit for measuring the intensity of a sound. Abbrev.: **dB.**

decide ⓣ (dɪˈsaɪd) *vb* **decides, deciding, decided. 1** (*may take a clause or an infinitive as object;* when *intr*, sometimes foll. by *on* or *about*) to reach a decision: *decide what you want; he decided to go.* **2** (*tr*) to cause to reach a decision. **3** (*tr*) to determine or settle (a contest or question). **4** (*tr*) to influence decisively the outcome of (a contest or question). **5** (*intr;* foll. by *for* or *against*) to pronounce a formal verdict. [C14: from OF, from L *dēcīdere*, lit.: to cut off, from *caedere* to cut]
▸**deˈcidable** *adj*

decided ⓣ (dɪˈsaɪdɪd) *adj* (*prenominal*) **1** unmistakable. **2** determined; resolute: *a girl of decided character.*
▸**deˈcidedly** *adv*

decider (dɪˈsaɪdə) *n* the point, goal, game, etc., that determines who wins a match or championship.

deciduous (dɪˈsɪdjʊəs) *adj* **1** (of trees and shrubs) shedding all leaves annually at the end of the growing season. Cf. **evergreen. 2** (of antlers, teeth, etc.) being shed at the end of a period of growth. [C17: from L: falling off, from *dēcidere* to fall down, from *cadere* to fall]
▸**deˈciduousness** *n*

decilitre *or US* **deciliter** (ˈdɛsɪˌliːtə) *n* a metric measure of volume equivalent to one tenth of a litre.

decillion (dɪˈsɪljən) *n* **1** (in Britain, France, and Germany) the number represented as one followed by 60 zeros (10^{60}). **2** (in the US and Canada) the number represented as one followed by 33 zeros (10^{33}). [C19: from L *decem* ten + *-illion* as in *million*]
▸**deˈcillionth** *adj*

decimal (ˈdɛsɪməl) *n* **1** Also called: **decimal fraction.** a fraction that has an unwritten denominator of a power of ten. It is indicated by a decimal point to the left of the numerator: *.2=2/10.* **2** any number used in the decimal system. ◆ *adj* **3a** relating to or using powers of ten. **3b** of the base ten. **4** (*prenominal*) expressed as a decimal. [C17: from Med. L *decimālis* of tithes, from L *decima* a tenth]
▸ˈ**decimally** *adv*

decimal classification *n* another term for **Dewey Decimal System.**

decimal currency *n* a system of currency in which the monetary units are parts or powers of ten.

decimalize *or* **decimalise** (ˈdɛsɪməˌlaɪz) *vb* **decimalizes, decimalizing, decimalized** *or* **decimalises, decimalising, decimalised.** to change (a system, number, etc.) to the decimal system.
▸ˌ**decimaliˈzation** *or* ˌ**decimaliˈsation** *n*

decimal place *n* **1** the position of a digit after the decimal point. **2** the number of digits to the right of the decimal point.

decimal point *n* a full stop or a raised full stop placed between the integral and fractional parts of a number in the decimal system.

> **USAGE NOTE** Conventions relating to the use of the decimal point are confused. The IX General Conference on Weights and Measures resolved in 1948 that the decimal point should be a point on the line or a comma, but not a centre dot. It also resolved that figures could be grouped in threes about the decimal point, but that no point or comma should be used for this purpose. These conventions are adopted in this dictionary. However, the Decimal Currency Board recommended that for sums of money the centre dot should be used as the decimal point and that the comma should be used as the thousand marker. Moreover, in some countries the position is reversed, the comma being used as the decimal point and the dot as the thousand marker.

decimal system *n* **1** the number system in general use, having a base of ten, in which numbers are expressed by combinations of the ten digits 0 to 9. **2** a system of measurement in which the multiple and submultiple units are related to a basic unit by powers of ten.

decimate ⓣ (ˈdɛsɪˌmeɪt) *vb* **decimates, decimating, decimated.** (*tr*) **1** to destroy or kill a large proportion of. **2** (esp. in the ancient Roman army) to kill every tenth man of (a mutinous section). [C17: from L *decimāre*, from *decem* ten]
▸ˌ**deciˈmation** *n* ▸ˈ**deciˌmator** *n*

> **USAGE NOTE** One talks about the whole of something being *decimated*, not a part: *disease decimated the population*, not *disease decimated most of the population.*

decimetre *or US* **decimeter** (ˈdɛsɪˌmiːtə) *n* one tenth of a metre. Symbol: **dm.**

decipher ⓣ (dɪˈsaɪfə) *vb* (*tr*) **1** to determine the meaning of (something obscure or illegible). **2** to convert from code into plain text; decode.
▸**deˈcipherable** *adj* ▸**deˈcipherment** *n*

decision ⓣ (dɪˈsɪʒən) *n* **1** a judgment, conclusion, or resolution reached or given; verdict. **2** the act of making up one's mind. **3** firmness of purpose or character; determination. [C15: from OF, from L *dēcīsiō*, lit.: a cutting off; see DECIDE]

decision tree *n* a treelike diagram illustrating the choices available to a decision maker, each possible decision and its estimated outcome being shown as a separate branch of the tree.

decisive ⓣ (dɪˈsaɪsɪv) *adj* **1** influential; conclusive. **2** characterized by the ability to make decisions, esp. quickly; resolute.
▸**deˈcisively** *adv* ▸**deˈcisiveness** *n*

deck ⓣ (dɛk) *n* **1** *Naut.* any of various platforms built into a vessel. **2** a similar platform, as in a bus. **3a** the horizontal platform that supports the turntable and pick-up of a record player. **3b** See **tape deck. 4** *Chiefly US.* a pack of playing cards. **5** *Computing.* a collection of punched cards relevant to a particular program. **6 clear the decks.** *Inf.* to prepare for action, as by removing obstacles. **7 hit the deck.** *Inf.* **7a** to fall to the ground, esp. to avoid injury. **7b** to prepare for action. **7c** to get out of bed. ◆ *vb* (*tr*) **8** (often foll. by *out*) to dress or decorate. **9** to build a deck on (a vessel). **10** *Sl.* to knock (someone) to the floor or ground. [C15: from MDu. *dec* a covering]

deck-access *adj* (of a block of flats) having a continuous balcony at each level onto which the front door of each flat opens.

deck chair *n* a folding chair consisting of a wooden frame suspending a length of canvas.

-decker *adj* (*in combination*) having a certain specified number of levels or layers: *a double-decker bus.*

deck hand *n* **1** a seaman assigned duties on the deck of a ship. **2** (in Britain) a seaman who has seen sea duty for at least one year. **3** a helper aboard a yacht.

deckle *or* **deckel** (ˈdɛkᵊl) *n* **1** a frame used to contain pulp on the mould in the making of handmade paper. **2** a strap on a paper-making machine that fixes the width of the paper. [C19: from G *Deckel* lid, from *decken* to cover]

deckle edge *n* **1** the rough edge of paper made using a deckle, often left as ornamentation. **2** an imitation of this.
▸ˈ**deckle-**ˈ**edged** *adj*

declaim ⓣ (dɪˈkleɪm) *vb* **1** to make (a speech, etc.) loudly and in a rhetorical manner. **2** to speak lines from (a play, poem, etc.) with studied

THESAURUS

deceit, deceitfulness, deceptiveness, dissimulation, duplicity, fraud, fraudulence, guile, hypocrisy, imposition, insincerity, legerdemain, treachery **2** = **trick**, artifice, bluff, canard, cheat, decoy, feint, fraud, hoax, hokum (*sl., chiefly US. & Canad.*), illusion, imposture, leg-pull (*Brit. inf.*), lie, pork pie, porky (*Brit. sl.*), ruse, sham, snare, snow job (*sl., chiefly US. & Canad.*), stratagem, subterfuge, wile
Antonyms *n* ≠ **trickery:** artlessness, candour, fidelity, frankness, honesty, openness, scrupulousness, straightforwardness, trustworthiness, truthfulness

deceptive *adj* = **misleading**, ambiguous, deceitful, delusive, dishonest, fake, fallacious, false, fraudulent, illusory, mock, specious, spurious, unreliable

decide *vb* **1-5** = **reach** *or* **come to a decision**, adjudge, adjudicate, choose, come to a conclusion, commit oneself, conclude, decree, determine, elect, end, make a decision, make up one's mind, purpose, resolve, settle, tip the balance
Antonyms *vb* be indecisive, be unable to decide, blow hot and cold (*inf.*), dither (*chiefly Brit.*), falter, fluctuate, hesitate, hum and haw, seesaw, shillyshally (*inf.*), swither (*Scot.*), vacillate

decided *adj* **1** = **definite**, absolute, categorical, certain, clear-cut, distinct, express, indisputable, positive, pronounced, unambiguous, undeniable, undisputed, unequivocal, unquestionable **2** = **determined**, assertive, decisive, deliberate, emphatic, firm, resolute, strong-willed, unfaltering, unhesitating
Antonyms *adj* ≠ **definite:** doubtful, dubious, questionable, undetermined ≠ **determined:** hesitant, indecisive, irresolute, undetermined, weak

decidedly *adv* **1** = **definitely**, absolutely, certainly, clearly, decisively, distinctly, downright, positively, unequivocally, unmistakably

deciding *adj* **4** = **determining**, chief, conclusive, critical, crucial, decisive, influential, prime, principal, significant

decimate *vb* **1** = **devastate**, destroy, lay waste, ravage, wreak havoc on

decipher *vb* **1, 2** = **figure out** (*inf.*), construe, crack, decode, deduce, explain, interpret, make out, read, reveal, solve, suss (out) (*sl.*), understand, unfold, unravel

decision *n* **1** = **judgment**, arbitration, conclusion, finding, outcome, resolution, result, ruling, sentence, settlement, verdict **3** = **decisiveness**, determination, firmness, purpose, purposefulness, resoluteness, resolution, resolve, strength of mind *or* will

decisive *adj* **1** = **crucial**, absolute, conclusive, critical, definite, definitive, fateful, final, influential, momentous, positive, significant **2** = **resolute**, decided, determined, firm, forceful, incisive, strong-minded, trenchant
Antonyms *adj* ≠ **crucial:** doubtful, indecisive, uncertain, undecided ≠ **resolute:** hesitant, hesitating, indecisive, in two minds (*inf.*), irresolute, pussy-footing (*inf.*), uncertain, undecided, vacillating

deck *vb* **8** = **decorate**, adorn, apparel (*arch.*), array, attire, beautify, bedeck, bedight (*arch.*), bedizen (*arch.*), clothe, dress, embellish, engarland, festoon, garland, grace, ornament, trim **8 deck up** *or* **out** = **dress up**, doll up (*sl.*), get ready, prettify, pretty up, prink, rig out, tog up *or* out, trick out

declaim *vb* **1, 2** = **orate**, harangue, hold forth, lecture, perorate, proclaim, rant, recite, speak, spiel (*inf.*) **3 declaim against** = **protest against**, attack, decry, denounce, inveigh, rail

eloquence. **3** (*intr;* foll. by *against*) to protest (against) loudly and publicly. [C14: from L *dēclāmāre,* from *clāmāre* to call out]
▸**deˈclaimer** *n* ▸**declamatory** (dɪˈklæmətərɪ) *adj*

declamation ❶ (ˌdɛkləˈmeɪʃən) *n* **1** a rhetorical or emotional speech, made esp. in order to protest; tirade. **2** a speech, verse, etc., that is or can be spoken. **3** the act or art of declaiming.

declaration ❶ (ˌdɛkləˈreɪʃən) *n* **1** an explicit or emphatic statement. **2** a formal statement or announcement. **3** the act of declaring. **4** the ruling of a judge or court on a question of law. **5** *Law.* an unsworn statement of a witness admissible in evidence under certain conditions. **6** *Cricket.* the voluntary closure of an innings before all ten wickets have fallen. **7** *Contract bridge.* the final contract. **8** a statement or inventory of goods, etc., submitted for tax assessment.

declarative ❶ (dɪˈklærətɪv) *or* **declaratory** (dɪˈklærətərɪ, -trɪ) *adj* making or having the nature of a declaration.
▸**deˈclaratively** *or* **deˈclaratorily** *adv*

declare ❶ (dɪˈklɛə) *vb* **declares, declaring, declared.** (*mainly tr*) **1** (*may take a clause as object*) to make clearly known or announce officially: *war was declared.* **2** to state officially that (a person, fact, etc.) is as specified: *he declared him fit.* **3** (*may take a clause as object*) to state emphatically; assert. **4** to show, reveal, or manifest. **5** (*intr;* often foll. by *for* or *against*) to make known one's choice or opinion. **6** to make a statement of (dutiable goods, etc.). **7** (*also intr*) *Cards.* **7a** to display (cards) on the table so as to add to one's score. **7b** to decide (the trump suit) by making the winning bid. **8** (*intr*) *Cricket.* to close an innings voluntarily before all ten wickets have fallen. **9** to authorize payment of (a dividend). [C14: from L *dēclārāre* to make clear, from *clārus* clear]
▸**deˈclarable** *adj* ▸**deˈclarer** *n*

declassify (diːˈklæsɪˌfaɪ) *vb* **declassifies, declassifying, declassified.** (*tr*) to release (a document or information) from the security list.
▸**deˌclassifiˈcation** *n*

declension ❶ (dɪˈklɛnʃən) *n* **1** *Grammar.* **1a** inflection of nouns, pronouns, or adjectives for case, number, and gender. **1b** the complete set of the inflections of such a word. **2** a decline or deviation. **3** a downward slope. [C15: from L *dēclīnātiō,* lit.: a bending aside, hence variation; see DECLINE]
▸**deˈclensional** *adj*

declination (ˌdɛklɪˈneɪʃən) *n* **1** *Astron.* the angular distance of a star, planet, etc., north or south from the celestial equator. Symbol: δ. **2** the angle made by a compass needle with the direction of the geographical north pole. **3** a refusal, esp. a courteous or formal one.
▸ˌ**decliˈnational** *adj*

decline ❶ (dɪˈklaɪn) *vb* **declines, declining, declined. 1** to refuse to do or accept (something), esp. politely. **2** (*intr*) to grow smaller; diminish. **3** to slope or cause to slope downwards. **4** (*intr*) to deteriorate gradually. **5** *Grammar.* to list the inflections of (a noun, adjective, or pronoun), or (of a noun, adjective, or pronoun) to be inflected for number, case, or gender. ◆ *n* **6** gradual deterioration or loss. **7** a movement downward; diminution. **8** a downward slope. **9** *Arch.* any slowly progressive disease, such as tuberculosis. [C14: from OF *decliner,* from L *dēclīnāre* to bend away, inflect grammatically]
▸**deˈclinable** *adj* ▸**deˈcliner** *n*

declivity (dɪˈklɪvɪtɪ) *n, pl* **declivities.** a downward slope, esp. of the ground. [C17: from L *dēclīvitās,* from DE- + *clīvus* a slope, hill]
▸**deˈclivitous** *adj*

declutch (dɪˈklʌtʃ) *vb* (*intr*) to disengage the clutch of a motor vehicle.

decoct (dɪˈkɒkt) *vb* to extract the essence or active principle from (a medicinal or similar substance) by boiling. [C15: see DECOCTION]

decoction (dɪˈkɒkʃən) *n* **1** *Pharmacol.* the extraction of the water-soluble substances of a drug or medicinal plants by boiling. **2** the liquor resulting from this. [C14: from OF, from LL, from *dēcoquere* to boil down, from *coquere* to cook]

decode ❶ (diːˈkəʊd) *vb* **decodes, decoding, decoded.** to convert from code into ordinary language.
▸**deˈcoder** *n*

decoke (diːˈkəʊk) *vb* **decokes, decoking, decoked.** (*tr*) another word for **decarbonize.**

décolletage (ˌdeɪkɒlˈtɑːʒ) *n* a low-cut dress or neckline. [C19: from F; see DÉCOLLETÉ]

décolleté (deɪˈkɒlteɪ) *adj* **1** (of a woman's garment) low-cut. **2** wearing a low-cut garment. ◆ *n* **3** a low-cut neckline. [C19: from F *décolleter* to cut out the neck (of a dress), from *collet* collar]

decolonize *or* **decolonise** (diːˈkɒləˌnaɪz) *vb* **decolonizes, decolonizing, decolonized** *or* **decolonises, decolonising, decolonised.** (*tr*) to grant independence to (a colony).
▸**deˌcoloniˈzation** *or* ▸**deˌcoloniˈsation** *n*

decolour (diːˈkʌlə), **decolorize,** *or* **decolorise** *vb* **decolorizes, decolorizing, decolorized** *or* **decolorises, decolorising, decolorised.** (*tr*) to deprive of colour.
▸**deˌcoloriˈzation** *or* **deˌcoloriˈsation** *n*

decommission (ˌdiːkəˈmɪʃən) *vb* (*tr*) to dismantle or remove from service (a nuclear reactor, weapon, ship, etc. which is no longer required).

decompose ❶ (ˌdiːkəmˈpəʊz) *vb* **decomposes, decomposing, decomposed. 1** to break down or be broken down into constituent elements by bacterial or fungal action; rot. **2** *Chem.* to break down or cause to break down into simpler chemical compounds. **3** to break up or separate into constituent parts.
▸**decomposition** (ˌdiːkɒmpəˈzɪʃən) *n*

decomposer (ˌdiːkəmˈpəʊzə) *n* a person or thing that causes decomposition, esp. any of the organisms, such as bacteria, that do so in an ecosystem.

decompress (ˌdiːkəmˈprɛs) *vb* **1** to relieve or be relieved of pressure. **2** to return (a diver, etc.) to a condition of normal atmospheric pressure or to be returned to such a condition.
▸ˌ**decomˈpression** *n*

decompression chamber *n* a chamber in which the pressure of air can be varied slowly for returning people safely from abnormal pressures to atmospheric pressure.

decompression sickness *or* **illness** *n* a disorder characterized by severe pain, cramp, and difficulty in breathing, caused by a sudden and sustained decrease in atmospheric pressure.

decongestant (ˌdiːkənˈdʒɛstənt) *adj* **1** relieving congestion, esp. nasal congestion. ◆ *n* **2** a decongestant drug.

deconsecrate (diːˈkɒnsɪˌkreɪt) *vb* **deconsecrates, deconsecrating, deconsecrated.** (*tr*) to transfer (a church, etc.) to secular use.
▸**deˌconseˈcration** *n*

deconstruct (ˌdiːkənˈstrʌkt) *vb* (*tr*) **1** to apply the theories of deconstruction to (a text, film, etc.). **2** to expose or dismantle the existing structure in (a system, organization, etc.).

deconstruction (ˌdiːkənˈstrʌkʃən) *n* a technique of literary analysis that regards meaning as resulting from the differences between words rather than their reference to the things they stand for.

decontaminate ❶ (ˌdiːkənˈtæmɪˌneɪt) *vb* **decontaminates, decontaminating, decontaminated.** (*tr*) to render harmless by the removal or neutralization of poisons, radioactivity, etc.
▸ˌ**deconˌtamiˈnation** *n*

decontrol (ˌdiːkənˈtrəʊl) *vb* **decontrols, decontrolling, decontrolled.** (*tr*) to free of restraints or controls, esp. government controls: *to decontrol prices.*

décor ❶ *or* **decor** (ˈdeɪkɔː) *n* **1** a style or scheme of interior decoration, furnishings, etc., as in a room or house. **2** stage decoration; scenery. [C19: from F, from *décorer* to DECORATE]

decorate ❶ (ˈdɛkəˌreɪt) *vb* **decorates, decorating, decorated. 1** (*tr*) to ornament; adorn. **2** to paint or wallpaper. **3** (*tr*) to confer a mark of distinction, esp. a medal, upon. [C16: from L *decorāre,* from *decus* adornment]
▸ˈ**decorative** *adj*

Decorated style *n* a 14th-century style of English architecture characterized by geometrical tracery and floral decoration.

decoration ❶ (ˌdɛkəˈreɪʃən) *n* **1** an addition that renders something

THESAURUS

declamation *n* **1, 2** = **oration**, address, harangue, lecture, rant, recitation, speech, tirade

declamatory *adj* **1, 2** = **rhetorical**, bombastic, discursive, fustian, grandiloquent, high-flown, incoherent, inflated, magniloquent, orotund, pompous, stagy, stilted, theatrical, turgid

declaration *n* **1** = **statement**, acknowledgment, affirmation, assertion, attestation, averment, avowal, deposition, disclosure, protestation, revelation, testimony **2** = **announcement**, edict, manifesto, notification, proclamation, profession, promulgation, pronouncement, pronunciamento

declarative *adj* = **affirmative**, definite, demonstrative, enunciatory, explanatory, expository, expressive, positive

declare *vb* **1, 3** = **state**, affirm, announce, assert, asseverate, attest, aver, avow, certify, claim, confirm, maintain, notify, proclaim, profess, pronounce, swear, testify, utter, validate **4** = **make known**, confess, convey, disclose, manifest, reveal, show

declension *n* **1, 2** = **inflection**, variation

decline *vb* **1** = **refuse**, abstain, avoid, deny, forgo, reject, say 'no', send one's regrets, turn down **2** = **lessen**, decrease, diminish, drop, dwindle, ebb, fade, fail, fall, fall off, flag, shrink, sink, wane **3** = **slope**, descend, dip, sink, slant **4** = **deteriorate**, decay, degenerate, droop, languish, pine, weaken, worsen ◆ *n* **6** = **deterioration**, decay, decrepitude, degeneration, enfeeblement, failing, senility, weakening, worsening **7** = **lessening**, abatement, diminution, downturn, drop, dwindling, falling off, recession, slump **8** = **slope**, declivity, hill, incline **9** *Archaic* = **consumption**, phthisis, tuberculosis
Antonyms *vb* ≠ **lessen:** increase, rise ≠ **deteriorate:** improve ≠ **refuse:** accept, agree, consent ◆ *n* ≠ **lessening:** rise, upswing ≠ **deterioration:** improvement

decode *vb* = **decipher**, crack, decrypt, descramble, interpret, solve, unscramble, work out
Antonyms *vb* encipher, encode, encrypt, scramble

decompose *vb* **1** = **rot**, break up, crumble, decay, fall apart, fester, putrefy, spoil **2, 3** = **break down**, analyse, atomize, break up, decompound, disintegrate, dissect, dissolve, distil, separate

decomposition *n* **1** = **rot**, corruption, decay, putrefaction, putrescence, putridity **2, 3** = **breakdown**, atomization, disintegration, dissolution, division

decontaminate *vb* = **sterilize**, clean, cleanse, deodorize, disinfect, disinfest, fumigate, make safe, purify, sanitize
Antonyms *vb* contaminate, infect, infest, poison, pollute

décor *n* **1** = **decoration**, colour scheme, furnishing style, ornamentation

decorate *vb* **1** = **adorn**, beautify, bedeck, deck, embellish, engarland, enrich, festoon, grace, ornament, trim **2** = **do up** (*inf.*), colour, furbish, paint, paper, renovate, wallpaper **3** = **pin a medal on**, cite, confer an honour on *or* upon

decoration *n* **1** = **ornament**, arabesque, bauble, cartouch(e), curlicue, falderal, festoon, flounce, flourish, frill, furbelow, garnish, scroll,

DICTIONARY

more attractive or ornate. **2** the act or art of decorating. **3** a medal, etc., conferred as a mark of honour.

decorator (ˈdɛkəˌreɪtə) *n* **1** *Brit.* a person whose profession is the painting and wallpapering of buildings or their interiors. **2** a person who decorates.

decorous Ⓣ (ˈdɛkərəs) *adj* characterized by propriety in manners, conduct, etc. [C17: from L, from *decor* elegance]
▸**ˈdecorously** *adv* ▸**ˈdecorousness** *n*

decorum Ⓣ (dɪˈkɔːrəm) *n* **1** propriety, esp. in behaviour or conduct. **2** a requirement of correct behaviour in polite society. [C16: from L: propriety]

decoupage (ˌdeɪkuːˈpɑːʒ) *n* the decoration of a surface with cutout shapes or illustrations. [C20: from F, from *découper,* from DE- + *couper* to cut]

decoy Ⓣ *n* (ˈdiːkɔɪ, dɪˈkɔɪ). **1** a person or thing used to lure someone into danger. **2** *Mil.* something designed to deceive an enemy. **3** a bird or animal, or an image of one, used to lure game into a trap or within shooting range. **4** a place into which game can be lured for capture. **5** *Canad.* another word for **deke** (sense 2). ◆ *vb* (dɪˈkɔɪ). **6** to lure or be lured by or as if by means of a decoy. **7** *(tr) Canad.* another word for **deke** (sense 1). [C17: prob. from Du. *de kooi,* lit.: the cage, from L *cavea* CAGE]

decrease Ⓣ *vb* (dɪˈkriːs). **decreases, decreasing, decreased. 1** to diminish or cause to diminish in size, strength, etc. ◆ *n* (ˈdiːkriːs, dɪˈkriːs). **2** a diminution; reduction. **3** the amount by which something has been diminished. [C14: from OF, from L *dēcrescere* to grow less, from DE- + *crescere* to grow]
▸**deˈcreasing** *adj* ▸**deˈcreasingly** *adv*

decree Ⓣ (dɪˈkriː) *n* **1** an edict, law, etc., made by someone in authority. **2** an order or judgment of a court. ◆ *vb* **decrees, decreeing, decreed. 3** to order, adjudge, or ordain by decree. [C14: from OF, from L *dēcrētum* ordinance, from *dēcrētus* decided, p.p. of *dēcernere*]

decree absolute *n* the final decree in divorce proceedings, which leaves the parties free to remarry.

decree nisi (ˈnaɪsaɪ) *n* a provisional decree, esp. in divorce proceedings, which will later be made absolute unless cause is shown why it should not.

decrement (ˈdɛkrɪmənt) *n* **1** the act of decreasing; diminution. **2** *Maths.* a negative increment. **3** *Physics.* a measure of the damping of an oscillator or oscillation, expressed by the ratio of amplitudes in successive cycles. [C17: from L *dēcrēmentum,* from *dēcrescere* to DECREASE]

decrepit Ⓣ (dɪˈkrɛpɪt) *adj* **1** enfeebled by old age; infirm. **2** broken down or worn out by hard or long use; dilapidated. [C15: from L *dēcrepitus,* from *crepāre* to creak]
▸**deˈcrepiˌtude** *n*

decrescendo (ˌdiːkrɪˈʃɛndəʊ) *n, adj* another word for **diminuendo.** [It., from *decrescere* to DECREASE]

decrescent (dɪˈkrɛsənt) *adj* (esp. of the moon) decreasing; waning. [C17: from L *dēcrescēns* growing less; see DECREASE]
▸**deˈcrescence** *n*

decretal (dɪˈkriːtᵊl) *n* **1** *RC Church.* a papal decree; edict on doctrine or church law. ◆ *adj* **2** of or relating to a decree. [C15: from OF, from LL *dēcrētālis;* see DECREE]

decriminalize *or* **decriminalise** (diːˈkrɪmɪnᵊˌlaɪz) *vb* **decriminalizes, decriminalizing, decriminalized** *or* **decriminalises, decriminalising, decriminalised.** *(tr)* to remove (an action) from the legal category of criminal offence: *to decriminalize the possession of marijuana.*

decry Ⓣ (dɪˈkraɪ) *vb* **decries, decrying, decried.** *(tr)* **1** to express open disapproval of; disparage. **2** to depreciate by proclamation: *to decry obsolete coinage.* [C17: from OF *descrier,* from *des-* DIS-[1] + *crier* to CRY]

decumbent (dɪˈkʌmbənt) *adj* **1** lying down. **2** *Bot.* (of stems) lying flat with the tip growing upwards. [C17: from L, present participle of *dēcumbere* to lie down]
▸**deˈcumbency** *n*

dedicate Ⓣ (ˈdɛdɪˌkeɪt) *vb* **dedicates, dedicating, dedicated.** *(tr)* **1** (often foll. by *to*) to devote (oneself, one's time, etc.) wholly to a special purpose or cause. **2** (foll. by *to*) to address a book, performance, etc., to a person, cause, etc., as a token of affection or respect. **3** (foll. by *to*) to request or play (a record) on radio for another person as a greeting. **4** to assign or allocate to a particular project, function, etc. **5** to set apart for a deity or for sacred uses. [C15: from L *dēdicāre* to announce, from *dicāre* to make known]
▸**ˈdediˌcator** *n* ▸**dedicatory** (ˈdɛdɪˌkeɪtərɪ, ˈdɛdɪkətərɪ) *or* **ˈdediˌcative** *adj*

dedicated Ⓣ (ˈdɛdɪˌkeɪtɪd) *adj* **1** devoted to a particular purpose or cause. **2** assigned or allocated to a particular project, function, etc.: *a dedicated transmission line.* **3** *Computing.* designed to fulfil one function.

dedication Ⓣ (ˌdɛdɪˈkeɪʃən) *n* **1** the act of dedicating or being dedicated. **2** an inscription prefixed to a book, etc., dedicating it to a person or thing. **3** wholehearted devotion, esp. to a career, ideal, etc.
▸**ˌdediˈcational** *adj*

deduce Ⓣ (dɪˈdjuːs) *vb* **deduces, deducing, deduced.** *(tr)* **1** *(may take a clause as object)* to reach (a conclusion) by reasoning; conclude (that); infer. **2** *Arch.* to trace the origin or derivation of. [C15: from L *dēdūcere* to lead away, derive, from DE- + *dūcere* to lead]
▸**deˈducible** *adj*

deduct Ⓣ (dɪˈdʌkt) *vb (tr)* to take away or subtract (a number, quantity, part, etc.). [C15: from L *dēductus,* p.p. of *dēdūcere* to DEDUCE]

deductible (dɪˈdʌktɪbᵊl) *adj* **1** capable of being deducted. **2** *US.* short for **tax-deductible.** ◆ *n* **3** *Insurance.* the US name for **excess** (sense 5).

deduction Ⓣ (dɪˈdʌkʃən) *n* **1** the act or process of deducting or subtracting. **2** something that is or may be deducted. **3** *Logic.* **3a** a process of reasoning by which a specific conclusion necessarily follows from a set of general premises. **3b** a logical conclusion reached by this process.
▸**deˈductive** *adj*

deed Ⓣ (diːd) *n* **1** something that is done or performed; act. **2** a notable achievement. **3** action as opposed to words. **4** *Law.* a legal document signed, witnessed, and delivered to effect a conveyance or transfer of property or to create a legal contract. ◆ *vb* **5** *(tr) US.* to convey or transfer (property) by deed. [OE *dēd*]

deed box *n* a strong box in which deeds and other documents are kept.

deed poll *n Law.* a deed made by one party only, esp. one by which a person changes his name.

deejay (ˈdiːˌdʒeɪ) *n* an informal name for **disc jockey.** [C20: from the initials DJ (disc jockey)]

THESAURUS

spangle, trimmings, trinket **2** = **adornment,** beautification, elaboration, embellishment, enrichment, garnishing, ornamentation, trimming **3** = **medal,** award, badge, colours, emblem, garter, order, ribbon, star

decorative *adj* **1** = **ornamental,** adorning, arty-crafty, beautifying, enhancing, fancy, nonfunctional, pretty

decorous *adj* = **proper,** appropriate, becoming, befitting, comely, *comme il faut,* correct, decent, dignified, fit, fitting, mannerly, polite, refined, sedate, seemly, staid, suitable, well-behaved
Antonyms *adj* inapposite, inappropriate, malapropos, out of keeping, unbefitting, undignified, unseemly

decorum *n* **1, 2** = **propriety,** behaviour, breeding, courtliness, decency, deportment, dignity, etiquette, gentility, good grace, good manners, gravity, politeness, politesse, protocol, punctilio, respectability, seemliness
Antonyms *n* bad manners, churlishness, impoliteness, impropriety, indecorum, rudeness, unseemliness

decoy *n* **1** = **lure,** attraction, bait, ensnarement, enticement, inducement, pretence, trap ◆ *vb* **6** = **lure,** allure, bait, deceive, ensnare, entice, entrap, inveigle, seduce, tempt

decrease *vb* **1** = **lessen,** abate, contract, curtail, cut down, decline, diminish, drop, dwindle, ease, fall off, lower, peter out, reduce, shrink, slacken, subside, wane ◆ *n* **2** = **lessening,** abatement, contraction, cutback, decline, diminution, downturn, dwindling, ebb, falling off, loss, reduction, shrinkage, subsidence
Antonyms *vb* ≠ **lessen:** enlarge, expand, extend, increase ◆ *n* ≠ **lessening:** expansion, extension, growth

decreasingly *adv* **1** = **less and less,** at a declining rate, diminishingly, ever less, to a lesser or smaller extent
Antonyms *adv* ever more, increasingly, more and more, to a greater extent

decree *n* **1, 2** = **law,** act, canon, command, demand, dictum, edict, enactment, mandate, order, ordinance, precept, proclamation, regulation, ruling, statute ◆ *vb* **3** = **order,** command, decide, demand, determine, dictate, enact, establish, lay down, ordain, prescribe, proclaim, pronounce, rule

decrepit *adj* **1** = **weak,** aged, crippled, debilitated, doddering, effete, feeble, frail, incapacitated, infirm, past it, superannuated, wasted **2** = **worn-out,** antiquated, battered, beat-up (*inf.*), broken-down, deteriorated, dilapidated, ramshackle, rickety, run-down, tumbledown, weather-beaten

decrepitude *n* **1** = **weakness,** debility, dotage, eld (*arch.*), feebleness, incapacity, infirmity, invalidity, old age, senility, wasting **2** = **dilapidation,** decay, degeneration, deterioration

decry *vb* **1** = **condemn,** abuse, asperse, belittle, blame, blast, censure, criticize, cry down, denigrate, denounce, depreciate, derogate, detract, devalue, discredit, disparage, excoriate, lambast(e), put down, rail against, run down, tear into (*inf.*), traduce, underestimate, underrate, undervalue

dedicate *vb* **1** = **devote,** commit, give over to, pledge, surrender **2** = **inscribe,** address, assign, offer **5** = **consecrate,** bless, hallow, sanctify, set apart

dedicated *adj* **1** = **devoted,** committed, enthusiastic, given over to, purposeful, single-minded, sworn, wholehearted, zealous
Antonyms *adj* indifferent, uncaring, uncommitted, unconcerned, uninterested, unresponsive

dedication *n* **2** = **inscription,** address, message **3** = **devotion,** adherence, allegiance, commitment, devotedness, faithfulness, loyalty, single-mindedness, wholeheartedness
Antonyms *n* ≠ **devotion:** apathy, coolness, indifference, insensibility, torpor, unconcern, uninterestedness

deduce *vb* **1** = **conclude,** derive, draw, gather, glean, infer, put two and two together, read between the lines, reason, take to mean, understand

deducible *adj* **1** = **inferable,** derivable, to be inferred, traceable

deduct *vb* = **subtract,** decrease by, knock off, reduce by, remove, take away, take from, take off, take out, withdraw
Antonyms *vb* add, add to, enlarge

deduction *n* **1** = **subtraction,** abatement, allowance, decrease, diminution, discount, reduction, withdrawal **3b** = **conclusion,** assumption, consequence, corollary, finding, inference, reasoning, result

deed *n* **1** = **action,** achievement, act, exploit, fact, feat, performance, reality, truth **4** *Law* =

deem Ⓣ (diːm) *vb* (*tr*) to judge or consider. [OE *dēman*]

de-emphasize *or* **de-emphasise** (diːˈɛmfəˌsaɪz) *vb* **de-emphasizes, de-emphasizing, de-emphasized** *or* **de-emphasises, de-emphasising, de-emphasised.** (*tr*) to remove emphasis from.

deemster (ˈdiːmstə) *n* the title of one of the two justices in the Isle of Man. Also called: **dempster.**

de-energize *or* **de-energise** (diːˈɛnəˌdʒaɪz) *vb* **de-energizes, de-energizing, de-energized** *or* **de-energises, de-energising, de-energised.** (*tr*) *Electrical engineering.* to disconnect (an electrical circuit) from its source.
▸**de-ˌenergiˈzation** *or* **de-ˌenergiˈsation** *n*

deep Ⓣ (diːp) *adj* **1** extending or situated far down from a surface: *a deep pool.* **2** extending or situated far inwards, backwards, or sideways. **3** *Cricket.* far from the pitch: *the deep field.* **4** (*postpositive*) of a specified dimension downwards, inwards, or backwards: *six feet deep.* **5** coming from or penetrating to a great depth. **6** difficult to understand; abstruse. **7** intellectually demanding: *a deep discussion.* **8** of great intensity: *deep trouble.* **9** (*postpositive;* foll. by *in*) absorbed (by); immersed (in): *deep in study.* **10** very cunning; devious. **11** mysterious: *a deep secret.* **12** (of a colour) having an intense or dark hue. **13** low in pitch: *a deep voice.* **14 go off the deep end.** *Inf.* **14a** to lose one's temper; react angrily. **14b** *Chiefly US.* to act rashly. **15 in deep water.** *Inf.* in a tricky position or in trouble. ◆ *n* **16** any deep place on land or under water. **17 the deep. 17a** a poetic term for the **ocean. 17b** *Cricket.* the area of the field relatively far from the pitch. **18** the most profound, intense, or central part: *the deep of winter.* **19** a vast extent, as of space or time. ◆ *adv* **20** far on in time; late: *they worked deep into the night.* **21** profoundly or intensely. **22 deep down.** *Inf.* in reality, esp. as opposed to appearance. [OE *dēop*]
▸ˈ**deeply** *adv* ▸ˈ**deepness** *n*

deep-discount bond *n* a fixed-interest security that pays little or no interest but is issued at a substantial discount to its redemption value, thus largely substituting capital gain for income.

deepen Ⓣ (ˈdiːpᵊn) *vb* to make or become deep, deeper, or more intense.
▸ˈ**deepener** *n*

deepfreeze (ˌdiːpˈfriːz) *n* **1** another name for **freezer. 2** storage in a freezer. **3** *Inf.* a state of suspended activity. ◆ *vb* **deep-freeze, deep-freezes, deep-freezing, deep-froze, deep-frozen. 4** (*tr*) to freeze (food) or keep (food) in a freezer.

deep-fry *vb* **deep-fries, deep-frying, deep-fried.** to cook (fish, etc.) in sufficient hot fat to cover the food.

deep-laid *adj* (of a plot or plan) carefully worked out and kept secret.

deep-rooted Ⓣ *or* **deep-seated** *adj* (of ideas, beliefs, etc.) firmly fixed or held; ingrained.

deep-sea *n* (*modifier*) of, found in, or characteristic of the deep parts of the sea.

deep-set *adj* (esp. of eyes) deeply set.

deep space *n* any region of outer space beyond the system of the earth and moon.

deep structure *n Generative grammar.* a representation of a sentence at a level where logical or grammatical relations are made explicit. Cf. **surface structure.**

deer (dɪə) *n, pl* **deer** *or* **deers.** any of a family of hoofed, ruminant mammals including reindeer, elk, and roe deer, typically having antlers in the male. Related adj: **cervine.** [OE *dēor* beast]

deer lick *n* a naturally or artificially salty area of ground where deer come to lick the salt.

deerskin (ˈdɪəˌskɪn) *n* **a** the hide of a deer. **b** (*as modifier*): *a deerskin jacket.*

deerstalker (ˈdɪəˌstɔːkə) *n* **1** a person who stalks deer, esp. in order to shoot them. **2** a hat, peaked in front and behind, with earflaps usually tied together on the top.
▸ˈ**deerˌstalking** *adj, n*

de-escalate Ⓣ (diːˈɛskəˌleɪt) *vb* **de-escalates, de-escalating, de-escalated.** to reduce the level or intensity of (a crisis, etc.) or (of a crisis, etc.) to decrease in level or intensity.
▸**de-ˌescaˈlation** *n*

def (dɛf) *adj Sl.* very good. [C20: ?from *definitive*]

def. *abbrev. for:* **1** defective. **2** defence. **3** defendant. **4** deferred. **5** definite. **6** definition.

deface Ⓣ (dɪˈfeɪs) *vb* **defaces, defacing, defaced.** (*tr*) to spoil or mar the surface or appearance of; disfigure.
▸**deˈfaceable** *adj* ▸**deˈfacement** *n* ▸**deˈfacer** *n*

de facto Ⓣ (deɪ ˈfæktəʊ) *adv* **1** in fact. ◆ *adj* **2** existing in fact, whether legally recognized or not: *a de facto regime.* Cf. **de jure.** ◆ *n, pl* **de factos. 3** *Austral. & NZ.* a de facto wife or husband. [C17: L]

defalcate (ˈdiːfælˌkeɪt) *vb* **defalcates, defalcating, defalcated.** (*intr*) *Law.* to misuse or misappropriate property or funds entrusted to one. [C15: from Med. L *dēfalcāre* to cut off, from L DE- + *falx* sickle]
▸ˈ**defalˌcator** *n*

defame Ⓣ (dɪˈfeɪm) *vb* **defames, defaming, defamed.** (*tr*) to attack the good name or reputation of; slander; libel. [C14: from OF, from L, from *diffāmāre* to spread by unfavourable report, from *fāma* FAME]
▸**defamation** (ˌdɛfəˈmeɪʃən) *n* ▸**defamatory** (dɪˈfæmətərɪ) *adj*

default Ⓣ (dɪˈfɔːlt) *n* **1** a failure to act, esp. a failure to meet a financial obligation or to appear in a court of law at a time specified. **2** absence or lack. **3 by default.** in the absence of opposition or a better alternative: *he became prime minister by default.* **4 in default of.** through or in the lack or absence of. **5 judgment by** *or* **in default.** *Law.* a judgment in the plaintiff's favour when the defendant fails to plead or to appear. **6** (*also* ˈdiːfɔːlt). *Computing.* **6a** the preset selection of an option offered by a system, which will always be followed except when explicitly altered. **6b** (*as modifier*): *default setting.* ◆ *vb* **7** (*intr;* often foll. by *on* or *in*) to fail to make payment when due. **8** (*intr*) to fail to fulfil an obligation. **9** *Law.* to lose (a case) by failure to appear in court. [C13: from OF *defaute,* from *defaillir* to fail, from Vulgar L *dēfallīre* (unattested) to be lacking]

defaulter Ⓣ (dɪˈfɔːltə) *n* **1** a person who defaults. **2** *Chiefly Brit.* a person, esp. a soldier, who has broken the disciplinary code of his service.

defeat Ⓣ (dɪˈfiːt) *vb* (*tr*) **1** to overcome; win a victory over. **2** to thwart or frustrate. **3** *Law.* to render null and void. ◆ *n* **4** a defeating or being defeated. [C14: from OF, from *desfaire* to undo, ruin, from *des-* DIS-[1] + *faire* to do, from L *facere*]

defeatism (dɪˈfiːtɪzəm) *n* a ready acceptance or expectation of defeat.
▸**deˈfeatist** *n, adj*

THESAURUS

document, contract, indenture, instrument, title, title deed, transaction

deem *vb* = **consider**, account, believe, conceive, esteem, estimate, hold, imagine, judge, reckon, regard, suppose, think

deep *adj* **1** = **wide**, abyssal, bottomless, broad, far, profound, unfathomable, yawning **6** = **mysterious**, abstract, abstruse, arcane, esoteric, hidden, obscure, recondite, secret **7** = **wise**, acute, discerning, learned, penetrating, sagacious **8** = **intense**, extreme, grave, great, profound, serious (*inf.*), unqualified **9** = **absorbed**, engrossed, immersed, lost, preoccupied, rapt **10** = **cunning**, artful, astute, canny, designing, devious, insidious, knowing, scheming, shrewd **12** = **dark**, intense, rich, strong, vivid **13** = **low**, bass, booming, full-toned, low-pitched, resonant, sonorous ◆ *n* **17 the deep** *Poetic* = **ocean**, briny (*inf.*), high seas, main, sea **18** = **middle**, culmination, dead, mid point ◆ *adv* **20** = **far into**, deeply, far down, late
Antonyms *adj* ≠ **wide:** shallow ≠ **mysterious:** shallow ≠ **intense:** shallow, superficial ≠ **wise:** simple ≠ **cunning:** shallow, simple ≠ **dark:** light, pale ≠ **low:** high, sharp

deepen *vb* = **intensify**, grow, increase, magnify, reinforce, strengthen

deeply *adv* **21** = **thoroughly**, completely, gravely, profoundly, seriously, severely, to the core, to the heart, to the quick **21** = **intensely**, acutely, affectingly, distressingly, feelingly, mournfully, movingly, passionately, sadly

deep-rooted *adj* = **fixed**, confirmed, dyed-in-the-wool, entrenched, ineradicable, ingrained, inveterate, rooted, settled, subconscious, unconscious
Antonyms *adj* eradicable, exterior, external, on the surface, peripheral, shallow, skin-deep, slight, superficial, surface

de-escalate *vb* = **reduce**, check, contain, curb, damp down, decrease, defuse, diminish, lessen, limit, minimize, take the heat *or* sting out
Antonyms *vb* escalate, heighten, increase, intensify, magnify

deface *vb* = **vandalize**, blemish, damage, deform, destroy, disfigure, impair, injure, mar, mutilate, obliterate, spoil, sully, tarnish, total (*sl.*), trash (*sl.*)

defacement *n* = **vandalism**, blemish, damage, destruction, disfigurement, distortion, impairment, injury, mutilation

de facto *adv* **1** = **in fact**, actually, in effect, in reality, really ◆ *adj* **2** = **actual**, existing, real

defamation *n* = **slander**, aspersion, calumny, character assassination, denigration, disparagement, libel, obloquy, opprobrium, scandal, slur, smear, traducement, vilification

defamatory *adj* = **slanderous**, abusive, calumnious, contumelious, denigrating, derogatory, disparaging, injurious, insulting, libellous, vilifying, vituperative

defame *vb* = **slander**, asperse, bad-mouth (*sl., chiefly US & Canad.*), belie, besmirch, blacken, calumniate, cast a slur on, cast aspersions on, denigrate, detract, discredit, disgrace, dishonour, disparage, knock (*inf.*), libel, malign, rubbish (*inf.*), slag (off) (*sl.*), smear, speak evil of, stigmatize, traduce, vilify, vituperate

default *n* **2** = **failure**, absence, defect, deficiency, dereliction, evasion, fault, lack, lapse, neglect, nonpayment, omission, want ◆ *vb* **7, 8** = **fail**, bilk, defraud, dodge, evade, levant (*Brit.*), neglect, rat (*inf.*), swindle, welsh (*sl.*)

defaulter *n* **7, 8** = **nonpayer**, delinquent, embezzler, levanter (*Brit.*), offender, peculator, welsher (*sl.*)

defeat *vb* **1** = **beat**, blow out of the water (*sl.*), clobber (*sl.*), conquer, crush, lick (*inf.*), make mincemeat of (*inf.*), master, outplay, overpower, overthrow, overwhelm, pip at the post, quell, repulse, rout, run rings around (*inf.*), stuff (*sl.*), subdue, subjugate, tank (*sl.*), trounce, undo, vanquish, wipe the floor with (*inf.*), worst **2** = **frustrate**, baffle, balk, confound, disappoint, discomfit, foil, get the better of, ruin, thwart ◆ *n* **4** = **conquest**, beating, debacle, overthrow, pasting (*sl.*), repulse, rout, trouncing, vanquishment **4** = **frustration**, disappointment, discomfiture, failure, rebuff, repulse, reverse, setback, thwarting
Antonyms *vb* ≠ **beat:** bow, cave in (*inf.*), lose, submit, succumb, surrender, yield ◆ *n* ≠ **conquest:** success, triumph, victory

defeated *adj* **1, 2** = **beaten**, balked, bested, checkmated, conquered, crushed, licked (*inf.*), overcome, overpowered, overwhelmed, routed, thrashed, thwarted, trounced, vanquished, worsted
Antonyms *adj* conquering, dominant, glorious, successful, triumphal, triumphant, undefeated, victorious, winning

defeatist *n* = **pessimist**, prophet of doom, quitter, submitter, yielder ◆ *adj* = **pessimistic**

defecate ⓣ ('dɛfɪˌkeɪt) *vb* **defecates, defecating, defecated. 1** (*intr*) to discharge waste from the body through the anus. **2** (*tr*) to remove impurities from. [C16: from L *dēfaecāre* to cleanse from dregs, from DE- + *faex* dregs]
▸ˌ**defe'cation** *n* ▸'**defeˌcator** *n*

defect ⓣ *n* ('diːfɛkt). **1** a lack of something necessary for completeness; deficiency. **2** an imperfection or blemish. ◆ *vb* (dɪ'fɛkt). **3** (*intr*) to desert one's country, cause, etc., esp. in order to join the opposing forces. [C15: from L, from *dēficere* to forsake, fail]
▸**de'fector** *n*

defection ⓣ (dɪ'fɛkʃən) *n* **1** abandonment of duty, allegiance, principles, etc. **2** a shortcoming.

defective ⓣ (dɪ'fɛktɪv) *adj* **1** having a defect or flaw; imperfect. **2** (of a person) below the usual standard or level, esp. in intelligence. **3** *Grammar.* lacking the full range of inflections characteristic of its form class.
▸**de'fectiveness** *n*

defence ⓣ *or US* **defense** (dɪ'fɛns) *n* **1** resistance against danger or attack. **2** a person or thing that provides such resistance. **3** a plea, essay, etc., in support of something. **4** a country's military measures or resources. **5** *Law.* a defendant's denial of the truth of the allegations or charge against him. **6** *Law.* the defendant and his legal advisers collectively. **7** *Sport.* **7a** the action of protecting oneself or part of the playing area against an opponent's attacks. **7b** (usually preceded by *the*) the players in a team whose function is to do this. **8** *American football.* (usually preceded by *the*) **8a** the team that does not have possession of the ball. **8b** the members of a team that play in such circumstances. **9** (*pl*) fortifications. [C13: from OF, from LL *dēfensum,* p.p. of *dēfendere* to DEFEND]
▸**de'fenceless** *or US* **de'fenseless** *adj*

defence mechanism *n* **1** *Psychoanalysis.* an unconscious mental process designed to reduce anxiety or shame. **2** *Physiol.* the protective response of the body against disease.

defend ⓣ (dɪ'fɛnd) *vb* **1** (*tr*) to protect from harm or danger. **2** (*tr*) to support in the face of criticism, esp. by argument. **3** to represent (a defendant) in court. **4** *Sport.* to guard (one's goal, etc.) against attack. **5** (*tr*) to protect (a title, etc.) against a challenge. [C13: from OF, from L *dēfendere* to ward off, from DE- + *-fendere* to strike]
▸**de'fender** *n*

defendant ⓣ (dɪ'fɛndənt) *n* **1** a person against whom an action or claim is brought in a court of law. Cf. **plaintiff.** ◆ *adj* **2** defending.

defenestration (diːˌfɛnɪ'streɪʃən) *n* the act of throwing someone out of a window. [C17: from NL *dēfenestrātiō,* from L DE- + *fenestra* window]

defensible ⓣ (dɪ'fɛnsɪbᵊl) *adj* capable of being defended, as in war, an argument, etc.
▸**deˌfensi'bility** *or* **de'fensibleness** *n*

defensive ⓣ (dɪ'fɛnsɪv) *adj* **1** intended for defence. **2** rejecting criticisms of oneself. ◆ *n* **3** a position of defence. **4 on the defensive.** in a position of defence, as in being ready to reject criticism.
▸**de'fensively** *adv*

defer[1] ⓣ (dɪ'fɜː) *vb* **defers, deferring, deferred.** (*tr*) to delay until a future time; postpone. [C14: from OF *differer* to be different, postpone; see DIFFER]
▸**de'ferment** *or* **de'ferral** *n* ▸**de'ferrer** *n*

defer[2] ⓣ (dɪ'fɜː) *vb* **defers, deferring, deferred.** (*intr*; foll. by *to*) to yield to or comply with the wishes or judgments (of). [C15: from L *dēferre,* lit.: to bear down, from DE- + *ferre* to bear]

deference ⓣ ('dɛfərəns) *n* **1** compliance with the wishes of another. **2** courteous regard; respect. [C17: from F *déférence;* see DEFER[2]]

deferent[1] ('dɛfərənt) *adj* another word for **deferential.**

deferent[2] ('dɛfərənt) *adj* (esp. of a nerve or duct) conveying an impulse, fluid, etc., down or away; efferent. [C17: from L *dēferre;* see DEFER[2]]

deferential ⓣ (ˌdɛfə'rɛnʃəl) *adj* showing deference; respectful.
▸ˌ**defer'entially** *adv*

defiance ⓣ (dɪ'faɪəns) *n* **1** open or bold resistance to authority, opposition, or power. **2** a challenge.
▸**de'fiant** *adj*

defibrillation (dɪˌfaɪbrɪ'leɪʃən) *n Med.* the application of an electric current to the heart to restore normal contractions after a heart attack caused by fibrillation.

defibrillator (dɪ'faɪbrɪˌleɪtə) *n Med.* an apparatus for stopping fibrillation of the heart by application of an electric current.

deficiency ⓣ (dɪ'fɪʃənsɪ) *n, pl* **deficiencies. 1** the state or quality of being deficient. **2** a lack or insufficiency; shortage. **3** a deficit. **4** *Biol.* the absence of a gene or a region of a chromosome normally present.

deficiency disease *n* **1** *Med.* any condition, such as pellagra, beriberi, or scurvy, produced by a lack of vitamins or other essential substances. **2** *Bot.* any disease caused by lack of essential minerals.

deficient ⓣ (dɪ'fɪʃənt) *adj* **1** lacking some essential; incomplete; defective. **2** inadequate in quantity or supply; insufficient. [C16: from L *dēficiēns* lacking, from *dēficere* to fall short]
▸**de'ficiently** *adv*

deficit ⓣ ('dɛfɪsɪt, dɪ'fɪsɪt) *n* **1** the amount by which an actual sum is lower than that expected or required. **2a** an excess of liabilities over assets. **2b** an excess of expenditures over revenues. [C18: from L, lit.: there is lacking, from *dēficere*]

deficit financing *n* government spending in excess of revenues so that a budget deficit is incurred, which is financed by borrowing.

defile[1] ⓣ (dɪ'faɪl) *vb* **defiles, defiling, defiled.** (*tr*) **1** to make foul or dirty; pollute. **2** to taint; corrupt. **3** to damage or sully (someone's reputation, etc.). **4** to make unfit for ceremonial use. **5** to violate the chastity

THESAURUS

defecate *vb* **1** = **excrete**, crap, egest, empty, evacuate (*Physiology*), move, open the bowels, pass a motion, shit (*taboo sl.*), void excrement

defecation *n* **1** = **excretion**, egestion, elimination, emptying *or* opening of the bowels, evacuation (*Physiology*), excrement, motion, movement, voiding excrement

defect *n* **1** = **deficiency**, absence, default, frailty, inadequacy, lack, shortcoming, weakness **2** = **imperfection**, blemish, blotch, error, failing, fault, flaw, foible, mistake, spot, taint, want ◆ *vb* **3** = **desert**, abandon, apostatize, break faith, change sides, go over, rebel, revolt, tergiversate, walk out on (*inf.*)

defection *n* **1** = **desertion**, abandonment, apostasy, backsliding, dereliction, rebellion, revolt

defective *adj* **1** = **faulty**, broken, deficient, flawed, imperfect, inadequate, incomplete, insufficient, not working, on the blink (*sl.*), out of order, scant, short **2** = **abnormal**, mentally deficient, retarded, subnormal
Antonyms *adj* ≠ **faulty:** adequate, intact, perfect, whole, working ≠ **abnormal:** normal

defector *n* **3** = **deserter**, apostate, rat (*inf.*), recreant (*arch.*), renegade, runagate (*arch.*), tergiversator, turncoat

defence *n* **1** = **protection**, armament, cover, deterrence, guard, immunity, resistance, safeguard, security, shelter **2** = **shield**, barricade, bastion, buckler, bulwark, buttress, fastness, fortification, rampart **3** = **argument**, apologia, apology, excuse, exoneration, explanation, extenuation, justification, plea, vindication **5** *Law* = **plea**, alibi, case, declaration, denial, pleading, rebuttal, testimony

defenceless *adj* **1, 2** = **helpless**, endangered, exposed, naked, powerless, unarmed, unguarded, unprotected, vulnerable, wide open
Antonyms *adj* free from harm, guarded, out of harm's way, protected, safe, safe and sound, secure

defend *vb* **1** = **protect**, cover, fortify, guard, keep safe, preserve, safeguard, screen, secure, shelter, shield, ward off, watch over **2** = **support**, assert, champion, endorse, espouse, justify, maintain, plead, speak up for, stand by, stand up for, stick up for (*inf.*), sustain, uphold, vindicate

defendant *n* **1** = **the accused**, appellant, defence, litigant, offender, prisoner at the bar, respondent

defender *n* **1** = **protector**, bodyguard, escort, guard **2** = **supporter**, advocate, champion, patron, sponsor, vindicator

defensible *adj* = **secure**, holdable, impregnable, safe, unassailable = **justifiable**, pardonable, permissible, plausible, tenable, valid, vindicable
Antonyms *adj* ≠ **justifiable:** faulty, inexcusable, insupportable, unforgivable, unjustifiable, unpardonable, untenable, wrong

defensive *adj* **1** = **on guard**, averting, defending, on the defensive, opposing, protective, safeguarding, uptight (*inf.*), watchful, withstanding

defensively *adv* **1** = **in self-defence**, at bay, in defence, on guard, on the defensive, suspiciously

defer[1] *vb* = **postpone**, adjourn, delay, hold over, procrastinate, prorogue, protract, put off, put on ice (*inf.*), put on the back burner (*inf.*), set aside, shelve, suspend, table, take a rain check on (*US & Canad. inf.*)

defer[2] *vb* = **comply**, accede, bow, capitulate, give in, give way to, respect, submit, yield

deference *n* **1** = **obedience**, acquiescence, capitulation, complaisance, compliance, obeisance, submission, yielding **2** = **respect**, attention, civility, consideration, courtesy, esteem, homage, honour, obeisance, politeness, regard, reverence, thoughtfulness, veneration
Antonyms *n* ≠ **respect:** contempt, discourtesy, dishonour, disregard, disrespect, impertinence, impoliteness, impudence, incivility, insolence, irreverence, lack of respect, rudeness ≠ **obedience:** disobedience, insubordination, non-compliance, nonobservance, revolt

deferential *adj* = **respectful**, civil, complaisant, considerate, courteous, dutiful, ingratiating, obedient, obeisant, obsequious, polite, regardful, reverential, submissive

deferment *n* = **postponement**, adjournment, delay, moratorium, putting off, stay, suspension

defiance *n* **1, 2** = **resistance**, challenge, confrontation, contempt, contumacy, disobedience, disregard, insolence, insubordination, opposition, provocation, rebelliousness, recalcitrance, spite
Antonyms *n* accordance, acquiescence, compliance, deference, obedience, observance, regard, respect, subservience

defiant *adj* **1, 2** = **resisting**, aggressive, audacious, bold, challenging, contumacious, daring, disobedient, insolent, insubordinate, mutinous, provocative, rebellious, recalcitrant, refractory, truculent
Antonyms *adj* cowardly, meek, obedient, respectful, submissive

deficiency *n* **1** = **resisting**, frailty, imperfection, weakness **2, 3** = **lack**, absence, dearth, deficit, inadequacy, insufficiency, scantiness, scarcity, shortage
Antonyms *n* ≠ **lack:** abundance, adequacy, sufficiency, superfluity, surfeit

deficient *adj* **1** = **unsatisfactory**, defective, faulty, flawed, impaired, imperfect, incomplete, inferior, weak **2** = **lacking**, exiguous, inadequate, insufficient, meagre, pathetic, scant, scanty, scarce, short, skimpy, wanting

deficit *n* **1** = **shortfall**, arrears, default, deficiency, loss, shortage

defile[1] *vb* **1, 2** = **dirty**, befoul, contaminate, corrupt, make foul, pollute, smear, smirch, soil, taint, tarnish, vitiate **3** = **degrade**, besmirch, de-

of. [C14: from earlier *defoilen*, from OF *defouler* to trample underfoot, abuse, from DE- + *fouler* to tread upon; see FULL[2]]
▸**de'filement** *n*

defile[2] Ⓣ ('di:faɪl, dɪ'faɪl) *n* **1** a narrow pass or gorge. **2** a single file of soldiers, etc. ◆ *vb* **defiles, defiling, defiled. 3** (*intr*) to march in single file. [C17: from F, from *défiler* to file off, from *filer* to march in a column, from OF, from L *fīlum* thread]

define Ⓣ (dɪ'faɪn) *vb* **defines, defining, defined.** (*tr*) **1** to state precisely the meaning of (words, terms, etc.). **2** to describe the nature, properties, or essential qualities of. **3** to determine the boundary or extent of. **4** (*often passive*) to delineate the form or outline of: *the shape of the tree was clearly defined by the light behind it.* **5** to fix with precision; specify. [C14: from OF: to determine, from L *dēfīnīre* to set bounds to, from *fīnīre* to FINISH]
▸**de'finable** *adj* ▸**de'finer** *n*

definite Ⓣ ('dɛfɪnɪt) *adj* **1** clearly defined; exact. **2** having precise limits or boundaries. **3** known for certain. [C15: from L *dēfīnītus* limited, distinct; see DEFINE]
▸**'definiteness** *n*

> **USAGE NOTE** *Definite* and *definitive* should be carefully distinguished. *Definite* indicates precision and firmness, as in *a definite decision. Definitive* includes these senses but also indicates conclusiveness. *A definite answer* indicates a clear and firm answer to a particular question; *a definitive answer* implies an authoritative resolution of a complex question.

definite article *n Grammar.* a determiner that expresses specificity of reference, such as *the* in English. Cf. **indefinite article.**

definite integral *n* See **integral.**

definitely Ⓣ ('dɛfɪnɪtlɪ) *adv* **1** in a definite manner. **2** (*sentence modifier*) certainly: *he said he was coming, definitely.* ◆ *sentence substitute.* **3** unquestionably.

definition Ⓣ (ˌdɛfɪ'nɪʃən) *n* **1** a formal and concise statement of the meaning of a word, phrase, etc. **2** the act of defining. **3** specification of the essential properties of something. **4** the act of making clear or definite. **5** the state of being clearly defined. **6** a measure of the clarity of an optical, photographic, or television image as characterized by its sharpness and contrast.

definitive Ⓣ (dɪ'fɪnɪtɪv) *adj* **1** serving to decide or settle finally. **2** most reliable or authoritative. **3** serving to define or outline. **4** *Zool.* fully developed. **5** (of postage stamps) permanently on sale. ◆ *n* **6** *Grammar.* a word indicating specificity of reference.
▸**de'finitively** *adv*

deflate Ⓣ (di:'fleɪt) *vb* **deflates, deflating, deflated. 1** to collapse through the release of gas. **2** (*tr*) to take away the self-esteem or conceit from. **3** (*tr*) to take away the enthusiasm or excitement from. **4** *Econ.* to cause deflation of (an economy, the money supply, etc.). [C19: from DE- + (IN)FLATE]
▸**de'flator** *n*

deflation (di:'fleɪʃən) *n* **1** the act of deflating or the state of being deflated. **2** *Econ.* a reduction in spending and economic activity resulting in lower levels of output, employment, investment, trade, profits, and prices. **3** the removal of loose rock material, etc., by wind.
▸**de'flationary** *adj* ▸**de'flationist** *n, adj*

deflect Ⓣ (dɪ'flɛkt) *vb* to turn or cause to turn aside from a course. [C17: from L *dēflectere*, from *flectere* to bend]
▸**de'flector** *n*

deflection Ⓣ *or* **deflexion** (dɪ'flɛkʃən) *n* **1** a deflecting or being deflected. **2** the amount of deviation. **3** the change in direction of a light beam as it crosses a boundary between two media with different refractive indexes. **4** a deviation of the indicator of a measuring instrument from its zero position.
▸**de'flective** *adj*

deflocculate (di:'flɒkjuˌleɪt) *vb* **deflocculates, deflocculating, deflocculated.** (*tr*) to cause (an aggregate) to separate into particles.
▸**deˌflocculation** *n* ▸**de'flocculant** *n*

deflower Ⓣ (di:'flaʊə) *vb* (*tr*) **1** to deprive (esp. a woman) of virginity. **2** to despoil of beauty, innocence, etc. **3** to rob or despoil of flowers.
▸ˌ**deflo'ration** *n*

defoliant (di:'fəʊlɪənt) *n* a chemical sprayed or dusted onto trees to cause their leaves to fall, esp. to remove cover from an enemy in warfare.

defoliate (di:'fəʊlɪˌeɪt) *vb* **defoliates, defoliating, defoliated.** to deprive (a plant) of its leaves. [C18: from Med. L *dēfoliāre*, from L DE- + *folium* leaf]
▸**deˌfoli'ation** *n*

deforest (di:'fɒrɪst) *vb* (*tr*) to clear of trees. Also: **disforest.**
▸**deˌfores'tation** *n*

deform Ⓣ (dɪ'fɔ:m) *vb* **1** to make or become misshapen or distorted. **2** (*tr*) to mar the beauty of; disfigure. **3** (*tr*) to subject or be subjected to a stress that causes a change of dimensions. [C15: from L *dēformāre*, from DE- + *forma* shape, beauty]
▸**de'formable** *adj* ▸ˌ**defor'mation** *n*

deformed Ⓣ (dɪ'fɔ:md) *adj* **1** disfigured or misshapen. **2** morally perverted; warped.

deformity Ⓣ (dɪ'fɔ:mɪtɪ) *n, pl* **deformities. 1** a deformed condition. **2** *Pathol.* a distortion of an organ or part. **3** a deformed person or thing. **4** a defect, esp. of the mind or morals; depravity.

defraud Ⓣ (dɪ'frɔ:d) *vb* (*tr*) to take away or withhold money, rights, property, etc., from (a person) by fraud; swindle.
▸**de'frauder** *n*

defray Ⓣ (dɪ'freɪ) *vb* (*tr*) to provide money for (costs, expenses, etc.); pay. [C16: from OF *deffroier* to pay expenses, from *de-* DIS-[1] + *frai* expenditure]
▸**de'frayable** *adj* ▸**de'frayal** *or* **de'frayment** *n*

defrock (di:'frɒk) *vb* (*tr*) to deprive (a person in holy orders) of ecclesiastical status; unfrock.

defrost Ⓣ (di:'frɒst) *vb* **1** to make or become free of frost or ice. **2** to thaw, esp. through removal from a deepfreeze.

defroster (di:'frɒstə) *n* a device by which a de-icing process, as of a refrigerator, is accelerated.

deft Ⓣ (dɛft) *adj* quick and neat in movement; nimble; dexterous. [C13 (in the sense: gentle): see DAFT]
▸**'deftly** *adv* ▸**'deftness** *n*

THESAURUS

base, disgrace, dishonour, smirch, stain, sully **4** = **desecrate**, profane, treat sacrilegiously **5** = **violate**, abuse, deflower, molest, rape, ravish, seduce

defile[2] *n* **1** = **gorge**, gully, pass, passage, ravine, way through

defiled *adj* **3** = **unclean**, besmirched, dirtied, impure, polluted, spoilt, tainted **4** = **desecrated**, profaned **5** = **dishonoured**, ravished, violated
Antonyms *adj* ≠ **unclean:** clean, immaculate, spotless, uncontaminated, uncorrupted, undefiled, unstained, unsullied, untainted ≠ **dishonoured:** chaste, innocent

defilement *n* **1-3** = **contamination**, corruption, pollution, sullying **4** = **desecration**, profanation **5** = **violation**, debasement, degradation, depravity, disgrace

definable *adj* **1-5** = **specific**, apparent, definite, describable, determinable, explicable, perceptible

define *vb* **2** = **describe**, characterize, designate, detail, determine, explain, expound, interpret, specify, spell out **3** = **mark out**, bound, circumscribe, delimit, delineate, demarcate, limit, outline

definite *adj* **1** = **clear**, black-and-white, clear-cut, clearly defined, cut-and-dried (*inf.*), determined, exact, explicit, express, fixed, marked, obvious, particular, precise, specific **3** = **certain**, assured, decided, guaranteed, positive, settled, sure
Antonyms *adj* ≠ **clear:** confused, fuzzy, general, hazy, ill-defined, imprecise, indefinite, indeterminate, indistinct, inexact, loose, obscure, unclear, undetermined, vague ≠ **certain:** uncertain, undecided

definitely *adv* **1-3** = **certainly**, absolutely, beyond any doubt, categorically, clearly, come hell or high water (*inf.*), decidedly, easily, far and away, finally, indubitably, needless to say, obviously, plainly, positively, surely, undeniably, unequivocally, unmistakably, unquestionably, without doubt, without fail, without question

definition *n* **1-3** = **explanation**, clarification, elucidation, exposition, statement of meaning **4** = **description**, delimitation, delineation, demarcation, determination, fixing, outlining, settling **6** = **sharpness**, clarity, contrast, distinctness, focus, precision

definitive *adj* **1** = **final**, absolute, complete, conclusive, decisive **2** = **authoritative**, exhaustive, mother of all (*inf.*), perfect, reliable, ultimate

deflate *vb* **1** = **collapse**, contract, empty, exhaust, flatten, puncture, shrink, void **2, 3** = **humiliate**, chasten, dash, debunk (*inf.*), disconcert, dispirit, humble, mortify, put down (*sl.*), squash, take the wind out of (someone's) sails **4** *Economics* = **reduce**, decrease, depreciate, depress, devalue, diminish
Antonyms *vb* ≠ **collapse:** aerate, balloon, bloat, blow up, dilate, distend, enlarge, expand, increase, inflate, puff up *or* out, pump up, swell ≠ **humiliate:** boost, expand, increase, inflate

deflect *vb* = **turn aside**, bend, deviate, diverge, glance off, ricochet, shy, sidetrack, slew, swerve, turn, twist, veer, wind

deflection *n* = **deviation**, aberration, bend, declination, divergence, drift, refraction, swerve, turning aside, veer

deflower *vb Literary* **1** = **ravish**, assault, force, molest, rape, ruin, seduce, violate

deform *vb* **1** = **distort**, buckle, contort, gnarl, malform, mangle, misshape, twist, warp **2** = **disfigure**, cripple, deface, injure, maim, mar, mutilate, ruin, spoil

deformation *n* **1** = **distortion**, contortion, disfiguration, malformation, misshapenness, warping

deformed *adj* **1** = **distorted**, bent, blemished, crooked, disfigured, malformed, mangled, misshapen, twisted, warped

deformity *n* **1** = **abnormality**, defect, disfigurement, malformation

defraud *vb* = **cheat**, beguile, bilk, con (*inf.*), cozen, delude, diddle (*inf.*), do (*sl.*), dupe, embezzle, fleece, gull (*arch.*), gyp (*sl.*), outwit, pilfer, pull a fast one on (*inf.*), rip off (*sl.*), rob, rook (*sl.*), skin (*sl.*), stiff (*sl.*), stitch up (*sl.*), swindle, trick

defray *vb* = **pay**, clear, cover, discharge, foot the bill, liquidate, meet, settle

defrayal *n* = **payment**, clearance, discharge, liquidation, settlement

defrost *vb* **1, 2** = **thaw**, de-ice, unfreeze
Antonyms *vb* freeze (up), frost, ice over *or* up

deft *adj* = **skilful**, able, adept, adroit, agile, clever, dexterous, expert, handy, neat, nimble, proficient
Antonyms *adj* awkward, bumbling, cack-handed (*inf.*), clumsy, gauche, inept, maladroit, unskilful

deftness *n* = **skill**, ability, adeptness, adroitness, agility, cleverness, competence, coordination, dexterity, expertise, facility, finesse, neatness, nimbleness, proficiency, touch
Antonyms *n* awkwardness, cack-handedness

defunct ❶ (dɪˈfʌŋkt) *adj* **1** no longer living; dead or extinct. **2** no longer operative or valid. [C16: from L *dēfungī* to discharge (one's obligations), die; see DE-, FUNCTION]
▸**deˈfunctness** *n*

defuse ❶ *or US (sometimes)* **defuze** (diːˈfjuːz) *vb* **defuses, defusing, defused** *or US (sometimes)* **defuzes, defuzing, defuzed.** *(tr)* **1** to remove the triggering device of (a bomb, etc.). **2** to remove the cause of tension from (a crisis, etc.).

USAGE NOTE Avoid confusion with **diffuse.**

defy ❶ (dɪˈfaɪ) *vb* **defies, defying, defied.** *(tr)* **1** to resist openly and boldly. **2** to elude, esp. in a baffling way. **3** *Formal.* to challenge (someone to do something); dare. **4** *Arch.* to invite to do battle or combat. [C14: from OF *desfier,* from *des-* DE- + *fier* to trust, from L *fidere*]
▸**deˈfier** *n*

deg. *abbrev. for* degree.

degauss (diːˈgaʊs) *vb (tr)* to neutralize by producing an opposing magnetic field.
▸**deˈgausser** *n*

degeneracy ❶ (dɪˈdʒɛnərəsɪ) *n, pl* **degeneracies. 1** the act or state of being degenerate. **2** the process of becoming degenerate.

degenerate ❶ *vb* (dɪˈdʒɛnəˌreɪt). **degenerates, degenerating, degenerated.** *(intr)* **1** to become degenerate. **2** *Biol.* (of organisms or their parts) to become less specialized or functionally useless. ◆ *adj* (dɪˈdʒɛnərɪt). **3** having declined or deteriorated to a lower mental, moral, or physical level; degraded; corrupt. ◆ *n* (dɪˈdʒɛnərɪt). **4** a degenerate person. [C15: from L, from *dēgener* departing from its kind, ignoble, from DE- + *genus* race]
▸**deˈgenerately** *adv* ▸**deˈgenerateness** *n* ▸**deˈgenerative** *adj*

degenerate matter *n Astrophysics.* the highly compressed state of a star's matter when its atoms virtually touch in the final stage of its evolution into a white dwarf.

degeneration ❶ (dɪˌdʒɛnəˈreɪʃən) *n* **1** the process of degenerating. **2** the state of being degenerate. **3** *Biol.* the loss of specialization, function, or structure by organisms and their parts. **4** impairment or loss of the function and structure of cells or tissues, as by disease or injury. **5** *Electronics.* negative feedback of a signal.

degradable (dɪˈgreɪdəbᵊl) *adj* **1** capable of being decomposed chemically or biologically. **2** capable of being degraded.

degradation ❶ (ˌdɛgrəˈdeɪʃən) *n* **1** a degrading or being degraded. **2** a state of degeneration or squalor. **3** some act, constraint, etc., that is degrading. **4** the wearing down of the surface of rocks, cliffs, etc., by erosion. **5** *Chem.* a breakdown of a molecule into atoms or smaller molecules. **6** *Physics.* an irreversible process in which the energy available to do work is decreased. **7** *RC Church.* the permanent unfrocking of a priest.

degrade ❶ (dɪˈgreɪd) *vb* **degrades, degrading, degraded. 1** *(tr)* to reduce in worth, character, etc.; disgrace. **2** (diːˈgreɪd) *(tr)* to reduce in rank or status; demote. **3** *(tr)* to reduce in strength, quality, etc. **4** to reduce or be reduced by erosion or down-cutting, as a land surface or bed of a river. **5** *Chem.* to decompose into atoms or smaller molecules. [C14: from LL *dēgradāre,* from L DE- + *gradus* rank, degree]
▸**deˈgrader** *n*

degrading ❶ (dɪˈgreɪdɪŋ) *adj* causing humiliation; debasing.
▸**deˈgradingly** *adv*

degree ❶ (dɪˈgriː) *n* **1** a stage in a scale of relative amount or intensity: *a high degree of competence.* **2** an academic award conferred by a university or college on successful completion of a course or as an honorary distinction (**honorary degree**). **3** any of three categories of seriousness of a burn. **4** (in the US) any of the categories into which a crime is divided according to its seriousness. **5** *Genealogy.* a step in a line of descent. **6** *Grammar.* any of the forms of an adjective used to indicate relative amount or intensity: in English they are *positive, comparative,* and *superlative.* **7** *Music.* any note of a diatonic scale relative to the other notes in that scale. **8** a unit of temperature on a specified scale. Symbol: °. See also **Celsius scale, Fahrenheit scale. 9** a measure of angle equal to one three-hundred-and-sixtieth of the angle traced by one complete revolution of a line about one of its ends. Symbol: °. **10** a unit of latitude or longitude used to define points on the earth's surface. Symbol: °. **11** a unit on any of several scales of measurement, as for specific gravity. Symbol: °. **12** *Maths.* **12a** the highest power or the sum of the powers of any term in a polynomial or by itself: *$x^4 + x + 3$ and xyz^2 are of the fourth degree.* **12b** the greatest power of the highest order derivative in a differential equation. **13** *Obs.* a step; rung. **14** *Arch.* a stage in social status or rank. **15 by degrees.** little by little; gradually. **16 one degree under.** *Inf.* off colour; ill. **17 to a degree.** somewhat; rather. [C13: from OF *degre,* from L DE- + *gradus* step]

degree of freedom *n* **1** *Chem.* the least number of independently variable properties needed to determine the state of a system. See also **phase rule. 2** one of the independent components of motion (translation, vibration, and rotation) of an atom or molecule.

dehisce (dɪˈhɪs) *vb* **dehisces, dehiscing, dehisced.** *(intr)* (of fruits, anthers, etc.) to burst open spontaneously, releasing seeds, pollen, etc. [C17: from L *dēhiscere* to split open, from DE- + *hiscere* to yawn, gape]
▸**deˈhiscent** *adj*

dehorn (diːˈhɔːn) *vb (tr)* to remove the horns of (cattle, sheep, or goats).

dehumanize *or* **dehumanise** (diːˈhjuːməˌnaɪz) *vb* **dehumanizes, dehumanizing, dehumanized** *or* **dehumanises, dehumanising, dehumanised.** *(tr)* **1** to deprive of human qualities. **2** to render mechanical, artificial, or routine.
▸**deˌhumaniˈzation** *or* **deˌhumaniˈsation** *n*

dehumidify (ˌdiːhjuːˈmɪdɪˌfaɪ) *vb* **dehumidifies, dehumidifying, dehumidified.** *(tr)* to remove water from (the air, etc.)
▸**ˌdehuˌmidifiˈcation** *n* ▸**ˌdehuˈmidiˌfier** *n*

dehydrate ❶ (diːˈhaɪdreɪt, ˌdiːhaɪˈdreɪt) *vb* **dehydrates, dehydrating, dehydrated. 1** to lose or cause to lose water. **2** to lose or deprive of water, as the body or tissues.
▸**ˌdehyˈdration** *n* ▸**deˈhydrator** *n*

dehydrogenate (diːˈhaɪdrədʒəˌneɪt), **dehydrogenize,** *or* **dehydrogenise** (diːˈhaɪdrədʒəˌnaɪz) *vb* **dehydrogenates, dehydrogenating, dehydrogenated, dehydrogenizes, dehydrogenizing, dehydrogenized** *or* **dehydrogenises, dehydrogenising, dehydrogenised.** *(tr)* to remove hydrogen from.
▸**deˌhydrogeˈnation, deˌhydrogeniˈzation,** *or* **deˌhydrogeniˈsation** *n*

de-ice (diːˈaɪs) *vb* **de-ices, de-icing, de-iced.** to free or be freed of ice.

de-icer (diːˈaɪsə) *n* **1** a mechanical or thermal device designed to melt or stop the formation of ice on an aircraft. **2** a substance used for this purpose, esp. an aerosol that can be sprayed on car windscreens to remove ice or frost.

deictic (ˈdaɪktɪk) *adj* **1** *Logic.* proving by direct argument. Cf. **elenctic** (see **elenchus**). ◆ *n* **2** another word for **indexical** (sense 2). [C17: from Gk *deiktikos* concerning proof, from *deiknunai* to show]

deify ❶ (ˈdiːɪˌfaɪ, ˈdeɪɪ-) *vb* **deifies, deifying, deified.** *(tr)* **1** to exalt to the position of a god or personify as a god. **2** to accord divine honour or worship to. [C14: from OF, from LL *deificāre,* from L *deus* god + *facere* to make]
▸**ˌdeifiˈcation** *n* ▸**ˈdeiˌfier** *n*

deign ❶ (deɪn) *vb* **1** *(intr)* to think it fit or worthy of oneself (to do something); condescend. **2** *(tr) Arch.* to vouchsafe. [C13: from OF, from L *dignārī* to consider worthy, from *dignus*]

deindividuation (diːˌɪndɪˌvɪdjuˈeɪʃən) *n Psychol.* the loss of a person's sense of individuality and responsibility.

de-industrialization *or* **de-industrialisation** (diːɪndʌstrɪəlaɪˈzeɪʃən) *n* a decline in importance of a country's manufacturing industry.

de-ionize *or* **de-ionise** (diːˈaɪəˌnaɪz) *vb* **de-ionizes, de-ionizing, de-ionized**

THESAURUS

(*inf.*), clumsiness, ham-fistedness (*inf.*), incompetence, ineptitude

defunct *adj* **1** = **dead,** deceased, departed, extinct, gone **2** = **obsolete,** a dead letter, bygone, expired, inoperative, invalid, nonexistent, not functioning, out of commission

defuse *vb* **1** = **deactivate,** disable, disarm, make safe **2** = **calm,** contain, cool, damp down, settle, smooth, stabilize, take the heat *or* sting out
Antonyms *vb* ≠ **deactivate:** activate, arm ≠ **calm:** aggravate, escalate, exacerbate, inflame, intensify, magnify, make worse, worsen

defy *vb* **1** = **resist,** beard, brave, confront, contemn, despise, disobey, disregard, face, flout, hurl defiance at, scorn, slight, spurn **2** = **foil,** baffle, call (someone's) bluff, defeat, elude, frustrate, repel, repulse, thwart, withstand **3** *Formal* = **challenge,** dare, provoke

degeneracy *n* **1** = **depravity,** corruption, decadence, degradation, dissoluteness, immorality, inferiority, meanness, poorness, turpitude **2** = **worsening,** debasement, decay, decline, decrease, depravation, deterioration

degenerate *vb* **1** = **worsen,** decay, decline, decrease, deteriorate, fall off, go to pot, lapse, regress, retrogress, rot, sink, slip ◆ *adj* **3** = **depraved,** base, corrupt, debased, debauched, decadent, degenerated, degraded, deteriorated, dissolute, fallen, immoral, low, mean, perverted

degeneration *n* **1, 2** = **deterioration,** debasement, decline, degeneracy, descent, dissipation, dissolution, regression

degradation *n* **1** = **deterioration,** abasement, debasement, decadence, decline, degeneracy, degeneration, demotion, derogation, downgrading, perversion **2** = **disgrace,** discredit, dishonour, humiliation, ignominy, mortification, shame

degrade *vb* **1** = **demean,** cheapen, corrupt, debase, discredit, disgrace, dishonour, humble, humiliate, impair, injure, pervert, shame, vitiate **2** = **demote,** break, cashier, depose, downgrade, lower, reduce to inferior rank **3** = **adulterate,** dilute, doctor, mix, thin, water, water down, weaken
Antonyms *vb* ≠ **demean:** dignify, enhance, ennoble, honour, improve ≠ **demote:** elevate, promote, raise

degraded *adj* **1** = **disgraced,** abandoned, base, corrupt, debased, debauched, decadent, depraved, despicable, disreputable, dissolute, low, mean, profligate, sordid, vicious, vile

degrading *adj* = **demeaning,** cheapening, contemptible, debasing, disgraceful, dishonourable, humiliating, infra dig (*inf.*), lowering, shameful, undignified, unworthy

degree *n* **1** = **stage,** division, extent, gradation, grade, interval, limit, mark, measure, notch, point, rung, scale, step, unit **1** = **rank,** class, grade, level, order, position, standing, station, status **1** = **extent,** ambit, calibre, intensity, level, measure, proportion, quality, quantity, range, rate, ratio, scale, scope, severity, standard **15 by degrees** = **little by little,** bit by bit, gently, gradually, imperceptibly, inch by inch, slowly, step by step

dehydrate *vb* **1** = **dry,** desiccate, drain, evaporate, exsiccate, parch

deification *n* **1, 2** = **worship,** apotheosis, elevation, ennoblement, exaltation, glorification, idolization

deify *vb* **1, 2** = **worship,** apotheosize, elevate, ennoble, enthrone, exalt, extol, glorify, idealize, idolize, immortalize, venerate

deign *vb* **1** = **condescend,** consent, deem worthy, lower oneself, see fit, stoop, think fit

or **de-ionises, de-ionising, de-ionised.** (*tr*) to remove ions from (water, etc.), esp. by ion exchange.
▸**deˌioniˈzation** *or* **deˌioniˈsation** *n*

deism (ˈdiːɪzəm, ˈdeɪ-) *n* belief in the existence of God based on natural reason, without revelation. Cf. **theism.** [C17: from F *déisme,* from L *deus* god]
▸**ˈdeist** *n, adj* ▸**deˈistic** *or* **deˈistical** *adj* ▸**deˈistically** *adv*

deity Ⓣ (ˈdiːɪtɪ, ˈdeɪ-) *n, pl* **deities. 1** a god or goddess. **2** the state of being divine; godhead. **3** the rank of a god. **4** the nature or character of God. [C14: from OF, from LL *deitās,* from L *deus* god]

Deity (ˈdiːɪtɪ, ˈdeɪ-) *n* **the.** God.

déjà vu (ˈdeɪʒæ ˈvuː) *n* the experience of perceiving a new situation as if it had occurred before. [from F, lit.: already seen]

deject Ⓣ (dɪˈdʒɛkt) *vb* (*tr*) to have a depressing effect on; dispirit; dishearten. [C15: from L *dēicere* to cast down, from DE- + *iacere* to throw]

dejected Ⓣ (dɪˈdʒɛktɪd) *adj* miserable; despondent; downhearted.
▸**deˈjectedly** *adv*

dejection Ⓣ (dɪˈdʒɛkʃən) *n* **1** lowness of spirits; depression. **2a** faecal matter. **2b** defecation.

de jure Ⓣ (deɪ ˈdʒʊəreɪ) *adv* according to law; by right; legally. Cf. **de facto.** [L]

deka- *or* **dek-** *combining form.* variants of **deca-.**

deke (diːk) *Canad. sl.* ◆ *vb* **dekes, deking, deked. 1** (*tr*) (in ice hockey or box lacrosse) to draw a defending player out of position by faking a shot or movement. ◆ *n* **2** such a shot or movement. ◆ Also: **decoy.** [C20: from DECOY]

dekko (ˈdɛkəʊ) *n, pl* **dekkos.** *Brit. sl.* a look; glance. [C19: from Hindi *dekho!* look! from *dekhnā* to see]

del (dɛl) *n Maths.* the differential operator $\mathbf{i}(\partial/\partial x) + \mathbf{j}(\partial/\partial y) + \mathbf{k}(\partial/\partial z)$, where $\mathbf{i}$, $\mathbf{j}$, and $\mathbf{k}$ are unit vectors in the *x*, *y*, and *z* directions. Symbol: ∇ Also called: **nabla.**

del. *abbrev. for* delegate.

Del. *abbrev. for* Delaware.

Delaware (ˈdɛləˌwɛə) *n* **1** (*pl* **Delawares** *or* **Delaware**) a member of a North American Indian people formerly living near the Delaware River. **2** the language of this people.

delay Ⓣ (dɪˈleɪ) *vb* **1** (*tr*) to put off to a later time; defer. **2** (*tr*) to slow up or cause to be late. **3** (*intr*) to be irresolute or put off doing something. **4** (*intr*) to linger; dawdle. ◆ *n* **5** a delaying or being delayed. **6** the interval between one event and another. [C13: from OF, from *des-* off + *laier* to leave, from L *laxāre* to loosen]
▸**deˈlayer** *n*

delayed action *or* **delay action** *n* a device for operating a mechanism, such as a camera shutter, a short time after setting.

delayed drop *n Aeronautics.* a parachute descent in which the opening of the parachute is delayed for a predetermined time.

delayering (diːˈleɪərɪŋ) *n* the process of pruning the administrative structure of a large organization by reducing the number of tiers in its hierarchy.

dele (ˈdiːlɪ) *n, pl* **deles. 1** a sign (δ) indicating that typeset matter is to be deleted. ◆ *vb* **deles, deleing, deled. 2** (*tr*) to mark (matter to be deleted) with a dele. [C18: from L: delete (imperative), from *dēlēre* to destroy, obliterate]

delectable Ⓣ (dɪˈlɛktəbᵊl) *adj* highly enjoyable, esp. pleasing to the taste; delightful. [C14: from L *dēlectābilis,* from *dēlectāre* to DELIGHT]
▸**deˈlectableness** *or* **deˌlectaˈbility** *n*

delectation Ⓣ (ˌdiːlɛkˈteɪʃən) *n* pleasure; enjoyment.

delegate Ⓣ *n* (ˈdɛlɪˌgeɪt, -gɪt). **1** a person chosen to act for another or others, esp. at a conference or meeting. ◆ *vb* (ˈdɛlɪˌgeɪt), **delegates, delegating, delegated. 2** to give (duties, powers, etc.) to another as representative; depute. **3** (*tr*) to authorize (a person) as representative. [C14: from L *dēlēgāre* to send on a mission, from *lēgāre* to send, depute]
▸**ˈdelegable** *adj*

delegation Ⓣ (ˌdɛlɪˈgeɪʃən) *n* **1** a person or group chosen to represent another or others. **2** a delegating or being delegated.

delete Ⓣ (dɪˈliːt) *vb* **deletes, deleting, deleted.** (*tr*) to remove (something printed or written); erase; strike out. [C17: from L *dēlēre* to destroy, obliterate]
▸**deˈletion** *n*

deleterious (ˌdɛlɪˈtɪərɪəs) *adj* harmful; injurious; hurtful. [C17: from NL, from Gk *dēlētērios,* from *dēleisthai* to hurt]
▸**ˌdeleˈteriousness** *n*

Delft (dɛlft) *n* tin-glazed earthenware that originated in Delft, a town in the SW Netherlands, typically having blue decoration on a white ground. Also called: **delftware.**

deli (ˈdɛlɪ) *n, pl* **delis.** an informal word for **delicatessen.**

deliberate Ⓣ *adj* (dɪˈlɪbərɪt). **1** carefully thought out in advance; intentional. **2** careful or unhurried: *a deliberate pace.* ◆ *vb* (dɪˈlɪbəˌreɪt). **deliberates, deliberating, deliberated. 3** to consider (something) deeply; think over. [C15: from L *dēlīberāre,* from *lībrāre* to weigh, from *lībra* scales]
▸**deˈliberately** *adv* ▸**deˈliberateness** *n* ▸**deˈliberˌator** *n*

deliberation Ⓣ (dɪˌlɪbəˈreɪʃən) *n* **1** careful consideration. **2** (*often pl*) formal discussion, as of a committee. **3** care or absence of hurry.

deliberative (dɪˈlɪbərətɪv) *adj* **1** of or for deliberating: *a deliberative assembly.* **2** characterized by deliberation.
▸**deˈliberatively** *adv* ▸**deˈliberativeness** *n*

delicacy Ⓣ (ˈdɛlɪkəsɪ) *n, pl* **delicacies. 1** fine or subtle quality, character, construction, etc. **2** fragile or graceful beauty. **3** something that is considered choice to eat, such as caviar. **4** fragile construction or constitution. **5** refinement of feeling, manner, or appreciation. **6** fussy or squeamish refinement, esp. in matters of taste, propriety, etc. **7** need for tactful or sensitive handling. **8** sensitivity of response, as of an instrument.

delicate Ⓣ (ˈdɛlɪkɪt) *adj* **1** fine or subtle in quality, character, construction, etc. **2** having a soft or fragile beauty. **3** (of colour, tone, taste, etc.) pleasantly subtle. **4** easily damaged or injured; fragile. **5** precise or sensitive in action: *a delicate mechanism.* **6** requiring tact. **7** showing regard for the feelings of others. **8** excessively refined; squeamish. [C14: from L *dēlicātus* affording pleasure, from *dēliciae* (pl) delight, pleasure]
▸**ˈdelicately** *adv* ▸**ˈdelicateness** *n*

THESAURUS

deity *n* **1, 2** = **god**, celestial being, divine being, divinity, goddess, godhead, idol, immortal, supreme being

deject *vb* = **depress**, cast down, dampen, daunt, demoralize, discourage, dishearten, dismay, dispirit

dejected *adj* = **downhearted**, blue, cast down, crestfallen, depressed, despondent, disconsolate, disheartened, dismal, doleful, down, downcast, down in the dumps (*inf.*), gloomy, glum, low, low-spirited, melancholy, miserable, morose, sad, sick as a parrot (*inf.*), woebegone, wretched
Antonyms *adj* blithe, cheerful, chirpy (*inf.*), encouraged, genial, happy, joyous, light-hearted, upbeat (*inf.*)

dejection *n* **1** = **low spirits**, blues, depression, despair, despondency, doldrums, downheartedness, dumps (*inf.*), gloom, gloominess, heavy-heartedness, melancholy, sadness, sorrow, the hump (*Brit. inf.*), unhappiness

de jure *adv* = **legally**, according to the law, by right, rightfully

delay *vb* **1** = **put off**, beat about the bush, defer, hold over, play for time, postpone, procrastinate, prolong, protract, put on the back burner (*inf.*), shelve, stall, suspend, table, take a rain check on (*US & Canad. inf.*), temporize **2** = **hold up**, arrest, bog down, check, detain, halt, hinder, hold back, impede, obstruct, retard, set back, slow up, stop, throw a spanner in the works **4** = **drag one's feet** *or* **heels** (*inf.*), dawdle, dilly-dally (*inf.*), drag, lag, linger, loiter, tarry ◆ *n* **5** = **putting off**, deferment, postponement, procrastination, stay, suspension **6** = **hold-up**, check, detention, hindrance, impediment, interruption, interval, obstruction, setback, stoppage, wait
Antonyms *vb* ≠ **hold up**: accelerate, advance, dispatch, expedite, facilitate, forward, hasten, hurry, precipitate, press, promote, quicken, rush, speed (up), urge

delaying *adj* **2** = **hindering**, halting, moratory, obstructive, retardant **3** = **procrastinating**, temporizing **4** = **dawdling**, dallying, dilatory, lingering, slow, tardy, tarrying
Antonyms *adj* ≠ **procrastinating, dawdling**: expeditious, hasty, precipitate, prompt, urgent

delectable *adj* = **delicious**, adorable, agreeable, appetizing, charming, dainty, delightful, enjoyable, enticing, gratifying, inviting, luscious, lush, pleasant, pleasurable, satisfying, scrumptious (*inf.*), tasty, toothsome, yummy (*sl.*)
Antonyms *adj* awful, disagreeable, disgusting, distasteful, dreadful, horrible, horrid, nasty, offensive, terrible, unappetizing, unpleasant, yucky *or* yukky (*sl.*)

delectation *n Formal* = **enjoyment**, amusement, delight, diversion, entertainment, gratification, happiness, jollies (*sl.*), pleasure, refreshment, relish, satisfaction

delegate *n* **1** = **representative**, agent, ambassador, commissioner, deputy, envoy, legate, vicar ◆ *vb* **2** = **entrust**, assign, consign, devolve, give, hand over, pass on, relegate, transfer **3** = **appoint**, accredit, authorize, commission, designate, empower, mandate

delegation *n* **1** = **deputation**, commission, contingent, embassy, envoys, legation, mission **2** = **devolution**, assignment, commissioning, committal, deputizing, entrustment, relegation

delete *vb* = **remove**, blot out, blue-pencil, cancel, cross out, cut out, dele, edit, edit out, efface, erase, excise, expunge, obliterate, rub out, strike out

deliberate *adj* **1** = **intentional**, calculated, conscious, considered, designed, planned, prearranged, premeditated, purposeful, studied, thoughtful, wilful **2** = **unhurried**, careful, cautious, circumspect, heedful, measured, methodical, ponderous, prudent, slow, thoughtful, wary ◆ *vb* **3** = **consider**, cogitate, consult, debate, discuss, meditate, mull over, ponder, reflect, think, weigh
Antonyms *adj* ≠ **intentional**: accidental, inadvertent, unconscious, unintended, unpremeditated, unthinking ≠ **unhurried**: fast, haphazard, hasty, heedless, hurried, impetuous, impulsive, rash

deliberately *adv* **1** = **intentionally**, by design, calculatingly, consciously, determinedly, emphatically, in cold blood, knowingly, on purpose, pointedly, resolutely, studiously, wilfully, wittingly

deliberation *n* **1** = **consideration**, calculation, care, carefulness, caution, circumspection, cogitation, coolness, forethought, meditation, prudence, purpose, reflection, speculation, study, thought, wariness **2** = **discussion**, conference, consultation, debate

delicacy *n* **1** = **fineness**, accuracy, daintiness, elegance, exquisiteness, lightness, nicety, precision, subtlety **3** = **treat**, *bonne bouche,* dainty, luxury, relish, savoury, titbit **4** = **fragility**, debility, flimsiness, frailness, frailty, infirmity, slenderness, tenderness, weakness **5** = **fastidiousness**, discrimination, finesse, purity, refinement, sensibility, taste **7** = **sensitivity**, sensitiveness, tact

delicate *adj* **1** = **fine**, accurate, deft, detailed, elegant, exquisite, graceful, minute, precise, skilled, subtle **3** = **soft**, faint, muted, pastel, subdued, subtle **4** = **fragile**, flimsy, frail, slender,

delicatessen (ˌdɛlɪkəˈtɛsᵊn) *n* **1** a shop selling various foods, esp. unusual or imported foods, already cooked or prepared. **2** such foods. [C19: from G *Delikatessen*, lit.: delicacies, from F *délicatesse*]

delicious ❶ (dɪˈlɪʃəs) *adj* **1** very appealing, esp. to taste or smell. **2** extremely enjoyable. [C13: from OF, from LL *dēliciōsus*, from L *dēliciae* delights, from *dēlicere* to entice; see DELIGHT]
▸**deˈliciously** *adv* ▸**deˈliciousness** *n*

delight ❶ (dɪˈlaɪt) *vb* **1** (*tr*) to please greatly. **2** (*intr*; foll. by *in*) to take great pleasure (in). ◆ *n* **3** extreme pleasure. **4** something that causes this. [C13: from OF, from *deleitier* to please, from L *dēlectāre*, from *dēlicere* to allure, from DE- + *lacere* to entice]
▸**deˈlighted** *adj* ▸**deˈlightedly** *adv*

delightful ❶ (dɪˈlaɪtfʊl) *adj* giving great delight; very pleasing, beautiful, charming, etc.
▸**deˈlightfully** *adv* ▸**deˈlightfulness** *n*

Delilah (dɪˈlaɪlə) *n* **1** Samson's Philistine mistress, who betrayed him (Judges 16). **2** a voluptuous and treacherous woman; temptress.

delimit ❶ (diːˈlɪmɪt) *or* **delimitate** *vb* **delimits, delimiting, delimited** *or* **delimitates, delimitating, delimitated.** (*tr*) to mark or prescribe the limits or boundaries of.
▸**deˌlimiˈtation** *n* ▸**deˈlimitative** *adj*

delineate ❶ (dɪˈlɪnɪˌeɪt) *vb* **delineates, delineating, delineated.** (*tr*) **1** to trace the outline of. **2** to represent pictorially; depict. **3** to portray in words; describe. [C16: from L *dēlīneāre* to sketch out, from *līnea* LINE[1]]
▸**deˌlineˈation** *n* ▸**deˈlineative** *adj*

delinquency ❶ (dɪˈlɪŋkwənsɪ) *n, pl* **delinquencies. 1** an offence or misdeed, esp. one committed by a young person. See **juvenile delinquency. 2** failure or negligence in duty or obligation. **3** a delinquent nature or delinquent behaviour. [C17: from LL *dēlinquentia* fault, offence, from L *dēlinquere* to transgress, from DE- + *linquere* to forsake]

delinquent ❶ (dɪˈlɪŋkwənt) *n* **1** someone, esp. a young person, guilty of delinquency. ◆ *adj* **2** guilty of an offence or misdeed. **3** failing in or neglectful of duty or obligation. [C17: from L *dēlinquēns* offending; see DELINQUENCY]

deliquesce (ˌdɛlɪˈkwɛs) *vb* **deliquesces, deliquescing, deliquesced.** (*intr*) (esp. of certain salts) to dissolve gradually in water absorbed from the air. [C18: from L *dēliquēscere*, from DE- + *liquēscere* to melt, from *liquēre* to be liquid]
▸**ˌdeliˈquescence** *n* ▸**ˌdeliˈquescent** *adj*

delirious ❶ (dɪˈlɪrɪəs) *adj* **1** affected with delirium. **2** wildly excited, esp. with joy or enthusiasm.
▸**deˈliriously** *adv*

delirium ❶ (dɪˈlɪrɪəm) *n, pl* **deliriums** *or* **deliria** (-ˈlɪrɪə). **1** a state of excitement and mental confusion, often accompanied by hallucinations, caused by high fever, poisoning, brain injury, etc. **2** violent excitement or emotion; frenzy. [C16: from L: madness, from *dēlīrāre*, lit.: to swerve from a furrow, hence be crazy, from DE- + *līra* furrow]

delirium tremens (ˈtrɛmɛnz, ˈtriː-) *n* a severe psychotic condition occurring in some persons with chronic alcoholism, characterized by delirium, tremor, anxiety, and vivid hallucinations. Abbrevs.: **DT's** (informal), **dt.** [C19: NL, lit.: trembling delirium]

deliver ❶ (dɪˈlɪvə) *vb* (*mainly tr*) **1** to carry to a destination, esp. to distribute (goods, mail, etc.) to several places. **2** (often foll. by *over* or *up*) to hand over or transfer. **3** (often foll. by *from*) to release or rescue (from captivity, harm, etc.). **4** (*also intr*) **4a** to aid in the birth of (offspring). **4b** to give birth to (offspring). **4c** (usually foll. by *of*) to aid (a female) in the birth (of offspring). **4d** (*passive*; foll. by *of*) to give birth (to offspring). **5** to present (a speech, idea, etc.). **6** to utter: *to deliver a cry of exultation*. **7** to discharge or release (something, such as a blow or shot) suddenly. **8** (*intr*) *Inf.* Also: **deliver the goods.** to produce something promised or expected. **9** *Chiefly US.* to cause (voters, etc.) to support a given candidate, cause, etc. **10 deliver oneself of.** to speak with deliberation or at length. [C13: from OF, from LL *dēlīberāre* to set free, from L DE- + *līberāre* to free]
▸**deˈliverable** *adj* ▸**deˈliverer** *n*

deliverance ❶ (dɪˈlɪvərəns) *n* **1** a formal expression of opinion. **2** rescue from moral corruption or evil; salvation.

delivery ❶ (dɪˈlɪvərɪ) *n, pl* **deliveries. 1a** the act of delivering or distributing goods, mail, etc. **1b** something that is delivered. **2** the act of giving birth to a child. **3** manner or style of utterance, esp. in public speaking: *the chairman had a clear delivery*. **4** the act of giving or transferring or the state of being given or transferred. **5** a rescuing or being rescued; liberation. **6** *Sport.* the act or manner of bowling or throwing a ball. **7** the handing over of property, a deed, etc.

dell (dɛl) *n* a small, esp. wooded hollow. [OE]

delouse (diːˈlaʊs, -ˈlaʊz) *vb* **delouses, delousing, deloused.** (*tr*) to rid (a person or animal) of lice as a sanitary measure.

Delphic (ˈdɛlfɪk) *or* **Delphian** *adj* **1** of or relating to the ancient Greek city of Delphi or its oracle or temple. **2** obscure or ambiguous.

delphinium (dɛlˈfɪnɪəm) *n, pl* **delphiniums** *or* **delphinia** (-ɪə). a plant with spikes of blue, pink, or white spurred flowers. See also **larkspur.** [C17: NL, from Gk *delphinion* larkspur, from *delphis* dolphin, referring to the shape of the nectary]

delta (ˈdɛltə) *n* **1** the fourth letter in the Greek alphabet (Δ or δ). **2** (*cap. when part of name*) the flat alluvial area at the mouth of some rivers where the mainstream splits up into several distributaries. **3** *Maths.* a finite increment in a variable. [C16: via L from Gk, of Semitic origin]
▸**deltaic** (dɛlˈteɪɪk) *or* **ˈdeltic** *adj*

delta connection *n* a connection used in a three-phase electrical system in which three elements in series form a triangle, the supply being input and output at the three junctions.

delta particle *n Physics* a very short-lived type of hyperon.

delta ray *n* a particle, esp. an electron, ejected from matter by ionizing radiation.

delta rhythm *or* **wave** *n Physiol.* the normal electrical activity of the cerebral cortex during deep sleep. See also **brain wave.**

delta stock *n* any of the fourth rank of active securities on the London stock exchange. Market makers need not display prices of these securities continuously.

delta wing *n* a triangular swept-back aircraft wing.

deltiology (ˌdɛltɪˈɒlədʒɪ) *n* the collection and study of postcards. [C20: from Gk *deltion*, dim. of *deltos* a writing tablet + -LOGY]
▸**ˌdeltiˈologist** *n*

deltoid (ˈdɛltɔɪd) *n* a thick muscle of the shoulder that acts to raise the arm. [C18: from Gk *deltoeidēs* triangular, from DELTA]

delude ❶ (dɪˈluːd) *vb* **deludes, deluding, deluded.** (*tr*) to deceive; mislead; beguile. [C15: from L *dēlūdere* to mock, play false, from DE- + *lūdere* to play]
▸**deˈludable** *adj* ▸**deˈluder** *n*

deluge ❶ (ˈdɛljuːdʒ) *n* **1** a great flood of water. **2** torrential rain. **3** an overwhelming rush or number. ◆ *vb* **deluges, deluging, deluged.** (*tr*) **4** to

THESAURUS

slight, tender, weak **7** = **considerate**, diplomatic, discreet, sensitive, tactful **8** = **fastidious**, careful, critical, discriminating, nice, prudish, pure, refined, scrupulous, squeamish
Antonyms *adj* ≠ **fine:** coarse, crude, indelicate, unrefined ≠ **subtle:** harsh, strong ≠ **soft:** bright, harsh, rough ≠ **considerate:** harsh, inconsiderate, indelicate, insensitive, rough ≠ **fastidious:** careless, crude, rough

delicately *adv* **1** = **finely**, carefully, daintily, deftly, elegantly, exquisitely, gracefully, lightly, precisely, skilfully, softly, subtly **6** = **tactfully**, diplomatically, sensitively

delicious *adj* **1** = **delectable**, ambrosial, appetizing, choice, dainty, luscious, mouthwatering, nectareous, palatable, savoury, scrumptious (*inf.*), tasty, toothsome, yummy (*sl.*) **2** = **delightful**, agreeable, charming, enjoyable, entertaining, exquisite, pleasant, pleasing
Antonyms *adj* ≠ **delectable:** disagreeable, distasteful, unpleasant

delight *n* **1** = **pleasure**, ecstasy, enjoyment, felicity, gladness, glee, gratification, happiness, jollies (*sl.*), joy, rapture, transport ◆ *vb* **1** = **please**, amuse, charm, cheer, divert, enchant, gratify, ravish, rejoice, satisfy, thrill **2 delight in** = **take pleasure in**, appreciate, enjoy, feast on, glory in, indulge in, like, love, luxuriate in, relish, revel in, savour
Antonyms *n* ≠ **pleasure:** disapprobation, disfavour, dislike, displeasure, dissatisfaction, distaste ◆ *vb* ≠ **please:** disgust, displease, dissatisfy, gall, irk, offend, upset, vex

delighted *adj* **1** = **pleased**, blissed out, captivated, charmed, cock-a-hoop, ecstatic, elated, enchanted, gladdened, happy, in seventh heaven, joyous, jubilant, overjoyed, over the moon (*inf.*), rapt, sent, thrilled

delightful *adj* = **pleasant**, agreeable, amusing, captivating, charming, congenial, delectable, enchanting, engaging, enjoyable, entertaining, fascinating, gratifying, heavenly, pleasing, pleasurable, rapturous, ravishing, thrilling
Antonyms *adj* disagreeable, displeasing, distasteful, horrid, nasty, unpleasant

delimit *vb* = **define**, bound, demarcate, determine, fix, mark (out)

delineate *vb* **1-3** = **outline**, characterize, chart, contour, depict, describe, design, draw, figure, map out, paint, picture, portray, render, sketch, trace

delineation *n* **1-3** = **outline**, account, chart, depiction, description, design, diagram, drawing, picture, portrait, portrayal, representation, tracing

delinquency *n* **1** = **crime**, fault, misbehaviour, misconduct, misdeed, misdemeanour, offence, wrongdoing

delinquent *n* **1** = **criminal**, culprit, defaulter, juvenile delinquent, lawbreaker, malefactor, miscreant, offender, villain, wrongdoer, young offender

delirious *adj* **1** = **mad**, crazy, demented, deranged, incoherent, insane, light-headed, raving, unhinged **2** = **ecstatic**, beside oneself, blissed out, carried away, excited, frantic, frenzied, hysterical, sent, wild
Antonyms *adj* calm, clear-headed, coherent, *compos mentis*, in one's right mind, lucid, rational, sane, sensible

delirium *n* **1** = **madness**, aberration, derangement, hallucination, insanity, lunacy, raving **2** = **frenzy**, ecstasy, fever, fury, hysteria, passion, rage

deliver *vb* **1** = **carry**, bear, bring, cart, convey, distribute, transport **2** = **hand over**, cede, commit, give up, grant, make over, relinquish, resign, surrender, transfer, turn over, yield **3** = **release**, acquit, discharge, emancipate, free, liberate, loose, ransom, redeem, rescue, save **5** = **give**, announce, declare, give forth, present, proclaim, pronounce, publish, read, utter **7** = **strike**, administer, aim, deal, direct, give, inflict, launch, throw

deliverance *n* **2** = **release**, emancipation, escape, liberation, ransom, redemption, rescue, salvation

delivery *n* **1a** = **handing over**, consignment, conveyance, dispatch, distribution, surrender, transfer, transmission, transmittal **2** = **childbirth**, confinement, labour, parturition **3** = **speech**, articulation, elocution, enunciation, intonation, utterance **5** = **release**, deliverance, escape, liberation, rescue

delude *vb* = **deceive**, bamboozle (*inf.*), beguile, cheat, con (*inf.*), cozen, dupe, fool, gull (*arch.*), hoax, hoodwink, impose on, kid (*inf.*), lead up the garden path (*inf.*), misguide, mislead, pull the wool over someone's eyes, take for a ride (*inf.*), take in (*inf.*), trick

deluge *n* **1, 2** = **flood**, cataclysm, downpour, inundation, overflowing, spate, torrent **3** = **rush**,

flood. **5** to overwhelm; inundate. [C14: from OF, from L *dīluvium*, from *dīluere* to wash away, drench, from *di-* DIS-[1] + *-luere*, from *lavere* to wash]

Deluge ('dɛljuːdʒ) *n* **the.** another name for the **Flood.**

delusion Ⓣ (dɪ'luːʒən) *n* **1** a mistaken idea, belief, etc. **2** *Psychiatry.* a belief held in the face of evidence to the contrary, that is resistant to all reason. **3** a deluding or being deluded.
▸**de'lusional** *adj* ▸**de'lusive** *adj* ▸**delusory** (dɪ'luːsərɪ) *adj*

de luxe Ⓣ (də 'lʌks, 'lʊks) *adj* **1** rich or sumptuous; superior in quality: *the de luxe model of a car.* ◆ *adv* **2** *Chiefly US.* in a luxurious manner. [C19: from F, lit.: of luxury]

delve Ⓣ (dɛlv) *vb* **delves, delving, delved.** (*mainly intr;* often foll. by *in* or *into*) **1** to research deeply or intensively (for information, etc.). **2** to search or rummage. **3** to dig or burrow deeply. **4** (*also tr*) *Arch. or Brit. dialect.* to dig. [OE *delfan*]
▸**'delver** *n*

Dem. (in the US) *abbrev. for* Democrat(ic).

demagnetize *or* **demagnetise** (diː'mægnəˌtaɪz) *vb* **demagnetizes, demagnetizing, demagnetized** *or* **demagnetises, demagnetising, demagnetised.** to remove or lose magnetic properties. Also: **degauss.**
▸**deˌmagneti'zation** *or* **deˌmagneti'sation** *n* ▸**de'magnetˌizer** *or* **de'magnetˌiser** *n*

demagogue Ⓣ *or US* (*sometimes*) **demagog** ('dɛməˌgɒg) *n* **1** a political agitator who appeals with crude oratory to the prejudice and passions of the mob. **2** (esp. in the ancient world) any popular political leader or orator. [C17: from Gk *dēmagōgos* people's leader, from *dēmos* people + *agein* to lead]
▸ˌ**dema'gogic** *adj* ▸ˌ**dema'goguery** *n*

demagogy ('dɛməˌgɒgɪ) *n, pl* **demagogies. 1** demagoguery. **2** rule by a demagogue or by demagogues. **3** a group of demagogues.

demand Ⓣ (dɪ'mɑːnd) *vb* (*tr; may take a clause as object or an infinitive*) **1** to request peremptorily or urgently. **2** to require as just, urgent, etc.: *the situation demands attention.* **3** to claim as a right; exact. **4** *Law.* to make a formal legal claim to (property). ◆ *n* **5** an urgent or peremptory requirement or request. **6** something that requires special effort or sacrifice. **7** the act of demanding something or the thing demanded. **8** an insistent question. **9** *Econ.* **9a** willingness and ability to purchase goods and services. **9b** the amount of a commodity that consumers are willing and able to purchase at a specified price. Cf. **supply**[1] (sense 9). **10** *Law.* a formal legal claim, esp. to real property. **11 in demand.** sought after. **12 on demand.** as soon as requested. [C13: from Anglo-F, from Med. L *dēmandāre*, from L: to commit to, from DE- + *mandāre* to command, entrust]
▸**de'mandable** *adj* ▸**de'mander** *n*

demand feeding *n* the practice of feeding a baby whenever it is hungry, rather than at set intervals.

demanding Ⓣ (dɪ'mɑːndɪŋ) *adj* requiring great patience, skill, etc.: *a demanding job.*

demarcate Ⓣ ('diːmɑːˌkeɪt) *vb* **demarcates, demarcating, demarcated.** (*tr*) **1** to mark the boundaries, limits, etc., of. **2** to separate; distinguish.
▸**'demarˌcator** *n*

demarcation Ⓣ *or* **demarkation** (ˌdiːmɑː'keɪʃən) *n* **1** the act of establishing limits or boundaries. **2** a limit or boundary. **3a** a strict separation of the kinds of work performed by members of different trade unions. **3b** (*as modifier*): *demarcation dispute.* **4** separation or distinction (as in **line of demarcation**). [C18: from Sp. *demarcar* to appoint the boundaries of, from *marcar* to mark, from It., of Gmc origin]

démarche *French.* (demarʃ) *n* a move, step, or manoeuvre, esp. in diplomatic affairs. [C17: lit.: walk, gait, from OF *demarcher* to tread, trample]

dematerialize *or* **dematerialise** (diːmə'tɪərɪəˌlaɪz) *vb* **dematerializes, dematerializing, dematerialized** *or* **dematerialises, dematerialising, dematerialised.** (*intr*) **1** to cease to have material existence, as in science fiction or spiritualism. **2** to vanish.
▸**demaˌteriali'zation** *or* **demaˌteriali'sation** *n*

deme (diːm) *n* **1** (in ancient Attica) a geographical unit of local government. **2** *Biol.* a group of individuals within a species that possess particular characteristics of cytology, genetics, etc. [C19: from Gk *dēmos* district in local government, the populace]

demean[1] Ⓣ (dɪ'miːn) *vb* (*tr*) to lower (oneself) in dignity, status, or character; humble; debase. [C17: see DE-, MEAN[2]]

demean[2] (dɪ'miːn) *vb* (*tr*) *Rare.* to behave or conduct (oneself). [C13: from OF, from DE- + *mener* to lead, from L *mināre* to drive (animals), from *minārī* to use threats]

demeanour Ⓣ *or US* **demeanor** (dɪ'miːnə) *n* **1** the way a person behaves towards others. **2** bearing or mien. [C15: see DEMEAN[2]]

dement (dɪ'mɛnt) *vb* **1** (*intr*) to deteriorate mentally, esp. because of old age. **2** (*tr*) *Rare.* to drive mad; make insane. [C16: from LL *dēmentāre* to drive mad, from L DE- + *mēns* mind]

demented Ⓣ (dɪ'mɛntɪd) *adj* mad; insane.
▸**de'mentedly** *adv* ▸**de'mentedness** *n*

dementia (dɪ'mɛnʃə, -ʃɪə) *n* a state of serious mental deterioration, of organic or functional origin. [C19: from L: madness; see DEMENT]

dementia praecox ('priːkɒks) *n* a former name for **schizophrenia.** [C19: NL, lit.: premature dementia]

demerara (ˌdɛmə'rɛərə, -'rɑːrə) *n* brown crystallized cane sugar from the Caribbean. [C19: after *Demerara*, a region of Guyana]

demerit (diː'mɛrɪt) *n* **1** something that deserves censure. **2** *US & Canad.* a mark given against a student, etc., for failure or misconduct. **3** a fault. [C14 (orig.: worth, desert, ult.: something worthy of blame): from L *dēmerērī* to deserve]
▸**deˌmeri'torious** *adj*

demersal (dɪ'mɜːsᵊl) *adj* living or occurring in deep water or on the bottom of a sea or lake. [C19: from L *dēmersus* submerged (from *mergere* to dip) + -AL[1]]

demesne (dɪ'meɪn, -'miːn) *n* **1** land surrounding a house or manor. **2** *Property law.* the possession and use of one's own property or land. **3** realm; domain. **4** a region or district. [C14: from OF *demeine;* see DOMAIN]

demi- *prefix* **1** half: *demirelief.* **2** of less than full size, status, or rank: *demigod.* [via F from Med. L, from L *dīmīdius* half, from *dis-* apart + *medius* middle]

demigod ('dɛmɪˌgɒd) *n* **1a** a being who is part mortal, part god. **1b** a lesser deity. **2** a person with godlike attributes. [C16: translation of L *sēmideus*]
▸**'demiˌgoddess** *fem n*

demijohn ('dɛmɪˌdʒɒn) *n* a large bottle with a short narrow neck, often encased in wickerwork. [C18: prob. from F *dame-jeanne*, from *dame* lady + *Jeanne* Jane]

demilitarize *or* **demilitarise** (diː'mɪlɪtəˌraɪz) *vb* **demilitarizes, demilitarizing, demilitarized** *or* **demilitarises, demilitarising, demilitarised.** (*tr*) **1** to remove and prohibit any military presence or function in (an area): *demilitarized zone.* **2** to free of military character, purpose, etc.
▸**deˌmilitari'zation** *or* **deˌmilitari'sation** *n*

demimondaine (ˌdɛmɪ'mɒndeɪn) *n* a woman of the demimonde. [C19: from F]

demimonde (ˌdɛmɪ'mɒnd) *n* **1** (esp. in the 19th century) those women considered to be outside respectable society, esp. on account of sexual promiscuity. **2** any group considered to be not wholly respectable. [C19: from F, lit.: half-world]

demise Ⓣ (dɪ'maɪz) *n* **1** failure or termination. **2** a euphemistic or formal word for **death. 3** *Property law.* a transfer of an estate by lease or on the death of the owner. **4** the transfer of sovereignty to a successor upon the death, abdication, etc., of a ruler (esp. in **demise of the crown**).

THESAURUS

avalanche, barrage, flood, spate, torrent ◆ *vb* **4** = **flood**, douse, drench, drown, inundate, soak, submerge, swamp **5** = **overwhelm**, engulf, inundate, overload, overrun, swamp

delusion *n* **1-3** = **misconception**, deception, error, fallacy, false impression, fancy, hallucination, illusion, misapprehension, misbelief, mistake, phantasm, self-deception

delusive *adj* **1** = **deceptive**, chimerical, fallacious, illusive, illusory, misleading, specious, spurious

delusory **1** *adj* = **deceptive**, deluded, erroneous, fallacious, false, fictitious, illusory, imaginary, imagined, misguided, mistaken, unfounded
Antonyms *adj* actual, authentic, genuine, real, true

de luxe *adj* **1** = **luxurious**, choice, costly, elegant, exclusive, expensive, gorgeous, grand, opulent, palatial, plush (*inf.*), rich, select, special, splendid, splendiferous (*facetious*), sumptuous, superior

delve *vb* **1-3** = **research**, burrow, dig into, examine, explore, ferret out, forage, investigate, look into, probe, ransack, rummage, search, unearth

demagogue *n* **1** = **agitator**, firebrand, haranguer, rabble-rouser, soapbox orator

demand *vb* **1** = **request**, ask, challenge, inquire, interrogate, question **2** = **require**, call for, cry out for, entail, involve, necessitate, need, take, want **3** = **claim**, exact, expect, insist on, order ◆ *n* **5** = **request**, bidding, charge, inquiry, interrogation, order, question, requisition **9a** = **need**, call, claim, market, necessity, requirement, want **11 in demand** = **sought after**, fashionable, in vogue, like gold dust, needed, popular, requested
Antonyms *vb* ≠ **require, claim:** come up with, contribute, furnish, give, grant, produce, provide, supply, yield

demanding *adj* = **difficult**, challenging, exacting, exhausting, exigent, hard, taxing, tough, trying, wearing
Antonyms *adj* ≠ **difficult:** a piece of cake (*inf.*), child's play (*inf.*), easy, easy-peasy (*sl.*), effortless, facile, no bother, painless, simple, straightforward, uncomplicated, undemanding

demarcate *vb* **1, 2** = **delimit**, define, determine, differentiate, distinguish between, fix, mark, separate

demarcation *n* **1** = **delimitation**, differentiation, distinction, division, separation **2** = **limit**, bound, boundary, confine, enclosure, margin, pale

demean[1] *vb* = **lower**, abase, debase, degrade, descend, humble, stoop

demeaning *adj* = **humiliating**, beneath one's dignity, cheapening, contemptible, debasing, degrading, disgraceful, dishonourable, infra dig (*inf.*), shameful, undignified, unworthy

demeanour *n* **1, 2** = **behaviour**, air, bearing, carriage, comportment, conduct, deportment, manner, mien

demented *adj* = **mad**, barking (*sl.*), barking mad, crackbrained, crackpot (*inf.*), crazed, crazy, daft (*inf.*), deranged, distraught, doolally (*sl.*), dotty (*sl., chiefly Brit.*), foolish, frenzied, idiotic, insane, loopy (*inf.*), lunatic, maniacal, manic, *non compos mentis*, not the full shilling (*inf.*), off one's trolley (*sl.*), out to lunch (*inf.*), unbalanced, unhinged, up the pole (*inf.*)
Antonyms *adj* all there (*inf.*), *compos mentis*, in one's right mind, lucid, mentally sound, normal, of sound mind, rational, reasonable, sensible, sound

demise *n* **1** = **failure**, collapse, dissolution, downfall, end, fall, ruin, termination **2** *Euphemistic* = **death**, decease, departure, expiration **3** *Property law* = **death**, alienation, conveyance,

◆ *vb* **demises, demising, demised. 5** to transfer or be transferred by inheritance, will, or succession. **6** (*tr*) *Property law.* to transfer for a limited period; lease. **7** (*tr*) to transfer (sovereignty, a title, etc.) [C16: from OF, fem of *demis* dismissed, from *demettre* to send away, from L *dīmittere*]
▸**de'misable** *adj*

demi-sec (ˌdɛmɪ'sɛk) *adj* (of wine) medium-dry. [C20: from F, from *demi* half + *sec* dry]

demisemiquaver ('dɛmɪˌsɛmɪˌkweɪvə) *n Music.* a note having the time value of one thirty-second of a semibreve. Usual US and Canad. name: **thirty-second note.**

demist (diː'mɪst) *vb* to free or become free of condensation.
▸**de'mister** *n*

demitasse ('dɛmɪˌtæs) *n* **1** a small cup used to serve coffee, esp. after a meal. **2** the coffee itself. [C19: F, lit.: half-cup]

demiurge ('dɛmɪˌɜːdʒ) *n* **1** (in the philosophy of Plato) the creator of the universe. **2** (in Gnostic philosophy) the creator of the universe, supernatural but subordinate to the Supreme Being. [C17: from Church L, from Gk *dēmiourgos* skilled workman, lit.: one who works for the people, from *dēmos* people + *ergon* work]
▸ˌ**demi'urgic** *or* ˌ**demi'urgical** *adj*

demiveg ('dɛmɪˌvɛdʒ) *Inf.* ◆ *n* **1** a person who eats poultry and fish, but no red meat. ◆ *adj* **2** denoting a person who eats poultry and fish, but no red meat. [C20: from DEMI- + VEG(ETARIAN)]

demo ('dɛməʊ) *n, pl* **demos.** *Inf.* **1** short for **demonstration** (sense 4). **2** a demonstration record or tape.

demo- *or before a vowel* **dem-** *combining form.* indicating people or population: *demography.* [from Gk *dēmos*]

demob *Brit. inf.* ◆ *vb* (diː'mɒb), **demobs, demobbing, demobbed. 1** to demobilize. ◆ *n* ('diːmɒb). **2** demobilization.

demobilize ⓘ *or* **demobilise** (diː'məʊbɪˌlaɪz) *vb* **demobilizes, demobilizing, demobilized** *or* **demobilises, demobilising, demobilised.** to disband, as troops, etc.
▸**deˌmobili'zation** *or* **deˌmobili'sation** *n*

Demochristian (ˌdɛməʊ'krɪstʃən) *n* an informal name for a **Christian Democrat.**

democracy ⓘ (dɪ'mɒkrəsɪ) *n, pl* **democracies. 1** government by the people or their elected representatives. **2** a political or social unit governed ultimately by all its members. **3** the practice or spirit of social equality. **4** a social condition of classlessness and equality. [C16: from F, from LL, from Gk *dēmokratia* government by the people]

democrat ('dɛməˌkræt) *n* **1** an advocate of democracy. **2** a member or supporter of a democratic party or movement.

Democrat ('dɛməˌkræt) *n* (in the US) a member or supporter of the Democratic Party.
▸ˌ**Demo'cratic** *adj*

democratic ⓘ (ˌdɛmə'krætɪk) *adj* **1** of or relating to the principles of democracy. **2** upholding democracy or the interests of the common people. **3** popular with or for the benefit of all.
▸ˌ**demo'cratically** *adv*

democratic centralism *n* the Leninist principle that policy should be decided centrally by officials, who are nominally democratically elected.

democratize *or* **democratise** (dɪ'mɒkrəˌtaɪz) *vb* **democratizes, democratizing, democratized** *or* **democratises, democratising, democratised.** (*tr*) to make democratic.
▸**deˌmocrati'zation** *or* **deˌmocrati'sation** *n*

démodé *French.* (demɔde) *adj* outmoded. [F, from *dé-* out of + *mode* fashion]

demodulate (diː'mɒdjʊˌleɪt) *vb* **demodulates, demodulating, demodulated.** to carry out demodulation on.
▸**de'moduˌlator** *n*

demodulation (ˌdiːmɒdjʊ'leɪʃən) *n Electronics.* the act or process by which an output wave or signal is obtained having the characteristics of the original modulating wave or signal; the reverse of modulation.

demographic timebomb *n Chiefly Brit.* a predicted shortage of school-leavers and consequently of available workers, caused by an earlier drop in the birth rate.

demography (dɪ'mɒgrəfɪ) *n* the scientific study of human populations, esp. of their size, distribution, etc. [C19: from F, from Gk *dēmos* the populace; see -GRAPHY]
▸**de'mographer** *n* ▸**demographic** (ˌdiːmə'græfɪk, ˌdɛmə-) *adj*

demoiselle (dəmwɑː'zɛl) *n* **1** a small crane of central Asia, N Africa, and SE Europe, having a grey plumage with black breast feathers and white ear tufts. **2** a less common name for a **damselfly. 3** a literary word for **damsel.** [C16: from F: young woman; see DAMSEL]

demolish ⓘ (dɪ'mɒlɪʃ) *vb* (*tr*) **1** to tear down or break up (buildings, etc.). **2** to put an end to (an argument, etc.). **3** *Facetious.* to eat up. [C16: from F, from L *dēmōlīrī* to throw down, from DE- + *mōlīrī* to construct, from *mōles* mass]
▸**de'molisher** *n*

demolition ⓘ (ˌdɛmə'lɪʃən, ˌdiː-) *n* **1** a demolishing or being demolished. **2** *Chiefly mil.* destruction by explosives.
▸ˌ**demo'litionist** *n, adj*

demon ⓘ ('diːmən) *n* **1** an evil spirit or devil. **2** a person, obsession, etc., thought of as evil or cruel. **3** Also called: **daemon, daimon.** an attendant or ministering spirit; genius: *the demon of inspiration.* **4a** a person extremely skilful in or devoted to a given activity, esp. a sport: *a demon at cycling.* **4b** (*as modifier*): *a demon cyclist.* **5** a variant spelling of **daemon** (senses 1, 2). **6** *Austral. & NZ sl.* a detective or policeman, esp. one in plain clothes. [C15: from L *daemōn* (evil) spirit, from Gk *daimōn* spirit, deity, fate]
▸**demonic** (dɪ'mɒnɪk) *adj*

demonetize *or* **demonetise** (diː'mʌnɪˌtaɪz) *vb* **demonetizes, demonetizing, demonetized** *or* **demonetises, demonetising, demonetised.** (*tr*) **1** to deprive (a metal) of its capacity as a monetary standard. **2** to withdraw from use as currency.
▸**deˌmoneti'zation** *or* **deˌmoneti'sation** *n*

demoniac (dɪ'məʊnɪˌæk) *adj also* **demoniacal** (ˌdiːmə'naɪək[ə]l). **1** of or like a demon. **2** suggesting inner possession or inspiration. **3** frantic; frenzied. ◆ *n* **4** a person possessed by a demon.
▸ˌ**demo'niacally** *adv*

demonism ('diːməˌnɪzəm) *n* **1** belief in the existence and power of demons. **2** another name for **demonology** (sense 1).
▸**'demonist** *n*

demonolatry (ˌdiːmə'nɒlətrɪ) *n* the worship of demons. [C17: see DEMON, -LATRY]

demonology (ˌdiːmə'nɒlədʒɪ) *n* **1** Also called: **demonism.** the study of demons or demonic beliefs. **2** a set of people or things that are disliked or feared: *Adolf Hitler's place in contemporary demonology.*
▸ˌ**demon'ologist** *n*

demonstrable ⓘ ('dɛmənstrəb[ə]l, dɪ'mɒn-) *adj* able to be demonstrated or proved.
▸ˌ**demonstra'bility** *n* ▸**'demonstrably** *adv*

demonstrate ⓘ ('dɛmənˌstreɪt) *vb* **demonstrates, demonstrating, demonstrated. 1** (*tr*) to show or prove, esp. by reasoning, evidence, etc. **2** (*tr*) to evince; reveal the existence of. **3** (*tr*) to explain by experiment, example, etc. **4** (*tr*) to display and explain the workings of (a machine, product, etc.). **5** (*intr*) to manifest support, protest, etc., by public parades or rallies. **6** (*intr*) to be employed as a demonstrator of machinery, etc. **7** (*intr*) *Mil.* to make a show of force. [C16: from L *dēmonstrāre* to point out, from *monstrāre* to show]

demonstration ⓘ (ˌdɛmən'streɪʃən) *n* **1** the act of demonstrating. **2** proof or evidence leading to proof. **3** an explanation, illustration, or experiment showing how something works. **4** Also: **demo.** a manifestation of support or protest by public rallies, parades, etc. **5** a manifestation of emotion. **6** a show of military force.
▸ˌ**demon'strational** *adj* ▸ˌ**demon'strationist** *n*

demonstration model *n* a nearly new product, such as a car, that has been used to demonstrate its performance by a dealer and is offered at a discount.

demonstrative ⓘ (dɪ'mɒnstrətɪv) *adj* **1** tending to express one's feelings easily or unreservedly. **2** (*postpositive;* foll. by *of*) serving as proof; indicative. **3** involving or characterized by demonstration. **4** conclusive. **5** *Grammar.* denoting or belonging to a class of determiners used to point out the individual referent or referents intended, such as *this*

THESAURUS

transfer, transmission ◆ *vb* **5** = **transfer,** bequeath, convey, grant, leave, will

demobilize *vb* = **discharge,** deactivate, decommission, demob (*Brit. inf.*), disband, release
Antonyms *vb* call up, conscript, draft (*US.*), enlist, enrol, mobilize, muster, recruit

democracy *n* **1, 2** = **self-government,** commonwealth, government by the people, representative government, republic

democratic *adj* **1-3** = **self-governing,** autonomous, egalitarian, popular, populist, representative, republican

demolish *vb* **1** = **knock down,** bulldoze, destroy, dismantle, flatten, level, overthrow, pulverize, raze, ruin, tear down, total (*sl.*), trash (*sl.*) **2** = **defeat,** annihilate, blow out of the water (*sl.*), destroy, lick (*inf.*), master, overthrow, overturn, stuff (*sl.*), tank (*sl.*), undo, wipe the floor with (*inf.*), wreck **3** *Facetious* = **devour,** consume, eat, gobble up, put away
Antonyms *vb* ≠ **knock down:** build, construct, create, repair, restore, strengthen

demolition *n* **1** = **knocking down,** bulldozing, destruction, explosion, levelling, razing, tearing down, wrecking

demon *n* **1** = **evil spirit,** devil, fiend, ghoul, goblin, malignant spirit **2** = **monster,** devil, fiend, ghoul, rogue, villain **4a** = **wizard,** ace (*inf.*), addict, fanatic, fiend, master

demonic *adj* **1** = **devilish,** diabolic, diabolical, fiendish, hellish, infernal, satanic **2** = **frenzied,** crazed, frantic, frenetic, furious, hectic, like one possessed, mad, maniacal, manic

demonstrable *adj* = **provable,** attestable, axiomatic, certain, evident, evincible, incontrovertible, indubitable, irrefutable, obvious, palpable, positive, self-evident, undeniable, unmistakable, verifiable

demonstrate *vb* **1** = **prove,** display, establish, evidence, evince, exhibit, indicate, manifest, show, testify to **3** = **show how,** describe, explain, illustrate, make clear, teach **5** = **march,** parade, picket, protest, rally

demonstration *n* **2** = **proof,** affirmation, confirmation, display, evidence, exhibition, expression, illustration, manifestation, substantiation, testimony, validation **3** = **explanation,** description, exposition, presentation, test, trial **4** = **march,** mass lobby, parade, picket, protest, rally, sit-in

demonstrative *adj* **1** = **open,** affectionate, effusive, emotional, expansive, expressive, gushing, loving, unreserved, unrestrained **3** = **indicative,** evincive, explanatory, expository, illustrative, symptomatic
Antonyms *adj* ≠ **open:** aloof, cold, contained, distant, formal, impassive, reserved, restrained, stiff, unaffectionate, undemonstrative, unemotional, unresponsive

demoralization *n* **1** = **lowering** *or* **loss of morale,** agitation, crushing, devitalization, dis-

and *those*. Cf. **interrogative, relative.** ◆ *n* **6** *Grammar.* a demonstrative word.
▸**de'monstratively** *adv* ▸**de'monstrativeness** *n*

demonstrator ('dɛmənˌstreɪtə) *n* **1** a person who demonstrates equipment, machines, products, etc. **2** a person who takes part in a public demonstration.

demoralize ➊ *or* **demoralise** (dɪ'mɒrəˌlaɪz) *vb* **demoralizes, demoralizing, demoralized** *or* **demoralises, demoralising, demoralised.** (*tr*) **1** to undermine the morale of; dishearten. **2** to corrupt. **3** to throw into confusion.
▸**deˌmorali'zation** *or* **deˌmorali'sation** *n*

demote ➊ (dɪ'məʊt) *vb* **demotes, demoting, demoted.** (*tr*) to lower in rank or position; relegate. [C19: from DE- + (PRO)MOTE]
▸**de'motion** *n*

demotic (dɪ'mɒtɪk) *adj* **1** of or relating to the common people; popular. **2** of or relating to a simplified form of hieroglyphics used in ancient Egypt. Cf. **hieratic.** ◆ *n* **3** the demotic script of ancient Egypt. [C19: from Gk *dēmotikos* of the people, from *dēmotēs* a man of the people, commoner]
▸**de'motist** *n*

dempster ('dɛmpstə) *n* a variant spelling of **deemster.**

demulcent (dɪ'mʌlsᵊnt) *adj* **1** soothing. ◆ *n* **2** a drug or agent that soothes irritation. [C18: from L *dēmulcēre*, from DE- + *mulcēre* to stroke]

demur ➊ (dɪ'mɜː) *vb* **demurs, demurring, demurred.** (*intr*) **1** to show reluctance. **2** *Law.* to raise an objection by entering a demurrer. ◆ *n also* **demurral** (dɪ'mʌrəl). **3** the act of demurring. **4** an objection raised. [C13: from OF, from L *dēmorārī*, from *morārī* to delay]
▸**de'murrable** *adj*

demure ➊ (dɪ'mjʊə) *adj* **1** sedate; decorous; reserved. **2** affectedly modest or prim; coy. [C14: ?from OF *demorer* to delay, linger; ? infl. by *meur* ripe, MATURE]
▸**de'murely** *adv* ▸**de'mureness** *n*

demurrage (dɪ'mʌrɪdʒ) *n* **1** the delaying of a ship, etc., caused by the charterer's failure to load, unload, etc., before the time of scheduled departure. **2** the extra charge required for such delay. [C14: from OF *demorage, demourage*; see DEMUR]

demurrer (dɪ'mʌrə) *n* **1** *Law.* a pleading that admits an opponent's point but denies that it is relevant or valid. **2** any objection raised.

demutualize *or* **demutualise** (diː'mjuːtjʊəˌlaɪz) *vb* **demutualizes, demutualizing, demutualized** *or* **demutualises, demutualising, demutualised.** (*intr*) (of a mutual savings or life-assurance organization) to convert to a public limited company.
▸ˌ**demutuali'zation** *or* ˌ**demutuali'sation** *n*

demy (dɪ'maɪ) *n, pl* **demies. 1** a size of printing paper, 17½ by 22½ inches (444.5 × 571.5 mm). **2** a size of writing paper, 15½ by 20 inches (Brit.) (393.7 × 508 mm) or 16 by 21 inches (US) (406.4 × 533.4 mm). [C16: see DEMI-]

demystify (diː'mɪstɪˌfaɪ) *vb* **demystifies, demystifying, demystified.** (*tr*) to remove the mystery from.
▸**deˌmystifi'cation** *n*

demythologize *or* **demythologise** (ˌdiːmɪ'θɒləˌdʒaɪz) *vb* **demythologizes, demythologizing, demythologized** *or* **demythologises, demythologising, demythologised.** (*tr*) **1** to eliminate mythical elements from (a piece of writing, esp. the Bible). **2** to restate (a religious message) in rational terms.

den ➊ (dɛn) *n* **1** the habitat or retreat of a wild animal; lair. **2** a small or secluded room in a home, often used for carrying on a hobby. **3** a squalid room or retreat. **4** a site or haunt: *a den of vice.* **5** *Scot.* a small wooded valley. ◆ *vb* **dens, denning, denned. 6** (*intr*) to live in or as if in a den. [OE *denn*]

Den. *abbrev. for* Denmark.

denar (dɪ'nɑː) *n* the standard monetary unit of (the Former Yugoslav Republic of) Macedonia.

denarius (dɪ'nɛərɪəs) *n, pl* **denarii** (-'nɛərɪˌaɪ). **1** a silver coin of ancient Rome, often called a penny in translation. **2** a gold coin worth 25 silver denarii. [C16: from L: coin orig. equal to ten asses, from *dēnārius* (adj) containing ten, from *decem* ten]

denary ('diːnərɪ) *adj* **1** calculated by tens; decimal. **2** containing ten parts; tenfold. [C16: from L *dēnārius*; see DENARIUS]

denationalize *or* **denationalise** (diː'næʃənᵊˌlaɪz) *vb* **denationalizes, denationalizing, denationalized** *or* **denationalises, denationalising, denationalised. 1** to transfer (an industry, etc.) from public to private ownership. **2** to deprive of national character or nationality.
▸**deˌnationali'zation** *or* **deˌnationali'sation** *n*

denaturalize *or* **denaturalise** (diː'nætʃrəˌlaɪz) *vb* **denaturalizes, denaturalizing, denaturalized** *or* **denaturalises, denaturalising, denaturalised.** (*tr*) **1** to deprive of nationality. **2** to make unnatural.
▸**deˌnaturali'zation** *or* **deˌnaturali'sation** *n*

denature (diː'neɪtʃə) *or* **denaturize, denaturise** (diː'neɪtʃəˌraɪz) *vb* **denatures, denaturing, denatured** *or* **denaturizes, denaturizing, denaturized; denaturises, denaturising, denaturised.** (*tr*) **1** to change the nature of. **2** to change the properties of (a protein), as by the action of acid or heat. **3** to render (something, such as alcohol) unfit for consumption by adding nauseous substances. **4** to render (fissile material) unfit for use in nuclear weapons by addition of an isotope.
▸**de'naturant** *n* ▸**deˌnatur'ation** *n*

dendrite ('dɛndraɪt) *n* **1** Also called: **dendron.** any of the branched extensions of a nerve cell, which conduct impulses towards the cell body. **2** a branching mosslike crystalline structure in some rocks and minerals. **3** a crystal that has branched during growth. [C18: from Gk *dendritēs* relating to a tree]
▸**dendritic** (dɛn'drɪtɪk) *adj*

dendro-, dendri-, *or before a vowel* **dendr-** *combining form.* tree: *dendrochronology.* [NL, from Gk, from *dendron* tree]

dendrochronology (ˌdɛndrəʊkrə'nɒlədʒɪ) *n* the study of the annual rings of trees, used esp. to date past events.

dendrology (dɛn'drɒlədʒɪ) *n* the branch of botany that is concerned with the natural history of trees.
▸**dendrological** (ˌdɛndrə'lɒdʒɪkᵊl) *or* ˌ**dendro'logic** *adj* ▸**den'drologist** *n*

dene[1] *or* **dean** (diːn) *n Brit.* a narrow wooded valley. [OE *denu* valley]

dene[2] *or* **dean** (diːn) *n Dialect, chiefly southern English.* a sandy stretch of land or dune near the sea. [C13: prob. rel. to OE *dūn* hill]

denervate ('dɛnəˌveɪt) *vb* **denervates, denervating, denervated.** (*tr*) to deprive (a tissue or organ) of its nerve supply.
▸ˌ**dener'vation** *n*

dengue ('dɛŋgɪ) *or* **dandy** ('dændɪ) *n* an acute viral disease transmitted by mosquitoes, characterized by headache, fever, pains in the joints, and skin rash. [C19: from Sp., prob. of African origin]

deniable (dɪ'naɪəbᵊl) *adj* able to be denied; questionable.
▸**de'niably** *adv*

denial ➊ (dɪ'naɪəl) *n* **1** a refusal to agree or comply with a statement. **2** the rejection of the truth of a proposition, doctrine, etc. **3** a rejection of a request. **4** a refusal to acknowledge; disavowal. **5** a psychological process by which painful truths are not admitted into an individual's consciousness. **6** abstinence; self-denial.

denier[1] *n* **1** ('dɛnɪˌeɪ, 'dɛnjə). a unit of weight used to measure the fineness of silk and man-made fibres, esp. when woven into women's tights, etc. **2** (də'njeɪ, -'nɪə). any of several former European coins of various denominations. [C15: from OF: coin, from L *dēnārius* DENARIUS]

denier[2] (dɪ'naɪə) *n* a person who denies.

denigrate ➊ ('dɛnɪˌgreɪt) *vb* **denigrates, denigrating, denigrated.** (*tr*) to belittle or disparage the character of; defame. [C16: from L *dēnigrāre* to make very black, from *nigrāre*, from *niger* black]
▸ˌ**deni'gration** *n* ▸'**deniˌgrator** *n*

denim ('dɛnɪm) *n* **1** a hard-wearing twill-weave cotton fabric used for trousers, work clothes, etc. **2** a similar lighter fabric used in upholstery. [C17: from F (*serge*) *de Nîmes* (serge) of Nîmes, in S France]

denims ('dɛnɪmz) *pl n* jeans or overalls made of denim.

denizen ➊ ('dɛnɪzən) *n* **1** an inhabitant; resident. **2** *Brit.* an individual permanently resident in a foreign country where he enjoys certain rights of citizenship. **3** a plant or animal established in a place to which it is not native. **4** a naturalized foreign word. [C15: from Anglo-F *denisein*, from OF *denzein*, from *denz* within, from L *de intus* from within]

THESAURUS

comfiture, enervation, panic, perturbation, trepidation, unmanning, weakening

demoralize *vb* **1** = **dishearten**, cripple, daunt, deject, depress, disconcert, discourage, dispirit, enfeeble, psych out (*inf.*), rattle (*inf.*), sap, shake, undermine, unnerve, weaken
Antonyms *vb* boost, cheer, egg on, encourage, gee up, hearten, spur

demoralized *adj* **1** = **disheartened**, broken, crushed, depressed, discouraged, dispirited, downcast, sick as a parrot (*inf.*), subdued, unmanned, unnerved, weakened

demoralizing *adj* **1** = **disheartening**, crushing, dampening, daunting, depressing, disappointing, discouraging, dispiriting
Antonyms *adj* cheering, comforting, encouraging, heartening, reassuring

demote *vb* = **downgrade**, declass, degrade, disrate (*Naval*), kick downstairs (*sl.*), lower in rank, relegate
Antonyms *vb* advance, elevate, kick upstairs (*inf.*), prefer, promote, raise, upgrade

demur *vb* **1** = **object**, balk, cavil, disagree, dispute, doubt, hesitate, pause, protest, refuse, take exception, waver

demure *adj* **1** = **shy**, decorous, diffident, grave, modest, reserved, reticent, retiring, sedate, sober, staid, unassuming **2** = **coy**, affected, bashful, niminy-piminy, priggish, prim, prissy (*inf.*), prudish, strait-laced
Antonyms *adj* brash, brazen, forward, immodest, impudent, shameless

den *n* **1** = **lair**, cave, cavern, haunt, hide-out, hole, shelter **2** = **study**, cloister, cubbyhole, hideaway, retreat, sanctuary, sanctum, snuggery

denial *n* **1** = **negation**, adjuration, contradiction, disavowal, disclaimer, dismissal, dissent, renunciation, repudiation, retraction **3** = **refusal**, prohibition, rebuff, rejection, repulse, veto
Antonyms *n* ≠ **negation:** acknowledgment, admission, affirmation, avowal, confession, declaration, disclosure, divulgence, profession, revelation

denigrate *vb* = **disparage**, asperse, bad-mouth (*sl., chiefly US & Canad.*), belittle, besmirch, blacken, calumniate, decry, defame, impugn, knock (*inf.*), malign, revile, rubbish (*inf.*), run down, slag (off) (*sl.*), slander, vilify
Antonyms *vb* acclaim, admire, approve, cheer, compliment, eulogize, extol, honour, laud, praise, take one's hat off to

denigration *n* = **disparagement**, aspersion, backbiting, defamation, detraction, obloquy, scandal, scurrility, slander, vilification

denizen *n* **1** = **inhabitant**, citizen, dweller, occupant, resident

denominate *vb* (dɪˈnɒmɪˌneɪt). **denominates, denominating, denominated.** **1** *(tr)* to give a specific name to; designate. ◆ *adj* (dɪˈnɒmɪnɪt, -ˌneɪt). **2** *Maths.* (of a number) representing a multiple of a unit of measurement: *4 is the denominate number in 4 miles.* [C16: from L *denōminare* from DE- (intensive) + *nōminare* to name]

denomination (dɪˌnɒmɪˈneɪʃən) *n* **1** a group having a distinctive interpretation of a religious faith and usually its own organization. **2** a grade or unit in a series of designations of value, weight, measure, etc. **3** a name given to a class or group; classification. **4** the act of giving a name. **5** a name; designation.
▸**deˌnomiˈnational** *adj*

denominative (dɪˈnɒmɪnətɪv) *adj* **1** giving or constituting a name. **2** *Grammar.* **2a** formed from or having the same form as a noun. **2b** *(as n): the verb "to mushroom" is a denominative.*

denominator (dɪˈnɒmɪˌneɪtə) *n* the divisor of a fraction, as 8 in ⅞. Cf. **numerator.**

denotation (ˌdiːnəʊˈteɪʃən) *n* **1** a denoting; indication. **2** a particular meaning given by a sign or symbol. **3** specific meaning as distinguished from suggestive meaning and associations. **4** *Logic.* another word for **extension** (sense 10).

denote (dɪˈnəʊt) *vb* **denotes, denoting, denoted.** *(tr; may take a clause as object)* **1** to be a sign of; designate. **2** (of words, phrases, etc.) to have as a literal or obvious meaning. [C16: from L *dēnotāre* to mark, from *notāre* to mark, NOTE]
▸**deˈnotative** *adj*

denouement (deɪˈnuːmɒn) *or* **dénouement** *(French* denumɑ̃) *n* **1** the clarification or resolution of a plot in a play or other work. **2** final outcome; solution. [C18: from F, lit.: an untying, from OF *desnoer,* from *des-* DE- + *noer* to tie, from L *nōdus* a knot]

denounce (dɪˈnaʊns) *vb* **denounces, denouncing, denounced.** *(tr)* **1** to condemn openly or vehemently. **2** to give information against; accuse. **3** to announce formally the termination of (a treaty, etc.). [C13: from OF *denoncier,* from L *dēnuntiāre* to make an official proclamation, threaten, from DE- + *nuntiāre* to announce]
▸**deˈnouncement** *n* ▸**deˈnouncer** *n*

de novo *Latin.* (diː ˈnəʊvəʊ) *adv* from the beginning; anew.

dense (dɛns) *adj* **1** thickly crowded or closely set. **2** thick; impenetrable. **3** *Physics.* having a high density. **4** stupid; dull. **5** (of a photographic negative) having many dark or exposed areas. [C15: from L *densus* thick]
▸**ˈdensely** *adv* ▸**ˈdenseness** *n*

densimeter (dɛnˈsɪmɪtə) *n Physics.* any instrument for measuring density.
▸**densimetric** (ˌdɛnsɪˈmɛtrɪk) *adj* ▸**denˈsimetry** *n*

density (ˈdɛnsɪtɪ) *n, pl* **densities. 1** the degree to which something is filled or occupied: *high density of building in towns.* **2** stupidity. **3** a measure of the compactness of a substance, expressed as its mass per unit volume. Symbol: ρ. See also **relative density. 4** a measure of a physical quantity per unit of length, area, or volume. **5** *Physics, photog.* a measure of the extent to which a substance or surface transmits or reflects light.

dent (dɛnt) *n* **1** a hollow in a surface, as one made by pressure or a blow. **2** an appreciable effect, esp. of lessening: *a dent in our resources.* ◆ *vb (tr)* **3** to make a dent in. [C13 (in the sense: a stroke, blow): var. of DINT]

dental (ˈdɛntᵊl) *adj* **1** of or relating to the teeth or dentistry. **2** *Phonetics.* pronounced with the tip of the tongue touching the backs of the upper teeth, as for *t* in French *tout.* ◆ *n* **3** *Phonetics.* a dental consonant. [C16: from Med. L *dentālis,* from L *dens* tooth]

dental floss *n* a waxed thread used to remove food particles from between the teeth.

dental plaque *n* a filmy deposit on the surface of a tooth consisting of a mixture of mucus, bacteria, food, etc.

dental surgeon *n* another name for **dentist.**

dentate (ˈdɛnteɪt) *adj* **1** having teeth or toothlike processes. **2** (of leaves) having a toothed margin. [C19: from L *dentātus*]
▸**ˈdentately** *adv*

denti- *or before a vowel* **dent-** *combining form.* indicating a tooth: *dentine.* [from L *dens, dent-*]

denticulate (dɛnˈtɪkjʊlɪt, -ˌleɪt) *adj* **1** *Biol.* very finely toothed: *denticulate leaves.* **2** *Arch.* having dentils. [C17: from L *denticulātus* having small teeth]

dentifrice (ˈdɛntɪfrɪs) *n* any substance, esp. paste or powder, for use in cleaning the teeth. [C16: from L *dentifricium,* from *dent-, dens* tooth + *fricāre* to rub]

dentil (ˈdɛntɪl) *n* one of a set of small square or rectangular blocks evenly spaced to form an ornamental row. [C17: from F, from obs. *dentille* a little tooth, from *dent* tooth]

dentine (ˈdɛntiːn) *or* **dentin** (ˈdɛntɪn) *n* the calcified tissue comprising the bulk of a tooth. [C19: from DENTI- + -IN]
▸**ˈdentinal** *adj*

dentist (ˈdɛntɪst) *n* a person qualified to practise dentistry. [C18: from F *dentiste,* from *dent* tooth]

dentistry (ˈdɛntɪstrɪ) *n* the branch of medical science concerned with the diagnosis and treatment of disorders of the teeth and gums.

dentition (dɛnˈtɪʃən) *n* **1** the arrangement, type, and number of the teeth in a particular species. **2** the time or process of teething. [C17: from L *dentītiō* a teething]

denture (ˈdɛntʃə) *n (usually pl)* **1** a partial or full set of artificial teeth. **2** *Rare.* a set of natural teeth. [C19: from F, from *dent* tooth + -URE]

denuclearize *or* **denuclearise** (diːˈnjuːklɪəˌraɪz) *vb* **denuclearizes, denuclearizing, denuclearized** *or* **denuclearises, denuclearising, denuclearised.** *(tr)* to deprive (a state, etc.) of nuclear weapons.
▸**deˌnucleariˈzation** *or* **deˌnucleariˈsation** *n*

denudate (ˈdɛnjʊˌdeɪt, dɪˈnjuːdeɪt) *vb* **denudates, denudating, denudated. 1** a less common word for **denude.** ◆ *adj* **2** denuded.

denude (dɪˈnjuːd) *vb* **denudes, denuding, denuded.** *(tr)* **1** to make bare; strip. **2** to expose (rock) by the erosion of the layers above.
▸**denudation** (ˌdɛnjʊˈdeɪʃən) *n*

denumerable (dɪˈnjuːmərəbᵊl) *adj Maths.* capable of being put into a one-to-one correspondence with the positive integers; countable.
▸**deˈnumerably** *adv*

denunciate (dɪˈnʌnsɪˌeɪt) *vb* **denunciates, denunciating, denunciated.** *(tr)* to condemn; denounce. [C16: from L *dēnuntiāre;* see DENOUNCE]
▸**deˈnunciˌator** *n* ▸**deˈnunciatory** *adj*

denunciation (dɪˌnʌnsɪˈeɪʃən) *n* **1** open condemnation; denouncing. **2** *Law, obsolete.* a charge or accusation of crime made before a public prosecutor or tribunal. **3** a formal announcement of the termination of a treaty.

Denver boot *n* a slang name for **wheel clamp.** [C20: from *Denver,* Colorado, where the device was first used]

deny (dɪˈnaɪ) *vb* **denies, denying, denied.** *(tr)* **1** to declare (a statement, etc.) to be untrue. **2** to reject as false. **3** to withhold. **4** to refuse to fulfil the expectations of: *it is hard to deny a child.* **5** to refuse to acknowledge; disown. **6** to refuse (oneself) things desired. [C13: from OF *denier,* from L *dēnegāre,* from *negāre*]

deodar (ˈdiːəʊˌdɑː) *n* **1** a Himalayan cedar with drooping branches. **2** the durable fragrant highly valued wood of this tree. [C19: from Hindi, from Sansk. *devadāru,* lit.: wood of the gods]

deodorant (diːˈəʊdərənt) *n* **1** a substance applied to the body to suppress or mask the odour of perspiration. **2** any substance for destroying or masking odours.

deodorize *or* **deodorise** (diːˈəʊdəˌraɪz) *vb* **deodorizes, deodorizing, deodorized** *or* **deodorises, deodorising, deodorised.** *(tr)* to remove, disguise, or absorb the odour of, esp. when unpleasant.
▸**deˌodoriˈzation** *or* **deˌodoriˈsation** *n* ▸**deˈodorˌizer** *or* **deˈodorˌiser** *n*

deontic (diːˈɒntɪk) *adj Logic.* **a** of such ethical concepts as obligation and permissibility. **b** designating the branch of logic that deals with the formalization of these concepts. [C19: from Gk *deon* duty, from impersonal *dei* it behoves, it is binding]
▸**ˌdeonˈtology** *n*

deoxidize *or* **deoxidise** (diːˈɒksɪˌdaɪz) *vb* **deoxidizes, deoxidizing, deoxidized** *or* **deoxidises, deoxidising, deoxidised. 1** *(tr)* to remove oxygen

THESAURUS

denominate *vb* **1 = name,** call, christen, designate, dub, entitle, phrase, style, term

denomination *n* **1 = religious group,** belief, communion, creed, persuasion, school, sect **2 = unit,** grade, size, value **3 = classification,** body, category, class, group **5 = name,** appellation, designation, label, style, term, title

denotation *n* **1 = indication,** designation, meaning, signification, specification

denote *vb* **1 = indicate,** betoken, designate, express, imply, import, mark, mean, show, signify, typify

denouement *n* **1, 2 = outcome,** climax, conclusion, culmination, finale, resolution, solution, termination, upshot

denounce *vb* **1, 2 = condemn,** accuse, arraign, attack, brand, castigate, censure, declaim against, decry, denunciate, excoriate, impugn, point a *or* the finger at, proscribe, revile, stigmatize, vilify

dense *adj* **1, 2 = thick,** close, close-knit, compact, compressed, condensed, heavy, impenetrable, opaque, solid, substantial, thickset **4** *Informal* **= stupid,** blockish, braindead *(inf.),* crass, dead from the neck up *(inf.),* dozy *(Brit. inf.),* dull, dumb *(inf.),* obtuse, slow, slow-witted, stolid, thick, thick-witted
Antonyms *adj* ≠ **thick:** light, scattered, sparse, thin, transparent ≠ **stupid:** alert, bright, clever, intelligent, quick

density *n* **1 = tightness,** body, bulk, closeness, compactness, consistency, crowdedness, denseness, impenetrability, mass, solidity, thickness **2** *Informal* **= stupidity,** crassness, dullness, obtuseness, slowness, stolidity, thickness

dent *n* **1 = hollow,** chip, concavity, crater, depression, dimple, dip, impression, indentation, pit ◆ *vb* **3 = make a dent in,** depress, dint, gouge, hollow, imprint, make concave, press in, push in

denude *vb* **1 = strip,** bare, divest, expose, lay bare, uncover

denunciate *vb* **= condemn,** castigate, curse, damn, denounce, stigmatize, vituperate

denunciation *n* **1 = condemnation,** accusation, castigation, censure, character assassination, criticism, denouncement, fulmination, incrimination, invective, obloquy, stick *(sl.),* stigmatization

denunciatory *adj* **= condemnatory,** accusatory, censorious, comminatory, fulminatory, incriminatory, recriminatory, reproachful

deny *vb* **1, 2 = contradict,** disagree with, disprove, gainsay *(arch. or literary),* oppose, rebuff, rebut, refute **3 = refuse,** begrudge, decline, disallow, forbid, negate, reject, turn down, veto, withhold **5 = renounce,** abjure, disavow, discard, disclaim, disown, recant, renege, repudiate, retract, revoke
Antonyms *vb* ≠ **contradict:** accept, acknowledge, admit, affirm, agree, allow, concede, confirm, recognize, take on board ≠ **refuse:** accept, grant, let, permit, receive

deodorant *n* **1, 2 = antiperspirant,** air freshener, deodorizer, disinfectant, fumigant

deodorize *vb* **= purify,** aerate, disinfect, freshen, fumigate, refresh, ventilate

atoms from (a compound, molecule, etc.). **2** another word for **reduce** (sense 12).
▸**deˌoxidiˈzation** *or* **deˌoxidiˈsation** *n* ▸**deˈoxiˌdizer** *or* **deˈoxiˌdiser** *n*

deoxygenate (diːˈɒksɪdʒɪˌneɪt) *or* **deoxygenize, deoxygenise** (diːˈɒksɪdʒɪˌnaɪz) *vb* **deoxygenates, deoxygenating, deoxygenated** *or* **deoxygenizes, deoxygenizing, deoxygenized; deoxygenises, deoxygenising, deoxygenised.** (*tr*) to remove oxygen from.
▸**deˌoxygenˈation** *n*

deoxyribonuclease (diːˌɒksɪˌraɪbəʊˈnjuːklɪeɪz) *n* the full name for **DNAase.**

deoxyribonucleic acid (diːˌɒksɪˌraɪbəʊnjuːˈkleɪɪk) *or* **desoxyribonucleic acid** *n* the full name for **DNA.**

dep. *abbrev. for:* **1** department. **2** departure. **3** deposed. **4** deposit. **5** depot. **6** deputy.

depart Ⓣ (dɪˈpɑːt) *vb* (*mainly intr*) **1** to leave. **2** to set forth. **3** (usually foll. by *from*) to differ; vary: *to depart from normal procedure.* **4** (*tr*) to quit (arch., except in **depart this life**). [C13: from OF *departir,* from DE- + *partir* to go away, divide, from L *partīrī* to divide, distribute, from *pars* a part]

departed Ⓣ (dɪˈpɑːtɪd) *adj Euphemistic.* **a** dead. **b** (*as sing or collective n; preceded by the*): *the departed.*

department Ⓣ (dɪˈpɑːtmənt) *n* **1** a specialized division of a large concern, such as a business, store, or university. **2** a major subdivision of the administration of a government. **3** a branch of learning. **4** an administrative division in several countries, such as France. **5** *Inf.* a specialized sphere of skill or activity: *wine-making is my wife's department.* [C18: from F *département,* from *départir* to divide; see DEPART]
▸**departmental** (ˌdiːpɑːtˈmentᵊl) *adj*

departmentalize *or* **departmentalise** (ˌdiːpɑːtˈmentᵊˌlaɪz) *vb* **departmentalizes, departmentalizing, departmentalized** *or* **departmentalises, departmentalising, departmentalised.** (*tr*) to organize into departments, esp. excessively.
▸**ˌdepartˌmentaliˈzation** *or* **ˌdepartˌmentaliˈsation** *n*

department store *n* a large shop divided into departments selling a great many kinds of goods.

departure Ⓣ (dɪˈpɑːtʃə) *n* **1** the act or an instance of departing. **2** a variation from previous custom. **3** a course of action, venture, etc.: *selling is a new departure for him.* **4** *Naut.* the net distance travelled due east or west by a vessel. **5** a euphemistic word for **death.**

depend Ⓣ (dɪˈpend) *vb* (*intr*) **1** (foll. by *on* or *upon*) to put trust (in); rely (on). **2** (usually foll. by *on* or *upon*) to be influenced or determined (by): *it all depends on you.* **3** (foll. by *on* or *upon*) to rely (on) for income, support, etc. **4** (foll. by *from*) *Rare.* to hang down. **5** to be undecided. [C15: from OF, from L *dēpendēre* to hang from, from DE- + *pendēre*]

dependable Ⓣ (dɪˈpendəbᵊl) *adj* able to be depended on; reliable.
▸**deˌpendaˈbility** *or* **deˈpendableness** *n* ▸**deˈpendably** *adv*

dependant Ⓣ (dɪˈpendənt) *n* a person who depends on another person, organization, etc., for support, aid, or sustenance, esp. financial support.

> **USAGE NOTE** Avoid confusion with **dependent.**

dependence Ⓣ *or US* (*sometimes*) **dependance** (dɪˈpendəns) *n* **1** the state or fact of being dependent, esp. for support or help. **2** reliance; trust; confidence.

dependency Ⓣ *or US* (*sometimes*) **dependancy** (dɪˈpendənsɪ) *n, pl* **dependencies** *or US* (*sometimes*) **dependancies. 1** a territory subject to a state on which it does not border. **2** a dependent or subordinate person or thing. **3** *Psychol.* overreliance on another person or on a drug, etc. **4** another word for **dependence.**

dependent Ⓣ *or US* (*sometimes*) **dependant** (dɪˈpendənt) *adj* **1** depending on a person or thing for aid, support, etc. **2** (*postpositive;* foll. by *on* or *upon*) influenced or conditioned (by); contingent (on). **3** subordinate; subject. **4** *Obs.* hanging down. ◆ *n* **5** a variant spelling (esp. US) of **dependant.**
▸**deˈpendently** *adv*

> **USAGE NOTE** Avoid confusion with **dependant.**

dependent clause *n Grammar.* another term for **subordinate clause.**

dependent variable *n* a variable in a mathematical equation or statement whose value depends on that taken on by the independent variable.

depersonalize *or* **depersonalise** (dɪˈpɜːsnᵊˌlaɪz) *vb* **depersonalizes, depersonalizing, depersonalized** *or* **depersonalises, depersonalising, depersonalised.** (*tr*) **1** to deprive (a person, organization, etc.) of individual or personal qualities. **2** to cause (someone) to lose his sense of identity.
▸**deˌpersonaliˈzation** *or* **deˌpersonaliˈsation** *n*

depict Ⓣ (dɪˈpɪkt) *vb* (*tr*) **1** to represent by drawing, sculpture, painting, etc.; delineate; portray. **2** to represent in words; describe. [C17: from L *dēpingere,* from *pingere* to paint]
▸**deˈpicter** *or* **deˈpictor** *n* ▸**deˈpiction** *n* ▸**deˈpictive** *adj*

depilate (ˈdepɪˌleɪt) *vb* **depilates, depilating, depilated.** (*tr*) to remove the hair from. [C16: from L *dēpilāre,* from *pilāre* to make bald, from *pilus* hair]
▸**ˌdepiˈlation** *n* ▸**ˈdepiˌlator** *n*

depilatory (dɪˈpɪlətərɪ, -trɪ) *adj* **1** able or serving to remove hair. ◆ *n, pl* **depilatories. 2** a chemical used to remove hair from the body.

deplane (diːˈpleɪn) *vb* **deplanes, deplaning, deplaned.** (*intr*) *Chiefly US. & Canad.* to disembark from an aeroplane. [C20: from DE- + PLANE[1]]

deplete Ⓣ (dɪˈpliːt) *vb* **depletes, depleting, depleted.** (*tr*) **1** to use up (supplies, money, etc.); exhaust. **2** to empty entirely or partially. [C19: from L *dēplēre* to empty out, from DE- + *plēre* to fill]
▸**deˈpletion** *n*

depletion layer *n* a region at the interface between dissimilar zones of conductivity in a semiconductor, in which there are few charge carriers.

deplorable Ⓣ (dɪˈplɔːrəbᵊl) *adj* **1** lamentable. **2** worthy of censure or reproach; very bad.
▸**deˈplorably** *adv*

deplore Ⓣ (dɪˈplɔː) *vb* **deplores, deploring, deplored.** (*tr*) **1** to express or feel sorrow about. **2** to express or feel strong disapproval of; censure. [C16: from OF, from L *dēplōrāre* to weep bitterly, from *plōrāre* to weep]
▸**deˈploringly** *adv*

deploy Ⓣ (dɪˈplɔɪ) *vb Chiefly mil.* **1** to adopt or cause to adopt a battle formation. **2** (*tr*) to redistribute (forces) to or within a given area. [C18: from F, from L *displicāre* to unfold; see DISPLAY]
▸**deˈployment** *n*

THESAURUS

depart *vb* **1, 2** = **leave**, absent (oneself), decamp, disappear, escape, exit, go, go away, hook it (*sl.*), make tracks, migrate, pack one's bags (*inf.*), quit, remove, retire, retreat, set forth, slope off, start out, take (one's) leave, vanish, withdraw **3** = **deviate**, differ, digress, diverge, stray, swerve, turn aside, vary, veer
Antonyms *vb* ≠ **leave:** arrive, remain, show up (*inf.*), stay, turn up

departed *adj* **a** *Euphemistic* = **dead**, deceased, expired, late

department *n* **1** = **section**, branch, bureau, division, office, station, subdivision, unit **2** = **region**, district, division, province, sector **5** *Informal* = **speciality**, area, domain, function, line, province, realm, responsibility, sphere

departure *n* **1** = **leaving**, exit, exodus, going, going away, leave-taking, removal, retirement, withdrawal **2** = **divergence**, abandonment, branching off, deviation, digression, variation, veering **3** = **shift**, branching out, change, difference, innovation, novelty, whole new ball game (*inf.*)
Antonyms *n* ≠ **leaving:** advent, appearance, arrival, coming, entrance, return

depend *vb* **1** = **trust in**, bank on, build upon, calculate on, confide in, count on, lean on, reckon on, rely upon, turn to **2** = **be determined by**, be based on, be contingent on, be subject to, be subordinate to, hang on, hinge on, rest on, revolve around

dependable *adj* = **reliable**, faithful, reputable, responsible, staunch, steady, sure, trustworthy, trusty, unfailing
Antonyms *adj* irresponsible, undependable, unreliable, unstable, untrustworthy

dependant *n* = **relative**, child, client, cohort (*chiefly US.*), hanger-on, henchman, minion, minor, protégé, retainer, subordinate, vassal

dependence *n* **1** = **overreliance**, addiction, attachment, helplessness, need, subordination, subservience, vulnerability, weakness **2** = **reliance**, assurance, belief, confidence, expectation, faith, hope, trust

dependency *n Psychology* **3** = **overreliance**, addiction, attachment, helplessness, need, vulnerability, weakness

dependent *adj* **1** = **reliant**, counting on, defenceless, helpless, immature, relying on, vulnerable, weak **2 dependent on** *or* **upon** = **determined by**, conditional on, contingent on, depending on, influenced by, liable to, relative to, subject to
Antonyms *adj* ≠ **reliant:** autarkic, autonomous, independent, self-determining, self-governing, self-reliant

depict *vb* **1** = **draw**, delineate, illustrate, limn, outline, paint, picture, portray, render, reproduce, sculpt, sketch **2** = **describe**, characterize, detail, narrate, outline, represent, sketch

depiction *n* **1, 2** = **representation**, delineation, description, drawing, illustration, image, likeness, outline, picture, portrayal, sketch

deplete *vb* **1, 2** = **use up**, bankrupt, consume, decrease, drain, empty, evacuate, exhaust, expend, impoverish, lessen, milk, reduce
Antonyms *vb* add to, augment, enhance, expand, increase, raise, step up (*inf.*), swell

depleted *adj* **1, 2** = **used (up)**, consumed, decreased, depreciated, devoid of, drained, effete, emptied, exhausted, lessened, out of, reduced, short of, spent, wasted, weakened, worn out

depletion *n* **1, 2** = **using up**, attenuation, consumption, decrease, deficiency, diminution, drain, dwindling, exhaustion, expenditure, lessening, lowering, reduction

deplorable *adj* **1** = **terrible**, calamitous, dire, disastrous, distressing, grievous, heartbreaking, lamentable, melancholy, miserable, pitiable, regrettable, sad, unfortunate, wretched **2** = **disgraceful**, blameworthy, dishonourable, disreputable, execrable, opprobrious, reprehensible, scandalous, shameful
Antonyms *adj* ≠ **terrible:** A1 *or* A-one (*inf.*), bad (*sl.*), bodacious (*sl., chiefly US.*), brilliant, excellent, fantastic, great (*inf.*), marvellous, outstanding, super (*inf.*), superb ≠ **disgraceful:** admirable, laudable, notable, praiseworthy

deplore *vb* **1** = **lament**, bemoan, bewail, grieve for, mourn, regret, rue, sorrow over **2** = **disapprove of**, abhor, censure, condemn, denounce, deprecate, excoriate, object to, take a dim view of

deploy *vb* **2** = **position**, arrange, dispose, extend, redistribute, set out, set up, spread out, station, use, utilize

depolarize *or* **depolarise** (diːˈpəʊləˌraɪz) *vb* **depolarizes, depolarizing, depolarized** *or* **depolarises, depolarising, depolarised.** to undergo or cause to undergo a loss of polarity or polarization.
▸**deˌpolariˈzation** *or* **deˌpolariˈsation** *n*

deponent (dɪˈpəʊnənt) *adj* **1** *Grammar.* (of a verb, esp. in Latin) having the inflectional endings of a passive verb but the meaning of an active verb. ◆ *n* **2** *Grammar.* a deponent verb. **3** *Law.* a person who makes an affidavit or a deposition. [C16: from L *dēpōnēns* putting aside, putting down, from *dēpōnere*]

depopulate (dɪˈpɒpjʊˌleɪt) *vb* **depopulates, depopulating, depopulated.** to be or cause to be reduced in population.
▸**deˌpopuˈlation** *n*

deport ⓣ (dɪˈpɔːt) *vb (tr)* **1** to remove forcibly from a country; expel. **2** to conduct, hold, or behave (oneself) in a specified manner. [C15: from F, from L *dēportāre* to carry away, banish, from DE- + *portāre* to carry]
▸**deˈportable** *adj*

deportation ⓣ (ˌdiːpɔːˈteɪʃən) *n* the act of expelling someone from a country.

deportee (ˌdiːpɔːˈtiː) *n* a person deported or awaiting deportation.

deportment ⓣ (dɪˈpɔːtmənt) *n* the manner in which a person behaves, esp. in physical bearing: *military deportment.* [C17: from F, from OF *deporter* to conduct (oneself); see DEPORT]

depose ⓣ (dɪˈpəʊz) *vb* **deposes, deposing, deposed. 1** *(tr)* to remove from an office or position of power. **2** *Law.* to testify or give (evidence, etc.) on oath. [C13: from OF: to put away, put down, from LL *dēpōnere* to depose from office, from L: to put aside]

deposit ⓣ (dɪˈpɒzɪt) *vb (tr)* **1** to put or set down, esp. carefully; place. **2** to entrust for safekeeping. **3** to place (money) in a bank or similar institution to earn interest or for safekeeping. **4** to give (money) in part payment or as security. **5** to lay down naturally: *the river deposits silt.* ◆ *n* **6a** an instance of entrusting money or valuables to a bank or similar institution. **6b** the money or valuables so entrusted. **7** money given in part payment or as security. **8** an accumulation of sediments, minerals, coal, etc. **9** any deposited material, such as a sediment. **10** a depository or storehouse. **11 on deposit.** payable as the first instalment, as when buying on hire-purchase. [C17: from Med. L *dēpositāre,* from L *dēpositus* put down]

deposit account *n Brit.* a bank account that earns interest and usually requires notice of withdrawal.

depositary ⓣ (dɪˈpɒzɪtərɪ, -trɪ) *n, pl* **depositaries. 1** a person or group to whom something is entrusted for safety. **2** a variant spelling of **depository.**

deposition ⓣ (ˌdɛpəˈzɪʃən) *n* **1** *Law.* **1a** the giving of testimony on oath. **1b** the testimony given. **1c** the sworn statement of a witness used in court in his absence. **2** the act or an instance of deposing. **3** the act or an instance of depositing. **4** something deposited. [C14: from LL *dēpositiō* a laying down, disposal, burying, testimony]

depositor (dɪˈpɒzɪtə) *n* a person who places or has money on deposit, esp. in a bank.

depository ⓣ (dɪˈpɒzɪtərɪ, -trɪ) *n, pl* **depositories. 1** a store for furniture, valuables, etc.; repository. **2** a variant spelling of **depositary.** [C17 (in the sense: place of a deposit): from Med. L *dēpositōrium;* C18 (in the sense: depositary): see DEPOSIT, -ORY[1]]

depot ⓣ (ˈdɛpəʊ; *US & Canad.* ˈdiːpəʊ) *n* **1** a storehouse or warehouse. **2** *Mil.* **2a** a store for supplies. **2b** a training and holding centre for recruits and replacements. **3** *Chiefly Brit.* a building used for the storage and servicing of buses or railway engines. **4** *US & Canad.* a bus or railway station. [C18: from F *dépôt,* from L *dēpositum* a deposit, trust]

deprave ⓣ (dɪˈpreɪv) *vb* **depraves, depraving, depraved.** *(tr)* to make morally bad; corrupt. [C14: from L *dēprāvāre* to distort, corrupt, from DE- + *prāvus* crooked]
▸**depravation** (ˌdɛprəˈveɪʃən) *n* ▸**deˈpraved** *adj*

depravity ⓣ (dɪˈprævɪtɪ) *n, pl* **depravities.** the state or an instance of moral corruption.

deprecate ⓣ (ˈdɛprɪˌkeɪt) *vb* **deprecates, deprecating, deprecated.** *(tr)* **1** to express disapproval of; protest against. **2** to depreciate; belittle. [C17: from L *dēprecārī* to avert, ward off by entreaty, from DE- + *precārī* to PRAY]
▸**ˈdepreˌcating** *adj* ▸**ˈdepreˌcatingly** *adv* ▸**ˌdepreˈcation** *n* ▸**ˈdeprecative** *adj* ▸**ˈdepreˌcator** *n*

> **USAGE NOTE** Avoid confusion with **depreciate.**

deprecatory ⓣ (ˈdɛprɪkətərɪ) *adj* **1** expressing disapproval; protesting. **2** expressing apology; apologetic.
▸**ˈdeprecatorily** *adv*

depreciate ⓣ (dɪˈpriːʃɪˌeɪt) *vb* **depreciates, depreciating, depreciated. 1** to reduce or decline in value or price. **2** *(tr)* to lessen the value of by derision, criticism, etc. [C15: from LL *dēpretiāre* to lower the price of, from L DE- + *pretium* PRICE]
▸**deˈpreciˌatingly** *adv* ▸**depreciatory** (dɪˈpriːʃɪətərɪ) *or* **deˈpreciative** *adj*

> **USAGE NOTE** Avoid confusion with **deprecate.**

depreciation ⓣ (dɪˌpriːʃɪˈeɪʃən) *n* **1** *Accounting.* **1a** the reduction in value of a fixed asset due to use, obsolescence, etc. **1b** the amount deducted from gross profit to allow for this. **2** the act or an instance of depreciating or belittling. **3** a decrease in the exchange value of a currency brought about by excess supply of that currency under conditions of fluctuating exchange rates.

depredation ⓣ (ˌdɛprɪˈdeɪʃən) *n* the act or an instance of plundering; pillage. [C15: from LL *dēpraedārī* to ravage]

depress ⓣ (dɪˈprɛs) *vb (tr)* **1** to lower in spirits; make gloomy. **2** to weaken the force, or energy of. **3** to lower prices of. **4** to press or push down. [C14: from OF *depresser,* from L *dēprimere* from DE- + *premere* to PRESS[1]]
▸**deˈpressing** *adj* ▸**deˈpressingly** *adv*

depressant (dɪˈprɛsᵊnt) *adj* **1** *Med.* able to reduce nervous or functional activity. **2** causing gloom; depressing. ◆ *n* **3** a depressant drug.

depressed ⓣ (dɪˈprɛst) *adj* **1** low in spirits; downcast. **2** lower than the surrounding surface. **3** pressed down or flattened. **4** Also: **distressed.** characterized by economic hardship, such as unemployment: *a depressed area.* **5** lowered in force, intensity, or amount. **6** *Bot., zool.* flattened.

THESAURUS

deployment *n* **2** = **position,** arrangement, disposition, organization, setup, spread, stationing, use, utilization

deport *vb* **1** = **expel,** banish, exile, expatriate, extradite, oust **2 deport oneself** = **behave,** acquit oneself, act, bear oneself, carry oneself, comport oneself, conduct oneself, hold oneself

deportation *n* = **expulsion,** banishment, eviction, exile, expatriation, extradition, transportation

deportment *n* = **bearing,** air, appearance, aspect, behaviour, carriage, cast, comportment, conduct, demeanour, manner, mien, posture, stance

depose *vb* **1** = **remove from office,** break, cashier, degrade, demote, dethrone, dismiss, displace, downgrade, oust **2** *Law* = **testify,** avouch, declare, make a deposition

deposit *vb* **1** = **put,** drop, lay, locate, place, precipitate, settle, sit down **3** = **store,** amass, bank, consign, entrust, hoard, lodge, save ◆ *n* **7** = **down payment,** instalment, money (*in bank*), part payment, pledge, retainer, security, stake, warranty **8** = **sediment,** accumulation, alluvium, deposition, dregs, lees, precipitate, silt

depositary *n* **1** = **trustee,** fiduciary (*Law*), guardian, steward

deposition *n* **1** *Law* = **sworn statement,** affidavit, declaration, evidence, testimony **2** = **removal,** dethronement, dismissal, displacement, ousting

depository *n* **1** = **storehouse,** depot, repository, safe-deposit box, store, warehouse

depot *n* **1** = **storehouse,** depository, repository, warehouse **2a** *Military* = **arsenal,** dump **4** *Chiefly U.S. & Canad.* = **bus station,** garage, terminus

deprave *vb* = **corrupt,** brutalize, debase, debauch, degrade, demoralize, lead astray, pervert, seduce, subvert, vitiate

depraved *adj* = **corrupt,** abandoned, debased, debauched, degenerate, degraded, dissolute, evil, immoral, lascivious, lewd, licentious, perverted, profligate, shameless, sinful, sink, vicious, vile, wicked
Antonyms *adj* chaste, decent, ethical, good, honourable, innocent, moral, principled, proper, pure, upright, virtuous, wholesome

depravity *n* = **corruption,** baseness, contamination, criminality, debasement, debauchery, degeneracy, depravation, evil, immorality, iniquity, profligacy, sinfulness, turpitude, vice, viciousness, vitiation, wickedness

deprecate *vb* **1** = **disapprove of,** condemn, deplore, frown on, object to, protest against, take exception to **2** = **disapprove of,** belittle, denigrate, depreciate, detract, disparage

deprecatory *adj* **1** = **disapproving,** censuring, condemnatory, opprobrious, reproachful **2** = **apologetic,** contrite, penitent, regretful, remorseful, rueful

depreciate *vb* **1** = **decrease,** deflate, devaluate, devalue, lessen, lose value, lower, reduce **2** = **disparage,** belittle, decry, denigrate, deride, detract, look down on, ridicule, run down, scorn, sneer at, traduce, underestimate, underrate, undervalue
Antonyms *vb* ≠ **decrease:** add to, appreciate, augment, enhance, enlarge, expand, grow, increase, rise ≠ **disparage:** admire, appreciate, cherish, esteem, like, prize, rate highly, regard, respect, value

depreciation *n* **1a, 3** = **devaluation,** drop, fall, slump **2** = **disparagement,** belittlement, denigration, deprecation, derogation, detraction, pejoration

depredation *n* = **plunder,** desolation, despoiling, destruction, devastation, harrying, laying waste, marauding, pillage, ransacking, rapine, ravaging, robbery, spoliation, theft

depress *vb* **1** = **sadden,** cast down, chill, damp, daunt, deject, desolate, discourage, dishearten, dispirit, make despondent, oppress, weigh down **3** = **lower,** cheapen, depreciate, devaluate, devalue, diminish, downgrade, impair, lessen, reduce **4** = **press down,** flatten, level, lower, push down
Antonyms *vb* ≠ **sadden:** cheer, elate, hearten, heighten, increase, lift, raise, strengthen, uplift ≠ **lower:** heighten, increase, raise, strengthen

depressed *adj* **1** = **low-spirited,** blue, crestfallen, dejected, despondent, discouraged, dispirited, down, downcast, downhearted, down in the dumps (*inf.*), fed up, glum, low, melancholy, moody, morose, pessimistic, sad, unhappy **2** = **sunken,** concave, hollow, indented, recessed, set back **4** = **poverty-stricken,** deprived, destitute, disadvantaged, distressed, grey, needy, poor, run-down **5** = **lowered,** cheapened, depreciated, devalued, impaired, weakened

depressing *adj* **1** = **bleak,** black, daunting, dejecting, depressive, discouraging, disheartening, dismal, dispiriting, distressing, dreary,

depression ⓘ (dɪˈprɛʃən) *n* **1** a depressing or being depressed. **2** a sunken place. **3** a mental disorder characterized by feelings of gloom and inadequacy. **4** *Pathol.* an abnormal lowering of the rate of any physiological activity or function. **5** an economic condition characterized by unemployment, low investment, etc.; slump. **6** Also called: **cyclone, low.** *Meteorol.* a body of moving air below normal atmospheric pressure, which often brings rain. **7** (esp. in surveying and astronomy) the angular distance of an object below the horizontal plane.

Depression (dɪˈprɛʃən) *n* (usually preceded by *the*) the worldwide economic depression of the early 1930s, when there was mass unemployment.

depressive (dɪˈprɛsɪv) *adj* **1** tending to depress. **2** *Psychol.* tending to be subject to periods of depression.
▸**deˈpressively** *adv*

depressor (dɪˈprɛsə) *n* **1** a person or thing that depresses. **2** any muscle that draws down a part. **3** *Med.* an instrument used to press down or aside an organ or part.

depressurize *or* **depressurise** (dɪˈprɛʃəˌraɪz) *vb* **depressurizes, depressurizing, depressurized** *or* **depressurises, depressurising, depressurised.** (*tr*) to reduce the pressure of a gas inside (an enclosed space), as in an aircraft cabin.
▸**deˌpressuriˈzation** *or* **deˌpressuriˈsation** *n*

deprive ⓘ (dɪˈpraɪv) *vb* **deprives, depriving, deprived.** (*tr*) **1** (foll. by *of*) to prevent from possessing or enjoying; dispossess (of). **2** *Arch.* to depose; demote. [C14: from OF, from Med. L *dēprīvāre*, from L DE- + *prīvāre* to deprive of]
▸**deˈprival** *n* ▸**deprivation** (ˌdɛprɪˈveɪʃən) *n*

deprived ⓘ (dɪˈpraɪvd) *adj* lacking adequate food, shelter, education, etc.: *deprived inner-city areas.*

dept *abbrev. for* department.

depth ⓘ (dɛpθ) *n* **1** the distance downwards, backwards, or inwards. **2** the quality of being deep; deepness. **3** intensity of emotion. **4** profundity of moral character; sagacity; integrity. **5** complexity or abstruseness, as of thought. **6** intensity, as of silence, colour, etc. **7** lowness of pitch. **8** (*often pl*) a deep, inner, or remote part, such as an inaccessible region of a country. **9** (*often pl*) the most intense or severe part: *the depths of winter.* **10** (*usually pl*) a low moral state. **11** (*often pl*) a vast space or abyss. **12 beyond** *or* **out of one's depth. 12a** in water deeper than one is tall. **12b** beyond the range of one's competence or understanding. [C14: from *dep* DEEP + -TH[1]]

depth charge *or* **bomb** *n* a bomb used to attack submarines that explodes at a preset depth of water.

depth gauge *n* a device attached to a drill bit to prevent the hole from exceeding a predetermined depth.

depth of field *n* the range of distance in front of and behind an object focused by an optical instrument, such as a camera or microscope, within which other objects will also appear sharply defined in the resulting image.

depth psychology *n Psychol.* the study of unconscious motives and attitudes.

depuration (ˌdɛpjʊˈreɪʃən) *n* the act or process of eliminating impurities; self-purification. [C17: from F or Med. L, ult. from L *pūrus* pure]

deputation ⓘ (ˌdɛpjʊˈteɪʃən) *n* **1** the act of appointing a person or body of people to represent others. **2** a person or body of people so appointed; delegation.

depute ⓘ *vb* (dɪˈpjuːt), **deputes, deputing, deputed.** (*tr*) **1** to appoint as an agent. **2** to assign (authority, duties, etc.) to a deputy. ◆ *n* (ˈdɛpjuːt). **3** *Scot.* **3a** a deputy. **3b** (*as modifier, usually postpositive*): *a sheriff-depute.* [C15: from OF, from LL *dēputāre* to assign, allot, from L DE- + *putāre* to think, consider]

deputize ⓘ *or* **deputise** (ˈdɛpjʊˌtaɪz) *vb* **deputizes, deputizing, deputized** *or* **deputises, deputising, deputised.** to appoint or act as deputy.

deputy ⓘ (ˈdɛpjʊtɪ) *n, pl* **deputies. 1a** a person appointed to act on behalf of or represent another. **1b** (*as modifier*): *the deputy chairman.* **2** a member of a legislative assembly in various countries, such as France. [C16: from OF, from *deputer* to appoint; see DEPUTE]

der. *abbrev. for:* **1** derivation. **2** derivative.

deracinate (dɪˈræsɪˌneɪt) *vb* **deracinates, deracinating, deracinated.** (*tr*) to pull up by or as if by the roots; uproot. [C16: from OF *desraciner*, from *des-* DIS-[1] + *racine* root, from LL, from L *rādīx* a root]
▸**deˌraciˈnation** *n*

derail (dɪˈreɪl) *vb* to go or cause to go off the rails, as a train, tram, etc.
▸**deˈrailment** *n*

derange ⓘ (dɪˈreɪndʒ) *vb* **deranges, deranging, deranged.** (*tr*) **1** to throw into disorder; disarrange. **2** to disturb the action of. **3** to make insane. [C18: from OF *desrengier*, from des- DIS-[1] + *reng* row, order]
▸**deˈrangement** *n*

derby (ˈdɜːrbɪ) *n, pl* **derbies.** the US and Canad. name for **bowler**[2].

Derby (ˈdɑːbɪ; *US* ˈdɜːrbɪ) *n, pl* **Derbies. 1 the.** an annual horse race run at Epsom Downs, Surrey, since 1780. **2** (*usually not cap.*) any of various other horse races. **3 local derby.** a football match between two teams from the same area. [C18: after the twelfth Earl of *Derby* (died 1834), who founded the race in 1780]

derecognize *or* **derecognise** (diːˈrɛkəgˌnaɪz) *vb* **derecognizes, derecognizing, derecognized** *or* **derecognises, derecognising, derecognised.** (*tr*) to cease to recognize (a trade union) as having special negotiating rights within a company or industry.
▸ˌ**derecogˈnition** *n*

deregulate (diːˈrɛgjʊˌleɪt) *vb* **deregulates, deregulating, deregulated.** (*tr*) to remove regulations from.
▸**deˌreguˈlation** *n*

derelict ⓘ (ˈdɛrɪlɪkt) *adj* **1** deserted or abandoned, as by an owner, occupant, etc. **2** falling into ruins. **3** neglectful of duty; remiss. ◆ *n* **4** a social outcast or vagrant. **5** property deserted or abandoned by an owner, occupant, etc. **6** a vessel abandoned at sea. **7** a person who is neglectful of duty. [C17: from L, from *dērelinquere* to abandon, from DE- + *relinquere* to leave]

dereliction ⓘ (ˌdɛrɪˈlɪkʃən) *n* **1** conscious or wilful neglect (esp. in **dereliction of duty**). **2** an abandoning or being abandoned. **3** *Law.* accretion of dry land gained by the gradual receding of the sea.

derestrict (ˌdiːrɪˈstrɪkt) *vb* (*tr*) to render or leave free from restriction, esp. a road from speed limits.
▸ˌ**dereˈstriction** *n*

deride ⓘ (dɪˈraɪd) *vb* **derides, deriding, derided.** (*tr*) to speak of or treat with contempt or ridicule; scoff at. [C16: from L *dērīdēre* to laugh to scorn, from DE- + *rīdēre* to laugh, smile]
▸**deˈrider** *n* ▸**deˈridingly** *adv*

de rigueur ⓘ *French.* (də rigœr) *adj* required by etiquette or fashion. [lit.: of strictness]

derision ⓘ (dɪˈrɪʒən) *n* the act of deriding; mockery; scorn. [C15: from LL *dērīsiō*, from L *dērīsus*; see DERIDE]
▸**deˈrisible** *adj*

THESAURUS

funereal, gloomy, harrowing, heartbreaking, hopeless, melancholy, sad, saddening, sombre

depression *n* **2** = **hollow**, bowl, cavity, concavity, dent, dimple, dip, excavation, impression, indentation, pit, sag, sink, valley **3** = **low spirits**, dejection, despair, despondency, dolefulness, downheartedness, dumps (*inf.*), gloominess, hopelessness, melancholia, melancholy, sadness, the blues, the hump (*Brit. inf.*) **5** = **recession**, dullness, economic decline, hard *or* bad times, inactivity, lowness, slump, stagnation

deprivation *n* **1** = **want**, destitution, detriment, disadvantage, distress, hardship, need, privation

deprive *vb* **1** = **withhold**, bereave, despoil, dispossess, divest, expropriate, rob, strip, wrest

deprived *adj* = **poor**, bereft, denuded, destitute, disadvantaged, down at heel, forlorn, in need, in want, lacking, necessitous, needy
Antonyms *adj* born with a silver spoon in one's mouth, favoured, fortunate, golden, happy, having a charmed life, lucky, prosperous, sitting pretty (*inf.*), successful, well-off

depth *n* **2** = **deepness**, drop, extent, measure, profoundness, profundity **4** = **profoundness**, astuteness, discernment, insight, penetration, profundity, sagacity, wisdom **5** = **complexity**, abstruseness, obscurity, reconditeness **6** = **intensity**, richness, strength **11** *often plural* = **deepest part**, abyss, bowels of the earth, furthest part, innermost part, middle, midst, most intense part, remotest part
Antonyms *n* ≠ **deepness:** apex, apogee, crest, crown, height, peak, pinnacle, summit, top, vertex, zenith ≠ **profoundness:** emptiness, lack of depth *or* substance, superficiality, triviality

deputation *n* **1** = **appointment**, assignment, commission, designation, nomination **2** = **delegation**, commission, delegates, deputies, embassy, envoys, legation

depute *vb* **1** = **appoint**, accredit, authorize, charge, commission, delegate, empower, entrust, mandate

deputize *vb* = **appoint**, commission, delegate, depute = **stand in for**, act for, take the place of, understudy

deputy *n* **1a** = **substitute**, agent, ambassador, commissioner, delegate, legate, lieutenant, number two, nuncio, proxy, representative, second-in-command, surrogate, vicegerent ◆ *modifier* **1b** = **assistant**, depute (*Scot.*), subordinate

derange *vb* **1** = **disorder**, confound, confuse, disarrange, disarray, discompose, disconcert, displace, disturb, ruffle, unsettle, upset **3** = **drive mad**, craze, dement (*rare*), madden, make insane, unbalance, unhinge

deranged *adj* **3** = **mad**, barking (*sl.*), barking mad (*sl.*), berserk, crackpot (*inf.*), crazed, crazy, delirious, demented, distracted, doolally (*sl.*), frantic, frenzied, insane, irrational, loopy (*inf.*), lunatic, maddened, not the full shilling (*inf.*), off one's trolley (*sl.*), out to lunch (*inf.*), unbalanced, unhinged, up the pole (*inf.*)
Antonyms *adj* all there (*inf.*), calm, *compos mentis*, in one's right mind, lucid, mentally sound, normal, of sound mind

derangement *n* **1, 2** = **disorder**, confusion, disarrangement, disarray, disturbance, irregularity, jumble, muddle **3** = **madness**, aberration, alienation, delirium, dementia, hallucination, insanity, loss of reason, lunacy, mania

derelict *adj* **1, 2** = **abandoned**, deserted, dilapidated, discarded, forsaken, neglected, ruined **3** = **negligent**, careless, irresponsible, lax, remiss, slack ◆ *n* **4** = **tramp**, bag lady, bum (*inf.*), down-and-out, good-for-nothing, ne'er-do-well, outcast, vagrant, wastrel

dereliction *n* **1** = **negligence**, delinquency, evasion, failure, faithlessness, fault, neglect, nonperformance, remissness **2** = **abandonment**, abdication, desertion, forsaking, relinquishment, renunciation

deride *vb* = **mock**, chaff, contemn, detract, disdain, disparage, flout, gibe, insult, jeer, knock (*inf.*), pooh-pooh, ridicule, scoff, scorn, sneer, take the piss out of (*taboo sl.*), taunt

de rigueur *adj* = **necessary**, *comme il faut*, conventional, correct, decent, decorous, done, fitting, proper, required, right, the done thing

derision *n* = **mockery**, contempt, contumely, denigration, disdain, disparagement, disrespect, insult, laughter, raillery, ridicule, satire, scoffing, scorn, sneering

derisive ❶ (dɪˈraɪsɪv) *adj* characterized by derision; mocking; scornful. ▸**deˈrisively** *adv* ▸**deˈrisiveness** *n*

derisory ❶ (dɪˈraɪsərɪ) *adj* **1** subject to or worthy of derision. **2** another word for **derisive.**

deriv. *abbrev. for:* **1** derivation. **2** derivative. **3** derived.

derivation ❶ (ˌdɛrɪˈveɪʃən) *n* **1** a deriving or being derived. **2** the origin or descent of something, such as a word. **3** something derived; a derivative. **4a** the process of deducing a mathematical theorem, formula, etc., as a necessary consequence of a set of accepted statements. **4b** this sequence of statements. ▸ˌ**deriˈvational** *adj*

derivative ❶ (dɪˈrɪvətɪv) *adj* **1** derived. **2** based on other sources; not original. ◆ *n* **3** a term, idea, etc., that is based on or derived from another in the same class. **4** a word derived from another word. **5** *Chem.* a compound that is formed from, or can be regarded as formed from, a structurally related compound. **6** *Maths.* **6a** Also called: **differential coefficient, first derivative.** the change of a function, f(*x*), with respect to an infinitesimally small change in the independent variable, *x*. **6b** the rate of change of one quantity with respect to another. **7** *Finance.* a financial instrument, such as a futures contract or option, the price of which is largely determined by the commodity, currency, share price, interest rate, etc., to which it is linked. ▸**deˈrivatively** *adv*

derive ❶ (dɪˈraɪv) *vb* **derives, deriving, derived. 1** (usually foll. by *from*) to draw or be drawn (from) in source or origin. **2** (*tr*) to obtain by reasoning; deduce; infer. **3** (*tr*) to trace the source or development of. **4** (usually foll. by *from*) to produce or be produced (from) by a chemical reaction. [C14: from OF: to spring from, from L *dērīvāre* to draw off, from DE- + *rīvus* a stream] ▸**deˈrivable** *adj* ▸**deˈriver** *n*

derived unit *n* a unit of measurement obtained by multiplication or division of the base units of a system without the introduction of numerical factors.

-derm *n combining form.* indicating skin: *endoderm.* [via F from Gk *derma* skin]

derma (ˈdɜːmə) *n* another name for **corium.** Also: **derm.** [C18: NL, from Gk: skin]

dermal (ˈdɛːməl) *adj* of or relating to the skin.

dermatitis (ˌdɜːməˈtaɪtɪs) *n* inflammation of the skin.

dermato-, derma- *or before a vowel* **dermat-, derm-** *combining form.* indicating skin: *dermatitis.* [from Gk *derma* skin]

dermatology (ˌdɜːməˈtɒlədʒɪ) *n* the branch of medicine concerned with the skin and its diseases. ▸**dermatological** (ˌdɜːmətəˈlɒdʒɪkˀl) *adj* ▸ˌ**dermaˈtologist** *n*

dermis (ˈdɜːmɪs) *n* another name for **corium.** [C19: NL, from EPIDERMIS] ▸ˈ**dermic** *adj*

dernier cri *French.* (dɛrnje kri) *n* **le** (lə). the latest fashion; the last word. [lit.: last cry]

derogate (ˈdɛrəˌgeɪt) *vb* **derogates, derogating, derogated. 1** (*intr;* foll. by *from*) to cause to seem inferior; detract. **2** (*intr;* foll. by *from*) to deviate in standard or quality. **3** (*tr*) to cause to seem inferior, etc.; disparage. **4** (*tr*) to curtail the application of (a law or regulation). [C15: from L *dērogāre* to repeal some part of a law, modify it, from DE- + *rogāre* to ask, propose a law] ▸ˌ**deroˈgation** *n* ▸**derogative** (dɪˈrɒgətɪv) *adj*

derogatory ❶ (dɪˈrɒgətərɪ) *adj* tending or intended to detract, disparage, or belittle; intentionally offensive. ▸**deˈrogatorily** *adv*

derrick (ˈdɛrɪk) *n* **1** a simple crane having lifting tackle slung from a boom. **2** the framework erected over an oil well to enable drill tubes to be raised and lowered. [C17 (in the sense: gallows): from *Derrick,* celebrated hangman at Tyburn, London]

derrière (ˌdɛrɪˈɛə) *n* a euphemistic word for **buttocks.** [C18: lit.: behind (prep), from OF *deriere,* from L *dē retrō* from the back]

derring-do (ˈdɛrɪŋˈduː) *n Arch. or literary.* boldness or bold action. [C16: from ME *durring don* daring to do, from *durren* to dare + *don* to do]

derringer *or* **deringer** (ˈdɛrɪndʒə) *n* a short-barrelled pocket pistol of large calibre. [C19: after Henry *Deringer,* US gunsmith, who invented it]

derris (ˈdɛrɪs) *n* **1** an East Indian woody climbing plant. **2** an insecticide made from its powdered roots. [C19: NL, from Gk: covering, leather, from *deros* skin, hide, from *derein* to skin]

derv (dɜːv) *n* a Brit. name for **diesel oil** when used for road transport. [C20: from *d(iesel) e(ngine) r(oad) v(ehicle)*]

dervish (ˈdɜːvɪʃ) *n* a member of any of various Muslim orders of ascetics, some of which (**whirling dervishes**) are noted for a frenzied, ecstatic, whirling dance. [C16: from Turkish, from Persian *darvīsh* mendicant monk]

DES (in Britain) *abbrev. for* (the former) Department of Education and Science.

desalination (diːˌsælɪˈneɪʃən) *or* **desalinization, desalinisation** *n* the process of removing salt, esp. from sea water.

descale (ˌdiːˈskeɪl) *vb* **descales, descaling, descaled.** (*tr*) to remove the hard deposit formed by chemicals in water from (a kettle, pipe, etc.).

descant ❶ (ˈdɛskænt) *n* **1** Also called: **discant.** a decorative counterpoint added above a basic melody. **2** a comment or discourse. ◆ *adj* **3** Also: **discant.** of the highest member in common use in a family of musical instruments: *a descant recorder.* ◆ *vb* (*intr*) **4** Also: **discant.** (often foll. by *on* or *upon*) to perform a descant. **5** (often foll. by *on* or *upon*) to discourse or make comments. **6** *Arch.* to sing sweetly. [C14: from OF, from Med. L *discanthus,* from L DIS-[1] + *cantus* song] ▸**desˈcanter** *n*

descend ❶ (dɪˈsɛnd) *vb* (*mainly intr*) **1** (*also tr*) to move down (a slope, staircase, etc.). **2** to lead or extend down; slope. **3** to move to a lower level, pitch, etc.; fall. **4** (often foll. by *from*) to be connected by a blood relationship (to a dead or extinct individual, species, etc.). **5** to be inherited. **6** to sink or come down in morals or behaviour. **7** (often foll. by *on* or *upon*) to arrive or attack in a sudden or overwhelming way. **8** (of the sun, moon, etc.) to move towards the horizon. [C13: from OF, from L *dēscendere,* from DE- + *scandere* to climb] ▸**desˈcendable** *or* **desˈcendible** *adj*

descendant ❶ (dɪˈsɛndənt) *n* **1** a person, animal, or plant when described as descended from an individual, race, species, etc. **2** something that derives from an earlier form. ◆ *adj* **3** a variant spelling of **descendent.**

descendent (dɪˈsɛndənt) *adj* descending.

descender (dɪˈsɛndə) *n* **1** *Printing.* the part of certain lower-case letters, such as j, p, or y, that extends below the body of the letter. **2** a person or thing that descends.

descent ❶ (dɪˈsɛnt) *n* **1** the act of descending. **2** a downward slope. **3** a path or way leading downwards. **4** derivation from an ancestor; lineage. **5** a generation in a particular lineage. **6** a decline or degeneration. **7** a movement or passage in degree or state from higher to lower. **8** (often foll. by *on*) a sudden and overwhelming arrival or attack. **9** *Property law.* (formerly) the transmission of real property to the heir.

deschool (ˌdiːˈskuːl) *vb* (*tr*) to separate education from the institution of school and operate through the pupil's life experience as opposed to a set curriculum.

describe ❶ (dɪˈskraɪb) *vb* **describes, describing, described.** (*tr*) **1** to give an account or representation of in words. **2** to pronounce or label. **3** to draw a line or figure, such as a circle. [C15: from L *dēscrībere* to copy off, write out, from DE- + *scrībere* to write] ▸**deˈscribable** *adj* ▸**deˈscriber** *n*

description ❶ (dɪˈskrɪpʃən) *n* **1** a statement or account that describes. **2** the act, process, or technique of describing. **3** sort or variety: *reptiles of every description.*

descriptive ❶ (dɪˈskrɪptɪv) *adj* **1** characterized by or containing description. **2** *Grammar.* (of an adjective) serving to describe the referent of the noun modified, as for example the adjective *brown* as con-

THESAURUS

derisive *adj* = **mocking**, contemptuous, jeering, ridiculing, scoffing, scornful, taunting

derisory *adj* **1** = **ridiculous**, contemptible, insulting, laughable, ludicrous, outrageous, preposterous

derivation *n* **1** = **obtaining**, acquiring, deriving, extraction, getting **2** = **origin**, ancestry, basis, beginning, descent, etymology, foundation, genealogy, root, source

derivative *adj* **2** = **unoriginal**, copied, imitative, plagiaristic, plagiarized, rehashed, secondary, second-hand, uninventive ◆ *n* **3** = **by-product**, derivation, descendant, offshoot, outgrowth, spin-off
Antonyms *adj* ≠ **unoriginal:** archetypal, authentic, first-hand, genuine, master, original, prototypical, seminal

derive *vb* **1** *foll. by* **from** = **come from**, arise from, descend from, emanate from, flow from, issue from, originate from, proceed from, spring from, stem from **2** = **obtain**, collect, deduce, draw, elicit, extract, follow, gain, gather, get, glean, infer, procure, receive, trace

derogatory *adj* = **disparaging**, belittling, damaging, defamatory, depreciative, detracting, discreditable, dishonouring, injurious, offensive, slighting, uncomplimentary, unfavourable, unflattering
Antonyms *adj* appreciative, complimentary, flattering, fulsome, laudatory

descant *n* **1** = **counterpoint**, decoration, melody, song, tune

descend *vb* **1, 3** = **move down**, alight, dismount, drop, fall, go down, plummet, plunge, sink, subside, tumble **2** = **slope**, dip, gravitate, incline, slant **4** *often foll. by* **from** = **originate**, be handed down, be passed down, derive, issue, proceed, spring **6** = **lower oneself**, abase oneself, condescend, degenerate, deteriorate, stoop **7 descend on** = **attack**, arrive, assail, assault, come in force, invade, pounce, raid, swoop
Antonyms *vb* ≠ **move down:** ascend, climb, go up, mount, rise, scale, soar

descendant *n* **1** = **successor**, child, daughter, heir, inheritor, issue, offspring, progeny, scion, son
Antonyms *n* ancestor, antecedent, forebear, forefather, forerunner, precursor, predecessor, progenitor

descent *n* **1** = **coming down**, drop, fall, plunge, swoop **2** = **slope**, declination, declivity, dip, drop, incline, slant **4** = **ancestry**, extraction, family tree, genealogy, heredity, lineage, origin, parentage **6** = **decline**, debasement, decadence, degeneration, degradation, deterioration

describe *vb* **1** = **relate**, characterize, define, depict, detail, explain, express, illustrate, narrate, portray, recount, report, specify, tell **3** = **trace**, delineate, draw, mark out, outline

description *n* **1** = **account**, characterization, delineation, depiction, detail, explanation, narration, narrative, portrayal, report, representation, sketch **3** = **kind**, brand, breed, category, class, genre, genus, ilk, kidney, order, sort, species, type, variety

descriptive *adj* **1** = **graphic**, circumstantial,

trasted with *my*. **3** relating to description or classification rather than explanation or prescription.
▸**de'scriptively** *adv* ▸**de'scriptiveness** *n*

descry (dɪ'skraɪ) *vb* **descries, descrying, descried.** (*tr*) **1** to catch sight of. **2** to discover by looking carefully. [C14: from OF *descrier* to proclaim, DECRY]

desecrate 🅣 ('dɛsɪˌkreɪt) *vb* **desecrates, desecrating, desecrated.** (*tr*) **1** to violate the sacred character of (an object or place) by destructive, blasphemous, or sacrilegious action. **2** to deconsecrate. [C17: from DE- + CONSECRATE]
▸**'deseˌcrator** *or* **'deseˌcrater** *n* ▸**ˌdese'cration** *n*

desegregate (diː'sɛgrɪˌgeɪt) *vb* **desegregates, desegregating, desegregated.** to end racial segregation in (a school or other public institution).
▸**ˌdesegre'gation** *n*

deselect (ˌdiːsɪ'lɛkt) *vb* (*tr*) *Brit. politics.* (of a constituency organization) to refuse to select (an existing MP) for re-election.
▸**ˌdese'lection** *n*

desensitize *or* **desensitise** (diː'sɛnsɪˌtaɪz) *vb* **desensitizes, desensitizing, desensitized** *or* **desensitises, desensitising, desensitised.** (*tr*) to render less sensitive or insensitive: *the patient was desensitized to the allergen.*
▸**deˌsensiti'zation** *or* **deˌsensiti'sation** *n* ▸**de'sensiˌtizer** *or* **de'sensiˌtiser** *n*

desert[1] 🅣 ('dɛzət) *n* **1** a region that is devoid or almost devoid of vegetation, esp. because of low rainfall. **2** an uncultivated uninhabited region. **3** a place which lacks some desirable feature or quality: *a cultural desert.* **4** (*modifier*) of, relating to, or like a desert. [C13: from OF, from Church L *dēsertum,* from L *dēserere* to abandon, lit.: to sever one's links with, from DE- + *serere* to bind together]

desert[2] 🅣 (dɪ'zɜːt) *vb* **1** (*tr*) to abandon (a person, place, etc.) without intending to return, esp. in violation of a promise or obligation. **2** *Mil.* to abscond from (a post or duty) with no intention of returning. **3** (*tr*) to fail (someone) in time of need. [C15: from F *déserter,* from LL *dēsertāre,* from L *dēserere* to forsake; see DESERT[1]]
▸**de'serted** *adj* ▸**de'serter** *n*

desert[3] 🅣 (dɪ'zɜːt) *n* **1** (*often pl*) just reward or punishment. **2** the state of deserving a reward or punishment. [C13: from OF *deserte,* from *deservir* to DESERVE]

desert boots *pl n* ankle-high boots, often of suede, with laces and soft soles.

desertification (dɪˌzɜːtɪfɪ'keɪʃən) *n* the transformation of fertile land into an arid or semiarid region as a result of intensive farming, soil erosion, etc.

desertion 🅣 (dɪ'zɜːʃən) *n* **1** a deserting or being deserted. **2** *Law.* wilful abandonment, esp. of one's spouse or children.

desert island *n* a small remote tropical island.

desert pea *n* an Australian trailing leguminous plant with scarlet flowers.

desert rat *n* **1** a jerboa inhabiting the deserts of N Africa. **2** *Brit. inf.* a soldier who served in North Africa with the British 7th Armoured Division in 1941–42.

deserve 🅣 (dɪ'zɜːv) *vb* **deserves, deserving, deserved.** **1** (*tr*) to be entitled to or worthy of; merit. **2** (*intr;* foll. by *of*) *Obs.* to be worthy. [C13: from OF *deservir,* from L *dēservīre* to serve devotedly, from DE- + *servīre* to SERVE]

deserved 🅣 (dɪ'zɜːvd) *adj* rightfully earned; justified; warranted.
▸**deservedly** (dɪ'zɜːvɪdlɪ) *adv* ▸**deservedness** (dɪ'zɜːvɪdnɪs) *n*

deserving 🅣 (dɪ'zɜːvɪŋ) *adj* (often *postpositive* and foll. by *of*) worthy, esp. of praise or reward.
▸**de'servingly** *adv* ▸**de'servingness** *n*

deshabille (ˌdeɪzæ'biːl) *or* **dishabille** *n* the state of being partly or carelessly dressed. [C17: from F *déshabillé,* from *dés* DIS-[1] + *habiller* to dress]

desiccant ('dɛsɪkənt) *adj* **1** drying. ◆ *n* **2** a substance that absorbs water and is used to remove moisture. [C17: from L *dēsiccāns* drying up; see DESICCATE]

desiccate 🅣 ('dɛsɪˌkeɪt) *vb* **desiccates, desiccating, desiccated.** **1** (*tr*) to remove most of the water from; dehydrate. **2** (*tr*) to preserve (food) by removing moisture; dry. **3** (*intr*) to become dried up. [C16: from L *dēsiccāre* to dry up, from DE- + *siccāre,* from *siccus* dry]
▸**'desicˌcated** *adj* ▸**ˌdesic'cation** *n*

desiderate (dɪ'zɪdəˌreɪt) *vb* **desiderates, desiderating, desiderated.** (*tr*) to feel the lack of or need for; miss. [C17: from L *dēsīderāre,* from DE- + *sīdus* star; see DESIRE]
▸**deˌsider'ation** *n*

desideratum (dɪˌzɪdə'rɑːtəm) *n, pl* **desiderata** (-tə). something lacked and wanted. [C17: from L; see DESIDERATE]

design 🅣 (dɪ'zaɪn) *vb* **1** to work out the structure or form of (something), as by making a sketch or plans. **2** to plan and make (something) artistically or skilfully. **3** (*tr*) to invent. **4** (*tr*) to intend, as for a specific purpose; plan. ◆ *n* **5** a plan or preliminary drawing. **6** the arrangement, elements, or features of an artistic or decorative work: *the design of the desk is Chippendale.* **7** a finished artistic or decorative creation. **8** the art of designing. **9** a plan or project. **10** an intention; purpose. **11** (*often pl;* often foll. by *on* or *against*) a plot, often to gain possession of (something) by illegitimate means. [C16: from L *dēsignāre* to mark out, describe, from DE- + *signāre,* from *signum* a mark]
▸**de'signable** *adj*

designate 🅣 *vb* ('dɛzɪgˌneɪt). **designates, designating, designated.** (*tr*) **1** to indicate or specify. **2** to give a name to; style; entitle. **3** to select or name for an office or duty; appoint. ◆ *adj* ('dɛzɪgnɪt, -ˌneɪt). **4** (*immediately postpositive*) appointed, but not yet in office: *a minister designate.* [C15: from L *dēsignātus* marked out, defined; see DESIGN]
▸**'desigˌnator** *n*

designation 🅣 (ˌdɛzɪg'neɪʃən) *n* **1** something that designates, such as a name. **2** the act of designating or the fact of being designated.

designedly 🅣 (dɪ'zaɪnɪdlɪ) *adv* by intention or design; on purpose.

designer 🅣 (dɪ'zaɪnə) *n* **1** a person who devises and executes designs, as for clothes, machines, etc. **2** (*modifier*) designed by and bearing the label of a well-known fashion designer: *designer jeans.* **3** (*modifier*) (of things, ideas, etc.) fashionably trendy: *designer stubble.* **4** (*modifier*) (of cells, chemicals, etc.) designed or produced to perform a specific function or combat a specific problem: *designer insecticide.* **5** a person who devises plots; intriguer.

designer drug *n* **1** *Med.* a synthetic antibiotic designed to be effective against a particular bacterium. **2** a synthetic drug that has the same properties as an illegal narcotic or hallucinogen but can be manufactured legally.

designing 🅣 (dɪ'zaɪnɪŋ) *adj* artful and scheming.

desirable 🅣 (dɪ'zaɪərəbᵊl) *adj* **1** worthy of desire: *a desirable residence.* **2** arousing desire, esp. sexual desire; attractive.
▸**deˌsira'bility** *or* **de'sirableness** *n* ▸**de'sirably** *adv*

THESAURUS

depictive, detailed, explanatory, expressive, illustrative, pictorial, picturesque, vivid

desecrate *vb* **1** = **commit sacrilege**, abuse, blaspheme, contaminate, defile, despoil, dishonour, pervert, pollute, profane, violate
Antonyms *vb* esteem, exalt, glorify, hallow, prize, respect, revere, value, venerate, worship

desecration *n* **1** = **sacrilege**, blasphemy, debasement, defilement, impiety, profanation, violation

desert[1] *n* **1, 2** = **wilderness**, solitude, waste, wasteland, wilds ◆ *modifier* **4** = **barren**, arid, bare, desolate, infertile, lonely, solitary, uncultivated, uninhabited, unproductive, untilled, waste, wild

desert[2] *vb* **1-3** = **abandon**, abscond, betray, decamp, defect, forsake, give up, go over the hill (*Military sl.*), jilt, leave, leave high and dry, leave (someone) in the lurch, leave stranded, maroon, quit, rat (on) (*inf.*), relinquish, renounce, resign, run out on (*inf.*), strand, throw over, vacate, walk out on (*inf.*)
Antonyms *vb* be a source of strength to, look after, maintain, provide for, succour, sustain, take care of

desert[3] *n* **1** *often plural* = **due**, comeuppance, guerdon (*poetic*), meed (*arch.*), payment, punishment, recompense, requital, retribution, return, reward, right

deserted *adj* **1** = **abandoned**, bereft, cast off, derelict, desolate, empty, forlorn, forsaken, godforsaken, isolated, left in the lurch, left stranded, lonely, neglected, solitary, unfriended, unoccupied, vacant

deserter *n* **1, 2** = **defector**, absconder, apostate, escapee, fugitive, rat (*inf.*), renegade, runaway, traitor, truant

desertion *n* **1, 2** = **abandonment**, absconding, apostasy, betrayal, defection, departure, dereliction, escape, evasion, flight, forsaking, relinquishment, truancy

deserve *vb* **1** = **merit**, be entitled to, be worthy of, earn, gain, justify, procure, rate, warrant, win

deserved *adj* = **well-earned**, appropriate, condign, due, earned, fair, fitting, just, justifiable, justified, meet (*arch.*), merited, proper, right, rightful, suitable, warranted

deservedly *adv* = **by rights**, according to one's due, appropriately, condignly, duly, fairly, fittingly, justifiably, justly, properly, rightfully, rightly
Antonyms *adv* inappropriately, undeservedly, unduly, unfairly, unfittingly, unjustifiably, unjustly, unwarrantedly, wrongfully, wrongly

deserving *adj* = **worthy**, commendable, estimable, laudable, meritorious, praiseworthy, righteous
Antonyms *adj* not deserving of, not good enough, not worth, undeserving, unworthy

desiccate *vb* **1** = **dry**, dehydrate, drain, evaporate, exsiccate, parch

desiccated *adj* **2** = **dried**, dehydrated, dry, powdered

design *vb* **1** = **plan**, delineate, describe, draft, draw, outline, sketch, trace **2, 3** = **create**, conceive, fabricate, fashion, invent, originate, think up **4** = **intend**, aim, contrive, destine, devise, make, mean, plan, project, propose, purpose, scheme, tailor ◆ *n* **5** = **plan**, blueprint, delineation, draft, drawing, model, outline, scheme, sketch **6** = **arrangement**, configuration, construction, figure, form, motif, organization, pattern, shape, style **10** = **intention**, aim, end, goal, intent, meaning, object, objective, point, purport, purpose, target, view

designate *vb* **1** = **specify**, characterize, define, denote, describe, earmark, indicate, pinpoint, show, stipulate **2** = **name**, call, christen, dub, entitle, label, nominate, style, term **3** = **appoint**, allot, assign, choose, delegate, depute, nominate, select

designation *n* **1** = **name**, denomination, description, epithet, label, mark, title **2** = **appointment**, classification, delegation, indication, selection, specification

designedly *adv* = **intentionally**, by design, calculatedly, deliberately, knowingly, on purpose, purposely, studiously, wilfully, wittingly

designer *n* **1** = **creator**, architect, artificer, couturier, deviser, inventor, originator, planner, stylist

designing *adj* = **scheming**, artful, astute, conniving, conspiring, crafty, crooked (*inf.*), cunning, deceitful, devious, intriguing, Machiavellian, plotting, sharp, shrewd, sly, treacherous, tricky, unscrupulous, wily

desirability *n* **1** = **worth**, advantage, benefit, merit, profit, usefulness, value

desirable *adj* **1** = **agreeable**, advantageous, advisable, beneficial, covetable, eligible, enviable, good, pleasing, preferable, profitable, to

desire ➊ (dɪˈzaɪə) *vb* **desires, desiring, desired.** (*tr*) **1** to wish or long for; crave. **2** to request; ask for. ◆ *n* **3** a wish or longing. **4** an expressed wish; request. **5** sexual appetite. **6** a person or thing that is desired. [C13: from OF, from L *dēsīderāre* to desire earnestly; see DESIDERATE]
▸**deˈsirer** *n*

desirous ➊ (dɪˈzaɪərəs) *adj* (usually *postpositive* and foll. by *of*) having or expressing desire (for).

desist ➊ (dɪˈzɪst) *vb* (*intr*; often foll. by *from*) to cease, as from an action; stop or abstain. [C15: from OF, from L *dēsistere* to leave off, stand apart, from DE- + *sistere* to stand, halt]

desk (dɛsk) *n* **1** a piece of furniture with a writing surface and usually drawers or other compartments. **2** a service counter or table in a public building, such as a hotel. **3** a support for the book from which services are read in a church. **4** the editorial section of a newspaper, etc., responsible for a particular subject: *the news desk.* **5** a music stand shared by two orchestral players. [C14: from Med. L *desca* table, from L *discus* disc, dish]

desk-bound *adj* obliged by one's occupation to work sitting at a desk.

desk editor *n* (in a publishing house) an editor responsible for the preparation and checking of manuscripts for printing.

deskill (diːˈskɪl) *vb* (*tr*) **1** to mechanize or computerize (a job) so that little skill is required to do it. **2** to deprive (employees) of the opportunity for skilled work.

desktop (ˈdɛsk,tɒp) *n* (*modifier*) denoting a computer system, esp. for word processing, that is small enough to use at a desk.

desktop publishing *n* a means of publishing reports, advertising material, etc., to near-typeset quality using a desktop computer and a laser printer. Abbrev.: **DTP**.

desman (ˈdɛsmən) *n*, *pl* **desmans.** either of two molelike amphibious mammals, the Russian desman or the Pyrenean desman, with dense fur and webbed feet. [C18: from Swedish *desmansråtta,* from *desman* musk + *råtta* rat]

desolate ➊ *adj* (ˈdɛsəlɪt). **1** uninhabited; deserted. **2** made uninhabitable; laid waste; devastated. **3** without friends, hope, or encouragement. **4** dismal; depressing. ◆ *vb* (ˈdɛsə,leɪt), **desolates, desolating, desolated.** (*tr*) **5** to deprive of inhabitants; depopulate. **6** to lay waste; devastate. **7** to make wretched or forlorn. **8** to forsake or abandon. [C14: from L *dēsōlāre* to leave alone, from DE- + *sōlāre* to make lonely, lay waste, from *sōlus* alone]
▸ˈ**deso,later** *or* ˈ**deso,lator** *n* ▸ˈ**desolately** *adv* ▸ˈ**desolateness** *n*

desolation ➊ (,dɛsəˈleɪʃən) *n* **1** a desolating or being desolated; ruin or devastation. **2** solitary misery; wretchedness. **3** a desolate region.

despair ➊ (dɪˈspɛə) *vb* **1** (*intr*; often foll. by *of*) to lose or give up hope: *I despair of his coming.* ◆ *n* **2** total loss of hope. **3** a person or thing that causes hopelessness or for which there is no hope. [C14: from OF *despoir* hopelessness, from *desperer* to despair, from L *dēspērāre,* from DE- + *spērāre* to hope]

despairing ➊ (dɪˈspɛərɪŋ) *adj* hopeless, despondent; feeling or showing despair.
▸**deˈspairingly** *adv*

despatch ➊ (dɪˈspætʃ) *vb* (*tr*), *n* a less common spelling of **dispatch.**
▸**desˈpatcher** *n*

desperado ➊ (,dɛspəˈrɑːdəʊ) *n*, *pl* **desperadoes** *or* **desperados.** a reckless or desperate person, esp. one ready to commit any violent illegal act. [C17: prob. pseudo-Spanish var. of obs. *desperate* (n)]

desperate ➊ (ˈdɛspərɪt, -prɪt) *adj* **1** careless of danger, as from despair. **2** (of an act) reckless; risky. **3** used or undertaken as a last resort. **4** critical; very grave: *in desperate need.* **5** (often *postpositive* and foll. by *for*) in distress and having a great need or desire. **6** moved by or showing despair. [C15: from L *dēspērāre* to have no hope; see DESPAIR]
▸ˈ**desperately** *adv* ▸ˈ**desperateness** *n*

desperation ➊ (,dɛspəˈreɪʃən) *n* **1** desperate recklessness. **2** the state of being desperate.

despicable ➊ (ˈdɛspɪkəbᵊl, dɪˈspɪk-) *adj* worthy of being despised; contemptible; mean. [C16: from LL *dēspicābilis,* from *dēspicārī* to disdain; cf. DESPISE]
▸ˈ**despicably** *adv*

despise ➊ (dɪˈspaɪz) *vb* **despises, despising, despised.** (*tr*) to look down on with contempt; scorn: *he despises flattery.* [C13: from OF *despire,* from L *dēspicere* to look down, from DE- + *specere* to look]
▸**deˈspiser** *n*

despite ➊ (dɪˈspaɪt) *prep* **1** in spite of; undeterred by. ◆ *n* **2** *Arch.* contempt; insult. **3 in despite of.** (*prep*) *Rare.* in spite of. [C13: from OF *despit,* from L *dēspectus* contempt; see DESPISE]

despoil ➊ (dɪˈspɔɪl) *vb* (*tr*) to deprive by force; plunder; loot. [C13: from OF, from L *dēspoliāre,* from DE- + *spoliāre* to rob (esp. of clothing)]
▸**deˈspoiler** *n* ▸**deˈspoilment** *n*

despoliation (dɪ,spəʊlɪˈeɪʃən) *n* **1** plunder or pillage. **2** the state of being despoiled.

despond (dɪˈspɒnd) *vb* (*intr*) **1** to become disheartened; despair. ◆ *n* **2** *Arch.* despondency. [C17: from L *dēspondēre* to promise, make over to, yield, lose heart, from DE- + *spondēre* to promise]
▸**deˈspondingly** *adv*

despondent ➊ (dɪˈspɒndənt) *adj* downcast or disheartened; dejected.
▸**deˈspondence** *or* **deˈspondency** *n* ▸**deˈspondently** *adv*

despot ➊ (ˈdɛspɒt) *n* **1** an absolute or tyrannical ruler. **2** any person in power who acts tyrannically. [C16: from Med. L *despota,* from Gk *despotēs* lord, master]
▸**despotic** (dɛsˈpɒtɪk) *or* **desˈpotical** *adj* ▸**desˈpotically** *adv*

THESAURUS

die for (*inf.*), worthwhile **2** = **attractive**, adorable, alluring, fascinating, fetching, glamorous, seductive, sexy (*inf.*)
Antonyms *adj* ≠ **agreeable:** disagreeable, distasteful, unacceptable, unappealing, unattractive, undesirable, unpleasant, unpopular ≠ **attractive:** unappealing, unattractive, undesirable, unsexy (*inf.*)

desire *vb* **1** = **want**, aspire to, covet, crave, desiderate, fancy, hanker after, hope for, long for, set one's heart on, thirst for, wish for, yearn for **2** = **request**, ask, entreat, importune, petition, solicit ◆ *n* **3** = **wish**, ache, appetite, aspiration, craving, hankering, hope, longing, need, thirst, want, yearning, yen (*inf.*) **4** = **request**, appeal, entreaty, importunity, petition, solicitation, supplication **5** = **lust**, appetite, concupiscence, lasciviousness, lechery, libido, lustfulness, passion

desirous *adj* = **wishing**, ambitious, anxious, aspiring, avid, craving, desiring, eager, hopeful, hoping, keen, longing, ready, willing, yearning
Antonyms *adj* averse, disinclined, grudging, indisposed, loath, opposed, reluctant, unenthusiastic, unwilling

desist *vb* = **stop**, abstain, belay (*Nautical*), break off, cease, discontinue, end, forbear, give over (*inf.*), give up, have done with, kick (*inf.*), leave off, pause, refrain from, remit, suspend

desolate *adj* **1** = **uninhabited**, bare, barren, bleak, desert, dreary, godforsaken, ruined, solitary, unfrequented, waste, wild **3** = **miserable**, abandoned, bereft, cheerless, comfortless, companionless, dejected, depressing, despondent, disconsolate, dismal, downcast, down in the dumps (*inf.*), forlorn, forsaken, gloomy, lonely, melancholy, wretched ◆ *vb* **5, 6** = **lay waste**, depopulate, despoil, destroy, devastate, lay low, pillage, plunder, ravage, ruin **7** = **deject**, daunt, depress, discourage, dishearten, dismay, distress, grieve
Antonyms *adj* ≠ **uninhabited:** inhabited, populous ≠ **miserable:** cheerful, happy, joyous, light-hearted ◆ *vb* ≠ **lay waste:** develop ≠ **deject:** cheer, encourage, hearten, nourish

desolation *n* **1** = **ruin**, destruction, devastation, havoc, ravages, ruination **2** = **misery**, anguish, dejection, despair, distress, gloom, gloominess, melancholy, sadness, unhappiness, woe, wretchedness

despair *vb* **1** = **lose hope**, despond, give up, lose heart ◆ *n* **2** = **despondency**, anguish, dejection, depression, desperation, disheartenment, gloom, hopelessness, melancholy, misery, wretchedness **3** = **hardship**, burden, cross, ordeal, pain, trial, tribulation

despairing *adj* = **hopeless**, anxious, at the end of one's tether, broken-hearted, dejected, depressed, desperate, despondent, disconsolate, dismal, downcast, down in the dumps (*inf.*), frantic, grief-stricken, inconsolable, melancholy, miserable, suicidal, wretched

despatch *see* **dispatch**

desperado *n* = **criminal**, bandit, cut-throat, gangster, gunman, heavy (*sl.*), hoodlum (*chiefly US*), lawbreaker, mugger (*inf.*), outlaw, ruffian, thug, villain

desperate *adj* **2** = **reckless**, audacious, dangerous, daring, death-defying, determined, foolhardy, frantic, furious, hasty, hazardous, headstrong, impetuous, madcap, precipitate, rash, risky, violent, wild **4** = **grave**, acute, critical, dire, drastic, extreme, great, urgent, very grave **6** = **hopeless**, at the end of one's tether, despairing, despondent, forlorn, inconsolable, irrecoverable, irremediable, irretrievable, wretched

desperately *adv* **4** = **gravely**, badly, dangerously, perilously, seriously, severely **6** = **hopelessly**, appallingly, fearfully, frightfully, shockingly

desperation *n* **1** = **recklessness**, defiance, foolhardiness, frenzy, heedlessness, impetuosity, madness, rashness **2** = **misery**, agony, anguish, anxiety, despair, despondency, distraction, heartache, hopelessness, pain, sorrow, torture, trouble, unhappiness, worry

despicable *adj* = **contemptible**, abject, base, beyond contempt, cheap, degrading, detestable, disgraceful, disreputable, hateful, ignominious, infamous, low, mean, pitiful, reprehensible, scurvy, shameful, sordid, vile, worthless, wretched
Antonyms *adj* admirable, estimable, ethical, exemplary, good, honest, honourable, moral, noble, praiseworthy, righteous, upright, virtuous, worthy

despise *vb* = **look down on**, abhor, contemn, deride, detest, disdain, disregard, flout, have a down on (*inf.*), loathe, neglect, revile, scorn, slight, spurn, undervalue
Antonyms *vb* admire, adore, be fond of, be keen on, cherish, dig (*sl.*), esteem, fancy (*inf.*), love, relish, revel in, take to

despite *prep* **1** = **in spite of**, against, even with, in contempt of, in defiance of, in the face of, in the teeth of, notwithstanding, regardless of, undeterred by

despoil *vb Formal* = **plunder**, denude, deprive, destroy, devastate, dispossess, divest, loot, pillage, ravage, rifle, rob, strip, total (*sl.*), trash (*sl.*), vandalize, wreak havoc upon, wreck

despondency *n* = **dejection**, depression, despair, desperation, disconsolateness, discouragement, dispiritedness, downheartedness, gloom, hopelessness, low spirits, melancholy, misery, sadness, the hump (*Brit. inf.*), wretchedness

despondent *adj* = **dejected**, blue, depressed, despairing, disconsolate, discouraged, disheartened, dismal, dispirited, doleful, down, downcast, downhearted, down in the dumps (*inf.*), gloomy, glum, hopeless, in despair, low, low-spirited, melancholy, miserable, morose, sad, sick as a parrot (*inf.*), sorrowful, woebegone, wretched
Antonyms *adj* buoyant, cheerful, cheery, chirpy (*inf.*), genial, glad, happy, hopeful, joyful, light-hearted, optimistic, upbeat (*inf.*)

despot *n* **1, 2** = **tyrant**, autocrat, dictator, monocrat, oppressor

despotism ❶ (ˈdɛspəˌtɪzəm) *n* **1** the rule of a despot; absolute or tyrannical government. **2** arbitrary or tyrannical authority or behaviour.

des res (ˈdɛz ˈrɛz) *n* (in estate agents' jargon) a desirable residence.

dessert ❶ (dɪˈzɜːt) *n* **1** the sweet, usually last course of a meal. **2** *Chiefly Brit.* (esp. formerly) fruit, dates, nuts, etc., served at the end of a meal. [C17: from F, from *desservir* to clear a table, from *des-* DIS-[1] + *servir* to SERVE]

dessertspoon (dɪˈzɜːtˌspuːn) *n* a spoon intermediate in size between a tablespoon and a teaspoon.

destination ❶ (ˌdɛstɪˈneɪʃən) *n* **1** the predetermined end of a journey. **2** the end or purpose for which something is created or a person is destined.

destine ❶ (ˈdɛstɪn) *vb* **destines, destining, destined.** (*tr*) to set apart (for a certain purpose or person); intend; design. [C14: from OF, from L *dēstināre* to appoint, from DE- + *-stināre*, from *stāre* to stand]

destined ❶ (ˈdɛstɪnd) *adj* (*postpositive*) **1** foreordained; meant. **2** (usually foll. by *for*) heading (towards a specific destination).

destiny ❶ (ˈdɛstɪnɪ) *n, pl* **destinies. 1** the future destined for a person or thing. **2** the predetermined or inevitable course of events. **3** the power that predetermines the course of events. [C14: from OF, from *destiner* to DESTINE]

destitute ❶ (ˈdɛstɪˌtjuːt) *adj* **1** lacking the means of subsistence; totally impoverished. **2** (*postpositive;* foll. by *of*) completely lacking: *destitute of words.* [C14: from L, from *dēstituere* to leave alone, from *statuere* to place]

destitution ❶ (ˌdɛstɪˈtjuːʃən) *n* the state of being destitute; utter poverty.

destrier (ˈdɛstrɪə) *n Arch.* a warhorse. [C13: from OF, from *destre* right hand, from L *dextra;* from the fact that a squire led a knight's horse with his right hand]

destroy ❶ (dɪˈstrɔɪ) *vb* (*mainly tr*) **1** to ruin; spoil. **2** to tear down or demolish. **3** to put an end to. **4** to kill or annihilate. **5** to crush or defeat. **6** (*intr*) to be destructive or cause destruction. [C13: from OF, from L *dēstruere* to pull down, from DE- + *struere* to pile up, build]

destroyer (dɪˈstrɔɪə) *n* **1** a small fast lightly armoured but heavily armed warship. **2** a person or thing that destroys.

destruct (dɪˈstrʌkt) *vb* **1** to destroy (one's own missile, etc.) for safety. **2** (*intr*) (of a missile, etc.) to be destroyed, for safety, by those controlling it. ◆ *n* **3** the act of destructing. ◆ *adj* **4** designed to be capable of destroying itself or the object containing it: *destruct mechanism.*

destructible (dɪˈstrʌktɪbᵊl) *adj* capable of being or liable to be destroyed.

destruction ❶ (dɪˈstrʌkʃən) *n* **1** the act of destroying or state of being destroyed; demolition. **2** a cause of ruin or means of destroying. [C14: from L *dēstructiō* a pulling down; see DESTROY]

destructive ❶ (dɪˈstrʌktɪv) *adj* **1** (often *postpositive* and foll. by *of* or *to*) causing or tending to cause the destruction (of). **2** intended to discredit, esp. without positive suggestions or help; negative: *destructive criticism.*
▸**deˈstructively** *adv* ▸**deˈstructiveness** *n*

destructive distillation *n* the decomposition of a complex substance, such as wood or coal, by heating it in the absence of air and collecting the volatile products.

destructor (dɪˈstrʌktə) *n* **1** a furnace or incinerator for the disposal of refuse. **2** a device used to blow up a defective missile.

desuetude (dɪˈsjuːɪˌtjuːd, ˈdɛswɪˌtjuːd) *n Formal.* the condition of not being in use or practice; disuse. [C15: from L, from *dēsuescere* to lay aside a habit, from DE- + *suescere* to grow accustomed]

desulphurize *or* **desulphurise** (diːˈsʌlfjʊˌraɪz) *vb* **desulphurizes, desulphurizing, desulphurized** *or* **desulphurises, desulphurising, desulphurised.** to free or become free from sulphur.

desultory ❶ (ˈdɛsəltərɪ, -trɪ) *adj* **1** passing from one thing to another, esp. in a fitful way; unmethodical; disconnected. **2** random or incidental: *a desultory thought.* [C16: from L: relating to one who vaults or jumps, hence superficial, from *dēsilīre* to jump down, from DE- + *salīre*]
▸**ˈdesultorily** *adv* ▸**ˈdesultoriness** *n*

Det. *abbrev. for* Detective.

detach ❶ (dɪˈtætʃ) *vb* (*tr*) **1** to disengage and separate or remove; unfasten; disconnect. **2** *Mil.* to separate (a small unit) from a larger, esp. for a special assignment. [C17: from OF *destachier,* from *des-* DIS-[1] + *atachier* to ATTACH]
▸**deˈtachable** *adj* ▸**deˌtachaˈbility** *n*

detached ❶ (dɪˈtætʃt) *adj* **1** disconnected or standing apart; not attached: *a detached house.* **2** showing no bias or emotional involvement. **3** *Ophthalmol.* (of the retina) separated from the choroid layer of the eyeball to which it is normally attached, resulting in loss of vision in the affected part.

detachment ❶ (dɪˈtætʃmənt) *n* **1** indifference; aloofness. **2** freedom from self-interest or bias; disinterest. **3** the act of detaching something. **4** the condition of being detached; disconnection. **5** *Mil.* **5a** the separation of a small unit from its main body. **5b** the unit so detached.

detail ❶ (ˈdiːteɪl) *n* **1** an item that is considered separately; particular. **2** an item that is unimportant: *passengers' comfort was regarded as a detail.* **3** treatment of particulars: *this essay includes too much detail.* **4** items collectively; particulars. **5** a small section or element in a painting, building, statue, etc., esp. when considered in isolation. **6** *Mil.* **6a** the act of assigning personnel for a specific duty. **6b** the personnel selected. **6c** the duty. **7 in detail.** including all or most particulars or items thoroughly. ◆ *vb* (*tr*) **8** to list or relate fully. **9** *Mil.* to select (personnel) for a specific duty. [C17: from F, from OF *detailler* to cut in pieces, from *de-* DIS-[1] + *tailler* to cut]

detailed ❶ (ˈdiːteɪld) *adj* having many details or giving careful attention to details.

detain ❶ (dɪˈteɪn) *vb* (*tr*) **1** to delay; hold back. **2** to confine or hold in custody. [C15: from OF, from L *dētinēre* to hold off, keep back, from DE- + *tenēre* to hold]
▸**deˈtainable** *adj* ▸**detainee** (ˌdiːteɪˈniː) *n* ▸**deˈtainment** *n*

detect ❶ (dɪˈtɛkt) *vb* (*tr*) **1** to perceive or notice. **2** to discover the existence or presence of (esp. something likely to elude observation). **3**

THESAURUS

despotic *adj* **1, 2 = tyrannical,** absolute, arbitrary, arrogant, authoritarian, autocratic, dictatorial, domineering, imperious, monocratic, oppressive, unconstitutional

despotism *n* **1, 2 = tyranny,** absolutism, autarchy, autocracy, dictatorship, monocracy, oppression, totalitarianism

dessert *n* **1, 2 = pudding,** afters (*Brit. inf.*), last course, second course, sweet, sweet course

destination *n* **1 = journey's end,** harbour, haven, landing-place, resting-place, station, stop, terminus **2 = objective,** aim, ambition, design, end, goal, intention, object, purpose, target

destine *vb* **= fate,** allot, appoint, assign, consecrate, decree, design, devote, doom, earmark, intend, mark out, ordain, predetermine, preordain, purpose, reserve

destined *adj* **1 = fated,** bound, certain, designed, doomed, foreordained, ineluctable, inescapable, inevitable, intended, meant, ordained, predestined, unavoidable **2 = bound for,** assigned, booked, directed, en route, heading for, on the road to, routed, scheduled

destiny *n* **1–3 = fate,** cup, divine decree, doom, fortune, karma, kismet, lot, portion

destitute *adj* **1 = penniless,** dirt-poor (*inf.*), distressed, down and out, flat broke (*inf.*), impecunious, impoverished, indigent, in queer street (*inf.*), insolvent, moneyless, necessitous, needy, on one's uppers, on the breadline (*inf.*), on the rocks, penurious, poor, poverty-stricken, short, without two pennies to rub together (*inf.*) **2 = lacking,** bereft of, deficient in, depleted, deprived of, devoid of, drained, empty of, in need of, wanting, without

destitution *n* **= pennilessness,** beggary, dire straits, distress, impecuniousness, indigence, neediness, pauperism, penury, privation, utter poverty, want
Antonyms *n* affluence, fortune, good fortune, life of luxury, luxury, plenty, prosperity, riches, wealth

destroy *vb* **= ruin,** annihilate, blow sky-high, blow to bits, break down, crush, demolish, desolate, devastate, dismantle, dispatch, eradicate, extinguish, extirpate, gut, kill, put paid to, ravage, raze, shatter, slay, smash, torpedo, total (*sl.*), trash (*sl.*), waste, wipe out, wreck

destruction *n* **1 = ruin,** annihilation, crushing, demolition, devastation, downfall, end, eradication, extermination, extinction, havoc, liquidation, massacre, overthrow, overwhelming, ruination, shattering, slaughter, undoing, wreckage, wrecking

destructive *adj* **1 = damaging,** baleful, baneful, calamitous, cataclysmic, catastrophic, deadly, deleterious, detrimental, devastating, fatal, harmful, hurtful, injurious, lethal, maleficent, noxious, pernicious, ruinous **2 = negative,** adverse, antagonistic, contrary, derogatory, discouraging, discrediting, disparaging, hostile, invalidating, opposed, undermining, vicious

desultory *adj* **1, 2 = random,** aimless, capricious, cursory, disconnected, discursive, disorderly, erratic, fitful, haphazard, inconsistent, inconstant, inexact, irregular, loose, maundering, off and on, rambling, roving, spasmodic, unmethodical, unsettled, unsystematic, vague

detach *vb* **1 = separate,** cut off, disconnect, disengage, disentangle, disjoin, disunite, divide, free, isolate, loosen, remove, segregate, sever, tear off, unbridle, uncouple, unfasten, unhitch
Antonyms *vb* attach, bind, connect, fasten

detached *adj* **1 = separate,** disconnected, discrete, disjoined, divided, free, loosened, severed, unconnected **2 = uninvolved,** aloof, disinterested, dispassionate, impartial, impersonal, neutral, objective, reserved, unbiased, uncommitted, unprejudiced
Antonyms *adj* ≠ **uninvolved:** biased, concerned, interested, involved, partisan, prejudiced

detachment *n* **1 = indifference,** aloofness, coolness, nonchalance, remoteness, unconcern **2 = impartiality,** disinterestedness, fairness, neutrality, nonpartisanship, objectivity **4 = separation,** disconnection, disengagement, disjoining, severing **5b** *Military* **= unit,** body, detail, force, party, patrol, squad, task force

detail *n* **1 = point,** aspect, component, count, element, fact, factor, feature, item, particular, respect, specific, technicality **2 = fine point,** minutiae, nicety, part, particular, triviality **6b** *Military* **= party,** assignment, body, detachment, duty, fatigue, force, squad **7 in detail = comprehensively,** exhaustively, inside out, item by item, point by point, thoroughly ◆ *vb* **8 = list,** catalogue, delineate, depict, describe, enumerate, individualize, itemize, narrate, particularize, portray, recite, recount, rehearse, relate, specify, tabulate **9 = appoint,** allocate, assign, charge, commission, delegate, detach, send

detailed *adj* **= comprehensive,** blow-by-blow, circumstantial, elaborate, exact, exhaustive, full, intricate, itemized, meticulous, minute, particular, particularized, specific, thorough
Antonyms *adj* brief, compact, concise, condensed, limited, pithy, short, slight, succinct, summary, superficial, terse

detain *vb* **1 = delay,** check, hinder, hold up, impede, keep, keep back, retard, slow up (*or* down), stay, stop **2 = hold,** arrest, confine, intern, restrain

detect *vb* **1 = notice,** ascertain, catch, descry, distinguish, identify, note, observe, perceive,

Obs. to discover, or reveal (a crime, criminal, etc.). **4** to extract information from (an electromagnetic wave). [C15: from L *dētectus*, from *dētegere* to uncover, from DE- + *tegere* to cover]
▸**de'tectable** *or* **de'tectible** *adj*

detection ⓣ (dɪ'tɛkʃən) *n* **1** the act of discovering or the fact of being discovered. **2** the act or process of extracting information, esp. at audio or video frequencies, from an electromagnetic wave; demodulation.

detective ⓣ (dɪ'tɛktɪv) *n* **1a** a police officer who investigates crimes. **1b** See **private detective. 1c** (*as modifier*): *a detective story.* ◆ *adj* **2** of or for detection.

detector (dɪ'tɛktə) *n* **1** a person or thing that detects. **2** any mechanical sensing device. **3** *Electronics.* a device used in the detection of radio signals.

detent (dɪ'tɛnt) *n* the locking piece of a mechanism, often spring-loaded to check the movement of a wheel in only one direction. [C17: from OF *destente* a loosening, trigger; see DÉTENTE]

détente (deɪ'tɑːnt; *French* detɑ̃t) *n* the relaxing or easing of tension, esp. between nations. [F, lit.: a loosening, from OF *destendre* to release, from *tendre* to stretch]

detention ⓣ (dɪ'tɛnʃən) *n* **1** a detaining or being detained. **2a** custody or confinement, esp. of a suspect awaiting trial. **2b** (*as modifier*): *a detention order.* **3** a form of punishment in which a pupil is detained after school. [C16: from L *dētentiō* a keeping back; see DETAIN]

detention centre *n* (formerly) a place in which young persons could be detained for short periods by order of a court.

deter ⓣ (dɪ'tɜː) *vb* **deters, deterring, deterred.** (*tr*) to discourage (from acting) or prevent (from occurring), usually by instilling fear, doubt, or anxiety. [C16: from L *dēterrēre*, from DE- + *terrēre* to frighten]
▸**de'terment** *n*

deterge (dɪ'tɜːdʒ) *vb* **deterges, deterging, deterged.** (*tr*) to cleanse: *to deterge a wound.* [C17: from L *dētergēre* to wipe away, from DE- + *tergēre* to wipe]

detergent ⓣ (dɪ'tɜːdʒənt) *n* **1** a cleansing agent, esp. a chemical such as an alkyl sulphonate, widely used in industry, laundering, etc. ◆ *adj* **2** having cleansing power. [C17: from L *dētergēns* wiping off; see DETERGE]

deteriorate ⓣ (dɪ'tɪərɪəˌreɪt) *vb* **deteriorates, deteriorating, deteriorated. 1** to make or become worse; depreciate. **2** (*intr*) to wear away or disintegrate. [C16: from LL *dēteriōrāre*, from L *dēterior* worse]
▸**deˌterio'ration** *n* ▸**de'teriorative** *adj*

determinacy (dɪ'tɜːmɪnəsɪ) *n* **1** the quality of being defined or fixed. **2** the condition of being predicted or deduced.

determinant (dɪ'tɜːmɪnənt) *adj* **1** serving to determine. ◆ *n* **2** a factor that influences or determines. **3** *Maths.* a square array of elements that represents the sum of certain products of these elements, used to solve simultaneous equations, in vector studies, etc.

determinate ⓣ (dɪ'tɜːmɪnɪt) *adj* **1** definitely limited, defined, or fixed. **2** determined. **3** able to be predicted or deduced. **4** *Bot.* having the main and branch stems ending in flowers.
▸**de'terminateness** *n*

determination ⓣ (dɪˌtɜːmɪ'neɪʃən) *n* **1** the act of making a decision. **2** the condition of being determined; resoluteness. **3** an ending of an argument by the decision of an authority. **4** the act of fixing the quality, limit, position, etc., of something. **5** a decision or opinion reached. **6** a resolute movement towards some object or end. **7** *Law.* the termination of an estate or interest. **8** *Law.* the decision reached by a court of justice on a disputed matter.

determinative (dɪ'tɜːmɪnətɪv) *adj* **1** serving to settle or determine; deciding. ◆ *n* **2** a factor, circumstance, etc., that settles or determines.
▸**de'terminatively** *adv* ▸**de'terminativeness** *n*

determine ⓣ (dɪ'tɜːmɪn) *vb* **determines, determining, determined. 1** to settle or decide (an argument, question, etc.) conclusively. **2** (*tr*) to conclude, esp. after observation or consideration. **3** (*tr*) to influence; give direction to. **4** (*tr*) to fix in scope, variety, etc.: *the river determined the edge of the property.* **5** to make or cause to make a decision. **6** (*tr*) *Logic.* to define or limit (a notion) by adding or requiring certain features or characteristics. **7** (*tr*) *Geom.* to fix or specify the position or form of. **8** *Chiefly law.* to come or bring to an end, as an estate. [C14: from OF, from L *dētermināre* to set boundaries to, from DE- + *termināre* to limit]
▸**de'terminable** *adj*

determined ⓣ (dɪ'tɜːmɪnd) *adj* of unwavering mind; resolute; firm.
▸**de'terminedly** *adv*

determiner (dɪ'tɜːmɪnə) *n* **1** a word, such as a number, article, or personal pronoun, that determines (limits) the meaning of a noun phrase, e.g. *their* in 'their black cat'. **2** a person or thing that determines.

determinism (dɪ'tɜːmɪˌnɪzəm) *n* the philosophical doctrine that all events, including human actions, are fully determined by preceding events, and so freedom of choice is illusory. Also called: **necessitarianism.** Cf. **free will.**
▸**de'terminist** *n, adj* ▸**deˌtermin'istic** *adj*

deterrent ⓣ (dɪ'tɛrənt) *n* **1** something that deters. **2** a weapon, esp. nuclear, held by one state, etc., to deter attack by another. ◆ *adj* **3** tending or used to deter. [C19: from L *dēterrēns* hindering; see DETER]
▸**de'terrence** *n*

detest ⓣ (dɪ'tɛst) *vb* (*tr*) to dislike intensely; loathe. [C16: from L *dētestārī* to curse (while invoking a god as witness), from DE- + *testārī*, from *testis* a witness]
▸**de'tester** *n*

detestable ⓣ (dɪ'tɛstəbᵊl) *adj* being or deserving to be abhorred or detested.
▸**deˌtesta'bility** *or* **de'testableness** *n* ▸**de'testably** *adv*

detestation ⓣ (ˌdiːtɛs'teɪʃən) *n* **1** intense hatred; abhorrence. **2** a person or thing that is detested.

dethrone ⓣ (dɪ'θrəʊn) *vb* **dethrones, dethroning, dethroned.** (*tr*) to remove from a throne or deprive of any high position or title.
▸**de'thronement** *n* ▸**de'throner** *n*

detonate ⓣ ('dɛtəˌneɪt) *vb* **detonates, detonating, detonated.** to cause (a bomb, mine, etc.) to explode or (of a bomb, mine, etc.) to explode. [C18: from L *dētonāre* to thunder down, from DE- + *tonāre* to THUNDER]
▸ˌ**deto'nation** *n*

detonator ('dɛtəˌneɪtə) *n* **1** a small amount of explosive, as in a percussion cap, used to initiate a larger explosion. **2** a device, such as an electrical generator, used to set off an explosion from a distance. **3** an explosive.

detour ⓣ ('diːtʊə) *n* **1** a deviation from a direct route or course of action. ◆ *vb* **2** to deviate or cause to deviate from a direct route or

THESAURUS

recognize, scent, spot **2** = **discover**, catch, disclose, expose, find, reveal, track down, uncover, unmask

detection *n* **1** = **discovery**, exposé, exposure, ferreting out, revelation, tracking down, uncovering, unearthing, unmasking

detective *n* **1a, 1b** = **investigator**, bizzy, C.I.D. man, constable, cop (*sl.*), copper (*sl.*), dick (*sl., chiefly US*), gumshoe (*US sl.*), private eye, private investigator, sleuth (*inf.*), tec (*sl.*)

detention *n* **1, 2a** = **imprisonment**, confinement, custody, delay, hindrance, holding back, incarceration, keeping in, porridge (*sl.*), quarantine, restraint, withholding
Antonyms *n* acquittal, discharge, emancipation, freedom, liberation, liberty, release

deter *vb* = **discourage**, caution, check, damp, daunt, debar, dissuade, frighten, hinder, inhibit from, intimidate, prevent, prohibit, put off, restrain, stop, talk out of

detergent *n* **1** = **cleaner**, cleanser ◆ *adj* **2** = **cleansing**, abstergent, cleaning, purifying

deteriorate *vb* **1** = **decline**, corrupt, debase, degenerate, degrade, deprave, depreciate, go downhill (*inf.*), go to pot, go to the dogs (*inf.*), impair, injure, lower, slump, spoil, worsen **2** = **disintegrate**, be the worse for wear (*inf.*), break down, crumble, decay, decline, decompose, ebb, fade, fall apart, lapse, retrogress, weaken, wear away
Antonyms *vb* ≠ **decline:** advance, ameliorate, get better, improve

deterioration *n* **1** = **decline**, debasement, degeneration, degradation, depreciation, descent, downturn, drop, fall, retrogression, slump, vitiation, worsening **2** = **disintegration**, atrophy, corrosion, dilapidation, lapse, meltdown (*inf.*)

determinable *adj* **2** = **ascertainable**, answerable, assessable, definable, describable, discoverable

determinate *adj* **1, 2** = **definite**, absolute, certain, conclusive, decided, decisive, defined, definitive, determined, distinct, established, explicit, express, fixed, limited, positive, precise, quantified, settled, specified

determination *n* **2** = **resolution**, backbone, constancy, conviction, dedication, doggedness, drive, firmness, fortitude, indomitability, perseverance, persistence, resoluteness, resolve, single-mindedness, steadfastness, tenacity, willpower **5** = **decision**, conclusion, judgment, purpose, resolve, result, settlement, solution, verdict
Antonyms *n* ≠ **resolution:** doubt, hesitancy, hesitation, indecision, instability, irresolution, vacillation

determine *vb* **1** = **settle**, arbitrate, conclude, decide, end, finish, fix upon, ordain, regulate, terminate **2** = **find out**, ascertain, certify, check, detect, discover, establish, learn, verify, work out **3** = **affect**, condition, control, decide, dictate, direct, govern, impel, impose, incline, induce, influence, lead, modify, regulate, rule, shape **5** = **decide**, choose, elect, establish, fix, make up one's mind, purpose, resolve

determined *adj* = **resolute**, bent on, constant, dogged, firm, fixed, immovable, intent, persevering, persistent, purposeful, set on, single-minded, stalwart, steadfast, strong-minded, strong-willed, tenacious, unflinching, unwavering

determining *adj* **1** = **deciding**, conclusive, critical, crucial, decisive, definitive, essential, final, important, settling

deterrent *n* **1** = **discouragement**, check, curb, defensive measures, determent, disincentive, hindrance, impediment, obstacle, restraint
Antonyms *n* bait, carrot (*inf.*), enticement, incentive, inducement, lure, motivation, spur, stimulus

detest *vb* = **hate**, abhor, abominate, despise, dislike intensely, execrate, feel aversion towards, feel disgust towards, feel hostility towards, feel repugnance towards, loathe, recoil from
Antonyms *vb* adore, cherish, dig (*sl.*), dote on, love, relish

detestable *adj* = **hateful**, abhorred, abominable, accursed, despicable, disgusting, execrable, heinous, loathsome, obnoxious, obscene, odious, offensive, repugnant, repulsive, revolting, shocking, vile, yucky *or* yukky (*sl.*)

detestation *n* **1** = **hatred**, abhorrence, abomination, animosity, animus, antipathy, aversion, disgust, dislike, execration, hostility, loathing, odium, repugnance, revulsion

dethrone *vb* = **depose**, oust, uncrown, unseat

detonate *vb* = **explode**, blast, blow up, discharge, fulminate, set off, touch off, trigger

detonation *n* = **explosion**, bang, blast, blowup, boom, discharge, fulmination, report

detour *n* **1** = **diversion**, bypass, byway, circuitous route, deviation, indirect course, roundabout way

course of action. [C18: from F, from OF *destorner* to divert, turn away, from *des-* DE- + *torner* to TURN]
detox ('di:ˌtɒks) *Inf.* ◆ *n* **1** treatment designed to rid the body of poisonous substances, esp. alcohol and drugs. ◆ *vb* (*intr*) **2** to undergo treatment to rid the body of poisonous substances, esp. alcohol and drugs.
detoxification centre *n* a place that specializes in the treatment of alcoholism or drug addiction.
detoxify (di:'tɒksɪˌfaɪ) *vb* **detoxifies, detoxifying, detoxified.** (*tr*) **1** to remove poison from. **2** to treat (a person) for alcoholism or drug dependency.
▸**deˌtoxifi'cation** *n*
detract ❶ (dɪ'trækt) *vb* **1** (when *intr,* usually foll. by *from*) to take away a part (of); diminish: *her anger detracts from her beauty.* **2** (*tr*) to distract or divert. **3** (*tr*) *Obs.* to belittle or disparage. [C15: from L *dētractus,* from *dētrahere* to pull away, disparage, from DE- + *trahere* to drag]
▸**de'tractive** *adj* ▸**de'tractor** *n* ▸**de'traction** *n*

USAGE NOTE *Detract* is sometimes wrongly used where *distract* is meant: *a noise distracted* (not *detracted*) *my attention.*

detrain (di:'treɪn) *vb* to leave or cause to leave a railway train.
▸**de'trainment** *n*
detriment ❶ ('dɛtrɪmənt) *n* **1** disadvantage or damage. **2** a cause of disadvantage or damage. [C15: from L *dētrīmentum,* a rubbing off, hence damage, from *dēterere,* from DE- + *terere* to rub]
detrimental ❶ (ˌdɛtrɪ'mɛntᵊl) *adj* (when *postpositive,* foll. by *to*) harmful; injurious.
detritus ❶ (dɪ'traɪtəs) *n* **1** a loose mass of stones, silt, etc., worn away from rocks. **2** the organic debris formed from the decay of organisms. [C18: from F, from L: a rubbing away; see DETRIMENT]
▸**de'trital** *adj*
de trop *French.* (də tro) *adj* (*postpositive*) not wanted; in the way. [lit.: of too much]
detumescence (ˌdi:tju'mɛsəns) *n* the subsidence of a swelling. [C17: from L *dētumescere* to cease swelling, from DE- + *tumescere,* from *tumēre* to swell]
deuce[1] (dju:s) *n* **1a** a playing card or dice with two spots. **1b** a throw of two in dice. **2** *Tennis, etc.* a tied score that requires one player to gain two successive points to win the game. [C15: from OF *deus* two, from L *duos,* from *duo* two]
deuce[2] (dju:s) *Inf.* ◆ *interj* **1** an expression of annoyance or frustration. ◆ *n* **2 the deuce.** (intensifier) used in such phrases as **what the deuce, where the deuce,** etc. [C17: prob. special use of DEUCE[1] (in the sense: lowest throw at dice)]
deuced ('dju:sɪd, dju:st) *Brit. inf.* ◆ *adj* **1** (intensifier) confounded: *he's a deuced idiot.* ◆ *adv* **2** (intensifier): *deuced good luck.*
Deus *Latin.* ('deɪʊs) *n* God. [rel. to Gk *Zeus*]
deus ex machina *Latin.* ('deɪʊs ɛks 'mækɪnə) *n* **1** (in ancient Greek and Roman drama) a god introduced into a play to resolve the plot. **2** any unlikely device serving this purpose. [lit.: god out of a machine]
Deut. *Bible. abbrev. for* Deuteronomy.
deuteride ('dju:təˌraɪd) *n* a compound of deuterium and another element.
deuterium (dju:'tɪərɪəm) *n* a stable isotope of hydrogen, occurring in natural hydrogen and in heavy water. Symbol: D or ^{2}H; atomic no.: 1; atomic wt.: 2.014. [C20: NL; see DEUTERO-, -IUM; from the fact that it is the second heaviest hydrogen isotope]
deuterium oxide *n* the compound D_2O; water in which the normal hydrogen atoms are replaced by deuterium atoms. See also **heavy water.**
deutero-, deuto- *or before a vowel* **deuter-, deut-** *combining form.* second or secondary: *deuterium.* [from Gk *deuteros* second]
deuteron ('dju:təˌrɒn) *n* the nucleus of a deuterium atom.
Deutschmark ('dɔɪtʃˌmɑ:k) *or* **Deutsche Mark** ('dɔɪtʃə) *n* the standard monetary unit of Germany.
deutzia ('dju:tsɪə, 'dɔɪtsɪə) *n* any of various shrubs with white, pink, or purplish flowers in early summer. [C19: NL, after J. *Deutz,* 18th-cent. Du. patron of botany]
devalue (di:'vælju:) *or* **devaluate** (di:'vælju:ˌeɪt) *vb* **devalues, devaluing, devalued** *or* **devaluates, devaluating, devaluated. 1** to reduce (a currency) or (of a currency) be reduced in exchange value. **2** (*tr*) to reduce the value of.
▸**deˌvalu'ation** *n*
Devanagari (ˌdeɪvə'nɑ:gərɪ) *n* a syllabic script in which Sanskrit, Hindi, and other modern languages of India are written. [C18: from Sansk.: alphabet of the gods]
devastate ❶ ('dɛvəˌsteɪt) *vb* **devastates, devastating, devastated.** (*tr*) **1** to lay waste or make desolate; ravage; destroy. **2** to confound or overwhelm. [C17: from L *dēvastāre,* from DE- + *vastāre* to ravage; rel. to *vastus* waste, empty]
▸ˌ**devas'tation** *n* ▸'**devasˌtator** *n*
develop ❶ (dɪ'vɛləp) *vb* **1** to come or bring to a later or more advanced or expanded stage; grow or cause to grow gradually. **2** (*tr*) to work out in detail. **3** to disclose or unfold (thoughts, a plot, etc.) gradually or (of thoughts, etc.) to be gradually disclosed or unfolded. **4** to come or bring into existence: *he developed a new faith in God.* **5** (*intr*) to follow as a result of something; ensue: *a row developed after her remarks.* **6** (*tr*) to contract (a disease or illness). **7** (*tr*) to improve the value or change the use of (land). **8** to exploit or make available the natural resources of (a country or region). **9** (*tr*) *Photog.* to treat (exposed film, plate, or paper) with chemical solutions in order to produce a visible image. **10** *Biol.* to progress or cause to progress from simple to complex stages in the growth of an individual or the evolution of a species. **11** (*tr*) to elaborate upon (a musical theme) by varying the melody, key, etc. **12** (*tr*) *Maths.* to expand (a function or expression) in the form of a series. **13** (*tr*) *Geom.* to project or roll out (a surface) onto a plane without stretching or shrinking any element. **14** *Chess.* to bring (a piece) into play from its initial position on the back rank. [C19: from OF *desveloper* to unwrap, from *des-* DIS-[1] + *veloper* to wrap; see ENVELOP]
▸**de'velopable** *adj*
developer (dɪ'vɛləpə) *n* **1** a person or thing that develops something, esp. a person who develops property. **2** Also called: **developing agent.** *Photog.* a chemical used to convert the latent image recorded in the emulsion of a film or paper into a visible image.
developing country *n* a poor or non-industrial country that is seeking to develop its resources by industrialization.
development ❶ (dɪ'vɛləpmənt) *n* **1** the act or process of growing or developing. **2** the product of developing. **3** a fact or event, esp. one that changes a situation. **4** an area of land that has been developed. **5** the section of a movement, usually in sonata form, in which the basic musical themes are developed. **6** *Chess.* the process of developing pieces.
▸**deˌvelop'mental** *adj*
developmental disorder *n Psychiatry.* any condition, such as autism or dyslexia, that appears in childhood and is characterized by delay in the development of one or more psychological functions, such as language skill.
development area *n* (in Britain) an area which has experienced economic depression because of the decline of its main industry or industries, and which is given government assistance to establish new industry.
deviance ('di:vɪəns) *n* **1** Also called: **deviancy.** the act or state of being deviant. **2** *Statistics.* a measure of the degree of fit of a statistical model compared to that of a more complete model.
deviant ❶ ('di:vɪənt) *adj* **1** deviating, as from what is considered acceptable behaviour. ◆ *n* **2** a person whose behaviour, esp. sexual behaviour, deviates from what is considered to be acceptable.
deviate ❶ *vb* ('di:vɪˌeɪt), **deviates, deviating, deviated. 1** (*usually intr*) to differ or cause to differ, as in belief or thought. **2** (*usually intr*) to turn aside or cause to turn aside. **3** (*intr*) *Psychol.* to depart from an accepted standard. ◆ *n, adj* ('di:vɪɪt). **4** another word for **deviant.** [C17: from LL *dēviāre* to turn aside from the direct road, from DE- + *via* road]
▸'**deviˌator** *n* ▸'**deviatory** *adj*

THESAURUS

detract *vb* **1** = **lessen**, derogate, devaluate, diminish, lower, reduce, take away from **2** = **divert**, deflect, distract, shift
Antonyms *vb* ≠ **lessen:** add to, augment, boost, complement, enhance, improve, reinforce, strengthen
detraction *n* **3** = **disparagement**, abuse, aspersion, belittlement, calumny, defamation, denigration, deprecation, innuendo, insinuation, misrepresentation, muckraking, running down, scandalmongering, scurrility, slander, traducement, vituperation
detractor *n* **3** = **slanderer**, backbiter, belittler, defamer, denigrator, disparager, muckraker, scandalmonger, traducer
detriment *n* **1** = **damage**, disadvantage, disservice, harm, hurt, impairment, injury, loss, mischief, prejudice
detrimental *adj* = **damaging**, adverse, baleful, deleterious, destructive, disadvantageous, harmful, inimical, injurious, mischievous, pernicious, prejudicial, unfavourable
Antonyms *adj* advantageous, beneficial, efficacious, favourable, good, helpful, salutary
detritus *n* **1, 2** = **debris**, fragments, litter, remains, rubbish, waste
devastate *vb* **1** = **destroy**, demolish, desolate, despoil, lay waste, level, pillage, plunder, ravage, raze, ruin, sack, spoil, total (*sl.*), trash (*sl.*), waste, wreck **2** = **overwhelm**, chagrin, confound, discomfit, discompose, disconcert, floor (*inf.*), nonplus, overpower, take aback
devastating *adj* **2** = **overwhelming**, caustic, cutting, effective, incisive, keen, mordant, overpowering, ravishing, sardonic, satirical, savage, stunning, trenchant, vitriolic, withering
devastation *n* **1** = **destruction**, demolition, depredation, desolation, havoc, pillage, plunder, ravages, ruin, ruination, spoliation
develop *vb* **1** = **advance**, blossom, cultivate, evolve, flourish, foster, grow, mature, progress, promote, prosper, ripen **2** = **expand**, amplify, augment, broaden, dilate upon, elaborate, enlarge, unfold, work out **4** = **form**, acquire, begin, breed, commence, contract, establish, generate, invent, originate, pick up, start **5** = **result**, be a direct result of, break out, come about, ensue, follow, happen
development *n* **1** = **growth**, advance, advancement, evolution, expansion, improvement, increase, maturity, progress, progression, spread, unfolding, unravelling **3** = **event**, change, circumstance, happening, incident, issue, occurrence, outcome, phenomenon, result, situation, turn of events, upshot
deviant *adj* **1** = **perverted**, aberrant, abnormal, bent, deviate, devious, freaky (*sl.*), heretical, kinky (*sl.*), perverse, queer (*inf., derogatory*), sick (*inf.*), twisted, warped, wayward ◆ *n* **2** = **pervert**, deviate, freak, misfit, odd type, queer (*inf., derogatory*), sicko (*inf.*)
Antonyms *adj* ≠ **perverted:** conventional, normal, orthodox, straight, straightforward
deviate *vb* **2** = **differ**, avert, bend, deflect, depart, digress, diverge, drift, err, meander, part,

deviation Ⓣ (ˌdiːvɪˈeɪʃən) *n* **1** an act or result of deviating. **2** *Statistics.* the difference between an observed value in a series of such values and their arithmetic mean. **3** the error of a compass due to local magnetic disturbances.

device Ⓣ (dɪˈvaɪs) *n* **1** a machine or tool used for a specific task. **2** *Euphemistic.* a bomb. **3** a plan, esp. a clever or evil one; trick. **4** any ornamental pattern or picture, as in embroidery. **5** computer hardware designed for a specific function. **6** a design or figure, used as a heraldic sign, emblem, etc. **7** a particular pattern of words, figures of speech, etc., used in literature to produce an effect on the reader. **8 leave (someone) to his own devices.** to leave (someone) alone to do as he wishes. [C13: from OF *devis* purpose, contrivance & *devise* difference, intention, from *deviser* to divide, control; see DEVISE]

devil Ⓣ (ˈdɛvᵊl) *n* **1** (*often cap.*) *Theol.* the chief spirit of evil and enemy of God, often depicted as a human figure with horns, cloven hoofs, and tail. **2** any subordinate evil spirit. **3** a person or animal regarded as wicked or ill-natured. **4** a person or animal regarded as unfortunate or wretched. **5** a person or animal regarded as daring, mischievous, or energetic. **6** *Inf.* something difficult or annoying. **7** *Christian Science.* an error, lie, or false belief. **8** (in Malaysia) a ghost. **9** a portable furnace or brazier. **10** any of various mechanical devices, such as a machine for making wooden screws or a rag-tearing machine. **11** See **printer's devil. 12** *Law.* (in England) a junior barrister who does work for another in order to gain experience, usually for a half fee. **13** *Meteorol.* a small whirlwind in arid areas that raises dust or sand in a column. **14 between the devil and the deep blue sea.** between equally undesirable alternatives. **15 devil of 15a** *Inf.* (intensifier): *a devil of a fine horse.* **16 give the devil his due.** to acknowledge the talent or success of an unpleasant person. **17 go to the devil. 17a** to fail or become dissipated. **17b** (*interj*) used to express annoyance with the person causing it. **18 (let) the devil take the hindmost.** look after oneself and leave others to their fate. **19 talk** (*or* **speak**) **of the devil!** used when an absent person who has been the subject of conversation appears. **20 the devil!** (intensifier): **20a** used in **what the devil, where the devil,** etc. **20b** an exclamation of anger, surprise, disgust, etc. **21 the devil to pay.** trouble to be faced as a consequence of an action. ◆ *vb* **devils, devilling, devilled** *or US* **devils, deviling, deviled. 22** (*tr*) to prepare (food) by coating with a highly flavoured spiced paste or mixture of condiments before cooking. **23** (*tr*) to tear (rags) with a devil. **24** (*intr*) to serve as a printer's devil. **25** (*intr*) *Chiefly Brit.* to do hackwork, esp. for a lawyer or author. **26** (*tr*) *US inf.* to harass, vex, etc. [OE *dēofol,* from L *diabolus,* from Gk *diabolos* enemy, accuser, slanderer]

devilfish (ˈdɛvᵊlˌfɪʃ) *n, pl* **devilfish** *or* **devilfishes. 1** Also called: **devil ray.** another name for **manta** (the fish). **2** another name for **octopus.**

devilish Ⓣ (ˈdɛvəlɪʃ) *adj* **1** of, resembling, or befitting a devil; diabolic; fiendish. ◆ *adv, adj* **2** *Inf.* (intensifier): *devilish good food.*
▸ **ˈdevilishly** *adv* ▸ **ˈdevilishness** *n*

devil-may-care Ⓣ *adj* careless or reckless; happy-go-lucky: *a devil-may-care attitude.*

devilment Ⓣ (ˈdɛvᵊlmənt) *n* devilish or mischievous conduct.

devilry Ⓣ (ˈdɛvᵊlrɪ) *or* **deviltry** *n, pl* **devilries** *or* **deviltries. 1** reckless or malicious fun or mischief. **2** wickedness. **3** black magic or other forms of diabolism. [C18: from F *diablerie,* from *diable* DEVIL]

devil's advocate *n* **1** a person who advocates an opposing or unpopular view, often for the sake of argument. **2** *RC Church.* the official appointed to put the case against the beatification or canonization of a candidate. [translation of NL *advocātus diabolī*]

devil's coach-horse *n* a large black beetle with large jaws and ferocious habits.

devil's food cake *n Chiefly US & Canad.* a rich chocolate cake.

devious Ⓣ (ˈdiːvɪəs) *adj* **1** not sincere or candid; deceitful. **2** (of a route or course of action) rambling; indirect. **3** going astray; erring. [C16: from L *dēvius* lying to one side of the road, from DE- + *via* road]
▸ **ˈdeviously** *adv* ▸ **ˈdeviousness** *n*

devise Ⓣ (dɪˈvaɪz) *vb* **devises, devising, devised. 1** to work out or plan (something) in one's mind. **2** (*tr*) *Law.* to dispose of (real property) by will. ◆ *n Law.* **3** a disposition of property by will. **4** a will or clause in a will disposing of real property. [C15: from OF *deviser* to divide, apportion, intend, from L *dīvidere* to DIVIDE]
▸ **deˈviser** *n*

devitalize *or* **devitalise** (diːˈvaɪtəˌlaɪz) *vb* **devitalizes, devitalizing, devitalized** *or* **devitalises, devitalising, devitalised.** (*tr*) to lower or destroy the vitality of; make weak or lifeless.
▸ **deˌvitaliˈzation** *or* **deˌvitaliˈsation** *n*

devoid Ⓣ (dɪˈvɔɪd) *adj* (*postpositive;* foll. by *of*) destitute or void (of); free (from). [C15: orig. p.p. of *devoid* (*vb*) to remove, from OF *devoider* from DE- + *voider* to void]

devoirs (dəˈvwɑː) *pl n* (*sometimes sing*) compliments or respects. [C13: from OF: duty, from *devoir* to be obliged to, owe, from L *dēbēre*]

devolution Ⓣ (ˌdiːvəˈluːʃən) *n* **1** a devolving. **2** a passing onwards or downwards from one stage to another. **3** a transfer of authority from a central government to regional governments. [C16: from Med. L *dēvolūtiō* a rolling down, from L *dēvolvere;* see DEVOLVE]
▸ **ˌdevoˈlutionary** *adj* ▸ **ˌdevoˈlutionist** *n, adj*

devolve Ⓣ (dɪˈvɒlv) *vb* **devolves, devolving, devolved. 1** (foll. by *on, upon, to,* etc.) to pass or cause to pass to a successor or substitute, as duties, power, etc. **2** (*intr;* foll. by *on* or *upon*) *Law.* (of an estate, etc.) to pass to another by operation of law. [C15: from L *dēvolvere* to roll down, fall into, from DE- + *volvere* to roll]
▸ **deˈvolvement** *n*

Devonian (dəˈvəunɪən) *adj* **1** of, denoting, or formed in the fourth period of the Palaeozoic era, between the Silurian and Carboniferous periods. **2** of or relating to Devon. ◆ *n* **3 the.** the Devonian period or rock system.

Devonshire split (ˈdɛvᵊnʃə) *n* a kind of yeast bun split open and served with cream or jam.

devoré (dəvɒˈreɪ) *n* a velvet fabric with a raised pattern created by disintegrating some of the pile with chemicals. [from F, p.p. of *dévorer* to devour]

devote Ⓣ (dɪˈvəut) *vb* **devotes, devoting, devoted.** (*tr*) to apply or dedicate (oneself, money, etc.) to some pursuit, cause, etc. [C16: from L *dēvōtus* devoted, solemnly promised, from *dēvovēre* to vow; see DE-, VOW]

devoted Ⓣ (dɪˈvəutɪd) *adj* **1** feeling or demonstrating loyalty or devotion; devout. **2** (*postpositive;* foll. by *to*) dedicated or consecrated.
▸ **deˈvotedly** *adv* ▸ **deˈvotedness** *n*

devotee Ⓣ (ˌdɛvəˈtiː) *n* **1** a person ardently enthusiastic about something, such as a sport or pastime. **2** a zealous follower of a religion.

devotion Ⓣ (dɪˈvəuʃən) *n* **1** (often foll. by *to*) strong attachment (to) or affection (for a cause, person, etc.) marked by dedicated loyalty. **2** religious zeal; piety. **3** (*often pl*) religious observance or prayers.
▸ **deˈvotional** *adj*

devour Ⓣ (dɪˈvauə) *vb* (*tr*) **1** to eat up greedily or voraciously. **2** to waste or destroy; consume. **3** to consume greedily or avidly with the senses

THESAURUS

stray, swerve, turn, turn aside, vary, veer, wander

deviation *n* **1** = **departure,** aberration, alteration, change, deflection, digression, discrepancy, disparity, divergence, fluctuation, inconsistency, irregularity, shift, variance, variation

device *n* **1** = **gadget,** apparatus, appliance, contraption, contrivance, gimmick, gizmo *or* gismo (*sl., chiefly US & Canad.*), implement, instrument, invention, machine, tool, utensil, waldo **3** = **ploy,** artifice, design, dodge, expedient, gambit, improvisation, manoeuvre, plan, project, purpose, ruse, scheme, shift, stratagem, strategy, stunt, trick, wile **4** = **emblem,** badge, colophon, crest, design, figure, insignia, logo, motif, motto, symbol, token

devil *n* **1 the Devil** = **Satan,** Apollyon, archfiend, Beelzebub, Belial, deil, demon, Deuce, Evil One, fiend, Foul Fiend, Lord of the Flies, Lucifer, Mephisto, Mephistopheles, Old Gentleman (*inf.*), Old Harry (*inf.*), Old Nick (*inf.*), Old One, Old Scratch (*inf.*), Prince of Darkness, Tempter, Wicked One **3** = **brute,** beast, demon, fiend, ghoul, monster, ogre, rogue, savage, terror, villain **4** = **person,** beggar, creature, thing, unfortunate, wretch **5** = **scamp,** imp, monkey (*inf.*), pickle (*Brit. inf.*), rascal, rogue, scoundrel

devilish *adj* **1** = **fiendish,** accursed, atrocious, damnable, detestable, diabolic, diabolical, execrable, hellish, infernal, satanic, wicked

devil-may-care *adj* = **happy-go-lucky,** careless, casual, easy-going, flippant, heedless, insouciant, nonchalant, reckless, swaggering, swashbuckling, unconcerned

devilment *n* = **mischief,** devilry, knavery, mischievousness, naughtiness, rascality, roguery, roguishness

devilry *n* **1** = **mischief,** devilment, jiggery-pokery (*inf., chiefly Brit.*), knavery, mischievousness, monkey-business (*inf.*), rascality, roguery **2** = **wickedness,** cruelty, evil, malevolence, malice, vice, viciousness, villainy **3** = **sorcery,** black magic, diablerie, diabolism

devious *adj* **1** = **sly,** calculating, crooked (*inf.*), deceitful, dishonest, double-dealing, evasive, indirect, insidious, insincere, not straightforward, scheming, surreptitious, treacherous, tricky, underhand, wily **2** = **indirect,** circuitous, confusing, crooked, deviating, erratic, excursive, misleading, rambling, roundabout, tortuous, wandering
Antonyms *adj* ≠ **sly:** blunt, candid, direct, downright, forthright, frank, honest, straight, straightforward ≠ **indirect:** blunt, direct, downright, forthright, straight, straightforward, undeviating, unswerving

devise *vb* = **work out,** arrange, conceive, concoct, construct, contrive, design, dream up, form, formulate, frame, imagine, invent, plan, plot, prepare, project, scheme, think up

devoid *adj* = **lacking,** barren, bereft, deficient, denuded, destitute, empty, free from, sans (*arch.*), vacant, void, wanting, without

devolution *n* **1-3** = **decentralization,** delegation

devolve *vb* **1** = **fall upon** *or* **to,** be transferred, commission, consign, delegate, depute, entrust, rest with, transfer **2** *Law* = **be handed down,** alienate, convey

devote *vb* = **dedicate,** allot, apply, appropriate, assign, commit, concern oneself, consecrate, enshrine, give, occupy oneself, pledge, reserve, set apart

devoted *adj* **1** = **dedicated,** ardent, caring, committed, concerned, constant, devout, faithful, fond, loving, loyal, staunch, steadfast, true
Antonyms *adj* disloyal, inconstant, indifferent, uncommitted, undedicated, unfaithful

devotee *n* **1, 2** = **enthusiast,** addict, adherent, admirer, aficionado, buff (*inf.*), disciple, fan, fanatic, follower, supporter, votary

devotion *n* **1** = **dedication,** adherence, affection, allegiance, ardour, commitment, consecration, constancy, earnestness, faithfulness, fervour, fidelity, fondness, intensity, love, loyalty, passion, zeal **2** = **devoutness,** adoration, godliness, holiness, piety, prayer, religiousness, reverence, sanctity, spirituality, worship **3** *often plural* = **prayers,** church service, divine office, religious observance
Antonyms *n* ≠ **dedication:** carelessness, disregard, inattention, indifference, laxity, laxness, neglect, thoughtlessness ≠ **devoutness:** derision, disrespect, impiety, irreverence

devotional *adj* **2** = **religious,** devout, holy, pious, reverential, sacred, solemn, spiritual

devour *vb* **1** = **eat,** bolt, consume, cram, dispatch, gobble, gorge, gulp, guzzle, pig out on

or mind. **4** to engulf or absorb. [C14: from OF, from L *dēvorāre* to gulp down, from DE- + *vorāre;* see VORACIOUS]
▸**de'vourer** *n* ▸**de'vouring** *adj*

devout ❶ (dɪ'vaʊt) *adj* **1** deeply religious; reverent. **2** sincere; earnest; heartfelt. [C13: from OF *devot,* from LL *dēvōtus,* from L: faithful; see DEVOTE]
▸**de'voutly** *adv* ▸**de'voutness** *n*

dew (djuː) *n* **1** drops of water condensed on a cool surface, esp. at night, from vapour in the air. **2** something like this, esp. in freshness: *the dew of youth.* **3** small drops of moisture, such as tears. ◆ *vb* **4** (*tr*) to moisten with or as with dew. [OE *dēaw*]

dewberry ('djuːbərɪ, -brɪ) *n, pl* **dewberries. 1** any trailing bramble having blue-black fruits. **2** the fruit of any such plant.

dewclaw ('djuːˌklɔː) *n* **1** a nonfunctional claw in dogs. **2** an analogous rudimentary hoof in deer, goats, etc.
▸**'dewˌclawed** *adj*

dewdrop ('djuːˌdrɒp) *n* a drop of dew.

Dewey Decimal System ('djuːɪ) *n* a system of library book classification with ten main subject classes. Also called: **decimal classification.** [C19: after Melvil *Dewey* (1851–1931), US educator]

dewlap ('djuːˌlæp) *n* **1** a loose fold of skin hanging from beneath the throat in cattle, dogs, etc. **2** loose skin on an elderly person's throat. [C14 *dewlappe,* from DEW (prob. from an earlier form of different meaning) + LAP[1] (from OE *læppa* hanging flap), ?from ON]

DEW line (djuː) *n acronym for* distant early warning line, a network of radar stations situated mainly in Arctic regions of North America.

dew point *n* the temperature at which dew begins to form.

dew pond *n* a shallow pond, usually man-made, that is kept full by dew and mist.

dewy ('djuːɪ) *adj* **dewier, dewiest. 1** moist with or as with dew. **2** of or resembling dew. **3** *Poetic.* suggesting, falling, or refreshing like dew: *dewy sleep.*
▸**'dewily** *adv* ▸**'dewiness** *n*

dexter ('dɛkstə) *adj* **1** *Arch.* of or located on the right side. **2** (*usually postpositive*) *Heraldry.* of, on, or starting from the right side of a shield from the bearer's point of view and therefore on the spectator's left. ◆ Cf. **sinister.** [C16: from L; cf. Gk *dexios* on the right hand]

dexterity ❶ (dɛk'stɛrɪtɪ) *n* **1** physical, esp. manual, skill or nimbleness. **2** mental skill or adroitness. [C16: from L *dexteritās* aptness, readiness; see DEXTER]

dexterous ❶ ('dɛkstrəs) *adj* possessing or done with dexterity.
▸**'dexterously** *adv* ▸**'dexterousness** *n*

dextral ('dɛkstrəl) *adj* **1** of or located on the right side, esp. of the body. **2** of a person who prefers to use his right foot, hand, or eye; right-handed. **3** (of shells) coiling in an anticlockwise direction from the apex.
▸**dextrality** (dɛk'strælɪtɪ) *n* ▸**'dextrally** *adv*

dextran ('dɛkstrən) *n Biochem.* a chainlike polymer of glucose produced by the action of bacteria on sucrose: used as a substitute for plasma in blood transfusions. [C19: from DEXTRO- + -AN]

dextrin ('dɛkstrɪn) *or* **dextrine** ('dɛkstrɪn, -triːn) *n* any of a group of sticky substances obtained from starch: used as thickening agents in foods and as gums. [C19: from F *dextrine;* see DEXTRO-, -IN]

dextro- *or before a vowel* **dextr-** *combining form.* on or towards the right: *dextrorotation.* [from L, from *dexter* on the right side]

dextrorotation (ˌdɛkstrəʊrəʊ'teɪʃən) *n* a rotation to the right; clockwise rotation, esp. of the plane of polarization of plane-polarized light. Cf. **laevorotation.**
▸**dextrorotatory** (ˌdɛkstrəʊ'rəʊtətərɪ, -trɪ) *or* ˌ**dextro'rotary** *adj*

dextrorse ('dɛkstrɔːs) *or* **dextrorsal** (dɛk'strɔːsᵊl) *adj* (of some climbing plants) growing upwards in a spiral from left to right or anticlockwise. [C19: from L *dextrorsum* towards the right, from DEXTRO- + *vorsus,* var. of *versus,* from *vertere* to turn]
▸**'dextrorsely** *adv*

dextrose ('dɛkstrəʊz, -trəʊs) *n* a glucose occurring widely in fruit, honey, and in the blood and tissue of animals. Formula: $C_6H_{12}O_6$. Also called: **grape sugar, dextroglucose.**

dextrous ('dɛkstrəs) *adj* a variant spelling of **dexterous.**
▸**'dextrously** *adv* ▸**'dextrousness** *n*

DF *abbrev. for* Defender of the Faith.

D/F *or* **DF** *Telecomm.* ◆ *abbrev. for:* **1** direction finder. **2** direction finding.

DFC *abbrev. for* Distinguished Flying Cross.

DfEE (in Britain) *abbrev. for* Department for Education and Employment.

DFM *abbrev. for* Distinguished Flying Medal.

dg *symbol for* decigram.

DH (in Britain) *abbrev. for* Department of Health.

dhal, dal, *or* **dholl** (dɑːl) *n* **1** a tropical African and Asian shrub cultivated for its nutritious pealike seeds. **2** the seed of this shrub. **3** a curry made from lentils or other pulses. [C17: from Hindi, from Sansk. *dal* to split]

dharma ('dɑːmə) *n* **1** *Hinduism.* social custom regarded as a religious and moral duty. **2** *Hinduism.* **2a** the essential principle of the cosmos; natural law. **2b** conduct that conforms with this. **3** *Buddhism.* ideal truth. [Sansk.: habit, usage, law]

dhobi ('dəʊbɪ) *n, pl* **dhobis.** (in India, E Africa, etc.) a washerman. [C19: from Hindi, from *dhōb* washing]

dhoti ('dəʊtɪ), **dhooti, dhootie,** *or* **dhuti** ('duːtɪ) *n, pl* **dhotis.** a long loincloth worn by men in India. [C17: from Hindi]

dhow (daʊ) *n* a lateen-rigged coastal Arab sailing vessel. [C19: from Ar.]

DHSS (formerly, in Britain) *abbrev. for* Department of Health and Social Security.

DI *abbrev. for* donor insemination.

di. *or* **dia.** *abbrev. for* diameter.

di-[1] *prefix* **1** twice; two; double: *dicotyledon.* **2a** containing two specified atoms or groups of atoms: *carbon dioxide.* **2b** a nontechnical equivalent of **bi-** (sense 5). [via L from Gk, from *dis* twice, double, rel. to *duo* two. Cf. BI-]

di-[2] *combining form.* a variant of **dia-** before a vowel: *dioptre.*

dia- *or* **di-** *prefix* **1** through or during: *diachronic.* **2** across: *diactinic.* **3** apart: *diacritic.* [from Gk *dia* through, between, across, by]

diabetes (ˌdaɪə'biːtɪs, -tiːz) *n* any of various disorders, esp. diabetes mellitus, characterized by excessive thirst and excretion of an abnormally large amount of urine. [C16: from L: siphon, from Gk, lit.: a passing through]

diabetes mellitus (mə'laɪtəs) *n* a form of diabetes, caused by a deficiency of insulin, in which the body is unable to metabolize sugars. [C18: NL, lit.: honey-sweet diabetes]

diabetic (ˌdaɪə'bɛtɪk) *adj* **1** of, relating to, or having diabetes. **2** for the use of diabetics. ◆ *n* **3** a person who has diabetes.

diablerie (dɪ'ɑːblərɪ) *n* **1** magic or witchcraft connected with devils. **2** esoteric knowledge of devils. **3** devilry; mischief. [C18: from OF, from *diable* devil, from L *diabolus;* see DEVIL]

diabolic ❶ (ˌdaɪə'bɒlɪk) *adj* **1** of the devil; satanic. **2** extremely cruel or wicked; fiendish. **3** very difficult or unpleasant. [C14: from LL, from Gk *diabolikos,* from *diabolos* DEVIL]
▸ˌ**dia'bolically** *adv* ▸ˌ**dia'bolicalness** *n*

diabolical ❶ (ˌdaɪə'bɒlɪkᵊl) *adj Inf.* **1** excruciatingly bad. **2** (intensifier): *a diabolical liberty.*
▸ˌ**dia'bolically** *adv* ▸ˌ**dia'bolicalness** *n*

diabolism (daɪ'æbəˌlɪzəm) *n* **1a** witchcraft or sorcery. **1b** worship of devils or beliefs concerning them. **2** character or conduct that is devilish.
▸**di'abolist** *n*

diabolo (dɪ'æbəˌləʊ) *n, pl* **diabolos. 1** a game in which one throws and catches a top on a cord fastened to two sticks. **2** the top used in this. [C20: from It., lit.: devil]

diachronic (ˌdaɪə'krɒnɪk) *adj* of, relating to, or studying the development of a phenomenon through time; historical. Cf. **synchronic.** [C19: from DIA- + Gk *khronos* time]

diacidic (ˌdaɪə'sɪdɪk) *adj* (of a base) capable of neutralizing two protons with one of its molecules. Also: **diacid.**

diaconal (daɪ'ækənᵊl) *adj* of or associated with a deacon or the diaconate. [C17: from LL *diāconālis,* from *diāconus* DEACON]

diaconate (daɪ'ækənɪt, -ˌneɪt) *n* the office, sacramental status, or period of office of a deacon. [C17: from LL *diāconātus;* see DEACON]

diacritic (ˌdaɪə'krɪtɪk) *n* **1** a sign placed above or below a character or letter to indicate that it has a different phonetic value, is stressed, or for some other reason. ◆ *adj* **2** another word for **diacritical.** [C17: from Gk *diakritikos* serving to distinguish, from *diakrinein,* from DIA- + *krinein* to separate]

diacritical (ˌdaɪə'krɪtɪkᵊl) *adj* **1** of or relating to a diacritic. **2** showing up a distinction.

diadem ❶ ('daɪəˌdɛm) *n* **1** a royal crown, esp. a light jewelled circlet. **2** royal dignity or power. [C13: from L, from Gk: fillet, royal headdress, from *diadein,* from DIA- + *dein* to bind]

diaeresis *or* **dieresis** (daɪ'ɛrɪsɪs) *n, pl* **diaereses** *or* **diereses** (-ˌsiːz). **1** the mark ¨ placed over the second of two adjacent vowels to indicate that

THESAURUS

(*sl.*), polish off (*inf.*), stuff, swallow, wolf **2** = **destroy**, annihilate, consume, ravage, spend, waste, wipe out **3** = **enjoy**, absorb, appreciate, be engrossed by, be preoccupied, delight in, drink in, feast on, go through, read compulsively *or* voraciously, relish, revel in, take in

devouring *adj* **3** = **overwhelming**, consuming, excessive, flaming, insatiable, intense, passionate, powerful

devout *adj* **1** = **religious**, godly, holy, orthodox, pious, prayerful, pure, reverent, saintly **2** = **sincere**, ardent, deep, devoted, earnest, fervent, genuine, heartfelt, intense, passionate, profound, serious, zealous

Antonyms *adj* ≠ **religious:** impious, irreligious, irreverent, sacrilegious ≠ **sincere:** indifferent, passive

devoutly *adv* **2** = **with all one's heart**, fervently, heart and soul, profoundly, sincerely

dexterity *n* **1** = **skill**, adroitness, artistry, craft, deftness, effortlessness, expertise, facility, finesse, handiness, knack, mastery, neatness, nimbleness, proficiency, smoothness, touch **2** = **cleverness**, ability, address, adroitness, aptitude, aptness, art, expertness, ingenuity, readiness, skilfulness, tact

Antonyms *n* clumsiness, gaucheness, inability, incapacity, incompetence, ineptitude, uselessness

dexterous *adj* = **skilful**, able, active, acute, adept, adroit, agile, apt, clever, deft, expert, handy, ingenious, masterly, neat, nimble, nimble-fingered, proficient, prompt, quick

diabolic *adj* **1** = **satanic**, demoniac, demonic, devilish, fiendish, hellish, infernal **2** = **wicked**, atrocious, cruel, evil, fiendish, monstrous, nefarious, vicious, villainous

diabolical *adj Informal* = **dreadful**, abysmal, appalling, atrocious, damnable, difficult, disastrous, excruciating, fiendish, from hell (*inf.*), hellacious (*US sl.*), hellish, nasty, outrageous, shocking, terrible, tricky, unpleasant, vile

diadem *n* **1** = **coronet**, circlet, crown, tiara

it is to be pronounced separately, as in some spellings of *coöperate, naïve,* etc. **2** this mark used for any other purpose, such as to indicate a special pronunciation for a particular vowel. **3** a pause in a line of verse when the end of a foot coincides with the end of a word. [C17: from L, from Gk: a division, from *diairein,* from DIA- + *hairein* to take; cf. HERESY]
▸**diaeretic** *or* **dieretic** (ˌdaɪəˈrɛtɪk) *adj*

diag. *abbrev. for* diagram.

diagnose ⓣ (ˈdaɪəgˌnəʊz) *vb* **diagnoses, diagnosing, diagnosed. 1** to determine by diagnosis. **2** (*tr*) to examine (a person or thing), as for a disease.
▸ˌ**diagˈnosable** *adj*

diagnosis ⓣ (ˌdaɪəgˈnəʊsɪs) *n, pl* **diagnoses** (-siːz). **1a** the identification of diseases from the examination of symptoms. **1b** an opinion so reached. **2a** thorough analysis of facts or problems in order to gain understanding. **2b** an opinion reached through such analysis. [C17: NL, from Gk: a distinguishing, from *diagignōskein,* from *gignōskein* to perceive, KNOW]
▸**diagnostic** (ˌdaɪəgˈnɒstɪk) *adj*

diagonal ⓣ (daɪˈægənᵊl) *adj* **1** *Maths.* connecting any two vertices that in a polygon are not adjacent and in a polyhedron are not in the same face. **2** slanting; oblique. **3** marked with slanting lines or patterns. ◆ *n* **4** a diagonal line, plane, or pattern. **5** something put, set, or drawn obliquely. [C16: from L, from Gk *diagōnios,* from DIA- + *gōnia* angle]
▸**diˈagonally** *adv*

diagram ⓣ (ˈdaɪəˌgræm) *n* **1** a sketch or plan demonstrating the form or workings of something. **2** *Maths.* a pictorial representation of a quantity or of a relationship. ◆ *vb* **diagrams, diagramming, diagrammed** *or US* **diagrams, diagraming, diagramed. 3** to show in or as if in a diagram. [C17: from L, from Gk, from *diagraphein,* from *graphein* to write]
▸**diagrammatic** (ˌdaɪəgrəˈmætɪk) *adj*

dial (ˈdaɪəl) *n* **1** the face of a watch, clock, etc., marked with divisions representing units of time. **2** the graduated disc of various measuring instruments. **3a** the control on a radio or television set used to change the station or channel. **3b** the panel on a radio on which the frequency, wavelength, or station is indicated. **4** a numbered disc on a telephone that is rotated a set distance for each digit of a number being called. **5** *Brit.* a slang word for **face.** ◆ *vb* **dials, dialling, dialled** *or US* **dials, dialing, dialed. 6** to try to establish a telephone connection with (a subscriber) by operating the dial or buttons on a telephone. **7** (*tr*) to indicate, measure, or operate with a dial. [C14: from Med. L *diālis* daily, from L *diēs* day]
▸ˈ**dialler** *or US* ˈ**dialer** *n*

dial. *abbrev. for* dialect(al).

dialect ⓣ (ˈdaɪəˌlɛkt) *n* **a** a form of a language spoken in a particular geographical area or by members of a particular social class or occupational group, distinguished by its vocabulary, grammar, and pronunciation. **b** a form of a language that is considered inferior. [C16: from L, from Gk *dialektos* speech, dialect, discourse, from *dialegesthai* to converse, from *legein* to talk, speak]
▸ˌ**diaˈlectal** *adj*

dialectic ⓣ (ˌdaɪəˈlɛktɪk) *n* **1** disputation or debate, esp. when intended to resolve differences between two views. **2** logical argumentation. **3** a variant of **dialectics** (sense 1). **4** *Philosophy.* an interpretive method used by Hegel in which contradictions are resolved at a higher level of truth (synthesis). ◆ *adj* **5** of or relating to logical disputation. [C17: from L, from Gk *dialektikē* (*tekhnē*) (the art) of argument; see DIALECT]
▸ˌ**dialecˈtician** *n*

dialectical (ˌdaɪəˈlɛktɪkᵊl) *adj* of or relating to dialectic or dialectics.
▸ˌ**diaˈlectically** *adv*

dialectical materialism *n* the economic, political, and philosophical system of Marx and Engels that combines traditional materialism and Hegelian dialectic.

dialectics (ˌdaɪəˈlɛktɪks) *n* (*functioning as pl or* (*sometimes*) *sing*) **1** the study of reasoning. **2** a particular methodology or system. **3** the application of the Hegelian dialectic or the rationale of dialectical materialism.

dialling code *n* a sequence of numbers which is dialled for connection with another exchange before an individual subscriber's telephone number is dialled.

dialling tone *or US & Canad.* **dial tone** *n* a continuous sound, either purring or high-pitched, heard over a telephone indicating that a number can be dialled.

dialogue ⓣ *or US* (*often*) **dialog** (ˈdaɪəˌlɒg) *n* **1** conversation between two or more people. **2** an exchange of opinions; discussion. **3** the lines spoken by characters in drama or fiction. **4** a passage of conversation in a literary or dramatic work. **5** a literary composition in the form of a dialogue. **6** a political discussion between representatives of two nations or groups. [C13: from OF, from L, from Gk, from *dialegesthai;* see DIALECT]

dialyse *or US* **dialyze** (ˈdaɪəˌlaɪz) *vb* **dialyses, dialysing, dialysed** *or US* **dialyzes, dialyzing, dialyzed.** (*tr*) to separate by dialysis.
▸ˌ**dialyˈsation** *or US* ˌ**dialyˈzation** *n*

dialyser *or US* **dialyzer** (ˈdaɪəˌlaɪzə) *n* a machine that performs dialysis, esp. one that removes impurities from the blood of patients with malfunctioning kidneys; kidney machine.

dialysis (daɪˈælɪsɪs) *n, pl* **dialyses** (-ˌsiːz). **1** the separation of small molecules from large molecules and colloids in a solution by the selective diffusion of the small molecules through a semipermeable membrane. **2** *Med.* the filtering of blood through a semipermeable membrane to remove waste products. [C16: from LL: a separation, from Gk *dialusis,* from *dialuein* to tear apart, dissolve, from *luein* to loosen]
▸**dialytic** (ˌdaɪəˈlɪtɪk) *adj*

diam. *abbrev. for* diameter.

diamagnetic (ˌdaɪəmægˈnɛtɪk) *adj* of, exhibiting, or concerned with diamagnetism.

diamagnetism (ˌdaɪəˈmægnɪˌtɪzəm) *n* the phenomenon exhibited by substances that have a relative permeability less than unity and a negative susceptibility; caused by the orbital motion of electrons in the atoms of the material.

diamanté (ˌdaɪəˈmæntɪ) *adj* **1** decorated with glittering ornaments, such as sequins. ◆ *n* **2** a fabric so covered. [C20: from F, from *diamanter* to adorn with diamonds]

diameter (daɪˈæmɪtə) *n* **1a** a straight line connecting the centre of a circle, sphere, etc. with two points on the perimeter or surface. **1b** the length of such a line. **2** the thickness of something, esp. with circular cross section. [C14: from Med. L, from Gk: diameter, diagonal, from DIA- + *metron* measure]

diametric ⓣ (ˌdaɪəˈmɛtrɪk) *or* **diametrical** *adj* **1** Also: **diametral.** of, related to, or along a diameter. **2** completely opposed.

diametrically ⓣ (ˌdaɪəˈmɛtrɪkəlɪ) *adv* completely; utterly (esp. in **diametrically opposed**).

diamond (ˈdaɪəmənd) *n* **1a** a usually colourless exceptionally hard form of carbon in cubic crystalline form. It is used as a precious stone and for industrial cutting or abrading. **1b** (*as modifier*): *a diamond ring.* **2** *Geom.* a figure having four sides of equal length forming two acute angles and two obtuse angles; rhombus. **3a** a red lozenge-shaped symbol on a playing card. **3b** a card with one or more of these symbols or (*when pl*) the suit of cards so marked. **4** *Baseball.* **4a** the whole playing field. **4b** the square formed by the four bases. ◆ *vb* **5** (*tr*) to decorate with or as with diamonds. [C13: from OF *diamant,* from Med. L *diamas,* from L *adamas* the hardest iron or steel, diamond; see ADAMANT]
▸**diamantine** (ˌdaɪəˈmæntaɪn) *adj*

diamond anniversary *n* a 60th, or occasionally 75th, anniversary.

diamondback (ˈdaɪəməndˌbæk) *n* **1** Also called: **diamondback terrapin** *or* **turtle.** any edible North American terrapin having diamond-shaped markings on the shell. **2** a large North American rattlesnake having diamond-shaped markings.

diamond wedding *n* the 60th, or occasionally the 75th, anniversary of a marriage.

diamorphine (ˌdaɪəˈmɔːfiːn) *n* a technical name for **heroin.**

dianthus (daɪˈænθəs) *n, pl* **dianthuses.** any Eurasian plant of the widely cultivated genus *Dianthus,* such as the carnation, pink, and sweet william. [C19: NL, from Gk DI-[1] + *anthos* flower]

diapason (ˌdaɪəˈpeɪzᵊn) *n Music.* **1** either of two stops (**open** and **stopped diapason**) found throughout the compass of a pipe organ that give it its characteristic tone colour. **2** the compass of an instrument or voice. **3a** a standard pitch used for tuning. **3b** a tuning fork or pitch pipe. **4** (in classical Greece) an octave. [C14: from L: the whole octave, from Gk: (*hē*) *dia pasōn* (*khordōn sumphōnia*) (concord) through all (the notes)]

diapause (ˈdaɪəˌpɔːz) *n* a period of suspended development and growth accompanied by decreased metabolism in insects and some other animals. [C19: from Gk *diapausis* pause, from *diapauein* to pause, bring to an end, from DIA- + *pauein* to stop]

diaper (ˈdaɪəpə) *n* **1** the US and Canad. word for **nappy**[1]. **2a** a fabric having a pattern of a small repeating design, esp. diamonds. **2b** such a pattern, used as decoration. ◆ *vb* **3** (*tr*) to decorate with such a pat-

THESAURUS

diagnose *vb* **1** = **identify,** analyse, determine, distinguish, interpret, investigate, pinpoint, pronounce, put one's finger on, recognize

diagnosis *n* **1a, 2a** = **examination,** analysis, investigation, scrutiny **1b, 2b** = **opinion,** conclusion, interpretation, pronouncement

diagnostic *adj* **1, 2** = **symptomatic,** demonstrative, distinctive, distinguishing, idiosyncratic, indicative, particular, peculiar, recognizable

diagonal *adj* **2** = **slanting,** angled, cater-cornered (*US inf.*), cornerways, cross, crossways, crosswise, oblique

diagonally *adv* **2** = **aslant,** at an angle, cornerwise, crosswise, obliquely, on the bias, on the cross

diagram *n* **1** = **plan,** chart, drawing, figure, graph, layout, outline, representation, sketch

dialect *n* = **language,** accent, brogue, idiom, jargon, lingo (*inf.*), localism, patois, pronunciation, provincialism, speech, tongue, vernacular

dialectal *n* = **regional,** dialect, idiomatic, local, nonstandard, restricted, vernacular

dialectic *n* **1, 2** = **debate,** argumentation, contention, discussion, disputation, logic, polemics, ratiocination, reasoning ◆ *adj* **5** = **logical,** analytic, argumentative, dialectical, polemical, rational, rationalistic

dialogue *n* **1, 2** = **conversation,** colloquy, communication, confabulation, conference, converse, discourse, discussion, duologue, exchange, interlocution **3** = **lines,** conversation, script, spoken part

diametric *adj* **2** = **opposed,** antipodal, antithetical, conflicting, contrary, contrasting, counter, opposite, poles apart

diametrically *adv* = **completely,** absolutely, entirely, totally, utterly

tern. [C14: from OF *diaspre,* from Med. L *diasprus* made of diaper, from Med. Gk *diaspros* pure white, from DIA- + *aspros* white, shining]

diaphanous ❶ (daɪ'æfənəs) *adj* (usually of fabrics) fine and translucent. [C17: from Med. L, from Gk *diaphanēs* transparent, from DIA- + *phainein* to show]
▸**di'aphanously** *adv*

diaphoresis (ˌdaɪəfə'riːsɪs) *n* perspiration, esp. when perceptible and excessive. [C17: via LL from Gk, from *diaphorein* to disperse by perspiration, from DIA- + *phorein* to carry]

diaphoretic (ˌdaɪəfə'retɪk) *adj* **1** relating to or causing perspiration. ◆ *n* **2** a diaphoretic drug.

diaphragm ('daɪəˌfræm) *n* **1** *Anat.* any separating membrane, esp. the muscular partition that separates the abdominal and thoracic cavities in mammals. **2** another name for **cap** (sense 11). **3** any thin dividing membrane. **4** Also called: **stop.** a device to control the amount of light entering an optical instrument, such as a camera. **5** a thin vibrating disc used to convert sound signals to electrical signals or vice versa in telephones, etc. [C17: from LL, from Gk, from DIA- + *phragma* fence]
▸**diaphragmatic** (ˌdaɪəfræg'mætɪk) *adj*

diapositive (ˌdaɪə'pɒzɪtɪv) *n* a positive transparency; slide.

diarist ('daɪərɪst) *n* a person who writes a diary, esp. one that is subsequently published.

diarrhoea ❶ *or esp. US* **diarrhea** (ˌdaɪə'rɪə) *n* frequent and copious discharge of abnormally liquid faeces. [C16: from LL, from Gk, from *diarrhein,* from DIA- + *rhein* to flow]
▸ˌ**diar'rhoeal,** ˌ**diar'rhoeic** *or esp. US* ˌ**diar'rheal,** ˌ**diar'rheic** *adj*

diary ❶ ('daɪərɪ) *n, pl* **diaries. 1** a personal record of daily events, appointments, observations, etc. **2** a book for this. [C16: from L *diārium* daily allocation of food or money, journal, from *diēs* day]

Diaspora (daɪ'æspərə) *n* **1a** the dispersion of the Jews after the Babylonian and Roman conquests of Palestine. **1b** the Jewish people and communities outside Israel. **2** (*often not cap.*) a dispersion, as of people originally belonging to one nation. [C19: from Gk: a scattering, from *diaspeirein,* from DIA- + *speirein* to scatter, sow]

diastalsis (ˌdaɪə'stælsɪs) *n, pl* **diastalses** (-siːz). *Physiol.* a downward wave of contraction occurring in the intestine during digestion. [C20: NL, from DIA- + (PERI)STALSIS]
▸ˌ**dia'staltic** *adj*

diastase ('daɪəˌsteɪs, -ˌsteɪz) *n* any of a group of enzymes that hydrolyse starch to maltose. They are present in germinated barley and in the pancreas. [C19: from F, from Gk *diastasis* a separation]
▸ˌ**dia'stasic** *adj*

diastole (daɪ'æstəlɪ) *n* the dilation of the chambers of the heart that follows each contraction, during which they refill with blood. Cf. **systole.** [C16: via LL from Gk, from *diastellein* to expand, from DIA- + *stellein* to place, bring together, make ready]
▸**diastolic** (ˌdaɪə'stɒlɪk) *adj*

diastrophism (daɪ'æstrəˌfɪzəm) *n* the process of movement of the earth's crust that gives rise to mountains, continents, and other large-scale features. [C19: from Gk *diastrophē* a twisting; see DIA-, STROPHE]
▸**diastrophic** (ˌdaɪə'strɒfɪk) *adj*

diathermancy (ˌdaɪə'θɜːmənsɪ) *n, pl* **diathermancies.** the property of transmitting infrared radiation. [C19: from F, from DIA- + Gk *thermansis* heating, from *thermos* hot]
▸ˌ**dia'thermanous** *adj*

diathermy ('daɪəˌθɜːmɪ) *or* **diathermia** (ˌdaɪə'θɜːmɪə) *n* local heating of the body tissues with an electric current for medical purposes. [C20: from NL, from DIA- + Gk *thermē* heat]

diatom ('daɪətəm) *n* a microscopic unicellular alga having a cell wall impregnated with silica. [C19: from NL, from Gk *diatomos* cut in two, from DIA- + *temnein* to cut]

diatomaceous (ˌdaɪətə'meɪʃəs) *adj* of or containing diatoms or their fossil remains.

diatomic (ˌdaɪə'tɒmɪk) *adj* (of a compound or molecule) containing two atoms.

diatomite (daɪ'ætəˌmaɪt) *n* a soft whitish rock consisting of the siliceous remains of diatoms.

diatonic (ˌdaɪə'tɒnɪk) *adj* **1** of, relating to, or based upon any scale of five tones and two semitones produced by playing the white keys of a keyboard instrument. **2** not involving the sharpening or flattening of the notes of the major or minor scale nor the use of such notes as modified by accidentals. [C16: from LL, from Gk, from *diatonos* extending, from DIA- + *teinein* to stretch]

diatonic scale *n Music.* the major and minor scales, made up of both tones and semitones.

diatribe ❶ ('daɪəˌtraɪb) *n* a bitter or violent criticism or attack. [C16: from L *diatriba* learned debate, from Gk *diatribē* discourse, pastime, from *diatribein* to while away, from DIA- + *tribein* to rub]

diazepam (daɪ'æzəˌpæm) *n* a chemical compound used as a tranquillizer and muscle relaxant. [C20: from DI-[1] + *azo-* + *ep*(*oxide*) + *-am*]

diazo (daɪ'eɪzəʊ) *adj* **1** of, consisting of, or containing the divalent group, =N:N, or the divalent group, -N:N-. **2** of the reproduction of documents using the bleaching action of ultraviolet radiation on diazonium salts. ◆ *n, pl* **diazos** *or* **diazoes. 3** a document produced by this method.

diazonium (ˌdaɪə'zəʊnɪəm) *n* (*modifier*) of, consisting of, or containing the group ArN:N–, where Ar is an aryl group: *a diazonium salt.*

dibasic (daɪ'beɪsɪk) *adj* **1** (of an acid) containing two acidic hydrogen atoms. **2** (of a salt) derived by replacing two acidic hydrogen atoms.
▸**dibasicity** (ˌdaɪbeɪ'sɪsɪtɪ) *n*

dibble ('dɪbᵊl) *n* **1** Also: **dibber.** a small hand tool used to make holes in the ground for bulbs, seeds, or roots. ◆ *vb* **dibbles, dibbling, dibbled. 2** to make a hole in (the ground) with a dibble. **3** to plant (seeds, etc.) with a dibble. [C15: from ?]

dibs (dɪbz) *pl n* **1** another word for **jacks. 2** *Sl.* money. **3** (foll. by *on*) *Inf.* rights (to) or claims (on): used mainly by children. [C18: from *dibstones* game played with knucklebones or pebbles, prob. from *dib* to tap]

dice (daɪs) *pl n* **1** cubes of wood, plastic, etc., each of whose sides has a different number of spots (1 to 6), used in games of chance. **2** (*functioning as sing*) Also called: **die.** one of these cubes. **3** small cubes as of vegetables, meat, etc. **4 no dice.** *Sl., chiefly US & Canad.* an expression of refusal. ◆ *vb* **dices, dicing, diced. 5** to cut (food, etc.) into small cubes. **6** (*intr*) to gamble or play with dice. **7** (*intr*) to take a chance or risk (esp. in **dice with death**). **8** (*tr*) *Austral. inf.* to abandon or reject. [C14: pl of DIE[2]]
▸'**dicer** *n*

dicey ❶ ('daɪsɪ) *adj* **dicier, diciest.** *Inf., chiefly Brit.* difficult or dangerous; risky; tricky.

dichloride (daɪ'klɔːraɪd) *n* a compound in which two atoms of chlorine are combined with another atom or group. Also called: **bichloride.**

dichlorodiphenyltrichloroethane (daɪˌklɔːrəʊdaɪˌfiːnaɪltraɪˌklɔːrəʊ'iːθeɪn) *n* the full name for **DDT.**

dichloromethane (daɪˌklɔːrəʊ'miːθeɪn) *n* a noxious colourless liquid widely used as a solvent, e.g. in paint strippers. Formula: CH_2Cl_2. Traditional name: **methylene dichloride.**

dichotomy ❶ (daɪ'kɒtəmɪ) *n, pl* **dichotomies. 1** division into two parts or classifications, esp. when they are sharply distinguished or opposed. **2** *Bot.* a simple method of branching by repeated division into two equal parts.
▸**di'chotomous** *adj*

> **USAGE NOTE** *Dichotomy* should always refer to a division of some kind into two groups. It is sometimes used to refer to a puzzling situation which seems to involve a contradiction, but this use is generally thought to be incorrect.

dichroism ('daɪkrəʊˌɪzəm) *n* a property of a uniaxial crystal of showing a difference in colour when viewed along two different axes (in transmitted white light). Also called: **dichromaticism.** See also **pleochroism.**
▸**di'chroic** *adj*

dichromate (daɪ'krəʊmeɪt) *n* any salt or ester of dichromic acid. Also called: **bichromate.**

dichromatic (ˌdaɪkrəʊ'mætɪk) *adj* **1** Also: **dichroic.** having two colours. **2** (of animal species) having two different colour varieties. **3** able to perceive only two colours (and mixes of them).
▸**dichromatism** (daɪ'krəʊməˌtɪzəm) *n*

dichromic (daɪ'krəʊmɪk) *adj* of or involving only two colours; dichromatic.

dick (dɪk) *n Sl.* **1** *Brit.* a fellow or person. **2 clever dick.** *Brit.* an opinionated person; know-all. **3** a taboo word for **penis.** [C16 (meaning: fellow): from *Dick,* familiar form of *Richard,* applied to any fellow, lad, etc.; hence, C19: penis]

dickens ('dɪkɪnz) *n Inf.* a euphemistic word for **devil** (used as intensifier in **what the dickens**). [C16: from the name *Dickens*]

Dickensian (dɪ'kenzɪən) *adj* **1** of Charles Dickens (1812–70), English novelist, or his novels. **2a** denoting poverty, distress, and exploitation as depicted in the novels of Dickens. **2b** grotesquely comic, as some of the characters of Dickens.

dicker ('dɪkə) *vb* **1** to trade (goods) by bargaining; barter. ◆ *n* **2** a petty bargain or barter. [C12: ult. from L *decuria* company of ten, from *decem* ten]

dickhead ('dɪkˌhed) *n Sl.* a stupid or despicable man or boy. [C20: from DICK (in the sense: penis) + HEAD]

dicky[1] *or* **dickey** ('dɪkɪ) *n, pl* **dickies** *or* **dickeys. 1** a false blouse or shirt front. **2** Also called: **dicky bow.** *Brit.* a bow tie. **3** Also called: **dicky-bird, dickeybird.** a child's word for a bird. **4** a folding outside seat at the rear of some early cars. [C18 (in the sense: shirt front): from *Dickey,* dim. of *Dick* (name)]

dicky[2] *or* **dickey** ❶ ('dɪkɪ) *adj* **dickier, dickiest.** *Brit. inf.* shaky, unsteady,

THESAURUS

diaphanous *n* = **fine,** chiffon, clear, cobwebby, delicate, filmy, gauzy, gossamer, light, pellucid, see-through, sheer, thin, translucent, transparent

diarrhoea *n* = **the runs,** dysentery, gippy tummy, holiday tummy, looseness, Montezuma's revenge (*inf.*), Spanish tummy, the skits (*inf.*), the skitters (*inf.*), the trots (*inf.*)

diary *n* **1, 2** = **journal,** appointment book, chronicle, daily record, day-to-day account, engagement book, Filofax (*Trademark*)

diatribe *n* = **tirade,** abuse, castigation, criticism, denunciation, disputation, harangue, invective, philippic, reviling, stream of abuse, stricture, verbal onslaught, vituperation

dicey *adj Informal, chiefly Brit.* = **dangerous,** chancy (*inf.*), difficult, hairy (*sl.*), risky, ticklish, tricky

dichotomy *n* **1** = **division,** bisection, disjunction, divorce, separation, split (in two)

dicky[2] *adj Brit. informal* = **weak,** fluttery, queer, shaky, unreliable, unsound, unsteady

or unreliable: *I feel a bit dicky today*. [C18: ?from *as queer as Dick's hatband* feeling ill]

diclinous ('daɪklɪnəs) *adj* (of flowering plants) unisexual. Cf. **monoclinous**.
► **'diclinism** *n*

dicotyledon (ˌdaɪkɒtɪ'liːdᵊn) *n* a flowering plant having two embryonic seed leaves.
► **ˌdicoty'ledonous** *adj*

dict. *abbrev. for:* **1** dictation. **2** dictator. **3** dictionary.

dicta ('dɪktə) *n* a plural of **dictum**.

Dictaphone ('dɪktəˌfəʊn) *n Trademark*. a tape recorder designed for recording dictation for subsequent typing.

dictate Ⓣ *vb* (dɪk'teɪt), **dictates, dictating, dictated. 1** to say (letters, speeches, etc.) aloud for mechanical recording or verbatim transcription by another person. **2** (*tr*) to prescribe (commands, etc.) authoritatively. **3** (*intr*) to seek to impose one's will on others. ◆ *n* ('dɪkteɪt). **4** an authoritative command. **5** a guiding principle: *the dictates of reason*. [C17: from L *dictāre* to say repeatedly, order, from *dīcere* to say]

dictation (dɪk'teɪʃən) *n* **1** the act of dictating material to be recorded or taken down in writing. **2** the material dictated. **3** authoritative commands or the act of giving them.

dictator Ⓣ (dɪk'teɪtə) *n* **1a** a ruler who is not effectively restricted by a constitution, laws, etc. **1b** an absolute, esp. tyrannical, ruler. **2** (in ancient Rome) a person appointed during a crisis to exercise supreme authority. **3** a person who makes pronouncements, which are regarded as authoritative. **4** a person who behaves in an authoritarian or tyrannical manner.

dictatorial Ⓣ (ˌdɪktə'tɔːrɪəl) *adj* **1** of or characteristic of a dictator. **2** tending to dictate; tyrannical; overbearing.
► **ˌdicta'torially** *adv*

dictatorship Ⓣ (dɪk'teɪtəˌʃɪp) *n* **1** the rank, office, or period of rule of a dictator. **2** government by a dictator. **3** a country ruled by a dictator. **4** absolute power or authority.

diction Ⓣ ('dɪkʃən) *n* **1** the choice of words in writing or speech. **2** the manner of enunciating words and sounds. [C15: from L *dictiō* a saying, mode of expression, from *dīcere* to speak, say]

dictionary Ⓣ ('dɪkʃənərɪ) *n, pl* **dictionaries. 1a** a book that consists of an alphabetical list of words with their meanings, parts of speech, pronunciations, etymologies, etc. **1b** a similar book giving equivalent words in two or more languages. **2** a reference book listing words or terms and giving information about a particular subject or activity. **3** a collection of information or examples with the entries alphabetically arranged: *a dictionary of quotations*. [C16: from Med. L *dictiōnārium* collection of words, from LL *dictiō* word; see DICTION]

dictum Ⓣ ('dɪktəm) *n, pl* **dictums** *or* **dicta. 1** a formal or authoritative statement; pronouncement. **2** a popular saying or maxim. **3** *Law*. See **obiter dictum**. [C16: from L, from *dīcere* to say]

did (dɪd) *vb* the past tense of **do**[1].

didactic Ⓣ (dɪ'dæktɪk) *adj* **1** intended to instruct, esp. excessively. **2** morally instructive. **3** (of works of art or literature) containing a political or moral message to which aesthetic considerations are subordinated. [C17: from Gk *didaktikos* skilled in teaching, from *didaskein*]
►**di'dactically** *adv* ►**di'dacticism** *n*

didactics (dɪ'dæktɪks) *n* (*functioning as sing*) the art or science of teaching.

diddle ('dɪdᵊl) *vb* **diddles, diddling, diddled.** (*tr*) *Inf.* to cheat or swindle. [C19: back formation from Jeremy *Diddler*, a scrounger in J. Kenney's farce *Raising the Wind* (1803)]
► **'diddler** *n*

didgeridoo (ˌdɪdʒərɪ'duː) *n Music*. a native deep-toned Australian wind instrument. [C20: imit.]

didn't ('dɪdᵊnt) *contraction of* did not.

dido ('daɪdəʊ) *n, pl* **didos** *or* **didoes.** (*usually pl*) *Inf.* an antic; prank; trick. [C19: from ?]

didst (dɪdst) *vb Arch.* (used with *thou*) a form of the past tense of **do**[1].

didymium (daɪ'dɪmɪəm) *n* a mixture of the metallic rare earths neodymium and praseodymium, once thought to be an element. [C19: from NL, from Gk *didumos* twin + -IUM]

die[1] Ⓣ (daɪ) *vb* **dies, dying, died.** (*mainly intr*) **1** (of an organism, organs, etc.) to cease all biological activity permanently. **2** (of something inanimate) to cease to exist. **3** (often foll. by *away, down,* or *out*) to lose strength, power, or energy, esp. by degrees. **4** (often foll. by *away* or *down*) to become calm; subside. **5** to stop functioning: *the engine died*. **6** to languish, as with love, longing, etc. **7** (usually foll. by *of*) *Inf.* to be nearly overcome (with laughter, boredom, etc.). **8** *Christianity*. to lack spiritual life within the soul. **9** (*tr*) to suffer (a death of a specified kind): *he died a saintly death*. **10 be dying.** (foll. by *for* or an infinitive) to be eager or desperate (for something or to do something). **11 die hard.** to cease to exist after a struggle: *old habits die hard*. **12 die in harness.** to die while still working or active. **13 never say die.** *Inf.* never give up. ◆ See also **die down, die out.** [OE *dīegan*, prob. of Scand. origin]

> **USAGE NOTE** It was formerly considered incorrect to use the preposition *from* after *die*, but *of* and *from* are now both acceptable: *he died of/from his injuries*.

die[2] (daɪ) *n* **1a** a shaped block used to cut or form metal in a drop forge, press, etc. **1b** a tool with a conical hole through which wires, etc. are drawn to reduce their diameter. **2** an internally-threaded tool for cutting external threads. **3** a casting mould. **4** *Archit.* the dado of a pedestal, usually cubic. **5** another name for **dice** (sense 2). **6 the die is cast.** the irrevocable decision has been taken. [C13 *dee*, from OF *de*, ?from Vulgar L *datum* (unattested) a piece in games, from L *dare* to give, play]

die-cast *vb* **die-casts, die-casting, die-cast.** (*tr*) to shape or form (an object) by introducing molten metal or plastic into a reusable mould, esp. under pressure.
► **'die-ˌcasting** *n*

die down *vb* (*intr, adv*) **1** (of plants) to wither above ground, leaving only the root alive during the winter. **2** to lose strength or power, esp. by degrees. **3** to become calm.

die-hard Ⓣ *n* **1** a person who resists change or who holds onto an untenable position. **2** (*modifier*) obstinately resistant to change.

dieldrin ('diːldrɪn) *n* a crystalline substance, consisting of a chlorinated derivative of naphthalene: a contact insecticide the use of which is now restricted. [C20: from *Diel(s-Al)d(e)r* (*reaction*) + -IN; Diels & Alder were G chemists]

dielectric (ˌdaɪɪ'lektrɪk) *n* **1** a substance that can sustain an electric field. **2** a substance of very low electrical conductivity; insulator. ◆ *adj* **3** concerned with or having the properties of a dielectric. [from DIA- + ELECTRIC]
► **ˌdie'lectrically** *adv*

diene ('daɪiːn) *n Chem.* a hydrocarbon that contains two carbon-to-carbon double bonds in its molecules. [from DI-[1] + -ENE]

die out *or* **off** *vb* (*intr, adv*) **1** to die one after another until few or none are left. **2** to become extinct, esp. after a period of gradual decline.

dieresis (daɪ'ɛrɪsɪs) *n, pl* **diereses** (-ˌsiːz). a variant spelling of **diaeresis**.

diesel ('diːzᵊl) *n* **1** See **diesel engine. 2** a ship, locomotive, lorry, etc., driven by a diesel engine. **3** *Inf.* short for **diesel oil** (*or* **fuel**). [after R. *Diesel* (1858–1913), G engineer]

diesel-electric *n* **1** a locomotive fitted with a diesel engine driving an electric generator that feeds electric traction motors. ◆ *adj* **2** of or relating to such a locomotive or system.

diesel engine *or* **motor** *n* a type of internal-combustion engine in which atomized fuel oil is ignited by compression alone.

diesel oil *or* **fuel** *n* a fuel obtained from petroleum distillation that is used in diesel engines. Also called (Brit.): **derv**.

Dies Irae *Latin.* ('diːeɪz 'ɪəraɪ) *n* **1** a Latin hymn of the 13th century, describing the Last Judgment. It is used in the Mass for the dead. **2** a musical setting of this. [lit.: day of wrath]

diesis ('daɪɪsɪs) *n, pl* **dieses** (-ˌsiːz). *Printing*. another name for **double dagger.** [C16: via L from Gk: a quarter tone, lit.: a sending through, from *diienai;* the double dagger was orig. used in musical notation]

diestock ('daɪˌstɒk) *n* the device holding the dies used to cut an external screw thread.

diet[1] Ⓣ ('daɪət) *n* **1** a specific allowance or selection of food, esp. prescribed to control weight or for health reasons: *a salt-free diet*. **2** the

THESAURUS

dictate *vb* **1** = **speak**, read out, say, transmit, utter **2** = **order**, command, decree, demand, direct, enjoin, establish, impose, lay down, lay down the law, ordain, prescribe, pronounce ◆ *n* **4** = **command**, behest, bidding, decree, demand, direction, edict, fiat, injunction, mandate, order, ordinance, requirement, statute, ultimatum, word **5** = **principle**, canon, code, dictum, law, precept, rule

dictator *n* = **absolute ruler**, autocrat, despot, oppressor, tyrant

dictatorial *adj* **1** = **absolute**, arbitrary, autocratic, despotic, totalitarian, tyrannical, unlimited, unrestricted **2** = **domineering**, authoritarian, bossy (*inf.*), dogmatical, imperious, iron-handed, magisterial, oppressive, overbearing
Antonyms *adj* ≠ **absolute:** constitutional, democratic, egalitarian, restricted ≠ **domineering:** humble, servile, suppliant, tolerant

dictatorship *n* **2, 4** = **absolute rule**, absolutism, authoritarianism, autocracy, despotism, reign of terror, totalitarianism, tyranny

diction *n* **2** = **pronunciation**, articulation, delivery, elocution, enunciation, fluency, inflection, intonation, speech

dictionary *n* **1** = **wordbook**, concordance, encyclopedia, glossary, lexicon, vocabulary

dictum *n* **1** = **decree**, canon, command, demand, dictate, edict, fiat, order, pronouncement, statement **2** = **saying**, adage, axiom, gnome, maxim, precept, proverb, saw

didactic *adj* **1, 2** = **instructive**, edifying, educational, enlightening, homiletic, moral, moralizing, pedagogic, pedantic, preceptive

die[1] *vb* **1** = **pass away**, breathe one's last, buy it (*US. sl.*), buy the farm (*US. sl.*), check out (*US. sl.*), croak (*sl.*), decease, depart, expire, finish, give up the ghost, go belly-up (*sl.*), hop the twig (*sl.*), kick it (*sl.*), kick the bucket (*sl.*), peg it (*inf.*), peg out (*inf.*), perish, pop one's clogs (*inf.*), snuff it (*sl.*) **3** = **dwindle**, decay, decline, disappear, ebb, end, fade, lapse, pass, sink, subside, vanish, wane, wilt, wither **5** = **stop**, break down, fade out *or* away, fail, fizzle out, halt, lose power, peter out, run down **7** *foll. by* **of** *Informal* = **be overcome with**, collapse with, succumb to **10 be dying** *foll. by* **for** = **long for**, ache for, be eager for, desire, hunger for, languish for, pine for, set one's heart on, swoon over, yearn for
Antonyms *vb* ≠ **pass away:** be born, begin, come to life, exist, live, survive ≠ **dwindle, stop:** flourish, grow, increase

die-hard *n* **1** = **reactionary**, fanatic, intransigent, old fogey, stick-in-the-mud (*inf.*), ultraconservative, zealot ◆ *modifier* **2** = **reactionary**, dyed-in-the-wool, immovable, inflexible, intransigent, ultraconservative, uncompromising, unreconstructed (*chiefly US*)

diet[1] *n* **1** = **regime**, abstinence, dietary, fast, regimen **2** = **food**, aliment, comestibles, commons, edibles, fare, nourishment, nutriment, provi-

food and drink that a person or animal regularly consumes. **3** regular activities or occupations. ◆ *vb* **4** (*usually intr*) to follow or cause to follow a dietary regimen. [C13: from OF *diete,* from L *diaeta,* from Gk *diaita* mode of living, from *diaitan* to direct one's own life]
▸ **'dieter** *n*

diet[2] ⓣ ('daɪət) *n* **1** (*sometimes cap.*) a legislative assembly in various countries. **2** (*sometimes cap.*) the assembly of the estates of the Holy Roman Empire. **3** *Scots Law.* a single session of a court. [C15: from Med. L *diēta* public meeting, prob. from L *diaeta* DIET[1] but associated with L *diēs* day]

dietary ('daɪətərɪ, -trɪ) *adj* **1** of or relating to a diet. ◆ *n, pl* **dietaries. 2** a regulated diet. **3** a system of dieting.

dietary fibre *n* fibrous substances in fruits and vegetables, such as the structural polymers of cell walls, which aid digestion. Also called: **roughage.**

dietetic (ˌdaɪɪ'tɛtɪk) *or* **dietetical** *adj* **1** denoting or relating to diet. **2** prepared for special dietary requirements.
▸ **ˌdie'tetically** *adv*

dietetics (ˌdaɪɪ'tɛtɪks) *n* (*functioning as sing*) the scientific study and regulation of food intake and preparation.

diethylene glycol *n* a colourless soluble liquid used as an antifreeze and solvent.

dietitian *or* **dietician** (ˌdaɪɪ'tɪʃən) *n* a person who specializes in dietetics.

differ ⓣ ('dɪfə) *vb* (*intr*) **1** (often foll. by *from*) to be dissimilar in quality, nature, or degree (to); vary (from). **2** (often foll. by *from* or *with*) to disagree (with). **3** *Dialect.* to quarrel or dispute. [C14: from L *differre,* to scatter, put off, be different, from *dis-* apart + *ferre* to bear]

difference ⓣ ('dɪfərəns) *n* **1** the state or quality of being unlike. **2** a specific instance of being unlike. **3** a distinguishing mark or feature. **4** a significant change. **5** a disagreement or argument. **6** a degree of distinctness, as between two people or things. **7** Also called: **remainder.** the result of the subtraction of one number, quantity, etc., from another. **8** *Maths.* (of two sets) the set of members of the first that are not members of the second. **9** *Heraldry.* an addition to the arms of a family to represent a younger branch. **10 make a difference. 10a** to have an effect. **10b** to treat differently. **11 split the difference. 11a** to compromise. **11b** to divide a remainder equally. **12 with a difference.** with some distinguishing quality, good or bad.

different ⓣ ('dɪfərənt) *adj* **1** partly or completely unlike. **2** not identical or the same; other. **3** unusual.
▸ **'differently** *adv* ▸ **'differentness** *n*

> **USAGE NOTE** The constructions *different from, different to,* and *different than* are all found in the works of writers of English during the past. Nowadays, however, the most widely acceptable preposition to use after *different* is *from. Different to* is common in British English, but is considered by some people to be incorrect, or less acceptable. *Different than* is a standard construction in American English, and has the advantage of conciseness when a clause or phrase follows, as in *this result is only slightly different than in the US.* As, however, this idiom is not regarded as totally acceptable in British usage, it is preferable either to use *different from: this result is only slightly different from that obtained in the US* or to rephrase the sentence: *this result differs only slightly from that in the US.*

differentia (ˌdɪfə'rɛnʃɪə) *n, pl* **differentiae** (-ʃɪˌiː). *Logic.* a feature by which two subclasses of the same class of named objects can be distinguished. [C19: from L: diversity]

differential ⓣ (ˌdɪfə'rɛnʃəl) *adj* **1** of, relating to, or using a difference. **2** constituting a difference; distinguishing. **3** *Maths.* involving one or more derivatives or differentials. **4** *Physics, engineering.* relating to, operating on, or based on the difference between two opposing effects, motions, forces, etc. ◆ *n* **5** a factor that differentiates between two comparable things. **6** *Maths.* **6a** an increment in a given function, expressed as the product of the derivative of that function and the corresponding increment in the independent variable. **6b** an increment in a given function of two or more variables, $f(x_1, x_2, \ldots x_n)$, expressed as the sum of the products of each partial derivative and the increment in the corresponding variable. **7** See **differential gear. 8** *Chiefly Brit.* the difference between rates of pay for different types of labour, esp. when forming a pay structure within an industry. **9** (in commerce) a difference in rates, esp. between comparable services.
▸ **ˌdiffer'entially** *adv*

differential calculus *n* the branch of calculus concerned with the study, evaluation, and use of derivatives and differentials.

differential equation *n* an equation containing differentials or derivatives of a function of one independent variable.

differential gear *n* the epicyclic gear mounted in the driving axle of a road vehicle that permits one driving wheel to rotate faster than the other, as when cornering.

differential operator *n* the mathematical operator del, ∇, used in vector analysis.

differentiate ⓣ (ˌdɪfə'rɛnʃɪˌeɪt) *vb* **differentiates, differentiating, differentiated. 1** (*tr*) to serve to distinguish between. **2** (when *intr,* often foll. by *between*) to perceive, show, or make a difference (in or between); discriminate. **3** (*intr*) to become dissimilar or distinct. **4** *Maths.* to perform a differentiation on (a quantity, expression, etc.). **5** (*intr*) (of unspecialized cells, etc.) to change during development to more specialized forms.
▸ **ˌdiffer'entiˌator** *n*

differentiation (ˌdɪfəˌrɛnʃɪ'eɪʃən) *n* **1** the act, process, or result of differentiating. **2** *Maths.* an operation used in calculus in which the derivative of a function or variable is determined.

difficult ⓣ ('dɪfɪkᵊlt) *adj* **1** not easy to do; requiring effort. **2** not easy to understand or solve. **3** troublesome: *a difficult child.* **4** not easily convinced, pleased, or satisfied. **5** full of hardships or trials. [C14: back formation from DIFFICULTY]
▸ **'difficultly** *adv*

difficulty ⓣ ('dɪfɪkᵊltɪ) *n, pl* **difficulties. 1** the state or quality of being difficult. **2** a task, problem, etc., that is hard to deal with. **3** (*often pl*) a troublesome or embarrassing situation, esp. a financial one. **4** a disagreement. **5** (*often pl*) an objection or obstacle. **6** a trouble or source of trouble; worry. **7** lack of ease; awkwardness. [C14: from L *difficultās,* from *difficilis,* from *dis-* not + *facilis* easy]

diffident ⓣ ('dɪfɪdənt) *adj* lacking self-confidence; shy. [C15: from L *diffīdere,* from *dis-* not + *fīdere* to trust]
▸ **'diffidence** *n* ▸ **'diffidently** *adv*

diffract (dɪ'frækt) *vb* to undergo or cause to undergo diffraction.
▸ **dif'fractive** *adj* ▸ **dif'fractively** *adv* ▸ **dif'fractiveness** *n*

diffraction (dɪ'frækʃən) *n* **1** *Physics.* a deviation in the direction of a wave at the edge of an obstacle in its path. **2** any phenomenon caused by diffraction, such as the formation of light and dark fringes by the

THESAURUS

sions, rations, subsistence, sustenance, viands, victuals ◆ *vb* **4** = **slim**, abstain, eat sparingly, fast, lose weight

Antonyms *vb* ≠ **slim:** get fat, glut, gobble, gormandize, guzzle, indulge, overindulge, pig out (*sl.*), stuff oneself

diet[2] *n* = **council**, chamber, congress, convention, legislative assembly, legislature, meeting, parliament, sitting

dieter *n* = **slimmer**, calorie counter, faster, reducer, weight watcher

differ *vb* **1** = **be dissimilar**, be distinct, contradict, contrast, depart from, diverge, run counter to, stand apart, vary **2** = **disagree**, clash, contend, debate, demur, dispute, dissent, oppose, take exception, take issue

Antonyms *vb* ≠ **be dissimilar:** accord, coincide, harmonize ≠ **disagree:** accord, acquiesce, agree, assent, concur, cooperate

difference *n* **1** = **dissimilarity**, alteration, change, contrast, deviation, differentiation, discrepancy, disparity, distinction, distinctness, divergence, diversity, unlikeness, variation, variety **3** = **distinction**, exception, idiosyncrasy, particularity, peculiarity, singularity **5** = **disagreement**, argument, clash, conflict, contention, contrariety, contretemps, controversy, debate, discordance, dispute, quarrel, row, set-to (*inf.*), strife, tiff, wrangle **7** = **remainder**, balance, rest, result

Antonyms *n* ≠ **dissimilarity:** affinity, comparability, conformity, congruence, likeness, relation, resemblance, sameness, similarity, similitude ≠ **disagreement:** agreement, concordance

different *adj* **1** = **unlike**, altered, at odds, at variance, changed, clashing, contrasting, deviating, discrepant, disparate, dissimilar, divergent, diverse, inconsistent, opposed, streets apart **2** = **other**, another, discrete, distinct, individual, separate **3** = **unusual**, another story, atypical, bizarre, distinctive, extraordinary, left-field (*inf.*), out of the ordinary, peculiar, rare, singular, something else, special, strange, uncommon, unconventional, unique

differential *adj* **2** = **distinctive**, diacritical, discriminative, distinguishing ◆ *n* **5** = **difference**, amount of difference, discrepancy, disparity

differentiate *vb* **1** = **distinguish**, contrast, discern, discriminate, make a distinction, mark off, separate, set off *or* apart, tell apart

differently *adv* **1** = **otherwise**, contrastingly, in another way, in contrary fashion

Antonyms *adv* ≠ **otherwise:** in like manner, in the same way, likewise, similarly

difficult *adj* **1** = **hard**, arduous, burdensome, demanding, formidable, laborious, like getting blood out of a stone, no picnic (*inf.*), onerous, painful, strenuous, toilsome, uphill, wearisome **2** = **problematical**, abstract, abstruse, baffling, complex, complicated, delicate, enigmatical, intricate, involved, knotty, obscure, perplexing, thorny, ticklish **4** = **troublesome**, demanding, fastidious, fractious, fussy, hard to please, intractable, obstreperous, perverse, refractory, rigid, tiresome, trying, unaccommodating, unamenable, unmanageable **5** = **tough**, dark, full of hardship, grim, hard, straitened, trying

Antonyms *adj* ≠ **hard:** easy, easy-peasy (*sl.*), light, manageable, obvious, plain, simple, straightforward, uncomplicated ≠ **troublesome:** accommodating, amenable, cooperative, pleasant ≠ **tough:** easy, pleasant

difficulty *n* **1** = **laboriousness**, arduousness, awkwardness, hardship, labour, pain, painfulness, strain, strenuousness, tribulation **3** = **predicament**, deep water, dilemma, distress, embarrassment, fix (*inf.*), hot water (*inf.*), jam (*inf.*), mess, perplexity, pickle (*inf.*), plight, quandary, spot (*inf.*), straits, tight spot, trial, trouble **5** = **problem**, complication, hassle (*inf.*), hazard, hindrance, hurdle, impediment, objection, obstacle, opposition, pitfall, protest, snag, stumbling block

diffidence *n* = **shyness**, backwardness, bashfulness, constraint, doubt, fear, hesitancy, hesitation, humility, insecurity, lack of self-confidence, meekness, modesty, reluctance, reserve, self-consciousness, sheepishness, timidity, timidness, timorousness, unassertiveness

Antonyms *n* assurance, boldness, confidence, courage, firmness, self-confidence, self-possession

diffident *adj* = **shy**, backward, bashful, constrained, distrustful, doubtful, hesitant, insecure, meek, modest, reluctant, reserved, self-

passage of light through a small aperture. [C17: from NL *diffractiō* a breaking to pieces, from L *diffringere* to shatter, from *dis-* apart + *frangere* to break]

diffuse ❶ *vb* (dɪˈfjuːz), **diffuses, diffusing, diffused. 1** to spread in all directions. **2** to undergo or cause to undergo diffusion. **3** to scatter; disperse. ◆ *adj* (dɪˈfjuːs). **4** spread out over a wide area. **5** lacking conciseness. **6** characterized by diffusion. [C15: from L *diffūsus* spread abroad, from *diffundere* to pour forth, from *dis-* away + *fundere* to pour]
▸**diffusely** (dɪˈfjuːslɪ) *adv* ▸**difˈfuseness** *n* ▸**diffusible** (dɪˈfjuːzɪbᵊl) *adj*

USAGE NOTE Avoid confusion with **defuse.**

diffuser *or* **diffusor** (dɪˈfjuːzə) *n* **1** a person or thing that diffuses. **2** a part of a lighting fixture, as a translucent covering, used to scatter the light and prevent glare. **3** a cone, wedge, or baffle placed in front of the diaphragm of a loudspeaker to diffuse the sound waves. **4** a duct, esp. in a wind tunnel or jet engine, that reduces the speed and increases the pressure of the air or fluid. **5** *Photog.* a light-scattering medium, such as a screen of fine fabric, used to reduce the sharpness of shadows and thus soften the lighting. **6** a device attached to a hair dryer that diffuses the warm air as it comes out.

diffusion ❶ (dɪˈfjuːʒən) *n* **1** a diffusing or being diffused; dispersion. **2** verbosity. **3** *Physics.* **3a** the random thermal motion of atoms, molecules, etc., in gases, liquids, and some solids. **3b** the transfer of atoms or molecules by their random motion from one part of a medium to another. **4** *Physics.* the transmission or reflection of electromagnetic radiation, esp. light, in which the radiation is scattered in many directions. **5** *Anthropol.* the transmission of social institutions, skills, and myths from one culture to another.

diffusionism (dɪˈfjuːʒənˌɪzəm) *n Anthropol.* the theory that diffusion is responsible for the similarities between different cultures.
▸**difˈfusionist** *n, adj*

diffusive (dɪˈfjuːsɪv) *adj* characterized by diffusion.
▸**difˈfusively** *adv* ▸**difˈfusiveness** *n*

dig ❶ (dɪg) *vb* **digs, digging, dug. 1** (when *tr*, often foll. by *up*) to cut into, break up, and turn over or remove (earth, etc.), esp. with a spade. **2** to excavate (a hole, tunnel, etc.) by digging, usually with an implement or (of animals) with claws, etc. **3** (often foll. by *through*) to make or force (one's way): *he dug his way through the crowd.* **4** (*tr*; often foll. by *out* or *up*) to obtain by digging. **5** (*tr*; often foll. by *out* or *up*) to find by effort or searching: *to dig out facts.* **6** (*tr*; foll. by *in* or *into*) to thrust or jab. **7** (*tr*; foll. by *in* or *into*) to mix (compost, etc.) with soil by digging. **8** (*intr*; foll. by *in* or *into*) *Inf.* to begin vigorously to do something. **9** (*tr*) *Inf.* to like, understand, or appreciate. **10** (*intr*) *US sl.* to work hard, esp. for an examination. ◆ *n* **11** the act of digging. **12** a thrust or poke. **13** a cutting remark. **14** *Inf.* an archaeological excavation. **15** *Austral. & NZ inf.* short for **digger** (sense 4). ◆ See also **dig in.** [C13 *diggen*, from ?]

digest ❶ *vb* (dɪˈdʒɛst, daɪ-). **1** to subject (food) to a process of digestion. **2** (*tr*) to assimilate mentally. **3** *Chem.* to soften or disintegrate by the action of heat, moisture, or chemicals. **4** (*tr*) to arrange in a methodical order; classify. **5** (*tr*) to reduce to a summary. ◆ *n* (ˈdaɪdʒɛst). **6** a comprehensive and systematic compilation of information or material, often condensed. **7** a magazine, periodical, etc., that summarizes news. **8** a compilation of rules of law. [C14: from LL *dīgesta* writings grouped under various heads, from L *dīgerere* to divide, from *di-* apart + *gerere* to bear]

Digest (ˈdaɪdʒɛst) *n Roman law.* the books of law compiled by order of Justinian in the sixth century A.D.

digestible (dɪˈdʒɛstɪbᵊl, daɪ-) *adj* capable of being digested.
▸**diˌgestiˈbility** *n*

digestion ❶ (dɪˈdʒɛstʃən, daɪ-) *n* **1** the act or process in living organisms of breaking down food into easily absorbed substances by the action of enzymes, etc. **2** mental assimilation, esp. of ideas. **3** the decomposition of sewage by bacteria. **4** *Chem.* the treatment of material with heat, solvents, etc., to cause decomposition. [C14: from OF, from L *digestiō* a dissolving, digestion]
▸**diˈgestional** *adj*

digestive (dɪˈdʒɛstɪv, daɪ-) *or* **digestant** (daɪˈdʒɛstənt) *adj* **1** relating to, aiding, or subjecting to digestion. ◆ *n* **2** any substance that aids digestion.
▸**diˈgestively** *adv*

digestive biscuit *n* a round semisweet biscuit made from wholemeal flour.

digger (ˈdɪgə) *n* **1** a person, animal, or machine that digs. **2** a miner. **3** a tool or machine used for excavation. **4** (*sometimes cap.*) *Austral. & NZ inf.* an Australian or New Zealander, esp. a soldier: often used as a friendly term of address.

diggings (ˈdɪgɪŋz) *pl n* **1** (*functioning as pl*) material that has been dug out. **2** (*functioning as sing or pl*) a place where mining has taken place. **3** (*functioning as pl*) *Brit. inf.* a less common name for **digs.**

dight (daɪt) *vb* **dights, dighting, dight** *or* **dighted.** (*tr*) *Arch.* to adorn or equip, as for battle. [OE *dihtan* to compose, from L *dictāre* to DICTATE]

dig in ❶ *vb* (*adv*) **1** *Mil.* to dig foxholes, trenches, etc. **2** *Inf.* to entrench (oneself). **3** (*intr*) *Inf.* to defend a position firmly, as in an argument. **4** (*intr*) *Inf.* to begin to eat vigorously: *don't wait, just dig in.* **5 dig one's heels in.** *Inf.* to refuse to move or be persuaded.

digit ❶ (ˈdɪdʒɪt) *n* **1** a finger or toe. **2** any of the ten Arabic numerals from 0 to 9. [C15: from L *digitus* toe, finger]

digital (ˈdɪdʒɪtᵊl) *adj* **1** of, resembling, or possessing a digit or digits. **2** performed with the fingers. **3** representing data as a series of numerical values. **4** displaying information as numbers rather than by a pointer moving over a dial. ◆ *n* **5** *Music.* a key on a piano, harpsichord, etc.
▸ˈ**digitally** *adv*

digital audio tape *n* magnetic tape on which sound is recorded digitally, giving high-fidelity reproduction. Abbrev.: **DAT.**

digital camera *n* a camera that produces digital images, which can be stored on a computer, displayed on a screen, and printed.

digital clock *or* **watch** *n* a clock or watch in which the time is indicated by digits rather than by hands on a dial.

digital compact cassette *n* a magnetic tape cassette on which sound can be recorded in digital format. Abbrev.: **DCC.**

digital computer *n* an electronic computer in which the input is discrete, consisting of numbers, letters, etc. that are represented internally in binary notation.

digitalin (ˌdɪdʒɪˈteɪlɪn) *n* a poisonous glycoside extracted from digitalis and used in treating heart disease. [C19: from DIGITAL(IS) + -IN]

digitalis (ˌdɪdʒɪˈteɪlɪs) *n* **1** any of a genus of Eurasian plants such as the foxglove, having long spikes of bell-shaped flowers. **2** a drug prepared from the dried leaves of the foxglove: used medicinally as a heart stimulant. [C17: from NL, from L: relating to a finger; based on G *Fingerhut* foxglove, lit.: finger-hat]

digitalize *or* **digitalise** (ˈdɪdʒɪtəˌlaɪz) *vb* **digitalizes, digitalizing, digitalized** *or* **digitalises, digitalising, digitalised.** (*tr*) another word for **digitize.**

digital mapping *n* a method of preparing maps in which the data is stored in a computer for ease of access and updating.
▸**digital map** *n*

digital recording *n* a sound recording process that converts audio or analogue signals into a series of pulses that correspond to the voltage level.

digital television *n* television in which the picture information is transmitted in digital form and decoded at the receiver.

digital video *n* video output based on digital rather than analogue signals.

digitate (ˈdɪdʒɪˌteɪt) *or* **digitated** *adj* **1** (of leaves) having the leaflets in the form of a spread hand. **2** (of animals) having digits.
▸ˈ**digiˌtately** *adv* ▸ˌ**digiˈtation** *n*

digitigrade (ˈdɪdʒɪtɪˌgreɪd) *adj* **1** (of dogs, cats, horses, etc.) walking so that only the toes touch the ground. ◆ *n* **2** a digitigrade animal.

digitize *or* **digitise** (ˈdɪdʒɪˌtaɪz) *vb* **digitizes, digitizing, digitized** *or* **digitises, digitising, digitised.** (*tr*) to transcribe (data) into a digital form for processing by a computer.
▸ˌ**digitiˈzation** *or* ˌ**digitiˈsation** *n* ▸ˈ**digiˌtizer** *or* ˈ**digiˌtiser** *n*

dignified ❶ (ˈdɪgnɪˌfaɪd) *adj* characterized by dignity of manner or appearance; stately; noble.
▸ˈ**digniˌfiedly** *adv* ▸ˈ**digniˌfiedness** *n*

dignify ❶ (ˈdɪgnɪˌfaɪ) *vb* **dignifies, dignifying, dignified.** (*tr*) **1** to invest with honour or dignity. **2** to add distinction to. **3** to add a semblance of

THESAURUS

conscious, self-effacing, sheepish, shrinking, suspicious, timid, timorous, unassertive, unassuming, unobtrusive, unsure, withdrawn

diffuse *vb* **1-3** = **spread**, circulate, dispel, dispense, disperse, disseminate, dissipate, distribute, propagate, scatter ◆ *adj* **4** = **spread out**, dispersed, scattered, unconcentrated **5** = **rambling**, circumlocutory, copious, diffusive, digressive, discursive, long-winded, loose, maundering, meandering, prolix, vague, verbose, waffling (*inf.*), wordy
Antonyms *adj* ≠ **spread out:** concentrated ≠ **rambling:** apposite, brief, compendious, concise, succinct, terse, to the point

diffusion *n* **1** = **spread**, circulation, dispersal, dispersion, dissemination, dissipation, distribution, expansion, propaganda, propagation, scattering **2** = **rambling**, circuitousness, diffuseness, digressiveness, discursiveness, long-windedness, prolixity, verbiage, verbosity, wandering, wordiness

dig *vb* **1, 2** = **excavate**, break up, burrow, delve, gouge, grub, hoe, hollow out, mine, penetrate, pierce, quarry, scoop, till, tunnel, turn over **4** *with* **out** *or* **up** = **find**, bring to light, come across, come up with, discover, expose, extricate, retrieve, root (*inf.*), rootle, uncover, unearth, uproot **5** = **investigate**, delve, dig down, go into, probe, research, search **6** = **poke**, drive, jab, prod, punch, thrust **9** *Informal* = **like**, appreciate, enjoy, follow, groove (*dated sl.*), understand ◆ *n* **12** = **poke**, jab, prod, punch, thrust **13** = **cutting remark**, barb, crack, gibe, insult, jeer, quip, sneer, taunt, wisecrack (*inf.*)

digest *vb* **1** = **ingest**, absorb, assimilate, concoct, dissolve, incorporate, macerate **2** = **take in**, absorb, assimilate, con, consider, contemplate, grasp, master, meditate, ponder, study, understand ◆ *n* **6** = **summary**, abridgment, abstract, compendium, condensation, epitome, précis, résumé, synopsis

digestion *n* **1** = **ingestion**, absorption, assimilation, conversion, incorporation, transformation

dig in *vb* **1-3** = **entrench**, defend, establish, fortify, maintain *Informal* **4** = **start eating**, begin, fall to, set about, tuck in (*inf.*)

digit *n* **1** = **finger**, toe **2** = **number**, figure, numeral

dignified *adj* = **distinguished**, august, decorous, exalted, formal, grave, honourable, imposing, lofty, lordly, noble, reserved, solemn, stately, upright
Antonyms *adj* crass, inelegant, unbecoming, undignified, unseemly, vulgar

dignify *vb* **1, 2** = **distinguish**, adorn, advance,

dignity to, esp. by the use of a pretentious name or title. [C15: from OF *dignifier*, from LL *dignificāre*, from L *dignus* worthy + *facere* to make]

dignitary 🅣 (ˈdɪgnɪtərɪ) *n, pl* **dignitaries.** a person of high official position or rank.

dignity 🅣 (ˈdɪgnɪtɪ) *n, pl* **dignities. 1** a formal, stately, or grave bearing. **2** the state or quality of being worthy of honour. **3** relative importance; rank. **4** sense of self-importance (often in **stand** (*or* **be**) **on one's dignity, beneath one's dignity**). **5** high rank, esp. in government or the church. [C13: from OF *dignite*, from L *dignitās* merit, from *dignus* worthy]

digoxin (daɪˈdʒɒksɪn) *n* a glycoside extracted from digitalis leaves and used in the treatment of heart failure.

digraph (ˈdaɪgrɑːf) *n* a combination of two letters used to represent a single sound such as *gh* in *tough*.
▸**digraphic** (daɪˈgræfɪk) *adj*

digress 🅣 (daɪˈgrɛs) *vb* (*intr*) **1** to depart from the main subject in speech or writing. **2** to wander from one's path. [C16: from L *dīgressus* turned aside, from *dīgredī*, from *dis-* apart + *gradī* to go]
▸**diˈgresser** *n* ▸**diˈgression** *n*

digressive (daɪˈgrɛsɪv) *adj* characterized by digression or tending to digress.
▸**diˈgressively** *adv* ▸**diˈgressiveness** *n*

digs 🅣 (dɪgz) *pl n Brit. inf.* lodgings. [C19: from DIGGINGS, ? referring to where one *digs* or works, but see also DIG IN]

dihedral (daɪˈhiːdrəl) *adj* **1** having or formed by two intersecting planes. ◆ *n* **2** Also called: **dihedron, dihedral angle.** the figure formed by two intersecting planes. **3** the upward inclination of an aircraft wing in relation to the lateral axis.

dik-dik (ˈdɪkˌdɪk) *n* any of several small antelopes inhabiting semiarid regions of Africa. [C19: E African, prob. imit.]

dike (daɪk) *n, vb* **dikes, diking, diked.** a variant spelling of **dyke**[1].

diktat (ˈdɪktɑːt) *n* **1** a decree or settlement imposed, esp. by a ruler or a victorious nation. **2** a dogmatic statement. [from G: dictation, from L *dictātum*, from *dictāre* to DICTATE]

dilapidate 🅣 (dɪˈlæpɪˌdeɪt) *vb* **dilapidates, dilapidating, dilapidated.** to fall or cause to fall into ruin. [C16: from L *dīlapidāre* to waste, from *dis-* apart + *lapidāre* to stone, from *lapis* stone]
▸**diˌlapiˈdation** *n*

dilapidated 🅣 (dɪˈlæpɪˌdeɪtɪd) *adj* falling to pieces or in a state of disrepair; shabby.

dilate 🅣 (daɪˈleɪt, dɪ-) *vb* **dilates, dilating, dilated. 1** to make or become wider or larger. **2** (*intr*; often foll. by *on* or *upon*) to speak or write at length. [C14: from L *dīlātāre* to spread out, from *dis-* apart + *lātus* wide]
▸**diˈlatable** *adj* ▸**diˌlataˈbility** *n* ▸**diˈlation** *or* **dilatation** (ˌdaɪləˈteɪʃən) *n*
▸**dilative** (daɪˈleɪtɪv) *adj*

dilatory 🅣 (ˈdɪlətərɪ, -trɪ) *adj* **1** tending to delay or waste time. **2** intended to waste time or defer action. [C15: from LL *dīlātōrius* inclined to delay, from *differre* to postpone; see DIFFER]
▸**ˈdilatorily** *adv* ▸**ˈdilatoriness** *n*

dildo *or* **dildoe** (ˈdɪldəʊ) *n, pl* **dildos** *or* **dildoes.** an object used as a substitute for an erect penis. [C16: from ?]

dilemma 🅣 (dɪˈlɛmə, daɪ-) *n* **1** a situation necessitating a choice between two equally undesirable alternatives. **2** a problem that seems incapable of a solution. **3** *Logic.* a type of argument which forces the maintainer of a proposition to accept one of two conclusions each of which contradicts the original assertion. **4 on the horns of a dilemma. 4a** faced with the choice between two equally unpalatable alternatives. **4b** in an awkward situation. [C16: via L from Gk, from DI-[1] + *lēmma* proposition, from *lambanein* to grasp]
▸**dilemmatic** (ˌdɪlɪˈmætɪk) *adj*

> **USAGE NOTE** The use of *dilemma* to refer to a problem that seems incapable of a solution is considered by some people to be incorrect.

dilettante 🅣 (ˌdɪlɪˈtɑːntɪ) *n, pl* **dilettantes** *or* **dilettanti** (-ˈtɑːntɪ). **1** a person whose interest in a subject is superficial rather than professional. **2** a person who loves the arts. ◆ *adj* **3** of or characteristic of a dilettante. [C18: from It., from *dilettare* to delight, from L *dēlectāre*]
▸**ˌdiletˈtantish** *or* **ˌdiletˈtanteish** *adj* ▸**ˌdiletˈtantism** *or* **ˌdiletˈtanteism** *n*

diligence[1] 🅣 (ˈdɪlɪdʒəns) *n* **1** steady and careful application. **2** proper attention or care. [C14: from L *dīligentia* care]

diligence[2] (ˈdɪlɪdʒəns) *n History.* a stagecoach. [C18: from F, shortened from *carosse de diligence*, lit.: coach of speed]

diligent 🅣 (ˈdɪlɪdʒənt) *adj* **1** careful and persevering in carrying out tasks or duties. **2** carried out with care and perseverance: *diligent work.* [C14: from OF, from L *dīligere* to value, from *dis-* apart + *legere* to read]
▸**ˈdiligently** *adv*

dill[1] (dɪl) *n* **1** an aromatic Eurasian plant with umbrella-shaped clusters of yellow flowers. **2** the leaves or fruits of this plant, used for flavouring and in medicine. [OE *dile*]

dill[2] (dɪl) *n Austral. & NZ sl.* a fool. [C20: from DILLY[2]]

dill pickle *n* a pickled cucumber flavoured with dill.

dilly[1] (ˈdɪlɪ) *n, pl* **dillies.** *Sl., chiefly US & Canad.* a person or thing that is remarkable. [C20: ?from girl's name *Dilly*]

dilly[2] (ˈdɪlɪ) *adj* **dillier, dilliest.** *Austral. sl.* silly. [C20: from E dialect, ?from SILLY]

dilly bag *n Austral.* a small bag, esp., formerly, one made of plaited grass, etc., often used for carrying food. [from Abor. *dilly* small bag or basket]

dilly-dally 🅣 (ˌdɪlɪˈdælɪ) *vb* **dilly-dallies, dilly-dallying, dilly-dallied.** (*intr*) *Inf.* to loiter or vacillate. [C17: by reduplication from DALLY]

dilute 🅣 (daɪˈluːt) *vb* **dilutes, diluting, diluted. 1** to make or become less concentrated, esp. by adding water or a thinner. **2** to make or become weaker in force, effect, etc. ◆ *adj* **3** *Chem.* **3a** (of a solution, etc.) having a low concentration. **3b** (of a substance) present in solution, esp. a weak solution in water: *dilute acetic acid.* [C16: from L *dīluere*, from *dis-* apart + *-luere*, from *lavāre* to wash]
▸**diˈluter** *n*

dilution (daɪˈluːʃən) *n* **1** the act of diluting or state of being diluted. **2** a diluted solution.

diluvial (daɪˈluːvɪəl, dɪ-) *or* **diluvian** *adj* of or connected with a deluge, esp. with the great Flood described in Genesis. [C17: from LL *dīluviālis*, from L *dīluere* to wash away; see DILUTE]

dim 🅣 (dɪm) *adj* **dimmer, dimmest. 1** badly illuminated. **2** not clearly seen; faint. **3** having weak or indistinct vision. **4** mentally dull. **5** not clear in the mind; obscure: *a dim memory.* **6** lacking in brightness or

THESAURUS

aggrandize, elevate, ennoble, exalt, glorify, grace, honour, promote, raise

dignitary *n* = **public figure**, bigwig (*inf.*), celeb (*inf.*), high-up (*inf.*), notability, notable, personage, pillar of society, pillar of the church, pillar of the state, V.I.P., worthy

dignity *n* **1** = **decorum**, courtliness, grandeur, gravity, hauteur, loftiness, majesty, nobility, propriety, solemnity, stateliness **3** = **honour**, elevation, eminence, excellence, glory, greatness, importance, nobleness, rank, respectability, standing, station, status **4** = **self-importance**, *amour-propre*, pride, self-esteem, self-possession, self-regard, self-respect

digress *vb* **1** = **wander**, be diffuse, depart, deviate, diverge, drift, expatiate, get off the point *or* subject, go off at a tangent, meander, ramble, stray, turn aside

digression *n* **1** = **departure**, apostrophe, aside, detour, deviation, divergence, diversion, footnote, obiter dictum, parenthesis, straying, wandering

digs *pl n Brit. informal* = **lodgings**, accommodation, quarters, rooms

dilapidated *adj* = **ruined**, battered, beat-up, broken-down, crumbling, decayed, decaying, decrepit, fallen in, falling apart, gone to rack and ruin, in ruins, neglected, ramshackle, rickety, ruinous, run-down, shabby, shaky, tumbledown, uncared for, worn-out

dilapidation *n* = **ruin**, collapse, decay, demolition, destruction, deterioration, disintegration, disrepair, dissolution, downfall, waste, wear and tear

dilate *vb* **1** = **enlarge**, broaden, distend, expand, extend, puff out, stretch, swell, widen **2** = **expand**, amplify, be profuse, be prolix, descant, detail, develop, dwell on, enlarge, expatiate, expound, spin out
Antonyms *vb* ≠ **enlarge:** compress, constrict, contract, narrow, shrink

dilation *n* **1** = **enlargement**, broadening, dilatation, distension, expansion, extension, increase, spread

dilatory *adj* **1, 2** = **time-wasting**, backward, behindhand, dallying, delaying, laggard, lingering, loitering, procrastinating, putting off, slack, slow, sluggish, snail-like, tardy, tarrying
Antonyms *adj* on-the-ball (*inf.*), prompt, punctual, sharp (*inf.*)

dilemma *n* **2** = **predicament**, difficulty, embarrassment, fix (*inf.*), how-do-you-do (*inf.*), jam (*inf.*), mess, perplexity, pickle (*inf.*), plight, problem, puzzle, quandary, spot (*inf.*), strait, tight corner *or* spot **4a on the horns of a dilemma** = **between the devil and the deep blue sea**, between a rock and a hard place (*inf.*), between Scylla and Charybdis

dilettante *n* **1** = **amateur**, aesthete, dabbler, nonprofessional, trifler

diligence[1] *n* **1, 2** = **application**, activity, assiduity, assiduousness, attention, attentiveness, care, constancy, earnestness, heedfulness, industry, intentness, laboriousness, perseverance, sedulousness

diligent *adj* **1, 2** = **hard-working**, active, assiduous, attentive, busy, careful, conscientious, constant, earnest, indefatigable, industrious, laborious, painstaking, persevering, persistent, sedulous, studious, tireless
Antonyms *adj* careless, dilatory, good-for-nothing, inconstant, indifferent, lazy

dilly-dally *vb Informal* = **dawdle**, dally, delay, dither (*chiefly Brit.*), falter, fluctuate, hesitate, hover, hum and haw, linger, loiter, potter, procrastinate, shillyshally (*inf.*), trifle, vacillate, waver

dilute *vb* **1** = **water down**, adulterate, cut, make thinner, thin (out), weaken **2** = **reduce**, attenuate, decrease, diffuse, diminish, lessen, mitigate, temper, weaken
Antonyms *vb* ≠ **water down:** concentrate, condense, strengthen, thicken ≠ **reduce:** intensify, strengthen

diluted *adj* **1, 2** = **watered down**, adulterated, cut, dilute, thinned, watery, weak, weakened, wishy-washy (*inf.*)

dim *adj* **1** = **poorly lit**, caliginous (*arch.*), cloudy, dark, darkish, dusky, grey, overcast, shadowy, tenebrous, unilluminated **2** = **unclear**, bleary, blurred, faint, fuzzy, ill-defined, indistinct, obscured, shadowy **4** *Informal* = **stupid**, braindead (*inf.*), dense, doltish, dozy (*Brit. inf.*), dull, dumb (*inf.*), obtuse, slow, slow on the uptake (*inf.*), thick **5** = **obscure**, confused, hazy, imperfect, indistinct, intangible, remote, shadowy, vague **6** = **dull**, dingy, feeble, lacklustre, muted, opaque, pale, sullied, tarnished, weak **7 take a dim view** = **disapprove**, be displeased, be sceptical, look askance, reject, suspect, take exception, view with disfavour ◆ *vb* **8** = **dull**, bedim, blur, cloud, darken, fade, lower, obscure, tarnish, turn down
Antonyms *adj* ≠ **poorly lit:** bright, clear, cloudless, fair, limpid, pleasant, sunny, unclouded ≠ **un-**

lustre. **7** unfavourable, gloomy or disapproving (esp. in **take a dim view**). ◆ *vb* **dims, dimming, dimmed. 8** to become or cause to become dim. **9** (*tr*) to cause to seem less bright. **10** the US and Canad. word for **dip** (sense 5). [OE *dimm*]
▸'**dimly** *adv* ▸'**dimness** *n*

dim. *abbrev. for:* **1** dimension. **2** Also: **dimin.** *Music.* diminuendo. **3** Also: **dimin.** diminutive.

dime (daɪm) *n* **1** a coin of the US and Canada, worth one tenth of a dollar or ten cents. **2 a dime a dozen.** very cheap or common. [C14: from OF *disme,* from L *decimus* tenth, from *decem* ten]

dimenhydrinate (ˌdaɪmɛnˈhaɪdrɪˌneɪt) *n* a crystalline substance, used as an antihistamine and for the prevention of nausea, esp. in travel sickness. [from DI-[1] + ME(THYL) + (AMI)N(E) + (*diphen*)*hydr*(*am*)*in*(*e*) + -ATE[1]]

dime novel *n US.* (formerly) a cheap melodramatic novel, usually in paperback.

dimension ➊ (dɪˈmɛnʃən) *n* **1** (*often pl*) a measurement of the size of something in a particular direction, such as the length, width, height, or diameter. **2** (*often pl*) scope; size; extent. **3** aspect: *a new dimension to politics.* **4** *Maths.* the number of coordinates required to locate a point in space. ◆ *vb* **5** (*tr*) *Chiefly US.* to cut to or mark with specified dimensions. [C14: from OF, from L *dīmensiō* an extent, from *dīmētīrī* to measure out, from *mētīrī*]
▸**di'mensional** *adj* ▸**di'mensionless** *adj*

dimer (ˈdaɪmə) *n Chem.* a compound the molecule of which is formed by the linking of two identical molecules. [C20: from DI-[1] + -MER]
▸**dimeric** (daɪˈmɛrɪk) *adj*

dimerize *or* **dimerise** (ˈdaɪməˌraɪz) *vb* **dimerizes, dimerizing, dimerized** *or* **dimerises, dimerising, dimerised.** to react or cause to react to form a dimer.
▸ˌ**dimeri'zation** *or* ˌ**dimeri'sation** *n*

dimeter (ˈdɪmɪtə) *n Prosody.* a line of verse consisting of two metrical feet or a verse written in this metre.

dimethylformamide (daɪˌmiːθaɪlˈfɔːməˌmaɪd) *n* a colourless liquid widely used as a solvent and sometimes as a catalyst. Formula: $(CH_3)_2NCHO$. Abbrev.: **DMF.**

dimethylsulphoxide (daɪˌmiːθaɪlsʌlˈfɒksaɪd) *n* a liquid used as a solvent and in medicine to improve the penetration of drugs applied to the skin. Abbrev.: **DMSO.**

diminish ➊ (dɪˈmɪnɪʃ) *vb* **1** to make or become smaller, fewer, or less. **2** (*tr*) *Archit.* to cause to taper. **3** (*tr*) *Music.* to decrease (a minor or perfect interval) by a semitone. **4** to reduce in authority, status, etc. [C15: blend of *diminuen* to lessen (from L *dēminuere,* from *minuere*) + archaic *minish* to lessen]
▸**di'minishable** *adj*

diminished (dɪˈmɪnɪʃt) *adj* **1** reduced or lessened; made smaller. **2** *Music.* denoting any minor or perfect interval reduced by a semitone.

diminished responsibility *n Law.* a plea under which mental derangement is submitted as demonstrating lack of criminal responsibility.

diminishing returns *pl n Econ.* progressively smaller increases in output resulting from equal increases in production.

diminuendo (dɪˌmɪnjuˈɛndəʊ) *Music.* ◆ *n, pl* **diminuendos. 1a** a gradual decrease in loudness. Symbol: 5 **1b** a musical passage affected by a diminuendo. ◆ *adj* **2** gradually decreasing in loudness. **3** with a diminuendo. [C18: from It., from *diminuire* to DIMINISH]

diminution ➊ (ˌdɪmɪˈnjuːʃən) *n* **1** reduction; decrease. **2** *Music.* the presentation of the subject of a fugue, etc., in which the note values are reduced in length. [C14: from L *dēminūtiō*; see DIMINISH]

diminutive ➊ (dɪˈmɪnjʊtɪv) *adj* **1** very small; tiny. **2** *Grammar.* **2a** denoting an affix added to a word to convey the meaning *small* or *unimportant* or to express affection. **2b** denoting a word formed by the addition of a diminutive affix. ◆ *n* **3** *Grammar.* a diminutive word or affix. **4** a tiny person or thing.
▸**di'minutively** *adv* ▸**di'minutiveness** *n*

dimissory (dɪˈmɪsərɪ) *adj* **1** granting permission to be ordained: *a bishop's dimissory letter.* **2** granting permission to depart.

dimity (ˈdɪmɪtɪ) *n, pl* **dimities.** a light strong cotton fabric with woven stripes or squares. [C15: from Med. L *dimitum,* from Gk *dimiton,* from DI-[1] + *mitos* thread of the warp]

dimmer (ˈdɪmə) *n* **1** a device for dimming an electric light. **2** (*often pl*) *US.* **2a** a dipped headlight on a road vehicle. **2b** a parking light on a car.

dimorphism (daɪˈmɔːfɪzəm) *n* **1** the occurrence within a plant of two distinct forms of any part. **2** the occurrence in an animal species of two distinct types of individual. **3** a property of certain substances that enables them to exist in two distinct crystalline forms.
▸**di'morphic** *or* **di'morphous** *adj*

dimple (ˈdɪmpᵊl) *n* **1** a small natural dent, esp. on the cheeks or chin. **2** any slight depression in a surface. ◆ *vb* **dimples, dimpling, dimpled. 3** to make or become dimpled. **4** (*intr*) to produce dimples by smiling. [C13 *dympull*]
▸'**dimply** *adj*

dim sum (ˌdɪm ˈsʌm) *n* a Chinese appetizer of steamed dumplings containing various fillings. [Cantonese]

dimwit ➊ (ˈdɪmˌwɪt) *n Inf.* a stupid or silly person.
▸ˌ**dim-'witted** *adj* ▸ˌ**dim-'wittedness** *n*

din ➊ (dɪn) *n* **1** a loud discordant confused noise. ◆ *vb* **dins, dinning, dinned. 2** (*tr;* usually foll. by *into*) to instil by constant repetition. **3** (*tr*) to subject to a din. **4** (*intr*) to make a din. [OE *dynn*]

DIN *n* **1** a formerly used logarithmic expression of the speed of a photographic film, plate, etc.; high-speed films have high numbers. **2** a system of standard plugs, sockets, etc. formerly used for interconnecting domestic audio and video equipment. [C20: from G *D*(*eutsche*) *I*(*ndustrie*) *N*(*ormen*) German Industry Standards]

dinar (ˈdiːnɑː) *n* the standard monetary unit of Algeria, Bahrain, Bosnia-Herzegovina, Iraq, Jordan, Kuwait, Libya, Sudan, Tunisia, and Yugoslavia. [C17: from Ar., from LGk *dēnarion,* from L *dēnārius* DENARIUS]

dine ➊ (daɪn) *vb* **dines, dining, dined. 1** (*intr*) to eat dinner. **2** (*intr;* often foll. by *on, off,* or *upon*) to make one's meal (of): *the guests dined upon roast beef.* **3** (*tr*) *Inf.* to entertain to dinner (esp. in **wine and dine someone**). [C13: from OF *disner,* from Vulgar L *disjējūnāre* (unattested), from *dis-* not + LL *jējūnāre* to fast]

dine out *vb* (*intr, adv*) **1** to dine away from home. **2** (foll. by *on*) to have dinner at the expense of someone else mainly for the sake of one's conversation about (a subject or story).

diner (ˈdaɪnə) *n* **1** a person eating a meal, esp. in a restaurant. **2** *Chiefly US & Canad.* a small cheap restaurant. **3** a fashionable bar, or a section of one, where food is served.

dinette (daɪˈnɛt) *n* an alcove or small area for use as a dining room.

ding (dɪŋ) *vb* **1** to ring, esp. with tedious repetition. **2** (*tr*) another word for **din** (sense 2). ◆ *n* **3** an imitation of the sound of a bell. [C13: prob. imit., but infl. by DIN + RING[2]]

dingbat (ˈdɪŋˌbæt) *n Austral. sl.* a crazy or stupid person.

dingbats (ˈdɪŋˌbæts) *pl n Austral. & NZ sl.* an attack of nervousness, irritation, or loathing: *he had the dingbats.*

ding-dong *n* **1** the sound of a bell or bells. **2** an imitation of the sound of a bell. **3a** a violent exchange of blows or words. **3b** (*as modifier*): *a ding-dong battle.* ◆ *adj* **4** sounding or ringing repeatedly. [C16: imit.; see DING]

dinges (ˈdɪŋəs) *n S. African inf.* a jocular word for something whose name is unknown or forgotten; thingumabob. [from Afrik., from Du. *dinges* thing]

dinghy (ˈdɪŋɪ, ˈdɪŋgɪ) *n, pl* **dinghies.** any small boat, powered by sail, oars, or outboard motor. Also (esp. formerly): **dingy, dingey.** [C19: from Hindi or Bengali *dingi*]

dingle ➊ (ˈdɪŋgᵊl) *n* a small wooded dell. [C13: from ?]

dingo (ˈdɪŋgəʊ) *n, pl* **dingoes.** a wild dog of Australia, having a yellowish-brown coat and resembling a wolf. [C18: from Abor.]

dingy ➊ (ˈdɪndʒɪ) *adj* **dingier, dingiest. 1** lacking light or brightness; drab. **2** dirty; discoloured. [C18: perhaps from an earlier dialect word rel. to OE *dynge* dung]
▸'**dingily** *adv* ▸'**dinginess** *n*

dining car *n* a railway coach in which meals are served at tables. Also called: **restaurant car.**

dining room *n* a room where meals are eaten.

dinitrogen oxide (daɪˈnaɪtrədʒən) *n* the systematic name for **nitrous oxide.**

dinkie (ˈdɪŋkɪ) *n* **1** an affluent married childless person. ◆ *adj* **2** designed for or appealing to dinkies. [C20: from *d*(*ouble*) *i*(*ncome*) *n*(*o*) *k*(*ids*) + -IE]

THESAURUS

clear: bright, brilliant, clear, distinct, limpid, palpable ≠ **stupid:** acute, astute, aware, brainy, bright, clever, intelligent, keen, quick-witted, sharp, smart

dimension *n* **1, 2** *often plural* = **measurement,** amplitude, bulk, capacity, extent, proportions, size, volume

diminish *vb* **1** = **decrease,** abate, contract, curtail, cut, downsize, lessen, lower, reduce, retrench, shrink, taper, weaken **4** = **belittle,** cheapen, demean, depreciate, devalue
Antonyms *vb* ≠ **decrease:** amplify, augment, enhance, enlarge, expand, grow, heighten, increase

diminution *n* **1** = **decrease,** abatement, contraction, curtailment, cut, cutback, decay, decline, deduction, lessening, reduction, retrenchment, weakening

diminutive *adj* **1** = **small,** bantam, Lilliputian, little, midget, mini, miniature, minute, petite, pocket(-sized), pygmy *or* pigmy, teensy-weensy, teeny-weeny, tiny, undersized, wee
Antonyms *adj* big, colossal, enormous, giant, gigantic, great, immense, jumbo (*inf.*), king-size, massive (*inf.*)

dimwit *n Informal* = **idiot,** blockhead, bonehead (*sl.*), booby, dullard, dumb-ass (*sl.*), dunce, dunderhead, fathead (*inf.*), gobshite (*Irish taboo sl.*), ignoramus, lamebrain (*inf.*), nitwit (*inf.*), numbskull *or* numskull

dim-witted *adj Informal* = **stupid,** braindead (*inf.*), dense, dim, doltish, dopey (*inf.*), dozy (*Brit. inf.*), dull, dumb (*inf.*), dumb-ass (*sl.*), obtuse, slow, slow on the uptake, thick (*inf.*), thick-skulled, unperceptive
Antonyms *adj* alert, astute, bright, clever, keen, perceptive, quick on the uptake, quick-witted, sharp, shrewd, smart

din *n* **1** = **noise,** babel, clamour, clangour, clash, clatter, commotion, crash, hubbub, hullabaloo, outcry, pandemonium, racket, row, shout, uproar ◆ *vb* **2** *usually foll. by* **into** = **instil,** drum into, go on at, hammer into, inculcate, instruct, teach
Antonyms *n* ≠ **noise:** calm, calmness, hush, peace, quiet, quietness, silence, tranquillity

dine *vb* **1** = **eat,** banquet, chow down (*sl.*), feast, lunch, sup **2 dine on** *or* **off** = **eat,** consume, feed on

dingle *n* = **dell,** dale, glen, hollow, vale, valley

dingy *adj* **1** = **dull,** bedimmed, colourless, dark, dim, drab, dreary, dusky, faded, gloomy, murky, obscure, sombre **2** = **discoloured,** dirty, grimy, seedy, shabby, soiled, tacky (*inf.*)

dinkum ('dɪŋkəm) *adj Austral. & NZ inf.* **1** genuine or right: *a fair dinkum offer.* **2 dinkum oil.** the truth. [C19: from E dialect: work, from ?]
dinky ⓘ ('dɪŋkɪ) *adj* **dinkier, dinkiest.** *Inf.* **1** *Brit.* small and neat; dainty. **2** *US.* inconsequential; insignificant. [C18: from Scot. & N English dialect *dink* neat, neatly dressed]
dinky-di ('dɪŋkɪ'daɪ) *adj Austral. inf.* typical: *dinky-di Pom idleness.* [C20: var. of DINKUM]
dinner ⓘ ('dɪnə) *n* **1** a meal taken in the evening. **2** a meal taken at midday, esp. when it is the main meal of the day; lunch. **3** a formal meal or banquet in honour of someone or something. **4** (*as modifier*): *dinner table; dinner hour.* [C13: from OF *disner;* see DINE]
dinner dance *n* a formal dinner followed by dancing.
dinner jacket *n* a man's semiformal evening jacket without tails, usually black. US and Canad. name: **tuxedo.**
dinner service *n* a set of matching plates, dishes, etc., suitable for serving a meal.
dinosaur ('daɪnəˌsɔː) *n* **1** any of a large order of extinct reptiles many of which were of gigantic size and abundant in the Mesozoic era. **2** a person or thing that is considered to be out of date. [C19: from NL *dinosaurus,* from Gk *deinos* fearful + *sauros* lizard]
▸ˌ**dino'saurian** *adj*
dint ⓘ (dɪnt) *n* **1 by dint of.** by means or use of: *by dint of hard work.* **2** *Arch.* a blow or a mark made by a blow. ◆ *vb* **3** (*tr*) to mark with dints. [OE *dynt*]
dioc. *abbrev. for:* **1** diocesan. **2** diocese.
diocesan (daɪ'ɒsɪsᵊn) *adj* **1** of or relating to a diocese. ◆ *n* **2** the bishop of a diocese.
diocese ⓘ ('daɪəsɪs) *n* the district under the jurisdiction of a bishop. [C14: from OF, from LL *diocēsis,* from Gk *dioikēsis* administration, from *dioikein* to manage a household, from *oikos* house]
diode ('daɪəʊd) *n* **1** a semiconductor device used in circuits for converting alternating current to direct current. **2** the earliest type of electronic valve having two electrodes between which a current can flow only in one direction. [C20: from DI-[1] + -ODE[2]]
dioecious (daɪ'iːʃəs) *adj* (of plants) having the male and female reproductive organs on separate plants. [C18: from NL *Dioecia* name of class, from DI-[1] + Gk *oikia* house]
Dionysian (ˌdaɪə'nɪzɪən) *adj* **1** of or relating to Dionysus, the Greek god of wine and revelry. **2** (*often not cap.*) wild or orgiastic.
Diophantine equation (ˌdaɪəʊ'fæntaɪn) *n* (in number theory) an equation in more than one variable, for which integral solutions are sought. [from *Diophantus,* 3rd century A.D., Gk mathematician]
dioptre *or US* **diopter** (daɪ'ɒptə) *n* a unit for measuring the refractive power of a lens: the reciprocal of the focal length of the lens expressed in metres. [C16: from L *dioptra* optical instrument, from Gk, from *dia-* through + *opsesthai* to see]
▸**di'optral** *adj*
dioptrics (daɪ'ɒptrɪks) *n* (*functioning as sing*) the branch of geometrical optics concerned with the formation of images by lenses. [C20: from DIOPTRE + -ICS]
diorama (ˌdaɪə'rɑːmə) *n* **1** a miniature three-dimensional scene, in which models of figures are seen against a background. **2** a picture made up of illuminated translucent curtains, viewed through an aperture. **3** a museum display, as of an animal, of a specimen in its natural setting. [C19: from F, from Gk *dia-* through + *horama* view, from *horan* to see]
▸**dioramic** (ˌdaɪə'ræmɪk) *adj*
dioxide (daɪ'ɒksaɪd) *n* any oxide containing two oxygen atoms per molecule, both of which are bonded to an atom of another element.
dioxin (daɪ'ɒksɪn) *n* any of various chemical by-products of the manufacture of certain herbicides and bactericides, esp. the extremely toxic tetrachlorodibenzoparadioxin (TCDD).
dip ⓘ (dɪp) *vb* **dips, dipping, dipped. 1** to plunge or be plunged quickly or briefly into a liquid, esp. to wet or coat. **2** (*intr*) to undergo a slight decline, esp. temporarily: *sales dipped in November.* **3** (*intr*) to slope downwards. **4** (*intr*) to sink quickly. **5** (*tr*) to switch (car headlights) from the main to the lower beam. US and Canad. word: **dim. 6** (*tr*) **6a** to immerse (sheep, etc.) briefly in a chemical to rid them of or prevent infestation by insects, etc. **6b** to immerse (grain, vegetables, or wood) in a preservative liquid. **7** (*tr*) to dye by immersing in a liquid. **8** (*tr*) to baptize (someone) by immersion. **9** (*tr*) to plate or galvanize (a metal, etc.) by immersion in an electrolyte or electrolytic cell. **10** (*tr*) to scoop up a liquid or something from a liquid in the hands or in a container. **11** to lower or be lowered briefly. **12** (*tr*) to make (a candle) by plunging the wick into melted wax. **13** (*intr*) to plunge a container, the hands, etc., into something, esp. to obtain an object. **14** (*intr*) (of an aircraft) to drop suddenly and then regain height. ◆ *n* **15** the act of dipping or state of being dipped. **16** a brief swim in water. **17a** any liquid chemical in which sheep, etc. are dipped. **17b** any liquid preservative into which objects are dipped. **18** a dye into which fabric is immersed. **19** a depression, esp. in a landscape. **20** something taken up by dipping. **21** a container used for dipping; dipper. **22** a momentary sinking down. **23** the angle of slope of rock strata, etc., from the horizontal plane. **24** the angle between the direction of the earth's magnetic field and the plane of the horizon; the angle that a magnetic needle free to swing in a vertical plane makes with the horizontal. **25** a creamy savoury mixture into which pieces of food are dipped before being eaten. **26** *Surveying.* the angular distance of the horizon below the plane of observation. **27** a candle made by plunging a wick into wax. **28** a momentary loss of altitude when flying. ◆ See also **dip into.** [OE *dyppan*]
dip. *or* **Dip.** *abbrev. for* diploma.
DipAD *abbrev. for* Diploma in Art and Design.
DipEd (in Britain) *abbrev. for* Diploma in Education.
diphtheria (dɪp'θɪərɪə) *n* an acute contagious disease caused by a bacillus, producing fever, severe prostration, and difficulty in breathing and swallowing as the result of swelling of the throat and the formation of a false membrane. [C19: NL, from F *diphthérie,* from Gk *diphthera* leather; from the nature of the membrane]
▸**diph'therial, diphtheritic** (ˌdɪpθə'rɪtɪk), *or* **diphtheric** (dɪp'θɛrɪk) *adj*
diphthong ('dɪfθɒŋ) *n* **1** a vowel sound, occupying a single syllable, during the articulation of which the tongue moves continuously from one position to another, as in the pronunciation of *a* in *late.* **2** a digraph or ligature representing a composite vowel such as this, as *ae* in *Caesar.* [C15: from LL *diphthongus,* from Gk *diphthongos,* from DI-[1] + *phthongos* sound]
▸**diph'thongal** *adj*
diphthongize *or* **diphthongise** ('dɪfθɒŋˌaɪz) *vb* **diphthongizes, diphthongizing, diphthongized** *or* **diphthongises, diphthongising, diphthongised.** (*often passive*) to make (a simple vowel) into a diphthong.
▸ˌ**diphthongi'zation** *or* ˌ**diphthongi'sation** *n*
dip into ⓘ *vb* (*intr, prep*) **1** to draw upon: *he dipped into his savings.* **2** to dabble (in); play at. **3** to read passages at random from (a book, newspaper, etc.).
diplodocus (ˌdɪpləʊ'dəʊkəs, dɪ'plɒdəkəs) *n, pl* **diplodocuses.** a herbivorous dinosaur characterized by a very long neck and tail and a total body length of 27 metres. [C19: from NL, from Gk *diplo-,* (from *diploos,* from DI-[1] + *-ploos* -fold) + *dokos* beam]
diploid ('dɪplɔɪd) *adj* **1** *Biol.* (of cells or organisms) having paired homologous chromosomes so that twice the haploid number is present. **2** double or twofold. ◆ *n* **3** a diploid cell or organism.
▸**dip'loidic** *adj*
diploma (dɪ'pləʊmə) *n* **1** a document conferring a qualification, recording success in examinations or successful completion of a course of study. **2** an official document that confers an honour or privilege. [C17: from L: official letter or document, lit.: letter folded double, from Gk]
diplomacy ⓘ (dɪ'pləʊməsɪ) *n, pl* **diplomacies. 1** the conduct of the relations of one state with another by peaceful means. **2** skill in the management of international relations. **3** tact, skill, or cunning in dealing with people. [C18: from F *diplomatie,* from *diplomatique* DIPLOMATIC]
diplomat ⓘ ('dɪpləˌmæt) *n* **1** an official such as an ambassador, engaged in diplomacy. **2** a person who deals with people tactfully or skilfully. ◆ Also called: **diplomatist** (dɪ'pləʊmətɪst).
diplomatic ⓘ (ˌdɪplə'mætɪk) *adj* **1** of or relating to diplomacy or diplomats. **2** skilled in negotiating, esp. between states or people. **3** tactful in dealing with people. [C18: from F *diplomatique* concerning the documents of diplomacy, from NL *diplōmaticus;* see DIPLOMA]
▸ˌ**diplo'matically** *adv*
diplomatic bag *n* a container or bag in which official mail is sent, free from customs inspection, to and from an embassy or consulate.
diplomatic corps *or* **body** *n* the entire body of diplomats accredited to a given state.
diplomatic immunity *n* the immunity from local jurisdiction and exemption from taxation in the country to which they are accredited afforded to diplomats.
Diplomatic Service *n* **1** (in Britain) the division of the Civil Service which provides diplomats to represent the UK abroad. **2** (*not caps.*) the equivalent institution of any other country.
dipole ('daɪˌpəʊl) *n* **1** two equal but opposite electric charges or magnetic poles separated by a small distance. **2** a molecule in which the centre of positive charge does not coincide with the centre of nega-

THESAURUS

dinky *adj* **1** *Brit. informal* = **cute,** dainty, mini, miniature, natty (*inf.*), neat, petite, small, trim
dinner *n* **1, 3** = **meal,** banquet, beanfeast (*Brit. inf.*), blowout (*sl.*), collation, feast, main meal, refection, repast, spread (*inf.*)
dint *n* **1** *As in* **by dint of** = **means,** force, power, use, virtue
diocese *n* = **bishopric,** see
dip *vb* **1** = **plunge,** bathe, douse, duck, dunk, immerse, rinse, souse **3** = **slope,** decline, descend, disappear, droop, drop (down), fade, fall, lower, sag, set, sink, slump, subside, tilt ◆ *n* **15** = **plunge,** douche, drenching, ducking, immersion, soaking **16** = **bathe,** dive, plunge, swim **17b** = **mixture,** concoction, dilution, infusion, preparation, solution, suspension **19** = **hollow,** basin, concavity, depression, hole, incline, slope **22** = **drop,** decline, fall, lowering, sag, slip, slump
dip into *vb* **1** = **draw upon,** reach into **2, 3** = **sample,** browse, dabble, glance at, peruse, play at, run over, skim, try
diplomacy *n* **1** = **statesmanship,** international negotiation, statecraft **2** = **tact,** artfulness, craft, delicacy, discretion, finesse, savoir-faire, skill, subtlety
Antonyms *n* ≠ **tact:** awkwardness, clumsiness, ineptness, tactlessness, thoughtlessness
diplomat *n* **2** = **negotiator,** conciliator, go-between, mediator, moderator, politician, public relations expert, tactician
diplomatic *adj* **3** = **tactful,** adept, discreet, polite, politic, prudent, sensitive, subtle
Antonyms *adj* impolitic, insensitive, rude, tactless, thoughtless, undiplomatic, unsubtle

tive charge. **3** a directional aerial consisting of two metal rods with a connecting wire fixed between them in the form of a T.
▸di'polar *adj*

dipole moment *n Chem.* a measure of the polarity in a chemical bond or molecule, equal to the product of one charge and the distance between the charges. Symbol: μ

dipper ('dɪpə) *n* **1** a ladle used for dipping. **2** Also called: **water ouzel.** any of a genus of aquatic songbirds that inhabit fast-flowing streams. **3** a person or thing that dips. **4** *Arch.* an Anabaptist. ◆ See also **big dipper.**

dippy ('dɪpɪ) *adj* **dippier, dippiest.** *Sl.* odd, eccentric, or crazy. [C20: from ?]

dipsomania (ˌdɪpsəʊ'meɪnɪə) *n* a compulsive desire to drink alcoholic beverages. [C19: NL, from Gk *dipsa* thirst + -MANIA]
▸ˌdipso'maniac *n, adj*

dipstick ('dɪpˌstɪk) *n* **1** a graduated rod or strip dipped into a container to indicate the fluid level. **2** *Brit. sl.* a fool.

dip switch *n* a device for dipping car headlights.

dipteran ('dɪptərən) *or* **dipteron** ('dɪptəˌrɒn) *n* **1** any dipterous insect. ◆ *adj* **2** another word for **dipterous** (sense 1).

dipterous ('dɪptərəs) *adj* **1** Also: **dipteran.** of a large order of insects having a single pair of wings and sucking or piercing mouthparts. The group includes flies, mosquitoes, and midges. **2** *Bot.* having two winglike parts. [C18: from Gk *dipteros* two-winged]

diptych ('dɪptɪk) *n* **1** a pair of hinged wooden tablets with waxed surfaces for writing. **2** a painting or carving on two hinged panels. [C17: from Gk *diptukhos* folded together, from DI-[1] + *ptukhos* fold]

dire Ⓣ ('daɪə) *adj* (*usually prenominal*) **1** Also: **direful.** disastrous; fearful. **2** desperate; urgent: *a dire need.* **3** foreboding disaster; ominous. [C16: from L *dīrus* ominous]
▸'direly *adv* ▸'direness *n*

direct Ⓣ (dɪ'rɛkt, daɪ-) *vb* (*mainly tr*) **1** to conduct or control the affairs of. **2** (*also intr*) to give commands or orders with authority to (a person or group). **3** to tell or show (someone) the way to a place. **4** to aim, point, or cause to move towards a goal. **5** to address (a letter, etc.). **6** to address (remarks, etc.). **7** (*also intr*) **7a** to provide guidance to (actors, cameramen, etc.) in a play or film. **7b** to supervise the making or staging of (a film or play). **8** (*also intr*) to conduct (a piece of music or musicians), usually while performing oneself. ◆ *adj* **9** without delay or evasion; straightforward. **10** without turning aside; shortest; straight: *a direct route.* **11** without intervening persons or agencies: *a direct link.* **12** honest; frank. **13** (*usually prenominal*) precise; exact: *a direct quotation.* **14** diametrical: *the direct opposite.* **15** in an unbroken line of descent: *a direct descendant.* **16** (of government, decisions, etc.) by or from the electorate rather than through representatives. **17** *Logic, maths.* (of a proof) progressing from the premises to the conclusion, rather than eliminating the possibility of the falsehood of the conclusion. Cf. **indirect proof. 18** *Astron.* moving from west to east. Cf. **retrograde. 19** of or relating to direct current. **20** *Music.* (of an interval or chord) in root position; not inverted. ◆ *adv* **21** directly; straight. [C14: from L *dīrectus,* from *dīrigere* to guide, from *dis-* apart + *regere* to rule]
▸di'rectness *n*

direct access *n* a method of reading data from a computer file without reading through the file from the beginning.

direct action *n* action such as strikes or civil disobedience employed to obtain demands from an employer, government, etc.

direct current *n* a continuous electric current that flows in one direction only.

direct debit *n* an order given to a bank or building society by a holder of an account, instructing it to pay to a specified person or organization any sum demanded by that person or organization. Cf. **standing order.**

direct-grant school *n* (in Britain, formerly) a school financed by endowment, fees, and a state grant conditional upon admittance of a percentage of nonpaying pupils.

direction Ⓣ (dɪ'rɛkʃən, daɪ-) *n* **1** the act of directing or the state of being directed. **2** management, control, or guidance. **3** the work of a stage or film director. **4** the course or line along which a person or thing moves, points, or lies. **5** the place towards which a person or thing is directed. **6** a line of action; course. **7** the name and address on a letter, parcel, etc. **8** *Music.* the process of conducting an orchestra, choir, etc. **9** *Music.* an instruction to indicate tempo, dynamics, mood, etc.

directional (dɪ'rɛkʃənᵊl, daɪ-) *adj* **1** of or relating to a spatial direction. **2** *Electronics.* **2a** having or relating to an increased sensitivity to radio waves, nuclear particles, etc., coming from a particular direction. **2b** (of an aerial) transmitting or receiving radio waves more effectively in some directions than in others. **3** *Physics, electronics.* concentrated in, following, or producing motion in a particular direction.
▸diˌrection'ality *n*

directional drilling *n* a method of drilling for oil in which the well is not drilled vertically, as when a number of wells are to be drilled from a single platform. Also called: **deviated drilling.**

direction finder *n* a device to determine the direction of incoming radio signals, used esp. as a navigation aid.

directions Ⓣ (dɪ'rɛkʃənz, daɪ-) *pl n* (*sometimes sing*) instructions for doing something or for reaching a place.

directive Ⓣ (dɪ'rɛktɪv, daɪ-) *n* **1** an instruction; order. ◆ *adj* **2** tending to direct; directing. **3** indicating direction.

directly Ⓣ (dɪ'rɛktlɪ, daɪ-) *adv* **1** in a direct manner. **2** at once; without delay. **3** (foll. by *before* or *after*) immediately; just. ◆ *conj* **4** (*subordinating*) as soon as.

direct marketing *n* selling goods directly to consumers rather than through retailers, as by mail order, telephone selling, etc. Also called: **direct selling.**

direct object *n Grammar.* a noun, pronoun, or noun phrase whose referent receives the direct action of a verb. For example, *a book* in *They bought Anne a book.*

directoire (dɪ'rɛktwɑː) *adj* (of ladies' knickers) knee-length, with elastic at waist and knees. [C19: after fashions of the period of the French *Directoire* Directorate (1795–99)]

director Ⓣ (dɪ'rɛktə, daɪ-) *n* **1** a person or thing that directs, controls, or regulates. **2** a member of the governing board of a business concern. **3** a person who directs the affairs of an institution, trust, etc. **4** the person responsible for the artistic and technical aspects of the making of a film or television programme or the staging of a play. Cf. **producer** (sense 3). **5** *Music.* another word (esp. US) for **conductor.**
▸ˌdirec'torial *adj* ▸ˌdi'rectorˌship *n* ▸di'rectress *fem n*

directorate (dɪ'rɛktərɪt, daɪ-) *n* **1** a board of directors. **2** Also: **directorship.** the position of director.

director-general *n, pl* **directors-general.** the head of a large organization such as the CBI or BBC.

Director of Public Prosecutions *n* (in Britain) an official who, as head of the Crown Prosecution Service, is responsible for conducting all criminal prosecutions initiated by the police. Abbrev.: **DPP.**

director's chair *n* a light wooden folding chair with arm rests and a canvas seat and back, as used by film directors.

directory (dɪ'rɛktərɪ, -trɪ; daɪ-) *n, pl* **directories. 1** a book listing names, addresses, telephone numbers, etc., of individuals or firms. **2** a book giving directions. **3** a book containing the rules to be observed in the forms of worship used in churches. **4** a directorate. **5** *Computing.* an area of a disk, Winchester disk, or floppy disk that contains the names and locations of files currently held on that disk. ◆ *adj* **6** directing.

Directory (dɪ'rɛktərɪ, -trɪ; daɪ-) *n* **the.** *History.* the body of five directors in power in France from 1795 until their overthrow by Napoleon in 1799. Also called: **French Directory.**

direct primary *n US government.* a primary in which voters directly select the candidates who will run for office.

direct selling *n* another name for **direct marketing.**

direct speech *or esp. US* **direct discourse** *n* the reporting of what someone has said or written by quoting his exact words.

direct tax *n* a tax paid by the person or organization on which it is levied.

dirge Ⓣ (dɜːdʒ) *n* **1** a chant of lamentation for the dead. **2** the funeral service in its solemn or sung forms. **3** any mourning song or melody. [C13: from L *dīrigē* direct (imperative), opening word of antiphon used in the office of the dead]
▸'dirgeful *adj*

THESAURUS

dire *adj* **1** = **disastrous**, alarming, appalling, awful, calamitous, cataclysmic, catastrophic, cruel, horrible, horrid, ruinous, terrible, woeful **2** = **desperate**, critical, crucial, crying, drastic, exigent, extreme, now or never, pressing, urgent **3** = **grim**, dismal, dreadful, fearful, gloomy, ominous, portentous

direct *vb* **1** = **control**, administer, advise, call the shots, call the tune, conduct, dispose, govern, guide, handle, lead, manage, mastermind, oversee, preside over, regulate, rule, run, superintend, supervise **2** = **order**, bid, charge, command, demand, dictate, enjoin, instruct **3** = **guide**, indicate, lead, point in the direction of, point the way, show **5** = **address**, label, mail, route, send, superscribe **6** = **aim**, address, cast, fix, focus, intend, level, mean, point, train, turn ◆ *adj* **10** = **straight**, nonstop, not crooked, shortest, through, unbroken, undeviating, uninterrupted **11** = **first-hand**, face-to-face, head-on, immediate, personal **12** = **straightforward**, candid, downright, frank, honest, man-to-man, matter-of-fact, open, outspoken, plain-spoken, round, sincere, straight, upfront (*inf.*)
Antonyms *adj* ≠ **straight:** circuitous, crooked, indirect ≠ **first-hand:** indirect, mediated ≠ **straightforward:** circuitous, crooked, devious, indirect, sly, subtle ≠ **explicit:** ambiguous, circuitous, indirect

direction *n* **2** = **management**, administration, charge, command, control, government, guidance, leadership, order, oversight, superintendence, supervision **4** = **way**, aim, bearing, course, line, path, road, route, track

directions *pl n* = **instructions**, briefing, guidance, guidelines, indication, plan, recommendation, regulations

directive *n* **1** = **order**, canon, charge, command, decree, dictate, edict, fiat, imperative, injunction, instruction, mandate, notice, ordinance, regulation, ruling

directly *adv* **1** = **straight**, by the shortest route, exactly, in a beeline, precisely, unswervingly, without deviation **1** = **honestly**, candidly, face-to-face, in person, openly, overtly, personally, plainly, point-blank, straightforwardly, truthfully, unequivocally, without prevarication **2** = **at once**, as soon as possible, dead, due, forthwith, immediately, in a second, instantaneously, instantly, posthaste, presently, promptly, pronto (*inf.*), quickly, right away, soon, speedily, straightaway

directness *n* **12** = **honesty**, bluntness, candour, forthrightness, frankness, outspokenness, plain speaking, sincerity, straightforwardness

director *n* **1-4** = **controller**, administrator, boss (*inf.*), chairman, chief, executive, governor, head, leader, manager, organizer, principal, producer, supervisor

dirge *n* **1, 3** = **lament**, coronach (*Scot. & Irish*),

dirham ('dɪəræm) *n* **1** the standard monetary unit of Morocco and the United Arab Emirates. **2** a monetary unit of Kuwait, Libya, Qatar, and Tunisia. **3** any of various N African coins. [C18: from Ar., from L: DRACHMA]

dirigible ('dɪrɪdʒɪbᵊl) *adj* **1** able to be steered or directed. ◆ *n* **2** another name for **airship.** [C16: from L *dīrigere* to DIRECT]
▸ˌ**dirigi'bility** *n*

dirigisme (diːriː'ʒiːzəm) *n* control by the state of economic and social matters. [C20: from F]
▸**diri'giste** *adj*

dirk (dɜːk) *n* **1** a dagger, esp. as formerly worn by Scottish Highlanders. ◆ *vb* **2** (*tr*) to stab with a dirk. [C16: from Scot. *durk,* ?from G *Dolch* dagger]

dirndl ('dɜːndᵊl) *n* **1** a woman's dress with a full gathered skirt and fitted bodice; originating from Tyrolean peasant wear. **2** a gathered skirt of this kind. [G (Bavarian and Austrian): from *Dirndlkleid,* from *Dirndl* little girl + *Kleid* dress]

dirt ❶ (dɜːt) *n* **1** any unclean substance, such as mud, etc.; filth. **2** loose earth; soil. **3a** packed earth, gravel, cinders, etc., used to make a racetrack. **3b** (*as modifier*): *a dirt track.* **4** *Mining.* the gravel or soil from which minerals are extracted. **5** a person or thing regarded as worthless. **6** obscene or indecent speech or writing. **7** *Sl.* gossip; scandalous information. **8** moral corruption. **9 do (someone) dirt.** *Sl.* to do something vicious to (someone). **10 eat dirt.** *Sl.* to accept insult without complaining. [C13: from ON *drit* excrement]

dirt-cheap *adj, adv Inf.* at an extremely low price.

dirty ❶ ('dɜːtɪ) *adj* **dirtier, dirtiest. 1** covered or marked with dirt; filthy. **2a** obscene: *dirty books.* **2b** sexually clandestine: *a dirty weekend.* **3** causing one to become grimy: *a dirty job.* **4** (of a colour) not clear and bright. **5** unfair; dishonest. **6** mean; nasty: *a dirty cheat.* **7** scandalous; unkind. **8** revealing dislike or anger. **9** (of weather) rainy or squally; stormy. **10** (of a nuclear weapon) producing a large quantity of radioactive fallout. **11 dirty linen.** *Inf.* intimate secrets, esp. those that might give rise to gossip. **12 dirty work.** unpleasant or illicit activity. ◆ *n* **13 do the dirty on.** *Inf.* to behave meanly towards. ◆ *vb* **dirties, dirtying, dirtied. 14** to make or become dirty; stain; soil.
▸'**dirtily** *adv* ▸'**dirtiness** *n*

dis (dɪs) *vb* a variant spelling of **diss.**

dis-[1] *prefix* **1** indicating reversal: *disconnect.* **2** indicating negation, lack, or deprivation: *dissimilar; disgrace.* **3** indicating removal or release: *disembowel.* **4** expressing intensive force: *dissever.* [from L *dis-* apart; in some cases, via OF *des-*. In compound words of L origin, *dis-* becomes *dif-* before *f,* and *di-* before some consonants]

dis-[2] *combining form.* a variant of **di-**[1] before *s: dissyllable.*

disability ❶ (ˌdɪsə'bɪlɪtɪ) *n, pl* **disabilities. 1** the condition of being physically or mentally impaired. **2** something that disables; handicap. **3** lack of necessary intelligence, strength, etc. **4** an incapacity in the eyes of the law to enter into certain transactions.

disable ❶ (dɪs'eɪbᵊl) *vb* **disables, disabling, disabled.** (*tr*) **1** to make ineffective, unfit, or incapable, as by crippling. **2** to make or pronounce legally incapable. **3** to switch off (an electronic device).
▸**dis'ablement** *n*

disabled ❶ (dɪ'seɪbᵊld) *adj* **a** lacking one or more physical powers, such as the ability to walk or to coordinate one's movements. **b** (*as collective n; preceded by the*): *the disabled.* See usage note below.

> **USAGE NOTE** The use of *the disabled, the blind,* etc. can be offensive and should be avoided. Instead one should talk about *disabled people, blind people,* etc.

disabuse ❶ (ˌdɪsə'bjuːz) *vb* **disabuses, disabusing, disabused.** (*tr; usually foll. by of*) to rid of a mistaken idea; set right.

disadvantage ❶ (ˌdɪsəd'vɑːntɪdʒ) *n* **1** an unfavourable circumstance, thing, person, etc. **2** injury, loss, or detriment. **3** an unfavourable situation (esp. in **at a disadvantage**). ◆ *vb* **disadvantages, disadvantaging, disadvantaged. 4** (*tr*) to put at a disadvantage; handicap.

disadvantaged ❶ (ˌdɪsəd'vɑːntɪdʒd) *adj* socially or economically deprived or discriminated against.

disadvantageous ❶ (ˌdɪsædvɑːn'teɪdʒəs, dɪsˌædvən'teɪdʒəs) *adj* unfavourable; detrimental.
▸ˌ**disadvan'tageously** *adv* ▸ˌ**disadvan'tageousness** *n*

disaffect ❶ (ˌdɪsə'fɛkt) *vb* (*tr; often passive*) to cause to lose loyalty or affection; alienate.
▸ˌ**disaf'fectedly** *adv* ▸ˌ**disaf'fection** *n*

disaffiliate (ˌdɪsə'fɪlɪˌeɪt) *vb* **disaffiliates, disaffiliating, disaffiliated.** to sever an affiliation (with).
▸ˌ**disafˌfili'ation** *n*

disafforest (ˌdɪsə'fɒrɪst) *vb* (*tr*) *Law.* to reduce (land) from the status of a forest to the state of ordinary ground.
▸ˌ**disafˌfores'tation** *n*

disaggregate (dɪs'ægrɪˌgeɪt) *vb* **disaggregates, disaggregating, disaggregated. 1** to separate from a group or mass. **2** to divide into parts.
▸ˌ**disaggre'gation** *n*

disagree ❶ (ˌdɪsə'griː) *vb* **disagrees, disagreeing, disagreed.** (*intr; often foll. by with*) **1** to dissent in opinion or dispute (about an idea, fact, etc.). **2** to fail to correspond; conflict. **3** to be unacceptable (to) or unfavourable (for): *curry disagrees with me.* **4** to be opposed (to).

disagreeable ❶ (ˌdɪsə'griːəbᵊl) *adj* **1** not likable; bad-tempered, esp. disobliging, etc. **2** not to one's liking; unpleasant.
▸ˌ**disa'greeableness** *n* ▸ˌ**disa'greeably** *adv*

disagreement ❶ (ˌdɪsə'griːmənt) *n* **1** refusal or failure to agree. **2** a failure to correspond. **3** an argument or dispute.

disallow ❶ (ˌdɪsə'laʊ) *vb* (*tr*) **1** to reject as untrue or invalid. **2** to cancel.
▸ˌ**disal'lowable** *adj* ▸ˌ**disal'lowance** *n*

disappear ❶ (ˌdɪsə'pɪə) *vb* **1** (*intr*) to cease to be visible; vanish. **2** (*intr*) to go away or become lost, esp. without explanation. **3** (*intr*) to cease to exist; become extinct or lost. **4** (*tr*) (esp. in South and Central

THESAURUS

dead march, elegy, funeral song, requiem, threnody

dirt *n* **1** = **filth**, crap (*sl.*), crud (*sl.*), dust, excrement, grime, grot (*sl.*), impurity, mire, muck, mud, shit (*taboo sl.*), slime, slob (*Irish*), smudge, stain, tarnish **2** = **soil**, clay, earth, loam **6** = **obscenity**, indecency, pornography, sleaze, smut

dirty *adj* **1** = **filthy**, begrimed, foul, grimy, grotty (*sl.*), grubby, grungy (*sl., chiefly US*), messy, mucky, muddy, nasty, polluted, scuzzy (*sl., chiefly US*), soiled, sullied, unclean **2a** = **obscene**, blue, indecent, off-colour, pornographic, risqué, salacious, sleazy, smutty, vulgar, X-rated (*inf.*) **4** = **dark**, clouded, dull, miry, muddy, not clear **5** = **dishonest**, corrupt, crooked, fraudulent, illegal, treacherous, unfair, unscrupulous, unsporting **6** = **despicable**, base, beggarly, contemptible, cowardly, ignominious, low, low-down (*inf.*), mean, nasty, scurvy, shabby, sordid, squalid, vile **9** = **stormy**, gusty, louring *or* lowering, rainy, squally ◆ *vb* **14** = **soil**, begrime, blacken, defile, foul, mess up, muddy, pollute, smear, smirch, smudge, spoil, stain, sully
Antonyms *adj* ≠ **filthy:** clean, pure ≠ **dishonest:** decent, honest, moral, reputable, respectable, upright ≠ **obscene:** clean, decent ≠ **stormy:** pleasant ◆ *vb* ≠ **soil:** clean, tidy up

disability *n* **1, 2** = **handicap**, affliction, ailment, complaint, defect, disablement, disorder, impairment, infirmity, malady **4** = **incapacity**, disqualification, impotency, inability, incompetency, unfitness, weakness

disable *vb* **1** = **handicap**, cripple, damage, debilitate, enfeeble, hamstring, immobilize, impair, incapacitate, paralyse, prostrate, put out of action, render *hors de combat*, render inoperative, unfit, unman, weaken **2** = **disqualify**, disenable, invalidate, render *or* declare incapable

disabled *adj* **a** = **handicapped**, bedridden, crippled, incapacitated, infirm, lame, maimed, mangled, mutilated, paralysed, weak, weakened, wrecked
Antonyms *adj* able-bodied, fit, hale, healthy, hearty, robust, sound, strong, sturdy

disabuse *vb* = **enlighten**, correct, free from error, open the eyes of, set right, set straight, shatter (someone's) illusions, undeceive

disadvantage *n* **1** = **drawback**, burden, downside, flaw, fly in the ointment (*inf.*), handicap, hardship, hindrance, impediment, inconvenience, liability, minus (*inf.*), nuisance, privation, snag, trouble, weakness, weak point **2** = **harm**, damage, detriment, disservice, hurt, injury, loss, prejudice **3 at a disadvantage** = **vulnerable**, boxed in, cornered, handicapped, in a corner, with one's hands tied behind one's back
Antonyms *n* ≠ **harm, drawback:** advantage, aid, benefit, convenience, gain, help, merit, profit

disadvantaged *adj* = **deprived**, discriminated against, handicapped, impoverished, struggling, underprivileged

disadvantageous *adj* = **unfavourable**, adverse, damaging, deleterious, detrimental, harmful, hurtful, ill-timed, inconvenient, inexpedient, injurious, inopportune, prejudicial

disaffected *adj* = **alienated**, antagonistic, discontented, disloyal, dissatisfied, estranged, hostile, mutinous, rebellious, seditious, uncompliant, unsubmissive

disaffection *n* = **alienation**, animosity, antagonism, antipathy, aversion, breach, disagreement, discontent, dislike, disloyalty, dissatisfaction, estrangement, hostility, ill will, repugnance, resentment, unfriendliness

disagree *vb* **1** = **differ (in opinion)**, argue, be at sixes and sevens, bicker, clash, contend, contest, cross swords, debate, dispute, dissent, fall out (*inf.*), have words (*inf.*), object, oppose, quarrel, take issue with, wrangle **2** = **conflict**, be discordant, be dissimilar, contradict, counter, depart, deviate, differ, diverge, run counter to, vary **3** = **make ill**, be injurious, bother, discomfort, distress, hurt, nauseate, sicken, trouble, upset
Antonyms *vb* ≠ **differ (in opinion):** agree, concur, get on (together) ≠ **conflict:** accord, coincide, harmonize

disagreeable *adj* **1** = **ill-natured**, bad-tempered, brusque, churlish, contrary, cross, difficult, disobliging, irritable, nasty, peevish, ratty (*Brit. & NZ inf.*), rude, surly, tetchy, unfriendly, ungracious, unlikable *or* unlikeable, unpleasant **2** = **nasty**, disgusting, displeasing, distasteful, horrid, objectionable, obnoxious, offensive, repellent, repugnant, repulsive, uninviting, unpalatable, unpleasant, unsavoury, yucky *or* yukky (*sl.*)
Antonyms *adj* ≠ **nasty:** agreeable, delightful, enjoyable, lovely, nice, pleasant ≠ **ill-natured:** agreeable, congenial, delightful, friendly, good-natured, lovely, nice, pleasant

disagreement *n* **3** = **argument**, altercation, clash, conflict, debate, difference, discord, dispute, dissent, division, falling out, misunderstanding, quarrel, row, squabble, strife, tiff, wrangle
Antonyms *n* ≠ **argument:** accord, agreement, assent, consensus, unison, unity

disallow *vb* **1** = **reject**, abjure, disavow, disclaim, dismiss, disown, rebuff, refuse, repudiate **2** = **cancel**, ban, boycott, embargo, forbid, prohibit, proscribe, veto

disappear *vb* **1** = **vanish**, be lost to view, drop out of sight, ebb, evanesce, fade away, pass, recede, vanish off the face of the earth, wane **2** =

America) to arrest secretly and presumably imprison or kill (a member of an opposing political group).
▸ˌ**disapˈpearance** *n*

disapplication (ˌdɪsæplɪˈkeɪʃən) *n Brit. education.* a provision for exempting schools or individuals from the requirements of the National Curriculum in special circumstances.

disappoint Ⓣ (ˌdɪsəˈpɔɪnt) *vb (tr)* **1** to fail to meet the expectations, hopes, etc. of; let down. **2** to prevent the fulfilment of (a plan, etc.); frustrate. [C15 (orig. meaning: to remove from office): from OF *desapointier;* see DIS-[1], APPOINT]
▸ˌ**disapˈpointed** *adj* ▸ˌ**disapˈpointing** *adj* ▸ˌ**disapˈpointingly** *adv*

disappointment Ⓣ (ˌdɪsəˈpɔɪntmənt) *n* **1** a disappointing or being disappointed. **2** a person or thing that disappoints.

disapprobation Ⓣ (ˌdɪsæprəʊˈbeɪʃən) *n* moral or social disapproval.

disapproval Ⓣ (ˌdɪsəˈpruːvᵊl) *n* the act or a state or feeling of disapproving; censure.

disapprove Ⓣ (ˌdɪsəˈpruːv) *vb* **disapproves, disapproving, disapproved. 1** (*intr;* often foll. by *of*) to consider wrong, bad, etc. **2** (*tr*) to withhold approval from.
▸ˌ**disapˈproving** *adj* ▸ˌ**disapˈprovingly** *adv*

disarm Ⓣ (dɪsˈɑːm) *vb* **1** (*tr*) to remove defensive or offensive capability from (a country, army, etc.). **2** (*tr*) to deprive of weapons. **3** (*tr*) to win the confidence or affection of. **4** (*intr*) (of a nation, etc.) to decrease the size and capability of one's armed forces. **5** (*intr*) to lay down weapons.
▸**disˈarmer** *n*

disarmament Ⓣ (dɪsˈɑːməmənt) *n* **1** the reduction of fighting capability, as by a nation. **2** a disarming or being disarmed.

disarming Ⓣ (dɪsˈɑːmɪŋ) *adj* tending to neutralize hostility, suspicion, etc.
▸**disˈarmingly** *adv*

disarrange Ⓣ (ˌdɪsəˈreɪndʒ) *vb* **disarranges, disarranging, disarranged.** (*tr*) to throw into disorder.
▸ˌ**disarˈrangement** *n*

disarray Ⓣ (ˌdɪsəˈreɪ) *n* **1** confusion, dismay, and lack of discipline. **2** (esp. of clothing) disorderliness; untidiness. ◆ *vb (tr)* **3** to throw into confusion. **4** *Arch.* to undress.

disassemble Ⓣ (ˌdɪsəˈsɛmbᵊl) *vb* **disassembles, disassembling, disassembled.** (*tr*) to take apart (a piece of machinery, etc.); dismantle.

disassembler (ˌdɪsəˈsɛmblə) *n Computing.* a computer program that translates machine code into assembly language.

disassociate (ˌdɪsəˈsəʊʃɪˌeɪt, -sɪ-) *vb* **disassociates, disassociating, disassociated.** a less common word for **dissociate.**
▸ˌ**disasˌsociˈation** *n*

disaster Ⓣ (dɪˈzɑːstə) *n* **1** an occurrence that causes great distress or destruction. **2** a thing, project, etc., that fails or has been ruined. [C16 (orig. in the sense: malevolent astral influence): from It. *disastro,* from *dis-* (pejorative) + *astro* star, ult. from Gk *astron*]
▸**disˈastrous** *adj*

disavow Ⓣ (ˌdɪsəˈvaʊ) *vb (tr)* to deny knowledge of, connection with, or responsibility for.
▸ˌ**disaˈvowal** *n* ▸**disavowedly** (ˌdɪsəˈvaʊɪdlɪ) *adv*

disband Ⓣ (dɪsˈbænd) *vb* to cease to function or cause to stop functioning, as a unit, group, etc.
▸**disˈbandment** *n*

disbar (dɪsˈbɑː) *vb* **disbars, disbarring, disbarred.** (*tr*) *Law.* to deprive of the status of barrister; expel from the Bar.
▸**disˈbarment** *n*

> **USAGE NOTE** *Disbar* is sometimes wrongly used where *debar* is meant: *he was debarred* (not *disbarred*) *from attending meetings.*

disbelief Ⓣ (ˌdɪsbɪˈliːf) *n* refusal or reluctance to believe.

disbelieve Ⓣ (ˌdɪsbɪˈliːv) *vb* **disbelieves, disbelieving, disbelieved. 1** (*tr*) to reject as false or lying. **2** (*intr;* usually foll. by *in*) to have no faith (in).
▸ˌ**disbeˈliever** *n* ▸ˌ**disbeˈlieving** *adj*

disbud (dɪsˈbʌd) *or* **debud** (diːˈbʌd) *vb* **disbuds, disbudding, disbudded** *or* **debuds, debudding, debudded. 1** to remove superfluous buds from (a plant). **2** *Vet. science.* to remove the horn buds of (calves, lambs, and kids).

disburden Ⓣ (dɪsˈbɜːdᵊn) *vb* **1** to remove a load from. **2** (*tr*) to relieve (one's mind, etc.) of a distressing worry.

disburse Ⓣ (dɪsˈbɜːs) *vb* **disburses, disbursing, disbursed.** (*tr*) to pay out. [C16: from OF *desborser,* from *des-* DIS-[1] + *borser* to obtain money, from *borse* bag, from LL *bursa*]
▸**disˈbursable** *adj* ▸**disˈbursement** *n* ▸**disˈburser** *n*

> **USAGE NOTE** *Disburse* is sometimes wrongly used where *disperse* is meant: *the police used a water cannon to disperse* (not *disburse*) *the crowd.*

disc Ⓣ (dɪsk) *n* **1** a flat circular plate. **2** something resembling this. **3** a gramophone record. **4** *Anat.* any approximately circular flat structure in the body, esp. an intervertebral disc. **5** the flat receptacle of composite flowers, such as the daisy. **6a** Also called: **parking disc.** a marker or device for display in a parked vehicle showing the time of arrival or the latest permitted time of departure or both. **6b** (*as modifier*): *disc parking.* **7** *Computing.* a variant spelling of **disk.** [C18: from L *discus* DISCUS]
▸ˈ**discal** *adj*

disc. *abbrev. for:* **1** discount. **2** discovered.

THESAURUS

flee, abscond, depart, escape, fly, go, retire, withdraw **3** = **cease**, cease to be known, cease to exist, die out, dissolve, end, evaporate, expire, fade, leave no trace, melt away, pass away, perish, vanish
Antonyms *vb* appear, arrive, materialize, reappear

disappearance *n* **2** = **vanishing**, departure, desertion, disappearing, disappearing trick, eclipse, evanescence, evaporation, fading, flight, going, loss, melting, passing, vanishing point

disappoint *vb* **1** = **let down**, chagrin, dash, deceive, delude, disenchant, disgruntle, dishearten, disillusion, dismay, dissatisfy, fail, sadden, vex **2** = **frustrate**, baffle, balk, defeat, disconcert, foil, hamper, hinder, thwart

disappointed *adj* **1, 2** = **let down**, balked, cast down, choked, depressed, despondent, discontented, discouraged, disenchanted, disgruntled, disillusioned, dissatisfied, distressed, downhearted, foiled, frustrated, saddened, thwarted, upset
Antonyms *adj* content, contented, fulfilled, happy, pleased, satisfied

disappointing *adj* **1** = **unsatisfactory**, depressing, disagreeable, disconcerting, discouraging, failing, inadequate, inferior, insufficient, lame, not much cop (*Brit. sl.*), pathetic, sad, second-rate, sorry, unexpected, unhappy, unworthy, upsetting

disappointment *n* **1** = **frustration**, chagrin, discontent, discouragement, disenchantment, disillusionment, displeasure, dissatisfaction, distress, failure, ill-success, mortification, regret, unfulfilment **2** = **letdown**, blow, calamity, choker (*inf.*), disaster, failure, fiasco, miscarriage, misfortune, setback, washout (*inf.*), whammy (*inf., chiefly US*)

disapprobation *n* = **disapproval**, blame, censure, condemnation, disfavour, dislike, displeasure, dissatisfaction, reproof, stricture

disapproval *n* = **displeasure**, censure, condemnation, criticism, denunciation, deprecation, disapprobation, dissatisfaction, objection, reproach, stick (*sl.*)

disapprove *vb* **1** = **condemn**, blame, censure, deplore, deprecate, discountenance, dislike, find unacceptable, frown on, have a down on (*inf.*), look down one's nose at (*inf.*), object to, raise an *or* one's eyebrow, reject, take a dim view of, take exception to **2** = **turn down**, disallow, reject, set aside, spurn, veto
Antonyms *vb* ≠ **condemn:** applaud, approve, commend, compliment (*inf.*), like ≠ **turn down:** endorse, give the go-ahead (to), O.K. *or* okay (*inf.*)

disapproving *adj* **1** = **critical**, censorious, condemnatory, denunciatory, deprecatory, disapprobatory, discouraging, disparaging, frowning, reproachful
Antonyms *adj* approbatory, approving, commendatory, encouraging

disarm *vb* **1, 2** = **render defenceless**, disable, unarm **3** = **win over**, persuade, set at ease **4** = **demilitarize**, deactivate, demobilize, disband

disarmament *n* **1** = **arms reduction**, arms limitation, de-escalation, demilitarization, demobilization

disarming *adj* = **charming**, irresistible, likable *or* likeable, persuasive, winning

disarrange *vb* = **disorder**, confuse, derange, discompose, disorganize, disturb, jumble (up), mess (up), scatter, shake (up), shuffle, unsettle, untidy

disarray *n* **1** = **confusion**, discomposure, disharmony, dismay, disorder, disorderliness, disorganization, disunity, indiscipline, unruliness, upset **2** = **untidiness**, chaos, clutter, dishevelment, hodgepodge (*US*), hotchpotch, jumble, mess, mix-up, muddle, pig's breakfast (*inf.*), shambles, state, tangle
Antonyms *n* arrangement, harmony, method, neatness, order, orderliness, organization, pattern, plan, regularity, symmetry, system, tidiness

disassemble *vb* = **take apart**, deconstruct, dismantle, dismount, knock down, strike, take down

disaster *n* **1** = **catastrophe**, accident, act of God, adversity, blow, bummer (*sl.*), calamity, cataclysm, misadventure, mischance, misfortune, mishap, reverse, ruin, ruination, stroke, tragedy, trouble, whammy (*inf., chiefly US*)

disastrous *adj* **1** = **terrible**, adverse, calamitous, cataclysmal, cataclysmic, catastrophic, destructive, detrimental, devastating, dire, dreadful, fatal, hapless, harmful, ill-fated, ill-starred, ruinous, tragic, unfortunate, unlucky, unpropitious, untoward

disavow *vb* = **deny**, abjure, contradict, disclaim, disown, forswear, gainsay (*arch. or literary*), rebut, reject, repudiate, retract

disavowal *n* = **denial**, abjuration, contradiction, disclaimer, gainsaying (*arch. or literary*), recantation, rejection, renunciation, repudiation, retraction

disband *vb* = **break up**, demobilize, dismiss, disperse, dissolve, go (their) separate ways, let go, part company, scatter, send home, separate

disbelief *n* = **scepticism**, distrust, doubt, dubiety, incredulity, mistrust, unbelief
Antonyms *n* belief, credence, credulity, faith, trust

disbelieve *vb* **1** = **doubt**, discount, discredit, give no credence to, mistrust, not accept, not buy (*sl.*), not credit, not swallow (*inf.*), reject, repudiate, scoff at, suspect

disbeliever *n* **2** = **sceptic**, agnostic, atheist, doubter, doubting Thomas, questioner, scoffer
Antonyms *n* adherent, believer, devotee, disciple, follower, proselyte, supporter, upholder, zealot

disburden *vb* **1, 2** = **relieve**, alleviate, diminish, discharge, disencumber, ease, free, lighten, take a load off one's mind, unburden, unload

disburse *vb* = **pay out**, expend, fork out (*sl.*), lay out, shell out (*inf.*), spend

disbursement *n* = **payment**, disposal, expenditure, outlay, spending

disc *n* **1, 2** = **circle**, discus, plate, saucer **3** = **record**, gramophone record, phonograph record (*US & Canad.*), platter (*US sl.*), vinyl

discard Ⓣ *vb* (dɪsˈkɑːd). **1** (*tr*) to get rid of as useless or undesirable. **2** *Cards.* to throw out (a card or cards) from one's hand. **3** *Cards.* to play (a card not of the suit led nor a trump) when unable to follow suit. ◆ *n* (ˈdɪskɑːd). **4** a person or thing that has been cast aside. **5** *Cards.* a discarded card. **6** the act of discarding.

disc brake *n* a type of brake in which two pads rub against a flat disc attached to the wheel hub when the brake is applied.

discern Ⓣ (dɪˈsɜːn) *vb* **1** (*tr*) to recognize or perceive clearly. **2** to recognize or perceive (differences). [C14: from OF *discerner*, from L *discernere* to divide, from DIS-[1] apart + *cernere* to separate]
▸**disˈcernible** *adj* ▸**disˈcernibly** *adv*

discerning Ⓣ (dɪˈsɜːnɪŋ) *adj* having or showing good taste or judgment; discriminating.

discernment Ⓣ (dɪˈsɜːnmənt) *n* keen perception or judgment.

disc flower *or* **floret** *n* any of the small tubular flowers at the centre of the flower head of certain composite plants, such as the daisy.

discharge Ⓣ *vb* (dɪsˈtʃɑːdʒ). **discharges, discharging, discharged. 1** (*tr*) to release or allow to go. **2** (*tr*) to dismiss from or relieve of duty, employment, etc. **3** to fire or be fired, as a gun. **4** to pour forth or cause to pour forth: *the boil discharges pus.* **5** (*tr*) to remove (the cargo) from (a boat, etc.); unload. **6** (*tr*) to perform the duties of or meet the demands of (an office, obligation, etc.). **7** (*tr*) to relieve (oneself) of (a responsibility, debt, etc.). **8** (*intr*) *Physics.* **8a** to lose or remove electric charge. **8b** to form an arc, spark, or corona in a gas. **8c** to take or supply electrical current from a cell or battery. **9** (*tr*) *Law.* to release (a prisoner from custody, etc.). ◆ *n* (ˈdɪstʃɑːdʒ, dɪsˈtʃɑːdʒ). **10** a person or thing that is discharged. **11a** dismissal or release from an office, job, institution, etc. **11b** the document certifying such release. **12** the fulfilment of an obligation or release from a responsibility or liability. **13** the act of removing a load, as of cargo. **14** a pouring forth of a fluid; emission. **15a** the act of firing a projectile. **15b** the volley, bullet, etc., fired. **16** *Law.* **16a** a release, as of a person held under legal restraint. **16b** an annulment, as of a court order. **17** *Physics.* **17a** the act or process of removing or losing charge. **17b** a conduction of electricity through a gas by the formation and movement of electrons and ions in an applied electric field.
▸**disˈchargeable** *adj* ▸**disˈcharger** *n*

discharge tube *n Electronics.* an electrical device in which current flow is by electrons and ions in an ionized gas, as in a fluorescent light or neon tube.

disc harrow *n* a harrow with sharp-edged discs used to cut clods on the surface of the soil or to cover seed after planting.

disciple Ⓣ (dɪˈsaɪpᵊl) *n* **1** a follower of the doctrines of a teacher or a school of thought. **2** one of the personal followers of Christ (including his 12 apostles) during his earthly life. [OE *discipul*, from L *discipulus* pupil, from *discere* to learn]
▸**disˈciple,ship** *n* ▸**discipular** (dɪˈsɪpjʊlə) *adj*

disciplinarian Ⓣ (ˌdɪsɪplɪˈnɛərɪən) *n* a person who imposes or advocates strict discipline.

disciplinary (ˈdɪsɪˌplɪnərɪ) *adj* **1** of, promoting, or used for discipline; corrective. **2** relating to a branch of learning.

discipline Ⓣ (ˈdɪsɪplɪn) *n* **1** training or conditions imposed for the improvement of physical powers, self-control, etc. **2** systematic training in obedience. **3** the state of improved behaviour, etc., resulting from such training. **4** punishment or chastisement. **5** a system of rules for behaviour, etc. **6** a branch of learning or instruction. **7** the laws governing members of a Church. ◆ *vb* **disciplines, disciplining, disciplined.** (*tr*) **8** to improve or attempt to improve the behaviour, orderliness, etc., of by training, conditions, or rules. **9** to punish or correct. [C13: from L *disciplīna* teaching, from *discipulus* DISCIPLE]
▸ˈ**disci,plinable** *adj* ▸**disciplinal** (ˌdɪsɪˈplaɪnᵊl) *adj* ▸ˈ**disci,pliner** *n*

disc jockey *n* a person who announces and plays recorded music, esp. pop music, on a radio programme, etc.

disclaim Ⓣ (dɪsˈkleɪm) *vb* **1** (*tr*) to deny or renounce (any claim, connection, etc.). **2** (*tr*) to deny the validity or authority of. **3** *Law.* to renounce or repudiate (a legal claim or right).

disclaimer Ⓣ (dɪsˈkleɪmə) *n* a repudiation or denial.

disclose Ⓣ (dɪsˈkləʊz) *vb* **discloses, disclosing, disclosed.** (*tr*) **1** to make known. **2** to allow to be seen.
▸**disˈcloser** *n*

disclosure Ⓣ (dɪsˈkləʊʒə) *n* **1** something that is disclosed. **2** the act of disclosing; revelation.

disco (ˈdɪskəʊ) *n, pl* **discos. 1a** an occasion at which people dance to pop records. **1b** (*as modifier*): *disco music.* **2** a nightclub or other public place where such dances are held. **3** mobile equipment for providing music for a disco. [C20: from DISCOTHEQUE]

discobolus (dɪsˈkɒbələs) *n, pl* **discoboli** (-ˌlaɪ). a discus thrower. [C18: from L, from Gk, from *diskos* DISCUS + *-bolos*, from *ballein* to throw]

discography (dɪsˈkɒgrəfɪ) *n* a classified list of gramophone records.
▸**disˈcographer** *n*

discoid (ˈdɪskɔɪd) *adj also* **discoidal. 1** like a disc. ◆ *n* **2** a disclike object.

discolour Ⓣ *or US* **discolor** (dɪsˈkʌlə) *vb* to change in colour; fade or stain.
▸**dis,colorˈation** *or* **dis,colourˈation** *n*

discombobulate (ˌdɪskəmˈbɒbjʊˌleɪt) *vb* **discombobulates, discombobulating, discombobulated.** (*tr*) *Inf., chiefly US & Canad.* to throw into confusion. [C20: prob. a whimsical alteration of DISCOMPOSE or DISCOMFIT]

discomfit Ⓣ (dɪsˈkʌmfɪt) *vb* (*tr*) **1** to make uneasy or confused. **2** to frustrate the plans or purpose of. **3** *Arch.* to defeat. [C14: from OF *desconfire* to destroy, from *des-* (indicating reversal) + *confire* to make, from L *conficere* to produce]
▸**disˈcomfiture** *n*

discomfort Ⓣ (dɪsˈkʌmfət) *n* **1** an inconvenience, distress, or mild pain. **2** something that disturbs or deprives of ease. ◆ *vb* **3** (*tr*) to make uncomfortable or uneasy.

THESAURUS

discard *vb* **1 = get rid of**, abandon, axe (*inf.*), cast aside, chuck (*inf.*), dispense with, dispose of, ditch (*sl.*), drop, dump (*inf.*), jettison, junk (*inf.*), reject, relinquish, remove, repudiate, scrap, shed, throw away *or* out
Antonyms *vb* hang *or* hold on to, hold back, keep, reserve, retain, save

discern *vb* **1 = see**, behold, catch sight of, descry, discover, espy, make out, notice, observe, perceive, recognize, suss (out) (*sl.*) **2 = distinguish**, detect, determine, differentiate, discriminate, judge, make a distinction, pick out

discernible *adj* **1, 2 = perceptible**, apparent, appreciable, detectable, discoverable, distinct, distinguishable, noticeable, observable, obvious, plain, recognizable, visible

discerning *adj* **= discriminating**, acute, astute, clear-sighted, critical, ingenious, intelligent, judicious, knowing, penetrating, perceptive, percipient, perspicacious, piercing, sagacious, sensitive, sharp, shrewd, subtle, wise

discernment *n* **= judgment**, acumen, acuteness, astuteness, awareness, clear-sightedness, cleverness, discrimination, ingenuity, insight, intelligence, keenness, penetration, perception, perceptiveness, percipience, perspicacity, sagacity, sharpness, shrewdness, understanding

discharge *vb* **1 = release**, absolve, acquit, allow to go, clear, exonerate, free, liberate, pardon, set free **2 = dismiss**, cashier, discard, eject, expel, fire (*inf.*), give (someone) the boot (*sl.*), give (someone) the sack (*inf.*), oust, remove, sack (*inf.*) **3 = fire**, detonate, explode, let loose (*inf.*), let off, set off, shoot **4 = pour forth**, disembogue, dispense, emit, empty, excrete, exude, give off, gush, leak, ooze, release, void **5 = off-load**, disburden, lighten, remove, unburden, unload **6 = carry out**, accomplish, do, execute, fulfil, observe, perform **7 = pay**, clear, honour, meet, relieve, satisfy, settle, square up ◆ *n* **11a = dismissal**, congé, demobilization, ejection, the boot (*sl.*), the (old) heave-ho (*inf.*), the order of the boot (*sl.*), the sack (*inf.*) **11a = release**, acquittal, clearance, exoneration, liberation, pardon, remittance **12 = carrying out**, accomplishment, achievement, execution, fulfilment, observance, performance **13 = unloading**, disburdening, emptying, unburdening **14 = emission**, emptying, excretion, flow, ooze, pus, secretion, seepage, suppuration, vent, voiding **15 = firing**, blast, burst, detonation, discharging, explosion, fusillade, report, salvo, shot, volley

disciple *n* **1 = follower**, adherent, apostle, believer, catechumen, convert, devotee, learner, partisan, proselyte, pupil, student, supporter, votary
Antonyms *n* guru, leader, master, swami, teacher

disciplinarian *n* **= authoritarian**, despot, drill sergeant, hard master, martinet, stickler, strict teacher, taskmaster, tyrant

discipline *n* **1 = training**, drill, exercise, method, practice, regimen, regulation **3 = self-control**, conduct, control, orderliness, regulation, restraint, strictness **4 = punishment**, castigation, chastisement, correction **6 = field of study**, area, branch of knowledge, course, curriculum, speciality, subject ◆ *vb* **8 = train**, break in, bring up, check, control, drill, educate, exercise, form, govern, instruct, inure, prepare, regulate, restrain **9 = punish**, bring to book, castigate, chasten, chastise, correct, penalize, reprimand, reprove

disclaim *vb* **1-3 = deny**, abandon, abjure, abnegate, decline, disaffirm, disallow, disavow, disown, forswear, rebut, reject, renege, renounce, repudiate, retract

disclaimer *n* **= denial**, abjuration, contradiction, disavowal, rejection, renunciation, repudiation, retraction

disclose *vb* **1 = make known**, blow wide open (*sl.*), broadcast, communicate, confess, divulge, get off one's chest (*inf.*), impart, leak, let slip, make public, out (*inf.*), publish, relate, reveal, spill one's guts about (*sl.*), spill the beans about (*inf.*), tell, unveil, utter **2 = show**, bring to light, discover, exhibit, expose, lay bare, reveal, take the wraps off, uncover, unveil
Antonyms *vb* conceal, cover, dissemble, hide, keep dark, keep secret, mask, obscure, secrete, veil

disclosure *n* **1, 2 = revelation**, acknowledgment, admission, announcement, broadcast, confession, declaration, discovery, divulgence, exposé, exposure, leak, publication, uncovering

discoloration *n* **= stain**, blemish, blot, blotch, mark, patch, smirch, splotch, spot

discolour *vb* **= stain**, fade, mar, mark, rust, soil, streak, tarnish, tinge

discoloured *adj* **= stained**, besmirched, blotched, etiolated, faded, foxed, pale, tainted, tarnished, wan, washed out

discomfit *vb* **1 = embarrass**, abash, confound, confuse, demoralize, discompose, disconcert, faze, flurry, fluster, perplex, perturb, rattle (*inf.*), ruffle, take aback, take the wind out of someone's sails, unnerve, unsettle, worry **2 = frustrate**, baffle, balk, beat, checkmate, defeat, foil, outwit, overcome, thwart, trump, worst

discomfiture *n* **1 = embarrassment**, abashment, chagrin, confusion, demoralization, discomposure, humiliation, shame, unease **2 = frustration**, beating, defeat, disappointment, failure, overthrow, rout, ruin, undoing

discomfort *n* **1 = pain**, ache, hurt, irritation, malaise, soreness **2 = uneasiness**, annoyance, disquiet, distress, gall, hardship, inquietude, ir-

discommode Ⓣ (ˌdɪskəˈməʊd) *vb* **discommodes, discommoding, discommoded.** (*tr*) to cause inconvenience to; disturb.
▸ˌ**discomˈmodious** *adj*

discompose Ⓣ (ˌdɪskəmˈpəʊz) *vb* **discomposes, discomposing, discomposed.** (*tr*) **1** to disturb the composure of; disconcert. **2** *Now rare.* to disarrange.
▸ˌ**discomˈposure** *n*

disconcert Ⓣ (ˌdɪskənˈsɜːt) *vb* (*tr*) **1** to disturb the composure of. **2** to frustrate or upset.
▸ˌ**disconˈcerted** *adj* ▸ˌ**disconˈcerting** *adj* ▸ˌ**disconˈcertion** *n*

disconformity (ˌdɪskənˈfɔːmɪtɪ) *n, pl* **disconformities. 1** lack of conformity; discrepancy. **2** the junction between two parallel series of stratified rocks.

disconnect Ⓣ (ˌdɪskəˈnɛkt) *vb* (*tr*) to undo or break the connection of or between (something, as a plug and a socket).
▸ˌ**disconˈnection** *n*

disconnected Ⓣ (ˌdɪskəˈnɛktɪd) *adj* **1** not rationally connected; confused or incoherent. **2** not connected or joined.

disconsolate Ⓣ (dɪsˈkɒnsəlɪt) *adj* **1** sad beyond comfort; inconsolable. **2** disappointed; dejected. [C14: from Med. L *disconsōlātus,* from DIS-[1] + *consōlātus* comforted]
▸**disˈconsolately** *adv* ▸**disˈconsolateness** *or* **disˌconsoˈlation** *n*

discontent Ⓣ (ˌdɪskənˈtɛnt) *n* **1** Also called: **discontentment.** lack of contentment, as with one's condition or lot in life. ◆ *vb* **2** (*tr*) to make dissatisfied.
▸ˌ**disconˈtented** *adj* ▸ˌ**disconˈtentedness** *n*

discontinue Ⓣ (ˌdɪskənˈtɪnjuː) *vb* **discontinues, discontinuing, discontinued. 1** to come or bring to an end; interrupt or be interrupted; stop. **2** (*tr*) *Law.* to terminate or abandon (an action, suit, etc.).
▸ˌ**disconˈtinuance** *n* ▸ˌ**disconˌtinuˈation** *n*

discontinuity Ⓣ (ˌdɪskɒntɪˈnjuːɪtɪ, dɪsˌkɒntɪ-) *n, pl* **discontinuities. 1** lack of rational connection or cohesion. **2** a break or interruption.

discontinuous Ⓣ (ˌdɪskənˈtɪnjʊəs) *adj* characterized by interruptions or breaks; intermittent.
▸ˌ**disconˈtinuously** *adv* ▸ˌ**disconˈtinuousness** *n*

discord Ⓣ *n* (ˈdɪskɔːd). **1** lack of agreement or harmony. **2** harsh confused mingling of sounds. **3** a combination of musical notes, esp. one containing one or more dissonant intervals. ◆ *vb* (dɪsˈkɔːd). **4** (*intr*) to disagree; clash. [C13: from OF *descort,* from *descorder* to disagree, from L *discordāre,* from *discors* at variance, from DIS-[1] + *cor* heart]

discordant Ⓣ (dɪsˈkɔːdᵊnt) *adj* **1** at variance; disagreeing. **2** harsh in sound; inharmonious.
▸**disˈcordance** *n* ▸**disˈcordantly** *adv*

discotheque (ˈdɪskəˌtɛk) *n* the full term for **disco.** [C20: from F *discothèque,* from Gk *diskos* disc + *-o-* + Gk *thēkē* case]

discount Ⓣ *vb* (dɪsˈkaʊnt, ˈdɪskaʊnt). (*mainly tr*) **1** to leave out of account as being unreliable, prejudiced, or irrelevant. **2** to anticipate and make allowance for. **3a** to deduct (an amount or percentage) from the price, cost, etc. **3b** to reduce (the regular price, etc.) by a percentage or amount. **4** to sell or offer for sale at a reduced price. **5** to buy or sell (a bill of exchange, etc.) before maturity, with a deduction for interest. **6** (*also intr*) to loan money on (a negotiable instrument) with a deduction for interest. ◆ *n* (ˈdɪskaʊnt). **7** a deduction from the full amount of a price or debt. See also **cash discount, trade discount. 8** Also called: **discount rate. 8a** the amount of interest deducted in the purchase or sale of or the loan of money on unmatured negotiable instruments. **8b** the rate of interest deducted. **9** (in the issue of shares) a percentage deducted from the par value to give a reduced amount payable by subscribers. **10** a discounting. **11 at a discount. 11a** below the regular price. **11b** held in low regard. **12** (*modifier*) offering or selling at reduced prices: *a discount shop.*
▸**disˈcountable** *adj* ▸ˈ**discounter** *n*

discounted cash flow *n* the cash flow of an organization taking into account the future values of benefits and assets in addition to their present values.

discountenance (dɪsˈkaʊntɪnəns) *vb* **discountenances, discountenancing, discountenanced.** (*tr*) **1** to make ashamed or confused. **2** to disapprove of. ◆ *n* **3** disapproval.

discount house *n* **1** *Chiefly Brit.* a financial organization engaged in discounting bills of exchange, etc., on a large scale. **2** Also called: **discount store.** *Chiefly US.* a shop offering for sale most of its merchandise at prices below the recommended prices.

discount market *n* the part of the money market consisting of banks, discount houses, and brokers on which bills are discounted.

discourage Ⓣ (dɪsˈkʌrɪdʒ) *vb* **discourages, discouraging, discouraged.** (*tr*) **1** to deprive of the will to persist in something. **2** to inhibit; prevent: *this solution discourages rust.* **3** to oppose by expressing disapproval.
▸**disˈcouragement** *n* ▸**disˈcouragingly** *adv*

discourse Ⓣ *n* (ˈdɪskɔːs, dɪsˈkɔːs). **1** verbal communication; talk; conversation. **2** a formal treatment of a subject in speech or writing. **3** a

THESAURUS

ritation, nuisance, trouble, unpleasantness, vexation ◆ *vb* **3** = **make uncomfortable**, discomfit, discompose, disquiet, distress, disturb, embarrass
Antonyms *n* ≠ **pain:** comfort, ease ≠ **uneasiness:** ease, reassurance, solace ◆ *vb* ≠ **make uncomfortable:** alleviate, assuage, comfort, ease, reassure, solace, soothe

discommode *vb* = **inconvenience**, annoy, bother, burden, disquiet, disturb, harass, hassle, incommode, molest, put out, trouble

discompose *vb* **1** = **disturb**, agitate, annoy, bewilder, confuse, discomfit, disconcert, displease, embarrass, faze, flurry, fluster, fret, hassle (*inf.*), irritate, nettle, perplex, perturb, provoke, rattle (*inf.*), ruffle, unnerve, unsettle, upset, vex, worry

discomposure *n* **1** = **disturbance**, agitation, anxiety, confusion, discomfiture, disquiet, disquietude, distraction, embarrassment, fluster, inquietude, malaise, nervousness, perturbation, trepidation, uneasiness

disconcert *vb* **1** = **disturb**, abash, agitate, bewilder, discompose, faze, flummox, flurry, fluster, nonplus, perplex, perturb, put out of countenance, rattle (*inf.*), ruffle, shake up (*inf.*), take aback, throw off balance, trouble, unbalance, unnerve, unsettle, upset, worry **2** = **frustrate**, baffle, balk, confuse, defeat, disarrange, hinder, put off, thwart, undo

disconcerted *adj* **1, 2** = **disturbed**, annoyed, at sea, bewildered, caught off balance, confused, distracted, embarrassed, fazed, flummoxed, flurried, flustered, mixed-up, nonplussed, out of countenance, perturbed, rattled (*inf.*), ruffled, shook up (*inf.*), taken aback, thrown (*inf.*), troubled, unsettled, upset, worried

disconcerting *adj* **1, 2** = **disturbing**, alarming, awkward, baffling, bewildering, bothersome, confusing, dismaying, distracting, embarrassing, off-putting (*Brit. inf.*), perplexing, upsetting

disconnect *vb* = **cut off**, detach, disengage, divide, part, separate, sever, take apart, uncouple

disconnected *adj* **1** = **illogical**, confused, disjointed, garbled, incoherent, irrational, jumbled, mixed-up, rambling, uncoordinated, unintelligible, wandering

disconnection *n* = **cutting off**, cessation, cut-off, discontinuation, discontinuity, interruption, separation, severance, stoppage, suspension

disconsolate *adj* **1, 2** = **inconsolable**, crushed, dejected, desolate, despairing, dismal, down in the dumps (*inf.*), forlorn, gloomy, grief-stricken, heartbroken, hopeless, low, melancholy, miserable, sad, unhappy, woeful, wretched

discontent *n* **1** = **dissatisfaction**, discontentment, displeasure, envy, fretfulness, regret, restlessness, uneasiness, unhappiness, vexation

discontented *adj* **2** = **dissatisfied**, brassed off (*Brit. sl.*), cheesed off, complaining, disaffected, disgruntled, displeased, exasperated, fed up, fretful, miserable, pissed off (*taboo sl.*), unhappy, vexed, with a chip on one's shoulder (*inf.*)
Antonyms *adj* cheerful, content, contented, happy, pleased, satisfied

discontinuance *n* **1** = **stopping**, adjournment, cessation, discontinuation, disjunction, intermission, interruption, separation, stop, stoppage, suspension, termination

discontinue *vb* **1** = **stop**, abandon, axe (*inf.*), belay (*Nautical*), break off, cease, drop, end, finish, give up, halt, interrupt, kick (*inf.*), leave off, pause, pull the plug on, put an end to, quit, refrain from, suspend, terminate, throw in the sponge, throw in the towel

discontinued *adj* **1** = **stopped**, abandoned, ended, finished, given up *or* over, halted, no longer made, terminated

discontinuity *n* **1, 2** = **disconnectedness**, disconnection, disjointedness, disruption, disunion, incoherence, interruption, lack of coherence, lack of unity

discontinuous *adj* = **intermittent**, broken, disconnected, fitful, interrupted, irregular, spasmodic

discord *n* **1** = **disagreement**, clashing, conflict, contention, difference, discordance, dispute, dissension, disunity, division, friction, incompatibility, lack of concord, opposition, row, rupture, strife, variance, wrangling **2** = **disharmony**, cacophony, din, dissonance, harshness, jangle, jarring, racket, tumult
Antonyms *n* ≠ **disagreement:** accord, agreement, concord, friendship, harmony, peace, understanding, unison, unity ≠ **disharmony:** concord, euphony, harmony, melody, tunefulness, unison

discordant *adj* **1** = **disagreeing**, at odds, clashing, conflicting, contradictory, contrary, different, divergent, incompatible, incongruous, inconsistent, opposite **2** = **inharmonious**, cacophonous, dissonant, grating, harsh, jangling, jarring, shrill, strident, unmelodious

discount *vb* **1** = **leave out**, brush off (*sl.*), disbelieve, disregard, ignore, overlook, pass over **3, 4** = **deduct**, lower, mark down, rebate, reduce, take off ◆ *n* **7** = **deduction**, abatement, allowance, concession, cut, cut price, drawback, percentage (*inf.*), rebate, reduction

discourage *vb* **1** = **dishearten**, abash, awe, cast down, cow, damp, dampen, dash, daunt, deject, demoralize, depress, dismay, dispirit, frighten, intimidate, overawe, psych out (*inf.*), put a damper on, scare, unman, unnerve **2** = **prevent**, check, curb, deter, hinder, inhibit **3** = **put off**, check, curb, deprecate, deter, discountenance, disfavour, dissuade, divert from, hinder, inhibit, prevent, restrain, talk out of, throw cold water on (*inf.*)
Antonyms *vb* ≠ **dishearten:** embolden, encourage, gee up, hearten, inspire ≠ **put off:** bid, countenance, encourage, urge

discouraged *adj* **1** = **put off**, crestfallen, dashed, daunted, deterred, disheartened, dismayed, dispirited, downcast, down in the mouth, glum, pessimistic, sick as a parrot (*inf.*)

discouragement *n* **1** = **loss of confidence**, cold feet (*inf.*), dejection, depression, despair, despondency, disappointment, discomfiture, dismay, downheartedness, hopelessness, low spirits, pessimism **2** = **deterrent**, constraint, curb, damper, disincentive, hindrance, impediment, obstacle, opposition, rebuff, restraint, setback

discouraging *adj* **1** = **disheartening**, dampening, daunting, depressing, disappointing, dispiriting, off-putting (*Brit. inf.*), unfavourable, unpropitious

discourse *n* **1** = **conversation**, chat, communication, converse, dialogue, discussion, seminar,

unit of text used by linguists for the analysis of linguistic phenomena that range over more than one sentence. **4** *Arch.* the ability to reason. ◆ *vb* (dɪsˈkɔːs), **discourses, discoursing, discoursed. 5** (*intr;* often foll. by *on* or *upon*) to speak or write (about) formally. **6** (*intr*) to hold a discussion. **7** (*tr*) *Arch.* to give forth (music). [C14: from Med. L *discursus* argument, from L: a running to and fro, from *discurrere,* from DIS-[1] + *currere* to run]

discourteous ⓣ (dɪsˈkɜːtɪəs) *adj* showing bad manners; impolite; rude. ▸**disˈcourteously** *adv* ▸**disˈcourteousness** *n*

discourtesy ⓣ (dɪsˈkɜːtɪsɪ) *n, pl* **discourtesies. 1** bad manners; rudeness. **2** a rude remark or act.

discover ⓣ (dɪˈskʌvə) *vb* (*tr; may take a clause as object*) **1** to be the first to find or find out about. **2** to learn about for the first time; realize. **3** to find after study or search. **4** to reveal or make known. ▸**disˈcoverable** *adj* ▸**disˈcoverer** *n*

discovery ⓣ (dɪˈskʌvərɪ) *n, pl* **discoveries. 1** the act, process, or an instance of discovering. **2** a person, place, or thing that has been discovered. **3** *Law.* the compulsory disclosure by a party to an action of relevant documents in his possession.

discredit ⓣ (dɪsˈkrɛdɪt) *vb* (*tr*) **1** to damage the reputation of. **2** to cause to be disbelieved or distrusted. **3** to reject as untrue. ◆ *n* **4** something that causes disgrace. **5** damage to a reputation. **6** lack of belief or confidence.

discreditable ⓣ (dɪsˈkrɛdɪtəbᵊl) *adj* tending to bring discredit; shameful or unworthy.

discreet ⓣ (dɪˈskriːt) *adj* **1** careful to avoid embarrassment, esp. by keeping confidences secret; tactful. **2** unobtrusive. [C14: from OF *discret,* from Med. L *discrētus,* from L *discernere* to DISCERN] ▸**disˈcreetly** *adv* ▸**disˈcreetness** *n*

USAGE NOTE Avoid confusion with **discrete.**

discrepancy ⓣ (dɪˈskrɛpənsɪ) *n, pl* **discrepancies.** a conflict or variation, as between facts, figures, or claims. [C15: from L *discrepāns,* from *discrepāre* to differ in sound, from DIS-[1] + *crepāre* to be noisy] ▸**disˈcrepant** *adj*

USAGE NOTE *Discrepancy* is sometimes wrongly used where *disparity* is meant. A *discrepancy* exists between things which ought to be the same; it can be small but is usually significant. A *disparity* is a large difference between measurable things such as age, rank, or wages.

discrete ⓣ (dɪsˈkriːt) *adj* **1** separate or distinct. **2** consisting of distinct or separate parts. [C14: from L *discrētus* separated; see DISCREET] ▸**disˈcretely** *adv* ▸**disˈcreteness** *n*

USAGE NOTE Avoid confusion with **discreet.**

discretion ⓣ (dɪˈskrɛʃən) *n* **1** the quality of behaving so as to avoid social embarrassment or distress. **2** freedom or authority to make judgments and to act as one sees fit (esp. in **at one's own discretion, at the discretion of**). **3 age** *or* **years of discretion.** the age at which a person is thought able to manage his own affairs.

discretionary ⓣ (dɪˈskrɛʃənərɪ, -ənrɪ) *or* **discretional** *adj* having or using the ability to decide at one's own discretion: *discretionary powers.*

discretionary trust *n* a trust in which the beneficiaries' shares are not fixed in the trust deed but are left to the discretion of other persons, often the trustees.

discriminate ⓣ *vb* (dɪˈskrɪmɪˌneɪt). **discriminates, discriminating, discriminated. 1** (*intr;* usually foll. by *in favour of* or *against*) to single out a particular person, group, etc., for special favour or, esp., disfavour. **2** (when *intr,* foll. by *between* or *among*) to recognize or understand the difference (between); distinguish. **3** (*intr*) to constitute or mark a difference. **4** (*intr*) to be discerning in matters of taste. ◆ *adj* (dɪˈskrɪmɪnɪt). **5** showing or marked by discrimination. [C17: from L *discrīmināre* to divide, from *discrīmen* a separation, from *discernere* to DISCERN] ▸**disˈcriminately** *adv*

discriminating ⓣ (dɪˈskrɪmɪˌneɪtɪŋ) *adj* **1** able to see fine distinctions and differences. **2** discerning in matters of taste. **3** (of a tariff, import duty, etc.) levied at differential rates.

discrimination ⓣ (dɪˌskrɪmɪˈneɪʃən) *n* **1** unfair treatment of a person, racial group, minority, etc.; action based on prejudice. **2** subtle appreciation in matters of taste. **3** the ability to see fine distinctions and differences.

discriminatory ⓣ (dɪˈskrɪmɪnətərɪ, -trɪ) *or* **discriminative** (dɪˈskrɪmɪnətɪv) *adj* **1** based on or showing prejudice; biased. **2** capable of making fine distinctions.

discursive (dɪˈskɜːsɪv) *adj* **1** passing from one topic to another; digressive. **2** *Philosophy.* of or relating to knowledge obtained by reason and argument rather than intuition. [C16: from Med. L *discursīvus,* from LL *discursus* DISCOURSE] ▸**disˈcursively** *adv* ▸**disˈcursiveness** *n*

discus (ˈdɪskəs) *n, pl* **discuses** *or* **disci** (ˈdɪskaɪ). **1** (originally) a circular stone or plate used in throwing competitions by the ancient Greeks. **2** *Field sports.* a similar disc-shaped object with a heavy middle, thrown by athletes. **3** (preceded by *the*) the event or sport of throwing the discus. [C17: from L, from Gk *diskos,* from *dikein* to throw]

discuss ⓣ (dɪˈskʌs) *vb* (*tr*) **1** to have a conversation about; consider by talking over. **2** to treat (a subject) in speech or writing. [C14: from LL *discussus* examined, from *discutere,* from L: to dash to pieces, from DIS-[1] + *quatere* to shake] ▸**disˈcussant** *or* **disˈcusser** *n* ▸**disˈcussible** *or* **disˈcussable** *adj*

discussion ⓣ (dɪˈskʌʃən) *n* the examination or consideration of a matter in speech or writing.

disdain ⓣ (dɪsˈdeɪn) *n* **1** a feeling or show of superiority and dislike; contempt; scorn. ◆ *vb* **2** (*tr; may take an infinitive*) to refuse or reject

THESAURUS

speech, talk **2** = **speech**, address, disquisition, dissertation, essay, homily, lecture, oration, sermon, talk, treatise ◆ *vb* **5, 6** = **hold forth**, confer, converse, debate, declaim, discuss, expatiate, speak, talk

discourteous *adj* = **rude**, abrupt, bad-mannered, boorish, brusque, curt, disrespectful, ill-bred, ill-mannered, impolite, insolent, offhand, uncivil, uncourteous, ungentlemanly, ungracious, unmannerly
Antonyms *adj* civil, courteous, courtly, gracious, mannerly, polite, respectful, well-mannered

discourtesy *n* **1** = **rudeness**, bad manners, disrespectfulness, ill-breeding, impertinence, impoliteness, incivility, insolence, ungraciousness, unmannerliness **2** = **insult**, affront, cold shoulder, kick in the teeth (*sl.*), rebuff, slight, snub

discover *vb* **1** = **find**, bring to light, come across, come upon, dig up, light upon, locate, turn up, uncover, unearth **2** = **find out**, ascertain, descry, detect, determine, discern, disclose, espy, get wise to (*inf.*), learn, notice, perceive, realize, recognize, reveal, see, spot, suss (out) (*sl.*), turn up, uncover

discoverer *n* **1** = **inventor**, author, explorer, founder, initiator, originator, pioneer

discovery *n* **1** = **finding**, ascertainment, detection, disclosure, espial, exploration, introduction, locating, location, origination, revelation, uncovering

discredit *vb* **1** = **disgrace**, blame, bring into disrepute, censure, defame, degrade, detract from, dishonour, disparage, reproach, slander, slur, smear, vilify **2** = **doubt**, challenge, deny, disbelieve, discount, dispute, distrust, mistrust, question ◆ *n* **5** = **disgrace**, aspersion, censure, dishonour, disrepute, ignominy, ill-repute, imputation, odium, reproach, scandal, shame, slur, smear, stigma **6** = **doubt**, distrust, mistrust, question, scepticism, suspicion
Antonyms *vb* ≠ **disgrace:** acclaim, applaud, commend, honour, laud, pay tribute to, praise ◆ *n* ≠ **disgrace:** acclaim, acknowledgment, approval, commendation, credit, honour, merit, praise

discreditable *adj* = **disgraceful**, blameworthy, degrading, dishonourable, humiliating, ignominious, improper, infamous, reprehensible, scandalous, shameful, unprincipled, unworthy

discredited *adj* **2, 3** = **debunked**, discarded, exploded, exposed, obsolete, outworn, refuted, rejected

discreet *adj* **1** = **tactful**, careful, cautious, circumspect, considerate, diplomatic, discerning, guarded, judicious, politic, prudent, reserved, sagacious, sensible, wary
Antonyms *adj* incautious, indiscreet, injudicious, rash, tactless, undiplomatic, unthinking, unwise

discrepancy *n* = **disagreement**, conflict, contradiction, contrariety, difference, discordance, disparity, dissimilarity, dissonance, divergence, incongruity, inconsistency, variance, variation

discrete *adj* **1** = **separate**, detached, disconnected, discontinuous, distinct, individual, unattached

discretion *n* **1** = **tact**, acumen, care, carefulness, caution, circumspection, consideration, diplomacy, discernment, good sense, heedfulness, judgment, judiciousness, maturity, prudence, sagacity, wariness **2** = **choice**, disposition, inclination, liking, mind, option, pleasure, predilection, preference, responsibility, volition, will, wish
Antonyms *n* ≠ **tact:** carelessness, indiscretion, insensitivity, rashness, tactlessness, thoughtlessness

discretionary *adj* = **optional**, arbitrary, elective, nonmandatory, open, open to choice, unrestricted

discriminate *vb* **1** = **show prejudice**, disfavour, favour, show bias, single out, treat as inferior, treat differently, victimize **2, 4** = **differentiate**, assess, discern, distinguish, draw a distinction, evaluate, segregate, separate, separate the wheat from the chaff, sift, tell the difference

discriminating *adj* **1, 2** = **discerning**, acute, astute, critical, cultivated, fastidious, keen, particular, refined, selective, sensitive, tasteful
Antonyms *adj* careless, desultory, general, hit or miss (*inf.*), indiscriminate, random, undiscriminating, unselective, unsystematic

discrimination *n* **1** = **prejudice**, bias, bigotry, favouritism, inequity, intolerance, unfairness **2** = **discernment**, acumen, acuteness, clearness, insight, judgment, keenness, penetration, perception, refinement, sagacity, subtlety, taste

discriminatory *adj* **1** = **prejudiced**, biased, favouring, inequitable, one-sided, partial, partisan, preferential, prejudicial, unjust, weighted **2** = **discerning**, analytical, astute, differentiating, discriminating, perceptive, perspicacious

discuss *vb* **1** = **talk about**, argue, confer, consider, consult with, converse, debate, deliberate, examine, exchange views on, get together, go into, reason about, review, sift, thrash out, ventilate, weigh up the pros and cons

discussion *n* = **talk**, analysis, argument, colloquy, confabulation, conference, consideration, consultation, conversation, debate, deliberation, dialogue, discourse, examination, exchange, review, scrutiny, seminar, symposium

disdain *n* **1** = **contempt**, arrogance, contumely,

with disdain. [C13 *dedeyne,* from OF *desdeign,* from *desdeigner* to reject as unworthy, from L *dēdignārī;* see DIS-[1], DEIGN]
▸**dis'dainful** *adj*

disease ⓘ (dɪ'zi:z) *n* **1** any impairment of normal physiological function affecting an organism, esp. a change caused by infection, stress, etc., producing characteristic symptoms; illness or sickness in general. **2** a corresponding condition in plants. **3** any condition likened to this. [C14: from OF *desaise;* see DIS-[1], EASE]
▸**dis'eased** *adj*

diseconomy (ˌdɪsɪ'kɒnəmɪ) *n Econ.* disadvantage, such as lower efficiency or higher costs, resulting from the scale on which an enterprise operates.

disembark ⓘ (ˌdɪsɪm'bɑ:k) *vb* to land or cause to land from a ship, aircraft, etc.
▸**disembarkation** (dɪsˌɛmbɑ:'keɪʃən) *n*

disembarrass (ˌdɪsɪm'bærəs) *vb (tr)* **1** to free from embarrassment, entanglement, etc. **2** to relieve or rid of something burdensome.

disembodied ⓘ (ˌdɪsɪm'bɒdɪd) *adj* **1** lacking a body or freed from the body. **2** lacking in substance or any firm relation to reality.

disembody (ˌdɪsɪm'bɒdɪ) *vb* **disembodies, disembodying, disembodied.** *(tr)* to free from the body or from physical form.
▸ˌ**disem'bodiment** *n*

disembogue (ˌdɪsɪm'bəʊg) *vb* **disembogues, disemboguing, disembogued. 1** (of a river, stream, etc.) to discharge (water) at the mouth. **2** *(intr)* to flow out. [C16: from Sp. *desembocar,* from *des-* DIS-[1] + *embocar* to put into the mouth]
▸ˌ**disem'boguement** *n*

disembowel ⓘ (ˌdɪsɪm'baʊəl) *vb* **disembowels, disembowelling, disembowelled** *or US* **disembowels, disemboweling, disemboweled.** *(tr)* to remove the entrails of.
▸ˌ**disem'bowelment** *n*

disempower (ˌdɪsɪm'paʊə) *vb (tr)* to deprive (a person) of power or authority.
▸ˌ**disem'powerment** *n*

disenchant ⓘ (ˌdɪsɪn'tʃɑ:nt) *vb (tr)* to free from or as if from an enchantment; disillusion.
▸ˌ**disen'chantingly** *adv* ▸ˌ**disen'chantment** *n*

disencumber ⓘ (ˌdɪsɪn'kʌmbə) *vb (tr)* to free from encumbrances.
▸ˌ**disen'cumberment** *n*

disenfranchise (ˌdɪsɪn'fræntʃaɪz) *or* **disfranchise** *vb* **disenfranchises, disenfranchising, disenfranchised** *or* **disfranchises, disfranchising, disfranchised.** *(tr)* **1** to deprive (a person) of the right to vote or other rights of citizenship. **2** to deprive (a place) of the right to send representatives to an elected body. **3** to deprive (a person, place, etc.) of any franchise or right.
▸**disenfranchisement** (ˌdɪsɪn'fræntʃɪzmənt) *or* **dis'franchisement** *n*

disengage ⓘ (ˌdɪsɪn'geɪdʒ) *vb* **disengages, disengaging, disengaged. 1** to release or become released from a connection, obligation, etc. **2** *Mil.* to withdraw (forces) from close action. **3** *Fencing.* to move (one's blade) from one side of an opponent's blade to another in a circular motion.
▸ˌ**disen'gaged** *adj* ▸ˌ**disen'gagement** *n*

disentangle ⓘ (ˌdɪsɪn'tæŋgᵊl) *vb* **disentangles, disentangling, disentangled. 1** to release or become free from entanglement or confusion. **2** *(tr)* to unravel or work out.
▸ˌ**disen'tanglement** *n*

disequilibrium (ˌdɪsi:kwɪ'lɪbrɪəm) *n* a loss or absence of equilibrium, esp. in an economy.

disestablish (ˌdɪsɪ'stæblɪʃ) *vb (tr)* to deprive (a church, custom, institution, etc.) of established status.
▸ˌ**dises'tablishment** *n*

disesteem (ˌdɪsɪ'sti:m) *vb* **1** *(tr)* to think little of. ◆ *n* **2** lack of esteem.

disfavour ⓘ *or US* **disfavor** (dɪs'feɪvə) *n* **1** disapproval or dislike. **2** the state of being disapproved of or disliked. **3** an unkind act. ◆ *vb* **4** *(tr)* to treat with disapproval or dislike.

disfigure ⓘ (dɪs'fɪgə) *vb* **disfigures, disfiguring, disfigured.** *(tr)* **1** to spoil the appearance or shape of; deface. **2** to mar the effect or quality of.
▸**dis'figurement** *n*

disforest (dɪs'fɒrɪst) *vb (tr)* **1** another word for **deforest. 2** *English law.* a less common word for **disafforest.**
▸**disˌfores'tation** *n*

disfranchise (dɪs'fræntʃaɪz) *vb* another word for **disenfranchise.**

disgorge ⓘ (dɪs'gɔ:dʒ) *vb* **disgorges, disgorging, disgorged. 1** to throw out (food, etc.) from the throat or stomach; vomit. **2** to discharge or empty of (contents). **3** *(tr)* to yield up unwillingly.
▸**dis'gorgement** *n*

disgrace ⓘ (dɪs'greɪs) *n* **1** a condition of shame, loss of reputation, or dishonour. **2** a shameful person or thing. **3** exclusion from confidence or trust: *he is in disgrace with his father.* ◆ *vb* **disgraces, disgracing, disgraced.** *(tr)* **4** to bring shame upon. **5** to treat or cause to be treated with disfavour.

disgraceful ⓘ (dɪs'greɪsfʊl) *adj* shameful; scandalous.
▸**dis'gracefully** *adv*

disgruntle ⓘ (dɪs'grʌntᵊl) *vb* **disgruntles, disgruntling, disgruntled.** *(tr)* to make sulky or discontented. [C17: DIS-[1] + obs. *gruntle* to complain]
▸**dis'gruntled** *adj* ▸**dis'gruntlement** *n*

disguise ⓘ (dɪs'gaɪz) *vb* **disguises, disguising, disguised. 1** to modify the appearance or manner in order to conceal the identity of (someone or something). **2** *(tr)* to misrepresent in order to obscure the actual nature or meaning. ◆ *n* **3** a mask, costume, or manner that disguises. **4** a disguising or being disguised. [C14: from OF *desguisier,* from *des-* DIS-[1] + *guise* manner]
▸**dis'guised** *adj*

disgust ⓘ (dɪs'gʌst) *vb (tr)* **1** to sicken or fill with loathing. **2** to offend the moral sense of. ◆ *n* **3** a great loathing or distaste. **4 in disgust.** as a

THESAURUS

derision, dislike, haughtiness, hauteur, indifference, scorn, sneering, snobbishness, superciliousness ◆ *vb* **2** = **scorn**, belittle, contemn, deride, despise, disregard, look down on, look down one's nose at (*inf.*), misprize, pooh-pooh, reject, slight, sneer at, spurn, undervalue

disdainful *adj* = **contemptuous**, aloof, arrogant, derisive, haughty, high and mighty (*inf.*), hoity-toity (*inf.*), insolent, looking down one's nose (at), on one's high horse (*inf.*), proud, scornful, sneering, supercilious, superior, turning up one's nose (at)

disease *n* **1** = **illness**, affliction, ailment, complaint, condition, disorder, ill health, indisposition, infection, infirmity, lurgy (*inf.*), malady, sickness, upset **3** = **malady**, blight, cancer, canker, contagion, contamination, disorder, plague

diseased *adj* **1** = **sick**, ailing, infected, rotten, sickly, tainted, unhealthy, unsound, unwell, unwholesome

disembark *vb* = **land**, alight, arrive, get off, go ashore, step out of

disembodied *adj* **1, 2** = **bodiless**, ghostly, immaterial, incorporeal, intangible, phantom, spectral, spiritual, unbodied

disembowel *vb* = **eviscerate**, draw, gut, paunch

disenchant *vb* = **disillusion**, break the spell, bring (someone) down to earth, destroy (someone's) illusions, disabuse, open (someone's) eyes, undeceive

disenchanted *adj* = **disillusioned**, blasé, cynical, disappointed, indifferent, jaundiced, let down, out of love, sick of, soured, undeceived

disenchantment *n* = **disillusionment**, disappointment, disillusion, revulsion, rude awakening

disencumber *vb* = **unburden**, disburden, discharge, disembarrass, disembroil, extricate, lighten, unhamper, unload

disengage *vb* **1** = **detach**, disconnect, disentangle, disjoin, disunite, divide, ease, extricate, free, liberate, loosen, release, separate, set free, unbridle, undo, unloose, untie, withdraw

disengaged *adj* **1** = **unconnected**, apart, detached, free, loose, out of gear, released, separate, unattached, uncoupled

disengagement *n* **1** = **disconnection**, detachment, disentanglement, division, separation, withdrawal

disentangle *vb* **1** = **untangle**, detach, disconnect, disengage, extricate, free, loose, separate, sever, unfold, unravel, unsnarl, untwist **2** = **sort out**, clarify, clear (up), resolve, simplify, work out

disfavour *n* **1** = **disapproval**, disapprobation, dislike, displeasure

disfigure *vb* **1** = **damage**, blemish, deface, deform, disfeature, distort, injure, maim, make ugly, mar, mutilate, scar

disfigurement *n* **1** = **damage**, blemish, defacement, defect, deformity, distortion, impairment, injury, mutilation, scar, spot, stain, trauma (*Pathology*)

disgorge *vb* **1** = **vomit**, barf (*US sl.*), belch, blow lunch (*US sl.*), chuck (up) (*sl., chiefly US*), chunder (*sl., chiefly Austral.*), discharge, do a technicolour yawn (*sl.*), eject, empty, expel, lose one's lunch (*US sl.*), regurgitate, spew, spit up, spout, throw up, toss one's cookies (*US sl.*) **3** = **give up**, cede, relinquish, renounce, resign, surrender, yield

disgrace *n* **1** = **shame**, baseness, degradation, dishonour, disrepute, ignominy, infamy, odium, opprobrium **3** = **discredit**, contempt, disesteem, disfavour, obloquy ◆ *vb* **4** = **bring shame upon**, abase, defame, degrade, discredit, disfavour, dishonour, disparage, humiliate, reproach, shame, slur, stain, stigmatize, sully, taint

Antonyms *n* ≠ **shame:** credit, esteem, favour, grace, honour, repute ◆ *vb* ≠ **bring shame upon:** credit, grace, honour

disgraced *adj* **4** = **shamed**, branded, degraded, discredited, dishonoured, humiliated, in disgrace, in the doghouse (*inf.*), mortified, stigmatized, under a cloud

disgraceful *adj* = **shameful**, blameworthy, contemptible, degrading, detestable, discreditable, dishonourable, disreputable, ignominious, infamous, low, mean, opprobrious, scandalous, shocking, unworthy

disgruntled *adj* = **discontented**, annoyed, cheesed off (*Brit. sl.*), displeased, dissatisfied, grumpy, hacked (off) (*US sl.*), huffy, irritated, malcontent, peeved, peevish, petulant, pissed off (*taboo sl.*), put out, sulky, sullen, testy, vexed

disguise *vb* **1** = **hide**, camouflage, cloak, conceal, cover, mask, screen, secrete, shroud, veil **2** = **misrepresent**, deceive, dissemble, dissimulate, fake, falsify, fudge, gloss over ◆ *n* **3** = **costume**, camouflage, cloak, cover, get-up (*inf.*), mask, screen, veil **4** = **façade**, deception, dissimulation, front, pretence, semblance, trickery, veneer

disguised *adj* **1** = **in disguise**, camouflaged, cloaked, covert, fake, false, feigned, incognito, masked, pretend, undercover, unrecognizable

disgust *vb* **1, 2** = **sicken**, cause aversion, displease, fill with loathing, gross out (*US. sl.*), nauseate, offend, outrage, put off, repel, revolt, turn one's stomach ◆ *n* **3** = **loathing**, abhorrence, abomination, antipathy, aversion, detestation, dislike, distaste, hatefulness, hatred, nausea, odium, repugnance, repulsion, revulsion

Antonyms *n* ≠ **loathing:** liking, love, pleasure, satisfaction, taste ◆ *vb* ≠ **sicken:** delight, impress, please

result of disgust. [C16: from OF *desgouster*, from *des-* DIS-[1] + *gouster* to taste, from L *gustus* taste]
▸**dis'gustedly** *adv* ▸**dis'gustedness** *n*

dish Ⓣ (dɪʃ) *n* **1** a container used for holding or serving food, esp. an open shallow container. **2** the food in a dish. **3** a particular kind of food. **4** Also called: **dishful.** the amount contained in a dish. **5** something resembling a dish. **6** a concavity. **7** short for **dish aerial. 8** *Inf.* an attractive person. ◆ *vb (tr)* **9** to put into a dish. **10** to make concave. **11** *Brit. inf.* to ruin or spoil. ◆ See also **dish out, dish up.** [OE *disc*, from L *discus* quoit]
▸**'dish,like** *adj*

dishabille (ˌdɪsæ'biːl) *n* a variant of **deshabille.**

dish aerial *n* a microwave aerial, used esp. in radar, radio telescopes, and satellite broadcasting (**satellite dish aerial**), consisting of a parabolic reflector. Formal name: **parabolic aerial.** ◆ Also called: **dish antenna.** Often shortened to **dish.**

disharmony Ⓣ (dɪs'hɑːmənɪ) *n, pl* **disharmonies. 1** lack of accord or harmony. **2** a situation, circumstance, etc., that is inharmonious.
▸**disharmonious** (ˌdɪshɑː'məʊnɪəs) *adj*

dishcloth ('dɪʃˌklɒθ) *n* a cloth or rag for washing or drying dishes.

dishearten Ⓣ (dɪs'hɑːtᵊn) *vb (tr)* to weaken or destroy the hope, courage, enthusiasm, etc., of.
▸**dis'hearteningly** *adv* ▸**dis'heartenment** *n*

dished (dɪʃt) *adj* **1** shaped like a dish. **2** (of wheels) closer to one another at the bottom than at the top. **3** *Inf.* exhausted or defeated.

dishevel (dɪ'ʃɛvᵊl) *vb* **dishevels, dishevelling, dishevelled** *or US* **dishevels, disheveling, disheveled.** to disarrange (the hair or clothes) of (someone). [C15: back formation from DISHEVELLED]
▸**di'shevelment** *n*

dishevelled Ⓣ *or US* **disheveled** (dɪ'ʃɛvᵊld) *adj* **1** (esp. of hair) hanging loosely. **2** unkempt; untidy. [C15 *dischevelee*, from OF *deschevelé*, from *des-* DIS-[1] + *chevel* hair, from L *capillus*]

dishonest Ⓣ (dɪs'ɒnɪst) *adj* not honest or fair; deceiving or fraudulent.
▸**dis'honestly** *adv*

dishonesty Ⓣ (dɪs'ɒnɪstɪ) *n, pl* **dishonesties. 1** lack of honesty. **2** a deceiving act or statement.

dishonour Ⓣ *or US* **dishonor** (dɪs'ɒnə) *vb (tr)* **1** to treat with disrespect. **2** to fail or refuse to pay (a cheque, etc.). **3** to cause the disgrace of (a woman) by seduction or rape. ◆ *n* **4** a lack of honour or respect. **5** a state of shame or disgrace. **6** a person or thing that causes a loss of honour. **7** an insult; affront. **8** refusal or failure to accept or pay a commercial paper.

dishonourable Ⓣ *or US* **dishonorable** (dɪs'ɒnərəbᵊl) *adj* **1** characterized by or causing dishonour or discredit. **2** having little or no integrity; unprincipled.
▸**dis'honourableness** *or US* **dis'honorableness** *n* ▸**dis'honourably** *or US* **dis'honorably** *adv*

dish out Ⓣ *vb (tr, adv)* **1** *Inf.* to distribute. **2 dish it out.** to inflict punishment.

dishtowel ('dɪʃˌtaʊəl) *n* another name (esp. Scot., US and Canad.) for a **tea towel.**

dish up Ⓣ *vb (adv)* **1** to serve (a meal, food, etc.). **2** *(tr) Inf.* to prepare or present, esp. in an attractive manner.

dishwasher ('dɪʃˌwɒʃə) *n* **1** a machine for washing dishes, etc. **2** a person who washes dishes, etc.

dishwater ('dɪʃˌwɔːtə) *n* **1** water in which dishes have been washed. **2** something resembling this.

dishy ('dɪʃɪ) *adj* **dishier, dishiest.** *Inf., chiefly Brit.* good-looking or attractive.

disillusion Ⓣ (ˌdɪsɪ'luːʒən) *vb* **1** *(tr)* to destroy the ideals, illusions, or false ideas of. ◆ *n also* **disillusionment. 2** the act of disillusioning or the state of being disillusioned.

disincentive Ⓣ (ˌdɪsɪn'sentɪv) *n* **1** something that acts as a deterrent. ◆ *adj* **2** acting as a deterrent: *a disincentive effect on productivity.*

disincline Ⓣ (ˌdɪsɪn'klaɪn) *vb* **disinclines, disinclining, disinclined.** to make or be unwilling, reluctant, or averse.
▸**disinclination** (ˌdɪsɪnklɪ'neɪʃən) *n*

disinfect Ⓣ (ˌdɪsɪn'fɛkt) *vb (tr)* to rid of microorganisms potentially harmful to man, esp. by chemical means.
▸**ˌdisin'fection** *n*

disinfectant Ⓣ (ˌdɪsɪn'fɛktənt) *n* an agent that destroys or inhibits the activity of microorganisms that cause disease.

disinfest (ˌdɪsɪn'fɛst) *vb (tr)* to rid of vermin.
▸**ˌdisinfes'tation** *n*

disinflation (ˌdɪsɪn'fleɪʃən) *n Econ.* a reduction or stabilization of the general price level intended to improve the balance of payments without incurring reductions in output, employment, etc.

disinformation (ˌdɪsɪnfə'meɪʃən) *n* false information intended to deceive or mislead.

disingenuous (ˌdɪsɪn'dʒɛnjʊəs) *adj* not sincere; lacking candour.
▸**ˌdisin'genuously** *adv* ▸**ˌdisin'genuousness** *n*

disinherit Ⓣ (ˌdɪsɪn'hɛrɪt) *vb (tr)* **1** *Law.* to deprive (an heir or next of kin) of inheritance or right to inherit. **2** to deprive of a right or heritage.
▸**ˌdisin'heritance** *n*

disintegrate Ⓣ (dɪs'ɪntɪˌgreɪt) *vb* **disintegrates, disintegrating, disintegrated. 1** to break or be broken into fragments or parts; shatter. **2** to lose or cause to lose cohesion. **3** *(intr)* to lose judgment or control. **4** *Physics.* **4a** to induce or undergo nuclear fission. **4b** another word for **decay** (sense 3).
▸**disˌinte'gration** *n* ▸**dis'inteˌgrator** *n*

disinter Ⓣ (ˌdɪsɪn'tɜː) *vb* **disinters, disinterring, disinterred.** *(tr)* **1** to remove or dig up; exhume. **2** to bring to light; expose.
▸**ˌdisin'terment** *n*

disinterest Ⓣ (dɪs'ɪntrɪst, -tərɪst) *n* **1** freedom from bias or involvement. **2** lack of interest.

disinterested Ⓣ (dɪs'ɪntrɪstɪd, -tərɪs-) *adj* **1** free from bias or partiality; objective. **2** not interested.
▸**dis'interestedly** *adv* ▸**dis'interestedness** *n*

> **USAGE NOTE** Many people consider that the use of *disinterested* to mean not interested is incorrect and *uninterested* should be used.

THESAURUS

disgusted *adj* **1, 2** = **sickened**, appalled, nauseated, offended, outraged, repelled, repulsed, scandalized, sick and tired of (*inf.*), sick of (*inf.*)

disgusting *adj* **1, 2** = **sickening**, abominable, cringe-making (*Brit. inf.*), detestable, distasteful, foul, gross, grotty (*sl.*), hateful, loathsome, nasty, nauseating, nauseous, noisome, objectionable, obnoxious, odious, offensive, repellent, repugnant, revolting, shameless, stinking, vile, vulgar, yucky *or* yukky (*sl.*)

dish *n* **1** = **bowl**, plate, platter, salver **2** = **food**, fare, recipe ◆ *vb* **11** *Brit. informal* = **ruin**, finish, muck up, spoil, torpedo, wreck

disharmony *n* **1, 2** = **discord**, clash, conflict, disaccord, discordance, dissonance, friction, inharmoniousness

dishearten *vb* = **discourage**, cast down, crush, damp, dampen, dash, daunt, deject, depress, deter, dismay, dispirit, put a damper on
Antonyms *vb* buck up (*inf.*), cheer up, encourage, gee up, hearten, lift, perk up, rally

disheartened *adj* = **discouraged**, choked, crestfallen, crushed, daunted, dejected, depressed, disappointed, dismayed, dispirited, downcast, downhearted, sick as a parrot (*inf.*)

dishevelled *adj* = **untidy**, bedraggled, blowsy, disarranged, disarrayed, disordered, frowzy, hanging loose, messy, ruffled, rumpled, tousled, uncombed, unkempt
Antonyms *adj* chic, dapper, neat, smart, soigné *or* soignée, spick-and-span, spruce, tidy, trim, well-groomed

dishonest *adj* = **deceitful**, bent (*sl.*), cheating, corrupt, crafty, crooked (*inf.*), deceiving, deceptive, designing, disreputable, double-dealing, false, fraudulent, guileful, knavish (*arch.*), lying, mendacious, perfidious, shady (*inf.*), swindling, treacherous, unfair, unprincipled, unscrupulous, untrustworthy, untruthful
Antonyms *adj* honest, honourable, law-abiding, lawful, principled, true, trustworthy, upright

dishonesty *n* **1** = **deceit**, cheating, chicanery, corruption, craft, criminality, crookedness, duplicity, falsehood, falsity, fraud, fraudulence, graft (*inf.*), improbity, mendacity, perfidy, sharp practice, stealing, treachery, trickery, unscrupulousness, wiliness

dishonour *vb* **1** = **disgrace**, abase, blacken, corrupt, debase, debauch, defame, degrade, discredit, shame, sully **3** = **seduce**, defile, deflower, pollute, rape, ravish ◆ *n* **5** = **disgrace**, abasement, degradation, discredit, disfavour, disrepute, ignominy, infamy, obloquy, odium, opprobrium, reproach, scandal, shame **7** = **insult**, abuse, affront, discourtesy, indignity, offence, outrage, sacrilege, slight
Antonyms *vb* ≠ **disgrace:** esteem, exalt, respect, revere, worship ◆ *n* ≠ **disgrace:** decency, goodness, honour, integrity, morality, principles, rectitude

dishonourable *adj* **1** = **shameful**, base, contemptible, despicable, discreditable, disgraceful, ignoble, ignominious, infamous, not cricket (*inf.*), scandalous **2** = **untrustworthy**, blackguardly, corrupt, disreputable, shameless, treacherous, unprincipled, unscrupulous

dish out *vb* **1** *Informal* = **distribute**, allocate, dole out, hand out **2 dish it out** = **mete out**, inflict

dish up *vb* = **serve**, hand out, ladle, prepare, present, produce, scoop, spoon

disillusion *vb* **1** = **shatter one's illusions**, break the spell, bring down to earth, disabuse, disenchant, open the eyes of, undeceive

disillusioned *adj* **1** = **disenchanted**, disabused, disappointed, enlightened, indifferent, out of love, sadder and wiser, undeceived

disillusionment *n* **2** = **disenchantment**, disappointment, disillusion, enlightenment, lost innocence, rude awakening

disincentive *n* **1** = **discouragement**, damper, determent, deterrent, dissuasion, impediment

disinclination *n* = **reluctance**, alienation, antipathy, aversion, demur, dislike, hesitance, lack of desire, lack of enthusiasm, loathness, objection, opposition, repugnance, resistance, unwillingness

disinclined *adj* = **reluctant**, antipathetic, averse, balking, hesitating, indisposed, loath, not in the mood, opposed, resistant, unwilling

disinfect *vb* = **sterilize**, clean, cleanse, decontaminate, deodorize, fumigate, purify, sanitize
Antonyms *vb* contaminate, defile, infect, poison, pollute, taint

disinfectant *n* = **antiseptic**, germicide, sanitizer, sterilizer

disinherit *vb Law* **1** = **cut off**, cut off without a penny, disown, dispossess, oust, repudiate

disintegrate *vb* **1-3** = **break up**, break apart, crumble, disunite, fall apart, fall to pieces, go to pieces, go to seed, reduce to fragments, separate, shatter, splinter

disinter *vb* **1** = **dig up**, disentomb, exhume, unearth **2** = **expose**, bring to light, disclose, discover, uncover, unearth

disinterest *n* **1** = **impartiality**, candidness, detachment, disinterestedness, dispassionateness, equity, fairness, justice, neutrality, unbiasedness

disinterested *adj* **1** = **impartial**, candid, detached, dispassionate, equitable, even-handed,

disintermediation (dɪsˌɪntəˌmiːdɪˈeɪʃən) *n Finance.* the elimination of such financial intermediaries as banks and brokers in transactions between principals, often as a result of deregulation and the use of computing.

disinvest (dɪsɪnˈvɛst) *vb Econ.* **1** (usually foll. by *in*) to remove investment (from). **2** (*intr*) to reduce the capital stock of an economy or enterprise, as by not replacing obsolete machinery.
▸ **ˌdisinˈvestment** *n*

disjoin (dɪsˈdʒɔɪn) *vb* to disconnect or become disconnected; separate.
▸ **disˈjoinable** *adj*

disjoint (dɪsˈdʒɔɪnt) *vb* **1** to take apart or come apart at the joints. **2** (*tr*) to disunite or disjoin. **3** to dislocate or become dislocated. **4** (*tr; usually passive*) to end the unity, sequence, or coherence of.

disjointed Ⓣ (dɪsˈdʒɔɪntɪd) *adj* **1** having no coherence; disconnected. **2** separated at the joint. **3** dislocated.
▸ **disˈjointedly** *adv*

disjunct (ˈdɪsdʒʌŋkt) *n Logic.* one of the propositions in a disjunction.

disjunction (dɪsˈdʒʌŋkʃən) *n* **1** Also called: **disjuncture.** a disconnecting or being disconnected; separation. **2** *Logic.* **2a** the operator that forms a compound sentence from two given sentences and corresponds to the English *or.* **2b** the relation between such sentences.

disjunctive (dɪsˈdʒʌŋktɪv) *adj* **1** serving to disconnect or separate. **2** *Grammar.* denoting a word, esp. a conjunction, that serves to express opposition or contrast: *but* in *She was poor but she was honest.* **3** *Logic.* relating to, characterized by, or containing disjunction. ◆ *n* **4** *Grammar.* a disjunctive word, esp. a conjunction. **5** *Logic.* a disjunctive proposition.
▸ **disˈjunctively** *adv*

disk (dɪsk) *n* **1** a variant spelling (esp. US and Canad.) of **disc. 2** Also called: **magnetic disk, hard disk.** *Computing.* a direct-access storage device consisting of a stack of plates coated with a magnetic layer, the whole assembly rotating rapidly as a single unit.

disk drive *n Computing.* the controller and mechanism for reading and writing data on computer disks.

diskette (dɪsˈkɛt) *n* another name for **floppy disk.**

disk operating system *n* an operating system used on a computer system with one or more disk drives. Often shortened to: **DOS.**

dislike Ⓣ (dɪsˈlaɪk) *vb* **dislikes, disliking, disliked. 1** (*tr*) to consider unpleasant or disagreeable. ◆ *n* **2** a feeling of aversion or antipathy.
▸ **disˈlikable** *or* **disˈlikeable** *adj*

dislocate Ⓣ (ˈdɪsləˌkeɪt) *vb* **dislocates, dislocating, dislocated.** (*tr*) **1** to disrupt or shift out of place. **2** to displace from its normal position, esp. a bone from its joint.

dislocation Ⓣ (ˌdɪsləˈkeɪʃən) *n* **1** a displacing or being displaced. **2** the state or condition of being dislocated.

dislodge Ⓣ (dɪsˈlɒdʒ) *vb* **dislodges, dislodging, dislodged.** to remove from or leave a lodging place, hiding place, or previously fixed position.
▸ **disˈlodgment** *or* **disˈlodgement** *n*

disloyal Ⓣ (dɪsˈlɔɪəl) *adj* not loyal or faithful; deserting one's allegiance.
▸ **disˈloyally** *adv*

disloyalty Ⓣ (dɪsˈlɔɪəltɪ) *n, pl* **disloyalties.** the condition or an instance of being unfaithful or disloyal.

dismal Ⓣ (ˈdɪzməl) *adj* **1** causing gloom or depression. **2** causing dismay or terror. **3** of poor quality or a low standard; feeble. [C13: from *dismal* (n) list of 24 unlucky days in the year, from Med. L *diēs malī,* from L *diēs* day + *malus* bad]
▸ **ˈdismally** *adv* ▸ **ˈdismalness** *n*

dismantle Ⓣ (dɪsˈmæntᵊl) *vb* **dismantles, dismantling, dismantled.** (*tr*) **1** to take apart. **2** to demolish or raze. **3** to strip of covering. [C17: from OF *desmanteler* to remove a cloak from]
▸ **disˈmantlement** *n*

dismast (dɪsˈmɑːst) *vb* (*tr*) to break off the mast or masts of (a sailing vessel).

dismay Ⓣ (dɪsˈmeɪ) *vb* (*tr*) **1** to fill with apprehension or alarm. **2** to fill with depression or discouragement. ◆ *n* **3** consternation or agitation. [C13: from OF *desmaiier* (unattested), from *des-* DIS-[1] + *esmayer* to frighten, ult. of Gmc origin]
▸ **disˈmaying** *adj*

dismember Ⓣ (dɪsˈmɛmbə) *vb* (*tr*) **1** to remove the limbs or members of. **2** to cut to pieces. **3** to divide or partition (something, such as an empire).
▸ **disˈmemberment** *n*

dismiss Ⓣ (dɪsˈmɪs) *vb* (*tr*) **1** to remove or discharge from employment or service. **2** to send away or allow to go. **3** to dispel from one's mind; discard. **4** to cease to consider (a subject). **5** to decline further hearing to (a claim or action). **6** *Cricket.* to bowl out a side for a particular number of runs. [C15: from Med. L *dismissus* sent away, from *dīmittere,* from *dī-* DIS-[1] + *mittere* to send]
▸ **disˈmissal** *n* ▸ **disˈmissible** *adj* ▸ **disˈmissive** *adj*

dismount Ⓣ (dɪsˈmaʊnt) *vb* **1** to get off a horse, bicycle, etc. **2** (*tr*) to disassemble or remove from a mounting. ◆ *n* **3** the act of dismounting.

Disneyfication (ˌdɪznɪfɪˈkeɪʃən) *n Derog.* the process by which historical places, local customs, etc. are transformed into trivial entertainment for tourists: *the Disneyfication of Britain's heritage.* [C20: from the *Disneyland* amusement park in California]
▸ **ˌDisneyˈfy** *vb* (*tr*).

disobedience Ⓣ (ˌdɪsəˈbiːdɪəns) *n* lack of obedience.

disobedient Ⓣ (ˌdɪsəˈbiːdɪənt) *adj* not obedient; neglecting or refusing to obey.
▸ **ˌdisoˈbediently** *adv*

disobey Ⓣ (ˌdɪsəˈbeɪ) *vb* to neglect or refuse to obey (someone, an order, etc.).
▸ **ˌdisoˈbeyer** *n*

disoblige Ⓣ (ˌdɪsəˈblaɪdʒ) *vb* **disobliges, disobliging, disobliged.** (*tr*) **1** to disregard the desires of. **2** to slight; insult. **3** *Inf.* to cause trouble or inconvenience to.
▸ **ˌdisoˈbliging** *adj*

disorder Ⓣ (dɪsˈɔːdə) *n* **1** a lack of order; confusion. **2** a disturbance of public order. **3** an upset of health; ailment. **4** a deviation from the

THESAURUS

free from self-interest, impersonal, neutral, objective, outside, unbiased, uninvolved, unprejudiced, unselfish
Antonyms *adj* biased, involved, partial, prejudiced, selfish

disjointed *adj* **1** = **incoherent**, aimless, confused, disconnected, disordered, fitful, loose, rambling, spasmodic, unconnected **3** = **disconnected**, dislocated, displaced, disunited, divided, separated, split

dislike *vb* **1** = **be averse to**, abhor, abominate, despise, detest, disapprove, disfavour, disrelish, hate, have a down on (*inf.*), have no taste *or* stomach for, loathe, not be able to bear *or* abide *or* stand, object to, scorn, shun, take a dim view of ◆ *n* **2** = **aversion**, animosity, animus, antagonism, antipathy, detestation, disapprobation, disapproval, disgust, disinclination, displeasure, distaste, enmity, hatred, hostility, loathing, odium, repugnance
Antonyms *vb* ≠ **be averse to:** esteem, favour, like ◆ *n* ≠ **aversion:** admiration, attraction, delight, esteem, inclination, liking

dislocate *vb* **1** = **shift**, disorder, displace, disrupt, disturb, misplace **2** = **put out of joint**, disarticulate, disconnect, disengage, disjoint, disunite, luxate, unhinge

dislocation *n* **1** = **shift**, disarray, disorder, disorganization, disruption, disturbance, misplacement **2** = **putting out of joint**, disarticulation, disconnection, disengagement, luxation (*Medical*), unhinging

dislodge *vb* = **displace**, dig out, disentangle, disturb, eject, extricate, force out, knock loose, oust, remove, uproot

disloyal *adj* = **treacherous**, apostate, disaffected, faithless, false, perfidious, seditious, subversive, traitorous, treasonable, two-faced, unfaithful, unpatriotic, untrustworthy
Antonyms *adj* constant, dependable, dutiful, faithful, loyal, steadfast, true, trustworthy, trusty

disloyalty *n* = **treachery**, betrayal of trust, breach of trust, breaking of faith, deceitfulness, double-dealing, falseness, falsity, inconstancy, infidelity, perfidy, Punic faith, treason, unfaithfulness

dismal *adj* **1** = **gloomy**, black, bleak, cheerless, dark, depressing, despondent, discouraging, dolorous, dreary, forlorn, funereal, lonesome, louring *or* lowering, lugubrious, melancholy, sad, sombre, sorrowful, wretched
Antonyms *adj* bright, cheerful, cheery, glad, happy, joyful, light-hearted, sunny

dismantle *vb* **1-3** = **take apart**, demolish, disassemble, dismount, raze, strike, strip, take to pieces, unrig

dismay *vb* **1** = **alarm**, affright, appal, distress, fill with consternation, frighten, horrify, paralyse, scare, terrify, unnerve **2** = **disappoint**, daunt, discourage, dishearten, disillusion, dispirit, put off ◆ *n* **3** = **alarm**, agitation, anxiety, apprehension, consternation, distress, dread, fear, fright, horror, panic, terror, trepidation

dismember *vb* **1, 2** = **cut into pieces**, amputate, anatomize, disjoint, dislocate, dissect, divide, mutilate, rend, sever

dismiss *vb* **1** = **sack** (*inf.*), axe (*inf.*), cashier, discharge, fire (*inf.*), give notice to, give (someone) their marching orders, give the boot to (*sl.*), give the bullet to (*Brit. sl.*), kiss off (*sl., chiefly US & Canad.*), lay off, oust, remove, send packing (*inf.*) **2** = **let go**, disband, disperse, dissolve, free, release, send away **3, 4** = **put out of one's mind**, banish, discard, dispel, disregard, drop, lay aside, pooh-pooh, reject, relegate, repudiate, set aside, shelve, spurn

dismissal *n* **1** = **the sack** (*inf.*), discharge, expulsion, kiss-off (*sl., chiefly US & Canad.*), marching orders (*inf.*), notice, one's books *or* cards, removal, the boot (*sl.*), the bum's rush (*sl.*), the (old) heave-ho (*inf.*), the order of the boot (*sl.*), the push (*sl.*) **2** = **permission to go**, adjournment, congé, end, freedom to depart, release

dismount *vb* **1** = **get off**, alight, descend, get down, light

disobedience *n* = **defiance**, indiscipline, infraction, insubordination, mutiny, noncompliance, nonobservance, recalcitrance, revolt, unruliness, waywardness

disobedient *adj* = **defiant**, contrary, contumacious, disorderly, froward (*arch.*), insubordinate, intractable, mischievous, naughty, noncompliant, nonobservant, obstreperous, refractory, undisciplined, unruly, wayward, wilful
Antonyms *adj* biddable, compliant, dutiful, manageable, obedient, submissive, well-behaved

disobey *vb* = **refuse to obey**, contravene, defy, dig one's heels in, disregard, flout, go counter to, ignore, infringe, overstep, rebel, resist, transgress, violate

disoblige *vb* **2** = **offend**, affront, displease, insult, slight **3** = **inconvenience**, annoy, bother, discommode, disturb, put out, trouble, upset

disobliging *adj* **3** = **unhelpful**, awkward, bloody-minded (*Brit. inf.*), cussed (*inf.*), disagreeable, discourteous, ill-disposed, rude, unaccommodating, uncivil, uncooperative, unobliging, unpleasant

disorder *n* **1** = **untidiness**, chaos, clutter, confusion, derangement, disarray, disorderliness,

normal system or order. ◆ *vb* (*tr*) **5** to upset the order of. **6** to disturb the health or mind of.

disorderly ❶ (dɪsˈɔːdəlɪ) *adj* **1** untidy; irregular. **2** uncontrolled; unruly. **3** *Law.* violating public peace or order.
▸**disˈorderliness** *n*

disorderly house *n Law.* an establishment in which unruly behaviour habitually occurs, esp. a brothel or a gaming house.

disorganize ❶ *or* **disorganise** (dɪsˈɔːgəˌnaɪz) *vb* **disorganizes, disorganizing, disorganized** *or* **disorganises, disorganising, disorganised.** (*tr*) to disrupt the arrangement, system, or unity of.
▸**disˌorganiˈzation** *or* **disˌorganiˈsation** *n*

disorientate ❶ (dɪsˈɔːrɪenˌteɪt) *or* **disorient** *vb* **disorientates, disorientating, disorientated** *or* **disorients, disorienting, disoriented.** (*tr*) **1** to cause (someone) to lose his bearings. **2** to perplex; confuse.
▸**disˌorienˈtation** *n*

disown ❶ (dɪsˈəʊn) *vb* (*tr*) to deny any connection with; refuse to acknowledge.
▸**disˈowner** *n*

disparage ❶ (dɪˈspærɪdʒ) *vb* **disparages, disparaging, disparaged.** (*tr*) **1** to speak contemptuously of; belittle. **2** to damage the reputation of. [C14: from OF *desparagier*, from *des-* DIS-[1] + *parage* equality, from L *par* equal]
▸**disˈparagement** *n* ▸**disˈparaging** *adj*

disparate ❶ (ˈdɪspərɪt) *adj* **1** utterly different or distinct in kind. ◆ *n* **2** (*pl*) unlike things or people. [C16: from L *disparāre* to divide, from DIS-[1] + *parāre* to prepare; also infl. by L *dispar* unequal]
▸ˈ**disparately** *adv* ▸ˈ**disparateness** *n*

disparity ❶ (dɪˈspærɪtɪ) *n, pl* **disparities. 1** inequality or difference, as in age, rank, wages, etc. **2** dissimilarity.

> **USAGE NOTE** See at **discrepancy.**

dispassionate ❶ (dɪsˈpæʃənɪt) *adj* devoid of or uninfluenced by emotion or prejudice; objective; impartial.
▸**disˈpassionately** *adv*

dispatch ❶ *or* **despatch** (dɪˈspætʃ) *vb* (*tr*) **1** to send off promptly, as to a destination or to perform a task. **2** to discharge or complete (a duty, etc.) promptly. **3** *Inf.* to eat up quickly. **4** to murder or execute. ◆ *n* **5** the act of sending off a letter, messenger, etc. **6** prompt action or speed (often in **with dispatch**). **7** an official communication or report, sent in haste. **8** a report sent to a newspaper, etc., by a correspondent. **9** murder or execution. [C16: from It. *dispacciare*, from Provençal *despachar*, from OF *despeechier* to set free, from *des-* DIS-[1] + *-peechier*, ult. from L *pedica* a fetter]
▸**disˈpatcher** *n*

dispatch box *n* a case or box used to hold valuables or documents, esp. official state documents.

dispatch case *n* a case used for carrying papers, documents, books, etc.

dispatch rider *n* a horseman or motorcyclist who carries dispatches.

dispel ❶ (dɪˈspɛl) *vb* **dispels, dispelling, dispelled.** (*tr*) to disperse or drive away. [C17: from L *dispellere*, from DIS-[1] + *pellere* to drive]
▸**disˈpeller** *n*

dispensable ❶ (dɪˈspɛnsəbəl) *adj* **1** not essential; expendable. **2** (of a law, vow, etc.) able to be relaxed.
▸**disˌpensaˈbility** *n*

dispensary (dɪˈspɛnsərɪ) *n, pl* **dispensaries.** a place where medicine, etc., is dispensed.

dispensation ❶ (ˌdɪspɛnˈseɪʃən) *n* **1** the act of distributing or dispensing. **2** something distributed or dispensed. **3** a system or plan of administering or dispensing. **4** *Chiefly RC Church.* permission to dispense with an obligation of church law. **5** any exemption from an obligation. **6a** the ordering of life and events by God. **6b** a religious system or code of prescriptions for life and conduct regarded as of divine origin.
▸ˌ**dispenˈsational** *adj*

dispensatory (dɪˈspɛnsətərɪ, -trɪ) *n, pl* **dispensatories.** a book listing the composition, preparation, and application of various drugs.

dispense ❶ (dɪˈspɛns) *vb* **dispenses, dispensing, dispensed. 1** (*tr*) to give out or distribute in portions. **2** (*tr*) to prepare and distribute (medicine), esp. on prescription. **3** (*tr*) to administer (the law, etc.). **4** (*intr*; foll. by *with*) to do away (with) or manage (without). **5** to grant a dispensation to. **6** to exempt or excuse from a rule or obligation. [C14: from Med. L *dispensāre* to pardon, from L *dispendere* to weigh out, from DIS-[1] + *pendere*]

> **USAGE NOTE** *Dispense with* is sometimes wrongly used where *dispose of* is meant: *the task can be disposed of* (not *dispensed with*) *quickly and easily.*

dispenser (dɪˈspɛnsə) *n* **1** a device that automatically dispenses a single item or a measured quantity. **2** a person or thing that dispenses.

dispensing optician *n* See **optician.**

THESAURUS

disorganization, hodgepodge (*US*), hotchpotch, irregularity, jumble, mess, muddle, pig's breakfast (*inf.*), shambles, state **2 = disturbance**, brawl, clamour, commotion, fight, fracas, hubbub, hullabaloo, quarrel, riot, rumpus, scrimmage, shindig (*inf.*), shindy (*inf.*), tumult, turbulence, turmoil, unrest, unruliness, upheaval, uproar **3 = illness**, affliction, ailment, complaint, disease, indisposition, malady, sickness ◆ *vb* **5 = disorganize**, clutter, confound, confuse, derange, disarrange, discompose, disturb, jumble, make hay of, mess up, mix up, muddle, scatter, unsettle, upset

disordered *adj* **5 = untidy**, all over the place, confused, deranged, disarranged, disarrayed, dislocated, disorganized, displaced, higgledy-piggledy (*inf.*), in a mess, in confusion, jumbled, misplaced, muddled, out of kilter, out of place

disorderly *adj* **1 = untidy**, chaotic, confused, disorganized, higgledy-piggledy (*inf.*), indiscriminate, irregular, jumbled, messy, shambolic (*inf.*), unsystematic **2 = unruly**, boisterous, disruptive, indisciplined, lawless, obstreperous, rebellious, refractory, riotous, rowdy, stormy, tumultuous, turbulent, ungovernable, unlawful, unmanageable
Antonyms *adj* ≠ **untidy:** arranged, neat, orderly, organized, tidy

disorganization *n* **= disorder**, chaos, confusion, derangement, disarray, disjointedness, disruption, incoherence, unconnectedness

disorganize *vb* **= disrupt**, break up, confuse, convulse, derange, destroy, disarrange, discompose, disorder, disturb, jumble, make a shambles of, muddle, turn topsy-turvy, unsettle, upset

disorganized *adj* **= muddled**, chaotic, confused, disordered, haphazard, jumbled, off the rails, shuffled, unmethodical, unorganized, unsystematic

disorientate *vb* **1, 2 = confuse**, cause to lose one's bearings, dislocate, mislead, perplex, upset

disorientated *adj* **1, 2 = confused**, adrift, all at sea, astray, bewildered, lost, mixed up, not adjusted, off-beam, off-course, out of joint, perplexed, unbalanced, unhinged, unsettled, unstable

disown *vb* **= deny**, abandon, abnegate, cast off, disallow, disavow, disclaim, rebut, refuse to acknowledge *or* recognize, reject, renounce, repudiate, retract

disparage *vb* **1, 2 = run down**, asperse, bad-mouth (*sl., chiefly US & Canad.*), belittle, blast, criticize, decry, defame, degrade, denigrate, deprecate, depreciate, deride, derogate, detract from, discredit, disdain, dismiss, knock (*inf.*), lambast(e), malign, minimize, put down, ridicule, rubbish (*inf.*), scorn, slag (off) (*sl.*), slander, tear into (*inf.*), traduce, underestimate, underrate, undervalue, vilify

disparagement *n* **1, 2 = contempt**, aspersion, belittlement, condemnation, contumely, criticism, debasement, degradation, denigration, denunciation, depreciation, derision, derogation, detraction, discredit, disdain, impairment, lessening, prejudice, reproach, ridicule, scorn, slander, underestimation

disparaging *adj* **1, 2 = contemptuous**, abusive, belittling, contumelious, critical, damaging, defamatory, deprecatory, derisive, derogatory, disdainful, dismissive, fault-finding, insulting, libellous, malign, offensive, scathing, scornful, slanderous, slighting, uncomplimentary, unfavourable, unflattering
Antonyms *adj* appreciative, approving, commendatory, complimentary, favourable, flattering, laudatory

disparate *adj* **1 = different**, at odds, at variance, contrary, contrasting, discordant, discrepant, dissimilar, distinct, diverse, unlike

disparity *n* **1, 2 = difference**, discrepancy, disproportion, dissimilarity, dissimilitude, distinction, gap, imbalance, incongruity, inequality, unevenness, unlikeness

dispassionate *adj* **= unemotional**, calm, collected, composed, cool, imperturbable, moderate, quiet, serene, sober, temperate, unexcitable, unexcited, unfazed (*inf.*), unmoved, unruffled **= objective**, candid, detached, disinterested, fair, impartial, impersonal, indifferent, neutral, unbiased, uninvolved, unprejudiced
Antonyms *adj* ≠ **unemotional:** ablaze, ardent, emotional, excited, fervent, impassioned, intense, passionate ≠ **objective:** biased, concerned, interested, involved, partial, prejudiced

dispatch *vb* **1 = send**, accelerate, consign, dismiss, express, forward, hasten, hurry, quicken, remit, transmit **2 = carry out**, conclude, discharge, dispose of, expedite, finish, make short work of (*inf.*), perform, settle **4 = murder**, assassinate, blow away (*sl., chiefly US*), bump off (*sl.*), butcher, eliminate (*sl.*), execute, finish off, kill, put an end to, slaughter, slay, take out (*sl.*) ◆ *n* **6** *As in* **with dispatch = promptness**, alacrity, celerity, expedition, haste, precipitateness, promptitude, quickness, rapidity, speed, swiftness **7, 8 = message**, account, bulletin, communication, communiqué, document, instruction, item, letter, missive, news, piece, report, story

dispel *vb* **= drive away**, allay, banish, chase away, dismiss, disperse, dissipate, eliminate, expel, resolve, rout, scatter

dispensable *adj* **1 = expendable**, disposable, inessential, needless, nonessential, superfluous, unnecessary, unrequired, useless
Antonyms *adj* crucial, essential, important, indispensable, necessary, requisite, vital

dispensation *n* **1 = distribution**, allotment, appointment, apportionment, bestowal, conferment, consignment, dealing out, disbursement, endowment, supplying **5 = exemption**, exception, immunity, indulgence, licence, permission, privilege, relaxation, relief, remission, reprieve

dispense *vb* **1 = distribute**, allocate, allot, apportion, assign, deal out, disburse, dole out, mete out, share **2 = prepare**, measure, mix, supply **3 = administer**, apply, carry out, direct, discharge, enforce, execute, implement, operate, undertake **4 dispense with = do away with**, abolish, abstain from, brush aside, cancel, dispose of, disregard, do without, forgo, get rid of, give up, ignore, omit, pass over, relinquish, render needless, shake off, waive **6 = exempt**, except,

dispersal ⓣ (dɪˈspɜːsᵊl) *n* **1** a dispersing or being dispersed. **2** the spread of animals, plants, or seeds to new areas.

dispersant (dɪsˈpɜːsənt) *n* a liquid or gas used to disperse small particles or droplets, as in an aerosol.

disperse ⓣ (dɪˈspɜːs) *vb* **disperses, dispersing, dispersed.** **1** to scatter; distribute over a wide area. **2** to dissipate. **3** to leave or cause to leave a gathering. **4** to separate or be separated by dispersion. **5** (*tr*) to spread (news, etc.). **6** to separate (particles) throughout a solid, liquid, or gas. ◆ *adj* **7** of or consisting of the particles in a colloid or suspension: *disperse phase*. [C14: from L *dispersus*, from *dispergere* to scatter widely, from DI-[2] + *spargere* to strew]
▸**disˈperser** *n*

USAGE NOTE See at **disburse.**

dispersion (dɪˈspɜːʃən) *n* **1** another word for **dispersal. 2** *Physics.* **2a** the separation of electromagnetic radiation into constituents of different wavelengths. **2b** a measure of the ability of a substance to separate by refraction. **3** *Statistics.* the degree to which values of a frequency distribution are scattered around some central point, usually the arithmetic mean or median. **4** *Chem.* a system containing particles dispersed in a solid, liquid, or gas. **5** *Ecology.* the distribution pattern of a population of animals or plants.

dispirit ⓣ (dɪˈspɪrɪt) *vb* (*tr*) to lower the spirit of; make downhearted; discourage.
▸**disˈpirited** *adj* ▸**disˈpiritedness** *n* ▸**disˈpiriting** *adj*

displace ⓣ (dɪsˈpleɪs) *vb* **displaces, displacing, displaced.** (*tr*) **1** to move from the usual or correct location. **2** to remove from office or employment. **3** to occupy the place of; replace; supplant.

displaced person *n* a person forced from his or her home or country, esp. by war or revolution.

displacement (dɪsˈpleɪsmənt) *n* **1** a displacing or being displaced. **2** the weight or volume displaced by a body in a fluid. **3** *Psychoanal.* the transferring of emotional feelings from their original object to one that disguises their real nature. **4** *Maths.* the distance measured in a particular direction from a reference point. Symbol: *s*

displacement activity *n Psychol.* behaviour that occurs typically when there is a conflict of motives and that has no relevance to either motive: e.g. head scratching.

display ⓣ (dɪˈspleɪ) *vb* **1** (*tr*) to show or make visible. **2** (*tr*) to put out to be seen; exhibit. **3** (*tr*) to disclose; reveal. **4** (*tr*) to flaunt in an ostentatious way. **5** (*tr*) to spread out; unfold. **6** (*tr*) to give prominence to. **7** (*intr*) *Zool.* to engage in a display. ◆ *n* **8** an exhibiting or displaying; show. **9** something exhibited or displayed. **10** an ostentatious exhibition. **11** an arrangement of certain typefaces to give prominence to headings, etc. **12** *Electronics.* **12a** a device capable of representing information visually, as on a cathode-ray tube screen. **12b** the information so presented. **13** *Zool.* a pattern of behaviour by which the animal attracts attention while it is courting the female, defending its territory, etc. **14** (*modifier*) designating typefaces that give prominence to the words they are used to set. [C14: from Anglo-F *despleier* to unfold, from LL *displicāre* to scatter, from DIS-[1] + *plicāre* to fold]
▸**disˈplayer** *n*

displease ⓣ (dɪsˈpliːz) *vb* **displeases, displeasing, displeased.** to annoy, offend, or cause displeasure to (someone).
▸**disˈpleasing** *adj* ▸**disˈpleasingly** *adv*

displeasure ⓣ (dɪsˈplɛʒə) *n* **1** the condition of being displeased. **2** *Arch.* **2a** pain. **2b** an act or cause of offence.

disport (dɪˈspɔːt) *vb* **1** (*tr*) to indulge (oneself) in pleasure. **2** (*intr*) to frolic or gambol. ◆ *n* **3** *Arch.* amusement. [C14: from Anglo-F *desporter,* from *des-* DIS-[1] + *porter* to carry]

disposable ⓣ (dɪˈspəʊzəbᵊl) *adj* **1** designed for disposal after use: *disposable cups.* **2** available for use if needed: *disposable assets.* ◆ *n* **3** something, such as a baby's nappy, that is designed for disposal. **4** (*pl*) short for **disposable goods.**
▸**dis͵posaˈbility** *or* **disˈposableness** *n*

disposable goods *pl n* consumer goods that are used up a short time after purchase, including perishables, newspapers, clothes, etc. Also called: **disposables.**

disposable income *n* **1** the money a person has available to spend after paying taxes, pension contributions, etc. **2** the total amount of money that the individuals in a community, country, etc., have available to buy consumer goods.

disposal ⓣ (dɪˈspəʊzᵊl) *n* **1** the act or means of getting rid of something. **2** arrangement in a particular order. **3** a specific method of tending to matters, as in business. **4** the act or process of transferring something to or providing something for another. **5** the power or opportunity to make use of someone or something (esp. in **at one's disposal**).

dispose ⓣ (dɪˈspəʊz) *vb* **disposes, disposing, disposed.** **1** (*intr;* foll. by *of*) **1a** to deal with or settle. **1b** to give, sell, or transfer to another. **1c** to throw out or away. **1d** to consume, esp. hurriedly. **1e** to kill. **2** to arrange or settle (matters). **3** (*tr*) to make willing or receptive. **4** (*tr*) to place in a certain order. **5** (*tr;* often foll. by *to*) to accustom or condition. [C14: from OF *disposer,* from L *dispōnere* to set in different places, from DIS-[1] + *pōnere* to place]
▸**disˈposer** *n*

disposed ⓣ (dɪˈspəʊzd) *adj* **a** having an inclination as specified (towards something). **b** (*in combination*): *well-disposed.*

disposition ⓣ (͵dɪspəˈzɪʃən) *n* **1** a person's usual temperament or frame of mind. **2** a tendency, inclination, or habit. **3** another word for **disposal** (senses 2–5). **4** *Arch.* manner of placing or arranging.

dispossess ⓣ (͵dɪspəˈzɛs) *vb* (*tr*) to take away possession of something, esp. property; expel.
▸͵**disposˈsession** *n* ▸͵**disposˈsessor** *n*

dispraise (dɪsˈpreɪz) *vb* **dispraises, dispraising, dispraised.** **1** (*tr*) to express disapproval or condemnation of. ◆ *n* **2** the disapproval, etc., expressed.
▸**disˈpraiser** *n*

disproof (dɪsˈpruːf) *n* **1** facts that disprove something. **2** the act of disproving.

disproportion ⓣ (͵dɪsprəˈpɔːʃən) *n* **1** lack of proportion or equality. **2** an instance of disparity or inequality. ◆ *vb* **3** (*tr*) to cause to become exaggerated or unequal.
▸͵**disproˈportional** *adj*

disproportionate ⓣ (͵dɪsprəˈpɔːʃənɪt) *adj* out of proportion; unequal.
▸͵**disproˈportionately** *adv* ▸͵**disproˈportionateness** *n*

THESAURUS

excuse, exonerate, let off (*inf.*), release, relieve, reprieve

dispersal *n* **1 = scattering**, broadcast, circulation, diffusion, dissemination, dissipation, distribution, spread

disperse *vb* **1 = scatter**, broadcast, circulate, diffuse, disseminate, dissipate, distribute, spread, strew **4 = break up**, disappear, disband, dismiss, dispel, dissolve, rout, scatter, send off, separate, vanish
Antonyms *vb* amass, assemble, collect, concentrate, congregate, convene, gather, muster, pool

dispirit *vb* **= dishearten**, cast down, damp, dampen, dash, deject, depress, deter, discourage, disincline, sadden

dispirited *adj* **= disheartened**, crestfallen, dejected, depressed, despondent, discouraged, down, downcast, gloomy, glum, in the doldrums, low, morose, sad, sick as a parrot (*inf.*)

dispiriting *adj* **= disheartening**, crushing, dampening, daunting, demoralizing, depressing, disappointing, discouraging, saddening, sickening
Antonyms *adj* cheering, comforting, encouraging, heartening, reassuring

displace *vb* **1 = move**, derange, disarrange, disturb, misplace, shift, transpose **2 = dismiss**, cashier, depose, discard, discharge, fire (*inf.*), remove, sack (*inf.*) **3 = replace**, crowd out, oust, succeed, supersede, supplant, take the place of

display *vb* **1-3 = show**, betray, demonstrate, disclose, evidence, evince, exhibit, expose, manifest, open, open to view, present, reveal, take the wraps off, unveil **4 = show off**, boast, flash (*inf.*), flaunt, flourish, parade, vaunt **5 = spread out**, expand, extend, model, open out, stretch out, unfold, unfurl ◆ *n* **9 = exhibition**, array, demonstration, exposition, exposure, manifestation, presentation, revelation, show **10 = show**, flourish, ostentation, pageant, parade, pomp, spectacle
Antonyms *vb* ≠ **show:** conceal, cover, hide, keep dark, keep secret, mask, secrete, veil

displease *vb* **= annoy**, aggravate (*inf.*), anger, disgust, dissatisfy, exasperate, gall, hassle (*inf.*), incense, irk, irritate, nark (*Brit., Austral., & NZ sl.*), nettle, offend, pique, piss one off (*taboo sl.*), provoke, put one's back up, put out, rile, upset, vex

displeasure *n* **1 = annoyance**, anger, disapprobation, disapproval, disfavour, disgruntlement, dislike, dissatisfaction, distaste, indignation, irritation, offence, pique, resentment, vexation, wrath
Antonyms *n* approval, endorsement, pleasure, satisfaction

disposable *adj* **1 = throwaway**, biodegradable, compostable, decomposable, nonreturnable, paper **2 = available**, at one's service, consumable, expendable, free for use, spendable

disposal *n* **1 = throwing away**, clearance, discarding, dumping (*inf.*), ejection, jettisoning, parting with, relinquishment, removal, riddance, scrapping **2 = arrangement**, array, dispensation, disposition, distribution, grouping, placing, position **5 at one's disposal = available**, at one's service, consumable, expendable, free for use, spendable

dispose *vb* **1a** *foll. by* **of = deal with**, decide, determine, end, finish with, settle **1b** *foll. by* **of = give**, bestow, make over, part with, sell, transfer **1c** *foll. by* **of = get rid of**, bin (*inf.*), chuck (*inf.*), destroy, discard, dump (*inf.*), get shot of, jettison, junk (*inf.*), scrap, throw out *or* away, unload **3 = lead**, actuate, adapt, bias, condition, incline, induce, influence, motivate, move, predispose, prompt, tempt

disposed *adj* **a = inclined**, apt, given, liable, likely, of a mind to, predisposed, prone, ready, subject, tending towards

disposition *n* **1 = character**, constitution, make-up, nature, spirit, temper, temperament **2 = tendency**, bent, bias, habit, inclination, leaning, predisposition, proclivity, proneness, propensity, readiness **3 = arrangement**, adjustment, classification, direction, disposal, distribution, grouping, management, ordering, organization, placement, regulation

dispossess *vb* **= expel**, deprive, dislodge, divest, drive out, eject, evict, oust, strip, take away, turn out

dispossessed *adj* **= expelled**, destitute, evicted, exiled, homeless, landless

disproportion *n* **1 = inequality**, asymmetry, discrepancy, disparity, imbalance, inadequacy, insufficiency, lopsidedness, unevenness, unsuitableness
Antonyms *n* balance, congruity, harmony, proportion, symmetry

disproportionate *adj* **= unequal**, excessive,

disprove Ⓣ (dɪsˈpruːv) *vb* **disproves, disproving, disproved.** (*tr*) to show (an assertion, claim, etc.) to be incorrect.
▸disˈ**provable** *adj* ▸disˈ**proval** *n*

disputable Ⓣ (dɪˈspjuːtəbᵊl, ˈdɪspjʊtə-) *adj* capable of being argued; debatable.
▸dis,**putaˈbility** *or* **disˈputableness** *n* ▸**disˈputably** *adv*

disputant Ⓣ (dɪˈspjuːtᵊnt, ˈdɪspjʊtənt) *n* **1** a person who argues; contestant. ◆ *adj* **2** engaged in argument.

disputation (ˌdɪspjʊˈteɪʃən) *n* **1** the act or an instance of arguing. **2** a formal academic debate on a thesis. **3** an obsolete word for **conversation.**

disputatious (ˌdɪspjʊˈteɪʃəs) *or* **disputative** (dɪˈspjuːtətɪv) *adj* inclined to argument.
▸ˌ**dispuˈtatiousness** *or* **disˈputativeness** *n*

dispute Ⓣ *vb* (dɪˈspjuːt) **disputes, disputing, disputed. 1** to argue, debate, or quarrel about (something). **2** (*tr; may take a clause as object*) to doubt the validity, etc., of. **3** (*tr*) to seek to win; contest for. **4** (*tr*) to struggle against; resist. ◆ *n* (dɪˈspjuːt, ˈdɪspjuːt). **5** an argument or quarrel. **6** *Rare.* a fight. [C13: from LL *disputāre* to contend verbally, from L: to discuss, from DIS-[1] + *putāre* to think]
▸**disˈputer** *n*

disqualify Ⓣ (dɪsˈkwɒlɪˌfaɪ) *vb* **disqualifies, disqualifying, disqualified.** (*tr*) **1** to make unfit or unqualified. **2** to make ineligible, as for entry to an examination. **3** to debar from a contest. **4** to deprive of rights, powers, or privileges.
▸**dis,qualifiˈcation** *n*

disquiet Ⓣ (dɪsˈkwaɪət) *n* **1** a feeling or condition of anxiety or uneasiness. ◆ *vb* **2** (*tr*) to make anxious or upset.
▸**disˈquieting** *adj*

disquietude (dɪsˈkwaɪɪˌtjuːd) *n* a feeling or state of anxiety or uneasiness.

disquisition (ˌdɪskwɪˈzɪʃən) *n* a formal examination of a subject. [C17: from L *disquīsītiō*, from *disquīrere* to make an investigation, from DIS-[1] + *quaerere* to seek]
▸ˌ**disquiˈsitional** *adj*

disregard Ⓣ (ˌdɪsrɪˈgɑːd) *vb* (*tr*) **1** to give little or no attention to; ignore. **2** to treat as unworthy of consideration or respect. ◆ *n* **3** lack of attention or respect.
▸ˌ**disreˈgardful** *adj*

disremember (ˌdɪsrɪˈmɛmbə) *vb Inf., chiefly US.* to fail to recall.

disrepair Ⓣ (ˌdɪsrɪˈpɛə) *n* the condition of being worn out or in poor working order; a condition requiring repairs.

disreputable Ⓣ (dɪsˈrɛpjʊtəbᵊl) *adj* **1** having or causing a lack of repute. **2** disordered in appearance.
▸**disˈreputably** *adv*

disrepute Ⓣ (ˌdɪsrɪˈpjuːt) *n* a loss or lack of credit or repute.

disrespect Ⓣ (ˌdɪsrɪˈspɛkt) *n* contempt; rudeness; lack of respect.
▸ˌ**disreˈspectful** *adj*

disrobe Ⓣ (dɪsˈrəʊb) *vb* **disrobes, disrobing, disrobed. 1** to undress. **2** (*tr*) to divest of authority, etc.
▸**disˈrobement** *n*

disrupt Ⓣ (dɪsˈrʌpt) *vb* **1** (*tr*) to throw into turmoil or disorder. **2** (*tr*) to interrupt the progress of. **3** to break or split apart. [C17: from L *disruptus* burst asunder, from *dīrumpere* to dash to pieces, from DIS-[1] + *rumpere* to burst]
▸**disˈrupter** *or* **disˈruptor** *n* ▸**disˈruption** *n*

disruptive Ⓣ (dɪsˈrʌptɪv) *adj* involving, causing, or tending to cause disruption.

diss *or* **dis** (dɪs) *vb* **disses, dissing, dissed.** *Sl., chiefly US.* to treat (someone) with contempt. [C20: orig. US Black rap slang, short for DISRESPECT]

dissatisfy Ⓣ (dɪsˈsætɪsˌfaɪ) *vb* **dissatisfies, dissatisfying, dissatisfied.** (*tr*) to fail to satisfy; disappoint.
▸ˌ**dissatisˈfaction** *n* ▸ˌ**dissatisˈfactory** *adj*

dissect Ⓣ (dɪˈsɛkt, daɪ-) *vb* **1** to cut open and examine the structure of (a dead animal or plant). **2** (*tr*) to examine critically and minutely. [C17: from L *dissecāre*, from DIS-[1] + *secāre* to cut]
▸**disˈsection** *n* ▸**disˈsector** *n*

dissected (dɪˈsɛktɪd, daɪ-) *adj* **1** *Bot.* in the form of narrow lobes or segments. **2** *Geol.* cut by erosion into hills and valleys.

disselboom (ˈdɪsᵊlˌbuːm) *n S. African.* the single shaft of a wagon, esp. an ox wagon. [from Du. *dissel* shaft + *boom* beam]

dissemble Ⓣ (dɪˈsɛmbᵊl) *vb* **dissembles, dissembling, dissembled. 1** to conceal (one's real motives, emotions, etc.) by pretence. **2** (*tr*) to pretend; simulate. [C15: from earlier *dissimulen*, from L *dissimulāre*; prob. infl. by obs. *semble* to resemble]
▸**disˈsemblance** *n* ▸**disˈsembler** *n*

disseminate Ⓣ (dɪˈsɛmɪˌneɪt) *vb* **disseminates, disseminating, disseminated.** (*tr*) to distribute or scatter about; diffuse. [C17: from L *dissēmināre*, from DIS-[1] + *sēmināre* to sow, from *sēmen* seed]
▸**dis,semiˈnation** *n* ▸**disˈsemi,nator** *n*

disseminated sclerosis *n* another name for **multiple sclerosis.**

dissension Ⓣ (dɪˈsɛnʃən) *n* disagreement, esp. when leading to a quarrel. [C13: from L *dissēnsiō*, from *dissentīre* to DISSENT]

dissent Ⓣ (dɪˈsɛnt) *vb* (*intr*) **1** to have a disagreement or withhold as-

THESAURUS

incommensurate, inordinate, out of proportion, too much, unbalanced, uneven, unreasonable

disprove *vb* = **prove false**, blow out of the water (*sl.*), confute, contradict, controvert, discredit, expose, give the lie to, invalidate, make a nonsense of, negate, rebut, refute
Antonyms *vb* ascertain, bear out, confirm, evince, prove, show, substantiate, verify

disputable *adj* = **debatable**, arguable, controversial, doubtful, dubious, iffy (*inf.*), moot, open to discussion, questionable, uncertain

disputant *n* **1** = **contestant**, adversary, antagonist, arguer, contender, debater, opponent

dispute *vb* **1** = **argue**, altercate, brawl, clash, contend, cross swords, debate, discuss, quarrel, row, spar, squabble, wrangle **2** = **doubt**, challenge, contest, contradict, controvert, deny, impugn, question, rebut ◆ *n* **5** = **disagreement**, altercation, argument, brawl, conflict, contention, controversy, debate, discord, discussion, dissension, disturbance, feud, friction, quarrel, shindig (*inf.*), shindy (*inf.*), strife, wrangle

disqualification *n* **1** = **unfitness**, disability, disablement, incapacitation, incapacity **2, 3** = **ban**, debarment, disenablement, disentitlement, elimination, exclusion, incompetence, ineligibility, rejection

disqualified *adj* **2, 3** = **ineligible**, debarred, eliminated, knocked out, out of the running

disqualify *vb* **1** = **invalidate**, disable, incapacitate, unfit (*rare*) **3** = **ban**, debar, declare ineligible, disentitle, preclude, prohibit, rule out

disquiet *n* **1** = **uneasiness**, alarm, angst, anxiety, concern, disquietude, distress, disturbance, fear, foreboding, fretfulness, nervousness, restlessness, trepidation, trouble, unrest, worry ◆ *vb* **2** = **make uneasy**, agitate, annoy, bother, concern, discompose, distress, disturb, fret, harass, hassle (*inf.*), incommode, perturb, pester, plague, trouble, unsettle, upset, vex, worry

disquieting *adj* **2** = **worrying**, annoying, bothersome, disconcerting, distressing, disturbing, harrowing, irritating, perturbing, troubling, unnerving, unsettling, upsetting, vexing

disregard *vb* **1, 2** = **ignore**, brush aside *or* away, discount, disobey, laugh off, leave out of account, make light of, neglect, overlook, pass over, pay no attention to, pay no heed to, take no notice of, turn a blind eye to ◆ *n* **3** = **inattention**, brushoff (*sl.*), contempt, disdain, disrespect, heedlessness, ignoring, indifference, neglect, negligence, oversight, slight, the cold shoulder
Antonyms *vb* ≠ **ignore:** attend, heed, listen to, mind, note, pay attention to, regard, respect, take into consideration, take notice of

disrepair *n* = **dilapidation**, collapse, decay, deterioration, ruination

disreputable *adj* **1** = **discreditable**, base, contemptible, derogatory, disgraceful, dishonourable, disorderly, ignominious, infamous, louche, low, mean, notorious, opprobrious, scandalous, shady (*inf.*), shameful, shocking, unprincipled, vicious, vile **2** = **scruffy**, bedraggled, dilapidated, dingy, dishevelled, down at heel, seedy, shabby, threadbare, worn
Antonyms *adj* ≠ **discreditable:** decent, reputable, respectable, respected, upright, worthy

disrepute *n* = **discredit**, disesteem, disfavour, disgrace, dishonour, ignominy, ill favour, ill repute, infamy, obloquy, shame, unpopularity

disrespect *n* = **contempt**, cheek, discourtesy, dishonour, disregard, impertinence, impoliteness, impudence, incivility, insolence, irreverence, lack of respect, lese-majesty, rudeness, sauce, unmannerliness
Antonyms *n* esteem, regard, respect

disrespectful *adj* = **contemptuous**, bad-mannered, cheeky, discourteous, ill-bred, impertinent, impolite, impudent, insolent, insulting, irreverent, misbehaved, rude, uncivil

disrobe *vb* **1** = **undress**, bare, denude, divest, doff, remove, shed, strip, take off, unclothe, uncover

disrupt *vb* **1** = **disturb**, agitate, confuse, convulse, disorder, disorganize, spoil, throw into disorder, upset **2** = **interrupt**, break up *or* into, interfere with, intrude, obstruct, unsettle, upset

disruption *n* **1, 2** = **disturbance**, confusion, disarray, disorder, disorderliness, interference, interruption, stoppage

disruptive *adj* = **disturbing**, confusing, disorderly, distracting, obstreperous, troublemaking, troublesome, unruly, unsettling, upsetting
Antonyms *adj* biddable, compliant, cooperative, docile, obedient, well-behaved

dissatisfaction *n* = **discontent**, annoyance, chagrin, disappointment, discomfort, dislike, dismay, displeasure, distress, exasperation, frustration, irritation, regret, resentment, unhappiness

dissatisfied *adj* = **discontented**, disappointed, disgruntled, displeased, fed up, frustrated, not satisfied, unfulfilled, ungratified, unhappy, unsatisfied
Antonyms *adj* content, contented, pleased, satisfied

dissatisfy *vb* = **discontent**, annoy, disappoint, disgruntle, displease, give cause for complaint, irritate, leave dissatisfied, not pass muster, not suffice, put out, vex

dissect *vb* **1** = **cut up** *or* **apart**, anatomize, dismember, lay open **2** = **analyse**, break down, explore, inspect, investigate, research, scrutinize, study

dissection *n* **1** = **cutting up**, anatomization, anatomy, autopsy, dismemberment, necropsy, postmortem (examination) **2** = **analysis**, breakdown, examination, inspection, investigation, research, scrutiny

dissemble *vb* **1** = **hide**, camouflage, cloak, conceal, cover up, disguise, dissimulate, mask **2** = **pretend**, affect, counterfeit, falsify, feign, sham, simulate

dissembler *n* **1, 2** = **fraud**, charlatan, con man (*inf.*), deceiver, dissimulator, feigner, hypocrite, impostor, pretender, trickster, whited sepulchre

disseminate *vb* = **spread**, broadcast, circulate, diffuse, disperse, dissipate, distribute, proclaim, promulgate, propagate, publicize, publish, scatter, sow

dissemination *n* = **spread**, broadcasting, circulation, diffusion, distribution, promulgation, propagation, publication, publishing

dissension *n* = **disagreement**, conflict, conflict of opinion, contention, difference, discord, discordance, dispute, dissent, friction, quarrel, row, strife, variance

dissent *vb* **1** = **disagree**, decline, differ, object,

sent. **2** *Christianity.* to reject the doctrines, beliefs, or practices of an established church, and to adhere to a different system of beliefs. ◆ *n* **3** a difference of opinion. **4** *Christianity.* separation from an established church; Nonconformism. **5** the voicing of a minority opinion in the decision on a case at law. **[**C16: from L *dissentīre* to disagree, from DIS-[1] + *sentīre* to feel**]**
▸**dis'senter** *n* ▸**dis'senting** *adj*

Dissenter (dɪ'sɛntə) *n Christianity, chiefly Brit.* a Nonconformist or a person who refuses to conform to the established church.

dissentient (dɪ'sɛnʃənt) *adj* **1** dissenting, esp. from the opinion of the majority. ◆ *n* **2** a dissenter.
▸**dis'sentience** *or* **dis'sentiency** *n*

dissertation Ⓣ (ˌdɪsə'teɪʃən) *n* **1** a written thesis, often based on original research, usually required for a higher degree. **2** a formal discourse. **[**C17: from L *dissertāre* to debate, from *disserere* to examine, from DIS-[1] + *serere* to arrange**]**
▸ˌ**disser'tational** *adj*

disserve (dɪs'sɜːv) *vb* **disserves, disserving, disserved.** (*tr*) *Arch.* to do a disservice to.

disservice Ⓣ (dɪs'sɜːvɪs) *n* an ill turn; wrong; injury, esp. when trying to help.

dissever (dɪ'sɛvə) *vb* **1** to break off or become broken off. **2** (*tr*) to divide up into parts. **[**C13: from OF *dessevrer*, from LL DIS-[1] + *sēparāre* to SEPARATE**]**
▸**dis'severance** *or* **dis'severment** *n*

dissident Ⓣ ('dɪsɪdənt) *adj* **1** disagreeing; dissenting. ◆ *n* **2** a person who disagrees, esp. one who disagrees with the government. **[**C16: from L *dissidēre* to be remote from, from DIS-[1] + *sedēre* to sit**]**
▸**'dissidence** *n* ▸**'dissidently** *adv*

dissimilar Ⓣ (dɪ'sɪmɪlə) *adj* not alike; not similar; different.
▸**dis'similarly** *adv* ▸ˌ**dissimi'larity** *n*

dissimilate (dɪ'sɪmɪˌleɪt) *vb* **dissimilates, dissimilating, dissimilated. 1** to make or become dissimilar. **2** (usually foll. by *to*) *Phonetics.* to change or displace (a consonant) or (of a consonant) to be changed to or displaced by (another consonant) so that its manner of articulation becomes less similar to a speech sound in the same word. Thus (r) in the final syllable of French *marbre* is dissimilated to (l) in its English form *marble.* **[**C19: from DIS-[1] + ASSIMILATE**]**

dissimilation (ˌdɪsɪmɪ'leɪʃən) *n* **1** the act or an instance of making dissimilar. **2** *Phonetics.* the alteration or omission of a consonant as a result of being dissimilated.

dissimilitude Ⓣ (ˌdɪsɪ'mɪlɪˌtjuːd) *n* **1** dissimilarity; difference. **2** a point of difference.

dissimulate Ⓣ (dɪ'sɪmjʊˌleɪt) *vb* **dissimulates, dissimulating, dissimulated.** to conceal (one's real feelings) by pretence.
▸**disˌsimu'lation** *n* ▸**dis'simuˌlator** *n*

dissipate Ⓣ ('dɪsɪˌpeɪt) *vb* **dissipates, dissipating, dissipated. 1** to exhaust or be exhausted by dispersion. **2** (*tr*) to scatter or break up. **3** (*intr*) to indulge in the pursuit of pleasure. **[**C15: from L *dissipāre* to disperse, from DIS-[1] + *supāre* to throw**]**
▸**'dissiˌpater** *or* **'dissiˌpator** *n* ▸**'dissiˌpative** *adj*

dissipated Ⓣ ('dɪsɪˌpeɪtɪd) *adj* **1** indulging without restraint in the pursuit of pleasure; debauched. **2** wasted, scattered, or exhausted.

dissipation Ⓣ (ˌdɪsɪ'peɪʃən) *n* **1** a dissipating or being dissipated. **2** unrestrained indulgence in physical pleasures. **3** excessive expenditure; wastefulness.

dissociate Ⓣ (dɪ'səʊʃɪˌeɪt, -sɪ-) *vb* **dissociates, dissociating, dissociated. 1** to break or cause to break the association between (people, organizations, etc.). **2** (*tr*) to regard or treat as separate or unconnected. **3** to undergo or subject to dissociation.
▸**dis'sociative** *adj*

dissociation Ⓣ (dɪˌsəʊsɪ'eɪʃən, -ʃɪ-) *n* **1** a dissociating or being dissociated. **2** *Chem.* the decomposition of the molecules of a single compound into two or more other compounds, atoms, ions, or radicals. **3** *Psychiatry.* the separation of a group of mental processes or ideas from the rest of the personality, so that they lead an independent existence, as in cases of multiple personality.

dissoluble (dɪ'sɒljʊbᵊl) *adj* a less common word for **soluble. [**C16: from L *dissolūbilis*, from *dissolvere* to DISSOLVE**]**
▸**disˌsolu'bility** *n*

dissolute Ⓣ ('dɪsəˌluːt) *adj* given to dissipation; debauched. **[**C14: from L *dissolūtus* loose, from *dissolvere* to DISSOLVE**]**
▸**'dissoˌlutely** *adv* ▸**'dissoˌluteness** *n*

dissolution Ⓣ (ˌdɪsə'luːʃən) *n* **1** separation into component parts; disintegration. **2** destruction by breaking up and dispersing. **3** the termination of a meeting or assembly, such as Parliament. **4** the termination of a formal or legal relationship, such as a business, marriage, etc. **5** the act or process of dissolving.

dissolve Ⓣ (dɪ'zɒlv) *vb* **dissolves, dissolving, dissolved. 1** to go or cause to go into solution. **2** to become or cause to become liquid; melt. **3** to disintegrate or disperse. **4** to come or bring to an end. **5** to dismiss (a meeting, Parliament, etc.) or (of a meeting, etc.) to be dismissed. **6** to collapse or cause to collapse emotionally: *to dissolve into tears.* **7** to lose or cause to lose distinctness. **8** (*tr*) to terminate legally, as a marriage, etc. **9** (*intr*) *Films, television.* to fade out one scene and replace with another to make two scenes merge imperceptibly or slowly overlap. ◆ *n* **10** *Films, television.* a scene filmed or televised by dissolving. **[**C14: from L *dissolvere* to make loose, from DIS-[1] + *solvere* to release**]**
▸**dis'solvable** *adj*

dissonance Ⓣ ('dɪsənəns) *or* **dissonancy** *n* **1** a discordant combination of sounds. **2** lack of agreement or consistency. **3** *Music.* **3a** a sensation of harshness and incompleteness associated with certain intervals and chords. **3b** an interval or chord of this kind.

dissonant Ⓣ ('dɪsənənt) *adj* **1** discordant. **2** incongruous or discrepant. **3** *Music.* characterized by dissonance. **[**C15: from L *dissonāre* to be discordant, from DIS-[1] + *sonāre* to sound**]**

dissuade Ⓣ (dɪ'sweɪd) *vb* **dissuades, dissuading, dissuaded.** (*tr*) **1** (often foll. by *from*) to deter (someone) by persuasion from a course of action, policy, etc. **2** to advise against (an action, etc.). **[**C15: from L *dissuādēre*, from DIS-[1] + *suādēre* to persuade**]**
▸**dis'suader** *n* ▸**dis'suasion** *n* ▸**dis'suasive** *adj*

THESAURUS

protest, refuse, withhold assent *or* approval ◆ *n* **3 = disagreement**, difference, discord, dissension, dissidence, nonconformity, objection, opposition, refusal, resistance
Antonyms *vb* ≠ **disagree:** agree, assent, concur ◆ *n* ≠ **disagreement:** accord, agreement, assent, concurrence, consensus

dissenter *n* **1, 2 = objector**, disputant, dissident, nonconformist, protestant

dissenting *adj* **1 = disagreeing**, conflicting, differing, dissident, opposing, protesting

dissertation *n* = **thesis**, critique, discourse, disquisition, essay, exposition, treatise

disservice *n* = **bad turn**, disfavour, harm, ill turn, injury, injustice, unkindness, wrong
Antonyms *n* courtesy, good turn, indulgence, kindness, obligement (*Scot. or arch.*), service

dissidence *n* = **dissent**, difference of opinion, disagreement, discordance, dispute, feud, rupture, schism

dissident *adj* **1 = dissenting**, differing, disagreeing, discordant, dissentient, heterodox, nonconformist, schismatic ◆ *n* **2 = protester**, agitator, dissenter, rebel, recusant

dissimilar *adj* = **different**, disparate, divergent, diverse, heterogeneous, manifold, mismatched, not alike, not capable of comparison, not similar, unlike, unrelated, various
Antonyms *adj* alike, comparable, congruous, corresponding, in agreement, much the same, resembling, uniform

dissimilarity *n* = **difference**, discrepancy, disparity, dissimilitude, distinction, divergence, heterogeneity, incomparability, nonuniformity, unlikeness, unrelatedness

dissimilitude *n* **1 = difference**, discrepancy, disparity, dissimilarity, diversity, heterogeneity, incomparability, nonuniformity, unlikeness, unrelatedness

dissimulate *vb* = **pretend**, camouflage, cloak, conceal, disguise, dissemble, feign, hide, mask

dissimulation *n* = **pretence**, concealment, deceit, deception, dissembling, double-dealing, duplicity, feigning, hypocrisy, play-acting, sham, wile

dissipate *vb* **2 = disperse**, disappear, dispel, dissolve, drive away, evaporate, scatter, vanish **3 = squander**, burn up, consume, deplete, expend, fritter away, indulge oneself, lavish, misspend, run through, spend, waste

dissipated *adj* **1 = debauched**, abandoned, dissolute, intemperate, profligate, rakish, self-indulgent **2 = squandered**, consumed, destroyed, exhausted, scattered, wasted

dissipation *n* **1 = dispersal**, disappearance, disintegration, dissemination, dissolution, scattering, vanishing **2 = debauchery**, abandonment, dissoluteness, drunkenness, excess, extravagance, indulgence, intemperance, lavishness, prodigality, profligacy, squandering, wantonness, waste

dissociate *vb* **1 = break away**, break off, disband, disrupt, part company, quit **2 = separate**, detach, disconnect, distance, divorce, isolate, segregate, set apart

dissociation *n* **1 = separation**, break, detachment, disconnection, disengagement, distancing, disunion, division, divorce, isolation, segregation, severance

dissolute *adj* = **immoral**, abandoned, corrupt, debauched, degenerate, depraved, dissipated, lax, lewd, libertine, licentious, loose, profligate, rakish, unrestrained, vicious, wanton, wild
Antonyms *adj* chaste, clean-living, good, moral, squeaky-clean, upright, virtuous, worthy

dissolution *n* **1 = breaking up**, disintegration, division, divorce, parting, resolution, separation **3 = adjournment**, conclusion, disbandment, discontinuation, dismissal, end, ending, finish, suspension, termination
Antonyms *n* ≠ **breaking up:** alliance, amalgamation, coalition, combination, unification, union

dissolve *vb* **2 = melt**, deliquesce, flux, fuse, liquefy, soften, thaw **3 = disappear**, break down, crumble, decompose, diffuse, disintegrate, disperse, dissipate, dwindle, evanesce, evaporate, fade, melt away, perish, vanish, waste away **5 = end**, break up, discontinue, dismiss, suspend, terminate, wind up **8 = break up**, collapse, disorganize, disunite, divorce, loose, resolve into, separate, sever

dissonance *n* **1 = discordance**, cacophony, discord, harshness, jangle, jarring, lack of harmony, unmelodiousness **2 = disagreement**, difference, discord, discrepancy, disparity, dissension, incongruity, inconsistency, variance

dissonant *adj* **1 = discordant**, cacophonous, grating, harsh, inharmonious, jangling, jarring, out of tune, raucous, strident, tuneless, unmelodious **2 = disagreeing**, anomalous, at variance, different, differing, discrepant, dissentient, incompatible, incongruous, inconsistent, irreconcilable, irregular

dissuade *vb* **1, 2 = deter**, advise against, discourage, disincline, divert, expostulate, persuade not to, put off, remonstrate, talk out of, urge not to, warn
Antonyms *vb* bring round (*inf.*), coax, convince, persuade, sway, talk into

dissuasion *n* **1, 2 = deterrence**, caution, damper, determent, deterrent, discouragement, disincentive, expostulation, hindrance, remonstrance, setback

DICTIONARY

dissyllable (dɪˈsɪləbᵊl) *or* **disyllable** *n* a word of two syllables.
▸**dissyllabic** (ˌdɪsɪˈlæbɪk) *or* **disyllabic** (ˌdaɪsɪˈlæbɪk) *adj*

dissymmetry (dɪˈsɪmɪtrɪ, dɪsˈsɪm-) *n, pl* **dissymmetries. 1** lack of symmetry. **2** the relationship between two objects when one is the mirror image of the other.
▸**dissymmetric** (ˌdɪsɪˈmɛtrɪk, ˌdɪssɪ-) *or* ˌ**dissymˈmetrical** *adj*

dist. *abbrev. for:* **1** distant. **2** distinguish(ed). **3** district.

distaff (ˈdɪstɑːf) *n* **1** the rod on which flax is wound preparatory to spinning. **2** *Figurative.* women's work. [OE *distæf,* from *dis-* bunch of flax + *stæf* STAFF[1]]

distaff side *n* the female side of a family.

distal (ˈdɪstᵊl) *adj Anat.* situated farthest from the centre or point of attachment or origin. [C19: from DISTANT + -AL[1]]
▸ˈ**distally** *adv*

distance 🅣 (ˈdɪstəns) *n* **1** the space between two points. **2** the length of this gap. **3** the state of being apart in space; remoteness. **4** an interval between two points in time. **5** the extent of progress. **6** a distant place or time. **7** a separation or remoteness in relationship. **8** (preceded by *the*) the most distant or a faraway part of the visible scene. **9** *Horse racing.* **9a** *Brit.* a point on a racecourse 240 yards from the winning post. **9b** *US.* the part of a racecourse that a horse must reach before the winner passes the finishing line in order to qualify for later heats. **10 go the distance. 10a** *Boxing.* to complete a bout without being knocked out. **10b** to be able to complete an assigned task or responsibility. **11 keep one's distance.** to maintain a reserve in respect of another person. **12 middle distance.** halfway between the foreground or the observer and the horizon. ◆ *vb* **distances, distancing, distanced.** (*tr*) **13** to hold or place at a distance. **14** to separate (oneself) mentally from something. **15** to outdo; outstrip.

distance learning *n* a teaching system consisting of video, audio, and written material designed for a person to use in studying a subject at home.

distant 🅣 (ˈdɪstənt) *adj* **1** far apart in space or time. **2** (*postpositive*) separated in space or time by a specified distance. **3** apart in relationship: *a distant cousin.* **4** coming from or going to a faraway place. **5** remote in manner; aloof. **6** abstracted; absent: *a distant look.* [C14: from L *distāre* to be distant, from DIS-[1] + *stāre* to stand]
▸ˈ**distantly** *adv* ▸ˈ**distantness** *n*

distaste 🅣 (dɪsˈteɪst) *n* (often foll. by *for*) a dislike (of); aversion (to).

distasteful 🅣 (dɪsˈteɪstfʊl) *adj* unpleasant or offensive.
▸**disˈtastefulness** *n*

distemper[1] (dɪsˈtɛmpə) *n* **1** any of various infectious diseases of animals, esp. **canine distemper,** a highly contagious viral disease of dogs. **2** *Arch.* **2a** a disorder. **2b** disturbance. **2c** discontent. [C14: from LL *distemperāre* to derange the health of, from L DIS-[1] + *temperāre* to mix in correct proportions]

distemper[2] (dɪsˈtɛmpə) *n* **1** a technique of painting in which the pigments are mixed with water, glue, size, etc.: used for poster, mural, and scene painting. **2** the paint used in this technique or any of various water-based paints. ◆ *vb* **3** to paint (something) with distemper. [C14: from Med. L *distemperāre* to soak, from L DIS-[1] + *temperāre* to mingle]

distend 🅣 (dɪˈstɛnd) *vb* **1** to expand by or as if by pressure from within; swell; inflate. **2** (*tr*) to stretch out or extend. [C14: from L *distendere,* from DIS-[1] + *tendere* to stretch]
▸**disˈtensible** *adj* ▸**disˈtension** *or* **disˈtention** *n*

distich (ˈdɪstɪk) *n Prosody.* a unit of two verse lines, usually a couplet. [C16: from Gk *distikhos* having two lines, from DI-[1] + *stikhos* row, line]

distil 🅣 *or US* **distill** (dɪsˈtɪl) *vb* **distils, distilling, distilled** *or US* **distills, distilling, distilled. 1** to subject to or undergo distillation. **2** (sometimes foll. by *out* or *off*) to purify, separate, or concentrate, or be purified, separated, or concentrated by distillation. **3** to obtain or be obtained by distillation. **4** to exude or give off (a substance) in drops. **5** (*tr*) to extract the essence of. [C14: from L *dēstillāre* to distil, from DE- + *stillāre* to drip]

distillate (ˈdɪstɪlɪt) *n* **1** the product of distillation. **2** a concentrated essence.

distillation 🅣 (ˌdɪstɪˈleɪʃən) *n* **1** a distilling. **2** the process of evaporating or boiling a liquid and condensing its vapour. **3** purification or separation of mixtures by using different evaporation rates or boiling points of their components. **4** the process of obtaining the essence or an extract of a substance, usually by heating it in a solvent. **5** a distillate. **6** a concentrated essence.
▸**disˈtillatory** *adj*

distiller (dɪˈstɪlə) *n* a person or organization that distils, esp. a company that makes spirits.

distillery (dɪˈstɪlərɪ) *n, pl* **distilleries.** a place where alcoholic drinks, etc., are made by distillation.

distinct 🅣 (dɪˈstɪŋkt) *adj* **1** easily sensed or understood; clear. **2** (when *postpositive,* foll. by *from*) not the same (as); separate (from). **3** not alike; different. **4** sharp; clear. **5** recognizable; definite. **6** explicit; unequivocal. **7** *Bot.* (of parts of a plant) not joined together; separate. [C14: from L *distinctus,* from *distinguere* to DISTINGUISH]
▸**disˈtinctly** *adv* ▸**disˈtinctness** *n*

distinction 🅣 (dɪˈstɪŋkʃən) *n* **1** the act or an instance of distinguishing or differentiating. **2** a distinguishing feature. **3** the state of being different or distinguishable. **4** special honour, recognition, or fame. **5** excellence of character; distinctive qualities. **6** distinguished appearance. **7** a symbol of honour or rank.

distinctive 🅣 (dɪˈstɪŋktɪv) *adj* serving or tending to distinguish; characteristic.
▸**disˈtinctively** *adv* ▸**disˈtinctiveness** *n*

distingué *French.* (distɛ̃ge) *adj* distinguished or noble.

distinguish 🅣 (dɪˈstɪŋgwɪʃ) *vb* (*mainly tr*) **1** (when *intr,* foll. by *between* or *among*) to make, show, or recognize a difference (between or among); differentiate (between). **2** to be a distinctive feature of; characterize. **3** to make out; perceive. **4** to mark for a special honour. **5** to make (oneself) noteworthy. **6** to classify. [C16: from L *distinguere* to separate]
▸**disˈtinguishable** *adj* ▸**disˈtinguishing** *adj*

distinguished 🅣 (dɪˈstɪŋgwɪʃt) *adj* **1** noble or dignified in appearance or behaviour. **2** eminent; famous; celebrated.

distort 🅣 (dɪˈstɔːt) *vb* (*tr*) **1** (*often passive*) to twist or pull out of shape; contort; deform. **2** to alter or misrepresent (facts, etc.). **3** *Electronics.* to reproduce or amplify (a signal) inaccurately. [C16: from L

THESAURUS

dissuasive *adj* **1, 2** = **deterring,** admonitory, cautionary, discouraging, disincentive, dissuading, monitory, off-putting (*Brit. inf.*), remonstrative, warning

distance *n* **3** = **space,** absence, extent, gap, interval, lapse, length, range, reach, remoteness, remove, separation, span, stretch, width **7** = **reserve,** aloofness, coldness, coolness, frigidity, remoteness, restraint, stiffness **10 go the distance** = **finish,** bring to an end, complete, see through, stay the course **11 keep one's distance** = **be reserved,** avoid, be aloof, be indifferent, keep (someone) at arm's length, shun

distant *adj* **1** = **apart,** disparate, dispersed, distinct, scattered, separate **4** = **far-off,** abroad, afar, far, faraway, far-flung, outlying, out-of-the-way, remote, removed **5** = **reserved,** aloof, at arm's length, ceremonious, cold, cool, formal, haughty, restrained, reticent, standoffish, stiff, unapproachable, unfriendly, withdrawn
Antonyms *adj* ≠ **far-off:** adjacent, adjoining, at hand, close, handy, imminent, just round the corner, near, nearby, neighbouring, nigh, proximate, within sniffing distance (*inf.*) ≠ **reserved:** close, friendly, intimate, warm

distaste *n* = **dislike,** abhorrence, antipathy, aversion, detestation, disfavour, disgust, disinclination, displeasure, disrelish, dissatisfaction, horror, loathing, odium, repugnance, revulsion

distasteful *adj* = **unpleasant,** abhorrent, disagreeable, displeasing, loathsome, nauseous, objectionable, obnoxious, obscene, offensive, repugnant, repulsive, undesirable, uninviting, unpalatable, unsavoury
Antonyms *adj* agreeable, charming, enjoyable, pleasing, pleasurable

distend *vb* **1, 2** = **swell,** balloon, bloat, bulge, dilate, enlarge, expand, increase, inflate, puff, stretch, widen

distended *adj* **1** = **swollen,** bloated, dilated, enlarged, expanded, inflated, puffy, stretched, tumescent

distension *n* **1** = **swelling,** dilatation, dilation, enlargement, expansion, extension, inflation, intumescence, spread

distil *vb* **1-5** = **extract,** condense, draw out, evaporate, express, press out, purify, rectify, refine, sublimate, vaporize

distillation *n* **1, 6** = **essence,** elixir, extract, quintessence, spirit

distinct *adj* **3** = **different,** detached, discrete, dissimilar, individual, separate, unconnected **4** = **definite,** apparent, black-and-white, blatant, bold, clear, clear-cut, decided, evident, lucid, manifest, marked, noticeable, obvious, palpable, patent, plain, recognizable, sharp, unambiguous, unmistakable, well-defined
Antonyms *adj* ≠ **different:** common, connected, identical, indistinct, similar ≠ **definite:** fuzzy, indefinite, indistinct, obscure, unclear, vague

distinction *n* **1** = **differentiation,** discernment, discrimination, penetration, perception, separation **2** = **feature,** characteristic, distinctiveness, individuality, mark, particularity, peculiarity, quality **4** = **excellence,** account, celebrity, consequence, credit, eminence, fame, greatness, honour, importance, merit, name, note, prominence, quality, rank, renown, reputation, repute, superiority, worth

distinctive *adj* = **characteristic,** different, distinguishing, extraordinary, idiosyncratic, individual, original, peculiar, singular, special, typical, uncommon, unique
Antonyms *adj* common, ordinary, run-of-the-mill, typical

distinctly *adv* **4** = **definitely,** clearly, decidedly, evidently, manifestly, markedly, noticeably, obviously, palpably, patently, plainly, precisely, sharply, unmistakably

distinctness *n* **3** = **difference,** detachment, discreteness, disparateness, dissimilarity, dissociation, distinctiveness, individuality, separation **4** = **clearness,** clarity, lucidity, obviousness, plainness, sharpness, vividness

distinguish *vb* **1** = **differentiate,** ascertain, decide, determine, discriminate, judge, tell apart, tell between, tell the difference **3** = **make out,** discern, know, perceive, pick out, recognize, see, tell **4** = **make famous,** celebrate, dignify, honour, immortalize, signalize **6** = **characterize,** categorize, classify, individualize, make distinctive, mark, separate, set apart, single out

distinguishable *adj* **1** = **recognizable,** bold, clear, conspicuous, discernible, evident, manifest, noticeable, obvious, perceptible, plain, well-marked

distinguished *adj* **2** = **eminent,** acclaimed, celebrated, conspicuous, famed, famous, illustrious, notable, noted, renowned, well-known
Antonyms *adj* common, inferior, undistinguished, unknown

distinguishing *adj* **1** = **characteristic,** different, differentiating, distinctive, individualistic, marked, peculiar, typical

distort *vb* **1** = **deform,** bend, buckle, contort, disfigure, misshape, twist, warp, wrench, wrest

distortus, from *distorquēre* to turn different ways, from DIS-[1] + *torquēre* to twist]
▸**dis'torted** *adj*

distortion ❶ (dɪ'stɔːʃən) *n* **1** a distorting or being distorted. **2** something that is distorted. **3** *Electronics*. an undesired change in the shape of an electrical wave or signal resulting in a loss of clarity in radio reception or sound reproduction.
▸**dis'tortional** *adj*

distract ❶ (dɪ'strækt) *vb* (*tr*) **1** (*often passive*) to draw the attention of (a person) away from something. **2** to divide or confuse the attention of (a person). **3** to amuse or entertain. **4** to trouble greatly. **5** to make mad. [C14: from L *distractus* perplexed, from *distrahere* to pull in different directions, from DIS-[1] + *trahere* to drag]

distracted ❶ (dɪ'stræktɪd) *adj* **1** bewildered; confused. **2** mad.
▸**dis'tractedly** *adv*

distraction ❶ (dɪ'strækʃən) *n* **1** a distracting or being distracted. **2** something that serves as a diversion or entertainment. **3** an interruption; obstacle to concentration. **4** mental turmoil or madness.

distrain (dɪ'streɪn) *vb Law*. to seize (personal property) as security or indemnity for a debt. [C13: from OF *destreindre*, from L *distringere* to impede, from DIS-[1] + *stringere* to draw tight]
▸**dis'trainment** *n* ▸**dis'trainor** *or* **dis'trainer** *n*

distraint (dɪ'streɪnt) *n Law*. the act or process of distraining; distress.

distrait (dɪ'streɪ; *French* distrɛ) *adj* absent-minded; abstracted. [C18: from F, from *distraire* to DISTRACT]

distraught ❶ (dɪ'strɔːt) *adj* **1** distracted or agitated. **2** *Rare*. mad. [C14: changed from obs. *distract* through influence of obs. *straught*, p.p. of STRETCH]

distress ❶ (dɪ'strɛs) *vb* (*tr*) **1** to cause mental pain to; upset badly. **2** (*usually passive*) to subject to financial or other trouble. **3** to treat (something, esp. furniture or fabric) in order to make it appear older than it is. **4** *Law*. a less common word for **distrain**. ◆ *n* **5** mental pain; anguish. **6** a distressing or being distressed. **7** physical or financial trouble. **8 in distress**. (of a ship, etc.) in dire need of help. **9** *Law*. **9a** the seizure of property as security for or in satisfaction of a debt, claim, etc.; distraint. **9b** the property thus seized. **9c** *US* (*as modifier*): distress merchandise. [C13: from OF *destresse*, via Vulgar L, from L *districtus* divided in mind]
▸**dis'tressful** *adj* ▸**dis'tressing** *adj* ▸**dis'tressingly** *adv*

distressed ❶ (dɪ'strɛst) *adj* **1** much troubled; upset; afflicted. **2** in financial straits; poor. **3** (of furniture, fabric, etc.) having signs of ageing artificially applied. **4** *Econ*. another word for **depressed**.

distress signal *n* a signal by radio, Very light, etc., from a ship in need of immediate assistance.

distribute ❶ (dɪ'strɪbjuːt) *vb* **distributes, distributing, distributed**. (*tr*) **1** to give out in shares; dispense. **2** to hand out or deliver. **3** (*often passive*) to spread throughout an area. **4** (*often passive*) to divide into classes or categories. **5** *Printing*. to return (used type) to the correct positions in the typecase. **6** *Logic*. to incorporate in a distributed term of a categorical proposition. **7** *Maths*. to expand an expression containing two operators so as to change the order, as in expressing $a(b + c)$ as $ab + ac$. [C15: from L *distribuere*, from DIS-[1] + *tribuere* to give]
▸**dis'tributable** *adj*

distributed logic *n* a computer system in which remote terminals and electronic devices supplement the main computer by doing some of the computing or decision making.

distributed term *n Logic*. a term applying equally to every member of the class it designates, as *men* in *all men are mortal*.

distribution ❶ (ˌdɪstrɪ'bjuːʃən) *n* **1** the act of distributing or the state or manner of being distributed. **2** a thing or portion distributed. **3** arrangement or location. **4** the process of physically satisfying the demand for goods and services. **5** *Econ*. the division of the total income of a community among its members. **6** *Statistics*. the set of possible values of a random variable, considered in terms of theoretical or observed frequency. **7** *Law*. the apportioning of the estate of a deceased intestate. **8** *Law*. the lawful division of the assets of a bankrupt among his creditors. **9** *Finance*. **9a** the division of part of a company's profit as a dividend to its shareholders. **9b** the amount paid by dividend in a particular distribution. **10** *Engineering*. the way in which the fuel-air mixture is supplied to each cylinder of a multicylinder internal-combustion engine.
▸ˌ**distri'butional** *adj*

distributive (dɪ'strɪbjʊtɪv) *adj* **1** characterized by or relating to distribution. **2** *Grammar*. referring separately to the individual people or items in a group, as the words *each* and *every*. ◆ *n* **3** *Grammar*. a distributive word.
▸**dis'tributively** *adv* ▸**dis'tributiveness** *n*

distributive law *n Maths, logic*. a theorem asserting that one operator can validly be distributed over another. See **distribute** (sense 7).

distributor (dɪ'strɪbjʊtə) *n* **1** a person or thing that distributes. **2** a wholesaler or middleman engaged in the distribution of a category of goods, esp. to retailers in a specific area. **3** the device in a petrol engine that distributes the high-tension voltage to the sparking plugs.

district ❶ ('dɪstrɪkt) *n* **1a** an area of land marked off for administrative or other purposes. **1b** (*as modifier*): *district nurse*. **2** a locality separated by geographical attributes; region. **3** any subdivision of a territory, region, etc. **4** a political subdivision of a county, region, etc., that elects a council responsible for certain local services. ◆ *vb* **5** (*tr*) to divide into districts. [C17: from Med. L *districtus* area of jurisdiction, from L *distringere* to stretch out]

district attorney *n* (in the US) the state prosecuting officer in a specified judicial district.

District Court *n* **1** (in Scotland) a court of summary jurisdiction which deals with minor criminal offences. **2** (in the US) **2a** a Federal trial court in each US district. **2b** in some states, a court of general jurisdiction. **3** (in New Zealand) a court lower than a High Court. Formerly called: **magistrates' court**.

district high school *n* (in New Zealand) a school in a rural area providing both primary and secondary education.

district nurse *n* (in Britain) a nurse appointed to attend patients within a particular district, usually in the patients' homes.

distrust ❶ (dɪs'trʌst) *vb* **1** to regard as untrustworthy or dishonest. ◆ *n* **2** suspicion; doubt.
▸**dis'truster** *n* ▸**dis'trustful** *adj*

disturb ❶ (dɪ'stɜːb) *vb* (*tr*) **1** to intrude on; interrupt. **2** to destroy the quietness or peace of. **3** to disarrange; muddle. **4** (*often passive*) to

THESAURUS

2 = **misrepresent**, bias, colour, falsify, garble, pervert, slant, twist

distorted *adj* **1** = **deformed**, bent, buckled, contorted, crooked, disfigured, irregular, misshapen, twisted, warped **2** = **misrepresented**, biased, coloured, false, garbled, one-sided, partial, perverted, slanted, twisted

distortion *n* **1** = **misrepresentation**, bias, colouring, falsification, perversion, slant **2** = **deformity**, bend, buckle, contortion, crookedness, malformation, twist, twistedness, warp

distract *vb* **1** = **divert**, draw away, sidetrack, turn aside **3** = **amuse**, beguile, engross, entertain, occupy **4, 5** = **agitate**, bewilder, confound, confuse, derange, discompose, disconcert, disturb, harass, madden, perplex, puzzle, torment, trouble

distracted *adj* **1** = **agitated**, at sea, bemused, bewildered, confounded, confused, flustered, harassed, in a flap (*inf.*), perplexed, puzzled, troubled **2** = **frantic**, at the end of one's tether, crazy, deranged, desperate, distraught, frenzied, grief-stricken, insane, mad, overwrought, raving, wild

distracting *adj* **4** = **disturbing**, bewildering, bothering, confusing, disconcerting, dismaying, off-putting (*Brit. inf.*), perturbing

distraction *n* **2** = **entertainment**, amusement, beguilement, diversion, divertissement, pastime, recreation **3** = **diversion**, disturbance, interference, interruption **4** = **frenzy**, aberration, abstraction, agitation, alienation, bewilderment, commotion, confusion, delirium, derangement, desperation, discord, disorder, disturbance, hallucination, incoherence, insanity, mania

distraught *adj* **1, 2** = **frantic**, agitated, anxious, at the end of one's tether, beside oneself, crazed, desperate, distracted, distressed, hysterical, mad, out of one's mind, overwrought, raving, wild, worked-up, wrought-up

distress *vb* **1** = **upset**, afflict, agonize, bother, disturb, grieve, harass, harrow, pain, perplex, sadden, torment, trouble, worry, wound ◆ *n* **5** = **worry**, affliction, agony, anguish, anxiety, desolation, discomfort, grief, heartache, misery, pain, sadness, sorrow, suffering, torment, torture, woe, wretchedness **7** = **need**, adversity, calamity, destitution, difficulties, hardship, indigence, misfortune, poverty, privation, straits, trial, trouble

distressed *adj* **1** = **upset**, afflicted, agitated, anxious, distracted, distraught, saddened, tormented, troubled, worried, wretched **2** = **poverty-stricken**, destitute, down at heel, indigent, needy, poor, straitened

distressing *adj* **1** = **upsetting**, affecting, afflicting, distressful, disturbing, grievous, gut-wrenching, harrowing, heart-breaking, hurtful, lamentable, nerve-racking, painful, sad, worrying

distribute *vb* **1** = **share**, administer, allocate, allot, apportion, assign, deal, dispense, dispose, divide, dole out, give, measure out, mete **2** = **hand out**, circulate, convey, deliver, pass round **3** = **spread**, diffuse, disperse, disseminate, scatter, strew **4** = **classify**, arrange, assort, categorize, class, file, group

distribution *n* **1** = **spreading**, allocation, allotment, apportionment, circulation, diffusion, dispensation, dispersal, dispersion, dissemination, division, dole, partition, propagation, scattering, sharing **3** = **classification**, arrangement, assortment, disposition, grouping, location, organization, placement **4** = **delivery**, dealing, handling, mailing, marketing, trading, transport, transportation

district *n* **1-4** = **area**, community, locale, locality, neck of the woods (*inf.*), neighbourhood, parish, quarter, region, sector, vicinity, ward

distrust *vb* **1** = **suspect**, be sceptical of, be suspicious of, be wary of, disbelieve, discredit, doubt, misbelieve, mistrust, question, smell a rat (*inf.*), wonder about ◆ *n* **2** = **suspicion**, disbelief, doubt, dubiety, lack of faith, misgiving, mistrust, qualm, question, scepticism, wariness
Antonyms *vb* ≠ **suspect**: believe, depend, have confidence, have faith, trust ◆ *n* ≠ **suspicion**: confidence, faith, reliance, trust

distrustful *adj* **2** = **suspicious**, chary, cynical, disbelieving, distrusting, doubtful, doubting, dubious, leery (*sl.*), mistrustful, sceptical, uneasy, wary

disturb *vb* **1** = **interrupt**, bother, butt in on, disrupt, interfere with, intrude on, pester, rouse, startle **3** = **muddle**, confuse, derange, disarrange, disorder, disorganize, unsettle **4** = **upset**, agitate, alarm, annoy, confound, discompose, distract, distress, excite, fluster, harass, hassle (*inf.*), perturb, ruffle, shake, trouble, unnerve, unsettle, worry
Antonyms *vb* ≠ **upset**: calm, compose, lull, pacify, quiet, quieten, reassure, relax, relieve, settle, soothe

upset; trouble. **5** to inconvenience; put out. [C13: from L *disturbāre,* from DIS-[1] + *turbāre* to confuse]
▸**dis'turber** *n* ▸**dis'turbing** *adj* ▸**dis'turbingly** *adv*

disturbance Ⓣ (dɪ'stɜ:bəns) *n* **1** a disturbing or being disturbed. **2** an interruption or intrusion. **3** an unruly outburst or tumult. **4** *Law.* an interference with another's rights. **5** *Geol.* a minor movement of the earth causing a small earthquake. **6** *Meteorol.* a small depression. **7** *Psychiatry.* a mental or emotional disorder.

disturbed Ⓣ (dɪ'stɜ:bd) *adj Psychiatry.* emotionally upset, troubled, or maladjusted.

disulphide (daɪ'sʌlfaɪd) *n* any chemical compound containing two sulphur atoms per molecule.

disunite Ⓣ (ˌdɪsju'naɪt) *vb* **disunites, disuniting, disunited. 1** to separate; disrupt. **2** (*tr*) to set at variance; estrange.
▸**dis'union** *n* ▸**dis'unity** *n*

disuse Ⓣ (dɪs'ju:s) *n* the condition of being unused; neglect (often in **in** *or* **into disuse**).

disutility (ˌdɪsju:'tɪlɪtɪ) *n, pl* **disutilities.** *Econ.* the shortcomings of a commodity or activity in satisfying human wants. Cf. **utility** (sense 4).

disyllable ('daɪˌsɪləbᵊl) *n* a variant of **dissyllable.**

ditch Ⓣ (dɪtʃ) *n* **1** a narrow channel dug in the earth, usually used for drainage, irrigation, or as a boundary marker. ◆ *vb* **2** to make a ditch in. **3** (*intr*) to edge with a ditch. **4** *Sl.* to crash, esp. deliberately, as to avoid more unpleasant circumstances: *he had to ditch the car.* **5** (*tr*) *Sl.* to abandon. **6** *Sl.* to land (an aircraft) on water in an emergency. **7** (*tr*) *US sl.* to evade. [OE *dīc*]
▸**'ditcher** *n*

ditchwater ('dɪtʃˌwɔ:tə) *n* **1** stagnant water, esp. found in ditches. **2 as dull as ditchwater.** very dull; very uninteresting.

dither Ⓣ ('dɪðə) *vb* (*intr*) **1** *Chiefly Brit.* to be uncertain or indecisive. **2** *Chiefly US.* to be in an agitated state. **3** to tremble, as with cold. ◆ *n* **4** *Chiefly Brit.* a state of indecision. **5** a state of agitation. [C17: var. of C14 (N English dialect) *didder,* from ?]
▸**'ditherer** *n* ▸**'dithery** *adj*

dithyramb ('dɪθɪˌræm, -ˌræmb) *n* **1** (in ancient Greece) a passionate choral hymn in honour of Dionysus. **2** any utterance or a piece of writing that resembles this. [C17: from L *dīthyrambus,* from Gk *dithurambos*]
▸**ˌdithy'rambic** *adj*

dittany ('dɪtənɪ) *n, pl* **dittanies. 1** an aromatic Cretan plant with pink flowers: formerly credited with medicinal properties. **2** a North American plant with purplish flowers. [C14: from OF *ditan,* from L *dictamnus,* from Gk *diktamnon,* ?from *Diktē,* mountain in Crete]

ditto ('dɪtəʊ) *n, pl* **dittos. 1** the aforementioned; the above; the same. Used in accounts, lists, etc., to avoid repetition, and symbolized by two small marks („) known as **ditto marks,** placed under the thing repeated. **2** *Inf.* a duplicate. ◆ *adv* **3** in the same way. ◆ *sentence substitute.* **4** *Inf.* used to avoid repeating or to confirm agreement with an immediately preceding sentence. ◆ *vb* **dittos, dittoing, dittoed. 5** (*tr*) to copy; repeat. [C17: from It. (dialect): var. of *detto* said, from *dicere* to say, from L]

ditty ('dɪtɪ) *n, pl* **ditties.** a short simple song or poem. [C13: from OF *ditie* poem, from *ditier* to compose, from L *dictāre* to DICTATE]

ditty bag *or* **box** *n* a sailor's bag or box for personal belongings or tools. [C19: ?from obs. *dutty* calico, from Hindi *dhōtī* loincloth]

ditzy *or* **ditsy** ('dɪtzɪ, 'dɪtsɪ) *adj* **ditzier, ditziest** *or* **ditsier, ditsiest.** *Sl.* silly and scatterbrained. [C20: perhaps from DOTTY + DIZZY]

diuretic (ˌdaɪju'rɛtɪk) *adj* **1** acting to increase the flow of urine. ◆ *n* **2** a drug or agent that increases the flow of urine. [ME, from LL, from Gk, from *dia-* through + *ourein* to urinate]
▸**diuresis** (ˌdaɪju'ri:sɪs) *n*

diurnal Ⓣ (daɪ'ɜ:nᵊl) *adj* **1** happening during the day or daily. **2** (of flowers) open during the day and closed at night. **3** (of animals) active during the day. ◆ Cf. **nocturnal.** [C15: from LL *diurnālis,* from L *diurnus,* from *diēs* day]
▸**di'urnally** *adv*

div (dɪv) *n Sl.* a shortened form of **divvy**[1].

div. *abbrev. for:* **1** divide(d). **2** dividend. **3** division. **4** divorce(d).

diva Ⓣ ('di:və) *n, pl* **divas** *or* **dive** (-vɪ). a highly distinguished female singer; prima donna. [C19: via It. from L: a goddess, from *dīvus* DIVINE]

divagate ('daɪvəˌgeɪt) *vb* **divagates, divagating, divagated.** (*intr*) *Rare.* to digress or wander. [C16: from L DI-[2] + *vagārī* to wander]
▸**ˌdiva'gation** *n*

divalent (daɪ'veɪlənt, 'daɪˌveɪ-) *adj Chem.* **1** having a valency of two. **2** having two valencies. ◆ Also: **bivalent.**
▸**di'valency** *n*

divan (dɪ'væn) *n* **1a** a backless sofa or couch. **1b** a bed resembling such a couch. **2** (esp. formerly) a smoking room. **3a** a Muslim law court, council chamber, or counting house. **3b** a Muslim council of state. [C16: from Turkish *dīvān,* from Persian *dīwān*]

dive Ⓣ (daɪv) *vb* **dives, diving, dived** *or US* **dove** (dəʊv), **dived.** (*mainly intr*) **1** to plunge headfirst into water. **2** (of a submarine, etc.) to submerge under water. **3** (*also tr*) to fly in a steep nose-down descending path. **4** to rush, go, or reach quickly, as in a headlong plunge: *he dived for the ball.* **5** (*also tr;* foll. by *in* or *into*) to dip or put (one's hand) quickly or forcefully (into). **6** (usually foll. by *in* or *into*) to involve oneself (in something), as in eating food. ◆ *n* **7** a headlong plunge into water. **8** an act or instance of diving. **9** a steep nose-down descent of an aircraft. **10** *Sl.* a disreputable bar or club. **11** *Boxing sl.* the act of a boxer pretending to be knocked down or out. [OE *dȳfan*]

dive bomber *n* a military aircraft designed to release its bombs on a target during a steep dive.
▸**'dive-bomb** *vb* (*tr*)

diver ('daɪvə) *n* **1** a person or thing that dives. **2** a person who works or explores underwater. **3** any of various aquatic birds of northern oceans: noted for skill in diving. US and Canad. name: **loon. 4** any of various other diving birds.

diverge Ⓣ (daɪ'vɜ:dʒ) *vb* **diverges, diverging, diverged. 1** to separate or cause to separate and go in different directions from a point. **2** (*intr*) to be at variance; differ. **3** (*intr*) to deviate from a prescribed course. **4** (*intr*) *Maths.* (of a series) to have no limit. [C17: from Med. L *dīvergere,* from L DI-[2] + *vergere* to turn]

divergence Ⓣ (daɪ'vɜ:dʒəns) *or* **divergency** *n* **1** the act or result of diverging or the amount by which something diverges. **2** the condition of being divergent.

divergent Ⓣ (daɪ'vɜ:dʒənt) *adj* **1** diverging or causing divergence. **2** *Maths.* (of a series) having no limit.
▸**di'vergently** *adv*

> **USAGE NOTE** The use of *divergent* to mean different as in *they hold widely divergent views* is considered by some people to be incorrect.

divergent thinking *n Psychol.* thinking in an unusual and unstereotyped way, for instance to generate several possible solutions to a problem.

divers Ⓣ ('daɪvəz) *determiner Arch. or literary.* various; sundry; some. [C13: from OF, from L *dīversus* turned in different directions]

diverse Ⓣ (daɪ'vɜ:s, 'daɪvɜ:s) *adj* **1** having variety; assorted. **2** distinct in kind. [C13: from L *dīversus;* see DIVERS]
▸**di'versely** *adv*

THESAURUS

disturbance *n* **1, 2 = interruption**, agitation, annoyance, bother, confusion, derangement, disorder, distraction, hindrance, intrusion, molestation, perturbation, upset **3 = disorder**, bother (*inf.*), brawl, commotion, fracas, fray, hubbub, riot, ruckus (*inf.*), ruction (*inf.*), rumpus, shindig (*inf.*), shindy (*inf.*), tumult, turmoil, upheaval, uproar

disturbed *adj Psychiatry* **= unbalanced**, disordered, maladjusted, neurotic, troubled, upset
Antonyms *adj* balanced, untroubled

disturbing *adj* **4 = worrying**, agitating, alarming, disconcerting, discouraging, dismaying, disquieting, distressing, frightening, harrowing, perturbing, startling, threatening, troubling, unsettling, upsetting

disunion *n* **1 = separation**, abstraction, detachment, disconnection, disjunction, division, partition, severance **2 = disagreement**, alienation, breach, discord, dissension, dissidence, estrangement, feud, rupture, schism, split

disunite *vb* **1 = separate**, detach, disband, disconnect, disengage, disjoin, disrupt, divide, part, segregate, sever, split, sunder **2 = set at odds**, alienate, embroil, estrange, set at variance

disunity *n* **2 = disagreement**, alienation, breach, discord, discordance, dissension, dissent, estrangement, rupture, schism, split, variance

disuse *n* **= neglect**, abandonment, decay, desuetude, discontinuance, idleness, nonemployment, nonuse
Antonyms *n* application, employment, practice, service, usage, use

ditch *n* **1 = channel**, drain, dyke, furrow, gully, moat, trench, watercourse ◆ *vb* **5** *Slang* **= get rid of**, abandon, axe (*inf.*), bin (*inf.*), chuck (*inf.*), discard, dispose of, drop, dump (*inf.*), jettison, junk (*inf.*), scrap, throw out *or* overboard

dither *Chiefly Brit.* ◆ *vb* **1 = vacillate**, faff about (*Brit. inf.*), falter, haver, hesitate, hum and haw, oscillate, shillyshally (*inf.*), swither (*Scot.*), teeter, waver ◆ *n* **4 = flutter**, bother, flap (*inf.*), fluster, pother, stew (*inf.*), tiz-woz (*inf.*), tizzy (*inf.*), twitter (*inf.*)
Antonyms *vb* ≠ **vacillate:** come to a conclusion, conclude, decide, make a decision, make up one's mind, reach *or* come to a decision, resolve, settle

dithery *adj* **1 = indecisive**, agitated, all of a dither *or* fluster, bothered, dithering, flustered, hesitant, in a flap *or* tizzy (*inf.*), irresolute, swithering (*Scot.*), tentative, uncertain, unsure, vacillating, wavering
Antonyms *adj* certain, decisive, firm, positive, resolute, sure, unhesitating

diurnal *adj* **1 = daily**, circadian, daytime, everyday, quotidian, regular

diva *n* **= prima donna**, opera singer, singer

dive *vb* **1-4 = plunge**, descend, dip, disappear, drop, duck, fall, go underwater, jump, leap, nose-dive, pitch, plummet, submerge, swoop ◆ *n* **7-9 = plunge**, dash, header (*inf.*), jump, leap, lunge, nose dive, spring **10** *Slang* **= sleazy bar**, honky-tonk (*US sl.*), joint (*sl.*)

diverge *vb* **1 = separate**, bifurcate, branch, divaricate, divide, fork, part, radiate, split, spread **2 = be at variance**, be at odds, conflict, differ, disagree, dissent **3 = deviate**, depart, digress, meander, stray, turn aside, wander

divergence *n* **1, 2 = separation**, branching out, deflection, departure, deviation, difference, digression, disparity, divagation, ramification, varying

divergent *adj* **1 = separate**, conflicting, deviating, different, differing, disagreeing, dissimilar, diverging, diverse, variant

divers *determiner Archaic or literary* **= various**, different, manifold, many, multifarious, numerous, several, some, sundry, varied

diverse *adj* **1 = various**, assorted, diversified, manifold, miscellaneous, of every description,

diversify ⓘ (daɪˈvɜːsɪˌfaɪ) *vb* **diversifies, diversifying, diversified.** **1** (*tr*) to create different forms of; variegate; vary. **2** (of an enterprise) to vary (products, operations, etc.) in order to spread risk, expand, etc. **3** to distribute (investments) among several securities in order to spread risk. [C15: from OF *diversifier*, from Med. L *dīversificāre*, from L *dīversus* DIVERSE + *facere* to make]
▸**diˌversifiˈcation** *n*

diversion ⓘ (daɪˈvɜːʃən) *n* **1** the act of diverting from a specified course. **2** *Chiefly Brit.* an official detour used by traffic when a main route is closed. **3** something that distracts from business, etc.; amusement. **4** *Mil.* a feint attack designed to draw an enemy away from the main attack.
▸**diˈversional** *or* **diˈversionary** *adj*

diversity ⓘ (daɪˈvɜːsɪtɪ) *n* **1** the state or quality of being different or varied. **2** a point of difference.

divert ⓘ (daɪˈvɜːt) *vb* **1** to turn aside; deflect. **2** (*tr*) to entertain; amuse. **3** (*tr*) to distract the attention of. [C15: from F *divertir*, from L *dīvertere* to turn aside, from DI-[2] + *vertere* to turn]
▸**diˈverting** *adj* ▸**diˈvertingly** *adv*

diverticulitis (ˌdaɪvəˌtɪkjʊˈlaɪtɪs) *n* inflammation of one or more diverticula, esp. of the colon.

diverticulum (ˌdaɪvəˈtɪkjʊləm) *n, pl* **diverticula** (-lə). any sac or pouch formed by herniation of the wall of a tubular organ or part, esp. the intestines. [C16: from NL, from L *dēverticulum* by-path, from *dēvertere* to turn aside, from *vertere* to turn]

divertimento (dɪˌvɜːtɪˈmɛntəʊ) *n, pl* **divertimenti** (-tɪ). **1** a piece of entertaining music, often scored for a mixed ensemble and having no fixed form. **2** an episode in a fugue. [C18: from It.]

divertissement (dɪˈvɜːtɪsmənt) *n* a brief entertainment or diversion, usually between the acts of a play. [C18: from F: entertainment]

Dives (ˈdaɪviːz) *n* **1** a rich man in the parable in Luke 16:19–31. **2** a very rich man.

divest ⓘ (daɪˈvɛst) *vb* (*tr*; usually foll. by *of*) **1** to strip (of clothes). **2** to deprive or dispossess. [C17: changed from earlier *devest*]
▸**divestiture** (daɪˈvɛstɪtʃə), **divesture** (daɪˈvɛstʃə), *or* **diˈvestment** *n*

divi (ˈdɪvɪ) *n* an alternative spelling of **divvy**[1].

divide ⓘ (dɪˈvaɪd) *vb* **divides, dividing, divided.** **1** to separate into parts; split up. **2** to share or be shared out in parts; distribute. **3** to diverge or cause to diverge in opinion or aim. **4** (*tr*) to keep apart or be a boundary between. **5** (*intr*) to vote by separating into two groups. **6** to categorize; classify. **7** to calculate the quotient of (one number or quantity) and (another number or quantity) by division. **8** (*intr*) to diverge: *the roads divide*. **9** (*tr*) to mark increments of (length, angle, etc.). ◆ *n* **10** *Chiefly US & Canad.* an area of relatively high ground separating drainage basins; watershed. **11** a division; split. [C14: from L *dīvidere* to force apart, from DIS-[1] + *vid-* separate, from the source of *viduus* bereaved]

divided (dɪˈvaɪdɪd) *adj* **1** *Bot.* another word for **dissected** (sense 1). **2** split; not united.

dividend ⓘ (ˈdɪvɪˌdɛnd) *n* **1a** a distribution from the net profits of a company to its shareholders. **1b** a portion of this distribution received by a shareholder. **2** the share of a cooperative society's surplus allocated to members. **3** *Insurance.* a sum of money distributed from a company's net profits to the holders of certain policies. **4** something extra; a bonus. **5** a number or quantity to be divided by another number or quantity. **6** *Law.* the proportion of an insolvent estate payable to the creditors. [C15: from L *dīvidendum* what is to be divided]

divider (dɪˈvaɪdə) *n* **1** Also called: **room divider.** a screen or piece of furniture placed so as to divide a room into separate areas. **2** a person or thing that divides. **3** *Electronics.* an electrical circuit with an output that is a well-defined fraction of a given input: *a voltage divider.*

dividers (dɪˈvaɪdəz) *pl n* a type of compass with two pointed arms, used for measuring lines or dividing them.

divination ⓘ (ˌdɪvɪˈneɪʃən) *n* **1** the art or practice of discovering future events or unknown things, as though by supernatural powers. **2** a prophecy. **3** a guess.
▸**divinatory** (dɪˈvɪnətərɪ, -trɪ) *adj*

divine ⓘ (dɪˈvaɪn) *adj* **1** of God or a deity. **2** godlike. **3** of or associated with religion or worship. **4** of supreme excellence or worth. **5** *Inf.* splendid; perfect. ◆ *n* **6** (*often cap.*; preceded by *the*) another term for **God.** **7** a priest, esp. one learned in theology. ◆ *vb* **divines, divining, divined.** **8** to perceive (something) by intuition. **9** to conjecture (something); guess. **10** to discern (a hidden or future reality) as though by supernatural power. **11** (*tr*) to search for (water, metal, etc.) using a divining rod. [C14: from L *dīvīnus*, from *dīvus* a god]
▸**diˈvinely** *adv* ▸**diˈviner** *n*

divine office *n* (*sometimes cap.*) the canonical prayers recited daily by priests, etc. Also called: **Liturgy of the Hours.**

divine right of kings *n History.* the concept that the right to rule derives from God and that kings are answerable for their actions to God alone.

diving bell *n* an early diving submersible having an open bottom and being supplied with compressed air.

diving board *n* a platform or springboard from which swimmers may dive.

diving suit *or* **dress** *n* a waterproof suit used by divers, having a heavy detachable helmet and an air supply.

divining rod *n* a forked twig said to move when held over ground in which water, metal, etc., is to be found. Also called: **dowsing rod.**

divinity ⓘ (dɪˈvɪnɪtɪ) *n, pl* **divinities.** **1** the nature of a deity or the state of being divine. **2** a god. **3** (*often cap.*; preceded by *the*) another term for **God.** **4** another word for **theology.**

divisible ⓘ (dɪˈvɪzɪbᵊl) *adj* capable of being divided, usually with no remainder.
▸**diˌvisiˈbility** *or* **diˈvisibleness** *n* ▸**diˈvisibly** *adv*

division ⓘ (dɪˈvɪʒən) *n* **1** a dividing or being divided. **2** the act of sharing out; distribution. **3** something that divides; boundary. **4** one of the parts, groups, etc., into which something is divided. **5** a part of a government, business, etc., that has been made into a unit for administrative or other reasons. **6** a formal vote in Parliament or a similar legislative body. **7** a difference of opinion. **8** (in sports) a section or class organized according to age, weight, skill, etc. **9** a mathematical operation in which the quotient of two numbers or quantities is calculated. Usually written: $a \div b$, a/b, $\frac{a}{b}$. **10** *Army.* a major formation, larger than a brigade but smaller than a corps, containing the necessary arms to sustain independent combat. **11** *Biol.* (in traditional classification systems) a major category of the plant kingdom that contains one or more related classes. Cf. **phylum** (sense 1). [C14: from L *dīvīsiō*, from *dīvidere* to DIVIDE]
▸**diˈvisional** *or* **diˈvisionary** *adj* ▸**diˈvisionally** *adv*

division sign *n* the symbol ÷, placed between the dividend and the divisor to indicate division, as in $12 \div 6 = 2$.

divisive ⓘ (dɪˈvaɪsɪv) *adj* tending to cause disagreement or dissension.
▸**diˈvisively** *adv* ▸**diˈvisiveness** *n*

divisor (dɪˈvaɪzə) *n* **1** a number or quantity to be divided into another number or quantity (the dividend). **2** a number that is a factor of another number.

divorce ⓘ (dɪˈvɔːs) *n* **1** the legal dissolution of a marriage. **2** a judicial

THESAURUS

several, sundry, varied **2** = **different**, differing, discrete, disparate, dissimilar, distinct, divergent, separate, unlike, varying

diversify *vb* **1** = **vary**, alter, assort, branch out, change, expand, have a finger in every pie, mix, modify, spread out, transform, variegate

diversion *n* **1** = **detour**, alteration, change, deflection, departure, deviation, digression, variation **3** = **pastime**, amusement, beguilement, delight, distraction, divertissement, enjoyment, entertainment, game, gratification, jollies (*sl.*), play, pleasure, recreation, relaxation, sport

diversity *n* **1** = **difference**, assortment, dissimilarity, distinctiveness, divergence, diverseness, diversification, heterogeneity, medley, multiplicity, range, unlikeness, variance, variegation, variety

divert *vb* **1** = **redirect**, avert, deflect, switch, turn aside **2** = **entertain**, amuse, beguile, delight, gratify, recreate, regale **3** = **distract**, detract, draw *or* lead away from, lead astray, sidetrack

diverted *adj* **1** = **redirected**, changed, deflected, made use of, rebudgeted, rechannelled, reclassified, taken over, turned aside **2** = **entertained**, amused, taken out of oneself, tickled

diverting *adj* **2** = **entertaining**, amusing, beguiling, enjoyable, fun, humorous, pleasant

divest *vb* **1** = **strip**, denude, disrobe, doff, remove, take off, unclothe, undress **2** = **deprive**, despoil, dispossess, strip

divide *vb* **1** = **separate**, bisect, cleave, cut (up), detach, disconnect, part, partition, segregate, sever, shear, split, subdivide, sunder **2** = **share**, allocate, allot, apportion, deal out, dispense, distribute, divvy (up) (*inf.*), dole out, measure out, portion **3** = **cause to disagree**, alienate, break up, come between, disunite, estrange, set at variance *or* odds, set *or* pit against one another, sow dissension, split **6** = **classify**, arrange, categorize, grade, group, put in order, separate, sort
Antonyms *vb* ≠ **separate:** combine, come together, connect, join, knit, marry, splice, unite

dividend *n* **4** = **bonus**, cut (*inf.*), divvy (*inf.*), extra, gain, plus, portion, share, surplus

divination *n* **1** = **prediction**, augury, clairvoyance, divining, foretelling, fortune-telling, presage, prognostication, prophecy, soothsaying, sortilege

divine *adj* **1, 2** = **heavenly**, angelic, celestial, godlike, holy, spiritual, superhuman, supernatural **3** = **sacred**, consecrated, holy, religious, sanctified, spiritual **5** *Informal* = **wonderful**, beautiful, excellent, glorious, marvellous, perfect, splendid, superlative ◆ *n* **7** = **priest**, churchman, clergyman, cleric, ecclesiastic, minister, pastor, reverend ◆ *vb* **8-10** = **infer**, apprehend, conjecture, deduce, discern, foretell, guess, intuit, perceive, prognosticate, suppose, surmise, suspect, understand **11** = **dowse**

diviner *n* **8-10** = **seer**, astrologer, augur, oracle, prophet, sibyl, soothsayer **11** = **dowser**

divinity *n* **1** = **godliness**, deity, divine nature, godhead, godhood, holiness, sanctity **2** = **god** *or* **goddess**, daemon, deity, genius, guardian spirit, spirit **4** = **theology**, religion, religious studies

divisible *adj* = **dividable**, fractional, separable, splittable

division *n* **1, 2** = **separation**, bisection, cutting up, detaching, dividing, partition, splitting up **3** = **dividing line**, border, boundary, demarcation, divide, divider, partition **4** = **sharing**, allotment, apportionment, distribution **5** = **part**, branch, category, class, compartment, department, group, head, portion, section, sector, segment **7** = **disagreement**, breach, difference of opinion, discord, disunion, estrangement, feud, rupture, split, variance
Antonyms *n* ≠ **disagreement:** accord, agreement, concord, harmony, peace, union, unity

divisive *adj* = **disruptive**, alienating, damaging, detrimental, discordant, estranging, inharmonious, pernicious, troublesome, unsettling

divorce *n* **1** = **separation**, annulment, breach, break, decree nisi, dissolution, disunion, rupture, severance, split-up ◆ *vb* **4, 5** = **separate**,

decree declaring a marriage to be dissolved. **3** a separation, esp. one that is total or complete. ◆ *vb* **divorces, divorcing, divorced. 4** to separate or be separated by divorce; give or obtain a divorce. **5** (*tr*) to remove or separate, esp. completely. [C14: from OF, from L *dīvortium*, from *dīvertere* to separate]
▸**di'vorceable** *adj*

divorcée (dɪvɔː'siː) *or* (*masc*) **divorcé** (dɪ'vɔːseɪ) *n* a person who has been divorced.

divot ('dɪvət) *n* a piece of turf dug out of a grass surface, esp. by a golf club or by horses' hooves. [C16: from Scot., from ?]

divulge Ⓣ (daɪ'vʌldʒ) *vb* **divulges, divulging, divulged.** (*tr; may take a clause as object*) to make known; disclose. [C15: from L *dīvulgāre*, from DI-[2] + *vulgāre* to spread among people, from *vulgus* the common people]
▸**di'vulgence** *or* **di'vulgement** *n* ▸**di'vulger** *n*

divvy[1] Ⓣ ('dɪvɪ) *Inf.* ◆ *n, pl* **divvies. 1** *Brit.* short for **dividend**, esp. (formerly) one paid by a cooperative society. **2** *US & Canad.* a share; portion. ◆ *vb* **divvies, divvying, divvied. 3** (*tr;* usually foll. by *up*) to divide and share.

divvy[2] ('dɪvɪ) *n, pl* **divvies.** *Sl.* a stupid or odd person; misfit. [C20: ? from DEVIANT]

Diwali (dɪ'wɑːlɪ) *n* a major Hindu religious festival, honouring Lakshmi, the goddess of wealth. Held over the New Year according to the Vikrama calendar, it is marked by feasting, gifts, and the lighting of lamps.

dixie ('dɪksɪ) *n* **1** *Chiefly mil.* a large metal pot for cooking, brewing tea, etc. **2** a mess tin. [C19: from Hindi *degcī*, dim. of *degcā* pot]

Dixie ('dɪksɪ) *n* **1** Also called: **Dixieland.** the southern states of the US. ◆ *adj* **2** of the southern states of the US. [C19: ?from the nickname of New Orleans, from *dixie* a ten-dollar bill printed there, from F *dix* ten]

Dixieland ('dɪksɪˌlænd) *n* **1** a form of jazz that originated in New Orleans in the 1920s. **2** a revival of this style in the 1950s. **3** See **Dixie** (sense 1).

DIY *or* **d.i.y.** *Brit., Austral., & NZ abbrev. for* do-it-yourself.

dizzy Ⓣ ('dɪzɪ) *adj* **dizzier, dizziest. 1** affected with a whirling or reeling sensation; giddy. **2** mentally confused or bewildered. **3** causing or tending to cause vertigo or bewilderment. **4** *Inf.* foolish or flighty. ◆ *vb* **dizzies, dizzying, dizzied. 5** (*tr*) to make dizzy. [OE *dysig* silly]
▸**'dizzily** *adv* ▸**'dizziness** *n*

DJ *or* **dj** ('diːˌdʒeɪ) *n* **1** a variant of **deejay. 2** an informal term for **dinner jacket.**

djellaba, djellabah *or* **jellaba, jellabah** ('dʒɛləbə) *n* a kind of loose cloak with a hood, worn by men esp. in N Africa and the Middle East. [from Ar. *jallabah*]

djinni *or* **djinny** (dʒɪ'niː, 'dʒɪnɪ) *n, pl* **djinn** (dʒɪn). variant spellings of **jinni.**

dl *symbol for* decilitre.

DLitt *or* **DLit** *abbrev. for:* **1** Doctor of Letters. **2** Doctor of Literature. [L *Doctor Litterarum*]

dm *symbol for* decimetre.

DM *abbrev. for* Deutschmark.

DMA *Computing. abbrev. for* direct memory access.

D-mark *or* **D-Mark** *n* short for **Deutschmark.**

DMF *abbrev. for* dimethylformamide.

DMs *Inf. abbrev. for* Doc Martens.

DMus *abbrev. for* Doctor of Music.

DNA *n* deoxyribonucleic acid, the main constituent of the chromosomes of all organisms (except some viruses) in the form of a double helix. DNA is self-replicating and is responsible for the transmission of hereditary characteristics.

DNAase (ˌdiːæn'eɪeɪz) *or* **DNase** (ˌdiːɛn'eɪz) *n* deoxyribonuclease; any of a number of enzymes that hydrolyse DNA.

DNA fingerprinting *or* **profiling** *n* another name for **genetic fingerprinting.**

D-notice *n Brit.* an official notice sent to newspapers prohibiting the publication of certain security information. [C20: from their administrative classification letter]

do[1] Ⓣ (duː; *unstressed* dʊ, də) *vb* **does, doing, did, done. 1** to perform or complete (a deed or action): *to do a portrait.* **2** (often *intr;* foll. by *for*) to serve the needs of; be suitable for; suffice. **3** (*tr*) to arrange or fix. **4** (*tr*) to prepare or provide; serve: *this restaurant doesn't do lunch on Sundays.* **5** (*tr*) to make tidy, elegant, ready, etc.: *to do one's hair.* **6** (*tr*) to improve (esp. in **do something to** *or* **for**). **7** (*tr*) to find an answer to (a problem or puzzle). **8** (*tr*) to translate or adapt the form or language of: *the book was done into a play.* **9** (*intr*) to conduct oneself: *do as you please.* **10** (*intr*) to fare or manage. **11** (*tr*) to cause or produce: *complaints do nothing to help.* **12** (*tr*) to give or render: *do me a favour.* **13** (*tr*) to work at, esp. as a course of study or a profession. **14** (*tr*) to perform (a play, etc.); act. **15** (*tr*) to mimic or play the part of: *she does a wonderful elderly aunt.* **16** (*tr*) to travel at a specified speed, esp. as a maximum. **17** (*tr*) to travel or traverse (a distance). **18** (takes an infinitive without *to*) used as an auxiliary **18a** before the subject of an interrogative sentence as a way of forming a question: *do you agree?* **18b** to intensify positive statements and commands: *I do like your new house; do hurry!* **18c** before a negative adverb to form negative statements or commands: *do not leave me here alone!* **18d** in inverted constructions: *little did he realize that.* **19** used as an auxiliary to replace an earlier verb or verb phrase: *he likes you as much as I do.* **20** (*tr*) *Inf.* to visit as a sightseer or tourist. **21** (*tr*) to wear out; exhaust. **22** (*intr*) to happen (esp. in **nothing doing**). **23** (*tr*) *Sl.* to serve (a period of time) as a prison sentence. **24** (*tr*) *Inf.* to cheat or swindle. **25** (*tr*) *Sl.* to rob. **26** (*tr*) *Sl.* **26a** to arrest. **26b** to convict of a crime. **27** (*tr*) *Austral. sl.* to spend (money). **28** (*tr*) *Sl., chiefly Brit.* to treat violently; assault. **29** *Sl.* to take or use (a drug). **30** (*tr*) *Taboo sl.* (of a male) to have sexual intercourse with. **31 do or die.** to make a final or supreme effort. **32 make do.** to manage with whatever is available. ◆ *n, pl* **dos** *or* **do's. 33** *Sl.* an act or instance of cheating or swindling. **34** *Inf., chiefly Brit. & NZ.* a formal or festive gathering; party. **35 do's and don'ts.** *Inf.* rules. ◆ See also **do away with, do by,** etc. [OE *dōn*]

do[2] (dəʊ) *n, pl* **dos.** a variant spelling of **doh.**

do. *abbrev. for* ditto.

DOA *abbrev. for* dead on arrival.

doable ('duːəbəl) *adj* capable of being done.

do away with Ⓣ *vb* (*intr, adv + prep*) **1** to kill or destroy. **2** to discard or abolish.

dobbin ('dɒbɪn) *n* a name for a horse, esp. a workhorse. [C16: from *Robin*, pet form of *Robert*]

Doberman pinscher ('dəʊbəmən 'pɪnʃə) *or* **Doberman** *n* a breed of large dog with a glossy black-and-tan coat. Also: **Dobermann.** [C19: after L. *Dobermann* (19th-cent. G dog breeder) who bred it + *Pinscher*, ? after *Pinzgau*, district in Austria]

dob in *vb* **dobs, dobbing, dobbed.** (*adv*) *Austral. & NZ sl.* **1** (*tr*) to inform against, esp. to the police. **2** to contribute to a fund.

dobra ('dəʊbrə) *n* the standard monetary unit of São Tomé e Principe.

do by *vb* (*intr, prep*) to treat in the manner specified.

doc (dɒk) *n Inf.* short for **doctor.**

DOC *abbrev. for* Denominazione di Origine Controllata: used of wines. [It., lit.: name of origin controlled]

docent ('dəʊsənt) *n* a voluntary worker acting as a guide in a museum, art gallery, etc. [C19: from G *Dozent*, from L *docēns* from *docēre* to teach]

DOCG *abbrev. for* Denominazione di Origine Controllata Garantita: used of wines. [It., lit: name of origin guaranteed controlled]

docile Ⓣ ('dəʊsaɪl) *adj* **1** easy to manage or discipline; submissive. **2** *Rare.* easy to teach. [C15: from L *docilis* easily taught, from *docēre* to teach]
▸**'docilely** *adv* ▸**docility** (dəʊ'sɪlɪtɪ) *n*

dock[1] Ⓣ (dɒk) *n* **1** a wharf or pier. **2** a space between two wharves or piers for the mooring of ships. **3** an area of water that can accommodate a ship and can be closed off to allow regulation of the water level. **4** short for **dry dock. 5 in** *or* **into dock.** *Brit. inf.* **5a** (of people) in hospital. **5b** (of cars, etc.) in a repair shop. **6** *Chiefly US & Canad.* a platform from which lorries, goods trains, etc., are loaded and unloaded. ◆ *vb* **7** to moor or be moored at a dock. **8** to put (a vessel) into, or (of a

THESAURUS

annul, disconnect, dissociate, dissolve (*marriage*), disunite, divide, part, sever, split up, sunder

divulge *vb* = **make known**, betray, blow wide open (*sl.*), communicate, confess, cough (*sl.*), declare, disclose, exhibit, expose, get off one's chest (*inf.*), impart, leak, let slip, out (*inf.*), proclaim, promulgate, publish, reveal, spill (*inf.*), spill one's guts about (*sl.*), tell, uncover
Antonyms *vb* conceal, hide, keep secret

divvy[1] *Informal* ◆ *n* **1** = **share**, cut (*inf.*), dividend, percentage, portion, quota, whack (*inf.*) ◆ *vb* **3** *Informal* = **share (out)**, apportion, cut, distribute, divide, parcel out, split

dizzy *adj* **1** = **giddy**, faint, light-headed, off balance, reeling, shaky, staggering, swimming, vertiginous, weak at the knees, wobbly, woozy (*inf.*) **2** = **confused**, at sea, befuddled, bemused, bewildered, dazed, dazzled, muddled **3** = **steep**, lofty, vertiginous **4** *Informal* = **scatterbrained**, capricious, ditzy *or* ditsy, fickle, flighty, foolish, frivolous, giddy, light-headed, silly

do[1] *vb* **1** = **perform**, accomplish, achieve, act, carry out, complete, conclude, discharge, end, execute, produce, transact, undertake, work **2** = **be adequate**, answer, be enough, be of use, be sufficient, cut the mustard, pass muster, satisfy, serve, suffice, suit **3** = **get ready**, arrange, be responsible for, fix, look after, make, make ready, organize, prepare, see to, take on **7** = **solve**, decipher, decode, figure out, puzzle out, resolve, work out **9** = **behave**, bear oneself, carry oneself, comport oneself, conduct oneself **10** = **get on**, fare, get along, make out, manage, proceed **11** = **cause**, bring about, create, effect, produce **14** = **perform**, act, give, present, produce, put on **20** *Informal* = **visit**, cover, explore, journey through *or* around, look at, stop in, tour, travel **24** *Informal* = **cheat**, con (*inf.*), cozen, deceive, defraud, diddle (*inf.*), dupe, fleece, hoax, pull a fast one on (*inf.*), skin (*sl.*), stiff (*sl.*), swindle, take (someone) for a ride (*inf.*), trick **32 make do** = **manage**, cope, get along *or* by, improvise, muddle through, scrape along *or* by ◆ *n* **34** *Informal, chiefly Brit. & NZ* = **event**, affair, function, gathering, occasion, party **35 do's and don'ts** *Informal* = **rules**, code, customs, etiquette, instructions, regulations, standards

do away with *vb* **1** = **kill**, blow away (*sl., chiefly US*), bump off (*sl.*), destroy, do in, exterminate, liquidate, murder, slay, take out (*sl.*) **2** = **get rid of**, abolish, axe (*inf.*), chuck (*inf.*), discard, discontinue, eliminate, junk (*inf.*), pull, put an end to, put paid to, remove

docile 1 *adj* = **submissive**, amenable, biddable, compliant, ductile, manageable, obedient, pliant, tractable
Antonyms *adj* difficult, intractable, obstreperous, troublesome, trying, uncooperative, unmanageable

docility *n* **1** = **submissiveness**, amenability, biddableness, compliance, ductility, manageability, meekness, obedience, pliancy, tractability

dock[1] *n* **1** = **wharf**, harbour, pier, quay, waterfront ◆ *vb* **7** = **moor**, anchor, berth, drop an-

vessel) to come into a dry dock. **9** (of two spacecraft) to link together in space or link together (two spacecraft) in space. [C14: from MDu. *docke;* ? rel. to L *ducere* to lead]

dock[2] (dɒk) *n* **1** the bony part of the tail of an animal. **2** the part of an animal's tail left after the major part of it has been cut off. ◆ *vb (tr)* **3** to remove (the tail or part of the tail) of (an animal) by cutting through the bone. **4** to deduct (an amount) from (a person's wages, pension, etc.). [C14: *dok* from ?]

dock[3] (dɒk) *n* an enclosed space in a court of law where the accused sits or stands during his trial. [C16: from Flemish *dok* sty]

dock[4] (dɒk) *n* any of various weedy plants having greenish or reddish flowers and broad leaves. [OE *docce*]

dockage (ˈdɒkɪdʒ) *n* **1** a charge levied upon a vessel for using a dock. **2** facilities for docking vessels. **3** the practice of docking vessels.

docker (ˈdɒkə) *n Brit.* a man employed in the loading or unloading of ships. US and Canad. equivalent: **longshoreman.** Austral. and NZ equivalent: **watersider, wharfie.** See also **stevedore.**

docket (ˈdɒkɪt) *n* **1** *Chiefly Brit.* a piece of paper accompanying or referring to a package or other delivery, stating contents, delivery instructions, etc., sometimes serving as a receipt. **2** *Law.* **2a** a summary of the proceedings in a court. **2b** a register containing this. **3** *Brit.* **3a** a customs certificate declaring that duty has been paid. **3b** a certificate giving particulars of a shipment. **4** a summary of contents, as in a document. **5** *US.* a list of things to be done. **6** *US law.* a list of cases awaiting trial. ◆ *vb* **dockets, docketing, docketed.** *(tr)* **7** to fix a docket to (a package, etc.). **8** *Law.* **8a** to make a summary of (a judgment, etc.). **8b** to abstract and enter in a register. **9** to endorse (a document, etc.) with a summary. [C15: from ?]

dockland (ˈdɒkˌlænd) *n* the area around the docks.

dockside (ˈdɒkˌsaɪd) *n* an area beside a dock.

dockyard (ˈdɒkˌjɑːd) *n* a naval establishment with docks, workshops, etc., for the building, fitting out, and repair of vessels.

Doc Martens (dɒk ˈmɑːtənz) *pl n Trademark.* a brand of lace-up boots with thick lightweight resistant soles. In full: **Doctor Martens.** Abbrev.: **DMs.**

doctor (ˈdɒktə) *n* **1** a person licensed to practise medicine. **2** a person who has been awarded a higher academic degree in any field of knowledge. **3** *Chiefly US & Canad.* a person licensed to practise dentistry or veterinary medicine. **4** *(often cap.)* Also called: **Doctor of the Church.** a title given to any of several of the early Fathers of the Christian Church. **5** *Angling.* any of various artificial flies. **6** *Inf.* a person who mends or repairs things. **7** *Sl.* a cook on a ship or at a camp. **8** *Arch.* a man, esp. a teacher, of learning. **9 go for the doctor.** *Austral. sl.* to make a great effort or move very fast. **10 what the doctor ordered.** something needed or desired. ◆ *vb* **11** *(tr)* to give medical treatment to. **12** *(intr) Inf.* to practise medicine. **13** *(tr)* to repair or mend. **14** *(tr)* to make different in order to deceive. **15** *(tr)* to adapt. **16** *(tr) Inf.* to castrate (a cat, dog, etc.). [C14: from L: teacher, from *docēre* to teach]
▸ **ˈdoctoral** *or* **doctorial** (dɒkˈtɔːrɪəl) *adj*

doctorate (ˈdɒktərɪt, -trɪt) *n* the highest academic degree in any field of knowledge.

Doctor of Philosophy *n* a doctorate awarded for original research in any subject except law, medicine, or theology.

doctrinaire (ˌdɒktrɪˈnɛə) *adj* **1** stubbornly insistent on the observation of the niceties of a theory, esp. without regard to practicality, suitability, etc. **2** theoretical; impractical. ◆ *n* **3** a person who stubbornly attempts to apply a theory without regard to practical difficulties.
▸ **ˌdoctriˈnairism** *n* ▸ **ˌdoctriˈnarian** *n*

doctrine (ˈdɒktrɪn) *n* **1** a creed or body of teachings of a religious, political, or philosophical group presented for acceptance or belief; dogma. **2** a principle or body of principles that is taught or advocated. [C14: from OF, from L *doctrīna* teaching, from *doctor;* see DOCTOR]
▸ **doctrinal** (dɒkˈtraɪnˀl) *adj* ▸ **docˈtrinally** *adv*

docudrama (ˈdɒkjuˌdrɑːmə) *n* a film or television programme based on true events, presented in a dramatized form.

document *n* (ˈdɒkjʊmənt). **1** a piece of paper, booklet, etc., providing information, esp. of an official nature. **2** a piece of text or graphics, such as a letter or article, stored in a computer as a file for manipulation by document processing software. **3** *Arch.* proof. ◆ *vb* (ˈdɒkjuˌmɛnt). *(tr)* **4** to record or report in detail, as in the press, on television, etc. **5** to support (statements in a book) with references, etc. **6** to support (a claim, etc.) with evidence. **7** to furnish (a vessel) with documents specifying its registration, dimensions, etc. [C15: from L *documentum* a lesson, from *docēre* to teach]

documentary (ˌdɒkjuˈmɛntərɪ) *adj* **1** Also: **documental.** consisting of or relating to documents. **2** presenting factual material with few or no fictional additions. ◆ *n, pl* **documentaries. 3** a factual film or television programme about an event, person, etc., presenting the facts with little or no fiction.
▸ **ˌdocuˈmentarily** *adv*

documentation (ˌdɒkjumɛnˈteɪʃən) *n* **1** the act of supplying with or using documents or references. **2** the documents or references supplied.

document reader *n Computing.* a device that reads and inputs into a computer marks and characters on a special form, as by optical or magnetic character recognition.

docu-soap *or* **docusoap** (ˈdɒkjuˌsəʊp) *n* a television documentary series in which the lives of the people filmed are presented as entertainment or drama. [C20: from DOCU(MENTARY) + SOAP (OPERA)]

dodder[1] (ˈdɒdə) *vb (intr)* **1** to move unsteadily; totter. **2** to shake or tremble, as from age. [C17: var. of earlier *dadder*]
▸ **ˈdodderer** *n* ▸ **ˈdoddery** *adj*

dodder[2] (ˈdɒdə) *n* any of a genus of rootless parasitic plants lacking chlorophyll and having suckers for drawing nourishment from the host plant. [C13: of Gmc origin]

doddle (ˈdɒdˀl) *n Brit. inf.* something easily accomplished. [C20: ?from *doddle* (vb) to totter]

dodeca- *combining form.* indicating twelve: *dodecaphonic.* [from Gk *dōdeka* twelve]

dodecagon (dəʊˈdɛkəˌgɒn) *n* a polygon having twelve sides.

dodecahedron (ˌdəʊdɛkəˈhiːdrən) *n* a solid figure having twelve plane faces.
▸ **ˌdodecaˈhedral** *adj*

dodecaphonic (ˌdəʊdɛkəˈfɒnɪk) *adj* of or relating to the twelve-tone system of serial music.

dodge (dɒdʒ) *vb* **dodges, dodging, dodged. 1** to avoid or attempt to avoid (a blow, discovery, etc.), as by moving suddenly. **2** to evade by cleverness or trickery. **3** *(intr) Change-ringing.* to make a bell change places with its neighbour when sounding in successive changes. **4** *(tr) Photog.* to lighten or darken (selected areas on a print). ◆ *n* **5** a plan contrived to deceive. **6** a sudden evasive movement. **7** a clever contrivance. **8** *Change-ringing.* the act of dodging. [C16: from ?]

Dodgem (ˈdɒdʒəm) *n Trademark.* an electrically propelled vehicle driven and bumped against similar cars in a rink at a funfair.

dodger (ˈdɒdʒə) *n* **1** a person who evades or shirks. **2** a shifty dishonest person. **3** a canvas shelter on a ship's bridge, etc., to protect the helmsman from bad weather. **4** *Dialect & Austral.* food, esp. bread.

dodgy (ˈdɒdʒɪ) *adj* **dodgier, dodgiest.** *Brit., Austral. & NZ inf.* **1** risky, difficult, or dangerous. **2** uncertain or unreliable; tricky.

dodo (ˈdəʊdəʊ) *n, pl* **dodos** *or* **dodoes. 1** any of a now extinct family of flightless birds formerly found on Mauritius. They had a hooked bill and short stout legs. **2** *Inf.* an intensely conservative person who is unaware of changing fashions, ideas, etc. **3 (as) dead as a dodo.** irretrievably defunct or out of date. [C17: from Port. *doudo,* from *duodo* stupid]

do down *vb (tr, adv)* **1** to belittle or humiliate. **2** to deceive or cheat.

doe (dəʊ) *n, pl* **does** *or* **doe.** the female of the deer, hare, rabbit, and certain other animals. [OE *dā*]

Doe (dəʊ) *n* **John.** *Law.* **1** (formerly) the plaintiff in a fictitious action, Doe versus Roe, to test a point of law. See also **Roe. 2** Also: **Jane Doe.** *US.* an unknown or unidentified person.

DOE (formerly, in Britain) *abbrev. for* Department of the Environment.

doek (dʊk) *n S. African inf.* a square of cloth worn mainly by African women to cover the head. [C18: from Afrik.: cloth]

doer (ˈduːə) *n* **1** a person or thing that does something. **2** an active or energetic person. **3** a thriving animal, esp. a horse.

does (dʌz) *vb* (used with a singular noun or the pronouns *he, she,* or *it*) a form of the present tense (indicative mood) of **do**[1].

doeskin (ˈdəʊˌskɪn) *n* **1** the skin of a deer, lamb, or sheep. **2** a very supple leather made from this. **3** a heavy smooth cloth.

THESAURUS

chor, land, put in, tie up **9 = link up,** couple, hook up, join, rendezvous, unite

dock[2] *vb* **3 = cut off,** clip, crop, curtail, cut short, diminish, lessen, shorten **4 = deduct,** decrease, diminish, lessen, reduce, subtract, withhold
Antonyms *vb* ≠ **deduct:** augment, boost, increase, raise

docket *n* **1 = label,** bill, certificate, chit, chitty, counterfoil, receipt, tab, tag, tally, ticket, voucher ◆ *vb* **7 = label,** catalogue, file, index, mark, register, tab, tag, ticket

doctor *n* **1 = G.P.,** general practitioner, medic (*inf.*), medical practitioner, physician ◆ *vb* **14 = change,** alter, disguise, falsify, fudge, misrepresent, pervert, tamper with

doctrinaire *adj* **1 = dogmatic,** biased, fanatical, inflexible, insistent, opinionated, rigid **2 = impractical,** hypothetical, ideological, speculative, theoretical, unpragmatic, unrealistic

doctrine *n* **1 = teaching,** article, article of faith, belief, canon, concept, conviction, creed, dogma, opinion, precept, principle, tenet

document *n* **1 = paper,** certificate, instrument, legal form, record, report ◆ *vb* **5, 6 = support,** authenticate, back up, certify, cite, corroborate, detail, give weight to, instance, particularize, substantiate, validate, verify

dodder[1] *vb* **1, 2 = totter,** quake, quaver, quiver, shake, shamble, shiver, shuffle, stagger, sway, teeter, tremble

doddering *adj* **1, 2 = tottering,** aged, decrepit, doddery, faltering, feeble, floundering, infirm, senile, shaky, shambling, trembly, unsteady, weak

doddle *n Brit. informal* **= piece of cake** (*inf.*), cakewalk (*inf.*), child's play (*inf.*), cinch (*sl.*), easy-peasy (*sl.*), money for old rope, no sweat (*sl.*), picnic (*inf.*), pushover (*sl.*)

dodge *vb* **1 = duck,** body-swerve (*Scot.*), dart, shift, sidestep, swerve, turn aside **2 = evade,** avoid, body-swerve (*Scot.*), deceive, elude, equivocate, fend off, flannel (*Brit. inf.*), fudge, get out of, hedge, parry, shirk, shuffle, trick ◆ *n* **5 = trick,** contrivance, device, feint, flannel (*Brit. inf.*), machination, ploy, ruse, scheme, stratagem, subterfuge, wheeze (*Brit. sl.*), wile

dodgy *adj* **1, 2** *Brit., Austral., & NZ* **= risky,** chancy (*inf.*), dangerous, delicate, dicey (*inf., chiefly Brit.*), dicky (*Brit. inf.*), difficult, problematic(al), ticklish, tricky, uncertain, unreliable

doer *n* **2 = achiever,** active person, activist, bustler, dynamo, go-getter (*inf.*), live wire (*sl.*),

doff ❶ (dɒf) *vb (tr)* **1** to take off or lift (one's hat) in salutation. **2** to remove (clothing). [OE *dōn of;* see DO[1], OFF; cf. DON[1]]
▸ **'doffer** *n*

do for ❶ *vb (prep) Inf.* **1** *(tr)* to convict of a crime or offence. **2** *(intr)* to cause the ruin, death, or defeat of. **3** *(intr)* to do housework for. **4 do well for oneself.** to thrive or succeed.

dog ❶ (dɒg) *n* **1** a domesticated canine mammal occurring in many breeds that show a great variety in size and form. **2** any other carnivore of the dog family, such as the dingo and coyote. **3** the male of animals of the dog family. **4** *(modifier)* spurious, inferior, or useless. **5** a mechanical device for gripping or holding. **6** *Inf.* a fellow; chap. **7** *Inf.* a man or boy regarded as unpleasant or wretched. **8** *Sl.* an unattractive girl or woman. **9** *US & Canad. inf.* something unsatisfactory or inferior. **10** short for **firedog. 11 a dog's chance.** no chance at all. **12 a dog's dinner** *or* **breakfast.** *Inf.* something messy or bungled. **13 a dog's life.** a wretched existence. **14 dog eat dog.** ruthless competition. **15 like a dog's dinner.** dressed smartly or ostentatiously. **16 put on the dog.** *US & Canad. inf.* to behave or dress in an ostentatious manner. ◆ *vb* **dogs, dogging, dogged.** *(tr)* **17** to pursue or follow after with determination. **18** to trouble; plague. **19** to chase with a dog. **20** to grip or secure by a mechanical device. ◆ *adv* **21** *(usually in combination)* thoroughly; utterly: *dog-tired.* ◆ See also **dogs.** [OE *docga,* from ?]

dog biscuit *n* a hard biscuit for dogs.

dog box *n NZ inf.* disgrace; disfavour: *in the dog box.*

dogcart ('dɒg,kɑːt) *n* a light horse-drawn two-wheeled vehicle.

dog-catcher *n Now chiefly US & Canad.* a local official whose job is to impound and dispose of stray dogs.

dog collar *n* **1** a collar for a dog. **2** *Inf.* a clerical collar. **3** *Inf.* a tight-fitting necklace.

dog days *pl n* the hot period of the summer reckoned in ancient times from the heliacal rising of Sirius (the Dog Star). [C16: translation of LL *diēs caniculārēs,* translation of Gk *hēmerai kunades*]

doge (dəʊdʒ) *n* (formerly) the chief magistrate in the republics of Venice and Genoa. [C16: via F from It. (Venetian dialect), from L *dux* leader]

dog-ear *vb* **1** *(tr)* to fold down the corner of (a page). ◆ *n also* **dog's-ear. 2** a folded-down corner of a page.

dog-eared *adj* **1** having dog-ears. **2** shabby or worn.

dog-end *n Inf.* a cigarette end.

dogfight ('dɒg,faɪt) *n* **1** close-quarters combat between fighter aircraft. **2** any rough fight.

dogfish ('dɒg,fɪʃ) *n, pl* **dogfish** *or* **dogfishes. 1** any of several small sharks. **2** a less common name for the **bowfin.**

dogged ❶ ('dɒgɪd) *adj* obstinately determined; wilful or tenacious.
▸ **'doggedly** *adv* ▸ **'doggedness** *n*

doggerel ('dɒgərəl) *or* **dogrel** ('dɒgrəl) *n* **1a** comic verse, usually irregular in measure. **1b** *(as modifier): a doggerel rhythm.* **2** nonsense. [C14 *dogerel* worthless, ?from *dogge* DOG]

doggish ('dɒgɪʃ) *adj* **1** of or like a dog. **2** surly; snappish.

doggo ('dɒgəʊ) *adv Brit. inf.* in hiding and keeping quiet (esp. in **lie doggo**). [C19: prob. from DOG]

doggone ('dɒgɒn) *US & Canad.* ◆ *interj* **1** an exclamation of annoyance, etc. ◆ *adj (prenominal), adv* **2** Also: **doggoned.** another word for **damn.** [C19: euphemism for *God damn*]

doggy *or* **doggie** ('dɒgɪ) *n, pl* **doggies. 1** a child's word for a **dog.** ◆ *adj* **doggier, doggiest. 2** of, like, or relating to a dog. **3** fond of dogs.

doggy bag *n* a bag in which leftovers from a meal may be taken away, supposedly for the diner's dog.

doggy paddle *or* **doggie paddle** *n, vb* another word for **dog paddle.**

doghouse ('dɒg,haʊs) *n* **1** the US and Canad. name for **kennel. 2** *Inf.* disfavour (in **in the doghouse**).

dogie, dogy, *or* **dogey** ('dəʊgɪ) *n, pl* **dogies** *or* **dogeys.** *US & Canad.* a motherless calf. [C19: from *dough-guts,* because they were fed on flour-and-water paste]

dog in the manger *n* a person who prevents others from using something he has no use for.

dog Latin *n* spurious or incorrect Latin.

dogleg ('dɒg,lɛg) *n* **1** a sharp bend or angle. ◆ *vb* **doglegs, doglegging, doglegged. 2** *(intr)* to go off at an angle. ◆ *adj* **3** of or with the shape of a dogleg.
▸ **doglegged** (,dɒg'lɛgɪd, 'dɒg,lɛgd) *adj*

dogma ❶ ('dɒgmə) *n, pl* **dogmas** *or* **dogmata** (-mətə). **1** a religious doctrine or system of doctrines proclaimed by ecclesiastical authority as true. **2** a belief, principle, or doctrine or a code of beliefs, principles, or doctrines. [C17: via L from Gk: opinion, from *dokein* to seem good]

dogman ('dɒgmən) *n, pl* **dogmen.** *Austral.* a person who directs the operation of a crane whilst riding on an object being lifted by it.

dogmatic ❶ (dɒg'mætɪk) *or* **dogmatical** *adj* **1a** (of a statement, opinion, etc.) forcibly asserted as if authoritative and unchallengeable. **1b** (of a person) prone to making such statements. **2** of or constituting dogma. **3** based on assumption rather than observation.
▸ **dog'matically** *adv*

dogmatics (dɒg'mætɪks) *n (functioning as sing)* the study of religious dogmas and doctrines. Also called: **dogmatic** *(or* **doctrinal) theology.**

dogmatize ❶ *or* **dogmatise** ('dɒgmə,taɪz) *vb* **dogmatizes, dogmatizing, dogmatized** *or* **dogmatises, dogmatising, dogmatised.** to say or state (something) in a dogmatic manner.
▸ **'dogmatism** *n* ▸ **'dogmatist** *n*

do-gooder *n Inf.* a well-intentioned person, esp. a naive or impractical one.
▸ **,do-'gooding** *n, adj*

dog paddle *n* **1** a swimming stroke in which the swimmer paddles his hands in imitation of a swimming dog. ◆ *vb* **dog-paddle, dog-paddles, dog-paddling, dog-paddled. 2** *(intr)* to swim using the dog paddle. ◆ Also: **doggy paddle** *or* **doggie paddle.**

dog rose *n* a prickly wild European rose that has pink or white scentless flowers. [from belief that its root was effective against the bite of a mad dog]

dogs ❶ (dɒgz) *pl n* **1** *Sl.* the feet. **2** *Marketing inf.* goods with a low market share, which are unlikely to yield substantial profits. **3 go to the dogs.** *Inf.* to go to ruin physically or morally. **4 let sleeping dogs lie.** to leave things undisturbed. **5 the dogs.** *Brit. inf.* greyhound racing.

dogsbody ❶ ('dɒgz,bɒdɪ) *Inf.* ◆ *n, pl* **dogsbodies. 1** a person who carries out menial tasks for others. ◆ *vb* **dogsbodies, dogsbodying, dogsbodied.** *(intr)* **2** to act as a dogsbody.

dog's disease *n Austral. inf.* influenza.

dogsled ('dɒg,slɛd) *n Chiefly US & Canad.* a sleigh drawn by dogs. Also called (Brit.): **dog sledge.**

Dog Star *n* **the.** another name for **Sirius.**

dog-tired *adj (usually postpositive) Inf.* exhausted.

dogtooth ('dɒg,tuːθ) *n, pl* **dogteeth.** *Archit.* a carved ornament in the form of a series of four-cornered pyramids set diagonally and often decorated with leaf shapes along each edge, used in England in the 13th century.

dogtooth violet *n* any of a genus of plants, esp. a European plant with purple flowers.

dogtrot ('dɒg,trɒt) *n* a gently paced trot.

dog violet *n* any of three wild violets found in Britain and northern Europe.

dogwatch ('dɒg,wɒtʃ) *n* either of two two-hour watches aboard ship, from four to six p.m. or from six to eight p.m.

dogwood ('dɒg,wʊd) *n* any of various trees or shrubs, esp. a European shrub with small white flowers and black berries.

dogy ('dəʊgɪ) *n, pl* **dogies.** a variant of **dogie.**

doh (dəʊ) *n Music.* (in tonic sol-fa) the first degree of any major scale. [C18: from It., replacing *ut;* see GAMUT]

doily *or* **doyley** ('dɔɪlɪ) *n, pl* **doilies** *or* **doileys.** a decorative mat of lace or lacelike paper, etc., laid on plates. [C18: after *Doily,* a London draper]

do in ❶ *vb (tr, adv) Sl.* **1** to kill. **2** to exhaust.

doing ❶ ('duːɪŋ) *n* **1** an action or the performance of an action: *whose doing is this?* **2** *Inf.* a beating or castigation.

doings ❶ ('duːɪŋz) *n* **1** *(functioning as pl)* deeds, actions, or events. **2** *(functioning as sing) Inf.* anything of which the name is not known, or euphemistically left unsaid, etc.

do-it-yourself *n* **a** the hobby or process of constructing and repairing things oneself. **b** *(as modifier): a do-it-yourself kit.*

dol. *abbrev. for:* **1** *Music.* dolce. **2** *(pl* **dols.)** dollar.

Dolby ('dɒlbɪ) *n Trademark.* any of various specialized electronic circuits, esp. those used in tape recorders for noise reduction in high-frequency signals. [after R. *Dolby* (born 1933), US inventor]

THESAURUS

organizer, powerhouse *(sl.)*, wheeler- dealer *(inf.)*

doff *vb* **1 = tip,** lift, raise, remove, take off, touch **2 = take off,** cast off, discard, remove, shed, slip off, slip out of, throw off, undress

do for *vb* **2** *Informal* **= destroy,** defeat, finish (off), kill, ruin, shatter, slay, undo

dog *n* **1 = hound,** bitch, canine, cur, kuri *or* goorie *(NZ)*, man's best friend, mongrel, mutt *(sl.)*, pooch *(sl.)*, pup, puppy, tyke **7** *Informal* **= scoundrel,** beast, blackguard, cur, heel, knave *(arch.)*, villain ◆ *vb* **17, 18 = trouble,** follow, haunt, hound, plague, pursue, shadow, tail *(inf.)*, track, trail

dogged *adj* **= determined,** firm, immovable, indefatigable, obstinate, persevering, persistent, pertinacious, resolute, single-minded, staunch, steadfast, steady, stiff-necked, stubborn, tenacious, unflagging, unshakable, unyielding

Antonyms *adj* doubtful, half-hearted, hesitant, irresolute, undetermined, unsteady

doggedness *n* **= determination,** bulldog tenacity, endurance, obstinacy, perseverance, persistence, pertinacity, relentlessness, resolution, single-mindedness, steadfastness, steadiness, stubbornness, tenaciousness, tenacity

dogma *n* **1, 2 = doctrine,** article, article of faith, belief, credo, creed, opinion, precept, principle, teachings, tenet

dogmatic *adj* **1 = opinionated,** arbitrary, arrogant, assertive, categorical, dictatorial, doctrinaire, downright, emphatic, imperious, magisterial, obdurate, overbearing, peremptory **2 = doctrinal,** authoritative, canonical, categorical, ex cathedra, oracular, positive

dogmatism *n* **= opinionatedness,** arbitrariness, arrogance, dictatorialness, imperiousness, peremptoriness, positiveness, presumption

dogs *pl n* **3 go to the dogs** *Informal* **= go to ruin,** degenerate, deteriorate, go down the drain, go to pot

dogsbody *n* **1** *Informal* **= drudge,** general factotum, maid *or* man of all work, menial, skivvy *(chiefly Brit.)*, slave

do in *vb Slang* **1 = kill,** blow away, butcher, dispatch, eliminate *(sl.)*, execute, liquidate, murder, slaughter, slay, take out *(sl.)* **2 = exhaust,** fag *(inf.)*, fatigue, knacker *(sl.)*, shatter *(inf.)*, tire, wear out, weary

doing *n* **1 = carrying out** *or* **through,** achievement, act, action, deed, execution, exploit, handiwork, implementation, performance

doings *pl n* **1 = deeds,** actions, affairs, concerns, dealings, events, exploits, goings-on *(inf.)*, handiwork, happenings, proceedings, transactions

dolce (ˈdɒltʃɪ) *adj, adv Music.* (to be performed) gently and sweetly. [It.]
Dolcelatte (ˌdɒltʃiːˈlɑːtɪ) *n* a soft creamy blue-veined Italian cheese. [It., lit: sweet milk]
dolce vita (ˈdɒltʃɪ ˈviːtə) *n* a life of luxury. [It., lit.: sweet life]
doldrums Ⓣ (ˈdɒldrəmz) *n* **the. 1** a depressed or bored state of mind. **2** a state of inactivity or stagnation. **3** a belt of light winds or calms along the equator. [C19: prob. from OE *dol* DULL, infl. by TANTRUM]
dole[1] Ⓣ (dəʊl) *n* **1** (usually preceded by *the*) *Brit. & Austral. inf.* money received from the state while out of work. **2 on the dole.** *Brit. & Austral. inf.* receiving such money. **3** a small portion of money or food given to a poor person. **4** the act of distributing such portions. **5** *Arch.* fate. ◆ *vb* **doles, doling, doled. 6** (*tr;* usually foll. by *out*) to distribute, esp. in small portions. [OE *dāl* share]
dole[2] (dəʊl) *n Arch.* grief or mourning. [C13: from OF, from LL *dolus,* from L *dolēre* to lament]
dole-bludger *n Austral. sl.* a person who draws unemployment benefit without making any attempt to get work.
doleful Ⓣ (ˈdəʊlfʊl) *adj* dreary; mournful.
▸ **ˈdolefully** *adv* ▸ **ˈdolefulness** *n*
dolerite (ˈdɒləˌraɪt) *n* **1** a dark basic igneous rock; a coarse-grained basalt. **2** any dark igneous rock whose composition cannot be determined with the naked eye. [C19: from F *dolérite,* from Gk *doleros* deceitful; from the difficulty in determining its composition]
dolichocephalic (ˌdɒlɪkəʊsɪˈfælɪk) *or* **dolichocephalous** (ˌdɒlɪkəʊˈsɛfələs) *adj* having a head much longer than it is broad. [C19: from Gk *dolichos* long + -CEPHALIC]
doll (dɒl) *n* **1** a small model or dummy of a human being, used as a toy. **2** *Sl.* a pretty girl or woman of little intelligence. [C16: prob. from *Doll,* pet name for *Dorothy*]
dollar (ˈdɒlə) *n* **1** the standard monetary unit of the US, divided into 100 cents. **2** the standard monetary unit, comprising 100 cents, of various other countries including: Australia, the Bahamas, Canada, Jamaica, Malaysia, New Zealand, Singapore, Taiwan, and Zimbabwe. [C16: from Low G *daler,* from G *Taler, Thaler,* short for *Joachimsthaler,* coin made from metal mined in *Joachimsthal* Jachymov, town in the Czech Republic]
dollarbird (ˈdɒləˌbɜːd) *n* a bird of S and SE Asia and Australia with a round white spot on each wing.
dollar diplomacy *n Chiefly US.* **1** a foreign policy that encourages and protects commercial and financial involvement abroad. **2** use of financial power as a diplomatic weapon.
dollop Ⓣ (ˈdɒləp) *Inf.* ◆ *n* **1** a semisolid lump. **2** a measure or serving. ◆ *vb* **3** (*tr;* foll. by *out*) to serve out (food). [C16: from ?]
doll up Ⓣ *vb (tr, adv) Sl.* to dress in a stylish or showy manner.
dolly (ˈdɒlɪ) *n, pl* **dollies. 1** a child's word for a **doll. 2** *Films, etc.* a wheeled support on which a camera may be mounted. **3** a cup-shaped anvil used to hold a rivet. **4** *Cricket.* **4a** a simple catch. **4b** a full toss bowled in a slow high arc. **5** Also called: **dolly bird.** *Sl., chiefly Brit.* an attractive and fashionable girl. ◆ *vb* **dollies, dollying, dollied. 6** *Films, etc.* to wheel (a camera) backwards or forwards on a dolly.
dolly mixture *n* **1** a mixture of tiny coloured sweets. **2** one such sweet.
dolma (ˈdɒlmə) *n, pl* **dolmas** *or* **dolmades** (dɒlˈmɑːdiːz). a vine leaf stuffed with a filling of meat and rice. [C19: Turkish *dolma* lit. something filled]
dolman sleeve (ˈdɒlmən) *n* a sleeve that is very wide at the armhole and tapers to a tight wrist. [C19: from *dolman,* a type of Turkish robe, ult. from Turkish *dolamak* to wind]
dolmen (ˈdɒlmɛn) *n* a Neolithic stone formation, consisting of a horizontal stone supported by several vertical stones, and thought to be a tomb. [C19: from F, prob. from OBreton *tol* table, from L *tabula* board + Breton *mēn* stone, of Celtic origin]
dolomite (ˈdɒləˌmaɪt) *n* **1** a mineral consisting of calcium magnesium carbonate. **2** a rock resembling limestone but consisting principally of the mineral dolomite. [C18: after Déodat de *Dolomieu* (1750–1801), F mineralogist]
▸ **dolomitic** (ˌdɒləˈmɪtɪk) *adj*
doloroso (ˌdɒləˈrəʊsəʊ) *adj, adv Music.* (to be performed) in a sorrowful manner. [It.]
dolorous Ⓣ (ˈdɒlərəs) *adj* causing or involving pain or sorrow.
▸ **ˈdolorously** *adv*
dolos (ˈdɒlɒs) *n, pl* **dolosse.** *S. African.* a knucklebone of a sheep, buck, etc., used esp. by diviners. [from ?]
dolour *or US* **dolor** (ˈdɒlə) *n Poetic.* grief or sorrow. [C14: from L, from *dolēre* to grieve]
dolphin (ˈdɒlfɪn) *n* **1** any of various marine mammals that are typically smaller than whales and larger than porpoises and have a beaklike snout. **2 river dolphin.** any of various freshwater mammals inhabiting rivers of North and South America and S Asia. **3** Also called: **dorado.** either of two large marine fishes that have an iridescent coloration. **4** *Naut.* a post or buoy for mooring a vessel. [C13: from OF *dauphin,* via L, from Gk *delphin-, delphis*]
dolphinarium (ˌdɒlfɪˈnɛərɪəm) *n, pl* **dolphinariums** *or* **dolphinaria** (-ɪə). a pool or aquarium for dolphins, esp. one in which they give public displays.
dolt Ⓣ (dəʊlt) *n* a slow-witted or stupid person. [C16: prob. rel. to OE *dol* stupid]
▸ **ˈdoltish** *adj* ▸ **ˈdoltishness** *n*
dom. *abbrev. for:* **1** domain. **2** domestic.
-dom *suffix forming nouns.* **1** state or condition: *freedom.* **2** rank, office, or domain of: *earldom.* **3** a collection of persons: *officialdom.* [OE *-dōm*]
domain Ⓣ (dəˈmeɪn) *n* **1** land governed by a ruler or government. **2** land owned by one person or family. **3** a field or scope of knowledge or activity. **4** a region having specific characteristics. **5** *Austral. & NZ.* a park or recreation reserve maintained by a public authority, often the government. **6** *Law.* the absolute ownership and right to dispose of land. **7** *Maths.* the set of values of the independent variable of a function for which the functional value exists. **8** *Logic.* another term for **universe of discourse. 9** *Philosophy.* range of significance. **10** *Physics.* one of the regions in a ferromagnetic solid in which all the atoms have their magnetic moments aligned in the same direction. **11** *Computing.* a group of computers that have the same suffix (**domain name**) in their names on the Internet, specifying the country, type of institution, etc. where they are located. [C17: from F *domaine,* from L *dominium* property, from *dominus* lord]
dome (dəʊm) *n* **1** a hemispherical roof or vault. **2** something shaped like this. **3** a slang word for the **head.** ◆ *vb* **domes, doming, domed.** (*tr*) **4** to cover with or as if with a dome. **5** to shape like a dome. [C16: from F, from It. *duomo* cathedral, from L *domus* house]
▸ **ˈdomeˌlike** *adj* ▸ **domical** (ˈdəʊmɪkᵊl, ˈdɒm-) *adj*
Domesday Book *or* **Doomsday Book** (ˈduːmzˌdeɪ) *n History.* the record of a survey of the land of England carried out by the commissioners of William I in 1086.
domestic Ⓣ (dəˈmɛstɪk) *adj* **1** of the home or family. **2** enjoying or accustomed to home or family life. **3** (of an animal) bred or kept by man as a pet or for purposes such as the supply of food. **4** of one's own country or a specific country: *domestic and foreign affairs.* ◆ *n* **5** a household servant. [C16: from OF *domestique,* from L *domesticus* belonging to the house, from *domus* house]
▸ **doˈmestically** *adv*
domesticate Ⓣ (dəˈmɛstɪˌkeɪt) *or US (sometimes)* **domesticize** (dəˈmɛstɪˌsaɪz) *vb* **domesticates, domesticating, domesticated** *or US* **domesticizes, domesticizing, domesticized.** (*tr*) **1** to bring or keep (wild animals or plants) under control or cultivation. **2** to accustom to home life. **3** to adapt to an environment.
▸ **doˈmesticable** *adj* ▸ **doˌmestiˈcation** *n*
domesticity Ⓣ (ˌdəʊmɛˈstɪsɪtɪ) *n, pl* **domesticities. 1** home life. **2** devotion to or familiarity with home life. **3** (*usually pl*) a domestic duty or matter.
domestic science *n* the study of cooking, needlework, and other subjects concerned with household skills.

THESAURUS

doldrums *n* **1, 2 the doldrums = inactivity,** apathy, blues, boredom, depression, dullness, dumps (*inf.*), ennui, gloom, inertia, lassitude, listlessness, malaise, stagnation, tedium, the hump (*Brit. inf.*), torpor
dole[1] *n* **1** *Brit. & Austral. informal* = **benefit,** allowance, alms, donation, gift, grant, gratuity, handout, modicum, parcel, pittance, portion, quota, share ◆ *vb* **6 dole out = give out,** administer, allocate, allot, apportion, assign, deal, dispense, distribute, divide, hand out, mete, share
doleful *adj* = **mournful,** cheerless, depressing, dismal, distressing, dolorous, down in the mouth, dreary, forlorn, funereal, gloomy, low, lugubrious, melancholy, painful, pitiful, rueful, sad, sombre, sorrowful, woebegone, woeful, wretched
dollop *n* **1, 2** = **lump,** gob, helping, portion, scoop, serving
doll up *vb Slang* = **dress up,** deck out, get ready, preen, primp, prink, tart up (*sl.*), titivate, trick out
dolorous *adj* = **sorrowful,** anguished, dismal, distressing, doleful, grievous, harrowing, heart-rending, melancholy, miserable, mournful, painful, rueful, sad, woebegone, woeful, wretched
dolt *n* = **idiot,** ass, berk (*Brit. sl.*), blockhead, booby, charlie (*Brit. inf.*), chump (*inf.*), clot (*Brit. inf.*), coot, dimwit (*inf.*), dipstick (*Brit. sl.*), dope (*inf.*), dork (*sl.*), dullard, dumb-ass (*sl.*), dunce, fathead (*inf.*), fool, geek (*sl.*), gobshite (*Irish taboo sl.*), ignoramus, jerk (*sl., chiefly US & Canad.*), lamebrain (*inf.*), nerd *or* nurd (*sl.*), nitwit (*inf.*), numbskull *or* numskull, oaf, plank (*Brit. sl.*), plonker (*sl.*), prat (*sl.*), prick (*sl.*), schmuck (*US. sl.*), simpleton, thickhead, twit (*inf., chiefly Brit.*), wally (*sl.*)
doltish *adj* = **stupid,** asinine, boneheaded (*sl.*), brainless, clottish (*Brit. inf.*), dense, dim-witted (*inf.*), dopey (*inf.*), dumb (*inf.*), dumb-ass (*sl.*), foolish, goofy (*inf.*), halfwitted, idiotic, inane, mindless, silly
domain *n* **1** = **kingdom,** demesne, dominion, empire, estate, lands, policies (*Scot.*), province, realm, region, territory **3** = **area,** authority, bailiwick, concern, department, discipline, field, jurisdiction, orbit, power, realm, scope, speciality, sphere, sway
domestic *adj* **1** = **home,** domiciliary, family, household, private **2** = **home-loving,** domesticated, homely, housewifely, stay-at-home **3** = **domesticated,** house, house-trained, pet, tame, trained **4** = **native,** indigenous, internal, not foreign ◆ *n* **5** = **servant,** char (*inf.*), charwoman, daily, daily help, help, maid, woman (*inf.*)
domesticate *vb* **1** = **tame,** break, gentle, house-train, train **3** = **accustom,** acclimatize, familiarize, habituate, naturalize
domesticated *adj* **1** = **tame,** broken (in), naturalized, tamed **2** = **home-loving,** domestic, homely, house-trained (*jocular*), housewifely
Antonyms *adj* ≠ **tame:** feral, ferocious, savage, unbroken, undomesticated, untamed, wild
domesticity *n* **1, 2** = **home life,** domestication, home-lovingness, homemaking, housekeeping, housewifery

domicile Ⓣ ('dɒmɪˌsaɪl) *or* **domicil** ('dɒmɪsɪl) *Formal.* ◆ *n* **1** a dwelling place. **2** a permanent legal residence. **3** *Commerce, Brit.* the place where a bill of exchange is to be paid. ◆ *vb also* **domiciliate** (ˌdɒmɪ'sɪlɪˌeɪt), **domiciles, domiciling, domiciled** *or* **domiciliates, domiciliating, domiciliated. 4** to establish or be established in a dwelling place. [C15: from L *domicilium*, from *domus* house]
▸**domiciliary** (ˌdɒmɪ'sɪlɪərɪ) *adj*

dominance Ⓣ ('dɒmɪnəns) *n* control; ascendancy.

dominant Ⓣ ('dɒmɪnənt) *adj* **1** having primary authority or influence; governing; ruling. **2** predominant or primary: *the dominant topic of the day.* **3** occupying a commanding position. **4** *Genetics.* (of a gene) producing the same phenotype in the organism whether its allele is identical or dissimilar. Cf. **recessive. 5** *Music.* of or relating to the fifth degree of a scale. **6** *Ecology.* (of a plant or animal species) more prevalent than any other species and determining the appearance and composition of the community. ◆ *n* **7** *Genetics.* a dominant gene. **8** *Music.* **8a** the fifth degree of a scale. **8b** a key or chord based on this. **9** *Ecology.* a dominant plant or animal in a community.
▸'**dominantly** *adv*

dominant seventh chord *n Music.* a chord consisting of the dominant and the major third, perfect fifth, and minor seventh above it.

dominate Ⓣ ('dɒmɪˌneɪt) *vb* **dominates, dominating, dominated. 1** to control, rule, or govern. **2** to tower above (surroundings, etc.). **3** (*tr; usually passive*) to predominate in. [C17: from L *dominārī* to be lord over, from *dominus* lord]
▸'**domiˌnating** *adj* ▸ˌ**domi'nation** *n*

dominatrix (ˌdɒmɪ'neɪtrɪks) *n, pl* **dominatrices** (ˌdɒmɪnə'traɪsiːz). **1** a woman who is the dominant sexual partner in a sadomasochistic relationship. **2** a dominant woman. [C16: from L, fem of *dominātor*, from *dominārī* to be lord over]

dominee ('duːmɪnɪ, 'dʊə-) *n* (in South Africa) a minister in any of the Afrikaner Churches. [from Afrik., from Du.; cf. DOMINIE]

domineer Ⓣ (ˌdɒmɪ'nɪə) *vb* (*intr;* often foll. by *over*) to act with arrogance or tyranny; behave imperiously. [C16: from Du. *domineren*, from F *dominer* to DOMINATE]
▸ˌ**domi'neering** *adj*

dominical (də'mɪnɪk°l) *adj* **1** of Jesus Christ as Lord. **2** of Sunday as the Lord's Day. [C15: from LL *dominicālis*, from L *dominus* lord]

Dominican[1] (də'mɪnɪkən) *n* **1a** a member of an order of preaching friars founded by Saint Dominic in 1215; a Blackfriar. **1b** a nun of one of the orders founded under his patronage. ◆ *adj* **2** of Saint Dominic or the Dominican order.

Dominican[2] (də'mɪnɪkən) *adj* **1** of or relating to the Dominican Republic or Dominica. ◆ *n* **2** a native or inhabitant of the Dominican Republic or Dominica.

dominie ('dɒmɪnɪ) *n* **1** a Scots word for **schoolmaster. 2** a minister or clergyman. [C17: from L *dominē*, vocative case of *dominus* lord]

dominion Ⓣ (də'mɪnjən) *n* **1** rule; authority. **2** the land governed by one ruler or government. **3** sphere of influence; area of control. **4** a name formerly applied to self-governing divisions of the British Empire. **5 the Dominion.** New Zealand. [C15: from OF, from L *dominium* ownership, from *dominus* master]

Dominion Day *n* the former name for **Canada Day.**

domino[1] ('dɒmɪˌnəʊ) *n, pl* **dominoes.** a small rectangular block marked with dots, used in dominoes. [C19: from F, from It., ?from *domino!* master!, said by the winner]

domino[2] ('dɒmɪˌnəʊ) *n, pl* **dominoes** *or* **dominos. 1** a large hooded cloak worn with an eye mask at a masquerade. **2** the eye mask worn with such a cloak. [C18: from F or It., prob. from L *dominus* lord, master]

domino effect *n* a series of similar or related events occurring as a direct and inevitable result of one initial event. [C20: alluding to a row of dominoes, each standing on end, all of which fall when one is pushed]

dominoes ('dɒmɪˌnəʊz) *n* (*functioning as sing*) any of several games in which dominoes with matching halves are laid together.

don[1] Ⓣ (dɒn) *vb* **dons, donning, donned.** (*tr*) to put on (clothing). [C14: from DO[1] + ON; cf. DOFF]

don[2] (dɒn) *n* **1** *Brit.* a member of the teaching staff at a university or college, esp. at Oxford or Cambridge. **2** the head of a student dormitory at certain Canadian universities and colleges. **3** a Spanish gentleman or nobleman. **4** (in the Mafia) the head of the family. **5** *Arch.* a person of rank. [C17: ult. from L *dominus* lord]

Don (dɒn) *n* a Spanish title equivalent to *Mr.* [C16: via Sp., from L *dominus* lord]

Doña ('dɒnjə) *n* a Spanish title of address equivalent to *Mrs* or *Madam.* [C17: via Sp., from L *domina*]

donate Ⓣ (dəʊ'neɪt) *vb* **donates, donating, donated.** to give (money, time, etc.), esp. to a charity.
▸**do'nator** *n*

donation Ⓣ (dəʊ'neɪʃən) *n* **1** the act of donating. **2** a contribution. [C15: from L *dōnātiō* a presenting, from *dōnāre* to give, from *dōnum* gift]

donative ('dəʊnətɪv) *n* **1** a gift or donation. **2** a benefice capable of being conferred as a gift. ◆ *adj* **3** of or like a donation. **4** being or relating to a benefice. [C15: from L *dōnātīvum* a donation made to soldiers by a Roman emperor, from *dōnāre* to present]

donder ('dɒndə) *S. African sl.* ◆ *vb* **1** (*tr*) to beat (someone) up. ◆ *n* **2** a wretch; swine. [from Afrik., from Du. *donderen* to swear, bully]

done Ⓣ (dʌn) *vb* **1** the past participle of **do**[1]. **2 be** *or* **have done with.** to end relations with. **3 have done.** to be completely finished: *have you done?* ◆ *interj* **4** an expression of agreement, as on the settlement of a bargain. ◆ *adj* **5** completed. **6** cooked enough. **7** used up. **8** socially acceptable. **9** *Inf.* cheated; tricked. **10 done for.** *Inf.* **10a** dead or almost dead. **10b** in serious difficulty. **11 done in** *or* **up.** *Inf.* exhausted.

donee (dəʊ'niː) *n* a person who receives a gift. [C16: from DON(OR) + -EE]

doner kebab ('dɒnə) *n* a fast-food dish comprising grilled meat and salad served in pitta bread with chilli sauce. [from Turkish *döner* rotating + KEBAB]

dong (dɒŋ) *n* **1** an imitation of the sound of a bell. **2** *Austral. & NZ inf.* a heavy blow. ◆ *vb* **3** (*intr*) to make such a sound. **4** *Austral. & NZ inf.* to strike or punch. [C19: imit.]

donga ('dɒŋgə) *n S. African, Austral., & NZ.* a steep-sided gully created by soil erosion. [C19: from Afrik., from Zulu]

donjon ('dʌndʒən, 'dɒn-) *n* the heavily fortified central tower or keep of a medieval castle. Also: **dungeon.** [C14: arch. var. of *dungeon*]

Don Juan ('dɒn 'dʒuːən) *n* **1** a legendary Spanish nobleman and philanderer: hero of many poems, plays, and operas. **2** a successful seducer of women.

donkey ('dɒŋkɪ) *n* **1** a long-eared member of the horse family. **2** a stupid or stubborn person. **3 talk the hind leg(s) off a donkey.** to talk endlessly. [C18: ?from *dun* dark + *-key*, as in *monkey*]

donkey jacket *n* a thick hip-length jacket, usually navy blue, with a waterproof panel across the shoulders.

donkey's years *pl n Inf.* a long time.

donkey vote *n Austral.* a vote in which the voter's order of preference follows the order in which the candidates are listed.

donkey-work *n* **1** groundwork. **2** drudgery.

Donna ('dɒnə) *n* an Italian title of address equivalent to *Madam.* [C17: from It., from L *domina* lady]

donnish Ⓣ ('dɒnɪʃ) *adj* of or resembling a university don, esp. denoting pedantry or fussiness.
▸'**donnishness** *n*

donnybrook ('dɒnɪˌbrʊk) *n* a rowdy brawl. [C19: after *Donnybrook Fair*, an annual event until 1855 near Dublin]

donor Ⓣ ('dəʊnə) *n* **1** a person who makes a donation. **2** *Med.* any per-

THESAURUS

domicile *n* **1, 2** = **dwelling**, abode, habitation, home, house, legal residence, mansion, pad (*sl.*), residence, residency, settlement

dominance *n* = **control**, ascendancy, authority, command, domination, government, mastery, paramountcy, power, rule, supremacy, sway

dominant *adj* **1** = **controlling**, ascendant, assertive, authoritative, commanding, governing, leading, presiding, ruling, superior, supreme **2** = **main**, chief, influential, outstanding, paramount, predominant, pre-eminent, prevailing, prevalent, primary, principal, prominent

Antonyms *adj* ≠ **controlling, main:** ancillary, auxiliary, inferior, junior, lesser, lower, minor, secondary, subservient, subsidiary

dominate *vb* **1** = **control**, direct, domineer, govern, have the upper hand over, have the whip hand over, keep under one's thumb, lead, lead by the nose (*inf.*), master, monopolize, overbear, rule, rule the roost, tyrannize **2** = **tower above**, bestride, loom over, overlook, stand head and shoulders above, stand over, survey **3** = **predominate**, detract from, eclipse, outshine, overrule, overshadow, prevail over

domination *n* **1** = **control**, ascendancy, authority, command, influence, mastery, power, rule, superiority, supremacy, sway

domineer *vb* = **boss around** *or* **about** (*inf.*), bluster, browbeat, bully, hector, intimidate, lord it over, menace, overbear, ride roughshod over, swagger, threaten, tyrannize

domineering *adj* = **overbearing**, arrogant, authoritarian, autocratic, bossy (*inf.*), coercive, despotic, dictatorial, high-handed, imperious, iron-handed, magisterial, masterful, oppressive, tyrannical

Antonyms *adj* meek, obsequious, servile, shy, submissive, subservient

dominion *n* **1** = **control**, ascendancy, authority, command, domination, government, jurisdiction, mastery, power, rule, sovereignty, supremacy, sway **2** = **kingdom**, country, domain, empire, patch, province, realm, region, territory, turf (*US. sl.*)

don[1] *vb* = **put on**, clothe oneself in, dress in, get into, pull on, slip on *or* into

donate *vb* = **give**, bequeath, bestow, chip in (*inf.*), contribute, gift, hand out, make a gift of, present, subscribe

donation *n* **2** = **contribution**, alms, benefaction, boon, gift, grant, gratuity, hand-out, largesse *or* largess, offering, present, stipend, subscription

done *interjection* **4** = **agreed**, it's a bargain, O.K. *or* okay (*inf.*), settled, you're on (*inf.*) ◆ *adj* **5** = **finished**, accomplished, completed, concluded, consummated, ended, executed, in the can (*inf.*), over, perfected, realized, terminated, through **6** = **cooked enough**, cooked, cooked sufficiently, cooked to a turn, ready **7** = **used up**, depleted, exhausted, finished, spent **8** = **acceptable**, conventional, *de rigueur*, proper **9** *Informal* = **cheated**, conned (*inf.*), duped, taken for a ride (*inf.*), tricked **10 done for** *Informal* = **finished**, beaten, broken, dashed, defeated, destroyed, doomed, foiled, lost, ruined, undone, wrecked **11 done in** *or* **up** *Informal* = **exhausted**, all in (*sl.*), bushed (*inf.*), clapped out (*Austral. & NZ inf.*), dead, dead beat (*inf.*), dog-tired (*inf.*), fagged out (*inf.*), knackered (*sl.*), on one's last legs, ready to drop, tired out, worn out, worn to a frazzle (*inf.*), zonked (*sl.*)

donnish *adj* = **scholarly**, bookish, erudite, formalistic, pedagogic, pedantic, precise, scholastic

donor *n* **1** = **giver**, almsgiver, benefactor, con-

son who gives blood, organs, etc., for use in the treatment of another person. **3** the atom supplying both electrons in a coordinate bond. [C15: from OF *doneur*, from L *dōnātor*, from *dōnāre* to give]

donor card *n* a card carried to show that the bodily organs specified on it may be used for transplants after the carrier's death.

Don Quixote ('dɒn kiː'həʊtiː, 'kwɪksət) *n* an impractical idealist. [after the hero of Cervantes' *Don Quixote de la Mancha* (1605)]

don't (dəʊnt) *contraction of* do not.

don't know *n* a person who has no definite opinion, esp. as a response to a questionnaire.

doodah ('duːdɑː) *or US & Canad.* **doodad** ('duːdæd) *n Inf.* an unnamed thing, esp. an object the name of which is unknown or forgotten. [C20: from ?]

doodle ('duːdᵊl) *Inf.* ◆ *vb* **doodles, doodling, doodled. 1** to scribble or draw aimlessly. **2** to play or improvise idly. **3** (*intr; often foll. by away*) *US.* to dawdle or waste time. ◆ *n* **4** a shape, picture, etc., drawn aimlessly. [C20: ?from C17: a foolish person, but infl. in meaning by DAWDLE]
▸ **'doodler** *n*

doodlebug ('duːdᵊl,bʌg) *n* **1** another name for the **V-1. 2** a diviner's rod. **3** a US name for an **antlion** (the larva). [C20: prob. from DOODLE + BUG]

doo-doo ('duː,duː) *n US & Canad. inf.* a child's word for **excrement.**

doohickey ('duː,hɪkɪ) *n US & Canad. inf.* another name for **doodah.**

doom Ⓣ (duːm) *n* **1** death or a terrible fate. **2** a judgment. **3** (*sometimes cap.*) another term for the **Last Judgment.** ◆ *vb* **4** (*tr*) to destine or condemn to death or a terrible fate. [OE *dōm*]

doomsday *or* **domesday** ('duːmz,deɪ) *n* **1** (*sometimes cap.*) the day on which the Last Judgment will occur. **2** any day of reckoning. **3** (*modifier*) characterized by predictions of disaster: *doomsday scenario.* [OE *dōmes dæg* Judgment Day]

doona ('duːnə) *n* the Austral. name for **continental quilt.** [from a trademark]

door Ⓣ (dɔː) *n* **1** a hinged or sliding panel for closing the entrance to a room, cupboard, etc. **2** a doorway or entrance. **3** a means of access or escape: *a door to success.* **4 lay at someone's door.** to lay (the blame or responsibility) on someone. **5 out of doors.** in or into the open air. **6 show someone the door.** to order someone to leave. [OE *duru*]

do-or-die Ⓣ *adj* (*prenominal*) of a determined and sometimes reckless effort to succeed.

door furniture *n* locks, handles, etc., designed for use on doors.

doorjamb ('dɔː,dʒæm) *n* one of the two vertical members forming the sides of a doorframe. Also called: **doorpost.**

doorkeeper ('dɔː,kiːpə) *n* a person attending or guarding a door or gateway.

doorman ('dɔː,mæn, -mən) *n, pl* **doormen.** a man employed to attend the doors of certain buildings.

doormat ('dɔː,mæt) *n* **1** a mat, placed at an entrance, for wiping dirt from shoes. **2** *Inf.* a person who offers little resistance to ill-treatment.

doornail ('dɔː,neɪl) *n* (**as**) **dead as a doornail.** dead beyond any doubt.

doorsill ('dɔː,sɪl) *n* a horizontal member of wood, stone, etc., forming the bottom of a doorframe.

doorstep ('dɔː,stɛp) *n* **1** a step in front of a door. **2** *Inf.* a thick slice of bread. ◆ *vb* **doorsteps, doorstepping, doorstepped.** (*tr*) **3** to canvass (a district or member of the public) by or in the course of door-to-door visiting. **4** (of journalists) to wait outside the house of (someone) in order to obtain an interview or photograph when he or she emerges.

doorstop ('dɔː,stɒp) *n* **1** any device which prevents an open door from moving. **2** a piece of rubber, etc., fixed to the floor to stop a door striking a wall.

door to door *adj* (**door-to-door** *when prenominal*), *adv* **1** (of selling, etc.) from one house to the next. **2** (of journeys, etc.) direct.

doorway ('dɔː,weɪ) *n* **1** an opening into a building, room, etc., esp. one that has a door. **2** a means of access or escape: *a doorway to freedom.*

do over *vb* (*tr, adv*) **1** *Inf.* to redecorate. **2** *Brit., Austral. & NZ sl.* to beat up; thrash.

doo-wop ('duː,wɒp) *n* vocalizing based on rhythm-and-blues harmony. [C20: imit.]

dop (dɒp) *n S. African sl.* **1** Cape brandy. **2** a tot of this. [from Afrik., from ?]

dope Ⓣ (dəʊp) *n* **1** any of a number of preparations applied to fabric in order to improve strength, tautness, etc. **2** an additive, such as an antiknock compound added to petrol. **3** a thick liquid, such as a lubricant, applied to a surface. **4** a combustible absorbent material used to hold the nitroglycerine in dynamite. **5** *Sl.* an illegal drug, usually cannabis. **6** a drug administered to a racehorse or greyhound to affect its performance. **7** *Inf.* a stupid or slow-witted person. **8** *Inf.* news or facts, esp. confidential information. ◆ *vb* **dopes, doping, doped.** (*tr*) **9** *Electronics.* to add impurities to (a semiconductor) in order to produce or modify its properties. **10** to apply or add dope to. **11** to administer a drug to (oneself or another). [C19: from Du. *doop* sauce, from *doopen* to dip]

dopey Ⓣ *or* **dopy** ('dəʊpɪ) *adj* **dopier, dopiest. 1** *Sl.* silly. **2** *Inf.* half-asleep or semiconscious, as when under the influence of a drug.

doppelgänger ('dɒpᵊl,gɛŋə) *n Legend.* a ghostly duplicate of a living person. [from G *Doppelgänger,* lit.: double-goer]

Doppler effect ('dɒplə) *n* a change in the apparent frequency of a sound or light wave, etc., as a result of relative motion between the observer and the source. Also called: **Doppler shift.** [C19: after C. J. *Doppler* (1803–53), Austrian physicist]

Doric ('dɒrɪk) *adj* **1** of the inhabitants of Doris in ancient Greece or their dialect. **2** of or denoting one of the five classical orders of architecture: characterized by a heavy fluted column and a simple capital. **3** (*sometimes not cap.*) rustic. ◆ *n* **4** one of four chief dialects of Ancient Greek. **5** any rural dialect of English, esp. a Scots one.

dorm (dɔːm) *n Inf.* short for **dormitory.**

dormant Ⓣ ('dɔːmənt) *adj* **1** quiet and inactive, as during sleep. **2** latent or inoperative. **3** (of a volcano) neither extinct nor erupting. **4** *Biol.* alive but in a resting condition with reduced metabolism. **5** (*usually postpositive*) *Heraldry.* (of a beast) in a sleeping position. [C14: from OF *dormant,* from *dormir* to sleep, from L *dormīre*]
▸ **'dormancy** *n*

dormer ('dɔːmə) *n* a construction with a gable roof and a window that projects from a sloping roof. Also called: **dormer window.** [C16: from OF *dormoir,* from L *dormītōrium* DORMITORY]

dormie *or* **dormy** ('dɔːmɪ) *adj Golf.* as many holes ahead of an opponent as there are still to play: *dormie three.* [C19: from ?]

dormitory ('dɔːmɪtərɪ, -trɪ) *n, pl* **dormitories. 1** a large room, esp. at a school, containing several beds. **2** *US.* a building, esp. at a college or camp, providing living and sleeping accommodation. **3** (*modifier*) *Brit.* denoting or relating to an area from which most of the residents commute to work (esp. in **dormitory suburb**). [C15: from L *dormītōrium,* from *dormīre* to sleep]

Dormobile ('dɔːməʊ,biːl) *n Trademark.* a vanlike vehicle specially equipped for living in while travelling.

dormouse ('dɔː,maʊs) *n, pl* **dormice.** a small Eurasian rodent resembling a mouse with a furry tail. [C15: *dor-*, ?from OF *dormir* to sleep, (from L *dormīre*) + MOUSE]

dorp (dɔːp) *n S. African.* a small town or village. [C16: from Du.]

dorsal ('dɔːsᵊl) *adj Anat., zool.* relating to the back or spinal part of the body. [C15: from Med. L *dorsālis,* from L *dorsum* back]
▸ **'dorsally** *adv*

dorsal fin *n* an unpaired fin on the back of a fish that maintains balance during locomotion.

dory[1] ('dɔːrɪ) *n, pl* **dories.** any of various spiny-finned food fishes, esp. the John Dory. [C14: from F *dorée* gilded, from LL *deaurāre* to gild, ult. from L *aurum* gold]

dory[2] ('dɔːrɪ) *n, pl* **dories.** *US & Canad.* a flat-bottomed rowing boat with a high bow, stern, and sides. [C18: from Amerind *dóri* dugout]

DOS (dɒs) *n Computers, trademark. acronym for* disk-operating system, often prefixed, as in MS-DOS and PC-DOS; a computer operating system.

dosage ('dəʊsɪdʒ) *n* **1** the administration of a drug or agent in prescribed amounts. **2** the optimum therapeutic dose and interval between doses. **3** another name for **dose** (senses 3, 4).

dose Ⓣ (dəʊs) *n* **1** *Med.* a specific quantity of a therapeutic drug or agent taken at any one time or at specified intervals. **2** *Inf.* something unpleasant to experience: *a dose of influenza.* **3** Also called: **dosage.** the total energy of ionizing radiation absorbed by unit mass of material, esp. of living tissue; usually measured in grays (SI unit) or rads. **4** Also called: **dosage.** a small amount of syrup added to wine during bottling. **5** *Sl.* a sexually transmitted infection. ◆ *vb* **doses, dosing, dosed.** (*tr*) **6** to administer a dose to (someone). **7** *Med.* to prescribe (a drug) in appropriate quantities. **8** to add syrup to (wine) during bottling. [C15: from F, from LL *dosis,* from Gk: a giving, from *didonai* to give]

THESAURUS

tributor, donator, grantor (*Law*), philanthropist
Antonyms *n* assignee, beneficiary, inheritor, legatee, payee, receiver, recipient

doom *n* **1** = **destruction**, catastrophe, death, destiny, downfall, fate, fortune, lot, portion, ruin **2** = **sentence**, condemnation, decision, decree, judgment, verdict ◆ *vb* **4** = **condemn**, consign, damn, decree, destine, foreordain, judge, predestine, preordain, sentence, sound the death knell, threaten

doomed *adj* **4** = **condemned**, bedevilled, bewitched, cursed, fated, hopeless, ill-fated, ill-omened, luckless, star-crossed

door *n* **1** = **opening**, doorway, egress, entrance, entry, exit, ingress **4 lay at someone's door** = **blame**, censure, charge, hold responsible, impute to **5 out of doors** = **in the open air**, alfresco, out, outdoors, outside **6 show someone the door** = **throw out**, ask to leave, boot out, bounce (*sl.*), eject, oust, show out

do-or-die *adj* = **desperate**, death-or-glory, going for broke, hazardous, kill-or-cure, risky, win-or-bust

dope *n* **5** *Slang* = **drug**, narcotic, opiate **7** *Informal* = **idiot**, berk, blockhead, charlie (*Brit. inf.*), coot, dickhead (*sl.*), dimwit (*inf.*), dipstick (*Brit. sl.*), divvy (*Brit. sl.*), dolt, dork (*sl.*), dumb-ass (*sl.*), dunce, fathead (*inf.*), fool, geek (*sl.*), gobshite (*Irish taboo sl.*), jerk (*sl., chiefly US & Canad.*), lamebrain (*inf.*), nerd *or* nurd (*sl.*), nitwit (*inf.*), numbskull *or* numskull, oaf, pillock (*Brit. sl.*), plank (*Brit. sl.*), plonker (*sl.*), prat (*sl.*), prick (*sl.*), schmuck (*US sl.*), simpleton, twit (*inf., chiefly Brit.*), wally (*sl.*) **8** = **information**, details, facts, gen (*Brit. inf.*), info (*inf.*), inside information, lowdown (*inf.*), news, tip ◆ *vb* **11** = **drug**, anaesthetize, doctor, inject, knock out, narcotize, sedate, stupefy

dopey *adj* **1** *Informal* = **stupid**, asinine, dense, dozy, dumb (*inf.*), dumb-ass (*sl.*), foolish, goofy (*inf.*), idiotic, senseless, silly, simple, slow, thick **2** = **drowsy**, dazed, drugged, groggy (*inf.*), half-asleep, muzzy, stupefied, woozy (*inf.*)

dormant *adj* **1-4** = **inactive**, asleep, comatose, fallow, hibernating, inert, inoperative, latent, quiescent, sleeping, sluggish, slumbering, suspended, torpid
Antonyms *adj* active, alert, alive and kicking, aroused, awake, awakened, conscious, wakeful, wide-awake

dose *n* **1** = **quantity**, dosage, draught, drench, measure, portion, potion, prescription

dosh (dɒʃ) *n Brit.* a slang word for **money**. [C20: of unknown origin]
dosimeter (dəʊˈsɪmɪtə) *n* an instrument for measuring the dose of radiation absorbed by matter or the intensity of a source of radiation.
▸**dosimetric** (ˌdəʊsɪˈmɛtrɪk) *adj*
dosing strip *n* (in New Zealand) an area set aside for treating dogs suspected of having hydatid disease.
doss (dɒs) *Brit. sl.* ◆ *vb* **1** (*intr;* often foll. by *down*) to sleep, esp. in a dosshouse. **2** (*intr;* often foll. by *around*) to pass time aimlessly. ◆ *n* **3** a bed, esp. in a dosshouse. **4** another word for **sleep**. **5** short for **dosshouse**. **6** a task or pastime requiring little effort: *making a film is a bit of a doss.* [C18: from ?]
dosser (ˈdɒsə) *n* **1** *Brit. sl.* a person who sleeps in dosshouses. **2** *Brit. sl.* another word for **dosshouse**. **3** *Sl.* a lazy person.
dosshouse (ˈdɒsˌhaʊs) *n Brit. sl.* a cheap lodging house, esp. one used by tramps. US name: **flophouse**.
dossier (ˈdɒsɪˌeɪ) *n* a collection of papers about a subject or person. [C19: from F: a file with a label on the back, from *dos* back, from L *dorsum*]
dost (dʌst) *vb Arch. or dialect.* (used with *thou*) a singular form of the present tense (indicative mood) of **do**[1].
dot[1] ❶ (dɒt) *n* **1** a small round mark; spot; point. **2** anything resembling a dot; a small amount. **3** the mark (˙) above the letters *i, j*. **4** *Music.* **4a** the symbol (·) placed after a note or rest to increase its time value by half. **4b** this symbol written above or below a note indicating staccato. **5** *Maths, logic.* **5a** the symbol (.) indicating multiplication or logical conjunction. **5b** a decimal point. **6** the symbol (·) used, in combination with the symbol for *dash* (—), in Morse and other codes. **7 on the dot.** at exactly the arranged time. ◆ *vb* **dots, dotting, dotted.** **8** (*tr*) to mark or form with a dot. **9** (*tr*) to scatter or intersperse (as with dots): *bushes dotting the plain.* **10** (*intr*) to make a dot or dots. **11 dot one's i's and cross one's t's.** *Inf.* to pay meticulous attention to detail. [OE *dott* head of a boil]
▸ˈ**dotter** *n*
dot[2] (dɒt) *n* a woman's dowry. [C19: from F from L *dōs;* rel. to *dōtāre* to endow, *dāre* to give]
dotage ❶ (ˈdəʊtɪdʒ) *n* **1** feebleness of mind, esp. as a result of old age. **2** foolish infatuation. [C14: from DOTE + -AGE]
dotard (ˈdəʊtəd) *n* a person who is weak-minded, esp. through senility. [C14: from DOTE + -ARD]
▸ˈ**dotardly** *adj*
dote ❶ (dəʊt) *vb* **dotes, doting, doted.** (*intr*) **1** (foll. by *on* or *upon*) to love to an excessive or foolish degree. **2** to be foolish or weak-minded, esp. as a result of old age. [C13: rel. to MDu. *doten* to be silly]
▸ˈ**doter** *n*
doth (dʌθ) *vb Arch. or dialect.* (used with *he, she,* or *it*) a singular form of the present tense of **do**[1].
dot-matrix printer *n Computing.* a printer in which each character is produced by a subset of an array of needles.
dotterel *or* **dottrel** (ˈdɒtrəl) *n* **1** a rare Eurasian plover with white bands around the head and neck. **2** *Dialect.* a person who is foolish or easily duped. [C15 *dotrelle;* see DOTE]
dottle (ˈdɒtᵊl) *n* the plug of tobacco left in a pipe after smoking. [C15: dim. of *dot* lump]
dotty ❶ (ˈdɒtɪ) *adj* **dottier, dottiest.** **1** *Sl., chiefly Brit.* feeble-minded; slightly crazy. **2** *Brit. sl.* (foll. by *about*) extremely fond (of). **3** marked with dots. [C19: from DOT[1]]
▸ˈ**dottily** *adv* ▸ˈ**dottiness** *n*
Douay Bible *or* **Version** (ˈduːeɪ) *n* an English translation of the Bible from the Vulgate by Catholic scholars at Douai, a city in N France, in 1610.
double ❶ (ˈdʌbᵊl) *adj* (*usually prenominal*) **1** as much again in size, strength, number, etc.: *a double portion.* **2** composed of two equal or similar parts. **3** designed for two users: *a double room.* **4** folded in two; composed of two layers. **5** stooping; bent over. **6** having two aspects; ambiguous: *a double meaning.* **7** false, deceitful, or hypocritical: *a double life.* **8** (of flowers) having more than the normal number of petals. **9** *Music.* **9a** (of an instrument) sounding an octave lower: *a double bass.* **9b** (of time) duple. ◆ *adv* **10** twice over; twofold. **11** two together; two at a time (esp. in **see double**). ◆ *n* **12** twice the number, amount, size, etc. **13** a double measure of spirits. **14** a duplicate or counterpart, esp. a person who closely resembles another; understudy. **15** a ghostly apparition of a living person; doppelgänger. **16** a sharp turn, esp. a return on one's own tracks. **17** *Bridge.* a call that increases certain scoring points if the last preceding bid becomes the contract. **18** *Billiards, etc.* a strike in which the object ball is struck so as to make it rebound against the cushion to an opposite pocket. **19** a bet on two horses in different races in which any winnings from the first race are placed on the horse in the later race. **20a** the narrow outermost ring on a dartboard. **20b** a hit on this ring. **21 at** *or* **on the double. 21a** at twice normal marching speed. **21b** quickly or immediately. ◆ *vb* **doubles, doubling, doubled.** **22** to make or become twice as much. **23** to bend or fold (material, etc.). **24** (*tr;* sometimes foll. by *up*) to clench (a fist). **25** (*tr;* often foll. by *together* or *up*) to join or couple. **26** (*tr*) to repeat exactly; copy. **27** (*intr*) to play two parts or serve two roles. **28** (*intr*) to turn sharply; follow a winding course. **29** *Naut.* to sail around (a headland or other point). **30** *Music.* **30a** to duplicate (a part) either in unison or at the octave above or below it. **30b** (*intr;* usually foll. by *on*) to be capable of performing (upon an additional instrument). **31** *Bridge.* to make a call that will double certain scoring points if the preceding bid becomes the contract. **32** *Billiards, etc.* to cause (a ball) to rebound or (of a ball) to rebound from a cushion. **33** (*intr;* foll. by *for*) to act as substitute. **34** (*intr*) to go or march at twice the normal speed. ◆ See also **double back, doubles, double up.** [C13: from OF, from L *duplus* twofold, from *duo* two + *-plus* -FOLD]
▸ˈ**doubler** *n*
double agent *n* a spy employed by two mutually antagonistic countries, companies, etc.
double back ❶ *vb* (*intr, adv*) to go back in the opposite direction (esp. in **double back on one's tracks**).
double-bank *vb Austral. & NZ inf.* to carry (a second person) on (a horse, bicycle, etc.). Also: **dub.**
double bar *n Music.* a symbol, consisting of two ordinary bar lines or a single heavy one, that marks the end of a composition or section.
double-barrelled *or US* **double-barreled** *adj* **1** (of a gun) having two barrels. **2** extremely forceful. **3** *Brit.* (of a surname) having hyphenated parts. **4** serving two purposes; ambiguous: *a double-barrelled remark.*
double bass (beɪs) *n* **1** Also called (US): **bass viol.** a stringed instrument, the largest and lowest member of the violin family with a range of almost three octaves. Inf. name: **bass fiddle.** ◆ *adj* **double-bass.** **2** of an instrument whose pitch lies below the bass; contrabass.
double bassoon *n Music.* the lowest and largest instrument in the oboe class; contrabassoon.
double-blind *adj* of or denoting an experimental study of a new drug in which neither the experimenters nor the patients know which are the test subjects and which are the controls.
double boiler *n* the US and Canad. name for **double saucepan.**
double-breasted *adj* (of a garment) having overlapping fronts.
double-check *vb* **1** to check again; verify. ◆ *n* **double check.** **2** a second examination or verification. **3** *Chess.* a simultaneous check from two pieces.
double chin *n* a fold of fat under the chin.
▸ˌ**double-ˈchinned** *adj*
double concerto *n* a concerto for two solo instruments and orchestra.
double cream *n Brit.* thick cream with a high fat content.
double-cross ❶ *vb* **1** (*tr*) to cheat or betray. ◆ *n* **2** the act or an instance of double-crossing; betrayal.
▸ˌ**double-ˈcrosser** *n*
double dagger *n* a character (‡) used in printing to indicate a cross-reference. Also called: **diesis, double obelisk.**
double-dealing ❶ *n* **a** action characterized by treachery or deceit. **b** (*as modifier*): *double-dealing treachery.*
▸ˌ**double-ˈdealer** *n*
double-decker *n* **1** *Chiefly Brit.* a bus with two passenger decks. **2** *Inf.* **2a** a thing or structure having two decks, layers, etc. **2b** (*as modifier*): *a double-decker sandwich.*
double-declutch *vb* (*intr*) *Brit., Austral, & NZ.* to change to a lower gear in a motor vehicle by first placing the gear lever into neutral before engaging the desired gear. US term: **double-clutch.**
double Dutch *n Brit. inf.* incomprehensible talk; gibberish.
double-edged *adj* **1** acting in two ways. **2** (of a remark, etc.) having two possible interpretations, esp. applicable both for and against, or

THESAURUS

dot[1] *n* **1** = **spot**, atom, circle, dab, fleck, full stop, iota, jot, mark, mite, mote, point, speck, speckle **7 on the dot** = **on time**, exactly, on the button (*inf.*), precisely, promptly, punctually, to the minute ◆ *vb* **8** = **spot**, dab, dabble, fleck, speckle, sprinkle, stipple, stud
dotage *n* **1** = **senility**, decrepitude, eld (*arch.*), feebleness, imbecility, old age, second childhood, weakness
dote on *vb* **1** = **adore**, admire, hold dear, idolize, lavish affection on, prize, treasure
doting *adj* **1** = **adoring**, devoted, fond, foolish, indulgent, lovesick
dotty *adj* **1** *Slang, chiefly Brit.* = **crazy**, batty, crackpot (*inf.*), doolally (*sl.*), eccentric, feeble-minded, loopy (*inf.*), oddball (*inf.*), off one's trolley (*sl.*), off-the-wall (*sl.*), outré, out to lunch (*inf.*), peculiar, potty (*Brit. inf.*), touched, up the pole (*inf.*) **2 dotty about** = **keen on**, crazy about (*inf.*), daft about (*inf.*), fond of, mad about (*inf.*)
double *adj* **1** = **twice**, binate (*Botany*), coupled, doubled, dual, duplicate, in pairs, paired, twin, twofold **7** = **deceitful**, dishonest, false, hypocritical, insincere, Janus-faced, knavish (*arch.*), perfidious, treacherous, two-faced, vacillating ◆ *n* **14** = **twin**, clone, copy, counterpart, dead ringer (*sl.*), Doppelgänger, duplicate, fellow, impersonator, lookalike, mate, replica, ringer (*sl.*), spitting image (*inf.*) **21 at** *or* **on the double** = **quickly**, at full speed, briskly, immediately, in double-quick time, posthaste, without delay ◆ *vb* **22** = **multiply**, duplicate, enlarge, fold, grow, increase, magnify, plait, repeat
double back *vb* = **backtrack**, circle, dodge, loop, retrace one's steps, return, reverse
double-cross *vb* **1** = **betray**, cheat, cozen, defraud, hoodwink, mislead, sell down the river (*inf.*), swindle, trick, two-time (*inf.*)
double-dealer *n* = **cheat**, betrayer, con man (*inf.*), cozener, deceiver, dissembler, double-crosser (*inf.*), fraud, fraudster, hypocrite, rogue, snake in the grass (*inf.*), swindler, traitor, two-timer (*inf.*)
double-dealing *n* **a** = **treachery**, bad faith, betrayal, cheating, deceit, deception, dishonesty, duplicity, foul play, hypocrisy, mendacity, perfidy, trickery, two-timing (*inf.*) ◆ *modifier* **b** = **treacherous**, cheating, crooked (*inf.*), deceitful, dishonest, duplicitous, fraudulent, hypocritical, lying, perfidious, sneaky, swindling, tricky, two-faced, two-timing (*inf.*), underhanded, untrustworthy, wily

being malicious though apparently innocuous. **3** (of a knife, etc.) having a cutting edge on either side of the blade.

double entendre Ⓣ (ɑːnˈtɑːndrə) *n* **1** a word, phrase, etc., that can be interpreted in two ways, esp. one having one meaning that is indelicate. **2** the type of humour that depends upon this. [C17: from obs. F: double meaning]

double entry *n* **a** a book-keeping system in which any commercial transaction is entered as a debit in one account and as a credit in another. **b** (*as modifier*): *double-entry book-keeping.*

double exposure *n* **1** the act or process of recording two superimposed images on a photographic medium. **2** the photograph resulting from such an act.

double-faced *adj* **1** (of textiles) having a finished nap on each side; reversible. **2** insincere or deceitful.

double feature *n Films.* a programme showing two full-length films. Inf. name (US): **twin bill.**

double first *n Brit.* a first-class honours degree in two subjects.

double glazing *n* **1** two panes of glass in a window, fitted to reduce heat loss, etc. **2** the fitting of glass in such a manner.

double-header *n* **1** a train drawn by two locomotives coupled together. **2** Also called: **twin bill.** *Sport, US & Canad.* two games played consecutively. **3** *Austral. & NZ inf.* a coin with the impression of a head on each side. **4** *Austral. inf.* a double ice-cream cone.

double helix *n* the form of the molecular structure of DNA, consisting of two helical chains coiled around the same axis.

double-jointed *adj* having unusually flexible joints permitting an abnormal degree of motion.

double knitting *n* a widely used medium thickness of knitting wool.

double negative *n* a construction, often considered ungrammatical, in which two negatives are used where one is needed, as in *I wouldn't never have believed it.*

> **USAGE NOTE** There are two contexts where double negatives are found. An adjective with negative force is often used with a negative in order to express a nuance of meaning somewhere between the positive and the negative: *he was a not infrequent visitor; it is not an uncommon sight.* Two negatives are also found together where they reinforce each other rather than conflict: *he never went back, not even to collect his belongings.* These two uses of what is technically a double negative are acceptable. A third case, illustrated by *I shouldn't wonder if it didn't rain today,* has the force of a weak positive statement (*I expect it to rain today*) and is common in informal English.

double-park *vb* to park (a vehicle) alongside or opposite another already parked by the roadside, thereby causing an obstruction.

double pneumonia *n* pneumonia affecting both lungs.

double-quick *adj* **1** very quick; rapid. ◆ *adv* **2** in a very quick or rapid manner.

double-reed *adj* relating to or denoting a wind instrument having two reeds that vibrate against each other.

double refraction *n* the splitting of a ray of unpolarized light into two unequally refracted rays polarized in mutually perpendicular planes. Also called: **birefringence.**

doubles (ˈdʌbᵊlz) *n* (*functioning as sing or pl*) **a** a game between two pairs of players. **b** (*as modifier*): *a doubles match.*

double saucepan *n Brit.* a cooking utensil consisting of two saucepans: the lower pan is used to boil water to heat food in the upper pan. US and Canad. name: **double boiler.**

double-space *vb* **double-spaces, double-spacing, double-spaced.** to type (copy) with a full space between lines.

double spread *n Printing.* two facing pages of a publication treated as a single unit.

double standard *n* a set of principles that allows greater freedom to one person or group than to another.

double-stop *vb* **double-stops, double-stopping, double-stopped.** to play (two notes or parts) simultaneously on a violin or related instrument.

doublet Ⓣ (ˈdʌblɪt) *n* **1** (formerly) a man's close-fitting jacket, with or without sleeves (esp. in **doublet and hose**). **2a** a pair of similar things, esp. two words deriving ultimately from the same source. **2b** one of such a pair. **3** *Jewellery.* a false gem made by welding or fusing stones together. **4** *Physics.* a closely spaced pair of related spectral lines. **5** (*pl*) two dice each showing the same number of spots on one throw. [C14: from OF, from DOUBLE]

double take *n* (esp. in comedy) a delayed reaction by a person to a remark, situation, etc.

double talk *n* **1** rapid speech with a mixture of nonsense syllables and real words; gibberish. **2** empty, deceptive, or ambiguous talk.

doublethink (ˈdʌbᵊlˌθɪŋk) *n* deliberate, perverse, or unconscious acceptance or promulgation of conflicting facts, principles, etc.

double time *n* **1** a doubled wage rate, paid for working on public holidays, etc. **2** *Music.* two beats per bar. **3** a slow running pace, keeping in step. **4** *US Army.* a fast march.

double up *vb* (*adv*) **1** to bend or cause to bend in two. **2** (*intr*) to share a room or bed designed for one person, family, etc. **3** (*intr*) *Brit.* to use the winnings from one bet as the stake for another. US and Canad. term: **parlay.**

double whammy *n Inf., chiefly US.* a devastating setback made up of two elements.

doubloon (dʌˈbluːn) *n* **1** a former Spanish gold coin. **2** (*pl*) *Sl.* money. [C17: from Sp. *doblón,* from *dobla,* from L *dupla,* fem. of *duplus* twofold]

doubly Ⓣ (ˈdʌblɪ) *adv* **1** to or in a double degree, quantity, or measure. **2** in two ways.

doubt Ⓣ (daʊt) *n* **1** uncertainty about the truth, fact, or existence of something (esp. in **in doubt, without doubt,** etc.). **2** (*often pl*) lack of belief in or conviction about something. **3** an unresolved difficulty, point, etc. **4** *Obs.* fear. **5 give (someone) the benefit of the doubt.** to presume (someone suspected of guilt) innocent. **6 no doubt.** almost certainly. ◆ *vb* **7** (*tr; may take a clause as object*) to be inclined to disbelieve. **8** (*tr*) to distrust or be suspicious of. **9** (*intr*) to feel uncertainty or be undecided. **10** (*tr*) *Arch.* to fear. [C13: from OF *douter,* from L *dubitāre*] ▸ˈ**doubtable** *adj* ▸ˈ**doubter** *n* ▸ˈ**doubtingly** *adv*

> **USAGE NOTE** Where a clause follows *doubt* in a positive sentence, it was formerly considered correct to use *whether*: (*I doubt whether he will come*), but now *if* and *that* are also acceptable. In negative statements, *doubt* is followed by *that*: *I do not doubt that he is telling the truth.* In such sentences, *but* (*I do not doubt but that he is telling the truth*) is redundant.

doubtful Ⓣ (ˈdaʊtfʊl) *adj* **1** unlikely; improbable. **2** uncertain: *a doubtful answer.* **3** unsettled; unresolved. **4** of questionable reputation or morality. **5** having reservations or misgivings. ▸ˈ**doubtfully** *adv* ▸ˈ**doubtfulness** *n*

> **USAGE NOTE** It was formerly considered correct to use *whether* after *doubtful* (*it is doubtful whether he will come*), but now *if* and *that* are also acceptable.

doubting Thomas (ˈtɒməs) *n* a person who insists on proof before he will believe anything. [after *Thomas* (the apostle), who did not believe that Jesus had been resurrected until he had proof]

doubtless Ⓣ (ˈdaʊtlɪs) *adv also* **doubtlessly** (*sentence modifier*), *sentence substitute.* **1** certainly. **2** probably. ◆ *adj* **3** certain; assured. ▸ˈ**doubtlessness** *n*

douche (duːʃ) *n* **1** a stream of water directed onto or into the body for cleansing or medical purposes. **2** the application of such a stream of water. **3** an instrument for applying a douche. ◆ *vb* **douches, douching, douched. 4** to cleanse or treat or be cleansed or treated by means of a douche. [C18: from F, from It. *doccia* pipe]

dough (dəʊ) *n* **1** a thick mixture of flour or meal and water or milk, used for making bread, pastry, etc. **2** any similar pasty mass. **3** a slang word for **money.** [OE *dāg*]

doughboy (ˈdəʊˌbɔɪ) *n* **1** *US inf.* an infantryman, esp. in World War I. **2** dough that is boiled or steamed as a dumpling.

doughnut (ˈdəʊnʌt) *n* **1** a small cake of sweetened dough, often ring-shaped, cooked in hot fat. **2** anything shaped like a ring, such as the reaction vessel of a thermonuclear reactor. ◆ *vb* **doughnuts, doughnutting, doughnutted. 3** (*tr*) *Inf.* (of Members of Parliament) to surround (a speaker) during the televising of Parliament to give the impression that the chamber is crowded or the speaker is well supported.

doughty Ⓣ (ˈdaʊtɪ) *adj* **doughtier, doughtiest.** hardy; resolute. [OE *dohtig*] ▸ˈ**doughtily** *adv* ▸ˈ**doughtiness** *n*

THESAURUS

double entendre *n* **1** = **double meaning,** ambiguity, innuendo, play on words, pun

doublet *n* **1** *History* = **jacket,** jerkin, vest, waistcoat

doubly *adv* **1, 2** = **twice,** again, as much again, in double measure, in two ways, once more, over again, twofold

doubt *n* **1** = **suspicion,** apprehension, disquiet, distrust, fear, incredulity, lack of faith, misgiving, mistrust, qualm, scepticism **2** = **uncertainty,** dubiety, hesitancy, hesitation, indecision, irresolution, lack of conviction, suspense, vacillation **3** = **difficulty,** ambiguity, can of worms (*inf.*), confusion, dilemma, perplexity, problem, quandary **6 no doubt** = **certainly,** admittedly, assuredly, doubtless, doubtlessly, probably, surely ◆ *vb* **8** = **suspect,** discredit, distrust, fear, lack confidence in, misgive, mistrust, query, question **9** = **be uncertain,** be dubious, demur, fluctuate, hesitate, scruple, vacillate, waver **Antonyms** *n* ≠ **suspicion:** confidence, trust ≠ **uncertainty:** belief, certainty, confidence, conviction ◆ *vb* ≠ **suspect:** accept, believe, buy (*sl.*), have faith in, swallow (*inf.*), take on board, trust

doubter *n* **7, 8** = **sceptic,** agnostic, disbeliever, doubting Thomas, questioner, unbeliever

doubtful *adj* **1** = **unlikely,** ambiguous, debatable, dodgy (*Brit., Austral., & NZ inf.*), dubious, equivocal, hazardous, iffy (*inf.*), improbable, inconclusive, indefinite, indeterminate, inexact, obscure, precarious, problematic(al), questionable, unclear, unconfirmed, unsettled, vague **2, 3** = **unsure,** distrustful, hesitating, in two minds (*inf.*), irresolute, leery (*sl.*), perplexed, sceptical, suspicious, tentative, uncertain, unconvinced, undecided, unresolved, unsettled, vacillating, wavering **4** = **questionable,** disreputable, dodgy (*Brit., Austral., & NZ inf.*), dubious, shady (*inf.*), suspect, suspicious **Antonyms** *adj* ≠ **unlikely:** certain, definite, indubitable ≠ **unsure:** certain, decided, positive, resolute

doubtless *adv* **1** = **certainly,** assuredly, clearly, indisputably, of course, precisely, surely, truly, undoubtedly, unquestionably, without doubt **2** = **probably,** apparently, most likely, ostensibly, presumably, seemingly, supposedly

doughty *adj Old-fashioned* = **intrepid,** bold,

doughy ('dəʊɪ) *adj* **doughier, doughiest.** resembling dough; soft, pallid, or flabby.

Douglas fir, spruce, *or* **hemlock** *n* a North American pyramidal coniferous tree, widely planted for ornament and for timber. [C19: after David *Douglas* (1798–1834), Scot. botanist]

Doukhobor *or* **Dukhobor** ('duːkəʊˌbɔː) *n* a member of a Russian sect of Christians that originated in the 18th century. In the late 19th century a large number emigrated to W Canada, where most Doukhobors now live. [C19: from Russian *dukhoborets* spirit wrestlers]

do up *vb* (*adv; mainly tr*) **1** to wrap and make into a bundle: *to do up a parcel.* **2** to beautify or adorn. **3** (*also intr*) to fasten or be fastened. **4** *Inf.* to renovate or redecorate. **5** *Sl.* to assault. **6** *Inf.* to cause the downfall of (a person).

dour ⓣ (dʊə, 'daʊə) *adj* **1** sullen. **2** hard or obstinate. [C14: prob. from L *dūrus* hard]
▸ **'dourly** *adv* ▸ **'dourness** *n*

douroucouli (ˌduːruː'kuːlɪ) *n* a nocturnal New World monkey of Central and South America with thick fur and large eyes. [from Amerind]

douse ⓣ *or* **dowse** (daʊs) *vb* **douses, dousing, doused** *or* **dowses, dowsing, dowsed. 1** to plunge or be plunged into liquid; duck. **2** (*tr*) to drench with water. **3** (*tr*) to put out (a light, candle, etc.). ◆ *n* **4** an immersion. [C16: ? rel. to obs. *douse* to strike, from ?]

dove (dʌv) *n* **1** any of a family of birds having a heavy body, small head, short legs, and long pointed wings. **2** *Politics.* a person opposed to war. **3** a gentle or innocent person: used as a term of endearment. **4a** a greyish-brown colour. **4b** (*as adj*): *dove walls.* [OE *dūfe* (unattested except as a fem proper name)]
▸ **'doveˌlike** *adj*

Dove (dʌv) *n* **the.** *Christianity.* a manifestation of the Holy Spirit (John 1:32).

dovecote ('dʌvˌkəʊt) *or* **dovecot** ('dʌvˌkɒt) *n* a structure for housing pigeons.

dovetail ⓣ ('dʌvˌteɪl) *n* **1** a wedge-shaped tenon. **2** Also called: **dovetail joint.** a joint containing such tenons. ◆ *vb* **3** (*tr*) to join by means of dovetails. **4** to fit or cause to fit together closely or neatly.

dowager ('daʊədʒə) *n* **1a** a widow possessing property or a title obtained from her husband. **1b** (*as modifier*): *the dowager duchess.* **2** a wealthy or dignified elderly woman. [C16: from OF *douagiere,* from *douage* DOWER]

dowdy ⓣ ('daʊdɪ) *adj* **dowdier, dowdiest. 1** (esp. of a woman or a woman's dress) shabby or old-fashioned. ◆ *n, pl* **dowdies. 2** a dowdy woman. [C14: *dowd* slut, from ?]
▸ **'dowdily** *adv* ▸ **'dowdiness** *n* ▸ **'dowdyish** *adj*

dowel ('daʊəl) *n* a wooden or metal peg that fits into two corresponding holes to join two adjacent parts. [C14: from MLow G *dövel* plug, from OHG *tubili*]

dower ('daʊə) *n* **1** the life interest in a part of her husband's estate allotted to a widow by law. **2** an archaic word for **dowry** (sense 1). **3** a natural gift. ◆ *vb* **4** (*tr*) to endow. [C14: from OF *douaire,* from Med. L *dōtārium,* from L *dōs* gift]

dower house *n* a house for the use of a widow, often on her deceased husband's estate.

do with *vb* **1 could** *or* **can do with.** to find useful; benefit from. **2 have to do with.** to be involved in or connected with. **3 to do with.** concerning; related to. **4 what...do with. 4a** to put or place: *what did you do with my coat?* **4b** to handle or treat. **4c** to fill one's time usefully: *she didn't know what to do with herself when the project was finished.*

do without ⓣ *vb* (*intr*) **1** to forgo; manage without. **2** (*prep*) not to require (uncalled-for comments): *we can do without your criticisms.*

Dow-Jones average ('daʊ'dʒəʊnz) *n US.* a daily index of average stock-exchange prices. [C20: after Charles H. *Dow* (died 1902) & Edward D. *Jones* (died 1920), American financial statisticians]

down[1] ⓣ (daʊn) *prep* **1** used to indicate movement from a higher to a lower position. **2** at a lower or further level or position on, in, or along: *he ran down the street.* ◆ *adv* **3** downwards; at or to a lower level or position. **4** (*particle*) used with many verbs when the result of the verb's action is to lower or destroy its object: *knock down.* **5** (*particle*) used with several verbs to indicate intensity or completion: *calm down.* **6** immediately: *cash down.* **7** on paper: *write this down.* **8** arranged; scheduled. **9** in a helpless position. **10a** away from a more important place. **10b** away from a more northerly place. **10c** (of a member of some British universities) away from the university. **10d** in a particular part of a country: *down south.* **11** *Naut.* (of a helm) having the rudder to windward. **12** reduced to a state of lack or want: *down to the last pound.* **13** lacking a specified amount. **14** lower in price. **15** including all intermediate grades. **16** from an earlier to a later time. **17** to a finer or more concentrated state: *to grind down.* **18** *Sport.* being a specified number of points, goals, etc., behind another competitor, team, etc. **19** (of a person) being inactive, owing to illness: *down with flu.* **20** (*functioning as imperative*) (to dogs): *down, Rover!* **21** (*functioning as imperative*) **down with.** wanting the end of somebody or something: *down with the king!* **22 get down on something.** *Austral. & NZ.* to procure something, esp. in advance of needs or in anticipation of someone else. ◆ *adj* **23** (*postpositive*) depressed. **24** (*prenominal*) of or relating to a train or trains from a more important place or one regarded as higher: *the down line.* **25** (*postpositive*) (of a device, machine, etc., esp. a computer) temporarily out of action. **26** made in cash: *a down payment.* **27 down to.** the responsibility or fault of: *this defeat was down to me.* ◆ *vb* (*tr*) **28** to knock, push, or pull down. **29** to cause to go or come down. **30** *Inf.* to drink, esp. quickly. **31** to bring (someone) down, esp. by tackling. ◆ *n* **32** a descent; downward movement. **33** a lowering or a poor period (esp. in **ups and downs**). **34** (in American football) any of a series of four attempts to advance the ball ten yards. **35 have a down on.** *Inf.* to bear ill will towards. [OE *dūne,* short for *adūne,* var. of *of dūne,* lit.: from the hill]

down[2] (daʊn) *n* **1** soft fine feathers. **2** another name for **eiderdown** (sense 1). **3** *Bot.* a fine coating of soft hairs, as on certain leaves, fruits, and seeds. **4** any growth or coating of soft fine hair. [C14: from ON]

down[3] (daʊn) *n Arch.* a hill, esp. a sand dune. See also **downs.** [OE *dūn*]

down-and-out ⓣ *adj* **1** without any means of livelihood; poor and, often, socially outcast. ◆ *n* **2** a person who is destitute and, often, homeless.

downbeat ⓣ ('daʊnˌbiːt) *n* **1** *Music.* the first beat of a bar or the downward gesture of a conductor's baton indicating this. ◆ *adj Inf.* **2** depressed; gloomy. **3** relaxed.

downcast ⓣ ('daʊnˌkɑːst) *adj* **1** dejected. **2** (esp. of the eyes) directed downwards. ◆ *n* **3** *Mining.* a ventilation shaft.

downer ('daʊnə) *n Sl.* **1** a barbiturate, tranquillizer, or narcotic. **2** a depressing experience. **3** a state of depression.

downfall ⓣ ('daʊnˌfɔːl) *n* **1** a sudden loss of position, health, or reputation. **2** a fall of rain, snow, etc., esp. a sudden heavy one.

downgrade ⓣ ('daʊnˌgreɪd) *vb* **downgrades, downgrading, downgraded.** (*tr*) **1** to reduce in importance or value, esp. to demote (a person) to a poorer job. **2** to speak of disparagingly. ◆ *n* **3** *Chiefly US & Canad.* a downward slope. **4 on the downgrade.** waning in importance, health, etc.

downhearted ⓣ (ˌdaʊn'hɑːtɪd) *adj* discouraged; dejected.
▸ **ˌdown'heartedly** *adv*

downhill ('daʊn'hɪl) *adj* **1** going or sloping down. ◆ *adv* **2** towards the bottom of a hill; downwards. **3 go downhill.** *Inf.* to decline; deteriorate. ◆ *n* **4** the downward slope of a hill; a descent. **5** a skiing race downhill.

downhole ('daʊnˌhəʊl) *adj* (in the oil industry) denoting any piece of equipment used in the well itself.

downhome (ˌdaʊn'həʊm) *adj Sl., chiefly US.* of, relating to, or reminiscent of rural life, esp. in the southern US; unsophisticated; homely.

Downing Street ('daʊnɪŋ) *n* **1** a street in W central London: official

THESAURUS

brave, courageous, daring, dauntless, fearless, gallant, gritty, hardy, heroic, redoubtable, resolute, stouthearted, valiant, valorous

dour *adj* **1** = **gloomy**, dismal, dreary, forbidding, grim, morose, sour, sullen, unfriendly
Antonyms *adj* carefree, cheerful, cheery, chirpy (*inf.*), genial, good-humoured, happy, jovial, pleasant, sunny

douse *vb* **1, 2** = **drench**, duck, dunk, immerse, plunge into water, saturate, soak, souse, steep, submerge **3** = **put out**, blow out, extinguish, smother, snuff (out)

dovetail *vb* **3** = **fit together**, fit, interlock, join, link, mortise, tenon, unite **4** = **correspond**, accord, agree, coincide, conform, harmonize, match, tally

dowdy *adj* **1** = **frumpy**, dingy, drab, frowzy, frumpish, ill-dressed, old-fashioned, scrubby (*Brit. inf.*), shabby, slovenly, tacky (*US inf.*), unfashionable
Antonyms *adj* chic, dressy, fashionable, neat, smart, spruce, trim, well-dressed

do without *vb* **1** = **manage without**, abstain from, dispense with, forgo, get along without, give up, kick (*inf.*)

down[1] *adj* **23** = **depressed**, blue, dejected, disheartened, dismal, downcast, down in the dumps (*inf.*), low, miserable, sad, sick as a parrot (*inf.*), unhappy ◆ *vb* **28, 29** = **bring down**, deck (*sl.*), fell, floor, knock down, overthrow, prostrate, subdue, tackle, throw, trip **30** *Informal* = **swallow**, drain, drink (down), gulp, put away, toss off ◆ *n* **32** = **drop**, decline, descent, dropping, fall, falling, reverse **35 have a down on** *Informal* = **be antagonistic** *or* **hostile to**, be anti (*inf.*), bear a grudge towards, be contra (*inf.*), be prejudiced against, be set against, feel ill will towards, have it in for (*sl.*)

down-and-out *adj* **1** = **destitute**, derelict, dirt-poor (*inf.*), flat broke (*inf.*), impoverished, on one's uppers (*inf.*), penniless, ruined, short, without two pennies to rub together (*inf.*) ◆ *n* **2** = **tramp**, bag lady, beggar, bum (*inf.*), derelict, dosser (*Brit. sl.*), loser, outcast, pauper, vagabond, vagrant

downbeat *adj* **2** *Informal* = **gloomy**, depressed, discouraging, disheartening, flat, low-key, muted, negative, pessimistic, sober, sombre, subdued, unfavourable
Antonyms *adj* buoyant, cheerful, encouraging, favourable, heartening, optimistic, positive, upbeat

downcast *adj* **1** = **dejected**, cheerless, choked, crestfallen, daunted, depressed, despondent, disappointed, disconsolate, discouraged, disheartened, dismal, dismayed, dispirited, down in the dumps (*inf.*), miserable, sad, sick as a parrot (*inf.*), unhappy
Antonyms *adj* cheerful, cheery, chirpy (*inf.*), contented, elated, genial, happy, joyful, light-hearted, optimistic

downfall *n* **1** = **ruin**, breakdown, collapse, comedown, comeuppance (*sl.*), debacle, descent, destruction, disgrace, fall, overthrow, undoing **2** = **rainstorm**, cloudburst, deluge, downpour

downgrade *vb* **1** = **demote**, degrade, humble, lower *or* reduce in rank, take down a peg (*inf.*) **2** = **run down**, decry, denigrate, detract from, disparage
Antonyms *vb* ≠ **demote:** advance, ameliorate, better, elevate, enhance, improve, promote, raise, upgrade

downhearted *adj* = **dejected**, blue, chapfallen, crestfallen, depressed, despondent, discouraged, disheartened, dismayed, dispirited, downcast, low-spirited, sad, sick as a parrot (*inf.*), sorrowful, unhappy

residences of the prime minister of Great Britain and the Chancellor of the Exchequer. **2** the office of the prime minister. [after Sir George *Downing* (1623–84), E statesman]

download ('daʊn,ləʊd) *vb* (*tr*) to copy or transfer (data or a program) from one computer's memory to that of another, esp. in a network of computing.

down-market ⓣ *adj* relating to commercial products, services, etc., that are cheap, unfashionable, or poor quality.

down payment *n* the deposit paid on an item purchased on hire-purchase, mortgage, etc.

downpipe ('daʊn,paɪp) *n Brit. and NZ.* a pipe for carrying rainwater from a roof gutter to ground level. Usual US & Canad. name: **downspout.**

downpour ⓣ ('daʊn,pɔː) *n* a heavy continuous fall of rain.

downrange ('daʊn'reɪndʒ) *adj, adv* in the direction of the intended flight path of a rocket or missile.

downright ⓣ ('daʊn,raɪt) *adj* **1** frank or straightforward; blunt. ◆ *adv, adj* (*prenominal*) **2** (intensifier): *downright rude.*
▸'**down,rightly** *adv* ▸'**down,rightness** *n*

downs (daʊnz) *pl n* **1** rolling upland, esp. in the chalk areas of S Britain, characterized by lack of trees and used mainly as pasture. **2** *Austral. & NZ.* a flat grassy area, not necessarily of uplands.

downshifting ('daʊn,ʃɪftɪŋ) *n* the practice of simplifying one's lifestyle and becoming less materialistic.

downside ⓣ ('daʊn,saɪd) *n* the disadvantageous aspect of a situation: *the downside of twentieth-century living.*

downsize ('daʊn,saɪz) *vb* **downsizes, downsizing, downsized.** (*tr*) **1** to reduce the number of people employed by (a company). **2** to upgrade (a computer system) by replacing a mainframe or minicomputer with a network of microcomputing. Cf. **rightsize.**

Down's syndrome (daʊnz) *n* **a** *Pathol.* a chromosomal abnormality resulting in a flat face and nose, a vertical fold of skin at the inner edge of the eye, and mental retardation. Former name: **mongolism. b** (*as modifier*): *a Down's syndrome baby.* [C19: after John *Langdon-Down* (1828–96), Brit. physician]

downstage ('daʊn'steɪdʒ) *Theatre.* ◆ *adv* **1** at or towards the front of the stage. ◆ *adj* **2** of or relating to the front of the stage.

downstairs ('daʊn'steəz) *adv* **1** down the stairs; to or on a lower floor. ◆ *n* **2a** a lower or ground floor. **2b** (*as modifier*): *a downstairs room.* **3** *Brit. inf., old-fashioned.* the servants of a household collectively.

downstream ('daʊn'striːm) *adv, adj* in or towards the lower part of a stream; with the current. Cf. **upstream** (sense 1).

downswing ('daʊn,swɪŋ) *n* a statistical downward trend in business activity, the death rate, etc.

downtime ('daʊn,taɪm) *n Commerce.* time during which a computer or machine is not working, as when under repair.

down-to-earth ⓣ *adj* sensible; practical; realistic.

downtown ('daʊn'taʊn) *Chiefly US, Canad., & NZ.* ◆ *n* **1** the central or lower part of a city, esp. the main commercial area. ◆ *adv* **2** towards, to, or into this area. ◆ *adj* **3** of, relating to, or situated in the downtown area: *a downtown cinema.*

downtrodden ⓣ ('daʊn,trɒdᵊn) *adj* **1** subjugated; oppressed. **2** trodden down.

downturn ('daʊn,tɜːn) *n* a drop or reduction in the success of a business or economy.

down under *Inf.* ◆ *n* **1** Australia or New Zealand. ◆ *adv* **2** in or to Australia or New Zealand.

downward ⓣ ('daʊnwəd) *adj* **1** descending from a higher to a lower level, condition, position, etc. **2** descending from a beginning. ◆ *adv* **3** a variant of **downwards.**
▸'**downwardly** *adv*

downwards ('daʊnwədz) *or* **downward** *adv* **1** from a higher to a lower place, level, etc. **2** from an earlier time or source to a later.

downwind ('daʊn'wɪnd) *adv, adj* in the same direction towards which the wind is blowing; with the wind from behind.

downy ⓣ ('daʊnɪ) *adj* **downier, downiest. 1** covered with soft fine hair or feathers. **2** light, soft, and fluffy. **3** made from or filled with down. **4** *Brit. sl.* sharp-witted.
▸'**downiness** *n*

dowry ('daʊərɪ) *n, pl* **dowries. 1** the property brought by a woman to her husband at marriage. **2** a natural talent or gift. [C14: from Anglo-F *douarie,* from Med. L *dōtārium;* see DOWER]

dowse (daʊz) *vb* **dowses, dowsing, dowsed.** (*intr*) to search for underground water, minerals, etc., using a divining rod; divine. [C17: from ?]
▸'**dowser** *n*

doxology (dɒk'sɒlədʒɪ) *n, pl* **doxologies.** a hymn, verse, or form of words in Christian liturgy glorifying God. [C17: from Med. L *doxologia,* from Gk, from *doxologos* uttering praise, from *doxa* praise; see -LOGY]
▸**doxological** (,dɒksə'lɒdʒɪkᵊl) *adj*

doxy ('dɒksɪ) *n, pl* **doxies.** *Arch. sl.* a prostitute or mistress. [C16: prob. from MFlemish *docke* doll]

doyen ('dɔɪən) *n* the senior member of a group, profession, or society. [C17: from F, from LL *decānus* leader of a group of ten]
▸**doyenne** (dɔɪ'ɛn) *fem n*

doyley ('dɔɪlɪ) *n* a variant spelling of **doily.**

doz. *abbrev. for* dozen.

doze ⓣ (dəʊz) *vb* **dozes, dozing, dozed.** (*intr*) **1** to sleep lightly or intermittently. **2** (often foll. by *off*) to fall into a light sleep. ◆ *n* **3** a short sleep. [C17: prob. from ON *dūs* lull]
▸'**dozer** *n*

dozen ('dʌzᵊn) *determiner* **1** (preceded by *a* or a numeral) twelve or a group of twelve. ◆ *n, pl* **dozens** *or* **dozen. 2 by the dozen.** in large quantities. **3 daily dozen.** *Brit.* regular physical exercises. **4 talk nineteen to the dozen.** to talk without stopping. [C13: from OF *douzaine,* from *douze* twelve, from L *duodecim,* from *duo* two + *decem* ten]
▸'**dozenth** *adj*

dozy ⓣ ('dəʊzɪ) *adj* **dozier, doziest. 1** drowsy. **2** *Brit. inf.* stupid.
▸'**dozily** *adv* ▸'**doziness** *n*

DP *abbrev. for:* **1** data processing. **2** displaced person.

DPB (in New Zealand) *abbrev. for* domestic purposes benefit: an allowance paid to single parents.

DPhil *or* **DPh** *abbrev. for* Doctor of Philosophy. Also: **PhD.**

dpi *abbrev. for* dots per inch: a measure of the resolution of a typesetting machine, computer screen, etc.

DPP (in Britain) *abbrev. for* Director of Public Prosecutions.

dpt *abbrev. for:* **1** department. **2** depot.

dr *abbrev. for:* **1** Also: **dr.** dram. **2** debtor.

Dr *abbrev. for:* **1** Doctor. **2** Drive.

DR *abbrev. for* dry riser.

dr. *abbrev. for:* **1** debit. **2** drachma.

drab[1] ⓣ (dræb) *adj* **drabber, drabbest. 1** dull; dingy. **2** cheerless; dreary. **3** of the colour drab. ◆ *n* **4** a light olive-brown colour. [C16: from OF *drap* cloth, from LL *drappus,* ? of Celtic origin]
▸'**drably** *adv* ▸'**drabness** *n*

drab[2] (dræb) *Arch.* ◆ *n* **1** a slatternly woman. **2** a whore. ◆ *vb* **drabs, drabbing, drabbed. 3** (*intr*) to consort with prostitutes. [C16: of Celtic origin]

drachm (dræm) *n* **1** Also called: **fluid dram.** *Brit.* one eighth of a fluid ounce. **2** *US.* another name for **dram** (sense 2). **3** another name for **drachma.** [C14: learned var. of DRAM]

drachma ('drækmə) *n, pl* **drachmas** *or* **drachmae** (-miː). **1** the standard monetary unit of Greece. **2** *US.* another name for **dram** (sense 2). **3** a silver coin of ancient Greece. [C16: from L, from Gk *drakhmē* a handful, from *drassesthai* to seize]

drack *or* **drac** (dræk) *adj Austral. sl.* (of a woman) unattractive. [C20: ?from *Dracula's* daughter]

Draconian ⓣ (dreɪ'kəʊnɪən) *or* **Draconic** (dreɪ'kɒnɪk) *adj* (*sometimes not cap.*) **1** of or relating to Draco (Athenian statesman, 7th century B.C.) or his code of laws. **2** harsh.
▸**Dra'conianism** *n* ▸**Dra'conically** *adv*

Dracula ('drækjʊlə) *n* **1** a cruel or bloodthirsty person. **2** a person who preys ruthlessly on others. [C20: from the vampire in Bram Stoker's Gothic novel *Dracula* (1897)]

draff (dræf) *n* the residue of husks after fermentation of the grain in brewing, used as cattle fodder. [C13: from ON *draf*]

THESAURUS

down-market *adj* = **second-rate**, bush-league (*Austral. & NZ inf.*), cheap, cheap and nasty, inferior, lowbrow, low-grade, low-quality, shoddy, tacky (*inf.*), tawdry, two-bit (*US & Canad. sl.*)
Antonyms *adj* elite, exclusive, first-rate, high-brow, high-class, high-quality, posh (*inf., chiefly Brit.*), superior, top-quality, up-market

downpour *n* = **rainstorm**, cloudburst, deluge, flood, inundation, torrential rain

downright *adj* **1** = **blunt**, candid, forthright, frank, honest, open, outspoken, plain, sincere, straightforward, straight-from-the-shoulder, upfront (*inf.*) **2** = **complete**, absolute, arrant, blatant, categorical, clear, deep-dyed (*usually derogatory*), explicit, out-and-out, outright, plain, positive, simple, thoroughgoing, total, undisguised, unequivocal, unqualified, utter

downside *n* = **drawback**, bad *or* weak point, disadvantage, flip side, minus (*inf.*), other side of the coin (*inf.*), problem, snag, trouble
Antonyms *n* advantage, benefit, good *or* strong point, plus (*inf.*)

down-to-earth *adj* = **sensible**, common-sense, hard-headed, matter-of-fact, mundane, no-nonsense, plain-spoken, practical, realistic, sane, unsentimental

downtrodden *adj* **1** = **oppressed**, abused, afflicted, distressed, exploited, helpless, subjugated, subservient, tyrannized

downward *adj* **1** = **descending**, declining, earthward, heading down, sliding, slipping

downy *adj* **1** = **fluffy**, feathery, fleecy, plumate (*Zoology, Botany*), silky, soft, velvety, woolly

doze *vb* **1, 2** = **nap**, catnap, drop off (*inf.*), drowse, kip (*Brit. sl.*), nod, nod off (*inf.*), sleep, sleep lightly, slumber, snooze (*inf.*), zizz (*Brit. inf.*) ◆ *n* **3** = **nap**, catnap, forty winks (*inf.*), kip (*Brit. sl.*), little sleep, shuteye (*sl.*), siesta, snooze (*inf.*), zizz (*Brit. inf.*)

dozy *adj* **1** = **drowsy**, dozing, half asleep, nodding, sleepy **2** *Brit. informal* = **stupid**, daft (*inf.*), goofy (*inf.*), not all there, senseless, silly, simple, slow, slow-witted, witless

drab[1] *adj* **1, 2** = **dull**, cheerless, colourless, dingy, dismal, dreary, flat, gloomy, grey, lack-lustre, shabby, sombre, uninspired, vapid
Antonyms *adj* bright, cheerful, colourful, jazzy (*inf.*), vibrant, vivid

drabness *n* **1, 2** = **dullness**, banality, cheerlessness, colourlessness, dinginess, dreariness, flatness, gloom, gloominess, greyness, insipidity, monotony, sobriety, tediousness, vapidity
Antonyms *n* brightness, brilliance, character, cheerfulness, colour, colourfulness, gaiety, interest, liveliness, vividness

Draconian *adj* **2** *sometimes not cap.* = **severe**,

DICTIONARY

draft Ⓣ (drɑːft) *n* **1** a plan, sketch, or drawing of something. **2** a preliminary outline of a book, speech, etc. **3** another word for **bill of exchange.** **4** a demand or drain on something. **5** *US & Austral.* selection for compulsory military service. **6** detachment of military personnel from one unit to another. **7** *Austral. & NZ.* a group of livestock separated from the rest of the herd or flock. ◆ *vb (tr)* **8** to draw up an outline or sketch for. **9** to prepare a plan or design of. **10** to detach (military personnel) from one unit to another. **11** *US & Austral.* to select for compulsory military service. **12** *Austral. & NZ.* **12a** to select (cattle or sheep) from a herd or flock. **12b** to select (farm stock) for sale. ◆ *n, vb* **13** the usual US spelling of **draught.** [C16: var. of DRAUGHT]
▸ **'drafter** *n*

draftee (drɑːf'tiː) *n US.* a conscript.

drafty ('drɑːftɪ) *adj* **draftier, draftiest.** the usual US spelling of **draughty.**

drag Ⓣ (dræg) *vb* **drags, dragging, dragged. 1** to pull or be pulled with force, esp. along the ground. **2** *(tr; often foll. by away or from)* to persuade to come away. **3** to trail or cause to trail on the ground. **4** *(tr)* to move with effort or difficulty. **5** to linger behind. **6** (often foll. by *on* or *out*) to prolong or be prolonged unnecessarily or tediously: *his talk dragged on for hours.* **7** (when *intr,* usually foll. by *for*) to search (the bed of a river, etc.) with a dragnet or hook. **8** *(tr;* foll. by *out* or *from)* to crush (clods) or level (a soil surface) by use of a drag. **9** (of hounds) to follow (a fox or its trail). **10** *(intr) Sl.* to draw (on a cigarette, etc.). **11** *Computing.* to move (a graphics image) from one place to another on the screen using a mouse. **12 drag anchor.** (of a vessel) to move away from its mooring because the anchor has failed to hold. **13 drag one's feet** *or* **heels.** *Inf.* to act with deliberate slowness. ◆ *n* **14** the act of dragging or the state of being dragged. **15** an implement, such as a dragnet, dredge, etc., used for dragging. **16** a type of harrow used to crush clods, level soil, etc. **17** a coach with seats inside and out, usually drawn by four horses. **18** a braking device. **19** a person or thing that slows up progress. **20** slow progress or movement. **21** *Aeronautics.* the resistance to the motion of a body passing through a fluid, esp. through air. **22** the trail of scent left by a fox, etc. **23** an artificial trail of scent drawn over the ground for hounds to follow. **24** See **drag hunt. 25** *Inf.* a person or thing that is very tedious. **26** *Sl.* a car. **27** short for **drag race. 28** *Sl.* **28a** women's clothes worn by a man (esp. in **in drag**). **28b** *(as modifier): a drag show.* **28c** clothes collectively. **29** *Inf.* a draw on a cigarette, etc. **30** *US sl.* influence. **31** *Chiefly US sl.* a street (esp. in **main drag**). ◆ See also **drag out of, drag up.** [OE *dragan* to DRAW]

dragée (dræ'ʒeɪ) *n* **1** a sweet coated with a hard sugar icing. **2** a tiny beadlike sweet used for decorating cakes, etc. **3** a medicinal pill coated with sugar. [C19: from F; see DREDGE[2]]

draggle ('dræg^{ə}l) *vb* **draggles, draggling, draggled. 1** to make or become wet or dirty by trailing on the ground; bedraggle. **2** *(intr)* to lag; dawdle. [ME, prob. frequentative of DRAG]

drag hunt *n* **1** a hunt in which hounds follow an artificial trail of scent. **2** a club that organizes such hunts.
▸ **'drag-ˌhunt** *vb*

dragnet ('drægˌnɛt) *n* **1** a net used to scour the bottom of a pond, river, etc., as when searching for something. **2** any system of coordinated efforts to track down wanted persons.

dragoman ('drægəʊmən) *n, pl* **dragomans** *or* **dragomen.** (in some Middle Eastern countries, esp. formerly) a professional interpreter or guide. [C14: from F, from It., from Med. Gk *dragoumanos,* from Ar. *targumān,* ult. from Akkadian]

dragon ('drægən) *n* **1** a mythical monster usually represented as breathing fire and having a scaly reptilian body, wings, claws, and a long tail. **2** *Inf.* a fierce person, esp. a woman. **3** any of various very large lizards, esp. the Komodo dragon. **4** *Commerce.* a newly industrialized country, esp. one in SE Asia. **5 chase the dragon.** *Sl.* to smoke opium or heroin. [C13: from OF, from L *dracō,* from Gk *drakōn*]

dragonet ('drægənɪt) *n* a small fish with spiny fins, a flat head, and a tapering brighty coloured body. [C14 (meaning: small dragon): from F; applied to fish C18]

dragonfly ('drægənˌflaɪ) *n, pl* **dragonflies.** a predatory insect having a long slender body and two pairs of iridescent wings that are outspread at rest.

dragon light *n* an extremely powerful light used by police to dazzle and immobilize criminal suspects.

dragonnade (ˌdrægə'neɪd) *n* **1** *History.* the persecution of French Huguenots during the reign of Louis XIV by dragoons quartered in their villages and homes. **2** subjection by military force. ◆ *vb* **dragonnades, dragonnading, dragonnaded. 3** *(tr)* to subject to persecution by military troops. [C18: from F, from *dragon* DRAGOON]

dragoon Ⓣ (drə'guːn) *n* **1** (originally) a mounted infantryman armed with a carbine. **2** *(sometimes cap.)* a domestic fancy pigeon. **3a** a type of cavalryman. **3b** *(pl; cap. when part of a name): the Royal Dragoons.* ◆ *vb (tr)* **4** to coerce; force. **5** to persecute by military force. [C17: from F *dragon* (special use of DRAGON), soldier armed with a carbine]

drag out of *vb (tr, adv + prep)* to obtain or extract (a confession, statement, etc.), esp. by force. Also: **drag from.**

drag race *n* a type of motor race in which specially built or modified cars or motorcycles are timed over a measured course.
▸ **drag racing** *n*

dragster ('drægstə) *n* a car specially built or modified for drag racing.

drag up *vb (tr, adv) Inf.* **1** to rear (a child) poorly and in an undisciplined manner. **2** to introduce or revive (an unpleasant fact or story).

drain Ⓣ (dreɪn) *n* **1** a pipe or channel that carries off water, sewage, etc. **2** an instance or cause of continuous diminution in resources or energy; depletion. **3** *Surgery.* a device, such as a tube, to drain off pus, etc. **4 down the drain.** wasted. ◆ *vb* **5** *(tr;* often foll. by *off)* to draw off or remove (liquid) from. **6** *(intr;* often foll. by *away)* to flow (away) or filter (off). **7** *(intr)* to dry or be emptied as a result of liquid running off or flowing away. **8** *(tr)* to drink the entire contents of (a glass, etc.). **9** *(tr)* to consume or make constant demands on (resources, energy, etc.); exhaust. **10** *(intr)* to disappear or leave, esp. gradually. **11** (of a river, etc.) to carry off the surface water from (an area). **12** *(intr)* (of an area) to discharge its surface water into rivers, streams, etc. [OE *drēahnian*]
▸ **'drainer** *n*

drainage Ⓣ ('dreɪnɪdʒ) *n* **1** the process or a method of draining. **2** a system of watercourses or drains. **3** liquid, sewage, etc., that is drained away.

drainage basin *or* **area** *n* another name for **catchment area.**

draining board *n* a sloping grooved surface at the side of a sink, used for draining washed dishes, etc. Also called: **drainer.**

drainpipe ('dreɪnˌpaɪp) *n* a pipe for carrying off rainwater, sewage, etc.; downpipe.

drainpipes ('dreɪnˌpaɪps) *pl n* trousers with very narrow legs, worn esp. by teddy boys in the 1950s.

drake (dreɪk) *n* the male of any duck. [C13: ?from Low G]

Dralon ('dreɪlɒn) *n Trademark.* an acrylic fibre fabric used esp. for upholstery.

dram Ⓣ (dræm) *n* **1** one sixteenth of an ounce (avoirdupois). 1 dram is equivalent to 0.0018 kilogram. **2** *US.* one eighth of an apothecaries' ounce; 60 grains. 1 dram is equivalent to 0.0039 kilogram. **3** a small amount of an alcoholic drink, esp. a spirit; tot. **4** the standard monetary unit of Armenia. [C15: from OF *dragme,* from LL *dragma,* from Gk *drakhmē;* see DRACHMA]

DRAM *or* **D-RAM** ('diːræm) *n acronym for* dynamic random access memory: **a** a widely used type of random access memory. See **RAM**[1]. **b** a chip containing such a memory.

drama Ⓣ ('drɑːmə) *n* **1** a work to be performed by actors; play. **2** the genre of literature represented by works intended for the stage. **3** the art of the writing and production of plays. **4** a situation that is highly emotional, tragic, or turbulent. [C17: from LL: a play, from Gk: something performed, from *drān* to do]

dramatic Ⓣ (drə'mætɪk) *adj* **1** of drama. **2** like a drama in suddenness, emotional impact, etc. **3** striking; effective. **4** acting or performed in a flamboyant way.
▸ **dra'matically** *adv*

dramatic irony *n Theatre.* the irony occurring when the implications of a situation, speech, etc., are understood by the audience but not by the characters in the play.

dramatics (drə'mætɪks) *n* **1** *(functioning as sing or pl)* **1a** the art of acting or producing plays. **1b** dramatic productions. **2** *(usually functioning as pl)* histrionic behaviour.

dramatis personae ('drɑːmətɪs pə'səʊnaɪ) *pl n (often functioning as sing)* the characters in a play. [C18: from NL]

dramatist Ⓣ ('dræmətɪst) *n* a playwright.

THESAURUS

austere, drastic, hard, harsh, pitiless, punitive, stern, stringent

draft *n* **1, 2 = outline**, abstract, delineation, plan, preliminary form, rough, sketch, version **3 = order**, bill (*of exchange*), cheque, postal order ◆ *vb* **8, 9 = outline**, compose, delineate, design, draw, draw up, formulate, plan, sketch

drag *vb* **1 = pull**, draw, hale, haul, lug, tow, trail, tug, yank **4 = go slowly**, crawl, creep, inch, limp along, shamble, shuffle **5 = lag behind**, dawdle, draggle, linger, loiter, straggle, trail behind **6 drag on** *or* **out = last**, draw out, extend, keep going, lengthen, persist, prolong, protract, spin out, stretch out **13 drag one's feet** *or* **heels** *Informal* **= stall**, block, hold back, obstruct, procrastinate ◆ *n* **25** *Informal* **= nuisance**, annoyance, bore, bother, pain (*inf.*), pain in the arse (*taboo sl.*), pest

dragging *adj* **6 = tedious**, boring, dull, going slowly, humdrum, mind-numbing, monotonous, tiresome, wearisome

dragoon *vb* **4 = force**, browbeat, bully, coerce, compel, constrain, drive, impel, intimidate, railroad (*inf.*), strong-arm (*inf.*)

drain *n* **1 = pipe**, channel, conduit, culvert, ditch, duct, outlet, sewer, sink, trench, watercourse **2 = reduction**, depletion, drag, exhaustion, expenditure, sap, strain, withdrawal **4 down the drain = wasted**, gone, gone for good, lost, ruined ◆ *vb* **5 = remove**, bleed, draw off, dry, empty, evacuate, milk, pump off *or* out, tap, withdraw **6 = flow out**, discharge, effuse, exude, leak, ooze, seep, trickle, well out **8 = drink up**, finish, gulp down, quaff, swallow **9 = exhaust**, consume, deplete, dissipate, empty, sap, strain, tax, use up, weary

drainage *n* **3 = sewerage**, bilge (water), seepage, sewage, waste

dram *n* **3 = shot** (*inf.*), drop, glass, measure, slug, snifter (*inf.*), snort (*sl.*), tot

drama *n* **1 = play**, dramatization, show, stage play, stage show, theatrical piece **2 = theatre**, acting, dramatic art, dramaturgy, stagecraft, Thespian art **4 = excitement**, crisis, dramatics, histrionics, scene, spectacle, theatrics, turmoil

dramatic *adj* **1 = theatrical**, dramaturgic, dramaturgical, Thespian **2 = powerful**, affecting, effective, expressive, impressive, moving, striking, vivid **4 = exciting**, breathtaking, climactic, electrifying, emotional, high-octane (*inf.*), melodramatic, sensational, shock-horror (*facetious*), startling, sudden, suspenseful, tense, thrilling

Antonyms *adj* ≠ **powerful**: ordinary, run-of-the-mill, unexceptional, unmemorable

dramatist *n* **= playwright**, dramaturge, screenwriter, scriptwriter

dramatize Ⓣ *or* **dramatise** (ˈdræməˌtaɪz) *vb* **dramatizes, dramatizing, dramatized** *or* **dramatises, dramatising, dramatised. 1** (*tr*) to put into dramatic form. **2** to express (something) in a dramatic or exaggerated way.
▸ **ˌdramatiˈzation** *or* **ˌdramatiˈsation** *n*

dramaturge (ˈdræməˌtɜːdʒ) *n* **1** Also called: **dramaturgist.** a dramatist. **2** Also called: **dramaturg.** a literary adviser on the staff of a theatre, film company, etc. [C19: prob. from F, from Gk *dramatourgos* playwright, from DRAMA + *ergon* work]

dramaturgy (ˈdræməˌtɜːdʒɪ) *n* the art and technique of the theatre; dramatics.
▸ **ˌdramaˈturgic** *or* **ˌdramaˈturgical** *adj*

drank (dræŋk) *vb* the past tense of **drink**.

drape Ⓣ (dreɪp) *vb* **drapes, draping, draped. 1** (*tr*) to hang or cover with material or fabric, usually in folds. **2** to hang or arrange or be hung or arranged, esp. in folds. **3** (*tr*) to place casually and loosely. ◆ *n* **4** (*often pl*) a cloth or hanging that covers something in folds. **5** the way in which fabric hangs. [C15: from OF *draper,* from *drap* piece of cloth; see DRAB[1]]

draper (ˈdreɪpə) *n* **1** *Brit.* a dealer in fabrics and sewing materials. **2** *Arch.* a maker of cloth.

drapery (ˈdreɪpərɪ) *n, pl* **draperies. 1** fabric or clothing arranged and draped. **2** (*often pl*) curtains or hangings that drape. **3** *Brit.* the occupation or shop of a draper. **4** fabrics and cloth collectively.
▸ **ˈdraperied** *adj*

drapes (dreɪps) *or* **draperies** (ˈdreɪpərɪz) *pl n Chiefly US & Canad.* curtains, esp. ones of heavy fabric.

drastic Ⓣ (ˈdræstɪk) *adj* extreme or forceful; severe. [C17: from Gk *drastikos,* from *drān* to do, act]
▸ **ˈdrastically** *adv*

drat (dræt) *interj Sl.* an exclamation of annoyance. [C19: prob. alteration of *God rot*]

draught Ⓣ *or US* **draft** (drɑːft) *n* **1** a current of air, esp. in an enclosed space. **2a** the act of pulling a load, as by a vehicle or animal. **2b** (*as modifier*): *a draught horse.* **3** the load or quantity drawn. **4** a portion of liquid to be drunk, esp. a dose of medicine. **5** the act or an instance of drinking; a gulp or swallow. **6** the act or process of drawing air, etc., into the lungs. **7** the amount of air, etc., inhaled. **8a** beer, wine, etc., stored in bulk, esp. in a cask. **8b** (*as modifier*): *draught beer.* **8c on draught.** drawn from a cask or keg. **9** any one of the flat discs used in the game of draughts. US and Canad. equivalent: **checker. 10** the depth of a loaded vessel in the water. **11 feel the draught.** to be short of money. [C14: prob. from ON *drahtr,* of Gmc origin]

draughtboard (ˈdrɑːftˌbɔːd) *n* a square board divided into 64 squares of alternating colours, used for playing draughts or chess.

draughts (drɑːfts) *n* (*functioning as sing*) a game for two players using a draughtboard and 12 draughtsmen each. US and Canad. name: **checkers.** [C14: pl of DRAUGHT (in obs. sense: a chess move)]

draughtsman *or US* **draftsman** (ˈdrɑːftsmən) *n, pl* **draughtsmen** *or US* **draftsmen. 1** a person employed to prepare detailed scale drawings of machinery, buildings, etc. **2** a person skilled in drawing. **3** *Brit.* any of the flat discs used in the game of draughts. US and Canad. equivalent: **checker.**
▸ **ˈdraughtsmanˌship** *or US* **ˈdraftsmanˌship** *n*

draughty *or US* **drafty** (ˈdrɑːftɪ) *adj* **draughtier, draughtiest** *or US* **draftier, draftiest.** characterized by or exposed to draughts of air.
▸ **ˈdraughtily** *or US* **ˈdraftily** *adv* ▸ **ˈdraughtiness** *or US* **ˈdraftiness** *n*

Dravidian (drəˈvɪdɪən) *n* **1** a family of languages spoken in S and central India and Sri Lanka, including Tamil, Malayalam, etc. **2** a member of one of the aboriginal races of India, pushed south by the Indo-Europeans and now mixed with them. ◆ *adj* **3** of or denoting this family of languages or these peoples.

draw Ⓣ (drɔː) *vb* **draws, drawing, drew, drawn. 1** to cause (a person or thing) to move towards or away by pulling. **2** to bring, take, or pull (something) out, as from a drawer, holster, etc. **3** (*tr*) to extract or pull or take out: *to draw teeth.* **4** (*tr;* often foll. by *off*) to take (liquid) out of a cask, etc., by means of a tap. **5** (*intr*) to move, esp. in a specified direction: *to draw alongside.* **6** (*tr*) to attract: *to draw attention.* **7** (*tr*) to cause to flow: *to draw blood.* **8** to depict or sketch (a figure, picture, etc.) in lines, as with a pencil or pen. **9** (*tr*) to make, formulate, or derive: *to draw conclusions.* **10** (*tr*) to write (a legal document) in proper form. **11** (*tr;* sometimes foll. by *in*) to suck or take in (air, etc.). **12** (*intr*) to induce or allow a draught to carry off air, smoke, etc. **13** (*tr*) to take or receive from a source: *to draw money from the bank.* **14** (*tr*) to earn: *draw interest.* **15** (*tr*) to write out (a bill of exchange, etc.). **16** (*tr*) to choose at random. **17** (*tr*) to reduce the diameter of (a wire) by pulling it through a die. **18** (*tr*) to shape (metal or glass) by rolling, by pulling through a die, or by stretching. **19** *Archery.* to bend (a bow) by pulling the string. **20** to steep (tea) or (of tea) to steep in boiling water. **21** (*tr*) to disembowel. **22** (*tr*) to cause (pus, etc.) to discharge from an abscess or wound. **23** (*intr*) (of two teams, etc.) to finish a game with an equal number of points, goals, etc.; tie. **24** (*tr*) *Bridge, whist.* to keep leading a suit in order to force out (all outstanding cards). **25 draw trumps.** *Bridge, whist.* to play the trump suit until the opponents have none left. **26** (*tr*) *Billiards.* to cause (the cue ball) to spin back after a direct impact with another ball. **27** (*tr*) to search (a place) in order to find wild animals, etc., for hunting. **28** *Golf.* to cause (a golf ball) to move with a controlled right-to-left trajectory or (of a golf ball) to veer gradually from right to left. **29** (*tr*) *Naut.* (of a vessel) to require (a certain depth) in which to float. **30 draw and quarter.** to disembowel and dismember (a person) after hanging. **31 draw stumps.** *Cricket.* to close play. **32 draw the shot.** *Bowls.* to deliver the bowl in such a way that it approaches the jack. ◆ *n* **33** the act of drawing. **34** *US.* a sum of money advanced to finance anticipated expenses. **35** *Inf.* an event, act, etc., that attracts a large audience. **36** a raffle or lottery. **37** something taken at random, as a ticket in a lottery. **38** a contest or game ending in a tie. **39** *US & Canad.* a small natural drainage way or gully. ◆ See also **drawback, draw in,** etc. [OE *dragan*]

drawback Ⓣ (ˈdrɔːˌbæk) *n* **1** a disadvantage or hindrance. **2** a refund of customs or excise paid on goods that are being exported or used in making goods for export. ◆ *vb* **draw back.** (*intr, adv;* often foll. by *from*) **3** to retreat; move backwards. **4** to turn aside from an undertaking.

drawbridge (ˈdrɔːˌbrɪdʒ) *n* a bridge that may be raised to prevent access or to enable vessels to pass.

drawee (drɔːˈiː) *n* the person or organization on which an order for payment is drawn.

drawer (ˈdrɔːə) *n* **1** a person or thing that draws, esp. a draughtsman. **2** a person who draws a cheque. See **draw** (sense 15). **3** a person who draws up a commercial paper. **4** *Arch.* a person who draws beer, etc., in a bar. **5** (drɔː). a boxlike container in a chest, table, etc., made for sliding in and out.

drawers (drɔːz) *pl n* a legged undergarment for either sex, worn below the waist.

draw in *vb* (*intr, adv*) **1** (of hours of daylight) to become shorter. **2** (of a train) to arrive at a station.

drawing Ⓣ (ˈdrɔːɪŋ) *n* **1** a picture or plan made by means of lines on a surface, esp. one made with a pencil or pen. **2** a sketch or outline. **3** the art of making drawings; draughtsmanship.

drawing pin *n Brit.* a short tack with a broad smooth head for fastening papers to a drawing board, etc. US and Canad. name: **thumbtack.**

drawing room *n* **1** a room where visitors are received and entertained; living room; sitting room. **2** *Arch.* a formal reception.

drawknife (ˈdrɔːˌnaɪf) *or* **drawshave** *n, pl* **drawknives** *or* **drawshaves.** a tool with two handles, used to shave wood. US name: **spokeshave.**

drawl Ⓣ (drɔːl) *vb* **1** to speak or utter (words) slowly, esp. prolonging the vowel sounds. ◆ *n* **2** the way of speech of someone who drawls. [C16: prob. frequentative of DRAW]
▸ **ˈdrawling** *adj*

drawn Ⓣ (drɔːn) *vb* **1** the past participle of **draw.** ◆ *adj* **2** haggard, tired, or tense in appearance.

drawn work *n* ornamental needlework done by drawing threads out of the fabric and using the remaining threads to form lacelike patterns. Also called: **drawn-thread work.**

draw off *vb* (*adv*) **1** (*tr*) to cause (a liquid) to flow from something. **2** to withdraw (troops).

draw on Ⓣ *vb* **1** (*intr, prep*) to use or exploit (a source, fund, etc.). **2** (*intr, adv*) to come near. **3** (*tr, prep*) to withdraw (money) from (an account). **4** (*tr, adv*) to put on (clothes). **5** (*tr, adv*) to lead further; entice.

draw out Ⓣ *vb* (*adv*) **1** to extend. **2** (*tr*) to cause (a person) to talk freely. **3** (*tr;* foll. by *of*) Also: **draw from.** to elicit (information) (from). **4** (*tr*) to withdraw (money) as from a bank account. **5** (*intr*) (of hours of daylight) to become longer. **6** (*intr*) (of a train) to leave a station. **7** (*tr*) to extend (troops) in line. **8** (*intr*) (of troops) to proceed from camp.

THESAURUS

dramatize *vb* **2** = **exaggerate**, act, lay it on (thick) (*sl.*), make a performance of, overdo, overstate, play-act, play to the gallery

drape *vb* **1** = **cover**, adorn, array, cloak, fold, swathe, wrap **2** = **hang**, dangle, droop, drop, lean over, let fall, suspend

drastic *adj* = **extreme**, desperate, dire, forceful, harsh, radical, severe, strong

draught *n* **1** = **breeze**, current, flow, influx, movement, puff **2a** = **pulling**, dragging, drawing, haulage, traction **4** = **drink**, cup, dose, drench, potion, quantity

draw *vb* **1** = **pull**, drag, haul, tow, tug **3** = **take out**, extort, extract, pull out **6** = **attract**, allure, bring forth, call forth, elicit, engage, entice, evoke, induce, influence, invite, persuade **8** = **sketch**, delineate, depict, design, map out, mark out, outline, paint, portray, trace **9** = **deduce**, derive, get, infer, make, take **11** = **inhale**, breathe in, drain, inspire, puff, pull, respire, suck **16** = **choose**, pick, select, single out, take **18** = **stretch**, attenuate, elongate, extend, lengthen ◆ *n* **35** *Informal* = **attraction**, enticement, lure, pull (*inf.*) **38** = **tie**, dead heat, deadlock, impasse, stalemate

drawback *n* **1** = **disadvantage**, defect, deficiency, detriment, difficulty, downside, fault, flaw, fly in the ointment (*inf.*), handicap, hazard, hindrance, hitch, impediment, imperfection, nuisance, obstacle, snag, stumbling block, trouble
Antonyms *n* advantage, asset, benefit, gain, help, service, use

draw back *vb* **3** = **recoil**, back off, retract, retreat, shrink, start back, withdraw

drawing *n* **1, 2** = **picture**, cartoon, delineation, depiction, illustration, outline, portrayal, representation, sketch, study

drawl *vb* **1** = **draw out**, drag out, extend, lengthen, prolong, protract

drawling *adj* **1** = **droning**, dragging, drawly, dull, twanging, twangy

drawn *adj* **2** = **tense**, fatigued, fraught, haggard, harassed, harrowed, pinched, sapped, strained, stressed, taut, tired, worn

draw on *vb* **1** = **make use of**, employ, exploit, extract, fall back on, have recourse to, rely on, take from, use

draw out *vb* **1** = **extend**, drag out, lengthen, make longer, prolong, protract, spin out, stretch, string out
Antonyms *vb* curtail, cut, cut short, dock, pare down, reduce, shorten, trim, truncate

drawstring ('drɔːˌstrɪŋ) *n* a cord, etc., run through a hem around an opening, so that when it is pulled tighter, the opening closes.

draw up Ⓣ *vb* (*adv*) **1** to come or cause to come to a halt. **2** (*tr*) **2a** to prepare a draft of (a document, etc.). **2b** to formulate and write out: *to draw up a contract.* **3** (*used reflexively*) to straighten oneself. **4** to form or arrange (a body of soldiers, etc.) in order or formation.

dray[1] (dreɪ) *n* **a** a low cart used for carrying heavy loads. **b** (*in combination*): *a drayman.* [OE *dræge* dragnet]

dray[2] (dreɪ) *n* a variant spelling of **drey.**

dread Ⓣ (drɛd) *vb* (*tr*) **1** to anticipate with apprehension or terror. **2** to fear greatly. **3** *Arch.* to be in awe of. ◆ *n* **4** great fear. **5** an object of terror. **6** *Sl.* a Rastafarian. **7** *Arch.* deep reverence. [OE *ondrǣdan*]

dreadful Ⓣ ('drɛdful) *adj* **1** extremely disagreeable, shocking, or bad. **2** (intensifier): *a dreadful waste of time.* **3** causing dread; terrifying. **4** *Arch.* inspiring awe.

dreadfully Ⓣ ('drɛdfulɪ) *adv* **1** in a shocking or disagreeable manner. **2** (intensifier): *you're dreadfully kind.*

dreadlocks ('drɛdˌlɒks) *pl n Inf.* hair worn in the Rastafarian style of long tightly-curled strands.

dreadnought ('drɛdˌnɔːt) *n* **1** a battleship armed with heavy guns of uniform calibre. **2** an overcoat made of heavy cloth.

dream Ⓣ (driːm) *n* **1a** mental activity, usually an imagined series of events, occurring during sleep. **1b** (*as modifier*): *a dream sequence.* **1c** (*in combination*): *dreamland.* **2a** a sequence of imaginative thoughts indulged in while awake; daydream; fantasy. **2b** (*as modifier*): *a dream world.* **3** a person or thing seen or occurring in a dream. **4** a cherished hope; aspiration. **5** a vain hope. **6** a person or thing that is as pleasant or seemingly unreal as a dream. **7 go like a dream.** to move, develop, or work very well. ◆ *vb* **dreams, dreaming, dreamed** *or* **dreamt. 8** (*may take a clause as object*) to undergo or experience (a dream or dreams). **9** (*intr*) to indulge in daydreams. **10** (*intr*) to suffer delusions; be unrealistic. **11** (when *intr,* foll. by *of* or *about*) to have an image (of) or fantasy (about) in or as if in a dream. **12** (*intr;* foll. by *of*) to consider the possibility (of). ◆ *adj* **13** too good to be true; ideal: *dream kitchen.* [OE *drēam* song]
▸'**dreamer** *n*

dreamboat ('driːmˌbəʊt) *n Sl.* an ideal or desirable person, esp. one of the opposite sex.

dreamt (drɛmt) *vb* a past tense and past participle of **dream.**

dream ticket *n* a combination of two people, usually candidates in an election, that is considered to be ideal.

Dreamtime ('driːmˌtaɪm) *n* **1** Also called: **alcheringa.** (in the mythology of Australian Aboriginal peoples) a mythical golden age of the past, when the first men were created. **2** *Austral. inf.* any remote period, out of touch with the realities of the present.

dream up Ⓣ *vb* (*tr, adv*) to invent by ingenuity and imagination: *to dream up an excuse.*

dreamy Ⓣ ('driːmɪ) *adj* **dreamier, dreamiest. 1** vague or impractical. **2** resembling a dream. **3** relaxing; gentle. **4** *Inf.* wonderful. **5** having dreams, esp. daydreams.
▸'**dreamily** *adv* ▸'**dreaminess** *n*

dreary Ⓣ ('drɪərɪ) *adj* **drearier, dreariest. 1** sad or dull. **2** wearying; boring. ◆ Also (literary): **drear.** [OE *drēorig* gory]
▸'**drearily** *adv* ▸'**dreariness** *n*

dredge[1] (drɛdʒ) *n* **1** a machine used to scoop or suck up material from a riverbed, channel, etc. **2** another name for **dredger.** ◆ *vb* **dredges, dredging, dredged. 3** to remove (material) from a riverbed, etc., by means of a dredge. **4** (*tr*) to search for (a submerged object) with or as if with a dredge; drag. [C16: ? ult. from OE *dragan* to DRAW]

dredge[2] (drɛdʒ) *vb* **dredges, dredging, dredged.** to sprinkle or coat (food) with flour, etc. [C16: from OF *dragie,* ?from L *tragēmata* spices, from Gk]
▸'**dredger** *n*

dredger ('drɛdʒə) *n* **1** a vessel used for dredging. **2** another name for **dredge**[1] (sense 1).

dredge up Ⓣ *vb* (*tr, adv*) **1** *Inf.* to bring to notice, esp. with effort and from an obscure source. **2** to raise, as with a dredge.

dree (driː) *Scot., literary.* ◆ *vb* **drees, dreeing, dreed. 1** (*tr*) to endure. ◆ *adj* **2** dreary. [OE *drēogan*]

D region *or* **layer** *n* the lowest region of the ionosphere, extending from a height of about 60 km to about 90 km.

dregs Ⓣ (drɛgz) *pl n* **1** solid particles that settle at the bottom of some liquids. **2** residue or remains. **3 the dregs.** *Brit. sl.* a despicable person or people. [C14 *dreg,* from ON *dregg*]

dreich *or* **dreigh** (driːx) *adj Scot. dialect.* dreary. [ME *dreig, drih* enduring, from OE *drēog* (unattested)]

drench Ⓣ (drɛntʃ) *vb* (*tr*) **1** to make completely wet; soak. **2** to give liquid medicine to (an animal). ◆ *n* **3** a drenching. **4** a dose of liquid medicine given to an animal. [OE *drencan* to cause to drink]
▸'**drenching** *n, adj*

Dresden china *n n* porcelain ware, esp. delicate and elegantly decorative objects and figures of high quality, made at Meissen, near Dresden, Germany, since 1710.

dress Ⓣ (drɛs) *vb* **1** to put clothes on; attire. **2** (*intr*) to put on more formal attire. **3** (*tr*) to provide (someone) with clothing; clothe. **4** (*tr*) to arrange merchandise in (a shop window). **5** (*tr*) to arrange (the hair). **6** (*tr*) to apply protective or therapeutic covering to (a wound, sore, etc.). **7** (*tr*) to prepare (food, esp. fowl and fish) by cleaning, gutting, etc. **8** (*tr*) to put a finish on (stone, metal, etc.). **9** (*tr*) to cultivate (land), esp. by applying fertilizer. **10** (*tr*) to trim (trees, etc.). **11** (*tr*) to groom (a horse). **12** (*tr*) to convert (tanned hides) into leather. **13** *Angling.* to tie (a fly). **14** *Mil.* to bring (troops) into line or (of troops) to come into line (esp. in **dress ranks**). **15 dress ship.** *Naut.* to decorate a vessel by displaying signal flags on lines. ◆ *n* **16** a one-piece garment for a woman, consisting of a skirt and bodice. **17** complete style of clothing; costume: *military dress.* **18** (*modifier*) suitable for a formal occasion: *a dress shirt.* **19** outer covering or appearance. ◆ See also **dress down, dress up.** [C14: from OF *drecier,* ult. from L *dīrigere* to DIRECT]

dressage ('drɛsɑːʒ) *n* **a** the training of a horse to perform manoeuvres in response to the rider's body signals. **b** the manoeuvres performed. [F: preparation, from OF *dresser* to prepare; see DRESS]

dress circle *n* a tier of seats in a theatre or other auditorium, usually the first gallery, in which evening dress formerly had to be worn.

dress code *n* a set of rules or guidelines regarding the manner of dress acceptable in an office, restaurant, etc.

dress down Ⓣ *vb* (*adv*) **1** (*tr*) *Inf.* to reprimand severely or scold (a person). **2** (*intr*) to dress in casual clothes.

dresser[1] ('drɛsə) *n* **1** a set of shelves, usually also with cupboards, for storing or displaying dishes, etc. **2** *US.* a chest of drawers for storing clothing, often having a mirror on top. [C14 *dressour,* from OF *dreceore,* from *drecier* to arrange; see DRESS]

dresser[2] ('drɛsə) *n* **1** a person who dresses in a specified way: *a fashionable dresser.* **2** *Theatre.* a person employed to assist actors with their costumes. **3** a tool used for dressing stone, etc. **4** *Brit.* a person who assists a surgeon during operations. **5** *Brit.* See **window-dresser.**

THESAURUS

draw up *vb* **1** = **halt**, bring to a stop, pull up, run in, stop, stop short **2** = **draft**, compose, formulate, frame, prepare, write out

dread *vb* **1** = **fear**, anticipate with horror, cringe at, have cold feet (*inf.*), quail, shrink from, shudder, tremble ◆ *n* **4** = **fear**, affright, alarm, apprehension, aversion, awe, dismay, fright, funk (*inf.*), heebie-jeebies (*sl.*), horror, terror, trepidation

dreadful *adj* **1** = **terrible**, abysmal, alarming, appalling, atrocious, awful, dire, distressing, fearful, formidable, frightful, from hell (*inf.*), ghastly, grievous, hellacious (*US sl.*), hideous, horrendous, horrible, monstrous, shocking, tragic, tremendous

dreadfully *adv* **1** = **terribly**, abysmally, alarmingly, appallingly, awfully, badly, disgracefully, disreputably, frightfully, horrendously, horribly, inadequately, monstrously, reprehensibly, shockingly, unforgivably, wickedly, woefully, wretchedly **2** = **extremely**, awfully (*inf.*), badly, deeply, desperately, exceedingly, exceptionally, excessively, greatly, immensely, terribly, tremendously, very, very much

dream *n* **1a** = **vision**, delusion, hallucination, illusion, imagination, reverie, speculation, trance, vagary **2a** = **daydream**, fantasy, pipe dream **4** = **ambition**, aim, aspiration, design, desire, goal, Holy Grail (*inf.*), hope, notion, thirst, wish **6** = **delight**, beauty, gem, joy, marvel, pleasure, treasure ◆ *vb* **8** = **have dreams**, conjure up, envisage, fancy, hallucinate, imagine, think, visualize **9** = **daydream**, build castles in the air *or* in Spain, fantasize, stargaze

dreamer *n* **9** = **idealist**, daydreamer, Don Quixote, escapist, fantasist, fantasizer, fantast, romancer, theorizer, utopian, visionary, Walter Mitty

dream up *vb* = **invent**, concoct, contrive, cook up (*inf.*), create, devise, hatch, imagine, spin, think up

dreamy *adj* **1** = **impractical**, airy-fairy, dreamlike, fanciful, imaginary, quixotic, speculative, surreal, vague, visionary **3** = **relaxing**, calming, gentle, lulling, romantic, soothing **5** = **vague**, absent, abstracted, daydreaming, faraway, in a reverie, musing, pensive, preoccupied, with one's head in the clouds
Antonyms *adj* ≠ **impractical, vague:** *adj* commonsense, down-to-earth, feet-on-the-ground, practical, pragmatic, realistic, unromantic

dreary *adj* **1** = **dismal**, bleak, cheerless, comfortless, depressing, doleful, downcast, forlorn, funereal, gloomy, glum, joyless, lonely, lonesome, melancholy, mournful, sad, solitary, sombre, sorrowful, wretched **2** = **dull**, as dry as dust, boring, colourless, drab, ho-hum (*inf.*), humdrum, lifeless, mind-numbing, monotonous, routine, tedious, tiresome, uneventful, uninteresting, wearisome
Antonyms *adj* ≠ **dismal:** cheerful, happy, joyful ≠ **dull:** bright, interesting

dredge up *vb* **1** *Informal* = **dig up**, discover, drag up, draw up, fish up, raise, rake up, uncover, unearth

dregs *pl n* **1** = **sediment**, deposit, draff, dross, grounds, lees, residue, residuum, scourings, scum, trash, waste **3** = **scum**, *canaille,* down-and-outs, good-for-nothings, outcasts, rabble, ragtag and bobtail, riffraff

drench *vb* **1** = **soak**, drown, duck, flood, imbrue, inundate, saturate, souse, steep, swamp, wet ◆ *n* **4** *Veterinary* = **dose**, physic, purge

dress *vb* **1** = **put on**, attire, change, clothe, don, garb, robe, slip on *or* into **5** = **arrange**, adjust, comb (out), do (up), groom, prepare, set, straighten **6** = **bandage**, bind up, plaster, treat ◆ *n* **16** = **frock**, costume, ensemble, garment, get-up (*inf.*), gown, outfit, rigout (*inf.*), robe, suit **17** = **clothing**, apparel, attire, clothes, costume, garb, garments, gear (*inf.*), guise, habiliment, raiment (*arch. or poetic*), threads (*sl.*), togs, vestment
Antonyms *vb* ≠ **put on:** disrobe, divest oneself of, peel off (*sl.*), shed, strip, take off one's clothes

dress down *vb* **1** *Informal* = **reprimand**, bawl out (*inf.*), berate, carpet, castigate, chew out (*US & Canad. inf.*), give a rocket (*Brit. & NZ inf.*), haul over the coals, rap over the knuckles, read the riot act, rebuke, reprove, scold, slap on the wrist, tear into (*inf.*), tear (someone) off a strip (*Brit. inf.*), tell off (*inf.*), upbraid

dressing ('drɛsɪŋ) *n* **1** a sauce for food, esp. for salad. **2** the US and Canad. name for **stuffing** (sense 2). **3** a covering for a wound, etc. **4** fertilizer spread on land. **5** size used for stiffening textiles. **6** the processes in the conversion of hides into leather.
dressing-down *n Inf.* a severe scolding.
dressing gown *n* a full robe worn before dressing or for lounging.
dressing room *n* **1** *Theatre.* a room backstage for an actor to change clothing and to make up. **2** any room used for changing clothes.
dressing station *n Mil.* a first-aid post close to a combat area.
dressing table *n* a piece of bedroom furniture with a mirror and a set of drawers for clothes, cosmetics, etc.
dressmaker **T** ('drɛsˌmeɪkə) *n* a person whose occupation is making clothes, esp. for women.
▸ **'dressˌmaking** *n*
dress parade *n Mil.* a formal parade in dress uniform.
dress rehearsal *n* **1** the last rehearsal of a play, etc., using costumes, lighting, etc., as for the first night. **2** any full-scale practice.
dress shirt *n* a man's evening shirt, worn as part of formal evening dress.
dress suit *n* a man's evening suit, esp. tails.
dress uniform *n Mil.* formal ceremonial uniform.
dress up **T** *vb* (*adv*) **1** to attire (oneself or another) very smartly or elaborately. **2** to put fancy dress, etc., on. **3** (*tr*) to improve the appearance or impression of: *to dress up the facts.*
dressy **T** ('drɛsɪ) *adj* **dressier, dressiest. 1** (of clothes) elegant. **2** (of persons) dressing stylishly. **3** overelegant.
▸ **'dressiness** *n*
drew (druː) *vb* the past tense of **draw**.
drey *or* **dray** (dreɪ) *n* a squirrel's nest. [C17: from ?]
dribble **T** ('drɪbᵊl) *vb* **dribbles, dribbling, dribbled. 1** (*usually intr*) to flow or allow to flow in a thin stream or drops; trickle. **2** (*intr*) to allow saliva to trickle from the mouth. **3** (in soccer, basketball, hockey, etc.) to propel (the ball) by repeatedly tapping it with the hand, foot, or a stick. ◆ *n* **4** a small quantity of liquid falling in drops or flowing in a thin stream. **5** a small quantity or supply. **6** an act or instance of dribbling. [C16: frequentative of *drib*, var. of DRIP]
▸ **'dribbler** *n* ▸ **'dribbly** *adj*
driblet *or* **dribblet** ('drɪblɪt) *n* a small amount. [C17: from obs. *drib* to fall bit by bit + -LET]
dribs and drabs (drɪbz) *pl n Inf.* small sporadic amounts.
dried (draɪd) *vb* the past tense and past participle of **dry**.
drier[1] ('draɪə) *adj* a comparative of **dry**.
drier[2] ('draɪə) *n* a variant spelling of **dryer**[1].
driest ('draɪɪst) *adj* a superlative of **dry**.
drift **T** (drɪft) *vb* (*mainly intr*) **1** (*also tr*) to be carried along as by currents of air or water or (of a current) to carry (a vessel, etc.) along. **2** to move aimlessly from one place or activity to another. **3** to wander away from a fixed course or point; stray. **4** (*also tr*) (of snow, etc.) to accumulate in heaps or to drive (snow, etc.) into heaps. ◆ *n* **5** something piled up by the wind or current, as a snowdrift. **6** tendency or meaning: *the drift of the argument.* **7** a state of indecision or inaction. **8** the extent to which a vessel, aircraft, etc., is driven off course by winds, etc. **9** a general tendency of surface ocean water to flow in the direction of the prevailing winds. **10** a driving movement, force, or influence; impulse. **11** a controlled four-wheel skid used to take bends at high speed. **12** a deposit of sand, gravel, etc., esp. one transported and deposited by a glacier. **13** a horizontal passage in a mine that follows the mineral vein. **14** something, esp. a group of animals, driven along. **15** a steel tool driven into holes to enlarge or align them. **16** an uncontrolled slow change in some operating characteristic of a piece of equipment. **17** *S. African.* a ford. [C13: from ON: snowdrift]
driftage ('drɪftɪdʒ) *n* **1** the act of drifting. **2** matter carried along by drifting. **3** the amount by which an aircraft or vessel has drifted.
drifter **T** ('drɪftə) *n* **1** a person or thing that drifts. **2** a person who moves aimlessly from place to place. **3** a boat used for drift-net fishing.
drift ice *n* masses of ice floating in the sea.
drift net *n* a large fishing net that is allowed to drift with the tide or current.
driftwood ('drɪftˌwʊd) *n* wood floating on or washed ashore by the sea or other body of water.
drill[1] **T** (drɪl) *n* **1** a machine or tool for boring holes. **2** *Mil.* **2a** training in procedures or movements, as for parades or the use of weapons. **2b** (*as modifier*): *drill hall.* **3** strict and often repetitious training or exercises used in teaching. **4** *Inf.* correct procedure. **5** a marine mollusc that preys on oysters. ◆ *vb* **6** to pierce, bore, or cut (a hole) in (material) with or as if with a drill. **7** to instruct or be instructed in military procedures or movements. **8** (*tr*) to teach by rigorous exercises or training. **9** (*tr*) *Inf.* to riddle with bullets. [C17: from MDu. *drillen*]
▸ **'driller** *n*
drill[2] (drɪl) *n* **1** a machine for planting seeds in rows. **2** a furrow in which seeds are sown. **3** a row of seeds planted by means of a drill. ◆ *vb* **4** to plant (seeds) by means of a drill. [C18: from ?; cf. G *Rille* furrow]
▸ **'driller** *n*
drill[3] (drɪl) *n* a hard-wearing twill-weave cotton cloth, used for uniforms, etc. [C18: var. of G *Drillich*, from L *trilīx*, from TRI- + *līcium* thread]
drill[4] (drɪl) *n* an Old World monkey of W Africa, related to the mandrill. [C17: from a West African word]
drilling fluid *n* a fluid, usually consisting of a suspension of clay in water, pumped down when an oil well is being drilled. Also called: **mud**.
drilling platform *n* a structure, either fixed to the sea bed or mobile, which supports the drilling rig, stores, etc., required for drilling an offshore oil well.
drilling rig *n* **1** the complete machinery, equipment, and structures needed to drill an oil well. **2** a mobile drilling platform used for exploratory offshore drilling.
drillmaster ('drɪlˌmɑːstə) *n* **1** Also called: **drill sergeant.** a military drill instructor. **2** a person who instructs in a strict manner.
drill press *n* a machine tool for boring holes.
drily *or* **dryly** ('draɪlɪ) *adv* in a dry manner.
drink **T** (drɪŋk) *vb* **drinks, drinking, drank, drunk. 1** to swallow (a liquid). **2** (*tr*) to soak up (liquid); absorb. **3** (*tr; usually foll. by in*) to pay close attention to. **4** (*tr*) to bring (oneself) into a certain condition by consuming alcohol. **5** (*tr; often foll. by away*) to dispose of or ruin by excessive expenditure on alcohol. **6** (*intr*) to consume alcohol, esp. to excess. **7** (when *intr*, foll. by *to*) to drink (a toast). **8 drink the health of.** to salute or celebrate with a toast. **9 drink with the flies.** *Austral. inf.* to drink alone. ◆ *n* **10** liquid suitable for drinking. **11** alcohol or its habitual or excessive consumption. **12** a portion of liquid for drinking; draught. **13 the drink.** *Inf.* the sea. [OE *drincan*]
▸ **'drinkable** *adj* ▸ **'drinker** *n*
drink-driving *n* (*modifier*) of or relating to driving a car after drinking alcohol: *drink-driving offences.*
drinking fountain *n* a device for providing a flow or jet of drinking water, esp. in public places.
drinking-up time *n* (in Britain) a short time for finishing drinks after last orders in a public house.
drinking water *n* water reserved or suitable for drinking.
drip **T** (drɪp) *vb* **drips, dripping, dripped. 1** to fall or let fall in drops. ◆ *n* **2** the formation and falling of drops of liquid. **3** the sound made by falling drops. **4** a projection at the edge of a sill or cornice designed to throw water clear of the wall. **5** *Inf.* an inane, insipid person. **6** *Med.* **6a** the apparatus used for the intravenous drop-by-drop administration of a solution. **6b** the solution so administered. [OE *dryppan*, from *dropa* DROP]
drip-dry *adj* **1** designating clothing or a fabric that will dry relatively free of creases if hung up when wet. ◆ *vb* **drip-dries, drip-drying, drip-dried. 2** to dry or become dry thus.
drip-feed *vb* **drip-feeds, drip-feeding, drip-fed.** (*tr*) **1** to feed (someone) a liquid drop by drop, esp. intravenously. **2** *Inf.* to fund (a new company) in stages rather than by injecting a large sum at its inception. ◆ *n* **drip feed. 3** another term for **drip** (sense 6).

THESAURUS

dressmaker *n* = **seamstress**, couturier, modiste, sewing woman, tailor
dress up *vb* **1** = **dress formally**, doll up (*sl.*), dress for dinner, put on one's best bib and tucker (*inf.*), put on one's glad rags (*inf.*) **2** = **put on fancy dress**, disguise, play-act, wear a costume
dressy *adj* **1** = **elegant**, classy (*sl.*), elaborate, formal, ornate, ritzy (*sl.*), smart, stylish, swish (*inf., chiefly Brit.*)
dribble *vb* **1** = **run**, drip, drop, fall in drops, leak, ooze, seep, trickle **2** = **drool**, drip saliva, drivel, slaver, slobber
drift *vb* **1** = **float**, be carried along, coast, go (aimlessly), meander, stray, waft, wander **4** = **pile up**, accumulate, amass, bank up, drive, gather ◆ *n* **5** = **pile**, accumulation, bank, heap, mass, mound **6** = **meaning**, aim, design, direction, gist, implication, import, intention, object, purport, scope, significance, tendency, tenor, thrust **9** = **current**, course, direction, flow, impulse, movement, rush, sweep, trend
drifter *n* **2** = **wanderer**, bag lady (*chiefly US*), beachcomber, bum (*inf.*), hobo (*US*), itinerant, rolling stone, tramp, vagabond, vagrant
drill[1] *n* **1** = **boring tool**, bit, borer, gimlet, rotary tool **2a** = **training**, discipline, exercise, instruction, practice, preparation, repetition ◆ *vb* **6** = **bore**, penetrate, perforate, pierce, puncture, sink in **7, 8** = **train**, coach, discipline, exercise, instruct, practise, rehearse, teach
drink *vb* **1** = **swallow**, absorb, drain, gulp, guzzle, imbibe, partake of, quaff, sip, suck, sup, swig (*inf.*), swill, toss off, wash down, wet one's whistle (*inf.*) **3** *usually foll. by* **in** = **pay attention**, absorb, assimilate, be all ears (*inf.*), be fascinated by, be rapt, hang on (someone's) words, hang on the lips of **6** = **booze** (*inf.*), bend the elbow (*inf.*), bevvy (*dialect*), carouse, go on a binge *or* bender (*inf.*), hit the bottle (*inf.*), indulge, pub-crawl (*inf., chiefly Brit.*), revel, tipple, tope, wassail **7** *foll. by* **to** = **toast**, pledge, pledge the health of, salute ◆ *n* **10** = **beverage**, liquid, potion, refreshment, thirst quencher **11** = **alcohol**, booze (*inf.*), Dutch courage, hooch *or* hootch (*inf., chiefly US & Canad.*), liquor, spirits, the bottle (*inf.*) **12** = **glass**, cup, draught, gulp, noggin, sip, snifter (*inf.*), swallow, swig (*inf.*), taste, tipple **13 the drink** *Informal* = **the sea**, the briny (*inf.*), the deep, the main, the ocean
drinkable *adj* **1** = **fit to drink**, drinking, potable, quaffable
drinker *n* **4–6** = **alcoholic**, bibber, boozer (*inf.*), dipsomaniac, drunk, drunkard, guzzler, inebriate, lush (*sl.*), soak (*sl.*), sot, sponge (*inf.*), tippler, toper, wino (*inf.*)
drip *vb* **1** = **drop**, dribble, drizzle, exude, filter, plop, splash, sprinkle, trickle ◆ *n* **2** = **drop**, dribble, dripping, leak, trickle **5** *Informal* = **weakling**, milksop, mummy's boy (*inf.*),

dripping ('drɪpɪŋ) *n* **1** the fat exuded by roasting meat. **2** (*often pl*) liquid that falls in drops. ◆ *adv* **3** (intensifier): *dripping wet.*

drippy ('drɪpɪ) *adj* **drippier, drippiest. 1** *Inf.* mawkish, insipid, or inane. **2** tending to drip.

drive ⓘ (draɪv) *vb* **drives, driving, drove, driven. 1** to push, propel, or be pushed or propelled. **2** to guide the movement of (a vehicle, animal, etc.). **3** (*tr*) to compel or urge to work or act, esp. excessively. **4** (*tr*) to goad into a specified attitude or state: *work drove him mad.* **5** (*tr*) to cause (an object) to make (a hole, crack, etc.). **6** to move rapidly by striking or throwing with force. **7** *Sport.* to hit (a ball) very hard and straight. **8** *Golf.* to strike (the ball) with a driver. **9** (*tr*) to chase (game) from cover. **10** to transport or be transported in a vehicle. **11** (*intr*) to rush or dash violently, esp. against an obstacle. **12** (*tr*) to transact with vigour (esp. in **drive a hard bargain**). **13** (*tr*) to force (a component) into or out of its location by means of blows or a press. **14** (*tr*) *Mining.* to excavate horizontally. **15 drive home. 15a** to cause to penetrate to the fullest extent. **15b** to make clear by special emphasis. ◆ *n* **16** the act of driving. **17** a journey in a driven vehicle. **18** a road for vehicles, esp. a private road leading to a house. **19** vigorous pressure, as in business. **20** a united effort, esp. towards a common goal. **21** *Brit.* a large gathering of persons to play cards, etc. **22** energy, ambition, or initiative. **23** *Psychol.* a motive or interest, such as sex or ambition. **24** a sustained and powerful military offensive. **25a** the means by which force, motion, etc., is transmitted in a mechanism. **25b** (*as modifier*): *a drive shaft.* **26** *Sport.* a hard straight shot or stroke. **27** a search for and chasing of game towards waiting guns. **28** *Electronics.* the signal applied to the input of an amplifier. [OE *drīfan*]
▸'**drivable** *or* '**driveable** *adj*

drive at ⓘ *vb* (*intr, prep*) *Inf.* to intend or mean: *what are you driving at?*

drive-in *adj* **1** denoting a public facility or service designed to be used by patrons seated in their cars: *a drive-in bank.* ◆ *n* **2** *Chiefly US & Canad.* a cinema designed to be used in such a manner.

drivel ⓘ ('drɪvᵊl) *vb* **drivels, drivelling, drivelled** *or US* **drivels, driveling, driveled. 1** to allow (saliva) to flow from the mouth; dribble. **2** (*intr*) to speak foolishly. ◆ *n* **3** foolish or senseless talk. **4** saliva flowing from the mouth; slaver. [OE *dreflian* to slaver]
▸'**driveller** *or US* '**driveler** *n*

driven ('drɪvᵊn) *vb* the past participle of **drive.**

driver ('draɪvə) *n* **1** a person who drives a vehicle. **2 in the driver's seat.** in a position of control. **3** a person who drives animals. **4** a mechanical component that exerts a force on another to produce motion. **5** *Golf.* a club, a No. 1 wood, used for tee shots. **6** *Electronics.* a circuit whose output provides the input of another circuit. **7** *Computing.* a computer program that controls a device.
▸'**driverless** *adj*

drive-thru *n* **a** a takeaway restaurant, bank, etc., designed so that customers can use it without leaving their cars. **b** (*as modifier*): *a drive-thru restaurant.*

drive-time *n* **a** the time of day when many people are driving to or from work, considered as a broadcasting slot. **b** (*as modifier*): *the daily drive-time show.*

driveway ('draɪvˌweɪ) *n* a path for vehicles, often connecting a house with a public road.

driving chain *n Engineering.* a roller chain that transmits power from one toothed wheel to another. Also called: **drive chain.**

driving licence *n* an official document authorizing a person to drive a motor vehicle.

drizzle ⓘ ('drɪzᵊl) *n* **1** very light rain. ◆ *vb* **drizzles, drizzling, drizzled. 2** (*intr*) to rain lightly. [OE *drēosan* to fall]
▸'**drizzly** *adj*

drogue (drəʊg) *n* **1** any funnel-like device used as a sea anchor. **2a** a small parachute released behind an aircraft to reduce its landing speed. **2b** a small parachute released during the landing of a spacecraft. **3** a device towed behind an aircraft as a target for firing practice. **4** a device on the end of the hose of a tanker aircraft, to assist location of the probe of the receiving aircraft. **5** a windsock. [C18: prob. based ult. on OE *dragan* to DRAW]

droll ⓘ (drəʊl) *adj* amusing in a quaint or odd manner; comical. [C17: from F *drôle* scamp, from MDu.: imp]
▸'**drollness** *n* ▸'**drolly** *adv*

drollery ⓘ ('drəʊlərɪ) *n, pl* **drolleries. 1** humour; comedy. **2** *Rare.* a droll act, story, or remark.

-drome *n combining form.* **1** a course or race-course: *hippodrome.* **2** a large place for a special purpose: *aerodrome.* [via L from Gk *dromos* race, course]

dromedary ('drʌmədərɪ) *n, pl* **dromedaries.** a type of Arabian camel bred for racing and riding, having a single hump. [C14: from LL *dromedārius (camēlus),* from Gk *dromas* running]

-dromous *adj combining form.* moving or running: *anadromous; catadromous.* [via NL from Gk *-dromos,* from *dromos* a running]

drone[1] ⓘ (drəʊn) *n* **1** a male honeybee whose sole function is to mate with the queen. **2** a person who lives off the work of others. **3** a pilotless radio-controlled aircraft. [OE *drān;* see DRONE[2]]

drone[2] ⓘ (drəʊn) *vb* **drones, droning, droned. 1** (*intr*) to make a monotonous low dull sound. **2** (when *intr,* often foll. by *on*) to utter (words) in a monotonous tone, esp. to talk without stopping. ◆ *n* **3** a monotonous low dull sound. **4** *Music.* a sustained bass note or chord. **5** one of the single-reed pipes in a set of bagpipes. **6** a person who speaks in a low monotonous tone. [C16: rel. to DRONE[1] & MDu. *drōnen,* G *dröhnen*]
▸'**droning** *adj*

drongo ('drɒŋgəʊ) *n, pl* **drongos. 1** any of various songbirds of the Old World tropics, having a glossy black plumage. **2** *Austral. & NZ sl.* a slow-witted person. [C19: from Malagasy]

drool ⓘ (druːl) *vb* **1** (*intr;* often foll. by *over*) to show excessive enthusiasm (for) or pleasure (in); gloat (over). ◆ *vb, n* **2** another word for **drivel** (senses 1, 2, 4). [C19: prob. alteration of DRIVEL]

droop ⓘ (druːp) *vb* **1** to sag or allow to sag, as from weakness. **2** (*intr*) to be overcome by weariness. **3** (*intr*) to lose courage. ◆ *n* **4** the act or state of drooping. [C13: from ON *drūpa*]
▸'**drooping** *adj* ▸'**droopy** *adj*

drop ⓘ (drɒp) *n* **1** a small quantity of liquid that forms or falls in a spherical mass. **2** a very small quantity of liquid. **3** a very small quantity of anything. **4** something resembling a drop in shape or size. **5** the act or an instance of falling; descent. **6** a decrease in amount or value. **7** the vertical distance that anything may fall. **8** a steep incline or slope. **9** short for **fruit drop. 10** the act of unloading troops, etc., by parachute. **11** (in cable television) a short spur from a trunk cable that feeds signals to an individual house. **12** *Theatre.* See **drop curtain. 13** another word for **trap door** or **gallows. 14** *Chiefly US & Canad.* a slot through which an object can be dropped into a receptacle. **15** *Austral. cricket sl.* a fall of the wicket. **16** See **drop shot. 17 at the drop of a hat.** without hesitation or delay. **18 have the drop on (someone).** *US & NZ.* to have the advantage over (someone). ◆ *vb* **drops, dropping, dropped. 19** (of liquids) to fall or allow to fall in globules. **20** to fall or allow to fall vertically. **21** (*tr*) to allow to fall by letting go of. **22** to sink or fall or cause to sink to the ground, as from a blow, weariness, etc. **23** (*intr;* foll. by *back, behind,* etc.) to move in a specified manner, direction, etc. **24** (*intr;* foll. by *in, by,* etc.) *Inf.* to pay a casual visit (to). **25** to decrease in amount or value. **26** to sink or cause to sink to a lower position. **27** to make or become less in strength, volume, etc. **28** (*intr*) to decline in

THESAURUS

namby-pamby, ninny, softie (*inf.*), weed (*inf.*), wet (*Brit. inf.*)

drive *vb* **1** = **push**, herd, hurl, impel, propel, send, urge **2** = **operate**, direct, go, guide, handle, manage, motor, ride, steer, travel **4** = **goad**, actuate, coerce, compel, constrain, dragoon, force, harass, impel, motivate, oblige, overburden, overwork, press, prick, prod, prompt, railroad (*inf.*), rush, spur **5** = **thrust**, dig, hammer, plunge, push, ram, sink, stab ◆ *n* **17** = **run**, excursion, hurl (*Scot.*), jaunt, journey, outing, ride, spin (*inf.*), trip, turn **20** = **campaign**, action, advance, appeal, crusade, effort, push (*inf.*), surge **22** = **initiative**, ambition, effort, energy, enterprise, get-up-and-go (*inf.*), motivation, pep, pressure, push (*inf.*), vigour, zip (*inf.*)

drive at *vb Informal* = **mean**, aim, allude to, get at, have in mind, hint at, imply, indicate, insinuate, intend, intimate, refer to, signify, suggest

drivel *vb* **1** = **dribble**, drool, slaver, slobber **2** = **babble**, blether, gab (*inf.*), gas (*inf.*), maunder, prate, ramble, waffle (*inf., chiefly Brit.*) ◆ *n* **3** = **nonsense**, balderdash, balls (*taboo sl.*), bilge (*inf.*), blah (*sl.*), bosh (*inf.*), bull (*sl.*), bullshit (*taboo sl.*), bunk (*inf.*), bunkum *or* buncombe (*chiefly US*), cobblers (*Brit. taboo sl.*), crap (*sl.*), dross, eyewash (*inf.*), fatuity, garbage (*inf.*), gibberish, guff (*sl.*), hogwash, hokum (*sl., chiefly US & Canad.*), hot air (*inf.*), moonshine, pap, piffle (*inf.*), poppycock (*inf.*), prating, rot, rubbish, shit (*taboo sl.*), stuff, tommyrot, tosh (*sl., chiefly Brit.*), trash, tripe (*inf.*), twaddle, waffle (*inf., chiefly Brit.*) **4** = **saliva**, slaver, slobber

driving *adj* **22** = **forceful**, compelling, dynamic, energetic, galvanic, storming (*inf.*), sweeping, vigorous, violent

drizzle *n* **1** = **fine rain**, Scotch mist, smir (*Scot.*) ◆ *vb* **2** = **rain**, mizzle, shower, spot *or* spit with rain, spray, sprinkle

droll *adj* = **amusing**, clownish, comic, comical, diverting, eccentric, entertaining, farcical, funny, humorous, jocular, laughable, ludicrous, odd, oddball (*inf.*), off-the-wall (*sl.*), quaint, ridiculous, risible, waggish, whimsical

drollery *n* **1** = **humour**, absurdity, archness, buffoonery, farce, fun, jocularity, pleasantry, waggishness, whimsicality, wit

drone[1] *n* **2** = **parasite**, couch potato (*sl.*), idler, leech, loafer, lounger, scrounger (*inf.*), skiver (*Brit. sl.*), sluggard, sponger (*inf.*)

drone[2] *vb* **1** = **hum**, buzz, purr, thrum, vibrate, whirr **2 drone on** = **speak monotonously**, be boring, chant, drawl, intone, prose about, spout, talk interminably ◆ *n* **3** = **hum**, buzz, murmuring, purr, thrum, vibration, whirr, whirring

droning *adj* **1** = **humming**, buzzing, murmuring, purring, thrumming, vibrating, whirring **2** = **monotonous**, boring, drawling, soporific, tedious

drool *vb* **1 drool over** = **gloat over**, dote on, fondle, gush, make much of, pet, rave about (*inf.*), slobber over, spoil **2** = **dribble**, drivel, salivate, slaver, slobber, water at the mouth

droop *vb* **1** = **sag**, bend, dangle, drop, fall down, hang (down), sink **2** = **flag**, decline, diminish, fade, faint, languish, slump, wilt, wither

droopy *adj* **1** = **sagging**, drooping, flabby, floppy, languid, languorous, lassitudinous, limp, pendulous, stooped, wilting

drop *n* **1** = **droplet**, bead, bubble, driblet, drip, globule, pearl, tear **2, 3** = **dash**, dab, mouthful, nip, pinch, shot (*inf.*), sip, spot, taste, tot, trace, trickle **5, 6** = **decrease**, cut, decline, deterioration, downturn, fall-off, lowering, reduction, slump **7, 8** = **fall**, abyss, chasm, declivity, descent, plunge, precipice, slope ◆ *vb* **19** = **drip**, dribble, fall in drops, trickle **20** = **fall**, decline, depress, descend, diminish, dive, droop, lower, plummet, plunge, sink, tumble **24** *foll. by* **in** *Informal* = **visit**, blow in (*inf.*), call, call in, look in, look up, pop in, roll up (*inf.*), stop, turn up **33** = **set down**, deposit, leave, let off, unload **35** = **discontinue**, abandon, axe (*inf.*), cease, desert, forsake, give up, kick (*inf.*), leave, quit, relinquish, remit, terminate **36** *Informal* = **reject**, dis-

health or condition. **29** (*intr; sometimes foll. by into*) to pass easily into a condition: *to drop into a habit.* **30** (*intr*) to move gently as with a current of air. **31** (*tr*) to mention casually: *to drop a hint.* **32** (*tr*) to leave out (a word or letter). **33** (*tr*) to set down (passengers or goods). **34** (*tr*) to send or post: *drop me a line.* **35** (*tr*) to discontinue: *let's drop the matter.* **36** (*tr*) to cease to associate with. **37** (*tr*) *Sl., chiefly US.* to cease to employ. **38** (*tr; sometimes foll. by in, off, etc.*) *Inf.* to leave or deposit. **39** (of animals) to give birth to (offspring). **40** *Sl., chiefly US & Canad.* to lose (money). **41** (*tr*) to lengthen (a hem, etc.). **42** (*tr*) to unload (troops, etc.) by parachute. **43** (*tr*) *Naut.* to sail out of sight of. **44** (*tr*) *Sport.* to omit (a player) from a team. **45** (*tr*) to lose (a game, etc.). **46** (*tr*) *Golf, basketball, etc.* to hit or throw (a ball) into a goal. **47** (*tr*) to hit (a ball) with a drop shot. ◆ *n, vb* **48** *Rugby.* short for **drop kick** or **drop-kick.** ◆ See also **drop off, dropout, drops.** [OE *dropian*]

drop curtain *n Theatre.* a curtain that can be raised and lowered onto the stage.

drop-dead *adv Sl.* outstandingly or exceptionally: *drop-dead gorgeous.*

drop forge *n* a device for forging metal between two dies, one of which is fixed, the other acting by gravity or by pressure.
▸**'drop-ˌforge** *vb (tr)*

drop goal *n Rugby.* a goal scored with a drop kick during the run of play.

drop hammer *n* another name for **drop forge.**

drop-in centre *n* (in Britain) a daycentre run by the social services or a charity that clients may attend on an informal basis.

drop kick *n* **1** a kick in which the ball is dropped and kicked as it bounces from the ground. **2** a wrestling attack in which a wrestler leaps in the air and kicks his opponent. ◆ *vb* **drop-kick. 3** to kick (a ball, a wrestling opponent, etc.) by the use of a drop kick.

drop leaf *n* **a** a hinged flap on a table that can be raised to extend the surface. **b** (*as modifier*): *a drop-leaf table.*

droplet ('drɒplɪt) *n* a tiny drop.

drop lock *n Finance.* a variable-rate bank loan that is automatically replaced by a fixed-rate long-term bond if the long-term interest rates fall to a specified level.

drop off Ⓣ *vb (adv)* **1** (*intr*) to grow smaller or less. **2** (*tr*) to set down. **3** (*intr*) *Inf.* to fall asleep. ◆ *n* **drop-off. 4** a steep descent. **5** a sharp decrease.

dropout Ⓣ ('drɒpˌaʊt) *n* **1** a student who fails to complete a course. **2** a person who rejects conventional society. **3 drop-out.** *Rugby.* a drop kick taken to restart play. ◆ *vb* **drop out.** (*intr, adv; often foll. by of*) **4** to abandon or withdraw from (a school, job, etc.).

dropper ('drɒpə) *n* **1** a small tube having a rubber bulb at one end for dispensing drops of liquid. **2** a person or thing that drops.

droppings Ⓣ ('drɒpɪŋz) *pl n* the dung of certain animals, such as rabbits, sheep, and birds.

drops (drɒps) *pl n* any liquid medication applied by means of a dropper.

drop scone *n* a flat spongy cake made by dropping a spoonful of batter on a hot griddle.

drop shot *n* **a** *Tennis.* a softly played return that drops abruptly after clearing the net. **b** *Squash.* a shot that stops abruptly after hitting the front wall of the court.

dropsy ('drɒpsɪ) *n* **1** *Pathol.* a condition characterized by an accumulation of watery fluid in the tissues or in a body cavity. **2** *Sl.* a tip or bribe. [C13: from *ydropesie,* from L *hydrōpisis,* from Gk *hudrōps,* from *hudōr* water]
▸**dropsical** ('drɒpsɪkᵊl) *adj*

droshky ('drɒʃkɪ) *or* **drosky** ('drɒskɪ) *n, pl* **droshkies** *or* **droskies.** an open four-wheeled carriage, formerly used in Russia. [C19: from Russian, dim. of *drogi* wagon]

drosophila (drɒ'sɒfɪlə) *n, pl* **drosophilas** *or* **drosophilae** (-ˌliː). any of a genus of small flies that are widely used in laboratory genetics studies. Also called: **fruit fly.** [C19: NL, from Gk *drosos* dew + *-phila* -PHILE]

dross Ⓣ (drɒs) *n* **1** the scum formed on the surfaces of molten metals. **2** worthless matter; waste. [OE *drōs* dregs]
▸**'drossy** *adj* ▸**'drossiness** *n*

drought Ⓣ (draʊt) *n* **1** a prolonged period of scanty rainfall. **2** a prolonged shortage. [OE *drūgoth*]
▸**'droughty** *adj*

drove[1] (drəʊv) *vb* the past tense of **drive.**

drove[2] Ⓣ (drəʊv) *n* **1** a herd of livestock being driven together. **2** (*often pl*) a moving crowd of people. ◆ *vb* **droves, droving, droved.** (*tr*) **3** to drive (livestock), usually for a considerable distance. [OE *drāf* herd]

drover ('drəʊvə) *n* a person who drives sheep or cattle, esp. to and from market.

drown Ⓣ (draʊn) *vb* **1** to die or kill by immersion in liquid. **2** (*tr*) to get rid of: *he drowned his sorrows in drink.* **3** (*tr*) to drench thoroughly. **4** (*tr; sometimes foll. by out*) to render (a sound) inaudible by making a loud noise. [C13: prob. from OE *druncnian*]

drowse Ⓣ (draʊz) *vb* **drowses, drowsing, drowsed. 1** to be or cause to be sleepy, dull, or sluggish. ◆ *n* **2** the state of being drowsy. [C16: prob. from OE *drūsian* to sink]

drowsy Ⓣ ('draʊzɪ) *adj* **drowsier, drowsiest. 1** heavy with sleepiness; sleepy. **2** inducing sleep; soporific. **3** sluggish or lethargic; dull.
▸**'drowsily** *adv* ▸**'drowsiness** *n*

drub (drʌb) *vb* **drubs, drubbing, drubbed.** (*tr*) **1** to beat as with a stick. **2** to defeat utterly, as in a contest. **3** to drum or stamp (the feet). **4** to instil with force or repetition. ◆ *n* **5** a blow, as from a stick. [C17: prob. from Ar. *dáraba* to beat]

drubbing Ⓣ ('drʌbɪŋ) *n* **1** a beating. **2** a total defeat.

drudge Ⓣ (drʌdʒ) *n* **1** a person who works hard at wearisome menial tasks. ◆ *vb* **drudges, drudging, drudged. 2** (*intr*) to toil at such tasks. [C16: ?from *druggen* to toil]
▸**'drudger** *n* ▸**'drudgingly** *adv*

drudgery Ⓣ ('drʌdʒərɪ) *n, pl* **drudgeries.** hard, menial, and monotonous work.

drug Ⓣ (drʌg) *n* **1** any substance used in the treatment, prevention, or diagnosis of disease. Related adj: **pharmaceutical. 2** a chemical substance, esp. a narcotic, taken for the effects it produces. **3 drug on the market.** a commodity available in excess of demand. ◆ *vb* **drugs, drugging, drugged.** (*tr*) **4** to mix a drug with (food, etc.). **5** to administer a drug to. **6** to stupefy or poison with or as if with a drug. [C14: from OF *drogue,* prob. of Gmc origin]

drug addict Ⓣ *n* any person who is abnormally dependent on narcotic drugs.

drugget ('drʌgɪt) *n* a coarse fabric used as a protective floor covering, etc. [C16: from F *droguet* useless fabric, from *drogue* trash]

druggie ('drʌgɪ) *n Inf.* a drug addict.

druggist ('drʌgɪst) *n* a US and Canad. term for **pharmacist.**

drugstore ('drʌgˌstɔː) *n US & Canad.* a shop where medical prescriptions are made up and a wide variety of goods and sometimes light meals are sold.

druid ('druːɪd) *n* (*sometimes cap.*) **1** a member of an ancient order of priests in Gaul, Britain, and Ireland in the pre-Christian era. **2** a member of any of several modern movements attempting to revive druidism. [C16: from L *druides,* of Gaulish origin]
▸**'druidess** *fem n* ▸**dru'idic** *or* **dru'idical** *adj* ▸**'druidˌism** *n*

drum Ⓣ (drʌm) *n* **1** a percussion instrument sounded by striking a membrane stretched across the opening of a hollow cylinder or hemisphere. **2** the sound produced by a drum or any similar sound. **3**

THESAURUS

own, ignore, jilt, renounce, repudiate, throw over

drop off *vb* **1** = **decrease**, decline, diminish, dwindle, fall off, lessen, slacken **2** = **set down**, allow to alight, deliver, leave, let off **3** *Informal* = **fall asleep**, catnap, doze (off), drowse, have forty winks (*inf.*), nod (off), snooze (*inf.*)

drop out *vb* **4** = **leave**, abandon, back out, cop out (*sl.*), fall by the wayside, forsake, give up, quit, renege, stop, withdraw

droppings *pl n* = **excrement**, crap (*taboo sl.*), doo-doo (*inf.*), dung, excreta, faeces, guano, manure, ordure, shit (*taboo sl.*), stool, turd

dross *n* **1, 2** = **scum**, crust, debris, dregs, impurity, lees, recrement, refuse, remains, scoria, waste

drought *n* **1** = **dry spell**, aridity, dehydration, drouth (*Scot.*), dryness, dry weather, parchedness **2** = **shortage**, dearth, deficiency, insufficiency, lack, need, scarcity, want
Antonyms *n* ≠ **dry spell:** deluge, downpour, flood, flow, inundation, outpouring, rush, stream, torrent ≠ **shortage:** abundance, profusion

drove[2] *n* **1, 2** = **herd**, collection, company, crowd, flock, gathering, horde, mob, multitude, press, swarm, throng

drown *vb* **1** = **drench**, deluge, engulf, flood, go down, go under, immerse, inundate, sink, submerge, swamp **4** = **overpower**, deaden, engulf, muffle, obliterate, overcome, overwhelm, stifle, swallow up, wipe out

drowse *vb* **1** = **be sleepy**, be drowsy, be lethargic, doze, drop off (*inf.*), kip (*Brit. sl.*), nap, nod, sleep, slumber, snooze (*inf.*), zizz (*Brit. inf.*) ◆ *n* **2** = **sleep**, doze, forty winks (*inf.*), kip (*Brit. sl.*), nap, slumber, zizz (*Brit. inf.*)

drowsiness *n* **1** = **sleepiness**, doziness, heavy eyelids, languor, lethargy, oscitancy, sluggishness, somnolence, tiredness, torpidity, torpor
Antonyms *n* alertness, brightness, liveliness, perkiness, wakefulness

drowsy *adj* **1** = **sleepy**, comatose, dazed, dopey (*sl.*), dozy, drugged, half asleep, heavy, lethargic, nodding, somnolent, tired, torpid **2** = **peaceful**, dreamy, lulling, quiet, restful, sleepy, soothing, soporific
Antonyms *adj* ≠ **sleepy:** alert, awake, bright-eyed and bushy-tailed, full of beans (*inf.*), lively, perky

drubbing *n* **1** = **beating**, clobbering (*sl.*), flogging, hammering (*inf.*), licking (*inf.*), pasting (*sl.*), pounding, pummelling, thrashing, walloping (*inf.*), whipping **2** = **defeat**, clobbering, hammering (*inf.*), licking (*inf.*), pasting (*sl.*), thrashing, trouncing

drudge *n* **1** = **menial**, dogsbody (*inf.*), factotum, hack, maid *or* man of all work, plodder, scullion (*arch.*), servant, skivvy (*chiefly Brit.*), slave, toiler, worker ◆ *vb* **2** = **toil**, grind (*inf.*), keep one's nose to the grindstone, labour, moil (*arch. or dialect*), plod, plug away (*inf.*), slave, work

drudgery *n* = **menial labour**, chore, donkey-work, fag (*inf.*), grind (*inf.*), hack work, hard work, labour, skivvying (*Brit.*), slavery, slog, sweat (*inf.*), sweated labour, toil

drug *n* **1** = **medication**, medicament, medicine, physic, poison, remedy **2** = **dope** (*sl.*), narcotic, opiate, stimulant ◆ *vb* **5** = **dose**, administer a drug, dope (*sl.*), medicate, treat **6** = **knock out**, anaesthetize, deaden, numb, poison, stupefy

drug addict *n* = **junkie** (*inf.*), acid head (*inf.*), crack-head, dope-fiend (*sl.*), head (*inf.*), hophead (*inf.*), tripper (*inf.*)

drugged *adj* **2** = **stoned** (*sl.*), bombed (*sl.*), comatose, doped (*sl.*), dopey (*sl.*), flying (*sl.*), high (*inf.*), on a trip (*inf.*), out of it (*sl.*), out of one's mind (*sl.*), out to it (*Austral. & NZ sl.*), smashed (*sl.*), spaced out (*sl.*), stupefied, tripping (*inf.*), turned on (*sl.*), under the influence (*inf.*), wasted (*sl.*), wrecked (*sl.*), zonked (*sl.*)

drum *vb* **11** = **beat**, pulsate, rap, reverberate, tap, tattoo, throb **14** *foll. by* **into** = **drive home**, din into, hammer away, harp on, instil into, reiterate

an object that resembles a drum in shape, such as a large spool or a cylindrical container. **4** *Archit.* a cylindrical block of stone used to construct the shaft of a column. **5** short for **eardrum. 6** any of various North American fishes that utter a drumming sound. **7** a type of hollow rotor for steam turbines or axial compressors. **8** *Arch.* a drummer. **9 beat the drum for.** *Inf.* to attempt to arouse interest in. **10 the drum.** *Austral. inf.* the necessary information (esp. in **give (someone) the drum**). ◆ *vb* **drums, drumming, drummed. 11** to play (music) on or as if on a drum. **12** to tap rhythmically or regularly. **13** (*tr;* sometimes foll. by *up*) to summon or call by drumming. **14** (*tr*) to instil by constant repetition. ◆ See also **drum up.** [C16: prob. from MDu. *tromme,* imit.]

drumbeat ('drʌmˌbiːt) *n* the sound made by beating a drum.

drum brake *n* a type of brake used on the wheels of vehicles, consisting of two shoes that rub against the brake drum when the brake is applied.

drumhead ('drʌmˌhɛd) *n* **1** the part of a drum that is actually struck. **2** the head of a capstan. **3** another name for **eardrum.**

drumlin ('drʌmlɪn) *n* a streamlined mound of glacial drift. [C19: from Irish Gaelic *druim* ridge + *-lin* -LING[1]]

drum machine *n* a synthesizer specially programmed to reproduce the sound of drums and other percussion instruments in variable rhythms and combinations selected by the musician; the resulting beat is produced continually until stopped or changed.

drum major *n* the noncommissioned officer, usually of warrant officer's rank, who commands the corps of drums of a military band and who is in command of both the drums and the band when paraded together.

drum majorette *n* a girl who marches at the head of a procession, twirling a baton.

drummer ('drʌmə) *n* **1** a drum player. **2** *Chiefly US.* a travelling salesman.

drumstick ('drʌmˌstɪk) *n* **1** a stick used for playing a drum. **2** the lower joint of the leg of a cooked fowl.

drum up Ⓣ *vb* (*tr, adv*) to obtain (support, business, etc.) by solicitation or canvassing.

drunk Ⓣ (drʌŋk) *adj* **1** intoxicated with alcohol to the extent of losing control over normal functions. **2** overwhelmed by strong influence or emotion. ◆ *n* **3** a person who is drunk. **4** *Inf.* a drinking bout. [OE *druncen,* p.p. of *drincan* to drink]

drunkard Ⓣ ('drʌŋkəd) *n* a person who is frequently or habitually drunk.

drunken Ⓣ ('drʌŋkən) *adj* **1** intoxicated. **2** habitually drunk. **3** (*prenominal*) caused by or relating to alcoholic intoxication: *a drunken brawl.*
▸ **'drunkenly** *adv* ▸ **'drunkenness** *n*

drupe (druːp) *n* any fruit that has a fleshy or fibrous part around a stone that encloses a seed, as the peach, plum, and cherry. [C18: from L *druppa* wrinkled overripe olive, from Gk: olive]
▸ **drupaceous** (druːˈpeɪʃəs) *adj*

drupelet ('druːplɪt) *or* **drupel** ('druːpᵊl) *n* a small drupe, usually one of a number forming a compound fruit.

Druse *or* **Druze** (druːz) *n, pl* **Druse** *or* **Druze. a** a member of a religious sect, mainly living in Syria, Lebanon, and Israel, having certain characteristics in common with Muslims. **b** (*as modifier*): *Druse customs.* [C18: from Arabic *Durūz,* after Ismail al-*Darazi,* 11th-century founder of the sect]

dry Ⓣ (draɪ) *adj* **drier, driest** *or* **dryer, dryest. 1** lacking moisture; not damp or wet. **2** having little or no rainfall. **3** not in or under water. **4** having the water drained away or evaporated: *a dry river.* **5** not providing milk: *a dry cow.* **6** (of the eyes) free from tears. **7a** *Inf.* thirsty. **7b** causing thirst. **8** eaten without butter, jam, etc.: *dry toast.* **9** *Electronics* (of a soldered joint) imperfect because the solder has not adhered to the metal. **10** (of wine, etc.) not sweet. **11** not producing a mucous or watery discharge: *a dry cough.* **12** consisting of solid as opposed to liquid substances. **13** without adornment; plain: *dry facts.* **14** lacking interest: *a dry book.* **15** lacking warmth: *a dry greeting.* **16** (of humour) shrewd and keen in an impersonal, sarcastic, or laconic way. **17** *Inf.* opposed to or prohibiting the sale of alcoholic liquor: *a dry country.* ◆ *vb* **dries, drying, dried. 18** (when *intr,* often foll. by *off*) to make or become dry. **19** (*tr*) to preserve (fruit, etc.) by removing the moisture. ◆ *n, pl* **drys** *or* **dries. 20** *Brit. inf.* a Conservative politician who is a hard-liner. **21 the dry.** (*sometimes cap.*) *Austral. inf.* the dry season. ◆ See also **dry out, dry up.** [OE *drȳge*]
▸ **'dryness** *n*

dryad ('draɪəd, -æd) *n, pl* **dryads** *or* **dryades** (-əˌdiːz). *Greek myth.* a nymph or divinity of the woods. [C14: from L *Dryas,* from Gk *Druas,* from *drus* tree]

dry battery *n* an electric battery consisting of two or more dry cells.

dry cell *n* a primary cell in which the electrolyte is in the form of a paste or is treated in some way to prevent it from spilling.

dry-clean *vb* (*tr*) to clean (fabrics, etc.) with a solvent other than water.
▸ **ˌdry-'cleaner** *n* ▸ **ˌdry-'cleaning** *n*

dry dock *n* a dock that can be pumped dry for work on a ship's bottom.

dryer[1] ('draɪə) *n* **1** a person or thing that dries. **2** an apparatus for removing moisture by forced draught, heating, or centrifuging. **3** any of certain chemicals added to oils to accelerate their drying when used in paints, etc.

dryer[2] ('draɪə) *adj* a variant spelling of **drier**[1].

dry fly *n Angling.* **a** an artificial fly designed to be floated on the surface of the water. **b** (*as modifier*): *dry-fly fishing.*

dry hole *n* (in the oil industry) a well which proves unsuccessful.

dry ice *n* solid carbon dioxide used as a refrigerant, and to create billows of smoke in stage shows. Also called: **carbon dioxide snow.**

drying ('draɪɪŋ) *n* the processing of timber until it has a moisture content suitable for the purposes for which it is to be used.

dryly ('draɪlɪ) *adv* a variant spelling of **drily.**

dry measure *n* a unit or system of units for measuring dry goods, such as fruit, grains, etc.

dry out *vb* (*adv*) **1** to make or become dry. **2** to undergo or cause to undergo treatment for alcoholism or drug addiction.

dry point *n* **1** a technique of intaglio engraving with a hard steel needle, without acid, on a copper plate. **2** the sharp steel needle used. **3** the engraving or print produced.

dry riser *n* a vertical pipe, not containing water, having connections on different floors of a building for a fireman's hose to be attached. A fire tender can be connected at the lowest level to make water rise under pressure within the pipe. Abbrev.: **DR.**

dry rot *n* **1** crumbling and drying of timber, bulbs, potatoes, or fruit, caused by certain fungi. **2** any fungus causing this decay. **3** moral degeneration or corruption.

dry run *n* **1** *Mil.* practice in firing without live ammunition. **2** *Inf.* a rehearsal.

drysalter ('draɪˌsɔːltə) *n Obs.* a dealer in dyestuffs and gums, and in dried, tinned, or salted foods and edible oils.

dry-stone *adj* (of a wall) made without mortar.

dry up Ⓣ *vb* (*adv*) **1** (*intr*) to become barren or unproductive; fail. **2** to dry (dishes, cutlery, etc.) with a tea towel after they have been washed. **3** (*intr*) *Inf.* to stop talking or speaking.

DS *or* **ds** *Music. abbrev. for* dal segno.

DSc *abbrev. for* Doctor of Science.

DSC *Mil. abbrev. for* Distinguished Service Cross.

DSM *Mil. abbrev. for* Distinguished Service Medal.

DSO *Brit. mil. abbrev. for* Distinguished Service Order.

DSS *Brit. abbrev. for:* **1** Department of Social Security. **2** Director of Social Services.

DST *abbrev. for* Daylight Saving Time.

DSW (in New Zealand) *abbrev. for* Department of Social Welfare.

DTI (in Britain) *abbrev. for* Department of Trade and Industry.

DTP *abbrev for* desktop publishing.

DT's *Inf. abbrev. for* delirium tremens.

Du. *abbrev. for* Dutch.

dual Ⓣ ('djuːəl) *adj* **1** relating to or denoting two. **2** twofold; double. **3** (in the grammar of some languages) denoting a form of a word indicating that exactly two referents are being referred to. **4** *Maths, logic.* (of a pair of operators) convertible into one another by the distribution of negation over either. ◆ *n* **5** *Grammar.* **5a** the dual number. **5b** a dual form of a word. [C17: from L *duālis* concerning two, from *duo* two]
▸ **'dually** *adv* ▸ **duality** (djuːˈælɪtɪ) *n*

THESAURUS

drum up *vb* = **canvass**, attract, bid for, obtain, petition, round up, solicit

drunk *adj* **1** = **intoxicated**, babalas (*S. Afr.*), bacchic, bevvied (*dialect*), blitzed (*sl.*), blotto (*sl.*), bombed (*sl.*), Brahms and Liszt (*sl.*), canned (*sl.*), drunken, flying (*sl.*), fu' (*Scot.*), fuddled, half seas over (*inf.*), inebriated, legless (*inf.*), lit up (*sl.*), loaded (*sl., chiefly US & Canad.*), maudlin, merry (*Brit. inf.*), muddled, out of it (*sl.*), out to it (*Austral. & NZ sl.*), paralytic (*inf.*), pickled (*inf.*), pie-eyed (*sl.*), pissed (*taboo sl.*), plastered (*sl.*), rat-arsed (*taboo sl.*), sloshed (*sl.*), smashed (*sl.*), soaked (*inf.*), steamboats (*Scot. sl.*), steaming (*sl.*), stewed (*sl.*), stoned (*sl.*), tanked up (*sl.*), tiddly (*sl., chiefly Brit.*), tight (*inf.*), tipsy, tired and emotional (*euphemistic*), under the influence (*inf.*), wasted (*sl.*), well-oiled (*sl.*), wrecked (*sl.*), zonked (*sl.*) ◆ *n* **3** = **drunkard**, alcoholic, boozer (*inf.*), inebriate, lush (*sl.*), soak (*sl.*), sot, toper, wino (*inf.*)

drunkard *n* = **drinker**, alcoholic, carouser, dipsomaniac, drunk, lush (*sl.*), soak (*sl.*), sot, tippler, toper, wino (*inf.*)

drunken *adj* **1** = **intoxicated**, bevvied (*dialect*), bibulous, blitzed, blotto (*sl.*), bombed (*sl.*), boozing (*inf.*), Brahms and Liszt (*sl.*), drunk, flying (*sl.*), (gin-)sodden, inebriate, legless (*inf.*), lit up (*sl.*), out of it (*sl.*), out to it (*Austral. & NZ sl.*), paralytic (*inf.*), pissed (*taboo sl.*), rat-arsed (*taboo sl.*), red-nosed, smashed (*sl.*), sottish, steamboats (*Scot. sl.*), steaming (*sl.*), tippling, toping, under the influence (*inf.*), wasted (*sl.*), wrecked (*sl.*), zonked (*sl.*) **3** = **debauched**, bacchanalian, bacchic, boozy (*inf.*), dionysian, dissipated, orgiastic, riotous, saturnalian

drunkenness *n* **1-3** = **intoxication**, alcoholism, bibulousness, dipsomania, inebriation, insobriety, intemperance, sottishness, tipsiness

dry *adj* **1, 2** = **dehydrated**, arid, barren, desiccated, dried up, juiceless, moistureless, parched, sapless, thirsty, torrid, waterless **14** = **dull**, boring, dreary, ho-hum (*inf.*), monotonous, plain, tedious, tiresome, uninteresting **16** = **sarcastic**, cutting, deadpan, droll, keen, low-key, quietly humorous, sharp, sly ◆ *vb* **18** = **dehydrate**, dehumidify, desiccate, drain, make dry, parch, sear
Antonyms *adj* ≠ **dehydrated:** damp, humid, moist, wet ≠ **dull:** entertaining, interesting, lively ◆ *vb* ≠ **dehydrate:** moisten, wet

dryness *n* **1, 2** = **aridity**, aridness, dehumidification, dehydration, drought, thirst, thirstiness

dry up *vb* **1** = **become dry**, become unproductive, harden, mummify, shrivel up, wilt, wither, wizen

dual *adj* **1, 2** = **twofold**, binary, coupled, double, duplex, duplicate, matched, paired, twin

duality *n* **1** = **dualism**, dichotomy, doubleness, duplexity, polarity

dual carriageway *n Brit.* a road on which traffic travelling in opposite directions is separated by a central strip of turf, etc. US and Canad. name: **divided highway.**

dualism ('dju:əˌlɪzəm) *n* **1** the state of being twofold or double. **2** *Philosophy.* the doctrine that reality consists of two basic types of substance, usually taken to be mind and matter or mental and physical entities. Cf. **monism** (sense 1). **3a** the theory that the universe has been ruled from its origins by two conflicting powers, one good and one evil. **3b** the theory that there are two personalities, one human and one divine, in Christ.
▸**'dualist** *n* ▸**dual'istic** *adj*

dub[1] Ⓣ (dʌb) *vb* **dubs, dubbing, dubbed. 1** (*tr*) to invest (a person) with knighthood by tapping on the shoulder with a sword. **2** (*tr*) to invest with a title, name, or nickname. **3** (*tr*) to dress (leather) by rubbing. **4** *Angling.* to dress (a fly). [OE *dubbian*]

dub[2] (dʌb) *vb* **dubs, dubbing, dubbed. 1** to alter the soundtrack of (a film, etc.). **2** (*tr*) to provide (a film) with a new soundtrack, esp. in a different language. **3** (*tr*) to provide (a film or tape) with a soundtrack. ◆ *n* **4** the new sounds added. **5** *Music.* a style of record production associated with reggae, involving the use of echo, delay, etc. [C20: shortened from DOUBLE]

dub[3] (dʌb) *vb* **dubs, dubbing, dubbed.** *Austral. & NZ inf.* short for **double- bank.**

dubbin ('dʌbɪn) *n Brit.* a greasy preparation applied to leather to soften it and make it waterproof. [C18: from *dub* to dress leather]

dubbing[1] ('dʌbɪŋ) *n Films.* **1** the replacement of a soundtrack, esp. by one in another language. **2** the combination of several soundtracks. **3** the addition of a soundtrack to a film, etc.

dubbing[2] ('dʌbɪŋ) *n* **1** *Angling.* fibrous material used for the body of an artificial fly. **2** a variant of **dubbin.**

dubiety Ⓣ (dju:'baɪɪtɪ) *n, pl* **dubieties. 1** the state of being doubtful. **2** a doubtful matter. [C18: from LL *dubietās,* from L *dubius* DUBIOUS]

dub in *or* **up** *vb* (*adv*) *Sl.* to contribute to the cost of something: *we'll all dub in a fiver for the trip.*

dubious Ⓣ ('dju:bɪəs) *adj* **1** marked by or causing doubt. **2** uncertain; doubtful. **3** of doubtful quality; untrustworthy. **4** not certain in outcome. [C16: from L *dubius* wavering]
▸**'dubiously** *adv* ▸**'dubiousness** *n*

Dublin Bay prawn ('dʌblɪn) *n* a large prawn used in a dish of scampi.

dubnium ('dʌbˌnɪəm) *n* a synthetic transactinide element produced in minute quantities by bombarding plutonium with high-energy neon ions. Symbol: Du; atomic no. 105. [C20: from *Dubna,* city in Russia where it was first reported]

ducal ('dju:kᵊl) *adj* of a duke or duchy. [C16: from F, from LL *ducālis* of a leader, from L *dux* leader]

ducat ('dʌkət) *n* **1** any of various former European gold or silver coins. **2** (*often pl*) money. [C14: from OF, from OIt. *ducato* coin stamped with the doge's image]

duce ('du:tʃɪ) *n* leader. [C20: from It., from L *dux*]

Duce (*Italian* 'du:tʃe) *n* **Il** (il). the title assumed by Mussolini as leader of Fascist Italy (1922–43).

Duchenne dystrophy (du'ʃɛn) *or* **Duchenne muscular dystrophy** *n* the most common form of muscular dystrophy, usually affecting only boys. [after Guillaume *Duchenne* (1806–75), F neurologist]

duchess ('dʌtʃɪs) *n* **1** the wife or widow of a duke. **2** a woman who holds the rank of duke in her own right. ◆ *vb* **3** (*tr*) *Austral. inf.* to overwhelm with flattering attention. [C14: from OF *duchesse*]

duchy ('dʌtʃɪ) *n, pl* **duchies.** the territory of a duke or duchess; dukedom. [C14: from OF *duche,* from *duc* DUKE]

duck[1] (dʌk) *n, pl* **ducks** *or* **duck. 1** any of a family of aquatic birds, esp. those having short legs, webbed feet, and a broad blunt bill. **2** the flesh of this bird, used as food. **3** the female of such a bird, as opposed to the male (drake). **4** Also: **ducks.** *Brit. inf.* dear or darling: used as a term of address. See also **ducky. 5** *Cricket.* a score of nothing by a batsman. **6 like water off a duck's back.** *Inf.* without effect. [OE *dūce* duck, diver; rel. to DUCK[2]]

duck[2] Ⓣ (dʌk) *vb* **1** to move (the head or body) quickly downwards or away, esp. to escape observation or evade a blow. **2** to plunge suddenly under water. **3** (when *intr,* often foll. by *out*) *Inf.* to dodge or escape (a person, duty, etc.). **4** (*intr*) *Bridge.* to play a low card rather than try to win a trick. ◆ *n* **5** the act or an instance of ducking. [C14: rel. to OHG *tūhhan* to dive, MDu. *dūken*]
▸**'ducker** *n*

duck[3] (dʌk) *n* a heavy cotton fabric of plain weave, used for clothing, tents, etc. [C17: from MDu. *doek*]

duck[4] (dʌk) *n* an amphibious vehicle used in World War II. [C20: from code name DUKW]

duck-billed platypus *n* an amphibious egg-laying mammal of E Australia having dense fur, a broad bill and tail, and webbed feet.

duckboard ('dʌkˌbɔ:d) *n* a board or boards laid so as to form a path over wet or muddy ground.

ducking stool *n History.* a chair used for punishing offenders by plunging them into water.

duckling ('dʌklɪŋ) *n* a young duck.

ducks and drakes *n* (*functioning as sing*) **1** a game in which a flat stone is bounced across the surface of water. **2 make ducks and drakes of** *or* **play (at) ducks and drakes with.** *Inf.* to use recklessly; squander.

duck's arse *n* a hairstyle in which the hair is swept back to a point at the nape of the neck, resembling a duck's tail. Abbrev.: **DA.**

duck soup *n US sl.* something that is easy to do.

duckweed ('dʌkˌwi:d) *n* any of various small stemless aquatic plants that occur floating on still water in temperate regions.

ducky *or* **duckie** ('dʌkɪ) *Inf.* ◆ *n, pl* **duckies. 1** *Brit.* darling or dear: a term of endearment. ◆ *adj* **duckier, duckiest. 2** delightful; fine.

duct Ⓣ (dʌkt) *n* **1** a tube, pipe, or canal by means of which a substance, esp. a fluid or gas, is conveyed. **2** any bodily passage, esp. one conveying secretions or excretions. **3** a narrow tubular cavity in plants. **4** a channel or pipe carrying electric wires. **5** a passage through which air can flow, as in air conditioning. [C17: from L *ductus* a leading (in Med. L: aqueduct), from *dūcere* to lead]
▸**'ductless** *adj*

ductile Ⓣ ('dʌktaɪl) *adj* **1** (of a metal) able to sustain large deformations without fracture and able to be hammered into sheets or drawn out into wires. **2** able to be moulded. **3** easily led or influenced. [C14: from OF, from L *ductilis,* from *dūcere* to lead]
▸**ductility** (dʌk'tɪlɪtɪ) *n*

ductless gland *n Anat.* See **endocrine gland.**

dud Ⓣ (dʌd) *Inf.* ◆ *n* **1** a person or thing that proves ineffectual. **2** a shell, etc., that fails to explode. **3** (*pl*) *Old-fashioned.* clothes or belongings. ◆ *adj* **4** failing in its purpose or function. [C15 (in the sense: an article of clothing, a thing, used disparagingly): from ?]

dude (du:d, dju:d) *n Inf.* **1** *Western US & Canad.* a city dweller, esp. one holidaying on a ranch. **2** *US & Canad.* a dandy. **3** *US & Canad.* any person: often used to any male in direct address. [C19: from ?]
▸**'dudish** *adj* ▸**'dudishly** *adv*

dude ranch *n US & Canad.* a ranch used as a holiday resort.

dudgeon Ⓣ ('dʌdʒən) *n* anger or resentment (arch., except in **in high dudgeon**). [C16: from ?]

due Ⓣ (dju:) *adj* **1** (*postpositive*) immediately payable. **2** (*postpositive*) owed as a debt. **3** fitting; proper. **4** (*prenominal*) adequate or sufficient. **5** (*postpositive*) expected or appointed to be present or arrive. **6 due to.** attributable to or caused by. ◆ *n* **7** something that is owed, required, or due. **8 give (a person) his due.** to give or allow what is deserved or right. ◆ *adv* **9** directly or exactly. [C13: from OF *deu,* from *devoir* to owe, from L *debēre*]

> **USAGE NOTE** The use of *due to* as a compound preposition (*the performance has been cancelled due to bad weather*) was formerly considered incorrect, but is now acceptable.

duel Ⓣ ('dju:əl) *n* **1** a formal prearranged combat with deadly weapons between two people in the presence of seconds, usually to settle a quarrel. **2** a contest or conflict between two persons or parties. ◆ *vb* **duels, duelling, duelled** *or US* **duels, dueling, dueled.** (*intr*) **3** to fight in a duel. **4** to contest closely. [C15: from Med. L *duellum,* from L, poetical var. of *bellum* war; associated with L *duo* two]
▸**'dueller, 'duellist** *or US* **'dueler, 'duelist** *n*

duenna (dju:'ɛnə) *n* (in Spain and Portugal, etc.) an elderly woman retained by a family to act as governess and chaperon to girls. [C17: from Sp. *dueña,* from L *domina* lady]

due process of law *n* the administration of justice in accordance with established rules and principles.

dues Ⓣ (dju:z) *pl n* (*sometimes sing*) charges, as for membership of a club or organization; fees.

THESAURUS

dub[1] *vb* **1 = knight,** bestow, confer, confer knighthood upon, entitle **2 = name,** call, christen, denominate, designate, label, nickname, style, term

dubiety *n* **1, 2 = doubtfulness,** doubt, dubiosity, incertitude, indecision, misgiving, mistrust, qualm, scepticism, uncertainty

dubious *adj* **1 = doubtful,** ambiguous, debatable, dodgy (*Brit., Austral., & NZ inf.*), equivocal **2 = unsure,** doubtful, hesitant, iffy (*inf.*), leery, sceptical, uncertain, unconvinced, undecided, wavering **3 = suspect,** dodgy (*Brit., Austral., & NZ inf.*), fishy (*inf.*), questionable, shady (*inf.*), suspicious, undependable, unreliable, untrustworthy
Antonyms *adj* ≠ **unsure:** certain, definite, positive, sure ≠ **suspect:** dependable, reliable, trustworthy

duck[2] *vb* **1 = bob,** bend, bow, crouch, dodge, drop, lower, stoop **2 = plunge,** dip, dive, douse, dunk, immerse, souse, submerge, wet **3** *Informal* **= dodge,** avoid, body-swerve (*Scot.*), escape, evade, shirk, shun, sidestep

duct *n* **1 = pipe,** canal, channel, conduit, funnel, passage, tube

ductile *adj* **1, 2 = pliable,** extensible, flexible, malleable, plastic, pliant, tensile **3 = docile,** amenable, biddable, compliant, manageable, tractable, yielding

dud *Informal* ◆ *n* **1 = failure,** clinker (*sl., chiefly US*), flop (*inf.*), washout (*inf.*) ◆ *adj* **4 = useless,** broken, bust (*inf.*), duff (*Brit. inf.*), failed, inoperative, kaput (*inf.*), not functioning, valueless, worthless

dudgeon *n* **in high dudgeon = indignant,** angry, choked, fuming, offended, resentful, vexed

due *adj* **1, 2 = payable,** in arrears, outstanding, owed, owing, unpaid **3 = fitting,** appropriate, becoming, bounden, deserved, fit, just, justified, merited, obligatory, proper, requisite, right, rightful, suitable, well-earned **5 = expected,** expected to arrive, scheduled ◆ *n* **7 = right(s),** comeuppance, deserts, merits, prerogative, privilege ◆ *adv* **9 = directly,** dead, direct, exactly, straight, undeviatingly

duel *n* **1 = single combat,** affair of honour **2 = contest,** clash, competition, encounter, engagement, fight, head-to-head, rivalry ◆ *vb* **3, 4 = fight,** clash, compete, contend, contest, lock horns, rival, struggle, vie with

dues *pl n* **= membership fee,** charge, charges, contribution, fee, levy

duet (djuː'ɛt) *n* **1** a musical composition for two performers or voices. **2** a pair of closely connected individuals; duo. [C18: from It. *duetto* a little duet, from *duo* duet, from L: two]
▸**du'ettist** *n*

duff[1] (dʌf) *n* **1** a thick flour pudding boiled in a cloth bag. **2 up the duff.** *Sl.* pregnant. [C19: N English var. of DOUGH]

duff[2] ❶ (dʌf) *vb (tr)* **1** *Sl.* to give a false appearance to (old or stolen goods); fake. **2** (foll. by *up*) *Brit. sl.* to beat (a person) severely. **3** *Austral. sl.* to steal (cattle), altering the brand. **4** *Golf. inf.* to bungle a shot by hitting the ground behind the ball. ◆ *adj* **5** *Brit., Austral., & NZ inf.* bad or useless. [C19: prob. back formation from DUFFER]

duffel *or* **duffle** ('dʌfᵊl) *n* **1** a heavy woollen cloth. **2** *Chiefly US & Canad.* equipment or supplies. [C17: after *Duffel*, Belgian town]

duffel bag *n* a cylindrical drawstring canvas bag, originally used esp. by sailors for carrying personal articles.

duffel coat *n* a usually knee-length wool coat, usually with a hood and fastened with toggles.

duffer ❶ ('dʌfə) *n* **1** *Inf.* a dull or incompetent person. **2** *Sl.* something worthless. **3** *Austral. sl.* **3a** an unproductive mine. **3b** a person who steals cattle. [C19: from ?]

dug[1] (dʌg) *vb* the past tense and past participle of **dig.**

dug[2] (dʌg) *n* a nipple, teat, udder, or breast. [C16: of Scand. origin]

dugong ('duːgɒŋ) *n* a whalelike mammal occurring in shallow tropical waters from E Africa to Australia. [C19: from Malay *duyong*]

dugout ('dʌg,aʊt) *n* **1** a canoe made by hollowing out a log. **2** *Mil.* a covered excavation dug to provide shelter. **3** (at a sports ground) the covered bench where managers, substitutes, etc., sit. **4** (in the Canadian prairies) a reservoir dug on a farm in which water from rain and snow is collected for use in irrigation, watering livestock, etc.

duiker *or* **duyker** ('daɪkə) *n, pl* **duikers, duiker** *or* **duykers, duyker. 1** Also: **duikerbok.** any of various small African antelopes. **2** *S. African.* any of several cormorants, esp. the long-tailed shag. [C18: via Afrik., from Du. *duiker* diver, from *duiken* to dive]

duke (djuːk) *n* **1** a nobleman of high rank: in the British Isles standing above the other grades of the nobility. **2** the prince or ruler of a small principality or duchy. [C12: from OF *duc*, from L *dux* leader]
▸**'dukedom** *n*

dukes (djuːks) *pl n Sl.* the fists. [C19: from *Duke of Yorks* rhyming sl. for *forks* (fingers)]

dulcet ❶ ('dʌlsɪt) *adj* (of a sound) soothing or pleasant; sweet. [C14: from L *dulcis* sweet]

dulcimer ('dʌlsɪmə) *n* **1** a tuned percussion instrument consisting of a set of strings stretched over a sounding board and struck with hammers. **2** an instrument used in US folk music, with an elliptical body and usually three strings plucked with a goose quill. [C15: from OF *doulcemer*, from OIt. *dolcimelo*, from *dolce* (from L *dulcis* sweet) + *-melo*, ?from Gk *melos* song]

dull ❶ (dʌl) *adj* **1** slow to think or understand; stupid. **2** lacking in interest. **3** lacking in perception; insensitive. **4** lacking sharpness. **5** not acute, intense, or piercing. **6** (of weather) not bright or clear. **7** not active, busy, or brisk. **8** lacking in spirit; listless. **9** (of colour) lacking brilliance; sombre. **10** not loud or clear; muffled. ◆ *vb* **11** to make or become dull. [OE *dol*]
▸**'dullish** *adj* ▸**'dullness** *or* **'dulness** *n* ▸**'dully** *adv*

dullard ❶ ('dʌləd) *n* a dull or stupid person.

dulse (dʌls) *n* any of several seaweeds that occur on rocks and have large red edible fronds. [C17: from OIrish *duilesc* seaweed]

duly ❶ ('djuːlɪ) *adv* **1** in a proper manner. **2** at the proper time. [C14: see DUE, -LY[2]]

duma *Russian.* ('duːmə) *n Russian history.* **1** (*usually cap.*) the elective legislative assembly established by Tsar Nicholas II in 1905: overthrown in 1917. **2** (before 1917) any official assembly or council. **3** short for **State Duma**, the lower chamber of the Russian parliament. [C20: from *duma* thought, of Gmc origin]

dumb ❶ (dʌm) *adj* **1** lacking the power to speak; mute. **2** lacking the power of human speech: *dumb animals.* **3** temporarily bereft of the power to speak: *struck dumb.* **4** refraining from speech; uncommunicative. **5** producing no sound: *a dumb piano.* **6** made, done, or performed without speech. **7** *Inf.* **7a** dim-witted. **7b** foolish. ◆ See also **dumb down.** [OE]
▸**'dumbly** *adv* ▸**'dumbness** *n*

dumbbell ('dʌm,bɛl) *n* **1** an exercising weight consisting of a short bar with a heavy ball or disc at either end, used for single-arm movements. **2** a small wooden or rubber object of a similar shape used to train dogs in retrieval. **3** *Sl., chiefly US & Canad.* a fool.

dumb down *vb (tr)* to make less intellectually demanding or sophisticated: *the alleged dumbing down of BBC radio.*

dumbfound ❶ *or* **dumfound** (dʌm'faʊnd) *vb (tr)* to strike dumb with astonishment; amaze. [C17: from DUMB + (CON)FOUND]

dumb show *n* **1** formerly, a part of a play acted in pantomime. **2** meaningful gestures.

dumbstruck ('dʌm,strʌk) *adj* temporarily deprived of speech through shock or surprise.

dumbwaiter ('dʌm,weɪtə) *n* **1** *Brit.* **1a** a stand placed near a dining table to hold food. **1b** a revolving circular tray placed on a table to hold food. US and Canad. name: **lazy Susan. 2** a lift for carrying food, rubbish, etc., between floors.

dumdum ('dʌm,dʌm) *n* a soft-nosed bullet that expands on impact and inflicts extensive laceration. [C19: after *Dum-Dum*, town near Calcutta where orig. made]

dummy ❶ ('dʌmɪ) *n, pl* **dummies. 1** a figure representing the human form, used for displaying clothes, as a target, etc. **2a** a copy of an object, often lacking some essential feature of the original. **2b** (*as modifier*): *a dummy drawer.* **3** *Sl.* a stupid person. **4** *Derog., sl.* a person without the power of speech. **5** *Inf.* a person who says or does nothing. **6a** a person who appears to act for himself while acting on behalf of another. **6b** (*as modifier*): *a dummy buyer.* **7** *Mil.* a weighted round without explosives. **8** *Bridge.* **8a** the hand exposed on the table by the declarer's partner and played by the declarer. **8b** the declarer's partner. **9a** a prototype of a book, indicating the appearance of the finished product. **9b** a designer's layout of a page. **10** *Sport.* a feigned pass or move. **11** *Brit.* a rubber teat for babies to suck or bite on. US and Canad. equivalent: **pacifier. 12** (*modifier*) counterfeit; sham. **13** (*modifier*) (of a card game) played with one hand exposed or unplayed. **14 sell (someone) a dummy.** *Sport.* to trick (an opponent) with a dummy pass. [C16: see DUMB, -Y[3]]

dummy run ❶ *n* an experimental run; practice; rehearsal.

dump ❶ (dʌmp) *vb* **1** to drop, fall, or let fall heavily or in a mass. **2** (*tr*) to empty (objects or material) out of a container. **3** to unload or empty (a container), as by overturning. **4** (*tr*) **4a** *Inf.* to dispose of without subtlety or proper care. **4b** to dispose of (nuclear waste). **5** *Commerce.* to market (goods) in bulk and at low prices, esp. abroad, in

THESAURUS

duff[2] *adj* **5** *Brit., Austral., & NZ informal* = **useless**, bad, counterfeit, dud (*inf.*), fake, false, not working, worthless

duffer *n* **1** *Informal* = **clot** (*Brit. inf.*), blunderer, booby, bungler, clod, galoot (*sl., chiefly US*), lubber, lummox (*inf.*), oaf

dulcet *adj* = **sweet**, agreeable, charming, delightful, euphonious, harmonious, honeyed, mellifluent, mellifluous, melodious, musical, pleasant, pleasing, soothing

dull *adj* **1** = **stupid**, braindead (*inf.*), daft, dense, dim, dim-witted (*inf.*), doltish, dozy (*Brit. inf.*), obtuse, slow, stolid, thick, unintelligent **2** = **boring**, as dry as dust, commonplace, dozy, dreary, dry, flat, ho-hum (*inf.*), humdrum, mind-numbing, monotonous, plain, prosaic, run-of-the-mill, tedious, tiresome, unimaginative, uninteresting, vapid **4, 5** = **blunt**, blunted, dulled, edgeless, not keen, not sharp, unsharpened **6** = **cloudy**, dim, dismal, gloomy, leaden, opaque, overcast, turbid **8** = **lifeless**, apathetic, blank, callous, dead, empty, heavy, indifferent, insensible, insensitive, listless, passionless, slow, sluggish, unresponsive, unsympathetic, vacuous **9** = **drab**, faded, feeble, murky, muted, sombre, subdued, subfusc, toned-down ◆ *vb* **11** = **dampen**, deject, depress, discourage, dishearten, dispirit, sadden **11** = **relieve**, allay, alleviate, assuage, blunt, lessen, mitigate, moderate, palliate, paralyse, soften, stupefy, take the edge off **11** = **cloud**, darken, dim, fade, obscure, stain, sully, tarnish
Antonyms *adj* ≠ **stupid:** bright, clever, intelligent, sharp ≠ **boring:** exciting, interesting ≠ **blunt:** sharp ≠ **cloudy:** bright ≠ **lifeless:** active, full of beans (*inf.*), lively

dullard *n Old-fashioned* = **dolt**, blockhead, clod, dimwit (*inf.*), dope (*inf.*), dunce, fathead (*inf.*), gobshite (*Irish taboo sl.*), lamebrain (*inf.*), nitwit (*inf.*), numbskull *or* numskull, oaf

dullness *n* **1** = **stupidity**, dimness, dim-wittedness, dopiness (*sl.*), doziness, obtuseness, slowness, thickness **2** = **tediousness**, banality, dreariness, flatness, insipidity, monotony, vapidity **9** = **drabness**, colourlessness, dimness, dinginess, gloominess, greyness
Antonyms *n* ≠ **stupidity:** brightness, cleverness, intelligence, quickness, sharpness, smartness ≠ **tediousness:** colour, interest, liveliness ≠ **drabness:** brightness, brilliance, effulgence, incandescence, shine, sparkle

duly *adv* **1** = **properly**, accordingly, appropriately, befittingly, correctly, decorously, deservedly, fittingly, rightfully, suitably **2** = **on time**, at the proper time, punctually

dumb *adj* **1** = **mute**, at a loss for words, inarticulate, mum, silent, soundless, speechless, tongue-tied, voiceless, wordless **7** *Informal* = **stupid**, asinine, braindead (*inf.*), dense, dim-witted (*inf.*), dozy (*Brit. inf.*), dull, foolish, obtuse, thick, unintelligent
Antonyms *adj* ≠ **mute:** articulate ≠ **stupid:** bright, clever, intelligent, quick-witted, smart

dumbfound *vb* = **amaze**, astonish, astound, bewilder, bowl over (*inf.*), confound, confuse, flabbergast (*inf.*), flummox, nonplus, overwhelm, stagger, startle, stun, take aback

dumbfounded *adj* = **amazed**, astonished, astounded, at sea, bewildered, bowled over (*inf.*), breathless, confounded, confused, dumb, flabbergasted (*inf.*), flummoxed, gob- smacked (*Brit. sl.*), knocked for six (*inf.*), knocked sideways (*inf.*), lost for words, nonplussed, overcome, overwhelmed, speechless, staggered, startled, stunned, taken aback, thrown, thunderstruck

dummy *n* **1** = **model**, figure, form, lay figure, manikin, mannequin **2a** = **copy**, counterfeit, duplicate, imitation, sham, substitute **3** *Slang* = **fool**, berk, blockhead, charlie (*Brit. inf.*), coot, dickhead (*sl.*), dimwit (*inf.*), dipstick (*Brit. sl.*), divvy (*Brit. sl.*), dolt, dork (*sl.*), dullard, dumbass (*sl.*), dunce, fathead (*inf.*), geek (*sl.*), gobshite (*Irish taboo sl.*), idiot, jerk (*sl., chiefly US & Canad.*), lamebrain (*inf.*), nerd *or* nurd (*sl.*), nitwit (*inf.*), numbskull *or* numskull, oaf, pillock (*Brit. sl.*), plank (*Brit. sl.*), plonker (*sl.*), prat (*sl.*), prick (*sl.*), schmuck (*US sl.*), simpleton, wally (*sl.*), weenie (*US inf.*) ◆ *modifier* **12** = **imitation**, artificial, bogus, fake, false, mock, phoney *or* phony (*inf.*), sham, simulated

dummy run *n* = **practice**, mock, simulated, trial

dump *vb* **1** = **drop**, deposit, fling down, let fall, throw down **2–4** = **get rid of**, coup (*Scot.*), discharge, dispose of, ditch (*sl.*), empty out, jettison, scrap, throw away *or* out, tip, unload ◆ *n* **11** = **rubbish tip**, junkyard, refuse heap, rubbish

order to maintain a high price in the home market and obtain a share of the foreign markets. **6** (*tr*) to store (supplies, etc.) temporarily. **7** (*intr*) *Sl., chiefly US.* to defecate. **8** (*tr*) *Surfing.* (of a wave) to hurl a swimmer or surfer down. **9** (*tr*) *Austral. & NZ.* to compact (bales of wool) by hydraulic pressure. **10** (*tr*) *Computing.* to record (the contents of the memory) on a storage device at a series of points during a computer run. ◆ *n* **11** a place or area where waste materials are dumped. **12** a pile or accumulation of rubbish. **13** the act of dumping. **14** *Inf.* a dirty or unkempt place. **15** *Mil.* a place where weapons, supplies, etc., are stored. **16** *Sl., chiefly US.* an act of defecation. [C14: prob. from ON]

dumper ('dʌmpə) *n* **1** a person or thing that dumps. **2** *Surfing.* a wave that hurls a swimmer or surfer down.

dumpling ('dʌmplɪŋ) *n* **1** a small ball of dough cooked and served with stew. **2** a pudding consisting of a round pastry case filled with fruit: *apple dumpling.* **3** *Inf.* a short plump person. [C16: *dump-*, ? var. of LUMP[1] + -LING[1]]

dumps ⓣ (dʌmps) *pl n Inf.* a state of melancholy or depression (esp. in **down in the dumps**). [C16: prob. from MDu. *domp* haze]

dump truck *or* **dumper-truck** *n* a small truck used on building sites, having a load-bearing container at the front that can be tipped up to dump the contents.

dumpy ⓣ ('dʌmpɪ) *adj* **dumpier, dumpiest.** short and plump; squat. [C18: ? rel. to DUMPLING]
▸ **'dumpily** *adv* ▸ **'dumpiness** *n*

dun[1] ⓣ (dʌn) *vb* **duns, dunning, dunned. 1** (*tr*) to press (a debtor) for payment. ◆ *n* **2** a person, esp. a hired agent, who importunes another for the payment of a debt. **3** a demand for payment. [C17: from ?]

dun[2] (dʌn) *n* **1** a brownish-grey colour. **2** a horse of this colour. **3** *Angling.* **3a** an immature adult mayfly. **3b** an artificial fly resembling this. ◆ *adj* **dunner, dunnest. 4** of a dun colour. **5** gloomy. [OE *dunn*]

dunce ⓣ (dʌns) *n* a person who is stupid or slow to learn. [C16: from *Dunses* or *Dunsmen,* term of ridicule applied to the followers of John *Duns Scotus* (?1265–1308), Scot. scholastic theologian, esp. by 16th-cent. humanists]

dunce cap *or* **dunce's cap** *n* a conical paper hat, formerly placed on the head of a dull child at school.

Dundee cake (dʌn'diː) *n Chiefly Brit.* a fairly rich fruit cake decorated with almonds. [after *Dundee,* a port in E Scotland]

dunderhead ('dʌndəˌhɛd) *n* a slow-witted person. [C17: prob. from Du. *donder* thunder + HEAD]
▸ **'dunderˌheaded** *adj*

dune (djuːn) *n* a mound or ridge of drifted sand. [C18: via OF from MDu. *dūne*]

dung (dʌŋ) *n* **1** excrement, esp. of animals; manure. **2** something filthy. ◆ *vb* **3** (*tr*) to cover with manure. [OE: prison; rel. to OHG *tunc* cellar roofed with dung, ON *dyngja* manure heap]

dungaree (ˌdʌŋgə'riː) *n* **1** a coarse cotton fabric used chiefly for work clothes, etc. **2** (*pl*) **2a** a suit of workman's overalls made of this material, consisting of trousers with a bib attached. **2b** a casual garment resembling this, usually worn by women or children. **3** (*pl*) *US.* jeans. [C17: from Hindi, after *Dungrī,* district of Bombay, where this fabric originated]

dungeon ⓣ ('dʌndʒən) *n* **1** a prison cell, often underground. **2** a variant spelling of **donjon.** [C14: from OF *donjon*]

dunghill ('dʌŋˌhɪl) *n* **1** a heap of dung. **2** a foul place, condition, or person.

dunk (dʌŋk) *vb* **1** to dip (bread, etc.) in tea, soup, etc., before eating. **2** to submerge or be submerged. [C20: from Pennsylvania Du., from MHG *dunken,* from OHG *dunkōn*]
▸ **'dunker** *n*

dunlin ('dʌnlɪn) *n* a small sandpiper of northern and arctic regions, having a brown back and black breast in summer. [C16: DUN[2] + -LING[1]]

dunnage ('dʌnɪdʒ) *n* loose material used for packing cargo. [C14: from ?]

dunno (dʌ'nəʊ, də-) *Sl. contraction of* (I) do not know.

dunnock ('dʌnək) *n* another name for a **hedge sparrow.** [C15: from DUN[2] + -OCK]

dunny ('dʌnɪ) *n, pl* **dunnies. 1** *Scot. dialect.* a cellar or basement. **2** *Austral. & NZ inf.* a lavatory, esp. one which is outside. [C20: from ?]

duo ('djuːəʊ) *n, pl* **duos** *or* **dui** ('djuːiː). **1** *Music.* **1a** a pair of performers. **1b** a duet. **2** a pair of actors, etc. **3** *Inf.* a pair of closely connected individuals. [C16: via It. from L: two]

duo- *combining form.* indicating two. [from L]

duodecimal (ˌdjuːəʊ'dɛsɪməl) *adj* **1** relating to twelve or twelfths. ◆ *n* **2** a twelfth. **3** one of the numbers in a duodecimal number system.
▸ **ˌduo'decimally** *adv*

duodecimo (ˌdjuːəʊ'dɛsɪˌməʊ) *n, pl* **duodecimos. 1** Also called: **twelvemo.** a book size resulting from folding a sheet of paper into twelve leaves. **2** a book of this size. [C17: from L *in duodecimō* in twelfth]

duodenum (ˌdjuːəʊ'diːnəm) *n, pl* **duodena** (-nə) *or* **duodenums.** the first part of the small intestine, between the stomach and the jejunum. [C14: from Med. L, from *intestinum duodenum digitorum* intestine of twelve fingers' length]
▸ **ˌduo'denal** *adj*

duologue *or US (sometimes)* **duolog** ('djuːəˌlɒg) *n* **1** a part or all of a play in which the speaking roles are limited to two actors. **2** a less common word for **dialogue.**

duopoly (dju'ɒpəlɪ) *n, pl* **duopolies.** a situation in which control of a commodity or service in a particular market is vested in two producers or suppliers.
▸ **duˌopo'listic** *adj*

dup. *abbrev. for* duplicate.

dupe ⓣ (djuːp) *n* **1** a person who is easily deceived. ◆ *vb* **dupes, duping, duped. 2** (*tr*) to deceive; cheat; fool. [C17: from F, from OF *duppe,* contraction of *de huppe* of (a) hoopoe; from the bird's reputation for stupidity]
▸ **'dupable** *adj* ▸ **'duper** *n* ▸ **'dupery** *n*

duple ('djuːp[ə]l) *adj* **1** a less common word for **double. 2** *Music.* (of time or music) having two beats in a bar. [C16: from L *duplus* twofold]

duplex ('djuːplɛks) *n* **1** *US & Canad.* a duplex apartment or house. **2** *Biochem.* a double-stranded region in a nucleic acid molecule. ◆ *adj* **3** having two parts. **4** having pairs of components of independent but identical function. **5** permitting the transmission of simultaneous signals in both directions. [C19: from L: twofold, from *duo* two + *-plex* -FOLD]
▸ **du'plexity** *n*

duplex apartment *n US & Canad.* an apartment on two floors.

duplex house *n US & Canad.* a house divided into two separate dwellings. Also called (US): **semidetached.**

duplicate ⓣ *adj* ('djuːplɪkɪt). **1** copied exactly from an original. **2** identical. **3** existing as a pair or in pairs. ◆ *n* ('djuːplɪkɪt). **4** an exact copy. **5** something extra of the same kind. **6** two exact copies (esp. in **in duplicate**). ◆ *vb* ('djuːplɪˌkeɪt), **duplicates, duplicating, duplicated.** (*tr*) **7** to make a replica of. **8** to do or make again. **9** to make in a pair; make double. [C15: from L *duplicāre* to double, from *duo* two + *plicāre* to fold]
▸ **'duplicable** *adj*

duplication (ˌdjuːplɪ'keɪʃən) *n* **1** the act of duplicating or the state of being duplicated. **2** a copy; duplicate. **3** *Genetics.* a mutation in which there are two or more copies of a gene or of a segment of a chromosome.

duplicator ('djuːplɪˌkeɪtə) *n* an apparatus for making replicas of an original, such as a machine using a stencil wrapped on an ink-loaded drum.

duplicity ⓣ (djuː'plɪsɪtɪ) *n, pl* **duplicities.** deception; double-dealing. [C15: from OF *duplicite,* from LL *duplicitās* a being double, from L DUPLEX]

durable ⓣ ('djʊərəb[ə]l) *adj* long-lasting; enduring. [C14: from OF, from L *dūrābilis,* from *dūrāre* to last]
▸ **ˌdura'bility** *n* ▸ **'durably** *adv*

durable goods *pl n* goods that require infrequent replacement. Also called: **durables.**

dural ('djʊərəl) *adj* relating to or affecting the dura mater.

Duralumin (djʊ'ræljʊmɪn) *n Trademark.* a light strong aluminium alloy containing copper, silicon, magnesium, and manganese.

dura mater ('djʊərə 'meɪtə) *n* the outermost and toughest of the three membranes covering the brain and spinal cord. Often shortened to **dura.** [C15: from Med. L: hard mother]

duramen (djʊ'reɪmɛn) *n* another name for **heartwood.** [C19: from L: hardness, from *dūrāre* to harden]

THESAURUS

heap, tip **14** *Informal* = **pigsty**, hole (*inf.*), hovel, joint, mess, shack, shanty, slum

dumps *pl n As in* **down in the dumps** = **low spirits**, blues, dejection, depression, despondency, dolour, gloom, gloominess, melancholy, mopes, sadness, the hump (*Brit. inf.*), unhappiness, woe

dumpy *adj* = **podgy**, chubby, chunky, fubsy (*arch. or dialect*), homely, plump, pudgy, roly-poly, short, squab, squat, stout, tubby

dun[1] *vb* **1** = **pester**, beset, importune, plague, press, urge

dunce *n* = **simpleton**, ass, blockhead, bonehead, dimwit (*inf.*), dolt, donkey, duffer (*inf.*), dullard, dunderhead, fathead (*inf.*), goose (*inf.*), halfwit, ignoramus, lamebrain (*inf.*), loon (*inf.*), moron, nincompoop, nitwit (*inf.*), numbskull *or* numskull, oaf, thickhead

dungeon *n* **1** = **prison**, cage, calaboose (*US. inf.*), cell, donjon, lockup, oubliette, vault

dupe *n* **1** = **victim**, fall guy (*inf.*), gull, mug (*Brit. sl.*), pigeon (*sl.*), pushover, sap (*sl.*), simpleton, sucker (*sl.*) ◆ *vb* **2** = **deceive**, bamboozle (*inf.*), beguile, cheat, con (*inf.*), cozen, defraud, delude, gull (*arch.*), hoax, hoodwink, humbug, kid (*inf.*), outwit, overreach, pull a fast one on (*inf.*), rip off (*sl.*), swindle, take for a ride (*inf.*), trick

duplicate *adj* **1-3** = **identical**, corresponding, matched, matching, twin, twofold ◆ *n* **4, 5** = **copy**, carbon copy, clone, dead ringer (*sl.*), double, facsimile, fax, likeness, lookalike, match, mate, photocopy, Photostat (*Trademark*), replica, reproduction, ringer (*sl.*), twin, Xerox (*Trademark*) ◆ *vb* **7-9** = **copy**, clone, double, echo, fax, photocopy, Photostat (*Trademark*), reinvent the wheel, repeat, replicate, reproduce, Xerox (*Trademark*)

duplicity *n* = **deceit**, artifice, chicanery, deception, dishonesty, dissimulation, double-dealing, falsehood, fraud, guile, hypocrisy, perfidy
Antonyms *n* candour, honesty, straightforwardness

durability *n* = **durableness**, constancy, endurance, imperishability, lastingness, permanence, persistence

durable *adj* = **long-lasting**, abiding, constant, dependable, enduring, fast, firm, fixed, hard-wearing, lasting, permanent, persistent, reliable, resistant, sound, stable, strong, sturdy, substantial, tough
Antonyms *adj* breakable, brittle, delicate, fragile, impermanent, perishable, weak

durance ('djʊərəns) *n Arch. or literary.* **1** imprisonment. **2** duration. [C15: from OF, from *durer* to last, from L *dūrāre*]

duration ❶ (djʊ'reɪʃən) *n* the length of time that something lasts or continues. [C14: from Med. L *dūrātiō*, from L *dūrāre* to last]
▸**du'rational** *adj*

durative ('djʊərətɪv) *Grammar.* ◆ *adj* **1** denoting an aspect of verbs that includes the imperfective and the progressive. ◆ *n* **2a** the durative aspect of a verb. **2b** a verb in this aspect.

durbar ('dɜːbɑː, ˌdɜː'bɑː) *n* **a** (formerly) the court of a native ruler or a governor in India. **b** a levee at such a court. [C17: from Hindi *darbār*, from Persian, from *dar* door + *bār* entry, audience]

duress ❶ (djʊ'rɛs, djʊə-) *n* **1** compulsion by use of force or threat; coercion (often in **under duress**). **2** imprisonment. [C14: from OF *duresse*, from L *dūritia* hardness, from *dūrus* hard]

Durga Puja (ˌdʊəgə 'puːdʒə) *n* another name for **Navaratri.** [from Sanskr. *Durga* (Hindu goddess) and *puja* worship]

during ('djʊərɪŋ) *prep* **1** concurrently with (some other activity). **2** within the limit of (a period of time). [C14: from *duren* to last, ult. from L *dūrare* to last]

durmast *or* **durmast oak** ('dɜːˌmɑːst) *n* a large Eurasian oak tree with lobed leaves and sessile acorns. Also called: **sessile oak.** [C18: prob. from DUN[2] + MAST[2]]

durra ('dʌrə) *n* an Old World variety of sorghum, cultivated for grain and fodder. [C18: from Ar. *dhurah* grain]

durry ('dʌrɪ) *n, pl* **durries.** *Austral. sl.* a cigarette. [from *durrie* a type of Indian carpet]

durst (dɜːst) *vb* an archaic past tense of **dare.**

durum *or* **durum wheat** ('djʊərəm) *n* a variety of wheat with a high gluten content, used chiefly to make pastas. [C20: from NL *trīticum dūrum*, lit.: hard wheat]

dusk ❶ (dʌsk) *n* **1** the darker part of twilight. **2** *Poetic.* gloom; shade. ◆ *adj* **3** *Poetic.* shady. ◆ *vb* **4** *Poetic.* to make or become dark. [OE *dox*]

dusky ❶ ('dʌskɪ) *adj* **duskier, duskiest. 1** dark in colour; swarthy or dark-skinned. **2** dim.
▸**'duskily** *adv* ▸**'duskiness** *n*

dust ❶ (dʌst) *n* **1** dry fine powdery material, such as particles of dirt, earth, or pollen. **2** a cloud of such fine particles. **3a** the mortal body of man. **3b** the corpse of a dead person. **4** the earth; ground. **5** *Inf.* a disturbance; fuss (esp. in **kick up a dust, raise a dust**). **6** something of little worth. **7** short for **gold dust. 8** ashes or household refuse. **9 dust and ashes.** something that is very disappointing. **10 shake the dust off** (*or* **from**) **one's feet.** to depart angrily or contemptuously. **11 throw dust in the eyes of.** to confuse or mislead. ◆ *vb* **12** (*tr*) to sprinkle or cover (something) with (dust or some other powdery substance). **13** to remove dust (from) by wiping, sweeping, or brushing. **14** *Arch.* to make or become dirty with dust. ◆ See also **dust down, dust-up.** [OE *dūst*]
▸**'dustless** *adj*

dustbin ('dʌstˌbɪn) *n* a large container for rubbish, esp. one used by a household. US and Canad. names: **garbage can, trash can.**

dust bowl *n* a semiarid area in which the surface soil is exposed to wind erosion.

dustcart ('dʌstˌkɑːt) *n* a road vehicle for collecting refuse. US and Canad. name: **garbage truck.**

dust cover *n* **1** another name for **dustsheet. 2** another name for **dust jacket. 3** a Perspex cover for the turntable of a record player.

dust devil *n* a strong miniature whirlwind that whips up dust, litter, leaves, etc., into the air.

dust down *vb* (*tr, adv*). **1** to remove dust from by brushing or wiping. **2** to reprimand severely.
▸**dusting down** *n*

duster ('dʌstə) *n* **1** a cloth used for dusting. US name: **dust cloth. 2** a machine for blowing out dust. **3** a person or thing that dusts.

dusting-powder *n* fine powder (such as talcum powder) used to absorb moisture, etc.

dust jacket *or* **cover** *n* a removable paper cover used to protect a bound book.

dustman ('dʌstmən) *n, pl* **dustmen.** *Brit.* a man whose job is to collect domestic refuse.

dustpan ('dʌstˌpæn) *n* a short-handled hooded shovel into which dust is swept from floors, etc.

dustsheet ('dʌstˌʃiːt) *n Brit.* a large cloth to protect furniture from dust.

dust storm *n* a windstorm that whips up clouds of dust.

dust-up ❶ *Inf.* ◆ *n* **1** a fight or argument. ◆ *vb* **dust up. 2** (*tr, adv*) to attack (someone).

dusty ❶ ('dʌstɪ) *adj* **dustier, dustiest. 1** covered with or involving dust. **2** like dust. **3** (of a colour) tinged with grey; pale. **4 give** (*or* **get**) **a dusty answer.** to give (*or* get) an unhelpful or bad-tempered reply.
▸**'dustily** *adv* ▸**'dustiness** *n*

Dutch (dʌtʃ) *n* **1** the language of the Netherlands. **2 the Dutch.** (*functioning as pl*) the natives, citizens, or inhabitants of the Netherlands. **3** See **double Dutch. 4 in Dutch.** *Sl.* in trouble. ◆ *adj* **5** of the Netherlands, its inhabitants, or their language. ◆ *adv* **6 go Dutch.** *Inf.* to share expenses equally.

Dutch auction *n* an auction in which the price is lowered by stages until a buyer is found.

Dutch barn *n Brit.* a farm building consisting of a steel frame and a curved roof.

Dutch courage *n* **1** false courage gained from drinking alcohol. **2** alcoholic drink.

Dutch door *n* the US and Canad. name for **stable door.**

Dutch elm disease *n* a fungal disease of elm trees characterized by withering of the foliage and stems and eventual death of the tree.

Dutchman ('dʌtʃmən) *n, pl* **Dutchmen. 1** a native, citizen, or inhabitant of the Netherlands. **2** *S. African derog.* an Afrikaner.

Dutch medicine *n S. African.* patent medicine, esp. made of herbs.

Dutch oven *n* **1** an iron or earthenware container with a cover, used for stews, etc. **2** a metal box, open in front, for cooking in front of an open fire.

Dutch treat *n Inf.* an entertainment, meal, etc., where each person pays for himself.

Dutch uncle *n Inf.* a person who criticizes frankly and severely.

duteous ('djuːtɪəs) *adj Formal or arch.* dutiful; obedient.
▸**'duteously** *adv*

dutiable ('djuːtɪəbᵊl) *adj* (of goods) liable to duty.
▸**ˌdutia'bility** *n*

dutiful ❶ ('djuːtɪfʊl) *adj* **1** exhibiting or having a sense of duty. **2** characterized by or resulting from a sense of duty: *a dutiful answer.*

duty ❶ ('djuːtɪ) *n, pl* **duties. 1** a task or action that a person is bound to perform for moral or legal reasons. **2** respect or obedience due to a superior, older persons, etc. **3** the force that binds one morally or legally to one's obligations. **4** a government tax, esp. on imports. **5** *Brit.* **5a** the quantity of work for which a machine is designed. **5b** a measure of the efficiency of a machine. **6a** a job or service allocated. **6b** (*as modifier*): *duty rota.* **7 do duty for.** to act as a substitute for. **8 on** (*or* **off**) **duty.** at (*or* not at) work. [C13: from Anglo-F *dueté*, from OF *deu* DUE]

duty-bound *adj* morally obliged.

duty-free *adj, adv* **1** with exemption from customs or excise duties. ◆ *n* **2** goods sold in a duty-free shop.

duty-free shop *n* a shop, esp. one at an airport or on board a ship, that sells perfume, tobacco, etc., at duty-free prices.

duumvir (djuː'ʌmvə) *n, pl* **duumvirs** *or* **duumviri** (-vɪˌriː). **1** *Roman history.* one of two coequal magistrates. **2** either of two men who exercise a joint authority. [C16: from L, from *duo* two + *vir* man]
▸**duumvirate** (djuː'ʌmvɪrɪt) *n*

duvet ('duːveɪ) *n* **1** another name for **continental quilt. 2** Also called: **duvet jacket.** a down-filled jacket. [C18: from F, from earlier *dumet*, from OF *dum* DOWN[2]]

dux (dʌks) *n* (esp. in Scottish schools) the top pupil in a class or school. [L: leader]

DV *abbrev. for:* **1** Deo volente. [L: God willing] **2** Douay Version (of the Bible).

DVD *abbrev. for* Digital Versatile Disk or (formerly) Digital Video Disk.

DVLA *abbrev. for* Driver and Vehicle Licensing Agency.

dwaal (dwɑːl) *n S. African.* a state of befuddlement; daze. [from Afrik. *dwaal* wander]

dwale (dweɪl) *n* another name for **deadly nightshade.** [C14: ?from ON]

dwarf ❶ (dwɔːf) *n, pl* **dwarfs** *or* **dwarves** (dwɔːvz). **1** an abnormally undersized person. **2a** an animal or plant much below the average height for the species. **2b** (*as modifier*): *a dwarf tree.* **3** (in folklore) a small ugly manlike creature, often possessing magical powers. **4** *Astron.* short for **dwarf star.** ◆ *vb* **5** to become or cause to become com-

THESAURUS

duration *n* = **length**, continuance, continuation, extent, period, perpetuation, prolongation, span, spell, stretch, term, time

duress *n* **1** = **pressure**, coercion, compulsion, constraint, threat **2** = **imprisonment**, captivity, confinement, constraint, hardship, incarceration, restraint

dusk *n* **1** = **twilight**, dark, evening, eventide, gloaming (*Scot. or poetic*), nightfall, sundown, sunset **2** *Poetic* = **shade**, darkness, gloom, murk, obscurity, shadowiness
Antonyms *n* ≠ **twilight:** aurora (*poetic*), cockcrow, dawn, dawning, daybreak, daylight, morning, sunlight, sunup

dusky *adj* **1** = **dark**, dark-complexioned, dark-hued, sable, swarthy **2** = **dim**, caliginous, cloudy, crepuscular, darkish, gloomy, murky, obscure, overcast, shadowy, shady, tenebrous, twilight, twilit, veiled

dust *n* **1, 2** = **grime**, dirt, earth, fine fragments, grit, ground, particles, powder, powdery dirt, soil **11 throw dust in the eyes of** = **mislead**, con (*sl.*), confuse, deceive, fool, have (someone) on, hoodwink, take in (*inf.*) ◆ *vb* **12** = **sprinkle**, cover, dredge, powder, scatter, sift, spray, spread

dust-up *n* **1** *Informal* = **fight**, argument, brush, conflict, encounter, fracas, punch-up (*Brit. inf.*), quarrel, scrap (*inf.*), set-to (*inf.*), shindig (*inf.*), skirmish, tussle

dusty *adj* **1** = **dirty**, grubby, sooty, unclean, undusted, unswept **2** = **powdery**, chalky, crumbly, friable, granular, sandy

dutiful *adj* **1** = **conscientious**, compliant, deferential, devoted, docile, duteous (*arch.*), filial, obedient, punctilious, respectful, reverential, submissive
Antonyms *adj* disobedient, disrespectful, insubordinate, remiss, uncaring

duty *n* **1** = **responsibility**, assignment, business, calling, charge, engagement, function, job, mission, obligation, office, onus, pigeon (*inf.*), province, role, service, task, work **2** = **loyalty**, allegiance, deference, obedience, respect, reverence **4** = **tax**, customs, due, excise, impost, levy, tariff, toll **8 off duty** = **off work**, at leisure, free, off, on holiday **8 on duty** = **at work**, busy, engaged, on active service

dwarf *n* **1** = **midget**, bantam, homunculus, hop-o'-my-thumb, Lilliputian, manikin, pygmy *or* pigmy, Tom Thumb **2b** *as modifier* = **miniature**, baby, bonsai, diminutive, dwarfed, Lilliputian, petite, pint-sized, pocket, small, teensy-

paratively small in size, importance, etc. **6** (*tr*) to stunt the growth of. [OE *dweorg*]
▸**'dwarfish** *adj*

dwarf star *n* any unevolved star, such as the sun, lying in the main sequence of the Hertzsprung-Russell diagram. Also called: **main sequence star.** See also **red dwarf, white dwarf.**

dwell Ⓣ (dwɛl) *vb* **dwells, dwelling, dwelt** *or* **dwelled.** (*intr*) **1** *Formal, literary.* to live as a permanent resident. **2** to live (in a specified state): *to dwell in poverty.* ◆ *n* **3** a regular pause in the operation of a machine. [OE *dwellan* to seduce, get lost]
▸**'dweller** *n*

dwelling Ⓣ ('dwɛlɪŋ) *n Formal, literary.* a place of residence.

dwell on Ⓣ *or* **upon** *vb* (*intr, prep*) to think, speak, or write at length about.

dwelt (dwɛlt) *vb* a past tense and past participle of **dwell.**

dwindle Ⓣ ('dwɪndᵊl) *vb* **dwindles, dwindling, dwindled.** to grow or cause to grow less in size, intensity, or number. [C16: from OE *dwīnan* to waste away]

Dy *the chemical symbol for* dysprosium.

dyad ('daɪæd) *n* **1** *Maths.* an operator that is the unspecified product of two vectors. **2** an atom or group that has a valency of two. **3** a group of two; couple. [C17: from LL *dyas,* from Gk *duas* two]
▸**dy'adic** *adj*

Dyak *or* **Dayak** ('daɪæk) *n, pl* **Dyaks, Dyak** *or* **Dayaks, Dayak.** a member of a Malaysian people of Borneo. [from Malay: upcountry, from *darat* land]

dybbuk ('dɪbək) *n, pl* **dybbuks** *or* **dybbukkim.** *Judaism.* (in folklore) the soul of a dead sinner that has transmigrated into the body of a living person. [from Yiddish: devil, from Heb.]

dye Ⓣ (daɪ) *n* **1** a staining or colouring substance. **2** a liquid that contains a colouring material and can be used to stain fabrics, skins, etc. **3** the colour produced by dyeing. ◆ *vb* **dyes, dyeing, dyed. 4** (*tr*) to impart a colour or stain to (fabric, hair, etc.) by or as if by the application of a dye. [OE *dēagian,* from *dēag* a dye]
▸**'dyable** *or* **'dyeable** *adj* ▸**'dyer** *n*

dyed-in-the-wool Ⓣ *adj* **1** uncompromising or unchanging in attitude, opinion, etc. **2** (of a fabric) made of dyed yarn.

dyeing ('daɪɪŋ) *n* the process or industry of colouring yarns, fabric, etc.

dyestuff ('daɪˌstʌf) *n* a substance that can be used as a dye or which yields a dye.

dying Ⓣ ('daɪɪŋ) *vb* **1** the present participle of **die**[1]. ◆ *adj* **2** relating to or occurring at the moment of death: *a dying wish.*

dyke[1] *or* **dike** (daɪk) *n* **1** an embankment constructed to prevent flooding, keep out the sea, or confine a river to a particular course. **2** a ditch or watercourse. **3** a bank made of earth alongside a ditch. **4** *Scot.* a wall, esp. a dry-stone wall. **5** a barrier or obstruction. **6** a wall-like mass of igneous rock in older sedimentary rock. **7** *Austral. & NZ inf.* a lavatory. ◆ *vb* **dykes, dyking, dyked. 8** (*tr*) to protect, enclose, or drain (land) with a dyke. [C13: from OE *dīc* ditch]

dyke[2] *or* **dike** (daɪk) *n Sl.* a lesbian. [C20: from ?]

dynamic Ⓣ (daɪ'næmɪk) *adj* **1** of or concerned with energy or forces that produce motion, as opposed to *static.* **2** of or concerned with dynamics. **3** Also: **dynamical.** characterized by force of personality, ambition, energy, etc. **4** *Computing.* (of a memory) needing its contents refreshed periodically. [C19: from F *dynamique,* from Gk *dunamikos* powerful, from *dunamis* power, from *dunasthai* to be able]
▸**dy'namically** *adv*

dynamics (daɪ'næmɪks) *n* **1** (*functioning as sing*) the branch of mechanics concerned with the forces that change or produce the motions of bodies. **2** (*functioning as sing*) the branch of mechanics that includes statics and kinetics. **3** (*functioning as sing*) the branch of any science concerned with forces. **4** (*functioning as pl*) those forces that produce change in any field or system. **5** (*functioning as pl*) *Music.* **5a** the various degrees of loudness called for in performance. **5b** directions and symbols used to indicate degrees of loudness.

dynamism Ⓣ ('daɪnəˌmɪzəm) *n* **1** *Philosophy.* any of several theories that attempt to explain phenomena in terms of an immanent force or energy. **2** the forcefulness of an energetic personality.
▸**'dynamist** *n* ▸**ˌdyna'mistic** *adj*

dynamite ('daɪnəˌmaɪt) *n* **1** an explosive consisting of nitroglycerine mixed with an absorbent. **2** *Inf.* a spectacular or potentially dangerous person or thing. ◆ *vb* **dynamites, dynamiting, dynamited. 3** (*tr*) to blow up with dynamite. [C19 (coined by Alfred Nobel): from DYNAMO- + -ITE[1]]
▸**'dynaˌmiter** *n*

dynamo ('daɪnəˌməʊ) *n, pl* **dynamos. 1** a device for converting mechanical energy into electrical energy. **2** *Inf.* an energetic hard-working person. [C19: short for *dynamoelectric machine*]

dynamo- *or sometimes before a vowel* **dynam-** *combining form.* indicating power: *dynamite.* [from Gk, from *dunamis* power]

dynamoelectric (ˌdaɪnəməʊɪ'lɛktrɪk) *or* **dynamoelectrical** *adj* of or concerned with the interconversion of mechanical and electrical energy.

dynamometer (ˌdaɪnə'mɒmɪtə) *n* an instrument for measuring power or force.

dynamotor ('daɪnəˌməʊtə) *n* an electrical machine having two independent armature windings, one acting as a motor and the other a generator: used to convert direct current into alternating current.

dynast ('dɪnəst, -æst) *n* a ruler, esp. a hereditary one. [C17: from L *dynastēs,* from Gk, from *dunasthai* to be powerful]

dynasty Ⓣ ('dɪnəstɪ) *n, pl* **dynasties. 1** a sequence of hereditary rulers. **2** any sequence of powerful leaders of the same family. [C15: via LL from Gk, from *dunastēs* DYNAST]
▸**dynastic** (dɪ'næstɪk) *adj*

dyne (daɪn) *n* the cgs unit of force; the force that imparts an acceleration of 1 centimetre per second per second to a mass of 1 gram. 1 dyne is equivalent to 10^{-5} newton or 7.233×10^{-5} poundal. [C19: from F, from Gk *dunamis* power, force]

dys- *prefix* **1** diseased, abnormal, or faulty. **2** difficult or painful. **3** unfavourable or bad. [via L from Gk *dus-*]

dysentery ('dɪsᵊntrɪ) *n* infection of the intestine marked by severe diarrhoea with the passage of mucus and blood. [C14: via L from Gk, from *dusentera,* lit.: bad bowels, from DYS- + *enteron* intestine]
▸**dysenteric** (ˌdɪsᵊn'tɛrɪk) *adj*

dysfunction (dɪs'fʌŋkʃən) *n* **1** *Med.* any disturbance or abnormality in the function of an organ or part. **2** (esp. of a family) failure to show the characteristics or fulfil the purposes held as normal or beneficial.

dysgraphia (dɪs'græfɪə) *n* inability to write correctly, caused by disease of part of the brain.

dyslexia (dɪs'lɛksɪə) *n* a developmental disorder which can cause learning difficulty in one or more of the areas of reading, writing, and numeracy. [C19: NL, from DYS- + *-lexia,* from Gk *lexis* word]
▸**dyslectic** (dɪs'lɛktɪk) *adj* ▸**dys'lexic** *adj, n*

dysmenorrhoea *or esp. US* **dysmenorrhea** (ˌdɪsmɛnə'rɪə) *n* abnormally difficult or painful menstruation. [C19: from DYS- + Gk *mēn* month + *rhoiā* a flowing]

dyspepsia (dɪs'pɛpsɪə) *n* indigestion or upset stomach. [C18: from L, from Gk *duspepsia,* from DYS- + *pepsis* digestion]

dyspeptic (dɪs'pɛptɪk) *adj* **1** relating to or suffering from dyspepsia. **2** irritable. ◆ *n* **3** a person suffering from dyspepsia.

dysphasia (dɪs'feɪzɪə) *n* a disorder of language caused by a brain lesion.
▸**dys'phasic** *adj, n*

dysphoria (dɪs'fɔːrɪə) *n* a feeling of being ill at ease. [C20: NL, from Gk DYS- + *-phoria,* from *pherein* to bear]

dyspnoea *or US* **dyspnea** (dɪsp'niːə) *n* difficulty in breathing or in catching the breath. [C17: via L from Gk *duspnoia,* from DYS- + *pnoē* breath, from *pnein* to breathe]
▸**dysp'noeal, dysp'noeic** *or US* **dysp'neal, dysp'neic** *adj*

dysprosium (dɪs'prəʊsɪəm) *n* a metallic element of the lanthanide series: used in laser materials and as a neutron absorber in nuclear control rods. Symbol: Dy; atomic no.: 66; atomic wt.: 162.50. [C20: NL, from Gk *dusprositos* difficult to get near + -IUM]

dysthymia (dɪs'θaɪmɪə) *n Psychiatry.* the characteristics of the neurotic and introverted, including anxiety, depression, and compulsive behaviour. [C19: NL, from Gk *dusthumia,* from DYS- + *thumos* mind]
▸**dys'thymic** *adj*

dysthymic disorder *n* a psychiatric disorder characterized by generalized depression that lasts for at least a year.

dystrophy ('dɪstrəfɪ) *n* any of various bodily disorders, characterized by wasting of tissues. See also **muscular dystrophy.** [C19: NL *dystrophia,* from DYS- + Gk *trophē* food]
▸**dystrophic** (dɪs'trɒfɪk) *adj*

dz. *abbrev. for* dozen.

dzo (zəʊ) *n, pl* **dzos** *or* **dzo.** a variant spelling of **zo.**

THESAURUS

weensy, teeny-weeny, tiny, undersized **3** = **gnome**, goblin ◆ *vb* **5** = **tower above** *or* **over**, dim, diminish, dominate, minimize, overshadow **6** = **stunt**, check, cultivate by bonsai, lower, retard

dwarfish *adj* **1, 2** = **undersized**, diminutive, dwarfed, knee high to a grasshopper (*inf.*), low, miniature, minute, pint-size (*inf.*), pygmaean, pygmy *or* pigmy, runtish, runty, short, small, stunted, teensy-weensy, teeny-weeny, tiny

dwell *vb* **1** *Formal, literary* = **live**, abide, establish oneself, hang out (*inf.*), inhabit, lodge, quarter, remain, reside, rest, settle, sojourn, stay, stop

dwelling *n Formal, literary* = **home**, abode, domicile, dwelling house, establishment, habitation, house, lodging, pad (*sl.*), quarters, residence

dwell on *vb* = **go on about** (*inf.*), be engrossed in, continue, elaborate, emphasize, expatiate, harp on, linger over, tarry over

dwindle *vb* = **lessen**, abate, contract, decay, decline, decrease, die away, die down, die out, diminish, ebb, fade, fall, grow less, peter out, pine, shrink, shrivel, sink, subside, taper off, wane, waste away, weaken, wither
Antonyms *vb* advance, amplify, develop, dilate, enlarge, escalate, expand, grow, heighten, increase, magnify, multiply, swell, wax

dye *n* **1, 2** = **colouring**, colorant, colour, pigment, stain, tinge, tint ◆ *vb* **4** = **colour**, pigment, stain, tincture, tinge, tint

dyed-in-the-wool *adj* **1** = **confirmed**, complete, deep-dyed (*usually derogatory*), deep-rooted, die-hard, entrenched, established, inveterate, through-and-through

dying *adj* **2** = **expiring**, at death's door, ebbing, fading, failing, final, going, *in extremis,* moribund, mortal, not long for this world, passing, perishing, sinking

dynamic *adj* **3** = **energetic**, active, alive and kicking, driving, electric, forceful, full of beans (*inf.*), go-ahead, go-getting (*inf.*), high-octane (*inf.*), high-powered, lively, magnetic, powerful, storming (*inf.*), vigorous, vital, zippy (*inf.*)
Antonyms *adj* apathetic, couldn't-care-less (*inf.*), impassive, inactive, listless, sluggish, torpid, undynamic, unenergetic

dynamism *n* **2** = **energy**, brio, drive, enterprise, forcefulness, get-up-and-go (*inf.*), go (*inf.*), initiative, liveliness, pep, push (*inf.*), vigour, zap (*sl.*), zip (*inf.*)

dynasty *n* **1, 2** = **lineage**, family, house, line

Ee

e *or* **E** (iː) *n, pl* **e's, E's,** *or* **Es. 1** the fifth letter and second vowel of the English alphabet. **2** any of several speech sounds represented by this letter, as in *he, bet,* or *below*.
e *symbol for:* **1** *Maths.* a transcendental number used as the base of natural logarithms. Approximate value: 2.718 282... **2** electron.
E *symbol for:* **1** *Music.* **1a** the third note of the scale of C major. **1b** the major or minor key having this note as its tonic. **2** earth. **3** East. **4** English. **5** Egypt(ian). **6** *Physics.* **6a** energy. **6b** electromotive force. **7** exa-. **8a** a person without a regular income, or who is dependent on the state on a long-term basis because of unemployment, sickness, old age, etc. **8b** (*as modifier*): *E worker.* ◆ See also **occupation groupings. 9** the drug ecstasy.
e. *abbrev. for* engineer(ing).
E. *abbrev. for* Earl.
e- *prefix* electronic: *e-mail; e-money.*
E- *prefix* used with numbers indicating a standardized system within the European Union, as of food additives. See also **E number.**
ea. *abbrev. for* each.
each Ⓣ (iːtʃ) *determiner* **1a** every (one) of two or more considered individually: *each day; each person.* **1b** (*as pron*): *each gave according to his ability.* ◆ *adv* **2** for, to, or from each one; apiece: *four apples each.* [OE *ǣlc*]

> **USAGE NOTE** *Each* is a singular pronoun and should be used with a singular form of a verb: *each of the candidates was* (not *were*) *interviewed separately.* See also at **either.**

eager Ⓣ (ˈiːgə) *adj* **1** (*postpositive;* often foll. by *to* or *for*) impatiently desirous (of); anxious or avid (for). **2** characterized by or feeling expectancy or great desire: *an eager look.* **3** *Arch.* biting; sharp. [C13: from OF *egre,* from L *acer* sharp, keen]
▸ˈ**eagerly** *adv* ▸ˈ**eagerness** *n*
eager beaver *n Inf.* a person who displays conspicuous diligence.
eagle (ˈiːgᵊl) *n* **1** any of various birds of prey having large broad wings and strong soaring flight. Related adj: **aquiline. 2** a representation of an eagle used as an emblem, etc., esp. representing power: *the Roman eagle.* **3** a standard, seal, etc., bearing the figure of an eagle. **4** *Golf.* a score of two strokes under par for a hole. **5** a former US gold coin worth ten dollars. ◆ *vb* **6** *Golf.* to score two strokes under par for a hole. [C14: from OF *aigle,* from OProvençal *aigla,* from L *aquila*]
eagle-eyed *adj* having keen or piercing eyesight.
eagle-hawk *n* a large brown Australian eagle. Also called: **wedge-tailed eagle.**
eagle owl *n* a large Eurasian owl with brownish speckled plumage and large ear tufts.
eaglet (ˈiːglɪt) *n* a young eagle.
ealdorman (ˈɔːldəmən) *n, pl* **ealdormen.** an official of Anglo-Saxon England, appointed by the king, and responsible for law and order in his shire and for leading local militia. [OE *ealdor* lord + MAN]
-ean *suffix forming adjectives and nouns.* a variant of **-an:** *Caesarean.*
ear[1] Ⓣ (ɪə) *n* **1** the organ of hearing and balance in higher vertebrates (see **middle ear**). Related adj: **aural. 2** the outermost cartilaginous part of the ear in mammals, esp. man. **3** the sense of hearing. **4** sensitivity to musical sounds, poetic diction, etc.: *he has an ear for music.* **5** attention; consideration (esp. in **give ear to, lend an ear**). **6** an object resembling the external ear. **7 all ears.** very attentive; listening carefully. **8 a thick ear.** *Inf.* a blow on the ear. **9 fall on deaf ears.** to be ignored or pass unnoticed. **10 in one ear and out the other.** heard but unheeded. **11 keep** (*or* **have**) **one's ear to the ground.** to be or try to be well informed about current trends and opinions. **12 out on one's ear.** *Inf.* dismissed unceremoniously. **13 play by ear. 13a** *Inf.* to act according to the demands of a situation; improvise. **13b** to perform a musical piece on an instrument without written music. **14 turn a deaf ear.** to be deliberately unresponsive. **15 up to one's ears.** *Inf.* deeply involved, as in work or debt. [OE *ēare*]
▸**eared** *adj* ▸ˈ**earless** *adj*
ear[2] (ɪə) *n* **1** the part of a cereal plant, such as wheat or barley, that contains the seeds, grains, or kernels. ◆ *vb* **2** (*intr*) (of cereal plants) to develop such parts. [OE *ēar*]
earache (ˈɪərˌeɪk) *n* pain in the ear.
eardrum (ˈɪəˌdrʌm) *n* the nontechnical name for **tympanic membrane.**
earful (ˈɪəfʊl) *n Inf.* **1** something heard or overheard. **2** a rebuke or scolding.
earl (ɜːl) *n* (in Britain) a nobleman ranking below a marquess and above a viscount. Female equivalent: **countess.** [OE *eorl*]
▸ˈ**earldom** *n*
Earl Grey *n* a variety of China tea flavoured with oil of bergamot.
Earl Marshal *n* an officer of the English peerage who presides over the College of Heralds and organizes royal processions and other important ceremonies.
early Ⓣ (ˈɜːlɪ) *adj, adv* **earlier, earliest. 1** before the expected or usual time. **2** occurring in or characteristic of the first part of a period or sequence. **3** occurring in or characteristic of a period far back in time. **4** occurring in the near future. **5 in the early days.** during the first years of any enterprise, such as marriage. [OE *ǣrlīce,* from *ǣr* ERE + *-līce* -LY[2]]
▸ˈ**earliness** *n*
early closing *n Brit.* the shutting of shops in a town one afternoon each week.
Early English *n* a style of architecture used in England in the 12th and 13th centuries, characterized by lancet arches and plate tracery.
early music *n* **1** music of the Middle Ages and Renaissance, sometimes also including music of the baroque and early classical periods. ◆ (*modifier*) **early-music. 2** of or denoting an approach to musical performance emphasizing the use of period instruments and historically researched scores and playing techniques: *the early-music movement.*
early warning *n* advance notice of some impending event.
earmark Ⓣ (ˈɪəˌmɑːk) *vb* (*tr*) **1** to set aside or mark out for a specific purpose. **2** to make an identification mark on the ear of (a domestic animal). ◆ *n* **3** such a mark of identification. **4** any distinguishing mark or characteristic.
earmuff (ˈɪəˌmʌf) *n* one of a joined pair of pads of fur or cloth for keeping the ears warm.
earn Ⓣ (ɜːn) *vb* **1** to gain or be paid (money or other payment) in return for work or service. **2** (*tr*) to acquire or deserve through behaviour or action. **3** (*tr*) (of securities, investments, etc.) to gain (interest, profit, etc.). [OE *earnian*]
earned income *n* income derived from paid employment.
earner (ˈɜːnə) *n* **1** a person who earns money. **2** *Sl.* an activity or thing that produces income, esp. illicitly: *a nice little earner.*
earnest[1] Ⓣ (ˈɜːnɪst) *adj* **1** serious in mind or intention. **2** characterized by sincerity of intention. **3** demanding or receiving serious attention. ◆ *n* **4 in earnest.** with serious or sincere intentions. [OE *eornost*]
▸ˈ**earnestly** *adv* ▸ˈ**earnestness** *n*
earnest[2] Ⓣ (ˈɜːnɪst) *n* **1** a part of something given in advance as a guarantee of the remainder. **2** Also called: **earnest money.** *Contract law.* something given, usually a nominal sum of money, to confirm a contract. **3** any token of something to follow. [C13: from OF *erres* pledges, pl of *erre* earnest money, from L *arrha,* from *arrabō* pledge, from Gk *arrabōn,* from Heb. *ʿērābhōn* pledge]

THESAURUS

each *determiner* **1a** = **every** ◆ *pron* **1b** = **every one,** each and every one, each one, one and all ◆ *adv* **2** = **apiece,** for each, from each, individually, per capita, per head, per person, respectively, singly, to each
eager *adj* **1, 2** = **keen,** agog, anxious, ardent, athirst, avid, earnest, enthusiastic, fervent, fervid, greedy, hot, hungry, impatient, intent, longing, raring, vehement, yearning, zealous
Antonyms *adj* apathetic, blasé, impassive, indifferent, lazy, nonchalant, opposed, unambitious, unconcerned, unenthusiastic, unimpressed, uninterested
eagerness *n* = **keenness,** ardour, avidity, earnestness, enthusiasm, fervour, greediness, heartiness, hunger, impatience, impetuosity, intentness, longing, thirst, vehemence, yearning, zeal
ear[1] *n* **4** = **sensitivity,** appreciation, discrimination, musical perception, taste **5** = **attention,** consideration, hearing, heed, notice, regard
13a play by ear *Informal* = **improvise,** ad lib, extemporize, rise to the occasion, take it as it comes
early *adj* **1** = **premature,** advanced, forward, untimely ◆ *adv* **1** = **too soon,** ahead of time, beforehand, betimes, in advance, in good time, prematurely ◆ *adj* **3** = **primitive,** primeval, primordial, undeveloped, young
Antonyms *adj* ≠ **premature:** developed, mature, ripe, seasoned ◆ *adv* ≠ **too soon:** behind, belated, late, overdue, tardy
earmark *vb* **1** = **set aside,** allocate, designate, flag, keep back, label, mark out, reserve, tag ◆ *n* **4** = **characteristic,** attribute, feature, hallmark, label, quality, signature, stamp, tag, token, trademark, trait
earn *vb* **1** = **make,** bring in, collect, draw, gain, get, gross, net, obtain, procure, realize, reap, receive **2** = **deserve,** acquire, attain, be entitled to, be worthy of, merit, rate, warrant, win
earnest[1] *adj* **1** = **serious,** close, constant, determined, firm, fixed, grave, intent, resolute, resolved, sincere, solemn, stable, staid, steady, thoughtful **2** = **heartfelt,** ablaze, ardent, devoted, eager, enthusiastic, fervent, fervid, impassioned, keen, keen as mustard, passionate, purposeful, urgent, vehement, warm, zealous ◆ *n* **4** *As in* **in earnest** = **seriousness,** determination, reality, resolution, sincerity, truth
Antonyms *adj* ≠ **serious:** flippant, frivolous, insincere, trifling ≠ **heartfelt:** apathetic, couldn't-care-less, half-hearted, indifferent, unconcerned, unenthusiastic, uninterested ◆ *n* ≠ **seriousness:** apathy, indifference, unconcern
earnest[2] *n* **1-3** = **down payment,** assurance, deposit, foretaste, guarantee, pledge, promise, security, token
earnestness *n* = **seriousness,** ardour, determination, devotion, eagerness, enthusiasm, fervour, gravity, intentness, keenness, passion, purposefulness, resolution, sincerity, urgency, vehemence, warmth, zeal

earnings ❶ ('ɜːnɪŋz) *pl n* **1** money or other payment earned. **2** the profits of an enterprise.

EAROM ('ɪərɒm) *n Computing. acronym for* electrically alterable read only memory.

earphone ('ɪəˌfəʊn) *n* a device for converting electric currents into sound waves, held close to or inserted into the ear.

ear piercing *n* **1** the making of a hole in the lobe of an ear, using a sterilized needle, so that earrings may be worn fastened in the hole. ◆ *adj* **ear-piercing. 2** so loud or shrill as to hurt the ears.

earplug ('ɪəˌplʌg) *n* a piece of soft material placed in the ear to keep out noise or water.

earring ('ɪəˌrɪŋ) *n* an ornament for the ear, usually clipped onto the lobe or fastened through a hole pierced in the lobe.

earshot ('ɪəˌʃɒt) *n* the range or distance within which sound may be heard (esp. in **out of earshot,** etc.)

ear-splitting *adj* so loud or shrill as to hurt the ears.

earth ❶ (ɜːθ) *n* **1** (*sometimes cap.*) the third planet from the sun, the only planet on which life is known to exist. Related adjs.: **terrestrial, telluric. 2** the inhabitants of this planet: *the whole earth rejoiced.* **3** the dry surface of this planet; land; ground. **4** the loose soft material on the surface of the ground that consists of disintegrated rock particles, mould, clay, etc.; soil. **5** worldly or temporal matters as opposed to the concerns of the spirit. **6** the hole in which a burrowing animal, esp. a fox, lives. **7** *Chem.* See **rare earth, alkaline earth. 8** Also (US and Canad.): **ground. 8a** a connection between an electric circuit or device and the earth, which is at zero potential. **8b** a terminal to which this connection is made. **9** (*modifier*) *Astrol.* of or relating to a group of three signs of the zodiac: Taurus, Virgo, and Capricorn. **10 come back** *or* **down to earth.** to return to reality from a fantasy or daydream. **11 on earth.** used as an intensifier in **what on earth, who on earth,** etc. **12 run to earth. 12a** to hunt (an animal, esp. a fox) to its earth and trap it there. **12b** to find (someone) after hunting. ◆ *vb* **13** Also (US and Canad.): **ground.** (*tr*) to connect (a circuit, device, etc.) to earth. ◆ See also **earth up.** [OE *eorthe*]

earthbound ('ɜːθˌbaʊnd) *adj* **1** confined to the earth. **2** heading towards the earth.

earth closet *n* a type of lavatory in which earth is used to cover excreta.

earthen ('ɜːθən) *adj* (*prenominal*) **1** made of baked clay: *an earthen pot.* **2** made of earth.

earthenware ❶ ('ɜːθənˌwɛə) *n* **a** vessels, etc., made of baked clay. **b** (*as adj*): *an earthenware pot.*

earth-grazer *n* an asteroid in an orbit that takes it close to the earth. Also called: **near-earth asteroid.**

earthly ❶ ('ɜːθlɪ) *adj* **earthlier, earthliest. 1** of or characteristic of the earth as opposed to heaven; materialistic; worldly. **2** (*usually with a negative*) *Inf.* conceivable or possible (in **not an earthly** (**chance**), etc.).
▸'**earthliness** *n*

earthman ('ɜːθˌmæn) *n, pl* **earthmen.** (esp. in science fiction) an inhabitant or native of the earth. Also called: **earthling.**

earthnut ('ɜːθˌnʌt) *n* **1** a perennial umbelliferous plant of Europe and Asia, having edible dark brown tubers. **2** any of various plants having an edible root, tuber, or underground pod, such as the peanut or truffle.

earthquake ('ɜːθˌkweɪk) *n* a series of vibrations at the earth's surface caused by movement along a fault plane, volcanic activity, etc. Related adj: **seismic.**

earth science *n* any of various sciences, such as geology and geography, that are concerned with the structure, age, etc., of the earth.

earth up *vb* (*tr, adv*) to cover (part of a plant) with soil to protect from frost, light, etc.

earthward ('ɜːθwəd) *adj* **1** directed towards the earth. ◆ *adv* **2** a variant of **earthwards.**

earthwards ('ɜːθwədz) *or* **earthward** *adv* towards the earth.

earthwork ('ɜːθˌwɜːk) *n* **1** excavation of earth, as in engineering construction. **2** a fortification made of earth.

earthworm ('ɜːθˌwɜːm) *n* any of numerous worms which burrow in the soil and help aerate and break up the ground.

earthy ❶ ('ɜːθɪ) *adj* **earthier, earthiest. 1** of, composed of, or characteristic of earth. **2** unrefined, coarse, or crude.
▸'**earthily** *adv* ▸'**earthiness** *n*

ear trumpet *n* a trumpet-shaped instrument held to the ear: an old form of hearing aid.

earwax ('ɪəˌwæks) *n* the nontechnical name for **cerumen.**

earwig ('ɪəˌwɪg) *n* **1** any of various insects that typically have an elongated body with small leathery forewings, semicircular membranous hindwings, and curved forceps at the tip of the abdomen. ◆ *vb* **earwigs, earwigging, earwigged. 2** (*intr*) *Inf.* to eavesdrop. **3** (*tr*) *Arch.* to attempt to influence (a person) by private insinuation. [OE *ēarwicga,* from *ēare* ear + *wicga* beetle, insect; prob. from superstition that the insect crept into human ears]

earwigging ('ɪəˌwɪgɪŋ) *n Inf.* a scolding or harangue: *I'll give him an earwigging about that.*

ease ❶ (iːz) *n* **1** freedom from discomfort, worry, or anxiety. **2** lack of difficulty, labour, or awkwardness. **3** rest, leisure, or relaxation. **4** freedom from poverty; affluence: *a life of ease.* **5** lack of restraint, embarrassment, or stiffness: *ease of manner.* **6 at ease. 6a** *Mil.* (of a standing soldier, etc.) in a relaxed position with the feet apart, rather than at attention. **6b** a command to adopt such a position. **6c** in a relaxed attitude or frame of mind. ◆ *vb* **eases, easing, eased. 7** to make or become less burdensome. **8** (*tr*) to relieve (a person) of worry or care; comfort. **9** (*tr*) to make comfortable or give rest to. **10** (*tr*) to make less difficult; facilitate. **11** to move or cause to move into, out of, etc., with careful manipulation. **12** (when *intr,* often foll. by *off* or *up*) to lessen or cause to lessen in severity, pressure, tension, or strain. **13 ease oneself** *or* **ease nature.** *Arch., euphemistic.* to urinate or defecate. [C13: from OF *aise* ease, opportunity, from L *adjacēns* neighbouring (area); see ADJACENT]
▸'**easeful** *adj*

easel ('iːzᵊl) *n* a frame, usually an upright tripod, for supporting or displaying an artist's canvas, a blackboard, etc. [C17: from Du. *ezel;* ult. from L *asinus* ass]

easement ('iːzmənt) *n* **1** *Property law.* the right enjoyed by a landowner of making limited use of his neighbour's land, as by crossing it to reach his own property. **2** the act of easing or something that brings ease.

easily ❶ ('iːzɪlɪ) *adv* **1** with ease; without difficulty or exertion. **2** by far; undoubtedly: *easily the best.* **3** probably; almost certainly.

USAGE NOTE See at **easy.**

easiness ('iːzɪnɪs) *n* **1** the quality or condition of being easy to accomplish, do, obtain, etc. **2** ease or relaxation of manner; nonchalance.

east (iːst) *n* **1** the direction along a parallel towards the sunrise, at 90° to north; the direction of the earth's rotation. **2 the east.** (*often cap.*) any area lying in or towards the east. Related adj: **oriental. 3** (*usually cap.*) *Cards.* the player or position at the table corresponding to east on the compass. ◆ *adj* **4** situated in, moving towards, or facing the east. **5** (esp. of the wind) from the east. ◆ *adv* **6** in, to, or towards the east. **7 back East.** *Canad.* in or to E Canada, esp. east of Quebec. ◆ Symbol: E [OE *ēast*]

East (iːst) *n* **the. 1** the continent of Asia regarded as culturally distinct from Europe and the West; the Orient. **2** the countries under Communist rule and those under Communist rule until *c.* 1991, lying mainly in the E hemisphere. ◆ *adj* **3** of or denoting the eastern part of a specified country, area, etc.

eastbound ('iːstˌbaʊnd) *adj* going or leading towards the east.

east by north *n* one point on the compass north of east.

east by south *n* one point on the compass south of east.

Easter ('iːstə) *n* **1** a festival of the Christian Church commemorating the Resurrection of Christ: falls on the Sunday following the first full moon after the vernal equinox. **2** Also called: **Easter Sunday, Easter Day.** the day on which this festival is celebrated. **3** the period between Good Friday and Easter Monday. ◆ Related adj: **Paschal.** [OE *ēastre*]

Easter cactus *n* a Brazilian cactus, *Rhipsalidopsis gaertneri,* widely cultivated as an ornamental for its showy red flowers.

THESAURUS

earnings *pl n* **1, 2** = **income,** emolument, gain, pay, proceeds, profits, receipts, remuneration, return, reward, salary, stipend, takings, wages

earth *n* **1** = **world,** globe, orb, planet, sphere, terrestrial sphere **3, 4** = **soil,** clay, clod, dirt, ground, land, loam, mould, sod, topsoil, turf

earthenware *n* = **crockery,** ceramics, crocks, pots, pottery, terracotta

earthiness *n* **2** = **crudeness,** bawdiness, coarseness, crudity, lustiness, naturalness, ribaldry, robustness, uninhibitedness

earthly *adj* **1** = **worldly,** human, material, materialistic, mortal, non-spiritual, physical, profane, secular, temporal **2** *Informal* = **possible,** conceivable, feasible, imaginable, likely, practical

Antonyms *adj* ≠ **worldly:** ethereal, heavenly, immaterial, immortal, otherworldly, spiritual, supernatural, unearthly

earthy *adj* **2** = **crude,** bawdy, coarse, down-to-earth, homely, lusty, natural, raunchy (*sl.*), ribald, robust, rough, simple, uninhibited, unrefined, unsophisticated

ease *n* **1** = **peace of mind,** calmness, comfort, content, contentment, enjoyment, happiness, peace, quiet, quietude, serenity, tranquillity **2** = **effortlessness,** easiness, facility, readiness, simplicity **3** = **leisure,** relaxation, repose, rest, restfulness **5** = **freedom,** flexibility, informality, liberty, naturalness, unaffectedness, unconstraint, unreservedness ◆ *vb* **7, 8, 12** = **relieve,** abate, allay, alleviate, appease, assuage, calm, comfort, disburden, lessen, lighten, mitigate, moderate, mollify, pacify, palliate, quiet, relax, relent, slacken, soothe, still, tranquillize **10** = **make easier,** aid, assist, expedite, facilitate, forward, further, give a leg up (*inf.*), lessen the labour of, simplify, smooth, speed up **11** = **move carefully,** edge, guide, inch, manoeuvre, slide, slip, squeeze, steer

Antonyms *n* ≠ **peace of mind:** agitation, awkwardness, clumsiness, discomfort, disturbance, tension ≠ **effortlessness:** arduousness, awkwardness, clumsiness, difficulty, effort, exertion, toil ≠ **leisure:** difficulty, discomfort, hardship, irritation, pain, poverty, tribulation ≠ **freedom:** awkwardness, clumsiness, constraint, formality ◆ *vb* ≠ **relieve:** aggravate, discomfort, exacerbate, irritate, worsen ≠ **make easier:** hinder, retard

easily *adv* **1** = **without difficulty,** comfortably, effortlessly, facilely, like a knife through butter, readily, simply, smoothly, standing on one's head, with ease, with one hand tied behind one's back, with one's eyes closed *or* shut, without trouble **2** = **without a doubt,** absolutely, beyond question, by far, certainly, clearly, definitely, doubtlessly, far and away, indisputably, indubitably, plainly, surely, undeniably, undoubtedly, unequivocally, unquestionably

Easter egg *n* an egg given to children at Easter, usually a chocolate egg or a hen's egg with its shell painted.

easterly ('i:stəlɪ) *adj* **1** of or in the east. ◆ *adv, adj* **2** towards the east. **3** from the east: *an easterly wind.* ◆ *n, pl* **easterlies. 4** a wind from the east.

eastern ('i:stən) *adj* **1** situated in or towards the east. **2** facing or moving towards the east.

Eastern Church *n* **1** any of the Christian Churches of the former Byzantine Empire. **2** any Church owing allegiance to the Orthodox Church. **3** any Church having Eastern forms of liturgy and institutions.

Easterner ('i:stənə) *n* (*sometimes not cap.*) a native or inhabitant of the east of any specified region.

eastern hemisphere *n* (*often caps.*) **1** that half of the globe containing Europe, Asia, Africa, and Australia, lying east of the Greenwich meridian. **2** the lands in this, esp. Asia.

Eastern Orthodox Church *n* another name for the **Orthodox Church.**

Eastertide ('i:stə,taɪd) *n* the Easter season.

easting ('i:stɪŋ) *n* **1** *Naut.* the net distance eastwards made by a vessel moving towards the east. **2** *Cartography.* the distance eastwards of a point from a given meridian indicated by the first half of a map grid reference.

east-northeast *n* **1** the point on the compass or the direction midway between northeast and east. ◆ *adj, adv* **2** in, from, or towards this direction.

east-southeast *n* **1** the point on the compass or the direction midway between east and southeast. ◆ *adj, adv* **2** in, from, or towards this direction.

eastward ('i:stwəd) *adj* **1** situated or directed towards the east. ◆ *adv* **2** a variant of **eastwards.** ◆ *n* **3** the eastward part, direction, etc.
▸'**eastwardly** *adv, adj*

eastwards ('i:stwədz) *or* **eastward** *adv* towards the east.

easy ➊ ('i:zɪ) *adj* **easier, easiest. 1** not requiring much labour or effort; not difficult. **2** free from pain, care, or anxiety. **3** not restricting; lenient: *easy laws.* **4** tolerant and undemanding; easy-going: *an easy disposition.* **5** readily influenced; pliant: *an easy victim.* **6** not constricting; loose: *an easy fit.* **7** not strained or extreme; moderate: *an easy pace.* **8** *Inf.* ready to fall in with any suggestion made; not predisposed: *he is easy about what to do.* **9** *Sl.* sexually available. ◆ *adv* **10** *Inf.* in an easy or relaxed manner. **11 easy does it.** *Inf.* go slowly and carefully; be careful. **12 go easy.** (*usually imperative;* often foll. by *on*) to exercise moderation. **13 stand easy.** *Mil.* a command to soldiers standing at ease that they may relax further. **14 take it easy. 14a** to avoid stress or undue hurry. **14b** to remain calm. [C12: from OF *aisié*, p.p. of *aisier* to relieve, EASE]

> **USAGE NOTE** *Easy* is not used as an adverb by careful speakers and writers except in certain set phrases: *to take it easy; easy does it.* Where a fixed expression is not involved, the usual adverbial form of *easily* is preferred: *this polish goes on more easily* (not *easier*) *than the other.*

easy-care *adj* (esp. of a fabric or garment) hard-wearing and requiring no special treatment during washing, etc.

easy chair *n* a comfortable upholstered armchair.

easy-going ➊ ('i:zɪ'gəʊɪŋ) *adj* **1** relaxed in manner or attitude; excessively tolerant. **2** moving at a comfortable pace: *an easy-going horse.*

easy meat *n Inf.* **1** someone easily seduced or deceived. **2** something easy.

easy money *n* **1** money made with little effort, sometimes dishonestly. **2** *Commerce.* money that can be borrowed at a low interest rate.

Easy Street *n* (*sometimes not caps.*) *Inf.* a state of financial security.

eat ➊ (i:t) *vb* **eats, eating, ate, eaten. 1** to take into the mouth and swallow (food, etc.), esp. after biting and chewing. **2** (*tr;* often foll. by *away* or *up*) to destroy as if by eating: *the damp had eaten away the woodwork.* **3** (often foll. by *into*) to use up or waste: *taxes ate into his inheritance.* **4** (often foll. by *into* or *through*) to make (a hole, passage, etc.) by eating or gnawing: *rats ate through the floor.* **5** to take or have (a meal or meals): *we eat at six.* **6** (*tr*) to include as part of one's diet: *he doesn't eat fish.* **7** (*tr*) *Inf.* to cause to worry: *what's eating you?* ◆ See also **eat out, eats, eat up.** [OE *etan*]
▸'**eater** *n*

eatable ➊ ('i:təb[ə]l) *adj* fit or suitable for eating; edible.

eatables ('i:təb[ə]lz) *pl n* food.

eating ('i:tɪŋ) *n* **1** food, esp. in relation to quality or taste: *this fruit makes excellent eating.* ◆ *adj* **2** suitable for eating uncooked: *eating apples.* **3** relating to or for eating: *an eating house.*

eat out *vb* (*intr, adv*) to eat away from home, esp. in a restaurant.

eats (i:ts) *pl n Inf.* articles of food; provisions.

eat up *vb* (*adv, mainly tr*) **1** (*also intr*) to eat or consume entirely. **2** *Inf.* to listen to with enthusiasm or appreciation: *the audience ate up his every word.* **3** (*often passive*) *Inf.* to affect grossly: *she was eaten up by jealousy.* **4** *Inf.* to travel (a distance) quickly: *we just ate up the miles.*

eau de Cologne (,əʊ də kə'ləʊn) *n* See **cologne.** [F, lit.: water of Cologne]

eau de nil (,əʊ də 'ni:l) *n, adj* (of) a pale yellowish-green colour. [F, lit.: water of (the) Nile]

eau de vie (,əʊ də 'vi:) *n* brandy or other spirits. [F, lit.: water of life]

eaves (i:vz) *pl n* the edge of a roof that projects beyond the wall. [OE *efes*]

eavesdrop ➊ ('i:vz,drɒp) *vb* **eavesdrops, eavesdropping, eavesdropped.** (*intr*) to listen secretly to the private conversation of others. [C17: back formation from *evesdropper*, from OE *yfesdrype* water dripping from the eaves]
▸'**eaves,dropper** *n*

ebb ➊ (ɛb) *vb* (*intr*) **1** (of tide water) to flow back or recede. Cf. **flow** (sense 8). **2** to fall away or decline. ◆ *n* **3a** the flowing back of the tide from high to low water or the period in which this takes place. **3b** (*as modifier*): *the ebb tide.* Cf. **flood** (sense 3). **4 at a low ebb.** in a state of weakness or decline. [OE *ebba*]

EBCDIC ('ɛpsɪ,dɪk) *n acronym for* extended binary-coded decimal-interchange code: a computer code for representing alphanumeric characters.

ebon ('ɛb[ə]n) *adj, n* a poetic word for **ebony.** [C14: from L *hebenus;* see EBONY]

ebonite ('ɛbə,naɪt) *n* another name for **vulcanite.**

ebonize *or* **ebonise** ('ɛbə,naɪz) *vb* **ebonizes, ebonizing, ebonized** *or* **ebonises, ebonising, ebonised.** (*tr*) to stain or otherwise finish in imitation of ebony.

ebony ('ɛbənɪ) *n, pl* **ebonies. 1** any of various tropical and subtropical trees that have hard dark wood. **2** the wood of such a tree. **3a** a black colour. **3b** (*as adj*): *an ebony skin.* [C16 *hebeny*, from LL, from Gk, from *ebenos* ebony, from Egyptian]

Ebor. ('i:bɔ:) *abbrev. for* Eboracensis. [L.: (Archbishop) of York]

EBRD *abbrev. for* European Bank for Reconstruction and Development.

ebullient ➊ (ɪ'bʌljənt, ɪ'bʊl-) *adj* **1** overflowing with enthusiasm or excitement. **2** boiling. [C16: from L *ēbullīre* to bubble forth, be boisterous, from *bullīre* to BOIL[1]]
▸**e'bullience** *or* **e'bulliency** *n*

ebulliometer (ɪ,bʌlɪ'ɒmɪtə) *n Physics.* a device used to determine the boiling point of a solution.

ebullition (,ɛbə'lɪʃən) *n* **1** the process of boiling. **2** a sudden outburst, as of intense emotion. [C16: from LL *ēbullītiō;* see EBULLIENT]

EC *abbrev. for:* **1** European Community (now called European Union). **2** (in London postal codes) East Central.

ec- *combining form.* out from; away from: *eccentric; ecdysis.* [from Gk *ek* (before a vowel *ex*) out of, away from; see EX-[1]]

ECB *abbrev. for* European Central Bank.

eccentric ➊ (ɪk'sɛntrɪk) *adj* **1** deviating or departing from convention;

THESAURUS

easy *adj* **1 = not difficult**, a bed of roses, a piece of cake (*inf.*), child's play (*inf.*), clear, effortless, facile, light, no bother, no trouble, painless, plain sailing, simple, smooth, straightforward, uncomplicated, undemanding **2 = carefree**, calm, comfortable, contented, cushy (*inf.*), easeful, leisurely, peaceful, pleasant, quiet, relaxed, satisfied, serene, tranquil, undisturbed, untroubled, unworried, well-to-do **3 = tolerant**, easy-going, flexible, indulgent, lenient, liberal, light, mild, permissive, unburdensome, unoppressive **4 = relaxed**, affable, casual, easy-going, friendly, gentle, graceful, gracious, informal, laid-back, mild, natural, open, pleasant, smooth, tolerant, unaffected, unceremonious, unconstrained, undemanding, unforced, unpretentious **5 = accommodating**, amenable, biddable, compliant, docile, gullible, manageable, pliant, soft, submissive, suggestible, susceptible, tractable, trusting, yielding
Antonyms *adj* ≠ **not difficult:** arduous, complex, demanding, difficult, exacting, exhausting, formidable, hard, impossible, onerous, stiff ≠ **carefree:** difficult, insecure, stressful, uncomfortable, worried ≠ **tolerant:** demanding, dictatorial, difficult, exacting, hard, harsh, inflexible, intolerant, rigid, stern, strict, unyielding ≠ **relaxed:** affected, anxious, forced, formal, self-conscious, stiff, uncomfortable, unnatural, worried ≠ **accommodating:** difficult, impossible, unyielding

easy-going *adj* **1 = relaxed**, amenable, calm, carefree, casual, complacent, easy, easy-oasy (*sl.*), even-tempered, flexible, happy-go-lucky, indulgent, insouciant, laid-back (*inf.*), lenient, liberal, mild, moderate, nonchalant, permissive, placid, serene, tolerant, unconcerned, uncritical, undemanding, unhurried
Antonyms *adj* anxious, edgy, fussy, hung-up (*sl.*), intolerant, irritated, nervy (*Brit. inf.*), neurotic, on edge, strict, tense, uptight (*inf.*)

eat *vb* **1 = consume**, chew, devour, gobble, ingest, munch, scoff (*sl.*), swallow **2 = destroy**, corrode, crumble, decay, dissolve, erode, rot, waste away, wear away **5 = have a meal**, break bread, chow down (*sl.*), dine, feed, take food, take nourishment

eatable *adj* **= edible**, comestible (*rare*), digestible, esculent, fit to eat, good, harmless, palatable, wholesome

eavesdrop *vb* **= listen in**, bug (*inf.*), earwig (*inf.*), monitor, overhear, snoop (*inf.*), spy, tap

eavesdropper *n* **= listener**, monitor, snooper (*inf.*), spy

ebb *vb* **1 = flow back**, abate, fall away, fall back, go out, recede, retire, retreat, retrocede, sink, subside, wane, withdraw **2 = decline**, decay, decrease, degenerate, deteriorate, diminish, drop, dwindle, fade away, fall away, flag, lessen, peter out, shrink, sink, slacken, weaken ◆ *n* **3 = flowing back**, ebb tide, going out, low tide, low water, reflux, regression, retreat, retrocession, subsidence, wane, waning, withdrawal

ebullience *n* **1 = exuberance**, brio, buoyancy, effervescence, effusiveness, elation, enthusiasm, excitement, exhilaration, high spirits, vivacity, zest

ebullient *adj* **1 = exuberant**, buoyant, effervescent, effusive, elated, enthusiastic, excited, exhilarated, frothy, gushing, in high spirits, irrepressible, vivacious, zestful

eccentric *adj* **1 = odd**, aberrant, abnormal, anomalous, bizarre, capricious, erratic, freakish, idiosyncratic, irregular, oddball (*inf.*), out-

irregular or odd. **2** situated away from the centre or the axis. **3** not having a common centre: *eccentric circles.* **4** not precisely circular. ◆ *n* **5** a person who deviates from normal forms of behaviour. **6** a device for converting rotary motion to reciprocating motion. [C16: from Med. L *eccentricus,* from Gk *ekkentros,* from *ek-* EX-[1] + *kentron* centre]
▸**ec'centrically** *adv*

eccentricity ❶ (ˌɛksɛn'trɪsɪtɪ) *n, pl* **eccentricities. 1** unconventional or irregular behaviour. **2** the state of being eccentric. **3** deviation from a circular path or orbit. **4** *Geom.* a number that expresses the shape of a conic section. **5** the degree of displacement of the geometric centre of a part from the true centre, esp. of the axis of rotation of a wheel.

eccl. *or* **eccles.** *abbrev. for* ecclesiastic(al).

Eccles. *or* **Eccl.** *Bible. abbrev. for* Ecclesiastes.

ecclesiastic ❶ (ɪˌkliːzɪ'æstɪk) *n* **1** a clergyman or other person in holy orders. ◆ *adj* **2** of or associated with the Christian Church or clergy.

ecclesiastical (ɪˌkliːzɪ'æstɪkᵊl) *adj* of or relating to the Christian Church.
▸**ecˌclesi'astically** *adv*

ecclesiasticism (ɪˌkliːzɪ'æstɪˌsɪzəm) *n* exaggerated attachment to the practices or principles of the Christian Church.

ecclesiology (ɪˌkliːzɪ'ɒlədʒɪ) *n* **1** the study of the Christian Church. **2** the study of Church architecture and decoration.
▸**ecclesiological** (ɪˌkliːzɪə'lɒdʒɪkᵊl) *adj*

eccrine ('ɛkrɪn) *adj* of or denoting glands that secrete externally, esp. the sweat glands. Cf. **apocrine.** [from Gk *ekkrinein,* from *ek-* EC- + *krinein* to separate]
▸**eccrinology** (ˌɛkrɪ'nɒlədʒɪ) *n*

ecdemic (ɛk'dɛmɪk) *adj* not indigenous or endemic; foreign: *an ecdemic disease.*

ecdysis ('ɛkdɪsɪs) *n, pl* **ecdyses** (-ˌsiːz). the periodic shedding of the cuticle in insects and other arthropods or the outer epidermal layer in reptiles. [C19: NL, from Gk *ekdusis,* from *ekduein* to strip, from *ek-* EX-[1] + *duein* to put on]

ECG *abbrev. for:* **1** electrocardiogram. **2** electrocardiograph.

echelon ❶ ('ɛʃəˌlɒn) *n* **1** a level of command, responsibility, etc. (esp. in **the upper echelons**). **2** *Mil.* **2a** a formation in which units follow one another but are offset sufficiently to allow each unit a line of fire ahead. **2b** a group formed in this way. ◆ *vb* **3** to assemble in echelon. [C18: from F *échelon,* lit.: rung of a ladder, from OF *eschiele* ladder, from L *scāla*]

echidna (ɪ'kɪdnə) *n, pl* **echidnas** *or* **echidnae** (-niː). a spine-covered monotreme mammal of Australia and New Guinea, having a long snout and claws. Also called: **spiny anteater.** [C19: from NL, from L: viper, from Gk *ekhidna*]

echinoderm (ɪ'kaɪnəʊˌdɜːm) *n* any of various marine invertebrates characterized by tube feet, a calcite body-covering, and a five-part symmetrical body. The group includes the starfish, sea urchins, and sea cucumbers.

echinus (ɪ'kaɪnəs) *n, pl* **echini** (-naɪ). **1** *Archit.* a moulding between the shaft and the abacus of a Doric column. **2** any sea urchin of the genus *Echinus,* such as the Mediterranean edible sea urchin. [C14: from L, from Gk *ekhinos*]

echo ❶ ('ɛkəʊ) *n, pl* **echoes. 1a** the reflection of sound or other radiation by a reflecting medium, esp. a solid object. **1b** the sound so reflected. **2** a repetition or imitation, esp. an unoriginal reproduction of another's opinions. **3** something that evokes memories. **4** (*sometimes pl*) an effect that continues after the original cause has disappeared: *echoes of the French Revolution.* **5** a person who copies another, esp. one who obsequiously agrees with another's opinions. **6a** the signal reflected by a radar target. **6b** the trace produced by such a signal on a radar screen. ◆ *vb* **echoes, echoing, echoed. 7** to resound or cause to resound with an echo. **8** (*intr*) (of sounds) to repeat or resound by echoes; reverberate. **9** (*tr*) (of persons) to repeat (words, opinions, etc.) in imitation, agreement, or flattery. **10** (*tr*) (of things) to resemble or imitate (another style, an earlier model, etc.). [C14: via L from Gk *ēkhō;* rel. to Gk *ēkhē* sound]
▸**'echoing** *adj* ▸**'echoless** *adj* ▸**'echo-ˌlike** *adj*

echocardiography (ˌɛkəʊˌkɑːdɪ'ɒgrəfɪ) *n* examination of the heart using ultrasound techniques.

echo chamber *n* a room with walls that reflect sound. It is used to make acoustic measurements and as a recording studio when echo effects are required. Also called: **reverberation chamber.**

echography (ɛ'kɒgrəfɪ) *n* medical examination of the internal structures of the body by means of ultrasound.

echoic ❶ (ɛ'kəʊɪk) *adj* **1** characteristic of or resembling an echo. **2** onomatopoeic; imitative.

echolalia (ˌɛkəʊ'leɪlɪə) *n Psychiatry.* the tendency to repeat mechanically words just spoken by another person. [C19: from NL, from ECHO + Gk *lalia* talk, chatter]

echolocation (ˌɛkəʊləʊ'keɪʃən) *n* determination of the position of an object by measuring the time taken for an echo to return from it and its direction.

echo sounder *n* a navigation device that determines depth by measuring the time taken for a pulse of sound to reach the sea bed or a submerged object and for the echo to return.
▸**echo sounding** *n*

echovirus *or* **ECHO virus** ('ɛkəʊˌvaɪrəs) *n* any of a group of viruses that can cause symptoms of mild meningitis, the common cold, or infections of the intestinal and respiratory tracts. [C20: from initials of *Enteric Cytopathic Human Orphan* ("orphan" because orig. believed to be unrelated to any disease) + VIRUS]

éclair (eɪ'klɛə, ɪ'klɛə) *n* a finger-shaped cake of choux pastry, usually filled with cream and covered with chocolate. [C19: from F, lit.: lightning (prob. because it does not last long)]

eclampsia (ɪ'klæmpsɪə) *n Pathol.* a toxic condition that sometimes develops in the last three months of pregnancy, characterized by high blood pressure, weight gain, and convulsions. [C19: from NL, from Gk *eklampsis* a shining forth]

éclat ❶ (eɪ'klɑː) *n* **1** brilliant or conspicuous success, effect, etc. **2** showy display; ostentation. **3** social distinction. **4** approval; acclaim; applause. [C17: from F, from *éclater* to burst]

eclectic ❶ (ɪ'klɛktɪk, ɛ'klɛk-) *adj* **1** selecting from various styles, ideas, methods, etc. **2** composed of elements drawn from a variety of sources, styles, etc. ◆ *n* **3** a person who favours an eclectic approach. [C17: from Gk *eklektikos,* from *eklegein* to select, from *legein* to gather]
▸**e'clectically** *adv* ▸**e'clecticism** *n*

eclipse ❶ (ɪ'klɪps) *n* **1** the total or partial obscuring of one celestial body by another (**total eclipse** *or* **partial eclipse**). A **solar eclipse** occurs when the moon passes between the sun and the earth; a **lunar eclipse** when the earth passes between the sun and the moon. **2** the period of time during which such a phenomenon occurs. **3** any dimming or obstruction of light. **4** a loss of importance, power, fame, etc., esp. through overshadowing by another. ◆ *vb* **eclipses, eclipsing, eclipsed.** (*tr*) **5** to cause an eclipse of. **6** to cast a shadow upon; obscure. **7** to overshadow or surpass. [C13: back formation from OE *eclypsis,* from L, from Gk *ekleipsis* a forsaking, from *ekleipein* to abandon]
▸**e'clipser** *n*

eclipsing binary *n* a binary star whose orbital plane lies in or near the line of sight so that one component is regularly eclipsed by its companion.

ecliptic (ɪ'klɪptɪk) *n* **1** *Astron.* **1a** the great circle on the celestial sphere representing the apparent annual path of the sun relative to the stars. **1b** (*as modifier*): *the ecliptic plane.* **2** an equivalent great circle on the terrestrial globe. ◆ *adj* **3** of or relating to an eclipse.
▸**e'cliptically** *adv*

eclogue ('ɛklɒg) *n* a pastoral or idyllic poem, usually in the form of a conversation. [C15: from L *ecloga* short poem, collection of extracts, from Gk *eklogē* selection]

eclosion (ɪ'kləʊʒən) *n* the emergence of an insect larva from the egg or an adult from the pupal case. [C19: from F, from *éclore* to hatch, ult. from L *exclūdere* to shut out]

eco- *combining form.* denoting ecology or ecological: *ecocide; ecosphere.*

ecocentric (ˌiːkəʊ'sɛntrɪk) *adj* having a serious concern for environmental issues: *ecocentric management.*

ecofriendly ('iːkəʊˌfrɛndlɪ) *adj* having a beneficial effect on the environment or at least not causing environmental damage.

ecol. *abbrev. for:* **1** ecological. **2** ecology.

E. coli (iː'kəʊlaɪ) *n* short for *Escherichia coli,* see **Escherichia.**

ecological (ˌiːkə'lɒdʒɪkᵊl) *adj* **1** of or relating to ecology. **2** (of a practice,

THESAURUS

landish, outré, peculiar, queer (*inf.*), quirky, rum (*Brit. sl.*), singular, strange, uncommon, unconventional, weird, whimsical ◆ *n* **5** = **crank** (*inf.*), card (*inf.*), case (*inf.*), character (*inf.*), freak (*inf.*), loose cannon, nonconformist, oddball (*inf.*), oddity, queer fish (*Brit. inf.*), weirdo (*inf.*)
Antonyms *adj* ≠ **odd:** average, conventional, normal, ordinary, regular, run-of-the-mill, straightforward, typical

eccentricity *n* **1, 2** = **oddity**, aberration, abnormality, anomaly, bizarreness, caprice, capriciousness, foible, freakishness, idiosyncrasy, irregularity, nonconformity, oddness, outlandishness, peculiarity, queerness (*inf.*), quirk, singularity, strangeness, unconventionality, waywardness, weirdness, whimsicality, whimsicalness

ecclesiastic *n* **1** = **clergyman**, churchman, cleric, divine, holy man, man of the cloth, minister, parson, pastor, priest ◆ *adj* **2** = **clerical**, church, churchly, divine, holy, pastoral, priestly, religious, spiritual

echelon *n* **1** = **level**, degree, grade, office, place, position, rank, tier

echo *n* **1** = **repetition**, answer, reverberation **2** = **copy**, imitation, mirror image, parallel, reflection, reiteration, reproduction **3** = **reminder**, allusion, evocation, hint, intimation, memory, suggestion, trace **4** *sometimes plural* = **repercussion**, aftereffect, aftermath, consequence ◆ *vb* **7, 8** = **repeat**, resound, reverberate **9, 10** = **copy**, ape, imitate, mirror, parallel, parrot, recall, reflect, reiterate, reproduce, resemble, ring, second

echoic *adj* **2** = **imitative**, onomatopoeic

éclat *n* **1** = **brilliance**, effect, success **2** = **showmanship**, display, lustre, ostentation, pomp, show, splendour **3** = **renown**, celebrity, distinction, fame, glory **4** = **acclaim**, acclamation, applause, approval, plaudits

eclectic *adj* **1, 2** = **comprehensive**, all-embracing, broad, catholic, dilettantish, diverse, diversified, general, heterogeneous, liberal, manifold, many-sided, multifarious, selective, varied, wide-ranging

eclipse *n* **1, 3** = **obscuring**, darkening, dimming, extinction, occultation, shading **4** = **decline**, diminution, failure, fall, loss ◆ *vb* **5, 6** = **obscure**, blot out, cloud, darken, dim, extinguish, overshadow, shroud, veil **7** = **surpass**, exceed, excel, outdo, outshine, put in the shade (*inf.*), transcend

policy, product, etc.) tending to benefit or cause minimal damage to the environment.
▸ˌ**ecoˈlogically** *adv*

ecology (ɪˈkɒlədʒɪ) *n* **1** the study of the relationships between living organisms and their environment. **2** the set of relationships of a particular organism with its environment. [C19: from G *Ökologie,* from Gk *oikos* house (hence, environment)]
▸**eˈcologist** *n*

econ. *abbrev. for:* **1** economical. **2** economics. **3** economy.

econometrics (ɪˌkɒnəˈmetrɪks) *n* (*functioning as sing*) the application of mathematical and statistical techniques to economic theories.
▸**eˌconoˈmetric** *or* **eˌconoˈmetrical** *adj* ▸**econometrician** (ɪˌkɒnəməˈtrɪʃən) *or* **econometrist** (ˌiːkəˈnɒmətrɪst, -ˌɛkə-) *n*

economic ⓣ (ˌiːkəˈnɒmɪk, ˌɛkə-) *adj* **1** of or relating to an economy, economics, or finance. **2** *Brit.* capable of being produced, operated, etc., for profit; profitable. **3** concerning or affecting material resources or welfare: *economic pests.* **4** concerned with or relating to the necessities of life; utilitarian. **5** a variant of **economical. 6** *Inf.* inexpensive; cheap.

economical ⓣ (ˌiːkəˈnɒmɪkᵊl, ˌɛkə-) *adj* **1** using the minimum required; not wasteful. **2** frugal; thrifty. **3** a variant of **economic** (senses 1–4). **4** *Euphemistic.* deliberately withholding information (esp. in **economical with the truth**).
▸ˌ**ecoˈnomically** *adv*

economic indicator *n* a statistical measure representing an economic variable: *the retail price index is an economic indicator of the actual level of prices.*

economic migrant *or* **refugee** *n* a person who emigrates from a poor country to a developed one in the hope of improving his or her standard of living.

economics ⓣ (ˌiːkəˈnɒmɪks, ˌɛkə-) *n* **1** (*functioning as sing*) the social science concerned with the production and consumption of goods and services and the analysis of the commercial activities of a society. **2** (*functioning as pl*) financial aspects.

economic sanctions *pl n* any actions taken by one nation or group of nations to harm the economy of another nation or group, often to force a political change.

economist (ɪˈkɒnəmɪst) *n* a specialist in economics.

economize ⓣ *or* **economise** (ɪˈkɒnəˌmaɪz) *vb* **economizes, economizing, economized** *or* **economises, economising, economised.** (often foll. by *on*) to limit or reduce (expense, waste, etc.).
▸**eˌconomiˈzation** *or* **eˌconomiˈsation** *n*

economy ⓣ (ɪˈkɒnəmɪ) *n, pl* **economies. 1** careful management of resources to avoid unnecessary expenditure or waste; thrift. **2** a means or instance of this; saving. **3** sparing, restrained, or efficient use. **4a** the complex of activities concerned with the production, distribution, and consumption of goods and services. **4b** a particular type or branch of this: *a socialist economy.* **5** the management of the resources, finances, income, and expenditure of a community, business enterprise, etc. **6a** a class of travel in aircraft, cheaper and less luxurious than first class. **6b** (*as modifier*): *economy class.* **7** (*modifier*) purporting to offer a larger quantity for a lower price: *economy pack.* **8** the orderly interplay between the parts of a system or structure. [C16: via L from Gk *oikonomia* domestic management, from *oikos* house + *-nomia,* from *nemein* to manage]

ecosphere (ˈiːkəʊˌsfɪə, ˈɛkəʊ-) *n* the parts of the universe, esp. on earth, where life can exist.

écossaise (ˌeɪkɒˈseɪz) *n* **1** a lively dance in two-four time. **2** the tune for such a dance. [C19: F, lit.: Scottish (dance)]

ecosystem (ˈiːkəʊˌsɪstəm, ˈɛkəʊ-) *n Ecology.* a system involving the interactions between a community and its nonliving environment. [C20: from ECO- + SYSTEM]

ecoterrorist (ˈiːkəʊˌtɛrərɪst) *n* a person who uses violence in order to achieve environmentalist aims.

ecotourism (ˈiːkəʊˌtʊərɪzəm) *n* tourism which is designed to contribute to the protection of the environment or at least minimize damage to it, often involving travel to areas of natural interest in developing countries or participation in environmental projects.
▸ˈ**ecoˌtourist** *n*

ecru (ˈɛkruː, ˈeɪkruː) *n, adj* (of) a greyish-yellow to a light greyish colour. [C19: from F, from *é-* (intensive) + *cru* raw, from L *crūdus;* see CRUDE]

ecstasy ⓣ (ˈɛkstəsɪ) *n, pl* **ecstasies. 1** (*often pl*) a state of exalted delight, joy, etc.; rapture. **2** intense emotion of any kind: *an ecstasy of rage.* **3** *Psychol.* overpowering emotion sometimes involving temporary loss of consciousness: often associated with mysticism. **4** *Sl.* 3,4-methylenedioxymethamphetamine: a powerful drug that acts as a stimulant and can produce hallucinations. [C14: from OF via Med. L from Gk *ekstasis* displacement, trance, from *ex-* out + *histanai* to cause to stand]

ecstatic ⓣ (ɛkˈstætɪk) *adj* **1** in a trancelike state of rapture or delight. **2** showing or feeling great enthusiasm. ◆ *n* **3** a person who has periods of intense trancelike joy.
▸**ecˈstatically** *adv*

ECT *abbrev. for* electroconvulsive therapy.

ecto- *combining form.* indicating outer, outside. [from Gk *ektos* outside, from *ek, ex* out]

ectoblast (ˈɛktəʊˌblæst) *n* another name for **ectoderm.**
▸ˌ**ectoˈblastic** *adj*

ectoderm (ˈɛktəʊˌdɜːm) *or* **exoderm** *n* the outer germ layer of an animal embryo, which gives rise to epidermis and nervous tissue.
▸ˌ**ectoˈdermal** *or* ˌ**ectoˈdermic** *adj*

ectomorph (ˈɛktəʊˌmɔːf) *n* a type of person having a body build characterized by thinness, weakness, and a lack of weight.
▸ˌ**ectoˈmorphic** *adj* ▸ˈ**ectoˌmorphy** *n*

-ectomy *n combining form.* indicating surgical excision of a part: *appendectomy.* [from NL *-ectomia,* from Gk *ek-* out + -TOMY]

ectopic pregnancy (ɛkˈtɒpɪk) *n Pathol.* the abnormal development of a fertilized egg outside the uterus, usually within a Fallopian tube.

ectoplasm (ˈɛktəʊˌplæzəm) *n* **1** *Cytology.* the outer layer of cytoplasm. **2** *Spiritualism.* the substance supposedly emanating from the body of a medium during trances.
▸ˌ**ectoˈplasmic** *adj*

ECU (*also* ˈeɪkjuː, ˈɛkjuː) *abbrev. for* European Currency Unit.

ecumenical ⓣ, **oecumenical** (ˌiːkjʊˈmɛnɪkᵊl, ˌɛk-) *or* **ecumenic, oecumenic** *adj* **1** of or relating to the Christian Church throughout the world, esp. with regard to its unity. **2** tending to promote unity among Churches. [C16: via LL from Gk *oikoumenikos,* from *oikein* to inhabit, from *oikos* house]
▸ˌ**ecuˈmenically** *or* ˌ**oecuˈmenically** *adv*

ecumenism (ɪˈkjuːməˌnɪzəm, ˈɛkjʊm-), **ecumenicism** (ˌiːkjʊˈmɛnɪˌsɪzəm, ˌɛk-) *or* **ecumenicalism** (ˌiːkjʊˈmɛnɪkəˌlɪzəm, ˌɛk-) *n* the aim of unity among all Christian churches throughout the world.

eczema (ˈɛksɪmə) *n Pathol.* a skin inflammation with lesions that scale, crust, or ooze a serous fluid, often accompanied by intense itching. [C18: from NL, from Gk *ekzema,* from *ek-* out + *zein* to boil]
▸**eczematous** (ɛkˈsɛmətəs) *adj*

ed. *abbrev. for:* **1** edited. **2** (*pl* **eds.**) edition. **3** (*pl* **eds.**) editor. **4** education.

-ed[1] *suffix.* forming the past tense of most English verbs. [OE *-de, -ede, -ode, -ade*]

-ed[2] *suffix.* forming the past participle of most English verbs. [OE *-ed, -od, -ad*]

-ed[3] *suffix forming adjectives from nouns.* possessing or having the characteristics of: *salaried; red-blooded.* [OE *-ede*]

Edam (ˈiːdæm) *n* a round yellow cheese with a red outside covering. [after *Edam,* in Holland]

EDC *abbrev. for* European Defence Community.

Edda (ˈɛdə) *n* **1** Also called: **Elder Edda, Poetic Edda.** a 12th-century collection of mythological Old Norse poems. **2** Also called: **Younger Edda, Prose Edda.** a treatise on versification together with a collection of Scandinavian myths, legends, and poems (?1222). [C18: ON]
▸**Eddaic** (ɛˈdeɪɪk) *adj*

eddo (ˈɛdəʊ) *n, pl* **eddoes.** another name for **taro.**

eddy ⓣ (ˈɛdɪ) *n, pl* **eddies. 1** a movement in air, water, or other fluid in which the current doubles back on itself causing a miniature whirlwind or whirlpool. **2** a deviation from or disturbance in the main trend of thought, life, etc. ◆ *vb* **eddies, eddying, eddied. 3** to move or cause to move against the main current. [C15: prob. from ON]

eddy current *n* an electric current induced in a massive conductor by an alternating magnetic field.

edelweiss (ˈeɪdᵊlˌvaɪs) *n* a small alpine flowering plant having white woolly oblong leaves and a tuft of floral leaves surrounding the flowers. [C19: G, lit.: noble white]

edema (ɪˈdiːmə) *n, pl* **edemata** (-mətə). the usual US spelling of **oedema.**

Eden (ˈiːdᵊn) *n* **1** Also called: **Garden of Eden.** *Bible.* the garden in which Adam and Eve were placed at the Creation. **2** a place or state of great

THESAURUS

economic *adj* **1** = **financial**, business, commercial, industrial, mercantile, trade **2** = **profitable**, money-making, productive, profit-making, remunerative, solvent, viable **3** = **monetary**, bread-and-butter (*inf.*), budgetary, financial, fiscal, material, pecuniary **6** *Informal* = **inexpensive**, cheap, fair, low, low-priced, modest, reasonable

economical *adj* **1** = **cost-effective**, efficient, money-saving, neat, sparing, time-saving, unwasteful, work-saving **2** = **thrifty**, careful, economizing, frugal, prudent, saving, scrimping, sparing
Antonyms *adj* ≠ **cost-effective:** loss-making, uneconomical, unprofitable, wasteful ≠ **thrifty:** extravagant, generous, imprudent, lavish, profligate, spendthrift, uneconomical, unthrifty, wasteful

economics *n* **1** = **finance**, commerce, the dismal science

economize *vb* = **cut back**, be economical, be frugal, be on a shoestring, be sparing, draw in one's horns, husband, pull in one's horns, retrench, save, scrimp, tighten one's belt
Antonyms *vb* be extravagant, push the boat out (*inf.*), spend, splurge, squander

economy *n* **1, 3** = **thrift**, frugality, husbandry, parsimony, providence, prudence, restraint, retrenchment, saving, sparingness, thriftiness

ecstasy *n* **1** = **rapture**, bliss, delight, elation, enthusiasm, euphoria, exaltation, fervour, frenzy, joy, ravishment, rhapsody, seventh heaven, trance, transport
Antonyms *n* affliction, agony, anguish, distress, hell, misery, pain, suffering, torment, torture

ecstatic *adj* **1, 2** = **rapturous**, blissful, cock-a-hoop, delirious, elated, enraptured, enthusiastic, entranced, euphoric, fervent, floating on air, frenzied, in seventh heaven, in transports of delight, joyful, joyous, on cloud nine (*inf.*), overjoyed, over the moon (*inf.*), rhapsodic, transported, walking on air

ecumenical *adj* **1, 2** = **unifying**, catholic, general, universal, worldwide

eddy *n* **1** = **swirl**, counter-current, counterflow, tideway, undertow, vortex, whirlpool ◆ *vb* **3** = **swirl**, whirl

delight or contentment. [C14: from LL, from Heb. *'ēdhen* place of pleasure]
▸**Edenic** (iːˈdɛnɪk) *adj*

edentate (iːˈdɛnteɪt) *n* **1** any mammal of the order *Edentata,* of tropical Central and South America, which have few or no teeth. The order includes anteaters, sloths, and armadillos. ◆ *adj* **2** of or relating to the order *Edentata.* [C19: from L *ēdentātus* lacking teeth, from *ēdentāre* to render toothless, from *e-* out + *dēns* tooth]

edge Ⓣ (ɛdʒ) *n* **1** a border, brim, or margin. **2** a brink or verge. **3** a line along which two faces or surfaces of a solid meet. **4** the sharp cutting side of a blade. **5** keenness, sharpness, or urgency. **6** force, effectiveness, or incisiveness: *the performance lacked edge.* **7** a ridge. **8 have the edge on** *or* **over.** to have a slight advantage or superiority over. **9 on edge. 9a** nervously irritable; tense. **9b** nervously excited or eager. **10 set (someone's) teeth on edge.** to make (someone) acutely irritated or uncomfortable. ◆ *vb* **edges, edging, edged. 11** *(tr)* to provide an edge or border for. **12** *(tr)* to shape or trim the edge or border of (something). **13** to push (one's way, someone, something, etc.) gradually, esp. edgeways. **14** *(tr) Cricket.* to hit (a bowled ball) with the edge of the bat. **15** *(tr)* to sharpen (a knife, etc.). [OE *ecg*]
▸**ˈedger** *n*

edgeways (ˈɛdʒˌweɪz) *or esp. US & Canad.* **edgewise** (ˈɛdʒˌwaɪz) *adv* **1** with the edge forwards or uppermost. **2** on, by, with, or towards the edge. **3 get a word in edgeways.** *(usually with a negative)* to interrupt a conversation in which someone else is talking incessantly.

edging (ˈɛdʒɪŋ) *n* **1** anything placed along an edge to finish it, esp. as an ornament. **2** the act of making an edge. ◆ *adj* **3** used for making an edge: *edging shears.*

edgy Ⓣ (ˈɛdʒɪ) *adj* **edgier, edgiest.** *(usually postpositive)* nervous, irritable, tense, or anxious.
▸**ˈedgily** *adv* ▸**ˈedginess** *n*

edh (ɛð) *or* **eth** (ɛθ, ɛð) *n* a character of the runic alphabet (ð) used to represent the voiced dental fricative as in *then, mother, bathe.*

edible Ⓣ (ˈɛdɪbᵊl) *adj* fit to be eaten; eatable. [C17: from LL *edibilis,* from L *edere* to eat]
▸**ˌediˈbility** *n*

edibles (ˈɛdɪbᵊlz) *pl n* articles fit to eat; food.

edict Ⓣ (ˈiːdɪkt) *n* **1** a decree or order issued by any authority. **2** any formal or authoritative command, proclamation, etc. [C15: from L *ēdictum,* from *ēdīcere* to declare]
▸**eˈdictal** *adj*

edifice Ⓣ (ˈɛdɪfɪs) *n* **1** a building, esp. a large or imposing one. **2** a complex or elaborate institution or organization. [C14: from OF, from L *aedificium,* from *aedificāre* to build; see EDIFY]

edify Ⓣ (ˈɛdɪˌfaɪ) *vb* **edifies, edifying, edified.** *(tr)* to improve the morality, intellect, etc., of, esp. by instruction. [C14: from OF, from L *aedificāre* to construct, from *aedēs* a dwelling, temple + *facere* to make]
▸**ˌedifiˈcation** *n* ▸**ˈediˌfying** *adj*

edit Ⓣ (ˈɛdɪt) *vb* **edits, editing, edited.** *(tr)* **1** to prepare (text) for publication by checking and improving its accuracy, clarity, etc. **2** to be in charge of (a publication, esp. a periodical). **3** to prepare (a film, tape, etc.) by rearrangement or selection of material. **4** *(tr)* to modify (a computer file). **5** (often foll. by *out*) to remove, as from a manuscript or film. [C18: back formation from EDITOR]

edit. *abbrev. for:* **1** edited. **2** edition. **3** editor.

edition Ⓣ (ɪˈdɪʃən) *n* **1** *Printing.* **1a** the entire number of copies of a book or other publication printed at one time. **1b** a copy from this number: *a first edition.* **2** one of a number of printings of a book or other publication, issued at separate times with alterations, amendments, etc. **3a** an issue of a work identified by its format: *a leather-bound edition.* **3b** an issue of a work identified by its editor or publisher: *the Oxford edition.* [C16: from L *ēditiō* a bringing forth, publishing, from *ēdere* to give out; see EDITOR]

editor (ˈɛdɪtə) *n* **1** a person who edits written material for publication. **2** a person in overall charge of a newspaper or periodical. **3** a person in charge of one section of a newspaper or periodical: *the sports editor.* **4** *Films.* a person who makes a selection and arrangement of shots. **5** a person in overall control of a television or radio programme that consists of various items. [C17: from LL: producer, exhibitor, from *ēdere* to give out, publish, from *ē-* out + *dāre* to give]
▸**ˈeditorˌship** *n*

editorial (ˌɛdɪˈtɔːrɪəl) *adj* **1** of or relating to editing or editors. **2** of, relating to, or expressed in an editorial. **3** of or relating to the content of a publication. ◆ *n* **4** an article in a newspaper, etc., expressing the opinion of the editor or the publishers.
▸**ˌediˈtorially** *adv*

editorialize *or* **editorialise** (ˌɛdɪˈtɔːrɪəˌlaɪz) *vb* **editorializes, editorializing, editorialized** *or* **editorialises, editorialising, editorialised.** *(intr)* to express an opinion as in an editorial.
▸**ˌediˌtorialiˈzation** *or* **ˌediˌtorialiˈsation** *n*

EDT (in the US and Canada) *abbrev. for* Eastern Daylight Time.

educate Ⓣ (ˈɛdjʊˌkeɪt) *vb* **educates, educating, educated.** *(mainly tr)* **1** *(also intr)* to impart knowledge by formal instruction to (a pupil); teach. **2** to provide schooling for. **3** to improve or develop (a person, taste, skills, etc.). **4** to train for some particular purpose or occupation. [C15: from L *ēducāre* to rear, educate, from *dūcere* to lead]
▸**ˈeducable** *or* **ˈeduˌcatable** *adj* ▸**ˌeducaˈbility** *or* **ˌeduˌcataˈbility** *n* ▸**ˈeducative** *adj*

educated Ⓣ (ˈɛdjʊˌkeɪtɪd) *adj* **1** having an education, esp. a good one. **2** displaying culture, taste, and knowledge; cultivated. **3** *(prenominal)* based on experience or information (esp. in **an educated guess**).

education Ⓣ (ˌɛdjʊˈkeɪʃən) *n* **1** the act or process of acquiring knowledge. **2** the knowledge or training acquired by this process. **3** the act or process of imparting knowledge, esp. at a school, college, or university. **4** the theory of teaching and learning. **5** a particular kind of instruction or training: *a university education.*
▸**ˌeduˈcational** *adj* ▸**ˌeduˈcationalist** *or* **ˌeduˈcationist** *n*

educator Ⓣ (ˈɛdjʊˌkeɪtə) *n* **1** a person who educates; teacher. **2** a specialist in education.

educe (ɪˈdjuːs) *vb* **educes, educing, educed.** *(tr) Rare.* **1** to evolve or develop. **2** to draw out or elicit (information, solutions, etc.). [C15: from L *ēdūcere,* from *ē-* out + *dūcere* to lead]
▸**eˈducible** *adj* ▸**eductive** (ɪˈdʌktɪv) *adj*

Edwardian (ɛdˈwɔːdɪən) *adj* of or characteristic of the reign of Edward VII, king of Great Britain and Ireland (1901–10).
▸**Edˈwardianˌism** *n*

-ee *suffix forming nouns.* **1** indicating a recipient of an action (as opposed, esp. in legal terminology, to the agent): *assignee; lessee.* **2** indicating a person in a specified state or condition: *absentee.* **3** indicating a diminutive form of something: *bootee.* [via OF *-é, -ée,* p.p. endings, from L *-ātus, -āta* -ATE[1]]

EEC *abbrev. for* (the former) European Economic Community.

EEG *abbrev. for:* **1** electroencephalogram. **2** electroencephalograph.

eel (iːl) *n* **1** any teleost fish such as the European freshwater eel, having a long snakelike body, a smooth slimy skin, and reduced fins. **2** any of various similar animals, such as the mud eel and the electric eel. **3** an evasive or untrustworthy person. [OE *ǣl*]
▸**ˈeel-ˌlike** *adj* ▸**ˈeely** *adj*

eelgrass (ˈiːlˌgrɑːs) *n* any of several perennial submerged marine plants having grasslike leaves.

THESAURUS

edge *n* **1, 2 = border,** bound, boundary, brim, brink, contour, flange, fringe, limit, line, lip, margin, outline, perimeter, periphery, rim, side, threshold, verge **5, 6 = sharpness,** acuteness, animation, bite, effectiveness, force, incisiveness, interest, keenness, point, pungency, sting, urgency, zest **8** *As in* **have the edge on** *or* **over = advantage,** ascendancy, dominance, lead, superiority, upper hand **9 on edge = nervous,** apprehensive, eager, edgy, excited, ill at ease, impatient, irritable, keyed up, on tenterhooks, tense, tetchy, twitchy *(inf.),* uptight *(inf.),* wired *(sl.)* ◆ *vb* **11, 12 = border,** bind, fringe, hem, rim, shape, trim **13 = inch,** creep, ease, sidle, steal, work, worm **15 = sharpen,** hone, strop, whet

edginess *n* **= nervousness,** anxiety, irascibility, irritability, jitters *(inf.),* nerves, nervous tension, prickliness, restiveness, tenseness, tetchiness, touchiness, twitchiness

edgy *adj* **= nervous,** anxious, ill at ease, irascible, irritable, keyed up, nervy *(Brit. inf.),* neurotic, on edge, on pins and needles, on tenterhooks, restive, tense, tetchy, touchy, twitchy *(inf.),* uptight *(inf.),* wired *(sl.)*

edible *adj* **= eatable,** comestible *(rare),* digestible, esculent, fit to eat, good, harmless, palatable, wholesome
Antonyms *adj* baneful, harmful, indigestible, inedible, noxious, pernicious, poisonous, uneatable

edict *n* **1, 2 = decree,** act, canon, command, demand, dictate, dictum, enactment, fiat, injunction, law, mandate, manifesto, order, ordinance, proclamation, pronouncement, pronunciamento, regulation, ruling, statute, ukase *(rare)*

edification *n* **= instruction,** education, elevation, enlightenment, guidance, improvement, information, nurture, schooling, teaching, tuition, uplifting

edifice *n* **1 = building,** construction, erection, fabric *(rare),* habitation, house, pile, structure

edify *vb* **= instruct,** educate, elevate, enlighten, guide, improve, inform, nurture, school, teach, uplift

edifying *adj* **= instructional,** elevating, enlightening, improving, inspiring, uplifting

edit *vb* **1 = revise,** adapt, annotate, censor, check, condense, correct, emend, polish, redact, rephrase, rewrite **2, 3 = put together,** assemble, compose, rearrange, reorder, select

edition *n* **2, 3 = version,** copy, impression, issue, number, printing, volume

educate *vb* **1-4 = teach,** civilize, coach, cultivate, develop, discipline, drill, edify, enlighten, exercise, foster, improve, indoctrinate, inform, instruct, mature, rear, school, train, tutor

educated *adj* **1 = taught,** coached, informed, instructed, nurtured, schooled, tutored **2 = cultured,** civilized, cultivated, enlightened, experienced, informed, knowledgeable, learned, lettered, literary, polished, refined, sophisticated, tasteful
Antonyms *adj* **≠ taught:** ignorant, illiterate, uneducated, unlettered, unread, unschooled, untaught **≠ cultured:** benighted, lowbrow, philistine, uncultivated, uncultured, uneducated

education *n* **1-5 = teaching,** breeding, civilization, coaching, cultivation, culture, development, discipline, drilling, edification, enlightenment, erudition, improvement, indoctrination, instruction, knowledge, nurture, scholarship, schooling, training, tuition, tutoring

educational *adj* **1-5 = instructive,** cultural, didactic, edifying, educative, enlightening, heuristic, improving, informative

educative *adj* **1-4 = instructive,** didactic, edifying, educational, enlightening, heuristic, improving, informative

educator *n* **1 = teacher,** coach, edifier, educationalist *or* educationist, instructor, pedagogue, schoolmaster *or* schoolmistress, schoolteacher, trainer, tutor

eelpout (ˈiːlˌpaʊt) *n* **1** a marine eel-like fish. **2** another name for **burbot**. [OE *ǣlepūte*]

eelworm (ˈiːlˌwɜːm) *n* any of various nematode worms, esp. the wheatworm and the vinegar eel.

e'en (iːn) *adv, n Poetic or arch.* contraction of **even**[2] or **evening**.

e'er (ɛə) *adv Poetic or arch.* contraction of **ever**.

-eer *or* **-ier** *suffix.* **1** (*forming nouns*) indicating a person who is concerned with or who does something specified: *auctioneer; engineer; profiteer; mutineer.* **2** (*forming verbs*) to be concerned with something specified: *electioneer.* [from OF *-ier*, from L *-arius* -ARY]

eerie Ⓣ (ˈɪərɪ) *adj* **eerier, eeriest.** uncannily frightening or disturbing; weird. [C13: orig. Scot. & N English, prob. from OE *earg* cowardly]
▸ **ˈeerily** *adv* ▸ **ˈeeriness** *n*

EETPU (in Britain) *abbrev. for* Electrical, Electronic, Telecommunications, and Plumbing Union.

eff (ɛf) *vb* **1** euphemism for **fuck** (esp. in **eff off**). **2 eff and blind.** *Sl.* to use obscene language.
▸ **ˈeffing** *n, adj, adv*

efface Ⓣ (ɪˈfeɪs) *vb* **effaces, effacing, effaced.** (*tr*) **1** to obliterate or make dim. **2** to make (oneself) inconspicuous or humble. **3** to rub out; erase. [C15: from F *effacer*, lit.: to obliterate the face; see FACE]
▸ **efˈfaceable** *adj* ▸ **efˈfacement** *n* ▸ **efˈfacer** *n*

effect Ⓣ (ɪˈfɛkt) *n* **1** something produced by a cause or agent; result. **2** power to influence or produce a result. **3** the condition of being operative (esp. in **in** *or* **into effect**). **4 take effect.** to become operative or begin to produce results. **5** basic meaning or purpose (esp. in **to that effect**). **6** an impression, usually contrived (esp. in **for effect**). **7** a scientific phenomenon: *the Doppler effect.* **8 in effect. 8a** in fact; actually. **8b** for all practical purposes. **9** the overall impression or result. ◆ *vb* **10** (*tr*) to cause to occur; accomplish. [C14: from L *effectus* a performing, tendency, from *efficere* to accomplish, from *facere* to do]
▸ **efˈfecter** *n* ▸ **efˈfectible** *adj*

effective Ⓣ (ɪˈfɛktɪv) *adj* **1** productive of or capable of producing a result. **2** in effect; operative. **3** impressive: *an effective entrance.* **4** (*prenominal*) actual rather than theoretical. **5** (of a military force, etc.) equipped and prepared for action. ◆ *n* **6** a serviceman equipped and prepared for action.
▸ **efˈfectively** *adv* ▸ **efˈfectiveness** *n*

effects Ⓣ (ɪˈfɛkts) *pl n* **1** Also called: **personal effects.** personal belongings. **2** lighting, sounds, etc., to accompany a stage, film, or broadcast production.

effectual Ⓣ (ɪˈfɛktjʊəl) *adj* **1** capable of or successful in producing an intended result; effective. **2** (of documents, etc.) having legal force.
▸ **efˌfectuˈality** *or* **efˈfectualness** *n*

effectually (ɪˈfɛktjʊəlɪ) *adv* **1** with the intended effect. **2** in effect.

effectuate Ⓣ (ɪˈfɛktjʊˌeɪt) *vb* **effectuates, effectuating, effectuated.** (*tr*) to cause to happen; effect; accomplish.
▸ **efˌfectuˈation** *n*

effeminate Ⓣ (ɪˈfɛmɪnɪt) *adj* (of a man or boy) displaying characteristics regarded as typical of a woman; not manly. [C14: from L *effēmināre* to make into a woman, from *fēmina* woman]
▸ **efˈfeminacy** *or* **efˈfeminateness** *n*

effendi (ɛˈfɛndɪ) *n, pl* **effendis. 1** (in the Ottoman Empire) a title of respect. **2** (in Turkey since 1934) the oral title of address equivalent to *Mr.* [C17: from Turkish *efendi* master, from Mod. Gk *aphentēs*, from Gk *authentēs* lord, doer]

efferent (ˈɛfərənt) *adj Physiol.* carrying or conducting outwards, esp. from the brain or spinal cord. Cf. **afferent.** [C19: from L *efferre* to bear off, from *ferre* to bear]
▸ **ˈefference** *n*

effervesce Ⓣ (ˌɛfəˈvɛs) *vb* **effervesces, effervescing, effervesced.** (*intr*) **1** (of a liquid) to give off bubbles of gas. **2** (of a gas) to issue in bubbles from a liquid. **3** to exhibit great excitement, vivacity, etc. [C18: from L *effervescere* to foam up, ult. from *fervēre* to boil, ferment]
▸ **ˌefferˈvescingly** *adv*

effervescent Ⓣ (ˌɛfəˈvɛsᵊnt) *adj* **1** (of a liquid) giving off bubbles of gas. **2** high-spirited; vivacious.
▸ **ˌefferˈvescence** *n*

effete Ⓣ (ɪˈfiːt) *adj* **1** weak or decadent. **2** exhausted; spent. **3** (of animals or plants) no longer capable of reproduction. [C17: from L *effētus* exhausted by bearing, from *fētus* having brought forth; see FETUS]
▸ **efˈfeteness** *n*

efficacious Ⓣ (ˌɛfɪˈkeɪʃəs) *adj* capable of or successful in producing an intended result; effective. [C16: from L *efficāx* powerful, efficient, from *efficere* to achieve]
▸ **efficacy** (ˈɛfɪkəsɪ) *or* **ˌeffiˈcaciousness** *n*

efficiency Ⓣ (ɪˈfɪʃənsɪ) *n, pl* **efficiencies. 1** the quality or state of being efficient. **2** the ratio of the useful work done by a machine, etc., to the energy input, often expressed as a percentage.

efficient Ⓣ (ɪˈfɪʃənt) *adj* **1** functioning or producing effectively and with the least waste of effort; competent. **2** *Philosophy.* producing a direct effect. [C14: from L *efficiēns* effecting]

effigy Ⓣ (ˈɛfɪdʒɪ) *n, pl* **effigies. 1** a portrait, esp. as a monument. **2** a crude representation of someone, used as a focus for contempt or ridicule (often in **burn** *or* **hang in effigy**). [C18: from L *effigiēs*, from *effingere* to form, portray, from *fingere* to shape]

effleurage (ˌɛflɜːˈrɑːʒ) *n Med.* a light stroking movement used in massage. [C19: from F]

effloresce (ˌɛflɔːˈrɛs) *vb* **effloresces, efflorescing, effloresced.** (*intr*) **1** to burst forth as into flower; bloom. **2** to become powdery by loss of water or crystallization. **3** to become encrusted with powder or crystals as a result of chemical change or evaporation. [C18: from L *efflōrēscere* to blossom, from *flōrēscere*, from *flōs* flower]

efflorescence (ˌɛflɔːˈrɛsᵊns) *n* **1** a bursting forth or flowering. **2** *Chem.*,

THESAURUS

eerie *adj* = **frightening**, awesome, creepy (*inf.*), eldritch (*poetic*), fearful, ghostly, mysterious, scary (*inf.*), spectral, spooky (*inf.*), strange, uncanny, unearthly, uneasy, weird

efface *vb* **1, 3** = **obliterate**, annihilate, blot out, cancel, cross out, delete, destroy, dim, eradicate, erase, excise, expunge, extirpate, raze, rub out, wipe out **2 efface oneself** = **make oneself inconspicuous**, be bashful, be diffident, be modest, be retiring, be timid, be unassertive, humble oneself, lower oneself, withdraw

effect *n* **1** = **result**, aftermath, conclusion, consequence, end result, event, fruit, issue, outcome, upshot **2** = **power**, clout (*inf.*), effectiveness, efficacy, efficiency, fact, force, influence, reality, strength, use, validity, vigour, weight **3** = **operation**, action, enforcement, execution, force, implementation **4 take effect** = **produce results**, become operative, begin, come into force, work **5** = **impression**, drift, essence, impact, import, meaning, purport, purpose, sense, significance, tenor **8 in effect** = **in fact**, actually, effectively, essentially, for practical purposes, in actuality, in reality, in truth, really, to all intents and purposes, virtually ◆ *vb* **10** = **bring about**, accomplish, achieve, actuate, carry out, cause, complete, consummate, create, effectuate, execute, fulfil, give rise to, initiate, make, perform, produce

effective *adj* **1** = **efficient**, able, active, adequate, capable, competent, effectual, efficacious, energetic, operative, productive, serviceable, useful **2** = **in operation**, active, actual, current, in effect, in execution, in force, operative, real **3** = **powerful**, cogent, compelling, convincing, emphatic, forceful, forcible, impressive, moving, persuasive, potent, striking, telling
Antonyms *adj* ≠ **efficient:** futile, inadequate, incompetent, ineffective, inefficient, insufficient, otiose, unimpressive, unproductive, useless, vain, worthless ≠ **in operation:** inactive, inoperative ≠ **powerful:** feeble, ineffectual, pathetic, powerless, tame, weak

effectiveness *n* **1** = **power**, bottom, capability, clout (*inf.*), cogency, effect, efficacy, efficiency, force, influence, potency, strength, success, use, validity, vigour, weight

effects *pl n* **1** = **belongings**, chattels, furniture, gear, goods, movables, paraphernalia, possessions, property, things, trappings

effectual *adj* **1** = **effective**, capable, efficacious, efficient, forcible, influential, potent, powerful, productive, serviceable, successful, telling, useful **2** = **binding**, authoritative, in force, lawful, legal, licit (*rare*), sound, valid

effectuate *vb* = **bring about**, accomplish, achieve, carry out *or* through, cause, complete, create, do, effect, execute, fulfil, make, perform, procure, produce

effeminacy *n* = **womanliness**, delicacy, femininity, softness, tenderness, unmanliness, weakness, womanishness

effeminate *adj* = **womanly**, camp (*inf.*), delicate, feminine, poofy (*sl.*), sissy, soft, tender, unmanly, weak, wimpish *or* wimpy (*inf.*), womanish, womanlike
Antonyms *adj* butch (*sl.*), he-man (*inf.*), macho, manly, virile

effervesce *vb* **1** = **bubble**, ferment, fizz, foam, froth, sparkle

effervescence *n* **1** = **bubbling**, ferment, fermentation, fizz, foam, foaming, froth, frothing, sparkle **2** = **liveliness**, animation, brio, buoyancy, ebullience, enthusiasm, excitedness, excitement, exhilaration, exuberance, gaiety, high spirits, pizzazz *or* pizazz (*inf.*), vim (*sl.*), vitality, vivacity, zing (*inf.*)

effervescent *adj* **1** = **bubbling**, bubbly, carbonated, fermenting, fizzing, fizzy, foaming, foamy, frothing, frothy, sparkling **2** = **lively**, animated, bubbly, buoyant, ebullient, enthusiastic, excited, exhilarated, exuberant, gay, in high spirits, irrepressible, merry, vital, vivacious, zingy (*inf.*)
Antonyms *adj* ≠ **bubbling:** flat, flavourless, insipid, stale, watery, weak ≠ **lively:** boring, dull, flat, insipid, jejune, lacklustre, lifeless, spiritless, stale, unexciting, vapid

effete *adj* **1** = **decadent**, corrupt, debased, decayed, decrepit, degenerate, dissipated, enervated, enfeebled, feeble, ineffectual, overrefined, spoiled, weak **2** = **worn out**, burnt out, drained, enervated, exhausted, played out, spent, used up, wasted **3** = **sterile**, barren, fruitless, infecund, infertile, unfruitful, unproductive, unprolific

efficacious *adj* = **effective**, active, adequate, capable, competent, effectual, efficient, energetic, operative, potent, powerful, productive, serviceable, successful, useful
Antonyms *adj* abortive, futile, ineffective, ineffectual, inefficacious, unavailing, unproductive, unsuccessful, useless

efficacy *n* = **effectiveness**, ability, capability, competence, effect, efficaciousness, efficiency, energy, force, influence, potency, power, strength, success, use, vigour, virtue, weight

efficiency *n* **1** = **competence**, ability, adeptness, capability, economy, effectiveness, efficacy, power, productivity, proficiency, readiness, skilfulness, skill

efficient *adj* **1** = **competent**, able, adept, businesslike, capable, economic, effective, effectual, organized, powerful, productive, proficient, ready, skilful, well-organized, workmanlike
Antonyms *adj* cowboy (*inf.*), disorganized, incompetent, ineffectual, inefficient, inept, slipshod, sloppy, unbusinesslike, unproductive, wasteful

effigy *n* **1, 2** = **likeness**, dummy, figure, guy,

geol. **2a** the process of efflorescing. **2b** the powdery substance formed as a result of this process. **3** any skin rash or eruption.
▸ ˌefflo'rescent *adj*

effluence 🅣 ('ɛfluəns) *or* **efflux** ('ɛflʌks) *n* **1** the act or process of flowing out. **2** something that flows out.

effluent 🅣 ('ɛfluənt) *n* **1** liquid discharged as waste, as from an industrial plant or sewage works. **2** radioactive waste released from a nuclear power station. **3** a stream that flows out of another body of water. **4** something that flows out or forth. ◆ *adj* **5** flowing out or forth. [C18: from L *effluere* to run forth, from *fluere* to flow]

effluvium 🅣 (ɛ'flu:vɪəm) *n, pl* **effluvia** (-vɪə) *or* **effluviums.** an unpleasant smell or exhalation, as of gaseous waste or decaying matter. [C17: from L: a flowing out; see EFFLUENT]
▸ ef'fluvial *adj*

effort 🅣 ('ɛfət) *n* **1** physical or mental exertion. **2** a determined attempt. **3** achievement; creation. [C15: from OF *esfort*, from *esforcier* to force, ult. from L *fortis* strong]
▸ 'effortful *adj* ▸ 'effortless *adj*

effrontery 🅣 (ɪ'frʌntərɪ) *n, pl* **effronteries.** shameless or insolent boldness. [C18: from F, from OF *esfront* barefaced, shameless, from LL *effrons*, lit.: putting forth one's forehead]

effulgent (ɪ'fʌldʒənt) *adj* radiant; brilliant. [C18: from L *effulgēre* to shine forth, from *fulgēre* to shine]
▸ ef'fulgence *n* ▸ ef'fulgently *adv*

effuse *vb* (ɪ'fju:z), **effuses, effusing, effused.** **1** to pour or flow out. **2** to spread out; diffuse. ◆ *adj* (ɪ'fju:s). **3** *Bot.* (esp. of an inflorescence) spreading out loosely. [C16: from L *effūsus* poured out, from *effundere* to shed]

effusion 🅣 (ɪ'fju:ʒən) *n* **1** an unrestrained outpouring in speech or words. **2** the act or process of being poured out. **3** something that is poured out. **4** *Med.* **4a** the escape of blood or other fluid into a body cavity or tissue. **4b** the fluid that has escaped.

effusive 🅣 (ɪ'fju:sɪv) *adj* **1** extravagantly demonstrative of emotion; gushing. **2** (of rock) formed by the solidification of magma.
▸ ef'fusively *adv* ▸ ef'fusiveness *n*

EFL *abbrev. for* English as a Foreign Language.

eft (ɛft) *n* a dialect or archaic name for a **newt.** [OE *efeta*]

EFTA ('ɛftə) *n acronym for* European Free Trade Association; established in 1960 to eliminate trade tariffs on industrial products; the current members are Austria, Iceland, Norway, Sweden, and Switzerland.

EFTPOS ('ɛftpɒs) *n acronym for* electronic funds transfer at point of sale.

EFTS *abbrev. for* electronic funds transfer system.

Eg. *abbrev. for:* **1** Egypt(ian). **2** Egyptology.

e.g., eg, *or* **eg.** *abbrev. for* exempli gratia. [L: for example]

egad (ɪ'gæd, i:'gæd) *interj Arch.* a mild oath. [C17: prob. var. of *Ah God!*]

egalitarian (ɪˌgælɪ'tɛərɪən) *adj* **1** of or upholding the doctrine of the equality of mankind. ◆ *n* **2** an adherent of egalitarian principles. [C19: alteration of *equalitarian*, through infl. of F *égal* equal]
▸ eˌgali'tarianˌism *n*

egg[1] (ɛg) *n* **1** the oval or round reproductive body laid by the females of birds, reptiles, fishes, insects, and some other animals, consisting of a developing embryo, its food store, and sometimes jelly or albumen, all surrounded by an outer shell or membrane. **2** Also called: **egg cell.** any female gamete; ovum. **3** the egg of the domestic hen used as food. **4** something resembling an egg, esp. in shape. **5 good** (*or* **bad**) **egg.** *Old-fashioned inf.* a good (or bad) person. **6 put** *or* **have all one's eggs in one basket.** to stake everything on a single venture. **7 teach one's grandmother to suck eggs.** *Inf.* to presume to teach someone something that he knows already. **8 with egg on one's face.** *Inf.* made to look ridiculous. [C14: from ON *egg*; rel. to OE *ǣg*]

egg[2] 🅣 (ɛg) *vb* (*tr*; usually foll. by *on*) to urge or incite, esp. to daring or foolish acts. [OE *eggian*]

egg-and-spoon race *n* a race in which runners carry an egg balanced in a spoon.

eggbeater ('ɛgˌbi:tə) *n* **1** Also called: **eggwhisk.** a utensil for beating eggs; whisk. **2** *Chiefly US & Canad.* an informal name for **helicopter.**

egger *or* **eggar** ('ɛgə) *n* any of various European moths having brown bodies and wings. [C18: from EGG[1], from the egg-shaped cocoon]

egghead ('ɛgˌhɛd) *n Inf.* an intellectual.

eggnog (ˌɛg'nɒg) *n* a drink made of eggs, milk, sugar, spice, and brandy, rum, or other spirit. Also called: **egg flip.** [C19: from EGG[1] + NOG]

eggplant ('ɛgˌplɑ:nt) *n* another name (esp. US, Canad., & Austral.) for **aubergine.**

eggshell ('ɛgˌʃɛl) *n* **1** the hard porous outer layer of a bird's egg. **2** (*modifier*) (of paint) having a very slight sheen.

eggshell porcelain *or* **china** *n* a very thin translucent porcelain originally from China.

egg tooth *n* (in embryo reptiles) a temporary tooth or (in birds) projection of the beak used for piercing the eggshell.

eglantine ('ɛglənˌtaɪn) *n* another name for **sweetbrier.** [C14: from OF *aiglent*, ult. from L *acus* needle, from *acer* sharp, keen]

EGM *abbrev. for* extraordinary general meeting.

ego ('i:gəu, 'ɛgəu) *n, pl* **egos.** **1** the self of an individual person; the conscious subject. **2** *Psychoanalysis.* the conscious mind, based on perception of the environment: modifies the antisocial instincts of the id and is itself modified by the conscience (superego). **3** one's image of oneself; morale. **4** egotism; conceit. [C19: from L: I]

egocentric 🅣 (ˌi:gəu'sɛntrɪk, ˌɛg-) *adj* **1** regarding everything only in relation to oneself; self-centred. ◆ *n* **2** a self-centred person; egotist.
▸ ˌegocen'tricity *n* ▸ ˌego'centrism *n*

egoism ('i:gəuˌɪzəm, 'ɛg-) *n* **1** concern for one's own interests and welfare. **2** *Ethics.* the theory that the pursuit of one's own welfare is the highest good. **3** self-centredness; egotism.
▸ 'egoist *n* ▸ ˌego'istic *or* ˌego'istical *adj*

egomania (ˌi:gəu'meɪnɪə, ˌɛg-) *n Psychiatry.* obsessive love for oneself.
▸ ˌego'maniˌac *n* ▸ egomaniacal (ˌi:gəumə'naɪkᵊl, ˌɛg-) *adj*

egotism 🅣 ('i:gəˌtɪzəm, 'ɛgə-) *n* **1** an inflated sense of self-importance or superiority; self-centredness. **2** excessive reference to oneself. [C18: from L *ego* I + -ISM]
▸ 'egotist *n* ▸ ˌego'tistic *or* ˌego'tistical *adj*

ego trip *n Inf.* something undertaken to boost or draw attention to a person's own image or appraisal of himself.

egregious (ɪ'gri:dʒəs, -dʒɪəs) *adj* **1** outstandingly bad; flagrant. **2** *Arch.* distinguished; eminent. [C16: from L *ēgregius* outstanding (lit.: standing out from the herd), from *ē-* out + *grex* flock, herd]
▸ e'gregiousness *n*

egress 🅣 ('i:grɛs) *n* **1** Also: **egression.** the act of going or coming out; emergence. **2** a way out; exit. **3** the right to go out or depart. [C16: from L *ēgredī* to come forth, depart, from *gradī* to move, step]

egret ('i:grɪt) *n* any of various wading birds similar to herons but usually having white plumage and, in the breeding season, long feathery plumes. [C15: from OF *aigrette*, of Gmc origin]

Egyptian (ɪ'dʒɪpʃən) *adj* **1** of or relating to Egypt, a republic in NE Africa, its inhabitants, or their dialect of Arabic. **2** of or characteristic of the ancient Egyptians, their language, or culture. ◆ *n* **3** a native or inhabitant of Egypt. **4** a member of a people who established an advanced civilization in Egypt that flourished from the late fourth millennium B.C. **5** the extinct language of the ancient Egyptians.

Egyptology (ˌi:dʒɪp'tɒlədʒɪ) *n* the study of the archaeology and language of ancient Egypt.
▸ ˌEgyp'tologist *n*

eh (eɪ) *interj* an exclamation used to express questioning surprise or to seek the repetition or confirmation of a statement or question.

EHF *abbrev. for* extremely high frequency.

eider *or* **eider duck** ('aɪdə) *n* any of several sea ducks of the N hemisphere. See **eiderdown.** [C18: from ON *æthr*]

eiderdown ('aɪdəˌdaun) *n* **1** the breast down of the female eider duck, used for stuffing pillows, quilts, etc. **2** a thick, warm cover for a bed, enclosing a soft filling.

eidetic (aɪ'dɛtɪk) *adj Psychol.* **1** (of visual, or sometimes auditory, im-

THESAURUS

icon, idol, image, picture, portrait, representation, statue

effluence *n* **1, 2** = **outflow**, discharge, effluent, effluvium, efflux, emanation, emission, exhalation, flow, issue, outpouring, secretion

effluent *n* **1** = **waste**, effluvium, pollutant, sewage **4** = **outflow**, discharge, effluence, efflux, emanation, emission, exhalation, flow, issue, outpouring ◆ *adj* **5** = **outflowing**, discharged, emanating, emitted

effluvium *n* = **smell**, exhalation, exhaust, fumes, malodour, mephitis, miasma, niff (*Brit. sl.*), odour, pong (*Brit. inf.*), reek, stench, stink

effort *n* **1** = **exertion**, application, blood, sweat, and tears (*inf.*), elbow grease (*facetious*), endeavour, energy, force, labour, pains, power, strain, stress, stretch, striving, struggle, toil, travail (*literary*), trouble, work **2** = **attempt**, endeavour, essay, go (*inf.*), shot (*inf.*), stab (*inf.*), try **3** = **creation**, accomplishment, achievement, act, deed, feat, job, product, production

effortless *adj* **1** = **easy**, easy-peasy (*sl.*), facile, painless, plain sailing, simple, smooth, uncomplicated, undemanding, untroublesome
Antonyms *adj* demanding, difficult, formidable, hard, onerous, uphill

effrontery *n* = **insolence**, arrogance, assurance, audacity, boldness, brashness, brass neck (*Brit. inf.*), brazenness, cheek (*inf.*), cheekiness, chutzpah (*US & Canad. inf.*), disrespect, front, gall (*inf.*), impertinence, impudence, incivility, nerve, presumption, rudeness, shamelessness, temerity

effusion *n* **1** = **talk**, address, outpouring, speech, utterance, writing **2** = **outpouring**, discharge, effluence, efflux, emission, gush, issue, outflow, shedding, stream

effusive *adj* **1** = **demonstrative**, ebullient, enthusiastic, expansive, extravagant, exuberant, free-flowing, fulsome, gushing, lavish, overflowing, profuse, talkative, unreserved, unrestrained, wordy

egg[2] *usually with* **on** *vb* = **encourage**, exhort, goad, incite, prod, prompt, push, spur, urge
Antonyms *vb* deter, discourage, dissuade, hold back, put off, talk out of

egocentric *adj* **1** = **self-centred**, egoistic, egoistical, egotistic, egotistical, selfish

egotism *n* **1** = **self-centredness**, conceitedness, egocentricity, egomania, narcissism, self-absorption, self-admiration, self-conceit, self-esteem, self-importance, self-interest, selfishness, self-love, self-praise, self-regard, self-seeking, superiority, vainglory, vanity

egotist *n* **1** = **egomaniac**, bighead (*inf.*), blowhard (*inf.*), boaster, braggadocio, braggart, narcissist, self-admirer, self-seeker, swaggerer

egotistic *adj* **1** = **self-centred**, boasting, bragging, conceited, egocentric, egomaniacal, full of oneself, narcissistic, opinionated, self-absorbed, self-admiring, self-important, self-seeking, superior, vain, vainglorious

egress *n* **1, 2** = **exit**, departure, emergence,

ages) very vivid and allowing detailed recall of something previously perceived: thought to be common in children. **2** relating to or subject to such imagery. [C20: from Gk *eidētikos*, from *eidos* shape, form]

▸**ei'detically** *adv*

Eid-ul-Adha ('iːdʊlˌɑːdə) *n* an annual Muslim festival marking the end of the pilgrimage to Mecca. Animals are sacrificed and their meat shared among the poor. [from Ar. *id ul adha* festival of sacrifice]

Eid-ul-Fitr ('iːdʊlˌfiːtə) *n* an annual Muslim festival marking the end of Ramadan, involving the exchange of gifts and a festive meal. [from Ar. *id ul fitr* festival of fast-breaking]

eight (eɪt) *n* **1** the cardinal number that is the sum of one and seven and the product of two and four. **2** a numeral, 8, VIII, etc., representing this number. **3** the amount or quantity that is one greater than seven. **4** something representing, represented by, or consisting of eight units. **5** *Rowing*. **5a** a racing shell propelled by eight oarsmen. **5b** the crew of such a shell. **6** Also called: **eight o'clock**. eight hours after noon or midnight. **7 have one over the eight**. *Sl*. to be drunk. ◆ *determiner* **8a** amounting to eight. **8b** (*as pron*): *I could only find eight*. [OE *eahta*]

eighteen ('eɪ'tiːn) *n* **1** the cardinal number that is the sum of ten and eight and the product of two and nine. **2** a numeral, 18, XVIII, etc., representing this number. **3** the amount or quantity that is eight more than ten. **4** something represented by, representing, or consisting of 18 units. ◆ *determiner* **5a** amounting to eighteen: *eighteen weeks*. **5b** (*as pron*): *eighteen of them knew*. [OE *eahtatēne*]

▸**'eigh'teenth** *adj, n*

eightfold ('eɪtˌfəʊld) *adj* **1** equal to or having eight times as many or as much. **2** composed of eight parts. ◆ *adv* **3** by eight times as much.

eighth (eɪtθ) *adj* **1** (*usually prenominal*) **1a** coming after the seventh and before the ninth in numbering, position, etc.; being the ordinal number of *eight*: often written 8th. **1b** (*as n*): *the eighth in line*. ◆ *n* **2a** one of eight equal parts of something. **2b** (*as modifier*): *an eighth part*. **3** the fraction one divided by eight (1/8). **4** another word for **octave**. ◆ *adv* **5** Also: **eighthly**. after the seventh person, position, event, etc.

eighth note *n Music*. the usual US and Canad. name for **quaver**.

eightsome reel ('eɪtsəm) *n* a Scottish dance for eight people.

eighty ('eɪtɪ) *n, pl* **eighties**. **1** the cardinal number that is the product of ten and eight. **2** a numeral, 80, LXXX, etc., representing this number. **3** (*pl*) the numbers 80-89, esp. the 80th to the 89th year of a person's life or of a century. **4** the amount or quantity that is eight times ten. **5** something represented by, representing, or consisting of 80 units. ◆ *determiner* **6a** amounting to eighty: *eighty pages of nonsense*. **6b** (*as pron*): *eighty are expected*. [OE *eahtatig*]

▸**'eightieth** *adj, n*

einsteinium (aɪn'staɪnɪəm) *n* a radioactive metallic transuranic element artificially produced from plutonium. Symbol: Es; atomic no.: 99; half-life of most stable isotope, ^{252}Es: 276 days. [C20: NL, after Albert *Einstein* (1879–1955), German-born US physicist and mathematician]

EIS *abbrev. for* Educational Institute of Scotland.

eisteddfod (aɪ'stɛdfəd) *n, pl* **eisteddfods** *or* **eisteddfodau** (*Welsh* aɪˌstɛð'vɒdaɪ). any of a number of annual festivals in Wales in which competitions are held in music, poetry, drama, and the fine arts. [C19: from Welsh, lit.: session, from *eistedd* to sit + *-fod*, from *bod* to be]

either ('aɪðə, 'iːðə) *determiner* **1a** one or the other (of two). **1b** (*as pron*): *either is acceptable*. **2** both one and the other: *at either end of the table*. ◆ *conj* **3** (*coordinating*) used preceding two or more possibilities joined by *"or"*. ◆ *adv* (*sentence modifier*) **4** (*with a negative*) used to indicate that the clause immediately preceding is a partial reiteration of a previous clause: *John isn't a liar, but he isn't exactly honest either*. [OE *ǣgther*, short for *ǣghwæther* each of two; see WHETHER]

USAGE NOTE *Either* is followed by a singular verb in good usage: *either is good; either of these books is useful*. Care should be taken to avoid ambiguity when using *either* to mean *both* or *each*, as in the following sentence: *a ship could be moored on either side of the channel*. Agreement between verb and subject in *either...or...* constructions follows the pattern for *neither...nor...* See at **neither**.

ejaculate ❶ (ɪ'dʒækjʊˌleɪt) *vb* **ejaculates, ejaculating, ejaculated**. **1** to eject or discharge (semen) in orgasm. **2** (*tr*) to utter abruptly; blurt out. ◆ *n* (ɪ'dʒækjʊlɪt). **3** another word for **semen**. [C16: from L *ējaculārī* to hurl out, from *jaculum* javelin, from *jacere* to throw]

▸**eˌjacu'lation** *n* ▸**e'jaculatory** *or* **e'jaculative** *adj* ▸**e'jacuˌlator** *n*

eject ❶ (ɪ'dʒɛkt) *vb* **1** (*tr*) to force out; expel or emit. **2** (*tr*) to compel (a person) to leave; evict. **3** (*tr*) to dismiss, as from office. **4** (*intr*) to leave an aircraft rapidly, using an ejection seat or capsule. [C15: from L *ejicere*, from *jacere* to throw]

▸**e'jection** *n* ▸**e'jective** *adj* ▸**e'jector** *n*

ejection seat *or* **ejector seat** *n* a seat, esp. in military aircraft, fired by a cartridge or rocket to eject the occupant in an emergency.

eke (iːk) *sentence connector. Arch*. also; moreover. [OE *eac*]

eke out ❶ (iːk) *vb* (*tr, adv*) **1** to make (a supply) last, esp. by frugal use. **2** to support (existence) with difficulty and effort. **3** to add to (something insufficient), esp. with effort. [from obs. *eke* to enlarge]

elaborate ❶ *adj* (ɪ'læbərɪt). **1** planned with care and exactness. **2** marked by complexity or detail. ◆ *vb* (ɪ'læbəˌreɪt), **elaborates, elaborating, elaborated**. **3** (*intr; usually foll. by on or upon*) to add detail (to an account); expand (upon). **4** (*tr*) to work out in detail; develop. **5** (*tr*) to produce by careful labour. **6** (*tr*) *Physiol*. to change (food or simple substances) into more complex substances for use in the body. [C16: from L *ēlabōrāre* to take pains, from *labōrāre* to toil]

▸**e'laborateness** *n* ▸**eˌlabo'ration** *n* ▸**elaborative** (ɪ'læbərətɪv) *adj* ▸**e'laboˌrator** *n*

élan ❶ (eɪ'lɑːn) *n* a combination of style and vigour. [C19: from F, from *élancer* to throw forth, ult. from L *lancea* LANCE]

eland ('iːlənd) *n* **1** a large spiral-horned antelope inhabiting bushland in eastern and southern Africa. **2 giant eland**. a similar but larger animal of central and W Africa. [C18: via Afrik., from Du. *eland* elk]

elapse ❶ (ɪ'læps) *vb* **elapses, elapsing, elapsed**. (*intr*) (of time) to pass by. [C17: from L *ēlābī* to slip away]

elasmobranch (ɪ'læsməˌbræŋk) *n* **1** any cartilaginous fish of the subclass *Elasmobranchii*, which includes sharks, rays, and skates. ◆ *adj* **2** of or relating to the *Elasmobranchii*. [C19: from NL *elasmobranchii*, from Gk *elasmos* metal plate + *brankhia* gills]

elastane (ɪ'læsteɪn) *n* a synthetic fibre characterized by its ability to revert to its original shape after being stretched.

elastic ❶ (ɪ'læstɪk) *adj* **1** (of a body or material) capable of returning to its original shape after compression, stretching, or other deformation. **2** capable of adapting to change. **3** quick to recover from fatigue, dejection, etc. **4** springy or resilient. **5** made of elastic. ◆ *n* **6** tape, cord, or fabric containing flexible rubber or similar substance allowing it to stretch and return to its original shape. [C17: from NL *elasticus* impulsive, from Gk *elastikos*, from *elaunein* to beat, drive]

▸**e'lastically** *adv* ▸**elas'ticity** *n*

elasticate (ɪ'læstɪˌkeɪt) *vb* **elasticates, elasticating, elasticated**. (*tr*) to insert elastic into (a fabric or garment).

▸**eˌlasti'cation** *n*

elastic band *n* another name for **rubber band**.

elasticize *or* **elasticise** (ɪ'læstɪˌsaɪz) *vb* **elasticizes, elasticizing, elasticized** *or* **elasticises, elasticising, elasticised**. **1** to make elastic. **2** another word for **elasticate**.

elastomer (ɪ'læstəmə) *n* any material, such as rubber, able to resume its original shape when a deforming force is removed. [C20: from ELASTIC + -MER]

▸**elastomeric** (ɪˌlæstə'mɛrɪk) *adj*

Elastoplast (ɪ'læstəˌplɑːst) *n Trademark*. a gauze surgical dressing backed by adhesive tape.

elate ❶ (ɪ'leɪt) *vb* **elates, elating, elated**. (*tr*) to fill with high spirits, exhila-

THESAURUS

escape, exodus, issue, outlet, passage out, vent, way out, withdrawal

ejaculate *vb* **1** = **discharge**, eject, emit, spurt **2** = **exclaim**, blurt out, burst out, cry out, shout

ejaculation *n* **1** = **discharge**, ejection, emission, spurt **2** = **exclamation**, cry, shout

eject *vb* **1** = **emit**, cast out, discharge, disgorge, expel, spew, spout, throw out, vomit **2** = **throw out**, banish, boot out (*inf*.), bounce, deport, dispossess, drive out, evacuate, evict, exile, expel, give the bum's rush (*sl*.), oust, relegate, remove, show one the door, throw out on one's ear (*inf*.), turn out **3** = **dismiss**, discharge, dislodge, fire (*inf*.), get rid of, kick out (*inf*.), oust, sack (*inf*.), throw out

ejection *n* **1** = **emission**, casting out, disgorgement, expulsion, spouting, throwing out **2** = **expulsion**, banishment, deportation, dispossession, evacuation, eviction, exile, ouster (*Law*), removal, the bum's rush (*sl*.) **3** = **dismissal**, discharge, dislodgement, firing (*inf*.), sacking (*inf*.), the boot (*sl*.), the sack (*inf*.)

eke out *vb* **1** = **be sparing with**, be economical with, be frugal with, economize on, husband, stretch out

elaborate *adj* **1** = **detailed**, careful, exact, intricate, laboured, minute, painstaking, perfected, precise, skilful, studied, thorough **2** = **complicated**, complex, decorated, detailed, extravagant, fancy, fussy, involved, ornamented, ornate, ostentatious, showy ◆ *vb* **3, 4** = **expand (upon)**, add detail, amplify, complicate, decorate, develop, devise, embellish, enhance, enlarge, flesh out, garnish, improve, ornament, polish, produce, refine, work out

Antonyms *adj* ≠ **complicated**: basic, minimal, modest, plain, severe, simple, unadorned, unembellished, unfussy ◆ *vb* ≠ **expand (upon)**: abbreviate, condense, put in a nutshell, reduce to essentials, simplify, streamline, summarize, truncate

élan *n* = **style**, animation, brio, dash, esprit, flair, impetuosity, panache, spirit, verve, vigour, vivacity, zest

elapse *vb* = **pass**, glide by, go, go by, lapse, pass by, roll by, roll on, slip away, slip by

elastic *adj* **1, 4** = **flexible**, ductile, plastic, pliable, pliant, resilient, rubbery, springy, stretchable, stretchy, supple, tensile, yielding **2** = **adaptable**, accommodating, adjustable, complaisant, compliant, flexible, supple, tolerant, variable, yielding

Antonyms *adj* ≠ **flexible**: firm, immovable, inflexible, rigid, set, stiff, unyielding ≠ **adaptable**: firm, immovable, inflexible, intractable, obdurate, resolute, rigid, set, stiff, strict, stringent, unyielding

elasticity *n* **1, 4** = **flexibility**, ductileness, ductility, give (*inf*.), plasticity, pliability, pliancy, pliantness, resilience, rubberiness, springiness, stretch, stretchiness, suppleness **2** = **adaptability**, adjustability, complaisance, compliantness, flexibility, suppleness, tolerance, variability

elated *adj* = **joyful**, animated, cheered, cock-

ration, pride, or optimism. [C16: from p.p. of L *efferre* to bear away, from *ferre* to carry]
▸**e'lated** *adj* ▸**e'latedly** *adv* ▸**e'latedness** *n*
elation Ⓣ (ɪ'leɪʃən) *n* joyfulness or exaltation of spirit, as from success, pleasure, or relief.
E layer *n* another name for **E region.**
elbow Ⓣ ('ɛlbəʊ) *n* **1** the joint between the upper arm and the forearm. **2** the corresponding joint of birds or mammals. **3** the part of a garment that covers the elbow. **4** something resembling an elbow, such as a sharp bend in a road. **5 at one's elbow.** within easy reach. **6 out at elbow(s).** ragged or impoverished. ◆ *vb* **7** to make (one's way) by shoving, jostling, etc. **8** (*tr*) to knock or shove as with the elbow. **9** (*tr*) to reject; dismiss (esp. in **give** or **get the elbow**). [OE *elnboga*]
elbow grease *n Facetious.* vigorous physical labour, esp. hard rubbing.
elbowroom Ⓣ ('ɛlbəʊˌruːm, -ˌrʊm) *n* sufficient scope to move or function.
elder[1] Ⓣ ('ɛldə) *adj* **1** born earlier; senior. Cf. **older. 2** (in certain card games) denoting or relating to the nondealer (the **elder hand**), who has certain advantages in the play. **3** *Arch.* **3a** prior in rank or office. **3b** of a previous time. ◆ *n* **4** an older person; one's senior. **5** *Anthropol.* a senior member of a tribe who has authority. **6** (in certain Protestant Churches) a lay office. **7** another word for **presbyter.** [OE *eldra*, comp. of *eald* OLD]
▸**'elderˌship** *n*
elder[2] ('ɛldə) *n* any of various shrubs or small trees having clusters of small white flowers and red, purple, or black berry-like fruits. Also called: **elderberry.** [OE *ellern*]
elderberry ('ɛldəˌbɛrɪ) *n, pl* **elderberries. 1** the fruit of the elder. **2** another name for **elder**[2].
elder brother *n* one of the senior members of Trinity House.
elderly ('ɛldəlɪ) *adj* (of people) quite old; past middle age.
▸**'elderliness** *n*
eldest ('ɛldɪst) *adj* being the oldest, esp. the oldest surviving child of the same parents. [OE *eldesta*, sup. of *eald* OLD]
El Dorado (ɛl dɒ'rɑːdəʊ) *n* **1** a fabled city in South America, rich in treasure. **2** Also: **eldorado.** any place of great riches or fabulous opportunity. [C16: from Sp., lit.: the gilded (place)]
eldritch *or* **eldrich** ('ɛldrɪtʃ) *adj Poetic, Scot.* unearthly; weird. [C16: ?from OE *ælf* elf + *rīce* realm]
elect Ⓣ (ɪ'lɛkt) *vb* **1** (*tr*) to choose (someone) to be (a representative or official) by voting. **2** to select; choose. **3** (*tr*) (of God) to predestine for the grace of salvation. ◆ *adj* **4** (*immediately postpositive*) voted into office but not yet installed: *president elect.* **5a** chosen; elite. **5b** (*as collective n;* preceded by *the*): *the elect.* **6** *Christian theol.* **6a** predestined by God to receive salvation. **6b** (*as collective n;* preceded by *the*): *the elect.* [C15: from L *ēligere* to select, from *legere* to choose]
▸**e'lectable** *adj*
elect. *or* **elec.** *abbrev. for:* **1** electric(al). **2** electricity.
election Ⓣ (ɪ'lɛkʃən) *n* **1** the selection by vote of a person or persons for a position, esp. a political office. **2** a public vote. **3** the act or an instance of choosing. **4** *Christian theol.* **4a** the doctrine that God chooses individuals for salvation without reference to faith or works. **4b** the doctrine that God chooses for salvation those who, by grace, persevere in faith and works.
electioneer (ɪˌlɛkʃə'nɪə) *vb* (*intr*) **1** to be active in a political election or campaign. ◆ *n* **2** a person who engages in this activity.
▸**eˌlection'eering** *n, adj*
elective (ɪ'lɛktɪv) *adj* **1** of or based on selection by vote. **2** selected by vote. **3** having the power to elect. **4** open to choice; optional. ◆ *n* **5** an optional course or hospital placement undertaken by a medical student.
▸**electivity** (ˌiːlɛk'tɪvɪtɪ) *or* **e'lectiveness** *n*
elector Ⓣ (ɪ'lɛktə) *n* **1** someone who is eligible to vote in the election of a government. **2** (*often cap.*) a member of the US electoral college. **3** (*often cap.*) (in the Holy Roman Empire) any of the German princes entitled to take part in the election of a new emperor.
▸**e'lectoral** *adj* ▸**e'lectorˌship** *n* ▸**e'lectress** *fem n*
electoral college *n* (*often cap.*) **1** *US.* a body of electors chosen by the voters who formally elect the president and vice president. **2** any body of electors with similar functions.
electorate (ɪ'lɛktərɪt) *n* **1** the body of all qualified voters. **2** the rank, position, or territory of an elector of the Holy Roman Empire. **3** *Austral. & NZ.* the area represented by a Member of Parliament. **4** *Austral. & NZ.* the voters in a constituency.
electret (ɪ'lɛktrət) *n* a permanently polarized dielectric material; its field is similar to that of a permanent magnet. [C20: from *electr(icity + magn)et*]
electric Ⓣ (ɪ'lɛktrɪk) *adj* **1** of, derived from, produced by, producing, transmitting, or powered by electricity. **2** (of a musical instrument) amplified electronically. **3** very tense or exciting; emotionally charged. ◆ *n* **4** *Inf.* an electric train, car, etc. **5** (*pl*) an electric circuit or electric appliances. [C17: from NL *electricus* amber-like (because friction causes amber to become charged), from L *ēlectrum* amber, from Gk *ēlektron*, from ?]

USAGE NOTE See at **electronic.**

electrical (ɪ'lɛktrɪkᵊl) *adj* of, relating to, or concerned with electricity.
▸**e'lectrically** *adv*

USAGE NOTE See at **electronic.**

electrical engineering *n* the branch of engineering concerned with practical applications of electricity.
▸**electrical engineer** *n*
electric blanket *n* a blanket that contains an electric heating element, used to warm a bed.
electric chair *n* (in the US) **a** an electrified chair for executing criminals. **b** (usually preceded by *the*) execution by this method.
electric circuit *n Physics.* another name for **circuit** (sense 3a).
electric constant *n* the permittivity of free space, which has the value 8.854 185 × 10^{-12} farad per metre.
electric discharge *n Physics.* another name for **discharge** (sense 17b).
electric displacement *n Physics.* the charge per unit area displaced across a layer of conductor in an electric field. Symbol: *D* Also called: **electric flux density.**
electric eel *n* an eel-like freshwater fish of N South America, having electric organs in the body.
electric eye *n* another name for **photocell.**
electric field *n* a field of force surrounding a charged particle within which another charged particle experiences a force.
electric flux *n* the amount of electricity displaced across a given area in a dielectric. Symbol: Ψ
electric flux density *n* another name for **electric displacement.**
electric guitar *n* an electrically amplified guitar, used mainly in pop music.
electrician (ɪlɛk'trɪʃən, ˌiːlɛk-) *n* a person whose occupation is the installation, maintenance, and repair of electrical devices.
electricity (ɪlɛk'trɪsɪtɪ, ˌiːlɛk-) *n* **1** any phenomenon associated with stationary or moving electrons, ions, or other charged particles. **2** the science of electricity. **3** an electric current or charge. **4** emotional tension or excitement.
electric motor *n* a device that converts electrical energy to mechanical torque.
electric organ *n* **1** *Music.* **1a** a pipe organ operated by electrical means. **1b** another name for **electronic organ. 2** a group of cells on certain fishes, such as the electric eel, that gives an electric shock to any animal touching them.
electric potential *n* **a** the work required to transfer a unit positive electric charge from an infinite distance to a given point. **b** the potential difference between the point and some other point. Sometimes shortened to **potential.**
electric ray *n* any ray of tropical and temperate seas, having a flat rounded body and an organ for producing electricity in each fin.
electric shock *n* the physiological reaction, characterized by pain and muscular spasm, to the passage of an electric current through the body. It can affect the respiratory system and heart rhythm. Sometimes shortened to **shock.**
electric susceptibility *n* another name for **susceptibility** (sense 4a).
electrify Ⓣ (ɪ'lɛktrɪˌfaɪ) *vb* **electrifies, electrifying, electrified.** (*tr*) **1** to adapt or equip (a system, device, etc.) for operation by electrical power. **2** to charge with or subject to electricity. **3** to startle or excite intensely.
▸**e'lectriˌfiable** *adj* ▸**eˌlectrifi'cation** *n* ▸**e'lectriˌfier** *n*
electro (ɪ'lɛktrəʊ) *n, pl* **electros.** short for **electroplate** or **electrotype.**
electro- *or sometimes before a vowel* **electr-** *combining form.* **1** electric or

THESAURUS

a-hoop, delighted, ecstatic, euphoric, excited, exhilarated, exultant, floating *or* walking on air, gleeful, in high spirits, in seventh heaven, joyous, jubilant, overjoyed, over the moon (*inf.*), proud, puffed up, rapt, roused
Antonyms *adj* dejected, depressed, discouraged, dispirited, downcast, down in the dumps (*inf.*), miserable, sad, unhappy, woebegone
elation *n* = **joy**, bliss, delight, ecstasy, euphoria, exaltation, exhilaration, exultation, glee, high spirits, joyfulness, joyousness, jubilation, rapture
elbow *n* **4** = **joint**, angle, bend, corner, turn **5 at one's elbow** = **within reach**, at hand, close by, handy, near, to hand **6 out at elbow(s)** = **impoverished**, beggarly, down at heel, in rags, ragged, seedy, shabby, tattered ◆ *vb* **7, 8** = **push**, bump, crowd, hustle, jostle, knock, nudge, shoulder, shove
elbowroom *n* = **scope**, freedom, latitude, leeway, play, room, space
elder[1] *adj* **1** = **older**, ancient, earlier born, first-born, senior ◆ *n* **4** = **older person**, senior **6** = **church official**, office bearer, presbyter
elect *vb* **1, 2** = **choose**, appoint, decide upon, designate, determine, opt for, pick, pick out, prefer, select, settle on, vote ◆ *adj* **5** = **selected**, choice, chosen, elite, hand-picked, picked, preferred, select
election *n* **1-3** = **voting**, appointment, choice, choosing, decision, determination, judgment, preference, selection, vote
elector *n* **1-2** = **voter**, chooser, constituent, selector
electric *adj* **3** = **charged**, dynamic, exciting, high-octane (*inf.*), rousing, stimulating, stirring, tense, thrilling
electrify *vb* **3** = **startle**, amaze, animate, astonish, astound, excite, fire, galvanize, invigorate, jolt, rouse, shock, stimulate, stir, take one's breath away, thrill
Antonyms *vb* be tedious, bore, exhaust, fatigue, jade, send to sleep, tire, weary

electrically: *electrodynamic*. **2** electrolytic: *electrodialysis*. [from NL, from L *ēlectrum* amber, from Gk *ēlektron*]

electroacoustic (ɪˌlɛktrəʊə'ku:stɪk) *adj* (of music) combining both computer-generated and acoustic sounds.

electrocardiograph (ɪˌlɛktrəʊ'kɑ:dɪəʊˌgrɑ:f) *n* an instrument for making tracings (**electrocardiograms**) recording the electrical activity of the heart.
▸**eˌlectroˌcardio'graphic** *or* **eˌlectroˌcardio'graphical** *adj* ▸**electrocardiography** (ɪˌlɛktrəʊˌkɑ:dɪ'ɒgrəfɪ) *n*

electrochemistry (ɪˌlɛktrəʊ'kɛmɪstrɪ) *n* the branch of chemistry concerned with electric cells and electrolysis.
▸**ˌelectro'chemical** *adj* ▸**eˌlectro'chemist** *n*

electroconvulsive therapy (ɪˌlɛktrəʊkən'vʌlsɪv) *n Med.* the treatment of certain psychotic conditions by passing an electric current through the brain to induce coma or convulsions. See also **shock therapy**.

electrocute (ɪ'lɛktrəˌkju:t) *vb* **electrocutes, electrocuting, electrocuted.** (*tr*) **1** to kill as a result of an electric shock. **2** *US.* to execute in the electric chair. [C19: from ELECTRO- + (EXE)CUTE]
▸**eˌlectro'cution** *n*

electrode (ɪ'lɛktrəʊd) *n* **1** a conductor through which an electric current enters or leaves an electrolyte, an electric arc, or an electronic valve or tube. **2** an element in a semiconducting device that emits, collects, or controls the movement of electrons or holes.

electrodeposit (ɪˌlɛktrəʊdɪ'pɒzɪt) *vb* **1** (*tr*) to deposit (a metal) by electrolysis. ◆ *n* **2** the deposit so formed.
▸**electrodeposition** (ɪˌlɛktrəʊˌdɛpə'zɪʃən) *n*

electrodynamics (ɪˌlɛktrəʊdaɪ'næmɪks) *n* (*functioning as sing*) the branch of physics concerned with the interactions between electrical and mechanical forces.

electroencephalograph (ɪˌlɛktrəʊɛn'sɛfələˌgrɑ:f) *n* an instrument for making tracings (**electroencephalograms**) recording the electrical activity of the brain, usually by means of electrodes placed on the scalp. See also **brain wave**.
▸**eˌlectroenˌcephalo'graphic** *adj* ▸**electroencephalography** (ɪˌlɛktrəʊɛn-ˌsɛfə'lɒgrəfɪ) *n*

electrolyse *or US* **electrolyze** (ɪ'lɛktrəʊˌlaɪz) *vb* **electrolyses, electrolysing, electrolysed** *or US* **electrolyzes, electrolyzing, electrolyzed.** (*tr*) **1** to decompose (a chemical compound) by electrolysis. **2** to destroy (living tissue, such as hair roots) by electrolysis.
▸**e'lectroˌlyser** *or US* **e'lectroˌlyzer** *n*

electrolysis (ɪlɛk'trɒlɪsɪs) *n* **1** the conduction of electricity by an electrolyte, esp. the use of this process to induce chemical changes. **2** the destruction of living tissue, such as hair roots, by an electric current, usually for cosmetic reasons.

electrolyte (ɪ'lɛktrəʊˌlaɪt) *n* **1** a solution or molten substance that conducts electricity. **2a** a chemical compound that dissociates in solution into ions. **2b** any of the ions themselves.

electrolytic (ɪˌlɛktrəʊ'lɪtɪk) *adj* **1** *Physics.* **1a** of, concerned with, or produced by electrolysis or electrodeposition. **1b** of, relating to, or containing an electrolyte. ◆ *n* **2** *Electronics.* Also called: **electrolytic capacitor.** a small capacitor consisting of two electrodes separated by an electrolyte.
▸**eˌlectro'lytically** *adv*

electromagnet (ɪˌlɛktrəʊ'mægnɪt) *n* a magnet consisting of an iron or steel core wound with a coil of wire, through which a current is passed.

electromagnetic (ɪˌlɛktrəʊmæg'nɛtɪk) *adj* **1** of, containing, or operated by an electromagnet. **2** of, relating to, or consisting of electromagnetism. **3** of or relating to electromagnetic radiation.
▸**eˌlectromag'netically** *adv*

electromagnetic radiation *n* radiation consisting of an electric and magnetic field at right angles to each other and to the direction of propagation.

electromagnetics (ɪˌlɛktrəʊmæg'nɛtɪks) *n* (*functioning as sing*) *Physics.* another name for **electromagnetism** (sense 2).

electromagnetic spectrum *n* the complete range of electromagnetic radiation from the longest radio waves to the shortest gamma radiation.

electromagnetic unit *n* any unit of a system of electrical cgs units in which the magnetic constant is given the value of unity.

electromagnetic wave *n* a wave of energy propagated in an electromagnetic field.

electromagnetism (ɪˌlɛktrəʊ'mægnɪˌtɪzəm) *n* **1** magnetism produced by electric current. **2** Also called: **electromagnetics.** the branch of physics concerned with this magnetism and with the interaction of electric and magnetic fields.

electrometer (ɪlɛk'trɒmɪtə, ˌi:lɛk-) *n* an instrument for detecting or measuring a potential difference or charge by the electrostatic forces between charged bodies.
▸**electrometric** (ɪˌlɛktrəʊ'mɛtrɪk) *or* **eˌlectro'metrical** *adj* ▸**elec'trometry** *n*

electromotive (ɪˌlɛktrəʊ'məʊtɪv) *adj* of, concerned with, or producing an electric current.

electromotive force *n Physics.* **a** a source of energy that can cause current to flow in an electrical circuit. **b** the rate at which energy is drawn from this source when unit current flows through the circuit, measured in volts.

electromyography (ɪˌlɛktrəʊmaɪ'ɒgrəfɪ) *n Med.* a technique for recording the electrical activity of muscles: used in the diagnosis of nerve and muscle disorders.

electron (ɪ'lɛktrɒn) *n* an elementary particle in all atoms, orbiting the nucleus in numbers equal to the atomic number of the element. [C19: from ELECTRO- + -ON]

electronegative (ɪˌlɛktrəʊ'nɛgətɪv) *adj* **1** having a negative electric charge. **2** (of an atom, molecule, etc.) tending to attract electrons and form negative ions or polarized bonds.

electron gun *n* a heated cathode for producing and focusing a beam of electrons, used esp. in cathode-ray tubes.

electronic (ɪlɛk'trɒnɪk, ˌi:lɛk-) *adj* **1** of, concerned with, using, or operated by devices, such as transistors, in which electrons are conducted through a semiconductor, free space, or gas. **2** of or concerned with electronics. **3** of or concerned with electrons. **4** involving or concerned with the representation, storage, or transmission of information by electronic systems: *electronic mail; electronic shopping.*
▸**elec'tronically** *adv*

> **USAGE NOTE** *Electronic* is used to refer to equipment, such as television sets, computers, etc., in which current is controlled by transistors, valves, and similar components and also to the components themselves. *Electrical* is used in a more general sense, often to refer to the use of electricity as opposed to other forms of energy: *electrical engineering; an electrical appliance. Electric,* in many cases used interchangeably with *electrical,* is often restricted to the description of devices or to concepts relating to the flow of current: *electric fire; electric charge.*

electronic flash *n Photog.* an electronic device for producing a very bright flash of light by means of an electric discharge in a gas-filled tube.

electronic funds transfer at point of sale *n* a system for debiting a retail sale direct to the customer's bank, building-society, or credit-card account by means of a computer link using the telephone network. The customer inserts his debit card or credit card into the computer at the point of sale. Acronym: **EFTPOS.**

electronic ignition *n* any system that uses an electronic circuit to supply the voltage to the sparking plugs of an internal-combustion engine.

electronic keyboard *n* a typewriter keyboard used to operate an electronic device such as a computer.

electronic mail *n* the transmission of information, messages, facsimiles, etc., from one computer terminal to another. Often shortened to **E-mail, e-mail, email.**

electronic music *n* music consisting of sounds produced by electric currents either controlled from an instrument panel or keyboard or prerecorded on magnetic tape.

electronic organ *n Music.* an instrument played by means of a keyboard, in which sounds are produced by electronic or electrical means.

electronic organizer *n* a computerized personal organizer.

electronic point of sale *n* a computerized system for recording sales in retail shops, using a laser scanner at the cash till to read bar codes on the packages of the items sold. The retailer's stock record is automatically adjusted and the customer receives an itemized bill. Acronym: **EPOS.**

electronic publishing *n* the publication of information on magnetic tape, discs, etc., so that it can be accessed by a computer.

electronics (ɪlɛk'trɒnɪks, ˌi:lɛk-) *n* **1** (*functioning as sing*) the science and technology concerned with the development, behaviour, and applications of electronic devices and circuits. **2** (*functioning as pl*) the circuits and devices of a piece of electronic equipment.

electronic surveillance *n* **1** the use of such electronic devices as television monitors, video cameras, etc., to prevent burglary, shop lifting, break-ins, etc. **2** monitoring events, conversations, etc. at a distance by electronic means, esp. by such covert means as wire tapping or bugging.

electronic tag *n* another name for **tag**[1] (sense 2).

electronic transfer of funds *n* the transfer of money from one bank or building-society account to another by means of a computer link using the telephone network. Abbrev.: **ETF.**

electron lens *n* a system, such as an arrangement of electrodes or magnets, that produces a field for focusing a beam of electrons.

electron micrograph *n* a photograph of a specimen taken through an electron microscope.

electron microscope *n* a powerful microscope that uses electrons, rather than light, and electron lenses to produce a magnified image.

electron tube *n* an electrical device, such as a valve, in which a flow of electrons between electrodes takes place.

electronvolt (ɪˌlɛktrɒn'vəʊlt) *n* a unit of energy equal to the work done on an electron accelerated through a potential difference of 1 volt.

electrophoresis (ɪˌlɛktrəʊfə'ri:sɪs) *n* the motion of charged particles in a colloid under the influence of an applied electric field.
▸**electrophoretic** (ɪˌlɛktrəʊfə'rɛtɪk) *adj*

electrophorus (ɪlɛk'trɒfərəs, ˌi:lɛk-) *n* an apparatus for generating static electricity by induction. [C18: from ELECTRO- + *-phorus,* from Gk, from *pherein* to bear]

electroplate (ɪ'lɛktrəʊˌpleɪt) *vb* **electroplates, electroplating, electroplated.** **1** (*tr*) to plate (an object) by electrolysis. ◆ *n* **2** electroplated articles collectively, esp. when plated with silver.
▸**e'lectroˌplater** *n*

electropositive (ɪˌlɛktrəʊ'pɒzɪtɪv) *adj* **1** having a positive electric charge. **2** (of an atom, molecule, etc.) tending to release electrons and form positive ions or polarized bonds.

electrorheology (ɪˌlɛktrəʊrɪˈɒlədʒɪ) *n* **1** the study of the flow of fluids under the influence of electric fields. **2** the way in which fluid flow is influenced by an electric field.
▸**eˌlectroˌrheoˈlogical** *adj*

electroscope (ɪˈlɛktrəʊˌskəʊp) *n* an apparatus for detecting an electric charge, typically consisting of a rod holding two gold foils that separate when a charge is applied.
▸**electroscopic** (ɪˌlɛktrəʊˈskɒpɪk) *adj*

electroshock therapy (ɪˈlɛktrəʊˌʃɒk) *n* another name for **electroconvulsive therapy.**

electrostatics (ɪˌlɛktrəʊˈstætɪks) *n* (*functioning as sing*) the branch of physics concerned with static electricity.
▸**eˌlectroˈstatic** *adj*

electrostatic unit *n* any unit of a system of electrical cgs units in which the electric constant is given the value of unity.

electrotherapeutics (ɪˌlɛktrəʊˌθɛrəˈpjuːtɪks) *n* (*functioning as sing*) the branch of medical science concerned with the use of electrotherapy.
▸**eˌlectroˌtheraˈpeutic** *or* **eˌlectroˌtheraˈpeutical** *adj*

electrotherapy (ɪˌlɛktrəʊˈθɛrəpɪ) *n* treatment in which electric currents are passed through the tissues to stimulate muscle function in paralysed patients.
▸**eˌlectroˈtherapist** *n*

electrotype (ɪˈlɛktrəʊˌtaɪp) *n* **1** a duplicate printing plate made by electrolytically depositing a layer of copper or nickel onto a mould of the original. ◆ *vb* **electrotypes, electrotyping, electrotyped. 2** (*tr*) to make an electrotype of (printed matter, etc.).
▸**eˈlectroˌtyper** *n*

electrovalent bond (ɪˌlɛktrəʊˈveɪlənt) *n* a type of chemical bond in which one atom loses an electron to form a positive ion and the other atom gains the electron to form a negative ion. The resulting ions are held together by electrostatic attraction.
▸**eˌlectroˈvalency** *n*

electroweak (ɪˌlɛktrəʊˈwiːk) *adj Physics.* involving both electromagnetic interaction and weak interaction.

electrum (ɪˈlɛktrəm) *n* an alloy of gold and silver. [C14: from L, from Gk *ēlektron* amber]

electuary (ɪˈlɛktjʊərɪ) *n, pl* **electuaries.** *Med.* a paste taken orally, containing a drug mixed with syrup or honey. [C14: from LL *ēlēctuārium,* prob. from Gk *ekleikton,* from *leikhein* to lick]

eleemosynary (ˌɛlɪiːˈmɒsɪnərɪ) *adj* **1** of or dependent on charity. **2** given as an act of charity. [C17: from Church L *eleēmosyna* ALMS]

elegance ➊ (ˈɛlɪgəns) *or* **elegancy** *n, pl* **elegances** *or* **elegancies. 1** dignified grace. **2** good taste in design, style, arrangement, etc. **3** something elegant; a refinement.

elegant ➊ (ˈɛlɪgənt) *adj* **1** tasteful in dress, style, or design. **2** dignified and graceful. **3** cleverly simple; ingenious: *an elegant solution.* [C16: from L *ēlegāns* tasteful; see ELECT]

elegiac ➊ (ˌɛlɪˈdʒaɪək) *adj* **1** resembling, characteristic of, relating to, or appropriate to an elegy. **2** lamenting; mournful. **3** denoting or written in elegiac couplets (which consist of a dactylic hexameter followed by a dactylic pentameter) or elegiac stanzas (which consist of a quatrain in iambic pentameters with alternate lines rhyming). ◆ *n* **4** (*often pl*) an elegiac couplet or stanza.
▸**ˌeleˈgiacally** *adv*

elegize *or* **elegise** (ˈɛlɪˌdʒaɪz) *vb* **elegizes, elegizing, elegized** *or* **elegises, elegising, elegised. 1** to compose an elegy (in memory of). **2** (*intr*) to write elegiacally.
▸**ˈelegist** *n*

elegy ➊ (ˈɛlɪdʒɪ) *n, pl* **elegies. 1** a mournful poem or song, esp. a lament for the dead. **2** poetry written in elegiac couplets or stanzas. [C16: via F & L from Gk, from *elegos* lament sung to flute accompaniment]

USAGE NOTE Avoid confusion with **eulogy.**

elem. *abbrev. for:* **1** element(s). **2** elementary.

element ➊ (ˈɛlɪmənt) *n* **1** any of the 109 known substances that consist of atoms with the same number of protons in their nuclei. **2** one of the fundamental or irreducible components making up a whole. **3** a cause that contributes to a result; factor. **4** any group that is part of a larger unit, such as a military formation. **5** a small amount; hint. **6** a distinguishable section of a social group. **7** the most favourable environment for an animal or plant. **8** the situation in which a person is happiest or most effective (esp. in **in** *or* **out of one's element**). **9** the resistance wire that constitutes the electrical heater in a cooker, heater, etc. **10** one of the four substances thought in ancient and medieval cosmology to constitute the universe (earth, air, water, or fire). **11** (*pl*) atmospheric conditions, esp. wind, rain, and cold. **12** (*pl*) the basic principles. **13** *Christianity.* the bread or wine consecrated in the Eucharist. [C13: from L *elementum* a first principle, element]

elemental ➊ (ˌɛlɪˈmentᵊl) *adj* **1** fundamental; basic. **2** motivated by or symbolic of primitive powerful natural forces or passions. **3** of or relating to earth, air, water, and fire considered as elements. **4** of or relating to atmospheric forces, esp. wind, rain, and cold. **5** of or relating to a chemical element. ◆ *n* **6** *Rare.* a spirit or force that is said to appear in physical form.
▸**ˌeleˈmentalˌism** *n*

elementary ➊ (ˌɛlɪˈmentərɪ) *adj* **1** not difficult; rudimentary. **2** of or concerned with the first principles of a subject; introductory or fundamental. **3** *Chem.* another word for **elemental** (sense 5).
▸**ˌeleˈmentariness** *n*

elementary particle *n* any of several entities, such as electrons, neutrons, or protons, that are less complex than atoms.

elementary school *n* **1** *Brit.* a former name for **primary school. 2** *US & Canad.* a state school for the first six to eight years of a child's education.

elenchus (ɪˈlɛŋkəs) *n, pl* **elenchi** (-kaɪ). *Logic.* refutation of an argument by proving the contrary of its conclusion, esp. syllogistically. [C17: from L, from Gk, from *elenkhein* to refute]
▸**eˈlenctic** *adj*

elephant (ˈɛlɪfənt) *n, pl* **elephants** *or* **elephant.** either of two proboscidean mammals. The **African elephant** is the larger species, with large flapping ears and a less humped back than the **Indian elephant,** of S and SE Asia. [C13: from L, from Gk *elephas* elephant, ivory]

elephantiasis (ˌɛlɪfənˈtaɪəsɪs) *n Pathol.* a complication of chronic filariasis, in which nematode worms block the lymphatic vessels, usually in the legs or scrotum, causing extreme enlargement of the affected area. [C16: via L from Gk, from *elephas* ELEPHANT + -IASIS]

elephantine ➊ (ˌɛlɪˈfæntaɪn) *adj* **1** denoting, relating to, or characteristic of an elephant or elephants. **2** huge, clumsy, or ponderous.

elephant seal *n* either of two large earless seals, of southern oceans or of the N Atlantic, the males of which have a trunklike snout.

Eleusinian mysteries *pl n* a mystical religious festival, held at Eleusis in classical times, to celebrate the gods Persephone, Demeter, and Dionysus.

elev. *or* **el.** *abbrev. for* elevation.

elevate ➊ (ˈɛlɪˌveɪt) *vb* **elevates, elevating, elevated.** (*tr*) **1** to move to a higher place. **2** to raise in rank or status. **3** to put in a cheerful mood; elate. **4** to put on a higher cultural plane; uplift. **5** to raise the axis of a gun. **6** to raise the intensity or pitch of (the voice). [C15: from L *ēlevāre,* from *levāre* to raise, from *levis* (adj) light]
▸**ˈeleˌvatory** *adj*

elevated ➊ (ˈɛlɪˌveɪtɪd) *adj* **1** raised to or being at a higher level. **2** inflated or lofty; exalted. **3** in a cheerful mood. **4** *Inf.* slightly drunk.

elevation ➊ (ˌɛlɪˈveɪʃən) *n* **1** the act of elevating or the state of being elevated. **2** the height of something above a given place, esp. above sea level. **3** a raised area; height. **4** nobleness or grandeur. **5** a drawing to scale of the external face of a building or structure. **6** a ballet dancer's ability to leap high. **7** *Astron.* another name for **altitude** (sense 3). **8** the angle formed between the muzzle of a gun and the horizontal.
▸**ˌeleˈvational** *adj*

elevator (ˈɛlɪˌveɪtə) *n* **1** a person or thing that elevates. **2** a mechanical hoist, often consisting of a chain of scoops linked together on a conveyor belt. **3** the US and Canad. name for **lift** (sense 14a). **4** *Chiefly US & Canad.* a granary equipped with an elevator and, usually, facilities for cleaning and grading the grain. **5** a control surface on the tailplane of

THESAURUS

elegance *n* **1-2** = **style**, beauty, courtliness, dignity, exquisiteness, gentility, grace, gracefulness, grandeur, luxury, polish, politeness, refinement, sumptuousness, taste

elegant *adj* **1-2** = **stylish**, à la mode, artistic, beautiful, chic, choice, comely, courtly, cultivated, delicate, exquisite, fashionable, fine, genteel, graceful, handsome, luxurious, modish, nice, polished, refined, sumptuous, tasteful, urbane **3** = **ingenious**, appropriate, apt, clever, effective, neat, simple
Antonyms *adj* ≠ **stylish:** awkward, clumsy, clunky (*inf.*), coarse, gauche, graceless, inelegant, misshapen, plain, tasteless, tawdry, ugly, uncouth, undignified, ungraceful, unrefined

elegiac *adj* = **lamenting**, dirgeful, funereal, keening, melancholy, mournful, nostalgic, plaintive, sad, threnodial, threnodic, valedictory

elegy *n* **1** = **lament**, coronach (*Scot. & Irish*), dirge, keen, plaint (*arch.*), requiem, threnody

element *n* **2-4** = **component**, basis, constituent, essential factor, factor, feature, ingredient, member, part, section, subdivision, unit **8** *As in* **in one's element** = **environment**, domain, field, habitat, medium, milieu, sphere **11** *plural* = **weather conditions**, atmospheric conditions, atmospheric forces, powers of nature **12** *plural* = **basics**, essentials, foundations, fundamentals, nuts and bolts (*inf.*), principles, rudiments

elemental *adj* **1** = **basic**, elementary, essential, fundamental **2** = **primal**, original, primitive, primordial **4** = **atmospheric**, meteorological, natural

elementary *adj* **1** = **simple**, clear, easy, facile, plain, rudimentary, straightforward, uncomplicated **2** = **basic**, bog-standard (*inf.*), elemental, fundamental, initial, introductory, original, primary, rudimentary
Antonyms *adj* ≠ **simple:** complex, complicated, sophisticated ≠ **basic:** advanced, higher, highly-developed, progressive, secondary

elephantine *adj* **2** = **massive**, bulky, clumsy, enormous, heavy, huge, hulking, humongous *or* humungous (*US sl.*), immense, laborious, lumbering, monstrous, ponderous, weighty

elevate *vb* **1** = **raise**, heighten, hoist, lift, lift up, uplift, upraise **2** = **promote**, advance, aggrandize, exalt, prefer, upgrade **3** = **cheer**, animate, boost, brighten, buoy up, elate, excite, exhilarate, hearten, lift up, perk up, raise, rouse, uplift

elevated *adj* **2** = **high-minded**, dignified, exalted, grand, high, high-flown, inflated, lofty, noble, sublime **3** = **in high spirits**, animated, bright, cheerful, cheery, elated, excited, exhilarated, gleeful, overjoyed
Antonyms *adj* ≠ **high-minded:** humble, lowly, modest, simple

elevation *n* **1** = **promotion**, advancement, aggrandizement, exaltation, preferment, upgrading **2** = **altitude**, height **3** = **rise**, acclivity, eminence, height, hill, hillock, mountain, rising ground

an aircraft, for making it climb or descend. **6** any muscle that raises a part of the body.

eleven (ɪˈlɛvᵊn) *n* **1** the cardinal number that is the sum of ten and one. **2** a numeral, 11, XI, etc., representing this number. **3** something representing, represented by, or consisting of 11 units. **4** (*functioning as sing or pl*) a team of 11 players in football, cricket, etc. **5** Also called: **eleven o'clock**. eleven hours after noon or midnight. ◆ *determiner* **6a** amounting to eleven. **6b** (*as pron*): *another eleven*. [OE *endleofan*]
▸**eˈleventh** *adj, n*

eleven-plus *n* (in Britain, esp. formerly) an examination taken by children aged 10 or 11 that determines the type of secondary education a child will be given.

elevenses (ɪˈlɛvᵊnzɪz) *pl n* (*sometimes functioning as sing*) *Brit. inf.* a light snack taken in mid-morning.

eleventh hour *n* the latest possible time; last minute.

elf (ɛlf) *n, pl* **elves. 1** (in folklore) one of a kind of legendary beings, usually characterized as small, manlike, and mischievous. **2** a mischievous or whimsical child. [OE *ælf*]
▸ˈ**elfish** *or* ˈ**elvish** *adj*

elfin ❶ (ˈɛlfɪn) *adj* **1** of or like an elf or elves. **2** small, delicate, and charming.

elflock (ˈɛlfˌlɒk) *n* a lock of hair, fancifully regarded as having been tangled by the elves.

elicit ❶ (ɪˈlɪsɪt) *vb* (*tr*) **1** to give rise to; evoke. **2** to bring to light. [C17: from L *ēlicere*, from *licere* to entice]
▸**eˈlicitable** *adj* ▸**eˌliciˈtation** *n* ▸**eˈlicitor** *n*

elide (ɪˈlaɪd) *vb* **elides, eliding, elided.** to undergo or cause to undergo elision. [C16: from L *ēlīdere* to knock, from *laedere* to hit, wound]
▸**eˈlidible** *adj*

eligible ❶ (ˈɛlɪdʒəbᵊl) *adj* **1** fit, worthy, or qualified, as for office. **2** desirable, esp. as a spouse. [C15: from LL *ēligere* to ELECT]
▸ˌ**eligiˈbility** *n* ▸ˈ**eligibly** *adv*

eliminate ❶ (ɪˈlɪmɪˌneɪt) *vb* **eliminates, eliminating, eliminated.** (*tr*) **1** to remove or take out. **2** to reject; omit from consideration. **3** to remove (a competitor, team, etc.) from a contest, usually by defeat. **4** *Sl.* to murder in cold blood. **5** *Physiol.* to expel (waste) from the body. **6** *Maths.* to remove (an unknown variable) from simultaneous equations. [C16: from L *ēlīmināre* to turn out of the house, from *e-* out + *līmen* threshold]
▸**eˈliminable** *adj* ▸**eˌlimiˈnation** *n* ▸**eˈliminative** *adj* ▸**eˈlimiˌnator** *n*

> **USAGE NOTE** *Eliminate* is sometimes wrongly used to talk about avoiding the repetition of something undesirable: *we must prevent* (not *eliminate*) *further mistakes of this kind.*

ELISA (ɪˈlaɪzə) *n acronym for* enzyme-linked immunosorbent assay: an immunological technique for accurately measuring the amount of a substance, for example in a blood sample.

elision (ɪˈlɪʒən) *n* **1** omission of a syllable or vowel from a word. **2** omission of parts of a book, etc. [C16: from L *ēlīdere* to ELIDE]

elite ❶ *or* **élite** (ɪˈliːt, eɪ-) *n* **1** (*sometimes functioning as pl*) the most powerful, rich, or gifted members of a group, community, etc. **2** a typewriter type size having 12 characters to the inch. ◆ *adj* **3** of or suitable for an elite. [C18: from F, from OF *eslit* chosen, from L *ēligere* to ELECT]

elitism ❶ (ɪˈliːtɪzəm, eɪ-) *n* **1a** the belief that society should be governed by an elite. **1b** such government. **2** pride in or awareness of being one of an elite group.
▸**eˈlitist** *adj, n*

elixir ❶ (ɪˈlɪksə) *n* **1** an alchemical preparation supposed to be capable of prolonging life (**elixir of life**) or of transmuting base metals into gold. **2** anything that purports to be a sovereign remedy. **3** a quintessence. **4** a liquid containing a medicine with syrup, glycerine, or alcohol added to mask its unpleasant taste. [C14: from Med. L, from Ar., prob. from Gk *xērion* powder used for drying wounds]

Elizabethan (ɪˌlɪzəˈbiːθən) *adj* **1** of, characteristic of, or relating to the reigns of Elizabeth I (queen of England, 1558–1603) or Elizabeth II (queen of Great Britain and N Ireland since 1952). **2** of, relating to, or designating a style of architecture used in England during the reign of Elizabeth I. ◆ *n* **3** a person who lived in England during the reign of Elizabeth I.

Elizabethan sonnet *n* another term for **Shakespearean sonnet.**

elk (ɛlk) *n, pl* **elks** *or* **elk. 1** a large deer of N Europe and Asia: also occurs in N America, where it is called a moose. **2 American elk.** another name for **wapiti.** [OE *eolh*]

ell (ɛl) *n* an obsolete unit of length, approximately 45 inches. [OE *eln* forearm (the measure orig. being from elbow to fingertips)]

ellipse (ɪˈlɪps) *n* a closed conic section shaped like a flattened circle and formed by an inclined plane that does not cut the base of the cone. [C18: back formation from ELLIPSIS]

ellipsis (ɪˈlɪpsɪs) *n, pl* **ellipses** (-siːz). **1** omission of parts of a word or sentence. **2** *Printing.* a sequence of three dots (...) indicating an omission in text. [C16: from L, from Gk, from *en* in + *leipein* to leave]

ellipsoid (ɪˈlɪpsɔɪd) *n* **a** a geometric surface, symmetrical about the three coordinate axes, whose plane sections are ellipses or circles. **b** a solid having this shape.
▸**ellipsoidal** (ɪlɪpˈsɔɪdᵊl, ˌɛl-) *adj*

ellipsoid of revolution *n* a geometric surface produced by rotating an ellipse about one of its two axes and having circular plane sections perpendicular to the axis of revolution.

elliptical ❶ (ɪˈlɪptɪkᵊl) *adj* **1** relating to or having the shape of an ellipse. **2** relating to or resulting from ellipsis. **3** (of speech, literary style, etc.) **3a** very concise, often so as to be obscure or ambiguous. **3b** circumlocutory. ◆ Also (for senses 1 and 2): **elliptic.**
▸**elˈlipticalness** *n*

> **USAGE NOTE** The use of *elliptical* to mean *circumlocutory* should be avoided as it may be interpreted wrongly as meaning *condensed* or *concise*.

elm (ɛlm) *n* **1** any tree of the genus *Ulmus*, occurring in the N hemisphere, having serrated leaves and winged fruits (samaras). **2** the hard heavy wood of this tree. [OE *elm*]

El Niño (ɛl ˈniːnjəʊ) *n Meteorol.* a warming of the eastern tropical Pacific occurring every few years, which disrupts the weather pattern of the region. [from Sp.: The Child, i.e. Christ, referring to its original occurrence at Christmas time]

elocution ❶ (ˌɛləˈkjuːʃən) *n* the art of public speaking. [C15: from L *ēloquī*, from *loquī* to speak]
▸ˌ**eloˈcutionary** *adj* ▸ˌ**eloˈcutionist** *n* [C17: from Hebrew *'Elōhim*, plural (used to indicate uniqueness) of *'Elōah* God; probably related to *'El* God]

Elohist (ɛˈləʊhɪst) *n Bible.* the supposed author or authors of the Pentateuch, identified chiefly by the use of the word *Elohim* for God.

elongate ❶ (ˈiːlɒŋgeɪt) *vb* **elongates, elongating, elongated. 1** to make or become longer; stretch. ◆ *adj* **2** long and narrow. **3** lengthened or tapered. [C16: from LL *ēlongāre* to keep at a distance, from *ē-* away + L *longē* (adv) far]
▸ˌ**elonˈgation** *n*

elope ❶ (ɪˈləʊp) *vb* **elopes, eloping, eloped.** (*intr*) to run away secretly with a lover, esp. in order to marry. [C16: from Anglo-F *aloper*, ?from MDu. *lōpen* to run; see LOPE]
▸**eˈlopement** *n* ▸**eˈloper** *n*

eloquence ❶ (ˈɛləkwəns) *n* **1** ease in using language. **2** powerful and effective language. **3** the quality of being persuasive or moving.

eloquent ❶ (ˈɛləkwənt) *adj* **1** (of speech, writing, etc.) fluent and persuasive. **2** visibly or vividly expressive: *an eloquent yawn*. [C14: from L *ēloquēns*, from *loquī* to speak]
▸ˈ**eloquentness** *n*

Elsan (ˈɛlsæn) *n Trademark.* a type of portable chemical lavatory. [C20: from initials of *E. L.* Jackson, manufacturer + SAN(ITATION)]

else (ɛls) *determiner* (*postpositive; used after an indefinite pronoun or an interrogative*) **1** in addition; more: *there is nobody else here*. **2** other; different: *where else could he be?* ◆ *adv* **3 or else. 3a** if not, then: *go away or else I won't finish my work today*. **3b** or something terrible will result: used as a threat: *sit down, or else!* [OE *elles*, genitive of *el-* strange, foreign]

THESAURUS

elfin *adj* **1** = **rise**, elfish, elflike, elvish **2** = **small**, arch, charming, frolicsome, impish, mischievous, playful, prankish, puckish, sprightly

elicit *vb* **1, 2** = **bring about**, bring forth, bring out, bring to light, call forth, cause, derive, evolve, give rise to

eligible *adj* **1, 2** = **qualified**, acceptable, appropriate, desirable, fit, preferable, proper, suitable, suited, worthy
Antonyms *adj* inappropriate, ineligible, unacceptable, unqualified, unsuitable, unsuited

eliminate *vb* **1** = **get rid of**, cut out, dispose of, do away with, eradicate, exterminate, get shot of, remove, stamp out, take out, wipe from the face of the earth **2, 3** = **drop**, axe (*inf.*), dispense with, disregard, eject, exclude, expel, ignore, knock out, leave out, omit, put out, reject, throw out **4** *Slang* = **murder**, annihilate, blow away (*sl., chiefly US*), bump off (*sl.*), kill, liquidate, rub out (*US sl.*), slay, take out (*sl.*), terminate, waste (*inf.*)

elite *n* **1** = **best**, aristocracy, cream, *crème de la crème*, elect, flower, gentry, high society, nobility, pick, upper class ◆ *adj* **3** = **best**, aristocratic, choice, crack (*sl.*), elect, exclusive, first-class, noble, pick, selected, upper-class
Antonyms *n* ≠ **best:** dregs, hoi polloi, rabble, riff-raff

elitist *adj* **2** = **snobbish**, exclusive, selective ◆ *n* **2** = **snob**

elixir *n* **2** = **panacea**, cure-all, nostrum, sovereign remedy **3** = **essence**, concentrate, extract, pith, principle, quintessence **4** = **syrup**, mixture, potion, solution, tincture

elliptical *adj* **1** = **oval 3a** = **obscure**, abstruse, ambiguous, concentrated, concise, condensed, cryptic, laconic, recondite, terse

elocution *n* = **diction**, articulation, declamation, delivery, enunciation, oratory, pronunciation, public speaking, rhetoric, speech, speechmaking, utterance, voice production

elongate *vb* **1** = **make longer**, draw out, extend, lengthen, prolong, protract, stretch

elongated *adj* **1** = **drawn out**, extended, long, long-drawn-out, prolonged, protracted, stretched

elope *vb* = **run away**, abscond, bolt, decamp, disappear, escape, leave, run off, slip away, steal away

eloquence *n* **1-3** = **expressiveness**, expression, fluency, forcefulness, oratory, persuasiveness, rhetoric, way with words

eloquent *adj* **1** = **silver-tongued**, articulate, fluent, forceful, graceful, moving, persuasive, stirring, well-expressed **2** = **expressive**, meaningful, pregnant, revealing, suggestive, telling, vivid
Antonyms *adj* ≠ **silver-tongued:** faltering, halting, hesitant, inarticulate, speechless, stumbling, tongue-tied, wordless

elsewhere ⓣ (ˌɛlsˈwɛə) *adv* in or to another place; somewhere else. [OE *elles hwǣr;* see ELSE, WHERE]

ELT *abbrev. for* English Language Teaching.

eluate (ˈɛljuːˌeɪt) *n* a solution of adsorbed material in the eluant obtained during the process of elution.

elucidate ⓣ (ɪˈluːsɪˌdeɪt) *vb* **elucidates, elucidating, elucidated.** to make clear (something obscure or difficult); clarify. [C16: from LL *ēlūcidāre* to enlighten; see LUCID]
▸**eˌluciˈdation** *n* ▸**eˈluciˌdative** *or* **eˈluciˌdatory** *adj* ▸**eˈluciˌdator** *n*

elude ⓣ (ɪˈluːd) *vb* **eludes, eluding, eluded.** (*tr*) **1** to escape from or avoid, esp. by cunning. **2** to avoid fulfilment of (a responsibility, obligation, etc.); evade. **3** to escape discovery or understanding by; baffle. [C16: from L *ēlūdere* to deceive, from *lūdere* to play]
▸**eˈluder** *n* ▸**eˈlusion**

USAGE NOTE *Elude* is sometimes wrongly used where *allude* is meant: *he was alluding* (not *eluding*) *to his previous visit to the city.*

eluent *or* **eluant** (ˈɛljʊənt) *n* a solvent used for eluting.

elusive ⓣ (ɪˈluːsɪv) *adj* **1** difficult to catch. **2** preferring or living in solitude and anonymity. **3** difficult to remember.
▸**eˈlusiveness** *n*

USAGE NOTE See at **illusory.**

elute (iːˈluːt, ɪˈluːt) *vb* **elutes, eluting, eluted.** (*tr*) to wash out (a substance) by the action of a solvent, as in chromatography. [C18: from L *ēlūtus* rinsed out, from *luere* to wash, LAVE]
▸**eˈlution** *n*

elutriate (ɪˈluːtrɪˌeɪt) *vb* **elutriates, elutriating, elutriated.** (*tr*) to purify or separate (a substance or mixture) by washing and straining or decanting. [C18: from L *ēluere,* from *ē-* out + *lavere* to wash]
▸**eˌlutriˈation** *n*

elver (ˈɛlvə) *n* a young eel, esp. one migrating up a river. [C17: var. of *eelfare,* lit.: eel-journey; see EEL, FARE]

elves (ɛlvz) *n* the plural of **elf.**

elvish (ˈɛlvɪʃ) *adj* a variant of **elfish:** see **elf.**

Elysium (ɪˈlɪzɪəm) *n* **1** Also called: **Elysian fields.** *Greek myth.* the dwelling place of the blessed after death. **2** a state or place of perfect bliss. [C16: from L, from Gk *Ēlusion pedion* Elysian (that is, blessed) fields]

elytron (ˈɛlɪˌtrɒn) *or* **elytrum** (ˈɛlɪtrəm) *n, pl* **elytra** (-trə). either of the horny front wings of beetles and some other insects. [C18: from Gk *elutron* sheath]

em (ɛm) *n Printing.* **1** the square of a body of any size of type, used as a unit of measurement. **2** Also called: **pica em, pica.** a unit of measurement in printing, equal to twelve points or one sixth of an inch. [C19: from the name of the letter *M*]

em- *prefix* a variant of **en-**[1] and **en-**[2] before *b, m,* and *p.*

'em (əm) *pron* an informal variant of **them.**

emaciate ⓣ (ɪˈmeɪsɪˌeɪt) *vb* **emaciates, emaciating, emaciated.** (*usually tr*) to become or cause to become abnormally thin. [C17: from L, from *macer* thin]
▸**eˈmaciˌated** *adj* ▸**eˌmaciˈation** *n*

E-mail, e-mail, *or* **email** (ˈiːmeɪl) *n* **1** short for **electronic mail.** ◆ *vb* (*tr*) **2** to contact (a person) by electronic mail. **3** to send (a message, document, etc.) by electronic mail.

emanate ⓣ (ˈɛməˌneɪt) *vb* **emanates, emanating, emanated. 1** (*intr;* often foll. by *from*) to issue or proceed from or as from a source. **2** (*tr*) to send forth; emit. [C18: from L *ēmānāre* to flow out, from *mānāre* to flow]
▸**emanative** (ˈɛmənətɪv) *adj* ▸**ˈemaˌnator** *n* ▸**ˈemaˌnatory** *adj*

emanation ⓣ (ˌɛməˈneɪʃən) *n* **1** an act or instance of emanating. **2** something that emanates or is produced. **3** a gaseous product of radioactive decay.
▸**ˌemaˈnational** *adj*

emancipate ⓣ (ɪˈmænsɪˌpeɪt) *vb* **emancipates, emancipating, emancipated.** (*tr*) **1** to free from restriction or restraint, esp. social or legal restraint. **2** (*often passive*) to free from the inhibitions of conventional morality. **3** to liberate (a slave) from bondage. [C17: from L *ēmancipāre* to give independence (to a son), from *mancipāre* to transfer property; see MANCIPLE]
▸**eˈmanciˌpated** *adj* ▸**eˌmanciˈpation** *n* ▸**eˈmanciˌpator** *n* ▸**emancipatory** (ɪˈmænsɪpətərɪ, -trɪ) *adj*

emasculate ⓣ *vb* (ɪˈmæskjʊˌleɪt), **emasculates, emasculating, emasculated.** (*tr*) **1** to remove the testicles of; castrate; geld. **2** to deprive of vigour, effectiveness, etc. **3** *Bot.* to remove the stamens from (a flower) to prevent self-pollination for the purposes of plant breeding. ◆ *adj* (ɪˈmæskjʊlɪt, -ˌleɪt). **4** castrated; gelded. **5** Also: **emasculated.** deprived of strength, effectiveness, etc. [C17: from L *ēmasculāre,* from *masculus* male; see MASCULINE]
▸**eˌmascuˈlation** *n* ▸**eˈmascuˌlator** *n* ▸**eˈmasculatory** *adj*

embalm ⓣ (ɪmˈbɑːm) *vb* (*tr*) **1** to treat (a dead body) with preservatives to retard putrefaction. **2** to preserve or cherish the memory of. **3** *Poetic.* to give a sweet fragrance to. [C13: from OF *embaumer;* see BALM]
▸**emˈbalmer** *n* ▸**emˈbalmment** *n*

embank (ɪmˈbæŋk) *vb* (*tr*) to protect, enclose, or confine with an embankment.

embankment (ɪmˈbæŋkmənt) *n* a man-made ridge of earth or stone that carries a road or railway or confines a waterway.

embargo ⓣ (ɛmˈbɑːgəʊ) *n, pl* **embargoes. 1** a government order prohibiting the departure or arrival of merchant ships in its ports. **2** any legal stoppage of commerce. **3** a restraint or prohibition. ◆ *vb* **embargoes, embargoing, embargoed.** (*tr*) **4** to lay an embargo upon. **5** to seize for use by the state. [C16: from Sp., from *embargar,* from L IM- + *barra* BAR[1]]

embark ⓣ (ɛmˈbɑːk) *vb* **1** to board (a ship or aircraft). **2** (*intr;* usually foll. by *on* or *upon*) to commence or engage (in) a new project, venture, etc. [C16: via F from OF, from EM- + *barca* boat, BARQUE]
▸**ˌembarˈkation** *n*

embarrass ⓣ (ɪmˈbærəs) *vb* (*mainly tr*) **1** to cause to feel confusion or self-consciousness; disconcert. **2** (*usually passive*) to involve in financial difficulties. **3** *Arch.* to complicate. **4** *Arch.* to impede or hamper. [C17 (in the sense: to impede): via F & Sp. from It., from *imbarrare* to confine within bars]
▸**emˈbarrassed** *adj* ▸**emˈbarrassing** *adj* ▸**emˈbarrassment** *n*

embassy (ˈɛmbəsɪ) *n, pl* **embassies. 1** the residence or place of business of an ambassador. **2** an ambassador and his entourage collectively. **3** the position, business, or mission of an ambassador. **4** any important or official mission. [C16: from OF *ambaisada;* see AMBASSADOR]

embattle (ɪmˈbætᵊl) *vb* **embattles, embattling, embattled.** (*tr*) **1** to deploy (troops) for battle. **2** to fortify (a position, town, etc.). **3** to provide with battlements. [C14: from OF *embataillier;* see EN-[1] BATTLE]

embay (ɪmˈbeɪ) *vb* (*tr*) (*usually passive*) **1** to form into a bay. **2** to enclose in or as if in a bay.

embed ⓣ (ɪmˈbɛd) *vb* **embeds, embedding, embedded. 1** (usually foll. by *in*)

THESAURUS

elsewhere *adv* = **in** *or* **to another place,** abroad, away, hence (*arch.*), not here, somewhere else

elucidate *vb* = **clarify,** annotate, clear the air, clear up, explain, explicate, expound, gloss, illuminate, illustrate, interpret, make plain, shed *or* throw light upon, spell out, unfold

elucidation *n* = **clarification,** annotation, comment, commentary, explanation, explication, exposition, gloss, illumination, illustration, interpretation

elude *vb* **1, 2** = **escape,** avoid, body-swerve, circumvent, dodge, duck (*inf.*), evade, flee, get away from, outrun, shirk, shun, slip through one's fingers, slip through the net **3** = **baffle,** be beyond (someone), confound, escape, foil, frustrate, puzzle, stump, thwart

elusive *adj* **1** = **difficult to catch,** shifty, slippery, tricky **3** = **indefinable,** baffling, fleeting, intangible, puzzling, subtle, transient, transitory

emaciated *adj* = **skeletal,** atrophied, attenuate, attenuated, cadaverous, gaunt, haggard, lank, lean, meagre, pinched, scrawny, thin, undernourished, wasted

emaciation *n* = **thinness,** atrophy, attenuation, gauntness, haggardness, leanness, meagreness, scrawniness, wasting away

emanate *vb* **1** = **flow,** arise, come forth, derive, emerge, issue, originate, proceed, spring, stem **2** = **give out,** discharge, emit, exhale, give off, issue, radiate, send forth

emanation *n* **1** = **flow,** arising, derivation, emergence, origination, proceeding **2** = **emission,** discharge, effluent, efflux, effusion, exhalation **3** = **radiation**

emancipate *vb* **1-3** = **free,** deliver, discharge, disencumber, disenthral, enfranchise, liberate, manumit, release, set free, unbridle, unchain, unfetter, unshackle
Antonyms *vb* bind, capture, enchain, enslave, enthral, fetter, shackle, subjugate, yoke

emancipation *n* **1-3** = **freedom,** deliverance, discharge, enfranchisement, liberation, liberty, manumission, release
Antonyms *n* bondage, captivity, confinement, detention, enthralment, imprisonment, servitude, slavery, thraldom, vassalage

emasculate *vb* **1** = **castrate,** geld **2** = **weaken,** cripple, debilitate, deprive of force, enervate, impoverish, soften

embalm *vb* **1** = **preserve,** mummify **2** = **enshrine,** cherish, consecrate, conserve, immortalize, store, treasure

embargo *n* **1-3** = **ban,** bar, barrier, block, blockage, boycott, check, hindrance, impediment, interdict, interdiction, prohibition, proscription, restraint, restriction, stoppage ◆ *vb* **4** = **ban,** bar, block, boycott, check, impede, interdict, prohibit, proscribe, restrict, stop

embark *vb* **1** = **go aboard,** board ship, put on board, take on board, take ship **2** *usually with* **on** *or* **upon** = **begin,** broach, commence, engage, enter, get the show on the road (*inf.*), initiate, launch, plunge into, set about, set out, start, take up, undertake
Antonyms *vb* ≠ **go aboard:** alight, arrive, get off, go ashore, land, step out of

embarrass *vb* **1** = **shame,** abash, chagrin, confuse, discomfit, discompose, disconcert, discountenance, distress, faze, fluster, humiliate, mortify, put out of countenance, show up (*inf.*)

embarrassed *adj* **1** = **ashamed,** awkward, blushing, caught with egg on one's face, chagrined, confused, discomfited, disconcerted, discountenanced, flustered, humiliated, mortified, not knowing where to put oneself, put out of countenance, red-faced, self-conscious, sheepish, shown-up, thrown, upset, wishing the earth would swallow one up

embarrassing *adj* **1** = **humiliating,** awkward, blush-making, compromising, discomfiting, disconcerting, distressing, mortifying, sensitive, shameful, shaming, toe-curling (*sl.*), touchy, tricky, uncomfortable

embarrassment *n* **1** = **shame,** awkwardness, bashfulness, chagrin, confusion, discomfiture, discomposure, distress, humiliation, mortification, self-consciousness, showing up (*inf.*) **2** = **predicament,** bind (*inf.*), difficulty, mess, pickle (*inf.*), scrape (*inf.*)

embed *vb* **1** = **fix,** dig in, drive in, hammer in, implant, plant, ram in, root, set, sink

DICTIONARY

to fix or become fixed firmly and deeply in a surrounding solid mass. **2** (*tr*) to surround closely. **3** (*tr*) to fix or retain (a thought, idea, etc.) in the mind. ◆ Also: **imbed.**
▸**em'bedment** *n*

embellish Ⓣ (ɪm'bɛlɪʃ) *vb* (*tr*) **1** to beautify; adorn. **2** to make (a story, etc.) more interesting by adding detail. [C14: from OF *embelir*, from *bel* beautiful, from L *bellus*]
▸**em'bellisher** *n* ▸**em'bellishment** *n*

ember Ⓣ ('ɛmbə) *n* **1** a glowing or smouldering piece of coal or wood, as in a dying fire. **2** the remains of a past emotion. [OE *ǣmyrge*]

Ember days *pl n RC & Anglican Church.* any of four groups in the year of three days (always Wednesday, Friday, and Saturday) of prayer and fasting. [OE *ymbrendǣg*, from *ymb* around + *ryne* a course + *dǣg* day]

embezzle Ⓣ (ɪm'bɛz°l) *vb* **embezzles, embezzling, embezzled.** to convert (money or property entrusted to one) fraudulently to one's own use. [C15: from Anglo-F *embeseiller* to destroy, from OF *beseiller* to make away with, from ?]
▸**em'bezzlement** *n* ▸**em'bezzler** *n*

embitter Ⓣ (ɪm'bɪtə) *vb* (*tr*) **1** to make (a person) bitter. **2** to aggravate (a hostile feeling, difficult situation, etc.).
▸**em'bittered** *adj* ▸**em'bitterment** *n*

emblazon Ⓣ (ɪm'bleɪz°n) *vb* (*tr*) **1** to portray heraldic arms on (a shield, one's notepaper, etc.). **2** to make bright or splendid, as with colours, flowers, etc. **3** to glorify, praise, or extol.
▸**em'blazonment** *n*

emblem Ⓣ ('ɛmbləm) *n* a visible object or representation that symbolizes a quality, type, group, etc. [C15: from L *emblēma*, from Gk, from *emballein* to insert, from *en* in + *ballein* to throw]
▸ˌ**emblem'atic** *or* ˌ**emblem'atical** *adj* ▸ˌ**emblem'atically** *adv*

embody Ⓣ (ɪm'bɒdɪ) *vb* **embodies, embodying, embodied.** (*tr*) **1** to give a tangible, bodily, or concrete form to (an abstract concept). **2** to be an example of or express (an idea, principle, etc.). **3** (often foll. by *in*) to collect or unite in a comprehensive whole. **4** to invest (a spiritual entity) with bodily form.
▸**em'bodiment** *n*

embolden Ⓣ (ɪm'bəʊld°n) *vb* (*tr*) to encourage; make bold.

embolism ('ɛmbəˌlɪzəm) *n* the occlusion of a blood vessel by an embolus. [C14: from Med. L, from LGk *embolismos*; see EMBOLUS]
▸**embolic** (ɛm'bɒlɪk) *adj*

embolus ('ɛmbələs) *n*, *pl* **emboli** (-ˌlaɪ). material, such as part of a blood clot or an air bubble, that becomes lodged within a small blood vessel and impedes the circulation. [C17: via L from Gk *embolos* stopper; see EMBLEM]

embonpoint *French.* (ɑ̃bɔ̃pwɛ̃) *n* **1** plumpness or stoutness. ◆ *adj* **2** plump; stout. [C18: from *en bon point* in good condition]

embosom (ɪm'bʊzəm) *vb* (*tr*) *Arch.* **1** to enclose or envelop, esp. protectively. **2** to clasp to the bosom; hug. **3** to cherish.

emboss (ɪm'bɒs) *vb* **1** to mould or carve (a decoration) on (a surface) so that it is raised above the surface in low relief. **2** to cause to bulge; make protrude. [C14: from OF *embocer*, from EM- + *boce* BOSS[2]]
▸**em'bossed** *adj* ▸**em'bosser** *n* ▸**em'bossment** *n*

embouchure (ˌɒmbʊ'ʃʊə) *n* **1** the mouth of a river or valley. **2** *Music.* **2a** the correct application of the lips and tongue in playing a wind instrument. **2b** the mouthpiece of a wind instrument. [C18: from F, from OF, from *bouche* mouth, from L *bucca* cheek]

embower (ɪm'baʊə) *vb* (*tr*) *Arch.* to enclose in or as in a bower.

embrace Ⓣ (ɪm'breɪs) *vb* **embraces, embracing, embraced.** (*mainly tr*) **1** (*also intr*) (of a person) to take or clasp (another person) in the arms, or (of two people) to clasp each other, as in affection, greeting, etc.; hug. **2** to accept willingly or eagerly. **3** to take up (a new idea, faith, etc.); adopt. **4** to comprise or include as an integral part. **5** to encircle or enclose. **6** *Rare.* to perceive or understand. ◆ *n* **7** the act of embracing. [C14: from OF, from EM- + *brace* a pair of arms, from L *bracchia* arms]
▸**em'braceable** *adj* ▸**em'bracement** *n* ▸**em'bracer** *n*

embrasure (ɪm'breɪʒə) *n* **1** *Fortifications.* an opening or indentation, as in a battlement, for shooting through. **2** a door or window having splayed sides that increase the width of the opening in the interior. [C18: from F, from obs. *embraser* to widen]
▸**em'brasured** *adj*

embrocate ('ɛmbrəʊˌkeɪt) *vb* **embrocates, embrocating, embrocated.** (*tr*) to apply a liniment or lotion to (a part of the body). [C17: from Med. L *embrocha* poultice, from Gk, from *brokhē* a moistening]

embrocation (ˌɛmbrəʊ'keɪʃən) *n* a drug or agent for rubbing into the skin; liniment.

embroider (ɪm'brɔɪdə) *vb* **1** to do decorative needlework (upon). **2** to add fictitious or exaggerated detail to (a story, etc.). [C15: from OF *embroder*]
▸**em'broiderer** *n*

embroidery (ɪm'brɔɪdərɪ) *n*, *pl* **embroideries. 1** decorative needlework done usually on loosely woven cloth or canvas, often being a picture or pattern. **2** elaboration or exaggeration, esp. in writing or reporting; embellishment.

embroil Ⓣ (ɪm'brɔɪl) *vb* (*tr*) **1** to involve (a person, oneself, etc.) in trouble, conflict, or argument. **2** to throw (affairs, etc.) into a state of confusion or disorder; complicate; entangle. [C17: from F *embrouiller*, from *brouiller* to mingle, confuse]
▸**em'broiler** *n* ▸**em'broilment** *n*

embryo Ⓣ ('ɛmbrɪˌəʊ) *n*, *pl* **embryos. 1** an animal in the early stages of development up to birth or hatching. **2** the human product of conception up to approximately the end of the second month of pregnancy. Cf. **fetus. 3** a plant in the early stages of development. **4** an undeveloped or rudimentary state (esp. in **in embryo**). **5** something in an early stage of development. [C16: from LL, from Gk *embruon*, from *bruein* to swell]

embryology (ˌɛmbrɪ'ɒlədʒɪ) *n* **1** the scientific study of embryos. **2** the structure and development of the embryo of a particular organism.
▸**embryological** (ˌɛmbrɪə'lɒdʒɪk°l) *or* ˌ**embryo'logic** *adj* ▸ˌ**embry'ologist** *n*

embryonic Ⓣ (ˌɛmbrɪ'ɒnɪk) *or* **embryonal** ('ɛmbrɪən°l) *adj* **1** of or relating to an embryo. **2** in an early stage; rudimentary; undeveloped.
▸ˌ**embry'onically** *adv*

emcee (ˌɛm'siː) *Inf.* ◆ *n* **1** a master of ceremonies. ◆ *vb* **emcees, emceeing, emceed. 2** to act as master of ceremonies (for or at). [C20: from MC]

-eme *suffix forming nouns. Linguistics.* indicating a minimal distinctive unit of a specified type in a language: *morpheme; phoneme.* [C20: via F, abstracted from PHONEME]

emend Ⓣ (ɪ'mɛnd) *vb* (*tr*) to make corrections or improvements in (a text) by critical editing. [C15: from L, from *ē-* out + *mendum* a mistake]
▸**e'mendable** *adj*

emendation Ⓣ (ˌiːmɛn'deɪʃən) *n* **1** a correction or improvement in a text. **2** the act or process of emending.
▸**'emenˌdator** *n* ▸**emendatory** (ɪ'mɛndətərɪ, -trɪ) *adj*

emerald ('ɛmərəld, 'ɛmrəld) *n* **1** a green transparent variety of beryl: highly valued as a gem. **2a** its clear green colour. **2b** (*as adj*): *an emerald carpet.* [C13: from OF *esmeraude*, from L *smaragdus*, from Gk *smaragdos*]

Emerald Isle *n* a poetic name for Ireland.

emerge Ⓣ (ɪ'mɜːdʒ) *vb* **emerges, emerging, emerged.** (*intr*; often foll. by

THESAURUS

embellish *vb* **1, 2 = decorate**, adorn, beautify, bedeck, deck, dress up, elaborate, embroider, enhance, enrich, exaggerate, festoon, garnish, gild, gild the lily, grace, ornament, tart up (*sl.*), varnish

embellishment *n* **1, 2 = decoration**, adornment, elaboration, embroidery, enhancement, enrichment, exaggeration, gilding, ornament, ornamentation, trimming

ember *n* **1 = cinder**, ash, live coal

embezzle *vb* **= misappropriate**, abstract, appropriate, defalcate (*Law*), filch, have one's hand in the till (*inf.*), misapply, misuse, peculate, pilfer, purloin, rip off (*sl.*), steal

embezzlement *n* **= misappropriation**, abstraction, appropriation, defalcation (*Law*), filching, fraud, larceny, misapplication, misuse, peculation, pilferage, pilfering, purloining, stealing, theft, thieving

embitter *vb* **1 = make bitter** *or* **resentful**, alienate, anger, disaffect, disillusion, envenom, poison, sour **2 = aggravate**, exacerbate, exasperate, worsen

embittered *adj* **1 = resentful**, acid, angry, at daggers drawn (*inf.*), bitter, disaffected, disillusioned, nursing a grudge, rancorous, sour, soured, venomous, with a chip on one's shoulder (*inf.*)

emblazon *vb* **1, 2 = decorate**, adorn, blazon, colour, embellish, illuminate, ornament, paint **3 = publicize**, crack up (*inf.*), extol, glorify, laud (*literary*), praise, proclaim, publish, trumpet

emblem *n* **= symbol**, badge, crest, device, figure, image, insignia, mark, representation, sigil, sign, token, type

emblematic *adj* **= symbolic**, figurative, representative

embodiment *n* **1, 2 = personification**, epitome, example, exemplar, exemplification, expression, incarnation, incorporation, manifestation, realization, reification, representation, symbol, type **3 = incorporation**, bringing together, codification, collection, combination, comprehension, concentration, consolidation, inclusion, integration, organization, systematization

embody *vb* **1, 2 = personify**, concretize, exemplify, express, incarnate, incorporate, manifest, realize, reify, represent, stand for, symbolize, typify **3 = incorporate**, bring together, codify, collect, combine, comprehend, comprise, concentrate, consolidate, contain, include, integrate, organize, systematize

embolden *vb* **= encourage**, animate, cheer, fire, gee up, hearten, inflame, inspirit, invigorate, nerve, reassure, rouse, stimulate, stir, strengthen, vitalize

embrace *vb* **1 = hug**, clasp, cuddle, encircle, enfold, envelop, grasp, hold, neck (*inf.*), seize, squeeze, take *or* hold in one's arms **2, 3 = accept**, adopt, avail oneself of, espouse, grab, make use of, receive, seize, take on board, take up, welcome **4 = include**, comprehend, comprise, contain, cover, deal with, embody, encompass, involve, provide for, subsume, take in, take into account ◆ *n* **7 = hug**, canoodle (*sl.*), clasp, clinch (*sl.*), cuddle, squeeze

embroil *vb* **1, 2 = involve**, complicate, compromise, confound, confuse, disorder, disturb, encumber, enmesh, ensnare, entangle, implicate, incriminate, mire, mix up, muddle, perplex, stitch up (*sl.*), trouble

embryo *n* **5 = germ**, beginning, nucleus, root, rudiment

embryonic *adj* **2 = early**, beginning, germinal, immature, inchoate, incipient, primary, rudimentary, seminal, undeveloped
Antonyms *adj* advanced, developed, progressive

emend *vb* **= revise**, amend, correct, edit, improve, rectify, redact

emendation *n* **1, 2 = revision**, amendment, correction, editing, improvement, rectification, redaction

emerge *vb* **1, 2 = come into view**, appear, arise, become visible, come forth, come out, come up, emanate, issue, proceed, rise, spring up,

from) **1** to come up to the surface of or rise from water or other liquid. **2** to come into view, as from concealment or obscurity. **3** (foll. by *from*) to come out (of) or live (through (a difficult experience, etc.)). **4** to become apparent. [C17: from L *ēmergere* to rise up from, from *mergere* to dip]
▸**e'mergence** *n* ▸**e'merging** *adj*

emergency 🅣 (ɪ'mɜːdʒənsɪ) *n, pl* **emergencies. 1a** an unforeseen or sudden occurrence, esp. of danger demanding immediate action. **1b** (*as modifier*): *an emergency exit.* **2a** a patient requiring urgent treatment. **2b** (*as modifier*): *an emergency ward.* **3** *NZ.* a player selected to stand by to replace an injured member of a team; reserve. **4 state of emergency.** a condition, declared by a government, in which martial law applies, usually because of civil unrest or natural disaster.

emergent 🅣 (ɪ'mɜːdʒənt) *adj* **1** coming into being or notice. **2** (of a nation) recently independent.
▸**e'mergently** *adv*

emeritus (ɪ'merɪtəs) *adj* (*usually postpositive*) retired or honourably discharged from full-time work, but retaining one's title on an honorary basis: *a professor emeritus.* [C19: from L, from *merēre* to deserve; see MERIT]

emersion (ɪ'mɜːʃən) *n* **1** the act or an instance of emerging. **2** *Astron.* the reappearance of a celestial body after an eclipse or occultation. [C17: from L *ēmersus;* see EMERGE]

emery ('ɛmərɪ) *n* **a** a hard greyish-black mineral consisting of corundum with either magnetite or haematite: used as an abrasive and polishing agent. **b** (*as modifier*): *emery paper.* [C15: from OF *esmeril,* ult. from Gk *smuris* powder for rubbing]

emery board *n* a strip of cardboard or wood with a rough surface of crushed emery, for filing one's nails.

emetic 🅣 (ɪ'metɪk) *adj* **1** causing vomiting. ◆ *n* **2** an emetic agent or drug. [C17: from LL, from Gk *emetikos,* from *emein* to vomit]

emf *or* **EMF** *abbrev. for* electromotive force.

-emia *n combining form.* a US variant of **-aemia.**

emigrant ('ɛmɪgrənt) *n* **a** a person who leaves one place, esp. his native country, to settle in another. **b** (*as modifier*): *an emigrant worker.*

emigrate 🅣 ('ɛmɪˌgreɪt) *vb* **emigrates, emigrating, emigrated.** (*intr*) to leave one place, esp. one's native country, to settle in another. [C18: from L *ēmīgrāre,* from *mīgrāre* to depart, MIGRATE]
▸**ˌemi'gration** *n* ▸**'emiˌgratory** *adj*

émigré ('ɛmɪˌgreɪ) *n* an emigrant, esp. one forced to leave his native country for political reasons. [C18: from F, from *émigrer* to EMIGRATE]

eminence 🅣 ('ɛmɪnəns) *n* **1** a position of superiority or fame. **2** a high or raised piece of ground. ◆ Also: **eminency.** [C17: from F, from L *ēminentia* a standing out; see EMINENT]

Eminence ('ɛmɪnəns) *or* **Eminency** *n, pl* **Eminences** *or* **Eminencies.** (preceded by *Your* or *His*) a title used to address or refer to a cardinal.

éminence grise *French.* (eminɑ̃s griz) *n, pl* ***éminences grises*** (eminɑ̃s griz). a person who wields power and influence unofficially or behind the scenes. [lit.: grey eminence, orig. applied to Père Joseph, F monk, secretary of Cardinal Richelieu (1585–1642), F statesman]

eminent 🅣 ('ɛmɪnənt) *adj* **1** above others in rank, merit, or reputation; distinguished. **2** (*prenominal*) noteworthy or outstanding. **3** projecting or protruding; prominent. [C15: from L *ēminēre* to project, stand out, from *minēre* to stand]

eminent domain *n Law.* the right of a state to confiscate private property for public use, payment usually being made in compensation.

emir (ɛ'mɪə) *n* (in the Islamic world) **1** an independent ruler or chieftain. **2** a military commander or governor. **3** a descendant of Mohammed. [C17: via F from Sp., from Ar. *'amīr* commander]
▸**e'mirate** *n*

emissary 🅣 ('ɛmɪsərɪ, -ɪsrɪ) *n, pl* **emissaries. 1a** an agent sent on a mission, esp. one who represents a government or head of state. **1b** (*as modifier*): *an emissary delegation.* **2** an agent sent on a secret mission, as a spy. ◆ *adj* **3** (of veins) draining blood from sinuses in the dura mater to veins outside the skull. [C17: from L *ēmissārius,* from *ēmittere* to send out; see EMIT]

emission 🅣 (ɪ'mɪʃən) *n* **1** the act of emitting or sending forth. **2** energy, in the form of heat, light, radio waves, etc., emitted from a source. **3** a substance, fluid, etc., that is emitted; discharge. **4** *Physiol.* any bodily discharge, esp. of semen. [C17: from L *ēmissiō,* from *ēmittere* to send forth, EMIT]
▸**e'missive** *adj*

emission spectrum *n* the spectrum or pattern of bright lines or bands seen when the electromagnetic radiation emitted by a substance is passed into a spectrometer.

emissivity (ˌiːmɪ'sɪvɪtɪ, ˌɛm-) *n* a measure of the ability of a surface to radiate energy; the ratio of the radiant flux emitted per unit area to that emitted by a black body at the same temperature.

emit 🅣 (ɪ'mɪt) *vb* **emits, emitting, emitted.** (*tr*) **1** to give or send forth; discharge. **2** to give voice to; utter. **3** *Physics.* to give off (radiation or particles). [C17: from L *ēmittere* to send out, from *mittere* to send]

emitter (ɪ'mɪtə) *n* **1** a person or thing that emits. **2** a substance that emits radiation. **3** the region in a transistor in which the charge-carrying holes or electrons originate.

Emmenthal, Emmental ('ɛmənˌtɑːl), *or* **Emmenthaler** *n* a hard Swiss cheese with holes in it. [C20: after *Emmenthal,* valley in Switzerland]

Emmy ('ɛmɪ) *n, pl* **Emmys** *or* **Emmies.** (in the US) one of the statuettes awarded annually for outstanding television performances and productions. [C20: from *Immy,* short for *image orthicon tube*]

emollient (ɪ'mɒljənt) *adj* **1** softening or soothing, esp. to the skin. **2** helping to avoid confrontation; calming. ◆ *n* **3** any preparation or substance that has this effect. [C17: from L *ēmollīre* to soften, from *mollis* soft]
▸**e'mollience** *n*

emolument 🅣 (ɪ'mɒljʊmənt) *n* the profit arising from an office or employment; fees or wages. [C15: from L *ēmolumentum* benefit; orig., fee paid to a miller, from *molere* to grind]

emote (ɪ'məʊt) *vb* **emotes, emoting, emoted.** (*intr*) to display exaggerated emotion, as in acting. [C20: back formation from EMOTION]
▸**e'moter** *n*

emotion 🅣 (ɪ'məʊʃən) *n* any strong feeling, as of joy, sorrow, or fear. [C16: from F, from OF, from L *ēmovēre* to disturb, from *movēre* to MOVE]

emotional 🅣 (ɪ'məʊʃənᵊl) *adj* **1** of, characteristic of, or expressive of emotion. **2** readily or excessively affected by emotion. **3** appealing to or arousing emotion. **4** caused or determined by emotion rather than reason: *an emotional argument.*
▸**eˌmotion'ality** *n*

emotionalism (ɪ'məʊʃənəˌlɪzəm) *n* **1** emotional nature or quality. **2** a tendency to yield readily to the emotions. **3** an appeal to the emotions, esp. as to an audience.
▸**e'motionalist** *n* ▸**eˌmotional'istic** *adj*

emotionalize *or* **emotionalise** (ɪ'məʊʃənəˌlaɪz) *vb* **emotionalizes, emotionalizing, emotionalized** *or* **emotionalises, emotionalising, emotionalised.** (*tr*) to make emotional; subject to emotional treatment.

emotive 🅣 (ɪ'məʊtɪv) *adj* **1** tending or designed to arouse emotion. **2** of or characterized by emotion.
▸**e'motiveness** *or* **ˌemo'tivity** *n*

USAGE NOTE *Emotional* is preferred to *emotive* when describing a display of emotion: *he was given an emotional* (not *emotive*) *welcome.*

THESAURUS

surface **4** = **become apparent**, become known, come out, come out in the wash, come to light, crop up, develop, materialize, transpire, turn up
Antonyms *vb* ≠ **come into view:** depart, disappear, fade, fall, recede, retreat, sink, submerge, vanish from sight, wane, withdraw

emergence *n* **2, 4** = **coming**, advent, apparition, appearance, arrival, dawn, development, disclosure, emanation, issue, materialization, rise

emergency *n* **1** = **crisis**, danger, difficulty, exigency, extremity, necessity, panic stations (*inf.*), pass, pinch, plight, predicament, quandary, scrape (*inf.*), strait

emergent *adj* **1** = **developing**, appearing, budding, coming, rising

emetic *adj* **1** = **vomitory**, vomitive

emigrate *vb* = **move abroad**, migrate, move, remove

emigration *n* = **departure**, exodus, migration, removal

eminence *n* **1** = **prominence**, celebrity, dignity, distinction, esteem, fame, greatness, illustriousness, importance, notability, note, pre-eminence, prestige, rank, renown, reputation, repute, superiority **2** = **high ground**, elevation, height, hill, hillock, knoll, rise, summit

eminent *adj* **1, 2** = **prominent**, big-time (*inf.*), celebrated, conspicuous, distinguished, elevated, esteemed, exalted, famous, grand, great, high, high-ranking, illustrious, important, major league (*inf.*), notable, noted, noteworthy, outstanding, paramount, pre-eminent, prestigious, renowned, signal, superior, well-known
Antonyms *adj* anonymous, commonplace, infamous, lowly, ordinary, undistinguished, unheard-of, unimportant, unknown, unremarkable, unsung

emissary *n* **1** = **messenger**, agent, ambassador, courier, delegate, deputy, envoy, go-between, herald, legate, representative, scout **2** = **spy**, agent, secret agent

emission *n* **1** = **giving off** *or* **out**, diffusion, discharge, ejaculation, ejection, emanation, exhalation, exudation, issuance, issue, radiation, shedding, transmission, utterance, venting

emit *vb* **1-3** = **give off**, breathe forth, cast out, diffuse, discharge, eject, emanate, exhale, exude, give out, give vent to, issue, radiate, send forth, send out, shed, throw out, transmit, utter, vent
Antonyms *vb* absorb, assimilate, consume, devour, digest, drink in, incorporate, ingest, receive, soak up, suck up, take in

emolument *n* = **fee**, benefit, compensation, earnings, gain, hire, pay, payment, profits, recompense, remuneration, return, reward, salary, stipend, wages

emotion *n* = **feeling**, agitation, ardour, excitement, fervour, passion, perturbation, sensation, sentiment, vehemence, warmth

emotional *adj* **2** = **sensitive**, demonstrative, excitable, feeling, hot-blooded, passionate, responsive, sentimental, susceptible, temperamental, tender, touchy-feely (*inf.*), warm **3** = **moving**, affecting, emotive, exciting, heart-warming, pathetic, poignant, sentimental, stirring, tear-jerking (*inf.*), three-hankie (*inf.*), thrilling, touching
Antonyms *adj* ≠ **sensitive:** apathetic, cold, detached, insensitive, phlegmatic, undemonstrative, unemotional, unfeeling, unmoved, unsentimental ≠ **passionate:** dispassionate, unenthusiastic, unexcitable, unruffled

emotive *adj* **1** = **sensitive**, argumentative, controversial, delicate, touchy

Emp. *abbrev. for:* **1** Emperor. **2** Empire. **3** Empress.

empanel *or* **impanel** (ɪm'pænᵊl) *vb* **empanels, empanelling, empanelled** *or US* **empanels, empaneling, empaneled** *or* **impanels, impanelling, impanelled** *or US* **impanels, impaneling, impaneled.** (*tr*) *Law.* **1** to enter on a list (names of persons to be summoned for jury service). **2** to select (a jury) from such a list.
▸**em'panelment** *or* **im'panelment** *n*

empathize ⓣ *or* **empathise** ('ɛmpəˌθaɪz) *vb* **empathizes, empathizing, empathized** *or* **empathises, empathising, empathised.** (*intr*) to engage in or feel empathy.

empathy ('ɛmpəθɪ) *n* **1** the power of understanding and imaginatively entering into another person's feelings. **2** the attribution to an object, such as a work of art, of one's own feelings about it. [C20: from Gk *empatheia* affection, passion]
▸**em'pathic** *or* ˌ**empa'thetic** *adj*

emperor ('ɛmpərə) *n* a monarch who rules or reigns over an empire. [C13: from OF, from L *imperāre* to command, from IM- + *parāre* to make ready]
▸'**emperor**ˌ**ship** *n*

emperor penguin *n* an Antarctic penguin with orange-yellow patches on the neck: the largest penguin, reaching a height of 1.3 m (4 ft).

emphasis ⓣ ('ɛmfəsɪs) *n, pl* **emphases** (-siːz). **1** special importance or significance. **2** an object, idea, etc., that is given special importance or significance. **3** stress on a particular syllable, word, or phrase in speaking. **4** force or intensity of expression. **5** sharpness or clarity of form or outline. [C16: via L from Gk: meaning, (in rhetoric) significant stress; see EMPHATIC]

emphasize ⓣ *or* **emphasise** ('ɛmfəˌsaɪz) *vb* **emphasizes, emphasizing, emphasized** *or* **emphasises, emphasising, emphasised.** (*tr*) to give emphasis or prominence to; stress.

emphatic ⓣ (ɪm'fætɪk) *adj* **1** expressed, spoken, or done with emphasis. **2** forceful and positive; definite; direct. **3** sharp or clear in form, contour, or outline. **4** important or significant; stressed. [C18: from Gk, from *emphainein* to display, from *phainein* to show]
▸**em'phatically** *adv*

emphysema (ˌɛmfɪ'siːmə) *n Pathol.* **1** a condition in which the air sacs of the lungs are grossly enlarged, causing breathlessness and wheezing. **2** the abnormal presence of air in a tissue or part. [C17: from NL, from Gk *emphusēma* a swelling up, from *phusan* to blow]

empire ⓣ ('ɛmpaɪə) *n* **1** an aggregate of peoples and territories under the rule of a single person, oligarchy, or sovereign state. **2** any monarchy that has an emperor as head of state. **3** the period during which a particular empire exists. **4** supreme power; sovereignty. **5** a large industrial organization with many ramifications. [C13: from OF, from L, from *imperāre* to command, from *parāre* to prepare]

Empire ('ɛmpaɪə) *n* **the. 1.** the British Empire. **2** *French history.* **2a** the period of imperial rule in France from 1804 to 1815 under Napoleon Bonaparte. **2b** Also called: **Second Empire.** the period from 1852 to 1870 when Napoleon III ruled as emperor. ◆ *adj* **3** denoting, characteristic of, or relating to the British Empire. **4** denoting, characteristic of, or relating to either French Empire, esp. the first.

empire-builder *n Inf.* a person who seeks extra power, esp. by increasing the number of his staff.
▸'**empire-**ˌ**building** *n, adj*

Empire Day *n* the former name of **Commonwealth Day.**

empiric (ɛm'pɪrɪk) *n* **1** a person who relies on empirical methods. **2** a medical quack. ◆ *adj* **3** a variant of **empirical.** [C16: from L, from Gk *empeirikos* practised, from *peiran* to attempt]

empirical ⓣ (ɛm'pɪrɪkᵊl) *adj* **1** derived from or relating to experiment and observation rather than theory. **2** (of medical treatment) based on practical experience rather than scientific proof. **3** *Philosophy.* (of knowledge) derived from experience rather than by logic from first principles. **4** of or relating to medical quackery.
▸**em'piricalness** *n*

empiricism (ɛm'pɪrɪˌsɪzəm) *n* **1** *Philosophy.* the doctrine that all knowledge derives from experience. **2** the use of empirical methods. **3** medical quackery.
▸**em'piricist** *n, adj*

emplace ⓣ (ɪm'pleɪs) *vb* **emplaces, emplacing, emplaced.** (*tr*) to put in position.

emplacement ⓣ (ɪm'pleɪsmənt) *n* **1** a prepared position for a gun or other weapon. **2** the act of putting or state of being put in place. [C19: from F, from obs. *emplacer* to put in position, from PLACE]

emplane (ɪm'pleɪn) *vb* **emplanes, emplaning, emplaned.** to board or put on board an aeroplane.

employ ⓣ (ɪm'plɔɪ) *vb* (*tr*) **1** to engage or make use of the services of (a person) in return for money; hire. **2** to provide work or occupation for; keep busy. **3** to use as a means. ◆ *n* **4** the state of being employed (esp. in **in someone's employ**). [C15: from OF *emploier,* from L *implicāre* to entangle, engage, from *plicāre* to fold]
▸**em'ployable** *adj* ▸**em**ˌ**ploya'bility** *n*

employee ⓣ *or US* **employe** (ɛm'plɔɪiː, ˌɛmplɔɪ'iː) *n* a person who is hired to work for another or for a business, firm, etc., in return for payment.

employer ⓣ (ɪm'plɔɪə) *n* **1** a person, firm, etc., that employs workers. **2** a person who employs.

employment ⓣ (ɪm'plɔɪmənt) *n* **1** the act of employing or state of being employed. **2** a person's work or occupation.

employment exchange *n Brit.* a former name for **employment office.**

employment office *n Brit.* any government office established to collect and supply to the unemployed information about job vacancies and to employers information about availability of prospective workers. See also **Jobcentre.**

emporium ⓣ (ɛm'pɔːrɪəm) *n, pl* **emporiums** *or* **emporia** (-rɪə). a large retail shop offering for sale a wide variety of merchandise. [C16: from L, from Gk, from *emporos* merchant, from *poros* a journey]

empower ⓣ (ɪm'paʊə) *vb* (*tr*) **1** to give power or authority to; authorize. **2** to give ability to; enable or permit.
▸**em'powerment** *n*

empress ('ɛmprɪs) *n* **1** the wife or widow of an emperor. **2** a woman who holds the rank of emperor in her own right. [C12: from OF *empereriz,* from L *imperātrix;* see EMPEROR]

empty ⓣ ('ɛmptɪ) *adj* **emptier, emptiest. 1** containing nothing. **2** without inhabitants; vacant or unoccupied. **3** carrying no load, passengers, etc. **4** without purpose, substance, or value: *an empty life.* **5** insincere or trivial: *empty words.* **6** not expressive or vital; vacant: *an empty look.* **7** *Inf.* hungry. **8** (*postpositive;* foll. by *of*) devoid; destitute. **9** *Inf.* drained of energy or emotion. **10** *Maths, logic.* (of a set or class) containing no members. ◆ *vb* **empties, emptying, emptied. 11** to make or become empty. **12** (when *intr,* foll. by *into*) to discharge (contents). **13** (*tr;* often foll. by *of*) to unburden or rid (oneself). ◆ *n, pl* **empties. 14** an empty container, esp. a bottle. [OE *ǣmtig*]
▸'**emptiable** *adj* ▸'**emptier** *n* ▸'**emptily** *adv* ▸'**emptiness** *n*

THESAURUS

empathize *vb* = **relate to,** feel for, identify with, put oneself in someone else's shoes (*inf.*)

emphasis *n* **1, 3, 4** = **stress,** accent, accentuation, attention, decidedness, force, importance, impressiveness, insistence, intensity, moment, positiveness, power, pre-eminence, priority, prominence, significance, strength, underscoring, weight

emphasize *vb* = **stress,** accent, accentuate, dwell on, foreground, give priority to, highlight, insist on, lay stress on, play up, press home, put the accent on, underline, underscore, weight
Antonyms *vb* gloss over, make light of, make little of, minimize, play down, soft-pedal (*inf.*), underplay

emphatic *adj* **2, 4** = **forceful,** absolute, categorical, certain, decided, definite, direct, distinct, earnest, energetic, forcible, important, impressive, insistent, in spades, marked, momentous, positive, powerful, pronounced, resounding, significant, striking, strong, telling, unequivocal, unmistakable, vigorous
Antonyms *adj* commonplace, equivocal, hesitant, insignificant, tame, tentative, uncertain, undecided, unremarkable, unsure, weak

empire *n* **1** = **kingdom,** commonwealth, domain, imperium (*rare*), realm **4** = **power,** authority, command, control, dominion, government, rule, sovereignty, supremacy, sway

empirical *adj* **1** = **first-hand,** experiential, experimental, observed, practical, pragmatic
Antonyms *adj* academic, assumed, conjectural, hypothetical, putative, speculative, theoretic(al)

emplace *vb* = **position,** insert, place, put, put in place, set up, station

emplacement *n* **1** = **position,** location, lodgment, platform, site, situation, station **2** = **positioning,** placement, placing, putting in place, setting up, stationing

employ *vb* **1** = **hire,** commission, engage, enlist, retain, take on **2** = **keep busy,** engage, fill, make use of, occupy, spend, take up, use up **3** = **use,** apply, bring to bear, exercise, exert, make use of, ply, put to use, utilize ◆ *n* **4** *As in* **in someone's employ** = **service,** employment, engagement, hire

employed *adj* **1** = **working,** active, busy, engaged, in a job, in employment, in work, occupied
Antonyms *adj* idle, jobless, laid off, on the dole (*Brit. inf.*), out of a job, out of work, redundant, unoccupied

employee *n* = **worker,** hand, job-holder, staff member, wage-earner, workman

employer *n* **1** = **boss** (*inf.*), business, company, establishment, firm, gaffer (*inf., chiefly Brit.*), organization, outfit (*inf.*), owner, patron, proprietor

employment *n* **1** = **use,** application, engagement, enlistment, exercise, hire, taking on, utilization **2** = **job,** avocation (*arch.*), business, calling, craft, employ, line, métier, occupation, profession, pursuit, service, trade, vocation, work

emporium *n* = **shop,** bazaar, market, mart, store, warehouse

empower *vb* **1, 2** = **enable,** allow, authorize, commission, delegate, entitle, license, permit, qualify, sanction, warrant

emptiness *n* **1, 2** = **bareness,** blankness, desertedness, desolation, destitution, vacancy, vacantness, vacuum, void, waste **4** = **purposelessness,** aimlessness, banality, barrenness, frivolity, futility, hollowness, inanity, ineffectiveness, meaninglessness, senselessness, silliness, unreality, unsatisfactoriness, unsubstantiality, vainness, valuelessness, vanity, worthlessness **5** = **insincerity,** cheapness, hollowness, idleness, triviality, trivialness **6** = **blankness,** absentness, expressionlessness, unintelligence, vacancy, vacantness, vacuity, vacuousness

empty *adj* **1, 2** = **bare,** blank, clear, deserted, desolate, destitute, hollow, unfurnished, uninhabited, unoccupied, untenanted, vacant, void, waste **4** = **purposeless,** aimless, banal, bootless, frivolous, fruitless, futile, hollow, inane, ineffective, meaningless, otiose, senseless, silly, unreal, unsatisfactory, unsubstantial, vain, valueless, worthless **5** = **insincere,** cheap, hollow, idle, trivial **6** = **blank,** absent, expres-

empty-handed *adj* **1** carrying nothing in the hands. **2** having gained nothing.
empty-headed Ⓣ *adj* lacking sense; frivolous.
empty-nester (-'nɛstə) *n Inf.* a married person whose children have grown up and left home.
empyema (ˌɛmpaɪ'iːmə) *n, pl* **empyemata** (-'iːmətə) *or* **empyemas.** a collection of pus in a body cavity, esp. in the chest. [C17: from Med. L, from Gk *empuēma* abscess, from *empuein* to suppurate, from *puon* pus]
▸ˌ**empy'emic** *adj*
empyrean (ˌɛmpaɪ'riːən) *n* **1** *Arch.* the highest part of the heavens, thought in ancient times to contain the pure element of fire and by early Christians to be the abode of God. **2** *Poetic.* the heavens or sky. ◆ *adj also* **empyreal. 3** of or relating to the sky. **4** heavenly or sublime. [C17: from LL, from Gk *empurios* fiery]
empyreuma (ˌɛmpɪ'ruːmə) *n, pl* **empyreumata** (-mətə). the smell and taste associated with burning vegetable and animal matter. [C17: from Gk, from *empureuein* to set on fire]
EMS *abbrev. for* European Monetary System.
emu ('iːmjuː) *n* a large Australian flightless bird, similar to the ostrich. [C17: changed from Port. *ema* ostrich, from Arab. *Na-'amah* ostrich]
EMU 1 *abbrev. for* European monetary union. **2** See **e.m.u.**
e.m.u. *or* **EMU** *abbrev. for* electromagnetic unit.
emu-bob *Austral. inf.* ◆ *vb* **emu-bobs, emu-bobbing, emu-bobbed. 1** (*intr*) to bend over to collect litter or small pieces of wood. ◆ *n* **2** Also called: **emu parade.** a parade of soldiers or schoolchildren for litter collection.
▸'**emu-ˌbobbing** *n*
emulate Ⓣ ('ɛmjʊˌleɪt) *vb* **emulates, emulating, emulated.** (*tr*) **1** to attempt to equal or surpass, esp. by imitation. **2** to rival or compete with. [C16: from L *aemulus* competing with]
▸'**emulative** *adj* ▸ˌ**emu'lation** *n* ▸'**emuˌlator** *n*
emulous ('ɛmjʊləs) *adj* **1** desiring or aiming to equal or surpass another. **2** characterized by or arising from emulation. [C14: from L; see EMULATE]
▸'**emulousness** *n*
emulsifier (ɪ'mʌlsɪˌfaɪə) *n* an agent that forms an emulsion, esp. a food additive that prevents separation of processed foods.
emulsify (ɪ'mʌlsɪˌfaɪ) *vb* **emulsifies, emulsifying, emulsified.** to make or form into an emulsion.
▸**eˌmulsi'fiable** *or* **e'mulsible** *adj* ▸**eˌmulsifi'cation** *n*
emulsion (ɪ'mʌlʃən) *n* **1** *Photog.* a light-sensitive coating on a base, such as paper or film, consisting of silver bromide suspended in gelatine. **2** *Chem.* a colloid in which both phases are liquids. **3** a type of paint in which the pigment is suspended in a vehicle that is dispersed in water as an emulsion. **4** *Pharmacol.* a mixture in which an oily medicine is dispersed in another liquid. **5** any liquid resembling milk. [C17: from NL *ēmulsiō*, from L, from *ēmulgēre* to milk out, from *mulgēre* to milk]
▸**e'mulsive** *adj*
emu-wren *n* an Australian wren having long plumy tail feathers.
en (ɛn) *n Printing.* a unit of measurement, half the width of an em.
EN (in Britain) *abbrev. for:* **1** enrolled nurse. **2** English Nature.
en-[1] *or* **em-** *prefix forming verbs.* **1** (*from nouns*) **1a** put in or on: *entomb; enthrone.* **1b** go on or into: *enplane.* **1c** surround or cover with: *enmesh.* **1d** furnish with: *empower.* **2** (*from adjectives and nouns*) cause to be in a certain condition: *enable; enslave.* [via OF from L *in-* IN-[2]]
en-[2] *or* **em-** *prefix forming nouns and adjectives.* in; into; inside: *endemic.* [from Gk (often via L); cf. IN-[1], IN-[2]]
-en[1] *suffix forming verbs from adjectives and nouns.* cause to be; become; cause to have: *blacken; heighten.* [OE *-n-*, as in *fæst-n-ian* to fasten, of Gmc origin]
-en[2] *suffix forming adjectives from nouns.* of; made of; resembling: *ashen; wooden.* [OE *-en*]
enable Ⓣ (ɪn'eɪbᵊl) *vb* **enables, enabling, enabled.** (*tr*) **1** to provide (someone) with adequate power, means, opportunity, or authority (to do something). **2** to make possible.
▸**en'ablement** *n* ▸**en'abler** *n*
enabling act *n* a legislative act conferring certain specified powers on a person or organization.
enact Ⓣ (ɪn'ækt) *vb* (*tr*) **1** to make into an act or statute. **2** to establish by law; decree. **3** to represent or perform as in a play.
▸**en'actable** *adj* ▸**en'active** *or* **en'actory** *adj* ▸**en'actment** *or* **en'action** *n* ▸**en'actor** *n*
enamel (ɪ'næməl) *n* **1** a coloured glassy substance, translucent or opaque, fused to the surface of articles made of metal, glass, etc., for ornament or protection. **2** an article or articles ornamented with enamel. **3** an enamel-like paint or varnish. **4** any coating resembling enamel. **5** the hard white substance that covers the crown of each tooth. **6** (*modifier*) decorated or covered with enamel. ◆ *vb* **enamels, enamelling, enamelled** *or US* **enamels, enameling, enameled.** (*tr*) **7** to decorate with enamel. **8** to ornament with glossy variegated colours, as if with enamel. **9** to portray in enamel. [C15: from OF *esmail*, of Gmc origin]
▸**e'nameller, e'namellist** *or US* **e'nameler, e'namelist** *n* ▸**e'namelˌwork** *n*
enamour Ⓣ *or US* **enamor** (ɪn'æmə) *vb* (*tr; usually passive* and foll. by *of*) to inspire with love; captivate. [C14: from OF, from *amour* love, from L *amor*]
▸**en'amoured** *or US* **en'amored** *adj*
en bloc *French.* (ɑ̃ blɔk) *adv* in a lump or block; as a body or whole; all together.
en brosse *French.* (ɑ̃ brɔs) *adj, adv* (of the hair) cut very short so that the hair stands up stiffly. [lit.: in the style of a brush]
enc. *abbrev. for:* **1** enclosed. **2** enclosure.
encamp (ɪn'kæmp) *vb* to lodge or cause to lodge in a camp.
encampment Ⓣ (ɪn'kæmpmənt) *n* **1** the act of setting up a camp. **2** the place where a camp, esp. a military camp, is set up.
encapsulate Ⓣ *or* **incapsulate** (ɪn'kæpsjʊˌleɪt) *vb* **encapsulates, encapsulating, encapsulated** *or* **incapsulates, incapsulating, incapsulated. 1** to enclose or be enclosed as in a capsule. **2** (*tr*) to sum up in a short or concise form.
▸**enˌcapsu'lation** *or* **inˌcapsu'lation** *n*
encase *or* **incase** (ɪn'keɪs) *vb* **encases, encasing, encased.** (*tr*) to place or enclose as in a case.
▸**en'casement** *or* **in'casement** *n*
encash (ɪn'kæʃ) *vb* (*tr*) *Brit., formal.* to exchange (a cheque) for cash.
▸**en'cashable** *adj* ▸**en'cashment** *n*
encaustic (ɪn'kɒstɪk) *Ceramics, etc.* ◆ *adj* **1** decorated by any process involving burning in colours, esp. by inlaying coloured clays and baking or by fusing wax colours to the surface. ◆ *n* **2** the process of burning in colours. **3** a product of such a process. [C17: from L *encausticus*, from Gk, from *enkaiein* to burn in, from *kaiein* to burn]
▸**en'caustically** *adv*
-ence *or* **-ency** *suffix forming nouns.* indicating an action, state, condition, or quality: *benevolence; residence; patience.* [via OF from L *-entia*, from *-ēns*, present participial ending]
enceinte (ɒn'sænt) *adj* another word for **pregnant.** [C17: from F, from L *inciēns* pregnant]
encephalic (ˌɛnsɪ'fælɪk) *adj* of or relating to the brain.
encephalin (ɛn'sɛfəlɪn) *n* a variant of **enkephalin.**
encephalitis (ˌɛnsɛfə'laɪtɪs) *n* inflammation of the brain.
▸**encephalitic** (ˌɛnsɛfə'lɪtɪk) *adj*
encephalitis lethargica (lɪ'θɑːdʒɪkə) *n* a technical name for **sleeping sickness** (sense 2).
encephalo- *or before a vowel* **encephal-** *combining form.* indicating the brain: *encephalogram; encephalitis.* [from NL, from Gk *enkephalos*, from *en-* in + *kephalē* head]
encephalogram (ɛn'sɛfələˌgræm) *n* **1** an X-ray photograph of the brain, esp. one (a **pneumoencephalogram**) taken after replacing some of the cerebrospinal fluid with air or oxygen. **2** short for **electroencephalogram;** see **electroencephalograph.**
encephalon (ɛn'sɛfəˌlɒn) *n, pl* **encephala** (-lə). a technical name for **brain.** [C18: from NL, from Gk *enkephalos* brain, from EN-[2] + *kephalē* head]
▸**en'cephalous** *adj*
encephalopathy (ˌɛnsɛfə'lɒpəθɪ) *n* any degenerative disease of the brain, often associated with toxic conditions. See also **BSE.**
enchain Ⓣ (ɪn'tʃeɪn) *vb* (*tr*) **1** to bind with chains. **2** to hold fast or captivate (the attention, etc.).
▸**en'chainment** *n*
enchant Ⓣ (ɪn'tʃɑːnt) *vb* (*tr*) **1** to cast a spell on; bewitch. **2** to delight or

THESAURUS

sionless, unintelligent, vacant, vacuous **7** *Informal* = **hungry**, esurient, famished, ravenous, starving (*inf.*), unfed, unfilled ◆ *vb* **11-13** = **evacuate**, clear, consume, deplete, discharge, drain, dump, exhaust, gut, pour out, unburden, unload, use up, vacate, void
Antonyms *adj* ≠ **bare:** full, inhabited, occupied, packed, stuffed ≠ **purposeless:** busy, fulfilled, full, interesting, meaningful, occupied, purposeful, satisfying, serious, significant, useful, valuable, worthwhile ◆ *vb* ≠ **evacuate:** cram, fill, pack, replenish, stock, stuff
empty-headed *adj* = **scatterbrained**, brainless, ditzy *or* ditsy (*sl.*), dizzy (*inf.*), featherbrained, flighty, frivolous, giddy, goofy (*inf.*), harebrained, inane, silly, skittish, vacuous
emulate *vb* **1** = **imitate**, copy, echo, follow, follow in the footsteps of, follow suit, follow the example of, mimic, take after, take a leaf out of someone's book **2** = **compete with**, challenge, contend with, rival, vie with
emulation *n* **1** = **imitation**, copying, following, mimicry **2** = **rivalry**, challenge, competition, contention, contest, envy, jealousy, strife
enable *vb* **1** = **allow**, authorize, capacitate, commission, empower, entitle, facilitate, fit, license, permit, prepare, qualify, sanction, warrant
Antonyms *vb* bar, block, hinder, impede, obstruct, prevent, stop, thwart
enact *vb* **2** = **establish**, authorize, command, decree, legislate, ordain, order, pass, proclaim, ratify, sanction **3** = **perform**, act, act out, appear as, depict, personate, play, play the part of, portray, represent
enactment *n* **2** = **decree**, authorization, canon, command, commandment, dictate, edict, law, legislation, order, ordinance, proclamation, ratification, regulation, statute **3** = **portrayal**, acting, depiction, performance, personation, play-acting, playing, representation
enamoured *adj* = **in love**, bewitched, captivated, charmed, crazy about (*inf.*), enchanted, enraptured, entranced, fascinated, fond, infatuated, smitten, swept off one's feet, taken, wild about (*inf.*)
encampment *n* **2** = **camp**, base, bivouac, camping ground, campsite, cantonment, quarters, tents
encapsulate *vb* **2** = **sum up**, abridge, compress, condense, digest, epitomize, précis, summarize
enchain *vb* **1** = **shackle**, bind, enslave, fetter, hold, hold fast, manacle, pinion, put in irons
enchant *vb* **1, 2** = **fascinate**, beguile, bewitch,

captivate utterly. [C14: from OF, from L *incantāre*, from *cantāre* to chant]
▸**en'chanted** *adj* ▸**en'chanter** *n* ▸**en'chantress** *fem n*

enchanting ⓘ (ɪn'tʃɑːntɪŋ) *adj* pleasant; delightful.
▸**en'chantingly** *adv*

enchantment ⓘ (ɪn'tʃɑːntmənt) *n* **1** the act of enchanting or state of being enchanted. **2** a magic spell. **3** great charm or fascination.

enchase (ɪn'tʃeɪs) *vb* **enchases, enchasing, enchased.** (*tr*) a less common word for **chase**[3]. [C15: from OF *enchasser* to enclose, set, from EN-[1] + *casse* CASE[2]]
▸**en'chaser** *n*

enchilada (ˌentʃɪ'lɑːdə) *n* a Mexican dish of a tortilla filled with meat, served with a chilli sauce. [American Sp., from *enchilado*, from *enchilar* to spice with chilli]

-enchyma *n combining form.* denoting cellular tissue. [C20: abstracted from PARENCHYMA]

encipher (ɪn'saɪfə) *vb* (*tr*) to convert (a message, etc.) into code or cipher.
▸**en'cipherer** *n* ▸**en'cipherment** *n*

encircle ⓘ (ɪn'sɜːk[ə]l) *vb* **encircles, encircling, encircled.** (*tr*) to form a circle around; enclose within a circle; surround.
▸**en'circlement** *n*

enclave ('enkleɪv) *n* a part of a country entirely surrounded by foreign territory: viewed from the position of the surrounding territories. [C19: from F, from OF *enclaver* to enclose, from Vulgar L *inclāvāre* (unattested) to lock up, from L IN-[2] + *clavis* key]

enclitic (ɪn'klɪtɪk) *adj* **1** denoting or relating to a monosyllabic word or form that is treated as a suffix of the preceding word. ◆ *n* **2** an enclitic word or form. [C17: from LL, from Gk, from *enklinein* to cause to lean, from EN-[2] + *klinein* to lean]
▸**en'clitically** *adv*

enclose ⓘ *or* **inclose** (ɪn'kləʊz) *vb* **encloses, enclosing, enclosed** *or* **incloses, inclosing, inclosed.** (*tr*) **1** to close; hem in; surround. **2** to surround (land) with or as if with a fence. **3** to put in an envelope or wrapper, esp. together with a letter. **4** to contain or hold.
▸**en'closable** *or* **in'closable** *adj* ▸**en'closer** *or* **in'closer** *n*

enclosed order *n* a Christian religious order that does not permit its members to go into the outside world.

enclosure *or* **inclosure** (ɪn'kləʊʒə) *n* **1** the act of enclosing or state of being enclosed. **2** an area enclosed as by a fence. **3** the act of appropriating land by setting up a fence, hedge, etc., around it. **4** a fence, wall, etc., that encloses. **5** something enclosed within an envelope or wrapper, esp. together with a letter. **6** *Brit.* a section of a sports ground, racecourse, etc., allotted to certain spectators.

encode (ɪn'kəʊd) *vb* **encodes, encoding, encoded.** (*tr*) to convert (a message) into code.
▸**en'codement** *n* ▸**en'coder** *n*

encomiast (en'kəʊmɪˌæst) *n* a person who speaks or writes an encomium. [C17: from Gk, from *enkōmiazein* to utter an ENCOMIUM]
▸**enˌcomi'astic** *or* **enˌcomi'astical** *adj*

encomium (en'kəʊmɪəm) *n, pl* **encomiums** *or* **encomia** (-mɪə). a formal expression of praise; eulogy. [C16: from L, from Gk, from EN-[2] + *kōmos* festivity]

encompass ⓘ (ɪn'kʌmpəs) *vb* (*tr*) **1** to enclose within a circle; surround. **2** to bring about: *he encompassed the enemy's ruin.* **3** to include entirely or comprehensively.
▸**en'compassment** *n*

encore ('ɒŋkɔː) *sentence substitute.* **1** again: used by an audience to demand an extra or repeated performance. ◆ *n* **2** an extra or repeated performance given in response to enthusiastic demand. ◆ *vb* **encores, encoring, encored. 3** (*tr*) to demand an extra or repeated performance of (a work, piece of music, etc.) by (a performer). [C18: from F: still, again, ?from L *in hanc hōram* until this hour]

encounter ⓘ (ɪn'kaʊntə) *vb* **1** to come upon or meet casually or unexpectedly. **2** to meet (an enemy, army, etc.) in battle or contest. **3** (*tr*) to be faced with; contend with. ◆ *n* **4** a casual or unexpected meeting. **5** a hostile meeting; contest. [C13: from OF, from Vulgar L *incontrāre* (unattested), from L IN-[2] + *contrā* against, opposite]

encounter group *n* a group of people who meet in order to develop self-awareness and mutual understanding by openly expressing their feelings, by confrontation, etc.

encourage ⓘ (ɪn'kʌrɪdʒ) *vb* **encourages, encouraging, encouraged.** (*tr*) **1** to inspire (someone) with the courage or confidence (to do something). **2** to stimulate (something or someone) by approval or help.
▸**en'couragement** *n* ▸**en'courager** *n* ▸**en'couraging** *adj* ▸**en'couragingly** *adv*

encroach ⓘ (ɪn'krəʊtʃ) *vb* (*intr*) **1** (often foll. by *on* or *upon*) to intrude gradually or stealthily upon the rights, property, etc., of another. **2** to advance beyond certain limits. [C14: from OF *encrochier* to seize, lit.: fasten upon with hooks, of Gmc origin]
▸**en'croacher** *n* ▸**en'croachment** *n*

encrust *or* **incrust** (ɪn'krʌst) *vb* **1** (*tr*) to cover or overlay with or as with a crust or hard coating. **2** to form or cause to form a crust or hard coating. **3** (*tr*) to decorate lavishly, as with jewels.
▸ˌ**encrus'tation** *or* ˌ**incrus'tation** *n*

encumber ⓘ *or* **incumber** (ɪn'kʌmbə) *vb* (*tr*) **1** to hinder or impede; hamper. **2** to fill with superfluous or useless matter. **3** to burden with debts, obligations, etc. [C14: from OF, from EN-[1] + *combre* a barrier, from LL *combrus*]

encumbrance ⓘ *or* **incumbrance** (ɪn'kʌmbrəns) *n* **1** a thing that impedes or is burdensome; hindrance. **2** *Law.* a burden or charge upon property, such as a mortgage or lien.

ency., encyc., *or* **encycl.** *abbrev. for* encyclopedia.

-ency *suffix forming nouns.* a variant of **-ence:** *fluency; permanency.*

encyclical (en'sɪklɪk[ə]l) *n* **1** a letter sent by the pope to all Roman Catholic bishops. ◆ *adj also* **encyclic. 2** (of letters) intended for general circulation. [C17: from LL, from Gk, from *kuklos* circle]

encyclopedia ⓘ *or* **encyclopaedia** (enˌsaɪkləʊ'piːdɪə) *n* a book, often in many volumes, containing articles, often arranged in alphabetical order, dealing either with the whole range of human knowledge or with one particular subject. [C16: from NL, erroneously for Gk *enkuklios paideia* general education]
▸**enˌcyclo'pedic** *or* **enˌcyclo'paedic** *adj*

encyclopedist *or* **encyclopaedist** (enˌsaɪkləʊ'piːdɪst) *n* a person who compiles or contributes to an encyclopedia.
▸**enˌcyclo'pedism** *or* **enˌcyclo'paedism** *n*

encyst (en'sɪst) *vb Biol.* to enclose or become enclosed by a cyst, thick membrane, or shell.
▸**en'cystment** *or* ˌ**encys'tation** *n*

end ⓘ (end) *n* **1** the extremity of the length of something, such as a road, line, etc. **2** the surface at either extremity of an object. **3** the extreme extent, limit, or degree of something. **4** the most distant place or time that can be imagined: *the ends of the earth.* **5** the time at which

THESAURUS

captivate, cast a spell on, charm, delight, enamour, enrapture, enthral, hypnotize, mesmerize, ravish, spellbind

enchanter *n* **1 = sorcerer**, conjuror, magician, magus, necromancer, spellbinder, warlock, witch, wizard

enchanting *adj* **= fascinating**, alluring, appealing, attractive, bewitching, captivating, charming, delightful, endearing, entrancing, lovely, Orphean, pleasant, ravishing, winsome

enchantment *n* **1, 3 = fascination**, allure, allurement, beguilement, bliss, charm, delight, hypnotism, mesmerism, rapture, ravishment, transport **2 = spell**, charm, conjuration, incantation, magic, necromancy, sorcery, witchcraft, wizardry

enchantress *n* **1 = sorceress**, conjuror, lamia, magician, necromancer, spellbinder, witch **2 = seductress**, charmer, *femme fatale*, siren, vamp (*inf.*)

encircle *vb* **= surround**, begird (*poetic*), circle, circumscribe, compass, enclose, encompass, enfold, envelop, environ, enwreath, gird in, girdle, hem in, ring

enclose *vb* **1, 2 = surround**, bound, circumscribe, cover, encase, encircle, encompass, environ, fence, hedge, hem in, impound, pen, pound, shut in, wall in, wrap **3 = send with**, include, insert, put in **4 = include**, comprehend, contain, embrace, hold, incorporate

encompass *vb* **1 = surround**, circle, circumscribe, encircle, enclose, envelop, environ, enwreath, girdle, hem in, ring **3 = include**, admit, comprehend, comprise, contain, cover, embody, embrace, hold, incorporate, involve, subsume, take in

encounter *vb* **1 = meet**, bump into (*inf.*), chance upon, come upon, confront, experience, face, happen on *or* upon, run across, run into (*inf.*) **2 = battle with**, attack, clash with, combat, come into conflict with, contend, cross swords with, do battle with, engage, face off (*sl.*), fight, grapple with, join battle with, strive, struggle ◆ *n* **4 = meeting**, brush, confrontation, rendezvous **5 = battle**, action, clash, collision, combat, conflict, contest, dispute, engagement, face-off (*sl.*), fight, head-to-head, run-in (*inf.*), set to (*inf.*), skirmish

encourage *vb* **1 = inspire**, animate, buoy up, cheer, comfort, console, embolden, gee up, hearten, incite, inspirit, rally, reassure, rouse, stimulate **2 = spur**, abet, advance, advocate, aid, boost, commend, egg on, favour, forward, foster, further, help, promote, prompt, strengthen, succour, support, urge

Antonyms *vb* **≠ inspire:** daunt, depress, deter, discourage, dishearten, dispirit, dissuade, hinder, inhibit, intimidate, prevent, retard, scare, throw cold water on (*inf.*)

encouragement *n* **1, 2 = inspiration**, advocacy, aid, boost, cheer, clarion call, consolation, favour, gee-up, help, incitement, inspiritment, promotion, reassurance, security blanket (*inf.*), stimulation, stimulus, succour, support, urging

encouraging *adj* **1 = promising**, bright, cheerful, cheering, comforting, good, heartening, hopeful, reassuring, rosy, satisfactory, stimulating

Antonyms *adj* daunting, depressing, disappointing, discouraging, disheartening, dispiriting, off-putting (*inf.*), unfavourable, unpropitious

encroach *vb* **1 = intrude**, appropriate, arrogate, impinge, infringe, invade, make inroads, overstep, trench, trespass, usurp

encroachment *n* **1 = intrusion**, appropriation, arrogation, impingement, incursion, infringement, inroad, invasion, trespass, usurpation, violation

encumber *vb* **1 = burden**, clog, cramp, embarrass, hamper, handicap, hinder, impede, incommode, inconvenience, make difficult, obstruct, oppress, overload, retard, saddle, slow down, trammel, weigh down

encumbrance *n* **1 = burden**, albatross, clog, difficulty, drag, embarrassment, handicap, hindrance, impediment, inconvenience, liability, load, millstone, obstacle, obstruction

encyclopedic *adj* **= comprehensive**, all-embracing, all-encompassing, all-inclusive, complete, exhaustive, thorough, universal, vast, wide-ranging

end *n* **1-4 = extremity**, bound, boundary, edge, extent, extreme, limit, point, terminus, tip **5 = finish**, cessation, close, closure, ending, expiration, expiry, stop, termination, wind-up **6 = conclusion**, attainment, completion, consequence, consummation, culmination, denouement, ending, end result, finale, issue,

something is concluded. **6** the last section or part. **7** a share or part. **8** (*often pl*) a remnant or fragment (esp. in **odds and ends**). **9** a final state, esp. death; destruction. **10** the purpose of an action or existence. **11** *Sport.* either of the two defended areas of a playing field, rink, etc. **12** *Bowls, etc.* a section of play from one side of the rink to the other. **13 at an end.** exhausted or completed. **14 come to an end.** to become completed or exhausted. **15 have one's end away.** *sl.* to have sexual intercourse. **16 in the end.** finally. **17 keep one's end up. 17a** to sustain one's part in a joint undertaking. **17b** to hold one's own in an argument, contest, etc. **18 make (both) ends meet.** to spend no more than the money one has. **19 no end (of).** *Inf.* (intensifier): *I had no end of work.* **20 on end.** *Inf.* without pause or interruption. **21 the end.** *Sl.* the worst, esp. something that goes beyond the limits of endurance. ◆ *vb* **22** to bring or come to a finish; conclude. **23** to die or cause to die. **24** (*tr*) to surpass or outdo: *a novel to end all novels.* **25 end it all.** *Inf.* to commit suicide. ◆ See also **end up.** [OE *ende*]
▸**'ender** *n*

end- *combining form.* a variant of **endo-** before a vowel.

-end *suffix forming nouns.* See **-and.**

endamoeba *or US* **endameba** (ˌɛndəˈmiːbə) *n* variant spellings of **entamoeba.**

endanger ❶ (ɪnˈdeɪndʒə) *vb* (*tr*) to put in danger or peril; imperil.
▸**en'dangerment** *n*

endangered (ɪnˈdeɪndʒəd) *adj* in danger, esp. of extinction: *an endangered species.*

endear ❶ (ɪnˈdɪə) *vb* (*tr*) to cause to be beloved or esteemed.
▸**en'dearing** *adj*

endearment ❶ (ɪnˈdɪəmənt) *n* something that endears, such as an affectionate utterance.

endeavour ❶ *or US* **endeavor** (ɪnˈdɛvə) *vb* **1** to try (to do something). ◆ *n* **2** an effort to do or attain something. [C14 *endeveren,* from EN-[1] + *-deveren* from *dever* duty, from OF *deveir;* see DEVOIRS]
▸**en'deavourer** *or US* **en'deavorer** *n*

endemic (ɛnˈdɛmɪk) *adj also* **endemial** (ɛnˈdɛmɪəl) *or* **endemical. 1** present within a localized area or peculiar to persons in such an area. ◆ *n* **2** an endemic disease or plant. [C18: from NL *endēmicus,* from Gk *endēmos* native, from EN-[2] + *dēmos* the people]
▸**en'demically** *adv* ▸**'endemism** *or* **ˌende'micity** *n*

endermic (ɛnˈdɜːmɪk) *adj* (of a medicine, etc.) acting by absorption through the skin. [C19: from EN-[2] + Gk *derma* skin]

endgame (ˈɛndˌgeɪm) *n* the closing stage of any of certain games, esp. chess, when there are only a few pieces left in play.

ending ❶ (ˈɛndɪŋ) *n* **1** the act of bringing to or reaching an end. **2** the last part of something. **3** the final part of a word, esp. a suffix.

endive (ˈɛndaɪv) *n* a plant cultivated for its crisp curly leaves, which are used in salads. Cf. **chicory.** [C15: from OF, from Med. L, from var. of L *intubus, entubus*]

endless ❶ (ˈɛndlɪs) *adj* **1** having or seeming to have no end; eternal or infinite. **2** continuing too long or continually recurring. **3** formed with the ends joined.
▸**'endlessness** *n*

endmost (ˈɛndˌməʊst) *adj* nearest the end; most distant.

endo- *or before a vowel* **end-** *combining form.* inside; within: *endocrine.* [from Gk, from *endon* within]

endoblast (ˈɛndəʊˌblæst) *n* **1** *Embryol.* a less common name for **endoderm. 2** another name for **hypoblast.**
▸**ˌendo'blastic** *adj*

endocarditis (ˌɛndəʊkɑːˈdaɪtɪs) *n* inflammation of the lining of the heart. [C19: from NL, from ENDO- + Gk *kardia* heart + -ITIS]
▸**endocarditic** (ˌɛndəʊkɑːˈdɪtɪk) *adj*

endocarp (ˈɛndəˌkɑːp) *n* the inner layer of the pericarp of a fruit, such as the stone of a peach.
▸**ˌendo'carpal** *or* **ˌendo'carpic** *adj*

endocrine (ˈɛndəʊˌkraɪn) *adj also* **ˌendo'crinal, endocrinic** (ˌɛndəʊˈkrɪnɪk). **1** of or denoting endocrine glands or their secretions. ◆ *n* **2** an endocrine gland. [C20: from ENDO- + *-crine,* from Gk *krinein* to separate]

endocrine gland *n* any of the glands that secrete hormones directly into the bloodstream, e.g. the pituitary, pineal, and thyroid.

endocrinology (ˌɛndəʊkraɪˈnɒlədʒɪ, -krɪ-) *n* the branch of medical science concerned with the endocrine glands and their secretions.
▸**ˌendocri'nologist** *n*

endoderm (ˈɛndəʊˌdɜːm) *or* **entoderm** *n* the inner germ layer of an animal embryo, which gives rise to the lining of the digestive and respiratory tracts.
▸**ˌendo'dermal, ˌendo'dermic** *or* **ˌento'dermal, ˌento'dermic** *adj*

end of steel *n Canad.* **1** a point up to which railway tracks have been laid. **2** a town located at such a point.

endogamy (ɛnˈdɒgəmɪ) *n* **1** *Anthropol.* marriage within one's own tribe or similar unit. **2** pollination between two flowers on the same plant.
▸**en'dogamous** *or* **endogamic** (ˌɛndəʊˈgæmɪk) *adj*

endogenous (ɛnˈdɒdʒɪnəs) *adj* **1** *Biol.* developing or originating within an organism or part of an organism. **2** having no apparent external cause: *endogenous depression.*
▸**en'dogeny** *n*

endometritis (ˌɛndəʊmɪˈtraɪtɪs) *n* inflammation of the endometrium, which is caused by infection, as by bacteria, foreign bodies, etc.

endometrium (ˌɛndəʊˈmiːtrɪəm) *n, pl* **endometria** (-trɪə). the mucous membrane that lines the uterus. [C19: NL, from ENDO- + Greek *mētra* uterus]
▸**ˌendo'metrial** *adj*

endomorph (ˈɛndəʊˌmɔːf) *n* **1** a type of person having a body build characterized by fatness and heaviness. **2** a mineral that naturally occurs enclosed within another mineral.
▸**ˌendo'morphic** *adj* ▸**'endoˌmorphy** *n*

endomorphism (ˌɛndəʊˈmɔːˌfɪzəm) *n Geol.* metamorphism in which changes are induced in cooling molten rock by contact with older rocks.

endophyte (ˈɛndəʊˌfaɪt) *n* any plant, parasitic fungus, or alga that lives within a plant.
▸**endophytic** (ˌɛndəʊˈfɪtɪk) *adj*

endoplasm (ˈɛndəʊˌplæzəm) *n Cytology.* the inner cytoplasm of a cell.
▸**ˌendo'plasmic** *adj*

end organ *n Anat.* the expanded end of a peripheral motor or sensory nerve.

endorphin (ɛnˈdɔːfɪn) *n* any of a class of chemicals occurring in the brain, including enkephalin, which have a similar effect to morphine.

endorsation (ˌɛndɔːˈseɪʃən) *n Canad.* approval or support.

endorse ❶ *or* **indorse** (ɪnˈdɔːs) *vb* **endorses, endorsing, endorsed** *or* **indorses, indorsing, indorsed.** (*tr*) **1** to give approval or sanction to. **2** to sign (one's name) on the back of (a cheque, etc.) to specify oneself as payee. **3** *Commerce.* **3a** to sign the back of (a document) to transfer ownership of the rights to a specified payee. **3b** to specify (a sum) as transferable to another as payee. **4** to write (a qualifying comment, etc.) on the back of a document. **5** to sign a document, as when confirming receipt of payment. **6** *Chiefly Brit.* to record a conviction on (a driving licence). [C16: from OF *endosser* to put on the back, from EN-[1] + *dos* back]
▸**en'dorsable** *or* **in'dorsable** *adj* ▸**en'dorser, en'dorsor** *or* **in'dorser, in'dorsor** *n* ▸**enˌdor'see** *or* **inˌdor'see** *n*

endorsement ❶ *or* **indorsement** (ɪnˈdɔːsmənt) *n* **1** the act or an instance of endorsing. **2** something that endorses, such as a signature. **3** approval or support. **4** a record of a motoring offence on a driving licence.

endoscope (ˈɛndəʊˌskəʊp) *n* a medical instrument for examining the interior of hollow organs such as the stomach or bowel.
▸**endoscopic** (ˌɛndəʊˈskɒpɪk) *adj*

THESAURUS

outcome, resolution, result, sequel, upshot **8** = **remnant**, bit, butt, fragment, leftover, oddment, remainder, scrap, stub, tag end, tail end **9** = **destruction**, annihilation, death, demise, dissolution, doom, extermination, extinction, ruin, ruination **10** = **purpose**, aim, aspiration, design, drift, goal, intent, intention, object, objective, point, reason **21 the end** *Slang* = **the worst**, beyond endurance, insufferable, intolerable, the final blow, the last straw, the limit (*inf.*), too much (*inf.*), unbearable, unendurable ◆ *vb* **22** = **finish**, axe (*inf.*), belay (*Nautical*), bring to an end, cease, close, complete, conclude, culminate, dissolve, expire, nip in the bud, pull the plug on, put paid to, resolve, stop, terminate, wind up **23** = **destroy**, abolish, annihilate, exterminate, extinguish, kill, put to death, ruin

Antonyms *n* ≠ **finish:** beginning, birth, commencement, inception, launch, opening, origin, outset, prelude, source, start ◆ *vb* ≠ **finish:** begin, come into being, commence, initiate, launch, originate, start

endanger *vb* = **put at risk**, compromise, hazard, imperil, jeopardize, put in danger, risk, threaten

Antonyms *vb* defend, guard, preserve, protect, safeguard, save, secure

endear *vb* = **attract**, attach, bind, captivate, charm, engage, win

endearing *adj* = **attractive**, adorable, captivating, charming, cute, engaging, lovable, sweet, winning, winsome

endearment *n* = **loving word**, affectionate utterance, sweet nothing

endeavour *vb* **1** = **try**, aim, aspire, attempt, bend over backwards (*inf.*), do one's best, essay, give it one's best shot (*inf.*), have a go, knock oneself out (*inf.*), labour, make an effort, strive, struggle, take pains, undertake ◆ *n* **2** = **effort**, aim, attempt, crack (*inf.*), enterprise, essay, go (*inf.*), shot (*inf.*), stab (*inf.*), trial, try, undertaking, venture

ending *n* **1, 2** = **finish**, cessation, close, completion, conclusion, consummation, culmination, denouement, end, finale, resolution, termination, wind-up

Antonyms *n* birth, commencement, inauguration, inception, onset, opening, origin, preface, source, start, starting point

endless *adj* **1** = **eternal**, boundless, ceaseless, constant, continual, everlasting, immortal, incessant, infinite, interminable, limitless, measureless, perpetual, unbounded, unbroken, undying, unending, uninterrupted, unlimited **2** = **interminable**, monotonous, overlong **3** = **continuous**, unbroken, undivided, whole

Antonyms *adj* ≠ **eternal:** bounded, brief, circumscribed, finite, limited, passing, restricted, temporary, terminable, transient, transitory

endorse *vb* **1** = **approve**, advocate, affirm, authorize, back, champion, confirm, espouse, favour, prescribe, promote, ratify, recommend, sanction, subscribe to, support, sustain, vouch for, warrant **2-5** = **sign**, countersign, superscribe, undersign

endorsement *n* **1, 3** = **approval**, advocacy, affirmation, approbation, authorization, backing, championship, confirmation, espousal, favour, fiat, O.K. *or* okay (*inf.*), promotion, ratification, recommendation, sanction, seal of approval, subscription to, support, warrant **2** = **signature**,

endoskeleton (ˌɛndəʊˈskɛlɪtən) *n* an internal skeleton, esp. the bony or cartilaginous skeleton of vertebrates.
▸ **ˌendoˈskeletal** *adj*

endosperm (ˈɛndəʊˌspɜːm) *n* the tissue within the seed of a flowering plant that surrounds and nourishes the embryo.
▸ **ˌendoˈspermic** *adj*

endothermic (ˌɛndəʊˈθɜːmɪk) *or* **endothermal** *adj* (of a chemical reaction or compound) occurring or formed with the absorption of heat.
▸ **ˌendoˈthermically** *adv* ▸ **ˌendoˈthermism** *n*

endow Ⓣ (ɪnˈdaʊ) *vb (tr)* **1** to provide with or bequeath a source of permanent income. **2** (usually foll. by *with*) to provide (with qualities, characteristics, etc.). [C14: from OF, from EN-[1] + *douer*, from L *dōtāre*, from *dōs* dowry]

endowment Ⓣ (ɪnˈdaʊmənt) *n* **1** the income with which an institution, etc., is endowed. **2** the act or process of endowing. **3** (*usually pl*) natural talents or qualities.

endowment assurance *or* **insurance** *n* a form of life insurance that provides for the payment of a specified sum directly to the policyholder at a designated date or to his beneficiary should he die before this date.

endpaper (ˈɛndˌpeɪpə) *n* either of two leaves at the front and back of a book pasted to the inside of the board covers and the first leaf of the book.

end point *n* **1** *Chem.* the point at which a titration is complete. **2** the point at which anything is complete.

end product *n* the final result of a process, series, etc., esp. in manufacturing.

endue Ⓣ *or* **indue** (ɪnˈdjuː) *vb* **endues, enduing, endued** *or* **indues, induing, indued.** (*tr*) (usually foll. by *with*) to invest or provide, as with some quality or trait. [C15: from OF, from L *indūcere*, from *dūcere* to lead]

end up Ⓣ *vb (adv)* **1** (*copula*) to become eventually; turn out to be. **2** (*intr*) to arrive, esp. by a circuitous or lengthy route or process.

endurance Ⓣ (ɪnˈdjʊərəns) *n* **1** the capacity, state, or an instance of enduring. **2** something endured; a hardship, strain, or privation.

endure Ⓣ (ɪnˈdjʊə) *vb* **endures, enduring, endured. 1** to undergo (hardship, strain, etc.) without yielding; bear. **2** (*tr*) to permit or tolerate. **3** (*intr*) to last or continue to exist. [C14: from OF, from L *indūrāre* to harden, from *dūrus* hard]
▸ **enˈdurable** *adj*

enduring Ⓣ (ɪnˈdjʊərɪŋ) *adj* **1** permanent; lasting. **2** having forbearance; long-suffering.
▸ **enˈduringly** *adv* ▸ **enˈduringness** *n*

end user *n* **1** (in international trading) the person, organization, or nation that will be the ultimate user of goods such as arms. **2** *Computing.* the ultimate destination of information that is being transferred within a system.

endways (ˈɛndˌweɪz) *or esp. US & Canad.* **endwise** (ˈɛndˌwaɪz) *adv* **1** having the end forwards or upwards. ◆ *adj* **2** vertical or upright. **3** lengthways. **4** standing or lying end to end.

end zone *n American football.* the area behind the goals at each end of the field that the ball must cross for a touchdown to be awarded.

ENE *symbol for* east-northeast.

-ene *n combining form.* (in chemistry) indicating an unsaturated compound containing double bonds: *benzene; ethylene.* [from Gk *-ēnē*, fem. patronymic suffix]

enema (ˈɛnɪmə) *n, pl* **enemas** *or* **enemata** (-mətə). *Med.* **1** the introduction of liquid into the rectum to evacuate the bowels, medicate, or nourish. **2** the liquid so introduced. [C15: from NL, from Gk: injection, from *enienai* to send in]

enemy Ⓣ (ˈɛnəmɪ) *n, pl* **enemies. 1** a person hostile or opposed to a policy, cause, person, or group. **2a** an armed adversary; opposing military force. **2b** (*as modifier*): *enemy aircraft.* **3a** a hostile nation or people. **3b** (*as modifier*): *an enemy alien.* **4** something that harms or opposes.
◆ Related adj: **inimical.** [C13: from OF, from L *inimīcus* hostile, from IN-[1] + *amīcus* friend]

energetic Ⓣ (ˌɛnəˈdʒɛtɪk) *adj* having or showing energy; vigorous.
▸ **ˌenerˈgetically** *adv*

energize Ⓣ *or* **energise** (ˈɛnəˌdʒaɪz) *vb* **energizes, energizing, energized** *or* **energises, energising, energised. 1** to have or cause to have energy; invigorate. **2** (*tr*) to apply electric current or electromotive force to (a circuit, etc.).
▸ **ˈenerˌgizer** *or* **ˈenerˌgiser** *n*

energy Ⓣ (ˈɛnədʒɪ) *n, pl* **energies. 1** intensity or vitality of action or expression; forcefulness. **2** capacity or tendency for intense activity; vigour. **3** *Physics.* **3a** the capacity of a body or system to do work. **3b** a measure of this capacity, measured in joules (SI units). [C16: from LL, from Gk *energeia* activity, from EN-[2] + *ergon* work]

energy band *n Physics.* a range of energies associated with the quantum states of electrons in a crystalline solid.

energy conversion *n* the process of changing one form of energy into another, such as nuclear energy into heat or solar energy into electrical energy.

enervate Ⓣ *vb* (ˈɛnəˌveɪt), **enervates, enervating, enervated. 1** (*tr*) to deprive of strength or vitality. ◆ *adj* (ɪˈnɜːvɪt). **2** deprived of strength or vitality. [C17: from L *ēnervāre* to remove the nerves from, from *nervus* nerve]
▸ **ˈenerˌvating** *adj* ▸ **ˌenerˈvation** *n*

en famille *French.* (ɑ̃ famij) *adv* **1** with one's family; at home. **2** in a casual way; informally.

enfant terrible *French.* (ɑ̃fɑ̃ tɛriblə) *n, pl* ***enfants terribles*** (ɑ̃fɑ̃ tɛriblə). a person given to unconventional conduct or indiscreet remarks. [C19: lit.: terrible child]

enfeeble Ⓣ (ɪnˈfiːbəl) *vb* **enfeebles, enfeebling, enfeebled.** (*tr*) to make weak.
▸ **enˈfeeblement** *n* ▸ **enˈfeebler** *n*

en fête *French.* (ɑ̃ fɛt) *adv* dressed for or engaged in a festivity. [C19: lit.: in festival]

enfilade (ˌɛnfɪˈleɪd) *Mil.* ◆ *n* **1** gunfire directed along the length of a position or formation. **2** a position or formation subject to such fire. ◆ *vb* **enfilades, enfilading, enfiladed.** (*tr*) **3** to attack (a position or formation) with enfilade. [C18: from F: suite, from *enfiler* to thread on string, from *fil* thread]

enfold Ⓣ *or* **infold** (ɪnˈfəʊld) *vb (tr)* **1** to cover by enclosing. **2** to embrace.
▸ **enˈfolder** *or* **inˈfolder** *n* ▸ **enˈfoldment** *or* **inˈfoldment** *n*

enforce Ⓣ (ɪnˈfɔːs) *vb* **enforces, enforcing, enforced.** (*tr*) **1** to ensure obedience to (a law, decision, etc.). **2** to impose (obedience, etc.) as by force. **3** to emphasize or reinforce (an argument, etc.).
▸ **enˈforceable** *adj* ▸ **enˌforceaˈbility** *n* ▸ **enforcedly** (ɪnˈfɔːsɪdlɪ) *adv* ▸ **enˈforcement** *n* ▸ **enˈforcer** *n*

THESAURUS

comment, countersignature, qualification, superscription

endow *vb* **1, 2** = **provide**, award, bequeath, bestow, confer, donate, endue, enrich, favour, finance, fund, furnish, give, grant, invest, leave, make over, purvey, settle on, supply, will

endowment *n* **1** = **income**, award, bequest, boon, donation, fund, gift, grant, hand-out, largesse *or* largess, legacy, property, revenue, stipend **2** = **provision**, award, benefaction, bestowal, donation, gift, presentation **3** *usually plural* = **talent**, ability, aptitude, attribute, capability, capacity, faculty, flair, genius, gift, power, qualification, quality

endue *vb* = **provide**, endow, fill, furnish, invest, supply

end up *vb* **1** = **turn out to be**, become eventually, finish as, finish up, pan out (*inf.*) **2** = **arrive**, come to a halt, fetch up (*inf.*), finish up, stop, wind up

endurable *adj* **1** = **bearable**, acceptable, sufferable, supportable, sustainable, tolerable
Antonyms *adj* insufferable, insupportable, intolerable, too much (*inf.*), unbearable, unendurable

endurance *n* **1** = **staying power**, bearing, fortitude, patience, perseverance, persistence, pertinacity, resignation, resolution, stamina, strength, submission, sufferance, tenacity, toleration

endure *vb* **1** = **bear**, brave, cope with, experience, go through, stand, stick it out (*inf.*), suffer, support, sustain, take it (*inf.*), thole (*Scot.*), undergo, weather, withstand **2** = **put up with**, abide, allow, bear, brook, countenance, hack (*sl.*), permit, stand, stick (*sl.*), stomach, submit to, suffer, swallow, take patiently, tolerate **3** = **last**, abide, be durable, continue, have a good innings, hold, live, live on, persist, prevail, remain, stand, stay, survive, wear well

enduring *adj* **1** = **long-lasting**, abiding, continuing, durable, eternal, firm, immortal, immovable, imperishable, lasting, living, perennial, permanent, persistent, persisting, prevailing, remaining, steadfast, steady, surviving, unfaltering, unwavering
Antonyms *adj* brief, ephemeral, fleeting, momentary, passing, short, short-lived, temporary, transient, transitory

enemy *n* **1-4** = **foe**, adversary, antagonist, competitor, opponent, rival, the opposition, the other side
Antonyms *n* ally, confederate, friend, supporter

energetic *adj* = **vigorous**, active, alive and kicking, animated, brisk, dynamic, forceful, forcible, full of beans (*inf.*), high-powered, indefatigable, lively, potent, powerful, spirited, storming (*inf.*), strenuous, strong, tireless
Antonyms *adj* debilitated, dull, enervated, inactive, lazy, lethargic, lifeless, listless, slow, sluggish, torpid, weak

energize *vb* **1** = **stimulate**, activate, animate, enliven, inspirit, invigorate, liven up, motivate, pep up, quicken, vitalize **2** = **stimulate**, activate, electrify, kick-start, start up, switch on, turn on

energy *n* **1, 2** = **vigour**, activity, animation, ardour, brio, drive, efficiency, élan, elbow grease (*facetious*), exertion, fire, force, forcefulness, get-up-and-go (*inf.*), go (*inf.*), intensity, life, liveliness, pep, pluck, power, spirit, stamina, strength, strenuousness, verve, vim (*sl.*), vitality, vivacity, zeal, zest, zip (*inf.*)

enervate *vb* **1** = **weaken**, debilitate, devitalize, enfeeble, exhaust, fatigue, incapacitate, paralyse, prostrate, sap, tire, unnerve, wash out, wear out

enervation *n* **1** = **weakness**, debilitation, debility, enfeeblement, exhaustedness, exhaustion, fatigue, feebleness, impotence, incapacity, infirmity, lassitude, paralysis, powerlessness, prostration, tiredness, weakening

enfeeble *vb* = **weaken**, debilitate, deplete, devitalize, diminish, exhaust, fatigue, render feeble, sap, undermine, unhinge, unnerve, wear out

enfold *vb* **1, 2** = **wrap**, clasp, embrace, enclose, encompass, envelop, enwrap, fold, hold, hug, shroud, swathe, wrap up

enforce *vb* **1, 2** = **impose**, administer, apply, carry out, coerce, compel, constrain, exact, execute, implement, insist on, oblige, prosecute, put in force, put into effect, reinforce, require, urge

enforced *adj* **1, 2** = **imposed**, compelled, compulsory, constrained, dictated, involuntary, necessary, ordained, prescribed, required, unavoidable, unwilling

enforcement *n* **1, 2** = **imposition**, administration, application, carrying out, exaction, execution, implementation, prosecution, reinforcement

enfranchise Ⓣ (ɪn'fræntʃaɪz) *vb* **enfranchises, enfranchising, enfranchised.** (*tr*) **1** to grant the power of voting to. **2** to liberate, as from servitude. **3** (in England) to invest (a town, city, etc.) with the right to be represented in Parliament.
▸**en'franchisement** *n* ▸**en'franchiser** *n*

ENG *abbrev. for* electronic news gathering: TV news obtained at the point of action by means of modern video equipment.

Eng. *abbrev. for:* **1** England. **2** English.

engage Ⓣ (ɪn'geɪdʒ) *vb* **engages, engaging, engaged.** (*mainly tr*) **1** to secure the services of. **2** to secure for use; reserve. **3** to involve (a person or his attention) intensely. **4** to attract (the affection) of (a person). **5** to draw (somebody) into conversation. **6** (*intr*) to take part; participate. **7** to promise (to do something). **8** (*also intr*) *Mil.* to begin an action with (an enemy). **9** to bring (a mechanism) into operation. **10** (*also intr*) to undergo or cause to undergo interlocking, as of the components of a driving mechanism. **11** *Machinery.* to locate (a locking device) in its operative position or to advance (a tool) into a workpiece to commence cutting. [C15: from OF, from EN-[1] + *gage* a pledge; see GAGE[1]]
▸**en'gager** *n*

engagé *or* (*fem*) ***engagée*** *French.* (ɑ̃gaʒe) *adj* (of an artist) committed to some ideology.

engaged Ⓣ (ɪn'geɪdʒd) *adj* **1** pledged to be married; betrothed. **2** occupied or busy. **3** *Archit.* built against or attached to a wall or similar structure. **4** (of a telephone line) in use.

engaged tone *n Brit.* a repeated single note heard on a telephone when the number called is already in use.

engagement Ⓣ (ɪn'geɪdʒmənt) *n* **1** a pledge of marriage; betrothal. **2** an appointment or arrangement, esp. for business or social purposes. **3** the act of engaging or condition of being engaged. **4** a promise, obligation, or other condition that binds. **5** a period of employment, esp. a limited period. **6** an action; battle.

engagement ring *n* a ring given by a man to a woman as a token of their betrothal.

engaging Ⓣ (ɪn'geɪdʒɪŋ) *adj* pleasing, charming, or winning.
▸**en'gagingness** *n*

en garde *French.* (ɑ̃ gard) *sentence substitute.* **1** on guard; a call to a fencer to adopt a defensive stance in readiness for an attack or bout. ◆ *adj* **2** (of a fencer) in such a stance.

engender Ⓣ (ɪn'dʒendə) *vb* (*tr*) to bring about or give rise to; cause to be born. [C14: from OF, from L *ingenerāre,* from *generāre* to beget]

engin. *abbrev. for* engineering.

engine Ⓣ ('ɛndʒɪn) *n* **1** any machine designed to convert energy into mechanical work. **2** a railway locomotive. **3** *Mil.* any piece of equipment formerly used in warfare, such as a battering ram. **4** *Obs.* any instrument or device. [C13: from OF, from L *ingenium* nature, talent, ingenious contrivance, from IN-[2] + *-genium,* rel. to *gignere* to beget, produce]

engine driver *n Chiefly Brit.* a man who drives a railway locomotive; train driver.

engineer Ⓣ (ˌɛndʒɪ'nɪə) *n* **1** a person trained in any branch of engineering. **2** the originator or manager of a situation, system, etc. **3** *US & Canad.* the driver of a railway locomotive. **4** an officer responsible for a ship's engines. **5** a member of the armed forces trained in engineering and construction work. ◆ *vb* (*tr*) **6** to originate, cause, or plan in a clever or devious manner. **7** to design, plan, or construct as a professional engineer. [C14 *enginer,* from OF, from *engignier* to contrive, ult. from L *ingenium* skill, talent; see ENGINE]

engineering (ˌɛndʒɪ'nɪərɪŋ) *n* the profession of applying scientific principles to the design, construction, and maintenance of engines, cars, machines, etc. (**mechanical engineering**), buildings, bridges, roads, etc. (**civil engineering**), electrical machines and communication systems (**electrical engineering**), chemical plant and machinery (**chemical engineering**), or aircraft (**aeronautical engineering**).

English ('ɪŋglɪʃ) *n* **1** the official language of Britain, the US, most of the Commonwealth, and certain other countries. **2 the English.** (*functioning as pl*) the natives or inhabitants of England collectively. **3** (*often not cap.*) the usual US & Canad. term for **side** (in billiards). ◆ *adj* **4** of or relating to the English language. **5** relating to or characteristic of England or the English. ◆ *vb* (*tr*) **6** *Arch.* to translate or adapt into English.
▸**'Englishness** *n*

English horn *n Music.* another name for **cor anglais.**

Englishman ('ɪŋglɪʃmən) *or* (*fem*) **Englishwoman** *n, pl* **Englishmen** *or* **Englishwomen.** a native or inhabitant of England.

engorge Ⓣ (ɪn'gɔːdʒ) *vb* **engorges, engorging, engorged.** (*tr*) **1** *Pathol.* to congest with blood. **2** to eat (food) greedily. **3** to gorge (oneself); glut.
▸**en'gorgement** *n*

engr *abbrev. for:* **1** engineer. **2** engraver.

engraft Ⓣ *or* **ingraft** (ɪn'grɑːft) *vb* (*tr*) **1** to graft (a shoot, bud, etc.) onto a stock. **2** to incorporate in a firm or permanent way; implant.
▸ˌ**engraf'tation,** ˌ**ingraf'tation** *or* **en'graftment, in'graftment** *n*

engrain Ⓣ (ɪn'greɪn) *vb* a variant spelling of **ingrain.**

engrave Ⓣ (ɪn'greɪv) *vb* **engraves, engraving, engraved.** (*tr*) **1** to inscribe (a design, writing, etc.) onto (a block, plate, or other printing surface) by carving, etching, or other process. **2** to print (designs or characters) from a plate so made. **3** to fix deeply or permanently in the mind. [C16: from EN-[1] + GRAVE[3], on the model of F *engraver*]
▸**en'graver** *n*

engraving Ⓣ (ɪn'greɪvɪŋ) *n* **1** the art of a person who engraves. **2** a printing surface that has been engraved. **3** a print made from this.

engross Ⓣ (ɪn'grəʊs) *vb* (*tr*) **1** to occupy one's attention completely; absorb. **2** to write or copy (manuscript) in large legible handwriting. **3** *Law.* to write or type out formally (a document) preparatory to execution. [C14 (in the sense: to buy up wholesale); C15 (in the sense: to write in large letters): from L *grossus* thick, GROSS]
▸**en'grossed** *adj* ▸**en'grossing** *adj* ▸**en'grossment** *n*

engulf Ⓣ *or* **ingulf** (ɪn'gʌlf) *vb* (*tr*) **1** to immerse, plunge, bury, or swallow up. **2** (*often passive*) to overwhelm.
▸**en'gulfment** *n*

enhance Ⓣ (ɪn'hɑːns) *vb* **enhances, enhancing, enhanced.** (*tr*) to intensify or increase in quality, value, power, etc.; improve; augment. [C14: from OF, from EN-[1] + *haucier* to raise, from Vulgar L *altiāre* (unattested), from L *altus* high]
▸**en'hancement** *n* ▸**en'hancer** *n*

enharmonic (ˌɛnhɑː'mɒnɪk) *adj Music.* **1** denoting or relating to a small difference in pitch between two notes, such as A flat and G sharp: not present in instruments of equal temperament, but significant in the

THESAURUS

enfranchise *vb* **1 = give the vote to,** grant suffrage to, grant the franchise to, grant voting rights to **2 = free,** emancipate, liberate, manumit, release, set free

enfranchisement *n* **1 = giving the vote,** granting suffrage *or* the franchise, granting voting rights **2 = freeing,** emancipation, freedom, liberating, liberation, manumission, release, setting free

engage *vb* **1 = employ,** appoint, commission, enlist, enrol, hire, retain, take on **2 = book,** bespeak, charter, hire, lease, prearrange, rent, reserve, secure **3 = occupy,** absorb, busy, engross, grip, involve, preoccupy, tie up **4 = captivate,** allure, arrest, attach, attract, catch, charm, draw, enamour, enchant, fascinate, fix, gain, win **6 = participate,** embark on, enter into, join, partake, practise, set about, take part, undertake **7 = promise,** agree, bind, commit, contract, covenant, guarantee, obligate, oblige, pledge, undertake, vouch, vow **8** *Military* **= begin battle with,** assail, attack, combat, come to close quarters with, encounter, face off (*sl.*), fall on, fight with, give battle to, join battle with, meet, take on **9 = set going,** activate, apply, bring into operation, energize, switch on **10 = interlock,** dovetail, interact, interconnect, join, mesh
Antonyms *vb* ≠ **employ:** axe (*inf.*), discharge, dismiss, fire (*inf.*), give notice to, lay off, oust, remove, sack (*inf.*)

engaged *adj* **1 = betrothed** (*arch.*), affianced, pledged, promised, spoken for **2 = occupied,** absorbed, busy, committed, employed, engrossed, in use, involved, preoccupied, tied up, unavailable
Antonyms *adj* ≠ **betrothed:** available, fancy-free, free, unattached, uncommitted, unengaged ≠ **occupied:** available, free, uncommitted, unengaged

engagement *n* **1 = betrothal,** troth (*arch.*) **2 = appointment,** arrangement, commitment, date, meeting **4 = promise,** assurance, bond, compact, contract, oath, obligation, pact, pledge, undertaking, vow, word **5 = job,** commission, employment, gig (*inf.*), post, situation, stint, work **6 = battle,** action, combat, conflict, confrontation, contest, encounter, face-off (*sl.*), fight

engaging *adj* **= charming,** agreeable, appealing, attractive, captivating, cute, enchanting, fascinating, fetching (*inf.*), likable *or* likeable, lovable, pleasant, pleasing, winning, winsome
Antonyms *adj* disagreeable, objectionable, obnoxious, offensive, repulsive, unattractive, unlikable *or* unlikeable, unlovely, unpleasant

engender *vb* **= produce,** beget, breed, bring about, cause, create, excite, foment, generate, give rise to, hatch, incite, induce, instigate, lead to, make, occasion, precipitate, provoke

engine *n* **1 = machine,** mechanism, motor **4** *Obsolete* **= device,** agency, agent, apparatus, appliance, contrivance, implement, instrument, means, tool, weapon

engineer *vb* **6 = bring about,** cause, concoct, contrive, control, create, devise, effect, encompass, finagle (*inf.*), manage, manoeuvre, mastermind, originate, plan, plot, scheme, wangle (*inf.*)

engorge *vb* **2, 3 = gorge,** bolt, cram, devour, eat, fill, glut, gobble, gulp, guzzle, pig out (*sl.*), satiate, stuff, wolf

engraft *vb* **1, 2 = incorporate,** graft, implant, inculcate, infix, infuse, ingrain, instil

engrain *see* **ingrain**

engrave *vb* **1 = carve,** chase, chisel, cut, enchase (*rare*), etch, grave (*arch.*), inscribe **2 = imprint,** impress, print **3 = fix,** embed, impress, imprint, infix, ingrain, lodge

engraving *n* **1 = cutting,** carving, chasing, chiselling, dry point, enchasing (*rare*), etching, inscribing, inscription **2 = carving,** block, etching, inscription, plate, woodcut **3 = print,** etching, impression

engross *vb* **1 = absorb,** arrest, engage, engulf, hold, immerse, involve, occupy, preoccupy

engrossed *adj* **1 = absorbed,** captivated, caught up, deep, enthralled, fascinated, gripped, immersed, intent, intrigued, lost, preoccupied, rapt, riveted

engrossing *adj* **1 = absorbing,** captivating, compelling, enthralling, fascinating, gripping, interesting, intriguing, riveting

engulf *vb* **1, 2 = immerse,** absorb, bury, consume, deluge, drown, encompass, engross, envelop, flood (out), inundate, overrun, overwhelm, plunge, submerge, swallow up, swamp

enhance *vb* **= improve,** add to, augment, boost, complement, elevate, embellish, exalt, heighten, increase, intensify, lift, magnify, raise, reinforce, strengthen, swell
Antonyms *vb* debase, decrease, depreciate, devalue, diminish, lower, minimize, reduce, spoil

enhancement *n* **= improvement,** addition, augmentation, boost, embellishment, enrichment, heightening, increase, increment, rise

intonation of stringed instruments. **2** denoting or relating to enharmonic modulation. [C17: from L, from Gk, from EN-[2] + *harmonia;* see HARMONY]
▸ˌ**enharˈmonically** *adv*

enigma ⓣ (ɪˈnɪgmə) *n* a person, thing, or situation that is mysterious, puzzling, or ambiguous. [C16: from L, from Gk, from *ainissesthai* to speak in riddles, from *ainos* fable, story]
▸**enigmatic** (ˌɛnɪgˈmætɪk) *or* ˌ**enigˈmatical** *adj* ▸ˌ**enigˈmatically** *adv*

enjambment *or* **enjambement** (ɪnˈdʒæmmənt) *n Prosody.* the running over of a sentence from one line of verse into the next. [C19: from F, lit.: a straddling, from EN-[1] + *jambe* leg; see JAMB]
▸**enˈjambed** *adj*

enjoin ⓣ (ɪnˈdʒɔɪn) *vb (tr)* **1** to order (someone) to do something. **2** to impose or prescribe (a mode of behaviour, etc.). **3** *Law.* to require (a person) to do or refrain from some act, esp. by an injunction. [C13: from OF *enjoindre,* from L *injungere* to fasten to, from IN-[2] + *jungere* to JOIN]
▸**enˈjoiner** *n* ▸**enˈjoinment** *n*

enjoy ⓣ (ɪnˈdʒɔɪ) *vb (tr)* **1** to receive pleasure from; take joy in. **2** to have the benefit of; use. **3** to have as a condition; experience. **4 enjoy oneself.** to have a good time. [C14: from OF, from EN-[1] + *joir* to find pleasure in, from L *gaudēre* to rejoice]
▸**enˈjoyable** *adj* ▸**enˈjoyableness** *n* ▸**enˈjoyably** *adv* ▸**enˈjoyer** *n*

enjoyment ⓣ (ɪnˈdʒɔɪmənt) *n* **1** the act or condition of receiving pleasure from something. **2** the use or possession of something that is satisfying. **3** something that provides joy or satisfaction.

enkephalin (ɛnˈkɛfəlɪn) *or* **encephalin** (ɛnˈsɛfəlɪn) *n* a chemical occurring in the brain, having effects similar to those of morphine.

enkindle ⓣ (ɪnˈkɪndᵊl) *vb* **enkindles, enkindling, enkindled.** *(tr)* **1** to set on fire; kindle. **2** to excite to activity or ardour; arouse.

enlace (ɪnˈleɪs) *vb* **enlaces, enlacing, enlaced.** *(tr)* **1** to bind or encircle with or as with laces. **2** to entangle; intertwine.
▸**enˈlacement** *n*

enlarge ⓣ (ɪnˈlɑːdʒ) *vb* **enlarges, enlarging, enlarged. 1** to make or grow larger; increase or expand. **2** *(tr)* to make (a photographic print) of a larger size than the negative. **3** *(intr;* foll. by *on* or *upon)* to speak or write (about) in greater detail.
▸**enˈlargeable** *adj* ▸**enˈlargement** *n* ▸**enˈlarger** *n*

enlighten ⓣ (ɪnˈlaɪtᵊn) *vb (tr)* **1** to give information or understanding to; instruct. **2** to free from prejudice, superstition, etc. **3** to give spiritual or religious revelation to. **4** *Poetic.* to shed light on.
▸**enˈlightening** *adj*

enlightened ⓣ (ɪnˈlaɪtᵊnd) *adj* **1** well-informed, tolerant, and guided by rational thought: *an enlightened administration.* **2** claiming a spiritual revelation of truth.

enlightenment ⓣ (ɪnˈlaɪtᵊnmənt) *n* the act or means of enlightening or the state of being enlightened.

Enlightenment (ɪnˈlaɪtᵊnmənt) *n* **the.** an 18th-century philosophical movement stressing the importance of reason.

enlist ⓣ (ɪnˈlɪst) *vb* **1** to enter or persuade to enter the armed forces. **2** *(tr)* to engage or secure (a person or his support) for a venture, cause, etc. **3** *(intr;* foll. by *in)* to enter into or join an enterprise, cause, etc.
▸**enˈlister** *n* ▸**enˈlistment** *n*

enlisted man *n US.* a serviceman who holds neither a commission nor a warrant.

enliven ⓣ (ɪnˈlaɪvᵊn) *vb (tr)* **1** to make active, vivacious, or spirited. **2** to make cheerful or bright; gladden.
▸**enˈlivening** *adj* ▸**enˈlivenment** *n*

en masse ⓣ *(French* ɑ̃ mas) *adv* in a group or mass; as a whole; all together. [C19: from F]

enmesh ⓣ (ɪnˈmɛʃ) *vb (tr)* to catch or involve in or as if in a net or snare; entangle.
▸**enˈmeshment** *n*

enmity ⓣ (ˈɛnmɪtɪ) *n, pl* **enmities.** a feeling of hostility or ill will, as between enemies. [C13: from OF; see ENEMY]

ennoble ⓣ (ɪˈnəʊbᵊl) *vb* **ennobles, ennobling, ennobled.** *(tr)* **1** to make noble, honourable, or excellent; dignify; exalt. **2** to raise to a noble rank.
▸**enˈnoblement** *n* ▸**enˈnobler** *n* ▸**enˈnobling** *adj*

ennui ⓣ (ˈɒnwiː) *n* a feeling of listlessness and general dissatisfaction resulting from lack of activity or excitement. [C18: from F: apathy, from OF *enui* annoyance, vexation; see ANNOY]

enology (iːˈnɒlədʒɪ) *n* the usual US spelling of **oenology.**

enormity ⓣ (ɪˈnɔːmɪtɪ) *n, pl* **enormities. 1** the quality or character of extreme wickedness. **2** an act of great wickedness; atrocity. **3** *Inf.* vastness of size or extent. [C15: from OF, from LL *ēnormitās* hugeness; see ENORMOUS]

> **USAGE NOTE** In modern English, it is common to talk about the *enormity* of something such as a task or a problem, but one should not talk about the *enormity* of an object or area: *distribution is a problem because of India's enormous size* (not *India's enormity*).

enormous ⓣ (ɪˈnɔːməs) *adj* **1** unusually large in size, extent, or degree; immense; vast. **2** *Arch.* extremely wicked; heinous. [C16: from L, from *ē-* out of, away from + *norma* rule, pattern]
▸**eˈnormously** *adv* ▸**eˈnormousness** *n*

enosis (ˈɛnəʊsɪs) *n* the union of Greece and Cyprus: the aim of a group of Greek Cypriots. [C20: Mod. Gk: from Gk *henoun* to unite, from *heis* one]

enough ⓣ (ɪˈnʌf) *determiner* **1a** sufficient to answer a need, demand or supposition. **1b** *(as pron): enough is now known.* **2 that's enough!** that will

THESAURUS

enigma *n* = **mystery,** conundrum, problem, puzzle, riddle, teaser

enigmatic *adj* = **mysterious,** ambiguous, cryptic, Delphic, doubtful, equivocal, incomprehensible, indecipherable, inexplicable, inscrutable, obscure, oracular, perplexing, puzzling, recondite, sphinxlike, uncertain, unfathomable, unintelligible
Antonyms *adj* clear, comprehensible, simple, straightforward, uncomplicated

enjoin *vb* **1, 2** = **order,** advise, bid, call upon, charge, command, counsel, demand, direct, instruct, prescribe, require, urge, warn **3** *Law* = **prohibit,** ban, bar, disallow, forbid, interdict, place an injunction on, preclude, proscribe, restrain

enjoy *vb* **1** = **take pleasure in** *or* **from,** appreciate, be entertained by, be pleased with, delight in, like, rejoice in, relish, revel in, take joy in **2, 3** = **have,** be blessed *or* favoured with, experience, have the benefit of, have the use of, own, possess, reap the benefits of, use **4 enjoy oneself** = **have a good time,** have a ball *(inf.),* have a field day, have fun, let one's hair down, make merry
Antonyms *vb* ≠ **take pleasure in** *or* **from:** abhor, despise, detest, dislike, hate, have no taste *or* stomach for, loathe

enjoyable *adj* **1** = **pleasurable,** agreeable, amusing, delectable, delicious, delightful, entertaining, gratifying, pleasant, pleasing, satisfying, to one's liking
Antonyms *adj* despicable, disagreeable, displeasing, hateful, loathsome, obnoxious, offensive, repugnant, unenjoyable, unpleasant, unsatisfying, unsavoury

enjoyment *n* **1** = **pleasure,** amusement, beer and skittles *(inf.),* delectation, delight, diversion, entertainment, fun, gladness, gratification, gusto, happiness, indulgence, joy, recreation, relish, satisfaction, zest

enkindle *vb* **1** = **set on fire,** fire, ignite, kindle, light, put a match to, put to the torch, set ablaze, set alight, set fire to, torch **2** = **arouse,** awake, excite, foment, incite, inflame, inspire, provoke, stir

enlarge *vb* **1, 2** = **increase,** add to, amplify, augment, blow up *(inf.),* broaden, diffuse, dilate, distend, elongate, expand, extend, grow, heighten, inflate, lengthen, magnify, make *or* grow larger, multiply, stretch, swell, wax, widen **3** *with* **on** *or* **upon** = **expand on,** descant on, develop, elaborate on, expatiate on, give further details about
Antonyms *vb* ≠ **increase:** compress, condense, curtail, decrease, diminish, lessen, narrow, reduce, shorten, shrink, trim, truncate ≠ **expand on:** abbreviate, abridge, condense, shorten

enlighten *vb* **1** = **inform,** advise, apprise, cause to understand, civilize, counsel, edify, educate, instruct, make aware, teach

enlightened *adj* **1** = **informed,** aware, broad-minded, civilized, cultivated, educated, knowledgeable, liberal, literate, open-minded, reasonable, refined, sophisticated
Antonyms *adj* ignorant, narrow-minded, short-sighted, small-minded, unaware, uneducated, unenlightened

enlightenment *n* = **understanding,** awareness, broad-mindedness, civilization, comprehension, cultivation, edification, education, information, insight, instruction, knowledge, learning, literacy, open-mindedness, refinement, sophistication, teaching, wisdom

enlist *vb* **1, 3** = **join up,** enrol, enter (into), join, muster, register, sign up, volunteer **2** = **obtain,** engage, procure, recruit, secure

enliven *vb* **1, 2** = **cheer up,** animate, brighten, buoy up, cheer, excite, exhilarate, fire, gladden, hearten, inspire, inspirit, invigorate, pep up, perk up, quicken, rouse, spark, stimulate, vitalize, vivify, wake up
Antonyms *vb* chill, dampen, deaden, depress, put a damper on, repress, subdue

en masse *adv* = **all together,** all at once, as a group, as a whole, as one, ensemble, in a body, in a group, in a mass, together

enmesh *vb* = **entangle,** catch, embroil, ensnare, implicate, incriminate, involve, net, snare, snarl, tangle, trammel, trap

enmity *n* = **hostility,** acrimony, animosity, animus, antagonism, antipathy, aversion, bad blood, bitterness, hate, hatred, ill will, malevolence, malice, malignity, rancour, spite, venom
Antonyms *n* affection, amity, cordiality, friendliness, friendship, geniality, goodwill, harmony, love, warmth

ennoble *vb* **1** = **dignify,** aggrandize, elevate, enhance, exalt, glorify, honour, magnify, raise

ennui *n* = **boredom,** dissatisfaction, lassitude, listlessness, tedium, the doldrums

enormity *n* **1** = **wickedness,** atrociousness, atrocity, depravity, disgrace, evilness, heinousness, monstrousness, nefariousness, outrageousness, turpitude, viciousness, vileness, villainy **2** = **atrocity,** abomination, crime, disgrace, evil, horror, monstrosity, outrage, villainy **3** *Informal* = **hugeness,** enormousness, greatness, immensity, magnitude, massiveness, vastness

enormous *adj* **1** = **huge,** astronomic, Brobdingnagian, colossal, elephantine, excessive, gargantuan, gigantic, ginormous *(inf.),* gross, humongous *or* humungous *(US sl.),* immense, jumbo *(inf.),* mammoth, massive, monstrous, mountainous, prodigious, stellar *(inf.),* titanic, tremendous, vast **2** *Archaic* = **wicked,** abominable, atrocious, depraved, disgraceful, evil, heinous, monstrous, nefarious, odious, outrageous, vicious, vile, villainous
Antonyms *adj* ≠ **huge:** diminutive, dwarf, infinitesimal, insignificant, Lilliputian, little, meagre, microscopic, midget, minute, petite, pint-sized *(inf.),* small, tiny, trivial, wee

enough *determiner* **1a** = **sufficient,** abundant, adequate, ample, plenty ◆ *pron* **1b** = **sufficiency,** abundance, adequacy, ample supply,

do: used to put an end to an action, speech, performance, etc. ◆ *adv* **3** so as to be sufficient; as much as necessary. **4** (*not used with a negative*) very or quite; rather. **5** (intensifier): *oddly enough.* **6** just adequately; tolerably. [OE *genōh*]

en passant (ɒn pæ'sɑːnt) *adv* in passing: in chess, said of capturing a pawn that has made an initial move of two squares. The capture is made as if the captured pawn had moved one square instead of two. [C17: from F]

enprint ('ɛnprɪnt) *n* a standard photographic print (5 × 3·5 in.) produced from a negative.

enquire Ⓣ (ɪn'kwaɪə) *vb* **enquires, enquiring, enquired.** a variant of **inquire.**
►**en'quirer** *n* ►**en'quiry** *n*

enrage Ⓣ (ɪn'reɪdʒ) *vb* **enrages, enraging, enraged.** (*tr*) to provoke to fury; put into a rage.
►**en'raged** *adj* ►**en'ragement** *n*

en rapport *French.* (ɑ̃ rapɔr) *adj* (*postpositive*), *adv* in sympathy, harmony, or accord.

enrapture Ⓣ (ɪn'ræptʃə) *vb* **enraptures, enrapturing, enraptured.** (*tr*) to fill with delight; enchant.

enrich Ⓣ (ɪn'rɪtʃ) *vb* (*tr*) **1** to increase the wealth of. **2** to endow with fine or desirable qualities. **3** to make more beautiful; adorn; decorate. **4** to improve in quality, colour, flavour, etc. **5** to increase the food value of by adding nutrients. **6** to fertilize (soil). **7** *Physics.* to increase the concentration or abundance of one component or isotope in (a solution or mixture).
►**en'riched** *adj* ►**en'richment** *n*

enrol Ⓣ *or US* **enroll** (ɪn'rəʊl) *vb* **enrols** *or US* **enrolls, enrolling, enrolled.** (*mainly tr*) **1** to record or note in a roll or list. **2** (*also intr*) to become or cause to become a member; enlist; register. **3** to put on record.
►**ˌenrol'lee** *n* ►**en'roller** *n*

enrolment Ⓣ *or US* **enrollment** (ɪn'rəʊlmənt) *n* **1** the act of enrolling or state of being enrolled. **2** a list of people enrolled. **3** the total number of people enrolled.

en route Ⓣ (ɒn 'ruːt) *adv* on or along the way. [C18: from F]

Ens. *abbrev. for* Ensign.

ENSA ('ɛnsə) *n acronym for* Entertainments National Service Association.

ensconce Ⓣ (ɪn'skɒns) *vb* **ensconces, ensconcing, ensconced.** (*tr; often passive*) **1** to establish or settle firmly or comfortably. **2** to place in safety; hide. [C16: see EN-[1], SCONCE[2]]

ensemble Ⓣ (ɒn'sɒmbᵊl) *n* **1** all the parts of something considered together. **2** a person's complete costume; outfit. **3** the cast of a play other than the principals. **4** *Music.* a group of soloists singing or playing together. **5** *Music.* the degree of precision and unity exhibited by a group of instrumentalists or singers performing together. **6** the general effect of something made up of individual parts. ◆ *adv* **7** all together or at once. [C15: from F: together, from L, from IN-[2] + *simul* at the same time]

enshrine Ⓣ *or* **inshrine** (ɪn'ʃraɪn) *vb* **enshrines, enshrining, enshrined.** (*tr*) **1** to place or enclose as in a shrine. **2** to hold as sacred; cherish; treasure.
►**en'shrinement** *n*

enshroud Ⓣ (ɪn'ʃraʊd) *vb* (*tr*) to cover or hide as with a shroud.

ensign Ⓣ ('ɛnsaɪn) *n* **1** (*also* 'ɛnsən). a flag flown by a ship, branch of the armed forces, etc., to indicate nationality, allegiance, etc. See also **Red Ensign, White Ensign. 2** any flag, standard, or banner. **3** a standard-bearer. **4** a symbol or emblem; sign. **5** (in the US Navy) a commissioned officer of the lowest rank. **6** (in the British infantry) a colours bearer. **7** (formerly in the British infantry) a commissioned officer of the lowest rank. [C14: from OF *enseigne,* from L INSIGNIA]
►**'ensignˌship** *or* **'ensigncy** *n*

ensilage ('ɛnsɪlɪdʒ) *n* **1** the process of ensiling green fodder. **2** a less common name for **silage.**

ensile (ɛn'saɪl, 'ɛnsaɪl) *vb* **ensiles, ensiling, ensiled.** (*tr*) **1** to store and preserve (green fodder) in a silo. **2** to turn (green fodder) into silage by causing it to ferment in a silo. [C19: from F, from Sp., from EN-[1] + *silo* SILO]

enslave Ⓣ (ɪn'sleɪv) *vb* **enslaves, enslaving, enslaved.** (*tr*) to make a slave of; subjugate.
►**en'slavement** *n* ►**en'slaver** *n*

ensnare Ⓣ *or* **insnare** (ɪn'snɛə) *vb* **ensnares, ensnaring, ensnared** *or* **insnares, insnaring, insnared.** (*tr*) **1** to catch or trap as in a snare. **2** to trap or gain power over (someone) by dishonest or underhand means.
►**en'snarement** *n* ►**en'snarer** *n*

ensue Ⓣ (ɪn'sjuː) *vb* **ensues, ensuing, ensued. 1** (*intr*) to come next or afterwards. **2** (*intr*) to occur as a consequence; result. **3** (*tr*) *Obs.* to pursue. [C14: from Anglo-F, from OF, from EN-[1] + *suivre* to follow, from L *sequī*]
►**en'suing** *adj*

en suite *French.* (ɑ̃ sɥit) *adv* forming a unit: *a room with bathroom en suite.* [lit.: in sequence]

ensure Ⓣ (ɛn'ʃʊə, -'ʃɔː) *or esp. US* **insure** *vb* **ensures, ensuring, ensured** *or US* **insures, insuring, insured.** (*tr*) **1** (*may take a clause as object*) to make certain or sure; guarantee. **2** to make safe or secure; protect.
►**en'surer** *n*

ENT *Med. abbrev. for* ear, nose, and throat.

-ent *suffix forming adjectives and nouns.* causing or performing an action or existing in a certain condition; the agent that performs an action: *astringent; dependent.* [from L *-ent-, -ens,* present participial ending]

entablature (ɛn'tæblətʃə) *n Archit.* **1** the part of a classical temple above the columns, having an architrave, a frieze, and a cornice. **2** any similar construction. [C17: from F, from It. *intavolatura* something put on a table, hence, something laid flat, from *tavola* table]

entablement (ɪn'teɪbᵊlmənt) *n* the platform of a pedestal, above the dado, that supports a statue. [C17: from OF]

entail Ⓣ (ɪn'teɪl) *vb* (*tr*) **1** to bring about or impose inevitably: *this task entails careful thought.* **2** *Property law.* to restrict (the descent of an estate) to designated heirs. **3** *Logic.* to have as a necessary consequence. ◆ *n* **4** *Property law.* **4a** the restriction imposed by entailing an estate. **4b** an entailed estate. [C14 *entaillen,* from EN-[1] + *taille* limitation, TAIL[2]]
►**en'tailer** *n* ►**en'tailment** *n*

entamoeba (ˌɛntə'miːbə), **endamoeba** *or US* **entameba, endameba** *n, pl* **entamoebae** (-biː), **entamoebas, endamoebae, endamoebas** *or US* **entamebae, entamebas, endamebae, endamebas.** any parasitic amoeba of the genus *Entamoeba* (or *Endamoeba*) which lives in the intestines of man and causes amoebic dysentery.

entangle Ⓣ (ɪn'tæŋgᵊl) *vb* **entangles, entangling, entangled.** (*tr*) **1** to catch or involve in or as if in a tangle; ensnare or enmesh. **2** to make tangled or twisted; snarl. **3** to make complicated; confuse. **4** to involve in difficulties.
►**en'tanglement** *n* ►**en'tangler** *n*

entasis ('ɛntəsɪs) *n, pl* **entasises** (-siːz). a slightly convex curve given to the shaft of a column, or similar structure, to correct the illusion of concavity produced by a straight shaft. [C18: from Gk, from *enteinein* to stretch tight, from *teinein* to stretch]

entellus (ɛn'tɛləs) *n* an Old World monkey of S Asia. [C19: NL, apparently after a character in Virgil's *Aeneid*]

THESAURUS

plenty, right amount ◆ *adv* **3, 4** = **sufficiently,** abundantly, adequately, amply, fairly, moderately, passably, reasonably, satisfactorily, tolerably

enquire *see* **inquire**

enquiry *see* **inquiry**

enrage *vb* = **anger,** aggravate (*inf.*), exasperate, gall, get one's back up, incense, incite, inflame, infuriate, irritate, madden, make one's blood boil, make one see red (*inf.*), nark (*Brit., Austral., & NZ sl.*), provoke, put one's back up
Antonyms *vb* appease, assuage, calm, conciliate, mollify, pacify, placate, soothe

enraged *adj* = **furious,** aggravated (*inf.*), angered, angry, boiling mad, choked, cross, exasperated, fit to be tied (*sl.*), fuming, incandescent, incensed, inflamed, infuriated, irate, irritated, livid (*inf.*), mad (*inf.*), on the warpath, pissed (*taboo sl.*), pissed off (*taboo sl.*), raging, raging mad, wild

enrapture *vb* = **enchant,** absorb, beguile, bewitch, captivate, charm, delight, enamour, enthral, entrance, fascinate, ravish, spellbind, transport

enrich *vb* **1** = **make rich,** make wealthy **2, 4** = **enhance,** aggrandize, ameliorate, augment, cultivate, develop, endow, improve, refine, supplement

enrol *vb* **1, 3** = **record,** chronicle, inscribe, list, note **2** = **enlist,** accept, admit, engage, join up, matriculate, recruit, register, sign up *or* on, take on

enrolment *n* **1** = **enlistment,** acceptance, admission, engagement, matriculation, recruitment, registration

en route *adv* = **on** *or* **along the way,** in transit, on the road

ensconce *vb* **1** = **settle,** curl up, establish, install, nestle, snuggle up **2** = **hide,** conceal, cover, protect, screen, shelter, shield

ensemble *n* **1** = **whole,** aggregate, assemblage, collection, entirety, set, sum, total, totality, whole thing **2** = **outfit,** costume, get-up (*inf.*), suit **3** = **group,** band, cast, chorus, company, supporting cast, troupe ◆ *adv* **7** = **all together,** all at once, as a group, as a whole, at once, at the same time, en masse, in concert

enshrine *vb* **2** = **preserve,** apotheosize, cherish, consecrate, dedicate, embalm, exalt, hallow, revere, sanctify, treasure

enshroud *vb* = **cover,** cloak, cloud, conceal, enclose, enfold, envelop, enwrap, hide, obscure, pall, shroud, veil, wrap

ensign *n* **1, 2** = **flag,** badge, banner, colours, jack, pennant, pennon, standard, streamer

enslave *vb* = **subjugate,** bind, dominate, enchain, enthral, reduce to slavery, yoke

ensnare *vb* **1, 2** = **trap,** catch, embroil, enmesh, entangle, entrap, net, snare, snarl

ensue *vb* **1, 2** = **follow,** arise, attend, be consequent on, befall, come after, come next, come to pass (*arch.*), derive, flow, issue, proceed, result, stem, succeed, supervene, turn out *or* up
Antonyms *vb* antecede, come first, forerun, go ahead of, go before, introduce, lead, pave the way, precede, usher

ensure *vb* **1** = **make certain,** certify, confirm, effect, guarantee, make sure, secure, warrant **2** = **protect,** guard, make safe, safeguard, secure

entail *vb* **1** = **involve,** bring about, call for, cause, demand, encompass, give rise to, impose, lead to, necessitate, occasion, require, result in

entangle *vb* **1** = **tangle,** catch, compromise, embroil, enmesh, ensnare, entrap, foul, implicate, involve, knot, mat, mix up, ravel, snag, snare, trammel, trap **3** = **mix up,** bewilder, complicate, confuse, jumble, muddle, perplex, puzzle, snarl, twist
Antonyms *vb* ≠ **tangle:** detach, disconnect, disengage, disentangle, extricate, free, loose, separate, sever, unfold, unravel, unsnarl, untangle, untwist ≠ **mix up:** clarify, clear (up), resolve, simplify, work out

entanglement *n* **1-3** = **tangle,** complication, confusion, ensnarement, entrapment, imbroglio, involvement, jumble, knot, mesh, mess, mix-up, muddle, snare, snarl-up (*inf., chiefly Brit.*), toils, trap **4** = **difficulty,** embarrassment,

entente (*French* ɑ̃tɑ̃t) *n* **1** short for **entente cordiale. 2** the parties to an entente cordiale collectively. [C19: F: understanding]

entente cordiale Ⓣ (*French* ɑ̃tɑ̃t kɔrdjal) *n* **1** a friendly understanding between political powers. **2** (*often caps.*) the understanding reached by France and Britain in 1904, over colonial disputes. [C19: F: cordial understanding]

enter Ⓣ ('ɛntə) *vb* **1** to come or go into (a place, house, etc.). **2** to penetrate or pierce. **3** (*tr*) to introduce or insert. **4** to join (a party, organization, etc.). **5** (when *intr,* foll. by *into*) to become involved or take part (in). **6** (*tr*) to record (an item) in a journal, account, etc. **7** (*tr*) to record (a name, etc.) on a list. **8** (*tr*) to present or submit: *to enter a proposal.* **9** (*intr*) *Theatre.* to come on stage: used as a stage direction: *enter Juliet.* **10** (when *intr,* often foll. by *into, on,* or *upon*) to begin; start: *to enter upon a new career.* **11** (*intr;* often foll. by *upon*) to come into possession (of). **12** (*tr*) to place (evidence, etc.) before a court of law. [C13: from OF, from L *intrāre,* from *intrā* within]
▸**'enterable** *adj* ▸**'enterer** *n*

enteric (ɛn'tɛrɪk) *or* **enteral** ('ɛntərəl) *adj* intestinal. [C19: from Gk, from *enteron* intestine]

enter into *vb* (*intr, prep*) **1** to be considered as a necessary part of (one's plans, calculations, etc.). **2** to be in sympathy with.

enteritis (ˌɛntə'raɪtɪs) *n* inflammation of the intestine.

entero- *or before a vowel* **enter-** *combining form.* indicating an intestine: *enterovirus; enteritis.* [from NL, from Gk *enteron* intestine]

enterobiasis (ˌɛntərəʊ'baɪəsɪs) *n* a disease, common in children, caused by infestation of the large intestine with pinworms. [C20: NL, from *enterobius* (generic name of worm) + -IASIS]

enterprise Ⓣ ('ɛntəˌpraɪz) *n* **1** a project or undertaking, esp. one that requires boldness or effort. **2** participation in such projects. **3** readiness to embark on new ventures; boldness and energy. **4a** initiative in business. **4b** (*as modifier*): *the enterprise culture.* **5** a company or firm. [C15: from OF *entreprise* (n), from *entreprendre* from *entre-* between (from L: INTER-) + *prendre* to take, from L *prehendere* to grasp]
▸**'enterˌpriser** *n*

Enterprise Allowance Scheme *n* (in Britain) a scheme to provide a weekly allowance to an unemployed person who wishes to set up a business and is willing to invest a specified amount in it during its first year.

enterprise zone *n* one of several areas in the UK in which industrial development is encouraged by tax and other concessions.

enterprising Ⓣ ('ɛntəˌpraɪzɪŋ) *adj* ready to embark on new ventures; full of boldness and initiative.
▸**'enterˌprisingly** *adv*

entertain Ⓣ (ˌɛntə'teɪn) *vb* **1** to provide amusement for (a person or audience). **2** to show hospitality to (guests). **3** (*tr*) to hold in the mind. [C15: from OF, from *entre-* mutually + *tenir* to hold]

entertainer (ˌɛntə'teɪnə) *n* **1** a professional performer in public entertainments. **2** any person who entertains.

entertaining Ⓣ (ˌɛntə'teɪnɪŋ) *adj* serving to entertain or give pleasure; diverting; amusing.

entertainment Ⓣ (ˌɛntə'teɪnmənt) *n* **1** the act or art of entertaining or state of being entertained. **2** an act, production, etc., that entertains; diversion; amusement.

enthral Ⓣ *or US* **enthrall** (ɪn'θrɔːl) *vb* **enthrals** *or US* **enthralls, enthralling, enthralled.** (*tr*) **1** to hold spellbound; enchant; captivate. **2** *Obs.* to hold as thrall; enslave.
▸**en'thraller** *n* ▸**en'thralling** *adj* ▸**en'thralment** *or US* **en'thrallment** *n*

enthrone (ɛn'θrəʊn) *vb* **enthrones, enthroning, enthroned.** (*tr*) **1** to place on a throne. **2** to honour or exalt. **3** to assign authority to.
▸**en'thronement** *n*

enthuse (ɪn'θjuːz) *vb* **enthuses, enthusing, enthused.** to feel or show or cause to feel or show enthusiasm.

enthusiasm Ⓣ (ɪn'θjuːzɪˌæzəm) *n* **1** ardent and lively interest or eagerness. **2** an object of keen interest. **3** *Arch.* extravagant religious fervour. [C17: from LL, from Gk, from *enthousiazein* to be possessed by a god, from EN-[2] + *theos* god]

enthusiast Ⓣ (ɪn'θjuːzɪˌæst) *n* **1** a person motivated by enthusiasm; fanatic. **2** *Arch.* one whose zeal for religion is extravagant.
▸**enˌthusi'astic** *adj* ▸**enˌthusi'astically** *adv*

enthymeme ('ɛnθɪˌmiːm) *n Logic.* a syllogism in which one or more premises are unexpressed. [C16: via L from Gk *enthumeisthai* to infer, from EN-[2] + *thumos* mind]

entice Ⓣ (ɪn'taɪs) *vb* **entices, enticing, enticed.** (*tr*) to attract by exciting hope or desire; tempt; allure. [C13: from OF, from Vulgar L *intitiāre* (unattested) to incite]
▸**en'ticement** *n* ▸**en'ticer** *n* ▸**en'ticing** *adj* ▸**en'ticingly** *adv*

entire Ⓣ (ɪn'taɪə) *adj* **1** (*prenominal*) whole; complete. **2** (*prenominal*) without reservation or exception. **3** not broken or damaged. **4** undivided; continuous. **5** (of leaves, petals, etc.) having a smooth margin not broken up into teeth or lobes. **6** not castrated: *an entire horse.* **7** *Obs.* unmixed; pure. ◆ *n* **8** an uncastrated horse. [C14: from OF, from L *integer* whole, from IN-[1] + *tangere* to touch]
▸**en'tireness** *n*

entirely Ⓣ (ɪn'taɪəlɪ) *adv* **1** wholly; completely. **2** solely or exclusively.

entirety Ⓣ (ɪn'taɪərɪtɪ) *n, pl* **entireties. 1** the state of being entire or whole; completeness. **2** a thing, sum, amount, etc., that is entire; whole; total.

entitle Ⓣ (ɪn'taɪt(ə)l) *vb* **entitles, entitling, entitled.** (*tr*) **1** to give (a person) the right to do or have something; qualify; allow. **2** to give a name or title to. **3** to confer a title of rank or honour upon. [C14: from OF *entituler,* from LL, from L *titulus* TITLE]
▸**en'titlement** *n*

entity Ⓣ ('ɛntɪtɪ) *n, pl* **entities. 1** something having real or distinct existence. **2** existence or being. [C16: from Med. L, from *ēns* being, from L *esse* to be]
▸**'entitative** *adj*

THESAURUS

imbroglio, involvement, liaison, predicament, tie

entente cordiale *n* **1** = **agreement**, arrangement, compact, deal, friendship, pact, treaty, understanding

enter *vb* **1-3** = **come** *or* **go in** *or* **into**, arrive, insert, introduce, make an entrance, pass into, penetrate, pierce **4, 5, 10** = **join**, become a member of, begin, commence, commit oneself to, embark upon, enlist, enrol, participate in, set about, set out on, sign up, start, take part in, take up **6, 7** = **record**, inscribe, list, log, note, register, set down, take down **8** = **put forward**, offer, present, proffer, register, submit, tender
Antonyms *vb* ≠ **come** *or* **go in** *or* **into:** depart, exit, go, issue from, leave, take one's leave, withdraw ≠ **join:** drop out, go, leave, pull out, resign, retire, withdraw

enterprise *n* **1** = **undertaking**, adventure, effort, endeavour, essay, operation, plan, programme, project, venture **3** = **initiative**, activity, adventurousness, alertness, audacity, boldness, daring, dash, drive, eagerness, energy, enthusiasm, get-up-and-go (*inf.*), gumption (*inf.*), pep, push (*inf.*), readiness, resource, resourcefulness, spirit, vigour, zeal **5** = **firm**, business, company, concern, establishment, operation

enterprising *adj* = **resourceful**, active, adventurous, alert, audacious, bold, daring, dashing, eager, energetic, enthusiastic, go-ahead, intrepid, keen, ready, spirited, stirring, up-and-coming, venturesome, vigorous, zealous

entertain *vb* **1** = **amuse**, charm, cheer, delight, divert, occupy, please, recreate (*rare*), regale **2** = **show hospitality to**, accommodate, be host to, harbour, have company, have guests *or* visitors, lodge, put up, treat **3** = **consider**, cogitate on, conceive, contemplate, foster, harbour, hold, imagine, keep in mind, maintain, muse over, ponder, support, think about, think over

entertaining *adj* = **enjoyable**, amusing, charming, cheering, delightful, diverting, funny, humorous, interesting, pleasant, pleasing, pleasurable, recreative (*rare*), witty

entertainment *n* **1, 2** = **enjoyment**, amusement, beer and skittles (*inf.*), cheer, distraction, diversion, fun, good time, leisure activity, pastime, play, pleasure, recreation, satisfaction, sport, treat

enthral *vb* **1** = **fascinate**, absorb, beguile, captivate, charm, enchant, enrapture, entrance, grip, hold spellbound, hypnotize, intrigue, mesmerize, ravish, rivet, spellbind

enthralling *adj* **1** = **fascinating**, beguiling, captivating, charming, compelling, compulsive, enchanting, entrancing, gripping, hypnotizing, intriguing, mesmerizing, riveting, spellbinding

enthusiasm *n* **1** = **keenness**, ardour, avidity, devotion, eagerness, earnestness, excitement, fervour, frenzy, interest, passion, relish, vehemence, warmth, zeal, zest, zing (*inf.*) **2** = **passion**, craze, fad (*inf.*), hobby, hobbyhorse, interest, mania, rage

enthusiast *n* **1** = **lover**, admirer, aficionado, buff (*inf.*), devotee, fan, fanatic, fiend, follower, freak (*inf.*), supporter, zealot

enthusiastic *adj* **1** = **keen**, ablaze, ardent, avid, bright-eyed and bushy-tailed (*inf.*), devoted, eager, earnest, ebullient, excited, exuberant, fervent, fervid, forceful, full of beans (*inf.*), hearty, keen as mustard, lively, passionate, spirited, unqualified, unstinting, vehement, vigorous, warm, wholehearted, zealous
Antonyms *adj* apathetic, blasé, bored, cool, dispassionate, half-hearted, indifferent, nonchalant, unconcerned, unenthusiastic, uninterested

entice *vb* = **attract**, allure, beguile, cajole, coax, dangle a carrot in front of (someone's) nose, decoy, draw, inveigle, lead on, lure, persuade, prevail on, seduce, tempt, wheedle

enticement *n* = **attraction**, allurement, bait, blandishments, cajolery, coaxing, come-on (*inf.*), decoy, incentive, inducement, inveiglement, lure, persuasion, seduction, temptation

enticing *adj* = **attractive**, alluring, beguiling, captivating, come-hither (*inf.*), intriguing, inviting, irresistible, persuasive, seductive, tempting, yummy (*inf.*)
Antonyms *adj* distasteful, off-putting (*Brit. inf.*), repellent, unappealing, unattractive

entire *adj* **1** = **whole**, complete, full, gross, total **2** = **total**, absolute, full, outright, thorough, undiminished, unmitigated, unreserved, unrestricted **3** = **intact**, perfect, sound, unbroken, undamaged, unmarked, unmarred, whole, without a scratch **4** = **continuous**, integrated, unbroken, undivided, unified

entirely *adv* **1** = **completely**, absolutely, altogether, every inch, fully, in every respect, lock, stock and barrel, perfectly, thoroughly, totally, unreservedly, utterly, wholly, without exception, without reservation **2** = **only**, exclusively, solely
Antonyms *adv* ≠ **completely:** incompletely, moderately, partially, partly, piecemeal, slightly, somewhat, to a certain extent *or* degree

entirety *n* **1** = **wholeness**, absoluteness, completeness, fullness, totality, undividedness, unity **2** = **whole**, aggregate, sum, total, unity

entitle *vb* **1** = **give the right to**, accredit, allow, authorize, empower, enable, enfranchise, fit for, license, make eligible, permit, qualify for, warrant **2** = **call**, characterize, christen, denominate, designate, dub, label, name, style, term, title

entity *n* **1** = **thing**, being, body, creature, existence, individual, object, organism, presence, quantity, substance **2** = **essential nature**, es-

ento- *combining form.* inside; within: *entoderm.* [NL, from Gk *entos* within]

entomb Ⓣ (ɪn'tuːm) *vb* (*tr*) **1** to place in or as if in a tomb; bury; inter. **2** to serve as a tomb for.
▸**en'tombment** *n*

entomo- *combining form.* indicating an insect: *entomology.* [from Gk *entomon* insect]

entomol. *or* **entom.** *abbrev. for* entomology.

entomology (ˌɛntə'mɒlədʒɪ) *n* the branch of science concerned with the study of insects.
▸ˌ**entomo'logical** *adj* ▸ˌ**ento'mologist** *n*

entophyte ('ɛntəʊˌfaɪt) *n Bot.* a variant spelling of **endophyte.**
▸**entophytic** (ˌɛntəʊ'fɪtɪk) *adj*

entourage Ⓣ (ɒntu'rɑːʒ) *n* **1** a group of attendants or retainers; retinue. **2** surroundings. [C19: from F, from *entourer* to surround, from *tour* circuit; see TOUR, TURN]

entr'acte (ɒn'trækt) *n* **1** an interval between two acts of a play or opera. **2** (esp. formerly) an entertainment during such an interval. [C19: F, lit.: between-act]

entrails Ⓣ ('ɛntreɪlz) *pl n* **1** the internal organs of a person or animal; intestines; guts. **2** the innermost parts of anything. [C13: from OF, from Med. L *intrālia*, changed from L *interānea* intestines]

entrain (ɪn'treɪn) *vb* to board or put aboard a train.
▸**en'trainment** *n*

entrance[1] Ⓣ ('ɛntrəns) *n* **1** the act or an instance of entering; entry. **2** a place for entering, such as a door. **3a** the power, liberty, or right of entering. **3b** (*as modifier*): *an entrance fee.* **4** the coming of an actor or other performer onto a stage. [C16: from F, from *entrer* to ENTER]

entrance[2] Ⓣ (ɪn'trɑːns) *vb* **entrances, entrancing, entranced.** (*tr*) **1** to fill with wonder and delight; enchant. **2** to put into a trance; hypnotize.
▸**en'trancement** *n* ▸**en'trancing** *adj*

entrant Ⓣ ('ɛntrənt) *n* a person who enters. [C17: from F, lit.: entering, from *entrer* to ENTER]

entrap Ⓣ (ɪn'træp) *vb* **entraps, entrapping, entrapped.** (*tr*) **1** to catch or snare as in a trap. **2** to trick into danger, difficulty, or embarrassment.
▸**en'trapment** *n* ▸**en'trapper** *n*

entreat Ⓣ *or* **intreat** (ɪn'triːt) *vb* **1** to ask (a person) earnestly; beg or plead with; implore. **2** to make an earnest request or petition for (something). **3** an archaic word for **treat** (sense 4). [C15: from OF, from EN-[1] + *traiter* to TREAT]
▸**en'treatment** *or* **in'treatment** *n*

entreaty Ⓣ (ɪn'triːtɪ) *n, pl* **entreaties.** an earnest request or petition; supplication; plea.

entrechat (*French* ɑ̃trəʃa) *n* a leap in ballet during which the dancer repeatedly crosses his feet or beats them together. [C18: from F *entrechase*, changed by folk etymology from It. (*capriola*) *intrecciata*, lit.: entwined (caper)]

entrecôte (*French* ɑ̃trəkot) *n* a beefsteak cut from between the ribs. [F, from *entre-* INTER- + *côte* rib]

entrée ('ɒntreɪ) *n* **1** a dish served before a main course. **2** *Chiefly US.* the main course of a meal. **3** the power or right of entry. [C18: from F, from *entrer* to ENTER; in cookery, so called because formerly the course was served after an intermediate course called the *relevé* (remove)]

entremets (*French* ɑ̃trəmɛ) *n, pl* **entremets** (*French* -mɛ). **1** a dessert. **2** a light dish formerly served between the main course and the dessert. [C18: from F, from OF, from *entre-* between + *mes* dish]

entrench Ⓣ *or* **intrench** (ɪn'trɛntʃ) *vb* **1** (*tr*) to construct a defensive position by digging trenches around it. **2** (*tr*) to fix or establish firmly. **3** (*intr; foll. by on or upon*) to trespass or encroach.
▸**en'trenched** *or* **in'trenched** *adj* ▸**en'trenchment** *or* **in'trenchment** *n*

entrepôt (*French* ɑ̃trəpo) *n* **1** a warehouse for commercial goods. **2a** a trading centre or port at which goods are imported and re-exported without incurring duty. **2b** (*as modifier*): *an entrepôt trade.* [C18: F, from *entreposer*, from *entre* between + *poser* to place; formed on the model of DEPOT]

entrepreneur Ⓣ (ˌɒntrəprə'nɜː) *n* **1** the owner or manager of a business enterprise who, by risk and initiative, attempts to make profits. **2** a middleman or commercial intermediary. [C19: from F, from *entreprendre* to undertake; see ENTERPRISE]
▸ˌ**entrepre'neurial** *adj* ▸ˌ**entrepre'neurship** *n*

entropy ('ɛntrəpɪ) *n, pl* **entropies. 1** a thermodynamic quantity that changes in a reversible process by an amount equal to the heat absorbed or emitted divided by the thermodynamic temperature. It is measured in joules per kelvin. **2** lack of pattern or organization; disorder. [C19: from EN-[2] + -TROPE]

entrust Ⓣ *or* **intrust** (ɪn'trʌst) *vb* (*tr*) **1** (usually foll. by *with*) to invest or charge (with a duty, responsibility, etc.). **2** (often foll. by *to*) to put into the care or protection of someone.
▸**en'trustment** *or* **in'trustment** *n*

> **USAGE NOTE** It is usually considered incorrect to talk about *entrusting* someone *to do* something: *the army cannot be trusted* (not *entrusted*) *to carry out orders.*

entry Ⓣ ('ɛntrɪ) *n, pl* **entries. 1** the act or an instance of entering; entrance. **2** a point or place for entering, such as a door, etc. **3a** the right or liberty of entering. **3b** (*as modifier*): *an entry permit.* **4** the act of recording an item in a journal, account, etc. **5** an item recorded, as in a diary, dictionary, or account. **6** a person, horse, car, etc., entering a competition or contest. **7** the competitors entering a contest considered collectively. **8** the action of an actor in going on stage. **9** *Property law.* the act of going upon land with the intention of asserting the right to possession. **10** any point in a piece of music at which a performer commences or resumes singing or playing. **11** *Bridge, etc.* a card that enables one to transfer the lead from one's own hand to that of one's partner or to the dummy hand. **12** *Dialect.* a passage between the backs of two rows of houses. [C13: from OF *entree*, p.p. of *entrer* to ENTER]

entryism ('ɛntrɪɪzəm) *n* the policy or practice of joining an existing political party with the intention of changing it instead of forming a new party.
▸**'entryist** *n, adj*

entry-level *adj* **1** (of a job or worker) at the most elementary level in a career structure. **2** (of a product) characterized by being at the most appropriate level for use by a beginner: *an entry-level camera.*

entwine Ⓣ *or* **intwine** (ɪn'twaɪn) *vb* **entwines, entwining, entwined** *or* **intwines, intwining, intwined.** (of two or more things) to twine together or (of one or more things) to twine around (something else).
▸**en'twinement** *or* **in'twinement** *n*

E number *n* any of a series of numbers with the prefix E indicating a specific food additive recognized by the European Union.

enumerate Ⓣ (ɪ'njuːməˌreɪt) *vb* **enumerates, enumerating, enumerated.** (*tr*) **1** to name one by one; list. **2** to determine the number of; count. [C17: from L, from *numerāre* to count, reckon; see NUMBER]
▸**e'numerable** *adj* ▸**eˌnumer'ation** *n* ▸**e'numerative** *adj*

enumerator (ɪ'njuːməˌreɪtə) *n* **1** a person or thing that enumerates. **2** *Brit.* a person who issues and retrieves census forms.

enunciable (ɪ'nʌnsɪəb°l) *adj* capable of being enunciated.

enunciate Ⓣ (ɪ'nʌnsɪˌeɪt) *vb* **enunciates, enunciating, enunciated. 1** to articulate or pronounce (words), esp. clearly and distinctly. **2** (*tr*) to

THESAURUS

sence, quiddity (*Philosophy*), quintessence, real nature

entomb *vb* **1** = **bury**, inhume, inter, inurn, lay to rest, sepulchre

entombment *n* **1** = **burial**, inhumation, interment, inurnment, sepulture

entourage *n* **1** = **retinue**, associates, attendants, companions, company, cortege, court, escort, followers, following, retainers, staff, suite, train **2** = **surroundings**, ambience, environment, environs, milieu

entrails *pl n* **1** = **intestines**, bowels, guts, innards (*inf.*), insides, offal, viscera

entrance[1] *n* **1, 4** = **appearance**, arrival, coming in, entry, ingress, introduction **2** = **way in**, access, avenue, door, doorway, entry, gate, ingress, inlet, opening, passage, portal **3** = **admission**, access, admittance, entrée, entry, ingress, permission to enter
Antonyms *n* ≠ **appearance:** departure, egress, exit, exodus, leave-taking ≠ **way in:** exit, outlet, way out

entrance[2] *vb* **1** = **enchant**, absorb, bewitch, captivate, charm, delight, enrapture, enthral, fascinate, gladden, ravish, spellbind, transport **2** = **mesmerize**, hypnotize, put in a trance
Antonyms *vb* ≠ **enchant:** bore, disenchant, irritate, offend, put off, turn off (*inf.*)

entrant *n* = **competitor**, candidate, contestant, entry, participant, player

entrap *vb* **1** = **catch**, capture, ensnare, net, snare, trap **2** = **trick**, allure, beguile, decoy, embroil, enmesh, ensnare, entangle, entice, implicate, inveigle, involve, lead on, lure, seduce

entreat *vb* **1, 2** = **beg**, appeal to, ask, ask earnestly, beseech, conjure, crave, enjoin, exhort, implore, importune, petition, plead with, pray, request, supplicate

entreaty *n* = **plea**, appeal, earnest request, exhortation, importunity, petition, prayer, request, solicitation, suit, supplication

entrench *vb* **1** = **fortify**, construct defences, dig in, dig trenches **2** = **fix**, anchor, dig in, embed, ensconce, establish, implant, ingrain, install, lodge, plant, root, seat, set, settle **3** = **encroach**, impinge, infringe, interlope, intrude, make inroads, trespass

entrenched *adj* **2** = **fixed**, deep-rooted, deep-seated, firm, indelible, ineradicable, ingrained, rooted, set, unshakable, well-established

entrepreneur *n* **1** = **businessman** *or* **businesswoman**, contractor, director, financier, impresario, industrialist, magnate, tycoon

entrust *vb* **1, 2** = **give custody of**, assign, authorize, charge, commend, commit, confide, consign, delegate, deliver, hand over, invest, trust, turn over

entry *n* **1** = **coming in**, appearance, entering, entrance, initiation, introduction **2** = **way in**, access, avenue, door, doorway, entrance, gate, ingress, inlet, opening, passage, passageway, portal **3** = **admission**, access, entrance, entrée, free passage, permission to enter **5** = **record**, account, item, jotting, listing, memo, memorandum, minute, note, registration **6** = **competitor**, attempt, candidate, contestant, effort, entrant, participant, player, submission
Antonyms *n* ≠ **coming in:** departure, egress, exit, leave, leave-taking, withdrawal ≠ **way in:** exit, way out

entwine *vb* = **twist**, braid, embrace, encircle, entwist (*arch.*), interlace, intertwine, interweave, knit, plait, ravel, surround, twine, weave, wind
Antonyms *vb* disentangle, extricate, free, separate, straighten out, undo, unravel, untangle, unwind

enumerate *vb* **1** = **list**, cite, detail, itemize, mention, name, quote, recapitulate, recite, recount, rehearse, relate, specify, spell out, tell **2** = **count**, add up, calculate, compute, number, reckon, sum up, tally, total

enunciate *vb* **1** = **pronounce**, articulate, enounce, say, sound, speak, utter, vocalize,

state precisely or formally. [C17: from L *ēnuntiāre* to declare, from *nuntiāre* to announce]
▸**e͵nunci'ation** *n* ▸**e'nunciative** *or* **e'nunciatory** *adj* ▸**e'nunci͵ator** *n*

enuresis (͵ɛnjʊ'riːsɪs) *n* involuntary discharge of urine, esp. during sleep. [C19: from NL, from Gk EN-[2] + *ouron* urine]
▸**enuretic** (͵ɛnjʊ'rɛtɪk) *adj*

envelop Ⓣ (ɪn'vɛləp) *vb* **envelops, enveloping, enveloped.** (*tr*) **1** to wrap or enclose as in a covering. **2** to conceal or obscure. **3** to surround (an enemy force). [C14: from OF *envoluper,* from EN-[1] + *voluper, voloper,* from ?]
▸**en'velopment** *n*

envelope Ⓣ ('ɛnvə͵ləʊp, 'ɒn-) *n* **1** a flat covering of paper, usually rectangular and with a flap that can be sealed, used to enclose a letter, etc. **2** any covering or wrapper. **3** *Biol.* any enclosing structure, such as a membrane, shell, or skin. **4** the bag enclosing gas in a balloon. **5** *Maths.* a curve or surface that is tangential to each one of a group of curves or surfaces. [C18: from F, from *envelopper* to wrap around; see ENVELOP]

envenom (ɪn'vɛnəm) *vb* (*tr*) **1** to fill or impregnate with venom; make poisonous. **2** to fill with bitterness or malice.

enviable Ⓣ ('ɛnvɪəbᵊl) *adj* exciting envy; fortunate or privileged.
▸**'enviableness** *n*

envious Ⓣ ('ɛnvɪəs) *adj* feeling, showing, or resulting from envy. [C13: from Anglo-Norman, ult. from L *invidiōsus* full of envy, INVIDIOUS; see ENVY]
▸**'enviously** *adv* ▸**'enviousness** *n*

environ Ⓣ (ɪn'vaɪrən) *vb* (*tr*) to encircle or surround. [C14: from OF *environner* to surround, from EN-[1] + *viron* a circle, from *virer* to turn, VEER]

environment Ⓣ (ɪn'vaɪrənmənt) *n* **1** external conditions or surroundings. **2** *Ecology.* the external surroundings in which a plant or animal lives, which influence its development and behaviour. **3** *Computing.* an operating system, program, or integrated suite of programs that provides all the facilities necessary for a particular application: *a word-processing environment.*
▸**en͵viron'mental** *adj*

environmentalist Ⓣ (ɪn͵vaɪrən'mɛntəlɪst) *n* **1** a specialist in the maintenance of ecological balance and the conservation of the environment. **2** a person concerned with issues that affect the environment, such as pollution.

environs Ⓣ (ɪn'vaɪrənz) *pl n* a surrounding area or region, esp. the suburbs or outskirts of a city.

envisage Ⓣ (ɪn'vɪzɪdʒ) *vb* **envisages, envisaging, envisaged.** (*tr*) **1** to form a mental image of; visualize. **2** to conceive of as a possibility in the future. [C19: from F, from EN-[1] + *visage* face, VISAGE]
▸**en'visagement** *n*

> **USAGE NOTE** It was formerly considered incorrect to use a clause after *envisage* as in *it is envisaged that the new centre will cost £40 million,* but this use is now acceptable.

envision Ⓣ (ɪn'vɪʒən) *vb* (*tr*) to conceive of as a possibility, esp. in the future; foresee.

envoy[1] Ⓣ ('ɛnvɔɪ) *n* **1** Also called: **minister, minister plenipotentiary.** a diplomat ranking between an ambassador and a minister resident. **2** an accredited agent or representative. [C17: from F, from *envoyer* to send, from Vulgar L *inviāre* (unattested) to send on a journey, from IN-[2] + *via* road]
▸**'envoyship** *n*

envoy[2] *or* **envoi** ('ɛnvɔɪ) *n* **1** a brief concluding stanza, notably in ballades. **2** a postscript in other forms of verse or prose. [C14: from OF, from *envoyer* to send; see ENVOY[1]]

envy Ⓣ ('ɛnvɪ) *n, pl* **envies. 1** a feeling of grudging or somewhat admiring discontent aroused by the possessions, achievements, or qualities of another. **2** the desire to have something possessed by another; covetousness. **3** an object of envy. ◆ *vb* **envies, envying, envied. 4** to be envious of (a person or thing). [C13: via OF from L *invidia,* from *invidēre* to eye maliciously, from IN-[2] + *vidēre* to see]
▸**'envier** *n* ▸**'envyingly** *adv*

enwrap *or* **inwrap** (ɪn'ræp) *vb* **enwraps, enwrapping, enwrapped.** (*tr*) **1** to wrap or cover up; envelop. **2** (*usually passive*) to engross or absorb.

enwreath (ɪn'riːð) *vb* (*tr*) to surround or encircle with or as with a wreath or wreaths.

enzootic (͵ɛnzəʊ'ɒtɪk) *adj* **1** (of diseases) affecting animals within a limited region. ◆ *n* **2** an enzootic disease. [C19: from EN-[2] + Gk *zōion* animal + -OTIC]
▸**͵enzo'otically** *adv*

enzyme ('ɛnzaɪm) *n* any of a group of complex proteins produced by living cells, that act as catalysts in specific biochemical reactions. [C19: from Med. Gk *enzumos* leavened, from Gk EN-[2] + *zumē* leaven]
▸**enzymatic** (͵ɛnzaɪ'mætɪk, -zɪ-) *or* **enzymic** (ɛn'zaɪmɪk, -'zɪm-) *adj*

enzyme-linked immunosorbent assay (͵ɪmjʊnəʊ'sɔːbənt) *n* the full name for **ELISA.**

eo- *combining form.* early or primeval: *Eocene; eohippus.* [from Gk, from *ēōs* dawn]

EOC *abbrev. for* Equal Opportunities Commission.

Eocene ('iːəʊ͵siːn) *adj* **1** of or denoting the second epoch of the Tertiary period, during which hooved mammals appeared. ◆ *n* **2 the.** the Eocene epoch or rock series. [C19: from EO- + -CENE]

eohippus (͵iːəʊ'hɪpəs) *n, pl* **eohippuses.** the earliest horse: an extinct Eocene dog-sized animal. [C19: NL, from EO- + Gk *hippos* horse]

Eolithic (͵iːəʊ'lɪθɪk) *adj* denoting or relating to the early part of the Stone Age, characterized by the use of crude stone tools (**eoliths**).

eon ('iːən, 'iːɒn) *n* **1** the usual US spelling of **aeon. 2** *Geol.* the longest division of geological time, comprising two or more eras.

eosin ('iːəʊsɪn) *or* **eosine** ('iːəʊsɪn, -͵siːn) *n* **1** a red fluorescent crystalline water-insoluble compound. Its soluble salts are used as dyes. **2** any of several similar dyes. [C19: from Gk *ēōs* dawn + -IN; referring to colour it gives to silk]

-eous *suffix forming adjectives.* relating to or having the nature of: *gaseous.* [from L *-eus*]

EP *n* an extended-play gramophone record, usually 7 inches (18 cm) in diameter: a longer recording than a single.

EPA *abbrev. for* eicosapentaenoic acid: a fatty acid, found in certain fish oils, that can reduce blood cholesterol.

epact ('iːpækt) *n* **1** the difference in time, about 11 days, between the solar year and the lunar year. **2** the number of days between the beginning of the calendar year and the new moon immediately preceding this. [C16: via LL from Gk *epaktē,* from *epagein* to bring in, intercalate]

eparch ('ɛpɑːk) *n* **1** a bishop or metropolitan in the Orthodox Church. **2** a governor of a subdivision of a province of modern Greece. [C17: from Gk *eparkhos,* from *epi-* over, on + -ARCH]
▸**'eparchy** *n*

epaulette *or US* **epaulet** ('ɛpə͵lɛt, -lɪt) *n* a piece of ornamental material on the shoulder of a garment, esp. a military uniform. [C18: from F, from *épaule* shoulder, from L *spatula* shoulder blade]

épée ('ɛpeɪ) *n* a sword similar to the foil but with a heavier blade. [C19: from F: sword, from L *spatha,* from Gk *spathē* blade; see SPADE[1]]
▸**'épéeist** *n*

epeirogeny (͵ɛpaɪ'rɒdʒɪnɪ) *or* **epeirogenesis** (ɪ͵paɪrəʊ'dʒɛnɪsɪs) *n* the formation of continents by relatively slow displacements of the earth's crust. [C19: from Gk *ēpeiros* continent + -GENY]
▸**epeirogenic** (ɪ͵paɪrəʊ'dʒɛnɪk) *or* **epeirogenetic** (ɪ͵paɪrəʊdʒɪ'nɛtɪk) *adj*

epergne (ɪ'pɜːn) *n* an ornamental centrepiece for a table, holding fruit, flowers, etc. [C18: prob. from F *épargne* a saving, from *épargner* to economize, of Gmc origin]

epexegesis (ɛ͵pɛksɪ'dʒiːsɪs) *n, pl* **epexegesises** (-͵siːz). *Rhetoric.* **1** the addition of a phrase, clause, or sentence to a text to provide further explanation. **2** the phrase, clause, or sentence added for this purpose. [C17: from Gk; see EPI-, EXEGESIS]
▸**epexegetic** (ɛ͵pɛksɪ'dʒɛtɪk) *or* **ep͵exe'getical** *adj*

Eph. *or* **Ephes.** *Bible. abbrev. for* Ephesians.

ephah *or* **epha** ('iːfə) *n* a Hebrew unit of measure equal to approximately one bushel or about 33 litres. [C16: from Heb., from Egyptian]

ephedrine *or* **ephedrin** (ɪ'fɛdrɪn, 'ɛfɪ͵driːn, -drɪn) *n* a white crystalline alkaloid used for the treatment of asthma and hay fever. [C19: from NL from L from Gk, from EPI- + *hedra* seat + -INE[2]]

ephemera (ɪ'fɛmərə) *n, pl* **ephemeras** *or* **ephemerae** (-ə͵riː). **1** a mayfly, esp. one of the genus *Ephemera.* **2** something transitory or short-lived. **3** (*functioning as pl*) collectable items not originally intended to be

THESAURUS

voice **2** = **state**, declare, proclaim, promulgate, pronounce, propound, publish

envelop *vb* **1, 2** = **enclose**, blanket, cloak, conceal, cover, embrace, encase, encircle, encompass, enfold, engulf, enwrap, hide, obscure, sheathe, shroud, surround, swaddle, swathe, veil, wrap

envelope *n* **2** = **wrapping**, case, casing, coating, cover, covering, jacket, sheath, shell, skin, wrapper

enviable *adj* = **desirable**, advantageous, blessed, covetable, favoured, fortunate, lucky, much to be desired, privileged, to die for (*inf.*)
Antonyms *adj* disagreeable, painful, thankless, uncomfortable, undesirable, unenviable, unpleasant

envious *adj* = **covetous**, begrudging, green-eyed, green with envy, grudging, jaundiced, jealous, malicious, resentful, spiteful

environ *vb* = **surround**, beset, besiege, encircle, enclose, encompass, engird, envelop, gird, hem, invest (*rare*), ring

environment *n* **1** = **surroundings**, atmosphere, background, conditions, context, domain, element, habitat, locale, medium, milieu, scene, setting, situation, territory

environmental *adj* **2** = **ecological**, green

environmentalist *n* **1, 2** = **conservationist**, ecologist, friend of the earth, green

environs *pl n* = **surrounding area**, district, locality, neighbourhood, outskirts, precincts, purlieus, suburbs, vicinity

envisage *vb* **1** = **imagine**, conceive (of), conceptualize, contemplate, fancy, picture, think up, visualize **2** = **foresee**, anticipate, envision, predict, see

envision *vb* = **conceive of**, anticipate, contemplate, envisage, foresee, predict, see, visualize

envoy[1] *n* **2** = **messenger**, agent, ambassador, courier, delegate, deputy, diplomat, emissary, intermediary, legate, minister, plenipotentiary, representative

envy *n* **1, 2** = **covetousness**, enviousness, grudge, hatred, ill will, jealousy, malice, malignity, resentfulness, resentment, spite, the green-eyed monster (*inf.*) ◆ *vb* **4** = **covet**, be envious (of), begrudge, be jealous (of), grudge, resent

long-lasting, such as tickets, posters, etc. **4** a plural of **ephemeron.** [C16: see EPHEMERAL]

ephemeral ⓣ (ɪ'fɛmərəl) *adj* **1** transitory; short-lived: *ephemeral pleasure.* ◆ *n* **2** a short-lived organism, such as the mayfly. [C16: from Gk *ephēmeros* lasting only a day, from *hēmera* day]
▸**e,phemer'ality** *or* **e'phemeralness** *n*

ephemerid (ɪ'fɛmərɪd) *n* any insect of the order *Ephemeroptera* (or *Ephemerida*), which comprises the mayflies. Also: **ephemeropteran.** [C19: from NL, from Gk *ephēmeros* short-lived + -ID[1]]

ephemeris (ɪ'fɛmərɪs) *n, pl* **ephemerides** (,ɛfɪ'mɛrɪ,di:z). a table giving the future positions of a planet, comet, or satellite during a specified period. [C16: from L, from Gk: diary, journal; see EPHEMERAL]

ephemeron (ɪ'fɛmə,rɒn) *n, pl* **ephemera** (-ərə) *or* **ephemerons.** (*usually pl*). something transitory or short-lived. [C16: see EPHEMERAL]

ephod ('i:fɒd) *n Bible.* an embroidered vestment worn by priests in ancient Israel. [C14: from Heb.]

ephor ('ɛfɔ:) *n, pl* **ephors** *or* **ephori** (-ə,raɪ) (in ancient Greece) a senior magistrate, esp. one of the five Spartan ephors, who wielded effective power. [C16: from Gk, from *ephoran* to supervise, from EPI- + *horan* to look]
▸**'ephoral** *adj* ▸**'ephorate** *n*

epi-, eph-, *or before a vowel* **ep-** *prefix* **1** upon; above; over: *epidermis; epicentre.* **2** in addition to: *epiphenomenon.* **3** after: *epilogue.* **4** near; close to: *epicalyx.* [from Gk, from *epi* (prep)]

epic ('ɛpɪk) *n* **1** a long narrative poem recounting in elevated style the deeds of a legendary hero. **2** the genre of epic poetry. **3** any work of literature, film, etc., having qualities associated with the epic. **4** an episode in the lives of men in which heroic deeds are performed. ◆ *adj* **5** denoting, relating to, or characteristic of an epic or epics. **6** of heroic or impressive proportions. [C16: from L, from Gk *epikos,* from *epos* speech, word, song]

epicalyx (,ɛpɪ'keɪlɪks, -'kæl-) *n, pl* **epicalyxes** *or* **epicalyces** (-lɪ,si:z). *Bot.* a series of small sepal-like bracts forming an outer calyx beneath the true calyx in some flowers.

epicanthus (,ɛpɪ'kænθəs) *n, pl* **epicanthi** (-θaɪ). a fold of skin extending vertically over the inner angle of the eye: characteristic of Mongolian peoples. [C19: NL, from EPI- + L *canthus* corner of the eye, from Gk *kanthos*]
▸**,epi'canthic** *adj*

epicardium (,ɛpɪ'kɑ:dɪəm) *n, pl* **epicardia** (-dɪə). *Anat.* the innermost layer of the pericardium. [C19: NL, from EPI- + Gk *kardia* heart]
▸**,epi'cardiac** *or* **,epi'cardial** *adj*

epicarp ('ɛpɪ,kɑ:p) *or* **exocarp** *n* the outermost layer of the pericarp of fruits. [C19: from F, from EPI- + Gk *karpos* fruit]

epicene ('ɛpɪ,si:n) *adj* **1** having the characteristics of both sexes. **2** of neither sex; sexless. **3** effeminate. **4** *Grammar.* **4a** denoting a noun that may refer to a male or a female. **4b** (in Latin, Greek, etc.) denoting a noun that retains the same gender regardless of the sex of the referent. [C15: from L *epicoenus* of both genders, from Gk *epikoinos* common to many, from *koinos* common]
▸**,epi'cenism** *n*

epicentre *or US* **epicenter** ('ɛpɪ,sɛntə) *n* the point on the earth's surface immediately above the origin of an earthquake. [C19: from NL, from Gk *epikentros* over the centre, from EPI- + CENTRE]
▸**,epi'central** *adj*

epicure ⓣ ('ɛpɪ,kjʊə) *n* **1** a person who cultivates a discriminating palate for good food and drink. **2** a person devoted to sensual pleasures. [C16: from Med. L *epicūrus,* after *Epicurus;* see EPICUREAN]
▸**'epicur,ism** *n*

epicurean ⓣ (,ɛpɪkjʊ'ri:ən) *adj* **1** devoted to sensual pleasures, esp. food and drink. **2** suitable for an epicure. ◆ *n* **3** an epicure; gourmet.
▸**,epicu'rean,ism** *n*

Epicurean (,ɛpɪkjʊ'ri:ən) *adj* **1** of or relating to the philosophy of Epicurus (341–270 B.C.), Greek philosopher, who held that the highest good is pleasure or freedom from pain. ◆ *n* **2** a follower of the philosophy of Epicurus.
▸**,Epicu'rean,ism** *n*

epicycle ('ɛpɪ,saɪk[ə]l) *n* a circle that rolls around the inside or outside of another circle. [C14: from LL, from Gk; see EPI-, CYCLE]
▸**epicyclic** (,ɛpɪ'saɪklɪk, -'sɪklɪk) *or* **,epi'cyclical** *adj*

epicyclic train *n* a cluster of gears consisting of a central gearwheel, a coaxial gearwheel of greater diameter, and one or more planetary gears engaging with both of them.

epicycloid (,ɛpɪ'saɪklɔɪd) *n* the curve described by a point on the circumference of a circle as this circle rolls around the outside of another fixed circle.
▸**,epicy'cloidal** *adj*

epideictic (,ɛpɪ'daɪktɪk) *adj* designed to display something, esp. the skill of the speaker in rhetoric. Also: **epidictic** (,ɛpɪ'dɪktɪk). [C18: from Gk, from *epideiknunai* to display, from *deiknunai* to show]

epidemic ⓣ (,ɛpɪ'dɛmɪk) *adj* **1** (esp. of a disease) attacking or affecting many persons simultaneously in a community or area. ◆ *n* **2** a widespread occurrence of a disease. **3** a rapid development, spread, or growth of something. [C17: from F, via LL from Gk *epidēmia,* lit.: among the people, from EPI- + *dēmos* people]
▸**,epi'demically** *adv*

epidemiology (,ɛpɪ,di:mɪ'ɒlədʒɪ) *n* the branch of medical science concerned with the occurrence, distribution, and control of diseases in populations.
▸**epidemiological** (,ɛpɪ,di:mɪə'lɒdʒɪk[ə]l) *adj* ▸**,epi,demi'ologist** *n*

epidermis (,ɛpɪ'dɜ:mɪs) *n* **1** the thin protective outer layer of the skin. **2** the outer layer of cells of an invertebrate. **3** the outer protective layer of cells of a plant. [C17: via LL from Gk, from EPI- + *derma* skin]
▸**,epi'dermal, ,epi'dermic,** *or* **,epi'dermoid** *adj*

epidiascope (,ɛpɪ'daɪə,skəʊp) *n* an optical device for projecting a magnified image onto a screen.

epididymis (,ɛpɪ'dɪdɪmɪs) *n, pl* **epididymides** (-dɪ'dɪmɪ,di:z). *Anat.* a convoluted tube behind each testis, in which spermatozoa are stored and conveyed to the vas deferens. [C17: from Gk *epididumis,* from EPI- + *didumos* twin, testicle]

epidural (,ɛpɪ'djʊərəl) *adj* **1** Also: **extradural.** upon or outside the dura mater. ◆ *n* **2** Also: **epidural anaesthesia, spinal anaesthesia. 2a** injection of anaesthetic into the space outside the dura mater enveloping the spinal cord. **2b** anaesthesia induced by this method. [C19: from EPI- + DUR(A MATER) + -AL[1]]

epigamic (,ɛpɪ'gæmɪk) *adj Zool.* attractive to the opposite sex: *epigamic coloration.*

epigeal (,ɛpɪ'dʒi:əl), **epigean,** *or* **epigeous** *adj* **1** of or relating to seed germination in which the cotyledons appear above the ground. **2** living or growing on or close to the surface of the ground. [C19: from Gk *epigeios* of the earth, from EPI- + *gē* earth]

epiglottis (,ɛpɪ'glɒtɪs) *n, pl* **epiglottises** *or* **epiglottides** (-tɪ,di:z). a thin cartilaginous flap that covers the entrance to the larynx during swallowing, preventing food from entering the trachea.
▸**,epi'glottal** *or* **,epi'glottic** *adj*

epigram ⓣ ('ɛpɪ,græm) *n* **1** a witty, often paradoxical remark, concisely expressed. **2** a short poem, esp. one having a witty and ingenious ending. [C15: from L *epigramma,* from Gk: inscription, from *graphein* to write]
▸**,epigram'matic** *adj* ▸**,epigram'matically** *adv*

epigrammatize *or* **epigrammatise** (,ɛpɪ'græmə,taɪz) *vb* **epigrammatizes, epigrammatizing, epigrammatized** *or* **epigrammatises, epigrammatising, epigrammatised.** to make an epigram (about).
▸**,epi'grammatism** *n* ▸**,epi'grammatist** *n*

epigraph ('ɛpɪ,grɑ:f) *n* **1** a quotation at the beginning of a book, chapter, etc. **2** an inscription on a monument or building. [C17: from Gk; see EPIGRAM]
▸**epigraphic** (,ɛpɪ'græfɪk) or **,epi'graphical** *adj*

epigraphy (ɪ'pɪgrəfɪ) *n* **1** the study of ancient inscriptions. **2** epigraphs collectively.
▸**e'pigraphist** *or* **e'pigrapher** *n*

epilator ('ɛpɪ,leɪtə) *n* an electrical appliance consisting of a metal spiral head that rotates at high speed, plucking unwanted hair.

epilepsy ('ɛpɪ,lɛpsɪ) *n* a disorder of the central nervous system characterized by periodic loss of consciousness with or without convulsions. [C16: from LL *epilēpsia,* from Gk, from *epilambanein* to attack, seize]

epileptic (,ɛpɪ'lɛptɪk) *adj* **1** of, relating to, or having epilepsy. ◆ *n* **2** a person who has epilepsy.
▸**,epi'leptically** *adv*

epilogue ⓣ ('ɛpɪ,lɒg) *n* **1a** a speech addressed to the audience by an actor at the end of a play. **1b** the actor speaking this. **2** a short postscript to any literary work. **3** *Brit.* the concluding programme of the day on a radio or television station. [C15: from L, from Gk *epilogos,* from *logos* word, speech]
▸**epilogist** (ɪ'pɪlədʒɪst) *n*

epinephrine (,ɛpɪ'nɛfrɪn, -ri:n) *or* **epinephrin** *n* a US name for **adrenaline.** [C19: from EPI- + *nephro-* + -INE[2]]

epiphany (ɪ'pɪfənɪ) *n, pl* **epiphanies. 1** the manifestation of a supernatural or divine reality. **2** any moment of great or sudden revelation.
▸**epiphanic** (,ɛpɪ'fænɪk) *adj*

Epiphany (ɪ'pɪfənɪ) *n, pl* **Epiphanies.** a Christian festival held on Jan. 6, commemorating, in the Western Church, the manifestation of Christ to the Magi. [C17: via Church L from Gk *epiphaneia* an appearing, from EPI- + *phainein* to show]

epiphenomenon (,ɛpɪfɪ'nɒmɪnən) *n, pl* **epiphenomenona** (-nə). **1** a sec-

THESAURUS

ephemeral *adj* **1** = **brief,** evanescent, fleeting, flitting, fugacious, fugitive, impermanent, momentary, passing, short, short-lived, temporary, transient, transitory
Antonyms *adj* abiding, durable, enduring, eternal, immortal, lasting, long-lasting, persisting, steadfast

epicure *n* **1** = **gourmet,** *bon vivant,* epicurean, foodie, gastronome **2** = **hedonist,** glutton, gourmand, sensualist, sybarite, voluptuary

epicurean *adj* **1** = **hedonistic,** bacchanalian, gluttonous, libertine, luscious, lush, luxurious, pleasure-seeking, self-indulgent, sensual, sybaritic, voluptuous ◆ *n* **3** = **gourmet,** *bon vivant,* epicure, foodie, gastronome

epidemic *adj* **1** = **widespread,** general, pandemic, prevailing, prevalent, rampant, rife, sweeping, wide-ranging ◆ *n* **2** = **spread,** contagion, growth, outbreak, plague, rash, upsurge, wave

epigram *n* **1** = **witticism,** aphorism, bon mot, quip

epigrammatic *adj* **1** = **witty,** concise, laconic, piquant, pithy, pointed, pungent, sharp, short, succinct, terse

epilogue *n* **1, 2** = **conclusion,** afterword, coda, concluding speech, postscript
Antonyms *n* exordium, foreword, introduction, preamble, preface, prelude, prologue

ondary or additional phenomenon. **2** *Philosophy.* mind or consciousness regarded as a by-product of the biological activity of the human brain. **3** *Pathol.* an unexpected symptom or occurrence during the course of a disease.
▸ **ˌepipheˈnomenal** *adj*

epiphyte (ˈɛpɪˌfaɪt) *n* a plant that grows on another plant but is not parasitic on it. [C19: via NL from Gk, from EPI- + *phusis* growth]
▸ **epiphytic** (ˌɛpɪˈfɪtɪk), **ˌepiˈphytal,** *or* **ˌepiˈphytical** *adj*

Epis. *abbrev. for:* **1** Also: **Episc.** Episcopal *or* Episcopalian. **2** *Bible.* Also: **Epist.** Epistle.

episcopacy (ɪˈpɪskəpəsɪ) *n, pl* **episcopacies. 1** government of a Church by bishops. **2** another word for **episcopate.**

episcopal (ɪˈpɪskəpᵊl) *adj* of, denoting, governed by, or relating to a bishop or bishops. [C15: from Church L, from *episcopus* BISHOP]

Episcopal (ɪˈpɪskəpᵊl) *adj* of or denoting the Episcopal Church, an autonomous church of Scotland and the US which is in full communion with the Church of England.

episcopalian (ɪˌpɪskəˈpeɪlɪən) *adj also* **episcopal. 1** practising or advocating the principle of Church government by bishops. ◆ *n* **2** an advocate of such Church government.
▸ **eˌpiscoˈpalianism** *n*

Episcopalian (ɪˌpɪskəˈpeɪlɪən) *adj* **1** belonging to or denoting the Episcopal Church. ◆ *n* **2** a member or adherent of this Church.

episcopate (ɪˈpɪskəpɪt, -ˌpeɪt) *n* **1** the office, status, or term of office of a bishop. **2** bishops collectively.

episiotomy (ɪˌpiːzɪˈɒtəmɪ) *n, pl* **episiotomies.** surgical incision into the perineum during labour to prevent its laceration during childbirth. [C20: from Gk *epision* pubic region + -TOMY]

episode ⓘ (ˈɛpɪˌsəʊd) *n* **1** an event or series of events. **2** any of the sections into which a serialized novel or radio or television programme is divided. **3** an incident or sequence that forms part of a narrative but may be a digression from the main story. **4** (in ancient Greek tragedy) a section between two choric songs. **5** *Music.* a contrasting section between statements of the subject, as in a fugue. [C17: from Gk *epeisodion* something added, from *epi-* (in addition) + *eisodios* coming in, from *eis-* in + *hodos* road]

episodic ⓘ (ˌɛpɪˈsɒdɪk) *or* **episodical** *adj* **1** resembling or relating to an episode. **2** divided into episodes. **3** irregular or sporadic.
▸ **ˌepiˈsodically** *adv*

epistaxis (ˌɛpɪˈstæksɪs) *n* the technical name for **nosebleed.** [C18: from Gk: a dropping, from *epistazein* to drop on, from *stazein* to drip]

epistemology (ɪˌpɪstɪˈmɒlədʒɪ) *n* the theory of knowledge, esp. the critical study of its validity, methods, and scope. [C19: from Gk *epistēmē* knowledge]
▸ **epistemological** (ɪˌpɪstɪməˈlɒdʒɪkᵊl) *adj* ▸ **eˌpisteˈmologist** *n*

epistle ⓘ (ɪˈpɪsᵊl) *n* **1** a letter, esp. one that is long, formal, or didactic. **2** a literary work in letter form, esp. a verse letter. [OE *epistol,* via L from Gk *epistolē*]

Epistle (ɪˈpɪsᵊl) *n* **1** *Bible.* any of the letters of the apostles. **2** a reading from one of the Epistles, part of the Eucharistic service in many Christian Churches.

epistolary (ɪˈpɪstələrɪ) *or (arch.)* **epistolatory** *adj* **1** relating to, denoting, conducted by, or contained in letters. **2** (of a novel, etc.) in the form of a series of letters.

epistyle (ˈɛpɪˌstaɪl) *n* another name for **architrave** (sense 1). [C17: via L from Gk, from EPI- + *stulos* column, STYLE]

epitaph ⓘ (ˈɛpɪˌtɑːf) *n* **1** a commemorative inscription on a tombstone or monument. **2** a commemorative speech or written passage. **3** a final judgment on a person or thing. [C14: via L from Gk, from EPI- + *taphos* tomb]
▸ **epitaphic** (ˌɛpɪˈtæfɪk) *adj* ▸ **ˈepiˌtaphist** *n*

epitaxy (ˈɛpɪˌtæksɪ) *n* the growth of a layer of one substance on the surface of a crystal so that the layer has the same structure as the underlying crystal.
▸ **epitaxial** (ˌɛpɪˈtæksɪəl) *adj*

epithalamium (ˌɛpɪθəˈleɪmɪəm) *or* **epithalamion** *n, pl* **epithalamia** (-mɪə). a poem or song written to celebrate a marriage. [C17: from L, from Gk *epithalamion* marriage song, from *thalamos* bridal chamber]
▸ **epithalamic** (ˌɛpɪθəˈlæmɪk) *adj*

epithelium (ˌɛpɪˈθiːlɪəm) *n, pl* **epitheliums** *or* **epithelia** (-lɪə). an animal cellular tissue covering the external and internal surfaces of the body. [C18: NL, from EPI- + Gk *thēlē* nipple]
▸ **ˌepiˈthelial** *adj*

epithet ⓘ (ˈɛpɪˌθɛt) *n* a descriptive word or phrase added to or substituted for a person's name. [C16: from L, from Gk, from *epitithenai* to add, from *tithenai* to put]
▸ **ˌepiˈthetic** *or* **ˌepiˈthetical** *adj*

epitome ⓘ (ɪˈpɪtəmɪ) *n* **1** a typical example of a characteristic or class; embodiment; personification. **2** a summary of a written work; abstract. [C16: via L from Gk, from *epitemnein* to abridge, from EPI- + *temnein* to cut]
▸ **epitomical** (ˌɛpɪˈtɒmɪkᵊl) *or* **ˌepiˈtomic** *adj*

epitomize ⓘ *or* **epitomise** (ɪˈpɪtəˌmaɪz) *vb* **epitomizes, epitomizing, epitomized** *or* **epitomises, epitomising, epitomised.** (*tr*) **1** to be a personification of; typify. **2** to make an epitome of.
▸ **eˈpitomist** *n* ▸ **eˌpitomiˈzation** *or* **eˌpitomiˈsation** *n*

epizootic (ˌɛpɪzəʊˈɒtɪk) *adj* **1** (of a disease) suddenly and temporarily affecting a large number of animals. ◆ *n* **2** an epizootic disease.

EPNS *abbrev. for* electroplated nickel silver.

epoch ⓘ (ˈiːpɒk) *n* **1** a point in time beginning a new or distinctive period. **2** a long period of time marked by some predominant characteristic; era. **3** *Astron.* a precise date to which information relating to a celestial body is referred. **4** a unit of geological time within a period during which a series of rocks is formed. [C17: from NL, from Gk *epokhē* cessation]
▸ **epochal** (ˈɛpˌɒkᵊl) *adj*

epode (ˈɛpəʊd) *n Greek prosody.* **1** the part of a lyric ode that follows the strophe and the antistrophe. **2** a type of lyric poem composed of couplets in which a long line is followed by a shorter one. [C16: via L from Gk, from *epaidein* to sing after, from *aidein* to sing]

eponym (ˈɛpənɪm) *n* **1** a name, esp. a place name, derived from the name of a real or mythical person. **2** the name of the person from which such a name is derived. [C19: from Gk *epōnumos* giving a significant name]
▸ **eˈponymy** *n*

eponymous (ɪˈpɒnɪməs) *adj* **1** (of a person) being the person after whom a literary work, film, etc., is named: *the eponymous heroine in the film of Jane Eyre.* **2** (of a literary work, film, etc.) named after its central character or creator: *The Stooges' eponymous debut album.*
▸ **eˈponymously** *adv*

EPOS (ˈiːpɒs) *n acronym for* electronic point of sale.

epoxidize *or* **epoxidise** *vb* **epoxidizes, epoxidizing, epoxidized** *or* **epoxidises, epoxidising, epoxidised.** (*tr*) to convert into or treat with an epoxy resin.

epoxy (ɪˈpɒksɪ) *adj Chem.* **1** of, consisting of, or containing an oxygen atom joined to two different groups that are themselves joined to other groups: *epoxy group.* **2** of, relating to, or consisting of an epoxy resin. ◆ *n, pl* **epoxies. 3** short for **epoxy resin.** [C20: from EPI- + OXY-[2]]

epoxy *or* **epoxide resin** (ɪˈpɒksaɪd) *n* any of various tough resistant thermosetting synthetic resins containing epoxy groups: used in surface coatings, laminates, and adhesives.

eps *abbrev. for* earnings per share.

epsilon (ˈɛpsɪˌlɒn) *n* the fifth letter of the Greek alphabet (Ε, ε). [Gk *e psilon,* lit.: simple *e*]

Epsom salts (ˈɛpsəm) *n* (*functioning as sing or pl*) a medicinal preparation of hydrated magnesium sulphate, used as a purgative, etc. [C18: after *Epsom,* a town in England, where they occur in the water]

equable ⓘ (ˈɛkwəbᵊl) *adj* **1** even-tempered; placid. **2** unvarying; uniform: *an equable climate.* [C17: from L *aequābilis,* from *aequāre* to make equal]
▸ **ˌequaˈbility** *or* **ˈequableness** *n*

equal ⓘ (ˈiːkwəl) *adj* **1** (often foll. by *to* or *with*) identical in size, quantity, degree, intensity, etc. **2** having identical privileges, rights, status, etc. **3** having uniform effect or application: *equal opportunities.* **4** evenly balanced or proportioned. **5** (usually foll. by *to*) having the necessary or adequate strength, ability, means, etc. (for). ◆ *n* **6** a person or thing equal to another, esp. in merit, ability, etc. ◆ *vb* **equals, equalling, equalled** *or US* **equals, equaling, equaled. 7** (*tr*) to be equal to; match. **8** (*intr;* usually foll. by *out*) to become equal. **9** (*tr*) to make or do something equal to. [C14: from L *aequālis,* from *aequus* level]
▸ **ˈequally** *adv*

> **USAGE NOTE** The use of *more equal* as in *from now on their relationship will be a more equal one* is acceptable in modern English usage. *Equally* is preferred to *equally as* in sentences such as *reassuring the victims is equally important. Just as* is preferred to *equally as* in sentences such as *their surprise was just as great as his.*

THESAURUS

episode *n* **1** = **event**, adventure, affair, business, circumstance, escapade, experience, happening, incident, matter, occurrence **2** = **part**, chapter, instalment, passage, scene, section

episodic *adj* **3** = **irregular**, anecdotal, digressive, disconnected, discursive, disjointed, intermittent, occasional, picaresque, rambling, sporadic, wandering

epistle *n* **1, 2** = **letter**, communication, message, missive, note

epitaph *n* **1** = **monument**, inscription

epithet *n* = **name**, appellation, description, designation, moniker *or* monicker (*sl.*), nickname, sobriquet, tag, title

epitome *n* **1** = **personification**, archetype, embodiment, essence, exemplar, norm, quintessence, representation, type, typical example **2** = **summary**, abbreviation, abridgment, abstract, compendium, condensation, conspectus, contraction, digest, précis, résumé, syllabus, synopsis

epitomize *vb* **1** = **typify**, embody, exemplify, illustrate, incarnate, personify, represent, symbolize **2** = **summarize**, abbreviate, abridge, abstract, condense, contract, curtail, cut, encapsulate, précis, reduce, shorten, synopsize

epoch *n* **2** = **era**, age, date, period, time

equable *adj* **1** = **even-tempered**, agreeable, calm, composed, easy-going, imperturbable, level-headed, placid, serene, temperate, unexcitable, unfazed (*inf.*), unflappable (*inf.*), unruffled **2** = **constant**, consistent, even, on an even keel, regular, smooth, stable, steady, temperate, tranquil, unchanging, uniform, unvarying
Antonyms *adj* ≠ **even-tempered:** excitable, nervous, temperamental ≠ **constant:** changeable, fitful, inconsistent, irregular, temperamental, uneven, unstable, volatile

equal *adj* **1** = **identical**, alike, commensurate, corresponding, equivalent, like, matched, one and the same, proportionate, tantamount, the same, uniform **4** = **even**, balanced, evenly bal-

equalitarian (ɪˌkwɒlɪˈtɛərɪən) *adj, n* a less common word for **egalitarian.** ▸**eˌqualiˈtarianism** *n*

equality Ⓣ (ɪˈkwɒlɪtɪ) *n, pl* **equalities.** the state of being equal.

equalize Ⓣ *or* **equalise** (ˈiːkwəˌlaɪz) *vb* **equalizes, equalizing, equalized** *or* **equalises, equalising, equalised. 1** (*tr*) to make equal or uniform. **2** (*intr*) (in sports) to reach the same score as one's opponent or opponents. ▸ˌ**equaliˈzation** *or* ˌ**equaliˈsation** *n*

equal opportunity *n* **a** the offering of employment, pay, or promotion without discrimination as to sex, race, etc. **b** (*as modifier*): *an equal-opportunities employer.*

equal sign *or* **equals sign** *n* the symbol =, used to indicate a mathematical equality.

equanimity Ⓣ (ˌiːkwəˈnɪmɪtɪ, ˌɛkwə-) *n* calmness of mind or temper; composure. [C17: from L, from *aequus* even, EQUAL + *animus* mind, spirit]
▸**equanimous** (ɪˈkwænɪməs) *adj*

equate Ⓣ (ɪˈkweɪt) *vb* **equates, equating, equated.** (*mainly tr*) **1** to make or regard as equivalent or similar. **2** *Maths.* to indicate the equality of; form an equation from. **3** (*intr*) to be equal. [C15: from L *aequāre* to make EQUAL]
▸**eˈquatable** *adj* ▸**eˌquataˈbility** *n*

equation Ⓣ (ɪˈkweɪʒən, -ʃən) *n* **1** a mathematical statement that two expressions are equal. **2** the act of equating. **3** the state of being equal, equivalent, or equally balanced. **4** a representation of a chemical reaction using symbols of the elements. **5** a situation or problem in which a number of factors need to be considered.
▸**eˈquational** *adj* ▸**eˈquationally** *adv*

equator (ɪˈkweɪtə) *n* **1** the great circle of the earth, equidistant from the poles, dividing the N and S hemispheres. **2** a circle dividing a sphere into two equal parts. **3** *Astron.* See **celestial equator.** [C14: from Med. L (*circulus*) *aequātor* (*diei et noctis*) (circle) that equalizes (the day and night), from L *aequāre* to make EQUAL]

equatorial (ˌɛkwəˈtɔːrɪəl) *adj* **1** of, like, or existing at or near the equator. **2** *Astron.* of or referring to the celestial equator. **3** (of a telescope) mounted on perpendicular axes, one of which is parallel to the earth's axis. ◆ *n* **4** an equatorial mounting for a telescope.

equerry (ˈɛkwərɪ; *at the British court* ɪˈkwɛrɪ) *n, pl* **equerries. 1** an officer attendant upon the British sovereign. **2** (formerly) an officer in a royal household responsible for the horses. [C16: alteration (through infl. of L *equus* horse) of earlier *escuirie*, from OF: stable]

equestrian Ⓣ (ɪˈkwɛstrɪən) *adj* **1** of or relating to horses and riding. **2** on horseback; mounted. **3** of, relating to, or composed of knights. ◆ *n* **4** a person skilled in riding and horsemanship. [C17: from L *equestris*, from *equus* horse]
▸**eˈquestrianˌism** *n*

equi- *combining form.* equal or equally: *equidistant; equilateral.*

equiangular (ˌiːkwɪˈæŋɡjʊlə) *adj* having all angles equal.

equidistant (ˌiːkwɪˈdɪstənt) *adj* equally distant.
▸ˌ**equiˈdistance** *n* ▸ˌ**equiˈdistantly** *adv*

equilateral (ˌiːkwɪˈlætərəl) *adj* **1** having all sides of equal length. ◆ *n* **2** a geometric figure having all sides of equal length. **3** a side that is equal in length to other sides.

equilibrant (ɪˈkwɪlɪbrənt) *n* a force capable of balancing another force.

equilibrate (ˌiːkwɪˈlaɪbreɪt, ɪˈkwɪlɪˌbreɪt) *vb* **equilibrates, equilibrating, equilibrated.** to bring to or be in equilibrium; balance. [C17: from LL, from *aequilībris* in balance; see EQUILIBRIUM]
▸ˌ**equiliˈbration** *n*

equilibrist (ɪˈkwɪlɪbrɪst) *n* a person who performs balancing feats, esp. on a high wire.
▸**eˌquiliˈbristic** *adj*

equilibrium Ⓣ (ˌiːkwɪˈlɪbrɪəm) *n, pl* **equilibriums** *or* **equilibria** (-rɪə). **1** a stable condition in which forces cancel one another. **2** a state or feeling of mental balance; composure. **3** any unchanging state of a body, system, etc., resulting from the balance of the influences to which it is subjected. **4** *Physiol.* a state of bodily balance, maintained primarily by receptors in the inner ear. [C17: from L, from *aequi-* EQUI- + *lībra* pound, balance]

equine (ˈɛkwaɪn) *adj* of, relating to, or resembling a horse. [C18: from L, from *equus* horse]

equinoctial (ˌiːkwɪˈnɒkʃəl) *adj* **1** relating to or occurring at either or both equinoxes. **2** *Astron.* of or relating to the celestial equator. ◆ *n* **3** a storm or gale at or near an equinox. **4** another name for **celestial equator.** [C14: from L: see EQUINOX]

equinoctial circle *or* **line** *n* another name for **celestial equator.**

equinoctial point *n* either of two points at which the celestial equator intersects the ecliptic.

equinox (ˈiːkwɪˌnɒks) *n* **1** either of the two occasions, six months apart, when day and night are of equal length. In the N hemisphere the **vernal equinox** occurs around March 21 (Sept. 23 in the S hemisphere). The **autumnal equinox** occurs around Sept. 23 in the N hemisphere (March 21 in the S hemisphere). **2** another name for **equinoctial point.** [C14: from Med. L *equinoxium*, changed from L *aequinoctium*, from *aequi-* EQUI- + *nox* night]

equip Ⓣ (ɪˈkwɪp) *vb* **equips, equipping, equipped.** (*tr*) **1** to furnish (with necessary supplies, etc.). **2** (*usually passive*) to provide with abilities, understanding, etc. **3** to dress out; attire. [C16: from OF *eschiper* to embark, fit out (a ship), of Gmc origin]
▸**eˈquipper** *n*

equipage Ⓣ (ˈɛkwɪpɪdʒ) *n* **1** a horse-drawn carriage, esp. one attended by liveried footmen. **2** the stores and equipment of a military unit. **3** *Arch.* a set of useful articles.

equipment Ⓣ (ɪˈkwɪpmənt) *n* **1** an act or instance of equipping. **2** the items provided. **3** a set of tools, kit, etc., assembled for a specific purpose.

equipoise (ˈɛkwɪˌpɔɪz) *n* **1** even balance of weight; equilibrium. **2** a counterbalance; counterpoise. ◆ *vb* **equipoises, equipoising, equipoised. 3** (*tr*) to offset or balance.

equipollent (ˌiːkwɪˈpɒlənt) *adj* **1** equal or equivalent in significance, power, or effect. ◆ *n* **2** something that is equipollent. [C15: from L *aequipollēns* of equal importance, from EQUI- + *pollēre* to be able, be strong]
▸ˌ**equiˈpollence** *or* ˌ**equiˈpollency** *n*

equisetum (ˌɛkwɪˈsiːtəm) *n, pl* **equisetums** *or* **equiseta** (-tə). any plant of the horsetail genus. [C19: NL, from L, from *equus* horse + *saeta* bristle]

equitable Ⓣ (ˈɛkwɪtəbᵊl) *adj* **1** fair; just. **2** *Law.* relating to or valid in equity, as distinct from common law or statute law. [C17: from F, from *équité* EQUITY]
▸ˈ**equitableness** *n*

equitation (ˌɛkwɪˈteɪʃən) *n* the study and practice of riding and horsemanship. [C16: from L *equitātiō*, from *equitāre* to ride, from *equus* horse]

equities (ˈɛkwɪtɪz) *pl n* another name for **ordinary shares.**

equity Ⓣ (ˈɛkwɪtɪ) *n, pl* **equities. 1** the quality of being impartial; fairness. **2** an impartial or fair act, decision, etc. **3** *Law.* a system of jurisprudence founded on principles of natural justice and fair conduct. It supplements common law, as by providing a remedy where none exists at law. **4** *Law.* an equitable right or claim. **5** the interest of ordinary shareholders in a company. **6** the value of a debtor's property in excess of debts to which it is liable. [C14: from OF, from L *aequitās*, from *aequus* level, EQUAL]

Equity (ˈɛkwɪtɪ) *n* the actors' trade union.

equity capital *n* the part of the share capital of a company owned by ordinary shareholders or in certain circumstances by other classes of shareholder.

equity-linked policy *n* an insurance or assurance policy in which premiums are invested partially or wholly in ordinary shares for the eventual benefit of the beneficiaries of the policy.

THESAURUS

anced, evenly matched, evenly proportioned, fifty-fifty (*inf.*), level pegging (*Brit. inf.*) **5** *usually with* **to** = **capable of,** able to, adequate for, competent to, fit for, good enough for, ready for, strong enough, suitable for, up to ◆ *n* **6** = **match,** brother, compeer, counterpart, equivalent, fellow, mate, parallel, peer, rival, twin ◆ *vb* **7** = **match,** agree with, amount to, balance, be equal to, be even with, be level with, be tantamount to, come up to, correspond to, equalize, equate, even, level, parallel, rival, square with, tally with, tie with
Antonyms *adj* ≠ **identical:** different, disproportionate, dissimilar, diverse, unequal, unlike ≠ **even:** unbalanced, unequal, uneven, unmatched ≠ **capable of:** inadequate, incapable, incompetent, not good enough, not up to, unequal, unfit ◆ *vb* ≠ **match:** be different, be unequal, disagree

equality *n* = **sameness,** balance, coequality, correspondence, equatability, equivalence, evenness, identity, likeness, similarity, uniformity
Antonyms *n* disparity, lack of balance, unevenness

equalize *vb* **1** = **make equal,** balance, equal, equate, even up, level, match, regularize, smooth, square, standardize

equanimity *n* = **composure,** aplomb, calm, calmness, coolness, imperturbability, level-headedness, peace, phlegm, placidity, poise, presence of mind, sang-froid, self-possession, serenity, steadiness, tranquillity

equate *vb* **1, 3** = **make** *or* **be equal,** agree, balance, be commensurate, compare, correspond with *or* to, equalize, liken, match, mention in the same breath, offset, pair, parallel, square, tally, think of together

equation *n* **2, 3** = **equating,** agreement, balancing, comparison, correspondence, equality, equalization, equivalence, likeness, match, pairing, parallel

equestrian *adj* **2** = **on horseback,** in the saddle, mounted ◆ *n* **4** = **rider,** cavalier (*arch.*), horseman, knight

equilibrium *n* **1, 3** = **stability,** balance, counterpoise, equipoise, evenness, rest, steadiness, symmetry **2** = **composure,** calm, calmness, collectedness, coolness, equanimity, poise, self-possession, serenity, stability, steadiness

equip *vb* **1-3** = **supply,** accoutre, arm, array, attire, deck out, dress, endow, fit out, fit up, furnish, kit out, outfit, prepare, provide, rig, stock

equipage *n* **1** = **carriage,** coach **2** = **equipment,** accoutrements, apparatus, baggage, gear, materiel, munitions, stores

equipment *n* **2, 3** = **apparatus,** accoutrements, appurtenances, baggage, equipage, furnishings, furniture, gear, materiel, outfit, paraphernalia, rig, stuff, supplies, tackle, tools

equitable *adj* **1** = **fair,** candid, disinterested, dispassionate, due, even-handed, honest, impartial, just, nondiscriminatory, proper, proportionate, reasonable, right, rightful, unbiased, unprejudiced

equity *n* **1** = **fairness,** disinterestedness, equitableness, even-handedness, fair-mindedness, fair play, honesty, impartiality, integrity, justice, reasonableness, rectitude, righteousness, uprightness
Antonyms *n* bias, discrimination, injustice, partiality, preference, prejudice, unfairness

equivalence ⓣ (ɪ'kwɪvələns) *or* **equivalency** *n* **1** the state of being equivalent. **2** *Logic, maths.* another term for **biconditional.**

equivalent ⓣ (ɪ'kwɪvələnt) *adj* **1** equal in value, quantity, significance, etc. **2** having the same or a similar effect or meaning. **3** *Logic, maths.* (of two propositions) having a biconditional between them. ◆ *n* **4** something that is equivalent. **5** Also called: **equivalent weight.** the weight of a substance that will combine with or displace 8 grams of oxygen or 1.007 97 grams of hydrogen. [C15: from LL, from L *aequi-* EQUI- + *valēre* to be worth]
▸**e'quivalently** *adv*

equivocal ⓣ (ɪ'kwɪvək°l) *adj* **1** capable of varying interpretations; ambiguous. **2** deliberately misleading or vague. **3** of doubtful character or sincerity. [C17: from LL, from L EQUI- + *vōx* voice]
▸**e,quivo'cality** *or* **e'quivocalness** *n*

equivocate ⓣ (ɪ'kwɪvə,keɪt) *vb* **equivocates, equivocating, equivocated.** (*intr*) to use equivocal language, esp. to avoid speaking directly or honestly. [C15: from Med. L, from LL *aequivocus* ambiguous, EQUIVOCAL]
▸**e'quivo,catingly** *adv* ▸**e,quivo'cation** *n* ▸**e'quivo,cator** *n* ▸**e'quivocatory** *adj*

er (ə, ɜː) *interj* a sound made when hesitating in speech.

Er *the chemical symbol for* erbium.

ER *abbrev. for:* **1** Elizabeth Regina. [L: Queen Elizabeth] **2** Eduardus Rex. [L: King Edward]

-er[1] *suffix forming nouns.* **1** a person or thing that performs a specified action: *reader; lighter.* **2** a person engaged in a profession, occupation, etc.: *writer; baker.* **3** a native or inhabitant of: *Londoner; villager.* **4** a person or thing having a certain characteristic: *newcomer; fiver.* [OE *-ere*]

-er[2] *suffix.* forming the comparative degree of adjectives (*deeper, freer,* etc.) and adverbs (*faster, slower,* etc.). [OE *-rd, -re* (adj), *-or* (adv)]

era ⓣ ('ɪərə) *n* **1** a period of time considered as being of a distinctive character; epoch. **2** an extended period of time the years of which are numbered from a fixed point: *the Christian era.* **3** a point in time beginning a new or distinctive period. **4** a major division of geological time, divided into periods. [C17: from L *aera* counters, pl of *aes* brass, pieces of brass money]

ERA ('ɪərə) *n* (in Britain) *acronym for* Education Reform Act: the 1988 act which established the key elements of the National Curriculum and the Basic Curriculum.

eradicate ⓣ (ɪ'rædɪ,keɪt) *vb* **eradicates, eradicating, eradicated.** (*tr*) **1** to obliterate. **2** to pull up by the roots. [C16: from L *ērādīcāre* to uproot, from EX-[1] + *rādīx* root]
▸**e'radicable** *adj* ▸**e,radi'cation** *n* ▸**e'radicative** *adj*

erase ⓣ (ɪ'reɪz) *vb* **erases, erasing, erased. 1** to obliterate or rub out (something written, typed, etc.). **2** (*tr*) to destroy all traces of. **3** to remove (a recording) from (magnetic tape). [C17: from L, from EX-[1] + *rādere* to scratch, scrape]
▸**e'rasable** *adj*

eraser (ɪ'reɪzə) *n* an object, such as a piece of rubber, for erasing something written, typed, etc.

erasure (ɪ'reɪʒə) *n* **1** the act or an instance of erasing. **2** the place or mark, as on a piece of paper, where something has been erased.

Erato ('ɛrə,təʊ) *n Greek myth.* the Muse of love poetry.

erbium ('ɜːbɪəm) *n* a soft malleable silvery-white element of the lanthanide series of metals. Symbol: Er; atomic no.: 68; atomic wt.: 167.26. [C19: from NL, from (*Ytt*)*erb*(*y*), Sweden, where it was first found + -IUM]

ERDF *abbrev. for* European Regional Development Fund: a fund to provide money for specific projects for work on the infrastructure in countries of the European Union.

ere (ɛə) *conj, prep* a poetic word for **before.** [OE *ǣr*]

erect ⓣ (ɪ'rɛkt) *adj* **1** upright in posture or position. **2** *Physiol.* (of the penis, clitoris, or nipples) firm or rigid after swelling with blood, esp. as a result of sexual excitement. **3** (of plant parts) growing vertically or at right angles to the parts from which they arise. ◆ *vb* (*mainly tr*) **4** to put up; build. **5** to raise to an upright position. **6** to found or form; set up. **7** (*also intr*) *Physiol.* to become or cause to become firm or rigid by filling with blood. **8** to exalt. **9** to draw or construct (a line, figure, etc.) on a given line or figure. [C14: from L *ērigere* to set up, from *regere* to control, govern]
▸**e'rectable** *adj* ▸**e'recter** *or* **e'rector** *n* ▸**e'rectness** *n*

erectile (ɪ'rɛktaɪl) *adj* **1** *Physiol.* (of tissues or organs, such as the penis or clitoris) capable of becoming erect. **2** capable of being erected.
▸**erectility** (ɪrɛk'tɪlɪtɪ, ,iːrɛk-) *n*

erection ⓣ (ɪ'rɛkʃən) *n* **1** the act of erecting or the state of being erected. **2** a building or construction. **3** *Physiol.* the enlarged state of erectile tissues or organs, esp. the penis, when filled with blood. **4** an erect penis.

E region *or* **layer** *n* a region of the ionosphere, extending from a height of 90 to about 150 kilometres. It reflects radio waves of medium wavelength.

eremite ('ɛrɪ,maɪt) *n* a Christian hermit or recluse. [C13: see HERMIT]
▸**eremitic** (,ɛrɪ'mɪtɪk) *or* ,**ere'mitical** *adj* ▸**'eremit,ism** *n*

erepsin (ɪ'rɛpsɪn) *n* a mixture of proteolytic enzymes secreted by the small intestine. [C20: *er-,* from L *ēripere* to snatch + (P)EPSIN]

erethism ('ɛrɪ,θɪzəm) *n* **1** *Physiol.* an abnormal irritability or sensitivity in any part of the body. **2** *Psychiatry.* **2a** a personality disorder resulting from mercury poisoning. **2b** an abnormal tendency to become aroused quickly, esp. sexually, as the result of a verbal or psychic stimulus. [C18: from F, from Gk, from *erethizein* to excite, irritate]

erf (ɜːf) *n, pl* **erven** ('ɜːvən). *S. African.* a plot of land, usually urban. [from Afrik., from Du.: inheritance]

Erf (ɜːf) *n acronym for* electrorheological fluid: a man-made liquid that thickens or solidifies when an electric current passes through it and returns to a liquid when the current ceases.

erg[1] (ɜːg) *n* the cgs unit of work or energy. [C19: from Gk *ergon* work]

erg[2] (ɜːg) *n, pl* **ergs** *or* **areg** (ə'rɛg). an area of shifting sand dunes, esp. in the Sahara Desert in N Africa. [C19: from Ar. *'irj*]

ergo ⓣ ('ɜːgəʊ) *sentence connector.* therefore; hence. [C14: from L: therefore]

ergonomic (,ɜːgə'nɒmɪk) *adj* **1** of or relating to ergonomics. **2** designed to minimize physical effort and discomfort, and hence maximize efficiency.

ergonomics (,ɜːgə'nɒmɪks) *n* (*functioning as sing*) the study of the relationship between workers and their environment, esp. the equipment they use. [C20: from Gk *ergon* work + (ECO)NOMICS]
▸**ergonomist** (ɜː'gɒnəmɪst) *n*

ergosterol (ɜː'gɒstə,rɒl) *n* a plant sterol that is converted into vitamin D by the action of ultraviolet radiation.

ergot ('ɜːgət, -gɒt) *n* **1** a disease of cereals and other grasses caused by fungi of the genus *Claviceps.* **2** any fungus causing this disease. **3** the dried fungus, used as the source of certain alkaloids used in medicine. [C17: from F: spur (of a cock), from ?]

ergotism ('ɜːgə,tɪzəm) *n* ergot poisoning, producing either burning pains and eventually gangrene or itching skin and convulsions.

erica ('ɛrɪkə) *n* any shrub of the ericaceous genus *Erica,* including the heaths and some heathers. [C19: via L from Gk *ereikē* heath]

ericaceous (,ɛrɪ'keɪʃəs) *adj* of or relating to the Ericaceae, a family of trees and shrubs with typically bell-shaped flowers: includes heather, rhododendron, azalea, and arbutus.

erigeron (ɪ'rɪdʒərən, -'rɪg-) *n* any plant of the genus *Erigeron,* whose flowers resemble asters. [C17: via L from Gk, from *ēri* early + *gerōn* old man; from the white down of some species]

Erin ('ɪərɪn, 'ɛərɪn) *n* an archaic or poetic name for Ireland. [from Irish Gaelic *Éirinn,* dative of Ireland]

Erinyes (ɪ'rɪnɪ,iːz) *pl n, sing* **Erinys** (ɪ'rɪnɪs, ɪ'raɪ-). *Myth.* another name for the **Furies.** [Gk]

erk (ɜːk) *n Brit. sl.* an aircraftman or naval rating. [C20: ? a corruption of *AC* (aircraftman)]

ERM *abbrev. for* Exchange Rate Mechanism.

ermine ('ɜːmɪn) *n, pl* **ermines** *or* **ermine. 1** the stoat in northern regions, where it has a white winter coat with a black-tipped tail. **2** the fur of this animal. **3** the dignity or office of a judge, noble, etc., whose state

THESAURUS

equivalence *n* **1** = **equality,** agreement, alikeness, conformity, correspondence, evenness, identity, interchangeableness, likeness, match, parallel, parity, sameness, similarity, synonymy

equivalent *adj* **1, 2** = **equal,** alike, commensurate, comparable, correspondent, corresponding, even, homologous, interchangeable, of a kind, of a piece, same, similar, synonymous, tantamount ◆ *n* **4** = **equal,** correspondent, counterpart, match, opposite number, parallel, peer, twin
Antonyms *adj* ≠ **equal:** different, dissimilar, incomparable, unequal, unlike

equivocal *adj* **1-2** = **ambiguous,** ambivalent, doubtful, dubious, evasive, indefinite, indeterminate, misleading, oblique, obscure, oracular, prevaricating, questionable, suspicious, uncertain, vague
Antonyms *adj* absolute, certain, clear, clear-cut, cut-and-dried (*inf.*), decisive, definite, evident, explicit, incontrovertible, indubitable, manifest, plain, positive, straight, unambiguous, unequivocal

equivocate *vb* = **be evasive,** avoid the issue, beat about the bush (*inf.*), dodge, evade, fence, flannel (*Brit. inf.*), fudge, hedge, parry, prevaricate, pussyfoot (*inf.*), quibble, shuffle, sidestep, tergiversate, waffle (*inf., chiefly Brit.*)

equivocation *n* = **ambiguity,** double talk, doubtfulness, evasion, hedging, prevarication, quibbling, shuffling, tergiversation, waffle (*inf., chiefly Brit.*), weasel words (*inf., chiefly US*)

era *n* **1** = **age,** aeon, cycle, date, day *or* days, epoch, generation, period, stage, time

eradicate *vb* **1** = **wipe out,** abolish, annihilate, deracinate, destroy, efface, eliminate, erase, excise, expunge, exterminate, extinguish, extirpate, get rid of, obliterate, put paid to, remove, root out, stamp out, uproot, weed out, wipe from the face of the earth

eradication *n* **1** = **wiping out,** abolition, annihilation, deracination, destruction, effacement, elimination, erasure, expunction, extermination, extinction, extirpation, obliteration, removal

erase *vb* **1-3** = **wipe out,** blot, cancel, delete, efface, excise, expunge, obliterate, remove, rub out, scratch out

erect *adj* **1** = **upright,** elevated, firm, perpendicular, pricked-up, raised, rigid, standing, stiff, straight, vertical ◆ *vb* **4, 5** = **build,** construct, elevate, lift, mount, pitch, put up, raise, rear, set up, stand up **6** = **found,** create, establish, form, initiate, institute, organize, set up
Antonyms *adj* ≠ **upright:** bent, flaccid, horizontal, leaning, limp, prone, recumbent, relaxed, supine ◆ *vb* ≠ **build:** demolish, destroy, dismantle, raze, tear down

erection *n* **1** = **building,** assembly, construction, creation, elevation, establishment, fabrication, manufacture **2** = **structure,** building, construction, edifice, pile

ergo *sentence connector* = **therefore,** accordingly, consequently, for that reason, hence, in consequence, so, then, thus

robes are trimmed with ermine. [C12: from OF, from Med. L *Armenius* (*mūs*) Armenian (mouse)]

erne *or* **ern** (ɜːn) *n* a fish-eating sea eagle. [OE *earn*]

Ernie (ˈɜːnɪ) *n* (in Britain) a machine that randomly selects winning numbers of Premium Bonds. [C20: acronym of *E*lectronic *R*andom *N*umber *I*ndicator *E*quipment]

erode ❶ (ɪˈrəʊd) *vb* **erodes, eroding, eroded. 1** to grind or wear down or away or become ground or worn down or away. **2** to deteriorate or cause to deteriorate. [C17: from L, from EX-[1] + *rōdere* to gnaw]
▸**eˈrodible** *adj*

erogenous (ɪˈrɒdʒɪnəs) *or* **erogenic** (ˌɛrəˈdʒɛnɪk) *adj* **1** sensitive to sexual stimulation. **2** arousing sexual desire or giving sexual pleasure. [C19: from Gk *erōs* love, desire + -GENOUS]
▸**erogeneity** (ˌɛrədʒɪˈniːɪtɪ) *n*

erosion ❶ (ɪˈrəʊʒən) *n* **1** the wearing away of rocks, soil, etc., by the action of water, ice, wind, etc. **2** the act or process of eroding or the state of being eroded.
▸**eˈrosive** *or* **eˈrosional** *adj*

erotic ❶ (ɪˈrɒtɪk) *adj* **1** of, concerning, or arousing sexual desire or giving sexual pleasure. **2** marked by strong sexual desire or being especially sensitive to sexual stimulation. Also: **erotical.** [C17: from Gk *erōtikos*, from *erōs* love]
▸**eˈrotically** *adv*

erotica (ɪˈrɒtɪkə) *pl n* explicitly sexual literature or art. [C19: from Gk: see EROTIC]

eroticism (ɪˈrɒtɪˌsɪzəm) *or* **erotism** (ˈɛrəˌtɪzəm) *n* **1** erotic quality or nature. **2** the use of sexually arousing or pleasing symbolism in literature or art. **3** sexual excitement or desire.

erotogenic (ɪˌrɒtəˈdʒɛnɪk) *adj* originating from or causing sexual stimulation; erogenous.

err ❶ (ɜː) *vb* (*intr*) **1** to make a mistake; be incorrect. **2** to deviate from a moral standard. **3** to act with bias, esp. favourable bias: *to err on the right side.* [C14 *erren* to wander, stray, from OF, from L *errāre*]
▸**ˈerrancy** *n*

errand ❶ (ˈɛrənd) *n* **1** a short trip undertaken to perform a task or commission (esp. in **run errands**). **2** the purpose or object of such a trip. [OE *ǣrende*]

errant ❶ (ˈɛrənt) *adj* (*often postpositive*) **1** *Arch. or literary.* wandering in search of adventure. **2** erring or straying from the right course or accepted standards. [C14: from OF: journeying, from Vulgar L *iterāre* (unattested), from L *iter* journey; infl. by L *errāre* to err]
▸**ˈerrantry** *n*

erratic ❶ (ɪˈrætɪk) *adj* **1** irregular in performance, behaviour, or attitude; unpredictable. **2** having no fixed or regular course. ◆ *n* **3** a piece of rock that has been transported from its place of origin, esp. by glacial action. [C14: from L, from *errāre* to wander, err]
▸**erˈratically** *adv*

erratum ❶ (ɪˈrɑːtəm) *n, pl* **errata** (-tə). **1** an error in writing or printing. **2** another name for **corrigendum.** [C16: from L: mistake, from *errāre* to err]

erroneous ❶ (ɪˈrəʊnɪəs) *adj* based on or containing error; incorrect. [C14 (in the sense: deviating from what is right), from L, from *errāre* to wander]
▸**erˈroneousness** *n*

error ❶ (ˈɛrə) *n* **1** a mistake or inaccuracy. **2** an incorrect belief or wrong judgment. **3** the condition of deviating from accuracy or correctness. **4** deviation from a moral standard; wrongdoing. **5** *Maths, statistics.* a measure of the difference between some quantity and an approximation of it, often expressed as a percentage. [C13: from L, from *errāre* to err]
▸**ˈerror-ˌfree** *adj*

ersatz ❶ (ˈɛəzæts, ˈɜː-) *adj* **1** made in imitation; artificial. ◆ *n* **2** an ersatz substance or article. [C20: G, from *ersetzen* to substitute]

Erse (ɜːs) *n* **1** another name for Irish **Gaelic.** ◆ *adj* **2** of or relating to the Irish Gaelic language. [C14: from Lowland Scots *Erisch* Irish]

erst (ɜːst) *adv Arch.* **1** long ago; formerly. **2** at first. [OE *ǣrest* earliest, sup. of *ǣr* early]

erstwhile ❶ (ˈɜːstˌwaɪl) *adj* **1** former; one-time. ◆ *adv* **2** *Arch.* long ago; formerly.

eruct (ɪˈrʌkt) *or* **eructate** *vb* **eructs, eructing, eructed** *or* **eructates, eructating, eructated. 1** to belch. **2** (of a volcano) to pour out (fumes or volcanic matter). [C17: from L, from *ructāre* to belch]
▸**eructation** (ɪˌrʌkˈteɪʃən, ˌiːrʌk-) *n*

erudite ❶ (ˈɛrʊˌdaɪt) *adj* having or showing extensive scholarship; learned. [C15: from L, from *ērudīre* to polish]
▸**erudition** (ˌɛrʊˈdɪʃən) *or* **ˈeruˌditeness** *n*

erupt ❶ (ɪˈrʌpt) *vb* **1** to eject (steam, water, and volcanic material) violently or (of volcanic material, etc.) to be so ejected. **2** (*intr*) (of a blemish) to appear on the skin. **3** (*intr*) (of a tooth) to emerge through the gum during normal tooth development. **4** (*intr*) to burst forth suddenly and violently. [C17: from L *ēruptus* having burst forth, from *ērumpere*, from *rumpere* to burst]
▸**eˈruptive** *adj* ▸**eˈruption** *n*

-ery *or* **-ry** *suffix forming nouns.* **1** indicating a place of business or activity: *bakery; refinery.* **2** indicating a class or collection of things: *cutlery.* **3** indicating qualities or actions: *snobbery; trickery.* **4** indicating a practice or occupation: *husbandry.* **5** indicating a state or condition: *slavery.* [from OF *-erie*; see -ER[1], -Y[3]]

erysipelas (ˌɛrɪˈsɪpɪləs) *n* an acute streptococcal infectious disease of the skin, characterized by fever and purplish lesions. [C16: from L, from Gk, from *erusi-* red + *-pelas* skin]

erythro- *or before a vowel* **erythr-** *combining form.* red: *erythrocyte.* [from Gk *eruthros* red]

erythrocyte (ɪˈrɪθrəʊˌsaɪt) *n* a blood cell of vertebrates that transports oxygen and carbon dioxide, combined with haemoglobin.
▸**erythrocytic** (ɪˌrɪθrəʊˈsɪtɪk) *adj*

erythromycin (ɪˌrɪθrəʊˈmaɪsɪn) *n* an antibiotic used in treating certain bacterial infections. [C20: from ERYTHRO- + Gk *mukēs* fungus + -IN]

erythropoiesis (ɪˌrɪθrəʊpɔɪˈiːsɪs) *n Physiol.* the formation of red blood cells. [C19: from ERYTHRO- + Gk *poiēs* a making, from *poiein* to make]
▸**erythropoietic** (ɪˌrɪθrəʊpɔɪˈɛtɪk) *adj*

Es *the chemical symbol for* einsteinium.

-es *suffix.* **1** a variant of **-s**[1] for nouns ending in *ch, s, sh, z,* postconsonantal *y*, for some nouns ending in a vowel, and nouns in *f* with *v* in the plural: *ashes; heroes; calves.* **2** a variant of **-s**[2] for verbs ending in *ch, s, sh, z,* postconsonantal *y*, or a vowel: *preaches; steadies; echoes.*

escadrille (ˌɛskəˈdrɪl) *n* a French squadron of aircraft, esp. in World War I. [from F: flotilla, from Sp., from *escuadra* SQUADRON]

escalade (ˌɛskəˈleɪd) *n* **1** an assault using ladders, esp. on a fortification. ◆ *vb* **escalades, escalading, escaladed. 2** to gain access to (a place) by ladders. [C16: from F, from It., from *scalare* to mount, SCALE[3]]

escalate ❶ (ˈɛskəˌleɪt) *vb* **escalates, escalating, escalated.** to increase or be increased in extent, intensity, or magnitude. [C20: back formation from ESCALATOR]
▸**ˌescaˈlation** *n*

escalator (ˈɛskəˌleɪtə) *n* **1** a moving staircase consisting of stair treads fixed to a conveyor belt. **2** short for **escalator clause.** [C20: orig. a trademark]

escalator clause *n* a clause in a contract stipulating an adjustment in wages, prices, etc., in the event of specified changes in conditions, such as a large rise in the cost of living.

THESAURUS

erode *vb* **1, 2** = **wear down** *or* **away**, abrade, consume, corrode, destroy, deteriorate, disintegrate, eat away, grind down, spoil

erosion *n* **1, 2** = **deterioration**, abrasion, attrition, consumption, corrasion, corrosion, destruction, disintegration, eating away, grinding down, spoiling, wear, wearing down *or* away

erotic *adj* **1** = **sexual**, amatory, aphrodisiac, carnal, erogenous, lustful, rousing, seductive, sensual, sexy (*inf.*), steamy (*inf.*), stimulating, suggestive, titillating, voluptuous

err *vb* **1** = **make a mistake**, be inaccurate, be incorrect, be in error, blot one's copybook (*inf.*), blunder, drop a brick *or* clanger (*inf.*), go astray, go wrong, misapprehend, miscalculate, misjudge, mistake, put one's foot in it (*inf.*), slip up (*inf.*) **2** = **sin**, be out of order, blot one's copybook (*inf.*), deviate, do wrong, fall, go astray, lapse, misbehave, offend, transgress, trespass

errand *n* **1** = **job**, charge, commission, message, mission, task

errant *adj* **1** *Archaic or literary* = **wandering**, itinerant, journeying, nomadic, peripatetic, rambling, roaming, roving **2** = **sinning**, aberrant, deviant, erring, offending, straying, wayward, wrong

erratic *adj* **1** = **unpredictable**, aberrant, abnormal, capricious, changeable, desultory, eccentric, fitful, inconsistent, inconstant, irregular, shifting, uneven, unreliable, unstable, variable, wayward **2** = **wandering**, directionless, meandering, planetary
Antonyms *adj* ≠ **unpredictable:** certain, consistent, constant, dependable, invariable, natural, normal, predictable, regular, reliable, stable, steady, straight, unchanging, undeviating

erratum *n* **1, 2** = **misprint**, corrigendum, error, literal, omission, typo (*inf.*)

erroneous *adj* = **incorrect**, amiss, fallacious, false, faulty, flawed, inaccurate, inexact, invalid, mistaken, spurious, unfounded, unsound, untrue, wide of the mark, wrong
Antonyms *adj* accurate, correct, factual, faultless, flawless, precise, right, true, veracious

error *n* **1** = **mistake**, bloomer (*Brit. inf.*), blunder, boner (*sl.*), boob (*Brit. sl.*), delusion, erratum, fallacy, fault, flaw, howler (*inf.*), inaccuracy, misapprehension, miscalculation, misconception, oversight, slip, solecism **4** = **wrongdoing**, delinquency, deviation, fault, lapse, misdeed, offence, sin, transgression, trespass, wrong

ersatz *adj* **1** = **artificial**, bogus, counterfeit, fake, imitation, phoney *or* phony (*inf.*), pretended, sham, simulated, spurious, substitute, synthetic

erstwhile *adj* **1** = **former**, bygone, ex (*inf.*), late, old, once, one-time, past, previous, quondam, sometime

erudite *adj* = **learned**, cultivated, cultured, educated, knowledgeable, lettered, literate, scholarly, well-educated, well-read
Antonyms *adj* ignorant, illiterate, shallow, uneducated, uninformed, unlettered, unschooled, untaught, unthinking

erudition *n* = **learning**, education, knowledge, letters, lore, scholarship

erupt *vb* **1** = **explode**, be ejected, belch forth, blow up, break out, burst forth, burst into, burst out, discharge, flare up, gush, pour forth, spew forth *or* out, spit out, spout, throw off, vent, vomit **2** = **break out**, appear

eruption *n* **1** = **explosion**, discharge, ejection, flare-up, outbreak, outburst, sally, venting **2** = **inflammation**, outbreak, rash

escalate *vb* = **increase**, amplify, ascend, be increased, enlarge, expand, extend, grow, heighten, intensify, magnify, mount, raise, rise, step up
Antonyms *vb* abate, contract, decrease, descend, diminish, fall, lessen, limit, lower, shrink, wane, wind down

escalation *n* = **increase**, acceleration, amplifi-

escallop (ɛ'skɒləp, ɛ'skæl-) *n, vb* another word for **scallop.**

escalope ('ɛskəˌlɒp) *n* a thin slice of meat, usually veal. [C19: from OF: shell]

escapade ('ɛskəˌpeɪd, ˌɛskə'peɪd) *n* **1** an adventure, esp. one that is mischievous or unlawful. **2** a prank; romp. [C17: from F, from OIt., from Vulgar L *excappāre* (unattested) to ESCAPE]

escape (ɪ'skeɪp) *vb* **escapes, escaping, escaped. 1** to get away or break free from (confinement, etc.). **2** to manage to avoid (danger, etc.). **3** (*intr;* usually foll. by *from*) (of gases, liquids, etc.) to issue gradually, as from a crack; seep; leak. **4** (*tr*) to elude; be forgotten by: *the figure escapes me.* **5** (*tr*) to be articulated inadvertently or involuntarily from: *a roar escaped his lips.* ◆ *n* **6** the act of escaping or state of having escaped. **7** avoidance of injury, harm, etc. **8a** a means or way of escape. **8b** (*as modifier*): *an escape route.* **9** a means of distraction or relief. **10** a gradual outflow; leakage; seepage. **11** Also called: **escape valve, escape cock.** a valve that releases air, steam, etc., above a certain pressure. **12** a plant originally cultivated but now growing wild. [C14: from OF, from Vulgar L *excappāre* (unattested) to escape (lit.: to slip out of one's cloak, hence free oneself), from EX-[1] + LL *cappa* cloak]
▸**es'capable** *adj* ▸**es'caper** *n*

escapee (ɪˌskeɪ'piː) *n* a person who has escaped, esp. an escaped prisoner.

escapement (ɪ'skeɪpmənt) *n* **1** a mechanism consisting of a toothed wheel (**escape wheel**) and anchor, used in timepieces to provide periodic impulses to the pendulum or balance. **2** any similar mechanism that regulates movement. **3** in pianos, the mechanism which allows the hammer to clear the string after striking, so the string can vibrate. **4** *Rare.* an act or means of escaping.

escape road *n* a road provided on a hill for a driver to drive into if his brakes fail or on a bend if he loses control of the turn.

escape velocity *n* the minimum velocity necessary for a body to escape from the gravitational field of the earth or other celestial body.

escapism (ɪ'skeɪpɪzəm) *n* an inclination to retreat from unpleasant reality, as through diversion or fantasy.
▸**es'capist** *n, adj*

escapologist (ˌɛskə'pɒlədʒɪst) *n* an entertainer who specializes in freeing himself from confinement.
▸**ˌesca'pology** *n*

escargot *French.* (ɛskargo) *n* a variety of edible snail.

escarpment (ɪ'skɑːpmənt) *n* **1** the long continuous steep face of a ridge or plateau formed by erosion or faulting; scarp. **2** a steep artificial slope made immediately in front of a fortified place. [C19: from F *escarpe;* see SCARP]

-escent *suffix forming adjectives.* beginning to be, do, show, etc.: *convalescent; luminescent.* [via OF from L *-ēscent-*, stem of present participial suffix of *-ēscere,* ending of inceptive verbs]
▸**-escence** *suffix forming nouns.*

eschatology (ˌɛskə'tɒlədʒɪ) *n* the branch of theology concerned with the end of the world. [C19: from Gk *eskhatos* last]
▸**eschatological** (ˌɛskətə'lɒdʒɪk'l) *adj* ▸**ˌescha'tologist** *n*

escheat (ɪs'tʃiːt) *Law.* ◆ *n* **1** (in England before 1926) the reversion of property to the Crown in the absence of legal heirs. **2** *Feudalism.* the reversion of property to the feudal lord in the absence of legal heirs. **3** the property so reverting. ◆ *vb* **4** to take (land) by escheat or (of land) to revert by escheat. [C14: from OF, from *escheoir* to fall to the lot of, from LL *excadere* (unattested), from L *cadere* to fall]
▸**es'cheatable** *adj* ▸**es'cheatage** *n*

Escherichia (ˌɛʃə'rɪkɪə) *n* a genus of bacteria that form acid and gas in the presence of carbohydrates and are found in the intestines of humans and many animals, esp. *E. coli,* which is sometimes pathogenic and is widely used in genetic research. [C19: after Theodor *Escherich* (1857–1911), G paediatrician]

eschew (ɪs'tʃuː) *vb* (*tr*) to keep clear of or abstain from (something disliked, injurious, etc.); shun; avoid. [C14: from OF *eschiver,* of Gmc origin; see SHY[1], SKEW]
▸**es'chewal** *n* ▸**es'chewer** *n*

eschscholzia *or* **eschscholtzia** (ɪs'kɒlʃə) *n* another name for **California poppy.** [C19: after J. F. von *Eschscholtz* (1793–1831), G botanist]

escort *n* ('ɛskɔːt). **1** one or more persons, soldiers, vehicles, etc., accompanying another or others for protection, as a mark of honour, etc. **2** a man or youth who accompanies a woman or girl on a social occasion. ◆ *vb* (ɪs'kɔːt). **3** (*tr*) to accompany or attend as an escort. [C16: from F, from It., from *scorgere* to guide, from L *corrigere* to straighten; see CORRECT]

escritoire (ˌɛskrɪ'twɑː) *n* a writing desk with compartments and drawers. [C18: from F, from Med. L *scriptōrium* writing room in a monastery, from L *scrībere* to write]

escrow ('ɛskrəʊ, ɛ'skrəʊ) *Law.* ◆ *n* **1** money, goods, or a written document, held by a third party pending fulfilment of some condition. **2** the state or condition of being an escrow (esp. in **in escrow**). ◆ *vb* (*tr*) **3** to place (money, a document, etc.) in escrow. [C16: from OF *escroe,* of Gmc origin; see SCREED, SHRED, SCROLL]

escudo (ɛ'skuːdəʊ) *n, pl* **escudos. 1** the standard monetary unit of Cape Verde and Portugal. **2** a former standard monetary unit of Chile. **3** an old Spanish silver coin. [C19: Sp., lit.: shield, from L *scūtum*]

esculent ('ɛskjʊlənt) *n* **1** any edible substance. ◆ *adj* **2** edible. [C17: from L *ēsculentus* good to eat, from *ēsca* food, from *edere* to eat]

escutcheon (ɪ'skʌtʃən) *n* **1** a shield, esp. a heraldic one that displays a coat of arms. **2** a plate or shield around a keyhole, door handle, etc. **3** the place on the stern of a vessel where the name is shown. **4 blot on one's escutcheon.** a stain on one's honour. [C15: from OF *escuchon,* ult. from L *scūtum* shield]
▸**es'cutcheoned** *adj*

ESE *symbol for* east-southeast.

-ese *suffix forming adjectives and nouns.* indicating place of origin, language, or style: *Cantonese; Japanese; journalese.*

ESG (in Britain) *abbrev. for* Educational Support Grant: a government grant given to a Local Education Authority to fund educational schemes dealing with social issues, such as drug abuse.

esker ('ɛskə) *or* **eskar** ('ɛskɑː, -kə) *n* a long winding ridge of gravel, sand, etc., originally deposited by a meltwater stream running under a glacier. [C19: from OIrish *escir* ridge]

Eskimo ('ɛskɪˌməʊ) *n* **1** (*pl* **Eskimos** *or* **Eskimo**) a member of a group of peoples inhabiting N Canada, Greenland, Alaska, and E Siberia. The Eskimos are more properly referred to as the **Inuit. 2** the language of these peoples. ◆ *adj* **3** of or relating to the Eskimos. [C18 *Esquimawes:* rel. to *esquimantsic* (from a native language) eaters of raw flesh]

> **USAGE NOTE** *Eskimo* is considered by many people to be offensive, and in North America the term *Inuit* is often used.

Eskimo dog *n* a large powerful breed of dog with a long thick coat and curled tail, developed for hauling sledges.

Esky ('ɛskɪ) *n, pl* **Eskies.** (*sometimes not cap.*) *Austral. trademark.* a portable insulated container for keeping food and drink cool. [C20: from ESKIMO, alluding to the Eskimos' cold habitat]

ESN *abbrev. for* educationally subnormal; formerly used to designate a person of limited intelligence who needs special schooling.

esophagus (iː'sɒfəgəs) *n* the US spelling of **oesophagus.**

esoteric (ˌɛsəʊ'tɛrɪk) *adj* **1** restricted to or intended for an enlightened or initiated minority. **2** difficult to understand; abstruse. **3** not openly admitted; private. [C17: from Gk, from *esōterō* inner]
▸**ˌeso'terically** *adv* ▸**ˌeso'teriˌcism** *n*

ESP *abbrev. for* extrasensory perception.

esp. *abbrev. for* especially.

espadrille (ˌɛspə'drɪl) *n* a light shoe with a canvas upper, esp. with a braided cord sole. [C19: from F, from Provençal *espardilho,* dim. of *espart* ESPARTO; from use of esparto for the soles]

espalier (ɪ'spæljə) *n* **1** an ornamental shrub or fruit tree trained to grow flat, as against a wall. **2** the trellis or framework on which such plants are trained. ◆ *vb* **3** (*tr*) to train (a plant) on an espalier. [C17: from F: trellis, from OIt.: shoulder supports, from *spalla* shoulder]

esparto *or* **esparto grass** (ɛ'spɑːtəʊ) *n, pl* **espartos.** any of various grasses of S Europe and N Africa, used to make ropes, mats, etc. [C18: from Sp., via L from Gk *spartos* a kind of rush]

especial (ɪ'spɛʃəl) *adj* (*prenominal*) **1** unusual; notable. **2** applying to one person or thing in particular; specific; peculiar: *he had an especial dislike of relatives.* [C14: from OF, from L *speciālis* individual; see SPECIAL]
▸**es'pecially** *adv*

> **USAGE NOTE** *Especial* and *especially* have a more limited use than *special* and *specially. Special* is always used in preference to

THESAURUS

cation, build-up, expansion, heightening, intensification, rise, upsurge

escapade *n* **1, 2 = adventure,** antic, caper, fling, lark (*inf.*), mischief, prank, romp, scrape (*inf.*), spree, stunt, trick

escape *vb* **1 = get away,** abscond, bolt, break free *or* out, decamp, do a bunk (*Brit. sl.*), do a runner (*sl.*), flee, fly, make one's getaway, make *or* effect one's escape, run away *or* off, skedaddle (*inf.*), skip, slip away, slip through one's fingers **2 = avoid,** body-swerve (*Scot.*), circumvent, dodge, duck, elude, evade, pass, shun, slip **3 = leak,** discharge, drain, emanate, exude, flow, gush, issue, pour forth, seep, spurt **4 = be forgotten by,** baffle, be beyond (someone), elude, puzzle, stump ◆ *n* **6 = getaway,** bolt, break, break-out, decampment, flight **7 = avoidance,** circumvention, elusion, evasion **9 = relaxation,** distraction, diversion, pastime, recreation, relief **10 = leak,** discharge, drain, effluence, efflux, emanation, emission, gush, leakage, outflow, outpour, seepage, spurt

eschew *vb* **= avoid,** abandon, abjure, abstain from, elude, fight shy of, forgo, forswear, give a wide berth to, give up, have nothing to do with, keep *or* steer clear of, kick (*inf.*), refrain from, renounce, shun, swear off

escort *n* **1 = guard,** bodyguard, company, convoy, cortege, entourage, protection, retinue, safeguard, train **2 = companion,** attendant, beau, chaperon, guide, partner, protector, squire (*rare*) ◆ *vb* **3 = accompany,** chaperon, conduct, convoy, guard, guide, hold (someone's) hand, lead, partner, protect, shepherd, squire, usher

esoteric *adj* **1-3 = obscure,** abstruse, arcane, cabbalistic, cryptic, hidden, inner, inscrutable, mysterious, mystic, mystical, occult, private, recondite, secret

especial *adj* **1 = exceptional,** chief, distinguished, extraordinary, marked, notable, noteworthy, outstanding, principal, signal, special, uncommon, unusual **2 = particular,** exclusive, express, individual, peculiar, personal, private, singular, special, specific, unique

especially *adv* **1 = exceptionally,** chiefly, conspicuously, extraordinarily, largely, mainly, markedly, notably, outstandingly, principally,

especial when the sense is one of being out of the ordinary: *a special lesson; he has been specially trained. Special* is also used when something is referred to as being for a particular purpose: *the word was specially underlined for you.* Where an idea of pre-eminence or individuality is involved, either *especial* or *special* may be used: *he is my especial* (or *special*) *friend; he is especially* (or *specially*) *good at his job.* In informal English, however, *special* is usually preferred in all contexts.

Esperanto (ˌɛspəˈræntəʊ) *n* an international artificial language based on words common to the chief European languages. [C19: lit.: the one who hopes, pseudonym of Dr L. L. Zamenhof (1859–1917), its Polish inventor]
▸ˌ**Espeˈrantist** *n, adj*

espial (ɪˈspaɪəl) *n Arch.* **1** the act or fact of being seen or discovered. **2** the act of noticing. **3** the act of spying upon; secret observation.

espionage ➊ (ˈɛspɪəˌnɑːʒ) *n* **1** the use of spies to obtain secret information, esp. by governments. **2** the act of spying. [C18: from F, from *espion* spy]

esplanade (ˌɛspləˈneɪd) *n* **1** a long open level stretch of ground for walking along, esp. beside the seashore. Cf. **promenade** (sense 1). **2** an open area in front of a fortified place. [C17: from F, from OIt. *spianata,* from *spianare* to make level, from L *explānāre;* see EXPLAIN]

espousal ➊ (ɪˈspaʊzᵊl) *n* **1** adoption or support: *an espousal of new beliefs.* **2** (*sometimes pl*) *Arch.* a marriage or betrothal ceremony.

espouse ➊ (ɪˈspaʊz) *vb* **espouses, espousing, espoused.** (*tr*) **1** to adopt or give support to (a cause, ideal, etc.): *to espouse socialism.* **2** *Arch.* (esp. of a man) to take as spouse; marry. [C15: from OF *espouser,* from L *spōnsāre* to affiance, espouse]
▸**esˈpouser** *n*

espressivo (ˌɛspreˈsiːvəʊ) *adv Music.* in an expressive manner. [It.]

espresso (ɛˈsprɛsəʊ) *n, pl* **espressos. 1** coffee made by forcing steam or boiling water through ground coffee beans. **2** an apparatus for making coffee in this way. [C20: It., lit.: pressed]

esprit ➊ (ɛˈspriː) *n* spirit and liveliness, esp. in wit. [C16: from F, from L *spīritus* a breathing, SPIRIT[1]]

esprit de corps (ɛˈspriː də ˈkɔː) *n* consciousness of and pride in belonging to a particular group; the sense of shared purpose and fellowship.

espy ➊ (ɪˈspaɪ) *vb* **espies, espying, espied.** (*tr*) to catch sight of or perceive; detect. [C14: from OF *espier* to SPY, of Gmc origin]
▸**esˈpier** *n*

Esq. *abbrev. for* esquire.

-esque *suffix forming adjectives.* indicating a specified character, manner, style, or resemblance: *picturesque; Romanesque; statuesque.* [via F from It. *-esco*]

Esquimau (ˈɛskɪˌməʊ) *n, pl* **Esquimaus** *or* **Esquimau,** *adj* a former spelling of **Eskimo.**

esquire (ɪˈskwaɪə) *n* **1** *Chiefly Brit.* a title of respect, usually abbreviated *Esq.,* placed after a man's name. **2** (in medieval times) the attendant of a knight, subsequently often knighted himself. [C15: from OF *escuier,* from LL *scūtārius* shield bearer, from L *scūtum* shield]

ESRC (in Britain) *abbrev. for* Economic and Social Research Council.

ESRO (ˈɛzrəʊ) *n acronym for* European Space Research Organization.

-ess *suffix forming nouns.* indicating a female: *waitress; lioness.* [via OF from LL *-issa,* from Gk]

USAGE NOTE The suffix *-ess* in such words as *poetess, authoress* is now often regarded as disparaging; a sexually neutral term *poet, author* is preferred.

essay ➊ *n* (ˈɛseɪ; *senses 2, 3 also* ɛˈseɪ). **1** a short literary composition. **2** an attempt; effort. **3** a test or trial. ◆ *vb* (ɛˈseɪ). (*tr*) **4** to attempt or try. **5** to test or try out. [C15: from OF *essai* an attempt, from LL *exagium* a weighing, from L *agere* to do, infl. by *exigere* to investigate]

essayist (ˈɛseɪɪst) *n* a person who writes essays.

essence ➊ (ˈɛsᵊns) *n* **1** the characteristic or intrinsic feature of a thing, which determines its identity; fundamental nature. **2** a perfect or complete form of something. **3** *Philosophy.* the unchanging and unchangeable inward nature of something. **4a** the constituent of a plant, usually an oil, alkaloid, or glycoside, that determines its chemical properties. **4b** an alcoholic solution of such a substance. **5** a substance containing the properties of a plant or foodstuff in concentrated form: *vanilla essence.* **6** a rare word for **perfume. 7 in essence.** essentially; fundamentally. **8 of the essence.** indispensable; vitally important. [C14: from Med. L *essentia,* from L: the being (of something), from *esse* to be]

Essene (ˈɛsiːn, ɛˈsiːn) *n Judaism.* a member of an ascetic sect that flourished in Palestine from the second century B.C. to the second century A.D.
▸**Essenian** (ɛˈsiːnɪən) *or* **Essenic** (ɛˈsɛnɪk) *adj*

essential ➊ (ɪˈsɛnʃəl) *adj* **1** vitally important; absolutely necessary. **2** basic; fundamental. **3** absolute; perfect. **4** derived from or relating to an extract of a plant, drug, etc.: *an essential oil.* **5** *Biochem.* (of an amino acid or a fatty acid) necessary for the normal growth of an organism but not synthesized by the organism and therefore required in the diet. **6** *Pathol.* (of a disease) having no obvious external cause: *essential hypertension.* ◆ *n* **7** something fundamental or indispensable.
▸**essentiality** (ɪˌsɛnʃɪˈælɪtɪ) *or* **esˈsentialness** *n* ▸**esˈsentially** *adv*

essential element *n Biochem.* any chemical element required by an organism for healthy growth. It may be required in large amounts (**macronutrient**) or in very small amounts (**trace element**).

essentialism (ɪˈsɛnʃəˌlɪzəm) *n Philosophy.* any doctrine that material objects have an essence distinguishable from their attributes and existence.
▸**esˈsentialist** *n*

essential oil *n* any of various volatile oils in plants, having the odour or flavour of the plant from which they are extracted.

Essex Man (ˈɛsɪks) *n Inf., derog.* a self-made man, esp. of working-class origins, characterized by philistinism and bigoted right-wing views. [C20: from the supposed prevalence of such people in *Essex,* county of SE England]

EST *abbrev. for:* **1** (in the US and Canada) Eastern Standard Time. **2** electric-shock treatment.

est. *abbrev. for:* **1** established. **2** estimate(d).

-est[1] *suffix.* forming the superlative degree of adjectives and adverbs: *fastest.* [OE *-est, -ost*]

-est[2] *or* **-st** *suffix.* forming the archaic second person singular present and past indicative tense of verbs: *thou goest; thou hadst.* [OE *-est, -ast*]

establish ➊ (ɪˈstæblɪʃ) *vb* (*tr*) **1** to make secure or permanent in a certain place, condition, job, etc. **2** to create or set up (an organization, etc.) as on a permanent basis. **3** to prove correct; validate: *establish a fact.* **4** to cause (a principle, theory, etc.) to be accepted: *establish a precedent.* **5** to give (a Church) the status of a national institution. **6** to cause (a person) to become recognized and accepted. **7** (in works of imagination) to cause (a character, place, etc.) to be credible and recognized. [C14: from OF, from L *stabilis* STABLE[2]]
▸**esˈtablisher** *n*

Established Church *n* a Church that is officially recognized as a national institution, esp. the Church of England.

establishment ➊ (ɪˈstæblɪʃmənt) *n* **1** the act of establishing or state of being established. **2a** a business organization or other large institution. **2b** a place of business. **3** the staff and equipment of an organization. **4** any large organization or system. **5** a household; residence. **6** a

THESAURUS

remarkably, seriously (*inf.*), signally, specially, strikingly, supremely, uncommonly, unusually **2** = **particularly,** exclusively, expressly, peculiarly, singularly, specifically, uniquely

espionage *n* **1, 2** = **spying,** counter-intelligence, intelligence, surveillance, undercover work

espousal *n* **1** = **support,** adoption, advocacy, backing, championing, championship, defence, embracing, maintenance, promotion, taking up **2** *Archaic* = **engagement,** affiancing, betrothal, betrothing (*arch.*), espousing (*arch.*), marriage, nuptials, plighting, wedding

espouse *vb* **1** = **support,** adopt, advocate, back, champion, defend, embrace, maintain, promote, stand up for, take up, uphold **2** *Archaic* = **marry,** betroth (*arch.*), plight one's troth (*old-fashioned*), take as spouse, take to wife, wed

esprit *n* = **spirit,** animation, brio, élan, liveliness, quickness, sparkle, sprightliness, verve, vitality, vivacity, wit, zest

espy *vb* = **catch sight of,** behold, catch a glimpse of, descry, detect, discern, discover, glimpse, make out, notice, observe, perceive, sight, spot, spy

essay *n* **1** = **composition,** article, discourse, disquisition, dissertation, paper, piece, tract, treatise **2** = **attempt,** aim, bid, crack (*inf.*), effort, endeavour, go (*inf.*), shot (*inf.*), stab (*inf.*), try, undertaking, venture **3** = **test,** experiment, trial ◆ *vb* **4** = **attempt,** aim, endeavour, have a bash (*inf.*), have a crack (*inf.*), have a go, have a shot (*inf.*), strive, take on, try, undertake **5** = **test,** put to the test, try out

essence *n* **1** = **fundamental nature,** being, bottom line, core, crux, entity, heart, kernel, life, lifeblood, meaning, nature, pith, principle, quiddity, quintessence, significance, soul, spirit, substance **5** = **concentrate,** distillate, elixir, extract, spirits, tincture **7 in essence** = **essentially,** basically, fundamentally, in effect, in substance, in the main, materially, substantially, to all intents and purposes, virtually **8 of the essence** = **vitally important,** crucial, essential, indispensable, of the utmost importance, vital

essential *adj* **1** = **vital,** crucial, important, indispensable, necessary, needed, requisite **2** = **fundamental,** basic, cardinal, constitutional, elemental, elementary, immanent, inherent, innate, intrinsic, key, main, principal, radical **3** = **perfect,** absolute, complete, ideal, quintessential **4** = **concentrated,** distilled, extracted, rectified, refined, volatile ◆ *n* **7** = **prerequisite,** basic, fundamental, must, necessity, principle, requisite, rudiment, *sine qua non,* vital part
Antonyms *adj* ≠ **vital, fundamental:** accessory, dispensable, expendable, extra, extraneous, incidental, inessential, lesser, minor, nonessential, optional, secondary, superfluous, surplus, trivial, unimportant, unnecessary

establish *vb* **1, 2** = **create,** base, constitute, decree, enact, ensconce, entrench, fix, form, found, ground, implant, inaugurate, install, institute, organize, plant, put down roots, root, secure, settle, set up, sow the seeds, start **3** = **prove,** authenticate, certify, confirm, corroborate, demonstrate, ratify, show, substantiate, validate, verify

establishment *n* **1** = **creation,** enactment, formation, foundation, founding, inauguration, installation, institution, organization, setting up **2a** = **organization,** business, company, concern, corporation, enterprise, firm, house, institute, institution, outfit (*inf.*), setup (*inf.*), structure, system **2b** = **office,** building, factory, house, plant, quarters **5** = **house,** abode, domi-

body of employees or servants. **7** (*modifier*) belonging to or characteristic of the Establishment.

Establishment ❶ (ɪˈstæblɪʃmənt) *n* **the.** a group or class having institutional authority within a society: usually seen as conservative.

estate ❶ (ɪˈsteɪt) *n* **1** a large piece of landed property, esp. in the country. **2** *Chiefly Brit.* a large area of property development, esp. of new houses or (**trading estate**) of factories. **3** *Law.* **3a** property or possessions. **3b** the nature of interest that a person has in land or other property. **3c** the total extent of the property of a deceased person or bankrupt. **4** Also called: **estate of the realm.** an order or class in a political community, regarded as a part of the body politic: the lords spiritual (**first estate**), lords temporal or peers (**second estate**), and commons (**third estate**). See also **fourth estate. 5** state, period, or position in life: *youth's estate; a poor man's estate.* [C13: from OF *estat,* from L *status* condition, STATE]

estate agent *n* **1** *Brit.* an agent concerned with the valuation, management, lease, and sale of property. **2** the administrator of a large landed property; estate manager.

estate car *n Brit.* a car containing a large carrying space, reached through a rear door: usually the back seats fold forward to increase the carrying space.

estate duty *n* another name for **death duty.**

esteem ❶ (ɪˈstiːm) *vb* (*tr*) **1** to have great respect or high regard for. **2** *Formal.* to judge or consider; deem. ◆ *n* **3** high regard or respect; good opinion. **4** *Arch.* judgment; opinion. [C15: from OF *estimer,* from L *aestimāre* ESTIMATE]
▸**esˈteemed** *adj*

ester (ˈɛstə) *n Chem.* any of a class of compounds produced by reaction between acids and alcohols with the elimination of water. [C19: from G, prob. a contraction of *Essigäther* acetic ether, from *Essig* vinegar (ult. from L *acētum*) + *Äther* ETHER]

Esth. *Bible. abbrev.for* Esther.

esthesia (iːsˈθiːzɪə) *n* a US spelling of **aesthesia.**

esthete (ˈiːsθiːt) *n* a US spelling of **aesthete.**

estimable ❶ (ˈɛstɪməbᵊl) *adj* worthy of respect; deserving of admiration.
▸**ˈestimableness** *n* ▸**ˈestimably** *adv*

estimate ❶ *vb* (ˈɛstɪˌmeɪt), **estimates, estimating, estimated. 1** to form an approximate idea of (size, cost, etc.); calculate roughly. **2** (*tr; may take a clause as object*) to form an opinion about; judge. **3** to submit (an approximate price) for (a job) to a prospective client. ◆ *n* (ˈɛstɪmɪt). **4** an approximate calculation. **5** a statement of the likely charge for certain work. **6** a judgment; appraisal. [C16: from L *aestimāre* to assess the worth of, from ?]
▸**ˈestiˌmator** *n* ▸**ˈestimative** *adj*

estimation ❶ (ˌɛstɪˈmeɪʃən) *n* **1** a considered opinion; judgment. **2** esteem; respect. **3** the act of estimating.

estival (iːˈstaɪvᵊl, ˈɛstɪ-) *adj* the usual US spelling of **aestival.**

estivate (ˈiːstɪˌveɪt, ˈɛs-) *vb* **estivates, estivating, estivated.** (*intr*) the usual US spelling of **aestivate.**

Estonian *or* **Esthonian** (ɛˈstəʊnɪən, ɛˈsθəʊ-) *adj* **1** of, relating to, or characteristic of Estonia, a republic on the Gulf of Finland and the Baltic Sea. ◆ *n* **2** the official language of Estonia. **3** a native or inhabitant of Estonia.

estop (ɪˈstɒp) *vb* **estops, estopping, estopped.** (*tr*) **1** *Law.* to preclude by estoppel. **2** *Arch.* to stop. [C15: from OF *estoper* to plug, ult. from L *stuppa* tow; see STOP]
▸**esˈtoppage** *n*

estoppel (ɪˈstɒpᵊl) *n Law.* a rule of evidence whereby a person is precluded from denying the truth of a statement he has previously asserted. [C16: from OF *estoupail* plug; see ESTOP]

estovers (ɛˈstəʊvəz) *pl n Law.* necessaries allowed to tenants of land, esp. wood for fuel and repairs. [C15: from Anglo-F., pl of *estover,* from OF *estovoir* to be necessary, from L *est opus* there is need]

estradiol (ˌɛstrəˈdaɪɒl, ˌiːstrə-) *n* the usual US spelling of **oestradiol.**

estrange ❶ (ɪˈstreɪndʒ) *vb* **estranges, estranging, estranged.** (*tr*) to antagonize or lose the affection of (someone previously friendly); alienate. [C15: from OF *estranger,* from LL *extrāneāre* to treat as a stranger, from L *extrāneus* foreign]
▸**esˈtranged** *adj* ▸**esˈtrangement** *n*

estrogen (ˈɛstrədʒən, ˈiːstrə-) *n* the usual US spelling of **oestrogen.**

estrus (ˈɛstrəs, ˈiːstrəs) *n* the usual US spelling of **oestrus.**

estuary ❶ (ˈɛstjʊərɪ) *n, pl* **estuaries.** the widening channel of a river where it nears the sea. [C16: from L *aestuārium* marsh, channel, from *aestus* tide]
▸**estuarial** (ˌɛstjʊˈɛərɪəl) *adj* ▸**ˈestuarine** *adj*

e.s.u. *or* **ESU** *abbrev. for* electrostatic unit.

ET (in Britain) *abbrev. for* Employment Training: a government scheme offering training in technology and business to unemployed people.

-et *suffix of nouns.* small or lesser: *islet; baronet.* [from OF *-et, -ete*]

eta (ˈiːtə) *n* the seventh letter in the Greek alphabet (Η, η). [Gk, from Phoenician]

ETA *abbrev. for* estimated time of arrival.

et al. *abbrev. for:* **1** et alibi. [L: and elsewhere] **2** et alii. [L: and others]

etalon (ˈɛtəˌlɒn) *n Physics.* a device used in spectroscopy to measure wavelengths by interference effects produced by multiple reflections between parallel half-silvered glass plates. [C20: F *étalon* a standard of weights & measures]

etc. *abbrev. for* et cetera.

et cetera ❶ *or* **etcetera** (ɪt ˈsɛtrə) *n and vb substitute.* **1** and the rest; and others; and so forth. **2** or the like; or something similar. [from L *et* and + *cetera* the other (things)]

> **USAGE NOTE** It is unnecessary to use *and* before *etc.* as *etc.* (*et cetera*) already means *and other things.* The repetition of *etc.,* as in *he brought paper, ink, notebooks, etc., etc.,* is avoided except in informal contexts.

etceteras (ɪtˈsɛtrəz) *pl n* miscellaneous extra things or persons.

etch ❶ (ɛtʃ) *vb* **1** (*tr*) to wear away the surface of (a metal, glass, etc.) by the action of an acid. **2** to cut or corrode (a design, etc.) on (a metal or other printing plate) by the action of acid on parts not covered by an acid-resistant coating. **3** (*tr*) to cut as with a sharp implement. **4** (*tr; usually passive*) to imprint vividly. [C17: from Du. *etsen,* from OHG *azzen* to feed, bite]
▸**ˈetcher** *n*

etching ❶ (ˈɛtʃɪŋ) *n* **1** the art, act, or process of preparing etched surfaces or of printing designs from them. **2** an etched plate. **3** an impression made from an etched plate.

ETD *abbrev. for* estimated time of departure.

eternal ❶ (ɪˈtɜːnᵊl) *adj* **1a** without beginning or end; lasting forever. **1b** (*as n*): *the eternal.* **2** (*often cap.*) a name applied to God. **3** unchanged by time; immutable: *eternal truths.* **4** seemingly unceasing. [C14: from LL, from L *aeternus;* rel. to L *aevum* age]
▸**ˌeterˈnality** *or* **eˈternalness** *n* ▸**eˈternally** *adv*

eternalize (ɪˈtɜːnəˌlaɪz), **eternize** (ɪˈtɜːnaɪz), *or* **eternalise, eternise** *vb* **eternalizes, eternalizing, eternalized; eternizes, eternizing, eternized** *or* **eternalises, eternalising, eternalised; eternises, eternising, eternised.** (*tr*) **1** to make eternal. **2** to make famous forever; immortalize.
▸**eˌternaliˈzation, eˌterniˈzation** *or* **eˌternaliˈsation, eternisation** *n*

eternal triangle *n* an emotional relationship usually involving three people, two of whom are rival lovers of the third person.

eternity ❶ (ɪˈtɜːnɪtɪ) *n, pl* **eternities. 1** endless or infinite time. **2** the quality, state, or condition of being eternal. **3** (*usually pl*) any aspect of

THESAURUS

cile, dwelling, home, household, pad (*sl.*), residence

Establishment *n* = **the authorities**, established order, institutionalized authority, ruling class, the powers that be, the system

estate *n* **1** = **lands**, area, demesne, domain, holdings, manor, property **3** *Law* = **property**, assets, belongings, effects, fortune, goods, possessions, wealth **4** = **class**, caste, order, rank **5** = **status**, condition, lot, period, place, position, quality, rank, situation, standing, state, station

esteem *vb* **1** = **respect**, admire, be fond of, cherish, honour, like, love, prize, regard highly, revere, reverence, take off one's hat to, think highly of, treasure, value, venerate **2** *Formal* = **consider**, account, believe, calculate, deem, estimate, hold, judge, rate, reckon, regard, think, view ◆ *n* **3** = **respect**, admiration, Brownie points, consideration, credit, estimation, good opinion, honour, regard, reverence, veneration

estimable *adj* = **respectable**, admirable, esteemed, excellent, good, honourable, honoured, meritorious, reputable, respected, valuable, valued, worthy

estimate *vb* **1** = **calculate roughly**, appraise, assess, evaluate, gauge, guess, judge, number, reckon, value **2** = **form an opinion**, assess, believe, conjecture, consider, guess, judge, rank, rate, reckon, surmise, think ◆ *n* **4** = **approximate calculation**, appraisal, appraisement, assessment, ballpark estimate (*inf.*), ballpark figure (*inf.*), evaluation, guess, guesstimate (*inf.*), judgment, reckoning, valuation **6** = **opinion**, appraisal, appraisement, assessment, belief, conjecture, educated guess, estimation, judgment, surmise, thought(s)

estimation *n* **1** = **opinion**, appraisal, appreciation, assessment, belief, consideration, considered opinion, estimate, evaluation, judgment, view **2** = **respect**, admiration, Brownie points, credit, esteem, good opinion, honour, regard, reverence, veneration

estrange *vb* = **alienate**, antagonize, disaffect, disunite, divide, drive apart, lose *or* destroy the affection of, make hostile, part, separate, set at odds, withdraw, withhold
Antonyms *vb* ally, associate, coalesce, couple, fuse, join, link, marry, unite

estrangement *n* = **alienation**, antagonization, breach, break-up, disaffection, dissociation, disunity, division, hostility, parting, separation, split, withdrawal, withholding

estuary *n* = **inlet**, creek, firth, fjord, mouth

et cetera *n* **1** = **and the rest**, and others, and the like, et al.

etch *vb* **2** = **cut**, carve, corrode, eat into, engrave, furrow, impress, imprint, incise, ingrain, inscribe, stamp

etching *n* **1-3** = **print**, carving, engraving, impression, imprint, inscription

eternal *adj* **1** = **everlasting**, abiding, ceaseless, constant, deathless, endless, immortal, infinite, interminable, never-ending, perennial, perpetual, sempiternal (*literary*), timeless, unceasing, undying, unending, unremitting, without end **3** = **permanent**, deathless, enduring, everlasting, immortal, immutable, imperishable, indestructible, lasting, unchanging
Antonyms *adj* ≠ **everlasting:** finite, fleeting, infrequent, irregular, mortal, occasional, random, rare, temporal ≠ **permanent:** changing, ephemeral, evanescent, perishable, transient, transitory

eternity *n* **1, 2** = **infinity**, age, ages, endlessness, immortality, infinitude, perpetuity, timelessness, time without end **4** = **the afterlife**, heaven, paradise, the hereafter, the next world

life and thought considered timeless. **4** the timeless existence, believed by some to characterize the afterlife. **5** a seemingly endless period of time.

eternity ring *n* a ring given as a token of lasting affection, esp. one set all around with stones to symbolize continuity.

etesian (ɪ'ti:ʒɪən) *adj* (of NW winds) recurring annually in the summer in the E Mediterranean. [C17: from L *etēsius* yearly, from Gk *etos* year]

ETF *abbrev. for* electronic transfer of funds.

Eth. *abbrev. for:* **1** Ethiopia(n). **2** Ethiopic.

-eth[1] *suffix.* forming the archaic third person singular present indicative tense of verbs: *goeth; taketh.* [OE *-eth, -th*]

-eth[2] *suffix forming ordinal numbers.* a variant of **-th**[2]: *twentieth.*

ethanal ('ɛθəˌnæl) *n* the systematic name for **acetaldehyde.**

ethane ('i:θeɪn, 'ɛθ-) *n* a colourless odourless flammable gaseous alkane obtained from natural gas and petroleum: used as a fuel. Formula: C_2H_6. [C19: from ETH(YL)+ -ANE]

ethanediol ('i:θeɪnˌdaɪɒl, 'ɛθ-) *n* a colourless soluble liquid used as an antifreeze and solvent. Formula: $C_2H_4(OH)_2$. [C20: from ETHANE + DI-[1] + -OL[1]]

ethanoic acid (ˌɛθə'nəʊɪk, ˌi:θə-) *n* the systematic name for **acetic acid.**

ethanol ('ɛθəˌnɒl, 'i:θə-) *n* the systematic name for **alcohol** (sense 1).

ethene ('ɛθi:n) *n* the systematic name for **ethylene.**

ether ('i:θə) *n* **1** Also called: **diethyl ether, ethyl ether, ethoxyethane.** a colourless volatile highly flammable liquid: used as a solvent and anaesthetic. Formula: $C_2H_5OC_2H_5$. **2** any of a class of organic compounds with the general formula ROR′, as in methyl ethyl ether, $CH_3OC_2H_5$. **3** the medium formerly believed to fill all space and to support the propagation of electromagnetic waves. **4** *Greek myth.* the upper atmosphere; clear sky or heaven. ◆ Also (for senses 3 and 4): **aether.** [C17: from L, from Gk *aithein* to burn]
▸**e'theric** *adj*

ethereal ❶ (ɪ'θɪərɪəl) *adj* **1** extremely delicate or refined. **2** almost as light as air; airy. **3** celestial or spiritual. **4** of, containing, or dissolved in an ether, esp. diethyl ether. **5** of or relating to the ether. [C16: from L, from Gk *aithēr* ETHER]
▸**eˌthere'ality** *or* **e'therealness** *n*

etherealize *or* **etherealise** (ɪ'θɪərɪəˌlaɪz) *vb* **etherealizes, etherealizing, etherealized** *or* **etherealises, etherealising, etherealised.** (*tr*) **1** to make or regard as being ethereal. **2** to add ether to or make into ether.
▸**eˌthereali'zation** *or* **eˌthereali'sation** *n*

etherize *or* **etherise** ('i:θəˌraɪz) *vb* **etherizes, etherizing, etherized** *or* **etherises, etherising, etherised.** (*tr*) *Obs.* to subject (a person) to the anaesthetic influence of ether fumes; anaesthetize.
▸ˌ**etheri'zation** *or* ˌ**etheri'sation** *n* ▸'**etherˌizer** *or* '**etherˌiser** *n*

Ethernet ('i:θəˌnɛt) *n Trademark, computing.* a widely used type of local area network.

ethic ('ɛθɪk) *n* **1** a moral principle or set of moral values held by an individual or group. ◆ *adj* **2** another word for **ethical.** [C15: from L, from Gk *ēthos* custom]

ethical ❶ ('ɛθɪk[ə]l) *adj* **1** in accordance with principles of conduct that are considered correct, esp. those of a given profession or group. **2** of or relating to ethics. **3** (of a medicinal agent) available legally only with a doctor's prescription.
▸'**ethically** *adv* ▸'**ethicalness** *or* ˌ**ethi'cality** *n*

ethical investment *n* an investment in a company whose activities or products are not considered by the investor to be unethical.

ethics ❶ ('ɛθɪks) *n* **1** (*functioning as sing*) the philosophical study of the moral value of human conduct and of the rules and principles that ought to govern it. **2** (*functioning as pl*) a code of behaviour considered correct, esp. that of a particular group, profession, or individual. **3** (*functioning as pl*) the moral fitness of a decision, course of action, etc.
▸**ethicist** ('ɛθɪsɪst) *n*

Ethiopian (ˌi:θɪ'əʊpɪən) *adj* **1** of or relating to Ethiopia (a state in NE Africa), its people, or any of their languages. ◆ *n* **2** a native or inhabitant of Ethiopia. **3** any of the languages of Ethiopia, esp. Amharic. ◆ *n, adj* **4** an archaic word for **Black.**

Ethiopic (ˌi:θɪ'ɒpɪk, -'əʊpɪk) *n* **1** the ancient Semitic language of Ethiopia: a Christian liturgical language. **2** the group of languages developed from this language, including Amharic. ◆ *adj* **3** denoting or relating to this language or group of languages. **4** a less common word for **Ethiopian.**

ethnic ❶ ('ɛθnɪk) *or* **ethnical** *adj* **1** of or relating to a human group having racial, religious, linguistic, and other traits in common. **2** relating to the classification of mankind into groups, esp. on the basis of racial characteristics. **3** denoting or deriving from the cultural traditions of a group of people. **4** characteristic of another culture, esp. a peasant one. ◆ *n* **5** *Chiefly US.* a member of an ethnic group, esp. a minority one. [C14 (in the senses: heathen, Gentile): from LL *ethnicus,* from Gk *ethnos* race]
▸'**ethnically** *adv* ▸**ethnicity** (ɛθ'nɪsɪtɪ) *n*

ethno- *combining form.* indicating race, people, or culture. [via F from Gk *ethnos* race]

ethnocentrism (ˌɛθnəʊ'sɛnˌtrɪzəm) *n* belief in the intrinsic superiority of the nation, culture, or group to which one belongs.
▸ˌ**ethno'centric** *adj* ▸ˌ**ethno'centrically** *adv* ▸ˌ**ethnocen'tricity** *n*

ethnography (ɛθ'nɒgrəfɪ) *n* the branch of anthropology that deals with the scientific description of individual human societies.
▸ˌ**eth'nographer** *n* ▸**ethnographic** (ˌɛθnəʊ'græfɪk) *or* ˌ**ethno'graphical** *adj*

ethnology (ɛθ'nɒlədʒɪ) *n* the branch of anthropology that deals with races and peoples, their origins, characteristics, etc.
▸**ethnologic** (ˌɛθnə'lɒdʒɪk) *or* ˌ**ethno'logical** *adj* ▸**eth'nologist** *n*

ethnomusicology (ˌɛθnəʊˌmju:zɪ'kɒlədʒɪ) *n* the study of the origins of music, esp. from non-European cultures.

ethology (ɪ'θɒlədʒɪ) *n* the study of the behaviour of animals in their normal environment. [C17 (in the obs. sense: mimicry): via L from Gk *ēthos* character; current sense, C19]
▸**ethological** (ˌɛθə'lɒdʒɪk[ə]l) *adj* ▸**e'thologist** *n*

ethos ❶ ('i:θɒs) *n* the distinctive character, spirit, and attitudes of a people, culture, era, etc.: *the revolutionary ethos.* [C19: from LL: habit, from Gk]

ethyl ('i:θaɪl, 'ɛθɪl) *n* (*modifier*) of, consisting of, or containing the monovalent group C_2H_5–. [C19: from ETH(ER) + -YL]
▸**ethylic** (ɪ'θɪlɪk) *adj*

ethyl acetate *n* a colourless volatile flammable liquid ester: used in perfumes and flavourings and as a solvent. Formula: $CH_3COOC_2H_5$.

ethyl alcohol *n* another name for **alcohol** (sense 1).

ethylene ('ɛθɪˌli:n) *or* **ethene** ('ɛθi:n) *n* a colourless flammable gaseous alkene used in the manufacture of polythene and other chemicals. Formula: $CH_2{:}CH_2$.
▸**ethylenic** (ˌɛθɪ'li:nɪk) *adj*

ethylene glycol *n* another name for **ethanediol.**

ethylene group *or* **radical** *n Chem.* the divalent group, $-CH_2CH_2-$, derived from ethylene.

ethylene series *n Chem.* another name for **alkene series.**

ethyne ('ɛθaɪn) *n Chem.* the systematic name for **acetylene.**

ethyne series *n Chem.* another name for **acetylene series.**

etiolate ('i:tɪəʊˌleɪt) *vb* **etiolates, etiolating, etiolated. 1** *Bot.* to whiten (a green plant) through lack of sunlight. **2** to become or cause to become pale and weak. [C18: from F *étioler* to make pale, prob. from OF *estuble* straw, from L *stipula*]
▸ˌ**etio'lation** *n*

etiology (ˌi:tɪ'ɒlədʒɪ) *n, pl* **etiologies.** a variant spelling of **aetiology.**

etiquette ❶ ('ɛtɪˌkɛt, ˌɛtɪ'kɛt) *n* **1** the customs or rules governing behaviour regarded as correct in social life. **2** a conventional code of practice followed in certain professions or groups. [C18: from F, from OF *estiquette* label, from *estiquier* to attach; see STICK[2]]

Eton collar ('i:t[ə]n) *n* (formerly) a broad stiff white collar worn outside a boy's jacket.

Eton crop *n* a very short mannish hairstyle worn by women in the 1920s.

Eton jacket *n* a waist-length jacket with a V-shaped back, open in front, formerly worn by pupils of Eton College, a public school for boys in S England.

Etruscan (ɪ'trʌskən) *or* **Etrurian** (ɪ'trʊərɪən) *n* **1** a member of an ancient people of Etruria, in central Italy, whose civilization greatly influenced the Romans. **2** the language of the ancient Etruscans. ◆ *adj* **3** of or relating to Etruria, the Etruscans, their culture, or their language.

et seq. *abbrev. for:* **1** et sequens [L: and the following] **2** Also: **et seqq.** et sequentia [L: and those that follow]

-ette *suffix of nouns.* **1** small: *cigarette.* **2** female: *majorette.* **3** (esp. in trade names) imitation: *Leatherette.* [from F, fem of -ET]

étude ('eɪtju:d) *n* a short musical composition for a solo instrument, esp. one designed as an exercise or exploiting virtuosity. [C19: from F: STUDY]

étui (ɛ'twi:) *n, pl* **étuis.** a small usually ornamented case for holding needles, cosmetics, or other small articles. [C17: F, from OF *estuier* to enclose; see TWEEZERS]

etymology (ˌɛtɪ'mɒlədʒɪ) *n, pl* **etymologies. 1** the study of the sources and development of words. **2** an account of the source and development of a word. [C14: via L from Gk; see ETYMON, -LOGY]
▸**etymological** (ˌɛtɪmə'lɒdʒɪk[ə]l) *adj* ▸ˌ**ety'mologist** *n* ▸ˌ**ety'moloˌgize** *or* ˌ**ety'moloˌgise** *vb*

etymon ('ɛtɪˌmɒn) *n, pl* **etymons** *or* **etyma** (-mə). a form of a word, usually the earliest recorded form or a reconstructed form, from which an-

THESAURUS

ethereal *adj* **1** = **delicate**, dainty, exquisite, fine, light, rarefied, refined, subtle, tenuous **2** = **insubstantial**, aerial, airy, fairy, impalpable, intangible, light, rarefied **3** = **spiritual**, celestial, empyreal, heavenly, sublime, unearthly, unworldly

ethical *adj* **1** = **moral**, conscientious, correct, decent, fair, fitting, good, honest, honourable, just, principled, proper, right, righteous, upright, virtuous

Antonyms *adj* dishonourable, disreputable, immoral, improper, indecent, low-down (*inf.*), not cricket (*inf.*), underhand, unethical, unfair, unscrupulous, unseemly

ethics *n* **2** *plural* = **moral code**, conscience, morality, moral philosophy, moral values, principles, rules of conduct, standards

ethnic *adj* **3** = **cultural**, folk, indigenous, national, native, racial, traditional

ethos *n* = **spirit**, attitude, beliefs, character, disposition, ethic, tenor

etiquette *n* **1** = **good** *or* **proper behaviour**, civility, code, convention, courtesy, customs, decorum, formalities, manners, politeness, politesse, propriety, protocol, p's and q's, rules, usage

other word is derived. [C16: via L from Gk *etumon* basic meaning, from *etumos* true, actual]
Eu *the chemical symbol for* europium.
EU *abbrev. for* European Union.
eu- *combining form.* well, pleasant, or good: *eupeptic; euphony.* [via L from Gk, from *eus* good]
eucalyptus (ˌjuːkəˈlɪptəs) *or* **eucalypt** (ˈjuːkəˌlɪpt) *n, pl* **eucalyptuses, eucalypti** (-ˈlɪptaɪ), *or* **eucalypts.** any tree of the mostly Australian genus *Eucalyptus,* widely cultivated for timber and gum, as ornament, and for the medicinal oil in their leaves (**eucalyptus oil**). [C19: NL, from EU- + Gk *kaluptos* covered, from *kaluptein* to cover, hide]
Eucharist (ˈjuːkərɪst) *n* **1** the Christian sacrament in which Christ's Last Supper is commemorated by the consecration of bread and wine. **2** the consecrated elements of bread and wine offered in the sacrament. [C14: via Church L from Gk *eukharistos* thankful, from EU- + *kharis* favour]
▸ˌ**Euchaˈristic** *or* ˌ**Euchaˈristical** *adj*
euchre (ˈjuːkə) *n* **1** a US and Canad. card game for two, three, or four players, using a poker pack. **2** an instance of euchring another player. ◆ *vb* **euchres, euchring, euchred.** (*tr*) **3** to prevent (a player) from making his contracted tricks. **4** (usually foll. by *out*) *US, Canad., Austral., & NZ inf.* to outwit or cheat. [C19: from ?]
Euclidean *or* **Euclidian** (juːˈklɪdɪən) *adj* denoting a system of geometry based on the axioms of Euclid, 3rd-century B.C. Greek mathematician, esp. the axiom that parallel lines meet at infinity.
eucryphia (juːˈkrɪfɪə) *n* any of various mostly evergreen trees and shrubs of S America and Australia. [NL, from EU- + Gk *kryphios* covered]
eudiometer (ˌjuːdɪˈɒmɪtə) *n* a graduated glass tube used in the study and volumetric analysis of gas reactions. [C18: from Gk *eudios,* lit.: clear-skied + -METER]
eugenics (juːˈdʒɛnɪks) *n* (*functioning as sing*) the study of methods of improving the quality of the human race, esp. by selective breeding. [C19: from Gk *eugenēs* well-born, from EU- + *-genēs* born; see -GEN]
▸**euˈgenic** *adj* ▸**euˈgenically** *adv* ▸**euˈgenicist** *n* ▸**eugenist** (ˈjuːdʒənɪst) *n*
eukaryote *or* **eucaryote** (juˈkærɪəʊt) *n* an organism having cells each with a nucleus within which the genetic material is contained. Cf. **prokaryote.** [from EU- + KARYO- + *-ote* as in *zygote*]
▸**eukaryotic** *or* **eucaryotic** (juˌkærɪˈɒtɪk) *adj*
eulogize ➊ *or* **eulogise** (ˈjuːləˌdʒaɪz) *vb* **eulogizes, eulogizing, eulogized** *or* **eulogises, eulogising, eulogised.** to praise (a person or thing) highly in speech or writing.
▸ˈ**eulogist,** ˈ**euloˌgizer,** *or* ˈ**euloˌgiser** *n* ▸ˌ**euloˈgistic** *or* ˌ**euloˈgistical** *adj*
eulogy ➊ (ˈjuːlədʒɪ) *n, pl* **eulogies. 1** a speech or piece of writing praising a person or thing, esp. a person who has recently died. **2** high praise or commendation. ◆ Also called (archaic): **eulogium** (juːˈləʊdʒɪəm). [C16: from LL, from Gk: praise, from EU- + -LOGY]

> **USAGE NOTE** Avoid confusion with **elegy.**

Eumenides (juːˈmɛnɪˌdiːz) *pl n* another name for the **Furies,** used by the Greeks as a euphemism. [from Gk, lit: the benevolent ones]
eunuch (ˈjuːnək) *n* **1** a man who has been castrated, esp. (formerly) for some office such as a guard in a harem. **2** *Inf.* an ineffective man. [C15: via L from Gk *eunoukhos* bedchamber attendant]
euonymus (juːˈɒnɪməs) *or* **evonymus** (ɛˈvɒnɪməs) *n* any tree or shrub of the N temperate genus *Euonymus,* such as the spindle tree. [C18: from L: spindle tree, from Gk *euōnumos* fortunately named, from EU- + *onoma* NAME]
eupepsia (juːˈpɛpsɪə) *or* **eupepsy** (juːˈpɛpsɪ) *n Physiol.* good digestion. [C18: from NL, from Gk, from EU- + *pepsis* digestion]
▸**eupeptic** (juːˈpɛptɪk) *adj*
euphemism (ˈjuːfɪˌmɪzəm) *n* **1** an inoffensive word or phrase substituted for one considered offensive or hurtful. **2** the use of such inoffensive words or phrases. [C17: from Gk, from EU- + *phēmē* speech]
▸ˌ**eupheˈmistic** *adj* ▸ˌ**eupheˈmistically** *adv*
euphemize *or* **euphemise** (ˈjuːfɪˌmaɪz) *vb* **euphemizes, euphemizing, euphemized** *or* **euphemises, euphemising, euphemised.** to speak in euphemisms or refer to by means of a euphemism.
▸ˈ**eupheˌmizer** *or* ˈ**eupheˌmiser** *n*
euphonic (juːˈfɒnɪk) *or* **euphonious** (juːˈfəʊnɪəs) *adj* **1** denoting or relating to euphony. **2** (of speech sounds) altered for ease of pronunciation.
▸**euˈphonically** *or* **euˈphoniously** *adv* ▸**euˈphoniousness** *n*
euphonium (juːˈfəʊnɪəm) *n* a brass musical instrument with four valves. [C19: NL, from EUPH(ONY + HARM)ONIUM]
euphonize *or* **euphonise** (ˈjuːfəˌnaɪz) *vb* **euphonizes, euphonizing, euphonized** *or* **euphonises, euphonising, euphonised. 1** to make pleasant to hear. **2** to change (speech sounds) so as to facilitate pronunciation.
euphony (ˈjuːfənɪ) *n, pl* **euphonies. 1** the alteration of speech sounds, esp. by assimilation, so as to make them easier to pronounce. **2** a pleasing sound, esp. in speech. [C17: from LL, from Gk, from EU- + *phōnē* voice]
euphorbia (juːˈfɔːbɪə) *n* any plant of the genus *Euphorbia,* such as the spurges. [C14 *euforbia,* from L *euphorbea* African plant, after *Euphorbus,* first-cent. A.D. Gk physician]
euphoria ➊ (juːˈfɔːrɪə) *n* a feeling of great elation, esp. when exaggerated. [C19: from Gk: good ability to endure, from EU- + *pherein* to bear]
▸**euphoric** (juːˈfɒrɪk) *adj*
euphoriant (juːˈfɔːrɪənt) *adj* **1** able to produce euphoria. ◆ *n* **2** a euphoriant drug or agent.
euphotic (juːˈfəʊtɪk, -ˈfɒt-) *adj* denoting or relating to the uppermost part of a sea or lake, which receives enough light for photosynthesis to take place. [C20: from EU- + PHOTIC]
euphrasy (ˈjuːfrəsɪ) *n, pl* **euphrasies.** another name for **eyebright.** [C15: *eufrasie,* from Med. L, from Gk *euphrasia* gladness, from EU- + *phrēn* mind]
euphuism (ˈjuːfjuːˌɪzəm) *n* **1** an artificial prose style of the Elizabethan period, marked by extreme use of antithesis, alliteration, and extended similes and allusions. **2** any stylish affectation in speech or writing. [C16: after *Euphues,* prose romance by John Lyly]
▸ˈ**euphuist** *n* ▸ˌ**euphuˈistic** *or* ˌ**euphuˈistical** *adj*
eur. *or* **Eur.** *abbrev. for* Europe(an).
eur- *combining form.* (*sometimes cap.*) a variant of **euro-** before a vowel.
Eurasian (juəˈreɪʃən, -ʒən) *adj* **1** of or relating to Europe and Asia considered as a whole. **2** of mixed European and Asian descent. ◆ *n* **3** a person of mixed European and Asian descent.
Euratom (juəˈrætəm) *n* short for **European Atomic Energy Community;** an authority established by the EEC (now the EU) to develop peaceful uses of nuclear energy.
eureka (juˈriːkə) *interj* an exclamation of triumph on discovering or solving something. [C17: from Gk *heurēka* I have found (it), from *heuriskein* to find; traditionally the exclamation of Archimedes when he realized, during bathing, that the volume of an irregular solid could be calculated by measuring the water displaced when it was immersed]
eurhythmic (juːˈrɪðmɪk), **eurhythmical,** *or esp. US* **eurythmic, eurythmical** *adj* **1** having a pleasing and harmonious rhythm, order, or structure. **2** of or relating to eurhythmics. [C19: from L, from Gk, from EU- + *rhuthmos* proportion, RHYTHM]
eurhythmics *or esp. US* **eurythmics** (juːˈrɪðmɪks) *n* (*functioning as sing*) **1** a system of training through physical movement to music. **2** dancing of this style. [C20: from EURHYTHMIC]
▸**euˈrhythmy** *or* **euˈrythmy** *n*
euro (ˈjuərəu) *n* the currency unit of the member countries of the European Union who have adopted European Monetary Union.
euro- (ˈjuərəu) *or before a vowel* **eur-** *combining form.* (*sometimes cap.*) Europe *or* European.
eurobond (ˈjuərəuˌbɒnd) *n* (*sometimes cap.*) a bond issued in a eurocurrency.
Eurocentric (ˌjuərəuˈsɛntrɪk) *adj* chiefly concerned with or concentrating on Europe and European culture: *the Eurocentric curriculum.*
eurocheque (ˈjuərəuˌtʃɛk) *n* (*sometimes cap.*) a cheque drawn on a European bank that can be cashed at any bank or bureau de change displaying the EU sign or that can be used to pay for goods or services at any outlet displaying this sign.
Eurocommunism (ˌjuərəuˈkɒmjuˌnɪzəm) *n* the policies, doctrines, and practices of Communist Parties in Western Europe in the 1970s and 1980s, esp. those rejecting democratic centralism and favouring nonalignment with the Soviet Union and China.
▸ˌ**Euroˈcommunist** *n, adj*
eurocrat (ˈjuərəˌkræt) *n* (*sometimes cap.*) a member of the administration of the European Union.
eurocurrency (ˈjuərəuˌkʌrənsɪ) *n* (*sometimes cap.*) the currency of any country held on deposit in Europe outside its home market: used as a source of short- or medium-term finance because of easy convertibility.
eurodollar (ˈjuərəuˌdɒlə) *n* (*sometimes cap.*) a US dollar as part of a European holding. See **eurocurrency.**
euromarket (ˈjuərəuˌmɑːkɪt) *n* **1** a market for financing international trade backed by the central banks and commercial banks of the European Union. **2** the European Union treated as one large market for the sale of goods and services.
Euro MP *n Inf.* a member of the European Parliament.
euronote (ˈjuərəuˌnəut) *n* a form of euro-commercial paper consisting of short-term negotiable bearer notes.
European (ˌjuərəˈpɪən) *adj* **1** of or relating to Europe or its inhabitants. **2** native to or derived from Europe. ◆ *n* **3** a native or inhabitant of Europe. **4** a person of European descent. **5** *S. African.* any White person.
▸ˌ**Euroˈpeanˌism** *n*
European Commission *n* the executive body of the European Union,

THESAURUS

eulogize *vb* = **praise,** acclaim, applaud, commend, compliment, crack up (*inf.*), cry up, exalt, extol, glorify, laud, magnify (*arch.*), panegyrize, pay tribute to, sing *or* sound the praises of
eulogy *n* **1** = **tribute,** accolade, encomium, paean, panegyric **2** = **praise,** acclaim, acclamation, applause, commendation, compliment, exaltation, glorification, laudation, plaudits
euphoria *n* = **elation,** bliss, ecstasy, exaltation, exhilaration, exultation, glee, high spirits, intoxication, joy, joyousness, jubilation, rapture, transport
Antonyms *n* depression, despair, despondency, dolefulness, downheartedness, dumps (*inf.*), gloominess, hopelessness, low spirits, melancholia, melancholy, sadness, the blues

formed in 1967 to initiate action in the union and mediate between member governments.

European Community *or* **Communities** *n* the former name (until 1993) of the **European Union.**

European Council *n* an executive body of the European Union, made up of the President of the European Commission and representatives of the member states, including foreign and other ministers. The Council acts at the request of the Commission.

European Currency Unit *n* See **ECU.**

European Economic Community *n* the former W European economic association created by the Treaty of Rome (1957); in 1967 it merged with the European Coal and Steel Community and the European Atomic Energy Community to form the European Community, which was replaced in 1993 by the European Union. Informal name: **Common Market.** Abbrev.: **EEC.**

Europeanize *or* **Europeanise** (ˌjuərəˈpɪəˌnaɪz) *vb* **Europeanizes, Europeanizing, Europeanized** *or* **Europeanises, Europeanising, Europeanised.** (*tr*) **1** to make European. **2** to integrate (a country, economy, etc.) into the European Union.
▸**ˌEuroˌpeaniˈzation** *or* **ˌEuroˌpeaniˈsation** *n*

European Monetary System *n* the system used in the European Union for stabilizing exchange rates between the currencies of member states. It relies on the Exchange Rate Mechanism and the balance-of-payments support mechanism. Abbrev.: **EMS.**

European Parliament *n* the assembly of the European Union in Strasbourg.

European Union *n* the economic and political organization of European states created in 1967 (as the European Community) by the merger of the European Economic Community with the European Coal and Steel Community and the European Atomic Energy Community. The current members are Belgium, Denmark, France, Germany, Greece, Ireland, Italy, Luxembourg, the Netherlands, Portugal, Spain, and the UK; Austria, Finland, and Sweden joined in 1995. Abbrev.: **EU.**

Europhile (ˈjuərəuˌfaɪl) (*sometimes not cap.*) ◆ *n* **1** a person who admires Europe, Europeans, or the European Union. ◆ *adj* **2** marked by admiration for Europe, Europeans, or the European Union.

europium (juˈrəupɪəm) *n* a silvery-white element of the lanthanide series of metals. Symbol: Eu; atomic no.: 63; atomic wt.: 151.96. [C20: after *Europe* + -IUM]

Eurotunnel (ˈjuərəuˌtʌnᵊl) *n* another name for **Channel Tunnel.**

eurythmics (juːˈrɪðmɪks) *n* a variant spelling (esp. US) of **eurhythmics.**

Eustachian tube (juːˈsteɪʃən) *n* a tube that connects the middle ear with the pharynx and equalizes the pressure between the two sides of the eardrum. [C18: after Bartolomeo *Eustachio,* 16th-cent. It. anatomist]

eustatic (juːˈstætɪk) *adj* denoting or relating to worldwide changes in sea level, caused by the melting of ice sheets, sedimentation, etc. [C20: from Gk, from EU- + STATIC]

eutectic (juːˈtɛktɪk) *adj* **1** (of a mixture of substances) having the lowest freezing point of all possible mixtures of the substances. **2** concerned with or suitable for the formation of eutectic mixtures. ◆ *n* **3** a eutectic mixture. **4** the temperature at which a eutectic mixture forms. [C19: from Gk *eutēktos* melting readily, from EU- + *tēkein* to melt]

Euterpe (juːˈtɜːpɪ) *n Greek myth.* the Muse of lyric poetry and music.
▸**Euˈterpean** *adj*

euthanasia (ˌjuːθəˈneɪzɪə) *n* the act of killing someone painlessly, esp. to relieve suffering from an incurable illness. [C17: via NL from Gk: easy death]

euthenics (juːˈθɛnɪks) *n* (*functioning as sing*) the study of the control of the environment, esp. with a view to improving the health and living standards of the human race. [C20: from Gk *euthēnein* to thrive]
▸**euˈthenist** *n*

eutrophic (juːˈtrɒfɪk, -ˈtrəu-) *adj* (of lakes, etc.) rich in organic and mineral nutrients and supporting an abundant plant life. [C18: prob. from *eutrophy,* from Gk, from *eutrophos* well-fed]
▸**ˈeutrophy** *n*

eV *abbrev. for* electronvolt.

EVA *Astronautics. abbrev. for* extravehicular activity.

evacuate ➊ (ɪˈvækjuˌeɪt) *vb* **evacuates, evacuating, evacuated.** (*mainly tr*) **1** (*also intr*) to withdraw or cause to withdraw (from a place of danger) to a place of safety. **2** to make empty. **3** (*also intr*) *Physiol.* **3a** to eliminate or excrete (faeces). **3b** to discharge (any waste) from (the body). **4** (*tr*) to create a vacuum in (a bulb, flask, etc.). [C16: from L *ēvacuāre* to void, from *vacuus* empty]
▸**eˌvacuˈation** *n* ▸**eˈvacuative** *adj* ▸**eˈvacuˌator** *n* ▸**eˌvacuˈee** *n*

evade ➊ (ɪˈveɪd) *vb* **evades, evading, evaded.** (*mainly tr*) **1** to get away from or avoid (imprisonment, captors, etc.). **2** to get around, shirk, or dodge (the law, a duty, etc.). **3** (*also intr*) to avoid answering (a question). [C16: from F, from L *ēvādere* to go forth]
▸**eˈvadable** *adj* ▸**eˈvader** *n*

evaginate (ɪˈvædʒɪˌneɪt) *vb* **evaginates, evaginating, evaginated.** (*tr*) *Med.* to turn (an organ or part) inside out. [C17: from LL *ēvāgīnare* to unsheathe, from L *vāgīna* sheath]

evaluate ➊ (ɪˈvæljuˌeɪt) *vb* **evaluates, evaluating, evaluated.** (*tr*) **1** to ascertain or set the amount or value of. **2** to judge or assess the worth of. [C19: back formation from *evaluation,* from F, from *évaluer;* see VALUE]
▸**eˌvaluˈation** *n* ▸**eˈvaluative** *adj* ▸**eˈvaluˌator** *n*

evanesce (ˌɛvəˈnɛs) *vb* **evanesces, evanescing, evanesced.** (*intr*) (of smoke, mist, etc.) to fade gradually from sight; vanish. [C19: from L *ēvānēscere* to disappear; see VANISH]

evanescent ➊ (ˌɛvəˈnɛsᵊnt) *adj* **1** passing out of sight; fading away; vanishing. **2** ephemeral or transitory.
▸**ˌevaˈnescence** *n*

evangel (ɪˈvændʒəl) *n* **1** *Arch.* the gospel of Christianity. **2** (*often cap.*) any of the four Gospels of the New Testament. **3** any body of teachings regarded as basic. **4** *US.* an evangelist. [C14: from Church L, from Gk *evangelion* good news, from EU- + *angelos* messenger; see ANGEL]

evangelical ➊ (ˌiːvænˈdʒɛlɪkᵊl) *Christianity.* ◆ *adj* **1** of or following from the Gospels. **2** denoting or relating to any of certain Protestant sects, which emphasize personal conversion and faith in atonement through the death of Christ as a means of salvation. **3** denoting or relating to an evangelist. ◆ *n* **4** a member of an evangelical sect.
▸**ˌevanˈgelicalism** *n* ▸**ˌevanˈgelically** *adv*

evangelism (ɪˈvændʒɪˌlɪzəm) *n* **1** the practice of spreading the Christian gospel. **2** ardent or missionary zeal for a cause.

evangelist (ɪˈvændʒɪlɪst) *n* **1** an occasional preacher, sometimes itinerant. **2** a preacher of the Christian gospel.
▸**eˌvangeˈlistic** *adj*

Evangelist (ɪˈvændʒɪlɪst) *n* any of the writers of the New Testament Gospels: Matthew, Mark, Luke, or John.

evangelize *or* **evangelise** (ɪˈvændʒɪˌlaɪz) *vb* **evangelizes, evangelizing, evangelized** *or* **evangelises, evangelising, evangelised. 1** to preach the Christian gospel (to). **2** (*intr*) to advocate a cause with the object of making converts.
▸**eˌvangeliˈzation** *or* **eˌvangeliˈsation** *n* ▸**eˈvangeˌlizer** *or* **eˈvangeˌliser** *n*

evaporate ➊ (ɪˈvæpəˌreɪt) *vb* **evaporates, evaporating, evaporated. 1** to change or cause to change from a liquid or solid state to a vapour. **2** to lose or cause to lose liquid by vaporization leaving a more concentrated residue. **3** to disappear or cause to disappear. [C16: from LL, from L *vapor* steam; see VAPOUR]
▸**eˈvaporable** *adj* ▸**eˌvapoˈration** *n* ▸**eˈvaporative** *adj* ▸**eˈvapoˌrator** *n*

evaporated milk *n* thick unsweetened tinned milk from which some of the water has been evaporated.

evasion ➊ (ɪˈveɪʒən) *n* **1** the act of evading, esp. a distasteful duty, responsibility, etc., by cunning or by illegal means: *tax evasion.* **2** cunning or deception used to dodge a question, duty, etc.; means of evading. [C15: from LL *ēvāsio;* see EVADE]

evasive ➊ (ɪˈveɪsɪv) *adj* **1** tending or seeking to evade; not straightforward. **2** avoiding or seeking to avoid trouble or difficulties. **3** hard to catch or obtain; elusive.
▸**eˈvasively** *adv* ▸**eˈvasiveness** *n*

eve ➊ (iːv) *n* **1** the evening or day before some special event. **2** the period immediately before an event: *the eve of war.* **3** an archaic word for **evening.** [C13: var. of EVEN[2]]

THESAURUS

evacuate *vb* **1** = **clear,** abandon, decamp, depart, desert, forsake, leave, move out, pull out, quit, relinquish, remove, vacate, withdraw **3** *Physiology* = **excrete,** crap (*taboo sl.*), defecate, discharge, eject, eliminate, empty, expel, shit (*taboo sl.*), void

evacuation *n* **1** = **clearance,** abandonment, departure, exodus, flight, leaving, moving out, pulling out, removal, vacation, withdrawal **3** *Physiology* = **excretion,** crap (*taboo sl.*), defecation, discharge, ejection, elimination, purging, shit (*taboo sl.*), voiding

evade *vb* **1, 2** = **avoid,** body-swerve (*Scot.*), circumvent, decline, dodge, duck, elude, escape, escape the clutches of, eschew, get away from, shirk, shun, sidestep, slip through one's fingers, slip through the net, steer clear of **3** = **avoid answering,** balk, beat about the bush, circumvent, cop out (*sl.*), equivocate, fence, fend off, flannel (*Brit. inf.*), fudge, hedge, parry, prevaricate, quibble, waffle (*inf., chiefly Brit.*)

Antonyms *vb* ≠ **avoid:** brave, confront, encounter, face, meet, meet face to face

evaluate *vb* **1, 2** = **assess,** appraise, assay, calculate, estimate, gauge, judge, rank, rate, reckon, size up (*inf.*), value, weigh

evaluation *n* **1, 2** = **assessment,** appraisal, calculation, estimate, estimation, judgment, opinion, rating, valuation

evanescent *adj* **1, 2** = **ephemeral,** brief, fading, fleeting, fugacious, fugitive, impermanent, momentary, passing, short-lived, transient, transitory, vanishing

evangelical *adj* **2** = **crusading,** missionary, propagandizing, proselytizing, zealous

evaporate *vb* **1** = **dry up,** dehydrate, desiccate, dry, vaporize **3** = **disappear,** dematerialize, dispel, disperse, dissipate, dissolve, evanesce, fade, fade away, melt, melt away, vanish

evaporation *n* **1** = **drying up,** dehydration, desiccation, drying, vaporization **3** = **disappearance,** dematerialization, dispelling, dispersal, dissipation, dissolution, evanescence, fading, fading away, melting, melting away, vanishing

evasion *n* **1** = **avoidance,** circumvention, dodging, elusion, escape **2** = **deception,** artifice, cop-out (*sl.*), cunning, equivocation, evasiveness, excuse, fudging, obliqueness, pretext, prevarication, ruse, shift, shirking, shuffling, sophism, sophistry, subterfuge, trickery, waffle (*inf., chiefly Brit.*)

evasive *adj* **1** = **deceptive,** cagey (*inf.*), casuistic, casuistical, cunning, deceitful, devious, dissembling, equivocating, indirect, misleading, oblique, prevaricating, shifty, shuffling, slippery, sophistical, tricky

Antonyms *adj* candid, direct, frank, guileless, honest, open, straight, straightforward, truthful, unequivocating

eve *n* **1** = **night before,** day before, vigil **2** = **brink,** edge, point, threshold, verge

even[1] Ⓣ ('iːvᵊn) *adj* **1** level and regular; flat. **2** (*postpositive*; foll. by *with*) on the same level or in the same plane (as). **3** without variation or fluctuation; regular; constant. **4** not readily moved or excited; calm: *an even temper.* **5** equally balanced between two sides: *an even game.* **6** equal or identical in number, quantity, etc. **7a** (of a number) divisible by two. **7b** characterized or indicated by such a number: *the even pages.* Cf. **odd** (sense 4). **8** relating to or denoting two or either of two alternatives, events, etc., that have an equal probability: *an even chance of missing or catching a train.* **9** having no balance of debt; neither owing nor being owed. **10** just and impartial; fair. **11** exact in number, amount, or extent: *an even pound.* **12** equal, as in score; level. **13 even money. 13a** a bet in which the winnings are the same as the amount staked. **13b** (*as modifier*): *the even-money favourite.* **14 get even (with).** *Inf.* to exact revenge (on); settle accounts (with). ◆ *adv* **15** (intensifier; used to suggest that the content of a statement is unexpected or paradoxical): *even an idiot can do that.* **16** (intensifier; used with comparative forms): *even better.* **17** notwithstanding; in spite of. **18** used to introduce a more precise version of a word, phrase, or statement: *he is base, even depraved.* **19** used preceding a clause of supposition or hypothesis to emphasize that whether or not the condition in it is fulfilled, the statement in the main clause remains valid: *even if she died he wouldn't care.* **20** *Arch.* all the way; fully: *I love thee even unto death.* **21 even as.** (*conj*) at the very same moment or in the very same way that. **22 even so.** in spite of any assertion to the contrary: nevertheless. ◆ See also **even out, evens, even up.** [OE *efen*]
▸**'evener** *n* ▸**'evenly** *adv* ▸**'evenness** *n*

even[2] ('iːvᵊn) *n* an archaic word for **eve** or **evening.** [OE *ǣfen*]

even-handed Ⓣ *adj* fair; impartial.
▸**ˌeven-'handedly** *adv* ▸**ˌeven-'handedness** *n*

evening Ⓣ ('iːvnɪŋ) *n* **1** the latter part of the day, esp. from late afternoon until nightfall. **2** the latter or concluding period: *the evening of one's life.* **3** the early part of the night spent in a specified way: *an evening at the theatre.* **4** (*modifier*) of, used in, or occurring in the evening: *the evening papers.* [OE *ǣfnung*]

evening dress *n* attire for a formal occasion during the evening.

evening primrose *n* any plant of the genus *Oenothera,* typically having yellow flowers that open in the evening.

evening primrose oil *n* an oil, obtained from the seeds of the evening primrose, that is claimed to stimulate the production of prostaglandins.

evenings ('iːvnɪŋz) *adv Inf.* in the evening, esp. regularly.

evening star *n* a planet, usually Venus, seen just after sunset during the time that the planet is east of the sun.

even out Ⓣ *vb* (*adv*) to make or become even, as by the removal of bumps, inequalities, etc.

evens ('iːvənz) *adj, adv* **1** (of a bet) winning the same as the amount staked if successful. **2** (of a runner) offered at such odds.

evensong ('iːvᵊnˌsɒŋ) *n* **1** Also called: **Evening Prayer, vespers.** *Church of England.* the daily evening service. **2** *RC Church, arch.* another name for **vespers.**

event Ⓣ (ɪ'vɛnt) *n* **1** anything that takes place, esp. something important; an incident. **2** the actual or final outcome (esp. in **in the event, after the event**). **3** any one contest in a programme of sporting or other contests. **4 in any event** *or* **at all events.** regardless of circumstances; in any case. **5 in the event of.** in case of; if (such a thing) happens. **6 in the event that.** if it should happen that. [C16: from L *ēvenīre* to come forth, happen]

even-tempered Ⓣ *adj* not easily angered or excited; calm.

eventful Ⓣ (ɪ'vɛntfʊl) *adj* full of events.
▸**e'ventfully** *adv* ▸**e'ventfulness** *n*

event horizon *n Astron.* the spherical boundary of a black hole: objects passing through it would disappear completely and for ever, as no information can escape across the event horizon from the interior.

eventide ('iːvᵊnˌtaɪd) *n Arch. or poetic.* another word for **evening.**

eventide home *n Euphemistic.* an old people's home.

eventing (ɪ'vɛntɪŋ) *n Chiefly Brit.* taking part in equestrian competitions (esp. **three-day events**), usually involving cross-country riding, jumping, and dressage.

eventual Ⓣ (ɪ'vɛntʃʊəl) *adj* **1** (*prenominal*) happening in due course of time; ultimate. **2** *Arch.* contingent or possible.

eventuality Ⓣ (ɪˌvɛntʃʊ'ælɪtɪ) *n, pl* **eventualities.** a possible event, occurrence, or result; contingency.

eventually Ⓣ (ɪ'vɛntʃʊəlɪ) *adv* **1** at the very end; finally. **2** (*sentence modifier*) after a long time or long delay: *eventually, he arrived.*

eventuate (ɪ'vɛntʃʊˌeɪt) *vb* **eventuates, eventuating, eventuated.** (*intr*) **1** (often foll. by *in*) to result ultimately (in). **2** to come about as a result.
▸**eˌventu'ation** *n*

even up Ⓣ *vb* (*adv*) to make or become equal, esp. in respect of claims or debts.

ever Ⓣ ('ɛvə) *adv* **1** at any time. **2** by any chance; in any case: *how did you ever find out?* **3** at all times; always. **4** in any possible way or manner: *come as fast as ever you can.* **5** *Inf., chiefly Brit.* (intensifier, in **ever so, ever such,** and **ever such a**). **6 is he** *or* **she ever!** *US & Canad. sl.* he *or* she displays the quality concerned in abundance. ◆ See also **forever.** [OE *ǣfre,* from ?]

evergreen ('ɛvəˌgriːn) *adj* **1** (of certain trees and shrubs) bearing foliage throughout the year. Cf. **deciduous. 2** remaining fresh and vital. ◆ *n* **3** an evergreen tree or shrub.

evergreen fund *n* a fund that provides capital for new companies and makes regular injections of capital to support their development.

everlasting Ⓣ (ˌɛvə'lɑːstɪŋ) *adj* **1** never coming to an end; eternal. **2** lasting for an indefinitely long period. **3** lasting so long or occurring so often as to become tedious. ◆ *n* **4** eternity. **5** Also called: **everlasting flower.** another name for **immortelle.**
▸**ˌever'lastingly** *adv*

evermore Ⓣ (ˌɛvə'mɔː) *adv* (often preceded by *for*) all time to come.

evert (ɪ'vɜːt) *vb* (*tr*) to turn (an eyelid or other bodily part) outwards or inside out. [C16: from L *ēvertere* to overthrow, from *vertere* to turn]
▸**e'versible** *adj* ▸**e'version** *n*

every Ⓣ ('ɛvrɪ) *determiner* **1** each one (of the class specified), without exception. **2** (*not used with a negative*) the greatest or best possible: *every hope.* **3** each: used before a noun phrase to indicate the recurrent, intermittent, or serial nature of a thing: *every third day.* **4 every bit.** (used in comparisons with *as*) quite; just; equally. **5 every other.** each alternate; every second. **6 every which way.** *US & Canad.* **6a** in all directions; everywhere. **6b** from all sides. [C15 *everich,* from OE *ǣfre ǣlc,* from *ǣfre* EVER + *ǣlc* EACH]

THESAURUS

even[1] *adj* **1** = **level,** flat, flush, horizontal, parallel, plane, plumb, smooth, steady, straight, true, uniform **3** = **regular,** constant, metrical, smooth, steady, unbroken, uniform, uninterrupted, unvarying, unwavering **4** = **calm,** composed, cool, equable, equanimous, even-tempered, imperturbable, peaceful, placid, serene, stable, steady, tranquil, undisturbed, unexcitable, unruffled, well-balanced **5, 6** = **equal,** coequal, commensurate, comparable, drawn, equalized, equally balanced, fifty-fifty (*inf.*), identical, level, level pegging (*Brit. inf.*), like, matching, neck and neck, on a par, parallel, similar, square, the same, tied, uniform **10** = **fair,** balanced, disinterested, dispassionate, equitable, fair and square, impartial, just, unbiased, unprejudiced **14 get even (with)** *Informal* = **pay back,** be revenged *or* revenge oneself, even the score, get one's own back, give tit for tat, pay (someone) back in his *or* her own coin, reciprocate, repay, requite, return like for like, settle the score, take an eye for an eye, take vengeance ◆ *adv* **17** = **despite,** disregarding, in spite of, notwithstanding **21 even as** = **while,** at the same time as, at the time that, during the time that, exactly as, just as, whilst **22 even so** = **nevertheless,** all the same, be that as it may, despite (that), however, in spite of (that), nonetheless, notwithstanding (that), still, yet
Antonyms *adj* ≠ **level:** asymmetrical, awry, bumpy, curving, rough, twisting, undulating, uneven, wavy ≠ **regular:** broken, changeable, changing, different, fluctuating, irregular, odd, uneven, variable ≠ **calm:** agitated, changeable, emotional, excitable, quick-tempered, unpredictable ≠ **equal:** disproportionate, ill-matched, imbalanced, irregular, unequal, uneven ≠ **fair:** biased, partial, prejudiced, unbalanced, unequal, unfair

even-handed *adj* = **fair,** balanced, disinterested, equitable, fair and square, impartial, just, unbiased, unprejudiced

evening *n* **1** = **dusk,** e'en (*arch. or poetic*), eve, even (*arch.*), eventide (*arch. or poetic*), gloaming (*Scot. or poetic*), twilight, vesper (*arch.*)

even out *vb* = **make** *or* **become level,** align, flatten, level, regularize, smooth, square, stabilize, steady

event *n* **1** = **incident,** adventure, affair, business, circumstance, episode, escapade, experience, fact, happening, matter, milestone, occasion, occurrence **2** *As in* **in the event** = **outcome,** conclusion, consequence, effect, end, issue, result, termination, upshot **3** = **competition,** bout, contest, game, tournament **4 in any event** *or* **at all events** = **whatever happens,** at any rate, come what may, in any case, regardless

even-tempered *adj* = **calm,** composed, cool, cool-headed, equable, imperturbable, level-headed, peaceful, placid, serene, steady, tranquil, unexcitable, unruffled
Antonyms *adj* emotional, excitable, hasty, highly-strung, hot-headed, hot-tempered, irascible, quick-tempered, temperamental, touchy, volatile

eventful *adj* = **exciting,** active, busy, consequential, critical, crucial, decisive, dramatic, fateful, full, historic, important, lively, memorable, momentous, notable, noteworthy, remarkable, significant
Antonyms *adj* commonplace, dull, humdrum, insignificant, ordinary, trivial, uneventful, unexceptional, unexciting, unimportant, uninteresting, unremarkable

eventual *adj* **1** = **final,** concluding, consequent, ensuing, future, later, overall, prospective, resulting, ultimate

eventuality *n* = **possibility,** case, chance, contingency, event, likelihood, probability

eventually *adv* **1** = **in the end,** after all, at the end of the day, finally, in the course of time, in the fullness of time, in the long run, one day, some day, some time, sooner or later, ultimately, when all is said and done

even up *vb* = **equalize,** balance, equal, match

ever *adv* **1, 2** = **at any time,** at all, at any period, at any point, by any chance, in any case, on any occasion **3** = **always,** at all times, aye (*Scot.*), constantly, continually, endlessly, eternally, everlastingly, evermore, for ever, incessantly, perpetually, relentlessly, to the end of time, unceasingly, unendingly

everlasting *adj* **1** = **eternal,** abiding, deathless, endless, immortal, imperishable, indestructible, infinite, interminable, never-ending, perpetual, timeless, undying **2** = **continual,** ceaseless, constant, continuous, endless, incessant, interminable, never-ending, unceasing, uninterrupted, unremitting
Antonyms *adj* ≠ **eternal:** brief, ephemeral, fleeting, impermanent, passing, short-lived, temporary, transient, transitory

evermore *adv* = **for ever,** always, eternally, ever, *in perpetuum,* to the end of time

every *determiner* **1** = **each,** all, each one, the whole number

everybody ➊ ('ɛvrɪˌbɒdɪ) *pron* every person; everyone.

USAGE NOTE See at **everyone.**

everyday ➊ ('ɛvrɪˌdeɪ) *adj* **1** happening each day. **2** commonplace or usual. **3** suitable for or used on ordinary days.
Everyman ('ɛvrɪˌmæn) *n* **1** a medieval English morality play in which the central figure represents mankind. **2** (*often not cap.*) the ordinary person; common man.
everyone ➊ ('ɛvrɪˌwʌn, -wən) *pron* every person; everybody.

USAGE NOTE *Everyone* and *everybody* are interchangeable, as are *no one* and *nobody,* and *someone* and *somebody.* Care should be taken to distinguish between *everyone* and *someone* as single words and *every one* and *some one* as two words, the latter form correctly being used to refer to each individual person or thing in a particular group: *every one of them is wrong.*

every one *pron* each person or thing in a group, without exception.
everything ➊ ('ɛvrɪˌθɪŋ) *pron* **1** the entirety of a specified or implied class. **2** a great deal, esp. of something very important.
everywhere ➊ ('ɛvrɪˌwɛə) *adv* to or in all parts or places.
evict ➊ (ɪ'vɪkt) *vb* (*tr*) **1** to expel (a tenant) from property by process of law; turn out. **2** to recover (property or the title to property) by judicial process or by virtue of a superior title. [C15: from LL *ēvincere,* from L: to vanquish utterly]
▸**e'viction** *n* ▸**e'victor** *n*
evidence ➊ ('ɛvɪdəns) *n* **1** ground for belief or disbelief; data on which to base proof or to establish truth or falsehood. **2** a mark or sign that makes evident. **3** *Law.* matter produced before a court of law in an attempt to prove or disprove a point in issue. **4 in evidence.** on display; apparent. ◆ *vb* **evidences, evidencing, evidenced.** (*tr*) **5** to make evident; show clearly. **6** to give proof of or evidence for.
evident ➊ ('ɛvɪdənt) *adj* easy to see or understand; apparent. [C14: from L *ēvidēns,* from *vidēre* to see]
evidential (ˌɛvɪ'dɛnʃəl) *adj* relating to, serving as, or based on evidence.
▸ˌ**evi'dentially** *adv*
evidently ➊ ('ɛvɪdəntlɪ) *adv* **1** without question; clearly. **2** to all appearances; apparently.
evil ➊ ('iːvᵊl) *adj* **1** morally wrong or bad; wicked. **2** causing harm or injury. **3** marked or accompanied by misfortune: *an evil fate.* **4** (of temper, disposition, etc.) characterized by anger or spite. **5** infamous: *an evil reputation.* **6** offensive or unpleasant: *an evil smell.* **7** *Sl., chiefly US.* excellent or outstanding. ◆ *n* **8** the quality or an instance of being morally wrong; wickedness. **9** (*sometimes cap.*) a force or power that brings about wickedness or harm. ◆ *adv* **10** (*now usually in combination*) in an evil manner; badly: *evil-smelling.* [OE *yfel*]
▸**'evilly** *adv* ▸**'evilness** *n*
evildoer ➊ ('iːvᵊlˌduːə) *n* a person who does evil.
▸**'evilˌdoing** *n*
evil eye *n* **the. 1** a look or glance superstitiously supposed to have the power of inflicting harm or injury. **2** the power to inflict harm, etc., by such a look.
▸ˌ**evil-'eyed** *adj*
evil-minded ➊ *adj* inclined to evil thoughts; malicious or spiteful.
▸ˌ**evil-'mindedly** *adv* ▸ˌ**evil-'mindedness** *n*
evince ➊ (ɪ'vɪns) *vb* **evinces, evincing, evinced.** (*tr*) to make evident; show (something) clearly. [C17: from L *ēvincere* to overcome; see EVICT]
▸**e'vincible** *adj*

USAGE NOTE *Evince* is sometimes wrongly used where *evoke* is meant: *the proposal evoked* (not *evinced*) *a storm of protest.*

eviscerate (ɪ'vɪsəˌreɪt) *vb* **eviscerates, eviscerating, eviscerated.** (*tr*) **1** to remove the internal organs of; disembowel. **2** to deprive of meaning or significance. [C17: from L *ēviscerāre,* from *viscera* entrails]
▸**eˌviscer'ation** *n* ▸**e'viscerˌator** *n*
evocation (ˌɛvə'keɪʃən) *n* the act or an instance of evoking. [C17: from L: see EVOKE]
▸**evocative** (ɪ'vɒkətɪv) *adj*
evoke ➊ (ɪ'vəʊk) *vb* **evokes, evoking, evoked.** (*tr*) **1** to call or summon up (a memory, feeling, etc.), esp. from the past. **2** to provoke; elicit. **3** to cause (spirits) to appear; conjure up. [C17: from L *ēvocāre* to call forth, from *vocāre* to call]
▸**evocable** ('ɛvəkəbᵊl) *adj* ▸**e'voker** *n*

USAGE NOTE See at **evince** and **invoke.**

evolute ('ɛvəˌluːt) *n* **1** a geometric curve that describes the locus of the centres of curvature of another curve (the **involute**). ◆ *adj* **2** *Biol.* having the margins rolled outwards. [C19: from L *ēvolūtus* unrolled, from *ēvolvere* to roll out, EVOLVE]
evolution ➊ (ˌiːvə'luːʃən) *n* **1** *Biol.* a gradual change in the characteristics of a population of animals or plants over successive generations. **2** a gradual development, esp. to a more complex form: *the evolution of modern art.* **3** the act of throwing off, as heat, gas, vapour, etc. **4** a pattern formed by a series of movements or something similar. **5** an algebraic operation in which the root of a number, expression, etc., is extracted. **6** *Mil.* an exercise carried out in accordance with a set procedure or plan. [C17: from L *ēvolūtiō* an unrolling, from *ēvolvere* to EVOLVE]
▸ˌ**evo'lutionary** *or* ˌ**evo'lutional** *adj*
evolutionist (ˌiːvə'luːʃənɪst) *n* **1** a person who believes in a theory of evolution. ◆ *adj* **2** of or relating to a theory of evolution.
▸ˌ**evo'lutionism** *n* ▸ˌ**evolution'istic** *adj*
evolve ➊ (ɪ'vɒlv) *vb* **evolves, evolving, evolved. 1** to develop or cause to develop gradually. **2** (of animal or plant species) to undergo evolution of (organs or parts). **3** (*tr*) to yield, emit, or give off (heat, gas, vapour, etc.). [C17: from L *ēvolvere* to unfold, from *volvere* to roll]
▸**e'volvable** *adj* ▸**e'volvement** *n*
evzone ('ɛvzəʊn) *n* a soldier in an elite Greek infantry regiment. [C19: from Mod. Gk, from Gk *euzōnos,* lit.: well-girt, from EU- + *zōne* girdle]

THESAURUS

everybody *pron* = **everyone**, all and sundry, each one, each person, every person, one and all, the whole world

everyday *adj* **1** = **daily**, quotidian **2** = **ordinary**, accustomed, banal, bog-standard (*Brit. & Irish sl.*), common, common or garden (*inf.*), commonplace, conventional, customary, dime-a-dozen (*inf.*), dull, familiar, frequent, habitual, informal, mundane, routine, run-of-the-mill, stock, unexceptional, unimaginative, usual, vanilla (*sl.*), wonted, workaday
Antonyms *adj* ≠ **daily:** infrequent, irregular, now and then, occasional, periodic ≠ **ordinary:** best, exceptional, exciting, extraordinary, incidental, individual, infrequent, interesting, irregular, now and then, occasional, original, outlandish, periodic, special, uncommon, unusual

everyone *pron* = **everybody**, all and sundry, each one, each person, every person, one and all, the whole world

everything *pron* **1** = **all**, each thing, the aggregate, the entirety, the lot, the sum, the total, the whole, the whole caboodle (*inf.*), the whole kit and caboodle (*inf.*), the whole lot

everywhere *adv* = **to** *or* **in every place**, all around, all over, far and wide *or* near, high and low, in each place, in every nook and cranny, omnipresent, the world over, ubiquitous, ubiquitously

evict *vb* **1** = **expel**, boot out (*inf.*), chuck out (*inf.*), dislodge, dispossess, eject, kick out (*inf.*), oust, put out, remove, show the door (to), throw on to the streets, throw out, turf out (*inf.*), turn out

eviction *n* **1** = **expulsion**, clearance, dislodgement, dispossession, ejection, ouster (*Law*), removal

evidence *n* **1, 2** = **proof**, affirmation, attestation, averment, confirmation, corroboration, data, declaration, demonstration, deposition, grounds, indication, manifestation, mark, sign, substantiation, testimony, token, witness ◆ *vb* **5, 6** = **show**, demonstrate, denote, display, evince, exhibit, indicate, manifest, prove, reveal, signify, testify to, witness

evident *adj* = **obvious**, apparent, blatant, bold, clear, conspicuous, incontestable, incontrovertible, indisputable, manifest, noticeable, palpable, patent, perceptible, plain, plain as the nose on your face, salient, tangible, unmistakable, visible
Antonyms *adj* ambiguous, concealed, doubtful, dubious, hidden, imperceptible, obscure, questionable, secret, uncertain, unclear, unknown, vague

evidently *adv* **1** = **obviously**, clearly, doubtless, doubtlessly, incontestably, incontrovertibly, indisputably, manifestly, patently, plainly, undoubtedly, unmistakably, without question **2** = **apparently**, it seems, it would seem, ostensibly, outwardly, seemingly, to all appearances

evil *adj* **1** = **wicked**, bad, base, corrupt, depraved, heinous, immoral, iniquitous, maleficent, malevolent, malicious, malignant, nefarious, reprobate, sinful, unholy, vicious, vile, villainous, wrong **2** = **harmful**, baneful (*arch.*), calamitous, catastrophic, deleterious, destructive, detrimental, dire, disastrous, hurtful, inauspicious, injurious, mischievous, painful, pernicious, ruinous, sorrowful, unfortunate, unlucky, woeful **6** = **offensive**, foul, mephitic, noxious, pestilential, putrid, unpleasant, vile ◆ *n* **8** = **wickedness**, badness, baseness, corruption, curse, depravity, heinousness, immorality, iniquity, maleficence, malignity, sin, sinfulness, turpitude, vice, viciousness, villainy, wrong, wrongdoing

evildoer *n* = **sinner**, bad hat (*inf., chiefly Brit*), blackguard, criminal, crook (*inf.*), culprit, delinquent, malefactor, mischief-maker, miscreant, offender, reprobate, rogue, villain, wrongdoer, wrong 'un (*inf.*)

evildoing *n* = **sin**, abomination, badness, crime, devilry, evil, fiendishness, harm, iniquity, injury, mischief-making, vice, viciousness, vileness, villainy, wickedness, wrongdoing

evil-minded *adj* = **nasty**, bitchy (*inf.*), depraved, dirty-minded, filthy, foul-mouthed, gossip-mongering, lewd, malicious, poisonous, salacious, snide, spiteful, venomous

evince *vb* = **show**, attest, bespeak, betoken, demonstrate, display, establish, evidence, exhibit, express, indicate, make clear, make evident, manifest, reveal, signify

evoke *vb* **1** = **arouse**, awaken, call, excite, give rise to, induce, recall, rekindle, stimulate, stir up, summon up **2** = **provoke**, call forth, educe (*rare*), elicit, produce **3** = **conjure up**, arouse, call, call forth, invoke, raise, summon
Antonyms *vb* ≠ **arouse:** contain, hold in check, inhibit, muffle, repress, restrain, smother, stifle, suppress

evolution *n* **2** = **development**, enlargement, evolvement, expansion, growth, increase, maturation, progress, progression, unfolding, unrolling, working out

evolve *vb* **1** = **develop**, disclose, educe, elabo-

DICTIONARY

ewe (juː) *n* **a** a female sheep. **b** *(as modifier): a ewe lamb.* [OE *ēowu*]

ewer (ˈjuːə) *n* a large jug or pitcher with a wide mouth. [C14: from OF *evier,* from L *aquārius* water carrier, from *aqua* water]

ex[1] (ɛks) *prep* **1** *Finance.* excluding; without: *ex dividend.* **2** *Commerce.* without charge to the buyer until removed from: *ex warehouse.* [C19: from L: out of, from]

ex[2] (ɛks) *n Inf.* (a person's) former wife, husband, etc.

Ex. *Bible. abbrev. for* Exodus.

ex-[1] *prefix* **1** out of; outside of; from: *exclosure; exurbia.* **2** former: *ex-wife.* [from L, from *ex* (prep), identical with Gk *ex, ek;* see EC-]

ex-[2] *combining form.* a variant of **exo-** before a vowel: *exergonic.*

exa- *prefix* denoting 10^{18}: *exametres.* Symbol: E

exacerbate ❶ (ɪgˈzæsəˌbeɪt, ɪkˈsæs-) *vb* **exacerbates, exacerbating, exacerbated.** *(tr)* **1** to make (pain, disease, etc.) more intense; aggravate. **2** to irritate (a person). [C17: from L *exacerbāre* to irritate, from *acerbus* bitter]
▸**exˌacerˈbation** *n*

exact ❶ (ɪgˈzækt) *adj* **1** correct in every detail; strictly accurate. **2** precise, as opposed to approximate. **3** *(prenominal)* specific; particular. **4** operating with very great precision. **5** allowing no deviation from a standard; rigorous; strict. **6** based on measurement and the formulation of laws, as opposed to description and classification: *an exact science.* ◆ *vb (tr)* **7** to force or compel (payment, etc.); extort: *to exact tribute.* **8** to demand as a right; insist upon. **9** to call for or require. [C16: from L *exactus* driven out, from *exigere* to drive forth, from *agere* to drive]
▸**exˈactable** *adj* ▸**exˈactness** *n* ▸**exˈactor** *or* **exˈacter** *n*

exacting ❶ (ɪgˈzæktɪŋ) *adj* making rigorous or excessive demands.
▸**exˈactingness** *n*

exaction ❶ (ɪgˈzækʃən) *n* **1** the act or an instance of exacting. **2** an excessive or harsh demand, esp. for money. **3** a sum or payment exacted.

exactitude ❶ (ɪgˈzæktɪˌtjuːd) *n* the quality of being exact; precision; accuracy.

exactly ❶ (ɪgˈzæktlɪ) *adv* **1** in an exact manner; accurately or precisely. **2** in every respect; just. ◆ *sentence substitute.* **3** just so!, precisely! **4 not exactly.** *Ironical.* not at all; by no means.

exacum (ˈɛksəkəm) *n* any of various Asian flowering herbs. [NL, from EX-[1] + Gk *ago* to arrive]

exaggerate ❶ (ɪgˈzædʒəˌreɪt) *vb* **exaggerates, exaggerating, exaggerated. 1** to regard or represent as larger or greater, more important or more successful, etc., than is true. **2** *(tr)* to make greater, more noticeable, etc. [C16: from L *exaggerāre* to magnify, from *aggerāre* to heap, from *agger* heap]
▸**exˈaggerˌated** *adj* ▸**exˌaggerˈation** *n* ▸**exˈaggerˌator** *n*

ex all *adv, adj Finance.* without the right to any benefits: *shares quoted ex all.*

exalt ❶ (ɪgˈzɔːlt) *vb (tr)* **1** to elevate in rank, dignity, etc. **2** to praise highly; extol. **3** to stimulate; excite. **4** to fill with joy or delight; elate. [C15: from L *exaltāre* to raise, from *altus* high]
▸**exˈalted** *adj* ▸**exˈalter** *n*

> **USAGE NOTE** *Exalt* is sometimes wrongly used where *exult* is meant: *he was exulting* (not *exalting*) *in his win earlier that day.*

exaltation ❶ (ˌɛgzɔːlˈteɪʃən) *n* **1** the act of exalting or state of being exalted. **2** exhilaration; elation; rapture.

exam (ɪgˈzæm) *n* short for **examination.**

examination ❶ (ɪgˌzæmɪˈneɪʃən) *n* **1** the act of examining or state of being examined. **2** *Education.* **2a** written exercises, oral questions, etc., set to test a candidate's knowledge and skill. **2b** *(as modifier): an examination paper.* **3** *Med.* **3a** physical inspection of a patient. **3b** laboratory study of secretory or excretory products, tissue samples, etc. **4** *Law.* the formal interrogation of a person on oath.
▸**exˌamiˈnational** *adj*

examine ❶ (ɪgˈzæmɪn) *vb* **examines, examining, examined.** *(tr)* **1** to inspect or scrutinize carefully or in detail; investigate. **2** *Education.* to test the knowledge or skill of (a candidate) in (a subject or activity) by written or oral questions, etc. **3** *Law.* to interrogate (a person) formally on oath. **4** *Med.* to investigate the state of health of (a patient). [C14: from OF, from L *exāmināre* to weigh, from *exāmen* means of weighing]
▸**exˈaminable** *adj* ▸**exˌamiˈnee** *n* ▸**exˈaminer** *n* ▸**exˈamining** *adj*

example ❶ (ɪgˈzɑːmpᵊl) *n* **1** a specimen or instance that is typical of its group or set; sample. **2** a person, action, thing, etc., that is worthy of imitation; pattern. **3** a precedent, illustration of a principle, or model. **4** a punishment or the recipient of a punishment intended to serve as a warning. **5 for example.** as an illustration; for instance. ◆ *vb* **examples, exampling, exampled. 6** *(tr; now usually passive)* to present an example of; exemplify. [C14: from OF, from L *exemplum* pattern, from *eximere* to take out]

exanthema (ˌɛksænˈθiːmə) *n, pl* **exanthemata** (-ˈθiːmətə) *or* **exanthemas.** a skin rash occurring in a disease such as measles. [C17: via LL from Gk, from *exanthein* to burst forth, from *anthein* to blossom]

exasperate ❶ (ɪgˈzɑːspəˌreɪt) *vb* **exasperates, exasperating, exasperated.** *(tr)* **1** to cause great irritation or anger to. **2** to cause (something unpleasant) to worsen; aggravate. [C16: from L *exasperāre* to make rough, from *asper* rough]
▸**exˈasperˌatedly** *adv* ▸**exˈasperˌatingly** *adv* ▸**exˌasperˈation** *n*

THESAURUS

rate, enlarge, expand, grow, increase, mature, open, progress, unfold, unroll, work out

exacerbate *vb* **1 = make worse,** aggravate, inflame, intensify, worsen **2 = irritate,** aggravate *(inf.)*, embitter, enrage, envenom, exasperate, infuriate, madden, provoke, vex

exact *adj* **1-3 = accurate,** careful, correct, definite, explicit, express, faithful, faultless, identical, literal, methodical, on the money *(US)*, orderly, particular, precise, right, specific, true, unequivocal, unerring, veracious, very **5 = meticulous,** careful, exacting, painstaking, punctilious, rigorous, scrupulous, severe, strict ◆ *vb* **7-9 = demand,** call for, claim, command, compel, extort, extract, force, impose, insist upon, require, squeeze, wrest, wring
Antonyms *adj* ≠ **accurate:** approximate, careless, imprecise, inaccurate, incorrect, indefinite, inexact, loose, rough, slovenly

exacting *adj* **= demanding,** difficult, hard, harsh, imperious, oppressive, painstaking, rigid, rigorous, severe, stern, strict, stringent, taxing, tough, unsparing
Antonyms *adj* easy, easy-peasy *(sl.)*, effortless, no bother, simple, undemanding

exaction *n* **1 = demand,** compulsion, contribution, extortion, imposition, oppression, rapacity, requirement, requisition, shakedown *(US sl.)*, squeeze *(inf.)*, tribute

exactitude *n* **= precision,** accuracy, carefulness, correctness, exactness, faithfulness, faultlessness, nicety, orderliness, painstakingness, preciseness, promptitude, regularity, rigorousness, rigour, scrupulousness, strictness, truth, unequivocalness, veracity

exactly *adv* **1 = precisely,** accurately, carefully, correctly, definitely, explicitly, faithfully, faultlessly, literally, methodically, rigorously, scrupulously, severely, strictly, truly, truthfully, unequivocally, unerringly, veraciously **2 = in every respect,** absolutely, bang, explicitly, expressly, indeed, just, on the button *(inf.)*, particularly, precisely, prompt *(inf.)*, quite, specifically, to the letter ◆ *sentence substitute* **3 = precisely,** absolutely, assuredly, as you say, certainly, indeed, just so, of course, quite, quite so, spot-on *(Brit. inf.)*, truly **4 not exactly** *Ironical* **= not at all,** by no means, certainly not, hardly, in no manner, in no way, not by any means, not quite, not really

exactness *n* **1 = precision,** accuracy, carefulness, correctness, exactitude, faithfulness, faultlessness, nicety, orderliness, painstakingness, preciseness, promptitude, regularity, rigorousness, rigour, scrupulousness, strictness, truth, unequivocalness, veracity
Antonyms *n* imprecision, inaccuracy, incorrectness, inexactness, unfaithfulness

exaggerate *vb* **1 = overstate,** amplify, blow out of all proportion, embellish, embroider, emphasize, enlarge, exalt, hyperbolize, inflate, lay it on thick *(inf.)*, magnify, make a federal case of *(US inf.)*, make a mountain out of a molehill *(inf.)*, make a production (out) of *(inf.)*, overdo, overemphasize, overestimate

exaggerated *adj* **1 = overstated,** amplified, exalted, excessive, extravagant, fulsome, highly coloured, hyped, hyperbolic, inflated, overblown, overdone, overestimated, over the top *(inf.)*, pretentious, tall *(inf.)*

exaggeration *n* **1 = overstatement,** amplification, embellishment, emphasis, enlargement, exaltation, excess, extravagance, hyperbole, inflation, magnification, overemphasis, overestimation, pretension, pretentiousness
Antonyms *n* litotes, meiosis, restraint, underplaying, understatement

exalt *vb* **1 = raise,** advance, aggrandize, dignify, elevate, ennoble, honour, promote, upgrade **2 = praise,** acclaim, apotheosize, applaud, bless, crack up *(inf.)*, extol, glorify, idolize, laud, magnify *(arch.)*, pay homage to, pay tribute to, reverence, set on a pedestal, worship **3 = stimulate,** animate, arouse, electrify, elevate, excite, fire the imagination (of), heighten, inspire, inspirit, uplift **4 = elate,** delight, exhilarate, fill with joy, thrill

exaltation *n* **1 = glorification,** acclamation, advancement, aggrandizement, apotheosis, elevation, ennoblement, lionization, magnification, praise, promotion, tribute, worship **2 = elation,** bliss, delight, ecstasy, exhilaration, exultation, joy, joyousness, jubilation, rapture, transport

exalted *adj* **1 = high-ranking,** august, dignified, elevated, eminent, grand, high, honoured, lofty, prestigious **4 = elated,** blissful, ecstatic, elevated, exhilarated, exultant, in seventh heaven, inspired, jubilant, rapturous, transported, uplifted

examination *n* **1 = inspection,** analysis, assay, checkup, exploration, interrogation, investigation, observation, once-over *(inf.)*, perusal, recce *(sl.)*, research, review, scrutiny, search, study, survey, test, trial **4 = questioning,** catechism, inquiry, inquisition, probe, quiz, test

examine *vb* **1 = inspect,** analyse, appraise, assay, check, check out, consider, explore, go over *or* through, investigate, look over, peruse, ponder, pore over, probe, recce *(sl.)*, research, review, scan, scrutinize, sift, study, survey, take stock of, test, vet, weigh, work over **3 = question,** catechize, cross-examine, grill *(inf.)*, inquire, interrogate, quiz, test

example *n* **1 = specimen,** case, case in point, exemplification, illustration, instance, sample **2, 3 = model,** archetype, exemplar, ideal, illustration, norm, paradigm, paragon, pattern, precedent, prototype, standard **4 = warning,** admonition, caution, lesson **5 for example = as an illustration,** by way of illustration, e.g., *exempli gratia,* for instance, to cite an instance, to illustrate

exasperate *vb* **1 = irritate,** aggravate, anger, annoy, bug *(inf.)*, embitter, enrage, exacerbate, excite, gall, get on one's nerves *(inf.)*, get on one's wick *(Brit. sl.)*, hassle *(inf.)*, incense, inflame, infuriate, irk, madden, nark *(Brit., Austral., & NZ sl.)*, needle *(inf.)*, nettle, peeve *(inf.)*, pique, provoke, rankle, rile *(inf.)*, rouse, try the patience of, vex
Antonyms *vb* appease, assuage, calm, conciliate, mollify, pacify, placate, soothe

exasperating *adj* **1 = irritating,** aggravating *(inf.)*, annoying, enough to drive one up the

ex cathedra (ɛks kəˈθiːdrə) *adj, adv* **1** with authority. **2** *RC Church.* (of doctrines of faith or morals) defined by the pope as infallibly true, to be accepted by all Catholics. [L, lit.: from the chair]

excavate ● (ˈɛkskəˌveɪt) *vb* **excavates, excavating, excavated. 1** to remove (soil, earth, etc.) by digging; dig out. **2** to make (a hole or tunnel) in (solid matter) by hollowing. **3** to unearth (buried objects) methodically to discover information about the past. [C16: from L *cavāre* to make hollow, from *cavus* hollow]
▸ **ˌexcaˈvation** *n* ▸ **ˈexcaˌvator** *n*

exceed ● (ɪkˈsiːd) *vb* **1** to be superior (to); excel. **2** (*tr*) to go beyond the limit or bounds of. **3** (*tr*) to be greater in degree or quantity than. [C14: from L *excēdere* to go beyond]
▸ **exˈceedable** *adj* ▸ **exˈceeder** *n*

exceeding ● (ɪkˈsiːdɪŋ) *adj* **1** very great; exceptional or excessive. ◆ *adv* **2** *Arch.* to a great or unusual degree.
▸ **exˈceedingly** *adv*

excel ● (ɪkˈsɛl) *vb* **excels, excelling, excelled. 1** to be superior to (another or others); surpass. **2** (*intr;* foll. by *in* or *at*) to be outstandingly good or proficient. [C15: from L *excellere* to rise up]

excellence ● (ˈɛksələns) *n* **1** the state or quality of excelling or being exceptionally good; extreme merit. **2** an action, feature, etc., in which a person excels.
▸ **ˈexcellent** *adj* ▸ **ˈexcellently** *adv*

Excellency (ˈɛksələnsɪ) *or* **Excellence** *n, pl* **Excellencies** *or* **Excellences. 1** (usually preceded by *Your, His,* or *Her*) a title used to address or refer to a high-ranking official, such as an ambassador. **2** *RC Church.* a title of bishops and archbishops in many non-English-speaking countries.

excelsior (ɪkˈsɛlsɪˌɔː) *interj, n* **1** excellent: used as a motto and as a trademark for various products. **2** upward. [C19: from L: higher]

except ● (ɪkˈsɛpt) *prep* **1** Also: **except for.** other than; apart from. **2 except that.** (*conj*) but for the fact that; were it not true that. ◆ *conj* **3** an archaic word for **unless. 4** *Inf. (not standard in the US)* except that; but for the fact that. ◆ *vb* **5** (*tr*) to leave out; omit; exclude. **6** (*intr;* often foll. by *to*) *Rare.* to take exception; object. [C14: from OF *excepter* to leave out, from L *excipere* to take out]

excepting (ɪkˈsɛptɪŋ) *prep* **1** except; except for (esp. in **not excepting**). ◆ *conj* **2** an archaic word for **unless.**

> **USAGE NOTE** The use of *excepting* is considered by many people to be acceptable only after *not, only, always,* or *without.* Elsewhere *except* is preferred: *every country agreed to the proposal except* (not *excepting*) *Spain; he was well again except for* (not *excepting*) *a slight pain in his chest.*

exception ● (ɪkˈsɛpʃən) *n* **1** the act of excepting or fact of being excepted; omission. **2** anything excluded from or not in conformance with a general rule, principle, class, etc. **3** criticism, esp. adverse; objection. **4** *Law.* (formerly) a formal objection in legal proceedings. **5 take exception. 5a** (usually foll. by *to*) to make objections (to); demur (at). **5b** (often foll. by *at*) to be offended (by); be resentful (at).

exceptionable ● (ɪkˈsɛpʃənəbᵊl) *adj* open to or subject to objection; objectionable.
▸ **exˈceptionableness** *n* ▸ **exˈceptionably** *adv*

exceptional ● (ɪkˈsɛpʃənᵊl) *adj* **1** forming an exception; not ordinary. **2** having much more than average intelligence, ability, or skill.

excerpt ● *n* (ˈɛksɜːpt). **1** a part or passage taken from a book, speech, etc.; extract. ◆ *vb* (ɛkˈsɜːpt). **2** (*tr*) to take (a part or passage) from a book, speech, etc. [C17: from L *excerptum,* lit.: (something) picked out, from *excerpere* to select, from *carpere* to pluck]
▸ **exˈcerptible** *adj* ▸ **exˈcerption** *n* ▸ **exˈcerptor** *n*

excess ● *n* (ɪkˈsɛs, ˈɛksɛs). **1** the state or act of going beyond normal, sufficient, or permitted limits. **2** an immoderate or abnormal amount. **3** the amount, number, etc., by which one thing exceeds another. **4** overindulgence or intemperance. **5** *Insurance, chiefly Brit.* a specified contribution towards the cost of a claim, payable by the policyholder. US name: **deductible. 6 in excess of.** of more than; over. **7 to excess.** to an inordinate extent; immoderately. ◆ *adj* (ˈɛksɛs, ɪkˈsɛs). (*usually prenominal*) **8** more than normal, necessary, or permitted; surplus: *excess weight.* **9** payable as a result of previous underpayment: *excess postage.* [C14: from L *excēdere* to go beyond; see EXCEED]

excessive ● (ɪkˈsɛsɪv) *adj* exceeding the normal or permitted limits; immoderate; inordinate.
▸ **exˈcessively** *adv* ▸ **exˈcessiveness** *n*

excess luggage *or* **baggage** *n* luggage that is more in weight or number of pieces than an airline, etc., will carry free.

exchange ● (ɪksˈtʃeɪndʒ) *vb* **exchanges, exchanging, exchanged. 1** (*tr*) to give up or transfer (one thing) for an equivalent. **2** (*tr*) to give and receive (information, ideas, etc.); interchange. **3** (*tr*) to replace (one thing) with another, esp. to replace unsatisfactory goods. **4** to hand over (goods) in return for the equivalent value in kind; barter; trade. ◆ *n* **5** the act or process of exchanging. **6a** anything given or received as an equivalent or substitute for something else. **6b** (*as modifier*): *an exchange student.* **7** an argument or quarrel. **8** Also called: **telephone exchange.** a switching centre in which telephone lines are interconnected. **9** a place where securities or commodities are sold, bought, or traded, esp. by brokers or merchants. **10a** the system by which commercial debts are settled by commercial documents, esp. bills of exchange, instead of by direct payment of money. **10b** the percentage or fee charged for accepting payment in this manner. **11** a transfer or interchange of sums of money of equivalent value, as between different currencies. **12 win** (*or* **lose**) **the exchange.** *Chess.* to win (*or* lose) a rook in return for a bishop or knight. ◆ See also **bill of exchange, exchange rate, labour exchange.** [C14: from Anglo-French *eschaungier,* from Vulgar L *excambiāre* (unattested), from L *cambīre* to barter]
▸ **exˈchangeable** *adj* ▸ **exˌchangeaˈbility** *n* ▸ **exˈchangeably** *adv* ▸ **exˈchanger** *n*

exchange rate *n* the rate at which the currency unit of one country may be exchanged for that of another.

Exchange Rate Mechanism *n* the mechanism used in the European Monetary System in which participating governments commit themselves to maintain the values of their currencies in relation to the ECU. Abbrev.: **ERM.**

THESAURUS

wall (*inf.*), enough to try the patience of a saint, galling, infuriating, irksome, maddening, provoking, vexing

exasperation *n* **1** = **irritation,** aggravation (*inf.*), anger, annoyance, exacerbation, fury, ire (*literary*), passion, pique, provocation, rage, vexation, wrath

excavate *vb* **1-3** = **dig out,** burrow, cut, delve, dig, dig up, gouge, hollow, mine, quarry, scoop, trench, tunnel, uncover, unearth

excavation *n* **1-3** = **hole,** burrow, cavity, cut, cutting, dig, diggings, ditch, dugout, hollow, mine, pit, quarry, shaft, trench, trough

exceed *vb* **1** = **surpass,** beat, be superior to, better, cap (*inf.*), eclipse, excel, go beyond, knock spots off, outdistance, outdo, outreach, outrun, outshine, outstrip, overtake, pass, put in the shade (*inf.*), run rings around (*inf.*), surmount, top, transcend **2** = **go over the limit of,** go beyond the bounds of, go over the top, overstep

exceeding *adj* **1** = **extraordinary,** enormous, exceptional, excessive, great, huge, preeminent, streets ahead, superior, superlative, surpassing, vast

exceedingly *adv* **1** = **extremely,** enormously, especially, exceptionally, excessively, extraordinarily, greatly, highly, hugely, inordinately, seriously (*inf.*), superlatively, surpassingly, to a fault, to the nth degree, unusually, vastly, very

excel *vb* **1** = **be superior,** beat, better, cap (*inf.*), eclipse, exceed, go beyond, outdo, outrival, outshine, pass, put in the shade (*inf.*), run rings around (*inf.*), steal the show (*inf.*), surmount, surpass, top, transcend **2** *with* **in** *or* **at** = **be good at,** be master of, be proficient in, be skilful at, be talented at, have (something) down to a fine art, predominate in, shine at, show talent in

excellence *n* **1** = **high quality,** distinction, eminence, fineness, goodness, greatness, merit, perfection, pre-eminence, purity, superiority, supremacy, transcendence, virtue, worth

excellent *adj* **1** = **outstanding,** admirable, brilliant, capital, champion, choice, cracking, distinguished, estimable, exemplary, exquisite, fine, first-class, first-rate, good, great, meritorious, notable, noted, prime, select, sovereign, sterling, superb, superior, superlative, tiptop, top-notch (*inf.*), world-class, worthy
Antonyms *adj* abysmal, bad, dreadful, faulty, imperfect, incompetent, inexpert, inferior, lousy (*sl.*), mediocre, no great shakes (*inf.*), poor, rotten (*inf.*), second-class, second-rate, substandard, terrible, unskilled

except *prep* **1** = **apart from,** bar, barring, besides, but, excepting, excluding, exclusive of, omitting, other than, save (*arch.*), saving, with the exception of ◆ *vb* **5** = **exclude,** ban, bar, disallow, leave out, omit, pass over, reject, rule out

exception *n* **1** = **exclusion,** debarment, disallowment, excepting, leaving out, omission, passing over, rejection **2** = **special case,** anomaly, departure, deviation, freak, inconsistency, irregularity, oddity, peculiarity, quirk **5 take exception** = **object to,** be offended at, be resentful of, demur at, disagree with, quibble at, take offence at, take umbrage at

exceptionable *adj* = **objectionable,** disagreeable, inappropriate, unacceptable, unbearable, undesirable, unsatisfactory, unwelcome

exceptional *adj* **1** = **unusual,** aberrant, abnormal, anomalous, atypical, deviant, extraordinary, inconsistent, irregular, odd, peculiar, rare, singular, special, strange, uncommon **2** = **remarkable,** excellent, extraordinary, marvellous, notable, one in a million, outstanding, phenomenal, prodigious, special, superior
Antonyms *adj* ≠ **unusual:** average, common, customary, familiar, normal, ordinary, regular, straightforward, typical, unexceptional, unremarkable, usual ≠ **remarkable:** average, awful, bad, lousy (*sl.*), mediocre, no great shakes (*inf.*), second-rate

excerpt *n* **1** = **extract,** citation, fragment, part, passage, pericope, piece, portion, quotation, quote (*inf.*), section, selection ◆ *vb* **2** = **extract,** cite, cull, pick out, quote, select, take

excess *n* **2, 3** = **surfeit,** glut, leftover, overabundance, overdose, overflow, overload, plethora, remainder, superabundance, superfluity, surplus, too much **4** = **overindulgence,** debauchery, dissipation, dissoluteness, exorbitance, extravagance, immoderation, intemperance, prodigality, unrestraint ◆ *adj* **8** = **spare,** extra, leftover, redundant, remaining, residual, superfluous, surplus
Antonyms *n* ≠ **surfeit:** dearth, deficiency, insufficiency, lack, shortage, want ≠ **overindulgence:** moderation, restraint, self-control, self-discipline, self-restraint, temperance

excessive *adj* = **immoderate,** disproportionate, enormous, exaggerated, exorbitant, extravagant, extreme, fulsome, inordinate, intemperate, needless, O.T.T. (*sl.*), overdone, overmuch, over the odds, over the top (*sl.*), prodigal, profligate, superfluous, too much, unconscionable, undue, unfair, unreasonable

exchange *vb* **1** = **interchange,** bandy, barter, change, commute, convert into, reciprocate, swap, switch, trade, truck ◆ *n* **5** = **interchange,** barter, dealing, quid pro quo, reciprocity, sub-

exchequer (ɪks'tʃɛkə) *n* **1** (*often cap.*) *Government.* (in Britain and certain other countries) the accounting department of the Treasury. **2** *Inf.* personal funds; finances. [C13 (in the sense: chessboard, counting table): from OF *eschequier,* from *eschec* CHECK]

excisable (ɪk'saɪzəbᵊl) *adj* **1** liable to an excise tax. **2** suitable for deletion.

excise[1] Ⓣ *n* ('ɛksaɪz, ɛk'saɪz). **1** Also called: **excise tax.** a tax on goods, such as spirits, produced for the home market. **2** a tax paid for a licence to carry out various trades, sports, etc. **3** *Brit.* that section of the government service responsible for the collection of excise, now the Board of Customs and Excise. ◆ *vb* (ɪk'saɪz), **excises, excising, excised. 4** (*tr*) *Rare.* to compel (a person) to pay excise. [C15: prob. from MDu. *excijs,* prob. from OF *assise* a sitting, assessment, from L *assidēre* to sit beside, assist in judging]
▸**ex'cisable** *adj*

excise[2] Ⓣ (ɪk'saɪz) *vb* **excises, excising, excised.** (*tr*) **1** to delete (a passage, sentence, etc.). **2** to remove (an organ or part) surgically. [C16: from L *excīdere* to cut down]
▸**excision** (ɪk'sɪʒən) *n*

exciseman ('ɛksaɪz,mæn) *n, pl* **excisemen.** *Brit.* (formerly) a government agent whose function was to collect excise and prevent smuggling.

excitable Ⓣ (ɪk'saɪtəbᵊl) *adj* **1** easily excited; volatile. **2** (esp. of a nerve) ready to respond to a stimulus.
▸**ex,cita'bility** *or* **ex'citableness** *n*

excitation (,ɛksɪ'teɪʃən) *n* **1** the act or process of exciting or state of being excited. **2** a means of exciting or cause of excitement. **3** the current in a field coil of a generator, motor, etc., or the magnetizing current in a transformer. **4** the action of a stimulus on an animal or plant organ, inducing it to respond.

excite Ⓣ (ɪk'saɪt) *vb* **excites, exciting, excited.** (*tr*) **1** to arouse (a person), esp. to pleasurable anticipation or nervous agitation. **2** to arouse or elicit (an emotion, response, etc.); evoke. **3** to cause or bring about; stir up. **4** to arouse sexually. **5** *Physiol.* to cause a response in or increase the activity of (an organ, tissue, or part); stimulate. **6** to raise (an atom, molecule, etc.) from the ground state to a higher energy level. **7** to supply electricity to (the coils of a generator or motor) in order to create a magnetic field. [C14: from L *excīēre* to stimulate, from *ciēre* to set in motion, rouse]
▸**ex'citant** *n* ▸**ex'citative** *or* **ex'citatory** *adj* ▸**ex'citer** *or* **ex'citor** *n*

excited Ⓣ (ɪk'saɪtɪd) *adj* **1** emotionally aroused, esp. to pleasure or agitation. **2** characterized by excitement. **3** sexually aroused. **4** (of an atom, molecule, etc.) having an energy level above the ground state.
▸**ex'citedness** *n*

excitement Ⓣ (ɪk'saɪtmənt) *n* **1** the state of being excited. **2** a person or thing that excites.

exciting Ⓣ (ɪk'saɪtɪŋ) *adj* causing excitement; stirring; stimulating.
▸**ex'citingly** *adv*

exclaim Ⓣ (ɪk'skleɪm) *vb* to cry out or speak suddenly or excitedly, as from surprise, delight, horror, etc. [C16: from L *exclāmāre,* from *clāmāre* to shout]
▸**ex'claimer** *n*

exclamation Ⓣ (,ɛksklə'meɪʃən) *n* **1** an abrupt or excited cry or utterance; ejaculation. **2** the act of exclaiming.
▸**,excla'mational** *adj* ▸**ex'clamatory** *adj*

exclamation mark *or US* **point** *n* **1** the punctuation mark ! used after exclamations and vehement commands. **2** this mark used for any other purpose, as to draw attention to an obvious mistake, in road warning signs, etc.

exclave ('ɛkskleɪv) *n* a part of a country entirely surrounded by foreign territory: viewed from the position of the home country. [C20: from EX-[1] + *-clave,* on the model of ENCLAVE]

exclosure (ɪk'skləʊʒə) *n* an area of land fenced round to keep out unwanted animals.

exclude Ⓣ (ɪk'sklu:d) *vb* **excludes, excluding, excluded.** (*tr*) **1** to keep out; prevent from entering. **2** to reject or not consider; leave out. **3** to expel forcibly; eject. [C14: from L *exclūdere,* from *claudere* to shut]
▸**ex'cludable** *or* **ex'cludible** *adj* ▸**ex'cluder** *n*

exclusion Ⓣ (ɪk'sklu:ʒən) *n* the act or an instance of excluding or the state of being excluded.
▸**ex'clusionary** *adj*

exclusion principle *n* See **Pauli exclusion principle.**

exclusive Ⓣ (ɪk'sklu:sɪv) *adj* **1** excluding all else; rejecting other considerations, events, etc. **2** belonging to a particular individual or group and to no other; not shared. **3** belonging to or catering for a privileged minority, esp. a fashionable clique. **4** (*postpositive;* foll. by *to*) limited (to); found only (in). **5** single; unique; only. **6** separate and incompatible. **7** (*immediately postpositive*) not including the numbers, dates, letters, etc., mentioned. **8** (*postpositive;* foll. by *of*) except (for); not taking account (of). **9** *Logic.* (of a disjunction) true if only one rather than both of its component propositions is true. ◆ *n* **10** an exclusive story; a story reported in only one newspaper.
▸**ex'clusively** *adv* ▸**exclusivity** (,ɛksklu:'sɪvɪtɪ) *or* **ex'clusiveness** *n*

exclusive OR circuit *or* **gate** *n Electronics.* a computer logic circuit having two or more input wires and one output wire and giving a high-voltage output signal if a low-voltage signal is fed to one or more, but not all, of the input wires. Cf. **OR circuit.**

excommunicate Ⓣ *RC Church.* ◆ *vb* (,ɛkskə'mju:nɪ,keɪt), **excommunicates, excommunicating, excommunicated. 1** (*tr*) to sentence (a member of the Church) to exclusion from the communion of believers and from the privileges and public prayers of the Church. ◆ *adj* (,ɛkskə'mju:nɪkɪt, -,keɪt). **2** having incurred such a sentence. ◆ *n* (,ɛkskə'mju:nɪkɪt, -,keɪt). **3** an excommunicated person. [C15: from LL *excommūnicāre,* lit.: to exclude from the community, from L *commūnis* COMMON]
▸**,excom,muni'cation** *n* ▸**,excom'muni,cator** *n*

excoriate (ɪk'skɔ:rɪ,eɪt) *vb* **excoriates, excoriating, excoriated.** (*tr*) **1** to strip the skin from (a person or animal). **2** to denounce vehemently. [C15: from LL *excoriāre* to strip, flay, from L *corium* skin, hide]
▸**ex,cori'ation** *n*

excrement Ⓣ ('ɛkskrɪmənt) *n* waste matter discharged from the body, esp. faeces; excreta. [C16: from L *excernere* to sift, EXCRETE]
▸**excremental** (,ɛkskrɪ'mɛntᵊl) *or* **excrementitious** (,ɛkskrɪmɛn'tɪʃəs) *adj*

excrescence Ⓣ (ɪk'skrɛsᵊns) *n* a projection or protuberance, esp. an outgrowth from an organ or part of the body.
▸**ex'crescent** *adj* ▸**excrescential** (,ɛkskrɪ'sɛnʃəl) *adj*

excreta (ɪk'skri:tə) *pl n* waste matter, such as urine, faeces, or sweat, discharged from the body. [C19: NL, from L: see EXCRETE]
▸**ex'cretal** *adj*

excrete Ⓣ (ɪk'skri:t) *vb* **excretes, excreting, excreted. 1** to discharge (waste matter, such as urine, sweat, or faeces) from the body. **2** (of plants) to eliminate (waste matter) through the leaves, roots, etc. [C17: from L *excernere* to separate, discharge, from *cernere* to sift]
▸**ex'creter** *n* ▸**ex'cretion** *n* ▸**ex'cretive** *or* **ex'cretory** *adj*

THESAURUS

stitution, swap, switch, tit for tat, trade, traffic, truck **9** = **market,** Bourse

excise[1] *n* **1** = **tax,** customs, duty, impost, levy, surcharge, tariff, toll

excise[2] *vb* **1** = **delete,** cross out, cut, destroy, eradicate, erase, expunge, exterminate, extirpate, strike out, wipe from the face of the earth **2** = **cut off** *or* **out,** extract, remove

excision *n* **1** = **deletion,** destruction, eradication, extermination, extirpation, removal

excitability *n* **1** = **nervousness,** high spirits, hot-headedness, restiveness, restlessness, volatility

excitable *adj* **1** = **nervous,** edgy, emotional, hasty, highly strung, hot-headed, hot-tempered, irascible, mercurial, passionate, quick-tempered, sensitive, susceptible, temperamental, testy, touchy, uptight (*inf.*), violent, volatile
Antonyms *adj* calm, cool, cool-headed, even-tempered, imperturbable, laid-back (*inf.*), placid, unexcitable, unruffled

excite *vb* **1-3** = **arouse,** agitate, animate, awaken, elicit, evoke, fire, foment, galvanize, incite, inflame, inspire, instigate, kindle, move, provoke, quicken, rouse, stimulate, stir up, waken, whet, work up

excited *adj* **1** = **worked up,** aflame, agitated, animated, aroused, awakened, discomposed, disturbed, enthusiastic, feverish, flurried, moved, nervous, overwrought, roused, stimulated, stirred, thrilled, tumultuous, wild

excitement *n* **1** = **agitation,** action, activity, ado, adventure, animation, commotion, discomposure, elation, enthusiasm, ferment, fever, flurry, furore, heat, kicks (*inf.*), passion, perturbation, thrill, tumult, warmth **2** = **stimulus,** impulse, incitement, instigation, motivation, motive, provocation, stimulation, urge

exciting *adj* = **stimulating,** dramatic, electrifying, exhilarating, inspiring, intoxicating, moving, provocative, rip-roaring, rousing, sensational, sexy (*inf.*), stirring, thrilling, titillating
Antonyms *adj* boring, dreary, dull, flat, humdrum, mind-numbing, monotonous, unexciting, uninspiring, uninteresting

exclaim *vb* = **cry out,** call, call out, cry, declare, ejaculate, proclaim, shout, utter, vociferate, yell

exclamation *n* **1** = **cry,** call, ejaculation, expletive, interjection, outcry, shout, utterance, vociferation, yell

exclude *vb* **1** = **keep out,** ban, bar, black, blackball, boycott, debar, disallow, embargo, forbid, interdict, ostracize, prohibit, proscribe, refuse, shut out, veto **2** = **leave out,** count out, eliminate, except, ignore, not count, omit, pass over, preclude, reject, repudiate, rule out, set aside **3** = **remove,** bounce (*sl.*), drive out, eject, evict, expel, force out, get rid of, oust, throw out
Antonyms *vb* ≠ **keep out, remove:** accept, admit, allow, let in, permit, receive, welcome ≠ **leave out:** accept, count, include

exclusion *n* = **ban,** bar, boycott, debarment, disqualification, embargo, forbiddance, interdict, nonadmission, preclusion, prohibition, proscription, refusal, rejection, removal, veto

exclusive *adj* **2** = **sole,** absolute, complete, entire, full, only, private, single, total, undivided, unique, unshared, whole **3** = **select,** aristocratic, chic, choice, cliquish, closed, elegant, fashionable, high-toned, limited, narrow, posh (*inf., chiefly Brit.*), private, restricted, restrictive, ritzy (*sl.*), snobbish, top-drawer, up-market **4** = **limited,** confined, peculiar, restricted, unique **8** *with* **of** = **except for,** debarring, excepting, excluding, leaving aside, not counting, omitting, restricting, ruling out
Antonyms *adj* ≠ **sole, limited:** inclusive, nonexclusive, partial, shared ≠ **select:** common, communal, open, popular, public, unrestricted

excommunicate *vb* **1** = **expel,** anathematize, ban, banish, cast out, denounce, eject, exclude, proscribe, remove, repudiate, unchurch

excrement *n* = **faeces,** crap (*taboo sl.*), droppings, dung, excreta, mess (*especially of a domestic animal*), motion, ordure, shit (*taboo sl.*), stool, turd (*taboo sl.*)

excrescence *n* = **protrusion,** knob, lump, outgrowth, process, projection, prominence, protuberance

excrete *vb* **1** = **defecate,** crap (*taboo sl.*), discharge, egest, eject, eliminate, evacuate, expel, exude, shit (*taboo sl.*), void

DICTIONARY

excruciate (ɪkˈskruːʃɪˌeɪt) *vb* **excruciates, excruciating, excruciated.** (*tr*) to inflict mental suffering on; torment. [C16: from L *excruciāre*, from *cruciāre* to crucify, from *crux* cross]

excruciating ❶ (ɪkˈskruːʃɪˌeɪtɪŋ) *adj* **1** unbearably painful; agonizing. **2** intense; extreme. **3** *Inf.* irritating; trying. **4** *Humorous.* very bad: *an excruciating pun.*

exculpate ❶ (ˈɛkskʌlˌpeɪt, ɪkˈskʌlpeɪt) *vb* **exculpates, exculpating, exculpated.** (*tr*) to free from blame or guilt; vindicate or exonerate. [C17: from Med. L, from L EX-[1] + *culpa* fault, blame]
▸ˌ**exculˈpation** *n* ▸**exˈculpatory** *adj*

excursion ❶ (ɪkˈskɜːʃən, -ʒən) *n* **1** a short outward and return journey, esp. for sightseeing, etc.; outing. **2** a group going on such a journey. **3** (*modifier*) of or relating to reduced rates offered on certain journeys by rail: *an excursion ticket.* **4** a digression or deviation; diversion. **5** (formerly) a raid or attack. [C16: from L *excursiō* an attack, from *excurrere* to run out, from *currere* to run]
▸**exˈcursionist** *n*

excursive (ɪkˈskɜːsɪv) *adj* **1** tending to digress. **2** involving detours; rambling. [C17: from L *excursus*, from *excurrere* to run forth]
▸**exˈcursively** *adv* ▸**exˈcursiveness** *n*

excuse ❶ *vb* (ɪkˈskjuːz), **excuses, excusing, excused.** (*tr*) **1** to pardon or forgive. **2** to seek pardon or exemption for (a person, esp. oneself). **3** to make allowances for: *to excuse someone's ignorance.* **4** to serve as an apology or explanation for; justify: *her age excuses her.* **5** to exempt from a task, obligation, etc. **6** to dismiss or allow to leave. **7** to seek permission for (someone, esp. oneself) to leave. **8 be excused.** *Euphemistic.* to go to the lavatory. **9 excuse me!** an expression used to catch someone's attention or to apologize for an interruption, disagreement, etc. ◆ *n* (ɪkˈskjuːs). **10** an explanation offered in defence of some fault or as a reason for not fulfilling an obligation, etc. **11** *Inf.* an inferior example of something; makeshift substitute: *she is a poor excuse for a hostess.* **12** the act of excusing. [C13: from L, from EX-[1] + *causa* cause, accusation]
▸**exˈcusable** *adj* ▸**exˈcusableness** *n* ▸**exˈcusably** *adv*

excuse-me *n* a dance in which a person may take another's partner.

ex-directory *adj Chiefly Brit.* not listed in a telephone directory, by request, and not disclosed to inquirers.

ex dividend *adj, adv* without the right to the current dividend: *to quote shares ex dividend.*

exeat (ˈɛksɪət) *n Brit.* **1** leave of absence from school or some other institution. **2** a bishop's permission for a priest to leave his diocese in order to take up an appointment elsewhere. [C18: L, lit.: he may go out, from *exīre*]

exec. *abbrev. for:* **1** executive. **2** executor.

execrable ❶ (ˈɛksɪkrəbᵊl) *adj* **1** deserving to be execrated; abhorrent. **2** of very poor quality. [C14: from L: see EXECRATE]
▸ˈ**execrableness** *n* ▸ˈ**execrably** *adv*

execrate ❶ (ˈɛksɪˌkreɪt) *vb* **execrates, execrating, execrated.** **1** (*tr*) to loathe; detest; abhor. **2** (*tr*) to denounce; deplore. **3** to curse (a person or thing); damn. [C16: from L *exsecrārī* to curse, from EX-[1] + *-secrārī* from *sacer* SACRED]
▸ˌ**exeˈcration** *n* ▸ˈ**exeˌcrative** *or* ˈ**exeˌcratory** *adj*

execute ❶ (ˈɛksɪˌkjuːt) *vb* **executes, executing, executed.** (*tr*) **1** to put (a condemned person) to death; inflict capital punishment upon. **2** to carry out; complete. **3** to perform; accomplish; effect. **4** to make or produce: *to execute a drawing.* **5** to carry into effect (a judicial sentence, the law, etc.). **6** *Law.* to render (a deed, etc.) effective, as by signing, sealing, and delivering. **7** to carry out the terms of (a contract, will, etc.). [C14: from OF *executer*, back formation from *executeur* EXECUTOR]
▸ˈ**exeˌcutable** *adj* ▸**executant** (ɪgˈzɛkjʊtənt) *n* ▸ˈ**exeˌcuter** *n*

execution ❶ (ˌɛksɪˈkjuːʃən) *n* **1** the act or process of executing. **2** the carrying out or undergoing of a sentence of death. **3** the style or manner in which something is accomplished or performed; technique. **4a** the enforcement of the judgment of a court of law. **4b** the writ ordering such enforcement.

executioner ❶ (ˌɛksɪˈkjuːʃənə) *n* an official charged with carrying out the death sentence passed upon a condemned person.

executive ❶ (ɪgˈzɛkjʊtɪv) *n* **1** a person or group responsible for the administration of a project, activity, or business. **2a** the branch of government responsible for carrying out laws, decrees, etc. **2b** any administration. ◆ *adj* **3** having the function of carrying plans, orders, laws, etc., into effect. **4** of or relating to an executive. **5** *Inf.* very expensive or exclusive: *executive housing.*
▸**exˈecutively** *adv*

Executive Council *n* (in Australia and New Zealand) a body of ministers of the Crown presided over by the governor or governor-general that formally approves cabinet decisions, etc.

executive director *n* a member of the board of directors of a company who is also an employee (usually full-time) and who often has a specified area of responsibility, such as finance or production. Cf. **nonexecutive director.**

executive officer *n* the second-in-command of any of certain military units.

executor (ɪgˈzɛkjʊtə) *n* **1** *Law.* a person appointed by a testator to carry out his will. **2** a person who executes. [C14: from Anglo-F *executour*, from L *execūtor*]
▸**exˌecuˈtorial** *adj* ▸**exˈecutory** *adj* ▸**exˈecutorˌship** *n*

executrix (ɪgˈzɛkjʊtrɪks) *n, pl* **executrices** (ɪgˌzɛkjʊˈtraɪsiːz) *or* **executrixes.** *Law.* a female executor.

exegesis (ˌɛksɪˈdʒiːsɪs) *n, pl* **exegeses** (-siːz). explanation or critical interpretation of a text, esp. of the Bible. [C17: from Gk, from *exēgeisthai* to interpret, from EX-[1] + *hēgeisthai* to guide]
▸**exegetic** (ˌɛksɪˈdʒɛtɪk) *adj*

exegete (ˈɛksɪˌdʒiːt) *or* **exegetist** (ˌɛksɪˈdʒiːtɪst, -ˈdʒɛt-) *n* a person who practises exegesis.

exemplar ❶ (ɪgˈzɛmplə, -plɑː) *n* **1** a person or thing to be copied or imitated; model. **2** a typical specimen or instance; example. [C14: from L, from *exemplum* EXAMPLE]

exemplary ❶ (ɪgˈzɛmplərɪ) *adj* **1** fit for imitation; model. **2** serving as a warning; admonitory. **3** representative; typical.
▸**exˈemplarily** *adv* ▸**exˈemplariness** *n*

exemplary damages *pl n Law.* damages awarded to a plaintiff above the value of actual loss sustained so that they serve also as a punishment to the defendant.

exemplify ❶ (ɪgˈzɛmplɪˌfaɪ) *vb* **exemplifies, exemplifying, exemplified.** (*tr*) **1** to show by example. **2** to serve as an example of. **3** *Law.* to make an official copy of (a document) under seal. [C15: via OF from Med. L *exemplificāre*, from L *exemplum* EXAMPLE + *facere* to make]
▸**exˈempliˌfiable** *adj* ▸**exˌemplifiˈcation** *n* ▸**exˈempliˌcative** *adj* ▸**exˈempliˌfier** *n*

exempt ❶ (ɪgˈzɛmpt) *vb* **1** (*tr*) to release from an obligation, tax, etc.; excuse. ◆ *adj* **2a** freed from or not subject to an obligation, tax, etc.; excused. **2b** (*in combination*): *tax-exempt.* ◆ *n* **3** a person who is ex-

THESAURUS

excruciating *adj* **1 = agonizing**, acute, burning, exquisite, extreme, harrowing, insufferable, intense, piercing, racking, searing, severe, tormenting, torturous, unbearable, unendurable, violent

exculpate *vb* **= absolve**, acquit, clear, discharge, dismiss, excuse, exonerate, free, justify, pardon, release, vindicate

excursion *n* **1 = trip**, airing, day trip, expedition, jaunt, journey, outing, pleasure trip, ramble, tour **4 = digression**, detour, deviation, episode, excursus, wandering

excusable *adj* **1 = forgivable**, allowable, defensible, justifiable, minor, pardonable, permissible, slight, understandable, venial, warrantable

excuse *vb* **1, 3 = forgive**, absolve, acquit, bear with, exculpate, exonerate, extenuate, indulge, make allowances for, overlook, pardon, pass over, tolerate, turn a blind eye to, wink at **4 = justify**, apologize for, condone, defend, explain, mitigate, vindicate **5 = free**, absolve, discharge, exempt, let off, liberate, release, relieve, spare ◆ *n* **10 = justification**, apology, defence, explanation, grounds, mitigation, plea, pretext, reason, vindication **11** *Informal* **= poor substitute**, apology, makeshift, mockery, travesty
Antonyms *vb* ≠ **justify:** accuse, blame, censure, chasten, chastise, compel, condemn, correct, criticize, hold responsible, oblige, point a *or* the finger at, punish ≠ **free:** arraign, charge, convict, indict, sentence ◆ *n* ≠ **justification:** accusation, charge, imputation, indictment

execrable *adj* **1 = repulsive**, abhorrent, abominable, accursed, atrocious, damnable, deplorable, despicable, detestable, disgusting, foul, hateful, heinous, horrible, loathsome, nauseous, obnoxious, obscene, odious, offensive, revolting, sickening, vile

execrate *vb* **1, 2 = loathe**, abhor, abominate, condemn, denounce, deplore, despise, detest, excoriate, hate, revile, slam (*sl.*), vilify **3 = curse**, anathematize, damn, imprecate

execration *n* **1, 2 = loathing**, abhorrence, abomination, condemnation, contempt, detestation, excoriation, hate, hatred, odium, vilification **3 = curse**, anathema, damnation, imprecation, malediction

execute *vb* **1 = put to death**, behead, electrocute, guillotine, hang, kill, shoot **2-5 = carry out**, accomplish, achieve, administer, bring off, complete, consummate, discharge, do, effect, enact, enforce, finish, fulfil, implement, perform, prosecute, put into effect, realize, render **6** *Law* **= validate**, deliver, seal, serve, sign

execution *n* **1 = carrying out**, accomplishment, achievement, administration, completion, consummation, discharge, effect, enactment, enforcement, implementation, operation, performance, prosecution, realization, rendering **2 = killing**, capital punishment, hanging, necktie party (*inf.*) **3 = technique**, delivery, manner, mode, performance, rendition, style **4b = writ**, warrant

executioner *n* **= hangman**, headsman

executive *n* **1 = administrator**, director, manager, official **2 = administration**, directorate, directors, government, hierarchy, leadership, management ◆ *adj* **3 = administrative**, controlling, decision-making, directing, governing, managerial

exemplar *n* **1 = model**, criterion, epitome, example, ideal, paradigm, paragon, pattern, standard **2 = example**, exemplification, illustration, instance, prototype, specimen, type

exemplary *adj* **1 = ideal**, admirable, commendable, correct, estimable, excellent, fine, good, honourable, laudable, meritorious, model, praiseworthy, punctilious, sterling **2 = warning**, admonitory, cautionary, monitory **3 = typical**, characteristic, illustrative, representative

exemplification *n* **1, 2 = example**, embodiment, epitome, exemplar, illustration, manifestation, paradigm, personification, prototype, representation

exemplify *vb* **1, 2 = show**, demonstrate, depict, display, embody, evidence, exhibit, illustrate, instance, manifest, represent, serve as an example of

exempt *vb* **1 = grant immunity**, absolve, discharge, except, excuse, exonerate, free, let off, liberate, release, relieve, spare ◆ *adj* **2 = immune**, absolved, clear, discharged, excepted, excused, favoured, free, liberated, not liable, not subject, privileged, released, spared
Antonyms *adj* ≠ **immune:** accountable, answer-

empt. [C14: from L *exemptus* removed, from *eximere* to take out, from *emere* to buy, obtain]
▸ex'emption *n*

exequies ('ɛksɪkwɪz) *pl n, sing* **exequy**. the rites and ceremonies used at funerals. [C14: from L *exequiae* (pl) funeral procession, rites, from *exequī* to follow to the end]

exercise ➊ ('ɛksəˌsaɪz) *vb* **exercises, exercising, exercised.** (*mainly tr*) **1** to put into use; employ. **2** (*intr*) to take exercise or perform exercises. **3** to practise using in order to develop or train. **4** to perform or make use of: *to exercise one's rights*. **5** to bring to bear: *to exercise one's influence*. **6** (*often passive*) to occupy the attentions of, esp. so as to worry or vex: *to be exercised about a decision*. **7** *Mil.* to carry out or cause to carry out simulated combat, manoeuvres, etc. ◆ *n* **8** physical exertion, esp. for development, training, or keeping fit. **9** mental or other activity or practice, esp. to develop a skill. **10** a set of movements, tasks, etc., designed to train, improve, or test one's ability: *piano exercises*. **11** a performance or work of art done as practice or to demonstrate a technique. **12** the performance of a function: *the exercise of one's rights*. **13** (*usually pl*) *Mil.* a manoeuvre or simulated combat operation. **14** *Gymnastics.* a particular event, such as the horizontal bar. [C14: from OF, from L, from *exercēre* to drill, from EX-[1] + *arcēre* to ward off]
▸'exerˌcisable *adj* ▸'exerˌciser *n*

exercise bike *or* **cycle** *n* a stationary exercise machine that is pedalled like a bicycle as a method of increasing cardiovascular fitness.

exercise book *n* a notebook used by pupils and students.

exercise price *n Stock Exchange.* the price at which the holder of a traded option may exercise his right to buy (or sell) a security.

exert ➊ (ɪg'zɜːt) *vb* (*tr*) **1** to use (influence, authority, etc.) forcefully or effectively. **2** to apply (oneself) diligently; make a strenuous effort. [C17 (in the sense: push forth, emit): from L *exserere* to thrust out, from EX-[1] + *serere* to bind together, entwine]
▸ex'ertion *n* ▸ex'ertive *adj*

exeunt ('ɛksɪˌʌnt) *Latin.* they go out: used as a stage direction.

exeunt omnes ('ɒmneɪz) *Latin.* they all go out: used as a stage direction.

exfoliate (ɛks'fəʊlɪˌeɪt) *vb* **exfoliates, exfoliating, exfoliated.** (of bark, skin, minerals, etc.) to peel off in layers, flakes, or scales. [C17: from LL *exfoliāre* to strip off leaves, from L *folium* leaf]
▸exˌfoli'ation *n* ▸ex'foliative *adj*

ex gratia ('greɪʃə) *adj* given as a favour or gratuitously where no legal obligation exists: *an ex gratia payment*. [NL, lit.: out of kindness]

exhale ➊ (ɛks'heɪl, ɪg'zeɪl) *vb* **exhales, exhaling, exhaled. 1** to expel (breath, smoke, etc.) from the lungs; breathe out. **2** to give off (air, fumes, etc.) or (of air, etc.) to be given off. [C14: from L *exhālāre*, from *hālāre* to breathe]
▸ex'halable *adj* ▸ˌexha'lation *n*

exhaust ➊ (ɪg'zɔːst) *vb* (*mainly tr*) **1** to drain the energy of; tire out. **2** to deprive of resources, etc. **3** to deplete totally; consume. **4** to empty (a container) by drawing off or pumping out (the contents). **5** to develop or discuss thoroughly so that no further interest remains. **6** to remove gas from (a vessel, etc.) in order to reduce pressure or create a vacuum. **7** (*intr*) (of steam or other gases) to be emitted or to escape from an engine after being expanded. ◆ *n* **8** gases ejected from an engine as waste products. **9** the expulsion of expanded gas or steam from an engine. **10a** the parts of an engine through which exhausted gases or steam pass. **10b** (*as modifier*): *exhaust pipe*. [C16: from L *exhaustus* made empty, from *exhaurīre* to draw out, from *haurīre* to draw, drain]
▸ex'hausted *adj* ▸ex'haustible *adj* ▸ex'hausting *adj*

exhaustion ➊ (ɪg'zɔːstʃən) *n* **1** extreme tiredness. **2** the condition of being used up. **3** the act of exhausting or the state of being exhausted.

exhaustive ➊ (ɪg'zɔːstɪv) *adj* **1** comprehensive; thorough. **2** tending to exhaust.
▸ex'haustively *adv* ▸ex'haustiveness *n*

exhibit ➊ (ɪg'zɪbɪt) *vb* (*mainly tr*) **1** (*also intr*) to display (something) to the public. **2** to manifest; display; show. **3** *Law.* to produce (a document or object) in court as evidence. ◆ *n* **4** an object or collection exhibited to the public. **5** *Law.* a document or object produced in court as evidence. [C15: from L *exhibēre* to hold forth, from *habēre* to have]
▸ex'hibitor *n* ▸ex'hibitory *adj*

exhibition ➊ (ˌɛksɪ'bɪʃən) *n* **1** a public display of art, skills, etc. **2** the act of exhibiting or the state of being exhibited. **3 make an exhibition of oneself.** to behave so foolishly that one excites notice or ridicule. **4** *Brit.* an allowance or scholarship awarded to a student at a university or school.

exhibitioner (ˌɛksɪ'bɪʃənə) *n Brit.* a student who has been awarded an exhibition.

exhibitionism (ˌɛksɪ'bɪʃəˌnɪzəm) *n* **1** a compulsive desire to attract attention to oneself, esp. by exaggerated behaviour. **2** a compulsive desire to expose one's genital organs publicly.
▸ˌexhi'bitionist *n* ▸ˌexhiˌbition'istic *adj*

exhibitive (ɪg'zɪbɪtɪv) *adj* (*usually postpositive* and foll. by *of*) illustrative or demonstrative.

exhilarate ➊ (ɪg'zɪləˌreɪt) *vb* **exhilarates, exhilarating, exhilarated.** (*tr*) to make lively and cheerful; elate. [C16: from L *exhilarāre*, from *hilarāre* to cheer]
▸ex'hilaˌrating *adj* ▸exˌhila'ration *n* ▸ex'hilarative *adj*

exhort ➊ (ɪg'zɔːt) *vb* to urge or persuade (someone) earnestly; advise strongly. [C14: from L *exhortārī*, from *hortārī* to urge]
▸ex'hortative *or* ex'hortatory *adj* ▸ˌexhor'tation *n* ▸ex'horter *n*

exhume ➊ (ɛks'hjuːm) *vb* **exhumes, exhuming, exhumed.** (*tr*) **1** to dig up (something buried, esp. a corpse); disinter. **2** to reveal; disclose. [C18: from Med. L, from L EX-[1] + *humāre* to bury, from *humus* the ground]
▸exhumation (ˌɛkshjʊ'meɪʃən) *n* ▸ex'humer *n*

ex hypothesi (ɛks haɪ'pɒθəsɪ) *adv* in accordance with the hypothesis stated. [C17: NL]

exigency ➊ ('ɛksɪdʒənsɪ, ɪg'zɪdʒənsɪ) *or* **exigence** ('ɛksɪdʒəns) *n, pl* **exi-**

THESAURUS

able, chargeable, liable, obligated, responsible, subject

exemption *n* **1** = **immunity**, absolution, discharge, dispensation, exception, exoneration, freedom, privilege, release

exercise *vb* **1** = **put to use**, apply, bring to bear, employ, enjoy, exert, practise, use, utilize, wield **3** = **train**, discipline, drill, habituate, inure, practise, work out **6** = **worry**, afflict, agitate, annoy, burden, distress, disturb, occupy, pain, perturb, preoccupy, trouble, try, vex ◆ *n* **8** = **exertion**, action, activity, discipline, drill, drilling, effort, labour, toil, training, work, work-out **10** = **task**, drill, lesson, practice, problem, schooling, schoolwork, work **12** = **use**, accomplishment, application, discharge, employment, enjoyment, exertion, fulfilment, implementation, practice, utilization

exert *vb* **1** = **use**, apply, bring into play, bring to bear, employ, exercise, expend, make use of, put forth, utilize, wield **2 exert oneself** = **make an effort**, apply oneself, bend over backwards (*inf.*), break one's neck (*inf.*), bust a gut (*inf.*), do one's best, endeavour, go for broke (*sl.*), knock oneself out (*inf.*), labour, pull one's finger out (*Brit. inf.*), strain, strive, struggle, toil, try hard, work

exertion *n* **1** = **use**, application, employment, utilization **2** = **effort**, action, attempt, elbow grease (*facetious*), endeavour, exercise, industry, labour, pains, strain, stretch, struggle, toil, travail (*literary*), trial

exhalation *n* **1** = **breathing out**, breath, expiration **2** = **giving off**, discharge, effluvium, emanation, emission, evaporation, exhaust, fog, fume, mist, smoke, steam, vapour

exhale *vb* **1** = **breathe out**, breathe, expel, respire **2** = **give off**, discharge, eject, emanate, emit, evaporate, issue, steam

exhaust *vb* **1** = **tire out**, bankrupt, cripple, debilitate, disable, drain, enervate, enfeeble, fatigue, impoverish, prostrate, sap, tire, weaken, wear out **3** = **use up**, consume, deplete, dissipate, expend, finish, run through, spend, squander, waste **4** = **empty**, drain, dry, strain, void **7** = **be emitted**, discharge, emanate, escape, issue

exhausted *adj* **1** = **worn out**, all in, beat (*sl.*), dead beat (*inf.*), debilitated, dog-tired (*inf.*), done in (*inf.*), drained, enervated, enfeebled, fatigued, jaded, knackered (*sl.*), on one's last legs (*inf.*), out on one's feet (*inf.*), prostrated, ready to drop, sapped, spent, tired out, wasted, weak (*inf.*) **3** = **used up**, at an end, consumed, depleted, dissipated, done, expended, finished, gone, spent, squandered, wasted **4** = **empty**, bare, drained, dry, void
Antonyms *adj* ≠ **worn out:** active, alive and kicking, animated, enlivened, invigorated, refreshed, rejuvenated, restored, revived, stimulated ≠ **used up:** conserved, kept, preserved, replenished, restored

exhaustible *adj* **3** = **limited**, delimited, finite

exhausting *adj* **1** = **tiring**, arduous, backbreaking, crippling, debilitating, difficult, draining, enervating, fatiguing, gruelling, hard, laborious, punishing, sapping, strenuous, taxing, testing

exhaustion *n* **1** = **tiredness**, debilitation, enervation, fatigue, feebleness, lassitude, prostration, weariness **3** = **depletion**, consumption, emptying, using up

exhaustive *adj* **1** = **thorough**, all-embracing, all-inclusive, all-out (*inf.*), complete, comprehensive, detailed, encyclopedic, extensive, far-reaching, full, full-scale, in-depth, intensive, sweeping, thoroughgoing, total
Antonyms *adj* casual, cursory, desultory, incomplete, perfunctory, sketchy, superficial

exhibit *vb* **1, 2** = **display**, air, demonstrate, disclose, evidence, evince, expose, express, flaunt, indicate, make clear *or* plain, manifest, offer, parade, present, put on view, reveal, show ◆ *n* **4** = **display**, exhibition, illustration, model, show

exhibition *n* **1, 2** = **display**, airing, demonstration, exhibit, expo (*inf.*), exposition, fair, manifestation, performance, presentation, representation, show, showing, spectacle

exhilarate *vb* = **excite**, animate, cheer, delight, elate, enliven, exalt, gladden, inspirit, invigorate, lift, pep *or* perk up, rejoice, stimulate, thrill

exhilarating *adj* = **exciting**, breathtaking, cheering, enlivening, exalting, exhilarant, exhilarative, exhilaratory, gladdening, invigorating, stimulating, thrilling, vitalizing

exhilaration *n* = **excitement**, animation, cheerfulness, delight, elation, exaltation, gaiety, gladness, gleefulness, high spirits, hilarity, joy, joyfulness, liveliness, mirth, sprightliness, vivacity
Antonyms *n* dejection, depression, despondency, gloom, low spirits, melancholy, misery, sadness

exhort *vb* = **urge**, admonish, advise, beseech, bid, call upon, caution, counsel, encourage, enjoin, entreat, goad, incite, persuade, press, prompt, spur, warn

exhortation *n* = **urging**, admonition, advice, beseeching, bidding, caution, clarion call, counsel, encouragement, enjoinder (*rare*), entreaty, goading, incitement, lecture, persuasion, sermon, warning

exhume *vb* **1** = **dig up**, disentomb, disinter, unbury, unearth
Antonyms *vb* bury, entomb, inearth, inhume, inter

exigency *n* **1** = **urgency**, acuteness, constraint, criticalness, demandingness, difficulty, distress, emergency, imperativeness, necessity, needful-

gencies or **exigences. 1** urgency. **2** (*often pl*) an urgent demand; pressing requirement. **3** an emergency.

exigent ❶ ('ɛksɪdʒənt) *adj* **1** urgent; pressing. **2** exacting; demanding. [C15: from L *exigere* to drive out, weigh out, from *agere* to drive, compel]

exiguous (ɪg'zɪgjʊəs, ɪk'sɪg-) *adj* scanty or slender; meagre. [C17: from L *exiguus,* from *exigere* to weigh out; see EXIGENT]
▸**exiguity** (,ɛksɪ'gjuːɪtɪ) *or* **ex'iguousness** *n*

exile ❶ ('ɛgzaɪl, 'ɛksaɪl) *n* **1** a prolonged, usually enforced absence from one's home or country. **2** the official expulsion of a person from his native land. **3** a person banished or living away from his home or country; expatriate. ◆ *vb* **exiles, exiling, exiled. 4** (*tr*) to expel from home or country, esp. by official decree; banish. [C13: from L *exsilium* banishment, from *exsul* banished person]
▸**exilic** (ɛg'zɪlɪk, ɛk'sɪlɪk) *adj*

exist ❶ (ɪg'zɪst) *vb* (*intr*) **1** to have being or reality; be. **2** to eke out a living; stay alive. **3** to be living; live. **4** to be present under specified conditions or in a specified place. [C17: from L *exsistere* to step forth, from EX-[1] + *sistere* to stand]
▸**ex'istent** *adj* ▸**ex'isting** *adj*

existence ❶ (ɪg'zɪstəns) *n* **1** the fact or state of existing; being. **2** the continuance or maintenance of life; living, esp. in adverse circumstances. **3** something that exists; a being or entity. **4** everything that exists.

existential (,ɛgzɪ'stɛnʃəl) *adj* **1** of or relating to existence, esp. human existence. **2** *Philosophy.* known by experience rather than reason. **3** of a formula or proposition asserting the existence of at least one object fulfilling a given condition. **4** of or relating to existentialism.

existentialism (,ɛgzɪ'stɛnʃə,lɪzəm) *n* a modern philosophical movement stressing personal experience and responsibility and their demands on the individual, who is seen as a free agent in a deterministic and seemingly meaningless universe.
▸,**exis'tentialist** *adj, n*

exit ❶ ('ɛgzɪt, 'ɛksɪt) *n* **1** a way out. **2** the act or an instance of going out. **3a** the act of leaving or right to leave a particular place. **3b** (*as modifier*): *an exit visa.* **4** departure from life; death. **5** *Theatre.* the act of going offstage. **6** *Brit.* a point at which vehicles may leave or join a motorway. ◆ *vb* **exits, exiting, exited. 7** (*intr*) to go away or out; depart. **8** (*intr*) *Theatre.* to go offstage: used as a stage direction: *exit Hamlet.* **9** *Computing.* to leave (a computer program or system). [C17: from L *exitus* a departure, from *exīre* to go out, from EX-[1] + *īre* to go]

exitance ('ɛksɪtəns) *n* a measure of the ability of a surface to emit radiation. [C20: from EXIT + -ANCE]

exit poll *n* a poll taken by asking people how they voted in an election as they leave a polling station.

ex libris (ɛks 'liːbrɪs) *prep* **1** from the collection or library of. ◆ *n* **ex-libris,** *pl* **ex-libris. 2** a bookplate bearing the owner's name, coat of arms, etc. [C19: from L, lit.: from the books (of)]

ex new *adv, adj* (of shares, etc.) without the right to take up any scrip issue or rights issue. Cf. **cum new.**

exo- *combining form.* external, outside, or beyond: *exothermal.* [from Gk *exō* outside]

exobiology (,ɛksəʊbaɪ'ɒlədʒɪ) *n* another name for **astrobiology.**
▸,**exobi'ologist** *n*

exocarp ('ɛksəʊ,kɑːp) *n* another name for **epicarp.**

exocrine ('ɛksəʊ,kraɪn, -krɪn) *adj* **1** of or relating to exocrine glands or their secretions. ◆ *n* **2** an exocrine gland. [C20: EXO- + *-crine* from Gk *krinein* to separate]

exocrine gland *n* any gland, such as a salivary or sweat gland, that secretes its products through a duct onto an epithelial surface.

Exod. *Bible. abbrev. for* Exodus.

exodus ❶ ('ɛksədəs) *n* the act or an instance of going out. [C17: via L from Gk *exodos,* from EX-[1] + *hodos* way]

Exodus ('ɛksədəs) *n* **1 the.** the departure of the Israelites from Egypt. **2** the second book of the Old Testament, recounting the events connected with this.

ex officio ('ɛks ə'fɪʃɪəʊ, ə'fɪsɪəʊ) *adv, adj* by right of position or office. [L]

exogamy (ɛk'sɒgəmɪ) *n Anthropol., sociol.* marriage outside one's own tribe or similar unit.
▸**ex'ogamous** *or* **exogamic** (,ɛksəʊ'gæmɪk) *adj*

exogenous (ɛk'sɒdʒɪnəs) *adj* **1** having an external origin. **2** *Biol.* **2a** originating outside an organism. **2b** of or relating to external factors, such as light, that influence an organism. **3** *Psychiatry* (of a mental illness) caused by external factors.

exon ('ɛksɒn) *n Brit.* one of the four officers who command the Yeomen of the Guard. [C17: a pronunciation spelling of F *exempt* EXEMPT]

exonerate ❶ (ɪg'zɒnə,reɪt) *vb* **exonerates, exonerating, exonerated.** (*tr*) **1** to absolve from blame or a criminal charge. **2** to relieve from an obligation. [C16: from L *exonerāre* to free from a burden, from *onus* a burden]
▸**ex,oner'ation** *n* ▸**ex'onerative** *adj* ▸**ex'oner,ator** *n*

exophthalmos (,ɛksɒf'θælmɒs), **exophthalmus** (,ɛksɒf'θælməs), *or* **exophthalmia** (,ɛksɒf'θælmɪə) *n* abnormal protrusion of the eyeball, as caused by hyperthyroidism. [C19: via NL from Gk, from EX-[1] + *ophthalmos* eye]
▸,**exoph'thalmic** *adj*

exorbitant ❶ (ɪg'zɔːbɪtᵊnt) *adj* (of prices, demands, etc.) excessive; extravagant; immoderate. [C15: from LL *exorbitāre* to deviate, from L *orbita* track]
▸**ex'orbitance** *n* ▸**ex'orbitantly** *adv*

exorcize ❶ *or* **exorcise** ('ɛksɔː,saɪz) *vb* **exorcizes, exorcizing, exorcized** *or* **exorcises, exorcising, exorcised.** (*tr*) to expel (evil spirits) from (a person or place), by adjurations and religious rites. [C15: from LL, from Gk, from EX-[1] + *horkizein* to adjure]
▸**'exorcism** *n* ▸**'exorcist** *n* ▸**'exor,cizer** *or* **'exor,ciser** *n*

exordium (ɛk'sɔːdɪəm) *n, pl* **exordiums** *or* **exordia** (-dɪə). an introductory part or beginning, esp. of an oration or discourse. [C16: from L, from *exōrdīrī* to begin, from *ōrdīrī* to begin]
▸**ex'ordial** *adj*

exoskeleton (,ɛksəʊ'skɛlɪtᵊn) *n* the protective or supporting structure covering the outside of the body of many animals, such as the thick cuticle of arthropods.
▸,**exo'skeletal** *adj*

exosphere ('ɛksəʊ,sfɪə) *n* the outermost layer of the earth's atmosphere. It extends from about 400 kilometres above the earth's surface.

exothermic (,ɛksəʊ'θɜːmɪk) *or* **exothermal** *adj* (of a chemical reaction or compound) occurring or formed with the evolution of heat.
▸,**exo'thermically** *or* ,**exo'thermally** *adv*

exotic ❶ (ɪg'zɒtɪk) *adj* **1** originating in a foreign country, esp. one in the tropics; not native: *an exotic plant.* **2** having a strange or bizarre allure, beauty, or quality. ◆ *n* **3** an exotic person or thing. [C16: from L, from Gk *exōtikos* foreign, from *exō* outside]
▸**ex'otically** *adv* ▸**ex'oti,cism** *n* ▸**ex'oticness** *n*

exotica (ɪg'zɒtɪkə) *pl n* exotic objects, esp. when forming a collection. [C19: L, neuter pl of *exōticus;* see EXOTIC]

exotic dancer *n* a striptease or belly dancer.

expand ❶ (ɪk'spænd) *vb* **1** to make or become greater in extent, volume, size, or scope. **2** to spread out; unfold; stretch out. **3** (*intr; often*

THESAURUS

ness, pressingness, pressure, stress **2** = **need**, constraint, demand, necessity, requirement, wont **3** = **emergency**, crisis, difficulty, extremity, fix (*inf.*), hardship, jam (*inf.*), juncture, panic stations (*inf.*), pass, pickle (*inf.*), pinch, plight, predicament, quandary, scrape (*inf.*), strait

exigent *adj* **1** = **urgent**, acute, constraining, critical, crucial, imperative, importunate, insistent, necessary, needful, pressing **2** = **demanding**, arduous, difficult, exacting, hard, harsh, rigorous, severe, stiff, strict, stringent, taxing, tough

exile *n* **2** = **banishment**, deportation, expatriation, expulsion, ostracism, proscription, separation **3** = **expatriate**, deportee, émigré, outcast, refugee ◆ *vb* **4** = **banish**, deport, drive out, eject, expatriate, expel, ostracize, oust, proscribe

exist *vb* **1, 3** = **be**, abide, be extant, be living, be present, breathe, continue, endure, happen, last, live, obtain, occur, prevail, remain, stand, survive **2** = **survive**, eke out a living, get along *or* by, keep one's head above water, stay alive, subsist

existence *n* **1** = **being**, actuality, animation, breath, continuance, continuation, duration, endurance, life, subsistence, survival **3** = **creature**, being, entity, thing **4** = **creation**, life, reality, the world

existent *adj* **1, 3** = **in existence**, abiding, alive, around, current, enduring, existing, extant, living, obtaining, present, prevailing, remaining, standing, surviving, to the fore (*Scot.*)

existing *adj* **3** = **in existence**, alive, alive and kicking, extant, living, remaining, surviving
Antonyms *adj* dead, defunct, died out, extinct, gone, lost, vanished

exit *n* **1** = **way out**, door, egress, gate, outlet, passage out, vent **2, 3** = **departure**, adieu, evacuation, exodus, farewell, going, goodbye, leave-taking, retirement, retreat, withdrawal **4** = **death**, decease, demise, expiry, passing away ◆ *vb* **7** = **depart**, bid farewell, go away, go offstage (*Theatre*), go out, issue, leave, make tracks, retire, retreat, say goodbye, take one's leave, withdraw
Antonyms *n* ≠ **way out**: entrance, entry, ingress, inlet, opening, way in ◆ *vb* ≠ **depart**: arrive, come *or* go in *or* into, enter, make an entrance

exodus *n* = **departure**, evacuation, exit, flight, going out, leaving, migration, retirement, retreat, withdrawal

exonerate *vb* **1** = **clear**, absolve, acquit, discharge, dismiss, exculpate, excuse, justify, pardon, vindicate **2** = **exempt**, discharge, dismiss, except, excuse, free, let off, liberate, release, relieve

exoneration *n* **1** = **acquittal**, absolution, amnesty, discharge, dismissal, exculpation, justification, pardon, vindication **2** = **exemption**, deliverance, discharge, dismissal, exception, freeing, liberation, release, relief

exorbitant *adj* = **excessive**, enormous, extortionate, extravagant, extreme, immoderate, inordinate, outrageous, preposterous, ridiculous, unconscionable, undue, unreasonable, unwarranted
Antonyms *adj* cheap, fair, moderate, reasonable

exorcism *n* = **driving out**, adjuration, casting out, deliverance, expulsion, purification

exorcize *vb* = **drive out**, adjure, cast out, deliver (from), expel, purify

exotic *adj* **1** = **foreign**, alien, external, extraneous, extrinsic, imported, introduced, naturalized, not native **2** = **unusual**, beyond one's ken, bizarre, colourful, curious, different, extraordinary, fascinating, glamorous, mysterious, outlandish, peculiar, strange, striking, unfamiliar
Antonyms *adj* ≠ **unusual**: conventional, familiar, ordinary, pedestrian, plain, run-of-the-mill, unmemorable, unremarkable

expand *vb* **1** = **increase**, amplify, augment, bloat, blow up, broaden, develop, dilate, distend, enlarge, extend, fatten, fill out, grow, heighten, inflate, lengthen, magnify, multiply,

DICTIONARY

foll. by *on*) to enlarge or expatiate (on a story, topic, etc.). **4** (*intr*) to become increasingly relaxed, friendly, or talkative. **5** *Maths.* to express (a function or expression) as the sum or product of terms. **[C15:** from L *expandere* to spread out**]**
▸**ex'pandable** *adj*

expanded (ɪk'spændɪd) *adj* (of a plastic) having been foamed during manufacture by a gas to make a light packaging material or heat insulator: *expanded polystyrene.*

expanded metal *n* an open mesh of metal used for reinforcing brittle or friable materials and in fencing.

expander (ɪk'spændə) *n* **1** a device for exercising and developing the muscles of the body. **2** an electronic device for increasing the variations in signal amplitude in a transmission system according to a specified law.

expanse Ⓣ (ɪk'spæns) *n* **1** an uninterrupted surface of something that extends, esp. over a wide area; stretch. **2** expansion or extension. **[C17:** from NL *expansum* the heavens, from L *expansus* spread out, from *expandere* to expand**]**

expansible (ɪk'spænsəbᵊl) *adj* able to expand or be expanded.
▸**ex,pansi'bility** *n*

expansion Ⓣ (ɪk'spænʃən) *n* **1** the act of expanding or the state of being expanded. **2** something expanded. **3** the degree or amount by which something expands. **4** an increase or development, esp. in the activities of a company. **5** the increase in the dimensions of a body or substance when subjected to an increase in temperature, internal pressure, etc.
▸**ex'pansionary** *adj*

expansionism (ɪk'spænʃə,nɪzəm) *n* the doctrine or practice of expanding the economy or territory of a country.
▸**ex'pansionist** *n, adj* ▸**ex,pansion'istic** *adj*

expansive Ⓣ (ɪk'spænsɪv) *adj* **1** able or tending to expand or characterized by expansion. **2** wide; extensive. **3** friendly, open, or talkative. **4** grand or extravagant.
▸**ex'pansiveness** *n*

expansivity (,ɛkspæn'sɪvɪtɪ) *n* the fractional increase in length or volume of a substance or body on being heated through a one degree rise in temperature; coefficient of expansion.

ex parte (ɛks 'pɑːtɪ) *adj Law.* (of an application in a judicial proceeding) on behalf of one side or party only: *an ex parte injunction.*

expat (,ɛks'pæt) *n, adj Inf.* short for **expatriate.**

expatiate (ɪk'speɪʃɪ,eɪt) *vb* **expatiates, expatiating, expatiated.** (*intr*) **1** (foll. by *on* or *upon*) to enlarge (on a theme, topic, etc.); elaborate (on). **2** *Rare.* to wander about. **[C16:** from L *exspatiārī* to digress, from *spatiārī* to walk about**]**
▸**ex,pati'ation** *n* ▸**ex'pati,ator** *n*

expatriate Ⓣ *adj* (ɛks'pætrɪɪt, -,eɪt). **1** resident outside one's native country. **2** exiled or banished from one's native country. ◆ *n* (ɛks'pætrɪɪt, -,eɪt). **3** a person living outside his native country **4** an exile; expatriate person. ◆ *vb* (ɛks'pætrɪ,eɪt), **expatriates, expatriating, expatriated.** (*tr*) **5** to exile (oneself) from one's native country or cause (another) to go into exile. **[C18:** from Med. L, from L EX-[1] + *patria* native land**]**
▸**ex,patri'ation** *n*

expect Ⓣ (ɪk'spɛkt) *vb* (*tr; may take a clause as object or an infinitive*) **1** to regard as likely; anticipate. **2** to look forward to or be waiting for. **3** to decide that (something) is necessary; require: *the teacher expects us to work late.* ◆ See also **expecting. [C16:** from L *exspectāre* to watch for, from *spectāre* to look at**]**
▸**ex'pectable** *adj*

expectancy Ⓣ (ɪk'spɛktənsɪ) *or* **expectance** *n* **1** something expected, esp. on the basis of a norm or average: *his life expectancy was 30 years.* **2** anticipation; expectation. **3** the prospect of a future interest or possession.

expectant Ⓣ (ɪk'spɛktənt) *adj* **1** expecting, anticipating, or hopeful. **2** having expectations, esp. of possession of something. **3** pregnant. ◆ *n* **4** a person who expects something.
▸**ex'pectantly** *adv*

expectation Ⓣ (,ɛkspɛk'teɪʃən) *n* **1** the act or state of expecting or the state of being expected. **2** (*usually pl*) something looked forward to, whether feared or hoped for. **3** an attitude of expectancy or hope. **4** *Statistics.* **4a** the numerical probability that an event will occur. **4b** another term for **expected value.**

expected frequency *n Statistics.* the number of occasions on which an event may be presumed to occur on average in a given number of trials.

expected value *n Statistics.* the sum or integral of all possible values of a random variable, or any given function of it, multiplied by the respective probabilities of the values of the variable.

expecting Ⓣ (ɪk'spɛktɪŋ) *adj Inf.* pregnant.

expectorant (ɪk'spɛktərənt) *Med.* ◆ *adj* **1** promoting the secretion, liquefaction, or expulsion of sputum from the respiratory passages. ◆ *n* **2** an expectorant drug or agent.

expectorate (ɪk'spɛktə,reɪt) *vb* **expectorates, expectorating, expectorated.** to cough up and spit out (sputum from the respiratory passages). **[C17:** from L *expectorāre,* lit.: to drive from the breast, expel, from *pectus* breast**]**
▸**ex,pecto'ration** *n* ▸**ex'pecto,rator** *n*

expediency Ⓣ (ɪk'spiːdɪənsɪ) *or* **expedience** *n, pl* **expediencies** *or* **expediences. 1** appropriateness; suitability. **2** the use of or inclination towards methods that are advantageous rather than fair or just. **3** another word for **expedient** (sense 3).

expedient Ⓣ (ɪk'spiːdɪənt) *adj* **1** suitable to the circumstances; appropriate. **2** inclined towards methods that are advantageous rather than fair or just. ◆ *n also* **expediency. 3** something suitable or appropriate, esp. during an urgent situation. **[C14:** from L *expediēns* setting free; see EXPEDITE**]**

expedite Ⓣ ('ɛkspɪ,daɪt) *vb* **expedites, expediting, expedited.** (*tr*) **1** to hasten or assist the progress of. **2** to do or process with speed and efficiency. **[C17:** from L *expedīre,* lit.: to free the feet (as from a snare), hence, liberate, from EX-[1] + *pēs* foot**]**
▸**'expe,diter** *or* **'expe,ditor** *n*

expedition Ⓣ (,ɛkspɪ'dɪʃən) *n* **1** an organized journey or voyage, esp. for exploration or for a scientific or military purpose. **2** the people and equipment comprising an expedition. **3** promptness; dispatch. **[C15:** from L *expedīre* to prepare, EXPEDITE**]**
▸**,expe'ditionary** *adj*

expeditious Ⓣ (,ɛkspɪ'dɪʃəs) *adj* characterized by or done with speed and efficiency; prompt; quick.
▸**,expe'ditiously** *adv* ▸**,expe'ditiousness** *n*

expel Ⓣ (ɪk'spɛl) *vb* **expels, expelling, expelled.** (*tr*) **1** to eject or drive out

THESAURUS

prolong, protract, swell, thicken, wax, widen **2** = **spread (out)**, diffuse, open (out), outspread, stretch (out), unfold, unfurl, unravel, unroll **3** *with* **on** = **go into detail about**, amplify, develop, dilate, elaborate on, embellish, enlarge on, expatiate on, expound on, flesh out
Antonyms *vb* ≠ **increase:** condense, contract, decrease, reduce, shorten, shrink ≠ **go into detail about:** abbreviate, condense, shorten

expanse *n* **1** = **area**, breadth, extent, field, plain, range, space, stretch, sweep, tract

expansion *n* **1** = **increase**, amplification, augmentation, development, diffusion, dilatation, distension, enlargement, expanse, growth, inflation, magnification, multiplication, opening out, spread, swelling, unfolding, unfurling

expansive *adj* **1** = **expanding**, dilating, distending, elastic, enlargeable, extendable, inflatable, stretching, stretchy, swelling **2** = **wide**, all-embracing, broad, comprehensive, extensive, far-reaching, inclusive, thorough, voluminous, wide-ranging, widespread **3** = **talkative**, affable, communicative, easy, effusive, free, friendly, garrulous, genial, loquacious, open, outgoing, sociable, unreserved, warm

expatriate *adj* **1, 2** = **exiled**, banished, emigrant, émigré ◆ *n* **3, 4** = **exile**, emigrant, émigré, refugee ◆ *vb* **5** = **exile**, banish, expel, ostracize, proscribe

expect *vb* **1** = **think**, assume, believe, calculate, conjecture, forecast, foresee, imagine, presume, reckon, suppose, surmise, trust **2** = **look forward to**, anticipate, await, bargain for, contemplate, envisage, hope for, look ahead to, look for, predict, watch for **3** = **require**, call for, count on, demand, insist on, look for, rely upon, want, wish

expectancy *n* **1** = **likelihood**, outlook, prospect **2** = **expectation**, anticipation, assumption, belief, conjecture, hope, looking forward, prediction, presumption, probability, supposition, surmise, suspense, waiting

expectant *adj* **1** = **expecting**, anticipating, anxious, apprehensive, awaiting, eager, hopeful, in suspense, ready, watchful **3** = **pregnant**, enceinte, expecting (*inf.*), gravid

expectation *n* **1** = **anticipation**, apprehension, chance, expectancy, fear, hope, looking forward, outlook, possibility, prediction, promise, prospect, suspense

expected *adj* **1, 2** = **anticipated**, awaited, counted on, forecast, hoped-for, long-awaited, looked-for, predicted, promised, wanted

expecting *adj* = **pregnant**, enceinte, expectant, gravid, in the club (*Brit. sl.*), in the family way (*inf.*), with child

expediency *n* **1** = **suitability**, advantageousness, advisability, appropriateness, aptness, benefit, convenience, desirability, effectiveness, fitness, helpfulness, judiciousness, meetness, practicality, pragmatism, profitability, properness, propriety, prudence, usefulness, utilitarianism, utility **3** = **means**, contrivance, device, expedient, makeshift, manoeuvre, measure, method, resort, resource, scheme, shift, stopgap, stratagem, substitute

expedient *adj* **1** = **advantageous**, advisable, appropriate, beneficial, convenient, desirable, effective, fit, helpful, judicious, meet, opportune, politic, practical, pragmatic, profitable, proper, prudent, suitable, useful, utilitarian, worthwhile ◆ *n* **3** = **means**, contrivance, device, expediency, makeshift, manoeuvre, measure, method, resort, resource, scheme, shift, stopgap, stratagem, substitute
Antonyms *adj* ≠ **advantageous:** detrimental, disadvantageous, futile, harmful, ill-advised, impractical, imprudent, inadvisable, inappropriate, ineffective, inexpedient, unwise, wrong

expedite *vb* **1** = **speed (up)**, accelerate, advance, assist, dispatch, facilitate, forward, hasten, hurry, precipitate, press, promote, quicken, rush, urge
Antonyms *vb* block, curb, decelerate, delay, handicap, hold up, obstruct, restrict, slow up *or* down

expedition *n* **1** = **journey**, enterprise, excursion, exploration, mission, quest, safari, tour, trek, trip, undertaking, voyage **2** = **team**, company, crew, explorers, travellers, voyagers, wayfarers **3** = **speed**, alacrity, celerity, dispatch, expeditiousness, haste, hurry, promptness, quickness, rapidity, readiness, swiftness

expeditious *adj* = **quick**, active, alert, brisk, diligent, efficient, fast, hasty, immediate, instant, nimble, prompt, rapid, ready, speedy, swift

expel *vb* **1** = **drive out**, belch, cast out, discharge, dislodge, eject, remove, spew, throw out **2** = **dismiss**, ban, banish, bar, black, blackball, discharge, drum out, evict, exclude, exile,

DICTIONARY

with force. **2** to deprive of participation in or membership of a school, club, etc. [C14: from L *expellere* to drive out, from *pellere* to thrust, drive]
►**ex'pellable** *adj* ►**expellee** (ˌɛkspɛ'liː) *n* ►**ex'peller** *n*

expellant *or* **expellent** (ɪk'spɛlənt) *adj* **1** forcing out or able to force out. ◆ *n* **2** a medicine used to expel undesirable substances or organisms from the body.

expend ❶ (ɪk'spɛnd) *vb* (*tr*) **1** to spend; disburse. **2** to consume or use up. [C15: from L *expendere*, from *pendere* to weigh]
►**ex'pender** *n*

expendable ❶ (ɪk'spɛndəbᵊl) *adj* **1** that may be expended or used up. **2** able to be sacrificed to achieve an objective, esp. a military one. ◆ *n* **3** something expendable.
►**exˌpenda'bility** *n*

expenditure ❶ (ɪk'spɛndɪtʃə) *n* **1** something expended, esp. money. **2** the act of expending.

expense ❶ (ɪk'spɛns) *n* **1** a particular payment of money; expenditure. **2** money needed for individual purchases; cost; charge. **3** (*pl*) money spent in the performance of a job, etc., usually reimbursed by an employer or allowable against tax. **4** something requiring money for its purchase or upkeep. **5 at the expense of.** to the detriment of. [C14: from LL, from L *expēnsus* weighed out; see EXPEND]

expense account *n* **1** an arrangement by which an employee's expenses are refunded by his employer or deducted from his income for tax purposes. **2** a record of such expenses.

expensive ❶ (ɪk'spɛnsɪv) *adj* high-priced; costly; dear.
►**ex'pensiveness** *n*

experience ❶ (ɪk'spɪərɪəns) *n* **1** direct personal participation or observation. **2** a particular incident, feeling, etc., that a person has undergone. **3** accumulated knowledge, esp. of practical matters. ◆ *vb* **experiences, experiencing, experienced.** (*tr*) **4** to participate in or undergo. **5** to be moved by; feel. [C14: from L *experīrī* to prove; rel. to L *perīculum* PERIL]
►**ex'perienceable** *adj*

experienced ❶ (ɪk'spɪərɪənst) *adj* having become skilful or knowledgeable from extensive participation or observation.

experiential (ɪkˌspɪərɪ'ɛnʃəl) *adj Philosophy.* relating to or derived from experience; empirical.

experiment ❶ *n* (ɪk'spɛrɪmənt). **1** a test or investigation, esp. one planned to provide evidence for or against a hypothesis. **2** the act of conducting such an investigation or test; research. **3** an attempt at something new or original. ◆ *vb* (ɪk'spɛrɪˌmɛnt). **4** (*intr*) to make an experiment or experiments. [C14: from L *experīmentum* proof, trial, from *experīrī* to test; see EXPERIENCE]
►**ex'periˌmenter** *n*

experimental ❶ (ɪkˌspɛrɪ'mɛntᵊl) *adj* **1** relating to, based on, or having the nature of experiment. **2** based on or derived from experience; empirical. **3** tending to experiment. **4** tentative or provisional.
►**exˌperi'mentalism** *n*

experimentation (ɪkˌspɛrɪmɛn'teɪʃən) *n* the act, process, or practice of experimenting.

expert ❶ ('ɛkspɜːt) *n* **1** a person who has extensive skill or knowledge in a particular field. ◆ *adj* **2** skilful or knowledgeable. **3** of, involving, or done by an expert: *an expert job.* [C14: from L *expertus* known by experience; see EXPERIENCE]
►**'expertly** *adv* ►**'expertness** *n*

expertise ❶ (ˌɛkspɜː'tiːz) *n* special skill, knowledge, or judgment; expertness. [C19: from F: expert skill, from EXPERT]

expiate ('ɛkspɪˌeɪt) *vb* **expiates, expiating, expiated.** (*tr*) to atone for (sin or wrongdoing); make amends for. [C16: from L *expiāre*, from *pius* dutiful; see PIOUS]
►**'expiable** *adj* ►**ˌexpi'ation** *n* ►**'expiˌator** *n*

expiatory ('ɛkspɪətərɪ, -trɪ) *adj* **1** capable of making expiation. **2** offered in expiation.

expiration ❶ (ˌɛkspɪ'reɪʃən) *n* **1** the finish of something; expiry. **2** the act, process, or sound of breathing out.

expire ❶ (ɪk'spaɪə) *vb* **expires, expiring, expired. 1** (*intr*) to finish or run out; come to an end. **2** to breathe out (air). **3** (*intr*) to die. [C15: from OF, from L *exspīrāre* to breathe out, from *spīrāre* to breathe]
►**ex'pirer** *n*

expiry ❶ (ɪk'spaɪərɪ) *n, pl* **expiries. 1a** a coming to an end, esp. of a contract period; termination. **1b** (*as modifier*): *the expiry date.* **2** death.

explain ❶ (ɪk'spleɪn) *vb* **1** (when *tr, may take a clause as object*) to make (something) comprehensible, esp. by giving a clear and detailed account of it. **2** (*tr*) to justify or attempt to justify (oneself) by reasons for one's actions. [C15: from L *explānāre* to flatten, from *plānus* level]
►**ex'plainable** *adj* ►**ex'plainer** *n*

explain away *vb* (*tr, adv*) to offer excuses or reasons for (bad conduct, mistakes, etc.).

explanation ❶ (ˌɛksplə'neɪʃən) *n* **1** the act or process of explaining. **2** something that explains. **3** a clarification of disputed points.

explanatory ❶ (ɪk'splænətərɪ, -trɪ) *or* **explanative** *adj* serving or intended to serve as an explanation.
►**ex'planatorily** *adv*

expletive (ɪk'spliːtɪv) *n* **1** an exclamation or swearword; an oath or sound expressing emotion rather than meaning. **2** any syllable, word, or phrase conveying no independent meaning, esp. one inserted in verse for the sake of metre. ◆ *adj also* **expletory** (ɪk'spliːtərɪ, -trɪ). **3** without particular meaning, esp. when filling out a line of verse. [C17: from LL *explētīvus* for filling out, from *explēre*, from *plēre* to fill]

explicable ('ɛksplɪkəbᵊl, ɪk'splɪk-) *adj* capable of being explained.

explicate ❶ ('ɛksplɪˌkeɪt) *vb* **explicates, explicating, explicated.** (*tr*) *Formal.* **1** to make clear or explicit; explain. **2** to formulate or develop (a theory, hypothesis, etc.). [C16: from L *explicāre* to unfold]
►**ˌexpli'cation** *n*

explicit ❶ (ɪk'splɪsɪt) *adj* **1** precisely and clearly expressed, leaving nothing to implication; fully stated. **2** leaving little to the imagina-

THESAURUS

expatriate, oust, proscribe, relegate, send packing, show one the door, throw out, turf out (*inf.*)
Antonyms *vb* ≠ **dismiss:** admit, allow to enter, give access, let in, receive, take in, welcome

expend *vb* **1 = spend**, disburse, fork out (*sl.*), lay out (*inf.*), pay out, shell out **2 = use (up)**, consume, dissipate, employ, exhaust, go through

expendable *adj* **2 = dispensable**, inessential, nonessential, replaceable, unimportant, unnecessary
Antonyms *adj* crucial, essential, indispensable, key, necessary, vital

expenditure *n* **2 = spending**, application, charge, consumption, cost, disbursement, expense, outgoings, outlay, output, payment, use

expense *n* **2 = cost**, charge, expenditure, outlay, payment

expensive *adj* **= dear**, costly, excessive, exorbitant, extravagant, high-priced, inordinate, lavish, overpriced, rich, steep (*inf.*), stiff
Antonyms *adj* bargain, budget, cheap, cut-price, economical, inexpensive, low-cost, low-priced, reasonable

experience *n* **1, 3 = knowledge**, contact, doing, evidence, exposure, familiarity, involvement, know-how (*inf.*), observation, participation, practice, proof, training, trial, understanding **2 = event**, adventure, affair, encounter, episode, happening, incident, occurrence, ordeal, test, trial ◆ *vb* **4, 5 = undergo**, apprehend, become familiar with, behold, encounter, endure, face, feel, go through, have, know, live through, meet, observe, participate in, perceive, sample, sense, suffer, sustain, taste, try

experienced *adj* **= knowledgeable**, accomplished, adept, capable, competent, expert, familiar, master, practised, professional, qualified, seasoned, skilful, tested, trained, tried, veteran, well-versed
Antonyms *adj* apprentice, green, incompetent, inexperienced, new, unqualified, unskilled, untrained, untried

experiment *n* **1, 2 = test**, assay, attempt, examination, experimentation, investigation, procedure, proof, research, trial, trial and error, trial run, venture ◆ *vb* **4 = test**, assay, examine, investigate, put to the test, research, sample, try, verify

experimental *adj* **1-4 = test**, empirical, exploratory, pilot, preliminary, probationary, provisional, speculative, tentative, trial, trial-and-error

expert *n* **1 = master**, ace (*inf.*), adept, authority, buff (*inf.*), connoisseur, dab hand (*Brit. inf.*), guru, maven (*US*), past master, pro (*inf.*), professional, specialist, virtuoso, whizz (*inf.*), wizard ◆ *adj* **2 = skilful**, able, adept, adroit, apt, clever, deft, dexterous, experienced, facile, handy, knowledgeable, master, masterly, practised, professional, proficient, qualified, skilled, trained, virtuoso
Antonyms *n* ≠ **master:** amateur, dabbler, ham, layman, nonprofessional, novice ◆ *adj* ≠ **skilful:** amateurish, cack-handed (*inf.*), clumsy, incompetent, inexperienced, unpractised, unqualified, unskilled, untrained

expertise *n* **= skill**, ableness, adroitness, aptness, cleverness, command, craft, deftness, dexterity, expertness, facility, grasp, grip, judgment, knack, know-how (*inf.*), knowing inside out, knowledge, masterliness, mastery, proficiency, skilfulness

expertness *n* **2 = skill**, ableness, adroitness, aptness, command, craft, deftness, dexterity, expertise, facility, grasp, grip, judgment, know-how (*inf.*), knowing inside out, knowledge, masterliness, mastery, proficiency, skilfulness

expiration *n* **1 = finish**, cessation, close, conclusion, end, expiry, finis, termination

expire *vb* **1 = finish**, cease, close, come to an end, conclude, end, lapse, run out, stop, terminate **2 = breathe out**, emit, exhale, expel **3 = die**, croak, decease, depart, kick the bucket (*inf.*), pass away *or* on, peg out (*inf.*), perish, pop one's clogs (*inf.*), snuff it (*inf.*)

expiry *n* **1 = ending**, cessation, close, conclusion, demise, end, expiration, lapsing, termination

explain *vb* **1 = make clear** *or* **plain**, clarify, clear up, define, demonstrate, describe, disclose, elucidate, explicate (*formal*), expound, illustrate, interpret, resolve, solve, teach, unfold **2 = account for**, excuse, give an explanation for, give a reason for, justify

explanation *n* **2 = reason**, account, answer, cause, excuse, justification, meaning, mitigation, motive, sense, significance, the why and wherefore, vindication **3 = description**, clarification, definition, demonstration, elucidation, explication, exposition, illustration, interpretation, resolution

explanatory *adj* **= descriptive**, demonstrative, elucidatory, explicative, expository, illuminative, illustrative, interpretive, justifying

explicable *adj* **= explainable**, accountable, definable, intelligible, interpretable, justifiable, resolvable, understandable

explicate *vb Formal* **1 = explain**, clarify, clear up, elucidate, expound, interpret, make clear *or* explicit, make plain, unfold, untangle **2 = develop**, construct, devise, evolve, formulate, work out

explicit *adj* **1, 3 = clear**, absolute, categorical, certain, definite, direct, distinct, exact, express, frank, open, outspoken, patent, plain, posi-

tion; graphically detailed. **3** openly expressed without reservations; unreserved. [C17: from L *explicitus* unfolded]
▸**ex'plicitly** *adv* ▸**ex'plicitness** *n*

explode ❶ (ɪk'spləʊd) *vb* **explodes, exploding, exploded. 1** to burst or cause to burst with great violence, esp. through detonation of an explosive; blow up. **2** to destroy or be destroyed in this manner. **3** (of a gas) to undergo or cause (a gas) to undergo a sudden violent expansion, as a result of a fast exothermic chemical or nuclear reaction. **4** (*intr*) to react suddenly or violently with emotion, etc. **5** (*intr*) (esp. of a population) to increase rapidly. **6** (*tr*) to show (a theory, etc.) to be baseless. [C16: from L *explōdere* to drive off by clapping]
▸**ex'ploder** *n*

exploded view *n* a drawing or photograph of a mechanism that shows its parts separately, usually indicating their relative positions.

exploit ❶ *n* ('ɛksplɔɪt). **1** a notable deed or feat, esp. one that is heroic. ◆ *vb* (ɪk'splɔɪt). (*tr*) **2** to take advantage of (a person, situation, etc.) for one's own ends. **3** to make the best use of. [C14: from OF: accomplishment, from L *explicitum* (something) unfolded, from *explicāre* to EXPLICATE]
▸**ex'ploitable** *adj* ▸ˌ**exploi'tation** *n* ▸**ex'ploitive** *or* **ex'ploitative** *adj*

exploration ❶ (ˌɛksplə'reɪʃən) *n* **1** the act or process of exploring. **2** an organized trip into unfamiliar regions, esp. for scientific purposes.
▸**exploratory** (ɪk'splɒrətərɪ, -trɪ) *or* **ex'plorative** *adj*

explore ❶ (ɪk'splɔː) *vb* **explores, exploring, explored. 1** (*tr*) to examine or investigate, esp. systematically. **2** to travel into (unfamiliar regions), esp. for scientific purposes. **3** (*tr*) *Med.* to examine (an organ or part) for diagnostic purposes. [C16: from L, from EX-[1] + *plōrāre* to cry aloud; prob. from the shouts of hunters sighting prey]
▸**ex'plorer** *n*

explosion ❶ (ɪk'spləʊʒən) *n* **1** the act or an instance of exploding. **2** a violent release of energy resulting from a rapid chemical or nuclear reaction. **3** a sudden or violent outburst of activity, noise, emotion, etc. **4** a rapid increase, esp. in a population. [C17: from L *explōsiō*, from *explōdere* to EXPLODE]

explosive ❶ (ɪk'spləʊsɪv) *adj* **1** of, involving, or characterized by explosion. **2** capable of exploding or tending to explode. **3** potentially violent or hazardous: *an explosive situation.* ◆ *n* **4** a substance capable of exploding or tending to explode.
▸**ex'plosiveness** *n*

expo ('ɛkspəʊ) *n, pl* **expos.** short for **exposition** (sense 3).

exponent ❶ (ɪk'spəʊnənt) *n* **1** (usually foll. by *of*) a person or thing that acts as an advocate (of an idea, cause, etc.). **2** a person or thing that explains or interprets. **3** a performer or artist. **4** Also called: **power, index.** *Maths.* a number or variable placed as a superscript to another number or quantity to indicate the number of times the designated number or quantity should appear in a repeated multiplication, as in $x^3 = x \times x \times x$, where 3 is the exponent. ◆ *adj* **5** offering a declaration, explanation, or interpretation. [C16: from L *expōnere* to set out, expound]

exponential (ˌɛkspəʊ'nɛnʃəl) *adj* **1** *Maths.* (of a function, curve, etc.) of or involving numbers or quantities raised to an exponent, esp. e^x. **2** *Maths.* raised to the power of e, the base of natural logarithms. **3** of or involving an exponent or exponents. **4** *Inf.* very rapid. ◆ *n* **5** *Maths.* an exponential function, etc.

exponential distribution *n Statistics.* a continuous single-parameter distribution used esp. when making statements about the length of life of materials or times between random events.

export *n* ('ɛkspɔːt). **1** (*often pl*) **1a** goods (**visible exports**) or services (**invisible exports**) sold to a foreign country or countries. **1b** (*as modifier*): *an export licence.* ◆ *vb* (ɪk'spɔːt, 'ɛkspɔːt). **2** to sell (goods or services) or ship (goods) to a foreign country. **3** (*tr*) to transmit or spread (an idea, institution, etc.) abroad. [C15: from L *exportāre* to carry away]
▸**ex'portable** *adj* ▸**ex**ˌ**porta'bility** *n* ▸ˌ**expor'tation** *n* ▸**ex'porter** *n*

export reject *n* an article that fails to meet a standard of quality required for export and that is sold on the home market.

expose ❶ (ɪk'spəʊz) *vb* **exposes, exposing, exposed.** (*tr*) **1** to display for viewing; exhibit. **2** to bring to public notice; disclose. **3** to divulge the identity of; unmask. **4** (foll. by *to*) to make subject or susceptible (to attack, criticism, etc.). **5** to abandon (a child, etc.) in the open to die. **6** (foll. by *to*) to introduce (to) or acquaint (with). **7** *Photog.* to subject (a film or plate) to light, X-rays, etc. **8 expose oneself.** to display one's sexual organs in public. [C15: from OF *exposer*, from L *expōnere* to set out]
▸**ex'posable** *adj* ▸**ex'posal** *n* ▸**ex'poser** *n*

exposé ❶ (ɛks'pəʊzeɪ) *n* the act or an instance of bringing a scandal, crime, etc., to public notice.

exposed ❶ (ɪk'spəʊzd) *adj* **1** not concealed; displayed for viewing. **2** without shelter from the elements. **3** susceptible to attack or criticism; vulnerable.

exposition ❶ (ˌɛkspə'zɪʃən) *n* **1** a systematic, usually written statement about or explanation of a subject. **2** the act of expounding or setting forth information or a viewpoint. **3** a large public exhibition, esp. of industrial products or arts and crafts. **4** the act of exposing or the state of being exposed. **5** *Music.* the first statement of the subjects or themes of a movement in sonata form or a fugue. **6** *RC Church.* the exhibiting of the consecrated Eucharistic Host or a relic for public veneration. [C14: from L *expositiō* a setting forth, from *expōnere* to display]
▸ˌ**expo'sitional** *adj*

expositor (ɪk'spɒzɪtə) *n* a person who expounds.

expository ❶ (ɪk'spɒzɪtərɪ, -trɪ) *or* **expositive** *adj* of or involving exposition; explanatory.

ex post facto (ɛks pəʊst 'fæktəʊ) *adj* having retrospective effect. [C17: from L *ex* from + *post* afterwards + *factus* done, from *facere* to do]

expostulate ❶ (ɪk'spɒstjʊˌleɪt) *vb* **expostulates, expostulating, expostulated.** (*intr*; usually foll. by *with*) to argue or reason (with), esp. in order to dissuade. [C16: from L *expostulāre* to require, from *postulāre* to demand; see POSTULATE]
▸**ex**ˌ**postu'lation** *n* ▸**ex'postu**ˌ**lator** *n*

exposure ❶ (ɪk'spəʊʒə) *n* **1** the act of exposing or the condition of being exposed. **2** the position or outlook of a house, building, etc.: *a southern exposure.* **3** lack of shelter from the weather, esp. the cold. **4** a surface that is exposed. **5** *Photog.* **5a** the act of exposing a film or plate to light, X-rays, etc. **5b** an area on a film or plate that has been exposed. **6** *Photog.* **6a** the intensity of light falling on a film or plate multiplied by the time for which it is exposed. **6b** a combination of lens aperture and shutter speed used in taking a photograph. **7** appearance before the public, as in a theatre, on television, etc.

exposure meter *n Photog.* an instrument for measuring the intensity of light so that suitable camera settings can be determined. Also called: **light meter.**

expound ❶ (ɪk'spaʊnd) *vb* (when *intr*, foll. by *on* or *about*) to explain or set forth (an argument, theory, etc.) in detail. [C13: from OF, from L *expōnere* to set forth, from *pōnere* to put]
▸**ex'pounder** *n*

express ❶ (ɪk'sprɛs) *vb* (*tr*) **1** to transform (ideas) into words; utter; verbalize. **2** to show or reveal. **3** to communicate (emotion, etc.) without words, as through music, painting, etc. **4** to indicate through a sym-

THESAURUS

tive, precise, specific, stated, straightforward, unambiguous, unequivocal, unqualified, unreserved, upfront (*inf.*)
Antonyms *adj* ambiguous, cryptic, general, implicit, implied, indefinite, indirect, inexact, obscure, oracular, suggested, uncertain, vague

explode *vb* **1, 2** = **blow up**, burst, detonate, discharge, erupt, go off, set off, shatter, shiver **6** = **disprove**, belie, blow out of the water (*sl.*), debunk, discredit, give the lie to, invalidate, refute, repudiate

exploit *n* **1** = **feat**, accomplishment, achievement, adventure, attainment, deed, escapade, stunt ◆ *vb* **2** = **take advantage of**, abuse, dump on (*sl., chiefly US*), impose upon, manipulate, milk, misuse, play on *or* upon, shit on (*taboo sl.*) **3** = **make the best use of**, capitalize on, cash in on (*inf.*), live off the backs of, make capital out of, profit by *or* from, put to use, turn to account, use, use to advantage, utilize

exploitation *n* **2** = **misuse**, abuse, imposition, manipulation, trading upon, using **3** = **capitalization**, utilization

exploration *n* **1** = **investigation**, analysis, examination, inquiry, inspection, once-over (*inf.*), probe, research, scrutiny, search, study **2** = **expedition**, recce (*sl.*), reconnaissance, survey, tour, travel, trip

exploratory *adj* **1** = **investigative**, analytic, experimental, fact-finding, probing, searching, trial

explore *vb* **1** = **investigate**, analyse, examine, inquire into, inspect, look into, probe, prospect, research, scrutinize, search, work over **2** = **travel**, case (*sl.*), have *or* take a look around, range over, recce, reconnoitre, scout, survey, tour, traverse

explosion *n* **1** = **bang**, blast, burst, clap, crack, detonation, discharge, outburst, report **3** = **outburst**, eruption, fit, outbreak, paroxysm

explosive *adj* **2** = **unstable**, volatile **3** = **dangerous**, charged, hazardous, overwrought, perilous, tense, ugly

exponent *n* **1** = **advocate**, backer, champion, defender, promoter, propagandist, proponent, spokesman, spokeswoman, supporter, upholder **2** = **interpreter**, commentator, demonstrator, elucidator, expositor, expounder, illustrator **3** = **performer**, executant, interpreter, player, presenter

expose *vb* **1** = **uncover**, display, exhibit, manifest, present, put on view, reveal, show, take the wraps off, unveil **2, 3** = **reveal**, air, betray, blow wide open (*sl.*), bring to light, denounce, detect, disclose, divulge, lay bare, let out, make known, out (*inf.*), show up, smoke out, uncover, unearth, unmask **4** = **make vulnerable**, endanger, hazard, imperil, jeopardize, lay open, leave open, risk, subject **6** *with* **to** = **introduce to**, acquaint with, bring into contact with, familiarize with, make conversant with
Antonyms *vb* ≠ **uncover**: conceal, cover, hide, mask, protect, screen, shelter, shield ≠ **reveal**: conceal, cover, hide, keep secret

exposé *n* = **exposure**, disclosure, divulgence, revelation, uncovering

exposed *adj* **1** = **unconcealed**, bare, exhibited, laid bare, made manifest, made public, on display, on show, on view, revealed, shown, uncovered, unveiled **2** = **unsheltered**, open, open to the elements, unprotected **3** = **vulnerable**, in danger, in peril, laid bare, laid open, left open, liable, open, susceptible, wide open

exposition *n* **1** = **explanation**, account, commentary, critique, description, elucidation, exegesis, explication, illustration, interpretation, presentation **3** = **exhibition**, demonstration, display, expo (*inf.*), fair, presentation, show

expository *adj* = **explanatory**, descriptive, elucidative, exegetic, explicative, explicatory, hermeneutic, illustrative, interpretive

expostulate *vb* = **reason (with)**, argue (with), dissuade, protest, remonstrate (with)

exposure *n* **1** = **publicity**, baring, display, exhibition, manifestation, presentation, revelation, showing, uncovering, unveiling **2** = **position**, aspect, frontage, location, outlook, setting, view

expound *vb* = **explain**, describe, elucidate, explicate (*formal*), illustrate, interpret, set forth, spell out, unfold

express *vb* **1** = **state**, articulate, assert, asseverate, communicate, couch, declare, enunciate,

bol, formula, etc. **5** to squeeze out: *to express the juice from an orange.* **6** **express oneself.** to communicate one's thoughts or ideas. ◆ *adj* (*prenominal*) **7** clearly indicated; explicitly stated. **8** done or planned for a definite reason; particular. **9** of or designed for rapid transportation of people, mail, etc.: *express delivery.* ◆ *n* **10a** a system for sending mail, money, etc., rapidly. **10b** mail, etc., conveyed by such a system. **10c** *Chiefly US & Canad.* an enterprise operating such a system. **11** Also: **express train.** a fast train stopping at no or only a few stations between its termini. ◆ *adv* **12** by means of express delivery. **[**C14: from L *expressus*, lit.: squeezed out, hence, prominent, from *exprimere* to force out, from EX-[1] + *premere* to press**]**
▸**ex'presser** *n* ▸**ex'pressible** *adj*

expression Ⓣ (ɪk'sprɛʃən) *n* **1** the act or an instance of transforming ideas into words. **2** a manifestation of an emotion, feeling, etc., without words. **3** communication of emotion through music, painting, etc. **4** a look on the face that indicates mood or emotion. **5** the choice of words, intonation, etc., in communicating. **6** a particular phrase used conventionally to express something. **7** the act or process of squeezing out a liquid. **8** *Maths.* a variable, function, or some combination of these.
▸**ex'pressional** *adj* ▸**ex'pressionless** *adj*

expressionism (ɪk'sprɛʃəˌnɪzəm) *n* (*sometimes cap.*) an artistic and literary movement originating in the early 20th century, which sought to express emotions rather than to represent external reality: characterized by symbolism and distortion.
▸**ex'pressionist** *n, adj* ▸**exˌpression'istic** *adj*

expression mark *n* one of a set of musical directions, usually in Italian, indicating how a piece or passage is to be performed.

expressive Ⓣ (ɪk'sprɛsɪv) *adj* **1** of, involving, or full of expression. **2** (*postpositive;* foll. by *of*) indicative or suggestive (of). **3** having a particular meaning or force; significant.
▸**ex'pressiveness** *n*

expressly Ⓣ (ɪk'sprɛslɪ) *adv* **1** for an express purpose. **2** plainly, exactly, or unmistakably.

expresso (ɪk'sprɛsəʊ) *n, pl* **expressos.** a variant of **espresso.**

expressway (ɪk'sprɛsˌweɪ) *n* a motorway.

expropriate Ⓣ (ɛks'prəʊprɪˌeɪt) *vb* **expropriates, expropriating, expropriated.** (*tr*) to deprive (an owner) of (property), esp. by taking it for public use. **[**C17: from Med. L *expropriāre* to deprive of possessions, from *proprius* own**]**
▸**exˌpropri'ation** *n* ▸**ex'propriˌator** *n*

expulsion Ⓣ (ɪk'spʌlʃən) *n* the act of expelling or the fact or condition of being expelled. **[**C14: from L *expulsiō* a driving out, from *expellere* to EXPEL**]**
▸**ex'pulsive** *adj*

expunge Ⓣ (ɪk'spʌndʒ) *vb* **expunges, expunging, expunged.** (*tr*) to delete or erase; blot out; obliterate. **[**C17: from L *expungere* to blot out, from *pungere* to prick**]**
▸**expunction** (ɪk'spʌŋkʃən) *n* ▸**ex'punger** *n*

expurgate Ⓣ ('ɛkspəˌgeɪt) *vb* **expurgates, expurgating, expurgated.** (*tr*) to amend (a book, text, etc.) by removing (offensive sections). **[**C17: from L *expurgāre* to clean out, from *purgāre* to purify; see PURGE**]**
▸ˌ**expur'gation** *n* ▸**'expurˌgator** *n*

exquisite Ⓣ (ɪk'skwɪzɪt, 'ɛkskwɪzɪt) *adj* **1** possessing qualities of unusual delicacy and craftsmanship. **2** extremely beautiful. **3** outstanding or excellent. **4** sensitive; discriminating. **5** fastidious and refined. **6** intense or sharp in feeling. ◆ *n* **7** *Obs.* a dandy. **[**C15: from L *exquīsītus* excellent, from *exquīrere* to search out, from *quaerere* to seek**]**
▸**ex'quisitely** *adv* ▸**ex'quisiteness** *n*

ex-serviceman *or* (*fem*) **ex-servicewoman** *n, pl* **ex-servicemen** *or* **ex-servicewomen.** a person who has served in the armed forces.

extant Ⓣ (ɛk'stænt, 'ɛkstənt) *adj* still in existence; surviving. **[**C16: from L *exstāns* standing out, from *exstāre*, from *stāre* to stand**]**

> **USAGE NOTE** *Extant* is sometimes wrongly used simply to say that something exists, without any connotation of survival: *plutonium is perhaps the deadliest element in existence* (not *the deadliest element extant*).

extemporaneous Ⓣ (ɪkˌstɛmpə'reɪnɪəs) *or* **extemporary** (ɪk'stɛmpərərɪ) *adj* **1** spoken, performed, etc., without preparation; extempore. **2** done in a temporary manner; improvised.
▸**exˌtempo'raneously** *or* **ex'temporarily** *adv* ▸**exˌtempo'raneousness** *or* **ex'temporariness** *n*

extempore Ⓣ (ɪk'stɛmpərɪ) *adv, adj* without planning or preparation. **[**C16: from L *ex tempore* instantaneously, from EX-[1] out of + *tempus* time**]**

extemporize Ⓣ *or* **extemporise** (ɪk'stɛmpəˌraɪz) *vb* **extemporizes, extemporizing, extemporized** *or* **extemporises, extemporising, extemporised. 1** to perform, speak, or compose (an act, speech, music, etc.) without preparation. **2** to use a temporary solution; improvise.
▸**exˌtempori'zation** *or* **exˌtempori'sation** *n* ▸**ex'tempoˌrizer** *or* **ex'tempoˌriser** *n*

extend Ⓣ (ɪk'stɛnd) *vb* **1** to draw out or be drawn out; stretch. **2** to last or cause to last for a certain time. **3** (*intr*) to reach a certain point in time or distance. **4** (*intr*) to exist or occur. **5** (*tr*) to increase (a building, etc.) in size; add to or enlarge. **6** (*tr*) to broaden the meaning or scope of: *the law was extended.* **7** (*tr*) to present or offer. **8** to stretch forth (an arm, etc.). **9** (*tr*) to lay out (a body) at full length. **10** (*tr*) to strain or exert (a person or animal) to the maximum. **11** (*tr*) to prolong (the time) for payment of (a debt or loan), completion of (a task), etc. **[**C14: from L *extendere* to stretch out, from *tendere* to stretch**]**
▸**ex'tendible** *or* **ex'tendable** *adj* ▸**exˌtendi'bility** *or* **exˌtenda'bility** *n*

extended family *n Sociol., anthropol.* the nuclear family together with relatives, often spanning three or more generations.

extended-play *adj* denoting an EP record.

extender (ɪk'stɛndə) *n* **1** a person or thing that extends. **2** a substance added to paints to give body and decrease their rate of settlement. **3** a substance added to glues and resins to dilute them or to modify their viscosity.

THESAURUS

phrase, pronounce, put, put across, put into words, say, speak, tell, utter, verbalize, voice, word **2** = **show**, bespeak, convey, denote, depict, designate, disclose, divulge, embody, evince, exhibit, indicate, intimate, make known, manifest, represent, reveal, signify, stand for, symbolize, testify **5** = **squeeze out**, extract, force out, press out ◆ *adj* **7** = **explicit**, accurate, categorical, certain, clear, definite, direct, distinct, exact, outright, plain, pointed, precise, unambiguous **8** = **specific**, clear-cut, deliberate, especial, particular, singular, special **9** = **fast**, direct, high-speed, nonstop, quick, quickie (*inf.*), rapid, speedy, swift

expression *n* **1** = **statement**, announcement, assertion, asseveration, communication, declaration, enunciation, mention, pronouncement, speaking, utterance, verbalization, voicing **2** = **indication**, demonstration, embodiment, exhibition, manifestation, representation, show, sign, symbol, token **4** = **look**, air, appearance, aspect, countenance, face, mien (*literary*) **5** = **choice of words**, delivery, diction, emphasis, execution, intonation, language, phraseology, phrasing, speech, style, wording **6** = **phrase**, idiom, locution, remark, set phrase, term, turn of phrase, word

expressionless *adj* **4** = **blank**, deadpan, dull, empty, inscrutable, poker-faced (*inf.*), straight-faced, vacuous, wooden

expressive *adj* **1** = **vivid**, eloquent, emphatic, energetic, forcible, lively, mobile, moving, poignant, striking, strong, sympathetic, telling **2** = **meaningful**, allusive, demonstrative, indicative, pointed, pregnant, revealing, significant, suggestive, thoughtful
Antonyms *adj* ≠ **vivid:** blank, dead-pan, dull, empty, impassive, inscrutable, poker-faced (*inf.*), straight-faced, vacuous, wooden

expressly *adv* **1** = **specifically**, deliberately, especially, exactly, intentionally, on purpose, particularly, precisely, purposely, specially **2** = **definitely**, absolutely, categorically, clearly, decidedly, distinctly, explicitly, in no uncertain terms, manifestly, outright, plainly, pointedly, positively, unambiguously, unequivocally, unmistakably

expropriate *vb* = **seize**, appropriate, arrogate, assume, commandeer, confiscate, impound, requisition, take, take over

expropriation *n* = **seizure**, commandeering, confiscation, disseisin (*Law*), impounding, requisitioning, sequestration, takeover

expulsion *n* = **ejection**, banishment, debarment, discharge, dislodgment, dismissal, eviction, exclusion, exile, expatriation, extrusion, proscription, removal

expunge *vb* = **erase**, abolish, annihilate, annul, blot out, cancel, delete, destroy, efface, eradicate, excise, exterminate, extinguish, extirpate, obliterate, raze, remove, strike out, wipe from the face of the earth, wipe out

expurgate *vb* = **censor**, blue-pencil, bowdlerize, clean up (*inf.*), cut, purge, purify, sanitize

exquisite *adj* **1** = **fine**, beautiful, dainty, delicate, elegant, lovely, precious **2** = **beautiful**, attractive, charming, comely, lovely, pleasing, striking **3** = **excellent**, admirable, choice, consummate, delicious, divine, fine, flawless, incomparable, matchless, outstanding, peerless, perfect, rare, select, splendid, superb, superlative **4, 5** = **refined**, appreciative, consummate, cultivated, discerning, discriminating, fastidious, impeccable, meticulous, polished, selective, sensitive **6** = **intense**, acute, excruciating, keen, piercing, poignant, sharp
Antonyms *adj* ≠ **beautiful:** ill-favoured, ugly, unattractive, unlovely, unsightly ≠ **excellent:** flawed, imperfect

extant *adj* = **in existence**, existent, existing, living, remaining, subsisting, surviving, undestroyed

extemporaneous *adj* **1** = **improvised**, ad-lib, extempore, free, impromptu, improvisatory, made-up, offhand, off-the-cuff (*inf.*), off the top of one's head, spontaneous, unplanned, unpremeditated, unprepared, unrehearsed **2** = **makeshift**, expedient, improvised, on-the-spot, temporary

extempore *adv, adj* = **impromptu**, ad lib, extemporaneous, extemporary, freely, improvised, offhand, off the cuff (*inf.*), off the top of one's head, on the spot, spontaneously, unplanned, unpremeditated, unprepared

extemporize *vb* **1** = **improvise**, ad-lib, busk, make up, play (it) by ear, vamp, wing it (*inf.*)

extend *vb* **1** = **make longer**, carry on, continue, drag out, draw out, elongate, lengthen, prolong, protract, spin out, spread out, stretch, unfurl, unroll **2** = **last**, carry on, continue, go on, take **3** = **reach**, amount to, attain, go as far as, spread **5, 6** = **widen**, add to, amplify, augment, broaden, develop, dilate, enhance, enlarge, expand, increase, spread, supplement **7** = **offer**, advance, bestow, confer, give, grant, hold out, impart, present, proffer, put forth, reach out, stretch out, yield
Antonyms *vb* ≠ **make longer:** condense, contract, curtail, cut, decrease, limit, reduce, restrict, shorten, take back ≠ **widen:** abbreviate, abridge, condense, contract, cut, decrease, reduce, restrict, shorten ≠ **offer:** take back, withdraw

extensible (ɪk'stɛnsɪbᵊl) *or* **extensile** (ɪk'stɛnsaɪl) *adj* capable of being extended.
▸**ex,tensi'bility** *or* **ex'tensibleness** *n*

extension Ⓣ (ɪk'stɛnʃən) *n* **1** the act of extending or the condition of being extended. **2** something that can be extended or that extends another object. **3** the length, range, etc., over which something is extended. **4** an additional telephone set connected to the same telephone line as another set. **5** a room or rooms added to an existing building. **6** a delay in the date originally set for payment of a debt or completion of a contract. **7** the property of matter by which it occupies space. **8a** the act of straightening or extending an arm or leg. **8b** its position after being straightened or extended. **9a** a service by which the facilities of an educational establishment, library, etc., are offered to outsiders. **9b** (*as modifier*): *a university extension course.* **10** *Logic.* the class of entities to which a given word correctly applies. [C14: from LL *extensiō* a stretching out; see EXTEND]
▸**ex'tensional** *adj* ▸**ex,tension'ality** *or* **ex'tensional,ism** *n*

extensive Ⓣ (ɪk'stɛnsɪv) *adj* **1** having a large extent, area, degree, etc. **2** widespread. **3** *Agriculture.* involving or farmed with minimum expenditure of capital or labour, esp. depending on a large extent of land. Cf. **intensive** (sense 3). **4** of or relating to logical extension.
▸**ex'tensiveness** *n*

extensor (ɪk'stɛnsə, -sɔː) *n* any muscle that stretches or extends an arm, leg, or other bodily part. Cf. **flexor.** [C18: from NL, from L *extensus* stretched out]

extent Ⓣ (ɪk'stɛnt) *n* **1** the range over which something extends; scope. **2** an area or volume. [C14: from OF, from L *extentus* extensive, from *extendere* to EXTEND]

extenuate Ⓣ (ɪk'stɛnjʊ,eɪt) *vb* **extenuates, extenuating, extenuated.** (*tr*) **1** to represent (an offence, fault, etc.) as being less serious than it appears, as by showing mitigating circumstances. **2** to cause to be or appear less serious; mitigate. **3** *Arch.* **3a** to emaciate or weaken. **3b** to dilute or thin out. [C16: from L *extenuāre* to make thin, from *tenuis* thin, frail]
▸**ex'tenu,ating** *adj* ▸**ex,tenu'ation** *n* ▸**ex'tenu,ator** *n*

exterior Ⓣ (ɪk'stɪərɪə) *n* **1** a part, surface, or region that is on the outside. **2** the outward behaviour or appearance of a person. **3** a film or scene shot outside a studio. ◆ *adj* **4** of, situated on, or suitable for the outside. **5** coming or acting from without. [C16: from L, comp. of *exterus* on the outside, from *ex* out of]
▸**ex'teriorly** *adv*

exterior angle *n* **1** an angle of a polygon contained between one side extended and the adjacent side. **2** any of the four angles made by a transversal that are outside the region between the two intersected lines.

exteriorize *or* **exteriorise** (ɪk'stɪərɪə,raɪz) *vb* **exteriorizes, exteriorizing, exteriorized** *or* **exteriorises, exteriorising, exteriorised.** (*tr*) **1** *Surgery.* to expose (an attached organ or part) outside the body. **2** another word for **externalize.**
▸**ex,teriori'zation** *or* **ex,teriori'sation** *n*

exterminate Ⓣ (ɪk'stɜːmɪ,neɪt) *vb* **exterminates, exterminating, exterminated.** (*tr*) to destroy (living things, esp. pests or vermin) completely; annihilate; eliminate. [C16: from L *extermināre* to drive away, from *terminus* boundary]
▸**ex'terminable** *adj* ▸**ex,termi'nation** *n* ▸**ex'termi,nator** *n*

external Ⓣ (ɪk'stɜːnᵊl) *adj* **1** of, situated on, or suitable for the outside; outer. **2** coming or acting from without. **3** of or involving foreign nations. **4** of, relating to, or designating a medicine that is applied to the outside of the body. **5** *Anat.* situated on or near the outside of the body. **6** (of a student) studying a university subject extramurally. **7** *Philosophy.* (of objects, etc.) taken to exist independently of a perceiving mind. ◆ *n* **8** (*often pl*) an external circumstance or aspect, esp. one that is superficial. **9** *Austral. & NZ.* an extramural student. [C15: from L *externus* outward, from *exterus* on the outside, from *ex* out of]
▸**ex'ternally** *adv* ▸**,exter'nality** *n*

externalize *or* **externalise** (ɪk'stɜːnə,laɪz) *vb* **externalizes, externalizing, externalized** *or* **externalises, externalising, externalised.** (*tr*) **1** to make external; give outward shape to. **2** *Psychol.* to attribute (one's feelings) to one's surroundings.
▸**ex,ternali'zation** *or* **ex,ternali'sation** *n*

extinct Ⓣ (ɪk'stɪŋkt) *adj* **1** (of an animal or plant species) having died out. **2** quenched or extinguished. **3** (of a volcano) no longer liable to erupt; inactive. [C15: from L *exstinctus* quenched, from *exstinguere* to EXTINGUISH]

extinction Ⓣ (ɪk'stɪŋkʃən) *n* **1** the act of making extinct or the state of being extinct. **2** the act of extinguishing or the state of being extinguished. **3** complete destruction; annihilation. **4** *Physics.* reduction of the intensity of radiation as a result of absorption or scattering by matter.

extinguish Ⓣ (ɪk'stɪŋgwɪʃ) *vb* (*tr*) **1** to put out or quench (a light, flames, etc.). **2** to remove or destroy entirely; annihilate. **3** *Arch.* to eclipse or obscure. [C16: from L *exstinguere,* from *stinguere* to quench]
▸**ex'tinguishable** *adj* ▸**ex'tinguisher** *n* ▸**ex'tinguishment** *n*

extirpate Ⓣ ('ɛkstə,peɪt) *vb* **extirpates, extirpating, extirpated.** (*tr*) **1** to remove or destroy completely. **2** to pull up or out; uproot. [C16: from L *exstirpāre* to root out, from *stirps* root, stock]
▸**,extir'pation** *n* ▸**'extir,pator** *n*

extol Ⓣ *or US* **extoll** (ɪk'stəʊl) *vb* **extols** *or US* **extolls, extolling, extolled.** (*tr*) to praise lavishly; exalt. [C15: from L *extollere* to elevate, from *tollere* to raise]
▸**ex'toller** *n* ▸**ex'tolment** *n*

extort Ⓣ (ɪk'stɔːt) *vb* (*tr*) **1** to secure (money, favours, etc.) by intimidation, violence, or the misuse of authority. **2** to obtain by importunate demands. [C16: from L *extortus* wrenched out, from *extorquēre* to wrest away, from *torquēre* to twist, wrench]
▸**ex'tortion** *n* ▸**ex'tortioner, ex'tortionist,** *or* **ex'torter** *n* ▸**ex'tortive** *adj*

extortionate Ⓣ (ɪk'stɔːʃənɪt) *adj* **1** (of prices, etc.) excessive; exorbitant. **2** (of persons) using extortion.
▸**ex'tortionately** *adv*

extra Ⓣ ('ɛkstrə) *adj* **1** being more than what is usual or expected; additional. ◆ *n* **2** a person or thing that is additional. **3** something for which an additional charge is made. **4** an additional edition of a newspaper, esp. to report a new development. **5** *Films.* a person temporarily engaged, usually for crowd scenes. **6** *Cricket.* a run not scored from the bat, such as a wide, no-ball, or bye. ◆ *adv* **7** unusually; exceptionally: *an extra fast car.* [C18: ? shortened from EXTRAORDINARY]

extra- *prefix* outside or beyond an area or scope: *extrasensory; extraterri-*

THESAURUS

extendible *adj* **1 = flexible,** elastic, stretchy

extension *n* **1 = lengthening,** amplification, augmentation, broadening, continuation, delay, development, dilatation, distension, elongation, enlargement, expansion, extent, increase, postponement, prolongation, protraction, spread, stretching, widening **2 = annexe,** addendum, addition, add-on, adjunct, appendage, appendix, branch, ell, supplement, wing

extensive *adj* **1, 2 = wide,** all-inclusive, broad, capacious, commodious, comprehensive, expanded, extended, far-flung, far-reaching, general, great, huge, humongous *or* humungous (*US sl.*), large, large-scale, lengthy, long, pervasive, prevalent, protracted, spacious, sweeping, thorough, universal, vast, voluminous, wholesale, widespread
Antonyms *adj* circumscribed, confined, constricted, limited, narrow, restricted, tight

extent *n* **1 = range,** ambit, bounds, compass, play, reach, scope, sphere, sweep **2 = size,** amount, amplitude, area, breadth, bulk, degree, duration, expanse, expansion, length, magnitude, measure, quantity, stretch, term, time, volume, width

extenuate *vb* **1 = make light of,** discount, underestimate, underrate, undervalue **2 = mitigate,** decrease, diminish, excuse, lessen, make allowances for, minimize, moderate, palliate, play down, qualify, reduce, soften, temper, weaken

extenuating *adj* **2 = mitigating,** justifying, moderating, qualifying, serving as an excuse

exterior *n* **1 = outside,** appearance, aspect, coating, covering, façade, face, finish, shell, skin, surface ◆ *adj* **4 = outside,** external, outer, outermost, outward, superficial, surface **5 = external,** alien, exotic, extraneous, extrinsic, foreign, outside
Antonyms *n* ≠ **outside:** inner, inside, interior ◆ *adj* ≠ **outside:** immanent, inherent, inside, interior, internal, intrinsic ≠ **external:** domestic, internal, intrinsic

exterminate *vb* **= destroy,** abolish, annihilate, eliminate, eradicate, extirpate

extermination *n* **= destruction,** annihilation, elimination, eradication, extirpation, genocide, massacre, mass murder, murder, slaughter, wiping out

external *adj* **1 = outer,** apparent, exterior, outermost, outside, outward, superficial, surface, visible **2 = outside,** alien, exotic, exterior, extramural, extraneous, extrinsic, foreign, independent
Antonyms *adj* ≠ **outer:** immanent, inherent, inner, inside, interior, internal, intrinsic ≠ **outside:** inside, interior, intrinsic

extinct *adj* **1 = dead,** defunct, gone, lost, vanished **2 = inactive,** doused, extinguished, out, quenched, snuffed out
Antonyms *adj* ≠ **dead:** active, alive, existing, extant, flourishing, living, surviving, thriving

extinction *n* **1, 3 = dying out,** abolition, annihilation, death, destruction, eradication, excision, extermination, extirpation, obliteration, oblivion

extinguish *vb* **1 = put out,** blow out, douse, quench, smother, snuff out, stifle **2 = destroy,** abolish, annihilate, eliminate, end, eradicate, erase, expunge, exterminate, extirpate, kill, obscure, put paid to, remove, suppress, wipe out

extirpate *vb* **1 = wipe out,** abolish, annihilate, deracinate, destroy, eliminate, eradicate, erase, excise, expunge, exterminate, extinguish, pull up by the roots, remove, root out, uproot, wipe from the face of the earth

extol *vb* **= praise,** acclaim, applaud, celebrate, commend, crack up (*inf.*), cry up, eulogize, exalt, glorify, laud, magnify (*arch.*), panegyrize, pay tribute to, sing the praises of

extort *vb* **1 = force,** blackmail, bleed (*inf.*), bully, coerce, exact, extract, squeeze, wrest, wring

extortion *n* **1 = force,** blackmail, coercion, compulsion, demand, exaction, oppression, rapacity, shakedown (*US sl.*)

extortionate *adj* **1 = exorbitant,** excessive, extravagant, immoderate, inflated, inordinate, outrageous, preposterous, sky-high, unreasonable **2 = grasping,** blood-sucking (*inf.*), exacting, hard, harsh, oppressive, rapacious, rigorous, severe, usurious
Antonyms *adj* ≠ **exorbitant:** fair, inexpensive, moderate, modest, reasonable

extra *adj* **1 = additional,** added, auxiliary, further, more, spare, supererogatory, superfluous, supernumerary, supplemental, supplementary, surplus ◆ *n* **2 = addition,** accessory, addendum, add-on, adjunct, affix, appendage, appurtenance, attachment, bonus, complement, extension, supernumerary, supplement ◆ *adv* **7 = exceptionally,** especially, extraordinarily, extremely, particularly, remarkably, uncommonly, unusually
Antonyms *adj* ≠ **additional:** compulsory, essential, mandatory, necessary, needed, obligatory, required, requisite, vital ◆ *n* ≠ **addition:** essential,

torial. [from L *extrā* outside, beyond, from *extera,* from *exterus* outward]

extra cover *n Cricket.* a fielding position between cover and mid-off.

extract ❶ *vb* (ɪk'strækt). (*tr*) **1** to pull out or uproot by force. **2** to remove or separate. **3** to derive (pleasure, information, etc.) from some source. **4** to deduce or develop (a doctrine, policy, etc.). **5** *Inf.* to extort (money, etc.). **6** to obtain (a substance) from a mixture or material by a process, such as digestion, distillation, mechanical separation, etc. **7** to cut out or copy out (an article, passage, etc.) from a publication. **8** to determine the value of (the root of a number). ◆ *n* ('ɛkstrækt). **9** something extracted, such as a passage from a book, etc. **10** a preparation containing the active principle or concentrated essence of a material. [C15: from L *extractus* drawn forth, from *extrahere,* from *trahere* to drag]
▸**ex'tractable** *adj* ▸**ex,tracta'bility** *n* ▸**ex'tractive** *adj*

> **USAGE NOTE** *Extract* is sometimes wrongly used where *extricate* would be better: *he will find it difficult extricating* (not *extracting*) *himself from this situation.*

extraction ❶ (ɪk'strækʃən) *n* **1** the act of extracting or the condition of being extracted. **2** something extracted. **3** the act or an instance of extracting a tooth. **4** origin or ancestry.

extractor (ɪk'stræktə) *n* **1** a person or thing that extracts. **2** an instrument for pulling something out or removing tight-fitting components. **3** short for **extractor fan.**

extractor fan *or* **extraction fan** *n* a fan used in kitchens, bathrooms, workshops, etc., to remove stale air or fumes.

extracurricular (,ɛkstrəkə'rɪkjʊlə) *adj* **1** taking place outside the normal school timetable. **2** beyond the regular duties, schedule, etc.

extradite ('ɛkstrə,daɪt) *vb* **extradites, extraditing, extradited.** (*tr*) **1** to surrender (an alleged offender) for trial to a foreign state. **2** to procure the extradition of. [C19: back formation from EXTRADITION]
▸**'extra,ditable** *adj*

extradition (,ɛkstrə'dɪʃən) *n* the surrender of an alleged offender to the state where the alleged offence was committed. [C19: from F, from L *trāditiō* a handing over]

extrados (ɛk'streɪdɒs) *n, pl* **extrados** (-dəʊz) *or* **extradoses.** *Archit.* the outer curve of an arch or vault. [C18: from F, from EXTRA- + *dos* back]

extradural (,ɛkstrə'djʊərəl) *adj* another word for **epidural** (sense 1).

extragalactic (,ɛkstrəgə'læktɪk) *adj* occurring or existing beyond the Galaxy.

extramarital (,ɛkstrə'mærɪtᵊl) *adj* (esp. of sexual relations) occurring outside marriage.

extramural (,ɛkstrə'mjʊərəl) *adj* **1** connected with but outside the normal courses of a university, college, etc. **2** beyond the boundaries or walls of a city, castle, etc.

extraneous ❶ (ɪk'streɪnɪəs) *adj* **1** not essential. **2** not pertinent; irrelevant. **3** coming from without. **4** not belonging. [C17: from L *extrāneus* external, from *extrā* outside]
▸**ex'traneousness** *n*

extraordinary ❶ (ɪk'strɔːdᵊnrɪ) *adj* **1** very unusual or surprising. **2** not in an established manner or order. **3** employed for particular purposes. **4** (*usually postpositive*) (of an official, etc.) additional or subordinate. [C15: from L *extraordinārius* beyond what is usual; see ORDINARY]
▸**ex'traordinarily** *adv* ▸**ex'traordinariness** *n*

extraordinary general meeting *n* a meeting specially called to discuss an important item of a company's business. It may be called by a group of shareholders or by the directors. Abbrev.: **EGM.**

extrapolate (ɪk'stræpə,leɪt) *vb* **extrapolates, extrapolating, extrapolated. 1** *Maths.* to estimate (a value of a function etc.) beyond the known values, by the extension of a curve. Cf. **interpolate** (sense 4). **2** to infer (something) by using but not strictly deducing from known facts. [C19: EXTRA- + *-polate,* as in INTERPOLATE]
▸**ex,trapo'lation** *n* ▸**ex'trapolative** *or* **ex'trapolatory** *adj* ▸**ex'trapo,lator** *n*

extrasensory (,ɛkstrə'sɛnsərɪ) *adj* of or relating to extrasensory perception.

extrasensory perception *n* the supposed ability of certain individuals to obtain information about the environment without the use of normal sensory channels.

extraterritorial (,ɛkstrə,tɛrɪ'tɔːrɪəl) *or* **exterritorial** *adj* **1** beyond the limits of a country's territory. **2** of, relating to, or possessing extraterritoriality.

extraterritoriality (,ɛkstrə,tɛrɪ,tɔːrɪ'ælɪtɪ) *n* **1** the privilege granted to some aliens, esp. diplomats, of being exempt from the jurisdiction of the state in which they reside. **2** the right of a state to exercise authority in certain circumstances beyond the limits of its territory.

extra time *n Sport.* an additional period played at the end of a match, to compensate for time lost through injury or (in certain circumstances) to allow the teams to achieve a conclusive result.

extravagance ❶ (ɪk'strævɪgəns) *n* **1** excessive outlay of money; wasteful spending. **2** immoderate or absurd speech or behaviour.

extravagant ❶ (ɪk'strævɪgənt) *adj* **1** spending money excessively or immoderately. **2** going beyond usual bounds; unrestrained. **3** ostentatious; showy. **4** exorbitant in price; overpriced. [C14: from Med. L *extravagāns,* from L EXTRA- + *vagārī* to wander]

extravaganza ❶ (ɪk,strævə'gænzə) *n* **1** an elaborately staged light entertainment. **2** any lavish or fanciful display, literary composition, etc. [C18: from It.: extravagance]

extravasate (ɪk'strævə,seɪt) *vb* **extravasates, extravasating, extravasated.** *Pathol.* to cause (blood or lymph) to escape or (of blood or lymph) to escape into the surrounding tissues from their proper vessels. [C17: from L EXTRA- + *vās* vessel]
▸**ex,trava'sation** *n*

extravehicular (,ɛkstrəvɪ'hɪkjʊlə) *adj* occurring or used outside a spacecraft, either in space or on the surface of a planet.

extraversion (,ɛkstrə'vɜːʃən) *n* a variant spelling of **extroversion.**
▸**'extra,vert** *n, adj*

extra virgin *adj* (of olive oil) of the highest quality, extracted by cold pressing rather than chemical treatment.

extreme ❶ (ɪk'striːm) *adj* **1** being of a high or of the highest degree or intensity. **2** exceeding what is usual or reasonable; immoderate. **3** very strict or severe; drastic. **4** (*prenominal*) farthest or outermost. ◆ *n* **5** the highest or furthest degree (often in **in the extreme, go to extremes**). **6** (*often pl*) either of the two limits or ends of a scale or range. **7** *Maths.* the first or last term of a series or a proportion. [C15: from L *extrēmus* outermost, from *exterus* on the outside; see EXTERIOR]
▸**ex'tremely** *adv* ▸**ex'tremeness** *n*

> **USAGE NOTE** See at **very.**

extreme unction *n RC Church.* the former name for **anointing of the sick.**

THESAURUS

must, necessity, precondition, prerequisite, requirement, requisite

extract *vb* **1** = **pull out**, draw, extirpate, pluck out, pull, remove, take out, uproot, withdraw **3** = **derive**, bring out, draw, elicit, evoke, exact, gather, get, glean, obtain, reap, wrest, wring **4** = **develop**, deduce, derive, educe, elicit, evolve **6** = **obtain**, distil, draw out, express, press out, separate out, squeeze, take out **7** = **copy out**, abstract, choose, cite, cull, cut out, quote, select ◆ *n* **9** = **passage**, abstract, citation, clipping, cutting, excerpt, quotation, selection **10** = **essence**, concentrate, decoction, distillate, distillation, juice

extraction *n* **1** = **taking out**, drawing, extirpation, pulling, removal, uprooting, withdrawal **4** = **origin**, ancestry, birth, blood, derivation, descent, family, lineage, parentage, pedigree, race, stock

extraneous *adj* **1** = **nonessential**, accidental, additional, adventitious, extra, incidental, inessential, needless, peripheral, redundant, superfluous, supplementary, unessential, unnecessary, unneeded **2** = **irrelevant**, beside the point, immaterial, impertinent, inadmissible, inapplicable, inapposite, inappropriate, inapt, off the subject, unconnected, unrelated **3, 4** = **external**, adventitious, alien, exotic, extrinsic, foreign, out of place, strange

extraordinary *adj* **1** = **unusual**, amazing, beyond one's ken, bizarre, curious, exceptional, notable, odd, out of this world (*inf.*), outstanding, particular, peculiar, phenomenal, rare, remarkable, singular, special, strange, surprising, uncommon, unfamiliar, unheard-of, unique, unprecedented, unwonted, weird, wonderful, wondrous (*arch. or literary*)
Antonyms *adj* banal, common, commonplace, customary, everyday, ordinary, unexceptional, unremarkable, usual

extravagance *n* **1** = **waste**, improvidence, lavishness, overspending, prodigality, profligacy, profusion, squandering, wastefulness **2** = **excess**, absurdity, dissipation, exaggeration, exorbitance, folly, immoderation, outrageousness, preposterousness, recklessness, unreasonableness, unrestraint, wildness

extravagant *adj* **1** = **wasteful**, excessive, having money to burn, improvident, imprudent, lavish, prodigal, profligate, spendthrift **2** = **excessive**, absurd, exaggerated, exorbitant, fanciful, fantastic, foolish, immoderate, inordinate, outrageous, outré, over the top (*sl.*), preposterous, reckless, unreasonable, unrestrained, wild **3** = **showy**, fancy, flamboyant, flashy, garish, gaudy, grandiose, ornate, ostentatious, pretentious **4** = **overpriced**, costly, excessive, exorbitant, expensive, extortionate, inordinate, steep (*inf.*), unreasonable
Antonyms *adj* ≠ **wasteful:** careful, close, economical, frugal, miserly, moderate, prudent, sensible, sparing, thrifty, tight-fisted (*inf.*) ≠ **excessive:** conservative, down-to-earth, moderate, prudent, realistic, reasonable, restrained, sensible, sober ≠ **showy:** conservative, moderate, restrained, sober ≠ **overpriced:** economical, moderate, reasonable

extravaganza *n* **1** = **show**, display, flight of fancy, pageant, spectacle, spectacular

extreme *adj* **1** = **maximum**, acute, great, greatest, high, highest, intense, severe, supreme, ultimate, utmost, uttermost, worst **2** = **excessive**, exaggerated, exceptional, extraordinary, extravagant, fanatical, immoderate, inordinate, intemperate, out-and-out, outrageous, over the top (*sl.*), radical, remarkable, sheer, uncommon, unconventional, unreasonable, unusual **3** = **severe**, dire, drastic, harsh, radical, rigid, stern, strict, unbending, uncompromising **4** = **farthest**, faraway, far-off, final, last, most distant, outermost, remotest, terminal, ultimate, utmost, uttermost ◆ *n* **5** = **limit**, acme, apex, apogee, boundary, climax, consummation, depth, edge, end, excess, extremity, height, maximum, minimum, nadir, pinnacle, pole, termination, top, ultimate, zenith
Antonyms *adj* ≠ **maximum:** average, common, mild, moderate, modest, ordinary, reasonable, traditional, unremarkable ≠ **farthest:** nearest

extremely *adv* **1** = **very**, acutely, awfully (*inf.*), exceedingly, exceptionally, excessively, extraordinarily, greatly, highly, inordinately, intensely, markedly, quite, severely, terribly, to a

extremist ➊ (ɪk'stri:mɪst) *n* **1** a person who favours immoderate or fanatical methods, esp. in being politically radical. ◆ *adj* **2** of or characterized by immoderate or excessive actions, opinions, etc.
▸**ex'tremism** *n*

extremity ➊ (ɪk'strɛmɪtɪ) *n, pl* **extremities. 1** the farthest or outermost point or section. **2** the greatest degree. **3** an extreme condition or state, as of adversity. **4** a limb, such as a leg or wing, or the end of such a limb. **5** (*usually pl*) *Arch.* a drastic or severe measure.

extricate ➊ ('ɛkstrɪˌkeɪt) *vb* **extricates, extricating, extricated.** (*tr*) to remove or free from complication, hindrance, or difficulty; disentangle. [C17: from L *extrīcāre* to disentangle]
▸**'extricable** *adj* ▸**ˌextri'cation** *n*

USAGE NOTE See at **extract.**

extrinsic ➊ (ɛk'strɪnsɪk) *adj* **1** not contained or included within; extraneous. **2** originating or acting from outside. [C16: from LL *extrinsecus* (adj) outward, from L (adv), ult. from *exter* outward + *secus* alongside]
▸**ex'trinsically** *adv*

extroversion *or* **extraversion** (ˌɛkstrə'vɜ:ʃən) *n Psychol.* the directing of one's interest outwards, esp. towards social contacts. [C17: from *extro-* (var. of EXTRA-, contrasting with *intro-*) + *-version,* from L *vertere* to turn]
▸**ˌextro'versive** *or* **ˌextra'versive** *adj*

extrovert ➊ *or* **extravert** ('ɛkstrəˌvɜ:t) *Psychol.* ◆ *n* **1** a person concerned more with external reality than inner feelings. ◆ *adj* **2** of or characterized by extroversion. [C20: from *extro-* (var. of EXTRA-, contrasting with *intro-*) + *-vert,* from L *vertere* to turn]
▸**'extroˌverted** *or* **'extraˌverted** *adj*

extrude ➊ (ɪk'stru:d) *vb* **extrudes, extruding, extruded.** (*tr*) **1** to squeeze or force out. **2** to produce (moulded sections of plastic, metal, etc.) by ejection from a shaped nozzle or die. **3** to chop up or pulverize (an item of food) and re-form it to look like a whole. [C16: from L *extrūdere* to thrust out, from *trūdere* to push, thrust]
▸**ex'truded** *adj*

extrusion (ɪk'stru:ʒən) *n* **1** the act or process of extruding. **2a** the movement of magma through volcano craters and cracks in the earth's crust, forming igneous rock. **2b** any igneous rock formed in this way. **3** anything formed by the process of extruding.
▸**ex'trusive** *adj*

exuberant ➊ (ɪg'zju:bərənt) *adj* **1** abounding in vigour and high spirits. **2** lavish or effusive; excessively elaborate. **3** growing luxuriantly or in profusion. [C15: from L *exūberāns,* from *ūberāre* to be fruitful]
▸**ex'uberance** *n*

exuberate (ɪg'zju:bəˌreɪt) *vb* **exuberates, exuberating, exuberated.** (*intr*) *Rare.* **1** to be exuberant. **2** to abound. [C15: from L *exūberāre* to be abundant; see EXUBERANT]

exude ➊ (ɪg'zju:d) *vb* **exudes, exuding, exuded. 1** to release or be released through pores, incisions, etc., as sweat or sap. **2** (*tr*) to make apparent by mood or behaviour. [C16: from L *exsūdāre,* from *sūdāre* to sweat]
▸**exudation** (ˌɛksju'deɪʃən) *n*

exult ➊ (ɪg'zʌlt) *vb* (*intr*) **1** to be joyful or jubilant, esp. because of triumph or success. **2** (often foll. by *over*) to triumph (over). [C16: from L *exsultāre* to jump or leap for joy, from *saltāre* to leap]
▸**exultation** (ˌɛgzʌl'teɪʃən) *n* ▸**ex'ultingly** *adv*

USAGE NOTE See at **exalt.**

exultant ➊ (ɪg'zʌltənt) *adj* elated or jubilant, esp. because of triumph or success.
▸**ex'ultantly** *adv*

exurbia (ɛks'ɜ:bɪə) *n Chiefly US.* the region outside the suburbs of a city, consisting of residential areas (**exurbs**) occupied predominantly by rich commuters (**exurbanites**). [C20: from EX-[1] + L *urbs* city]
▸**ex'urban** *adj*

exuviate (ɪg'zju:vɪˌeɪt) *vb* **exuviates, exuviating, exuviated.** to shed (a skin or similar outer covering). [C17: from L *exuere* to strip off]
▸**exˌuvi'ation** *n*

-ey *suffix.* a variant of **-y**[1] and **-y**[2].

eyas ('aɪəs) *n* a nestling hawk or falcon, esp. one reared for falconry. [C15: mistaken division of earlier *a nyas,* from OF *niais* nestling, from L *nīdus* nest]

eye[1] ➊ (aɪ) *n* **1** the organ of sight of animals. Related adjs.: **ocular, ophthalmic. 2** (*often pl*) the ability to see; sense of vision. **3** the external part of an eye, often including the area around it. **4** a look, glance, expression, or gaze. **5** a sexually inviting or provocative look (esp. in **give (someone) the (glad) eye, make eyes at**). **6** attention or observation (often in **catch someone's eye, keep an eye on, cast an eye over**). **7** ability to recognize, judge, or appreciate. **8** (*often pl*) opinion, judgment, point of view, or authority: *in the eyes of the law.* **9** a structure or marking resembling an eye, such as the bud on a potato tuber or a spot on a butterfly wing. **10** a small loop or hole, as at one end of a needle. **11** a small area of low pressure and calm in the centre of a storm, hurricane, or tornado. **12 electric eye.** another name for **photocell. 13 all eyes.** *Inf.* acutely vigilant or observant. **14 (all) my eye.** *Inf.* rubbish; nonsense. **15 an eye for an eye.** retributive or vengeful justice; retaliation. **16 get one's eye in.** *Chiefly sport.* to become accustomed to the conditions, light, etc., with a consequent improvement in one's performance. **17 go eyes out.** *Austral. & NZ.* to make every possible effort. **18 half an eye.** a modicum of perceptiveness. **19 have eyes for.** to be interested in. **20 in one's mind's eye.** pictured within the mind; imagined or remembered vividly. **21 in the public eye.** exposed to public curiosity or publicity. **22 keep an eye open** *or* **out (for).** to watch with special attention (for). **23 keep one's eyes peeled** (*or* **skinned**). to watch vigilantly (for). **24 lay, clap,** *or* **set eyes on.** (*usually with a negative*) to see. **25 look (someone) in the eye.** to look openly and without shame or embarrassment at (someone). **26 make sheep's eyes (at).** *Old-fashioned.* to ogle amorously. **27 more than meets the eye.** hidden motives, meaning, or facts. **28 see eye to eye (with).** to agree (with). **29 turn a blind eye to** *or* **close one's eyes to.** to pretend not to notice or to ignore deliberately. **30 up to one's eyes (in).** extremely busy (with). **31 with** *or* **having an eye to.** (*prep*) **31a** regarding; with reference to. **31b** with the intention or purpose of. **32 with one's eyes open.** in the full knowledge of all relevant facts. **33 with one's eyes shut. 33a** with great ease, esp. as a result of thorough familiarity. **33b** without being aware of all the facts. ◆ *vb* **eyes, eyeing** *or* **eying, eyed.** (*tr*) **34** to look at carefully or warily. **35** Also: **eye up.** to look at in a manner indicating sexual interest; ogle. [OE *ēage*]
▸**'eyeless** *adj* ▸**'eyeˌlike** *adj*

eye[2] (aɪ) *n* another word for **nye.**

eyeball ('aɪˌbɔ:l) *n* **1** the entire ball-shaped part of the eye. **2 eyeball to eyeball.** in close confrontation. ◆ *vb* **3** (*tr*) *Sl.* to stare at.

eyebank ('aɪˌbæŋk) *n* a place in which corneas are stored for use in corneal grafts.

eyebath ('aɪˌbɑ:θ) *n* a small vessel for applying medicated or cleansing solutions to the eye. Also called (US and Canad.): **eyecup.**

eyeblack ('aɪˌblæk) *n* another name for **mascara.**

eyebright ('aɪˌbraɪt) *n* an annual plant having small white-and-purple flowers: formerly used in the treatment of eye disorders.

eyebrow ('aɪˌbraʊ) *n* **1** the transverse bony ridge over each eye. **2** the arch of hair that covers this ridge. **3 raise an eyebrow.** to give rise to doubt or disapproval.

eyebrow pencil *n* a cosmetic in pencil form for applying colour and shape to the eyebrows.

THESAURUS

fault, to *or* in the extreme, to the nth degree, ultra, uncommonly, unusually, utterly

extremist *n* **1** = **fanatic,** die-hard, radical, ultra, zealot

extremity *n* **1** = **limit,** acme, apex, apogee, border, bound, boundary, brim, brink, edge, end, extreme, farthest point, frontier, margin, maximum, minimum, nadir, pinnacle, pole, rim, terminal, termination, terminus, tip, top, ultimate, verge, zenith **3** = **crisis,** adversity, dire straits, disaster, emergency, exigency, hardship, pass, pinch, plight, setback, trouble

extricate *vb* = **free,** clear, deliver, disembarrass, disengage, disentangle, get out, get (someone) off the hook (*sl.*), liberate, release, relieve, remove, rescue, withdraw, wriggle out of

extrinsic *adj* **1, 2** = **external,** alien, exotic, exterior, extraneous, foreign, imported, outside, superficial

extrovert *adj* **2** = **outgoing,** amiable, exuberant, gregarious, hearty, sociable, social
Antonyms *adj* introspective, introverted, inward-looking, self-contained, withdrawn

extrude *vb* **1** = **force out,** eject, expel, press out, squeeze out, thrust out

exuberance *n* **1** = **high spirits,** animation, brio, buoyancy, cheerfulness, eagerness, ebullience, effervescence, energy, enthusiasm, excitement, exhilaration, life, liveliness, pep, spirit, sprightliness, vigour, vitality, vivacity, zest **2** = **fulsomeness,** effusiveness, exaggeration, excessiveness, lavishness, prodigality, superfluity **3** = **luxuriance,** abundance, copiousness, lavishness, lushness, plenitude, profusion, rankness, richness, superabundance

exuberant *adj* **1** = **high-spirited,** animated, buoyant, cheerful, chirpy (*inf.*), eager, ebullient, effervescent, elated, energetic, enthusiastic, excited, exhilarated, full of beans (*inf.*), full of life, in high spirits, lively, sparkling, spirited, sprightly, upbeat (*inf.*), vigorous, vivacious, zestful **2** = **fulsome,** effusive, exaggerated, excessive, lavish, overdone, prodigal, superfluous **3** = **luxuriant,** abundant, copious, lavish, lush, overflowing, plenteous, plentiful, profuse, rank, rich, superabundant, teeming
Antonyms *adj* ≠ **high-spirited:** apathetic, dull, lifeless, subdued, unenthusiastic

exude *vb* **1** = **seep,** bleed, discharge, emanate, emit, excrete, filter through, issue, leak, ooze, secrete, sweat, trickle, weep, well forth **2** = **radiate,** display, emanate, exhibit, manifest, show

exult *vb* **1** = **be joyful,** be delighted, be elated, be in high spirits, be jubilant, be overjoyed, celebrate, jubilate, jump for joy, make merry, rejoice **2** = **triumph,** boast, brag, crow, drool, gloat, glory (in), revel, take delight in, taunt, vaunt

exultant *adj* = **joyful,** cock-a-hoop, delighted, elated, exulting, flushed, gleeful, joyous, jubilant, overjoyed, over the moon (*inf.*), rapt, rejoicing, revelling, transported, triumphant

exultation *n* **1** = **joy,** celebration, delight, elation, glee, high spirits, joyousness, jubilation, merriness, rejoicing, transport **2** = **triumph,** boasting, bragging, crowing, gloating, glory, glorying, revelling

eye[1] *n* **1** = **eyeball,** optic (*inf.*), orb (*poetic*), peeper (*sl.*) **6 keep an eye on** = **watch,** guard, keep in view, keep tabs on (*inf.*), keep under surveillance, look after, look out for, monitor, observe, pay attention to, regard, scrutinize, supervise, survey, watch like a hawk, watch over **7** = **appreciation,** discernment, discrimination, judgment, perception, recognition, taste **8** *often plural* = **opinion,** belief, judgment, mind, point of view, viewpoint **15 an eye for an eye** = **retaliation,** justice, reprisal, requital, retribution, revenge, vengeance **24 lay, clap,** *or* **set eyes on** = **see,** behold, come across, encounter,

eye-catching 🅣 *adj* tending to attract attention; striking.
eye contact *n* a direct look between two people; meeting of eyes.
eyed (aɪd) *adj* **a** having an eye or eyes (as specified). **b** (*in combination*): *brown-eyed.*
eye dog *n NZ.* a dog trained to control sheep by staring fixedly at them. Also called: **strong-eye dog.**
eyeful 🅣 ('aɪfʊl) *n Inf.* **1** a view, glance, or gaze. **2** a beautiful or attractive sight, esp. a woman.
eyeglass ('aɪˌglɑːs) *n* **1** a lens for aiding or correcting defective vision, esp. a monocle. **2** another word for **eyepiece** or **eyebath.**
eyeglasses ('aɪˌglɑːsɪz) *pl n Now chiefly US.* another word for **spectacles.**
eyehole ('aɪˌhəʊl) *n* **1** a hole through which a rope, hook, etc., is passed. **2** the cavity that contains the eyeball. **3** another word for **peephole.**
eyelash ('aɪˌlæʃ) *n* **1** any one of the short curved hairs that grow from the edge of the eyelids. **2** a row or fringe of these hairs.
eyelet ('aɪlɪt) *n* **1** a small hole for a lace, cord, or hook to be passed through. **2** a small metal ring or tube reinforcing an eyehole in fabric. **3** a small opening, such as a peephole. **4** *Embroidery.* a small hole with finely stitched edges. **5** a small eye or eyelike marking. ◆ *vb* **6** (*tr*) to supply with an eyelet or eyelets. [C14: from OF *oillet,* lit.: a little eye, from *oill* eye, from L *oculus* eye]
eyelevel ('aɪˌlɛvᵊl) *adj* level with a person's eyes when looking straight ahead: *an eyelevel grill.*
eyelid ('aɪˌlɪd) *n* either of the two muscular folds of skin that can be moved to cover the exposed portion of the eyeball.
eyeliner ('aɪˌlaɪnə) *n* a cosmetic used to outline the eyes.
eye-opener *n Inf.* **1** something startling or revealing. **2** *US & Canad.* an alcoholic drink taken early in the morning.
eyepiece ('aɪˌpiːs) *n* the lens or lenses in an optical instrument nearest the eye of the observer.
eye rhyme *n* a rhyme involving words that are similar in spelling but not in sound, such as *stone* and *none.*
eye shadow *n* a coloured cosmetic put around the eyes.
eyeshot ('aɪˌʃɒt) *n* range of vision; view.
eyesight 🅣 ('aɪˌsaɪt) *n* the ability to see; faculty of sight.
eyesore 🅣 ('aɪˌsɔː) *n* something very ugly.
eyespot ('aɪˌspɒt) *n* **1** a small area of light-sensitive pigment in some simple organisms. **2** an eyelike marking, as on a butterfly wing.
eyestrain ('aɪˌstreɪn) *n* fatigue or irritation of the eyes, resulting from excessive use or uncorrected defects of vision.
Eyetie ('aɪtaɪ) *n, adj Brit. sl., offensive.* Italian. [C20: from jocular mispronunciation of *Italian*]
eyetooth (ˌaɪ'tuːθ) *n, pl* **eyeteeth. 1** either of the two canine teeth in the upper jaw. **2 give one's eyeteeth for.** to go to any lengths to achieve or obtain (something).
eyewash ('aɪˌwɒʃ) *n* **1** a lotion for the eyes. **2** *Inf.* nonsense; rubbish.
eyewitness 🅣 ('aɪˌwɪtnɪs) *n* a person present at an event who can describe what happened.
eyot (aɪt) *n Brit., obs. except in place names.* island. [var. of AIT]
eyrie ('ɪərɪ, 'ɛərɪ, 'aɪərɪ) *or* **aerie** *n* **1** the nest of an eagle or other bird of prey, built in a high inaccessible place. **2** any high isolated position or place. [C16: from Med. L *airea,* from L *ārea* open field, hence, nest]
eyrir ('eɪrɪə) *n, pl* **aurar** ('ɔɪrɑː). an Icelandic monetary unit worth one hundredth of a krona. [ON: ounce (of silver), money; rel. to L *aureus* golden]
Ez. *or* **Ezr.** *Bible. abbrev. for* Ezra.
Ezek. *Bible. abbrev. for* Ezekiel.

THESAURUS

meet, notice, observe, run into **28 see eye to eye** = **agree**, accord, back, be in unison, coincide, concur, fall in, get on, go along, harmonize, jibe (*inf.*), speak the same language, subscribe to **30 up to one's eyes** = **busy**, caught up, engaged, flooded out, fully occupied, inundated, overwhelmed, up to here, up to one's elbows, wrapped up in ◆ *vb* **34** = **look at**, behold, check out (*inf.*), contemplate, eyeball (*sl.*), get a load of (*inf.*), glance at, have *or* take a look at, inspect, peruse, regard, scan, scrutinize, stare at, study, survey, view, watch **35** = **ogle**, eye up (*inf.*), give (someone) the (glad) eye, leer at, make eyes at

eye-catching *adj* = **striking**, arresting, attractive, captivating, dramatic, showy, spectacular

eyeful *n* **1** = **look**, butcher's (*Brit. sl.*), gander (*inf.*), gaze, glance, shufti (*Brit. sl.*), sight, view **2** = **spectacle**, beauty, dazzler, humdinger (*sl.*), knockout (*inf.*), show, sight, sight for sore eyes (*inf.*), stunner (*inf.*), vision

eyesight *n* = **vision**, observation, perception, range of vision, sight

eyesore *n* = **mess**, atrocity, blemish, blight, blot, disfigurement, disgrace, horror, monstrosity, sight (*inf.*), ugliness

eyewitness *n* = **observer**, bystander, looker-on, onlooker, passer-by, spectator, viewer, watcher, witness

Ff

f *or* **F** (ɛf) *n, pl* **f's, F's,** *or* **Fs. 1** the sixth letter of the English alphabet. **2** a speech sound represented by this letter, as in *fat*.

f *symbol for:* **1** *Music.* forte: an instruction to play loudly. **2** *Physics.* frequency. **3** *Maths.* function (of). **4** *Physics.* femto-.

f, f/, *or* **f:** *symbol for* f-number.

F *symbol for:* **1** *Music.* **1a** the fourth note of the scale of C major. **1b** the major or minor key having this note as its tonic. **2** Fahrenheit. **3** farad(s). **4** *Chem.* fluorine. **5** *Physics.* force. **6** franc(s). **7** *Genetics.* a generation of filial offspring, F_1 being the first generation of offspring.

f. *or* **F.** *abbrev. for:* **1** fathom(s). **2** female. **3** *Grammar.* feminine. **4** (*pl* **ff.** *or* **FF.**) folio. **5** (*pl* **ff.**) following (page).

F- (of US military aircraft) *abbrev. for* fighter.

fa (fɑː) *n Music.* the syllable used in the fixed system of solmization for the note F. [C14: see GAMUT]

FA (in Britain) *abbrev. for* Football Association.

f.a. *or* **FA** *abbrev. for* fanny adams.

FAB *abbrev. for* fuel air bomb.

Fabian Ⓣ ('feɪbɪən) *adj* **1** of or resembling the delaying tactics of Q. Fabius Maximus, Roman general who wore out the strength of Hannibal while avoiding a pitched battle; cautious. ◆ *n* **2** a member of or sympathizer with the Fabian Society. [C19: from L *Fabiānus* of Fabius]
▸ **'Fabia,nism** *n*

Fabian Society *n* an association of British socialists advocating the establishment of socialism by gradual reforms.

fable Ⓣ ('feɪbᵊl) *n* **1** a short moral story, esp. one with animals as characters. **2** a false, fictitious, or improbable account. **3** a story or legend about supernatural or mythical characters or events. **4** legends or myths collectively. ◆ *vb* **fables, fabling, fabled. 5** to relate or tell (fables). **6** (*intr*) to tell lies. **7** (*tr*) to talk about or describe in the manner of a fable. [C13: from L *fābula* story, narrative, from *fārī* to speak, say]
▸ **'fabler** *n*

fabled Ⓣ ('feɪbᵊld) *adj* **1** made famous in fable. **2** fictitious.

fabliau ('fæblɪ,əʊ) *n, pl* **fabliaux** ('fæblɪ,əʊz). a comic usually ribald verse tale, popular in France in the 12th and 13th centuries. [C19: from F: a little tale, from *fable* tale]

Fablon ('fæblən, -lɒn) *n Trademark.* a brand of adhesive-backed plastic material used to cover and decorate shelves, worktops, etc.

fabric Ⓣ ('fæbrɪk) *n* **1** any cloth made from yarn or fibres by weaving, knitting, felting, etc. **2** the texture of a cloth. **3** a structure or framework: *the fabric of society.* **4** a style or method of construction. **5** *Rare.* a building. [C15: from L *fabrica* workshop, from *faber* craftsman]

fabricate Ⓣ ('fæbrɪ,keɪt) *vb* **fabricates, fabricating, fabricated.** (*tr*) **1** to make, build, or construct. **2** to devise or concoct (a story, etc.). **3** to fake or forge. [C15: from L, from *fabrica* workshop; see FABRIC]
▸ **,fabri'cation** *n* ▸ **'fabri,cator** *n*

fabulist ('fæbjʊlɪst) *n* **1** a person who invents or recounts fables. **2** a person who lies.

fabulous Ⓣ ('fæbjʊləs) *adj* **1** almost unbelievable; astounding; legendary: *fabulous wealth.* **2** *Inf.* extremely good: *a fabulous time at the party.* **3** of, relating to, or based upon fable: *a fabulous beast.* [C15: from L *fābulōsus* celebrated in fable, from *fābula* FABLE]
▸ **'fabulously** *adv* ▸ **'fabulousness** *n*

Fac. *abbrev. for* Faculty.

façade Ⓣ *or* **facade** (fə'sɑːd, fæ-) *n* **1** the face of a building, esp. the main front. **2** a front or outer appearance, esp. a deceptive one. [C17: from F, from It., from *faccia* FACE]

face Ⓣ (feɪs) *n* **1a** the front of the head from the forehead to the lower jaw. **1b** (*as modifier*): *face flannel.* **2a** the expression of the countenance: *a sad face.* **2b** a distorted expression, esp. to indicate disgust. **3** *Inf.* make-up (esp. in **put one's face on**). **4** outward appearance: *the face of the countryside is changing.* **5** appearance or pretence (esp. in **put a bold, good, bad,** etc., **face on**). **6** dignity (esp. in **lose** *or* **save face**). **7** *Inf.* impudence or effrontery. **8** the main side of an object, building, etc., or the front: *a cliff face.* **9** the marked surface of an instrument, esp. the dial of a timepiece. **10** the functional or working side of an object, as of a tool or playing card. **11a** the exposed area of a mine from which coal, ore, etc., may be mined. **11b** (*as modifier*): *face worker.* **12** the uppermost part or surface: *the face of the earth.* **13** Also called: **side.** any one of the plane surfaces of a crystal or other solid figure. **14** Also called: **typeface.** *Printing.* **14a** the printing surface of any type character. **14b** the style or design of the character on the type. **15** *NZ.* the exposed slope of a hill. **16** *Brit. sl.* a well-known or important person. **17 in (the) face of.** despite. **18 on the face of it.** to all appearances. **19 set one's face against.** to oppose with determination. **20 show one's face.** to make an appearance. **21 to someone's face.** in someone's presence: *I told him the truth to his face.* ◆ *vb* **faces, facing, faced. 22** (when *intr*, often foll. by *to, towards,* or *on*) to look or be situated or placed (in a specified direction): *the house faces onto the square.* **23** to be opposite: *facing page 9.* **24** (*tr*) to be confronted by: *he faces many problems.* **25** (*tr*) to provide with a surface of a different material. **26** to dress the surface of (stone or other material). **27** (*tr*) to expose (a card) with the face uppermost. **28** *Mil.* to order (a formation) to turn in a certain direction or (of a formation) to turn as required: *right face!* ◆ See also **face down, face up to.** [C13: from OF, from Vulgar L *facia* (unattested), from L *faciēs* form]

face card *n* the usual US and Canad. term for **court card.**

face cloth *or* **face flannel** *n Brit.* a small piece of cloth used to wash the face and hands. US equivalent: **washcloth.**

facedown ('feɪsdaʊn) *n Inf.* another word for **face-off** (sense 2).

face down *vb* (*tr, adv*) to confront and force (someone or something) to back down.

faceless Ⓣ ('feɪslɪs) *adj* **1** without a face. **2** without identity; anonymous.
▸ **'facelessness** *n*

face-lift Ⓣ *n* **1** a cosmetic surgical operation for tightening sagging skin and smoothing wrinkles on the face. **2** any improvement or renovation. ◆ *vb* (*tr*) **3** to improve the appearance of, as by a face-lift.

face-off *n* **1** *Ice hockey.* the method of starting a game, in which the referee drops the puck, etc. between two opposing players. **2** Also called **facedown.** a confrontation, esp. one in which each party attempts to make the other back down. ◆ *vb* **face off.** (*intr, adv*) **3** to start play by a face-off.

face powder *n* a cosmetic powder worn to make the face look less shiny, softer, etc.

facer Ⓣ ('feɪsə) *n* **1** a person or thing that faces. **2** *Brit. inf.* a difficulty or problem.

face-saving *adj* maintaining dignity or prestige.
▸ **'face-,saver** *n*

facet Ⓣ ('fæsɪt) *n* **1** any of the surfaces of a cut gemstone. **2** an aspect or phase, as of a subject or personality. ◆ *vb* **facets, faceting** *or* **facetting,**

THESAURUS

Fabian *adj* **1 = cautious,** attritional, circumspect, delaying, procrastinating

fable *n* **1, 3 = story,** allegory, apologue, legend, myth, parable, tale **2 = fiction,** fabrication, fairy story (*inf.*), falsehood, fantasy, fib, figment, invention, lie, romance, tall story (*inf.*), untruth, urban legend, urban myth, white lie, yarn (*inf.*)
Antonyms *n* actuality, certainty, fact, reality, truth, verity

fabled *adj* **1, 2 = legendary,** fabulous, famed, famous, fictional, mythical, storied

fabric *n* **1 = cloth,** material, stuff, textile, web **3, 4 = framework,** constitution, construction, foundations, infrastructure, make-up, organization, structure

fabricate *vb* **1 = build,** assemble, construct, erect, fashion, form, frame, make, manufacture, shape **2, 3 = make up,** coin, concoct, devise, fake, falsify, feign, forge, form, invent, trump up

fabrication *n* **1 = construction,** assemblage, assembly, building, erection, manufacture, production **2, 3 = forgery,** cock-and-bull story (*inf.*), concoction, fable, fairy story (*inf.*), fake, falsehood, fiction, figment, invention, lie, myth, pork pie (*Brit. sl.*), porky (*Brit. sl.*), untruth

fabulous *adj* **1 = astounding,** amazing, breathtaking, fictitious, immense, inconceivable, incredible, legendary, phenomenal, unbelievable **2** *Informal* **= wonderful,** brilliant, fantastic, magic (*inf.*), marvellous, out-of-this-world (*inf.*), sensational (*inf.*), spectacular, superb **3 = legendary,** apocryphal, fantastic, fictitious, imaginary, invented, made-up, mythical, unreal
Antonyms *adj* actual, common, commonplace, credible, genuine, natural, ordinary, real

façade *n* **1, 2 = appearance,** exterior, face, front, frontage, guise, mask, pretence, semblance, show, veneer

face *n* **1 = countenance,** clock, dial (*Brit. sl.*), features, kisser (*sl.*), lineaments, mug (*sl.*), phiz *or* phizog (*sl.*), physiognomy, visage **2 = scowl,** frown, grimace, *moue,* pout, smirk **4 = expression,** appearance, aspect, look **5** *As in* **put a good face on = façade,** air, appearance, disguise, display, exterior, front, mask, pretence, semblance, show **6** *As in* **save** *or* lose face **= self-respect,** authority, dignity, honour, image, prestige, reputation, standing, status **7** *Informal* **= impudence,** assurance, audacity, boldness, brass neck (*Brit. inf.*), cheek (*inf.*), chutzpah (*US & Canad. inf.*), confidence, effrontery, front, gall (*inf.*), neck (*inf.*), nerve, presumption, sauce (*inf.*) **12, 13 = side,** aspect, cover, exterior, facet, front, outside, right side, surface **18 on the face of it = to all appearances,** apparently, at first sight, seemingly, to the eye **20 = turn up,** appear **show one's face** approach, be seen, come, put in *or* make an appearance, show up (*inf.*) **21 to one's face = directly,** in one's presence, openly, straight ◆ *vb* **23 = look onto,** be opposite, front onto, give towards *or* onto, overlook **24 = confront,** be confronted by, brave, come up against, cope with, deal with, defy, encounter, experience, face off (*sl.*), meet, oppose, tackle **25, 26 = coat,** clad, cover, dress, finish, level, line, overlay, sheathe, surface, veneer

faceless *adj* **2 = impersonal,** anonymous, remote, unidentified, unknown

face-lift *n* **1 = cosmetic surgery,** plastic surgery **2 = renovation,** restoration

facer *n* **2** *Brit. informal* **= problem,** difficulty, dilemma, how-do-you-do (*inf.*), poser, puzzle, teaser

facet *n* **1 = aspect,** angle, face, part, phase, plane, side, slant, surface

facetious *adj* **1, 2 = funny,** amusing, comical,

faceted *or* **facetted. 3** (*tr*) to cut facets in (a gemstone). [C17: from F *facette* a little FACE]

facetiae (fəˈsiːʃɪˌiː) *pl n* **1** humorous or witty sayings. **2** obscene or coarsely witty books. [C17: from L: jests, pl of *facētia* witticism, from *facētus* elegant]

facetious ⓣ (fəˈsiːʃəs) *adj* **1** characterized by love of joking. **2** jocular or amusing, esp. at inappropriate times: *facetious remarks.* [C16: from OF *facetieux,* from *facetie* witticism; see FACETIAE]
▸**faˈcetiously** *adv* ▸**faˈcetiousness** *n*

face to face ⓣ *adv, adj* (**face-to-face** *as adj*) **1** opposite one another. **2** in confrontation.

face up to ⓣ *vb* (*intr, adv + prep*) to accept (an unpleasant fact, reality, etc.).

face value *n* **1** the value written or stamped on the face of a commercial paper or coin. **2** apparent worth or value.

facia (ˈfeɪʃɪə) *n* a variant spelling of **fascia.**

facial (ˈfeɪʃəl) *adj* **1** of or relating to the face. ◆ *n* **2** a beauty treatment for the face involving massage and cosmetic packs.
▸**ˈfacially** *adv*

-facient *suffix forming adjectives and nouns.* indicating a state or quality: *absorbefacient.* [from L *facient-, faciēns,* present participle of *facere* to do]

facies (ˈfeɪʃɪˌiːz) *n, pl* **facies. 1** the general form and appearance of an individual or a group. **2** the characteristics of a rock or rocks reflecting their appearance and conditions of formation. **3** *Med.* the general facial expression of a patient. [C17: from L: appearance, FACE]

facile ⓣ (ˈfæsaɪl) *adj* **1** easy to perform or achieve. **2** working or moving easily or smoothly. **3** superficial: *a facile solution.* [C15: from L *facilis* easy, from *facere* to do]
▸**ˈfacilely** *adv* ▸**ˈfacileness** *n*

facilitate ⓣ (fəˈsɪlɪˌteɪt) *vb* **facilitates, facilitating, facilitated.** (*tr*) to assist the progress of.
▸**faˌciliˈtation** *n*

facility ⓣ (fəˈsɪlɪtɪ) *n, pl* **facilities. 1** ease of action or performance. **2** ready skill or ease deriving from practice or familiarity. **3** (*often pl*) the means or equipment facilitating the performance of an action. **4** *Rare.* easy-going disposition. **5** (*usually pl*) a euphemistic word for **lavatory.** [C15: from L *facilitās,* from *facilis* easy; see FACILE]

facing ⓣ (ˈfeɪsɪŋ) *n* **1** a piece of material used esp. to conceal the seam of a garment and prevent fraying. **2** (*usually pl*) the collar, cuffs, etc., of the jacket of a military uniform. **3** an outer layer or coat of material applied to the surface of a wall.

facsimile ⓣ (fækˈsɪmɪlɪ) *n* **1** an exact copy or reproduction. **2** an image produced by facsimile transmission; fax. ◆ *vb* **facsimiles, facsimileing, facsimiled. 3** (*tr*) to make an exact copy of. [C17: from L *fac simile!* make something like it!, from *facere* to make + *similis* similar, like]

facsimile transmission *n* an international system of transmitting a written, printed, or pictorial document over the telephone system by scanning it photoelectrically and reproducing the image xerographically after transmission. Often shortened to **fax.**

fact ⓣ (fækt) *n* **1** an event or thing known to have happened or existed. **2** a truth verifiable from experience or observation. **3** a piece of information: *get me all the facts of this case.* **4** (*often pl*) *Law.* an actual event, happening, etc., as distinguished from its legal consequences. **5 after** (*or* **before**) **the fact.** *Criminal law.* after (or before) the commission of the offence. **6 as a matter of fact, in fact, in point of fact.** in reality or actuality. **7 fact of life.** an inescapable truth, esp. an unpleasant one. See also **facts of life.** [C16: from L *factum* something done, from *factus* made, from *facere* to do, make]

faction[1] ⓣ (ˈfækʃən) *n* **1** a group of people forming a minority within a larger body, esp. a dissentious group. **2** strife or dissension within a group. [C16: from L *factiō* a making, from *facere* to do, make]
▸**ˈfactional** *adj*

faction[2] (ˈfækʃən) *n* a television programme, film, or literary work comprising a dramatized presentation of actual events. [C20: a blend of FACT & FICTION]

faction fight *n* conflict between different groups within a larger body, esp. in S Africa a fight between Blacks of different tribes.

factious ⓣ (ˈfækʃəs) *adj* given to, producing, or characterized by faction.
▸**ˈfactiously** *adv*

> **USAGE NOTE** See at **fractious.**

factitious ⓣ (fækˈtɪʃəs) *adj* **1** artificial rather than natural. **2** not genuine; sham: *factitious enthusiasm.* [C17: from L *factīcius,* from *facere* to do, make]
▸**facˈtitiously** *adv* ▸**facˈtitiousness** *n*

factitive (ˈfæktɪtɪv) *adj Grammar.* denoting a verb taking a direct object as well as a noun in apposition, as for example *elect* in *They elected John president,* where *John* is the direct object and *president* is the complement. [C19: from NL, from L *factitāre* to do frequently, from *facere* to do, make]

factoid (ˈfæktɔɪd) *n* a piece of unreliable information believed to be true because of the way it is presented or repeated in print. [C20: coined by Norman Mailer (born 1923), US author, from FACT + -OID]

factor ⓣ (ˈfæktə) *n* **1** an element or cause that contributes to a result. **2** *Maths.* one of two or more integers or polynomials whose product is a given integer or polynomial: *2 and 3 are factors of 6.* **3** (foll. by identifying numeral) *Med.* any of several substances that participate in the clotting of blood: *factor VIII.* **4** a person who acts on another's behalf, esp. one who transacts business for another. **5** former name for a **gene. 6** *Commercial law.* a person to whom goods are consigned for sale and who is paid a commission. **7** (in Scotland) the manager of an estate. ◆ *vb* **8** (*intr*) to engage in the business of a factor. [C15: from L: one who acts, from *facere* to do, make]
▸**ˈfactorable** *adj* ▸**ˈfactorship** *n*

> **USAGE NOTE** *Factor* (sense 1) should only be used to refer to something which contributes to a result. It should not be used to refer to a part of something such as a plan or arrangement; instead a word such as *component* or *element* should be used.

factor VIII *n* a protein that participates in the clotting of blood. It is extracted from donated serum and used in the treatment of haemophilia.

factorial (fækˈtɔːrɪəl) *Maths.* ◆ *n* **1** the product of all the positive integers from one up to and including a given integer: *factorial four is* $1 \times 2 \times 3 \times 4$. ◆ *adj* **2** of or involving factorials or factors.
▸**facˈtorially** *adv*

factorize *or* **factorise** (ˈfæktəˌraɪz) *vb* **factorizes, factorizing, factorized** *or* **factorises, factorising, factorised.** (*tr*) *Maths.* to resolve (an integer or polynomial) into factors.
▸**ˌfactoriˈzation** *or* **ˌfactoriˈsation** *n*

factory ⓣ (ˈfæktərɪ) *n, pl* **factories. a** a building or group of buildings containing a plant assembly for the manufacture of goods. **b** (*as modifier*): *a factory worker.* [C16: from LL *factorium;* see FACTOR]
▸**ˈfactory-ˌlike** *adj*

factory farm *n* a farm in which animals are intensively reared using modern industrial methods.
▸**factory farming** *n*

THESAURUS

droll, flippant, frivolous, humorous, jesting, jocose, jocular, merry, playful, pleasant, tongue in cheek, unserious, waggish, witty
Antonyms *adj* earnest, genuine, grave, lugubrious, pensive, sedate, serious, sincere, sober, thoughtful

face to face *adv, adj* **1, 2 = facing,** *à deux,* confronting, eyeball to eyeball, in confrontation, opposite, tête-à-tête, vis-à-vis

face up to *vb* **= accept,** acknowledge, come to terms with, confront, cope with, deal with, face the music, meet head-on, tackle

facile *adj* **1, 2 = easy,** adept, adroit, dexterous, effortless, fluent, light, proficient, quick, ready, simple, skilful, smooth, uncomplicated **3 = superficial,** cursory, glib, hasty, shallow, slick
Antonyms *adj* ≠ **easy:** awkward, careful, clumsy, difficult, intractable, maladroit, slow, thoughtful, unskilful

facilitate *vb* **= promote,** assist the progress of, ease, expedite, forward, further, help, make easy, oil the wheels, pave the way for, smooth the path of, speed up
Antonyms *vb* delay, encumber, frustrate, hamper, handicap, hinder, hold up *or* back, impede, obstruct, prevent, restrain, thwart

facility *n* **1, 2 = ease,** ability, adroitness, craft, dexterity, efficiency, effortlessness, expertness, fluency, gift, knack, proficiency, quickness, readiness, skilfulness, skill, smoothness, talent **3** *often plural* **= equipment,** advantage, aid, amenity, appliance, convenience, means, opportunity, resource
Antonyms *n* ≠ **ease:** awkwardness, clumsiness, difficulty, hardship, ineptness, maladroitness, pains

facing *n* **3 = overlay,** cladding, coating, façade, false front, front, plaster, reinforcement, revetment, stucco, surface, trimming, veneer

facsimile *n* **1, 2 = copy,** carbon, carbon copy, duplicate, fax, photocopy, Photostat (*Trademark*), print, replica, reproduction, transcript, Xerox (*Trademark*)

fact *n* **1 = event,** act, deed, *fait accompli,* happening, incident, occurrence, performance **2 = truth,** actuality, certainty, gospel (truth), naked truth, reality **3 = detail,** circumstance, feature, item, particular, point, specific **6 in fact = actually,** indeed, in point of fact, in reality, in truth, really, truly
Antonyms *n* ≠ **truth:** delusion, fable, fabrication, falsehood, fiction, invention, lie, tall story, untruth, yarn (*inf.*)

faction[1] *n* **1 = group,** bloc, cabal, camp, caucus, clique, coalition, combination, confederacy, contingent, coterie, division, gang, ginger group, junta, lobby, minority, party, pressure group, schism, section, sector, set, splinter group **2 = dissension,** conflict, disagreement, discord, disharmony, disunity, division, divisiveness, friction, infighting, rebellion, sedition, strife, tumult, turbulence
Antonyms *n* ≠ **dissension:** accord, agreement, amity, assent, concord, consensus, friendship, goodwill, harmony, peace, rapport, unanimity, unity

factious *adj* **= contentious,** conflicting, disputatious, dissident, divisive, insurrectionary, litigious, malcontent, mutinous, partisan, rebellious, refractory, rival, sectarian, seditious, troublemaking, tumultuous, turbulent, warring

factitious *adj* **1, 2 = artificial,** affected, assumed, counterfeited, engineered, fabricated, fake, false, imitation, insincere, made-up, manufactured, mock, phoney *or* phony (*inf.*), pinchbeck, pseudo (*inf.*), put-on, sham, simulated, spurious, synthetic, unnatural, unreal

factor *n* **1 = element,** aspect, cause, circumstance, component, consideration, determinant, influence, item, part, point, thing **7** *Scot.* **= agent,** deputy, estate manager, middleman, reeve, steward

factory *n* **= works,** manufactory, mill, plant

factory ship *n* a vessel that processes fish supplied by a fleet.

factotum ➊ (fæk'təʊtəm) *n* a person employed to do all kinds of work. [C16: from Med. L, from L *fac!* do! + *tōtum,* from *tōtus* (adj) all]

facts and figures ➊ *pl n* details.

factsheet ('fækt,ʃiːt) *n* a printed sheet containing information relating to items covered in a television or radio programme.

facts of life *pl n* **the.** the details of sexual behaviour and reproduction.

factual ➊ ('fæktʃʊəl) *adj* **1** of, relating to, or characterized by facts. **2** real; actual.
▸**'factually** *adv* ▸**'factualness** *or* **,factu'ality** *n*

facula ('fækjʊlə) *n, pl* **faculae** (-,liː). any of the bright areas on the sun's surface, usually appearing just before a sunspot. [C18: from L: little torch, from *fax* torch]
▸**'facular** *adj*

facultative ('fækəltətɪv) *adj* **1** empowering but not compelling the doing of an act. **2** that may or may not occur. **3** *Biol.* able to exist under more than one set of environmental conditions. **4** of or relating to a faculty.
▸**'facultatively** *adv*

faculty ➊ ('fækəltɪ) *n, pl* **faculties. 1** one of the inherent powers of the mind or body, such as memory, sight, or hearing. **2** any ability or power, whether acquired or inherent. **3** a conferred power or right. **4a** a department within a university or college devoted to a particular branch of knowledge. **4b** the staff of such a department. **4c** *Chiefly US & Canad.* all the teaching staff at a university, school, etc. **5** all members of a learned profession. [C14 (in the sense: department of learning): from L *facultās* capability; rel. to L *facilis* easy]

FA Cup *n Soccer.* (in England and Wales) **1** an annual knockout competition among member teams of the Football Association. **2** the trophy itself.

fad ➊ (fæd) *n Inf.* **1** an intense but short-lived fashion. **2** a personal idiosyncrasy. [C19: from ?]
▸**'faddish** *or* **'faddy** *adj*

fade ➊ (feɪd) *vb* **fades, fading, faded. 1** to lose or cause to lose brightness, colour, or clarity. **2** (*intr*) to lose vigour or youth. **3** (*intr;* usually foll. by *away* or *out*) to vanish slowly. **4a** to decrease the brightness or volume of (a television or radio programme) or (of a television programme, etc.) to decrease in this way. **4b** to decrease the volume of (a sound) in a recording system or (of a sound) to be so reduced in volume. **5** (*intr*) (of the brakes of a vehicle) to lose power. **6** to cause (a golf ball) to veer from a straight line or (of a golf ball) to veer from a straight flight. ◆ *n* **7** the act or an instance of fading. [C14: from *fade* (adj) dull, from OF, from Vulgar L *fatidus* (unattested), prob. blend of L *vapidus* VAPID + L *fatuus* FATUOUS]
▸**'fadeless** *adj* ▸**'fadedness** *n* ▸**'fader** *n*

fade-in *n* **1** *Films.* an optical effect in which a shot appears gradually out of darkness. ◆ *vb* **fade in.** (*adv*) **2** to increase or cause to increase gradually, as vision or sound in a film or broadcast.

fade-out *n* **1** *Films.* an optical effect in which a shot slowly disappears into darkness. **2** a gradual and temporary loss of a radio or television signal. **3** a slow or gradual disappearance. ◆ *vb* **fade out.** (*adv*) **4** to decrease or cause to decrease gradually, as vision or sound in a film or broadcast.

faeces ➊ *or esp. US* **feces** ('fiːsiːz) *pl n* bodily waste matter discharged through the anus. [C15: from L *faecēs,* pl. of *faex* sediment, dregs]
▸**faecal** *or esp. US* **fecal** ('fiːkəl) *adj*

faerie *or* **faery** ('feɪərɪ, 'feərɪ) *n, pl* **faeries.** *Arch. or poetic.* **1** the land of fairies. ◆ *adj, n* **2** a variant spelling of **fairy.**

Faeroese *or* **Faroese** (,feərəʊ'iːz) *adj* **1** of or characteristic of the Faeroes, islands in the N Atlantic, their inhabitants, or their language. ◆ *n* **2** the language of the Faeroes, closely related to Icelandic. **3** (*pl* **Faeroese** *or* **Faroese**) a native or inhabitant of the Faeroes.

faff (fæf) *vb* (*intr;* often foll. by *about*) *Brit. inf.* to dither or fuss. [C19: from ?]

fag[1] ➊ (fæg) *n* **1** *Inf.* a boring or wearisome task. **2** *Brit.* (esp. formerly) a young public school boy who performs menial chores for an older boy or prefect. ◆ *vb* **fags, fagging, fagged. 3** (when *tr,* often foll. by *out*) *Inf.* to become or cause to become exhausted by hard work **4** (*usually intr*) *Brit.* to do or cause to do menial chores in a public school. [C18: from ?]

fag[2] (fæg) *n Brit. sl.* a cigarette. [C16 (in the sense: something hanging loose, flap): from ?]

fag[3] ➊ (fæg) *n Sl., chiefly US & Canad.* short for **faggot**[2].

fag end *n* **1** the last and worst part. **2** *Brit. inf.* the stub of a cigarette. [C17: see FAG[2]]

faggot[1] *or esp. US* **fagot** ('fægət) *n* **1** a bundle of sticks or twigs, esp. when used as fuel. **2** a bundle of iron bars, esp. to be forged into wrought iron. **3** a ball of chopped meat bound with herbs and bread and eaten fried. ◆ *vb* (*tr*) **4** to collect into a bundle or bundles. **5** *Needlework.* to do faggoting on (a garment, etc.). [C14: from OF, ?from Gk *phakelos* bundle]

faggot[2] ('fægət) *n Sl., chiefly US & Canad.* a male homosexual. [C20: special use of FAGGOT[1]]

faggoting *or esp. US* **fagoting** ('fægətɪŋ) *n* **1** decorative needlework done by tying vertical threads together in bundles. **2** a decorative way of joining two hems by crisscross stitches.

fag hag *n US sl., usually derog.* a heterosexual woman who prefers the company of homosexual men.

fah *n Music.* (in tonic sol-fa) the fourth degree of any major scale. [C14: later variant of *fa;* see GAMUT]

Fah. *or* **Fahr.** *abbrev. for* Fahrenheit.

Fahrenheit ('færən,haɪt) *adj* of or measured according to the Fahrenheit scale of temperature. Symbol: F [C18: after Gabriel *Fahrenheit* (1686–1736), G physicist]

Fahrenheit scale *n* a scale of temperatures in which 32° represents the melting point of ice and 212° represents the boiling point of pure water under standard atmospheric pressure. Cf. **Celsius scale.**

faïence (faɪ'ɑːns, feɪ-) *n* tin-glazed earthenware, usually that of French, German, Italian, or Scandinavian origin. [C18: from F, strictly: pottery from *Faenza,* N Italy]

fail ➊ (feɪl) *vb* **1** to be unsuccessful in an attempt (at something or to do something). **2** (*intr*) to stop operating or working properly: *the steering failed suddenly.* **3** to judge or be judged as being below the officially accepted standard required in (a course, examination, etc.). **4** (*tr*) to prove disappointing or useless to (someone). **5** (*tr*) to neglect or be unable (to do something). **6** (*intr*) to prove insufficient in quantity or extent. **7** (*intr*) to weaken. **8** (*intr*) to go bankrupt. ◆ *n* **9** a failure to attain the required standard. **10 without fail.** definitely. [C13: from OF *faillir,* ult. from L *fallere* to disappoint]

failing ➊ ('feɪlɪŋ) *n* **1** a weak point. ◆ *prep* **2** (*used to express a condition*) in default of: *failing a solution, the problem will have to wait until Monday.*

fail-safe *adj* **1** designed to return to a safe condition in the event of a failure or malfunction. **2** safe from failure; foolproof.

failure ➊ ('feɪljə) *n* **1** the act or an instance of failing. **2** a person or

THESAURUS

factotum *n* = **Man Friday** *or* **Girl Friday,** handyman, jack of all trades, man of all work, odd job man

facts and figures *pl n* = **information,** data, details, gen, info (*inf.*), ins and outs, the lowdown (*inf.*), the score (*inf.*), the whole story

factual *adj* **1, 2** = **true,** accurate, authentic, circumstantial, close, correct, credible, exact, faithful, genuine, literal, matter-of-fact, objective, precise, real, sure, true-to-life, unadorned, unbiased, veritable
Antonyms *adj* embellished, fanciful, fictitious, fictive, figurative, imaginary, unreal

faculty *n* **1** *usually plural* = **powers,** capabilities, intelligence, reason, senses, wits **2** = **ability,** adroitness, aptitude, bent, capability, capacity, cleverness, dexterity, facility, gift, knack, power, propensity, readiness, skill, talent, turn **3** = **right,** authorization, licence, prerogative, privilege **4** = **department,** branch of learning, discipline, profession, school, teaching staff (*chiefly US*)
Antonyms *n* ≠ **ability:** failing, inability, shortcoming, unskilfulness, weakness, weak point

fad *n* **1, 2** = **craze,** affectation, fancy, fashion, mania, mode, rage, trend, vogue, whim

fade *vb* **1** = **pale,** blanch, bleach, blench, dim, discolour, dull, grow dim, lose colour, lose lustre, wash out **2, 2** *As in* **fade away** *or* **out** = **dwindle,** decline, die away, die out, dim, disappear, disperse, dissolve, droop, ebb, etiolate, evanesce, fail, fall, flag, languish, melt away, perish, shrivel, vanish, vanish into thin air, wane, waste away, wilt, wither

faded *adj* **1** = **discoloured,** bleached, dim, dull, etiolated, indistinct, lustreless, pale, washed out

fading *adj* **2, 3** = **declining,** decreasing, disappearing, dying, on the decline, vanishing

faeces *pl n* = **excrement,** bodily waste, droppings, dung, excreta, ordure, stools

fag[1] *n* **1** *Informal* = **chore,** bind (*inf.*), bore, bother, drag (*inf.*), inconvenience, irritation, nuisance

fag[3] *n Slang, chiefly U.S. & Canad.* = **homosexual,** bender (*sl.*), catamite, fairy (*sl.*), gay, homo (*inf.*), nancy boy (*sl.*), poof (*sl.*), poofter (*sl.*), queen (*sl.*), queer (*inf., derogatory*), woofter (*sl.*)

fail *vb* **1, 3** = **be unsuccessful,** be defeated, be found lacking *or* wanting, be in vain, bite the dust, break down, come a cropper (*inf.*), come to grief, come to naught, come to nothing, come unstuck, fall, fall by the wayside, fall flat, fall flat on one's face, fall short, fall short of, fall through, fizzle out (*inf.*), flop (*inf.*), founder, go astray, go belly-up (*sl.*), go by the board, go down, go up in smoke, meet with disaster, miscarry, misfire, miss, not make the grade (*inf.*), run aground, turn out badly **2** = **give out,** be on one's last legs (*inf.*), cease, conk out, cut out, decline, die, disappear, droop, dwindle, fade, fall apart at the seams, give up, go phut, gutter, languish, peter out, sicken, sink, stop working, wane, weaken **4** = **disappoint,** abandon, break one's word, desert, forget, forsake, let down, neglect, omit, turn one's back on **8** = **go bankrupt,** become insolvent, close down, crash, fold, go broke (*inf.*), go bust (*inf.*), go into receivership, go out of business, go to the wall, go under, smash ◆ *n* **10 without fail** = **regularly,** conscientiously, constantly, dependably, like clockwork, punctually, religiously, without exception
Antonyms *vb* ≠ **be unsuccessful:** bloom, flourish, grow, pass, prosper, strengthen, succeed, thrive, triumph

failing *n* **1** = **weakness,** blemish, blind spot, defect, deficiency, drawback, error, failure, fault, flaw, foible, frailty, imperfection, lapse, miscarriage, misfortune, shortcoming ◆ *prep* **2** = **in the absence of,** in default of, lacking
Antonyms *n* ≠ **weakness:** advantage, asset, forte, métier, speciality, strength, strong suit

failure *n* **1** = **lack of success,** abortion, breakdown, collapse, defeat, downfall, fiasco, frustration, miscarriage, overthrow, wreck **2** = **loser,** black sheep, clinker (*sl., chiefly US*), dead duck (*sl.*), disappointment, dud (*inf.*), flop (*inf.*), incompetent, ne'er-do-well, no-good, no-hoper (*chiefly Austral.*), nonstarter, washout (*inf.*) **3, 4** = **shortcoming,** default, deficiency, dereliction, neglect, negligence, nonobser-

thing that is unsuccessful or disappointing. **3** nonperformance of something required or expected: *failure to attend will be punished.* **4** cessation of normal operation: *a power failure.* **5** an insufficiency: *a crop failure.* **6** a decline or loss, as in health. **7** the fact of not reaching the required standard in an examination, test, etc. **8** bankruptcy.

fain ❶ (feɪn) *adv* **1** (usually with *would*) *Arch.* gladly: *she would fain be dead.* ◆ *adj* **2** *Obs.* **2a** willing. **2b** compelled. [OE *fægen*; see FAWN[2]]

faint ❶ (feɪnt) *adj* **1** lacking clarity, brightness, volume, etc. **2** lacking conviction or force: *faint praise.* **3** feeling dizzy or weak as if about to lose consciousness. **4** timid (esp. in **faint-hearted**). **5 not the faintest (idea** *or* **notion)**. no idea whatsoever: *I haven't the faintest.* ◆ *vb (intr)* **6** to lose consciousness, as through weakness. **7** *Arch. or poetic.* to become weak, esp. in courage. ◆ *n* **8** a sudden spontaneous loss of consciousness caused by an insufficient supply of blood to the brain. [C13: from OF, from *faindre* to be idle]
▸ **'faintish** *adj* ▸ **'faintly** *adv* ▸ **'faintness** *n*

fair[1] ❶ (fɛə) *adj* **1** free from discrimination, dishonesty, etc. **2** in conformity with rules or standards: *a fair fight.* **3** (of the hair or complexion) light in colour. **4** beautiful to look at. **5** quite good: *a fair piece of work.* **6** unblemished; untainted. **7** (of the tide or wind) favourable to the passage of a vessel. **8** fine or cloudless. **9** pleasant or courteous. **10** apparently good or valuable: *fair words.* **11 fair and square.** in a correct or just way. ◆ *adv* **12** in a fair way: *act fair, now!* **13** absolutely or squarely; quite. ◆ *vb* **14** *(intr) Dialect.* (of the weather) to become fine. ◆ *n* **15** *Arch.* a person or thing that is beautiful or valuable. [OE *fæger*]
▸ **'fairish** *adj* ▸ **'fairness** *n*

fair[2] ❶ (fɛə) *n* **1** a travelling entertainment with sideshows, rides, etc. **2** a gathering of producers of and dealers in a given class of products to facilitate business: *a world fair.* **3** a regular assembly at a specific place for the sale of goods, esp. livestock. [C13: from OF *feire,* from LL *fēria* holiday, from L *fēriae* days of rest]

fair game *n* a legitimate object for ridicule or attack.

fairground ('fɛəˌgraʊnd) *n* an open space used for a fair or exhibition.

fairing[1] ('fɛərɪŋ) *n* an external metal structure fitted around parts of an aircraft, car, etc., to reduce drag. [C20: from *fair* to streamline + -ING[1]]

fairing[2] ('fɛərɪŋ) *n Arch.* a present, esp. from a fair.

Fair Isle *n* an intricate multicoloured pattern knitted with Shetland wool into various garments, such as sweaters. [C19: after one of the Shetland Islands where this type of pattern originated]

fairly ❶ ('fɛəlɪ) *adv* **1** *(not used with a negative)* moderately. **2** as deserved; justly. **3** *(not used with a negative)* positively: *the hall fairly rang with applause.*

fair-minded ❶ *adj* just or impartial.
▸ **ˌfair-'mindedness** *n*

fair play *n* **1** an established standard of decency, etc. **2** abidance by this standard.

fair sex *n* **the.** women collectively.

fair-spoken *adj* civil, courteous, or elegant in speech.
▸ **ˌfair-'spokenness** *n*

fairway ('fɛəˌweɪ) *n* **1** (on a golf course) the avenue approaching a green bordered by rough. **2** *Naut.* the navigable part of a river, harbour, etc.

fair-weather *adj* **1** suitable for use in fair weather only. **2** not reliable in situations of difficulty: *fair-weather friend.*

fairy ❶ ('fɛərɪ) *n, pl* **fairies. 1** an imaginary supernatural being, usually represented in diminutive human form and characterized as having magical powers. **2** *Sl.* a male homosexual. ◆ *adj (prenominal)* **3** of a fairy or fairies. **4** resembling a fairy or fairies. [C14: from OF *faerie* fairyland, from *feie* fairy, from L *Fāta* the Fates; see FATE, FAY]
▸ **'fairy-ˌlike** *adj*

fairy cycle *n* a child's bicycle.

fairyfloss ('fɛərɪˌflɒs) *n* the Australian word for **candyfloss.**

fairy godmother *n* a benefactress, esp. an unknown one.

fairyland ('fɛərɪˌlænd) *n* **1** the imaginary domain of the fairies. **2** a fantasy world, esp. one resulting from a person's wild imaginings.

fairy lights *pl n* small coloured electric bulbs strung together and used as decoration, esp. on a Christmas tree.

fairy penguin *n* a small penguin with a bluish head and back, found on the Australian coast. Also called: **little** or **blue penguin.**

fairy ring *n* a ring of dark luxuriant vegetation in grassy ground corresponding to the outer edge of an underground fungal mycelium.

fairy tale ❶ *or* **story** *n* **1** a story about fairies or other mythical or magical beings. **2** a highly improbable account.

fairy-tale *adj* **1** of or relating to a fairy tale. **2** resembling a fairy tale, esp. in being extremely happy or fortunate: *a fairy-tale ending.* **3** highly improbable: *a fairy-tale account.*

fait accompli *French.* (fɛt akɔ̃pli) *n, pl* ***faits accomplis*** (fɛz akɔ̃pli). something already done and beyond alteration. [lit.: accomplished fact]

faith ❶ (feɪθ) *n* **1** strong or unshakeable belief in something, esp. without proof. **2** a specific system of religious beliefs: *the Jewish faith.* **3** *Christianity.* trust in God and in his actions and promises. **4** a conviction of the truth of certain doctrines of religion. **5** complete confidence or trust in a person, remedy, etc. **6** loyalty, as to a person or cause (esp. in **keep faith, break faith**). **7 bad faith.** dishonesty. **8 good faith.** honesty. **9** *(modifier)* using or relating to the supposed ability to cure bodily ailments by means of religious faith: *a faith healer.* ◆ *interj* **10** *Arch.* indeed. [C12: from Anglo-F *feid,* from L *fidēs* trust, confidence]

faithful ❶ ('feɪθfʊl) *adj* **1** remaining true or loyal. **2** maintaining sexual loyalty to one's lover or spouse. **3** consistently reliable: *a faithful worker.* **4** reliable or truthful. **5** accurate in detail: *a faithful translation.* ◆ *n* **6 the faithful. 6a** the believers in a religious faith, esp. Christianity. **6b** any group of loyal and steadfast followers.
▸ **'faithfully** *adv* ▸ **'faithfulness** *n*

faithless ❶ ('feɪθlɪs) *adj* **1** unreliable or treacherous. **2** dishonest or disloyal. **3** lacking religious faith.
▸ **'faithlessness** *n*

fajitas (fə'hiːtəz) *pl n* a Mexican dish of soft tortillas wrapped round fried strips of meat, vegetables, etc. [Mexican Sp.]

fake ❶ (feɪk) *vb* **fakes, faking, faked. 1** *(tr)* to cause (something inferior or not genuine) to appear more valuable or real by fraud or pretence. **2**

THESAURUS

vance, nonperformance, nonsuccess, omission, remissness, stoppage **4 = breakdown,** decay, decline, deterioration, failing, loss **8 = bankruptcy,** crash, downfall, folding (*inf.*), insolvency, liquidation, ruin
Antonyms *n* ≠ **lack of success:** adequacy, effectiveness, success, triumph ≠ **shortcoming:** care, observance ≠ **bankruptcy:** fortune, prosperity

fain *adv Archaic* **1 = gladly,** as lief, as soon, cheerfully, eagerly, willingly ◆ *adj Obsolete* **2a = glad,** anxious, eager, well-pleased *Obsolete* **2b = compelled,** constrained, with no alternative but

faint *adj* **1 = dim,** bleached, delicate, distant, dull, faded, faltering, feeble, hazy, hushed, ill-defined, indistinct, light, low, muffled, muted, soft, subdued, thin, vague, whispered **2 = slight,** feeble, remote, unenthusiastic, weak **3 = dizzy,** drooping, enervated, exhausted, faltering, fatigued, giddy, languid, lethargic, light-headed, muzzy, vertiginous, weak, woozy (*inf.*) **4 = timid,** faint-hearted, lily-livered, spiritless, timorous ◆ *vb* **6 = pass out,** black out, collapse, fade, fail, flake out (*inf.*), keel over (*inf.*), languish, lose consciousness, swoon (*literary*), weaken ◆ *n* **8 = blackout,** collapse, swoon (*literary*), syncope (*Pathology*), unconsciousness
Antonyms *adj* ≠ **dim:** bright, clear, conspicuous, distinct, loud, powerful, strong ≠ **timid:** bold, brave, courageous ≠ **dizzy:** energetic, fresh, hearty, vigorous

faintly *adv* **1 = softly,** feebly, in a whisper, indistinctly, weakly

faintness *n* **1-3 = weakness,** dimness, dizziness, feebleness, giddiness, indistinctness, languor, loss of strength, shakiness

fair[1] *adj* **1, 2 = unbiased,** above board, according to the rules, clean, disinterested, dispassionate, equal, equitable, even-handed, honest, honourable, impartial, just, lawful, legitimate, objective, on the level (*inf.*), proper, square, trustworthy, unprejudiced, upright **3 = light,** blond, blonde, fair-haired, flaxen-haired, light-complexioned, tow-haired, towheaded **4 = beautiful,** beauteous, bonny, comely, handsome, lovely, pretty, well-favoured **5 = respectable,** adequate, all right, average, decent, mediocre, middling, moderate, not bad, O.K. *or* okay (*inf.*), passable, reasonable, satisfactory, so-so (*inf.*), tolerable **7, 8 = fine,** bright, clear, clement, cloudless, dry, favourable, sunny, sunshiny, unclouded **11 fair and square = just,** above board, correct, honest, kosher (*inf.*), on the level (*inf.*), straight
Antonyms *adj* ≠ **unbiased:** bad, biased, bigoted, discriminatory, dishonest, inequitable, one-sided, partial, partisan, prejudiced, unfair, unjust ≠ **beautiful:** homely, plain, ugly

fair[2] *n* **1-3 = carnival,** bazaar, expo (*inf.*), exposition, festival, fête, gala, market, show

fairly *adv* **1 = moderately,** adequately, pretty well, quite, rather, reasonably, somewhat, tolerably **2 = deservedly,** equitably, honestly, impartially, justly, objectively, properly, without fear or favour **3 = positively,** absolutely, in a manner of speaking, really, veritably

fair-minded *adj* **= impartial,** disinterested, even-handed, just, open-minded, unbiased, unprejudiced

fairness *n* **1, 2 = impartiality,** decency, disinterestedness, equitableness, equity, justice, legitimacy, rightfulness, uprightness

fairy *n* **1 = sprite,** brownie, elf, hob, leprechaun, peri, pixie, Robin Goodfellow

fairy tale *n* **1 = folk tale,** romance **2 = lie,** cock-and-bull story, fabrication, fantasy, fiction, invention, pork pie (*Brit. sl.*), porky (*Brit. sl.*), tall story, untruth

faith *n* **1, 4, 5 = confidence,** assurance, conviction, credence, credit, dependence, reliance, trust **2 = religion,** belief, church, communion, creed, denomination, dogma, persuasion **6 = allegiance,** constancy, faithfulness, fealty, fidelity, loyalty, troth (*arch.*), truth, truthfulness **8 good faith = honesty,** honour, pledge, promise, sincerity, vow, word, word of honour
Antonyms *n* ≠ **confidence:** apprehension, denial, disbelief, distrust, doubt, incredulity, misgiving, mistrust, rejection, scepticism, suspicion, uncertainty ≠ **religion:** agnosticism ≠ **allegiance:** infidelity

faithful *adj* **1, 3, 4 = loyal,** attached, constant, dependable, devoted, immovable, reliable, staunch, steadfast, true, true-blue, trusty, truthful, unswerving, unwavering **5 = accurate,** close, exact, just, precise, strict, true **6 the faithful = believers,** adherents, brethren, communicants, congregation, followers, the elect
Antonyms *adj* ≠ **loyal:** disloyal, doubting, faithless, false, false-hearted, fickle, inconstant, perfidious, recreant (*arch.*), traitorous, treacherous, unbelieving, unfaithful, unreliable, untrue, untrustworthy, untruthful

faithfulness *n* **1, 3, 4 = loyalty,** adherence, constancy, dependability, devotion, fealty, fidelity, trustworthiness **5 = accuracy,** closeness, exactness, justice, strictness, truth

faithless *adj* **1-3 = disloyal,** doubting, false, false-hearted, fickle, inconstant, perfidious, recreant (*arch.*), traitorous, treacherous, unbelieving, unfaithful, unreliable, untrue, untrustworthy, untruthful

faithlessness *n* **1, 2 = disloyalty,** betrayal, fickleness, inconstancy, infidelity, perfidy, treachery, unfaithfulness

fake *vb* **1, 2 = sham,** affect, assume, copy, counterfeit, fabricate, feign, forge, pretend, put on, simulate ◆ *n* **3 = impostor,** charlatan, copy,

to pretend to have (an illness, emotion, etc.). ◆ *n* **3** an object, person, or act that is not genuine; sham. ◆ *adj* **4** not genuine. [C18: prob. ult. from It. *facciare* to make or do]
▸ **'faker** *n* ▸ **'fakery** *n*

fakir ('feɪkɪə, fə'kɪə) *n* **1** a member of any religious order of Islam. **2** a Hindu ascetic mendicant. [C17: from Ar. *faqīr* poor]

falafel *or* **felafel** (fə'lɑ:fəl) *n* a ball or cake of ground spiced chickpeas, deep-fried and often served with pitta bread. [C20: from Arabic *felāfil*]

Falange ('fælændʒ) *n* the Fascist movement founded in Spain in 1933. [Sp.: PHALANX]
▸ **Fa'langist** *n, adj*

falcate ('fælkeɪt) *or* **falciform** ('fælsɪˌfɔ:m) *adj Biol.* shaped like a sickle. [C19: from L *falcātus*, from *falx* sickle]

falchion ('fɔ:ltʃən, 'fɔ:lʃən) *n* **1** a short and slightly curved medieval sword. **2** an archaic word for **sword.** [C14: from It., from *falce*, from L *falx* sickle]

falcon ('fɔ:lkən, 'fɔ:kən) *n* **1** a diurnal bird of prey such as the gyrfalcon, peregrine falcon, etc., having pointed wings and a long tail. **2a** any of these or related birds, trained to hunt small game. **2b** the female of such a bird (cf. **tercel**). [C13: from OF, from LL *falcō* hawk, prob. of Gmc origin; ? rel. to L *falx* sickle]

falconet ('fɔ:lkəˌnɛt, 'fɔ:kə-) *n* **1** any of various small falcons. **2** a small light cannon used from the 15th to 17th centuries.

falconry ('fɔ:lkənrɪ, 'fɔ:kən-) *n* the art of keeping falcons and training them to return from flight to a lure or to hunt quarry.
▸ **'falconer** *n*

falderal ('fældəˌræl) *or* **folderol** ('fɒldəˌrɒl) *n* **1** a showy but worthless trifle. **2** foolish nonsense. **3** a nonsensical refrain in old songs.

faldstool ('fɔ:ldˌstu:l) *n* a backless seat, sometimes capable of being folded, used by bishops and certain other prelates. [C11 *fyldestol*, prob. a translation of Med. L *faldistolium* folding stool, of Gmc origin; cf. OHG *faldstuol*]

fall Ⓣ (fɔ:l) *vb* **falls, falling, fell, fallen.** (*mainly intr*) **1** to descend by the force of gravity from a higher to a lower place. **2** to drop suddenly from an erect position. **3** to collapse to the ground, esp. in pieces. **4** to become less or lower in number, quality, etc.: *prices fell.* **5** to become lower in pitch. **6** to extend downwards: *her hair fell to her waist.* **7** to be badly wounded or killed. **8** to slope in a downward direction. **9** to yield to temptation or sin. **10** to diminish in status, estimation, etc. **11** to yield to attack: *the city fell under the assault.* **12** to lose power: *the government fell after the riots.* **13** to pass into or take on a specified condition: *to fall asleep.* **14** to adopt a despondent expression: *her face fell.* **15** to be averted: *her gaze fell.* **16** to come by chance or presumption: *suspicion fell on the butler.* **17** to occur; take place: *night fell.* **18** (foll. by *back, behind,* etc.) to move in a specified direction. **19** to occur at a specified place: *the accent falls on the last syllable.* **20** (foll. by *to*) to be inherited (by): *the estate falls to the eldest son.* **21** (often foll. by *into, under,* etc.) to be classified: *the subject falls into two main areas.* **22** to issue forth: *a curse fell from her lips.* **23** (*tr*) *Dialect, Austral. & NZ.* to fell (trees). **24** *Cricket.* (of a batsman's wicket) to be taken by the bowling side: *the sixth wicket fell for 96.* **25 fall short. 25a** to prove inadequate. **25b** (often foll. by *of*) to fail to reach or measure up to (a standard). ◆ *n* **26** an act or instance of falling. **27** something that falls: *a fall of snow.* **28** *Chiefly US.* autumn. **29** the distance that something falls: *a hundred-foot fall.* **30** a sudden drop from an upright position. **31** (*often pl*) **31a** a waterfall or cataract. **31b** (*cap. when part of a name*): *Niagara Falls.* **32** a downward slope or decline. **33** a decrease in value, number, etc. **34** a decline in status or importance. **35** a capture or overthrow: *the fall of the city.* **36** *Machinery, naut.* the end of a tackle to which power is applied to hoist it. **37** Also called: **pinfall.** *Wrestling.* a scoring move, pinning both shoulders of one's opponent to the floor for a specified period. **38a** the birth of an animal. **38b** the animals produced at a single birth. ◆ See also **fall about, fall away,** etc. [OE *feallan*: cf. FELL[2]]

Fall (fɔ:l) *n* **the.** *Theol.* Adam's sin of disobedience and the state of innate sinfulness ensuing from this for himself and all mankind.

fall about *vb* (*intr, adv*) to laugh in an uncontrolled manner: *we fell about at the sight.*

fallacious Ⓣ (fə'leɪʃəs) *adj* **1** containing or involving a fallacy. **2** tending to mislead. **3** delusive or disappointing.
▸ **fal'laciously** *adv*

fallacy Ⓣ ('fæləsɪ) *n, pl* **fallacies. 1** an incorrect or misleading notion or opinion based on inaccurate facts or invalid reasoning. **2** unsound reasoning. **3** the tendency to mislead. **4** *Logic.* an error in reasoning that renders an argument logically invalid. [C15: from L, from *fallax* deceitful, from *fallere* to deceive]

fall apart Ⓣ *vb* (*intr adv*) **1** to break owing to long use or poor construction: *the chassis is falling apart.* **2** to become disorganized and ineffective: *since you resigned, the office has fallen apart.*

fall away *vb* (*intr, adv*) **1** (of friendship, etc.) to be withdrawn. **2** to slope down.

fall back Ⓣ *vb* (*intr, adv*) **1** to recede or retreat. **2** (foll. by *on* or *upon*) to have recourse (to). ◆ *n* **fall-back. 3** a retreat. **4** a reserve, esp. money, that can be called upon in need. **5a** anything to which one can have recourse as a second choice. **5b** (*as modifier*): *a fall-back position.*

fall behind Ⓣ *vb* (*intr, adv*) **1** to drop back; fail to keep up. **2** to be in arrears, as with a payment.

fall down Ⓣ *vb* (*intr, adv*) **1** to drop suddenly or collapse. **2** (often foll. by *on*) *Inf.* to fail.

fallen Ⓣ ('fɔ:lən) *vb* **1** the past participle of **fall.** ◆ *adj* **2** having sunk in reputation or honour: *a fallen woman.* **3** killed in battle with glory.

fallen arch *n* collapse of the arch formed by the instep of the foot, resulting in flat feet.

fall for Ⓣ *vb* (*intr, prep*) **1** to become infatuated with (a person). **2** to allow oneself to be deceived by (a lie, trick, etc.).

fall guy *n Inf.* **1** a person who is the victim of a confidence trick. **2** a scapegoat.

fallible Ⓣ ('fælɪbᵊl) *adj* **1** capable of being mistaken. **2** liable to mislead. [C15: from Med. L *fallibilis*, from L *fallere* to deceive]
▸ **ˌfalli'bility** *n*

fall in Ⓣ *vb* (*intr, adv*) **1** to collapse. **2** to adopt a military formation, esp. as a soldier taking his place in a line. **3** (of a lease) to expire. **4** (often foll. by *with*) **4a** to meet and join. **4b** to agree with or support a person, suggestion, etc.

falling sickness *or* **evil** *n* a former name (nontechnical) for **epilepsy.**

falling star *n* an informal name for **meteor.**

fall off Ⓣ *vb* (*intr*) **1** to drop unintentionally to the ground from (a high object, bicycle, etc.), esp. after losing one's balance. **2** (*adv*) to diminish in size, intensity, etc. ◆ *n* **fall-off. 3** a decline or drop.

fall on Ⓣ *vb* (*intr, prep*) **1** Also: **fall upon.** to attack or snatch (an army,

THESAURUS

forgery, fraud, hoax, imitation, mountebank, phoney *or* phony (*inf.*), reproduction, sham ◆ *adj* **4 = artificial**, affected, assumed, counterfeit, false, forged, imitation, mock, phoney *or* phony (*inf.*), pinchbeck, pseudo (*inf.*), reproduction, sham
Antonyms *adj* ≠ **artificial:** actual, authentic, bona fide, faithful, genuine, honest, legitimate, real, true, veritable

faker *n* **1, 2 = fraud**, fake, humbug, impostor, phoney *or* phony (*inf.*), pretender, sham

fall *vb* **1-3 = descend**, be precipitated, cascade, collapse, come a cropper (*inf.*), crash, dive, drop, drop down, go head over heels, keel over, nose-dive, pitch, plummet, plunge, settle, sink, stumble, subside, topple, trip, trip over, tumble **4 = decrease**, abate, become lower, decline, depreciate, diminish, drop, dwindle, ebb, fall off, flag, go down, lessen, slump, subside **7 = die**, be a casualty, be killed, be lost, be slain, meet one's end, perish **8 = slope**, fall away, incline, incline downwards **9 = lapse**, backslide, err, go astray, offend, sin, transgress, trespass, yield to temptation **11 = be overthrown**, be taken, capitulate, give in *or* up, give way, go out of office, pass into enemy hands, resign, succumb, surrender, yield **17 = occur**, become, befall, chance, come about, come to pass, fall out, happen, take place **25 fall short = be lacking**, be deficient, be wanting, disappoint, fail, fall down on (*inf.*), miss, not come up to expectations *or* scratch (*inf.*), prove inadequate ◆ *n* **26, 30 = descent**, dive, drop, nose dive, plummet, plunge, slip, spill, tumble **31** *often plural* **= waterfall**, cascade, cataract, force (*N English dialect*), linn (*Scot.*), rapids **32 = slope**, declivity, descent, downgrade, incline, slant **33 = decrease**, cut, decline, diminution, dip, drop, dwindling, falling off, lessening, lowering, reduction, slump **35 = collapse**, capitulation, death, defeat, destruction, downfall, failure, overthrow, resignation, ruin, surrender
Antonyms *vb* ≠ **descend:** ascend, climb, go up, increase, mount, rise, scale, soar ≠ **decrease:** advance, appreciate, climb, escalate, extend, heighten, increase, wax ≠ **die:** endure, hold out, survive ≠ **be overthrown:** prevail, triumph

fallacious *adj* **1-3 = incorrect**, deceptive, delusive, delusory, erroneous, false, fictitious, illogical, illusory, misleading, mistaken, sophistic, sophistical, spurious, untrue, wrong

fallacy *n* **1, 2 = error**, casuistry, deceit, deception, delusion, falsehood, faultiness, flaw, illusion, inconsistency, misapprehension, misconception, mistake, sophism, sophistry, untruth

fall apart *vb* **1 = break up**, come apart at the seams, crumble, disband, disintegrate, disperse, dissolve, fall to bits, go *or* come to pieces, go to seed, lose cohesion, shatter

fall back *vb* **1 = retreat**, back off, draw back, recede, recoil, retire, withdraw **2** *foll. by* **on** *or* **upon = resort to**, call upon, employ, have recourse to, make use of, press into service

fall behind *vb* **1 = lag**, drop back, get left behind, lose one's place, trail **2 = be in arrears**

fall down *vb* **2 = fail**, disappoint, fail to make the grade, fall short, go wrong, prove unsuccessful

fallen *adj* **2 = dishonoured**, disgraced, immoral, loose, lost, ruined, shamed, sinful, unchaste **3 = killed**, dead, lost, perished, slain, slaughtered

fall for *vb* **1 = fall in love with**, become infatuated with, desire, lose one's head over, succumb to the charms of **2 = be fooled by**, accept, be deceived by, be duped by, be taken in by, buy (*sl.*), give credence to, swallow (*inf.*), take on board

fallible *adj* **1 = imperfect**, erring, frail, ignorant, mortal, prone to error, uncertain, weak
Antonyms *adj* divine, faultless, impeccable, infallible, omniscient, perfect, superhuman, unerring, unimpeachable

fall in *vb* **1 = collapse**, cave in, come down about one's ears, fall apart at the seams, sink **4b** *often foll. by* **with = go along with**, accept, agree with, assent, buy into (*inf.*), concur with, cooperate with, support, take on board

fall off *vb* **1 = tumble**, be unseated, come a cropper *or* purler (*inf.*), plummet, take a fall *or* tumble, topple **2 = decrease**, decline, diminish, drop, dwindle, ebb away, fade, fall away, go down *or* downhill, lessen, peter out, reduce, shrink, slacken, slump, subside, tail off (*inf.*), wane, weaken
Antonyms *vb* ≠ **decrease:** improve, increase, pick up, rally, recover, revive

fall on *vb* **1 = attack**, assail, assault, belabour,

booty, etc.). **2 fall on one's feet.** to emerge unexpectedly well from a difficult situation.

Fallopian tube (fəˈləʊpɪən) *n* either of a pair of slender tubes through which ova pass from the ovaries to the uterus in female mammals. [C18: after Gabriello *Fallopio* (1523–62), It. anatomist who first described the tubes]

fallout ❶ (ˈfɔːlˌaʊt) *n* **1** the descent of radioactive material following a nuclear explosion. **2** any particles that so descend. **3** secondary consequences. ◆ *vb* **fall out.** (*intr, adv*) **4** *Inf.* to disagree. **5** (*intr*) to occur. **6** *Mil.* to leave a disciplinary formation.

fallow[1] ❶ (ˈfæləʊ) *adj* **1** (of land) left unseeded after being ploughed to regain fertility for a crop. **2** (of an idea, etc.) undeveloped, but potentially useful. ◆ *n* **3** land treated in this way. ◆ *vb* **4** (*tr*) to leave (land) unseeded after ploughing it. [OE *fealga*]
▸ **ˈfallowness** *n*

fallow[2] (ˈfæləʊ) *n, adj* (of) a light yellowish-brown colour. [OE *fealu*]

fallow deer *n* either of two species of deer, one of which is native to the Mediterranean region and the other to Persia. The summer coat is reddish with white spots.

fall through ❶ *vb* (*intr, adv*) to fail.

fall to ❶ *vb* (*intr*) **1** (*adv*) to begin some activity, as eating, working, or fighting. **2** (*prep*) to devolve on (a person): *the task fell to me.*

false ❶ (fɔːls) *adj* **1** not in accordance with the truth or facts. **2** irregular or invalid: *a false start.* **3** untruthful or lying: *a false account.* **4** artificial; fake: *false teeth.* **5** being or intended to be misleading or deceptive: *a false rumour.* **6** treacherous: *a false friend.* **7** based on mistaken or irrelevant ideas or facts: *a false argument.* **8** (*prenominal*) (esp. of plants) superficially resembling the species specified: *false hellebore.* **9** serving to supplement or replace, often temporarily: *a false keel.* **10** *Music.* (of a note, interval, etc.) out of tune. ◆ *adv* **11** in a false or dishonest manner (esp. in **play (someone) false**). [OE *fals*]
▸ **ˈfalsely** *adv* ▸ **ˈfalseness** *n*

false colour *n* colour used in a computer or photographic display to help in interpreting the image, as in the use of red to show high temperatures and blue to show low temperatures in an infrared image converter.

false dawn *n* light appearing just before sunrise.

false diamond *n* any of a number of semiprecious stones that resemble diamond, such as zircon and white topaz.

falsehood ❶ (ˈfɔːlsˌhʊd) *n* **1** the quality of being untrue. **2** an untrue statement; lie. **3** the act of deceiving or lying.

false imprisonment *n Law.* the restraint of a person's liberty without lawful authority.

false pretences *pl n* a misrepresentation used to obtain anything, such as trust or affection (esp. in **under false pretences**).

false ribs *pl n* any of the lower five pairs of ribs in man, not attached directly to the breastbone.

false step *n* **1** an unwise action. **2** a stumble; slip.

falsetto (fɔːlˈsɛtəʊ) *n, pl* **falsettos.** a form of vocal production used by male singers to extend their range upwards by limiting the vibration of the vocal cords. [C18: from It., from *falso* false]

falsies (ˈfɔːlsɪz) *pl n Inf.* pads of soft material, such as foam rubber, worn to exaggerate the size of a woman's breasts.

falsify ❶ (ˈfɔːlsɪˌfaɪ) *vb* **falsifies, falsifying, falsified.** (*tr*) **1** to make (a report, evidence, etc.) false or inaccurate by alteration, esp. in order to deceive. **2** to prove false. [C15: from OF, from LL, from L *falsus* FALSE + *facere* to do, make]
▸ **ˈfalsiˌfiable** *adj* ▸ **falsification** (ˌfɔːlsɪfɪˈkeɪʃən) *n*

falsity ❶ (ˈfɔːlsɪtɪ) *n, pl* **falsities. 1** the state of being false or untrue. **2** a lie or deception.

Falstaffian (fɔːlˈstɑːfɪən) *adj* jovial, plump, and dissolute. [C19: after Sir John *Falstaff,* a character in Shakespeare's play *Henry IV*]

falter ❶ (ˈfɔːltə) *vb* **1** (*intr*) to be hesitant, weak, or unsure. **2** (*intr*) to move unsteadily or hesitantly. **3** to utter haltingly or hesitantly. ◆ *n* **4** hesitancy in speech or action. **5** a quavering sound. [C14: prob. from ON]
▸ **ˈfalterer** *n* ▸ **ˈfalteringly** *adv*

fame ❶ (feɪm) *n* **1** the state of being widely known or recognized. **2** *Arch.* rumour or public report. ◆ *vb* **fames, faming, famed. 3** (*tr; now usually passive*) to make famous: *he was famed for his ruthlessness.* [C13: from L *fāma* report; rel. to *fārī* to say]

familial (fəˈmɪlɪəl) *adj* **1** of or relating to the family. **2** occurring in the members of a family: *a familial disease.*

familiar ❶ (fəˈmɪlɪə) *adj* **1** well-known: *a familiar figure.* **2** frequent or customary: *a familiar excuse.* **3** (*postpositive;* foll. by *with*) acquainted. **4** friendly; informal. **5** close; intimate. **6** more intimate than is acceptable; presumptuous. ◆ *n* **7** Also called: **familiar spirit.** a supernatural spirit supposed to attend and aid a witch, wizard, etc. **8** a person attached to the household of the pope or a bishop, who renders service in return for support. **9** a friend. [C14: from L *familiāris* domestic, from *familia* FAMILY]
▸ **faˈmiliarly** *adv* ▸ **faˈmiliarness** *n*

familiarity ❶ (fəˌmɪlɪˈærɪtɪ) *n, pl* **familiarities. 1** knowledge, as of a subject or place. **2** close acquaintanceship. **3** undue intimacy. **4** (*sometimes pl*) an instance of unwarranted intimacy.

familiarize ❶ *or* **familiarise** (fəˈmɪljəˌraɪz) *vb* **familiarizes, familiarizing, familiarized** *or* **familiarises, familiarising, familiarised.** (*tr*) **1** to make (oneself or someone else) familiar, as with a particular subject. **2** to make (something) generally known.
▸ **faˌmiliariˈzation** *or* **faˌmiliariˈzatiˈsation** *n*

famille *French.* (famij) *n* a type of Chinese porcelain characterized either by a design on a background of yellow (***famille jaune***) or black (***famille noire***) or by a design in which the predominant colour is pink (***famille rose***) or green (***famille verte***). [C19: lit.: family]

family ❶ (ˈfæmɪlɪ, ˈfæmlɪ) *n, pl* **families. 1a** a primary social group consisting of parents and their offspring. **1b** (*as modifier*): *a family unit.* **2** one's wife or husband and one's children. **3** one's children, as distinguished from one's husband or wife. **4** a group descended from a common ancestor. **5** all the persons living together in one household.

THESAURUS

descend upon, lay into, pitch into (*inf.*), set upon *or* about, snatch, tear into (*inf.*)

fall out *vb* **4** *Informal* = **argue**, altercate, clash, come to blows, differ, disagree, fight, quarrel, squabble **5** = **happen**, chance, come to pass, occur, pan out (*inf.*), result, take place, turn out

fallow[1] *adj* **1** = **uncultivated**, dormant, idle, inactive, inert, resting, undeveloped, unplanted, untilled, unused

fall through *vb* = **fail**, come to nothing, fizzle out (*inf.*), go by the board, miscarry

fall to *vb* **1** = **begin**, apply oneself to, commence, set about, start **2** = **be the responsibility of**, be up to, come down to, devolve upon

false *adj* **1, 2** = **incorrect**, concocted, erroneous, faulty, fictitious, improper, inaccurate, inexact, invalid, mistaken, unfounded, unreal, wrong **3** = **untrue**, lying, mendacious, truthless, unreliable, unsound, untrustworthy, untruthful **4** = **artificial**, bogus, counterfeit, ersatz, fake, feigned, forged, imitation, mock, pretended, pseudo (*inf.*), sham, simulated, spurious, synthetic **5, 7** = **deceptive**, deceitful, deceiving, delusive, fallacious, fraudulent, hypocritical, misleading, trumped up **6** = **treacherous**, dishonest, dishonourable, disloyal, double-dealing, duplicitous, faithless, false-hearted, hypocritical, perfidious, treasonable, two-faced, unfaithful, untrustworthy ◆ *adv* **11 play (someone) false** = **deceive**, betray, cheat, double-cross, give the Judas kiss to, sell down the river (*inf.*), stab in the back

Antonyms *adj* ≠ **incorrect:** correct, exact, right, sound, valid ≠ **untrue:** reliable, true ≠ **artificial:** authentic, bona fide, genuine, honest, kosher (*inf.*), real, sincere ≠ **treacherous:** faithful, loyal, trustworthy

falsehood *n* **1, 3** = **untruthfulness**, deceit, deception, dishonesty, dissimulation, inveracity (*rare*), mendacity, perjury, prevarication **2** = **lie**, fabrication, fib, fiction, misstatement, pork pie (*Brit. sl.*), porky (*Brit. sl.*), story, untruth

falsification *n* **1** = **misrepresentation**, adulteration, deceit, dissimulation, distortion, forgery, perversion, tampering with

falsify *vb* **1** = **alter**, belie, cook (*sl.*), counterfeit, distort, doctor, fake, forge, garble, misrepresent, misstate, pervert, tamper with

falsity *n* **1** = **untruth**, deceit, deceptiveness, dishonesty, double-dealing, duplicity, fraudulence, hypocrisy, inaccuracy, mendacity, perfidy, treachery, unreality **2** = **lie**, cheating, deception, fraud, pork pie (*Brit. sl.*), porky (*Brit. sl.*)

falter *vb* **1-3** = **hesitate**, break, shake, speak haltingly, stammer, stumble, stutter, totter, tremble, vacillate, waver

Antonyms *vb* continue, endure, keep going, last, persevere, persist, proceed, stand firm, stick at, survive

faltering *adj* **1-3** = **hesitant**, broken, irresolute, stammering, tentative, timid, uncertain, weak

fame *n* **1** = **prominence**, celebrity, credit, eminence, glory, honour, illustriousness, name, public esteem, renown, reputation, repute, stardom

Antonyms *n* disgrace, dishonour, disrepute, ignominy, infamy, oblivion, obscurity, shame

famed *adj* **1** = **renowned**, acclaimed, celebrated, recognized, widely-known

familiar *adj* **1, 2** = **well-known**, accustomed, common, common or garden (*inf.*), conventional, customary, domestic, everyday, frequent, household, mundane, ordinary, recognizable, repeated, routine, stock **3** *foll. by* **with** = **acquainted with**, abreast of, at home with, *au courant with, au fait with,* aware of, conscious of, conversant with, introduced to, knowledgeable about, no stranger to, on speaking terms with, versed in, well up in **4, 5** = **friendly**, amicable, buddy-buddy, chummy (*inf.*), close, confidential, cordial, easy, free, free-and-easy, hail-fellow-well-met, informal, intimate, near, open, palsy-walsy (*inf.*), relaxed, unceremonious, unconstrained, unreserved **6** = **disrespectful**, bold, forward, impudent, intrusive, overfree, presuming, presumptuous

Antonyms *adj* ≠ **well-known:** infrequent, unaccustomed, uncommon, unfamiliar, unknown, unusual ≠ **acquainted with:** ignorant, unaccustomed, unacquainted, unfamiliar, uninformed, unskilled ≠ **friendly:** aloof, cold, detached, distant, formal, unfriendly

familiarity *n* **1** = **acquaintance**, acquaintanceship, awareness, experience, grasp, knowledge, understanding **2** = **friendliness**, absence of reserve, closeness, ease, fellowship, freedom, friendship, informality, intimacy, naturalness, openness, sociability, unceremoniousness **3, 4** = **disrespect**, boldness, forwardness, liberties, liberty, presumption

Antonyms *n* ≠ **acquaintance:** ignorance, inexperience, unfamiliarity ≠ **friendliness:** distance, formality, reserve ≠ **disrespect:** constraint, decorum, propriety, respect

familiarize *vb* **1** = **accustom**, bring into common use, coach, get to know (about), habituate, instruct, inure, make conversant, make used to, prime, school, season, train

family *n* **1-3, 5** = **relations**, brood, children, descendants, folk (*inf.*), household, issue, kin, kindred, kinsfolk, kinsmen, kith and kin, ménage, offspring, one's nearest and dearest, one's own flesh and blood, people, progeny, relatives **4** = **clan**, ancestors, ancestry, birth, blood, descent, dynasty, extraction, forebears, forefathers, ge-

6 any group of related things or beings, esp. when scientifically categorized. 7 *Biol.* any of the taxonomic groups into which an order is divided and which contains one or more genera. 8 a group of historically related languages assumed to derive from one original language. 9 *Maths.* a group of curves or surfaces whose equations differ from a given equation only in the values assigned to one or more constants. 10 **in the family way.** *Inf.* pregnant. [C15: from L *familia* a household, servants of the house, from *famulus* servant]

family allowance *n* 1 (in Britain) a former name for **child benefit.** 2 (*caps.*) the Canadian equivalent of **child benefit.**

family Bible *n* a large Bible in which births, marriages, and deaths of the members of a family are recorded.

Family Compact *n Canad.* 1 **the.** the ruling oligarchy in Upper Canada in the early 19th century. 2 (*often not cap.*) any influential clique.

family credit *n* (in Britain) a means-tested allowance paid to families who have at least one dependent child and whose earnings from full-time work are low. It replaced **family income supplement.**

family man *n* a man who is married and has children, esp. one who is devoted to his family.

family name *n* a surname, esp. when regarded as representing the family honour.

family planning *n* the control of the number of children in a family and of the intervals between them, esp. by the use of contraceptives.

family support *n NZ.* a means-tested allowance for families in need.

family therapy *n* a form of psychotherapy in which the members of a family participate, with the aim of improving communications between them and the ways in which they relate to each other.

family tree ➊ *n* a chart showing the genealogical relationships and lines of descent of a family. Also called: **genealogical tree.**

famine ➊ ('fæmɪn) *n* 1 a severe shortage of food, as through crop failure or overpopulation. 2 acute shortage of anything. 3 violent hunger. [C14: from OF, via Vulgar L, from L *famēs* hunger]

famish ➊ ('fæmɪʃ) *vb* (*now usually passive*) to be or make very hungry or weak. [C14: from OF, from L *famēs* FAMINE]

famous ➊ ('feɪməs) *adj* 1 known to or recognized by many people. 2 *Inf.* excellent; splendid. [C14: from L *fāmōsus;* see FAME]
▸ **'famously** *adv* ▸ **'famousness** *n*

fan[1] ➊ (fæn) *n* 1 any device for creating a current of air by movement of a surface or number of surfaces, esp. a rotating device consisting of a number of blades attached to a central hub. 2 any of various hand-agitated devices for cooling oneself, esp. a collapsible semicircular series of flat segments of paper, ivory, etc. 3 something shaped like such a fan, such as the tail of certain birds. 4 *Agriculture.* a kind of basket formerly used for winnowing grain. ◆ *vb* **fans, fanning, fanned.** (*mainly tr*) 5 to cause a current of air to blow upon, as by means of a fan: *to fan one's face.* 6 to agitate or move (air, etc.) with or as if with a fan. 7 to make fiercer, more ardent, etc.: *fan one's passion.* 8 (*also intr; often foll. by out*) to spread out or cause to spread out in the shape of a fan. 9 to winnow (grain) by blowing the chaff away from it. [OE *fann,* from L *vannus*]
▸ **'fanlike** *adj* ▸ **'fanner** *n*

fan[2] ➊ (fæn) *n* 1 an ardent admirer of a pop star, football team, etc. 2 a devotee of a sport, hobby, etc. [C17, re-formed C19: from FAN(ATIC)]

Fanagalo ('fænəgələʊ) *or* **Fanakalo** *n* (in South Africa) a Zulu-based pidgin with English and Afrikaans components. [C20: from Fanagalo *fana ga lo,* lit.: to be like this]

fanatic ➊ (fə'nætɪk) *n* 1 a person whose enthusiasm or zeal for something is extreme or beyond normal limits. 2 *Inf.* a person devoted to a particular hobby or pastime. ◆ *adj* 3 a variant of **fanatical.** [C16: from L *fānāticus* belonging to a temple, hence, inspired by a god, frenzied, from *fānum* temple]

fanatical ➊ (fə'nætɪkəl) *adj* surpassing what is normal or accepted in enthusiasm for or belief in something.
▸ **fa'natically** *adv*

fanaticism ➊ (fə'nætɪˌsɪzəm) *n* wildly excessive or irrational devotion, dedication, or enthusiasm.

fan belt *n* the belt that drives a cooling fan in a car engine.

fancied ('fænsɪd) *adj* 1 imaginary; unreal. 2 thought likely to win or succeed: *a fancied runner.*

fancier ➊ ('fænsɪə) *n* 1 a person with a special interest in something. 2 a person who breeds special varieties of plants or animals: *a pigeon fancier.*

fanciful ➊ ('fænsɪfʊl) *adj* 1 not based on fact: *fanciful notions.* 2 made or designed in a curious, intricate, or imaginative way. 3 indulging in or influenced by fancy.
▸ **'fancifully** *adv* ▸ **'fancifulness** *n*

fan club *n* 1 an organized group of admirers of a particular pop singer, film star, etc. 2 **be a member of someone's fan club.** *Inf.* to approve of someone strongly.

fancy ➊ ('fænsɪ) *adj* **fancier, fanciest.** 1 ornamented or decorative: *fancy clothes.* 2 requiring skill to perform: *a fancy dance routine.* 3 capricious or illusory. 4 (often used ironically) superior in quality. 5 higher than expected: *fancy prices.* 6 (of a domestic animal) bred for particular qualities. ◆ *n, pl* **fancies.** 7 a sudden capricious idea. 8 a sudden or irrational liking for a person or thing. 9 the power to conceive and represent decorative and novel imagery, esp. in poetry. 10 an idea or thing produced by this. 11 a mental image. 12 *Music.* a composition for solo lute, keyboard, etc., current during the 16th and 17th centuries. 13 **the fancy.** *Arch.* those who follow a particular sport, esp. prize fighting. ◆ *vb* **fancies, fancying, fancied.** (*tr*) 14 to picture in the imagination. 15 to imagine: *I fancy it will rain.* 16 (*often used with a negative*) to like: *I don't fancy your chances!* 17 (*reflexive*) to have a high or ill-founded opinion of oneself. 18 *Inf.* to have a wish for: *she fancied some chocolate.* 19 *Brit. inf.* to be physically attracted to (another person). 20 to breed (animals) for particular characteristics. ◆ *interj* 21 Also: **fancy that!** an exclamation of surprise. [C15 *fantsy,* shortened from *fantasie;* see FANTASY]
▸ **'fancily** *adv* ▸ **'fanciness** *n*

fancy dress *n* **a** costume worn at masquerades, etc., representing an historical figure, etc. **b** (*as modifier*): *a fancy-dress ball.*

fancy-free *adj* having no commitments.

fancy goods *pl n* small decorative gifts.

fancy man *n Sl.* 1 a woman's lover. 2 a pimp.

fancy woman *n Sl.* a mistress or prostitute.

fancywork ('fænsɪˌwɜːk) *n* any ornamental needlework, such as embroidery or crochet.

fan dance *n* a dance in which large fans are manipulated in front of the body, partially revealing or suggesting nakedness.

fandangle (fæn'dæŋgəl) *n Inf.* 1 elaborate ornament. 2 nonsense. [C19: ?from FANDANGO]

fandango (fæn'dæŋgəʊ) *n, pl* **fandangos.** 1 an old Spanish courtship dance in triple time. 2 a piece of music composed for or in the rhythm of this dance. [C18: from Sp., from ?]

fane (feɪn) *n Arch. or poetic.* a temple or shrine. [C14: from L *fānum*]

fanfare ➊ ('fænfɛə) *n* 1 a flourish or short tune played on brass instruments. 2 an ostentatious flourish or display. [C17: from F, back formation from *fanfarer,* from Sp, from *fanfarron* boaster, from Ar. *farfār* garrulous]

fang ➊ (fæŋ) *n* 1 the long pointed hollow or grooved tooth of a venom-

THESAURUS

nealogy, house, line, lineage, parentage, pedigree, race, sept, stemma, stirps, strain, tribe 6 = **group**, class, classification, genre, kind, network, subdivision, system

family tree *n* = **lineage**, ancestry, extraction, genealogy, line, line of descent, pedigree, stemma, stirps

famine *n* 1, 2 = **hunger**, dearth, destitution, scarcity, starvation

famished *adj* = **starving**, ravening, ravenous, starved, voracious

famous *adj* 1 = **well-known**, acclaimed, celebrated, conspicuous, distinguished, eminent, excellent, far-famed, glorious, honoured, illustrious, legendary, lionized, much-publicized, notable, noted, prominent, remarkable, renowned, signal
Antonyms *adj* forgotten, mediocre, obscure, uncelebrated, undistinguished, unexceptional, unknown, unremarkable

fan[1] *n* 1, 2 = **blower**, air conditioner, blade, propeller, punkah (*in India*), vane, ventilator ◆ *vb* 5, 6 = **blow**, air-condition, air-cool, cool, refresh, ventilate, winnow (*rare*) 7 = **stimulate**, add fuel to the flames, agitate, arouse, enkindle, excite, impassion, increase, provoke, rouse, stir up, whip up, work up 8 *often foll. by* **out** = **spread out**, disperse, lay out, open out, space out, spread, unfurl

fan[2] *n* 1, 2 = **supporter**, addict, adherent, admirer, aficionado, buff (*inf.*), devotee, enthusiast, fiend (*inf.*), follower, freak (*inf.*), groupie (*sl.*), lover, rooter (*US*), zealot

fanatic *n* 1, 2 = **extremist**, activist, addict, bigot, buff (*inf.*), devotee, energumen, enthusiast, militant, visionary, zealot

fanatical *adj* = **obsessive**, bigoted, burning, enthusiastic, extreme, fervent, frenzied, immoderate, mad, overenthusiastic, passionate, rabid, visionary, wild, zealous

fanaticism *n* = **immoderation**, bigotry, dedication, devotion, enthusiasm, extremism, infatuation, madness, monomania, obsessiveness, overenthusiasm, single-mindedness, zeal, zealotry

fancier *n* 1, 2 = **expert**, aficionado, amateur, breeder, connoisseur

fanciful *adj* 1, 3 = **unreal**, capricious, chimerical, curious, extravagant, fabulous, fairytale, fantastic, ideal, imaginary, imaginative, mythical, poetic, romantic, visionary, whimsical, wild
Antonyms *adj* conventional, down-to-earth, dry, dull, literal, matter of fact, ordinary, pedestrian, predictable, routine, sensible, sober, unimaginative, uninspired

fancy *adj* 1 = **elaborate**, baroque, decorated, decorative, elegant, embellished, extravagant, fanciful, intricate, ornamental, ornamented, ornate 3 = **illusory**, capricious, chimerical, delusive, fanciful, fantastic, far-fetched, whimsical ◆ *n* 7 = **whim**, caprice, desire, humour, idea, impulse, inclination, notion, thought, urge 8 = **partiality**, fondness, hankering, inclination, liking, predilection, preference, relish, thirst 9 = **imagination**, conception, image, impression 11 = **delusion**, chimera, daydream, dream, fantasy, nightmare, phantasm, vision ◆ *vb* 15 = **suppose**, be inclined to think, believe, conceive, conjecture, guess (*inf., chiefly US & Canad.*), imagine, infer, reckon, surmise, think, think likely 18 = **wish for**, be attracted to, crave, desire, dream of, hanker after, have a yen for, hope for, long for, relish, thirst for, would like, yearn for 19 *Brit. informal* = **be attracted to**, be captivated by, desire, favour, go for, have an eye for, like, lust after, prefer, take a liking to, take to
Antonyms *adj* ≠ **elaborate**: basic, cheap, common, inferior, ordinary, plain, simple, unadorned, undecorated, unfussy ◆ *n* ≠ **partiality**: aversion, disinclination, dislike

fanfare *n* 1 = **trumpet call**, fanfaronade, flourish, trump (*arch.*), tucket (*arch.*)

fang *n* 1, 2, 4 = **tooth**, tusk

ous snake through which venom is injected. **2** any large pointed tooth, esp. the canine tooth of a carnivorous mammal. **3** the root of a tooth. **4** (*usually pl*) *Brit. inf.* a tooth. [OE *fang* what is caught, prey]
▸**fanged** *adj* ▸**'fangless** *adj*

fan heater *n* a space heater consisting of an electrically heated element with an electrically driven fan to disperse the heat.

fanjet ('fæn,dʒɛt) *n* another name for **turbofan.**

fanlight ('fæn,laɪt) *n* **1** a semicircular window over a door or window, often having sash bars like the ribs of a fan. **2** a small rectangular window over a door. US name: **transom.**

fan mail *n* mail sent to a famous person, such as a pop musician or film star, by admirers.

fanny ('fænɪ) *n, pl* **fannies.** *Sl.* **1** *Taboo, Brit.* the female genitals. **2** *Chiefly US & Canad.* the buttocks. [C20: ?from *Fanny*, pet name from *Frances*]

fanny adams *n Brit. sl.* **1** (usually preceded by *sweet*) absolutely nothing at all. **2** *Chiefly naut.* (formerly) tinned meat. [C19: from the name of a young murder victim whose body was cut up into small pieces. For sense 1: a euphemism for *fuck all*]

fantail ('fæn,teɪl) *n* **1** a breed of domestic pigeon having a large tail that can be opened like a fan. **2** an Old World flycatcher of Australia, New Zealand, and SE Asia, having a broad fan-shaped tail. **3** a tail shaped like an outspread fan. **4** an auxiliary sail on the upper portion of a windmill. **5** *US.* a part of the deck projecting aft of the sternpost of a ship.
▸**'fan-,tailed** *adj*

fan-tan *n* **1** a Chinese gambling game. **2** a card game played in sequence, the winner being the first to use up all his cards. [C19: from Chinese (Cantonese) *fan t'an* repeated divisions, from *fan* times + *t'an* division]

fantasia (fæn'teɪzɪə) *n* **1** any musical composition of a free or improvisatory nature. **2** a potpourri of popular tunes woven loosely together. [C18: from It.: fancy; see FANTASY]

fantasize ⓣ *or* **fantasise** ('fæntə,saɪz) *vb* **fantasizes, fantasizing, fantasized** *or* **fantasises, fantasising, fantasised. 1** (when *tr*, takes a clause as object) to conceive extravagant or whimsical ideas, images, etc. **2** (*intr*) to conceive pleasant mental images.

fantastic ⓣ (fæn'tæstɪk) *adj also* **fantastical. 1** strange or fanciful in appearance, conception, etc. **2** created in the mind; illusory. **3** unrealistic: *fantastic plans.* **4** incredible or preposterous: *a fantastic verdict.* **5** *Inf.* very large or extreme: *a fantastic fortune.* **6** *Inf.* very good; excellent. **7** of or characterized by fantasy. **8** capricious; fitful. [C14 *fantastik* imaginary, via LL from Gk *phantastikos* capable of imagining, from *phantazein* to make visible]
▸**fan,tasti'cality** *or* **fan'tasticalness** *n* ▸**fan'tastically** *adv*

fantasy ⓣ *or* **phantasy** ('fæntəsɪ) *n, pl* **fantasies** *or* **phantasies. 1a** imagination unrestricted by reality. **1b** (*as modifier*): *a fantasy world.* **2** a creation of the imagination, esp. a weird or bizarre one. **3** *Psychol.* a series of pleasing mental images, usually serving to fulfil a need not gratified in reality. **4** a whimsical or far-fetched notion. **5** an illusion or phantom. **6** a highly elaborate imaginative design or creation. **7** *Music.* another word for **fantasia. 8** literature, etc., having a large fantasy content. ◆ *vb* **fantasies, fantasying, fantasied** *or* **phantasies, phantasying, phantasied. 9** a less common word for **fantasize.** [C14 *fantasie*, from L, from Gk *phantazein* to make visible]

fan vaulting *n Archit.* vaulting having ribs that radiate like those of a fan and spring from the top of a capital. Also called: **palm vaulting.**

fanzine ('fæn,zi:n) *n* a magazine produced by amateurs for fans of a specific interest, pop group, etc. [C20: from FAN[2] + (MAGA)ZINE]

FAO *abbrev. for:* **1** Food and Agriculture Organization (of the United Nations). **2** for the attention of.

f.a.q. *abbrev. for:* **1** *Commerce.* fair average quality. **2** free alongside quay.

far ⓣ (fɑ:) *adv* **farther** *or* **further, farthest** *or* **furthest. 1** at, to, or from a great distance. **2** at or to a remote time: *far in the future.* **3** to a considerable degree: *a far better plan.* **4 as far as. 4a** to the degree or extent that. **4b** to the distance or place of. **4c** *Inf.* with reference to; as for. **5 by far.** by a considerable margin. **6 far and away.** by a very great margin. **7 far and wide.** everywhere. **8 far be it from me.** on no account: *far be it from me to tell you what to do.* **9 go far. 9a** to be successful: *your son will go far.* **9b** to be sufficient or last long: *the wine didn't go far.* **10 go too far.** to exceed reasonable limits. **11 so far. 11a** up to the present moment. **11b** up to a certain point, extent, degree, etc. ◆ *adj* (*prenominal*) **12** remote in space or time: *in the far past.* **13** extending a great distance. **14** more distant: *the far end of the room.* **15 far from.** in a degree, state, etc. remote from: *he is far from happy.* [OE *feorr*]
▸**'farness** *n*

farad ('færəd) *n Physics.* the derived SI unit of electric capacitance; the capacitance of a capacitor between the plates of which a potential of 1 volt is created by a charge of 1 coulomb. Symbol: F [C19: see FARADAY]

faraday ('færə,deɪ) *n* a quantity of electricity, used in electrochemical calculations, equivalent to unit amount of substance of electrons. Symbol: *F* [C20: after Michael *Faraday*, (1791–1867), E physicist]

faradic (fə'rædɪk) *adj* of or concerned with an intermittent alternating current such as that induced in the secondary winding of an induction coil. [C19: from F *faradique*; see FARADAY]

farandole ('færən,dəʊl) *n* **1** a lively dance from Provence. **2** a piece of music composed for or in the rhythm of this dance. [C19: from F, from Provençal *farandoulo*, from ?]

faraway ⓣ ('fɑ:rə,weɪ) *adj* (**far away** *when postpositive*). **1** very distant. **2** absent-minded.

farce ⓣ (fɑ:s) *n* **1** a broadly humorous play based on the exploitation of improbable situations. **2** the genre of comedy represented by works of this kind. **3** a ludicrous situation or action. **4** another name for **forcemeat.** [C14 (in the sense: stuffing): from OF, from L *farcīre* to stuff, interpolate passages (in the mass, in religious plays, etc.)]

farcical ⓣ ('fɑ:sɪkᵊl) *adj* **1** absurd. **2** of or relating to farce.
▸**,farci'cality** *n* ▸**'farcically** *adv*

fardel ('fɑ:dᵊl) *n Arch.* a bundle or burden. [C13: from OF *farde*, ult. from Ar. *fardah*]

fare ⓣ (fɛə) *n* **1** the sum charged or paid for conveyance in a bus, train, etc. **2** a paying passenger, esp. when carried by taxi. **3** a range of food and drink. ◆ *vb* **fares, faring, fared.** (*intr*) **4** to get on (as specified): *he fared well.* **5** (with *it* as a subject) to happen as specified: *it fared badly with him.* **6** *Arch.* to eat: *we fared sumptuously.* **7** (often foll. by *forth*) *Arch.* to travel. [OE *faran*]
▸**'farer** *n*

Far East *n* **the.** the countries of E Asia, including China, Japan, North and South Korea, E Siberia, Indonesia, Malaysia, and the Philippines: sometimes extended to include all territories east of Afghanistan.
▸**Far Eastern** *adj*

fare stage *n* **1** a section of a bus journey for which a set charge is made. **2** the bus stop marking the end of such a section.

farewell ⓣ (,fɛə'wɛl) *sentence substitute.* **1** goodbye; adieu. ◆ *n* **2** a parting salutation. **3** an act of departure. **4** (*modifier*) expressing leave-taking: *a farewell speech.*

far-fetched ⓣ *adj* unlikely.

far-flung *adj* **1** widely distributed. **2** far distant; remote.

farina (fə'ri:nə) *n* **1** flour or meal made from any kind of cereal grain. **2** *Chiefly Brit.* starch. [C18: from L *fār* spelt, coarse meal]

farinaceous (,færɪ'neɪʃəs) *adj* **1** consisting or made of starch. **2** having a mealy texture or appearance. **3** containing starch: *farinaceous seeds.*

THESAURUS

fantasize *vb* **1, 2 = daydream**, build castles in the air, dream, envision, hallucinate, imagine, invent, live in a dream world, romance, see visions

fantastic *adj* **1 = strange**, comical, eccentric, exotic, fanciful, freakish, grotesque, imaginative, odd, oddball (*inf.*), off-the-wall (*sl.*), outlandish, outré, peculiar, phantasmagorical, quaint, queer, rococo, unreal, weird, whimsical, zany **2, 3 = unrealistic**, ambitious, chimerical, extravagant, far-fetched, grandiose, illusory, ludicrous, ridiculous, visionary, wild **4 = implausible**, absurd, capricious, cock-and-bull (*inf.*), incredible, irrational, mad, preposterous, unlikely **5** *Informal* = **enormous**, extreme, great, overwhelming, severe, tremendous **6** *Informal* = **wonderful**, awesome, brill (*inf.*), cracking (*Brit. inf.*), crucial (*sl.*), def (*sl.*), dope (*sl.*), excellent, first-rate, jim-dandy (*sl.*), marvellous, mega (*sl.*), out of this world (*inf.*), sensational (*inf.*), sovereign, superb, topping (*Brit. sl.*), world-class
Antonyms ≠ **unrealistic, implausible:** credible, moderate, rational, realistic, sensible *adj* ≠ **wonderful:** common, everyday, normal, ordinary, poor, typical

fantasy *n* **1 = imagination**, creativity, fancy, invention, originality **2 = daydream**, apparition, delusion, dream, fancy, figment of the imagination, flight of fancy, hallucination, illusion, mirage, nightmare, pipe dream, reverie, vision

far *adv* **1 = a long way**, afar, a good way, a great distance, deep, miles **3 = much**, considerably, decidedly, extremely, greatly, incomparably, very much **5 by far = very much**, by a long chalk (*inf.*), by a long shot, by a long way, easily, far and away, immeasurably, incomparably, to a great degree **7 far and wide = extensively**, broadly, everywhere, far and near, here, there and everywhere, in every nook and cranny, widely, worldwide **11a so far = up to now**, thus far, to date, until now, up to the present ◆ *adj* **12 = remote**, distant, faraway, far-flung, far-off, far-removed, long, outlying, out-of-the-way, removed
Antonyms *adj* ≠ **remote:** adjacent, adjoining, alongside, at close quarters, beside, bordering, close, contiguous, just round the corner, near, nearby, neighbouring, proximate, within sniffing distance (*inf.*)

faraway *adj* **1 = distant**, beyond the horizon, far, far-flung, far-off, far-removed, outlying, remote **2 = dreamy**, absent, abstracted, distant, lost, vague

farce *n* **1, 2 = comedy**, broad comedy, buffoonery, burlesque, satire, slapstick **3 = mockery**, absurdity, joke, nonsense, parody, ridiculousness, sham, travesty

farcical *adj* **1, 2 = ludicrous**, absurd, amusing, comic, custard-pie, derisory, diverting, droll, funny, laughable, nonsensical, preposterous, ridiculous, risible, slapstick

fare *n* **1 = charge**, passage money, price, ticket money, transport cost **2 = passenger**, pick-up (*inf.*), traveller **3 = food**, commons, diet, eatables, feed, meals, menu, nosebag (*sl.*), provisions, rations, sustenance, table, tack (*inf.*), victuals, vittles (*obs. or dialect*) ◆ *vb* **4 = get on**, do, get along, make out, manage, prosper **5** *used impersonally* = **happen**, go, pan out (*inf.*), proceed, turn out

farewell *n* **2, 3 = goodbye**, adieu, adieux *or* adieus, departure, leave-taking, parting, send-off (*inf.*), valediction

far-fetched *adj* = **unconvincing**, cock-and-bull (*inf.*), doubtful, dubious, fantastic, hard to swallow (*inf.*), implausible, improbable, incredible, preposterous, strained, unbelievable, unlikely, unnatural, unrealistic
Antonyms *adj* acceptable, authentic, believable, credible, feasible, imaginable, likely, plausible, possible, probable, realistic, reasonable

farm 🅣 (fɑːm) *n* **1a** a tract of land, usually with house and buildings, cultivated as a unit or used to rear livestock. **1b** (*as modifier*): *farm produce.* **1c** (*in combination*): *farmland.* **2** a unit of land or water devoted to the growing or rearing of some particular type of vegetable, fruit, animal, or fish: *a fish farm.* **3** an installation for storage or disposal: *a sewage farm.* ◆ *vb* **4** (*tr*) **4a** to cultivate (land). **4b** to rear (stock, etc.) on a farm. **5** (*intr*) to engage in agricultural work, esp. as a way of life. **6** (*tr*) to look after a child for a fixed sum. **7** to collect the moneys due and retain the profits from (a tax district, business, etc.) for a specified period. ◆ See also **farm out**. [C13: from OF *ferme* rented land, ult. from L *firmāre* to settle]
▸ **'farmable** *adj*

farmed (fɑːmd) *adj* (of fish and game) reared on a farm rather than caught in the wild.

farmer 🅣 ('fɑːmə) *n* **1** a person who operates or manages a farm. **2** a person who obtains the right to collect and retain a tax, rent, etc., on payment of a fee. **3** a person who looks after a child for a fixed sum.

farmer's lung *n* inflammation of the alveoli of the lungs caused by an allergic response to fungal spores in hay.

farm hand *n* a person who is hired to work on a farm.

farmhouse ('fɑːmˌhaʊs) *n* a house attached to a farm, esp. the dwelling from which the farm is managed.

farming 🅣 ('fɑːmɪŋ) *n* **a** the business or skill of agriculture. **b** (*as modifier*): *farming methods.*

farm out *vb* (*tr, adv*) **1** to send (work) to be done by another person, firm, etc. **2** to put (a child, etc.) into the care of a private individual. **3** to lease to another for a fee the right to collect (taxes).

farmstead ('fɑːmˌstɛd) *n* a farm or the part of a farm comprising its main buildings together with adjacent grounds.

farmyard ('fɑːmˌjɑːd) *n* an area surrounded by or adjacent to farm buildings.

Far North *n* **the.** the Arctic and sub-Arctic regions of the world.

faro ('fɛərəʊ) *n* a gambling game in which players bet against the dealer on what cards he will turn up. [C18: prob. spelling var. of *Pharoah*]

far-off *adj* (**far off** *when postpositive*). remote in space or time; distant.

farouche *French.* (faruʃ) *adj* sullen or shy. [C18: from F, from OF, from LL *forasticus* from without, from L *foras* out of doors]

far-out 🅣 *Sl.* ◆ *adj* (**far out** *when postpositive*) **1** bizarre or avant-garde. **2** wonderful. ◆ *interj* **far out. 3** an expression of amazement or delight.

farrago 🅣 (fə'rɑːgəʊ) *n, pl* **farragos** *or* **farragoes.** a hotchpotch. [C17: from L: mash for cattle (hence, a mixture), from *fār* spelt]
▸**farraginous** (fə'rædʒɪnəs) *adj*

far-reaching 🅣 *adj* extensive in influence, effect, or range.

farrier ('færɪə) *n Chiefly Brit.* **1** a person who shoes horses. **2** another name for **veterinary surgeon.** [C16: from OF, from L *ferrārius* smith, from *ferrum* iron]
▸ **'farriery** *n*

farrow ('færəʊ) *n* **1** a litter of piglets. ◆ *vb* **2** (of a sow) to give birth to (a litter). [OE *fearh*]

far-seeing *adj* having shrewd judgment.

Farsi ('fɑːsɪ) *n* a language spoken in Iran.

far-sighted 🅣 *adj* **1** possessing prudence and foresight. **2** another word for **long-sighted.**
▸ **ˌfar-'sightedly** *adv* ▸ **ˌfar-'sightedness** *n*

fart (fɑːt) *Taboo.* ◆ *n* **1** an emission of intestinal gas from the anus. **2** *Sl.* a contemptible person. ◆ *vb* (*intr*) **3** to break wind. **4 fart about** *or* **around.** *Sl.* **4a** to behave foolishly. **4b** to waste time. [ME *farten*]

farther ('fɑːðə) *adv* **1** to or at a greater distance in space or time. **2** in addition. ◆ *adj* **3** more distant or remote in space or time. **4** additional. [C13: see FAR, FURTHER]

> **USAGE NOTE** *Farther, farthest, further,* and *furthest* can all be used to refer to literal distance, but *further* and *furthest* are regarded as more correct for figurative senses denoting greater or additional amount, time, etc.: *further to my letter. Further* and *furthest* are also preferred for figurative distance.

farthermost ('fɑːðəˌməʊst) *adj* most distant or remote.

farthest ('fɑːðɪst) *adv* **1** to or at the greatest distance in space or time. ◆ *adj* **2** most distant in space or time. **3** most extended. [C14 *ferthest,* from *ferther* FURTHER]

farthing ('fɑːðɪŋ) *n* **1** a former British bronze coin worth a quarter of an old penny: withdrawn in 1961. **2** something of negligible value; jot. [OE *fēorthing* from *fēortha* FOURTH + -ING[1]]

farthingale ('fɑːðɪŋˌgeɪl) *n* a hoop or framework worn under skirts, esp. in the Elizabethan period, to shape and spread them. [C16: from F *verdugale,* from OSp. *verdugado,* from *verdugo* rod]

fasces ('fæsiːz) *pl n, sing* **fascis** (-sɪs). **1** (in ancient Rome) one or more bundles of rods containing an axe with its blade protruding; a symbol of a magistrate's power. **2** (in modern Italy) such an object used as the symbol of Fascism. [C16: from L, pl of *fascis* bundle]

fascia *or* **facia** ('feɪʃɪə) *n, pl* **fasciae** *or* **faciae** (-ʃɪˌiː). **1** the flat surface above a shop window. **2** *Archit.* a flat band or surface, esp. a part of an architrave. **3** ('fæʃɪə). fibrous connective tissue occurring in sheets between muscles. **4** *Biol.* a distinctive band of colour, as on an insect or plant. **5** *Brit.* the outer panel which covers the dashboard of a motor vehicle. [C16: from L: band: rel. to *fascis* bundle]
▸ **'fascial** *or* **'facial** *adj*

fasciate ('fæʃɪˌeɪt) *or* **fasciated** *adj* **1** *Bot.* (of stems and branches) abnormally flattened due to coalescence. **2** (of birds, insects, etc.) marked by bands of colour. [C17: prob. from NL *fasciātus* (unattested) having bands; see FASCIA]

fascicle ('fæsɪkᵊl) *n* **1** a bundle of branches, leaves, etc. **2** Also called: **fasciculus.** *Anat.* a small bundle of fibres, esp. nerve fibres. [C15: from L *fasciculus* a small bundle, from *fascis* a bundle]
▸ **'fascicled** *adj* ▸**fascicular** (fə'sɪkjʊlə) *or* **fasciculate** (fə'sɪkjʊˌleɪt) *adj* ▸**fasˌcicu'lation** *n*

fascicule ('fæsɪˌkjuːl) *n* one part of a printed work that is published in instalments. Also called: **fascicle, fasciculus.**

fascinate 🅣 ('fæsɪˌneɪt) *vb* **fascinates, fascinating, fascinated.** (*mainly tr*) **1** to attract and delight by arousing interest: *his stories fascinated me for hours.* **2** to render motionless, as by arousing terror or awe. **3** *Arch.* to put under a spell. [C16: from L, from *fascinum* a bewitching]
▸ **ˌfasci'nation** *n*

> **USAGE NOTE** A person can be fascinated *by* or *with* another person or thing. It is correct to speak of someone's fascination *with* a person or thing; one can also say a person or thing has a fascination *for* someone.

fascinating 🅣 ('fæsɪˌneɪtɪŋ) *adj* **1** arousing great interest. **2** enchanting or alluring.

fascinator ('fæsɪˌneɪtə) *n Rare.* a lace or crocheted head covering for women.

Fascism 🅣 ('fæʃɪzəm) *n* **1** the political movement, doctrine, system, or regime of Benito Mussolini in Italy (1922–43). Fascism encouraged militarism and nationalism, organizing the country along hierarchical authoritarian lines. **2** (*sometimes not cap.*) any ideology or movement modelled on or inspired by this. **3** *Inf.* (*often not cap.*) any doctrine, system, or practice, regarded as authoritarian, militaristic, or extremely right-wing. [C20: from It. *fascismo,* from *fascio* political group, from L *fascis* bundle; see FASCES]

Fascist ('fæʃɪst) *n* **1** a supporter or member of a Fascist movement. **2** (*sometimes not cap.*) any person regarded as having right-wing authoritarian views. ◆ *adj* **3** characteristic of or relating to Fascism.

fashion 🅣 ('fæʃən) *n* **1a** style in clothes, behaviour, etc., esp. the latest style. **1b** (*as modifier*): *a fashion magazine.* **2** (*modifier*) designed to be in the current fashion. **3a** manner of performance: *in a striking fashion.* **3b** (*in combination*): *crab-fashion.* **4** a way of life that revolves around the activities, dress, interests, etc., that are most fashionable. **5** shape or form. **6** sort; kind. **7 after** *or* **in a fashion.** in some manner, but not very well: *I mended it, after a fashion.* **8 of fashion.** of high social standing. ◆ *vb* (*tr*) **9** to give a particular form to. **10** to make suitable or fitting. **11** *Obs.* to contrive. [C13 *facioun* form, manner, from OF *faceon,* from L, from *facere* to make]
▸ **'fashioner** *n*

THESAURUS

farm *n* **1** = **smallholding,** acreage, acres, croft (*Scot.*), farmstead, grange, holding, homestead, land, plantation, ranch (*chiefly North American*), station (*Austral. & NZ*) ◆ *vb* **4** = **cultivate,** bring under cultivation, operate, plant, practise husbandry, till the soil, work

farmer *n* **1** = **agriculturist,** agronomist, husbandman, smallholder, yeoman

farming *n* = **agriculture,** agronomy, husbandry

far-out *adj* **1** = **strange,** advanced, avant-garde, bizarre, off-the-wall (*sl.*), outlandish, outré, unconventional, unusual, weird, wild

farrago *n* = **hotchpotch,** hash, hodgepodge, jumble, medley, *mélange,* miscellany, mishmash, mixed bag, mixture, potpourri

far-reaching *adj* = **extensive,** broad, important, momentous, pervasive, significant, sweeping, widespread

far-sighted *adj* **1** = **prudent,** acute, canny, cautious, discerning, far-seeing, judicious, politic, prescient, provident, sage, shrewd, wise

fascinate *vb* **1** = **entrance,** absorb, allure, beguile, bewitch, captivate, charm, delight, enamour, enchant, engross, enrapture, enthral, hold spellbound, hypnotize, infatuate, intrigue, mesmerize, ravish, rivet, spellbind, transfix
Antonyms *vb* alienate, bore, disenchant, disgust, irritate, jade, put one off, sicken, turn one off (*inf.*)

fascinated *adj* **1** = **entranced,** absorbed, beguiled, bewitched, captivated, charmed, engrossed, enthralled, hooked on, hypnotized, infatuated, smitten, spellbound, under a spell

fascinating *adj* **1** = **captivating,** alluring, bewitching, compelling, enchanting, engaging, engrossing, enticing, gripping, intriguing, irresistible, ravishing, riveting, seductive
Antonyms *adj* boring, dull, mind-numbing, unexciting, uninteresting

fascination *n* **1** = **attraction,** allure, charm, enchantment, glamour, lure, magic, magnetism, pull, sorcery, spell

Fascism *n* **2, 3** *sometimes not cap.* = **authoritarianism,** absolutism, autocracy, dictatorship, Hitlerism, totalitarianism

fashion *n* **1** = **style,** convention, craze, custom, fad, latest, latest style, look, mode, prevailing taste, rage, trend, usage, vogue **3** = **method,** attitude, demeanour, manner, mode, style, way **5** = **form,** appearance, configuration, cut, figure, guise (*arch.*), line, make, model, mould, pattern, shape, stamp **6** = **sort,** description, kind, stamp, type **7 after a fashion** = **to some extent,** in a manner of speaking, in a way, moderately, somehow, somehow or other, to a degree ◆ *vb* **9** = **make,** construct, contrive, create, design,

fashionable ❶ (ˈfæʃənəbᵊl) *adj* **1** conforming to fashion; in vogue. **2** of or patronized by people of fashion: *a fashionable café.* **3** (usually foll. by *with*) patronized (by).
▸ˈ**fashionableness** *n* ▸ˈ**fashionably** *adv*

fashion plate *n* **1** an illustration of the latest fashion in dress. **2** a fashionably dressed person.

fashion victim *n Inf.* a person who slavishly follows fashion.

fast[1] ❶ (fɑːst) *adj* **1** acting or moving or capable of acting or moving quickly. **2** accomplished in or lasting a short time: *a fast visit.* **3** (*prenominal*) adapted to or facilitating rapid movement: *the fast lane of a motorway.* **4** (of a clock, etc.) indicating a time in advance of the correct time. **5** given to an active dissipated life. **6** of or characteristic of such activity: *a fast life.* **7** not easily moved; firmly fixed; secure. **8** firmly fastened or shut. **9** steadfast; constant (esp. in **fast friends**). **10** *Sport.* (of a playing surface, running track, etc.) conducive to rapid speed, as of a ball used on it or of competitors racing on it. **11** that will not fade or change colour readily. **12** proof against fading. **13** *Photog.* **13a** requiring a relatively short time of exposure to produce a given density: *a fast film.* **13b** permitting a short exposure time: *a fast shutter.* **14 a fast one.** *Inf.* a deceptive or unscrupulous trick (esp. in **pull a fast one**). **15 fast worker.** a person who achieves results quickly, esp. in seductions. ◆ *adv* **16** quickly; rapidly. **17** soundly; deeply: *fast asleep.* **18** firmly; tightly. **19** in quick succession. **20** in advance of the correct time: *my watch is running fast.* **21** in a reckless or dissipated way. **22 fast by** *or* **beside.** *Arch.* close by. **23 play fast and loose.** *Inf.* to behave in an insincere or unreliable manner. [OE *fæst* strong, tight]

fast[2] ❶ (fɑːst) *vb* **1** (*intr*) to abstain from eating all or certain foods or meals, esp. as a religious observance. ◆ *n* **2a** an act or period of fasting. **2b** (*as modifier*): *a fast day.* [OE *fæstan*]
▸ˈ**faster** *n*

fastback (ˈfɑːstˌbæk) *n* a car having a back that forms one continuous slope from roof to rear.

fast-breeder reactor *n* a nuclear reactor that uses little or no moderator and produces more fissionable material than it consumes.

fasten ❶ (ˈfɑːsᵊn) *vb* **1** to make or become fast or secure. **2** to make or become attached or joined. **3** to close or become closed by fixing firmly in place, locking, etc. **4** (*tr*; foll. by *in* or *up*) to enclose or imprison. **5** (*tr*; usually foll. by *on*) to cause (blame, a nickname, etc.) to be attached (to). **6** (usually foll. by *on* or *upon*) to direct or be directed in a concentrated way. **7** (*intr*; usually foll. by *on*) to take a firm hold (of). [OE *fæstnian; see* FAST[1]]
▸ˈ**fastener** *n*

fastening ❶ (ˈfɑːsᵊnɪŋ) *n* something that fastens, such as a clasp or lock.

fast food *n* **a** food, esp. hamburgers, fried chicken, etc., that is prepared and served very quickly. **b** (*as modifier*): *a fast-food restaurant.*

fast-forward *n* **1** (*sometimes not hyphenated*) the control on a tape deck or video recorder used to wind the tape or video forwards at speed. **2** *Inf.* a state of urgency or rapid progress: *put the deal into fast-forward.* ◆ *vb* (*tr*) **3** to wind (a tape, etc.) forward using the fast-forward control. **4** *Inf.* **4a** to deal with or dispatch (something) rapidly: *fast-forward this to the press.* **4b** to skip (something): *fast-forward the small talk and get down to business.*

fastidious ❶ (fæˈstɪdɪəs) *adj* **1** hard to please. **2** excessively particular about details. **3** exceedingly delicate. [C15: from L *fastīdiōsus* scornful, from *fastīdium* loathing, from *fastus* pride + *taedium* weariness]
▸**fasˈtidiously** *adv* ▸**fasˈtidiousness** *n*

fastigiate (fæˈstɪdʒɪɪt) *or* **fastigiated** *adj Biol.* (of parts or organs) united in a tapering group. [C17: from Med. L *fastīgiātus* lofty, from L *fastīgium* height]

fast lane *n* **1** the outside lane on a motorway for vehicles overtaking or travelling at high speed. **2** *Inf.* the quickest but most competitive route to success.

fastness (ˈfɑːstnɪs) *n* **1** a stronghold; fortress. **2** the state or quality of being firm or secure. [OE *fæstnes; see* FAST[1]]

fast-track *adj* taking the quickest but most competitive route to success or personal advancement: *fast-track executives.*
▸ˌ**fast-ˈtracker** *n*

fat ❶ (fæt) *n* **1** any of a class of naturally occurring soft greasy solids that are present in some plants and animals, and are used in making soap and paint and in the food industry. **2** vegetable or animal tissue containing fat. **3** corpulence, obesity, or plumpness. **4** the best or richest part of something. **5 the fat is in the fire.** an irrevocable action has been taken from which dire consequences are expected. **6 the fat of the land.** the best that is obtainable. ◆ *adj* **fatter, fattest. 7** having much or too much flesh or fat. **8** consisting of or containing fat; greasy. **9** profitable; lucrative. **10** affording great opportunities: *a fat part in the play.* **11** fertile or productive: *a fat land.* **12** thick, broad, or extended: *a fat log of wood.* **13** *Sl.* very little or none (in **a fat chance, a fat lot of good,** etc.). ◆ *vb* **fats, fatting, fatted. 14** to make or become fat; fatten. [OE *fǣtt*, p.p. of *fǣtan* to cram]
▸ˈ**fatless** *adj* ▸ˈ**fatly** *adv* ▸ˈ**fatness** *n* ▸ˈ**fattish** *adj*

fatal ❶ (ˈfeɪtᵊl) *adj* **1** resulting in death: *a fatal accident.* **2** bringing ruin. **3** decisively important. **4** inevitable. [C14: from OF or L from L *fātum*; see FATE]
▸ˈ**fatally** *adv*

fatalism ❶ (ˈfeɪtəˌlɪzəm) *n* **1** the philosophical doctrine that all events are predetermined so that man is powerless to alter his destiny. **2** the acceptance of and submission to this doctrine.
▸ˈ**fatalist** *n* ▸ˌ**fatalˈistic** *adj*

fatality ❶ (fəˈtælɪtɪ) *n, pl* **fatalities. 1** an accident or disaster resulting in death. **2** a person killed in an accident or disaster. **3** the power of causing death or disaster. **4** the quality or condition of being fated. **5** something caused by fate.

fate ❶ (feɪt) *n* **1** the ultimate agency that predetermines the course of events. **2** the inevitable fortune that befalls a person or thing. **3** the end or final result. **4** death, destruction, or downfall. ◆ *vb* **fates, fating, fated. 5** (*tr; usually passive*) to predetermine: *he was fated to lose.* [C14: from L *fātum* oracular utterance, from *fārī* to speak]

fated ❶ (ˈfeɪtɪd) *adj* **1** destined. **2** doomed to death or destruction.

fateful ❶ (ˈfeɪtful) *adj* **1** having important consequences. **2** bringing death or disaster. **3** controlled by or as if by fate. **4** prophetic.
▸ˈ**fatefully** *adv* ▸ˈ**fatefulness** *n*

Fates (feɪts) *pl n Greek myth.* the three goddesses, Atropos, Clotho, and Lachesis, who control the destinies of the lives of man.

THESAURUS

forge, form, manufacture, mould, shape, work **10 = fit**, accommodate, adapt, adjust, suit, tailor

fashionable *adj* **1 = popular**, à la mode, all the go (*inf.*), all the rage, chic, cool (*sl.*), current, customary, genteel, happening (*inf.*), hip (*sl.*), in (*inf.*), in vogue, latest, modern, modish, prevailing, smart, stylish, trendsetting, trendy (*Brit. inf.*), up-to-date, up-to-the-minute, usual, voguish (*inf.*), with it (*inf.*)
Antonyms *adj* behind the times, dated, frumpy, obsolete, old-fashioned, old-hat, outmoded, out of date, out of the ark (*inf.*), uncool (*sl.*), unfashionable, unpopular, unstylish, untrendy (*Brit. inf.*)

fast[1] *adj* **1, 2 = quick**, accelerated, brisk, fleet, flying, hasty, hurried, mercurial, nippy (*Brit. inf.*), quickie (*inf.*), rapid, speedy, swift, winged **5, 6 = dissipated**, dissolute, extravagant, gadabout (*inf.*), giddy, immoral, intemperate, licentious, loose, profligate, promiscuous, rakish, reckless, self-indulgent, wanton, wild **7, 9 = fixed**, close, constant, fastened, firm, fortified, immovable, impregnable, lasting, loyal, permanent, secure, sound, stalwart, staunch, steadfast, tight, unwavering **14 pull a fast one** *Informal* **= trick**, bamboozle (*inf.*), cheat, con (*inf.*), deceive, defraud, hoodwink, put one over on (*inf.*), swindle, take advantage of, take for a ride (*inf.*) ◆ *adv* **16 = quickly**, apace, at a rate of knots, hastily, hell for leather (*inf.*), hotfoot, hurriedly, in haste, like a flash, like a shot (*inf.*), like lightning, posthaste, presto, rapidly, speedily, swiftly, with all haste **17, 18 = soundly**, deeply, firmly, fixedly, securely, tightly **21 = recklessly**, extravagantly, intemperately, loosely, promiscuously, rakishly, wildly
Antonyms *adj* ≠ **quick:** leisurely, plodding, slow, slow moving, unhurried ≠ **fixed:** inconstant, irresolute, unfaithful, unreliable, unstable, wavering, weak ◆ *adv* ≠ **quickly:** at a snail's pace, at one's leisure, gradually, leisurely, slowly, steadily, unhurriedly

fast[2] *vb* **1 = go hungry**, abstain, deny oneself, go without food, practise abstention, refrain from food *or* eating ◆ *n* **2 = fasting**, abstinence

fasten *vb* **1-3 = fix**, affix, anchor, attach, bind, bolt, chain, connect, grip, join, lace, link, lock, make fast, make firm, seal, secure, tie, unite **6 = direct**, aim, bend, concentrate, fix, focus, rivet

fastening *n* **= tie**, affixation, attachment, binding, bond, concatenation, connection, coupling, fusion, joint, junction, ligature, link, linking, union

fastidious *adj* **1-3 = particular**, choosy, critical, dainty, difficult, discriminating, finicky, fussy, hard to please, hypercritical, meticulous, nice, overdelicate, overnice, pernickety, picky (*inf.*), punctilious, squeamish
Antonyms *adj* careless, casual, disorderly, easy-going, lenient, slack, slipshod, sloppy, slovenly, unsystematic

fat *n* **3 = fatness**, adipose tissue, beef (*inf.*), blubber, bulk, cellulite, corpulence, flab, flesh, obesity, overweight, paunch, weight problem ◆ *adj* **7 = overweight**, beefy (*inf.*), broad in the beam (*inf.*), corpulent, elephantine, fleshy, gross, heavy, obese, plump, podgy, portly, roly-poly, rotund, solid, stout, tubby **8 = fatty**, adipose, greasy, lipid, oily, oleaginous, suety **9 = profitable**, affluent, cushy, fertile, flourishing, fruitful, jammy (*Brit. sl.*), lucrative, lush, productive, prosperous, remunerative, rich, thriving
Antonyms *adj* ≠ **overweight:** angular, bony, empty, gaunt, lank, lean, scrawny, skinny, slender, slight, slim, spare, thin ≠ **fatty:** lean ≠ **profitable:** barren, poor, scanty, scarce, unproductive, unprofitable, unrewarding

fatal *adj* **1 = lethal**, deadly, destructive, final, incurable, killing, malignant, mortal, pernicious, terminal **2 = disastrous**, baleful, baneful, calamitous, catastrophic, lethal, ruinous **3 = decisive**, critical, crucial, determining, fateful, final **4 = inevitable**, destined, doomed, foreordained, predestined
Antonyms *adj* ≠ **lethal:** beneficial, benign, harmless, innocuous, inoffensive, non-lethal, non-toxic, salutary, vitalizing, wholesome ≠ **disastrous:** inconsequential, minor

fatalism *n* **1, 2 = resignation**, acceptance, determinism, necessitarianism, passivity, predestinarianism, stoicism

fatality *n* **1, 3 = death**, casualty, deadliness, disaster, fatal accident, lethalness, loss, mortality

fate *n* **1 = destiny**, chance, divine will, fortune, kismet, nemesis, predestination, providence, weird (*arch.*) **2 = fortune**, cup, horoscope, lot, portion, stars **3 = outcome**, end, future, issue, upshot **4 = downfall**, death, destruction, doom, end, ruin

fated *adj* **1 = destined**, doomed, foreordained, ineluctable, inescapable, inevitable, marked down, predestined, pre-elected, preordained, sure, written

fateful *adj* **1 = crucial**, critical, decisive, important, portentous, significant **2 = disastrous**,

fat farm *n Sl.* a health farm or similar establishment to which people go to lose weight.

fathead ('fæt,hed) *n Inf.* a stupid person; fool.
▸**'fat,headed** *adj*

father Ⓣ ('fɑːðə) *n* **1** a male parent. **2** a person who founds a line or family; forefather. **3** any male acting in a paternal capacity. **4** (*often cap.*) a respectful term of address for an old man. **5** a male who originates something: *the father of modern psychology*. **6** a leader of an association, council, etc.: *a city father*. **7** *Brit.* the eldest or most senior member in a union, profession, etc. **8** (*often pl*) a senator in ancient Rome. ◆ *vb* (*tr*) **9** to procreate or generate (offspring). **10** to create, found, etc. **11** to act as a father to. **12** to acknowledge oneself as father or originator of. **13** (foll. by *on* or *upon*) to impose or foist upon. [OE *fæder*]
▸**'fatherhood** *n* ▸**'fatherless** *adj* ▸**'father-,like** *adj*

Father ('fɑːðə) *n* **1** God, esp. when considered as the first person of the Christian Trinity. **2** any of the early writers on Christian doctrine. **3** a title used for Christian priests.

father confessor *n* **1** *Christianity.* a priest who hears confessions. **2** any person to whom one tells private matters.

father-in-law *n, pl* **fathers-in-law.** the father of one's wife or husband.

fatherland Ⓣ ('fɑːðə,lænd) *n* **1** a person's native country. **2** the country of a person's ancestors.

fatherly Ⓣ ('fɑːðəlɪ) *adj* of, resembling, or suitable to a father, esp. in kindliness, encouragement, etc.
▸**'fatherliness** *n*

Father's Day *n* a day observed in honour of fathers; in Britain the third Sunday in June.

fathom Ⓣ ('fæðəm) *n* **1** a unit of length equal to six feet (1.829 metres), used to measure depths of water. ◆ *vb* (*tr*) **2** to measure the depth of, esp. with a sounding line. **3** to penetrate (a mystery, problem, etc.). [OE *fæthm*]
▸**'fathomable** *adj*

Fathometer (fə'ðɒmɪtə) *n Trademark.* a type of echo sounder used for measuring the depth of water.

fathomless Ⓣ ('fæðəmlɪs) *adj* another word for **unfathomable.**
▸**'fathomlessness** *n*

fatigue Ⓣ (fə'tiːg) *n* **1** physical or mental exhaustion due to exertion. **2** a tiring activity or effort. **3** *Physiol.* the temporary inability of an organ or part to respond to a stimulus because of overactivity. **4** the weakening of a material subjected to alternating stresses, esp. vibrations. **5** the temporary inability to respond to a situation resulting from overexposure to it: *compassion fatigue*. **6** any of the mainly domestic duties performed by military personnel, esp. as a punishment. **7** (*pl*) special clothing worn by military personnel to carry out such duties. ◆ *vb* **fatigues, fatiguing, fatigued. 8** to make or become weary or exhausted. [C17: from F, from *fatiguer* to tire, from L *fatīgāre*]
▸**fatigable** *or* **fatiguable** ('fætɪgəb°l) *adj*

fatshedera (fæts'hedərə) *n* a hybrid plant with five-lobed leaves. [from NL, from *Fatsia japonica* + *Hedera hibernica*]

fatsia ('fætsɪə) *n* an evergreen hardy shrub. Also known as the **false castor-oil plant.** [from NL]

fatso ('fætsəʊ) *n Sl.* a fat person.

fat-soluble *adj* soluble in substances, such as ether, chloroform, and oils. Fat-soluble compounds are often insoluble in water.

fat stock *n* livestock fattened and ready for market.

fatten Ⓣ ('fæt°n) *vb* **1** to grow or cause to grow fat or fatter. **2** (*tr*) to cause (an animal or fowl) to become fat by feeding it. **3** (*tr*) to make fuller or richer. **4** (*tr*) to enrich (soil).
▸**'fattening** *adj*

fatty Ⓣ ('fætɪ) *adj* **fattier, fattiest. 1** containing or derived from fat. **2** greasy; oily. **3** (esp. of tissues, organs, etc.) characterized by the excessive accumulation of fat. ◆ *n, pl* **fatties. 4** *Inf.* a fat person.
▸**'fattily** *adv* ▸**'fattiness** *n*

fatty acid *n* an aliphatic carboxylic acid, esp. one found in lipids, such as palmitic acid, stearic acid, and oleic acid.

fatty degeneration *n Pathol.* the abnormal formation of tiny globules of fat within the cytoplasm of a cell.

fatuity (fə'tjuːɪtɪ) *n, pl* **fatuities. 1** inanity. **2** a fatuous remark, act, sentiment, etc.
▸**fa'tuitous** *adj*

fatuous Ⓣ ('fætjuəs) *adj* complacently or inanely foolish. [C17: from L *fatuus*; rel. to *fatiscere* to gape]
▸**'fatuously** *adv* ▸**'fatuousness** *n*

fatwa *or* **fatwah** ('fætwə) *n* a religious decree issued by a Muslim leader. [Ar.]

fauces ('fɔːsiːz) *n, pl* **fauces.** *Anat.* the area between the cavity of the mouth and the pharynx. [C16: from L: throat]
▸**faucal** ('fɔːk°l) *or* **faucial** ('fɔːʃəl) *adj*

faucet ('fɔːsɪt) *n* **1** a tap fitted to a barrel. **2** the US and Canad. name for **tap**[2] (sense 1). [C14: from OF from Provençal *falsar* to bore]

fault Ⓣ (fɔːlt) *n* **1** a failing or defect; flaw. **2** a mistake or error. **3** a misdeed. **4** responsibility for a mistake or misdeed. **5** *Electronics.* a defect in a circuit, component, or line, such as a short circuit. **6** *Geol.* a fracture in the earth's crust resulting in the relative displacement of the rocks on either side of it. **7** *Tennis, squash, etc.* an invalid serve. **8** (in showjumping) a penalty mark given for failing to clear, or refusing, a fence, etc. **9 at fault.** guilty of error; culpable. **10 find fault (with).** to seek out minor imperfections or errors (in). **11 to a fault.** excessively. ◆ *vb* **12** *Geol.* to undergo or cause to undergo a fault. **13** (*tr*) to criticize or blame. **14** (*intr*) to commit a fault. [C13: from OF *faute* ult. from L *fallere* to fail]

fault-finding Ⓣ *n* **1** continual criticism. ◆ *adj* **2** given to finding fault.
▸**'fault-,finder** *n*

faultless Ⓣ ('fɔːltlɪs) *adj* perfect or blameless.
▸**'faultlessly** *adv* ▸**'faultlessness** *n*

faulty Ⓣ ('fɔːltɪ) *adj* **faultier, faultiest.** defective or imperfect.
▸**'faultily** *adv* ▸**'faultiness** *n*

faun (fɔːn) *n* (in Roman legend) a rural deity represented as a man with a goat's ears, horns, tail, and hind legs. [C14: back formation from *Faunes* (pl), from L *Faunus* deity of forests]
▸**'faun,like** *adj*

fauna ('fɔːnə) *n, pl* **faunas** *or* **faunae** (-niː). **1** all the animal life of a given place or time. **2** a descriptive list of such animals. [C18: from NL, from LL *Fauna* a goddess of living things]
▸**'faunal** *adj*

Fauvism ('fəʊvɪzəm) *n* a form of expressionist painting characterized

THESAURUS

deadly, destructive, fatal, lethal, ominous, ruinous
Antonyms *adj* ≠ **crucial:** inconsequential, insignificant, nugatory, ordinary, unimportant

father *n* **1 = daddy** (*inf.*), begetter, dad (*inf.*), governor (*inf.*), old boy (*inf.*), old man (*inf.*), pa (*inf.*), papa (*old-fashioned inf.*), pater, paterfamilias, patriarch, pop (*inf.*), sire **2 = forefather**, ancestor, forebear, predecessor, progenitor **5 = founder**, architect, author, creator, inventor, maker, originator, prime mover **6 = leader**, city father, elder, patriarch, patron, senator ◆ *vb* **9 = sire**, beget, get, procreate **10 = originate**, create, engender, establish, found, institute, invent

fatherland *n* **1, 2 = homeland**, land of one's birth, land of one's fathers, motherland, native land, old country

fatherly *adj* **= paternal**, affectionate, benevolent, benign, forbearing, indulgent, kind, kindly, patriarchal, protective, supportive, tender

fathom *vb* **2 = measure**, divine, estimate, gauge, penetrate, plumb, probe, sound **3 = understand**, comprehend, get to the bottom of, grasp, interpret

fathomless *adj* **= profound**, abysmal, bottomless, deep, immeasurable, impenetrable, incomprehensible, unfathomable, unplumbed

fatigue *n* **1 = tiredness**, debility, ennui, heaviness, languor, lethargy, listlessness, over- tiredness ◆ *vb* **8 = tire**, drain, drain of energy, exhaust, fag (out) (*inf.*), jade, knacker (*sl.*), overtire, poop (*inf.*), take it out of (*inf.*), weaken, wear out, weary, whack (*Brit. inf.*)
Antonyms *n* ≠ **tiredness:** alertness, animation, energy, freshness, get-up-and-go (*inf.*), go, indefatigability, life, vigour, zest ◆ *vb* ≠ **tire:** refresh, rejuvenate, relieve, rest, revive, stimulate

fatigued *adj* **8 = tired**, all in (*sl.*), bushed (*inf.*), clapped out (*Austral. & NZ inf.*), dead beat (*inf.*), exhausted, fagged (out) (*inf.*), jaded, jiggered (*inf.*), knackered (*sl.*), overtired, tired out, wasted, weary, whacked (*Brit. inf.*), zonked (*sl.*)

fatness *n* **3 = obesity**, beef (*inf.*), bulkiness, corpulence, *embonpoint*, flab, flesh, fleshiness, girth, grossness, heaviness, overweight, podginess, rotundity, size, stoutness, weight, weight problem

fatten *vb* **1 = grow fat**, broaden, coarsen, expand, gain weight, put on weight, spread, swell, thicken, thrive **2** *often with* **up = feed up**, bloat, build up, cram, distend, feed, nourish, overfeed, stuff

fatty *adj* **1, 2 = greasy**, adipose, fat, oily, oleaginous, rich

fatuous *adj* **= foolish**, absurd, asinine, brainless, dense, dull, idiotic, inane, ludicrous, lunatic, mindless, moronic, puerile, silly, stupid, vacuous, weak-minded, witless

fault *n* **1 = flaw**, blemish, defect, deficiency, demerit, drawback, failing, imperfection, infirmity, lack, shortcoming, snag, weakness, weak point **2 = mistake**, blunder, error, error of judgment, inaccuracy, indiscretion, lapse, negligence, offence, omission, oversight, slip, slip-up **3 = misdeed**, delinquency, frailty, lapse, misconduct, misdemeanour, offence, peccadillo, sin, transgression, trespass, wrong **4 = responsibility**, accountability, culpability, liability **9 at fault = guilty**, answerable, blamable, culpable, in the wrong, responsible, to blame **10 find fault (with) = criticize**, carp at, complain, pick holes in, pull to pieces, quibble, take to task **11 to a fault = excessively**, immoderately, in the extreme, needlessly, out of all proportion, overly (*US*), overmuch, preposterously, ridiculously, unduly ◆ *vb* **13 = criticize**, blame, call to account, censure, find fault with, find lacking, hold (someone) accountable, hold (someone) responsible, hold (someone) to blame, impugn
Antonyms *n* ≠ **flaw:** asset, attribute, credit, goodness, merit, perfection, strength, virtue

fault-finding *n* **1 = criticism**, carping, hairsplitting, nagging, niggling, nit-picking (*inf.*) ◆ *adj* **2 = critical**, captious, carping, censorious, hypercritical, on (someone's) back (*inf.*), pettifogging
Antonyms *adj* ≠ **critical:** complimentary, easily pleased, indiscriminate, uncritical, undiscerning, unexacting, unfussy, unperceptive

faultless *adj* **= flawless**, accurate, classic, correct, exemplary, faithful, foolproof, impeccable, model, perfect, unblemished **= blameless**, above reproach, guiltless, immaculate, impeccable, innocent, irreproachable, pure, sinless, spotless, squeaky-clean, stainless, unblemished, unspotted, unsullied

faulty *adj* **= defective**, bad, blemished, broken, damaged, erroneous, fallacious, flawed, impaired, imperfect, imprecise, inaccurate, incorrect, invalid, malfunctioning, not working, out of order, unsound, weak, wrong

by the use of bright colours and simplified forms. [C20: from F, from *fauve* wild beast]
▸**Fauve** *n, adj* ▸'**Fauvist** *n, adj*

faux pas Ⓣ (fəʊ pɑː) *n, pl* **faux pas** (fəʊ pɑːz). a social blunder. [C17: from F: false step]

favour Ⓣ *or US* **favor** ('feɪvə) *n* **1** an approving attitude; goodwill. **2** an act performed out of goodwill or mercy. **3** prejudice and partiality. **4** a condition of being regarded with approval (esp. in **in favour, out of favour**). **5** a token of love, goodwill, etc. **6** a small gift or toy given to a guest at a party. **7** *History.* a badge or ribbon worn or given to indicate loyalty. **8 find favour with.** to be approved of by someone. **9 in favour of. 9a** approving. **9b** to the benefit of. **9c** (of a cheque, etc.) made out to. **9d** in order to show preference for. ◆ *vb (tr)* **10** to regard with especial kindness. **11** to treat with partiality. **12** to support; advocate. **13** to oblige. **14** to help; facilitate. **15** *Inf.* to resemble: *he favours his father.* **16** to wear habitually: *she favours red.* **17** to treat gingerly: *a footballer favouring an injured leg.* [C14: from L, from *favēre* to protect]
▸'**favourer** *or US* '**favorer** *n*

favourable Ⓣ *or US* **favorable** ('feɪvərəbəl) *adj* **1** advantageous, encouraging or promising. **2** giving consent.
▸'**favourably** *or US* '**favorably** *adv*

-favoured *adj* (*in combination*) having an appearance (as specified): *ill-favoured.*

favourite Ⓣ *or US* **favorite** ('feɪvərɪt) *adj* **1** (*prenominal*) most liked. ◆ *n* **2** a person or thing regarded with especial preference or liking. **3** *Sport.* a competitor thought likely to win. [C16: from It., from *favorire* to favour, from L *favēre*]

favouritism Ⓣ *or US* **favoritism** ('feɪvərɪˌtɪzəm) *n* the practice of giving special treatment to a person or group.

fawn[1] Ⓣ (fɔːn) *n* **1** a young deer of either sex aged under one year. **2a** a light greyish-brown colour. **2b** (*as adj*): *a fawn raincoat.* ◆ *vb* **3** (of deer) to bear (young). [C14: from OF, from L *fētus* offspring; see FETUS]
▸'**fawn,like** *adj*

fawn[2] Ⓣ (fɔːn) *vb* (*intr*; often foll. by *on* or *upon*) **1** to seek attention and admiration (from) by cringing and flattering. **2** (of animals, esp. dogs) to try to please by a show of extreme friendliness. [OE *fægnian* to be glad, from *fægen* glad; see FAIN]
▸'**fawner** *n* ▸'**fawning** *adj*

fax (fæks) *n* **1** short for **facsimile transmission. 2** a message or document sent by facsimile transmission. **3** Also called: **fax machine, facsimile machine.** a machine which transmits and receives exact copies of documents. ◆ *vb* **4** (*tr*) to send (a message or document) by facsimile transmission.

fay (feɪ) *n* a fairy or sprite. [C14: from OF *feie*, ult. from L *fātum* FATE]

faze (feɪz) *vb* **fazes, fazing, fazed.** (*tr*) *Inf.* to disconcert; worry; disturb. [C19: var. of arch. *feeze* to beat off]

FBA *abbrev. for* Fellow of the British Academy.

FBI (in the US) *abbrev. for* Federal Bureau of Investigation; an agency responsible for investigating violations of Federal laws.

FC (in Britain) *abbrev. for:* **1** Football Club. **2** Free Church.

fcap *abbrev. for* foolscap.

F clef *n* another name for **bass clef.**

FD *abbrev. for* Fidei Defensor. [L: Defender of the Faith]

Fe *the chemical symbol for* iron. [from NL *ferrum*]

fealty Ⓣ ('fiːəltɪ) *n, pl* **fealties.** (in feudal society) the loyalty sworn to one's lord on becoming his vassal. [C14: from OF, from L *fidēlitās* FIDELITY]

fear Ⓣ (fɪə) *n* **1** a feeling of distress, apprehension, or alarm caused by impending danger, pain, etc. **2** a cause of this feeling. **3** awe; reverence: *fear of God.* **4** concern; anxiety. **5** possibility; chance. **6 for fear of, that** *or* **lest.** to forestall or avoid. **7 no fear.** certainly not. ◆ *vb* **8** to be afraid (to do something) or of (a person or thing). **9** (*tr*) to revere; respect. **10** (*tr; takes a clause as object*) to be sorry: *I fear that you have not won.* **11** (*intr*; foll. by *for*) to feel anxiety about something. [OE *fǣr*]
▸'**fearless** *adj* ▸'**fearlessly** *adv* ▸'**fearlessness** *n*

fearful Ⓣ ('fɪəfʊl) *adj* **1** afraid. **2** causing fear. **3** *Inf.* very unpleasant: *a fearful cold.*
▸'**fearfully** *adv* ▸'**fearfulness** *n*

fearsome Ⓣ ('fɪəsəm) *adj* **1** frightening. **2** timorous; afraid.
▸'**fearsomely** *adv*

feasibility study *n* a study designed to determine the practicability of a system or plan.

feasible Ⓣ ('fiːzəbəl) *adj* **1** able to be done or put into effect; possible. **2** likely; probable. [C15: from Anglo-F *faisable*, from *faire* to do, from L *facere*]
▸ˌ**feasi'bility** *n* ▸'**feasibly** *adv*

feast Ⓣ (fiːst) *n* **1** a large and sumptuous meal. **2** a periodic religious celebration. **3** something extremely pleasing: *a feast for the eyes.* **4 movable**

THESAURUS

faux pas *n* = **gaffe**, bloomer (*Brit. inf.*), blunder, breach of etiquette, clanger, gaucherie, impropriety, indiscretion, solecism

favour *n* **1** = **approval**, approbation, backing, bias, championship, espousal, esteem, favouritism, friendliness, good opinion, goodwill, grace, kindness, kind regard, partiality, patronage, promotion, support **2** = **good turn**, benefit, boon, courtesy, indulgence, kindness, obligement (*Scot. or arch.*), service **5, 6** = **memento**, gift, keepsake, love-token, present, souvenir, token **7** = **badge**, decoration, knot, ribbons, rosette **9a, 9b in favour of** = **for**, all for, backing, on the side of, pro, supporting, to the benefit of ◆ *vb* **10** = **prefer**, incline towards, single out **11** = **indulge**, be partial to, esteem, have in one's good books, pamper, pull strings for (*inf.*), reward, side with, smile upon, spoil, treat with partiality, value **12** = **support**, advocate, approve, back, be in favour of, champion, choose, commend, countenance, encourage, espouse, fancy, like, opt for, patronize **13, 14** = **help**, abet, accommodate, advance, aid, assist, befriend, do a kindness to, facilitate, oblige, promote, succour **15** *Informal* = **look like**, be the image *or* picture of, resemble, take after **17** = **ease**, extenuate, spare
Antonyms *n* ≠ **approval:** animosity, antipathy, disapproval, disfavour, ill will, malevolence ≠ **good turn:** disservice, harm, injury, wrong ◆ *vb* ≠ **prefer:** disapprove, disdain, dislike, object to ≠ **support:** oppose, thwart

favourable *adj* **1** = **advantageous**, appropriate, auspicious, beneficial, convenient, encouraging, fair, fit, good, helpful, hopeful, opportune, promising, propitious, suitable, timely **1** = **positive**, affirmative, agreeable, amicable, approving, benign, encouraging, enthusiastic, friendly, kind, reassuring, sympathetic, understanding, welcoming, well-disposed
Antonyms *adj* ≠ **advantageous:** disadvantageous, inauspicious, unfavourable, unhelpful, unpromising, useless ≠ **positive:** disapproving, ill-disposed, unfavourable, unfriendly, unsympathetic

favourably *adv* **1** = **advantageously**, auspiciously, conveniently, fortunately, opportunely, profitably, to one's advantage, well **1** = **positively**, agreeably, approvingly, enthusiastically, genially, graciously, helpfully, in a kindly manner, with approbation, with approval, with cordiality, without prejudice

favourite *adj* **1** = **preferred**, best-loved, choice, dearest, esteemed, fave (*inf.*), favoured ◆ *n* **2** = **darling**, beloved, blue-eyed boy (*inf.*), choice, dear, fave (*inf.*), idol, pet, pick, preference, teacher's pet, the apple of one's eye

favouritism *n* = **preferential treatment**, bias, cronyism, jobs for the boys (*inf.*), nepotism, one-sidedness, partiality, partisanship, preference
Antonyms *n* equality, equity, even-handedness, fairness, impartiality, neutrality, objectivity, open-mindedness

fawn[1] *adj* **2** = **beige**, buff, greyish-brown, neutral

fawn[2] *vb* **1** *often with* **on** *or* **upon** = **ingratiate oneself**, be obsequious, be servile, bow and scrape, brown-nose (*taboo sl.*), court, crawl, creep, cringe, curry favour, dance attendance, flatter, grovel, kneel, kowtow, lick (someone's) boots, pander to, pay court, toady, truckle

fawning[2] *adj* **1** = **obsequious**, abject, bootlicking (*inf.*), bowing and scraping, crawling, cringing, deferential, flattering, grovelling, prostrate, servile, slavish, sycophantic

fealty *n* = **loyalty**, allegiance, devotion, faith, faithfulness, fidelity, homage, obeisance, submission, troth (*arch.*)

fear *n* **1** = **dread**, alarm, apprehensiveness, awe, blue funk (*inf.*), consternation, cravenness, dismay, fright, horror, panic, qualms, terror, timidity, tremors, trepidation **2** = **bugbear**, bête noire, bogey, horror, nightmare, phobia, spectre **3** = **awe**, reverence, veneration, wonder **4** = **anxiety**, agitation, apprehension, concern, disquietude, distress, doubt, foreboding(s), misgiving(s), solicitude, suspicion, unease, uneasiness, worry ◆ *vb* **8** = **be afraid**, apprehend, be apprehensive, be frightened, be in a blue funk (*inf.*), be scared, dare not, dread, have a horror of, have a phobia about, have butterflies in one's stomach (*inf.*), have qualms, live in dread of, shake in one's shoes, shudder at, take fright, tremble at **9** = **revere**, respect, reverence, stand in awe of, venerate **11** *foll. by* **for** = **worry about**, be anxious about, be concerned about, be disquieted over, be distressed about, feel concern for, tremble for

fearful *adj* **1** = **scared**, afraid, alarmed, anxious, apprehensive, diffident, faint-hearted, frightened, hesitant, intimidated, jittery (*inf.*), jumpy, nervous, nervy (*Brit. inf.*), neurotic, panicky, pusillanimous, shrinking, tense, timid, timorous, uneasy, wired (*sl.*) **2** = **frightful**, appalling, atrocious, awful, dire, distressing, dreadful, ghastly, grievous, grim, gruesome, hair-raising, harrowing, hideous, horrendous, horrible, horrific, monstrous, shocking, terrible, unspeakable
Antonyms *adj* ≠ **scared:** bold, brave, confident, courageous, daring, dauntless, doughty, gallant, game (*inf.*), gutsy (*sl.*), heroic, indomitable, intrepid, lion-hearted, plucky, unabashed, unafraid, undaunted, unflinching, valiant, valorous

fearfully *adv* **1** = **nervously**, apprehensively, diffidently, in fear and trembling, timidly, timorously, uneasily, with bated breath, with many misgivings *or* forebodings, with one's heart in one's mouth

fearless *adj* **1** = **brave**, bold, confident, courageous, daring, dauntless, doughty, gallant, game (*inf.*), gutsy (*sl.*), heroic, indomitable, intrepid, lion-hearted, plucky, unabashed, unafraid, undaunted, unflinching, valiant, valorous

fearlessness *n* **1** = **bravery**, boldness, confidence, courage, dauntlessness, guts (*inf.*), indomitability, intrepidity, lion-heartedness, nerve, pluckiness

fearsome *adj* **1** = **terrifying**, alarming, appalling, awe-inspiring, awesome, awful, baleful, daunting, dismaying, formidable, frightening, hair-raising, horrendous, horrifying, menacing, unnerving

feasibility *n* **1, 2** = **possibility**, expediency, practicability, usefulness, viability, workability

feasible *adj* **1, 2** = **possible**, achievable, attainable, likely, practicable, realizable, reasonable, viable, workable
Antonyms *adj* impossible, impracticable, inconceivable, unreasonable, untenable, unviable, unworkable

feast *n* **1** = **banquet**, barbecue, beanfeast (*Brit. inf.*), beano (*Brit. sl.*), blowout (*sl.*), carousal, carouse, dinner, entertainment, festive board, jollification, junket, repast, revels, slap-up meal (*Brit. inf.*), spread (*inf.*), treat **2** = **festival**, cele-

feast. a festival of variable date. ◆ *vb* **5** (*intr*) **5a** to eat a feast. **5b** (usually foll. by *on*) to enjoy the eating (of): *to feast on cakes.* **6** (*tr*) to give a feast to. **7** (*intr;* foll. by *on*) to take great delight (in): *to feast on beautiful paintings.* **8** (*tr*) to regale or delight: *to feast one's eyes.* [C13: from OF, from L *festa,* neuter pl (later assumed to be fem sing) of *festus* joyful; rel. to L *fānum* temple, *fēriae* festivals]
▸ **ˈfeaster** *n*

Feast of Dedication *n* a literal translation of **Chanukah.**

Feast of Lights *n* an English name for **Chanukah.**

Feast of Tabernacles *n* a literal translation of **Sukkoth.**

Feast of Weeks *n* a literal translation of **Shavuot.**

feat ⓣ (fiːt) *n* a remarkable, skilful, or daring action. [C14: from Anglo-F *fait,* from L *factum* deed; see FACT]

feather ⓣ (ˈfɛðə) *n* **1** any of the flat light waterproof structures forming the plumage of birds, each consisting of a hollow shaft having a vane of barbs on either side. **2** something resembling a feather, such as a tuft of hair or grass. **3** *Archery.* **3a** a bird's feather or artificial substitute fitted to an arrow to direct its flight. **3b** the feathered end of an arrow. **4** *Rowing.* the position of an oar turned parallel to the water between strokes. **5** condition of spirits; fettle: *in fine feather.* **6** something of negligible value: *I don't care a feather.* **7 feather in one's cap.** a cause for pleasure at one's achievements. ◆ *vb* **8** (*tr*) to fit, cover, or supply with feathers. **9** *Rowing.* to turn (an oar) parallel to the water during recovery between strokes, in order to lessen wind resistance. **10** to change the pitch of (an aircraft propeller) so that the chord lines of the blades are in line with the airflow. **11** (*intr*) (of a bird) to grow feathers. **12 feather one's nest.** to provide oneself with comforts. [OE *fether*]
▸ **ˈfeathering** *n* ▸ **ˈfeather-ˌlike** *adj* ▸ **ˈfeathery** *adj*

feather bed *n* **1** a mattress filled with feathers or down. ◆ *vb* **featherbed, featherbeds, featherbedding, featherbedded. 2** (*tr*) to pamper; spoil.

featherbedding (ˈfɛðəˌbɛdɪŋ) *n* the practice of limiting production or of overmanning in order to prevent redundancies or create jobs.

featherbrain (ˈfɛðəˌbreɪn) *or* **featherhead** *n* a frivolous or forgetful person.
▸ **ˈfeatherˌbrained** *or* **ˈfeatherˌheaded** *adj*

featheredge (ˈfɛðərˌɛdʒ) *n* a board or plank that tapers to a thin edge at one side.

featherstitch (ˈfɛðəˌstɪtʃ) *n* **1** a zigzag embroidery stitch. ◆ *vb* **2** to decorate (cloth) with featherstitch.

featherweight (ˈfɛðəˌweɪt) *n* **1a** something very light or of little importance. **1b** (*as modifier*): *featherweight considerations.* **2a** a professional boxer weighing 118–126 pounds (53.5–57 kg). **2b** an amateur boxer weighing 54–57 kg (119–126 pounds). **3** an amateur wrestler weighing usually 127–137 pounds (58–62 kg).

feature ⓣ (ˈfiːtʃə) *n* **1** any one of the parts of the face, such as the nose, chin, or mouth. **2** a prominent or distinctive part, as of a landscape, book, etc. **3** the principal film in a programme at a cinema. **4** an item or article appearing regularly in a newspaper, magazine, etc.: *a gardening feature.* **5** Also called: **feature story.** a prominent story in a newspaper, etc.: *a feature on prison reform.* **6** a programme given special prominence on radio or television. **7** *Arch.* general form. ◆ *vb* **features, featuring, featured. 8** (*tr*) to have as a feature or make a feature of. **9** to give prominence to (an actor, famous event, etc.) in a film or (of an actor, etc.) to have prominence in a film. **10** (*tr*) *Arch.* to draw the main features or parts of. [C14: from Anglo-F *feture,* from L *factūra* a making, from *facere* to make]
▸ **ˈfeatureless** *adj*

-featured *adj* (*in combination*) having features as specified: *heavy-featured.*

Feb. *abbrev. for* February.

febri- *combining form.* indicating fever: *febrifuge.* [from L *febris* fever]

febrifuge (ˈfɛbrɪˌfjuːdʒ) *n* **1** any drug or agent for reducing fever. ◆ *adj* **2** serving to reduce fever. [C17: from Med. L *febrifugia* feverfew; see FEBRI-, -FUGE]
▸ **febrifugal** (fɪˈbrɪfjʊgᵊl) *adj*

febrile ⓣ (ˈfiːbraɪl) *adj* of or relating to fever; feverish. [C17: from Medical L *febrīlis,* from L *febris* fever]
▸ **febrility** (fɪˈbrɪlɪtɪ) *n*

February (ˈfɛbrʊərɪ) *n, pl* **Februaries.** the second month of the year, consisting of 28 or (in a leap year) 29 days. [C13: from L *Februārius mēnsis* month of expiation, from *februa* Roman festival of purification held on February 15, from pl of *februum* a purgation]

feces (ˈfiːsiːz) *pl n* the usual US spelling of **faeces.**
▸ **fecal** (ˈfiːkᵊl) *adj*

feckless ⓣ (ˈfɛklɪs) *adj* feeble; weak; ineffectual. [C16: from obs. *feck* value, effect + -LESS]
▸ **ˈfecklessly** *adv* ▸ **ˈfecklessness** *n*

feculent (ˈfɛkjʊlənt) *adj* **1** filthy or foul. **2** of or containing waste matter. [C15: from L *faeculentus;* see FAECES]
▸ **ˈfeculence** *n*

fecund ⓣ (ˈfiːkənd, ˈfɛk-) *adj* **1** fertile. **2** intellectually productive. [C14: from L *fēcundus*]
▸ **fecundity** (fɪˈkʌndɪtɪ) *n*

fecundate (ˈfiːkənˌdeɪt, ˈfɛk-) *vb* **fecundates, fecundating, fecundated.** (*tr*) **1** to make fruitful. **2** to fertilize. [C17: from L *fēcundāre* to fertilize]
▸ **ˌfecunˈdation** *n*

fed[1] (fɛd) *vb* **1** the past tense and past participle of **feed. 2 fed to death** *or* **fed (up) to the (back) teeth.** *Inf.* bored or annoyed.

fed[2] (fɛd) *n US sl.* an agent of the FBI.

Fed (fɛd) *n* short for **Federal Reserve System.**

Fed. *or* **fed.** *abbrev. for:* **1** Federal. **2** Federation. **3** Federated.

fedayee (fəˈdɑːjiː) *n, pl* **fedayeen** (-jiːn). **a** (*sometimes cap.*) (in Arab states) a commando, esp. one fighting against Israel. **b** (esp. in Iran and Afghanistan) a member of a guerrilla organization. [from Ar. *fidā'i* one who risks his life in a cause, from *fidā'* redemption]

federal (ˈfɛdərəl) *adj* **1** of or relating to a form of government or a country in which power is divided between one central and several regional governments. **2** of or relating to the central government of a federation. [C17: from L *foedus* league]
▸ **ˈfederaˌlism** *n* ▸ **ˈfederalist** *n, adj* ▸ **ˈfederally** *adv*

Federal (ˈfɛdərəl) *adj* **1** characteristic of or supporting the Union government during the American Civil War. ◆ *n* **2** a supporter of the Union government during the American Civil War.

Federal Government *n* the national government of a federated state, such as the Canadian national government located in Ottawa.

federalize *or* **federalise** (ˈfɛdərəˌlaɪz) *vb* **federalizes, federalizing, federalized** *or* **federalises, federalising, federalised.** (*tr*) **1** to unite in a federal union. **2** to subject to federal control.
▸ **ˌfederaliˈzation** *or* **ˌfederaliˈsation** *n*

Federal Reserve System *n* (in the US) a banking system consisting of twelve **Federal Reserve Banks** and their member banks. It performs functions similar to those of the Bank of England.

federate ⓣ *vb* (ˈfɛdəˌreɪt), **federates, federating, federated. 1** to unite or cause to unite in a federal union. ◆ *adj* (ˈfɛdərɪt). **2** federal; federated.
▸ **ˈfederative** *adj*

federation ⓣ (ˌfɛdəˈreɪʃən) *n* **1** the act of federating. **2** the union of several provinces, states, etc., to form a federal union. **3** a political unit formed in such a way. **4** any league, alliance, or confederacy.

fedora (fɪˈdɔːrə) *n* a soft felt brimmed hat, usually with a band. [C19: allegedly after *Fédora* (1882), play by Victorien Sardou (1831–1908)]

fed up ⓣ *adj* (*usually postpositive*) *Inf.* annoyed or bored: *I'm fed up with your conduct.*

fee ⓣ (fiː) *n* **1** a payment asked by professional people or public servants for their services: *school fees.* **2** a charge made for a privilege: *an entrance fee.* **3** *Property law.* an interest in land capable of being inherited. The interest can be with unrestricted rights of disposal (**fee simple**) or with restricted rights to one class of heirs (**fee tail**). **4** (in feudal Europe) the land granted by a lord to his vassal. **5 in fee.** *Law.* (of land) in absolute ownership. ◆ *vb* **fees, feeing, feed. 6** *Rare.* to give a fee to. **7** *Chiefly Scot.* to hire for a fee. [C14: from OF *fie,* of Gmc origin; see FIEF]

feeble ⓣ (ˈfiːbᵊl) *adj* **1** lacking in physical or mental strength. **2** uncon-

THESAURUS

bration, holiday, holy day, red-letter day, saint's day **3 = treat**, delight, enjoyment, gratification, pleasure ◆ *vb* **5 = eat one's fill**, eat to one's heart's content, fare sumptuously, gorge, gormandize, indulge, overindulge, pig out (*sl.*), stuff, stuff one's face (*sl.*), wine and dine **6 = treat**, entertain, hold a reception for, kill the fatted calf for, regale, wine and dine **7, 8 = delight**, gladden, gratify, rejoice, thrill

feat *n* = **accomplishment**, achievement, act, attainment, deed, exploit, feather in one's cap, performance

feather *n* **1** *plural* = **plumage**, down, plumes

feathery *adj* **1, 2 = downy**, feathered, fluffy, plumate *or* plumose (*Botany & Zoology*), plumed, plumy, wispy

feature 1 *plural* = **face**, countenance, lineaments, physiognomy *n* **2 = aspect**, attribute, characteristic, facet, factor, hallmark, mark, peculiarity, point, property, quality, trait **4 = article**, column, comment, item, piece, report, story ◆ *vb* **8, 9 = spotlight**, accentuate, call attention to, emphasize, foreground, give prominence to, give the full works (*sl.*), headline, play up, present, promote, set off, star

featured *adj* **8, 9 = highlighted**, given prominence, headlined, in the public eye, presented, promoted, recommended, specially presented, starred

featuring *adj* **8, 9 = highlighting**, calling attention to, displaying, drawing attention to, giving a star role, giving prominence to, giving the full works (*sl.*), making the main attraction, presenting, promoting, pushing, recommending, showing, showing off, starring, turning the spotlight on

febrile *adj* = **feverish**, delirious, fevered, fiery, flushed, hot, inflamed, pyretic (*Medical*)

feckless *adj* = **irresponsible**, aimless, feeble, futile, good-for-nothing, hopeless, incompetent, ineffectual, shiftless, useless, weak, worthless

fecund *adj* **1 = fertile**, fructiferous, fruitful, productive, prolific, teeming

fecundity *n* **1 = fertility**, fruitfulness, productiveness

federate *vb* **1 = unite**, amalgamate, associate, combine, confederate, integrate, syndicate, unify

federation *n* **2-4 = union**, alliance, amalgamation, association, *Bund,* coalition, combination, confederacy, copartnership, entente, federacy, league, syndicate

fed up *adj Informal* = **dissatisfied**, annoyed, blue, bored, brassed off (*Brit. sl.*), browned-off (*inf.*), depressed, discontented, dismal, down, down in the mouth, gloomy, glum, hacked (off) (*sl.*), pissed off (*taboo sl.*), sick and tired (*inf.*), tired, weary

fee *n* **1, 2 = charge**, account, bill, compensation, emolument, hire, honorarium, meed (*arch.*), pay, payment, recompense, remuneration, reward, toll

feeble *adj* **1 = weak**, debilitated, delicate, doddering, effete, enervated, enfeebled, etiolated, exhausted, failing, faint, frail, infirm, languid,

vincing: *feeble excuses.* **3** easily influenced. [C12: from OF *feble, fleible,* from L *flēbilis* to be lamented, from *flēre* to weep]
▸ˈ**feebleness** *n* ▸ˈ**feebly** *adv*

feeble-minded Ⓣ *adj* **1** lacking in intelligence. **2** mentally defective.

feed Ⓣ (fiːd) *vb* **feeds, feeding, fed.** (*mainly tr*) **1** to give food to: *to feed the cat.* **2** to give as food: *to feed meat to the cat.* **3** (*intr*) to eat food: *the horses feed at noon.* **4** to provide food for. **5** to gratify; satisfy. **6** (*also intr*) to supply (a machine, furnace, etc.) with (the necessary materials or fuel) for its operation, or (of such materials) to flow or move forwards into a machine, etc. **7** *Theatre, inf.* to cue (an actor, esp. a comedian) with lines. **8** *Sport.* to pass a ball to (a team-mate). **9** (*also intr;* foll. by *on* or *upon*) to eat or cause to eat. ◆ *n* **10** the act or an instance of feeding. **11** food, esp. that of animals or babies. **12** the process of supplying a machine or furnace with a material or fuel. **13** the quantity of material or fuel so supplied. **14** *Theatre, inf.* a performer, esp. a straight man, who provides cues. **15** *Inf.* a meal. [OE *fēdan*]
▸ˈ**feedable** *adj*

feedback (ˈfiːdˌbæk) *n* **1** information or an opinion in response to an inquiry, proposal, etc. **2a** the return of part of the output of an electronic circuit, device, or mechanical system to its input. In **negative feedback** a rise in output energy reduces the input energy; in **positive feedback** an increase in output energy reinforces the input energy. **2b** that part of the output signal fed back into the input. **3** the return of part of the sound output of a loudspeaker to the microphone or pick-up, so that a high-pitched whistle is produced. **4** the whistling noise so produced. **5** the effect of a product or action in a cyclic biological reaction on another stage in the same reaction.

feeder (ˈfiːdə) *n* **1** a person or thing that feeds or is fed. **2** a child's feeding bottle or bib. **3** a person or device that feeds the working material into a system or machine. **4** a tributary channel. **5** a road, service, etc., that links secondary areas to the main traffic network. **6** a power line for transmitting electrical power from a generating station to a distribution network.

feeding bottle *n* a bottle fitted with a rubber teat from which infants suck liquids.

feel Ⓣ (fiːl) *vb* **feels, feeling, felt. 1** to perceive (something) by touching. **2** to have a physical or emotional sensation of (something): *to feel anger.* **3** (*tr*) to examine (something) by touch. **4** (*tr*) to find (one's way) by testing or cautious exploration. **5** (*copula*) to seem in respect of the sensation given: *it feels warm.* **6** to sense (esp. in **feel (it) in one's bones**). **7** to consider; believe; think. **8** (*intr;* foll. by *for*) to show sympathy or compassion (towards): *I feel for you in your sorrow.* **9** (*tr;* often foll. by *up*) *Sl.* to pass one's hands over the sexual organs of. **10 feel like.** to have an inclination (for something or doing something): *I don't feel like going to the pictures.* **11 feel up to.** (*usually used with a negative or in a question*) to be fit enough for (something or doing something): *I don't feel up to going out.* ◆ *n* **12** the act or an instance of feeling. **13** the quality of or an impression from something perceived through feeling: *a homely feel.* **14** the sense of touch. **15** an instinctive aptitude; knack: *she's got a feel for this sort of work.* [OE *fēlan*]

feeler Ⓣ (ˈfiːlə) *n* **1** a person or thing that feels. **2** an organ in certain animals, such as an antenna, that is sensitive to touch. **3** a remark designed to probe the reactions or intentions of others.

feeler gauge *n* a thin metal strip of known thickness used to measure a narrow gap or to set a gap between two parts.

feel-good *adj* causing or characterized by a feeling of self-satisfaction: *feel-good factor.*

feeling Ⓣ (ˈfiːlɪŋ) *n* **1** the sense of touch. **2a** the ability to experience physical sensations, such as heat, etc. **2b** the sensation so experienced. **3** a state of mind. **4** a physical or mental impression: *a feeling of warmth.* **5** fondness; sympathy: *to have a great deal of feeling for someone.* **6** a sentiment: *a feeling that the project is feasible.* **7** an emotional disturbance, esp. anger or dislike: *a lot of bad feeling.* **8** intuitive appreciation and understanding: *a feeling for words.* **9** sensibility in the performance of something. **10** (*pl*) emotional or moral sensitivity (esp. in **hurt** *or* **injure the feelings of**). ◆ *adj* **11** sentient; sensitive. **12** expressing or containing emotion.
▸ˈ**feelingly** *adv*

feet (fiːt) *n* **1** the plural of **foot. 2 at (someone's) feet.** as someone's disciple. **3 be run** *or* **rushed off one's feet.** to be very busy. **4 carry** *or* **sweep off one's feet.** to fill with enthusiasm. **5 feet of clay.** a weakness that is not widely known. **6 have** (*or* **keep**) **one's feet on the ground.** to be practical and reliable. **7 on one's** *or* **its feet. 7a** standing up. **7b** in good health. **8 stand on one's own feet.** to be independent.

feign Ⓣ (feɪn) *vb* **1** to pretend: *to feign innocence.* **2** (*tr*) to invent: *to feign an excuse.* **3** (*tr*) to copy; imitate. [C13: from OF, from L *fingere* to form, shape, invent]
▸ˈ**feigningly** *adv*

feijoa (fiːˈdʒəʊə) *n* **1** an evergreen shrub of South America. **2** the fruit of this shrub. [C19: NL, after J. da Silva *Feijo*, 19th-cent. Sp. botanist]

feint[1] Ⓣ (feɪnt) *n* **1** a mock attack or movement designed to distract an adversary, as in boxing, fencing, etc. **2** a misleading action or appearance. ◆ *vb* **3** (*intr*) to make a feint. [C17: from F, from OF *feindre* to FEIGN]

feint[2] (feɪnt) *n Printing.* a narrow rule used in the production of ruled paper. [C19: var. of FAINT]

feisty (ˈfaɪstɪ) *adj* **feistier, feistiest.** *Inf.* **1** lively, resilient, and self-reliant. **2** *US & Canad.* frisky. **3** *US & Canad.* irritable. [C19: dialect *feist, fist* small dog]

felafel (fəˈlɑːfəl) *n* a variant spelling of **falafel.**

feldspar (ˈfɛldˌspɑː, ˈfɛlˌspɑː) *or* **felspar** *n* any of a group of hard rock-forming minerals consisting of aluminium silicates of potassium, sodium, calcium, or barium: the principal constituents of igneous rocks. [C18: from G, from *Feld* field + *Spat(h)* SPAR[3]]
▸**feldspathic** (fɛldˈspæθɪk, fɛlˈspæθ-) *or* **felˈspathic** *adj*

felicitate Ⓣ (fɪˈlɪsɪˌteɪt) *vb* **felicitates, felicitating, felicitated.** to congratulate.
▸**feˌliciˈtation** *n* ▸**feˈliciˌtator** *n*

felicitous Ⓣ (fɪˈlɪsɪtəs) *adj* **1** well-chosen; apt. **2** possessing an agreeable style. **3** marked by happiness.
▸**feˈlicitously** *adv*

felicity Ⓣ (fɪˈlɪsɪtɪ) *n, pl* **felicities. 1** happiness. **2** a cause of happiness. **3** an appropriate expression or style. **4** the display of such expressions or style. [C14: from L *fēlīcitās* happiness, from *fēlix* happy]

feline Ⓣ (ˈfiːlaɪn) *adj* **1** of, relating to, or belonging to a family of predatory mammals, including cats, lions, leopards, and cheetahs, having a round head and retractile claws. **2** resembling or suggestive of a cat, esp. in stealth or grace. ◆ *n* **3** any member of the cat family; a cat. [C17: from L, from *fēlēs* cat]
▸ˈ**felinely** *adv* ▸**felinity** (fɪˈlɪnɪtɪ) *n*

fell[1] (fɛl) *vb* the past tense of **fall.**

fell[2] Ⓣ (fɛl) *vb* (*tr*) **1** to cut or knock down: *to fell a tree.* **2** *Needlework.* to fold under and sew flat (the edges of a seam). ◆ *n* **3** *US & Canad.* the timber felled in one season. **4** a seam finished by felling. [OE *fellan;* cf. FALL]
▸ˈ**feller** *n*

THESAURUS

powerless, puny, shilpit (*Scot.*), sickly, weakened, weedy (*inf.*) **2** = **flimsy,** flat, inadequate, incompetent, indecisive, ineffective, ineffectual, inefficient, insignificant, insufficient, lame, paltry, pathetic, poor, slight, tame, thin, unconvincing, weak
Antonyms *adj* ≠ **weak:** energetic, hale, healthy, hearty, lusty, robust, stalwart, strong, sturdy, vigorous ≠ **flimsy:** effective, forceful, successful

feeble-minded *adj* **1, 2** = **half-witted,** addle-pated, bone-headed, braindead (*inf.*), deficient, dim-witted (*inf.*), dozy (*Brit. inf.*), dull, dumb (*inf.*), idiotic, imbecilic, lacking, moronic, obtuse, retarded, simple, slow on the uptake, slow-witted, soft in the head (*inf.*), stupid, vacant, weak-minded
Antonyms *adj* astute, aware, bright, clear-headed, clever, intelligent, keen, quick-witted, smart

feebleness *n* **1** = **weakness,** debility, delicacy, effeteness, enervation, etiolation, exhaustion, frailness, frailty, incapacity, infirmity, lack of strength, languor, lassitude, sickliness **2** = **flimsiness,** inadequacy, incompetence, indecisiveness, ineffectualness, insignificance, insufficiency, lameness, weakness

feed *vb* **1, 4** = **cater for,** nourish, provide for, provision, supply, sustain, victual, wine and dine **9** *foll. by* **on** = **eat,** devour, exist on, fare, graze, live on, nurture, partake of, pasture, subsist, take nourishment ◆ *n* **11** = **food,** fodder, forage, pasturage, provender, silage **15** *Informal* = **meal,** feast, nosh (*sl.*), nosh-up (*Brit. sl.*), repast, spread (*inf.*), tuck-in (*inf.*)

feel *vb* **1** = **touch,** caress, finger, fondle, handle, manipulate, maul, paw, run one's hands over, stroke **2** = **experience,** be aware of, be sensible of, endure, enjoy, go through, have, have a sensation of, know, notice, observe, perceive, suffer, take to heart, undergo **3, 4** = **explore,** fumble, grope, sound, test, try **5** = **seem,** appear, resemble, strike one as **6** = **sense,** be convinced, feel in one's bones, have a hunch, have the impression, intuit **7** = **believe,** be of the opinion that, consider, deem, hold, judge, think **8** *foll. by* **for** = **feel compassion for,** be moved by, be sorry for, bleed for, commiserate, compassionate, condole with, empathize, pity, sympathize with **10 feel like** = **fancy,** could do with, desire, feel inclined, feel the need for, feel up to, have the inclination, want ◆ *n* **13** = **impression,** air, ambience, atmosphere, feeling, quality, sense, vibes (*sl.*)

feeler *n* **2** = **antenna,** tentacle, whisker **3** = **probe,** advance, approach

feeling *n* **1** = **sense of touch,** feel, perception, sensation, sense, touch **4** = **impression,** apprehension, consciousness, hunch, idea, inkling, notion, presentiment, sense, suspicion **5, 6** = **emotion,** affection, ardour, fervour, fondness, heat, intensity, passion, sentiment, sentimentality, warmth **5** = **sympathy,** appreciation, compassion, concern, empathy, pity, sensibility, sensitivity, understanding **7** = **hostility,** anger, dislike, distrust, enmity, upset **10** *plural* = **emotions,** ego, self-esteem, sensitivities, susceptibilities

feign *vb* **1, 3** = **pretend,** act, affect, assume, counterfeit, devise, dissemble, fabricate, fake, forge, give the appearance of, imitate, make a show of, put on, sham, simulate

feigned *adj* **1, 3** = **pretended,** affected, artificial, assumed, counterfeit, ersatz, fabricated, fake, false, imitation, insincere, pseudo (*inf.*), sham, simulated, spurious

feint[1] *n* **2** = **bluff,** artifice, blind, distraction, dodge, expedient, gambit, manoeuvre, mock attack, play, pretence, ruse, stratagem, subterfuge, wile

felicitate *vb* = **congratulate,** compliment, wish joy to

felicitous *adj* **1, 3** = **fitting,** apposite, appropriate, apropos, apt, happy, inspired, neat, opportune, pat, propitious, suitable, timely, well-chosen, well-timed

felicity *n* **1** = **happiness,** blessedness, bliss, blissfulness, delectation, ecstasy, joy **3** = **aptness,** applicability, appropriateness, becomingness, effectiveness, grace, propriety, suitability, suitableness

feline *adj* **1** = **catlike,** leonine **2** = **graceful,** flowing, sinuous, sleek, slinky, smooth, stealthy

fell[2] *vb* **1** = **cut down,** cut, deck (*sl.*), demolish,

fell[3] Ⓣ (fɛl) *adj* **1** *Arch.* cruel or fierce. **2** *Arch.* destructive or deadly. **3 one fell swoop.** a single hasty action or occurrence. [C13 *fel,* from OF: cruel, from Med. L *fellō* villain; see FELON[1]]

fell[4] (fɛl) *n* an animal skin or hide. [OE]

fell[5] (fɛl) *n* (*often pl*) *Scot. & N English.* **a** a mountain, hill, or moor. **b** (*in combination*): *fell-walking.* [C13: from ON *fjall;* rel. to OHG *felis* rock]

fellah ('fɛlə) *n, pl* **fellahs, fellahin,** *or* **fellaheen** (ˌfɛlə'hiːn). a peasant in Arab countries. [C18: from Ar., dialect var. of *fallāh,* from *falaha* to cultivate]

fellatio (fɪ'leɪʃɪəʊ) *n* a sexual activity in which the penis is stimulated by the mouth. [C19: NL, from L *fellāre* to suck]

felloe ('fɛləʊ) *or* **felly** ('fɛlɪ) *n, pl* **felloes** *or* **fellies.** a segment or the whole rim of a wooden wheel to which the spokes are attached. [OE *felge*]

fellow Ⓣ ('fɛləʊ) *n* **1** a man or boy. **2** an informal word for **boyfriend. 3** *Inf.* one or oneself: *a fellow has to eat.* **4** a person considered to be of little worth. **5a** (*often pl*) a companion; associate. **5b** (*as modifier*): *fellow travellers.* **6** a member of the governing body at any of various universities or colleges. **7** a postgraduate student employed, esp. for a fixed period, to undertake research. **8a** a person in the same group, class, or condition: *the surgeon asked his fellows.* **8b** (*as modifier*): *a fellow sufferer.* **9** one of a pair; counterpart; mate. [OE *fēolaga*]

Fellow ('fɛləʊ) *n* a member of any of various learned societies: *Fellow of the British Academy.*

fellow feeling Ⓣ *n* **1** mutual sympathy or friendship. **2** an opinion held in common.

fellowship Ⓣ ('fɛləʊˌʃɪp) *n* **1** the state of sharing mutual interests, activities, etc. **2** a society of people sharing mutual interests, activities, etc. **3** companionship; friendship. **4** the state or relationship of being a fellow. **5** *Education.* **5a** a financed research post providing study facilities, privileges, etc., often in return for teaching services. **5b** an honorary title carrying certain privileges awarded to a postgraduate student.

fellow traveller *n* **1** a companion on a journey. **2** a non-Communist who sympathizes with Communism.

felon[1] ('fɛlən) *n* **1** *Criminal law.* (formerly) a person who has committed a felony. ◆ *adj* **2** *Arch.* evil. [C13: from OF: villain, from Med. L *fellō,* from ?]

felon[2] ('fɛlən) *n* a purulent inflammation of the end joint of a finger. [C12: from Med. L *fellō,* ?from L *fel* poison]

felonious (fɪ'ləʊnɪəs) *adj* **1** *Criminal law.* of, involving, or constituting a felony. **2** *Obs.* wicked.
▸**fe'loniously** *adv* ▸**fe'loniousness** *n*

felony ('fɛlənɪ) *n, pl* **felonies.** *Criminal law.* (formerly) a serious crime, such as murder or arson.

felspar ('fɛlˌspɑː) *n* a variant spelling (esp. Brit.) of **feldspar.**
▸**felspathic** (fɛl'spæθɪk) *adj*

felt[1] (fɛlt) *vb* the past tense and past participle of **feel.**

felt[2] (fɛlt) *n* **1** a matted fabric of wool, hair, etc., made by working the fibres together under pressure or by heat or chemical action. **2** any material, such as asbestos, made by a similar process of matting. ◆ *vb* **3** (*tr*) to make into or cover with felt. **4** (*intr*) to become matted. [OE]

felt-tip pen *n* a pen whose writing point is made from pressed fibres. Also called: **fibre-tip pen.**

felucca (fɛ'lʌkə) *n* a narrow lateen-rigged vessel of the Mediterranean. [C17: from It., prob. from obs. Sp. *faluca,* prob. from Ar. *fulūk* ships, from Gk, from *ephelkein* to tow]

fem. *abbrev. for:* **1** female. **2** feminine.

female ('fiːmeɪl) *adj* **1** of, relating to, or designating the sex producing gametes (ova) that can be fertilized by male gametes (spermatozoa). **2** of or characteristic of a woman. **3** for or composed of women or girls: *a female choir.* **4** (of reproductive organs such as the ovary and carpel) capable of producing female gametes. **5** (of flowers) lacking, or having nonfunctional, stamens. **6** having an internal cavity into which a projecting male counterpart can be fitted: *a female thread.* ◆ *n* **7** a female animal or plant. [C14: from earlier *femelle* (infl. by *male*), from L *fēmella* a young woman, from *fēmina* a woman]
▸**'femaleness** *n*

female impersonator *n* a male theatrical performer who acts as a woman.

feminine Ⓣ ('fɛmɪnɪn) *adj* **1** suitable to or characteristic of a woman. **2** possessing qualities or characteristics considered typical of or appropriate to a woman. **3** effeminate; womanish. **4** *Grammar.* **4a** denoting or belonging to a gender of nouns that includes all kinds of referents as well as some female animate referents. **4b** (*as n*): *German* Zeit *"time" and* Ehe *"marriage" are feminines.* [C14: from L, from *fēmina* woman]
▸**'femininely** *adv* ▸ˌ**femi'ninity** *or* **'feminineness** *n*

feminism ('fɛmɪˌnɪzəm) *n* a doctrine or movement that advocates equal rights for women.
▸**'feminist** *n, adj*

feminize *or* **feminise** ('fɛmɪˌnaɪz) *vb* **feminizes, feminizing, feminized** *or* **feminises, feminising, feminised. 1** to make or become feminine. **2** to cause (a male animal) to develop female characteristics.
▸ˌ**femini'zation** *or* ˌ**femini'sation** *n*

femme fatale Ⓣ *French.* (fam fatal) *n, pl* ***femmes fatales*** (fam fatal). an alluring or seductive woman, esp. one who causes men to love her to their own distress. [fatal woman]

femto- *prefix* denoting 10^{-15}: *femtometer.* Symbol: f [from Danish or Norwegian *femten* fifteen]

femur ('fiːmə) *n, pl* **femurs** *or* **femora** ('fɛmərə). **1** the longest thickest bone of the human skeleton, with the pelvis above and the knee below. Nontechnical name: **thighbone. 2** the corresponding bone in other vertebrates or the corresponding segment of an insect's leg. [C18: from L: thigh]
▸**'femoral** *adj*

fen Ⓣ (fɛn) *n* low-lying flat land that is marshy or artificially drained. [OE *fenn*]
▸**'fenny** *adj*

fence Ⓣ (fɛns) *n* **1** a structure that serves to enclose an area such as a garden or field, usually made of posts of timber, concrete, or metal connected by wire netting, rails, or boards. **2** *Sl.* a dealer in stolen property. **3** an obstacle for a horse to jump in steeplechasing or showjumping. **4** *Machinery.* a guard or guide, esp. in a circular saw or plane. **5** (**sit**) **on the fence.** (to be) unable or unwilling to commit oneself. ◆ *vb* **fences, fencing, fenced. 6** (*tr*) to construct a fence on or around (a piece of land, etc.). **7** (*tr;* foll. by *in* or *off*) to close (in) or separate (off) with or as if with a fence: *he fenced in the livestock.* **8** (*intr*) to fight using swords or foils. **9** (*intr*) to evade a question or argument. **10** (*intr*) *Sl.* to receive stolen property. [C14 *fens,* shortened from *defens* DEFENCE]
▸**'fenceless** *adj* ▸**'fencer** *n*

fencible ('fɛnsəb[ə]l) *n* (formerly) a person who undertook military service in immediate defence of his homeland only.

fencing ('fɛnsɪŋ) *n* **1** the practice, art, or sport of fighting with foils, épées, sabres, etc. **2a** wire, stakes, etc., used as fences. **2b** fences collectively.

fend Ⓣ (fɛnd) *vb* **1** (*intr;* foll. by *for*) to give support (to someone, esp. oneself). **2** (*tr;* usually foll. by *off*) to ward off or turn aside (blows, questions, etc.). ◆ *n* **3** *Scot. & N English dialect.* a shift or effort. [C13 *fenden,* shortened from *defenden* to DEFEND]

fender ('fɛndə) *n* **1** a low metal frame which confines falling coals to the hearth. **2** *Chiefly US.* a metal frame fitted to the front of locomotives to absorb shock, etc. **3** a cushion-like device, such as a car tyre hung over the side of a vessel to reduce damage resulting from collision. **4** the US and Canad. name for the wing of a car.

fenestra (fɪ'nɛstrə) *n, pl* **fenestrae** (-triː). **1** *Biol.* a small opening, esp. either of two openings between the middle and inner ears. **2** *Zool.* a transparent marking or spot, as on the wings of moths. **3** *Archit.* a window or window-like opening in the outside wall of a building. [C19: via NL from L: wall opening, window]

fenestrated (fɪ'nɛstreɪtɪd, 'fɛnɪˌstreɪtɪd) *or* **fenestrate** *adj* **1** *Archit.* having windows. **2** *Biol.* perforated or having fenestrae.

fenestration (ˌfɛnɪ'streɪʃən) *n* **1** the arrangement of windows in a building. **2** an operation to restore hearing by making an artificial opening into the labyrinth of the ear.

feng shui ('fʌŋ 'ʃweɪ) *n* the Chinese art of determining the most propitious design and placement of a grave, building, room, etc., so that the maximum harmony is achieved between the flow of chi of the

THESAURUS

flatten, floor, hew, knock down, level, prostrate, raze, strike down

fell[3] *adj* **1** *Archaic* = **cruel,** barbarous, bloody, ferocious, fierce, grim, implacable, inhuman, malicious, malignant, merciless, murderous, pitiless, relentless, ruthless, sanguinary, savage, vicious **2** *Archaic* = **deadly,** baneful, destructive, fatal, malign, mortal, noxious, pernicious, pestilential, ruinous

fellow *n* **1** = **man,** bloke (*Brit. inf.*), boy, chap (*inf.*), character, customer (*inf.*), guy (*inf.*), individual, person, punter (*inf.*) **5a** = **associate,** colleague, companion, compeer, comrade, co-worker, equal, friend, member, partner, peer ◆ *modifier* **5b, 8b** = **co-,** affiliated, akin, allied, associate, associated, like, related, similar ◆ *n* **9** = **counterpart,** brother, double, duplicate, match, mate, twin

fellow feeling *n* **1** = **sympathy,** compassion, empathy, friendship, pity, understanding

fellowship *n* **1, 3** = **camaraderie,** amity, brotherhood, communion, companionability, companionship, familiarity, fraternization, intercourse, intimacy, kindliness, sociability **2** = **society,** association, brotherhood, club, fraternity, guild, league, order, sisterhood, sodality

feminine *adj* **1, 2** = **womanly,** delicate, gentle, girlie, girlish, graceful, ladylike, modest, soft, tender **3** = **effeminate,** camp (*inf.*), effete, unmanly, unmasculine, weak, womanish
Antonyms *adj* Amazonian, butch, indelicate, manly, mannish, masculine, rough, unfeminine, unladylike, unwomanly, virile

femininity *n* **1, 2** = **womanliness,** delicacy, feminineness, gentleness, girlishness, muliebrity, softness, womanhood

femme fatale *n* = **seductress,** charmer, Circe, enchantress, siren, vamp (*inf.*)

fen *n* = **marsh,** bog, holm (*dialect*), morass, moss (*Scot.*), quagmire, slough, swamp

fence *n* **1** = **barrier,** barbed wire, barricade, defence, guard, hedge, paling, palisade, railings, rampart, shield, stockade, wall **5 on the fence** = **uncommitted,** between two stools, irresolute, uncertain, undecided, vacillating ◆ *vb* **6, 7** *often with* **in** *or* **off** = **enclose,** bound, circumscribe, confine, coop, defend, encircle, fortify, guard, hedge, impound, pen, pound, protect, restrict, secure, separate, surround **9** = **evade,** beat about the bush, cavil, dodge, equivocate, flannel (*Brit. inf.*), hedge, parry, prevaricate, quibble, shift, stonewall, tergiversate

fend *vb* **1** *foll. by* **for** = **look after,** make do, make provision for, provide for, shift for, support, sustain, take care of **2** *foll. by* **off** = **turn aside,** avert, beat off, deflect, drive back, hold *or* keep at bay, keep off, parry, repel, repulse, resist, stave off, ward off

environment and that of the user, believed to bring good fortune. [C20: from Chinese *feng* wind + *shui* water]

Fenian ('fi:nıən, 'fi:njən) *n* **1** (formerly) a member of an Irish revolutionary organization founded in the US in the 19th century to fight for an independent Ireland. ◆ *adj* **2** of or relating to the Fenians. [C19: from Irish Gaelic *fēinne,* after *Fiann* Irish folk hero]
▸**'Fenianism** *n*

fennec ('fɛnɛk) *n* a very small nocturnal fox inhabiting deserts of N Africa and Arabia, having enormous ears. [C18: from Ar. *fenek* fox]

fennel ('fɛn[ə]l) *n* a strong-smelling yellow-flowered umbelliferous plant whose seeds, feathery leaves, and bulbous aniseed-flavoured root are used in cookery. [OE *fenol*]

fenugreek ('fɛnjʊ,gri:k) *n* an annual heavily scented Mediterranean leguminous plant with hairy stems and white flowers. [OE *fēnogrēcum*]

feoff (fi:f) *History.* ◆ *n* **1** a variant spelling of **fief.** ◆ *vb* **2** (*tr*) to invest with a benefice or fief. [C13: from Anglo-F: a FIEF]
▸**'feoffee** *n* ▸**'feoffment** *n* ▸**'feoffor** *or* **'feoffer** *n*

-fer *n combining form.* indicating a person or thing that bears something specified: *crucifer; conifer.* [from L, from *ferre* to bear]

feral ❶ ('fıərəl) *adj* **1** (of animals and plants) existing in a wild or uncultivated state. **2** savage; brutal. [C17: from Med. L, from L, from *ferus* savage]

fer-de-lance (,fɛədə'lɑ:ns) *n* a large highly venomous tropical American snake with a greyish-brown mottled coloration. [C19: from F, lit.: iron (head) of a lance]

feretory ('fɛrıtərı, -trı) *n, pl* **feretories.** *Chiefly RC Church.* **1** a shrine, usually portable, for a saint's relics. **2** the chapel in which a shrine is kept. [C14: from MF *fiertre,* from L *feretrum* a bier, from Gk, from *pherein* to bear]

feria ('fıərıə) *n, pl* **ferias** *or* **feriae** (-rı,i:). *RC Church.* a weekday, other than Saturday, on which no feast occurs. [C19: from LL: day of the week (as in *prīma fēria* Sunday), sing of L *fēriae* festivals]
▸**'ferial** *adj*

fermata (fə'mɑ:tə) *n, pl* **fermatas** *or* **fermate** (-tı). *Music.* another word for **pause** (sense 5). [from It., from *fermare* to stop, from L *firmāre* to establish]

ferment ❶ *n* ('fɜ:mɛnt). **1** any agent or substance, such as a bacterium, mould, yeast, or enzyme, that causes fermentation. **2** another word for **fermentation. 3** commotion; unrest. ◆ *vb* (fə'mɛnt). **4** to undergo or cause to undergo fermentation. **5** to stir up or seethe with excitement. [C15: from L *fermentum* yeast, from *fervēre* to seethe]
▸**fer'mentable** *adj*

> **USAGE NOTE** See at **foment.**

fermentation (,fɜ:mɛn'teıʃən) *n* a chemical reaction in which an organic molecule splits into simpler substances, esp. the conversion of sugar to ethyl alcohol by yeast.
▸**fer'mentative** *adj*

fermentation lock *n* a valve placed on the top of bottles of fermenting wine to allow bubbles to escape.

fermi ('fɜ:mı) *n* a unit of length used in nuclear physics equal to 10^{-15} metre. [C20: see FERMION]

fermion ('fɜ:mı,ɒn) *n* any of a group of elementary particles, such as a nucleon, that has half-integral spin and obeys the Pauli exclusion principle. Cf. **boson.** [C20: after Enrico *Fermi* (1901–54), It. nuclear physicist; see -ON]

fermium ('fɜ:mıəm) *n* a transuranic element artificially produced by neutron bombardment of plutonium. Symbol: Fm; atomic no.: 100; half-life of most stable isotope, ^{257}Fm: 80 days (approx.). [C20: after Enrico *Fermi* (1901–54), It. nuclear physicist]

fern (fɜ:n) *n* **1** a plant having roots, stems, and fronds and reproducing by spores formed in structures (sori) on the fronds. **2** any of certain similar but unrelated plants, such as the sweet fern. [OE *fearn*]
▸**'ferny** *adj*

fernbird ('fɜ:n,bɜ:d) *n* a New Zealand swamp bird with a fernlike tail.

ferocious ❶ (fə'rəʊʃəs) *adj* savagely fierce or cruel: *a ferocious tiger.* [C17: from L *ferox* fierce, warlike]
▸**ferocity** (fə'rɒsıtı) *n*

-ferous *adj combining form.* bearing or producing: *coniferous.* [from -FER + -OUS]

ferrate ('fɛreıt) *n* a salt containing the divalent ion, FeO_4^{2-}. [C19: from L *ferrum* iron]

ferret ❶ ('fɛrıt) *n* **1** a domesticated albino variety of the polecat bred for hunting rats, rabbits, etc. **2** an assiduous searcher. ◆ *vb* **ferrets, ferreting, ferreted. 3** to hunt (rabbits, rats, etc.) with ferrets. **4** (*tr;* usually foll. by *out*) to drive from hiding: *to ferret out snipers.* **5** (*tr;* usually foll. by *out*) to find by persistent investigation. **6** (*intr*) to search around. [C14: from OF *furet,* from L *fur* thief]
▸**'ferreter** *n* ▸**'ferrety** *adj*

ferri- *combining form.* indicating the presence of iron, esp. in the trivalent state: *ferricyanide; ferriferous.* Cf. **ferro-.** [from L *ferrum* iron]

ferriage ('fɛrııdʒ) *n* **1** transportation by ferry. **2** the fee charged for passage on a ferry.

ferric ('fɛrık) *adj* of or containing iron in the trivalent state; designating an iron(III) compound. [C18: from L *ferrum* iron]

ferric oxide *n* a red crystalline insoluble oxide of iron that occurs as haematite and rust, used as a pigment and metal polish (**jeweller's rouge**), and as a sensitive coating on magnetic tape. Formula: Fe_2O_3. Systematic name: **iron(III) oxide.**

ferrimagnetism (,fɛrı'mægnı,tızəm) *n* a phenomenon exhibited by certain substances, such as ferrites, in which the magnetic moments of neighbouring ions are nonparallel and unequal in magnitude.
▸**ferrimagnetic** (,fɛrımæg'nɛtık) *adj*

Ferris wheel ('fɛrıs) *n* a fairground wheel having seats freely suspended from its rim. [C19: after G.W.G. *Ferris* (1859–96), American engineer]

ferrite ('fɛraıt) *n* any of a class of nonconducting magnetic mixed-oxide ceramics.

ferrite-rod aerial *n* a type of aerial, normally used in radio reception, consisting of a small coil of wire mounted on a ferromagnetic ceramic core, the coil serving as a tuning inductance.

ferro- *combining form.* **1** indicating a property of iron or the presence of iron: *ferromagnetism.* **2** indicating the presence of iron in the divalent state: *ferrocyanide.* Cf. **ferri-.** [from L *ferrum* iron]

ferrocene ('fɛrəʊ,si:n) *n* a reddish-orange compound in which the molecules have an iron atom sandwiched between two cyclopentadiene rings. Formula: $Fe(C_5H_5)_2$. [C20: from FERRO- + C(YCLOPENTADI)ENE]

ferroconcrete (,fɛrəʊ'kɒŋkri:t) *n* another name for **reinforced concrete.**

ferromagnetism (,fɛrəʊ'mægnı,tızəm) *n* the phenomenon exhibited by substances, such as iron, that have relative permeabilities much greater than unity and increasing magnetization with applied magnetizing field. Certain of these substances retain their magnetization in the absence of the applied field.
▸**ferromagnetic** (,fɛrəʊmæg'nɛtık) *adj*

ferromanganese (,fɛrəʊ'mæŋgə,ni:z) *n* an alloy of iron and manganese, used in making additions of manganese to cast iron and steel.

ferrous ('fɛrəs) *adj* of or containing iron in the divalent state; designating an iron(II) compound. [C19: from FERRI- + -OUS]

ferrous sulphate *n* an iron salt usually obtained as greenish crystals: used in inks, tanning, etc. Formula: $FeSO_4$. Systematic name: **iron(II) sulphate.** Also called: **copperas.**

ferruginous (fɛ'ru:dʒınəs) *adj* **1** (of minerals, rocks, etc.) containing iron: *a ferruginous clay.* **2** rust-coloured. [C17: from L *ferrūgineus* of a rusty colour, from *ferrum* iron]

ferrule ('fɛru:l) *n* **1** a metal ring, tube, or cap placed over the end of a stick or post for added strength or to increase wear. **2** a small length of tube, etc., esp. one used for making a joint. [C17: from ME *virole,* from OF, from L, from *viria* bracelet; infl. by L *ferrum* iron]

ferry ❶ ('fɛrı) *n, pl* **ferries. 1** Also called: **ferryboat.** a vessel for transporting passengers and usually vehicles across a body of water, esp. as a regular service. **2a** such a service. **2b** (*in combination*): *a ferryman.* **3** the delivering of aircraft by flying them to their destination. ◆ *vb* **ferries, ferrying, ferried. 4** to transport or go by ferry. **5** to deliver (an aircraft) by flying it to its destination. **6** (*tr*) to convey (passengers, goods, etc.). [OE *ferian* to carry, bring]

fertile ❶ ('fɜ:taıl) *adj* **1** capable of producing offspring. **2a** (of land) capable of sustaining an abundant growth of plants. **2b** (of farm animals) capable of breeding stock. **3** *Biol.* capable of undergoing growth and development: *fertile seeds; fertile eggs.* **4** producing many offspring; prolific. **5** highly productive: *a fertile brain.* **6** *Physics.* (of a substance) able to be transformed into fissile or fissionable material. [C15: from L *fertilis,* from *ferre* to bear]
▸**'fertilely** *adv* ▸**'fertileness** *n*

Fertile Crescent *n* an area of fertile land in the Middle East, extending

THESAURUS

feral *adj* **1** = **wild,** unbroken, uncultivated, undomesticated, untamed **2** = **savage,** bestial, brutal, fell, ferocious, fierce, vicious

ferment *n* **1** = **yeast,** bacteria, barm, fermentation agent, leaven, leavening, mother, mother-of-vinegar **3** = **commotion,** agitation, brouhaha, disruption, excitement, fever, frenzy, furore, glow, heat, hubbub, imbroglio, state of unrest, stew, stir, tumult, turbulence, turmoil, unrest, uproar ◆ *vb* **4** = **brew,** boil, bubble, concoct, effervesce, foam, froth, heat, leaven, rise, seethe, work **5** = **stir up,** agitate, boil, excite, fester, foment, heat, incite, inflame, provoke, rouse, seethe, smoulder

Antonyms *n* ≠ **commotion:** calmness, hush, peacefulness, quiet, restfulness, stillness, tranquillity

ferocious *adj* = **fierce,** feral, predatory, rapacious, ravening, savage, violent, wild = **cruel,** barbaric, barbarous, bloodthirsty, brutal, brutish, merciless, pitiless, relentless, ruthless, tigerish, vicious

Antonyms *adj* ≠ **fierce:** calm, docile, gentle, mild, subdued, submissive, tame

ferocity *n* = **savagery,** barbarity, bloodthirstiness, brutality, cruelty, ferociousness, fierceness, inhumanity, rapacity, ruthlessness, savageness, viciousness, wildness

ferret *vb* **5** *usually foll. by* **out** = **track down,** bring to light, dig up, disclose, discover, drive out, elicit, get at, nose out, root out, run to earth, search out, smell out, trace, unearth

ferry *n* **1** = **ferry boat,** packet, packet boat ◆ *vb* **6** = **carry,** chauffeur, convey, run, ship, shuttle, transport

fertile *adj* **1, 2, 4** = **productive,** abundant, fat, fecund, flowering, flowing with milk and honey, fruit-bearing, fruitful, generative, luxuriant, plenteous, plentiful, prolific, rich, teeming, yielding

Antonyms *adj* barren, dry, impotent, infecund, infertile, poor, sterile, unfruitful, unproductive

around the Rivers Tigris and Euphrates in a semicircle from Israel to the Persian Gulf.

fertility ❶ (fɜːˈtɪlɪtɪ) *n* **1** the ability to produce offspring. **2** the state or quality of being fertile.

fertility drug *n* any of a group of preparations used to stimulate ovulation in women hitherto infertile.

fertilize ❶ *or* **fertilise** (ˈfɜːtɪˌlaɪz) *vb* **fertilizes, fertilizing, fertilized** *or* **fertilises, fertilising, fertilised.** (*tr*) **1** to provide (an animal, plant, etc.) with sperm or pollen to bring about fertilization. **2** to supply (soil or water) with nutrients to aid the growth of plants. **3** to make fertile.
▸ **ˌfertiliˈzation** *or* **ˌfertiliˈsation** *n*

fertilizer ❶ *or* **fertiliser** (ˈfɜːtɪˌlaɪzə) *n* **1** any substance, such as manure, added to soil or water to increase its productivity. **2** an object or organism that fertilizes an animal or plant.

ferula (ˈfɛrʊlə) *n, pl* **ferulas** *or* **ferulae** (-ˌliː). a large umbelliferous plant having thick stems and dissected leaves. [C14: from L: giant fennel]

ferule (ˈfɛruːl) *n* **1** a flat piece of wood, such as a ruler, used in some schools to cane children on the hand. ◆ *vb* **ferules, feruling, feruled. 2** (*tr*) *Rare.* to punish with a ferule. [C16: from L *ferula* giant fennel]

fervent ❶ (ˈfɜːvənt) *or* **fervid** (ˈfɜːvɪd) *adj* **1** intensely passionate; ardent. **2** *Arch. or poetic.* burning or glowing. [C14: from L *fervēre* to boil, glow]
▸ **ˈfervency** *n* ▸ **ˈfervently** *or* **ˈfervidly** *adv*

fervour ❶ *or US* **fervor** (ˈfɜːvə) *n* **1** great intensity of feeling or belief. **2** *Rare.* intense heat. [C14: from L *fervor* heat, from *fervēre* to glow, boil]

fescue (ˈfɛskjuː) *or* **fescue grass** *n* a widely cultivated pasture and lawn grass, having stiff narrow leaves. [C14: from OF *festu,* ult. from L *festūca* stem, straw]

fesse *or* **fess** (fɛs) *n Heraldry.* an ordinary consisting of a horizontal band across a shield. [C15: from Anglo-F, from L *fascia* band, fillet]

festal (ˈfɛstᵊl) *adj* another word for **festive.** [C15: from L *festum* holiday]
▸ **ˈfestally** *adv*

fester ❶ (ˈfɛstə) *vb* **1** to form or cause to form pus. **2** (*intr*) to become rotten; decay. **3** to become or cause to become bitter, irritated, etc., esp. over a long period of time. ◆ *n* **4** a small ulcer or sore containing pus. [C13: from OF *festre* suppurating sore, from L: FISTULA]

festival ❶ (ˈfɛstɪvᵊl) *n* **1** a day or period set aside for celebration or feasting, esp. one of religious significance. **2** any occasion for celebration. **3** an organized series of special events and performances: *a festival of drama.* **4** *Arch.* a time of revelry. **5** (*modifier*) relating to or characteristic of a festival. [C14: from Church L *fēstivālis* of a feast, from L *festīvus* FESTIVE]

festive ❶ (ˈfɛstɪv) *adj* appropriate to or characteristic of a holiday, etc. [C17: from L *festīvus* joyful, from *festus* of a FEAST]
▸ **ˈfestively** *adv*

festivity ❶ (fɛsˈtɪvɪtɪ) *n, pl* **festivities. 1** merriment characteristic of a festival, etc. **2** any festival or other celebration. **3** (*pl*) celebrations.

festoon ❶ (fɛˈstuːn) *n* **1** a decorative chain of flowers, ribbons, etc., suspended in loops. **2** a carved or painted representation of this, as in architecture, furniture, or pottery. ◆ *vb* (*tr*) **3** to decorate or join together with festoons. **4** to form into festoons. [C17: from F, from It. *festone* ornament for a feast, from *festa* FEAST]

festoon blind *n* a window blind consisting of vertical rows of horizontally gathered fabric that may be drawn up to form a series of ruches.

feta (ˈfɛtə) *n* a white sheep or goat cheese popular in Greece. [Mod. Gk, from the phrase *turi pheta,* from *turi* cheese + *pheta,* from It. *fetta* a slice]

fetal *or* **foetal** (ˈfiːtᵊl) *adj* of, relating to, or resembling a fetus.

fetal alcohol syndrome *n* a condition in newborn babies caused by excessive intake of alcohol by the mother during pregnancy: characterized by various defects including mental retardation.

fetch[1] ❶ (fɛtʃ) *vb* (*mainly tr*) **1** to go after and bring back: *to fetch help.* **2** to cause to come; bring or draw forth. **3** (*also intr*) to cost or sell for (a certain price): *the table fetched six hundred pounds.* **4** to utter (a sigh, groan, etc.). **5** *Inf.* to deal (a blow, slap, etc.). **6** (used esp. as a command to dogs) to retrieve (an object thrown, etc.). **7 fetch and carry.** to perform menial tasks or run errands. ◆ *n* **8** the reach, stretch, etc., of a mechanism. **9** a trick or stratagem. [OE *feccan*]
▸ **ˈfetcher** *n*

fetch[2] (fɛtʃ) *n* the ghost or apparition of a living person. [C18: from ?]

fetching ❶ (ˈfɛtʃɪŋ) *adj Inf.* **1** attractively befitting. **2** charming.

fetch up ❶ *vb* (*adv*) **1** (*intr;* usually foll. by *at* or *in*) *Inf.* to arrive (at) or end up (in): *to fetch up in New York.* **2** *Sl.* to vomit (food, etc.).

fête ❶ *or* **fete** (feɪt) *n* **1** a gala, bazaar, or similar entertainment, esp. one held outdoors in aid of charity. **2** a feast day or holiday, esp. one of religious significance. ◆ *vb* **fêtes, fêting, fêted** *or* **fetes, feting, feted. 3** (*tr*) to honour or entertain with or as if with a fête [C18: from F: FEAST]

fetid ❶ *or* **foetid** (ˈfɛtɪd, ˈfiː-) *adj* having a stale nauseating smell, as of decay. [C16: from L, from *fētēre* to stink; rel. to *fūmus* smoke]
▸ **ˈfetidly** *or* **ˈfoetidly** *adv* ▸ **ˈfetidness** *or* **ˈfoetidness** *n*

fetish ❶ (ˈfɛtɪʃ, ˈfiːtɪʃ) *n* **1** something, esp. an inanimate object, that is believed to have magical powers. **2a** a form of behaviour involving fetishism. **2b** any object that is involved in fetishism. **3** any object, activity, etc., to which one is excessively devoted. [C17: from F, from Port. *feitiço* (n) sorcery, from adj: artificial, from L *factīcius* made by art, FACTITIOUS]

fetishism (ˈfɛtɪˌʃɪzəm, ˈfiː-) *n* **1** a condition in which the handling of an inanimate object or a part of the body other than the sexual organs is a source of sexual satisfaction. **2** belief in or recourse to a fetish for magical purposes.
▸ **ˈfetishist** *n* ▸ **ˌfetishˈistic** *adj*

fetlock (ˈfɛtˌlɒk) *n* **1** a projection behind and above a horse's hoof. **2** Also called: **fetlock joint.** the joint at this part of the leg. **3** the tuft of hair growing from this part. [C14 *fetlak*]

fetor *or* **foetor** (ˈfiːtə) *n* an offensive stale or putrid odour. [C15: from L, from *fētēre* to stink]

fetter ❶ (ˈfɛtə) *n* **1** (*often pl*) a chain or bond fastened round the ankle. **2** (*usually pl*) a check or restraint. ◆ *vb* (*tr*) **3** to restrict or confine. **4** to bind in fetters. [OE *fetor*]

fettle (ˈfɛtᵊl) *vb* **fettles, fettling, fettled.** (*tr*) **1** to line or repair (the walls of a furnace). **2** *Brit. dialect.* **2a** to prepare or arrange (a thing, oneself, etc.). **2b** to repair or mend (something). ◆ *n* **3** state of health, spirits, etc. (esp. in **in fine fettle**). [C14 (in the sense: to put in order): back formation from *fetled* girded up, from OE *fetel* belt]

fettler (ˈfɛtlə) *n Austral.* a person employed to maintain railway tracks.

fetus *or* **foetus** (ˈfiːtəs) *n, pl* **fetuses** *or* **foetuses.** the embryo of a mammal in the later stages of development, esp. a human embryo from the end of the second month of pregnancy until birth. [C14: from L: offspring]

feu (fjuː) *n* **1** *Scot. legal history.* **1a** a feudal tenure of land for which rent was paid in money or grain instead of by the performance of military service. **1b** the land so held. **2** *Scots Law.* a right to the use of land in return for a fixed annual payment (**feu duty**). [C15: from OF; see FEE]

feud[1] ❶ (fjuːd) *n* **1** long and bitter hostility between two families, clans, or individuals. **2** a quarrel or dispute. ◆ *vb* **3** (*intr*) to carry on a feud. [C13 *fede,* from OF, from OHG *fēhida;* rel. to OE *fæhth* hostility; see FOE]
▸ **ˈfeudist** *n*

feud[2] *or* **feod** (fjuːd) *n Feudal law.* land held in return for service. [C17: from Med. L *feodum,* of Gmc origin; see FEE]

THESAURUS

fertility *n* **1, 2** = **fruitfulness**, abundance, fecundity, luxuriance, productiveness, richness

fertilization *n* **1** = **propagation**, implantation, impregnation, insemination, pollination, procreation **2** = **manuring**, dressing, mulching, top dressing

fertilize *vb* **1** = **make fruitful**, fecundate, fructify, impregnate, inseminate, make pregnant, pollinate **2** = **feed**, compost, dress, enrich, manure, mulch, top-dress

fertilizer *n* **1** = **compost**, dressing, dung, guano, manure, marl

fervent *adj* **1** = **intense**, animated, ardent, devout, eager, earnest, ecstatic, emotional, enthusiastic, excited, fiery, flaming, heartfelt, impassioned, passionate, perfervid (*literary*), vehement, warm, zealous
Antonyms *adj* apathetic, cold, cool, detached, dispassionate, frigid, impassive, unfeeling, unimpassioned

fervour *n* **1** = **intensity**, animation, ardour, eagerness, earnestness, enthusiasm, excitement, fervency, passion, vehemence, warmth, zeal

fester *vb* **1, 2** = **putrefy**, become inflamed, decay, gather, maturate, suppurate, ulcerate **3** = **intensify**, aggravate, chafe, gall, irk, rankle, smoulder

festering *adj* **1** = **septic**, gathering, inflamed, maturating, poisonous, purulent, pussy, suppurating, ulcerated

festival *n* **1** = **holy day**, anniversary, commemoration, feast, fête, fiesta, holiday, red-letter day, saint's day **1, 2** = **celebration**, carnival, entertainment, -fest, festivities, fête, field day, gala, jubilee, treat

festive *adj* = **celebratory**, back-slapping, carnival, cheery, Christmassy, convivial, festal, gala, gay, gleeful, happy, hearty, holiday, jolly, jovial, joyful, joyous, jubilant, light-hearted, merry, mirthful, sportive
Antonyms *adj* depressing, drab, dreary, funereal, gloomy, lugubrious, mournful, sad

festivity *n* **1** = **merrymaking**, amusement, conviviality, fun, gaiety, jollification, joviality, joyfulness, merriment, mirth, pleasure, revelry, sport **3** *often plural* = **celebration**, beano (*Brit. sl.*), carousal, entertainment, festival, festive event, festive proceedings, fun and games, hooley or hoolie (*chiefly Irish & NZ*), jollification, party, rave (*Brit. sl.*), rave-up (*Brit. sl.*)

festoon *n* **1** = **decoration**, chaplet, garland, lei, swag, swathe, wreath ◆ *vb* **3** = **decorate**, array, bedeck, beribbon, deck, drape, engarland, garland, hang, swathe, wreathe

fetch[1] *vb* **1** = **bring**, carry, conduct, convey, deliver, escort, get, go for, lead, obtain, retrieve, transport **2** = **produce**, draw forth, elicit, give rise to **3** = **sell for**, bring in, earn, go for, make, realize, yield

fetching *adj* **1, 2** = **attractive**, alluring, captivating, charming, cute, enchanting, enticing, fascinating, intriguing, sweet, taking, winsome

fetch up *vb* **1** *Informal* = **end up**, arrive, come, finish up, halt, land, reach, stop, turn up

fête *n* **1** = **fair**, bazaar, festival, gala, garden party, sale of work ◆ *vb* **3** = **entertain**, hold a reception for (someone), honour, kill the fatted calf for (someone), lionize, make much of, treat, wine and dine

fetid *adj* = **stinking**, corrupt, foul, malodorous, mephitic, noisome, noxious, offensive, olid, rancid, rank, reeking

fetish *n* **1** = **talisman**, amulet, cult object **2, 3** = **fixation**, *idée fixe,* mania, obsession, thing (*inf.*)

fetter *n* **1** *often plural* = **chains**, bilboes, bonds, gyves (*arch.*), irons, leg irons, manacles, shackles **2** *usually plural* = **restraint**, bondage, captivity, check, curb, hindrance, obstruction ◆ *vb* **3** = **restrict**, bind, clip someone's wings, confine, curb, encumber, hamper, hamstring, restrain, straiten, trammel **4** = **chain**, gyve (*arch.*), hobble, hold captive, manacle, put a straitjacket on, shackle, tie, tie up

feud[1] *n* **1, 2** = **hostility**, argument, bad blood, bickering, broil, conflict, contention, disagreement, discord, dissension, enmity, estrange-

feudal ('fju:dəl) *adj* **1** of or characteristic of feudalism or its institutions. **2** of or relating to a fief. **3** *Disparaging.* old-fashioned. [C17: from Med. L, from *feudum* FEUD[2]]

feudalism ('fju:də,lɪzəm) *n* the legal and social system that evolved in W Europe in the 8th and 9th centuries, in which vassals were protected and maintained by their lords, usually through the granting of fiefs, and were required to serve under them in war. Also called: **feudal system.**
▸ **'feudalist** *n* ▸ **,feudal'istic** *adj*

feudality (fju:'dælɪtɪ) *n, pl* **feudalities. 1** the state or quality of being feudal. **2** a fief or fee.

feudalize *or* **feudalise** ('fju:də,laɪz) *vb* **feudalizes, feudalizing, feudalized** *or* **feudalises, feudalising, feudalised.** (*tr*) to create feudal institutions in (a society, etc.).
▸ **,feudali'zation** *or* **,feudali'sation** *n*

feudatory ('fju:dətərɪ) (in feudal Europe) ◆ *n, pl* **feudatories. 1** a person holding a fief; vassal. ◆ *adj* **2** relating to or characteristic of the relationship between lord and vassal. [C16: from Med. L *feudātor*]

feuilleton (*French* fœjtɔ̃) *n* **1** the part of a European newspaper carrying reviews, serialized fiction, etc. **2** such a review or article. [C19: from F, from *feuillet* sheet of paper, dim. of *feuille* leaf, from L *folium*]

fever ➊ ('fi:və) *n* **1** an abnormally high body temperature, accompanied by a fast pulse rate, dry skin, etc. Related adj: **febrile. 2** any of various diseases, such as yellow fever or scarlet fever, characterized by a high temperature. **3** intense nervous excitement. ◆ *vb* **4** (*tr*) to affect with or as if with fever. [OE *fēfor,* from L *febris*]
▸ **'fevered** *adj*

feverfew ('fi:və,fju:) *n* a bushy European strong-scented perennial plant with white flower heads, formerly used medicinally. [OE *feferfuge,* from LL, from L *febris* fever + *fugāre* to put to flight]

feverish ➊ ('fi:vərɪʃ) *or* **feverous** *adj* **1** suffering from fever. **2** in a state of restless excitement. **3** of, caused by, or causing fever.
▸ **'feverishly** *or* **'feverously** *adv*

fever pitch *n* a state of intense excitement.

fever therapy *n* a former method of treating disease by raising the body temperature.

few ➊ (fju:) *determiner* **1a** hardly any: *few men are so cruel.* **1b** (*as pronoun; functioning as pl*)*: many are called but few are chosen.* **2** (preceded by *a*) **2a** a small number of: *a few drinks.* **2b** (*as pronoun; functioning as pl*)*: a few of you.* **3 a good few.** *Inf.* several. **4 few and far between. 4a** widely spaced. **4b** scarce. **5 not** *or* **quite a few.** *Inf.* several. ◆ *n* **6 the few.** a small number of people considered as a class: *the few who fell at Thermopylae.* [OE *fēawa*]
▸ **'fewness** *n*

USAGE NOTE See at **less.**

fey (feɪ) *adj* **1** interested in or believing in the supernatural. **2** clairvoyant; visionary. **3** *Chiefly Scot.* fated to die; doomed. **4** *Chiefly Scot.* in a state of high spirits. [OE *fǣge* marked out for death]
▸ **'feyness** *n*

fez (fɛz) *n, pl* **fezzes.** an originally Turkish brimless felt or wool cap, shaped like a truncated cone. [C19: via F from Turkish, from *Fès* city in Morocco]

ff *Music. symbol for* fortissimo.

ff. 1 *abbrev. for* folios. **2** *symbol for* and the following (pages, lines, etc.).

fiacre (fɪ'ɑ:krə) *n* a small four-wheeled horse-drawn carriage. [C17: after the Hotel de St *Fiacre,* Paris, where these vehicles were first hired out]

fiancé ➊ *or* (*fem*) **fiancée** (fɪ'ɒnseɪ) *n* a person who is engaged to be married. [C19: from F, from OF *fiancier* to promise, betroth, from *fiance* a vow, from *fier* to trust, from L *fīdere*]

fiasco ➊ (fɪ'æskəʊ) *n, pl* **fiascos** *or* **fiascoes.** a complete failure, esp. one that is ignominious or humiliating. [C19: from It., lit.: FLASK; sense development obscure]

fiat ('faɪət) *n* **1** official sanction. **2** an arbitrary order or decree. [C17: from L, lit.: let it be done]

fib ➊ (fɪb) *n* **1** a trivial and harmless lie. ◆ *vb* **fibs, fibbing, fibbed. 2** (*intr*) to tell such a lie. [C17: ?from *fibble-fable* an unlikely story; see FABLE]
▸ **'fibber** *n*

Fibonacci sequence *or* **series** (,fɪbə'nɑ:tʃɪ) *n* the infinite sequence of numbers, 0, 1, 1, 2, 3, 5, 8, etc., in which each member (**Fibonacci number**) is the sum of the previous two. [after Leonardo *Fibonacci* (?1170–?1250), Florentine mathematician]

fibre ➊ *or US* **fiber** ('faɪbə) *n* **1** a natural or synthetic filament that may be spun into yarn, such as cotton or nylon. **2** cloth or other material made from such yarn. **3** a long fine continuous thread or filament. **4** the texture of any material or substance. **5** essential substance or nature. **6** strength of character (esp. in **moral fibre**). **7** *Bot.* **7a** a narrow elongated thick-walled cell. **7b** a very small root or twig. **8** a fibrous substance, such as bran, as part of someone's diet: *dietary fibre.* [C14: from L *fibra* filament, entrails]
▸ **'fibred** *or US* **'fibered** *adj*

fibreboard *or US* **fiberboard** ('faɪbə,bɔ:d) *n* a building material made of compressed wood or other plant fibres.

fibreglass *or US* **fiberglass** ('faɪbə,glɑ:s) *n* **1** material consisting of matted fine glass fibres, used as insulation in buildings, etc. **2** a light strong material made by bonding fibreglass with a synthetic resin; used for car bodies, etc.

fibre optics *or US* **fiber optics** *n* (*functioning as sing*) the transmission of information modulated on light down very thin flexible fibres of glass. See also **optical fibre.**
▸ **,fibre-'optic** *or US* **,fiber-'optic** *adj*

fibrescope *or US* **fiberscope** ('faɪbə,skəʊp) *n* a medical instrument using fibre optics used to examine internal organs, such as the stomach.

fibril ('faɪbrɪl) *or* **fibrilla** (faɪ'brɪlə) *n, pl* **fibrils** *or* **fibrillae** (-'brɪli:). **1** a small fibre or part of a fibre. **2** *Biol.* a root hair. [C17: from NL *fibrilla* a little FIBRE]
▸ **fi'brillar** *or* **fi'brillose** *adj*

fibrillation (,faɪbrɪ'leɪʃən, ,fɪb-) *n* **1** a local and uncontrollable twitching of muscle fibres. **2** irregular twitchings of the muscular wall of the heart.

fibrin ('fɪbrɪn) *n* a white insoluble elastic protein formed from fibrinogen when blood clots: forms a network that traps red cells and platelets.

fibrinogen (fɪ'brɪnədʒən) *n* a soluble protein in blood plasma, converted to fibrin by the action of the enzyme thrombin when blood clots.

fibro ('faɪbrəʊ) *n Austral. inf.* **a** short for **fibrocement. b** (*as modifier*)*: a fibro shack.*

fibro- *combining form.* **1** indicating fibrous tissue: *fibrosis.* **2** indicating fibre: *fibrocement.* [from L *fibra* FIBRE]

fibrocement (,faɪbrəʊsɪ'mɛnt) *n* cement combined with asbestos fibre, used esp. in sheets for building.

fibroid ('faɪbrɔɪd) *adj* **1** *Anat.* (of structures or tissues) containing or resembling fibres. ◆ *n* **2** a benign tumour, composed of fibrous and muscular tissue, occurring in the wall of the uterus and often causing heavy menstruation.

fibroin ('faɪbrəʊɪn) *n* a tough elastic protein that is the principal component of spiders' webs and raw silk.

fibroma (faɪ'brəʊmə) *n, pl* **fibromata** (-mətə) *or* **fibromas.** a benign tumour derived from fibrous connective tissue.

fibrosis (faɪ'brəʊsɪs) *n* the formation of an abnormal amount of fibrous tissue in an organ or part.

fibrositis (,faɪbrə'saɪtɪs) *n* inflammation of white fibrous tissue, esp. that of muscle sheaths.

fibrous ('faɪbrəs) *adj* consisting of or resembling fibres: *fibrous tissue.*
▸ **'fibrously** *adv*

fibula ('fɪbjʊlə) *n, pl* **fibulae** (-,li:) *or* **fibulas. 1** the outer and thinner of the two bones between the knee and ankle of the human leg. Cf. **tibia. 2** the corresponding bone in other vertebrates. **3** a metal brooch resembling a safety pin. [C17: from L: clasp, prob. from *fīgere* to fasten]
▸ **'fibular** *adj*

-fic *suffix forming adjectives.* making or producing: *honorific.* [from L *-ficus,* from *facere* to do, make]

fiche (fi:ʃ) *n* See **microfiche, ultrafiche.**

fichu ('fi:ʃu:) *n* a woman's shawl worn esp. in the 18th century. [C19: from F: small shawl, from *ficher* to fix with a pin, from L *fīgere* to fasten, FIX]

fickle ➊ ('fɪkəl) *adj* changeable in purpose, affections, etc. [OE *ficol* deceitful]
▸ **'fickleness** *n*

THESAURUS

ment, faction, falling out, grudge, quarrel, rivalry, row, strife, vendetta ◆ *vb* **3 = quarrel,** be at daggers drawn, be at odds, bicker, brawl, clash, contend, dispute, duel, fall out, row, squabble, war

fever *n* **1 = ague,** pyrexia (*Medical*) **3 = excitement,** agitation, delirium, ecstasy, ferment, fervour, flush, frenzy, heat, intensity, passion, restlessness, turmoil, unrest

feverish *adj* **1 = hot,** burning, febrile, fevered, flaming, flushed, hectic, inflamed, pyretic (*Medical*) **2 = excited,** agitated, desperate, distracted, frantic, frenetic, frenzied, impatient, obsessive, overwrought, restless
Antonyms *adj* ≠ **excited:** calm, collected, composed, cool, dispassionate, nonchalant, offhand, serene, tranquil, unemotional, unexcitable, unfazed (*inf.*), unruffled

few *adj* **1a = not many,** hardly any, inconsiderable, infrequent, insufficient, meagre, negligible, rare, scant, scanty, scarce, scarcely any, scattered, sparse, sporadic, thin ◆ *pron* **1b = small number,** handful, scarcely any, scattering, some ◆ *adj* **4 few and far between = scarce,** at great intervals, hard to come by, infrequent, in short supply, irregular, rare, scattered, seldom met with, thin on the ground, uncommon, unusual, widely spaced
Antonyms *adj* ≠ **not many, scarce:** abundant, bounteous, divers (*arch.*), inexhaustible, manifold, many, multifarious, plentiful, sundry

fiancé *n* **= husband-to-be,** betrothed, intended, prospective spouse

fiancée *n* **= wife-to-be,** betrothed, intended, prospective spouse

fiasco *n* **= flop** (*inf.*), balls-up (*taboo sl.*), catastrophe, cock-up, debacle, disaster, failure, mess, rout, ruin, washout (*inf.*)

fib *n* **1 = lie,** fiction, pork pie (*Brit. sl.*), porky (*Brit. sl.*), prevarication, story, untruth, white lie, whopper (*inf.*)

fibre *n* **1, 3 = thread,** fibril, filament, pile, staple, strand, texture, wisp **5 = essence,** nature, quality, spirit, substance **6** *As in* **moral fibre = strength of character,** resolution, stamina, strength, toughness

fickle *adj* **= changeable,** blowing hot and cold,

fictile ('fɪktaɪl) *adj* **1** moulded or capable of being moulded from clay. **2** made of clay by a potter. [C17: from L *fictilis* that can be moulded, from *fingere* to shape]

fiction ⓘ ('fɪkʃən) *n* **1** literary works invented by the imagination, such as novels or short stories. **2** an invented story or explanation. **3** the act of inventing a story. **4** *Law.* something assumed to be true for the sake of convenience, though probably false. [C14: from L *fictiō* a fashioning, hence something imaginary, from *fingere* to shape]
▸ **'fictional** *adj* ▸ **'fictionally** *adv* ▸ **'fictive** *adj*

fictionalize *or* **fictionalise** ('fɪkʃənəˌlaɪz) *vb* **fictionalizes, fictionalizing, fictionalized** *or* **fictionalises, fictionalising, fictionalised.** (*tr*) to make into fiction.
▸ **ˌfictionali'zation** *or* **ˌfictionali'sation** *n*

fictitious ⓘ (fɪk'tɪʃəs) *adj* **1** not genuine or authentic: *to give a fictitious address.* **2** of, related to, or characteristic of fiction.
▸ **fic'titiously** *adv* ▸ **fic'titiousness** *n*

fid (fɪd) *n Naut.* **1** a spike for separating strands of rope in splicing. **2** a wooden or metal bar for supporting the topmast. [C17: from ?]

-fid *adj combining form.* divided into parts or lobes: *bifid.* [from L *-fidus,* from *findere* to split]

fiddle ⓘ ('fɪdᵊl) *n* **1** *Inf. or disparaging.* the violin. **2** a violin played as a folk instrument. **3** *Naut.* a small railing around the top of a table to prevent objects from falling off it. **4** *Brit. inf.* an illegal transaction or arrangement. **5** *Brit. inf.* a manually delicate or tricky operation. **6 at** *or* **on the fiddle.** *Inf.* engaged in an illegal or fraudulent undertaking. **7 fit as a fiddle.** *Inf.* in very good health. **8 play second fiddle.** *Inf.* to play a minor part. ◆ *vb* **fiddles, fiddling, fiddled. 9** to play (a tune) on the fiddle. **10** (*intr;* often foll. by *with*) to make aimless movements with the hands. **11** (when *intr,* often foll. by *about* or *around*) *Inf.* to waste (time). **12** (often foll. by *with*) *Inf.* to interfere (with). **13** *Inf.* to contrive to do (something) by illicit means or deception. **14** (*tr*) *Inf.* to falsify (accounts, etc.). [OE *fithele;* see VIOLA[1]]

fiddle-faddle ('fɪdᵊlˌfædᵊl) *n, interj* **1** trivial matter; nonsense. ◆ *vb* **fiddle-faddles, fiddle-faddling, fiddle-faddled. 2** (*intr*) to fuss or waste time. [C16: reduplication of FIDDLE]
▸ **'fiddle-ˌfaddler** *n*

fiddler ('fɪdlə) *n* **1** a person who plays the fiddle. **2** See **fiddler crab. 3** *Inf.* a petty rogue.

fiddler crab *n* any of various burrowing crabs of American coastal regions, the males of which have one of their pincer-like claws enlarged. [C19: referring to the rapid fiddling movement of the enlarged anterior claw of the males, used to attract females]

fiddlestick ('fɪdᵊlˌstɪk) *n* **1** *Inf.* a violin bow. **2** any trifle. **3 fiddlesticks!** an expression of annoyance or disagreement.

fiddling ⓘ ('fɪdlɪŋ) *adj* **1** trifling or insignificant. **2** another word for **fiddly.**

fiddly ('fɪdlɪ) *adj* **fiddlier, fiddliest.** small and awkward to do or handle.

Fidei Defensor *Latin.* ('faɪdɪˌaɪ dɪ'fɛnsɔː) *n* defender of the faith; a title given to Henry VIII by Pope Leo X, and appearing on British coins as FID DEF (before decimalization) or FD (after decimalization).

fidelity ⓘ (fɪ'dɛlɪtɪ) *n, pl* **fidelities. 1** devotion to duties, obligations, etc. **2** loyalty or devotion, as to a person or cause. **3** faithfulness to one's spouse, lover, etc. **4** accuracy in reporting detail. **5** *Electronics.* the degree to which an amplifier or radio accurately reproduces the characteristics of the input signal. [C15: from L, from *fidēs* faith, loyalty]

fidget ⓘ ('fɪdʒɪt) *vb* **1** (*intr*) to move about restlessly. **2** (*intr;* often foll. by *with*) to make restless or uneasy movements (with something). **3** (*tr*) to cause to fidget. ◆ *n* **4** (*often pl*) a state of restlessness or unease: *he's got the fidgets.* **5** a person who fidgets. [C17: from earlier *fidge,* prob. from ON *fīkjast* to desire eagerly]
▸ **'fidgety** *adj*

fiducial (fɪ'djuːʃɪəl) *adj* **1** *Physics, etc.* used as a standard of reference or measurement: *a fiducial point.* **2** of or based on trust or faith. [C17: from LL *fīdūciālis,* from L *fīdūcia* confidence, from *fīdere* to trust]

fiduciary (fɪ'duːʃɪərɪ) *Law.* ◆ *n, pl* **fiduciaries. 1** a person bound to act for another's benefit, as a trustee. ◆ *adj* **2a** having the nature of a trust. **2b** of or relating to a trust or trustee. [C17: from L *fīdūciārius* relating to something held in trust, from *fīdūcia* trust]

fiduciary issue *n* an issue of banknotes not backed by gold.

fie (faɪ) *interj Obs. or facetious.* an exclamation of distaste or mock dismay. [C13: from OF *fi,* from L *fī,* exclamation of disgust]

fief *or* **feoff** (fiːf) *n* (in feudal Europe) the property or fee granted to a vassal for his maintenance by his lord in return for service. [C17: from OF *fie,* of Gmc origin; cf. OE *fēo* cattle, money, L *pecus* cattle, *pecūnia* money, Gk *pokos* fleece]

fiefdom ('fiːfdəm) *n* **1** (in feudal Europe) the property owned by a lord. **2** an area over which a person or organization exerts authority or influence.

field ⓘ (fiːld) *n* **1** an open tract of uncultivated grassland; meadow. **2** a piece of land cleared of trees and undergrowth used for pasture or growing crops: *a field of barley.* **3** a limited or marked off area on which any of various sports, athletic competitions, etc., are held: *a soccer field.* **4** an area that is rich in minerals or other natural resources: *a coalfield.* **5** short for **battlefield** or **airfield. 6** the mounted followers that hunt with a pack of hounds. **7a** all the runners in a race or competitors in a competition. **7b** the runners in a race or competitors in a competition excluding the favourite. **8** *Cricket.* the fielders collectively, esp. with regard to their positions. **9** a wide or open expanse: *a field of snow.* **10a** an area of human activity: *the field of human knowledge.* **10b** a sphere or division of knowledge, etc.: *his field is physics.* **11** a place away from the laboratory, office, library, etc., where practical work is done. **12** the surface or background, as of a flag, coin, or heraldic shield, on which a design is displayed. **13** Also called: **field of view.** the area within which an object may be observed with a telescope, etc. **14** *Physics.* See **field of force. 15** *Maths.* a set of entities, such as numbers, subject to two binary operations, addition and multiplication, such that the set is a commutative group under addition and the set, minus the zero, is a commutative group under multiplication. **16** *Computing.* a set of one or more characters comprising a unit of information. **17 play the field.** *Inf.* to disperse one's interests or attentions among a number of activities, people, or objects. **18 take the field.** to begin or carry on activity, esp. in sport or military operations. **19** (*modifier*) *Mil.* of or relating to equipment, personnel, etc., specifically trained for operations in the field: *a field gun.* ◆ *vb* **20** (*tr*) *Sport.* to stop, catch, or return (the ball) as a fielder. **21** (*tr*) *Sport.* to send (a player or team) onto the field to play. **22** (*intr*) *Sport.* (of a player or team) to act or take turn as a fielder or fielders. **23** (*tr*) to enter (a person) in a competition: *each party fielded a candidate.* **24** (*tr*) *Inf.* to deal with or handle: *to field a question.* [OE *feld*]

field artillery *n* artillery capable of deployment in support of front-line troops, due mainly to its mobility.

field day *n* **1** a day spent in some special outdoor activity, such as nature study. **2** *Mil.* a day devoted to manoeuvres or exercises, esp. before an audience. **3** *Inf.* a day or time of exciting activity: *the children had a field day with their new toys.*

field effect transistor *n* a unipolar transistor in which the transverse application of an electric field produces amplification.

fielder ('fiːldə) *n Cricket, etc.* **a** a player in the field. **b** a member of the fielding side.

field event *n* a competition, such as the discus, etc., that takes place on a field or similar area as opposed to those on the running track.

fieldfare ('fiːldˌfɛə) *n* a large Old World thrush having a pale grey head, brown wings and back, and a blackish tail. [OE *feldefare;* see FIELD, FARE]

field glasses *pl n* another name for **binoculars.**

THESAURUS

capricious, faithless, fitful, flighty, inconstant, irresolute, mercurial, mutable, quicksilver, temperamental, unfaithful, unpredictable, unstable, unsteady, vacillating, variable, volatile
Antonyms *adj* changeless, constant, faithful, firm, invariable, loyal, reliable, resolute, settled, stable, staunch, steadfast, true, trustworthy

fickleness *n* = **inconstancy,** capriciousness, fitfulness, flightiness, mutability, unfaithfulness, unpredictability, unsteadiness, volatility

fiction *n* **1** = **tale,** fable, fantasy, legend, myth, novel, romance, story, storytelling, work of imagination, yarn (*inf.*) **2** = **lie,** cock and bull story (*inf.*), concoction, fabrication, falsehood, fancy, fantasy, figment of the imagination, imagination, improvisation, invention, pork pie (*Brit. sl.*), porky (*Brit. sl.*), tall story, untruth, urban legend, urban myth

fictional *adj* **1** = **imaginary,** invented, legendary, made-up, nonexistent, unreal

fictitious *adj* **1** = **false,** apocryphal, artificial, assumed, bogus, counterfeit, fabricated, fanciful, feigned, imaginary, imagined, improvised, invented, made-up, make-believe, mythical, spurious, unreal, untrue
Antonyms *adj* actual, authentic, genuine, legitimate, real, true, truthful, veracious, veritable

fiddle *n* **1** *Informal or disparaging* = **violin 4** *Brit. informal* = **fraud,** fix, graft (*inf.*), piece of sharp practice, racket, scam (*sl.*), sting (*inf.*), swindle, wangle (*inf.*) **7 fit as a fiddle** *Informal* = **healthy,** blooming, hale and hearty, in fine fettle, in good form, in good shape, in rude health, in the pink, sound, strong ◆ *vb* **10, 12** = **fidget,** finger, interfere with, mess about *or* around, play, tamper with, tinker, toy, trifle **14** *Informal* = **cheat,** cook the books (*inf.*), diddle (*inf.*), finagle (*inf.*), fix, gerrymander, graft (*inf.*), manoeuvre, racketeer, sting (*inf.*), swindle, wangle (*inf.*)

fiddling *adj* **1** = **trivial,** futile, insignificant, nickel-and-dime (*US sl.*), pettifogging, petty, trifling

fidelity *n* **1-3** = **loyalty,** allegiance, constancy, dependability, devotedness, devotion, faith, faithfulness, fealty, integrity, lealty (*arch. or Scot.*), staunchness, troth (*arch.*), true-heartedness, trustworthiness **4** = **accuracy,** adherence, closeness, correspondence, exactitude, exactness, faithfulness, preciseness, precision, scrupulousness
Antonyms *n* ≠ **loyalty:** disloyalty, faithlessness, falseness, infidelity, perfidiousness, treachery, unfaithfulness, untruthfulness ≠ **accuracy:** inaccuracy, inexactness

fidget *vb* **1-3** = **move restlessly,** be like a cat on hot bricks, bustle, chafe, fiddle (*inf.*), fret, jiggle, jitter (*inf.*), squirm, twitch, worry ◆ *n* **4** *often plural* = **restlessness,** fidgetiness, jitters (*inf.*), nervousness, unease, uneasiness

fidgety *adj* **1, 2** = **restless,** impatient, jerky, jittery (*inf.*), jumpy, nervous, on edge, restive, twitchy (*inf.*), uneasy

field *n* **1, 2** = **meadow,** grassland, green, greensward (*arch. or literary*), lea (*poetic*), mead (*arch.*), pasture **7** = **competitors,** applicants, candidates, competition, contestants, entrants, possibilities, runners **10** = **speclality,** area, bailiwick, bounds, confines, department, discipline, domain, environment, limits, line, metier, pale, province, purview, range, scope, specialty, sphere of activity, sphere of influence, sphere of interest, sphere of study, territory ◆ *vb* **20** *Sport* = **retrieve,** catch, pick up, return, stop **24** *Informal* = **deal with,** deflect, handle, turn aside

field goal *n* **1** *Basketball.* a goal scored while the ball is in normal play rather than from a free throw. **2** *American & Canadian football.* a score of three points made by kicking the ball through the opponent's goalposts above the crossbar.
field hockey *n US & Canad.* hockey played on a field, as distinguished from ice hockey.
field hospital *n* a temporary hospital set up near a battlefield for emergency treatment.
field magnet *n* a permanent magnet or an electromagnet that produces the magnetic field in a generator, electric motor, or similar device.
field marshal *n* an officer holding the highest rank in certain armies.
fieldmouse ('fiːldˌmaʊs) *n, pl* **fieldmice.** a nocturnal mouse inhabiting woods, fields, and gardens of the Old World that has yellowish-brown fur.
field officer *n* an officer holding the rank of major, lieutenant colonel, or colonel.
field of force *n* the region of space surrounding a body, such as a charged particle or a magnet, within which it can exert a force on another similar body not in contact with it.
fieldsman ('fiːldzmən) *n, pl* **fieldsmen.** *Cricket.* another name for **fielder.**
field sports *pl n* sports carried on in the countryside, such as hunting or fishing.
field tile *n Brit. & NZ.* an earthenware drain used in farm drainage.
field trial *n (often pl)* a test to display performance, efficiency, or durability, as of a vehicle or invention.
field trip *n* an expedition, as by a group of students, to study something at first hand.
field winding ('waɪndɪŋ) *n* the current-carrying coils on a field magnet that produce the magnetic field intensity required to set up the electrical excitation in a generator or motor.
fieldwork ('fiːldˌwɜːk) *n Mil.* a temporary structure used in fortifying a place or position.
field work *n* an investigation or search for material, data, etc., made in the field as opposed to the classroom or laboratory.
▸**field worker** *n*
fiend ❶ (fiːnd) *n* **1** an evil spirit. **2** a cruel, brutal, or spiteful person. **3** *Inf.* **3a** a person who is intensely interested in or fond of something: *a fresh-air fiend.* **3b** an addict: *a drug fiend.* [OE *fēond*]
Fiend (fiːnd) *n* **the.** the devil; Satan.
fiendish ❶ ('fiːndɪʃ) *adj* **1** of or like a fiend. **2** diabolically wicked or cruel. **3** *Inf.* extremely difficult or unpleasant: *a fiendish problem.*
fierce ❶ (fɪəs) *adj* **1** having a violent and unrestrained nature: *a fierce dog.* **2** wild or turbulent in force, action, or intensity: *a fierce storm.* **3** intense or strong: *fierce competition.* **4** *Inf.* very unpleasant. [C13: from OF *fiers,* from L *ferus*]
▸'**fiercely** *adv* ▸'**fierceness** *n*
fiery ❶ ('faɪərɪ) *adj* **fierier, fieriest. 1** of, containing, or composed of fire. **2** resembling fire in heat, colour, ardour, etc.: *a fiery speaker.* **3** easily angered or aroused: *a fiery temper.* **4** (of food) producing a burning sensation: *a fiery curry.* **5** (of the skin or a sore) inflamed. **6** flammable.
▸'**fierily** *adv* ▸'**fieriness** *n*
fiesta ❶ (fɪ'ɛstə) *n* (esp. in Spain and Latin America) **1** a religious festival or celebration. **2** a holiday or carnival. [Sp., from L *festa;* see FEAST]
FIFA ('fiːfə) *n acronym for* Fédération Internationale de Football Association. [from F]
fife (faɪf) *n* **1** a small high-pitched flute similar to the piccolo, used esp. in military bands. ◆ *vb* **fifes, fifing, fifed. 2** to play (music) on a fife. [C16: from OHG *pfīfa;* see PIPE[1]]
▸'**fifer** *n*
FIFO ('faɪfəʊ) *n acronym for* first in, first out (as an accounting principle in costing stock). Cf. **LIFO.**
fifteen ('fɪf'tiːn) *n* **1** the cardinal number that is the sum of ten and five. **2** a numeral, 15, XV, etc., representing this number. **3** something represented by, representing, or consisting of 15 units. **4** a Rugby Union (football) team. ◆ *determiner* **5a** amounting to fifteen: *fifteen jokes.* **5b** *(as pronoun): fifteen of us danced.* [OE *fīftēne*]
▸'**fif'teenth** *adj, n*
fifth (fɪfθ) *adj (usually prenominal)* **1a** coming after the fourth in order, position, etc. Often written 5th. **1b** *(as n): he came on the fifth.* ◆ *n* **2a** one of five equal parts of an object, quantity, etc. **2b** *(as modifier): a fifth part.* **3** the fraction equal to one divided by five (1/5). **4** *Music.* **4a** the interval between one note and another five notes away from it in a diatonic scale. **4b** one of two notes constituting such an interval in relation to the other. ◆ *adv* **5** Also: **fifthly.** after the fourth person, position, event, etc. ◆ *sentence connector.* **6** Also: **fifthly.** as the fifth point. [OE *fifta*]
fifth column *n* **1** (originally) a group of Falangist sympathizers in Madrid during the Spanish Civil War who were prepared to join the insurgents marching on the city. **2** any group of hostile infiltrators.
▸**fifth columnist** *n*
fifth wheel *n* **1** a spare wheel for a four-wheeled vehicle. **2** a superfluous or unnecessary person or thing.
fifty ('fɪftɪ) *n, pl* **fifties. 1** the cardinal number that is the product of ten and five. **2** a numeral, 50, L, etc., representing this number. **3** something represented by, representing, or consisting of 50 units. ◆ *determiner* **4a** amounting to fifty: *fifty people.* **4b** *(as pronoun): fifty should be sufficient.* [OE *fīftig*]
▸'**fiftieth** *adj, n*
fifty-fifty *adj, adv Inf.* in equal parts.
fig (fɪg) *n* **1** a tree or shrub in which the flowers are borne inside a pear-shaped receptacle. **2** the fruit of any of these trees, which develops from the receptacle and has sweet flesh containing numerous seedlike structures. **3** *(used with a negative)* something of negligible value: *I don't care a fig for your opinion.* [C13: from OF, from *figa,* from L *fīcus* fig tree]
fig. *abbrev. for:* **1** figurative(ly). **2** figure.
fight ❶ (faɪt) *vb* **fights, fighting, fought. 1** to oppose or struggle against (an enemy) in battle. **2** to oppose or struggle against (a person, cause, etc.) in any manner. **3** *(tr)* to engage in or carry on (a battle, contest, etc.). **4** (when *intr,* often foll. by *for*) to uphold or maintain (a cause, etc.) by fighting or struggling: *to fight for freedom.* **5** *(tr)* to make or achieve (a way) by fighting. **6** to engage (another or others) in combat. **7 fight it out.** to contend until a decisive result is obtained. **8 fight shy.** to keep aloof from. ◆ *n* **9** a battle, struggle, or physical combat. **10** a quarrel, dispute, or contest. **11** resistance (esp. in **to put up a fight**). **12** a boxing match. ◆ See also **fight off.** [OE *feohtan*]
fighter ❶ ('faɪtə) *n* **1** a person who fights, esp. a professional boxer. **2** a person who has determination. **3** *Mil.* an armed aircraft designed for destroying other aircraft.
fighter-bomber *n* an aircraft that combines the roles of fighter and bomber.
fighting chance *n* a slight chance of success dependent on a struggle.
fighting cock *n* **1** a gamecock. **2** a pugnacious person.
fighting fish *n* any of various tropical fishes of the genus *Betta,* esp. the Siamese fighting fish.
fight off ❶ *vb (tr, adv)* **1** to repulse; repel. **2** to struggle to avoid or repress: *to fight off a cold.*
fight-or-flight *n (modifier)* involving or relating to an involuntary response to stress in which the hormone adrenaline is secreted into the blood in readiness for physical action, such as fighting or running away.
fig leaf *n* **1** a leaf from a fig tree. **2** a representation of a fig leaf used in sculpture, etc. to cover the genitals of nude figures. **3** a device to conceal something regarded as shameful.
figment ❶ ('fɪgmənt) *n* a fantastic notion or fabrication: *a figment of the*

THESAURUS

fiend *n* **1** = **demon**, devil, evil spirit, hellhound **2** = **brute**, barbarian, beast, degenerate, ghoul, monster, ogre, savage **3** *Informal* = **enthusiast**, addict, energumen, fanatic, freak (*inf.*), maniac
fiendish *adj* **1, 2** = **wicked**, accursed, atrocious, black-hearted, cruel, demoniac, devilish, diabolical, hellish, implacable, infernal, inhuman, malevolent, malicious, malignant, monstrous, satanic, savage, ungodly, unspeakable
fierce *adj* **1** = **wild**, baleful, barbarous, brutal, cruel, dangerous, fell (*arch.*), feral, ferocious, fiery, menacing, murderous, passionate, savage, threatening, tigerish, truculent, uncontrollable, untamed, vicious **2** = **stormy**, blustery, boisterous, furious, howling, inclement, powerful, raging, strong, tempestuous, tumultuous, uncontrollable, violent **3** = **intense**, cut-throat, keen, relentless, strong
Antonyms *adj* ≠ **wild**: affectionate, calm, civilized, cool, docile, domesticated, gentle, harmless, kind, mild, peaceful, submissive, tame ≠ **stormy**: temperate, tranquil
fiercely *adv* **1** = **ferociously**, frenziedly, furiously, in a frenzy, like cat and dog, menacingly, passionately, savagely, tempestuously, tigerishly, tooth and nail, uncontrolledly, viciously, with bared teeth, with no holds barred
fierceness *n* **1** = **ferocity**, fieriness, mercilessness, ruthlessness, savageness, viciousness, wildness **2** = **storminess**, bluster, destructiveness, roughness, tempestuousness, turbulence, violence **3** = **intensity**, avidity, fervidness, fervour, passion, relentlessness, strength
fiery *adj* **1** = **burning**, ablaze, afire, aflame, blazing, flaming, glowing, in flames, on fire, red-hot **3** = **excitable**, choleric, fierce, hot-headed, impetuous, irascible, irritable, passionate, peppery, violent **5** = **feverish**, burning, febrile, fevered, flushed, heated, hot, inflamed
fiesta *n* **1, 2** = **carnival**, bacchanal *or* bacchanalia, carousal, celebration, fair, feast, festival, festivity, fête, gala, holiday, jamboree, jubilee, Mardi Gras, merrymaking, party, revel, revelry, saint's day, Saturnalia
fight *vb* **1, 3** = **battle**, assault, bear arms against, box, brawl, carry on war, clash, close, combat, come to blows, conflict, contend, cross swords, do battle, engage, exchange blows, feud, go to war, grapple, joust, lock horns, row, spar, struggle, take the field, take up arms against, tilt, tussle, wage war, war, wrestle **2** = **quarrel**, argue, bicker, dispute, fall out (*inf.*), squabble, wrangle **4** = **oppose**, contest, defy, dispute, make a stand against, resist, stand up to, strive, struggle, withstand **8 fight shy** = **avoid**, duck out (*inf.*), keep aloof, keep at arm's length, shun, steer clear ◆ *n* **9** = **battle**, action, affray (*Law*), altercation, bout, brawl, brush, clash, combat, conflict, contest, dispute, dissension, dogfight, duel, encounter, engagement, fracas, fray, hostilities, joust, melee *or* mêlée, passage of arms, riot, row, scrap (*inf.*), set-to (*inf.*), shindig (*inf.*), shindy (*inf.*), skirmish, sparring match, struggle, tussle, war **11** = **resistance**, belligerence, gameness, mettle, militancy, pluck, spirit, will to resist
fighter *n* **1** = **boxer**, bruiser (*inf.*), prize fighter, pugilist **1** = **soldier**, fighting man, man-at-arms, warrior **1** = **combatant**, antagonist, battler, belligerent, contender, contestant, disputant, militant
fighting *n* **1** = **battle**, bloodshed, blows struck, combat, conflict, hostilities, warfare
fight off *vb* **1** = **repel**, beat off, drive away, keep *or* hold at bay, repress, repulse, resist, stave off, ward off
figment *n As in* **figment of one's imagination** =

imagination. [C15: from LL *figmentum* a fiction, from L *fingere* to shape]

figurant ('fɪgjʊrənt) *n* a ballet dancer who does group work but no solo roles. [C18: from F, from *figurer* to represent, appear, FIGURE]
▸**figurante** (ˌfɪgjʊ'rɒnt) *fem n*

figuration (ˌfɪgə'reɪʃən) *n* **1** *Music.* **1a** the employment of characteristic patterns of notes, esp. in variations on a theme. **1b** florid ornamentation. **2** the act or an instance of representing figuratively, as by means of allegory. **3** a figurative representation. **4** the act of decorating with a design.

figurative ➊ ('fɪgərətɪv) *adj* **1** involving a figure of speech; not literal; metaphorical. **2** using or filled with figures of speech. **3** representing by means of an emblem, likeness, etc.
▸ **'figuratively** *adv* ▸ **'figurativeness** *n*

figure ➊ ('fɪgə) *n* **1** any written symbol other than a letter, esp. a whole number. **2** another name for **digit** (sense 2). **3** an amount expressed numerically: *a figure of £1800 was suggested.* **4** (*pl*) calculations with numbers: *he's good at figures.* **5** visible shape or form; outline. **6** the human form: *a girl with a slender figure.* **7** a slim bodily shape (esp. in **keep** *or* **lose one's figure**). **8** a character or personage: *a figure in politics.* **9** the impression created by a person through behaviour (esp. in **to cut a fine, bold,** etc., **figure**). **10a** a person as impressed on the mind. **10b** (*in combination): father-figure.* **11** a representation in painting or sculpture, esp. of the human form. **12** an illustration or diagram in a text. **13** a representative object or symbol. **14** a pattern or design, as in wood. **15** a predetermined set of movements in dancing or skating. **16** *Geom.* any combination of points, lines, curves, or planes. **17** *Logic.* one of four possible arrangements of the terms in the major and minor premises of a syllogism that give the same conclusion. **18** *Music.* **18a** a numeral written above or below a note in a part. **18b** a characteristic short pattern of notes. ◆ *vb* **figures, figuring, figured. 19** (when *tr*, often foll. by *up*) to calculate or compute (sums, amounts, etc.). **20** (*tr; usually takes a clause as object*) *Inf., US, Canad., & NZ.* to consider. **21** (*tr*) to represent by a diagram or illustration. **22** (*tr*) to pattern or mark with a design. **23** (*tr*) to depict or portray in a painting, etc. **24** (*tr*) to imagine. **25** (*tr*) *Music.* to decorate (a melody line or part) with ornamentation. **26** (*intr;* usually foll. by *in*) to be included: *his name figures in the article.* **27** (*intr*) *Inf.* to accord with expectation: *it figures that he wouldn't come.* ◆ See also **figure out.** [C13: from L *figūra* a shape, from *fingere* to mould]
▸ **'figurer** *n*

figured ➊ ('fɪgəd) *adj* **1** depicted as a figure in painting or sculpture. **2** decorated with a design. **3** having a form. **4** *Music.* **4a** ornamental. **4b** (of a bass part) provided with numerals indicating accompanying harmonies.

figured bass (beɪs) *n* a shorthand method of indicating a thorough-bass part in which each bass note is accompanied by figures indicating the intervals to be played in the chord above it.

figurehead ➊ ('fɪgəˌhɛd) *n* **1** a person nominally having a prominent position, but no real authority. **2** a carved bust on the bow of some sailing vessels.

figure of speech ➊ *n* an expression of language, such as metaphor, by which the literal meaning of a word is not employed.

figure out ➊ *vb* (*tr, adv; may take a clause as object*) *Inf.* **1** to calculate. **2** to understand.

figure skating *n* **1** ice skating in which the skater traces outlines of selected patterns. **2** the whole art of skating, as distinct from skating at speed.
▸**figure skater** *n*

figurine (ˌfɪgə'riːn) *n* a small carved or moulded figure; statuette. [C19: from F, from It. *figurina* a little FIGURE]

figwort ('fɪgˌwɜːt) *n* a plant related to the foxglove having square stems and small greenish flowers.

Fijian (fiː'dʒiːən) *n* **1** a member of the indigenous people inhabiting Fiji. **2** the language of this people, belonging to the Malayo-Polynesian family. ◆ *adj* **3** of or characteristic of Fiji or its inhabitants. ◆ Also: **Fiji.**

filagree ('fɪləˌgriː) *n, adj* a less common spelling of **filigree.**

filament ➊ ('fɪləmənt) *n* **1** the thin wire, usually tungsten, inside a light bulb that emits light when heated to incandescence by an electric current. **2** *Electronics.* a high-resistance wire forming the cathode in some valves. **3** a single strand of a natural or synthetic fibre. **4** *Bot.* the stalk of a stamen. **5** any slender structure or part. [C16: from NL, from Med. L *filāre* to spin, from L *filum* thread]
▸**filamentary** (ˌfɪlə'mɛntərɪ) *or* ˌ**fila'mentous** *adj*

filaria (fɪ'lɛərɪə) *n, pl* **filariae** (-ɪˌiː). a parasitic nematode worm that lives in the blood of vertebrates and is transmitted by insects: the cause of filariasis. [C19: NL (former name of genus), from L *filum* thread]
▸**fi'larial** *adj*

filariasis (ˌfɪlə'raɪəsɪs, fɪˌlɛərɪ'eɪsɪs) *n* a disease common in tropical and subtropical countries resulting from infestation of the lymphatic system with nematode worms transmitted by mosquitoes: characterized by inflammation. See also **elephantiasis.** [C19: from NL; see FILARIA]

filbert ('fɪlbət) *n* **1** any of several N temperate shrubs that have edible rounded brown nuts. **2** Also called: **hazelnut, cobnut.** the nut of any of these shrubs. [C14: after St *Philbert,* 7th-century Frankish abbot, because the nuts are ripe around his feast day, Aug. 22]

filch ➊ (fɪltʃ) *vb* (*tr*) to steal or take in small amounts. [C16 *filchen* to steal, attack, ?from OE *gefylce* band of men]
▸ **'filcher** *n*

file[1] ➊ (faɪl) *n* **1** a folder, box, etc., used to keep documents or other items in order. **2** the documents, etc., kept in this way. **3** documents or information about a specific subject, person, etc. **4** a line of people in marching formation, one behind another. **5** any of the eight vertical rows of squares on a chessboard. **6** *Computing.* a named collection of information, in the form of text, programs, graphics, etc., held on a permanent storage device, such as a magnetic disk. **7 on file.** recorded or catalogued for reference, as in a file. ◆ *vb* **files, filing, filed. 8** to place (a document, etc.) in a file. **9** (*tr*) to place (a legal document) on public or official record. **10** (*tr*) to bring (a suit, esp. a divorce suit) in a court of law. **11** (*tr*) to submit (copy) to a newspaper. **12** (*intr*) to march or walk in a file or files: *the ants filed down the hill.* [C16 (in the sense: string on which documents are hung): from OF, from Med. L *filāre;* see FILAMENT]
▸ **'filer** *n*

file[2] ➊ (faɪl) *n* **1** a hand tool consisting of a steel blade with small cutting teeth on some or all of its faces. It is used for shaping or smoothing. ◆ *vb* **files, filing, filed. 2** (*tr*) to shape or smooth (a surface) with a file. [OE *fīl*]
▸ **'filer** *n*

filefish ('faɪlˌfɪʃ) *n, pl* **filefish** *or* **filefishes.** any tropical triggerfish having a narrow compressed body and a very long dorsal spine. [C18: referring to its file-like scales]

filename ('faɪlˌneɪm) *n* an arrangement of characters that enables a computer system to permit the user to have access to a particular file.

file server *n Computing.* the central unit of a local area network that controls its operation and provides access to separately stored data files.

filet ('fɪlɪt, 'fɪleɪ) *n* a variant spelling of **fillet** (senses 1–3). [C20: from F: net, from OF, from *fil* thread, from L *filum*]

filet mignon ('fɪleɪ 'miːnjɒn) *n* a small tender boneless cut of beef. [from F, lit.: dainty fillet]

filial ('fɪljəl) *adj* **1** of, resembling, or suitable to a son or daughter: *filial affection.* **2** *Genetics.* designating any of the generations following the parental generation. [C15: from LL *filiālis,* from L *filius* son]
▸ **'filially** *adv*

filibeg *or* **philibeg** ('fɪlɪˌbɛg) *n* the kilt worn by Scottish Highlanders. [C18: from Scot. Gaelic *fēileadhbeag,* from *fēileadh* kilt + *beag* small]

filibuster ➊ ('fɪlɪˌbʌstə) *n* **1** the process of obstructing legislation by means of delaying tactics. **2** Also called: **filibusterer.** a legislator who engages in such obstruction. **3** a freebooter or military adventurer, esp. in a foreign country. ◆ *vb* **4** to obstruct (legislation) with delaying tactics. **5** (*intr*) to engage in unlawful military action. [C16: from Sp., from F *flibustier,* prob. from Du. *vrijbuiter* pirate, lit.: one plundering freely; see FREEBOOTER]
▸ **'filiˌbusterer** *n*

filigree ➊ ('fɪlɪˌgriː) *or* **filagree** *n* **1** delicate ornamental work of twisted gold, silver, or other wire. **2** any fanciful delicate ornamentation.

THESAURUS

invention, creation, fable, fabrication, falsehood, fancy, fiction, improvisation, production

figurative *adj* **1** = **symbolical**, allegorical, emblematical, metaphorical, representative, typical **2** = **poetical**, descriptive, fanciful, florid, flowery, ornate, pictorial, tropical (*Rhetoric*)
Antonyms *adj* ≠ **symbolical:** accurate, exact, factual, faithful, literal ≠ **poetical**: prosaic, simple, true, unpoetical, unvarnished

figure *n* **1, 2** = **number**, character, cipher, digit, numeral, symbol **3** = **amount**, cost, price, sum, total, value **5** = **outline**, form, shadow, shape, silhouette **6** = **shape**, body, build, chassis (*sl.*), frame, physique, proportions, torso **8** = **character**, big name, celebrity, dignitary, face (*inf.*), force, leader, notability, notable, personage, personality, presence, somebody, worthy **12** = **diagram**, depiction, design, device, drawing, emblem, illustration, motif, pattern, representation, sketch ◆ *vb* **19** = **calculate**, add, compute, count, reckon, sum, tally, tot up, work out **26** *usually foll. by* **in** = **feature**, act, appear, be conspicuous, be featured, be included, be mentioned, contribute to, have a place in, play a part

figured *adj* **2** = **decorated**, adorned, embellished, marked, ornamented, patterned, variegated

figurehead *n* **1** = **front man**, cipher, dummy, leader in name only, man of straw, mouthpiece, name, nonentity, puppet, straw man (*chiefly US*), titular *or* nominal head, token

figure of speech *n* = **expression**, conceit, image, trope, turn of phrase

figure out *vb* **1** = **calculate**, compute, reckon, work out **2** = **understand**, comprehend, decipher, fathom, make head or tail of (*inf.*), make out, resolve, see, suss (out) (*sl.*)

filament *n* = **strand**, cilium (*Biology & Zoology*), fibre, fibril, pile, staple, string, thread, wire, wisp

filch *vb* = **steal**, abstract, crib (*inf.*), embezzle, lift (*inf.*), misappropriate, nick (*sl., chiefly Brit.*), pilfer, pinch (*inf.*), purloin, rip off (*sl.*), swipe (*sl.*), take, thieve, walk off with

file[1] *n* **1, 2** = **folder**, case, data, documents, dossier, information, portfolio **4** = **line**, column, list, queue, row, string ◆ *vb* **8** = **register**, document, enter, pigeonhole, put in place, record, slot in (*inf.*) **12** = **march**, parade, troop

file[2] *vb* **2** = **smooth**, abrade, burnish, furbish, polish, rasp, refine, rub, rub down, scrape, shape

filibuster *n* **1** = **obstruction**, delay, hindrance, postponement, procrastination **3** = **freebooter**, adventurer, buccaneer, corsair, pirate, sea robber, sea rover, soldier of fortune ◆ *vb* **4** = **obstruct**, delay, hinder, play for time, prevent, procrastinate, put off

filigree *n* **1** = **wirework**, lace, lacework, lattice, tracery

◆ *adj* **3** made of or as if with filigree. [C17: from earlier *filigreen*, from F *filigrane*, from L *filum* thread + *grānum* GRAIN]
▸ **'fili,greed** *adj*

filings ('faɪlɪŋz) *pl n* shavings or particles removed by a file: *iron filings*.

Filipino (,fɪlɪ'piːnəʊ) *n* **1** (*pl* **Filipinos**) Also (fem): **Filipina.** a native or inhabitant of the Philippines. **2** another name for **Tagalog.** ◆ *adj* **3** of or relating to the Philippines or their inhabitants.

fill ➊ (fɪl) *vb* (*mainly tr*; often foll. by *up*) **1** (*also intr*) to make or become full: *to fill up a bottle.* **2** to occupy the whole of: *the party filled the house.* **3** to plug (a gap, crevice, etc.). **4** to meet (a requirement or need) satisfactorily. **5** to cover (a page or blank space) with writing, drawing, etc. **6** to hold and perform the duties of (an office or position). **7** to appoint or elect an occupant to (an office or position). **8** (*also intr*) to swell or cause to swell with wind, as in manoeuvring the sails of a sailing vessel. **9** *Chiefly US & Canad.* to put together the necessary materials for (a prescription or order). **10 fill the bill.** *Inf.* to serve or perform adequately. ◆ *n* **11** material such as gravel, stones, etc., used to bring an area of ground up to a required level. **12 one's fill.** the quantity needed to satisfy one. ◆ See also **fill in, fill out,** etc. [OE *fyllan*]

filler ➊ ('fɪlə) *n* **1** a person or thing that fills. **2** an object or substance used to add weight or size to something or to fill in a gap. **3** a paste, used for filling in cracks, holes, etc., in a surface before painting. **4** the inner portion of a cigar. **5** *Journalism.* articles, photographs, etc., to fill space between more important articles in a newspaper or magazine.

fillet ('fɪlɪt) *n* **1a** Also called: **fillet steak.** a strip of boneless meat. **1b** the boned side of a fish. **2** a narrow strip of any material. **3** a thin strip of ribbon, lace, etc., worn in the hair or around the neck. **4** a narrow flat moulding, esp. one between other mouldings. **5** a narrow band between flutings on the shaft of a column. **6** *Heraldry.* a horizontal division of a shield. **7** a narrow decorative line, impressed on the cover of a book. ◆ *vb* **fillets, filleting, filleted.** (*tr*) **8** to cut or prepare (meat or fish) as a fillet. **9** to cut fillets from (meat or fish). **10** to bind or decorate with or as if with a fillet. ◆ Also (for senses 1–3): **filet.** [C14: from OF *filet*, from *fil* thread, from L *filum*]

fill in ➊ *vb* (*adv*) **1** (*tr*) to complete (a form, drawing, etc.). **2** (*intr*) to act as a substitute. **3** (*tr*) to put material into (a hole or cavity), esp. so as to make it level with a surface. **4** (*tr*) *Inf.* to inform with facts or news. ◆ *n* **fill-in. 5** a substitute.

filling ➊ ('fɪlɪŋ) *n* **1** the substance or thing used to fill a space or container: *pie filling.* **2** *Dentistry.* any of various substances (metal, plastic, etc.) for inserting into the prepared cavity of a tooth. **3** *Chiefly US.* the weft in weaving. ◆ *adj* **4** (of food or a meal) substantial and satisfying.

filling station *n* a place where petrol and other supplies for motorists are sold.

fillip ➊ ('fɪlɪp) *n* **1** something that adds stimulation or enjoyment. **2** the action of holding a finger towards the palm with the thumb and suddenly releasing it outwards to produce a snapping sound. **3** a quick blow or tap made by this. ◆ *vb* **4** (*tr*) to stimulate or excite. **5** (*tr*) to strike or project sharply with a fillip. **6** (*intr*) to make a fillip. [C15 *philippe*, imit.]

fill out *vb* (*adv*) **1** to make or become fuller, thicker, or rounder. **2** to make more substantial. **3** (*tr*) *Chiefly US & Canad.* to fill in (a form, etc.).

fill up *vb* (*adv*) **1** (*tr*) to complete (a form, application, etc.). **2** to make or become full. ◆ *n* **fill-up. 3** the act of filling something completely, esp. the petrol tank of a car.

filly ('fɪlɪ) *n, pl* **fillies.** a female horse or pony under the age of four. [C15: from ON *fylja*; see FOAL]

film ➊ (fɪlm) *n* **1a** a sequence of images of moving objects photographed by a camera and providing the optical illusion of continuous movement when projected onto a screen. **1b** a form of entertainment, etc., composed of such a sequence of images. **1c** (*as modifier*): *film techniques.* **2** a thin flexible strip of cellulose coated with a photographic emulsion, used to make negatives and transparencies. **3** a thin coating or layer. **4** a thin sheet of any material, as of plastic for packaging. **5** a fine haze, mist, or blur. **6** a gauzy web of filaments or fine threads. ◆ *vb* **7a** to photograph with a cine camera. **7b** to make a film of (a screenplay, event, etc.). **8** (often foll. by *over*) to cover or become covered or coated with a film. [OE *filmen* membrane]

filmic ('fɪlmɪk) *adj* **1** of or relating to films or the cinema. **2** suggestive of films or the cinema.
▸ **'filmically** *adv*

film noir (nwɑː) *n* a type of gangster thriller, made esp. in the 1940s in Hollywood, characterized by stark lighting, an involved plot, and an atmosphere of cynicism and corruption. [C20: F, lit.: black film]

filmography (fɪl'mɒgrəfɪ) *n* **1** a list of the films made by a particular director, actor, etc. **2** any writing that deals with films or the cinema.

filmset ('fɪlm,set) *vb* **filmsets, filmsetting, filmset.** (*tr*) *Brit.* to set (type matter) by filmsetting.
▸ **'film,setter** *n*

filmsetting ('fɪlm,setɪŋ) *n Brit., printing.* typesetting by exposing type characters onto photographic film from which printing plates are made.

film speed *n* **1** the sensitivity to light of a photographic film, specified in terms of the film's ISO rating. **2** the rate at which the film passes through a motion picture camera or projector.

film strip *n* a strip of film composed of different images projected separately as slides.

filmy ➊ ('fɪlmɪ) *adj* **filmier, filmiest. 1** transparent or gauzy. **2** hazy; blurred.
▸ **'filmily** *adv* ▸ **'filminess** *n*

filo ('fiːləʊ) *n* a type of Greek flaky pastry in very thin sheets. [C20: Mod. Gk *phullon* leaf]

Filofax ('faɪləʊ,fæks) *n Trademark.* a type of loose-leaf ring binder with sets of different-coloured paper, used as a portable personal filing system, including appointments, addresses, etc.

filter ➊ ('fɪltə) *n* **1** a porous substance, such as paper or sand, that allows fluid to pass but retains suspended solid particles. **2** any device containing such a porous substance for separating suspensions from fluids. **3** any of various porous substances built into the mouth end of a cigarette or cigar for absorbing impurities such as tar. **4** any electronic, optical, or acoustic device that blocks signals or radiations of certain frequencies while allowing others to pass. **5** any transparent disc of gelatine or glass used to eliminate or reduce the intensity of given frequencies from the light leaving a lamp, entering a camera, etc. **6** *Brit.* a traffic signal at a road junction which permits vehicles to turn either left or right when the main signals are red. ◆ *vb* **7** (often foll. by *out*) to remove or separate (suspended particles, etc.) from (a liquid, gas, etc.) by the action of a filter. **8** (*tr*) to obtain by filtering. **9** (*intr*; foll. by *through*) to pass (through a filter or something like a filter). **10** (*intr*) to flow slowly; trickle. [C16 *filtre*, from Med. L *filtrum* piece of felt used as a filter, of Gmc origin]

filterable ('fɪltərəbᵊl) *or* **filtrable** ('fɪltrəbᵊl) *adj* **1** capable of being filtered. **2** (of most viruses and certain bacteria) capable of passing through the pores of a fine filter.

filter bed *n* a layer of sand or gravel in a tank or reservoir through which a liquid is passed so as to purify it.

filter feeding *n Zool.* a method of feeding in some aquatic animals, such as whalebone whales, in which minute food particles are filtered from the surrounding water.
▸ **filter feeder** *n*

filter out *or* **through** *vb* (*intr, adv*) to become known gradually; leak.

filter paper *n* a porous paper used for filtering liquids.

filter tip *n* **1** an attachment to the mouth end of a cigarette for trapping impurities such as tar during smoking. **2** a cigarette having such an attachment.
▸ **'filter-,tipped** *adj*

filth ➊ (fɪlθ) *n* **1** foul or disgusting dirt; refuse. **2** extreme physical or moral uncleanliness. **3** vulgarity or obscenity. **4 the filth.** *Sl.* the police. [OE *fӯlth*]

filthy ➊ ('fɪlθɪ) *adj* **filthier, filthiest. 1** very dirty or obscene. **2** offensive or vicious: *that was a filthy trick to play.* **3** *Inf., chiefly Brit.* extremely unpleasant: *filthy weather.* ◆ *adv* **4** extremely; disgustingly (esp. in **filthy rich**).
▸ **'filthily** *adv* ▸ **'filthiness** *n*

THESAURUS

fill *vb* **1** = **stuff**, brim over, cram, crowd, furnish, glut, gorge, inflate, pack, pervade, replenish, sate, satiate, satisfy, stock, store, supply, swell **2** = **saturate**, charge, imbue, impregnate, overspread, pervade, suffuse **3** = **plug**, block, bung, close, cork, seal, stop **6, 7** = **perform**, assign, carry out, discharge, engage, execute, fulfil, hold, occupy, officiate, take up ◆ *n* **12 one's fill** = **sufficient**, all one wants, ample, a sufficiency, enough, plenty
Antonyms *vb* ≠ **stuff:** diminish, drain, empty, exhaust, shrink, subside, vacate, void

filler *n* **2** = **padding**, makeweight, stopgap

fill in *vb* **1** = **complete**, answer, fill out (*US*), fill up **2** = **replace**, deputize, represent, stand in, sub, substitute, take the place of **4** *Informal* = **inform**, acquaint, apprise, bring up to date, give the facts *or* background, put wise (*sl.*)

filling *n* **1** = **stuffing**, contents, filler, innards (*inf.*), inside, insides, padding, wadding ◆ *adj* **4** = **satisfying**, ample, heavy, square, substantial

fillip *n* **1** = **stimulus**, goad, incentive, prod, push, spice, spur, zest

film *n* **1** = **movie**, flick (*sl.*), motion picture **3** = **layer**, coat, coating, covering, dusting, gauze, integument, membrane, pellicle, scum, skin, tissue **5** = **haze**, blur, cloud, haziness, mist, mistiness, opacity, veil ◆ *vb* **7** = **photograph**, shoot, take, video, videotape **8** *often foll. by* **over** = **cloud**, blear, blur, dull, haze, mist, veil

filmy *adj* **1** = **transparent**, chiffon, cobwebby, delicate, diaphanous, fine, finespun, flimsy, floaty, fragile, gauzy, gossamer, insubstantial, see-through, sheer **2** = **transparent**, bleared, bleary, blurred, blurry, cloudy, dim, hazy, membranous, milky, misty, opalescent, opaque, pearly

filter *n* **1** = **sieve**, gauze, membrane, mesh, riddle, strainer ◆ *vb* **7** = **purify**, clarify, filtrate, refine, screen, sieve, sift, strain, winnow **9, 10** = **trickle**, dribble, escape, exude, leach, leak, ooze, penetrate, percolate, seep, well

filth *n* **1** = **dirt**, carrion, contamination, crud (*sl.*), defilement, dung, excrement, excreta, faeces, filthiness, foul matter, foulness, garbage, grime, grot (*sl.*), muck, nastiness, ordure, pollution, putrefaction, putrescence, refuse, sewage, slime, sludge, squalor, uncleanness **2, 3** = **obscenity**, corruption, dirty- mindedness, impurity, indecency, pornography, smut, vileness, vulgarity

filthy *adj* **1** = **dirty**, faecal, feculent, foul, nasty, polluted, putrid, scummy, scuzzy (*sl., chiefly US*), slimy, squalid, unclean, vile **1** = **obscene**, bawdy, coarse, corrupt, depraved, dirty-minded, foul, foul-mouthed, impure, indecent, lewd, licentious, pornographic, smutty, suggestive, X-rated (*inf.*) **1** = **muddy**, begrimed, black, blackened, grimy, grubby, miry, mucky, mud-encrusted, scuzzy (*sl., chiefly US*), smoky, sooty, unwashed **2** = **despicable**, base, contemptible, low, mean, offensive, scurvy, vicious, vile

filtrate ('fɪltreɪt) *n* **1** a liquid or gas that has been filtered. ◆ *vb* **filtrates, filtrating, filtrated. 2** to filter. [C17: from Med. L *filtrāre* to FILTER]
▸**fil'tration** *n*

fin (fɪn) *n* **1** any of the firm appendages that are the organs of locomotion and balance in fishes and some other aquatic animals. **2** a part or appendage that resembles a fin. **3a** *Brit.* a vertical surface to which the rudder is attached at the rear of an aeroplane. **3b** a tail surface fixed to a rocket or missile to give stability. **4** *Naut.* a fixed or adjustable blade projecting under water from the hull of a vessel to give it stability or control. **5** a projecting rib to dissipate heat from the surface of an engine cylinder or radiator. ◆ *vb* **fins, finning, finned. 6** (*tr*) to provide with fins. [OE *finn*]
▸**'finless** *adj* ▸**finned** *adj*

fin. *abbrev. for:* **1** finance. **2** financial.

Fin. *abbrev. for:* **1** Finland. **2** Finnish.

finable *or* **fineable** ('faɪnəbᵊl) *adj* liable to a fine.
▸**'finableness** *or* **'fineableness** *n*

finagle (fɪ'neɪgᵊl) *vb* **finagles, finagling, finagled.** *Inf.* **1** (*tr*) to get or achieve by craftiness or persuasion. **2** to use trickery on (a person). [C20: ?from dialect *fainaigue* cheat]
▸**fi'nagler** *n*

final ❶ ('faɪnᵊl) *adj* **1** of or occurring at the end; last. **2** having no possibility of further discussion, action, or change: *a final decree of judgment.* **3** relating to or constituting an end or purpose: *a final clause may be introduced by "in order to".* **4** *Music.* another word for **perfect** (sense 9b.). ◆ *n* **5** a last thing; end. **6** a deciding contest between the winners of previous rounds in a competition. ◆ See also **finals.** [C14: from L *fīnālis,* from *fīnis* limit, boundary]

finale ❶ (fɪ'nɑːlɪ) *n* **1** the concluding part of any performance or presentation. **2** the closing section or movement of a musical composition. [C18: from It., n use of adj *finale,* from L *fīnālis* FINAL]

finalist ('faɪnəlɪst) *n* a contestant who has reached the last stage of a competition.

finality ❶ (faɪ'nælɪtɪ) *n, pl* **finalities. 1** the condition or quality of being final or settled: *the finality of death.* **2** a final or conclusive act.

finalize ❶ *or* **finalise** ('faɪnəˌlaɪz) *vb* **finalizes, finalizing, finalized** *or* **finalises, finalising, finalised. 1** (*tr*) to put into final form; settle: *to finalize plans for the merger.* **2** to reach agreement on a transaction.
▸**ˌfinali'zation** *or* **ˌfinali'sation** *n*

> **USAGE NOTE** Although *finalize* has been in widespread use for some time, many speakers and writers still prefer to use *complete, conclude,* or *make final,* esp. in formal contexts.

finally ❶ ('faɪnəlɪ) *adv* **1** at last; eventually. **2** at the end or final point; lastly. **3** completely; conclusively. ◆ *sentence connector.* **4** in the end; lastly: *finally, he put his tie on.* **5** as the last or final point.

finals ('faɪnᵊlz) *pl n* **1** the deciding part of a competition. **2** *Education.* the last examinations in an academic or professional course.

finance ❶ (fɪ'næns, 'faɪnæns) *n* **1** the system of money, credit, etc., esp. with respect to government revenues and expenditures. **2** funds or the provision of funds. **3** (*pl*) financial condition. ◆ *vb* **finances, financing, financed. 4** (*tr*) to provide or obtain funds or credit for. [C14: from OF, from *finer* to end, settle by payment]

finance company *or* **house** *n* an enterprise engaged in the loan of money against collateral, esp. one specializing in the financing of hire-purchase contracts.

financial ❶ (fɪ'nænʃəl, faɪ-) *adj* **1** of or relating to finance or finances. **2** of or relating to persons who manage money, capital, or credit. **3** *Austral. & NZ inf.* having money; in funds. **4** *Austral. & NZ.* (of a club member) fully paid-up.
▸**fi'nancially** *adv*

financial futures *pl n* futures in a stock-exchange index, currency exchange rate, or interest rate enabling banks, building societies, brokers, and speculators to hedge their involvement in these markets.

Financial Ombudsman *n* any of five British ombudsmen: the **Banking Ombudsman**, set up in 1986 to investigate complaints from banking customers; the **Building Society Ombudsman**, set up in 1987 to investigate complaints from building society customers; the **Insurance Ombudsman**, set up in 1981 to investigate complaints by policyholders (since 1988 this ombudsman has also operated a **Unit Trust Ombudsman** scheme); the **Investment Ombudsman**, set up in 1989 to investigate complaints by investors (the **Personal Investment Authority Ombudsman** is responsible for investigating complaints by personal investors); and the **Pensions Ombudsman**, set up in 1993 to investigate complaints regarding pension schemes.

financial year *n Brit.* **1** any annual period at the end of which a firm's accounts are made up. **2** the annual period ending April 5, over which Budget estimates are made by the British Government. ◆ US and Canad. equivalent: **fiscal year.**

financier (fɪ'nænsɪə, faɪ-) *n* a person who is engaged in large-scale financial operations.

financing gap *n* the difference between a country's requirements for foreign exchange to finance its debts and imports and its income from overseas.

finback ('fɪnˌbæk) *n* another name for **rorqual.**

finch (fɪntʃ) *n* any of various songbirds having a short stout bill for feeding on seeds, such as the bullfinch, chaffinch, siskin, and canary. [OE *finc*]

find ❶ (faɪnd) *vb* **finds, finding, found.** (*mainly tr*) **1** to meet with or discover by chance. **2** to discover or obtain, esp. by search or effort: *to find happiness.* **3** (*may take a clause as object*) to realize: *he found that nobody knew.* **4** (*may take a clause as object*) to consider: *I find this wine a little sour.* **5** to look for and point out (something to be criticized). **6** (*also intr*) *Law.* to determine an issue and pronounce a verdict (upon): *the court found the accused guilty.* **7** to regain (something lost or not functioning): *to find one's tongue.* **8** to reach (a target): *the bullet found its mark.* **9** to provide, esp. with difficulty: *we'll find room for you too.* **10** to be able to pay: *I can't find that amount of money.* **11 find oneself.** to realize and accept one's true character; discover one's vocation. **12 find one's feet.** to become capable or confident. ◆ *n* **13** a person, thing, etc., that is found, esp. a valuable discovery. [OE *findan*]

finder ('faɪndə) *n* **1** a person or thing that finds. **2** *Physics.* a small telescope fitted to a more powerful larger telescope. **3** *Photog.* short for **viewfinder. 4 finders keepers.** *Inf.* whoever finds something has the right to keep it.

fin de siècle *French.* (fɛ̃ də sjɛklə) *n* **1** the end of the 19th century. ◆ *adj* ***fin-de-siècle.*** **2** of or relating to the close of the 19th century. **3** decadent, esp. in artistic tastes.

finding ❶ ('faɪndɪŋ) *n* **1** a thing that is found or discovered. **2** *Law.* the conclusion reached after a judicial inquiry; verdict.

find out ❶ *vb* (*adv*) **1** to gain knowledge of (something); learn. **2** to detect the crime, deception, etc., of (someone).

fine[1] ❶ (faɪn) *adj* **1** very good of its kind: *a fine speech.* **2** superior in skill or accomplishment: *a fine violinist.* **3** (of weather) clear and dry. **4** enjoyable or satisfying: *a fine time.* **5** (*postpositive*) *Inf.* quite well: *I feel fine.* **6** satisfactory; acceptable: *that's fine by me.* **7** of delicate composition or careful workmanship: *fine crystal.* **8** (of precious metals) pure or having a high degree of purity: *fine silver.* **9** discriminating: *a fine eye for antique brasses.* **10** abstruse or subtle: *a fine point.* **11** very thin or slender: *fine hair.* **12** very small: *fine print.* **13** (of edges, blades, etc.) sharp; keen. **14** ornate, showy, or smart. **15** good-looking: *a fine young woman.* **16** polished, elegant, or refined: *a fine gentleman.* **17** *Cricket.* (of a fielding position) oblique to and behind the wicket: *fine leg.* **18** (*prenominal*) *Inf.* disappointing or terrible: *a fine mess.* ◆ *adv* **19** *Inf.* all

THESAURUS

final *adj* **1** = **last**, closing, concluding, end, eventual, last-minute, latest, terminal, terminating, ultimate **2** = **conclusive**, absolute, decided, decisive, definite, definitive, determinate, finished, incontrovertible, irrevocable, settled
Antonyms *adj* ≠ **last:** earliest, first, initial, introductory, maiden, opening, original, precursory, prefatory, premier, preparatory

finale *n* **1** = **ending**, climax, close, conclusion, crowning glory, culmination, denouement, epilogue, finis, last act
Antonyms *n* commencement, exordium, foreword, intro (*inf.*), lead-in, opening, overture, preamble, preface, preliminaries, prelude, proem, prolegomenon, prologue

finality *n* **1** = **conclusiveness**, certitude, decidedness, decisiveness, definiteness, inevitableness, irrevocability, resolution, unavoidability

finalize *vb* **1, 2** = **complete**, agree, clinch, conclude, decide, settle, sew up (*inf.*), shake hands, tie up, work out, wrap up (*inf.*)

finally *adv* **1** = **eventually**, at last, at length, at long last, at the end of the day, at the last, at the last moment, in the end, in the fullness of time, in the long run, lastly, ultimately, when all is said and done **2** = **in conclusion**, in summary, lastly, to conclude **3** = **conclusively**, beyond the shadow of a doubt, completely, convincingly, decisively, for all time, for ever, for good, inescapably, inexorably, irrevocably, once and for all, permanently

finance *n* **1** = **economics**, accounts, banking, business, commerce, financial affairs, investment, money, money management **3** *plural* = **resources**, affairs, assets, capital, cash, financial condition, funds, money, wherewithal ◆ *vb* **4** = **fund**, back, bankroll (*US*), float, guarantee, pay for, provide security for, set up in business, subsidize, support, underwrite

financial *adj* **1** = **economic**, budgeting, fiscal, monetary, money, pecuniary

financing *n* **4** = **funding**, costs, expenditure, expense(s), operating expenses, outlay

find *vb* **1, 2** = **discover**, catch sight of, chance upon, come across, come up with, descry, encounter, espy, expose, ferret out, hit upon, lay one's hand on, light upon, locate, meet, recognize, run to earth, run to ground, spot, stumble upon, track down, turn up, uncover, unearth **2** = **get**, achieve, acquire, attain, earn, gain, obtain, procure, win **3** = **realise**, arrive at, ascertain, become aware, detect, discover, experience, learn, note, notice, observe, perceive, remark **7** = **regain**, get back, recover, repossess, retrieve **10** = **provide**, be responsible for, bring, contribute, cough up (*inf.*), furnish, purvey, supply ◆ *n* **13** = **discovery**, acquisition, asset, bargain, catch, good buy
Antonyms *vb* ≠ **discover:** lose, mislay, misplace, miss, overlook

finding *n* **2** = **conclusion**, award, decision, decree, judgment, pronouncement, recommendation, verdict

find out *vb* **1** = **learn**, detect, discover, note, observe, perceive, realize **2** = **detect**, bring to light, catch, disclose, expose, reveal, rumble (*Brit. inf.*), uncover, unmask

fine[1] *adj* **1, 2** = **excellent**, accomplished, admirable, beautiful, choice, divine, exceptional, exquisite, first-class, first-rate, great, magnificent, masterly, ornate, outstanding, rare, select, showy, skilful, splendid, sterling, superior, supreme, world-class **3** = **sunny**, balmy, bright, clear, clement, cloudless, dry, fair, pleasant **6** = **satisfactory**, acceptable, agreeable, all right, convenient, good, hunky-dory (*inf.*), O.K. *or* okay (*inf.*), suitable **7, 11** = **delicate**, dainty, elegant, expensive, exquisite, fragile, quality **7, 11** = **slender**, delicate, diaphanous, fine-grained,

right: *that suits me fine.* **20** finely. ◆ *vb* **fines, fining, fined. 21** to make or become finer; refine. **22** (often foll. by *down* or *away*) to make or become smaller. [C13: from OF *fin,* from L *fīnis* end, boundary, as in *fīnis honōrum* the highest degree of honour]
▸ **'finely** *adv* ▸ **'fineness** *n*

fine[2] ⓣ (faɪn) *n* **1** a certain amount of money exacted as a penalty: *a parking fine.* **2** a payment made by a tenant at the start of his tenancy to reduce his subsequent rent; premium. **3 in fine. 3a** in short. **3b** in conclusion. ◆ *vb* **fines, fining, fined. 4** (*tr*) to impose a fine on. [C12 (in the sense: conclusion, settlement): from OF *fin;* see FINE[1]]

fine[3] ('fiːneɪ) *n Music.* the point at which a piece is to end. [It., from L *fīnis* end]

fine art *n* **1** art produced chiefly for its aesthetic value. **2** (*often pl*) any of the fields in which such art is produced, such as painting, sculpture, and engraving.

fine-draw *vb* **fine-draws, fine-drawing, fine-drew, fine-drawn.** (*tr*) to sew together so finely that the join is scarcely noticeable.

fine-drawn *adj* **1** (of arguments, distinctions, etc.) precise or subtle. **2** (of wire, etc.) drawn out until very fine.

fine-grained *adj* (of wood, leather, etc.) having a fine smooth even grain.

finery[1] ⓣ ('faɪnərɪ) *n* elaborate or showy decoration, esp. clothing and jewellery.

finery[2] ('faɪnərɪ) *n, pl* **fineries.** a hearth for converting cast iron into wrought iron. [C17: from OF *finerie,* from *finer* to refine; see FINE[1]]

fines herbes (*French* finz ɛrb) *pl n* a mixture of finely chopped herbs, used to flavour omelettes, salads, etc.

finespun ('faɪn'spʌn) *adj* **1** spun or drawn out to a fine thread. **2** excessively subtle or refined.

finesse ⓣ (fɪ'nɛs) *n* **1** elegant skill in style or performance. **2** subtlety and tact in handling difficult situations. **3** *Bridge, whist.* an attempt to win a trick when opponents hold a high card in the suit led by playing a lower card. **4** a trick, artifice, or strategy. ◆ *vb* **finesses, finessing, finessed. 5** to bring about with finesse. **6** to play (a card) as a finesse. [C15: from OF, from *fin* fine, delicate; see FINE[1]]

fine-tooth comb *or* **fine-toothed comb** *n* **1** a comb with fine teeth set closely together. **2 go over** (*or* **through**) **with a fine-tooth(ed) comb.** to examine very thoroughly.

fine-tune *vb* **fine-tunes, fine-tuning, fine-tuned.** (*tr*) to make fine adjustments to (something) in order to obtain optimum performance.

finger ⓣ ('fɪŋgə) *n* **1a** any of the digits of the hand, often excluding the thumb. **1b** (*as modifier*): *a finger bowl.* **1c** (*in combination*): *a fingernail.* Related adj: **digital. 2** the part of a glove made to cover a finger. **3** something that resembles a finger in shape or function: *a finger of land.* **4** the length or width of a finger used as a unit of measurement. **5** a quantity of liquid in a glass, etc., as deep as a finger is wide. **6 get** *or* **pull one's finger out.** *Brit. inf.* to begin or speed up activity, esp. after initial delay. **7 have a** (*or* **one's**) **finger in the pie. 7a** to have an interest in or take part in some activity. **7b** to meddle or interfere. **8 lay** *or* **put one's finger on.** to indicate or locate accurately. **9 not lift** (*or* **raise**) **a finger.** (*foll. by an infinitive*) not to make any effort (to do something). **10 twist** *or* **wrap around one's little finger.** to have easy and complete control or influence over. **11 put the finger on.** *Inf.* to inform on or identify, esp. for the police. ◆ *vb* **12** (*tr*) to touch or manipulate with the fingers; handle. **13** (*tr*) *Inf., chiefly US.* to identify as a criminal or suspect. **14** to use one's fingers in playing (an instrument, such as a piano or clarinet). **15** to indicate on (a composition or part) the fingering required by a pianist, etc. [OE]
▸ **'fingerless** *adj*

fingerboard ('fɪŋgəˌbɔːd) *n* the long strip of hard wood on a violin, guitar, etc. upon which the strings are stopped by the fingers.

finger bowl *n* a small bowl filled with water for rinsing the fingers at the table after a meal.

finger buffet ('bʊfeɪ) *n* a buffet meal at which food that may be picked up in the fingers (**finger food**), such as canapés or vol-au-vents, is served.

fingered ('fɪŋgəd) *adj* **1** marked or dirtied by handling. **2a** having a finger or fingers. **2b** (*in combination*): *red-fingered.* **3** (of a musical part) having numerals indicating the fingering.

fingering ('fɪŋgərɪŋ) *n* **1** the technique or art of using one's fingers in playing a musical instrument, esp. the piano. **2** the numerals in a musical part indicating this.

fingerling ('fɪŋgəlɪŋ) *n* a very young fish, esp. the parr of salmon or trout.

fingermark ('fɪŋgəˌmɑːk) *n* a mark left by dirty or greasy fingers on paintwork, walls, etc.

fingernail ('fɪŋgəˌneɪl) *n* a thin horny translucent plate covering part of the dorsal surface of the end joint of each finger.

finger painting *n* the process or art of painting with **finger paints** of starch, glycerine, and pigments, using the fingers, hand, or arm.

finger post *n* a signpost showing a pointing finger or hand.

fingerprint ('fɪŋgəˌprɪnt) *n* **1** an impression of the pattern of ridges on the surface of the end joint of each finger and thumb. **2** any unique identifying characteristic. ◆ *vb* (*tr*) **3** to take an inked impression of the fingerprints of (a person). **4** to take a sample of (a person's) DNA.

fingerstall ('fɪŋgəˌstɔːl) *n* a protective covering for a finger. Also called: **cot.**

fingertip ('fɪŋgəˌtɪp) *n* **1** the end joint or tip of a finger. **2 at one's fingertips.** readily available.

finial ('faɪnɪəl) *n* **1** an ornament on top of a spire, etc., esp. in the form of a fleur-de-lys. **2** an ornament at the top of a piece of furniture, etc. [C14: from *finial* (adj), var. of FINAL]

finicky ⓣ ('fɪnɪkɪ) *or* **finicking** *adj* **1** excessively particular; fussy. **2** overelaborate. [C19: from *finical,* from FINE[1]]

finis ('fɪnɪs) *n* the end; finish: used at the end of books, films, etc. [C15: from L]

finish ⓣ ('fɪnɪʃ) *vb* (*mainly tr*) **1** to bring to an end; conclude or stop. **2** (*intr;* sometimes foll. by *up*) to be at or come to the end; use up. **3** to bring to a desired or complete condition. **4** to put a particular surface texture on (wood, cloth, etc.). **5** (often foll. by *off*) to destroy or defeat completely. **6** to train (a person) in social graces and talents. **7** (*intr;* foll. by *with*) to end a relationship or association. ◆ *n* **8** the final or last stage or part; end. **9** the death or absolute defeat of a person or one side in a conflict: *a fight to the finish.* **10** the surface texture or appearance of wood, cloth, etc.: *a rough finish.* **11** a thing, event, etc., that completes. **12** completeness and high quality of workmanship. **13** *Sport.* ability to sprint at the end of a race. [C14: from OF, from L *fīnīre;* see FINE[1]]
▸ **'finished** *adj* ▸ **'finisher** *n*

finishing school *n* a private school for girls that teaches social graces.

finite ⓣ ('faɪnaɪt) *adj* **1** bounded in magnitude or spatial or temporal extent. **2** *Maths, logic.* having a countable number of elements. **3** limited or restricted in nature: *human existence is finite.* **4** denoting any form of a verb inflected for grammatical features such as person, number, and tense. [C15: from L *fīnītus* limited, from *fīnīre* to limit, end]
▸ **'finitely** *adv* ▸ **'finiteness** *or* **finitude** ('faɪnɪˌtjuːd) *n*

fink (fɪŋk) *n Sl., chiefly US & Canad.* **1** a strikebreaker. **2** an unpleasant or contemptible person. [C20: from ?]

THESAURUS

flimsy, gauzy, gossamer, light, lightweight, powdered, powdery, pulverized, sheer, small, thin **8 = pure**, clear, refined, solid, sterling, unadulterated, unalloyed, unpolluted **10 = subtle**, abstruse, acute, critical, discriminating, fastidious, hairsplitting, intelligent, keen, minute, nice, precise, quick, refined, sensitive, sharp, tasteful, tenuous **13 = sharp**, brilliant, cutting, honed, keen, polished, razor-sharp **15 = good-looking**, attractive, bonny, handsome, lovely, smart, striking, stylish, well-favoured
Antonyms *adj* ≠ **excellent:** indifferent, inferior, poor, second rate, substandard ≠ **sunny:** cloudy, dull, overcast, unpleasant ≠ **delicate:** blunt, coarse, crude, dull, heavy, rough

fine[2] *n* **1 = penalty**, amercement (*obs.*), damages, forfeit, punishment ◆ *vb* **4 = penalize**, amerce (*arch.*), mulct, punish

finery[1] *n* **= splendour**, best bib and tucker (*inf.*), decorations, frippery, gear (*inf.*), gewgaws, glad rags (*inf.*), ornaments, showiness, Sunday best, trappings, trinkets

finesse *n* **1, 2 = skill**, adeptness, adroitness, artfulness, cleverness, craft, delicacy, diplomacy, discretion, know-how (*inf.*), polish, quickness, savoir-faire, sophistication, subtlety, tact **4 = stratagem**, artifice, bluff, feint, manoeuvre, ruse, trick, wile

finger *n* **8 put one's finger on = identify**, bring to mind, discover, find out, hit the nail on the head, hit upon, indicate, locate, pin down, place, recall, remember ◆ *vb* **12 = touch**, feel, fiddle with (*inf.*), handle, manipulate, maul, meddle with, paw (*inf.*), play about with, toy with

finicky *adj* **1 = fussy**, choosy (*inf.*), critical, dainty, difficult, fastidious, finicking, hard to please, nit-picking (*inf.*), overnice, overparticular, particular, picky (*inf.*), scrupulous, squeamish

finish *vb* **1 = stop**, accomplish, achieve, bring to a close *or* conclusion, carry through, cease, close, complete, conclude, culminate, deal with, discharge, do, end, execute, finalize, fulfil, get done, get out of the way, make short work of, put the finishing touch(es) to, put the tin lid on, round off, settle, terminate, wind up, wrap up (*inf.*) **2 = consume**, deplete, devour, dispatch, dispose of, drain, drink, eat, empty, exhaust, expend, spend, use, use up **4 = coat**, face, gild, lacquer, polish, smooth off, stain, texture, veneer, wax **5 = destroy**, annihilate, best, bring down, defeat, dispose of, drive to the wall, exterminate, get rid of, kill, move in for the kill, overcome, overpower, put an end to, put paid to, rout, ruin, worst **6 = perfect**, elaborate, polish, refine ◆ *n* **8 = end**, cessation, close, closing, completion, conclusion, culmination, denouement, ending, finale, last stage(s), run-in, termination, winding up (*inf.*), wind-up **9 = defeat**, annihilation, bankruptcy, curtains (*inf.*), death, end, end of the road, liquidation, ruin **10 = surface**, appearance, grain, lustre, patina, polish, shine, smoothness, texture
Antonyms *vb* ≠ **stop:** begin, commence, create, embark on, instigate, start, undertake ◆ *n* ≠ **end:** beginning, birth, commencement, conception, genesis, inauguration, inception, instigation, preamble, preface, prologue

finished *adj* **1 = over**, accomplished, achieved, closed, complete, completed, concluded, done, ended, entire, final, finalized, full, in the past, over and done with, sewed up (*inf.*), shut, terminated, through, tied up, wrapped up (*inf.*) **2 = spent**, done, drained, empty, exhausted, gone, played out (*inf.*), used up **5 = ruined**, bankrupt, defeated, devastated, done for (*inf.*), doomed, gone, liquidated, lost, through, undone, washed up (*inf., chiefly US*), wiped out, wound up, wrecked
Antonyms *adj* ≠ **over:** begun, incomplete

finite *adj* **1 = limited**, bounded, circumscribed, conditioned, delimited, demarcated, restricted, subject to limitations, terminable
Antonyms *adj* boundless, endless, eternal, ever-

Finlandization *or* **Finlandisation** (ˌfɪnləndaɪˈzeɪʃən) *n* neutralization of a small country by a superpower, using conciliation rather than confrontation, as the former Soviet Union did in relation to Finland.

Finn (fɪn) *n* a native, inhabitant, or citizen of Finland. [OE *Finnas* (pl)]

finnan haddock (ˈfɪnən) *or* **haddie** (ˈhædɪ) *n* smoked haddock. [C18: *finnan* after *Findon,* a village in NE Scotland]

Finnic (ˈfɪnɪk) *n* **1** one of the two branches of the Finno-Ugric family of languages, including Finnish and several languages of NE Europe. ◆ *adj* **2** of or relating to this group of languages or to the Finns.

Finnish (ˈfɪnɪʃ) *adj* **1** of or characteristic of Finland, the Finns, or their language. ◆ *n* **2** the official language of Finland, belonging to the Finno-Ugric family.

Finno-Ugric (ˈfɪnəʊˈuːgrɪk, -ˈjuː-) *or* **Finno-Ugrian** *n* **1** a family of languages spoken in Scandinavia, E Europe, and W Asia, including Finnish, Estonian, and Hungarian. ◆ *adj* **2** of, relating to, speaking, or belonging to this family of languages.

finny (ˈfɪnɪ) *adj* **finnier, finniest. 1** *Poetic.* relating to or containing many fishes. **2** having or resembling a fin or fins.

fino (ˈfiːnəʊ) *n* a very dry sherry. [Sp.: FINE[1]]

fiord (fjɔːd) *n* a variant spelling of **fjord.**

fioriture (ˌfjɔːrɪˈtʊəreɪ) *pl n Music.* flourishes; embellishments. [C19: It, from *fiorire* to flower]

fipple (ˈfɪpᵊl) *n* a wooden plug forming a flue in the end of a pipe, as the mouthpiece of a recorder. [C17: from ?]

fipple flute *n* an end-blown flute provided with a fipple, such as the recorder or flageolet.

fir (fɜː) *n* **1** any of a genus of pyramidal coniferous trees having single needle-like leaves and erect cones. **2** any of various other related trees, such as the Douglas fir. **3** the wood of any of these trees. [OE *furh*]

fire ❶ (ˈfaɪə) *n* **1** the state of combustion in which inflammable material burns, producing heat, flames, and often smoke. **2a** a mass of burning coal, wood, etc., used esp. in a hearth to heat a room. **2b** (*in combination*): *firelighter.* **3** a destructive conflagration, as of a forest, building, etc. **4** a device for heating a room, etc. **5** something resembling a fire in light or brilliance: *a diamond's fire.* **6** the act of discharging weapons, artillery, etc. **7** a burst or rapid volley: *a fire of questions.* **8** intense passion; ardour. **9** liveliness, as of imagination, etc. **10** fever and inflammation. **11** a severe trial or torment (esp. in **go through fire and water**). **12 between two fires.** under attack from two sides. **13 catch fire.** to ignite. **14 on fire. 14a** in a state of ignition. **14b** ardent or eager. **15 open fire.** to start firing a gun, artillery, etc. **16 play with fire.** to be involved in something risky. **17 set fire to** *or* **set on fire. 17a** to ignite. **17b** to arouse or excite. **18 under fire.** being attacked, as by weapons or by harsh criticism. **19** (*modifier*) *Astrol.* of or relating to a group of three signs of the zodiac, Aries, Leo, and Sagittarius. ◆ *vb* **fires, firing, fired. 20** to discharge (a firearm or projectile), or (of a firearm, etc.) to be discharged. **21** to detonate (an explosive charge or device), or (of such a charge or device) to be detonated. **22** (*intr*) (of an engine) to start working; ignite. **23** (*tr*) *Inf.* to dismiss from employment. **24** (*tr*) *Ceramics.* to bake in a kiln to harden the clay, etc. **25** to kindle or be kindled. **26** (*tr*) to provide with fuel: *oil fires the heating system.* **27** (*tr*) to subject to heat. **28** (*tr*) to heat slowly so as to dry. **29** (*tr*) to arouse to strong emotion. **30** to glow or cause to glow. ◆ *sentence substitute.* **31** a cry to warn others of a fire. **32** the order to begin firing a gun, artillery, etc. [OE *fӯr*]
▸ **ˈfirer** *n*

fire alarm *n* a device to give warning of fire, esp. a bell, siren, or hooter.

fire appliance *n* another name for fire engine.

firearm ❶ (ˈfaɪərˌɑːm) *n* a weapon from which a projectile can be discharged by an explosion caused by igniting gunpowder, etc.

fireback (ˈfaɪəˌbæk) *n* an ornamental iron slab against the back wall of a hearth.

fireball (ˈfaɪəˌbɔːl) *n* **1** a ball-shaped discharge of lightning. **2** the region of hot ionized gas at the centre of a nuclear explosion. **3** *Astron.* a large bright meteor. **4** *Sl.* an energetic person.

fire blight *n* a disease of apples, pears, and similar fruit trees, caused by a bacterium and characterized by blackening of the blossoms and leaves.

fireboat (ˈfaɪəˌbəʊt) *n* a motor vessel equipped with fire-fighting apparatus.

firebomb (ˈfaɪəˌbɒm) *n* another name for **incendiary** (sense 6).

firebox (ˈfaɪəˌbɒks) *n* the furnace chamber of a boiler in a steam locomotive.

firebrand ❶ (ˈfaɪəˌbrænd) *n* **1** a piece of burning wood. **2** a person who causes unrest.

firebreak (ˈfaɪəˌbreɪk) *n* a strip of open land in forest or prairie, serving to arrest the advance of a fire.

firebrick (ˈfaɪəˌbrɪk) *n* a refractory brick made of fire clay, used for lining furnaces, flues, etc.

fire brigade *n Chiefly Brit.* an organized body of firefighters.

firebug (ˈfaɪəˌbʌg) *n Inf.* a person who deliberately sets fire to property.

fire clay *n* a heat-resistant clay used in the making of firebricks, furnace linings, etc.

fire company *n* **1** an insurance company selling policies relating to fire risk. **2** *US.* an organized body of firemen.

fire control *n Mil.* the procedures by which weapons are brought to engage a target.

firecracker (ˈfaɪəˌkrækə) *n* a small cardboard container filled with explosive powder.

firecrest (ˈfaɪəˌkrest) *n* a small European warbler having a crown striped with yellow, black, and white.

firedamp (ˈfaɪəˌdæmp) *n* an explosive mixture of hydrocarbons, chiefly methane, formed in coal mines. See also **afterdamp.**

firedog (ˈfaɪəˌdɒg) *n* either of a pair of metal stands used to support logs in an open fire.

fire door *n* **1** a door made of noncombustible material that prevents a fire spreading within a building. **2** a similar door leading to the outside of a building that can be easily opened from inside; emergency exit.

fire-eater *n* **1** a performer who simulates the swallowing of fire. **2** a belligerent person.

fire engine *n* a vehicle that carries firemen and fire-fighting equipment to a fire.

fire escape *n* a means of evacuating persons from a building in the event of fire.

fire-extinguisher *n* a portable device for extinguishing fires, usually consisting of a canister with a directional nozzle used to direct a spray of water, etc., onto the fire.

firefighter (ˈfaɪəˌfaɪtə) *n* a person who assists in extinguishing fires and rescuing those endangered by them, usually a public employee or trained volunteer.
▸ **ˈfire-ˌfighting** *n, adj*

firefly (ˈfaɪəˌflaɪ) *n, pl* **fireflies.** a nocturnal beetle common in warm and tropical regions, having luminescent abdominal organs.

fireguard (ˈfaɪəˌgɑːd) *n* a meshed frame put before an open fire to protect against falling logs, sparks, etc.

fire hall *n Canad.* a fire station.

fire hydrant *n* a hydrant for use as an emergency supply for fighting fires.

fire insurance *n* insurance covering damage or loss caused by fire or lightning.

fire irons *pl n* metal fireside implements, such as poker, shovel, and tongs.

firelock (ˈfaɪəˌlɒk) *n* **1** an obsolete type of gunlock with a priming mechanism ignited by sparks. **2** a gun or musket having such a lock.

fireman (ˈfaɪəmən) *n, pl* **firemen. 1** a man who fights fires; firefighter. **2a** (on steam locomotives) the man who stokes the fire. **2b** (on diesel and electric locomotives) the driver's assistant. **3** a man who tends furnaces; stoker.

fire opal *n* an orange-red translucent variety of opal, valued as a gemstone.

fireplace (ˈfaɪəˌpleɪs) *n* **1** an open recess at the base of a chimney, etc., for a fire; hearth. **2** *Austral.* an authorized place or installation for outside cooking, esp. by a roadside.

fireplug (ˈfaɪəˌplʌg) *n* another name (esp. US and NZ) for **fire hydrant.**

fire power *n Mil.* **1** the amount of fire that can be delivered by a unit or weapon. **2** the capability of delivering fire.

fireproof (ˈfaɪəˌpruːf) *adj* **1** capable of resisting damage by fire. ◆ *vb* **2** (*tr*) to make resistant to fire.

fire raiser *n* a person who deliberately sets fire to property, etc.
▸ **fire raising** *n*

fire screen *n* **1** a decorative screen placed in the hearth when there is no fire. **2** a screen placed before a fire to protect the face.

fire ship *n* a vessel loaded with explosives and used, esp. formerly, as a bomb by igniting it and directing it to drift among an enemy's warships.

fireside (ˈfaɪəˌsaɪd) *n* **1** the hearth. **2** family life; the home.

fire station *n* a building where fire-fighting vehicles and equipment are stationed and where firefighters on duty wait. Also called (US): **firehouse, station house.**

firestorm (ˈfaɪəˌstɔːm) *n* an uncontrollable blaze sustained by violent winds that are drawn into the column of rising hot air over the burning area: often the result of heavy bombing.

THESAURUS

lasting, immeasurable, infinite, interminable, limitless, perpetual, unbounded

fire *n* **1-3** = **flames**, blaze, combustion, conflagration, inferno **6** = **bombardment**, barrage, cannonade, flak, fusillade, hail, salvo, shelling, sniping, volley **8** = **passion**, animation, ardour, brio, burning passion, dash, eagerness, élan, enthusiasm, excitement, fervency, fervour, force, heat, impetuosity, intensity, life, light, lustre, pizzazz *or* pizazz (*inf.*), radiance, scintillation, sparkle, spirit, splendour, verve, vigour, virtuosity, vivacity **14 on fire: a** = **ardent**, ablaze, aflame, alight, blazing, fiery, flaming, in flames **b** = **eager**, enthusiastic, excited, inspired, passionate ◆ *vb* **20, 21** = **shoot**, detonate, discharge, eject, explode, hurl, launch, let loose (*inf.*), let off, pull the trigger, set off, shell, touch off **23** *Informal* = **dismiss**, cashier, discharge, give marching orders, give the boot (*sl.*), give the bullet (*Brit. sl.*), give the push, make redundant, sack (*inf.*), show the door **25** = **set fire to**, enkindle, ignite, kindle, light, put a match to, set ablaze, set aflame, set alight, set on fire, torch **29** = **inspire**, animate, arouse, electrify, enliven, excite, galvanize, impassion, incite, inflame, inspirit, irritate, quicken, rouse, stir

firearm *n* = **weapon**, gun, handgun, heater (*US sl.*), piece (*sl.*), pistol, revolver, rod (*sl.*), shooter (*sl.*)

firebrand *n* **2** = **rabble-rouser**, agitator, demagogue, fomenter, incendiary, instigator, soapbox orator, tub-thumper

fire trail *n Austral.* a permanent track cleared through the bush to provide access for fire-fighting.

firetrap (ˈfaɪəˌtræp) *n* a building that would burn easily or one without fire escapes.

firewall (ˈfaɪəˌwɔːl) *n* **1** a fireproof wall or partition used to impede the progress of a fire. **2** *Computing.* a computer system that isolates another computer from the Internet in order to prevent unauthorized access.

firewater (ˈfaɪəˌwɔːtə) *n* any strong spirit, esp. whisky.

fireweed (ˈfaɪəˌwiːd) *n* any of various plants that appear as first vegetation in burnt-over areas.

firework (ˈfaɪəˌwɜːk) *n* a device, such as a Catherine wheel or rocket, in which combustible materials are ignited and produce coloured flames, sparks, and smoke.

fireworks Ⓣ (ˈfaɪəˌwɜːks) *pl n* **1** a show in which large numbers of fireworks are let off. **2** *Inf.* an exciting exhibition, as of musical virtuosity or wit. **3** *Inf.* a burst of temper.

firing (ˈfaɪərɪŋ) *n* **1** the process of baking ceramics, etc., in a kiln. **2** the act of stoking a fire or furnace. **3** a discharge of a firearm. **4** something used as fuel, such as coal or wood.

firing line *n* **1** *Mil.* the positions from which fire is delivered. **2** the leading or most advanced position in an activity.

firkin (ˈfɜːkɪn) *n* **1** a small wooden barrel. **2** *Brit.* a unit of capacity equal to nine gallons. [C14 *fir*, from MDu. *vierde* FOURTH + -KIN]

firm[1] Ⓣ (fɜːm) *adj* **1** not soft or yielding to a touch or pressure. **2** securely in position; stable or stationary. **3** decided; settled. **4** enduring or steady. **5** having determination or strength. **6** (of prices, markets, etc.) tending to rise. ◆ *adv* **7** in a secure or unyielding manner: *he stood firm.* ◆ *vb* **8** (sometimes foll. by *up*) to make or become firm. [C14: from L *firmus*]
▸ **ˈfirmly** *adv* ▸ **ˈfirmness** *n*

firm[2] Ⓣ (fɜːm) *n* **1** a business partnership. **2** any commercial enterprise. **3** a team of doctors and their assistants. **4 the.** (*often cap.*) *Sl.* any organized group of people, such as intelligence agents, criminals, or football hooligans. [C16 (in the sense: signature): from Sp. *firma* signature, from *firmar* to sign, from L *firmāre* to confirm, from *firmus* firm]

firmament Ⓣ (ˈfɜːməmənt) *n* the expanse of the sky; heavens. [C13: from LL *firmāmentum* sky (considered as fixed above the earth), from L: prop, support, from *firmāre* to make FIRM[1]]

firmware (ˈfɜːmˌwɛə) *n Computing.* a series of fixed instructions built into the hardware of a computer that can be changed only if the hardware itself is modified in some way.

first Ⓣ (fɜːst) *adj* (*usually prenominal*) **1a** coming before all others. **1b** (*as n*): *I was the first to arrive.* **2** preceding all others in numbering or counting order; the ordinal number of *one.* Often written: 1st. **3** rated, graded, or ranked above all other levels. **4** denoting the lowest forward ratio of a gearbox in a motor vehicle. **5** *Music.* **5a** denoting the highest part assigned to one of the voice parts in a chorus or one of the sections of an orchestra: *the first violins.* **5b** denoting the principal player in a specific orchestral section: *he plays first horn.* **6 first thing.** as the first action of the day: *I'll see you first thing tomorrow.* ◆ *n* **7** the beginning; outset: *I couldn't see at first because of the mist.* **8** *Education, chiefly Brit.* an honours degree of the highest class. Full term: **first-class honours degree. 9** the lowest forward ratio of a gearbox in a motor vehicle. ◆ *adv* **10** Also: **firstly.** before anything else in order, time, importance, etc.: *do this first.* **11 first and last.** on the whole. **12 from first to last.** throughout. **13** for the first time: *I've loved you since I first saw you.* **14** (*sentence modifier*) in the first place or beginning of a series of actions. [OE *fyrest*]

first aid *n* **a** immediate medical assistance given in an emergency. **b** (*as modifier*): *first-aid box.*

first-born *adj* **1** eldest of the children in a family. ◆ *n* **2** the eldest child in a family.

first class Ⓣ *n* **1** the class or grade of the best or highest value, quality, etc. ◆ *adj* (**first-class** *when prenominal*) **2** of the best or highest class or grade: *a first-class citizen.* **3** excellent. **4** of or denoting the most comfortable class of accommodation in a hotel, aircraft, train, etc. **5** (in Britain) of mail that is processed most quickly. ◆ *adv* **first-class. 6** by first-class mail, means of transportation, etc.

first-day cover *n Philately.* an envelope postmarked on the first day of the issue of its stamps.

first-degree burn *n Pathol.* the least severe type of burn, in which the skin surface is red and painful.

first-foot *Chiefly Scot.* ◆ *n also* **first-footer. 1** the first person to enter a household in the New Year. ◆ *vb* **2** to enter (a house) as first-foot.
▸ **ˈfirst-ˈfooting** *n*

first fruits *pl n* **1** the first results or profits of an undertaking. **2** fruit that ripens first.

first-hand Ⓣ *adj, adv* **1** from the original source: *he got the news first-hand.* **2 at first hand.** directly.

first lady *n* (*often caps.*) (in the US) the wife or official hostess of a state governor or a president.

firstling (ˈfɜːstlɪŋ) *n* the first, esp. the first offspring.

first-loss policy *n* an insurance policy for goods in which a total loss is extremely unlikely and the insurer agrees to provide cover for a sum less than the total value of the property.

firstly (ˈfɜːstlɪ) *adv* another word for **first.**

first mate *n* an officer second in command to the captain of a merchant ship.

First Minister *n* **1** the chief minister of the Northern Ireland Assembly. **2** the chief minister of the Scottish Parliament.

first mortgage *n* a mortgage that has priority over other mortgages on the same property.

first name *n* a name given to a person at birth, as opposed to a surname. Also called: **Christian name, forename, given name.**

First Nation *n Canad.* a formally recognized group of Indians on a reserve.

first night *n* **a** the first public performance of a play, etc. **b** (*as modifier*): *first-night nerves.*

first offender *n* a person convicted of a criminal offence for the first time.

first officer *n* **1** another name for **first mate. 2** the member of an aircraft crew who is second in command to the captain.

first-past-the-post *n* (*modifier*) of a voting system in which a candidate may be elected by a simple majority.

first person *n* a grammatical category of pronouns and verbs used by the speaker to refer to or talk about himself.

first-rate Ⓣ *adj* **1** of the best or highest rated class or quality. **2** *Inf.* very good; excellent.

first reading *n* the introduction of a bill into a legislative assembly.

first refusal *n* the right to buy something before it is offered to others.

first-strike *adj* (of a nuclear missile) intended for use in an opening attack calculated to destroy the enemy's nuclear weapons.

first water *n* **1** the finest quality of diamond or other precious stone. **2** the highest grade or best quality.

firth (fɜːθ) *or* **frith** *n* a narrow inlet of the sea, esp. in Scotland. [C15: from ON *fjörthr* FJORD]

fiscal Ⓣ (ˈfɪskᵊl) *adj* **1** of or relating to government finances, esp. tax revenues. **2** of or involving financial matters. ◆ *n* **3a** (in some countries) a public prosecutor. **3b** *Scot.* short for **procurator fiscal.** [C16: from L *fiscālis* concerning the state treasury, from *fiscus* public money]
▸ **ˈfiscally** *adv*

fiscal year *n* the US and Canad. term for **financial year.**

THESAURUS

fireworks *pl n* **1** = **pyrotechnics**, illuminations **3** *Informal* = **trouble**, fit of rage, hysterics, paroxysms, rage, row, storm, temper, uproar, wax (*inf., chiefly Brit.*)

firm[1] *adj* **1** = **hard**, close-grained, compact, compressed, concentrated, congealed, dense, inelastic, inflexible, jelled, jellified, rigid, set, solid, solidified, stiff, unyielding **2** = **secure**, anchored, braced, cemented, embedded, fast, fastened, fixed, immovable, motionless, riveted, robust, rooted, secured, stable, stationary, steady, strong, sturdy, taut, tight, unfluctuating, unmoving, unshakable **3-5** = **determined**, adamant, constant, definite, fixed, immovable, inflexible, obdurate, resolute, resolved, set on, settled, stalwart, staunch, steadfast, strict, true, unalterable, unbending, unfaltering, unflinching, unshakable, unshaken, unswerving, unwavering, unyielding
Antonyms *adj* ≠ **hard:** flabby, flaccid, limp, soft ≠ **secure:** flimsy, insecure, loose, shaky, unreliable, unstable, unsteady ≠ **determined:** inconstant, irresolute, wavering

firm[2] *n* **1, 2** = **company**, association, business, concern, conglomerate, corporation, enterprise, house, organization, outfit (*inf.*), partnership

firmament *n* = **sky**, empyrean (*poetic*), heaven, heavens, the blue, the skies, vault, vault of heaven, welkin (*arch.*)

firmly *adv* **4** = **securely**, enduringly, immovably, like a rock, motionlessly, steadily, tightly, unflinchingly, unshakably **4** = **resolutely**, determinedly, staunchly, steadfastly, strictly, through thick and thin, unchangeably, unwaveringly, with a rod of iron, with decision

firmness *n* **1** = **hardness**, compactness, density, fixedness, inelasticity, inflexibility, resistance, rigidity, solidity, stiffness **2** = **steadiness**, immovability, soundness, stability, strength, tautness, tensile strength, tension, tightness **3-5** = **resolve**, constancy, fixedness, fixity of purpose, inflexibility, obduracy, resolution, staunchness, steadfastness, strength of will, strictness

first *adj* **1** = **earliest**, initial, introductory, maiden, opening, original, premier, primeval, primitive, primordial, pristine **2** = **foremost**, chief, head, highest, leading, pre-eminent, prime, principal, ruling ◆ *n* **7** *As in* **from the first** = **start**, beginning, commencement, inception, introduction, outset, starting point, word go (*inf.*) ◆ *adv* **10** = **to begin with**, at the beginning, at the outset, before all else, beforehand, firstly, initially, in the first place, to start with

first class *adj* **first-class 2, 3** = **excellent**, A1 *or* A-one (*inf.*), ace (*inf.*), blue-chip, brilliant, capital, champion, choice, crack (*sl.*), elite, exceptional, exemplary, first-rate, five-star, great, marvellous, matchless, outstanding, premium, prime, second to none, sovereign, superb, superlative, tiptop, top, top-class, top-drawer, top-flight, top-notch (*inf.*), twenty-four carat, very good, world-class
Antonyms *adj* inferior, second-class, second-rate, shocking (*inf.*), terrible, third-rate

first-hand *adj, adv* **1** = **direct**, straight from the horse's mouth

first-rate *adj* **1, 2** = **excellent**, A1 *or* A-one, elite, exceptional, exclusive, first class, mean (*sl.*), mega (*sl.*), outstanding, prime, second to none, sovereign, superb, superlative, tiptop, top, top-notch (*inf.*), world-class

fiscal *adj* **2** = **financial**, budgetary, economic, monetary, money, pecuniary

fish ⓣ (fɪʃ) *n, pl* **fish** *or* **fishes. 1a** any of a large group of cold-blooded aquatic vertebrates having jaws, gills, and usually fins and a skin covered in scales: includes the sharks, rays, teleosts, lungfish, etc. **1b** (*in combination*): *fishpond*. Related adj: **piscine. 2** any of various similar but jawless vertebrates, such as the hagfish and lamprey. **3** (*not in technical use*) any of various aquatic invertebrates, such as the cuttlefish and crayfish. **4** the flesh of fish used as food. **5** *Inf.* a person of little emotion or intelligence: *a poor fish*. **6 drink like a fish.** to drink (esp. alcohol) to excess. **7 have other fish to fry.** to have other activities to do, esp. more important ones. **8 like a fish out of water.** out of one's usual place. **9 make fish of one and flesh of another.** *Irish.* to discriminate unfairly between people. **10 neither fish, flesh, nor fowl.** neither this nor that. ◆ *vb* **11** (*intr*) to attempt to catch fish, as with a line and hook or with nets, traps, etc. **12** (*tr*) to fish in (a particular area of water). **13** to search (a body of water) for something or to search for something, esp. in a body of water. **14** (*intr; foll. by for*) to seek something indirectly: *to fish for compliments*. ◆ See also **fish out.** [OE *fisc*]
▸ **'fish,like** *adj*

fish and chips *n* fish fillets coated with batter and deep-fried, eaten with potato chips.

fish cake *n* a fried flattened ball of flaked fish mixed with mashed potatoes.

fisher ('fɪʃə) *n* **1** a fisherman. **2** Also called: **pekan. 2a** a large North American marten having dark brown fur. **2b** the fur of this animal.

fisherman ('fɪʃəmən) *n, pl* **fishermen. 1** a person who fishes as a profession or for sport. **2** a vessel used for fishing.

fishery ('fɪʃərɪ) *n, pl* **fisheries. 1a** the industry of catching, processing, and selling fish. **1b** a place where this is carried on. **2** a place where fish are reared. **3** a fishing ground.

Fishes ('fɪʃɪz) *n* **the.** the constellation Pisces, the twelfth sign of the zodiac.

fisheye lens ('fɪʃ,aɪ) *n Photog.* a lens of small focal length, having a highly curved protruding front element that covers an angle of view of almost 180°.

fishfinger ('fɪʃ'fɪŋgə) *or US & Canad.* **fish stick** *n* an oblong piece of filleted or minced fish coated in breadcrumbs.

fish hawk *n* another name for the **osprey.**

fish-hook *n* a sharp hook used in angling, esp. one with a barb.

fishing ('fɪʃɪŋ) *n* **a** the occupation of catching fish. **b** (*as modifier*): *a fishing match*.

fishing ground *n* an area of water that is good for fishing.

fishing rod *n* a long tapered flexible pole for use with a fishing line and, usually, a reel.

fish joint *n* a connection formed by fishplates at the meeting point of two rails, beams, etc.

fishmeal ('fɪʃ,miːl) *n* ground dried fish used as feed for farm animals, as a fertilizer, etc.

fishmonger ('fɪʃ,mʌŋgə) *n Chiefly Brit.* a retailer of fish.

fishnet ('fɪʃ,net) *n* **a** an open mesh fabric resembling netting. **b** (*as modifier*): *fishnet tights*.

fish out ⓣ *vb* (*tr, adv*) to find or extract (something): *to fish keys out of a pocket*.

fishplate ('fɪʃ,pleɪt) *n* a flat piece of metal joining one rail or beam to the next, esp. on railway tracks.

fishtail ('fɪʃ,teɪl) *n* **1** an aeroplane manoeuvre in which the tail is moved from side to side to reduce speed. **2** a nozzle having a long narrow slot at the top, placed over a Bunsen burner to produce a thin fanlike flame.

fishwife ('fɪʃ,waɪf) *n, pl* **fishwives. 1** a woman who sells fish. **2** a coarse scolding woman.

fishy ⓣ ('fɪʃɪ) *adj* **fishier, fishiest. 1** of, involving, or suggestive of fish. **2** abounding in fish. **3** *Inf.* suspicious, doubtful, or questionable. **4** dull and lifeless: *a fishy look*.
▸ **'fishily** *adv*

fissile ('fɪsaɪl) *adj* **1** *Brit.* capable of undergoing nuclear fission. **2** fissionable. **3** tending to split or capable of being split. [C17: from L, from *fissus* split]

fission ⓣ ('fɪʃən) *n* **1** the act or process of splitting or breaking into parts. **2** *Biol.* a form of asexual reproduction involving a division into two or more equal parts. **3** short for **nuclear fission.** [C19: from L *fissiō* a cleaving]
▸ **'fissionable** *adj*

fission-track dating *n* the dating of samples of minerals by comparing the tracks in them made by fission fragments of the uranium nuclei they contain, before and after irradiation by neutrons.

fissiparous (fɪ'sɪpərəs) *adj Biol.* reproducing by fission.
▸ **fis'siparously** *adv*

fissure ⓣ ('fɪʃə) *n* **1** any long narrow cleft or crack, esp. in a rock. **2** a weakness or flaw. **3** *Anat.* a narrow split or groove that divides an organ such as the brain, lung, or liver into lobes. ◆ *vb* **fissures, fissuring, fissured. 4** to crack or split apart. [C14: from Medical L *fissūra*, from L *fissus* split]

fist (fɪst) *n* **1** a hand with the fingers clenched into the palm, as for hitting. **2** Also called: **fistful.** the quantity that can be held in a fist or hand. **3** *Inf.* handwriting. **4** an informal word for **index** (sense 9). ◆ *vb* **5** (*tr*) to hit with the fist. [OE *fȳst*]

fisticuffs ('fɪstɪ,kʌfs) *pl n* combat with the fists. [C17: prob. from *fisty* with the fist + CUFF[2]]

fistula ('fɪstjʊlə) *n, pl* **fistulas** *or* **fistulae** (-,liː). *Pathol.* an abnormal opening between one hollow organ and another or between a hollow organ and the surface of the skin, caused by ulceration, malformation, etc. [C14: from L: pipe, tube, hollow reed, ulcer]
▸ **'fistulous** *or* **'fistular** *adj*

fit[1] ⓣ (fɪt) *vb* **fits, fitting, fitted** *or US* **fit. 1** to be appropriate or suitable for (a situation, etc.). **2** to be of the correct size or shape for (a container, etc.). **3** (*tr*) to adjust in order to render appropriate. **4** (*tr*) to supply with that which is needed. **5** (*tr*) to try clothes on (someone) in order to make adjustments if necessary. **6** (*tr*) to make competent or ready. **7** (*tr*) to locate with care. **8** (*intr*) to correspond with the facts or circumstances. ◆ *adj* **fitter, fittest. 9** appropriate. **10** having the right qualifications; qualifying. **11** in good health. **12** worthy or deserving. **13** (*foll. by an infinitive*) *Inf.* ready (to); strongly disposed (to): *she was fit to scream*. ◆ *n* **14** the manner in which something fits. **15** the act or process of fitting. **16** *Statistics.* the correspondence between observed and predicted characteristics of a distribution or model. ◆ See also **fit in, fit out.** [C14: prob. from MDu. *vitten;* rel. to ON *fitja* to knit]
▸ **'fitly** *adv* ▸ **'fittable** *adj*

fit[2] ⓣ (fɪt) *n* **1** *Pathol.* a sudden attack or convulsion, such as an epileptic seizure. **2** a sudden spell of emotion: *a fit of anger*. **3** an impulsive period of activity or lack of activity. **4 have** *or* **throw a fit.** *Inf.* to become very angry. **5 in** *or* **by fits and starts.** in spasmodic spells. [OE *fitt* conflict]

fitch (fɪtʃ) *n* **1** a polecat. **2** the fur of the polecat. [C16: prob. from *ficheux*, from OF, from ?]

fitful ⓣ ('fɪtfʊl) *adj* characterized by or occurring in irregular spells.
▸ **'fitfully** *adv*

fit in *vb* **1** (*tr*) to give a place or time to. **2** (*intr, adv*) to belong or conform, esp. after adjustment: *he didn't fit in with their plans*.

fitment ('fɪtmənt) *n* **1** *Machinery.* an accessory attached to an assembly of parts. **2** *Chiefly Brit.* a detachable part of the furnishings of a room.

fitness ⓣ ('fɪtnɪs) *n* **1** the state of being fit. **2** *Biol.* **2a** the degree of adaptation of an organism to its environment, determined by its genetic constitution. **2b** the ability of an organism to produce viable offspring capable of surviving to the next generation.

fit out *vb* (*tr, adv*) to equip.

fitted ⓣ ('fɪtɪd) *adj* **1** designed for excellent fit: *a fitted suit*. **2** (of a carpet) cut or sewn to cover a floor completely. **3a** (of furniture) built to fit a particular space: *a fitted cupboard*. **3b** (of a room) equipped with fitted furniture: *a fitted kitchen*. **4** (of sheets) having ends that are elasticated and shaped to fit tightly over a mattress.

fitter ('fɪtə) *n* **1** a person who fits a garment, esp. when it is made for a

THESAURUS

fish *vb* **14** *foll. by* **for** = **seek**, angle for, elicit, hint at, hope for, hunt for, invite, look for, search for, solicit

fish out *vb* = **pull out**, extract, extricate, find, haul out, produce

fishy *adj* **1** = **fishlike**, piscatorial, piscatory, piscine **3** *Informal* = **suspicious**, cock-and-bull, dodgy (*Brit., Austral., & NZ inf.*), doubtful, dubious, funny (*inf.*), implausible, improbable, odd, queer, questionable, rum (*Brit. sl.*), suspect, unlikely **4** = **expressionless**, blank, deadpan, dull, glassy, glassy-eyed, inexpressive, lacklustre, lifeless, vacant, wooden

fission *n* **1** = **splitting**, breaking, cleavage, division, parting, rending, rupture, schism, scission

fissure *n* **1** = **crack**, breach, break, chink, cleavage, cleft, cranny, crevice, fault, fracture, gap, hole, interstice, opening, rent, rift, rupture, slit, split

fit[1] *vb* **2** = **suit**, accord, agree, be consonant, belong, concur, conform, correspond, dovetail, go, interlock, join, match, meet, tally **3** = **adapt**, adjust, alter, arrange, customize, dispose, fashion, modify, place, position, shape, tweak (*inf.*) **4** = **equip**, accommodate, accoutre, arm, fit out, kit out, outfit, prepare, provide, rig out ◆ *adj* **9, 10, 12** = **appropriate**, able, adapted, adequate, apposite, apt, becoming, capable, competent, convenient, correct, deserving, equipped, expedient, fitted, fitting, good enough, meet (*arch.*), prepared, proper, qualified, ready, right, seemly, suitable, trained, well-suited, worthy **11** = **healthy**, able-bodied, as right as rain, hale, in good condition, in good shape, in good trim, robust, strapping, toned up, trim, well
Antonyms *adj* ≠ **appropriate:** amiss, ill-fitted, ill-suited, improper, inadequate, inappropriate, unfit, unprepared, unseemly, unsuitable, untimely ≠ **healthy:** flabby, in poor condition, out of shape, out of trim, unfit, unhealthy

fit[2] *n* **1** = **seizure**, attack, bout, convulsion, paroxysm, spasm **2** = **outbreak**, bout, burst, outburst, spell **5 in** *or* **by fits and starts** = **spasmodically**, erratically, fitfully, intermittently, irregularly, on and off, sporadically, unsystematically

fitful *adj* = **irregular**, broken, desultory, disturbed, erratic, flickering, fluctuating, haphazard, impulsive, inconstant, intermittent, spasmodic, sporadic, uneven, unstable, variable
Antonyms *adj* constant, equable, even, orderly, predictable, regular, steady, systematic, unchanging, uniform

fitfully *adv* = **irregularly**, by fits and starts, desultorily, erratically, in fits and starts, in snatches, intermittently, interruptedly, off and on, spasmodically, sporadically

fitness *n* **1** = **appropriateness**, adaptation, applicability, aptness, competence, eligibility, pertinence, preparedness, propriety, qualifications, readiness, seemliness, suitability **1** = **health**, good condition, good health, robustness, strength, vigour, wellness

fitted *adj* **3** = **built-in**, permanent

particular person. **2** a person who is skilled in the assembly and adjustment of machinery, esp. of a specified sort.

fitting ('fɪtɪŋ) *adj* **1** appropriate or proper. ◆ *n* **2** an accessory or part: *an electrical fitting.* **3** (*pl*) furnishings or accessories in a building. **4** work carried out by a fitter. **5** the act of trying on clothes so that they can be adjusted to fit.
▸ **'fittingly** *adv*

Fitzgerald-Lorentz contraction *n Physics.* the contraction that a moving body exhibits when its velocity approaches that of light. [C19: after G. F. *Fitzgerald* (1851–1901), Irish physicist, and H. A. *Lorentz* (1853–1928), Du. physicist]

five (faɪv) *n* **1** the cardinal number that is the sum of four and one. **2** a numeral, 5, V, etc., representing this number. **3** the amount or quantity that is one greater than four. **4** something representing, represented by, or consisting of five units, such as a playing card with five symbols on it. **5 five o'clock.** five hours after noon or midnight. ◆ *determiner* **6a** amounting to five: *five nights.* **6b** (*as pronoun*): *choose any five you like.* ◆ See also **fives.** [OE *fīf*]

five-a-side *n* a version of soccer with five players on each side.

five-eighth *n Austral. & NZ.* a rugby player positioned between the halfbacks and three-quarters.

five-finger *n* any of various plants having five-petalled flowers or five lobed leaves, such as cinquefoil and Virginia creeper.

fivefold ('faɪvˌfəʊld) *adj* **1** equal to or having five times as many or as much. **2** composed of five parts. ◆ *adv* **3** by or up to five times as many or as much.

five-o'clock shadow *n* beard growth visible late in the day on a man's shaven face.

fivepins ('faɪvˌpɪnz) *n* (*functioning as sing*) a bowling game using five pins, played esp. in Canada.
▸ **'fiveˌpin** *adj*

fiver ('faɪvə) *n Brit. inf.* a five-pound note.

fives (faɪvz) *n* (*functioning as sing*) a ball game similar to squash but played with bats or the hands.

Five-Year Plan *n* (in socialist economies) a government plan for economic development over a period of five years.

fix (fɪks) *vb* (*mainly tr*) **1** (*also intr*) to make or become firm, stable, or secure. **2** to attach or place permanently. **3** (often foll. by *up*) to settle definitely; decide. **4** to hold or direct (eyes, etc.) steadily: *he fixed his gaze on the woman.* **5** to call to attention or rivet. **6** to make rigid: *to fix one's jaw.* **7** to place or ascribe: *to fix the blame.* **8** to mend or repair. **9** *Inf.* to provide or be provided with: *how are you fixed for supplies?* **10** *Inf.* to influence (a person, etc.) unfairly, as by bribery. **11** *Sl.* to take revenge on. **12** *Inf.* to give (someone) his just deserts: *that'll fix him.* **13** *Inf., chiefly US & Canad.* to prepare: *to fix a meal.* **14** *Dialect or inf.* to spay or castrate (an animal). **15** *Photog.* to treat (a film, plate, or paper) with fixer to make permanent the image rendered visible by developer. **16** to convert (atmospheric nitrogen) into nitrogen compounds, as in the manufacture of fertilizers or the action of bacteria in the soil. **17** to reduce (a substance) to a solid state or a less volatile state. **18** (*intr*) *Sl.* to inject a narcotic drug. ◆ *n* **19** *Inf.* a predicament; dilemma. **20** the ascertaining of the navigational position, as of a ship, by radar, etc. **21** *Sl.* an intravenous injection of a narcotic such as heroin. ◆ See also **fix up.** [C15: from Med. L *fixāre*, from L *fixus* fixed, from L *figere*]
▸ **'fixable** *adj*

fixate (fɪk'seɪt) *vb* **fixates, fixating, fixated. 1** to become or cause to become fixed. **2** *Psychol.* to engage in fixation. **3** (*tr; usually passive*) *Inf.* to obsess. [C19: from L *fixus* fixed + -ATE[1]]

fixation (fɪk'seɪʃən) *n* **1** the act of fixing or the state of being fixed. **2** a preoccupation or obsession. **3** *Psychol.* **3a** the situation of being set in a certain way of thinking or acting. **3b** a strong attachment of a person to another person or an object in early life. **4** *Chem.* the conversion of nitrogen in the air into a compound, esp. a fertilizer. **5** the reduction of a substance to a nonvolatile or solid form.

fixative ('fɪksətɪv) *adj* **1** serving or tending to fix. ◆ *n* **2** a fluid sprayed over drawings to prevent smudging or one that fixes tissues and cells for microscopic study. **3** a substance added to a liquid, such as a perfume, to make it less volatile.

fixed (fɪkst) *adj* **1** attached or placed so as to be immovable. **2** stable: *fixed prices.* **3** steadily directed: *a fixed expression.* **4** established as to relative position: *a fixed point.* **5** always at the same time: *a fixed holiday.* **6** (of ideas, etc.) firmly maintained. **7** (of an element) held in chemical combination: *fixed nitrogen.* **8** (of a substance) nonvolatile. **9** arranged. **10** *Inf.* equipped or provided for, as with money, possessions, etc. **11** *Inf.* illegally arranged: *a fixed trial.*
▸ **fixedly** ('fɪksɪdlɪ) *adv* ▸ **'fixedness** *n*

fixed assets *pl n* nontrading business assets of a relatively permanent nature, such as plant, fixtures, or goodwill. Also called: **capital assets.**

fixed oil *n* a natural animal or vegetable oil that is not volatile: a mixture of esters of fatty acids.

fixed-point representation *n Computing.* the representation of numbers by a single set of digits such that the radix point has a predetermined location. Cf. **floating-point representation.**

fixed satellite *n* a satellite revolving in a stationary orbit so that it appears to remain over a fixed point on the earth's surface.

fixed star *n* an extremely distant star whose position appears to be almost stationary over a long period of time.

fixer ('fɪksə) *n* **1** a person or thing that fixes. **2** *Photog.* a solution used to dissolve unexposed silver halides after developing. **3** *Sl.* a person who makes arrangements, esp. by underhand or illegal means.

fixing ('fɪksɪŋ) *n* a means of attaching one thing to another, as a pipe to a wall, a slate to a roof, etc.

fixity ('fɪksɪtɪ) *n, pl* **fixities. 1** the state or quality of being fixed. **2** a fixture.

fixture ('fɪkstʃə) *n* **1** an object firmly fixed in place, esp. a household appliance. **2** a person or thing regarded as fixed in a particular place or position. **3** *Property law.* an article attached to land and regarded as part of it. **4** *Chiefly Brit.* **4a** a sports match or social occasion. **4b** the date of such an event. [C17: from LL *fixūra* a fastening (with *-t-* by analogy with *mixture*)]

fix up *vb* (*tr, adv*) **1** to arrange: *let's fix up a date.* **2** (often foll. by *with*) to provide: *I'm sure we can fix you up with a room.*

fizgig ('fɪzˌgɪg) *n* **1** a frivolous or flirtatious girl. **2** a firework that fizzes as it moves. [C16: prob. from obs. *fise* a breaking of wind + *gig* girl]

fizz (fɪz) *vb* (*intr*) **1** to make a hissing or bubbling sound. **2** (of a drink) to produce bubbles of carbon dioxide. ◆ *n* **3** a hissing or bubbling sound. **4** the bubbly quality of a drink; effervescence. **5** any effervescent drink. [C17: imit.]
▸ **'fizzy** *adj* ▸ **'fizziness** *n*

fizzle ('fɪzᵊl) *vb* **fizzles, fizzling, fizzled.** (*intr*) **1** to make a hissing or bubbling sound. **2** (often foll. by *out*) *Inf.* to fail or die out, esp. after a promising start. ◆ *n* **3** a hissing or bubbling sound. **4** *Inf.* a failure. [C16: prob. from obs. *fist* to break wind]

fjord *or* **fiord** (fjɔːd) *n* a long narrow inlet of the sea between high steep cliffs, common in Norway. [C17: from Norwegian, from ON *fjörthr;* see FIRTH, FORD]

FL *abbrev. for:* **1** Flight Lieutenant. **2** Florida.

fl. *abbrev. for:* **1** floor. **2** floruit. **3** fluid.

Fl. *abbrev. for:* **1** Flanders. **2** Flemish.

flab (flæb) *n* unsightly or unwanted fat on the body. [C20: back formation from FLABBY]

flabbergast ('flæbəˌgɑːst) *vb* (*tr; usually passive*) *Inf.* to amaze utterly; astound. [C18: from ?]

THESAURUS

fitting *adj* **1** = **appropriate**, apposite, becoming, *comme il faut*, correct, decent, decorous, desirable, meet (*arch.*), proper, right, seemly, suitable ◆ *n* **2** = **accessory**, attachment, component, connection, part, piece, unit **3** *plural* = **furnishings**, accessories, accoutrements, appointments, appurtenances, bells and whistles, conveniences, equipment, extras, furniture, trimmings
Antonyms *adj* ≠ **appropriate:** ill-suited, improper, unfitting, unseemly, unsuitable

fix *vb* **1** = **place**, anchor, embed, establish, implant, install, locate, plant, position, root, set, settle **2** = **fasten**, attach, bind, cement, connect, couple, glue, link, make fast, pin, secure, stick, tie **3** = **decide**, agree on, appoint, arrange, arrive at, conclude, define, determine, establish, limit, name, resolve, set, settle, specify **4, 5** = **focus**, direct, level at, rivet **8** = **repair**, adjust, correct, mend, patch up, put to rights, regulate, see to, sort **10** *Informal* = **rig**, bribe, fiddle (*inf.*), influence, manipulate, manoeuvre, pull strings **11** *Slang* = **sort (someone) out** (*inf.*), cook (someone's) goose (*inf.*), get even with (*inf.*), get revenge on, pay back, settle (someone's) hash (*inf.*), take retribution on, wreak vengeance on **17** = **set**, congeal, consolidate, harden, rigidify, solidify, stiffen, thicken ◆ *n* **19** *Informal* = **predicament**, difficult situation, difficulty, dilemma, embarrassment, hole, hot water (*inf.*), jam (*inf.*), mess, pickle (*inf.*), plight, quandary, spot (*inf.*), ticklish situation, tight spot

fixated *adj* **3** = **obsessed**, absorbed, attached, besotted, captivated, caught up in, devoted, engrossed, fascinated, hung up on (*sl.*), hypnotized, infatuated, mesmerized, monomaniacal, preoccupied, prepossessed, single-minded, smitten, spellbound, taken up with, wrapped up in
Antonyms *adj* detached, disinterested, dispassionate, indifferent, open-minded, uncommitted, unconcerned, uninvolved, unprepossessed

fixation *n* **2** = **obsession**, addiction, complex, hang-up (*inf.*), *idée fixe*, infatuation, mania, preoccupation, thing (*inf.*)

fixed *adj* **1** = **immovable**, anchored, attached, established, made fast, permanent, rigid, rooted, secure, set **3** = **steady**, intent, level, resolute, unbending, unblinking, undeviating, unflinching, unwavering **9** = **agreed**, arranged, decided, definite, established, planned, resolved, settled **11** *Informal* = **rigged**, framed, manipulated, packed, put-up
Antonyms *adj* ≠ **immovable:** bending, mobile, motile, moving, pliant, unfixed ≠ **steady:** inconstant, varying, wavering

fixity *n* **1** = **steadiness**, doggedness, intentness, perseverance, persistence, stability

fix up *vb* **1** = **arrange**, agree on, fix, organize, plan, settle, sort out **2** *often with* **with** = **provide**, accommodate, arrange for, bring about, furnish, lay on

fizz *vb* **1, 2** = **bubble**, effervesce, fizzle, froth, hiss, sparkle, sputter

fizzle *vb* **2** *often foll. by* **out** *Informal* = **die away**, abort, collapse, come to nothing, end in disappointment, fail, fall through, fold (*inf.*), miss the mark, peter out

fizzy *adj* **1, 2** = **bubbly**, bubbling, carbonated, effervescent, gassy, sparkling

flab *n* = **fat**, beef (*inf.*), flabbiness, flesh, fleshiness, heaviness, overweight, plumpness, slackness, weight

flabbergasted *adj* = **astonished**, abashed,

flabby ⓘ ('flæbɪ) *adj* **flabbier, flabbiest. 1** loose or yielding: *flabby muscles.* **2** having flabby flesh, esp. through being overweight. **3** lacking vitality; weak. [C17: alteration of *flappy* from FLAP + -Y[1]; cf. Du. *flabbe* drooping lip]
▸'**flabbiness** *n*

flaccid ⓘ ('flæksɪd) *adj* lacking firmness; soft and limp. [C17: from L *flaccidus,* from *flaccus*]
▸**flac'cidity** *n*

flacon (*French* flakɔ̃) *n* a small stoppered bottle, esp. used for perfume. [C19: from F; see FLAGON]

flag[1] ⓘ (flæg) *n* **1** a piece of cloth, esp. bunting, often attached to a pole or staff, decorated with a design and used as an emblem, symbol, or standard or as a means of signalling. **2** a small piece of paper, etc., sold on flag days. **3** the conspicuously marked or shaped tail of a deer or of certain dogs. **4** anything used like a flag to attract attention, esp. a code inserted into a computer file to distinguish certain information. **5** *Brit., Austral., & NZ.* the part of a taximeter that is raised when a taxi is for hire. **6 show the flag. 6a** to assert a claim by military presence. **6b** *Inf.* to make an appearance. ◆ *vb* **flags, flagging, flagged.** (*tr*) **7** to decorate or mark with a flag or flags. **8** (often foll. by *down*) to warn or signal (a vehicle) to stop. **9** to send or communicate (messages, information, etc.) by flag. [C16: from ?]
▸'**flagger** *n*

flag[2] (flæg) *n* **1** any of various plants that have long swordlike leaves, esp. an iris (**yellow flag**). **2** the leaf of any such plant. [C14: prob. from ON]

flag[3] ⓘ (flæg) *vb* **flags, flagging, flagged.** (*intr*) **1** to hang down; droop. **2** to become weak or tired. [C16: from ?]

flag[4] (flæg) *n* **1** short for **flagstone.** ◆ *vb* **flags, flagging, flagged. 2** (*tr*) to furnish (a floor, etc.) with flagstones.

flag day *n Brit.* a day on which money is collected by a charity and small flags or emblems are given to contributors.

flagellant ('flædʒɪlənt, flə'dʒelənt) *or* **flagellator** ('flædʒɪˌleɪtə) *n* a person who whips himself or others either as part of a religious penance or for sexual gratification. [C16: from L *flagellāre* to whip, from FLAGELLUM]

flagellate ⓘ *vb* ('flædʒɪˌleɪt), **flagellates, flagellating, flagellated. 1** (*tr*) to whip; flog. ◆ *adj* ('flædʒɪlɪt), *also* **flagellated. 2** possessing one or more flagella. **3** whiplike. ◆ *n* ('flædʒɪlɪt). **4** a flagellate organism.
▸ˌ**flagel'lation** *n*

flagellum (flə'dʒeləm) *n, pl* **flagella** (-lə) *or* **flagellums. 1** *Biol.* a long whiplike outgrowth from a cell that acts as an organ of locomotion: occurs in some protozoans, gametes, etc. **2** *Bot.* a long thin shoot or runner. [C19: from L: a little whip, from *flagrum* a whip, lash]
▸**fla'gellar** *adj*

flageolet[1] (ˌflædʒə'let) *n* a high-pitched musical instrument of the recorder family. [C17: from F, modification of OF *flajolet* a little flute, from Vulgar L *flabeolum* (unattested), from L *flāre* to blow]

flageolet[2] (ˌflædʒə'let) *n* a type of kidney bean. [C19: from F, corruption of *fageolet,* dim. of *fageol,* from L *faseolus*]

flag fall *n Austral.* the minimum charge for hiring a taxi, to which the rate per kilometre is added.

flag of convenience *n* a national flag flown by a ship registered in that country to gain financial or legal advantage.

flag of truce *n* a white flag indicating an invitation to an enemy to negotiate.

flagon ('flægən) *n* **1** a large bottle of wine, cider, etc. **2** a vessel having a handle, spout, and narrow neck. [C15: from OF *flascon,* from LL *flascō,* prob. of Gmc origin; see FLASK]

flagpole ('flægˌpəʊl) *or* **flagstaff** ('flægˌstɑːf) *n, pl* **flagpoles, flagstaffs** *or* **flagstaves** (-ˌsteɪvz). a pole or staff on which a flag is hoisted and displayed.

flagrant ⓘ ('fleɪgrənt) *adj* openly outrageous. [C15: from L *flagrāre* to blaze, burn]
▸'**flagrancy** *n* ▸'**flagrantly** *adv*

flagrante delicto (flə'græntɪ dɪ'lɪktəʊ) *adv* See **in flagrante delicto.**

flagship ('flægˌʃɪp) *n* **1** a ship, esp. in a fleet, aboard which the commander of the fleet is quartered. **2** the most important ship belonging to a shipping company. **3** the item in a group considered most important esp. in establishing a public image: *costume drama is the flagship of the BBC.*

flagstone ⓘ ('flægˌstəʊn) *n* **1** a hard fine-textured rock that can be split up into slabs for paving. **2** a slab of such a rock. [C15 *flag* (in the sense: sod, turf), from ON *flaga* slab; cf. OE *flæcg* plaster, poultice]

flag-waving *n Inf.* an emotional appeal intended to arouse patriotic feeling.
▸'**flagˌwaver** *n*

flail ⓘ (fleɪl) *n* **1** an implement used for threshing grain, consisting of a wooden handle with a free-swinging metal or wooden bar attached to it. ◆ *vb* **2** (*tr*) to beat with or as if with a flail. **3** to thresh about: *with arms flailing.* [C12 *fleil,* ult. from LL *flagellum* flail, from L: whip]

flair ⓘ (flɛə) *n* **1** natural ability; talent. **2** perceptiveness. **3** *Inf.* stylishness or elegance: *to dress with flair.* [C19: from F, lit.: sense of smell, from OF: scent, ult. from L *frāgrāre* to smell sweet; see FRAGRANT]

flak ⓘ (flæk) *n* **1** anti-aircraft fire or artillery. **2** *Inf.* adverse criticism. [C20: from G *Fl(ieger)a(bwehr)k(anone),* lit.: aircraft defence gun]

flake[1] ⓘ (fleɪk) *n* **1** a small thin piece or layer chipped off or detached from an object or substance. **2** a small piece or particle: *a flake of snow.* **3** *Archaeol.* a fragment removed by chipping from a larger stone used as a tool or weapon. **4** *Chiefly US sl.* an eccentric, crazy, or unreliable person. ◆ *vb* **flakes, flaking, flaked. 5** to peel or cause to peel off in flakes. **6** to cover or become covered with or as with flakes. **7** (*tr*) to form into flakes. [C14: from ON]

flake[2] (fleɪk) *n* a rack or platform for drying fish. [C14: from ON *flaki;* rel. to Du. *vlaak* hurdle]

flake out ⓘ *vb* (*intr, adv*) *Inf.* to collapse or fall asleep as through extreme exhaustion.

flake white *n* a pigment made from flakes of white lead.

flak jacket *n* a reinforced jacket for protection against gunfire or shrapnel worn by soldiers, policemen, etc.

flaky ('fleɪkɪ) *adj* **flakier, flakiest. 1** like or made of flakes. **2** tending to break easily into flakes. **3** Also spelt: **flakey.** *US sl.* eccentric; crazy.
▸'**flakily** *adv* ▸'**flakiness** *n*

flambé ('flɑːmbeɪ) **1** *adj* (of food, such as steak or pancakes) served in flaming brandy ◆ *vb* **flambés, flambéing, flambéed. 2** (*tr*) to serve (food) in such a manner. [F, p.p. of *flamber* to FLAME]

flambeau ('flæmbəʊ) *n, pl* **flambeaux** (-bəʊ, -bəʊz) *or* **flambeaus.** a burning torch, as used in night processions, etc. [C17: from OF: torch, lit.: a little flame, from *flambe* FLAME]

flamboyant ⓘ (flæm'bɔɪənt) *adj* **1** elaborate or extravagant; showy. **2** rich or brilliant in colour. **3** exuberant or ostentatious. **4** of the French Gothic style of architecture characterized by flamelike tracery and elaborate carving. [C19: from F: flaming, from *flamboyer* to FLAME]
▸**flam'boyance** *or* **flam'boyancy** *n* ▸**flam'boyantly** *adv*

flame ⓘ (fleɪm) *n* **1** a hot usually luminous body of burning gas emanating in flickering streams from burning material or produced by a jet of ignited gas. **2** (*often pl*) the state or condition of burning with flames: *to burst into flames.* **3** a brilliant light. **4a** a strong reddish-orange colour. **4b** (*as adj*): *a flame carpet.* **5** intense passion or ardour. **6** *Inf.* a lover or sweetheart (esp. in **an old flame**). **7** *Inf.* an abusive message sent by electronic mail. ◆ *vb* **flames, flaming, flamed. 8** to burn or cause to burn brightly. **9** (*intr*) to become red or fiery: *his face flamed with anger.* **10** (*intr*) to become angry or excited. **11** (*tr*) to apply a flame to (something). **12** *Inf.* to send an abusive message by elec-

THESAURUS

amazed, astounded, bowled over (*inf.*), confounded, dazed, disconcerted, dumbfounded, gobsmacked (*Brit. sl.*), lost for words, nonplussed, overcome, overwhelmed, speechless, staggered, struck dumb, stunned

flabbiness *n* **1, 2** = **slackness**, bloatedness, flaccidity, limpness, looseness, pendulousness

flabby *adj* **1, 2** = **limp**, baggy, drooping, flaccid, floppy, hanging, lax, loose, pendulous, sagging, slack, sloppy, toneless, unfit, yielding **3** = **weak**, boneless, effete, enervated, feeble, impotent, ineffective, ineffectual, nerveless, spineless, wimpish *or* wimpy (*inf.*)
Antonyms *adj* ≠ **limp:** firm, hard, solid, strong, taut, tense, tight, tough

flaccid *adj* = **limp**, drooping, flabby, lax, loose, nerveless, slack, soft, weak

flaccidity *n* = **limpness**, flabbiness, looseness, nervelessness, slackness, softness

flag[1] *n* **1** = **banner**, banderole, colours, ensign, gonfalon, jack, pennant, pennon, standard, streamer ◆ *vb* **7** = **mark**, docket, indicate, label, note, tab **8** *often with* **down** = **hail**, salute, signal, warn, wave

flag[3] *vb* **1, 2** = **weaken**, abate, decline, die, droop, ebb, fade, fail, faint, fall, fall off, feel the pace, languish, peter out, pine, sag, sink, slump, succumb, taper off, wane, weary, wilt

flagellate *vb* **1** = **whip**, beat, castigate, chastise, flay, flog, lambast(e), lash, scourge, thrash

flagellation *n* **1** = **whipping**, beating, flogging, lashing, thrashing

flagrancy *n* = **outrageousness**, blatancy, enormity, heinousness, infamy, insolence, ostentation, public display, shamelessness

flagrant *adj* = **outrageous**, arrant, atrocious, awful, barefaced, blatant, bold, brazen, crying, dreadful, egregious, enormous, flagitious, flaunting, glaring, heinous, immodest, infamous, notorious, open, ostentatious, out-and-out, scandalous, shameless, undisguised
Antonyms *adj* delicate, faint, implied, indirect, insinuated, slight, subtle, understated

flagstone *n* **2** = **paving stone**, block, flag, slab

flail *vb* **2** = **thrash**, beat, thresh, windmill

flair *n* **1** = **ability**, accomplishment, aptitude, faculty, feel, genius, gift, knack, mastery, talent **3** = **style**, chic, dash, discernment, elegance, panache, stylishness, taste

flak *n* **2** *Informal* = **criticism**, abuse, bad press, brickbats (*inf.*), censure, complaints, condemnation, denigration, disapprobation, disapproval, disparagement, fault-finding, hostility, opposition, stick (*sl.*)

flake[1] *n* **1** = **chip**, disk, lamina, layer, peeling, scale, shaving, sliver, squama (*Biology*), wafer ◆ *vb* **5** = **chip**, blister, desquamate, peel (off), scale (off)

flake out *vb* = **collapse**, faint, keel over, lose consciousness, pass out, swoon (*literary*)

flamboyance *n* **1, 3** = **showiness**, bravura, brio, dash, élan, exhibitionism, extravagance, flair, flamboyancy, flashiness, floridity, glitz (*inf.*), ostentation, panache, pizzazz *or* pizazz (*inf.*), pomp, show, sparkle, style, stylishness, theatricality, verve
Antonyms *n* drabness, dullness, flatness, restraint, simplicity, unobtrusiveness

flamboyant *adj* **1, 3** = **showy**, actorly, baroque, camp (*inf.*), dashing, elaborate, extravagant, florid, ornate, ostentatious, over the top (*inf.*), rich, rococo, swashbuckling, theatrical

flame *n* **1** = **fire**, blaze, brightness, light **5** = **passion**, affection, ardour, enthusiasm, fervency, fervour, fire, intensity, keenness, warmth **6** *Informal* = **sweetheart**, beau, beloved, boyfriend, girlfriend, heart-throb (*Brit.*), ladylove, lover ◆ *vb* **8** = **burn**, blaze, flare, flash, glare, glow, shine

tronic mail. [C14: from Anglo-F, from OF *flambe*, from L *flammula* a little flame, from *flamma* flame]
▸ **'flame,like** *adj* ▸ **'flamy** *adj*

flame gun *n* a type of flame-thrower for destroying garden weeds, etc.

flamen ('fleɪmɛn) *n, pl* **flamens** *or* **flamines** ('flæmɪˌniːz). (in ancient Rome) any of 15 priests who each served a particular deity. [C14: from L; prob. rel. to OE *blōtan* to sacrifice, Gothic *blotan* to worship]

flamenco (flə'mɛŋkəʊ) *n, pl* **flamencos. 1** a type of dance music for vocal soloist and guitar, characterized by sad mood. **2** the dance performed to such music. [from Sp.: like a Gipsy, lit.: Fleming, from MDu. *Vlaminc* Fleming]

flameout ('fleɪmˌaʊt) *n* the failure of an aircraft jet engine in flight due to extinction of the flame.

flame-thrower *n* a weapon that ejects a stream or spray of burning fluid.

flame tree *n* any of various tropical trees with red or orange flowers.

flaming Ⓣ ('fleɪmɪŋ) *adj* **1** burning with or emitting flames. **2** glowing brightly. **3** intense or ardent: *a flaming temper.* **4** *Inf.* (intensifier): *you flaming idiot.*

flamingo (flə'mɪŋgəʊ) *n, pl* **flamingos** *or* **flamingoes.** a large wading bird having a pink-and-red plumage and downward-bent bill and inhabiting brackish lakes. [C16: from Port., from Provençal, from L *flamma* flame + Gmc suffix *-ing* denoting descent from; cf. -ING[3]]

flammable Ⓣ ('flæməb°l) *adj* readily combustible; inflammable.
▸ **ˌflamma'bility** *n*

> **USAGE NOTE** *Flammable* and *inflammable* are interchangeable when used of the properties of materials. *Flammable* is, however, often preferred for warning labels as there is less likelihood of misunderstanding (*inflammable* being sometimes taken to mean *not flammable*). *Inflammable* is preferred in figurative contexts: *this could prove to be an inflammable situation.*

flan (flæn) *n* **1** an open pastry or sponge tart filled with fruit or a savoury mixture. **2** a piece of metal ready to receive the die or stamp in the production of coins. [C19: from F, from OF *flaon*, from LL *fladō* flat cake, of Gmc origin]

flange (flændʒ) *n* **1** a radially projecting collar or rim on an object for strengthening it or for attaching it to another object. **2** a flat outer face of a rolled-steel joist. ◆ *vb* **flanges, flanging, flanged. 3** (*tr*) to provide (a component) with a flange. [C17: prob. changed from earlier *flaunche* curved segment at side of a heraldic field, from F *flanc* FLANK]
▸ **flanged** *adj* ▸ **'flangeless** *adj*

flank Ⓣ (flæŋk) *n* **1** the side of a man or animal between the ribs and the hip. **2** a cut of beef from the flank. **3** the side of anything, such as a mountain or building. **4** the side of a naval or military formation. ◆ *vb* **5** (when *intr*, often foll. by *on* or *upon*) to be located at the side of (an object, etc.). **6** *Mil.* to position or guard on or beside the flank of (a formation, etc.). [C12: from OF *flanc*, of Gmc origin]

flanker ('flæŋkə) *n* **1** one of a detachment of soldiers detailed to guard the flanks. **2** a fortification used to protect a flank. **3** Also called: **flank forward.** *Rugby.* another name for **winger.**

flannel Ⓣ ('flæn°l) *n* **1** a soft light woollen fabric with a slight nap, used for clothing, etc. **2** (*pl*) trousers or other garments made of flannel. **3** *Brit.* a small piece of cloth used to wash the face and hands; face flannel. US and Canad. equivalent: **washcloth. 4** *Brit. inf.* indirect or evasive talk. ◆ *vb* **flannels, flannelling, flannelled** *or US* **flannels, flanneling, flanneled.** (*tr*) **5** to cover or wrap with flannel. **6** to rub or polish with flannel. **7** *Brit. inf.* to flatter. [C14: prob. var. of *flanen* sackcloth, from Welsh, from *gwlân* wool]
▸ **'flannelly** *adj*

flannelette (ˌflæn°'lɛt) *n* a cotton imitation of flannel.

flap Ⓣ (flæp) *vb* **flaps, flapping, flapped. 1** to move (wings or arms) up and down, esp. in or as if in flying, or (of wings or arms) to move in this way. **2** to move or cause to move noisily back and forth or up and down: *the curtains flapped in the breeze.* **3** (*intr*) *Inf.* to become agitated or flustered. **4** to deal (a person or thing) a blow with a broad flexible object. ◆ *n* **5** the action, motion, or noise made by flapping: *with one flap of its wings the bird was off.* **6** a piece of material, etc., attached at one edge and usually used to cover an opening, as on a tent, envelope, or pocket. **7** a blow dealt with a flat object. **8** a movable surface fixed to an aircraft wing that increases lift during takeoff and drag during landing. **9** *Inf.* a state of panic or agitation. [C14: prob. imit.]

flapdoodle ('flæpˌduːd°l) *n Sl.* foolish talk; nonsense. [C19: from ?]

flapjack ('flæpˌdʒæk) *n* **1** a chewy biscuit made with rolled oats. **2** *Chiefly US & Canad.* another word for **pancake.**

flapper ('flæpə) *n* (in the 1920s) a young woman, esp. one flaunting her unconventional behaviour.

flare Ⓣ (flɛə) *vb* **flares, flaring, flared. 1** to burn or cause to burn with an unsteady or sudden bright flame. **2** to burn off excess gas or oil. **3** to spread or cause to spread outwards from a narrow to a wider shape. ◆ *n* **4** an unsteady flame. **5** a sudden burst of flame. **6a** a blaze of light or fire used to illuminate, signal distress, alert, etc. **6b** the device producing such a blaze. **7** a spreading shape or anything with a spreading shape: *a skirt with a flare.* **8** an open flame used to burn off unwanted gas at an oil well. **9** *Astron.* short for **solar flare.** [C16 (to spread out): from ?]

flares (flɛəz) *pl n Inf.* trousers with legs that widen below the knee.

flare-up Ⓣ *n* **1** a sudden burst of fire or light. **2** *Inf.* a sudden burst of emotion or violence. ◆ *vb* **flare up.** (*intr, adv*). **3** to burst suddenly into fire or light. **4** *Inf.* to burst into anger.

flash Ⓣ (flæʃ) *n* **1** a sudden short blaze of intense light or flame: *a flash of sunlight.* **2** a sudden occurrence or display, esp. one suggestive of brilliance: *a flash of understanding.* **3** a very brief space of time: *over in a flash.* **4** Also called: **newsflash.** a short news announcement concerning a new event. **5** Also called: **patch.** *Chiefly Brit.* an insignia or emblem worn on a uniform, vehicle, etc., to identify its military formation. **6** a sudden rush of water down a river or watercourse. **7** *Photog., inf.* short for **flashlight** (sense 2). **8** (*modifier*) involving, using, or produced by a flash of heat, light, etc.: *flash distillation.* **9 flash in the pan.** a project, person, etc., that enjoys only short-lived success. ◆ *adj* **10** *Inf.* ostentatious or vulgar. **11** sham or counterfeit. **12** *Inf.* relating to or characteristic of the criminal underworld. **13** brief and rapid: *flash freezing.* ◆ *vb* **14** to burst or cause to burst suddenly or intermittently into flame. **15** to emit or reflect or cause to emit or reflect light suddenly or intermittently. **16** (*intr*) to move very fast: *he flashed by on his bicycle.* **17** (*intr*) to come rapidly (into the mind or vision). **18** (*intr;* foll. by *out* or *up*) to appear like a sudden light. **19a** to signal or communicate very fast: *to flash a message.* **19b** to signal by use of a light, such as car headlights. **20** (*tr*) *Inf.* to display ostentatiously: *to flash money around.* **21** (*tr*) *Inf.* to show suddenly and briefly. **22** (*intr*) *Brit. sl.* to expose oneself indecently. **23** to send a sudden rush of water down (a river, etc.), or to carry (a vessel) down by this method. [C14 (in the sense: to rush, as of water): from ?]
▸ **'flasher** *n*

flashback ('flæʃˌbæk) *n* a transition in a novel, film, etc., to an earlier scene or event.

flashboard ('flæʃˌbɔːd) *n* a board or boarding that is placed along the top of a dam to increase its height and capacity.

flashbulb ('flæʃˌbʌlb) *n Photog.* a small expendable glass light bulb formerly used to produce a bright flash of light.

flashbulb memory *n Psychol.* the clear recollections that a person may have of the circumstances associated with a dramatic event.

flash burn *n Pathol.* a burn caused by momentary exposure to intense radiant heat.

flash card *n* a card on which are written or printed words for children to look at briefly, used as an aid to learning.

flashcube ('flæʃˌkjuːb) *n* a boxlike camera attachment, holding four flashbulbs, that turns so that each flashbulb can be used.

flash flood *n* a sudden short-lived torrent, usually caused by a heavy storm, esp. in desert regions.

flashgun ('flæʃˌgʌn) *n* a type of electronic flash, attachable to or sometimes incorporated in a camera, that emits a very brief flash of light when the shutter is open.

flashing ('flæʃɪŋ) *n* a weatherproof material, esp. thin sheet metal, used to cover the valleys between the slopes of a roof, the junction between a chimney and a roof, etc.

flashlight ('flæʃˌlaɪt) *n* **1** another word (esp. US and Canad.) for **torch. 2** *Photog.* the brief bright light emitted by an electronic flash unit. Often shortened to **flash.**

flash point *n* **1** the lowest temperature at which the vapour above a liquid can be ignited in air. **2** a critical time or place beyond which a situation will inevitably erupt into violence.

THESAURUS

flaming *adj* **1, 2** = **burning**, ablaze, afire, blazing, brilliant, fiery, glowing, ignited, in flames, raging, red, red-hot **3** = **intense**, angry, ardent, aroused, frenzied, hot, impassioned, raging, scintillating, vehement, vivid

flammable *adj* = **combustible**, ignitable, incendiary, inflammable

flank *n* **1, 2** = **side**, ham, haunch, hip, loin, quarter, thigh **3** = **wing**, side ◆ *vb* **5** = **border**, book-end, bound, edge, fringe, line, screen, skirt, wall

flannel *n* **4** *Brit. informal* = **prevarication**, baloney (*inf.*), blarney, equivocation, flattery, hedging, soft soap (*inf.*), sweet talk (*US inf.*), waffle (*inf., chiefly Brit.*) ◆ *vb* **7** *Brit. informal* = **prevaricate**, blarney, butter up, equivocate, flatter, hedge, pull the wool over (someone's) eyes, soft-soap (*inf.*), sweet-talk (*inf.*)

flap *vb* **2** = **flutter**, agitate, beat, flail, shake, swing, swish, thrash, thresh, vibrate, wag, wave **3** *Informal* = **panic**, dither (*chiefly Brit.*), fuss ◆ *n* **5** = **flutter**, bang, banging, beating, shaking, swinging, swish, waving **6** = **cover**, apron, fly, fold, lapel, lappet, overlap, skirt, tab, tail **9** *Informal* = **panic**, agitation, commotion, fluster, state (*inf.*), stew (*inf.*), sweat (*inf.*), tizzy (*inf.*), twitter (*inf.*)

flare *vb* **1** = **blaze**, burn up, dazzle, flicker, flutter, glare, waver **3** = **widen**, broaden, spread out ◆ *n* **4-6** = **flame**, blaze, burst, dazzle, flash, flicker, glare

flare up *vb* **4** = **lose one's temper**, blaze, blow one's top (*inf.*), boil over, break out, explode, fire up, fly off the handle (*inf.*), lose control, lose it (*inf.*), lose one's cool (*inf.*), lose the plot (*inf.*), throw a tantrum

flash *n* **1** = **blaze**, burst, coruscation, dazzle, flare, flicker, gleam, ray, scintillation, shaft, shimmer, spark, sparkle, streak, twinkle **2** = **burst**, demonstration, display, manifestation, outburst, show, sign, touch **3** = **moment**, bat of an eye, instant, jiffy (*inf.*), second, shake, split second, trice, twinkling, twinkling of an eye, two shakes of a lamb's tail (*inf.*) ◆ *adj* **10** *Informal* = **ostentatious**, cheap, glamorous, tacky (*inf.*), tasteless, vulgar ◆ *vb* **14, 15** = **blaze**, coruscate, flare, flicker, glare, gleam, glint, glisten, glitter, light, scintillate, shimmer, sparkle, twinkle **16** = **speed**, bolt, burn rubber (*inf.*), dart, dash, fly, race, shoot, sprint, streak, sweep,

flashy ➊ ('flæʃɪ) *adj* **flashier, flashiest. 1** brilliant and dazzling, esp. for a short time or in a superficial way. **2** cheap and ostentatious.
▸ **'flashily** *adv* ▸ **'flashiness** *n*

flask (flɑːsk) *n* **1** a bottle with a narrow neck, esp. used in a laboratory or for wine, oil, etc. **2** Also called: **hip flask.** a small flattened container of glass or metal designed to be carried in a pocket, esp. for liquor. **3** See **vacuum flask.** [C14: from OF, from Med. L *flasca, flasco,* ? of Gmc origin; cf. OE *flasce, flaxe*]

flat[1] ➊ (flæt) *adj* **flatter, flattest. 1** horizontal; level: *a flat roof.* **2** even or smooth, without projections or depressions: *a flat surface.* **3** lying stretched out at full length: *he lay flat on the ground.* **4** having little depth or thickness: *a flat dish.* **5** (*postpositive;* often foll. by *against*) having a surface or side in complete contact with another surface: *flat against the wall.* **6** (of a tyre) deflated. **7** (of shoes) having an unraised heel. **8** *Chiefly Brit.* **8a** (of races, racetracks, or racecourses) not having obstacles to be jumped. **8b** of, relating to, or connected with flat racing as opposed to steeplechasing and hurdling. **9** without qualification; total: *a flat denial.* **10** fixed: *a flat rate.* **11** (*prenominal or immediately postpositive*) neither more nor less; exact: *he did the journey in thirty minutes flat.* **12** unexciting: *a flat joke.* **13** without variation or resonance; monotonous: *a flat voice.* **14** (of beer, sparkling wines, etc.) having lost effervescence, as by exposure to air. **15** (of trade, business, etc.) commercially inactive. **16** (of a battery) fully discharged. **17** (of a print, photograph, or painting) lacking contrast. **18** (of paint) without gloss or lustre. **19** (of lighting) diffuse. **20** *Music.* **20a** (*immediately postpositive*) denoting a note of a given letter name (or the sound it represents) that has been lowered in pitch by one chromatic semitone: *B flat.* **20b** (of an instrument, voice, etc.) out of tune by being too low in pitch. Cf. **sharp** (sense 12). **21** *Phonetics.* **flat 21a** the vowel sound of *a* as in the usual US or S Brit. pronunciation of *hand, cat.* ◆ *adv* **22** in or into a prostrate, level, or flat state or position: *he held his hand out flat.* **23** completely or utterly; absolutely. **24** exactly; precisely: *in three minutes flat.* **25** *Music.* **25a** lower than a standard pitch. **25b** too low in pitch: *she sings flat.* Cf. **sharp** (sense 17). **26 fall flat (on one's face).** to fail to achieve a desired effect. **27 flat out.** *Inf.* **27a** with the maximum speed or effort. **27b** totally exhausted. ◆ *n* **28** a flat object, surface, or part. **29** (*often pl*) a low-lying tract of land, esp. a marsh or swamp. **30** (*often pl*) a mud bank exposed at low tide. **31** *Music.* **31a** an accidental that lowers the pitch of a note by one chromatic semitone. Usual symbol: ♭ **31b** a note affected by this accidental. Cf. **sharp** (sense 18). **32** *Theatre.* a wooden frame covered with painted canvas, etc., used to form part of a stage setting. **33** a punctured car tyre. **34** (*often cap.;* preceded by *the*) *Chiefly Brit.* **34a** flat racing, esp. as opposed to steeplechasing and hurdling. **34b** the season of flat racing. **35** *US & Canad.* a shallow box used for holding plants, etc. ◆ *vb* **flats, flatting, flatted. 36** to make or become flat. [C14: from ON *flatr*]
▸ **'flatly** *adv* ▸ **'flatness** *n* ▸ **'flattish** *adj*

flat[2] ➊ (flæt) *n* a set of rooms comprising a residence entirely on one floor of a building. Usual US and Canad. name: **apartment.** [OE *flett* floor, hall, house]

flatbed lorry ('flæt,bɛd) *n* a lorry with a flat platform for its body.

flatbed scanner *n Computing.* a computer-controlled device that electronically scans images placed on its flat glass, to produce digitized images for use in desktop publishing, etc.

flatboat ('flæt,bəʊt) *n* any boat with a flat bottom, usually for transporting goods on a canal.

flatette (,flæt'ɛt) *n Austral.* a very small flat.

flatfish ('flæt,fɪʃ) *n, pl* **flatfish** *or* **flatfishes.** any of an order of marine spiny-finned fish including the halibut, plaice, turbot, and sole, all of which have a flat body which has both eyes on the uppermost side.

flatfoot ('flæt,fʊt) *n* **1** Also called: **splayfoot.** a condition in which the instep arch of the foot is flattened. **2** (*pl* **flatfoots** *or* **flatfeet**) a slang word (usually derogatory) for a **policeman.**

flat-footed (,flæt'fʊtɪd) *adj* **1** having flatfoot. **2** *Inf.* **2a** awkward. **2b** downright. **3** *Inf.* off guard (often in **catch flat-footed**).
▸ **,flat-'footedly** *adv* ▸ **,flat-'footedness** *n*

flathead ('flæt,hɛd) *n, pl* **flathead** *or* **flatheads.** a Pacific food fish which resembles the gurnard.

flatiron ('flæt,aɪən) *n* (formerly) an iron for pressing clothes that was heated by being placed on a stove, etc.

flatlet ('flætlɪt) *n* a flat having only a few rooms.

flatmate ('flæt,meɪt) *n* a person with whom one shares a flat.

flat racing *n* **a** the racing of horses on racecourses without jumps. **b** (*as modifier*): *the flat-racing season.*

flat spin *n* **1** an aircraft spin in which the longitudinal axis is more nearly horizontal than vertical. **2** *Inf.* a state of confusion; dither.

flat spot *n* **1** *Engineering.* a region of poor acceleration over a narrow range of throttle openings, caused by a weak mixture in the carburettor. **2** any narrow region of poor performance in a mechanical device.

flatten ➊ ('flætᵊn) *vb* **1** (sometimes foll. by *out*) to make or become flat or flatter. **2** (*tr*) *Inf.* **2a** to knock down or injure. **2b** to crush or subdue. **3** (*tr*) *Music.* to lower the pitch of (a note) by one chromatic semitone.
▸ **'flattener** *n*

flatter ➊ ('flætə) *vb* **1** to praise insincerely, esp. in order to win favour or reward. **2** to show to advantage: *that dress flatters her.* **3** (*tr*) to make to appear more attractive, etc., than in reality. **4** to gratify the vanity of (a person). **5** (*tr*) to encourage, esp. falsely. **6** (*tr*) to deceive (oneself): *I flatter myself that I am the best.* [C13: prob. from OF *flater* to lick, fawn upon, of Frankish origin]
▸ **'flatterable** *adj* ▸ **'flatterer** *n*

flattery ➊ ('flætərɪ) *n, pl* **flatteries. 1** the act of flattering. **2** excessive or insincere praise.

flattie ('flætɪ) *n NZ inf.* a flounder or other flatfish.

flatties ('flætɪz) *pl n* shoes with flat heels.

flat top *n* a style of haircut in which the hair is cut shortest on the top of the head so that it stands up from the scalp and appears flat from the crown to the forehead.

flatulent ➊ ('flætjʊlənt) *adj* **1** suffering from or caused by an excessive amount of gas in the alimentary canal. **2** generating excessive gas in the alimentary canal. **3** pretentious. [C16: from NL *flātulentus,* from L *flatus,* from *flāre* to breathe, blow]
▸ **'flatulence** *or* **'flatulency** *n* ▸ **'flatulently** *adv*

flatus ('fleɪtəs) *n, pl* **flatuses.** gas generated in the alimentary canal. [C17: from L: a blowing, from *flāre* to breathe, blow]

flatworm ('flæt,wɜːm) *n* any parasitic or free-living invertebrate of the phylum *Platyhelminthes,* including flukes and tapeworms, having a flattened body.

flaunt ➊ (flɔːnt) *vb* **1** to display (possessions, oneself, etc.) ostentatiously. **2** to wave or cause to wave freely. ◆ *n* **3** the act of flaunting. [C16: ? of Scand. origin]

> **USAGE NOTE** *Flaunt* is sometimes wrongly used where *flout* is meant: *they must be prevented from flouting* (not *flaunting*) *the law.*

flautist ('flɔːtɪst) *or US & Canad.* **flutist** ('fluːtɪst) *n* a player of the flute. [C19: from It. *flautista,* from *flauto* FLUTE]

flavescent (flə'vɛsᵊnt) *adj* turning yellow; yellowish. [C19: from L *flāvēscere* to become yellow]

flavin *or* **flavine** ('fleɪvɪn) *n* **1** a heterocyclic ketone that forms the nucleus of certain natural yellow pigments, such as riboflavin. **2** any yellow pigment based on flavin. [C19: from L *flāvus* yellow]

THESAURUS

whistle, zoom **20** *Informal* = **show**, display, exhibit, expose, flaunt, flourish

flashy *adj* **2** = **showy**, brash, cheap, cheap and nasty, flamboyant, flaunting, garish, gaudy, glittery, glitzy (*sl.*), in poor taste, jazzy (*inf.*), loud, meretricious, ostentatious, over the top (*inf.*), snazzy (*inf.*), tacky (*inf.*), tasteless, tawdry, tinselly
Antonyms *adj* downbeat, low-key, modest, natural, plain, unaffected, understated

flat[1] *adj* **1, 2** = **even**, horizontal, level, levelled, low, planar, plane, smooth, unbroken **3** = **horizontal**, laid low, lying full length, outstretched, prone, prostrate, reclining, recumbent, supine **6** = **punctured**, blown out, burst, collapsed, deflated, empty **9** = **absolute**, categorical, direct, downright, explicit, final, fixed, out-and-out, peremptory, plain, positive, straight, unconditional, unequivocal, unmistakable, unqualified **12, 13** = **dull**, boring, dead, flavourless, ho-hum (*inf.*), insipid, jejune, lacklustre, lifeless, monotonous, pointless, prosaic, spiritless, stale, tedious, tiresome, uninteresting, vapid, watery, weak ◆ *adv* **23, 24** = **completely**, absolutely, categorically, exactly, point blank, precisely, utterly **27a flat out** *Informal* = **at full speed**, all out, at full gallop, at full tilt, for all one is worth, hell for leather (*inf.*), posthaste, under full steam ◆ *n* **29, 30** *often plural* = **plain**, lowland, marsh, mud flat, shallow, shoal, strand, swamp
Antonyms *adj* ≠ **even:** broken, hilly, irregular, rolling, rough, rugged, slanting, sloping, uneven, up and down ≠ **horizontal:** on end, perpendicular, straight, upright, vertical ≠ **dull:** bubbly, effervescent, exciting, fizzy, palatable, sparkling, tasty, zestful

flat[2] *n* = **apartment**, rooms

flatly *adv* **23** = **absolutely**, categorically, completely, positively, unhesitatingly

flatness *n* **1, 2** = **evenness**, horizontality, levelness, smoothness, uniformity **12, 13** = **dullness**, emptiness, insipidity, monotony, staleness, tedium, vapidity

flatten *vb* **1** = **level**, compress, even out, iron out, plaster, raze, roll, smooth off, squash, trample **2a** *Informal* = **knock down**, bowl over, deck (*sl.*), fell, floor, knock off one's feet, prostrate **2b** *Informal* = **crush**, subdue

flatter *vb* **1** = **praise**, blandish, butter up, cajole, compliment, court, fawn, flannel (*Brit. inf.*), humour, inveigle, lay it on (thick) (*sl.*), pander to, puff, soft-soap (*inf.*), sweet-talk (*inf.*), wheedle **2, 3** = **suit**, become, do something for, enhance, set off, show to advantage

flattering *adj* **1** = **ingratiating**, adulatory, complimentary, fawning, fulsome, gratifying, honeyed, honey-tongued, laudatory, sugary **2, 3** = **becoming**, effective, enhancing, kind, well-chosen
Antonyms *adj* ≠ **ingratiating:** blunt, candid, honest, straight, uncomplimentary ≠ **becoming:** not shown in the best light, not shown to advantage, plain, unattractive, unbecoming, unflattering, warts and all

flattery *n* **1, 2** = **obsequiousness**, adulation, blandishment, blarney, cajolery, false praise, fawning, flannel (*Brit. inf.*), fulsomeness, honeyed words, servility, soft-soap (*inf.*), sweet-talk (*inf.*), sycophancy, toadyism

flatulence *n* **1** = **wind**, borborygmus (*Medical*), eructation **3** = **pretentiousness**, boasting, bombast, claptrap, empty words, fustian, hot air (*inf.*), pomposity, prolixity, rodomontade, twaddle

flatulent *adj* **3** = **pretentious**, bombastic, inflated, long-winded, pompous, prolix, swollen, tedious, tiresome, turgid, wordy

flaunt *vb* **1** = **show off**, boast, brandish, display, disport, exhibit, flash about, flourish, make a (great) show of, make an exhibition of, parade, sport (*inf.*), vaunt

flavine ('fleɪvɪn) *n* another name for **acriflavine hydrochloride.**

flavone ('fleɪvəʊn) *n* **1** a crystalline compound occurring in plants. **2** any of a class of yellow plant pigments derived from flavone. [C19: from G, from L *flāvus* yellow + -ONE]

flavoprotein (ˌfleɪvəʊ'prəʊtiːn) *n* any of a group of enzymes that contain a derivative of riboflavin linked to a protein and catalyse oxidation in cells.

flavour Ⓣ *or US* **flavor** ('fleɪvə) *n* **1** taste perceived in food or liquid in the mouth. **2** a substance added to food, etc., to impart a specific taste. **3** a distinctive quality or atmosphere. **4** *Physics.* a property of quarks that distinguishes different types. ◆ *vb* **5** (*tr*) to impart a flavour or quality to. [C14: from OF *flaour,* from LL *flātor* (unattested) bad smell, breath, from L *flāre* to blow]
▸ **'flavourless** *or US* **'flavorless** *adj* ▸ **'flavourful** *or US* **'flavorful** *adj*

flavour enhancer *n* another term for **monosodium glutamate.**

flavouring *or US* **flavoring** ('fleɪvərɪŋ) *n* a substance used to impart a particular flavour to food.

flaw[1] Ⓣ (flɔː) *n* **1** an imperfection or blemish. **2** a crack or rift. **3** *Law.* an invalidating defect in a document or proceeding. ◆ *vb* **4** to make or become blemished or imperfect. [C14: prob. from ON *flaga* stone slab]
▸ **'flawless** *adj*

flaw[2] (flɔː) *n* a sudden short gust of wind; squall. [C16: of Scand. origin]

flax (flæks) *n* **1** a herbaceous plant or shrub that has blue flowers and is cultivated for its seeds (flaxseed) and for the fibres of its stems. **2** the fibre of this plant, made into thread and woven into linen fabrics. **3** any of various similar plants. **4** *NZ.* a swamp plant producing a fibre that is used by Maoris for clothing, baskets, etc. [OE *fleax*]

flaxen ('flæksən) *adj* **1** of or resembling flax. **2** of a soft yellow colour: *flaxen hair.*

flaxseed ('flæksˌsiːd) *n* the seed of the flax plant, which yields linseed oil. Also called: **linseed.**

flay Ⓣ (fleɪ) *vb* (*tr*) **1** to strip off the skin or covering of, esp. by whipping. **2** to attack with savage criticism. [OE *flēan*]
▸ **'flayer** *n*

flea (fliː) *n* **1** a small wingless parasitic blood-sucking jumping insect living on the skin of mammals and birds. **2 flea in one's ear.** *Inf.* a sharp rebuke. [OE *flēah*]

fleabane ('fliːˌbeɪn) *n* any of several plants, including one having purplish tubular flower heads with orange centres and one having yellow daisy-like flower heads, that are reputed to ward off fleas.

fleabite ('fliːˌbaɪt) *n* **1** the bite of a flea. **2** a slight or trifling annoyance or discomfort.

flea-bitten Ⓣ *adj* **1** bitten by or infested with fleas. **2** *Inf.* shabby or decrepit.

flea market *n* an open-air market selling cheap and often second-hand goods.

fleapit ('fliːˌpɪt) *n Inf.* a shabby cinema or theatre.

fleawort ('fliːˌwɜːt) *n* **1** any of various plants with yellow daisy-like flowers and rosettes of downy leaves. **2** a Eurasian plantain whose seeds were formerly used as a flea repellent.

flèche (fleɪʃ, flɛʃ) *n* a slender spire, esp. over the intersection of the nave and transept ridges of a church roof. Also called: **spirelet.** [C18: from F: spire (lit.: arrow), prob. of Gmc origin]

fleck Ⓣ (flɛk) *n* **1** a small marking or streak. **2** a speck: *a fleck of dust.* ◆ *vb* **3** (*tr*) Also: **flecker.** to speckle. [C16: prob. from ON *flekkr* stain, spot]

fled (flɛd) *vb* the past tense and past participle of **flee.**

fledge (flɛdʒ) *vb* **fledges, fledging, fledged.** (*tr*) **1** to feed and care for (a young bird) until it is able to fly. **2** Also called: **fletch.** to fit (something, esp. an arrow) with a feather or feathers. **3** to cover or adorn with or as if with feathers. [OE *-flycge,* as in *unflycge* unfledged; see FLY[1]]

fledgling Ⓣ *or* **fledgeling** ('flɛdʒlɪŋ) *n* **1** a young bird that has grown feathers. **2** a young and inexperienced person.

flee Ⓣ (fliː) *vb* **flees, fleeing, fled. 1** to run away from (a place, danger, etc.). **2** (*intr*) to run or move quickly. [OE *flēon*]
▸ **'fleer** *n*

fleece Ⓣ (fliːs) *n* **1** the coat of wool that covers the body of a sheep or similar animal. **2** the wool removed from a single sheep. **3** something resembling a fleece. **4** sheepskin or a fabric with soft pile, used as a lining for coats, etc. ◆ *vb* **fleeces, fleecing, fleeced.** (*tr*) **5** to defraud or charge exorbitantly. **6** another term for **shear** (sense 1). [OE *flēos*]

fleecie ('fliːsɪ) *n NZ.* a person who collects fleeces after shearing and prepares them for baling. Also called: **fleece-oh.**

fleecy Ⓣ ('fliːsɪ) *adj* **fleecier, fleeciest.** of or resembling fleece.
▸ **'fleecily** *adv*

fleer (flɪə) *Arch.* ◆ *vb* **1** to scoff; sneer. ◆ *n* **2** a derisory glance. [C14: from ON; cf. Norwegian *flire* to snigger]

fleet[1] Ⓣ (fliːt) *n* **1** a number of warships organized as a tactical unit. **2** all the warships of a nation. **3** a number of aircraft, ships, buses, etc., operating together or under the same ownership. [OE *flēot*]

fleet[2] (fliːt) *adj* **1** rapid in movement; swift. **2** *Poetic.* fleeting. ◆ *vb* **3** (*intr*) to move rapidly. **4** (*tr*) *Obs.* to cause (time) to pass rapidly. [prob. OE *flēotan* to float, glide rapidly]
▸ **'fleetly** *adv* ▸ **'fleetness** *n*

Fleet Air Arm *n* the aviation branch of the Royal Navy.

fleet chief petty officer *n* a noncommissioned officer in the Royal Navy comparable in rank to a warrant officer in the army or the Royal Air Force.

fleeting Ⓣ ('fliːtɪŋ) *adj* rapid and transient: *a fleeting glimpse of the sea.*
▸ **'fleetingly** *adv*

fleet rate *or* **rating** *n* a reduced rate quoted by an insurance company to underwrite the risks to a fleet of vehicles, aircraft, etc.

Fleet Street *n* **1** a street in central London in which many newspaper offices were formerly situated. **2** British journalism or journalists collectively.

Fleming ('flɛmɪŋ) *n* a native or inhabitant of Flanders, a medieval principality in the Low Countries, or of Flemish-speaking Belgium.

Flemish ('flɛmɪʃ) *n* **1** one of the two official languages of Belgium. **2 the Flemish.** (*functioning as pl*) the Flemings collectively. ◆ *adj* **3** of or characteristic of Flanders, the Flemings, or their language.

flense (flɛns), **flench** (flɛntʃ), *or* **flinch** (flɪntʃ) *vb* **flenses, flensing, flensed** *or* **flenches, flenching, flenched** *or* **flinches, flinching, flinched.** (*tr*) to strip (a whale, seal, etc.) of (its blubber or skin). [C19: from Danish *flense;* rel. to Du. *flensen*]

flesh Ⓣ (flɛʃ) *n* **1** the soft part of the body of an animal or human, esp. muscular tissue, as distinct from bone and viscera. **2** *Inf.* excess weight; fat. **3** *Arch.* the edible tissue of animals as opposed to that of fish or, sometimes, fowl. **4** the thick soft part of a fruit or vegetable. **5** the human body and its physical or sensual nature as opposed to the soul or spirit. Related adj: **carnal. 6** mankind in general. **7** animate creatures in general. **8** one's own family; kin (esp. in **one's own flesh and blood**). **9a** a yellowish-pink colour. **9b** (*as adj*): *flesh tights.* **10 in the flesh.** in person; actually present. **11 press the flesh.** *Inf.* to shake hands, usually with large numbers of people, esp. as a political campaigning ploy. ◆ *vb* **12** (*tr*) *Hunting.* to stimulate the hunting instinct of (hounds or falcons) by giving them small quantities of raw flesh. **13** *Arch. or poetic.* to accustom or incite to bloodshed or battle by initial experience. **14** to fatten; fill out. [OE *flǣsc*]

fleshings ('flɛʃɪŋz) *pl n* flesh-coloured tights.

fleshly Ⓣ ('flɛʃlɪ) *adj* **fleshlier, fleshliest. 1** relating to the body; carnal: *fleshly desire.* **2** worldly as opposed to spiritual. **3** fat.

THESAURUS

flavour *n* **1 = taste,** aroma, essence, extract, flavouring, odour, piquancy, relish, savour, seasoning, smack, tang, zest, zing (*inf.*) **2 = quality,** aspect, character, essence, feel, feeling, property, soupçon, stamp, style, suggestion, tinge, tone, touch ◆ *vb* **5 = season,** ginger up, imbue, infuse, lace, leaven, spice
Antonyms *n* ≠ **taste:** blandness, flatness, insipidity, odourlessness, tastelessness, vapidity

flaw[1] *n* **1 = weakness,** blemish, chink in one's armour, defect, disfigurement, failing, fault, imperfection, scar, speck, spot, weak spot **2 = crack,** breach, break, cleft, crevice, fissure, fracture, rent, rift, scission, split, tear

flawed *adj* **1, 2 = damaged,** blemished, broken, chipped, cracked, defective, erroneous, faulty, imperfect, unsound

flawless *adj* **1 = perfect,** faultless, impeccable, spotless, unblemished, unsullied **2 = intact,** sound, unbroken, undamaged, whole

flay *vb* **1 = skin,** excoriate **2 = upbraid,** castigate, excoriate, execrate, pull to pieces (*inf.*), revile, slam (*sl.*), tear a strip off, tear into (*inf.*)

flea-bitten *adj* **1, 2 = shabby,** crawling, decrepit, fetid, flea-ridden, frowsty, grotty (*sl.*), grubby, infested, insalubrious, lousy, mean, mucky, pediculous (*Medical*), run-down, scabby, scruffy, scurfy, sleazy, slummy, sordid, squalid, tatty, unhygienic

fleck *n* **1, 2 = mark,** dot, pinpoint, speck, speckle, spot, streak ◆ *vb* **3 = speckle,** bespeckle, besprinkle, dapple, dot, dust, mark, mottle, spot, stipple, streak, variegate

fledgling *n* **1 = chick,** nestling **2 = novice,** apprentice, beginner, learner, neophyte, newcomer, rookie (*inf.*), trainee, tyro

flee *vb* **1, 2 = run away,** abscond, avoid, bolt, cut and run (*inf.*), decamp, depart, do a runner (*sl.*), escape, fly, get away, hook it (*sl.*), leave, make a quick exit, make off, make oneself scarce (*inf.*), make one's escape, make one's getaway, scarper (*Brit. sl.*), skedaddle (*inf.*), slope off, split (*sl.*), take flight, take off (*inf.*), turn tail, vanish

fleece *n* **1, 2 = wool** ◆ *vb* **5 = cheat,** bleed, con (*inf.*), cozen, defraud, despoil, diddle (*inf.*), overcharge, plunder, rifle, rip off (*sl.*), rob, rook (*sl.*), skin (*sl.*), steal, stiff (*sl.*), swindle, take for a ride (*inf.*), take to the cleaners (*sl.*) **6 = shear,** clip

fleecy *adj* **= woolly,** downy, fluffy, shaggy, soft

fleet[1] *n* **1, 2 = navy,** argosy, armada, flotilla, naval force, sea power, squadron, task force, vessels, warships

fleet[2] *adj* **1 = swift,** fast, flying, mercurial, meteoric, nimble, nimble-footed, quick, rapid, speedy, winged

fleeting *adj* **= momentary,** brief, ephemeral, evanescent, flitting, flying, fugacious, fugitive, passing, short, short-lived, temporary, transient, transitory
Antonyms *adj* abiding, continuing, durable, enduring, eternal, imperishable, lasting, long-lasting, long-lived, permanent

fleetness *n* **1 = swiftness,** celerity, lightning speed, nimble-footedness, nimbleness, quickness, rapidity, speed, speediness, velocity

flesh *n* **1 = meat,** beef (*inf.*), body, brawn, fat, fatness, food, tissue, weight **5 = physical nature,** animality, body, carnality, flesh and blood, human nature, physicality, sensuality **6 = mankind,** homo sapiens, humankind, human race, living creatures, man, mortality, people, race, stock, world **8 one's own flesh and blood = family,** blood, kin, kindred, kinsfolk, kith and kin, relations, relatives

fleshiness *n* **1 = plumpness,** chubbiness, corpulence, flabbiness, heaviness, obesity, stoutness

fleshly *adj* **1 = carnal,** animal, bodily, erotic, lascivious, lecherous, lustful, sensual **2 =**

▸ 'fleshliness *n*

flesh out *vb (adv)* **1** *(tr)* to give substance to (an argument, description, etc.). **2** *(intr)* to expand or become more substantial.

fleshpots ('flɛʃ,pɒts) *pl n Often facetious.* **1** luxurious living. **2** places where bodily desires are gratified. [C16: from the Biblical use as applied to Egypt (Exodus 16:3)]

flesh wound (wu:nd) *n* a wound affecting superficial tissues.

fleshy Ⓣ ('flɛʃɪ) *adj* **fleshier, fleshiest. 1** plump. **2** related to or resembling flesh. **3** *Bot.* (of some fruits, etc.) thick and pulpy.
▸ '**fleshiness** *n*

fletcher ('flɛtʃə) *n* a person who makes arrows. [C14: from OF *flechier*, from *fleche* arrow; see FLÈCHE]

fleur-de-lys *or* **fleur-de-lis** (,flɜ:də'li:) *n, pl* **fleurs-de-lys** *or* **fleurs-de-lis** (,flɜ:də'li:z). **1** *Heraldry.* a charge representing a lily with three distinct petals. **2** another name for **iris** (sense 2). [C19: from OF *flor de lis*, lit.: lily flower]

fleurette *or* **fleuret** (fluə'rɛt) *n* an ornament or motif resembling a flower. [C19: F, lit.: a small flower, from *fleur* flower]

flew (flu:) *vb* the past tense of **fly**[1].

flews (flu:z) *pl n* the fleshy hanging upper lip of a bloodhound or similar dog. [C16: from ?]

flex Ⓣ (flɛks) *n* **1** *Brit.* a flexible insulated electric cable, used esp. to connect appliances to mains. US and Canad. name: **cord.** ◆ *vb* **2** to bend or be bent: *he flexed his arm.* **3** to contract (a muscle) or (of a muscle) to contract. **4** *(intr)* to work flexitime. [C16: from L *flexus* bent, winding, from *flectere* to bend, bow]

flexible Ⓣ ('flɛksɪbᵊl) *adj* **1** Also **flexile** ('flɛksaɪl). able to be bent easily without breaking. **2** adaptable or variable: *flexible working hours.* **3** able to be persuaded easily.
▸ ,**flexi'bility** *n* ▸ '**flexibly** *adv*

flexion ('flɛkʃən) *or* **flection** *n* **1** the act of bending a joint or limb. **2** the condition of the joint or limb so bent.
▸ '**flexional** *adj*

flexitime ('flɛksɪ,taɪm) *n* a system permitting flexibility of working hours at the beginning or end of the day, provided an agreed period (**core time**) is spent at work. Also called: **flextime.**

flexor ('flɛksə) *n* any muscle whose contraction serves to bend a joint or limb. Cf. **extensor.** [C17: NL; see FLEX]

flexuous ('flɛksjuəs) *adj* full of bends or curves; winding. [C17: from L *flexuōsus* full of bends, tortuous, from *flexus* a bending; see FLEX]
▸ '**flexuously** *adv*

flexure ('flɛkʃə) *n* **1** the act of flexing or the state of being flexed. **2** a bend, turn, or fold.

flex-wing *n Aeronautics.* a collapsible fabric delta wing, as used with hang-gliders.

flibbertigibbet ('flɪbətɪ,dʒɪbɪt) *n* an irresponsible, silly, or gossipy person. [C15: from ?]

flick[1] Ⓣ (flɪk) *vb* **1** *(tr)* to touch with or as if with the finger or hand in a quick jerky movement. **2** *(tr)* to propel or remove by a quick jerky movement, usually of the fingers or hand. **3** to move or cause to move quickly or jerkily. **4** *(intr; foll. by through)* to read or look at (a book, etc.) quickly or idly. ◆ *n* **5** a tap or quick stroke with the fingers, a whip, etc. **6** the sound made by such a stroke. **7** a fleck or particle. **8 give (someone) the flick.** to dismiss (someone) from consideration. [C15: imit.; cf. F *flicflac*]

flick[2] (flɪk) *n Sl.* **1** a cinema film. **2 the flicks.** the cinema: *what's on at the flicks tonight?*

flicker[1] Ⓣ ('flɪkə) *vb* **1** *(intr)* to shine with an unsteady or intermittent light. **2** *(intr)* to move quickly to and fro. **3** *(tr)* to cause to flicker. ◆ *n* **4** an unsteady or brief light or flame. **5** a swift quivering or fluttering movement. [OE *flicorian*]

flicker[2] ('flɪkə) *n* a North American woodpecker which has a yellow undersurface to the wings and tail. [C19: ? imit. of the bird's call]

flick knife *n* a knife with a retractable blade that springs out when a button is pressed.

flier Ⓣ ('flaɪə) *n* a variant spelling of **flyer.**

flight[1] Ⓣ (flaɪt) *n* **1** the act, skill, or manner of flying. **2** a journey made by a flying animal or object. **3** a group of flying birds or aircraft: *a flight of swallows.* **4** the basic tactical unit of a military air force. **5** a journey through space, esp. of a spacecraft. **6** an aircraft flying on a scheduled journey. **7** a soaring mental journey above or beyond the normal everyday world: *a flight of fancy.* **8** a single line of hurdles across a track in a race. **9** a feather or plastic attachment fitted to an arrow or dart to give it stability in flight. **10** a set of steps or stairs between one landing or floor and the next. ◆ *vb (tr)* **11** *Sport.* to cause (a ball, dart, etc.) to float slowly towards its target. **12** to shoot (a bird) in flight. **13** to fledge (an arrow or dart). [OE *flyht*]

flight[2] Ⓣ (flaɪt) *n* **1** the act of fleeing or running away, as from danger. **2 put to flight.** to cause to run away. **3 take (to) flight.** to run away; flee. [OE *flyht* (unattested)]

flight attendant *n* a person who attends to the needs of passengers on a commercial flight.

flight deck *n* **1** the crew compartment in an airliner. **2** the upper deck of an aircraft carrier from which aircraft take off.

flightless ('flaɪtlɪs) *adj* (of certain birds and insects) unable to fly. See also **ratite.**

flight lieutenant *n* an officer holding a commissioned rank senior to a flying officer and junior to a squadron leader in the Royal Air Force.

flight path *n* the course through the air of an aircraft, rocket, or projectile.

flight recorder *n* an electronic device fitted to an aircraft for collecting and storing information concerning its performance in flight. It is often used to determine the cause of a crash. Also called: **black box.**

flight sergeant *n* a noncommissioned officer in the Royal Air Force, junior in rank to that of master aircrew.

flight simulator *n* a ground-training device that reproduces exactly the conditions experienced on the flight deck of an aircraft.

flighty Ⓣ ('flaɪtɪ) *adj* **flightier, flightiest. 1** frivolous and irresponsible. **2** mentally erratic or wandering.
▸ '**flightiness** *n*

flimflam ('flɪm,flæm) *Inf.* ◆ *n* **1a** nonsense; rubbish; foolishness. **1b** *(as modifier): flimflam arguments.* **2** a deception; trick; swindle. ◆ *vb* **flimflams, flimflamming, flimflammed. 3** *(tr)* to deceive; trick; swindle; cheat. [C16: prob. of Scand. origin]
▸ '**flim,flammer** *n*

flimsy Ⓣ ('flɪmzɪ) *adj* **flimsier, flimsiest. 1** not strong or substantial: *a flimsy building.* **2** light and thin: *a flimsy dress.* **3** unconvincing; weak: *a flimsy excuse.* ◆ *n* **4** thin paper used for making carbon copies of a letter, etc. **5** a copy made on such paper. [C17: from ?]
▸ '**flimsiness** *n*

flinch Ⓣ (flɪntʃ) *vb (intr)* **1** to draw back suddenly, as from pain, shock, etc.; wince. **2** (often foll. by *from*) to avoid contact (with): *he never flinched from his duty.* [C16: from OF *flenchir;* rel. to MHG *lenken* to bend, direct]
▸ '**flinchingly** *adv*

flinders ('flɪndəz) *pl n Rare.* small fragments or splinters (esp. in **fly into flinders**). [C15: prob. from ON; cf. Norwegian *flindra* thin piece of stone]

fling Ⓣ (flɪŋ) *vb* **flings, flinging, flung.** *(mainly tr)* **1** to throw, esp. with force or abandon. **2** to put or send without warning or preparation: *to fling someone into jail.* **3** *(also intr)* to move (oneself or a part of the body) with abandon or speed. **4** (usually foll. by *into*) to apply (oneself) diligently and with vigour (to). **5** to cast aside: *she flung away her scruples.* ◆ *n* **6** the act or an instance of flinging. **7** a period or occasion of unrestrained or extravagant behaviour. **8** any of various vigorous Scottish

THESAURUS

worldly, corporal, corporeal, earthly, human, material, mundane, of this world, physical, secular, terrestrial

fleshy *adj* **1** = **plump**, ample, beefy *(inf.)*, brawny, chubby, chunky, corpulent, fat, hefty, meaty, obese, overweight, podgy, stout, tubby, well-padded

flex *vb* **2, 3** = **bend**, angle, contract, crook, curve, tighten

flexibility *n* **1** = **pliancy**, elasticity, give, pliability, resilience, springiness, tensility **2** = **adaptability**, adjustability, complaisance

flexible *adj* **1** = **pliable**, bendable, ductile, elastic, limber, lissom(e), lithe, mouldable, plastic, pliant, springy, stretchy, supple, tensile, willowy, yielding **2** = **adaptable**, adjustable, discretionary, open, variable **3** = **compliant**, amenable, biddable, complaisant, docile, gentle, manageable, responsive, tractable
Antonyms *adj* ≠ **pliable:** fixed, immovable, inflexible, rigid, stiff, tough, unyielding ≠ **adaptable:** absolute, inflexible ≠ **compliant:** determined, inexorable, inflexible, intractable, obdurate, staunch, unyielding

flick[1] *vb* **1** = **strike**, dab, fillip, flip, hit, jab, peck, rap, tap, touch **4** *foll. by* **through** = **browse**, flip through, glance at, skim, skip, thumb ◆ *n* **5** = **tap**, fillip, flip, jab, peck, rap, touch

flicker[1] *vb* **1** = **twinkle**, flare, flash, glimmer, gutter, shimmer, sparkle **2** = **flutter**, quiver, vibrate, waver ◆ *n* **4** = **glimmer**, flare, flash, gleam, spark

flickering *adj* **1** = **wavering**, fitful, guttering, twinkling, unsteady

flier *see* **flyer**

flight[1] *n* **1** = **flying**, mounting, soaring, winging **2** = **journey**, trip, voyage **4** = **flock**, cloud, formation, squadron, swarm, unit, wing

flight[2] *n* **1** = **escape**, departure, exit, exodus, fleeing, getaway, retreat, running away **2 put to flight** = **drive off**, chase off, disperse, rout, scare off, scatter, send packing, stampede **3 take (to) flight** = **run away** *or* **off**, abscond, beat a retreat, bolt, decamp, do a bunk *(Brit. sl.)*, do a runner *(sl.)*, fleet, skedaddle *(inf.)*, turn tail, withdraw hastily

flightiness *n* **1, 2** = **frivolity**, capriciousness, fickleness, flippancy, giddiness, irresponsibility, levity, lightness, mercurialness, volatility

flighty *adj* **1, 2** = **frivolous**, capricious, changeable, ditzy *or* ditsy *(sl.)*, dizzy, fickle, giddy, harebrained, impetuous, impulsive, irresponsible, light-headed, mercurial, scatterbrained, skittish, thoughtless, unbalanced, unstable, unsteady, volatile, wild

flimsy *adj* **1** = **fragile**, delicate, frail, gimcrack, insubstantial, makeshift, rickety, shaky, shallow, slight, superficial, unsubstantial **2** = **thin**, chiffon, gauzy, gossamer, light, sheer, transparent **3** = **unconvincing**, feeble, frivolous, implausible, inadequate, pathetic, poor, tenuous, thin, transparent, trivial, unsatisfactory, weak
Antonyms *adj* ≠ **fragile:** durable, heavy, robust, solid, sound, stout, strong, sturdy, substantial

flinch *vb* **1** = **recoil**, back off, baulk, blench, cower, cringe, draw back, duck, flee, quail, retreat, shirk, shrink, shy away, start, swerve, wince, withdraw

fling *vb* **1** = **throw**, cast, catapult, chuck *(inf.)*, heave, hurl, jerk, let fly, lob *(inf.)*, pitch, precipitate, propel, send, shy, sling, toss ◆ *n* **6** = **throw**, cast, lob, pitch, shot, toss **7** = **binge** *(inf.)*, bash, beano *(Brit. sl.)*, bit of fun, good time, hooley *or* hoolie *(chiefly Irish & NZ)*, indulgence, party, rave *(Brit. sl.)*, rave-up *(Brit. sl.)*, spree **9** = **try**, attempt, bash *(inf.)*, crack, gamble, go *(inf.)*, shot *(inf.)*, stab *(inf.)*, trial, venture, whirl *(inf.)*

reels full of leaps and turns, such as the Highland fling. **9** a trial; try: *to have a fling at something different.* [C13: from ON]
▸**'flinger** *n*

flint (flɪnt) *n* **1** an impure greyish-black form of quartz that occurs in chalk. It produces sparks when struck with steel and is used in the manufacture of pottery and road-construction materials. Formula: SiO_2. **2** any piece of flint, esp. one used as a primitive tool or for striking fire. **3** a small cylindrical piece of an iron alloy, used in cigarette lighters. **4** Also called: **flint glass.** colourless glass other than plate glass. [OE]

flintlock ('flɪnt,lɒk) *n* **1** an obsolete gunlock in which the charge is ignited by a spark produced by a flint in the hammer. **2** a firearm having such a lock.

flinty ❶ ('flɪntɪ) *adj* **flintier, flintiest. 1** of or resembling flint. **2** hard or cruel; unyielding.
▸**'flintily** *adv* ▸**'flintiness** *n*

flip ❶ (flɪp) *vb* **flips, flipping, flipped. 1** to throw (something light or small) carelessly or briskly. **2** to throw or flick (an object such as a coin) so that it turns or spins in the air. **3** to flick: *to flip a crumb across the room.* **4** (foll. by *through*) to read or look at (a book, etc.) quickly, idly, or incompletely. **5** (*intr*) to make a snapping movement or noise with the finger and thumb. **6** (*intr*) *Sl.* to fly into a rage or an emotional outburst (also in **flip one's lid, flip one's top, flip out**). ◆ *n* **7** a snap or tap, usually with the fingers. **8** a rapid jerk. **9** any alcoholic drink containing beaten egg. ◆ *adj* **10** *Inf.* flippant or pert. [C16: prob. imit.; see FILLIP]

flip chart *n* a pad, containing large sheets of paper that can be easily turned over, mounted on a stand and used to present reports, data, etc.

flip-flop *n* **1** a backward handspring. **2** Also called: **bistable.** an electronic device or circuit that can assume either of two states by the application of a suitable pulse. **3** a complete change of opinion, policy, etc. **4** a repeated flapping noise. **5** Also called (esp. US, Austral., NZ, and Canad.): **thong** or (S. Afr.) **slip-slop.** a rubber-soled sandal attached to the foot by a thong between the big toe and the next toe. ◆ *vb* **flip-flops, flip-flopping, flip-flopped. 6** (*intr*) to move with repeated flaps. [C16: reduplication of FLIP]

flippant ❶ ('flɪpənt) *adj* **1** marked by inappropriate levity; frivolous. **2** impertinent; saucy. [C17: ?from FLIP]
▸**'flippancy** *n* ▸**'flippantly** *adv*

flipper ('flɪpə) *n* **1** the flat broad limb of seals, whales, etc., specialized for swimming. **2** (*often pl*) either of a pair of rubber paddle-like devices worn on the feet as an aid in swimming.

flip side *n* **1** another term for **B-side. 2** another, less familiar, aspect of a person or thing.

flirt ❶ (flɜːt) *vb* **1** (*intr*) to behave or act amorously without emotional commitment. **2** (*intr; usually foll. by with*) to deal playfully or carelessly (with something dangerous or serious): *the motorcyclist flirted with death.* **3** (*intr; usually foll. by with*) to toy (with): *to flirt with the idea of leaving.* **4** (*intr*) to dart; flit. **5** (*tr*) to flick or toss. ◆ *n* **6** a person who acts flirtatiously. [C16: from ?]
▸**'flirter** *n* ▸**'flirty** *adj*

flirtation ❶ (flɜː'teɪʃən) *n* **1** behaviour intended to arouse sexual feelings or advances without emotional commitment. **2** any casual involvement.

flirtatious ❶ (flɜː'teɪʃəs) *adj* **1** given to flirtation. **2** expressive of playful sexual invitation: *a flirtatious glance.*
▸**flir'tatiously** *adv*

flit ❶ (flɪt) *vb* **flits, flitting, flitted.** (*intr*) **1** to move along rapidly and lightly. **2** to fly rapidly and lightly. **3** to pass quickly: *a memory flitted into his mind.* **4** *Scot. & N English dialect.* to move house. **5** *Brit. inf.* to depart hurriedly and stealthily in order to avoid obligations. ◆ *n* **6** the act or an instance of flitting. **7** *Brit. inf.* a hurried and stealthy departure in order to avoid obligations. [C12: from ON *flytja* to carry]
▸**'flitter** *n*

flitch (flɪtʃ) *n* **1** a side of pork salted and cured. **2** a piece of timber cut lengthways from a tree trunk. [OE *flicce;* cf. FLESH]

flitter ('flɪtə) *vb* a less common word for **flutter.**

flittermouse ('flɪtə,maʊs) *n, pl* **flittermice.** a dialect name for **bat**[2] (sense 1). [C16: translation of G *Fledermaus*]

float ❶ (fləʊt) *vb* **1** to rest or cause to rest on the surface of a fluid or in a fluid or space without sinking: *oil floats on water.* **2** to move or cause to move buoyantly, lightly, or freely across a surface or through air, water, etc. **3** to move about aimlessly, esp. in the mind: *thoughts floated before him.* **4** (*tr*) **4a** to launch or establish (a commercial enterprise, etc.). **4b** to offer for sale (stock or bond issues, etc.) on the stock market. **5** (*tr*) *Finance.* to allow (a currency) to fluctuate against other currencies in accordance with market forces. **6** (*tr*) to flood, inundate, or irrigate (land). ◆ *n* **7** something that floats. **8** *Angling.* an indicator attached to a baited line that sits on the water and moves when a fish bites. **9** a small hand tool with a rectangular blade used for smoothing plaster, etc. **10** Also called: **paddle.** a blade of a paddle wheel. **11** *Brit.* a buoyant garment or device to aid a person in staying afloat. **12** a structure fitted to the underside of an aircraft to allow it to land on water. **13** a motor vehicle used to carry a tableau or exhibit in a parade, esp. a civic parade. **14** a small delivery vehicle, esp. one powered by batteries: *a milk float.* **15** *Austral. & NZ.* a vehicle for transporting horses. **16** a sum of money used by shopkeepers to provide change at the start of the day's business. **17** the hollow floating ball of a ballcock. [OE *flotian;* see FLEET[2]]
▸**'floatable** *adj* ▸**,floata'bility** *n* ▸**'floaty** *adj*

floatage ('fləʊtɪdʒ) *n* a variant spelling of **flotage.**

floatation (fləʊ'teɪʃən) *n* a variant spelling of **flotation.**

floatel (fləʊ'tɛl) *n* a variant spelling of **flotel.**

floater ('fləʊtə) *n* **1** a person or thing that floats. **2** a dark spot that appears in one's vision as a result of dead cells or cell fragments in the eye. **3** *US & Canad.* a person of no fixed political opinion. **4** *US inf.* a person who often changes employment, residence, etc.

float glass *n* polished glass made by floating molten glass on liquid metal in a reservoir.

floating ❶ ('fləʊtɪŋ) *adj* **1** having little or no attachment. **2** (of an organ or part) displaced from the normal position or abnormally movable: *a floating kidney.* **3** uncommitted or unfixed: *floating voters.* **4** *Finance.* **4a** (of capital) available for current use. **4b** (of debt) short-term and unfunded, usually raised to meet current expenses. **4c** (of a currency) free to fluctuate against other currencies in accordance with market forces.
▸**'floatingly** *adv*

floating-point representation *n Computing.* the representation of numbers by two sets of digits (*a, b*), the set *a* indicating the significant digits, the set *b* giving the position of the radix point. Also called: **floating decimal point representation.** Cf. **fixed-point representation.**

floating rib *n* any rib of the lower two pairs of ribs in man, which are not attached to the breastbone.

floats (fləʊts) *pl n Theatre.* another word for **footlights.**

flob (flɒb) *vb* **flobs, flobbing, flobbed.** (*intr*) *Brit. sl.* to spit. [C20: from?]

flocculate ('flɒkjʊ,leɪt) *vb* **flocculates, flocculating, flocculated.** to form or be formed into an aggregated flocculent mass.
▸**,floccu'lation** *n*

flocculent ('flɒkjʊlənt) *adj* **1** like wool; fleecy. **2** *Chem.* aggregated in woolly cloudlike masses: *a flocculent precipitate.* **3** *Biol.* covered with tufts or flakes. [C19: from L *floccus* FLOCK[2] + -ULENT]
▸**'flocculence** *n*

flocculus ('flɒkjʊləs) *n, pl* **flocculi** (-,laɪ). **1** Also called: **plage.** a cloudy marking on the sun's surface. It consists of calcium when lighter than the surroundings and of hydrogen when darker. **2** *Anat.* a tiny prominence on each side of the cerebellum.

flock[1] ❶ (flɒk) *n* (*sometimes functioning as pl*) **1** a group of animals of one kind, esp. sheep or birds. **2** a large number of people. **3** a body of Christians regarded as the pastoral charge of a priest, bishop, etc. ◆ *vb* (*intr*) **4** to gather together or move in a flock. **5** to go in large numbers: *people flocked to the church.* [OE *flocc*]

flock[2] (flɒk) *n* **1** a tuft, as of wool, hair, cotton, etc. **2** waste from fabrics such as cotton or wool used for stuffing mattresses, etc. **3** Also called: **flocking.** very small tufts of wool applied to fabrics, wallpaper, etc., to give a raised pattern. [C13: from OF *floc,* from L *floccus*]
▸**'flocky** *adj*

floe (fləʊ) *n* See **ice floe.** [C19: prob. from Norwegian *flo* slab, layer, from ON; see FLAW[1]]

flog ❶ (flɒg) *vb* **flogs, flogging, flogged. 1** (*tr*) to beat harshly, esp. with a whip, strap, etc. **2** *Brit. sl.* to sell. **3** (*intr*) to make progress by painful work. **4 flog a dead horse.** *Chiefly Brit.* **4a** to harp on some long discarded subject. **4b** to pursue the solution of a problem long realized to be insoluble. [C17: prob. from L *flagellāre;* see FLAGELLANT]
▸**'flogger** *n*

THESAURUS

flinty *adj* **2** = **hard,** adamant, cruel, hard-hearted, harsh, heartless, inflexible, obdurate, pitiless, steely, stern, stony, unfeeling, unmerciful, unyielding

flip *vb, n* **1-3, 8** = **toss,** cast, flick, jerk, pitch, snap, spin, throw, twist

flippancy *n* **1, 2** = **frivolity,** cheek (*inf.*), cheekiness, disrespectfulness, impertinence, irreverence, levity, pertness, sauciness

flippant *adj* **1, 2** = **frivolous,** cheeky, disrespectful, flip (*inf.*), glib, impertinent, impudent, irreverent, offhand, pert, rude, saucy, superficial
Antonyms *adj* gracious, mannerly, polite, respectful, serious, sincere, solicitous, well-mannered

flirt *vb* **1** = **chat up** (*inf.*), coquet, dally, lead on, make advances, make eyes at, make sheep's eyes at, philander **2, 3** *usually foll. by* **with** = **toy with,** consider, dabble in, entertain, expose oneself to, give a thought to, play with, trifle with ◆ *n* **6** = **tease,** coquette, heart-breaker, philanderer, trifler, wanton

flirtation *n* **1** = **teasing,** coquetry, dalliance, intrigue, philandering, toying, trifling

flirtatious *adj* **1, 2** = **teasing,** amorous, arch, come-hither, come-on (*inf.*), coquettish, coy, enticing, flirty, provocative, sportive

flit *vb* **1-3** = **fly,** dart, flash, fleet, flutter, pass, skim, speed, whisk, wing

float *vb* **1, 2** = **be buoyant,** be *or* lie on the surface, displace water, hang, hover, poise, rest on water, stay afloat **2** = **glide,** bob, drift, move gently, sail, slide, slip along **4** = **launch,** get going, promote, push off, set up
Antonyms *vb* ≠ **be buoyant:** dip, drown, founder, go down, settle, sink, submerge ≠ **launch:** abolish, annul, cancel, dissolve, terminate

floating *adj* **3** = **free,** fluctuating, migratory, movable, unattached, uncommitted, unfixed, variable, wandering

flock[1] *n* **1** = **herd,** colony, drove, flight, gaggle, skein **2** = **crowd,** assembly, bevy, collection, company, congregation, convoy, gathering, group, herd, host, mass, multitude, throng ◆ *vb* **4** = **gather,** collect, congregate, converge, crowd, group, herd, huddle, mass, throng, troop

flog *vb* **1** = **beat,** castigate, chastise, flagellate, flay, lambast(e), lash, scourge, thrash, trounce, whack, whip **3** = **strain,** drive, oppress, overexert, overtax, overwork, punish, push, tax

flogging *n* **1** = **beating,** caning, flagellation,

flong (flɒŋ) *n Printing.* a material used for making moulds in stereotyping. [C20: var. of FLAN]

flood ⓣ (flʌd) *n* **1a** the inundation of land that is normally dry through the overflowing of a body of water, esp. a river. **1b** the state of a river that is at an abnormally high level. Related adj: **diluvial. 2** a great outpouring or flow: *a flood of words.* **3a** the rising of the tide from low to high water. **3b** (*as modifier*): *the flood tide.* Cf. **ebb** (sense 3). **4** *Theatre.* short for **floodlight.** ◆ *vb* **5** (of water) to inundate or submerge (land) or (of land) to be inundated or submerged. **6** to fill or be filled to overflowing, as with a flood. **7** (*intr*) to flow; surge: *relief flooded through him.* **8** to supply an excessive quantity of petrol to (a carburettor or petrol engine) or (of a carburettor, etc.) to be supplied with such an excess. **9** (*intr*) to overflow. **10** (*intr*) to bleed profusely from the uterus, as following childbirth. [OE *flōd;* see FLOW, FLOAT]

Flood (flʌd) *n Old Testament.* **the.** the flood from which Noah and his family and livestock were saved in the ark (Genesis 7–8).

floodgate (ˈflʌdˌɡeɪt) *n* **1** Also called: **head gate, water gate.** a gate in a sluice that is used to control the flow of water. **2** (*often pl*) a control or barrier against an outpouring or flow.

flooding (ˈflʌdɪŋ) *n* **1** *Psychol.* a method of eliminating anxiety in a given situation, by exposing a person to the situation until the anxiety subsides. **2** *Pathol.* excessive bleeding from the uterus.

floodlight (ˈflʌdˌlaɪt) *n* **1** a broad intense beam of artificial light, esp. as used in the theatre or to illuminate the exterior of buildings. **2** the lamp producing such light. ◆ *vb* **floodlights, floodlighting, floodlit. 3** (*tr*) to illuminate as by floodlight.

flood plain *n* the flat area bordering a river, composed of sediment deposited during flooding.

floor ⓣ (flɔː) *n* **1** Also called: **flooring.** the inner lower surface of a room. **2** a storey of a building: *the second floor.* **3** a flat bottom surface in or on any structure: *a dance floor.* **4** the bottom surface of a tunnel, cave, sea, etc. **5** that part of a legislative hall in which debate and other business is conducted. **6** the right to speak in a legislative body (esp. in **get, have,** *or* **be given the floor**). **7** the room in a stock exchange where trading takes place. **8** the earth; ground. **9** a minimum price charged or paid. **10 take the floor.** to begin dancing on a dance floor. ◆ *vb* **11** to cover with or construct a floor. **12** (*tr*) to knock to the floor or ground. **13** (*tr*) *Inf.* to disconcert, confound, or defeat. [OE *flōr*]

floorboard (ˈflɔːˌbɔːd) *n* one of the boards forming a floor.

flooring (ˈflɔːrɪŋ) *n* **1** the material used in making a floor. **2** another word for **floor** (sense 1).

floor manager *n* **1** the stage manager of a television programme. **2** a person in overall charge of one floor of a large shop.

floor plan *n* a drawing to scale of the arrangement of rooms on one floor of a building.

floor show *n* a series of entertainments, such as singing and dancing, performed in a nightclub.

floozy, floozie, *or* **floosie** (ˈfluːzɪ) *n, pl* **floozies** *or* **floosies.** *Sl.* a disreputable woman. [C20: from ?]

flop ⓣ (flɒp) *vb* **flops, flopping, flopped. 1** (*intr*) to bend, fall, or collapse loosely or carelessly: *his head flopped backwards.* **2** (when *intr,* often foll. by *into, onto,* etc.) to fall, cause to fall, or move with a sudden noise. **3** (*intr*) *Inf.* to fail: *the scheme flopped.* **4** (*intr*) to fall flat onto the surface of water. **5** (*intr;* often foll. by *out*) *Sl.* to go to sleep. ◆ *n* **6** the act of flopping. **7** *Inf.* a complete failure. [C17: var. of FLAP]

floppy ⓣ (ˈflɒpɪ) *adj* **floppier, floppiest. 1** limp or hanging loosely. ◆ *n, pl* **floppies. 2** short for **floppy disk.**
▸ˈ**floppily** *adv* ▸ˈ**floppiness** *n*

floppy disk *n* a flexible magnetic disk that stores information and can be used to store data in the memory of a digital computer.

flops *abbrev.* (*sometimes caps.*) *for* floating-point operations per second: a measure of computer processing power.

flora (ˈflɔːrə) *n, pl* **floras** *or* **florae** (-riː). **1** all the plant life of a given place or time. **2** a descriptive list of such plants, often including a key for identification. [C18: from NL, from *Flōra* goddess of flowers, from *flōs* FLOWER]

floral ⓣ (ˈflɔːrəl) *adj* **1** decorated with or consisting of flowers or patterns of flowers. **2** of or associated with flowers.
▸ˈ**florally** *adv*

Florentine (ˈflɒrənˌtaɪn) *adj* **1** of or relating to Florence, in Italy. ◆ *n* **2** a native or inhabitant of Florence.

florescence ⓣ (flɔːˈresəns) *n* the process, state, or period of flowering. [C18: from NL, from L *flōrēscere* to come into flower]

floret (ˈflɔːrɪt) *n* a small flower, esp. one of many making up the head of a composite flower. [C17: from OF, from *flor* FLOWER]

floriated *or* **floreated** (ˈflɔːrɪˌeɪtɪd) *adj Archit.* having ornamentation based on flowers and leaves. [C19: from L *flōs* FLOWER]

floribunda (ˌflɔːrɪˈbʌndə) *n* any of several varieties of cultivated hybrid roses whose flowers grow in large sprays. [C19: from NL, fem of *flōribundus* flowering freely]

floriculture (ˈflɔːrɪˌkʌltʃə) *n* the cultivation of flowering plants.
▸ˌ**floriˈcultural** *adj* ▸ˌ**floriˈculturist** *n*

florid ⓣ (ˈflɒrɪd) *adj* **1** having a red or flushed complexion. **2** excessively ornate; flowery: *florid architecture.* [C17: from L *flōridus* blooming]
▸**floˈridity** *n* ▸ˈ**floridly** *adv*

floriferous (flɔːˈrɪfərəs) *adj* bearing or capable of bearing many flowers.

florin (ˈflɒrɪn) *n* **1** a former British coin, originally silver, equivalent to ten (new) pence. **2** (formerly) another name for **guilder** (sense 1). [C14: from F, from OIt. *fiorino* Florentine coin, from *fiore* flower, from L *flōs*]

florist (ˈflɒrɪst) *n* a person who grows or deals in flowers.

floristic (flɒˈrɪstɪk) *adj* of or relating to flowers or a flora.
▸**floˈristically** *adv*

-florous *adj combining form.* indicating number or type of flowers: *tubuliflorous.*

floruit *Latin.* (ˈflɒruːɪt) *vb* (he or she) flourished: used to indicate the period when a figure, whose birth and death dates are unknown, was most active.

floss (flɒs) *n* **1** the mass of fine silky fibres obtained from cotton and similar plants. **2** any similar fine silky material. **3** untwisted silk thread used in embroidery, etc. **4** See **dental floss.** ◆ *vb* **5** (*tr*) to clean (between one's teeth) with dental floss. [C18: ?from OF *flosche* down]

flossy ⓣ (ˈflɒsɪ) *adj* **flossier, flossiest.** consisting of or resembling floss.

flotage *or* **floatage** (ˈfləʊtɪdʒ) *n* **1** the act or state of floating. **2** power or ability to float. **3** flotsam.

flotation *or* **floatation** (fləʊˈteɪʃən) *n* **1a** the launching or financing of a commercial enterprise by bond or share issues. **1b** the raising of a loan or new capital by bond or share issues. **2** power or ability to float. **3** Also called: **froth flotation.** a process to concentrate the valuable ore in low-grade ores by using induced differences in surface tension to carry the valuable fraction to the surface.

flotel *or* **floatel** (fləʊˈtel) *n* a rig used for accommodation of workers in off-shore oil fields. [C20: FLO(ATING) + (HO)TEL]

flotilla (fləˈtɪlə) *n* a small fleet or a fleet of small vessels. [C18: from Sp., from F *flotte,* ult. from ON *floti*]

flotsam ⓣ (ˈflɒtsəm) *n* **1** wreckage from a ship found floating. Cf. **jetsam. 2** odds and ends (esp. in **flotsam and jetsam**). **3** vagrants. [C16: from Anglo-F *floteson,* from *floter* to FLOAT]

flounce[1] ⓣ (flaʊns) *vb* **flounces, flouncing, flounced. 1** (*intr;* often foll. by *about, away, out,* etc.) to move or go with emphatic movements. ◆ *n* **2** the act of flouncing. [C16: of Scand. origin]

flounce[2] (flaʊns) *n* an ornamental gathered ruffle sewn to a garment by its top edge. [C18: from OF, from *froncir* to wrinkle, of Gmc origin]

flounder[1] ⓣ (ˈflaʊndə) *vb* (*intr*) **1** to move with difficulty, as in mud. **2** to make mistakes. ◆ *n* **3** the act of floundering. [C16: prob. a blend of FOUNDER[2] + BLUNDER; ? infl. by FLOUNDER[2]]

> **USAGE NOTE** *Flounder* is sometimes wrongly used where *founder* is meant: *the project foundered* (not *floundered*) *because of lack of funds.*

flounder[2] (ˈflaʊndə) *n, pl* **flounder** *or* **flounders.** a European flatfish having a greyish-brown body covered with prickly scales: an important food fish. [C14: from ON]

flour (ˈflaʊə) *n* **1** a powder, which may be either fine or coarse, prepared by grinding the meal of a grass, esp. wheat. **2** any finely powdered substance. ◆ *vb* (*tr*) **3** to make (grain, etc.) into flour. **4** to dredge or

THESAURUS

hiding (*inf.*), horsewhipping, lashing, scourging, thrashing, trouncing, whipping

flood *n* **1, 3** = **deluge**, downpour, flash flood, freshet, inundation, overflow, spate, tide, torrent **2** = **torrent**, abundance, flow, glut, multitude, outpouring, profusion, rush, stream ◆ *vb* **5, 6** = **immerse**, brim over, deluge, drown, inundate, overflow, pour over, submerge, swamp, teem **7, 9** = **engulf**, flow, gush, overwhelm, rush, surge, swarm, sweep **8** = **oversupply**, choke, fill, glut, saturate

floor *n* **2** = **tier**, level, stage, storey ◆ *vb* **12** = **knock down**, deck (*sl.*), prostrate **13** *Informal* = **disconcert**, baffle, beat, bewilder, bowl over (*inf.*), confound, conquer, defeat, discomfit, dumbfound, faze, nonplus, overthrow, perplex, puzzle, stump, throw (*inf.*)

flop *vb* **1, 2** = **fall**, collapse, dangle, droop, drop, hang limply, sag, slump, topple, tumble **3** *Informal* = **fail**, bomb (*US & Canad. sl.*), close, come to nothing, come unstuck, fall flat, fall short, fold (*inf.*), founder, go belly-up (*sl.*), misfire ◆ *n* **7** *Informal* = **failure**, debacle, disaster, fiasco, loser, nonstarter, washout (*inf.*)
Antonyms *vb* ≠ **fail:** flourish, make a hit, make it (*inf.*), prosper, succeed, triumph, work ◆ *n* ≠ **failure:** hit, success, triumph

floppy *adj* **1** = **droopy**, baggy, flaccid, flapping, flip-flop, hanging, limp, loose, pendulous, sagging, soft

floral *adj* **1** = **flowery**, flower-patterned

florescence *n* = **flowering**, blooming, blossoming, development, flourishing, fruition, maturity

florid *adj* **1** = **flushed**, blowsy, high-coloured, high-complexioned, rubicund, ruddy **2** = **ornate**, baroque, busy, embellished, euphuistic, figurative, flamboyant, flowery, fussy, grandiloquent, high-flown, overelaborate
Antonyms *adj* ≠ **flushed:** anaemic, bloodless, pale, pallid, pasty, wan, washed out ≠ **ornate:** bare, dull, plain, unadorned

flossy *adj* = **fluffy**, downy, feathery, satiny, silky, soft

flotsam *n* **1, 2** = **debris**, detritus, jetsam, junk, odds and ends, sweepings, wreckage

flounce[1] *vb* **1** = **bounce**, fling, jerk, spring, stamp, storm, throw, toss

flounder[1] *vb* **1** = **struggle**, blunder, fumble, grope, muddle, plunge, stumble, thrash, toss, tumble, wallow

sprinkle (food or utensils) with flour. [C13 *flur* finer portion of meal, FLOWER]
▸ 'floury *adj*

flourish ➊ ('flʌrɪʃ) *vb* **1** (*intr*) to thrive; prosper. **2** (*intr*) to be at the peak of condition. **3** (*intr*) to be healthy: *plants flourish in the light.* **4** to wave or cause to wave in the air with sweeping strokes. **5** to display or make a display. **6** to play (a fanfare, etc.) on a musical intrument. ◆ *n* **7** the act of waving or brandishing. **8** a showy gesture: *he entered with a flourish.* **9** an ornamental embellishment in writing. **10** a display of ornamental language or speech. **11** a grandiose passage of music. [C13: from OF, ult. from L *flōrēre* to flower, from *flōs* a flower]
▸ '**flourisher** *n*

flout ➊ (flaʊt) *vb* (when *intr*, usually foll. by *at*) to show contempt (for). [C16: ?from ME *flouten* to play the flute, from OF *flauter*]
▸ '**floutingly** *adv*

USAGE NOTE See at **flaunt.**

flow ➊ (fləʊ) *vb* (*mainly intr*) **1** (of liquids) to move or be conveyed as in a stream. **2** (of blood) to circulate around the body. **3** to move or progress freely as if in a stream: *the crowd flowed into the building.* **4** to be produced continuously and effortlessly: *ideas flowed from her pen.* **5** to be marked by smooth or easy movement. **6** to hang freely or loosely: *her hair flowed down her back.* **7** to be present in abundance: *wine flows at their parties.* **8** (of tide water) to advance or rise. Cf. **ebb** (sense 1). **9** (of rocks such as slate) to yield to pressure so that the structure and arrangement of the constituent minerals are altered. ◆ *n* **10** the act, rate, or manner of flowing: *a fast flow.* **11** a continuous stream or discharge. **12** continuous progression. **13** the advancing of the tide. **14** *Scot.* **14a** a marsh or swamp. **14b** an inlet or basin of the sea. **14c** (*cap. when part of a name*): *Scapa Flow.* [OE *flōwan*]

flow chart *or* **sheet** *n* a diagrammatic representation of the sequence of operations in an industrial process, computer program, etc.

flower ➊ ('flaʊə) *n* **1a** a bloom or blossom on a plant. **1b** a plant that bears blooms or blossoms. **2** the reproductive structure of angiosperm plants, consisting of stamens and carpels surrounded by petals and sepals. In some plants it is brightly coloured and attracts insects for pollination. Related adj: **floral. 3** any similar reproductive structure in other plants. **4** the prime; peak: *in the flower of his youth.* **5** the choice or finest product, part, or representative. **6** a decoration or embellishment. **7** (*pl*) fine powder, usually produced by sublimation: *flowers of sulphur.* ◆ *vb* **8** (*intr*) to produce flowers; bloom. **9** (*intr*) to reach full growth or maturity. **10** (*tr*) to deck or decorate with flowers or floral designs. [C13: from OF *flor*, from L *flōs*]
▸ '**flowerless** *adj* ▸ '**flower-,like** *adj*

flowered ('flaʊəd) *adj* **1** having flowers. **2** decorated with flowers or a floral design.

floweret ('flaʊərɪt) *n* another name for **floret.**

flower girl *n* a girl or woman who sells flowers in the street.

flowering ➊ ('flaʊərɪŋ) *adj* (of certain species of plants) capable of producing conspicuous flowers.

flowerpot ('flaʊə,pɒt) *n* a pot in which plants are grown.

flower power *n Inf.* a youth cult of the late 1960s advocating peace and love; associated with drug-taking. Its adherents were known as **flower children** or **flower people.**

flowery ➊ ('flaʊərɪ) *adj* **1** abounding in flowers. **2** decorated with flowers or floral patterns. **3** like or suggestive of flowers. **4** (of language or style) elaborate.
▸ '**floweriness** *n*

flown (fləʊn) *vb* the past participle of **fly**[1].

flow-on *n Austral. & NZ.* **a** a wage or salary increase granted to one group of workers as a consequence of a similar increase granted to another group. **b** (*as modifier*): *a flow-on effect.*

fl. oz. *abbrev. for* fluid ounce.

flu (flu:) *n Inf.* **1** (often preceded by *the*) short for **influenza. 2** any of various viral infections, esp. a respiratory or intestinal infection.

fluctuate ➊ ('flʌktjʊ,eɪt) *vb* **fluctuates, fluctuating, fluctuated. 1** to change or cause to change position constantly. **2** (*intr*) to rise and fall like a wave. [C17: from L, from *fluctus* a wave, from *fluere* to flow]
▸ '**fluctuant** *adj* ▸ ,**fluctu'ation** *n*

flue (flu:) *n* a shaft, tube, or pipe, esp. as used in a chimney, to carry off smoke, gas, etc. [C16: from ?]

fluent ➊ ('flu:ənt) *adj* **1** able to speak or write a specified foreign language with facility. **2** spoken or written with facility. **3** graceful in motion or shape. **4** flowing or able to flow freely. [C16: from L: flowing, from *fluere* to flow]
▸ '**fluency** *n* ▸ '**fluently** *adv*

flue pipe *or* **flue** *n* an organ pipe whose sound is produced by the passage of air across a fissure in the side, as distinguished from a **reed pipe.**

fluff ➊ (flʌf) *n* **1** soft light particles, such as the down or nap of cotton or wool. **2** any light downy substance. **3** *Inf.* a mistake, esp. in speaking or reading lines or performing music. **4** *Inf.* a young woman (esp. in **a bit of fluff**). ◆ *vb* **5** to make or become soft and puffy. **6** *Inf.* to make a mistake in performing (an action, music, etc.). [C18: ?from *flue* downy matter]

fluffy ➊ ('flʌfɪ) *adj* **fluffier, fluffiest. 1** of, resembling, or covered with fluff. **2** soft and light.
▸ '**fluffily** *adv* ▸ '**fluffiness** *n*

flugelhorn ('flu:gəl,hɔ:n) *n* a type of valved brass instrument consisting of a tube of conical bore with a cup-shaped mouthpiece, used esp. in brass bands. [G, from *Flügel* wing + *Horn* HORN]

fluid ➊ ('flu:ɪd) *n* **1** a substance, such as a liquid or gas, that can flow, has no fixed shape, and offers little resistance to an external stress. ◆ *adj* **2** capable of flowing and easily changing shape. **3** of or using a fluid or fluids. **4** constantly changing or apt to change. **5** flowing. [C15: from L, from *fluere* to flow]
▸ '**fluidal** *adj* ▸**flu'idity** *or* '**fluidness** *n*

fluidics (flu:'ɪdɪks) *n* (*functioning as sing*) the study and use of systems in which the flow of fluids in tubes simulates the flow of electricity in conductors.
▸**flu'idic** *adj*

fluidize *or* **fluidise** ('flu:ɪ,daɪz) *vb* **fluidizes, fluidizing, fluidized** *or* **fluidises, fluidising, fluidised.** (*tr*) to make fluid, esp. to make (solids) fluid by pulverizing them so that they can be transported in gas as if they were liquids.
▸ ,**fluidi'zation** *or* ,**fluidi'sation** *n*

fluid mechanics *n* (*functioning as sing*) the study of the mechanical and flow properties of fluids, esp. as they apply to practical engineering. Also called: **hydraulics.**

fluid ounce *n* **1** *Brit.* a unit of capacity equal to one twentieth of an Imperial pint. **2** *US.* a unit of capacity equal to one sixteenth of a US pint.

fluke[1] (flu:k) *n* **1** a flat bladelike projection at the end of the arm of an anchor. **2** either of the two lobes of the tail of a whale. **3** the barb of a harpoon, arrow, etc. [C16: ? a special use of FLUKE[3] (in the sense: a flounder)]

fluke[2] ➊ (flu:k) *n* **1** an accidental stroke of luck. **2** any chance happening. ◆ *vb* **flukes, fluking, fluked. 3** (*tr*) to gain, make, or hit by a fluke. [C19: from ?]

THESAURUS

flourish *vb* **1** = **thrive**, bear fruit, be in one's prime, be successful, be vigorous, bloom, blossom, boom, burgeon, develop, do well, flower, get ahead, get on, go great guns (*sl.*), go up in the world, grow, grow fat, increase, prosper, succeed **4, 5** = **wave**, brandish, display, flaunt, flutter, shake, sweep, swing, swish, twirl, vaunt, wag, wield ◆ *n* **7, 8** = **wave**, brandishing, dash, display, fanfare, parade, shaking, show, showy gesture, twirling **9** = **ornamentation**, curlicue, decoration, embellishment, plume, sweep
Antonyms *vb* ≠ **thrive:** decline, diminish, dwindle, fade, fail, grow less, pine, shrink, wane

flourishing *adj* **1** = **successful**, blooming, burgeoning, doing well, going places, going strong, in the pink, in top form, lush, luxuriant, mushrooming, on a roll, on the up and up (*inf.*), prospering, rampant, thriving

flout *vb* = **defy**, deride, gibe at, insult, jeer at, laugh in the face of, mock, outrage, ridicule, scoff at, scorn, show contempt for, sneer at, spurn, taunt, treat with disdain
Antonyms *vb* attend, esteem, heed, honour, mind, note, pay attention to, regard, respect, revere, value

flow *vb* **1, 5** = **run**, circulate, course, glide, move, purl, ripple, roll, slide **3, 7** = **pour**, cascade, deluge, flood, gush, inundate, issue, overflow, run, run out, rush, spew, spill, spurt, squirt, stream, surge, sweep, swirl, teem, well forth, whirl **4** = **issue**, arise, emanate, emerge, pour, proceed, result, spring ◆ *n* **10** = **stream**, course, current, drift, flood, flux, gush, issue, outflow, outpouring, spate, tide, tideway, undertow **11** = **outpouring**, abundance, deluge, effusion, emanation, outflow, plenty, plethora, succession, train

flower *n* **1** = **bloom**, blossom, efflorescence **4, 5** = **elite**, best, choicest part, cream, *crème de la crème*, freshness, greatest *or* finest point, height, pick, vigour ◆ *vb* **8, 9** = **bloom**, blossom, blow, burgeon, effloresce, flourish, mature, open, unfold

flowering *adj* = **blooming**, abloom, blossoming, in bloom, in blossom, in flower, open, out, ready

flowery *adj* **4** = **ornate**, baroque, embellished, euphuistic, fancy, figurative, florid, high-flown, overwrought, rhetorical
Antonyms *adj* austere, bare, basic, modest, muted, plain, restrained, simple, spartan, unadorned, unembellished

fluctuate *vb* **1, 2** = **change**, alter, alternate, ebb and flow, go up and down, hesitate, oscillate, rise and fall, seesaw, shift, swing, undulate, vacillate, vary, veer, waver

fluctuation *n* **1, 2** = **change**, alternation, fickleness, inconstancy, instability, oscillation, shift, swing, unsteadiness, vacillation, variation, wavering

fluency *n* **1, 2** = **ease**, articulateness, assurance, command, control, facility, glibness, readiness, slickness, smoothness, volubility

fluent *adj* **1, 2** = **effortless**, articulate, easy, facile, flowing, glib, natural, ready, smooth, smooth-spoken, voluble, well-versed
Antonyms *adj* faltering, halting, hesitant, hesitating, inarticulate, stammering, stumbling, tongue-tied

fluff *n* **1, 2** = **fuzz**, down, dust, dustball, lint, nap, oose (*Scot.*), pile ◆ *vb* **6** *Informal* = **mess up** (*inf.*), bungle, foul up (*inf.*), make a mess off, make a nonsense of, muddle, screw up (*inf.*), spoil

fluffy *adj* **1** = **soft**, downy, feathery, fleecy, flossy, fuzzy, gossamer, silky

fluid *n* **1** = **liquid**, liquor, solution ◆ *adj* **2, 5** = **liquid**, aqueous, flowing, in solution, liquefied, melted, molten, running, runny, watery **4** = **changeable**, adaptable, adjustable, flexible, floating, fluctuating, indefinite, mercurial, mobile, mutable, protean, shifting
Antonyms *adj* ≠ **liquid:** firm, hard, rigid, set, solid ≠ **changeable:** definite, firm, fixed, immobile, immutable

fluke[2] *n* **1, 2** = **stroke of luck**, accident, blessing, break, chance, chance occurrence, coinci-

fluke[3] (flu:k) *n* any parasitic flatworm, such as the blood fluke and liver fluke. [OE *flōc;* rel. to ON *flōki* flounder]

fluky ❶ *or* **flukey** ('flu:kɪ) *adj* **flukier, flukiest.** *Inf.* **1** done or gained by an accident, esp. a lucky one. **2** variable; uncertain.
► **'flukiness** *n*

flume (flu:m) *n* **1** a ravine through which a stream flows. **2** a narrow artificial channel made for providing water for power, floating logs, etc. **3** a slide in the form of a long and winding tube with a stream of water running through it that descends into a purpose-built pool. ◆ *vb* **flumes, fluming, flumed. 4** (*tr*) to transport (logs) in a flume. [C12: from OF, ult. from L *flūmen* stream, from *fluere* to flow]

flummery ('flʌmərɪ) *n, pl* **flummeries. 1** *Inf.* meaningless flattery. **2** *Chiefly Brit.* a cold pudding of oatmeal, etc. [C17: from Welsh *llymru*]

flummox ❶ ('flʌməks) *vb* (*tr*) to perplex or bewilder. [C19: from ?]

flung (flʌŋ) *vb* the past tense and past participle of **fling.**

flunk ❶ (flʌŋk) *vb Inf., US, Canad., & NZ.* **1** to fail or cause to fail to reach the required standard in (an examination, course, etc.). **2** (*intr;* foll. by *out*) to be dismissed from a school. [C19: ?from FLINCH + FUNK[1]]

flunky ❶ *or* **flunkey** ('flʌŋkɪ) *n, pl* **flunkies** *or* **flunkeys. 1** a servile person. **2** a person who performs menial tasks. **3** *Usually derog.* a manservant in livery. [C18: from ?]

fluor ('flu:ɔ:) *n* another name for **fluorspar.** [C17: from L: a flowing; so called from its use as a metallurgical flux]

fluor- *combining form.* a variant of **fluoro-** before a vowel: *fluorine.*

fluoresce (ˌfluə'rɛs) *vb* **fluoresces, fluorescing, fluoresced.** (*intr*) to exhibit fluorescence. [C19: back formation from FLUORESCENCE]

fluorescence (ˌfluə'rɛsəns) *n* **1** *Physics.* **1a** the emission of light or other radiation from atoms or molecules that are bombarded by particles, such as electrons, or by radiation from a separate source. **1b** such an emission of photons that ceases as soon as the bombarding radiation is discontinued. **2** the radiation emitted as a result of fluorescence. Cf. **phosphorescence.** [C19: FLUOR + *-escence* (as in *opalescence*)]
► ˌ**fluo'rescent** *adj*

fluorescent lamp *n* a type of lamp in which ultraviolet radiation from an electrical gas discharge causes a thin layer of phosphor on a tube's inside surface to fluoresce.

fluoridate ('fluərɪˌdeɪt) *vb* **fluoridates, fluoridating, fluoridated.** to subject (water) to fluoridation.

fluoridation (ˌfluərɪ'deɪʃən) *n* the addition of fluorides to the public water supply as a protection against tooth decay.

fluoride ('fluəˌraɪd) *n* **1** any salt of hydrofluoric acid, containing the fluoride ion, F^-. **2** any compound containing fluorine, such as methyl fluoride.

fluorinate ('fluərɪˌneɪt) *vb* **fluorinates, fluorinating, fluorinated.** to treat or combine with fluorine.
► ˌ**fluori'nation** *n*

fluorine ('fluəri:n) *n* a toxic pungent pale yellow gas of the halogen group that is the most electronegative and reactive of all the elements: used in the production of uranium, fluorocarbons, and other chemicals. Symbol: F; atomic no.: 9; atomic wt.: 18.998.

fluorite ('fluəraɪt) *n* the US and Canad. name for **fluorspar.**

fluoro- *or before a vowel* **fluor-** *combining form.* **1** indicating the presence of fluorine: *fluorocarbon.* **2** indicating fluorescence: *fluoroscope.*

fluorocarbon (ˌfluərəʊ'kɑ:bᵊn) *n* any compound derived by replacing all or some of the hydrogen atoms in hydrocarbons by fluorine atoms. Many of them are used as lubricants, solvents, coatings, and aerosol propellants. See also **Freon, CFC.**

fluorometer (ˌfluə'rɒmɪtə) *or* **fluorimeter** (ˌfluə'rɪmɪtə) *n* a device for detecting and measuring ultraviolet radiation by determining the amount of fluorescence that it produces from a phosphor.

fluoroscope ('fluərəˌskəʊp) *n* a device consisting of a fluorescent screen and an X-ray source that enables an X-ray image of an object, person, or part to be observed directly.

fluoroscopy (fluə'rɒskəpɪ) *n* examination of a person or object by means of a fluoroscope.

fluorosis (fluə'rəʊsɪs) *n* fluoride poisoning, due to ingestion of too much fluoride.

fluorspar ('fluəˌspɑ:), **fluor,** *or US & Canad.* **fluorite** *n* a white or colourless soft mineral, sometimes fluorescent or tinted by impurities, consisting of calcium fluoride (CaF) in crystalline form: the chief ore of fluorine.

flurry ❶ ('flʌrɪ) *n, pl* **flurries. 1** a sudden commotion. **2** a light gust of wind or rain or fall of snow. ◆ *vb* **flurries, flurrying, flurried. 3** to confuse or bewilder or be confused or bewildered. [C17: from obs. *flurr* to scatter, ? formed on analogy with HURRY]

flush[1] ❶ (flʌʃ) *vb* **1** to blush or cause to blush. **2** to flow or flood or cause to flow or flood with or as if with water. **3** to glow or shine or cause to glow or shine with a rosy colour. **4** to send a volume of water quickly through (a pipe, etc.) or into (a toilet) for the purpose of cleansing, etc. **5** (*tr; usually passive*) to excite or elate. ◆ *n* **6** a rosy colour, esp. in the cheeks. **7** a sudden flow or gush, as of water. **8** a feeling of excitement or elation: *the flush of success.* **9** freshness: *the flush of youth.* **10** redness of the skin, as from the effects of a fever, alcohol, etc. [C16: (in the sense: to gush forth): ?from FLUSH[3]]
► **'flusher** *n*

flush[2] ❶ (flʌʃ) *adj* (*usually postpositive*) **1** level or even with another surface. **2** directly adjacent; continuous. **3** *Inf.* having plenty of money. **4** *Inf.* abundant or plentiful, as money. **5** full to the brim. ◆ *adv* **6** so as to be level or even. **7** directly or squarely. ◆ *vb* (*tr*) **8** to cause (surfaces) to be on the same level or in the same plane. ◆ *n* **9** a period of fresh growth of leaves, shoots, etc. [C18: prob. from FLUSH[1] (in the sense: spring out)]
► **'flushness** *n*

flush[3] ❶ (flʌʃ) *vb* (*tr*) to rouse (game, etc.) and put to flight. [C13 *flusshen,* ? imit.]

flush[4] (flʌʃ) *n* (in poker and similar games) a hand containing only one suit. [C16: from OF, from L *fluxus* FLUX]

fluster ❶ ('flʌstə) *vb* **1** to make or become nervous or upset. ◆ *n* **2** a state of confusion or agitation. [C15: from ON]

flute (flu:t) *n* **1** a wind instrument consisting of an open cylindrical tube of wood or metal having holes in the side stopped either by the fingers or by pads controlled by keys. The breath is directed across a mouth hole cut in the side. **2** *Archit.* a rounded shallow concave groove on the shaft of a column, pilaster, etc. **3** a tall narrow wineglass. ◆ *vb* **flutes, fluting, fluted. 4** to produce or utter (sounds) in the manner or tone of a flute. **5** (*tr*) to make grooves or furrows in. [C14: from OF *flahute,* from Vulgar L *flabeolum* (unattested); ? also infl. by OF *laut* lute]
► **'fluteˌlike** *adj* ► **'fluty** *adj*

fluting ('flu:tɪŋ) *n* a design or decoration of flutes on a column, pilaster, etc.

flutist ('flu:tɪst) *n Now chiefly US & Canad.* a variant spelling of **flautist.**

flutter ❶ ('flʌtə) *vb* **1** to wave or cause to wave rapidly. **2** (*intr*) (of birds, butterflies, etc.) to flap the wings. **3** (*intr*) to move, esp. downwards, with an irregular motion. **4** (*intr*) *Pathol.* (of the heart) to beat abnormally rapidly, esp. in a regular rhythm. **5** to be or make nervous or restless. **6** (*intr*) to move about restlessly. ◆ *n* **7** a quick flapping or vibrating motion. **8** a state of nervous excitement or confusion. **9** excited interest; stir. **10** *Brit. inf.* a modest bet or wager. **11** *Pathol.* an abnormally rapid beating of the heart, esp. in a regular rhythm. **12** *Electronics.* a slow variation in pitch in a sound-reproducing system, similar to wow but occurring at higher frequencies. **13** a potentially dangerous oscillation of an aircraft, or part of an aircraft. **14** Also called: **flutter tonguing.** *Music.* a method of sounding a wind instrument, esp. the flute, with a rolling movement of the tongue. [OE *floterian* to float to and fro]
► **'flutterer** *n* ► **'fluttery** *adj*

THESAURUS

dence, fortuity, freak, lucky break, quirk, quirk of fate, serendipity, stroke, windfall

fluky *adj Informal* **1** = **lucky**, accidental, coincidental, fortuitous **2** = **uncertain**, at the mercy of events, chancy, incalculable, variable

flummox *vb* = **baffle**, bamboozle (*inf.*), bewilder, defeat, fox, mystify, nonplus, perplex, puzzle, stump, stymie

flummoxed *adj* = **baffled**, at a loss, at sea, bewildered, foxed, mystified, nonplussed, puzzled, stumped, stymied

flunk *Informal, U.S., Canad., & N.Z. vb* **1** = **fail**, be found lacking, be unsuccessful, bust, fall short, flop (*inf.*), founder, miss, not come up to scratch, not come up to the mark (*inf.*), not make the grade (*inf.*), underachieve, underperform, wash out **2** = **be expelled**, be dismissed, drop out (*inf.*), go down
Antonyms *vb* ≠ **fail:** be successful, come up to scratch (*inf.*), excel, get by *or* through, get pass marks, make it, make the grade, meet *or* satisfy requirements, pass, pass with flying colours, stand the test ≠ **be expelled:** graduate

flunky *n* **1, 2** = **minion**, assistant, cohort, drudge, hanger-on, menial, slave, toady, tool, underling, yes man **3** = **manservant**, footman, lackey, valet

flurry *n* **1** = **commotion**, ado, agitation, bustle, disturbance, excitement, ferment, flap, fluster, flutter, furore, fuss, hurry, stir, to-do, tumult, whirl **2** = **gust**, flaw, squall ◆ *vb* **3** = **confuse**, agitate, bewilder, bother, disconcert, disturb, faze, fluster, flutter, fuss, hassle (*inf.*), hurry, hustle, rattle (*inf.*), ruffle, unnerve, unsettle, upset

flush[1] *vb* **1** = **blush**, burn, colour, colour up, crimson, flame, glow, go as red as a beetroot, go red, redden, suffuse **2, 4** = **rinse out**, cleanse, douche, drench, eject, expel, flood, hose down, swab, syringe, wash out ◆ *n* **6, 10** = **blush**, bloom, colour, freshness, glow, redness, rosiness

flush[2] *adj* **1** = **level**, even, flat, plane, square, true **3** *Informal* = **wealthy**, in funds, in the money (*inf.*), moneyed, rich, rolling (*sl.*), well-heeled (*inf.*), well-off, well-supplied **4** *Informal* = **abundant**, affluent, full, generous, lavish, liberal, overflowing, prodigal ◆ *adv* **6, 7** = **level with**, even with, hard against, in contact with, squarely, touching

flush[3] *vb* = **drive out**, discover, disturb, put to flight, rouse, start, uncover

flushed *adj* **1** = **blushing**, burning, crimson, embarrassed, feverish, glowing, hot, red, rosy, rubicund, ruddy **5** *often foll. by* **with** = **exhilarated**, animated, aroused, elated, enthused, excited, high (*inf.*), inspired, intoxicated, thrilled

fluster *vb* **1** = **upset**, agitate, bother, bustle, confound, confuse, disturb, excite, flurry, hassle (*inf.*), heat, hurry, make nervous, perturb, rattle (*inf.*), ruffle, throw off balance, unnerve ◆ *n* **2** = **turmoil**, agitation, bustle, commotion, disturbance, dither (*chiefly Brit.*), flap (*inf.*), flurry, flutter, furore, perturbation, ruffle, state (*inf.*)

fluted *adj* **5** = **grooved**, channelled, corrugated, furrowed

flutter *vb* **1, 2, 4** = **beat**, agitate, bat, flap, flicker, flit, flitter, fluctuate, hover, palpitate, quiver, ripple, ruffle, shiver, tremble, vibrate, waver ◆ *n* **7, 11** = **vibration**, palpitation, quiver, quivering, shiver, shudder, tremble, tremor, twitching **8** = **agitation**, commotion, confusion, dither (*chiefly Brit.*), excitement, flurry, fluster, perturbation, state (*inf.*), state of nervous excitement, tremble, tumult

fluvial ('flu:vɪəl) *adj* of or occurring in a river: *fluvial deposits.* [C14: from L, from *fluvius* river, from *fluere* to flow]

flux 🅣 (flʌks) *n* **1** a flow or discharge. **2** continuous change; instability. **3** a substance, such as borax or salt, that gives a low melting-point mixture with a metal oxide to assist in fusion. **4** *Metallurgy.* a chemical used to increase the fluidity of refining slags. **5** *Physics.* **5a** the rate of flow of particles, energy, or a fluid, such as that of neutrons (**neutron flux**) or of light energy (**luminous flux**). **5b** the strength of a field in a given area: *magnetic flux.* **6** *Pathol.* an excessive discharge of fluid from the body, such as watery faeces in diarrhoea. ◆ *vb* **7** to make or become fluid. **8** (*tr*) to apply flux to (a metal, soldered joint, etc.). [C14: from L *fluxus* a flow, from *fluere* to flow]

flux density *n Physics.* the amount of flux per unit of cross-sectional area.

fluxion ('flʌkʃən) *n Maths., obs.* the rate of change of a function, especially the instantaneous velocity of a moving body; derivative. [C16: from LL *fluxiō* a flowing]

fly[1] 🅣 (flaɪ) *vb* **flies, flying, flew, flown. 1** (*intr*) (of birds, aircraft, etc.) to move through the air in a controlled manner using aerodynamic forces. **2** to travel over (an area of land or sea) in an aircraft. **3** to operate (an aircraft or spacecraft). **4** to float, flutter, or be displayed in the air or cause to float, etc., in this way: *they flew the flag.* **5** to transport or be transported by or through the air by aircraft, wind, etc. **6** (*intr*) to move or be moved very quickly, or suddenly: *the door flew open.* **7** (*intr*) to pass swiftly: *time flies.* **8** to escape from (an enemy, place, etc.); flee. **9** (*intr;* may be foll. by *at* or *upon*) to attack a person. **10 fly a kite. 10a** to procure money by an accommodation bill. **10b** to release information or take a step in order to test public opinion. **11 fly high.** *Inf.* **11a** to have a high aim. **11b** to prosper or flourish. **12 let fly.** *Inf.* **12a** to lose one's temper (with a person): *she really let fly at him.* **12b** to shoot or throw (an object). ◆ *n, pl* **flies. 13** (*often pl*) Also called: **fly front.** a closure that conceals a zip, buttons, or other fastening, by having one side overlapping, as on trousers. **14** Also called: **fly sheet. 14a** a flap forming the entrance to a tent. **14b** a piece of canvas drawn over the ridgepole of a tent to form an outer roof. **15** short for **flywheel. 16a** the outer edge of a flag. **16b** the distance from the outer edge of a flag to the staff. **17** *Brit.* a light one-horse covered carriage formerly let out on hire. **18** (*pl*) *Theatre.* the space above the stage out of view of the audience, used for storing scenery, etc. **19** *Rare.* the act of flying. [OE *flēogan*]
▸ **'flyable** *adj*

fly[2] 🅣 (flaɪ) *n, pl* **flies. 1** any dipterous insect, esp. the housefly, characterized by active flight. **2** any of various similar but unrelated insects, such as the caddis fly, firefly, and dragonfly. **3** *Angling.* a lure made from a fish-hook dressed with feathers, tinsel, etc., to resemble any of various flies or nymphs: used in fly-fishing. **4 fly in the ointment.** *Inf.* a slight flaw that detracts from value or enjoyment. **5 fly on the wall. 5a** a person who watches others, while not being noticed himself. **5b** (*as modifier*): *a fly-on-the-wall documentary.* **6 there are no flies on him, her,** etc. *Inf.* he, she, etc., is no fool. [OE *flēoge*]
▸ **'flyless** *adj*

fly[3] 🅣 (flaɪ) *adj Sl., chiefly Brit.* knowing and sharp; smart. [C19: from ?]

fly agaric *n* a woodland fungus having a scarlet cap with white warts and white gills: poisonous but rarely fatal. [so named from its use as a poison on flypaper]

fly ash *n* fine solid particles of ash carried into the air during combustion.

flyaway ('flaɪə,weɪ) *adj* **1** (of hair or clothing) loose and fluttering. **2** frivolous or flighty; giddy.

flyblow ('flaɪ,bləʊ) *vb* **flyblows, flyblowing, flyblew, flyblown. 1** (*tr*) to contaminate, esp. with the eggs or larvae of the blowfly; taint. ◆ *n* **2** (*usually pl*) the eggs or young larva of a blowfly.

flyblown ('flaɪ,bləʊn) *adj* **1** covered with flyblows. **2** contaminated; tainted.

flybook ('flaɪ,bʊk) *n* a small case or wallet used by anglers for storing artificial flies.

flyby ('flaɪ,baɪ) *n, pl* **flybys.** a flight past a particular position or target, esp. the close approach of a spacecraft to a planet or satellite.

fly-by-night 🅣 *Inf.* ◆ *adj* **1** unreliable or untrustworthy, esp. in finance. ◆ *n* **2** an untrustworthy person, esp. one who departs secretly or by night to avoid paying debts.

flycatcher ('flaɪ,kætʃə) *n* **1** a small insectivorous songbird of the Old World having a small slender bill fringed with bristles. **2** an American passerine bird.

fly-drive *adj, adv* describing a type of package-deal holiday in which the price includes outward and return flights and car hire while away.

flyer 🅣 *or* **flier** ('flaɪə) *n* **1** a person or thing that flies or moves very fast. **2** an aviator or pilot. **3** *Inf.* a large flying leap. **4** a rectangular step in a straight flight of stairs. Cf. **winder** (sense 5). **5** *Athletics inf.* a flying start. **6** *Chiefly US.* a speculative business transaction. **7** a small handbill.

fly-fish *vb* (*intr*) *Angling.* to fish using artificial flies as lures.
▸ **'fly-,fishing** *n*

fly half *n Rugby.* another name for **stand-off half.**

flying 🅣 ('flaɪɪŋ) *adj* **1** (*prenominal*) hurried; fleeting: *a flying visit.* **2** (*prenominal*) designed for fast action. **3** (*prenominal*) moving or passing quickly on or as if on wings: *flying hours.* **4** hanging, waving, or floating freely: *flying hair.* ◆ *n* **5** the act of piloting, navigating, or travelling in an aircraft. **6** (*modifier*) relating to, accustomed to, or adapted for flight: *a flying machine.*

flying boat *n* a seaplane in which the fuselage consists of a hull that provides buoyancy.

flying bridge *n* an auxiliary bridge of a vessel.

flying buttress *n* a buttress supporting a wall or other structure by an arch that transmits the thrust outwards and downwards.

flying colours *pl n* conspicuous success; triumph: *he passed his test with flying colours.*

flying doctor *n* (in areas of sparse or scattered population) a doctor who visits patients by aircraft.

flying fish *n* a fish common in warm and tropical seas, having enlarged winglike pectoral fins used for gliding above the surface of the water.

flying fox *n* **1** any large fruit bat of tropical Africa and Asia. **2** *Austral. & NZ.* a cable mechanism used for transportation across a river, gorge, etc.

flying gurnard *n* a marine spiny-finned gurnard-like fish having enlarged fan-shaped pectoral fins used to glide above the surface of the sea.

flying jib *n* the jib set furthest forward or outboard on a vessel with two or more jibs.

flying lemur *n* either of the two arboreal mammals of S and SE Asia that resemble lemurs but have a fold of skin between the limbs enabling movement by gliding leaps.

flying officer *n* an officer holding commissioned rank senior to a pilot officer but junior to a flight lieutenant in the British and certain other air forces.

flying phalanger *n* a nocturnal arboreal phalanger of E Australia and New Guinea, moving with gliding leaps using folds of skin between the hind limbs and forelimbs.

flying picket *n* (in industrial disputes) a member of a group of pickets organized to be able to move quickly from place to place.

flying saucer *n* any unidentified disc-shaped flying object alleged to come from outer space.

flying squad *n* a small group of police, soldiers, etc., ready to move into action quickly.

flying squirrel *n* a nocturnal rodent of Asia and North America, related to the squirrel. Furry folds of skin between the forelegs and hind legs enable these animals to move by gliding leaps.

flying start *n* **1** (in sprinting) a start by a competitor anticipating the starting signal. **2** a start to a race in which the competitor is already travelling at speed as he passes the starting line. **3** any promising beginning. **4** an initial advantage.

flying wing *n* **1** an aircraft consisting mainly of one large wing or tailplane and no fuselage. **2** (in Canadian football) the twelfth player, who has a variable position behind the scrimmage line.

flyleaf ('flaɪ,li:f) *n, pl* **flyleaves.** the inner leaf of the endpaper of a book, pasted to the first leaf.

flyover ('flaɪ,əʊvə) *n* **1** *Brit.* an intersection of two roads at which one is carried over the other by a bridge. **2** the US name for **fly-past.**

flypaper ('flaɪ,peɪpə) *n* paper with a sticky and poisonous coating, usually hung from the ceiling to trap flies.

fly-past *n* a ceremonial flight of aircraft over a given area.

THESAURUS

flux *n* **1** = **flow**, fluidity, motion **2** = **change**, alteration, fluctuation, instability, modification, mutability, mutation, transition, unrest

fly[1] *vb* **1** = **take wing**, flit, flutter, hover, mount, sail, soar, take to the air, wing **3** = **pilot**, aviate, be at the controls, control, manoeuvre, operate **4** = **display**, flap, float, flutter, show, wave **6** = **rush**, barrel (along), be off like a shot (*inf.*), bolt, burn rubber (*inf.*), career, dart, dash, hare (*Brit. inf.*), hasten, hurry, race, scamper, scoot, shoot, speed, sprint, tear, whizz (*inf.*), zoom **7** = **pass**, elapse, flit, glide, pass swiftly, roll on, run its course, slip away **8** = **flee**, abscond, avoid, beat a retreat, clear out, cut and run (*inf.*), decamp, disappear, do a runner (*sl.*), escape, get away, hasten away, make a getaway, make a quick exit, make one's escape, run, run for it, run from, shun, skedaddle (*inf.*), take flight, take off **9** = **attack**, assail, assault, belabour, fall upon, get stuck into (*inf.*), go for, go for the jugular, have a go at (*inf.*), lay about, pitch into (*inf.*), rush at **12 let fly** *Informal* **a** = **throw**, burst forth, give free reign, keep nothing back, lash out, let (someone) have it, tear into (*inf.*), vent **b** cast, chuck (*inf.*), fire, fling, heave, hurl, hurtle, launch, let off, lob (*inf.*), shoot, sling

fly[2] *n* **4** *Informal* **fly in the ointment** = **snag**, difficulty, drawback, flaw, hitch, problem, rub, small problem

fly[3] *adj Slang, chiefly Brit.* = **cunning**, astute, canny, careful, knowing, nobody's fool, not born yesterday, on the ball (*inf.*), sharp, shrewd, smart, wide-awake

fly-by-night *adj* **1** *Informal* = **unreliable**, cowboy (*inf.*), dubious, questionable, shady, undependable, untrustworthy

flyer *n* **1** = **goer**, racer, runner, scorcher (*inf.*), speed merchant (*inf.*), sprinter **2** = **pilot**, aeronaut, airman *or* airwoman, aviator *or* aviatrix **3** *Informal* = **jump**, bound, flying *or* running jump, hurdle, jeté, leap, spring, vault **7** = **leaflet**, advert, bill, booklet, circular, handbill, handout, leaf, literature (*inf.*), notice, pamphlet, promotional material, publicity material, release, throwaway (*US*)

flying *adj* **1** = **hurried**, brief, fleeting, fugacious, hasty, rushed, short-lived, transitory **2, 3** = **fast**, express, fleet, mercurial, mobile, rapid, speedy, winged **4** = **airborne**, flapping, floating, fluttering, gliding, hovering, in the air, soaring, streaming, volitant, waving, wind-borne, winging

flyposting ('flaɪˌpəʊstɪŋ) *n* the posting of advertising or political posters, etc., in unauthorized places.
flyscreen ('flaɪˌskriːn) *n* a wire-mesh screen over a window to prevent flies entering a room.
fly sheet *n* **1** another term for **fly**[1] (sense 14). **2** a short handbill.
flyspeck ('flaɪˌspɛk) *n* **1** the small speck of the excrement of a fly. **2** a small spot or speck. ◆ *vb* **3** (*tr*) to mark with flyspecks.
fly spray *n* a liquid used to destroy flies and other insects, sprayed from an aerosol.
fly-tipping *n* the deliberate dumping of rubbish in an unauthorized place.
flytrap ('flaɪˌtræp) *n* **1** any of various insectivorous plants. **2** a device for catching flies.
fly way *n* the usual route used by birds when migrating.
flyweight ('flaɪˌweɪt) *n* **1a** a professional boxer weighing not more than 112 pounds (51 kg). **1b** an amateur boxer weighing 48–51 kg (106–112 pounds). **2** an amateur wrestler weighing 107–115 pounds (49–52 kg).
flywheel ('flaɪˌwiːl) *n* a heavy wheel that stores kinetic energy and smooths the operation of a reciprocating engine by maintaining a constant speed of rotation over the whole cycle.
fm *abbrev. for:* **1** fathom. **2** from.
Fm *the chemical symbol for* fermium.
FM *abbrev. for:* **1** frequency modulation. **2** Field Marshal.
f-number, f number, f-stop, *or* **f stop** *n Photog.* the numerical value of the relative aperture. If the relative aperture is f8, 8 is the f-number.
FO *abbrev. for:* **1** *Army.* Field Officer. **2** *Air Force.* Flying Officer. **3** Foreign Office.
fo. *abbrev. for* folio.
foal (fəʊl) *n* **1** the young of a horse or related animal. ◆ *vb* **2** to give birth to (a foal). [OE *fola*]
foam 🅣 (fəʊm) *n* **1** a mass of small bubbles of gas formed on the surface of a liquid, such as the froth produced by a solution of soap or detergent in water. **2** frothy saliva sometimes formed in and expelled from the mouth, as in rabies. **3** the frothy sweat of a horse or similar animal. **4a** any of a number of light cellular solids made by creating bubbles of gas in the liquid material: used as insulation and packaging. **4b** (*as modifier*): *foam rubber; foam plastic.* ◆ *vb* **5** to produce or cause to produce foam; froth. **6** (*intr*) to be very angry (esp. in **foam at the mouth**). [OE *fām*]
▸ **'foamless** *adj*
foamy 🅣 ('fəʊmɪ) *adj* **foamier, foamiest.** of, resembling, consisting of, or covered with foam.
fob[1] (fɒb) *n* **1** a chain or ribbon by which a pocket watch is attached to a waistcoat. **2** any ornament hung on such a chain. **3** a small pocket in a man's waistcoat, etc., for holding a watch. [C17: prob. of Gmc origin]
fob[2] (fɒb) *vb* **fobs, fobbing, fobbed.** (*tr*) *Arch.* to cheat. [C15: prob. from G *foppen* to trick]
f.o.b. *or* **FOB** *Commerce. abbrev. for* free on board.
fob off 🅣 *vb* (*tr, adv*) **1** to trick (a person) with lies or excuses. **2** to dispose of (goods) by trickery.
focal ('fəʊkᵊl) *adj* **1** of or relating to a focus. **2** situated at or measured from the focus.
focalize *or* **focalise** ('fəʊkəˌlaɪz) *vb* **focalizes, focalizing, focalized** *or* **focalises, focalising, focalised.** a less common word for **focus.**
▸ **ˌfocaliˈzation** *or* **ˌfocaliˈsation** *n*
focal length *or* **distance** *n* the distance from the focal point of a lens or mirror to the reflecting surface of the mirror or the centre point of the lens.
focal plane *n* the plane that is perpendicular to the axis of a lens or mirror and passes through the focal point.
focal point *n* the point on the axis of a lens or mirror to which parallel rays of light converge or from which they appear to diverge after refraction or reflection. Also called: **focus.**
fo'c's'le *or* **fo'c'sle** ('fəʊksᵊl) *n* a variant spelling of **forecastle.**
focus 🅣 ('fəʊkəs) *n, pl* **focuses** *or* **foci** (-saɪ). **1** a point of convergence of light or sound waves, etc., or a point from which they appear to diverge. **2** another name for **focal point** or **focal length. 3** *Optics.* the state of an optical image when it is distinct and clearly defined or the state of an instrument producing this image: *the telescope is out of focus.* **4** a point upon which attention, activity, etc., is concentrated. **5** *Geom.* a fixed reference point on the concave side of a conic section, used when defining its eccentricity. **6** the point beneath the earth's surface at which an earthquake originates. **7** *Pathol.* the main site of an infection. ◆ *vb* **focuses, focusing, focused** *or* **focusses, focussing, focussed. 8** to bring or come to a focus or into focus. **9** (*tr;* often foll. by *on*) to concentrate. [C17: via NL from L: hearth, fireplace]
▸ **'focuser** *n*
focus group *n* a group of people gathered by a market research company to discuss and assess a product or service.
focus puller *n Films.* the member of a camera crew who adjusts the focus of the lens as the camera is tracked in or out.
fodder 🅣 ('fɒdə) *n* **1** bulk feed for livestock, esp. hay, straw, etc. ◆ *vb* **2** (*tr*) to supply (livestock) with fodder. [OE *fōdor*]
foe 🅣 (fəʊ) *n Formal or literary.* another word for **enemy.** [OE *fāh* hostile]
FoE *or* **FOE** *abbrev. for* Friends of the Earth.
foehn (fɜːn; *German* føːn) *n Meteorol.* a variant spelling of **föhn.**
foeman ('fəʊmən) *n, pl* **foemen.** *Arch. & poetic.* an enemy in war; foe.
foetal ('fiːtᵊl) *adj* a variant spelling of **fetal.**
foetid ('fɛtɪd, 'fiː-) *adj* a variant spelling of **fetid.**
▸ **'foetidly** *adv* ▸ **'foetidness** *n*
foetus ('fiːtəs) *n, pl* **foetuses.** a variant spelling of **fetus.**
fog[1] 🅣 (fɒg) *n* **1** a mass of droplets of condensed water vapour suspended in the air, often greatly reducing visibility. **2** a cloud of any substance in the atmosphere reducing visibility. **3** a state of mental uncertainty. **4** *Photog.* a blurred area on a developed negative, print, or transparency. ◆ *vb* **fogs, fogging, fogged. 5** to envelop or become enveloped with or as if with fog. **6** to confuse or become confused. **7** *Photog.* to produce fog on (a negative, print, or transparency) or (of a negative, print, or transparency) to be affected by fog. [C16: ? back formation from *foggy* damp, boggy, from FOG[2]]
fog[2] (fɒg) *n* a second growth of grass after the first mowing. [C14: prob. from ON]
fog bank *n* a distinct mass of fog, esp. at sea.
fogbound ('fɒgˌbaʊnd) *adj* prevented from operation by fog: *the airport was fogbound.*
fogbow ('fɒgˌbəʊ) *n* a faint arc of light sometimes seen in a fog bank.
fogey 🅣 *or* **fogy** ('fəʊgɪ) *n, pl* **fogeys** *or* **fogies.** an extremely fussy or conservative person (esp. in **old fogey**). [C18: from ?]
▸ **'fogeyish** *or* **'fogyish** *adj*
foggy 🅣 ('fɒgɪ) *adj* **foggier, foggiest. 1** thick with fog. **2** obscure or confused. **3 not the foggiest** (**idea** *or* **notion**). no idea whatsoever: *I haven't the foggiest.*
▸ **'fogginess** *n*
foghorn ('fɒgˌhɔːn) *n* **1** a mechanical instrument sounded at intervals to serve as a warning to vessels in fog. **2** *Inf.* a loud deep resounding voice.
fog signal *n* a signal used to warn railway engine drivers in fog, consisting of a detonator placed on the line.
föhn *or* **foehn** (fɜːn; *German* føːn) *n* a warm dry wind blowing down the northern slopes of the Alps. [G, from OHG, from L *favōnius;* rel. to *fovēre* to warm]
foible 🅣 ('fɔɪbᵊl) *n* **1** a slight peculiarity or minor weakness; idiosyncrasy. **2** the most vulnerable part of a sword's blade, from the middle to the tip. [C17: from obs. F, from obs. adj: FEEBLE]
foie gras (*French* fwa grɑ) *n* See **pâté de foie gras.**
foil[1] 🅣 (fɔɪl) *vb* (*tr*) **1** to baffle or frustrate (a person, attempt, etc.). **2** *Hunting.* (of hounds, hunters, etc.) to obliterate the scent left by a hunted animal or (of a hunted animal) to run back over its own trail. ◆ *n* **3** *Arch.* a setback or defeat. [C13 *foilen* to trample, from OF, *fuler* tread down]
▸ **'foilable** *adj*
foil[2] 🅣 (fɔɪl) *n* **1** metal in the form of very thin sheets: *tin foil.* **2** the thin metallic sheet forming the backing of a mirror. **3** a thin leaf of shiny metal set under a gemstone to add brightness or colour. **4** a person or thing that gives contrast to another. **5** *Archit.* a small arc between cusps. **6** short for **hydrofoil.** ◆ *vb* (*tr*) **7** Also: **foliate.** *Archit.* to ornament (windows, etc.) with foils. [C14: from OF, from L *folia* leaves]
foil[3] (fɔɪl) *n* a light slender flexible sword tipped by a button. [C16: from ?]
foist 🅣 (fɔɪst) *vb* (*tr*) **1** (often foll. by *off* or *on*) to sell or pass off (some-

THESAURUS

foam *n* **1** = **froth**, bubbles, head, lather, spray, spume, suds ◆ *vb* **5** = **bubble**, boil, effervesce, fizz, froth, lather
foamy *adj* = **bubbly**, foaming, frothy, lathery, spumescent, sudsy
fob off *vb* **1** = **put off**, appease, deceive, equivocate with, flannel (*Brit. inf.*), give (someone) the run-around (*inf.*), stall **2** = **pass off**, dump, foist, get rid of, inflict, palm off, unload
focus *n* **4** = **centre**, bull's eye, centre of activity, centre of attraction, core, cynosure, focal point, headquarters, heart, hub, meeting place, target ◆ *vb* **9** = **concentrate**, aim, bring to bear, centre, converge, direct, fix, join, meet, pinpoint, rivet, spotlight, zero in (*inf.*), zoom in
fodder *n* **1** = **feed**, food, foodstuff, forage, provender, rations, tack (*inf.*), victuals, vittles (*obs. or dialect*)
foe *n* = **enemy**, adversary, antagonist, foeman (*arch.*), opponent, rival
Antonyms *n* ally, companion, comrade, confederate, friend, partner
fog[1] *n* **1** = **mist**, gloom, miasma, murk, murkiness, peasouper (*inf.*), smog **3** = **obscurity**, blindness, confusion, daze, haze, mist, perplexity, stupor, trance ◆ *vb* **5** = **mist over** *or* **up**, cloud, steam up **6** = **obscure**, becloud, bedim, befuddle, bewilder, blear, blind, cloud, confuse, darken, daze, dim, muddle, muddy the waters, obfuscate, perplex, stupefy
fogey *n* = **fuddy-duddy** (*inf.*), anachronism, antique (*inf.*), back number (*inf.*), dinosaur, dodo (*inf.*), fossil (*inf.*), relic, square (*inf.*), stick-in-the-mud (*inf.*)
foggy *adj* **1** = **misty**, blurred, brumous (*rare*), cloudy, dim, grey, hazy, indistinct, murky, nebulous, obscure, smoggy, soupy, vaporous **2** = **unclear**, befuddled, bewildered, clouded, cloudy, confused, dark, dazed, dim, indistinct, muddled, obscure, stupefied, stupid, vague
Antonyms *adj* ≠ **misty:** bright, clear ≠ **unclear:** accurate, alert, awake, clear, decisive, distinct, lucid, palpable, sharp, shrewd, undimmed
foible *n* **1** = **idiosyncrasy**, defect, failing, fault, imperfection, infirmity, peculiarity, quirk, weakness, weak point
foil[1] *vb* **1** = **thwart**, baffle, balk, check, checkmate, circumvent, cook (someone's) goose (*inf.*), counter, defeat, disappoint, elude, frustrate, nip in the bud, nullify, outwit, stop
foil[2] *n* **4** = **contrast**, antithesis, background, complement, setting
foist *vb* **1, 2** = **impose**, fob off, get rid of, insert,

thing, esp. an inferior article) as genuine, valuable, etc. **2** (usually foll. by *in* or *into*) to insert surreptitiously or wrongfully. [C16: prob. from obs. Du. *vuisten* to enclose in one's hand, from MDu. *vuist* fist]

FOL (in New Zealand) *abbrev. for* Federation of Labour.

fol. *abbrev. for:* **1** folio. **2** following.

fold[1] Ⓣ (fəʊld) *vb* **1** to bend or be bent double so that one part covers another. **2** (*tr*) to bring together and intertwine (the arms, legs, etc.). **3** (*tr*) (of birds, insects, etc.) to close (the wings) together from an extended position. **4** (*tr;* often foll. by *up* or *in*) to enclose in or as if in a surrounding material. **5** (*tr;* foll. by *in*) to clasp (a person) in the arms. **6** (*tr;* usually foll. by *round, about,* etc.) to wind (around); entwine. **7** Also: **fold in.** (*tr*) to mix (a whisked mixture) with other ingredients by gently turning one part over the other with a spoon. **8** (*intr;* often foll. by *up*) *Inf.* to collapse; fail: *the business folded.* ◆ *n* **9** a piece or section that has been folded: *a fold of cloth.* **10** a mark, crease, or hollow made by folding. **11** a hollow in undulating terrain. **12** a bend in stratified rocks that results from movements within the earth's crust. **13** a coil, as in a rope, etc. [OE *fealdan*]
▸ **'foldable** *adj*

fold[2] (fəʊld) *n* **1a** a small enclosure or pen for sheep or other livestock, where they can be gathered. **1b** a flock of sheep. **2** a church or the members of it. ◆ *vb* **3** (*tr*) to gather or confine (sheep, etc.) in a fold. [OE *falod*]

-fold *suffix forming adjectives and adverbs.* having so many parts or being so many times as much or as many: *three-hundredfold.* [OE *-fald, -feald*]

foldaway ('fəʊldəˌweɪ) *adj* (*prenominal*) (of a bed, etc.) able to be folded away when not in use.

folded dipole *n* a type of aerial consisting of two parallel dipoles connected together at their outer ends and fed at the centre of one of them. The length is usually half the operating wavelength.

folder Ⓣ ('fəʊldə) *n* **1** a binder or file for holding loose papers, etc. **2** a folded circular. **3** a person or thing that folds.

folderol ('fɒldəˌrɒl) *n* a variant spelling of **falderal.**

folding door *n* a door in the form of two or more vertical hinged leaves that can be folded one against another.

folding money *n Inf.* paper money.

foley *or* **foley artist** ('fəʊlɪ) *n Films.* the US name for **footsteps editor.** [C20: after the inventor of the technique]

foliaceous (ˌfəʊlɪ'eɪʃəs) *adj* **1** having the appearance of the leaf of a plant. **2** bearing leaves or leaflike structures. **3** *Geol.* consisting of thin layers. [C17: from L *foliāceus*]

foliage ('fəʊlɪɪdʒ) *n* **1** the green leaves of a plant. **2** sprays of leaves used for decoration. **3** an ornamental leaflike design. [C15: from OF *fuellage,* from *fuelle* leaf; infl. in form by L *folium*]

foliar ('fəʊlɪə) *adj* of or relating to a leaf or leaves. [C19: from F, from L *folium* leaf]

foliate *adj* ('fəʊlɪɪt, -ˌeɪt). **1a** relating to, possessing, or resembling leaves. **1b** (*in combination*): *trifoliate.* ◆ *vb* ('fəʊlɪˌeɪt), **foliates, foliating, foliated. 2** (*tr*) to ornament with foliage or with leaf forms such as foils. **3** to hammer or cut (metal) into thin plates or foil. **4** (*tr*) to number the leaves of (a book, etc.). Cf. **paginate. 5** (*intr*) (of plants) to grow leaves. [C17: from L *foliātus* leaved, leafy]

foliation (ˌfəʊlɪ'eɪʃən) *n* **1** *Bot.* **1a** the process of producing leaves. **1b** the state of being in leaf. **1c** the arrangement of leaves in a leaf bud. **2** *Archit.* ornamentation consisting of cusps and foils. **3** the consecutive numbering of the leaves of a book. **4** *Geol.* the arrangement of the constituents of a rock in leaflike layers, as in schists.

folic acid ('fəʊlɪk) *n* any of a group of vitamins of the B complex, used in the treatment of anaemia. Also called: **folacin.** [C20: from L *folium* leaf; so called because it may be obtained from green leaves]

folio ('fəʊlɪəʊ) *n, pl* **folios. 1** a sheet of paper folded in half to make two leaves for a book. **2** a book of the largest common size made up of such sheets. **3a** a leaf of paper numbered on the front side only. **3b** the page number of a book. **4** *Law.* a unit of measurement of the length of legal documents, determined by the number of words, generally 72 or 90 in Britain and 100 in the US. ◆ *adj* **5** relating to or having the format of a folio: *a folio edition.* [C16: from L phrase *in foliō* in a leaf, from *folium* leaf]

folk Ⓣ (fəʊk) *n, pl* **folk** *or* **folks. 1** (*functioning as pl; often pl in form*) people in general, esp. those of a particular group or class: *country folk.* **2** (*functioning as pl; usually pl in form*) *Inf.* members of a family. **3** (*functioning as sing*) *Inf.* short for **folk music. 4** a people or tribe. **5** (*modifier*) originating from or traditional to the common people of a country: *a folk song.* [OE *folc*]
▸ **'folkish** *adj*

folk dance *n* **1** any of various traditional rustic dances. **2** a piece of music composed for or in the rhythm of such a dance.
▸ **folk dancing** *n*

folk etymology *n* the gradual change in the form of a word through the influence of a more familiar word or phrase with which it becomes associated, as for example *sparrow-grass* for *asparagus.*

folkie *or* **folky** ('fəʊkɪ) *n, pl* **folkies.** *Inf.* a devotee of folk music.

folklore ('fəʊkˌlɔː) *n* **1** the unwritten literature of a people as expressed in folk tales, songs, etc. **2** the body of stories and legends attached to a particular place, group, etc.: *rugby folklore.* **3** study of folkloric materials.
▸ **'folkˌloric** *adj* ▸ **'folkˌlorist** *n, adj*

folk medicine *n* medicine as practised among rustic communities and primitive peoples, consisting typically of the use of herbal remedies.

folk music *n* **1** music that is passed on from generation to generation. **2** any music composed in this idiom.

folk-rock *n* a style of rock music influenced by folk.

folk song *n* **1** a song which has been handed down among the common people. **2** a modern song which reflects the folk idiom.

folksy ('fəʊksɪ) *adj* **folksier, folksiest. 1** of or like ordinary people; sometimes used derogatorily to describe affected simplicity. **2** *Inf., chiefly US.* friendly; affable.

folk tale *or* **story** *n* a tale or legend originating among a people and becoming part of an oral tradition.

folk weave *n* a type of fabric with a loose weave.

follicle ('fɒlɪkᵊl) *n* **1** any small sac or cavity in the body having an excretory, secretory, or protective function: *a hair follicle.* **2** *Bot.* a dry fruit that splits along one side only to release its seeds. [C17: from L *folliculus* small bag, from *follis* pair of bellows, leather money-bag]
▸ **follicular** (fɒ'lɪkjʊlə), **folliculate** (fɒ'lɪkjʊˌleɪt), *or* **fol'licuˌlated** *adj*

follow Ⓣ ('fɒləʊ) *vb* **1** to go or come after in the same direction. **2** (*tr*) to accompany: *she followed her sister everywhere.* **3** to come after as a logical or natural consequence. **4** (*tr*) to keep to the course or track of: *she followed the towpath.* **5** (*tr*) to act in accordance with: *to follow instructions.* **6** (*tr*) to accept the ideas or beliefs of (a previous authority, etc.): *he followed Donne in most of his teachings.* **7** to understand (an explanation, etc.): *the lesson was difficult to follow.* **8** to watch closely or continuously: *she followed his progress.* **9** (*tr*) to have a keen interest in: *to follow athletics.* **10** (*tr*) to help in the cause of: *the men who followed Napoleon.* [OE *folgian*]

follower Ⓣ ('fɒləʊə) *n* **1** a person who accepts the teachings of another: *a follower of Marx.* **2** an attendant. **3** a supporter, as of a sport or team. **4** (esp. formerly) a male admirer.

following Ⓣ ('fɒləʊɪŋ) *adj* **1a** (*prenominal*) about to be mentioned, specified, etc.: *the following items.* **1b** (*as n*): *will the following please raise their hands?* **2** (of winds, currents, etc.) moving in the same direction as a vessel. ◆ *n* **3** a group of supporters or enthusiasts: *he attracted a large following.* ◆ *prep* **4** as a result of: *he was arrested following a tip-off.*

> **USAGE NOTE** The use of *following* to mean *as a result of* is very common in journalism, but should be avoided in other kinds of writing.

follow-on *Cricket.* ◆ *n* **1** an immediate second innings forced on a team scoring a prescribed number of runs fewer than its opponents in the first innings. ◆ *vb* **follow on. 2** (*intr, adv*) (of a team) to play a follow-on.

follow out *vb* (*tr, adv*) to implement (an idea or action) to a conclusion.

follow through Ⓣ *vb* (*adv*) **1** *Sport.* to complete (a stroke or shot) by continuing the movement to the end of its arc. **2** (*tr*) to pursue (an aim) to a conclusion. ◆ *n* **follow-through. 3** the act of following through.

follow up Ⓣ *vb* (*tr, adv*) **1** to pursue or investigate (a person, etc.)

THESAURUS

insinuate, interpolate, introduce, palm off, pass off, put over, sneak in, unload

fold[1] *vb* **1, 2** = **bend**, crease, crumple, dog-ear, double, double over, gather, intertwine, overlap, pleat, tuck, turn under **4** = **wrap**, do up, enclose, enfold, entwine, envelop, wrap up **8** *Informal* = **go bankrupt**, be ruined, close, collapse, crash, fail, go belly-up (*sl.*), go bust (*inf.*), go by the board, go to the wall, go under, shut down ◆ *n* **9, 10** = **crease**, bend, double thickness, folded portion, furrow, knife-edge, layer, overlap, pleat, turn, wrinkle

folder *n* **1** = **file**, binder, envelope, portfolio

folk *n* **1, 2, 4** = **people**, clan, ethnic group, family, kin, kindred, race, tribe

follow *vb* **1** = **come after**, come next, step into the shoes of, succeed, supersede, supplant, take the place of **1** = **pursue**, chase, dog, hound, hunt, run after, shadow, stalk, tail (*inf.*), track, trail **2** = **accompany**, attend, bring up the rear, come after, come *or* go with, escort, tag along, tread on the heels of **3** = **result**, arise, be consequent, develop, emanate, ensue, flow, issue, proceed, spring, supervene **5** = **obey**, act in accordance with, be guided by, comply, conform, give allegiance to, heed, mind, note, observe, regard, toe the line, watch **7** = **understand**, appreciate, catch, catch on (*inf.*), comprehend, fathom, get, get the hang of (*inf.*), get the picture, grasp, keep up with, realize, see, take in **9** = **be interested in**, be a devotee *or* supporter of, be devoted to, cultivate, keep abreast of, support
Antonyms *vb* ≠ **come after:** guide, lead, precede ≠ **pursue:** avoid, elude, escape ≠ **obey:** abandon, desert, disobey, flout, forsake, give up, ignore, reject, renounce, shun

follower *n* **1, 3** = **supporter**, adherent, admirer, apostle, backer, believer, cohort (*chiefly US*), convert, devotee, disciple, fan, fancier, habitué, henchman, partisan, protagonist, pupil, representative, votary, worshipper **2** = **attendant**, companion, hanger-on, helper, henchman, lackey, minion, retainer (*History*), sidekick (*sl.*)
Antonyms *n* ≠ **supporter:** guru, leader, mentor, svengali, swami, teacher, tutor ≠ **attendant:** antagonist, contender, enemy, foe, opponent, rival

following *adj* **1** = **next**, coming, consequent, consequential, ensuing, later, specified, subsequent, succeeding, successive ◆ *n* **3** = **supporters**, audience, circle, clientele, coterie, entourage, fans, patronage, public, retinue, suite, support, train

follow through *vb* **2** = **complete**, bring to a conclusion, conclude, consummate, pursue, see through

follow up *vb* **1** = **investigate**, check out, find

closely. **2** to continue (action) after a beginning, esp. to increase its effect. ◆ *n* **follow-up. 3a** something done to reinforce an initial action. **3b** (*as modifier*): *a follow-up letter.* **4** *Med.* an examination of a patient at intervals after treatment.

folly ⓣ ('fɒlɪ) *n, pl* **follies. 1** the state or quality of being foolish. **2** a foolish action, idea, etc. **3** a building in the form of a castle, temple, etc., built to satisfy a fancy or conceit. **4** (*pl*) *Theatre.* an elaborately costumed revue. [C13: from OF *folie* madness, from *fou* mad; see FOOL[1]]

foment ⓣ (fə'mɛnt) *vb* (*tr*) **1** to encourage or instigate (trouble, discord, etc.). **2** *Med.* to apply heat and moisture to (a part of the body) to relieve pain. [C15: from LL, from L *fōmentum* a poultice, ult. from *fovēre* to foster]
▸**fomentation** (ˌfəʊmɛn'teɪʃən) *n* ▸**fo'menter** *n*

> **USAGE NOTE** Both *foment* and *ferment* can be used to talk about stirring up trouble: *he was accused of fomenting/fermenting unrest.* Only *ferment* can be used intransitively or as a noun: *his anger continued to ferment* (not *foment*)*; rural areas were unaffected by the ferment in the cities.*

fond ⓣ (fɒnd) *adj* **1** (*postpositive;* foll. by *of*) having a liking (for). **2** loving; tender. **3** indulgent: *a fond mother.* **4** (of hopes, wishes, etc.) cherished but unlikely to be realized: *he had fond hopes of starting his own firm.* **5** *Arch. or dialect.* **5a** foolish. **5b** credulous. [C14 *fonned,* from *fonne* a fool]
▸**'fondly** *adv* ▸**'fondness** *n*

fondant ('fɒndənt) *n* **1** a thick flavoured paste of sugar and water, used in sweets and icings. **2** a sweet made of this mixture. ◆ *adj* **3** (of a colour) soft, pastel. [C19: from F, lit.: melting, from *fondre* to melt, from L *fundere;* see FOUND[3]]

fondle ⓣ ('fɒndᵊl) *vb* **fondles, fondling, fondled.** (*tr*) to touch or stroke tenderly. [C17: from (obs.) vb *fond* to fondle; see FOND]
▸**'fondler** *n*

fondue ('fɒndjuː; *French* fɔ̃dy) *n* a Swiss dish, consisting of melted cheese into which small pieces of bread are dipped. [C19: from F, fem of *fondu* melted; see FONDANT]

font[1] (fɒnt) *n* **1a** a large bowl for baptismal water. **1b** a receptacle for holy water. **2** the reservoir for oil in an oil lamp. **3** *Arch. or poetic.* a fountain or well. [OE, from Church L *fons,* from L: fountain]

font[2] (fɒnt) *n Printing.* another name (esp. US and Canad.) for **fount**[2].

fontanelle *or chiefly US* **fontanel** (ˌfɒntə'nɛl) *n Anat.* any of the soft membranous gaps between the bones of the skull in a fetus or infant. [C16 (in the sense: hollow between muscles): from OF *fontanele,* lit.: a little spring, from *fontaine* FOUNTAIN]

food ⓣ (fuːd) *n* **1** any substance that can be ingested by a living organism and metabolized into energy and body tissue. Related adj: **alimentary. 2** nourishment in more or less solid form: *food and drink.* **3** anything that provides mental nourishment or stimulus. [OE *fōda*]

food additive *n* any of various natural or synthetic substances, such as salt or citric acid, used in the commercial processing of food as preservatives, antioxidants, emulsifiers, etc.

food chain *n Ecology.* a series of organisms in a community, each member of which feeds on another in the chain and is in turn eaten.

foodie ⓣ *or* **foody** ('fuːdɪ) *n, pl* **foodies.** a person having an enthusiastic interest in the preparation and consumption of good food.

food poisoning *n* an acute illness caused by food that is either naturally poisonous or contaminated by bacteria.

food processor *n Cookery.* an electric domestic appliance for automatic chopping, grating, blending, etc.

foodstuff ('fuːdˌstʌf) *n* any material, substance, etc., that can be used as food.

food value *n* the relative degree of nourishment obtained from different foods.

fool[1] ⓣ (fuːl) *n* **1** a person who lacks sense or judgement. **2** a person who is made to appear ridiculous. **3** (formerly) a professional jester living in a royal or noble household. **4** *Obs.* an idiot or imbecile: *the village fool.* **5 play** *or* **act the fool.** to deliberately act foolishly. ◆ *vb* **6** (*tr*) to deceive (someone), esp. in order to make him look ridiculous. **7** (*intr;* foll. by *with, around with,* or *about with*) *Inf.* to act or play (with) irresponsibly or aimlessly. **8** (*intr*) to speak or act in a playful or jesting manner. **9** (*tr;* foll. by *away*) to squander; fritter. ◆ *adj* **10** *US inf.* short for **foolish.** [C13: from OF *fol* mad person, from LL *follis* empty-headed fellow, from L: bellows]

fool[2] (fuːl) *n Chiefly Brit.* a dessert made from a purée of fruit with cream. [C16: ?from FOOL[1]]

foolery ⓣ ('fuːlərɪ) *n, pl* **fooleries. 1** foolish behaviour. **2** an instance of this.

foolhardy ⓣ ('fuːlˌhɑːdɪ) *adj* **foolhardier, foolhardiest.** heedlessly rash or adventurous. [C13: from OF, from *fol* foolish + *hardi* bold]
▸**'foolˌhardily** *adv* ▸**'foolˌhardiness** *n*

foolish ⓣ ('fuːlɪʃ) *adj* **1** unwise; silly. **2** resulting from folly or stupidity. **3** ridiculous or absurd. **4** weak-minded; simple.
▸**'foolishly** *adv* ▸**'foolishness** *n*

foolproof ⓣ ('fuːlˌpruːf) *adj Inf.* **1** proof against failure. **2** (esp. of machines, etc.) proof against human misuse, error, etc.

foolscap ('fuːlzˌkæp) *n Chiefly Brit.* a size of writing or printing paper, 13½ by 17 inches. [C17: see FOOL[1], CAP; so called from the watermark formerly used on this kind of paper]

fool's cap *n* **1** a hood or cap with bells or tassels, worn by court jesters. **2** a dunce's cap.

fool's errand *n* a fruitless undertaking.

THESAURUS

out about, look into, make inquiries, pursue, research **2** = **continue**, consolidate, make sure, reinforce

folly *n* **1** = **foolishness**, absurdity, daftness, fatuity, idiocy, imbecility, imprudence, indiscretion, irrationality, lunacy, madness, nonsense, preposterousness, rashness, recklessness, silliness, stupidity
Antonyms *n* judgment, level-headedness, moderation, prudence, rationality, reason, sanity, sense, wisdom

foment *vb* **1** = **stir up**, abet, agitate, arouse, brew, encourage, excite, fan the flames, foster, goad, incite, instigate, promote, provoke, quicken, raise, rouse, sow the seeds of, spur, stimulate, whip up

fomenter *n* **1** = **instigator**, agitator, demagogue, firebrand, incendiary, inciter, rabble-rouser, stirrer (*inf.*), troublemaker

fond *adj* **1** *foll. by* **of** = **keen on**, addicted to, attached to, enamoured of, having a fancy for, having a liking for, having a soft spot for, having a taste for, hooked on, into (*inf.*), partial to, predisposed towards **2, 3** = **loving**, adoring, affectionate, amorous, caring, devoted, doting, indulgent, tender, warm **4** = **foolish**, absurd, credulous, deluded, delusive, delusory, empty, indiscreet, naive, overoptimistic, vain
Antonyms *adj* ≠ **loving:** aloof, austere, averse, disinterested, indifferent, unaffectionate, unconcerned, undemonstrative ≠ **foolish:** rational, sensible

fondle *vb* = **caress**, cuddle, dandle, pat, pet, stroke

fondly *adv* **2, 3** = **lovingly**, affectionately, dearly, indulgently, possessively, tenderly, with affection **4** = **foolishly**, credulously, naively, stupidly, vainly

fondness *n* **1** = **liking**, attachment, fancy, love, partiality, penchant, predilection, preference, soft spot, susceptibility, taste, weakness **2** = **devotion**, affection, attachment, kindness, love, tenderness

Antonyms *n* abhorrence, animosity, animus, antagonism, antipathy, aversion, bad blood, coldness, contempt, detestation, dislike, enmity, harshness, hatred, hostility, ill will, loathing, malevolence, malice, opposition, repugnance, repulsion, resentment, unfriendliness

food *n* **1** = **nourishment**, aliment, board, bread, chow (*inf.*), comestibles, commons, cooking, cuisine, diet, eatables (*sl.*), edibles, fare, feed, foodstuffs, grub (*sl.*), meat, nosh (*sl.*), nutriment, nutrition, provender, provisions, rations, refreshment, scoff (*sl.*), stores, subsistence, survival rations, sustenance, table, tuck (*inf.*), tucker (*Austral. & NZ inf.*), viands, victuals, vittles (*obs. or dialect*)

foodie *n* = **gourmet**, *bon vivant, bon viveur,* connoisseur, epicure, gastronome, gourmand

fool[1] *n* **1** = **simpleton**, ass, blockhead, bonehead (*sl.*), charlie (*Brit. inf.*), chump, coot, dimwit (*inf.*), dolt, dope (*inf.*), dork (*sl.*), dunce, fathead (*inf.*), goose (*inf.*), halfwit, idiot, ignoramus, illiterate, imbecile (*inf.*), jackass, jerk (*sl., chiefly US & Canad.*), loon, mooncalf, moron, nerd *or* nurd (*sl.*), nincompoop, ninny, nit (*inf.*), nitwit (*inf.*), numbskull *or* numskull, oaf, sap (*sl.*), schmuck (*US sl.*), silly, twerp *or* twirp (*inf.*), twit (*inf., chiefly Brit.*), wally (*sl.*) **2** = **dupe**, butt, chump (*inf.*), easy mark (*inf.*), fall guy (*inf.*), greenhorn (*inf.*), gull (*arch.*), laughing stock, mug (*Brit. sl.*), stooge (*sl.*), sucker (*sl.*) **3** = **clown**, buffoon, comic, harlequin, jester, merry-andrew, motley, pierrot, punchinello **5** **play** *or* act the fool = **clown**, act the goat, act up, be silly, cavort, cut capers, frolic, lark about (*inf.*), mess about, play (silly) games, show off (*inf.*) ◆ *vb* **6** = **deceive**, bamboozle, beguile, bluff, cheat, con, delude, dupe, gull (*arch.*), have (someone) on, hoax, hoodwink, kid (*inf.*), make a fool of, mislead, play a trick on, pull a fast one on (*inf.*), put one over on (*inf.*), stiff (*sl.*), take in, trick **7** *with* **with, around with,** *or* **about with** *Informal* = **play**, fiddle (*inf.*), meddle, mess, monkey, tamper, toy, trifle

Antonyms *n* ≠ **simpleton:** expert, genius, master, sage, savant, scholar, wise man

foolery *n* **1, 2** = **nonsense**, antics, capers, carry-on (*inf., chiefly Brit.*), childishness, clowning, folly, fooling, horseplay, larks, mischief, monkey tricks (*inf.*), practical jokes, pranks, shenanigans (*inf.*), silliness, tomfoolery

foolhardy *adj* = **rash**, adventurous, bold, hot-headed, impetuous, imprudent, incautious, irresponsible, madcap, precipitate, reckless, temerarious, venturesome, venturous
Antonyms *adj* alert, careful, cautious, chary, circumspect, heedful, judicious, prudent, shrewd, solicitous, thoughtful, wary, watchful

foolish *adj* **1** = **unwise**, absurd, asinine, ill-advised, ill-considered, ill-judged, imprudent, inane, incautious, indiscreet, injudicious, nonsensical, senseless, short-sighted, silly, unintelligent, unreasonable **3, 4** = **silly**, as daft as a brush (*inf., chiefly Brit.*), brainless, crackpot (*inf.*), crazy, daft (*inf.*), doltish, fatuous, goofy (*inf.*), half-baked (*inf.*), half-witted, hare-brained, idiotic, imbecilic, inane, loopy (*inf.*), ludicrous, mad, moronic, off one's head (*inf.*), potty (*Brit. inf.*), ridiculous, senseless, simple, stupid, weak, witless
Antonyms *adj* bright, cautious, clever, commonsensical, intelligent, judicious, prudent, rational, sagacious, sane, sensible, sharp, smart, sound, thoughtful, wise

foolishly *adv* **1** = **unwisely**, absurdly, idiotically, ill-advisedly, imprudently, incautiously, indiscreetly, injudiciously, like a fool, mistakenly, short-sightedly, stupidly, without due consideration

foolishness *n* **1, 2** = **stupidity**, absurdity, folly, idiocy, imprudence, inanity, indiscretion, irresponsibility, silliness, weakness **3** = **nonsense**, bunk (*inf.*), bunkum *or* buncombe (*chiefly US*), claptrap (*inf.*), foolery, rigmarole, rubbish, trash

foolproof *adj* **1** = **infallible**, certain, guaran-

fool's gold *n* any of various yellow minerals, esp. pyrite, that can be mistaken for gold.

fool's paradise *n* illusory happiness.

fool's-parsley *n* an evil-smelling Eurasian umbelliferous plant with small white flowers.

foot (fʊt) *n, pl* **feet. 1** the part of the vertebrate leg below the ankle joint that is in contact with the ground during standing and walking. Related adj: **pedal. 2** the part of a garment covering a foot. **3** any of various organs of locomotion or attachment in invertebrates, including molluscs. **4** *Bot.* the lower part of some plants or plant structures. **5** a unit of length equal to one third of a yard or 12 inches. 1 foot is equivalent to 0.3048 metre. **6** any part resembling a foot in form or function: *the foot of a chair.* **7** the lower part of something; bottom: *the foot of a hill.* **8** the end of a series or group: *the foot of the list.* **9** manner of walking or moving: *a heavy foot.* **10a** infantry, esp. in the British army. **10b** (*as modifier*): *a foot soldier.* **11** any of various attachments on a sewing machine that hold the fabric in position. **12** *Prosody.* a group of two or more syllables in which one syllable has the major stress, forming the basic unit of poetic rhythm. **13 my foot!** an expression of disbelief, often of the speaker's own preceding statement. **14 of foot.** *Arch.* in manner of movement: *fleet of foot.* **15 one foot in the grave.** *Inf.* near to death. **16 on foot. 16a** walking or running. **16b** astir; afoot. **17 put a foot wrong.** to make a mistake. **18 put one's best foot forward. 18a** to try to do one's best. **18b** to hurry. **19 put one's foot down.** *Inf.* to act firmly. **20 put one's foot in it.** *Inf.* to blunder. **21 underfoot.** on the ground; beneath one's feet. ◆ *vb* **22** to dance to music (esp. in **foot it**). **23** (*tr*) to walk over or set foot on (esp. in **foot it**). **24** (*tr*) to pay the entire cost of (esp. in **foot the bill**). [OE *fōt*] ◆ See also **feet.**
▸ **'footless** *adj*

> **USAGE NOTE** In front of another noun, the plural for the unit of length is *foot: a 20-foot putt; his 70-foot ketch. Foot* can also be used instead of *feet* when mentioning a quantity and in front of words like *tall: four foot of snow; he is at least six foot tall.*

footage ('fʊtɪdʒ) *n* **1** a length or distance measured in feet. **2** the extent of film material shot and exposed.

foot-and-mouth disease *n* an acute highly infectious viral disease of cattle, pigs, sheep, and goats, characterized by the formation of vesicular eruptions in the mouth and on the feet.

football ('fʊtˌbɔːl) *n* **1a** any of various games played with a round or oval ball and usually based on two teams competing to kick, head, carry, or otherwise propel the ball into each other's goal, territory, etc. **1b** (*as modifier*): *a football supporter.* **2** the ball used in any of these games or their variants. **3** a problem, issue, etc., that is continually passed from one group or person to another as a pretext for argument.
▸ **'footˌballer** *n*

footboard ('fʊtˌbɔːd) *n* **1** a board for a person to stand or rest his feet on. **2** a treadle or foot-operated lever on a machine. **3** a vertical board at the foot of a bed.

footbridge ('fʊtˌbrɪdʒ) *n* a narrow bridge for the use of pedestrians.

-footed *adj* **1** having a foot or feet as specified: *four-footed.* **2** having a tread as specified: *heavy-footed.*

footer[1] ('fʊtə) *n* (*in combination*) a person or thing of a specified length or height in feet: *a six-footer.*

footer[2] ('fʊtə) *n Brit. inf.* short for **football** (the game).

footfall ('fʊtˌfɔːl) *n* the sound of a footstep.

foot fault *n Tennis.* a fault that occurs when the server fails to keep both feet behind the baseline until he has served.

foothill ('fʊtˌhɪl) *n* (*often pl*) a relatively low hill at the foot of a mountain.

foothold ('fʊtˌhəʊld) *n* **1** a ledge or other place affording a secure grip, as during climbing. **2** a secure position from which further progress may be made.

footing ➊ ('fʊtɪŋ) *n* **1** the basis or foundation on which something is established: *the business was on a secure footing.* **2** the relationship or status existing between two persons, groups, etc. **3** a secure grip by or for the feet. **4** the lower part of a foundation of a column, wall, building, etc.

footle ('fuːtᵊl) *vb* **footles, footling, footled.** (*intr*; often foll. by *around* or *about*) *Inf.* to loiter aimlessly. [C19: prob. from F *foutre* to copulate with, from L *futuere*]
▸ **'footling** *adj*

footlights ('fʊtˌlaɪts) *pl n Theatre.* lights set in a row along the front of the stage floor.

footloose ('fʊtˌluːs) *adj* **1** free to go or do as one wishes. **2** restless: *to feel footloose.*

footman ('fʊtmən) *n, pl* **footmen. 1** a male servant, esp. one in livery. **2** (formerly) a foot soldier.

footnote ('fʊtˌnəʊt) *n* **1** a note printed at the bottom of a page, to which attention is drawn by means of a mark in the text. ◆ *vb* **footnotes, footnoting, footnoted. 2** (*tr*) to supply (a page, etc.) with footnotes.

footpad ('fʊtˌpæd) *n Arch.* a robber or highwayman, on foot rather than horseback.

footpath ('fʊtˌpɑːθ) *n* **1** a narrow path for walkers only. **2** *Chiefly Austral. & NZ.* another word for **pavement.**

footplate ('fʊtˌpleɪt) *n Chiefly Brit.* a platform in the cab of a locomotive on which the crew stand to operate the controls.

foot-pound-second *n* See **fps units.**

footprint ('fʊtˌprɪnt) *n* an indentation or outline of the foot of a person or animal on a surface.

footrest ('fʊtˌrest) *n* something that provides a support for the feet, such as a low stool, rail, etc.

foot rot *n Vet. science.* See **rot** (sense 10).

footsie ('fʊtsɪ) *n Inf.* flirtation involving the touching together of feet, etc.

Footsie ('fʊtsɪ) *n Brit. inf.* the Financial Times Stock Exchange 100 index. See **FT Index** (sense 2).

foot soldier *n* an infantryman.

footsore ('fʊtˌsɔː) *adj* having sore or tired feet, esp. from much walking.
▸ **'footˌsoreness** *n*

footstep ➊ ('fʊtˌstɛp) *n* **1** the action of taking a step in walking. **2** the sound made by walking. **3** the distance covered with a step. **4** a footmark. **5** a single stair. **6 follow in someone's footsteps.** to continue the example of another.

footsteps editor *n Brit. films.* the technician who adds sound effects, such as doors closing, rain falling, etc., during the postproduction sound-dubbing process. US name: **foley** *or* **foley artist.**

footstool ('fʊtˌstuːl) *n* a low stool used for supporting or resting the feet of a seated person.

footwear ➊ ('fʊtˌwɛə) *n* anything worn to cover the feet.

footwork ('fʊtˌwɜːk) *n* the use of the feet, esp. in sports, dancing, etc.

footy *or* **footie** ('fʊtɪ) *n Inf.* **a** football. **b** (*as modifier*): *footy boots.*

fop ➊ (fɒp) *n* a man who is excessively concerned with fashion and elegance. [C15: rel. to G *foppen* to trick]
▸ **'foppery** *n* ▸ **'foppish** *adj*

for (fɔː; *unstressed* fə) *prep* **1** directed or belonging to: *there's a phone call for you.* **2** to the advantage of: *I only did it for you.* **3** in the direction of: *heading for the border.* **4** over a span of (time or distance): *working for six days.* **5** in favour of: *vote for me.* **6** in order to get or achieve: *I do it for money.* **7** designed to meet the needs of: *these kennels are for puppies.* **8** at a cost of: *I got it for hardly any money.* **9** such as explains or results in: *his reason for changing his job was not given.* **10** in place of: *a substitute for the injured player.* **11** because of: *she wept for pure relief.* **12** with regard or consideration to the usual characteristics of: *it's cool for this time of year.* **13** concerning: *desire for money.* **14** as being: *I know that for a fact.* **15** at a specified time: *a date for the next evening.* **16** to do or partake of: *an appointment for supper.* **17** in the duty or task of: *that's for him to say.* **18** to allow of: *too big a job for us to handle.* **19** despite: *she's a good wife, for all her nagging.* **20** in order to preserve, retain, etc.: *to fight for survival.* **21** as a direct equivalent to: *word for word.* **22** in order to become or enter: *to train for the priesthood.* **23** in recompense for: *I paid for it last week.* **24 for it.** *Brit. inf.* liable for punishment or blame: *you'll be for it if she catches you.* ◆ *conj* **25** (*coordinating*) because; seeing that: *I couldn't stay, for the area was violent.* [OE]

for- *prefix* **1** indicating rejection or prohibition: *forbid.* **2** indicating falsity: *forswear.* **3** used to give intensive force: *forlorn.* [OE *for-*]

forage ➊ ('fɒrɪdʒ) *n* **1** food for horses or cattle, esp. hay or straw. **2** the act of searching for food or provisions. ◆ *vb* **forages, foraging, foraged. 3** to search (the countryside or a town) for food, etc. **4** (*intr*) *Mil.* to carry out a raid. **5** (*tr*) to obtain by searching about. **6** (*tr*) to give food or other provisions to. **7** (*tr*) to feed (cattle or horses) with such food. [C14: from OF *fourrage*, prob. of Gmc origin]
▸ **'forager** *n*

forage cap *n* a soldier's undress cap.

foramen (fɒ'reɪmɛn) *n, pl* **foramina** (-'ræmɪnə) *or* **foramens.** a natural hole, esp. one in a bone. [C17: from L, from *forāre* to bore, pierce]

foraminifer (ˌfɒrə'mɪnɪfə) *n* a protozoan of the phylum *Foraminifera*, having a shell with numerous openings through which the cytoplasmic processes protrude. [C19: from NL, from FORAMEN + -FER]

forasmuch as (fərəz'mʌtʃ) *conj* (*subordinating*) *Arch. or legal.* seeing that.

foray ➊ ('fɒreɪ) *n* **1** a short raid or incursion. ◆ *vb* **2** to raid or ravage (a town, district, etc.). [C14: from *forrayen* to pillage, from OF, from *fuerre* fodder]

THESAURUS

teed, never-failing, safe, sure-fire (*inf.*), unassailable, unbreakable

footing *n* **1** = **basis**, establishment, foot-hold, foundation, ground, groundwork, installation, settlement **2** = **relationship**, condition, grade, position, rank, relations, standing, state, status, terms

footling *adj* = **trivial**, fiddling, fussy, hairsplitting, immaterial, insignificant, irrelevant, minor, nickel-and-dime (*US sl.*), niggly, petty, pointless, silly, time-wasting, trifling, unimportant

footstep *n* **2** = **step**, footfall, tread **4** = **footprint**, footmark, trace, track

footwear *n* = **footgear**

fop *n* = **dandy**, beau, Beau Brummel, clotheshorse, coxcomb (*arch.*), fashion plate, peacock, popinjay, smoothie *or* smoothy (*sl.*), swell

foppish *adj* = **dandyish**, dandified, dapper, dressy (*inf.*), finical, natty (*inf.*), preening, primping, spruce, vain

forage *n* **1** = **fodder**, feed, food, foodstuffs, provender ◆ *vb* **3-5** = **search**, cast about, explore, hunt, look round, plunder, raid, ransack, rummage, scavenge, scour, scrounge (*inf.*), seek

foray *n* **1** = **raid**, depredation, descent, incursion, inroad, invasion, irruption, reconnaissance, sally, sortie, swoop

forbade (fə'bæd, -'beɪd) *or* **forbad** (fə'bæd) *vb* the past tense of **forbid**.
forbear[1] ➊ (fɔː'bɛə) *vb* **forbears, forbearing, forbore, forborne. 1** (when *intr*, often foll. by *from* or an infinitive) to cease or refrain (from doing something). **2** *Arch.* to tolerate (misbehaviour, etc.). [OE *forberan*]
forbear[2] ('fɔːˌbɛə) *n* a variant spelling of **forebear**.
forbearance ➊ (fɔː'bɛərəns) *n* **1** the act of forbearing. **2** self-control; patience.
forbid ➊ (fə'bɪd) *vb* **forbids, forbidding, forbade** *or* **forbad, forbidden** *or* **forbid.** (*tr*) **1** to prohibit (a person) in a forceful or authoritative manner (from doing or having something). **2** to make impossible. **3** to shut out or exclude. [OE *forbēodan;* see FOR-, BID]
▸**for'bidder** *n*

> **USAGE NOTE** It was formerly considered incorrect to talk of *forbidding* someone *from* doing something, but in modern usage either *from* or *to* can be used: *he was forbidden from entering/to enter the building.*

forbidden ➊ (fə'bɪdᵊn) *adj* **1** not permitted by order or law. **2** *Physics.* involving a change in quantum numbers that is not permitted by certain rules derived from quantum mechanics.
forbidden fruit *n* any pleasure or enjoyment regarded as illicit, esp. sexual indulgence.
forbidding ➊ (fə'bɪdɪŋ) *adj* **1** hostile or unfriendly. **2** dangerous or ominous.
forbore (fɔː'bɔː) *vb* the past tense of **forbear**[1].
forborne (fɔː'bɔːn) *vb* the past participle of **forbear**[1].
force[1] ➊ (fɔːs) *n* **1** strength or energy; power: *the force of the blow.* **2** exertion or the use of exertion against a person or thing that resists. **3** *Physics.* **3a** a dynamic influence that changes a body from a state of rest to one of motion or changes its rate of motion. **3b** a static influence that produces a strain in a body or system. Symbol: *F* **4a** intellectual, political, or moral influence or strength: *the force of his argument.* **4b** a person or thing with such influence: *he was a force in the land.* **5** vehemence or intensity: *she spoke with great force.* **6** a group of persons organized for military or police functions: *armed forces.* **7** (*sometimes cap.;* preceded by *the*) *Inf.* the police force. **8** a group of persons organized for particular duties or tasks: *a workforce.* **9** *Criminal law.* violence unlawfully committed or threatened. **10 in force. 10a** (of a law) having legal validity. **10b** in great strength or numbers. ◆ *vb* **forces, forcing, forced.** (*tr*) **11** to compel or cause (a person, group, etc.) to do something through effort, superior strength, etc. **12** to acquire or produce through effort, superior strength, etc.: *to force a confession.* **13** to propel or drive despite resistance. **14** to break down or open (a lock, door, etc.). **15** to impose or inflict: *he forced his views on them.* **16** to cause (plants or farm animals) to grow or fatten artificially at an increased rate. **17** to strain to the utmost: *to force the voice.* **18** to rape. **19** *Cards.* **19a** to compel a player by the lead of a particular suit to play (a certain card). **19b** (in bridge) to induce (a bid) from one's partner. [C13: from OF, from Vulgar L *fortia* (unattested), from L *fortis* strong]
▸**'forceable** *adj* ▸**'forceless** *adj* ▸**'forcer** *n*
force[2] (fɔːs) *n* (in N England) a waterfall. [C17: from ON *fors*]
forced ➊ (fɔːst) *adj* **1** done because of force: *forced labour.* **2** false or unnatural: *a forced smile.* **3** due to an emergency or necessity: *a forced landing.*
force de frappe (*French* fɔrs də frap) *n* a military strike force, esp. the independent nuclear strike force of France. [C20: F, lit.: striking force]
force-feed *vb* **force-feeds, force-feeding, force-fed.** (*tr*) to force (a person or animal) to eat or swallow food.
forceful ➊ ('fɔːsful) *adj* **1** powerful. **2** persuasive or effective.
▸**'forcefully** *adv* ▸**'forcefulness** *n*
forcemeat ('fɔːsˌmiːt) *n* a mixture of chopped ingredients used for stuffing. Also called: **farce.** [C17: from *force* (see FARCE) + MEAT]
forceps ('fɔːsɪps) *n, pl* **forceps. 1a** a surgical instrument in the form of a pair of pincers, used esp. in the delivery of babies. **1b** (*as modifier*): *a forceps baby.* **2** any part of an organism shaped like a forceps. [C17: from L, from *formus* hot + *capere* to seize]
force pump *n* a pump that ejects fluid under pressure. Cf. **lift pump.**
Forces ('fɔːsɪz) *pl n* (usually preceded by *the*) the armed services of a nation.
forcible ➊ ('fɔːsəbᵊl) *adj* **1** done by, involving, or having force. **2** convincing or effective: *a forcible argument.*
▸**'forcibly** *adv*
ford (fɔːd) *n* **1** a shallow area in a river that can be crossed by car, on horseback, etc. ◆ *vb* **2** (*tr*) to cross (a river, brook, etc.) over a shallow area. [OE]
▸**'fordable** *adj*
fore[1] (fɔː) *adj* **1** (*usually in combination*) located at, in, or towards the front: *the forelegs of a horse.* ◆ *n* **2** the front part. **3** something located at, or towards the front. **4 fore and aft.** located at both ends of a vessel: *a fore-and-aft rig.* **5 to the fore.** to the front or conspicuous position. ◆ *adv* **6** at or towards a ship's bow. **7** *Obs.* before. ◆ *prep, conj* **8** a less common word for **before.** [OE]
fore[2] (fɔː) *sentence substitute.* (in golf) a warning shout made by a player about to make a shot. [C19: prob. short for BEFORE]
fore- *prefix* **1** before in time or rank: *forefather.* **2** at or near the front: *forecourt.* [OE, from *fore* (adv)]
fore-and-after *n Naut.* **1** any vessel with a fore-and-aft rig. **2** a double-ended vessel.
forearm[1] ('fɔːrˌɑːm) *n* the part of the arm from the elbow to the wrist. [C18: from FORE- + ARM[1]]
forearm[2] (fɔːr'ɑːm) *vb* (*tr*) to prepare or arm (someone) in advance. [C16: from FORE- + ARM[2]]
forebear ➊ *or* **forbear** ('fɔːˌbɛə) *n* an ancestor.
forebode ➊ (fɔː'bəud) *vb* **forebodes, foreboding, foreboded. 1** to warn of or indicate (an event, result, etc.) in advance. **2** to have a premonition of (an event).
foreboding ➊ (fɔː'bəudɪŋ) *n* **1** a feeling of impending evil, disaster, etc. **2** an omen or portent. ◆ *adj* **3** presaging something.
forebrain ('fɔːˌbreɪn) *n* the nontechnical name for **prosencephalon.**
forecast ➊ ('fɔːˌkɑːst) *vb* **forecasts, forecasting, forecast** *or* **forecasted. 1** to predict or calculate (weather, events, etc.), in advance. **2** (*tr*) to serve as an early indication of. ◆ *n* **3** a statement of probable future weather calculated from meteorological data. **4** a prediction. **5** the practice or power of forecasting.
▸**'foreˌcaster** *n*
forecastle, fo'c's'le, *or* **fo'c'sle** ('fəuksᵊl) *n* the part of a vessel at the bow where the crew is quartered.
foreclose (fɔː'kləuz) *vb* **forecloses, foreclosing, foreclosed. 1** *Law.* to deprive (a mortgagor, etc.) of the right to redeem (a mortgage or

THESAURUS

forbear[1] *vb* **1 = refrain**, abstain, avoid, cease, decline, desist, eschew, hold back, keep from, omit, pause, resist the temptation to, restrain oneself, stop, withhold
forbearance *n* **1 = abstinence**, avoidance, refraining **2 = patience**, indulgence, leniency, lenity, longanimity (*rare*), long-suffering, mildness, moderation, resignation, restraint, self-control, temperance, tolerance
Antonyms *n* ≠ **patience:** anger, impatience, impetuosity, intolerance, irritability, shortness
forbearing *adj* **2 = patient**, clement, easy, forgiving, indulgent, lenient, long-suffering, merciful, mild, moderate, tolerant
forbid *vb* **1 = prohibit**, ban, debar, disallow, exclude, hinder, inhibit, interdict, outlaw, preclude, proscribe, rule out, veto
Antonyms *vb* allow, approve, authorize, bid, enable, endorse, grant, let, license, O.K. *or* okay (*inf.*), order, permit, sanction
forbidden *adj* **1 = prohibited**, banned, outlawed, out of bounds, proscribed, taboo, *verboten*, vetoed
forbidding *adj* **1, 2 = threatening**, baleful, daunting, foreboding, frightening, grim, hostile, menacing, ominous, sinister, unfriendly
Antonyms *adj* alluring, attractive, beguiling, enticing, inviting, magnetic, tempting, welcoming, winning
force[1] *n* **1 = power**, dynamism, energy, impact, impulse, life, might, momentum, muscle, potency, pressure, stimulus, strength, stress, vigour **2 = compulsion**, arm-twisting (*inf.*), coercion, constraint, duress, enforcement, pressure, violence **4 = influence**, bite, cogency, effect, effectiveness, efficacy, persuasiveness, power, punch (*inf.*), strength, validity, weight **5 = intensity**, drive, emphasis, fierceness, persistence, vehemence, vigour **6 = army**, battalion, body, corps, detachment, division, host, legion, patrol, regiment, squad, squadron, troop, unit **10 in force: a = valid**, binding, current, effective, in operation, on the statute book, operative, working **b = in great numbers**, all together, in full strength ◆ *vb* **11 = compel**, bring pressure to bear upon, coerce, constrain, dragoon, drive, impel, impose, make, necessitate, obligate, oblige, overcome, press, press-gang, pressure, pressurize, put the screws on (*inf.*), put the squeeze on (*inf.*), railroad (*inf.*), strong-arm (*inf.*), twist (someone's) arm, urge **12 = extort**, drag, exact, wring **13 = push**, propel, thrust **14 = break open**, blast, prise, use violence on, wrench, wrest
Antonyms *n* ≠ **power:** debility, enervation, feebleness, fragility, frailty, impotence, ineffectiveness, irresolution, powerlessness, weakness ◆ *vb* ≠ **extort:** coax, convince, induce, persuade, prevail, talk into
forced *adj* **1 = compulsory**, conscripted, enforced, involuntary, mandatory, obligatory, slave, unwilling **2 = false**, affected, artificial, contrived, insincere, laboured, stiff, strained, unnatural, wooden
Antonyms *adj* ≠ **compulsory:** spontaneous, voluntary ≠ **false:** easy, natural, simple, sincere, spontaneous, unforced, unpretending
forceful *adj* **1, 2 = powerful**, cogent, compelling, convincing, dynamic, effective, persuasive, pithy, potent, telling, vigorous, weighty
Antonyms *adj* enervated, exhausted, faint, feeble, frail, powerless, spent, weak
forcible *adj* **1 = violent**, aggressive, armed, coercive, compulsory, drastic **2 = compelling**, active, cogent, effective, efficient, energetic, forceful, impressive, mighty, potent, powerful, strong, telling, valid, weighty
forcibly *adv* **1 = by force**, against one's will, by main force, compulsorily, under compulsion, under protest, willy-nilly
forebear *n* **= ancestor**, father, forefather, forerunner, predecessor, progenitor
forebode *vb* **1 = portend**, augur, betoken, foreshadow, foreshow, foretell, foretoken, forewarn, indicate, predict, presage, prognosticate, promise, vaticinate (*rare*), warn of
foreboding *n* **1 = dread**, anxiety, apprehension, apprehensiveness, chill, fear, misgiving, premonition, presentiment **2 = omen**, augury, foreshadowing, foretoken, portent, prediction, presage, prognostication, sign, token, warning
forecast *vb* **1 = predict**, anticipate, augur, calculate, call, divine, estimate, foresee, foretell, plan, prognosticate, prophesy, vaticinate (*rare*) ◆ *n* **4 = prediction**, anticipation, conjecture, foresight, forethought, guess, outlook, planning, prognosis, projection, prophecy

pledge). **2** (*tr*) to shut out; bar. **3** (*tr*) to prevent or hinder. [C15: from OF, from *for-* out + *clore* to close, from L *claudere*]
►**fore'closable** *adj* ►**foreclosure** (fɔːˈkləʊʒə) *n*

forecourt (ˈfɔːˌkɔːt) *n* **1** a courtyard in front of a building, as one in a filling station. **2** the section of the court in tennis, badminton, etc., between the service line and the net.

foredoom (fɔːˈduːm) *vb* (*tr*) to doom or condemn beforehand.

forefather Ⓣ (ˈfɔːˌfɑːðə) *n* an ancestor, esp. a male.
►**'fore,fatherly** *adj*

forefinger (ˈfɔːˌfɪŋgə) *n* the finger next to the thumb. Also called: **index finger.**

forefoot (ˈfɔːˌfʊt) *n, pl* **forefeet.** either of the front feet of a quadruped.

forefront Ⓣ (ˈfɔːˌfrʌnt) *n* **1** the extreme front. **2** the position of most prominence or action.

foregather *or* **forgather** (fɔːˈgæðə) *vb* (*intr*) **1** to gather together. **2** (foll. by *with*) to socialize.

forego[1] Ⓣ (fɔːˈgəʊ) *vb* **foregoes, foregoing, forewent, foregone.** to precede in time, place, etc. [OE *foregān*]

forego[2] (fɔːˈgəʊ) *vb* **foregoes, foregoing, forewent, foregone.** (*tr*) a variant spelling of **forgo.**

foregoing Ⓣ (fɔːˈgəʊɪŋ) *adj* (*prenominal*) (esp. of writing or speech) going before; preceding.

foregone (fɔːˈgɒn, ˈfɔːˌgɒn) *adj* gone or completed; past.
►**fore'goneness** *n*

foregone conclusion *n* an inevitable result or conclusion.

foreground Ⓣ (ˈfɔːˌgraʊnd) *n* **1** the part of a scene situated towards the front or nearest to the viewer. **2** a conspicuous position.

forehand (ˈfɔːˌhænd) *adj* (*prenominal*) **1** *Tennis, squash, etc.* (of a stroke) made with the palm of the hand facing the direction of the stroke. ◆ *n* **2** *Tennis, squash, etc.* **2a** a forehand stroke. **2b** the side on which such strokes are made. **3** the part of a horse in front of the saddle.

forehead (ˈfɒrɪd, ˈfɔːˌhɛd) *n* the part of the face between the natural hairline and the eyes. Related adj: **frontal.** [OE *forhēafod*]

foreign Ⓣ (ˈfɒrɪn) *adj* **1** of, located in, or coming from another country, area, people, etc.: *a foreign resident.* **2** dealing or concerned with another country, area, people, etc.: *a foreign office.* **3** not pertinent or related: *a matter foreign to the discussion.* **4** not familiar; strange. **5** in an abnormal place or position: *foreign matter.* [C13: from OF, from Vulgar L *forānus* (unattested) on the outside, from L *foris* outside]
►**'foreignness** *n*

foreign affairs *pl n* matters abroad that involve the homeland, such as relations with another country.

foreigner Ⓣ (ˈfɒrɪnə) *n* **1** a person from a foreign country. **2** an outsider. **3** something from a foreign country, such as a ship or product.

foreign minister *or* **secretary** *n* (*often caps.*) a cabinet minister who is responsible for a country's dealings with other countries. US equivalent: **secretary of state.**

foreign office *n* the ministry of a country or state that is concerned with dealings with other states. US equivalent: **State Department.**

foreknowledge Ⓣ (fɔːˈnɒlɪdʒ) *n* knowledge of a thing before it exists or occurs; prescience.
►**fore'know** *vb* ►**fore'knowable** *adj*

foreland (ˈfɔːlənd) *n* **1** a headland, cape, or promontory. **2** land lying in front of something, such as water.

foreleg (ˈfɔːˌlɛg) *n* either of the front legs of a horse, sheep, or other quadruped.

forelimb (ˈfɔːˌlɪm) *n* either of the front or anterior limbs of a four-limbed vertebrate.

forelock (ˈfɔːˌlɒk) *n* a lock of hair growing or falling over the forehead.

foreman (ˈfɔːmən) *n, pl* **foremen. 1** a person, often experienced, who supervises other workmen. **2** *Law.* the principal juror, who presides at the deliberations of a jury.

foremast (ˈfɔːˌmɑːst; *Naut.* ˈfɔːməst) *n* the mast nearest the bow on vessels with two or more masts.

foremost Ⓣ (ˈfɔːˌməʊst) *adj, adv* first in time, place, rank, etc. [OE, from *forma* first]

forename Ⓣ (ˈfɔːˌneɪm) *n* another term for **first name.**

forenamed (ˈfɔːˌneɪmd) *adj* (*prenominal*) named or mentioned previously; aforesaid.

forenoon (ˈfɔːˌnuːn) *n* the daylight hours before or just before noon.

forensic (fəˈrɛnsɪk) *adj* used in, or connected with a court of law: *forensic science.* [C17: from L *forēnsis* public, from FORUM]
►**fo'rensically** *adv*

forensic medicine *n* the use of medical knowledge, esp. pathology, for the purposes of the law, as in determining the cause of death. Also called: **medical jurisprudence.**

foreordain Ⓣ (ˌfɔːrɔːˈdeɪn) *vb* (*tr; may take a clause as object*) to determine (events, etc.) in the future.
►**foreordination** (ˌfɔːrɔːdɪˈneɪʃən) *n*

forepaw (ˈfɔːˌpɔː) *n* either of the front feet of most land mammals that do not have hoofs.

foreplay (ˈfɔːˌpleɪ) *n* mutual sexual stimulation preceding sexual intercourse.

forequarter (ˈfɔːˌkwɔːtə) *n* the front portion, including the leg, of half of a carcass, as of beef.

forequarters (ˈfɔːˌkwɔːtəz) *pl n* the part of the body of a horse, etc. that consists of the forelegs, shoulders, and adjoining parts.

forerun (fɔːˈrʌn) *vb* **foreruns, forerunning, foreran, forerun.** (*tr*) **1** to serve as a herald for. **2** to precede. **3** to forestall.

forerunner Ⓣ (ˈfɔːˌrʌnə) *n* **1** a person or thing that precedes another. **2** a person or thing coming in advance to herald the arrival of someone or something. **3** an omen; portent.

foresail (ˈfɔːˌseɪl; *Naut.* ˈfɔːsᵊl) *n Naut.* **1** the aftermost headsail of a fore-and-aft rigged vessel. **2** the lowest sail set on the foremast of a square-rigged vessel.

foresee Ⓣ (fɔːˈsiː) *vb* **foresees, foreseeing, foresaw, foreseen.** (*tr; may take a clause as object*) to see or know beforehand: *he did not foresee that.*
►**fore'seeable** *adj* ►**fore'seer** *n*

foreshadow Ⓣ (fɔːˈʃædəʊ) *vb* (*tr*) to show, indicate, or suggest in advance; presage.

foreshank (ˈfɔːˌʃæŋk) *n* **1** the top of the front leg of an animal. **2** a cut of meat from this part.

foresheet (ˈfɔːˌʃiːt) *n* **1** the sheet of a foresail. **2** (*pl*) the part forward of the foremost thwart of a boat.

foreshock (ˈfɔːˌʃɒk) *n Chiefly US.* a relatively small earthquake heralding the arrival of a much larger one.

foreshore (ˈfɔːˌʃɔː) *n* **1** the part of the shore that lies between the limits for high and low tides. **2** the part of the shore that lies just above the high water mark.

foreshorten (fɔːˈʃɔːtᵊn) *vb* (*tr*) to represent (a line, form, object, etc.) as shorter than actual length in order to give an illusion of recession or projection.

foreshow (fɔːˈʃəʊ) *vb* **foreshows, foreshowing, foreshowed; foreshown** *or* **foreshowed.** (*tr*) *Arch.* to indicate in advance.

foresight Ⓣ (ˈfɔːˌsaɪt) *n* **1** provision for or insight into future problems, needs, etc. **2** the act or ability of foreseeing. **3** the act of looking forward. **4** *Surveying.* a reading taken looking forwards. **5** the front sight on a firearm.
►**ˌfore'sighted** *adj* ►**ˌfore'sightedly** *adv* ►**ˌfore'sightedness** *n*

foreskin (ˈfɔːˌskɪn) *n Anat.* the nontechnical name for **prepuce.**

forest (ˈfɒrɪst) *n* **1** a large wooded area having a thick growth of trees and plants. **2** the trees of such an area. **3** *NZ.* an area planted with pines or similar trees, not native trees. Cf. **bush**[1] (sense 4). **4** something resembling a large wooded area, esp. in density: *a forest of telegraph poles.* **5** *Law.* (formerly) an area of woodland, esp. one owned by the sovereign and set apart as a hunting ground. **6** (*modifier*) of, involving, or living in a forest or forests: *a forest glade.* ◆ *vb* **7** (*tr*) to create a forest. [C13: from OF, from Med. L *forestis* unfenced woodland, from L *foris* outside]
►**'forested** *adj*

forestall Ⓣ (fɔːˈstɔːl) *vb* (*tr*) **1** to delay, stop, or guard against beforehand. **2** to anticipate. **3** to buy up merchandise for profitable resale. [C14 *forestallen* to waylay, from OE, from *fore-* in front of + *steall* place]
►**fore'staller** *n* ►**fore'stalment** *n*

forestation (ˌfɒrɪˈsteɪʃən) *n* the planting of trees over a wide area.

forestay (ˈfɔːˌsteɪ) *n Naut.* an adjustable stay leading from the truck of the foremast to the deck, for controlling the bending of the mast.

forester (ˈfɒrɪstə) *n* **1** a person skilled in forestry or in charge of a forest.

THESAURUS

forefather *n* = **ancestor**, father, forebear, forerunner, predecessor, primogenitor, procreator, progenitor

forefront *n* **1, 2** = **lead**, centre, fore, foreground, front, prominence, spearhead, van, vanguard

forego[2] *see* **forgo**

foregoing *adj* = **preceding**, above, antecedent, anterior, former, previous, prior

foreground *n* **2** = **front**, centre, forefront, limelight, prominence

foreign *adj* **1, 4** = **alien**, beyond one's ken, borrowed, distant, exotic, external, imported, outlandish, outside, overseas, remote, strange, unfamiliar, unknown **3** = **extraneous**, extrinsic, incongruous, irrelevant, unassimilable, uncharacteristic, unrelated
Antonyms *adj* ≠ **alien:** customary, domestic, familiar, native, well-known ≠ **extraneous:** applicable, characteristic, intrinsic, pertinent, relevant, suited

foreigner *n* **1** = **alien**, immigrant, incomer, newcomer, outlander, stranger

foreknowledge *n* = **prior knowledge**, clairvoyance, foresight, forewarning, precognition, prescience, prevision

foremost *adj* = **leading**, chief, first, front, headmost, highest, inaugural, initial, paramount, pre-eminent, primary, prime, principal, supreme

forename *n* = **first name**, Christian name, given name

foreordain *vb* = **predestine**, doom, fate, foredoom, prearrange, predetermine, preordain, reserve

forerunner *n* **1, 2** = **precursor**, ancestor, announcer, envoy, forebear, foregoer, harbinger, herald, predecessor, progenitor, prototype **3** = **omen**, augury, foretoken, indication, portent, premonition, prognostic, sign, token

foresee *vb* = **predict**, anticipate, divine, envisage, forebode, forecast, foretell, prophesy, vaticinate (*rare*)

foreshadow *vb* = **predict**, adumbrate, augur, betoken, bode, forebode, imply, indicate, portend, prefigure, presage, promise, prophesy, signal

foresight *n* **1, 2** = **forethought**, anticipation, care, caution, circumspection, far-sightedness, precaution, premeditation, preparedness, prescience, prevision (*rare*), provision, prudence
Antonyms *n* carelessness, hindsight, imprudence, inconsideration, lack of foresight, neglect, retrospection, thoughtlessness, unpreparedness

forestall *vb* **1, 2** = **prevent**, anticipate, balk, circumvent, frustrate, head off, hinder, intercept, nip in the bud, obviate, parry, preclude, provide against, thwart

2 a person or animal that lives in a forest. 3 (*cap.*) a member of the Ancient Order of Foresters, a friendly society.

forest park *n NZ.* a recreational reserve which may include bush and exotic trees.

forestry Ⓣ ('fɒrɪstrɪ) *n* **1** the science of planting and caring for trees. **2** the planting and management of forests. **3** *Rare.* forest land.

foretaste Ⓣ ('fɔːˌteɪst) *n* an early but limited experience of something to come.

foretell Ⓣ (fɔː'tɛl) *vb* **foretells, foretelling, foretold.** (*tr; may take a clause as object*) to tell or indicate (an event, a result, etc.) beforehand.

forethought Ⓣ ('fɔːˌθɔːt) *n* **1** advance consideration or deliberation. **2** thoughtful anticipation of future events.

foretoken Ⓣ *n* ('fɔːˌtəʊkən). **1** a sign of a future event. ◆ *vb* (fɔː'təʊkən). **2** (*tr*) to foreshadow.

foretop ('fɔːˌtɒp; *Naut.* 'fɔːtəp) *n Naut.* a platform at the top of the foremast.

fore-topgallant (ˌfɔːtɒp'gælənt; *Naut.* ˌfɔːtə'gælənt) *adj Naut.* of, relating to, or being the topmost portion of a foremast.

fore-topmast (fɔː'tɒpˌmɑːst; *Naut.* fɔː'tɒpməst) *n Naut.* a mast stepped above a foremast.

fore-topsail (fɔː'tɒpˌseɪl; *Naut.* fɔː'tɒpsᵊl) *n Naut.* a sail set on a fore-topmast.

forever Ⓣ (fɔː'rɛvə, fə-) *adv* **1** Also: **for ever.** without end; everlastingly. **2** at all times. **3** *Inf.* for a very long time: *he went on speaking forever.* ◆ *n* **forever. 4** (*as object*) *Inf.* a very long time: *it took him forever to reply.*

> **USAGE NOTE** *Forever* and *for ever* can both be used to say that something is without end. For all other meanings, *forever* is the preferred form.

for evermore *or* **forevermore** (fɔːˌrɛvə'mɔː, fə-) *adv* a more emphatic or emotive term for **forever.**

forewarn Ⓣ (fɔː'wɔːn) *vb* (*tr*) to warn beforehand.
▸**fore'warner** *n*

forewent (fɔː'wɛnt) *vb* the past tense of **forego.**

forewing ('fɔːˌwɪŋ) *n* either wing of the anterior pair of an insect's two pairs of wings.

foreword Ⓣ ('fɔːˌwɜːd) *n* an introductory statement to a book. [C19: literal translation of G *Vorwort*]

forfaiting ('fɔːˌfeɪtɪŋ) *n* the financial service of discounting, without recourse, a promissory note, bill of exchange, letter of credit, etc., received from an overseas buyer by an exporter; a form of debt discounting. [C20: from F *forfaire* to forfeit or surrender]

forfeit Ⓣ ('fɔːfɪt) *n* **1** something lost or given up as a penalty for a fault, mistake, etc. **2** the act of losing or surrendering something in this manner. **3** *Law.* something confiscated as a penalty for an offence, etc. **4** (*sometimes pl*) **4a** a game in which a player has to give up an object, perform a specified action, etc., if he commits a fault. **4b** an object so given up. ◆ *vb* (*tr*) **5** to lose or be liable to lose in consequence of a mistake, fault, etc. **6** *Law.* to confiscate as punishment. ◆ *adj* **7** surrendered or liable to be surrendered as a penalty. [C13: from OF *forfet* offence, from *forfaire* to commit a crime, from Med. L, from L *foris* outside + *facere* to do]
▸**'forfeiter** *n*

forfeiture Ⓣ ('fɔːfɪtʃə) *n* **1** something forfeited. **2** the act of forfeiting or paying a penalty.

forfend *or* **forefend** (fɔː'fɛnd) *vb* (*tr*) **1** *US.* to protect or secure. **2** *Obs.* to prevent.

forgather (fɔː'gæðə) *vb* a variant spelling of **foregather.**

forgave (fə'geɪv) *vb* the past tense of **forgive.**

forge[1] Ⓣ (fɔːdʒ) *n* **1** a place in which metal is worked by heating and hammering; smithy. **2** a hearth or furnace used for heating metal. ◆ *vb* **forges, forging, forged. 3** (*tr*) to shape (metal) by heating and hammering. **4** (*tr*) to form, make, or fashion (objects, etc.). **5** (*tr*) to invent or devise (an agreement, etc.). **6** to make a fraudulent imitation of (a signature, etc.) or to commit forgery. [C14: from OF *forgier* to construct, from L *fabricāre*, from *faber* craftsman]
▸**'forger** *n*

forge[2] (fɔːdʒ) *vb* **forges, forging, forged.** (*intr*) **1** to move at a steady pace. **2** **forge ahead.** to increase speed. [C17: from ?]

forgery Ⓣ ('fɔːdʒərɪ) *n, pl* **forgeries. 1** the act of reproducing something for a fraudulent purpose. **2** something forged, such as an antique. **3** *Criminal law.* **3a** the false making or altering of a document, such as a cheque, etc., or any tape or disc storing information, with intent to defraud. **3b** something forged.

forget Ⓣ (fə'gɛt) *vb* **forgets, forgetting, forgot, forgotten** *or* (*Arch. or dialect*) **forgot. 1** (when *tr, may take a clause as object or an infinitive*) to fail to recall (someone or something once known). **2** (*tr; may take a clause as object or an infinitive*) to neglect, either as the result of an unintentional error or intentionally. **3** (*tr*) to leave behind by mistake. **4** **forget oneself. 4a** to act in an improper manner. **4b** to be unselfish. **4c** to be deep in thought. [OE *forgietan*]
▸**for'gettable** *adj* ▸**for'getter** *n*

forgetful Ⓣ (fə'gɛtfʊl) *adj* **1** tending to forget. **2** (*often postpositive; foll. by of*) inattentive (to) or neglectful (of).
▸**for'getfully** *adv* ▸**for'getfulness** *n*

forget-me-not *n* a temperate low-growing plant having clusters of small blue flowers.

forgive Ⓣ (fə'gɪv) *vb* **forgives, forgiving, forgave, forgiven. 1** to cease to blame (someone or something). **2** to grant pardon for (a mistake, etc.). **3** (*tr*) to free (someone) from penalty. **4** (*tr*) to free from the obligation of (a debt, etc.). [OE *forgiefan*]
▸**for'givable** *adj* ▸**for'giver** *n*

forgiveness Ⓣ (fə'gɪvnɪs) *n* **1** the act of forgiving or the state of being forgiven. **2** willingness to forgive.

forgiving Ⓣ (fə'gɪvɪŋ) *adj* willing to forgive.

forgo Ⓣ *or* **forego** (fɔː'gəʊ) *vb* **forgoes, forgoing, forwent, forgone.** (*tr*) to give up or do without. [OE *forgān*]

forgot (fə'gɒt) *vb* **1** the past tense of **forget. 2** *Arch. or dialect.* a past participle of **forget.**

forgotten Ⓣ (fə'gɒtᵊn) *vb* a past participle of **forget.**

forint (*Hungarian* 'forint) *n* the standard monetary unit of Hungary. [from Hungarian, from It. *fiorino* FLORIN]

fork Ⓣ (fɔːk) *n* **1** a small usually metal implement consisting of two, three, or four long thin prongs on the end of a handle, used for lifting food to the mouth, etc. **2** a similar-shaped agricultural tool, used for lifting, digging, etc. **3** a pronged part of any machine, device, etc. **4** (of a road, river, etc.) **4a** a division into two or more branches. **4b** the point where the division begins. **4c** such a branch. ◆ *vb* **5** (*tr*) to pick up, dig, etc., with a fork. **6** (*tr*) *Chess.* to place (two enemy pieces) under attack with one of one's own pieces. **7** (*intr*) to be divided into two or more branches. **8** to take one or other branch at a fork in a road, etc. [OE *forca*, from L *furca*]

THESAURUS

forestry *n* **1** = **woodcraft**, arboriculture, dendrology (*Botany*), silviculture, woodmanship

foretaste *n* = **sample**, example, foretoken, indication, prelude, preview, trailer, warning, whiff

foretell *vb* = **predict**, adumbrate, augur, bode, call, forebode, forecast, foreshadow, foreshow, forewarn, portend, presage, prognosticate, prophesy, signify, soothsay, vaticinate (*rare*)

forethought *n* **2** = **anticipation**, farsightedness, foresight, precaution, providence, provision, prudence
Antonyms *n* carelessness, imprudence, impulsiveness, inconsideration, neglect, unpreparedness

foretoken *vb* **2** = **portend**, augur, forebode, foreshadow, foreshow, give notice of, give warning of, presage, signify, warn of

forever *adv* **1** = **evermore**, always, for all time, for good and all (*inf.*), for keeps, in perpetuity, till Doomsday, till the cows come home (*inf.*), till the end of time, world without end **2** = **constantly**, all the time, continually, endlessly, eternally, everlastingly, incessantly, interminably, perpetually, unremittingly

forewarn *vb* = **caution**, admonish, advise, alert, apprise, dissuade, give fair warning, put on guard, put on the qui vive, tip off

foreword *n* = **introduction**, preamble, preface, preliminary, prolegomenon, prologue

forfeit *n* **1** = **penalty**, amercement, damages, fine, forfeiture, loss, mulct ◆ *vb* **5** = **lose**, be deprived of, be stripped of, give up, relinquish, renounce, say goodbye to, surrender

forfeiture *n* **2** = **loss**, confiscation, giving up, relinquishment, sequestration (*Law*), surrender

forge[1] *vb* **3, 4** = **create**, construct, contrive, devise, fabricate, fashion, form, frame, hammer out, invent, make, mould, shape, work **6** = **fake**, coin, copy, counterfeit, falsify, feign, imitate

forged *adj* **3, 4** = **formed**, beat out, cast, crafted, fashioned, founded, framed, hammered out, minted, modelled, moulded, shaped, stamped, worked **6** = **fake**, artificial, bogus, copy, copycat (*inf.*), counterfeit, duplicate, ersatz, fabricated, false, falsified, fraudulent, imitation, mock, phony *or* phoney (*inf.*), pretend, pseudo, quasi, reproduction, sham, simulated, synthetic, ungenuine, unoriginal
Antonyms *adj* ≠ **fake:** actual, authentic, bona fide, *echt*, genuine, honest, kosher (*inf.*), legitimate, original, real, true

forger *n* **6** = **counterfeiter**, coiner, falsifier

forgery *n* **1** = **falsification**, coining, counterfeiting, fraudulence, fraudulent imitation **2** = **fake**, counterfeit, falsification, imitation, phoney *or* phony (*inf.*), sham

forget *vb* **1** = **dismiss from one's mind**, consign to oblivion, let bygones be bygones, let slip from the memory **3** = **neglect**, leave behind, lose sight of, omit, overlook
Antonyms *vb* bring to mind, mind, recall, recollect, remember, retain

forgetful *adj* **1, 2** = **absent-minded**, apt to forget, careless, dreamy, having a memory like a sieve, heedless, inattentive, lax, neglectful, negligent, oblivious, slapdash, slipshod, unmindful, vague
Antonyms *adj* attentive, careful, mindful, retentive, unforgetful, unforgetting

forgetfulness *n* **1, 2** = **absent-mindedness**, abstraction, carelessness, dreaminess, heedlessness, inattention, lapse of memory, laxity, laxness, oblivion, obliviousness, woolgathering

forgive *vb* **1, 2** = **excuse**, absolve, accept (someone's) apology, acquit, bear no malice, condone, exonerate, let bygones be bygones, let off (*inf.*), pardon, remit
Antonyms *vb* blame, censure, charge, condemn, find fault with, reproach, reprove

forgiveness *n* **1** = **pardon**, absolution, acquittal, amnesty, condonation, exoneration, mercy, overlooking, remission

forgiving *adj* = **lenient**, clement, compassionate, forbearing, humane, magnanimous, merciful, mild, soft-hearted, tolerant

forgo *vb* = **give up**, abandon, abjure, cede, do without, kick (*inf.*), leave alone *or* out, relinquish, renounce, resign, sacrifice, say goodbye to, surrender, waive, yield

forgotten *adj* **1, 3** = **unremembered**, blotted out, buried, bygone, consigned to oblivion, gone (clean) out of one's mind, left behind, lost, obliterated, omitted, past, past recall

fork *vb* **7** = **branch**, bifurcate, branch off, diverge, divide, go separate ways, part, split

forked ➊ (fɔːkt) *adj* **1a** having a fork or forklike parts. **1b** (*in combination*): *two-forked*. **2** zigzag: *forked lightning*.
▸**forkedly** (ˈfɔːkɪdlɪ) *adv*

fork-lift truck *n* a vehicle having two power-operated horizontal prongs that can be raised and lowered for transporting and unloading goods. Sometimes shortened to **fork-lift**.

fork out, over, *or* **up** *vb* (*adv*) *Sl.* to pay (money, goods, etc.), esp. with reluctance.

forlorn ➊ (fəˈlɔːn) *adj* **1** miserable or cheerless. **2** forsaken. **3** (*postpositive*; foll. by *of*) bereft: *forlorn of hope*. **4** desperate: *the last forlorn attempt*. [OE *forloren* lost, from *forlēosan* to lose]
▸**forˈlornness** *n*

forlorn hope *n* **1** a hopeless enterprise. **2** a faint hope. **3** *Obs.* a group of soldiers assigned to an extremely dangerous duty. [C16 (in the obs. sense): changed (by folk etymology) from Du. *verloren hoop* lost troop, from *verloren*, p.p. of *verliezen* to lose + *hoop* troop (lit.: heap)]

form ➊ (fɔːm) *n* **1** the shape or configuration of something as distinct from its colour, texture, etc. **2** the particular mode, appearance, etc., in which a thing or person manifests itself: *water in the form of ice*. **3** a type or kind: *imprisonment is a form of punishment*. **4** a printed document, esp. one with spaces in which to insert facts or answers: *an application form*. **5** physical or mental condition, esp. good condition, with reference to ability to perform: *off form*. **6** the previous record of a horse, athlete, etc., esp. with regard to fitness. **7** *Brit. sl.* a criminal record. **8** a fixed mode of artistic expression or representation in literary, musical, or other artistic works: *sonata form*. **9** a mould, frame, etc., that gives shape to something. **10** *Education, chiefly Brit.* a group of children who are taught together. **11** behaviour or procedure, esp. as governed by custom or etiquette: *good form*. **12** formality or ceremony. **13** a prescribed set or order of words, terms, etc., as in a religious ceremony or legal document. **14** *Philosophy*. **14a** the structure of anything as opposed to its content. **14b** essence as opposed to matter. **15** See **logical form**. **16** *Brit., Austral., & NZ.* a bench, esp. one that is long, low, and backless. **17** a hare's nest. **18** any of the various ways in which a word may be spelt or inflected. ◆ *vb* **19** to give shape or form to or to take shape or form, esp. a particular shape. **20** to come or bring into existence: *a scum formed*. **21** to make or construct or be made or constructed. **22** to construct or develop in the mind: *to form an opinion*. **23** (*tr*) to train or mould by instruction or example. **24** (*tr*) to acquire or develop: *to form a habit*. **25** (*tr*) to be an element of or constitute: *this plank will form a bridge*. **26** (*tr*) to organize: *to form a club*. [C13: from OF, from L *forma* shape, model]

-form *adj combining form*. having the shape or form of or resembling: *cruciform; vermiform*. [from NL *-formis*, from L, from *fōrma* FORM]

formal ➊ (ˈfɔːməl) *adj* **1** of or following established forms, conventions, etc.: *a formal document*. **2** characterized by observation of conventional forms of ceremony, behaviour, etc.: *a formal dinner*. **3** methodical or stiff. **4** suitable for occasions organized according to conventional ceremony: *formal dress*. **5** denoting idiom, vocabulary, etc., used by educated speakers and writers of a language. **6** acquired by study in academic institutions. **7** symmetrical in form: *a formal garden*. **8** of or relating to the appearance, form, etc., of something as distinguished from its substance. **9** logically deductive: *formal proof*. **10** denoting a second-person pronoun in some languages: *in French the pronoun "vous" is formal, while "tu" is informal*. [C14: from L *formālis*]
▸ˈ**formally** *adv* ▸ˈ**formalness** *n*

formaldehyde (fɔːˈmældɪˌhaɪd) *n* a colourless poisonous irritating gas with a pungent characteristic odour, used as formalin and in the manufacture of synthetic resins. Formula: HCHO. Systematic name: **methanal**. [C19: FORM(IC) + ALDEHYDE; on the model of G *Formaldehyd*]

formalin (ˈfɔːməlɪn) *n* a solution of formaldehyde in water, used as a disinfectant, preservative for biological specimens, etc.

formalism (ˈfɔːməˌlɪzəm) *n* **1** scrupulous or excessive adherence to outward form at the expense of content. **2** the mathematical or logical structure of a scientific argument as distinguished from its subject matter. **3** *Theatre.* a stylized mode of production. **4** (in Marxist criticism, etc.) excessive concern with artistic technique at the expense of social values, etc.
▸ˈ**formalist** *n* ▸ˌ**formalˈistic** *adj*

formality ➊ (fɔːˈmælɪtɪ) *n, pl* **formalities. 1** a requirement of custom, etiquette, etc. **2** the quality of being formal or conventional. **3** strict or excessive observance of ceremony, etc.

formalize *or* **formalise** (ˈfɔːməˌlaɪz) *vb* **formalizes, formalizing, formalized** *or* **formalises, formalising, formalised. 1** to be or make formal. **2** (*tr*) to make official or valid. **3** (*tr*) to give a definite shape or form to.
▸ˌ**formaliˈzation** *or* ˌ**formaliˈsation** *n*

formal language *n* any of various languages designed for use in fields such as mathematics, logic, or computer programming, the symbols and formulas of which stand in precisely specified syntactic and semantic relations to one another.

formal logic *n* the study of systems of deductive argument in which symbols are used to represent precisely defined categories of expressions.

formant (ˈfɔːmənt) *n Acoustics, phonetics*. any of the constituents of a sound, esp. a vowel sound, that impart to the sound its own special quality, tone colour, or timbre.

format ➊ (ˈfɔːmæt) *n* **1** the general appearance of a publication, including type style, paper, binding, etc. **2** style, plan, or arrangement, as of a television programme. **3** *Computing*. **3a** the defined arrangement of data encoded in a file or, for example, on magnetic disk or CD-ROM, that is essential for the correct recording and recovery of data on different devices. **3b** the arrangement of text on printed output or on a display screen. ◆ *vb* **formats, formatting, formatted.** (*tr*) **4** to arrange (a book, page, etc.) into a specified format. [C19: via F from G, from L *liber formātus* volume formed]

formation ➊ (fɔːˈmeɪʃən) *n* **1** the act of giving or taking form or existence. **2** something that is formed. **3** the manner in which something is arranged. **4a** a formal arrangement of a number of persons or things acting as a unit, such as a troop of soldiers or a football team. **4b** (*as modifier*): *formation dancing*. **5** a series of rocks with certain characteristics in common.

formative ➊ (ˈfɔːmətɪv) *adj* **1** of or relating to formation, development, or growth: *formative years*. **2** shaping; moulding: *a formative experience*. **3** functioning in the formation of derived, inflected, or compound words. ◆ *n* **4** an inflectional or derivational affix.
▸ˈ**formatively** *adv* ▸ˈ**formativeness** *n*

form class *n* **1** another term for **part of speech**. **2** a group of words distinguished by common inflections, such as the weak verbs of English.

form criticism *n* literary criticism concerned esp. with analysing the Bible in terms of the literary forms used, such as proverbs, songs, or stories, and relating them to their historical forms and background.
▸**form critic** *n* ▸**form critical** *adj*

forme *or US* **form** (fɔːm) *n Printing*. type matter, blocks, etc., assembled in a chase and ready for printing. [C15: from F: FORM]

former[1] ➊ (ˈfɔːmə) *adj* (*prenominal*) **1** belonging to or occurring in an earlier time: *former glory*. **2** having been at a previous time: *a former colleague*. **3** denoting the first or first mentioned of two. ◆ *n* **4 the former.** the first or first mentioned of two: distinguished from *latter*.

former[2] (ˈfɔːmə) *n* **1** a person or thing that forms or shapes. **2** *Electrical engineering*. a tool for giving a coil or winding the required shape.

formerly ➊ (ˈfɔːməlɪ) *adv* at or in a former time; in the past.

formic (ˈfɔːmɪk) *adj* **1** of, relating to, or derived from ants. **2** of, containing, or derived from formic acid. [C18: from L *formīca* ant; the acid occurs naturally in ants]

Formica (fɔːˈmaɪkə) *n Trademark*. any of various laminated plastic sheets used esp. for heat-resistant surfaces.

THESAURUS

forked *adj* **1, 2** = **branching**, angled, bifurcate(d), branched, divided, pronged, split, tined, zigzag

forlorn *adj* **1, 2** = **miserable**, abandoned, bereft, cheerless, comfortless, deserted, desolate, destitute, disconsolate, down in the dumps (*inf.*), forgotten, forsaken, friendless, helpless, homeless, hopeless, lonely, lost, pathetic, pitiable, pitiful, unhappy, woebegone, wretched
Antonyms *adj* busy, cheerful, happy, hopeful, optimistic, thriving

form *n* **1** = **shape**, appearance, cast, configuration, construction, cut, fashion, formation, model, mould, pattern, stamp, structure **2** = **mode**, arrangement, character, design, guise, manifestation, semblance **3** = **type**, description, kind, manner, method, order, practice, sort, species, stamp, style, system, variety, way **4** = **document**, application, paper, sheet **5** = **condition**, fettle, fitness, good condition, good spirits, health, shape, trim **10** = **class**, grade, rank **11, 12** = **procedure**, behaviour, ceremony, conduct, convention, custom, done thing, etiquette, formality, manners, protocol, ritual, rule ◆ *vb* **20** = **take shape**, accumulate, appear, become visible, come into being, crystallize, grow, materialize, rise, settle, show up **21** = **make**, assemble, bring about, build, concoct, construct, contrive, create, devise, establish, fabricate, fashion, forge, found, invent, manufacture, model, mould, produce, put together, set up, shape, stamp **23** = **train**, bring up, discipline, educate, instruct, rear, school, teach **24** = **develop**, acquire, contract, cultivate, get into (*inf.*), pick up **25** = **constitute**, compose, comprise, make, make up, serve as **26** = **arrange**, combine, design, dispose, draw up, frame, organize, pattern, plan, think up

formal *adj* **1, 3** = **official**, approved, ceremonial, explicit, express, fixed, lawful, legal, methodical, prescribed, *pro forma*, regular, rigid, ritualistic, set, solemn, strict **3** = **conventional**, affected, aloof, ceremonious, correct, exact, precise, prim, punctilious, reserved, starched, stiff, unbending
Antonyms *adj* casual, easy-going, informal, laid-back (*inf.*), relaxed, unceremonious, unofficial

formality *n* **2** = **convention**, ceremony, conventionality, custom, form, gesture, matter of form, procedure, red tape, rite, ritual **3** = **correctness**, ceremoniousness, decorum, etiquette, politesse, protocol, p's and q's, punctilio

format *n* **1, 2** = **arrangement**, appearance, construction, form, layout, look, make-up, plan, style, type

formation *n* **1** = **development**, accumulation, compilation, composition, constitution, crystallization, establishment, evolution, forming, generation, genesis, manufacture, organization, production **3** = **arrangement**, configuration, design, disposition, figure, grouping, pattern, rank, structure

formative *adj* **1** = **impressionable**, malleable, mouldable, pliant, sensitive, susceptible **2** = **developmental**, determinative, influential, moulding, shaping

former[1] *adj* **1** = **past**, ancient, bygone, departed, long ago, long gone, of yore, old, old-time **2** = **previous**, antecedent, anterior, earlier, erstwhile, ex-, late, one-time, prior, quondam **3** = **aforementioned**, above, aforesaid, first mentioned, foregoing, preceding
Antonyms ≠ **past**: current, future, modern, present, present-day *adj* ≠ **previous**: coming, current, ensuing, following, future, latter, subsequent, succeeding

formerly *adv* = **previously**, aforetime (*arch.*),

formic acid *n* a colourless corrosive liquid carboxylic acid found in some insects, esp. ants, and many plants: used in the manufacture of insecticides. Formula: HCOOH. Systematic name: **methanoic acid.**

formidable Ⓣ ('fɔːmɪdəb^{ə}l) *adj* **1** arousing or likely to inspire fear or dread. **2** extremely difficult to defeat, overcome, manage, etc. **3** tending to inspire awe or admiration because of great size, excellence, etc. [C15: from L, from *formīdāre* to dread, from *formīdō* fear]
▸**'formidably** *adv*

formless Ⓣ ('fɔːmlɪs) *adj* without a definite shape or form; amorphous.
▸**'formlessly** *adv*

form letter *n* a single copy of a letter that has been mechanically reproduced in large numbers for circulation.

formula Ⓣ ('fɔːmjʊlə) *n, pl* **formulas** *or* **formulae** (-ˌliː). **1** an established form or set of words, as used in religious ceremonies, legal proceedings, etc. **2** *Maths., physics.* a general relationship, principle, or rule stated, often as an equation, in the form of symbols. **3** *Chem.* a representation of molecules, radicals, ions, etc., expressed in the symbols of the atoms of their constituent elements. **4a** a method, pattern, or rule for doing or producing something, often one proved to be successful. **4b** (*as modifier*): *formula fiction.* **5** *US & Canad.* a prescription for making up a medicine, baby's food, etc. **6** *Motor racing.* the category in which a type of car competes, judged according to engine size, weight, and fuel capacity. [C17: from L: dim. of *forma* FORM]
▸**formulaic** (ˌfɔːmjʊ'leɪɪk) *adj*

Formula One *n* **1** the top class of professional motor racing. **2** the most important world championship in motor racing.

formularize *or* **formularise** ('fɔːmjʊləˌraɪz) *vb* **formularizes, formularizing, formularized** *or* **formularises, formularising, formularised.** a less common word for **formulate** (sense 1).

formulary ('fɔːmjʊlərɪ) *n, pl* **formularies. 1** a book of prescribed formulas, esp. relating to religious procedure or doctrine. **2** a formula. **3** *Pharmacol.* a book containing a list of pharmaceutical products with their formulas. ◆ *adj* **4** of or relating to a formula.

formulate Ⓣ ('fɔːmjʊˌleɪt) *vb* **formulates, formulating, formulated.** (*tr*) **1** to put into or express in systematic terms; express in or as if in a formula. **2** to devise.
▸**ˌformu'lation** *n*

formwork ('fɔːmˌwɜːk) *n* an arrangement of wooden boards, etc., used to shape concrete while it is setting.

fornicate ('fɔːnɪˌkeɪt) *vb* **fornicates, fornicating, fornicated.** (*intr*) to commit fornication. [C16: from LL *fornicārī*, from L *fornix* vault, brothel situated therein]
▸**'forniˌcator** *n*

fornication Ⓣ (ˌfɔːnɪ'keɪʃən) *n* **1** voluntary sexual intercourse outside marriage. **2** *Bible.* sexual immorality in general, esp. adultery.

forsake Ⓣ (fə'seɪk) *vb* **forsakes, forsaking, forsook, forsaken.** (*tr*) **1** to abandon. **2** to give up (something valued or enjoyed). [OE *forsacan*]
▸**for'saker** *n*

forsaken Ⓣ (fə'seɪkən) *vb* **1** the past participle of **forsake.** ◆ *adj* **2** completely deserted or helpless.
▸**for'sakenly** *adv* ▸**for'sakenness** *n*

forsook (fə'sʊk) *vb* the past tense of **forsake.**

forsooth (fə'suːθ) *adv Arch.* in truth; indeed. [OE *forsōth*]

forswear Ⓣ (fɔː'swɛə) *vb* **forswears, forswearing, forswore, forsworn. 1** (*tr*) to reject or renounce with determination or as upon oath. **2** (*tr*) to deny or disavow absolutely or upon oath. **3** to perjure (oneself). [OE *forswearian*]
▸**for'swearer** *n*

forsworn (fɔː'swɔːn) *vb* the past participle of **forswear.**
▸**for'swornness** *n*

forsythia (fɔː'saɪθɪə) *n* a shrub native to China, Japan, and SE Europe but widely cultivated for its showy yellow bell-shaped flowers, which appear in spring before the foliage. [C19: NL, after William *Forsyth* (1737–1804), E botanist]

fort Ⓣ (fɔːt) *n* **1** a fortified enclosure, building, or position able to be defended against an enemy. **2 hold the fort.** *Inf.* to guard something temporarily. [C15: from OF, from *fort* (adj) strong, from L *fortis*]

fort. *abbrev. for:* **1** fortification. **2** fortified.

forte[1] Ⓣ (fɔːt, 'fɔːteɪ) *n* **1** something at which a person excels: *cooking is my forte.* **2** *Fencing.* the stronger section of a sword, between the hilt and the middle. [C17: from F, from *fort* (adj) strong, from L *fortis*]

forte[2] ('fɔːtɪ) *Music.* ◆ *adj, adv* **1** loud or loudly. Symbol: f ◆ *n* **2** a loud passage in music. [C18: from It., from L *fortis* strong]

forte-piano (ˌfɔːtɪ'pjɑːnəʊ) *Music.* ◆ *adj, adv* **1** loud and then immediately soft. Symbol: fp ◆ *n* **2** a note played in this way.

forth Ⓣ (fɔːθ) *adv* **1** forward in place, time, order, or degree. **2** out, as from concealment or inaction. **3** away, as from a place or country. **4 and so forth.** and so on. ◆ *prep* **5** *Arch.* out of. [OE]

forthcoming Ⓣ (ˌfɔːθ'kʌmɪŋ) *adj* **1** approaching in time: *the forthcoming debate.* **2** about to appear: *his forthcoming book.* **3** available or ready. **4** open or sociable.

forthright Ⓣ *adj* ('fɔːθˌraɪt). **1** direct and outspoken. ◆ *adv* (ˌfɔːθ'raɪt, 'fɔːθˌraɪt), *also* **forthrightly. 2** in a direct manner; frankly. **3** at once.
▸**'forthˌrightness** *n*

forthwith Ⓣ (ˌfɔːθ'wɪθ) *adv* at once.

fortification Ⓣ (ˌfɔːtɪfɪ'keɪʃən) *n* **1** the act, art, or science of fortifying or strengthening. **2a** a wall, mound, etc., used to fortify a place. **2b** such works collectively.

fortify Ⓣ ('fɔːtɪˌfaɪ) *vb* **fortifies, fortifying, fortified.** (*mainly tr*) **1** (*also intr*) to make (a place) defensible, as by building walls, etc. **2** to strengthen physically, mentally, or morally. **3** to add alcohol to (wine), in order to produce sherry, port, etc. **4** to increase the nutritious value of (a food), as by adding vitamins. **5** to confirm: *to fortify an argument.* [C15: from OF, from LL, from L *fortis* strong + *facere* to make]
▸**'fortiˌfiable** *adj* ▸**'fortiˌfier** *n*

fortissimo (fɔː'tɪsɪˌməʊ) *Music.* ◆ *adj, adv* **1** very loud. Symbol: ff ◆ *n* **2** a very loud passage in music. [C18: from It., from L, from *fortis* strong]

fortitude Ⓣ ('fɔːtɪˌtjuːd) *n* strength and firmness of mind. [C15: from L *fortitūdō* courage]

fortnight ('fɔːtˌnaɪt) *n* a period of 14 consecutive days; two weeks. [OE *fēowertīene niht* fourteen nights]

fortnightly ('fɔːtˌnaɪtlɪ) *Chiefly Brit.* ◆ *adj* **1** occurring or appearing once each fortnight. ◆ *adv* **2** once a fortnight. ◆ *n, pl* **fortnightlies. 3** a publication issued at intervals of two weeks.

Fortran ('fɔːtræn) *n* a high-level computer programming language for mathematical and scientific purposes. [C20: from *for(mula) tran(slation)*]

fortress Ⓣ ('fɔːtrɪs) *n* **1** a large fort or fortified town. **2** a place or source

THESAURUS

already, at one time, before, heretofore, lately, once

formidable *adj* **1** = **intimidating**, appalling, baleful, dangerous, daunting, dismaying, dreadful, fearful, frightful, horrible, menacing, shocking, terrifying, threatening **2** = **difficult**, arduous, challenging, colossal, mammoth, onerous, overwhelming, staggering, toilsome **3** = **impressive**, awesome, great, indomitable, mighty, powerful, puissant, redoubtable, terrific, tremendous
Antonyms *adj* ≠ **intimidating:** cheering, comforting, encouraging, genial, heartening, pleasant, reassuring ≠ **difficult:** easy

formless *adj* = **shapeless**, amorphous, disorganized, inchoate, incoherent, indefinite, nebulous, unformed, vague

formula *n* **1** = **form of words**, formulary, rite, ritual, rubric **4** = **method**, blueprint, modus operandi, precept, prescription, principle, procedure, recipe, rule, way

formulate *vb* **1** = **define**, codify, detail, express, frame, give form to, particularize, set down, specify, systematize **2** = **devise**, coin, develop, evolve, forge, invent, map out, originate, plan, work out

fornication *n* **1** = **adultery**, extra-curricular sex (*inf.*), extra-marital congress *or* relations *or* sex, infidelity, living in sin, pre-marital congress *or* relations *or* sex, unfaithfulness **2** = **immorality**, debauchery, dissipation, dissoluteness, easy virtue, immodesty, impurity, incontinence, indecency, indelicacy, lasciviousness, lechery, libertinism, loose morals, looseness, promiscuity, salaciousness, shamelessness, sin, sleeping around, unchastity, uncleanness

forsake *vb* **1** = **desert**, abandon, cast off, disown, jettison, jilt, leave, leave in the lurch, quit, repudiate, strand, throw over **2** = **give up**, abdicate, forgo, forswear, have done with, kick (*inf.*), relinquish, renounce, set aside, surrender, turn one's back on, yield

forsaken *adj* **2** = **deserted**, abandoned, cast off, destitute, disowned, ditched, forlorn, friendless, ignored, isolated, jilted, left behind, left in the lurch, lonely, marooned, outcast, solitary, stranded

forswear *vb* **1** = **renounce**, abandon, abjure, drop, forgo, forsake, give up, swear off **2** = **reject**, deny, disavow, disclaim, disown, recant, repudiate, retract **3** = **lie**, perjure oneself, renege, swear falsely

fort *n* **1** = **fortress**, blockhouse, camp, castle, citadel, fastness, fortification, garrison, redoubt, station, stronghold **2 hold the fort** *Informal* = **carry on**, keep things moving, keep things on an even keel, maintain the status quo, stand in, take over the reins

forte[1] *n* **1** = **speciality**, gift, long suit (*inf.*), métier, strength, strong point, talent
Antonyms *n* Achilles heel, chink in one's armour, defect, failing, imperfection, shortcoming, weak point

forth *adv* **1-3** = **forward**, ahead, away, into the open, onward, out, out of concealment, outward

forthcoming *adj* **1, 2** = **approaching**, coming, expected, future, imminent, impending, prospective, upcoming **3** = **available**, accessible, at hand, in evidence, obtainable, on tap (*inf.*), ready **4** = **communicative**, chatty, expansive, free, informative, open, sociable, talkative, unreserved

forthright *adj* **1** = **outspoken**, above-board, blunt, candid, direct, downright, frank, open, plain-spoken, straightforward, straight from the shoulder (*inf.*), upfront (*inf.*)
Antonyms *adj* dishonest, furtive, secret, secretive, sneaky, underhand, untruthful

forthwith *adv* = **at once**, directly, immediately, instantly, quickly, right away, straightaway, *tout de suite*, without delay

fortification *n* **1** = **strengthening**, embattlement, reinforcement **2** = **defence**, bastion, bulwark, castle, citadel, fastness, fort, fortress, keep, protection, stronghold

fortify *vb* **1** = **protect**, augment, brace, buttress, embattle, garrison, reinforce, secure, shore up, strengthen, support **2, 5** = **strengthen**, brace, cheer, confirm, embolden, encourage, hearten, invigorate, reassure, stiffen, sustain
Antonyms *vb* ≠ **strengthen:** debilitate, demoralize, dilute, dishearten, impair, reduce, sap the strength of, weaken

fortitude *n* = **courage**, backbone, bravery, dauntlessness, determination, endurance, fearlessness, firmness, grit, guts (*inf.*), hardihood, intrepidity, patience, perseverance, pluck, resolution, staying power, stoutheartedness, strength, strength of mind, valour

fortress *n* **1** = **castle**, citadel, fastness, fort, redoubt, stronghold

of refuge or support. ◆ *vb* **3** (*tr*) to protect. [C13: from OF, from Med. L *fortalitia,* from L *fortis* strong]

Fort Sumter ('sʌmtə) *n* a fort in SE South Carolina, guarding Charleston Harbour. Its capture by Confederate forces (1861) was the first action of the Civil War.

fortuitous ⊕ (fɔː'tjuːɪtəs) *adj* happening by chance, esp. by a lucky chance. [C17: from L *fortuitus* happening by chance, from *fors* chance, luck]
► **for'tuitously** *adv*

fortuity (fɔː'tjuːɪtɪ) *n, pl* **fortuities. 1** a chance or accidental occurrence. **2** chance or accident.

fortunate ⊕ ('fɔːtʃənɪt) *adj* **1** having good luck. **2** occurring by or bringing good fortune or luck.
► **'fortunately** *adv*

fortune ⊕ ('fɔːtʃən) *n* **1** an amount of wealth or material prosperity, esp. a great amount. **2 small fortune.** a large sum of money. **3** a power or force, often personalized, regarded as being responsible for human affairs. **4** luck, esp. when favourable. **5** (*often pl*) a person's destiny. ◆ *vb* **fortunes, fortuning, fortuned. 6** (*intr*) *Arch.* to happen by chance. [C13: from OF, from L, from *fors* chance]

fortune-hunter *n* a person who seeks to secure a fortune, esp. through marriage.

fortune-teller *n* a person who makes predictions about the future as by looking into a crystal ball, etc.
► **'fortune-ˌtelling** *adj, n*

forty ('fɔːtɪ) *n, pl* **forties. 1** the cardinal number that is the product of ten and four. **2** a numeral, 40, XL, etc., representing this number. **3** something representing, represented by, or consisting of 40 units. ◆ *determiner* **4a** amounting to forty: *forty thieves.* **4b** (*as pronoun*): *there were forty in the herd.* [OE *fēowertig*]
► **'fortieth** *adj, n*

forty-five *n* a gramophone record played at 45 revolutions per minute.

Forty-Five *n* **the.** *British history.* another name for the **Jacobite Rebellion** of 1745–46. See **Young Pretender.**

forty-niner *n* (*sometimes cap.*) *US history.* a prospector who took part in the California gold rush of 1849.

forty winks *n* (*functioning as sing or pl*) *Inf.* a short light sleep; nap.

forum ⊕ ('fɔːrəm) *n, pl* **forums** *or* **fora** (-rə). **1** a meeting for the open discussion of subjects of public interest. **2** a medium for open discussion, such as a magazine. **3** a public meeting place for open discussion. **4** a court; tribunal. **5** (in ancient Italy) an open space serving as a city's marketplace and centre of public business. [C15: from L: public place]

Forum *or* **Forum Romanum** (rəʊ'mɑːnəm) *n* **the.** the main forum of ancient Rome.

forward ⊕ ('fɔːwəd) *adj* **1** directed or moving ahead. **2** lying or situated in or near the front part of something. **3** presumptuous, pert, or impudent. **4** well developed or advanced, esp. in physical or intellectual development. **5a** of or relating to the future or favouring change. **5b** (*in combination*): *forward-looking.* **6** (*often postpositive*) *Arch.* ready, eager, or willing. **7** *Commerce.* relating to fulfilment at a future date. ◆ *n* **8** an attacking player in any of various sports, such as soccer. ◆ *adv* **9** a variant of **forwards. 10** ('fɔːwəd; *Naut.* 'fɒrəd). towards the front or bow of an aircraft or ship. **11** into a position of being subject to public scrutiny: *the witness came forward.* ◆ *vb* (*tr*) **12** to send forward or pass on to an ultimate destination: *the letter was forwarded.* **13** to advance or promote: *to forward one's career.* [OE *foreweard*]
► **'forwarder** *n* ► **'forwardly** *adv* ► **'forwardness** *n*

forwards ('fɔːwədz) *or* **forward** *adv* **1** towards or at a place ahead or in advance, esp. in space but also in time. **2** towards the front.

forwent (fɔː'wɛnt) *vb* the past tense of **forgo.**

forza ('fɔːtsə) *n Music.* force. [C19: It., lit.: force]

fossa ('fɒsə) *n, pl* **fossae** (-siː). an anatomical depression or hollow area. [C19: from L: ditch, from *fossus* dug up, from *fodere* to dig up]

fosse *or* **foss** (fɒs) *n* a ditch or moat, esp. one dug as a fortification. [C14: from OF, from L *fossa;* see FOSSA]

fossick ('fɒsɪk) *vb Austral. & NZ.* **1** (*intr*) to search for gold or precious stones in abandoned workings, rivers, etc. **2** to rummage or search for (something): *to fossick around for.* [C19: Austral., prob. from E dialect *fussock* to bustle about, from FUSS]
► **'fossicker** *n*

fossil ('fɒsᵊl) *n* **1a** a relic or representation of a plant or animal that existed in a past geological age, occurring in the form of mineralized bones, shells, etc. **1b** (*as modifier*): *fossil insects.* **2** *Inf., derog.* a person, idea, thing, etc., that is outdated or incapable of change. **3** *Linguistics.* a form once current but now appearing only in one or two special contexts. [C17: from L *fossilis* dug up, from *fodere* to dig]

fossil fuel *n* any naturally occurring fuel, such as coal, and natural gas, formed by the decomposition of prehistoric organisms.

fossiliferous (ˌfɒsɪ'lɪfərəs) *adj* (of sedimentary rocks) containing fossils.

fossilize *or* **fossilise** ('fɒsɪˌlaɪz) *vb* **fossilizes, fossilizing, fossilized** *or* **fossilises, fossilising, fossilised. 1** to convert or be converted into a fossil. **2** to become or cause to become antiquated or inflexible.
► **ˌfossili'zation** *or* **ˌfossili'sation** *n*

fossorial (fɒ'sɔːrɪəl) *adj* (of the forelimbs and skeleton of burrowing animals) adapted for digging. [C19: from Med. L, from L *fossor* digger, from *fodere* to dig]

foster ⊕ ('fɒstə) *vb* (*tr*) **1** to promote the growth or development of. **2** to bring up (a child, etc.). **3** to cherish (a plan, hope, etc.) in one's mind. **4** *Chiefly Brit.* **4a** to place (a child) in the care of foster parents. **4b** to bring up under fosterage. ◆ *adj* **5** indicating relationship through fostering and not through birth: *foster child, foster mother.* **6** of or involved in the rearing of a child by persons other than his natural parents: *foster home.* [OE *fōstrian* to feed, from *fōstor* FOOD]
► **'fosterer** *n* ► **'fostering** *n*

fosterage ('fɒstərɪdʒ) *n* **1** the act of caring for a foster child. **2** the state of being a foster child. **3** the act of encouraging.

fought (fɔːt) *vb* the past tense and past participle of **fight.**

foul ⊕ (faʊl) *adj* **1** offensive to the senses; revolting. **2** stinking. **3** charged with or full of dirt or offensive matter. **4** (of food) putrid; rotten. **5** morally or spiritually offensive. **6** obscene; vulgar: *foul language.* **7** unfair: *to resort to foul means.* **8** (esp. of weather) unpleasant or adverse. **9** blocked or obstructed with dirt or foreign matter: *a foul drain.* **10** (of the bottom of a vessel) covered with barnacles that slow forward motion. **11** *Inf.* unsatisfactory; bad: *a foul book.* ◆ *n* **12** *Sport.* **12a** a violation of the rules. **12b** (*as modifier*): *a foul blow.* **13** an entanglement or collision, esp. in sailing or fishing. ◆ *vb* **14** to make or become polluted. **15** to become or cause to become entangled. **16** (*tr*) to disgrace. **17** to become or cause to become clogged. **18** (*tr*) *Naut.* (of underwater growth) to cling to (the bottom of a vessel) so as to slow its motion. **19** (*tr*) *Sport.* to commit a foul against (an opponent). **20** (*intr*) *Sport.* to infringe the rules. **21** to collide (with a boat, etc.). ◆ *adv* **22** in a foul manner. **23 fall foul of. 23a** come into conflict with. **23b** *Naut.* to come into collision with. [OE *fūl*]
► **'foully** *adv* ► **'foulness** *n*

THESAURUS

fortuitous *adj* = **chance**, accidental, arbitrary, casual, contingent, incidental, random, unforeseen, unplanned = **lucky**, fluky (*inf.*), fortunate, happy, providential, serendipitous

fortunate *adj* **1** = **lucky**, bright, favoured, golden, happy, having a charmed life, in luck, jammy (*Brit. sl.*), on a roll, prosperous, rosy, sitting pretty (*inf.*), successful, well-off **2** = **providential**, advantageous, auspicious, convenient, encouraging, expedient, favourable, felicitous, fortuitous, helpful, opportune, profitable, promising, propitious, timely
Antonyms *adj* hapless, ill-fated, ill-starred, miserable, poor, unfortunate, unhappy, unlucky, unsuccessful, wretched

fortunately *adv* **2** = **luckily**, by a happy chance, by good luck, happily, providentially

fortune *n* **1** = **wealth**, affluence, an arm and a leg (*inf.*), big money, bomb (*Brit. sl.*), bundle (*sl.*), gold mine, king's ransom, megabucks (*US & Canad. sl.*), mint, opulence, packet (*sl.*), pile (*inf.*), possessions, pretty penny (*inf.*), property, prosperity, riches, tidy sum (*inf.*), treasure, wad (*US & Canad. sl.*) **3** = **luck**, accident, chance, contingency, destiny, fate, fortuity, hap (*arch.*), hazard, kismet, providence **5** *often plural* = **destiny**, adventures, circumstances, doom, expectation, experiences, history, life, lot, portion, star, success
Antonyms *n* ≠ **wealth:** destitution, hardship, indigence, penury, poverty, privation

forum *n* **1** = **meeting**, assemblage, assembly, body, caucus (*chiefly US & Canad.*), colloquium, conclave, conference, congregation, congress, convention, convergence, convocation, council, court, diet, gathering, get- together (*inf.*), moot, parliament, rally, seminar, senate, symposium, synod, tribunal (*arch. or literary*) **3** = **meeting**, amphitheatre, arena, chamber, court, meeting place, platform, pulpit, rostrum, stage

forward *adj* **2** = **leading**, advance, first, fore, foremost, front, head **3** = **presumptuous**, assuming, bare-faced, bold, brash, brass-necked (*Brit. inf.*), brazen, brazen-faced, cheeky, confident, familiar, fresh (*inf.*), impertinent, impudent, overassertive, overweening, pert, presuming, pushy (*inf.*), sassy (*US inf.*) **4** = **well-developed**, advanced, advancing, early, forward-looking, onward, precocious, premature, progressive ◆ *adv* **9** = **forth**, ahead, on, onward **11** = **to the front**, into consideration, into prominence, into the open, into view, out, to light, to the surface ◆ *vb* **12** = **send**, dispatch, freight, post, route, send on, ship, transmit **13** = **promote**, advance, aid, assist, back, encourage, expedite, favour, foster, further, hasten, help, hurry, speed, support
Antonyms *adj* ≠ **presumptuous:** backward, diffident, modest, regressive, retiring, shy ◆ *adv* ≠ **forth:** backward(s) ◆ *vb* ≠ **promote:** bar, block, hinder, hold up, impede, obstruct, retard, thwart

forwardness *n* **3** = **impertinence**, boldness, brashness, brazenness, cheek (*inf.*), cheekiness, chutzpah (*US & Canad. inf.*), impudence, overconfidence, pertness, presumption

foster *vb* **1** = **promote**, cultivate, encourage, feed, foment, nurture, stimulate, support, uphold **2** = **bring up**, mother, nurse, raise, rear, take care of **3** = **cherish**, accommodate, entertain, harbour, nourish, sustain
Antonyms *vb* ≠ **promote:** combat, curb, curtail, hold out against, inhibit, oppose, resist, restrain, subdue, suppress, withstand

foul *adj* **1, 2, 4** = **dirty**, contaminated, disgusting, fetid, filthy, grotty (*sl.*), impure, loathsome, malodorous, mephitic, nasty, nauseating, noisome, offensive, olid, polluted, putrid, rank, repulsive, revolting, rotten, squalid, stinking, sullied, tainted, unclean **5** = **offensive**, abhorrent, abominable, base, despicable, detestable, disgraceful, dishonourable, egregious, hateful, heinous, infamous, iniquitous, nefarious, notorious, scandalous, shameful, shitty (*taboo sl.*), vicious, vile, wicked **6** = **obscene**, abusive, blasphemous, blue, coarse, dirty, filthy, foul-mouthed, gross, indecent, lewd, low, profane, scatological, scurrilous, smutty, vulgar **7** = **unfair**, crooked, dirty, dishonest, fraudulent, inequitable, shady (*inf.*), underhand, unjust, unscrupulous, unsportsmanlike **8** = **stormy**, bad, blustery, disagreeable, foggy, murky, rainy, rough, wet, wild ◆ *vb* **14** =

foulard (fuːˈlɑːd) *n* a soft light fabric of plain-weave or twill-weave silk or rayon, usually with a printed design. [C19: from F, from ?]

foul play ⓣ *n* **1** violent or treacherous conduct, esp. murder. **2** a violation of the rules in a game or sport.

foul up ⓣ *vb* (*adv*) **1** (*tr*) to bungle. **2** (*tr*) to contaminate. **3** to be or cause to be blocked, choked, or entangled. ◆ *n* **foul-up. 4** a state of confusion or muddle caused by bungling.

found[1] (faʊnd) *vb* **1** the past tense and past participle of **find.** ◆ *adj* **2** furnished or fitted out. **3** *Brit.* with meals, heating, etc., provided without extra charge.

found[2] ⓣ (faʊnd) *vb* **1** (*tr*) to bring into being or establish (something, such as an institution, etc.). **2** (*tr*) to build or establish the foundation of. **3** (*also intr;* foll. by *on* or *upon*) to have a basis (in). [C13: from OF, from L, from *fundus* bottom]

found[3] (faʊnd) *vb* (*tr*) **1** to cast (a material, such as metal or glass) by melting and pouring into a mould. **2** to make (articles) in this way. [C14: from OF, from L *fundere* to melt]

foundation ⓣ (faʊnˈdeɪʃən) *n* **1** that on which something is founded. **2** (*often pl*) a construction below the ground that distributes the load of a building, wall, etc. **3** the base on which something stands. **4** the act of founding or establishing or the state of being founded or established. **5** an endowment for the support of an institution such as a school. **6** an institution supported by an endowment, often one that provides funds for charities, research, etc. **7** a cosmetic used as a base for make-up.
▸**founˈdational** *adj*

foundation garment *n* a woman's undergarment worn to shape and support the figure. Also called: **foundation.**

foundation stone *n* a stone laid at a ceremony to mark the foundation of a new building.

foundation subjects *pl n Brit. education.* the subjects studied as part of the National Curriculum, including the compulsory core subjects.

founder[1] ⓣ (ˈfaʊndə) *n* a person who establishes an institution, society, etc. [C14: see FOUND[2]]

founder[2] ⓣ (ˈfaʊndə) *vb* (*intr*) **1** (of a ship, etc.) to sink. **2** to break down or fail: *the project foundered.* **3** to sink into or become stuck in soft ground. **4** to collapse. **5** (of a horse) to stumble or go lame. [C13: from OF *fondrer* to submerge, from L *fundus* bottom]

> **USAGE NOTE** *Founder* is sometimes wrongly used where *flounder* is meant: *this unexpected turn of events left him floundering* (not *foundering*).

founder[3] (ˈfaʊndə) *n* **a** a person who makes metal castings. **b** (*in combination*): *an iron founder.* [C15: see FOUND[3]]

foundling ⓣ (ˈfaʊndlɪŋ) *n* an abandoned infant whose parents are not known. [C13 *foundeling;* see FIND]

foundry (ˈfaʊndrɪ) *n, pl* **foundries.** a place in which metal castings are produced. [C17: from OF, from *fondre;* see FOUND[3]]

fount[1] (faʊnt) *n* **1** *Poetic.* a spring or fountain. **2** source. [C16: back formation from FOUNTAIN]

fount[2] (faʊnt, fɒnt) *n Printing.* a complete set of type of one style and size. Also called (esp. US and Canad.): **font.** [C16: from OF *fonte* a founding, casting, from Vulgar L *funditus* (unattested) a casting, from L *fundere* to melt]

fountain ⓣ (ˈfaʊntɪn) *n* **1** a jet or spray of water or some other liquid. **2** a structure from which such a jet or a number of such jets spurt. **3** a natural spring of water, esp. the source of a stream. **4** a stream, jet, or cascade of sparks, lava, etc. **5** a principal source. **6** a reservoir, as for oil in a lamp. [C15: from OF, from LL, from L *fons* spring, source]
▸ˈ**fountained** *adj*

fountainhead ⓣ (ˈfaʊntɪn,hɛd) *n* **1** a spring that is the source of a stream. **2** a principal or original source.

fountain pen *n* a pen the nib of which is supplied with ink from a cartridge or a reservoir in its barrel.

four (fɔː) *n* **1** the cardinal number that is the sum of three and one. **2** a numeral, 4, IV, etc., representing this number. **3** something representing, represented by, or consisting of four units, such as a playing card with four symbols on it. **4** Also called: **four o'clock.** four hours after noon or midnight. **5** *Cricket.* **5a** a shot that crosses the boundary after hitting the ground. **5b** the four runs scored for such a shot. **6** *Rowing.* **6a** a racing shell propelled by four oarsmen. **6b** the crew of such a shell. ◆ *determiner* **7a** amounting to four: *four times.* **7b** (*as pronoun*): *four are ready.* [OE *fēower*]

four-by-four *n* a vehicle equipped with four-wheel drive.

four flush *n* a useless poker hand, containing four of a suit and one odd card.

fourfold (ˈfɔː,fəʊld) *adj* **1** equal to or having four times as many or as much. **2** composed of four parts. ◆ *adv* **3** by or up to four times as many or as much.

four-in-hand *n* **1** a road vehicle drawn by four horses and driven by one driver. **2** a four-horse team. **3** *US.* a long narrow tie tied in a flat slipknot with the ends dangling.

four-leaf clover *or* **four-leaved clover** *n* a clover with four leaves rather than three, supposed to bring good luck.

four-letter word *n* any of several short English words referring to sex or excrement: regarded generally as offensive or obscene.

four-o'clock *n* a tropical American plant, cultivated for its tubular yellow, red, or white flowers that open in late afternoon. Also called: **marvel-of-Peru.**

four-poster *n* a bed with posts at each corner supporting a canopy and curtains.

fourscore (,fɔːˈskɔː) *determiner* an archaic word for **eighty.**

foursome (ˈfɔːsəm) *n* **1** a set or company of four. **2** Also called: **four-ball.** *Golf.* a game between two pairs of players.

foursquare (,fɔːˈskweə) *adv* **1** squarely; firmly. ◆ *adj* **2** solid and strong. **3** forthright. **4** a rare word for **square.**

four-stroke *adj* designating an internal-combustion engine in which the piston makes four strokes for every explosion.

fourteen (ˈfɔːˈtiːn) *n* **1** the cardinal number that is the sum of ten and four. **2** a numeral, 14, XIV, etc., representing this number. **3** something represented by or consisting of 14 units. ◆ *determiner* **4a** amounting to fourteen: *fourteen cats.* **4b** (*as pronoun*): *the fourteen who remained.* [OE *fēowertīene*]
▸ˈ**fourˈteenth** *adj, n*

fourth (fɔːθ) *adj* (*usually prenominal*) **1a** coming after the third in order, position, time, etc. Often written: 4th. **1b** (*as n*): *the fourth in succession.* **2** denoting the highest forward ratio of a gearbox in most motor vehicles. ◆ *n* **3** *Music.* **3a** the interval between one note and another four notes away from it in a diatonic scale. **3b** one of two notes constituting such an interval in relation to the other. **4** the fourth forward ratio of a gearbox in a motor vehicle, usually the highest gear in cars. **5** a less common word for **quarter** (sense 2). ◆ *adv also:* **fourthly. 6** after the third person, position, event, etc. ◆ *sentence connector. also:* **fourthly. 7** as the fourth point.

fourth dimension *n* **1** the dimension of time, which in addition to three spatial dimensions specifies the position of a point or particle. **2** the concept in science fiction of a dimension in addition to three spatial dimensions.
▸,**fourth-diˈmensional** *adj*

fourth estate *n* (*sometimes caps.*) journalists or their profession; the press.

four-wheel drive *n* a system used in motor vehicles in which all four wheels are connected to the source of power.

fovea (ˈfəʊvɪə) *n, pl* **foveae** (-vɪ,iː). *Anat.* any small pit or depression in the surface of a bodily organ or part. [C19: from L: a small pit]

fowl (faʊl) *n* **1** Also called: **domestic fowl.** a domesticated gallinaceous bird occurring in many varieties. **2** any other bird that is used as food or hunted as game. **3** the flesh or meat of fowl, esp. of chicken. **4** an archaic word for any **bird.** ◆ *vb* **5** (*intr*) to hunt or snare wildfowl. [OE *fugol*]
▸ˈ**fowler** *n* ▸ˈ**fowling** *n, adj*

fowl pest *n* an acute and usually fatal viral disease of domestic fowl, characterized by discoloration of the comb and wattles.

fox (fɒks) *n, pl* **foxes** *or* **fox. 1** any canine mammal of the genus *Vulpes* and related genera. They are mostly predators and have a pointed muzzle and a bushy tail. **2** the fur of any of these animals, usually reddish-brown or grey in colour. **3** a person who is cunning and sly. ◆ *vb* **4** (*tr*) *Inf.* to perplex: *to fox a person with a problem.* **5** to cause (paper, wood, etc.) to become discoloured with spots, or (of paper, etc.) to be-

THESAURUS

dirty, begrime, besmear, besmirch, contaminate, defile, pollute, smear, smirch, soil, stain, sully, taint **15, 17** = **clog**, block, catch, choke, ensnare, entangle, jam, snarl, twist ◆ *adv* **23a** **fall foul of** = **come into conflict with**, brush with, cross swords with, have trouble with, make an enemy of
Antonyms *adj* ≠ **offensive:** admirable, attractive, decent, pleasant, respectable ≠ **dirty:** clean, clear, fair, fragrant, fresh, pure, spotless, undefiled ◆ *vb* ≠ **dirty:** clean, cleanse, clear, purge, purify, sanitize

foul play *n* **1** = **crime**, chicanery, corruption, deception, dirty work, double-dealing, duplicity, fraud, perfidy, roguery, sharp practice, skulduggery, treachery, villainy

foul up *vb* **1** = **bungle**, bodge (*inf.*), botch, cock up (*Brit. sl.*), make a mess of, make a nonsense of, make a pig's ear of (*inf.*), mismanage, muck up (*sl.*), put a spanner in the works (*Brit. inf.*), spoil

found[2] *vb* **1, 2** = **establish**, bring into being, constitute, construct, create, endow, erect, fix, inaugurate, institute, organize, originate, plant, raise, settle, set up, start **3** = **base**, bottom, build, ground, rest, root, sustain

foundation *n* **1, 3** = **basis**, base, bedrock, bottom, footing, groundwork, substructure, underpinning **4** = **setting up**, endowment, establishment, inauguration, institution, organization, settlement

founder[1] *n* = **initiator**, architect, author, beginner, benefactor, builder, constructor, designer, establisher, father, framer, generator, institutor, inventor, maker, organizer, originator, patriarch

founder[2] *vb* **1** = **sink**, be lost, go down, go to the bottom, submerge **2** = **fail**, abort, bite the dust, break down, collapse, come to grief, come to nothing, come unstuck, fall by the wayside, fall through, go belly-up (*sl.*), go down like a lead balloon (*inf.*), miscarry, misfire **4, 5** = **stumble**, collapse, fall, go lame, lurch, sprawl, stagger, trip

foundling *n* = **orphan**, outcast, stray, waif

fountain *n* **1, 3** = **jet**, font, fount, reservoir, spout, spray, spring, well **5** = **source**, beginning, cause, commencement, derivation, fount, fountainhead, genesis, origin, rise, wellhead, wellspring

fountainhead *n* **2** = **source**, *fons et origo*, fount, inspiration, mainspring, origin, spring, well, wellspring

come discoloured. **6** (*tr*) to trick; deceive. **7** (*intr*) to act deceitfully or craftily. [OE]
▸ **'fox,like** *adj*

foxfire ('fɒks,faɪə) *n* a luminescent glow emitted by certain fungi on rotting wood.

foxglove ('fɒks,glʌv) *n* a plant having spikes of purple or white thimble-like flowers. The soft wrinkled leaves are a source of digitalis. [OE]

foxhole ('fɒks,həʊl) *n Mil.* a small pit dug to provide shelter against hostile fire.

foxhound ('fɒks,haʊnd) *n* a breed of short-haired hound, usually kept for hunting foxes.

fox hunt *n* **1a** the hunting of foxes with hounds. **1b** an instance of this. **2** an organization for fox hunting within a particular area.
▸ **'fox-,hunter** *n* ▸ **'fox-,hunting** *n*

foxtail ('fɒks,teɪl) *n* any grass of Europe, Asia, and South America, having soft cylindrical spikes of flowers: cultivated as a pasture grass.

fox terrier *n* either of two breeds of small tan-black-and-white terrier, the wire-haired and the smooth.

foxtrot ('fɒks,trɒt) *n* **1** a ballroom dance in quadruple time, combining short and long steps in various sequences. ◆ *vb* **foxtrots, foxtrotting, foxtrotted. 2** (*intr*) to perform this dance.

foxy Ⓣ ('fɒksɪ) *adj* **foxier, foxiest. 1** of or resembling a fox, esp. in craftiness. **2** of a reddish-brown colour. **3** (of paper, etc.) spotted, esp. by mildew. **4** *Sl.* sexy; sexually attractive.
▸ **'foxily** *adv* ▸ **'foxiness** *n*

foyer Ⓣ ('fɔɪeɪ, 'fɔɪə) *n* a hall, lobby, or anteroom, as in a hotel, theatre, cinema, etc. [C19: from F: fireplace, from Med. L, from L *focus* fire]

fp *Music. abbrev. for* forte-piano.

FP *abbrev. for:* **1** fire plug. **2** former pupil. **3** Also: **fp.** freezing point.

FPA *abbrev. for* Family Planning Association.

fps *abbrev. for:* **1** feet per second. **2** foot-pound-second. **3** *Photog.* frames per second.

fps units *pl, n* an Imperial system of units based on the foot, pound, and second as the units of length, mass, and time.

Fr *abbrev. for:* **1** *Christianity:* **1a** Father. **1b** Frater. [L: brother] **2** *the chemical symbol for* francium.

fr. *abbrev. for:* **1** fragment. **2** franc. **3** from.

Fr. *abbrev. for:* **1** France. **2** French.

Fra (frɑː) *n* brother: a title given to an Italian monk or friar. [It., short for *frate* brother, from L *frāter* BROTHER]

fracas Ⓣ ('frækɑː) *n* a noisy quarrel; brawl. [C18: from F, from *fracasser* to shatter, from L *frangere* to break, infl. by *quassāre* to shatter]

fractal ('fræktəl) *n* any of various irregular and fragmented shapes or surfaces that are generated by a series of successive subdivisions. [C20: from L *frāctus,* p.p. of *frangere* to break]

fraction Ⓣ ('frækʃən) *n* **1** *Maths.* a ratio of two expressions or numbers other than zero. **2** any part or subdivision. **3** a small piece; fragment. **4** *Chem.* a component of a mixture separated by fractional distillation. **5** *Christianity.* the formal breaking of the bread in Communion. [C14: from LL, from L *fractus* broken, from *frangere* to break]
▸ **'fractional** *adj* ▸ **'fraction,ize** *or* **'fraction,ise** *vb*

fractional crystallization *n Chem.* the process of separating the components of a solution on the basis of their different solubilities, by means of evaporating the solution until the least soluble component crystallizes out.

fractional distillation *n* the process of separating the constituents of a liquid mixture by heating it and condensing separately the components according to their different boiling points. Sometimes shortened to **distillation.**

fractionate ('frækʃə,neɪt) *vb* **fractionates, fractionating, fractionated. 1** to separate or cause to separate into constituents. **2** (*tr*) *Chem.* to obtain (a constituent of a mixture) by a fractional process.
▸ **,fraction'ation** *n*

fractious Ⓣ ('frækʃəs) *adj* **1** irritable. **2** unruly. [C18: from (obs.) *fraction* discord + -OUS]
▸ **'fractiously** *adv* ▸ **'fractiousness** *n*

> **USAGE NOTE** *Fractious* is sometimes wrongly used where *factious* is meant: *this factious* (not *fractious*) *dispute has split the party still further.*

fracture Ⓣ ('fræktʃə) *n* **1** the act of breaking or the state of being broken. **2a** the breaking or cracking of a bone or the tearing of a cartilage. **2b** the resulting condition. **3** a division, split, or breach. **4** *Mineralogy.* **4a** the characteristic appearance of the surface of a freshly broken mineral or rock. **4b** the way in which a mineral or rock naturally breaks. ◆ *vb* **fractures, fracturing, fractured. 5** to break or cause to break. **6** to break or crack (a bone) or (of a bone) to become broken or cracked. [C15: from OF, from L, from *frangere* to break]
▸ **'fractural** *adj*

fraenum *or* **frenum** ('friːnəm) *n, pl* **fraena** *or* **frena** (-nə). a fold of membrane or skin, such as the fold beneath the tongue. [C18: from L: bridle]

fragile Ⓣ ('frædʒaɪl) *adj* **1** able to be broken easily. **2** in a weakened physical state. **3** delicate; light: *a fragile touch.* **4** slight; tenuous. [C17: from L *fragilis,* from *frangere* to break]
▸ **'fragilely** *adv* ▸ **fragility** (frə'dʒɪlɪtɪ) *n*

fragment Ⓣ *n* ('frægmənt). **1** a piece broken off or detached. **2** an incomplete piece: *fragments of a novel.* **3** a scrap; bit. ◆ *vb* (fræg'mɛnt). **4** to break or cause to break into fragments. [C15: from L *fragmentum,* from *frangere* to break]
▸ **,fragmen'tation** *n*

fragmentary Ⓣ ('frægməntərɪ) *adj* made up of fragments; disconnected. Also: **fragmental.**

fragrance Ⓣ ('freɪgrəns) *or* **fragrancy** *n, pl* **fragrances** *or* **fragrancies. 1** a pleasant or sweet odour. **2** the state of being fragrant.

fragrant Ⓣ ('freɪgrənt) *adj* having a pleasant or sweet smell. [C15: from L, from *frāgrāre* to emit a smell]
▸ **'fragrantly** *adv*

frail[1] Ⓣ (freɪl) *adj* **1** physically weak and delicate. **2** fragile: *a frail craft.* **3** easily corrupted or tempted. [C13: from OF *frele,* from L *fragilis,* FRAGILE]

frail[2] (freɪl) *n* **1** a rush basket for figs or raisins. **2** a quantity of raisins or figs equal to between 50 and 75 pounds. [C13: from OF *fraiel,* from ?]

frailty Ⓣ ('freɪltɪ) *n, pl* **frailties. 1** physical or moral weakness. **2** (*often pl*) a fault symptomatic of moral weakness.

framboesia *or US* **frambesia** (fræm'biːzɪə) *n Pathol.* another name for **yaws.** [C19: from NL, from F *framboise* raspberry; from its raspberry-like excrescences]

frame Ⓣ (freɪm) *n* **1** an open structure that gives shape and support to something, such as the ribs of a ship's hull or an aircraft's fuselage or the beams of a building. **2** an enclosing case or border into which something is fitted: *the frame of a picture.* **3** the system around which something is built up: *the frame of government.* **4** the structure of the human body. **5** a condition; state (esp. in **frame of mind**). **6a** one of a series of exposures on film used in making motion pictures. **6b** an exposure on a film used in still photography. **7** a television picture scanned by one or more electron beams at a particular frequency. **8** *Snooker, etc.* **8a** the wooden triangle used to set up the balls. **8b** the balls when set up. **8c** a single game finished when all the balls have been potted. **9** short for **cold frame. 10** one of the sections of which a beehive is composed, esp. one designed to hold a honeycomb. **11** *Sta-*

THESAURUS

foxy *adj* **1** = **crafty**, artful, astute, canny, cunning, devious, guileful, knowing, sharp, shrewd, sly, tricky, wily

foyer *n* = **entrance hall**, antechamber, anteroom, lobby, reception area, vestibule

fracas *n* = **brawl**, affray (*Law*), aggro, disturbance, donnybrook, fight, free-for-all (*inf.*), melee *or* mêlée, quarrel, riot, row, rumpus, scrimmage, scuffle, shindig (*inf.*), shindy (*inf.*), skirmish, trouble, uproar

fraction *n* **1, 2** = **piece**, cut, division, moiety, part, percentage, portion, proportion, quota, ratio, section, sector, segment, share, slice, subdivision **3** = **fragment**, atom, bit, bite, chip, crumb, drop, flake, grain, granule, iota, jot, morsel, mote, particle, scrap, shard, shred, sliver, smithereen (*inf.*), splinter, whit

fractious *adj* **1, 2** = **irritable**, awkward, captious, crabby, cross, fretful, froward (*arch.*), grouchy, peevish, pettish, petulant, querulous, ratty (*Brit. & NZ inf.*), recalcitrant, refractory, testy, tetchy, touchy, unruly
Antonyms *adj* affable, agreeable, amiable, biddable, complaisant, genial, good-natured, good-tempered, tractable

fracture *n* **3** = **break**, breach, cleft, crack, fissure, gap, opening, rent, rift, rupture, schism, split ◆ *vb* **5, 6** = **break**, crack, rupture, splinter, split

fragile *adj* **1** = **delicate**, breakable, brittle, dainty, feeble, fine, flimsy, frail, frangible, infirm, slight, weak
Antonyms *adj* durable, elastic, flexible, hardy, lasting, reliable, resilient, robust, strong, sturdy, tough

fragility *n* **1** = **delicacy**, brittleness, feebleness, frailty, frangibility, infirmity, weakness

fragment *n* **1-3** = **piece**, bit, chip, fraction, morsel, oddment, part, particle, portion, remnant, scrap, shiver, shred, sliver ◆ *vb* **4** = **break**, break up, come apart, come to pieces, crumble, disintegrate, disunite, divide, shatter, shiver, splinter, split, split up
Antonyms *vb* ≠ **break:** bond, combine, compound, fuse, join together, link, marry, merge, synthesize, unify

fragmentary *adj* = **incomplete**, bitty, broken, disconnected, discrete, disjointed, incoherent, partial, piecemeal, scattered, scrappy, sketchy, unsystematic

fragrance *n* **1** = **scent**, aroma, balm, bouquet, fragrancy, perfume, redolence, smell, sweet odour
Antonyms *n* effluvium, miasma, offensive smell, pong (*Brit. inf.*), reek, smell, stink, whiff (*Brit. sl.*)

fragrant *adj* = **aromatic**, ambrosial, balmy, odoriferous, odorous, perfumed, redolent, sweet-scented, sweet-smelling
Antonyms *adj* fetid, foul-smelling, malodorous, noisome, olid, pongy (*Brit. inf.*), reeking, smelling, smelly, stinking

frail[1] **1, 2** *adj* = **weak**, breakable, brittle, decrepit, delicate, feeble, flimsy, fragile, frangible, infirm, insubstantial, puny, slight, tender, unsound, vulnerable, wispy
Antonyms *adj* hale, healthy, robust, sound, stalwart, strong, sturdy, substantial, tough, vigorous

frailty *n* **1** = **weakness**, fallibility, feebleness, frailness, infirmity, peccability, puniness, susceptibility **2** = **fault**, blemish, chink in one's armour, defect, deficiency, failing, flaw, foible, imperfection, peccadillo, shortcoming, vice, weak point
Antonyms *n* ≠ **weakness:** fortitude, might, robustness, strength ≠ **fault:** asset, strong point, virtue

frame *n* **1** = **casing**, construction, fabric, form, framework, scheme, shell, structure, system **2** = **mounting**, mount, setting **4** = **physique**, anatomy, body, build, carcass, morphology, skeleton **5** = **mood**, attitude, disposition, fettle,

tistics. an enumeration of a population for the purposes of sampling. **12** *Sl.* another word for **frame-up. 13** *Obs.* shape; form. ◆ *vb* **frames, framing, framed.** (*mainly tr*) **14** to construct by fitting parts together. **15** to draw up the plans or basic details for: *to frame a policy.* **16** to compose or conceive: *to frame a reply.* **17** to provide, support, or enclose with a frame: *to frame a picture.* **18** to form (words) with the lips, esp. silently. **19** *Sl.* to conspire to incriminate (someone) on a false charge. [OE *framiae* to avail]
▸**'frameless** *adj* ▸**'framer** *n*

frame house *n* a house that has a timber framework and cladding.

frame of reference *n* **1** *Sociol.* a set of standards that determines and sanctions behaviour. **2** any set of planes or curves, such as the three coordinate axes, used to locate a point in space.

frame-up ❶ *n Sl.* **1** a conspiracy to incriminate someone on a false charge. **2** a plot to bring about a dishonest result, as in a contest.

framework ❶ ('freɪmˌwɜːk) *n* **1** a structural plan or basis of a project. **2** a structure or frame supporting or containing something.

franc (fræŋk; *French* frɑ̃) *n* **1** the standard monetary unit of France, French dependencies, and Monaco, divided into 100 centimes. Also called: **French franc. 2** the standard monetary and currency unit, comprising 100 centimes, of various countries including Belgium, the Central African Republic, Gabon, Guinea, Liechtenstein, Luxembourg, Mauritania, Niger, the Republic of Congo, Senegal, Switzerland, Togo, etc. **3** a Moroccan monetary unit worth one hundredth of a dirham. [C14: from OF; from L *Rex Francōrum* King of the Franks, inscribed on 14th-century francs]

franchise ❶ ('fræntʃaɪz) *n* **1** (usually preceded by *the*) the right to vote, esp. for representatives in a legislative body. **2** any exemption, privilege, or right granted to an individual or group by a public authority. **3** *Commerce.* authorization granted by a manufacturing enterprise to a distributor to market the manufacturer's products. **4** the full rights of citizenship. ◆ *vb* **franchises, franchising, franchised. 5** (*tr*) *Commerce, chiefly US & Canad.* to grant (a person, firm, etc.) a franchise. [C13: from OF, from *franchir* to set free, from *franc* free]
▸**ˌfranchi'see** *n* ▸**franchisement** ('fræntʃɪzmənt) *n* ▸**'franchiser** *n*

Franciscan (fræn'sɪskən) *n* **a** a member of a Christian religious order of friars or nuns tracing their origins back to Saint Francis of Assisi. **b** (*as modifier*): *a Franciscan friary.*

francium ('frænsɪəm) *n* an unstable radioactive element of the alkali-metal group, occurring in minute amounts in uranium ores. Symbol: Fr; atomic no.: 87; half-life of most stable isotope, ^{223}Fr: 22 minutes. [C20: from NL, from *France* + -IUM; because first found in France]

Franco- ('fræŋkəʊ-) *combining form.* indicating France or French: *Franco-Prussian.* [from Med. L *Francus*, from LL: FRANK]

francolin ('fræŋkəʊlɪn) *n* an African or Asian partridge. [C17: from F, from OIt. *francolino*, from ?]

Francophobe ('fræŋkəʊˌfəʊb) *n* **1** a person who hates or fears France or its people. **2** *Canad.* a person who hates or fears Canadian Francophones.

Francophone ('fræŋkəʊˌfəʊn) (*often not cap.*) ◆ *n* **1** a person who speaks French, esp. a native speaker. ◆ *adj* **2** speaking French as a native language. **3** using French as a lingua franca.

frangible ('frændʒɪbᵊl) *adj* breakable or fragile. [C15: from OF, ult. from L *frangere* to break]
▸**ˌfrangi'bility** *or* **'frangibleness** *n*

frangipane ('frændʒɪˌpeɪn) *n* **1** a pastry filled with cream and flavoured with almonds. **2** a variant of **frangipani** (the perfume).

frangipani (ˌfrændʒɪ'pɑːnɪ) *n, pl* **frangipanis** *or* **frangipani. 1** a tropical American shrub cultivated for its waxy white or pink flowers, which have a sweet overpowering scent. **2** a perfume prepared from this plant or resembling the odour of its flowers. **3 native frangipani.** *Austral.* an Australian evergreen tree with large fragrant yellow flowers. [C17: via F from It.: perfume for scenting gloves, after the Marquis Muzio *Frangipani*, 16th-century Roman nobleman who invented it]

Franglais (*French* frɑ̃glɛ) *n* informal French containing a high proportion of English. [C20: from F *français* French + *anglais* English]

frank ❶ (fræŋk) *adj* **1** honest and straightforward in speech or attitude: *a frank person.* **2** outspoken or blunt. **3** open and avowed: *frank interest.* ◆ *vb* (*tr*) **4** *Chiefly Brit.* to put a mark on (a letter, etc.), either cancelling the postage stamp or in place of a stamp, ensuring free carriage. **5** to mark (a letter, etc.) with an official mark or signature, indicating the right of free delivery. **6** to facilitate or assist (a person) to enter easily. **7** to obtain immunity for (a person). ◆ *n* **8** an official mark or signature affixed to a letter, etc., ensuring free delivery or delivery without stamps. [C13: from OF, from Med. L *francus* free; identical with FRANK (in Frankish Gaul only members of this people enjoyed full freedom)]
▸**'frankable** *adj* ▸**'franker** *n* ▸**'frankness** *n*

Frank (fræŋk) *n* a member of a group of West Germanic peoples who spread from the east in the late 4th century A.D., gradually conquering most of Gaul and Germany. [OE *Franca*; ?from the name of a Frankish weapon (cf. OE *franca* javelin)]

franked investment income *n* dividends from one UK company received by another on which the paying company has paid corporation tax.

Frankenstein ('fræŋkɪnˌstaɪn) *n* **1** a person who creates something that brings about his ruin. **2** Also called: **Frankenstein's monster.** a thing that destroys its creator. [C19: after Baron *Frankenstein*, who created a destructive monster from parts of corpses in the novel by Mary Shelley (1818)]
▸**ˌFranken'steinian** *adj*

frankfurter ('fræŋkˌfɜːtə) *n* a smoked sausage, made of finely minced pork or beef. [C20: short for G *Frankfurter Wurst* sausage from *Frankfurt am Main* in Germany]

frankincense ('fræŋkɪnˌsɛns) *n* an aromatic gum resin obtained from trees of the genus *Boswellia*, which occur in Asia and Africa. [C14: from OF *franc* free, pure + *encens* INCENSE[1]; see FRANK]

Frankish ('fræŋkɪʃ) *n* **1** the ancient West Germanic language of the Franks. ◆ *adj* **2** of or relating to the Franks or their language.

franklin ('fræŋklɪn) *n* (in 14th- and 15th-century England) a substantial landholder of free but not noble birth. [C13: from Anglo-F, from OF *franc* free, on the model of CHAMBERLAIN]

frankly ❶ ('fræŋklɪ) *adv* **1** (*sentence modifier*) to be honest. **2** in a frank manner.

frantic ❶ ('fræntɪk) *adj* **1** distracted with fear, pain, joy, etc. **2** marked by or showing frenzy: *frantic efforts.* [C14: from OF, from L *phrenēticus* mad]
▸**'frantically** *or* **'franticly** *adv*

frappé ('fræpeɪ) *n* **1** a drink consisting of a liqueur, etc., poured over crushed ice. ◆ *adj* **2** (*postpositive*) (esp. of drinks) chilled. [C19: from F, from *frapper* to strike, hence, chill]

frater ('freɪtə) *n Arch.* a refectory. [C13: from OF *fraiteur*, from *refreitor*, from LL *rĕfectōrium* REFECTORY]

fraternal (frə'tɜːnᵊl) *adj* **1** of or suitable to a brother; brotherly. **2** of a fraternity. **3** designating twins of the same or opposite sex that developed from two separate fertilized ova. Cf. **identical** (sense 3). [C15: from L, from *frāter* brother]
▸**fra'ternalism** *n*

fraternity ❶ (frə'tɜːnɪtɪ) *n, pl* **fraternities. 1** a body of people united in interests, aims, etc.: *the teaching fraternity.* **2** brotherhood. **3** *US & Canad.* a secret society joined by male students, functioning as a social club.

fraternize ❶ *or* **fraternise** ('frætəˌnaɪz) *vb* **fraternizes, fraternizing, fraternized** *or* **fraternises, fraternising, fraternised.** (*intr;* often foll. by *with*) to associate on friendly terms.
▸**ˌfraterni'zation** *or* **ˌfraterni'sation** *n* ▸**'fraterˌnizer** *or* **'fraterˌniser** *n*

fratricide ('frætrɪˌsaɪd, 'freɪ-) *n* **1** the act of killing one's brother. **2** a person who kills his brother. [C15: from L, from *frater* brother + -CIDE]
▸**ˌfratri'cidal** *adj*

Frau (fraʊ) *n, pl* **Frauen** ('fraʊən) *or* **Fraus.** a married German woman: usually used as a title equivalent to *Mrs.* [from OHG *frouwa*]

fraud ❶ (frɔːd) *n* **1** deliberate deception, trickery, or cheating intended to gain an advantage. **2** an act or instance of such deception. **3** *Inf.* a person who acts in a false or deceitful way. [C14: from OF, from L *fraus* deception]

THESAURUS

humour, outlook, spirit, state, temper ◆ *vb* **14 = construct**, assemble, build, constitute, fabricate, fashion, forge, form, institute, invent, make, manufacture, model, mould, put together, set up **15, 16 = devise**, block out, compose, conceive, concoct, contrive, cook up, draft, draw up, form, formulate, hatch, map out, plan, shape, sketch **17 = mount**, case, enclose, surround

frame-up *n* **1** *Slang* **= false charge**, fabrication, fit-up (*sl.*), put-up job, trumped-up charge

framework *n* **1, 2 = structure**, core, fabric, foundation, frame, frame of reference, groundwork, plan, schema, shell, skeleton, the bare bones

franchise *n* **1 = vote**, suffrage **2 = right**, authorization, charter, exemption, freedom, immunity, prerogative, privilege

frank *adj* **1, 2 = honest**, artless, blunt, candid, direct, downright, forthright, free, ingenuous, open, outright, outspoken, plain, plain-spoken, round, sincere, straightforward, straight from the shoulder (*inf.*), transparent, truthful, unconcealed, undisguised, unreserved, unrestricted, upfront (*inf.*)
Antonyms *adj* artful, crafty, cunning, evasive, indirect, inscrutable, reserved, reticent, secretive, shifty, shy, underhand

frankly *adv* **1 = honestly**, candidly, in truth, to be honest **2 = openly**, bluntly, directly, freely, overtly, plainly, straight, straight from the shoulder, without reserve

frankness *n* **1, 2 = outspokenness**, absence of reserve, bluntness, candour, forthrightness, ingenuousness, laying it on the line, openness, plain speaking, truthfulness

frantic *adj* **1 = distraught**, at one's wits' end, at the end of one's tether, berserk, beside oneself, distracted, furious, mad, overwrought, raging, raving, uptight (*inf.*), wild **2 = hectic**, desperate, fraught (*inf.*), frenetic, frenzied
Antonyms *adj* calm, collected, composed, cool, laid-back, poised, self-possessed, together (*sl.*), unfazed (*inf.*), unruffled

fraternity *n* **1 = association**, brotherhood, circle, clan, club, company, guild, league, order, set, sodality, union **2 = companionship**, brotherhood, camaraderie, comradeship, fellowship, kinship

fraternize *vb* **= associate**, concur, consort, cooperate, go around with, hang out (*inf.*), hobnob, keep company, mingle, mix, socialize, sympathize, unite
Antonyms *vb* avoid, eschew, keep away from, shun, steer clear of

fraud *n* **1, 2 = deception**, artifice, canard, cheat, chicane, chicanery, craft, deceit, double-dealing, duplicity, guile, hoax, humbug, imposture, scam (*sl.*), sharp practice, spuriousness, sting (*inf.*), stratagems, swindling, treachery, trickery **3** *Informal* **= impostor**, bluffer, charlatan, cheat, counterfeit, double-dealer, fake, forgery, fraudster, hoax, hoaxer, mountebank, phoney *or* phony (*inf.*), pretender, quack, sham, swindler
Antonyms *n* ≠ **deception**: fairness, good faith, hon-

fraudster ('frɔːdstə) *n* a swindler.

fraudulent Ⓣ ('frɔːdjʊlənt) *adj* **1** acting with or having the intent to deceive. **2** relating to or proceeding from fraud. [C15: from L *fraudulentus* deceitful]
▸**'fraudulence** *n* ▸**'fraudulently** *adv*

fraught Ⓣ (frɔːt) *adj* **1** (*usually postpositive* and foll. by *with*) filled or charged: *a venture fraught with peril.* **2** *Inf.* showing or producing tension or anxiety. [C14: from MDu. *vrachten,* from *vracht* FREIGHT]

Fräulein (*German* 'frɔylaɪn) *n, pl* **Fräulein** *or English* **Fräuleins.** an unmarried German woman: often used as a title equivalent to *Miss.* [from MHG *vrouwelīn,* dim. of *vrouwe* lady]

Fraunhofer lines ('fraunhəufə) *pl n* a set of dark lines appearing in the continuous emission spectrum of the sun. [C19: after Joseph von *Fraunhofer* (1787–1826), G physicist]

fraxinella (ˌfræksɪ'nɛlə) *n* another name for **gas plant.** [C17: from NL: a little ash tree, from L *frāxinus* ash]

fray[1] Ⓣ (freɪ) *n* **1** a noisy quarrel. **2** a fight or brawl. [C14: short for AFFRAY]

fray[2] Ⓣ (freɪ) *vb* **1** to wear or cause to wear away into loose threads, esp. at an edge or end. **2** to make or become strained or irritated. **3** to rub or chafe (another object). [C14: from F *frayer* to rub, from L *fricāre* to rub]

frazil ('freɪzɪl) *n* small pieces of ice that form in water moving turbulently enough to prevent the formation of a sheet of ice. [C19: from Canad. F, from F *fraisil* cinders, ult. from L *fax* torch]

frazzle ('fræzᵊl) *Inf.* ◆ *vb* **frazzles, frazzling, frazzled. 1** to make or become exhausted or weary. ◆ *n* **2** the state of being frazzled or exhausted. **3 to a frazzle.** completely (esp. in **burnt to a frazzle**). [C19: prob. from ME *faselen* to fray, from *fasel* fringe; infl. by FRAY[2]]

freak Ⓣ (friːk) *n* **1** a person, animal, or plant that is abnormal or deformed. **2a** an object, event, etc., that is abnormal. **2b** (*as modifier*): *a freak storm.* **3** a personal whim or caprice. **4** *Inf.* a person who acts or dresses in a markedly unconventional way. **5** *Inf.* a person who is ardently fond of something specified: *a jazz freak.* ◆ *vb* **6** See **freak out.** [C16: from ?]
▸**'freakish** *adj* ▸**'freaky** *adj*

freak out *vb* (*adv*) *Inf.* to be or cause to be in a heightened emotional state.

freckle ('frɛkᵊl) *n* **1** a small brownish spot on the skin developed by exposure to sunlight. Technical name: **lentigo. 2** any small area of discoloration. ◆ *vb* **freckles, freckling, freckled. 3** to mark or become marked with freckles or spots. [C14: from ON *freknur*]
▸**'freckled** *or* **'freckly** *adj*

free Ⓣ (friː) *adj* **freer, freest. 1** able to act at will; not under compulsion or restraint. **2a** not enslaved or confined. **2b** (*as n*): *land of the free.* **3** (*often postpositive* and foll. by *from*) not subject (to) or restricted (by some regulation, constraint, etc.): *free from pain.* **4** (of a country, etc.) autonomous or independent. **5** exempt from external direction: *free will.* **6** not subject to conventional constraints: *free verse.* **7** not exact or literal: *a free translation.* **8** provided without charge: *free entertainment.* **9** *Law.* (of property) **9a** not subject to payment of rent or performance of services; freehold. **9b** not subject to any burden or charge; unencumbered. **10** (*postpositive;* often foll. by *of* or *with*) ready or generous in using or giving: *free with advice.* **11** not occupied or in use; available: *a free cubicle.* **12** (of a person) not busy. **13** open or available to all. **14** without charge to the subscriber or user: *freepost; freephone.* **15** not fixed or joined; loose: *the free end of a chain.* **16** without obstruction or impediment: *free passage.* **17** *Chem.* chemically uncombined: *free nitrogen.* **18** *Logic.* denoting an occurrence of a variable not bound by a quantifier. Cf. **bound**[1] (sense 8). **19** (of routines in figure skating competitions) chosen by the competitor. **20** (of jazz) totally improvised. **21 for free.** *Nonstandard.* without charge or cost. **22 free and easy.** casual or tolerant; easy-going. **23 make free with.** to behave too familiarly towards. ◆ *adv* **24** in a free manner; freely. **25** without charge or cost. **26** *Naut.* with the wind blowing from the quarter. ◆ *vb* **frees, freeing, freed.** (*tr*) **27** to set at liberty; release. **28** to remove obstructions or impediments from. **29** (often foll. by *of* or *from*) to relieve or rid (of obstacles, pain, etc.). [OE *frēo*]
▸**'freely** *adv* ▸**'freeness** *n*

-free *adj combining form.* free from: *trouble-free; lead-free petrol.*

free alongside ship *adj* (of a shipment of goods) delivered to the dock without charge to the buyer, but excluding the cost of loading onto the vessel. Cf. **free on board.**

free association *n Psychoanal.* a method of exploring a person's unconscious by eliciting words and thoughts that are associated with key words provided by a psychoanalyst.

freebase ('friːˌbeɪs) *Sl.* ◆ *n* **1** cocaine that has been refined by heating it in ether or some other solvent. ◆ *vb* **freebases, freebasing, freebased. 2** to refine (cocaine) in this way. **3** to smoke or inhale the fumes from (refined cocaine).

freebie ('friːbɪ) *n Sl.* something provided without charge.

freeboard ('friːˌbɔːd) *n* the space or distance between the deck of a vessel and the waterline.

freebooter Ⓣ ('friːˌbuːtə) *n* a person, such as a pirate, living from plunder. [C16: from Du., from *vrijbuit* booty; see FILIBUSTER]
▸**'freeboot** *vb* (*intr*)

freeborn ('friːˌbɔːn) *adj* **1** not born in slavery. **2** of or suitable for people not born in slavery.

Free Church *n Chiefly Brit.* any Protestant Church, esp. the Presbyterian, other than the Established Church.

free city *n* a sovereign or autonomous city.

freedman ('friːdˌmæn) *n, pl* **freedmen.** a man who has been freed from slavery.

freedom Ⓣ ('friːdəm) *n* **1** personal liberty, as from slavery, serfdom, etc. **2** liberation, as from confinement or bondage. **3** the quality or state of being free, esp. to enjoy political and civil liberties. **4** (usually foll. by *from*) exemption or immunity: *freedom from taxation.* **5** the right or privilege of unrestricted use or access: *the freedom of a city.* **6** autonomy, self-government, or independence. **7** the power or liberty to order one's own actions. **8** *Philosophy.* the quality, esp. of the will or the individual, of not being totally constrained. **9** ease or frankness of manner: *she talked with complete freedom.* **10** excessive familiarity of manner. **11** ease and grace, as of movement. [OE *frēodōm*]

freedom fighter *n* a militant revolutionary.

free energy *n* a thermodynamic property that expresses the capacity of a system to perform work under certain conditions.

free enterprise *n* an economic system in which commercial organizations compete for profit with little state control.

THESAURUS

esty, integrity, probity, rectitude, trustworthiness, virtue

fraudulent *adj* **1 = deceitful,** counterfeit, crafty, criminal, crooked (*inf.*), deceptive, dishonest, double-dealing, duplicitous, false, knavish, phoney *or* phony (*inf.*), sham, spurious, swindling, treacherous
Antonyms *adj* above board, genuine, honest, honourable, lawful, principled, reputable, true, trustworthy, upright

fraught *adj* **1** *with* **with = filled,** abounding, accompanied, attended, bristling, charged, full, heavy, laden, replete, stuffed **2** *Informal* **= tense,** agitated, anxious, difficult, distracted, distressed, distressing, emotionally charged, emotive, hag-ridden, on tenterhooks, strung-up, tricky, trying, uptight (*inf.*), wired (*sl.*)

fray[1] *n* **1, 2 = fight,** affray (*Law*), battle, battle royal, brawl, broil, clash, combat, conflict, disturbance, donnybrook, melee *or* mêlée, quarrel, riot, row, ruckus (*inf.*), rumble (*US & NZ sl.*), rumpus, scrimmage, scuffle, set-to (*inf.*), shindig (*inf.*), shindy (*inf.*), skirmish

fray[2] *vb* **1, 3 = wear thin,** become threadbare, chafe, fret, rub, wear, wear away

frayed *adj* **1 = worn,** frazzled, out at elbows, ragged, tattered, threadbare

freak *n* **1, 2a = oddity,** aberration, abnormality, abortion, anomaly, grotesque, malformation, monster, monstrosity, mutant, queer fish (*Brit. inf.*), *rara avis,* sport (*Biology*), teratism, weirdo *or* weirdie (*inf.*) ◆ *modifier* **2b = abnormal,** aberrant, atypical, bizarre, erratic, exceptional, fluky (*inf.*), fortuitous, odd, queer, unaccountable, unexpected, unforeseen, unparalleled, unpredictable, unusual ◆ *n* **3 = whim,** caprice, crotchet, fad, fancy, folly, humour, irregularity, quirk, turn, twist, vagary, whimsy **5** *Informal* **= enthusiast,** addict, aficionado, buff (*inf.*), devotee, fan, fanatic, fiend (*inf.*), nut (*sl.*)

freakish *adj* **1, 2 = odd,** aberrant, abnormal, fantastic, freaky (*sl.*), grotesque, malformed, monstrous, outlandish, outré, preternatural, strange, teratoid (*Biology*), unconventional, weird **3 = whimsical,** arbitrary, capricious, changeable, erratic, fanciful, fitful, humorous, odd, unpredictable, vagarious (*rare*), wayward

freaky *adj* **1 = weird,** abnormal, bizarre, crazy, far-out (*sl.*), freakish, odd, queer, rum (*Brit. sl.*), strange, unconventional, wild

free *adj* **1 = allowed,** able, clear, disengaged, loose, open, permitted, unattached, unengaged, unhampered, unimpeded, unobstructed, unregulated, unrestricted, untrammelled **2 = at liberty,** at large, footloose, independent, liberated, loose, off the hook (*sl.*), on the loose, uncommitted, unconstrained, unengaged, unfettered, unrestrained **4 = independent,** autarchic, autonomous, democratic, emancipated, self-governing, self- ruling, sovereign **8 = complimentary,** buckshee (*Brit. sl.*), for free (*inf.*), for nothing, free of charge, gratis, gratuitous, on the house, unpaid, without charge **11, 12 = available,** at leisure, empty, extra, idle, not tied down, spare, unemployed, uninhabited, unoccupied, unused, vacant **22 free and easy = relaxed,** casual, easy-going, informal, laid-back (*inf.*), lax, lenient, liberal, tolerant, unceremonious ◆ *adv* **24 = freely,** abundantly, copiously, idly, loosely **25 = without charge,** at no cost, for love, gratis ◆ *vb* **27 = release,** deliver, discharge, disenthrall, emancipate, let go, let out, liberate, loose, manumit, set at liberty, set free, turn loose, unbridle, uncage, unchain, unfetter, unleash, untie **28, 29 = clear,** cut loose, deliver, disengage, disentangle, exempt, extricate, ransom, redeem, relieve, rescue, rid, unburden, undo, unshackle
Antonyms *adj* ≠ **at liberty:** bound, captive, confined, dependent, fettered, immured, incarcerated, restrained, restricted, secured ◆ *vb* ≠ **release:** confine, imprison, incarcerate, inhibit, limit, restrain, restrict, straiten

freebooter *n* **= pirate,** bandit, brigand, buccaneer, cateran (*Scot.*), highwayman, looter, marauder, pillager, plunderer, raider, reiver (*dialect*), robber, rover

freedom *n* **4 = exemption,** immunity, impunity, privilege **6 = liberty,** autonomy, deliverance, emancipation, home rule, independence, manumission, release, self-government **7 = licence,** ability, a free hand, blank cheque, carte blanche, discretion, elbowroom, facility, flexibility, free rein, latitude, leeway, opportunity, play, power, range, scope **9 = openness,** abandon, candour, directness, ease, familiarity, frankness, informality, ingenuousness, lack of restraint *or* reserve, unconstraint **10 = overfamiliarity,** boldness, brazenness, disrespect, forwardness, impertinence, laxity, licence, presumption
Antonyms *n* ≠ **liberty:** bondage, captivity, dependence, imprisonment, servitude, slavery, thraldom ≠ **licence:** limitation, restriction ≠ **open-**

free fall *n* **1** free descent of a body in which the gravitational force is the only force acting on it. **2** the part of a parachute descent before the parachute opens.

free flight *n* the flight of a rocket, missile, etc., when its engine has ceased to produce thrust.

free-for-all ⓘ *n Inf.* **1** a disorganized brawl or argument, usually involving all those present. **2a** a contest, discussion, etc., that is open to everyone. **2b** (*as modifier*): *a free-for-all contest.*

free-form *adj Arts.* freely flowing, spontaneous.

free hand ⓘ *n* **1** unrestricted freedom to act (esp. in **give (someone) a free hand**). ◆ *adj, adv* **freehand. 2** (done) by hand without the use of guiding instruments: *a freehand drawing.*

free-handed *adj* generous or liberal; unstinting.
▸ˌ**free-'handedly** *adv*

freehold ('fri:ˌhəuld) *Property law.* ◆ *n* **1a** tenure by which land is held in fee simple, fee tail, or for life. **1b** an estate held by such tenure. ◆ *adj* **2** relating to or having the nature of freehold.
▸'**freeholder** *n*

free house *n Brit.* a public house not bound to sell only one brewer's products.

free kick *n Soccer.* a place kick awarded for a foul or infringement.

freelance ('fri:ˌlɑ:ns) *n* **1a** Also called: **freelancer.** a self-employed person, esp. a writer or artist, who is hired to do specific assignments. **1b** (*as modifier*): *a freelance journalist.* **2** (in medieval Europe) a mercenary soldier or adventurer. ◆ *vb* **freelances, freelancing, freelanced. 3** to work as a freelance on (an assignment, etc.). ◆ *adv* **4** as a freelance. [C19 (in sense 2): later applied to politicians, writers, etc.]

free-living *adj* **1** given to ready indulgence of the appetites. **2** (of animals and plants) not parasitic.
▸ˌ**free-'liver** *n*

freeloader ('fri:ˌləudə) *n Sl.* a person who habitually depends on others for food, shelter, etc.

free love *n* the practice of sexual relationships without fidelity to a single partner.

freeman ('fri:mən) *n, pl* **freemen. 1** a person who is not a slave. **2** a person who enjoys political and civil liberties. **3** a person who enjoys a privilege, such as the freedom of a city.

free market *n* **a** an economic system that allows supply and demand to regulate prices, wages, etc., rather than government policy. **b** (*as modifier*): *a free-market economy.*

freemartin ('fri:ˌmɑ:tɪn) *n* the female of a pair of twin calves of unlike sex that is imperfectly developed and sterile. [C17: from ?]

Freemason ('fri:ˌmeɪsᵊn) *n* a member of the widespread secret order, constituted in London in 1717, of **Free and Accepted Masons,** pledged to brotherly love, faith, and charity. Sometimes shortened to **Mason.**

freemasonry ('fri:ˌmeɪsᵊnrɪ) *n* natural or tacit sympathy and understanding.

Freemasonry ('fri:ˌmeɪsᵊnrɪ) *n* **1** the institutions, rites, practices, etc., of Freemasons. **2** Freemasons collectively.

free on board *adj* (of a shipment of goods) delivered on board ship or other carrier without charge to the buyer. Cf. **free alongside ship.**

free port *n* **1** a port open to all commercial vessels on equal terms. **2** a port that permits the duty-free entry of foreign goods intended for re-export.

free radical *n* an atom or group of atoms containing at least one unpaired electron and existing for a brief period of time before reacting to produce a stable molecule.

free-range *adj Chiefly Brit.* kept or produced in natural conditions: *free-range eggs.*

free-select *vb* (*tr*) *Austral. history.* to select (areas of crown land) and acquire the freehold by a series of annual payments.
▸'**free-se'lection** *n* ▸'**free-se'lector** *n*

freesia ('fri:zɪə) *n* a plant of Southern Africa, cultivated for its white, yellow, or pink tubular fragrant flowers. [C19: NL, after F. H. T. *Freese* (died 1876), G physician]

free skating *n* either of two parts in a figure-skating competition in which the skater chooses the sequence of figures and the music and which are judged on technique and artistic presentation. The short programme consists of specified movements and the long programme is entirely the skater's own choice.

free space *n* a region that has no gravitational and electromagnetic fields. It is used as an absolute standard and was formerly referred to as a vacuum.

free-spoken *adj* speaking frankly or without restraint.
▸ˌ**free-'spokenly** *adv*

freestanding (ˌfri:'stændɪŋ) *adj* not attached to or supported by another object.

freestone ('fri:ˌstəun) *n* **1** any fine-grained stone, esp. sandstone or limestone, that can be worked in any direction without breaking. **2** *Bot.* a fruit, such as a peach, in which the flesh separates readily from the stone.

freestyle ('fri:ˌstaɪl) *n* **1** a competition or race, as in swimming, in which each participant may use a style of his or her choice instead of a specified style. **2a International freestyle.** an amateur style of wrestling with an agreed set of rules. **2b** Also called: **all-in wrestling.** a style of professional wrestling with no internationally agreed set of rules.

freethinker ⓘ (ˌfri:'θɪŋkə) *n* a person who forms his ideas and opinions independently of authority or accepted views, esp. in matters of religion.
▸**free thought** *n*

free trade *n* **1** international trade that is free of such government interference as protective tariffs. **2** *Arch.* smuggling.

free verse *n* unrhymed verse without a metrical pattern.

freeware ('fri:ˌwɛə) *n* computer software that may be distributed and used without payment.

freeway ('fri:ˌweɪ) *n US.* **1** an expressway. **2** a major road that can be used without paying a toll.

freewheel ⓘ (ˌfri:'wi:l) *n* **1** a ratchet device in the rear hub of a bicycle wheel that permits the wheel to rotate freely while the pedals are stationary. ◆ *vb* **2** (*intr*) to coast on a bicycle using the freewheel.

free will *n* **1a** the apparent human ability to make choices that are not externally determined. **1b** the doctrine that such human freedom of choice is not illusory. Cf. **determinism. 2** the ability to make a choice without outside coercion: *he left of his own free will.*

Free World *n* **the.** the non-Communist countries collectively.

freeze ⓘ (fri:z) *vb* **freezes, freezing, froze, frozen. 1** to change (a liquid) into a solid as a result of a reduction in temperature, or (of a liquid) to solidify in this way. **2** (when *intr*, sometimes foll. by *over* or *up*) to cover, clog, or harden with ice, or become so covered, clogged, or hardened. **3** to fix fast or become fixed (to something) because of the action of frost. **4** (*tr*) to preserve (food) by subjection to extreme cold, as in a freezer. **5** to feel or cause to feel the sensation or effects of extreme cold. **6** to die or cause to die of extreme cold. **7** to become or cause to become paralysed, fixed, or motionless, esp. through fear, shock, etc. **8** (*tr*) to cause (moving film) to stop at a particular frame. **9** to make or become formal, haughty, etc., in manner. **10** (*tr*) to fix (prices, incomes, etc.) at a particular level. **11** (*tr*) to forbid by law the exchange, liquidation, or collection of (loans, assets, etc.). **12** (*tr*) to stop (a process) at a particular stage of development. **13** (*intr;* foll. by *onto*) *Inf., chiefly US.* to cling. ◆ *n* **14** the act of freezing or state of being frozen. **15** *Meteorol.* a spell of temperatures below freezing point, usually over a wide area. **16** the fixing of incomes, prices, etc., by legislation. ◆ *sentence substitute.* **17** *Chiefly US.* a command to stop instantly or risk being shot. [OE *frēosan*]
▸'**freezable** *adj*

freeze-dry *vb* **freeze-dries, freeze-drying, freeze-dried.** (*tr*) to preserve (a substance) by rapid freezing and subsequently drying in a vacuum.

freeze-frame *n* **1** *Films, television.* a single frame of a film repeated to give an effect like a still photograph. **2** *Video.* a single frame of a video recording viewed as a still by stopping the tape.

freeze out *vb* (*tr, adv*) *Inf.* to exclude, as by unfriendly behaviour, etc.

freezer ('fri:zə) *n* an insulated cold-storage cabinet for long-term storage of perishable foodstuffs. Also called: **deepfreeze.**

freezing ⓘ ('fri:zɪŋ) *adj Inf.* extremely cold.

freezing point *n* the temperature below which a liquid turns into a solid.

freezing works *n Austral. & NZ.* a slaughterhouse at which animal carcasses are frozen for export.

freight ⓘ (freɪt) *n* **1a** commercial transport that is slower and cheaper than express. **1b** the price charged for such transport. **1c** goods transported by this means. **1d** (*as modifier*): *freight transport.* **2** *Chiefly Brit.* a ship's cargo or part of it. ◆ *vb* (*tr*) **3** to load with goods for transport. [C16: from MDu *vrecht,* var. of *vracht*]

freightage ('freɪtɪdʒ) *n* **1** the commercial conveyance of goods. **2** the goods so transported. **3** the price charged for such conveyance.

freighter ('freɪtə) *n* **1** a ship or aircraft designed for transporting cargo. **2** a person concerned with the loading of a ship.

freightliner ('freɪtˌlaɪnə) *n Trademark.* a type of goods train carrying containers that can be transferred onto lorries or ships.

French (frɛntʃ) *n* **1** the official language of France: also an official language of Switzerland, Belgium, Canada, and certain other countries. Historically, French is an Indo-European language belonging to the Romance group. **2 the French.** (*functioning as pl*) the natives, citizens, or inhabitants of France collectively. ◆ *adj* **3** relating to, denoting, or characteristic of France, the French, or their language. **4** (in Canada) of French Canadians. [OE *Frencisc* French, Frankish]
▸'**Frenchness** *n*

French bread *n* white bread in a long slender loaf that has a crisp brown crust.

THESAURUS

ness: caution, restraint ≠ **overfamiliarity:** respectfulness

free-for-all *n* **1** *Informal* = **fight,** affray (*Law*), brawl, donnybrook, dust-up (*inf.*), fracas, melee *or* mêlée, riot, row, scrimmage, shindig (*inf.*), shindy (*inf.*)

free hand *n* **1** = **freedom,** authority, blank cheque, carte blanche, discretion, latitude, liberty, scope

freethinker *n* = **unbeliever,** agnostic, deist, doubter, infidel, sceptic

freewheel *vb* **2** = **coast,** drift, float, glide

freeze *vb* **1, 5** = **chill,** benumb, congeal, glaciate, harden, ice over *or* up, stiffen **12** = **suspend,** fix, hold up, inhibit, peg, stop

freezing *adj Informal* = **icy,** arctic, biting, bitter, chill, chilled, cold as ice, cutting, frostbound, frosty, glacial, numbing, parky (*Brit. inf.*), penetrating, polar, raw, Siberian, wintry

freight *n* **1a** = **transportation,** carriage, conveyance, shipment **1c, 2** = **cargo,** bales, bulk, burden, consignment, contents, goods, haul, lading, load, merchandise, payload, tonnage

French *adj* **3** = **Gallic**

French Canadian *n* **1** a Canadian citizen whose native language is French. ◆ *adj* **French-Canadian. 2** of or relating to French Canadians or their language.
French chalk *n* a variety of talc used to mark cloth, remove grease stains, or as a dry lubricant.
French doors *pl n* the US and Canad. name for **French windows.**
French dressing *n* a salad dressing made from oil and vinegar with seasonings; vinaigrette.
French fried potatoes *pl n* a more formal name for chips. Often shortened to **French fries, fries.**
French horn *n Music.* a valved brass instrument with a funnel-shaped mouthpiece and a tube of conical bore coiled into a spiral.
Frenchify ('frɛntʃɪˌfaɪ) *vb* **Frenchifies, Frenchifying, Frenchified.** *Inf.* to make or become French in appearance, etc.
French kiss *n* a kiss involving insertion of the tongue into the partner's mouth.
French knickers *pl n* women's wide-legged underpants.
French leave *n* an unauthorized or unannounced absence or departure. [C18: alluding to a custom in France of leaving without saying goodbye to one's host or hostess]
French letter *n Brit.* a slang term for **condom.**
Frenchman ('frɛntʃmən) *n, pl* **Frenchmen.** a native, citizen, or inhabitant of France.
▸ **'French,woman** *fem n*
French mustard *n* a mild mustard paste made with vinegar rather than water.
French polish *n* **1** a varnish for wood consisting of shellac dissolved in alcohol. **2** the gloss finish produced by this polish.
French-polish *vb* to treat with French polish or give a French polish (to).
French seam *n* a seam in which the edges are not visible.
French toast *n* **1** *Brit.* toast cooked on one side only. **2** bread dipped in beaten egg and lightly fried.
French windows *pl n (sometimes sing) Brit.* a pair of casement windows extending to floor level and opening onto a balcony, garden, etc.
frenetic 🅣 (frɪ'nɛtɪk) *adj* distracted or frantic. [C14: via OF, from L, from Gk, from *phrenitis* insanity, from *phrēn* mind]
▸ **fre'netically** *adv*
frenum ('fri:nəm) *n, pl* **frena** (-nə). a variant spelling (esp. US) of **fraenum.**
frenzy 🅣 ('frɛnzɪ) *n, pl* **frenzies. 1** violent mental derangement. **2** wild excitement or agitation. **3** a bout of wild or agitated activity: *a frenzy of preparations.* ◆ *vb* **frenzies, frenzying, frenzied. 4** *(tr)* to drive into a frenzy. [C14: from OF, from LL *phrēnēsis* madness, from LGk, ult. from Gk *phrēn* mind]
▸ **'frenzied** *adj*
Freon ('fri:ˌɒn) *n Trademark.* any of a group of chemically unreactive gaseous or liquid derivatives of methane in which hydrogen atoms have been replaced by chlorine and fluorine atoms: used as aerosol propellants, refrigerants, and solvents.
freq. *abbrev. for:* **1** frequent(ly). **2** frequentative.
frequency 🅣 ('fri:kwənsɪ) *n, pl* **frequencies. 1** the state of being frequent. **2** the number of times that an event occurs within a given period. **3** *Physics.* the number of times that a periodic function or vibration repeats itself in a specified time, often 1 second. It is usually measured in hertz. **4** *Statistics.* **4a** the number of individuals in a class (**absolute frequency**). **4b** the ratio of this number to the total number of individuals under survey (**relative frequency**). **5** *Ecology.* the number of individuals of a species within a given area. [C16: from L, from *frequēns* crowded]
frequency distribution *n Statistics.* the function of the distribution of a sample corresponding to the probability density function of the underlying population and tending to it as the sample size increases.
frequency modulation *n* a method of transmitting information using a radio-frequency carrier wave. The frequency of the carrier wave is varied in accordance with the amplitude of the input signal, the amplitude of the carrier remaining unchanged. Cf. **amplitude modulation.**
frequent 🅣 *adj* ('fri:kwənt). **1** recurring at short intervals. **2** habitual. ◆ *vb* (frɪ'kwɛnt). **3** *(tr)* to visit repeatedly or habitually. [C16: from L *frequēns* numerous]
▸ **,frequen'tation** *n* ▸ **fre'quenter** *n* ▸ **'frequently** *adv*
frequentative (frɪ'kwɛntətɪv) *Grammar.* ◆ *adj* **1** denoting an aspect of verbs in some languages used to express repeated or habitual action. **2** (in English) denoting a verb or an affix meaning repeated action, such as the verb *wrestle,* from *wrest.* ◆ *n* **3** a frequentative verb or affix.
fresco ('frɛskəʊ) *n, pl* **frescoes** *or* **frescos. 1** a very durable method of wall-painting using watercolours on wet plaster. **2** a painting done in this way. [C16: from It.: fresh plaster, from *fresco* (adj) fresh, cool, of Gmc origin]
fresh 🅣 (frɛʃ) *adj* **1** newly made, harvested, etc.: *fresh bread; fresh strawberries.* **2** newly acquired, found, etc.: *fresh publications.* **3** novel; original: *a fresh outlook.* **4** most recent: *fresh developments.* **5** further; additional: *fresh supplies.* **6** not canned, frozen, or otherwise preserved: *fresh fruit.* **7** (of water) not salt. **8** bright or clear: *a fresh morning.* **9** chilly or invigorating: *a fresh breeze.* **10** not tired; alert. **11** not worn or faded: *fresh colours.* **12** having a healthy or ruddy appearance. **13** newly or just arrived: *fresh from the presses.* **14** youthful or inexperienced. **15** *Inf.* presumptuous or disrespectful; forward. ◆ *n* **16** the fresh part or time of something. **17** another name for **freshet.** ◆ *adv* **18** in a fresh manner. [OE *fersc* fresh, unsalted]
▸ **'freshly** *adv* ▸ **'freshness** *n*
fresh breeze *n* a wind of force 5 on the Beaufort scale, blowing at speeds between 19 and 24 mph.
freshen 🅣 ('frɛʃən) *vb* **1** to make or become fresh or fresher. **2** (often foll. by *up*) to refresh (oneself), esp. by washing. **3** *(intr)* (of the wind) to increase.
fresher ('frɛʃə) *or* **freshman** ('frɛʃmən) *n, pl* **freshers** *or* **freshmen.** a first-year student at college or university.
freshet ('frɛʃɪt) *n* **1** the sudden overflowing of a river caused by heavy rain or melting snow. **2** a stream of fresh water emptying into the sea.
freshwater ('frɛʃˌwɔ:tə) *n (modifier)* **1** of or living in fresh water. **2** (esp. of a sailor who has not sailed on the sea) inexperienced. **3** *US.* little known: *a freshwater school.*
fresnel ('freɪnɛl) *n* a unit of frequency equivalent to 10^{12} hertz. [C20: after A. J. *Fresnel* (1788–1827), F physicist]
fret[1] 🅣 (frɛt) *vb* **frets, fretting, fretted. 1** to distress or be distressed. **2** to rub or wear away. **3** to feel or give annoyance or vexation. **4** to eat away or be eaten away, as by chemical action. **5** *(tr)* to make by wearing away; erode. ◆ *n* **6** a state of irritation or anxiety. [OE *fretan* to eat]
fret[2] (frɛt) *n* **1** a repetitive geometrical figure, esp. one used as an ornamental border. **2** such a pattern made in relief; fretwork. ◆ *vb* **frets, fretting, fretted. 3** *(tr)* to ornament with fret or fretwork. [C14: from OF *frete* interlaced design used on a shield, prob. of Gmc origin]
▸ **'fretless** *adj*
fret[3] (frɛt) *n* any of several small metal bars set across the fingerboard of a musical instrument of the lute, guitar, or viol family at various points along its length so as to produce the desired notes. [C16: from ?]
▸ **'fretless** *adj*
fretboard ('frɛtbɔ:d) *n* a fingerboard with frets on a stringed instrument.

THESAURUS

frenetic *adj* = **wild**, demented, distraught, excited, fanatical, frantic, frenzied, hyped up (*sl.*), insane, mad, maniacal, obsessive, overwrought, unbalanced
frenzied *adj* **4** = **uncontrolled**, agitated, all het up (*inf.*), berserk, convulsive, distracted, distraught, excited, feverish, frantic, frenetic, furious, hysterical, mad, maniacal, rabid, wild
frenzy *n* **1, 2** = **fury**, aberration, agitation, delirium, derangement, distraction, hysteria, insanity, lunacy, madness, mania, paroxysm, passion, rage, seizure, transport, turmoil **3** = **fit**, bout, burst, convulsion, outburst, paroxysm, spasm
Antonyms *n* ≠ **fury:** calm, collectedness, composure, coolness, sanity
frequency *n* **1** = **recurrence**, constancy, frequentness, periodicity, prevalence, repetition
frequent *adj* **1, 2** = **common**, constant, continual, customary, everyday, familiar, habitual, incessant, numerous, persistent, recurrent, recurring, reiterated, repeated, usual ◆ *vb* **3** = **visit**, attend, be a regular customer of, be found at, hang out at (*inf.*), haunt, patronize, resort
Antonyms *adj* ≠ **common:** few, few and far between, infrequent, occasional, rare, scanty, sporadic ◆ *vb* ≠ **visit:** avoid, keep away, shun, spurn
frequenter *n* **3** = **regular visitor**, client, fan, habitué, haunter, patron, regular, regular customer
frequently *adv* **1, 2** = **often**, commonly, customarily, habitually, many a time, many times, much, not infrequently, oft, oftentimes (*arch.*), over and over again, repeatedly, thick and fast, very often
Antonyms *adv* hardly ever, infrequently, occasionally, once in a blue moon (*inf.*), rarely, seldom
fresh *adj* **3, 4** = **new**, different, groundbreakkng, latest, left-field (*inf.*), modern, modernistic, new-fangled, novel, original, recent, this season's, unconventional, unusual, up-to-date **5** = **additional**, added, auxiliary, extra, further, more, other, renewed, supplementary **6** = **natural**, crude, green, raw, uncured, undried, unprocessed, unsalted **8, 9** = **invigorating**, bracing, bright, brisk, clean, clear, cool, crisp, pure, refreshing, spanking, sparkling, stiff, sweet, unpolluted **10** = **lively**, alert, bouncing, bright, bright-eyed and bushy-tailed (*inf.*), chipper (*inf.*), energetic, full of beans (*inf.*), full of vim and vigour (*inf.*), invigorated, keen, like a new man, refreshed, rested, restored, revived, sprightly, spry, vigorous, vital **11** = **vivid**, dewy, undimmed, unfaded, unwearied, unwithered, verdant, young **12** = **rosy**, blooming, clear, fair, florid, glowing, good, hardy, healthy, ruddy, wholesome **14** = **inexperienced**, artless, callow, green, natural, new, raw, uncultivated, untrained, untried, youthful **15** *Informal* = **cheeky**, bold, brazen, disrespectful, familiar, flip (*inf.*), forward, impudent, insolent, pert, presumptuous, sassy (*US inf.*), saucy, smart-alecky (*inf.*)
Antonyms *adj* ≠ **new:** dull, old, ordinary, stereotyped, trite ≠ **natural:** frozen, pickled, preserved, salted, tinned ≠ **invigorating:** impure, musty, stale, warm ≠ **lively:** exhausted, weary ≠ **vivid:** old, weary ≠ **rosy:** pallid, sickly ≠ **inexperienced:** experienced, old ≠ **cheeky:** well-mannered
freshen *vb* **1, 2** = **refresh**, enliven, freshen up, liven up, restore, revitalize, rouse, spruce up, titivate
freshness *n* **3, 4** = **novelty**, innovativeness, inventiveness, newness, originality **11** = **cleanness**, bloom, brightness, clearness, dewiness, glow, shine, sparkle, vigour, wholesomeness
fret[1] *vb* **1** = **worry**, agonize, anguish, brood, lose sleep over, obsess about, upset *or* distress oneself **2** = **rub**, abrade, chafe, erode, fray, gall, wear, wear away **3** = **annoy**, agitate, bother, chagrin, distress, disturb, gall, goad, grieve, harass, irk, irritate, nag, nettle, peeve (*inf.*), pique, provoke, rankle with, rile, ruffle, torment, trouble, vex

fretful ⓣ ('fretful) *adj* peevish, irritable, or upset.
▸ **'fretfully** *adv* ▸ **'fretfulness** *n*

fret saw *n* a fine-toothed saw with a long thin narrow blade, used for cutting designs in thin wood or metal.

fretwork ('fret,wɜːk) *n* decorative geometrical carving or openwork.

Freudian ('frɔɪdɪən) *adj* **1** of or relating to Sigmund Freud (1856–1939), Austrian psychiatrist, or his ideas. ◆ *n* **2** a person who follows or believes in the basic ideas of Sigmund Freud.
▸ **'Freudian,ism** *n*

Freudian slip *n* any action, such as a slip of the tongue, that may reveal an unconscious thought.

Fri. *abbrev. for* Friday.

friable ⓣ ('fraɪəbᵊl) *adj* easily broken up; crumbly. [C16: from L, from *friāre* to crumble]
▸ **,fria'bility** *or* **'friableness** *n*

friar ('fraɪə) *n* a member of any of various chiefly mendicant religious orders of the Roman Catholic Church. [C13 *frere*, from OF: brother, from L *frāter* BROTHER]

friar's balsam *n* a compound containing benzoin, mixed with hot water and used as an inhalant to relieve colds and sore throats.

friary ('fraɪərɪ) *n, pl* **friaries.** *Christianity.* a convent or house of friars.

fricandeau ('frɪkən,dəʊ) *n, pl* **fricandeaus** *or* **fricandeaux** (-,dəʊz). a larded and braised veal fillet. [C18: from OF, prob. based on FRICASSEE]

fricassee (,frɪkə'siː, 'frɪkəsɪ) *n* **1** stewed meat, esp. chicken or veal, served in a thick white sauce. ◆ *vb* **fricassees, fricasseeing, fricasseed. 2** (*tr*) to prepare (meat, etc.) as a fricassee. [C16: from OF, from *fricasser* to fricassee]

fricative ('frɪkətɪv) *n* **1** a consonant produced by partial occlusion of the airstream, such as (f) or (z). ◆ *adj* **2** relating to or denoting a fricative. [C19: from NL, from L *fricāre* to rub]

friction ⓣ ('frɪkʃən) *n* **1** a resistance encountered when one body moves relative to another body with which it is in contact. **2** the act, effect, or an instance of rubbing one object against another. **3** disagreement or conflict. [C16: from F, from L *frictiō* a rubbing, from *fricāre* to rub]
▸ **'frictional** *adj* ▸ **'frictionless** *adj*

Friday ('fraɪdɪ) *n* **1** the sixth day of the week; fifth day of the working week. **2** See **man Friday.** [OE *Frīgedæg*]

fridge (frɪdʒ) *n* short for **refrigerator.**

fried (fraɪd) *vb* the past tense and past participle of **fry**[1].

friend ⓣ (frend) *n* **1** a person known well to another and regarded with liking, affection, and loyalty. **2** an acquaintance or associate. **3** an ally in a fight or cause. **4** a fellow member of a party, society, etc. **5** a patron or supporter. **6 be friends (with).** to be friendly (with). **7 make friends (with).** to become friendly (with). ◆ *vb* **8** (*tr*) an archaic word for **befriend.** [OE *frēond*]
▸ **'friendless** *adj* ▸ **'friendship** *n*

Friend (frend) *n* a member of the Religious Society of Friends; Quaker.

friend at court *n* an influential acquaintance who can promote one's interests.

friendly ⓣ ('frendlɪ) *adj* **friendlier, friendliest. 1** showing or expressing liking, goodwill, or trust. **2** on the same side; not hostile. **3** tending or disposed to help or support: *a friendly breeze helped them escape.* ◆ *n, pl* **friendlies. 4** Also: **friendly match.** *Sport.* a match played for its own sake.
▸ **'friendlily** *adv* ▸ **'friendliness** *n*

-friendly *adj combining form.* helpful, easy, or good for the person or thing specified: *ozone-friendly.*

friendly fire *n Mil.* firing by one's own side, esp. when it harms one's own personnel.

friendly society *n Brit.* an association of people who pay regular dues or other sums in return for old-age pensions, sickness benefits, etc.

Friends of the Earth *n* an organization of environmentalists and conservationists.

frier ('fraɪə) *n* a variant spelling of **fryer.** See **fry**[1].

fries (fraɪz) *pl n* short for **French fried potatoes;** chips.

Friesian ('friːʒən) *n* **1** *Brit.* any of several breeds of black-and-white dairy cattle having a high milk yield. **2** see **Frisian.**

frieze[1] (friːz) *n* **1** *Archit.* **1a** the horizontal band between the architrave and cornice of a classical entablature. **1b** the upper part of the wall of a room, below the cornice. **2** any ornamental band on a wall. [C16: from F *frise*, ?from Med. L *frisium*, changed from L *Phrygium* Phrygian (work), from Phrygia, famous for embroidery in gold]

frieze[2] (friːz) *n* a heavy woollen fabric used for coats, etc. [C15: from OF, from MDu. ?from *Vriese* Frisian]

frigate ('frɪgɪt) *n* **1** a medium-sized square-rigged warship of the 18th and 19th centuries. **2a** *Brit.* a warship smaller than a destroyer. **2b** *US.* (formerly) a warship larger than a destroyer. **2c** *US.* a small escort vessel. [C16: from F *frégate*, from It. *fregata*, from ?]

frigate bird *n* a bird of tropical and subtropical seas, having a long bill, a wide wingspan, and a forked tail.

fright ⓣ (fraɪt) *n* **1** sudden fear or alarm. **2** a sudden alarming shock. **3** *Inf.* a horrifying or ludicrous person or thing: *she looks a fright.* **4 take fright.** to become frightened. ◆ *vb* **5** a poetic word for **frighten.** [OE *fryhto*]

frighten ⓣ ('fraɪtᵊn) *vb* (*tr*) **1** to terrify; scare. **2** to drive or force to go (away, off, out, in, etc.) by making afraid.
▸ **'frightener** *n* ▸ **'frighteningly** *adv*

frightful ⓣ ('fraɪtfʊl) *adj* **1** very alarming or horrifying. **2** unpleasant, annoying, or extreme: *a frightful hurry.*
▸ **'frightfully** *adv* ▸ **'frightfulness** *n*

frigid ⓣ ('frɪdʒɪd) *adj* **1** formal or stiff in behaviour or temperament. **2** (esp. of women) lacking sexual responsiveness. **3** characterized by physical coldness: *a frigid zone.* [C15: from L *frigidus* cold, from *frīgēre* to be cold]
▸ **fri'gidity** *or* **'frigidness** *n* ▸ **'frigidly** *adv*

Frigid Zone *n* the cold region inside the Arctic or Antarctic Circle where the sun's rays are very oblique.

frijol (*Spanish* fri'xol) *n, pl* **frijoles** (*Spanish* -'xoles). a variety of bean extensively cultivated for food in Mexico. [C16: from Sp., ult. from L *phaseolus*, from Gk *phasēlos* bean with edible pod]

frill ⓣ (frɪl) *n* **1** a gathered, ruched, or pleated strip of cloth sewn on at one edge only, as on garments, as ornament, or to give extra body. **2** a

THESAURUS

fretful *adj* = **irritable**, captious, complaining, cross, crotchety (*inf.*), edgy, fractious, out of sorts, peevish, petulant, querulous, short-tempered, splenetic, testy, tetchy, touchy, uneasy

friable *adj* = **crumbly**, brittle, crisp, powdery, pulverizable

friction *n* **1, 2** = **rubbing**, abrasion, attrition, chafing, erosion, fretting, grating, irritation, rasping, resistance, scraping, wearing away **3** = **hostility**, animosity, antagonism, bad blood, bad feeling, bickering, conflict, disagreement, discontent, discord, disharmony, dispute, dissension, incompatibility, opposition, resentment, rivalry, wrangling

friend *n* **1** = **companion**, Achates, alter ego, boon companion, bosom friend, buddy (*inf.*), china (*Brit. sl.*), chum (*inf.*), cock (*Brit. inf.*), comrade, confidant, crony, familiar, homeboy (*sl., chiefly US*), intimate, mate (*inf.*), pal, partner, playmate, soul mate **2, 3, 5** = **supporter**, adherent, advocate, ally, associate, backer, benefactor, partisan, patron, protagonist, well-wisher
Antonyms *n* adversary, antagonist, competitor, enemy, foe, opponent, rival

friendless *adj* **1** = **alone**, abandoned, alienated, all alone, cut off, deserted, estranged, forlorn, forsaken, isolated, lonely, lonesome, ostracized, shunned, solitary, unattached, with no one to turn to, without a friend in the world, without ties

friendliness *n* **1-3** = **amiability**, affability, companionability, congeniality, conviviality, geniality, kindliness, mateyness *or* matiness (*Brit. inf.*), neighbourliness, open arms, sociability, warmth

friendly *adj* **1-3** = **amiable**, affable, affectionate, amicable, attached, attentive, auspicious, beneficial, benevolent, benign, chummy (*inf.*), close, clubby, companionable, comradely, conciliatory, confiding, convivial, cordial, familiar, favourable, fond, fraternal, genial, good, helpful, intimate, kind, kindly, neighbourly, on good terms, on visiting terms, outgoing, pally (*inf.*), peaceable, propitious, receptive, sociable, sympathetic, thick (*inf.*), welcoming, well-disposed
Antonyms *adj* antagonistic, belligerent, cold, contentious, distant, inauspicious, sinister, uncongenial, unfriendly

friendship *n* **1** = **friendliness**, affection, affinity, alliance, amity, attachment, benevolence, closeness, concord, familiarity, fondness, good-fellowship, goodwill, harmony, intimacy, love, rapport, regard
Antonyms *n* animosity, antagonism, antipathy, aversion, bad blood, conflict, enmity, hatred, hostility, resentment, strife, unfriendliness

fright *n* **1, 2** = **fear**, alarm, apprehension, (blue) funk (*inf.*), cold sweat, consternation, dismay, dread, fear and trembling, horror, panic, quaking, scare, shock, terror, the shivers, trepidation **3** *Informal* = **sight** (*inf.*), eyesore, frump, mess (*inf.*), scarecrow
Antonyms *n* ≠ **fear**: boldness, bravery, courage, pluck, valor

frighten *vb* **1** = **scare**, affright (*arch.*), alarm, appal, cow, daunt, dismay, freeze one's blood, get the wind up, intimidate, petrify, put the wind up (someone) (*inf.*), scare (someone) stiff, shock, startle, terrify, terrorize, throw into a fright, throw into a panic, unman, unnerve
Antonyms *vb* allay, assuage, calm, comfort, encourage, hearten, reassure, soothe

frightened *adj* **1** = **afraid**, abashed, affrighted (*arch.*), alarmed, cowed, dismayed, frozen, in a cold sweat, in a panic, in fear and trepidation, numb with fear, panicky, petrified, scared, scared shitless (*taboo sl.*), scared stiff, startled, terrified, terrorized, terror-stricken, unnerved

frightening *adj* **1** = **terrifying**, alarming, appalling, baleful, bloodcurdling, daunting, dismaying, dreadful, fearful, fearsome, hair-raising, horrifying, intimidating, menacing, scary (*inf.*), shocking, spooky (*inf.*), unnerving

frightful *adj* **1** = **terrifying**, alarming, appalling, awful, dire, dread, dreadful, fearful, from hell (*inf.*), ghastly, grim, grisly, gruesome, harrowing, hideous, horrendous, horrible, horrid, lurid, macabre, petrifying, shocking, terrible, traumatic, unnerving, unspeakable **2** = **dreadful**, annoying, awful, disagreeable, extreme, great, insufferable, terrible, terrific, unpleasant
Antonyms *adj* ≠ **terrifying**: attractive, beautiful, calming, lovely, nice, pleasant, soothing ≠ **dreadful**: moderate, pleasant, slight

frigid *adj* **1** = **unresponsive**, aloof, austere, cold as ice, cold-hearted, forbidding, formal, icy, lifeless, passionless, passive, repellent, rigid, stiff, unapproachable, unbending, unfeeling, unloving **3** = **cold**, arctic, chill, cool, frost-bound, frosty, frozen, gelid, glacial, icy, Siberian, wintry
Antonyms *adj* ≠ **unresponsive**: ardent, cordial, friendly, hospitable, hot, impassioned, passionate, responsive, sensual, warm ≠ **cold**: hot, stifling, sweltering, warm

frigidity *n* **1** = **unresponsiveness**, aloofness, austerity, chill, cold-heartedness, coldness, frostiness, iciness, impassivity, lack of response, lifelessness, passivity, touch-me-not attitude, unapproachability, wintriness

frill *n* **1, 2** = **ruffle**, flounce, furbelow, gathering,

ruff of hair or feathers around the neck of a dog or bird or a fold of skin around the neck of a reptile or amphibian. **3** (*often pl*) *Inf.* a superfluous or pretentious thing or manner; affectation: *he made a plain speech with no frills.* ◆ *vb* **4** (*tr*) to adorn or fit with a frill or frills. **5** to form into a frill or frills. [C14: ? of Flemish origin]
▸ **'frilliness** *n* ▸ **'frilly** *adj*

frilled lizard *n* a large arboreal insectivorous Australian lizard having an erectile fold of skin around the neck.

fringe ❶ (frɪndʒ) *n* **1** an edging consisting of hanging threads, tassels, etc. **2a** an outer edge; periphery. **2b** (*as modifier*): *a fringe area.* **3** (*modifier*) unofficial; not conventional in form: *fringe theatre.* **4** *Chiefly Brit.* a section of the front hair cut short over the forehead. **5** an ornamental border. **6** *Physics.* any of the light and dark bands produced by diffraction or interference of light. ◆ *vb* **fringes, fringing, fringed.** (*tr*) **7** to adorn with a fringe or fringes. **8** to be a fringe for. [C14: from OF *frenge,* ult. from L *fimbria* fringe, border]
▸ **'fringeless** *adj*

fringe benefit *n* an additional advantage, esp. a benefit provided by an employer to supplement an employee's regular pay.

fringing reef *n* a coral reef close to the shore to which it is attached, having a steep seaward edge.

frippery ❶ ('frɪpərɪ) *n, pl* **fripperies. 1** ornate or showy clothing or adornment. **2** ostentation. **3** trifles; trivia. [C16: from OF, from *frepe* frill, rag, from Med. L *faluppa* a straw, splinter, from ?]

Frisbee ('frɪzbɪ) *n Trademark.* a light plastic disc thrown with a spinning motion for recreation or in competition.

Frisian ('frɪʒən) *or* **Friesian** *n* **1** a language spoken in the NW Netherlands, parts of N Germany, and some of the adjacent islands. **2** a speaker of this language or a native or inhabitant of Friesland. ◆ *adj* **3** of or relating to this language, its speakers, or the peoples and culture of Friesland. [C16: from L *Frīsiī* people of northern Germany]

frisk ❶ (frɪsk) *vb* **1** (*intr*) to leap, move about, or act in a playful manner. **2** (*tr*) (esp. of animals) to whisk or wave briskly: *the dog frisked its tail.* **3** (*tr*) *Inf.* to search (someone) by feeling for concealed weapons, etc. ◆ *n* **4** a playful antic or movement. **5** *Inf.* an instance of frisking a person. [C16: from OF *frisque,* of Gmc origin]
▸ **'frisker** *n*

frisky ❶ ('frɪskɪ) *adj* **friskier, friskiest.** lively, high-spirited, or playful.
▸ **'friskily** *adv*

frisson *French.* (frisɔ̃) *n* a shiver; thrill. [C18 (but in common use only from C20): lit.: shiver]

frit (frɪt) *n* **1a** the basic materials, partially or wholly fused, for making glass, glazes for pottery, enamel, etc. **1b** a glassy substance used in some soft-paste porcelain. ◆ *vb* **frits, fritting, fritted. 2** (*tr*) to fuse (materials) in making frit. [C17: from It. *fritta,* lit.: fried, from *friggere* to fry, from L *frīgere*]

fritillary (frɪ'tɪlərɪ) *n, pl* **fritillaries. 1** a liliaceous plant having purple or white drooping bell-shaped flowers, typically marked in a chequered pattern. **2** any of various butterflies having brownish wings chequered with black and silver. [C17: from NL *fritillāria,* from L *fritillus* dice box; prob. with reference to the markings]

fritter[1] ❶ ('frɪtə) *vb* (*tr*) **1** (usually foll. by *away*) to waste: *to fritter away time.* **2** to break into small pieces. [C18: prob. from obs. *fitter* to break into small pieces, ult. from OE *fitt* a piece]

fritter[2] ('frɪtə) *n* a piece of food, such as apple, that is dipped in batter and fried in deep fat. [C14: from OF, from L *frictus* fried, from *frīgere* to fry]

frivolous ❶ ('frɪvələs) *adj* **1** not serious or sensible in content, attitude, or behaviour. **2** unworthy of serious or sensible treatment: *frivolous details.* [C15: from L *frīvolus*]
▸ **'frivolously** *adv* ▸ **'frivolousness** *or* **frivolity** (frɪ'vɒlɪtɪ) *n*

frizz (frɪz) *vb* **1** (of the hair, nap, etc.) to form or cause (the hair, etc.) to form tight curls or crisp tufts. ◆ *n* **2** hair that has been frizzed. **3** the state of being frizzed. [C19: from F *friser* to curl]

frizzle[1] ('frɪzᵊl) *vb* **frizzles, frizzling, frizzled. 1** to form (the hair) into tight crisp curls. ◆ *n* **2** a tight curl. [C16: prob. rel. to OE *frīs* curly]

frizzle[2] ❶ ('frɪzᵊl) *vb* **frizzles, frizzling, frizzled. 1** to scorch or be scorched, esp. with a sizzling noise. **2** (*tr*) to fry (bacon, etc.) until crisp. [C16: prob. blend of FRY[1] + SIZZLE]

frizzy ❶ ('frɪzɪ) *or* **frizzly** ('frɪzlɪ) *adj* **frizzier, frizziest** *or* **frizzlier, frizzliest.** (of the hair) in tight crisp wiry curls.
▸ **'frizziness** *or* **'frizzliness** *n*

fro (frəʊ) *adv* back or from. [C12: from ON *frā*]

frock (frɒk) *n* **1** a girl's or woman's dress. **2** a loose garment of several types, such as a peasant's smock. **3** a wide-sleeved outer garment worn by members of some religious orders. ◆ *vb* **4** (*tr*) to invest (a person) with the office of a cleric. [C14: from OF *froc*]

frock coat *n* a man's single- or double-breasted skirted coat, as worn in the 19th century.

Froebel ('frəʊbᵊl) *adj* of, denoting, or relating to a system of kindergarten education developed by Friedrich Froebel (1782–1852), German educator, or to the training and qualification of teachers to use this system.

frog[1] (frɒg) *n* **1** an insectivorous amphibian, having a short squat tailless body with a moist smooth skin and very long hind legs specialized for hopping. **2** any of various similar amphibians, such as the tree frog. **3** any spiked object that is used to support plant stems in a flower arrangement. **4 a frog in one's throat.** phlegm on the vocal cords that affects one's speech. [OE *frogga*]
▸ **'froggy** *adj*

frog[2] (frɒg) *n* **1** (*often pl*) a decorative fastening of looped braid or cord, as on a military uniform. **2** an attachment on a belt to hold the scabbard of a sword, etc. [C18: ? ult. from L *floccus* tuft of hair]
▸ **frogged** *adj* ▸ **'frogging** *n*

frog[3] (frɒg) *n* a tough elastic horny material in the centre of the sole of a horse's foot. [C17: from ?]

frog[4] (frɒg) *n* a plate of iron or steel to guide train wheels over an intersection of railway lines. [C19: from ?; ? a special use of FROG[1]]

Frog (frɒg) *or* **Froggy** ('frɒgɪ) *n, pl* **Frogs** *or* **Froggies.** *Brit. sl.* a derogatory word for a French person.

froghopper ('frɒg,hɒpə) *n* any small leaping insect whose larvae secrete a protective spittle-like substance around themselves.

frogman ('frɒgmən) *n, pl* **frogmen.** a swimmer equipped with a rubber suit, flippers, and breathing equipment for working underwater.

frogmarch ('frɒg,mɑːtʃ) *Chiefly Brit.* ◆ *n* **1** a method of carrying a resisting person in which each limb is held and the victim is carried horizontally and face downwards. **2** any method of making a person move against his will. ◆ *vb* **3** (*tr*) to carry in a frogmarch or cause to move forward unwillingly.

frogmouth ('frɒg,maʊθ) *n* a nocturnal insectivorous bird of SE Asia and Australia, similar to the nightjars.

frogspawn ('frɒg,spɔːn) *n* a mass of fertilized frogs' eggs surrounded by a protective nutrient jelly.

frog spit *or* **spittle** *n* **1** another name for **cuckoo spit. 2** a foamy mass of threadlike green algae floating on ponds.

frolic ❶ ('frɒlɪk) *n* **1** a light-hearted entertainment or occasion. **2** light-hearted activity; gaiety. ◆ *vb* **frolics, frolicking, frolicked. 3** (*intr*) to caper about. ◆ *adj* **4** *Arch.* full of fun; gay. [C16: from Du. *vrolijk,* from MDu. *vro* happy]
▸ **'frolicker** *n*

frolicsome ❶ ('frɒlɪksəm) *adj* merry and playful.
▸ **'frolicsomely** *adv*

from (frɒm; *unstressed* frəm) *prep* **1** used to indicate the original location, situation, etc.: *from behind the bushes.* **2** in a period of time starting at: *he lived from 1910 to 1970.* **3** used to indicate the distance between two things or places: *a hundred miles from here.* **4** used to indicate a lower amount: *from five to fifty pounds.* **5** showing the model of: *painted from life.* **6** used with the gerund to mark prohibition, etc.:

THESAURUS

purfle, ruche, ruching, ruff, tuck **3** *often plural* = **trimmings**, additions, affectation(s), bells and whistles, bits and pieces, decoration(s), dressing up, embellishments, extras, fanciness, fandangles, finery, frilliness, frippery, fuss, gewgaws, icing on the cake, jazz (*sl.*), mannerisms, nonsense, ornamentation, ostentation, superfluities, tomfoolery

frilly *adj* **1** = **ruffled**, fancy, flouncy, frothy, lacy, ruched

fringe *n* **1** = **border**, binding, edging, hem, tassel, trimming **2** = **edge**, borderline, limits, march, marches, margin, outskirts, perimeter, periphery ◆ *modifier* **3** = **unofficial**, unconventional, unorthodox ◆ *vb* **7, 8** = **border**, edge, enclose, skirt, surround, trim

fringed *adj* **8** = **edged**, befringed, bordered, margined, outlined, overhung

frippery *n* **1** = **decoration**, adornment, bauble, fandangle, gewgaw, icing on the cake, knickknack, ornament, toy, trinket **1, 2** = **frills**, fanciness, finery, flashiness, foppery, frilliness, fussiness, gaudiness, glad rags (*inf.*), meretriciousness, nonsense, ostentation, pretentiousness, showiness, tawdriness

frisk *vb* **1** = **frolic**, bounce, caper, cavort, curvet, dance, gambol, hop, jump, play, prance, rollick, romp, skip, sport, trip **3** *Informal* = **search**, check, inspect, run over, shake down (*US sl.*)

frisky *adj* = **lively**, bouncy, coltish, frolicsome, full of beans, full of joie de vivre, high-spirited, in high spirits, kittenish, playful, rollicking, romping, spirited, sportive
Antonyms *adj* demure, dull, lacklustre, pensive, sedate, stodgy, stolid, wooden

fritter[1] *vb* **1** *usually foll. by* **away** = **waste**, dally away, dissipate, fool away, idle away, misspend, run through, spend like water, squander

frivolity *n* **1, 2** = **flippancy**, childishness, desipience, flightiness, flummery, folly, frivolousness, fun, gaiety, giddiness, jest, levity, light-heartedness, lightness, nonsense, puerility, shallowness, silliness, superficiality, trifling, triviality
Antonyms *n* earnestness, gravity, humourlessness, importance, sedateness, seriousness, significance, soberness, sobriety

frivolous *adj* **1** = **flippant**, childish, ditzy *or* ditsy (*sl.*), dizzy, empty-headed, flighty, flip (*inf.*), foolish, giddy, idle, ill-considered, juvenile, light-minded, nonserious, puerile, silly, superficial **2** = **trivial**, extravagant, footling (*inf.*), impractical, light, minor, nickel-and-dime (*US sl.*), niggling, paltry, peripheral, petty, pointless, shallow, trifling, unimportant
Antonyms *adj* ≠ **flippant:** earnest, mature, practical, responsible, sensible, serious, solemn ≠ **trivial:** important, serious, vital

frizzle[2] *vb* **1, 2** = **crisp**, fry, hiss, roast, scorch, sizzle, sputter

frizzy *adj* = **tight-curled**, corrugated, crimped, crisp, frizzed, wiry

frolic *n* **1** = **revel**, antic, blast (*US sl.*), escapade, gambado, gambol, game, lark, prank, romp, spree **2** = **merriment**, amusement, drollery, fun, fun and games, gaiety, high jinks, skylarking (*inf.*), sport ◆ *vb* **3** = **play**, caper, cavort, cut capers, frisk, gambol, lark, make merry, rollick, romp, sport

frolicsome *adj* = **playful**, coltish, frisky, full of

nothing prevents him from leaving. **7** because of: *exhausted from his walk.* [OE *fram*]

fromage frais ('frɒmɑːʒ 'freɪ; *French* frɔmaʒ frɛ) *n* a low-fat soft cheese with a smooth light texture. [F, lit.: fresh cheese]

frond (frɒnd) *n* **1** the compound leaf of a fern. **2** the leaf of a palm. [C18: from L *frōns*]

front ⓣ (frʌnt) *n* **1** that part or side that is forward, or most often seen or used. **2** a position or place directly before or ahead: *a fountain stood at the front of the building.* **3** the beginning, opening, or first part. **4** the position of leadership: *in the front of scientific knowledge.* **5** land bordering a lake, street, etc. **6** land along a seashore or large lake, esp. a promenade. **7** *Mil.* **7a** the total area in which opposing armies face each other. **7b** the space in which a military unit is operating: *to advance on a broad front.* **8** *Meteorol.* the dividing line or plane between two air masses of different origins. **9** outward aspect or bearing, as when dealing with a situation: *a bold front.* **10** *Inf.* a business or other activity serving as a respectable cover for another, usually criminal, organization. **11** Also called: **front man.** a nominal leader of an organization etc.; figurehead. **12** *Inf.* outward appearance of rank or wealth. **13** a particular field of activity: *on the wages front.* **14** a group of people with a common goal: *a national liberation front.* **15** a false shirt front; a dicky. **16** *Arch.* the forehead or the face. ◆ *adj (prenominal)* **17** of, at, or in the front: *a front seat.* **18** *Phonetics.* of or denoting a vowel articulated with the tongue brought forward, as for the sound of *ee* in English *see* or *a* in English *hat.* ◆ *vb* **19** (when *intr*, foll. by *on* or *onto*) to face (onto): *this house fronts the river.* **20** (*tr*) to be a front of or for. **21** (*tr*) to appear as a presenter in a television show. **22** (*tr*) to be the lead singer or player in (a band). **23** (*tr*) to confront. **24** to supply a front for. **25** (*intr;* often foll. by *up*) *Austral. inf.* to appear (at): *to front up at the police station.* [C13 (in the sense: forehead, face): from L *frōns* forehead, foremost part]
▸ **'frontless** *adj*

frontage ('frʌntɪdʒ) *n* **1** the façade of a building or the front of a plot of ground. **2** the extent of the front of a shop, plot of land, etc. **3** the direction in which a building faces.

frontal ('frʌntᵊl) *adj* **1** of, at, or in the front. **2** of or relating to the forehead: *frontal artery.* ◆ *n* **3** a decorative hanging for the front of an altar. [C14 (in the sense: adornment for forehead, altarcloth): via OF *frontel,* from L *frōns* forehead]
▸ **'frontally** *adv*

frontal lobe *n Anat.* the anterior portion of each cerebral hemisphere.

front bench *n* **1** *Brit.* **1a** the foremost bench of either the Government or Opposition in the House of Commons. **1b** the leadership (**frontbenchers**) of either group, who occupy this bench. **2** the leadership of the government or opposition in various legislative assemblies.

front-end *adj* (of money, costs, etc.) required or incurred in advance of a project in order to get it under way.

frontier ⓣ ('frʌntɪə, frʌn'tɪə) *n* **1a** the region of a country bordering on another or a line, barrier, etc., marking such a boundary. **1b** *(as modifier): a frontier post.* **2** *US.* the edge of the settled area of a country. **3** (*often pl*) the limit of knowledge in a particular field: *the frontiers of physics have been pushed back.* [C14: from OF, from *front* (in the sense: part which is opposite)]

frontiersman ('frʌntɪəzmən, frʌn'tɪəz-) *or (fem)* **frontierswoman** (-ˌwʊmən) *n, pl* **frontiersmen** *or* **frontierswomen.** (formerly) a person living on a frontier, esp. in a newly pioneered territory of the US.

frontispiece ('frʌntɪsˌpiːs) *n* **1** an illustration facing the title page of a book. **2** the principal façade of a building. **3** a pediment over a door, window, etc. [C16 *frontispice,* from F, from LL *frontispicium* façade, from L *frōns* forehead + *specere* to look at; infl. by PIECE]

frontlet ('frʌntlɪt) *n Judaism.* a phylactery attached to the forehead. [C15: from OF *frontelet* a little FRONTAL]

front line *n* **1** *Military.* **1a** the most advanced military units in a battle. **1b** (*modifier*): of, relating to, or suitable for the military front line: *frontline troops.* **2** (*modifier*) close to a hostile country or scene of armed conflict: *the frontline states.*

front loader *n* a washing machine with a door at the front which opens one side of the drum into which washing is placed.

front-page *n* (*modifier*) important enough to be put on the front page of a newspaper.

frontrunner ('frʌntˌrʌnə) *n Inf.* the leader or a favoured contestant in a race, election, etc.

frontrunning ('frʌntˌrʌnɪŋ) *n Stock Exchange.* the practice by market makers of using advance information provided by their own investment analysts before it has been given to clients.

frost ⓣ (frɒst) *n* **1** a white deposit of ice particles, esp. one formed on objects out of doors at night. **2** an atmospheric temperature of below freezing point, characterized by the production of this deposit. **3 degrees of frost.** degrees below freezing point. **4** *Inf.* something given a cold reception; failure. **5** *Inf.* coolness of manner. **6** the act of freezing. ◆ *vb* **7** to cover or be covered with frost. **8** (*tr*) to give a frostlike appearance to (glass, etc.), as by means of a fine-grained surface. **9** (*tr*) *Chiefly US & Canad.* to decorate (cakes, etc.) with icing or frosting. **10** (*tr*) to kill or damage (crops, etc.) with frost. [OE *frost*]

frostbite ('frɒstˌbaɪt) *n* destruction of tissues, esp. those of the fingers, ears, toes, and nose, by freezing.
▸ **'frostˌbitten** *adj*

frosted ('frɒstɪd) *adj* **1** covered or injured by frost. **2** covered with icing, as a cake. **3** (of glass, etc.) having a surface roughened to prevent clear vision through it.

frost hollow *n* a depression in a hilly area in which cold air collects, becoming very cold at night.

frosting ('frɒstɪŋ) *n* **1** another word (esp. US and Canad.) for **icing. 2** a rough or matt finish on glass, silver, etc.

frosty ⓣ ('frɒstɪ) *adj* **frostier, frostiest. 1** characterized by frost: *a frosty night.* **2** covered by or decorated with frost. **3** lacking warmth or enthusiasm: *the new plan had a frosty reception.*
▸ **'frostily** *adv* ▸ **'frostiness** *n*

froth ⓣ (frɒθ) *n* **1** a mass of small bubbles of air or a gas in a liquid, produced by fermentation, etc. **2** a mixture of saliva and air bubbles formed at the lips in certain diseases, such as rabies. **3** trivial ideas or entertainment. ◆ *vb* **4** to produce or cause to produce froth. **5** (*tr*) to give out in the form of froth. [C14: from ON *frotha* or *frauth*]
▸ **'frothy** *adj* ▸ **'frothily** *adv*

froufrou ('fruːˌfruː) *n* a swishing sound, as made by a long silk dress. [C19: from F, imit.]

froward ('frəʊəd) *adj Arch.* obstinate; contrary. [C14: see FRO, -WARD]
▸ **'frowardly** *adv* ▸ **'frowardness** *n*

frown ⓣ (fraʊn) *vb* **1** (*intr*) to draw the brows together and wrinkle the forehead, esp. in worry, anger, or concentration. **2** (*intr;* foll. by *on* or *upon*) to look disapprovingly (upon). **3** (*tr*) to express (worry, etc.) by frowning. ◆ *n* **4** the act of frowning. **5** a show of dislike or displeasure. [C14: from OF *froigner,* of Celtic origin]
▸ **'frowner** *n* ▸ **'frowningly** *adv*

frowst (fraʊst) *n Brit. inf.* a hot and stale atmosphere; fug. [C19: back formation from *frowsty* musty, stuffy, var. of FROWZY]

frowsty ⓣ ('fraʊstɪ) *adj* **frowstier, frowstiest.** ill-smelling; stale; musty.
▸ **'frowstiness** *n*

frowzy ⓣ *or* **frowsy** ('fraʊzɪ) *adj* **frowzier, frowziest,** *or* **frowsier, frowsiest. 1** untidy or unkempt in appearance. **2** ill-smelling; frowsty. [C17: from ?]
▸ **'frowziness** *or* **'frowsiness** *n*

froze (frəʊz) *vb* the past tense of **freeze.**

frozen ⓣ ('frəʊzᵊn) *vb* **1** the past participle of **freeze.** ◆ *adj* **2** turned into or covered with ice. **3** killed or stiffened by extreme cold. **4** (of a region or climate) icy or snowy. **5** (of food) preserved by a freezing process. **6a** (of prices, wages, etc.) arbitrarily pegged at a certain level. **6b** (of business assets) not convertible into cash. **7** frigid or disdainful in manner. **8** motionless or unyielding: *he was frozen with horror.*
▸ **'frozenly** *adv*

frozen shoulder *n Pathol.* painful stiffness in a shoulder joint.

FRS (in Britain) *abbrev. for* Fellow of the Royal Society.

FRSNZ *abbrev. for* Fellow of the Royal Society of New Zealand.

fructify ('frʌktɪˌfaɪ) *vb* **fructifies, fructifying, fructified. 1** to bear or cause to bear fruit. **2** to make or become fruitful. [C14: from OF, from LL *frūctificāre,* from L *frūctus* fruit + *facere* to produce]
▸ **ˌfructifi'cation** *n* ▸ **fruc'tiferous** *adj* ▸ **'fructiˌfier** *n*

fructose ('frʌktəʊs) *n* a white crystalline sugar occurring in many fruits. Formula: $C_6H_{12}O_6$. [C19: from L *frūctus* fruit + -OSE[2]]

frugal ⓣ ('fruːgᵊl) *adj* **1** practising economy; thrifty. **2** not costly; meagre. [C16: from L, from *frūgī* useful, temperate, from *frux* fruit]
▸ **fru'gality** *n* ▸ **'frugally** *adv*

THESAURUS

beans (*inf.*), gay, kittenish, lively, merry, rollicking, sportive, sprightly, wanton (*arch.*)

front *n* **1** = **exterior**, anterior, façade, face, facing, foreground, forepart, frontage, obverse **2** = **forefront**, beginning, fore, front line, head, lead, top, van, vanguard **9** = **appearance**, air, aspect, bearing, countenance, demeanour, expression, exterior, face, manner, mien, show **10** *Informal* = **disguise**, blind, cover, cover-up, façade, mask, pretext, show ◆ *adj* **17** = **foremost**, first, head, headmost, lead, leading, topmost ◆ *vb* **19** = **face onto**, look over *or* onto, overlook
Antonyms *adj* ≠ **foremost:** aft, back, back end, behind, hindmost, nethermost, rear

frontier *n* **1, 3** = **boundary**, borderland, borderline, bound, confines, edge, limit, marches, perimeter, verge

frost *n* **1** = **hoarfrost**, freeze, freeze-up, Jack Frost, rime

frosty *adj* **1, 2** = **cold**, chilly, frozen, hoar (*rare*), ice-capped, icicled, icy, parky (*Brit. inf.*), rimy, wintry **3** = **unfriendly**, cold as ice, discouraging, frigid, off-putting (*Brit. inf.*), standoffish, unenthusiastic, unwelcoming

froth *n* **1** = **foam**, bubbles, effervescence, head, lather, scum, spume, suds ◆ *vb* **4** = **fizz**, bubble over, come to a head, effervesce, foam, lather

frothy *adj* **1** = **foamy**, foaming, spumescent, spumous, spumy, sudsy **3** = **trivial**, empty, frilly, frivolous, light, petty, slight, trifling, unnecessary, unsubstantial, vain

frown *vb* **1** = **scowl**, give a dirty look, glare, glower, knit one's brows, look daggers, lour *or* lower **2** *foll. by* **on** *or* **upon** = **disapprove of**, discountenance, discourage, dislike, look askance at, not take kindly to, show disapproval *or* displeasure, take a dim view of, view with disfavour

frowsty *adj* = **stale**, close, fuggy, fusty, ill-smelling, musty, stuffy

frowzy *adj* **1** = **slovenly**, blowsy, dirty, draggletailed (*arch.*), frumpy, messy, slatternly, sloppy, sluttish, ungroomed, unkempt, untidy, unwashed

frozen *adj* **2, 4** = **icy**, arctic, chilled, chilled to the marrow, frigid, frosted, icebound, ice-cold, ice-covered, numb **6** = **fixed**, pegged (*of prices*), stopped, suspended **8** = **motionless**, petrified, rooted, stock-still, turned to stone

frugal *adj* **1, 2** = **thrifty**, abstemious, careful, cheeseparing, economical, meagre, niggardly,

frugivorous (fruːˈdʒɪvərəs) *adj* fruit-eating. [C18: from *frugi-* (as in FRUGAL) + -VOROUS]

fruit ⓣ (fruːt) *n* **1** *Bot.* the ripened ovary of a flowering plant, containing one or more seeds. It may be dry, as in the poppy, or fleshy, as in the peach. **2** any fleshy part of a plant that supports the seeds and is edible, such as the strawberry. **3** any plant product useful to man, including grain, vegetables, etc. **4** (*often pl*) the result or consequence of an action or effort. **5** *Arch.* offspring of man or animals. **6** *Inf., chiefly US & Canad.* a male homosexual. ◆ *vb* **7** to bear or cause to bear fruit. [C12: from OF, from L *frūctus* enjoyment, fruit, from *fruī* to enjoy]
▸ **ˈfruit,like** *adj*

fruit bat *n* a large Old World bat occurring in tropical and subtropical regions and feeding on fruit.

fruitcake (ˈfruːt,keɪk) *n* a rich cake containing mixed dried fruit, lemon peel, etc.

fruit drop *n* **1** the premature shedding of fruit from a tree before fully ripe. **2** a boiled sweet with a fruity flavour.

fruiterer (ˈfruːtərə) *n Chiefly Brit.* a fruit dealer or seller.

fruit fly *n* **1** a small dipterous fly which feeds on and lays its eggs in plant tissues. **2** any dipterous fly of the genus *Drosophila.* See **drosophila.**

fruitful ⓣ (ˈfruːtfʊl) *adj* **1** bearing fruit in abundance. **2** productive or prolific. **3** producing results or profits: *a fruitful discussion.*
▸ **ˈfruitfully** *adv* ▸ **ˈfruitfulness** *n*

fruition ⓣ (fruːˈɪʃən) *n* **1** the attainment of something worked for or desired. **2** enjoyment of this. **3** the act or condition of bearing fruit. [C15: from LL, from L *fruī* to enjoy]

fruitless ⓣ (ˈfruːtlɪs) *adj* **1** yielding nothing or nothing of value; unproductive. **2** without fruit.
▸ **ˈfruitlessly** *adv* ▸ **ˈfruitlessness** *n*

fruit machine *n Brit.* a gambling machine that pays out when certain combinations of diagrams, usually of fruit, appear on a dial.

fruit salad *n* a dessert consisting of sweet fruits cut up and served in a syrup.

fruit sugar *n* another name for **fructose.**

fruit tree *n* any tree that bears edible fruit.

fruity ⓣ (ˈfruːtɪ) *adj* **fruitier, fruitiest. 1** of or resembling fruit. **2** (of a voice) mellow or rich. **3** *Inf., chiefly Brit.* erotically stimulating; salacious. **4** *Inf., chiefly US & Canad.* homosexual.
▸ **ˈfruitily** *adv* ▸ **ˈfruitiness** *n*

frumenty (ˈfruːməntɪ) *or* **furmenty** *n Brit.* a kind of porridge made from hulled wheat boiled with milk, sweetened, and spiced. [C14: from OF, from *frument* grain, from L *frūmentum*]

frump (frʌmp) *n* a woman who is dowdy, drab, or unattractive. [C16 (in the sense: to be sullen; C19: dowdy woman): from MDu. *verrompelen* to wrinkle]
▸ **ˈfrumpy** *or* **ˈfrumpish** *adj*

frustrate ⓣ (frʌˈstreɪt) *vb* **frustrates, frustrating, frustrated.** (*tr*) **1** to hinder or prevent (the efforts, plans, or desires) of. **2** to upset, agitate, or tire. ◆ *adj* **3** *Arch.* frustrated or thwarted. [C15: from L *frustrāre* to cheat, from *frustrā* in error]
▸ **frusˈtration** *n*

frustrated ⓣ (frʌˈstreɪtɪd) *adj* having feelings of dissatisfaction or lack of fulfilment.

frustum (ˈfrʌstəm) *n, pl* **frustums** *or* **frusta** (-tə). *Geom.* **a** the part of a solid, such as a cone or pyramid, contained between the base and a plane parallel to the base that intersects the solid. **b** the part of such a solid contained between two parallel planes intersecting the solid. [C17: from L: piece]

fry[1] (fraɪ) *vb* **fries, frying, fried. 1** (when *tr*, sometimes foll. by *up*) to cook or be cooked in fat, oil, etc., usually over direct heat. **2** *Sl., chiefly US.* to kill or be killed by electrocution. ◆ *n, pl* **fries. 3** a dish of something fried, esp. the offal of a specified animal: *pig's fry.* **4 fry-up.** *Brit. inf.* the act of preparing a mixed fried dish or the dish itself. [C13: from OF *frire,* from L *frīgere* to fry]
▸ **ˈfryer** *or* **ˈfrier** *n*

fry[2] (fraɪ) *pl n* **1** the young of various species of fish. **2** the young of certain other animals, such as frogs. [C14 (in the sense: young, offspring): from OF *freier* to spawn, from L *fricāre* to rub]

frying pan *n* **1** a long-handled shallow pan used for frying. **2 out of the frying pan into the fire.** from a bad situation to a worse one.

f-stop (ˈɛf,stɒp) *n* any of the settings for the f-number of a camera.

ft. *abbrev. for* foot *or* feet.

fth. *or* **fthm.** *abbrev. for* fathom.

FT Index *abbrev. for:* **1** Financial Times Industrial Ordinary Share Index: an index designed to show the general trend in share prices, produced daily by the *Financial Times* newspaper. **2** Financial Times Stock Exchange 100 Index: an index produced by the *Financial Times* based on an average of 100 securities and giving the best indication of daily movements. Also: **FTSE Index.** Informal name: **Footsie.**

FTP *abbrev.* (*sometimes not caps.*) *for* file transfer protocol: the standard mechanism used to transfer files between computer systems or across the Internet.

fuchsia (ˈfjuːʃə) *n* **1** a shrub widely cultivated for its showy drooping purple, red, or white flowers. **2a** a reddish-purple to purplish-pink colour. **2b** (*as adj*): *a fuchsia dress.* [C18: from NL, after Leonhard *Fuchs* (1501–66), G botanist]

fuchsin (ˈfuːksɪn) *or* **fuchsine** (ˈfuːksiːn, -sɪn) *n* an aniline dye forming a red solution in water: used as a textile dye and a biological stain. [C19: from FUCHS(IA) + -IN; from its similarity in colour to the flower]

fuck (fʌk) *Taboo.* ◆ *vb* **1** to have sexual intercourse with (someone). ◆ *n* **2** an act of sexual intercourse. **3** *Sl.* a partner in sexual intercourse. **4 not care** *or* **give a fuck.** not to care at all. ◆ *interj* **5** *Offens.* an expression of strong disgust or anger. [C16: of Gmc origin]

fucus (ˈfjuːkəs) *n, pl* **fuci** (-saɪ) *or* **fucuses.** a seaweed of the genus *Fucus,* having greenish-brown slimy fronds. [C16: from L: rock lichen, from Gk *phukos* seaweed, of Semitic origin]

fuddle (ˈfʌdᵊl) *vb* **fuddles, fuddling, fuddled. 1** (*tr; often passive*) to cause to be confused or intoxicated. ◆ *n* **2** a muddled or confused state. [C16: from ?]

fuddy-duddy ⓣ (ˈfʌdɪ,dʌdɪ) *n, pl* **fuddy-duddies.** *Inf.* a person, esp. an elderly one, who is extremely conservative or dull. [C20: from ?]

fudge[1] (fʌdʒ) *n* a soft variously flavoured sweet made from sugar, butter, etc. [C19: from ?]

fudge[2] (fʌdʒ) *n* **1** foolishness; nonsense. ◆ *interj* **2** a mild exclamation of annoyance. [C18: from ?]

fudge[3] ⓣ (fʌdʒ) *n* **1** a small section of type matter in a box in a newspaper allowing late news to be included without the whole page having to be remade. **2** the late news so inserted. **3** an unsatisfactory compromise reached to evade a difficult problem or controversial issue. ◆ *vb* **fudges, fudging, fudged. 4** (*tr*) to make or adjust in a false or clumsy way. **5** (*tr*) to misrepresent; falsify. **6** to evade (a problem, issue, etc.). [C19: ? rel. to arch. *fadge* to agree, succeed]

fuel ⓣ (fjʊəl) *n* **1** any substance burned as a source of heat or power, such as coal or petrol. **2** the material, containing a fissile substance such as uranium-235, that produces energy in a nuclear reactor. **3** something that nourishes or builds up emotion, action, etc. ◆ *vb* **fuels, fuelling, fuelled** *or US* **fuels, fueling, fueled. 4** to supply with or receive fuel. [C14: from OF, from *feu* fire, ult. from L *focus* hearth]

fuel air bomb *n* a type of bomb that spreads a cloud of gas, which is then detonated, over the target area, causing extensive destruction.

fuel cell *n* a cell in which chemical energy is converted directly into electrical energy.

fuel injection *n* a system for introducing fuel directly into the combustion chambers of an internal-combustion engine without the use of a carburettor.

THESAURUS

parsimonious, penny-wise, provident, prudent, saving, sparing
Antonyms *adj* excessive, extravagant, imprudent, lavish, luxurious, prodigal, profligate, spendthrift, wasteful

frugality *n* **1, 2** = **thrift,** carefulness, conservation, economizing, economy, good management, husbandry, moderation, providence, thriftiness

fruit *n* **1** = **produce,** crop, harvest, product, yield **4** *often plural* = **result,** advantage, benefit, consequence, effect, end result, outcome, profit, return, reward

fruitful *adj* **1** = **fertile,** fecund, fructiferous **2** = **plentiful,** abundant, copious, flush, plenteous, productive, profuse, prolific, rich, spawning **3** = **useful,** advantageous, beneficial, effective, gainful, productive, profitable, rewarding, successful, well-spent, worthwhile
Antonyms ≠ **fertile:** barren, fruitless, infertile, sterile, unfruitful, unproductive ≠ **plentiful:** scarce *adj* ≠ **useful:** fruitless, futile, ineffectual, pointless, unfruitful, unproductive, useless, vain

fruition *n* **1, 2** = **fulfilment,** actualization, attainment, completion, consummation, enjoyment, materialization, maturation, maturity, perfection, realization, ripeness

fruitless *adj* **1** = **useless,** abortive, bootless, futile, idle, ineffectual, in vain, pointless, profitless, to no avail, to no effect, unavailing, unfruitful, unproductive, unprofitable, unsuccessful, vain **2** = **barren,** unfruitful, unproductive, unprolific
Antonyms *adj* ≠ **useless:** effective, fruitful, productive, profitable, useful ≠ **barren:** abundant, fecund, fertile, fruitful, productive, prolific

fruity *adj* **2** = **rich,** full, mellow, resonant **3** *Informal, chiefly Brit.* = **risqué,** bawdy, blue, hot, indecent, indelicate, juicy, near the knuckle (*inf.*), racy, ripe, salacious, sexy, smutty, spicy (*inf.*), suggestive, titillating, vulgar

frumpy *adj* = **dowdy,** badly-dressed, dated, dingy, drab, dreary, mumsy, out of date

frustrate *vb* **1** = **thwart,** baffle, balk, block, check, circumvent, confront, counter, defeat, disappoint, foil, forestall, hobble, inhibit, neutralize, nullify, render null and void, stymie
Antonyms *vb* advance, encourage, endorse, forward, further, promote, satisfy, stimulate

frustrated *adj* = **disappointed,** choked, discontented, discouraged, disheartened, embittered, foiled, irked, resentful, sick as a parrot (*inf.*)

frustration *n* **1** = **annoyance,** disappointment, dissatisfaction, grievance, irritation, resentment, vexation

fuddled *adj* **1** = **confused,** muddled, muzzy **1** = **drunk,** babalas, bevvied (*dialect*), inebriated, intoxicated, legless (*inf.*), paralytic (*inf.*), smashed (*sl.*), sozzled (*inf.*), steamboats (*Scot. sl.*), steaming (*sl.*), stupefied, tipsy, wasted (*sl.*), woozy (*inf.*), wrecked (*sl.*)

fuddy-duddy *n Informal* = **conservative,** dinosaur, dodo (*inf.*), fossil, museum piece, (old) fogey, square (*inf.*), stick-in-the-mud (*inf.*), stuffed shirt (*inf.*)

fudge[3] *vb* **5, 6** = **misrepresent,** avoid, cook (*sl.*), dodge, equivocate, evade, fake, falsify, flannel (*Brit. inf.*), hedge, patch up, shuffle, slant, stall

fuel *n* **1, 3** = **incitement,** ammunition, encouragement, fodder, food, material, means, nourishment, provocation ◆ *vb* **4** = **inflame,** charge, fan, feed, fire, incite, nourish, stoke up, sustain

fuel oil *n* a liquid petroleum product used as a substitute for coal in industrial furnaces, ships, and locomotives.

fug ⓣ (fʌg) *n Chiefly Brit.* a hot, stale, or suffocating atmosphere. [C19: ? var. of FOG[1]]
▸ **'fuggy** *adj*

fugacity (fjuːˈgæsɪtɪ) *n Thermodynamics.* a property of a gas that expresses its tendency to escape or expand.

-fuge *n combining form.* indicating an agent or substance that expels or drives away: *vermifuge.* [from L *fugāre* to expel]

fugitive ⓣ (ˈfjuːdʒɪtɪv) *n* **1** a person who flees. **2** a thing that is elusive or fleeting. ◆ *adj* **3** fleeing, esp. from arrest or pursuit. **4** not permanent; fleeting. [C14: from L, from *fugere* to take flight]
▸ **'fugitively** *adv*

fugleman (ˈfjuːgᵊlmən) *n, pl* **fuglemen. 1** (formerly) a soldier used as an example for those learning drill. **2** a leader or example. [C19: from G *Flügelmann*, from *Flügel* wing + *Mann* MAN]

fugue (fjuːg) *n* **1** a musical form consisting of a theme repeated a fifth above or a fourth below the continuing first statement. **2** *Psychiatry.* a dreamlike altered state of consciousness, during which a person may lose his memory and wander away. [C16: from F, from It. *fuga*, from L: a running away]
▸ **'fugal** *adj*

Führer *or* ***Fuehrer*** *German.* (ˈfyːrər) *n* a leader: applied esp. to Adolf Hitler while he was Chancellor. [G, from *führen* to lead]

-ful *suffix.* **1** (*forming adjectives*) full of or characterized by: *painful; restful.* **2** (*forming adjectives*) able or tending to: *useful.* **3** (*forming nouns*) indicating as much as will fill the thing specified: *mouthful.* [OE *-ful, -full*, from FULL[1]]

> **USAGE NOTE** Where the amount held by a spoon, etc., is used as a rough unit of measurement, the correct form is *spoonful*, etc.: *take a spoonful of this medicine every day. Spoon full* is used in a sentence such as *he held out a spoon full of dark liquid*, where *full of* describes the spoon. A plural form such as *spoonfuls* is preferred by many speakers and writers to *spoonsful.*

fulcrum (ˈfʊlkrəm, ˈfʌl-) *n, pl* **fulcrums** *or* **fulcra** (-krə). **1** the pivot about which a lever turns. **2** something that supports or sustains; prop. [C17: from L: foot of a couch, from *fulcire* to prop up]

fulfil ⓣ *or US* **fulfill** (fʊlˈfɪl) *vb* **fulfils, fulfilling, fulfilled** *or US* **fulfills, fulfilling, fulfilled.** (*tr*) **1** to bring about the completion or achievement of (a desire, promise, etc.). **2** to carry out or execute (a request, etc.). **3** to conform with or satisfy (regulations, etc.). **4** to finish or reach the end of. **5 fulfil oneself.** to achieve one's potential or desires. [OE *fulfyllan*]
▸ **ful'filment** *or US* **ful'fillment** *n*

fulgent (ˈfʌldʒənt) *adj Poetic.* shining brilliantly; gleaming. [C15: from L *fulgēre* to shine]

fulgurate (ˈfʌlgjʊˌreɪt) *vb* **fulgurates, fulgurating, fulgurated.** (*intr*) *Rare.* to flash like lightning. [C17: from L, from *fulgur* lightning]

fulgurite (ˈfʌlgjʊˌraɪt) *n* glassy mineral matter found in sand and rock, formed by the action of lightning. [C19: from L *fulgur* lightning]

fuliginous (fjuːˈlɪdʒɪnəs) *adj* **1** sooty or smoky. **2** of the colour of soot. [C16: from LL *fūlīginōsus* full of soot, from L *fūlīgō* soot]

full[1] ⓣ (fʊl) *adj* **1** holding or containing as much as possible. **2** abundant in supply, quantity, number, etc.: *full of energy.* **3** having consumed enough food or drink. **4** (esp. of the face or figure) rounded or plump. **5** (*prenominal*) complete: *a full dozen.* **6** (*prenominal*) with all privileges, rights, etc.: *a full member.* **7** (*prenominal*) having the same parents: *a full brother.* **8** filled with emotion or sentiment: *a full heart.* **9** (*postpositive;* foll. by *of*) occupied or engrossed (with): *full of his own projects.* **10** *Music.* **10a** powerful or rich in volume and sound. **10b** completing a piece or section; concluding: *a full close.* **11** (of a garment, esp. a skirt) containing a large amount of fabric. **12** (of sails, etc.) distended by wind. **13** (of wine, such as a burgundy) having a heavy body. **14** (of a colour) rich; saturated. **15** *Inf.* drunk. **16 full of oneself.** full of pride or conceit. **17 full up.** filled to capacity. **18 in full swing.** at the height of activity: *the party was in full swing.* ◆ *adv* **19a** completely; entirely. **19b** (*in combination*): *full-fledged.* **20** directly; right: *he hit him full in the stomach.* **21** very; extremely (esp. in **full well**). ◆ *n* **22** the greatest degree, extent, etc. **23 in full.** without omitting or shortening: *we paid in full for our mistake.* **24 to the full.** thoroughly; fully. ◆ *vb* **25** (*tr*) *Needlework.* to gather or tuck. **26** (*intr*) (of the moon) to be fully illuminated. [OE]
▸ **'fullness** *or esp. US* **'fulness** *n*

full[2] (fʊl) *vb* (of cloth, yarn, etc.) to become or to make (cloth, yarn, etc.) more compact during manufacture through shrinking and pressing. [C14: from OF *fouler*, ult. from L *fullō* a FULLER]

fullback (ˈfʊlˌbæk) *n Soccer, hockey, rugby.* **a** a defensive player. **b** the position held by this player.

full-blooded ⓣ *adj* **1** (esp. of horses) of unmixed ancestry. **2** having great vigour or health; hearty.
▸ **ˌfull-'bloodedness** *n*

full-blown ⓣ *adj* **1** characterized by the fullest, strongest, or best development. **2** in full bloom.

full board *n* accommodation at a hotel, etc., that includes all meals.

full-bodied ⓣ *adj* having a full rich flavour or quality.

full-court press *n Basketball.* the tactic of harrying the opposing team in all areas of the court, as opposed to the more usual practice of trying to defend one's own basket.

full dress *n* **a** a formal style of dress, such as white tie and tails for a man. **b** (*as modifier*): *full-dress uniform.*

full employment *n* a state in which the labour force and other economic resources of a country are utilized to their maximum extent.

fuller (ˈfʊlə) *n* a person who fulls cloth for his living. [OE *fullere*]

fuller's earth *n* a natural absorbent clay used, after heating, for clarifying oils and fats, fulling cloth, etc.

full face *adj* facing towards the viewer, with the entire face visible.

full-fledged *adj* See **fully fledged.**

full-frontal *Inf.* ◆ *adj* **1** (of a nude person or a photograph of a nude person) exposing the genitals to full view. **2** all-out; unrestrained. ◆ *n* **full frontal. 3** a full-frontal photograph.

full house *n* **1** *Poker.* a hand with three cards of the same value and another pair. **2** a theatre, etc., filled to capacity. **3** (in bingo, etc.) the set of numbers needed to win.

full-length *n* (*modifier*) **1** showing the complete length. **2** not abridged.

full moon *n* one of the four phases of the moon when the moon is visible as a fully illuminated disc.

full monty (ˈmɒntɪ) *n* **the.** *Inf.* something in its entirety. [from ?]

full nelson *n* a wrestling hold in which a wrestler places both arms under his opponent's arms from behind and exerts pressure on the back of the neck.

full-on *adj Inf.* complete; unrestrained: *full-on military intervention; full-on hard rock.*

full sail *adv* **1** at top speed. ◆ *adj* (*postpositive*), *adv* **2** with all sails set.

full-scale ⓣ *n* (*modifier*) **1** (of a plan, etc.) of actual size. **2** using all resources; all-out.

full stop *or* **full point** *n* the punctuation mark (.) used at the end of a sentence that is not a question or exclamation, after abbreviations, etc. Also called (esp. US and Canad.): **period.**

full time *n* the end of a football or other match.

full-time *adj* **1** for the entire time appropriate to an activity: *a full-time job.* ◆ *adv* **full time. 2** on a full-time basis: *he works full time.* ◆ Cf. **part-time.**
▸ **ˌfull-'timer** *n*

full toss *or* **full pitch** *n Cricket.* a bowled ball that reaches the batsman without bouncing.

fully ⓣ (ˈfʊlɪ) *adv* **1** to the greatest degree or extent. **2** amply; adequately: *they were fully fed.* **3** at least: *it was fully an hour before she came.*

fully fashioned *adj* (of stockings, knitwear, etc.) shaped and seamed so as to fit closely.

THESAURUS

fug *n* = **stale air,** fetidity, fetor, frowst, frowstiness, fustiness, reek, staleness, stink

fuggy *adj* = **stuffy,** airless, fetid, foul, frowsty, noisome, noxious, stale, suffocating, unventilated

fugitive *n* **1** = **runaway,** deserter, escapee, refugee, runagate (*arch.*) ◆ *adj* **3, 4** = **momentary,** brief, ephemeral, evanescent, fleeing, fleeting, flitting, flying, fugacious, passing, short, short-lived, temporary, transient, transitory, unstable

fulfil *vb* **1, 2, 4** = **achieve,** accomplish, bring to completion, carry out, complete, conclude, discharge, effect, execute, finish, keep, perfect, perform, realise, satisfy **3** = **comply with,** answer, conform to, fill, meet, obey, observe
Antonyms *vb* disappoint, dissatisfy, fail in, fail to meet, fall short of, neglect

fulfilment *n* **1, 2, 4** = **achievement,** accomplishment, attainment, carrying out *or* through, completion, consummation, crowning, discharge, discharging, effecting, end, implementation, observance, perfection, realization

full[1] *adj* **1** = **crammed,** chock-a-block, chock-full, crowded, in use, jammed, occupied, packed, taken **2** = **extensive,** abundant, adequate, all-inclusive, ample, broad, comprehensive, copious, detailed, exhaustive, generous, maximum, plenary, plenteous, plentiful, thorough, unabridged **3** = **filled,** brimful, brimming, bursting at the seams, complete, entire, gorged, intact, loaded, replete, sated, satiated, satisfied, saturated, stocked, sufficient **4** = **plump,** buxom, curvaceous, rounded, voluptuous **10a** = **rich,** clear, deep, distinct, loud, resonant, rounded **11** = **voluminous,** baggy, balloon-like, capacious, large, loose, puffy ◆ *n* **23 in full** = **completely,** in its entirety, in total, *in toto,* without exception **24 to the full** = **thoroughly,** completely, entirely, fully, to the utmost, without reservation
Antonyms *adj* ≠ **extensive:** abridged, incomplete, limited, partial ≠ **filled, crammed:** blank, devoid, empty, vacant, void ≠ **rich:** faint, thin ≠ **voluminous:** restricted, tight

full-blooded *adj* **2** = **vigorous,** gutsy (*sl.*), hearty, lusty, mettlesome, red-blooded, virile

full-blown *adj* **1** = **fully developed,** advanced, complete, developed, entire, full, full-scale, full-sized, fully fledged, fully formed, fully grown, progressed, total, whole **2** = **in full bloom,** blossoming, flowering, full, opened out, unfolded
Antonyms *adj* ≠ **fully developed:** dormant, latent, potential, undeveloped

full-bodied *adj* = **rich,** fruity, full-flavoured, heady, heavy, mellow, redolent, strong, well-matured

fullness *n* **2** = **plenty,** abundance, adequateness, ampleness, copiousness, fill, glut, profusion, repletion, satiety, saturation, sufficiency **4** = **roundness,** curvaceousness, dilation, distension, enlargement, swelling, tumescence, voluptuousness **10a** = **richness,** clearness, loudness, resonance, strength

full-scale *adj* **2** = **major,** all-encompassing, all-out, comprehensive, exhaustive, extensive, full-dress, in-depth, proper, sweeping, thorough, thoroughgoing, wide-ranging

fully *adv* **1** = **totally,** absolutely, altogether, completely, entirely, every inch, from first to

fully fledged ❶ *or* **full-fledged** *adj* **1** (of a young bird) having acquired adult feathers, enabling it to fly. **2** developed to the fullest degree. **3** of full rank or status.

fulmar ('fʊlmə) *n* a heavily built short-tailed oceanic bird of polar regions. [C17: of Scand. origin]

fulminate ❶ ('fʌlmɪˌneɪt) *vb* **fulminates, fulminating, fulminated. 1** (*intr;* often foll. by *against*) to make severe criticisms or denunciations; rail. **2** to explode with noise and violence. ◆ *n* **3** any salt or ester of **fulminic acid**, an isomer of cyanic acid, which is used as a detonator. [C15: from Med. L, from L, from *fulmen* lightning that strikes]
▸ **'fulminant** *adj* ▸ **ˌfulmi'nation** *n* ▸ **'fulmiˌnatory** *adj*

fulsome ❶ ('fʊlsəm) *adj* **1** excessive or insincere, esp. in an offensive or distasteful way: *fulsome compliments*. **2** *Not standard*. extremely complimentary.
▸ **'fulsomely** *adv* ▸ **'fulsomeness** *n*

fulvous ('fʌlvəs) *adj* of a dull brownish-yellow colour. [C17: from L *fulvus* reddish yellow]

fumarole ('fju:məˌrəʊl) *n* a vent in or near a volcano from which hot gases, esp. steam, are emitted. [C19: from F, from LL *fūmāriolum* smoke hole, from L *fūmus* smoke]

fumble ❶ ('fʌmbᵊl) *vb* **fumbles, fumbling, fumbled. 1** (*intr;* often foll. by *for* or *with*) to grope about clumsily or blindly, esp. in searching. **2** (*intr;* foll. by *at* or *with*) to finger or play with, esp. in an absent-minded way. **3** to say or do awkwardly: *he fumbled the introduction badly*. **4** to fail to catch or grasp (a ball, etc.) cleanly. ◆ *n* **5** the act of fumbling. [C16: prob. of Scand. origin]
▸ **'fumbler** *n* ▸ **'fumblingly** *adv*

fume ❶ (fju:m) *vb* **fumes, fuming, fumed. 1** (*intr*) to be overcome with anger or fury. **2** to give off (fumes) or (of fumes) to be given off, esp. during a chemical reaction. **3** (*tr*) to fumigate. ◆ *n* **4** (*often pl*) a pungent or toxic vapour, gas, or smoke. **5** a sharp or pungent odour. [C14: from OF *fum*, from L *fūmus* smoke, vapour]
▸ **'fumeless** *adj* ▸ **'fumingly** *adv* ▸ **'fumy** *adj*

fumed (fju:md) *adj* (of wood, esp. oak) having a dark colour and distinctive grain from exposure to ammonia fumes.

fumigant ('fju:mɪgənt) *n* a substance used for fumigating.

fumigate ❶ ('fju:mɪˌgeɪt) *vb* **fumigates, fumigating, fumigated.** to treat (something contaminated or infected) with fumes or smoke. [C16: from L, from *fūmus* smoke + *agere* to drive]
▸ **ˌfumi'gation** *n* ▸ **'fumiˌgator** *n*

fuming sulphuric acid *n* a mixture of acids, made by dissolving sulphur trioxide in concentrated sulphuric acid. Also called: **oleum.**

fumitory ('fju:mɪtərɪ) *n, pl* **fumitories.** any plant of the genus *Fumaria* having spurred flowers and formerly used medicinally. [C14: from OF, from Med. L *fūmus terrae*, lit.: smoke of the earth]

fun ❶ (fʌn) *n* **1** a source of enjoyment, amusement, diversion, etc. **2** pleasure, gaiety, or merriment. **3** jest or sport (esp. in **in** *or* **for fun**). **4 fun and games.** *Ironic or facetious.* frivolous or hetic activity. **5 make fun of** *or* **poke fun at.** to ridicule or deride. **6** (*modifier*) full of amusement, diversion, gaiety, etc.: *a fun sport*. [C17: ?from obs. *fon* to make a fool of; see FOND]

funambulist (fju:'næmbjʊlɪst) *n* a tightrope walker. [C18: from L, from *fūnis* rope + *ambulāre* to walk]
▸ **fu'nambulism** *n*

function ❶ ('fʌŋkʃən) *n* **1** the natural action of a person or thing: *the function of the kidneys is to filter waste products from the blood*. **2** the intended purpose of a person or thing in a specific role: *the function of a hammer is to hit nails into wood*. **3** an official or formal social gathering or ceremony. **4** a factor dependent upon another or other factors. **5** Also called: **map, mapping.** *Maths, logic.* a relation between two sets that associates a unique element (the value) of the second (the range) with each element (the argument) of the first (the domain). Symbol: $f(x)$. The value of $f(x)$ for $x=2$ is $f(2)$. ◆ *vb* (*intr*) **6** to operate or perform as specified. **7** (foll. by *as*) to perform the action or role (of something or someone else): *a coin may function as a screwdriver*. [C16: from L *functiō*, from *fungī* to perform]

functional ❶ ('fʌŋkʃənᵊl) *adj* **1** of, involving, or containing a function or functions. **2** practical rather than decorative; utilitarian. **3** capable of functioning; working. **4** *Med.* affecting a function of an organ without structural change.
▸ **'functionally** *adv*

functionalism ('fʌŋkʃənəˌlɪzəm) *n* **1** the theory of design that the form of a thing should be determined by its use. **2** any doctrine that stresses purpose.
▸ **'functionalist** *n, adj*

functionary ❶ ('fʌŋkʃənərɪ) *n, pl* **functionaries.** a person acting in an official capacity, as for a government; an official.

fund ❶ (fʌnd) *n* **1** a reserve of money, etc., set aside for a certain purpose. **2** a supply or store of something; stock: *it exhausted his fund of wisdom*. ◆ *vb* (*tr*) **3** to furnish money to in the form of a fund. **4** to place or store up in a fund. **5** to convert (short-term floating debt) into long-term debt bearing fixed interest and represented by bonds. **6** to accumulate a fund for the discharge of (a recurrent liability): *to fund a pension plan*. ◆ See also **funds.** [C17: from L *fundus* the bottom, piece of land]
▸ **'funder** *n*

fundament ('fʌndəmənt) *n Euphemistic or facetious.* the buttocks. [C13: from L, from *fundāre* to FOUND[2]]

fundamental ❶ (ˌfʌndə'mɛntᵊl) *adj* **1** of, involving, or comprising a foundation; basic. **2** of, involving, or comprising a source; primary. **3** *Music.* denoting or relating to the principal or lowest note of a harmonic series. ◆ *n* **4** a principle, law, etc., that serves as the basis of an idea or system. **5a** the principal or lowest note of a harmonic series. **5b** the bass note of a chord in root position.
▸ **ˌfundamen'tality** *n* ▸ **ˌfunda'mentally** *adv*

fundamental interaction *n* any of the four basic interactions that occur in nature: the gravitational, electromagnetic, strong, and weak interactions.

fundamentalism (ˌfʌndə'mɛntəˌlɪzəm) *n* **1** *Christianity.* the view that the Bible is divinely inspired and is therefore literally true. **2** *Islam.* a movement favouring strict observance of the teachings of the Koran and Islamic law.
▸ **ˌfunda'mentalist** *n, adj*

fundamental particle *n* another name for **elementary particle.**

fundamental unit *n* one of a set of unrelated units that form the basis of a system of units. For example, the metre, kilogram, and second are fundamental SI units.

funded debt *n* that part of the British national debt that the government is not obliged to repay by a fixed date.

fundraiser ('fʌndˌreɪzə) *n* **1** a person engaged in fundraising. **2** an event held to raise money for a cause.

fundraising ('fʌndˌreɪzɪŋ) *n* **1** the activity involved in raising money for a cause. ◆ *adj* **2** of, for, or related to fundraising.

THESAURUS

last, heart and soul, in all respects, intimately, lock, stock and barrel, one hundred per cent, perfectly, positively, thoroughly, to the hilt, utterly, wholly **2** = **adequately**, abundantly, amply, comprehensively, enough, plentifully, satisfactorily, sufficiently **3** = **at least**, quite, without (any) exaggeration, without a word of a lie (*inf.*)

fully fledged *adj* **3** = **experienced**, mature, professional, proficient, qualified, senior, time-served, trained

fulminate *vb* **1** = **criticize**, animadvert upon, berate, blast, castigate, censure, curse, denounce, denunciate, excoriate, execrate, fume, inveigh against, lambast(e), protest against, put down, rage, rail against, reprobate, tear into (*inf.*), thunder, upbraid, vilify, vituperate

fulmination *n* **1** = **condemnation**, denunciation, diatribe, excoriation, invective, obloquy, philippic, reprobation, tirade

fulsome *adj* **1** = **extravagant**, adulatory, cloying, excessive, fawning, gross, immoderate, ingratiating, inordinate, insincere, nauseating, overdone, over the top, saccharine, sickening, smarmy (*Brit. inf.*), sycophantic, unctuous

fumble *vb* **1** = **grope**, bumble, feel around, flounder, paw (*inf.*), scrabble

fume *vb* **1** = **rage**, blow a fuse (*sl., chiefly US*), boil, chafe, crack up (*inf.*), fly off the handle (*inf.*), go ballistic (*sl.*), go off the deep end (*inf.*), go up the wall (*sl.*), rant, rave, see red (*inf.*), seethe, smoulder, storm ◆ *n* **4** *often plural* = **smoke**, effluvium, exhalation, exhaust, gas, haze, miasma, pollution, reek, smog, vapour

fumigate *vb* = **disinfect**, clean out *or* up, cleanse, purify, sanitize, sterilize

fuming *adj* **1** = **furious**, angry, at boiling point (*inf.*), choked, enraged, fit to be tied (*sl.*), foaming at the mouth, in a rage, incandescent, incensed, on the warpath (*inf.*), raging, roused, seething, up in arms

fun *n* **1** = **joking**, buffoonery, clowning, foolery, game, horseplay, jesting, jocularity, nonsense, play, playfulness, skylarking (*inf.*), sport, teasing, tomfoolery **2** = **enjoyment**, amusement, beer and skittles (*inf.*), cheer, distraction, diversion, entertainment, frolic, gaiety, good time, high jinks, jollification, jollity, joy, junketing, living it up, merriment, merrymaking, mirth, pleasure, recreation, romp, sport, treat, whoopee (*inf.*) **3 in** *or* **for fun** = **for a joke**, facetiously, for a laugh, in jest, jokingly, light-heartedly, mischievously, playfully, roguishly, teasingly, tongue in cheek, with a gleam *or* twinkle in one's eye, with a straight face **5 make fun of** = **mock**, deride, hold up to ridicule, lampoon, laugh at, make a fool of, parody, poke fun at, rag, rib (*inf.*), ridicule, satirize, scoff at, send up (*Brit. inf.*), sneer at, take off, taunt ◆ *modifier* **6** = **enjoyable**, amusing, convivial, diverting, entertaining, lively, witty
Antonyms *n* ≠ **enjoyment:** depression, desolation, despair, distress, gloom, grief, melancholy, misery, sadness, sorrow, unhappiness, woe

function *n* **2** = **purpose**, activity, business, capacity, charge, concern, duty, employment, exercise, job, mission, occupation, office, operation, part, post, province, *raison d'être*, responsibility, role, situation, task **3** = **reception**, affair, do (*inf.*), gathering, lig (*Brit. sl.*), social occasion ◆ *vb* **6** = **work**, act, act the part of, behave, be in business, be in commission, be in operation *or* action, be in running order, do duty, go, officiate, operate, perform, run, serve, serve one's turn

functional *adj* **2** = **practical**, hard-wearing, serviceable, useful, utilitarian, utility **3** = **working**, operative

functionary *n* = **officer**, dignitary, employee, office bearer, office holder, official

fund *n* **1** = **reserve**, capital, endowment, fall-back, foundation, kitty, pool, stock, store, supply, tontine **2** = **store**, hoard, mine, repository, reserve, reservoir, source, treasury, vein ◆ *vb* **3** = **finance**, capitalize, endow, float, pay for, promote, stake, subsidize, support

fundamental *adj* **1, 2** = **essential**, basic, cardinal, central, constitutional, crucial, elementary, first, important, indispensable, integral, intrinsic, key, necessary, organic, primary, prime, principal, radical, rudimentary, underlying, vital ◆ *n* **4** = **principle**, axiom, basic, cornerstone, essential, first principle, law, rudiment, rule, *sine qua non*
Antonyms *adj* ≠ **essential:** advanced, back-up, extra, incidental, lesser, secondary, subsidiary, superfluous

fundamentally *adv* **2** = **essentially**, at bot-

funds Ⓣ (fʌndz) *pl n* **1** money that is readily available. **2** British government securities representing national debt.

fundus ('fʌndəs) *n, pl* **fundi** (-daɪ). *Anat.* the base of an organ or the part farthest away from its opening. [C18: from L, lit.: the bottom]

funeral Ⓣ ('fjuːnərəl) *n* **1a** a ceremony at which a dead person is buried or cremated. **1b** (*as modifier*): *funeral service.* **2** a procession of people escorting a corpse to burial. **3** *Inf.* concern; affair: *it's your funeral.* [C14: from Med. L, from LL, from L *fūnus* funeral]
▸ **'funerary** *adj*

funeral director *n* an undertaker.

funeral parlour *n* a place where the dead are prepared for burial or cremation. Usual US name: **funeral home.**

funereal Ⓣ (fjuː'nɪərɪəl) *adj* suggestive of a funeral; gloomy or mournful. Also: **funebrial.** [C18: from L *fūnereus*]
▸ **fu'nereally** *adv*

funfair ('fʌn,fɛə) *n Brit.* an amusement park or fairground.

fungible ('fʌndʒɪbᵊl) *n Law.* (*often pl*) moveable perishable goods of a sort that may be estimated by number or weight, such as grain, wine, etc. [C18: from Med. L *fungibilis,* from L *fungī* to perform]
▸ **,fungi'bility** *n*

fungicide ('fʌndʒɪ,saɪd) *n* a substance or agent that destroys or is capable of destroying fungi.
▸ **,fungi'cidal** *adj*

fungoid ('fʌŋgɔɪd) *adj* resembling a fungus or fungi.

fungous ('fʌŋgəs) *adj* appearing suddenly and spreading quickly like a fungus.

fungus ('fʌŋgəs) *n, pl* **fungi** ('fʌŋgaɪ, 'fʌndʒaɪ, 'fʌndʒɪ) *or* **funguses. 1** any member of a kingdom of organisms, formerly classified as plants, that lack chlorophyll, leaves, true stems, and roots, reproduce by spores, and live as saprotrophs or parasites. **2** something resembling a fungus, esp. in suddenly growing. **3** *Pathol.* any soft tumorous growth. [C16: from L: mushroom, fungus]
▸ **'fungal** *adj*

funicular (fjuː'nɪkjʊlə) *n* **1** Also called: **funicular railway.** a railway up the side of a mountain, consisting of two cars at either end of a cable passing round a driving wheel at the summit. ◆ *adj* **2** relating to or operated by a rope, etc. [C17: from L, from *fūnis* rope]

funk[1] Ⓣ (fʌŋk) *Inf., chiefly Brit.* ◆ *n* **1** Also called: **blue funk.** a state of nervousness, fear, or depression. **2** a coward. ◆ *vb* **3** to flinch from (responsibility, etc.) through fear. **4** (*tr; usually passive*) to make afraid. [C18: university sl., ? rel. to *funk* to smoke]

funk[2] (fʌŋk) *n* a type of polyrhythmic Black dance music with heavy syncopation. [C20: back formation from FUNKY]

funky ('fʌŋkɪ) *adj* **funkier, funkiest.** *Inf.* (of jazz, pop, etc.) passionate; soulful. [C20: from *funk* to smoke (tobacco), ? alluding to music that was smelly, that is, earthy]

funnel Ⓣ ('fʌnᵊl) *n* **1** a hollow utensil with a wide mouth tapering to a small hole, used for pouring liquids, etc., into a narrow-necked vessel. **2** something resembling this in shape or function. **3** a smokestack for smoke and exhaust gases, as on a steam locomotive. ◆ *vb* **funnels, funnelling, funnelled** *or US* **funnels, funneling, funneled. 4** to move or cause to move or pour through or as if through a funnel. [C15: from OProvençal *fonilh,* ult. from L *infundibulum,* from *infundere* to pour in]
▸ **'funnel-,like** *adj*

funnel-web *n Austral.* a large poisonous black spider that constructs funnel-shaped webs.

funny Ⓣ ('fʌnɪ) *adj* **funnier, funniest. 1** causing amusement or laughter; humorous. **2** peculiar; odd. **3** suspicious or dubious (esp. in **funny business**). **4** *Inf.* faint or ill. ◆ *n, pl* **funnies. 5** *Inf.* a joke or witticism.
▸ **'funnily** *adv* ▸ **'funniness** *n*

funny bone *n* the area near the elbow where the ulnar nerve is close to the surface of the skin: when it is struck, a sharp tingling sensation is experienced.

fun run *n* a long run or part-marathon run for exercise and pleasure, often by large numbers of people.

fuoco (fuː'əʊkəʊ) *Music.* ◆ *n* **1** fire. ◆ *adv, adj* **2 con fuoco.** in a fiery manner. [C19: It., lit.: fire]

fur (fɜː) *n* **1** the dense coat of fine silky hairs on such mammals as the cat and mink. **2a** the dressed skin of certain fur-bearing animals, with the hair left on. **2b** (*as modifier*): *a fur coat.* **3** a garment made of fur, such as a stole. **4** a pile fabric made in imitation of animal fur. **5** *Heraldry.* any of various stylized representations of animal pelts used in coats of arms. **6 make the fur fly.** to cause a scene or disturbance. **7** *Inf.* a whitish coating on the tongue, caused by excessive smoking, illness, etc. **8** *Brit.* a whitish-grey deposit precipitated from hard water onto the insides of pipes, kettles, etc. ◆ *vb* **furs, furring, furred. 9** (*tr*) to line or trim a garment, etc., with fur. **10** (often foll. by *up*) to cover or become covered with a furlike lining or deposit. [C14: from OF *forrer* to line a garment, from *fuerre* sheath, of Gmc origin]
▸ **'furless** *adj*

fur. *abbrev. for* furlong.

furbelow ('fɜːbɪ,ləʊ) *n* **1** a flounce, ruffle, or other ornamental trim. **2** (*often pl*) showy ornamentation. ◆ *vb* **3** (*tr*) to put a furbelow on (a garment, etc.). [C18: by folk etymology from F dialect *farbella* a frill]

furbish Ⓣ ('fɜːbɪʃ) *vb* (*tr*) **1** to make bright by polishing. **2** (often foll. by *up*) to renovate; restore. [C14: from OF *fourbir* to polish, of Gmc origin]
▸ **'furbisher** *n*

furcate ('fɜːkeɪt) *vb* **furcates, furcating, furcated. 1** to divide into two parts. ◆ *adj* **2** forked: *furcate branches.* [C19: from LL, from L *furca* a fork]
▸ **fur'cation** *n*

furfuraceous (,fɜːfjʊ'reɪʃəs) *adj* **1** relating to or resembling bran. **2** *Med.* resembling dandruff. [C17: from L *furfur* bran, scurf + -ACEOUS]

Furies ('fjʊərɪz) *pl n, sing* **Fury.** *Classical myth.* the snake-haired goddesses of vengeance, usually three in number, who pursued unpunished criminals. Also called: **Erinyes, Eumenides.**

furioso (,fjʊərɪ'əʊsəʊ) *Music.* ◆ *adj, adv* **1** in a frantically rushing manner. ◆ *n* **2** a passage or piece to be performed in this way. [C19: It., lit.: furious]

furious Ⓣ ('fjʊərɪəs) *adj* **1** extremely angry or annoyed. **2** violent or unrestrained, as in speed, energy, etc.
▸ **'furiously** *adv* ▸ **'furiousness** *n*

furl (fɜːl) *vb* **1** to roll up (an umbrella, flag, etc.) neatly and securely or (of an umbrella, flag, etc.) to be rolled up in this way. ◆ *n* **2** the act or an instance of furling. **3** a single rolled-up section. [C16: from OF, from *ferm* tight (from L *firmus* FIRM[1]) + *lier* to bind, from L *ligāre*]
▸ **'furlable** *adj*

furlong ('fɜː,lɒŋ) *n* a unit of length equal to 220 yards (201.168 metres). [OE *furlang,* from *furh* furrow + *lang* long]

furlough ('fɜːləʊ) *n* **1** leave of absence from military duty. ◆ *vb* (*tr*) **2** to grant a furlough to. [C17: from Du. *verlof,* from *ver-* FOR- + *lof* leave, permission]

furnace ('fɜːnɪs) *n* **1** an enclosed chamber in which heat is produced to destroy refuse, smelt or refine ores, etc. **2** a very hot place. [C13: from OF, from L *fornax* oven, furnace]

furnish Ⓣ ('fɜːnɪʃ) *vb* (*tr*) **1** to provide (a house, room, etc.) with furniture, etc. **2** to equip with what is necessary. **3** to supply: *the records furnished the information.* [C15: from OF *fournir,* of Gmc origin]
▸ **'furnisher** *n*

furnishings ('fɜːnɪʃɪŋz) *pl n* furniture, carpets, etc., with which a room or house is furnished.

furniture Ⓣ ('fɜːnɪtʃə) *n* **1** the movable articles that equip a room, house, etc. **2** the equipment necessary for a ship, factory, etc. **3** *Printing.* lengths of wood, plastic, or metal, used in assembling formes to surround the type. ◆ See also **door furniture, street furniture.** [C16: from F, from *fournir* to equip]

furore Ⓣ (fjʊ'rɔːrɪ) *or esp. US* **furor** ('fjʊərɔː) *n* **1** a public outburst; uproar. **2** a sudden widespread enthusiasm; craze. **3** frenzy; rage. [C15: from L: frenzy, from *furere* to rave]

furphy ('fɜːfɪ) *n, pl* **furphies.** *Austral. sl.* a rumour or fictitious story. [C20: from *Furphy* carts (used for water or sewage in World War I), made at a foundry established by the Furphy family]

furred (fɜːd) *adj* **1** made of, lined with, or covered in fur. **2** wearing fur. **3** (of animals) having fur. **4** another word for **furry** (sense 3). **5** provided with furring strips. **6** (of a pipe, kettle, etc.) lined with hard lime.

furrier ('fʌrɪə) *n* a person whose occupation is selling, making, or repairing fur garments. [C14: *furour,* from OF *fourrer* to trim with FUR]

THESAURUS

tom, at heart, basically, intrinsically, primarily, radically

funds *pl n* **1 = money,** brass (*N English dialect*), bread (*sl.*), capital, cash, dosh (*Brit. & Austral. sl.*), dough (*sl.*), finance, hard cash, necessary (*inf.*), ready money, resources, savings, shekels (*inf.*), silver, spondulicks (*sl.*), the wherewithal, tin (*sl.*)

funeral *n* **1 = burial,** cremation, inhumation, interment, obsequies

funereal *adj* **= gloomy,** dark, deathlike, depressing, dirge-like, dismal, dreary, grave, lamenting, lugubrious, mournful, sad, sepulchral, solemn, sombre, woeful

funk[1] *vb* **3 = chicken out of** (*inf.*), dodge, duck out of (*inf.*), flinch from, recoil from, take fright, turn tail

funnel *vb* **4 = channel,** conduct, convey, direct, filter, move, pass, pour

funny *adj* **1 = humorous,** amusing, comic, comical, diverting, droll, entertaining, facetious, farcical, hilarious, jocose, jocular, jolly, killing (*inf.*), laughable, ludicrous, rich, ridiculous, riotous, risible, side-splitting, silly, slapstick, waggish, witty **2 = peculiar,** curious, dubious, mysterious, odd, perplexing, puzzling, queer, remarkable, rum (*Brit. sl.*), strange, suspicious, unusual, weird ◆ *n* **5** *Informal* **= joke,** crack (*sl.*), jest, play on words, pun, quip, wisecrack, witticism
Antonyms *adj* ≠ **humorous:** grave, humourless, melancholy, serious, sober, solemn, stern, unfunny

furbish *vb* **1, 2 = renovate,** brighten, burnish, polish, restore, rub, shine, smarten up, spruce up

furious *adj* **1 = angry,** beside oneself, boiling, choked, cross, enraged, frantic, frenzied, fuming, incandescent, incensed, infuriated, in high dudgeon, livid (*inf.*), mad, maddened, on the warpath (*inf.*), raging, up in arms, wrathful, wroth (*arch.*) **2 = violent,** boisterous, fierce, impetuous, intense, savage, stormy, tempestuous, tumultuous, turbulent, ungovernable, unrestrained, vehement, wild
Antonyms *adj* ≠ **angry:** calm, dispassionate, impassive, imperturbable, mild, placated, pleased, serene, tranquil

furnish *vb* **1, 2 = decorate,** appoint, equip, fit, fit out, fit up, outfit, provide, provision, purvey, rig, stock, store, supply **3 = supply,** afford, bestow, endow, give, grant, hand out, offer, present, provide, reveal

furniture *n* **1 = household goods,** appliances, appointments, chattels, effects, equipment, fittings, furnishings, goods, movable property, movables, possessions, things (*inf.*)

furore *n* **1 = commotion,** brouhaha, disturbance, excitement, flap (*inf.*), hullabaloo, out-

▸ **'furriery** *n*

furring ('fɜːrɪŋ) *n* **1** short for **furring strip**. **2** the formation of fur on the tongue. **3** trimming of animal fur, as on a coat.

furring strip *n* a strip of wood or metal fixed to a wall, floor, or ceiling to provide a surface for the fixing of plasterboard, floorboards, etc.

furrow ⓣ ('fʌrəʊ) *n* **1** a long narrow trench made in the ground by a plough. **2** any long deep groove, esp. a deep wrinkle on the forehead. ◆ *vb* **3** to develop or cause to develop furrows or wrinkles. **4** to make a furrow or furrows in (land). [OE *furh*]
▸ **'furrower** *n* ▸ **'furrowless** *adj* ▸ **'furrowy** *adj*

furry ('fɜːrɪ) *adj* **furrier, furriest. 1** covered with fur or something furlike. **2** of, relating to, or resembling fur. **3** Also: **furred.** (of the tongue) coated with whitish cellular debris.
▸ **'furrily** *adv* ▸ **'furriness** *n*

further ⓣ ('fɜːðə) *adv* **1** in addition; furthermore. **2** to a greater degree or extent. **3** to or at a more advanced point. **4** to or at a greater distance in time or space. ◆ *adj* **5** additional; more. **6** more distant or remote in time or space. ◆ *vb* **7** (*tr*) to assist the progress of. ◆ See also **far, furthest.** [OE *furthor*]

USAGE NOTE See at **farther.**

furtherance ⓣ ('fɜːðərəns) *n* **1** the act of furthering. **2** something that furthers.

further education *n* (in Britain) formal education beyond school other than at a university or polytechnic.

furthermore ⓣ ('fɜːðəˌmɔː) *adv* in addition; moreover.

furthermost ('fɜːðəˌməʊst) *adj* most distant; furthest.

furthest ⓣ ('fɜːðɪst) *adv* **1** to the greatest degree or extent. **2** to or at the greatest distance in time or space; farthest. ◆ *adj* **3** most distant or remote in time or space; farthest.

furtive ⓣ ('fɜːtɪv) *adj* characterized by stealth; sly and secretive. [C15: from L *furtīvus* stolen, from *furtum* a theft, from *fūr* a thief]
▸ **'furtively** *adv* ▸ **'furtiveness** *n*

furuncle ('fjʊərʌŋkᵊl) *n Pathol.* the technical name for **boil**[2]. [C17: from L *fūrunculus* pilferer, sore, from *fūr* thief]
▸**furuncular** (fjʊ'rʌŋkjʊlə) *or* **fu'runculous** *adj*

furunculosis (fjʊˌrʌŋkjʊ'ləʊsɪs) *n* **1** a skin condition characterized by the presence of multiple boils. **2** a disease of salmon and trout caused by a bacterium.

fury ⓣ ('fjʊərɪ) *n, pl* **furies. 1** violent or uncontrolled anger. **2** an outburst of such anger. **3** uncontrolled violence: *the fury of the storm.* **4** a person, esp. a woman, with a violent temper. **5** See **Furies. 6 like fury.** *Inf.* violently; furiously. [C14: from L, from *furere* to be furious]

furze (fɜːz) *n* another name for **gorse.** [OE *fyrs*]
▸ **'furzy** *adj*

fuscous ('fʌskəs) *adj* of a brownish-grey colour. [C17: from L *fuscus* dark, swarthy, tawny]

fuse[1] *or chiefly US* **fuze** (fjuːz) *n* **1** a lead of combustible black powder (**safety fuse**), or a lead containing an explosive (**detonating fuse**), used to fire an explosive charge. **2** any device by which an explosive charge is ignited. ◆ *vb* **fuses, fusing, fused** *or chiefly US* **fuzes, fuzing, fuzed. 3** (*tr*) to equip with such a fuse. [C17: from It. *fuso* spindle, from L *fūsus*]
▸ **'fuseless** *adj*

fuse[2] ⓣ (fjuːz) *vb* **fuses, fusing, fused. 1** to unite or become united by melting, esp. by the action of heat. **2** to become or cause to become liquid, esp. by the action of heat. **3** to join or become combined. **4** (*tr*) to equip (a plug, etc.) with a fuse. **5** *Brit.* to fail or cause to fail as a result of the blowing of a fuse: *the lights fused.* ◆ *n* **6** a protective device for safeguarding electric circuits, etc., containing a wire that melts and breaks the circuit when the current exceeds a certain value. [C17: from L *fūsus* melted, cast, from *fundere* to pour out; sense 5 infl. by FUSE[1]]

fusee *or* **fuzee** (fjuː'ziː) *n* **1** (in early clocks and watches) a spirally grooved spindle, functioning as an equalizing force on the unwinding of the mainspring. **2** a friction match with a large head. [C16: from F *fusée* spindleful of thread, from OF *fus* spindle, from L *fūsus*]

fuselage ('fjuːzɪˌlɑːʒ) *n* the main body of an aircraft. [C20: from F, from *fuseler* to shape like a spindle, from OF *fusel* spindle]

fusel oil *or* **fusel** ('fjuːzᵊl) *n* a poisonous by-product formed in the distillation of fermented liquors and used as a source of amyl alcohols. [C19: from G *Fusel* bad spirits]

fusible ('fjuːzəbᵊl) *adj* capable of being fused or melted.
▸ **ˌfusi'bility** *n* ▸ **'fusibly** *adv*

fusiform ('fjuːzɪˌfɔːm) *adj* elongated and tapering at both ends. [C18: from L *fūsus* spindle]

fusil ('fjuːzɪl) *n* a light flintlock musket. [C16 (in the sense: steel for a tinderbox): from OF, from Vulgar L *focīlis* (unattested), from L *focus* fire]

fusilier (ˌfjuːzɪ'lɪə) *n* **1** (formerly) an infantryman armed with a light musket. **2** Also: **fusileer. 2a** a soldier, esp. a private, serving in any of certain British or other infantry regiments. **2b** (*pl; cap. when part of a name*)*: the Royal Welch Fusiliers.* [C17: from F; see FUSIL]

fusillade ⓣ (ˌfjuːzɪ'leɪd) *n* **1** a rapid continual discharge of firearms. **2** a sudden outburst, as of criticism. ◆ *vb* **fusillades, fusillading, fusilladed. 3** (*tr*) to attack with a fusillade. [C19: from F, from *fusiller* to shoot; see FUSIL]

fusion ⓣ ('fjuːʒən) *n* **1** the act or process of fusing or melting together. **2** the state of being fused. **3** something produced by fusing. **4** a kind of popular music that is a blend of two or more styles, such as jazz and funk. **5** See **nuclear fusion. 6** a coalition of political parties. [C16: from L *fūsiō* a pouring out, melting, from *fundere* to pour out, FOUND[3]]

fusion bomb *n* a type of bomb in which most of the energy is provided by nuclear fusion. Also called: **thermonuclear bomb, fission-fusion bomb.**

fuss ⓣ (fʌs) *n* **1** nervous activity or agitation, esp. when unnecessary. **2** complaint or objection: *he made a fuss over the bill.* **3** an exhibition of affection or admiration: *they made a great fuss over the new baby.* **4** a quarrel. ◆ *vb* **5** (*intr*) to worry unnecessarily. **6** (*intr*) to be excessively concerned over trifles. **7** (when *intr*, usually foll. by *over*) to show great or excessive concern, affection, etc. (for). **8** (*tr*) to bother (a person). [C18: from ?]
▸ **'fusser** *n*

fusspot ⓣ ('fʌsˌpɒt) *n Brit. inf.* a person who fusses unnecessarily.

fussy ⓣ ('fʌsɪ) *adj* **fussier, fussiest. 1** inclined to fuss over minor points. **2** very particular about detail. **3** characterized by overelaborate detail.
▸ **'fussily** *adv* ▸ **'fussiness** *n*

fustanella (ˌfʌstə'nɛlə) *n* a white knee-length pleated skirt worn by men in Greece and Albania. [C19: from It., from Mod. Gk *phoustani*, prob. from It. *fustagno* FUSTIAN]

fustian ('fʌstɪən) *n* **1a** a hard-wearing fabric of cotton mixed with flax or wool. **1b** (*as modifier*)*: a fustian jacket.* **2** pompous talk or writing. ◆ *adj* **3** cheap; worthless. **4** bombastic. [C12: from OF, from Med. L *fustāneum*, from L *fustis* cudgel]

fustic ('fʌstɪk) *n* **1** Also called: **old fustic.** a large tropical American tree. **2** the yellow dye obtained from the wood of this tree. **3** any of various trees or shrubs that yield a similar dye, esp. a European sumach (**young fustic**). [C15: from F *fustoc*, from Sp., from Ar. *fustuq*, from Gk *pistakē* pistachio tree]

fusty ⓣ ('fʌstɪ) *adj* **fustier, fustiest. 1** smelling of damp or mould. **2**

THESAURUS

burst, outcry, stir, to-do, uproar **2** = **craze**, enthusiasm, mania, rage

furrow *n* **1, 2** = **groove**, channel, corrugation, crease, crow's-foot, fluting, hollow, line, rut, seam, trench, wrinkle ◆ *vb* **3** = **wrinkle**, corrugate, crease, draw together, flute, knit, seam

further *adv* **1** = **in addition**, additionally, also, as well as, besides, furthermore, into the bargain, moreover, on top of, over and above, to boot, what's more, yet ◆ *adj* **5** = **additional**, extra, fresh, more, new, other, supplementary ◆ *vb* **7** = **promote**, advance, aid, assist, champion, contribute to, encourage, expedite, facilitate, forward, foster, hasten, help, lend support to, patronize, pave the way for, plug (*inf.*), push, speed, succour, work for
Antonyms *vb* ≠ **promote:** foil, frustrate, hinder, hobble, impede, obstruct, oppose, prevent, retard, stop, thwart

furtherance *n* **1** = **promotion**, advancement, advocacy, backing, boosting, carrying-out, championship, prosecution, pursuit

furthermore *adv* = **besides**, additionally, as well, further, in addition, into the bargain, moreover, not to mention, to boot, too, what's more

furthest *adj* **3** = **most distant**, extreme, farthest, furthermost, outermost, outmost, remotest, ultimate, uttermost

furtive *adj* = **sly**, behind someone's back, clandestine, cloaked, conspiratorial, covert, hidden, secret, secretive, skulking, slinking, sneaking, sneaky, stealthy, surreptitious, underhand, under-the-table
Antonyms *adj* above-board, candid, forthright, frank, open, public, straightforward, undisguised, unreserved

fury *n* **1** = **anger**, frenzy, impetuosity, ire, madness, passion, rage, red mist (*inf.*), wrath **3** = **violence**, ferocity, fierceness, force, intensity, power, savagery, severity, tempestuousness, turbulence, vehemence **4** = **spitfire**, bacchante, hag, hellcat, shrew, termagant, virago, vixen
Antonyms *n* ≠ **anger:** calm, calmness, composure, equanimity ≠ **violence:** hush, peace, peacefulness, serenity, stillness, tranquillity

fuse[2] *vb* **1-3** = **join**, agglutinate, amalgamate, blend, coalesce, combine, commingle, dissolve, federate, integrate, intermingle, intermix, meld, melt, merge, run together, smelt, solder, unite, weld
Antonyms *vb* diffuse, dispense, disseminate, dissipate, disunite, scatter, separate, spread, strew

fusillade *n* **1, 2** = **barrage**, broadside, burst, fire, hail, outburst, salvo, volley

fusion *n* **1-3** = **merging**, alloy, amalgam, amalgamation, blend, blending, coalescence, commingling, commixture, federation, integration, liquefaction, meld, merger, mixture, smelting, synthesis, union, uniting, welding

fuss *n* **1** = **bother**, ado, agitation, bustle, commotion, confusion, excitement, fidget, flap (*inf.*), flurry, fluster, flutter, hue and cry, hurry, palaver, pother, stir, storm in a teacup (*Brit.*), to-do, upset, worry **2** = **argument**, altercation, bother, complaint, difficulty, display, furore, hassle (*inf.*), objection, row, squabble, trouble, unrest, upset ◆ *vb* **5** = **worry**, bustle, chafe, fidget, flap (*inf.*), fret, fume, get in a stew (*inf.*), get worked up, labour over, make a meal of (*inf.*), make a thing of (*inf.*), niggle, take pains

fusspot *n Brit. informal* = **perfectionist**, fidget, old woman, worrier

fussy *adj* **1, 2** = **particular**, choosy (*inf.*), dainty, difficult, discriminating, exacting, faddish, faddy, fastidious, finicky, hard to please, nit-picking (*inf.*), old-maidish, old womanish, overparticular, pernickety, picky (*inf.*), squeamish **3** = **overelaborate**, busy, cluttered, overdecorated, overembellished, overworked, rococo

fustiness *n* **1** = **staleness**, airlessness, damp-

old-fashioned in attitude. [C14: from *fust* wine cask, from OF: cask, from L *fūstis* cudgel]
▸ **'fustily** *adv* ▸ **'fustiness** *n*

fut. *abbrev. for* future.

futhark ('fu:θɑ:k) *or* **futhorc, futhork** ('fu:θɔ:k) *n* a phonetic alphabet consisting of runes. [C19: from the first six letters: *f, u, th, a, r, k*]

futile ❶ ('fju:taɪl) *adj* **1** having no effective result; unsuccessful. **2** pointless; trifling. **3** inane or foolish. [C16: from L *futtilis* pouring out easily, from *fundere* to pour out]
▸ **'futilely** *adv* ▸ **futility** (fju:'tɪlɪtɪ) *n*

futon ('fu:ˌtɒn) *n* a Japanese padded quilt, laid on the floor as a bed. [C19: from Japanese]

futtock ('fʌtək) *n Naut.* one of the ribs in the frame of a wooden vessel. [C13: ? var. of *foothook*]

future ❶ ('fju:tʃə) *n* **1** the time yet to come. **2** undetermined events that will occur in that time. **3** the condition of a person or thing at a later date: *the future of the school is undecided.* **4** likelihood of later improvement: *he has a future as a singer.* **5** *Grammar.* **5a** a tense of verbs used when the action or event described is to occur after the time of utterance. **5b** a verb in this tense. **6 in future.** from now on. ◆ *adj* **7** that is yet to come or be. **8** of or expressing time yet to come. **9** (*prenominal*) destined to become. **10** *Grammar.* in or denoting the future as a tense of verbs. ◆ See also **futures.** [C14: from L *fūtūrus* about to be, from *esse* to be]
▸ **'futureless** *adj*

future perfect *Grammar.* ◆ *adj* **1** denoting a tense of verbs describing an action that will have been performed by a certain time. ◆ *n* **2a** the future perfect tense. **2b** a verb in this tense.

futures ('fju:tʃəz) *pl n* **a** commodities or other financial products bought or sold at an agreed price for delivery at a specified future date. See also **financial futures. b** (*as modifier*): *futures contract; futures market.*

future value *n* the value that a sum of money invested at compound interest will have after a specified period.

futurism ('fju:tʃəˌrɪzəm) *n* an artistic movement that arose in Italy in 1909 to replace traditional aesthetic values with the characteristics of the machine age.
▸ **'futurist** *n, adj*

futuristic (ˌfju:tʃə'rɪstɪk) *adj* **1** denoting or relating to design, etc., that is thought likely to be fashionable at some future time. **2** of or relating to futurism.
▸ **ˌfutur'istically** *adv*

futurity (fju:'tjʊərɪtɪ) *n, pl* **futurities. 1** a less common word for **future. 2** the quality of being in the future. **3** a future event.

futurology (ˌfju:tʃə'rɒlədʒɪ) *n* the study or prediction of the future of mankind.
▸ **ˌfutur'ologist** *n*

fuze (fju:z) *n, vb* **fuzes, fuzing, fuzed.** *Chiefly US.* a variant spelling of **fuse**[1].

fuzee (fju:'zi:) *n* a variant spelling of **fusee.**

fuzz[1] ❶ (fʌz) *n* **1** a mass or covering of fine or curly hairs, fibres, etc. **2** a blur. ◆ *vb* **3** to make or become fuzzy. **4** to make or become indistinct. [C17: ?from Low G *fussig* loose]

fuzz[2] (fʌz) *n* a slang word for **police** or **policeman.** [C20: from ?]

fuzzy ❶ ('fʌzɪ) *adj* **fuzzier, fuzziest. 1** of, resembling, or covered with fuzz. **2** unclear or distorted. **3** (of the hair) tightly curled or very wavy.
▸ **'fuzzily** *adv* ▸ **'fuzziness** *n*

fuzzy logic *n* a branch of logic that allows degrees of imprecision in reasoning and knowledge to be represented in such a way that the information can be processed by computer.

fuzzy-wuzzy ('fʌzɪˌwʌzɪ) *n, pl* **fuzzy-wuzzies.** *Offens. arch. sl.* a Black fuzzy-haired native of any of various countries.

fwd *abbrev. for* forward.

f-word *n* **the.** (*sometimes cap.*) a euphemistic way of referring to the word **fuck.** [from F(UCK) + WORD]

FX *n Films, inf.* short for **special effects.** [C20: a phonetic respelling of EFFECTS]

-fy *suffix forming verbs.* to make or become: *beautify.* [from OF *-fier,* from L *-ficāre,* from *-ficus* -FIC]

fylfot ('faɪlfɒt) *n* a rare word for **swastika.** [C16 (apparently meaning: a sign or device for the lower part or foot of a painted window): from *fillen* to fill + *fot* foot]

THESAURUS

ness, frowstiness, fug, mouldiness, mustiness, smell of decay, stuffiness

fusty *adj* **1** = **stale**, airless, damp, frowsty, ill-smelling, malodorous, mildewed, mildewy, mouldering, mouldy, musty, rank, stuffy **2** = **old-fashioned**, antediluvian, antiquated, archaic, old-fogeyish, outdated, out-of-date, out of the ark (*inf.*), passé

futile *adj* **1** = **useless**, abortive, barren, bootless, empty, forlorn, fruitless, hollow, ineffectual, in vain, nugatory, otiose, profitless, sterile, to no avail, unavailing, unproductive, unprofitable, unsuccessful, vain, valueless, without rhyme or reason, worthless **2** = **trivial**, idle, pointless, trifling, unimportant
Antonyms *adj* ≠ **useless:** constructive, effective, fruitful, profitable, purposeful, successful, useful, valuable, worthwhile ≠ **trivial:** important, significant

futility *n* **1** = **uselessness**, bootlessness, emptiness, fruitlessness, hollowness, ineffectiveness, spitting in the wind **2** = **triviality**, pointlessness, unimportance, vanity

future *n* **1** = **time to come**, hereafter **3** = **prospect**, expectation, outlook ◆ *adj* **7, 9** = **forthcoming**, approaching, coming, destined, eventual, expected, fated, impending, in the offing, later, prospective, subsequent, to be, to come, ultimate, unborn
Antonyms *adj* ≠ **forthcoming:** bygone, erstwhile, ex-, former, late, past, preceding, previous, quondam

fuzz[1] *n* **1** = **fluff**, down, fibre, floss, hair, lint, nap, pile

fuzzy *adj* **1** = **fluffy**, down-covered, downy, flossy, frizzy, linty, napped, woolly **2** = **indistinct**, bleary, blurred, distorted, faint, ill-defined, muffled, out of focus, shadowy, unclear, unfocused, vague
Antonyms *adj* ≠ **indistinct:** clear, defined, detailed, distinct, in focus, precise

Gg

g *or* **G** (dʒiː) *n, pl* **g's, G's,** *or* **Gs. 1** the seventh letter of the English alphabet. **2** a speech sound represented by this letter, usually either as in *grass*, or as in *page*.

g *symbol for:* **1** gallon(s). **2** gram(s). **3** grav. **4** acceleration of free fall (due to gravity).

G *symbol for:* **1** *Music.* **1a** the fifth note of the scale of C major. **1b** the major or minor key having this note as its tonic. **2** gauss. **3** gravitational constant. **4** *Physics.* conductance. **5** *Biochem.* guanine. **6** German. **7** giga. **8** good. **9** *Sl., chiefly US.* grand (a thousand dollars or pounds). **10** (in Australia) **10a** general exhibition (used to describe a category of film certified as suitable for viewing by anyone). **10b** (*as modifier*): *a G film.*

G. *or* **g.** *abbrev. for:* **1** gauges. **2** gelding. **3** guilder(s). **4** guinea(s). **5** Gulf.

G3 *abbrev. for* Group of Three.

G5 *abbrev. for* Group of Five.

G7 *abbrev. for* Group of Seven.

G10 *abbrev. for* Group of Ten.

G24 *abbrev. for* Group of Twenty-Four.

G77 *abbrev. for* Group of Seventy-Seven.

Ga *the chemical symbol for* gallium.

GA *abbrev. for:* **1** General Assembly (of the United Nations). **2** general average. **3** Georgia.

gab Ⓣ (gæb) *Inf.* ◆ *vb* **gabs, gabbing, gabbed. 1** (*intr*) to talk excessively or idly; gossip. ◆ *n* **2** idle or trivial talk. **3 gift of the gab.** ability to speak glibly or persuasively. [C18: prob. from Irish Gaelic *gob* mouth]
▸ **'gabber** *n*

gabardine *or* **gaberdine** ('gæbəˌdiːn, ˌgæbə'diːn) *n* **1** a twill-weave worsted, cotton, or spun-rayon fabric. **2** an ankle-length loose coat or frock worn by men, esp. by Jews, in the Middle Ages. **3** any of various other garments made of gabardine, esp. a child's raincoat. [C16: from OF *gauvardine* pilgrim's garment, from MHG *wallewart* pilgrimage]

gabble Ⓣ ('gæbᵊl) *vb* **gabbles, gabbling, gabbled. 1** to utter (words, etc.) rapidly and indistinctly; jabber. **2** (*intr*) (of geese, etc.) to utter rapid cackling noises. ◆ *n* **3** rapid and indistinct speech or noises. [C17: from MDu. *gabbelen,* imit.]
▸ **'gabbler** *n*

gabbro ('gæbrəʊ) *n, pl* **gabbros.** a dark coarse-grained igneous rock consisting of feldspar, pyroxene, and often olivine. [C19: from It., prob. from L *glaber* smooth, bald]

gabby Ⓣ ('gæbɪ) *adj* **gabbier, gabbiest.** *Inf.* inclined to chatter; talkative.

gabfest ('gæbˌfɛst) *n Inf., chiefly US & Canad.* **1** prolonged gossiping or conversation. **2** an informal gathering for conversation. [C19: from GAB + FEST]

gabion ('geɪbɪən) *n* **1** a cylindrical metal container filled with stones, used in the construction of underwater foundations. **2** a wickerwork basket filled with stones or earth, used (esp. formerly) as part of a fortification. [C16: from F: basket, from It., from *gabbia* cage, from L *cavea;* see CAGE]

gable ('geɪbᵊl) *n* **1** the triangular upper part of a wall between the sloping ends of a pitched roof (**gable roof**). **2** a triangular ornamental feature, esp. as used over a door or window. [C14: OF, prob. from ON *gafl*]
▸ **'gabled** *adj*

gable end *n* the end wall of a building on the side which is topped by a gable.

gaboon (gə'buːn) *n* a dark mahogany-like wood from an African tree, used in plywood, for furniture, and as a veneer. [C20: altered from *Gabon*]

gaboon viper *n* a large venomous viper of African rainforests. It has brown and purple markings and hornlike projections on its snout.

gaby ('geɪbɪ) *n, pl* **gabies.** *Arch. or dialect.* a simpleton. [C18: from ?]

gad Ⓣ (gæd) *vb* **gads, gadding, gadded. 1** (*intr;* often foll. by *about* or *around*) to go out in search of pleasure; gallivant. ◆ *n* **2** carefree adventure (esp. in **on the gad**). [C15: back formation from obs. *gadling* companion, from OE, from *gæd* fellowship]
▸ **'gadder** *n*

gadabout Ⓣ ('gædəˌbaʊt) *n Inf.* a person who restlessly seeks amusement, etc.

Gadarene ('gædəˌriːn) *adj* relating to or engaged in a headlong rush. [C19: via LL from Gk *Gadarēnos,* of Gadara (Palestine), alluding to the Gadarene swine (Matthew 8:28ff.)]

gadfly ('gædˌflaɪ) *n, pl* **gadflies. 1** any of various large dipterous flies, esp. the horsefly, that annoy livestock by sucking their blood. **2** a constantly irritating person. [C16: from *gad* sting + FLY[2]]

gadget Ⓣ ('gædʒɪt) *n* **1** a small mechanical device or appliance. **2** any object that is interesting for its ingenuity. [C19: ?from F *gâchette* lock catch, dim. of *gâche* staple]

gadgetry ('gædʒɪtrɪ) *n* **1** gadgets collectively. **2** use of or preoccupation with gadgets.

gadoid ('geɪdɔɪd) *adj* **1** of or belonging to an order of marine soft-finned fishes typically having the pectoral and pelvic fins close together and small cycloid scales. The group includes cod and hake. ◆ *n* **2** any gadoid fish. [C19: from NL *Gadidae,* from *gadus* cod; see -OID]

gadolinium (ˌgædə'lɪnɪəm) *n* a ductile malleable silvery-white ferromagnetic element of the lanthanide series of metals. Symbol: Gd; atomic no.: 64; atomic wt.: 157.25. [C19: NL, after Johan *Gadolin* (1760–1852), Finnish mineralogist]

gadroon *or* **godroon** (gə'druːn) *n* a decorative moulding composed of a series of convex flutes and curves, used esp. as an edge to silver articles. [C18: from F *godron,* ?from OF *godet* cup, goblet]

gadwall ('gædˌwɔːl) *n, pl* **gadwalls** *or* **gadwall.** a duck related to the mallard. The male has a grey body and black tail. [C17: from ?]

gadzooks (gæd'zuːks) *interj Arch.* a mild oath. [C17: ?from *God's hooks* (the nails of the cross) from *Gad* arch. euphemism for God]

Gael (geɪl) *n* a person who speaks a Gaelic language, esp. a Highland Scot or an Irishman. [C19: from Gaelic *Gaidheal*]
▸ **'Gaeldom** *n*

Gaelic ('geɪlɪk, 'gæ-) *n* **1** any of the closely related languages of the Celts in Ireland, Scotland, or the Isle of Man. ◆ *adj* **2** of, denoting, or relating to the Celtic people of Ireland, Scotland, or the Isle of Man or their language or customs.

Gaelic coffee *n* another name for **Irish coffee.**

Gaeltacht ('geːltəxt) *n* any of the regions in Ireland in which Irish Gaelic is the vernacular speech. [C20: from Irish Gaelic]

gaff[1] (gæf) *n* **1** *Angling.* a stiff pole with a stout prong or hook attached for landing large fish. **2** *Naut.* a boom hoisted aft of a mast to support a fore-and-aft sail. **3** a metal spur fixed to the leg of a gamecock. ◆ *vb* **4** (*tr*) *Angling.* to hook or land (a fish) with a gaff. [C13: from F *gaffe,* from Provençal *gaf* boat hook]

gaff[2] (gæf) *n* **1** *Sl.* nonsense. **2 blow the gaff.** *Brit. sl.* to divulge a secret. [C19: from ?]

gaffe Ⓣ (gæf) *n* a social blunder, esp. a tactless remark. [C19: from F]

gaffer Ⓣ ('gæfə) *n* **1** an old man: often used affectionately or patronizingly. **2** *Inf., chiefly Brit.* a boss, foreman, or owner of a factory, etc. **3** *Inf.* the senior electrician on a television or film set. [C16: from GODFATHER]

gag[1] Ⓣ (gæg) *vb* **gags, gagging, gagged. 1** (*tr*) to stop up (a person's mouth), esp. with a piece of cloth, etc., to prevent him from speaking or crying out. **2** (*tr*) to suppress or censor (free expression, information, etc.). **3** to retch or cause to retch. **4** (*intr*) to struggle for breath; choke. ◆ *n* **5** a piece of cloth, rope, etc., stuffed into or tied across the mouth. **6** any restraint on or suppression of information, free speech, etc. **7** *Parliamentary procedure.* another word for **closure** (sense 4). [C15 *gaggen;* ? imit. of a gasping sound]

gag[2] Ⓣ (gæg) *Inf.* ◆ *n* **1** a joke or humorous story, esp. one told by a professional comedian. **2** a hoax, practical joke, etc. ◆ *vb* **gags, gagging, gagged. 3** (*intr*) to tell jokes or funny stories, as comedians in nightclubs, etc. [C19: ? special use of GAG[1]]

gaga ('gɑːgɑː) *adj Inf.* **1** senile; doting. **2** slightly crazy. [C20: from F, imit.]

gage[1] (geɪdʒ) *n* **1** something deposited as security against the fulfilment of an obligation; pledge. **2** (formerly) a glove or other object thrown down to indicate a challenge to combat. ◆ *vb* **gages, gaging,**

THESAURUS

gab *vb* **1** = **chatter,** babble, blabber, blather, buzz, chew the fat *or* rag (*sl.*), gossip, jabber, jaw (*sl.*), prattle, rabbit (*Brit. inf.*), spout, talk, waffle (*inf., chiefly Brit.*), yak (*sl.*) ◆ *n* **2** = **chatter,** blab, blarney, blather, chat, chitchat, conversation, gossip, loquacity, palaver, small talk, talk, tête-à-tête, tittle-tattle, tongue-wagging, waffle (*inf., chiefly Brit.*)

gabble *vb* **1** = **prattle,** babble, blab, blabber, cackle, chatter, gaggle, gibber, gush, jabber, rabbit (*Brit. inf.*), rattle, splutter, spout, sputter, waffle (*inf., chiefly Brit.*) ◆ *n* **3** = **gibberish,** babble, blabber, cackling, chatter, drivel, jargon, pap, prattle, twaddle, waffle (*inf., chiefly Brit.*)

gabby *adj* = **talkative,** chatty, effusive, garrulous, glib, gossiping, gushing, long-winded, loquacious, mouthy, prattling, prolix, verbose, voluble, windy, wordy

gad *vb* **1** *with* **about** *or* **around** = **gallivant,** ramble, range, roam, rove, run around, stravaig (*Scot. & N English dialect*), stray, traipse (*inf.*), wander

gadabout *n* = **pleasure-seeker,** gallivanter, rambler, rover, wanderer

gadget *n* **1** = **device,** appliance, contraption, contrivance, gimmick, gizmo (*sl., chiefly US*), instrument, invention, novelty, thing, tool, waldo

gaffe *n* = **blunder,** bloomer (*inf.*), boob (*Brit. sl.*), boo-boo (*inf.*), clanger (*inf.*), faux pas, gaucherie, howler, indiscretion, lapse, mistake, slip, solecism

gaffer *n* **1** = **old man,** granddad, greybeard, old boy, old fellow, old-timer (*US*) **2** *Informal* = **manager,** boss (*inf.*), foreman, ganger, overseer, superintendent, supervisor

gag[1] *vb* **1, 2** = **suppress,** curb, muffle, muzzle, quiet, silence, stifle, still, stop up, throttle **3** = **retch,** barf (*sl.*), disgorge, heave, puke (*sl.*), spew, throw up (*inf.*), vomit **4** = **choke,** gasp, pant, struggle for breath

gag[2] *n* **1, 2** = **joke,** crack, funny (*inf.*), hoax, jest, wisecrack (*inf.*), witticism

gaged. 3 (*tr*) *Arch.* to stake, pledge, or wager. [C14: from OF, of Gmc origin]

gage[2] (geɪdʒ) *n* short for **greengage.**

gage[3] (geɪdʒ) *n, vb* **gages, gaging, gaged.** *US.* a variant spelling (esp. in technical senses) of **gauge.**

gaggle ('gægᵊl) *vb* **gaggles, gaggling, gaggled. 1** (*intr*) (of geese) to cackle. ◆ *n* **2** a flock of geese. **3** *Inf.* a disorderly group of people. [C14: of Gmc origin; imit.]

Gaia hypothesis *or* **theory** ('gaɪə) *n* the theory that the earth and everything on it constitutes a single self-regulating living entity. [C20: *Gaia,* variant of *Gaea,* Gk goddess of the earth]

gaiety ➊ ('geɪətɪ) *n, pl* **gaieties. 1** the state or condition of being merry, bright, or lively. **2** festivity; merrymaking. **3** bright appearance.

USAGE NOTE See at **gay.**

gaillardia (geɪ'lɑːdɪə) *n* a plant of the composite family having ornamental flower heads with yellow or red rays and purple discs. [C19: from NL, after *Gaillard* de Marentonneau, 18th-cent. F amateur botanist]

gaily ➊ ('geɪlɪ) *adv* **1** in a gay manner; merrily. **2** with bright colours; showily.

gain ➊ (geɪn) *vb* **1** (*tr*) to acquire (something desirable); obtain. **2** (*tr*) to win in competition: *to gain the victory.* **3** to increase, improve, or advance: *the car gained speed.* **4** (*tr*) to earn (a wage, living, etc.). **5** (*intr; usually foll. by on or upon*) **5a** to get nearer (to) or catch up (on). **5b** to get farther away (from). **6** (*tr*) (esp. of ships) to get to; reach: *the steamer gained port.* **7** (of a timepiece) to operate too fast, so as to indicate a time ahead of the true time. ◆ *n* **8** something won, acquired, earned, etc.; profit; advantage. **9** an increase in size, amount, etc. **10** the act of gaining; attainment; acquisition. **11** Also called: **amplification.** *Electronics.* the ratio of the output signal of an amplifier to the input signal, usually measured in decibels. [C15: from OF *gaaignier,* of Gmc origin]

gainer ('geɪnə) *n* **1** a person or thing that gains. **2** a type of dive in which the diver leaves the board facing forward and completes a full backward somersault to enter the water feet first with his back to the diving board.

gainful ➊ ('geɪnfʊl) *adj* profitable; lucrative.
▸ **'gainfully** *adv* ▸ **'gainfulness** *n*

gainsay ➊ (geɪn'seɪ) *vb* **gainsays, gainsaying, gainsaid.** (*tr*) *Arch. or literary.* to deny (an allegation, statement, etc.); contradict. [C13 *gainsaien,* from *gain-* AGAINST + *saien* to SAY]
▸ **gain'sayer** *n*

'gainst *or* **gainst** (genst, geɪnst) *prep Poetic.* short for **against.**

gait ➊ (geɪt) *n* **1** manner of walking or running. **2** (used esp. of horses and dogs) the pattern of footsteps at a particular speed, as the walk, canter, etc. ◆ *vb* **3** (*tr*) to teach (a horse) a particular gait. [C16: var. of GATE]

gaiter ('geɪtə) *n* (*often pl*) **1** a cloth or leather covering for the leg or ankle. **2** Also called: **spat.** a similar covering extending from the ankle to the instep. [C18: from F *guêtre,* prob. of Gmc origin]

gal (gæl) *n Sl.* a girl.

gal. *or* **gall.** *abbrev. for* gallon.

Gal. *Bible. abbrev. for* Galatians.

gala ➊ ('gɑːlə, 'geɪlə) *n* **1a** a celebration; festive occasion. **1b** (*as modifier*): *a gala occasion.* **2** *Chiefly Brit.* a sporting occasion involving competitions in several events: *a swimming gala.* [C17: from F or It., from OF *gale,* from *galer* to make merry, prob. of Gmc origin]

galactic (gə'læktɪk) *adj* **1** *Astron.* of or relating to a galaxy, esp. the Galaxy. **2 galactic plane.** the plane passing through the spiral arms of the Galaxy, contained by the great circle of the celestial sphere (**galactic equator**) and perpendicular to an imaginary line joining opposite points (**galactic poles**) on the celestial sphere. **3** *Med.* of or relating to milk. [C19: from Gk *galaktikos;* see GALAXY]

galactic halo *n Astron.* a spheroidal aggregation of globular clusters, individual stars, dust, and gas that surrounds the Galaxy.

galago (gə'lɑːgəʊ) *n, pl* **galagos.** another name for **bushbaby.** [C19: from NL, ?from Wolof *golokh* monkey]

galah (gə'lɑː) *n* **1** an Australian cockatoo, having grey wings, back, and crest, and a pink body. **2** *Austral. sl.* a fool or simpleton. [C19: from Abor.]

Galahad ('gælə,hæd) *n* **1 Sir.** (in Arthurian legend) the most virtuous knight of the Round Table. **2** a pure or noble man.

galantine ('gælən,tiːn) *n* a cold dish of meat or poultry, which is boned, cooked, then pressed and glazed. [C14: from OF, from Med. L *galatina,* prob. from L *gelātus* frozen, set]

galaxy ('gæləksɪ) *n, pl* **galaxies. 1** any of a vast number of star systems held together by gravitational attraction. **2** a splendid gathering, esp. one of famous or distinguished people. [C14 (in the sense: the Milky Way): from Med. L *galaxia,* from L, from Gk, from *gala* milk]

Galaxy ('gæləksɪ) *n* **the.** the spiral galaxy that contains the solar system about three fifths of the distance from its centre. Also called: the **Milky Way System.**

galbanum ('gælbənəm) *n* a bitter aromatic gum resin extracted from any of several Asian umbelliferous plants. [C14: from L, from Gk, from Heb. *helbenāh*]

gale ➊ (geɪl) *n* **1** a strong wind, specifically one of force 8 on the Beaufort scale or from 39-46 mph. **2** (*often pl*) a loud outburst, esp. of laughter. **3** *Arch. & poetic.* a gentle breeze. [C16: from ?]

galea ('geɪlɪə) *n, pl* **galeae** (-lɪ,iː). a part shaped like a helmet, such as the petals of certain flowers. [C18: from L: helmet]
▸ **'gale,ate** *or* **'gale,ated** *adj*

galena (gə'liːnə) *or* **galenite** (gə'liːnaɪt) *n* a soft heavy bluish-grey or black mineral consisting of lead sulphide: the chief source of lead. Formula: PbS. [C17: from L: lead ore]

Galenic (geɪ'lɛnɪk, gə-) *adj* of or relating to Galen, 2nd-century Greek physician, or his teachings or methods.

Galilean[1] (,gælɪ'liːən) *n* **1** a native or inhabitant of Galilee. **2 the.** an epithet of Jesus Christ. ◆ *adj* **3** of Galilee.

Galilean[2] (,gælɪ'leɪən) *adj* of or relating to Galileo (1564–1642), It. astronomer and physicist.

galingale ('gælɪŋ,geɪl) *or* **galangal** (gə'læŋgᵊl) *n* a European plant with rough-edged leaves, reddish spikelets of flowers, and aromatic roots. [C13: from OF, from Ar., from Chinese]

galiot *or* **galliot** ('gælɪət) *n* **1** a small swift galley formerly sailed on the Mediterranean. **2** a ketch formerly used along the coasts of Germany and the Netherlands. [C14: from OF, from It., from Med. L *galea* GALLEY]

galipot ('gælɪ,pɒt) *n* a resin obtained from several species of pine. [C18: from F, from ?]

gall[1] ➊ (gɔːl) *n* **1** *Inf.* impudence. **2** bitterness; rancour. **3** something bitter or disagreeable. **4** *Physiol.* an obsolete term for **bile.** See also **gall bladder.** [from ON, replacing OE *gealla*]

gall[2] ➊ (gɔːl) *n* **1** a sore on the skin caused by chafing. **2** something that causes vexation or annoyance. **3** irritation; exasperation. ◆ *vb* **4** to abrade (the skin, etc.) as by rubbing. **5** (*tr*) to irritate or annoy; vex. [C14: of Gmc origin; rel. to OE *gealla* sore on a horse, & ? to GALL[1]]

gall[3] (gɔːl) *n* an abnormal outgrowth in plant tissue caused by certain parasitic insects, fungi, or bacteria. [C14: from OF, from L *galla*]

gall. *or* **gal.** *abbrev. for* gallon.

gallant ➊ *adj* ('gælənt). **1** brave and high-spirited; courageous and honourable: *a gallant warrior.* **2** (gə'lænt, 'gælənt). (of a man) attentive to women; chivalrous. **3** imposing; dignified; stately: *a gallant ship.* **4**

THESAURUS

gaiety *n* **1 = cheerfulness**, animation, blitheness, blithesomeness (*literary*), effervescence, elation, exhilaration, glee, good humour, high spirits, hilarity, *joie de vivre,* jollity, joviality, joyousness, light-heartedness, liveliness, merriment, mirth, sprightliness, vivacity **2 = merrymaking**, celebration, conviviality, festivity, fun, jollification, revelry, revels **3 = colour**, brightness, brilliance, colourfulness, gaudiness, glitter, show, showiness, sparkle
Antonyms *n* ≠ **cheerfulness:** despondency, gloom, melancholy, misery, sadness

gaily *adv* **1 = cheerfully**, blithely, gleefully, happily, joyfully, light-heartedly, merrily **2 = colourfully**, brightly, brilliantly, flamboyantly, flashily, gaudily, showily

gain *vb* **1, 2 = acquire**, achieve, attain, bag, bring in, capture, clear, collect, earn, gather, get, glean, harvest, land, make, net, obtain, procure, realize, reap, score (*sl.*), secure, win **3 = improve**, advance, build up, increase, pick up, profit **5a** *with* **on** *or* **upon = get nearer**, approach, catch up with, close, narrow the gap, overtake **6 = reach**, arrive at, attain, come to, get to ◆ *n* **8 = profit**, accretion, achievement, acquisition, advantage, attainment, benefit, dividend, earnings, emolument, headway, income, lucre, proceeds, produce, return, winnings, yield **9 = increase**, advance, advancement, growth, improvement, increment, progress, rise
Antonyms *vb* ≠ **acquire:** forfeit, lose ≠ **improve:** fail, worsen ◆ *n* ≠ **profit:** forfeiture, loss ≠ **increase:** damage, injury

gainful *adj* **= profitable**, advantageous, beneficial, expedient, fruitful, lucrative, money-making, paying, productive, remunerative, rewarding, useful, worthwhile

gainsay *vb* **= contradict**, contravene, controvert, deny, disaffirm, disagree with, dispute, rebut, retract
Antonyms *vb* agree with, back, confirm, support

gait *n* **1 = walk**, bearing, carriage, pace, step, stride, tread

gala *n* **1a = festival**, beano (*Brit. sl.*), carnival, celebration, festivity, fête, hooley *or* hoolie (*chiefly Irish & NZ*), jamboree, pageant, party, rave (*Brit. sl.*), rave-up (*Brit. sl.*) ◆ *modifier* **1b = festive**, celebratory, convivial, festal, gay, jovial, joyful, merry

gale *n* **1 = storm**, blast, cyclone, hurricane, squall, tempest, tornado, typhoon **2 = outburst**, burst, eruption, explosion, fit, howl, outbreak, paroxysm, peal, shout, shriek, storm

gall[1] *n* **1** *Informal* **= impudence**, brass neck (*Brit. inf.*), brazenness, cheek (*inf.*), chutzpah (*US & Canad. inf.*), effrontery, face (*inf.*), impertinence, insolence, neck (*inf.*), nerve (*inf.*) **2 = bitterness**, acrimony, animosity, animus, antipathy, bad blood, bile, enmity, hostility, malevolence, malice, malignity, rancour, sourness, spite, spleen, venom

gall[2] *n* **1 = sore**, abrasion, chafe, excoriation, raw spot, scrape, sore spot, wound **2, 3 = irritation**, aggravation (*inf.*), annoyance, bother, botheration (*inf.*), exasperation, harassment, irritant, nuisance, pest, provocation, vexation ◆ *vb* **4 = scrape**, abrade, bark, chafe, excoriate, fret, graze, irritate, rub raw, skin **5 = annoy**, aggravate (*inf.*), be on one's back (*sl.*), bother, exasperate, fret, get on one's nerves (*inf.*), harass, hassle (*inf.*), irk, irritate, nag, nark (*Brit., Austral., & NZ sl.*), nettle, peeve (*inf.*), pester, plague, provoke, rankle, rile (*inf.*), rub up the wrong way, ruffle, vex

gallant *adj* **1 = brave**, bold, courageous, daring, dashing, dauntless, doughty, fearless, game (*inf.*), heroic, high-spirited, honourable, intrepid, lion-hearted, manful, manly, mettlesome, noble, plucky, valiant, valorous **2 = courteous**, attentive, chivalrous, courtly, gentlemanly, gracious, magnanimous, noble,

Arch. showy in dress. ◆ *n* ('gælənt, gə'lænt). *Arch.* **5** a woman's lover or suitor. **6** a dashing or fashionable young man, esp. one who pursues women. **7** a brave, high-spirited, or adventurous man. ◆ *vb* (gə'lænt, 'gælənt). *Rare.* **8** (when *intr*, usually foll. by *with*) to court or flirt (with). [C15: from OF, from *galer* to make merry, from *gale* enjoyment, of Gmc origin]
▸ **'gallantly** *adv*

gallantry ❶ ('gæləntrɪ) *n, pl* **gallantries. 1** conspicuous courage, esp. in war. **2** polite attentiveness to women. **3** a gallant action, speech, etc.

gall bladder *n* a muscular sac, attached to the right lobe of the liver, that stores bile.

galleass ('gælɪˌæs) *n* a three-masted galley used as a warship in the Mediterranean from the 15th to the 18th centuries. [C16: from F, from It., from Med. L *galea* GALLEY]

galleon ('gælɪən) *n* a large sailing ship having three or more masts, used as a warship or trader from the 15th to the 18th centuries. [C16: from Sp. *galeón,* from F, from OF *galie* GALLEY]

gallery ('gælərɪ) *n, pl* **galleries. 1** a room or building for exhibiting works of art. **2** a covered passageway open on one side or on both sides. **3** a balcony running along or around the inside wall of a church, hall, etc. **4** *Theatre.* **4a** an upper floor that projects from the rear and contains the cheapest seats. **4b** the seats there. **4c** the audience seated there. **5** a long narrow room, esp. one used for a specific purpose: *a shooting gallery.* **6** an underground passage, as in a mine, etc. **7** a small ornamental railing, esp. one surrounding the top of a desk, table, etc. **8** any group of spectators, as at a golf match. **9** a glass-fronted soundproof room overlooking a television studio, used for lighting, etc. **10 play to the gallery.** to try to gain popular favour, esp. by crude appeals. [C15: from OF, from Med. L, prob. from *galilea* galilee, porch or chapel at entrance to medieval church]
▸ **'galleried** *adj*

galley ('gælɪ) *n* **1** any of various kinds of ship propelled by oars or sails used in ancient or medieval times. **2** the kitchen of a ship, boat, or aircraft. **3** any of various long rowing boats. **4** *Printing.* **4a** a tray for holding composed type. **4b** short for **galley proof.** [C13: from OF *galie,* from Med. L *galea,* from Gk *galaia,* from ?]

galley proof *n* a printer's proof, esp. one taken from type in a galley, used to make corrections before the matter has been split into pages. Often shortened to **galley.**

galley slave *n* **1** a criminal or slave condemned to row in a galley. **2** *Inf.* a drudge.

gallfly ('gɔːlˌflaɪ) *n, pl* **gallflies.** any of several small insects that produce galls in plant tissues.

galliard ('gæljəd) *n* **1** a spirited dance in triple time for two persons, popular in the 16th and 17th centuries. **2** a piece of music composed for or in the rhythm of this dance. [C14: from OF *gaillard* valiant, ? of Celtic origin]

Gallic ('gælɪk) *adj* **1** of or relating to France. **2** of or relating to ancient Gaul or the Gauls.

gallic acid *n* a colourless crystalline compound obtained from tannin: used as a tanning agent and in making inks and paper. [C18: from F *gallique;* see GALL[1]]

Gallicism ('gælɪˌsɪzəm) *n* a word or idiom borrowed from French.

Gallicize *or* **Gallicise** ('gælɪˌsaɪz) *vb* **Gallicizes, Gallicizing, Gallicized** *or* **Gallicises, Gallicising, Gallicised.** to make or become French in attitude, language, etc.

galligaskins (ˌgælɪ'gæskɪnz) *pl n* **1** loose wide breeches or hose, esp. as worn by men in the 17th century. **2** leather leggings, as worn in the 19th century. [C16: from obs. F, from It. *grechesco* Greek, from L *Graecus*]

gallimaufry (ˌgælɪ'mɔːfrɪ) *n, pl* **gallimaufries.** a jumble; hotchpotch. [C16: from F *galimafrée* ragout, hash, from ?]

gallinacean (ˌgælɪ'neɪʃən) *n* any gallinaceous bird.

gallinaceous (ˌgælɪ'neɪʃəs) *adj* of, relating to, or belonging to an order of birds, including domestic fowl, pheasants, grouse, etc., having a heavy rounded body, short bill, and strong legs. [C18: from L, from *gallīna* hen]

galling ❶ ('gɔːlɪŋ) *adj* irritating, exasperating, or bitterly humiliating.
▸ **'gallingly** *adv*

gallinule ('gælɪˌnjuːl) *n* any of various aquatic birds, typically having a dark plumage, red bill, and a red shield above the bill. [C18: from NL *Gallīnula,* from L *gallīna* hen]

galliot ('gælɪət) *n* a variant spelling of **galiot.**

gallipot ('gælɪˌpɒt) *n* a small earthenware pot used by pharmacists as a container for ointments, etc. [C16: prob. from GALLEY + POT[1]; because imported in galleys]

gallium ('gælɪəm) *n* a silvery metallic element that is liquid for a wide temperature range. It is used in high-temperature thermometers and low-melting alloys. **Gallium arsenide** is a semiconductor. Symbol: Ga; atomic no.: 31; atomic wt.: 69.72. [C19: from NL, from L *gallus* cock, translation of F *coq* in the name of its discoverer, *Lecoq* de Boisbaudran, 19th-cent. F chemist]

gallivant ❶ ('gælɪˌvænt) *vb* (*intr*) to go about in search of pleasure, etc.; gad about. [C19: ? whimsical from GALLANT]

galliwasp ('gælɪˌwɒsp) *n* a lizard of the Caribbean. [C18: from ?]

gallnut ('gɔːlˌnʌt) *or* **gall-apple** *n* a type of plant gall that resembles a nut.

Gallo- ('gæləʊ) *combining form.* denoting Gaul or France: *Gallo-Roman.* [from L *Gallus* a Gaul]

gallon ('gælən) *n* **1** Also called: **imperial gallon.** *Brit.* a unit of capacity equal to 277.42 cubic inches. 1 Brit. gallon is equivalent to 1.20 US gallons or 4.55 litres. **2** *US.* a unit of capacity equal to 231 cubic inches. 1 US gallon is equivalent to 0.83 imperial gallon or 3.79 litres. **3** (*pl*) *Inf.* great quantities. [C13: from ONorthern F *galon* (OF *jalon*), ? of Celtic origin]

gallonage ('gælənɪdʒ) *n* a capacity measured in gallons.

galloon (gə'luːn) *n* a narrow band of cord, embroidery, silver or gold braid, etc., used on clothes and furniture. [C17: from F, from OF *galonner* to trim with braid, from ?]

gallop ❶ ('gæləp) *vb* **gallops, galloping, galloped. 1** (*intr*) (of a horse or other quadruped) to run fast with a two-beat stride in which all four legs are off the ground at once. **2** to ride (a horse, etc.) at a gallop. **3** (*intr*) to move, read, progress, etc., rapidly. ◆ *n* **4** the fast two-beat gait of horses. **5** an instance of galloping. [C16: from OF *galoper,* from ?]
▸ **'galloper** *n*

gallows ('gæləʊz) *n, pl* **gallowses** *or* **gallows. 1** a wooden structure usually consisting of two upright posts with a crossbeam, used for hanging criminals. **2** any timber structure resembling this. **3 the gallows.** execution by hanging. [C13: from ON *galgi,* replacing OE *gealga*]

gallows bird *n Inf.* a person considered deserving of hanging.

gallows humour *n* sinister and ironic humour.

gallows tree *or* **gallow tree** *n* another name for **gallows** (sense 1).

gallsickness ('gɔːlˌsɪknɪs) *n* a disease of cattle and sheep, caused by infection with rickettsiae, resulting in anaemia and jaundice. Also called: **anaplasmosis.**

gallstone ('gɔːlˌstəʊn) *n* a small hard concretion formed in the gall bladder or its ducts.

Gallup Poll ('gæləp) *n* a sampling of the views of a representative cross section of the population, used esp. as a means of forecasting voting. [C20: after G. H. *Gallup* (1901–84), US statistician]

galluses ('gæləsɪz) *pl n Dialect.* braces for trousers. [C18: var. of *gallowses,* from GALLOWS (in the obs. sense: braces)]

gall wasp *n* any small solitary wasp that produces galls in plant tissue.

galoot *or* **galloot** (gə'luːt) *n Sl., chiefly US.* a clumsy or uncouth person. [C19: from ?]

galop ('gæləp) *n* **1** a 19th-century dance in quick duple time. **2** a piece of music for this dance. [C19: from F; see GALLOP]

galore ❶ (gə'lɔː) *determiner* (*immediately postpositive*) in great numbers or quantity: *there were daffodils galore in the park.* [C17: from Irish Gaelic *go leór* to sufficiency]

galoshes *or* **goloshes** (gə'lɒʃɪz) *pl n* (*sometimes sing*) a pair of waterproof overshoes. [C14 (in the sense: wooden shoe): from OF, from LL *gallicula* Gallic shoe]

galumph (gə'lʌmpf, -'lʌmf) *vb* (*intr*) *Inf.* to leap or move about clumsily or joyfully. [C19 (coined by Lewis Carroll): prob. a blend of GALLOP + TRIUMPH]

galvanic (gæl'vænɪk) *adj* **1** of, producing, or concerned with an electric current, esp. a direct current produced chemically. **2** *Inf.* resembling the effect of an electric shock; convulsive, startling, or energetic.
▸ **gal'vanically** *adv*

galvanism ('gælvəˌnɪzəm) *n* **1** *Obs.* electricity, esp. when produced by chemical means as in a cell or battery. **2** *Med.* treatment involving the application of electric currents to tissues. [C18: via F from It. *galvanismo,* after Luigi *Galvani* (1737–98), It. physiologist]

galvanize ❶ *or* **galvanise** ('gælvəˌnaɪz) *vb* **galvanizes, galvanizing, galvanized** *or* **galvanises, galvanising, galvanised.** (*tr*) **1** to stimulate to action; excite; startle. **2** to cover (iron, steel, etc.) with a protective zinc coating. **3** to stimulate by application of an electric current.
▸ **ˌgalvani'zation** *or* **ˌgalvani'sation** *n*

galvanized iron *or* **galvanised iron** *n Building trades.* iron, esp. a sheet of corrugated iron, covered with a protective coating of zinc.

THESAURUS

polite **3** = **elegant**, august, dignified, glorious, grand, imposing, lofty, magnificent, noble, splendid, stately ◆ *n* **6** = **ladies' man**, beau, blade (*arch.*), buck (*inf.*), dandy, fop, lady-killer (*inf.*), man about town, man of fashion
Antonyms *adj* ≠ **brave:** cowardly, fearful, ignoble ≠ **courteous:** churlish, discourteous, ill-mannered, impolite, rude

gallantry *n* **1** = **bravery**, audacity, boldness, courage, courageousness, daring, dauntlessness, derring-do (*arch.*), fearlessness, heroism, intrepidity, manliness, mettle, nerve, pluck, prowess, spirit, valiance, valour **2** = **courtesy**, attentiveness, chivalry, courteousness, courtliness, elegance, gentlemanliness, graciousness, nobility, politeness
Antonyms *n* ≠ **bravery:** cowardice, irresolution ≠ **courtesy:** churlishness, discourtesy, rudeness, ungraciousness

galling *adj* = **annoying**, aggravating (*inf.*), bitter, bothersome, exasperating, harassing, humiliating, irksome, irritating, nettlesome, plaguing, provoking, rankling, vexatious, vexing

gallivant *vb* = **wander**, gad about, ramble, range, roam, rove, run around, stravaig (*Scot. & N English dialect*), stray, traipse (*inf.*)

gallop *vb* **3** = **run**, barrel (along) (*inf., chiefly US & Canad.*), bolt, career, dart, dash, fly, hasten, hie (*arch.*), hurry, race, rush, scud, shoot, speed, sprint, tear along, zoom

galore *determiner* = **in abundance**, à gogo (*inf.*), all over the place, aplenty, everywhere, in great quantity, in numbers, in profusion, to spare

galvanize *vb* **1** = **stimulate**, arouse, awaken, electrify, excite, fire, inspire, invigorate, jolt,

galvano- *combining form.* indicating a galvanic current: *galvanometer.*
galvanometer (ˌgælvəˈnɒmɪtə) *n* any sensitive instrument for detecting or measuring small electric currents.
▸**galvanometric** (ˌgælvənəʊˈmɛtrɪk, gælˌvænəʊ-) *adj* ▸ˌ**galvaˈnometry** *n*
gam (gæm) *n Sl.* a leg. [C18: from F *jambe* leg]
gambier *or* **gambir** (ˈgæmbɪə) *n* an astringent resinous substance obtained from a tropical Asian plant: used as an astringent and tonic and in tanning. [C19: from Malay]
gambit (ˈgæmbɪt) *n* **1** *Chess.* an opening move in which a chessman, usually a pawn, is sacrificed to secure an advantageous position. **2** an opening comment, manoeuvre, etc., intended to secure an advantage. [C17: from F, from It. *gambetto* a tripping up, from *gamba* leg]
gamble **T** (ˈgæmbᵊl) *vb* **gambles, gambling, gambled. 1** (*intr*) to play games of chance to win money, etc. **2** to risk or bet (money, etc.) on the outcome of an event, sport, etc. **3** (*intr; often foll. by on*) to act with the expectation of: *to gamble on its being a sunny day.* **4** (often foll. by *away*) to lose by or as if by betting; squander. ◆ *n* **5** a risky act or venture. **6** a bet or wager. [C18: prob. var. of GAME[1]]
▸ˈ**gambler** *n* ▸ˈ**gambling** *n*
gamboge (gæmˈbəʊdʒ, -ˈbuːʒ) *n* **1a** a gum resin used as the source of a yellow pigment and as a purgative. **1b** the pigment made from this resin. **2 gamboge tree.** any of several tropical Asian trees that yield this resin. [C18: from NL *gambaugium,* from *Cambodia,* where first found]
gambol **T** (ˈgæmbᵊl) *vb* **gambols, gambolling, gambolled** *or US* **gambols, gamboling, gamboled. 1** (*intr*) to skip or jump about in a playful manner; frolic. ◆ *n* **2** a playful antic; frolic. [C16: from F *gambade;* see JAMB]
gambrel (ˈgæmbrəl) *n* **1** the hock of a horse or similar animal. **2** short for **gambrel roof.** [C16: from OF, from *gambe* leg]
gambrel roof *n* **1** *Chiefly Brit.* a hipped roof having a small gable at both ends. **2** *Chiefly US & Canad.* a roof having two slopes on both sides, the lower slopes being steeper than the upper.
game[1] **T** (geɪm) *n* **1** an amusement or pastime; diversion. **2** a contest with rules, the result being determined by skill, strength, or chance. **3** a single period of play in such a contest, sport, etc. **4** the score needed to win a contest. **5** a single contest in a series; match. **6** (*pl; often cap.*) an event consisting of various sporting contests, esp. in athletics: *Olympic Games.* **7** equipment needed for playing certain games. **8** short for **computer game. 9** style or ability in playing a game. **10** a scheme, proceeding, etc., practised like a game: *the game of politics.* **11** an activity undertaken in a spirit of levity; joke: *marriage is just a game to him.* **12a** wild animals, including birds and fish, hunted for sport, food, or profit. **12b** (*as modifier*): *game laws.* **13** the flesh of such animals, used as food. **14** an object of pursuit; quarry; prey (esp. in **fair game**). **15** *Inf.* work or occupation. **16** *Inf.* a trick, strategy, or device: *I can see through your little game.* **17** *Sl., chiefly Brit.* prostitution (esp. in **on the game**). **18 give the game away.** to reveal one's intentions or a secret. **19 make (a) game of.** to make fun of; ridicule; mock. **20 play the game.** to behave fairly or in accordance with the rules. **21 the game is up.** there is no longer a chance of success. ◆ *adj* **22** *Inf.* full of fighting spirit; plucky; brave. **23** (usually foll. by *for*) *Inf.* prepared or ready; willing: *I'm game for a try.* ◆ *vb* **games, gaming, gamed. 24** (*intr*) to play games of chance for money, stakes, etc.; gamble. [OE *gamen*]
▸ˈ**gamely** *adv* ▸ˈ**gameness** *n*
game[2] **T** (geɪm) *adj* a less common word for **lame** (esp. in **game leg**). [C18: prob. from Irish *cam* crooked]
gamecock (ˈgeɪmˌkɒk) *n* a cock bred and trained for fighting. Also called: **fighting cock.**
game fish *n* any fish providing sport for the angler.
gamekeeper (ˈgeɪmˌkiːpə) *n* a person employed to take care of game, as on an estate.
gamelan (ˈgæmɪˌlæn) *n* a type of percussion orchestra common in the East Indies. [from Javanese]
game laws *pl n* laws governing the hunting and preservation of game.
game plan *n* **1** a strategy. **2** a plan of campaign, esp. in politics.
game point *n Tennis, etc.* a stage at which winning one further point would enable one player or side to win a game.
gamesmanship (ˈgeɪmzmənˌʃɪp) *n Inf.* the art of winning games or defeating opponents by cunning practices without actually cheating.
gamesome (ˈgeɪmsəm) *adj* full of merriment; sportive.
▸ˈ**gamesomeness** *n*
gamester (ˈgeɪmstə) *n* a person who habitually plays games for money; gambler.
gametangium (ˌgæmɪˈtændʒɪəm) *n, pl* **gametangia** (-dʒɪə). *Biol.* an organ or cell in which gametes are produced, esp. in algae and fungi. [C19: NL, from GAMETO- + Gk *angeion* vessel]
gamete (ˈgæmiːt, gəˈmiːt) *n* a haploid germ cell that fuses with another during fertilization. [C19: from NL, from Gk *gametē* wife, from *gamos* marriage]
▸**gametic** (gəˈmɛtɪk) *adj*
gamete intrafallopian transfer (ˌɪntrəfəˈləʊpɪən) *n* See **GIFT.**
game theory *n* mathematical theory concerned with the optimum choice of strategy in situations involving a conflict of interest.
gameto- *or sometimes before a vowel* **gamet-** *combining form.* gamete: *gametophyte.*
gametophyte (gəˈmiːtəʊˌfaɪt) *n* the plant body, in species showing alternation of generations, that produces the gametes.
▸**gametophytic** (ˌgæmɪtəʊˈfɪtɪk) *adj*
gamey *or* **gamy** (ˈgeɪmɪ) *adj* **gamier, gamiest. 1** having the smell or flavour of game, esp. high game. **2** *Inf.* spirited; plucky; brave.
▸ˈ**gamily** *adv* ▸ˈ**gaminess** *n*
gamin **T** (ˈgæmɪn) *n* a street urchin. [from F]
gamine (ˈgæmiːn) *n* a slim and boyish girl or young woman; an elfish tomboy. [from F]
gaming (ˈgeɪmɪŋ) *n* **a** gambling on games of chance. **b** (*as modifier*): *gaming house.*
gamma (ˈgæmə) *n* **1** the third letter in the Greek alphabet (Γ, γ). **2** the third in a group or series. [C14: from Gk]
gamma distribution *n Statistics.* a continuous two-parameter distribution from which the chi-square and exponential distributions are derived.
gamma globulin *n* any of a group of proteins in blood plasma that includes most known antibodies.
gamma radiation *n* electromagnetic radiation of shorter wavelength and higher energy than X-rays.
gamma-ray astronomy *n* the investigation of cosmic gamma rays, such as those from quasars.
gamma rays *pl n* streams of gamma radiation.
gamma stock *n* any of the third rank of active securities on the London stock exchange. Prices displayed by market makers are given as an indication rather than an offer to buy or sell.
gammer (ˈgæmə) *n Rare, chiefly Brit.* a dialect word for an old woman: now chiefly humorous or contemptuous. [C16: prob. from GODMOTHER or GRANDMOTHER]
gammon[1] (ˈgæmən) *n* **1** a cured or smoked ham. **2** the hindquarter of a side of bacon, cooked either whole or in rashers. [C15: from OF *gambon,* from *gambe* leg]
gammon[2] (ˈgæmən) *n* **1** a double victory in backgammon in which one player throws off all his pieces before his opponent throws any. ◆ *vb* **2** (*tr*) to score such a victory over. [C18: prob. special use of ME *gamen* GAME[1]]
gammon[3] (ˈgæmən) *Brit. inf.* ◆ *n* **1** deceitful nonsense; humbug. ◆ *vb* **2** to deceive (a person). [C18: ? special use of GAMMON[1]]
gammy (ˈgæmɪ) *adj* **gammier, gammiest.** *Brit. sl.* (esp. of the leg) malfunctioning, injured, or lame; game. [C19: dialect var. of GAME[2]]
gamo- *or before a vowel* **gam-** *combining form.* **1** indicating sexual union or reproduction: *gamogenesis.* **2** united or fused: *gamopetalous.* [from Gk *gamos* marriage]
gamopetalous (ˌgæməʊˈpetələs) *adj* (of flowers) having petals that are united or partly united, as the primrose.
gamp (gæmp) *n Brit. inf.* an umbrella. [C19: after Mrs Sarah *Gamp,* a nurse in Dickens' *Martin Chuzzlewit,* who carried a faded cotton umbrella]
gamut **T** (ˈgæmət) *n* **1** entire range or scale, as of emotions. **2** *Music.* **2a** a scale, esp. (in medieval theory) one starting on the G on the bottom line of the bass staff. **2b** the whole range of notes. **3** *Physics.* the range of chromaticities that can be obtained by mixing three colours. [C14: from Med. L, from *gamma,* the lowest note of the hexachord as established by Guido d'Arezzo + *ut* (now, *doh*), the first of the notes of the scale *ut, re, mi, fa, sol, la, si*]
-gamy *n combining form.* denoting marriage or sexual union: *bigamy.* [from Gk, from *gamos* marriage]
▸**-gamous** *adj combining form.*
gander (ˈgændə) *n* **1** a male goose. **2** *Inf.* a quick look (esp. in **take** (*or* **have**) **a gander**). **3** *Inf.* a simpleton. [OE *gandra, ganra*]
Gandhian (ˈgændɪən) *adj* **1.** of or relating to the Indian political and

THESAURUS

kick-start, move, prod, provoke, quicken, shock, spur, startle, stir, thrill, vitalize, wake

gamble *vb* **1, 2** = **bet,** back, game, have a flutter (*inf.*), lay *or* make a bet, play, punt, put one's shirt on, stake, try one's luck, wager **3** = **risk,** back, chance, hazard, put one's faith *or* trust in, skate on thin ice, speculate, stake, stick one's neck out (*inf.*), take a chance, take the plunge, venture ◆ *n* **5** = **risk,** chance, leap in the dark, lottery, speculation, uncertainty, venture **6** = **bet,** flutter (*inf.*), punt, wager
Antonyms *n* ≠ **risk:** banker, certainty, foregone conclusion, safe bet, sure thing

gambol *vb* **1** = **frolic,** caper, cavort, curvet, cut a caper, frisk, hop, jump, prance, rollick, skip ◆ *n* **2** = **frolic,** antic, caper, gambado, hop, jump, prance, skip, spring

game[1] *n* **1** = **pastime,** amusement, distraction, diversion, entertainment, frolic, fun, jest, joke, lark, merriment, play, recreation, romp, sport **2** = **match,** competition, contest, event, head-to-head, meeting, round, tournament **10** = **undertaking,** adventure, business, enterprise, line, occupation, plan, proceeding, scheme **12** = **wild animals,** chase, prey, quarry **16** = **scheme,** design, device, plan, plot, ploy, stratagem, strategy, tactic, trick **20 play the game** = **play fair,** conform, follow the rules, go along with, keep in step, play by the rules, toe the line ◆ *adj* **22** = **brave,** bold, courageous, dauntless, dogged, fearless, feisty (*inf., chiefly US & Canad.*), gallant, gritty, have-a-go (*inf.*), heroic, intrepid, persevering, persistent, plucky, resolute, spirited, unflinching, valiant, valorous **23** = **willing,** desirous, disposed, eager, inclined, interested, keen, prepared, ready, up for it (*inf.*)
Antonyms *n* ≠ **pastime:** business, chore, duty, job, labour, toil, work ◆ *adj* ≠ **brave:** cowardly, fearful, irresolute

game[2] *adj* = **lame,** bad, crippled, deformed, disabled, gammy (*Brit. sl.*), incapacitated, injured, maimed

gamin *n* = **(street) urchin,** guttersnipe, mudlark (*sl.*), ragamuffin, street Arab (*offens.*), waif

gamut *n* **1** = **range,** area, catalogue, compass, field, scale, scope, series, sweep

spiritual leader Mahatma Gandhi (1869–1948) or his ideas. ◆ *n* **2** a follower of Gandhi or his ideas.

gang[1] ⓣ (gæŋ) *n* **1** a group of people who associate together or act as an organized body, esp. for criminal or illegal purposes. **2** an organized group of workmen. **3** a series of similar tools arranged to work simultaneously in parallel. ◆ *vb* **4** to form into, become part of, or act as a gang. ◆ See also **gang up**. [OE: journey]

gang[2] (gæŋ) *n* a variant spelling of **gangue**.

gang[3] (gæŋ) *vb* (*intr*) *Scot.* to go or walk. [OE *gangan*]

gangbang ('gæŋˌbæŋ) *n Sl.* an instance of sexual intercourse between one woman and several men one after the other, esp. against her will.

gang-banger *n US sl.* a member of a street gang.
▸ **'gang-ˌbanging** *n*

ganger ('gæŋə) *n Chiefly Brit.* the foreman of a gang of labourers.

gangland ('gæŋˌlænd, -lənd) *n* the criminal underworld.

gangling ⓣ ('gæŋglɪŋ) *or* **gangly** *adj* tall, lanky, and awkward in movement. [see GANG[3]]

ganglion ('gæŋglɪən) *n, pl* **ganglia** (-glɪə) *or* **ganglions. 1** an encapsulated collection of nerve-cell bodies, usually located outside the brain and spinal cord. **2** any concentration or centre of energy, activity, or strength. **3** a cystic tumour on a tendon sheath. [C17: from LL: swelling, from Gk: cystic tumour]
▸ **'gangliar** *adj* ▸ **ˌgangli'onic** *or* **'gangliˌated** *adj*

gangplank ('gæŋˌplæŋk) *or* **gangway** *n Naut.* a portable bridge for boarding and leaving a vessel at dockside.

gangrene ('gæŋgriːn) *n* **1** death and decay of tissue due to an interrupted blood supply, disease, or injury. ◆ *vb* **gangrenes, gangrening, gangrened. 2** to become or cause to become affected with gangrene. [C16: from L, from Gk *gangraina* an eating sore]
▸ **gangrenous** ('gæŋgrɪnəs) *adj*

gang-saw *n* a multiple saw used in a timber mill to cut planks from logs.

gangster ⓣ ('gæŋstə) *n* a member of an organized gang of criminals.

gangue *or* **gang** (gæŋ) *n* valueless and undesirable material in an ore. [C19: from F, from G *Gang* vein of metal, course]

gang up *vb* (*intr, adv;* often foll. by *on* or *against*) *Inf.* to combine in a group (against).

gangway ('gæŋˌweɪ) *n* **1** another word for **gangplank. 2** an opening in a ship's side to take a gangplank. **3** *Brit.* an aisle between rows of seats. **4** temporary planks over mud, as on a building site. ◆ *sentence substitute.* **5** clear a path!

ganister *or* **gannister** ('gænɪstə) *n* a refractory siliceous sedimentary rock occurring beneath coal seams: used for lining furnaces. [C20: from ?]

gannet ('gænɪt) *n* **1** any of several heavily built marine birds having a long stout bill and typically white plumage with dark markings. **2** *Sl.* a greedy person. [OE *ganot*]

ganoid ('gænɔɪd) *adj* **1** (of the scales of certain fishes) consisting of an inner bony layer and an outer layer of an enamel-like substance (**ganoin**). **2** denoting fishes, including the sturgeon, having such scales. ◆ *n* **3** a ganoid fish. [C19: from F, from Gk *ganos* brightness + -OID]

gantry ('gæntrɪ) *n, pl* **gantries. 1** a bridgelike framework used to support a travelling crane, signals over a railway track, etc. **2** Also called: **gantry scaffold.** the framework tower used to attend to a large rocket on its launch pad. **3** a supporting framework for a barrel. **4a** the area behind a bar where bottles, esp. spirit bottles mounted in optics, are kept. **4b** the range or quality of the spirits on display there. [C16 (in the sense: wooden platform for barrels): from OF *chantier,* from Med. L, from L *canthērius* supporting frame, pack ass]

Gantt chart (gænt) *n* a chart showing, in horizontal lines, activity planned to take place during specified periods, which are indicated in vertical bands. [C20: named after Henry L. *Gantt* (1861–1919), US management consultant]

gaol ⓣ (dʒeɪl) *n, vb* (*tr*) *Brit.* a variant spelling of **jail**.
▸ **'gaoler** *n*

gap ⓣ (gæp) *n* **1** a break or opening in a wall, fence, etc. **2** a break in continuity; interruption; hiatus. **3** a break in a line of hills or mountains affording a route through. **4** *Chiefly US.* a gorge or ravine. **5** a divergence or difference; disparity: *the generation gap.* **6** *Electronics.* **6a** a break in a magnetic circuit that increases the inductance and saturation point of the circuit. **6b** See **spark gap. 7 bridge, close, fill,** *or* **stop a gap.** to remedy a deficiency. ◆ *vb* **gaps, gapping, gapped. 8** (*tr*) to make a breach or opening in. [C14: from ON *gap* chasm]
▸ **'gappy** *adj*

gape ⓣ (geɪp) *vb* **gapes, gaping, gaped.** (*intr*) **1** to stare in wonder, esp. with the mouth open. **2** to open the mouth wide, esp. involuntarily, as in yawning. **3** to be or become wide open: *the crater gaped under his feet.* ◆ *n* **4** the act of gaping. **5** a wide opening. **6** the width of the widely opened mouth of a vertebrate. **7** a stare of astonishment. [C13: from ON *gapa*]
▸ **'gaper** *n* ▸ **'gaping** *adj*

gapes (geɪps) *n* (*functioning as sing*) **1** a disease of young domestic fowl, characterized by gaping and caused by parasitic worms (**gapeworms**). **2** *Inf.* a fit of yawning.

gap year *n* a year's break taken by a student between leaving school and starting further education.

gar (gɑː) *n, pl* **gar** *or* **gars.** short for **garpike.**

garage ('gærɑːʒ, -rɪdʒ) *n* **1** a building used to house a motor vehicle. **2** a commercial establishment in which motor vehicles are repaired, serviced, bought, and sold, and which usually also sells motor fuels. ◆ *vb* **garages, garaging, garaged. 3** (*tr*) to put into or keep in a garage. [C20: from F, from OF: to protect, from OHG *warōn*]

garage band *n* a rough-and-ready amateurish rock group. [?from the practice of such bands rehearsing in a garage]

garage sale *n* a sale of personal belongings or household effects held at a person's home, usually in the garage.

garb ⓣ (gɑːb) *n* **1** clothes, esp. the distinctive attire of an occupation: *clerical garb.* **2** style of dress; fashion. **3** external appearance, covering, or attire. ◆ *vb* **4** (*tr*) to clothe; attire. [C16: from OF: graceful contour, from OIt. *garbo* grace, prob. of Gmc origin]

garbage ⓣ ('gɑːbɪdʒ) *n* **1** worthless, useless, or unwanted matter. **2** another word (esp. US and Canad.) for **rubbish. 3** *Computing.* invalid data. **4** *Inf.* nonsense. [C15: prob. from Anglo-F *garbelage* removal of discarded matter, from ?]

garble ⓣ ('gɑːbᵊl) *vb* **garbles, garbling, garbled.** (*tr*) **1** to jumble (a story, quotation, etc.), esp. unintentionally. **2** to distort the meaning of (an account, text, etc.), as by making misleading omissions; corrupt. ◆ *n* **3a** the act of garbling. **3b** garbled matter. [C15: from OIt. *garbellare* to strain, sift, from Ar., from LL *crībellum* small sieve]
▸ **'garbler** *n*

garboard ('gɑːˌbɔːd) *n Naut.* the bottommost plank of a vessel's hull. Also called: **garboard strake.** [C17: from Du. *gaarboord,* prob. from MDu. *gaderen* to GATHER + *boord* BOARD]

garbology (gɑː'bɒlədʒɪ) *n Chiefly US.* **1** analysis of refuse as a means of investigating the lifestyle of the person or people who produced it. **2** the study of waste disposal. [C20: from GARBAGE + -OLOGY]
▸ **gar'bologist** *n*

garçon (*French* garsɔ̃) *n* a waiter or male servant, esp. if French. [C19: from OF *gars* lad, prob. of Gmc origin]

garda ('gɑːrdə) *n, pl* **gardaí** ('gɑːrdɪ). a member of the **Garda Síochána,** the police force of the Republic of Ireland.

garden ('gɑːdᵊn) *n* **1** *Brit.* **1a** an area of land, usually planted with grass, trees, flowerbeds, etc., adjoining a house. US and Canad. word: **yard. 1b** (*as modifier*): *a garden chair.* **2a** an area of land used for the cultivation of ornamental plants, herbs, fruit, vegetables, trees, etc. **2b** (*as modifier*): *garden tools.* Related adj: **horticultural. 3** (*often pl*) such an area of land that is open to the public, sometimes part of a park: *botanical gardens.* **4** a fertile and beautiful region. **5 lead (a person) up the garden path.** *Inf.* to mislead or deceive. ◆ *vb* **6** to work in, cultivate, or take care of (a garden, plot of land, etc.). [C14: from OF *gardin,* of Gmc origin]
▸ **'gardener** *n* ▸ **'gardening** *n*

garden centre *n* a place where gardening tools and equipment, plants, seeds, etc., are sold.

garden city *n Brit.* a planned town of limited size surrounded by a rural belt.

gardenia (gɑː'diːnɪə) *n* **1** any evergreen shrub or tree of the Old World tropical genus *Gardenia,* cultivated for their large fragrant waxlike typically white flowers. **2** the flower of any of these shrubs. [C18: NL, after Dr Alexander *Garden* (1730–91), American botanist]

garderobe ('gɑːdˌrəʊb) *n Arch.* **1** a wardrobe or its contents. **2** a private room. **3** a privy. [C14: from F, from *garder* to keep + *robe* dress, clothing; see WARDROBE]

THESAURUS

gang[1] *n* **2** = **group**, band, bevy, camp, circle, clique, club, company, coterie, crew (*inf.*), crowd, herd, horde, lot, mob, pack, party, posse (*sl.*), ring, set, shift, squad, team, troupe

gangling *adj* = **tall**, angular, awkward, lanky, loose-jointed, rangy, rawboned, skinny, spindly

gangster *n* = **racketeer**, bandit, brigand, crook (*inf.*), desperado, gang member, heavy (*sl.*), hood, hoodlum (*chiefly US*), mobster (*US sl.*), robber, ruffian, thug, tough, tsotsi (*S. Afr.*)

gaol *see* **jail**

gap *n* **1** = **opening**, blank, breach, break, chink, cleft, crack, cranny, crevice, discontinuity, divide, hole, interstice, rent, rift, space, vacuity, void **2** = **interval**, breathing space, entr'acte, hiatus, interlude, intermission, interruption, lacuna, lull, pause, recess, respite **5** = **difference**, disagreement, disparity, divergence, inconsistency

gape *vb* **1** = **stare**, gawk, gawp (*Brit. sl.*), goggle, wonder **3** = **open**, crack, split, yawn

gaping *adj* **3** = **wide**, broad, cavernous, great, open, vast, wide open, yawning

garb *n* **1** = **clothes**, apparel, array, attire, clothing, costume, dress, garment, gear (*sl.*), habiliment, habit, outfit, raiment (*arch.*), robes, uniform, vestments, wear **2** = **fashion**, cut, look, mode, style **3** = **appearance**, aspect, attire, covering, guise, outward form ◆ *vb* **4** = **clothe**, apparel, attire, cover, dress, rig out, robe

garbage *n* **1** = **junk**, bits and pieces, debris, detritus, litter, odds and ends, rubbish, scraps **2** = **waste**, dreck (*sl., chiefly US*), dross, filth, muck, offal, refuse, rubbish, scourings, slops, sweepings, swill, trash (*chiefly US*), wack (*US sl.*) **4** = **nonsense**, bunkum *or* buncombe (*chiefly US*), claptrap (*inf.*), codswallop (*Brit. sl.*), drivel, gibberish, guff (*sl.*), hogwash, hokum (*sl., chiefly US & Canad.*), hot air (*inf.*), moonshine, piffle (*inf.*), poppycock (*inf.*), rot, stuff and nonsense, tommyrot, tosh (*inf.*), trash, tripe (*inf.*), twaddle

garble *vb* **1** = **jumble**, confuse, mix up **2** = **distort**, corrupt, doctor, falsify, misinterpret, misquote, misreport, misrepresent, misstate, mistranslate, mutilate, pervert, slant, tamper with, twist
Antonyms *vb* clarify, decipher, make intelligible

garbled *adj* **1** = **jumbled**, confused, distorted, double-Dutch, incomprehensible, mixed up, unintelligible

garfish ('gɑːˌfɪʃ) *n, pl* **garfish** *or* **garfishes. 1** another name for **garpike** (sense 1). **2** an elongated marine teleost fish with long toothed jaws: related to the flying fishes. [OE *gār* spear + FISH]

garganey ('gɑːgənɪ) *n* a small Eurasian duck closely related to the mallard. The male has a white stripe over each eye. [C17: from It. dialect *garganei,* imit.]

gargantuan ❶ (gɑː'gæntjuən) *adj* (*sometimes cap.*) huge; enormous. [after *Gargantua,* a giant in Rabelais' satire *Gargantua and Pantagruel* (1534)]

> **USAGE NOTE** Some people think that *gargantuan* should only be used to describe things connected with food: *a gargantuan meal; his gargantuan appetite.*

gargle ('gɑːgᵊl) *vb* **gargles, gargling, gargled. 1** to rinse the mouth and throat with (a liquid, esp. a medicinal fluid) by slowly breathing out through the liquid. ◆ *n* **2** the liquid used for gargling. **3** the sound produced by gargling. [C16: from OF, from *gargouille* throat, ? imit.]

gargoyle ('gɑːgɔɪl) *n* **1** a waterspout carved in the form of a grotesque face or creature and projecting from a roof gutter. **2** a person with a grotesque appearance. [C15: from OF *gargouille* gargoyle, throat; see GARGLE]

garibaldi (ˌgærɪ'bɔːldɪ) *n Brit.* a type of biscuit having a layer of currants in the centre.

garish ❶ ('gɛərɪʃ) *adj* gay or colourful in a crude manner; gaudy. [C16: from earlier *gaure* to stare + -ISH]
▸**'garishly** *adv* ▸**'garishness** *n*

garland ❶ ('gɑːlənd) *n* **1** a wreath of flowers, leaves, etc., worn round the head or neck or hung up. **2** a collection of short literary pieces, such as poems; anthology. ◆ *vb* **3** (*tr*) to adorn with a garland or garlands. [C14: from OF *garlande,* ? of Gmc origin]

garlic ('gɑːlɪk) *n* **1** a hardy widely cultivated Asian alliaceous plant having whitish flowers. **2** the bulb of this plant, made up of small segments (cloves) that have a strong odour and pungent taste and are used in cooking. [OE *gārlēac,* from *gār* spear + *lēac* LEEK]
▸**'garlicky** *adj*

garment ❶ ('gɑːmənt) *n* **1** (*often pl*) an article of clothing. **2** outer covering. ◆ *vb* **3** (*tr; usually passive*) to cover or clothe. [C14: from OF *garniment,* from *garnir* to equip; see GARNISH]

garner ❶ ('gɑːnə) *vb* (*tr*) **1** to gather or store as in a granary. ◆ *n* **2** an archaic word for **granary. 3** *Arch.* a place for storage. [C12: from OF: granary, from L *grānārium,* from *grānum* grain]

garnet ('gɑːnɪt) *n* any of a group of hard glassy red, yellow, or green minerals consisting of silicates in cubic crystalline form: used as a gemstone and abrasive. [C13: from OF, from *grenat* (adj) red, from *pome grenate* POMEGRANATE]

garnish ❶ ('gɑːnɪʃ) *vb* (*tr*) **1** to decorate; trim. **2** to add something to (food) in order to improve its appearance or flavour. **3** *Law.* **3a** to serve with notice of proceedings; warn. **3b** to attach (a debt). ◆ *n* **4** a decoration; trimming. **5** something, such as parsley, added to a dish for its flavour or decorative effect. [C14: from OF *garnir* to adorn, equip, of Gmc origin]
▸**'garnisher** *n*

garnishee (ˌgɑːnɪ'ʃiː) *Law.* ◆ *n* **1** a person upon whom a garnishment has been served. ◆ *vb* **garnishees, garnisheeing, garnisheed.** (*tr*) **2** to attach (a debt or other property) by garnishment. **3** to serve (a person) with a garnishment.

garnishment ('gɑːnɪʃmənt) *n* **1** decoration or embellishment. **2** *Law.* **2a** a notice or warning. **2b** *Obs.* a summons to court proceedings already in progress. **2c** a notice warning a person holding money or property belonging to a debtor whose debt has been attached to hold such property until directed by the court to apply it.

garniture ('gɑːnɪtʃə) *n* decoration or embellishment. [C16: from F, from *garnir* to GARNISH]

garpike ('gɑːˌpaɪk) *n* **1** Also called: **garfish, gar.** any primitive freshwater elongated bony fish of North and Central America, having very long toothed jaws and a body covering of thick scales. **2** another name for **garfish** (sense 2).

garret ('gærɪt) *n* another word for **attic** (sense 1). [C14: from OF: watchtower, from *garir* to protect, of Gmc origin]

garret window *n* a skylight that lies along the slope of the roof.

garrison ❶ ('gærɪsᵊn) *n* **1** the troops who maintain and guard a base or fortified place. **2** the place itself. ◆ *vb* **3** (*tr*) to station (troops) in (a fort, etc.). [C13: from OF, from *garir* to defend, of Gmc origin]

garron ('gærən) *n* a small sturdy pony bred and used chiefly in Scotland and Ireland. [C16: from Gaelic *gearran*]

garrotte *or* **garotte** (gə'rɒt) *n* **1** a Spanish method of execution by strangulation. **2** the device, usually an iron collar, used in such executions. **3** *Obs.* strangulation of one's victim while committing robbery. ◆ *vb* **garrottes, garrotting, garrotted** *or* **garottes, garotting, garotted.** (*tr*) **4** to execute by means of the garrotte. **5** to strangle, esp. in order to commit robbery. [C17: from Sp. *garrote,* ?from OF *garrot* cudgel; from ?]
▸**gar'rotter** *or* **ga'rotter** *n*

garrulous ❶ ('gærʊləs) *adj* **1** given to constant chatter; talkative. **2** wordy or diffuse. [C17: from L, from *garrīre* to chatter]
▸**'garrulously** *adv* ▸**'garrulousness** *or* **garrulity** (gæ'ruːlɪtɪ) *n*

garryowen (ˌgærɪ'əʊɪn) *n* (in rugby union) another term for **up-and-under.** [from *Garryowen* RFC, Ireland]

garter ('gɑːtə) *n* **1** a band, usually of elastic, worn round the leg to hold up a sock or stocking. **2** the US and Canad. word for **suspender.** ◆ *vb* **3** (*tr*) to fasten or secure as with a garter. [C14: from OF *gartier,* from *garet* bend of the knee, prob. of Celtic origin]

Garter ('gɑːtə) *n* **the. 1 Order of the Garter.** the highest order of British knighthood, open to women since 1987. **2** (*sometimes not cap.*) **2a** the badge of this Order. **2b** membership of this Order.

garter snake *n* a nonvenomous North American snake, typically marked with longitudinal stripes.

garter stitch *n* knitting in which all the rows are knitted in plain stitch.

garth (gɑːθ) *n* **1** a courtyard surrounded by a cloister. **2** *Arch.* a yard or garden. [C14: from ON *garthr*]

gas (gæs) *n, pl* **gases** *or* **gasses. 1** a substance in a physical state in which it does not resist change of shape and will expand indefinitely to fill any container. Cf. **liquid** (sense 1), **solid** (sense 1). **2** any substance that is gaseous at room temperature and atmospheric pressure. **3** any gaseous substance that is above its critical temperature and therefore not liquefiable by pressure alone. Cf. **vapour** (sense 2). **4a** a fossil fuel in the form of a gas, used as a source of domestic and industrial heat. **4b** (*as modifier): a gas cooker; gas fire.* **5** a gaseous anaesthetic, such as nitrous oxide. **6** *Mining.* firedamp or the explosive mixture of firedamp and air. **7** the usual US, Canad., Austral., and NZ word for **petrol,** a shortened form of **gasoline. 8 step on the gas.** *Inf.* **8a** to accelerate a motor vehicle. **8b** to hurry. **9** a toxic, etc., substance in suspension in air used against an enemy, etc. **10** *Inf.* idle talk or boasting. **11** *Sl.* a delightful or successful person or thing: *his latest record is a gas.* **12** *US.* an informal name for **flatus.** ◆ *vb* **gases** *or* **gasses, gassing, gassed. 13** (*tr*) to provide or fill with gas. **14** (*tr*) to subject to gas fumes, esp. so as to asphyxiate or render unconscious. **15** (*intr; foll. by to*) *Inf.* to talk in an idle or boastful way (to a person). [C17 (coined by J. B. van Helmont (1577–1644), Flemish chemist): from Gk *khaos* atmosphere]

gasbag ('gæsˌbæg) *n Inf.* a person who talks in a voluble way, esp. about unimportant matters.

gas chamber *or* **oven** *n* an airtight room into which poison gas is introduced to kill people or animals.

gas chromatography *n* a technique for analysing a mixture of volatile substances in which the mixture is carried by an inert gas through a column packed with a selective adsorbent or absorbent and a detector records on a moving strip the conductivity of the gas leaving the tube.

Gascon ('gæskən) *n* **1** a native or inhabitant of Gascony. **2** the dialect of French spoken in Gascony. ◆ *adj* **3** of or relating to Gascony, its inhabitants, or their dialect of French.

gasconade (ˌgæskə'neɪd) *Rare.* ◆ *n* **1** boastful talk or bluster. ◆ *vb* **gasconades, gasconading, gasconaded. 2** (*intr*) to boast, brag, or bluster. [C18: from F, from *gasconner* to chatter, boast like a GASCON]

gas constant *n* the constant in the gas equation, having the value 8.3143 joules per kelvin per mole. Symbol *R* Also called: **universal gas constant.**

gas-cooled reactor *n* a nuclear reactor using a gas as the coolant.

gas-discharge tube *n Electronics.* any tube in which an electric discharge takes place through a gas.

THESAURUS

gargantuan *adj* = **huge,** big, colossal, elephantine, enormous, giant, gigantic, ginormous (*inf.*), humongous *or* humungous (*US sl.*), immense, mammoth, massive, monstrous, monumental, mountainous, prodigious, titanic, towering, tremendous, vast
Antonyms *adj* little, meagre, miniature, minute, paltry, petite, puny, pygmy *or* pigmy, small, tiny

garish *adj* = **gaudy,** brash, brassy, brummagem, cheap, flash (*inf.*), flashy, flaunting, glaring, glittering, loud, meretricious, naff (*Brit. sl.*), raffish, showy, tacky (*inf.*), tasteless, tawdry, vulgar
Antonyms *adj* conservative, elegant, modest, plain, refined, sedate, sombre, unobtrusive

garland *n* **1** = **wreath,** bays, chaplet, coronal, crown, festoon, honours, laurels ◆ *vb* **3** = **adorn,** crown, deck, festoon, wreathe

garment *n* **1** *plural* = **clothes,** apparel, array, articles of clothing, attire, clothing, costume, dress, duds (*inf.*), garb, gear (*sl.*), habiliment, habit, outfit, raiment (*arch.*), robes, threads (*sl.*), togs, uniform, vestments, wear

garner *vb* **1** = **collect,** accumulate, amass, assemble, deposit, gather, hoard, husband, lay in *or* up, put by, reserve, save, stockpile, store, stow away, treasure ◆ *n* **2, 3** *Archaic* = **storehouse,** depository, granary, store, vault

garnish *vb* **1** = **decorate,** adorn, beautify, bedeck, deck, embellish, enhance, festoon, grace, ornament, set off, trim ◆ *n* **4** = **decoration,** adornment, embellishment, enhancement, festoon, garniture, ornament, ornamentation, trim, trimming
Antonyms *vb* ≠ **decorate:** denude, spoil, strip

garrison *n* **1** = **troops,** armed force, command, detachment, unit **2** = **fort,** base, camp, encampment, fortification, fortress, post, station, stronghold ◆ *vb* **3** = **station,** assign, mount, position, post, put on duty

garrulous *adj* **1** = **talkative,** babbling, chattering, chatty, effusive, gabby (*inf.*), glib, gossiping, gushing, loquacious, mouthy, prating, prattling, verbose, voluble **2** = **long-winded,** diffuse, gassy (*sl.*), prolix, prosy, verbose, windy, wordy
Antonyms *adj* ≠ **talkative:** reserved, reticent, taciturn, tight-lipped, uncommunicative ≠ **long-winded:** concise, succinct, terse

garrulousness *n* **1** = **talkativeness,** babble, babbling, chatter, chattering, chattiness, effusiveness, gabbiness (*inf.*), garrulity, gift of the gab (*inf.*), glibness, loquacity, mouthiness, prating, prattle, verbosity, volubility **2** =

gaseous ('gæsɪəs, -ʃəs, -ʃɪəs, 'geɪ-) *adj* of, concerned with, or having the characteristics of a gas.
▸'**gaseousness** *n*

gas equation *n* an equation relating the product of the pressure and the volume of an ideal gas to the product of its thermodynamic temperature and the gas constant.

gas gangrene *n* gangrene resulting from infection of a wound by anaerobic bacteria that cause gas bubbles in the surrounding tissues.

gas guzzler *n Sl., chiefly US.* a car that consumes large quantities of petrol.

gash ⓘ (gæʃ) *vb* **1** (*tr*) to make a long deep cut in; slash. ◆ *n* **2** a long deep cut. [C16: from OF *garser* to scratch, from Vulgar L, from Gk *kharassein*]

gasholder ('gæs,həʊldə) *n* **1** Also called: **gasometer.** a large tank for storing coal gas or natural gas prior to distribution to users. **2** any vessel for storing or measuring a gas.

gasify ('gæsɪ,faɪ) *vb* **gasifies, gasifying, gasified.** to make into or become a gas.
▸,**gasifi'cation** *n*

gasket ('gæskɪt) *n* **1** a compressible packing piece of paper, rubber, asbestos, etc., sandwiched between the faces of a metal joint to provide a seal. **2** *Naut.* a piece of line used as a sail stop. [C17 (in the sense: rope lashing a furled sail): prob. from F *garcette* rope's end, lit.: little girl, from OF]

gaslight ('gæs,laɪt) *n* **1** a type of lamp in which the illumination is produced by an incandescent mantle heated by a jet of gas. **2** the light produced by such a lamp.

gasman ('gæs,mæn) *n, pl* **gasmen.** a man employed to read household gas meters, supervise gas fittings, etc.

gas mantle *n* a mantle for use in a gaslight. See **mantle** (sense 4).

gas mask *n* a mask fitted with a chemical filter to enable the wearer to breathe air free of poisonous or corrosive gases.

gas meter *n* an apparatus for measuring and recording the amount of gas passed through it.

gasoline *or* **gasolene** ('gæsə,liːn) *n* a US and Canad. name for **petrol.**

gasometer (gæs'ɒmɪtə) *n* a nontechnical name for **gasholder.**

gasp ⓘ (gɑːsp) *vb* **1** (*intr*) to draw in the breath sharply or with effort, esp. in expressing awe, horror, etc. **2** (*intr; foll. by after or for*) to crave. **3** (*tr; often foll. by out*) to utter breathlessly. ◆ *n* **4** a short convulsive intake of breath. **5 at the last gasp. 5a** at the point of death. **5b** at the last moment. [C14: from ON *geispa* to yawn]

gasper ('gɑːspə) *n* **1** a person who gasps. **2** *Brit. dated sl.* a cheap cigarette.

gas plant *n* an aromatic white-flowered Eurasian plant that emits vapour capable of being ignited. Also called: **burning bush, dittany, fraxinella.**

gas ring *n* a circular assembly of gas jets, used esp. for cooking.

gassy ('gæsɪ) *adj* **gassier, gassiest. 1** filled with, containing, or resembling gas. **2** *Inf.* full of idle or vapid talk.
▸'**gassiness** *n*

gasteropod ('gæstərə,pɒd) *n, adj* a variant spelling of **gastropod.**

gas thermometer *n* a device for measuring temperature by observing the pressure of gas at a constant volume or the volume of a gas kept at a constant pressure.

gastric ('gæstrɪk) *adj* of, relating to, near, or involving the stomach.

gastric juice *n* a digestive fluid secreted by the stomach, containing hydrochloric acid, pepsin, rennin, etc.

gastric ulcer *n* an ulcer of the mucous membrane lining the stomach.

gastritis (gæs'traɪtɪs) *n* inflammation of the stomach.

gastro- *or often before a vowel* **gastr-** *combining form.* stomach: *gastroenteritis; gastritis.* [from Gk *gastēr*]

gastrocolic (,gæstrəʊ'kɒlɪk) *adj* of or relating to the stomach and colon: *gastrocolic reflex.*

gastroenteritis (,gæstrəʊ,ɛntə'raɪtɪs) *n* inflammation of the stomach and intestines.

gastrointestinal (,gæstrəʊɪn'tɛstɪn°l) *adj* of or relating to the stomach and intestinal tract.

gastronome ('gæstrə,nəʊm), **gastronomer** (gæs'trɒnəmə), *or* **gastronomist** *n* less common words for **gourmet.**

gastronomy (gæs'trɒnəmɪ) *n* the art of good eating. [C19: from F, from Gk, from *gastēr* stomach; see -NOMY]
▸**gastronomic** (,gæstrə'nɒmɪk) *or* ,**gastro'nomical** *adj* ▸,**gastro'nomically** *adv*

gastropod ('gæstrə,pɒd) *or* **gasteropod** *n* any of a class of molluscs typically having a flattened muscular foot for locomotion and a head that bears stalked eyes. The class includes the snails, whelks, and slugs.
▸**gastropodan** (gæs'trɒpəd°n) *adj, n*

gastroscope ('gæstrə,skəʊp) *n* a medical instrument for examining the interior of the stomach.

gastrula ('gæstrʊlə) *n, pl* **gastrulas** *or* **gastrulae** (-,liː). a saclike animal embryo consisting of three layers of cells surrounding a central cavity with a small opening to the exterior. [C19: NL: little stomach, from Gk *gastēr* belly]

gas turbine *n* an internal-combustion engine in which the expanding gases emerging from one or more combustion chambers drive a turbine.

gasworks ('gæs,wɜːks) *n* (*functioning as sing*) a plant in which gas, esp. coal gas, is made.

gat (gæt) *vb Arch.* a past tense of **get.**

gate ⓘ (geɪt) *n* **1** a movable barrier, usually hinged, for closing an opening in a wall, fence, etc. **2** an opening to allow passage into or out of an enclosed place. **3** any means of entrance or access. **4** a mountain pass or gap, esp. one providing entry into another country or region. **5a** the number of people admitted to a sporting event or entertainment. **5b** the total entrance money received from them. **6** *Electronics.* a logic circuit having one or more input terminals and one output terminal, the output being switched between two voltage levels determined by the combination of input signals. **7** a component in a motion-picture camera or projector that holds each frame flat and momentarily stationary behind the lens. **8** a slotted metal frame that controls the positions of the gear lever in a motor vehicle. ◆ *vb* **gates, gating, gated. 9** (*tr*) *Brit.* to restrict (a student) to the school or college grounds as a punishment. [OE *geat*]

gâteau ('gætəʊ) *n, pl* **gâteaux** (-təʊz). a rich cake usually layered with cream and elaborately decorated. [F: cake]

gate-crash *vb Inf.* to gain entry to (a party, concert, etc.) without invitation or payment.
▸'**gate-,crasher** *n*

gatefold ('geɪt,fəʊld) *n* an oversize page in a book or magazine that is folded in. Also called: **foldout.**

gatehouse ('geɪt,haʊs) *n* **1** a building at or above a gateway, used by a porter or guard, or, formerly, as a fortification. **2** a small house at the entrance to the grounds of a country mansion.

gatekeeper ('geɪt,kiːpə) *n* **1** a person who has charge of a gate and controls who may pass through it. **2** a manager in a large organization who controls the flow of information, esp. to parent and subsidiary companies. **3** any of several Eurasian butterflies having brown-bordered orange wings.

gate-leg table *or* **gate-legged table** *n* a table with one or two leaves supported by a hinged leg swung out from the frame.

gatepost ('geɪt,pəʊst) *n* **1a** the post on which a gate is hung. **1b** the post to which a gate is fastened when closed. **2 between you, me, and the gatepost.** confidentially.

gateway ('geɪt,weɪ) *n* **1** an entrance that may be closed by or as by a gate. **2** a means of entry or access: *Bombay, gateway to India.* **3** *Computing.* hardware and software that connect incompatible computer networks.

gather ⓘ ('gæðə) *vb* **1** to assemble or cause to assemble. **2** to collect or be collected gradually; muster. **3** (*tr*) to learn from information given; conclude or assume. **4** (*tr*) to pick or harvest (flowers, fruit, etc.). **5** (*tr*) to bring close (to). **6** to increase or cause to increase gradually, as in force, speed, intensity, etc. **7** to contract (the brow) or (of the brow) to become contracted into wrinkles; knit. **8** (*tr*) to assemble (sections of a book) in the correct sequence for binding. **9** (*tr*) to prepare or make ready: *to gather one's wits.* **10** to draw (material) into a series of small tucks or folds. **11** (*intr*) (of a boil or other sore) to come to a head; form pus. ◆ *n* **12a** the act of gathering. **12b** the amount gathered. **13** a small fold in material, as made by a tightly pulled stitch; tuck. [OE *gadrian*]
▸'**gatherer** *n*

gathering ⓘ ('gæðərɪŋ) *n* **1** a group of people, things, etc., that are gathered together; assembly. **2** *Sewing.* a series of gathers in material. **3** *Inf.* **3a** the formation of pus in a boil. **3b** the pus so formed. **4** *Printing.* an informal name for **section** (sense 16).

Gatling gun ('gætlɪŋ) *n* a machine gun equipped with a rotating cluster of barrels that are fired in succession. [C19: after R. J. *Gatling* (1818–1903), its US inventor]

GATT (gæt) *n acronym for* General Agreement on Tariffs and Trade: a multilateral international treaty signed in 1947 to promote trade; replaced in 1995 by the World Trade Organization.

gauche ⓘ (gəʊʃ) *adj* lacking ease of manner; tactless. [C18: F: awkward, left, from OF *gauchir* to swerve, ult. of Gmc origin]
▸'**gauchely** *adv* ▸'**gaucheness** *n*

THESAURUS

long-windedness, diffuseness, prolixity, prosiness, verbosity, windiness, wordiness

gash *vb* **1** = **cut**, cleave, gouge, incise, lacerate, rend, slash, slit, split, tear, wound ◆ *n* **2** = **cut**, cleft, gouge, incision, laceration, rent, slash, slit, split, tear, wound

gasp *vb* **1** = **gulp**, blow, catch one's breath, choke, fight for breath, pant, puff ◆ *n* **4** = **gulp**, blow, ejaculation, exclamation, intake of breath, pant, puff, sharp intake of breath

gate *n* **1-3** = **barrier**, access, door, doorway, egress, entrance, exit, gateway, opening, passage, port (*Scot.*), portal

gather *vb* **1, 2** = **assemble**, accumulate, amass, bring *or* get together, collect, congregate, convene, flock, foregather, garner, group, heap, hoard, marshal, mass, muster, pile up, round up, stack up, stockpile **3** = **learn**, assume, be led to believe, conclude, deduce, draw, hear, infer, make, surmise, understand **4** = **pick**, crop, cull, garner, glean, harvest, pluck, reap, select **5** = **enfold**, clasp, draw, embrace, hold, hug **6** = **intensify**, build, deepen, enlarge, expand, grow, heighten, increase, rise, swell, thicken, wax **10** = **fold**, pleat, pucker, ruffle, shirr, tuck
Antonyms *vb* ≠ **assemble:** diffuse, disperse, dissipate, scatter, separate

gathering *n* **1** = **assembly**, assemblage, collection, company, conclave, concourse, congregation, congress, convention, convocation, crowd, flock, get-together (*inf.*), group, knot, mass, meeting, muster, party, rally, throng, turnout **3** *Informal* = **pimple**, abscess, boil, carbuncle, pustule, sore, spot, tumour, ulcer

gauche *adj* = **awkward**, clumsy, graceless, ig-

gaucherie ◑ (ˌgəʊʃəˈriː, ˈgəʊʃərɪ) *n* **1** the quality of being gauche. **2** a gauche act.

gaucho (ˈgaʊtʃəʊ) *n, pl* **gauchos.** a cowboy of the South American pampas, usually one of mixed Spanish and Indian descent. [C19: from American Sp., prob. from Quechuan *wáhcha* orphan, vagabond]

gaud (gɔːd) *n* an article of cheap finery. [C14: prob. from OF *gaudir* to be joyful, from L *gaudēre*]

gaudy[1] ◑ (ˈgɔːdɪ) *adj* **gaudier, gaudiest.** bright or colourful in a crude or vulgar manner. [C16: from GAUD]
▸ˈ**gaudily** *adv* ▸ˈ**gaudiness** *n*

gaudy[2] (ˈgɔːdɪ) *n, pl* **gaudies.** *Brit.* a celebratory feast held at some schools and colleges. [C16: from L *gaudium* joy, from *gaudēre* to rejoice]

gauge ◑ *or* **gage** (geɪdʒ) *vb* **gauges, gauging, gauged** *or* **gages, gaging, gaged.** (*tr*) **1** to measure or determine the amount, quantity, size, condition, etc., of. **2** to estimate or appraise; judge. **3** to check for conformity or bring into conformity with a standard measurement, etc. ◆ *n* **4** a standard measurement, dimension, capacity, or quantity. **5** any of various instruments for measuring a quantity: *a pressure gauge.* **6** any of various devices used to check for conformity with a standard measurement. **7** a standard or means for assessing; test; criterion. **8** scope, capacity, or extent. **9** the diameter of the barrel of a gun, esp. a shotgun. **10** the thickness of sheet metal or the diameter of wire. **11** the distance between the rails of a railway track. **12** the distance between two wheels on the same axle of a vehicle, truck, etc. **13** *Naut.* the position of a vessel in relation to the wind and another vessel. **14** a measure of the fineness of woven or knitted fabric. **15** the width of motion-picture film or magnetic tape. ◆ *adj* **16** (of a pressure measurement) measured on a pressure gauge that registers zero at atmospheric pressure. [C15: from OF, prob. of Gmc origin]
▸ˈ**gaugeable** *or* ˈ**gageable** *adj*

gauge boson *n Physics.* a boson that mediates the interaction between elementary particles. There are four types: photons for electromagnetic interactions, gluons for strong interactions, intermediate vector bosons for weak interactions, and gravitons for gravitational interactions.

gauge theory *n Physics.* a type of theory of elementary particles designed to explain the strong, weak, and electromagnetic interactions in terms of exchange of virtual particles.

Gaul (gɔːl) *n* **1** a native of ancient Gaul, a region in Roman times stretching from what is now N Italy to the S Netherlands. **2** a Frenchman.

Gauleiter (ˈgaʊˌlaɪtə) *n* **1** a provincial governor in Germany under Hitler. **2** (*sometimes not cap.*) a person in a position of petty authority who behaves in an overbearing manner. [G, from *Gau* district + *Leiter* leader]

Gaulish (ˈgɔːlɪʃ) *n* **1** the extinct Celtic language of the pre-Roman Gauls. ◆ *adj* **2** of ancient Gaul, the Gauls, or their language.

gaunt ◑ (gɔːnt) *adj* **1** bony and emaciated in appearance. **2** (of places) bleak or desolate. [C15: ?from ON]
▸ˈ**gauntly** *adv* ▸ˈ**gauntness** *n*

gauntlet[1] (ˈgɔːntlɪt) *n* **1** a medieval armoured leather glove. **2** a heavy glove with a long cuff. **3 take up** (*or* **throw down**) **the gauntlet.** to accept (*or* offer) a challenge. [C15: from OF *gantelet,* dim. of *gant* glove, of Gmc origin]

gauntlet[2] (ˈgɔːntlɪt) *n* **1** a punishment in which the victim is forced to run between two rows of men who strike at him as he passes: formerly a military punishment. **2 run the gauntlet. 2a** to suffer this punishment. **2b** to endure an onslaught, as of criticism. **3** a testing ordeal. [C15: changed (through infl. of GAUNTLET[1]) from earlier *gantlope,* from Swedish *gatlopp* passageway]

gaur (ˈgaʊə) *n* a large wild ox of mountainous regions of S Asia. [C19: from Hindi, from Sansk. *gāura*]

gauss (gaʊs) *n, pl* **gauss.** the cgs unit of magnetic flux density. 1 gauss is equivalent to 10^{-4} tesla. [after K. F. *Gauss* (1777–1855), G mathematician]

Gaussian distribution (ˈgaʊsɪən) *n* another name for **normal distribution.**

gauze (gɔːz) *n* **1** a transparent cloth of loose weave. **2** a surgical dressing of muslin or similar material. **3** any thin openwork material, such as wire. **4** a fine mist or haze. [C16: from F *gaze,* ?from *Gaza,* Israel, where it was believed to originate]

gauzy ◑ (ˈgɔːzɪ) *adj* **gauzier, gauziest.** resembling gauze; thin and transparent.
▸ˈ**gauzily** *adv* ▸ˈ**gauziness** *n*

gave (geɪv) *vb* the past tense of **give.**

gavel (ˈgævᵊl) *n* a small hammer used by a chairman, auctioneer, etc., to call for order or attention. [C19: from ?]

gavial (ˈgeɪvɪəl), **gharial,** *or* **garial** (ˈgærɪəl) *n* a large fish-eating Indian crocodile with a very long slender snout. [C19: from F, from Hindi]

gavotte *or* **gavot** (gəˈvɒt) *n* **1** an old formal dance in quadruple time. **2** a piece of music composed for or in the rhythm of this dance. [C17: from F, from Provençal, from *gavot* mountaineer, dweller in the Alps (where the dance originated)]

gawk ◑ (gɔːk) *n* **1** a clumsy stupid person; lout. ◆ *vb* **2** (*intr*) to stare in a stupid way; gape. [C18: from ODanish *gaukr;* prob. rel. to GAPE]

gawky ◑ (ˈgɔːkɪ) *adj* **gawkier, gawkiest.** clumsy or ungainly; awkward. Also: **gawkish.**
▸ˈ**gawkily** *adv* ▸ˈ**gawkiness** *n*

gawp *or* **gaup** (gɔːp) *vb* (*intr;* often foll. by *at*) *Brit. sl.* to stare stupidly; gape. [C14 *galpen;* prob. rel. to OE *gielpan* to boast, YELP]
▸ˈ**gawper** *n*

gay ◑ (geɪ) *adj* **1a** homosexual. **1b** of or for homosexuals: *a gay club.* **2** carefree and merry: *a gay temperament.* **3** brightly coloured; brilliant: *a gay hat.* **4** given to pleasure, esp. in social entertainment: *a gay life.* ◆ *n* **5** a homosexual. [C13: from OF *gai,* from OProvençal, of Gmc origin]
▸ˈ**gayness** *n*

> **USAGE NOTE** *Gayness* is the state of being homosexual. The noun which refers to the state of being carefree and merry is *gaiety.*

gazania (gæˈzeɪnɪə) *n* any of a genus of S. African plants of the composite family having large showy flowers. [? after Theodore of *Gaza* (1398–1478), who translated the botanical works of Theophrastus into Latin]

gaze ◑ (geɪz) *vb* **gazes, gazing, gazed. 1** (*intr*) to look long and fixedly, esp. in wonder. ◆ *n* **2** a fixed look. [C14: from Swedish dialect *gasa* to gape at]
▸ˈ**gazer** *n*

gazebo (gəˈziːbəʊ) *n, pl* **gazebos** *or* **gazeboes.** a summerhouse, garden pavilion, or belvedere, sited to command a view. [C18: ? a pseudo-Latin coinage based on GAZE]

gazelle (gəˈzɛl) *n, pl* **gazelles** *or* **gazelle.** any small graceful usually fawn-coloured antelope of Africa and Asia. [C17: from OF, from Ar. *ghazāl*]

gazette ◑ (gəˈzɛt) *n* **1** a newspaper or official journal. **2** *Brit.* an official

THESAURUS

norant, ill-bred, ill-mannered, inelegant, inept, insensitive, lacking in social graces, maladroit, tactless, uncultured, unpolished, unsophisticated
Antonyms *adj* elegant, gracious, polished, polite, refined, sophisticated, tasteful, urbane, well-mannered

gaucherie *n* **1** = **awkwardness**, bad taste, clumsiness, gaucheness, gracelessness, ignorance, ill-breeding, inelegance, ineptness, insensitivity, lack of polish, maladroitness, tactlessness, unsophisticatedness **2** = **blunder**, bloomer, boob (*sl.*), breach of etiquette, clanger (*inf.*), faux pas, gaffe, indiscretion, lapse, mistake, slip, solecism

gaudiness *n* = **garishness**, brashness, flashiness, loudness, naffness, ostentation, poor taste, tastelessness, tawdriness, vulgarity

gaudy[1] *adj* = **garish**, brash, bright, brilliant, brummagem, flash (*inf.*), flashy, florid, gay, gimcrack, glaring, jazzy (*inf.*), loud, meretricious, naff (*Brit. sl.*), ostentatious, raffish, showy, tacky (*inf.*), tasteless, tawdry, vulgar
Antonyms *adj* colourless, conservative, dull, elegant, modest, quiet, refined, sedate, subtle, tasteful

gauge *vb* **1** = **measure**, ascertain, calculate, check, compute, count, determine, weigh **2** = **judge**, adjudge, appraise, assess, estimate, evaluate, guess, rate, reckon, value ◆ *n* **4, 7** = **indicator**, basis, criterion, example, exemplar, guide, guideline, measure, meter, model, par, pattern, rule, sample, standard, test, touchstone, yardstick **9-12** = **size**, bore, capacity, degree, depth, extent, height, magnitude, measure, scope, span, thickness, width

gaunt *adj* **1** = **thin**, angular, attenuated, bony, cadaverous, emaciated, haggard, lank, lean, meagre, pinched, rawboned, scraggy, scrawny, skeletal, skin and bone, skinny, spare, wasted **2** = **bleak**, bare, desolate, dismal, dreary, forbidding, forlorn, grim, harsh, stark
Antonyms *adj* ≠ **thin:** chubby, corpulent, fat, lush, obese, plump, stout, well-fed ≠ **bleak:** inviting, lush, luxurious

gauntness *n* **1** = **thinness**, angularity, boniness, cadaverousness, emaciation, leanness, scragginess, scrawniness, wasted frame **2** = **bleakness**, desolation, forlornness, grimness, harshness, starkness

gauzy *adj* = **delicate**, diaphanous, filmy, flimsy, gossamer, insubstantial, light, see-through, sheer, thin, translucent, transparent

gawk *n* **1** = **oaf**, boor, churl, clod, clodhopper (*inf.*), dolt, dunderhead, galoot (*sl.*), ignoramus, lout, lubber, lummox (*inf.*) ◆ *vb* **2** = **stare**, gape, gawp (*sl.*), gaze open-mouthed, goggle

gawky *adj* = **awkward**, clownish, clumsy, gauche, loutish, lumbering, lumpish, maladroit, oafish, uncouth, ungainly
Antonyms *adj* elegant, graceful, self-assured, well-coordinated

gay *adj* **1** = **homosexual**, bent, dykey (*sl.*), lesbian, pink (*inf.*), queer (*inf., derogatory*) **2** = **cheerful**, animated, blithe, carefree, debonair, full of beans (*inf.*), glad, gleeful, happy, hilarious, insouciant, jolly, jovial, joyful, joyous, light-hearted, lively, merry, sparkling, sunny, vivacious **3** = **colourful**, bright, brilliant, flamboyant, flashy, fresh, garish, gaudy, rich, showy, vivid **4** = **merry**, convivial, festive, frivolous, frolicsome, fun-loving, gamesome, playful, pleasure-seeking, rakish, rollicking, sportive, waggish ◆ *n* **5** = **homosexual**, bull dyke (*offens. sl.*), dyke (*offens. sl.*), faggot (*US offens. sl.*), fairy, invert, lesbian, poof (*offens. sl.*), queer (*offens. sl.*)
Antonyms *adj, n* ≠ **homosexual:** heterosexual, straight ◆ *adj* ≠ **cheerful:** cheerless, down in the dumps (*inf.*), grave, grim, melancholy, miserable, sad, sedate, serious, sober, solemn, sombre, unhappy ≠ **colourful:** colourless, conservative, drab, dull, sombre

gaze *vb* **1** = **stare**, contemplate, eyeball (*sl.*), gape, look, look fixedly, regard, view, watch, wonder ◆ *n* **2** = **stare**, fixed look, look

gazette *n* **1** = **newspaper**, journal, news-sheet, organ, paper, periodical

document containing public notices, appointments, etc. ◆ *vb* **gazettes, gazetting, gazetted. 3** (*tr*) *Brit.* to announce or report (facts or an event) in a gazette. [C17: from F, from It., from Venetian dialect *gazeta* news-sheet costing one *gazet,* small copper coin]

gazetteer (ˌgæzɪˈtɪə) *n* **1** a book or section of a book that lists and describes places. **2** *Arch.* a writer for a gazette.

gazpacho (gəzˈpɑːtʃəʊ, gæs-) *n* a Spanish soup made from tomatoes, peppers, etc., and served cold. [from Sp.]

gazump (gəˈzʌmp) *Brit.* ◆ *vb* **1** to raise the price of something, esp. a house, after agreeing a price verbally with (an intending buyer). **2** (*tr*) to swindle or overcharge. ◆ *n* **3** an instance of gazumping. [C20: from ?]
▸**gaˈzumper** *n*

gazunder (gəˈzʌndə) *Brit.* ◆ *vb* **1** to reduce an offer on a property immediately before exchanging contracts, having previously agreed to a higher price with (the seller). ◆ *n* **2** an act or instance of gazundering. [C20: modelled on GAZUMP]
▸**gaˈzunderer** *n*

GB *abbrev. for* Great Britain.

GBE *abbrev. for* (Knight or Dame) Grand Cross of the British Empire (a Brit. title).

GBH *abbrev. for* grievous bodily harm.

GC *abbrev. for* George Cross (a Brit. award for bravery).

GCB *abbrev. for* (Knight) Grand Cross of the Bath (a Brit. title).

gcd *or* **GCD** *abbrev. for* greatest common divisor.

GCE (in Britain) *abbrev. for* General Certificate of Education: a public examination in specified subjects taken as qualifying examinations for entry into a university, college, etc. The GCSE has replaced it at O level. See also **A level, S level.**

GCHQ (in Britain) *abbrev. for* Government Communications Headquarters.

G clef *n* another name for **treble clef.**

GCMG *abbrev. for* (Knight or Dame) Grand Cross of the Order of St Michael and St George (a Brit. title).

GCSE (in Britain) *abbrev. for* General Certificate of Secondary Education: a public examination in specified subjects for 16-year-old schoolchildren. It replaced GCE O level and CSE.

GCVO *abbrev. for* (Knight or Dame) Grand Cross of the Royal Victorian Order (a Brit. title).

Gd *the chemical symbol for* gadolinium.

g'day *or* **gidday** (gəˈdaɪ) *sentence substitute.* an Australian and NZ informal variant of **good day.**

Gdns *abbrev. for* Gardens.

Ge *the chemical symbol for* germanium.

gean (giːn) *n* a white-flowered tree of the rose family of Europe, W Asia, and N Africa; the ancestor of the cultivated sweet cherries.

gear ❶ (gɪə) *n* **1** a toothed wheel that engages with another toothed wheel or with a rack in order to change the speed or direction of transmitted motion. **2** a mechanism for transmitting motion by gears. **3** the engagement or specific ratio of a system of gears: *in gear; high gear.* **4** personal belongings. **5** equipment and supplies for a particular operation, sport, etc. **6** *Naut.* all equipment or appurtenances belonging to a certain vessel, sailor, etc. **7** short for **landing gear. 8** *Inf.* up-to-date clothes and accessories. **9** *Sl.* drugs of any type. **10** a less common word for **harness** (sense 1). **11 out of gear.** out of order; not functioning properly. ◆ *vb* **12** (*tr*) to adjust or adapt (one thing) so as to fit in or work with another: *to gear our output to current demand.* **13** (*tr*) to equip with or connect by gears. **14** (*intr*) to be in or come into gear. **15** (*tr*) to equip with a harness. [C13: from ON *gervi*]

gearbox (ˈgɪəˌbɒks) *n* **1** the metal casing within which a train of gears is sealed. **2** this metal casing and its contents, esp. in a motor vehicle.

gearing (ˈgɪərɪŋ) *n* **1** an assembly of gears designed to transmit motion. **2** the act or technique of providing gears to transmit motion. **3** Also called: **capital gearing.** *Accounting, Brit.* the ratio of a company's debt capital to its equity capital. US word: **leverage.**

gear lever *or US & Canad.* **gearshift** (ˈgɪəˌʃɪft) *n* a lever used to move gearwheels relative to each other, esp. in a motor vehicle.

gear train *n Engineering.* a system of gears that transmits power from one shaft to another.

gearwheel (ˈgɪəˌwiːl) *n* another name for **gear** (sense 1).

gecko (ˈgekəʊ) *n, pl* **geckos** *or* **geckoes.** a small insectivorous terrestrial lizard of warm regions. [C18: from Malay *ge'kok,* imit.]

gee[1] (dʒiː) *interj* **1** Also: **gee up!** an exclamation, as to a horse or draught animal, to encourage it to turn to the right, go on, or go faster. ◆ *vb* **gees, geeing, geed. 2** (usually foll. by *up*) to move (an animal, esp. a horse) ahead; urge on. [C17: from ?]

gee[2] (dʒiː) *interj US & Canad. inf.* a mild exclamation of surprise, admiration, etc. Also: **gee whizz.** [C20: euphemism for JESUS]

geebung (ˈdʒiːbʌŋ) *n* **1** any of several Australian trees or shrubs with edible but tasteless fruit. **2** the fruit of these trees. [from Abor.]

geek (giːk) *n Sl.* **1** a boring or unattractive social misfit. **2** a degenerate. [C19: prob. from Scot. *geck* fool]
▸ˈ**geeky** *adj*

geelbek (ˈxiːlˌbɛk) *n S. African.* an edible marine fish with yellow jaws. Also called: **Cape salmon.** [from Afrik. *geel* yellow + *bek* mouth]

geese (giːs) *n* the plural of **goose**[1].

geezer (ˈgiːzə) *n Inf.* a man. [C19: prob. from dialect pronunciation of GUISER]

Gehenna (gɪˈhɛnə) *n* **1** *Old Testament.* the valley below Jerusalem, where children were sacrificed and, later, unclean things were burnt. **2** *New Testament, Judaism.* a place where the wicked are punished after death. **3** a place or state of pain and torment. [C16: from LL, from Gk, from Heb. *Gê' Hinnōm,* lit.: valley of Hinnom, symbolic of hell]

Geiger counter (ˈgaɪgə) *or* **Geiger-Müller counter** (ˈmʊlə) *n* an instrument for detecting and measuring the intensity of ionizing radiation. [C20: after Hans *Geiger* and W. *Müller,* 20th-cent. G physicists]

geisha (ˈgeɪʃə) *n, pl* **geisha** *or* **geishas.** a professional female companion for men in Japan, trained in music, dancing, and the art of conversation. [C19: from Japanese, from Ancient Chinese]

Geissler tube (ˈgaɪslə) *n* a glass or quartz vessel for maintaining an electric discharge in a low-pressure gas as a source of visible or ultraviolet light for spectroscopy, etc. [C19: after Heinrich *Geissler* (1814–79), G mechanic]

gel (dʒɛl) *n* **1** a semirigid jelly-like colloid in which a liquid is dispersed in a solid: *nondrip paint is a gel.* **2** a jelly-like substance applied to the hair before styling in order to retain the style. ◆ *vb* **gels, gelling, gelled. 3** to become or cause to become a gel. **4** a variant spelling of **jell.** [C19: from GELATINE]

gelatine (ˈdʒɛləˌtiːn) *or* **gelatin** (ˈdʒɛlətɪn) *n* **1** a colourless or yellowish water-soluble protein prepared by boiling animal hides and bones: used in foods, glue, photographic emulsions, etc. **2** an edible jelly made of this substance. [C19: from F *gélatine,* from Med. L, from L *gelāre* to freeze]

gelatinize *or* **gelatinise** (dʒɪˈlætɪˌnaɪz) *vb* **gelatinizes, gelatinizing, gelatinized** *or* **gelatinises, gelatinising, gelatinised. 1** to make or become gelatinous. **2** (*tr*) *Photog.* to coat (glass, paper, etc.) with gelatine.
▸**geˌlatiniˈzation** *or* ▸**geˌlatiniˈsation** *n*

gelatinous ❶ (dʒɪˈlætɪnəs) *adj* **1** consisting of or resembling jelly; viscous. **2** of, containing, or resembling gelatine.
▸**geˈlatinously** *adv* ▸**geˈlatinousness** *n*

gelation[1] (dʒɪˈleɪʃən) *n* the act or process of freezing a liquid. [C19: from L *gelātiō* a freezing; see GELATINE]

gelation[2] (dʒɪˈleɪʃən) *n* the act or process of forming into a gel. [C20: from GEL]

geld (geld) *vb* **gelds, gelding, gelded** *or* **gelt** (gelt). (*tr*) **1** to castrate (a horse or other animal). **2** to deprive of virility or vitality; emasculate; weaken. [C13: from ON, from *geldr* barren]

gelding (ˈgeldɪŋ) *n* a castrated male horse. [C14: from ON *geldingr;* see GELD, -ING[1]]

gelid (ˈdʒɛlɪd) *adj* very cold, icy, or frosty. [C17: from L *gelidus,* from *gelu* frost]
▸**geˈlidity** *n*

gelignite (ˈdʒɛlɪgˌnaɪt) *n* a type of dynamite in which the nitrogelatine is absorbed in a base of wood pulp and potassium or sodium nitrate. Also called (informal): **gelly.** [C19: from GEL(ATINE) + L *ignis* fire + -ITE[1]]

gem ❶ (dʒɛm) *n* **1** a precious or semiprecious stone used in jewellery as a decoration; jewel. **2** a person or thing held to be a perfect example; treasure. ◆ *vb* **gems, gemming, gemmed. 3** (*tr*) to set or ornament with gems. [C14: from OF, from L *gemma* bud, precious stone]
▸ˈ**gemˌlike** *adj* ▸ˈ**gemmy** *adj*

Gemara (geˈmɑːrə; *Hebrew* gemaˈra) *n Judaism.* the later main part of the Talmud, being a commentary on the Mishnah: the primary source of Jewish religious law. [C17: from Aramaic *gemārā* completion]

geminate *adj* (ˈdʒɛmɪnɪt, -ˌneɪt) *also* **geminated. 1** combined in pairs; doubled: *a geminate leaf.* ◆ *vb* (ˈdʒɛmɪˌneɪt), **geminates, geminating, geminated. 2** to arrange or be arranged in pairs: *the "t"s in "fitted" are geminated.* [C17: from L *gemināre* to double, from *geminus* twin]
▸ˈ**geminately** *adv* ▸ˌ**gemiˈnation** *n*

Gemini (ˈdʒɛmɪˌnaɪ, -ˌniː) *n* **1** *Astron.* a zodiacal constellation in the N hemisphere containing the stars Castor and Pollux. **2** *Astrol.* Also called: the **Twins.** the third sign of the zodiac. The sun is in this sign between about May 21 and June 20.

gemma (ˈdʒɛmə) *n, pl* **gemmae** (-miː). **1** a small asexual reproductive structure in mosses, etc., that becomes detached from the parent and develops into a new individual. **2** *Zool.* another name for **gemmule.** [C18: from L: bud, GEM]

gemmate (ˈdʒɛmeɪt) *adj* **1** (of some plants and animals) having or reproducing by gemmae. ◆ *vb* **gemmates, gemmating, gemmated. 2** (*intr*) to produce or reproduce by gemmae.
▸**gemˈmation** *n*

gemmiparous (dʒɛˈmɪpərəs) *adj* (of plants and animals) reproducing by gemmae or buds. Also: **gemmiferous.**

gemmule (ˈdʒɛmjuːl) *n* **1** *Zool.* a cell or mass of cells produced asexually by sponges and developing into a new individual; bud. **2** *Bot.* a small gemma. [C19: from F, from L *gemmula* a little bud; see GEM]

THESAURUS

gear *n* **1 = cog,** cogwheel, gearwheel, toothed wheel **2 = mechanism,** cogs, gearing, machinery, works **4 = belongings,** baggage, effects, kit, luggage, stuff, things **5 = equipment,** accessories, accoutrements, apparatus, harness, instruments, outfit, paraphernalia, supplies, tackle, tools, trappings **8 = clothing,** apparel, array, attire, clothes, costume, dress, garb, garments, habit, outfit, rigout (*inf.*), threads (*sl.*), togs, wear ◆ *vb* **12 = equip,** adapt, adjust, fit, rig, suit, tailor

gelatinous *adj* **1 = jelly-like,** gluey, glutinous, gummy, mucilaginous, sticky, viscid, viscous

gem *n* **1 = precious stone,** jewel, semiprecious stone, stone **2 = prize,** flower, jewel, masterpiece, pearl, pick, treasure

gemology *or* **gemmology** (dʒɛˈmɒlədʒɪ) *n* the branch of mineralogy concerned with gems and gemstones.
▸**gemological** *or* **gemmological** (ˌdʒɛməˈlɒdʒɪkᵊl) *adj* ▸**gemˈologist** *or* **gemˈmologist** *n*

gemsbok *or* **gemsbuck** (ˈgɛmzˌbʌk) *n, pl* **gemsbok, gemsboks** *or* **gemsbuck, gemsbucks.** an oryx of southern Africa, marked with a broad black band along its flanks. [C18: from Afrik., from G *Gemsbock,* from *Gemse* chamois + *Bock* BUCK[1]]

gemstone (ˈdʒɛmˌstəʊn) *n* a precious or semiprecious stone, esp. one cut and polished.

gen (dʒɛn) *n Brit., Austral., & NZ inf.* information: *give me the gen on your latest project.* See also **gen up.** [C20: from *gen(eral information)*]

gen. *abbrev. for:* **1** gender. **2** general(ly). **3** generic. **4** genitive. **5** genus.

Gen. *abbrev. for:* **1** General. **2** *Bible.* Genesis.

-gen *suffix forming nouns.* **1** producing or that which produces: *hydrogen.* **2** something produced: *carcinogen.* [via F *-gène,* from Gk *-genēs* born]

gendarme (ˈʒɒndɑːm) *n* **1** a member of the police force in France or in countries influenced or controlled by France. **2** a sharp pinnacle of rock on a mountain ridge. [C16: from F, from *gens d'armes* people of arms]

gendarmerie *or* **gendarmery** (ʒɒnˈdɑːmərɪ) *n* **1** the whole corps of gendarmes. **2** the headquarters of a body of gendarmes.

gender (ˈdʒɛndə) *n* **1** a set of two or more grammatical categories into which the nouns of certain languages are divided. **2** any of the categories, such as masculine, feminine, neuter, or common, within such a set. **3** *Inf.* the state of being male, female, or neuter. **4** *Inf.* all the members of one sex: *the female gender.* [C14: from OF, from L *genus* kind]

gender-bender *n Inf.* a person who adopts an androgynous style of dress, hair, etc.

gene (dʒiːn) *n* a unit of heredity composed of DNA occupying a fixed position on a chromosome and transmitted from parent to offspring during reproduction. [C20: from G *Gen,* shortened from *Pangen;* see PAN-, -GEN]

-gene *suffix forming nouns.* a variant of **-gen.**

genealogy Ⓣ (ˌdʒiːnɪˈælədʒɪ) *n, pl* **genealogies.** **1** the direct descent of an individual or group from an ancestor. **2** the study of the evolutionary development of animals and plants from earlier forms. **3** a chart showing the relationships and descent of an individual, group, etc. [C13: from OF, from LL, from Gk, from *genea* race]
▸**genealogical** (ˌdʒiːnɪəˈlɒdʒɪkᵊl) *adj* ▸**ˌgeneaˈlogically** *adv* ▸**ˌgeneˈalogist** *n*

gene bank *n Bot.* a collection of seeds, plants, tissue cultures, etc., of potentially useful species, esp. species containing genes of significance to the breeding of crops.

gene clone *n* See **clone** (sense 2).

genecology (ˌdʒɛnɪˈkɒlədʒɪ) *n* the study of the gene frequency of a species in relation to its population distribution within a particular environment.

gene library *n* a collection of gene clones that represents the genetic material of an organism: used in genetic engineering.

gene pool *n* the total of all the genes and their alleles in a population of a plant or animal species.

genera (ˈdʒɛnərə) *n* a plural of **genus.**

general Ⓣ (ˈdʒɛnərəl, ˈdʒɛnrəl) *adj* **1** common; widespread. **2** of, applying to, or participated in by all or most of the members of a group, category, or community. **3** relating to various branches of an activity, profession, etc.; not specialized: *general office work.* **4** including various or miscellaneous items: *general knowledge; a general store.* **5** not specific as to detail; overall: *a general description.* **6** not definite; vague: *the general idea.* **7** applicable or true in most cases; usual. **8** (*prenominal or immediately postpositive*) having superior or extended authority or rank: *general manager; consul general.* ◆ *n* **9** an officer of a rank senior to lieutenant general, esp. one who commands a large military formation. **10** any person acting as a leader and applying strategy or tactics. **11** a general condition or principle: opposed to *particular.* **12** a title for the head of a religious order, congregation, etc. **13** *Arch.* the people; public. **14 in general.** generally; mostly or usually. [C13: from L *generālis* of a particular kind, from *genus* kind]

general anaesthetic *n* See **anaesthesia.**

General Assembly *n* **1** the deliberative assembly of the United Nations. Abbrev.: **GA. 2** *NZ.* an older name for **parliament. 3** the supreme governing body of certain religious denominations, esp. of the Presbyterian Church.

general average *n Insurance.* loss or damage to a ship or its cargo that is shared among the shipowners and all the cargo owners. Abbrev.: **GA.** Cf. **particular average.**

General Certificate of Education *n* See **GCE.**

General Certificate of Secondary Education *n* See **GCSE.**

general election *n* **1** an election in which representatives are chosen in all constituencies of a state. **2** *US.* a final election from which successful candidates are sent to a legislative body. **3** *US & Canad.* a national, state, or provincial election.

generalissimo (ˌdʒɛnərəˈlɪsɪˌməʊ, ˌdʒɛnrə-) *n, pl* **generalissimos.** a supreme commander of combined military, naval, and air forces. [C17: from It., sup. of *generale* GENERAL]

generality Ⓣ (ˌdʒɛnəˈrælɪtɪ) *n, pl* **generalities. 1** a principle or observation having general application. **2** the state or quality of being general. **3** *Arch.* the majority.

generalization *or* **generalisation** (ˌdʒɛnrəlaɪˈzeɪʃən) *n* **1** a principle, theory, etc., with general application. **2** the act or an instance of generalizing. **3** *Logic.* the derivation of a general statement from a particular one, formally by prefixing a quantifier and replacing a subject term by a bound variable. If the quantifier is universal (**universal generalization**) the argument is not in general valid; if it is existential (**existential generalization**) it is valid.

generalize *or* **generalise** (ˈdʒɛnrəˌlaɪz) *vb* **generalizes, generalizing, generalized** *or* **generalises, generalising, generalised. 1** to form (general principles or conclusions) from (detailed facts, experience, etc.); infer. **2** (*intr*) to think or speak in generalities, esp. in a prejudiced way. **3** (*tr; usually passive*) to cause to become widely used or known.

generally Ⓣ (ˈdʒɛnrəlɪ) *adv* **1** usually; as a rule. **2** commonly or widely. **3** without reference to specific details or facts; broadly.

general practitioner *n* a physician who does not specialize but has a medical practice (**general practice**) in which he treats all illnesses. Informal name: **family doctor.** Abbrev.: **GP.**

general-purpose *adj* having a range of uses; not restricted to one function.

generalship (ˈdʒɛnrəlˌʃɪp) *n* **1** the art or duties of exercising command of a major military formation or formations. **2** tactical or administrative skill.

general staff *n* officers assigned to advise commanders in the planning and execution of military operations.

general strike *n* a strike by all or most of the workers of a country, province, city, etc.

General Synod *n* the governing body, under Parliament, of the Church of England, made up of the bishops and elected clerical and lay representatives.

generate Ⓣ (ˈdʒɛnəˌreɪt) *vb* **generates, generating, generated.** (*mainly tr*) **1** to produce or bring into being; create. **2** (*also intr*) to produce (electricity). **3** to produce (a substance) by a chemical process. **4** *Maths, linguistics.* to provide a precise criterion for membership in (a set). **5** *Geom.* to trace or form by moving a point, line, or plane in a specific way: *circular motion of a line generates a cylinder.* [C16: from L *generāre* to beget, from *genus* kind]
▸ˈ**generable** *adj*

generation Ⓣ (ˌdʒɛnəˈreɪʃən) *n* **1** the act or process of bringing into being; production or reproduction, esp. of offspring. **2** a successive stage in natural descent of people or animals or the individuals produced at each stage. **3** the average time between two such generations of a species: about 35 years for humans. **4** all the people of approximately the same age, esp. when considered as sharing certain attitudes, etc. **5** production of electricity, heat, etc. **6** (*modifier, in combination*) **6a** belonging to a generation specified as having been born in or as having parents, grandparents, etc., born in a given country: *a third-generation American.* **6b** belonging to a specified stage of development in manufacture: *a second-generation computer.*

generation gap *n* the years separating one generation from the next, esp. when regarded as representing the difference in outlook and the lack of understanding between them.

generative (ˈdʒɛnərətɪv) *adj* **1** of or relating to the production of offspring, parts, etc. **2** capable of producing or originating.

generative grammar *n* a description of a language in terms of ex-

THESAURUS

genealogy *n* **1** = **ancestry,** blood line, derivation, descent, extraction, family tree, line, lineage, pedigree, stemma, stirps, stock, strain

general *adj* **1** = **common,** accepted, broad, extensive, popular, prevailing, prevalent, public, universal, widespread **5** = **universal,** across-the-board, all-inclusive, blanket, broad, catholic, collective, comprehensive, encyclopedic, generic, indiscriminate, miscellaneous, overall, overarching, panoramic, sweeping, total **6** = **imprecise,** approximate, ill-defined, inaccurate, indefinite, inexact, loose, undetailed, unspecific, vague **7** = **ordinary,** accustomed, conventional, customary, everyday, habitual, normal, regular, typical, usual
Antonyms *adj* ≠ **common, universal:** distinctive, exceptional, extraordinary, individual, peculiar, special, unusual ≠ **imprecise:** definite, exact, particular, precise, specific ≠ **ordinary:** infrequent, rare

generality *n* **1** = **generalization,** abstract principle, loose statement, sweeping statement, vague notion **2** = **commonness,** acceptedness, breadth, comprehensiveness, extensiveness, popularity, prevalence, ubiquity, universality

generally *adv* **1** = **usually,** almost always, as a rule, by and large, conventionally, customarily, for the most part, habitually, in most cases, largely, mainly, normally, on average, on the whole, ordinarily, regularly, typically **2** = **commonly,** extensively, popularly, publicly, universally, widely **3** = **broadly,** approximately, chiefly, for the most part, in the main, largely, mainly, mostly, on the whole, predominantly, principally
Antonyms *adv* ≠ **usually:** especially, occasionally, rarely, unusually ≠ **commonly:** individually, particularly

generate *vb* **1** = **produce,** beget, breed, bring about, cause, create, engender, form, give rise to, initiate, make, originate, procreate, propagate, spawn, whip up
Antonyms *vb* annihilate, crush, destroy, end, extinguish, kill, terminate

generation *n* **1** = **production,** begetting, breeding, creation, engenderment, formation, genesis, origination, procreation, propagation, reproduction **2** = **age group,** breed, crop **3** = **age,** day, days, epoch, era, period, time, times

plicit rules that ideally generate all and only the grammatical sentences of the language.

generator ('dʒɛnəˌreɪtə) *n* **1** *Physics.* **1a** any device for converting mechanical energy into electrical energy. **1b** a device for producing a voltage electrostatically. **2** an apparatus for producing a gas. **3** a person or thing that generates.

generatrix ('dʒɛnəˌreɪtrɪks) *n, pl* **generatrices** ('dʒɛnəˌreɪtrɪˌsiːz). a point, line, or plane moved in a specific way to produce a geometric figure.

generic Ⓣ (dʒɪ'nɛrɪk) *adj* **1** applicable or referring to a whole class or group; general. **2** *Biol.* of, relating to, or belonging to a genus: *the generic name.* **3** (of a drug, food product, etc.) not having a trademark. [C17: from F; see GENUS]
▸**ge'nerically** *adv*

generic advertising *n* advertising designed to promote a class of product rather than a particular brand.

generosity Ⓣ (ˌdʒɛnə'rɒsɪtɪ) *n, pl* **generosities. 1** willingness and liberality in giving away one's money, time, etc.; magnanimity. **2** freedom from pettiness in character and mind. **3** a generous act. **4** abundance; plenty.

generous Ⓣ ('dʒɛnərəs, 'dʒɛnrəs) *adj* **1** willing and liberal in giving away one's money, time, etc.; munificent. **2** free from pettiness in character and mind. **3** full or plentiful: *a generous portion.* **4** (of wine) rich in alcohol. [C16: via OF from L *generōsus* nobly born, from *genus* race]
▸**'generously** *adv* ▸**'generousness** *n*

genesis Ⓣ ('dʒɛnɪsɪs) *n, pl* **geneses** (-ˌsiːz). a beginning or origin of anything. [OE: via L from Gk; rel. to Gk *gignesthai* to be born]

Genesis ('dʒɛnɪsɪs) *n* the first book of the Old Testament recounting the Creation of the world.

-genesis *n combining form.* indicating genesis, development, or generation: *parthenogenesis.* [NL, from L: GENESIS]
▸**-genetic** *or* **-genic** *adj combining form.*

genet[1] ('dʒɛnɪt) *or* **genette** (dʒɪ'nɛt) *n* **1** an agile catlike mammal of Africa and S Europe, having thick spotted fur and a very long tail. **2** the fur of such an animal. [C15: from OF, from Ar. *jarnayt*]

genet[2] ('dʒɛnɪt) *n* an obsolete spelling of **jennet.**

gene therapy *n* the replacement or alteration of defective genes in order to prevent the occurrence of such inherited diseases as haemophilia. Effected by genetic engineering techniques, it is still at an early stage of development.

genetic (dʒɪ'nɛtɪk) *or* **genetical** *adj* of or relating to genetics, genes, or the origin of something. [C19: from GENESIS]
▸**ge'netically** *adv*

genetic code *n Biochem.* the order in which the four nitrogenous bases of DNA are arranged in the molecule, which determines the type and amount of protein synthesized in the cell.

genetic counselling *n* the provision of advice for couples with a history of inherited disorders who wish to have children, including the likelihood of having affected children, the course and management of the disorder, etc.

genetic engineering *n* alteration of the DNA of a cell as a means of manufacturing animal proteins, making improvements to plants and animals bred by man, etc.

genetic fingerprint *n* the pattern of DNA unique to each individual, that can be analysed in a sample of blood, saliva, or tissue: used as a means of identification.
▸**genetic fingerprinting** *n*

genetic map *n* a graphic representation of the order of genes within chromosomes by means of detailed analysis of the DNA. See also **chromosome map.**
▸**genetic mapping** *n*

genetics (dʒɪ'nɛtɪks) *n* **1** (*functioning as sing*) the study of heredity and variation in organisms. **2** (*functioning as pl*) the genetic features and constitution of a single organism, species, or group.
▸**ge'neticist** *n*

Geneva bands (dʒɪ'niːvə) *pl n* a pair of white linen strips hanging from the front of the collar of some ecclesiastical robes. [C19: after *Geneva*, Switzerland, where orig. worn by Swiss Calvinist clergy]

Geneva Convention *n* the international agreement, first formulated in 1864 at Geneva, establishing a code for wartime treatment of the sick or wounded: revised and extended to cover maritime warfare and prisoners of war.

Geneva gown *n* a black gown with wide sleeves worn by Protestant clerics. [C19: after *Geneva*; see GENEVA BANDS]

Geneva protocol *n* the agreement in 1925 to ban the use of asphyxiating, poisonous, or other gases in war. It does not ban the development or manufacture of such gases.

genial[1] Ⓣ ('dʒiːnjəl, -nɪəl) *adj* **1** cheerful, easy-going, and warm in manner. **2** pleasantly warm, so as to give life, growth, or health. [C16: from L *geniālis* relating to birth or marriage, from *genius* tutelary deity; see GENIUS]
▸**geniality** (ˌdʒiːnɪ'ælɪtɪ) *n* ▸**'genially** *adv*

genial[2] (dʒɪ'niːəl) *adj Anat.* of or relating to the chin. [C19: from Gk, from *genus* jaw]

genic ('dʒɛnɪk) *adj* of or relating to a gene or genes.

-genic *adj combining form.* **1** relating to production or generation: *carcinogenic.* **2** suited to or suitable for: *photogenic.* [from -GEN + -IC]

genie ('dʒiːnɪ) *n* **1** (in fairy tales and stories) a servant who appears by magic and fulfils a person's wishes. **2** another word for **jinni.** [C18: from F, from Ar. *jinni* demon, infl. by L *genius* attendant spirit; see GENIUS]

genista (dʒɪ'nɪstə) *n* any of a genus of leguminous deciduous shrubs, usually having yellow, often fragrant, flowers; broom. [C17: from L]

genital ('dʒɛnɪtᵊl) *adj* **1** of or relating to the sexual organs or to reproduction. **2** *Psychoanal.* relating to the mature stage of psychosexual development. [C14: from L *genitālis* concerning birth, from *gignere* to beget]

genital herpes *n* a sexually transmitted disease caused by the herpes simplex virus, in which painful blisters occur in the genital region.

genitals Ⓣ ('dʒɛnɪtᵊlz) *or* **genitalia** (ˌdʒɛnɪ'teɪlɪə, -'teɪljə) *pl n* the external sexual organs.

genitive ('dʒɛnɪtɪv) *Grammar.* ◆ *adj* **1** denoting a case of nouns, pronouns, and adjectives in inflected languages used to indicate a relation of ownership or association. ◆ *n* **2a** the genitive case. **2b** a word or speech element in this case. [C14: from L *genetīvus* relating to birth, from *gignere* to produce]
▸**genitival** (ˌdʒɛnɪ'taɪvᵊl) *adj*

genitourinary (ˌdʒɛnɪtəʊ'jʊərɪnərɪ) *adj* of or relating to both the reproductive and excretory organs; urogenital: *genitourinary medicine.*

genius Ⓣ ('dʒiːnɪəs, -njəs) *n, pl* **geniuses** *or* (*for senses 5, 6*) **genii** ('dʒiːnɪˌaɪ). **1** a person with exceptional ability, esp. of a highly original kind. **2** such ability. **3** the distinctive spirit of a nation, era, language, etc. **4** a person considered as exerting influence of a certain sort: *an evil genius.* **5** *Roman myth.* **5a** the guiding spirit who attends a person from birth to death. **5b** the guardian spirit of a place. **6** (*usually pl*) *Arabic myth.* a demon; jinn. [C16: from L, from *gignere* to beget]

genizah (gɛ'niːzə) *n, pl* **genizahs** *or* **genizoth** (gɛ'niːzəθ). *Judaism.* a repository for sacred objects which can no longer be used but which may not be destroyed. [C19: from Heb., lit.: a hiding place]

genoa ('dʒɛnəʊə) *n Yachting.* a large jib sail.

genocide ('dʒɛnəʊˌsaɪd) *n* the policy of deliberately killing a nationality or ethnic group. [C20: from Gk *genos* race + -CIDE]
▸ˌ**geno'cidal** *adj*

Genoese (ˌdʒɛnəʊ'iːz) *or* **Genovese** (ˌdʒɛnə'viːz) *n, pl* **Genoese** *or* **Genovese. 1** a native or inhabitant of Genoa. ◆ *adj* **2** of or relating to Genoa or its inhabitants.

genome ('dʒɛˌnəʊm) *n* the complete set of haploid chromosomes that an organism passes on to its offspring in its reproductive cells. [C20: from GEN(E) + (CHROMOS)OME]

genotype ('dʒɛnəʊˌtaɪp) *n* **1** the genetic constitution of an organism. **2** a group of organisms with the same genetic constitution.
▸**genotypic** (ˌdʒɛnəʊ'tɪpɪk) *adj*

-genous *adj combining form.* **1** yielding or generating: *erogenous.* **2** generated by or issuing from: *endogenous.* [from -GEN + -OUS]

genre Ⓣ ('ʒɑːnrə) *n* **1a** kind, category, or sort, esp. of literary or artistic work. **1b** (*as modifier*): *genre fiction.* **2** a category of painting in which incidents from everyday life are depicted. [C19: from F, from OF *gendre;* see GENDER]

THESAURUS

generic *adj* **1** = **collective**, all-encompassing, blanket, common, comprehensive, general, inclusive, sweeping, universal, wide
Antonyms *adj* individual, particular, precise, specific

generosity *n* **1** = **liberality**, beneficence, benevolence, bounteousness, bounty, charity, kindness, largesse *or* largess, munificence, open-handedness **2** = **unselfishness**, disinterestedness, goodness, high-mindedness, magnanimity, nobleness

generous *adj* **1** = **liberal**, beneficent, benevolent, bounteous, bountiful, charitable, free, hospitable, kind, lavish, munificent, open-handed, princely, prodigal, ungrudging, unstinting **2** = **unselfish**, big-hearted, disinterested, good, high-minded, lofty, magnanimous, noble **3** = **plentiful**, abundant, ample, copious, full, fulsome, lavish, liberal, overflowing, rich, unstinting
Antonyms *adj* ≠ **liberal**: avaricious, close-fisted, greedy, mean, miserly, parsimonious, selfish, stingy, tight ≠ **plentiful**: cheap, minimal, scanty, small, tiny

genesis *n* = **beginning**, birth, commencement, creation, dawn, engendering, formation, generation, inception, origin, outset, propagation, root, source, start
Antonyms *n* completion, conclusion, end, finish, termination

genial[1] *adj* **1** = **cheerful**, affable, agreeable, amiable, cheery, congenial, convivial, cordial, easy-going, enlivening, friendly, glad, good-natured, happy, hearty, jolly, jovial, joyous, kind, kindly, merry, pleasant, sunny, warm, warm-hearted
Antonyms *adj* cheerless, cool, discourteous, frigid, morose, rude, sardonic, sullen, unfriendly, ungracious, unpleasant

geniality *n* **1** = **cheerfulness**, affability, agreeableness, amiability, cheeriness, congenialness, conviviality, cordiality, friendliness, gladness, good cheer, good nature, happiness, heartiness, jollity, joviality, joy, joyousness, kindliness, kindness, mirth, pleasantness, sunniness, warm-heartedness, warmth

genitals *pl n* = **sex organs**, genitalia, loins, private parts, pudenda, reproductive organs

genius *n* **1** = **master**, adept, brainbox, buff (*inf.*), expert, hotshot, intellect (*inf.*), maestro, master-hand, mastermind, maven (*US*), virtuoso, whiz (*inf.*) **2** = **brilliance**, ability, aptitude, bent, capacity, creative power, endowment, faculty, flair, gift, inclination, knack, propensity, talent, turn
Antonyms *n* ≠ **master**: dolt, dunce, fool, half-wit, idiot, imbecile, nincompoop, simpleton

genre *n* **1** = **type**, brand, category, character, class, fashion, genus, group, kind, school, sort, species, stamp, style

gens (dʒɛnz) *n, pl* **gentes** ('dʒɛntiːz). **1** (in ancient Rome) any of a group of families, having a common name and claiming descent from a common ancestor in the male line. **2** *Anthropol.* a group based on descent in the male line. [C19: from L: race]

gent (dʒɛnt) *n Inf.* short for **gentleman.**

genteel ❶ (dʒɛn'tiːl) *adj* **1** affectedly proper or refined; excessively polite. **2** respectable, polite, and well-bred. **3** appropriate to polite or fashionable society. [C16: from F *gentil* well-born; see GENTLE]
▸**gen'teelly** *adv* ▸**gen'teelness** *n*

gentian ('dʒɛnʃən) *n* **1** any plant of the genus *Gentiana,* having blue, yellow, white, or red showy flowers. **2** the bitter-tasting roots of the yellow gentian, which can be used as a tonic. [C14: from L *gentiāna;* ? after *Gentius,* a second-century B.C. Illyrian king, reputedly the first to use it medicinally]

gentian violet *n* a greenish crystalline substance that forms a violet solution in water, used as an indicator, antiseptic, and in the treatment of burns.

Gentile ('dʒɛntaɪl) *n* **1** a person, esp. a Christian, who is not a Jew. **2** a Christian, as contrasted with a Jew. **3** a person who is not a member of one's own church: used esp. by Mormons. **4** a heathen or pagan. ◆ *adj* **5** of or relating to a race or religion that is not Jewish. **6** Christian, as contrasted with Jewish. **7** not being a member of one's own church: used esp. by Mormons. **8** pagan or heathen. [C15 *gentil,* from LL *gentīlis,* from L: one belonging to the same tribe]

gentility ❶ (dʒɛn'tɪlɪtɪ) *n, pl* **gentilities. 1** respectability and polite good breeding. **2** affected politeness. **3** noble birth or ancestry. **4** people of noble birth. [C14: from OF, from L *gentīlitās* relationship of those belonging to the same tribe or family; see GENS]

gentle ❶ ('dʒɛntᵊl) *adj* **1** having a mild or kindly nature or character. **2** soft or temperate; mild; moderate. **3** gradual: *a gentle slope.* **4** easily controlled; tame. **5** *Arch.* of good breeding; noble: *gentle blood.* **6** *Arch.* gallant; chivalrous. ◆ *vb* **gentles, gentling, gentled.** (*tr*) **7** to tame or subdue (a horse, etc.). **8** to appease or mollify. ◆ *n* **9** a maggot, esp. when used as bait in fishing. [C13: from OF *gentil* noble, from L *gentīlis* belonging to the same family; see GENS]
▸**'gentleness** *n* ▸**'gently** *adv*

gentle breeze *n* a wind of force 3 on the Beaufort scale, blowing at 8-12 mph.

gentlefolk ('dʒɛntᵊlˌfəʊk) *or* **gentlefolks** *pl n* persons regarded as being of good breeding.

gentleman ❶ ('dʒɛntᵊlmən) *n, pl* **gentlemen. 1** a man regarded as having qualities of refinement associated with a good family. **2** a man who is cultured, courteous, and well-educated. **3** a polite name for a man. **4** the personal servant of a gentleman (esp. in **gentleman's gentleman**).
▸**'gentlemanly** *adj* ▸**'gentlemanliness** *n*

gentleman-farmer *n, pl* **gentlemen-farmers. 1** a person who engages in farming but does not depend on it for his living. **2** a person who owns farmland but does not farm it personally.

gentlemen's agreement *or* **gentleman's agreement** *n* an understanding or arrangement based on honour and not legally binding.

gentlewoman ('dʒɛntᵊlˌwʊmən) *n, pl* **gentlewomen. 1** *Arch.* a woman regarded as being of good family or breeding; lady. **2** (formerly) a woman in personal attendance on a high-ranking lady.

gentrification (ˌdʒɛntrɪfɪ'keɪʃən) *n Brit.* a process by which middle-class people take up residence in a traditionally working-class area, changing its character. [C20: from *gentrify* (to become GENTRY)]
▸**'gentriˌfier** *n*

gentry ❶ ('dʒɛntrɪ) *n* **1** *Brit.* persons just below the nobility in social rank. **2** people of a particular class, esp. one considered to be inferior. [C14: from OF *genterie,* from *gentil* GENTLE]

gents (dʒɛnts) *n* (*functioning as sing*) *Brit. inf.* a men's public lavatory.

genuflect ('dʒɛnjʊˌflɛkt) *vb* (*intr*) **1** to act in a servile or deferential manner. **2** *RC Church.* to bend one or both knees as a sign of reverence. [C17: from Med. L, from L *genu* knee + *flectere* to bend]
▸ˌ**genu'flection** *or* (*esp. Brit.*) ˌ**genu'flexion** *n* ▸**'genuˌflector** *n*

genuine ❶ ('dʒɛnjʊɪn) *adj* **1** not fake or counterfeit; original; real; authentic. **2** not pretending; frank; sincere. **3** being of authentic or original stock. [C16: from L *genuīnus* inborn, hence (in LL) authentic]
▸**'genuinely** *adv* ▸**'genuineness** *n*

gen up *vb* **gens, genning, genned.** (*adv; often passive;* when *intr,* usually foll. by *on*) *Brit. inf.* to make or become fully conversant (with).

genus ❶ ('dʒiːnəs) *n, pl* **genera** *or* **genuses. 1** *Biol.* any of the taxonomic groups into which a family is divided and which contains one or more species. **2** *Logic.* a class of objects or individuals that can be divided into two or more groups or species. **3** a class, group, etc., with common characteristics. [C16: from L: race]

-geny *n combining form.* origin or manner of development: *phylogeny.* [from Gk, from *-genēs* born]
▸**-genic** *adj combining form.*

geo- *combining form.* indicating earth: *geomorphology.* [from Gk, from *gē* earth]

geocentric (ˌdʒiːəʊ'sɛntrɪk) *adj* **1** having the earth at its centre. **2** measured as from the centre of the earth.
▸ˌ**geo'centrically** *adv*

geochronology (ˌdʒiːəʊkrə'nɒlədʒɪ) *n* the branch of geology concerned with ordering and dating events in the earth's history.
▸**geochronological** (ˌdʒiːəʊˌkrɒnə'lɒdʒɪkᵊl) *adj*

geode ('dʒiːəʊd) *n* a cavity, usually lined with crystals, within a rock mass or nodule. [C17: from L *geōdēs* a precious stone, from Gk: earthlike; see GEO-, -ODE[1]]
▸**geodic** (dʒɪ'ɒdɪk) *adj*

geodesic (ˌdʒiːəʊ'dɛsɪk, -'diː-) *adj* **1** Also: **geodetic.** relating to the geometry of curved surfaces. ◆ *n* **2** Also called: **geodesic line.** the shortest line between two points on a curved surface.

geodesic dome *n* a light structural framework arranged as a set of polygons in the form of a shell.

geodesy (dʒɪ'ɒdɪsɪ) *n* the branch of science concerned with determining the exact position of geographical points and the shape and size of the earth. [C16: from F, from Gk *geōdaisia,* from GEO- + *daiein* to divide]
▸**ge'odesist** *n*

geodetic (ˌdʒiːəʊ'dɛtɪk) *adj* **1** of or relating to geodesy. **2** another word for **geodesic.**
▸ˌ**geo'detically** *adv*

geog. *abbrev. for:* **1** geographer. **2** geographic(al). **3** geography.

geographical mile *n* a former name for **nautical mile.**

geography (dʒɪ'ɒgrəfɪ) *n, pl* **geographies. 1** the study of the natural features of the earth's surface, including topography, climate, soil, vegetation, etc., and man's response to them. **2** the natural features of a region.
▸**ge'ographer** *n* ▸**geographical** (ˌdʒɪə'græfɪkᵊl) *or* ˌ**geo'graphic** *adj* ▸ˌ**geo'graphically** *adv*

geoid ('dʒiːɔɪd) *n* **1** a hypothetical surface that corresponds to mean sea level and extends under the continents. **2** the shape of the earth.

geol. *abbrev. for:* **1** geologic(al). **2** geologist. **3** geology.

geology (dʒɪ'ɒlədʒɪ) *n* **1** the scientific study of the origin, structure, and composition of the earth. **2** the geological features of a district or country.
▸**geological** (ˌdʒɪə'lɒdʒɪkᵊl) *or* ˌ**geo'logic** *adj* ▸ˌ**geo'logically** *adv* ▸**ge'ologist** *n*

geom. *abbrev. for:* **1** geometric(al). **2** geometry.

geomagnetism (ˌdʒiːəʊ'mægnɪˌtɪzəm) *n* **1** the magnetic field of the earth. **2** the branch of physics concerned with this.
▸**geomagnetic** (ˌdʒiːəʊmæg'nɛtɪk) *adj*

geometric (ˌdʒɪə'mɛtrɪk) *or* **geometrical** *adj* **1** of, relating to, or following the methods and principles of geometry. **2** consisting of, formed by, or characterized by points, lines, curves, or surfaces. **3** (of design or ornamentation) composed predominantly of simple geometric forms, such as circles, triangles, etc.
▸ˌ**geo'metrically** *adv*

geometric mean *n* the average value of a set of *n* integers, terms, or quantities, expressed as the *n*th root of their product.

THESAURUS

genteel *adj* **2** = **refined,** aristocratic, civil, courteous, courtly, cultivated, cultured, elegant, fashionable, formal, gentlemanly, ladylike, mannerly, polished, polite, respectable, sophisticated, stylish, urbane, well-bred, well-mannered
Antonyms *adj* discourteous, ill-bred, impolite, inelegant, low-bred, natural, plebeian, rude, unaffected, uncultured, unmannerly, unpolished, unrefined

gentility *n* **1** = **nobility,** blue blood, gentle birth, good family, high birth, rank **2** = **refinement,** breeding, civility, courtesy, courtliness, cultivation, culture, decorum, elegance, etiquette, formality, good breeding, good manners, mannerliness, polish, politeness, propriety, respectability, sophistication, urbanity **4** = **aristocracy,** elite, gentlefolk, gentry, nobility, nobles, ruling class, upper class

gentle *adj* **1** = **mild,** amiable, benign, bland, compassionate, dove-like, humane, kind, kindly, lenient, meek, merciful, pacific, peaceful, placid, quiet, soft, sweet-tempered, tender **2** = **moderate,** balmy, calm, clement, easy, light, low, mild, muted, placid, quiet, serene, slight, smooth, soft, soothing, temperate, tranquil, untroubled **3** = **gradual,** easy, imperceptible, light, mild, moderate, slight, slow **4** = **tame,** biddable, broken, docile, manageable, placid, tractable **5** *Archaic* = **well-bred,** aristocratic, civil, courteous, cultured, elegant, genteel, gentlemanlike, gentlemanly, high-born, ladylike, noble, polished, polite, refined, upper-class, well-born
Antonyms *adj* ≠ **mild:** aggressive, cruel, fierce, hard, harsh, heartless, impolite, rough, savage, sharp, unkind ≠ **moderate:** powerful, strong, violent, wild ≠ **gradual:** sudden ≠ **tame:** fierce, savage, unmanageable, wild

gentlemanly *adj* **2** = **polite,** civil, civilized, courteous, cultivated, debonair, gallant, genteel, gentlemanlike, honourable, mannerly, noble, obliging, polished, refined, reputable, suave, urbane, well-bred, well-mannered

gentleness *n* **1** = **tenderness,** compassion, kindliness, kindness, lightness of touch, mansuetude (*arch.*), mildness, softness, sweetness

gentry *n* **1** = **nobility,** aristocracy, elite, gentility, gentlefolk, nobles, ruling class, upper class, upper crust (*inf.*)

genuine *adj* **1** = **authentic,** actual, bona fide, honest, legitimate, natural, on the level, original, pure, real, sound, sterling, the real McCoy, true, unadulterated, unalloyed, veritable **2** = **sincere,** artless, candid, earnest, frank, heartfelt, honest, unaffected, unfeigned
Antonyms *adj* ≠ **authentic:** artificial, bogus, counterfeit, fake, false, fraudulent, imitation, phoney, pseudo (*inf.*), sham, simulated, spurious ≠ **sincere:** affected, false, feigned, hypocritical, insincere, phoney

genus *n* **3** = **type,** breed, category, class, genre, group, kind, order, race, set, sort

geometric progression *n* **1** a sequence of numbers, each of which differs from the succeeding one by a constant ratio, as 1, 2, 4, 8, … Cf. **arithmetic progression. 2 geometric series.** such numbers written as a sum.

geometrid (dʒɪˈɒmɪtrɪd) *n* any of a family of moths, the larvae of which are called measuring worms, inchworms, or loopers. [C19: from NL, from L, from Gk *geometrēs* land measurer, from the looping gait of the larvae]

geometry (dʒɪˈɒmɪtrɪ) *n* **1** the branch of mathematics concerned with the properties, relationships, and measurement of points, lines, curves, and surfaces. **2** a shape, configuration, or arrangement. [C14: from L, from Gk, from *geōmetrein* to measure the land]
▸**geˌomeˈtrician** *n*

geomorphology (ˌdʒiːəʊmɔːˈfɒlədʒɪ) *n* the branch of geology that is concerned with the structure, origin, and development of the topographical features of the earth's crust.
▸**geomorphological** (ˌdʒiːəʊˌmɔːfəˈlɒdʒɪkᵊl) *or* **ˌgeoˌmorphoˈlogic** *adj*

geophysics (ˌdʒiːəʊˈfɪzɪks) *n* (*functioning as sing*) the study of the earth's physical properties and of the physical processes acting upon, above, and within the earth. It includes seismology, meteorology, and oceanography.
▸**ˌgeoˈphysical** *adj* ▸**ˌgeoˈphysicist** *n*

geopolitics (ˌdʒiːəʊˈpɒlɪtɪks) *n* **1** (*functioning as sing*) the study of the effect of geographical factors on politics. **2** (*functioning as pl*) the combination of geographical and political factors affecting a country or area. **3** (*functioning as pl*) politics as they affect the whole world; global politics.
▸**geopolitical** (ˌdʒiːəʊpəˈlɪtɪkᵊl) *adj*

Geordie (ˈdʒɔːdɪ) *Brit.* ◆ *n* **1** a person who comes from or lives in Tyneside. **2** the dialect spoken by these people. ◆ *adj* **3** of or relating to these people or their dialect. [C19: a dim. of *George*]

George Cross (dʒɔːdʒ) *n* a British award for bravery, esp. of civilians. Abbrev.: **GC.**

georgette *or* **georgette crepe** (dʒɔːˈdʒɛt) *n* a thin silk or cotton crepe fabric. [C20: from Mme *Georgette,* a F modiste]

Georgian (ˈdʒɔːdʒjən) *adj* **1** of or relating to any or all of the four kings who ruled Great Britain from 1714 to 1830, or to their reigns. **2** of or relating to George V of Great Britain or his reign (1910–36): *the Georgian poets.* **3** of or relating to Georgia, its people, or their language. **4** of or relating to the American State of Georgia or its inhabitants. **5** (of furniture, architecture, etc.) in or imitative of the style prevalent in Britain during the 18th century. ◆ *n* **6** the official language of Georgia, belonging to the South Caucasian family. **7** a native or inhabitant of Georgia. **8** a native or inhabitant of the American State of Georgia.

geostatics (ˌdʒiːəʊˈstætɪks) *n* (*functioning as sing*) the branch of physics concerned with the statics of rigid bodies, esp. the balance of forces within the earth.

geostationary (ˌdʒiːəʊˈsteɪʃənərɪ) *adj* (of a satellite, etc.) in a circular equatorial orbit in which it circles the earth once in 24 hours so that it appears stationary in relation to the earth's surface.

geostrophic (ˌdʒiːəʊˈstrɒfɪk) *adj* of, relating to, or caused by the force produced by the rotation of the earth: *geostrophic wind.*

geosynchronous (ˌdʒiːəʊˈsɪŋkrənəs) *n* (of a satellite) in an orbit in which it circles the earth once in 24 hours.

geosyncline (ˌdʒiːəʊˈsɪŋklaɪn) *n* a broad elongated depression in the earth's crust.

geotextile (ˌdʒiːəʊˈtɛkstaɪl) *n* any strong synthetic fabric used in civil engineering, as to retain an embankment.

geothermal (ˌdʒiːəʊˈθɜːməl) *or* **geothermic** *adj* of or relating to the heat in the interior of the earth.

geotropism (dʒɪˈɒtrəˌpɪzəm) *n* the response of a plant part to the stimulus of gravity. Plant stems, which grow upwards irrespective of the position in which they are placed, show **negative geotropism.**
▸**geotropic** (ˌdʒiːəʊˈtrɒpɪk) *adj*

Ger. *abbrev. for:* **1** German. **2** Germany.

geranium (dʒɪˈreɪnɪəm) *n* **1** a cultivated plant of the genus *Pelargonium* having scarlet, pink, or white showy flowers. See also **pelargonium. 2** any plant such as cranesbill and herb Robert, having divided leaves and pink or purplish flowers. [C16: from L: cranesbill, from Gk, from *geranos* CRANE]

gerbera (ˈdʒɜːbərə) *n* a genus of African or Asian plants belonging to the composite family, esp. the Transvaal daisy. [C19: from NL, after T. *Gerber* (died 1743), G naturalist]

gerbil *or* **gerbille** (ˈdʒɜːbɪl) *n* a burrowing rodent inhabiting hot dry regions of Asia and Africa. [C19: from F, from NL *gerbillus* a little JERBOA]

gerfalcon (ˈdʒɜːˌfɔːlkən, -ˌfɔːkən) *n* a variant spelling of **gyrfalcon.**

geriatric (ˌdʒɛrɪˈætrɪk) *adj* **1** of or relating to geriatrics or to elderly people. **2** *Inf.* old, decrepit, or useless. ◆ *n* **3** an elderly person. [C20: from Gk *gēras* old age + IATRIC]

geriatrics (ˌdʒɛrɪˈætrɪks) *n* (*functioning as sing*) the branch of medical science concerned with the diagnosis and treatment of diseases affecting elderly people.
▸**ˌgeriaˈtrician** *n*

germ ❶ (dʒɜːm) *n* **1** a microorganism, esp. one that produces disease. **2** (*often pl*) the rudimentary or initial form of something: *the germs of revolution.* **3** a simple structure that is capable of developing into a complete organism. [C17: from F, from L *germen* sprout, seed]

german (ˈdʒɜːmən) *adj* **1** (used in combination) **1a** having the same parents as oneself: *a brother-german.* **1b** having a parent that is a brother or sister of either of one's own parents: *cousin-german.* **2** a less common word for **germane.** [C14: via OF, from L *germānus* of the same race, from *germen* sprout, offshoot]

German (ˈdʒɜːmən) *n* **1** the official language of Germany and Austria and one of the official languages of Switzerland. **2** a native, inhabitant, or citizen of Germany. **3** a person whose native language is German. ◆ *adj* **4** denoting, relating to, or using the German language. **5** relating to, denoting, or characteristic of any German state or its people.

germander (dʒɜːˈmændə) *n* any of several plants of Europe, having two-lipped flowers with a very small upper lip. [C15: from Med. L, ult. from Gk *khamai* on the ground + *drus* oak tree]

germane ❶ (dʒɜːˈmeɪn) *adj* (*postpositive;* usually foll. by *to*) related (to the topic being considered); akin; relevant. [var. of GERMAN]
▸**gerˈmanely** *adv* ▸**gerˈmaneness** *n*

Germanic (dʒɜːˈmænɪk) *n* **1** a branch of the Indo-European family of languages that includes English, Dutch, German, the Scandinavian languages, and Gothic. Abbrev.: **Gmc. 2** Also called: **Proto-Germanic.** the unrecorded language from which all of these languages developed. ◆ *adj* **3** of, denoting, or relating to this group of languages. **4** of, relating to, or characteristic of the German language or any people that speaks a Germanic language. **5** (formerly) of the German people.

germanium (dʒɜːˈmeɪnɪəm) *n* a brittle crystalline grey element that is a semiconducting metalloid: used in transistors, and to strengthen alloys. Symbol: Ge; atomic no.: 32; atomic wt.: 72.59. [C19: NL, after *Germany*]

German measles *n* (*functioning as sing*) a nontechnical name for **rubella.**

German shepherd dog *n* another name for **Alsatian.**

German silver *n* another name for **nickel silver.**

germ cell *n* a sexual reproductive cell.

germicide (ˈdʒɜːmɪˌsaɪd) *n* any substance that kills germs.
▸**ˌgermiˈcidal** *adj*

germinal (ˈdʒɜːmɪnᵊl) *adj* **1** of, relating to, or like germs or a germ cell. **2** of or in the earliest stage of development. [C19: from NL, from L *germen* bud; see GERM]
▸**ˈgerminally** *adv*

germinate ❶ (ˈdʒɜːmɪˌneɪt) *vb* **germinates, germinating, germinated. 1** to cause (seeds or spores) to sprout or (of seeds or spores) to sprout. **2** to grow or cause to grow; develop. **3** to come or bring into existence; originate: *the idea germinated with me.* [C17: from L *germināre* to sprout; see GERM]
▸**ˈgerminative** *adj* ▸**ˌgermiˈnation** *n* ▸**ˈgermiˌnator** *n*

germ plasm *n* **a** the part of a germ cell that contains hereditary material. **b** the germ cells collectively.

germ warfare *n* the military use of disease-spreading bacteria against an enemy.

gerontology (ˌdʒɛrɒnˈtɒlədʒɪ) *n* the scientific study of ageing and the problems associated with elderly people.
▸**gerontological** (ˌdʒɛrɒntəˈlɒdʒɪkᵊl) *adj* ▸**ˌgeronˈtologist** *n*

-gerous *adj combining form.* bearing or producing: *armigerous.* [from L *-ger* bearing + -OUS]

gerrymander (ˈdʒɛrɪˌmændə) *vb* **1** to divide the constituencies of (a voting area) so as to give one party an unfair advantage. **2** to manipulate or adapt to one's advantage. ◆ *n* **3** an act or result of gerrymandering. [C19: from Elbridge *Gerry,* US politician + (SALA)MANDER; from the salamander-like outline of an electoral district reshaped (1812) for political purposes while Gerry was governor of Massachusetts]

gerund (ˈdʒɛrənd) *n* a noun formed from a verb, ending in *-ing,* denoting an action or state: *the living is easy.* [C16: from LL, from L *gerundum* something to be carried on, from *gerere* to wage]
▸**gerundial** (dʒɪˈrʌndɪəl) *adj*

gerundive (dʒɪˈrʌndɪv) *n* **1** (in Latin grammar) an adjective formed from a verb, expressing the desirability, etc., of the activity denoted by the verb. ◆ *adj* **2** of or relating to the gerund or gerundive. [C17: from LL, from *gerundium* GERUND]
▸**gerundival** (ˌdʒɛrənˈdaɪvᵊl) *adj*

gesso (ˈdʒɛsəʊ) *n* **1** a white ground of plaster and size, used to prepare panels or canvas for painting or gilding. **2** any white substance, esp. plaster of Paris, that forms a ground when mixed with water. [C16: from It.: chalk, GYPSUM]

gest *or* **geste** (dʒɛst) *n Arch.* **1** a notable deed or exploit. **2** a tale of adventure or romance, esp. in verse. [C14: from OF, from L *gesta* deeds, from *gerere* to carry out]

Gestalt psychology (gəˈʃtælt) *n* a system of thought that regards all mental phenomena as being arranged in patterns or structures (**gestalts**) perceived as a whole and not merely as the sum of their parts. [C20: from G *Gestalt* form]

THESAURUS

germ *n* **1** = **microbe,** bacterium, bug (*inf.*), microorganism, virus **2** = **beginning,** bud, cause, embryo, origin, root, rudiment, seed, source, spark **3** = **embryo,** bud, egg, nucleus, ovule, ovum, seed, spore, sprout

germane *adj* = **relevant,** akin, allied, apposite, appropriate, apropos, apt, cognate, connected, fitting, kindred, material, pertinent, proper, related, suitable, to the point *or* purpose

Antonyms *adj* extraneous, foreign, immaterial, inappropriate, irrelevant, unrelated

germinate *vb* **1** = **sprout,** bud, develop, generate, grow, originate, pullulate, shoot, swell, vegetate

Gestapo (ge'stɑːpəʊ) *n* the secret state police in Nazi Germany. [from G *Ge(heime) Sta(ats)po(lizei)*, lit.: secret state police]

gestate ➊ ('dʒesteɪt) *vb* **gestates, gestating, gestated. 1** (*tr*) to carry (developing young) in the uterus during pregnancy. **2** (*tr*) to develop (a plan or idea) in the mind. **3** (*intr*) to be in the process of gestating. [C19: from L p.p. of *gestare*, from *gerere* to bear]
▸**ges'tation** *n*

gesticulate ➊ (dʒe'stɪkjʊˌleɪt) *vb* **gesticulates, gesticulating, gesticulated.** to express by or make gestures. [C17: from L, from *gesticulus* (unattested except in LL) gesture, from *gerere* to bear, conduct]
▸**geˌsticu'lation** *n* ▸**ge'sticulative** *adj* ▸**ges'ticuˌlator** *n* ▸**ges'ticulatory** *adj*

gesture ➊ ('dʒestʃə) *n* **1** a motion of the hands, head, or body to express or emphasize an idea or emotion. **2** something said or done as a formality or as an indication of intention. ◆ *vb* **gestures, gesturing, gestured. 3** to express by or make gestures; gesticulate. [C15: from Med. L *gestūra* bearing, from L *gestus*, p.p. of *gerere* to bear]
▸**'gestural** *adj*

get ➊ (get) *vb* **gets, getting, got; got** *or esp. US* **gotten.** (*mainly tr*) **1** to come into possession of; receive or earn. **2** to bring or fetch. **3** to contract or be affected by: *he got a chill.* **4** to capture or seize: *the police got him.* **5** (*also intr*) to become or cause to become or act as specified: *to get one's hair cut; get wet.* **6** (*intr;* foll. by a preposition or adverbial particle) to succeed in going, coming, leaving, etc.: *get off the bus.* **7** (*takes an infinitive*) to manage or contrive: *how did you get to be captain?* **8** to make ready or prepare: *to get a meal.* **9** to hear, notice, or understand: *I didn't get your meaning.* **10** to learn or master by study. **11** (*intr;* often foll. by *to*) to come (to) or arrive (at): *we got home safely; to get to London.* **12** to catch or enter: *to get a train.* **13** to induce or persuade: *get him to leave.* **14** to reach by calculation: *add 2 and 2 and you will get 4.* **15** to receive (a broadcast signal). **16** to communicate with (a person or place), as by telephone. **17** (*also intr;* foll. by *to*) *Inf.* to have an emotional effect (on): *that music really gets me.* **18** *Inf.* to annoy or irritate: *her voice gets me.* **19** *Inf.* to bring a person into a difficult position from which he cannot escape. **20** *Inf.* to puzzle; baffle. **21** *Inf.* to hit: *the blow got him in the back.* **22** *Inf.* to be revenged on, esp. by killing. **23** *Inf.* to have the better of: *your extravagant habits will get you in the end.* **24** (*intr;* foll. by present participle) *Inf.* to begin: *get moving.* **25** (used as a command) *Inf.* go! leave now! **26** *Arch.* to beget or conceive. **27 get with child.** *Arch.* to make pregnant. ◆ *n* **28** *Rare.* the act of begetting. **29** *Rare.* something begotten; offspring. **30** *Brit. sl.* a variant of **git.** ◆ See also **get about, get across,** etc. [OE *gietan*]
▸**'getable** *or* **'gettable** *adj* ▸**'getter** *n*

> **USAGE NOTE** The use of *off* after *get* as in *I got this chair off an antique dealer* is acceptable in conversation, but should not be used in formal writing.

get about *or* **around** *vb* (*intr, adv*) **1** to move around, as when recovering from an illness. **2** to be socially active. **3** (of news, rumour, etc.) to become known; spread.

get across ➊ *vb* **1** to cross or cause to cross. **2** (*adv*) to be or cause to be understood.

get at ➊ *vb* (*intr, prep*) **1** to gain access to. **2** to mean or intend: *what are you getting at?* **3** to irritate or annoy persistently; criticize: *she is always getting at him.* **4** to influence or seek to influence, esp. illegally by bribery, intimidation, etc.: *someone had got at the witness before the trial.*

get away ➊ *vb* (*adv, mainly intr*) **1** to make an escape; leave. **2** to make a start. **3 get away with. 3a** to steal and escape with (money, goods, etc.). **3b** to do (something wrong, illegal, etc.) without being discovered or punished. ◆ *interj* **4** an exclamation indicating mild disbelief. ◆ *n* **getaway. 5** the act of escaping, esp. by criminals. **6** a start or acceleration. **7** a short holiday away from home. **8** (*modifier*) used for escaping: *a getaway car.*

get back ➊ *vb* (*adv*) **1** (*tr*) to recover or retrieve. **2** (*intr;* often foll. by *to*) to return, esp. to a former position or activity. **3** (*intr;* foll. by *at*) to retaliate (against); wreak vengeance (on). **4 get one's own back.** *Inf.* to obtain one's revenge.

get by ➊ *vb* **1** to pass; go past or overtake. **2** (*intr, adv*) *Inf.* to manage, esp. in spite of difficulties. **3** (*intr*) to be accepted or permitted: *that book will never get by the authorities.*

get in ➊ *vb* (*mainly adv*) **1** (*intr*) to enter a car, train, etc. **2** (*intr*) to arrive, esp. at one's home or place of work. **3** (*tr*) to bring in or inside: *get the milk in.* **4** (*tr*) to insert or slip in: *he got his suggestion in before anyone else.* **5** (*tr*) to gather or collect (crops, debts, etc.). **6** to be elected or cause to be elected. **7** (*intr*) to obtain a place at university, college, etc. **8** (foll. by *on*) to join or cause to join (an activity or organization).

get off ➊ *vb* **1** (*intr, adv*) to escape the consequences of an action: *he got off very lightly.* **2** (*adv*) to be or cause to be acquitted: *a good lawyer got him off.* **3** (*adv*) to depart or cause to depart: *to get the children off to school.* **4** (*intr*) to descend (from a bus, train, etc.); dismount: *she got off at the terminus.* **5** to move or cause to move to a distance (from): *get off the field.* **6** (*tr, adv*) to remove; take off: *get your coat off.* **7** (*adv*) to go or send to sleep. **8** (*adv*) to send (letters) or (of letters) to be sent. **9 get off with.** *Brit. inf.* to establish an amorous or sexual relationship (with).

get on ➊ *vb* (*mainly adv*) **1** Also (*when prep*): **get onto.** to board or cause or help to board (a bus, train, etc.). **2** (*tr*) to dress in (clothes as specified). **3** (*intr*) to grow late or (of time) to elapse: *it's getting on and I must go.* **4** (*intr*) (of a person) to grow old. **5** (*intr;* foll. by *for*) to approach (a time, age, amount, etc.): *she is getting on for seventy.* **6** (*intr*) to make progress, manage, or fare: *how did you get on in your exam?* **7** (*intr;* often foll. by *with*) to establish a friendly relationship: *he gets on well with other people.* **8** (*intr;* foll. by *with*) to continue to do: *get on with your homework!*

get out ➊ *vb* (*adv*) **1** to leave or escape or cause to leave or escape: used in the imperative when dismissing a person. **2** to make or become known; publish or be published. **3** (*tr*) to express with difficulty. **4** (*tr;* often foll. by *of*) to extract (information or money) (from a person): *to get a confession out of a criminal.* **5** (*tr*) to gain or receive something, esp. something of significance or value. **6** (foll. by *of*) to avoid or cause to avoid: *she always gets out of swimming.* **7** *Cricket.* to dismiss or be dismissed.

get over ➊ *vb* **1** to cross or surmount (something). **2** (*intr, prep*) to recover from (an illness, shock, etc.). **3** (*intr, prep*) to overcome or master (a problem). **4** (*intr, prep*) to appreciate fully: *I just can't get over seeing you again.* **5** (*tr, adv*) to communicate effectively. **6** (*tr, adv;* sometimes foll. by *with*) to bring (something necessary but unpleasant) to an end: *let's get this job over with quickly.*

get round ➊ *or* **around** *vb* (*intr*) **1** (*prep*) to circumvent or overcome. **2** (*prep*) *Inf.* to have one's way with; cajole: *that girl can get round anyone.* **3** (*prep*) to evade (a law or rules). **4** (*adv;* foll. by *to*) to reach or come to at length: *I'll get round to that job in an hour.*

get through *vb* **1** to succeed or cause or help to succeed in an examination, test, etc. **2** to bring or come to a destination, esp. after overcoming problems: *we got through the blizzards to the survivors.* **3** (*intr, adv*) to contact, as by telephone. **4** (*intr, prep*) to use, spend, or consume (money, supplies, etc.). **5** to complete or cause to complete (a task, process, etc.): *to get a bill through Parliament.* **6** (*adv;* foll. by *to*) to reach the awareness and understanding (of a person): *I just can't get the message through to him.*

THESAURUS

gestation *n* **1, 2** = **development**, evolution, incubation, maturation, pregnancy, ripening

gesticulate *vb* = **signal**, gesture, indicate, make a sign, motion, sign, wave

gesticulation *n* = **signalling**, arm-waving, gestures, waving

gesture *n* **1** = **signal**, action, gesticulation, indication, motion, sign ◆ *vb* **3** = **signal**, gesticulate, indicate, motion, sign, wave

get *vb* **1** = **obtain**, achieve, acquire, attain, bag, bring, come by, come into possession of, earn, fall heir to, fetch, gain, glean, inherit, land, make, net, pick up, procure, realize, reap, receive, score (*sl.*), secure, succeed to, win **3** = **contract**, be afflicted with, become infected with, be smitten by, catch, come down with, fall victim to, take **4** = **capture**, arrest, collar (*inf.*), grab, lay hold of, nab (*inf.*), nail (*inf.*), seize, take, trap **5** = **become**, come to be, grow, turn, wax **7** = **arrange**, contrive, fix, manage, succeed, wangle (*inf.*) **9** = **understand**, catch, comprehend, fathom, follow, get the picture, hear, notice, perceive, see, suss (out) (*sl.*), take in, work out **11** = **arrive**, come, make it (*inf.*), reach **13** = **persuade**, coax, convince, induce, influence, prevail upon, sway, talk into, wheedle, win over **16** = **contact**, communicate with, get in touch with, reach **17** *Informal* = **impress**, affect, arouse, excite, have an effect on, impact on, move, stimulate, stir, touch, tug at (someone's) heartstrings (*often facetious*) **18** *Informal* = **annoy**, bother, bug (*inf.*), gall, get (someone's) goat (*sl.*), irk, irritate, nark (*Brit., Austral., & NZ sl.*), pique, rub (someone) up the wrong way, upset, vex **20** = **puzzle**, baffle, confound, mystify, nonplus, perplex, stump

get across *vb* **1** = **cross**, ford, negotiate, pass over, traverse **2** = **communicate**, bring home to, convey, get (something) through to, impart, make clear *or* understood, put over, transmit

get at *vb* **1** = **gain access to**, acquire, attain, come to grips with, get, get hold of, reach **2** = **imply**, hint, intend, lead up to, mean, suggest **3** = **criticize**, annoy, attack, be on one's back (*sl.*), blame, carp, find fault with, hassle (*inf.*), irritate, nag, nark (*Brit., Austral., & NZ sl.*), pick on, put the boot into (*sl.*), taunt **4** = **corrupt**, bribe, buy off, influence, suborn, tamper with

get away *vb* **1** = **escape**, abscond, break free, break out, decamp, depart, disappear, flee, leave, make good one's escape, slope off ◆ *n* **getaway 5** = **escape**, break, break-out, decampment, flight

get back *vb* **1** = **regain**, recoup, recover, repossess, retrieve **2** = **return**, arrive home, come back *or* home, revert, revisit **3** *with* **at** = **retaliate**, be avenged, get even with, get one's own back, give tit for tat, hit back, settle the score with, take vengeance on

get by *vb* **1** = **pass**, circumvent, get ahead of, go around, go past, overtake, round **2** = **manage**, contrive, cope, exist, fare, get along, keep one's head above water, make both ends meet, subsist, survive

get in *vb* **1** = **enter**, embark, mount, penetrate **2** = **arrive**, alight, appear, come, land

get off *vb* **3, 4** = **leave**, alight, depart, descend, disembark, dismount, escape, exit **6** = **remove**, detach, shed, take off

get on *vb* **1** = **board**, ascend, climb, embark, mount **6** = **progress**, advance, cope, cut it (*inf.*), fare, get along, make out (*inf.*), manage, prosper, succeed **7** = **be friendly**, agree, be compatible, concur, get along, harmonize, hit it off (*inf.*)

get out *vb* **1** = **leave**, alight, break out, clear out, decamp, escape, evacuate, extricate oneself, free oneself, vacate, withdraw **6** *with* **of** = **avoid**, body-swerve (*Scot.*), dodge, escape, evade, shirk

get over *vb* **1** = **cross**, ford, get across, pass, pass over, surmount, traverse **2** = **recover from**, come round, get better, mend, pull through, rally, revive, survive **3** = **overcome**, defeat, get the better of, master, shake off **5** = **communicate**, convey, get *or* put across, impart, make clear *or* understood

get round *vb* **1** = **bypass**, circumvent, edge, evade, outmanoeuvre, skirt **2** *Informal* = **win over**, cajole, coax, convert, persuade, prevail upon, talk round, wheedle

get-together *n* **1** *Inf.* a small informal meeting or social gathering. ◆ *vb* **get together.** (*adv*) **2** (*tr*) to gather or collect. **3** (*intr*) (of people) to meet socially. **4** (*intr*) to discuss, esp. in order to reach an agreement.

get up *vb* (*mainly adv*) **1** to wake and rise from one's bed or cause to wake and rise from bed. **2** (*intr*) to rise to one's feet; stand up. **3** (*also prep*) to ascend or cause to ascend. **4** to increase or cause to increase in strength: *the wind got up at noon.* **5** (*tr*) *Inf.* to dress (oneself) in a particular way, esp. elaborately. **6** (*tr*) *Inf.* to devise or create: *to get up an entertainment for Christmas.* **7** (*tr*) *Inf.* to study or improve one's knowledge of: *I must get up my history.* **8** (*intr*; foll. by *to*) *Inf.* to be involved in: *he's always getting up to mischief.* ◆ *n* **get-up.** *Inf.* **9** a costume or outfit. **10** the arrangement or production of a book, etc.

get-up-and-go *n Inf.* energy or drive.

geum ('dʒiːəm) *n* any herbaceous plant of the rose type, having compound leaves and red, orange, yellow, or white flowers. [C19: NL, from L: herb bennet, avens]

gewgaw ('gjuːgɔː, 'guː-) *n* a showy but valueless trinket. [C15: from ?]

geyser ('giːzə; *US* 'gaɪzər) *n* **1** a spring that discharges steam and hot water. **2** *Brit.* a domestic gas water heater. [C18: from Icelandic *Geysir,* from ON *geysa* to gush]

G-force *n* the force of gravity.

gharry *or* **gharri** ('gærɪ) *n, pl* **gharries.** a horse-drawn vehicle used in India. [C19: from Hindi *gāṛī*]

ghastly ('gɑːstlɪ) *adj* **ghastlier, ghastliest. 1** *Inf.* very bad or unpleasant. **2** deathly pale; wan. **3** *Inf.* extremely unwell; ill. **4** terrifying; horrible. ◆ *adv* **5** unhealthily; sickly: *ghastly pale.* [OE *gāstlīc* spiritual]
▸'**ghastliness** *n*

ghat (gɔːt) *n* (in India) **1** stairs or a passage leading down to a river. **2** a mountain pass. **3** a place of cremation. [C17: from Hindi, from Sansk.]

ghazi ('gɑːzɪ) *n, pl* **ghazis. 1** a Muslim fighter against infidels. **2** (*often cap.*) a Turkish warrior of high rank. [C18: from Ar., from *ghazā* he made war]

ghee (giː) *n* a clarified butter used in Indian cookery. [C17: from Hindi *ghī,* from Sansk. *ghri* sprinkle]

gherkin ('gɜːkɪn) *n* **1** the small immature fruit of any of various cucumbers, used for pickling. **2a** a tropical American climbing plant. **2b** its small spiny edible fruit. [C17: from Du., dim. of *gurk,* ult. from Gk *angourion*]

ghetto ('getəʊ) *n, pl* **ghettos** *or* **ghettoes. 1** a densely populated slum area of a city inhabited by a socially and economically deprived minority. **2** an area or community that is segregated or isolated. **3** an area in a European city in which Jews were formerly required to live. [C17: from It., ?from *borghetto,* dim. of *borgo* settlement outside a walled city, or from *ghetto* foundry, because one occupied the site of the later Venetian ghetto]

ghettoblaster ('getəʊˌblɑːstə) *n Inf.* a large portable cassette recorder with built-in speakers.

ghettoize *or* **ghettoise** ('getəʊˌaɪz) *vb* **ghettoizes, ghettoizing, ghettoized** *or* **ghettoises, ghettoising, ghettoised.** (*tr*) to confine or restrict to a particular area, activity, or category: *to ghettoize women as housewives.*
▸ˌ**ghettoi'zation** *or* ˌ**ghettoi'sation** *n*

ghillie ('gɪlɪ) *n* a variant spelling of **gillie.**

ghost (gəʊst) *n* **1** the disembodied spirit of a dead person, supposed to haunt the living as a pale or shadowy vision; phantom. Related adj: **spectral. 2** a haunting memory: *the ghost of his former life rose up before him.* **3** a faint trace or possibility of something; glimmer: *a ghost of a smile.* **4** the spirit; soul (archaic, except in **the Holy Ghost**). **5** *Physics.* **5a** a faint secondary image produced by an optical system. **5b** a similar image on a television screen. **6** (*modifier*) falsely recorded as doing a particular job or fulfilling a particular function in order that some benefit, esp. money, may be obtained: *a ghost worker.* **7 give up the ghost.** to die. ◆ *vb* **8** See **ghostwrite. 9** (*tr*) to haunt. [OE *gāst*]
▸'**ghostˌlike** *adj* ▸'**ghostly** *adj*

ghost town *n* a deserted town, esp. one in the western US that was formerly a boom town.

ghost word *n* a word that has entered the language through the perpetuation, in dictionaries, etc., of an error.

ghostwrite ('gəʊstˌraɪt) *vb* **ghostwrites, ghostwriting, ghostwrote, ghostwritten.** to write (an article, etc.) on behalf of a person who is then credited as the author. Often shortened to **ghost.**
▸'**ghostˌwriter** *n*

ghoul (guːl) *n* **1** a malevolent spirit or ghost. **2** a person interested in morbid or disgusting things. **3** a person who robs graves. **4** (in Muslim legend) an evil demon thought to eat corpses. [C18: from Ar. *ghūl,* from *ghāla* he seized]
▸'**ghoulish** *adj* ▸'**ghoulishly** *adv* ▸'**ghoulishness** *n*

GHQ *Mil. abbrev. for* General Headquarters.

ghyll (gɪl) *n* a variant spelling of **gill**[3].

GI *US inf.* ◆ *n* **1** (*pl* **GIs** *or* **GI's**) a soldier in the US Army, esp. an enlisted man. ◆ *adj* **2** conforming to US Army regulations. [C20: abbrev. of *government issue*]

gi. *abbrev. for* gill (unit of measure).

giant ('dʒaɪənt) *n* **1** Also (fem): **giantess** ('dʒaɪəntɪs). a mythical figure of superhuman size and strength, esp. in folklore or fairy tales. **2** a person or thing of exceptional size, reputation, etc. ◆ *adj* **3** remarkably or supernaturally large. [C13: from OF *geant,* from L *gigant-, gigās,* from Gk]

giant hogweed *n* a species of cow parsley that grows up to 3½ metres (10 ft) and whose irritant hairs and sap can cause a severe reaction.

giantism ('dʒaɪənˌtɪzəm) *n* another term for **gigantism** (sense 1).

giant panda *n* See **panda** (sense 1).

giant slalom *n Skiing.* a type of slalom in which the course is longer and the obstacles are further apart than in a standard slalom.

giant star *n* any of a class of stars that have swelled and brightened as they approach the end of their life, their energy supply having changed.

giaour ('dʒaʊə) *n* a derogatory term for a non-Muslim, esp. a Christian. [C16: from Turkish: unbeliever, from Persian *gaur*]

gib (gɪb) *n* **1** a metal wedge, pad, or thrust bearing, esp. a brass plate let into a steam engine crosshead. ◆ *vb* **gibs, gibbing, gibbed. 2** (*tr*) to fasten or supply with a gib. [C18: from ?]

gibber[1] ('dʒɪbə) *vb* **1** to utter rapidly and unintelligibly; prattle. **2** (*intr*) (of monkeys and related animals) to make characteristic chattering sounds. [C17: imit.]

gibber[2] ('gɪbə) *n Austral.* **1** a stone or boulder. **2** (*modifier*) of or relating to a dry flat area of land covered with wind-polished stones: *gibber plains.* [C19: from Abor.]

gibberellin (ˌdʒɪbə'relɪn) *n* any of several plant hormones whose main action is to cause elongation of the stem. [C20: from NL *Gibberella,* lit.: a little hump, from L *gibber* hump + -IN]

gibberish ('dʒɪbərɪʃ) *n* **1** rapid chatter. **2** incomprehensible talk; nonsense.

gibbet ('dʒɪbɪt) *n* **1a** a wooden structure resembling a gallows, from which the bodies of executed criminals were formerly hung to public view. **1b** a gallows. ◆ *vb* (*tr*) **2** to put to death by hanging on a gibbet. **3** to hang (a corpse) on a gibbet. **4** to expose to public ridicule. [C13: from OF: gallows, lit.: little cudgel, from *gibe* cudgel; from ?]

gibbon ('gɪbən) *n* a small agile arboreal anthropoid ape inhabiting forests in S Asia. [C18: from F, prob. from an Indian dialect word]

gibbous ('gɪbəs) *or* **gibbose** ('gɪbəʊs) *adj* **1** (of the moon or a planet) more than half but less than fully illuminated. **2** hunchbacked. **3** bulging. [C17: from LL *gibbōsus* humpbacked, from L *gibba* hump]
▸'**gibbously** *adv* ▸'**gibbousness** *or* **gibbosity** (gɪ'bɒsɪtɪ) *n*

gibe[1] *or* **jibe** (dʒaɪb) *vb* **gibes, gibing, gibed** *or* **jibes, jibing, jibed. 1** to make jeering or scoffing remarks (at); taunt. ◆ *n* **2** a derisive or provoking remark. [C16: ?from OF *giber* to treat roughly, from ?]
▸'**giber** *or* '**jiber** *n*

gibe[2] (dʒaɪb) *vb* **gibes, gibing, gibed,** *n Naut.* a variant spelling of **gybe.**

giblets ('dʒɪblɪts) *pl n* (*sometimes sing*) the gizzard, liver, heart, and neck of a fowl. [C14: from OF *gibelet* stew of game birds, prob. from *gibier* game, of Gmc origin]

gidday (gə'daɪ) *sentence substitute.* a variant spelling of **g'day.**

giddy ('gɪdɪ) *adj* **giddier, giddiest. 1** affected with a reeling sensation and feeling as if about to fall; dizzy. **2** causing or tending to cause vertigo. **3** impulsive; scatterbrained. ◆ *vb* **giddies, giddying, giddied. 4** to

THESAURUS

get-together *n* **1 = gathering,** celebration, conference, do (*inf.*), function, knees-up (*Brit. inf.*), meeting, party, reception, social ◆ *vb* **get together 2 = collect,** accumulate, assemble, gather **3 = meet,** congregate, convene, converge, gather, join, muster, rally

get up *vb* **2-4 = arise,** ascend, climb, increase, mount, rise, scale, stand

ghastly *adj* **2 = pale,** ashen, cadaverous, deathlike, deathly pale, like death warmed up (*inf.*), livid, pallid, spectral, wan **4 = horrible,** dreadful, frightful, from hell (*inf.*), grim, grisly, gruesome, hideous, horrendous, horrid, loathsome, repellent, shocking, terrible, terrifying
Antonyms *adj* ≠ **pale:** appealing, attractive, beautiful, blooming, charming, healthy, lovely, pleasing

ghost *n* **1 = spirit,** apparition, eidolon, manes, phantasm, phantom, revenant, shade (*literary*), soul, spectre, spook (*inf.*), wraith **3 = trace,** glimmer, hint, possibility, semblance, shadow, suggestion

ghostly *adj* **1 = supernatural,** eerie, ghostlike, illusory, insubstantial, phantasmal, phantom, spectral, spooky (*inf.*), uncanny, unearthly, weird, wraithlike

ghoulish *adj* **2 = macabre,** disgusting, grisly, gruesome, morbid, sick (*inf.*), unwholesome

giant *n* **1 = ogre,** behemoth, colossus, Hercules, leviathan, monster, titan ◆ *adj* **3 = huge,** colossal, elephantine, enormous, gargantuan, gigantic, ginormous, immense, jumbo (*inf.*), large, mammoth, monstrous, prodigious, stellar (*inf.*), titanic, vast
Antonyms *adj* ≠ **huge:** dwarf, Lilliputian, miniature, pygmy *or* pigmy, tiny

gibber[1] *vb* **1 = gabble,** babble, blab, blabber, blather, cackle, chatter, jabber, prattle, rabbit (*Brit. inf.*), waffle (*inf., chiefly Brit.*)

gibberish *n* **2 = nonsense,** all Greek (*inf.*), babble, balderdash, blather, bunkum *or* buncombe (*chiefly US*), double talk, drivel, gabble, garbage (*inf.*), gobbledegook (*inf.*), guff (*sl.*), hogwash, hokum (*sl., chiefly US & Canad.*), jabber, moonshine, mumbo jumbo, poppycock (*inf.*), prattle, tommyrot, tosh (*sl., chiefly Brit.*), tripe (*inf.*), twaddle

gibbous *adj* **1, 3 = bulging,** convex, protuberant, rounded **2 = hunchbacked,** crookbacked, humpbacked, humped, hunched

gibe[1] *vb* **1 = taunt,** deride, flout, jeer, make fun of, mock, poke fun at, ridicule, scoff, scorn, sneer, take the piss out of (*sl.*), twit ◆ *n* **2 = taunt,** barb, crack (*sl.*), cutting remark, derision, dig, jeer, mockery, ridicule, sarcasm, scoffing, sneer

giddiness *n* **1 = dizziness,** faintness, lightheadedness, vertigo

giddy *adj* **1 = dizzy,** faint, light-headed, reeling, unsteady, vertiginous **3 = scatterbrained,** capri-

make or become giddy. [OE *gydig* mad, frenzied, possessed by God; rel. to GOD]
▸'**giddily** *adv* ▸'**giddiness** *n*

gidgee *or* **gidjee** ('gɪdʒiː) *n Austral.* **1** a small acacia tree yielding useful timber. **2** a spear made of this. [C19: from Abor.]

gie (giː) *vb* **gies, gi'ing, gi'ed.** a Scot. word for **give.**

gift Ⓣ (gɪft) *n* **1** something given; a present. **2** a special aptitude, ability, or power; talent. **3** the power or right to give or bestow (esp. in **in the gift of, in (someone's) gift**). **4** the act or process of giving. **5 look a gift-horse in the mouth.** (*usually negative*) to find fault with a free gift or chance benefit. ◆ *vb (tr)* **6** to present (something) as a gift to (a person). [OE *gift* payment for a wife, dowry; see GIVE]

GIFT (gɪft) *n acronym for* gamete intrafallopian transfer: a technique, similar to IVF, that enables some women who cannot conceive to bear children.

gifted Ⓣ ('gɪftɪd) *adj* having or showing natural talent or aptitude: *a gifted musician.*
▸'**giftedly** *adv* ▸'**giftedness** *n*

gift of tongues *n* an utterance, partly or wholly unintelligible, produced under the influence of ecstatic religious emotion. Also called: **glossolalia.**

giftwrap ('gɪftˌræp) *vb* **giftwraps, giftwrapping, giftwrapped.** to wrap (a gift) attractively.

gig[1] (gɪg) *n* **1** a light two-wheeled one-horse carriage without a hood. **2** *Naut.* a light tender for a vessel. **3** a long light rowing boat, used esp. for racing. ◆ *vb* **gigs, gigging, gigged. 4** (*intr*) to travel in a gig. [C13 (in the sense: flighty girl, spinning top): ?from ON]

gig[2] (gɪg) *n* **1** a cluster of barbless hooks drawn through a shoal of fish to try to impale them. ◆ *vb* **gigs, gigging, gigged. 2** to catch (fish) with a gig. [C18: ? shortened from obs. *fishgig* or *fizgig* kind of harpoon]

gig[3] (gɪg) *n* **1** a job, esp. a single booking for jazz or pop musicians. **2** the performance itself. ◆ *vb* **gigs, gigging, gigged. 3** (*intr*) to perform at a gig or gigs. [C20: from ?]

giga- ('gɪgə, 'gaɪgə) *combining form.* **1** denoting 10^9: *gigahertz.* **2** *Computing.* denoting 2^{30}: *gigabyte.* Symbol: G [from Gk *gigas* GIANT]

gigaflop ('gaɪgəˌflɒp) *n Computing.* a measure of processing speed, consisting of a thousand million floating-point operations a second. [C20: from GIGA- + *flo(ating) p(oint)*]

gigantic Ⓣ (dʒaɪ'gæntɪk) *adj* **1** very large; enormous. **2** Also: **gigantesque** (ˌdʒaɪgæn'tɛsk). of or suitable for giants. [C17: from Gk *gigantikos,* from *gigas* GIANT]
▸**gi'gantically** *adv*

gigantism ('dʒaɪgænˌtɪzəm, dʒaɪ'gæntɪzəm) *n* **1** Also called: **giantism.** excessive growth of the entire body, caused by overproduction of growth hormone by the pituitary gland. **2** the state or quality of being gigantic.

giggle Ⓣ ('gɪgᵊl) *vb* **giggles, giggling, giggled. 1** (*intr*) to laugh nervously or foolishly. ◆ *n* **2** such a laugh. **3** *Inf.* something or someone that causes amusement. [C16: imit.]
▸'**giggler** *n* ▸'**giggling** *adj, n* ▸'**giggly** *adj*

gigolo ('ʒɪgəˌləʊ) *n, pl* **gigolos. 1** a man who is kept by a woman, esp. an older woman. **2** a man who is paid to dance with or escort women. [C20: from F, back formation from *gigolette* girl for hire as a dancing partner, prostitute, ult. from *gigue* a fiddle]

gigot ('dʒɪgət) *n* **1** a leg of lamb or mutton. **2** a leg-of-mutton sleeve. [C16: from OF: leg, a small fiddle, from *gigue* a fiddle, of Gmc origin]

gigue (ʒiːg) *n* a piece of music, usually in six-eight time, incorporated into the classical suite. [C17: from F, from It. *giga,* lit.: a fiddle; see GIGOT]

Gila monster ('hiːlə) *n* a large venomous brightly coloured lizard inhabiting deserts of the southwestern US and Mexico. [C19: after the *Gila,* a river in New Mexico and Arizona]

gilbert ('gɪlbət) *n* the cgs unit of magnetomotive force. Symbol: Gb, Gi [C19: after William *Gilbert* (1540–1603), E scientist]

gild[1] Ⓣ (gɪld) *vb* **gilds, gilding, gilded** *or* **gilt.** (*tr*) **1** to cover with or as if with gold. **2 gild the lily. 2a** to adorn unnecessarily something already beautiful. **2b** to praise someone inordinately. **3** to give a falsely attractive or valuable appearance to. [OE *gyldan,* from *gold* GOLD]
▸'**gilder** *n*

gild[2] (gɪld) *n* a variant spelling of **guild.**

gilding ('gɪldɪŋ) *n* **1** the act or art of applying gilt to a surface. **2** the surface so produced. **3** another word for **gilt**[1] (sense 2).

gilet (dʒɪ'leɪ) *n* a garment resembling a waistcoat. [C20: F, lit.: waistcoat]

gill[1] (gɪl) *n* **1** the respiratory organ in many aquatic animals. **2** any of the radiating leaflike spore-producing structures on the undersurface of the cap of a mushroom. [C14: from ON]
▸**gilled** *adj*

gill[2] (dʒɪl) *n* a unit of liquid measure equal to one quarter of a pint. [C14: from OF *gille* vat, tub, from LL *gillō,* from ?]

gill[3] *or* **ghyll** (gɪl) *n Dialect.* **1** a narrow stream; rivulet. **2** a wooded ravine. [C11: from ON *gil* steep-sided valley]

gillie, ghillie, *or* **gilly** ('gɪlɪ) *n, pl* **gillies** *or* **ghillies.** *Scot.* **1** an attendant or guide for hunting or fishing. **2** (formerly) a Highland chieftain's male attendant. [C17: from Scot. Gaelic *gille* boy, servant]

gills (gɪlz) *pl n* **1** (*sometimes sing*) the wattle of birds such as domestic fowl. **2** the cheeks and jowls of a person. **3 green about the gills.** *Inf.* looking or feeling nauseated.

gillyflower *or* **gilliflower** ('dʒɪlɪˌflaʊə) *n* **1** any of several plants having fragrant flowers, such as the stock and wallflower. **2** an archaic name for **carnation.** [C14: from *gilofre,* from OF *girofle,* from Med. L, from Gk: clove tree, from *karuon* nut + *phullon* leaf]

gilt[1] (gɪlt) *vb* **1** a past tense and past participle of **gild**[1]. ◆ *n* **2** gold or a substance simulating it, applied in gilding. **3** another word for **gilding** (senses 1, 2). **4** superficial or false appearance of excellence. **5** a gilt-edged security. **6 take the gilt off the gingerbread.** to destroy the part of something that gives it its appeal. ◆ *adj* **7** covered with or as if with gold or gilt; gilded.

gilt[2] (gɪlt) *n* a young female pig, esp. one that has not had a litter. [C15: from ON *gyltr*]

gilt-edged *adj* **1** denoting government securities on which interest payments will certainly be met and that will certainly be repaid at par on the due date. **2** of the highest quality: *the last track on the album is a gilt-edged classic.* **3** (of books, papers, etc.) having gilded edges.

gimbals ('dʒɪmbᵊlz, 'gɪm-) *pl n* a device, consisting of two or three pivoted rings at right angles to each other, that provides free suspension in all planes for a compass, chronometer, etc. Also called: **gimbal ring.** [C16: var. of earlier *gimmal,* from OF *gemel* double finger ring, from L *gemellus,* dim. of *geminus* twin]

gimcrack ('dʒɪmˌkræk) *adj* **1** cheap; shoddy. ◆ *n* **2** a cheap showy trifle or gadget. [C18: from C14 *gibecrake* little ornament, from ?]
▸'**gimˌcrackery** *n*

gimlet ('gɪmlɪt) *n* **1** a small hand tool consisting of a pointed spiral tip attached at right angles to a handle, used for boring small holes in wood. **2** *US.* a cocktail consisting of half gin or vodka and half lime juice. ◆ *vb* **3** (*tr*) to make holes in (wood) using a gimlet. ◆ *adj* **4** penetrating; piercing (esp. in **gimlet-eyed**). [C15: from OF *guimbelet,* of Gmc origin, see WIMBLE]

gimmick Ⓣ ('gɪmɪk) *n Inf.* **1** something designed to attract extra attention, interest, or publicity. **2** any clever device, gadget, or stratagem, esp. one used to deceive. [C20: orig. US sl., from ?]
▸'**gimmickry** *n* ▸'**gimmicky** *adj*

gimp *or* **guimpe** (gɪmp) *n* a tapelike trimming. [C17: prob. from Du. *gimp,* from ?]

gin[1] (dʒɪn) *n* an alcoholic drink obtained by distillation of the grain of malted barley, rye, or maize, flavoured with juniper berries. [C18: from Du. *genever,* via OF from L *jūniperus* JUNIPER]

gin[2] (dʒɪn) *n* **1** a primitive engine in which a vertical shaft is turned by horses driving a horizontal beam in a circle. **2** Also called: **cotton gin.** a machine of this type used for separating seeds from raw cotton. **3** a trap for catching small mammals, consisting of a noose of thin strong wire. ◆ *vb* **gins, ginning, ginned.** (*tr*) **4** to free (cotton) of seeds with a gin. **5** to trap or snare (game) with a gin. [C13 *gyn,* from ENGINE]

gin[3] (gɪn) *vb* **gins, ginning, gan** (gæn), **gun** (gʌn). an archaic word for **begin.**

gin[4] (dʒɪn) *n Austral. offens. sl.* an Aboriginal woman. [C19: from Abor.]

ginger ('dʒɪndʒə) *n* **1** any of several plants of the East Indies, cultivated throughout the tropics for their spicy hot-tasting underground stems. **2** the underground stem of this plant, which is used fresh or powdered as a flavouring or crystallized as a sweetmeat. **3a** a reddish-brown or yellowish-brown colour. **3b** (*as adj*): *ginger hair.* **4** *Inf.* liveliness; vigour. [C13: from OF *gingivre,* ult. from Sansk. *śṛṅgaveram,* from *śṛṅga-* horn + *vera-* body, referring to its shape]
▸'**gingery** *adj*

ginger ale *n* a sweetened effervescent nonalcoholic drink flavoured with ginger extract.

ginger beer *n* a slightly alcoholic drink made by fermenting a mixture of syrup and root ginger.

gingerbread ('dʒɪndʒəˌbrɛd) *n* **1** a moist brown cake, flavoured with ginger and treacle. **2a** a biscuit, similarly flavoured, cut into various shapes. **2b** (*as modifier*): *gingerbread man.* **3** an elaborate but unsubstantial ornamentation.

THESAURUS

cious, careless, changeable, changeful, ditzy *or* ditsy (*sl.*), dizzy, erratic, fickle, flighty, frivolous, heedless, impulsive, inconstant, irresolute, irresponsible, reckless, silly, thoughtless, unbalanced, unstable, unsteady, vacillating, volatile, wild
Antonyms *adj* ≠ **scatterbrained:** calm, constant, determined, earnest, resolute, serious, steady

gift *n* **1** = **donation,** benefaction, bequest, bonus, boon, bounty, contribution, grant, gratuity, hand-out, largesse *or* largess, legacy, offering, present **2** = **talent,** ability, aptitude, attribute, bent, capability, capacity, endowment, faculty, flair, genius, knack, power, turn

gifted *adj* = **talented,** able, accomplished, adroit, brilliant, capable, clever, expert, ingenious, intelligent, masterly, skilled
Antonyms *adj* amateur, backward, dull, incapable, inept, retarded, slow, talentless, unskilled

gigantic *adj* **1** = **enormous,** Brobdingnagian, colossal, Cyclopean, elephantine, gargantuan, giant, herculean, huge, immense, mammoth, monstrous, prodigious, stellar (*inf.*), stupendous, titanic, tremendous, vast
Antonyms *adj* diminutive, insignificant, little, miniature, puny, small, tiny, weak

giggle *vb* **1** = **laugh,** cackle, chortle, chuckle, snigger, tee-hee, titter, twitter ◆ *n* **2** = **laugh,** cackle, chortle, chuckle, snigger, tee-hee, titter, twitter

gild[1] *vb* **3** = **embellish,** adorn, beautify, bedeck, brighten, coat, deck, dress up, embroider, enhance, enrich, garnish, grace, ornament

gimmick *n* **1, 2** = **stunt,** contrivance, device, dodge, gadget, gambit, gizmo (*sl., chiefly US*), ploy, scheme, stratagem, trick

ginger group *n Chiefly Brit.* a group within a party, association, etc., that enlivens or radicalizes its parent body.

gingerly Ⓣ (ˈdʒɪndʒəlɪ) *adv* **1** in a cautious, reluctant, or timid manner. ◆ *adj* **2** cautious, reluctant, or timid. [C16: ?from OF *gensor* dainty, from *gent* of noble birth; see GENTLE]

ginger nut *or* **snap** *n* a crisp biscuit flavoured with ginger.

gingham (ˈgɪŋəm) *n* a cotton fabric, usually woven of two coloured yarns in a checked or striped design. [C17: from F, from Malay *ginggang* striped cloth]

gingili (ˈdʒɪndʒɪlɪ) *n* **1** the oil obtained from sesame seeds. **2** another name for **sesame.** [C18: from Hindi *jingalī*]

gingiva (ˈdʒɪndʒɪvə, dʒɪnˈdʒaɪvə) *n, pl* **gingivae** (-dʒɪˌviː, -ˈdʒaɪviː). *Anat.* the technical name for the **gum**[2]. [from L]
►ˈ**gingival** *adj*

gingivitis (ˌdʒɪndʒɪˈvaɪtɪs) *n* inflammation of the gums.

ginglymus (ˈdʒɪŋglɪməs, ˈgɪŋ-) *n, pl* **ginglymi** (-ˌmaɪ). *Anat.* a hinge joint. [C17: NL, from Gk *ginglumos* hinge]

gink (gɪŋk) *n Sl.* a man or boy, esp. one considered to be odd. [C20: from ?]

ginkgo (ˈgɪŋkgəʊ) *or* **gingko** (ˈgɪŋkəʊ) *n, pl* **ginkgoes** *or* **gingkoes.** a widely planted ornamental Chinese tree with fan-shaped deciduous leaves and fleshy yellow fruit. Also called: **maidenhair tree.** [C18: from Japanese, from Ancient Chinese: silver + apricot]

ginormous (dʒaɪˈnɔːməs) *adj Inf.* very large. [C20: blend of *giant* or *gigantic* & *enormous*]

gin palace (dʒɪn) *n* (formerly) a gaudy drinking house.

gin rummy (dʒɪn) *n* a version of rummy in which a player may go out if the odd cards outside his sequences total less than ten points. [C20: from GIN[1] + RUMMY]

ginseng (ˈdʒɪnsɛŋ) *n* **1** either of two plants of China or of North America, whose forked aromatic roots are used medicinally. **2** the root of either of these plants or a substance obtained from the roots, believed to possess tonic and energy-giving properties. [C17: from Mandarin Chinese *jen shen*]

Gioconda (*Italian* dʒoˈkonda) *n* **1 La.** Also called: **Mona Lisa.** the portrait by Leonardo da Vinci of a young woman with an enigmatic smile. ◆ *adj* **2** mysterious or enigmatic. [It.: the smiling (lady)]

giocoso (dʒəˈkəʊzəʊ) *adj Music.* jocose. [It.]

gip (dʒɪp) *vb* **gips, gipping, gipped. 1** a variant spelling of **gyp**[1]. ◆ *n* **2** a variant spelling of **gyp**[2].

Gipsy (ˈdʒɪpsɪ) *n, pl* **Gipsies.** (*sometimes not cap.*) a variant spelling of **Gypsy.**

gipsy moth *n* a variant spelling of **gypsy moth.**

giraffe (dʒɪˈrɑːf, -ˈræf) *n, pl* **giraffes** *or* **giraffe.** a large ruminant mammal inhabiting savannas of tropical Africa: the tallest mammal, with very long legs and neck. [C17: from It. *giraffa,* from Ar. *zarāfah,* prob. of African origin]

girandole (ˈdʒɪrənˌdəʊl) *n* **1** a branched wall candleholder. **2** an earring or pendant having a central gem surrounded by smaller ones. **3** a revolving firework. **4** *Artillery.* a group of connected mines. [C17: from F, from It. *girandola,* from L *gȳrāre* to GYRATE]

girasol *or* **girasole** (ˈdʒɪrəˌsɒl, -ˌsəʊl) *n* a type of opal that has a red or pink glow; fire opal. [C16: from It., from *girare* to revolve (see GYRATE) + *sole* the sun]

gird[1] Ⓣ (gɜːd) *vb* **girds, girding, girded** *or* **girt.** (*tr*) **1** to put a belt, girdle, etc., around (the waist or hips). **2** to bind or secure with or as if with a belt: *to gird on one's armour.* **3** to surround; encircle. **4** to prepare (oneself) for action (esp. in **gird (up) one's loins**). [OE *gyrdan,* of Gmc origin]

gird[2] (gɜːd) *N English dialect.* ◆ *vb* **1** (when *intr,* foll. by *at*) to jeer (at someone); mock. ◆ *n* **2** a taunt; gibe. [C13 *girden* to strike, cut, from ?]

girder (ˈgɜːdə) *n* a large beam, esp. one made of steel, used in the construction of bridges, buildings, etc.

girdle[1] Ⓣ (ˈgɜːdᵊl) *n* **1** a woman's elastic corset covering the waist to the thigh. **2** anything that surrounds or encircles. **3** a belt or sash. **4** *Jewellery.* the outer edge of a gem. **5** *Anat.* any encircling structure or part. **6** the mark left on a tree trunk after the removal of a ring of bark. ◆ *vb* **girdles, girdling, girdled.** (*tr*) **7** to put a girdle on or around. **8** to surround or encircle. **9** to remove a ring of bark from (a tree). [OE *gyrdel,* of Gmc origin; see GIRD[1]]

girdle[2] (ˈgɜːdᵊl) *n Scot. & N English dialect.* another word for **griddle.**

girl Ⓣ (gɜːl) *n* **1** a female child from birth to young womanhood. **2** a young unmarried woman; lass; maid. **3** *Inf.* a sweetheart or girlfriend. **4** *Inf.* a woman of any age. **5** a female employee, esp. a female servant. **6** *S. African derog.* a Black female servant. [C13: from ?; ? rel. to Low G *Göre* boy, girl]
►ˈ**girlish** *adj*

girlfriend (ˈgɜːlˌfrɛnd) *n* **1** a female friend with whom a person is romantically or sexually involved. **2** any female friend.

Girl Guide *n* See **Guide.**

girlhood (ˈgɜːlˌhʊd) *n* the state or time of being a girl.

girlie (ˈgɜːlɪ) *adj* **1** *Inf.* featuring nude or scantily dressed women: *a girlie magazine.* **2** suited to or designed to appeal to young women: *a real girlie night out.*

giro (ˈdʒaɪrəʊ) *n, pl* **giros. 1** a system of transferring money within a financial organization, such as a bank or post office, directly from the account of one person into that of another. **2** *Brit. inf.* a jobseeker's allowance or income support payment by giro cheque. [C20: ult. from Gk *guros* circuit]

girt[1] (gɜːt) *vb* a past tense and past participle of **gird**[1].

girt[2] (gɜːt) *vb* **1** (*tr*) to bind or encircle; gird. **2** to measure the girth of (something).

girth Ⓣ (gɜːθ) *n* **1** the distance around something; circumference. **2** a band around a horse's belly to keep the saddle in position. ◆ *vb* **3** (usually foll. by *up*) to fasten a girth on (a horse). **4** (*tr*) to encircle or surround. [C14: from ON *gjörth* belt; see GIRD[1]]

gist Ⓣ (dʒɪst) *n* the point or substance of an argument, speech, etc. [C18: from Anglo-F, as in *cest action gist en* this action consists in, lit.: lies in, from OF *gésir,* from L *jacēre*]

git (gɪt) *n Brit. sl.* **1** a contemptible person, often a fool. **2** a bastard. [C20: from GET (in the sense: *to beget,* hence a bastard, fool)]

gîte (ʒiːt) *n* a self-catering holiday cottage for let in France. [C20: F]

gittern (ˈgɪtɜːn) *n* an obsolete medieval stringed instrument resembling the guitar. [C14: from OF, ult. from OSp. *guitarra* GUITAR; see CITTERN]

giusto (ˈdʒuːstəʊ) *adj Music.* (of tempo) exact; strict. [It.]

give Ⓣ (gɪv) *vb* **gives, giving, gave, given.** (*mainly tr*) **1** (*also intr*) to present or deliver voluntarily (something that is one's own) to another. **2** (often foll. by *for*) to transfer (something that is one's own, esp. money) to the possession of another as part of an exchange: *to give fifty pounds for a painting.* **3** to place in the temporary possession of another: *I gave him my watch while I went swimming.* **4** (when *intr,* foll. by *of*) to grant, provide, or bestow: *give me some advice.* **5** to administer: *to give a reprimand.* **6** to award or attribute: *to give blame, praise,* etc. **7** to be a source of: *he gives no trouble.* **8** to impart or communicate: *to give news.* **9** to utter or emit: *to give a shout.* **10** to perform, make, or do: *the car gave a jolt.* **11** to sacrifice or devote: *he gave his life for his country.* **12** to surrender: *to give place to others.* **13** to concede or yield: *I will give you this game.* **14** (*intr*) *Inf.* to happen: *what gives?* **15** (often foll. by *to*) to cause; lead: *she gave me to believe that she would come.* **16** to perform or present as an entertainment: *to give a play.* **17** to act as a host of (a party, etc.). **18** (*intr*) to yield or break under force or pressure: *this surface will give if you sit on it.* **19 give as good as one gets.** to respond to verbal or bodily blows to at least an equal extent as those received. **20 give or take.** plus or minus: *three thousand people came, give or take a few hundred.* ◆ *n* **21** tendency to yield under pressure; resilience. ◆ See also **give away, give in,** etc. [OE *giefan*]
►ˈ**givable** *or* ˈ**giveable** *adj* ►ˈ**giver** *n*

give-and-take *n* **1** mutual concessions, shared benefits, and cooperation. **2** a smoothly flowing exchange of ideas and talk. ◆ *vb* **give and take.** (*intr*) **3** to make mutual concessions.

give away Ⓣ *vb* (*tr, adv*) **1** to donate or bestow as a gift, prize, etc. **2** to sell very cheaply. **3** to reveal or betray. **4** to fail to use (an opportunity) through folly or neglect. **5** to present (a bride) formally to her husband in a marriage ceremony. ◆ *n* **giveaway. 6** a betrayal or disclosure esp. when unintentional. **7** (*modifier*) **7a** very cheap (esp. in **giveaway prices**). **7b** free of charge: *a giveaway property magazine.*

give in Ⓣ *vb* (*adv*) **1** (*intr*) to yield; admit defeat. **2** (*tr*) to submit or deliver (a document).

given Ⓣ (ˈgɪvᵊn) *vb* **1** the past participle of **give.** ◆ *adj* **2** (*postpositive;* foll. by *to*) tending (to); inclined or addicted (to). **3** specific or previously stated. **4** assumed as a premise. **5** *Maths.* known or determined independently: *a given volume.* **6** (on official documents) issued or executed, as on a stated date.

THESAURUS

gingerly *adv* **1** = **cautiously,** carefully, charily, circumspectly, daintily, delicately, fastidiously, hesitantly, reluctantly, squeamishly, suspiciously, timidly, warily ◆ *adj* **2** = **cautious,** careful, chary, circumspect, dainty, delicate, fastidious, hesitant, reluctant, squeamish, suspicious, timid, wary
Antonyms *adv* ≠ **cautiously:** boldly, carelessly, confidently, rashly

gird[1] *vb* **1, 2** = **girdle,** belt, bind **3** = **surround,** blockade, encircle, enclose, encompass, enfold, environ, hem in, pen, ring **4** *As in* **gird (up) one's loins** = **prepare,** brace, fortify, make ready, ready, steel

girdle[1] *n* **3** = **belt,** band, cincture, cummerbund, fillet, sash, waistband ◆ *vb* **8** = **surround,** bind, bound, encircle, enclose, encompass, environ, enwreath, gird, hem, ring

girl *n* **1, 2** = **female child,** bird (*sl.*), chick (*sl.*), colleen (*Irish*), damsel (*arch.*), daughter, lass, lassie (*inf.*), maid (*arch.*), maiden (*arch.*), miss, wench

girth *n* **1** = **circumference,** bulk, measure, size

gist *n* = **point,** core, drift, essence, force, idea, import, marrow, meaning, nub, pith, quintessence, sense, significance, substance

give *vb* **1** = **present,** accord, administer, allow, award, bestow, commit, confer, consign, contribute, deliver, donate, entrust, furnish, grant, hand over *or* out, make over, permit, provide, purvey, supply, vouchsafe **7** = **produce,** cause, do, engender, lead, make, occasion, perform **8** = **announce,** be a source of, communicate, emit, impart, issue, notify, pronounce, publish, render, transmit, utter **12** = **surrender,** cede, devote, hand over, lend, relinquish, yield **13** = **concede,** allow, grant **18** = **break,** bend, collapse, fall, recede, retire, sink
Antonyms *vb* ≠ **present:** accept, get, hold, keep, receive, take, withdraw

give away *vb* **3** = **reveal,** betray, disclose, divulge, expose, grass (*Brit. sl.*), grass up (*sl.*), inform on, leak, let out, let slip, let the cat out of the bag (*inf.*), put the finger on (*inf.*), shop (*sl., chiefly Brit.*), uncover

give in *vb* **1** = **admit defeat,** capitulate, cave in (*inf.*), collapse, comply, concede, quit, submit, succumb, surrender, yield

given *adj* **2** = **inclined,** addicted, apt, disposed, liable, likely, prone

given name *n* another term (esp. US) for **first name.**

give off ⓣ *vb* (*tr, adv*) to emit or discharge: *the mothballs gave off an acrid odour.*

give out ⓣ *vb* (*adv*) **1** (*tr*) to emit or discharge. **2** (*tr*) to publish or make known: *the chairman gave out that he would resign.* **3** (*tr*) to hand out or distribute: *they gave out free chewing gum.* **4** (*intr*) to become exhausted; fail: *the supply of candles gave out.*

give over *vb* (*adv*) **1** (*tr*) to transfer, esp. to the care or custody of another. **2** (*tr*) to assign or resign to a specific purpose or function: *the day was given over to pleasure.* **3** *Inf.* to cease (an activity): *give over fighting, will you!*

give up ⓣ *vb* (*adv*) **1** to abandon hope (for). **2** (*tr*) to renounce (an activity, belief, etc.): *I have given up smoking.* **3** (*tr*) to relinquish or resign from: *he gave up the presidency.* **4** (*tr; usually reflexive*) to surrender: *the escaped convict gave himself up.* **5** (*intr*) to admit one's defeat or inability to do something. **6** (*tr; often passive or reflexive*) to devote completely (to): *she gave herself up to caring for the sick.*

gizmo *or* **gismo** ('gɪzməʊ) *n, pl* **gizmos, gismos.** *Sl.* a device; gadget. [C20: from ?]

gizzard ('gɪzəd) *n* **1** the thick-walled part of a bird's stomach, in which hard food is broken up. **2** *Inf.* the stomach and entrails generally. [C14: from OF *guisier* fowl's liver, from L *gigēria* entrails of poultry when cooked, from ?]

Gk *abbrev. for* Greek.

glabella (glə'bɛlə) *n, pl* **glabellae** (-li:). *Anat.* a smooth elevation of the frontal bone just above the bridge of the nose. [C19: NL, from L, from *glaber* bald, smooth]
▸**gla'bellar** *adj*

glabrous ('gleɪbrəs) *adj Biol.* without hair or a similar growth; smooth. [C17 *glabrous,* from L *glaber*]

glacé ('glæseɪ) *adj* **1** crystallized or candied: *glacé cherries.* **2** covered in icing. **3** (of leather, silk, etc.) having a glossy finish. ◆ *vb* **glacés, glacéing, glacéed. 4** (*tr*) to ice or candy (cakes, fruits, etc.). [C19: from F *glacé,* lit.: iced, from *glacer* to freeze, from L *glaciēs* ice]

glacial ⓣ ('gleɪsɪəl, -ʃəl) *adj* **1** characterized by the presence of masses of ice. **2** relating to, caused by, or deposited by a glacier. **3** extremely cold; icy. **4** cold or hostile in manner. **5** (of a chemical compound) of or tending to form crystals that resemble ice.
▸**'glacially** *adv*

glacial acetic acid *n* pure acetic acid.

glacial period *n* **1** any period of time during which a large part of the earth's surface was covered with ice, due to the advance of glaciers. **2** (*often caps.*) the Pleistocene epoch. ◆ Also called: **glacial epoch, ice age.**

glaciate ('gleɪsɪ,eɪt) *vb* **glaciates, glaciating, glaciated. 1** to cover or become covered with glaciers or masses of ice. **2** (*tr*) to subject to the effects of glaciers, such as denudation and erosion.
▸**,glaci'ation** *n*

glacier ('glæsɪə, 'gleɪs-) *n* a slowly moving mass of ice originating from an accumulation of snow. [C18: from F (dialect), from OF *glace* ice, from LL, from L *glaciēs* ice]

glaciology (,glæsɪ'ɒlədʒɪ, ,gleɪ-) *n* the study of the distribution, character, and effects of glaciers.
▸**glaciological** (,glæsɪə'lɒdʒɪkᵊl, ,gleɪ-) *adj* ▸**,glaci'ologist** *n*

glacis ('glæsɪs, 'glæsɪ, 'gleɪ-) *n, pl* **glacises** *or* **glacis** (-i:z, -ɪz). **1** a slight incline; slope. **2** an open slope in front of a fortified place. [C17: from F, from OF *glacier* to freeze, slip, from L, from *glaciēs* ice]

glad[1] ⓣ (glæd) *adj* **gladder, gladdest. 1** happy and pleased; contented. **2** causing happiness or contentment. **3** (*postpositive;* foll. by *to*) very willing: *he was glad to help.* **4** (*postpositive;* foll. by *of*) happy or pleased to have: *glad of her help.* ◆ *vb* **glads, gladding, gladded. 5** (*tr*) an archaic word for **gladden.** [OE *glæd*]
▸**'gladly** *adv* ▸**'gladness** *n*

glad[2] (glæd) *n Inf.* short for **gladiolus.**

gladden ⓣ ('glædᵊn) *vb* to make or become glad and joyful.
▸**'gladdener** *n*

glade (gleɪd) *n* an open place in a forest; clearing. [C16: from ?; ? rel. to GLAD[1] (in obs. sense: bright); see GLEAM]

glad eye *n Inf.* an inviting or seductive glance (esp. in **give (someone) the glad eye**).

gladiator ('glædɪ,eɪtə) *n* **1** (in ancient Rome) a man trained to fight in arenas to provide entertainment. **2** a person who supports and fights publicly for a cause. [C16: from L: swordsman, from *gladius* sword]
▸**gladiatorial** (,glædɪə'tɔ:rɪəl) *adj*

gladiolus (,glædɪ'əʊləs) *n, pl* **gladiolus, gladioli** (-laɪ), *or* **gladioluses.** any plant of a widely cultivated genus having sword-shaped leaves and spikes of funnel-shaped brightly coloured flowers. Also called: **gladiola.** [C16: from L: a small sword, sword lily, from *gladius* a sword]

glad rags *pl n Inf.* best clothes or clothes used on special occasions.

gladsome ('glædsəm) *adj* an archaic word for **glad**[1].
▸**'gladsomely** *adv* ▸**'gladsomeness** *n*

Gladstone bag ('glædstən) *n* a piece of hand luggage consisting of two equal-sized hinged compartments. [C19: after W. E. *Gladstone* (1809–98), Brit. statesman]

Glagolitic (,glægə'lɪtɪk) *adj* of, relating to, or denoting a Slavic alphabet whose invention is attributed to Saint Cyril. [C19: from NL, from Serbo-Croat *glagolica* the Glagolitic alphabet]

glair (glɛə) *n* **1** white of egg, esp. when used as a size or adhesive. **2** any substance resembling this. ◆ *vb* **3** (*tr*) to apply glair to (something). [C14: from OF *glaire,* from Vulgar L *clāria* (unattested) CLEAR, from L *clārus*]
▸**'glairy** *or* **'glaireous** *adj*

glam (glæm) *adj Inf.* short for **glamorous.**

glamorize, glamorise, *or US* (*sometimes*) **glamourize** ('glæmə,raɪz) *vb* **glamorizes, glamorizing, glamorized; glamorises, glamorising, glamorised** *or US (sometimes)* **glamourizes, glamourizing, glamourized.** (*tr*) to cause to be or seem glamorous; romanticize or beautify.
▸**,glamori'zation** *or* **,glamori'sation** *n*

glamorous ⓣ ('glæmərəs) *adj* **1** possessing glamour; alluring and fascinating. **2** beautiful and smart, esp. in a showy way: *a glamorous woman.*
▸**'glamorously** *adv*

glamour ⓣ *or US* (*sometimes*) **glamor** ('glæmə) *n* **1** charm and allure; fascination. **2a** fascinating or voluptuous beauty. **2b** (*as modifier*): *a glamour girl.* **3** *Arch.* a magic spell; charm. [C18: Scot. var. of GRAMMAR (hence a magic spell, because occult practices were popularly associated with learning)]

glance[1] ⓣ (glɑ:ns) *vb* **glances, glancing, glanced. 1** (*intr*) to look hastily or briefly. **2** (*intr;* foll. by *over, through,* etc.) to look over briefly: *to glance through a report.* **3** (*intr*) to reflect, glint, or gleam: *the sun glanced on the water.* **4** (*intr;* usually foll. by *off*) to depart (from an object struck) at an oblique angle: *the arrow glanced off the tree.* ◆ *n* **5** a hasty or brief look; peep. **6** a flash or glint of light; gleam. **7** the act or an instance of an object glancing off another. **8** a brief allusion. [C15: from *glacen* to strike obliquely, from OF *glacier* to slide (see GLACIS)]
▸**'glancing** *adj* ▸**'glancingly** *ad*

> **USAGE NOTE** *Glance* is sometimes wrongly used where *glimpse* is meant: *he caught a glimpse* (not *glance*) *of her making her way through the crowd.*

glance[2] (glɑ:ns) *n* any mineral having a metallic lustre. [C19: from G *Glanz* brightness, lustre]

gland[1] (glænd) *n* **1** a cell or organ in man and other animals that synthesizes chemical substances and secretes them for the body to use or eliminate, either through a duct (exocrine gland) or directly into the bloodstream (endocrine gland). **2** a structure, such as a lymph node, that resembles a gland in form. **3** a cell or organ in plants that synthesizes and secretes a particular substance. [C17: from L *glāns* acorn]

gland[2] (glænd) *n* a device that prevents leakage of fluid along a rotating shaft or reciprocating rod passing between areas of high and low

THESAURUS

give off *vb* = **emit**, discharge, exhale, exude, produce, release, send out, throw out, vent

give out *vb* **1** = **emit**, discharge, exhale, exude, produce, release, send out, throw out, vent **2** = **make known**, announce, broadcast, communicate, disseminate, impart, notify, publish, shout from the rooftops (*inf.*), transmit, utter

give up *vb* **2-5** = **abandon**, call it a day *or* night, capitulate, cave in (*inf.*), cease, cede, cut out, desist, despair, fall by the wayside, forswear, hand over, kick (*inf.*), kiss (something) goodbye, leave off, quit, relinquish, renounce, resign, say goodbye to, step down (*inf.*), stop, surrender, throw in the sponge, throw in the towel, waive

glacial *adj* **3** = **icy**, arctic, biting, bitter, chill, chilly, cold, freezing, frigid, frosty, frozen, gelid, piercing, polar, raw, wintry **4** = **unfriendly**, antagonistic, cold, frigid, hostile, icy, inimical

glad[1] *adj* **1** = **happy**, cheerful, chuffed (*sl.*), contented, delighted, gay, gleeful, gratified, jocund, jovial, joyful, overjoyed, pleased **2** = **pleasing**, animated, cheerful, cheering, cheery, delightful, felicitous, gratifying, joyous, merry, pleasant
Antonyms *adj* ≠ **happy:** depressed, discontented, displeased, melancholy, miserable, sad, sorrowful, unhappy

gladden *vb* = **please**, cheer, delight, elate, enliven, exhilarate, gratify, hearten, rejoice

gladly *adv* **3** = **happily**, cheerfully, freely, gaily, gleefully, jovially, joyfully, joyously, lief (*rare*), merrily, readily, willingly, with (a) good grace, with pleasure
Antonyms *adv* dolefully, grudgingly, reluctantly, sadly, unenthusiastically, unwillingly

gladness *n* **1** = **happiness**, animation, blitheness, cheerfulness, delight, felicity, gaiety, glee, high spirits, hilarity, jollity, joy, joyousness, mirth, pleasure

glamorous *adj* **1, 2** = **elegant**, alluring, attractive, beautiful, bewitching, captivating, charming, dazzling, enchanting, entrancing, exciting, fascinating, glittering, glitzy (*sl.*), glossy, lovely, prestigious, smart
Antonyms *adj* colourless, dull, plain, unattractive, unexciting, unglamorous

glamour *n* **1** = **charm**, allure, appeal, attraction, beauty, bewitchment, enchantment, fascination, magnetism, prestige, ravishment, witchery

glance[1] *vb* **1** = **peek**, check, check out (*inf.*), clock (*Brit. inf.*), gaze, glimpse, look, peep, scan, take a dekko at (*Brit. sl.*), view **2** *with* **over, through,** *etc.* = **scan**, browse, dip into, flip through, leaf through, riffle through, run over *or* through, skim through, thumb through **3** = **gleam**, flash, glimmer, glint, glisten, glitter, reflect, shimmer, shine, twinkle **4** = **graze**, bounce, brush, rebound, ricochet, skim ◆ *n* **5** = **peek**, brief look, butcher's (*Brit. sl.*), dekko (*sl.*), gander (*inf.*), glimpse, look, peep, quick look, shufti (*Brit. sl.*), squint, view **6** = **gleam**, flash, glimmer, glint, reflection, sparkle, twinkle **8** = **allusion**, passing mention, reference
Antonyms *vb* ≠ **peek:** peruse, scrutinize, study ◆ *n* ≠ **peek:** examination, good look, inspection, perusal

pressure. It often consists of a flanged metal sleeve bedding into a stuffing box. [C19: from ?]

glanders ('glændəz) *n* (*functioning as sing*) a highly infectious bacterial disease of horses, sometimes communicated to man, characterized by inflammation and ulceration of the mucous membranes of the air passages, skin and lymph glands. [C16: from OF *glandres*, from L *glandulae*, lit.: little acorns, from *glāns* acorn; see GLAND[1]]

glandular ('glændjʊlə) *or* **glandulous** ('glændjʊləs) *adj* of, relating to, containing, functioning as, or affecting a gland. [C18: from L *glandula*, lit.: a little acorn; see GLANDERS]
▸ **'glandularly** *or* **'glandulously** *adv*

glandular fever *n* another name for **infectious mononucleosis.**

glandule ('glændjuːl) *n* a small gland.

glans (glænz) *n, pl* **glandes** ('glændiːz). *Anat.* any small rounded body or glandlike mass, such as the head of the penis (**glans penis**). [C17: from L: acorn; see GLAND[1]]

glare ❶ (glɛə) *vb* **glares, glaring, glared. 1** (*intr*) to stare angrily; glower. **2** (*tr*) to express by glowering. **3** (*intr*) (of light, colour, etc.) to be very bright and intense. **4** (*intr*) to be dazzlingly ornamented or garish. ◆ *n* **5** an angry stare. **6** a dazzling light or brilliance. **7** garish ornamentation or appearance. [C13: prob. from MLow G, MDu. *glaren* to gleam]

glaring ❶ ('glɛərɪŋ) *adj* **1** conspicuous: *a glaring omission.* **2** dazzling or garish.
▸ **'glaringly** *adv* ▸ **'glaringness** *n*

glasnost ('glæsˌnɒst) *n* the policy of public frankness and accountability developed in the former Soviet Union under the leadership of Mikhail Gorbachov. [C20: Russian, lit.: publicity, openness]

glass (glɑːs) *n* **1a** a hard brittle transparent or translucent noncrystalline solid, consisting of metal silicates or similar compounds. It is made from a fused mixture of oxides, such as lime, silicon dioxide, phosphorus pentoxide, etc. **1b** (*as modifier*): *a glass bottle.* Related adj: **vitreous. 2** something made of glass, esp. a drinking vessel, a barometer, or a mirror. **3** Also called: **glassful.** the amount or volume contained in a drinking glass: *he drank a glass of wine.* **4** glassware collectively. **5** See **fibreglass.** ◆ *vb* **6** (*tr*) to cover with, enclose in, or fit with glass. [OE *glæs*]
▸ **'glassless** *adj* ▸ **'glassˌlike** *adj*

glass-blowing *n* the process of shaping a mass of molten glass by blowing air into it through a tube.
▸ **'glass-ˌblower** *n*

glass ceiling *n* a situation in which progress, esp. promotion, appears to be possible but restrictions or discrimination create a barrier that prevents it.

glasses ('glɑːsɪz) *pl n* a pair of lenses for correcting faulty vision, in a frame that rests on the bridge of the nose and hooks behind the ears. Also called: **spectacles, eyeglasses.**

glass fibre *n* another name for **fibreglass.**

glass harmonica *n* a musical instrument of the 18th century consisting of a set of glass bowls of graduated pitches, played by rubbing the fingers over the moistened rims or by a keyboard mechanism. Sometimes shortened to **harmonica.** Also called: **musical glasses.**

glasshouse ('glɑːsˌhaʊs) *n* **1** *Brit.* a glass building, esp. a greenhouse, used for growing plants in protected or controlled conditions. **2** *Inf., chiefly Brit.* a military detention centre.

glassine (glæ'siːn) *n* a glazed translucent paper.

glass snake *n* any snakelike lizard of Europe, Asia, or North America, with vestigial hind limbs and a tail that breaks off easily.

glassware ('glɑːsˌwɛə) *n* articles made of glass, esp. drinking glasses.

glass wool *n* fine spun glass massed into a wool-like bulk, used in insulation, filtering, etc.

glasswort ('glɑːsˌwɜːt) *n* **1** any plant of salt marshes having fleshy stems and scalelike leaves: formerly used as a source of soda for glass-making. **2** another name for **saltwort.**

glassy ❶ ('glɑːsɪ) *adj* **glassier, glassiest. 1** resembling glass, esp. in smoothness or transparency. **2** void of expression, life, or warmth: *a glassy stare.*
▸ **'glassily** *adv* ▸ **'glassiness** *n*

Glaswegian (glæz'wiːdʒən) *adj* **1.** of or relating to Glasgow, a city in Scotland, or its inhabitants. ◆ *n* **2** a native or inhabitant of Glasgow. [C19: infl. by NORWEGIAN]

Glauber's salt ('glaʊbəz) *or* **Glauber salt** *n* the crystalline decahydrate of sodium sulphate: used in making glass, detergents, and pulp. [C18: after J. R. *Glauber* (1604–68), G chemist]

glaucoma (glɔː'kəʊmə) *n* a disease of the eye in which increased pressure within the eyeball causes impaired vision, sometimes progressing to blindness. [C17: from L, from Gk, from *glaukos;* see GLAUCOUS]
▸ **glau'comatous** *adj*

glaucous ('glɔːkəs) *adj* **1** *Bot.* covered with a waxy or powdery bloom. **2** bluish-green. [C17: from L *glaucus* silvery, bluish-green, from Gk *glaukos*]

glaze ❶ (gleɪz) *vb* **glazes, glazing, glazed. 1** (*tr*) to fit or cover with glass. **2** (*tr*) *Ceramics.* to cover with a vitreous solution, rendering impervious to liquid. **3** (*tr*) to cover (foods) with a shiny coating by applying beaten egg, sugar, etc. **4** (*tr*) to make glossy or shiny. **5** (when *intr*, often foll. by *over*) to become or cause to become glassy: *his eyes were glazing over.* ◆ *n* **6** *Ceramics.* **6a** a vitreous coating. **6b** the substance used to produce such a coating. **7** a smooth lustrous finish on a fabric produced by applying various chemicals. **8** something used to give a glossy surface to foods: *a syrup glaze.* [C14 *glasen*, from *glas* GLASS]
▸ **glazed** *adj* ▸ **'glazer** *n*

glaze ice *n Brit.* a thin clear layer of ice caused by the freezing of rain in the air or by refreezing after a thaw.

glazier ('gleɪzɪə) *n* a person who fits windows, doors, etc., with glass.
▸ **'glaziery** *n*

glazing ('gleɪzɪŋ) *n* **1** the surface of a glazed object. **2** glass fitted, or to be fitted, in a door, frame, etc.

GLC *abbrev. for* Greater London Council; abolished 1986.

gleam ❶ (gliːm) *n* **1** a small beam or glow of light, esp. reflected light. **2** a brief or dim indication: *a gleam of hope.* ◆ *vb* (*intr*) **3** to send forth or reflect a beam of light. **4** to appear, esp. briefly. [OE *glǣm*]
▸ **'gleaming** *adj* ▸ **'gleamingly** *adv* ▸ **'gleamy** *adj*

glean ❶ (gliːn) *vb* **1** to gather (something) slowly and carefully in small pieces: *to glean information.* **2** to gather (the useful remnants of a crop) from the field after harvesting. [C14: from OF *glener*, from LL *glennāre*, prob. of Celtic origin]
▸ **'gleaner** *n*

gleanings ('gliːnɪŋz) *pl n* the useful remnants of a crop that can be gathered from the field after harvesting.

glebe (gliːb) *n* **1** *Brit.* land granted to a clergyman as part of his benefice. **2** *Poetic.* land, esp. for growing things. [C14: from L *glaeba*]

glee ❶ (gliː) *n* **1** great merriment or delight, often caused by someone else's misfortune. **2** a type of song originating in 18th-century England, sung by three or more unaccompanied voices. [OE *gléo*]

glee club *n Now chiefly US & Canad.* a society organized for the singing of choral music.

gleeful ❶ ('gliːfʊl) *adj* full of glee; merry.
▸ **'gleefully** *adv* ▸ **'gleefulness** *n*

gleeman ('gliːmən) *n, pl* **gleemen.** *Obs.* a minstrel.

glen (glɛn) *n* a narrow and deep mountain valley, esp. in Scotland or Ireland. [C15: from Scot. Gaelic *gleann*, from OIrish *glend*]

glengarry (glɛn'gærɪ) *n, pl* **glengarries.** a brimless Scottish cap with a crease down the crown, often with ribbons at the back. Also called: **glengarry bonnet.** [C19: after *Glengarry*, Scotland]

glia ('gliːə) *n* the delicate web of connective tissue that surrounds and supports nerve cells. Also called: **neuroglia.**
▸ **'glial** *adj*

glib ❶ (glɪb) *adj* **glibber, glibbest.** fluent and easy, often in an insincere or deceptive way. [C16: prob. from MLow G *glibberich* slippery]
▸ **'glibly** *adv* ▸ **'glibness** *n*

glide ❶ (glaɪd) *vb* **glides, gliding, glided. 1** to move or cause to move easily without jerks or hesitations. **2** (*intr*) to pass slowly or without perceptible change: *to glide into sleep.* **3** to cause (an aircraft) to come into land without engine power, or (of an aircraft) to land in this way. **4** (*intr*) to fly a glider. **5** (*intr*) *Music.* to execute a portamento from one note to another. **6** (*intr*) *Phonetics.* to produce a glide. ◆ *n* **7** a smooth easy movement. **8a** any of various dances featuring gliding steps. **8b** a step in such a dance. **9** a manoeuvre in which an aircraft makes a gen-

THESAURUS

glare *vb* **1** = **scowl**, frown, give a dirty look, glower, look daggers, lour *or* lower, stare angrily **3** = **dazzle**, blaze, flame, flare ◆ *n* **5** = **scowl**, angry stare, black look, dirty look, frown, glower, lour *or* lower **6** = **dazzle**, blaze, brilliance, flame, flare, glow

glaring *adj* **1** = **conspicuous**, audacious, blatant, egregious, flagrant, gross, manifest, obvious, open, outrageous, outstanding, overt, patent, rank, unconcealed, visible **2** = **dazzling**, blazing, bright, flashy, florid, garish, glowing, loud
Antonyms *adj* ≠ **conspicuous:** concealed, hidden, inconspicuous, obscure ≠ **dazzling:** soft, subdued, subtle

glassy *adj* **1** = **transparent**, clear, glossy, icy, shiny, slick, slippery, smooth **2** = **expressionless**, blank, cold, dazed, dull, empty, fixed, glazed, lifeless, vacant

glaze *vb* **2** = **coat**, burnish, enamel, furbish, gloss, lacquer, polish, varnish ◆ *n* **6a** = **coat**, enamel, finish, gloss, lacquer, lustre, patina, polish, shine, varnish

gleam *n* **1** = **glow**, beam, flash, glimmer, ray, sparkle **2** = **trace**, flicker, glimmer, hint, inkling, ray, suggestion ◆ *vb* **3** = **shine**, coruscate, flare, flash, glance, glimmer, glint, glisten, glitter, glow, scintillate, shimmer, sparkle

gleaming *adj* **3** = **bright**, bright as a button, brilliant, burnished, catching the light, glimmering, glistening, glowing, lustrous, scintillating, shining, sparkling
Antonyms *adj* dull, lustreless, unpolished

glean *vb* **1, 2** = **gather**, accumulate, amass, collect, cull, garner, harvest, learn, pick, pick up, reap, select

glee *n* **1** = **delight**, cheerfulness, elation, exhilaration, exuberance, exultation, fun, gaiety, gladness, hilarity, jocularity, jollity, joviality, joy, joyfulness, joyousness, liveliness, merriment, mirth, sprightliness, triumph, verve
Antonyms *n* depression, gloom, melancholy, misery, sadness

gleeful *adj* = **delighted**, cheerful, chirpy, cock-a-hoop, elated, exuberant, exultant, gay, gratified, happy, jocund, jovial, joyful, joyous, jubilant, merry, mirthful, overjoyed, over the moon (*inf.*), pleased, rapt, triumphant

glib *adj* = **smooth**, artful, easy, fast-talking, fluent, garrulous, insincere, plausible, quick, ready, slick, slippery, smooth-tongued, suave, talkative, voluble
Antonyms *adj* halting, hesitant, implausible, sincere, tongue-tied

glibness *n* = **smoothness**, fluency, gift of the gab, patter, plausibility, readiness, slickness

glide *vb* **1** = **slide**, coast, drift, float, flow, fly, roll, run, sail, skate, skim, slip, soar

tle descent without engine power. **10** the act or process of gliding. **11** *Music.* a portamento or slur. **12** *Phonetics.* a transitional sound as the speech organs pass from the articulatory position of one speech sound to that of the next. [OE *glīdan*]
▸ **'glidingly** *adv*

glide path *n* the path of an aircraft as it descends to land.

glider ('glaɪdə) *n* **1** an aircraft capable of gliding and soaring in air currents without the use of an engine. **2** a person or thing that glides.

glide time *n* the NZ term for **flexitime.**

glimmer Ⓣ ('glɪmə) *vb* (*intr*) **1** (of a light) to glow faintly or flickeringly. **2** to be indicated faintly: *hope glimmered in his face.* ◆ *n* **3** a glow or twinkle of light. **4** a faint indication. [C14: cf. MHG *glimmern*]
▸ **'glimmeringly** *adv*

glimpse Ⓣ (glɪmps) *n* **1** a brief or incomplete view: *to catch a glimpse of the sea.* **2** a vague indication. **3** *Arch.* a glimmer of light. ◆ *vb* **glimpses, glimpsing, glimpsed. 4** (*tr*) to catch sight of momentarily. [C14: of Gmc origin; cf. MHG *glimsen* to glimmer]
▸ **'glimpser** *n*

USAGE NOTE *Glimpse* is sometimes wrongly used where *glance* is meant: *he gave a quick glance* (not *glimpse*) *at his watch.*

glint Ⓣ (glɪnt) *vb* **1** to gleam or cause to gleam brightly. ◆ *n* **2** a bright gleam or flash. **3** brightness or gloss. **4** a brief indication. [C15: prob. from ON]

glioma (glaɪ'əumə) *n, pl* **gliomata** (-mətə) *or* **gliomas.** a tumour of the brain and spinal cord, composed of glia cells and fibres. [C19: from NL, from Gk *glia* glue + -OMA]

glissade (glɪ'sɑːd, -'seɪd) *n* **1** a gliding step in ballet. **2** a controlled slide down a snow slope. ◆ *vb* **glissades, glissading, glissaded. 3** (*intr*) to perform a glissade. [C19: from F, from *glisser* to slip, from OF *glicier*, of Frankish origin]

glissando (glɪ'sændəu) *n, pl* **glissandi** (-diː) *or* **glissandos.** a rapidly executed series of notes, each of which is discretely audible. [C19: prob. It. var. of GLISSADE]

glisten Ⓣ ('glɪsᵊn) *vb* (*intr*) **1** (of a wet or glossy surface) to gleam by reflecting light. **2** (of light) to reflect with brightness: *the sunlight glistens on wet leaves.* ◆ *n* **3** *Rare.* a gleam or gloss. [OE *glisnian*]

glister ('glɪstə) *vb, n* an archaic word for **glitter.** [C14: prob. from MDu. *glisteren*]

glitch Ⓣ (glɪtʃ) *n* **1** a sudden instance of malfunctioning in an electronic system. **2** a change in the rotation rate of a pulsar. [C20: from ?]

glitter Ⓣ ('glɪtə) *vb* (*intr*) **1** (of a hard, wet, or polished surface) to reflect light in bright flashes. **2** (of light) to be reflected in bright flashes. **3** (usually foll. by *with*) to be decorated or enhanced by the glamour (of): *the show glitters with famous actors.* ◆ *n* **4** sparkle or brilliance. **5** show and glamour. **6** tiny pieces of shiny decorative material. **7** *Canad.* Also called: **silver thaw.** ice formed from freezing rain. [C14: from ON *glitra*]
▸ **'glitteringly** *adv* ▸ **'glittery** *adj*

glitterati (ˌglɪtə'rɑːtiː) *pl n Inf.* the leaders of society, esp. the rich and beautiful. [C20: from GLITTER + *-ati* as in LITERATI]

glitzy ('glɪtsɪ) *adj* **glitzier, glitziest.** *Sl.* showily attractive; flashy or glittery. [C20: prob. via Yiddish from G *glitzern* to glitter]

gloaming Ⓣ ('gləumɪŋ) *n Scot. or poetic.* twilight or dusk. [OE *glōmung*, from *glōm*]

gloat Ⓣ (gləut) *vb* **1** (*intr;* often foll. by *over*) to dwell (on) with malevolent smugness or exultation. ◆ *n* **2** the act of gloating. [C16: prob. of Scand. origin; cf. ON *glotta* to grin, MHG *glotzen* to stare]
▸ **'gloater** *n*

glob (glɒb) *n Inf.* a rounded mass of some thick fluid substance. [C20: prob. from GLOBE, infl. by BLOB]

global Ⓣ ('gləubᵊl) *adj* **1** covering or relating to the whole world. **2** comprehensive; total.
▸ **'globally** *adv*

globalization *or* **globalisation** (ˌgləubᵊlaɪ'zeɪʃən) *n* **1** the process enabling financial and investment markets to operate internationally, largely as a result of deregulation and improved communications. **2** the process by which a company, etc., expands to operate internationally.

globalize *or* **globalise** ('gləubᵊˌlaɪz) *vb* **globalizes, globalizing, globalized** *or* **globalises, globalising, globalised.** (*tr*) to put into effect or spread worldwide.

global product *n* a commercial product, such as Coca Cola, that is marketed throughout the world under the same brand name.

global warming *n* an increase in the average temperature worldwide believed to be caused by the greenhouse effect.

globe Ⓣ (gləub) *n* **1** a sphere on which a map of the world is drawn. **2** **the globe.** the world; the earth. **3** a planet or some other astronomical body. **4** an object shaped like a sphere, such as a glass lampshade or fishbowl. **5** an orb, usually of gold, symbolic of sovereignty. ◆ *vb* **globes, globing, globed. 6** to form or cause to form into a globe. [C16: from OF, from L *globus*]
▸ **'globeˌlike** *adj*

globefish ('gləubˌfɪʃ) *n, pl* **globefish** *or* **globefishes.** another name for **puffer.**

globeflower ('gləubˌflauə) *n* a plant having pale yellow, white, or orange globe-shaped flowers.

globetrotter ('gləubˌtrɒtə) *n* a habitual worldwide traveller, esp. a tourist.
▸ **'globeˌtrotting** *n, adj*

globigerina (gləuˌbɪdʒə'raɪnə) *n, pl* **globigerinas** *or* **globigerinae** (-niː). **1** a marine protozoan having a rounded shell with spiny processes. **2** **globigerina ooze.** a deposit on the ocean floor consisting of the shells of these protozoans. [C19: from NL, from L *globus* GLOBE + *gerere* to bear]

globoid ('gləubɔɪd) *adj* **1** shaped like a globe. ◆ *n* **2** a globoid body.

globose ('gləubəus, gləu'bəus) *or* **globous** ('gləubəs) *adj* spherical or approximately spherical. [C15: from L *globōsus;* see GLOBE]
▸ **'globosely** *adv*

globular Ⓣ ('glɒbjulə) *or* **globulous** *adj* **1** shaped like a globe or globule. **2** having or consisting of globules.

globule Ⓣ ('glɒbjuːl) *n* a small globe, esp. a drop of liquid. [C17: from L *globulus*, dim. of *globus* GLOBE]

globulin ('glɒbjulɪn) *n* any of a group of simple proteins that are generally insoluble in water but soluble in salt solutions.

glockenspiel ('glɒkənˌspiːl, -ˌʃpiːl) *n* a percussion instrument consisting of a set of tuned metal plates played with a pair of small hammers. [C19: G, from *Glocken* bells + *Spiel* play]

glomerate ('glɒmərɪt) *adj* **1** gathered into a compact rounded mass. **2** *Anat.* (esp. of glands) conglomerate in structure. [C18: from L *glomerāre*, from *glomus* ball]
▸ **ˌglome'ration** *n*

glomerule ('glɒməˌruːl) *n Bot.* an inflorescence in the form of a ball-like cluster of flowers. [C18: from NL *glomerulus*]

gloom Ⓣ (gluːm) *n* **1** partial or total darkness. **2** a state of depression or melancholy. **3** an appearance or expression of despondency or melancholy. **4** *Poetic.* a dim or dark place. ◆ *vb* **5** (*intr*) to look sullen or depressed. **6** to make or become dark or gloomy. [C14 *gloumben* to look sullen]

gloomy Ⓣ ('gluːmɪ) *adj* **gloomier, gloomiest. 1** dark or dismal. **2** causing depression or gloom: *gloomy news.* **3** despairing; sad.
▸ **'gloomily** *adv* ▸ **'gloominess** *n*

gloop (gluːp) *or esp. US* **glop** (glɒp) *n Inf.* any messy sticky fluid or substance. [C20: from ?]
▸ **'gloopy** *or esp. US* **'gloppy** *adj*

THESAURUS

glimmer *vb* **1** = **flicker,** blink, gleam, glisten, glitter, glow, shimmer, shine, sparkle, twinkle ◆ *n* **3** = **gleam,** blink, flicker, glow, ray, shimmer, sparkle, twinkle **4** = **trace,** flicker, gleam, grain, hint, inkling, ray, suggestion

glimpse *n* **1** = **look,** brief view, butcher's (*Brit. sl.*), gander (*inf.*), glance, peek, peep, quick look, shufti (*Brit. sl.*), sight, sighting, squint ◆ *vb* **4** = **catch sight of,** clock (*Brit. inf.*), descry, espy, sight, spot, spy, view

glint *vb* **1** = **gleam,** flash, glimmer, glitter, shine, sparkle, twinkle ◆ *n* **2** = **gleam,** flash, glimmer, glitter, shine, sparkle, twinkle, twinkling

glisten *vb* **1, 2** = **gleam,** coruscate, flash, glance, glare, glimmer, glint, glitter, scintillate, shimmer, shine, sparkle, twinkle

glitch *n* **1** = **problem,** blip, bug (*inf.*), difficulty, fault, flaw, fly in the ointment, gremlin, hitch, interruption, kink, malfunction, snag

glitter *vb* **1, 2** = **shine,** coruscate, flare, flash, glare, gleam, glimmer, glint, glisten, scintillate, shimmer, sparkle, twinkle ◆ *n* **4** = **shine,** beam, brightness, brilliance, flash, glare, gleam, lustre, radiance, scintillation, sheen, shimmer, sparkle **5** = **glamour,** display, gaudiness, gilt, pageantry, show, showiness, splendour, tinsel

gloaming *n* = **twilight,** dusk, eventide (*arch.*), half-light, nightfall

gloat *vb* **1** = **relish,** crow, drool, exult, glory, revel in, rub it in (*inf.*), rub one's hands, rub someone's nose in it, triumph, vaunt

global *adj* **1** = **worldwide,** international, pandemic, planetary, universal, world **2** = **comprehensive,** all-encompassing, all-inclusive, all-out, encyclopedic, exhaustive, general, thorough, total, unbounded, unlimited
Antonyms *adj* ≠ **comprehensive:** limited, narrow, parochial, restricted, sectional

globe *n* **2** = **earth,** planet, world **4** = **sphere,** ball, orb, round

globular *adj* **1** = **spherical,** globate, globelike, globoid, globose, globous, globulous, orbicular, round, spheroid

globule *n* = **droplet,** bead, bubble, drop, particle, pearl, pellet

gloom *n* **1** = **darkness,** blackness, cloud, cloudiness, dark, dimness, dullness, dusk, duskiness, gloominess, murk, murkiness, obscurity, shade, shadow, twilight **2** = **depression,** blues, dejection, desolation, despair, despondency, downheartedness, low spirits, melancholy, misery, sadness, sorrow, the hump (*Brit. inf.*), unhappiness, woe
Antonyms *n* ≠ **darkness:** daylight, light, radiance ≠ **depression:** brightness, cheerfulness, delight, happiness, high spirits, jollity, joy, mirth

gloomy *adj* **1** = **dark,** black, crepuscular, dim, dismal, dreary, dull, dusky, grey, murky, obscure, overcast, shadowy, sombre, Stygian, tenebrous **2** = **depressing,** bad, black, cheerless, comfortless, disheartening, dismal, dispiriting, dreary, funereal, joyless, sad, saddening, sombre **3** = **miserable,** blue, chapfallen, cheerless, crestfallen, dejected, despondent, dismal, dispirited, down, downcast, downhearted, down in the dumps (*inf.*), down in the mouth, glum, in low spirits, low, melancholy, moody, morose, pessimistic, sad, saturnine, sullen
Antonyms *adj* ≠ **dark:** brilliant, light, radiant, sunny ≠ **miserable:** blithe, bright, cheerful, chirpy (*inf.*), happy, high-spirited, jolly, jovial, light, merry, upbeat (*inf.*)

gloria ('glɔːrɪə) *n* a halo or nimbus, esp. as represented in art. [C16: from L: GLORY]

Gloria ('glɔːrɪə, -ˌɑː) *n* **1** any of several doxologies beginning with the word *Gloria*. **2** a musical setting of one of these.

glorify ❶ ('glɔːrɪˌfaɪ) *vb* **glorifies, glorifying, glorified.** (*tr*) **1** to make glorious. **2** to make more splendid; adorn. **3** to worship, exalt, or adore. **4** to extol. **5** to cause to seem more splendid or imposing than reality.
▸ˌ**glorifiˈcation** *n*

gloriole ('glɔːrɪˌəʊl) *n* another name for a **halo.** [C19: from L *glōriola*, lit.: a small GLORY]

glorious ❶ ('glɔːrɪəs) *adj* **1** having or full of glory; illustrious. **2** conferring glory or renown: *a glorious victory.* **3** brilliantly beautiful. **4** delightful or enjoyable.
▸ˈ**gloriously** *adv* ▸ˈ**gloriousness** *n*

glory ❶ ('glɔːrɪ) *n, pl* **glories. 1** exaltation, praise, or honour. **2** something that brings or is worthy of praise (esp. in **crowning glory**). **3** thanksgiving, adoration, or worship: *glory be to God.* **4** pomp; splendour: *the glory of the king's reign.* **5** radiant beauty; resplendence: *the glory of the sunset.* **6** the beauty and bliss of heaven. **7** a state of extreme happiness or prosperity. **8** another word for **halo** or **nimbus.** ◆ *vb* **glories, glorying, gloried. 9** (*intr;* often foll. by *in*) to triumph or exalt. ◆ *interj* **10** *Inf.* a mild interjection to express pleasure or surprise (often **glory be!**). [C13: from OF *glorie*, from L *glōria*, from ?]

glory box *n Austral. & NZ.* (esp. formerly) a box in which a young woman stores clothes, etc., in preparation for marriage.

glory hole *n* **1** a cupboard or storeroom, esp. one which is very untidy. **2** *Naut.* another term for **lazaretto** (sense 1).

Glos *abbrev. for* Gloucestershire.

gloss[1] ❶ (glɒs) *n* **1a** lustre or sheen, as of a smooth surface. **1b** (*as modifier*): *gloss paint.* **2** a superficially attractive appearance. **3** a cosmetic used to give a sheen. ◆ *vb* **4** to give a gloss to or obtain a gloss. **5** (*tr;* often foll. by *over*) to hide under a deceptively attractive surface or appearance. [C16: prob. of Scand. origin]
▸ˈ**glosser** *n*

gloss[2] ❶ (glɒs) *n* **1** a short or expanded explanation or interpretation of a word, expression, or foreign phrase in the margin or text of a manuscript, etc. **2** an intentionally misleading explanation. **3** short for **glossary.** ◆ *vb* (*tr*) **4** to add glosses to. **5** (often foll. by *over*) to give a false or misleading interpretation of. [C16: from L *glōssa* unusual word requiring explanatory note, from Ionic Gk]

glossary ('glɒsərɪ) *n, pl* **glossaries.** an alphabetical list of terms peculiar to a field of knowledge with explanations. [C14: from LL *glossārium;* see GLOSS[2]]
▸**glossarial** (glɒ'sɛərɪəl) *adj* ▸ˈ**glossarist** *n*

glosseme ('glɒsiːm) *n* the smallest meaningful unit of a language, such as stress, form, etc. [C20: from Gk; see GLOSS[2], -EME]

glossitis (glɒ'saɪtɪs) *n* inflammation of the tongue.
▸**glossitic** (glɒ'sɪtɪk) *adj*

glosso- *or before a vowel* **gloss-** *combining form.* indicating a tongue or language: *glossolaryngeal.* [from Gk *glossa* tongue]

glossolalia (ˌglɒsə'leɪlɪə) *n* another term for **gift of tongues.** [C19: NL, from GLOSSO- + Gk *lalein* to babble]

glossy ❶ ('glɒsɪ) *adj* **glossier, glossiest. 1** smooth and shiny; lustrous. **2** superficially attractive; plausible. **3** (of a magazine) lavishly produced on shiny paper. ◆ *n, pl* **glossies. 4** Also called (US): **slick.** an expensively produced magazine, printed on shiny paper and containing high-quality colour photography. **5** a photograph printed on paper that has a smooth shiny surface.
▸ˈ**glossily** *adv* ▸ˈ**glossiness** *n*

glottal ('glɒtᵊl) *adj* **1** of or relating to the glottis. **2** *Phonetics.* articulated or pronounced at or with the glottis.

glottal stop *n* a plosive speech sound produced by tightly closing the glottis and allowing the air pressure to build up before opening the glottis, causing the air to escape with force.

glottis ('glɒtɪs) *n, pl* **glottises** *or* **glottides** (-tɪˌdiːz). the vocal apparatus of the larynx, consisting of the two true vocal cords and the opening between them. [C16: from NL, from Gk, from Attic form of Ionic *glōssa* tongue; see GLOSS[2]]

glove (glʌv) *n* **1** (*often pl*) a shaped covering for the hand with individual sheaths for the fingers and thumb, made of leather, fabric, etc. **2** any of various large protective hand covers worn in sports, such as a boxing glove. ◆ *vb* **gloves, gloving, gloved. 3** (*tr*) to cover or provide with or as if with gloves. [OE *glōfe*]

glove box *n* a closed box in which toxic or radioactive substances can be handled by an operator who places his hands through protective gloves sealed to the box.

glove compartment *n* a small compartment in a car dashboard for the storage of miscellaneous articles.

glover ('glʌvə) *n* a person who makes or sells gloves.

glow ❶ (gləʊ) *n* **1** light emitted by a substance or object at a high temperature. **2** a steady even light without flames. **3** brilliance of colour. **4** brightness of complexion. **5** a feeling of wellbeing or satisfaction. **6** intensity of emotion. ◆ *vb* (*intr*) **7** to emit a steady even light without flames. **8** to shine intensely, as if from great heat. **9** to be exuberant, as from excellent health or intense emotion. **10** to experience a feeling of wellbeing or satisfaction: *to glow with pride.* **11** (esp. of the complexion) to show a strong bright colour, esp. red. **12** to be very hot. [OE *glōwan*]

glow discharge *n* a silent luminous discharge of electricity through a low-pressure gas.

glower ❶ ('glaʊə) *vb* **1** (*intr*) to stare hard and angrily. ◆ *n* **2** a sullen or angry stare. [C16: prob. of Scand. origin]
▸ˈ**gloweringly** *adv*

glowing ❶ ('gləʊɪŋ) *adj* **1** emitting light without flames: *glowing embers.* **2** warm and rich in colour: *glowing shades of gold and orange.* **3** flushed and rosy: *glowing cheeks.* **4** displaying or indicative of extreme pride or emotion: *a glowing account of his son's achievements.*

glow-worm *n* a European beetle, the females and larvae of which bear luminescent organs producing a soft greenish light.

gloxinia (glɒk'sɪnɪə) *n* any of several tropical plants cultivated for their large white, red, or purple bell-shaped flowers. [C19: after Benjamin P. *Gloxin*, 18th-cent. G physician & botanist]

gloze (gləʊz) *vb* **glozes, glozing, glozed.** *Arch.* **1** (*tr;* often foll. by *over*) to explain away; minimize the effect or importance of. **2** to make explanatory notes or glosses on (a text). **3** to use flattery (on). [C13: from OF *glosser* to comment; see GLOSS[2]]

glucose ('gluːkəʊz, -kəʊs) *n* **1** a white crystalline sugar, the most abundant form being dextrose. Formula: $C_6H_{12}O_6$. **2** a yellowish syrup obtained by incomplete hydrolysis of starch: used in confectionery, fermentation, etc. [C19: from F, from Gk *gleukos* sweet wine; rel. to Gk *glukus* sweet]

glucoside ('gluːkəʊˌsaɪd) *n Biochem.* any of a large group of glycosides that yield glucose on hydrolysis.
▸**glucosidic** (ˌgluːkəʊ'sɪdɪk) *adj*

glue ❶ (gluː) *n* **1** any natural or synthetic adhesive, esp. a sticky gelatinous substance prepared by boiling animal products such as bones, skin, and horns. **2** any other sticky or adhesive substance. ◆ *vb* **glues,**

THESAURUS

glorify *vb* **2** = **enhance**, add lustre to, adorn, aggrandize, augment, dignify, elevate, ennoble, illuminate, immortalize, lift up, magnify, raise **3** = **worship**, adore, apotheosize, beatify, bless, canonize, deify, enshrine, exalt, honour, idolize, pay homage to, revere, sanctify, venerate **4** = **praise**, celebrate, crack up (*inf.*), cry up (*inf.*), eulogize, extol, hymn, laud, lionize, magnify, panegyrize, sing *or* sound the praises of
Antonyms *vb* ≠ **enhance:** debase, defile, degrade ≠ **worship:** desecrate, dishonour ≠ **praise:** condemn, humiliate, mock

glorious *adj* **1** = **famous**, celebrated, distinguished, elevated, eminent, excellent, famed, grand, honoured, illustrious, magnificent, majestic, noble, noted, renowned, sublime, triumphant **3** = **splendid**, beautiful, bright, brilliant, dazzling, divine, effulgent, gorgeous, radiant, resplendent, shining, splendiferous (*facetious*), superb **4** = **delightful**, enjoyable, excellent, fine, gorgeous, great, heavenly (*inf.*), marvellous, pleasurable, splendid, splendiferous (*facetious*), wonderful
Antonyms *adj* ≠ **famous:** minor, ordinary, trivial, unimportant, unknown ≠ **splendid, delightful:** awful, dreary, dull, gloomy, horrible, unimpressive, unpleasant

glory *n* **1** = **honour**, celebrity, dignity, distinction, eminence, exaltation, fame, illustriousness, immortality, kudos, praise, prestige, renown **3** = **worship**, adoration, benediction, blessing, gratitude, homage, laudation, praise, thanksgiving, veneration **4** = **splendour**, éclat, grandeur, greatness, magnificence, majesty, nobility, pageantry, pomp, sublimity, triumph **5** = **beauty**, brilliance, effulgence, gorgeousness, lustre, radiance, resplendence ◆ *vb* **9** = **triumph**, boast, crow, drool, exult, gloat, pride oneself, relish, revel, take delight
Antonyms *n* ≠ **honour:** condemnation, disgrace, dishonour, disrepute, infamy, shame ≠ **worship:** blasphemy ≠ **splendour:** triviality ≠ **beauty:** ugliness

gloss[1] *n* **1** = **shine**, brightness, brilliance, burnish, gleam, lustre, patina, polish, sheen, varnish, veneer **2** = **façade**, appearance, front, mask, semblance, show, surface ◆ *vb* **4** = **glaze**, burnish, finish, furbish, lacquer, polish, shine, varnish, veneer **5** *with* **over** = **conceal**, camouflage, cover up, disguise, hide, mask, smooth over, sweep under the carpet (*inf.*), veil, whitewash (*inf.*)

gloss[2] *n* **1** = **comment**, annotation, commentary, elucidation, explanation, footnote, interpretation, note, scholium, translation ◆ *vb* **4** = **interpret**, annotate, comment, construe, elucidate, explain, translate

glossy *adj* **1** = **shiny**, bright, brilliant, burnished, glassy, glazed, lustrous, polished, sheeny, shining, silken, silky, sleek, smooth
Antonyms *adj* drab, dull, mat *or* matt, subfusc

glow *n* **1** = **light**, burning, gleam, glimmer, incandescence, lambency, luminosity, phosphorescence **3** = **radiance**, brightness, brilliance, effulgence, splendour, vividness **4** = **blush**, bloom, flush, reddening, rosiness **6** = **passion**, ardour, earnestness, enthusiasm, excitement, fervour, gusto, impetuosity, intensity, vehemence, warmth ◆ *vb* **7** = **shine**, brighten, burn, gleam, glimmer, redden, smoulder **10, 11** = **blush**, be suffused, colour, fill, flush, radiate, thrill, tingle
Antonyms *n* ≠ **radiance:** dullness, greyness ≠ **blush:** paleness, pallor, wanness ≠ **passion:** chill, coolness, half-heartedness, iciness, indifference

glower *vb* **1** = **scowl**, frown, give a dirty look, glare, look daggers, lour *or* lower ◆ *n* **2** = **scowl**, angry stare, black look, dirty look, frown, glare, lour *or* lower

glowing *adj* **1** = **bright**, aglow, beaming, flaming, florid, flushed, lambent, luminous, radiant, red, rich, ruddy, suffused, vibrant, vivid, warm **4** = **complimentary**, adulatory, ecstatic, enthusiastic, eulogistic, laudatory, panegyrical, rave (*inf.*), rhapsodic
Antonyms *adj* ≠ **bright:** colourless, cool, dull, grey, pale, pallid, wan ≠ **complimentary:** cruel, dispassionate, scathing, unenthusiastic

glue *n* **1, 2** = **adhesive**, cement, gum, mucilage, paste ◆ *vb* **3** = **stick**, affix, agglutinate, cement, fix, gum, paste, seal

gluing *or* **glueing, glued. 3** (*tr*) to join or stick together as with glue. [C14: from OF *glu,* from LL *glūs*]
▸'**glue,like** *adj* ▸'**gluer** *n* ▸'**gluey** *adj*

glue ear *n* accumulation of fluid in the middle ear in children, caused by infection and resulting in deafness.

glue-sniffing *n* the practice of inhaling the fumes of certain types of glue to produce intoxicating or hallucinatory effects.
▸'**glue-,sniffer** *n*

gluhwein ('glu:,vaɪn) *n* mulled wine. [G]

glum ❶ (glʌm) *adj* **glummer, glummest.** silent or sullen, as from gloom. [C16: var. of GLOOM]
▸'**glumly** *adv* ▸'**glumness** *n*

glume (glu:m) *n Bot.* one of a pair of dry membranous bracts at the base of the spikelet of grasses. [C18: from L *glūma* husk of corn]
▸**glu'maceous** *adj*

gluon ('glu:ɒn) *n* a hypothetical particle believed to be exchanged between quarks in order to bind them together to form particles. [C20: coined from GLUE + -ON]

glut ❶ (glʌt) *n* **1** an excessive amount, as in the production of a crop. **2** the act of glutting or state of being glutted. ◆ *vb* **gluts, glutting, glutted.** (*tr*) **3** to feed or supply beyond capacity. **4** to supply (a market, etc.) with a commodity in excess of the demand for it. [C14: prob. from OF *gloutir,* from L *gluttīre;* see GLUTTON[1]]

glutamic acid (glu:'tæmɪk) *n* an amino acid, occurring in proteins.

gluten ('glu:tᵊn) *n* a protein present in cereal grains, esp. wheat. [C16: from L: GLUE]
▸'**glutenous** *adj*

gluteus (glʊ'ti:əs) *n, pl* **glutei** (-'ti:aɪ). any one of the three large muscles that form the human buttock. [C17: from NL, from Gk *gloutos* buttock, rump]
▸**glu'teal** *adj*

glutinous ❶ ('glu:tɪnəs) *adj* resembling glue in texture; sticky.
▸'**glutinously** *adv*

glutton[1] ❶ ('glʌtᵊn) *n* **1** a person devoted to eating and drinking to excess; greedy person. **2** a person who has or appears to have a voracious appetite for something: *a glutton for punishment.* [C13: from OF *glouton,* from L from *gluttīre* to swallow]
▸'**gluttonous** *adj* ▸'**gluttonously** *adv*

glutton[2] ('glʌtᵊn) *n* another name for **wolverine.** [C17: from GLUTTON[1], apparently translating G *Vielfrass* great eater]

gluttony ❶ ('glʌtənɪ) *n* the act or practice of eating to excess.

glyceride ('glɪsə,raɪd) *n* any fatty-acid ester of glycerol.

glycerine ('glɪsəri:n, ,glɪsə'ri:n) *or* **glycerin** ('glɪsərɪn) *n* another name (not in technical usage) for **glycerol.** [C19: from F, from Gk *glukeros* sweet + *-ine* -IN; rel. to Gk *glukus* sweet]

glycerol ('glɪsə,rɒl) *n* a colourless odourless syrupy liquid: a by-product of soap manufacture, used as a solvent, antifreeze, plasticizer, and sweetener (**E422**). Formula: $CH_2OHCHOHCH_2OH$. [C19: from GLYCER(IN) + -OL[1]]

glycine ('glaɪsi:n, glaɪ'si:n) *n* a white sweet crystalline amino acid occurring in most proteins. [C19: GLYCO- + -INE[2]]

glyco- *or before a vowel* **glyc-** *combining form.* sugar: *glycogen.* [from Gk *glukus* sweet]

glycogen ('glaɪkəʊdʒən) *n* a polysaccharide consisting of glucose units: the form in which carbohydrate is stored in animals.
▸**glycogenic** (,glaɪkəʊ'dʒɛnɪk) *adj* ▸,**glyco'genesis** *n*

glycol ('glaɪkɒl) *n* another name (not in technical usage) for **ethanediol.**

glycolic acid (glaɪ'kɒlɪk) *n* a colourless crystalline compound found in sugar cane and sugar beet: used in the manufacture of pharmaceuticals, pesticides, and plasticizers.

glycolysis (glaɪ'kɒlɪsɪs) *n Biochem.* the breakdown of glucose by enzymes with the liberation of energy.

glycoside ('glaɪkəʊ,saɪd) *n* any of a group of substances derived from simple sugars by replacing the hydroxyl group by another group.
▸**glycosidic** (,glaɪkəʊ'sɪdɪk) *adj*

glycosuria (,glaɪkəʊ'sjʊərɪə) *n* the presence of excess sugar in the urine, as in diabetes. [C19: from NL, from F *glycose* GLUCOSE + -URIA]

glyph (glɪf) *n* **1** a carved channel or groove, esp. a vertical one. **2** *Now rare.* another word for **hieroglyphic.** [C18: from F, from Gk, from *gluphein* to carve]
▸'**glyphic** *adj*

glyptic ('glɪptɪk) *adj* of or relating to engraving or carving, esp. on precious stones. [C19: from F, from Gk, from *gluphein* to carve]

glyptodont ('glɪptə,dɒnt) *n* an extinct mammal of South America which resembled the giant armadillo. [C19: from Gk *gluptos* carved + -ODONT]

GM *abbrev. for:* **1** general manager. **2** genetically modified. **3** (in Britain) George Medal. **4** Grand Master. **5** grant-maintained.

G-man *n, pl* **G-men. 1** *US sl.* an FBI agent. **2** *Irish.* a political detective.

Gmc *abbrev. for* Germanic.

GMT *abbrev. for* Greenwich Mean Time.

GMWU (in Britain) *abbrev. for* National Union of General and Municipal Workers.

gnarl (nɑ:l) *n* **1** any knotty swelling on a tree. ◆ *vb* **2** (*tr*) to knot or cause to knot. [C19: back formation from *gnarled*]

gnarled ❶ (nɑ:ld) *or* **gnarly** *adj* **1** having gnarls: *the gnarled trunk of the old tree.* **2** (esp. of hands) rough, twisted, and weather-beaten.

gnash (næʃ) *vb* **1** to grind (the teeth) together, as in pain or anger. **2** (*tr*) to bite or chew as by grinding the teeth. ◆ *n* **3** the act of gnashing the teeth. [C15: prob. from ON; cf. *gnastan* gnashing of teeth]

gnat (næt) *n* any of various small fragile biting two-winged insects. [OE *gnætt*]

gnathic ('næθɪk) *adj Anat.* of or relating to the jaw. [C19: from Gk *gnathos* jaw]

-gnathous *adj combining form.* indicating or having a jaw of a specified kind: *prognathous.* [from NL, from Gk *gnathos* jaw]

gnaw ❶ (nɔ:) *vb* **gnaws, gnawing, gnawed; gnawed** *or* **gnawn. 1** (when *intr,* often foll. by *at* or *upon*) to bite (at) or chew (upon) constantly so as to wear away little by little. **2** (*tr*) to form by gnawing: *to gnaw a hole.* **3** to cause erosion of (something). **4** (when *intr,* often foll. by *at*) to cause constant distress or anxiety (to). ◆ *n* **5** the act or an instance of gnawing. [OE *gnagan*]

gnawing ('nɔ:ɪŋ) *n* a dull persistent pang or pain, esp. of hunger.

gneiss (naɪs) *n* any coarse-grained metamorphic rock that is banded or foliated. [C18: from G *Gneis,* prob. from MHG *ganeist* spark]
▸'**gneissic,** '**gneissoid,** *or* '**gneissose** *adj*

gnocchi ('nɒkɪ) *pl n* dumplings made of pieces of semolina pasta, or sometimes potato, served with sauce. [It., pl of *gnocco* lump, prob. of Gmc origin]

gnome (nəʊm) *n* **1** one of a species of legendary creatures, usually resembling small misshapen old men, said to live in the depths of the earth and guard buried treasure. **2** the statue of a gnome, esp. in a garden. **3** a very small or ugly person. **4** *Facetious or derog.* an international banker or financier (esp. in **gnomes of Zürich**). [C18: from F, from NL *gnomus,* coined by Paracelsus (1493-1541), Swiss alchemist, from ?]
▸'**gnomish** *adj*

gnomic ('nəʊmɪk, 'nɒm-) *adj* of or relating to aphorisms; pithy.
▸'**gnomically** *adv*

gnomon ('nəʊmɒn) *n* **1** the stationary arm that projects the shadow on a sundial. **2** a geometric figure remaining after a parallelogram has been removed from one corner of a larger parallelogram. [C16: from L, from Gk: interpreter, from *gignōskein* to know]
▸**gno'monic** *adj*

-gnosis *n combining form.* (esp. in medicine) recognition or knowledge: *diagnosis.* [via L from Gk: knowledge]
▸**-gnostic** *adj combining form.*

gnostic ('nɒstɪk) *adj* of, relating to, or possessing knowledge, esp. spiritual knowledge.

Gnostic ('nɒstɪk) *n* **1** an adherent of Gnosticism. ◆ *adj* **2** of or relating to Gnostics or to Gnosticism. [C16: from LL, from Gk *gnōstikos* relating to knowledge]

Gnosticism ('nɒstɪ,sɪzəm) *n* a religious movement characterized by a belief in intuitive spiritual knowledge: regarded as a heresy by the Christian Church.

gnotobiotic (,nəʊtəʊbaɪ'ɒtɪk) *adj* of or pertaining to germ-free conditions, esp. in a laboratory in which animals are injected with known strains of organisms. [C20: from Gk *gnōtos,* from *gignōskein* to know + BIOTIC]

GNP *abbrev. for* gross national product.

gnu (nu:) *n, pl* **gnus** *or* **gnu.** either of two sturdy antelopes inhabiting the savannas of Africa, having an oxlike head and a long tufted tail. Also called: **wildebeest.** [C18: from Xhosa *nqu*]

GNVQ (in Britain) *abbrev. for* general national vocational qualification: a qualification which rewards the development of skills likely to be of use to employers.

go ❶ (gəʊ) *vb* **goes, going, went, gone.** (*mainly intr*) **1** to move or proceed, esp. to or from a point or in a certain direction: *go home.* **2** (*tr; takes an infinitive,* often with *to* omitted or replaced by *and*) to proceed towards a particular person or place with some specified purpose: *I must go and*

THESAURUS

glum *adj* = **gloomy,** chapfallen, churlish, crabbed, crestfallen, crusty, dejected, doleful, down, gruff, grumpy, huffy, ill-humoured, low, moody, morose, pessimistic, saturnine, sour, sulky, sullen, surly
Antonyms *adj* cheerful, cheery, chirpy (*inf.*), jolly, joyful, merry, upbeat (*inf.*)

glut *n* **1** = **surfeit,** excess, overabundance, oversupply, plethora, saturation, superabundance, superfluity, surplus ◆ *vb* **3** = **overfeed,** cram, fill, gorge, satiate, stuff **4** = **saturate,** choke, clog, deluge, flood, inundate, overload, oversupply
Antonyms *n* ≠ **surfeit:** dearth, lack, paucity, scarcity, shortage, want

glutinous *adj* = **sticky,** adhesive, cohesive, gluey, gooey, gummy, mucilaginous, viscid, viscous

glutton[1] *n* **1** = **gourmand,** gannet (*sl.*), gobbler, gorger, gormandizer, pig (*inf.*)

gluttonous[1] *adj* **1** = **greedy,** edacious, gormandizing, hoggish, insatiable, piggish, rapacious, ravenous, voracious

gluttony *n* = **greed,** edacity, gormandizing, gourmandism, greediness, piggishness, rapacity, voraciousness, voracity

gnarled *adj* **1, 2** = **twisted,** contorted, knotted, knotty, knurled, leathery, rough, rugged, weather-beaten, wrinkled

gnaw *vb* **1** = **bite,** chew, munch, nibble **3** = **erode,** consume, devour, eat away *or* into, fret, wear away *or* down **4** = **distress,** fret, harry, haunt, nag, plague, prey on one's mind, trouble, worry

go *vb* **1** = **move,** advance, fare (*arch.*), journey, make for, pass, proceed, repair, set off, travel **3** = **leave,** decamp, depart, make tracks, move out, slope off, withdraw **6** = **function,** move, operate, perform, run, work **11** = **lead,** connect, extend, fit, give access, reach, run, span, spread, stretch **13** = **contribute,** avail, concur, conduce, incline, lead to, serve, tend, work towards **14** = **fare,** develop, eventuate, fall out,

get that book. **3** to depart: *we'll have to go at eleven.* **4** to start, as in a race: often used in commands. **5** to make regular journeys: *this train service goes to the east coast.* **6** to operate or function effectively: *the radio won't go.* **7** (*copula*) to become: *his face went red.* **8** to make a noise as specified: *the gun went bang.* **9** to enter into a specified state or condition: *to go into hysterics.* **10** to be or continue to be in a specified state or condition: *to go in rags; to go in poverty.* **11** to lead, extend, or afford access: *this route goes to the north.* **12** to proceed towards an activity: *to go to sleep.* **13** (*tr; takes an infinitive*) to serve or contribute: *this letter goes to prove my point.* **14** to follow a course as specified; fare: *the lecture went badly.* **15** to be applied or allotted to a particular purpose or recipient: *his money went on drink.* **16** to be sold: *the necklace went for three thousand pounds.* **17** to be ranked; compare: *this meal is good as my meals go.* **18** to blend or harmonize: *these chairs won't go with the rest of your furniture.* **19** (foll. by *by* or *under*) to be known (by a name or disguise). **20** to have a usual or proper place: *those books go on this shelf.* **21** (of music, poetry, etc.) to be sounded; expressed, etc.: *how does that song go?* **22** to fail or give way: *my eyesight is going.* **23** to break down or collapse abruptly: *the ladder went at the critical moment.* **24** to die: *the old man went at 2 a.m.* **25** (often foll. by *by*) **25a** (of time, etc.) to elapse: *the hours go by so slowly.* **25b** to travel past: *the train goes by her house.* **25c** to be guided (by). **26** to occur: *happiness does not always go with riches.* **27** to be eliminated, abolished, or given up: *this entry must go to save space.* **28** to be spent or finished: *all his money has gone.* **29** to attend: *go to school.* **30** to join a stated profession: *go on the stage.* **31** (foll. by *to*) to have recourse (to); turn: *to go to arbitration.* **32** (foll. by *to*) to subject or put oneself (to): *she goes to great pains to please him.* **33** to proceed, esp. up to or beyond certain limits: *you will go too far one day and then you will be punished.* **34** to be acceptable or tolerated: *anything goes.* **35** to carry the weight of final authority: *what the boss says goes.* **36** (*tr*) *Nonstandard.* to say: *Then she goes, "Give it to me!" and she just snatched it.* **37** (foll. by *into*) to be contained in: *four goes into twelve three times.* **38** (often foll. by *for*) to endure or last out: *we can't go for much longer without water.* **39** (*tr*) *Cards.* to bet or bid: *I go two hearts.* **40 be going.** to intend or be about to start (to do or be doing something): often used as an alternative future construction: *what's going to happen to us?* **41 go and.** *Inf.* to be so foolish or unlucky as to: *then she had to go and lose her hat.* **42 go it.** *Sl.* to do something or move energetically. **43 go it alone.** *Inf.* to act or proceed without allies or help. **44 go one better.** *Inf.* to surpass or outdo (someone). **45 let go. 45a** to relax one's hold (on); release. **45b** to discuss or consider no further. **46 let oneself go. 46a** to act in an uninhibited manner. **46b** to lose interest in one's appearance, manners, etc. **47 to go. 47a** remaining. **47b** *US & Canad. inf.* (of food served by a restaurant) for taking away. ◆ *n, pl* **goes. 48** the act of going. **49a** an attempt or try: *he had a go at the stamp business.* **49b** an attempt at stopping a person suspected of a crime: *the police are not always in favour of the public having a go.* **49c** an attack, esp. verbal: *she had a real go at them.* **50** a turn: *it's my go next.* **51** *Inf.* the quality of being active and energetic: *she has much more go than I have.* **52** *Inf.* hard or energetic work: *it's all go.* **53** *Inf.* a successful venture or achievement: *he made a go of it.* **54** *Inf.* a bargain or agreement. **55 from the word go.** *Inf.* from the very beginning. **56 no go.** *Inf.* impossible; abortive or futile: *it's no go, I'm afraid.* **57 on the go.** *Inf.* active and energetic. ◆ *adj* **58** (*postpositive*) *Inf.* functioning properly and ready for action: esp. used in astronautics: *all systems are go.* ◆ See also **go about, go against,** etc. [OE *gān*]

go about Ⓣ *vb* (*intr*) **1** (*prep*) to busy oneself with: *to go about one's duties.* **2** (*prep*) to tackle (a problem or task). **3** to circulate (in): *there's a lot of flu going about.* **4** (*adv*) (of a sailing ship) to change from one tack to another.

goad Ⓣ (gəʊd) *n* **1** a sharp pointed stick for urging on cattle, etc. **2** anything that acts as a spur or incitement. ◆ *vb* **3** (*tr*) to drive as if with a goad; spur; incite. [OE *gād*, of Gmc origin]

go against *vb* (*intr, prep*) **1** to be contrary to (principles or beliefs). **2** to be unfavourable to (a person): *the case went against him.*

go-ahead Ⓣ *n* **1** (usually preceded by *the*) *Inf.* permission to proceed. ◆ *adj* **2** enterprising or ambitious.

goal Ⓣ (gəʊl) *n* **1** the aim or object towards which an endeavour is directed. **2** the terminal point of a journey or race. **3** (in various sports) the net, basket, etc., into or over which players try to propel the ball, puck, etc., to score. **4** *Sport.* **4a** a successful attempt at scoring. **4b** the score so made. **5** (in soccer, hockey, etc.) the position of goalkeeper. [C16: ? rel. to ME *gol* boundary, OE *gǣlan* to hinder]
▸ ˈ**goalless** *adj*

goalball (ˈgəʊlˌbɔːl) *n* **1** a game played by two teams who compete to score goals by throwing a ball that emits sound when in motion. Players are blindfolded during play. **2** the ball used in this game.

goalie (ˈgəʊlɪ) *n Inf.* short for **goalkeeper.**

goalkeeper (ˈgəʊlˌkiːpə) *n Sport.* a player in the goal whose duty is to prevent the ball, puck, etc., from entering or crossing it.

goal kick *n Soccer.* a kick taken from the six-yard line by the defending team after the ball has been put out of play by an opposing player.

goal line *n Sport.* the line marking each end of the pitch, on which the goals stand.

go along Ⓣ *vb* (*intr, adv;* often foll. by *with*) to refrain from disagreement; assent.

goalpost (ˈgəʊlˌpəʊst) *n* **1** either of two upright posts supporting the crossbar of a goal. **2 move the goalposts.** to change the target required during negotiations, etc.

goanna (gəʊˈænə) *n* any of various Australian monitor lizards. [C19: from IGUANA]

goat (gəʊt) *n* **1** any sure-footed agile ruminant mammal with hollow horns, naturally inhabiting rough stony ground in Europe, Asia, and N Africa. **2** *Inf.* a lecherous man. **3** a foolish person. **4 get (someone's) goat.** *Sl.* to cause annoyance to (someone). [OE *gāt*]
▸ ˈ**goatish** *adj*

Goat (gəʊt) *n* **the.** the constellation Capricorn, the tenth sign of the zodiac.

go at Ⓣ *vb* (*intr, prep*) **1** to make an energetic attempt at (something). **2** to attack vehemently.

goatee (gəʊˈtiː) *n* a pointed tuftlike beard on the chin. [C19: from GOAT + -*ee* (see -Y[2])]

goatherd (ˈgəʊtˌhɜːd) *n* a person employed to tend or herd goats.

goatsbeard *or* **goat's-beard** (ˈgəʊtsˌbɪəd) *n* **1** Also called: **Jack-go-to-bed-at-noon.** a Eurasian plant of the composite family, with woolly stems and large heads of yellow rayed flowers. **2** an American plant with long spikes of small white flowers.

goatskin (ˈgəʊtˌskɪn) *n* **1** the hide of a goat. **2** something made from the hide of a goat, such as leather or a container for wine.

goatsucker (ˈgəʊtˌsʌkə) *n* the US and Canad. name for **nightjar.**

gob[1] Ⓣ (gɒb) *n* **1** a lump or chunk, esp. of a soft substance. **2** (*often pl*) *Inf.* a great quantity or amount. **3** *Inf.* a globule of spittle or saliva. **4** a lump of molten glass used to make a piece of glassware. ◆ *vb* **gobs, gobbing, gobbed. 5** (*intr*) *Brit. inf.* to spit. [C14: from OF *gobe* lump, from *gober;* see GOBBET]

gob[2] (gɒb) *n* a slang word (esp. Brit.) for the **mouth.** [C16: ?from Gaelic *gob*]

go back Ⓣ *vb* (*intr, adv*) **1** to return. **2** (often foll. by *to*) to originate (in): *the links with France go back to the Norman Conquest.* **3** (foll. by *on*) to change one's mind about; repudiate (esp. in **go back on one's word**).

gobbet (ˈgɒbɪt) *n* a chunk, lump, or fragment, esp. of raw meat. [C14: from OF *gobet*, from *gober* to gulp down]

gobble[1] Ⓣ (ˈgɒbᵊl) *vb* **gobbles, gobbling, gobbled. 1** (when *tr*, often foll. by *up*) to eat or swallow (food) hastily and in large mouthfuls. **2** (*tr;* often foll. by *up*) *Inf.* to snatch. [C17: prob. from GOB[1]]

gobble[2] (ˈgɒbᵊl) *n* **1** the loud rapid gurgling sound made by male turkeys. ◆ *vb* **gobbles, gobbling, gobbled. 2** (*intr*) (of a turkey) to make this sound. [C17: prob. imit.]

gobbledegook Ⓣ *or* **gobbledygook** (ˈgɒbᵊl dɪˌguːk) *n* pretentious or unintelligible jargon, such as that used by officials. [C20: whimsical formation from GOBBLE[2]]

gobbler (ˈgɒblə) *n Inf.* a male turkey.

Gobelin (ˈgəʊbəlɪn; *French* gɔblɛ̃) *adj* **1** of or resembling tapestry made at the Gobelins' factory in Paris, having vivid pictorial scenes. ◆ *n* **2** a tapestry of this kind. [C19: from the *Gobelin* family, who founded the factory]

go-between Ⓣ *n* a person who acts as agent or intermediary for two people or groups in a transaction or dealing.

goblet (ˈgɒblɪt) *n* **1** a vessel for drinking, with a base and stem but with-

THESAURUS

happen, pan out (*inf.*), proceed, result, turn out, work out **18** = **harmonize**, accord, agree, blend, chime, complement, correspond, fit, match, suit **24** = **die**, croak (*sl.*), expire, give up the ghost, kick the bucket (*sl.*), pass away, peg out (*inf.*), perish, pop one's clogs (*inf.*), snuff it (*inf.*) **25a** = **elapse**, expire, flow, lapse, pass, slip away ◆ *n* **49a** = **attempt**, bid, crack (*inf.*), effort, essay, shot (*inf.*), stab (*inf.*), try, turn, whack (*inf.*), whirl (*inf.*) **51** *Informal* = **energy**, activity, animation, brio, drive, force, get-up-and-go (*inf.*), life, oomph (*inf.*), pep, spirit, verve, vigour, vitality, vivacity **56 no go** *Informal* = **impossible**, futile, hopeless, not on (*inf.*), vain
Antonyms *vb* ≠ **move:** arrive, halt, reach, remain, stay, stop ≠ **function:** break (down), fail, malfunction, stop

go about *vb* **1** = **busy** *or* **occupy oneself with**, devote oneself to **2** = **tackle**, approach, begin, get the show on the road, set about, take the bit between one's teeth, undertake **3** = **move around**, circulate, pass around, wander

goad *n* **2** = **provocation**, impetus, incentive, incitement, irritation, motivation, pressure, spur, stimulation, stimulus, urge ◆ *vb* **3** = **provoke**, annoy, arouse, drive, egg on, exhort, harass, hound, impel, incite, instigate, irritate, lash, prick, prod, prompt, propel, spur, stimulate, sting, urge, worry

go-ahead *n* **1** *Informal* = **permission**, assent, authorization, consent, green light, leave, O.K. *or* okay (*inf.*) ◆ *adj* **2** = **enterprising**, ambitious, go-getting (*inf.*), pioneering, progressive, up-and-coming

goal *n* **1, 2** = **aim**, ambition, design, destination, end, Holy Grail (*inf.*), intention, limit, mark, object, objective, purpose, target

go along *vb* = **agree**, acquiesce, assent, concur, cooperate, follow

go at *vb* **2** = **attack**, argue, blame, blast, criticize, go for the jugular, impugn, lambast(e), put down, set about, tear into (*inf.*)

gob[1] *n* **1** = **piece**, blob, chunk, clod, gobbet, hunk, lump, nugget, wad, wodge (*Brit. inf.*)

go back *vb* **1** = **return**, retrocede, revert **3** *with* **on** = **repudiate**, change one's mind about, desert, forsake, renege on, retract

gobble[1] *vb* **1** = **devour**, bolt, cram, gorge, gulp, guzzle, pig out on (*US & Canad. sl.*), stuff, swallow, wolf

gobbledegook *n* = **nonsense**, babble, cant, double talk, gabble, gibberish, Greek (*inf.*), hocus-pocus, jabber, jargon, mumbo jumbo, officialese, rigmarole, twaddle

go-between *n* = **intermediary**, agent, broker,

out handles. **2** *Arch.* a large drinking cup. [C14: from OF *gobelet* a little cup, ult. of Celtic origin]

goblin ('gɒblɪn) *n* (in folklore) a small grotesque supernatural creature, regarded as malevolent towards human beings. [C14: from OF, from MHG *kobolt;* cf. COBALT]

gobo ('gəʊbəʊ) *n, pl* **gobos** *or* **goboes.** a shield placed round a microphone to exclude unwanted sounds, or round a camera lens, etc., to reduce the incident light. [C20: from ?]

gobshite ('gɒb,ʃaɪt) *n Irish taboo sl.* a stupid person. [C20: from GOB[2] + *shite* excrement; see SHIT]

gobsmacked ('gɒb,smækt) *adj Brit. sl.* astounded; astonished. [C20: from GOB[2] + SMACK]

goby ('gəʊbɪ) *n, pl* **goby** *or* **gobies.** a small spiny-finned fish of coastal or brackish waters, having a large head, an elongated tapering body, and the ventral fins modified as a sucker. [C18: from L *gōbius* gudgeon from Gk *kōbios*]

go-by *n Sl.* a deliberate snub or slight (esp. in **give (a person) the go-by**).

go by ❶ *vb* (*intr*) **1** to pass: *as the years go by.* **2** (*prep*) to be guided by: *in the darkness we could only go by the stars.* **3** (*prep*) to use as a basis for forming an opinion or judgment: *it's wise not to go only by appearances.*

go-cart *n* See **kart.**

god (gɒd) *n* **1** a supernatural being, who is worshipped as the controller of some part of the universe or some aspect of life in the world or is the personification of some force. **2** an image, idol, or symbolic representation of such a deity. **3** any person or thing to which excessive attention is given: *money was his god.* **4** a man who has qualities regarded as making him superior to other men. **5** (*pl*) the gallery of a theatre. [OE *god*]

God (gɒd) *n* **1** the sole Supreme Being, eternal, spiritual, and transcendent, who is the Creator and ruler of all and is infinite in all attributes; the object of worship in monotheistic religions. ◆ *interj* **2** an oath or exclamation used to indicate surprise, annoyance, etc. (and in such expressions as **My God!** or **God Almighty!**).

godchild ('gɒd,tʃaɪld) *n, pl* **godchildren.** a person who is sponsored by adults at baptism.

goddaughter ('gɒd,dɔːtə) *n* a female godchild.

goddess ('gɒdɪs) *n* **1** a female divinity. **2** a woman who is adored or idealized, esp. by a man.

godetia (gə'diːʃə) *n* any plant of the American genus *Godetia,* esp. one grown as a showy-flowered annual garden plant. [C19: after C. H. *Godet* (died 1879), Swiss botanist]

godfather ('gɒd,fɑːðə) *n* **1** a male godparent. **2** the head of a Mafia family or other criminal ring. **3** an originator or leading exponent: *the godfather of South African pop.*

godfather offer *n Inf.* a takeover bid pitched so high that the management of the target company is unable to dissuade shareholders from accepting it. [from the 1972 film *The Godfather,* in which a character was made an offer he could not refuse]

God-fearing *adj* pious; devout.

godforsaken ❶ ('gɒdfə,seɪkən) *adj* (*sometimes cap.*) **1** (*usually prenominal*) desolate; dreary; forlorn. **2** wicked.

Godhead ('gɒd,hɛd) *n* (*sometimes not cap.*) **1** the essential nature and condition of being God. **2 the Godhead.** God.

godhood ('gɒd,hʊd) *n* the state of being divine.

godless ❶ ('gɒdlɪs) *adj* **1** wicked or unprincipled. **2** lacking a god. **3** refusing to acknowledge God.
▶'**godlessly** *adv* ▶'**godlessness** *n*

godlike ❶ ('gɒd,laɪk) *adj* resembling or befitting a god or God; divine.

godly ❶ ('gɒdlɪ) *adj* **godlier, godliest.** having a religious character; pious; devout.
▶'**godliness** *n*

godmother ('gɒd,mʌðə) *n* a female godparent.

godown ('gəʊ,daʊn) *n* (in the East, esp. in India) a warehouse. [C16: from Malay *godong*]

go down ❶ *vb* (*intr, mainly adv*) **1** (*also prep*) to move or lead to or as if to a lower place or level; sink, decline, decrease, etc. **2** to be defeated; lose. **3** to be remembered or recorded (esp. in **go down in history**). **4** to be received: *his speech went down well.* **5** (of food) to be swallowed. **6** *Brit.* to leave a college or university at the end of a term. **7** (usually foll. by *with*) to fall ill; be infected. **8** (of a celestial body) to sink or set. **9 go down on.** *Taboo sl.* to perform cunnilingus or fellatio on.

godparent ('gɒd,pɛərənt) *n* a person who stands sponsor to another at baptism.

God's acre *n Literary.* a churchyard or burial ground. [C17: translation of G *Gottesacker*]

godsend ❶ ('gɒd,send) *n* a person or thing that comes unexpectedly but is particularly welcome. [C19: from C17 *God's send,* alteration of *goddes sand* God's message, from OE *sand;* see SEND]

godslot ('gɒd,slɒt) *n Inf.* a time in a television or radio schedule traditionally reserved for religious broadcasts.

godson ('gɒd,sʌn) *n* a male godchild.

Godspeed ('gɒd'spiːd) *sentence substitute, n* an expression of good wishes for a person's success and safety. [C15: from *God spede* may God prosper (you)]

godsquad ('gɒd,skwɒd) *n Inf., derog.* any group of evangelical Christians, members of which are regarded as intrusive and exuberantly pious.

godwit ('gɒdwɪt) *n* a large shore bird of the sandpiper family having long legs and a long upturned bill. [C16: from ?]

goer ('gəʊə) *n* **1a** a person who attends something regularly. **1b** (*in combination*): *filmgoer.* **2** a person or thing that goes, esp. one that goes very fast. **3** an energetic person. **4** *Austral. inf.* an acceptable or feasible idea, proposal, etc.

go-faster stripe *n Inf.* a decorative line, often suggestive of high speed, on the bodywork of a car.

gofer ('gəʊfə) *n Sl.* a person who runs errands. [C20: from GO + FOR]

goffer ('gəʊfə) *vb* (*tr*) **1** to press pleats into (a frill). **2** to decorate (the edges of a book). ◆ *n* **3** an ornamental frill made by pressing pleats. **4** the decoration formed by goffering books. **5** the iron or tool used in making goffers. [C18: from F *gaufrer* to impress a pattern, from *gaufre,* from MLow G *wāfel;* see WAFFLE[1], WAFER]

go for ❶ *vb* (*intr, prep*) **1** to go somewhere in order to have or fetch: *he went for a drink.* **2** to seek to obtain: *I'd go for that job if I were you.* **3** to prefer or choose; like: *I really go for that new idea of yours.* **4** to make a physical or verbal attack on. **5** to be considered to be of a stated importance or value: *his twenty years went for nothing when he was made redundant.* **6 go for it.** *Inf.* to make the maximum effort to achieve a particular goal.

go-getter *n Inf.* an ambitious enterprising person.
▶,**go-'getting** *adj*

gogga ('xɒxə) *n S. African inf.* any small animal that crawls or flies, esp. an insect. [C20: from Khoikhoi *xoxon* insects collectively]

goggle ❶ ('gɒg[ə]l) *vb* **goggles, goggling, goggled.** **1** (*intr*) to stare fixedly, as in astonishment. **2** to cause (the eyes) to roll or bulge or (of the eyes) to roll or bulge. ◆ *n* **3** a bulging stare. **4** (*pl*) spectacles, often of coloured glass or covered with gauze: used to protect the eyes. [C14: from *gogelen* to look aside, from ?; see AGOG]
▶'**goggle-**,**eyed** *adj*

gogglebox ('gɒg[ə]l,bɒks) *n Brit. sl.* a television set.

Go-Go *n* a form of soul music originating in Washington, DC, characterized by the use of funk rhythms and a brass section.

go-go dancer *n* a dancer, usually scantily dressed, who performs rhythmic and often erotic modern dance routines, esp. in a nightclub.

Goidelic (gɔɪ'dɛlɪk) *n* **1** the N group of Celtic languages, consisting of Irish Gaelic, Scottish Gaelic, and Manx. ◆ *adj* **2** of, relating to, or characteristic of this group of languages. [C19: from OIrish *Goidel* a Celt, from OWelsh, from *gwydd* savage]

go in ❶ *vb* (*intr, adv*) **1** to enter. **2** (*prep*) See **go into.** **3** (of the sun) to become hidden behind a cloud. **4 go in for. 4a** to enter as a competitor or contestant. **4b** to adopt as an activity, interest, or guiding principle: *she went in for nursing.*

going ('gəʊɪŋ) *n* **1** a departure or farewell. **2** the condition of a surface such as a road or field with regard to walking, riding, etc.: *muddy going.* **3** *Inf.* speed, progress, etc.: *we made good going on the trip.* ◆ *adj* **4** thriving (esp. in **a going concern**). **5** current or accepted: *the going rate.* **6** (*postpositive*) available: *the best going.*

going-over ❶ *n, pl* **goings-over.** *Inf.* **1** a check, examination, or investigation. **2** a castigation or thrashing.

goings-on *pl n Inf.* **1** actions or conduct, esp. when regarded with disapproval. **2** happenings or events, esp. when mysterious or suspicious.

go into ❶ *vb* (*intr, prep*) **1** to enter. **2** to start a career in: *to go into publishing.* **3** to investigate or examine. **4** to discuss: *we won't go into that now.* **5** to be admitted to, esp. temporarily: *she went into hospital.* **6** to enter a specified state: *she went into fits of laughter.*

goitre *or US* **goiter** ('gɔɪtə) *n Pathol.* a swelling of the thyroid gland, in

THESAURUS

dealer, factor, liaison, mediator, medium, middleman

go by *vb* **1** = **pass**, elapse, exceed, flow on, move onward, proceed **2, 3** = **follow**, adopt, be guided by, heed, judge from, observe, take as guide

godforsaken *adj* **1** = **desolate**, abandoned, backward, bleak, deserted, dismal, dreary, forlorn, gloomy, lonely, neglected, remote, wretched

godless *adj* **1** = **wicked**, depraved, evil, impious, unprincipled, unrighteous **3** = **profane**, atheistic, irreligious, ungodly

godlike *adj* = **divine**, celestial, deific, deiform, heavenly, superhuman, transcendent

godly *adj* = **devout**, god-fearing, good, holy, pious, religious, righteous, saintly

go down *vb* **2** = **fall**, be beaten, collapse, decline, decrease, drop, founder, go under, lose, set, sink, submerge, submit, suffer defeat **3** = **be recorded**, be commemorated, be recalled, be remembered

godsend *n* = **blessing**, boon, manna, stroke of luck, windfall

go for *vb* **2** = **seek**, clutch at, fetch, obtain, reach, stretch for **3** = **favour**, admire, be attracted to, be fond of, choose, hold with, like, prefer **4** = **attack**, assail, assault, launch oneself at, rush upon, set about *or* upon, spring upon

goggle *vb* **1** = **stare**, gape, gawk, gawp, peer, rubberneck (*sl.*)

go in *vb* **4 go in for** = **enter**, adopt, embrace, engage in, espouse, practise, pursue, take up, undertake

going-over *n* **1** = **examination**, analysis, check, inspection, investigation, perusal, recce (*sl.*), review, scrutiny, study, survey **2** = **beating**, buffeting, castigation, chastisement, doing (*inf.*), drubbing, pasting (*sl.*), rebuke, thrashing, thumping, whipping

go into *vb* **1, 2** = **enter**, begin, develop, participate in, undertake **3** = **investigate**, analyse, consider, delve into, discuss, examine, inquire into,

some cases nearly doubling the size of the neck. [C17: from F, from OF *goitron* ult. from L *guttur* throat]
▸'**goitred** *or US* '**goitered** *adj* ▸'**goitrous** *adj*

go-kart *or* **go-cart** *n* See **kart.**

Golconda (gɒl'kɒndə) *n* (*sometimes not cap.*) a source of wealth or riches, esp. a mine. [C18: from former city in India, renowned for its diamond mines]

gold (gəʊld) *n* **1a** a dense inert bright yellow element that is the most malleable and ductile metal, occurring in rocks and alluvial deposits: used as a monetary standard and in jewellery, dentistry, and plating. Symbol: Au; atomic no.: 79; atomic wt.: 196.97. Related adj: **auric. 1b** (*as modifier*): *a gold mine.* **2** a coin or coins made of this metal. **3** money; wealth. **4** something precious, beautiful, etc., such as a noble nature (esp. in **heart of gold**). **5a** a deep yellow colour, sometimes with a brownish tinge. **5b** (*as adj*): *a gold carpet.* **6** short for **gold medal.** [OE *gold*]

gold card *n* a credit card issued by credit-card companies to favoured clients, entitling them to high unsecured overdrafts, some insurance cover, etc.

goldcrest ('gəʊld,krest) *n* a small Old World warbler having a greenish plumage and a bright yellow-and-black crown.

gold-digger *n* **1** a person who prospects or digs for gold. **2** *Inf.* a woman who uses her sexual attractions to accumulate gifts and wealth.

gold disc *n* **1** (in Britain) an LP record certified to have sold 100 000 copies or a single certified to have sold 400 000 copies. **2** (in the US) an LP record or single certified to have sold 500 000 copies.

gold dust *n* gold in the form of small particles or powder.

golden ⓣ ('gəʊldən) *adj* **1** of the yellowish colour of gold: *golden hair.* **2** made from or largely consisting of gold: *a golden statue.* **3** happy or prosperous: *golden days.* **4** (*sometimes cap.*) (of anniversaries) the 50th in a series: *Golden Jubilee; golden wedding.* **5** *Inf.* very successful or destined for success: *the golden girl of tennis.* **6** extremely valuable or advantageous: *a golden opportunity.*
▸'**goldenly** *adv* ▸'**goldenness** *n*

golden age *n* **1** *Classical myth.* the first and best age of mankind, when existence was happy, prosperous, and innocent. **2** the most flourishing and outstanding period, esp. in the history of an art or nation: *the golden age of poetry.*

golden eagle *n* a large eagle of mountainous regions of the N hemisphere, having a plumage that is golden brown on the back.

goldeneye ('gəʊldən,aɪ) *n, pl* **goldeneyes** *or* **goldeneye.** either of two black-and-white diving ducks of northern regions.

Golden Fleece *n Greek myth.* the fleece of a winged ram stolen by Jason and the Argonauts.

golden goose *n* a goose in folklore that laid a golden egg every day until its greedy owner killed it in an attempt to get all the gold at once.

golden handcuffs *pl n* payments deferred over a number of years that induce a person to stay with a particular company or in a particular job.

golden handshake *n Inf.* a sum of money given to an employee, either on retirement or as compensation for loss of employment.

golden hello *n* a payment made to a sought-after recruit on signing a contract of employment with a company.

golden hour *n* the first hour after a serious accident, when it is crucial that the victim receives medical treatment in order to have a chance of surviving.

golden mean *n* **1** the middle course between extremes. **2** another term for **golden section.**

golden number *n* a number between 1 and 19, used to indicate the position of any year in the Metonic cycle: so called from its importance in fixing the date of Easter.

golden parachute *n Inf.* a clause in the employment contract of a senior executive providing for special benefits if the executive's employment is terminated as a result of a takeover.

golden retriever *n* a breed of retriever with a silky wavy coat of a golden colour.

goldenrod (,gəʊldən'rɒd) *n* a plant of the composite family of North America, Europe, and Asia, having spikes of small yellow flowers.

golden rule *n* **1** any of a number of rules of fair conduct, such as *Whatsoever ye would that men should do to you, do ye even so to them* (Matthew 7:12). **2** any important principle: *a golden rule of sailing is to wear a life jacket.* **3** another name for **rule of three.**

golden section *or* **mean** *n* the proportion of the two divisions of a straight line such that the smaller is to the larger as the larger is to the sum of the two.

golden share *n* a share in a company that controls at least 51% of the voting rights, esp. one retained by the UK government in some privatization issues.

Golden Starfish *n* an award given to a bathing beach that meets EU standards of cleanliness but that does not provide facilities.

golden syrup *n Brit.* a light golden-coloured treacle produced by the evaporation of cane sugar juice, used to flavour cakes, puddings, etc.

Golden Triangle *n* **the.** an opium-producing area of SE Asia, comprising parts of Myanmar, Laos, and Thailand.

golden wattle *n* **1** an Australian yellow-flowered plant that yields a useful gum and bark. **2** any of several similar and related Australian plants.

goldfinch ('gəʊld,fɪntʃ) *n* a common European finch, the adult of which has a red-and-white face and yellow-and-black wings.

goldfish ('gəʊld,fɪʃ) *n, pl* **goldfish** *or* **goldfishes.** a freshwater fish of E Europe and Asia, esp. China, widely introduced as a pond or aquarium fish. It resembles the carp and has a typically golden or orange-red coloration.

gold foil *n* thin gold sheet that is thicker than gold leaf.

gold leaf *n* very thin gold sheet produced by rolling or hammering gold and used for gilding woodwork, etc.

gold medal *n* a medal of gold, awarded to the winner of a competition or race.

gold plate *n* **1** a thin coating of gold, usually produced by electroplating. **2** vessels or utensils made of gold.
▸,**gold-'plate** *vb* (*tr*)

gold reserve *n* the gold reserved by a central bank to support domestic credit expansion, to cover balance of payments deficits, and to protect currency.

gold rush *n* a large-scale migration of people to a territory where gold has been found.

goldsmith ('gəʊld,smɪθ) *n* **1** a dealer in articles made of gold. **2** an artisan who makes such articles.

gold standard *n* a monetary system in which the unit of currency is defined with reference to gold.

golf (gɒlf) *n* **1** a game played on a large open course, the object of which is to hit a ball using clubs, with as few strokes as possible, into each of usually 18 holes. ◆ *vb* **2** (*intr*) to play golf. [C15: ?from MDu. *colf* CLUB]
▸'**golfer** *n*

golf ball *n* **1** a small resilient, usually white, ball of either two-piece or three-piece construction, the former consisting of a solid inner core with a thick covering of toughened material, the latter consisting of a liquid centre, rubber-wound core, and a thin layer of balata. **2** (in some electric typewriters) a small detachable metal sphere, around the surface of which type characters are arranged.

golf club *n* **1** any of various long-shafted clubs with wood or metal heads used to strike a golf ball. **2a** an association of golf players, usually having its own course and facilities. **2b** the premises of such an association.

golf course *or* **links** *n* an area of ground laid out for the playing of golf.

Goliath (gə'laɪəθ) *n Bible.* a Philistine giant who was killed by David with a stone from his sling (I Samuel 17).

golliwog ('gɒlɪ,wɒg) *n* a soft doll with a black face, usually made of cloth or rags. [C19: from a doll in a series of American children's books]

gollop ('gɒləp) *vb* **gollops, golloping, golloped.** to eat or drink (something) quickly or greedily. [dialect var. of GULP]

golly ('gɒlɪ) *interj* an exclamation of mild surprise. [C19: orig. a euphemism for GOD]

goloshes (gə'lɒʃɪz) *pl n* a less common spelling of **galoshes.**

-gon *n combining form.* indicating a figure having a specified number of angles: *pentagon.* [from Gk *-gōnon,* from *gōnia* angle]

gonad ('gɒnæd) *n* an animal organ in which gametes are produced, such as a testis or an ovary. [C19: from NL *gonas,* from Gk *gonos* seed]
▸'**gonadal** *or* **gonadial** (gɒ'neɪdɪəl) *adj*

gonadotrophin (,gɒnədəʊ'trəʊfɪn) *or* **gonadotropin** (-'trəʊpɪn) *n* any of several hormones that stimulate the gonads. See also **HCG.**
▸**gonadotrophic** (,gɒnədəʊ'trɒfɪk) *or* ,**gonado'tropic** *adj*

gondola ('gɒndələ) *n* **1** a long narrow flat-bottomed boat with a high ornamented stem: traditionally used on the canals of Venice. **2a** a car or cabin suspended from an airship or balloon. **2b** a moving cabin suspended from a cable across a valley, etc. **3** a flat-bottomed barge used on canals and rivers of the US. **4** *US & Canad.* a low open flat-bottomed railway goods wagon. **5** a set of island shelves in a self-service shop: used for displaying goods. **6** *Canad.* a broadcasting booth built close to the roof of an ice-hockey stadium. [C16: from It. (dialect), from Med. L, ? ult. from Gk *kondu* drinking vessel]

gondolier (,gɒndə'lɪə) *n* a man who propels a gondola.

Gondwanaland (gɒnd'wɑːnə,lænd) *n* one of the two ancient supercontinents comprising chiefly what are now Africa, South America, Australia, Antarctica, and the Indian subcontinent. [C19: from *Gondwana,* region in central north India, where the rock series was orig. found]

gone ⓣ (gɒn) *vb* **1** the past participle of **go.** ◆ *adj* (*usually postpositive*) **2** ended; past. **3** lost; ruined. **4** dead. **5** spent; consumed; used up. **6** *Inf.*

THESAURUS

look into, probe, pursue, research, review, scrutinize, study, work over

golden *adj* **1** = **yellow**, blond, blonde, bright, brilliant, flaxen, resplendent, shining **3** = **successful**, best, blissful, delightful, flourishing, glorious, halcyon, happy, joyful, joyous, precious, prosperous, rich **6** = **promising**, advantageous, auspicious, excellent, favourable, opportune, propitious, rosy, valuable
Antonyms *adj* ≠ **yellow:** black, brunette, dark, dull ≠ **successful:** poorest, sad, unfavourable, worst ≠ **promising:** black, dark, sad, unfavourable, untimely, wretched

gone *adj* **2** = **past**, elapsed, ended, finished, over **3** = **missing**, absent, astray, away, lacking, lost, vanished **4** = **dead**, deceased, defunct, departed, extinct, no more **5** = **used up**, consumed, done, finished, spent

faint or weak. **7** *Inf.* having been pregnant (for a specified time): *six months gone.* **8** (usually foll. by *on*) *Sl.* in love (with).

goner (ˈgɒnə) *n Sl.* a person or thing beyond help or recovery, esp. a person who is about to die.

gonfalon (ˈgɒnfələn) *n* **1** a banner hanging from a crossbar, used esp. by certain medieval Italian republics. **2** a battle flag suspended crosswise on a staff, usually having a serrated edge. [C16: from OIt., from OF, of Gmc origin]

gong (gɒŋ) *n* **1** a percussion instrument consisting of a metal platelike disc struck with a soft-headed drumstick. **2** a rimmed metal disc, hollow metal hemisphere, or metal strip, tube, or wire that produces a note when struck. **3** a fixed saucer-shaped bell, as on an alarm clock, struck by a mechanically operated hammer. **4** *Brit. sl.* a medal, esp. a military one. ◆ *vb* **5** (*intr*) to sound a gong. **6** (*tr*) (of traffic police) to summon (a driver) to stop by sounding a gong. [C17: from Malay, imit.]

goniometer (ˌgəʊnɪˈɒmɪtə) *n* **1** an instrument for measuring the angles between the faces of a crystal. **2** an instrument used to determine the bearing of a distant radio station. [C18: via F from Gk *gōnia* angle]
▸**goniometric** (ˌgəʊnɪəˈmɛtrɪk) *adj* ▸**ˌgoniˈometry** *n*

-gonium *n combining form.* indicating a seed or reproductive cell: *archegonium.* [from NL, from Gk *gonos* seed]

gonococcus (ˌgɒnəʊˈkɒkəs) *n, pl* **gonococci** (-ˈkɒksaɪ). a spherical bacterium that causes gonorrhoea.

gonorrhoea *or esp. US* **gonorrhea** (ˌgɒnəˈrɪə) *n* an infectious venereal disease characterized by a discharge of mucus from the urethra or vagina. [C16: from L, from Gk *gonos* semen + *rhoia* flux]
▸**ˌgonorˈrhoeal** *or esp. US* **ˌgonorˈrheal** *adj*

-gony *n combining form.* genesis, origin, or production: *cosmogony.* [from L, from Gk, from *gonos* seed, procreation]

gonzo (ˈgɒnzəʊ) *Sl.* ◆ *adj* **1** wild or crazy. **2** (of journalism) focusing on the eccentric personality or lifestyle of the reporter as much as on the events reported. ◆ *n, pl* **gonzos. 3** a wild or crazy person. [C20: coined by Hunter S. Thompson, US journalist, ? from It., lit.: fool, or Sp. *ganso* idiot (lit.: goose)]

goo (guː) *n Inf.* **1** a sticky substance. **2** coy or sentimental language or ideas. [C20: from ?]

good Ⓣ (gʊd) *adj* **better, best. 1** having admirable, pleasing, superior, or positive qualities; not negative, bad, or mediocre: *a good teacher.* **2a** morally excellent or admirable; virtuous; righteous: *a good man.* **2b** (*as collective n;* preceded by *the*): *the good.* **3** suitable or efficient for a purpose: *a good winter coat.* **4** beneficial or advantageous: *vegetables are good for you.* **5** not ruined or decayed: *the meat is still good.* **6** kindly or generous: *you are good to him.* **7** valid or genuine: *I would not do this without good reason.* **8** honourable or held in high esteem: *a good family.* **9** financially secure, sound, or safe: *a good investment.* **10** (of a draft, etc.) drawn for a stated sum. **11** (of debts) expected to be fully paid. **12** clever, competent, or talented: *he's good at science.* **13** obedient or well-behaved: *a good dog.* **14** reliable, safe, or recommended: *a good make of clothes.* **15** affording material pleasure: *the good life.* **16** having a well-proportioned or generally fine appearance: *a good figure.* **17** complete; full: *I took a good look round the house.* **18** propitious; opportune: *a good time to ask for a rise.* **19** satisfying or gratifying: *a good rest.* **20** comfortable: *did you have a good night?* **21** newest or of the best quality: *keep the good plates for guests.* **22** fairly large, extensive, or long: *a good distance away.* **23** sufficient; ample: *we have a good supply of food.* **24 a good one. 24a** an unbelievable assertion. **24b** a very funny joke. **25 as good as.** virtually; practically: *it's as good as finished.* **26 good and.** *Inf.* (intensifier): *good and mad.* ◆ *interj* **27** an exclamation of approval, agreement, pleasure, etc. ◆ *n* **28** moral or material advantage or use; benefit or profit: *for the good of our workers; what is the good of worrying?* **29** positive moral qualities; goodness; virtue; righteousness; piety. **30** (*sometimes cap.*) moral qualities seen as an abstract entity: *we must pursue the Good.* **31** a good thing. **32 for good (and all).** forever; permanently: *I have left them for good.* **33 good for** *or* **on you.** well done, well said, etc.: a term of congratulation. **34 make good. 34a** to recompense or repair damage or injury. **34b** to be successful. **34c** to prove the truth of (a statement or accusation). **34d** to secure and retain (a position). **34e** to effect or fulfil (something intended or promised). ◆ See also **goods.** [OE *gōd*]
▸**ˈgoodish** *adj*

Good Book *n* a name for the **Bible.**

goodbye Ⓣ (ˌgʊdˈbaɪ) *sentence substitute.* **1** farewell: a conventional expression used at leave-taking or parting with people. ◆ *n* **2** a leave-taking; parting: *they prolonged their goodbyes.* **3** a farewell: *they said goodbyes to each other.* [C16: from *God be with ye*]

good day *sentence substitute.* a conventional expression of greeting or farewell used during the day.

good-for-nothing Ⓣ *n* **1** an irresponsible or worthless person. ◆ *adj* **2** irresponsible; worthless.

Good Friday *n* the Friday before Easter, observed as a commemoration of the Crucifixion of Jesus.

good-humoured Ⓣ *adj* being in or expressing a pleasant, tolerant, and kindly state of mind.
▸**ˌgood-ˈhumouredly** *adv*

goodies (ˈgʊdɪz) *pl n* any objects, rewards, etc., considered particularly desirable.

good-looking Ⓣ *adj* handsome or pretty.

goodly Ⓣ (ˈgʊdlɪ) *adj* **goodlier, goodliest. 1** considerable: *a goodly amount of money.* **2** *Obs.* attractive, pleasing, or fine.
▸**ˈgoodliness** *n*

goodman (ˈgʊdmən) *n, pl* **goodmen.** *Arch.* **1** a husband. **2** a man not of gentle birth: used as a title. **3** a master of a household.

good morning *sentence substitute.* a conventional expression of greeting or farewell used in the morning.

good-natured Ⓣ *adj* of a tolerant and kindly disposition.
▸**ˌgood-ˈnaturedly** *adv*

goodness Ⓣ (ˈgʊdnɪs) *n* **1** the state or quality of being good. **2** generosity; kindness. **3** moral excellence; piety; virtue. **4** what is good in something; essence. ◆ *interj* **5** a euphemism for **God:** used as an exclamation of surprise.

goodness of fit *n Statistics.* the extent to which observed sample values of a variable approximate to values derived from a theoretical density.

good night *sentence substitute.* a conventional expression of farewell, used in the evening or at night, esp. when departing to bed.

good-oh *or* **good-o** (ˈgʊdˈəʊ) *interj Brit. & Austral. inf.* an exclamation of pleasure, agreement, etc.

good oil *n* (usually preceded by *the*) *Austral. sl.* true or reliable facts, information, etc.

goods Ⓣ (gʊdz) *pl n* **1** possessions and personal property. **2** (*sometimes sing*) *Econ.* commodities that are tangible, usually movable, and generally not consumed at the same time as they are produced. **3** articles of commerce; merchandise. **4** *Chiefly Brit.* **4a** merchandise when

THESAURUS

good *adj* **1 = excellent,** admirable, agreeable, capital, choice, commendable, divine, fine, first-class, first-rate, great, pleasant, pleasing, positive, precious, satisfactory, splendid, super (*inf.*), superior, tiptop, valuable, world-class, worthy **2 = honourable,** admirable, estimable, ethical, exemplary, honest, moral, praiseworthy, right, righteous, trustworthy, upright, virtuous, worthy **4 = favourable,** adequate, advantageous, auspicious, beneficial, convenient, fit, fitting, healthy, helpful, opportune, profitable, propitious, salubrious, salutary, suitable, useful, wholesome **5 = eatable,** fit to eat, sound, uncorrupted, untainted, whole **6 = kind,** altruistic, approving, beneficent, benevolent, charitable, friendly, gracious, humane, kind-hearted, kindly, merciful, obliging, well-disposed **7 = valid,** authentic, bona fide, dependable, genuine, honest, legitimate, proper, real, reliable, sound, true, trustworthy **12 = expert,** able, accomplished, adept, adroit, capable, clever, competent, dexterous, efficient, first-rate, proficient, reliable, satisfactory, serviceable, skilled, sound, suitable, talented, thorough, useful **13 = well-behaved,** decorous, dutiful, mannerly, obedient, orderly, polite, proper, seemly, well-mannered **15 = enjoyable,** agreeable, cheerful, congenial, convivial, gratifying, happy, pleasant, pleasing, pleasurable, satisfying **17, 23 = full,** adequate, ample, complete, considerable, entire, extensive, large, long, sizable *or* sizeable, solid, substantial, sufficient, whole **21 = best,** fancy, finest, newest, nicest, precious, smartest, special, valuable ◆ *n* **28 = benefit,** advantage, avail, behalf, gain, interest, mileage (*inf.*), profit, service, use, usefulness, welfare, wellbeing, worth **29 = virtue,** excellence, goodness, merit, morality, probity, rectitude, right, righteousness, uprightness, worth **32 for good = permanently,** finally, for ever, irrevocably, never to return, once and for all, *sine die*

Antonyms *adj* ≠ **excellent:** awful, bad, boring, disagreeable, dull, inadequate, rotten, tedious, unpleasant ≠ **honourable:** bad, base, corrupt, dishonest, dishonourable, evil, immoral, improper, sinful ≠ **favourable:** inappropriate, pathetic, unbecoming, unbefitting, unfavourable, unfitting, unsuitable, useless ≠ **eatable:** bad, decayed, mouldy, off, rotten, unsound ≠ **kind:** cruel, evil, mean (*inf.*), selfish, unkind, vicious, wicked ≠ **valid:** counterfeit, false, fraudulent, invalid, phoney ≠ **expert:** bad, incompetent, inefficient, unsatisfactory, unskilled ≠ **well-behaved:** ill-mannered, mischievous, naughty, rude ≠ **full:** scant, short ◆ *n* ≠ **benefit:** detriment, disadvantage, failure, ill-fortune, loss ≠ **virtue:** badness, baseness, corruption, cruelty, dishonesty, evil, immorality, meanness, wickedness

goodbye *n* **2 = farewell,** adieu, leave-taking, parting

good-for-nothing *n* **1 = layabout,** black sheep, idler, ne'er-do-well, numb-nut (*US sl.*), profligate, rapscallion, scapegrace, skiver (*Brit. sl.*), slacker (*inf.*), waster, wastrel ◆ *adj* **2 = worthless,** feckless, idle, irresponsible, useless

good-humoured *adj* **= cheerful,** affable, amiable, congenial, genial, good-tempered, happy, pleasant

good-looking *adj* **= attractive,** comely, fair, handsome, personable, pretty, well-favoured

goodly *adj* **1 = considerable,** ample, large, significant, sizable *or* sizeable, substantial, tidy (*inf.*) **2 = attractive,** agreeable, comely, desirable, elegant, fine, good-looking, graceful, handsome, personable, pleasant, pleasing, well-favoured

good-natured *adj* **= kindly,** agreeable, amiable, benevolent, friendly, good-hearted, helpful, kind, tolerant, warm-hearted, well-disposed, willing to please

goodness *n* **1 = excellence,** merit, quality, superiority, value, worth **2 = kindness,** beneficence, benevolence, friendliness, generosity, goodwill, graciousness, humaneness, kind-heartedness, kindliness, mercy, obligingness **3 = virtue,** honesty, honour, integrity, merit, morality, probity, rectitude, righteousness, uprightness **4 = benefit,** advantage, nourishment, nutrition, salubriousness, wholesomeness

Antonyms *n* ≠ **virtue:** badness, corruption, dishonesty, evil, immorality, wickedness, worthlessness ≠ **benefit:** detriment, disadvantage

goods *pl n* **1 = property,** appurtenances, belongings, chattels, effects, furnishings, furniture, gear, movables, paraphernalia, posses-

transported, esp. by rail; freight. **4b** (*as modifier*): *a goods train.* **5 the goods. 5a** *Inf.* that which is expected or promised: *to deliver the goods.* **5b** *Sl.* the real thing. **5c** *US & Canad. sl.* incriminating evidence (esp. in **have the goods on someone**).

Good Samaritan *n* **1** *New Testament.* a figure in one of Christ's parables (Luke 10:30–37) who is an example of compassion towards those in distress. **2** a kindly person who helps another in difficulty or distress.

Good Shepherd *n New Testament.* a title given to Jesus Christ in John 10:11–12.

good-sized *adj* quite large.

good-tempered *adj* of a kindly and generous disposition.

good turn *n* a helpful and friendly act; favour.

goodwife ('gʊd,waɪf) *n, pl* **goodwives.** *Arch.* **1** the mistress of a household. **2** a woman not of gentle birth: used as a title.

goodwill Ⓣ (,gʊd'wɪl) *n* **1** benevolence, approval, and kindly interest. **2** willingness or acquiescence. **3** an intangible asset of an enterprise reflecting its commercial reputation, customer connections, etc.

goody[1] ('gʊdɪ) *interj* **1** a child's exclamation of pleasure. ◆ *n, pl* **goodies. 2** short for **goody-goody. 3** *Inf.* the hero in a film, book, etc. **4** See **goodies.**

goody[2] ('gʊdɪ) *n, pl* **goodies.** *Arch. or literary.* a married woman of low rank: used as a title: *Goody Two-Shoes.* [C16: from GOODWIFE]

goody-goody *n, pl* **goody-goodies. 1** *Inf.* a smugly virtuous or sanctimonious person. ◆ *adj* **2** smug and sanctimonious.

gooey Ⓣ ('gu:ɪ) *adj* **gooier, gooiest.** *Inf.* **1** sticky, soft, and often sweet. **2** oversweet and sentimental.
▸ **'gooily** *adv*

goof (gu:f) *Inf.* ◆ *n* **1** a foolish error. **2** a stupid person. ◆ *vb* **3** to bungle (something); botch. **4** (*intr;* often foll. by *about* or *around*) to fool (around); mess (about). [C20: prob. from (dialect) *goff* simpleton, from OF *goffe* clumsy, from It. *goffo,* from ?]

go off Ⓣ *vb* (*intr*) **1** (*adv*) (of power, a water supply, etc.) to cease to be available or functioning: *the lights suddenly went off.* **2** (*adv*) to explode. **3** (*adv*) to occur as specified: *the meeting went off well.* **4** to leave (a place): *the actors went off stage.* **5** (*adv*) (of a sensation) to gradually cease to be felt. **6** (*adv*) to fall asleep. **7** (*adv*) (of concrete, mortar, etc.) to harden. **8** (*adv*) *Brit. inf.* (of food, etc.) to become stale or rotten. **9** (*prep*) *Brit. inf.* to cease to like.

goofy ('gu:fɪ) *adj* **goofier, goofiest.** *Inf.* foolish; silly.
▸ **'goofily** *adv* ▸ **'goofiness** *n*

goog (gʊg) *n Austral. sl.* an egg. [?from Du. *oog*]

googly ('gu:glɪ) *n, pl* **googlies.** *Cricket.* an off break bowled with a leg break action. [C20: Austral. from ?]

goolie *or* **gooly** ('gu:lɪ) *n, pl* **goolies. 1** (*usually pl*) *Taboo sl.* a testicle. **2** *Austral. sl.* a stone or pebble. [from Hindi *goli* ball]

goon (gu:n) *n* **1** a stupid or deliberately foolish person. **2** *US inf.* a thug hired to commit acts of violence or intimidation, esp. in an industrial dispute. [C20: partly from dialect *gooney* fool, partly after the character Alice the *Goon,* created by E. C. Segar (1894–1938), American cartoonist]

go on Ⓣ *vb* (*intr, mostly adv*) **1** to continue or proceed. **2** to happen: *there's something peculiar going on here.* **3** (*prep*) to ride on, esp. as a treat: *children love to go on donkeys at the seaside.* **4** *Theatre.* to make an entrance on stage. **5** to talk excessively; chatter. **6** to continue talking, esp. after a short pause. **7** to criticize or nag: *stop going on at me all the time!* ◆ *sentence substitute.* **8** I don't believe what you're saying.

gooney bird ('gu:nɪ) *n* an informal name for **albatross,** esp. the black-footed albatross. [C19 *gony* (orig. sailors' sl.), prob. from dialect *gooney* fool, from ?]

goop (gu:p) *n US & Canad. sl.* **1** a rude or ill-mannered person. **2** any sticky or semiliquid substance. [C20: coined by G. Burgess (1866–1951), American humorist]
▸ **'goopy** *adj*

goorie *or* **goory** ('gu:rɪ) *n, pl* **goories.** *NZ inf.* a mongrel dog. [from Maori *kuri*]

goosander (gu:'sændə) *n* a common merganser (a duck) of Europe and North America, having a dark head and white body in the male. [C17: prob. from GOOSE[1] + ON *önd* (genitive *andar*) duck]

goose[1] (gu:s) *n, pl* **geese. 1** any of various web-footed long-necked birds typically larger and less aquatic than ducks. They are gregarious and migratory. **2** the female of such a bird, as opposed to the male (gander). **3** *Inf.* a silly person. **4** (*pl* **gooses**) a pressing iron with a long curving handle, used esp. by tailors. **5** the flesh of the goose, used as food. **6 cook someone's goose.** *Inf.* **6a** to spoil someone's chances or plans completely. **6b** to bring about someone's downfall. **7 kill the goose that lays the golden eggs.** See **golden goose.** [OE *gōs*]

goose[2] (gu:s) *Sl.* ◆ *vb* **gooses, goosing, goosed. 1** (*tr*) to prod (a person) playfully in the bottom. ◆ *n, pl* **gooses. 2** such a prod. [C19: from GOOSE[1], prob. from a comparison with the jabbing of a goose's bill]

gooseberry ('gʊzbərɪ, -brɪ) *n, pl* **gooseberries. 1** a Eurasian shrub having ovoid yellow-green or red-purple berries. **2a** the berry of this plant. **2b** (*as modifier*): *gooseberry jam.* **3** *Brit. inf.* an unwanted single person, esp. a third person with a couple (often in **play gooseberry**).

goose flesh *n* the bumpy condition of the skin induced by cold, fear, etc., caused by contraction of the muscles at the base of the hair follicles with consequent erection of papillae. Also called: **goose bumps, goose pimples, goose skin.**

goosefoot ('gu:s,fʊt) *n, pl* **goosefoots.** any typically weedy plant having small greenish flowers and leaves shaped like a goose's foot.

goosegog ('gʊzgɒg) *n Brit.* a dialect or informal word for **gooseberry.** [from *goose* in GOOSEBERRY + *gog,* var. of GOB[1]]

goosegrass ('gu:s,grɑ:s) *n* another name for **cleavers.**

gooseneck ('gu:s,nɛk) *n* something, such as a jointed pipe, in the form of the neck of a goose.

goose step *n* **1** a military march step in which the leg is swung rigidly to an exaggerated height. ◆ *vb* **goose-step, goose-steps, goose-stepping, goose-stepped. 2** (*intr*) to march in goose step.

go out Ⓣ *vb* (*intr, adv*) **1** to depart from a room, house, country, etc. **2** to cease to illuminate, burn, or function: *the fire has gone out.* **3** to cease to be fashionable or popular: *that style went out ages ago!* **4** (of a broadcast) to be transmitted. **5** to go to entertainments, social functions, etc. **6** (usually foll. by *with* or *together*) to associate (with a person of the opposite sex) regularly. **7** (of workers) to begin to strike. **8** *Card games, etc.* to get rid of the last card, token, etc., in one's hand.

go over Ⓣ *vb* (*intr*) **1** to be received in a specified manner: *the concert went over very well.* **2** (*prep*) Also: **go through.** to examine and revise as necessary: *he went over the accounts.* **3** (*prep*) to check and repair: *can you go over my car, please?* **4** (*prep*) Also: **go through.** to rehearse: *I'll go over my lines before the play.*

gopak ('gəʊ,pæk) *n* a spectacular high-leaping Russian peasant dance for men. [from Russian]

gopher ('gəʊfə) *n* **1** Also called: **pocket gopher.** a burrowing rodent of North and Central America, having a thickset body, short legs, and cheek pouches. **2** another name for **ground squirrel. 3** a burrowing tortoise of SE North America. [C19: from earlier *megopher* or *magopher,* from ?]

goral ('gɔ:rəl) *n* a small goat antelope inhabiting mountainous regions of S Asia. [C19: from Hindi, prob. from Sansk.]

Gordian knot ('gɔ:dɪən) *n* **1** (in Greek legend) a complicated knot, tied by King Gordius of Phrygia, that Alexander the Great cut with a sword. **2** a complicated and intricate problem (esp. in **cut the Gordian knot**).

gore[1] Ⓣ (gɔ:) *n* **1** blood shed from a wound, esp. when coagulated. **2** *Inf.* killing, fighting, etc. [OE *gor* dirt]

gore[2] Ⓣ (gɔ:) *vb* **gores, goring, gored.** (*tr*) (of an animal, such as a bull) to pierce or stab (a person or another animal) with a horn or tusk. [C16: prob. from OE *gār* spear]

gore[3] (gɔ:) *n* **1** a tapering or triangular piece of material used in making a shaped skirt, umbrella, etc. ◆ *vb* **gores, goring, gored. 2** (*tr*) to make into or with a gore or gores. [OE *gāra*]
▸ **gored** *adj*

gorge Ⓣ (gɔ:dʒ) *n* **1** a deep ravine, esp. one through which a river runs. **2** the contents of the stomach. **3** feelings of disgust or resentment (esp. in **one's gorge rises**). **4** an obstructing mass: *an ice gorge.* **5** *Fortifications.* a narrow rear entrance to a work. **6** *Arch.* the throat or gullet. ◆ *vb* **gorges, gorging, gorged. 7** to swallow (food) ravenously. **8** (*tr*) to stuff (oneself) with food. [C14: from OF *gorger* to stuff, from *gorge* throat, from LL *gurga,* from L *gurges* whirlpool]

gorgeous Ⓣ ('gɔ:dʒəs) *adj* **1** strikingly beautiful or magnificent: *a gorgeous array; a gorgeous girl.* **2** *Inf.* extremely pleasing, fine, or good: *gorgeous weather.* [C15: from OF *gorgias* elegant, from *gorge;* see GORGE]
▸ **'gorgeously** *adv* ▸ **'gorgeousness** *n*

gorget ('gɔ:dʒɪt) *n* **1** a collar-like piece of armour worn to protect the throat. **2** a part of a wimple worn by women to cover the throat and chest, esp. in the 14th century. **3** a band of distinctive colour on the throat of an animal, esp. a bird. [C15: from OF, from *gorge;* see GORGE]

Gorgio ('gɔ:dʒɪəʊ) *n, pl* **Gorgios.** the Gypsy name for a non-Gypsy. [C19: from Romany]

THESAURUS

sions, things, trappings **3** = **merchandise,** commodities, stock, stuff, wares

goodwill *n* **1** = **friendliness,** amity, benevolence, favour, friendship, heartiness, kindliness, zeal

gooey *adj* **1** = **sticky,** gluey, glutinous, mucilaginous, soft, tacky, viscous **2** = **sentimental,** maudlin, mawkish, slushy (*inf.*), syrupy (*inf.*), tear-jerking (*inf.*)

go off *vb* **2** = **explode,** blow up, detonate, fire **3** = **happen,** occur, take place **4** = **leave,** decamp, depart, go away, hook it (*sl.*), move out, pack one's bags (*inf.*), part, quit, slope off **8** *Informal* = **rot,** go bad, go stale

go on *vb* **1** = **continue,** endure, happen, last, occur, persist, proceed, stay **5** = **chatter,** blether, carry on, prattle, rabbit (*Brit. inf.*), ramble on, waffle (*inf., chiefly Brit.*), witter (on) (*inf.*)

go out *vb* **1** = **leave,** depart, exit **2** = **be extinguished,** die out, expire, fade out

go over *vb* **2** = **examine,** inspect, rehearse, reiterate, review, revise, study, work over

gore[1] *n* **2** = **blood,** bloodshed, butchery, carnage, slaughter

gore[2] *vb* = **pierce,** impale, spit, stab, transfix, wound

gorge *n* **1** = **ravine,** canyon, chasm, cleft, clough (*dialect*), defile, fissure, pass ◆ *vb* **7, 8** = **overeat,** bolt, cram, devour, feed, fill, glut, gobble, gormandize, gulp, guzzle, pig out (*US & Canad. sl.*), raven, sate, satiate, stuff, surfeit, swallow, wolf

gorgeous *adj* **1** = **beautiful,** brilliant, dazzling, drop-dead (*sl.*), elegant, glittering, grand, luxuriant, magnificent, opulent, ravishing, resplendent, showy, splendid, splendiferous (*facetious*), stunning (*inf.*), sumptuous, superb **2** *Informal* = **pleasing,** attractive, bright, delightful, enjoyable, exquisite, fine, glorious, good, good-looking, lovely
Antonyms *adj* cheap, dismal, dreary, dull, gloomy, homely, plain, repulsive, shabby, shoddy, sombre, ugly, unattractive, unsightly

Gorgon ('gɔːgən) *n* **1** *Greek myth.* any of three winged monstrous sisters who had live snakes for hair, huge teeth, and brazen claws. **2** (*often not cap.*) *Inf.* a fierce or unpleasant woman. [via L *Gorgō* from Gk, from *gorgos* terrible]

gorgonian (gɔː'gəʊnɪən) *n* any of various corals having a horny or calcareous branching skeleton, such as the sea fans and red corals.

Gorgonzola (ˌgɔːgən'zəʊlə) *n* a semihard blue-veined cheese of sharp flavour, made from pressed milk. [C19: after *Gorgonzola,* It. town where it originated]

gorilla (gə'rɪlə) *n* **1** the largest anthropoid ape, inhabiting the forests of central W Africa. It is stocky with a short muzzle and coarse dark hair. **2** *Inf.* a large, strong, and brutal-looking man. [C19: NL, from Gk *Gorillai,* an African tribe renowned for their hirsute appearance]

gormand ('gɔːmənd) *n* a less common spelling of **gourmand.**

gormandize *or* **gormandise** ('gɔːmənˌdaɪz) *vb* **gormandizes, gormandizing, gormandized** *or* **gormandises, gormandising, gormandised.** to eat (food) greedily and voraciously.
▸'**gormandˌizer** *or* '**gormandˌiser** *n*

gormless ('gɔːmlɪs) *adj Brit. inf.* stupid; dull. [C19: var. of C18 *gaumless,* from dialect *gome,* from OE *gom, gome,* from ON *gaumr* heed]

go round *vb* (*intr*) **1** (*adv*) to be sufficient: *are there enough sweets to go round?* **2** to circulate (in): *measles is going round the school.* **3** to be long enough to encircle: *will that belt go round you?*

gorse (gɔːs) *n* an evergreen shrub which has yellow flowers and thick green spines instead of leaves. Also called: **furze, whin.** [OE *gors*]
▸'**gorsy** *adj*

gory ❶ ('gɔːrɪ) *adj* **gorier, goriest. 1** horrific or bloodthirsty: *a gory story.* **2** involving bloodshed and killing: *a gory battle.* **3** covered in gore.
▸'**gorily** *adv* ▸'**goriness** *n*

gosh (gɒʃ) *interj* an exclamation of mild surprise or wonder. [C18: euphemistic for GOD]

goshawk ('gɒsˌhɔːk) *n* a large hawk of Europe, Asia, and North America, having a bluish-grey back and wings and paler underparts: used in falconry. [OE *gōshafoc;* see GOOSE[1], HAWK[1]]

gosling ('gɒzlɪŋ) *n* **1** a young goose. **2** an inexperienced or youthful person. [C15: from ON *gæslingr;* rel. to Danish *gäsling;* see GOOSE[1], -LING[1]]

go-slow *n* **1** *Brit.* a deliberate slackening of the rate of production by organized labour as a tactic in industrial conflict. US and Canad. equivalent: **slowdown.** ◆ *vb* **go slow. 2** (*intr*) to work deliberately slowly as a tactic in industrial conflict.

gospel ❶ ('gɒspᵊl) *n* **1** Also called: **gospel truth.** an unquestionable truth: *to take someone's word as gospel.* **2** a doctrine maintained to be of great importance. **3** Black religious music originating in the churches of the Southern states of the United States. **4** the message or doctrine of a religious teacher. **5a** the story of Christ's life and teachings as narrated in the Gospels. **5b** the good news of salvation in Jesus Christ. **5c** (*as modifier*): *the gospel story.* [OE *gōdspell,* from *gōd* GOOD + *spell* message; see SPELL[2]]

Gospel ('gɒspᵊl) *n* **1** any of the first four books of the New Testament, namely Matthew, Mark, Luke, and John. **2** a reading from one of these in a religious service.

gossamer ('gɒsəmə) *n* **1** a gauze or silk fabric of the very finest texture. **2** a filmy cobweb often seen on foliage or floating in the air. **3** anything resembling gossamer in fineness or filminess. [C14 (in sense 2): prob. from *gos* GOOSE[1] + *somer* SUMMER; the phrase refers to *St Martin's summer,* a period in November when goose was traditionally eaten; from the prevalence of the cobweb in the autumn]
▸'**gossamery** *adj*

gossip ❶ ('gɒsɪp) *n* **1** casual and idle chat. **2** a conversation involving malicious chatter or rumours about other people. **3** Also called: **gossipmonger.** a person who habitually talks about others, esp. maliciously. **4** light easy communication: *to write a letter full of gossip.* **5** *Arch.* a close woman friend. ◆ *vb* **gossips, gossiping, gossiped. 6** (*intr;* often foll. by *about*) to talk casually or maliciously (about other people). [OE *godsibb* godparent, from GOD + SIB; came to be applied esp. to a woman's female friends at the birth of a child, hence a woman fond of light talk]
▸'**gossiper** *n* ▸'**gossipy** *adj*

gossypol ('gɒsɪˌpɒl) *n* a toxic crystalline pigment that is a constituent of cottonseed oil. [C19: from Mod. L *gossypium* cotton plant + -OL[1]]

got (gɒt) *vb* **1** the past tense and past participle of **get. 2 have got. 2a** to possess. **2b** (*takes an infinitive*) used as an auxiliary to express compulsion: *I've got to get a new coat.*

Goth (gɒθ) *n* **1** a member of an East Germanic people from Scandinavia who settled south of the Baltic early in the first millennium A.D. They moved on to the Ukrainian steppes and raided and later invaded many parts of the Roman Empire from the 3rd to the 5th century. **2** a rude or barbaric person. [C14: from LL (pl) *Gothī* from Gk *Gothoi*]

Gothic ('gɒθɪk) *adj* **1** denoting, relating to, or resembling the style of architecture that was used in W Europe from the 12th to the 16th centuries, characterized by the lancet arch, the ribbed vault, and the flying buttress. See also **Gothic Revival. 2** of or relating to the style of sculpture, painting, or other arts as practised in W Europe from the 12th to the 16th centuries. **3** (*sometimes not cap.*) of or relating to a literary style characterized by gloom, the grotesque, and the supernatural, popular esp. in the late 18th century: when used of modern literature, films, etc., sometimes spelt: **Gothick. 4** of, relating to, or characteristic of the Goths or their language. **5** (*sometimes not cap.*) primitive and barbarous in style, behaviour, etc. **6** of or relating to the Middle Ages. ◆ *n* **7** Gothic architecture or art. **8** the extinct language of the ancient Goths, known mainly from fragments of a translation of the Bible made in the 4th century by Bishop Wulfila. **9** Also called (esp. Brit): **black letter.** a family of heavy script typefaces.
▸'**Gothically** *adv*

Gothic Revival *n* a Gothic style of architecture popular between the late 18th and late 19th centuries, exemplified by the Houses of Parliament in London (1840). Also called: **neogothic.**

go through ❶ *vb* (*intr*) **1** (*adv*) to be approved or accepted: *the amendment went through.* **2** (*prep*) to consume; exhaust: *we went through our supplies in a day.* **3** (*prep*) Also: **go over.** to examine: *he went through the figures.* **4** (*prep*) to suffer: *she went through tremendous pain.* **5** (*prep*) Also: **go over.** to rehearse: *let's just go through the details again.* **6** (*prep*) to search: *she went through the cupboards.* **7** (*adv;* foll. by *with*) to come or bring to a successful conclusion, often by persistence.

go together ❶ *vb* (*intr, adv*) **1** to be mutually suited; harmonize: *the colours go well together.* **2** *Inf.* (of two people) to have a romantic or sexual relationship: *they had been going together for two years.*

gotten ('gɒtᵊn) *vb Chiefly US.* a past participle of **get.**

Götterdämmerung (ˌgɒtə'dɛməˌrʊŋ) *n German myth.* the twilight of the gods; their ultimate destruction in a battle with the forces of evil.

gouache (gʊ'ɑːʃ) *n* **1** Also called: **body colour.** a painting technique using opaque watercolour in which the pigments are bound with glue and lighter tones contain white. **2** the paint used in this technique. **3** a painting done by this method. [C19: from F, from It. *guazzo* puddle, from L, from *aqua* water]

Gouda ('gaʊdə) *n* a large round mild Dutch cheese, orig. made in the town of Gouda.

gouge ❶ (gaʊdʒ) *vb* **gouges, gouging, gouged.** (*mainly tr*) **1** (usually foll. by *out*) to scoop or force (something) out of its position. **2** (sometimes foll. by *out*) to cut (a hole or groove) in (something) with a sharp instrument or tool. **3** *US & Canad. inf.* to extort from. **4** (*also intr*) *Austral.* to dig for (opal). ◆ *n* **5** a type of chisel with a blade that has a concavo-convex section. **6** a mark or groove made as with a gouge. **7** *US & Canad. inf.* extortion; swindling. [C15: from F, from LL *gulbia* a chisel, of Celtic origin]
▸'**gouger** *n*

goujon ('guːʒɒn) *n* a small strip of fish or chicken, coated in breadcrumbs and deep-fried. [F, lit.: gudgeon]

goulash ('guːlæʃ) *n* **1** Also called: **Hungarian goulash.** a rich stew, originating in Hungary, made of beef, lamb, or veal highly seasoned with paprika. **2** *Bridge.* a method of dealing in threes and fours without first shuffling the cards, to produce freak hands. [C19: from Hungarian *gulyás hus* herdsman's meat]

go under ❶ *vb* (*intr, mainly adv*) **1** (*also prep*) to sink below (a surface). **2** to be overwhelmed: *the firm went under in the economic crisis.*

go up *vb* (*intr, mainly adv*) **1** (*also prep*) to move or lead as to a higher place or level; rise; increase: *prices are always going up.* **2** to be destroyed: *the house went up in flames.* **3** *Brit.* to go or return (to college or university) at the beginning of a term or academic year.

gourami ('gʊərəmɪ) *n, pl* **gourami** *or* **gouramis. 1** a large SE Asian labyrinth fish used for food. **2** any of various other labyrinth fishes, many of which are brightly coloured and popular aquarium fishes. [from Malay *gurami*]

gourd (gʊəd) *n* **1** the fruit of any of various plants of the cucumber family, esp. the bottle gourd and some squashes, whose dried shells are used for ornament, drinking cups, etc. **2** any plant that bears this fruit. **3** a bottle or flask made from the dried shell of the bottle gourd. [C14: from OF *gourde,* ult. from L *cucurbita*]

gourmand ('gʊəmənd) *or* **gormand** *n* a person devoted to eating and drinking, esp. to excess. [C15: from OF *gourmant,* from ?]
▸'**gourmandˌism** *n*

THESAURUS

gory *adj* **1-3** = **bloodthirsty**, blood-soaked, bloodstained, bloody, ensanguined (*literary*), murderous, sanguinary

gospel *n* **1** = **truth**, certainty, fact, the last word, verity **2** = **doctrine**, credo, creed, message, news, revelation, tidings

gossip *n* **1** = **idle talk**, blether, bush telegraph, buzz, chinwag (*Brit. inf.*), chitchat, clishmaclaver (*Scot.*), dirt (*US sl.*), gen (*Brit. inf.*), hearsay, jaw (*sl.*), latest (*inf.*), newsmongering (*old-fashioned*), prattle, scandal, scuttlebutt (*US sl.*), small talk, tittle-tattle **3** = **busybody**, babbler, blatherskite, blether, chatterbox (*inf.*), chatterer, flibbertigibbet, gossip-monger, newsmonger (*old-fashioned*), prattler, quidnunc, scandalmonger, tattler, telltale ◆ *vb* **6** = **chat**, blather, blether, chew the fat *or* rag (*sl.*), dish the dirt (*inf.*), gabble, jaw (*sl.*), prate, prattle, schmooze (*sl.*), shoot the breeze (*sl., chiefly US*), tattle

go through *vb* **2** = **use up**, consume, exhaust, squander **3** = **examine**, check, explore, forage, hunt, look, search, work over **4** = **suffer**, bear, brave, endure, experience, tolerate, undergo, withstand

go together *vb* **1** = **harmonize**, accord, agree, fit, make a pair, match **2** *Informal* = **go out**, court, date (*inf., chiefly US*), escort, go steady (*inf.*)

gouge *vb* **1, 2** = **scoop**, chisel, claw, cut, dig (out), gash, hollow (out), incise, score, scratch ◆ *n* **6** = **gash**, cut, furrow, groove, hollow, incision, notch, scoop, score, scratch, trench

go under *vb* **2** = **sink**, default, die, drown, fail, fold (*inf.*), founder, go down, submerge, succumb

gourmet ❶ (ˈɡʊəmeɪ) *n* a person who cultivates a discriminating palate for the enjoyment of good food and drink. [C19: from F, from OF *gromet* serving boy]

gout (ɡaʊt) *n* **1** a metabolic disease characterized by painful inflammation of certain joints, esp. of the big toe, caused by deposits of sodium urate. **2** *Arch.* a drop or splash, esp. of blood. [C13: from OF, from L *gutta* a drop]
►ˈ**gouty** *adj* ►ˈ**goutily** *adv* ►ˈ**goutiness** *n*

Gov. *or* **gov.** *abbrev. for:* **1** government. **2** governor.

govern ❶ (ˈɡʌvᵊn) *vb* (*mainly tr*) **1** (*also intr*) to direct and control the actions, affairs, policies, functions, etc., of (an organization, nation, etc.); rule. **2** to exercise restraint over; regulate or direct: *to govern one's temper.* **3** to decide or determine (something): *his injury governed his decision to avoid sports.* **4** to control the speed of (an engine, machine, etc.) using a governor. **5** (of a word) to determine the inflection of (another word): *Latin nouns govern adjectives that modify them.* [C13: from OF, from L *gubernāre* to steer, from Gk *kubernan*]
►ˈ**governable** *adj*

governance (ˈɡʌvənəns) *n* **1** government, control, or authority. **2** the action, manner, or system of governing.

governess (ˈɡʌvənɪs) *n* a woman teacher employed in a private household to teach and train the children.

government ❶ (ˈɡʌvənmənt, ˈɡʌvəmənt) *n* **1** the exercise of political authority over the actions, affairs, etc., of a political unit, people, etc.; the action of governing; political rule and administration. **2** the system or form by which a community, etc., is ruled: *tyrannical government.* **3a** the executive policy-making body of a political unit, community, etc.; ministry or administration. **3b** (*cap. when of a specific country*): *the British Government.* **4a** the state and its administration: *blame it on the government.* **4b** (*as modifier*): *a government agency.* **5** regulation; direction. **6** *Grammar.* the determination of the form of one word by another word.
►**governmental** (ˌɡʌvənˈmɛntᵊl, ˌɡʌvəˈmɛntᵊl) *adj* ►ˌ**governˈmentally** *adv*

governor ❶ (ˈɡʌvənə) *n* **1** a person who governs. **2** the ruler or chief magistrate of a colony, province, etc. **3** the representative of the Crown in a British colony. **4** *Brit.* the senior administrator of a society, prison, etc. **5** the chief executive of any state in the US. **6** a device that controls the speed of an engine, esp. by regulating the supply of fuel. **7** *Brit. inf.* a name or title of respect for a father, employer, etc.
►ˈ**governorˌship** *n*

governor general *n, pl* **governors general** *or* **governor generals. 1** the representative of the Crown in a dominion of the Commonwealth or a British colony; vicegerent. **2** *Brit.* a governor with jurisdiction or precedence over other governors.
►ˌ**governor-ˈgeneralˌship** *n*

Govt *or* **govt** *abbrev. for* government.

go with ❶ *vb* (*intr, prep*) **1** to accompany. **2** to blend or harmonize: *that new wallpaper goes well with the furniture.* **3** to be a normal part of: *three acres of land go with the house.* **4** (of two people of the opposite sex) to associate frequently with each other.

go without ❶ *vb* (*intr*) *Chiefly Brit.* to be denied or deprived of (something, esp. food): *if you don't like your tea you can go without.*

gowk (ɡaʊk) *n Scot. & N English dialect.* **1** a fool. **2** a cuckoo. [from ON *gaukr* cuckoo]

gown ❶ (ɡaʊn) *n* **1** any of various outer garments, such as a woman's elegant or formal dress, a dressing robe, or a protective garment, esp. one worn by surgeons during operations. **2** a loose wide garment indicating status, such as worn by academics. **3** the members of a university as opposed to the other residents of the university town. ◆ *vb* **4** (*tr*) to supply with or dress in a gown. [C14: from OF, from LL *gunna* garment made of leather or fur, of Celtic origin]

goy (ɡɔɪ) *n, pl* **goyim** (ˈɡɔɪɪm) *or* **goys.** a Jewish word for a **Gentile.** [from Yiddish, from Heb. *goi* people]
►ˈ**goyish** *adj*

GP *abbrev. for:* **1** Gallup Poll. **2** *Music.* general pause. **3** general practitioner. **4** (in Britain) graduated pension. **5** Grand Prix.

GPMU (in Britain) *abbrev. for* Graphical, Paper and Media Union.

GPO *abbrev. for* general post office.

Gr. *abbrev. for:* **1** Grecian. **2** Greece. **3** Greek.

Graafian follicle (ˈɡrɑːfɪən) *n* a fluid-filled vesicle in the mammalian ovary containing a developing egg cell. [C17: after R. de *Graaf* (1641–73), Du. anatomist]

grab ❶ (ɡræb) *vb* **grabs, grabbing, grabbed. 1** to seize hold of (something). **2** (*tr*) to seize illegally or unscrupulously. **3** (*tr*) to arrest; catch. **4** (*tr*) *Inf.* to catch the attention or interest of; impress. ◆ *n* **5** the act or an instance of grabbing. **6** a mechanical device for gripping objects, esp. the hinged jaws of a mechanical excavator. **7** something that is grabbed. [C16: prob. from MLow G or MDu. *grabben*]
►ˈ**grabber** *n*

grab bag *n* **1** a collection of miscellaneous things. **2** *US, Canad., & Austral.* a bag or other container from which gifts are drawn at random.

grabby (ˈɡræbɪ) *adj* **grabbier, grabbiest. 1** grasping or avaricious. **2** seizing the attention: *a grabby headline; a grabby performance.*

grace ❶ (ɡreɪs) *n* **1** elegance and beauty of movement, form, expression, or proportion. **2** a pleasing or charming quality. **3** goodwill or favour. **4** a delay granted for the completion of a task or payment of a debt. **5** a sense of propriety and consideration for others. **6** (*pl*) **6a** affectation of manner (esp. in **airs and graces**). **6b in (someone's) good graces.** regarded favourably and with kindness by (someone). **7** mercy; clemency. **8** *Christian theol.* **8a** the free and unmerited favour of God shown towards man. **8b** the divine assistance given to man in spiritual rebirth. **8c** the condition of being favoured or sanctified by God. **8d** an unmerited gift, favour, etc., granted by God. **9** a short prayer recited before or after a meal to give thanks for it. **10** *Music.* a melodic ornament or decoration. **11 with (a) bad grace.** unwillingly or grudgingly. **12 with (a) good grace.** willingly or cheerfully. ◆ *vb* **graces, gracing, graced. 13** (*tr*) to add elegance and beauty to: *flowers graced the room.* **14** (*tr*) to honour or favour: *to grace a party with one's presence.* **15** to ornament or decorate (a melody, part, etc.) with nonessential notes. [C12: from OF, from L *grātia,* from *grātus* pleasing]

Grace (ɡreɪs) *n* (preceded by *your, his,* or *her*) a title used to address or refer to a duke, duchess, or archbishop.

grace-and-favour *n* (*modifier*) *Brit.* (of a house, flat, etc.) owned by the sovereign and granted free of rent to a person to whom the sovereign wishes to express gratitude.

graceful ❶ (ˈɡreɪsfʊl) *adj* characterized by beauty of movement, style, form, etc.
►ˈ**gracefully** *adv* ►ˈ**gracefulness** *n*

graceless ❶ (ˈɡreɪslɪs) *adj* **1** lacking manners. **2** lacking elegance.
►ˈ**gracelessly** *adv* ►ˈ**gracelessness** *n*

grace note *n Music.* a note printed in small type to indicate that it is melodically and harmonically nonessential.

Graces (ˈɡreɪsɪz) *pl n Greek myth.* three sister goddesses, givers of charm and beauty.

gracious ❶ (ˈɡreɪʃəs) *adj* **1** characterized by or showing kindness and courtesy. **2** condescendingly courteous, benevolent, or indulgent. **3** characterized by or suitable for a life of elegance, ease, and indulgence: *gracious living.* **4** merciful or compassionate. ◆ *interj* **5** an expression of mild surprise or wonder.
►ˈ**graciously** *adv* ►ˈ**graciousness** *n*

grackle (ˈɡrækᵊl) *n* **1** an American songbird of the oriole family, having a dark iridescent plumage. **2** any of various starlings, such as the Indian grackle or hill myna. [C18: from NL, from L *grāculus* jackdaw]

THESAURUS

gourmet *n* = **connoisseur,** *bon vivant,* epicure, foodie (*inf.*), gastronome

govern *vb* **1** = **rule,** administer, be in power, call the shots, call the tune, command, conduct, control, direct, guide, handle, hold sway, lead, manage, order, oversee, pilot, reign, steer, superintend, supervise **3** = **determine,** decide, guide, influence, rule, sway, underlie **4** = **restrain,** bridle, check, contain, control, curb, direct, discipline, get the better of, hold in check, inhibit, keep a tight rein on, master, regulate, subdue, tame

government *n* **1** = **rule,** administration, authority, dominion, execution, governance, law, polity, sovereignty, state, statecraft **3** = **executive,** administration, ministry, powers-that-be, regime **5** = **guidance,** authority, command, control, direction, domination, management, regulation, restraint, superintendence, supervision, sway

governmental *adj* **1** = **administrative,** bureaucratic, executive, ministerial, official, political, sovereign, state

governor *n* **1** = **leader,** administrator, boss (*inf.*), chief, commander, comptroller, controller, director, executive, head, manager, overseer, ruler, superintendent, supervisor

go with *vb* **2** = **match,** agree, blend, complement, concur, correspond, fit, harmonize, suit

go without *vb* = **be deprived of,** abstain, be denied, deny oneself, do without, go short, lack, want

gown *n* **1** = **dress,** costume, frock, garb, garment, habit, robe

grab *vb* **1** = **snatch,** bag, capture, catch, catch *or* take hold of, clutch, grasp, grip, latch on to, nab (*inf.*), nail (*inf.*), pluck, seize, snap up

grace *n* **1, 2** = **elegance,** attractiveness, beauty, charm, comeliness, ease, finesse, gracefulness, loveliness, pleasantness, poise, polish, refinement, shapeliness, tastefulness **3** = **goodwill,** benefaction, beneficence, benevolence, favour, generosity, goodness, kindliness, kindness **5** = **manners,** breeding, consideration, cultivation, decency, decorum, etiquette, mannerliness, propriety, tact **7** = **indulgence,** charity, clemency, compassion, forgiveness, leniency, lenity, mercy, pardon, quarter, reprieve **9** = **prayer,** benediction, blessing, thanks, thanksgiving ◆ *vb* **13, 14** = **honour,** adorn, beautify, bedeck, deck, decorate, dignify, distinguish, elevate, embellish, enhance, enrich, favour, garnish, glorify, ornament, set off
Antonyms *n* ≠ **elegance:** awkwardness, clumsiness, inelegance, stiffness, tastelessness, ugliness, ungainliness ≠ **goodwill:** disfavour, ill will ≠ **manners:** bad manners, tactlessness ◆ *vb* ≠ **honour:** desecrate, dishonour, insult, ruin, spoil

graceful *adj* = **elegant,** agile, beautiful, becoming, charming, comely, easy, fine, flowing, gracile (*rare*), natural, pleasing, smooth, symmetrical, tasteful
Antonyms *adj* awkward, clumsy, gawky, inelegant, plain, ponderous, stiff, ugly, ungainly, ungraceful

graceless *adj* **1** = **ill-mannered,** barbarous, boorish, coarse, crude, improper, indecorous, loutish, rude, shameless, unmannerly, unsophisticated, vulgar **2** = **inelegant,** awkward, clumsy, forced, gauche, gawky, rough, uncouth, ungainly, untutored

gracious *adj* **1, 2, 4** = **kind,** accommodating, affable, amiable, beneficent, benevolent, benign, benignant, charitable, chivalrous, civil, compassionate, considerate, cordial, courteous, courtly, friendly, hospitable, indulgent, kindly, lenient, loving, merciful, mild, obliging, pleasing, polite, well-mannered
Antonyms *adj* brusque, cold, discourteous, gruff, haughty, impolite, mean, remote, rude, surly, unfriendly, ungracious, unpleasant

grad. *abbrev. for:* **1** *Maths.* gradient. **2** *Education.* graduate(d).

gradate (grəˈdeɪt) *vb* **gradates, gradating, gradated. 1** to change or cause to change imperceptibly, as from one colour, tone, or degree to another. **2** (*tr*) to arrange in grades or ranks.

gradation ❶ (grəˈdeɪʃən) *n* **1** a series of systematic stages; gradual progression. **2** (*often pl*) a stage or degree in such a series or progression. **3** the act or process of arranging or forming in stages, grades, etc., or of progressing evenly. **4** (in painting, drawing, or sculpture) transition from one colour, tone, or surface to another through a series of very slight changes. **5** *Linguistics.* any change in the quality or length of a vowel within a word indicating certain distinctions, such as inflectional or tense differentiations. See **ablaut.**
▸**graˈdational** *adj*

grade ❶ (greɪd) *n* **1** a position or degree in a scale, as of quality, rank, size, or progression: *high-grade timber.* **2** a group of people or things of the same category. **3** *Chiefly US.* a military or other rank. **4** a stage in a course of progression. **5** a mark or rating indicating achievement or the worth of work done, as at school. **6** *US & Canad.* a unit of pupils of similar age or ability taught together at school. **7 make the grade.** *Inf.* **7a** to reach the required standard. **7b** to succeed. ◆ *vb* **grades, grading, graded. 8** (*tr*) to arrange according to quality, rank, etc. **9** (*tr*) to determine the grade of or assign a grade to. **10** (*intr*) to achieve or deserve a grade or rank. **11** to change or blend (something) gradually; merge. **12** (*tr*) to level (ground, a road, etc.) to a suitable gradient. [C16: from F, from L *gradus* step, from *gradī* to step]

-grade *adj combining form.* indicating a kind or manner of movement or progression: *plantigrade; retrograde.* [via F from L *-gradus,* from *gradus* a step, from *gradī* to walk]

gradely (ˈgreɪdlɪ) *adj* **gradelier, gradeliest.** *Midland English dialect.* fine; excellent. [C13: from ON *greidhligr,* from *greidhr* ready]

grader (ˈgreɪdə) *n* **1** a person or thing that grades. **2** a machine that levels earth, rubble, etc., as in road construction.

gradient ❶ (ˈgreɪdɪənt) *n* **1** Also called (esp. US): **grade.** a part of a railway, road, etc., that slopes upwards or downwards; inclination. **2** Also called (esp. US and Canad.): **grade.** a measure of such a slope, esp. the ratio of the vertical distance between two points on the slope to the horizontal distance between them. **3** *Physics.* a measure of the change of some physical quantity, such as temperature or electric potential, over a specified distance. **4** *Maths.* (of a curve) the slope of the tangent at any point on a curve with respect to the horizontal axis. ◆ *adj* **5** sloping uniformly. [C19: from L *gradiēns* stepping, from *gradī* to go]

gradin (ˈgreɪdɪn) *or* **gradine** (grəˈdiːn) *n* **1** a ledge above or behind an altar for candles, etc., to stand on. **2** one of a set of steps or seats arranged on a slope, as in an amphitheatre. [C19: from F, from It. *gradino,* dim. of *grado* a step]

gradual ❶ (ˈgrædjʊəl) *adj* **1** occurring, developing, moving, etc., in small stages: *a gradual improvement in health.* **2** not steep or abrupt: *a gradual slope.* ◆ *n* **3** (*often cap.*) *Christianity.* **3a** an antiphon usually from the Psalms, sung or recited immediately after the epistle at Mass. **3b** a book of plainsong containing the words and music of the parts of the Mass that are sung by the cantors and choir. [C16: from Med. L: relating to steps, from L *gradus* a step]
▸**ˈgradually** *adv* ▸**ˈgradualness** *n*

gradualism (ˈgrædjʊəˌlɪzəm) *n* **1** the policy of seeking to change something gradually, esp. in politics. **2** the theory that explains major changes in fossils, rock strata, etc., in terms of gradual evolutionary processes rather than sudden violent catastrophes.
▸**ˈgradualist** *n, adj* ▸**ˌgradualˈistic** *adj*

graduand (ˈgrædjʊˌænd) *n Chiefly Brit.* a person who is about to graduate. [C19: from Med. L gerundive of *graduārī* to GRADUATE]

graduate ❶ *n* (ˈgrædjʊɪt). **1** a person who has been awarded a first degree from a university or college. **2** *US & Canad.* a student who has completed a course of studies at a high school and received a diploma. ◆ *vb* (ˈgrædjʊˌeɪt), **graduates, graduating, graduated. 3** to receive or cause to receive a degree or diploma. **4** *Chiefly US & Canad.* to confer a degree, diploma, etc., upon. **5** (*tr*) to mark (a thermometer, flask, etc.) with units of measurement; calibrate. **6** (*tr*) to arrange or sort into groups according to type, quality, etc. **7** (*intr; often foll. by to*) to change by degrees (from something to something else). [C15: from Med. L *graduārī* to take a degree, from L *gradus* a step]
▸**ˈgraduˌator** *n*

graduated pension *n* (in Britain) a national pension scheme in which employees' contributions are scaled in accordance with their wage rate.

graduation (ˌgrædjʊˈeɪʃən) *n* **1** the act of graduating or the state of being graduated. **2** the ceremony at which school or college degrees and diplomas are conferred. **3** a mark or division or all the marks or divisions that indicate measure on an instrument or vessel.

Graecism *or esp. US* **Grecism** (ˈgriːsɪzəm) *n* **1** Greek characteristics or style. **2** admiration for or imitation of these, as in sculpture or architecture. **3** a form of words characteristic of the idiom of the Greek language.

Graeco- *or esp. US* **Greco-** (ˈgriːkəʊ, ˈgrɛkəʊ) *combining form.* Greek: *Graeco-Roman.*

Graeco-Roman *or esp. US* **Greco-Roman** *adj* of, characteristic of, or relating to Greek and Roman influences.

graffiti (græˈfiːtɪ) *pl n* (*sometimes functioning as sing*) drawings, messages, etc., often obscene, scribbled on the walls of public lavatories, advertising posters, etc. [C19: see GRAFFITO]

graffito (græˈfiːtəʊ) *n, pl* **graffiti** (-tɪ). **1** *Archaeol.* any inscription or drawing scratched onto a surface, esp. rock or pottery. **2** See **graffiti.** [C19: from It.: a little scratch, from L *graphium* stylus, from Gk *grapheion;* see GRAFT[1]]

graft[1] ❶ (grɑːft) *n* **1** *Horticulture.* **1a** a small piece of plant tissue (the scion) that is made to unite with an established plant (the stock), which supports and nourishes it. **1b** the plant resulting from the union of scion and stock. **1c** the point of union between the scion and the stock. **2** *Surgery.* a piece of tissue transplanted from a donor or from the patient's own body to an area of the body in need of the tissue. **3** the act of joining one thing to another as by grafting. ◆ *vb* **4** *Horticulture.* **4a** to induce (a plant or part of a plant) to unite with another part or (of a plant or part of a plant) to unite in this way. **4b** to produce (fruit, flowers, etc.) by this means or (of fruit, etc.) to grow by this means. **5** to transplant (tissue) or (of tissue) to be transplanted. **6** to attach or incorporate or become attached or incorporated: *to graft a happy ending onto a sad tale.* [C15: from OF *graffe,* from Med. L *graphium,* from L: stylus, from Gk *grapheion,* from *graphein* to write]
▸**ˈgrafting** *n*

graft[2] (grɑːft) *n* **1** *Inf.* work (esp. in **hard graft**). **2a** the acquisition of money, power, etc., by dishonest or unfair means, esp. by taking advantage of a position of trust. **2b** something gained in this way. **2c** a payment made to a person profiting by such a practice. ◆ *vb* **3** (*intr*) *Inf.* to work, esp. hard. **4** to acquire by or practise graft. [C19: from ?]
▸**ˈgrafter** *n*

Grail (greɪl) *n* See **Holy Grail.**

grain ❶ (greɪn) *n* **1** the small hard seedlike fruit of a grass, esp. a cereal plant. **2** a mass of such fruits, esp. when gathered for food. **3** the plants, collectively, from which such fruits are harvested. **4** a small hard particle: *a grain of sand.* **5a** the general direction or arrangement of the fibres, layers, or particles in wood, leather, stone, etc. **5b** the pattern or texture resulting from such an arrangement. **6** the relative size of the particles of a substance: *sugar of fine grain.* **7** the granular texture of a rock, mineral, etc. **8** the outer layer of a hide or skin from which the hair or wool has been removed. **9** the smallest unit of weight in the avoirdupois, Troy, and apothecaries' systems: equal to 0.0648 gram. **10** the threads or direction of threads in a woven fabric. **11** *Photog.* any of a large number of particles in a photographic emulsion. **12** cleavage lines in crystalline material. **13** *Chem.* any of a large number of small crystals forming a solid. **14** a very small amount: *a grain of truth.* **15** natural disposition, inclination, or character (esp. in **go against the grain**). **16** *Astronautics.* a homogenous mass of solid propellant in a form designed to give the required combustion characteristics for a particular rocket. **17** (not in technical usage) kermes or a red dye made from this insect. ◆ *vb* (*mainly tr*) **18** (*also intr*) to form grains or cause to form into grains; granulate; crystallize. **19** to give a granular or roughened appearance or texture to. **20** to paint, stain, etc., in imitation of the grain of wood or leather. **21a** to remove the hair or wool from (a hide or skin) before tanning. **21b** to raise the grain pattern on (leather). [C13: from OF, from L *grānum*]

grain alcohol *n* ethanol containing about 10 per cent of water, made by the fermentation of grain.

grain elevator *n* a machine for raising grain to a higher level, esp. one having an endless belt fitted with scoops.

graining (ˈgreɪnɪŋ) *n* **1** the pattern or texture of the grain of wood, leather, etc. **2** the process of painting, printing, staining, etc., a surface in imitation of a grain. **3** a surface produced by such a process.

grainy (ˈgreɪnɪ) *adj* **grainier, grainiest. 1** resembling, full of, or composed of grain; granular. **2** resembling the grain of wood, leather, etc. **3** *Photog.* having poor definition because of large grain size.
▸**ˈgraininess** *n*

THESAURUS

gradation *n* **1 = progression**, array, sequence, series, succession **2 = stage**, degree, grade, level, mark, measurement, notch, place, point, position, rank, step **3 = classification**, arrangement, grouping, ordering, sorting

grade *n* **1, 4 = level**, brand, category, class, condition, degree, echelon, group, mark, notch, order, place, position, quality, rank, rung, size, stage, station, step **7 make the grade** *Informal* **= succeed**, come through with flying colours, come up to scratch (*inf.*), measure up, measure up to expectations, pass muster, prove acceptable, win through ◆ *vb* **8 = classify**, arrange, brand, class, evaluate, group, order, range, rank, rate, sequence, sort, value

gradient *n* **1 = slope**, acclivity, bank, declivity, grade, hill, incline, rise

gradual *adj* **1 = steady**, continuous, even, gentle, graduated, moderate, piecemeal, progressive, regular, slow, successive, unhurried
Antonyms *adj* abrupt, broken, instantaneous, overnight, sudden

gradually *adv* **1 = steadily**, bit by bit, by degrees, drop by drop, evenly, gently, little by little, moderately, piece by piece, piecemeal, progressively, slowly, step by step, unhurriedly

graduate *vb* **5 = mark off**, calibrate, grade, measure out, proportion, regulate **6 = classify**, arrange, grade, group, order, range, rank, sequence, sort

graft[1] *n* **1a = shoot**, bud, implant, scion, splice, sprout ◆ *vb* **4a = transplant**, affix, implant, ingraft, insert, join, splice

grain *n* **1 = seed**, grist, kernel **3 = cereals**, corn **10 = texture**, fibre, nap, pattern, surface, weave **14 = bit**, atom, crumb, fragment, granule, iota, jot, mite, modicum, molecule, morsel, mote, ounce, particle, piece, scrap, scruple, spark, speck, suspicion, trace, whit **15** *As in* **go against the grain = inclination**, character, disposition, humour, make-up, temper

grallatorial (ˌgrælə'tɔːrɪəl) *adj* of or relating to long-legged wading birds. [C19: from NL, from L *grallātor* one who walks on stilts, from *grallae* stilts]

gram[1] (græm) *n* a metric unit of mass equal to one thousandth of a kilogram. Symbol: g [C18: from F *gramme*, from LL *gramma*, from Gk: small weight, from *graphein* to write]

gram[2] (græm) *n* **1** any of several leguminous plants whose seeds are used as food in India. **2** the seed of any of these plants. [C18: from Port. *gram* (modern spelling: *grão*), from L *grānum* GRAIN]

gram. *abbrev. for:* **1** grammar. **2** grammatical.

-gram *n combining form.* indicating a drawing or something written or recorded: *hexagram; telegram.* [from L *-gramma*, from Gk, from *gramma* letter & *grammē* line]

gram atom *or* **gram-atomic weight** *n* an amount of an element equal to its atomic weight expressed in grams: now replaced by the mole.

gramineous (grə'mɪnɪəs) *adj* **1** of, relating to, or belonging to the grass family. **2** resembling a grass; grasslike. ◆ Also: **graminaceous** (ˌgræmɪ'neɪʃəs). [C17: from L, from *grāmen* grass]

graminivorous (ˌgræmɪ'nɪvərəs) *adj* (of animals) feeding on grass. [C18: from L *grāmen* grass + -VOROUS]

grammar ➊ ('græmə) *n* **1** the branch of linguistics that deals with syntax and morphology, sometimes also phonology and semantics. **2** the abstract system of rules in terms of which a person's mastery of his native language can be explained. **3** a systematic description of the grammatical facts of a language. **4** a book containing an account of the grammatical facts of a language or recommendations as to rules for the proper use of a language. **5** the use of language with regard to its correctness or social propriety, esp. in syntax: *the teacher told him to watch his grammar.* [C14: from OF, from L, from Gk *grammatikē* (*tekhnē*) the grammatical (art), from *grammatikos* concerning letters, from *gramma* letter]

grammarian (grə'mɛərɪən) *n* **1** a person whose occupation is the study of grammar. **2** the author of a grammar.

grammar school *n* **1** *Brit.* (esp. formerly) a state-maintained secondary school providing an education with an academic bias. **2** *US.* another term for **elementary school**. **3** *Austral.* a private school, esp. one controlled by a church. **4** *NZ.* a secondary school forming part of the public education system.

grammatical (grə'mætɪkᵊl) *adj* **1** of or relating to grammar. **2** (of a sentence) well formed; regarded as correct.
▸**gram'matically** *adv* ▸**gram'maticalness** *n*

gram molecule *or* **gram-molecular weight** *n* an amount of a compound equal to its molecular weight expressed in grams: now replaced by the mole. See **mole**[3].

Grammy ('græmɪ) *n, pl* **Grammys** *or* **Grammies.** (in the US) one of the gold-plated discs awarded annually for outstanding achievement in the record industry. [C20: from GRAM(OPHONE) + *-my* as in EMMY]

gramophone ('græməˌfəʊn) *n* **1a** Also called: **record player.** a device for reproducing the sounds stored on a record: now usually applied to the early type that uses an acoustic horn. US and Canad. word: **phonograph. 1b** (*as modifier*): *a gramophone record.* **2** the technique of recording sound on disc: *the gramophone has made music widely available.* [C19: orig. a trademark, ? based on an inversion of *phonogram;* see PHONO-, -GRAM]

grampus ('græmpəs) *n, pl* **grampuses. 1** a widely distributed slaty-grey dolphin with a blunt snout. **2** another name for **killer whale.** [C16: from OF *graspois,* from *gras* fat (from L *crassus*) + *pois* fish (from L *piscis*)]

Gram's method (græmz) *n Bacteriol.* **1** a technique used to classify bacteria by staining them with a violet iodine solution. **2 Gram-positive** (*or* **Gram-negative**). *adj* denoting bacteria that do (*or* do not) retain this stain. [C19: after H. C. J. *Gram* (1853–1938), Danish physician]

gran (græn) *n* an informal word for **grandmother.**

granadilla (ˌgrænə'dɪlə) *n* **1** any of various passionflowers that have edible egg-shaped fleshy fruit. **2** Also called: **passion fruit.** the fruit of such a plant. [C18: from Sp., dim. of *granada* pomegranate, from LL *grānātum*]

granary ('grænərɪ; *US* 'greɪnərɪ) *n, pl* **granaries. 1** a building for storing threshed grain. **2** a region that produces a large amount of grain. ◆ *adj* **3** (*cap.*) *Trademark.* (of bread, flour, etc.) containing malted wheat grain. [C16: from L *grānārium,* from *grānum* GRAIN]

grand ➊ (grænd) *adj* **1** large or impressive in size, extent, or consequence: *grand mountain scenery.* **2** characterized by or attended with magnificence or display; sumptuous: *a grand feast.* **3** of great distinction or pretension; dignified or haughty. **4** designed to impress: *grand gestures.* **5** very good; wonderful. **6** comprehensive; complete: *a grand total.* **7** worthy of respect; fine: *a grand old man.* **8** large or impressive in conception or execution: *grand ideas.* **9** most important; chief: *the grand arena.* ◆ *n* **10** See **grand piano. 11** (*pl* **grand**) *Sl.* a thousand pounds or dollars. [C16: from OF, from L *grandis*]
▸**'grandly** *adv* ▸**'grandness** *n*

grand- *prefix* (in designations of kinship) one generation removed in ascent or descent: *grandson; grandfather.* [from F *grand-,* on the model of L *magnus* in such phrases as *avunculus magnus* great-uncle]

grandad, granddad ('grænˌdæd) *or* **grandaddy, granddaddy** ('grænˌdædɪ) *n, pl* **grandads, granddads** *or* **grandaddies, granddaddies.** informal words for **grandfather.**

grandam ('grændəm, -dæm) *or* **grandame** ('grændeɪm, -dəm) *n* an archaic word for **grandmother.** [C13: from Anglo-F *grandame,* from OF GRAND- + *dame* lady, mother]

grandaunt ('grændˌɑːnt) *n* another name for **great-aunt.**

grandchild ('grænˌtʃaɪld) *n, pl* **grandchildren.** the son or daughter of one's child.

granddaughter ('grænˌdɔːtə) *n* a daughter of one's son or daughter.

grand duchess *n* **1** the wife or widow of a grand duke. **2** a woman who holds the rank of grand duke in her own right.

grand duchy *n* the territory, state, or principality of a grand duke or grand duchess.

grand duke *n* **1** a prince or nobleman who rules a territory, state, or principality. **2** a son or a male descendant in the male line of a Russian tsar. **3** a medieval Russian prince who ruled over other princes.

grande dame *French.* (grɑ̃d dam) *n* a woman regarded as the most experienced, prominent, or venerable member of her profession, etc.

grandee (græn'diː) *n* **1** a Spanish or Portuguese prince or nobleman of the highest rank. **2** a person of high station. [C16: from Sp. *grande*]

grandeur ➊ ('grændʒə) *n* **1** personal greatness, esp. when based on dignity, character, or accomplishments. **2** magnificence; splendour. **3** pretentious or bombastic behaviour.

grandfather ('grænˌfɑːðə, 'grænd-) *n* **1** the father of one's father or mother. **2** (*often pl*) a male ancestor. **3** (*often cap.*) a familiar term of address for an old man.
▸**'grandˌfatherly** *adj*

grandfather clock *n* a long-pendulum clock in a tall standing wooden case.

Grand Guignol *French.* (grɑ̃ giɲɔl) *n* **a** a brief sensational play intended to horrify. **b** (*modifier*) of or like plays of this kind. [C20: after *Le Grand Guignol,* a small theatre in Montmartre, Paris]

grandiloquent (græn'dɪləkwənt) *adj* inflated, pompous, or bombastic in style or expression. [C16: from L *grandiloquus,* from *grandis* great + *loquī* to speak]
▸**gran'diloquence** *n* ▸**gran'diloquently** *adv*

grandiose ➊ ('grændɪˌəʊs) *adj* **1** pretentiously grand or stately. **2** imposing in conception or execution. [C19: from F, from It., from *grande* great; see GRAND]
▸**'grandiˌosely** *adv* ▸**grandiosity** (ˌgrændɪ'ɒsɪtɪ) *n*

grand jury *n Law.* (esp. in the US and, now rarely, in Canada) a jury summoned to inquire into accusations of crime and ascertain whether the evidence is adequate to found an indictment. Abolished in Britain in 1948.

grand larceny *n* **1** (formerly, in England) the theft of property valued at over 12 pence. Abolished in 1827. **2** (in some states of the US) the theft of property of which the value is above a specified figure.

grandma ('grænˌmɑː), **grandmama,** *or* **grandmamma** ('grænməˌmɑː) *n* informal words for **grandmother.**

grand mal (grɒn mæl) *n* a form of epilepsy characterized by loss of consciousness for up to five minutes and violent convulsions. Cf. **petit mal.** [F: great illness]

grandmaster ('grændˌmɑːstə) *n* **1** *Chess.* one of the top chess players of a particular country. **2** a leading exponent of any of various arts.

Grand Master *n* the title borne by the head of any of various societies, orders, and other organizations, such as the Templars, Freemasons, or the various martial arts.

grandmother ('grænˌmʌðə, 'grænd-) *n* **1** the mother of one's father or mother. **2** (*often pl*) a female ancestor.
▸**'grandˌmotherly** *adj*

Grand National *n* **the.** an annual steeplechase run at Aintree, Liverpool, since 1839.

grandnephew ('grænˌnɛvjuː, -ˌnɛfjuː, 'grænd-) *n* another name for **great-nephew.**

grandniece ('grænˌniːs, 'grænd-) *n* another name for **great-niece.**

THESAURUS

grammar *n* **2** = **syntax**, rules of language

grand *adj* **1-3** = **impressive**, ambitious, august, dignified, elevated, eminent, exalted, fine, glorious, gorgeous, grandiose, great, haughty, illustrious, imposing, large, lofty, lordly, luxurious, magnificent, majestic, monumental, noble, opulent, ostentatious, palatial, pompous, pretentious, princely, regal, splendid, stately, striking, sublime, sumptuous, superb **5** = **excellent**, admirable, divine, fine, first-class, first-rate, great (*inf.*), marvellous (*inf.*), outstanding, smashing (*inf.*), splendid, super (*inf.*), superb, terrific (*inf.*), very good, wonderful, world-class **9** = **chief**, big-time (*inf.*), head, highest, lead, leading, main, major league (*inf.*), pre-eminent, principal, supreme
Antonyms *adj* ≠ **impressive:** undignified, unimposing ≠ **excellent:** awful, bad, common, contemptible, mean, petty, poor, terrible, worthless ≠ **chief:** inferior, insignificant, little, secondary, small, trivial, unimportant

grandeur *n* **1, 2** = **splendour**, augustness, dignity, greatness, importance, loftiness, magnificence, majesty, nobility, pomp, state, stateliness, sublimity
Antonyms *n* commonness, inferiority, insignificance, lowliness, pettiness, smallness, triviality, unimportance

grandiose *adj* **1** = **pretentious**, affected, ambitious, bombastic, extravagant, flamboyant, high-flown, ostentatious, pompous, showy **2** = **imposing**, ambitious, grand, impressive, lofty, magnificent, majestic, monumental, stately
Antonyms *adj* ≠ **pretentious:** down-to-earth, unpretentious ≠ **imposing:** humble, modest, small-scale

grand opera *n* an opera that has a serious plot and is entirely in musical form, with no spoken dialogue.

grandpa ('græn,pɑː) *or* **grandpapa** ('grænpə,pɑː) *n* informal words for **grandfather.**

grandparent ('græn,pɛərənt, 'grænd-) *n* the father or mother of either of one's parents.

grand piano *n* a form of piano in which the strings are arranged horizontally.

Grand Prix (*French* grɑ̃ pri) *n* **1** any of a series of formula motor races to determine the annual Driver's World Championship. **2** a very important competitive event in various other sports, such as athletics, snooker, or powerboating. [F: great prize]

grandsire ('græn,saɪə, 'grænd-) *n* an archaic word for **grandfather.**

grand slam *n* **1** *Bridge, etc.* the winning of 13 tricks by one player or side or the contract to do so. Cf. **little slam. 2** the winning of all major competitions in a season, esp. in tennis and golf. **3** (*often caps.*) *Rugby union.* the winning of all five games in the annual Six Nations Championship involving Scotland, England, Wales, Ireland, Italy, and France.

grandson ('grænsʌn, 'grænd-) *n* a son of one's son or daughter.

grandstand ('græn,stænd, 'grænd-) *n* **1** a terraced block of seats commanding the best view at racecourses, football pitches, etc. **2** the spectators in a grandstand.

grand tour *n* **1** (formerly) an extended tour through the major cities of Europe, esp. one undertaken by a rich or aristocratic Englishman to complete his education. **2** *Inf.* an extended sightseeing trip, tour of inspection, etc.

granduncle ('grænd,ʌŋkᵊl) *n* another name for **great-uncle.**

grand unified theory *n Physics.* any of a number of theories of elementary particles and fundamental interactions designed to explain the electromagnetic, strong, and weak interactions in terms of a single mathematical formalism. Abbrev.: **GUT.**

grange (greɪndʒ) *n* **1** *Chiefly Brit.* a farm, esp. a farmhouse or country house with its various outbuildings. **2** *Arch.* a granary or barn. [C13: from Anglo-F *graunge,* from Med. L *grānica,* from L *grānum* GRAIN]

granite ('grænɪt) *n* **1** a light-coloured coarse-grained acid plutonic igneous rock consisting of quartz and feldspars: widely used for building. **2** great hardness, endurance, or resolution. [C17: from It. *granito* grained, from *grano* grain, from L *grānum*]
▸**granitic** (grə'nɪtɪk) *adj*

graniteware ('grænɪt,wɛə) *n* **1** iron vessels coated with enamel of a granite-like appearance. **2** a type of pottery with a speckled glaze.

granivorous (græ'nɪvərəs) *adj* (of animals) feeding on seeds and grain.
▸**granivore** ('grænɪ,vɔː) *n*

granny *or* **grannie** ('grænɪ) *n, pl* **grannies. 1** informal words for **grandmother. 2** *Inf.* an irritatingly fussy person. **3** See **granny knot.**

granny bond *n Brit. inf.* a savings scheme available originally only to people over retirement age.

granny farm *n Derog. sl.* an old people's home, esp. one that charges high fees and offers poor care.

granny flat *n* self-contained accommodation within or built onto a house, suitable for an elderly parent.

granny knot *or* **granny's knot** *n* a reef knot with the ends crossed the wrong way, making it liable to slip or jam.

grant ❶ (grɑːnt) *vb* (*tr*) **1** to consent to perform or fulfil: *to grant a wish.* **2** (*may take a clause as object*) to permit as a favour, indulgence, etc.: *to grant an interview.* **3** (*may take a clause as object*) to acknowledge the validity of; concede: *I grant what you say is true.* **4** to bestow, esp. in a formal manner. **5** to transfer (property) to another, esp. by deed; convey. **6 take for granted. 6a** to accept or assume without question: *one takes certain amenities for granted.* **6b** to fail to appreciate the value, merit, etc., of (a person). ◆ *n* **7** a sum of money provided by a government, local authority, or public fund to finance educational study, building repairs, overseas aid, etc. **8** a privilege, right, etc., that has been granted. **9** the act of granting. **10** a transfer of property by deed; conveyance. [C13: from OF *graunter,* from Vulgar L *credentāre* (unattested), from L *crēdere* to believe]
▸'**grantable** *adj* ▸'**granter** *or* (*Law*) '**grantor** *n*

grantee (grɑːn'tiː) *n Law.* a person to whom a grant is made.

Granth (grʌnt) *n* the sacred scripture of the Sikhs. [from Hindi, from Sansk. *grantha* a book]

grant-in-aid *n, pl* **grants-in-aid.** a sum of money granted by one government to a lower level of government for a programme, etc.

grant-maintained *adj* (**grant maintained** *when postpositive*) (of schools or educational institutions) funded directly by central government.

gran turismo ('græn tʊə'rɪzməʊ) *n, pl* **gran turismos.** See **GT.** [C20: from It.]

granular ❶ ('grænjʊlə) *adj* **1** of, like, or containing granules. **2** having a grainy surface.
▸**granularity** (,grænjʊ'lærɪtɪ) *n* ▸'**granularly** *adv*

granulate ❶ ('grænjʊ,leɪt) *vb* **granulates, granulating, granulated. 1** (*tr*) to make into grains: *granulated sugar.* **2** to make or become roughened in surface texture.
▸,**granu'lation** *n* ▸'**granulative** *adj* ▸'**granu,lator** *or* '**granu,later** *n*

granule ❶ ('grænjuːl) *n* a small grain. [C17: from LL *grānulum* a small GRAIN]

granulocyte ('grænjʊlə,saɪt) *n* any of a group of unpigmented blood cells having cytoplasmic granules that take up various dyes.

grape (greɪp) *n* **1** the fruit of the grapevine, which has a purple or green skin and sweet flesh: eaten raw, dried to make raisins, currants, or sultanas, or used for making wine. **2** See **grapevine** (sense 1). **3 the grape.** *Inf.* wine. **4** See **grapeshot.** [C13: from OF *grape* bunch of grapes, of Gmc origin; rel. to CRAMP², GRAPPLE]
▸'**grapey** *or* '**grapy** *adj*

grapefruit ('greɪp,fruːt) *n, pl* **grapefruit** *or* **grapefruits. 1** a tropical or subtropical evergreen tree. **2** the large round edible fruit of this tree, which has yellow rind and juicy slightly bitter pulp.

grape hyacinth *n* any of various Eurasian bulbous plants of the lily family with clusters of rounded blue flowers resembling tiny grapes.

grapeshot ('greɪp,ʃɒt) *n* ammunition for cannons consisting of a cluster of iron balls that scatter after firing.

grape sugar *n* another name for **dextrose.**

grapevine ('greɪp,vaɪn) *n* **1** any of several vines of E Asia, widely cultivated for its fruit (grapes). **2** *Inf.* an unofficial means of relaying information, esp. from person to person.

graph (grɑːf) *n* **1** Also called: **chart.** a drawing depicting the relation between certain sets of numbers or quantities by means of a series of dots, lines, etc., plotted with reference to a set of axes. **2** *Maths.* a drawing depicting a functional relation between two or three variables by means of a curve or surface containing only those points whose coordinates satisfy the relation. **3** *Linguistics.* a symbol in a writing system not further subdivisible into other such symbols. ◆ *vb* **4** (*tr*) to draw or represent in a graph. [C19: short for *graphic formula*]

-graph *n combining form.* **1** an instrument that writes or records: *telegraph.* **2** a writing, record, or drawing: *autograph; lithograph.* [via L from Gk, from *graphein* to write]
▸**-graphic** *or* **-graphical** *adj combining form.* ▸**-graphically** *adv combining form.*

grapheme ('græfiːm) *n Linguistics.* the complete class of letters or combinations of letters that represent one speech sound: for instance, the *f* in *full,* the *gh* in *cough,* and the *ph* in *photo* are members of the same grapheme. [C20: from Gk *graphēma* a letter]
▸**gra'phemically** *adv*

-grapher *n combining form.* **1** indicating a person skilled in a subject: *geographer; photographer.* **2** indicating a person who writes or draws in a specified way: *stenographer; lithographer.*

graphic ❶ ('græfɪk) *or* **graphical** *adj* **1** vividly or clearly described: *a graphic account of the disaster.* **2** of or relating to writing: *graphic symbols.* **3** *Maths.* using, relating to, or determined by a graph: *a graphic representation of the figures.* **4** of or relating to the graphic arts. **5** *Geol.* having or denoting a texture resembling writing: *graphic granite.* [C17: from L *graphicus,* from Gk *graphikos,* from *graphein* to write]
▸'**graphically** *adv* ▸'**graphicness** *n*

graphicacy ('græfɪkəsɪ) *n* the ability to understand and use maps, symbols, etc. [C20: formed on the model of *literacy*]

graphical user interface *n* an interface between a user and a computer system that allows the user to operate the system by means of pictorial devices, such as menus and icons.

graphic arts *pl n* any of the fine or applied visual arts based on drawing or the use of line, esp. illustration and printmaking of all kinds.

graphic equalizer *n* a tone control that enables the output signal of an audio amplifier to be adjusted in each of a series of frequency bands by means of sliding contacts.

graphic novel *n* a novel in the form of a comic strip.

graphics ('græfɪks) *n* **1** (*functioning as sing*) the process or art of drawing in accordance with mathematical principles. **2** (*functioning as sing*) the study of writing systems. **3** (*functioning as pl*) the drawings, photographs, etc., in a magazine or book, or in a television or film production. **4** (*functioning as pl*) *Computing.* information displayed in the form of diagrams, graphs, etc.

graphite ('græfaɪt) *n* a blackish soft form of carbon used in pencils, electrodes, as a lubricant, as a moderator in nuclear reactors, and, in carbon fibre form, for tough lightweight sports equipment. [C18: from G *Graphit,* from Gk *graphein* to write + -ITE¹]
▸**graphitic** (grə'fɪtɪk) *adj*

graphology (græ'fɒlədʒɪ) *n* **1** the study of handwriting, esp. to analyse the writer's character. **2** *Linguistics.* the study of writing systems.
▸,**grapho'logical** *adj* ▸**gra'phologist** *n*

THESAURUS

grant *vb* **1, 2 = consent to,** accede to, accord, agree to, allow, permit **3 = admit,** acknowledge, cede, concede **4 = give,** allocate, allot, assign, award, bestow, confer, donate, hand out, impart, present, vouchsafe **5 = transfer,** assign, convey, transmit ◆ *n* **7 = award,** bequest, boon, bounty, donation, endowment, gift, hand-out, present, stipend, subsidy **9 = allowance,** admission, allocation, allotment, concession, endowment

granular *adj* **1 = grainy,** crumbly, granulated, gravelly, gritty, rough, sandy

granulate *vb* **1 = crystallize,** crumble, crush, grind, levigate (*Chemistry*), pound, powder, pulverize, triturate

granule *n* **= grain,** atom, crumb, fragment, iota, jot, molecule, particle, scrap, speck

graphic *adj* **1 = vivid,** clear, descriptive, detailed, explicit, expressive, forcible, illustrative, lively, lucid, picturesque, striking, telling, well-drawn **4 = pictorial,** delineated, diagrammatic, drawn, illustrative, representational, seen, visible, visual

Antonyms *adj* ≠ **vivid:** generalized, imprecise, unspecific, vague, woolly ≠ **pictorial:** impressionistic

graph paper *n* paper printed with intersecting lines for drawing graphs, diagrams, etc.

-graphy *n combining form.* **1** indicating a form of writing, representing, etc.: *calligraphy; photography.* **2** indicating an art or descriptive science: *choreography; oceanography.* [via L from Gk, from *graphein* to write]

grapnel ('græpnᵊl) *n* **1** a device with a multiple hook at one end and attached to a rope, which is thrown or hooked over a firm mooring to secure an object attached to the other end of the rope. **2** a light anchor for small boats. [C14: from OF *grapin,* from *grape* a hook; see GRAPE]

grappa ('græpə) *n* a spirit distilled from the fermented remains of grapes after pressing. [It.: grape stalk, of Gmc origin; see GRAPE]

grapple ❶ ('græpᵊl) *vb* **grapples, grappling, grappled. 1** to come to grips with (one or more persons), esp. to struggle in hand-to-hand combat. **2** (*intr;* foll. by *with*) to cope or contend: *to grapple with a financial problem.* **3** (*tr*) to secure with a grapple. ◆ *n* **4** any form of hook or metal instrument by which something is secured, such as a grapnel. **5a** the act of gripping or seizing, as in wrestling. **5b** a grip or hold. [C16: from OF *grappelle* a little hook, from *grape* hook; see GRAPNEL]
▸**'grappler** *n*

grappling iron *or* **hook** *n* a grapnel, esp. one used for securing ships.

graptolite ('græptəˌlaɪt) *n* an extinct Palaeozoic colonial animal: a common fossil. [C19: from Gk *graptos* written, from *graphein* to write + -LITE]

grasp ❶ (grɑːsp) *vb* **1** to grip (something) firmly as with the hands. **2** (when *intr,* often foll. by *at*) to struggle, snatch, or grope (for). **3** (*tr*) to understand, esp. with effort. ◆ *n* **4** the act of grasping. **5** a grip or clasp, as of a hand. **6** total rule or possession. **7** understanding; comprehension. [C14: from Low G *grapsen;* rel. to OE *græppian* to seize]
▸**'graspable** *adj* ▸**'grasper** *n*

grasping ❶ ('grɑːspɪŋ) *adj* greedy; avaricious.
▸**'graspingly** *adv* ▸**'graspingness** *n*

grass (grɑːs) *n* **1** any of a family of plants having jointed stems sheathed by long narrow leaves, flowers in spikes, and seedlike fruits. The family includes cereals, bamboo, etc. **2** such plants collectively, in a lawn, meadow, etc. Related adj: **verdant. 3** ground on which such plants grow; a lawn, field, etc. **4** ground on which animals are grazed; pasture. **5** a slang word for **marijuana. 6** *Brit. sl.* a person who informs, esp. on criminals. **7 let the grass grow under one's feet.** to squander time or opportunity. ◆ *vb* **8** to cover or become covered with grass. **9** to feed or be fed with grass. **10** (*tr*) to spread (cloth, etc.) out on grass for drying or bleaching in the sun. **11** (*intr;* usually foll. by *on*) *Brit. sl.* to inform, esp. to the police. ◆ See also **grass up.** [OE *græs*]
▸**'grassˌlike** *adj*

grass hockey *n* in W Canada, field hockey, as contrasted with ice hockey.

grasshopper ('grɑːsˌhɒpə) *n* an insect having hind legs adapted for leaping: typically terrestrial, feeding on plants, and producing a ticking sound by rubbing the hind legs against the leathery forewings.

grassland ('grɑːsˌlænd) *n* **1** land, such as a prairie, on which grass predominates. **2** land reserved for natural grass pasture.

grass roots *pl n* **1** ordinary people as distinct from the active leadership of a group or organization, esp. a political party. **2** the essentials.

grass snake *n* **1** a harmless nonvenomous European snake having a brownish-green body with variable markings. **2** any of several similar related European snakes.

grass tree *n* **1** Also called: **blackboy.** an Australian plant of the lily family, having a woody stem, stiff grasslike leaves, and a spike of small white flowers. **2** any of several similar Australasian plants.

grass up *vb* (*tr, adv*) *Sl.* to inform on (someone), esp. to the police.

grass widow *or* (*masc*) **grass widower** *n* a person whose spouse is regularly away for a short period. [C16: ? an allusion to a grass bed as representing an illicit relationship]

grassy ('grɑːsɪ) *adj* **grassier, grassiest.** covered with, containing, or resembling grass.
▸**'grassiness** *n*

grate[1] ❶ (greɪt) *vb* **grates, grating, grated. 1** (*tr*) to reduce to small shreds by rubbing against a rough or sharp perforated surface: *to grate carrots.* **2** to scrape (an object) against something or (objects) together, producing a harsh rasping sound, or (of objects) to scrape with such a sound. **3** (*intr;* foll. by *on* or *upon*) to annoy. [C15: from OF *grater* to scrape, of Gmc origin]
▸**'grater** *n*

grate[2] (greɪt) *n* **1** a framework of metal bars for holding fuel in a fireplace, stove, or furnace. **2** a less common word for **fireplace. 3** another name for **grating**[1]. ◆ *vb* **4** (*tr*) to provide with a grate or grates. [C14: from OF, from L *crātis* hurdle]

grateful ❶ ('greɪtfʊl) *adj* **1** thankful for gifts, favours, etc.; appreciative. **2** showing gratitude: *a grateful letter.* **3** favourable or pleasant: *a grateful rest.* [C16: from obs. *grate,* from L *grātus* + -FUL]
▸**'gratefully** *adv* ▸**'gratefulness** *n*

graticule ('grætɪˌkjuːl) *n* **1** the grid of intersecting lines of latitude and longitude on which a map is drawn. **2** another name for **reticle.** [C19: from F, from L *crāticula,* from *crātis* wickerwork]

gratify ❶ ('grætɪˌfaɪ) *vb* **gratifies, gratifying, gratified.** (*tr*) **1** to satisfy or please. **2** to yield to or indulge (a desire, whim, etc.). [C16: from L *grātificārī,* from *grātus* grateful + *facere* to make]
▸**ˌgratifi'cation** *n* ▸**'gratiˌfier** *n* ▸**'gratiˌfying** *adj* ▸**'gratiˌfyingly** *adv*

gratin (*French* gratɛ̃) See **au gratin.**

grating[1] ❶ ('greɪtɪŋ) *n* a framework of metal bars in the form of a grille set into a wall, pavement, etc., serving as a cover or guard but admitting air and sometimes light. Also called: **grate.**

grating[2] ❶ ('greɪtɪŋ) *adj* **1** (of sounds) harsh and rasping. **2** annoying; irritating. ◆ *n* **3** (*often pl*) something produced by grating.
▸**'gratingly** *adv*

gratis ❶ ('greɪtɪs, 'grætɪs, 'grɑːtɪs) *adv, adj* (*postpositive*) without payment; free of charge. [C15: from L: out of kindness, from *grātiīs,* ablative pl of *grātia* favour]

gratitude ❶ ('grætɪˌtjuːd) *n* a feeling of thankfulness, as for gifts or favours. [C16: from Med. L *grātitūdō,* from L *grātus* GRATEFUL]

gratuitous ❶ (grə'tjuːɪtəs) *adj* **1** given or received without payment or obligation. **2** without cause; unjustified. [C17: from L *grātuītus* from *grātia* favour]
▸**gra'tuitously** *adv* ▸**gra'tuitousness** *n*

gratuity ❶ (grə'tjuːɪtɪ) *n, pl* **gratuities. 1** a gift or reward, usually of money, for services rendered; tip. **2** *Mil.* a financial award granted for long or meritorious service.

gratulatory ('grætjʊlətərɪ) *adj* expressing congratulation. [C16: from L *grātulārī* to congratulate]

grav (græv) *n* a unit of acceleration equal to the standard acceleration of free fall. 1 grav is equivalent to 9.806 65 metres per second per second. Symbol: g

gravadlax ('grævədˌlæks) *n* another name for **gravlax.**

gravamen (grə'veɪmɛn) *n, pl* **gravamina** (-'væmɪnə). **1** *Law.* that part of an accusation weighing most heavily against an accused. **2** *Law.* the substance or material grounds of a complaint. **3** a rare word for **grievance.** [C17: from LL: trouble, from L *gravis* heavy]

grave[1] ❶ (greɪv) *n* **1** a place for the burial of a corpse, esp. beneath the ground and usually marked by a tombstone. Related adj: **sepulchral. 2** something resembling a grave or resting place: *the ship went to its grave.* **3** (often preceded by *the*) a poetic term for **death. 4 make (someone) turn in his grave.** to do something that would have shocked or distressed a person now dead. [OE *græf*]

grave[2] ❶ (greɪv) *adj* **1** serious and solemn: *a grave look.* **2** full of or sug-

THESAURUS

grapple *vb* **1 = grip,** catch, clasp, clutch, come to grips, fasten, grab, grasp, hold, hug, lay *or* take hold, make fast, seize, wrestle **2 = deal with,** address oneself to, attack, battle, clash, combat, confront, contend, cope, do battle, encounter, engage, face, fight, get to grips with, struggle, tackle, take on, tussle, wrestle

grasp *vb* **1 = grip,** catch, clasp, clinch, clutch, grab, grapple, hold, lay *or* take hold of, seize, snatch **3 = understand,** catch on, catch *or* get the drift of, comprehend, follow, get, get the hang of (*inf.*), get the message, get the picture, realize, see, take in ◆ *n* **5 = grip,** clasp, clutches, embrace, hold, possession, tenure **6 = control,** capacity, compass, extent, mastery, power, range, reach, scope, sway, sweep **7 = understanding,** awareness, comprehension, grip, ken, knowledge, mastery, perception, realization

grasping *adj* **= greedy,** acquisitive, avaricious, close-fisted, covetous, mean, miserly, niggardly, penny-pinching (*inf.*), rapacious, selfish, stingy, tightfisted, usurious, venal
Antonyms *adj* altruistic, generous, unselfish

grate[1] *vb* **1 = shred,** mince, pulverize, triturate **2 = scrape,** creak, grind, rasp, rub, scratch **3 = annoy,** chafe, exasperate, fret, gall, get one down, get on one's nerves (*inf.*), irk, irritate, jar, nark (*Brit., Austral., & NZ sl.*), nettle, peeve, rankle, rub one up the wrong way, set one's teeth on edge, vex

grateful *adj* **1 = thankful,** appreciative, beholden, indebted, obliged

gratification *n* **1 = satisfaction,** delight, enjoyment, fruition, fulfilment, glee, indulgence, joy, kick *or* kicks (*inf.*), pleasure, recompense, relish, reward, thrill
Antonyms *n* control, denial, disappointment, discipline, dissatisfaction, frustration, pain, restraint, sorrow

gratify *vb* **1, 2 = please,** cater to, delight, favour, fawn on, feed, fulfil, give pleasure, gladden, humour, indulge, pander to, recompense, requite, satisfy, thrill

grating[1] *n* **= grille,** grate, grid, gridiron, lattice, trellis

grating[2] *adj* **1, 2 = irritating,** annoying, disagreeable, discordant, displeasing, grinding, harsh, irksome, jarring, offensive, rasping, raucous, scraping, squeaky, strident, unpleasant, vexatious
Antonyms *adj* agreeable, calming, mellifluous, musical, pleasing, soft, soothing

gratis *adj* **= free,** buckshee (*Brit. sl.*), for nothing, freely, free of charge, gratuitously, on the house, unpaid

gratitude *n* **= thankfulness,** appreciation, gratefulness, indebtedness, obligation, recognition, sense of obligation, thanks
Antonyms *n* ingratitude, ungratefulness, unthankfulness

gratuitous *adj* **1 = voluntary,** buckshee (*Brit. sl.*), complimentary, free, gratis, spontaneous, unasked-for, unpaid, unrewarded **2 = unjustified,** assumed, baseless, causeless, groundless, irrelevant, needless, superfluous, uncalled-for, unfounded, unmerited, unnecessary, unprovoked, unwarranted, wanton
Antonyms *adj* ≠ **voluntary:** compulsory, involuntary, paid ≠ **unjustified:** justifiable, provoked, relevant, well-founded

gratuity *n* **1 = tip,** baksheesh, benefaction, bonus, boon, bounty, donation, gift, largesse *or* largess, perquisite, *pourboire,* present, recompense, reward

grave[1] *n* **1 = tomb,** burying place, crypt, last resting place, mausoleum, pit, sepulchre, vault

grave[2] *adj* **1 = solemn,** dignified, dour, dull, earnest, gloomy, grim-faced, heavy, leaden, long-

gesting danger: *a grave situation.* **3** important; crucial: *grave matters of state.* **4** (of colours) sober or dull. **5** (grɑːv). *Phonetics.* of or relating to an accent (`) over vowels, denoting a pronunciation with lower or falling musical pitch (as in ancient Greek), with certain special quality (as in French), or in a manner that gives the vowel status as a syllable (as in English *agèd*). ◆ *n* **6** (*also* grɑːv). a grave accent. [C16: from OF, from L *gravis*]
▸ **'gravely** *adv* ▸ **'graveness** *n*

grave[3] (greɪv) *vb* **graves, graving, graved; graved** *or* **graven.** (*tr*) *Arch.* **1** to carve or engrave. **2** to fix firmly in the mind. [OE *grafan*]

grave[4] ('grɑːveɪ) *adj Music.* solemn. [It.]

grave clothes (greɪv) *pl n* the wrappings in which a dead body is interred.

gravel ('grævᵊl) *n* **1** a mixture of rock fragments and pebbles that is coarser than sand. **2** *Pathol.* small rough calculi in the kidneys or bladder. ◆ *vb* **gravels, gravelling, gravelled** *or US* **gravels, graveling, graveled.** (*tr*) **3** to cover with gravel. **4** to confound or confuse. **5** *US inf.* to annoy or disturb. [C13: from OF *gravele,* dim. of *grave,* ? of Celtic origin]

gravel-blind *adj Literary.* almost completely blind. [C16: from GRAVEL + BLIND]

gravelly ('grævəlɪ) *adj* **1** consisting of or abounding in gravel. **2** of or like gravel. **3** (esp. of a voice) harsh and grating.

graven ('greɪvᵊn) *vb* **1** a past participle of **grave**[3]. ◆ *adj* **2** strongly fixed.

graven image *n Chiefly Bible.* a carved image used as an idol.

graver ('greɪvə) *n* any of various engraving or sculpting tools, such as a burin.

Graves (grɑːv) *n* (*sometimes not cap.*) a white or red wine from the district around Bordeaux, France.

gravestone ('greɪvˌstəʊn) *n* a stone marking a grave.

graveyard 🅣 ('greɪvˌjɑːd) *n* a place for graves; a burial ground, esp. a small one or one in a churchyard.

graveyard shift *n US.* the working shift between midnight and morning.

graveyard slot *n Television.* the hours from late night until early morning when the number of people watching television is at its lowest.

gravid ('grævɪd) *adj* the technical word for **pregnant.** [C16: from L *gravidus,* from *gravis* heavy]

gravimeter (grə'vɪmɪtə) *n* **1** an instrument for measuring the earth's gravitational field at points on its surface. **2** an instrument for measuring relative density. [C18: from F *gravimètre,* from L *gravis* heavy]
▸ **gra'vimetry** *n*

gravimetric (ˌgrævɪ'metrɪk) *adj* **1** of, concerned with, or using measurement by weight. **2** *Chem.* of analysis of quantities by weight.

graving dock *n* another term for **dry dock.**

gravitas 🅣 ('grævɪˌtæs) *n* seriousness or solemnity, esp. of conduct or demeanour; weight or authority. [C20: from L *gravitās* weight, from *gravis* heavy]

gravitate 🅣 ('grævɪˌteɪt) *vb* **gravitates, gravitating, gravitated.** (*intr*) **1** *Physics.* to move under the influence of gravity. **2** (usually foll. by *to* or *towards*) to be influenced or drawn, as by strong impulses. **3** to sink or settle.
▸ **'graviˌtater** *n* ▸ **'graviˌtative** *adj*

gravitation (ˌgrævɪ'teɪʃən) *n* **1** the force of attraction that bodies exert on one another as a result of their mass. **2** any process or result caused by this interaction. ◆ Also called: **gravity.**
▸ **ˌgravi'tational** *adj* ▸ **ˌgravi'tationally** *adv*

gravitational constant *n* the factor relating force to mass and distance in Newton's law of gravitation. Symbol: *G*

gravitational field *n* the field of force surrounding a body of finite mass in which another body would experience an attractive force that is proportional to the product of the masses and inversely proportional to the square of the distance between them.

gravitational mass *n* the mass of a body expressed in terms of the gravitational force between it and the earth. Cf. **inertial mass.**

graviton ('grævɪˌtɒn) *n* a postulated quantum of gravitational energy, usually considered to be a particle with zero charge and rest mass and a spin of 2.

gravity 🅣 ('grævɪtɪ) *n, pl* **gravities. 1** the force of attraction that moves or tends to move bodies towards the centre of a celestial body, such as the earth or moon. **2** the property of being heavy or having weight. **3** another name for **gravitation. 4** seriousness or importance, esp. as a consequence of an action or opinion. **5** manner or conduct that is solemn or dignified. **6** lowness in pitch. **7** (*modifier*) of or relating to gravity or gravitation or their effects: *gravity feed.* [C16: from L *gravitās* weight, from *gravis* heavy]

gravity wave *n Physics.* **1** a wave propagated in a gravitational field, predicted to occur as a result of an accelerating mass. **2** a surface wave on water or other liquid propagated because of the weight of liquid in the crests. ◆ Also called: **gravitational wave.**

gravlax ('grævˌlæks) *or* **gravadlax** *n* dry-cured salmon, marinated in salt, sugar, and spices, as served in Scandinavia. [C20: from Norwegian, from *grav* grave (because the salmon is left to ferment) + *laks* or Swedish *lax* salmon]

gravure (grə'vjʊə) *n* **1** a method of intaglio printing using a plate with many small etched recesses. See also **rotogravure. 2** See **photogravure. 3** matter printed by this process. [C19: from F, from *graver* to engrave]

gravy ('greɪvɪ) *n, pl* **gravies. 1a** the juices that exude from meat during cooking. **1b** the sauce made by thickening and flavouring such juices. **2** *Sl.* money or gain acquired with little effort, esp. above that needed for ordinary living. [C14: from OF *gravé,* from ?]

gravy boat *n* a small often boat-shaped vessel for serving gravy or other sauces.

gray[1] (greɪ) *adj, n, vb* a variant spelling (now esp. US) of **grey.**

gray[2] (greɪ) *n* the derived SI unit of the absorbed dose of ionizing radiation: equal to 1 joule per kilogram. Symbol: Gy [C20: after L. H. *Gray,* Brit. radiobiologist]

grayling ('greɪlɪŋ) *n, pl* **grayling** *or* **graylings. 1** a freshwater food fish of the salmon family of the N hemisphere, having a long spiny dorsal fin, a silvery back, and greyish-green sides. **2** any of various European butterflies having grey or greyish-brown wings.

graze[1] 🅣 (greɪz) *vb* **grazes, grazing, grazed. 1** to allow (animals) to consume the vegetation on (an area of land), or (of animals) to feed thus. **2** (*tr*) to tend (livestock) while at pasture. **3** (*intr*) *Inf.* to eat snacks throughout the day rather than formal meals. **4** (*intr*) *US.* to pilfer and eat sweets, vegetables, etc., from supermarket shelves while shopping. [OE *grasian,* from *græs* GRASS]

graze[2] 🅣 (greɪz) *vb* **grazes, grazing, grazed. 1** (when *intr,* often foll. by *against* or *along*) to brush or scrape (against) gently, esp. in passing. **2** (*tr*) to break the skin of (a part of the body) by scraping. ◆ *n* **3** the act of grazing. **4** a scrape or abrasion made by grazing. [C17: prob. special use of GRAZE[1]]

grazier ('greɪzɪə) *n* a rancher or farmer who rears or fattens cattle or sheep on grazing land.

grazing ('greɪzɪŋ) *n* **1** the vegetation on pastures that is available for livestock to feed upon. **2** the land on which this is growing.

grazioso (ˌgrɑːtsɪ'əʊsəʊ) *adj Music.* graceful. [It.]

grease 🅣 (griːs, griːz) *n* **1** animal fat in a soft or melted condition. **2** any thick fatty oil, esp. one used as a lubricant for machinery, etc. ◆ *vb* **greases, greasing, greased.** (*tr*) **3** to soil, coat, or lubricate with grease. **4 grease the palm** (*or* **hand**) **of.** *Sl.* to bribe; influence by giving money to. [C13: from OF *craisse,* from L *crassus* thick]
▸ **'greaser** *n*

grease gun *n* a device for forcing grease through nipples into bearings.

grease monkey *n Inf.* a mechanic, esp. one who works on cars or aircraft.

grease nipple *n* a metal nipple designed to engage with a grease gun for injecting grease into a bearing, etc.

greasepaint ('griːsˌpeɪnt) *n* **1** a waxy or greasy substance used as make-up by actors. **2** theatrical make-up.

greaseproof paper ('griːsˌpruːf) *n* any paper that is resistant to penetration by greases and oils.

greasy 🅣 ('griːsɪ, -zɪ) *adj* **greasier, greasiest. 1** coated or soiled with or as if with grease. **2** composed of or full of grease. **3** resembling grease. **4** unctuous or oily in manner.
▸ **'greasily** *adv* ▸ **'greasiness** *n*

greasy wool *n* untreated wool still retaining the lanolin; used for waterproof clothing.

great 🅣 (greɪt) *adj* **1** relatively large in size or extent; big. **2** relatively large in number; having many parts or members: *a great assembly.* **3** of relatively long duration: *a great wait.* **4** of larger size or more importance than others of its kind: *the great auk.* **5** extreme or more than usual: *great worry.* **6** of significant importance or consequence: *a great*

THESAURUS

faced, muted, quiet, sage (*obs.*), sedate, serious, sober, sombre, staid, subdued, thoughtful, unsmiling **2, 3** = **important**, acute, critical, crucial, dangerous, exigent, hazardous, life-and-death, momentous, of great consequence, perilous, pressing, serious, severe, significant, threatening, urgent, vital, weighty
Antonyms *adj* ≠ **solemn:** carefree, exciting, flippant, happy, joyous, merry, undignified ≠ **important:** frivolous, insignificant, mild, trifling, unimportant

graveyard *n* = **cemetery**, boneyard (*inf.*), burial ground, charnel house, churchyard, God's acre (*literary*), necropolis

gravitas *n* = **seriousness**, gravity, solemnity

gravitate *vb* **2** *with* **to** *or* **towards** = **be drawn**, be attracted, be influenced, be pulled, incline, lean, move, tend **3** = **fall**, be precipitated, descend, drop, precipitate, settle, sink

gravity *n* **4** = **importance**, acuteness, consequence, exigency, hazardousness, moment, momentousness, perilousness, pressingness, seriousness, severity, significance, urgency, weightiness **5** = **solemnity**, demureness, dignity, earnestness, gloom, gravitas, grimness, reserve, sedateness, seriousness, sobriety, thoughtfulness
Antonyms *n* ≠ **importance:** inconsequentiality, insignificance, triviality, unimportance ≠ **solemnity:** flippancy, frivolity, gaiety, happiness, joy, levity, merriment, thoughtlessness

graze[1] *vb* **1** = **feed**, browse, crop, pasture

graze[2] *vb* **1** = **touch**, brush, glance off, kiss, rub, scrape, shave, skim **2** = **scratch**, abrade, bark, chafe, scrape, skin ◆ *n* **4** = **scratch**, abrasion, scrape

grease *vb* **4 grease someone's palm** *Slang* = **bribe**, buy, corrupt, fix (*inf.*), give a backhander (*sl.*), induce, influence, pay off (*inf.*), square, suborn

greasy *adj* **1-3** = **fatty**, oily, oleaginous, slick, slimy, slippery **4** = **sycophantic**, fawning, glib, grovelling, ingratiating, oily, slick, smarmy (*Brit. inf.*), smooth, toadying, unctuous

great *adj* **1** = **large**, big, bulky, colossal, elephantine, enormous, extensive, gigantic, huge, immense, mammoth, prodigious, stellar (*inf.*), stupendous, tremendous, vast, voluminous **3** = **long**, extended, lengthy, prolonged, protracted **4** = **major**, big-time (*inf.*), capital, chief, grand, head, lead, leading, main, major league (*inf.*),

decision. **7a** of exceptional talents or achievements; remarkable: *a great writer.* **7b** (*as n*): *the great; one of the greats.* **8** doing or exemplifying (something) on a large scale: *she's a great reader.* **9** arising from or possessing idealism in thought, action, etc.; heroic: *great deeds.* **10** illustrious or eminent: *a great history.* **11** impressive or striking: *a great show of wealth.* **12** active or enthusiastic: *a great walker.* **13** (often foll. by *at*) skilful or adroit: *a great carpenter; you are great at singing.* **14** *Inf.* excellent; fantastic. ◆ *n* **15** Also called: **great organ.** the principal manual on an organ. [OE *grēat*]
▸ **'greatly** *adv* ▸ **'greatness** *n*

great- *prefix* **1** being the parent of a person's grandparent (in the combinations **great-grandfather, great-grandmother, great-grandparent**). **2** being the child of a person's grandchild (in the combinations **great-grandson, great-granddaughter, great-grandchild**).

great auk *n* a large flightless auk, extinct since the middle of the 19th century.

great-aunt *or* **grandaunt** *n* an aunt of one's father or mother; sister of one's grandfather or grandmother.

Great Bear *n* **the.** the English name for **Ursa Major.**

great circle *n* a circular section of a sphere that has a radius equal to that of the sphere.

greatcoat ('greɪtˌkəʊt) *n* a heavy overcoat.

Great Dane *n* one of a very large breed of dog with a short smooth coat.

great gross *n* a unit of quantity equal to one dozen gross (or 1728).

great-hearted *adj* benevolent or noble; magnanimous.
▸ **ˌgreat-'heartedness** *n*

great-nephew *or* **grandnephew** *n* a son of one's nephew or niece; grandson of one's brother or sister.

great-niece *or* **grandniece** *n* a daughter of one's nephew or niece; grand-daughter of one's brother or sister.

Great Red Spot *n* a large long-lived oval feature, south of Jupiter's equator, that is an anticyclonic disturbance in the atmosphere.

Great Russian *n* **1** *Linguistics.* the technical name for **Russian. 2** a member of the chief East Slavonic people of Russia. ◆ *adj* **3** of or relating to this people or their language.

Greats (greɪts) *pl n* (at Oxford University) **1** the Honour School of Literae Humaniores, involving the study of Greek and Roman history and literature and philosophy. **2** the final examinations at the end of this course.

great seal *n* (*often caps.*) the principal seal of a nation, sovereign, etc., used to authenticate documents of the highest importance.

great tit *n* a Eurasian tit with yellow-and-black underparts and a black-and-white head.

great-uncle *or* **granduncle** *n* an uncle of one's father or mother; brother of one's grandfather or grandmother.

Great War *n* another name for **World War I.**

greave (griːv) *n* (*often pl*) a piece of armour worn to protect the shin. [C14: from OF *greve,* ?from *graver* to part the hair, of Gmc origin]

grebe (griːb) *n* an aquatic bird, such as the great crested grebe and little grebe, similar to the divers but with lobate rather than webbed toes and a vestigial tail. [C18: from F *grèbe,* from ?]

Grecian ('griːʃən) *adj* **1** (esp. of beauty or architecture) conforming to Greek ideals. ◆ *n* **2** a scholar of Greek. ◆ *adj, n* **3** another word for **Greek.**

Grecism ('griːˌsɪzəm) *n* a variant spelling (esp. US) of **Graecism.**

Greco- ('griːkəʊ, 'grɛkəʊ) *combining form.* a variant (esp. US) of **Graeco-.**

greed ❶ (griːd) *n* **1** excessive consumption of or desire for food. **2** excessive desire, as for wealth or power. [C17: back formation from GREEDY]

greedy ❶ ('griːdɪ) *adj* **greedier, greediest. 1** excessively desirous of food or wealth, esp. in large amounts; voracious. **2** (*postpositive;* foll. by *for*) eager (for): *a man greedy for success.* [OE *grǣdig*]
▸ **'greedily** *adv* ▸ **'greediness** *n*

greegree ('griːgriː) *n* a variant spelling of **grigri.**

Greek ❶ (griːk) *n* **1** the official language of Greece, constituting the Hellenic branch of the Indo-European family of languages. **2** a native or inhabitant of Greece or a descendant of such a native. **3** a member of the Greek Orthodox Church. **4** *Inf.* anything incomprehensible (esp. in **it's (all) Greek to me**). ◆ *adj* **5** denoting, relating to, or characteristic of Greece, the Greeks, or the Greek language; Hellenic. **6** of, relating to, or designating the Greek Orthodox Church.
▸ **'Greekness** *n*

Greek cross *n* a cross with each of the four arms of the same length.

Greek fire *n* a Byzantine weapon consisting of an unknown mixture that caught fire when wetted.

Greek gift *n* a gift given with the intention of tricking and causing harm to the recipient. [C19: in allusion to Virgil's *Aeneid* ii 49; see also TROJAN HORSE]

Greek Orthodox Church *n* **1** Also called: **Greek Church.** the established Church of Greece, governed by the holy synod of Greece, in which the Metropolitan of Athens has primacy of honour. **2** another name for **Orthodox Church.**

green ❶ (griːn) *n* **1** any of a group of colours, such as that of fresh grass, that lie between yellow and blue in the visible spectrum. Related adj: **verdant. 2** a dye or pigment of or producing these colours. **3** something of the colour green. **4** a small area of grassland, esp. in the centre of a village. **5** an area of smooth turf kept for a special purpose: *a putting green.* **6** (*pl*) **6a** the edible leaves and stems of certain plants, eaten as a vegetable. **6b** freshly cut branches of ornamental trees, shrubs, etc., used as a decoration. **7** (*sometimes cap.*) a person, esp. a politician, who supports environmentalist issues. ◆ *adj* **8** of the colour green. **9** greenish in colour or having parts or marks that are greenish. **10** (*sometimes cap.*) of or concerned with conservation of natural resources and improvement of the environment: used esp. in a political context. **11** vigorous; not faded: *a green old age.* **12** envious or jealous. **13** immature, unsophisticated, or gullible. **14** characterized by foliage or green plants: *a green wood; a green salad.* **15** denoting a unit of account that is adjusted in accordance with fluctuations between the currencies of the EU nations and is used to make payments to agricultural producers within the EU: *green pound.* **16** fresh, raw, or unripe: *green bananas.* **17** unhealthily pale in appearance: *he was green after his boat trip.* **18** (of meat) not smoked or cured: *green bacon.* **19** (of timber) freshly felled; not dried or seasoned. ◆ *vb* **20** to make or become green. [OE *grēne*]
▸ **'greenish** *or* **'greeny** *adj* ▸ **'greenly** *adv* ▸ **'greenness** *n*

greenback ('griːnˌbæk) *n US.* **1** *Inf.* a legal-tender US currency note. **2** *Sl.* a dollar bill.

green ban *n Austral.* a trade-union ban on any development that might be considered harmful to the environment.

green bean *n* any bean plant, such as the French bean, having narrow green edible pods.

green belt *n* a zone of farmland, parks, and open country surrounding a town or city.

Green Cross Code *n Brit.* a code for children giving rules for road safety.

greenery ('griːnərɪ) *n, pl* **greeneries.** green foliage, esp. when used for decoration.

green-eyed *adj* **1** jealous or envious. **2 the green-eyed monster.** jealousy or envy.

greenfield ('griːnˌfiːld) *n* (*modifier*). denoting or located in a rural area which has not previously been built on.

greenfinch ('griːnˌfɪntʃ) *n* a European finch the male of which has a dull green plumage with yellow patches on the wings and tail.

THESAURUS

paramount, primary, principal, prominent, superior **5** = **extreme**, considerable, decided, excessive, extravagant, grievous, high, inordinate, prodigious, pronounced, serious (*inf.*), strong **6** = **important**, consequential, critical, crucial, grave, heavy, momentous, serious, significant, weighty **7** = **famous**, celebrated, distinguished, eminent, exalted, excellent, famed, glorious, illustrious, notable, noteworthy, outstanding, prominent, remarkable, renowned, superb, superlative, talented, world-class **9** = **noble**, august, chivalrous, dignified, distinguished, exalted, fine, glorious, grand, heroic, high-minded, idealistic, impressive, lofty, magnanimous, princely, sublime **12** = **enthusiastic**, active, devoted, keen, zealous **13** = **skilful**, able, adept, adroit, crack (*sl.*), expert, good, masterly, proficient, skilled **14** *Informal* = **excellent**, admirable, cracking (*Brit. inf.*), fantastic (*inf.*), fine, first-rate, good, hunky-dory (*inf.*), jim-dandy (*sl.*), marvellous (*inf.*), sovereign, superb, terrific (*inf.*), tremendous (*inf.*), wonderful
Antonyms *adj* ≠ **large:** diminutive, little, small ≠ **important:** inconsequential, inconsiderable, insignificant, petty, trivial, unimportant ≠ **noble:** base, hateful, ignoble, inhumane, mean, unkind ≠ **skilful:** inexperienced, unskilled, untrained ≠ **excellent:** average, inferior, poor, secondary, second-rate, undistinguished, unnotable

greatly *adv* **5** = **very much**, abundantly, by leaps and bounds, by much, considerably, enormously, exceedingly, extremely, highly, hugely, immensely, markedly, mightily, much, notably, powerfully, remarkably, seriously (*inf.*), to the nth degree, tremendously, vastly

greatness *n* **1** = **immensity**, bulk, enormity, hugeness, largeness, length, magnitude, mass, prodigiousness, size, vastness **6** = **importance**, gravity, heaviness, import, moment, momentousness, seriousness, significance, urgency, weight **7** = **fame**, celebrity, distinction, eminence, glory, grandeur, illustriousness, lustre, note, renown **9** = **grandeur**, chivalry, dignity, disinterestedness, generosity, heroism, high-mindedness, idealism, loftiness, majesty, nobility, nobleness, stateliness, sublimity

greed *n* **1** = **gluttony**, edacity, esurience, gormandizing, hunger, insatiableness, ravenousness, voracity **2** = **avarice**, acquisitiveness, avidity, covetousness, craving, cupidity, desire, eagerness, graspingness, longing, rapacity, selfishness
Antonyms *n* ≠ **avarice:** altruism, benevolence, generosity, largesse *or* largess, munificence, self-restraint, unselfishness

greedy *adj* **1** = **grasping**, acquisitive, avaricious, covetous, edacious, esurient, gluttonous, gormandizing, hoggish, hungry, insatiable, piggish, rapacious, ravenous, selfish, voracious **2** = **eager**, avid, craving, desirous, hungry, impatient
Antonyms *adj* ≠ **grasping:** altruistic, benevolent, generous, munificent, self-restrained, unselfish

Greek *n* **2** = **Hellene** ◆ *adj* **5** = **Hellenic**

green *n* **4** = **lawn**, common, sward, turf ◆ *adj* **10** = **ecological**, conservationist, ecologically sound, environment-friendly, non-polluting, ozone-friendly **12** = **jealous**, covetous, envious, grudging, resentful **13** = **inexperienced**, callow, credulous, gullible, ignorant, immature, inexpert, ingenuous, innocent, naive, new, raw, unpolished, unpractised, unskilful, unsophisticated, untrained, unversed, wet behind the ears (*inf.*) **14** = **leafy**, blooming, budding, flourishing, fresh, grassy, new, undecayed, verdant, verdurous **16** = **new**, fresh, immature, raw, recent, unripe **17** = **nauseous**, ill, pale, sick, under the weather, unhealthy, wan

green fingers *pl n* considerable talent or ability to grow plants.

greenfly (ˈgriːnˌflaɪ) *n, pl* **greenflies.** a greenish aphid commonly occurring as a pest on garden and crop plants.

greengage (ˈgriːnˌgeɪdʒ) *n* **1** a cultivated variety of plum tree with edible green plumlike fruits. **2** the fruit of this tree. [C18: GREEN + *-gage,* after Sir W. *Gage* (1777–1864), E botanist who brought it from France]

greengrocer (ˈgriːnˌgrəʊsə) *n Chiefly Brit.* a retail trader in fruit and vegetables.
▸ **ˈgreenˌgrocery** *n*

greenheart (ˈgriːnˌhɑːt) *n* **1** Also called: **bebeeru.** a tropical American tree that has dark green durable wood. **2** any of various similar trees. **3** the wood of any of these trees.

greenhorn ➊ (ˈgriːnˌhɔːn) *n* **1** an inexperienced person, esp. one who is extremely gullible. **2** *Chiefly US.* a newcomer. [C17: orig. an animal with *green* (that is, young) horns]

greenhouse (ˈgriːnˌhaʊs) *n* **1** a building with glass walls and roof for the cultivation of plants under controlled conditions. ◆ *adj* **2** relating to or contributing to the greenhouse effect: *greenhouse gases, such as carbon dioxide.*

greenhouse effect *n* **1** an effect occurring in greenhouses, etc., in which ultraviolet radiation from the sun passes through the glass warming the contents, the infrared radiation from inside being trapped by the glass. **2** the application of this effect to a planet's atmosphere, esp. the warming up of the earth as man-made carbon dioxide in the atmosphere traps the infrared radiation emitted by the earth's surface. The greenhouse effect is made more serious by damage to the ozone layer, which permits more ultraviolet radiation to reach the earth.

greenie (ˈgriːnɪ) *n Austral. inf.* a conservationist.

greenkeeper (ˈgriːnˌkiːpə) *n* a person responsible for maintaining a golf course or bowling green.

Greenland whale *n* another name for **bowhead.**

green leek *n* any of several Australian parrots with a green or mostly green plumage.

green light ➊ *n* **1** a signal to go, esp. a green traffic light. **2** permission to proceed with a project, etc. ◆ *vb* **greenlight, greenlights, greenlighting, greenlighted.** (*tr*) **3** to permit (a project, etc.) to proceed.

greenmail (ˈgriːnˌmeɪl) *n* (esp. in the US) the practice of a company buying sufficient shares in another company to threaten takeover and making a quick profit as a result of the threatened company buying back its shares at a higher price.

green monkey disease *n* another name for **Marburg disease.**

green paper *n* (*often caps.*) (in Britain) a government document containing policy proposals to be discussed, esp. by Parliament.

Green Party *n* a political party whose policies are based on concern for the environment.

Greenpeace (ˈgriːnˌpiːs) *n* a conservationist organization founded in 1971: members take active but nonviolent measures against what are regarded as threats to environmental safety, such as the dumping of nuclear waste at sea.

green pepper *n* the green unripe fruit of the sweet pepper, eaten raw or cooked.

green pound *n* a unit of account used in calculating Britain's contributions to and payments from the Community Agricultural Fund of the EU. See also **green** (sense 15).

greenroom (ˈgriːnˌruːm, -ˌrʊm) *n* (esp. formerly) a backstage room in a theatre where performers may rest or receive visitors. [C18: prob. from its original colour]

greensand (ˈgriːnˌsænd) *n* an olive-green sandstone consisting mainly of quartz and glauconite.

greenshank (ˈgriːnˌʃæŋk) *n* a large European sandpiper with greenish legs and a slightly upturned bill.

greensickness (ˈgriːnˌsɪknɪs) *n* an informal name for **chlorosis.**

greenstick fracture (ˈgriːnˌstɪk) *n* a fracture in children in which the bone is partly bent and splinters only on the convex side of the bend. [C20: alluding to the similar way in which a green stick splinters]

greenstone (ˈgriːnˌstəʊn) *n* **1** any basic dark green igneous rock. **2** a variety of jade formerly used in New Zealand by Maoris for ornaments and tools, now used for jewellery.

greensward (ˈgriːnˌswɔːd) *n Arch. or literary.* fresh green turf or an area of such turf.

green tea *n* a sharp tea made from tea leaves that have been dried quickly without fermenting.

green turtle *n* a mainly tropical edible turtle, with greenish flesh.

green-wellie *n* (*modifier*) characterizing or belonging to the upper-class set devoted to hunting, shooting, and fishing: *the green-wellie brigade.*

Greenwich Mean Time *or* **Greenwich Time** (ˈgrɪnɪdʒ, -ɪtʃ, ˈgrɛn-) *n* mean solar time on the 0° meridian passing through Greenwich, England, measured from midnight: formerly a standard time in Britain and a basis for calculating times throughout most of the world, it has been replaced by an atomic timescale. See **universal time.** Abbrev.: **GMT.**

> **USAGE NOTE** The name **Greenwich mean time** is ambiguous, having been measured from mean midday in astronomy up to 1925, and is not used for scientific purposes. It is generally and incorrectly used in the sense of **universal coordinated time**, an atomic timescale available since 1972 from broadcast signals, in addition to the earliest sense of **universal time**, adopted internationally in 1928 as the name for GMT measured from midnight.

greenwood (ˈgriːnˌwʊd) *n* a forest or wood when the leaves are green.

greet[1] ➊ (griːt) *vb* (*tr*) **1** to meet or receive with expressions of gladness or welcome. **2** to send a message of friendship to. **3** to receive in a specified manner: *her remarks were greeted by silence.* **4** to become apparent to: *the smell of bread greeted him.* [OE *grētan*]
▸ **ˈgreeter** *n*

greet[2] (griːt) *Scot. or dialect.* ◆ *vb* **1** (*intr*) to weep; lament. ◆ *n* **2** weeping; lamentation. [from OE *grētan,* N dialect var. of *grǣtan*]

greeting ➊ (ˈgriːtɪŋ) *n* **1** the act or an instance of welcoming or saluting on meeting. **2** (*often pl*) **2a** an expression of friendly salutation. **2b** (*as modifier*): *a greetings card.*

gregarious ➊ (grɪˈgɛərɪəs) *adj* **1** enjoying the company of others. **2** (of animals) living together in herds or flocks. **3** (of plants) growing close together. **4** of or characteristic of crowds or communities. [C17: from L, from *grex* flock]
▸**greˈgariously** *adv* ▸**greˈgariousness** *n*

Gregorian calendar (grɪˈgɔːrɪən) *n* the revision of the Julian calendar introduced in 1582 by Pope Gregory XIII and still in force, whereby the ordinary year is made to consist of 365 days.

Gregorian chant *n* another name for **plainsong.**

Gregorian telescope *n* a type of reflecting astronomical telescope with a concave secondary mirror and the eyepiece set in the centre of the parabolic primary mirror. [C18: after J. *Gregory* (died 1675), Scot. mathematician]

gremial (ˈgriːmɪəl) *n RC Church.* a cloth spread upon the lap of a bishop when seated during Mass. [C17: from L *gremium* lap]

gremlin (ˈgrɛmlɪn) *n* **1** an imaginary imp jokingly said to be responsible for mechanical troubles in aircraft, esp. in World War II. **2** any mischievous troublemaker. [C20: from ?]

grenade (grɪˈneɪd) *n* **1** a small container filled with explosive thrown by hand or fired from a rifle. **2** a sealed glass vessel that is thrown and shatters to release chemicals, such as tear gas. [C16: from F, from Sp.: pomegranate, from LL, from L *grānātus* seedy; see GRAIN]

grenadier (ˌgrɛnəˈdɪə) *n* **1** *Mil.* **1a** (in the British Army) a member of the senior regiment of infantry in the Household Brigade. **1b** (formerly) a member of a special formation, usually selected for strength and height. **1c** (formerly) a soldier trained to throw grenades. **2** any of various deep-sea fish, typically having a large head and a long tapering tail. [C17: from F; see GRENADE]

grenadine[1] (ˌgrɛnəˈdiːn) *n* a light thin fabric of silk, wool, rayon, or nylon, used for dresses, etc. [C19: from F]

grenadine[2] (ˌgrɛnəˈdiːn, ˈgrɛnəˌdiːn) *n* a syrup made from pomegranate juice, used as a sweetening and colouring agent in various drinks. [C19: from F: a little pomegranate; see GRENADE]

Gresham's law *or* **theorem** (ˈgrɛʃəmz) *n* the economic hypothesis that bad money drives good money out of circulation; the superior currency will tend to be hoarded and the inferior will thus dominate the circulation. [C16: after Sir T. *Gresham* (?1519–79), E financier]

gressorial (grɛˈsɔːrɪəl) *or* **gressorious** *adj* **1** (of the feet of certain birds) specialized for walking. **2** (of birds, such as the ostrich) having such feet. [C19: from NL, from *gressus* having walked, from *gradī* to step]

grew (gruː) *vb* the past tense of **grow.**

grey ➊ *or US* **gray** (greɪ) *adj* **1** of a neutral tone, intermediate between black and white, that has no hue and reflects and transmits only a little light. **2** greyish in colour or having greyish marks. **3** dismal or dark, esp. from lack of light; gloomy. **4** conventional or dull, esp. in character or opinion. **5** having grey hair. **6** of or relating to people of middle age or above: *grey power.* **7** ancient; venerable. ◆ *n* **8** any of a group of grey tones. **9** grey cloth or clothing. **10** an animal, esp. a horse, that is grey or whitish. ◆ *vb* **11** to become or make grey. [OE *grǣg*]
▸ **ˈgreyish** *or US* **ˈgrayish** *adj* ▸ **ˈgreyly** *or US* **ˈgrayly** *adv* ▸ **ˈgreyness** *or US* **ˈgrayness** *n*

grey area *n* **1** an area or part of something existing between two extremes and having mixed characteristics of both. **2** an area, situation, etc., lacking clearly defined characteristics.

THESAURUS

greenhorn *n* **1** = **novice**, apprentice, beginner, ignoramus, ingénue, learner, naïf, neophyte, newcomer, raw recruit, simpleton, tyro

green light *n* **2** = **permission**, approval, authorization, blessing, clearance, confirmation, go-ahead (*inf.*), imprimatur, O.K. *or* okay, sanction

greet[1] *vb* **1** = **welcome**, accost, address, compliment, hail, meet, nod to, receive, salute, tip one's hat to

greeting *n* **1** = **welcome**, address, hail, reception, salutation, salute **2** *plural* = **best wishes**, compliments, devoirs, good wishes, regards, respects, salutations

gregarious *adj* **1** = **outgoing**, affable, companionable, convivial, cordial, friendly, sociable, social
Antonyms *adj* antisocial, reserved, solitary, standoffish, unsociable, withdrawn

grey *adj* **3** = **dismal**, cheerless, cloudy, dark, depressing, dim, drab, dreary, dull, foggy, gloomy, misty, murky, overcast, sunless **4** = **characterless**, anonymous, colourless, dull, indistinct, neutral, unclear, unidentifiable **7** = **old**, aged, ancient, elderly, experienced, hoary, mature, venerable

greybeard *or US* **graybeard** ('greɪˌbɪəd) *n* **1** an old man, esp. a sage. **2** a large stoneware or earthenware jar or jug for spirits.

grey eminence *n* the English equivalent of ***éminence grise.***

Grey Friar *n* a Franciscan friar.

greyhen ('greɪˌhen) *n* the female of the black grouse.

greyhound ('greɪˌhaʊnd) *n* a tall slender fast-moving breed of dog.

grey knight *n Inf.* an ambiguous intervener in a takeover battle, who makes a counterbid for the shares of the target company without having made his intentions clear. Cf. **black knight, white knight.**

greylag *or* **greylag goose** ('greɪˌlæg) *n* a large grey Eurasian goose: the ancestor of many domestic breeds of goose. US spelling: **graylag.** [C18: from GREY + LAG[1], from its migrating later than other species]

grey market *n* **1** trade in newly-issued shares before they have been formally listed and traded on the Stock Exchange. **2** a practice in which supermarkets buy excess stock of branded goods from other retailers at a low margin and then sell them at discounted prices.

grey matter *n* **1** the greyish tissue of the brain and spinal cord, containing nerve cell bodies and fibres. **2** *Inf.* brains or intellect.

grey squirrel *n* a grey-furred squirrel, native to E North America but now widely established.

greywacke ('greɪˌwækə) *n* any dark sandstone or grit having a matrix of clay minerals. [C19: partial translation of G *Grauwacke;* see WACKE]

grey water *n* water that has been used for one purpose but can be used again for another without repurification (e.g. bathwater, which can be used to water plants).

grey wolf *n* another name for **timber wolf.**

grid (grɪd) *n* **1** See **gridiron. 2** a network of horizontal and vertical lines superimposed over a map, building plan, etc., for locating points. **3** a grating consisting of parallel bars. **4 the grid.** the national network of transmission lines, pipes, etc., by which electricity, gas, or water is distributed. **5** Also called: **control grid.** *Electronics.* an electrode usually consisting of a cylindrical mesh of wires, that controls the flow of electrons between the cathode and anode of a valve. **6** See **starting grid. 7** a plate in an accumulator that carries the active substance. **8** any interconnecting system of links: *the bus service formed a grid across the country.* [C19: back formation from GRIDIRON]

grid bias *n* the fixed voltage applied between the control grid and cathode of a valve.

griddle ('grɪdᵊl) *n* **1** Also called: **girdle.** *Brit.* a thick round iron plate with a half hoop handle over the top, for making scones, etc. **2** any flat heated surface, esp. on the top of a stove, for cooking food. ◆ *vb* **griddles, griddling, griddled. 3** *(tr)* to cook (food) on a griddle. [C13: from OF *gridil,* from LL *crātīculum* (unattested) fine wickerwork; see GRILL]

griddlecake ('grɪdᵊlˌkeɪk) *n* another name for **drop scone.**

gridiron ('grɪdˌaɪən) *n* **1** a utensil of parallel metal bars, used to grill meat, fish, etc. **2** any framework resembling this utensil. **3** a framework above the stage in a theatre from which suspended scenery, lights, etc., are manipulated. **4a** the field of play in American football. **4b** an informal name for **American football.** ◆ Often shortened to **grid.** [C13 *gredire,* ? a var. (through influence of *ire* IRON) of *gredile* GRIDDLE]

gridlock ⓣ ('grɪdˌlɒk) *Chiefly US.* ◆ *n* **1** obstruction of urban traffic caused by queues of vehicles forming across junctions and causing further queues to form in the intersecting streets. **2** a point in a dispute at which no agreement can be reached: *political gridlock.* ◆ *vb* **3** *(tr)* (of traffic) to block or obstruct (an area).

grief ⓣ (gri:f) *n* **1** deep or intense sorrow, esp. at the death of someone. **2** something that causes keen distress. **3 come to grief.** *Inf.* to end unsuccessfully or disastrously. [C13: from Anglo-F *gref,* from *grever* to GRIEVE]

grievance ⓣ ('gri:vᵊns) *n* **1** a real or imaginary wrong causing resentment and regarded as grounds for complaint. **2** a feeling of resentment or injustice at having been unfairly treated. [C15 *grevance,* from OF, from *grever* to GRIEVE]

grieve ⓣ (gri:v) *vb* **grieves, grieving, grieved.** to feel or cause to feel great sorrow or distress, esp. at the death of someone. [C13: from OF *grever,* from L *gravāre* to burden, from *gravis* heavy]
▸**'griever** *n* ▸**'grieving** *n, adj*

grievous ⓣ ('gri:vəs) *adj* **1** very severe or painful: *a grievous injury.* **2** very serious; heinous: *a grievous sin.* **3** showing or marked by grief. **4** causing great pain or suffering.
▸**'grievously** *adv* ▸**'grievousness** *n*

grievous bodily harm *n Criminal law.* serious injury caused by one person to another.

griffin ('grɪfɪn), **griffon,** *or* **gryphon** *n* a winged monster with an eagle-like head and the body of a lion. [C14: from OF *grifon,* from L *gryphus,* from Gk *grups,* from *grupos* hooked]

griffon ('grɪfᵊn) *n* **1** any of various small wire-haired breeds of dog, originally from Belgium. **2** a large vulture of Africa, S Europe, and SW Asia, having a pale plumage with black wings. [C19: from F: GRIFFIN] a variant of **griffin**[1]. a variant of **griffin.**

grifter ('grɪftə) *n Sl., chiefly US.* a petty criminal or gambler. [C20: a blend of GR(AFT)[2] (sense 2) + DRIFTER (sense 2)]

grigri, gris-gris, *or* **greegree** ('gri:gri:) *n, pl* **grigris, gris-gris** (-gri:z) *or* **greegrees.** an African talisman, amulet, or charm. [of African origin]

grill (grɪl) *vb* **1** to cook (meat, etc.) by direct heat, as under a grill or over a hot fire, or (of meat, etc.) to be cooked in this way. Usual US and Canad. word: **broil. 2** *(tr; usually passive)* to torment with or as if with extreme heat: *the travellers were grilled by the scorching sun.* **3** *(tr) Inf.* to subject to insistent or prolonged questioning. ◆ *n* **4** a device with parallel bars of thin metal on which meat, etc., may be cooked by a fire; gridiron. **5** a device on a cooker that radiates heat downwards for grilling meat, etc. **6** food cooked by grilling. **7** See **grillroom.** [C17: from F *gril* gridiron, from L *crātīcula* fine wickerwork; see GRILLE]
▸**grilled** *adj* ▸**'griller** *n*

grillage ('grɪlɪdʒ) *n* an arrangement of beams and crossbeams used as a foundation on soft ground. [C18: from F, from *griller* to furnish with a grille]

grille *or* **grill** (grɪl) *n* **1** a framework, esp. of metal bars arranged to form an ornamental pattern, used as a screen or partition. **2** Also called: **radiator grille.** a grating that admits cooling air to the radiator of a motor vehicle. **3** a metal or wooden openwork grating used as a screen or divider. **4** a protective screen, usually plastic or metal, in front of the loudspeaker in a radio, record player, etc. [C17: from OF, from L *crātīcula* fine hurdlework, from *crātis* a hurdle]

grillroom ('grɪlˌru:m, -ˌrʊm) *n* a restaurant where grilled steaks and other meat are served.

grilse (grɪls) *n, pl* **grilses** *or* **grilse.** a young salmon that returns to fresh water after one winter in the sea. [C15 *grilles* (pl), from ?]

grim ⓣ (grɪm) *adj* **grimmer, grimmest. 1** stern; resolute: *grim determination.* **2** harsh or formidable in manner or appearance. **3** harshly ironic or sinister: *grim laughter.* **4** cruel, severe, or ghastly: *a grim accident.* **5** *Arch. or poetic.* fierce: *a grim warrior.* **6** *Inf.* unpleasant; disagreeable. [OE *grimm*]
▸**'grimly** *adv* ▸**'grimness** *n*

grimace ⓣ (grɪ'meɪs) *n* **1** an ugly or distorted facial expression, as of wry humour, disgust, etc. ◆ *vb* **grimaces, grimacing, grimaced. 2** *(intr)* to contort the face. [C17: from F, of Gmc origin; rel. to Sp. *grimazo* caricature]
▸**gri'macer** *n*

grimalkin (grɪ'mælkɪn, -'mɔ:l-) *n* **1** an old cat, esp. an old female cat. **2** a crotchety or shrewish old woman. [C17: from GREY + *malkin,* dim. of female name *Maud*]

grime ⓣ (graɪm) *n* **1** dirt, soot, or filth, esp. when ingrained. ◆ *vb* **grimes, griming, grimed. 2** *(tr)* to make dirty or coat with filth. [C15: from MDu. *grime*]
▸**'grimy** *adj* ▸**'griminess** *n*

grin (grɪn) *vb* **grins, grinning, grinned. 1** to smile with the lips drawn back revealing the teeth or express (something) by such a smile: *to grin a welcome.* **2** *(intr)* to draw back the lips revealing the teeth, as in a snarl or grimace. **3 grin and bear it.** *Inf.* to suffer trouble or hardship without complaint. ◆ *n* **4** a broad smile. **5** a snarl or grimace. [OE *grennian*]
▸**'grinning** *adj, n*

grind ⓣ (graɪnd) *vb* **grinds, grinding, ground. 1** to reduce or be reduced to small particles by pounding or abrading: *to grind corn.* **2** *(tr)* to smooth, sharpen, or polish by friction or abrasion: *to grind a knife.* **3** to scrape or grate together (two things, esp. the teeth) with a harsh rasping sound or (of such objects) to be scraped together. **4** *(tr; foll. by out)* to speak or say something in a rough voice. **5** *(tr; often foll. by down)* to hold

THESAURUS

gridlock *n* **2** = **standstill**, deadlock, full stop, halt, impasse, stalemate

grief *n* **1** = **sadness**, affliction, agony, anguish, bereavement, dejection, distress, grievance, hardship, heartache, heartbreak, misery, mournfulness, mourning, pain, regret, remorse, sorrow, suffering, trial, tribulation, trouble, woe **3 come to grief** *Informal* = **fail**, come unstuck, fall flat on one's face, meet with disaster, miscarry
Antonyms *n* ≠ **sadness:** cheer, comfort, consolation, delight, gladness, happiness, joy, rejoicing, solace

grievance *n* **1** = **complaint**, affliction, beef, gripe (*inf.*), hardship, injury, injustice, protest, wrong **2** = **unhappiness**, axe to grind, chip on one's shoulder (*inf.*), distress, grief, resentment, sorrow, tribulation, trouble

grieve *vb* = **mourn**, ache, bemoan, bewail, complain, deplore, lament, regret, rue, sorrow, suffer, wail, weep = **sadden**, afflict, agonize, break the heart of, crush, distress, hurt, injure, make one's heart bleed, pain, wound
Antonyms *vb* ≠ **sadden:** cheer, comfort, console, ease, gladden, please, rejoice, solace

grievous *adj* **1** = **severe**, afflicting, calamitous, damaging, distressing, dreadful, grave, harmful, heavy, hurtful, injurious, lamentable, oppressive, painful, wounding **2** = **deplorable**, appalling, atrocious, dreadful, egregious, flagrant, glaring, heinous, intolerable, lamentable, monstrous, offensive, outrageous, shameful, shocking, unbearable
Antonyms *adj* ≠ **severe:** insignificant, mild, trivial, unimportant ≠ **deplorable:** delightful, glad, happy, joyous, pleasant

grim *adj* **1** = **stern**, hard, implacable, relentless, resolute, unrelenting, unyielding **2-4** = **forbidding**, cruel, ferocious, fierce, formidable, frightful, ghastly, grisly, gruesome, harsh, hideous, horrible, horrid, merciless, morose, ruthless, severe, shocking, sinister, terrible
Antonyms *adj* ≠ **forbidding:** amiable, attractive, benign, cheerful, easy, genial, gentle, happy, kind, pleasant, soft, sympathetic

grimace *n* **1** = **scowl**, face, frown, mouth, sneer, wry face ◆ *vb* **2** = **scowl**, frown, lour *or* lower, make a face *or* faces, mouth, sneer

grime *n* **1** = **dirt**, filth, grot (*sl.*), smut, soot

grimy *adj* **1** = **dirty**, begrimed, besmeared, besmirched, filthy, foul, grubby, scuzzy (*sl.*), smutty, soiled, sooty, unclean

grind *vb* **1** = **crush**, abrade, comminute, granulate, grate, kibble, mill, pound, powder, pulverize, triturate **2** = **smooth**, file, polish, sand, sharpen, whet **3** = **scrape**, gnash, grate, grit **5** *with* **down** = **oppress**, afflict, harass, hold down, hound, persecute, plague, trouble, tyrannize (over) ◆ *n* **9** *Informal* = **hard work**, chore, drudgery, labour, sweat (*inf.*), task, toil

down; oppress; tyrannize. **6** (*tr*) to operate (a machine) by turning a handle. **7** (*tr; foll. by out*) to produce in a routine or uninspired manner: *he ground out his weekly article for the paper.* **8** (*intr*) *Inf.* to study or work laboriously. ◆ *n* **9** *Inf.* laborious or routine work or study. **10** a specific grade of pulverization, as of coffee beans: *coarse grind.* **11** the act or sound of grinding. [OE *grindan*]
▸**'grindingly** *adv*

grinder ('graɪndə) *n* **1** a person who grinds, esp. one who grinds cutting tools. **2** a machine for grinding. **3** a molar tooth.

grindstone ('graɪnd,stəʊn) *n* **1a** a machine having a circular block of stone rotated for sharpening tools or grinding metal. **1b** the stone used in this machine. **1c** any stone used for sharpening; whetstone. **2 keep** *or* **have one's nose to the grindstone.** to work hard and perseveringly.

gringo ('grɪŋgəʊ) *n, pl* **gringos.** a person from an English-speaking country: used as a derogatory term by Latin Americans. [C19: from Sp.: foreigner, prob. from *griego* Greek, hence an alien]

grip ❶ (grɪp) *n* **1** the act or an instance of grasping and holding firmly: *he lost his grip on the slope.* **2** Also called: **handgrip.** the strength or pressure of such a grasp, as in a handshake. **3** the style or manner of grasping an object, such as a tennis racket. **4** understanding, control, or mastery of a subject, problem, etc. **5** a person who manoeuvres the cameras in a film or television studio. **6 get** *or* **come to grips.** (often foll. by *with*) **6a** to deal with (a problem or subject). **6b** to tackle (an assailant). **7** Also called: **handgrip.** a part by which an object is grasped; handle. **8** Also called: **handgrip.** a travelling bag or holdall. **9** See **hairgrip. 10** any device that holds by friction, such as certain types of brake. ◆ *vb* **grips, gripping, gripped. 11** to take hold of firmly or tightly, as by a clutch. **12** to hold the interest or attention of: *the thrilling performance gripped the audience.* [OE *gripe* grasp]
▸**'gripper** *n* ▸**'gripping** *adj*

gripe ❶ (graɪp) *vb* **gripes, griping, griped. 1** (*intr*) *Inf.* to complain, esp. in a persistent nagging manner. **2** to cause sudden intense pain in the intestines of (a person) or (of a person) to experience this pain. **3** *Arch.* to clutch; grasp. **4** (*tr*) *Arch.* to afflict. ◆ *n* **5** (*usually pl*) a sudden intense pain in the intestines; colic. **6** *Inf.* a complaint or grievance. **7** *Now rare.* **7a** the act of gripping. **7b** a firm grip. **7c** a device that grips. [OE *grīpan*]
▸**'griper** *n*

Gripe Water *n Brit., trademark.* a solution given to infants to relieve colic.

grippe *or* **grip** (grɪp) *n* a former name for **influenza.** [C18: from F *grippe,* from *gripper* to seize, of Gmc origin; see GRIP]

grisaille (grɪ'zeɪl) *n* **1** a technique of monochrome painting in shades of grey, imitating the effect of relief. **2** a painting, stained-glass window, etc., in this manner. [C19: from F, from *gris* grey]

griseofulvin (,grɪzɪəʊ'fʊlvɪn) *n* an antibiotic used to treat fungal infections of the skin and hair. [C20: from NL, ult. from Med. L *griseus* grey + L *fulvus* reddish-yellow]

grisette (grɪ'zɛt) *n* (esp. formerly) a French working girl. [C18: from F, from grey fabric used for dresses, from *gris* grey]

gris-gris ('gri:gri:) *n, pl* **gris-gris** (-gri:z). a variant spelling of **grigri.**

grisly ❶ ('grɪzlɪ) *adj* **grislier, grisliest.** causing horror or dread; gruesome. [OE *grislic*]
▸**'grisliness** *n*

> **USAGE NOTE** See at **grizzly.**

grist (grɪst) *n* **1a** grain intended to be or that has been ground. **1b** the quantity of such grain processed in one grinding. **2** *Brewing.* malt grains that have been cleaned and cracked. **3 grist to** (*or* **for**) **the** (*or* **one's**) **mill.** anything that can be turned to profit or advantage. [OE *grīst*]

gristle ('grɪsᵊl) *n* cartilage, esp. when in meat. [OE *gristle*]
▸**'gristly** *adj* ▸**'gristliness** *n*

grit ❶ (grɪt) *n* **1** small hard particles of sand, earth, stone, etc. **2** Also called: **gritstone.** any coarse sandstone that can be used as a grindstone or millstone. **3** indomitable courage, toughness, or resolution. ◆ *vb* **grits, gritting, gritted. 4** to clench or grind together (two objects, esp. the teeth). **5** to cover (a surface, such as icy roads) with grit. [OE *grēot*]
▸**'gritter** *n*

Grit (grɪt) *n, adj Canad.* an informal word for **Liberal.**

grits (grɪts) *pl n* **1** hulled or coarsely ground grain. **2** *US.* See **hominy grits.** [OE *grytt*]

gritty ❶ ('grɪtɪ) *adj* **grittier, grittiest. 1** courageous; hardy; resolute. **2** of, like, or containing grit.
▸**'grittily** *adv* ▸**'grittiness** *n*

grizzle[1] ('grɪzᵊl) *vb* **grizzles, grizzling, grizzled. 1** to make or become grey. ◆ *n* **2** a grey colour. **3** grey hair. [C15: from OF *grisel,* from *gris,* of Gmc origin]

grizzle[2] ❶ ('grɪzᵊl) *vb* **grizzles, grizzling, grizzled.** (*intr*) *Inf., chiefly Brit.* (esp. of a child) to fret; whine. [C18: of Gmc origin]
▸**'grizzler** *n*

grizzled ❶ ('grɪzᵊld) *adj* **1** streaked or mixed with grey; grizzly. **2** having grey hair.

grizzly ('grɪzlɪ) *adj* **grizzlier, grizzliest. 1** somewhat grey; grizzled. ◆ *n, pl* **grizzlies. 2** See **grizzly bear.**

> **USAGE NOTE** *Grizzly* is sometimes wrongly used where *grisly* is meant: *a grisly* (not *grizzly*) *murder.*

grizzly bear *n* a variety of the brown bear, formerly widespread in W North America; its brown fur has cream or white tips on the back, giving a grizzled appearance. Often shortened to **grizzly.**

groan ❶ (grəʊn) *n* **1** a prolonged stressed dull cry expressive of agony, pain, or disapproval. **2** a loud harsh creaking sound, as of a tree bending in the wind. **3** *Inf.* a grumble or complaint, esp. a persistent one. ◆ *vb* **4** to utter (low inarticulate sounds) expressive of pain, grief, disapproval, etc. **5** (*intr*) to make a sound like a groan. **6** (*intr; usually foll. by beneath or under*) to be weighed down (by) or suffer greatly (under). **7** (*intr*) *Inf.* to complain or grumble. [OE *grānian*]
▸**'groaner** *n* ▸**'groaning** *adj, n* ▸**'groaningly** *adv*

groat (grəʊt) *n* an obsolete English silver coin worth four pennies. [C14: from MDu. *groot,* from MLow G *gros,* from Med. L (*denarius*) *grossus* thick (coin); see GROSCHEN]

groats (grəʊts) *pl n* the hulled and crushed grain of oats, wheat, or certain other cereals. [OE *grot* particle]

grocer ('grəʊsə) *n* a dealer in foodstuffs and other household supplies. [C15: from OF *grossier,* from *gros* large; see GROSS]

groceries ('grəʊsərɪz) *pl n* merchandise, esp. foodstuffs, sold by a grocer.

grocery ('grəʊsərɪ) *n, pl* **groceries.** the business or premises of a grocer.

grog (grɒg) *n* **1** diluted spirit, usually rum, as an alcoholic drink. **2** *Austral. & NZ inf.* alcoholic drink in general, esp. spirits. [C18: from Old *Grog,* nickname of Edward Vernon (1684–1757), Brit. admiral, who in 1740 issued naval rum diluted with water; his nickname arose from his grogram cloak]

groggy ❶ ('grɒgɪ) *adj* **groggier, groggiest.** *Inf.* **1** dazed or staggering, as from exhaustion, blows, or drunkenness. **2** faint or weak.
▸**'groggily** *adv* ▸**'grogginess** *n*

grogram ('grɒgrəm) *n* a coarse fabric of silk, wool, or silk mixed with wool or mohair, often stiffened with gum, formerly used for clothing. [C16: from F *gros grain* coarse grain; see GROSGRAIN]

groin (grɔɪn) *n* **1** the depression or fold where the legs join the abdomen. **2** *Euphemistic.* the genitals, esp. the testicles. **3** a variant spelling (esp. US) of **groyne. 4** *Archit.* a curved arris formed where two intersecting vaults meet. ◆ *vb* **5** (*tr*) *Archit.* to provide or construct with groins. [C15: ?from E *grynde* abyss]

grommet ('grɒmɪt) *or* **grummet** *n* **1** a ring of rubber or plastic or a metal eyelet designed to line a hole to prevent a cable or pipe passed through it from chafing. **2** *Med.* a small tube inserted into the eardrum in order to drain fluid from the middle ear, as in glue ear. [C15: from obs. F *gourmette* chain linking the ends of a bit, from *gourmer* bridle, from ?]

groom ❶ (gru:m, grʊm) *n* **1** a person employed to clean and look after horses. **2** See **bridegroom. 3** any of various officers of a royal or noble

THESAURUS

grip *n* **1** = **clasp,** handclasp (*US*), hold, purchase **4** = **control,** command, comprehension, domination, grasp, mastery, tenure, understanding **6 get** *or* **come to grips** *often foll. by* **with** = **tackle,** close with, confront, contend with, cope with, deal with, encounter, face up to, grapple with, grasp, handle, meet, take on, take the bit between one's teeth, undertake ◆ *vb* **11** = **grasp,** clasp, clutch, hold, latch on to, seize, take hold of **12** = **engross,** absorb, catch up, compel, enthral, entrance, fascinate, hold, involve, mesmerize, rivet, spellbind

gripe *vb* **1** *Informal* = **complain,** beef (*sl.*), bellyache (*sl.*), bitch (*sl.*), bleat, carp, groan, grouch (*inf.*), grouse, grumble, kvetch (*US sl.*), moan, nag, whine **2** = **ache,** compress, cramp, hurt, pain, pinch, press, squeeze ◆ *n* **5** *usually plural* = **pain,** ache, aching, affliction, colic, cramps, distress, griping, pang, pinching, stomachache, twinge **6** *Informal* = **complaint,** beef (*sl.*), grievance, groan, grouch (*inf.*), grouse, grumble, moan, objection, protest

gripping *adj* **12** = **fascinating,** compelling, compulsive, engrossing, enthralling, entrancing, exciting, riveting, spellbinding, thrilling, unputdownable (*inf.*)

grisly *adj* = **gruesome,** abominable, appalling, awful, dreadful, frightful, ghastly, grim, hellacious (*US sl.*), hideous, horrible, horrid, macabre, shocking, sickening, terrible, terrifying
Antonyms *adj* agreeable, attractive, charming, innocuous, nice, pleasant

grit *n* **1** = **gravel,** dust, pebbles, sand **3** = **courage,** backbone, balls, determination, doggedness, fortitude, gameness, guts (*inf.*), hardihood, mettle, nerve, perseverance, pluck, resolution, spirit, tenacity, toughness ◆ *vb* **4** = **grind,** clench, gnash, grate

gritty *adj* **1** = **courageous,** ballsy (*taboo sl.*), brave, determined, dogged, feisty (*inf., chiefly US & Canad.*), game, hardy, mettlesome, plucky, resolute, spirited, steadfast, tenacious, tough **2** = **rough,** abrasive, dusty, grainy, granular, gravelly, rasping, sandy

grizzle[2] *vb* = **whine,** fret, girn (*Scot.*), pule, snivel, whimper, whinge (*inf.*)

grizzled *adj* **1, 2** = **grey,** canescent, grey-haired, grey-headed, greying, griseous, grizzly, hoary

groan *n* **1** = **moan,** cry, sigh, whine **3** *Informal* = **complaint,** beef (*sl.*), gripe (*inf.*), grouse, grumble, objection, protest ◆ *vb* **4** = **moan,** cry, sigh, whine **7** *Informal* = **complain,** beef (*sl.*), bemoan, bitch (*sl.*), gripe (*inf.*), grouse, grumble, lament, object

groggy *adj* **1, 2** = **dizzy,** befuddled, confused, dazed, faint, muzzy, punch-drunk, reeling, shaky, staggering, stunned, stupefied, unsteady, weak, wobbly, woozy (*inf.*)

groom *n* **1** = **stableman,** currier (*rare*), hostler *or*

household. **4** *Arch.* a male servant. ◆ *vb* (*tr*) **5** to make or keep (clothes, appearance, etc.) clean and tidy. **6** to rub down, clean, and smarten (a horse, dog, etc.). **7** to train or prepare for a particular task, occupation, etc.: *to groom someone for the Presidency.* [C13 *grom* manservant; ? rel. to OE *grōwan* to GROW]

groomsman ('gruːmzmən, 'grʊmz-) *n, pl* **groomsmen.** a man who attends the bridegroom at a wedding, usually the best man.

groove ⓣ (gruːv) *n* **1** a long narrow channel or furrow, esp. one cut into wood by a tool. **2** the spiral channel in a gramophone record. **3** a settled existence, routine, etc., to which one is suited or accustomed. **4** *Dated sl.* an experience, event, etc., that is groovy. **5** **in the groove. 5a** *Jazz.* playing well and apparently effortlessly, with a good beat, etc. **5b** *US.* fashionable. ◆ *vb* **grooves, grooving, grooved. 6** (*tr*) to form or cut a groove in. **7** (*intr*) *Dated sl.* to enjoy oneself or feel in rapport with one's surroundings. **8** (*intr*) *Jazz.* to play well, with a good beat, etc. [C15: from obs. Du. *groeve,* of Gmc origin]

groovy ('gruːvɪ) *adj* **groovier, grooviest.** *Sl., often jocular.* attractive, fashionable, or exciting.

grope ⓣ (grəʊp) *vb* **gropes, groping, groped. 1** (*intr;* usually foll. by *for*) to feel or search about uncertainly (for something) with the hands. **2** (*intr;* usually foll. by *for* or *after*) to search uncertainly or with difficulty (for a solution, answer, etc.). **3** (*tr*) to find (one's way) by groping. **4** (*tr*) *Sl.* to fondle the body of (someone) for sexual gratification. ◆ *n* **5** the act of groping. [OE *grāpian*]
▸ **'gropingly** *adv*

groper ('grəʊpə) *or* **grouper** *n, pl* **groper, gropers** *or* **grouper, groupers.** a large marine fish of warm and tropical seas. [C17: from Port. *garupa,* prob. from a South American Indian word]

grosbeak ('grəʊsˌbiːk, 'grɒs-) *n* any of various finches that have a massive powerful bill. [C17: from F *grosbec,* from OF *gros* large, thick + *bec* BEAK[1]]

groschen ('grəʊʃən) *n, pl* **groschen. 1** an Austrian monetary unit worth one hundredth of a schilling. **2** a German coin worth ten pfennigs. **3** a former German silver coin. [C17: from G: alteration of MHG *grosse,* from Med. L (*denarius*) *grossus* thick (penny); see GROSS, GROAT]

grosgrain ('grəʊˌgreɪn) *n* a heavy ribbed silk or rayon fabric or tape for trimming clothes, etc. [C19: from F *gros grain* coarse grain; see GROSS, GRAIN]

gros point ('grəʊ 'pɔɪnt; *French* gro pwɛ̃) *n* **1** a needlepoint stitch covering two horizontal and two vertical threads. **2** work done in this stitch. [OF: large point]

gross ⓣ (grəʊs) *adj* **1** repellently or excessively fat or bulky. **2** with no deductions for expenses, tax, etc.; total: *gross sales.* Cf. **net**[2]. **3** (of personal qualities, tastes, etc.) conspicuously coarse or vulgar. **4** obviously or exceptionally culpable or wrong; flagrant: *gross inefficiency.* **5** lacking in perception, sensitivity, or discrimination: *gross judgments.* **6** (esp. of vegetation) dense; thick; luxuriant. ◆ *n* **7** (*pl* **gross**). a unit of quantity equal to 12 dozen. **8** (*pl* **grosses**). **8a** the entire amount. **8b** the great majority. ◆ *interj* **9** *Sl.* an exclamation indicating disgust. ◆ *vb* (*tr*) **10** to earn as total revenue, before deductions for expenses, tax, etc. [C14: from OF *gros* large, from LL *grossus* thick]
▸ **'grossly** *adv* ▸ **'grossness** *n*

gross domestic product *n* the total value of all goods and services produced domestically by a nation during a year. It is equivalent to gross national product minus net investment incomes from foreign nations. Abbrev.: **GDP.**

gross national product *n* the total value of all final goods and services produced annually by a nation. Abbrev.: **GNP.**

gross profit *n Accounting.* the difference between total revenue from sales and the total cost of purchases or materials, with an adjustment for stock.

gross weight *n* total weight of an article inclusive of the weight of the container and packaging.

grot (grɒt) *n Sl.* rubbish; dirt. [C20: from GROTTY]

grotesque ⓣ (grəʊ'tɛsk) *adj* **1** strangely or fantastically distorted; bizarre. **2** of or characteristic of the grotesque in art. **3** absurdly incongruous; in a ludicrous context. ◆ *n* **4** a 16th-century decorative style in which parts of human, animal, and plant forms are distorted and mixed. **5** a decorative device, as in painting or sculpture, in this style. **6** *Printing.* the family of 19th-century sans serif display types. **7** any grotesque person or thing. [C16: from F, from OIt. (*pittura*) *grottesca* cave painting, from *grotta* cave; see GROTTO]
▸ **gro'tesquely** *adv* ▸ **gro'tesqueness** *n* ▸ **gro'tesquery** *or* **gro'tesquerie** *n*

grotto ('grɒtəʊ) *n, pl* **grottoes** *or* **grottos. 1** a small cave, esp. one with attractive features. **2** a construction in the form of a cave, esp. as in landscaped gardens during the 18th century. [C17: from OIt. *grotta,* from LL *crypta* vault; see CRYPT]

grotty ('grɒtɪ) *adj* **grottier, grottiest.** *Brit. sl.* **1** nasty or unattractive. **2** of poor quality or in bad condition. [C20: from GROTESQUE]

grouch ⓣ (grautʃ) *Inf.* ◆ *vb* (*intr*) **1** to complain; grumble. ◆ *n* **2** a complaint, esp. a persistent one. **3** a person who is always grumbling. [C20: from obs. *grutch,* from OF *grouchier* to complain; see GRUDGE]
▸ **'grouchy** *adj* ▸ **'grouchily** *adv* ▸ **'grouchiness** *n*

ground[1] ⓣ (graund) *n* **1** the land surface. **2** earth or soil. **3** (*pl*) the land around a dwelling house or other building. **4** (*sometimes pl*) an area of land given over to a purpose: *football ground.* **5** land having a particular characteristic: *high ground.* **6** matter for consideration or debate; field of research or inquiry: *the report covered a lot of ground.* **7** a position or viewpoint, as in an argument or controversy (esp. in **give ground, hold, stand,** *or* **shift one's ground**). **8** position or advantage, as in a subject or competition (esp. in **gain ground, lose ground,** etc.). **9** (*often pl*) reason; justification: *grounds for complaint.* **10** *Arts.* **10a** the prepared surface applied to a wall, canvas, etc., to prevent it reacting with or absorbing the paint. **10b** the background of a painting against which the other parts of a work of art appear superimposed. **11a** the first coat of paint applied to a surface. **11b** (*as modifier*): *ground colour.* **12** the bottom of a river or the sea. **13** (*pl*) sediment or dregs, esp. from coffee. **14** *Chiefly Brit.* the floor of a room. **15** *Cricket.* the area from the popping crease back past the stumps, in which a batsman may legally stand. **16** *Electrical.* the usual US and Canad. word for **earth** (sense 8). **17** **break new ground.** to do something that has not been done before. **18** **common ground.** an agreed basis for identifying issues in an argument. **19** **cut the ground from under someone's feet.** to anticipate someone's action or argument and thus make it irrelevant or meaningless. **20** (**down**) **to the ground.** *Brit. inf.* completely; absolutely: *it suited him down to the ground.* **21** **home ground.** a familiar area or topic. **22** **into the ground.** beyond what is requisite or can be endured; to exhaustion. **23** (*modifier*) on or concerned with the ground: *ground frost; ground forces.* ◆ *vb* **24** (*tr*) to put or place on the ground. **25** (*tr*) to instruct in fundamentals. **26** (*tr*) to provide a basis or foundation for; establish. **27** (*tr*) to confine (an aircraft, pilot, etc.) to the ground. **28** (*tr*) to confine (a teenager) to the house as a punishment. **29** the usual US and Canad. word for **earth** (sense 13). **30** (*tr*) *Naut.* to run (a vessel) aground. **31** (*intr*) to hit or reach the ground. [OE *grund*]

ground[2] (graund) *vb* **1** the past tense and past participle of **grind.** ◆ *adj* **2** having the surface finished, thickness reduced, or an edge sharpened by grinding. **3** reduced to fine particles by grinding.

groundage ('graundɪdʒ) *n Brit.* a fee levied on a vessel entering a port or anchored off a shore.

groundbait ('graundˌbeɪt) *n Angling.* bait, such as bread or maggots, thrown into an area of water to attract fish.

ground bass (beɪs) *n Music.* a short melodic bass line that is repeated over and over again.

ground-breaking *adj* innovative: *a ground-breaking novel.*

ground control *n* **1** the personnel, radar, computers, etc., on the ground that monitor the progress of aircraft or spacecraft. **2** a system

THESAURUS

ostler (*arch.*), stableboy ◆ *vb* **5** = **smarten up,** clean, dress, get up (*inf.*), preen, primp, spruce up, tidy, turn out **6** = **rub down,** brush, clean, curry, tend **7** = **train,** coach, drill, educate, make ready, nurture, prepare, prime, ready

groove *n* **1** = **indentation,** channel, cut, cutting, flute, furrow, gutter, hollow, rebate, rut, score, trench, trough

grope *vb* **1, 2** = **feel,** cast about, fish, flounder, forage, fumble, grabble, scrabble, search

gross *adj* **1** = **fat,** big, bulky, corpulent, dense, great, heavy, hulking, large, lumpish, massive, obese, overweight, thick **2** = **total,** aggregate, before deductions, before tax, entire, whole **3** = **vulgar,** coarse, crude, improper, impure, indecent, indelicate, lewd, low, obscene, offensive, ribald, rude, sensual, smutty, unseemly, X-rated (*inf.*) **4** = **blatant,** apparent, arrant, downright, egregious, flagrant, glaring, grievous, heinous, manifest, obvious, outrageous, plain, rank, serious, shameful, sheer, shocking, unmitigated, unqualified, utter **5** = **coarse,** boorish, callous, crass, dull, ignorant, imperceptive, insensitive, tasteless, uncultured, undiscriminating, unfeeling, unrefined, unsophisticated ◆ *vb* **10** = **earn,** bring in, make, rake in (*inf.*), take

Antonyms *adj* ≠ **fat:** delicate, little, petite, slim, small, svelte, thin ≠ **total:** net ≠ **vulgar:** decent, delicate, proper, pure ≠ **blatant:** partial, qualified ≠ **coarse:** cultivated, elegant

grossness *n* **1** = **obesity,** bigness, bulkiness, corpulence, fatness, greatness, heaviness, lumpishness, thickness **3** = **coarseness,** bestiality, crudity, impurity, indecency, indelicacy, licentiousness, obscenity, offensiveness, ribaldry, rudeness, sensuality, smut, smuttiness, unseemliness, vulgarity **4** = **blatancy,** egregiousness, flagrancy, grievousness, obviousness, rankness, seriousness, shamefulness **5** = **insensitivity,** coarseness, crassness, ignorance, lack of taste, pig-ignorance (*sl.*), tastelessness

grotesque *adj* **1, 3** = **unnatural,** absurd, bizarre, deformed, distorted, extravagant, fanciful, fantastic, freakish, incongruous, ludicrous, malformed, misshapen, odd, outlandish, preposterous, ridiculous, strange, weird, whimsical

Antonyms *adj* average, classic, graceful, natural, normal, realistic

grouch *vb* **1** = **complain,** beef (*sl.*), bellyache (*sl.*), bitch (*sl.*), bleat, carp, find fault, gripe (*inf.*), grouse, grumble, kvetch (*US sl.*), moan, whine, whinge (*inf.*) ◆ *n* **2** = **complaint,** beef (*sl.*), grievance, gripe (*inf.*), grouse, grumble, moan, objection, protest **3** = **moaner,** complainer, crab (*inf.*), crosspatch (*inf.*), curmudgeon, faultfinder, grouser, grumbler, malcontent, whiner

grouchy *adj* **3** = **bad-tempered,** cantankerous, cross, discontented, grumbling, grumpy, huffy, ill-tempered, irascible, irritable, liverish, peevish, petulant, querulous, ratty (*Brit. & NZ inf.*), sulky, surly, testy, tetchy

ground[1] *n* **1, 2** = **earth,** clod, dirt, dry land, dust, field, land, loam, mould, sod, soil, terra firma, terrain, turf **3** *plural* = **land,** area, country, district, domain, estate, fields, gardens, habitat, holding, property, realm, terrain, territory, tract **4** = **stadium,** arena, field, park (*inf.*), pitch **9** *often plural* = **reason,** account, argument, base, basis, call, cause, excuse, factor, foundation, inducement, justification, motive, occasion, premise, pretext, rationale **13** *plural* = **dregs,** deposit, grouts, lees, sediment, settlings ◆ *vb* **25** = **instruct,** acquaint with, coach, familiarize with, inform, initiate, prepare, teach, train, tutor **26** = **base,** establish, fix, found, set, settle

for feeding radio messages to an aircraft pilot to enable him to make a blind landing.

ground cover *n* dense low herbaceous plants and shrubs that grow over the surface of the ground.

ground elder *n* a widely naturalized Eurasian umbelliferous plant with white flowers and creeping underground stems. Also called: **bishop's weed, goutweed.**

ground floor *n* **1** the floor of a building level or almost level with the ground. **2 get in on the ground floor.** *Inf.* to be in a project, undertaking, etc., from its inception.

ground frost *n* the condition resulting from a temperature reading of 0°C or below on a thermometer in contact with a grass surface.

ground glass *n* **1** glass that has a rough surface produced by grinding, used for diffusing light. **2** glass in the form of fine particles produced by grinding, used as an abrasive.

groundhog ('graʊnd,hɒg) *n* another name for **woodchuck.**

grounding ('graʊndɪŋ) *n* a foundation, esp. the basic general knowledge of a subject.

ground ivy *n* a creeping or trailing Eurasian aromatic herbaceous plant with scalloped leaves and purplish-blue flowers.

groundless ❶ ('graʊndlɪs) *adj* without reason or justification: *his suspicions were groundless.*
▸**'groundlessly** *adv* ▸**'groundlessness** *n*

groundling ('graʊndlɪŋ) *n* **1** any animal or plant that lives close to the ground or at the bottom of a lake, river, etc. **2** (in Elizabethan theatre) a spectator standing in the yard in front of the stage and paying least. **3** a person on the ground as distinguished from one in an aircraft.

groundnut ('graʊnd,nʌt) *n* **1** a North American climbing leguminous plant with small edible underground tubers. **2** the tuber of this plant. **3** *Brit.* another name for **peanut.**

ground plan *n* **1** a drawing of the ground floor of a building, esp. one to scale. **2** a preliminary or basic outline.

ground rule *n* a procedural or fundamental principle.

groundsel ('graʊnsəl) *n* any of certain plants of the composite family, esp. a Eurasian weed with heads of small yellow flowers. [OE, from *gundeswilge,* from *gund* pus + *swelgan* to swallow; after its use in poultices]

groundsheet ('graʊnd,ʃi:t) *n* a waterproof rubber, plastic, or polythene sheet placed on the ground in a tent, etc., to keep out damp.

groundsill ('graʊnd,sɪl) *n* a joist forming the lowest member of a timber frame. Also called: **ground plate.**

groundsman ('graʊndzmən) *n, pl* **groundsmen.** a person employed to maintain a sports ground, park, etc.

groundspeed ('graʊnd,spi:d) *n* the speed of an aircraft relative to the ground.

ground squirrel *n* a burrowing rodent resembling a chipmunk and occurring in North America, E Europe, and Asia. Also called: **gopher.**

groundswell ('graʊnd,swɛl) *n* **1** a considerable swell of the sea, often caused by a distant storm or earthquake. **2** a rapidly developing general feeling or opinion.

ground water *n* underground water that is held in the soil and in pervious rocks.

groundwork ❶ ('graʊnd,wɜ:k) *n* **1** preliminary work as a foundation or basis. **2** the ground or background of a painting, etc.

ground zero *n* a point on the ground directly below the centre of a nuclear explosion.

group ❶ (gru:p) *n* **1** a number of persons or things considered as a collective unit. **2a** a number of persons bound together by common social standards, interests, etc. **2b** (*as modifier*): *group behaviour.* **3** a small band of players or singers, esp. of pop music. **4** a number of animals or plants considered as a unit because of common characteristics, habits, etc. **5** an association of companies under a single ownership and control. **6** two or more figures or objects forming a design in a painting or sculpture. **7** a military formation comprising complementary arms and services: *a brigade group.* **8** an air force organization of higher level than a squadron. **9** Also called: **radical.** *Chem.* two or more atoms that are bound together in a molecule and behave as a single unit: *a methyl group* $-CH_3$. **10** a vertical column of elements in the periodic table that all have similar electronic structures, properties, and valencies: *the halogen group.* **11** *Maths.* a set under an operation involving any two members of the set such that the set is closed, associative, and contains both an identity and the inverse of each member. **12** See **blood group.** ◆ *vb* **13** to arrange or place (things, people, etc.) in or into a group, or (of things, etc.) to form into a group. [C17: from F *groupe,* of Gmc origin; cf. It. *gruppo;* see CROP]

group captain *n* an officer holding commissioned rank senior to a wing commander but junior to an air commodore in the RAF and certain other air forces.

group dynamics *n* (*functioning as sing*) *Psychol.* a field of social psychology concerned with the nature of human groups, their development, and their interactions.

grouper ('gru:pə) *n* a variant spelling of **groper.**

groupie ('gru:pɪ) *n Sl.* **1** an ardent fan of a celebrity, esp. a girl who follows the members of a pop group on tour in order to have sexual relations with them. **2** an enthusiastic follower of some activity: *a political groupie.*

Group of Five *n* France, Japan, the UK, the US, and Germany acting as a group to stabilize their currency exchange rates. Abbrev.: **G5.**

Group of Seven *n* the seven leading industrial nations excepting Russia, i.e. Canada, France, Germany, Italy, Japan, the UK, and the US, whose heads of state and finance ministers meet regularly to coordinate economic policy. Abbrev.: **G7.**

Group of Seventy-Seven *n* the developing countries of the world. Abbrev.: **G77.**

Group of Ten *n* the ten nations who met in Paris in 1961 to arrange the special drawing rights of the IMF; Belgium, Canada, France, Italy, Japan, the Netherlands, Sweden, the UK, the US, and West Germany. Also called: **Paris Club.** Abbrev.: **G10.**

Group of Three *n* Japan, the US, and Germany, regarded as the largest industrialized nations. Abbrev.: **G3.**

group practice *n* a group of doctors who together run a general practice.

group therapy *n Psychol.* the simultaneous treatment of a number of individuals who are brought together to share their problems in group discussion.

groupuscule ('gru:pə,skju:l) *n Usually derog.* a small group within a political party or movement. [C20: a blend of GROUP + *corpuscule*; see CORPUSCLE]

groupware ('gru:p,wɛə) *n* software that enables a group of computers to work together, so that users may access shared files, exchange messages, etc.

grouse[1] (graʊs) *n, pl* **grouse** *or* **grouses.** a game bird occurring mainly in the N hemisphere, having a stocky body and feathered legs and feet. [C16: from ?]

grouse[2] ❶ (graʊs) *vb* **grouses, grousing, groused. 1** (*intr*) to grumble; complain. ◆ *n* **2** a persistent complaint. [C19: from ?]
▸**'grouser** *n*

grouse[3] (graʊs) *adj Austral. & NZ sl.* fine; excellent. [from ?]

grout (graʊt) *n* **1** a thin mortar for filling joints between tiles, masonry, etc. **2** a fine plaster used as a finishing coat. **3** (*pl*) sediment or dregs. ◆ *vb* **4** (*tr*) to fill (joints) or finish (walls, etc.) with grout. [OE *grūt*]
▸**'grouter** *n*

grove ❶ (grəʊv) *n* **1** a small wooded area. **2** a road lined with houses and trees, esp. in a suburban area. [OE *grāf*]

grovel ❶ ('grɒvᵊl) *vb* **grovels, grovelling, grovelled** *or US* **grovels, groveling, groveled.** (*intr*) **1** to humble or abase oneself, as in making apologies or showing respect. **2** to lie or crawl face downwards, as in fear or humility. **3** (often foll. by *in*) to indulge or take pleasure (in sensuality or vice). [C16: back formation from obs. *groveling* (adv), from ME *on grufe* on the face, of Scand. origin; see -LING[2]]
▸**'groveller** *or US* **,groveler** *n*

grow ❶ (grəʊ) *vb* **grows, growing, grew, grown. 1** (of an organism or part of an organism) to increase in size or develop (hair, leaves, or other structures). **2** (*intr;* usually foll. by *out of* or *from*) to originate, as from an initial cause or source: *the federation grew out of the Empire.* **3** (*intr*) to increase in size, number, degree, etc.: *the population is growing rapidly.* **4** (*intr*) to change in length or amount in a specified direction: *some plants grow downwards.* **5** (*copula; may take an infinitive*) (esp. of emotions, physical states, etc.) to develop or come into existence or being gradually: *to grow cold.* **6** (*intr;* foll. by *together*) to be joined gradually by or as by growth. **7** (when *intr,* foll. by *with*) to become covered with a growth: *the path grew with weeds.* **8** to produce (plants) by controlling or encouraging their growth, esp. for home consump-

THESAURUS

groundless *adj* = **unjustified,** baseless, chimerical, empty, false, idle, illusory, imaginary, unauthorized, uncalled-for, unfounded, unprovoked, unsupported, unwarranted
Antonyms *adj* justified, logical, proven, real, reasonable, substantial, supported, true, well-founded

groundwork *n* **1** = **preliminaries,** base, basis, cornerstone, footing, foundation, fundamentals, preparation, spadework, underpinnings

group *n* **1** = **set,** aggregation, assemblage, association, band, batch, bevy, bunch, camp, category, circle, class, clique, clump, cluster, collection, company, congregation, coterie, crowd, faction, formation, gang, gathering, organization, pack, party, posse (*sl.*), troop ◆ *vb* **13** = **arrange,** assemble, associate, assort, bracket, class, classify, congregate, dispose, gather, marshal, order, organize, put together, range, sort

grouse[2] *vb* **1** = **complain,** beef, bellyache (*sl.*), bitch (*sl.*), bleat, carp, find fault, gripe (*inf.*), grouch (*inf.*), grumble, kvetch (*US sl.*), moan, whine, whinge (*inf.*) ◆ *n* **2** = **complaint,** beef (*sl.*), grievance, gripe (*inf.*), grouch (*inf.*), grumble, moan, objection, protest

grove *n* **1** = **wood,** brake, coppice, copse, covert, hurst (*arch.*), plantation, spinney, thicket, woodland

grovel *vb* **1** = **humble oneself,** abase oneself, bootlick (*inf.*), bow and scrape, brown-nose (*taboo sl.*), cower, crawl, creep, cringe, crouch, demean oneself, fawn, flatter, kiss ass (*taboo sl.*), kowtow, lick someone's arse (*taboo sl.*), lick someone's boots, pander to, sneak, toady
Antonyms *vb* be proud, domineer, face, hold one's head high, intimidate

grow *vb* **1** = **spring up,** develop, flourish, germinate, shoot, sprout, vegetate **2** = **originate,** arise, issue, spring, stem **3** = **increase,** develop, enlarge, expand, extend, fill out, get bigger, get taller, heighten, multiply, spread, stretch, swell, thicken, widen **5** = **become,** come to be, develop (into), get, turn, wax **8** = **improve,** advance, expand, flourish, progress, prosper, succeed, thrive
Antonyms *vb* ≠ **increase:** decline, decrease, die, diminish, dwindle, fail, lessen, shrink, subside, wane

tion or on a commercial basis. ◆ See also **grow into, grow on,** etc. [OE *grōwan*]
▸ **'growable** *adj* ▸ **'grower** *n*

grow bag *n* a plastic bag containing a sterile growing medium that enables a plant to be grown to full size in it, usually for one season only. [C20: from *Gro-bag*, trademark for the first ones marketed]

growing pains *pl n* **1** pains in muscles or joints sometimes experienced by growing children. **2** difficulties besetting a new enterprise in its early stages.

grow into *vb* (*intr, prep*) to become big or mature enough for: *clothes big enough for him to grow into.*

growl (graul) *vb* **1** (of animals, esp. when hostile) to utter (sounds) in a low inarticulate manner: *the dog growled.* **2** to utter (words) in a gruff or angry manner. **3** (*intr*) to make sounds suggestive of an animal growling: *the thunder growled.* ◆ *n* **4** the act or sound of growling. [C18: from earlier *grolle*, from OF *grouller* to grumble]
▸ **'growler** *n*

grown (grəun) *adj* **a** developed or advanced: *fully grown.* **b** (*in combination*): *half-grown.*

grown-up ❶ *adj* **1** having reached maturity; adult. **2** suitable for or characteristic of an adult. ◆ *n* **3** an adult.

grow on *vb* (*intr, prep*) to become progressively more acceptable or pleasant to.

grow out of *vb* (*intr, adv + prep*) to become too big or mature for: *she soon grew out of her girlish ways.*

growth ❶ (grəuθ) *n* **1** the process or act of growing. **2** an increase in size, number, significance, etc. **3** something grown or growing: *a new growth of hair.* **4** a stage of development: *a full growth.* **5** any abnormal tissue, such as a tumour. **6** (*modifier*) of, relating to, causing, or characterized by growth: *a growth industry; growth hormone.*

growth curve *n* a curve on a graph in which a variable is plotted against time to illustrate the growth of the variable.

grow up *vb* (*intr, adv*) **1** to reach maturity; become adult. **2** to come into existence; develop.

groyne *or esp. US* **groin** (grɔɪn) *n* a wall or jetty built out from a riverbank or seashore to control erosion. Also called: **spur, breakwater.** [C16: ?from OF *groign* snout, promontory]

grub ❶ (grʌb) *vb* **grubs, grubbing, grubbed. 1** (when *tr*, often foll. by *up* or *out*) to search for and pull up (roots, stumps, etc.) by digging in the ground. **2** to dig up the surface of (ground, soil, etc.), esp. to clear away roots, stumps, etc. **3** (*intr;* often foll. by *in* or *among*) to search carefully. **4** (*intr*) to work unceasingly, esp. at a dull task. ◆ *n* **5** the short legless larva of certain insects, esp. beetles. **6** *Sl.* food; victuals. **7** a person who works hard, esp. in a dull plodding way. [C13: of Gmc origin; cf. OHG *grubilōn* to dig]
▸ **'grubber** *n*

grubby ❶ ('grʌbɪ) *adj* **grubbier, grubbiest. 1** dirty; slovenly. **2** mean; beggarly. **3** infested with grubs.
▸ **'grubbily** *adv* ▸ **'grubbiness** *n*

grub screw *n* a small headless screw used to secure a sliding component in position.

grubstake ('grʌb,steɪk) *US & Canad. inf.* ◆ *n* **1** supplies provided for a prospector on the condition that the donor has a stake in any finds. ◆ *vb* **grubstakes, grubstaking, grubstaked.** (*tr*) **2** to furnish with such supplies. **3** to supply (a person) with a stake in a gambling game.
▸ **'grub,staker** *n*

Grub Street *n* **1** a former street in London frequented by literary hacks and needy authors. **2** the world or class of literary hacks, etc. ◆ *adj also* **Grubstreet. 3** (*sometimes not cap.*) relating to or characteristic of hack literature.

grudge ❶ (grʌdʒ) *n* **1** a persistent feeling of resentment, esp. one due to an insult or injury. **2** (*modifier*) planned or carried out in order to settle a grudge: *a grudge fight.* ◆ *vb* **grudges, grudging, grudged. 3** (*tr*) to give unwillingly. **4** to feel resentful or envious about (someone else's success, etc.). [C15: from OF *grouchier* to grumble, prob. of Gmc origin]
▸ **'grudging** *adj* ▸ **'grudgingly** *adv*

gruel ('gru:əl) *n* a drink or thin porridge made by boiling meal, esp. oatmeal, in water or milk. [C14: from OF, of Gmc origin]

gruelling ❶ *or US* **grueling** ('gru:əlɪŋ) *adj* **1** extremely severe or tiring. ◆ *n* **2** *Inf.* a severe or tiring experience, esp. punishment. [C19: from obs. *gruel* (vb) to punish]

gruesome ❶ ('gru:səm) *adj* inspiring repugnance and horror; ghastly. [C16: orig. Northern E and Scot., of Scand. origin]
▸ **'gruesomely** *adv* ▸ **'gruesomeness** *n*

gruff ❶ (grʌf) *adj* **1** rough or surly in manner, speech, etc. **2** (of a voice, bark, etc.) low and throaty. [C16: orig. Scot., from Du. *grof*, of Gmc origin; rel. to OE *hrēof*]
▸ **'gruffly** *adv* ▸ **'gruffness** *n*

grumble ❶ ('grʌmbᵊl) *vb* **grumbles, grumbling, grumbled. 1** to utter (complaints) in a nagging way. **2** (*intr*) to make low rumbling sounds. ◆ *n* **3** a complaint. **4** a low rumbling sound. [C16: from MLow G *grommelen*, of Gmc origin]
▸ **'grumbler** *n* ▸ **'grumblingly** *adv* ▸ **'grumbly** *adj*

grumbling appendix *n Inf.* a condition in which the appendix causes intermittent pain or discomfort but appendicitis has not developed.

grummet ('grʌmɪt) *n* a variant of **grommet.**

grump (grʌmp) *Inf.* ◆ *n* **1** a surly or bad-tempered person. **2** (*pl*) a sulky or morose mood (esp. in **have the grumps**). ◆ *vb* **3** (*intr*) to complain or grumble. [C18: dialect: surly remark, prob. imit.]

grumpy ❶ ('grʌmpɪ) *or* **grumpish** *adj* **grumpier, grumpiest.** peevish; sulky. [C18: from GRUMP + -Y[1]]
▸ **'grumpily** *or* **'grumpishly** *adv* ▸ **'grumpiness** *or* **'grumpishness** *n*

Grundy ('grʌndɪ) *n* a narrow-minded person who keeps critical watch on the propriety of others. [C18: after Mrs *Grundy*, the character in T. Morton's play *Speed the Plough* (1798)]
▸ **'Grundy,ism** *n* ▸ **'Grundyist** *or* **'Grundyite** *n*

grungy ('grʌndʒɪ) *adj* **grungier, grungiest. 1** *Sl., chiefly US & Canad.* squalid, seedy, grotty. **2** (of pop music) characterized by a loud fuzzy guitar sound. [from ?]

grunion ('grʌnjən) *n* a Californian marine fish that spawns on beaches. [C20: prob. from Sp. *gruñón* a grunter]

grunt (grʌnt) *vb* **1** (*intr*) (esp. of pigs and some other animals) to emit a low short gruff noise. **2** (when *tr, may take a clause as object*) to express something gruffly: *he grunted his answer.* ◆ *n* **3** the characteristic low short gruff noise of pigs, etc., or a similar sound, as of disgust. **4** any of various mainly tropical marine fishes that utter a grunting sound when caught. [OE *grunnettan*, prob. imit.; cf. OHG *grunnizōn, grunni* moaning]
▸ **'grunter** *n*

Gruyère *or* **Gruyère cheese** ('gru:jɛə) *n* a hard flat whole-milk cheese, pale yellow in colour and with holes. [C19: after *Gruyère*, Switzerland, where it originated]

gr. wt. *abbrev. for* gross weight. a variant of **griffin**[1]. a variant of **griffin.**

grysbok ('graɪs,bɒk) *n* either of two small antelopes of central and southern Africa, having small straight horns. [C18: Afrik., from Du. *grijs* grey + *bok* BUCK[1]]

GS *abbrev. for:* **1** General Secretary. **2** General Staff.

GST (in New Zealand) *abbrev. for* goods and services tax.

G-string *n* **1** a piece of cloth worn by striptease artistes covering the pubic area and attached to a narrow waistband. **2** a strip of cloth attached to the front and back of a waistband and covering the loins. **3** *Music.* a string tuned to G.

G-suit *n* a close-fitting garment that is worn by the crew of high-speed aircraft and can be pressurized to prevent blackout during manoeuvres. [C20: from *g(ravity) suit*]

GSVQ (in Britain) *abbrev. for* General Scottish Vocational Qualification: the Scottish equivalent of GNVQ.

THESAURUS

grown-up *adj* **1 = mature**, adult, fully-grown, of age ◆ *n* **3 = adult**, man, woman

growth *n* **1 = cultivation**, crop, development, germination, produce, production, shooting, sprouting, vegetation **2 = increase**, advance, advancement, enlargement, expansion, extension, improvement, proliferation, rise **5 = tumour**, excrescence, lump
Antonyms *n* ≠ **increase:** decline, decrease, drop, dwindling, failure, fall, lessening, shrinkage, slackening, subsiding

grub *vb* **1 = search**, ferret, forage, hunt, rummage, scour, uncover, unearth **2 = dig up**, burrow, probe, pull up, root (*inf.*), rootle (*Brit.*), search for, uproot ◆ *n* **5 = larva**, caterpillar, maggot **6** *Slang* **= food**, eats (*sl.*), feed, nosebag (*sl.*), nosh (*sl.*), rations, sustenance, tack (*inf.*), victuals, vittles (*obs. or dialect*)

grubby *adj* **1 = dirty**, besmeared, filthy, frowzy, grimy, grungy (*sl., chiefly US & Canad.*), manky (*Scot. dialect*), mean, messy, mucky, scruffy, scuzzy (*sl.*), seedy, shabby, slovenly, smutty, soiled, sordid, squalid, unkempt, untidy, unwashed

grudge *n* **1 = resentment**, animosity, animus, antipathy, aversion, bitterness, chip on one's shoulder (*inf.*), dislike, enmity, grievance, hard feelings, hate, ill will, malevolence, malice, pique, rancour, spite, venom ◆ *vb* **4 = resent**, begrudge, be reluctant, complain, covet, envy, hold back, mind, stint
Antonyms *n* ≠ **resentment:** appreciation, goodwill, liking, thankfulness ◆ *vb* ≠ **resent:** be glad for, celebrate, welcome

gruelling *adj* **1 = exhausting**, arduous, backbreaking, brutal, crushing, demanding, difficult, fatiguing, fierce, grinding, hard, harsh, laborious, punishing, severe, stiff, strenuous, taxing, tiring, trying
Antonyms *adj* cushy (*inf.*), easy, enjoyable, light, pleasant, undemanding

gruesome *adj* **= horrific**, abominable, awful, fearful, from hell (*inf.*), ghastly, grim, grisly, hellacious (*US sl.*), hideous, horrendous, horrible, horrid, horrifying, loathsome, macabre, obscene, repugnant, repulsive, shocking, spine-chilling, terrible
Antonyms *adj* appealing, benign, cheerful, pleasant, sweet

gruff *adj* **1 = surly**, bad-tempered, bearish, blunt, brusque, churlish, crabbed, crusty, curt, discourteous, grouchy (*inf.*), grumpy, ill-humoured, ill-natured, impolite, rough, rude, sour, sullen, uncivil, ungracious, unmannerly **2 = hoarse**, croaking, guttural, harsh, husky, low, rasping, rough, throaty
Antonyms *adj* ≠ **surly:** courteous, good-tempered, gracious, kind, pleasant, polite ≠ **hoarse:** mellifluous, smooth, sweet

grumble *vb* **1 = complain**, beef (*sl.*), bellyache (*sl.*), bitch (*sl.*), bleat, carp, find fault, gripe (*inf.*), grouch (*inf.*), grouse, kvetch (*US sl.*), moan, repine, whine, whinge (*inf.*) **2 = rumble**, growl, gurgle, murmur, mutter, roar ◆ *n* **3 = complaint**, beef (*sl.*), grievance, gripe (*inf.*), grouch (*inf.*), grouse, moan, objection, protest **4 = rumble**, growl, gurgle, murmur, muttering, roar

grumpy *adj* **= irritable**, bad-tempered, cantankerous, crabbed, cross, crotchety (*inf.*), edgy, grouchy (*inf.*), grumbling, huffy, ill-tempered, liverish, peevish, petulant, querulous, sulky, sullen, surly, testy, tetchy

GT *abbrev. for* gran turismo: a touring car; usually a fast sports car with a hard fixed roof.

gtd *abbrev. for* guaranteed.

guaiacum ('gwaɪəkəm) *n* **1** any of a family of tropical American evergreen trees such as the lignum vitae. **2** the hard heavy wood of any of these trees. **3** a brownish resin obtained from the lignum vitae, used medicinally and in making varnishes. **[**C16: NL, from Sp. *guayaco,* of Amerind origin**]**

guanaco (gwɑː'nɑːkəʊ) *n, pl* **guanacos.** a cud-chewing South American mammal closely related to the domesticated llama. **[**C17: from Sp., from Quechuan *huanacu***]**

guanine ('gwɑːniːn, 'guːə,niːn) *n* a white almost insoluble compound: one of the purine bases in nucleic acids. **[**C19: from GUANO + -INE[2]**]**

guano ('gwɑːnəʊ) *n, pl* **guanos. 1** the dried excrement of fish-eating sea birds, deposited in rocky coastal regions of South America: used as a fertilizer. **2** any similar but artificially produced fertilizer. **[**C17: from Sp., from Quechuan *huano* dung**]**

Guarani (,gwɑːrə'niː) *n* **1** (*pl* **Guarani** *or* **Guaranis**) a member of a South American Indian people of Paraguay, S Brazil, and Bolivia. **2** the language of this people.

guarantee ❶ (,gærən'tiː) *n* **1** a formal assurance, esp. in writing, that a product, service, etc., will meet certain standards or specifications. **2** *Law.* a promise, esp. a collateral agreement, to answer for the debt, default, or miscarriage of another. **3a** a person, company, etc., to whom a guarantee is made. **3b** a person, company, etc., who gives a guarantee. **4** a person who acts as a guarantor. **5** something that makes a specified condition or outcome certain. **6** a variant spelling of **guaranty.** ◆ *vb* **guarantees, guaranteeing, guaranteed.** (*mainly tr*) **7** (*also intr*) to take responsibility for (someone else's debts, obligations, etc.). **8** to serve as a guarantee for. **9** to secure or furnish security for: *a small deposit will guarantee any dress.* **10** (usually foll. by *from* or *against*) to undertake to protect or keep secure, as against injury, loss, etc. **11** to ensure: *good planning will guarantee success.* **12** (*may take a clause as object or an infinitive*) to promise or make certain. **[**C17: ?from Sp. *garante* or F *garant,* of Gmc origin; cf. WARRANT**]**

guarantor ❶ (,gærən'tɔː) *n* a person who gives or is bound by a guarantee or guaranty; surety.

guaranty ('gærəntɪ) *n, pl* **guaranties. 1** a pledge of responsibility for fulfilling another person's obligations in case of that person's default. **2** a thing given or taken as security for a guaranty. **3** the act of providing security. **4** a person who acts as a guarantor. ◆ *vb* **guaranties, guarantying, guarantied. 5** a variant spelling of **guarantee. [**C16: from OF *garantie,* var. of *warantie,* of Gmc origin; see WARRANTY**]**

guard ❶ (gɑːd) *vb* **1** to watch over or shield (a person or thing) from danger or harm; protect. **2** to keep watch over (a prisoner or other potentially dangerous person or thing), as to prevent escape. **3** (*tr*) to control: *to guard one's tongue.* **4** (*intr;* usually foll. by *against*) to take precautions. **5** to control entrance and exit through (a gate, door, etc.). **6** (*tr*) to provide (machinery, etc.) with a device to protect the operator. **7** (*tr*) **7a** *Chess, cards.* to protect or cover (a chessman or card) with another. **7b** *Curling, bowling.* to protect or cover (a stone or bowl) by placing one's own stone or bowl between it and another player. ◆ *n* **8** a person or group who keeps a protecting, supervising, or restraining watch or control over people, such as prisoners, things, etc. Related adj: **custodial. 9** a person or group of people, such as soldiers, who form a ceremonial escort. **10** *Brit.* the official in charge of a train. **11a** the act or duty of protecting, restraining, or supervising. **11b** (*as modifier*): *guard duty.* **12** a device, part, or attachment on an object, such as a weapon or machine tool, designed to protect the user against injury. **13** anything that provides or is intended to provide protection: *a guard against infection.* **14** *Sport.* an article of light tough material worn to protect any of various parts of the body. **15** the posture of defence or readiness in fencing, boxing, cricket, etc. **16 mount guard. 16a** (of a sentry, etc.) to begin to keep watch. **16b** (with *over*) to take a protective or defensive stance (towards something). **17 off (one's) guard.** having one's defences down; unprepared. **18 on (one's) guard.** prepared to face danger, difficulties, etc. **19 stand guard.** (of a sentry, etc.) to keep watch. **[**C15: from OF, from *garder* to protect, of Gmc origin; see WARD**]**
▸**'guarder** *n*

guarded ❶ ('gɑːdɪd) *adj* **1** protected or kept under surveillance. **2** prudent, restrained, or noncommittal: *a guarded reply.*
▸**'guardedly** *adv* ▸**'guardedness** *n*

guard hair *n* any of the coarse hairs that form the outer fur in certain mammals.

guardhouse ('gɑːd,haʊs) *or* **guardroom** ('gɑːd,ruːm, -rʊm) *n Mil.* a building serving as headquarters for military police and in which military prisoners are detained.

guardian ❶ ('gɑːdɪən) *n* **1** one who looks after, protects, or defends: *the guardian of public morals.* **2** *Law.* someone legally appointed to manage the affairs of a person incapable of acting for himself, as a minor or person of unsound mind. ◆ *adj* **3** protecting or safeguarding.
▸**'guardian,ship** *n*

Guardian Angels *pl n* vigilante volunteers who patrol the New York Underground and elsewhere, wearing red berets, to deter violent crime.

guard ring *n* **1** Also called: **keeper ring.** a ring worn to prevent another from slipping off the finger. **2** an electrode used to counteract distortion of the electric fields at the edges of other electrodes.

Guards (gɑːdz) *pl n* (esp. in European armies) any of various regiments responsible for ceremonial duties and, formerly, the protection of the head of state: *the Life Guards.*

guardsman ('gɑːdzmən) *n, pl* **guardsmen. 1** (in Britain) a member of a Guards battalion or regiment. **2** (in the US) a member of the National Guard. **3** a guard.

guard's van *n Railways, Brit. & NZ.* the van in which the guard travels, usually attached to the rear of a train. US and Canad. equivalent: **caboose.**

guava ('gwɑːvə) *n* **1** any of various tropical American trees, grown esp. for their edible fruit. **2** the fruit of such a tree, having yellow skin and pink pulp. **[**C16: from Sp. *guayaba,* from a South American Indian word**]**

guayule (gwə'juːlɪ) *n* **1** a bushy shrub of the southwestern US. **2** rubber derived from the sap of this plant. **[**from American Sp., from Nahuatl *cuauhuli,* from *cuahuitl* tree + *uli* gum**]**

gubbins ('gʌbɪnz) *n* **1** (*functioning as sing*) an object of little value. **2** (*functioning as sing*) a small gadget. **3** (*functioning as pl*) odds and ends; rubbish. **4** (*functioning as sing*) a silly person. **[**C16 (meaning: fragments): from obs. *gobbon***]**

gubernatorial (,gjuːbənə'tɔːrɪəl, ,guː-) *adj Chiefly US.* of or relating to a governor. **[**C18: from L *gubernātor* governor**]**

guddle ('gʌd[ə]l) *Scot.* ◆ *vb* **guddles, guddling, guddled. 1** to catch (fish) by groping with the hands under the banks or stones of a stream. ◆ *n* **2** a muddle; confusion. **[**C19: from ?**]**

gudgeon[1] ('gʌdʒən) *n* **1** a small slender European freshwater fish with a barbel on each side of the mouth: used as bait by anglers. **2** any of various other fishes, such as the goby. **3** *Sl.* a person who is easy to trick or cheat. ◆ *vb* **4** (*tr*) *Sl.* to trick or cheat. **[**C15: from OF *gougon,* prob. from L *gōbius;* see GOBY**]**

gudgeon[2] ('gʌdʒən) *n* **1** the female or socket portion of a pinned hinge. **2** *Naut.* one of two or more looplike sockets, fixed to the transom of a boat, into which the pintles of a rudder are fitted. **[**C14: from OF *goujon,* ?from LL *gulbia* chisel**]**

gudgeon pin *n Brit.* the pin through the skirt of a piston in an internal-combustion engine, to which the little end of the connecting rod is attached. US and Canad. name: **wrist pin.**

guelder-rose ('gɛldə,rəʊz) *n* a Eurasian shrub with clusters of white flowers and small red fruits. **[**C16: from Du. *geldersche roos,* from *Gelderland* or *Gelders,* province of Holland**]**

guenon (gə'nɒn) *n* a slender agile Old World monkey inhabiting wooded regions of Africa and having long hind limbs and tail and long hair surrounding the face. **[**C19: from F, from ?**]**

guerdon ('gɜːd[ə]n) *Poetic.* ◆ *n* **1** a reward or payment. ◆ *vb* **2** (*tr*) to give a guerdon to. **[**C14: from OF *gueredon,* of Gmc origin; final element infl. by L *dōnum* gift**]**

Guernsey ('gɜːnzɪ) *n* **1** a breed of dairy cattle producing rich creamy milk, originating from the island of Guernsey, one of the Channel Islands. **2** (*sometimes not cap.*) a seaman's knitted woollen sweater. **3** (*not cap.*) *Austral.* a sleeveless woollen shirt or jumper worn by a football player. **4 get a guernsey.** *Austral.* to be selected or gain recognition for something.

guerrilla ❶ *or* **guerilla** (gə'rɪlə) *n* **a** a member of an irregular usually politically motivated armed force that combats stronger regular forces. **b** (*as modifier*): *guerrilla warfare.* **[**C19: from Sp., dim. of *guerra* WAR**]**

guess ❶ (gɛs) *vb* (when *tr, may take a clause as object*) **1** (when *intr,* often foll. by *at* or *about*) to form or express an uncertain estimate or conclusion (about something), based on insufficient information: *guess what we're having for dinner.* **2** to arrive at a correct estimate of (something) by guessing: *he guessed my age.* **3** *Inf., chiefly US & Canad.* to be-

THESAURUS

guarantee *n* **1** = **assurance**, bond, certainty, collateral, covenant, earnest, guaranty, pledge, promise, security, surety, undertaking, warranty, word, word of honour ◆ *vb* **7, 11** = **ensure**, answer for, assure, certify, insure, maintain, make certain, pledge, promise, protect, secure, stand behind, swear, vouch for, warrant

guarantor *n* = **underwriter**, backer, bailsman (*rare*), bondsman, guarantee, sponsor, supporter, surety, voucher, warrantor

guard *vb* **1** = **watch over**, cover, defend, escort, keep, mind, oversee, patrol, police, preserve, protect, safeguard, save, screen, secure, shelter, shield, supervise, tend, watch ◆ *n* **8** = **protector**, custodian, defender, lookout, picket, sentinel, sentry, warder, watch, watchman **9** = **escort**, convoy, patrol **11** = **watchfulness**, attention, care, caution, heed, vigilance, wariness **12, 13** = **protection**, buffer, bulwark, bumper, defence, pad, rampart, safeguard, screen, security, shield **17 off guard** = **unprepared**, napping, unready, unwary, with one's defences down **18 on guard** = **prepared**, alert, cautious, circumspect, on the alert, on the lookout, on the qui vive, ready, vigilant, wary, watchful

guarded *adj* **2** = **cautious**, cagey (*inf.*), careful, circumspect, discreet, leery (*sl.*), noncommittal, prudent, reserved, restrained, reticent, suspicious, wary

guardian *n* **1** = **keeper**, attendant, champion, curator, custodian, defender, escort, guard, preserver, protector, trustee, warden, warder

guerrilla *n* = **freedom fighter**, irregular, member of the underground *or* resistance, partisan, underground fighter

guess *vb* **1** = **estimate**, conjecture, fathom, hypothesize, penetrate, predict, solve, speculate, work out **3** = **suppose**, believe, conjecture, dare say, deem, divine, fancy, hazard, imagine, judge, reckon, surmise, suspect, think ◆ *n* **4** = **supposition**, ballpark figure (*inf.*), conjecture,

lieve, think, or suppose (something): *I guess I'll go now.* ◆ *n* **4** an estimate or conclusion arrived at by guessing: *a bad guess.* **5** the act of guessing. [C13: prob. from ON]
▸ **'guesser** *n*

guesstimate *or* **guestimate** *Inf.* ◆ *n* ('gɛstɪmɪt). **1** an estimate calculated mainly or only by guesswork. ◆ *vb* ('gɛstɪˌmeɪt), **guesstimates, guesstimating, guesstimated.** (*tr*) **2** to form a guesstimate of.

guesswork Ⓣ ('gɛsˌwɜːk) *n* **1** a set of conclusions, estimates, etc., arrived at by guessing. **2** the process of making guesses.

guest Ⓣ (gɛst) *n* **1** a person who is entertained, taken out to eat, etc., and paid for by another. **2a** a person who receives hospitality at the home of another. **2b** (*as modifier*): *the guest room.* **3a** a person who receives the hospitality of a government, establishment, or organization. **3b** (*as modifier*): *a guest speaker.* **4a** an actor, contestant, entertainer, etc., taking part as a visitor in a programme in which there are also regular participants. **4b** (*as modifier*): *a guest appearance.* **5** a patron of a hotel, boarding house, restaurant, etc. ◆ *vb* **6** (*intr*) (in theatre and broadcasting) to be a guest: *to guest on a show.* [OE *giest* guest, stranger, enemy]

guest beer *n* a draught beer stocked by a bar, often for a limited period, in addition to its usual range.

guesthouse ('gɛstˌhaʊs) *n* a private home or boarding house offering accommodation.

guest rope *n Naut.* any line trailed over the side of a vessel as a convenience for boats drawing alongside, as an aid in towing, etc.

guff Ⓣ (gʌf) *n Sl.* ridiculous or insolent talk. [C19: imit. of empty talk]

guffaw (gʌ'fɔː) *n* **1** a crude and boisterous laugh. ◆ *vb* **2** to laugh or express (something) in this way. [C18: imit.]

guidance Ⓣ ('gaɪdᵊns) *n* **1** leadership, instruction, or direction. **2a** counselling or advice on educational, vocational, or psychological matters. **2b** (*as modifier*): *the marriage-guidance counsellor.* **3** something that guides. **4** any process by which the flight path of a missile is controlled in flight.

guide Ⓣ (gaɪd) *vb* **guides, guiding, guided. 1** to lead the way for (a person). **2** to control the movement or course of (an animal, vehicle, etc.) by physical action; steer. **3** to supervise or instruct (a person). **4** (*tr*) to direct the affairs of (a person, company, nation, etc.). **5** (*tr*) to advise or influence (a person) in his standards or opinions: *let truth guide you.* ◆ *n* **6a** a person, animal, or thing that guides. **6b** (*as modifier*): *a guide dog.* **7** a person, usually paid, who conducts tour expeditions, etc. **8** a model or criterion, as in moral standards or accuracy. **9** Also called: **guidebook.** a handbook with information for visitors to a place. **10** a book that instructs or explains the fundamentals of a subject or skill. **11** any device that directs the motion of a tool or machine part. **12** a mark, sign, etc., that points the way. **13a** *Naval.* a ship in a formation used as a reference for manoeuvres. **13b** *Mil.* a soldier stationed to one side of a column or line to regulate alignment, show the way, etc. [C14: from (O)F *guider,* of Gmc origin]
▸ **'guidable** *adj* ▸ **'guider** *n*

Guide (gaɪd) *n* (*sometimes not cap.*) a member of an organization for girls equivalent to the Scouts. US equivalent: **Girl Scout.**

guided missile *n* a missile, esp. one that is rocket-propelled, having a flight path controlled either by radio signals or by internal preset or self-actuating homing devices.

guide dog *n* a dog that has been specially trained to accompany someone who is blind, enabling the blind person to move about safely.

guideline ('gaɪdˌlaɪn) *n* a principle put forward to set standards or determine a course of action.

guidepost ('gaɪdˌpəʊst) *n* **1** a sign on a post by a road indicating directions. **2** a principle or guideline.

Guider ('gaɪdə) *n* (*sometimes not cap.*) a woman leader of a company of Guides or of a pack of Brownie Guides.

guidon ('gaɪdᵊn) *n* **1** a small pennant, used as a marker or standard, esp. by cavalry regiments. **2** the man or vehicle that carries this. [C16: from F, from OProvençal *guidoo,* from *guida* GUIDE]

guild Ⓣ *or* **gild** (gɪld) *n* **1** an organization, club, or fellowship. **2** (esp. in medieval Europe) an association of men sharing the same interests, such as merchants or artisans: formed for mutual aid and protection and to maintain craft standards. [C14: from ON; cf. *gjald* payment, *gildi* guild; rel. to OE *gield* offering, OHG *gelt* money]
▸ **'guildsman, 'gildsman** *or* (*fem*) **'guildswoman, 'gildswoman** *n*

guilder ('gɪldə) *or* **gulden** *n, pl* **guilders, guilder** *or* **guldens, gulden. 1** Also: **gilder, florin.** the standard monetary unit of the Netherlands, divided into 100 cents. **2** any of various former gold or silver coins of Germany, Austria, or the Netherlands. [C15: from MDu. *gulden,* lit.: GOLDEN]

guildhall ('gɪldˌhɔːl) *n Brit.* **a** the hall of a guild or corporation. **b** a town hall.

guile Ⓣ (gaɪl) *n* clever or crafty character or behaviour. [C18: from OF *guile,* of Gmc origin; see WILE]
▸ **'guileful** *adj* ▸ **'guilefully** *adv* ▸ **'guilefulness** *n* ▸ **'guileless** *adj* ▸ **'guilelessly** *adv* ▸ **'guilelessness** *n*

guillemot ('gɪlɪˌmɒt) *n* a northern oceanic diving bird having a black-and-white plumage and long narrow bill. [C17: from F, dim. of *Guillaume* William]

guilloche (gɪ'lɒʃ) *n* an ornamental border with a repeating pattern of two or more interwoven wavy lines, as in architecture. [C19: from F: tool used in ornamental work, ?from *Guillaume* William]

guillotine *n* ('gɪləˌtiːn). **1a** a device for beheading persons, consisting of a weighted blade set between two upright posts. **1b the guillotine.** execution by this instrument. **2** a device for cutting or trimming sheet material, such as paper or sheet metal, consisting of a slightly inclined blade that descends onto the sheet. **3** a surgical instrument for removing tonsils, growths in the throat, etc. **4** (in Parliament, etc.) a form of closure under which a bill is divided into compartments, groups of which must be completely dealt with each day. ◆ *vb* (ˌgɪlə'tiːn), **guillotines, guillotining, guillotined.** (*tr*) **5** to behead (a person) by guillotine. **6** (in Parliament, etc.) to limit debate on (a bill, motion, etc.) by the guillotine. [C18: from F, after Joseph Ignace *Guillotin* (1738–1814), F physician, who advocated its use in 1789]
▸ **ˌguillo'tiner** *n*

guilt Ⓣ (gɪlt) *n* **1** the fact or state of having done wrong or committed an offence. **2** responsibility for a criminal or moral offence deserving punishment or a penalty. **3** remorse or self-reproach caused by feeling that one is responsible for a wrong or offence. **4** *Arch.* sin or crime. [OE *gylt,* from ?]

guiltless Ⓣ ('gɪltlɪs) *adj* free of all responsibility for wrongdoing or crime; innocent.
▸ **'guiltlessly** *adv* ▸ **'guiltlessness** *n*

guilty Ⓣ ('gɪltɪ) *adj* **guiltier, guiltiest. 1** responsible for an offence or misdeed. **2** *Law.* having committed an offence or adjudged to have done so: *the accused was found guilty.* **3** of, showing, or characterized by guilt.
▸ **'guiltily** *adv* ▸ **'guiltiness** *n*

guimpe (gɪmp) *n* a variant spelling of **gimp.**

guinea ('gɪnɪ) *n* **1a** a British gold coin taken out of circulation in 1813, worth 21 shillings. **1b** the sum of 21 shillings (1.05), still used in quoting professional fees. **2** See **guinea fowl.** [C16: the coin was orig. made of gold from Guinea]

guinea fowl *or* **guinea** *n* a domestic fowl of Africa and SW Asia, having a dark plumage mottled with white, a naked head and neck, and a heavy rounded body.

THESAURUS

feeling, hypothesis, judgment, notion, prediction, reckoning, shot in the dark, speculation, surmise, suspicion, theory
Antonyms *vb* ≠ **estimate, suppose:** be certain, be sure, know, prove, show ◆ *n* ≠ **supposition:** certainty, fact

guesswork *n* **1** = **speculation,** conjecture, estimation, presumption, supposition, surmise, suspicion, theory

guest *n* **2** = **visitor,** boarder, caller, company, lodger, visitant

guff *n* = **nonsense,** balderdash, bull (*sl.*), bunkum *or* buncombe (*chiefly US*), drivel, empty talk, eyewash (*inf.*), garbage (*inf.*), hogwash, hokum (*sl., chiefly US & Canad.*), hot air (*inf.*), humbug, moonshine, pap, piffle (*inf.*), poppycock (*inf.*), rot, rubbish, tommyrot, tosh (*sl., chiefly Brit.*), trash, tripe (*inf.*)

guidance *n* **1** = **advice,** auspices, conduct, control, counsel, counselling, direction, government, help, instruction, intelligence, leadership, management, teaching

guide *vb* **1** = **lead,** accompany, attend, conduct, convoy, direct, escort, pilot, shepherd, show the way, steer, usher **2** = **steer,** command, control, direct, handle, manage, manoeuvre **3, 5** = **supervise,** advise, counsel, educate, govern, influence, instruct, oversee, regulate, rule, superintend, sway, teach, train ◆ *n* **6** = **escort,** adviser, attendant, chaperon, cicerone, conductor, controller, counsellor, director, dragoman, guru, leader, mentor, monitor, pilot, steersman, teacher, torchbearer, usher **8** = **model,** criterion, example, exemplar, ideal, imago (*Psychoanalysis*), inspiration, lodestar, master, par, paradigm, standard **9, 10** = **guidebook,** Baedeker, catalogue, directory, handbook, instructions, key, manual, vade mecum **12** = **pointer,** beacon, clue, guiding light, key, landmark, lodestar, mark, marker, sign, signal, signpost

guild *n* **1** = **society,** association, brotherhood, club, company, corporation, fellowship, fraternity, league, lodge, order, organization, union

guile *n* = **cunning,** art, artfulness, artifice, cleverness, craft, craftiness, deceit, deception, duplicity, gamesmanship (*inf.*), knavery, ruse, sharp practice, slyness, treachery, trickery, trickiness, wiliness
Antonyms *n* candour, frankness, honesty, sincerity, truthfulness

guileful *adj* = **cunning,** artful, clever, crafty, deceitful, duplicitous, foxy, sly, sneaky, treacherous, tricky, underhand, wily

guileless *adj* = **artless,** above-board, candid, frank, genuine, honest, ingenuous, innocent, naive, natural, open, simple, simple-minded, sincere, straightforward, truthful, undesigning, unsophisticated, upfront (*inf.*)

guilt *n* **1, 2** = **culpability,** blame, blameworthiness, criminality, delinquency, guiltiness, iniquity, misconduct, responsibility, sinfulness, wickedness, wrong, wrongdoing **3** = **remorse,** bad conscience, contrition, disgrace, dishonour, guiltiness, guilty conscience, infamy, regret, self-condemnation, self-reproach, shame, stigma
Antonyms *n* ≠ **culpability:** blamelessness, innocence, righteousness, sinlessness, virtue ≠ **remorse:** honour, pride, self-respect

guiltless *adj* = **innocent,** blameless, clean (*sl.*), clear, immaculate, impeccable, irreproachable, pure, sinless, spotless, squeaky-clean, unimpeachable, unsullied, untainted, untarnished

guilty *adj* **1, 2** = **culpable,** at fault, blameworthy, convicted, criminal, delinquent, erring, evil, felonious, iniquitous, offending, reprehensible, responsible, sinful, to blame, wicked, wrong **3** = **remorseful,** ashamed, conscience-stricken, contrite, hangdog, regretful, rueful, shamefaced, sheepish, sorry
Antonyms *adj* ≠ **culpable:** blameless, innocent, moral, righteous, virtuous ≠ **remorseful:** proud

guinea hen *n* a guinea fowl, esp. a female.

guinea pig *n* **1** a domesticated cavy, commonly kept as a pet and used in scientific experiments. **2** a person or thing used for experimentation. [C17: from ?]

guipure (gɪ'pjʊə) *n* **1** Also called: **guipure lace.** any of many types of heavy lace that have their pattern connected by threads, rather than supported on a net mesh. **2** a heavy corded trimming; gimp. [C19: from OF, from *guiper* to cover with cloth, of Gmc origin]

guise ❶ (gaɪz) *n* **1** semblance or pretence: *under the guise of friendship.* **2** external appearance in general. **3** *Arch.* manner or style of dress. [C13: from OF *guise,* of Gmc origin]

guising ('gaɪzɪŋ) *n* (in Scotland and N England) the practice or custom of disguising oneself in fancy dress, often with mask, and visiting people's houses, esp. at Halloween.
▸'**guiser** *n*

guitar (gɪ'tɑː) *n* a plucked stringed instrument originating in Spain, usually having six strings, a flat sounding board with a circular sound hole in the centre, a flat back, and a fretted fingerboard. [C17: from Sp. *guitarra,* from Ar. *qītār,* from Gk: CITHARA]
▸**gui'tarist** *n*

Gulag ('guːlæg) *n* **1** (formerly) the central administrative department of the Soviet security service, responsible for maintaining prisons and labour camps. **2** (*not cap.*) any system used to silence dissidents. [C20: from Russian *G(lavnoye) U(pravleniye Ispravitelno-Trudovykh) Lag(erei)* Main Administration for Corrective Labour Camps]

gulch (gʌltʃ) *n US & Canad.* a narrow ravine cut by a fast stream. [C19: from ?]

gulden ('gʊldᵊn) *n, pl* **guldens** *or* **gulden.** a variant of **guilder.**

gules (gjuːlz) *adj* (*usually postpositive*), *n Heraldry.* red. [C14: from OF *gueules* red fur worn around the neck, from *gole* throat, from L *gula* GULLET]

gulf ❶ (gʌlf) *n* **1** a large deep bay. **2** a deep chasm. **3** something that divides or separates, such as a lack of understanding. **4** something that engulfs, such as a whirlpool. ◆ *vb* **5** (*tr*) to swallow up; engulf. [C14: from OF *golfe,* from It. *golfo,* from Gk *kolpos*]

Gulf States *pl n* **the. 1** the oil-producing states around the Persian Gulf: Iran, Iraq, Kuwait, Saudi Arabia, Bahrain, Qatar, the United Arab Emirates, and Oman. **2** the states of the US that border on the Gulf of Mexico: Alabama, Florida, Louisiana, Mississippi, and Texas.

Gulf Stream *n* a relatively warm ocean current flowing northeastwards from the Gulf of Mexico towards NW Europe. Also called: **North Atlantic Drift.**

Gulf War *n* **1** the war (1991) between US-led UN forces and Iraq, following Iraq's invasion of Kuwait. **2** See **Iran-Iraq War.**

Gulf War syndrome *n* a group of various debilitating symptoms experienced by many soldiers who served in the Gulf War of 1991. It is claimed to be associated with damage to the central nervous system, caused by exposure to pesticides containing organophosphates.

gulfweed ('gʌlf,wiːd) *n* a brown seaweed having air bladders and forming dense floating masses in tropical Atlantic waters, esp. the Gulf Stream. Also called: **sargasso, sargasso weed.**

gull[1] (gʌl) *n* an aquatic bird such as the common gull or mew having long pointed wings, short legs, and a mostly white plumage. [C15: of Celtic origin]

gull[2] ❶ (gʌl) *Arch.* ◆ *n* **1** a person who is easily fooled or cheated. ◆ *vb* **2** (*tr*) to fool, cheat, or hoax. [C16: ?from dialect *gull* unfledged bird, prob. from *gul,* from ON *gulr* yellow]

gullet ❶ ('gʌlɪt) *n* **1** a less formal name for the **oesophagus. 2** the throat or pharynx. [C14: from OF *goulet,* dim. of *goule,* from L *gula* throat]

gullible ❶ ('gʌlɪbᵊl) *adj* easily taken in or tricked.
▸,**gulli'bility** *n* ▸'**gullibly** *adv*

gully ❶ *or* **gulley** ('gʌlɪ) *n, pl* **gullies** *or* **gulleys. 1** a channel or small valley, esp. one cut by heavy rainwater. **2** *NZ.* a bush-clad small valley. **3** *Cricket.* **3a** a fielding position between the slips and point. **3b** a fielder in this position. ◆ *vb* **gullies, gullying, gullied** *or* **gulleys, gulleying, gulleyed. 4** (*tr*) to make channels in (the ground, sand, etc.). [C16: from F *goulet* neck of a bottle; see GULLET]

gulp ❶ (gʌlp) *vb* **1** (*tr;* often foll. by *down*) to swallow rapidly, esp. in large mouthfuls. **2** (*tr;* often foll. by *back*) to stifle or choke: *to gulp back sobs.* **3** (*intr*) to swallow air convulsively because of nervousness, surprise, etc. **4** (*intr*) to make a noise, as when swallowing too quickly. ◆ *n* **5** the act of gulping. **6** the quantity taken in a gulp. [C15: from MDu. *gulpen,* imit.]
▸'**gulper** *n* ▸'**gulpingly** *adv* ▸'**gulpy** *adj*

gum[1] ❶ (gʌm) *n* **1** any of various sticky substances that exude from certain plants, hardening on exposure to air and dissolving or forming viscous masses in water. **2** any of various products, such as adhesives, that are made from such substances. **3** any sticky substance used as an adhesive; mucilage; glue. **4** See **chewing gum, bubble gum,** and **gumtree. 5** *NZ.* See **kauri gum. 6** *Chiefly Brit.* a gumdrop. ◆ *vb* **gums, gumming, gummed. 7** to cover or become covered, clogged, or stiffened as with gum. **8** (*tr*) to stick together or in place with gum. **9** (*intr*) to emit or form gum. ◆ See also **gum up.** [C14: from OF *gomme,* from L *gummi,* from Gk *kommi,* from Egyptian *kemai*]

gum[2] (gʌm) *n* the fleshy tissue that covers the jawbones around the bases of the teeth. Technical name: **gingiva.** Related adj: **gingival.** [OE *gōma* jaw]

gum ammoniac *n* another name for **ammoniac.**

gum arabic *n* a gum exuded by certain acacia trees, used in the manufacture of ink, food thickeners, pills, emulsifiers, etc. Also called: **gum acacia.**

gumbo ('gʌmbəʊ) *n, pl* **gumbos.** *US.* **1** the mucilaginous pods of okra. **2** another name for **okra. 3** a soup or stew thickened with okra pods. **4** a fine soil in the W prairies that becomes muddy when wet. [C19: from Louisiana F *gombo,* of Bantu origin]

gumboil ('gʌm,bɔɪl) *n* an abscess on the gums.

gumboots ('gʌm,buːts) *pl n* another name for **Wellington boots** (sense 1).

gum-digger *n NZ.* a person who digs for fossilized kauri gum in a **gum-field,** an area where it is found buried.

gumdrop ('gʌm,drɒp) *n* a small jelly-like sweet containing gum arabic and various colourings and flavourings. Also called (esp. Brit.): **gum.**

gummy[1] ❶ ('gʌmɪ) *adj* **gummier, gummiest. 1** sticky or tacky. **2** consisting of, coated with, or clogged by gum or a similar substance. **3** producing gum. [C14: from GUM[1] + -Y[1]]
▸'**gumminess** *n*

gummy[2] ('gʌmɪ) *adj* **gummier, gummiest. 1** toothless. ◆ *n, pl* **gummies. 2** Also called: **gummy shark.** *Austral.* a small crustacean-eating shark with flat crushing teeth. [C20: from GUM[2] + -Y[1]]

gum nut *n Austral.* the hardened seed container of the gumtree *Eucalyptus gummifera.*

gumption ❶ ('gʌmpʃən) *n Inf.* **1** *Brit.* common sense or resourcefulness. **2** initiative or courage. [C18: orig. Scot., from ?]

gum resin *n* a mixture of resin and gum obtained from various plants and trees.

gumtree ('gʌm,triː) *n* **1** any of various trees that yield gum, such as the eucalyptus, sweet gum, and sour gum. Sometimes shortened to **gum. 2 up a gumtree.** *Inf.* in a very awkward position; in difficulties.

gum up *vb* (*tr, adv*) **1** to cover, dab, or stiffen with gum. **2** *Inf.* to make a mess of; bungle (often in **gum up the works**).

gun ❶ (gʌn) *n* **1a** a weapon with a metallic tube or barrel from which a missile is discharged, usually by force of an explosion. It may be portable or mounted. **1b** (*as modifier*): *a gun barrel.* **2** the firing of a gun as a salute or signal, as in military ceremonial. **3** a member of or a place in a shooting party or syndicate. **4** any device used to project something under pressure: *a spray gun.* **5** *US sl.* an armed criminal; gunman. **6** *Austral. & NZ sl.* **6a** an expert. **6b** (*as modifier*): *a gun shearer.* **7 give it the gun.** *Sl.* to increase speed, effort, etc., to a considerable or maximum degree. **8 go great guns.** *Sl.* to act or function with great speed, intensity, etc. **9 jump** *or* **beat the gun. 9a** (of a runner, etc.) to set off before the starting signal is given. **9b** *Inf.* to act prematurely. **10 stick to one's guns.** *Inf.* to maintain one's opinions or intentions in spite of opposition. ◆ *vb* **guns, gunning, gunned. 11** (when *tr,* often foll. by *down*) to shoot (someone) with a gun. **12** (*tr*) to press hard on the accelerator of (an engine): *to gun the engine.* **13** (*intr*) to hunt with a gun. ◆ See also **gun for.** [C14: prob. from a female pet name, from the Scand. name *Gunnhildr* (from ON *gunnr* war + *hildr* war)]

gunboat ('gʌn,bəʊt) *n* a small shallow-draft vessel carrying mounted guns and used by coastal patrols, etc.

gunboat diplomacy *n* diplomacy conducted by threats of military intervention.

guncotton ('gʌn,kɒtᵊn) *n* cellulose nitrate containing a relatively large amount of nitrogen: used as an explosive.

gun dog *n* **1** a dog trained to work with a hunter or gamekeeper, esp. in retrieving, pointing at, or flushing game. **2** a dog belonging to any breed adapted to these activities.

gunfight ('gʌn,faɪt) *n Chiefly US.* a fight between persons using firearms.
▸'**gun,fighter** *n*

THESAURUS

guise *n* **1, 2** = **form,** air, appearance, aspect, behaviour, demeanour, disguise, dress, façade, face, fashion, front, mask, mode, pretence, semblance, shape, show

gulf *n* **1** = **bay,** bight, sea inlet **2** = **chasm,** abyss, breach, cleft, gap, opening, rent, rift, separation, split, void, whirlpool

gull[2] *n* **1** = **dupe,** babe in arms (*inf.*), chump, easy mark (*sl.*), fool, mug (*sl.*), sap (*sl.*), simpleton, sucker (*sl.*) ◆ *vb* **2** = **deceive,** beguile, cheat, con (*sl.*), cozen, defraud, dupe, hoax, pull a fast one on (*inf.*), put one over on (*inf.*), rook (*sl.*), sell a pup to, skin (*sl.*), stiff (*sl.*), swindle, take for a ride (*inf.*), take in (*inf.*), trick

gullet *n* **1** = **oesophagus 2** = **throat,** craw, crop, maw

gullibility *n* = **credulity,** innocence, naïveté, simplicity, trustingness

gullible *adj* = **naive,** as green as grass, born yesterday, credulous, easily taken in, foolish, green, innocent, silly, simple, trusting, unsceptical, unsophisticated, unsuspecting, wet behind the ears (*inf.*)
Antonyms *adj* cynical, sophisticated, suspicious, untrusting, worldly

gully *n* **1** = **channel,** ditch, gutter, watercourse

gulp *vb* **1** = **swallow,** bolt, devour, gobble, guzzle, knock back (*inf.*), quaff, swig (*inf.*), swill, toss off, wolf **2** = **gasp,** choke, stifle, swallow ◆ *n* **6** = **swallow,** draught, mouthful, swig (*inf.*)

gum[1] *n* **3** = **glue,** adhesive, cement, exudate, mucilage, paste, resin ◆ *vb* **6** = **clog,** stiffen **7** = **stick,** affix, cement, glue, paste

gummy[1] *adj* **1** = **sticky,** adhesive, gluey, tacky, viscid

gumption *n* **1, 2** = **resourcefulness,** ability, acumen, astuteness, cleverness, common sense, discernment, enterprise, get-up-and-go (*inf.*), horse sense, initiative, mother wit, nous (*Brit. sl.*), sagacity, savvy (*sl.*), shrewdness, spirit, wit(s)

gun *n* **1** = **firearm,** handgun, heater (*US sl.*), piece (*sl.*), rod (*sl.*), shooter (*sl.*)

gunfire ('gʌn,faɪə) *n* **1** the firing of one or more guns, esp. when done repeatedly. **2** the use of firearms, as contrasted with other military tactics.

gun for *vb (intr, prep)* **1** to search for in order to reprimand, punish, or kill. **2** to try earnestly for: *he was gunning for promotion.*

gunge (gʌndʒ) *Inf.* ◆ *n* **1** sticky, rubbery, or congealed matter. ◆ *vb* **gunges, gunging, gunged. 2** *(tr; usually passive;* foll. by *up)* to block or encrust with gunge; clog. [C20: imit., ? infl. by GOO & SPONGE]
▸ '**gungy** *adj*

gunk (gʌŋk) *n Inf.* slimy, oily, or filthy matter. [C20: ? imit.]

gunlock ('gʌn,lɒk) *n* the mechanism in some firearms that causes the charge to be exploded.

gunman ❶ ('gʌnmən) *n, pl* **gunmen. 1** a man armed with a gun, esp. unlawfully. **2** a man skilled with a gun.

gunmetal ('gʌn,metᵊl) *n* **1** a type of bronze containing copper, tin, and zinc. **2a** a dark grey colour. **2b** *(as adj): gunmetal chiffon.*

gunnel[1] ('gʌnᵊl) *n* any eel-like fish occurring in coastal regions of northern seas. [C17: from ?]

gunnel[2] ('gʌnᵊl) *n* a variant spelling of **gunwale.**

gunner ('gʌnə) *n* **1** a serviceman who works with, uses, or specializes in guns. **2** *Naval.* (formerly) a warrant officer responsible for the training of gun crews, their performance in action, and accounting for ammunition. **3** (in the British Army) an artilleryman, esp. a private. **4** a person who hunts with a rifle or shotgun.

gunnery ('gʌnərɪ) *n* **1** the art and science of the efficient design and use of ordnance, esp. artillery. **2** guns collectively. **3** the use and firing of guns.

gunny ('gʌnɪ) *n, pl* **gunnies.** *Chiefly US.* **1** a coarse hard-wearing fabric usually made from jute and used for sacks, etc. **2** Also called: **gunny sack.** a sack made from this fabric. [C18: from Hindi, from Sansk. *gōnī* sack, prob. of Dravidian origin]

gunplay ('gʌn,pleɪ) *n Chiefly US.* the use of firearms, as by criminals, etc.

gunpoint ('gʌn,pɔɪnt) *n* **1** the muzzle of a gun. **2 at gunpoint.** being under or using the threat of being shot.

gunpowder ('gʌn,paʊdə) *n* an explosive mixture of potassium nitrate, charcoal, and sulphur: used in time fuses and in fireworks.

gun room *n* **1** (esp. in the Royal Navy) the mess allocated to junior officers. **2** a room where guns are stored.

gunrunning ('gʌn,rʌnɪŋ) *n* the smuggling of guns and ammunition or other weapons of war into a country.
▸ '**gun,runner** *n*

gunshot ('gʌn,ʃɒt) *n* **1a** shot fired from a gun. **1b** *(as modifier): gunshot wounds.* **2** the range of a gun. **3** the shooting of a gun.

gunslinger ('gʌn,slɪŋə) *n Sl.* a gunfighter or gunman, esp. in the Old West.

gunsmith ('gʌn,smɪθ) *n* a person who makes or repairs firearms, esp. portable guns.

gunstock ('gʌn,stɒk) *n* the wooden handle or support to which is attached the barrel of a rifle.

Gunter's chain ('gʌntəz) *n Surveying.* a measuring chain 22 yards in length, or this length as a unit. [C17: after E. *Gunter* (1581–1626), E mathematician]

gunwale *or* **gunnel** ('gʌnᵊl) *n Naut.* the top of the side of a boat or ship. [C15: from GUN + WALE from its use to support guns]

gunyah ('gʌnjə) *n Austral.* a bush hut or shelter. [C19: from Abor.]

guppy ('gʌpɪ) *n, pl* **guppies.** a small brightly coloured freshwater fish of N South America and the Caribbean: a popular aquarium fish. [C20: after R. J. L. *Guppy,* 19th-cent. clergyman of Trinidad who first presented specimens to the British Museum]

gurdwara ('gɜːdwɑːrə) *n* a Sikh place of worship. [C20: from Punjabi *gurduārā,* from Sansk. *guru* teacher + *dvārā* door]

gurgle ❶ ('gɜːgᵊl) *vb* **gurgles, gurgling, gurgled.** *(intr)* **1** (of liquids, esp. of streams, etc.) to make low bubbling noises when flowing. **2** to utter low throaty bubbling noises, esp. as a sign of contentment: *the baby gurgled with delight.* ◆ *n* **3** the act or sound of gurgling. [C16: ?from Vulgar L *gurgulāre,* from L *gurguliō* gullet]

Gurkha ('gɜːkə) *n* **1** a member of a Hindu people, descended from Brahmins and Rajputs, living chiefly in Nepal. **2** a member of a Gurkha regiment in the Indian or British army.

gurnard ('gɜːnəd) *or* **gurnet** ('gɜːnɪt) *n, pl* **gurnard, gurnards** *or* **gurnet, gurnets.** a European marine fish having a heavily armoured head and finger-like pectoral fins. [C14: from OF *gornard,* from *grognier* to grunt, from L *grunnīre*]

guru ❶ ('guruː, 'guːruː) *n* **1** a Hindu or Sikh religious teacher or leader, giving personal spiritual guidance to his disciples. **2** *Often derog.* a leader or chief theoretician of a movement, esp. a spiritual or religious cult. **3** *Often facetious.* a leading authority in a particular field: *a cricketing guru.* [C17: from Hindi *gurū,* from Sansk. *guruh* weighty]

gush ❶ (gʌʃ) *vb* **1** to pour out or cause to pour out suddenly and profusely, usually with a rushing sound. **2** to act or utter in an overeffusive, affected, or sentimental manner. ◆ *n* **3** a sudden copious flow or emission, esp. of liquid. **4** something that flows out or is emitted. **5** an extravagant and insincere expression of admiration, sentiment, etc. [C14: prob. imit.; cf. ON *gjósa*]
▸ '**gushing** *adj* ▸ '**gushingly** *adv*

gusher ('gʌʃə) *n* **1** a person who gushes, as in being effusive or sentimental. **2** something, such as a spurting oil well, that gushes.

gushy ❶ ('gʌʃɪ) *adj* **gushier, gushiest.** *Inf.* displaying excessive admiration or sentimentality.
▸ '**gushily** *adv* ▸ '**gushiness** *n*

gusset ('gʌsɪt) *n* **1** an inset piece of material used esp. to strengthen or enlarge a garment. **2** a triangular metal plate for strengthening a corner joist. ◆ *vb* **3** *(tr)* to put a gusset in (a garment). [C15: from OF *gousset* a piece of mail, dim. of *gousse* pod, from ?]
▸ '**gusseted** *adj*

gust ❶ (gʌst) *n* **1** a sudden blast of wind. **2** a sudden rush of smoke, sound, etc. **3** an outburst of emotion. ◆ *vb* **4** *(intr)* to blow in gusts. [C16: from ON *gustr;* rel. to *gjósa* to GUSH; see GEYSER]

gustation (gʌ'steɪʃən) *n* the act of tasting or the faculty of taste. [C16: from L *gustātiō,* from *gustāre* to taste]
▸**gustatory** ('gʌstətərɪ) *adj*

gusto ❶ ('gʌstəʊ) *n* vigorous enjoyment, zest, or relish: *the aria was sung with great gusto.* [C17: from Sp.: taste, from L *gustus* a tasting]

gusty ❶ ('gʌstɪ) *adj* **gustier, gustiest. 1** blowing in gusts or characterized by blustery weather: *a gusty wind.* **2** given to sudden outbursts, as of emotion.
▸ '**gustily** *adv* ▸ '**gustiness** *n*

gut ❶ (gʌt) *n* **1a** the lower part of the alimentary canal; intestine. **1b** the entire alimentary canal. Related adj: **visceral. 2** *(often pl)* the bowels or entrails, esp. of an animal. **3** *Sl.* the belly; paunch. **4** See **catgut. 5** a silky fibrous substance extracted from silkworms, used in the manufacture of fishing tackle. **6** a narrow channel or passage. **7** *(pl) Inf.* courage, willpower, or daring; forcefulness. **8** *(pl) Inf.* the essential part: *the guts of a problem.* ◆ *vb* **guts, gutting, gutted.** *(tr)* **9** to remove the entrails from (fish, etc.). **10** (esp. of fire) to destroy the inside of (a building). **11** to take out the central points of (an article, etc.), esp. in summary form. ◆ *adj* **12** *Inf.* instinctive, basic, or fundamental: *a gut feeling; capital punishment is a gut issue.* [OE *gutt;* rel. to *gēotan* to flow]

GUT (gʌt) *n acronym for* grand unified theory.

gutless ❶ ('gʌtlɪs) *adj Inf.* lacking courage or determination.

gut reaction *n* the first, instinctive, reaction to a situation.

gutsy ❶ ('gʌtsɪ) *adj* **gutsier, gutsiest.** *Sl.* **1** gluttonous; greedy. **2** full of courage or boldness. **3** passionate; lusty.

gutta-percha ('gʌtə'pɜːtʃə) *n* **1** any of several tropical trees with leathery leaves. **2** a whitish rubber substance derived from the coagulated milky latex of any of these trees: used in electrical insulation and dentistry. [C19: from Malay *getah* gum + *percha* tree that produces it]

guttate ('gʌteɪt) *adj Biol.* (esp. of plants) covered with small drops or droplike markings. [C19: from L *guttātus* dappled, from *gutta* a drop]

gutted ('gʌtɪd) *adj Inf.* disappointed and upset.

gutter ❶ ('gʌtə) *n* **1** a channel along the eaves or on the roof of a building, used to collect and carry away rainwater. **2** a channel running along the kerb or the centre of a road to collect and carry away rainwater. **3** either of the two channels running parallel to a tenpin bowling lane. **4** *Printing.* the white space between the facing pages of an open book. **5** *Surfing.* a dangerous deep channel formed by currents

THESAURUS

gunman *n* **1** = **terrorist**, assassin, bandit, bravo, desperado, gangster, gunslinger (*US sl.*), heavy (*sl.*), hit man (*sl.*), killer, mobster (*US sl.*), murderer, thug

gurgle *vb* **1** = **murmur**, babble, bubble, burble, crow, lap, plash, purl, ripple, splash ◆ *n* **3** = **murmur**, babble, purl, ripple

guru *n* **2** = **teacher**, authority, guiding light, leader, maharishi, mahatma, master, mentor, sage, Svengali, swami, torchbearer, tutor

gush *vb* **1** = **flow**, burst, cascade, flood, issue, jet, pour, run, rush, spout, spurt, stream **2** = **enthuse**, babble, blather, chatter, effervesce, effuse, jabber, overstate, spout ◆ *n* **3** = **stream**, burst, cascade, flood, flow, issue, jet, outburst, outflow, rush, spout, spurt, torrent **5** = **babble**, blather, chatter, effusion, exuberance

gushy *adj* = **effusive**, cloying, emotional, excessive, fulsome, gushing, mawkish, overdone, overenthusiastic, over the top, sentimental

gust *n* **1** = **blast**, blow, breeze, flurry, gale, puff, rush, squall **3** = **surge**, burst, eruption, explosion, fit, gale, outburst, paroxysm, passion, storm ◆ *vb* **4** = **blow**, blast, puff, squall

gusto *n* = **relish**, appetite, appreciation, brio, delight, enjoyment, enthusiasm, exhilaration, fervour, liking, pleasure, savour, verve, zeal, zest
Antonyms *n* apathy, coolness, disinterest, distaste, inertia

gusty *adj* **1** = **windy**, blowy, blustering, blustery, breezy, inclement, squally, stormy, tempestuous

gut *n* **2** *plural* = **intestines**, belly, bowels, entrails, innards (*inf.*), insides (*inf.*), inwards, stomach, viscera **3** *Slang* = **paunch**, belly, potbelly, spare tyre (*Brit. sl.*) **7** *plural Informal* = **courage**, audacity, backbone, boldness, bottle (*sl.*), daring, forcefulness, grit, hardihood, mettle, nerve, pluck, spirit, spunk (*inf.*), willpower ◆ *vb* **9** = **disembowel**, clean, draw, dress, eviscerate ◆ *adj* **12** = **instinctive**, basic, deep-seated, emotional, heartfelt, innate, intuitive, involuntary, natural, spontaneous, unthinking, visceral

gutless *adj* = **faint-hearted**, abject, boneless, chicken (*sl.*), cowardly, craven, feeble, irresolute, lily-livered, spineless, submissive, timid, weak
Antonyms *adj* bold, brave, courageous, determined, resolute

gutsy *adj* **2** = **brave**, bold, courageous, determined, feisty (*inf., chiefly US & Canad.*), gallant, game (*inf.*), gritty, have-a-go (*inf.*), indomitable, mettlesome, plucky, resolute, spirited, staunch

gutter *n* **1** = **drain**, channel, conduit, ditch, duct, pipe, sluice, trench, trough, tube

and waves. **6 the gutter.** a poverty-stricken, degraded, or criminal environment. ◆ *vb* **7** (*tr*) to make gutters in. **8** (*intr*) to flow in a stream. **9** (*intr*) (of a candle) to melt away as the wax forms channels and runs down in drops. **10** (*intr*) (of a flame) to flicker and be about to go out. [C13: from Anglo-F *goutiere*, from OF *goute* a drop, from L *gutta*]
▸ **'guttering** *n*

gutter press *n* the section of the popular press that seeks sensationalism in its coverage.

guttersnipe ❶ ('gʌtəˌsnaɪp) *n* a child who spends most of his time in the streets, esp. in a slum area.

guttural ❶ ('gʌtərəl) *adj* **1** *Anat.* of or relating to the throat. **2** *Phonetics.* pronounced in the throat or the back of the mouth. **3** raucous. ◆ *n* **4** *Phonetics.* a guttural consonant. [C16: from NL *gutturālis*, from L *guttur* gullet]
▸ **'gutturally** *adv*

guy[1] ❶ (gaɪ) *n* **1** *Inf.* a man or youth. **2** *Brit.* a crude effigy of Guy Fawkes, usually made of old clothes stuffed with straw or rags, that is burnt on top of a bonfire on Guy Fawkes Day. **3** *Brit.* a person in shabby or ludicrously odd clothes. **4** (*pl*) *Inf.* persons of either sex. ◆ *vb* **5** (*tr*) to make fun of; ridicule. [C19: short for *Guy* Fawkes, who plotted to blow up King James I and the Houses of Parliament (1605)]

guy[2] (gaɪ) *n* **1** a rope, chain, wire, etc., for anchoring an object in position or for steadying or guiding it. ◆ *vb* **2** (*tr*) to anchor, steady, or guide with a guy or guys. [C14: prob. from Low G; cf. OF *guie* guide, from *guier* to GUIDE]

guzzle ❶ ('gʌzᵊl) *vb* **guzzles, guzzling, guzzled.** to consume (food or drink) excessively or greedily. [C16: from ?]
▸ **'guzzler** *n*

gybe, gibe, *or* **jibe** (dʒaɪb) *Naut.* ◆ *vb* **gybes, gybing, gybed, gibes, gibing, gibed** *or* **jibes, jibing, jibed. 1** (*intr*) (of a fore-and-aft sail) to shift suddenly from one side of the vessel to the other when running before the wind. **2** to cause (a sailing vessel) to gybe or (of a sailing vessel) to undergo gybing. ◆ *n* **3** an instance of gybing. [C17: from obs. Du. *gijben* (now *gijpen*), from ?]

gym (dʒɪm) *n, adj* short for **gymnasium, gymnastics, gymnastic.**

gymkhana (dʒɪm'kɑːnə) *n* **1** *Chiefly Brit.* an event in which horses and riders display skill and aptitude in various races and contests. **2** (in Anglo-India) a place providing sporting and athletic facilities. [C19: from Hindi *gend-khānā*, lit.: ball house]

gymnasium (dʒɪm'neɪzɪəm) *n, pl* **gymnasiums** *or* **gymnasia** (-zɪə). **1** a large room or hall equipped with bars, weights, ropes, etc., for physical training. **2** (in various European countries) a secondary school that prepares pupils for university. [C16: from L: school for gymnastics, from Gk *gumnasion*, from *gumnazein* to exercise naked]

gymnast ('dʒɪmnæst) *n* a person who is skilled or trained in gymnastics.

gymnastic (dʒɪm'næstɪk) *adj* of, like, or involving gymnastics.
▸ **gym'nastically** *adv*

gymnastics (dʒɪm'næstɪks) *n* **1** (*functioning as sing*) practice or training in exercises that develop physical strength and agility or mental capacity. **2** (*functioning as pl*) gymnastic exercises.

gymno- *combining form.* naked, bare, or exposed: *gymnosperm.* [from Gk *gumnos* naked]

gymnosperm ('dʒɪmnəʊˌspɜːm, 'gɪm-) *n* any seed-bearing plant in which the ovules are borne naked on open scales, which are often arranged in cones; any conifer or related plant. Cf. **angiosperm.**
▸ **ˌgymno'spermous** *adj*

gympie ('gɪmpɪ) *n* a tall Australian tree with stinging hairs on its leaves. Also: **nettle tree.**

gym shoe *n* another name for **plimsoll.**

gymslip ('dʒɪmˌslɪp) *n* a tunic or pinafore dress worn by schoolgirls, often part of a school uniform.

gyn- *combining form.* a variant of **gyno-** before a vowel.

gynaeco- *or US* **gyneco-** *combining form.* relating to women; female: *gynaecology.* [from Gk, from *gunē*, *gunaik-* woman, female]

gynaecology *or US* **gynecology** (ˌgaɪnɪ'kɒlədʒɪ) *n* the branch of medicine concerned with diseases and conditions specific to women.
▸**gynaecological** (ˌgaɪnɪkə'lɒdʒɪkᵊl), **ˌgynaeco'logic** *or US* **ˌgyneco'logical, ˌgyneco'logic** *adj* ▸ **ˌgynae'cologist** *or US* **ˌgyne'cologist** *n*

gynandromorph (dʒɪ'nændrəʊˌmɔːf, gaɪ-) *n* an abnormal organism, esp. an insect, that has both male and female physical characteristics.

gynandrous (dʒaɪ'nændrəs, gaɪ-) *adj* (of flowers such as the orchid) having the stamens and styles united in a column. [C19: from Gk *gunandros* of uncertain sex, from *gunē* woman + *anēr* man]

gyno- *or before a vowel* **gyn-** *combining form.* **1** relating to women; female: *gynarchy.* **2** denoting a female reproductive organ: *gynophore.* [from Gk, from *gunē* woman]

gynoecium, gynaeceum, *or esp. US* **gynecium** (dʒaɪ'niːsɪəm, gaɪ-) *n, pl* **gynoecia, gynaecea** *or esp. US* **gynecia** (-sɪə). the carpels of a flowering plant collectively. [C18: NL, from Gk *gunaikeion* women's quarters, from *gunaik-*, *gunē* woman + *-eion*, suffix indicating place]

gynophore ('dʒaɪnəʊˌfɔː, 'gaɪ-) *n* a stalk in some plants that bears the gynoecium above the level of the other flower parts.

-gynous *adj combining form.* **1** of or relating to women or females: *androgynous; misogynous.* **2** relating to female organs: *epigynous.* [from NL, from Gk, from *gunē* woman]
▸**-gyny** *n combining form.*

gyp[1] *or* **gip** (dʒɪp) *Sl.* ◆ *vb* **gyps, gypping, gypped** *or* **gips, gipping, gipped. 1** (*tr*) to swindle, cheat, or defraud. ◆ *n* **2** an act of cheating. **3** a person who gyps. [C18: back formation from GYPSY]

gyp[2] *or* **gip** (dʒɪp) *n Brit. & NZ sl.* severe pain; torture: *his arthritis gave him gyp.* [C19: prob. a contraction of *gee up!*; see GEE[1]]

gyp[3] (dʒɪp) *n* a college servant at the universities of Cambridge or Durham. [C18: ?from obs. *gippo* scullion]

gypsophila (dʒɪp'sɒfɪlə) *n* any of a Mediterranean genus of plants, having small white or pink fragrant flowers. [C18: NL, from Gk *gupsos* chalk + *philos* loving]

gypsum ('dʒɪpsəm) *n* a mineral consisting of hydrated calcium sulphate that occurs in sedimentary rocks and clay and is used principally in making plasters and cements, esp. plaster of Paris. Formula: $CaSO_4.2H_2O$. [C17: from L, from Gk *gupsos* chalk, plaster, cement, of Semitic origin]
▸**gypseous** ('dʒɪpsɪəs) *adj*

Gypsy ❶ *or* **Gipsy** ('dʒɪpsɪ) *n, pl* **Gypsies** *or* **Gipsies.** (*sometimes not cap.*) **1a** a member of a people scattered throughout Europe and North America, who maintain a nomadic way of life in industrialized societies. They migrated from NW India about the 9th century onwards. **1b** (*as modifier*): *a Gypsy fortune-teller.* **2** the language of the Gypsies; Romany. **3** a person who looks or behaves like a Gypsy. [C16: from EGYPTIAN, since they were thought to have come orig. from Egypt]
▸ **'Gypsyish** *or* **'Gipsyish** *adj*

gypsy moth *or* **gipsy moth** *n* a European moth whose caterpillars are pests on deciduous trees.

gyrate ❶ *vb* (dʒaɪ'reɪt), **gyrates, gyrating, gyrated. 1** (*intr*) to rotate or spiral, esp. about a fixed point or axis. ◆ *adj* ('dʒaɪrɪt). **2** *Biol.* curved or coiled into a circle. [C19: from LL *gȳrāre*, from L *gȳrus* circle, from Gk *guros*]
▸**gy'ration** *n* ▸**gy'rator** *n* ▸**gyratory** ('dʒaɪrətərɪ) *adj*

gyre ('dʒaɪə) *Chiefly literary.* ◆ *n* **1** a circular or spiral movement or path. **2** a ring, circle, or spiral. ◆ *vb* **gyres, gyring, gyred. 3** (*intr*) to whirl. [C16: from L *gȳrus* circle, from Gk *guros*]

gyrfalcon *or* **gerfalcon** ('dʒɜːˌfɔːlkən, -ˌfɔːkən) *n* a very large rare falcon of northern and arctic regions. [C14: from OF *gerfaucon*, ?from ON *geirfalki*, from *geirr* spear + *falki* falcon]

gyro ('dʒaɪrəʊ) *n, pl* **gyros. 1** See **gyrocompass. 2** See **gyroscope.**

gyro- *or before a vowel* **gyr-** *combining form.* **1** indicating rotating or gyrating motion: *gyroscope.* **2** indicating a gyroscope: *gyrocompass.* [via L from Gk, from *guros* circle]

gyrocompass ('dʒaɪrəʊˌkʌmpəs) *n* a nonmagnetic compass that uses a motor-driven gyroscope to indicate true north.

gyrodyne ('dʒaɪrəʊˌdaɪn) *n* an aircraft that uses a powered rotor to take off and manoeuvre, but uses autorotation when cruising.

gyromagnetic (ˌdʒaɪrəʊmæg'netɪk) *adj* of or caused by magnetic properties resulting from the spin of a charged particle, such as an electron.

gyroscope ('dʒaɪrəˌskəʊp) *n* a device containing a disc rotating on an axis that can turn freely in any direction so that the disc maintains the same orientation irrespective of the movement of the surrounding structure.
▸**gyroscopic** (ˌdʒaɪrə'skɒpɪk) *adj* ▸ **ˌgyro'scopically** *adv*

gyrostabilizer *or* **gyrostabiliser** (ˌdʒaɪrəʊ'steɪbɪˌlaɪzə) *n* a gyroscopic device used to stabilize the rolling motion of a ship.

gyve (dʒaɪv) *Arch.* ◆ *vb* **gyves, gyving, gyved. 1** (*tr*) to shackle or fetter. ◆ *n* **2** (*usually pl*) fetter. [C13: from ?]

THESAURUS

guttersnipe *n* = **street urchin**, gamin, mudlark (*sl.*), ragamuffin, street Arab (*offens.*), waif

guttural *adj* **3** = **throaty**, deep, gravelly, gruff, hoarse, husky, low, rasping, rough, thick

guy[1] *n* **1** *Informal* = **man**, bloke (*Brit. inf.*), cat (*sl.*), chap, fellow, lad, person, youth ◆ *vb* **5** = **mock**, caricature, make fun of, poke fun at, rib (*inf.*), ridicule, send up (*Brit. inf.*), take off (*inf.*)

guzzle *vb* = **devour**, bolt, carouse, cram, drink, gobble, gorge, gormandize, knock back (*inf.*), pig out (*US & Canad. sl.*), quaff, stuff (oneself), swill, tope, wolf

Gypsy *n* **1** = **Romany 3** = **traveller**, Bohemian, nomad, rambler, roamer, rover, vagabond, vagrant, wanderer

gyrate *vb* **1** = **rotate**, circle, pirouette, revolve, spin, spiral, twirl, whirl

gyration *n* **1** = **rotation**, convolution, pirouette, revolution, spin, spinning, spiral, whirl, whirling

Hh

h *or* **H** (eɪtʃ) *n, pl* **h's, H's,** *or* **Hs. 1** the eighth letter of the English alphabet. **2** a speech sound represented by this letter. **3a** something shaped like an H. **3b** *(in combination): an H-beam.*

h *symbol for:* **1** *Physics.* Planck constant. **2** hecto-. **3** hour.

H *symbol for:* **1** *Chem.* hydrogen. **2** *Physics.* magnetic field strength. **3** *Electronics.* henry. **4** (on Brit. pencils, signifying degree of hardness of lead) hard.

h. *or* **H.** *abbrev. for:* **1** harbour. **2** height. **3** high. **4** hour. **5** hundred. **6** husband.

ha[1] *or* **hah** (hɑː) *interj* **1** an exclamation expressing derision, triumph, surprise, etc. **2** *(reiterated)* a representation of the sound of laughter.

ha[2] *symbol for* hectare.

haar (hɑː) *n Eastern Brit.* a cold sea mist or fog off the North Sea. [C17: rel. to Du. dialect *harig* damp]

Hab. *Bible. abbrev. for* Habakkuk.

habanera (ˌhæbəˈnɛərə) *n* **1** a slow Cuban dance in duple time. **2** a piece of music for this dance. [from Sp. *danza habanera* dance from Havana]

habeas corpus (ˈheɪbɪəs ˈkɔːpəs) *n Law.* a writ ordering a person to be brought before a court or judge, esp. so that the court may ascertain whether his detention is lawful. [C15: from the opening of the L writ, lit.: you may have the body]

haberdasher (ˈhæbəˌdæʃə) *n* **1** *Brit.* a dealer in small articles for sewing, such as buttons and ribbons. **2** *US.* a men's outfitter. [C14: from Anglo-F *hapertas* small items of merchandise, from ?]

haberdashery (ˈhæbəˌdæʃərɪ) *n, pl* **haberdasheries.** the goods or business kept by a haberdasher.

habergeon (ˈhæbədʒən) *n* a light sleeveless coat of mail worn in the 14th century under the plated hauberk. [C14: from OF *haubergeon* a little HAUBERK]

Haber process (ˈhɑːbə) *n* an industrial process for producing ammonia by reacting atmospheric nitrogen with hydrogen at high pressure and temperature in the presence of a catalyst. [after Fritz *Haber* (1868–1934), G chemist]

habiliment (həˈbɪlɪmənt) *n (often pl)* dress or attire. [C15: from OF *habillement,* from *habiller* to dress]

habilitate (həˈbɪlɪˌteɪt) *vb* **habilitates, habilitating, habilitated. 1** *(tr) US.* to equip and finance (a mine). **2** *(intr)* to qualify for office. [C17: from Med. L *habilitāre* to make fit, from L *habilitās* aptness]
▸**haˌbiliˈtation** *n*

habit Ⓣ (ˈhæbɪt) *n* **1** a tendency or disposition to act in a particular way. **2** established custom, usual practice, etc. **3** *Psychol.* a learned behavioural response to a particular situation. **4** mental disposition or attitude: *a good working habit of mind.* **5a** a practice or substance to which a person is addicted: *drink has become a habit with him.* **5b** the state of being dependent on something, esp. a drug. **6** *Bot., zool.* method of growth, type of existence, or general appearance: *a burrowing habit.* **7** the customary apparel of a particular occupation, rank, etc., now esp. the costume of a nun or monk. **8** Also called: **riding habit.** a woman's riding dress. ◆ *vb* **habits, habiting, habited.** *(tr)* **9** to clothe. **10** an archaic word for **inhabit.** [C13: from L *habitus* custom, from *habēre* to have]

habitable (ˈhæbɪtəbᵊl) *adj* able to be lived in.
▸ˌ**habitaˈbility** *or* ˈ**habitableness** *n* ▸ˈ**habitably** *adv*

habitant (ˈhæbɪtᵊnt) *n* **1** a less common word for **inhabitant. 2a** an early French settler in Canada or Louisiana. **2b** a descendant of these settlers, esp. a farmer.

habitat Ⓣ (ˈhæbɪˌtæt) *n* **1** the natural home of an animal or plant. **2** the place in which a person, group, class, etc., is normally found. [C18: from L: it inhabits, from *habitāre* to dwell, from *habēre* to have]

habitation Ⓣ (ˌhæbɪˈteɪʃən) *n* **1** a dwelling place. **2** occupation of a dwelling place.

habit-forming Ⓣ *adj* tending to become a habit or addiction.

habitual Ⓣ (həˈbɪtjʊəl) *adj* **1** *(usually prenominal)* done or experienced regularly and repeatedly: *the habitual Sunday walk.* **2** *(usually prenominal)* by habit: *a habitual drinker.* **3** customary; usual.
▸**haˈbitually** *adv* ▸**haˈbitualness** *n*

habituate Ⓣ (həˈbɪtjʊˌeɪt) *vb* **habituates, habituating, habituated. 1** to accustom; make used to. **2** *US & Canad. arch.* to frequent.
▸**haˌbituˈation** *n*

habitude (ˈhæbɪˌtjuːd) *n Rare.* habit; tendency.

habitué Ⓣ (həˈbɪtjʊˌeɪ) *n* a frequent visitor to a place. [C19: from F, from *habituer* to frequent]

HAC *abbrev. for* Honourable Artillery Company.

hachure (hæˈʃjʊə) *n* shading of short lines drawn on a relief map to indicate gradients. [C19: from F, from *hacher* to chop up]

hacienda (ˌhæsɪˈɛndə) *n* (in Spain or Spanish-speaking countries) **1a** a ranch or large estate. **1b** any substantial manufacturing establishment in the country. **2** the main house on such a ranch or establishment. [C18: from Sp., from L *facienda* things to be done, from *facere* to do]

hack[1] Ⓣ (hæk) *vb* **1** (when *intr,* usually foll. by *at* or *away*) to chop (at) roughly or violently. **2** to cut and clear (a way), as through undergrowth. **3** (in sport, esp. rugby) to foul (an opposing player) by kicking his shins. **4** *(intr)* to cough in short dry bursts. **5** *(tr)* to cut (a story, article, etc.) in a damaging way. **6** *(intr;* usually foll. by *into)* to manipulate a computer program skilfully, esp. to gain unauthorized access to another computer system. ◆ *n* **7** a cut or gash. **8** any tool used for shallow digging, such as a mattock or pick. **9** a chopping blow. **10** a dry spasmodic cough. **11** a kick on the shins, as in rugby. [OE *haccian*]

hack[2] Ⓣ (hæk) *n* **1** a horse kept for riding. **2** an old or overworked horse. **3** a horse kept for hire. **4** *Brit.* a country ride on horseback. **5** a drudge. **6** a person who produces mediocre literary work. **7** *US inf.* **7a** a cab driver. **7b** a taxi. ◆ *vb* **8** *Brit.* to ride (a horse) cross-country for pleasure. **9** *(tr) Inf.* to write (an article, etc.) in the manner of a hack. ◆ *adj* **10** *(prenominal)* banal, mediocre, or unoriginal: *hack writing.* [C17: short for HACKNEY]

hack[3] (hæk) *n* **1** a rack used for fodder for livestock. **2** a board on which meat is placed for a hawk. **3** a pile or row of unfired bricks stacked to dry. [C16: var. of HATCH[2]]

hackamore (ˈhækəˌmɔː) *n US & NZ.* a rope or rawhide halter used for unbroken foals. [C19: from Sp. *jáquima* headstall, ult. from Ar. *shaqīmah*]

hackberry (ˈhækˌbɛrɪ) *n, pl* **hackberries. 1** an American tree having edible cherry-like fruits. **2** the fruit. [C18: var. of C16 *hagberry,* of Scand. origin]

hacker (ˈhækə) *n* **1** a person that hacks. **2** *Sl.* a computer fanatic, esp. one who through a personal computer breaks into the computer system of a company, government, etc.

hackery (ˈhækərɪ) *n* **1** *Ironic.* journalism; hackwork. **2** *Inf.* a variant of **hacking**[2].

hacking[1] (ˈhækɪŋ) *adj* (of a cough) harsh, dry, and spasmodic.

hacking[2] (ˈhækɪŋ) *n* the practice of gaining illegal access to a computer system.

hackle (ˈhækᵊl) *n* **1** any of the long slender feathers on the neck of poultry and other birds. **2** *Angling.* parts of an artificial fly made from hackle feathers, representing the legs and sometimes the wings of a real fly. **3** a feathered ornament worn in the headdress of some British regiments. **4** a steel flax comb. ◆ *vb* **hackles, hackling, hackled.** *(tr)* **5** to comb (flax) using a hackle. [C15: *hakell* prob. from OE]

hackles (ˈhækᵊlz) *pl n* **1** the hairs on the back of the neck and the back of a dog, cat, etc., which rise when the animal is angry or afraid. **2** anger or resentment: *to make one's hackles rise.*

hackney (ˈhæknɪ) *n* **1** a compact breed of harness horse with a high-stepping trot. **2** a coach or carriage that is for hire. **3** a popular term for **hack**[2] (sense 1). ◆ *vb* **4** *(tr; usually passive)* to make com-

THESAURUS

habit *n* **1** = **mannerism,** bent, custom, disposition, manner, practice, proclivity, propensity, quirk, tendency, way **2** = **custom,** convention, mode, practice, routine, rule, tradition, usage, wont **5** = **addiction,** dependence, fixation, obsession, weakness **7** = **dress,** apparel, garb, garment, habiliment, riding dress ◆ *vb* **9** = **clothe,** array, attire, dress, equip

habitat *n* **1, 2** = **home,** abode, element, environment, home ground, locality, natural home, surroundings, terrain, territory

habitation *n* **1** = **dwelling,** abode, domicile, dwelling house, home, house, living quarters, lodging, pad (*sl.*), quarters, residence **2** = **occupation,** inhabitance, inhabitancy, occupancy, tenancy

habit-forming *adj* = **addictive,** compulsive, moreish (*inf.*)

habitual *adj* **1** = **customary,** accustomed, common, familiar, fixed, natural, normal, ordinary, regular, routine, standard, traditional, usual, wonted **2** = **persistent,** chronic, confirmed, constant, established, frequent, hardened, ingrained, inveterate, recurrent
Antonyms *adj* ≠ **customary:** abnormal, exceptional, extraordinary, irregular, rare, strange, uncommon, unusual ≠ **persistent:** infrequent, irregular, occasional

habituate *vb* **1** = **accustom,** acclimatize, acquaint, break in, condition, discipline, familiarize, harden, inure, make used to, school, season, train

habituated *adj* **1** = **accustomed,** acclimatized, adapted, broken in, conditioned, disciplined, familiarized, hardened, inured, schooled, seasoned, trained, used (to)
Antonyms *adj* unaccustomed, unfamiliar, unused (to)

habitué *n* = **frequent visitor,** constant customer, frequenter, regular (*inf.*), regular patron

hack[1] *vb* **1** = **cut,** chop, gash, hew, kick, lacerate, mangle, mutilate, notch, slash ◆ *n* **4** = **cough,** bark, rasp **7** = **cut,** chop, gash, notch, slash

hack[2] *n* **2** = **horse,** crock, jade, nag **5** = **drudge,** plodder, slave **6** = **scribbler,** literary hack ◆ *adj* **10** = **unoriginal,** banal, mediocre, pedestrian, poor, stereotyped, tired, undistinguished, uninspired

monplace and banal by too frequent use. [C14: prob. after *Hackney*, London, where horses were formerly raised]

hackneyed Ⓣ ('hæknɪd) *adj* used so often as to be trite, dull, and stereotyped.

hacksaw ('hæk,sɔː) *n* a handsaw for cutting metal, with a blade in a frame under tension.

hackwork ('hæk,wɜːk) *n* undistinguished literary work produced to order.

had (hæd) *vb* the past tense and past participle of **have**.

haddock ('hædək) *n, pl* **haddocks** *or* **haddock.** a North Atlantic gadoid food fish similar to but smaller than the cod. [C14: from ?]

hade (heɪd) *Geol.* ◆ *n* **1** the angle made to the vertical by the plane of a fault or vein. ◆ *vb* **hades, hading, haded. 2** (*intr*) to incline from the vertical. [C18: from ?]

hadedah ('hɑːdɪ,dɑː) *n* a large grey-green S. African ibis. [imit.]

Hades Ⓣ ('heɪdiːz) *n* **1** *Greek myth.* **1a** the underworld abode of the souls of the dead. **1b** Pluto, the god of the underworld. **2** (*often not cap.*) hell.

Hadith ('hædɪθ, hɑː'diːθ) *n* the body of tradition about Mohammed and his followers. [Ar.]

hadj (hædʒ) *n* a variant spelling of **hajj**.

hadji ('hædʒɪ) *n, pl* **hadjis.** a variant spelling of **hajji**.

hadn't ('hædᵊnt) *contraction of* had not.

hadron ('hædrɒn) *n* an elementary particle capable of taking part in a strong nuclear interaction. [C20: from Gk *hadros* heavy, from *hadēn* enough + -ON]

▸**had'ronic** *adj*

hadst (hædst) *vb Arch. or dialect.* (used with the pronoun *thou*) a singular form of the past tense (indicative mood) of **have**.

haecceity (hɛk'siːɪtɪ, hiːk-) *n, pl* **haecceities.** *Philosophy.* the property that uniquely identifies an object. [C17: from Med. L *haecceitas*, lit.: thisness, from *haec*, fem. of *hic* this]

haem *or US* **heme** (hiːm) *n Biochem.* a complex red organic pigment containing ferrous iron, present in haemoglobin. [C20: from HAEMATIN]

haem- *combining form.* a variant of **haemo-** before a vowel. Also (US): **hem-**.

haemal *or US* **hemal** ('hiːməl) *adj* **1** of the blood. **2** denoting or relating to the region of the body containing the heart.

haematemesis *or US* **hematemesis** (,hiːmə'tɛmɪsɪs) *n* vomiting of blood, esp. as the result of a bleeding ulcer. [C19: from HAEMATO- + Gk *emesis* vomiting]

haematic *or US* **hematic** (hiː'mætɪk) *adj* relating to, acting on, having the colour of, or containing blood. Also: **haemic** *or US* **hemic**.

haematin *or US* **hematin** ('hɛmətɪn, 'hiː-) *n Biochem.* a dark bluish or brownish pigment obtained by the oxidation of haem.

haematite ('hiːmə,taɪt, 'hɛm-) *n* a variant spelling of **hematite**.

haemato- *or before a vowel* **haemat-** *combining form.* indicating blood: *haematology*. Also: **haemo-** or (US) **hemato-, hemat-, hemo-**. [from Gk *haima, haimat-* blood]

haematocrit *or US* **hematocrit** ('hɛmətəʊkrɪt, 'hiː-) *n* **1** a centrifuge for separating blood cells from plasma. **2** the ratio of the volume occupied by these cells, esp. the red cells, to the total volume of blood, expressed as a percentage. [C20: from HAEMATO- + *-crit*, from Gk *kritēs* judge, from *krinein* to separate]

haematology *or US* **hematology** (,hiːmə'tɒlədʒɪ) *n* the branch of medical science concerned with diseases of the blood.

▸**haematologic** (,hiːmətə'lɒdʒɪk), **,haemato'logical** *or US* **,hemato'logic, ,hemato'logical** *adj*

haematoma *or US* **hematoma** (,hiːmə'təʊmə) *n, pl* **haematomas, haematomata** *or US* **hematomas, hematomata** (-mətə). *Pathol.* a tumour of clotted blood.

haematuria *or US* **hematuria** (,hiːmə'tjʊərɪə) *n Pathol.* the presence of blood or red blood cells in the urine.

-haemia *or esp. US* **-hemia** *n combining form.* variants of **-aemia**.

haemo-, haema-, *or before a vowel* **haem-** *combining form.* denoting blood. Also: (US) **hemo-, hema-,** or **hem-**. [from Gk *haima* blood]

haemocyanin *or US* **hemocyanin** (,hiːməʊ'saɪənɪn) *n* a blue copper-containing respiratory pigment in crustaceans and molluscs that functions as haemoglobin.

haemocytometer *or US* **hemocytometer** (,hiːməʊsaɪ'tɒmɪtə) *n Med.* an apparatus for counting the number of cells in a quantity of blood.

haemodialysis *or US* **hemodialysis** (,hiːməʊdaɪ'ælɪsɪs) *n, pl* **haemodialyses** *or US* **hemodialyses** (-,siːz). *Med.* the filtering of circulating blood through a membrane in an apparatus (**haemodialyser** or **artificial kidney**) to remove waste products: performed in cases of kidney failure. [C20: from HAEMO- + DIALYSIS]

haemoglobin *or US* **hemoglobin** (,hiːməʊ'gləʊbɪn) *n* a protein that gives red blood cells their characteristic colour. It combines reversibly with oxygen and is thus very important in the transportation of oxygen to tissues. [C19: shortened from *haematoglobulin*: see HAEMATIN + GLOBULIN]

haemolysis (hɪ'mɒlɪsɪs), **haematolysis** (,hiːmə'tɒlɪsɪs) *or US* **hemolysis, hematolysis** *n, pl* **haemolyses, haematolyses** *or US* **hemolyses, hematolyses** (-,siːz). the disintegration of red blood cells, with the release of haemoglobin.

▸**haemolytic** *or US* **hemolytic** (,hiːməʊ'lɪtɪk) *adj*

haemophilia *or US* **hemophilia** (,hiːməʊ'fɪlɪə) *n* an inheritable disease, usually affecting only males, characterized by loss or impairment of the normal clotting ability of blood.

▸**,haemo'philiac** *or US* **,hemo'philiac** *n* ▸**,haemo'philic** *or US* **,hemo'philic** *adj*

haemoptysis *or US* **hemoptysis** (hɪ'mɒptɪsɪs) *n, pl* **haemoptyses** *or US* **hemoptyses** (-,siːz). spitting or coughing up of blood, as in tuberculosis. [C17: from HAEMO- + *-ptysis*, from Gk *ptyein* to spit]

haemorrhage *or US* **hemorrhage** ('hɛmərɪdʒ) *n* **1** profuse bleeding from ruptured blood vessels. **2** a steady or severe loss or depletion of resources, staff, etc. ◆ *vb* **haemorrhages, haemorrhaging, haemorrhaged** *or US* **hemorrhages, hemorrhaging, hemorrhaged. 3** (*intr*) to bleed profusely. [C17: from L *haemorrhagia*; see HAEMO-, -RRHAGIA]

haemorrhoids *or US* **hemorrhoids** ('hɛmə,rɔɪdz) *pl n Pathol.* swollen and twisted veins in the region of the anus. Nontechnical name: **piles**. [C14: from L *haemorrhoidae* (pl), from Gk, from *haimorrhoos* discharging blood, from *haimo-* HAEMO- + *rhein* to flow]

▸**,haemor'rhoidal** *or US* **,hemor'rhoidal** *adj*

haemostasis *or US* **hemostasis** (,hiːməʊ'steɪsɪs) *n* the stopping of bleeding or of blood circulation, as during a surgical operation. [C18: from NL, from HAEMO- + Gk *stasis* a standing still]

▸**,haemo'static** *or US* **,hemo'static** *adj*

haemostat *or US* **hemostat** ('hiːməʊ,stæt) *n* a surgical instrument or chemical agent that retards or stops bleeding.

haeremai ('haɪrə,maɪ) *NZ.* ◆ *sentence substitute.* **1** an expression of greeting or welcome. ◆ *n* **2** the act of saying "haeremai". [C18: Maori, lit.: come hither]

hafiz ('hɑːfɪz) *n Islam.* **1** a title for a person who knows the Koran by heart. **2** the guardian of a mosque. [from Persian, from Ar., from *hafiza* to guard]

hafnium ('hæfnɪəm) *n* a bright metallic element found in zirconium ores. Symbol: Hf; atomic no.: 72; atomic wt.: 178.49. [C20: NL, after *Hafnia*, L name of Copenhagen + -IUM]

haft Ⓣ (hɑːft) *n* **1** the handle of an axe, knife, etc. ◆ *vb* **2** (*tr*) to provide with a haft. [OE *hæft*]

hag[1] Ⓣ (hæg) *n* **1** an unpleasant or ugly old woman. **2** a witch. **3** short for **hagfish**. [OE *hægtesse* witch]

▸**'haggish** *adj*

hag[2] (hæg) *n Scot. & N English dialect.* **1** a firm spot in a bog. **2** a soft place in a moor. [C13: from ON]

Hag. *Bible. abbrev. for* Haggai.

hagfish ('hæg,fɪʃ) *n, pl* **hagfish** *or* **hagfishes.** an eel-like marine vertebrate having a round sucking mouth and feeding on the tissues of other animals and on dead organic material.

Haggadah *or* **Haggodoh** (hə'gɑːdə) *n, pl* **Haggadahs, Haggadas** *or* **Haggadoth** (hægə'dəʊt). *Judaism.* **a** a book containing the order of service of the traditional Passover meal. **b** the narrative of the Exodus from Egypt that constitutes the main part of that service. ◆ See also **Seder**. [C19: from Heb.: story, from *hagged* to tell]

▸**haggadic** (hə'gædɪk, -'gɑː-) *adj*

haggard Ⓣ ('hægəd) *adj* **1** careworn or gaunt, as from anxiety or starvation. **2** wild or unruly. **3** (of a hawk) having reached maturity in the wild before being caught. ◆ *n* **4** *Falconry.* a haggard hawk. [C16: from OF *hagard*, ? rel. to HEDGE]

▸**'haggardly** *adv* ▸**'haggardness** *n*

haggis ('hægɪs) *n* a Scottish dish made from sheep's or calf's offal, oatmeal, suet, and seasonings boiled in a skin made from the animal's stomach. [C15: ?from *haggen* to HACK[1]]

haggle Ⓣ ('hægᵊl) *vb* **haggles, haggling, haggled.** (*intr*; often foll. by *over*) to bargain or wrangle (over a price, terms of an agreement, etc.); barter. [C16: of Scand. origin]

▸**'haggler** *n*

hagio- *or before a vowel* **hagi-** *combining form.* indicating a saint, saints, or holiness: *hagiography*. [via LL from Gk, from *hagios* holy]

Hagiographa (,hægɪ'ɒgrəfə) *n* the third of the three main parts into which the books of the Old Testament are divided in Jewish tradition (the other two parts being the Law and the Prophets).

hagiographer (,hægɪ'ɒgrəfə) *or* **hagiographist** *n* **1** a person who writes about the lives of the saints. **2** one of the writers of the Hagiographa.

hagiography (,hægɪ'ɒgrəfɪ) *n, pl* **hagiographies. 1** the writing of the lives of the saints. **2** a biography that idealizes or idolizes its subject.

▸**hagiographic** (,hægɪə'græfɪk) *or* **,hagio'graphical** *adj*

hagiolatry (,hægɪ'ɒlətrɪ) *n* worship or veneration of saints.

hagiology (,hægɪ'ɒlədʒɪ) *n, pl* **hagiologies.** literature concerned with the lives and legends of saints.

▸**hagiological** (,hægɪə'lɒdʒɪkᵊl) *adj* ▸**,hagi'ologist** *n*

hag-ridden *adj* tormented or worried, as if by a witch.

THESAURUS

hackneyed *adj* = **unoriginal**, banal, clichéd, common, commonplace, overworked, pedestrian, played out (*inf.*), run-of-the-mill, stale, stereotyped, stock, threadbare, timeworn, tired, trite, worn-out
Antonyms *adj* fresh, imaginative, new, novel, original, striking, unusual

Hades *n* **1** = **underworld**, hell, infernal regions, lower world, nether regions, realm of Pluto, (the) inferno

haft *n* **1** = **handle**, helve, shaft

hag[1] *n* **1** = **crone**, fury, harridan, shrew, termagant, virago, vixen **2** = **witch**

haggard *adj* **1** = **gaunt**, careworn, drawn, emaciated, ghastly, hollow-eyed, pinched, shrunken, thin, wan, wasted, wrinkled
Antonyms *adj* bright-eyed, brisk, energetic, fresh, hale, robust, sleek, vigorous

haggle *vb* = **bargain**, barter, beat down, dicker (*chiefly US*), drive a hard bargain, wrangle

hah (hɑː) *interj* a variant spelling of **ha**[1].

ha-ha[1] ('hɑː'hɑː) *or* **haw-haw** ('hɔː'hɔː) *interj* **1** a representation of the sound of laughter. **2** an exclamation expressing derision, mockery, etc.

ha-ha[2] ('hɑːhɑː) *or* **haw-haw** ('hɔːhɔː) *n* a wall or other boundary marker that is set in a ditch so as not to interrupt the landscape. [C18: from F *haha*, prob. based on *ha!* ejaculation denoting surprise]

hahnium ('hɑːnɪəm) *n* the former name for **hassium**. [C20: after Otto *Hahn* (1879–1968), G physicist]

haik *or* **haick** (haɪk, heɪk) *n* a traditional Arabian outer garment for the head and body. [C18: from Ar.]

haiku ('haɪkuː) *or* **hokku** ('hɒkuː) *n, pl* **haiku** *or* **hokku.** an epigrammatic Japanese verse form in 17 syllables. [from Japanese, from *hai* amusement + *ku* verse]

hail[1] Ⓣ (heɪl) *n* **1** small pellets of ice falling from cumulonimbus clouds when there are strong rising air currents. **2** a storm of such pellets. **3** words, ideas, missiles, etc., directed with force and in great quantity: *a hail of abuse.* ◆ *vb* **4** (*intr;* with *it* as subject) to be the case that hail is falling. **5** (often with *it* as subject) to fall or cause to fall as or like hail. [OE *hægl*]

hail[2] Ⓣ (heɪl) *vb* (*mainly tr*) **1** to greet, esp. enthusiastically: *the crowd hailed the actress with joy.* **2** to acclaim or acknowledge: *they hailed him as their hero.* **3** to attract the attention of by shouting or gesturing: *to hail a taxi.* **4** (*intr;* foll. by *from*) to be a native of: *she hails from India.* ◆ *n* **5** the act or an instance of hailing. **6** a distance across which one can attract attention (esp. in **within hail**). ◆ *sentence substitute.* **7** *Poetic.* an exclamation of greeting. [C12: from ON *heill* healthy]

hail-fellow-well-met Ⓣ *adj* genial and familiar, esp. in an offensive or ingratiating way.

Hail Mary *n* **1** Also called: **Ave Maria.** *RC Church.* a prayer to the Virgin Mary, based on the salutations of the angel Gabriel (Luke 1:28) and Elizabeth (Luke 1:42) to her. **2** *American football sl.* a very long high pass into the end zone, made in the final seconds of a half or of a game.

hailstone ('heɪl,stəun) *n* a pellet of hail.

hailstorm ('heɪl,stɔːm) *n* a storm during which hail falls.

hair Ⓣ (hɛə) *n* **1** any of the threadlike structures that grow from follicles beneath the skin of mammals. **2** a growth of such structures, as on an animal's body, which helps prevent heat loss. **3** *Bot.* any threadlike outgrowth, such as a root hair. **4** a fabric made from the hair of some animals. **5** another word for **hair's-breadth:** *to lose by a hair.* **6 get in someone's hair.** *Inf.* to annoy someone persistently. **7 hair of the dog (that bit one).** an alcoholic drink taken as an antidote to a hangover. **8 keep your hair on!** *Brit. inf.* keep calm. **9 let one's hair down.** to behave without reserve. **10 not turn a hair.** to show no surprise, anger, fear, etc. **11 split hairs.** to make petty and unnecessary distinctions. [OE *hær*]
▸**'hairless** *adj* ▸**'hair,like** *adj*

haircloth ('hɛə,klɒθ) *n* a cloth woven from horsehair, used (esp. formerly) in upholstery, etc.

haircut ('hɛə,kʌt) *n* **1** the act of cutting the hair. **2** the style in which hair has been cut.

hairdo ('hɛə,duː) *n, pl* **hairdos.** the arrangement of a person's hair, esp. after styling and setting.

hairdresser Ⓣ ('hɛə,drɛsə) *n* **1** a person whose business is cutting, dyeing, and arranging hair. **2** a hairdresser's establishment. ◆ Related adj: **tonsorial.**
▸**'hair,dressing** *n*

-haired *adj* having hair as specified: *long-haired.*

hair gel *n* a preparation used in hair styling.

hairgrip ('hɛə,grɪp) *n Chiefly Brit.* a small tightly bent metal hair clip. Also called (US, Canad., and NZ): **bobby pin.**

hairline ('hɛə,laɪn) *n* **1** the natural margin formed by hair on the head. **2a** a very narrow line. **2b** (*as modifier*): *a hairline crack.*

hairline fracture *n* a very fine crack in a bone.

hairnet ('hɛə,nɛt) *n* any of several kinds of light netting worn over the hair to keep it in place.

hairpiece Ⓣ ('hɛə,piːs) *n* **1** a wig or toupee. **2** a section of extra hair attached to a woman's real hair to give it greater bulk or length.

hairpin ('hɛə,pɪn) *n* **1** a thin double-pronged pin used to fasten the hair. **2** (*modifier*) (esp. of a bend in a road) curving very sharply.

hair-raising Ⓣ *adj* inspiring horror; terrifying.

hair's-breadth Ⓣ *n* **a** a very short or imperceptible margin or distance. **b** (*as modifier*): *a hair's-breadth escape.*

hair shirt *n* **1** a shirt made of haircloth worn next to the skin as a penance. **2** a secret trouble or affliction.

hair slide *n* a hinged clip with a tortoiseshell, bone, or similar back, used to fasten a girl's hair.

hairsplitting Ⓣ ('hɛə,splɪtɪŋ) *n* **1** the making of petty distinctions. ◆ *adj* **2** occupied with or based on petty distinctions.
▸**'hair,splitter** *n*

hairspring ('hɛə,sprɪŋ) *n* a fine spiral spring in some timepieces which, in combination with the balance wheel, controls the timekeeping.

hairstreak ('hɛə,striːk) *n* a small butterfly having fringed wings with narrow white streaks.

hairstyle Ⓣ ('hɛə,staɪl) *n* a particular mode of arranging the hair.
▸**'hair,stylist** *n*

hair trigger *n* **1** a trigger of a firearm that responds to very slight pressure. **2** *Inf.* any mechanism, reaction, etc., set in operation by slight provocation.

hairy Ⓣ ('hɛərɪ) *adj* **hairier, hairiest. 1** covered with hair. **2** *Sl.* **2a** difficult or problematic. **2b** dangerous or exciting.
▸**'hairiness** *n*

hajj *or* **hadj** (hædʒ) *n* the pilgrimage to Mecca that every Muslim is required to make at least once. [from Ar.]

hajji, hadji, *or* **haji** ('hædʒɪ) *n, pl* **hajjis, hadjis,** *or* **hajis. 1** a Muslim who has made a pilgrimage to Mecca: also used as a title. **2** a Christian who has visited Jerusalem.

haka ('hɑːkə) *n NZ.* **1** a Maori war chant accompanied by gestures. **2** a similar performance by, for instance, a rugby team.

hake (heɪk) *n, pl* **hake** *or* **hakes. 1** a gadoid food fish of the N hemisphere, having an elongated body with a large head and two dorsal fins. **2** a similar North American fish. [C15: ?from ON *haki* hook]

hakea ('hɑːkɪə, 'heɪkɪə) *n* any shrub or tree of the Australian genus *Hakea,* having a hard woody fruit and often yielding a useful wood. [C19: NL, after C. L. von *Hake* (died 1818), G botanist]

hakim *or* **hakeem** (hɑː'kiːm) *n* **1** a Muslim judge, ruler, or administrator. **2** a Muslim physician. [C17: from Ar., from *hakama* to rule]

Halakah *or* **Halacha** (,hɑːlə'kɑː, hə'lɑːkə) *n* that part of traditional Jewish literature concerned with the law, as contrasted with Haggadah. [C19: from Heb.: way, from *hālakh* to go]
▸**Halakic** *or* **Halachic** (hə'lækɪk) *adj*

halal *or* **hallal** (hɑː'lɑːl) *n* **1** meat from animals that have been killed according to Muslim law. ◆ *adj* **2** of or relating to such meat: *a halal butcher.* ◆ *vb* **halals, halalling, halalled** *or* **hallals, hallalling, hallalled.** (*tr*) **3** to kill (animals) according to Muslim law. [from Ar.: lawful]

halation (hə'leɪʃən) *n Photog.* fogging usually seen as a bright ring surrounding a source of light. [C19: from HALO + -ATION]

halberd ('hælbəd) *or* **halbert** ('hælbət) *n* a weapon consisting of a long shaft with an axe blade and a pick, topped by a spearhead: used in 15th- and 16th-century warfare. [C15: from OF *hallebarde,* from MHG *helm* handle + *barde* axe]
▸**,halber'dier** *n*

halcyon Ⓣ ('hælsɪən) *adj* **1** peaceful, gentle, and calm. **2 halcyon days. 2a** a fortnight of calm weather during the winter solstice. **2b** a period of peace and happiness. ◆ *n* **3** *Greek myth.* a fabulous bird associated with the winter solstice. **4** a poetic name for the **kingfisher.** [C14: from L *alcyon,* from Gk *alkuōn* kingfisher, from ?]

hale[1] Ⓣ (heɪl) *adj* healthy and robust (esp. in **hale and hearty**). [OE *hæl* WHOLE]
▸**'haleness** *n*

hale[2] (heɪl) *vb* **hales, haling, haled.** (*tr*) to pull or drag. [C13: from OF *haler,* of Gmc origin]
▸**'haler** *n*

half Ⓣ (hɑːf) *n, pl* **halves** (hɑːvz). **1a** either of two equal or corresponding parts that together comprise a whole. **1b** a quantity equalling such a

THESAURUS

hail[1] *n* **3** = **shower,** barrage, bombardment, downpour, pelting, rain, storm, volley ◆ *vb* **5** = **shower,** barrage, batter, beat down upon, bombard, pelt, rain, rain down on, storm, volley

hail[2] *vb* **1** = **salute,** greet, welcome **2** = **acclaim,** acknowledge, applaud, cheer, exalt, glorify, honour **3** = **flag down,** accost, address, call, halloo, shout to, signal to, sing out, speak to, wave down **4** *foll. by* **from** = **come from,** be a native of, be born in, originate in
Antonyms *vb* ≠ **salute:** avoid, cut (*inf.*), ignore, snub ≠ **acclaim:** boo, condemn, criticize, hiss, insult, jeer

hail-fellow-well-met *adj* = **overfriendly,** back-slapping, familiar, free-and-easy, genial, hearty, unceremonious

hair *n* **2** = **locks,** head of hair, mane, mop, shock, tresses **5** = **narrow margin,** fraction of an inch, hair's-breadth, split second, the skin of one's teeth, whisker **6 get in one's hair** *Informal* = **annoy,** aggravate (*inf.*), be on one's back (*sl.*), exasperate, get on one's nerves (*inf.*), harass, hassle (*inf.*), irritate, nark (*Brit., Austral., & NZ sl.*), pester, piss one off (*taboo sl.*), plague **9 let one's hair down** = **let oneself go,** chill out (*sl., chiefly US*), let it all hang out, let off steam (*inf.*), mellow out (*inf.*), relax, veg out (*sl., chiefly US*) **10 not turn a hair** = **remain calm,** keep one's cool (*sl.*), keep one's hair on (*Brit. inf.*), not bat an eyelid **11 split hairs** = **quibble,** cavil, find fault, overrefine, pettifog

hairdresser *n* **1** = **stylist,** barber, coiffeur *or* coiffeuse

hairless *adj* **2** = **bare,** bald, baldheaded, beardless, clean-shaven, depilated, shorn

hairpiece *n* **1** = **wig,** toupee

hair-raising *adj* = **frightening,** alarming, bloodcurdling, breathtaking, creepy, exciting, horrifying, petrifying, scary, shocking, spine-chilling, startling, terrifying, thrilling

hair's-breadth *n* **a** = **fraction,** hair, jot, narrow margin, whisker ◆ *modifier* **b** = **narrow,** close, hazardous

hairsplitting *adj* **2** = **fault-finding,** captious, carping, cavilling, fine, finicky, nice, niggling, nit-picking (*inf.*), overrefined, pettifogging, quibbling, subtle

hairstyle *n* = **haircut,** coiffure, cut, hairdo, style

hairy *adj* **1** = **shaggy,** bearded, bewhiskered, bushy, fleecy, furry, hirsute, pileous (*Biology*), pilose (*Biology*), stubbly, unshaven, woolly **2b** *Slang* = **dangerous,** hazardous, perilous, risky

halcyon *adj* **1** = **peaceful,** calm, gentle, mild, pacific, placid, quiet, serene, still, tranquil, undisturbed, unruffled **2b halcyon days** = **happy,** carefree, flourishing, golden, palmy, prosperous

hale[1] *adj* = **healthy,** able-bodied, blooming, fit, flourishing, hearty, in fine fettle, in the pink, right as rain (*Brit. inf.*), robust, sound, strong, vigorous, well

half *n* **1** = **equal part,** bisection, division, fifty per cent, fraction, hemisphere, portion, section **11 by halves** = **incompletely,** imperfectly, scrappily, skimpily ◆ *adj* **14** = **partial,** incomplete, limited,

part: *half a dozen.* **2** half a pint, esp. of beer. **3** *Scot.* a small drink of spirits, esp. whisky. **4** *Football, hockey, etc.* the half of the pitch regarded as belonging to one team. **5** *Golf.* an equal score with an opponent. **6** (in various games) either of two periods of play separated by an interval. **7** a half-price ticket on a bus, etc. **8** short for **half-hour. 9** *Sport.* short for **halfback. 10** *Obs.* a half-year period. **11 by halves.** (*used with a negative*) without being thorough: *we don't do things by halves.* **12 go halves.** (often foll. by *on, in,* etc.) **12a** to share expenses. **12b** to share the whole amount (of something): *to go halves on an orange.* ◆ *determiner* **13a** being a half or approximately a half: *half the kingdom.* **13b** (*as pron; functioning as sing or pl*): *half of them came.* ◆ *adj* **14** not perfect or complete: *he only did a half job on it.* ◆ *adv* **15** to the amount or extent of a half. **16** to a great amount or extent. **17** partially; to an extent. **18 by half.** to an excessive degree: *he's too arrogant by half.* **19 half two,** etc. *Inf.* 30 minutes after two o'clock, etc. **20 have half a mind to.** to have a vague intention to. **21 not half.** *Inf.* **21a** not in any way: *he's not half clever enough.* **21b** *Brit.* very: *he isn't half stupid.* **21c** yes, indeed. [OE *healf*]

half- *prefix* **1** one of two equal parts: *half-moon.* **2** related through one parent only: *half-brother.* **3** not completely; partly: *half-hardy.*

half-and-half *n* **1** a mixture of half one thing and half another thing. **2** a drink consisting of equal parts of beer and stout, or equal parts of bitter and mild.

halfback ('hɑːfˌbæk) *n* **1** *Soccer.* any of three players positioned behind the line of forwards and in front of the fullbacks. **2** *Rugby.* either the scrum half or the stand-off half. **3** any of certain similar players in other team sports.

half-baked ❶ *adj* **1** insufficiently baked. **2** *Inf.* foolish; stupid. **3** *Inf.* poorly planned.

halfbeak ('hɑːfˌbiːk) *n* a marine and freshwater teleost fish having an elongated body with a short upper jaw and a long protruding lower jaw.

half-binding *n* a type of bookbinding in which the backs are bound in one material and the sides in another.

half-blood *n* **1a** the relationship between individuals having only one parent in common. **1b** an individual having such a relationship. **2** a less common name for a **half-breed.**
▸ˌ**half-'blooded** *adj*

half board *n* accommodation at a hotel, etc., that includes breakfast and one main meal. Also called: **demi-pension.**

half-boot *n* a boot reaching to the midcalf.

half-bottle *n* a bottle of spirits or wine that contains half the quantity of a standard bottle.

half-breed *n* **1** *Often offens.* a person whose parents are of different races, esp. the offspring of a White person and an American Indian. ◆ *adj also* **half-bred. 2** of, relating to, or designating offspring of people or animals of different races or breeds.

half-brother *n* the son of either of one's parents by another partner.

half-butt *n* a snooker cue that is longer than an ordinary cue.

half-caste ◆ *Offens. n* **1** a person having parents of different races, esp. the offspring of a European and an Indian. ◆ *adj* **2** of, relating to, or designating such a person.

half-century *n* **1** a period of 50 years. **2** a score or grouping of 50: *he scored his first half-century for England.*

half-cock *n* **1** the halfway position of a firearm's hammer when the trigger is cocked by the hammer and the hammer cannot reach the primer to fire the weapon. **2 go off at half-cock** *or* **half-cocked.** to fail as a result of inadequate preparation or premature starting.

half-crown *n* a former British coin worth two shillings and sixpence (12½p). Also called: **half-a-crown.**

half-cut *adj Brit. sl.* rather drunk.

half-dozen *n* six.

half gainer *n* a type of dive in which the diver completes a half backward somersault to enter the water headfirst facing the diving board.

half-hardy *adj* (of a cultivated plant) able to survive out of doors except during severe frost.

half-hearted ❶ *adj* without enthusiasm or determination.
▸ˌ**half-'heartedly** *adv*

half-hitch *n* a knot made by passing the end of a piece of rope around itself and through the loop thus made.

half-hour *n* **1** a period of 30 minutes. **2** the point of time 30 minutes after the beginning of an hour.
▸ˌ**half-'hourly** *adv, adj*

half-hunter *n* a watch with a hinged lid in which a small circular opening or crystal allows the approximate time to be read.

half landing *n* a landing halfway up a flight of stairs.

half-life *n* the time taken for half of the atoms in a radioactive material to undergo decay.

half-light *n* a dim light, as at dawn or dusk.

half-mast *n* the lower than normal position to which a flag is lowered on a mast as a sign of mourning.

half measure *n* (*often pl*) an inadequate measure or action; compromise.

half-moon *n* **1** the moon at first or last quarter when half its face is illuminated. **2** the time at which a half-moon occurs. **3** something shaped like a half-moon.

half-nelson *n* a wrestling hold in which a wrestler places an arm under one of his opponent's arms from behind and exerts pressure with his palm on the back of his opponent's neck.

half-note *n* the usual US name for **minim** (sense 2).

halfpenny *or* **ha'penny** ('heɪpnɪ, *for sense 1* 'hɑːfˌpɛnɪ) *n* **1** (*pl* **halfpennies** *or* **ha'pennies**) a small British coin worth half a new penny (withdrawn 1985). **2** (*pl* **halfpennies** *or* **ha'pennies**) an old British coin worth half an old penny. **3** (*pl* **halfpence**) something of negligible value.
▸**halfpennyworth** *or* **ha'p'orth** ('heɪpəθ) *n*

half-pie *adj NZ inf.* ill planned; not properly thought out: *a half-pie scheme.* [from Maori *pai* good]

half-pint *n Sl.* a small or insignificant person.

half-plate *or* **half-print** *n Photog.* a size of plate measuring 6½ × 4½ inches.

half-rotten *adj* partially rotted or decomposed.

half seas over *adj Brit. inf.* drunk.

half-section *n Engineering.* a scale drawing of a section through a symmetrical object that shows only half the object.

half-sister *n* the daughter of either of one's parents by another partner.

half-size *n* any size, esp. in clothing, that is halfway between two sizes.

half-sole *n* a sole from the shank of a shoe to the toe.

half term *n Brit. education.* a short holiday midway through an academic term.

half-timbered *or* **half-timber** *adj* (of a building) having an exposed timber framework filled with brick, stone, or plastered laths, as in Tudor architecture.
▸ˌ**half-'timbering** *n*

half-time *n Sport.* **a** a rest period between the two halves of a game. **b** (*as modifier*): *the half-time score.*

half-title *n* **1** the short title of a book as printed on the right-hand page preceding the title page. **2** a title on a separate page preceding a section of a book.

halftone ('hɑːfˌtəʊn) *n* **1** a process used to reproduce an illustration by photographing it through a fine screen to break it up into dots. **2** the print obtained. **3** *Music.* the usual US and Canad. name for **semitone.**

half-track *n* a vehicle with caterpillar tracks on the wheels that supply motive power only.

half-truth *n* a partially true statement intended to mislead.
▸ˌ**half-'true** *adj*

half volley *n Sport.* a stroke or shot in which the ball is hit immediately after it bounces.

halfway ❶ (ˌhɑːf'weɪ) *adv, adj* **1** at or to half the distance. **2** in or of an incomplete manner. **3 meet halfway.** to compromise with.

halfway house *n* **1** a place to rest midway on a journey. **2** the halfway point in any progression. **3** a centre or hostel designed to facilitate the readjustment to private life of released prisoners, mental patients, etc.

halfwit ❶ ('hɑːfˌwɪt) *n* **1** a feeble-minded person. **2** a foolish or inane person.
▸ˌ**half'witted** *adj*

half-year *n* a period of six months.

halibut ('hælɪbət) *n, pl* **halibuts** *or* **halibut.** the largest flatfish: a dark green North Atlantic species that is a very important food fish. [C15: from *hali* HOLY (because it was eaten on holy days) + *butte* flat-fish, from MDu.]

halide ('hælaɪd) *or* **halid** ('hælɪd) *n* a binary compound containing a halogen atom or ion in combination with a more electropositive element.

halite ('hælaɪt) *n* a mineral consisting of sodium chloride in cubic crystalline form, occurring in sedimentary beds and dried salt lakes: an important source of table salt. Also called: **rock salt.** [C19: from NL *halītes,* from Gk *hals* salt + -ITE[2]]

halitosis (ˌhælɪ'təʊsɪs) *n* the state or condition of having bad breath. [C19: NL, from L *hālitus* breath, from *hālāre* to breathe]

hall ❶ (hɔːl) *n* **1** a room serving as an entry area. **2** (*sometimes cap.*) a

THESAURUS

moderate ◆ *adv* **17** = **partially**, after a fashion, all but, barely, inadequately, incompletely, in part, partly, pretty nearly, slightly **18 by half** = **excessively**, considerably, very much

half-baked *adj Informal* **2** = **stupid**, brainless, crackpot, crazy, dumb-ass (*sl.*), foolish, hare-brained, inane, loopy (*inf.*), senseless, silly *Informal* **3** = **poorly planned**, ill-conceived, ill-judged, impractical, short-sighted, unformed, unthought out *or* through

half-hearted *adj* = **unenthusiastic**, apathetic, cool, indifferent, lacklustre, listless, lukewarm, neutral, passive, perfunctory, spiritless, tame, uninterested
Antonyms *adj* ambitious, animated, avid, concerned, determined, eager, emotional, energetic, enthusiastic, excited, spirited, warm, wholehearted, zealous

halfway *adv* **1** = **midway**, to *or* in the middle, to the midpoint **2** = **partially**, incompletely, moderately, nearly, partly, rather **3 meet halfway** = **compromise**, accommodate, come to terms, concede, give and take, strike a balance, trade off

halfwit *n* **1** = **mental defective**, imbecile, moron, simpleton **2** = **fool**, berk (*Brit. sl.*), dimwit (*inf.*), divvy (*Brit. sl.*), dolt, dork (*sl.*), dullard, dunce, dunderhead, fathead (*inf.*), idiot, imbecile (*inf.*), jerk (*sl., chiefly US & Canad.*), nitwit (*inf.*), numbskull *or* numskull, pillock (*Brit. sl.*), twit (*inf., chiefly Brit.*), wally (*sl.*)

halfwitted *adj* **1** = **feeble-minded**, dull, dull-witted, simple, simple-minded **2** = **foolish**, barmy (*sl.*), batty, crazy, doltish, doolally (*sl.*), dumb (*inf.*), idiotic, moronic, obtuse, silly, stupid

hall *n* **1** = **entrance hall**, corridor, entry, foyer, hallway, lobby, passage, passageway, vestibule

building for public meetings. **3** (*often cap.*) the great house of an estate; manor. **4** a large building or room used for assemblies, dances, etc. **5** a residential building, esp. in a university; hall of residence. **6a** a large room, esp. for dining, in a college or university. **6b** a meal eaten in this room. **7** the large room of a house, castle, etc. **8** *US & Canad.* a corridor into which rooms open. **9** (*often pl*) *Inf.* short for **music hall.** [OE *heall*]

hallelujah, halleluiah (ˌhælɪˈluːjə), *or* **alleluia** (ˌælɪˈluːjə) *interj* **1** an exclamation of praise to God. ◆ *n* **2** an exclamation of "Hallelujah". **3** a musical composition that uses the word *Hallelujah* as its text. [C16: from Heb. *hellēl* to praise + *yāh* the Lord]

halliard (ˈhæljəd) *n* a variant spelling of **halyard.**

hallmark ⓣ (ˈhɔːlˌmɑːk) *n* **1** *Brit.* an official series of marks stamped by the London Guild of Goldsmiths on gold, silver, or platinum articles to guarantee purity, date of manufacture, etc. **2** a mark of authenticity or excellence. **3** an outstanding feature. ◆ *vb* **4** (*tr*) to stamp with or as if with a hallmark. [C18: after Goldsmiths' *Hall* in London, where items were graded and stamped]

hallo (həˈləʊ) *sentence substitute, n* **1** a variant spelling of **hello.** ◆ *sentence substitute, n, vb* **2** a variant spelling of **halloo.**

halloo ⓣ (həˈluː), **hallo,** *or* **halloa** (həˈləʊ) *sentence substitute.* **1** a shout to attract attention, esp. to call hounds at a hunt. ◆ *n, pl* **halloos, hallos,** *or* **halloas. 2** a shout of "halloo". ◆ *vb* **halloos, hallooing, hallooed; hallos, halloing, halloed;** *or* **halloas, halloaing, halloaed. 3** to shout. **4** (*tr*) to urge on (dogs) with shouts. [C16: ? var. of *hallow* to encourage hounds by shouting]

hallow (ˈhæləʊ) *vb* (*tr*) **1** to consecrate or set apart as being holy. **2** to venerate as being holy. [OE *hālgian,* from *hālig* HOLY]
▸ˈ**hallower** *n*

hallowed ⓣ (ˈhæləʊd; *liturgical* ˈhæləʊɪd) *adj* **1** set apart as sacred. **2** consecrated or holy.

Halloween *or* **Hallowe'en** (ˌhæləʊˈiːn) *n* the eve of All Saints' Day celebrated on Oct. 31; Allhallows Eve. [C18: see ALLHALLOWS, EVEN[2]]

hall stand *or esp. US* **hall tree** *n* a piece of furniture for hanging coats, hats, etc., on.

Hallstatt (ˈhælstæt) *adj* of a late Bronze Age culture extending from central Europe to Britain and lasting from the 9th to the 5th century B.C. [C19: after *Hallstatt,* Austrian village where remains were found]

hallucinate ⓣ (həˈluːsɪˌneɪt) *vb* **hallucinates, hallucinating, hallucinated.** (*intr*) to experience hallucinations. [C17: from L *ālūcinārī* to wander in mind]
▸**halˈluciˌnator** *n*

hallucination ⓣ (həˌluːsɪˈneɪʃən) *n* the alleged perception of an object when no object is present, occurring under hypnosis, in some mental disorders, etc.
▸**halˈlucinatory** *adj*

hallucinogen (həˈluːsɪnəˌdʒɛn) *n* any drug that induces hallucinations.
▸**hallucinogenic** (həˌluːsɪnəˈdʒɛnɪk) *adj*

hallux (ˈhæləks) *n* the first digit on the hind foot of a mammal, bird, reptile, or amphibian; the big toe of man. [C19: NL, from LL *allex* big toe]

hallway (ˈhɔːlˌweɪ) *n* a hall or corridor.

halm (hɔːm) *n* a variant spelling of **haulm.**

halma (ˈhælmə) *n* a board game in which players attempt to transfer their pieces from their own to their opponents' bases. [C19: from Gk *halma* leap]

halo ⓣ (ˈheɪləʊ) *n, pl* **haloes** *or* **halos. 1** a disc or ring of light around the head of an angel, saint, etc., as in painting. **2** the aura surrounding a famous or admired person, thing, or event. **3** a circle of light around the sun or moon, caused by the refraction of light by particles of ice. ◆ *vb* **haloes** *or* **halos, haloing, haloed. 4** to surround with or form a halo. [C16: from Med. L, from L *halōs* circular threshing floor, from Gk]

halogen (ˈhæləˌdʒɛn) *n* any of the chemical elements fluorine, chlorine, bromine, iodine, and astatine. They are all monovalent and readily form negative ions. [C19: from Swedish, from Gk *hals* salt + -GEN]
▸**halogenous** (həˈlɒdʒɪnəs) *adj*

halogenate (ˈhælədʒəˌneɪt) *vb* **halogenates, halogenating, halogenated.** *Chem.* to treat or combine with a halogen.
▸ˌ**halogenˈation** *n*

haloid (ˈhælɔɪd) *Chem.* ◆ *adj* **1** derived from a halogen: *a haloid salt.* ◆ *n* **2** a compound containing halogen atoms in its molecules.

halon (ˈhælɒn) *n* any of a class of chemical compounds derived from hydrocarbons by replacing one or more hydrogen atoms by bromine atoms and other hydrogen atoms by other halogen atoms (chlorine, fluorine, or iodine).

halt[1] ⓣ (hɔːlt) *n* **1** an interruption or end to movement or progress. **2** *Chiefly Brit.* a minor railway station, without permanent buildings. **3** **call a halt (to).** to put an end (to); stop. ◆ *n, sentence substitute.* **4** a command to halt, esp. as an order when marching. ◆ *vb* **5** to come or bring to a halt. [C17: from *to make halt,* translation of G *halt machen,* from *halten* to stop]

halt[2] ⓣ (hɔːlt) *vb* (*intr*) **1** (esp. of verse) to falter or be defective. **2** to be unsure. **3** *Arch.* to be lame. ◆ *adj* **4** *Arch.* **4a** lame. **4b** (*as collective n; preceded by the*): *the halt.* [OE *healt* lame]

halter (ˈhɔːltə) *n* **1** headgear for a horse, usually with a rope for leading. **2** Also: **halterneck.** a style of woman's top fastened behind the neck and waist, leaving the back and arms bare. **3** a rope having a noose for hanging a person. **4** death by hanging. ◆ *vb* (*tr*) **5** to put on a halter. **6** to hang (someone). [OE *hælfter*]

haltere (ˈhæltɪə) *n, pl* **halteres** (hælˈtɪəriːz). one of a pair of short projections in dipterous insects that are modified hind wings, used for maintaining equilibrium during flight. [C18: from Gk *haltēres* (pl) hand-held weights used as balancers or to give impetus in leaping, from *hallesthai* to leap]

halting ⓣ (ˈhɔːltɪŋ) *adj* **1** hesitant: *halting speech.* **2** lame.
▸ˈ**haltingly** *adv*

halvah, halva (ˈhælvɑː), *or* **halavah** (ˈhæləvɑː) *n* an Eastern sweetmeat made of honey and containing sesame seeds, nuts, etc. [from Yiddish *halva,* ult. from Ar. *halwā*]

halve ⓣ (hɑːv) *vb* **halves, halving, halved.** (*mainly tr*) **1** to divide into two approximately equal parts. **2** to share equally. **3** (*also intr*) to reduce by half, as by cutting. **4** *Golf.* to take the same number of strokes on (a hole or round) as one's opponent. [OE *hielfan*]

halyard *or* **halliard** (ˈhæljəd) *n Naut.* a line for hoisting or lowering a sail, flag, or spar. [C14 *halier,* infl. by YARD[1]; see HALE[2]]

ham[1] (hæm) *n* **1** the part of the hindquarters of a pig between the hock and the hip. **2** the meat of this part. **3** *Inf.* the back of the leg above the knee. [OE *hamm*]

ham[2] (hæm) *n* **1** *Theatre, inf.* **1a** an actor who overacts or relies on stock gestures. **1b** overacting or clumsy acting. **1c** (*as modifier*): *a ham actor.* **2** *Inf.* a licensed amateur radio operator. ◆ *vb* **hams, hamming, hammed. 3** *Inf.* to overact. [C19: special use of HAM[1]; in some senses prob. infl. by AMATEUR]

hamadryad (ˌhæməˈdraɪəd) *n* **1** *Classical myth.* a nymph who inhabits a tree and dies with it. **2** another name for **king cobra.** [C14: from L *Hamādryas,* from Gk *Hamadruas,* from *hama* together with + *drus* tree]

hamadryas (ˌhæməˈdraɪəs) *n* a baboon of Arabia and NE Africa, having long silvery hair on the head, neck, and chest. [C19: via NL from L; see HAMADRYAD]

hamba (ˈhæmbə) *sentence substitute. S. African, usually offens.* go away; be off. [from a Bantu language, from *ukuttamba* to go]

hamburger (ˈhæmˌbɜːgə) *n* a cake of minced beef, often served in a bread roll. Also called: **beefburger.** [C20: from *Hamburger steak* (steak in the fashion of *Hamburg,* Germany)]

hame (heɪm) *n* either of the two curved bars holding the traces of the harness, attached to the collar of a draught animal. [C14: from MDu. *hame*]

ham-fisted ⓣ *or* **ham-handed** *adj Inf.* lacking dexterity or elegance; clumsy.

Hamitic (hæˈmɪtɪk, hə-) *n* **1** a group of N African languages related to Semitic. ◆ *adj* **2** denoting or belonging to this group of languages. **3** denoting or characteristic of the Hamites, a group of peoples of N Africa, including the ancient Egyptians, supposedly descended from Noah's son Ham.

hamlet (ˈhæmlɪt) *n* a small village, esp. (in Britain) one without its own church. [C14: from OF *hamelet,* dim. of *hamel,* from *ham,* of Gmc origin]

hammer ⓣ (ˈhæmə) *n* **1** a hand tool consisting of a heavy usually steel head held transversely on the end of a handle, used for driving in nails, etc. **2** any tool or device with a similar function, such as the

THESAURUS

2, 4 = **meeting place**, assembly room, auditorium, chamber, concert hall

hallmark *n* **2** = **seal**, authentication, device, endorsement, mark, sign, signet, stamp, symbol **3** = **indication**, badge, emblem, sure sign, telltale sign

halloo *vb* **3** = **call**, cry, hail, shout

hallowed *adj* **1, 2** = **sanctified**, beatified, blessed, consecrated, dedicated, holy, honoured, inviolable, revered, sacred, sacrosanct

hallucinate *vb* = **imagine**, daydream, envision, fantasize, freak out (*inf.*), have hallucinations, trip (*inf.*)

hallucination *n* = **illusion**, apparition, delusion, dream, fantasy, figment of the imagination, mirage, phantasmagoria, vision

hallucinogenic *adj* = **psychedelic**, hallucinatory, mind-blowing (*inf.*), mind-expanding, psychoactive, psychotropic

halo *n* **3** = **ring of light**, aura, aureole *or* aureola, corona, nimbus, radiance

halt[1] *n* **1** = **stop**, arrest, break, close, end, impasse, interruption, pause, stand, standstill, stoppage, termination ◆ *vb* **5** = **stop**, arrest, belay (*Nautical*), block, break off, bring to an end, call it a day, cease, check, close down, come to an end, curb, cut short, desist, draw up, end, pull up, rest, stand still, wait
Antonyms *n* ≠ **stop:** beginning, commencement, continuation, resumption, start ◆ *vb* ≠ **stop:** begin, commence, continue, go ahead, maintain, proceed, resume, start

halt[2] *vb* **1** = **falter**, be defective, hobble, limp, stumble **2** = **be unsure**, boggle, dither (*chiefly Brit.*), haver, hesitate, pause, stammer, swither (*Scot.*), think twice, waver ◆ *adj* **3** *Archaic* = **lame**, crippled, limping

halting *adj* **1** = **faltering**, awkward, hesitant, imperfect, laboured, stammering, stumbling, stuttering

halve *vb* **1** = **bisect**, cut in half, divide equally, split in two **3** = **reduce by fifty per cent**

ham-fisted *adj Informal* = **clumsy**, all fingers and thumbs, awkward, bungling, butterfingered (*inf.*), cack-handed (*inf.*), ham-handed (*inf.*), inept, maladroit, unhandy

hammer *vb* **12** = **hit**, bang, beat, drive, knock, strike, tap **13** = **fashion**, beat out, forge, form, make, shape **15** *often with* **into** = **impress upon**, din into, drive home, drub into, drum into, grind into, instruct, repeat **16** *often with* **away** = **work**, beaver away (*Brit. inf.*), drudge, grind, keep on, peg away, persevere, persist, plug

striking head on a bell. **3** a power-driven striking tool, esp. one used in forging. **4** a part of a gunlock that strikes the primer or percussion cap when the trigger is pulled. **5** *Athletics*. **5a** a heavy metal ball attached to a flexible wire: thrown in competitions. **5b** the sport of throwing the hammer. **6** an auctioneer's gavel. **7** a device on a piano that is made to strike a string or group of strings causing them to vibrate. **8** *Anat.* the nontechnical name for **malleus. 9 go under the hammer.** to be offered for sale by an auctioneer. **10 hammer and tongs.** with great effort or energy. **11 on someone's hammer.** *Austral. & NZ sl.* persistently demanding and critical of someone. ◆ *vb* **12** to strike or beat with or as if with a hammer. **13** (*tr*) to shape with or as if with a hammer. **14** (*tr; foll. by in or into*) to force (facts, ideas, etc.) into (someone) through constant repetition. **15** (*intr*) to feel or sound like hammering. **16** (*intr; often foll. by away*) to work at constantly. **17** (*tr*) *Brit.* to criticize severely. **18** (*tr*) *Inf.* to defeat. **19** (*tr*) *Stock Exchange*. **19a** to announce the default of (a member). **19b** to cause prices of (securities, the market, etc.) to fall by bearish selling. [OE *hamor*]

▸ **'hammer-ˌlike** *adj*

hammer and sickle *n* the emblem on the flag of the former Soviet Union, representing the industrial workers and the peasants respectively.

hammer beam *n* either of a pair of short horizontal beams that project from opposite walls to support arched braces and struts.

hammerhead ('hæməˌhɛd) *n* **1** a shark having a flattened hammer-shaped head. **2** a tropical African wading bird having a dark plumage and a long backward-pointing crest. **3** a large African fruit bat with a hammer-shaped muzzle.

▸ **'hammerˌheaded** *adj*

hammerlock ('hæməˌlɒk) *n* a wrestling hold in which a wrestler twists his opponent's arm upwards behind his back.

hammer out ⓣ *vb* (*tr, adv*) **1** to shape or remove with or as if with a hammer. **2** to settle or reconcile (differences, problems, etc.).

hammertoe ('hæməˌtəʊ) *n* a deformity causing the toe to be bent in a clawlike arch.

hammock ('hæmək) *n* a length of canvas, net, etc., suspended at the ends and used as a bed. [C16: from Sp. *hamaca*, from Amerind]

hammy ('hæmɪ) *adj* **hammier, hammiest.** *Inf.* **1** (of an actor) tending to overact. **2** (of a play, performance, etc.) overacted or exaggerated.

hamper[1] ⓣ ('hæmpə) *vb* **1** (*tr*) to prevent the progress or free movement of. ◆ *n* **2** *Naut.* gear aboard a vessel that, though essential, is often in the way. [C14: from ?; ? rel. to OE *hamm* enclosure, *hemm* HEM[1]]

hamper[2] ('hæmpə) *n* **1** a large basket, usually with a cover. **2** *Brit.* a selection of food and drink packed in a hamper or other container. [C14: var. of earlier *hanaper* a small basket, from OF, of Gmc origin]

hamster ('hæmstə) *n* a Eurasian burrowing rodent having a stocky body, short tail, and cheek pouches: a popular pet. [C17: from G, from OHG *hamustro*, of Slavic origin]

hamstring ⓣ ('hæmˌstrɪŋ) *n* **1** one of the tendons at the back of the knee. **2** the large tendon at the back of the hind leg of a horse, etc. ◆ *vb* **hamstrings, hamstringing, hamstrung.** (*tr*) **3** to cripple by cutting the hamstring of. **4** to thwart. [C16: HAM[1] + STRING]

hamulus ('hæmjʊləs) *n, pl* **hamuli** (-ˌlaɪ). *Biol.* a hook or hooklike process, between the fore and hind wings of a bee. [C18: from L: a little hook, from *hāmus* hook]

hand ⓣ (hænd) *n* **1** the prehensile part of the body at the end of the arm, consisting of a thumb, four fingers, and a palm. Related adj: **manual. 2** the corresponding part in animals. **3** something resembling this in shape or function. **4a** the cards dealt in one round of a card game. **4b** a player holding such cards. **4c** one round of a card game. **5** agency or influence: *the hand of God*. **6** a part in something done: *he had a hand in the victory*. **7** assistance: *to give someone a hand*. **8** a pointer on a dial, indicator, or gauge, esp. on a clock. **9** acceptance or pledge of partnership, as in marriage. **10** a position indicated by its location to the side of an object or the observer: *on the right hand*. **11** a contrastive aspect, condition, etc.: *on the other hand*. **12** source or origin: *a story heard at third hand*. **13** a person, esp. one who creates something: *a good hand at painting*. **14** a manual worker. **15** a member of a ship's crew: *all hands on deck*. **16** a person's handwriting: *the letter was in his own hand*. **17** a round of applause: *give him a hand*. **18** a characteristic way of doing something: *the hand of a master*. **19** a unit of length equalling four inches, used for measuring the height of horses. **20** a cluster of bananas. **21** (*modifier*) **21a** of or involving the hand: *a hand grenade*. **21b** carried in or worn on the hand: *hand luggage*. **21c** operated by hand: *a hand drill*. **22** (*in combination*) made by hand rather than machine: *hand-sewn*. **23 a free hand.** freedom to do as desired. **24 a hand's turn.** (*usually used with a negative*) a small amount of work: *he hasn't done a hand's turn*. **25 a heavy hand.** tyranny or oppression: *he ruled with a heavy hand*. **26 a high hand.** a dictatorial manner. **27 by hand. 27a** by manual rather than mechanical means. **27b** by messenger or personally: *the letter was delivered by hand*. **28 force someone's hand.** to force someone to act. **29 from hand to mouth. 29a** in poverty: *living from hand to mouth*. **29b** without preparation or planning. **30 hand and foot.** in all ways possible; completely: *they waited on him hand and foot*. **31 hand in glove.** in close association. **32 hand over fist.** steadily and quickly: *he makes money hand over fist*. **33 hold one's hand.** to stop or postpone a planned action or punishment. **34 hold someone's hand.** to support, help, or guide someone, esp. by giving sympathy. **35 in hand. 35a** under control. **35b** receiving attention. **35c** available in reserve. **35d** with deferred payment: *he works a week in hand*. **36 keep one's hand in.** to maintain a limited involvement in an activity so as to preserve one's proficiency at it. **37** (**near**) **at hand.** very close, esp. in time. **38 on hand.** close by; present. **39 out of hand. 39a** beyond control. **39b** without reservation or deeper examination: *he condemned him out of hand*. **40 show one's hand.** to reveal one's stand, opinion, or plans. **41 take in hand.** to discipline; control. **42 throw one's hand in.** to give up a venture, game, etc. **43 to hand.** accessible. **44 try one's hand.** to attempt to do something. ◆ *vb* (*tr*) **45** to transmit or offer by the hand or hands. **46** to help or lead with the hand. **47** *Naut.* to furl (a sail). **48 hand it to someone.** to give credit to someone. ◆ See also **hand down, hand in,** etc., **hands.** [OE *hand*]

▸ **'handless** *adj*

handbag ('hændˌbæg) *n* **1** Also called: **bag, purse** (US and Canad.), **pocketbook** (chiefly US). a woman's small bag carried to contain personal articles. **2** a small suitcase that can be carried by hand.

handball ('hændˌbɔːl) *n* **1** a game in which two teams of seven players try to throw a ball into their opponent's goal. **2** a game in which two or four people strike a ball against a wall with the hand. **3** *Soccer.* the offence committed when a player other than a goalkeeper in his own penalty area touches the ball with a hand. ◆ *vb* **4** *Australian Rules football.* to pass (the ball) with a blow of the fist.

handbarrow ('hændˌbærəʊ) *n* a flat tray for transporting loads, usually carried by two men.

handbill ('hændˌbɪl) *n* a small printed notice for distribution by hand.

handbook ⓣ ('hændˌbʊk) *n* a reference book listing brief facts on a subject or place or directions for maintenance or repair, as of a car.

handbrake ('hændˌbreɪk) *n* **1** a brake operated by a hand lever. **2** the lever that operates the handbrake.

handbrake turn *n* a turn sharply reversing the direction of a vehicle by speedily applying the handbrake while turning the steering wheel.

handbreadth ('hændˌbrɛtθ, -ˌbrɛdθ) *or* **hand's-breadth** *n* the width of a hand used as an indication of length.

h and c *abbrev. for* hot and cold (water).

handcart ('hændˌkɑːt) *n* a simple cart, usually with one or two wheels, pushed or drawn by hand.

handcraft ('hændˌkrɑːft) *n* **1** another word for **handicraft.** ◆ *vb* **2** (*tr*) to make by handicraft.

▸ **'handˌcrafted** *adj*

handcuff ⓣ ('hændˌkʌf) *vb* **1** (*tr*) to put handcuffs on (a person); manacle. ◆ *n* **2** (*pl*) a pair of locking metal rings joined by a short bar or chain for securing prisoners, etc.

hand down ⓣ *vb* (*tr, adv*) **1** to bequeath. **2** to pass (an outgrown garment) on from one member of a family to a younger one. **3** *US & Canad. law.* to announce (a verdict).

-handed *adj* of, for, or using a hand or hands as specified: *left-handed; a four-handed game of cards*.

handful ⓣ ('hændfʊl) *n, pl* **handfuls. 1** the amount or number that can be held in the hand. **2** a small number or quantity. **3** *Inf.* a person or thing difficult to manage or control.

handgun ⓣ ('hændˌgʌn) *n US & Canad.* a firearm that can be fired with one hand, such as a pistol.

THESAURUS

away (*inf.*), pound away, stick at **18** *Informal* = **defeat**, beat, blow out of the water (*sl.*), clobber (*sl.*), drub, lick (*inf.*), master, run rings around (*inf.*), tank (*sl.*), thrash, trounce, undo, wipe the floor with (*inf.*), worst

hammer out *vb* **2** = **work out**, accomplish, bring about, come to a conclusion, complete, finish, form a resolution, make a decision, negotiate, produce, settle, sort out, thrash out

hamper[1] *vb* **1** = **hinder**, bind, cramp, curb, embarrass, encumber, entangle, fetter, frustrate, hamstring, handicap, hobble, hold up, impede, interfere with, obstruct, prevent, restrain, restrict, slow down, thwart, trammel

Antonyms *vb* aid, assist, boost, encourage, expedite, forward, further, help, promote, speed

hamstring *vb* **3** = **lame**, cripple, disable, hock, injure **4** = **thwart**, balk, foil, frustrate, prevent, ruin, stop

hamstrung *adj* **3** = **incapacitated**, crippled, disabled, helpless, *hors de combat*, paralysed

hand *n* **1** = **palm**, fist, hook, mitt (*sl.*), paw (*inf.*) **5** = **influence**, agency, direction, part, participation, share **7** = **assistance**, aid, help, support **14** = **worker**, artificer, artisan, craftsman, employee, hired man, labourer, operative, workman **16** = **penmanship**, calligraphy, chirography, handwriting, longhand, script **17** = **round of applause**, clap, ovation **29a from hand to mouth** = **in poverty**, by necessity, improvidently, insecurely, on the breadline (*inf.*), precariously, uncertainly **31 hand in glove** = **in league**, allied, in cahoots (*inf.*), in partnership **32 hand over fist** = **steadily**, by leaps and bounds, easily, swiftly **35 in hand: a** = **in reserve**, in order, receiving attention **c** available for use, put by, ready **37 (near) at hand** = **imminent**, approaching, close, just round the corner, near **38 on hand** = **nearby**, at one's fingertips, available, close, handy, near, on tap (*inf.*), ready, within reach ◆ *vb* **45** = **give**, deliver, hand over, pass **46** = **help**, aid, assist, conduct, convey, guide, lead

handbook *n* = **guidebook**, guide, instruction book, manual

handcuff *vb* **1** = **shackle**, fetter, manacle ◆ *pl n* **2** = **shackles**, bracelets (*sl.*), cuffs, fetters, manacles

hand down *vb* **1** = **pass on** *or* **down**, bequeath, give, grant, transfer, will

handful *n* **2** = **few**, small number, small quantity, smattering, sprinkling

Antonyms *n* a lot, crowd, heaps, horde, large number, large quantity, loads (*inf.*), masses (*inf.*), mob, plenty, scores, stacks

handgun *n* = **pistol**, automatic, derringer, piece (*US sl.*), revolver, rod (*US sl.*), shooter (*inf.*)

handicap ⓣ ('hændɪˌkæp) *n* **1** something that hampers or hinders. **2a** a contest, esp. a race, in which competitors are given advantages or disadvantages of weight, distance, etc., in an attempt to equalize their chances. **2b** the advantage or disadvantage prescribed. **3** *Golf.* the number of strokes by which a player's averaged score exceeds par for the course. **4** any disability or disadvantage resulting from physical, mental, or social impairment or abnormality. ◆ *vb* **handicaps, handicapping, handicapped.** (*tr*) **5** to be a hindrance or disadvantage to. **6** to assign a handicap to. **7** to organize (a contest) by handicapping. [C17: prob. from *hand in cap,* a lottery game in which players drew forfeits from a cap or deposited money in it]
▸ **'handiˌcapper** *n*

handicapped ('hændɪˌkæpt) *adj* **1a** physically or mentally disabled. **1b** (*as collective n; preceded by the*): *the handicapped.* **2** (of a competitor) assigned a handicap.

handicraft ⓣ ('hændɪˌkrɑːft) *n* **1** skill in working with the hands. **2** a particular skill performed with the hands, such as weaving. **3** the work so produced. ◆ Also called: **handcraft.** [C15: changed from HANDCRAFT through infl. of HANDIWORK]

hand in *vb* (*tr, adv*) to return or submit (something, such as an examination paper).

handiwork ⓣ ('hændɪˌwɜːk) *n* **1** work produced by hand. **2** the result of the action or endeavours of a person or thing. [OE *handgeweorc,* from HAND + *ge-* (collective prefix) + *weorc* WORK]

handkerchief ⓣ ('hæŋkətʃɪf, -tʃiːf) *n* a small square of soft absorbent material carried and used to wipe the nose, etc.

handle ⓣ ('hænd°l) *n* **1** the part of a utensil, drawer, etc., designed to be held in order to move, use, or pick up the object. **2** *Sl.* a person's name or title. **3** *CB radio.* a slang name for **call sign. 4** an excuse for doing something: *his background served as a handle for their mockery.* **5** the quality, as of textiles, perceived by feeling. **6** *NZ.* a glass beer mug with a handle. **7 fly off the handle.** *Inf.* to become suddenly extremely angry. ◆ *vb* **handles, handling, handled.** (*mainly tr*) **8** to hold, move, or touch with the hands. **9** to operate using the hands: *the boy handled the reins well.* **10** to control: *my wife handles my investments.* **11** to manage successfully: *a secretary must be able to handle clients.* **12** to discuss (a theme, subject, etc.). **13** to deal with in a specified way: *I was handled with great tact.* **14** to trade or deal in (specified merchandise). **15** (*intr*) to react in a specified way to operation: *the car handles well on bends.* [OE]
▸ **'handled** *adj* ▸ **'handling** *n*

handlebar moustache ('hænd°lˌbɑː) *n* a bushy extended moustache with curled ends.

handlebars ('hænd°lˌbɑːz) *pl n* (*sometimes sing*) a metal tube having its ends curved to form handles, used for steering a bicycle, etc.

handler ('hændlə) *n* **1** a person who trains and controls an animal, esp. a police dog. **2** the trainer or second of a boxer.

handmade (ˌhænd'meɪd) *adj* made by hand, not by machine, esp. with care or craftsmanship.

handmaiden ('hændˌmeɪd°n) *or* **handmaid** *n* **1** a person or thing that serves a useful but subordinate purpose. **2** *Arch.* a female servant.

hand-me-down *n Inf.* **1** something, esp. an outgrown garment, passed down from one person to another. **2** anything that has already been used by another.

hand-off *Rugby.* ◆ *n* **1** the act of warding off an opposing player with the open hand. ◆ *vb* **hand off. 2** (*tr, adv*) to ward off thus.

hand on *vb* (*tr, adv*) to pass to the next in a succession.

hand organ *n* another name for **barrel organ.**

hand-out ⓣ *n* **1** clothing, food, or money given to a needy person. **2** a leaflet, free sample, etc., given out to publicize something. **3** a statement distributed to the press or an audience to confirm or replace an oral presentation. ◆ *vb* **hand out. 4** (*tr, adv*) to distribute.

hand over ⓣ *vb* **1** (*tr, adv*) to surrender possession of; transfer. ◆ *n* **handover. 2** a transfer; surrender.

hand-pick ⓣ *vb* (*tr*) to select with great care, as for a special job.
▸ **ˌhand-'picked** *adj*

handrail ('hændˌreɪl) *n* a rail alongside a stairway, etc., to provide support.

hands ⓣ (hændz) *pl n* **1** power or keeping: *your welfare is in his hands.* **2** Also called: **handling.** *Soccer.* the infringement of touching the ball with the hand or arm. **3 change hands.** to pass from the possession of one person to another. **4 hands down.** without effort; easily. **5 have one's hands full. 5a** to be completely occupied. **5b** to be beset with problems. **6 have one's hands tied.** to be unable to act. **7 lay hands on** *or* **upon. 7a** to get possession of. **7b** to beat up; assault. **7c** to find. **7d** *Christianity.* to place hands on (someone) in order to confirm or ordain. **8 off one's hands.** for which one is no longer responsible. **9 on one's hands. 9a** for which one is responsible: *I've got too much on my hands to help.* **9b** to spare: *time on my hands.* **10 wash one's hands of.** to have nothing more to do with; refuse to accept responsibility for.

handsaw ('hændˌsɔː) *n* any saw for use in one hand only.

hand's-breadth *n* another name for **handbreadth.**

handsel *or* **hansel** ('hæns°l) *Arch. or dialect.* ◆ *n* **1** a gift for good luck at the beginning of a new year, new venture, etc. ◆ *vb* **handsels, handselling, handselled** *or* **hansels, hanselling, hanselled;** *or US* **handsels, handseling, handseled** *or* **hansels, hanseling, hanseled.** (*tr*) **2** to give a handsel to (a person). **3** to inaugurate. [OE *handselen* delivery into the hand]

handset ('hændˌsɛt) *n* a telephone mouthpiece and earpiece mounted as a single unit.

handshake ('hændˌʃeɪk) *n* the act of grasping and shaking a person's hand, as when being introduced or agreeing on a deal.

hands-off *adj* **1** (of a machine, device, etc.) without need of manual operation. **2** denoting a policy, etc., of deliberate noninvolvement: *a hands-off strategy towards industry.*

handsome ⓣ ('hænsəm) *adj* **1** (of a man) good-looking. **2** (of a woman) fine-looking in a dignified way. **3** well-proportioned; stately: *a handsome room.* **4** liberal: *a handsome allowance.* **5** gracious or generous: *a handsome action.* [C15 *handsom* easily handled]
▸ **'handsomely** *adv* ▸ **'handsomeness** *n*

hands-on *adj* involving practical experience of equipment, etc.: *hands-on training in computing.*

handspring ('hændˌsprɪŋ) *n* a gymnastic feat in which a person starts from a standing position and leaps forwards or backwards into a handstand and then onto his feet.

handstand ('hændˌstænd) *n* the act of supporting the body on the hands in an upside-down position.

hand-to-hand *adj, adv* at close quarters.

hand-to-mouth *adj, adv* with barely enough money or food to satisfy immediate needs.

handwork ('hændˌwɜːk) *n* work done by hand rather than by machine.
▸ **'handˌworked** *adj*

handwriting ⓣ ('hændˌraɪtɪŋ) *n* **1** writing by hand rather than by typing or printing. **2** a person's characteristic writing style: *that is in my handwriting.*
▸ **'handˌwritten** *adj*

handy ⓣ ('hændɪ) *adj* **handier, handiest. 1** conveniently within reach. **2** easy to handle or use. **3** skilful with one's hands.
▸ **'handily** *adv* ▸ **'handiness** *n*

THESAURUS

handicap *n* **1** = **disadvantage**, albatross, barrier, block, drawback, encumbrance, hazard, hindrance, impediment, limitation, millstone, obstacle, restriction, shortcoming, stumbling block **2b** = **advantage**, edge, head start, odds, penalty, upper hand **4** = **disability**, impairment ◆ *vb* **5** = **hinder**, burden, encumber, hamper, hamstring, hobble, hold back, impede, limit, place at a disadvantage, restrict, retard
Antonyms *n* ≠ **disadvantage:** advantage, asset, benefit, boost, edge ◆ *vb* ≠ **hinder:** aid, assist, benefit, boost, forward, further, help, promote

handicraft *n* **1** = **craftsmanship**, art, artisanship, craft, handiwork, skill, workmanship

handily *adv* **1** = **conveniently**, accessibly, advantageously, helpfully, readily, suitably **3** = **skilfully**, adroitly, capably, cleverly, deftly, dexterously, expertly, proficiently

handiness *n* **1** = **convenience**, accessibility, availability, closeness, practicality, proximity, usefulness **3** = **skill**, adroitness, aptitude, cleverness, deftness, dexterity, efficiency, expertise, knack, proficiency

handiwork *n* **1** = **handicraft**, craft, handwork **2** = **creation**, achievement, artefact, design, invention, product, production, result

handkerchief *n* = **hanky** (*inf.*), tissue

handle *n* **1** = **grip**, haft, handgrip, helve, hilt, knob, stock **7 fly off the handle** *Informal* = **lose one's temper**, blow one's top, explode, flip one's lid (*sl.*), fly into a rage, go ballistic (*sl., chiefly US*), have a tantrum, hit *or* go through the roof (*inf.*), let fly (*inf.*), lose it (*inf.*), lose one's cool (*sl.*), lose the plot (*inf.*) ◆ *vb* **8** = **hold**, feel, finger, fondle, grasp, maul, paw (*inf.*), pick up, poke, touch **9** = **control**, direct, guide, manage, manipulate, manoeuvre, operate, steer, use, wield **11** = **manage**, cope with, deal with, take care of **12** = **discuss**, discourse, treat **13** = **deal with**, treat **14** = **deal in**, carry, market, sell, stock, trade, traffic in

handling *n* **11, 13** = **management**, administration, approach, conduct, direction, running, treatment

hand-out *n* **1** = **charity**, alms, dole **2** = **leaflet**, bulletin, circular, free sample, literature (*inf.*), mailshot ◆ *vb* **hand out 4** = **distribute**, deal out, disburse, dish out (*inf.*), dispense, disseminate, give out, mete

hand over *vb* **1** = **give**, deliver, donate, fork out *or* up (*sl.*), present, release, surrender, transfer, turn over, yield

hand-picked *adj* = **selected**, choice, chosen, elect, elite, recherché, select
Antonyms *adj* haphazard, indiscriminate, random, run-of-the-mill, wholesale

hands *pl n* **1** = **control**, authority, care, charge, command, custody, disposal, guardianship, keeping, possession, power, supervision **4 hands down** = **easily**, effortlessly, with no contest, with no trouble **7 lay hands on: a** = **bless**, acquire, get, grab, grasp, seize **b** assault, beat up, lay into (*inf.*), set on, work over (*sl.*) **c** find, unearth **d** *Christianity* confirm, consecrate, ordain **10 wash one's hands of** = **have nothing to do with**, abandon, accept no responsibility for, give up on, leave to one's own devices

handsome *adj* **1** = **good-looking**, attractive, dishy (*inf., chiefly Brit.*), gorgeous **2** = **majestic**, comely, elegant, graceful, personable **4** = **generous**, abundant, ample, bountiful, considerable, large, liberal, plentiful, sizable *or* sizeable **5** = **gracious**, generous, magnanimous
Antonyms *adj* ≠ **good-looking:** ugly, unattractive, unprepossessing, unsightly ≠ **generous:** base, cheap, meagre, mean, miserly, selfish, small, stingy, ungenerous

handsomely *adv* **4** = **generously**, abundantly, amply, bountifully, liberally, munificently, plentifully, richly

handwriting *n* **2** = **penmanship**, calligraphy, chirography, fist, hand, scrawl, script

handy *adj* **1** = **convenient**, accessible, at hand, at one's fingertips, available, close, just round

handyman ❶ (ˈhændɪˌmæn) *n, pl* **handymen.** a man employed to do or skilled in odd jobs, etc.

hanepoot (ˈhɑːnəˌpɔːt) *n S. African.* a kind of grape for eating or wine making. [from Du.]

hang ❶ (hæŋ) *vb* **hangs, hanging, hung. 1** to fasten or be fastened from above, esp. by a cord, chain, etc. **2** to place or be placed in position as by a hinge so as to allow free movement: *to hang a door.* **3** (*intr; sometimes foll. by over*) to be suspended; hover: *a pall of smoke hung over the city.* **4** (*intr; sometimes foll. by over*) to threaten. **5** (*intr*) to be or remain doubtful (esp. in **hang in the balance**). **6** (*p.t. & p.p.* **hanged**) to suspend or be suspended by the neck until dead. **7** (*tr*) to decorate, furnish, or cover with something suspended. **8** (*tr*) to fasten to a wall: *to hang wallpaper.* **9** to exhibit or be exhibited in an art gallery, etc. **10** to droop or allow to droop: *to hang one's head.* **11** (of cloth, clothing, etc.) to drape, fall, or flow: *her skirt hangs well.* **12** (*tr*) to suspend (game such as pheasant) so that it becomes slightly decomposed and therefore more tasty. **13** (of a jury) to prevent or be prevented from reaching a verdict. **14** (*p.t. & p.p.* **hanged**) *Sl.* to damn or be damned: used in mild curses or interjections. **15** (*intr*) to pass slowly (esp. in **time hangs heavily**). **16 hang fire.** to be delayed or to procrastinate. ◆ *n* **17** the way in which something hangs. **18** (*usually used with a negative*) *Sl.* a damn: *I don't care a hang.* **19 get the hang of.** *Inf.* **19a** to understand the technique of doing something. **19b** to perceive the meaning of. ◆ See also **hang about, hang back,** etc. [OE *hangian*]

hang about ❶ *or* **around** *vb* (*intr*) **1** to waste time; loiter. **2** (*adv; foll. by with*) to frequent the company (of someone).

hangar (ˈhæŋə) *n* a large building for storing and maintaining aircraft. [C19: from F: shed, ?from Med. L *angārium* shed used as a smithy, from ?]

hang back ❶ *vb* (*intr, adv; often foll. by from*) to be reluctant to go forward or carry on.

hangdog ❶ (ˈhæŋˌdɒg) *adj* downcast, furtive, or guilty in appearance or manner.

hanger (ˈhæŋə) *n* **1a** any support, such as a peg or loop, on or by which something may be hung. **1b** See **coat hanger. 2a** a person who hangs something. **2b** (*in combination*): *paperhanger.* **3** a type of dagger worn on a sword belt. **4** *Brit.* a wood on a steep hillside.

hanger-on ❶ *n, pl* **hangers-on.** a sycophantic follower or dependant.

hang-glider *n* an unpowered aircraft consisting of a large wing made of cloth or plastic stretched over a light framework from which the pilot hangs in a harness.
▸ **ˈhang-ˌgliding** *n*

hangi (ˈhʌŋiː) *n NZ.* **1** an open-air cooking pit. **2** the food cooked in it. **3** the social gathering at the resultant meal. [from Maori]

hang in *vb* (*intr, prep*) *Inf., chiefly US & Canad.* to persist: *just hang in there for a bit longer.*

hanging ❶ (ˈhæŋɪŋ) *n* **1a** the putting of a person to death by suspending the body by the neck. **1b** (*as modifier*): *a hanging offence.* **2** (*often pl*) a decorative drapery hung on a wall or over a window. ◆ *adj* **3** not supported from below; suspended. **4** undecided; still under discussion. **5** projecting downwards; overhanging. **6** situated on a steep slope. **7** (*prenominal*) given to issuing death sentences: *a hanging judge.*

hanging valley *n Geog.* a tributary valley entering a main valley at a much higher level because of overdeepening of the main valley, esp. by glacial erosion.

hangman (ˈhæŋmən) *n, pl* **hangmen.** an official who carries out a sentence of hanging.

hangnail (ˈhæŋˌneɪl) *n* a piece of skin torn away from, but still attached to, the base or side of a fingernail. [C17: from OE *angnægl,* from *enge* tight + *nægl* nail; infl. by HANG]

hang on ❶ *vb* (*intr*) **1** (*adv*) to continue or persist, esp. with effort or difficulty. **2** (*adv*) to grasp or hold. **3** (*prep*) to depend on: *everything hangs on this deal.* **4** (*prep*) Also: **hang onto, hang upon.** to listen attentively to. **5** (*adv*) *Inf.* to wait: *hang on for a few minutes.*

hang out ❶ *vb* (*adv*) **1** to suspend, be suspended, or lean. **2** (*intr*) *Inf.* to frequent a place. **3 let it all hang out.** *Inf., chiefly US.* **3a** to relax completely in an unassuming way. **3b** to act or speak freely. ◆ *n* **hang-out. 4** *Inf.* a place that one frequents.

hangover ❶ (ˈhæŋˌəʊvə) *n* **1** the delayed aftereffects of drinking too much alcohol. **2** a person or thing left over from or influenced by a past age.

Hang Seng Index (hæŋ sɛŋ) *n* an index of share prices based on an average of 33 stocks quoted on the Hong Kong Stock Exchange. [name of a Hong Kong bank]

hang together *vb* (*intr, adv*) **1** to be cohesive or united. **2** to be consistent: *your statements don't quite hang together.*

hang up ❶ *vb* (*adv*) **1** (*tr*) to put on a hook, hanger, etc. **2** to replace (a telephone receiver) on its cradle at the end of a conversation. **3** (*tr; usually passive; usually foll. by on*) *Inf.* to cause to have an emotional or psychological preoccupation or problem: *he's really hung up on his mother.* ◆ *n* **hang-up.** *Inf.* **4** an emotional or psychological preoccupation or problem. **5** a persistent cause of annoyance.

hank ❶ (hæŋk) *n* **1** a loop, coil, or skein, as of rope. **2** *Naut.* a ringlike fitting that can be opened to admit a stay for attaching the luff of a sail. **3** a unit of measurement of cloth, such as a length of 840 yards (767 m) of cotton or 560 yards (512 m) of worsted yarn. [C13: from ON]

hanker ❶ (ˈhæŋkə) *vb* (foll. by *for, after,* or an infinitive) to have a yearning. [C17: prob. from Du. dialect *hankeren*]
▸ **ˈhankering** *n*

hanky *or* **hankie** (ˈhæŋkɪ) *n, pl* **hankies.** *Inf.* short for **handkerchief.**

hanky-panky ❶ (ˈhæŋkɪˈpæŋkɪ) *n Inf.* **1** dubious or foolish behaviour. **2** illicit sexual relations. [C19: var. of HOCUS-POCUS]

Hanoverian (ˌhænəˈvɪərɪən) *adj* of or relating to the British royal house ruling from 1714 to 1901. [from the princely House of *Hanover,* former province of Germany]

Hansard (ˈhænsɑːd) *n* **1** the official verbatim report of the proceedings of the British Parliament. **2** a similar report kept by the Canadian House of Commons and other legislative bodies. [C19: after L. *Hansard* (1752–1828) and his descendants, who compiled the reports until 1889]

Hanse (hæns) *n* **1** a medieval guild of merchants. **2** a fee paid by the new members of a medieval trading guild. **3** another name for the **Hanseatic League.** [C12: of Gmc origin]
▸ **Hanseatic** (ˌhænsɪˈætɪk) *adj*

Hanseatic League *n* a commercial organization of towns in N Germany formed in the mid-14th century to protect and control trade.

hansel (ˈhænsᵊl) *n, vb* a variant spelling of **handsel.**

hansom (ˈhænsəm) *n* (*sometimes cap.*) a two-wheeled one-horse carriage with a fixed hood. The driver sits on a high outside seat at the rear. Also called: **hansom cab.** [C19: after its designer J. A. *Hansom* (1803–82)]

Hants (hænts) *abbrev. for* Hampshire.

Hanukkah (ˈhɑːnəkə, -nʊˌkɑː) *n* a variant of **Chanukah.**

Hanuman (ˌhʌnʊˈmɑːn) *n* **1** (*pl* **Hanumans**) another word for **entellus** (the monkey). **2** the monkey chief of Hindu mythology. [from Hindi, from Sansk. *hanumant* having (conspicuous) jaws, from *hanu* jaw]

hap (hæp) *Arch.* ◆ *n* **1** luck; chance. **2** an occurrence. ◆ *vb* **haps, happing, happed. 3** (*intr*) to happen. [C13: from ON *happ* good luck]

ha'penny (ˈheɪpnɪ) *n, pl* **ha'pennies.** *Brit.* a variant spelling of **halfpenny.**

haphazard ❶ (hæpˈhæzəd) *adv, adj* **1** at random. ◆ *adj* **2** careless.
▸ **hapˈhazardly** *adv* ▸ **hapˈhazardness** *n*

hapless ❶ (ˈhæplɪs) *adj* unfortunate; wretched.

THESAURUS

the corner, near, nearby, on hand, within reach **2** = **useful**, convenient, easy to use, helpful, manageable, neat, practical, serviceable, user-friendly **3** = **skilful**, adept, adroit, clever, deft, dexterous, expert, nimble, proficient, ready, skilled
Antonyms *adj* ≠ **convenient**: awkward, inaccessible, inconvenient, out of the way, unavailable ≠ **useful**: awkward, inconvenient, unwieldy, useless ≠ **skilful**: clumsy, ham-fisted, incompetent, inept, inexpert, maladroit, unaccomplished, unskilful, unskilled, useless

handyman *n* = **odd-jobman**, DIY expert, handy Andy (*inf.*), jack-of-all-trades

hang *vb* **1** = **suspend**, be pendent, dangle, depend, droop, incline **3** = **hover**, be poised, drift, float, remain, swing **4** *sometimes with* **over** = **threaten**, be imminent, impend, loom, menace **6** = **execute**, gibbet, lynch, send to the gallows, string up (*inf.*) **7** = **fasten**, attach, cover, deck, decorate, drape, fix, furnish **10** = **droop**, bend downward, bend forward, bow, dangle, incline, lean over, let droop, loll, lower, sag, trail **16 hang fire** = **put off**, be slow, be suspended, delay, hang back, procrastinate, stall, stick, vacillate ◆ *n* **19 get the hang of** = **grasp**, comprehend, get the knack *or* technique, understand

hang about *vb* **1** = **loiter**, dally, linger, roam, tarry, waste time **2** = **associate with**, frequent, hang out (*inf.*), hang with (*inf., chiefly US*), haunt, resort

hang back *vb* = **be reluctant**, be backward, demur, hesitate, hold back, recoil

hangdog *adj* = **guilty**, abject, browbeaten, cowed, cringing, defeated, downcast, furtive, shamefaced, wretched

hanger-on *n* = **parasite**, cohort (*chiefly US*), dependant, follower, freeloader (*sl.*), lackey, leech, ligger (*sl.*), minion, sponger (*inf.*), sycophant

hanging *adj* **3** = **suspended**, dangling, drooping, flapping, flopping, floppy, loose, pendent, swinging, unattached, unsupported **4** = **undecided**, unresolved, unsettled, up in the air (*inf.*) **5** = **projecting**, beetle, beetling, jutting, overhanging, prominent

hang on *vb* **1** = **continue**, carry on, endure, go on, hold on, hold out, persevere, persist, remain, stay the course **2** = **grasp**, cling, clutch, grip, hold fast **3** = **depend on**, be conditional upon, be contingent on, be dependent on, be determined by, hinge, rest, turn on **4** = **listen attentively**, be rapt, give ear **5** *Informal* = **wait**, hold on, hold the line, remain, stop

hang out *n* **hang-out 4** *Informal* = **haunt**, den, dive (*sl.*), home, joint (*sl.*), resort

hangover *n* **1** = **aftereffects**, crapulence, head (*inf.*), morning after (*inf.*)

hang up *n* **hang-up** *Informal* **4** = **preoccupation**, block, difficulty, inhibition, obsession, problem, thing (*inf.*)

hank *n* **1** = **coil**, length, loop, piece, roll, skein

hanker *vb, with* **for** *or* **after** = **desire**, ache, covet, crave, eat one's heart out over, hope, hunger, itch, long, lust, pine, set one's heart on, thirst, want, wish, yearn

hankering *n* = **desire**, ache, craving, hope, hunger, itch, longing, pining, thirst, urge, wish, yearning, yen (*inf.*)

hanky-panky *n Informal* **1** = **mischief**, chicanery, deception, devilry, funny business (*inf.*), jiggery-pokery (*inf., chiefly Brit.*), knavery, machinations, monkey business (*inf.*), shenanigans (*inf.*), subterfuge, trickery

haphazard *adj* **1** = **random**, accidental, arbitrary, chance, fluky (*inf.*) **2** = **unsystematic**, aimless, careless, casual, disorderly, disorganized, hit or miss, indiscriminate, slapdash, slipshod, unmethodical
Antonyms *adj* ≠ **random**: arranged, deliberate, planned ≠ **unsystematic**: careful, considered, methodical, orderly, organized, systematic, thoughtful

hapless *adj* = **unlucky**, cursed, ill-fated, ill-

▸'**haplessly** *adv* ▸'**haplessness** *n*
haplography (hæp'lɒgrəfɪ) *n, pl* **haplographies.** the accidental omission of a letter or syllable which recurs, as in spelling *endodontics* as *endontics*. [C19: from Gk, from *haplous* single + -GRAPHY]
haploid ('hæplɔɪd) *Biol.* ◆ *adj* **1** (esp. of gametes) having a single set of unpaired chromosomes. ◆ *n* **2** a haploid cell or organism. [C20: from Gk *haploeidēs*, from *haplous* single]
▸'**haploidy** *n*
haplology (hæp'lɒlədʒɪ) *n* omission of a repeated occurrence of a sound or syllable in fluent speech, as for example in the pronunciation of *library* as ('laɪbrɪ).
haply ('hæplɪ) *adv* (*sentence modifier*) an archaic word for **perhaps.**
happen ❶ ('hæpᵊn) *vb* **1** (*intr*) to take place; occur. **2** (*intr*; foll. by *to*) (of some unforeseen event, esp. death) to fall to the lot (of): *if anything happens to me it'll be your fault.* **3** (*tr*) to chance (to be or do something): *I happen to know him.* **4** (*tr*; *takes a clause as object*) to be the case, esp. by chance: *it happens that I know him.* ◆ *adv, sentence substitute.* **5** *N English dialect.* another word for **perhaps.** [C14: see HAP, -EN[1]]

USAGE NOTE See at **occur.**

happening ❶ ('hæpənɪŋ, 'hæpnɪŋ) *n* **1** an event. **2** an improvised or spontaneous performance consisting of bizarre events. ◆ *adj* **3** *Inf.* fashionable and up-to-the-minute.
happen on ❶ *or* **upon** *vb* (*intr*; *prep*) to find by chance.
happy ❶ ('hæpɪ) *adj* **happier, happiest. 1** feeling or expressing joy; pleased. **2** willing: *I'd be happy to show you around.* **3** causing joy or gladness. **4** fortunate: *the happy position of not having to work.* **5** aptly expressed; appropriate: *a happy turn of phrase.* **6** (*postpositive*) *Inf.* slightly intoxicated. [C14: see HAP, -Y[1]]
▸'**happily** *adv* ▸'**happiness** *n*
happy event *n Inf.* the birth of a child.
happy-go-lucky ❶ *adj* carefree or easy-going.
happy hour *n* a period during which some public houses, bars, restaurants, etc., charge reduced prices.
happy hunting ground *n* **1** (in Amerind legend) the paradise to which a person passes after death. **2** a productive or profitable area to explore.
happy medium *n* a course or state that avoids extremes.
haptic ('hæptɪk) *adj* relating to or based on the sense of touch. [C19: from Gk, from *haptein* to touch]
hapuka *or* **hapuku** (hə'puːkə, 'hɑːpʊkə) *n NZ.* another name for **groper.** [from Maori]
hara-kiri ❶ (ˌhærə'kɪrɪ) *or* **hari-kari** (ˌhærɪ'kɑːrɪ) *n* (formerly, in Japan) ritual suicide by disembowelment when disgraced or under sentence of death. Also called: **seppuku.** [C19: from Japanese, from *hara* belly + *kiri* cutting]
harangue ❶ (hə'ræŋ) *vb* **harangues, haranguing, harangued. 1** to address (a person or crowd) in an angry, vehement, or forcefully persuasive way. ◆ *n* **2** a loud, forceful, or angry speech. [C15: from OF, from OIt. *aringa* public speech, prob. of Gmc origin]
▸**ha'ranguer** *n*
harass ❶ ('hærəs, hə'ræs) *vb* (*tr*) to trouble, torment, or confuse by continual persistent attacks, questions, etc. [C17: from F *harasser*, var. of OF *harer* to set a dog on, of Gmc origin]
▸'**harassed** *adj* ▸'**harassment** *n*
harbinger ❶ ('hɑːbɪndʒə) *n* **1** a person or thing that announces or indicates the approach of something; forerunner. ◆ *vb* **2** (*tr*) to announce the approach or arrival of. [C12: from OF *herbergere*, from *herberge* lodging, from OSaxon]
harbour ❶ *or US* **harbor** ('hɑːbə) *n* **1** a sheltered port. **2** a place of refuge or safety. ◆ *vb* **3** (*tr*) to give shelter to: *to harbour a criminal.* **4** (*tr*) to maintain secretly: *to harbour a grudge.* **5** to shelter (a vessel) in a harbour or (of a vessel) to seek shelter. [OE *herebeorg*, from *here* army + *beorg* shelter]
harbourage *or US* **harborage** ('hɑːbərɪdʒ) *n* shelter or refuge, as for a ship.
harbour master *n* an official in charge of a harbour.
hard ❶ (hɑːd) *adj* **1** firm or rigid. **2** toughened; not soft or smooth: *hard skin.* **3** difficult to do or accomplish: *a hard task.* **4** difficult to understand: *a hard question.* **5** showing or requiring considerable effort or application: *hard work.* **6** demanding: *a hard master.* **7** harsh; cruel: *a hard fate.* **8** inflicting pain, sorrow, or hardship: *hard times.* **9** tough or violent: *a hard man.* **10** forceful: *a hard knock.* **11** cool or uncompromising: *we took a long hard look at our profit factor.* **12** indisputable; real: *hard facts.* **13** *Chem.* (of water) impairing the formation of a lather by soap. **14** practical, shrewd, or calculating: *he is a hard man in business.* **15** harsh: *hard light.* **16a** (of currency) in strong demand, esp. as a result of a good balance of payments situation. **16b** (of credit) difficult to obtain; tight. **17** (of alcoholic drink) being a spirit rather than a wine, beer, etc. **18** (of a drug) highly addictive. **19** *Physics.* (of radiation) having high energy and the ability to penetrate solids. **20** *Chiefly US.* (of goods) durable. **21** short for **hard-core. 22** *Phonetics.* (not in technical usage) denoting the consonants *c* and *g* when they are pronounced as in *cat* and *got.* **23a** heavily fortified. **23b** (of nuclear missiles) located underground. **24** politically extreme: *the hard left.* **25** *Brit. & NZ inf.* incorrigible or disreputable (esp. in **a hard case**). **26 a hard nut to crack. 26a** a person not easily won over. **26b** a thing not easily done or understood. **27 hard by.** close by. **28 hard of hearing.** slightly deaf. **29 hard up.** *Inf.* **29a** in need of money. **29b** (foll. by *for*) in great need (of): *hard up for suggestions.* ◆ *adv* **30** with great energy, force, or vigour: *the team always played hard.* **31** as far as possible: *hard left.* **32** earnestly or intently: *she thought hard about the formula.* **33** with great intensity: *his son's death hit him hard.* **34** (foll. by *on, upon, by,* or *after*) close; near: *hard on his heels.* **35** (foll. by *at*) assiduously; devotedly. **36a** with effort or difficulty: *their victory was hard won.* **36b** (*in combination*): *hard-earned.* **37** slowly: *prejudice dies hard.* **38 go hard with.** to cause pain or difficulty to (someone). **39 hard put (to it).** scarcely having the capacity (to do something). ◆ *n* **40** *Brit.* a roadway across a foreshore. **41** *Sl.* hard labour. **42**

THESAURUS

starred, jinxed, luckless, miserable, unfortunate, unhappy, wretched
happen *vb* **1** = **occur**, appear, arise, come about, come off (*inf.*), come to pass, crop up (*inf.*), develop, ensue, eventuate, follow, materialize, present itself, result, see the light of day, take place, transpire (*inf.*) **2** = **befall**, become of, betide **4** = **chance**, fall out, have the fortune to be, pan out (*inf.*), supervene, turn out
happening *n* **1** = **event**, accident, adventure, affair, case, chance, episode, escapade, experience, incident, occasion, occurrence, phenomenon, proceeding, scene
happen on *vb* = **find**, chance upon, come upon, discover unexpectedly, hit upon, light upon, stumble on, turn up
happily *adv* **1** = **joyfully**, blithely, cheerfully, gaily, gleefully, joyously, merrily **2** = **willingly**, agreeably, contentedly, delightedly, enthusiastically, freely, gladly, heartily, lief (*rare*), with pleasure **4** = **luckily**, auspiciously, favourably, fortunately, opportunely, propitiously, providentially, seasonably **5** = **aptly**, appropriately, felicitously, successfully
happiness *n* **1** = **joy**, beatitude, blessedness, bliss, cheer, cheerfulness, cheeriness, contentment, delight, ecstasy, elation, enjoyment, exuberance, felicity, gaiety, gladness, high spirits, jubilation, light-heartedness, merriment, pleasure, prosperity, satisfaction, wellbeing
Antonyms *n* annoyance, bane, depression, despondency, distress, grief, low spirits, misery, misfortune, sadness, sorrow, unhappiness
happy *adj* **1** = **joyful**, blessed, blest, blissful, blithe, cheerful, cock-a-hoop, content, contented, delighted, ecstatic, elated, floating on air, glad, gratified, jolly, joyous, jubilant, merry, on cloud nine (*inf.*), overjoyed, over the moon (*inf.*), pleased, rapt, sunny, thrilled, walking on air (*inf.*) **4** = **fortunate**, advantageous, auspicious, convenient, enviable, favourable, felicitous, lucky, promising, propitious, satisfactory, successful **5** = **apt**, appropriate, befitting, opportune, seasonable, timely, well-timed
Antonyms *adj* ≠ **joyful:** depressed, despondent, discontented, displeased, down in the dumps (*inf.*), forlorn, gloomy, joyless, low, melancholy, miserable, mournful, sad, sombre, sorrowful, sorry, unhappy ≠ **fortunate:** unfortunate, unhappy, unlucky
happy-go-lucky *adj* = **carefree**, blithe, casual, devil-may-care, easy-going, heedless, improvident, insouciant, irresponsible, light-hearted, nonchalant, unconcerned, untroubled
Antonyms *adj* careworn, cheerless, gloomy, melancholy, morose, sad, serious, unhappy
hara-kiri *n* = **ritual suicide**, seppuku
harangue *vb* **1** = **rant**, address, declaim, exhort, hold forth, lecture, spout (*inf.*) ◆ *n* **2** = **speech**, address, declamation, diatribe, exhortation, lecture, oration, spiel (*inf.*), tirade
harass *vb* = **annoy**, badger, bait, beleaguer, be on one's back (*sl.*), bother, breathe down someone's neck, chivvy (*Brit.*), devil (*inf.*), disturb, exasperate, exhaust, fatigue, harry, hassle (*inf.*), hound, perplex, persecute, pester, plague, tease, tire, torment, trouble, vex, weary, worry
harassed *adj* = **hassled** (*inf.*), careworn, distraught, harried, plagued, strained, tormented, troubled, under pressure, under stress, vexed, worried
harassment *n* = **hassle** (*inf.*), aggravation (*inf.*), annoyance, badgering, bedevilment, bother, grief (*inf.*), irritation, molestation, nuisance, persecution, pestering, torment, trouble, vexation
harbinger *n* **1** = **herald**, forerunner, foretoken, indication, messenger, omen, portent, precursor, sign
harbour *n* **1** = **port**, anchorage, destination, haven **2** = **sanctuary**, asylum, covert, haven, refuge, retreat, sanctum, security, shelter ◆ *vb* **3** = **shelter**, conceal, hide, lodge, protect, provide refuge, secrete, shield **4** = **maintain**, brood over, cherish, cling to, entertain, foster, hold, nurse, nurture, retain
hard *adj* **1, 2** = **tough**, compact, dense, firm, impenetrable, inflexible, rigid, rocklike, solid, stiff, stony, strong, unyielding **3, 5** = **strenuous**, arduous, backbreaking, burdensome, exacting, exhausting, fatiguing, formidable, Herculean, laborious, rigorous, toilsome, tough, uphill, wearying **4** = **difficult**, baffling, complex, complicated, intricate, involved, knotty, perplexing, puzzling, tangled, thorny, unfathomable **7** = **harsh**, callous, cold, cruel, exacting, grim, hardhearted, implacable, obdurate, pitiless, ruthless, severe, stern, strict, stubborn, unfeeling, unjust, unkind, unrelenting, unsparing, unsympathetic **8** = **grim**, calamitous, dark, disagreeable, disastrous, distressing, grievous, intolerable, painful, unpleasant **10** = **forceful**, driving, fierce, heavy, powerful, strong, violent **12** = **indisputable**, actual, bare, cold, definite, plain, undeniable, unvarnished, verified **29a hard up** *Informal* = **poor**, bankrupt, broke (*inf.*), bust (*inf.*), cleaned out (*sl.*), dirt-poor (*inf.*), down and out, flat broke (*inf.*), impecunious, impoverished, in queer street, in the red (*inf.*), on one's uppers (*inf.*), on the breadline, out of pocket, penniless, short, short of cash *or* funds, skint (*Brit. sl.*), strapped for cash (*inf.*), without two pennies to rub together (*inf.*) ◆ *adv* **30** = **energetically**, fiercely, forcefully, forcibly, heavily, intensely, powerfully, severely, sharply, strongly, vigorously, violently, with all one's

Taboo sl. an erection of the penis (esp. in **get** or **have a hard on**). [OE *heard*]
▸**'hardness** *n*
hard and fast Ⓣ *adj* (**hard-and-fast** *when prenominal*). (of rules, etc.) invariable or strict.
hardback ('hɑːdˌbæk) *n* **1** a book with covers of cloth, cardboard, or leather. ◆ *adj* **2** Also: **casebound, hardbound, hardcover.** of or denoting a hardback or the publication of hardbacks.
hard-bitten Ⓣ *adj Inf.* tough and realistic.
hardboard ('hɑːdˌbɔːd) *n* a thin stiff sheet made of compressed sawdust and wood pulp bound together under heat and pressure.
hard-boiled *adj* **1** (of an egg) boiled until solid. **2** *Inf.* **2a** tough, realistic. **2b** cynical.
hard card *n* a hard disk, mounted on a card, that can be added to a personal computer.
hard cash *n* money or payment in money, as opposed to payment by cheque, credit, etc.
hard coal *n* another name for **anthracite.**
hard copy *n* computer output printed on paper, as contrasted with machine-readable output such as magnetic tape.
hardcore ('hɑːdˌkɔː) *n* **1** a style of rock music characterized by short fast songs with minimal melody and aggressive delivery. **2** a type of dance music with a very fast beat.
hard core Ⓣ *n* **1** the members of a group who form an intransigent nucleus resisting change. **2** material, such as broken stones, used to form a foundation for a road, etc. ◆ *adj* **hard-core. 3** (of pornography) describing or depicting sexual acts in explicit detail. **4** extremely committed or fanatical: *a hard-core Communist.*
hard disk *n Computing.* a disk of rigid magnetizable material that is used to store data for computers: it is permanently mounted in its disk drive and usually has a storage capacity of a few gigabytes.
harden Ⓣ ('hɑːdᵊn) *vb* **1** to make or become hard or harder; freeze, stiffen, or set. **2** to make or become tough or unfeeling. **3** to make or become stronger or firmer. **4** (*intr*) *Commerce.* **4a** (of prices, a market, etc.) to cease to fluctuate. **4b** (of price) to rise higher.
▸**'hardener** *n*
hardened Ⓣ ('hɑːdᵊnd) *adj* **1** rigidly set, as in a mode of behaviour. **2** toughened; seasoned.
harden off *vb* (*tr, adv*) to cause (plants) to become resistant to cold, frost, etc., by gradually exposing them to such conditions.
hard feeling *n* (*often pl; often used with a negative*) resentment; ill will: *no hard feelings?*
hard hat *n* **1** a hat made of a hard material for protection, worn esp. by construction workers, equestrians, etc. **2** *Inf., chiefly US.* a construction worker.
hard-headed Ⓣ *adj* tough, realistic, or shrewd; not moved by sentiment.
hardhearted Ⓣ (ˌhɑːd'hɑːtɪd) *adj* unkind or intolerant.
▸ˌ**hard'heartedness** *n*
hardihood Ⓣ ('hɑːdɪˌhʊd) *n* courage or daring.
hard labour *n Criminal law.* (formerly) the penalty of compulsory physical labour imposed in addition to a sentence of imprisonment.
hard landing *n* **1** a landing by a rocket or spacecraft in which the vehicle is destroyed on impact. **2** a solution to a problem, esp. an economic problem, that involves hardship.
hard line *n* an uncompromising course or policy.
▸ˌ**hard'liner** *n*
hardly Ⓣ ('hɑːdlɪ) *adv* **1** scarcely; barely: *we hardly knew the family.* **2** only just: *he could hardly hold the cup.* **3** *Often used ironically.* not at all: *he will hardly incriminate himself.* **4** with difficulty. **5** *Rare.* harshly or cruelly.

> **USAGE NOTE** Since *hardly, scarcely,* and *barely* already have negative force, it is redundant to use another negative in the same clause: *he had hardly had* (not *he hadn't hardly had*) *time to think; there was scarcely any* (not *scarcely no*) *bread left.*

hard-nosed Ⓣ *adj Inf.* tough, shrewd, and practical.
hard pad *n* (in dogs) an abnormal increase in the thickness of the foot pads: one of the clinical signs of canine distemper. See **distemper**[1].
hard palate *n* the anterior bony portion of the roof of the mouth.
hardpan ('hɑːdˌpæn) *n* a hard impervious layer of clay below the soil.
hard paste *n* **a** porcelain made with kaolin and petuntse, of Chinese origin and made in Europe from the early 18th century. **b** (*as modifier*): *hard-paste porcelain.*
hard-pressed Ⓣ *adj* **1** in difficulties. **2** subject to severe competition or attack. **3** closely pursued.
hard rock *n* rhythmically simple rock music that is very loud.
hard sauce *n* another name for **brandy butter.**
hard science *n* one of the natural or physical sciences, such as physics, chemistry, biology, geology, or astronomy.
▸**hard scientist** *n*
hard sell *n* an aggressive insistent technique of selling or advertising.
hard-shell *adj also* **hard-shelled. 1** *Zool.* having a shell or carapace that is thick, heavy, or hard. **2** *US.* strictly orthodox.
hardship Ⓣ ('hɑːdʃɪp) *n* **1** conditions of life difficult to endure. **2** something that causes suffering or privation.
hard shoulder *n Brit.* a surfaced verge running along the edge of a motorway for emergency stops.
hardtack ('hɑːdˌtæk) *n* a kind of hard saltless biscuit, formerly eaten esp. by sailors as a staple aboard ship. Also called: **ship's biscuit, sea biscuit.**
hardtop ('hɑːdˌtɒp) *n* a car with a metal or plastic roof that is sometimes detachable.
hardware ('hɑːdˌwɛə) *n* **1** metal tools, implements, etc., esp. cutlery or cooking utensils. **2** *Computing.* the physical equipment used in a computer system, such as the central processing unit, peripheral devices, and memory. Cf. **software. 3** mechanical equipment, components, etc. **4** heavy military equipment, such as tanks and missiles. **5** *Inf.* a gun.
hard-wired *adj* (of a circuit or instruction) permanently wired into a computer, replacing separate software.
hardwood ('hɑːdˌwʊd) *n* **1** the wood of any of numerous broad-leaved trees, such as oak, beech, ash, etc., as distinguished from the wood of a conifer. **2** any tree from which this wood is obtained.
hardy Ⓣ ('hɑːdɪ) *adj* **hardier, hardiest. 1** having or demanding a tough constitution; robust. **2** bold; courageous. **3** foolhardy; rash. **4** (of plants) able to live out of doors throughout the winter. [C13: from OF *hardi,* p.p. of *hardir* to become bold, of Gmc origin; cf. OE *hierdan* to HARDEN, ON *hertha,* OHG *herten*]
▸**'hardily** *adv* ▸**'hardiness** *n*

THESAURUS

might, with might and main **32** = **intently**, assiduously, determinedly, diligently, doggedly, earnestly, industriously, persistently, steadily, strenuously, untiringly **36** = **with difficulty**, agonizingly, badly, distressingly, harshly, laboriously, painfully, roughly, severely
Antonyms *adj* ≠ **tough:** flexible, malleable, pliable, soft, weak ≠ **strenuous:** easy, easy-peasy (*sl.*), lazy, light, soft ≠ **difficult:** clear, direct, easy, easy-peasy (*sl.*), simple, straightforward, uncomplicated ≠ **harsh:** agreeable, amiable, careless, flexible, friendly, gentle, good, humane, kind, lenient, merciful, mild, permissive, pleasant ≠ **poor:** affluent, comfortable (*inf.*), fortunate, loaded (*sl.*), rich, wealthy, well-heeled (*inf.*), well-off ◆ *adv* ≠ **energetically:** lazily, lightly, loosely, softly, weakly ≠ **intently:** easily, gently, softly
hard and fast *adj* = **fixed**, binding, immutable, incontrovertible, inflexible, invariable, rigid, set, strict, stringent, unalterable
hard-bitten *adj Informal* = **tough**, case-hardened, cynical, down-to-earth, hard-headed, hard-nosed (*inf.*), matter-of-fact, practical, realistic, shrewd, unsentimental
Antonyms *adj* benign, compassionate, gentle, humane, idealistic, merciful, mild, romantic, sympathetic
hard core *adj* **hard-core 3** = **explicit**, obscene, X-rated (*inf.*) **4** = **dyed-in-the-wool**, dedicated, die-hard, extreme, intransigent, obstinate, rigid, staunch, steadfast
harden *vb* **1** = **solidify**, anneal, bake, cake, freeze, set, stiffen **2** = **accustom**, brutalize, case-harden, habituate, inure, season, train **3** = **reinforce**, brace, buttress, fortify, gird, indurate, nerve, steel, strengthen, toughen
hardened *adj* **1** = **habitual**, chronic, fixed, incorrigible, inveterate, irredeemable, reprobate, set, shameless **2** = **seasoned**, accustomed, habituated, inured, toughened
Antonyms *adj* infrequent, irregular, occasional, rare, unaccustomed
hard-headed *adj* = **shrewd**, astute, cool, hard-boiled (*inf.*), level-headed, practical, pragmatic, realistic, sensible, tough, unsentimental
Antonyms *adj* idealistic, impractical, sentimental, unrealistic
hardhearted *adj* = **unsympathetic**, callous, cold, cruel, hard, hard as nails, heartless, indifferent, inhuman, insensitive, intolerant, merciless, pitiless, stony, uncaring, unfeeling, unkind
Antonyms *adj* compassionate, forgiving, gentle, humane, kind, loving, merciful, sensitive, soft-hearted, sympathetic, understanding, warm, warm-hearted
hardihood *n* = **courage**, backbone, boldness, bottle (*Brit. sl.*), bravery, daring, determination, firmness, grit, guts (*inf.*), intrepidity, mettle, nerve, pluck, resolution, spirit, spunk (*inf.*), strength
hardiness *n* **1** = **resilience**, robustness, ruggedness, sturdiness, toughness **2** = **boldness**, courage, fortitude, intrepidity, resolution, valour
hardly *adv* **1, 2** = **barely**, almost not, faintly, infrequently, just, not quite, only, only just, scarcely **3** = **not at all**, by no means, no way **4** = **with difficulty**, at a push
Antonyms *adv* ≠ **barely:** abundantly, amply, by all means, certainly, completely, fully, indubitably, more than, really, truly, undoubtedly, well over
hard-nosed *adj Informal* = **tough**, businesslike, down-to-earth, hard-headed, hardline, practical, pragmatic, realistic, shrewd, uncompromising, unsentimental
hard-pressed *adj* **1, 2** = **under pressure**, harried, in difficulties, pushed (*inf.*), under attack, up against it (*inf.*), with one's back to the wall
hardship *n* **1, 2** = **suffering**, adversity, affliction, austerity, burden, calamity, destitution, difficulty, fatigue, grievance, labour, misery, misfortune, need, oppression, persecution, privation, toil, torment, trial, tribulation, trouble, want
Antonyms *n* aid, blessing, boon, comfort, ease, good fortune, happiness, help, prosperity, relief
hardy *adj* **1** = **strong**, firm, fit, hale, healthy, hearty, in fine fettle, lusty, robust, rugged, sound, stalwart, stout, sturdy, tough, vigorous **2** = **courageous**, bold, brave, daring, feisty (*inf., chiefly US & Canad.*), gritty, heroic, intrepid, manly, plucky, resolute, stouthearted, valiant, valorous **3** = **rash**, audacious, brazen, foolhardy, headstrong, impudent, reckless
Antonyms *adj* ≠ **strong:** delicate, feeble, fragile, frail, sickly, soft, weak, weedy ≠ **courageous:** faint-hearted, feeble, soft, weak, weedy (*inf.*), wimpish *or* wimpy (*inf.*)

hare (hɛə) *n, pl* **hares** *or* **hare.** **1** a solitary mammal which is larger than a rabbit, has longer ears and legs, and lives in a shallow nest (form). **2** **run with the hare and hunt with the hounds.** to be on good terms with both sides. **3** **start a hare.** to raise a topic for conversation. ◆ *vb* **hares, haring, hared. 4** (*intr;* often foll. by *off, after,* etc.) *Brit. inf.* to run fast or wildly. [OE *hara*]
▸ **'hare,like** *adj*

hare and hounds *n* (*functioning as sing*) a game in which certain players (**hares**) run across country scattering pieces of paper that the other players (**hounds**) follow in an attempt to catch the hares.

harebell ('hɛə,bɛl) *n* a N temperate plant having slender stems and leaves, and bell-shaped blue flowers.

harebrained ⓣ *or* **hairbrained** ('hɛə,breɪnd) *adj* rash, foolish, or badly thought out.

Hare Krishna ('hɑːrɪ 'krɪʃnə) *n* **1** a Hindu sect devoted to a form of Hinduism (**Krishna Consciousness**) based on the worship of the god Krishna. **2** (*pl* **Hare Krishnas**) a member or follower of this sect. [C20: from Hindi, literally: Lord Krishna (vocative): the opening words of a sacred verse often chanted in public by adherents of the movement]

harelip ('hɛə,lɪp) *n* a congenital cleft or fissure in the midline of the upper lip, resembling the cleft upper lip of a hare, often occurring with cleft palate.
▸ **'hare,lipped** *adj*

harem ⓣ ('hɛərəm, hɑː'riːm) *or* **hareem** (hɑː'riːm) *n* **1** the part of an Oriental house reserved strictly for wives, concubines, etc. **2** a Muslim's wives and concubines collectively. **3** a group of female animals that are the mates of a single male. [C17: from Ar. *harīm* forbidden (place)]

hare's-foot *n* a plant that grows on sandy soils in Europe and NW Asia and has downy heads of white or pink flowers.

haricot ('hærɪkəʊ) *n* a variety of French bean with light-coloured edible seeds, which can be dried and stored. [C17: from F, ?from Amerind]

Harijan ('hʌrɪdʒən) *n* a member of certain classes in India, formerly considered inferior and untouchable. [Hindi, lit.: man of God (so called by Mahatma Gandhi)]

hari-kari (,hærɪ'kɑːrɪ) *n* a non-Japanese variant spelling of **hara-kiri.**

hark ⓣ (hɑːk) *vb* (*intr; usually imperative*) to listen; pay attention. [OE *heorcnian* to HEARKEN]

hark back ⓣ *vb* (*intr, adv*) to return to an earlier subject in speech or thought.

harken ('hɑːkən) *vb* a variant spelling (esp. US) of **hearken.**
▸ **'harkener** *n*

harl (hɑːl) *n Angling.* a variant of **herl.**

harlequin ('hɑːlɪkwɪn) *n* **1** (*sometimes cap.*) *Theatre.* a stock comic character originating in the commedia dell'arte; the foppish lover of Columbine in the English harlequinade. He is usually represented in diamond-patterned multicoloured tights, wearing a black mask. **2** a clown or buffoon. ◆ *adj* **3** varied in colour or decoration. [C16: from OF *Herlequin, Hellequin* leader of band of demon horsemen]

harlequinade (,hɑːlɪkwɪ'neɪd) *n* **1** (*sometimes cap.*) *Theatre.* a play in which harlequin has a leading role. **2** buffoonery.

Harley Street ('hɑːlɪ) *n* a street in central London famous for its large number of medical specialists' consulting rooms.

harlot ⓣ ('hɑːlət) *n* a prostitute. [C13: from OF *herlot* rascal, from ?]
▸ **'harlotry** *n*

harm ⓣ (hɑːm) *n* **1** physical or mental injury. **2** moral wrongdoing. ◆ *vb* **3** (*tr*) to injure physically, morally, or mentally. [OE *hearm*]

harmattan (hɑː'mætᵊn) *n* a dry dusty wind from the Sahara blowing towards the W African coast. [C17: from native African language *haramata,* ?from Ar. *harām* forbidden thing; see HAREM]

harmful ⓣ ('hɑːmfʊl) *adj* causing or tending to cause harm; injurious.
▸ **'harmfully** *adv*

harmless ⓣ ('hɑːmlɪs) *adj* **1** not causing or tending to cause harm. **2** unlikely to annoy or worry people: *a harmless sort of man.*
▸ **'harmlessly** *adv*

harmonic (hɑː'mɒnɪk) *adj* **1** of, producing, or characterized by harmony; harmonious. **2** *Music.* of or belonging to harmony. **3** *Maths.* **3a** capable of expression in the form of sine and cosine functions. **3b** of or relating to numbers whose reciprocals form an arithmetic progression. **4** *Physics.* of or concerned with a harmonic or harmonics. ◆ *n* **5** *Physics, music.* a component of a periodic quantity, such as a musical tone, with a frequency that is an integral multiple of the fundamental frequency. **6** *Music.* (not in technical use) overtone. ◆ See also **harmonics.** [C16: from L *harmonicus* relating to HARMONY]
▸ **har'monically** *adv*

harmonica (hɑː'mɒnɪkə) *n* **1** Also called: **mouth organ.** a small wind instrument in which reeds of graduated lengths set into a metal plate enclosed in a narrow oblong box are made to vibrate by blowing and sucking. **2** See **glass harmonica.** [C18: from L *harmonicus* relating to HARMONY]

harmonic analysis *n* the representation of a periodic function by means of the summation and integration of simple trigonometric functions.

harmonic mean *n* the reciprocal of the arithmetic mean of the reciprocals of a set of specified numbers: the harmonic mean of 2, 3, and 4 is $3/(\frac{1}{2} + \frac{1}{3} + \frac{1}{4}) = 36/13$.

harmonic minor scale *n Music.* a minor scale modified from the natural by the sharpening of the seventh degree.

harmonic motion *n* a periodic motion in which the displacement is symmetrical about a point or a periodic motion that is composed of such motions.

harmonic progression *n* a sequence of numbers whose reciprocals form an arithmetic progression, as $1, \frac{1}{2}, \frac{1}{3}, \ldots$.

harmonics (hɑː'mɒnɪks) *n* **1** (*functioning as sing*) the science of musical sounds and their acoustic properties. **2** (*functioning as pl*) the overtones of a fundamental note, as produced by lightly touching the string of a stringed instrument at one of its node points while playing.

harmonic series *n* **1** *Maths.* a series whose terms are in harmonic progression, as in $1 + \frac{1}{2} + \frac{1}{3} + \ldots$. **2** *Acoustics.* the series of tones with frequencies strictly related to one another and to the fundamental tone, as obtained by touching lightly the node points of a string while playing it.

harmonious ⓣ (hɑː'məʊnɪəs) *adj* **1** (esp. of colours or sounds) fitting together well. **2** having agreement. **3** tuneful or melodious.

harmonist ('hɑːmənɪst) *n* **1** a person skilled in the art and techniques of harmony. **2** a person who combines and collates parallel narratives.

harmonium (hɑː'məʊnɪəm) *n* a musical keyboard instrument in which air from pedal-operated bellows causes the reeds to vibrate. [C19: from F, from *harmonie* HARMONY]

harmonize ⓣ *or* **harmonise** ('hɑːmə,naɪz) *vb* **harmonizes, harmonizing, harmonized** *or* **harmonises, harmonising, harmonised. 1** to make or become harmonious. **2** (*tr*) *Music.* to provide a harmony for (a tune, etc.). **3** (*intr*) to sing in harmony, as with other singers. **4** to collate parallel narratives.
▸ **,harmoni'zation** *or* **,harmoni'sation** *n*

harmony ⓣ ('hɑːmənɪ) *n, pl* **harmonies. 1** agreement in action, opinion, feeling, etc. **2** order or congruity of parts to their whole or to one another. **3** agreeable sounds. **4** *Music.* **4a** any combination of notes sounded simultaneously. **4b** the vertically represented structure of a piece of music. Cf. **melody** (sense 1b). **4c** the art or science concerned with combinations of chords. **5** a collation of parallel narratives, esp. of the four Gospels. [C14: from L *harmonia* concord of sounds, from Gk: harmony, from *harmos* a joint]

harness ⓣ ('hɑːnɪs) *n* **1** an arrangement of straps fitted to a draught animal in order that the animal can be attached to and pull a cart. **2**

THESAURUS

harebrained *adj* = **foolish**, asinine, careless, empty-headed, flighty, giddy, half-baked (*inf.*), harum-scarum, heedless, inane, mindless, rash, reckless, scatterbrained, unstable, unsteady, wild

harem *n* **1** = **women's quarters**, seraglio

hark *vb* = **listen**, attend, give ear, give heed, hear, hearken (*arch.*), mark, notice, pay attention

hark back *vb* = **return**, look back, recall, recollect, regress, remember, revert, think back

harlot *n* = **prostitute**, call girl, fallen woman, hussy, loose woman, pro (*sl.*), scrubber (*Brit. & Austral. sl.*), slag (*Brit. sl.*), slapper (*Brit. sl.*), streetwalker, strumpet, tart (*inf.*), tramp (*sl.*), whore, working girl (*facetious sl.*)

harm *n* **1** = **injury**, abuse, damage, detriment, disservice, hurt, ill, impairment, loss, mischief, misfortune **2** = **sin**, evil, immorality, iniquity, sinfulness, vice, wickedness, wrong ◆ *vb* **3** = **injure**, abuse, blemish, damage, hurt, ill-treat, ill-use, impair, lay a finger on, maltreat, mar, molest, ruin, spoil, wound
Antonyms *n* ≠ **injury:** aid, assistance, benefit, blessing, boon, gain, good, help, improvement, reparation ≠ **sin:** good, goodness, righteousness ◆ *vb* ≠ **injure:** aid, alleviate, ameliorate, assist, benefit, better, cure, heal, help, improve, repair

harmful *adj* = **injurious**, baleful, baneful, damaging, deleterious, destructive, detrimental, disadvantageous, evil, hurtful, maleficent, noxious, pernicious
Antonyms *adj* beneficial, good, harmless, healthy, helpful, innocuous, safe, wholesome

harmless *adj* **1** = **safe**, innocent, nontoxic, not dangerous **2** = **inoffensive**, gentle, innocuous, unobjectionable
Antonyms *adj* ≠ **safe:** dangerous, destructive, harmful, unhealthy, unsafe, unwholesome

harmonious *adj* **1** = **compatible**, agreeable, congruous, consonant, coordinated, correspondent, matching **2** = **friendly**, agreeable, amicable, compatible, concordant, congenial, cordial, *en rapport,* fraternal, in accord, in harmony, in unison, of one mind, sympathetic **3** = **melodious**, concordant, dulcet, euphonic, euphonious, harmonic, harmonizing, mellifluous, musical, sweet-sounding, symphonious (*literary*), tuneful
Antonyms *adj* ≠ **compatible:** contrasting, discordant, incompatible, inconsistent, unlike ≠ **friendly:** discordant, unfriendly ≠ **melodious:** cacophonous, discordant, grating, harsh, unmelodious

harmonize *vb* **1** = **go together**, accord, adapt, agree, arrange, attune, be in unison, be of one mind, blend, chime with, cohere, coordinate, correspond, match, reconcile, suit, tally, tone in with

harmony *n* **1** = **agreement**, accord, amicability, amity, assent, compatibility, concord, conformity, consensus, cooperation, friendship, goodwill, like-mindedness, order, peace, rapport, sympathy, unanimity, understanding, unity **2** = **compatibility**, balance, concord, congruity, consistency, consonance, coordination, correspondence, fitness, suitability, symmetry **4a** = **tunefulness**, euphony, melodiousness, melody, tune, unison
Antonyms *n* ≠ **agreement:** antagonism, conflict, contention, disagreement, dissension, hostility, opposition ≠ **compatibility:** conflict, disagreement, incongruity, inconsistency, unsuitability ≠ **tunefulness:** cacophony

harness *n* **1, 2** = **equipment**, gear, tack, tackle,

something resembling this, esp. for attaching something to the body: *a parachute harness.* **3** *Weaving.* the part of a loom that raises and lowers the warp threads. **4** *Arch.* armour. **5 in harness.** at one's routine work. ◆ *vb (tr)* **6** to put a harness on (a horse). **7** (usually foll. by *to*) to attach (a draught animal) to (a cart, etc.). **8** to control so as to employ the energy or potential power of: *to harness the atom.* **9** to equip with armour. [C13: from OF *harneis* baggage, prob. from ON *hernest* (unattested), from *herr* army + *nest* provisions]
▸ **'harnesser** *n*

harness race *n Horse racing.* a trotting or pacing race for horses pulling sulkies.

harp ❶ (hɑːp) *n* **1** a large triangular plucked stringed instrument consisting of a soundboard connected to an upright pillar by means of a curved crossbar from which the strings extend downwards. ◆ *vb (intr)* **2** to play the harp. **3** (foll. by *on* or *upon*) to speak or write in a persistent and tedious manner. [OE *hearpe*]
▸ **'harper** *or* **'harpist** *n*

harpoon (hɑː'puːn) *n* **1a** a barbed missile attached to a long cord and hurled or fired from a gun when hunting whales, etc. **1b** (*as modifier*): *a harpoon gun.* ◆ *vb* **2** *(tr)* to spear with or as if with a harpoon. [C17: prob. from Du. *harpoen,* from OF *harpon* clasp, ? of Scand. origin]
▸ **har'pooner** *or* **,harpoon'eer** *n*

harp seal *n* a brownish-grey North Atlantic and Arctic seal, having a dark mark on its back.

harpsichord ('hɑːpsɪ,kɔːd) *n* a horizontally strung stringed keyboard instrument, triangular in shape, with strings plucked by pivoted plectra mounted on jacks. [C17: from NL *harpichordium,* from LL *harpa* HARP + L *chorda* CHORD[1]]
▸ **'harpsi,chordist** *n*

harpy ('hɑːpɪ) *n, pl* **harpies.** a cruel grasping woman. [C16: from L *Harpyia,* from Gk *Harpuiai* the Harpies, lit.: snatchers, from *harpazein* to seize]

Harpy ('hɑːpɪ) *n, pl* **Harpies.** *Greek myth.* a ravenous creature with a woman's head and trunk and a bird's wings and claws.

harquebus ('hɑːkwɪbəs) *n, pl* **harquebuses.** a variant spelling of **arquebus.**

harridan ❶ ('hærɪdᵊn) *n* a scolding old woman; nag. [C17: from ?; ? rel. to F *haridelle,* lit.: broken-down horse]

harrier[1] ('hærɪə) *n* **1** a person or thing that harries. **2** a diurnal bird of prey having broad wings and long legs and tail.

harrier[2] ('hærɪə) *n* **1** a smallish breed of hound used originally for hare-hunting. **2** a cross-country runner. [C16: from HARE + -ER[1]; infl. by HARRIER[1]]

Harris Tweed ('hærɪs) *n Trademark.* a loose-woven tweed made in the Outer Hebrides.

harrow ❶ ('hærəʊ) *n* **1** any of various implements used to level the ground, stir the soil, break up clods, destroy weeds, etc., in soil. ◆ *vb (tr)* **2** to draw a harrow over (land). **3** to distress; vex. [C13: from ON]
▸ **'harrower** *n* ▸ **'harrowing** *adj*

harrumph (hə'rʌmf) *vb (intr) Chiefly US & Canad.* to clear or make the noise of clearing the throat.

harry ❶ ('hærɪ) *vb* **harries, harrying, harried.** **1** *(tr)* to harass; worry. **2** to ravage (a town, etc.), esp. in war. [OE *hergian;* rel. to *here* army, ON *herja* to lay waste]

harsh ❶ (hɑːʃ) *adj* **1** rough or grating to the senses. **2** stern, severe, or cruel. [C16: prob. of Scand. origin]
▸ **'harshly** *adv* ▸ **'harshness** *n*

hart (hɑːt) *n, pl* **harts** *or* **hart.** the male of the deer, esp. the red deer aged five years or more. [OE *heorot*]

hartal (hɑː'tɑːl) *n* (in India) the act of closing shops or suspending work, esp. in political protest. [C20: from Hindi *hartāl,* from *hāt* shop + *tālā* bolt for a door, from Sansk.]

hartebeest ('hɑːtɪ,biːst) *or* **hartbeest** ('hɑːt,biːst) *n* either of two large African antelopes having an elongated muzzle, lyre-shaped horns, and a fawn-coloured coat. [C18: via Afrik. from Du.; see HART, BEAST]

hartshorn ('hɑːts,hɔːn) *n* an obsolete name for **sal volatile.** [OE *heortes horn* hart's horn (formerly a chief source of ammonia)]

hart's-tongue *n* an evergreen Eurasian fern with narrow undivided fronds.

harum-scarum ❶ ('hɛərəm'skɛərəm) *adj, adv* **1** in a reckless way or of a reckless nature. ◆ *n* **2** a person who is impetuous or rash. [C17: ?from *hare* (in obs. sense: harass) + *scare,* var. of STARE]

haruspex (hə'rʌspɛks) *n, pl* **haruspices** (hə'rʌspɪ,siːz). (in ancient Rome) a priest who practised divination, esp. by examining the entrails of animals. [C16: from L, prob. from *hīra* gut + *specere* to look]
▸ **haruspicy** (hə'rʌspɪsɪ) *n*

harvest ❶ ('hɑːvɪst) *n* **1** the gathering of a ripened crop. **2** the crop itself. **3** the season for gathering crops. **4** the product of an effort, action, etc.: *a harvest of love.* ◆ *vb* **5** to gather (a ripened crop) from (the place where it has been growing). **6** *(tr)* to receive (consequences). [OE *hærfest*]
▸ **'harvesting** *n*

harvester ('hɑːvɪstə) *n* **1** a person who harvests. **2** a harvesting machine, esp. a combine harvester.

harvest home *n* **1** the bringing in of the harvest. **2** *Chiefly Brit.* a harvest supper.

harvestman ('hɑːvɪstmən) *n, pl* **harvestmen.** **1** a person engaged in harvesting. **2** Also called (US and Canad.): **daddy-longlegs.** an arachnid having a small rounded body and very long thin legs.

harvest moon *n* the full moon occurring nearest to the autumnal equinox.

harvest mouse *n* a very small reddish-brown Eurasian mouse inhabiting cornfields, hedgerows, etc.

has (hæz) *vb* (used with *he, she, it,* or a singular noun) a form of the present tense (indicative mood) of **have.**

has-been *n Inf.* a person or thing that is no longer popular, successful, effective, etc.

hash[1] ❶ (hæʃ) *n* **1** a dish of diced cooked meat, vegetables, etc., reheated in a sauce. **2** a reuse or rework of old material. **3 make a hash of.** *Inf.* to mess up or destroy. **4 settle someone's hash.** *Inf.* to subdue or silence someone. ◆ *vb (tr)* **5** to chop into small pieces. **6** to mess up. [C17: from OF *hacher* to chop up, from *hache* HATCHET]

hash[2] (hæʃ) *n Sl.* short for **hashish.**

hashish ('hæʃiːʃ, -ɪʃ) *or* **hasheesh** *n* a resinous extract of the dried flower tops of the female hemp plant, used as a hallucinogenic. See also **cannabis.** [C16: from Ar. *hashīsh* hemp]

haslet ('hæzlɪt) *or* **harslet** *n* a loaf of cooked minced pig's offal, eaten cold. [C14: from OF *hastelet* piece of spit-roasted meat, from *haste* spit, of Gmc origin]

hasn't ('hæzᵊnt) *contraction of* has not.

hasp (hɑːsp) *n* **1** a metal fastening consisting of a hinged strap with a slot that fits over a staple and is secured by a pin, bolt, or padlock. ◆ *vb* **2** *(tr)* to secure (a door, window, etc.) with a hasp. [OE *hæpse*]

Hassid ('hæsɪd) *n* a variant spelling of **Chassid.**

hassium ('hæsɪəm) *n* a synthetic element produced in small quantities by high-energy ion bombardment. Symbol: Hs; atomic no. 108. Former name: **hahnium.** [C20: from L, from *Hesse,* German state where it was discovered]

hassle ❶ ('hæsᵊl) *Inf.* ◆ *n* **1** a great deal of trouble. **2** a prolonged argument. ◆ *vb* **hassles, hassling, hassled.** **3** *(tr)* to cause annoyance or trouble to (someone); harass. **4** *(intr)* to quarrel or wrangle. [C20: from ?]

hassock ('hæsək) *n* **1** a firm upholstered cushion used for kneeling on, esp. in church. **2** a thick clump of grass. [OE *hassuc* matted grass]

hast (hæst) *vb Arch. or dialect.* (used with the pronoun *thou*) a singular form of the present tense (indicative mood) of **have.**

hastate ('hæsteɪt) *adj* (of a leaf) having a pointed tip and two outward-pointing lobes at the base. [C18: from L *hastātus,* from *hasta* spear]

haste ❶ (heɪst) *n* **1** speed, esp. in an action. **2** the act of hurrying in a

THESAURUS

trappings **5 in harness** = **working,** active, at work, busy, in action ◆ *vb* **6** = **put in harness,** saddle **7** = **yoke,** couple, hitch up **8** = **exploit,** apply, channel, control, employ, make productive, mobilize, render useful, turn to account, utilize

harp *vb* **3** *with* **on** *or* **upon** = **go on,** dwell on, labour, press, reiterate, renew, repeat, rub it in

harridan *n* = **shrew,** ballbreaker (*sl.*), battle-axe (*inf.*), nag, scold, tartar, termagant, virago, witch

harried *adj* **1** = **harassed,** agitated, anxious, beset, bothered, distressed, hard-pressed, hassled (*inf.*), plagued, tormented, troubled, worried

harrow *vb* **3** = **distress,** agonize, harass, perturb, rack, tear, torment, torture, vex, wound

harrowing *adj* **3** = **distressing,** agonizing, alarming, chilling, disturbing, excruciating, frightening, gut-wrenching, heartbreaking, heart-rending, nerve-racking, painful, racking, scaring, terrifying, tormenting, traumatic

harry *vb* **1** = **pester,** annoy, badger, bedevil, be on one's back, bother, breathe down someone's neck, disturb, get in one's hair (*inf.*), harass, hassle (*inf.*), molest, persecute, plague, tease, torment, trouble, vex, worry **2** = **ravage,** despoil, devastate, pillage, plunder, raid, rob, sack

harsh *adj* **1** = **rough,** coarse, croaking, discordant, dissonant, grating, guttural, jarring, rasping, raucous, strident, unmelodious **2** = **severe,** abusive, austere, bitter, bleak, brutal, comfortless, cruel, Draconian, drastic, grim, hard, pitiless, punitive, relentless, ruthless, sharp, Spartan, stern, stringent, tough, unfeeling, unkind, unpleasant, unrelenting
Antonyms *adj* ≠ **raucous:** harmonious, mellifluous, smooth, soft, soothing, sweet ≠ **severe:** agreeable, gentle, kind, loving, merciful, mild, pleasant, sweet

harshly *adv* **2** = **severely,** brutally, cruelly, grimly, roughly, sharply, sternly, strictly

harshness *n* **2** = **severity,** acerbity, acrimony, asperity, austerity, bitterness, brutality, coarseness, hardness, ill-temper, rigour, roughness, sourness, sternness

harum-scarum *adj* **1** = **reckless,** careless, erratic, giddy, haphazard, harebrained, hasty, ill-considered, impetuous, imprudent, irresponsible, precipitate, rash, scatterbrained, scatty (*Brit. inf.*), wild

harvest *n* **1, 3** = **gathering,** harvesting, harvest-time, reaping **2** = **crop,** produce, yield **4** = **product,** consequence, effect, fruition, result, return ◆ *vb* **5** = **gather,** mow, pick, pluck, reap

hash[1] *n* **3 make a hash of** *Informal* = **mess up,** bodge, botch, bungle, cock up (*Brit. sl.*), jumble, make a nonsense of (*inf.*), make a pig's ear of (*inf.*), mishandle, mismanage, mix, muddle

hassle *Informal n* **1** = **trouble,** bother, difficulty, grief (*inf.*), inconvenience, problem, struggle, trial, upset **2** = **argument,** altercation, bickering, disagreement, dispute, fight, quarrel, row, squabble, tussle, wrangle ◆ *vb* **3** = **bother,** annoy, badger, be on one's back (*sl.*), breathe down someone's neck, bug (*inf.*), get in one's hair (*inf.*), get on one's nerves (*inf.*), harass, harry, hound, pester

hassled *adj* **3** = **bothered,** browbeaten, hot and bothered, hounded, hunted, pressured, stressed, under pressure, uptight, worried

haste *n* **1** = **speed,** alacrity, briskness, celerity,

careless manner. **3** a necessity for hurrying; urgency. **4 make haste.** to hurry. ◆ *vb* **hastes, hasting, hasted. 5** a poetic word for **hasten.** [C14: from OF *haste,* of Gmc origin]

hasten ⓣ (ˈheɪsᵊn) *vb* **1** (*may take an infinitive*) to hurry or cause to hurry; rush. **2** (*tr*) to be anxious (to say something).
▸ **ˈhastener** *n*

hasty ⓣ (ˈheɪstɪ) *adj* **hastier, hastiest. 1** rapid; swift; quick. **2** excessively or rashly quick. **3** short-tempered. **4** showing irritation or anger: *hasty words.*
▸ **ˈhastily** *adv* ▸ **ˈhastiness** *n*

hat (hæt) *n* **1** a head covering, esp. one with a brim and a shaped crown. **2** *Inf.* a role or capacity. **3 I'll eat my hat.** *Inf.* I will be greatly surprised if (something that proves me wrong) happens. **4 keep (something) under one's hat.** to keep (something) secret. **5 pass** (*or* **send**) **the hat round.** to collect money, as for a cause. **6 take off one's hat to.** to admire or congratulate. **7 talk through one's hat. 7a** to talk foolishly. **7b** to deceive or bluff. ◆ *vb* **hats, hatting, hatted. 8** (*tr*) to supply (a person, etc.) with a hat or put a hat on (someone). [OE *hætt*]
▸ **ˈhatless** *adj*

hatband (ˈhæt,bænd) *n* a band or ribbon around the base of the crown of a hat.

hatbox (ˈhæt,bɒks) *n* a box or case for a hat.

hatch[1] ⓣ (hætʃ) *vb* **1** to cause (the young of various animals, esp. birds) to emerge from the egg or (of young birds, etc.) to emerge from the egg. **2** to cause (eggs) to break and release the fully developed young or (of eggs) to break and release the young animal within. **3** (*tr*) to contrive or devise (a scheme, plot, etc.). ◆ *n* **4** the act or process of hatching. **5** a group of newly hatched animals. [C13: of Gmc origin]

hatch[2] (hætʃ) *n* **1** a covering for a hatchway. **2a** short for **hatchway. 2b** a door in an aircraft or spacecraft. **3** Also called: **serving hatch.** an opening in a wall separating a kitchen from a dining area. **4** the lower half of a divided door. **5** a sluice in a dam, dyke, or weir. **6 down the hatch.** *Sl.* (used as a toast) drink up! **7 under hatches. 7a** below decks. **7b** out of sight. **7c** dead. [OE *hæcc*]

hatch[3] (hætʃ) *vb Drawing, engraving, etc.* to mark (a figure, etc.) with fine parallel or crossed lines to indicate shading. [C15: from OF *hacher* to chop, from *hache* HATCHET]
▸ **ˈhatching** *n*

hatch[4] (hætʃ) *n Inf.* short for **hatchback.**

hatchback (ˈhætʃ,bæk) *n* **1** a sloping rear end of a car having a single door that is lifted to open. **2** a car having such a rear end.

hatchery (ˈhætʃərɪ) *n, pl* **hatcheries.** a place where eggs are hatched under artificial conditions.

hatchet ⓣ (ˈhætʃɪt) *n* **1** a short axe used for chopping wood, etc. **2** a tomahawk. **3** (*modifier*) of narrow dimensions and sharp features: *a hatchet face.* **4 bury the hatchet.** to cease hostilities and become reconciled. [C14: from OF *hachette,* from *hache* axe, of Gmc origin]

hatchet job *n Inf.* a malicious or devastating verbal or written attack.

hatchet man ⓣ *n Inf.* **1** a person carrying out unpleasant assignments for an employer or superior. **2** a severe or malicious critic.

hatchling (ˈhætʃlɪŋ) *n* a young animal that has newly emerged from the egg. [C19: from HATCH[1] + -LING[1]]

hatchment (ˈhætʃmənt) *n Heraldry.* a diamond-shaped tablet displaying the coat of arms of a dead person. [C16: changed from earlier use of *achievement* in this sense]

hatchway (ˈhætʃ,weɪ) *n* **1** an opening in the deck of a vessel to provide access below. **2** a similar opening in a wall, floor, ceiling, or roof.

hate ⓣ (heɪt) *vb* **hates, hating, hated. 1** to dislike (something) intensely; detest. **2** (*intr*) to be unwilling (to be or do something). ◆ *n* **3** intense dislike. **4** *Inf.* a person or thing that is hated (esp. in **pet hate**). **5** (*modifier*) expressing or arousing feelings of hatred: *hate mail.* [OE *hatian*]
▸ **ˈhateable** *or* **ˈhatable** *adj* ▸ **ˈhater** *n*

hateful ⓣ (ˈheɪtfʊl) *adj* **1** causing or deserving hate; loathsome; detestable. **2** *Arch.* full of hate.
▸ **ˈhatefully** *adv* ▸ **ˈhatefulness** *n*

hath (hæθ) *vb Arch. or dialect.* (used with the pronouns *he, she,* or *it* or a singular noun) a form of the present tense (indicative mood) of **have.**

hatred ⓣ (ˈheɪtrɪd) *n* intense dislike; enmity.

hat stand *or esp. US* **hat tree** *n* a pole equipped with hooks for hanging up hats, etc.

hatter (ˈhætə) *n* **1** a person who makes and sells hats. **2 mad as a hatter.** eccentric.

hat trick *n* **1** *Cricket.* the achievement of a bowler in taking three wickets with three successive balls. **2** any achievement of three successive points, victories, etc.

hauberk (ˈhɔːbɜːk) *n* a long coat of mail, often sleeveless. [C13: from OF *hauberc,* of Gmc origin; cf. OHG *halsberc,* OE *healsbeorg,* from *heals* neck + *beorg* protection]

haughty ⓣ (ˈhɔːtɪ) *adj* **haughtier, haughtiest.** having or showing arrogance. [C16: from OF *haut* lofty, from L *altus* high]
▸ **ˈhaughtily** *adv* ▸ **ˈhaughtiness** *n*

haul ⓣ (hɔːl) *vb* **1** to drag (something) with effort. **2** (*tr*) to transport, as in a lorry. **3** *Naut.* to alter the course of (a vessel), esp. so as to sail closer to the wind. **4** (*intr*) *Naut.* (of the wind) to blow from a direction nearer the bow. ◆ *n* **5** the act of dragging with effort. **6** (esp. of fish) the amount caught at a single time. **7** something that is hauled. **8** the goods obtained from a robbery. **9** a distance of hauling or travelling. **10** the amount of a contraband seizure: *arms haul, drugs haul.* [C16: from OF *haler,* of Gmc origin]
▸ **ˈhauler** *n*

haulage (ˈhɔːlɪdʒ) *n* **1** the act or labour of hauling. **2** a rate or charge levied for the transportation of goods, esp. by rail.

haulier (ˈhɔːljə) *n* **1** *Brit.* a person or firm that transports goods by road. **2** a mine worker who conveys coal from the workings to the foot of the shaft.

haulm *or* **halm** (hɔːm) *n* **1** the stalks of beans, peas, potatoes, grasses, etc., collectively. **2** a single stem of such a plant. [OE *healm*]

haul up *vb* (*adv*) **1** (*tr*) *Inf.* to call to account or criticize. **2** *Naut.* to sail (a vessel) closer to the wind.

haunch (hɔːntʃ) *n* **1** the human hip or fleshy hindquarter of an animal. **2** the leg and loin of an animal, used for food. **3** *Archit.* the part of an arch between the impost and apex. [C13: from OF *hanche;* rel. to Sp., It. *anca,* of Gmc origin]

haunt ⓣ (hɔːnt) *vb* **1** to visit (a person or place) in the form of a ghost. **2** (*tr*) to recur to (the memory, thoughts, etc.): *he was haunted by the fear of insanity.* **3** to visit (a place) frequently. **4** to associate with (someone) frequently. ◆ *n* **5** (*often pl*) a place visited frequently. **6** a place to which animals habitually resort for food, drink, shelter, etc. [C13: from OF *hanter,* of Gmc origin]

haunted ⓣ (ˈhɔːntɪd) *adj* **1** frequented or visited by ghosts. **2** (*postpositive*) obsessed or worried.

THESAURUS

dispatch, expedition, fleetness, nimbleness, promptitude, quickness, rapidity, rapidness, swiftness, urgency, velocity **2** = **rush**, bustle, hastiness, helter-skelter, hurry, hustle, impetuosity, precipitateness, rashness, recklessness
Antonyms *n* ≠ **speed:** slowness, sluggishness ≠ **rush:** calmness, care, delay, deliberation, leisureliness, sureness

hasten *vb* **1** = **hurry (up)**, accelerate, advance, barrel (along) (*inf., chiefly US & Canad.*), beetle, bolt, burn rubber (*inf.*), dash, dispatch, expedite, fly, get one's skates on (*inf.*), haste, make haste, precipitate, press, push forward, quicken, race, run, rush, scurry, scuttle, speed (up), sprint, step on it (*inf.*), step up (*inf.*), tear (along), urge
Antonyms *vb* ≠ **hurry (up):** crawl, creep, dawdle, decelerate, delay, hinder, impede, move slowly, retard, slow, slow down

hastily *adv* **1** = **quickly**, apace, double-quick, fast, hotfoot, posthaste, promptly, pronto (*inf.*), rapidly, speedily, straightaway **2** = **hurriedly**, heedlessly, impetuously, impulsively, on the spur of the moment, precipitately, rashly, recklessly, too quickly

hasty *adj* **1** = **speedy**, brief, brisk, cursory, eager, expeditious, fast, fleeting, hurried, passing, perfunctory, prompt, rapid, rushed, short, superficial, swift, urgent **2** = **rash**, foolhardy, headlong, heedless, impetuous, impulsive, indiscreet, precipitate, reckless, thoughtless, unduly quick **3** = **impatient**, brusque, excited, fiery, hot-headed, hot-tempered, irascible, irritable, passionate, quick-tempered, snappy
Antonyms *adj* ≠ **speedy:** leisurely, long, protracted ≠ **rash:** careful, cautious, detailed, thorough, thoughtful ≠ **impatient:** dispassionate

hatch[1] *vb* **1, 2** = **incubate**, breed, bring forth, brood **3** = **devise**, conceive, concoct, contrive, cook up, design, dream up (*inf.*), manufacture, plan, plot, project, scheme, think up, trump up

hatchet *n* **1** = **axe**, cleaver, machete **2** = **tomahawk**

hatchet man *n Informal* **2** = **detractor**, defamer, smear campaigner, traducer

hate *vb* **1** = **detest**, abhor, abominate, be hostile to, be repelled by, be sick of, despise, dislike, execrate, have an aversion to, loathe, recoil from **2** = **be unwilling**, be loath, be reluctant, be sorry, dislike, feel disinclined, have no stomach for, shrink from ◆ *n* **3** = **dislike**, abhorrence, abomination, animosity, animus, antagonism, antipathy, aversion, detestation, enmity, execration, hatred, hostility, loathing, odium
Antonyms *vb* ≠ **detest:** be fond of, cherish, dote on, enjoy, esteem, fancy, like, love, relish, treasure, wish ◆ *n* ≠ **dislike:** affection, amity, devotion, fondness, goodwill, liking, love

hateful *adj* **1** = **despicable**, abhorrent, abominable, detestable, disgusting, execrable, forbidding, foul, heinous, horrible, loathsome, obnoxious, obscene, odious, offensive, repellent, repugnant, repulsive, revolting, vile
Antonyms *adj* attractive, beautiful, charming, desirable, good, likable *or* likeable, lovable, pleasant, wonderful

hatred *n* = **dislike**, abomination, animosity, animus, antagonism, antipathy, aversion, detestation, enmity, execration, hate, ill will, odium, repugnance, revulsion
Antonyms *n* affection, amity, attachment, devotion, fondness, friendliness, goodwill, liking, love

haughtiness *n* = **pride**, airs, aloofness, arrogance, conceit, contempt, contemptuousness, disdain, hauteur, insolence, loftiness, pomposity, snobbishness, superciliousness

haughty *adj* = **proud**, arrogant, assuming, conceited, contemptuous, disdainful, high, high and mighty (*inf.*), hoity-toity (*inf.*), imperious, lofty, on one's high horse (*inf.*), overweening, scornful, snobbish, snooty (*inf.*), stuck-up (*inf.*), supercilious, uppish (*Brit. inf.*)
Antonyms *adj* humble, meek, mild, modest, self-effacing, subservient, wimpish *or* wimpy (*inf.*)

haul *vb* **1** = **drag**, draw, hale, heave, lug, pull, tow, trail, tug **2** = **transport**, carry, cart, convey, hump (*Brit. sl.*), move ◆ *n* **5** = **drag**, heave, pull, tug **10** = **yield**, booty, catch, find, gain, harvest, loot, spoils, takings

haunt *vb* **1** = **visit**, walk **2** = **plague**, beset, come back, obsess, possess, prey on, recur, stay with, torment, trouble, weigh on **3** = **frequent**, hang around *or* about, repair, resort, visit ◆ *n* **5** = **meeting place**, den, gathering place, hangout (*inf.*), rendezvous, resort, stamping ground

haunted *adj* **1** = **possessed**, cursed, eerie, ghostly, jinxed, spooky (*inf.*) **2** = **preoccupied**,

haunting Ⓣ ('hɔːntɪŋ) *adj* **1** (of memories) poignant or persistent. **2** poignantly sentimental; eerily evocative.
▸**'hauntingly** *adv*

Hausa ('haʊsə) *n* **1** (*pl* **Hausas** *or* **Hausa**) a member of a Negroid people of W Africa, living chiefly in N Nigeria. **2** the language of this people, widely used as a trading language throughout W Africa.

hausfrau ('haʊsˌfraʊ) *n* a German housewife. [G, from *Haus* house + *Frau* woman, wife]

hautboy ('əʊbɔɪ) *n* **1** a strawberry with large fruit. **2** an archaic word for **oboe.** [C16: from F *hautbois,* from *haut* high + *bois* wood, of Gmc origin]

haute couture *French.* (ot kutyr) *n* high fashion. [lit.: high dressmaking]

haute cuisine *French.* (ot kwizin) *n* high-class cooking. [lit.: high cookery]

haute école *French.* (ot ekɔl) *n* the classical art of riding. [lit.: high school]

hauteur Ⓣ (əʊ'tɜː) *n* pride; haughtiness. [C17: from F, from *haut* high; see HAUGHTY]

haut monde *French.* (o mɔ̃d) *n* high society. [lit.: high world]

Havana cigar (hə'vænə) *n* any of various cigars manufactured in Cuba, known esp. for their high quality. Also: **Havana.**

have Ⓣ (hæv) *vb* **has, having, had.** (*mainly tr*) **1** to be in possession of; own: *he has two cars.* **2** to possess as a quality or attribute: *he has dark hair.* **3** to receive, take, or obtain: *she had a present; have a look.* **4** to hold in the mind: *to have an idea.* **5** to possess a knowledge of: *I have no German.* **6** to experience: *to have a shock.* **7** to suffer from: *to have a cold.* **8** to gain control of or advantage over: *you have me on that point.* **9** (*usually passive*) *Sl.* to cheat or outwit: *he was had by that dishonest salesman.* **10** (foll. by *on*) to exhibit (mercy, etc., towards). **11** to take part in: *to have a conversation.* **12** to arrange or hold: *to have a party.* **13** to cause, compel, or require to (be, do, or be done): *have my shoes mended.* **14** (takes an infinitive with *to*) used as an auxiliary to express compulsion or necessity: *I had to run quickly to escape him.* **15** to eat, drink, or partake of. **16** *Taboo sl.* to have sexual intercourse with. **17** (*used with a negative*) to tolerate or allow: *I won't have all this noise.* **18** to state or assert: *rumour has it that they will marry.* **19** to place: *I'll have the sofa in this room.* **20** to receive as a guest: *to have people to stay.* **21** to be pregnant with or bear (offspring). **22** (*takes a past participle*) used as an auxiliary to form compound tenses expressing completed action: *I have gone; I had gone.* **23 had rather** *or* **sooner.** to consider preferable that: *I had rather you left at once.* **24 have had it.** *Inf.* **24a** to be exhausted, defeated, or killed. **24b** to have lost one's last chance. **24c** to become unfashionable. **25 have it away** (*or* **off**). *Taboo, Brit. sl.* to have sexual intercourse. **26 have it so good.** to have so many material benefits. **27 have to do with. 27a** to have dealings with. **27b** to be of relevance to. **28 let (someone) have it.** *Sl.* to launch an attack on (someone). ◆ *n* **29** (*usually pl*) *Inf.* a person or group in possession of wealth, security, etc.: *the haves and the have-nots.* ◆ See also **have at, have on,** etc. [OE *habban*]

have-a-go *adj Inf.* (of members of the public at the scene of a crime) intervening physically in an attempt to catch or thwart a criminal, esp. one who is armed: *a have-a-go pensioner.*

have at *vb* (*intr, prep*) *Arch.* to make an opening attack on, esp. in fencing.

havelock ('hævlɒk) *n* a light-coloured cover for a service cap with a flap extending over the back of the neck to protect the head and neck from the sun. [C19: after Sir H. *Havelock* (1795–1857), E general in India]

haven Ⓣ ('heɪvᵊn) *n* **1** a harbour or other sheltered place for shipping. **2** a place of safety; shelter. ◆ *vb* **3** (*tr*) to shelter as in a haven. [OE *hæfen,* from ON *höfn*]

have-not *n* (*usually pl*) a person or group in possession of relatively little material wealth.

haven't ('hævᵊnt) *contraction of* have not.

have on Ⓣ *vb* (*tr*) **1** (*usually adv*) to wear. **2** (*usually adv*) to have a commitment: *what does your boss have on this afternoon?* **3** (*adv*) *Inf.* to trick or tease (a person). **4** (*prep*) to have available (information, esp. when incriminating) about (a person).

have out *vb* (*tr, adv*) **1** to settle (a matter) or come to (a final decision), esp. by fighting or by frank discussion (often in **have it out**). **2** to have extracted or removed.

haver ('heɪvə) *vb* (*intr*) **1** *Scot. & N English dialect.* to babble; talk nonsense. **2** to dither. ◆ *n* **3** (*usually pl*) *Scot.* nonsense. [C18: from ?]

haversack ('hævəˌsæk) *n* a canvas bag for provisions or equipment, carried on the back or shoulder. [C18: from F *havresac,* from G *Habersack* oat bag, from OHG *habaro* oats + *Sack* SACK^{1}]

haversine ('hævəˌsaɪn) *n* half the value of the versed sine. [C19: combination of *half* + *versed* + *sine*^{1}]

have up *vb* (*tr, adv; usually passive*) to cause to appear for trial: *he was had up for breaking and entering.*

havildar ('hævɪlˌdɑː) *n* a noncommissioned officer in the Indian army, equivalent in rank to sergeant. [C17: from Hindi, from Persian *hawāldār* one in charge]

havoc Ⓣ ('hævək) *n* **1** destruction; devastation; ruin. **2** *Inf.* confusion; chaos. **3 cry havoc.** *Arch.* to give the signal for pillage and destruction. **4 play havoc.** (often foll. by *with*) to cause a great deal of damage, distress, or confusion (to). [C15: from OF *havot* pillage, prob. of Gmc origin]

haw^{1} (hɔː) *n* **1** the fruit of the hawthorn. **2** another name for **hawthorn.** [OE *haga,* identical with *haga* hedge]

haw^{2} (hɔː) *n, interj* **1** an inarticulate utterance, as of hesitation, embarrassment, etc.; hem. ◆ *vb* **2** (*intr*) to make this sound. [C17: imit.]

haw^{3} (hɔː) *n* the nictitating membrane of a horse or other domestic animal. [C15: from ?]

Hawaiian (hə'waɪən) *adj* **1** of or relating to Hawaii, a state of the US consisting of over 20 islands and atolls in the central Pacific, its people, or their language. ◆ *n* **2** a native or inhabitant of Hawaii. **3** a language of Hawaii belonging to the Malayo-Polynesian family.

hawfinch ('hɔːˌfɪntʃ) *n* an uncommon European finch having a very stout bill.

hawk^{1} (hɔːk) *n* **1** any of various diurnal birds of prey of the family Accipitridae, typically having short rounded wings and a long tail. **2** a person who advocates or supports war or warlike policies. Cf. **dove** (sense 2). **3** a ruthless or rapacious person. ◆ *vb* **4** (*intr*) to hunt with falcons, hawks, etc. **5** (*intr*) (of falcons or hawks) to fly in quest of prey. **6** to pursue or attack on the wing, as a hawk. [OE *hafoc*]
▸**'hawking** *n* ▸**'hawkish** *adj* ▸**'hawkˌlike** *adj*

hawk^{2} Ⓣ (hɔːk) *vb* **1** to offer (goods) for sale, as in the street. **2** (*tr; often* foll. by *about*) to spread (news, gossip, etc.). [C16: back formation from HAWKER^{1}]

hawk^{3} (hɔːk) *vb* **1** (*intr*) to clear the throat noisily. **2** (*tr*) to force (phlegm, etc.) up from the throat. [C16: imit.]

hawk^{4} (hɔːk) *n* a small square board with a handle underneath, for carrying wet mortar. Also called: **mortarboard.** [from ?]

hawker^{1} Ⓣ ('hɔːkə) *n* a person who travels from place to place selling goods. [C16: prob. from MLow G *hōker,* from *hōken* to peddle; see HUCKSTER]

hawker^{2} ('hɔːkə) *n* a person who hunts with hawks, falcons, etc. [OE *hafecere*]

hawk-eyed Ⓣ *adj* **1** having extremely keen sight. **2** vigilant, watchful, or observant.

hawk moth *n* any of various moths having long narrow wings and powerful flight, with the ability to hover over flowers when feeding from the nectar.

hawksbill turtle *or* **hawksbill** ('hɔːksˌbɪl) *n* a small tropical turtle with a hooked beaklike mouth: a source of tortoiseshell.

hawkweed ('hɔːkˌwiːd) *n* a hairy plant with clusters of dandelion-like flowers.

hawse (hɔːz) *n Naut.* **1** the part of the bows of a vessel where the hawseholes are. **2** short for **hawsehole** or **hawsepipe. 3** the distance from the bow of an anchored vessel to the anchor. **4** the arrangement of port and starboard anchor ropes when a vessel is riding on both anchors. [C14: from earlier *halse,* prob. from ON *háls* neck, ship's bow]

hawsehole ('hɔːzˌhəʊl) *n Naut.* one of the holes in the upper part of the bows of a vessel through which the anchor ropes pass.

hawsepipe ('hɔːzˌpaɪp) *n Naut.* a strong metal pipe through which an anchor rope passes.

hawser ('hɔːzə) *n Naut.* a large heavy rope. [C14: from Anglo-F *hauceour,* from OF *haucier* to hoist, ult. from L *altus* high]

hawthorn ('hɔːˌθɔːn) *n* any of various thorny trees or shrubs of a N temperate genus, having white or pink flowers and reddish fruits (haws). Also called (in Britain): **may, may tree, mayflower.** [OE *haguthorn,* from *haga* hedge + *thorn* thorn]

hay (heɪ) *n* **1a** grass, clover, etc., cut and dried as fodder. **1b** (*in combina-*

THESAURUS

obsessed, plagued, tormented, troubled, worried

haunting *adj* **1, 2** = **evocative**, disturbing, eerie, indelible, nostalgic, persistent, poignant, recurrent, recurring, unforgettable

hauteur *n* = **haughtiness**, affectedness, airs, arrogance, contempt, dignity, disdain, loftiness, pride, snobbishness, stateliness, superciliousness

have *vb* **1, 2** = **possess**, hold, keep, obtain, occupy, own, retain **3** = **receive**, accept, acquire, gain, get, obtain, procure, secure, take **6** = **experience**, endure, enjoy, feel, meet with, suffer, sustain, undergo **9** *Slang* = **cheat**, deceive, dupe, fool, outwit, stiff (*sl.*), swindle, take in (*inf.*), trick **14** = **be obliged**, be bound, be compelled, be forced, have got to, must, ought, should **17** = **put up with** (*inf.*), allow, consider, entertain, permit, think about, tolerate **21** = **give birth to**, bear, beget, bring forth, bring into the world, deliver **24 have had it** *Informal* **a** = **be exhausted**, be defeated, be finished, be pooped (*US sl.*)

haven *n* **1** = **harbour**, anchorage, port, roads (*Nautical*) **2** = **sanctuary**, asylum, refuge, retreat, sanctum, shelter

have on *vb* **1** = **wear**, be clothed in, be dressed in **2** = **have planned**, be committed to, be engaged to, have on the agenda **3** *Informal* = **tease**, deceive, kid (*inf.*), play a joke on, pull someone's leg, take the mickey, trick, wind up (*Brit. sl.*)

havoc *n* **1** = **devastation**, carnage, damage, desolation, despoliation, destruction, rack and ruin, ravages, ruin, slaughter, waste, wreck **2** *Informal* = **disorder**, chaos, confusion, disruption, mayhem, shambles **4 play havoc (with)** = **wreck**, bring into chaos, confuse, convulse, demolish, destroy, devastate, disorganize, disrupt

hawk^{2} *vb* **1** = **peddle**, bark (*inf.*), cry, market, sell, tout (*inf.*), vend **2** *often with* **about** = **spread**, bandy about (*inf.*), bruit about, buzz, noise abroad, put about, rumour

hawker *n*^{1} = **pedlar**, barrow boy (*Brit.*), cheap-jack (*inf.*), crier, huckster, vendor

hawk-eyed *adj* **1** = **sharp-eyed**, gimlet-eyed, keen-sighted, lynx-eyed **2** = **vigilant**, Argus-eyed, having eyes in the back of one's head (*inf.*), observant, perceptive

tion): a hayfield. **2 hit the hay.** *Sl.* to go to bed. **3 make hay of.** to throw into confusion. **4 make hay while the sun shines.** to take full advantage of an opportunity. **5 roll in the hay.** *Inf.* sexual intercourse or heavy petting. ◆ *vb* **6** to cut, dry, and store (grass, etc.) as fodder. [OE *hieg*]

haybox ('heɪ,bɒks) *n* an airtight box full of hay used for cooking preheated food by retained heat.

haycock ('heɪ,kɒk) *n* a small cone-shaped pile of hay left in the field until dry.

hay fever *n* an allergic reaction to pollen, dust, etc., characterized by sneezing, runny nose, and watery eyes due to inflammation of the mucous membranes of the eyes and nose.

haymaker ('heɪ,meɪkə) *n* **1** a person who helps to cut, turn, or carry hay. **2** either of two machines, one designed to crush stems of hay, the other to break and bend them, in order to cause more rapid and even drying. **3** *Boxing sl.* a wild swinging punch.
▸**'hay,making** *adj, n*

haymow ('heɪ,maʊ) *n* **1** a part of a barn where hay is stored. **2** a quantity of hay stored.

hayseed ('heɪ,siːd) *n* **1** seeds or fragments of grass or straw. **2** *US & Canad. inf., derog.* a yokel.

haystack ('heɪ,stæk) *or* **hayrick** *n* a large pile of hay, esp. one built in the open air and covered with thatch.

haywire ❶ ('heɪ,waɪə) *adj (postpositive) Inf.* **1** (of things) not functioning properly. **2** (of people) erratic or crazy. [C20: from the disorderly tangle of wire removed from bales of hay]

hazard ❶ ('hæzəd) *n* **1** exposure or vulnerability to injury, loss, etc. **2 at hazard.** at risk; in danger. **3** a thing likely to cause injury, etc. **4** *Golf.* an obstacle such as a bunker, a road, rough, water, etc. **5** chance; accident. **6** a gambling game played with two dice. **7** *Real Tennis.* **7a** the receiver's side of the court. **7b** one of the winning openings. **8** *Billiards.* a scoring stroke made either when a ball other than the striker's is pocketed (**winning hazard**) or the striker's cue ball itself (**losing hazard**). ◆ *vb (tr)* **9** to risk. **10** to venture (an opinion, guess, etc.). **11** to expose to danger. [C13: from OF *hasard,* from Ar. *az-zahr* the die]

hazard lights *pl n* the indicator lights of a motor vehicle when flashing simultaneously to indicate that the vehicle is stationary and temporarily obstructing the traffic. Also called: **hazard warning lights, hazards.**

hazardous ❶ ('hæzədəs) *adj* **1** involving great risk. **2** depending on chance.
▸**'hazardously** *adv* ▸**'hazardousness** *n*

hazard warning device *n* an appliance fitted to a motor vehicle that operates the hazard lights.

haze[1] ❶ (heɪz) *n* **1** *Meteorol.* reduced visibility in the air as a result of condensed water vapour, dust, etc., in the atmosphere. **2** obscurity of perception, feeling, etc. ◆ *vb* **hazes, hazing, hazed. 3** (when *intr,* often foll. by *over*) to make or become hazy. [C18: back formation from HAZY]

haze[2] (heɪz) *vb* **hazes, hazing, hazed.** *(tr)* **1** *Chiefly US & Canad.* to subject (fellow students) to ridicule or abuse. **2** *Naut.* to harass with humiliating tasks. [C17: from ?]

hazel ('heɪzᵊl) *n* **1** Also called: **cob.** any of several shrubs of a N temperate genus, having edible rounded nuts. **2** the wood of any of these trees. **3** short for **hazelnut. 4a** a light yellowish-brown colour. **4b** *(as adj): hazel eyes.* [OE *hæsel*]

hazelhen ('heɪzᵊl,hɛn) *n* a European woodland gallinaceous bird with a speckled brown plumage and slightly crested crown.

hazelnut ('heɪzᵊl,nʌt) *n* the nut of a hazel shrub, having a smooth shiny hard shell. Also called: **filbert,** (Brit.) **cobnut, cob.**

hazy ❶ ('heɪzɪ) *adj* **hazier, haziest.** misty; indistinct; vague. [C17: from ?]
▸**'hazily** *adv* ▸**'haziness** *n*

Hb *symbol for* haemoglobin.

HB (on Brit. pencils) *symbol for* hard-black: denoting a medium-hard lead.

HBC *abbrev. for* Hudson's Bay Company.

HBM (in Britain) *abbrev. for* His (*or* Her) Britannic Majesty.

H-bomb *n* short for **hydrogen bomb.**

HC *abbrev. for:* **1** Holy Communion. **2** (in Britain) House of Commons.

HCF *or* **hcf** *abbrev. for* highest common factor.

HCG *abbrev. for* human chorionic gonadotrophin; a hormone produced by the placenta during pregnancy: its presence in the urine is used as the basis of most pregnancy tests.

hcp *abbrev. for* handicap.

HD *abbrev. for* heavy duty.

hdqrs *abbrev. for* headquarters.

HDTV *abbrev. for* high definition television.

he (hiː; *unstressed* iː) *pron (subjective)* **1** refers to a male person or animal. **2** refers to an indefinite antecedent such as *whoever* or *anybody: everybody can do as he likes.* **3** refers to a person or animal of unknown or unspecified sex: *a member may vote as he sees fit.* ◆ *n* **4a** a male person or animal. **4b** *(in combination): he-goat.* **5** (in children's play) another name for **tag**[2] (sense 1), **it** (sense 7). [OE *hē*]

He *the chemical symbol for* helium.

HE *abbrev. for:* **1** high explosive. **2** His Eminence. **3** His (*or* Her) Excellency.

head ❶ (hɛd) *n* **1** the upper or front part of the body in vertebrates, including man, that contains and protects the brain, eyes, mouth, nose, and ears. Related adj: **cephalic. 2** the corresponding part of an invertebrate animal. **3** something resembling a head in form or function, such as the top of a tool. **4a** the person commanding most authority within a group, organization, etc. **4b** *(as modifier): head buyer.* **4c** *(in combination): headmaster.* **5** the position of leadership or command. **6** the most forward part of a thing; front: *the head of a queue.* **7** the highest part of a thing; upper end: *the head of the pass.* **8** the froth on the top of a glass of beer. **9** aptitude, intelligence, and emotions (esp. in **over one's head, lose one's head,** etc.): *she has a good head for figures.* **10** *(pl* **head***)* a person or animal considered as a unit: *the show was two pounds per head; six hundred head of cattle.* **11** the head considered as a measure: *he's a head taller than his mother.* **12** *Bot.* **12a** a dense inflorescence such as that of the daisy. **12b** any other compact terminal part of a plant, such as the leaves of a cabbage. **13** a culmination or crisis (esp. in **bring** or **come to a head**). **14** the pus-filled tip or central part of a pimple, boil, etc. **15** the source of a river or stream. **16** *(cap. when part of a name)* a headland or promontory. **17** the obverse of a coin, usually bearing a portrait of the head of a monarch, etc. **18** a main point of an argument, discourse, etc. **19** *(often pl)* a headline or heading. **20** *(often pl) Naut.* a lavatory. **21** the taut membrane of a drum, tambourine, etc. **22a** the height of the surface of liquid above a specific point, esp. as a measure of the pressure at that point: *a head of four feet.* **22b** pressure of water, caused by height or velocity, measured in terms of a vertical column of water. **22c** any pressure: *a head of steam in the boiler.* **23** *Sl.* **23a** a person who regularly takes drugs, esp. LSD or cannabis. **23b** *(in combination): an acidhead.* **24** *Mining.* a road driven into the coalface. **25a** the terminal point of a route. **25b** *(in combination): railhead.* **26** a device on a turning or boring machine equipped with one or more cutting tools held to the work by this device. **27 cylinder head.** See **cylinder** (sense 4). **28** an electromagnet that can read, write, or erase information on a magnetic medium, used in computers, tape recorders, etc. **29** *Inf.* short for **headmaster** *or* **headmistress. 30** a narrow margin of victory (esp. in (**win**) **by a head**). **31** *Inf.* short for **headache. 32 bite** *or* **snap someone's head off.** to speak sharply to someone. **33 give someone** (*or* **something**) **his** (*or* **its**) **head. 33a** to allow a person greater freedom or responsibility. **33b** to allow a horse to gallop by lengthening the reins. **34 go to one's head. 34a** to make one dizzy or confused, as might an alcoholic drink. **34b** to make one conceited: *his success has gone to his head.* **35 head and shoulders above.** greatly superior to. **36 head over heels. 36a** turning a complete somersault. **36b** completely; utterly (esp. in **head over heels in love**). **37 hold up one's head.** to be unashamed. **38 keep one's head.** to remain calm. **39 keep one's head above water.** to manage to survive difficulties, esp. financial ones. **40 make head or tail of.** *(used with a negative)* to attempt to understand (a problem, etc.). **41 off** (*or* **out of**) **one's head.** *Sl.* insane or delirious. **42 on one's (own) head.** at a one's (own) risk or responsibility. **43 over someone's head. 43a** without a person in the obvious position being considered: *the graduate was promoted over the heads of several of his seniors.* **43b** without consulting a person in the obvious position but referring to a higher authority: *he went straight to the director, over the head of his imme-*

THESAURUS

haywire *adj* **1** = **chaotic,** confused, disarranged, disordered, disorganized, mixed up, on the blink (*sl.*), out of commission, out of order, shambolic (*inf.*), tangled, topsy-turvy **2** = **crazy,** erratic, mad, wild

hazard *n* **1, 3** = **danger,** endangerment, imperilment, jeopardy, peril, pitfall, risk, threat **5** = **chance,** accident, coincidence, fluke, luck, misfortune, mishap, stroke of luck ◆ *vb* **9** = **gamble,** chance, dare, risk, stake **10** = **conjecture,** advance, offer, presume, proffer, speculate, submit, suppose, throw out, venture, volunteer **11** = **jeopardize,** endanger, expose, imperil, risk, threaten

hazardous *adj* **1** = **dangerous,** dicey (*inf., chiefly Brit.*), difficult, fraught with danger, hairy (*sl.*), insecure, perilous, precarious, risky, unsafe **2** = **unpredictable,** chancy, haphazard, precarious, uncertain

Antonyms *adj* reliable, safe, secure, sound, stable, sure

haze[1] *n* **1** = **mist,** cloud, dimness, film, fog, obscurity, smog, smokiness, steam, vapour

hazy *adj* = **unclear,** blurry, cloudy, dim, dull, faint, foggy, fuzzy, ill-defined, indefinite, indistinct, misty, muddled, muzzy, nebulous, obscure, overcast, smoky, uncertain, vague, veiled

Antonyms *adj* ≠ **unclear:** bright, certain, clear, detailed, well-defined

head *n* **1, 2** = **skull,** bean (*US & Canad. sl.*), conk (*sl.*), cranium, loaf (*sl.*), noddle (*inf., chiefly Brit.*), noggin, nut (*sl.*), pate **4a** = **leader,** boss (*inf.*), captain, chief, chieftain, commander, director, headmaster *or* headmistress, head teacher, manager, master, principal, superintendent, supervisor ◆ *modifier* **4b** = **chief,** arch, first, foremost, front, highest, leading, main, pre-eminent, premier, prime, principal, supreme, topmost ◆ *n* **6** = **front,** cutting edge, first place, fore, forefront, van, vanguard **7** = **top,** apex, crest, crown, height, peak, pinnacle, pitch, summit, tip, vertex **9** = **mind,** ability, aptitude, brain, brains (*inf.*), capacity, faculty, flair, intellect, intelligence, mentality, talent, thought, understanding **13** = **culmination,** climax, conclusion, crisis, end, turning point **15** = **source,** beginning, commencement, origin, rise, start **16** = **headland,** cape, foreland, point, promontory **go to one's head 34a** = **intoxicate,** dizzy **34b** = **excite,** make conceited, puff up **36b head over heels** = **completely,** intensely, thoroughly, uncontrollably, utterly, wholeheartedly **44 put (our, their,** *etc.***) heads together** *Informal* = **consult,** confab, confabulate, confer, deliberate, discuss, palaver, powwow, talk over ◆ *vb* **47** = **lead,** be *or* go first, cap, crown, lead the way, precede, top **48** = **be in charge of,** command, control, direct, govern, guide, lead, manage,

diate boss. **43c** beyond a person's comprehension. **44 put (our, their, etc.) heads together.** *Inf.* to consult together. **45 take it into one's head.** to conceive a notion (to do something). **46 turn someone's head.** to make someone vain, conceited, etc. ◆ *vb* **47** (*tr*) to be at the front or top of: *to head the field.* **48** (*tr;* often foll. by *up*) to be in the commanding or most important position. **49** (often foll. by *for*) to go or cause to go (towards): *where are you heading?* **50** to turn or steer (a vessel) as specified: *to head into the wind.* **51** *Soccer.* to propel (the ball) by striking it with the head. **52** (*tr*) to provide with or be a head or heading for. **53** (*tr*) to cut the top branches or shoots off a tree or plant. **54** (*intr*) to form a head, as a plant. **55** (*intr;* often foll. by *in*) (of streams, rivers, etc.) to originate or rise. ◆ See also **head off, heads.** [OE *hēafod*]
▸**'headless** *adj* ▸**'head,like** *adj*

-head *n combining form.* indicating a person having a preoccupation as specified: *breadhead.*

headache ⓣ ('hɛd,eɪk) *n* **1** a continuous pain in the head. **2** *Inf.* any cause of worry, difficulty, or annoyance.
▸**'head,achy** *adj*

headband ('hɛd,bænd) *n* **1** a ribbon or band worn around the head. **2** a narrow cloth band attached to the top of the spine of a book for protection or decoration.

headbang ('hɛd,bæŋ) *vb* (*intr*) *Sl.* to nod one's head violently to the beat of heavy-metal rock music.

head-banger *n Sl.* **1** a heavy-metal rock fan. **2** a crazy or stupid person.

headboard ('hɛd,bɔːd) *n* a vertical board or terminal at the head of a bed.

head-butt *vb* (*tr*) **1** to strike (someone) deliberately with the head. ◆ *n* **head butt. 2** an act or an instance of deliberately striking someone with the head.

headdress ('hɛd,drɛs) *n* any head covering, esp. an ornate one or one denoting a rank.

headed ('hɛdɪd) *adj* **1a** having a head or heads. **1b** (*in combination*): *two-headed; bullet-headed.* **2** having a heading: *headed notepaper.*

header ('hɛdə) *n* **1** a machine that trims the heads from castings, forgings, etc., or one that forms heads, as in wire, to make nails. **2** a person who operates such a machine. **3** Also called: **header tank.** a reservoir that maintains a gravity feed or a static fluid pressure in an apparatus. **4** a brick or stone laid across a wall so that its end is flush with the outer surface. **5** the action of striking a ball with the head. **6** *Inf.* a headlong fall or dive.

headfirst ⓣ ('hɛd'fɜːst) *adj, adv* **1** with the head foremost; headlong. ◆ *adv* **2** rashly.

headgear ('hɛd,gɪə) *n* **1** a hat. **2** any part of a horse's harness that is worn on the head. **3** the hoisting mechanism at the pithead of a mine.

headguard ('hɛd,gɑːd) *n* a lightweight helmet-like piece of equipment worn to protect the head in various sports.

head-hunting *n* **1** the practice among certain peoples of removing the heads of slain enemies and preserving them as trophies. **2** *US sl.* the destruction or neutralization of political opponents. **3** (of a company or corporation) the recruitment of, or a drive to recruit, new high-level personnel, esp. in management or in specialist fields.
▸**'head-,hunter** *n*

heading ⓣ ('hɛdɪŋ) *n* **1** a title for a page, chapter, etc. **2** a main division, as of a speech. **3** *Mining.* **3a** a horizontal tunnel. **3b** the end of such a tunnel. **4** the angle between the direction of an aircraft and a specified meridian, often due north. **5** the compass direction parallel to the keel of a vessel. **6** the act of heading.

headland ⓣ *n* **1** ('hɛdlənd). a narrow area of land jutting out into a sea, lake, etc. **2** ('hɛd,lænd). a strip of land along the edge of an arable field left unploughed to allow space for machines.

headlight ('hɛd,laɪt) *or* **headlamp** *n* a powerful light, equipped with a reflector and attached to the front of a motor vehicle, etc.

headline ('hɛd,laɪn) *n* **1a** a phrase at the top of a newspaper or magazine article indicating the subject of the article, usually in larger and heavier type. **1b** a line at the top of a page indicating the title, page number, etc. **2 hit the headlines.** to become prominent in the news. **3** (*usually pl*) the main points of a television or radio news broadcast, read out before the full broadcast. ◆ *vb* **headlines, headlining, headlined. 4** (*tr*) to furnish (a story or page) with a headline. **5** to have top billing (in).

headlong ⓣ ('hɛd,lɒŋ) *adv, adj* **1** with the head foremost; headfirst. **2** with great haste. ◆ *adj* **3** *Arch.* (of slopes, etc.) very steep; precipitous.

headman ('hɛdmən) *n, pl* **headmen. 1** *Anthropol.* a chief or leader. **2** a foreman or overseer.

headmaster ⓣ (,hɛd'mɑːstə) *or* (*fem*) **headmistress** *n* the principal of a school.

headmost ('hɛd,məʊst) *adj* foremost.

head off ⓣ *vb* (*tr, adv*) **1** to intercept and force to change direction. **2** to prevent or forestall.

head-on *adv, adj* **1** front foremost: *a head-on collision.* **2** with directness or without compromise: *in his usual head-on fashion.*

headphones ('hɛd,fəʊnz) *pl n* an electrical device consisting of two earphones held in position by a flexible metallic strap passing over the head. Informal name: **cans.**

headpiece ('hɛd,piːs) *n* **1** *Printing.* a decorative band at the top of a page, etc. **2** a helmet. **3** *Arch.* the intellect.

headpin ('hɛd,pɪn) *n Tenpin bowling.* another word for **kingpin** (sense 2).

headquarters (,hɛd'kwɔːtəz) *pl n* (*sometimes functioning as sing*) **1** any centre from which operations are directed, as in the police. **2** a military formation comprising the commander and his staff. ◆ Abbrev.: **HQ, h.q.**

headrace ('hɛd,reɪs) *n* a channel that carries water to a water wheel, turbine, etc.

headrest ('hɛd,rɛst) *n* a support for the head, as on a dentist's chair or car seat.

head restraint *n* an adjustable support for the head, attached to a car seat, to prevent the neck from being jolted backwards sharply in the event of a crash or sudden stop.

headroom ('hɛd,rʊm, -,ruːm) *or* **headway** *n* the height of a bridge, room, etc.; clearance.

heads (hɛdz) *interj, adv* with the obverse side of a coin uppermost, esp. if it has a head on it: used as a call before tossing a coin.

headscarf ('hɛd,skɑːf) *n, pl* **headscarves.** a scarf for the head, often worn tied under the chin.

headset ('hɛd,sɛt) *n* a pair of headphones, esp. with a microphone attached.

headship ('hɛdʃɪp) *n* **1** the position or state of being a leader; command. **2** *Brit.* the position of headmaster or headmistress of a school.

headshrinker ('hɛd,ʃrɪŋkə) *n* **1** a slang name for **psychiatrist.** Often shortened to **shrink. 2** a head-hunter who shrinks the heads of his victims.

headsman ('hɛdzmən) *n, pl* **headsmen.** (formerly) an executioner who beheaded condemned persons.

headstall ('hɛd,stɔːl) *n* the part of a bridle that fits round a horse's head.

head start *n* an initial advantage in a competitive situation.

headstock ('hɛd,stɒk) *n* the part of a machine that supports and transmits the drive.

headstone ('hɛd,stəʊn) *n* **1** a memorial stone at the head of a grave. **2** *Archit.* another name for **keystone.**

headstream ('hɛd,striːm) *n* a stream that is the source or a source of a river.

headstrong ⓣ ('hɛd,strɒŋ) *adj* **1** self-willed; obstinate. **2** (of an action) heedless; rash.

head-to-head *Inf.* ◆ *adj* **1** in direct competition. ◆ *n* **2** a competition involving two people, teams, etc.

head-up display *n* a projection of readings from instruments onto a windscreen, enabling a pilot or driver to see them without moving his eyes.

head voice *or* **register** *n* the high register of the human voice, in which the vibrations of sung notes are felt in the head.

headwaters ('hɛd,wɔːtəz) *pl n* the tributary streams of a river in the area in which it rises.

headway ⓣ ('hɛd,weɪ) *n* **1** motion forward: *the vessel made no headway.* **2** progress: *he made no headway with the problem.* **3** another name for **headroom. 4** the interval between consecutive trains, buses, etc., on the same route.

headwind ('hɛd,wɪnd) *n* a wind blowing directly against the course of an aircraft or ship.

headword ('hɛd,wɜːd) *n* a key word placed at the beginning of a line, paragraph, etc., as in a dictionary entry.

headwork ('hɛd,wɜːk) *n* **1** mental work. **2** the ornamentation of the keystone of an arch.

heady ⓣ ('hɛdɪ) *adj* **headier, headiest. 1** (of alcoholic drink) intoxicating. **2** strongly affecting the senses; extremely exciting. **3** rash; impetuous.
▸**'headily** *adv* ▸**'headiness** *n*

heal ⓣ (hiːl) *vb* **1** to restore or be restored to health. **2** (*intr;* often foll. by *over* or *up*) (of a wound) to repair by natural processes, as by scar for-

THESAURUS

rule, run, supervise **49** = **make for**, aim, go to, make a beeline for, point, set off for, set out, start towards, steer, turn

headache *n* **1** = **migraine**, head (*inf.*), neuralgia **2** *Informal* = **problem**, bane, bother, inconvenience, nuisance, trouble, vexation, worry

headfirst *adj, adv* **1** = **headlong**, diving, head-on **2** = **recklessly**, carelessly, hastily, head over heels, precipitately, rashly

heading *n* **1** = **title**, caption, headline, name, rubric **2** = **division**, category, class, section

headland *n* **1** = **promontory**, bill, bluff, cape, cliff, foreland, head, mull (*Scot.*), point

headlong *adv, adj* **1** = **headfirst**, headforemost, head-on ◆ *adv* **2** = **hastily**, heedlessly, helter-skelter, hurriedly, pell-mell, precipitately, rashly, thoughtlessly, wildly ◆ *adj* **3** *Archaic* = **steep**, breakneck, dangerous, precipitate

headmaster *or* **headmistress** *n* = **principal**, head, head teacher, rector

head off *vb* **1** = **intercept**, block off, cut off, deflect, divert, interpose, intervene **2** = **prevent**, avert, fend off, forestall, parry, stop, ward off

headstrong *adj* **1** = **self-willed**, contrary, intractable, mulish, obstinate, perverse, pig-headed, stiff-necked, stubborn, ungovernable, unruly, wilful **2** = **rash**, foolhardy, heedless, imprudent, impulsive, reckless
Antonyms *adj* ≠ **self-willed:** impressionable, manageable, pliant, subservient, tractable ≠ **rash:** cautious

headway *n* **1, 2** = **advance**, improvement, progress, progression, way

heady *adj* **1** = **intoxicating**, inebriating, potent, spirituous, strong **2** = **exciting**, exhilarating, intoxicating, overwhelming, stimulating, thrilling **3** = **rash**, hasty, impetuous, impulsive, inconsiderate, precipitate, reckless, thoughtless

heal *vb* **1, 3** = **cure**, make well, mend, remedy,

mation. **3** (*tr*) to cure (a disease or disorder). **4** to restore or be restored to friendly relations, harmony, etc. [OE *hælan;* see HALE[1], WHOLE]
▶'**healer** *n* ▶'**healing** *n, adj*

health ⓘ (hɛlθ) *n* **1** the state of being bodily and mentally vigorous and free from disease. **2** the general condition of body and mind: *in poor health.* **3** the condition of any unit, society, etc.: *the economic health of a nation.* **4** a toast to a person. **5** (*modifier*) of or relating to food or other goods reputed to be beneficial to the health: *health food.* **6** (*modifier*) of or relating to health: *health care; health service.* [OE *hǣlth;* rel. to *hāl* HALE[1]]

health centre *n* (in Britain) premises providing health care for a local community and usually housing a group practice, nursing staff, a child-health clinic, etc.

health farm *n* a residential establishment, often in the country, visited by those who wish to improve their health by losing weight, eating health foods, taking exercise, etc.

health food *n* **a** food eaten for its alleged benefits to health, esp. fruit, vegetables, etc., that are organically grown, high in dietary fibre, and without additives. **b** (*as modifier*): *a health-food shop.*

healthful ⓘ ('hɛlθfʊl) *adj* a less common word for **healthy** (senses 1–3).

health salts *pl n* magnesium sulphate or similar salts taken as a mild laxative.

health visitor *n* (in Britain) a nurse employed by a district health authority to visit people in their homes and give help and advice on health and social welfare, esp. to mothers of preschool children, and to handicapped and elderly people.

healthy ⓘ ('hɛlθɪ) *adj* **healthier, healthiest. 1** enjoying good health. **2** sound: *the company's finances are not very healthy.* **3** conducive to health. **4** indicating soundness of body or mind: *a healthy appetite.* **5** *Inf.* considerable: *a healthy sum.*
▶'**healthily** *adv* ▶'**healthiness** *n*

heap ⓘ (hi:p) *n* **1** a collection of articles or mass of material gathered in a pile. **2** (*often pl;* usually foll. by *of*) *Inf.* a large number or quantity. **3** *Inf.* a thing that is very old, unreliable, etc.: *the car was a heap.* ◆ *adv* **4 heaps.** (intensifier): *he was heaps better.* ◆ *vb* **5** (often foll. by *up* or *together*) to collect or be collected into or as if into a pile. **6** (*tr;* often foll. by *with, on,* or *upon*) to load (with) abundantly: *to heap with riches.* [OE *héap*]

hear ⓘ (hɪə) *vb* **hears, hearing, heard** (hɜ:d). **1** (*tr*) to perceive (a sound) with the sense of hearing. **2** (*tr; may take a clause as object*) to listen to: *did you hear what I said?* **3** (when *intr,* sometimes foll. by *of* or *about;* when *tr, may take a clause as object*) to be informed (of); receive information (about). **4** *Law.* to give a hearing to (a case). **5** (when *intr,* usually foll. by *of* and used with a negative) to listen (to) with favour, assent, etc.: *she wouldn't hear of it.* **6** (*intr;* foll. by *from*) to receive a letter (from). **7 hear! hear!** an exclamation of approval. **8 hear tell (of).** *Dialect.* to be told (about). [OE *hieran*]
▶'**hearer** *n*

hearing ⓘ ('hɪərɪŋ) *n* **1** the sense by which sound is perceived. **2** an opportunity to be listened to. **3** the range within which sound can be heard; earshot. **4** the investigation of a matter by a court of law, esp. the preliminary inquiry into an indictable crime by magistrates.

hearing aid *n* a device for assisting the hearing of partially deaf people, typically a small battery-powered amplifier worn in or behind the ear. Also called: **deaf aid.**

hearing dog *n* a dog that has been specially trained to help deaf or partially deaf people by alerting them to such sounds as a ringing doorbell, an alarm, etc.

hearken *or US* (*sometimes*) **harken** ('hɑ:kən) *vb Arch.* to listen to (something). [OE *heorcnian*]

hear out *vb* (*tr, adv*) to listen in regard to every detail and give a proper or full hearing to.

hearsay ⓘ ('hɪəˌseɪ) *n* gossip; rumour.

hearsay evidence *n Law.* evidence based on what has been reported to a witness by others rather than what he has himself observed.

hearse (hɜ:s) *n* a vehicle, such as a car or carriage, used to carry a coffin to the grave. [C14: from OF *herce,* from L *hirpex* harrow]

heart ⓘ (hɑ:t) *n* **1** the hollow muscular organ in vertebrates whose contractions propel the blood through the circulatory system. Related adj: **cardiac. 2** the corresponding organ in invertebrates. **3** this organ considered as the seat of emotions, esp. love. **4** emotional mood: *a change of heart.* **5** tenderness or pity: *you have no heart.* **6** courage or spirit. **7** the most central part: *the heart of the city.* **8** the most important part: *the heart of the matter.* **9** (of vegetables, such as cabbage) the inner compact part. **10** the breast: *she held him to her heart.* **11** a dearly loved person: *dearest heart.* **12** a conventionalized representation of the heart, having two rounded lobes at the top meeting in a point at the bottom. **13a** a red heart-shaped symbol on a playing card. **13b** a card with one or more of these symbols or (*when pl*) the suit of cards so marked. **14** a fertile condition in land (esp. in **in good heart**). **15 after one's own heart.** appealing to one's own disposition or taste. **16 break one's** (*or* **someone's**) **heart.** to grieve (or cause to grieve) very deeply, esp. through love. **17 by heart.** by committing to memory. **18 eat one's heart out.** to brood or pine with grief or longing. **19 from** (**the bottom of**) **one's heart.** very sincerely or deeply. **20 have a change of heart.** to experience a profound change of outlook, attitude, etc. **21 have one's heart in one's mouth** (*or* **throat**). to be full of apprehension, excitement, or fear. **22 have one's heart in the right place.** to be kind, thoughtful, or generous. **23 have the heart.** (*usually used with a negative*) to have the necessary will, callousness, etc. (to do something): *I didn't have the heart to tell him.* **24 heart of hearts.** the depths of one's conscience or emotions. **25 heart of oak.** a brave person. **26 lose heart.** to become despondent or disillusioned (over something). **27 lose one's heart to.** to fall in love with. **28 set one's heart on.** to have as one's ambition to obtain; covet. **29 take heart.** to become encouraged. **30 take to heart.** to take seriously or be upset about. **31 wear one's heart on one's sleeve.** to show one's feelings openly. **32 with all one's heart.** very willingly. ◆ *vb* (*intr*) **33** (of vegetables) to form a heart. ◆ See also **hearts.** [OE *heorte*]

heartache ⓘ ('hɑ:tˌeɪk) *n* intense anguish or mental suffering.

heart attack *n* any sudden severe instance of abnormal heart functioning, esp. coronary thrombosis.

heartbeat ('hɑ:tˌbi:t) *n* one complete pulsation of the heart.

heart block *n* impaired conduction of the impulse that regulates the heartbeat, resulting in a lack of coordination between the beating of the atria and the ventricles.

heartbreak ⓘ ('hɑ:tˌbreɪk) *n* intense and overwhelming grief, esp. through disappointment in love.
▶'**heartˌbreaker** *n* ▶'**heartˌbreaking** *adj*

heartburn ('hɑ:tˌbɜ:n) *n* a burning sensation beneath the breastbone caused by irritation of the oesophagus. Technical names: **cardialgia, pyrosis.**

-hearted *adj* having a heart or disposition as specified: *cold-hearted; heavy-hearted.*

THESAURUS

restore, treat **4** = **reconcile**, alleviate, ameliorate, compose, conciliate, harmonize, patch up, settle, soothe
Antonyms *vb* aggravate, exacerbate, harm, hurt, make worse, reopen

healing *adj* **1, 3** = **medicinal**, analeptic, curative, remedial, restorative, restoring, sanative, therapeutic **4** = **soothing**, assuaging, comforting, emollient, gentle, lenitive, mild, mitigative, palliative

health *n* **1** = **wellbeing**, fitness, good condition, haleness, healthiness, robustness, salubrity, soundness, strength, vigour, wellness **2, 3** = **condition**, constitution, fettle, form, shape, state, tone
Antonyms *n* ≠ **wellbeing:** debility, disease, frailty, illness, sickness, weakness

healthful *adj* = **healthy**, beneficial, bracing, good for one, health-giving, invigorating, nourishing, nutritious, salubrious, salutary, wholesome

healthy *adj* **1** = **well**, active, alive and kicking, blooming, fighting fit, fit, fit as a fiddle (*inf.*), flourishing, hale, hale and hearty, hardy, hearty, in fine feather, in fine fettle, in fine form, in good condition, in good shape (*inf.*), in the pink, physically fit, right as rain (*Brit. inf.*), robust, sound, strong, sturdy, vigorous **3** = **wholesome**, beneficial, bracing, good for one, healthful, health-giving, hygienic, invigorating, nourishing, nutritious, salubrious, salutary
Antonyms *adj* ≠ **well:** ailing, at death's door, debilitated, delicate, diseased, feeble, fragile, frail, ill, infirm, poorly (*inf.*), sick, sickly, unfit, unhealthy, unsound, unwell, weak, weedy (*inf.*) ≠ **wholesome:** unhealthy, unwholesome

heap *n* **1** = **pile**, accumulation, aggregation, collection, hoard, lot, mass, mound, mountain, rick, stack, stockpile, store **2** *often plural Informal* = **a lot**, abundance, great deal, lashings (*Brit. inf.*), load(s) (*inf.*), lots (*inf.*), mass, mint, ocean(s), oodles (*inf.*), plenty, pot(s) (*inf.*), quantities, stack(s), tons ◆ *vb* **5** = **pile**, accumulate, amass, augment, bank, collect, gather, hoard, increase, mound, stack, stockpile, store **6** = **load**, assign, bestow, burden, confer, shower upon

hear *vb* **2** = **listen to**, attend, be all ears (*inf.*), catch, eavesdrop, give attention, hark, hearken (*arch.*), heed, listen in, overhear **3** = **learn**, ascertain, be informed, be told of, discover, find out, gather, get wind of (*inf.*), hear tell (*dialect*), pick up, understand **4** *Law* = **try**, examine, investigate, judge

hearing *n* **1** = **perception**, audition, ear **2** = **chance to speak**, audience, audition, interview **3** = **earshot**, auditory range, hearing distance, range, reach, sound **4** = **inquiry**, industrial tribunal, investigation, review, trial

hearsay *n* = **rumour**, buzz, dirt, gossip, grapevine (*inf.*), idle talk, report, talk, talk of the town, tittle-tattle, word of mouth

heart *n* **3, 4** = **nature**, character, disposition, emotion, feeling, inclination, sentiment, soul, sympathy, temperament **5** = **tenderness**, affection, benevolence, compassion, concern, humanity, love, pity, understanding **6** = **courage**, balls (*taboo sl.*), boldness, bravery, fortitude, guts (*inf.*), mettle, mind, nerve, pluck, purpose, resolution, spirit, spunk (*inf.*), will **7** = **centre**, central part, core, crux, essence, hub, kernel, marrow, middle, nucleus, pith, quintessence, root **17 by heart** = **by memory**, by rote, off pat, parrot-fashion (*inf.*), pat, word for word **18 eat one's heart out** = **grieve**, agonize, brood, mope, mourn, obsess, pine, regret, repine, sorrow **19 from (the bottom of) one's heart** = **sincerely**, deeply, devoutly, fervently, heart and soul, heartily, with all one's heart **29 take heart** = **be encouraged**, be comforted, be heartened, brighten up, buck up (*inf.*), cheer up, perk up, revive

heartache *n* = **sorrow**, affliction, agony, anguish, bitterness, despair, distress, grief, heartbreak, heartsickness, pain, remorse, suffering, torment, torture

heartbreak *n* = **grief**, anguish, desolation, despair, misery, pain, sorrow, suffering

heartbreaking *adj* = **sad**, agonizing, bitter, desolating, disappointing, distressing, grievous, gut-wrenching, harrowing, heart-rending, pitiful, poignant, tragic
Antonyms *adj* cheerful, cheery, comic, glorious, happy, jolly, joyful, joyous, light-hearted

hearten ❶ (ˈhɑːtᵊn) *vb* to make or become cheerful.
▸ **ˈheartening** *adj*

heart failure *n* **1** a condition in which the heart is unable to pump an adequate amount of blood to the tissues. **2** sudden cessation of the heartbeat, resulting in death.

heartfelt ❶ (ˈhɑːtˌfɛlt) *adj* sincerely and strongly felt.

hearth (hɑːθ) *n* **1a** the floor of a fireplace, esp. one that extends outwards into the room. **1b** (*as modifier*): *hearth rug.* **2** this as a symbol of the home, etc. **3** the bottom part of a metallurgical furnace in which the molten metal is produced or contained. [OE *heorth*]

hearthstone (ˈhɑːθˌstəʊn) *n* **1** a stone that forms a hearth. **2** soft stone used (esp. formerly) to clean and whiten floors, steps, etc.

heartily ❶ (ˈhɑːtɪlɪ) *adv* **1** thoroughly or vigorously. **2** in a sincere manner.

heartland (ˈhɑːtˌlænd) *n* the central or most important region of a country or continent.

heartless ❶ (ˈhɑːtlɪs) *adj* unkind or cruel.
▸ **ˈheartlessly** *adv* ▸ **ˈheartlessness** *n*

heart-lung machine *n* a machine used to maintain the circulation and oxygenation of the blood during heart surgery.

heart-rending ❶ *adj* causing great mental pain and sorrow.
▸ **ˈheart-ˌrendingly** *adv*

hearts (hɑːts) *n* (*functioning as sing*) a card game in which players must avoid winning tricks containing hearts or the queen of spades. Also called: **Black Maria.**

heart-searching *n* examination of one's feelings or conscience.

heartsease *or* **heart's-ease** (ˈhɑːtsˌiːz) *n* **1** another name for the **wild pansy. 2** peace of mind.

heartsick ❶ (ˈhɑːtˌsɪk) *adj* deeply despondent.
▸ **ˈheartˌsickness** *n*

heartstrings (ˈhɑːtˌstrɪŋz) *pl n Often facetious.* deep emotions. [C15: orig. referring to the tendons supposed to support the heart]

heart-throb *n* **1** an object of infatuation. **2** a heartbeat.

heart-to-heart ❶ *adj* **1** (esp. of a conversation) concerned with personal problems or intimate feelings. ◆ *n* **2** an intimate conversation.

heart-warming ❶ *adj* **1** pleasing; gratifying. **2** emotionally moving.

heartwood (ˈhɑːtˌwʊd) *n* the central core of dark hard wood in tree trunks, consisting of nonfunctioning xylem tissue that has become blocked with resins, tannins, and oils.

hearty ❶ (ˈhɑːtɪ) *adj* **heartier, heartiest. 1** warm and unreserved in manner. **2** vigorous and heartfelt: *hearty dislike.* **3** healthy and strong (esp. in **hale and hearty**). **4** substantial and nourishing. ◆ *n, pl* **hearties.** *Inf.* **5** a comrade, esp. a sailor. **6** a vigorous sporting man: *a rugby hearty.*
▸ **ˈheartiness** *n*

heat ❶ (hiːt) *n* **1** the energy transferred as a result of a difference in temperature. Related adjs.: **thermal, calorific. 2** the sensation caused by heat energy; warmth. **3** the state of being hot. **4** hot weather: *the heat of summer.* **5** intensity of feeling: *the heat of rage.* **6** pressure: *the political heat on the government over the economy.* **7** the most intense part: *the heat of the battle.* **8** a period of sexual excitement in female mammals that occurs at oestrus. **9** *Sport.* **9a** a preliminary eliminating contest in a competition. **9b** a single section of a contest. **10** *Sl.* police activity after a crime: *the heat is off.* **11** *Sl., chiefly US.* criticism or abuse: *he took a lot of heat for that mistake.* **12 in the heat of the moment.** without pausing to think. **13 on** *or* **in heat. 13a** Also: **in season.** (of some female mammals) sexually receptive. **13b** in a state of sexual excitement. ◆ *vb* **14** to make or become hot or warm. **15** to make or become excited or intense. [OE *hǣtu*]

heat barrier *n* another name for **thermal barrier.**

heat capacity *n* the heat required to raise the temperature of a substance by unit temperature interval under specified conditions.

heat death *n Thermodynamics.* the condition of any closed system when its total entropy is a maximum and it has no available energy. If the universe is a closed system it should eventually reach this state.

heated ❶ (ˈhiːtɪd) *adj* **1** made hot. **2** impassioned or highly emotional.
▸ **ˈheatedly** *adv*

heat engine *n* an engine that converts heat energy into mechanical energy.

heater (ˈhiːtə) *n* **1** any device for supplying heat, such as a convector. **2** *US sl.* a pistol. **3** *Electronics.* a conductor carrying a current that indirectly heats the cathode in some types of valve.

heat exchanger *n* a device for transferring heat from one fluid to another without allowing them to mix.

heat exhaustion *n* a condition resulting from exposure to intense heat, characterized by dizziness, abdominal cramp, and prostration.

heath (hiːθ) *n* **1** *Brit.* a large open area, usually with sandy soil and scrubby vegetation, esp. heather. **2** Also called: **heather.** a low-growing evergreen shrub having small bell-shaped typically pink or purple flowers. **3** any of several heathlike plants, such as sea heath. [OE *hǣth*]
▸ **ˈheathˌlike** *adj* ▸ **ˈheathy** *adj*

heathen ❶ (ˈhiːðən) *n, pl* **heathens** *or* **heathen. 1** a person who does not acknowledge the God of Christianity, Judaism, or Islam; pagan. **2** an uncivilized or barbaric person. ◆ *adj* **3** irreligious; pagan. **4** uncivilized; barbaric. **5** of or relating to heathen peoples or their customs and beliefs. [OE *hǣthen*]
▸ **ˈheathendom** *n* ▸ **ˈheathenism** *or* **ˈheathenry** *n*

heathenize *or* **heathenise** (ˈhiːðəˌnaɪz) *vb* **heathenizes, heathenizing, heathenized** *or* **heathenises, heathenising, heathenised.** to render or become heathen.

heather (ˈhɛðə) *n* **1** Also called: **ling, heath.** a low-growing evergreen Eurasian shrub that grows in dense masses on open ground and has clusters of small bell-shaped typically pinkish-purple flowers. **2** a purplish-red to pinkish-purple colour. ◆ *adj* **3** of a heather colour. **4** of or relating to interwoven yarns of mixed colours: *heather mixture.* [C14: orig. Scot. & N English, prob. from HEATH]
▸ **ˈheathery** *adj*

Heath Robinson *adj* (of a mechanical device) absurdly complicated in design and having a simple function. [C20: after William *Heath Robinson* (1872–1944), E cartoonist who drew such contrivances]

heating (ˈhiːtɪŋ) *n* **1** a device or system for supplying heat, esp. central heating, to a building. **2** the heat supplied.

heat pump *n* a device for extracting heat from a source and delivering it elsewhere at a higher temperature.

heat rash *n* a nontechnical name for **miliaria.**

heat-seeking *adj* (of a missile, detecting device, etc.) able to detect a source of heat, as from an aircraft engine: *a heat-seeking missile.*
▸ **heat seeker** *n*

heat shield *n* a coating or barrier for shielding from excessive heat, such as that experienced by a spacecraft on re-entry into the earth's atmosphere.

heat sink *n* **1** a metal plate designed to conduct and radiate heat from an electrical component. **2** a layer within the outer skin of high-speed aircraft to absorb heat.

heatstroke (ˈhiːtˌstrəʊk) *n* a condition resulting from prolonged exposure to intense heat, characterized by high fever.

heat-treat *vb* (*tr*) to apply heat to (a metal or alloy) in one or more temperature cycles to give it desirable properties.
▸ **heat treatment** *n*

heat wave *n* **1** a continuous spell of abnormally hot weather. **2** an extensive slow-moving air mass at a relatively high temperature.

heave ❶ (hiːv) *vb* **heaves, heaving, heaved** *or* **hove. 1** (*tr*) to lift or move with a great effort. **2** (*tr*) to throw (something heavy) with effort. **3** to utter (sounds) noisily or unhappily: *to heave a sigh.* **4** to rise and fall or

THESAURUS

hearten *vb* = **encourage,** animate, assure, buck up (*inf.*), buoy up, cheer, comfort, console, embolden, gee up, incite, inspire, inspirit, raise someone's spirits, reassure, revivify, rouse, stimulate

heartfelt *adj* = **sincere,** ardent, cordial, deep, devout, earnest, fervent, genuine, hearty, honest, profound, unfeigned, warm, wholehearted
Antonyms *adj* false, feigned, flippant, fraudulent, frivolous, half-hearted, hypocritical, insincere, phoney *or* phony (*inf.*), pretended, put on, reserved, unenthusiastic, unimpassioned

heartily *adv* **1** = **thoroughly,** absolutely, completely, eagerly, earnestly, enthusiastically, resolutely, totally, very, vigorously, zealously **2** = **sincerely,** cordially, deeply, feelingly, genuinely, profoundly, unfeignedly, warmly

heartless *adj* = **cruel,** affectless, brutal, callous, cold, cold-blooded, cold-hearted, hard, hardhearted, harsh, inhuman, merciless, pitiless, uncaring, unfeeling, unkind
Antonyms *adj* compassionate, generous, humane, kind, merciful, sensitive, sympathetic, warm-hearted

heart-rending *adj* = **moving,** affecting, distressing, gut-wrenching, harrowing, heartbreaking, pathetic, piteous, pitiful, poignant, sad, tragic

heartsick *adj* = **despondent,** dejected, dispirited, downcast, heartsore, heavy-hearted, sick at heart

heart-to-heart *adj* **1** = **intimate,** candid, open, personal, sincere, unreserved ◆ *n* **2** = **cosy chat,** tête-à-tête

heart-warming *adj* **1** = **gratifying,** pleasing, rewarding, satisfying **2** = **moving,** affecting, cheering, encouraging, heartening, touching, warming

hearty *adj* **1** = **friendly,** affable, ardent, back-slapping, cordial, eager, ebullient, effusive, enthusiastic, generous, genial, jovial, unreserved, warm **2** = **wholehearted,** earnest, genuine, heartfelt, honest, real, sincere, true, unfeigned **3** = **healthy,** active, alive and kicking, energetic, hale, hardy, right as rain (*Brit. inf.*), robust, sound, strong, vigorous, well **4** = **substantial,** ample, filling, nourishing, sizable *or* sizeable, solid, square
Antonyms *adj* ≠ **friendly:** cold, cool, unfriendly ≠ **wholehearted:** half-hearted, insincere, mild ≠ **healthy:** delicate, feeble, frail, sickly, unhealthy, weak

heat *n* **2, 3** = **hotness,** calefaction, fever, fieriness, high temperature, warmness, warmth **4** = **hot weather,** high temperature, sultriness, swelter, torridity **5** = **passion,** agitation, ardour, earnestness, excitement, fervour, fever, fury, impetuosity, intensity, vehemence, violence, warmth, zeal ◆ *vb* **14** = **warm up,** become warm, chafe, flush, glow, grow hot, make hot, reheat **15** = **stimulate,** animate, excite, impassion, inflame, inspirit, rouse, stir, warm
Antonyms *n* ≠ **hotness:** cold, coldness, coolness ≠ **passion:** calmness, coldness, composure, coolness ◆ *vb* ≠ **warm up:** chill, cool, cool off, freeze

heated *adj* **2** = **impassioned,** angry, bitter, excited, fierce, fiery, frenzied, furious, intense, passionate, raging, stormy, tempestuous, vehement, violent
Antonyms *adj* calm, civilized, dispassionate, friendly, half-hearted, mellow, mild, peaceful, quiet, rational, reasoned, serene, subdued, unemotional, unfazed (*inf.*), unruffled

heathen *n* **1** = **pagan,** idolater, idolatress, infidel, unbeliever **2** = **barbarian,** philistine, savage ◆ *adj* **3** = **pagan,** godless, heathenish, idolatrous, infidel, irreligious **4** = **uncivilized,** barbaric, philistine, savage, unenlightened

heave *vb* **1** = **lift,** drag (up), elevate, haul (up), heft, hoist, lever, pull (up), raise, tug **2** = **throw,**

cause to rise and fall heavily. **5** (*p.t. & p.p.* **hove**) *Naut.* **5a** to move or cause to move in a specified direction: *to heave in sight.* **5b** (*intr*) (of a vessel) to pitch or roll. **6** (*tr*) to displace (rock strata, etc.) in a horizontal direction. **7** (*intr*) to retch. ◆ *n* **8** the act of heaving. **9** a horizontal displacement of rock strata at a fault. ◆ See also **heave to, heaves.** [OE *hebban*]
▸ **'heaver** *n*

heave-ho *interj* a sailors' cry, as when hoisting anchor.

heaven Ⓣ ('hɛvən) *n* **1** (*sometimes cap.*) *Christianity.* **1a** the abode of God and the angels. **1b** a state of communion with God after death. **2** (*usually pl*) the firmament surrounding the earth. **3** (in various mythologies) a place, such as Elysium or Valhalla, to which those who have died in the gods' favour are brought to dwell in happiness. **4** a place or state of happiness. **5** (*sing* or *pl; sometimes cap.*) God or the gods, used in exclamatory phrases: *for heaven's sake.* **6 move heaven and earth.** to do everything possible (to achieve something). [OE *heofon*]

heavenly Ⓣ ('hɛvənlɪ) *adj* **1** *Inf.* wonderful. **2** of or occurring in space: *a heavenly body.* **3** holy.
▸ **'heavenliness** *n*

heavenward ('hɛvənwəd) *adj* **1** directed towards heaven or the sky. ◆ *adv* **2** Also **heavenwards.** towards heaven or the sky.

heaves (hiːvz) *n* (*functioning as sing or pl*) a chronic respiratory disorder of animals of the horse family, of unknown cause. Also called: **broken wind.**

heave to *vb* (*adv*) to stop (a vessel) or (of a vessel) to stop, as by trimming the sails, etc.

Heaviside layer ('hɛvɪˌsaɪd) *n* another name for **E region** (of the ionosphere). [C20: after O. *Heaviside* (1850–1925), E physicist who predicted its existence (1902)]

heavy Ⓣ ('hɛvɪ) *adj* **heavier, heaviest. 1** of comparatively great weight. **2** having a relatively high density: *lead is a heavy metal.* **3** great in yield, quality, or quantity: *heavy traffic.* **4** considerable: *heavy emphasis.* **5** hard to bear or fulfil: *heavy demands.* **6** sad or dejected: *heavy at heart.* **7** coarse or broad: *heavy features.* **8** (of soil) having a high clay content; cloggy. **9** solid or fat: *heavy legs.* **10** (of an industry) engaged in the large-scale complex manufacture of capital goods or extraction of raw materials. **11** serious; grave. **12** *Mil.* **12a** equipped with large weapons, armour, etc. **12b** (of guns, etc.) of a large and powerful type. **13** (of a syllable) having stress or accentuation. **14** dull and uninteresting: *a heavy style.* **15** prodigious: *a heavy drinker.* **16** (of cakes, etc.) insufficiently leavened. **17** deep and loud: *a heavy thud.* **18** (of music, literature, etc.) **18a** dramatic and powerful. **18b** not immediately comprehensible or appealing. **19** *Sl.* (of rock music) having a powerful beat; hard. **20** burdened: *heavy with child.* **21 heavy on.** *Inf.* using large quantities of: *this car is very heavy on petrol.* **22** clumsy and slow: *heavy going.* **23** cloudy or overcast: *heavy skies.* **24** not easily digestible: *a heavy meal.* **25** (of an element or compound) being or containing an isotope with greater atomic weight than that of the naturally occurring element: *heavy water.* **26** (of the going on a racecourse) soft and muddy. **27** *Sl.* using, or prepared to use, violence or brutality. ◆ *n, pl* **heavies. 28a** a villainous role. **28b** an actor who plays such a part. **29** *Mil.* **29a** a large fleet unit, esp. an aircraft carrier or battleship. **29b** a large piece of artillery. **30** (*usually pl; often preceded by the*) *Inf.* a serious newspaper: *the Sunday heavies.* **31** *Inf.* a heavyweight boxer, wrestler, etc. **32** *Sl.* a man hired to threaten violence or deter others by his presence. ◆ *adv* **33a** in a heavy manner; heavily: *time hangs heavy.* **33b** (*in combination*): *heavy-laden.* [OE *hefig*]
▸ **'heavily** *adv* ▸ **'heaviness** *n*

heavy-duty *n* (*modifier*) made to withstand hard wear, bad weather, etc.

heavy-handed Ⓣ *adj* **1** clumsy. **2** harsh and oppressive.
▸ **ˌheavy-'handedly** *adv*

heavy-hearted Ⓣ *adj* sad; melancholy.

heavy hydrogen *n* another name for **deuterium.**

heavy metal *n* a type of rock music characterized by high volume, a driving beat, and extended guitar solos, often with violent, nihilistic, and misogynistic lyrics.

heavy middleweight *n* a professional wrestler weighing 177–187 pounds (81–85 kg).

heavy spar *n* another name for **barytes.**

heavy water *n* water that has been electrolytically decomposed to reduce the amount of normal hydrogen present and enrich it in deuterium in the form D_2O or HDO. See also **deuterium oxide.**

heavyweight ('hɛvɪˌweɪt) *n* **1** a person or thing that is heavier than average. **2a** a professional boxer weighing more than 175 pounds (79 kg). **2b** an amateur boxer weighing more than 81 kg (179 pounds). **3a** a professional wrestler weighing over 209 pounds (95 kg). **3b** an amateur wrestler weighing over 220 pounds (100kg). **4** *Inf.* an important or highly influential person.

Heb. *or* **Hebr.** *abbrev. for:* **1** Hebrew (language). **2** *Bible.* Hebrews.

hebdomadal (hɛb'dɒmədəl) *adj* weekly. [C18: from L, from Gk *hebdomas* seven (days), from *hepta* seven]

hebetate ('hɛbɪˌteɪt) *adj* **1** (of plant parts) having a blunt or soft point. ◆ *vb* **hebetates, hebetating, hebetated. 2** *Rare.* to make or become blunted. [C16: from L *hebetāre* to make blunt, from *hebes* blunt]
▸ **ˌhebe'tation** *n*

Hebraic (hɪ'breɪɪk) *or* **Hebraical** *adj* of, relating to, or characteristic of the Hebrews or their language or culture.
▸ **He'braically** *adv*

Hebraism ('hiːbreɪˌɪzəm) *n* a linguistic usage, custom, or other feature borrowed from or particular to the Hebrew language, or to the Jewish people or their culture.
▸ **'Hebraist** *n* ▸ **'Hebraˌize** *or* **'Hebraˌise** *vb*

Hebrew ('hiːbruː) *n* **1** the ancient language of the Hebrews, revived as the official language of Israel. **2** a member of an ancient Semitic people claiming descent from Abraham; an Israelite. **3** *Arch. or offens.* a Jew. ◆ *adj* **4** of or relating to the Hebrews or their language. **5** *Arch. or offens.* Jewish. [C13: from OF *Ebreu,* ult. from Heb. *'ibhrī* one from beyond (the river)]

hecatomb ('hɛkəˌtəʊm, -ˌtuːm) *n* **1** (in ancient Greece or Rome) any great public sacrifice and feast, originally one in which 100 oxen were sacrificed. **2** a great sacrifice. [C16: from L *hecatombē,* from Gk, from *hekaton* hundred + *bous* ox]

heck (hɛk) *interj* a mild exclamation of surprise, irritation, etc. [C19: euphemistic for *hell*]

heckelphone ('hɛkəlˌfəʊn) *n Music.* a type of bass oboe. [C20: after W. *Heckel* (1856-1909), G inventor]

heckle Ⓣ ('hɛkəl) *vb* **heckles, heckling, heckled. 1** to interrupt (a public speaker, etc.) by comments, questions, or taunts. **2** (*tr*) Also: **hackle, hatchel.** to comb (hemp or flax). ◆ *n* **3** an instrument for combing flax or hemp. [C15: N English & East Anglian form of HACKLE]
▸ **'heckler** *n*

hectare ('hɛktɑː) *n* one hundred ares (10 000 square metres or 2.471 acres). Symbol: ha [C19: from F; see HECTO-, ARE[2]]

hectic Ⓣ ('hɛktɪk) *adj* **1** characterized by extreme activity or excitement. **2** associated with or symptomatic of tuberculosis (esp. in **hectic fever, hectic flush**). ◆ *n* **3** a hectic fever or flush. **4** *Rare.* a person who is consumptive. [C14: from LL *hecticus,* from Gk *hektikos* habitual, from *hexis* state, from *ekhein* to have]
▸ **'hectically** *adv*

THESAURUS

cast, fling, hurl, pitch, send, sling, toss **3 = sigh**, breathe heavily, groan, puff, sob, utter wearily **4 = surge**, billow, breathe, dilate, exhale, expand, palpitate, pant, rise, swell, throb **7 = vomit**, barf (*US sl.*), be sick, chuck (up) (*sl., chiefly US*), chunder (*sl., chiefly Austral.*), do a technicolour yawn (*sl.*), gag, retch, spew, throw up (*inf.*), toss one's cookies (*US sl.*)

heaven *n* **1, 3 = paradise**, abode of God, bliss, Elysium *or* Elysian fields (*Greek myth*), happy hunting ground (*Native American legend*), Happy Valley, hereafter, life everlasting, life to come, next world, nirvana (*Buddhism, Hinduism*), Valhalla (*Norse myth*), Zion (*Christianity*) **2** *usually plural* **= sky**, empyrean (*poetic*), ether, firmament, welkin (*arch.*) **4 = happiness**, bliss, dreamland, ecstasy, enchantment, felicity, paradise, rapture, seventh heaven, sheer bliss, transport, utopia

heavenly *adj* **1** *Informal* **= wonderful**, alluring, beautiful, blissful, delightful, divine (*inf.*), entrancing, exquisite, glorious, lovely, rapturous, ravishing, sublime **2 = celestial**, empyrean (*poetic*), extraterrestrial **3 = holy**, angelic, beatific, blessed, blest, cherubic, divine, godlike, immortal, paradisaical, seraphic, superhuman, supernal (*literary*), supernatural
Antonyms *adj* ≠ **wonderful:** abominable, abysmal, appalling, awful, bad, depressing, dire, disagreeable, dreadful, dreary, dull, frightful, gloomy, grim, hellacious (*US sl.*), horrible, horrid, lousy (*sl.*), miserable, rotten (*inf.*), terrible, unpleasant, vile ≠ **holy:** earthly, human, secular, worldly

heavily *adv* **3 = densely**, closely, compactly, fast, hard, thick, thickly **5 = laboriously**, painfully, with difficulty **15 = excessively**, a great deal, considerably, copiously, frequently, to excess, very much **22 = ponderously**, awkwardly, clumsily, weightily

heaviness *n* **1 = weight**, gravity, heftiness, ponderousness **5 = onerousness**, arduousness, grievousness, oppressiveness, severity, weightiness **6 = sadness**, dejection, depression, despondency, gloom, gloominess, glumness, melancholy, seriousness

heavy *adj* **1 = weighty**, bulky, hefty, massive, ponderous, portly **4 = considerable**, abundant, copious, large, profuse **5 = onerous**, burdensome, difficult, grievous, hard, harsh, intolerable, laborious, oppressive, severe, tedious, vexatious, wearisome **6 = sad**, crestfallen, dejected, depressed, despondent, disconsolate, downcast, gloomy, grieving, melancholy, sorrowful **18b = serious**, complex, deep, difficult, grave, profound, solemn, weighty **20 = burdened**, encumbered, laden, loaded, oppressed, weighted **23 = overcast**, cloudy, dull, gloomy, leaden, louring *or* lowering
Antonyms *adj* ≠ **weighty:** agile, compact, handy, light, slight, small ≠ **considerable:** light, moderate, slight, sparse ≠ **onerous:** bearable, easy, gentle, light, mild, moderate, soft ≠ **sad:** calm, cheerful, happy, joyful ≠ **serious:** exciting, inconsequential, trivial, unimportant

heavy-handed *adj* **1 = clumsy**, awkward, bungling, graceless, ham-fisted (*inf.*), ham-handed (*inf.*), inept, inexpert, like a bull in a china shop (*inf.*), maladroit, unhandy **2 = oppressive**, autocratic, domineering, harsh, overbearing
Antonyms *adj* ≠ **clumsy:** adept, adroit, competent, dexterous, effectual, efficient, gentle, graceful, skilful, smooth ≠ **oppressive:** considerate, submissive, subservient

heavy-hearted *adj* **= sad**, crushed, depressed, despondent, discouraged, disheartened, dismal, downcast, downhearted, down in the dumps (*inf.*), forlorn, heartsick, melancholy, miserable, morose, mournful, sick as a parrot (*inf.*), sorrowful

heckle *vb* **1 = jeer**, bait, barrack (*inf.*), boo, disrupt, interrupt, pester, shout down, taunt

hectic *adj* **1 = frantic**, animated, boisterous, chaotic, excited, fevered, feverish, flurrying, flustering, frenetic, frenzied, furious, heated, riotous, rumbustious, tumultuous, turbulent, wild

hecto- *or before a vowel* **hect-** *prefix* denoting 100: *hectogram.* Symbol: h [via F from Gk *hekaton* hundred]

hectog *abbrev. for* hectogram.

hectogram *or* **hectogramme** ('hɛktəʊˌɡræm) *n* one hundred grams (3.527 ounces). Symbol: hg

hectograph ('hɛktəʊˌɡrɑːf) *n* **1** a process for copying type or manuscript from a glycerine-coated gelatine master to which the original has been transferred. **2** a machine using this process.

hector ⓣ ('hɛktə) *vb* **1** to bully or torment by teasing. ◆ *n* **2** a blustering bully. [C17: after *Hector* (son of Priam), in the sense: a bully]

he'd (hiːd; *unstressed* iːd, hɪd, ɪd) *contraction of* he had *or* he would.

heddle ('hɛdᵊl) *n* one of a set of frames of vertical wires on a loom, each wire having an eye through which a warp thread can be passed. [OE *hefeld* chain]

hedera ('hɛdərə) *n* the genus name of **ivy** (sense 1). [L]

hedge ⓣ (hɛdʒ) *n* **1** a row of shrubs or bushes forming a boundary. **2** a barrier or protection against something. **3** the act or a method of reducing the risk of loss on an investment, etc. **4** a cautious or evasive statement. **5** (*as modifier*) low, inferior, or illiterate: *hedge priest.* ◆ *vb* **hedges, hedging, hedged. 6** (*tr*) to enclose or separate with or as if with a hedge. **7** (*intr*) to make or maintain a hedge. **8** (*tr;* often foll. by *in, about,* or *around*) to hinder or restrict. **9** (*intr*) to evade decision, esp. by making noncommittal statements. **10** (*tr*) to guard against the risk of loss in (a bet, etc.), esp. by laying bets with other bookmakers. **11** (*intr*) to protect against loss through future price fluctuations, as by investing in futures. [OE *hecg*]
▸**'hedger** *n* ▸**'hedging** *n*

hedge fund *n* a largely unregulated speculative fund which offers substantial returns for high-risk investments.

hedgehog ('hɛdʒˌhɒɡ) *n* a small nocturnal Old World mammal having a protective covering of spines on the back.

hedgehop ('hɛdʒˌhɒp) *vb* **hedgehops, hedgehopping, hedgehopped.** (*intr*) (of an aircraft) to fly close to the ground, as in crop spraying.
▸**'hedgeˌhopping** *n, adj*

hedgerow ('hɛdʒˌrəʊ) *n* a hedge of shrubs or low trees, esp. one bordering a field.

hedge sparrow *n* a small brownish European songbird. Also called: **dunnock.**

hedonics (hiː'dɒnɪks) *n* (*functioning as sing*) **1** the branch of psychology concerned with the study of pleasant and unpleasant sensations. **2** (in philosophy) the study of pleasure.

hedonism ⓣ ('hiːdᵊˌnɪzəm, 'hɛd-) *n* **1** *Ethics.* **1a** the doctrine that moral value can be defined in terms of pleasure. **1b** the doctrine that the pursuit of pleasure is the highest good. **2** indulgence in sensual pleasures. [C19: from Gk *hēdonē* pleasure]
▸**ˌhedon'istic** *adj* ▸**'hedonist** *n*

-hedron *n combining form.* indicating a solid having a specified number of surfaces: *tetrahedron.* [from Gk *-edron* -sided, from *hedra* seat, base]
▸**-hedral** *adj combining form.*

heebie-jeebies ('hiːbɪ'dʒiːbɪz) *pl n* **the.** *Sl.* apprehension and nervousness. [C20: coined by W. De Beck (1890–1942), American cartoonist]

heed ⓣ (hiːd) *n* **1** careful attention; notice: *to take heed.* ◆ *vb* **2** to pay close attention to (someone or something). [OE *hēdan*]
▸**'heedful** *adj* ▸**'heedfully** *adv* ▸**'heedfulness** *n*

heedless ⓣ ('hiːdlɪs) *adj* taking no notice; careless or thoughtless.
▸**'heedlessly** *adv* ▸**'heedlessness** *n*

heehaw (ˌhiː'hɔː) *interj* an imitation or representation of the braying sound of a donkey.

heel[1] ⓣ (hiːl) *n* **1** the back part of the human foot. **2** the corresponding part in other vertebrates. **3** the part of a stocking, etc., designed to fit the heel. **4** the outer part of a shoe underneath the heel. **5** the end or back section of something: *the heel of a loaf.* **6** *Horticulture.* the small part of the parent plant that remains attached to a young shoot cut for propagation. **7** the back part of a golf club head where it bends to join the shaft. **8** *Sl.* a contemptible person. **9 at** (*or* **on**) **one's heels.** following closely. **10 down at heel. 10a** shabby or worn. **10b** slovenly. **11 kick** (*or* **cool**) **one's heels.** to wait or be kept waiting. **12 take to one's heels.** to run off. **13 to heel.** under control, as a dog walking by a person's heel. ◆ *vb* **14** (*tr*) to repair or replace the heel of (a shoe, etc.). **15** (*tr*) *Golf.* to strike (the ball) with the heel of the club. **16** to follow at the heels of (a person). [OE *hēla*]
▸**'heelless** *adj*

heel[2] ⓣ (hiːl) *vb* **1** (of a vessel) to lean over; list. ◆ *n* **2** inclined position from the vertical. [OE *hieldan*]

heelball ('hiːlˌbɔːl) *n* **a** a mixture of beeswax and lampblack used by shoemakers to blacken the edges of heels and soles. **b** a similar substance used to take rubbings, esp. brass rubbings.

heeler ('hiːlə) *n* **1** *US.* See **ward heeler. 2** a person or thing that heels. **3** *Austral. & NZ.* a dog that herds cattle, etc., by biting at their heels.

heel in *vb* (*tr, adv*) to insert (cuttings, shoots, etc.) into the soil before planting to keep them moist.

heeltap ('hiːlˌtæp) *n* **1** a layer of leather, etc., in the heel of a shoe. **2** a small amount of alcoholic drink left at the bottom of a glass.

heft (hɛft) *vb* (*tr*) *Brit. dialect. & US inf.* **1** to assess the weight of (something) by lifting. **2** to lift. ◆ *n* **3** weight. **4** *US.* the main part. [C19: prob. from HEAVE, by analogy with *thieve, theft, cleave, cleft*]

hefty ⓣ ('hɛftɪ) *adj* **heftier, heftiest.** *Inf.* **1** big and strong. **2** characterized by vigour or force: *a hefty blow.* **3** bulky or heavy. **4** sizable; involving a large amount of money: *a hefty bill.*
▸**'heftily** *adv*

Hegelian (hɪ'ɡeɪlɪən, heɪ'ɡiː-) *adj* relating to G. W. F. Hegel (1770–1831), German philosopher, or his system of thought, esp. his concept of dialectic, in which the contradiction between a proposition (thesis) and its antithesis is resolved at a higher level of truth (synthesis).

hegemony (hɪ'ɡemənɪ) *n, pl* **hegemonies.** ascendancy or domination of one power or state within a league, confederation, etc. [C16: from Gk *hēgemonia,* from *hēgemōn* leader, from *hēgeisthai* to lead]
▸**hegemonic** (ˌhɛɡə'mɒnɪk) *adj*

Hegira *or* **Hejira** ('hɛdʒɪrə) *n* **1** the flight of Mohammed from Mecca to Medina in 622 A.D.; the starting point of the Muslim era. **2** the Muslim era itself. **3** (*often not cap.*) an emigration, escape, or flight. [C16: from Med. L, from Ar. *hijrah* emigration or flight]

heifer ('hɛfə) *n* a young cow. [OE *heahfore*]

heigh-ho ('heɪ'həʊ) *interj* an exclamation of weariness, surprise, or happiness.

height ⓣ (haɪt) *n* **1** the vertical distance from the bottom of something to the top. **2** the vertical distance of a place above sea level. **3** relatively great altitude. **4** the topmost point; summit. **5** *Astron.* the angular distance of a celestial body above the horizon. **6** the period of greatest intensity: *the height of the battle.* **7** an extreme example: *the height of rudeness.* **8** (*often pl*) an area of high ground. [OE *hīehthu;* see HIGH]

heighten ⓣ ('haɪtᵊn) *vb* to make or become higher or more intense.
▸**'heightened** *adj*

height of land *n US & Canad.* a watershed.

heinous ⓣ ('heɪnəs, 'hiː-) *adj* evil; atrocious. [C14: from OF *haineus,* from *haine* hatred, of Gmc origin]
▸**'heinously** *adv*

THESAURUS

Antonyms *adj* calm, peaceful, relaxing, tranquil

hector *vb* **1** = **bully**, bluster, boast, browbeat, bullyrag, harass, huff and puff, intimidate, menace, provoke, ride roughshod over, roister, threaten, worry

hedge *n* **1** = **hedgerow**, quickset **2** = **barrier**, boundary, screen, windbreak **3** = **insurance cover**, compensation, counterbalance, guard, protection ◆ *vb* **6** = **enclose**, border, edge, fence, surround **8** = **restrict**, block, confine, hem about, hem around, hem in, hinder, obstruct **9** = **dodge**, beg the question, be noncommittal, duck, equivocate, evade, flannel (*Brit. inf.*), prevaricate, pussyfoot (*inf.*), quibble, sidestep, temporize, waffle (*inf., chiefly Brit.*) **10, 11** = **insure**, cover, fortify, guard, protect, safeguard, shield

hedonism *n* **1** = **pursuit of pleasure**, dolce vita, gratification, luxuriousness, pleasure-seeking, self-indulgence, sensualism, sensuality **2** = **sybaritism**, epicureanism, epicurism

hedonist *n* **2** = **pleasure seeker**, *bon vivant*, epicure, epicurean, sensualist, sybarite, voluptuary

hedonistic *adj* **2** = **pleasure-seeking**, bacchanalian, epicurean, luxurious, self-indulgent, sybaritic, voluptuous

heed *n* **1** = **care**, attention, caution, consideration, ear, heedfulness, mind, note, notice, regard, respect, thought, watchfulness ◆ *vb* **2** = **pay attention to**, attend, bear in mind, be guided by, consider, follow, give ear to, listen to, mark, mind, note, obey, observe, regard, take notice of, take to heart
Antonyms *n* ≠ **care:** carelessness, disregard, inattention, laxity, laxness, neglect, thoughtlessness ◆ *vb* ≠ **pay attention to:** be inattentive to, discount, disobey, disregard, flout, ignore, neglect, overlook, reject, shun, turn a deaf ear to

heedful *adj* **1** = **careful**, attentive, cautious, chary, circumspect, mindful, observant, prudent, vigilant, wary, watchful

heedless *adj* = **careless**, foolhardy, imprudent, inattentive, incautious, neglectful, negligent, oblivious, precipitate, rash, reckless, thoughtless, unmindful, unobservant, unthinking
Antonyms *adj* attentive, aware, careful, cautious, concerned, heedful, mindful, observant, thoughtful, vigilant, wary, watchful

heel[1] *n* **5** = **end**, crust, remainder, rump, stub, stump **8** *Slang* = **swine**, blackguard, bounder, cad (*Brit. inf.*), rotter (*sl., chiefly Brit.*), scally (*Northwest English dialect*), scoundrel, scumbag (*sl.*) **10 down at heel** = **shabby**, dowdy, impoverished, out at elbows, run-down, seedy, slipshod, slovenly, worn **12 take to one's heels** = **flee**, escape, hook it (*sl.*), run away *or* off, show a clean pair of heels, skedaddle (*inf.*), take flight, turn tail, vamoose (*sl., chiefly US*)

heel[2] *vb* **1** = **lean over**, cant, careen, incline, keel over, list, tilt

hefty *adj Informal* **1** = **big**, beefy (*inf.*), brawny, burly, hulking, husky (*inf.*), massive, muscular, robust, strapping, strong **2** = **forceful**, heavy, powerful, thumping (*sl.*), vigorous **3** = **heavy**, ample, awkward, bulky, colossal, cumbersome, large, massive, ponderous, substantial, tremendous, unwieldy, weighty
Antonyms *adj* ≠ **big:** diminutive, inconsequential, ineffectual, infinitesimal, insignificant, little, minute, narrow, pocket-sized, scanty, short, slight, slim, small, thin, tiny ≠ **forceful:** feeble, frail, mild, soft, weak, weedy (*inf.*), wimpish *or* wimpy (*inf.*) ≠ **heavy:** agile, light

height *n* **1** = **tallness**, highness, loftiness, stature **2, 3** = **altitude**, elevation **4** = **peak**, apex, apogee, crest, crown, elevation, hill, mountain, pinnacle, summit, top, vertex, zenith **6, 7** = **culmination**, climax, extremity, limit, maximum, *ne plus ultra*, ultimate, utmost degree, uttermost
Antonyms *n* ≠ **tallness:** depth, lowness, shortness, smallness ≠ **peak:** abyss, base, bottom, canyon, chasm, depth, lowland, nadir, ravine, valley ≠ **culmination:** low point, minimum, nadir

heighten *vb* = **intensify**, add to, aggravate, amplify, augment, enhance, improve, increase, magnify, sharpen, strengthen

heinous *adj* = **shocking**, abhorrent, abomina-

heir ❶ (ɛə) *n* **1** the person legally succeeding to all property of a deceased person. **2** any person or thing that carries on some tradition, circumstance, etc., from a forerunner. [C13: from OF, from L *hērēs*]
▸ **'heirdom** *or* **'heirship** *n*

heir apparent *n, pl* **heirs apparent.** a person whose right to succeed to certain property cannot be defeated, provided such person survives his ancestor.

heiress ('ɛərɪs) *n* **1** a woman who inherits or expects to inherit great wealth. **2** a female heir.

heirloom ('ɛə,luːm) *n* **1** an object that has been in a family for generations. **2** an item of personal property inherited in accordance with the terms of a will. [C15: from HEIR + *lome* tool; see LOOM[1]]

heir presumptive *n Property law.* a person who expects to succeed to an estate but whose right may be defeated by the birth of one nearer in blood to the ancestor.

heist (haɪst) *Sl., chiefly US & Canad.* ◆ *n* **1** a robbery. ◆ *vb* **2** (*tr*) to steal. [var. of HOIST]

Hejira ('hɛdʒɪrə) *n* a variant spelling of **Hegira.**

held (hɛld) *vb* the past tense and past participle of **hold**[1].

helenium (hɛ'liːnɪəm) *n* a perennial garden plant with yellow, bronze, or crimson flowers. [from Gk *helenion* name of a plant]

heliacal rising (hɪ'laɪək'l) *n* **1** the rising of a celestial object at the same time as the sun. **2** the date at which such a celestial object first becomes visible. [C17: from LL *hēliacus* relating to the sun, from Gk, from *hēlios* sun]

helianthemum (hiːlɪ'ænθəməm) *n* any of a genus of dwarf shrubs with brightly coloured flowers: often grown in rockeries. [from Gk *helios* sun + *anthemon* flower]

helianthus (,hiːlɪ'ænθəs) *n, pl* **helianthuses.** a plant of the composite family having large yellow daisy-like flowers with yellow, brown, or purple centres. [C18: NL, from Gk *hēlios* sun + *anthos* flower]

helical ('hɛlɪk'l) *adj* of or like a helix; spiral.

helical gear *n* a gearwheel having the tooth form generated on a helical path about the axis of the wheel.

helices ('hɛlɪ,siːz) *n* a plural of **helix.**

helichrysum (,hɛlɪ'kraɪzəm) *n* any plant of the genus *Helichrysum,* whose flowers retain their shape and colour when dried. [C16: from L, from Gk, from *helix* spiral + *khrusos* gold]

helicoid ('hɛlɪ,kɔɪd) *adj* **1** *Biol.* shaped like a spiral: *a helicoid shell.* ◆ *n* **2** *Geom.* any surface resembling that of a screw thread.

helicon ('hɛlɪkən) *n* a bass tuba made to coil over the shoulder of a band musician. [C19: prob. from *Helicon,* Gk mountain, believed to be source of poetic inspiration; associated with Gk *helix* spiral]

helicopter ('hɛlɪ,kɒptə) *n* an aircraft capable of hover, vertical flight, and horizontal flight in any direction. Most get their lift and propulsion from overhead rotating blades. [C19: from F, from Gk *helix* spiral + *pteron* wing]

helicopter gunship *n* a large heavily armed helicopter used for ground attack.

helio- *or before a vowel* **heli-** *combining form.* indicating the sun: *heliocentric.* [from Gk, from *hēlios* sun]

heliocentric (,hiːlɪəʊ'sɛntrɪk) *adj* **1** having the sun at its centre. **2** measured from or in relation to the sun.
▸ **,helio'centrically** *adv*

heliograph ('hiːlɪəʊ,grɑːf) *n* **1** an instrument with mirrors and a shutter used for sending messages in Morse code by reflecting the sun's rays. **2** a device used to photograph the sun.
▸ **,heli'ography** *n*

heliometer (,hiːlɪ'ɒmɪtə) *n* a refracting telescope used to determine angular distances between celestial bodies.
▸ **,heli'ometry** *n*

heliopsis (,hɛlɪ'ɒpsɪs) *n* a perennial plant with yellow daisy-like flowers.

heliostat ('hiːlɪəʊ,stæt) *n* an astronomical instrument used to reflect the light of the sun in a constant direction.
▸ **,helio'static** *adj*

heliotrope ('hiːlɪə,trəʊp, 'hɛljə-) *n* **1** any plant of the genus *Heliotropium,* esp. the South American variety, cultivated for its small fragrant purple flowers. **2a** a bluish-violet to purple colour. **2b** (*as adj*): *a heliotrope dress.* **3** another name for **bloodstone.** [C17: from L *hēliotropium,* from Gk, from *hēlios* sun + *trepein* to turn]

heliotropism (,hiːlɪ'ɒtrə,pɪzəm) *n* the growth of a plant in response to the stimulus of sunlight.
▸ **heliotropic** (,hiːlɪəʊ'trɒpɪk) *adj*

heliport ('hɛlɪ,pɔːt) *n* an airport for helicopters. [C20: from HELI(COPTER) + PORT[1]]

helium ('hiːlɪəm) *n* a very light nonflammable colourless odourless element that is an inert gas, occurring in certain natural gases. Symbol: He; atomic no.: 2; atomic wt.: 4.0026. [C19: NL, from HELIO- + -IUM; because first detected in the solar spectrum]

helix ('hiːlɪks) *n, pl* **helices** *or* **helixes. 1** a spiral. **2** the incurving fold that forms the margin of the external ear. **3** another name for **volute** (sense 2). **4** any terrestrial mollusc of the genus *Helix,* including the garden snail. [C16: from L, from Gk: spiral; prob. rel. to Gk *helissein* to twist]

hell ❶ (hɛl) *n* **1** (*sometimes cap.*) *Christianity.* **1a** the place or state of eternal punishment of the wicked after death. **1b** forces of evil regarded as residing there. **2** (*sometimes cap.*) (in various religions and cultures) the abode of the spirits of the dead. **3** pain, extreme difficulty, etc. **4** *Inf.* a cause of such suffering: *war is hell.* **5** *US & Canad.* high spirits or mischievousness. **6** *Now rare.* a gambling house. **7** (**come**) **hell or high water.** *Inf.* whatever difficulties may arise. **8 for the hell of it.** *Inf.* for the fun of it. **9 from hell.** *Inf.* denoting a person or thing that is particularly bad or alarming: *job from hell.* **10 give someone hell.** *Inf.* **10a** to give someone a severe reprimand or punishment. **10b** to be a source of torment to someone. **11 hell for leather.** at great speed. **12 hell to pay.** *Inf.* serious consequences, as of a foolish action. **13 the hell.** *Inf.* **13a** (intensifier): used in such phrases as **what the hell. 13b** an expression of strong disagreement: *the hell I will.* ◆ *interj* **14** *Inf.* an exclamation of anger, surprise, etc. [OE *hell*]

he'll (hiːl; *unstressed* iːl, hɪl, ɪl) *contraction of* he will *or* he shall.

hellacious (hɛ'leɪʃəs) *adj US sl.* **1** remarkable; horrifying. **2** wonderful; excellent. [C20: from HELL + *-acious* as in AUDACIOUS]

Helladic (hɛ'lædɪk) *adj* of or relating to the Bronze Age civilization that flourished about 2900 to 1100 B.C. on the Greek mainland and islands.

Hellas ('hɛləs) *n* transliteration of the Ancient Greek name for Greece.

hellbent ❶ (,hɛl'bɛnt) *adj* (*postpositive;* foll. by *on*) *Inf.* strongly or rashly intent.

hellcat ('hɛl,kæt) *n* a spiteful fierce-tempered woman.

hellebore ('hɛlɪ,bɔː) *n* **1** any plant of the Eurasian genus *Helleborus,* typically having showy flowers and poisonous parts. See also **Christmas rose. 2** any of various plants that yield alkaloids used in the treatment of heart disease. [C14: from Gk *helleboros,* from ?]

Hellene ('hɛliːn) *or* **Hellenian** (hɛ'liːnɪən) *n* another name for a **Greek.**

Hellenic (hɛ'lɛnɪk, -'liː-) *adj* **1** of or relating to the ancient or modern Greeks or their language. **2** of or relating to ancient Greece or the Greeks of the classical period (776–323 B.C.). Cf. **Hellenistic.** ◆ *n* **3** the Greek language in its various ancient and modern dialects.

Hellenism ('hɛlɪ,nɪzəm) *n* **1** the principles, ideals, and pursuits associated with classical Greek civilization. **2** the spirit or national character of the Greeks. **3** imitation of or devotion to the culture of ancient Greece.
▸ **'Hellenist** *n*

Hellenistic (,hɛlɪ'nɪstɪk) *or* **Hellenistical** *adj* **1** characteristic of or relating to Greek civilization in the Mediterranean world, esp. from the death of Alexander the Great (323 B.C.) to the defeat of Antony and Cleopatra (30 B.C.). **2** of or relating to the Greeks or to Hellenism.
▸ **,Hellen'istically** *adv*

Hellenize *or* **Hellenise** ('hɛlɪ,naɪz) *vb* **Hellenizes, Hellenizing, Hellenized** *or* **Hellenises, Hellenising, Hellenised.** to make or become like the ancient Greeks.
▸ **,Helleni'zation** *or* **,Helleni'sation** *n*

hellfire ('hɛl,faɪə) *n* **1** the torment of hell, envisaged as eternal fire. **2** (*modifier*) characterizing sermons that emphasize this.

hellion ('hɛljən) *n Chiefly US inf.* a rowdy person, esp. a child; troublemaker. [C19: prob. from dialect *hallion* rogue, from ?]

hellish ❶ ('hɛlɪʃ) *adj* **1** of or resembling hell. **2** wicked; cruel. **3** *Inf.* very unpleasant. ◆ *adv* **4** *Brit. inf.* (intensifier): *a hellish good idea.*

hello ❶**, hallo,** *or* **hullo** (hɛ'ləʊ, hə-; 'hɛləʊ) *sentence substitute.* **1** an expression of greeting. **2** a call used to attract attention. **3** an expression of surprise. ◆ *n, pl* **hellos, hallos** *or* **hullos. 4** the act of saying or calling "hello". [C19: see HOLLO]

Hell's Angel *n* a member of a motorcycle gang who typically dress in Nazi-style paraphernalia and are noted for their lawless behaviour.

helm[1] ❶ (hɛlm) *n* **1** *Naut.* **1a** the wheel or entire apparatus by which a vessel is steered. **1b** the position of the helm: that is, on the side of the keel opposite from that of the rudder. **2** a position of leadership or control (esp. in **at the helm**). ◆ *vb* **3** (*tr*) to steer. [OE *helma*]
▸ **'helmsman** *n*

helm[2] (hɛlm) *n* an archaic or poetic word for **helmet.** [OE *helm*]

helmet ('hɛlmɪt) *n* **1** a piece of protective or defensive armour for the head worn by soldiers, policemen, firemen, divers, etc. See also **crash**

THESAURUS

ble, atrocious, awful, evil, execrable, flagrant, grave, hateful, hideous, infamous, iniquitous, monstrous, nefarious, odious, outrageous, revolting, unspeakable, vicious, villainous

heir *n* **1** = **successor**, beneficiary, heiress (*fem.*), inheritor, inheritress *or* inheritrix, next in line, scion

hell *n* **1, 2** = **underworld**, Abaddon, abode of the damned, abyss, Acheron (*Greek myth*), bottomless pit, fire and brimstone, Gehenna, Hades (*Greek myth*), hellfire, infernal regions, inferno, lower world, nether world, Tartarus (*Greek myth*) **3** *Informal* = **torment**, affliction, agony, anguish, martyrdom, misery, nightmare, ordeal, suffering, trial, wretchedness **11 hell for leather** = **speedily**, at a rate of knots, at the double, full-tilt, headlong, hotfoot, hurriedly, like a bat out of hell (*sl.*), pell-mell, posthaste, quickly, swiftly

hellbent *adj Informal* = **intent**, bent, determined, fixed, resolved, set, settled

hellish *adj* **1** = **devilish**, damnable, damned, demoniacal, diabolical, fiendish, infernal **2** = **atrocious**, abominable, accursed, barbarous, cruel, detestable, execrable, inhuman, monstrous, nefarious, vicious, wicked
Antonyms *adj* ≠ **atrocious:** admirable, agreeable, benevolent, delightful, fine, gentle, good, harmless, honourable, humane, innocuous, kind, merciful, noble, pleasant, virtuous, wonderful

hello *sentence substitute* **1** = **hi** (*Informal*), good afternoon, good evening, good morning, greetings, how do you do?, welcome

helm[1] *n* **1a** *Nautical* = **tiller**, rudder, steering gear, wheel **2** = **control**, command, driving seat, saddle

helmet, pith helmet. 2 *Biol.* a part or structure resembling a helmet, esp. the upper part of the calyx of certain flowers. [C15: from OF, dim. of *helme,* of Gmc origin]
▸ **'helmeted** *adj*

helminth ('hɛlmɪnθ) *n* any parasitic worm, esp. a nematode or fluke. [C19: from Gk *helmins* parasitic worm]
▸ **hel'minthic** *or* **helminthoid** ('hɛlmɪn,θɔɪd, hɛl'mɪnθɔɪd) *adj*

helminthiasis (,hɛlmɪn'θaɪəsɪs) *n* infestation of the body with parasitic worms. [C19: from NL, from Gk *helminthian* to be infested with worms]

helot ('hɛlət, 'hi:-) *n* **1** (*cap.*) (in ancient Sparta) a member of the class of serfs owned by the state. **2** a serf or slave. [C16: from L *Hēlotēs,* from Gk *Heilōtes,* alleged to have meant orig.: inhabitants of Helos, who, after its conquest, were serfs of the Spartans]
▸ **'helotism** *n* ▸ **'helotry** *n*

help Ⓣ (hɛlp) *vb* **1** to assist (someone to do something), esp. by sharing the work, cost, or burden of something. **2** to alleviate the burden of (someone else) by giving assistance. **3** (*tr*) to assist (a person) to go in a specified direction: *help the old lady up.* **4** to contribute to: *to help the relief operations.* **5** to improve (a situation, etc.): *crying won't help.* **6** (*tr;* preceded by *can, could,* etc.; *usually used with a negative*) **6a** to refrain from: *we can't help wondering who he is.* **6b** (usually foll. by *it*) to be responsible for: *I can't help it if it rains.* **7** to alleviate (an illness, etc.). **8** (*tr*) to serve (a customer). **9** (*tr;* foll. by *to*) **9a** to serve (someone with food, etc.) (usually in **help oneself**). **9b** to provide (oneself with) without permission. **10 cannot help but.** to be unable to do anything else except: *I cannot help but laugh.* **11 so help me. 11a** on my honour. **11b** no matter what: *so help me, I'll get revenge.* ◆ *n* **12** the act of helping or being helped, or a person or thing that helps. **13a** a person hired for a job, esp. a farm worker or domestic servant. **13b** (*functioning as sing*) several employees collectively. **14** a remedy: *there's no help for it.* ◆ *sentence substitute.* **15** used to ask for assistance. ◆ See also **help out.** [OE *helpan*]
▸ **'helper** *n*

helpful Ⓣ ('hɛlpfʊl) *adj* giving help.
▸ **'helpfully** *adv* ▸ **'helpfulness** *n*

helping Ⓣ ('hɛlpɪŋ) *n* a single portion of food.

helping hand *n* assistance: *many people lent a helping hand in making arrangements.*

helpless Ⓣ ('hɛlplɪs) *adj* **1** unable to manage independently. **2** made weak: *they were helpless from giggling.*
▸ **'helplessly** *adv* ▸ **'helplessness** *n*

helpline ('hɛlp,laɪn) *n* a telephone line operated by a charitable organization for people in distress or by a commercial organization to provide information.

helpmate Ⓣ ('hɛlp,meɪt) *n* a companion and helper, esp. a wife.

helpmeet ('hɛlp,mi:t) *n* a less common word for **helpmate.** [C17: from *an helpe meet* (suitable) *for him* Genesis 2:18]

help out *vb* (*adv*) to assist, esp. by sharing the burden or cost of something with (another person).

helter-skelter Ⓣ ('hɛltə'skɛltə) *adj* **1** haphazard or careless. ◆ *adv* **2** in a helter-skelter manner. ◆ *n* **3** *Brit.* a high spiral slide, as at a fairground. **4** disorder. [C16: prob. imit.]

helve (hɛlv) *n* the handle of a hand tool such as an axe or pick. [OE *hielfe*]

Helvetian (hɛl'vi:ʃən) *adj* **1** Swiss. ◆ *n* **2** a native or citizen of Switzerland. [from L *Helvetia* Switzerland]

hem[1] Ⓣ (hɛm) *n* **1** an edge to a piece of cloth, made by folding the raw edge under and stitching it down. **2** short for **hemline.** ◆ *vb* **hems, hemming, hemmed.** (*tr*) **3** to provide with a hem. **4** (usually foll. by *in, around,* or *about*) to enclose or confine. [OE *hemm*]
▸ **'hemmer** *n*

hem[2] Ⓣ (hɛm) *n, interj* **1** a representation of the sound of clearing the throat, used to gain attention, etc. ◆ *vb* **hems, hemming, hemmed. 2** (*intr*) to utter this sound. **3 hem** (*or* **hum**) **and haw.** to hesitate in speaking.

he-man Ⓣ *n, pl* **he-men.** *Inf.* a strongly built muscular man.

hematite *or* **haematite** ('hɛmətaɪt, 'hi:m-) *n* a red, grey, or black mineral, found as massive beds and in veins and igneous rocks. It is the chief source of iron. Composition: iron (ferric) oxide. Crystal structure: hexagonal (rhombohedral). [C16: via L from Gk *haimatitēs* resembling blood, from *haima* blood]
▸ **hematitic** *or* **haematitic** (,hɛmə'tɪtɪk, ,hi:-) *adj*

hemato- *or before a vowel* **hemat-** *combining form.* US variants of **haemato-.**

hemeralopia (,hɛmərə'ləʊpɪə) *n* inability to see clearly in bright light. Nontechnical name: **day blindness.** [C18: NL, from Gk, from *hēmera* day + *alaos* blind + *ōps* eye]

hemerocallis (hɛmər'ɒkælɪs) *n* a N temperate plant with large funnel-shaped orange flowers: each single flower lasts for only one day. Also called: **day lily.** [C17: from Gk *hēmera* day + *kallos* beauty]

hemi- *prefix* half: *hemicycle; hemisphere.* [from L, from Gk *hēmi-*]

-hemia *n combining form.* a US variant of **-aemia.**

hemidemisemiquaver (,hɛmɪ,dɛmɪ'sɛmɪ,kweɪvə) *n Music.* a note having the time value of one sixty-fourth of a semibreve. Usual US & Canad. name: **sixty-fourth note.**

hemiplegia (,hɛmɪ'pli:dʒɪə) *n* paralysis of one side of the body.
▸ **,hemi'plegic** *adj*

hemipode ('hɛmɪ,pəʊd) *n* a small quail-like bird occurring in tropical and subtropical regions of the Old World. Also called: **button quail.**

hemipteran (hɪ'mɪptərən) *n* any hemipterous insect. [C19: from HEMI- + Gk *pteron* wing]

hemipterous (hɪ'mɪptərəs) *adj* of or belonging to a large order of insects having sucking or piercing mouthparts.

hemisphere ('hɛmɪ,sfɪə) *n* **1** one half of a sphere. **2a** half of the terrestrial globe, divided into **northern** and **southern hemispheres** by the equator or into **eastern** and **western hemispheres** by some meridians, usually 0° and 180°. **2b** a map or projection of one of the hemispheres. **3** *Anat.* short for **cerebral hemisphere,** a half of the cerebrum.
▸ **hemispheric** (,hɛmɪ'sfɛrɪk) *or* **,hemi'spherical** *adj*

hemistich ('hɛmɪ,stɪk) *n Prosody.* a half line of verse.

hemline ('hɛm,laɪn) *n* the level to which the hem of a skirt or dress hangs.

hemlock ('hɛm,lɒk) *n* **1** an umbelliferous poisonous Eurasian plant having finely divided leaves, spotted stems, and small white flowers. **2** a poisonous drug derived from this plant. **3** Also called: **hemlock spruce.** a coniferous tree of North America and Asia. [OE *hymlic*]

hemo- *combining form.* a US variant of **haemo-.**

hemp (hɛmp) *n* **1** Also called: **cannabis, marijuana.** an Asian plant having tough fibres, deeply lobed leaves, and small greenish flowers. See also **Indian hemp. 2** the fibre of this plant, used to make canvas, rope, etc. **3** any of several narcotic drugs obtained from some varieties of this plant, esp. from Indian hemp. [OE *hænep*]
▸ **'hempen** *or* **'hemp,like** *adj*

hemstitch ('hɛm,stɪtʃ) *n* **1** a decorative edging stitch, usually for a hem, in which the cross threads are stitched in groups. ◆ *vb* **2** to decorate (a hem, etc.) with hemstitches.

hen (hɛn) *n* **1** the female of any bird, esp. of the domestic fowl. **2** the female of certain other animals, such as the lobster. **3** *Scot. dialect.* a term of address used to women. [OE *henn*]

henbane ('hɛn,beɪn) *n* a poisonous Mediterranean plant with sticky hairy leaves: yields the drug hyoscyamine.

hence Ⓣ (hɛns) *sentence connector.* **1** for this reason; therefore. ◆ *adv* **2** from this time: *a year hence.* **3** *Arch.* from here; away. ◆ *sentence substitute.* **4** *Arch.* begone! away! [OE *hionane*]

henceforth Ⓣ ('hɛns'fɔ:θ), **henceforwards,** *or* **henceforward** *adv* from now on.

THESAURUS

help *vb* **1 = aid,** abet, assist, back, befriend, co-operate, encourage, give a leg up (*inf.*), lend a hand, lend a helping hand, promote, relieve, save, second, serve, stand by, succour, support **5 = improve,** mitigate, relieve **6a = refrain from,** abstain, avoid, control, eschew, forbear, hinder, keep from, prevent, resist, shun, withstand **7 = alleviate,** ameliorate, cure, heal, remedy, restore ◆ *n* **12 = assistance,** advice, aid, avail, benefit, cooperation, guidance, helping hand, promotion, service, support, use, utility **13a = assistant,** employee, hand, helper, worker **14 = remedy,** balm, corrective, cure, relief, restorative, salve, succour
Antonyms *vb* ≠ **aid:** bar, block, discourage, fight, foil, frustrate, hinder, hobble, impede, obstruct, oppose ≠ **improve:** aggravate, irritate, make worse ◆ *n* ≠ **assistance:** aggravation, bane, block, discouragement, hindrance, irritant, obstruction, opposition

helper *n* **1 = assistant,** abettor, adjutant, aide, aider, ally, attendant, auxiliary, coadjutor, collaborator, colleague, deputy, helpmate, henchman, mate, partner, protagonist, right-hand man, second, subsidiary, supporter

helpful *adj* **= useful,** accommodating, advantageous, beneficent, beneficial, benevolent, caring, considerate, constructive, cooperative, favourable, fortunate, practical, productive, profitable, serviceable, supportive, timely

helpfulness *n* **= usefulness,** advantage, assistance, benefit, cooperation, friendliness, kindness, neighbourliness, rallying round, support, sympathy

helping *n* **= portion,** dollop (*inf.*), piece, plateful, ration, serving

helpless *adj* **1 = vulnerable,** abandoned, defenceless, dependent, destitute, exposed, forlorn, stranded, unprotected, wide open **2 = powerless,** debilitated, disabled, feeble, impotent, incapable, incompetent, infirm, paralysed, unfit, weak
Antonyms *adj* ≠ **vulnerable:** invulnerable, safe, secure, well-protected ≠ **powerless:** able, capable, competent, equipped, fit, hardy, healthy, hearty, mighty, powerful, robust, solid, strong, sturdy, thriving, tough

helplessness *n* **1 = vulnerability,** defencelessness, exposed position, forlornness **2 = weakness,** disability, feebleness, impotence, infirmity, powerlessness

helpmate *n* **= partner,** assistant, associate, companion, consort, helper, helpmeet, husband, significant other (*US inf.*), spouse, support, wife

helter-skelter *adj* **1 = haphazard,** confused, disordered, higgledy-piggledy (*inf.*), hit-or-miss, jumbled, muddled, random, topsy-turvy ◆ *adv* **2 = carelessly,** anyhow, hastily, headlong, hurriedly, pell-mell, rashly, recklessly, wildly

hem[1] *n* **1 = edge,** border, fringe, margin, trimming ◆ *vb* **4** *usually with* **in = surround,** beset, border, circumscribe, confine, edge, enclose, environ, hedge in, restrict, shut in, skirt

hem[2] *vb* **3 hem and haw** *or* **hum and haw = hesitate,** falter, fumble, pause, stammer, stutter

he-man *n Informal* **= muscle man,** Atlas, beefcake, Hercules, hunk (*sl.*), Tarzan (*inf.*)

hence *sentence connector* **1 = therefore,** ergo, for this reason, on that account, thus

henceforth *adv* **= from now on,** from this day forward, hence, hereafter, hereinafter, in the future

henchman ⊙ (ˈhɛntʃmən) *n, pl* **henchmen. 1** a faithful attendant or supporter. **2** *Arch.* a squire; page. [C14 *hengestman,* from OE *hengest* stallion + MAN]

hendeca- *combining form.* eleven: *hendecagon; hendecasyllable.* [from Gk *hendeka,* from *hen,* neuter of *heis* one + *deka* ten]

hendecagon (hɛnˈdɛkəgən) *n* a polygon having 11 sides.
▸**hendecagonal** (ˌhɛndɪˈkægənˈl) *adj*

hendecasyllable (ˈhɛndɛkəˌsɪləbˈl) *n Prosody.* a verse line of 11 syllables. [C18: from Gk]

hendiadys (hɛnˈdaɪədɪs) *n* a rhetorical device by which two nouns joined by a conjunction are used instead of a noun and a modifier, as in *to run with fear and haste* instead of *to run with fearful haste.* [C16: from Med. L, from Gk *hen dia duoin,* lit.: one through two]

henequen, henequin, *or* **heniquen** (ˈhɛnɪkɪn) *n* **1** an agave plant that is native to Mexico. **2** the fibre of this plant, used in making rope, twine, and coarse fabrics. [C19: from American Sp. *henequén,* prob. of Amerind origin]

henge (hɛndʒ) *n* a circular monument, often containing a circle of stones, dating from the Neolithic and Bronze Ages. [back formation from *Stonehenge,* site of important megalithic ruins on Salisbury Plain, S England]

hen harrier *n* a common harrier that nests in marshes and open land.

henhouse (ˈhɛnˌhaʊs) *n* a coop for hens.

henna (ˈhɛnə) *n* **1** a shrub or tree of Asia and N Africa. **2** a reddish dye obtained from the powdered leaves of this plant, used as a cosmetic and industrial dye. **3a** a reddish-brown colour. **3b** (*as adj*): *henna tresses.* ◆ *vb* **hennas, hennaing, hennaed. 4** (*tr*) to dye with henna. [C16: from Ar. *hinnā'*; see ALKANET]

hen night *n Inf.* a party for women only, esp. held for a woman shortly before she is married. Cf. **hen party, stag night.**

henotheism (ˈhɛnəʊθiːˌɪzəm) *n* the worship of one deity (of several) as the special god of one's family, clan, or tribe. [C19: from Gk *heis* one + *theos* god]
▸ˌ**henotheˈistic** *adj*

hen party *n Inf.* a party at which only women are present. Cf. **hen night, stag night.**

henpeck ⊙ (ˈhɛnˌpɛk) *vb* (*tr*) (of a woman) to harass or torment (a man, esp. her husband) by persistent nagging.
▸ˈ**henˌpecked** *adj*

henry (ˈhɛnrɪ) *n, pl* **henry, henries,** *or* **henrys.** the derived SI unit of electric inductance; the inductance of a closed circuit in which an emf of 1 volt is produced when the current varies uniformly at the rate of 1 ampere per second. Symbol: H [C19: after Joseph *Henry* (1797–1878), US physicist]

hep (hɛp) *adj* **hepper, heppest.** *Sl.* an earlier word for **hip**[4].

heparin (ˈhɛpərɪn) *n* a polysaccharide, containing sulphate groups, present in most body tissues: an anticoagulant used in the treatment of thrombosis. [C20: from Gk *hēpar* the liver + -IN]

hepatic (hɪˈpætɪk) *adj* **1** of the liver. **2** having the colour of liver. ◆ *n* **3** any of various drugs for use in treating diseases of the liver. [C15: from L *hēpaticus,* from Gk *hēpar* liver]

hepatica (hɪˈpætɪkə) *n* a woodland plant of a N temperate genus, having three-lobed leaves and white, mauve, or pink flowers. [C16: from Med. L: liverwort, from L *hēpaticus* of the liver]

hepatitis (ˌhɛpəˈtaɪtɪs) *n* inflammation of the liver.

hepatitis A *n* a form of hepatitis caused by a virus transmitted in contaminated food or drink.

hepatitis B *n* a form of hepatitis caused by a virus transmitted by infected blood (as in transfusions), contaminated hypodermic needles, sexual contact, or by contact with any other body fluid. Former name: **serum hepatitis.**

Hepplewhite (ˈhɛpˈlˌwaɪt) *adj* of or in a style of ornamental and carved 18th-century English furniture. [C18: after George *Hepplewhite* (1727–86), E cabinetmaker]

hepta- *or before a vowel* **hept-** *combining form.* seven: *heptameter.* [from Gk]

heptad (ˈhɛptæd) *n* a group or series of seven. [C17: from Gk *heptas* seven]

heptagon (ˈhɛptəgən) *n* a polygon having seven sides.
▸**heptagonal** (hɛpˈtægənˈl) *adj*

heptahedron (ˌhɛptəˈhiːdrən) *n* a solid figure having seven plane faces.
▸ˌ**heptaˈhedral** *adj*

heptameter (hɛpˈtæmɪtə) *n Prosody.* a verse line of seven metrical feet.
▸**heptametrical** (ˌhɛptəˈmɛtrɪkˈl) *adj*

heptane (ˈhɛpteɪn) *n* an alkane which is found in petroleum and used as an anaesthetic. [C19: from HEPTA- + -ANE, because it has seven carbon atoms]

heptarchy (ˈhɛptɑːkɪ) *n, pl* **heptarchies. 1** government by seven rulers. **2** the seven kingdoms into which Anglo-Saxon England is thought to have been divided from about the 7th to the 9th centuries A.D.
▸ˈ**heptarch** *n* ▸**hepˈtarchic** *or* **hepˈtarchal** *adj*

heptathlon (hɛpˈtæθlɒn) *n* an athletic contest for women in which each athlete competes in seven different events. [C20: from HEPTA- + Gk *athlon* contest]
▸**hepˈtathlete** *n*

heptavalent (hɛpˈtævələnt, ˌhɛptəˈveɪlənt) *adj Chem.* having a valency of seven.

her (hɜː; *unstressed* hə, ə) *pron* (*objective*) **1** refers to a female person or animal: *he loves her.* **2** refers to things personified as feminine or traditionally to ships and nations. ◆ *determiner* **3** of, belonging to, or associated with her: *her hair.* [OE *hire,* genitive & dative of *hēo* SHE, fem. of *hē* HE]

> **USAGE NOTE** See at **me**[1].

herald ⊙ (ˈhɛrəld) *n* **1** a person who announces important news. **2** *Often literary.* a forerunner; harbinger. **3** the intermediate rank of heraldic officer, between king-of-arms and pursuivant. **4** (in the Middle Ages) an official at a tournament. ◆ *vb* (*tr*) **5** to announce publicly. **6** to precede or usher in. [C14: from OF *herault,* of Gmc origin]

heraldic (hɛˈrældɪk) *adj* of or relating to heraldry or heralds.
▸**heˈraldically** *adv*

heraldry (ˈhɛrəldrɪ) *n, pl* **heraldries. 1** the study concerned with the classification of armorial bearings, the tracing of genealogies, etc. **2** armorial bearings, insignia, etc. **3** the show and ceremony of heraldry.
▸ˈ**heraldist** *n*

herb (hɜːb; *US* ɜːrb) *n* **1** a plant whose aerial parts do not persist above ground at the end of the growing season; herbaceous plant. **2** any of various usually aromatic plants, such as parsley and rosemary, that are used in cookery and medicine. [C13: from OF *herbe,* from L *herba* grass, green plants]
▸ˈ**herbˌlike** *adj* ▸ˈ**herby** *adj*

herbaceous (hɜːˈbeɪʃəs) *adj* **1** designating or relating to plants that are fleshy as opposed to woody: *a herbaceous plant.* **2** (of petals and sepals) green and leaflike.

herbaceous border *n* a flower bed that contains perennials rather than annuals.

herbage (ˈhɜːbɪdʒ) *n* **1** herbaceous plants collectively, esp. the edible parts on which cattle, sheep, etc., graze. **2** the vegetation of pasture land; pasturage.

herbal (ˈhɜːbˈl) *adj* **1** of herbs. ◆ *n* **2** a book describing the properties of plants.

herbalist (ˈhɜːbˈlɪst) *n* **1** a person who grows or specializes in the use of herbs, esp. medicinal herbs. **2** (formerly) a descriptive botanist.

herbarium (hɜːˈbɛərɪəm) *n, pl* **herbariums** *or* **herbaria** (-ɪə). **1** a collection of dried plants that are mounted and classified systematically. **2** a room, etc., in which such a collection is kept.

herb bennet (ˈbɛnɪt) *n* a Eurasian and N African plant with yellow flowers. Also called: **wood avens, bennet.** [from OF *herbe benoite,* lit.: blessed herb, from Med. L *herba benedicta*]

herbicide (ˈhɜːbɪˌsaɪd) *n* a chemical that destroys plants, esp. one used to control weeds.

herbivore (ˈhɜːbɪˌvɔː) *n* **1** an animal that feeds on grass and other plants. **2** *Inf.* a liberal, idealistic, or nonmaterialistic person. [C19: from NL *herbivora* grass-eaters]
▸**herˈbivorous** *adj*

herb Paris (ˈpærɪs) *n, pl* **herbs Paris.** a Eurasian woodland plant with a whorl of four leaves and a solitary yellow flower. [C16: from Med. L *herba paris,* lit.: herb of a pair: because the four leaves on the stalk look like a true lovers' knot]

herb Robert (ˈrɒbət) *n, pl* **herbs Robert.** a low-growing N temperate plant with strongly scented divided leaves and small purplish flowers. [C13: from Med. L *herba Roberti* herb of Robert, prob. after St *Robert,* 11th-cent. F ecclesiastic]

herculean ⊙ (ˌhɜːkjʊˈliːən) *adj* **1** requiring tremendous effort, strength, etc. **2** (*sometimes cap.*) resembling Hercules, hero of classical myth, in strength, courage, etc.

herd[1] ⊙ (hɜːd) *n* **1** a large group of mammals living and feeding together, esp. cattle. **2** *Often disparaging.* a large group of people. ◆ *vb* **3** to collect or be collected into or as if into a herd. [OE *heord*]

herd[2] (hɜːd) *n* **1a** *Arch. or dialect.* a man who tends livestock; herdsman.

THESAURUS

henchman *n* **1** = **attendant**, aide, associate, bodyguard, cohort (*chiefly US*), crony, follower, heavy (*sl.*), minder (*sl.*), minion, right-hand man, satellite, sidekick (*sl.*), subordinate, supporter

henpeck *vb* = **nag**, browbeat, bully, carp, chide, criticize, find fault, harass, hector, intimidate, niggle, pester, pick at, scold, torment

henpecked *adj* = **dominated**, browbeaten, bullied, cringing, led by the nose, meek, subject, subjugated, tied to someone's apron strings, timid, treated like dirt

Antonyms *adj* aggressive, assertive, bossy (*inf.*), dominating, domineering, forceful, macho, overbearing, self-assertive, spirited, wilful

herald *n* **1** = **messenger**, bearer of tidings, crier **2** *Often literary* = **forerunner**, harbinger, indication, omen, precursor, sign, signal, token ◆ *vb* **5** = **announce**, advertise, broadcast, proclaim, publicize, publish, trumpet **6** = **precede**, foretoken, harbinger, indicate, pave the way, portend, presage, promise, show, usher in

herculean *adj* **1** = **arduous**, demanding, difficult, exhausting, formidable, gruelling, hard, heavy, laborious, onerous, prodigious, strenuous, toilsome, tough **2** = **strong**, athletic, brawny, husky (*inf.*), mighty, muscular, powerful, rugged, sinewy, stalwart, strapping, sturdy

herd[1] *n* **1** = **flock**, assemblage, collection, crowd, crush, drove, horde, mass, mob, multitude, press, swarm, throng **2** *Often disparaging* = **mob**, populace, rabble, riffraff, the hoi polloi, the masses, the plebs ◆ *vb* **3** = **collect**, assemble, associate, congregate, flock, force, gather, guide, huddle, lead, muster, rally, shepherd

1b (*in combination*): *goatherd.* ◆ *vb* (*tr*) **2** to drive forwards in a large group. **3** to look after (livestock). [OE *hirde:* see HERD[1]]

herd instinct *n Psychol.* the inborn tendency to associate with others and follow the group's behaviour.

herdsman Ⓣ ('hɜːdzmən) *n, pl* **herdsmen.** *Chiefly Brit.* a person who breeds or cares for cattle or (rarely) other livestock. US equivalent: **herder.**

here (hɪə) *adv* **1** in, at, or to this place, point, case, or respect: *we come here every summer; here comes Roy.* **2 here and there.** at several places in or throughout an area. **3 here's to.** a formula used in proposing a toast to someone or something. **4 neither here nor there.** of no relevance or importance. ◆ *n* **5** this place or point: *they leave here tonight.* [OE *hēr*]

hereabouts ('hɪərəˌbaʊts) *or* **hereabout** *adv* in this region or neighbourhood.

hereafter Ⓣ (ˌhɪər'ɑːftə) *adv* **1** *Formal or law.* in a subsequent part of this document, matter, case, etc. **2** a less common word for **henceforth. 3** at some time in the future. **4** in a future life after death. ◆ *n* (usually preceded by *the*) **5** life after death. **6** the future.

hereat (ˌhɪər'æt) *adv Arch.* because of this.

hereby (ˌhɪə'baɪ) *adv* (used in official statements, etc.) by means of or as a result of this.

hereditable (hɪ'rɛdɪtəbᵊl) *adj* a less common word for **heritable.**
▸**heˌredita'bility** *n*

hereditament (ˌhɛrɪ'dɪtəmənt) *n Property law.* any kind of property capable of being inherited.

hereditary Ⓣ (hɪ'rɛdɪtərɪ, -trɪ) *adj* **1** of or denoting factors that can be transmitted genetically from one generation to another. **2** *Law.* **2a** descending to succeeding generations by inheritance. **2b** transmitted according to established rules of descent. **3** derived from one's ancestors; traditional: *hereditary feuds.*
▸**he'reditarily** *adv* ▸**he'reditariness** *n*

heredity Ⓣ (hɪ'rɛdɪtɪ) *n, pl* **heredities. 1** the transmission from one generation to another of genetic factors that determine individual characteristics. **2** the sum total of the inherited factors in an organism. [C16: from OF *heredite,* from L *hērēditās* inheritance; see HEIR]

herein (ˌhɪər'ɪn) *adv* **1** *Formal or law.* in or into this place, thing, document, etc. **2** *Rare.* in this respect, circumstance, etc.

hereinafter (ˌhɪərɪn'ɑːftə) *adv Formal or law.* from this point on in this document, etc.

hereinto (ˌhɪər'ɪntuː) *adv Formal or law.* into this place, circumstance, etc.

hereof (ˌhɪər'ɒv) *adv Formal or law.* of or concerning this.

hereon (ˌhɪər'ɒn) *adv* an archaic word for **hereupon.**

heresiarch (hɪ'riːzɪˌɑːk) *n* the leader or originator of a heretical movement or sect.

heresy Ⓣ ('hɛrəsɪ) *n, pl* **heresies. 1a** an opinion contrary to the orthodox tenets of a religious body. **1b** the act of maintaining such an opinion. **2** any belief that is or is thought to be contrary to official or established theory. **3** adherence to unorthodox opinion. [C13: from OF *eresie,* from LL, from L: sect, from Gk, from *hairein* to choose]

heretic Ⓣ ('hɛrətɪk) *n* **1** *Now chiefly RC Church.* a person who maintains beliefs contrary to the established teachings of his Church. **2** a person who holds unorthodox opinions in any field.
▸**heretical** (hɪ'rɛtɪkᵊl) *adj* ▸**he'retically** *adv*

hereto (ˌhɪə'tuː) *adv Formal or law.* to this place, thing, matter, document, etc.

heretofore (ˌhɪətʊ'fɔː) *adv Formal or law.* until now; before this time.

hereunder (ˌhɪər'ʌndə) *adv Formal or law.* **1** (in documents, etc.) below this; subsequently; hereafter. **2** under the terms or authority of this.

hereupon (ˌhɪərə'pɒn) *adv* **1** following immediately after this; at this stage. **2** *Formal or law.* upon this thing, point, subject, etc.

herewith (ˌhɪə'wɪð, -'wɪθ) *adv Formal.* together with this: *we send you herewith your statement of account.*

heriot ('hɛrɪət) *n* (in medieval England) a death duty paid by villeins and free tenants to their lord, often consisting of the dead man's best beast or chattel. [OE *heregeatwa,* from *here* army + *geatwa* equipment]

heritable ('hɛrɪtəbᵊl) *adj* **1** capable of being inherited; inheritable. **2** *Chiefly law.* capable of inheriting. [C14: from OF, from *heriter* to INHERIT]
▸ˌ**herita'bility** *n* ▸**'heritably** *adv*

heritage Ⓣ ('hɛrɪtɪdʒ) *n* **1** something inherited at birth. **2** anything that has been transmitted from the past or handed down by tradition. **3** the evidence of the past, such as historical sites, and the unspoilt natural environment, considered as the inheritance of present-day society. **4** *Law.* any property, esp. land, that by law has descended or may descend to an heir. [C13: from OF; see HEIR]

herl (hɜːl) *or* **harl** *n Angling.* **1** the barb or barbs of a feather, used to dress fishing flies. **2** an artificial fly dressed with such barbs. [C15: from MLow G *herle,* from ?]

hermaphrodite Ⓣ (hɜː'mæfrəˌdaɪt) *n* **1** *Biol.* an animal or flower that has both male and female reproductive organs. **2** a person having both male and female sexual characteristics. **3** a person or thing in which two opposite qualities are combined. ◆ *adj* **4** having the characteristics of a hermaphrodite. [C15: from L *hermaphrodītus,* from Gk, after *Hermaphroditus,* a son of Hermes and Aphrodite, who merged with the nymph Salmacis to form one body]
▸**herˌmaphro'ditic** *or* **herˌmaphro'ditical** *adj* ▸**her'maphroditˌism** *n*

hermaphrodite brig *n* a sailing vessel with two masts, rigged square on the foremast and fore-and-aft on the aftermast.

hermeneutic (ˌhɜːmɪ'njuːtɪk) *or* **hermeneutical** *adj* **1** of or relating to the interpretation of Scripture. **2** interpretive.
▸ˌ**herme'neutically** *adv*

hermeneutics (ˌhɜːmɪ'njuːtɪks) *n* (*functioning as sing*) **1** the science of interpretation, esp. of Scripture. **2** *Philosophy.* **2a** the study and interpretation of human behaviour and social institutions. **2b** (in existentialist thought) discussion of the purpose of life. [C18: from Gk *hermēneutikos* expert in interpretation, from *hermēneuein* to interpret, from ?]

hermetic (hɜː'mɛtɪk) *or* **hermetical** *adj* **1a** (of a seal) airtight. **1b** (of a vessel, etc.) sealed so as to be airtight. **2** of or relating to alchemy or other forms of ancient science: *the hermetic arts.* **3** esoteric or recondite. **4** hidden or protected from the outside world: *the hermetic world of Vatican politics.* [C17: from Med. L *hermēticus* belonging to *Hermes Trismegistus* (Gk, lit.: Hermes thrice-greatest), traditionally the inventor of a magic seal]
▸**her'metically** *adv*

hermit Ⓣ ('hɜːmɪt) *n* **1** one of the early Christian recluses. **2** any person living in solitude. [C13: from OF *hermite,* from LL, from Gk *erēmitēs* living in the desert, from *erēmos* lonely]
▸**her'mitic** *or* **her'mitical** *adj*

hermitage ('hɜːmɪtɪdʒ) *n* **1** the abode of a hermit. **2** any retreat.

hermit crab *n* a small soft-bodied crustacean living in and carrying about the empty shells of whelks or similar molluscs.

hernia ('hɜːnɪə) *n, pl* **hernias** *or* **herniae** (-nɪˌiː). the projection of an organ or part through the lining of the cavity in which it is normally situated, esp. the intestine through the front wall of the abdominal cavity. Also called: **rupture.** [C14: from L]
▸**'hernial** *adj* ▸**'herniˌated** *adj*

hero Ⓣ ('hɪərəʊ) *n, pl* **heroes. 1** a man distinguished by exceptional courage, nobility, etc. **2** a man who is idealized for possessing superior qualities in any field. **3** *Classical myth.* a being of extraordinary strength and courage, often the offspring of a mortal and a god. **4** the principal male character in a novel, play, etc. [C14: from L *hērōs,* from Gk]

heroic Ⓣ (hɪ'rəʊɪk) *or* **heroical** *adj* **1** of, like, or befitting a hero. **2** courageous but desperate. **3** treating of heroes and their deeds. **4** of or resembling the heroes of classical mythology. **5** (of language, manner, etc.) extravagant. **6** *Prosody.* of or resembling heroic verse. **7** (of the arts, esp. sculpture) larger than life-size; smaller than colossal.
▸**he'roically** *adv*

heroic age *n* the period in an ancient culture, when legendary heroes are said to have lived.

heroic couplet *n Prosody.* a verse form consisting of two rhyming lines in iambic pentameter.

heroics (hɪ'rəʊɪks) *pl n* **1** *Prosody.* short for **heroic verse. 2** extravagant or melodramatic language, behaviour, etc.

heroic verse *n Prosody.* a type of verse suitable for epic or heroic subjects, such as the classical hexameter or the French Alexandrine.

heroin ('hɛrəʊɪn) *n* a white bitter-tasting crystalline powder derived from morphine: a highly addictive narcotic. [C19: coined in G as a trademark, prob. from HERO, referring to its aggrandizing effect on the personality]

heroine Ⓣ ('hɛrəʊɪn) *n* **1** a woman possessing heroic qualities. **2** a

THESAURUS

herdsman *n Chiefly Brit.* = **stockman,** cowherd, cowman, drover, grazier

hereafter *adv* **2** = **in future,** after this, from now on, hence, henceforth, henceforward ◆ *n* **5** = **afterlife,** future life, life after death, next world, the beyond

hereditary *adj* **1** = **genetic,** family, inborn, inbred, inheritable, transmissible **2** *Law* = **inherited,** bequeathed, handed down, patrimonial, transmitted, willed **3** = **traditional,** ancestral

heredity *n* **1, 2** = **genetics,** congenital traits, constitution, genetic make-up, inheritance

heresy *n* **1-3** = **unorthodoxy,** apostasy, dissidence, heterodoxy, iconoclasm, impiety, revisionism, schism

heretic *n* **1, 2** = **nonconformist,** apostate, dissenter, dissident, renegade, revisionist, schismatic, sectarian, separatist

heretical *adj* **1, 2** = **unorthodox,** freethinking, heterodox, iconoclastic, idolatrous, impious, revisionist, schismatic

heritage *n* **1, 2, 4** = **inheritance,** bequest, birthright, endowment, estate, legacy, lot, patrimony, portion, share, tradition

hermaphrodite *n* **2** = **androgyne,** bisexual, epicene

hermaphroditic *adj* **2** = **androgynous,** AC/DC, bisexual, epicene, gynandrous

hermit *n* **1** = **recluse,** anchorite, eremite, monk, stylite **2** = **recluse,** loner (*inf.*), recluse, solitary

hero *n* **2** = **idol,** celeb (*inf.*), celebrity, champion, conqueror, exemplar, great man, heart-throb (*Brit.*), man of the hour, megastar (*inf.*), popular figure, star, superstar, victor **4** = **leading man,** lead actor, male lead, principal male character, protagonist

heroic *adj* **1, 2** = **courageous,** bold, brave, daring, dauntless, doughty, fearless, gallant, intrepid, lion-hearted, stouthearted, undaunted, valiant, valorous **3, 4** = **classical,** Homeric, legendary, mythological **5** = **extravagant,** classic, elevated, epic, exaggerated, grand, grandiose, high-flown, inflated
Antonyms *adj* ≠ **courageous:** base, chicken (*sl.*), cowardly, craven, faint-hearted, ignoble, irresolute, mean, timid ≠ **extravagant:** lowbrow, simple, unadorned

heroine *n* **2** = **idol,** celeb (*inf.*), celebrity, goddess, megastar (*inf.*), woman of the hour **3** = **leading lady,** diva, female lead, lead actress,

woman idealized for possessing superior qualities. **3** the main female character in a novel, play, film, etc.

heroism ➊ ('hɛrəʊˌɪzəm) *n* the state or quality of being a hero.

heron ('hɛrən) *n* any of various wading birds having a long neck, slim body, and a plumage that is commonly grey or white. [C14: from OF *hairon,* of Gmc origin]

heronry ('hɛrənrɪ) *n, pl* **heronries.** a colony of breeding herons.

hero worship ➊ *n* **1** admiration for heroes or idealized persons. **2** worship by the ancient Greeks and Romans of heroes. ◆ *vb* **hero-worship, hero-worships, hero-worshipping, hero-worshipped** *or US* **hero-worships, hero-worshiping, hero-worshiped. 3** (*tr*) to feel admiration or adulation for.
▸ **'hero-ˌworshipper** *or US* **'hero-ˌworshiper** *n*

herpes ('hɜːpiːz) *n* any of several inflammatory diseases of the skin, esp. herpes simplex. [C17: via L from Gk, from *herpein* to creep]
▸ **herpetic** (hɜː'pɛtɪk) *adj, n*

herpes simplex ('sɪmplɛks) *n* an acute viral disease characterized by formation of clusters of watery blisters, esp. on the lips or the genitals. See **cold sore, genital herpes.** [NL: simple herpes]

herpes zoster ('zɒstə) *n* a technical name for **shingles.** [NL: girdle herpes, from HERPES + Gk *zōstēr* girdle]

herpetology (ˌhɜːpɪ'tɒlədʒɪ) *n* the study of reptiles and amphibians. [C19: from Gk *herpeton* creeping animal]
▸ **herpetologic** (ˌhɜːpɪtə'lɒdʒɪk) *or* ˌ**herpeto'logical** *adj*

Herr (*German* hɛr) *n, pl* **Herren** ('hɛrən). a German man: used before a name as a title equivalent to *Mr.* [G, from OHG *herro* lord]

Herrenvolk *German.* ('hɛrənfɔlk) *n* a race, nation, or group, such as the Germans or Nazis as viewed by Hitler, believed by themselves to be superior to other races. Also called: **master race.** [lit.: master race, from *Herren,* pl. of HERR + *Volk* folk]

herring ('hɛrɪŋ) *n, pl* **herrings** *or* **herring.** an important food fish of northern seas, having an elongated body covered with large silvery scales. [OE *hǣring*]

herringbone ('hɛrɪŋˌbəʊn) *n* **1a** a pattern consisting of two or more rows of short parallel strokes slanting in alternate directions to form a series of zigzags. **1b** (*as modifier*): *a herringbone pattern.* **2** *Skiing.* a method of ascending a slope by walking with the skis pointing outwards and one's weight on the inside edges. ◆ *vb* **herringbones, herringboning, herringboned. 3** to decorate (textiles, brickwork, etc.) with herringbone. **4** (*intr*) *Skiing.* to ascend a slope in herringbone fashion.

herring gull *n* a common gull that has a white plumage with black-tipped wings.

hers (hɜːz) *pron* **1** something or someone belonging to her: *hers is the nicest dress; that cat is hers.* **2 of hers.** belonging to her. [C14 *hires;* see HER]

herself (hə'sɛlf) *pron* **1a** the reflexive form of *she* or *her.* **1b** (intensifier): *the queen herself signed.* **2** (*preceded by a copula*) her normal self: *she looks herself again.*

hertz (hɜːts) *n, pl* **hertz.** the derived SI unit of frequency; the frequency of a periodic phenomenon that has a periodic time of 1 second; 1 cycle per second. Symbol: Hz [C20: after H. R. *Hertz* (1857–94), G physicist]

Hertzian wave ('hɜːtsɪən) *n* an electromagnetic wave with a frequency in the range from about 3×10^{10} hertz to about 1.5×10^5 hertz. [C19: after H. R. *Hertz*]

Hertzsprung-Russell diagram ('hɜːtssprʌŋ'rʌsəl) *n* a graph in which the spectral types of stars are plotted against their absolute magnitudes. Stars fall into different groupings in different parts of the graph. [C20: after E. *Hertzsprung* (1873–1967), Danish astronomer, and H. N. *Russell* (1877–1957), US astronomer]

he's (hiːz) *contraction of* he is *or* he has.

hesitant ➊ ('hɛzɪtənt) *adj* wavering, hesitating, or irresolute.
▸ **'hesitantly** *adv*

hesitate ➊ ('hɛzɪˌteɪt) *vb* **hesitates, hesitating, hesitated.** (*intr*) **1** to be slow in acting; be uncertain. **2** to be reluctant (to do something). **3** to stammer or pause in speaking. [C17: from L *haesitāre,* from *haerēre* to cling to]
▸ **hesitancy** ('hɛzɪtənsɪ) *or* ˌ**hesi'tation** *n* ▸ **'hesiˌtatingly** *adv*

Hesperian (hɛ'spɪərɪən) *adj* **1** *Poetic.* western. **2** of or relating to the Hesperides or Islands of the Blessed where, in Greek mythology, the souls of the good went after death.

hesperidium (ˌhɛspə'rɪdɪəm) *n Bot.* the fruit of citrus plants, in which the flesh consists of fluid-filled hairs and is protected by a tough rind. [C19: NL; alluding to the fruit in the garden of the *Hesperides,* nymphs in Gk myth (daughters of Hesperus)]

Hesperus ('hɛspərəs) *n* an evening star, esp. Venus. [from L, from Gk, from *hesperos* western]

hessian ('hɛsɪən) *n* a coarse jute fabric similar to sacking. [C18: from HESSIAN]

Hessian ('hɛsɪən) *n* **1** a native or inhabitant of Hesse, a state of Germany. **2** a Hessian soldier in any of the mercenary units of the British Army in the War of American Independence or the Napoleonic Wars. ◆ *adj* **3** of Hesse or its inhabitants.

Hessian fly *n* a small dipterous fly whose larvae damage wheat, barley, and rye. [C18: thought to have been introduced into America by Hessian soldiers]

hest (hest) *n* an archaic word for **behest.** [OE *hǣs*]

hetaera (hɪ'tɪərə) *or* **hetaira** (hɪ'taɪrə) *n, pl* **hetaerae** (-'tɪəriː) *or* **hetairai** (-'taɪraɪ). (esp. in ancient Greece) a prostitute, esp. an educated courtesan. [C19: from Gk *hetaira* concubine]

hetaerism (hɪ'tɪərɪzəm) *or* **hetairism** (hɪ'taɪrɪzəm) *n* **1** the state of being a concubine. **2** *Sociol., anthropol.* a social system attributed to some primitive societies, in which women are communally shared.

hetero- *combining form.* other, another, or different: *heterosexual.* [from Gk *heteros* other]

heteroclite ('hɛtərəˌklaɪt) *adj also* **heteroclitic** (ˌhɛtərə'klɪtɪk). **1** (esp. of the form of a word) irregular or unusual. ◆ *n* **2** an irregularly formed word. [C16: from LL *heteroclitus* declining irregularly, from Gk, from HETERO- + *klinein* to inflect]

heterocyclic (ˌhɛtərəʊ'saɪklɪk, -'sɪk-) *adj* (of an organic compound) containing a closed ring of atoms, at least one of which is not a carbon atom.

heterodox ➊ ('hɛtərəʊˌdɒks) *adj* **1** at variance with established or accepted doctrines or beliefs. **2** holding unorthodox opinions. [C17: from Gk *heterodoxos,* from HETERO- + *doxa* opinion]
▸ **'heteroˌdoxy** *n*

heterodyne ('hɛtərəʊˌdaɪn) *vb* **heterodynes, heterodyning, heterodyned. 1** *Electronics.* to combine by modulation (two alternating signals) to produce two signals having frequencies corresponding to the sum and the difference of the original frequencies. ◆ *adj* **2** produced by, operating by, or involved in heterodyning two signals.

heteroecious (ˌhɛtə'riːʃəs) *adj* (of parasites) undergoing different stages of the life cycle on different host species. [from HETERO- + *-oecious,* from Gk *oikia* house]
▸ **heteroecism** (ˌhɛtə'riːˌsɪzəm) *n*

heterogamete (ˌhɛtərəʊgæ'miːt) *n* a gamete that differs in size and form from the one with which it unites in fertilization.

heterogamy (ˌhɛtə'rɒgəmɪ) *n* **1** a type of sexual reproduction in which the gametes differ in both size and form. **2** a condition in which different types of reproduction occur in successive generations of an organism. **3** the presence of both male and female flowers in one inflorescence.
▸ ˌ**heter'ogamous** *adj*

heterogeneous ➊ (ˌhɛtərəʊ'dʒiːnɪəs) *adj* **1** composed of unrelated parts. **2** not of the same type. [C17: from Med. L *heterogeneus,* from Gk, from HETERO- + *genos* sort]
▸ **heterogeneity** (ˌhɛtərəʊdʒɪ'niːɪtɪ) *or* ˌ**hetero'geneousness** *n*

heterogony (ˌhɛtə'rɒgənɪ) *n* **1** *Biol.* the alternation of parthenogenetic and sexual generations in rotifers and similar animals. **2** the condition in plants, such as the primrose, of having flowers that differ from each other in the length of their stamens and styles.
▸ ˌ**heter'ogonous** *adj*

heterologous (ˌhɛtə'rɒləgəs) *adj* **1** *Pathol.* designating cells or tissues not normally present in a particular part of the body. **2** differing in structure or origin.
▸ ˌ**heter'ology** *n*

heteromerous (ˌhɛtə'rɒmərəs) *adj Biol.* having parts that differ, esp. in number.

heteromorphic (ˌhɛtərəʊ'mɔːfɪk) *or* **heteromorphous** *adj Biol.* **1** differing from the normal form. **2** (esp. of insects) having different forms at different stages of the life cycle.
▸ ˌ**hetero'morphism** *n*

heteronomous (ˌhɛtə'rɒnɪməs) *adj* **1** subject to an external law. **2** (of parts of an organism) differing in the manner of growth, development, or specialization.
▸ ˌ**heter'onomy** *n*

heteronym ('hɛtərəʊˌnɪm) *n* one of two or more words pronounced differently but spelt alike: *the two English words spelt "bow" are heteronyms.* Cf. **homograph.** [C17: from LGk *heteronumos,* from Gk HETERO- + *onoma* name]

THESAURUS

prima donna, principal female character, protagonist

heroism *n* = **bravery**, boldness, courage, courageousness, daring, fearlessness, fortitude, gallantry, intrepidity, prowess, spirit, valour

hero worship *n* **1** = **idolization**, admiration, adoration, adulation, idealization, putting on a pedestal, veneration

hesitant *adj* = **uncertain**, diffident, doubtful, half-hearted, halting, hanging back, hesitating, irresolute, lacking confidence, reluctant, sceptical, shy, timid, unsure, vacillating, wavering
Antonyms *adj* arrogant, avid, can-do (*inf.*), clear, confident, definite, determined, dogmatic, eager, enthusiastic, firm, forceful, keen, positive, resolute, self-assured, spirited, sure, unhesitating, unwavering

hesitate *vb* **1** = **waver**, be uncertain, delay, dither (*chiefly Brit.*), doubt, haver (*Brit.*), hum and haw, pause, shillyshally (*inf.*), swither (*Scot.*), vacillate, wait **2** = **be reluctant**, balk, be unwilling, boggle, demur, hang back, scruple, shrink from, think twice **3** = **falter**, fumble, hem and haw *or* hum and haw, stammer, stumble, stutter
Antonyms *vb* ≠ **waver:** be confident, be decisive, be firm, continue, decide ≠ **be reluctant:** be determined, resolve, welcome

hesitation *n* **1** = **indecision**, delay, doubt, dubiety, hesitancy, irresolution, uncertainty, vacillation **2** = **reluctance**, demurral, misgiving(s), qualm(s), scruple(s), unwillingness **3** = **faltering**, fumbling, hemming and hawing, stammering, stumbling, stuttering

heterodox *adj* **1, 2** = **unorthodox**, dissident, heretical, iconoclastic, revisionist, schismatic, unsound

heterogeneous *adj* **1, 2** = **diverse**, assorted, contrary, contrasted, different, discrepant, disparate, dissimilar, divergent, diversified, incongruous, manifold, miscellaneous, mixed, motley, opposed, unlike, unrelated, varied

heterophyllous (ˌhɛtərəʊˈfɪləs, ˌhɛtəˈrɒfɪləs) *adj* having more than one type of leaf on the same plant.
▸ ˈ**heteroˌphylly** *n*

heteropterous (ˌhɛtəˈrɒptərəs) *or* **heteropteran** *adj* of or belonging to a suborder of hemipterous insects, including bedbugs, water bugs, etc., in which the forewings are membranous but have leathery tips. [C19: from NL *Heteroptera,* from HETERO- + Gk *pteron* wing]

heterosexism (ˌhɛtərəʊˈsɛkˌsɪzəm) *n* discrimination on the basis of sexual orientation, practised by heterosexuals against homosexuals.
▸**heteroˈsexist** *adj, n*

heterosexual (ˌhɛtərəʊˈsɛksjʊəl) *n* **1** a person who is sexually attracted to the opposite sex. ◆ *adj* **2** of or relating to heterosexuality.
▸ ˌ**heteroˌsexuˈality** *n*

heterotaxis (ˌhɛtərəʊˈtæksɪs) *or* **heterotaxy** *n* an abnormal or asymmetrical arrangement of parts, as of the organs of the body.

heterotrophic (ˌhɛtərəʊˈtrɒfɪk) *adj* (of animals and some plants) using complex organic compounds to manufacture their own organic constituents. [C20: from HETERO- + Gk *trophikos* concerning food, from *trophē* nourishment]
▸ ˈ**heteroˌtroph** *n*

heterozygote (ˌhɛtərəʊˈzaɪgəʊt) *n* an animal or plant that is heterozygous; a hybrid.

heterozygous (ˌhɛtərəʊˈzaɪgəs) *adj Genetics.* (of an organism) having dissimilar alleles for any one gene: *heterozygous for eye colour.*

hetman (ˈhɛtmən) *n, pl* **hetmans.** an elected leader of the Cossacks. Also called: **ataman.** [C18: from Polish, from G *Hauptmann* headman]

het up *adj Inf.* angry; excited: *don't get het up.* [C19: from dialect p.p. of HEAT]

heuchera (ˈhɔɪkərə) *n* a North American shrub with red or pink flowers and ornamental foliage. [after J. H. *Heucher* (1677–1747), G botanist]

heuristic (hjʊəˈrɪstɪk) *adj* **1** helping to learn; guiding in investigation. **2** (of a method of teaching) allowing pupils to learn things for themselves. **3a** *Maths, science, philosophy.* using or obtained by exploration of possibilities rather than by following set rules. **3b** *Computing.* denoting a rule of thumb for solving a problem without the exhaustive application of an algorithm: *a heuristic solution.* ◆ *n* **4** (*pl*) the science of heuristic procedure. [C19: from NL *heuristicus,* from Gk *heuriskein* to discover]
▸**heuˈristically** *adv*

hew ❶ (hjuː) *vb* **hews, hewing, hewed, hewed** *or* **hewn. 1** to strike (something, esp. wood) with cutting blows, as with an axe. **2** (*tr;* often foll. by *out*) to carve from a substance. **3** (*tr;* often foll. by *away, off,* etc.) to sever from a larger portion. **4** (*intr;* often foll. by *to*) *US & Canad.* to conform. [OE *hēawan*]
▸ ˈ**hewer** *n*

hex[1] (hɛks) *n* **a** short for **hexadecimal (notation)**. **b** (*as modifier*): *hex code.*

hex[2] (hɛks) *US & Canad. inf.* ◆ *vb* **1** (*tr*) to bewitch. ◆ *n* **2** an evil spell. **3** a witch. [C19: via Pennsylvania Du. from G *Hexe* witch, from MHG *hecse,* ?from OHG *hagzissa*]

hex. *abbrev. for:* **1** hexachord. **2** hexagon(al).

hexa- *or before a vowel* **hex-** *combining form.* six: *hexachord; hexameter.* [from Gk, from *hex* SIX]

hexachlorophene (ˌhɛksəˈklɔːrəfiːn) *n* an insoluble white bactericidal substance used in antiseptic soaps, deodorants, etc. Formula: $(C_6HCl_3OH)_2CH_2$.

hexachord (ˈhɛksəˌkɔːd) *n* (in medieval musical theory) any of three diatonic scales based upon C, F, and G, each consisting of six notes, from which solmization was developed.

hexad (ˈhɛksæd) *n* a group or series of six. [C17: from Gk *hexas,* from *hex* six]

hexadecane (ˈhɛksədɛˌkeɪn, ˌhɛksəˈdɛkeɪn) *n* the systematic name for **cetane.**

hexadecanoic acid (ˌhɛksəˌdɛkəˈnəʊɪk) *n* the systematic name for **palmitic acid.**

hexadecimal notation *or* **hexadecimal** (ˌhɛksəˈdɛsɪməl) *n* a number system having a base 16; the symbols for the numbers 0 – 9 are the same as those used in the decimal system, and the numbers 10 – 15 are usually represented by the letters A – F. The system is used as a convenient way of representing the internal binary code of a computer.

hexagon (ˈhɛksəgən) *n* a polygon having six sides.
▸**hexˈagonal** *adj*

hexagram (ˈhɛksəˌgræm) *n* a star-shaped figure formed by extending the sides of a regular hexagon to meet at six points.

hexahedron (ˌhɛksəˈhiːdrən) *n* a solid figure having six plane faces.
▸ ˌ**hexaˈhedral** *adj*

hexameter (hɛkˈsæmɪtə) *n Prosody.* **1** a verse line consisting of six metrical feet. **2** (in Greek and Latin epic poetry) a verse line of six metrical feet, of which the first four are usually dactyls or spondees, the fifth almost always a dactyl, and the sixth a spondee or trochee.
▸**hexametric** (ˌhɛksəˈmɛtrɪk) *or* ˌ**hexaˈmetrical** *adj*

hexane (ˈhɛkseɪn) *n* a liquid alkane found in petroleum and used as a solvent. Formula: C_6H_{14}. [C19: from HEXA- + -ANE]

hexapla (ˈhɛksəplə) *n* an edition of the Old Testament compiled by Origen (?185–?254 A.D.), Christian theologian, containing six versions of the text. [C17: from Gk *hexaploos* sixfold]
▸ ˈ**hexaplar** *adj*

hexapod (ˈhɛksəˌpɒd) *n* an insect.

hexavalent (ˌhɛksəˈveɪlənt) *adj Chem.* having a valency of six. Also: **sexivalent.**

hexose (ˈhɛksəʊs, -əʊz) *n* a monosaccharide, such as glucose, that contains six carbon atoms per molecule.

hey (heɪ) *interj* **1** an expression indicating surprise, dismay, discovery, etc. **2 hey presto!** an exclamation used by conjurors to herald the climax of a trick. [C13: imit.]

heyday ❶ (ˈheɪˌdeɪ) *n* the time of most power, popularity, vigour, etc. [C16: prob. based on HEY]

hf *abbrev. for* half.

Hf *the chemical symbol for* hafnium.

HF *or* **h.f.** *abbrev. for* high frequency.

hg *abbrev. for* hectogram.

Hg *the chemical symbol for* mercury. [from NL *hydrargyrum*]

HG *abbrev. for* His (*or* Her) Grace.

hgt *abbrev. for* height.

HGV (formerly, in Britain) *abbrev. for* heavy goods vehicle.

HH *abbrev. for:* **1** His (*or* Her) Highness. **2** His Holiness (title of the Pope). ◆ **3** (on Brit. pencils) *symbol for* double hard.

hi (haɪ) *sentence substitute.* an informal word for **hello.** [C20: prob. from *how are you?*]

hiatus ❶ (haɪˈeɪtəs) *n, pl* **hiatuses** *or* **hiatus. 1** (esp. in manuscripts) a break or interruption in continuity. **2** a break between adjacent vowels in the pronunciation of a word. [C16: from L: gap, cleft, from *hiāre* to gape]

hiatus hernia *n* protrusion of part of the stomach through the diaphragm at the oesophageal opening.

Hib (hɪb) *n acronym for* Haemophilus influenzae type b: a vaccine against a type of bacterial meningitis, administered to children.

hibachi (hɪˈbɑːtʃɪ) *n* a portable brazier for heating and cooking food. [from Japanese, from *hi* fire + *bachi* bowl]

hibakusha (hɪˈbɑːkʊʃə) *n, pl* **hibakusha** *or* **hibakushas.** a survivor of either of the atomic-bomb attacks on Hiroshima and Nagasaki in 1945. [C20: from Japanese, from *hibaku* bombed + *-sha* -person]

hibernal (haɪˈbɜːnᵊl) *adj* of or occurring in winter. [C17: from L *hībernālis,* from *hiems* winter]

hibernate ❶ (ˈhaɪbəˌneɪt) *vb* **hibernates, hibernating, hibernated.** (*intr*) **1** (of some animals) to pass the winter in a dormant condition with metabolism greatly slowed down. **2** to cease from activity. [C19: from L *hībernāre* to spend the winter, from *hībernus* of winter]
▸ ˌ**hiberˈnation** *n* ▸ˈ**hiberˌnator** *n*

Hibernia (haɪˈbɜːnɪə) *n* the Roman name for Ireland: used poetically in later times.
▸**Hiˈbernian** *adj, n*

Hibernicism (haɪˈbɜːnɪˌsɪzəm) *n* an Irish expression, idiom, trait, custom, etc.

Hiberno- (haɪˈbɜːnəʊ) *combining form.* denoting Irish or Ireland: *Hiberno-English.*

hibiscus (hɪˈbɪskəs) *n, pl* **hibiscuses.** any plant of the chiefly tropical and subtropical genus *Hibiscus,* cultivated for its large brightly coloured flowers. [C18: from L, from Gk *hibiskos* marsh mallow]

hiccup (ˈhɪkʌp) *n* **1** a spasm of the diaphragm producing a sudden breathing in of air resulting in a characteristic sharp sound. **2** (*pl*) the state of having such spasms. **3** *Inf.* a minor difficulty. ◆ *vb* **hiccups, hiccuping, hiccuped** *or* **hiccups, hiccupping, hiccupped. 4** (*intr*) to make a hiccup or hiccups. **5** (*tr*) to utter with a hiccup. ◆ Also: **hiccough** (ˈhɪkʌp). [C16: imit.]

hic jacet *Latin.* (hɪk ˈjækɛt) (on gravestones, etc.) here lies.

hick (hɪk) *n Inf., chiefly US & Canad.* a country bumpkin. [C16: after *Hick,* familiar form of *Richard*]

hickory (ˈhɪkərɪ) *n, pl* **hickories. 1** a tree of a chiefly North American genus having nuts with edible kernels and hard smooth shells. **2** the hard tough wood of this tree. [C17: ult. from Algonquian *pawcohiccora* food made from ground hickory nuts]

hid (hɪd) *vb* the past tense and a past participle of **hide**[1].

hidalgo (hɪˈdælgəʊ) *n, pl* **hidalgos.** a member of the lower nobility in Spain. [C16: from Sp., from OSp. *fijo dalgo* nobleman, from L *filius* son + *dē* of + *aliquid* something]

hidden ❶ (ˈhɪdᵊn) *vb* **1** a past participle of **hide**[1]. ◆ *adj* **2** concealed or obscured: *a hidden cave; a hidden meaning.*

hidden agenda *n* a hidden motive or intention behind an overt action, policy, etc.

hide[1] ❶ (haɪd) *vb* **hides, hiding, hid, hidden** *or* **hid. 1** to conceal (oneself or an object) from view or discovery: *to hide a pencil; to hide from the police.* **2** (*tr*) to obscure: *clouds hid the sun.* **3** (*tr*) to keep secret. **4** (*tr*) to turn

THESAURUS

hew *vb* **1 = cut,** axe, chop, hack, lop, split **2 = carve,** fashion, form, make, model, sculpt, sculpture, shape, smooth

heyday *n* **= prime,** bloom, flowering, pink, prime of life, salad days

hiatus *n* **1 = interruption,** break, discontinuity, gap, interval, lacuna, pause

hibernate *vb* **1 = lie dormant,** hole up, overwinter, remain torpid, sleep snug, vegetate, winter

hidden *adj* **2 = concealed,** abstruse, clandestine, close, covered, covert, cryptic, dark, hermetic, hermetical, latent, masked, mysterious, mystic, mystical, obscure, occult, recondite, secret, shrouded, ulterior, under wraps, unrevealed, unseen, veiled

hide[1] *vb* **1 = conceal,** cache, go into hiding, go to ground, go underground, hole up, lie low, secrete, stash (*inf.*), take cover **2 = disguise,** blot out, bury, camouflage, cloak, conceal, cover, eclipse, mask, obscure, screen, shelter, shroud,

(one's eyes, etc.) away. ◆ *n* **5** *Brit.* a place of concealment, usually disguised to appear as part of the natural environment, used by hunters, birdwatchers, etc. US and Canad. equivalent: **blind.** [OE *hȳdan*]
▸ **'hider** *n*

hide[2] ⓣ (haɪd) *n* **1** the skin of an animal, either tanned or raw. **2** *Inf.* the human skin. ◆ *vb* **hides, hiding, hided. 3** *(tr) Inf.* to flog. [OE *hȳd*]

hide[3] (haɪd) *n* an obsolete Brit. land measure, varying from about 60 to 120 acres. [OE *hīgid*]

hide-and-seek *or US, Canad., & Scot.* **hide-and-go-seek** *n* a game in which one player covers his eyes while the others hide, and he then tries to find them.

hideaway ⓣ ('haɪdəˌweɪ) *n* a hiding place or secluded spot.

hidebound ⓣ ('haɪdˌbaʊnd) *adj* **1** restricted by petty rules, a conservative attitude, etc. **2** (of cattle, etc.) having the skin closely attached to the flesh as a result of poor feeding.

hideous ⓣ ('hɪdɪəs) *adj* **1** extremely ugly; repulsive. **2** terrifying and horrific. [C13: from OF *hisdos*, from *hisde* fear; from ?]
▸ **'hideously** *adv* ▸ **'hideousness** *n*

hide-out ⓣ *n* a hiding place, esp. a remote place used by outlaws, etc.; hideaway.

hiding[1] ('haɪdɪŋ) *n* **1** the state of concealment: *in hiding.* **2 hiding place.** a place of concealment.

hiding[2] ⓣ ('haɪdɪŋ) *n Inf.* a flogging; beating.

hidrosis (hɪ'drəʊsɪs) *n* a technical word for **perspiration** or **sweat.** [C18: via NL from Gk, from *hidrōs* sweat]
▸**hidrotic** (hɪ'drɒtɪk) *adj*

hidy-hole *or* **hidey-hole** *n Inf.* a hiding place.

hie (haɪ) *vb* **hies, hieing** *or* **hying, hied.** *Arch. or poetic.* to hurry; speed. [OE *hīgian* to strive]

hierarch ('haɪəˌrɑːk) *n* **1** a high priest. **2** a person at a high level in a hierarchy.
▸ **ˌhier'archal** *adj*

hierarchy ⓣ ('haɪəˌrɑːkɪ) *n, pl* **hierarchies. 1** a system of persons or things arranged in a graded order. **2** a body of persons in holy orders organized into graded ranks. **3** the collective body of those so organized. **4** a series of ordered groupings within a system, such as the arrangement of plants into classes, orders, etc. **5** government by a priesthood. [C14: from Med. L *hierarchia*, from LGk, from *hierarkhēs* high priest; see HIERO-, -ARCHY]
▸ **ˌhier'archical** *or* **ˌhier'archic** *adj* ▸ **'hierˌarchism** *n*

hieratic (ˌhaɪə'rætɪk) *adj* **1** of priests. **2** of a cursive form of hieroglyphics used by priests in ancient Egypt. **3** of styles in art that adhere to certain fixed types, as in ancient Egypt. ◆ *n* **4** the hieratic script of ancient Egypt. [C17: from L *hierāticus*, from Gk, from *hiereus* priest]
▸ **ˌhier'atically** *adv*

hiero- *or before a vowel* **hier-** *combining form.* holy or divine: *hierarchy.* [from Gk, from *hieros* holy]

hieroglyphic ⓣ (ˌhaɪərə'glɪfɪk) *adj also* **hieroglyphical. 1** of or relating to a form of writing using picture symbols, esp. as used in ancient Egypt. **2** difficult to decipher. ◆ *n also* **hieroglyph. 3** a picture or symbol representing an object, concept, or sound. **4** a symbol that is difficult to decipher. [C16: from LL *hieroglyphicus*, from Gk, from HIERO- + *gluphē*, from *gluphein* to carve]
▸ **ˌhiero'glyphically** *adv*

hieroglyphics (ˌhaɪərə'glɪfɪks) *n (functioning as sing or pl)* **1** a form of writing, esp. as used in ancient Egypt, in which pictures or symbols are used to represent objects, concepts, or sounds. **2** difficult or undecipherable writing.

hierophant ('haɪərəˌfænt) *n* **1** (in ancient Greece) a high priest of religious mysteries. **2** a person who interprets esoteric mysteries. [C17: from LL *hierophanta*, from Gk, from HIERO- + *phainein* to reveal]
▸ **ˌhiero'phantic** *adj*

hi-fi ('haɪˌfaɪ) *n Inf.* **1a** short for **high fidelity. 1b** *(as modifier): hi-fi equipment.* **2** a set of high-quality sound-reproducing equipment.

higgledy-piggledy ⓣ ('hɪgᵊldɪ'pɪgᵊldɪ) *Inf.* ◆ *adj, adv* **1** in a jumble. ◆ *n* **2** a muddle.

high ⓣ (haɪ) *adj* **1** being a relatively great distance from top to bottom; tall: *a high building.* **2** situated at a relatively great distance above sea level: *a high plateau.* **3** *(postpositive)* being a specified distance from top to bottom: *three feet high.* **4** extending from or performed at an elevation: *a high dive.* **5** *(in combination)* coming up to a specified level: *knee-high.* **6** being at its peak: *high noon.* **7** of greater than average height: *a high collar.* **8** greater than normal in intensity or amount: *a high wind; high mileage.* **9** (of sound) acute in pitch. **10** (of latitudes) relatively far north or south from the equator. **11** (of meat) slightly decomposed, regarded as enhancing the flavour of game. **12** very important: *the high priestess.* **13** exalted in style or character: *high drama.* **14** expressing contempt or arrogance: *high words.* **15** elated; cheerful: *high spirits.* **16** *Inf.* being in a state of altered consciousness induced by alcohol, narcotics, etc. **17** *Inf.* overexcited: *by Christmas the children are high.* **18** luxurious or extravagant: *high life.* **19** advanced in complexity: *high finance.* **20** (of a gear) providing a relatively great forward speed for a given engine speed. **21** *Phonetics.* denoting a vowel whose articulation is produced by raising the tongue, such as for the *ee* in *see* or *oo* in *moon.* **22** *(cap. when part of a name)* formal and elaborate: *High Mass.* **23** *(usually cap.)* relating to the High Church. **24** *Cards.* having a relatively great value in a suit. **25 high and dry.** stranded; destitute. **26 high and mighty.** *Inf.* arrogant. **27 high opinion.** a favourable opinion. ◆ *adv* **28** at or to a height: *he jumped high.* **29** in a high manner. **30** *Naut.* close to the wind with sails full. ◆ *n* **31** a high place or level. **32** *Inf.* a state of altered consciousness induced by alcohol, narcotics, etc. **33** another word for **anticyclone. 34 on high. 34a** at a height. **34b** in heaven. [OE *hēah*]

High Arctic *n* the regions of Canada, esp. the northern islands, within the Arctic Circle.

highball ('haɪˌbɔːl) *n Chiefly US.* a long iced drink consisting of spirits with soda water, etc.

highborn ⓣ ('haɪˌbɔːn) *adj* of noble birth.

highboy ('haɪˌbɔɪ) *n US & Canad.* a tallboy.

highbrow ⓣ ('haɪˌbraʊ) *Often disparaging.* ◆ *n* **1** a person of scholarly and erudite tastes. ◆ *adj also* **highbrowed. 2** appealing to highbrows.

highchair ('haɪˌtʃɛə) *n* a long-legged chair for a child, esp. one with a table-like tray.

High Church *n* **1** the party or movement within the Church of England stressing continuity with Catholic Christendom, the authority of bishops, and the importance of sacraments. ◆ *adj* **High-Church. 2** of or relating to this party or movement.
▸ **'High-'Churchman** *n*

high-class ⓣ *adj* **1** of very good quality: *a high-class grocer.* **2** belonging to or exhibiting the characteristics of an upper social class.

high-coloured *adj* (of the complexion) deep red or purplish; florid.

THESAURUS

veil **3** = **suppress**, draw a veil over, hush up, keep dark, keep secret, keep under one's hat, withhold
Antonyms *vb* admit, bare, confess, disclose, display, divulge, exhibit, expose, find, flaunt, reveal, show, uncover, unveil

hide[2] *n* **1** = **skin**, fell, pelt

hideaway *n* = **hiding place**, haven, hide-out, nest, refuge, retreat, sanctuary

hidebound *adj* **1** = **conventional**, brassbound, narrow, narrow-minded, puritan, rigid, set, set in one's ways, strait-laced, ultraconservative
Antonyms *adj* broad-minded, flexible, liberal, open, receptive, tolerant, unconventional, unorthodox

hideous *adj* **1** = **ugly**, ghastly, grim, grisly, grotesque, gruesome, monstrous, repulsive, revolting, unsightly **2** = **terrifying**, abominable, appalling, awful, detestable, disgusting, dreadful, horrendous, horrible, horrid, horrific, loathsome, macabre, obscene, odious, shocking, sickening, terrible
Antonyms *adj* ≠ **ugly:** appealing, beautiful, captivating, charming, entrancing, lovely, pleasant, pleasing

hide-out *n* = **hiding place**, den, hideaway, lair, secret place, shelter

hiding[2] *n* = **beating**, caning, drubbing, flogging, larruping (*Brit. dialect*), lathering (*inf.*), licking (*inf.*), spanking, tanning (*sl.*), thrashing, walloping (*inf.*), whaling, whipping

hierarchy *n* **1** = **grading**, pecking order, ranking

hieroglyphic *adj* **2** = **indecipherable**, enigmatical, figurative, obscure, runic, symbolical

higgledy-piggledy *Informal adj* **1** = **haphazard**, helter-skelter, indiscriminate, jumbled, muddled, pell-mell, topsy-turvy ◆ *adv* **2** = **haphazardly**, all over the place, all over the shop (*inf.*), anyhow, any old how, confusedly, helter-skelter, pell-mell, topsy-turvy

high *adj* **1** = **tall**, elevated, lofty, soaring, steep, towering **8** = **extreme**, excessive, extraordinary, great, intensified, sharp, strong **9** = **high-pitched**, acute, penetrating, piercing, piping, sharp, shrill, soprano, strident, treble **11** = **gamey**, niffy (*Brit. sl.*), pongy (*Brit. inf.*), strong-flavoured, tainted, whiffy (*Brit. sl.*) **12** = **important**, arch, big-time (*inf.*), chief, consequential, distinguished, eminent, exalted, influential, leading, major league (*inf.*), notable, powerful, prominent, ruling, significant, superior **14** = **haughty**, arrogant, boastful, bragging, despotic, domineering, lofty, lordly, ostentatious, overbearing, proud, tyrannical, vainglorious **15** = **cheerful**, boisterous, bouncy (*inf.*), elated, excited, exhilarated, exuberant, joyful, lighthearted, merry **16** *Informal* = **intoxicated**, freaked out (*inf.*), inebriated, on a trip (*inf.*), spaced out (*sl.*), stoned (*sl.*), tripping (*inf.*), turned on (*sl.*), zonked (*sl.*) **17** *Informal* = **euphoric**, delirious, hyped up (*sl.*) **18** = **luxurious**, extravagant, grand, lavish, rich **25 high and dry** = **abandoned**, bereft, destitute, helpless, stranded **26 high and mighty** *Informal* = **self-important**, arrogant, cavalier, conceited, disdainful, haughty, imperious, overbearing, snobbish, stuck-up (*inf.*), superior ◆ *adv* **28** = **aloft**, at great height, far up, way up ◆ *n* **31** = **peak**, apex, crest, height, record level, summit, top **32** *Informal* = **intoxication**, delirium, ecstasy, euphoria, trip (*inf.*)
Antonyms *adj* ≠ **tall:** dwarfed, low, short, stunted ≠ **extreme:** average, low, mild, moderate, reduced, restrained, routine, suppressed ≠ **high-pitched:** alto, bass, deep, gruff, low, low-pitched ≠ **important:** average, common, degraded, ignoble, inconsequential, insignificant, low, lowly, low-ranking, menial, routine, secondary, undistinguished, unimportant ≠ **cheerful:** angry, dejected, depressed, gloomy, low, melancholy, sad

highborn *adj* = **noble**, aristocratic, blue-blooded, gentle (*arch.*), patrician, pedigreed, thoroughbred, well-born

highbrow *Often disparaging n* **1** = **intellectual**, aesthete, Brahmin (*US*), brain (*inf.*), brainbox (*sl.*), egghead (*inf.*), mastermind, savant, scholar ◆ *adj* **2** = **intellectual**, bookish, brainy (*inf.*), cultivated, cultured, deep, highbrowed, sophisticated
Antonyms *n* ≠ **intellectual:** idiot, ignoramus, illiterate, imbecile (*inf.*), lowbrow, moron, philistine ◆ *adj* ≠ **intellectual:** ignorant, lowbrow, philistine, shallow, uncultivated, uninformed, unintellectual, unlearned, unsophisticated

high-class *adj* **1** = **high-quality**, A1 *or* A-one (*inf.*), choice, classy (*sl.*), elite, exclusive, first-rate, high-toned, posh (*inf., chiefly Brit.*),

high comedy *n* comedy set largely among cultured and articulate people and featuring witty dialogue.

high commissioner *n* the senior diplomatic representative sent by one Commonwealth country to another instead of an ambassador.

high country *n* (often preceded by *the*) *NZ.* sheep pastures in the foothills of the Southern Alps, New Zealand.

High Court *n* **1** Also called: **High Court of Justice.** (in England) the supreme court dealing with civil law cases. **2** (in Australia) the highest court of appeal, deciding esp. constitutional issues. **3** (in New Zealand) a court of law that is superior to a District Court. Former name: **Supreme Court.**

high definition television *n* a television system using 1000 or more scanning lines and a higher field repetition rate. Abbrev.: **HDTV.**

high-energy physics *n* (*functioning as sing*) another name for **particle physics.**

higher ('haɪə) *adj* **1** the comparative of **high.** ◆ *n* (*usually cap.*) (in Scotland) **2a** the advanced level of the Scottish Certificate of Education. **2b** (*as modifier*): *Higher Latin.* **3** a pass in a subject at Higher level: *she has four Highers.*

higher education *n* education and training at colleges, universities, etc.

higher mathematics *n* (*functioning as sing*) mathematics that is more abstract than normal arithmetic, algebra, geometry, and trigonometry.

higher-rate tax *n* (in Britain) a rate of income tax that is higher than the basic rate and becomes payable on taxable income in excess of a specified limit.

higher-up ❶ *n Inf.* a person of higher rank or in a superior position.

highest common factor *n* the largest number or quantity that is a factor of each member of a group of numbers or quantities.

high explosive *n* an extremely powerful chemical explosive, such as TNT or gelignite.

highfalutin ❶ (ˌhaɪfə'lu:tɪn) *or* **highfaluting** *adj Inf.* pompous or pretentious. [C19: from HIGH + *-falutin,* ? var. of *fluting,* from FLUTE]

high fidelity *n* **a** the reproduction of sound using electronic equipment that gives faithful reproduction with little or no distortion. **b** (*as modifier*): *a high-fidelity amplifier.* ◆ Often shortened to **hi-fi.**

high-five *n Sl.* a gesture of greeting or congratulation in which two people slap raised right palms together.

high-flown ❶ *adj* extravagant or pretentious in conception or intention: *high-flown ideas.*

high-flyer *or* **high-flier** *n* **1** a person who is extreme in aims, ambition, etc. **2** a person of great ability, esp. in a career.
▸ˌ**high-'flying** *adj, n*

high frequency *n* a radio frequency lying between 30 and 3 megahertz. Abbrev.: **HF.**

High German *n* the standard German language, historically developed from the form of West Germanic spoken in S Germany.

high-handed ❶ *adj* tactlessly overbearing and inconsiderate.
▸ˌ**high-'handedness** *n*

high-hat *Inf.* ◆ *adj* **1** snobbish and arrogant. ◆ *vb* **high-hats, high-hatting, high-hatted.** (*tr*) **2** *Chiefly US & Canad.* to treat in a snobbish or offhand way. ◆ *n* **3** a snobbish person.

high hurdles *n* (*functioning as sing*) a race in which competitors leap over hurdles 42 inches (107 cm) high.

highjack ('haɪˌdʒæk) *vb, n* a less common spelling of **hijack.**
▸'**highˌjacker** *n*

high jump *n* **1** (usually preceded by *the*) an athletic event in which a competitor has to jump over a high bar. **2 be for the high jump.** *Brit. inf.* to be liable to receive a severe reprimand or punishment.
▸**high jumper** *n* ▸**high jumping** *n*

high-key *adj* (of a painting, etc.) having a predominance of light tones or colours. Cf. **low-key** (sense 3).

highland ('haɪlənd) *n* **1** relatively high ground. **2** (*modifier*) of or relating to a highland.
▸'**highlander** *n*

Highland ('haɪlənd) *n* **1** a council area in N Scotland, formed in 1975 as Highland Region and reorganized in 1996. Administrative centre: Inverness. Pop.: 206 900 (1996 est.). Area: 25 149 sq. km (9710 sq. miles). **2** (*modifier*) of or denoting the Highlands of Scotland.
▸'**Highlander** *n*

Highland cattle *n* a breed of cattle with shaggy reddish-brown hair and long horns.

Highland dress *n* **1** the historical costume including the plaid and kilt, of Highland clansmen and soldiers. **2** a modern version of this worn for formal occasions.

Highland fling *n* a vigorous Scottish solo dance.

Highland Games *n* (*functioning as sing or pl*) a meeting in which competitions in sport, piping, and dancing are held: originating in the Highlands of Scotland.

Highlands ❶ ('haɪləndz) *n* **the. 1a** the part of Scotland that lies to the northwest of the great fault that runs from Dumbarton to Stonehaven. **1b** a mountainous region of NW Scotland: distinguished by Gaelic culture. **2** (*often not cap.*) the highland region of any country.

high-level *adj* (of conferences, talks, etc.) involving very important people.

high-level language *n Computing.* a programming language that resembles natural language or mathematical notation and is designed to reflect the requirements of a problem.

high-level waste *n* high-activity radioactive waste, such as spent nuclear fuel, needing cooling for several decades before disposal. Cf. **intermediate-level waste, low-level waste.**

highlight ❶ ('haɪˌlaɪt) *n* **1** an area of the lightest tone in a painting, photograph, etc. **2** Also called: **high spot.** the most exciting or memorable part or time. **3** (*pl*) a lightened or brightened effect produced in the hair by bleaching selected strands. ◆ *vb* (*tr*) **4** *Painting, photog., etc.* to mark with light tone. **5** to bring emphasis to. **6** to produce highlights in (the hair).

highlighter ('haɪˌlaɪtə) *n* **1** a cosmetic cream or powder applied to the face to highlight the cheekbones, eyes, etc. **2** a fluorescent felt-tip pen used as a marker to emphasize a section of text without obscuring it.

highly ❶ ('haɪlɪ) *adv* **1** (intensifier): *highly disappointed.* **2** with great approbation: *we spoke highly of it.* **3** in a high position: *placed highly in class.* **4** at or for a high cost.

highly strung ❶ *or US & Canad.* **high-strung** *adj* tense and easily upset; excitable; nervous.

High Mass *n* a solemn and elaborate sung Mass.

high-minded ❶ *adj* **1** having or characterized by high moral principles. **2** *Arch.* arrogant; haughty.
▸ˌ**high-'mindedness** *n*

highness ('haɪnɪs) *n* the condition of being high.

Highness ('haɪnɪs) *n* (preceded by *Your, His,* or *Her*) a title used to address or refer to a royal person.

high-octane *adj* **1** (of petrol) having a high octane number. **2** *Inf.* dynamic, forceful, or intense: *high-octane drive and efficiency.*

high-pass filter *n Electronics.* a filter that transmits all frequencies above a specified value, attenuating frequencies below this value.

high-pitched *adj* **1** pitched high in tone. **2** (of a roof) having steeply sloping sides. **3** (of an argument, style, etc.) lofty or intense.

high-powered ❶ *adj* **1** (of an optical instrument or lens) having a high magnification. **2** dynamic and energetic; highly capable.

high-pressure ❶ *adj* **1** having, using, or designed to withstand pressure above normal. **2** *Inf.* (of selling) persuasive in an aggressive and persistent manner.

high priest *n* **1** *Bible.* the priest of highest rank who alone was permitted to enter the holy of holies of the Temple. **2** Also (fem): **high priestess.** the head of a cult.
▸**high priesthood** *n*

high profile *n* a position or attitude characterized by a deliberate seeking of prominence or publicity.

high-rise *adj* **1** (*prenominal*) of or relating to a building that has many

THESAURUS

ritzy (*sl.*), select, superior, swish (*inf., chiefly Brit.*), tip-top, tops (*sl.*), up-market
Antonyms *adj* cheap, cheapo (*inf.*), common, inferior, mediocre, ordinary, run-of-the-mill

higher-up *n Informal* = **superior**, boss, director, executive, gaffer (*inf., chiefly Brit.*), manager, senior

highfalutin *adj Informal* = **pompous**, arty-farty (*inf.*), big, bombastic, florid, grandiose, high-flown, high-sounding, lofty, magniloquent, pretentious, supercilious, swanky (*inf.*)

high-flown *adj* = **extravagant**, arty-farty (*inf.*), elaborate, exaggerated, florid, grandiose, highfalutin (*inf.*), inflated, lofty, magniloquent, overblown, pretentious
Antonyms *adj* down-to-earth, moderate, modest, practical, pragmatic, realistic, reasonable, restrained, sensible, simple, straightforward, unpretentious

high-handed *adj* = **dictatorial**, arbitrary, autocratic, bossy (*inf.*), despotic, domineering, imperious, inconsiderate, oppressive, overbearing, peremptory, self-willed, tyrannical, wilful

Highlands *pl n* **2** *often not cap.* = **uplands**, heights, hill country, hills, mesa, mountainous region, plateau, tableland

highlight *n* **2** = **high point**, best part, climax, feature, focal point, focus, high spot, main feature, memorable part, peak ◆ *vb* **5** = **emphasize**, accent, accentuate, bring to the fore, feature, focus attention on, foreground, give prominence to, play up, set off, show up, spotlight, stress, underline
Antonyms *n* ≠ **high point**: disappointment, lowlight, low point ◆ *vb* ≠ **emphasize**: de-emphasize, gloss over, neglect, overlook, play down

highly *adv* **1** = **extremely**, decidedly, eminently, exceptionally, extraordinarily, greatly, immensely, seriously (*inf.*), supremely, tremendously, vastly, very, very much **2** = **favourably**, appreciatively, approvingly, enthusiastically, warmly, well

highly strung *adj* = **nervous**, easily upset, edgy, excitable, irascible, irritable, nervy (*Brit. inf.*), neurotic, on pins and needles, on tenterhooks, restless, sensitive, stressed, taut, temperamental, tense, tetchy, twitchy (*inf.*), wired (*sl.*)
Antonyms *adj* calm, collected, easy-going, even-tempered, laid-back (*inf.*), placid, relaxed, serene, unfazed (*inf.*)

high-minded *adj* **1** = **principled**, elevated, ethical, fair, good, honourable, idealistic, magnanimous, moral, noble, pure, righteous, upright, virtuous, worthy
Antonyms *adj* dishonest, dishonourable, unethical, unfair

high-mindedness *n* **1** = **integrity**, probity, rectitude, scrupulousness, uprightness

high-powered *adj* **2** = **dynamic**, aggressive, driving, effective, energetic, enterprising, fast-track, forceful, go-ahead, go-getting (*inf.*), highly capable, high-octane (*inf.*), vigorous

high-pressure *Informal* **2** *adj* = **forceful**, aggressive, bludgeoning, coercive, compelling, high-powered, importunate, insistent, intensive, in-your-face (*sl.*), persistent, persuasive, pushy (*inf.*)

storeys, esp. one used for flats or offices: *a high-rise block.* ◆ *n* **2** a high-rise building.
high-risk *adj (prenominal)* denoting a group, part, etc., that is particularly subject to a danger.
highroad ('haɪˌrəʊd) *n* **1** a main road; highway. **2** (usually preceded by *the*) the sure way: *the highroad to fame.*
high school *n* **1** *Brit.* another term for **grammar school. 2** *US, Canad., NZ, & Scot.* a secondary school.
high seas *pl n (sometimes sing)* the open seas, outside the jurisdiction of any one nation.
high season *n* the most popular time of year at a holiday resort, etc.
high-sounding ⓣ *adj* another term for **high-flown.**
high-spirited ⓣ *adj* vivacious, bold, or lively.
▸ˌ**high-'spiritedness** *n*
High Street *n (often not cap.;* usually preceded by *the) Brit.* the main street of a town, usually where the principal shops are situated.
high table *n (sometimes cap.)* the table in the dining hall of a school, college, etc., at which the principal teachers, fellows, etc., sit.
hightail ('haɪˌteɪl) *vb (intr) Inf., chiefly US & Canad.* to go or move in a great hurry.
high tea *n Brit.* See **tea** (sense 4b).
high tech (tɛk) *n* a variant spelling of **hi tech.**
high technology *n* any type of sophisticated industrial process, esp. electronic.
high-tension *n (modifier)* carrying or operating at a relatively high voltage.
high tide *n* **1** the tide at its highest level. **2** a culminating point.
high time *Inf.* ◆ *adv* **1** the latest possible time: *it's high time you left.* ◆ *n* **2** Also: **high old time.** an enjoyable and exciting time.
high-toned *adj* **1** having a superior social, moral, or intellectual quality. **2** affectedly superior. **3** high in tone.
high tops *pl n* training shoes that reach to above the ankles.
high treason *n* an act of treason directly affecting a sovereign or state.
high-up *n Inf.* a person who holds an important or influential position.
highveld ('haɪˌfɛlt) *n* **the.** the high grassland region of NE South Africa.
high water *n* **1** another name for **high tide. 2** the state of any stretch of water at its highest level, as during a flood. ◆ Abbrev.: **HW.**
high-water mark *n* **1** the level reached by sea water at high tide or by other stretches of water in flood. **2** the highest point.
highway ('haɪˌweɪ) *n* **1** a public road that all may use. **2** *Now chiefly US & Canad. except in legal contexts.* a main road, esp. one that connects towns. **3** a direct path or course.
Highway Code *n* (in Britain) a booklet compiled by the Department of Transport for the guidance of users of public roads.
highwayman ('haɪweɪmən) *n, pl* **highwaymen.** (formerly) a robber, usually on horseback, who held up travellers on public roads.
high wire *n* a tightrope stretched high in the air for balancing acts.
HIH *abbrev. for* His (*or* Her) Imperial Highness.
hijack ⓣ *or* **highjack** ('haɪˌdʒæk) *vb* **1** *(tr)* to seize or divert (a vehicle or the goods it carries) while in transit: *to hijack an aircraft.* ◆ *n* **2** the act or an instance of hijacking. [C20: from ?]
▸**'hiˌjacker** *or* **'highˌjacker** *n*
hike ⓣ (haɪk) *vb* **hikes, hiking, hiked. 1** *(intr)* to walk a long way, usually for pleasure, esp. in the country. **2** (usually foll. by *up)* to pull or be pulled; hitch. **3** *(tr;* usually foll. by *up)* to raise (prices). ◆ *n* **4** a long walk. **5** a rise in price. [C18: from ?]
▸**'hiker** *n*
hilarious ⓣ (hɪ'lɛərɪəs) *adj* very funny. [C19: from L *hilaris* glad, from Gk *hilaros*]
▸**hi'lariously** *adv* ▸**hi'lariousness** *n*
hilarity ⓣ (hɪ'lærɪtɪ) *n* mirth and merriment.
Hilary term *n* the spring term at Oxford University, the Inns of Court, and some other educational establishments. [C16: after Saint *Hilary* of Poitiers (?315–?367), F bishop]
hill ⓣ (hɪl) *n* **1a** a natural elevation of the earth's surface, less high or craggy than a mountain. **1b** *(in combination): a hillside.* **2a** a heap or mound. **2b** *(in combination): a dunghill.* **3** an incline; slope. **4 over the hill. 4a** *Inf.* beyond one's prime. **4b** *Mil. sl.* absent without leave or deserting. ◆ *vb (tr)* **5** to form into a hill. **6** to cover or surround with a heap of earth. [OE *hyll*]
▸**'hilly** *adj*
hillbilly ('hɪlˌbɪlɪ) *n, pl* **hillbillies. 1** *Usually disparaging.* an unsophisticated person, esp. from the mountainous areas in the southeastern US. **2** another name for **country and western.** [C20: from HILL + *Billy* (the nickname)]
hillock ⓣ ('hɪlək) *n* a small hill or mound. [C14 *hilloc*]
▸**'hillocked** *or* **'hillocky** *adj*
hills (hɪlz) *pl n* **1 as old as the hills.** very old. **2 the.** a hilly and often remote region.
hill station *n* (in northern India, etc.) a settlement or resort at a high altitude.
hilt ⓣ (hɪlt) *n* **1** the handle or shaft of a sword, dagger, etc. **2 to the hilt.** to the full. [OE]
hilum ('haɪləm) *n, pl* **hila** (-lə). *Bot.* a scar on a seed marking its point of attachment to the seed stalk. [C17: from L: trifle]
him (hɪm; *unstressed* ɪm) *pron (objective)* refers to a male person or animal: *they needed him; she baked him a cake; not him again!* [OE *him,* dative of *hē* HE]

> **USAGE NOTE** See at **me**[1].

HIM *abbrev. for* His (*or* Her) Imperial Majesty.
himation (hɪ'mætɪˌɒn) *n, pl* **himatia** (-ɪə). (in ancient Greece) a cloak draped around the body. [C19: from Gk, from *heima* dress, from *hennunai* to clothe]
himself (hɪm'self; *medially often* ɪm'sɛlf) *pron* **1a** the reflexive form of *he* or *him.* **1b** (intensifier): *the king himself waved to me.* **2** *(preceded by a copula)* his normal self: *he seems himself once more.* [OE *him selfum,* dative sing of *hē self;* see HE, SELF]
Hinayana (ˌhiːnə'jɑːnə) *n* any of various early forms of Buddhism. [from Sansk., from *hīna* lesser + *yāna* vehicle]
hind[1] ⓣ (haɪnd) *adj* **hinder, hindmost** *or* **hindermost.** *(prenominal)* (esp. of parts of the body) situated at the back: *a hind leg.* [OE *hindan* at the back, rel. to G *hinten*]
hind[2] (haɪnd) *n, pl* **hinds** *or* **hind. 1** the female of the deer, esp. the red deer when aged three years or more. **2** any of several marine fishes related to the groper. [OE *hind*]
hind[3] (haɪnd) *n* (formerly) **1** a simple peasant. **2** (in Scotland and N England) a skilled farm worker. **3** a steward. [OE *hīne,* from *hīgna,* genitive pl of *hīgan* servants]
hinder[1] ⓣ ('hɪndə) *vb* **1** to be or get in the way of (someone or something); hamper. **2** *(tr)* to prevent. [OE *hindrian*]
hinder[2] ('haɪndə) *adj (prenominal)* situated at or further towards the back; posterior. [OE]
Hindi ('hɪndɪ) *n* **1** a language or group of dialects of N central India. See also **Hindustani. 2** a formal literary dialect of this language, the official language of India. **3** a person whose native language is Hindi. [C18: from Hindi, from *Hind* India, from OPersian *Hindu* the river Indus]
hindmost ⓣ ('haɪndˌməʊst) *or* **hindermost** ('hɪndəˌməʊst) *adj* furthest back; last.
Hindoo ('hɪnduː, hɪn'duː) *n, pl* **Hindoos,** *adj* an older spelling of **Hindu.**
▸**'HindooˌIsm** *n*
hindquarter ('haɪndˌkwɔːtə) *n* **1** one of the two back quarters of a carcass of beef, lamb, etc. **2** *(pl)* the rear, esp. of a four-legged animal.
hindrance ⓣ ('hɪndrəns) *n* **1** an obstruction or snag; impediment. **2** the act of hindering.
hindsight ('haɪndˌsaɪt) *n* **1** the ability to understand, after something has happened, what should have been done. **2** a firearm's rear sight.
Hindu ('hɪnduː, hɪn'duː) *n, pl* **Hindus. 1** a person who adheres to Hinduism. **2** an inhabitant or native of Hindustan or India. ◆ *adj* **3** relating to Hinduism, Hindus, or India. [C17: from Persian *Hindū,* from *Hind* India; see HINDI]
Hinduism ('hɪnduˌɪzəm) *n* the complex of beliefs and customs comprising the dominant religion of India, characterized by the worship of many gods, a caste system, belief in reincarnation, etc.
Hindustani (ˌhɪndʊ'stɑːnɪ) *n* **1** the dialect of Hindi spoken in Delhi:

THESAURUS

high-sounding *adj* = **extravagant,** affected, artificial, bombastic, flamboyant, florid, grandiloquent, grandiose, high-flown, imposing, magniloquent, ostentatious, overblown, pompous, pretentious, stilted, strained

high-spirited *adj* = **lively,** alive and kicking, animated, boisterous, bold, bouncy, daring, dashing, ebullient, effervescent, energetic, exuberant, frolicsome, full of beans (*inf.*), full of life, fun-loving, gallant, mettlesome, sparky, spirited, spunky (*inf.*), vibrant, vital, vivacious

hijack *vb* **1** = **seize,** commandeer, expropriate, skyjack, take over

hike *vb* **1** = **walk,** back-pack, hoof it (*sl.*), leg it (*inf.*), ramble, tramp **2** *usually with* **up** = **raise,** hitch up, jack up, lift, pull up ◆ *n* **4** = **walk,** journey on foot, march, ramble, tramp, trek

hiker *n* **1** = **walker,** backpacker, rambler

hilarious *adj* = **funny,** amusing, comical, entertaining, humorous, mirthful, side-splitting, uproarious
Antonyms *adj* dull, gloomy, sad, serious

hilarity *n* = **merriment,** amusement, glee, laughter, levity, mirth

hill *n* **1** = **mount,** brae (*Scot.*), down (*arch.*), elevation, eminence, fell, height, hillock, hilltop, knoll, mound, prominence, tor **2** = **heap,** drift, hummock, mound, pile, rick, stack **3** = **slope,** acclivity, brae, climb, gradient, incline, rise

hillock *n* = **mound,** barrow, hummock, knap (*dialect*), knoll

hilly *adj* **1** = **mountainous,** rolling, steep, undulating

hilt *n* **1** = **handle,** grip, haft, handgrip, helve **2 to the hilt** = **fully,** completely, entirely, totally, wholly

hind[1] *adj* = **back,** after, hinder, posterior, rear

hinder[1] *vb* **1** = **obstruct,** arrest, block, check, debar, delay, deter, encumber, frustrate, hamper, hamstring, handicap, hobble, hold up *or* back, impede, interrupt, oppose, retard, slow down, stymie, throw a spanner in the works, thwart, trammel **2** = **stop,** prevent
Antonyms *vb* accelerate, advance, aid, benefit, encourage, expedite, facilitate, further, help, hurry, promote, quicken, speed, support

hindmost *adj* = **last,** concluding, final, furthest, furthest behind, most remote, rearmost, terminal, trailing, ultimate

hindrance *n* **1** = **obstacle,** bar, barrier, block, check, deterrent, difficulty, drag, drawback, encumbrance, handicap, hazard, hitch, impediment, interruption, limitation, obstruction, restraint, restriction, snag, stoppage, stumbling block, trammel
Antonyms *n* advantage, aid, asset, assistance, benefit, boon, boost, encouragement, furtherance, help, support

used as a lingua franca throughout India. **2** all the spoken forms of Hindi and Urdu considered together. ◆ *adj* **3** of or relating to these languages or Hindustan.

hinge ⓣ (hɪndʒ) *n* **1** a device for holding together two parts such that one can swing relative to the other. **2** a natural joint, such as the knee joint, that functions in only one plane. **3** a similar structure in invertebrate animals, such as the joint between the two halves of a bivalve shell. **4** something on which events, opinions, etc., turn. **5** Also called: **mount.** *Philately.* a small transparent strip of gummed paper for affixing a stamp to a page. ◆ *vb* **hinges, hinging, hinged. 6** (*tr*) to fit a hinge to (something). **7** (*intr;* usually foll. by *on* or *upon*) to depend (on). **8** (*intr*) to hang or turn on or as if on a hinge. [C13: prob. of Gmc origin]
▸**hinged** *adj*

hinny[1] ('hɪnɪ) *n, pl* **hinnies.** the sterile hybrid offspring of a male horse and a female donkey. [C19: from L *hinnus,* from Gk *hinnos*]

hinny[2] ('hɪnɪ) *n Scot. & N English dialect.* a term of endearment, esp. for a woman. [var. of HONEY]

Hi-NRG (ˌhaɪ'enədʒɪ) *n* a type of dance music, originating in the late 1980s, that has a very fast tempo and a strong beat. [C20: from HIGH + ENERGY]

hint ⓣ (hɪnt) *n* **1** a suggestion given in an indirect or subtle manner. **2** a helpful piece of advice. **3** a small amount; trace. ◆ *vb* **4** (when *intr,* often foll. by *at;* when *tr, takes a clause as object*) to suggest indirectly. [C17: from ?]

hinterland ('hɪntəˌlænd) *n* **1** land lying behind something, esp. a coast or the shore of a river. **2** remote or undeveloped areas. **3** an area near and dependent on a large city, esp. a port. [C19: from G, from *hinter* behind + *land* LAND]

hip[1] (hɪp) *n* **1** (*often pl*) either side of the body below the waist and above the thigh. **2** another name for **pelvis** (sense 1). **3** short for **hip joint. 4** the angle formed where two sloping sides of a roof meet. [OE *hype*]
▸**'hipless** *adj*

hip[2] (hɪp) *n* the berry-like brightly coloured fruit of a rose plant. Also called: **rosehip.** [OE *héopa*]

hip[3] (hɪp) *interj* an exclamation used to introduce cheers (in **hip, hip, hurrah**). [C18: from ?]

hip[4] ⓣ (hɪp) *adj* **hipper, hippest.** *Sl.* **1** aware of or following the latest trends. **2** (*often postpositive;* foll. by *to*) informed (about). [var. of earlier *hep*]

hip bath *n* a portable bath in which the bather sits.

hipbone ('hɪpˌbəʊn) *n* the nontechnical name for **innominate bone.**

hip flask *n* a small metal flask for spirits, etc.

hip-hop ('hɪpˌhɒp) *n* a US pop culture movement of the 1980s comprising rap music, graffiti, and break dancing.

hip joint *n* the ball-and-socket joint that connects each leg to the trunk of the body.

hippeastrum (ˌhɪpɪ'æstrəm) *n* any plant of a South American genus cultivated for their large funnel-shaped typically red flowers. [C19: NL, from Gk *hippeus* knight + *astron* star]

hipped[1] (hɪpt) *adj* **1a** having a hip or hips. **1b** (*in combination*): *broad-hipped.* **2** (esp. of cows, sheep, etc.) having an injury to the hip, such as a dislocation. **3** *Archit.* having a hip or hips: *hipped roof.*

hipped[2] (hɪpt) *adj* (*often postpositive;* foll. by *on*) *US & Canad. dated sl.* very enthusiastic. [C20: from HIP[4]]

hippie *n, pl* **hippies.** a variant of **hippy**[1].

hippo ('hɪpəʊ) *n, pl* **hippos.** *Inf.* short for **hippopotamus.**

hippocampus (ˌhɪpəʊ'kæmpəs) *n, pl* **hippocampi** (-paɪ). **1** a mythological sea creature with the forelegs of a horse and the tail of a fish. **2** any of various small sea fishes with a horselike head; sea horse. **3** an area of cerebral cortex that forms a ridge in the floor of the brain, which in cross section has the shape of a sea horse. It functions as part of the limbic system. [C16: from L, from Gk *hippos* horse + *kampos* a sea monster]

hippocras ('hɪpəʊˌkræs) *n* an old English drink of wine flavoured with spices. [C14 *ypocras,* from OF: *Hippocrates,* prob. referring to a filter called *Hippocrates' sleeve,* Hippocrates being regarded as the father of medicine]

Hippocratic oath (ˌhɪpəʊ'krætɪk) *n* an oath taken by a doctor to observe a code of medical ethics derived from that of Hippocrates (?460–?377 B.C.), Greek physician.

hippodrome ('hɪpəˌdrəʊm) *n* **1** a music hall, variety theatre, or circus. **2** (in ancient Greece or Rome) an open-air course for horse and chariot races. [C16: from L *hippodromos,* from Gk *hippos* horse + *dromos* race]

hippogriff *or* **hippogryph** ('hɪpəʊˌgrɪf) *n* a monster with a griffin's head, wings, and claws and a horse's body. [C17: from It. *ippogrifo,* from *ippo-* horse (from Gk) + *grifo* GRIFFIN]

hippopotamus (ˌhɪpə'pɒtəməs) *n, pl* **hippopotamuses** *or* **hippopotami** (-ˌmaɪ). a very large gregarious mammal living in or around the rivers of tropical Africa. [C16: from L, from Gk: river horse, from *hippos* horse + *potamos* river]

hippy[1] ⓣ *or* **hippie** ('hɪpɪ) *n, pl* **hippies.** (esp. during the 1960s) a person whose behaviour, dress, use of drugs, etc., implies a rejection of conventional values. [C20: see HIP[4]]

hippy[2] ('hɪpɪ) *adj* **hippier, hippiest.** *Inf.* (esp. of a woman) having large hips.

hip roof *n* a roof having sloping ends and sides.

hipster ('hɪpstə) *n* **1** *Sl., now rare.* **1a** an enthusiast of modern jazz. **1b** an outmoded word for **hippy**[1]. **2** (*modifier*) (of trousers) cut so that the top encircles the hips.

hipsters ('hɪpstəz) *pl n Brit.* trousers cut so that the top encircles the hips. Usual US word: **hip-huggers.**

hircine ('hɜːsaɪn, -sɪn) *adj* **1** *Arch.* of or like a goat. **2** *Literary.* lascivious. [C17: from L *hircīnus,* from *hircus* goat]

hire ⓣ ('haɪə) *vb* **hires, hiring, hired.** (*tr*) **1** to acquire the temporary use of (a thing) or the services of (a person) in exchange for payment. **2** to employ (a person) for wages. **3** (often foll. by *out*) to provide (something) or the services of (oneself or others) for payment, usually for an agreed period. **4** (foll. by *out*) *Chiefly Brit.* to pay independent contractors for (work to be done). ◆ *n* **5a** the act of hiring or the state of being hired. **5b** (*as modifier*): *a hire car.* **6** the price for a person's services or the temporary use of something. **7 for** *or* **on hire.** available for hire. [OE *hȳrian*]
▸**'hirable** *or* **'hireable** *adj* ▸**'hirer** *n*

hireling ('haɪəlɪŋ) *n Derog.* a person who works only for money. [OE *hȳrling*]

hire-purchase *n Brit.* a system in which a buyer takes possession of merchandise on payment of a deposit and completes the purchase by paying a series of instalments while the seller retains ownership until the final instalment is paid. Abbrev.: **HP, h.p.** US and Canad. equivalents: **installment plan, instalment plan.**

hirsute ⓣ ('hɜːsjuːt) *adj* **1** covered with hair. **2** (of plants) covered with long but not stiff hairs. **3** (of a person) having long, thick, or untrimmed hair. [C17: from L *hirsūtus* shaggy]
▸**'hirsuteness** *n*

his (hɪz; *unstressed* ɪz) *determiner* **1a** of, belonging to, or associated with him: *his knee; I don't like his being out so late.* **1b** (*as pron*): *his is on the left; that book is his.* **2 his and hers.** for a man and woman respectively. ◆ *pron* **3 of his.** belonging to him. [OE *his,* genitive of *hē* HE & of *hit* IT]

Hispanic (hɪ'spænɪk) *adj* **1** of or derived from Spain or the Spanish. ◆ *n* **2** *US.* a US citizen of Latin-American descent.
▸**His'panicism** *n*

hispid ('hɪspɪd) *adj Biol.* covered with stiff hairs or bristles. [C17: from L *hispidus* bristly]

hiss ⓣ (hɪs) *n* **1** a sound like that of a prolonged *s.* **2** such a sound as an exclamation of derision, contempt, etc. ◆ *vb* **3** (*intr*) to produce or utter a hiss. **4** (*tr*) to express with a hiss. **5** (*tr*) to show derision or anger towards (a speaker, performer, etc.) by hissing. [C14: imit.]

hist (hɪst) *interj* an exclamation used to attract attention or as a warning to be silent.

histamine ('hɪstəˌmiːn) *n* an amine released by the body tissues in allergic reactions, causing irritation. [C20: from HIST- + AMINE]
▸**histaminic** (ˌhɪstə'mɪnɪk) *adj*

histo- *or before a vowel* **hist-** *combining form.* indicating animal or plant tissue: *histology; histochemistry.* [from Gk, from *histos* web]

histogenesis (ˌhɪstəʊ'dʒɛnɪsɪs) *n* the formation of tissues and organs from undifferentiated cells.
▸**histogenetic** (ˌhɪstəʊdʒə'nɛtɪk) *or* ˌ**histo'genic** *adj*

histogram ('hɪstəˌgræm) *n* a statistical graph that represents the frequency of values of a quantity by vertical rectangles of varying heights and widths. [C20: ?from HISTO(RY) + -GRAM]

histology (hɪ'stɒlədʒɪ) *n* the study of the tissues of an animal or plant.
▸**histological** (ˌhɪstə'lɒdʒɪkᵊl) *or* ˌ**histo'logic** *adj*

histolysis (hɪ'stɒlɪsɪs) *n* the disintegration of organic tissues.
▸**histolytic** (ˌhɪstə'lɪtɪk) *adj*

historian ⓣ (hɪ'stɔːrɪən) *n* a person who writes or studies history, esp. one who is an authority on it.

historic ⓣ (hɪ'stɒrɪk) *adj* **1** famous in history; significant. **2** *Linguistics.* (of Latin, Greek, or Sanskrit verb tenses) referring to past time.

> **USAGE NOTE** A distinction is usually made between *historic* (important, significant) and *historical* (pertaining to history): *a historic decision; a historical perspective.*

THESAURUS

hinge *vb* **7** *usually with* **on** *or* **upon** = **depend on,** be contingent on, be subject to, hang on, pivot on, rest on, revolve around, turn on

hint *n* **1** = **indication,** allusion, clue, implication, inkling, innuendo, insinuation, intimation, mention, reminder, suggestion, tip-off, word to the wise **2** = **advice,** help, pointer, suggestion, tip, wrinkle (*inf.*) **3** = **trace,** breath, dash, *soupçon,* speck, suggestion, suspicion, taste, tinge, touch, undertone, whiff, whisper ◆ *vb* **4** = **suggest,** allude, cue, imply, indicate, insinuate, intimate, let it be known, mention, prompt, tip off, tip the wink (*inf.*)

hip[4] *adj Slang* **1** = **fashionable,** in, trendy (*Brit. inf.*), with it (*inf.*) **2** = **informed,** aware, clued-up (*inf.*), in on, knowledgeable, onto, wise (*sl.*)

hippy[1] *n* = **bohemian,** beatnik, dropout, flower child

hire *vb* **1** = **rent,** charter, engage, lease, let **2** = **employ,** appoint, commission, engage, sign up, take on ◆ *n* **6** = **rental,** charge, cost, fee, price, rent

hirsute *adj* **1, 3** = **hairy,** bearded, bewhiskered, bristly, shaggy, unshaven

hiss *n* **1** = **sibilation,** buzz, hissing, sibilance **2** = **catcall,** boo, contempt, derision, jeer, raspberry ◆ *vb* **3** = **whistle,** rasp, shrill, sibilate, wheeze, whirr, whiz **5** = **jeer,** blow a raspberry, boo, catcall, condemn, damn, decry, deride, hoot, mock, revile, ridicule

historian *n* = **chronicler,** annalist, biographer, historiographer, recorder

historic *adj* **1** = **significant,** celebrated, conse-

historical ⓘ (hɪˈstɒrɪkᵊl) *adj* **1** belonging to or typical of the study of history: *historical methods.* **2** concerned with events of the past: *historical accounts.* **3** based on or constituting factual material as distinct from legend or supposition. **4** based on history: *a historical novel.* **5** occurring in history.
▸**hisˈtorically** *adv*

USAGE NOTE See at **historic.**

historical-cost accounting *n* a method of accounting that values assets at the original cost. In times of high inflation profits can be overstated. Cf. **current-cost accounting.**
historical linguistics *n* (*functioning as sing*) the study of language as it changes in the course of time.
historical present *n* the present tense used to narrate past events, employed for effect or in informal use, as in *a week ago I see this accident.*
historicism (hɪˈstɒrɪˌsɪzəm) *n* **1** the belief that natural laws govern historical events. **2** the doctrine that each period of history has its own beliefs and values inapplicable to any other. **3** excessive emphasis on history, past styles, etc.
▸**hisˈtoricist** *n, adj*
historicity (ˌhɪstəˈrɪsɪtɪ) *n* historical authenticity.
historiographer (hɪˌstɔːrɪˈɒgrəfə) *n* **1** a historian, esp. one concerned with historical method. **2** a historian employed to write the history of a group or public institution.
▸**hiˌstoriˈography** *n*
history ⓘ (ˈhɪstərɪ) *n, pl* **histories. 1** a record or account of past events, developments, etc. **2** all that is preserved of the past, esp. in written form. **3** the discipline of recording and interpreting past events. **4** past events, esp. when considered as an aggregate. **5** an event in the past, esp. one that has been reduced in importance: *their quarrel was just history.* **6** the past, previous experiences, etc., of a thing or person: *the house had a strange history.* **7** a play that depicts historical events. **8** a narrative relating the events of a character's life: *the history of Joseph Andrews.* [C15: from L *historia,* from Gk: inquiry, from *historein* to narrate, from *histōr* judge]
histrionic ⓘ (ˌhɪstrɪˈɒnɪk) *adj* **1** excessively dramatic or artificial: *histrionic gestures.* **2** *Now rare.* dramatic. ◆ *n* **3** (*pl*) melodramatic displays of temperament. **4** *Rare.* (*pl; functioning as sing*) dramatics. [C17: from LL *histriōnicus,* from L *histriō* actor]
▸**ˌhistriˈonically** *adv*
hit ⓘ (hɪt) *vb* **hits, hitting, hit.** (*mainly tr*) **1** (*also intr*) to deal (a blow) to (a person or thing); strike. **2** to come into violent contact with: *the car hit the tree.* **3** to strike with a missile: *to hit a target.* **4** to knock or bump: *I hit my arm on the table.* **5** to propel by striking: *to hit a ball.* **6** *Cricket.* to score (runs). **7** to affect (a person, place, or thing), esp. suddenly or adversely: *his illness hit his wife very hard.* **8** to reach: *unemployment hit a new high.* **9** to experience: *I've hit a slight snag here.* **10** *Sl.* to murder (a rival criminal) in fulfilment of an underworld vendetta. **11** *Inf.* to set out on: *let's hit the road.* **12** *Inf.* to arrive: *he will hit town tomorrow.* **13** *Inf., chiefly US & Canad.* to demand or request from: *he hit me for a pound.* **14 hit the bottle.** *Sl.* to drink an excessive amount of alcohol. ◆ *n* **15** an impact or collision. **16** a shot, blow, etc., that reaches its object. **17** an apt, witty, or telling remark. **18** *Inf.* **18a** a person or thing that gains wide appeal: *she's a hit with everyone.* **18b** (*as modifier*): *a hit record.* **19** *Inf.* a stroke of luck. **20** *Sl.* **20a** a murder carried out as the result of an underworld vendetta. **20b** (*as modifier*): *a hit squad.* **21** *Computing sl.* a single visit to a website. **22 make a hit with.** *Inf.* to make a favourable impression on. ◆ See also **hit off, hit on, hit out.** [OE *hittan,* from ON *hitta*]
▸**ˈhitter** *n*
hit-and-miss ⓘ *adj Inf.* random; haphazard: *a hit-and-miss affair; the technique is very hit and miss.* Also: **hit or miss.**
hit-and-run *adj* (*prenominal*) **1** denoting a motor-vehicle accident in which the driver leaves the scene without stopping to give assistance, inform the police, etc. **2** (of an attack, raid, etc.) relying on surprise allied to a rapid departure from the scene of operations: *hit-and-run tactics.*
hitch ⓘ (hɪtʃ) *vb* **1** to fasten or become fastened with a knot or tie. **2** (*tr;* often foll. by *up*) to pull up (the trousers, etc.) with a quick jerk. **3** (*intr*) *Chiefly US.* to move in a halting manner. **4** (*tr; passive*) *Sl.* to marry (esp. in **get hitched**). **5** *Inf.* to obtain (a ride) by hitchhiking. ◆ *n* **6** an impediment or obstacle, esp. one that is temporary or minor. **7** a knot that can be undone by pulling against the direction of the strain that holds it. **8** a sudden jerk: *he gave it a hitch and it came loose.* **9** *Inf.* a ride obtained by hitchhiking. [C15: from ?]
▸**ˈhitcher** *n*
hitchhike (ˈhɪtʃˌhaɪk) *vb* **hitchhikes, hitchhiking, hitchhiked.** (*intr*) to travel by obtaining free lifts in motor vehicles.
▸**ˈhitchˌhiker** *n*
hi tech *or* **high tech** (tɛk) *n* **1** short for **high technology. 2** a style of interior design using features of industrial equipment. ◆ *adj* **hi-tech** *or* **high-tech. 3** designed for or using high technology. **4** of or in the interior design style. ◆ Cf. **low tech.**
hither ⓘ (ˈhɪðə) *adv* **1** to or towards this place (esp. in **come hither**). **2 hither and thither.** this way and that, as in confusion. ◆ *adj* **3** *Arch. or dialect.* (of a side or part) nearer; closer. [OE *hider*]
hithermost (ˈhɪðəˌməʊst) *adj Now rare.* nearest to this place or in this direction.
hitherto ⓘ (ˌhɪðəˈtuː) *adv, adj* until this time: *hitherto, there have been no problems; hitherto private aristocratic homes.*
Hitlerism (ˈhɪtləˌrɪzəm) *n* the policies, principles, and methods of the Nazi party as developed by Adolf Hitler.
hit list *n Inf.* **1** a list of people to be murdered: *a terrorist hit list.* **2** a list of targets to be eliminated in some way: *a hit list of pits to be closed.*
hit man *n* a hired assassin.
hit off ⓘ *vb* **1** (*tr, adv*) to represent or mimic accurately. **2 hit it off with.** *Inf.* to have a good relationship with.
hit on ⓘ *vb* (*prep*) **1** (*tr*) to discover unexpectedly or guess correctly. Also: **hit upon. 2** (*tr*) *US & Canad.* to make sexual advances to.
hit out ⓘ *vb* (*intr, adv;* often foll. by *at*) **1** to direct blows forcefully and vigorously. **2** to make a verbal attack (upon someone).
Hittite (ˈhɪtaɪt) *n* **1** a member of an ancient people of Anatolia, who built a great empire in N Syria and Asia Minor in the second millennium B.C. **2** the extinct language of this people. ◆ *adj* **3** of or relating to this people, their civilization, or their language.
hit wicket *n Cricket.* an instance of a batsman breaking the wicket with the bat or a part of the body while playing a stroke and so being out.
HIV *abbrev. for* human immunodeficiency virus; the cause of AIDS.
hive ⓘ (haɪv) *n* **1** a structure in which social bees live. **2** a colony of social bees. **3** a place showing signs of great industry (esp. in **a hive of activity**). **4** a teeming multitude. ◆ *vb* **hives, hiving, hived. 5** to cause (bees) to collect or (of bees) to collect inside a hive. **6** to live or cause to live in or as if in a hive. **7** (*tr;* often foll. by *up* or *away*) to store, esp. for future use. [OE *hȳf*]
hive off *vb* (*adv*) **1** to transfer or be transferred from a larger group or unit. **2** (*usually tr*) to transfer (profitable activities of a nationalized industry) back to private ownership.
hives (haɪvz) *n* (*functioning as sing or pl*) *Pathol.* a nontechnical name for **urticaria.** [C16: from ?]
hiya (ˈhaɪjə, ˌhaɪˈjɑː) *sentence substitute.* an informal term of greeting. [C20: shortened from *how are you?*]
hl *abbrev. for* hectolitre.
HL (in Britain) *abbrev. for* House of Lords.
hm *symbol for* hectometre.
h'm (*spelling pron* hmmm) *interj* used to indicate hesitation, doubt, assent, pleasure, etc.
HM *abbrev. for:* **1** His (*or* Her) Majesty. **2** headmaster; headmistress.
HMAS *abbrev. for* His (*or* Her) Majesty's Australian Ship.
HMCS *abbrev. for* His (*or* Her) Majesty's Canadian Ship.
HMI (in Britain) *abbrev. for* His (*or* Her) Majesty's Inspector; a government official who examines and supervises schools.

THESAURUS

quential, epoch-making, extraordinary, famous, ground-breaking, momentous, notable, outstanding, red-letter, remarkable
Antonyms *adj* ordinary, uncelebrated, unimportant, unknown
historical *adj* **3** = **factual**, actual, archival, attested, authentic, chronicled, documented, real, verifiable
Antonyms *adj* contemporary, current, fabulous, fictional, legendary, mythical, present-day
history *n* **1** = **chronicle**, account, annals, autobiography, biography, memoirs, narration, narrative, recapitulation, recital, record, relation, saga, story **4** = **the past**, ancient history, antiquity, bygone times, days of old, days of yore, olden days, the good old days, the old days, yesterday, yesteryear
histrionic *adj* **1** = **theatrical**, actorly, actressy, affected, artificial, bogus, camp (*inf.*), dramatic, forced, insincere, melodramatic, sensational, unnatural ◆ *n* **3** *plural* = **temperament**, dramatics, performance, scene, staginess, tantrums, theatricality
hit *vb* **1, 4** = **strike**, bang, bash (*inf.*), batter, beat, belt, clip (*inf.*), clobber (*sl.*), clout (*inf.*), cuff, deck (*sl.*), flog, knock, lay one on (*sl.*), lob, punch, slap, smack, smite (*arch.*), sock (*sl.*), swat, thump, tonk (*sl.*), wallop (*inf.*), whack **2** = **collide with**, bang into, bump, clash with, crash against, meet head-on, run into, smash into **7** = **affect**, damage, devastate, impact on, impinge on, influence, leave a mark on, make an impact *or* impression on, move, overwhelm, touch **8** = **reach**, accomplish, achieve, arrive at, attain, gain, secure, strike, touch ◆ *n* **15** = **stroke**, belt (*inf.*), blow, bump, clash, clout, collision, cuff, impact, knock, rap, shot, slap, smack, swipe (*inf.*), wallop (*inf.*) **18** = **success**, sellout, sensation, smash (*inf.*), triumph, winner
hit-and-miss *adj Informal* = **haphazard**, aimless, casual, cursory, disorganized, indiscriminate, perfunctory, random, undirected, uneven
Antonyms *adj* arranged, deliberate, organized, planned, systematic
hitch *vb* **1** = **fasten**, attach, connect, couple, harness, join, make fast, tether, tie, unite, yoke **2** *often foll. by* **up** = **pull up**, hoick, jerk, tug, yank **5** *Informal* = **hitchhike**, thumb a lift ◆ *n* **6** = **problem**, catch, check, delay, difficulty, drawback, hassle (*inf.*), hazard, hindrance, hold-up, impediment, mishap, obstacle, snag, stoppage, trouble
hither *adv* **1** = **here**, close, closer, near, nearer, nigh (*arch.*), over here, to this place
hitherto *adv* = **previously**, heretofore, so far, thus far, till now, until now, up to now
hit off *vb* **1** = **mimic**, capture, catch, impersonate, represent, take off (*inf.*) **2 hit it off with** *Informal* = **get on (well) with**, be on good terms with, click with (*sl.*), get on with like a house on fire (*inf.*), take to, warm to
hit on *vb* **1** = **think up**, arrive at, chance upon, come upon, discover, guess, invent, light upon, realize, strike upon, stumble on
hit out *vb* **2** = **attack**, assail, castigate, condemn, denounce, inveigh against, lash out, rail against, strike out at
hive *n* **2** = **colony**, cluster, swarm **3** *As in* **hive of activity** = **centre**, heart, hub, powerhouse (*sl.*)

H.M.S. *or* **HMS** *abbrev. for:* **1** His (*or* Her) Majesty's Service. **2** His (*or* Her) Majesty's Ship.

HMSO (in Britain) *abbrev. for* His (*or* Her) Majesty's Stationery Office.

HNC (in Britain) *abbrev. for* Higher National Certificate; a qualification recognized by many national technical and professional institutions.

HND (in Britain) *abbrev. for* Higher National Diploma; a qualification in technical subjects equivalent to a degree.

ho (həʊ) *interj* **1** Also: **ho-ho.** an imitation or representation of a deep laugh. **2** an exclamation used to attract attention, etc. [C13: imit.]

Ho *the chemical symbol for* holmium.

hoar (hɔː) *n* **1** short for **hoarfrost.** ◆ *adj* **2** *Rare.* covered with hoarfrost. **3** *Arch.* a poetic variant of **hoary.** [OE *hār*]

hoard Ⓣ (hɔːd) *n* **1** an accumulated store hidden away for future use. **2** a cache of ancient coins, etc. ◆ *vb* **3** to accumulate (a hoard). [OE *hord*]
▸'**hoarder** *n*

> **USAGE NOTE** *Hoard* is sometimes wrongly written where *horde* is meant: *hordes* (not *hoards*) *of tourists.*

hoarding ('hɔːdɪŋ) *n* **1** Also called (esp. US and Canad.): **billboard.** a large board used for displaying advertising posters, as by a road. **2** a temporary wooden fence erected round a building or demolition site. [C19: from C15 *hoard* fence, from OF *hourd* palisade, of Gmc origin]

hoarfrost ('hɔːˌfrɒst) *n* a deposit of needle-like ice crystals formed on the ground by direct condensation at temperatures below freezing point. Also called: **white frost.**

hoarhound ('hɔːˌhaʊnd) *n* a variant spelling of **horehound.**

hoarse Ⓣ (hɔːs) *adj* **1** gratingly harsh in tone. **2** having a husky voice, as through illness, shouting, etc. [C14: from ON]
▸'**hoarsely** *adv* ▸'**hoarseness** *n*

hoarsen ('hɔːsᵊn) *vb* to make or become hoarse.

hoary Ⓣ ('hɔːrɪ) *adj* **hoarier, hoariest. 1** having grey or white hair. **2** white or whitish-grey in colour. **3** ancient or venerable.
▸'**hoariness** *n*

hoatzin (həʊ'ætsɪn) *n* a unique South American bird with clawed wing digits in the young. [C17: from American Sp., from Nahuatl *uatzin* pheasant]

hoax Ⓣ (həʊks) *n* **1** a deception, esp. a practical joke. ◆ *vb* **2** (*tr*) to deceive or play a joke on (someone). [C18: prob. from HOCUS]
▸'**hoaxer** *n*

hob[1] (hɒb) *n* **1** the flat top part of a cooking stove, or a separate flat surface, containing hotplates or burners. **2** a shelf beside an open fire, for keeping kettles, etc., hot. **3** a steel pattern used in forming a mould or die in cold metal. [C16: var. of obs. *hubbe;* ? rel. to HUB]

hob[2] (hɒb) *n* **1** a hobgoblin or elf. **2 raise** *or* **play hob.** *US inf.* to cause mischief. **3** a male ferret. [C14: var. of *Rob*, short for *Robin* or *Robert*]

hobble Ⓣ ('hɒbᵊl) *vb* **hobbles, hobbling, hobbled. 1** (*intr*) to walk with a lame awkward movement. **2** (*tr*) to fetter the legs of (a horse) in order to restrict movement. **3** (*intr*) to progress with difficulty. ◆ *n* **4** a strap, rope, etc., used to hobble a horse. **5** a limping gait. ◆ Also (for senses 2, 4): **hopple.** [C14: prob. from Low G]
▸'**hobbler** *n*

hobbledehoy (ˌhɒbᵊldɪ'hɔɪ) *n* a clumsy or bad-mannered youth. [C16: from earlier *hobbard de hoy*, from ?]

hobby[1] Ⓣ ('hɒbɪ) *n, pl* **hobbies. 1** an activity pursued in spare time for pleasure or relaxation. **2** *Arch.* a small horse. **3** short for **hobbyhorse** (sense 1). **4** an early form of bicycle, without pedals. [C14 *hobyn*, prob. var. of name *Robin*]
▸'**hobbyist** *n*

hobby[2] ('hɒbɪ) *n, pl* **hobbies.** any of several small Old World falcons. [C15: from OF *hobet*, from *hobe* falcon]

hobbyhorse ('hɒbɪˌhɔːs) *n* **1** a toy consisting of a stick with a figure of a horse's head at one end. **2** a rocking horse. **3** a figure of a horse attached to a performer's waist in a morris dance, etc. **4** a favourite topic (esp. in **on one's hobbyhorse**). [C16: from HOBBY[1], orig. a small horse; then generalized to apply to any pastime]

hobgoblin Ⓣ (ˌhɒb'gɒblɪn) *n* **1** a mischievous goblin. **2** a bogey; bugbear. [C16: from HOB[2] + GOBLIN]

hobnail ('hɒbˌneɪl) *n* **a** a short nail with a large head for protecting the soles of heavy footwear. **b** (*as modifier*): *hobnail boots.* [C16: from HOB[1] (in archaic sense: peg) + NAIL]
▸'**hobˌnailed** *adj*

hobnob Ⓣ ('hɒbˌnɒb) *vb* **hobnobs, hobnobbing, hobnobbed.** (*intr;* often foll. by *with*) **1** to socialize or talk informally. **2** *Obs.* to drink (with). [C18: from *hob or nob* to drink to one another in turns, ult. from OE *habban* to HAVE + *nabban* not to have]

hobo ('həʊbəʊ) *n, pl* **hobos** *or* **hoboes.** *Chiefly US & Canad.* **1** a tramp; vagrant. **2** a migratory worker. [C19 (US): from ?]
▸'**hoboism** *n*

Hobson's choice ('hɒbsᵊnz) *n* the choice of taking what is offered or nothing at all. [C16: after Thomas *Hobson* (1544–1631), E liveryman who gave his customers no choice but had them take the nearest horse]

hock[1] (hɒk) *n* **1** the joint at the tarsus of a horse or similar animal, corresponding to the human ankle. ◆ *vb* **2** another word for **hamstring.** [C16: short for *hockshin*, from OE *hōhsinu* heel sinew]

hock[2] (hɒk) *n* any of several white wines from the German Rhine. [C17: short for obs. *hockamore* from G *Hochheimer*]

hock[3] (hɒk) *Inf., chiefly US & Canad.* ◆ *vb* **1** (*tr*) to pawn or pledge. ◆ *n* **2** the state of being in pawn. **3 in hock. 3a** in prison. **3b** in debt. **3c** in pawn. [C19: from Du. *hok* prison, debt]

hockey ('hɒkɪ) *n* **1** Also called (esp. US and Canad.): **field hockey.** a game played on a field by two opposing teams of 11 players each, who try to hit a ball into their opponents' goal using long sticks curved at the end. **2** See **ice hockey.** [C19: from earlier *hawkey*, from ?]

hocus ('həʊkəs) *vb* **hocuses, hocusing, hocused** *or* **hocuses, hocussing, hocussed.** (*tr*) *Now rare.* **1** to trick. **2** to stupefy, esp. with a drug. **3** to drug (a drink).

hocus-pocus Ⓣ ('həʊkəs'pəʊkəs) *n* **1** trickery or chicanery. **2** an incantation used by conjurors or magicians. **3** conjuring skill. ◆ *vb* **hocus-pocuses, hocus-pocusing, hocus-pocused** *or* **hocus-pocuses, hocus-pocussing, hocus-pocussed. 4** to deceive or trick (someone). [C17: ? dog Latin invented by jugglers]

hod (hɒd) *n* **1** an open wooden box attached to a pole, for carrying bricks, mortar, etc. **2** a tall narrow coal scuttle. [C14: ?from C13 dialect *hot*, from OF *hotte* pannier, prob. of Gmc origin]

hodgepodge ('hɒdʒˌpɒdʒ) *n* a variant spelling (esp. US and Canad.) of **hotchpotch.**

Hodgkin's disease ('hɒdʒkɪnz) *n* a malignant disease, a form of lymphoma, characterized by enlargement of the lymph nodes, spleen, and liver. [C19: after Thomas *Hodgkin* (1798–1866), London physician, who first described it]

hodograph ('hɒdəˌgrɑːf) *n* a curve of which the radius vector represents the velocity of a moving particle. [C19: from Gk *hodos* way + -GRAPH]

hodometer (hɒ'dɒmɪtə) *n* another name for **odometer.**
▸**ho'dometry** *n*

hoe (həʊ) *n* **1** any of several kinds of long-handled hand implement used to till the soil, weed, etc. ◆ *vb* **hoes, hoeing, hoed. 2** to dig, scrape, weed, or till (surface soil) with or as if with a hoe. [C14: via OF *houe*, of Gmc origin]
▸'**hoer** *n*

hoedown ('həʊˌdaʊn) *n US & Canad.* **1** a boisterous square dance. **2** a party at which hoedowns are danced.

hog Ⓣ (hɒg) *n* **1** a domesticated pig, esp. a castrated male. **2** *US & Canad.* any mammal of the family Suidae; pig. **3** Also: **hogg.** *Dialect, Austral. & NZ.* another name for **hogget. 4** *Inf.* a greedy person. **5 go the whole hog.** *Sl.* to do something thoroughly or unreservedly. ◆ *vb* **hogs, hogging, hogged.** (*tr*) **6** *Sl.* to take more than one's share of. **7** to arch (the back) like a hog. **8** to cut (the mane) of (a horse) very short. [OE *hogg*, of Celtic origin]
▸'**hogger** *n* ▸'**hogˌlike** *adj*

hogan ('həʊgən) *n* a wooden dwelling covered with earth, typical of the Navaho Indians of North America. [of Amerind origin]

hogback ('hɒgˌbæk) *n* **1** Also called: **hog's back.** a narrow ridge with steep sides. **2** *Archaeol.* a tomb with sloping sides.

hogfish ('hɒgˌfɪʃ) *n, pl* **hogfish** *or* **hogfishes.** a wrasse that occurs in the Atlantic. The head of the male resembles a pig's snout.

THESAURUS

hoard *n* **1** = **store**, accumulation, cache, fall-back, fund, heap, mass, pile, reserve, stash, stockpile, supply ◆ *vb* **3** = **save**, accumulate, amass, buy up, cache, collect, deposit, garner, gather, hive, lay up, put away, put by, stash away (*inf.*), stockpile, store, treasure

hoarder *n* **3** = **saver**, collector, magpie (*Brit.*), miser, niggard

hoarse *adj* **1** = **rough**, discordant, grating, gravelly, growling, harsh, rasping, raucous **2** = **husky**, croaky, gruff, guttural, throaty
Antonyms *adj* harmonious, mellifluous, mellow, melodious, smooth

hoarseness *n* **2** = **croakiness**, a frog in one's throat, gruffness, huskiness, rasping, sore throat, throatiness, wheeziness

hoary *adj* **1** = **white-haired**, grey, grey-haired, grizzled **2** = **white**, frosty, grey, hoar, silvery **3** = **old**, aged, ancient, antiquated, antique, venerable

hoax *n* **1** = **trick**, canard, cheat, con (*inf.*), deception, fast one (*inf.*), fraud, imposture, joke, practical joke, prank, ruse, spoof (*inf.*), swindle ◆ *vb* **2** = **deceive**, bamboozle (*inf.*), befool, bluff, con (*sl.*), delude, dupe, fool, gull (*arch.*), hoodwink, hornswoggle (*sl.*), kid (*inf.*), swindle, take in (*inf.*), take (someone) for a ride (*inf.*), trick, wind up (*Brit. sl.*)

hoaxer *adj* **2** = **trickster**, bamboozler (*inf.*), hoodwinker, humbug, joker, practical joker, prankster, spoofer (*inf.*)

hobble *vb* **1, 3** = **limp**, dodder, falter, halt, shamble, shuffle, stagger, stumble, totter **2** = **tie**, clog, fasten, fetter, hamstring, restrict, shackle

hobby[1] *n* **1** = **pastime**, diversion, favourite occupation, (leisure) activity, leisure pursuit, relaxation, sideline

hobgoblin *n* **1** = **imp**, apparition, goblin, hob, spectre, spirit, sprite

hobnob *vb* **1** = **socialize**, associate, consort, fraternize, hang about, hang out (*inf.*), keep company, mingle, mix

hocus-pocus *n* **1** *Informal* = **trickery**, artifice, cheat, chicanery, deceit, deception, delusion, hoax, humbug, imposture, swindle **2** = **mumbo jumbo**, abracadabra, cant, gibberish, gobbledegook (*inf.*), Greek (*inf.*), hokum (*sl., chiefly US & Canad.*), jargon, nonsense, rigmarole **3** = **conjuring**, jugglery, legerdemain, prestidigitation, sleight of hand

hog *vb* **6** *Slang* = **monopolize**, be a dog in the manger, corner, corner the market in, dominate, tie up

hogget ('hɒgɪt) *n Dialect, Austral. & NZ.* a young sheep that has yet to be sheared. Also: **hog, hogg.**
hoggish ❶ ('hɒgɪʃ) *adj* selfish, gluttonous, or dirty.
Hogmanay (ˌhɒgmə'neɪ) *n (sometimes not cap.)* New Year's Eve in Scotland. [C17: ?from Norman F *hoguinane*, from OF *aguillanneuf* a New Year's Eve gift]
hognose snake ('hɒgˌnəʊz) *n* a North American nonvenomous snake that has a trowel-shaped snout and inflates its body when alarmed. Also called: **puff adder.**
hogshead ('hɒgzˌhɛd) *n* **1** a unit of capacity, used esp. for alcoholic beverages. It has several values. **2** a large cask. [C14: from ?]
hogtie ('hɒgˌtaɪ) *vb* **hogties, hogtying, hogtied.** *(tr) Chiefly US.* **1** to tie together the legs or the arms and legs of. **2** to impede, hamper, or thwart.
hogwash ❶ ('hɒgˌwɒʃ) *n* **1** *Inf.* nonsense. **2** pigswill.
hogweed ('hɒgˌwiːd) *n* any of several coarse weedy plants.
ho-hum ('həʊ'hʌm) *adj Inf.* lacking interest or inspiration; dull; mediocre: *a ho-hum collection of new releases.*
hoick (hɔɪk) *vb* to rise or raise abruptly and sharply. [C20: from ?]
hoi polloi ❶ ('hɔɪ pə'lɔɪ) *n* **the.** *Often derog.* the masses; common people. [Gk, lit.: the many]
hoist ❶ (hɔɪst) *vb* **1** *(tr)* to raise or lift up, esp. by mechanical means. ◆ *n* **2** any apparatus or device for hoisting. **3** the act of hoisting. **4** *Naut.* a group of signal flags. **5** the inner edge of a flag next to the staff. [C16: var. of *hoise*, prob. from Low G]
▸ **'hoister** *n*
hoity-toity ❶ (ˌhɔɪtɪ'tɔɪtɪ) *adj Inf.* arrogant or haughty. [C17: rhyming compound based on C16 *hoit* to romp, from ?]
hokey cokey ('həʊkɪ 'kəʊkɪ) *n* a dance routine performed to a cockney song of the same name.
hokonui (ˌhəʊkə'nuːiː) *n NZ.* illicit whisky. [from *Hokonui*, district of Southland region, NZ]
hokum ('həʊkəm) *n Sl., chiefly US & Canad.* **1** claptrap; bunk. **2** obvious or hackneyed material of a sentimental nature in a play, film, etc. [C20: prob. a blend of HOCUS-POCUS & BUNKUM]
Holarctic (həʊ'lɑːktɪk) *adj* of or denoting a zoogeographical region consisting of the entire arctic regions. [C19: from HOLO- + ARCTIC]
hold[1] ❶ (həʊld) *vb* **holds, holding, held. 1** to have or keep (an object) with or within the hands, arms, etc.; clasp. **2** *(tr)* to support: *to hold a drowning man's head above water.* **3** to maintain or be maintained in a specified state: *to hold firm.* **4** *(tr)* to set aside or reserve: *they will hold our tickets until tomorrow.* **5** (when *intr, usually used in commands*) to restrain or be restrained from motion, action, departure, etc.: *hold that man until the police come.* **6** *(intr)* to remain fast or unbroken: *that cable won't hold much longer.* **7** *(intr)* (of the weather) to remain dry and bright. **8** *(tr)* to keep the attention of. **9** *(tr)* to engage in or carry on: *to hold a meeting.* **10** *(tr)* to have the ownership, possession, etc., of: *he holds a law degree; who's holding the ace?* **11** *(tr)* to have the use of or responsibility for: *to hold office.* **12** *(tr)* to have the capacity for: *the carton will hold eight books.* **13** *(tr)* to be able to control the outward effects of drinking beer, spirits, etc. **14** (often foll. by *to* or *by*) to remain or cause to remain committed (to): *hold him to his promise.* **15** *(tr; takes a clause as object)* to claim: *he holds that the theory is incorrect.* **16** *(intr)* to remain relevant, valid, or true: *the old philosophies don't hold nowadays.* **17** *(tr)* to consider in a specified manner: *I hold him very dear.* **18** *(tr)* to defend successfully: *hold the fort against the attack.* **19** (sometimes foll. by *on*) *Music.* to sustain the sound of (a note) throughout its specified duration. **20** *(tr) Computing.* to retain (data) in a storage device after copying onto another storage device or location. **21 hold (good) for.** to apply or be relevant to: *the same rules hold for everyone.* **22 there is no holding him.** he is so spirited that he cannot be restrained. ◆ *n* **23** the act or method of holding fast or grasping. **24** something to hold onto, as for support or control. **25** an object or device that holds fast or grips something else. **26** controlling influence: *she has a hold on him.* **27** a short pause. **28** a prison or a cell in a prison. **29** *Wrestling.* a way of seizing one's opponent. **30** *Music.* a pause or fermata. **31a** a tenure, esp. of land. **31b** *(in combination): freehold.* **32** *Arch.* a fortified place. **33 no holds barred.** all limitations removed. ◆ See also **hold back, hold down,** etc. [OE *healdan*]
▸ **'holdable** *adj*
hold[2] (həʊld) *n* the space in a ship or aircraft for storing cargo. [C16: var. of HOLE]
holdall ('həʊldˌɔːl) *n Brit.* a large strong bag or basket. Usual US and Canad. name: **carryall.**
hold back ❶ *vb (adv)* **1** to restrain or be restrained. **2** *(tr)* to withhold: *he held back part of the payment.*
hold down *vb (tr, adv)* **1** to restrain or control. **2** *Inf.* to manage to retain or keep possession of: *to hold down two jobs at once.*
holder ❶ ('həʊldə) *n* **1** a person or thing that holds. **2a** a person who has possession or control of something. **2b** *(in combination): householder.* **3** *Law.* a person who has possession of a bill of exchange, cheque, or promissory note that he is legally entitled to enforce.
holdfast ('həʊldˌfɑːst) *n* **1** the act of gripping strongly. **2** any device used to secure an object, such as a hook, clamp, etc. **3** the organ of attachment of a seaweed or related plant.
hold forth ❶ *vb (adv)* **1** *(intr)* to speak for a long time or in public. **2** *(tr)* to offer (an attraction or enticement).
hold in *vb (tr, adv)* **1** to curb, control, or keep in check. **2** to conceal (feelings).
holding ❶ ('həʊldɪŋ) *n* **1** land held under a lease. **2** *(often pl)* property to which the holder has legal title, such as land, stocks, shares, and other investments. **3** *Sport.* the obstruction of an opponent with the hands or arms, esp. in boxing. ◆ *adj* **4** *Austral. inf.* in funds; having money.
holding company *n* a company with controlling shareholdings in one or more other companies.
holding operation *n* a plan or procedure devised to prolong the existing situation.
holding paddock *n Austral. & NZ.* a paddock in which cattle or sheep are kept temporarily, as before shearing, etc.
holding pattern *n* the oval or circular path of an aircraft flying around an airport awaiting permission to land.
hold off ❶ *vb (adv)* **1** *(tr)* to keep apart or at a distance. **2** *(intr;* often foll. by *from)* to refrain (from doing something).
hold on *vb (intr, adv)* **1** to maintain a firm grasp. **2** to continue or persist. **3** (foll. by *to*) to keep or retain: *hold on to those stamps as they'll soon be valuable.* **4** *Inf.* to keep a telephone line open. ◆ *sentence substitute.* **5** *Inf.* stop! wait!
hold out ❶ *vb (adv)* **1** *(tr)* to offer. **2** *(intr)* to last or endure. **3** *(intr)* to continue to stand firm, as a person refusing to succumb to persuasion. **4** *Chiefly US.* to withhold (something due). **5 hold out for.** to wait patiently for (the fulfilment of one's demands). **6 hold out on.** *Inf.* to keep from telling (a person) some important information.
hold over ❶ *vb (tr, mainly adv)* **1** to defer or postpone. **2** *(prep)* to intimidate (a person) with (a threat).
hold-up ❶ *n* **1** a robbery, esp. an armed one. **2** a delay; stoppage. ◆ *vb* **hold up.** *(tr, adv)* **3.** to delay; hinder. **4** to support. **5** to waylay in order to rob, esp. using a weapon. **6** to exhibit or present.

THESAURUS

hoggish *adj* = **greedy**, brutish, dirty, edacious, filthy, gluttonous, gross, mean, piggish, rapacious, ravenous, selfish, sordid, squalid, swinish, unclean
hogwash *n* **1** *Informal* = **nonsense**, balderdash, bilge *(inf.)*, bosh *(inf.)*, bunk, bunkum *or* buncombe *(chiefly US)*, cobblers *(Brit. taboo sl.)*, crap *(sl.)*, drivel, garbage *(inf.)*, hokum *(sl., chiefly US & Canad.)*, hooey *(sl.)*, hot air *(inf.)*, piffle *(inf.)*, poppycock *(inf.)*, rot, rubbish, shit *(taboo sl.)*, tommyrot, tosh *(sl., chiefly Brit.)*, trash, tripe *(inf.)*, twaddle
hoi polloi *n Often derog.* = **the common people**, *canaille*, commonalty, riffraff, the (common) herd, the great unwashed *(inf. & derogatory)*, the lower orders, the masses, the plebs, the populace, the proles *(derogatory sl., chiefly Brit.)*, the proletariat, the rabble, the third estate, the underclass
hoist *vb* **1** = **raise**, elevate, erect, heave, lift, rear, upraise ◆ *n* **2** = **lift**, crane, elevator, tackle, winch
hoity-toity *adj Informal* = **haughty**, arrogant, conceited, disdainful, high and mighty *(inf.)*, lofty, overweening, proud, scornful, snobbish, snooty *(inf.)*, stuck-up *(inf.)*, supercilious, toffee-nosed *(sl., chiefly Brit.)*, uppish *(Brit. inf.)*
hold[1] *vb* **1** = **grasp**, clasp, cleave, clinch, cling, clutch, cradle, embrace, enfold, grip **2** = **support**, bear, brace, carry, prop, shoulder, sustain, take **3** = **continue**, endure, last, persevere, persist, remain, resist, stay, wear **5** = **restrain**, arrest, bind, check, confine, curb, detain, impound, imprison, pound, stay, stop, suspend **9** = **convene**, assemble, call, carry on, celebrate, conduct, have, officiate at, preside over, run, solemnize **10** = **own**, have, keep, maintain, occupy, possess, retain **12** = **accommodate**, comprise, contain, have a capacity for, seat, take **15** = **consider**, assume, believe, deem, judge, maintain, presume, reckon, regard, think, view **16** = **apply**, be in force, be the case, exist, hold good, operate, remain true, remain valid, stand up ◆ *n* **23** = **grip**, clasp, clutch, grasp **24** = **foothold**, anchorage, footing, leverage, prop, purchase, stay, support, vantage **26** = **control**, ascendancy, authority, clout *(inf.)*, dominance, dominion, influence, mastery, pull *(inf.)*, sway
Antonyms *vb* ≠ **support:** break, come undone, give way, loosen ≠ **restrain:** free, let go, let loose, release ≠ **convene:** call off, cancel, postpone ≠ **own:** bestow, give, give away, give up, hand over, offer, turn over ≠ **consider:** deny, disavow, disclaim, put down, refute, reject
hold back *vb* **1** = **restrain**, check, control, curb, inhibit, rein, repress, stem the flow, suppress **2** = **withhold**, desist, forbear, keep back, refuse
holder *n* **1** = **case**, container, cover, housing, receptacle, sheath **2** = **owner**, bearer, custodian, incumbent, keeper, occupant, possessor, proprietor, purchaser
hold forth *vb* **1** = **speak**, declaim, descant, discourse, go on, harangue, lecture, orate, preach, speechify, spiel *(inf.)*, spout *(inf.)*
holding *n* **2** *often plural* = **property**, assets, estate, investments, land interests, possessions, resources, securities, stocks and shares
hold off *vb* **1** = **fend off**, keep off, rebuff, repel, repulse, stave off **2** = **put off**, avoid, defer, delay, keep from, postpone, refrain
hold out *vb* **1** = **offer**, extend, give, present, proffer **2** = **last**, carry on, continue, endure, hang on, persevere, persist, stand fast, stay the course, withstand
hold over *vb* **1** = **postpone**, adjourn, defer, delay, put off, suspend, take a rain check on *(US & Canad. inf.)*, waive
hold-up *n* **1** = **robbery**, burglary, mugging *(inf.)*, steaming *(inf.)*, stick-up *(sl., chiefly US)*, theft **2** = **delay**, bottleneck, difficulty, hitch, obstruction, setback, snag, stoppage, traffic jam, trouble, wait ◆ *vb* **hold up 3** = **delay**, detain, hinder, impede, retard, set back, slow down, stop **4** = **support**, bolster, brace, buttress, jack up, prop, shore up, sustain **5** = **rob**, mug *(inf.)*, stick up *(sl., chiefly US)*, waylay **6** = **exhibit**, display, flaunt, present, show

hold with Ⓣ *vb (intr, prep)* to support; approve of.

hole Ⓣ (həʊl) *n* **1** an area hollowed out in a solid. **2** an opening in or through something. **3** an animal's burrow. **4** *Inf.* an unattractive place, such as a town. **5** a fault (esp. in **pick holes in**). **6** *Sl.* a difficult and embarrassing situation. **7** the cavity in various games into which the ball must be thrust. **8** (on a golf course) **8a** each of the divisions of a course (usually 18) represented by the distance between the tee and a green. **8b** the score made in striking the ball from the tee into the hole. **9** *Physics.* a vacancy in a nearly full band of quantum states of electrons in a semiconductor or an insulator. Under the action of an electric field holes behave as carriers of positive charge. **10 hole in the wall.** *Inf.* a small dingy place, esp. one difficult to find. **11 in holes.** so worn as to be full of holes. **12 make a hole in.** to consume or use a great amount of (food, drink, money, etc.). ◆ *vb* **holes, holing, holed. 13** to make a hole or holes in (something). **14** (when *intr,* often foll. by *out*) *Golf.* to hit (the ball) into the hole. [OE *hol*]
▸**'holey** *adj*

hole-and-corner Ⓣ *adj (usually prenominal) Inf.* furtive or secretive.

hole in one *n Golf.* a shot from the tee that finishes in the hole. Also (esp. US): **ace.**

hole in the heart *n* a defect of the heart in which there is an abnormal opening in any of the walls dividing the four heart chambers.

hole up Ⓣ *vb (intr, adv)* **1** (of an animal) to hibernate. **2** *Inf.* to hide or remain secluded.

Holi ('həʊlɪ) *n* a Hindu spring festival, celebrated for two to five days, commemorating Krishna's dalliance with the cowgirls. Bonfires are lit and coloured powder and water thrown over celebrants. [after *Holika,* legendary female demon]

-holic *suffix forming noun* indicating desire for or dependence on; *workaholic; chocoholic.* [C20: abstracted from *(alco)holic*]

holiday Ⓣ ('hɒlɪˌdeɪ) *n* **1** *(often pl) Chiefly Brit.* a period in which a break is taken from work or studies for rest, travel, or recreation. US and Canad. word: **vacation. 2** a day on which work is suspended by law or custom, such as a religious festival, bank holiday, etc. Related adj: **ferial.** ◆ *vb* **3** *(intr) Chiefly Brit.* to spend a holiday. [OE *hāligdæg,* lit.: holy day]

holiday camp *n Brit.* a place, esp. one at the seaside, providing accommodation, recreational facilities, etc., for holiday-makers.

holiday-maker *n Brit.* a person who goes on holiday. US and Canad. equivalents: **vacationer, vacationist.**

holily ('həʊlɪlɪ) *adv* in a holy, devout, or sacred manner.

holiness Ⓣ ('həʊlɪnɪs) *n* the state or quality of being holy.

Holiness ('həʊlɪnɪs) *n* (preceded by *His* or *Your*) a title reserved for the pope.

holism ('həʊlɪzəm) *n* **1** any doctrine that a system may have properties over and above those of its parts and their organization. **2** (in medicine) the consideration of the complete person in the treatment of disease. [C20: from HOLO- + -ISM]
▸**ho'listic** *adj*

holland ('hɒlənd) *n* a coarse linen cloth. [C15: after *Holland,* where it was made]

hollandaise sauce (ˌhɒlən'deɪz, 'hɒlənˌdeɪz) *n* a rich sauce of egg yolks, butter, vinegar, etc. [C19: from F *sauce hollandaise* Dutch sauce]

Hollands ('hɒləndz) *n (functioning as sing)* Dutch gin, often sold in stone bottles. [C18: from Du. *hollandsch genever*]

holler Ⓣ ('hɒlə) *Inf.* ◆ *vb* **1** to shout or yell (something). ◆ *n* **2** a shout; call. [var. of C16 *hollow,* from *holla,* from F *holà* stop! (lit.: ho there!)]

hollo ('hɒləʊ) *or* **holla** ('hɒlə) *n, pl* **hollos** *or* **hollas,** *interj* **1** a cry for attention, or of encouragement. ◆ *vb* **2** *(intr)* to shout. [C16: from F *holà* ho there!]

hollow Ⓣ ('hɒləʊ) *adj* **1** having a hole or space within; not solid. **2** having a sunken area; concave. **3** deeply set: *hollow cheeks.* **4** (of sounds) as if resounding in a hollow place. **5** without substance or validity. **6** hungry or empty. **7** insincere; cynical. ◆ *adv* **8 beat (someone) hollow.** *Brit. inf.* to defeat thoroughly. ◆ *n* **9** a cavity, opening, or space in or within something. **10** a depression in the land. ◆ *vb* (often foll. by *out,* usually when *tr*) **11** to make or become hollow. **12** to form (a hole, cavity, etc.) or (of a hole, etc.) to be formed. [C12: from *holu,* inflected form of OE *holh* cave]
▸**'hollowly** *adv* ▸**'hollowness** *n*

hollow-eyed *adj* with the eyes appearing to be sunk into the face, as from excessive fatigue.

holly ('hɒlɪ) *n, pl* **hollies. 1** a tree or shrub having bright red berries and shiny evergreen leaves with prickly edges. **2** its branches, used for Christmas decorations. **3 holly oak.** another name for **holm oak.** [OE *holegn*]

hollyhock ('hɒlɪˌhɒk) *n* a tall plant with stout hairy stems and spikes of white, yellow, red, or purple flowers. Also called (US): **rose mallow.** [C16: from HOLY + *hock,* from OE *hoc* mallow]

Hollywood ('hɒlɪˌwʊd) *n* **1** a NW suburb of Los Angeles, California: centre of the US film industry. **2a** the US film industry. **2b** *(as modifier)*: *a Hollywood star.*

holm[1] (həʊm) *n Dialect, chiefly northwestern English.* **1** an island in a river or lake. **2** low flat land near a river. [OE *holm* sea, island]

holm[2] (həʊm) *n* **1** short for **holm oak. 2** *Chiefly Brit.* a dialect word for **holly.** [C14: var. of obs. *holin,* from OE *holegn* holly]

holmium ('hɒlmɪəm) *n* a malleable silver-white metallic element of the lanthanide series. Symbol: Ho; atomic no.: 67; atomic wt.: 164.93. [C19: from NL *Holmia* Stockholm]

holm oak *n* an evergreen Mediterranean oak tree with prickly leaves resembling holly. Also called: **holm, holly oak, ilex.**

holo- *or before a vowel* **hol-** *combining form.* whole or wholly: *holograph.* [from Gk *holos*]

holocaust Ⓣ ('hɒləˌkɔːst) *n* **1** great destruction or loss of life or the source of such destruction, esp. fire. **2** *(usually cap.)* **the.** the mass murder of some six million European Jews by the Germans during World War II. **3** a rare word for **burnt offering.** [C13: from LL *holocaustum* whole burnt offering, from Gk, from HOLO- + *kaiein* to burn]

Holocene ('hɒləˌsiːn) *adj* **1** of, denoting, or formed in the second and most recent epoch of the Quaternary period, which began 10 000 years ago. ◆ *n* **2 the.** the Holocene epoch or rock series. ◆ Also: **Recent.**

hologram ('hɒləˌgræm) *n* a photographic record produced by illuminating the object with coherent light (as from a laser) and, without using lenses, exposing a film to light reflected from this object and to a direct beam of coherent light. When interference patterns on the film are illuminated by the coherent light a three-dimensional image is produced.

holograph ('hɒləˌgrɑːf) *n* a book or document handwritten by its author; original manuscript; autograph.

holography (hɒ'lɒgrəfɪ) *n* the science or practice of producing holograms.
▸**holographic** (ˌhɒlə'græfɪk) *adj* ▸ˌ**holo'graphically** *adv*

holohedral (ˌhɒlə'hiːdrəl) *adj* (of a crystal) exhibiting all the planes required for the symmetry of the crystal system.

holophytic (ˌhɒlə'fɪtɪk) *adj* (of plants) capable of synthesizing their food from inorganic molecules, esp. by photosynthesis.

holothurian (ˌhɒlə'θjʊərɪən) *n* **1** an echinoderm of the class *Holothuroidea,* having a leathery elongated body with a ring of tentacles around the mouth. ◆ *adj* **2** of the *Holothuroidea.* [C19: from NL *Holothūria,* name of type genus, from L: water polyp, from Gk, from ?]

hols (hɒlz) *pl n Brit. school sl.* holidays.

holster ('həʊlstə) *n* a sheathlike leather case for a pistol, attached to a belt or saddle. [C17: via Du., of Gmc origin]

holt[1] (həʊlt) *n Arch. or poetic.* a wood or wooded hill. [OE *holt*]

holt[2] (həʊlt) *n* the lair of an animal, esp. an otter. [C16: from HOLD[1]]

holy Ⓣ ('həʊlɪ) *adj* **holier, holiest. 1** of or associated with God or a deity; sacred. **2** endowed or invested with extreme purity. **3** devout or virtuous. **4 holier-than-thou.** offensively sanctimonious or self-righteous. ◆ *n, pl* **holies. 5** a sacred place. [OE *hālig, hǣlig*]

THESAURUS

hold with *vb* = **approve of,** agree to *or* with, be in favour of, countenance, subscribe to, support, take kindly to
Antonyms *vb* be against, disagree with, disapprove of, hold out against, oppose

hole *n* **1** = **cavity,** cave, cavern, chamber, depression, excavation, hollow, pit, pocket, scoop, shaft **2** = **opening,** aperture, breach, break, crack, fissure, gap, orifice, outlet, perforation, puncture, rent, split, tear, vent **3** = **burrow,** covert, den, earth, lair, nest, retreat, shelter **4** *Informal* = **hovel,** dive, dump *(inf.),* joint *(sl.),* slum **5** = **fault,** defect, discrepancy, error, fallacy, flaw, inconsistency, loophole **6** *Slang* = **predicament,** dilemma, fix *(inf.),* hot water *(inf.),* imbroglio, jam *(inf.),* mess, quandary, scrape *(inf.),* spot *(inf.),* tangle, tight spot

hole-and-corner *adj Informal* = **furtive,** backstairs, clandestine, secret, secretive, sneaky *(inf.),* stealthy, surreptitious, underhand, under the counter *(inf.)*
Antonyms *adj* above-board, candid, frank, open, public

hole up *vb* **1** = **hibernate 2** *Informal* = **hide,** go into hiding, go to earth, shelter, take cover, take refuge

holiday *n* **1** = **vacation,** away day, break, leave, recess, time off **2** = **festival,** anniversary, bank holiday, celebration, feast, festivity, fête, gala, public holiday, red-letter day, saint's day

holiness *n* = **sanctity,** blessedness, devoutness, divinity, godliness, piety, purity, religiousness, righteousness, sacredness, saintliness, spirituality, virtuousness

holler *Informal* ◆ *vb, n* **1, 2** = **yell,** bawl, bellow, call, cheer, clamour, cry, hail, halloo, hollo, hurrah, huzzah, roar, shout, whoop

hollow *adj* **1** = **empty,** not solid, unfilled, vacant, void **2, 3** = **sunken,** cavernous, concave, deep-set, depressed, indented **4** = **toneless,** deep, dull, expressionless, flat, low, muffled, muted, reverberant, rumbling, sepulchral **5** = **toneless,** empty, fruitless, futile, meaningless, pointless, Pyrrhic, specious, unavailing, useless, vain, worthless **6** = **hungry,** empty, esurient, famished, ravenous, starved **7** = **insincere,** artificial, cynical, deceitful, faithless, false, flimsy, hollow-hearted, hypocritical, treacherous, unsound, weak ◆ *adv* **8 beat (someone) hollow** *Brit. informal* = **defeat,** hammer *(inf.),* outdo, overcome, rout, thrash, trounce, worst ◆ *n* **9** = **cavity,** basin, bowl, cave, cavern, concavity, crater, cup, den, dent, depression, dimple, excavation, hole, indentation, pit, trough **10** = **valley,** bottom, dale, dell, dingle, glen ◆ *vb* **11** = **scoop,** channel, dig, dish, excavate, furrow, gouge, groove, pit
Antonyms *adj* ≠ **empty:** full, occupied, solid ≠ **sunken:** convex, rounded ≠ **toneless:** expressive, vibrant ≠ **worthless:** gratifying, meaningful, pleasing, satisfying, valuable, worthwhile ≠ **insincere:** genuine ◆ *n* ≠ **cavity:** bump, mound, projection ≠ **valley:** bluff, height, hill, knoll, mountain, rise

holocaust *n* **1** = **genocide,** annihilation, carnage, conflagration, destruction, devastation, fire, inferno, massacre, mass murder, pogrom

holy *adj* **1** = **sacred,** blessed, consecrated, dedicated, hallowed, sacrosanct, sanctified, vener-

Holy Communion *n* **1** the celebration of the Eucharist. **2** the consecrated elements.

holy day *n* a day on which a religious festival is observed.

Holy Father *n RC Church.* the pope.

Holy Ghost *n* another name for the **Holy Spirit.**

Holy Grail *n* **1** Also called: **Grail, Sangraal.** (in medieval legend) the bowl used by Jesus at the Last Supper. It was brought to Britain by Joseph of Arimathea, where it became the quest of many knights. **2** *Inf.* any desired ambition or goal: *the Holy Grail of infrared astronomy.* [C14: *grail* from OF *graal,* from Med. L *gradālis* bowl, from ?]

Holy Land *n* **the.** another name for Palestine.

holy of holies *n* **1** any place of special sanctity. **2** (*cap.*) the innermost compartment of the Jewish tabernacle, where the Ark was enshrined.

holy orders *pl n* **1** the sacrament whereby a person is admitted to the Christian ministry. **2** the grades of the Christian ministry. **3** the status of an ordained Christian minister.

Holy Roman Empire *n* the complex of European territories under the rule of the Frankish or German king who bore the title of Roman emperor, beginning with the coronation of Charlemagne in 800 A.D.

Holy Scripture *n* another term for **Scripture.**

Holy See *n RC Church.* **1** the see of the pope as bishop of Rome. **2** the Roman curia.

Holy Spirit *n Christianity.* the third person of the Trinity. Also called: **Holy Ghost.**

holystone ('həʊlɪˌstəʊn) *n* **1** a soft sandstone used for scrubbing the decks of a vessel. ◆ *vb* **holystones, holystoning, holystoned. 2** (*tr*) to scrub (a vessel's decks) with a holystone. [C19: ?from its being used in a kneeling position]

holy synod *n* the governing body of any of the Orthodox Churches.

holy water *n* water that has been blessed by a priest for use in symbolic rituals of purification.

Holy Week *n* the week preceding Easter Sunday.

Holy Willie ('wɪlɪ) *n* a person who is hypocritically pious. [C18: from Burns' *Holy Willie's Prayer*]

Holy Writ *n* another term for **Scripture.**

homage Ⓣ ('hɒmɪdʒ) *n* **1** a public show of respect or honour towards someone or something (esp. in **pay** *or* **do homage to**). **2** (in feudal society) the act of respect and allegiance made by a vassal to his lord. [C13: from OF, from *home* man, from L *homo*]

homburg ('hɒmbɜːg) *n* a man's hat of soft felt with a dented crown and a stiff upturned brim. [C20: after *Homburg,* in Germany, where orig. made]

home Ⓣ (həʊm) *n* **1** the place where one lives. **2** a house or other dwelling. **3** a family or other group living in a house. **4** a person's country, city, etc., esp. viewed as a birthplace or a place dear to one. **5** the habitat of an animal. **6** the place where something is invented, founded, or developed. **7** a building or organization set up to care for people in a certain category, such as orphans, the aged, etc. **8** *Sport.* one's own ground: *the match is at home.* **9a** the objective towards which a player strives in certain sports. **9b** an area where a player is safe from attack. **10 a home from home.** a place other than one's own home where one can be at ease. **11 at home. 11a** in one's own home or country. **11b** at ease. **11c** giving an informal party at one's own home. **12 at home in, on,** *or* **with.** familiar with. **13 home and dry.** *Brit. sl.* definitely safe or successful. Austral. and NZ equivalent: **home and hosed. 14 near home.** concerning one deeply. ◆ *adj* (*usually prenominal*) **15** of one's home, country, etc.; domestic. **16** (of an activity) done in one's house: *home taping.* **17** *Sport.* relating to one's own ground: *a home game.* **18** *US.* central; principal: *the company's home office.* ◆ *adv* **19** to or at home: *I'll be home tomorrow.* **20** to or on the point. **21** to the fullest extent: *hammer the nail home.* **22 bring home to. 22a** to make clear to. **22b** to place the blame on. **23 nothing to write home about.** *Inf.* of no particular interest: *the film was nothing to write home about.* ◆ *vb* **homes, homing, homed. 24** (*intr*) (of birds and other animals) to return home accurately from a distance. **25** (often foll. by *in on* or *onto*) to direct or be directed onto a point or target, esp. by automatic navigational aids. **26** to send or go home. **27** (*tr*) to furnish with a home. **28** (*intr*; often foll. by *in* or *in on*) to be directed towards a goal, target, etc. [OE *hām*]

home banking *n* a system whereby a person at home or in an office can use a computer with a modem to call up information from a bank or to transfer funds electronically.

homeboy ('həʊmˌbɔɪ) *n Sl., chiefly US.* **1** a close friend. **2** a person from one's home town or neighbourhood. **3** a member of a neighbourhood gang. [C20: US rap-music usage]
► **'homeˌgirl** *fem n*

home-brew *n* **1** a beer or other alcoholic drink brewed at home rather than commercially. **2** *Canad. inf.* a professional football player who was born in Canada and is not an import.
► **ˌhome-'brewed** *adj*

homecoming ('həʊmˌkʌmɪŋ) *n* **1** the act of coming home. **2** *US.* an annual celebration held by a university, college, or school for former students.

Home Counties *pl n* the counties surrounding London.

home economics *n* (*functioning as sing or pl*) the study of diet, budgeting, child care, and other subjects concerned with running a home.

home farm *n Brit.* (esp. formerly) a farm attached to and providing food for a large country house.

Home Guard *n* a volunteer part-time military force recruited to defend the United Kingdom in World War II.

home help *n Brit.* a woman employed, esp. by a local authority, to do housework in a person's home. NZ equivalent: **home aid.**

homeland Ⓣ ('həʊmˌlænd) *n* **1** the country in which one lives or was born. **2** the official name for a **Bantustan.**

homeless Ⓣ ('həʊmlɪs) *adj* **a** having nowhere to live. **b** (*as collective n*; preceded by *the*): *the homeless.*
► **'homelessness** *n*

homely Ⓣ ('həʊmlɪ) *adj* **homelier, homeliest. 1** characteristic of or suited to the ordinary home; unpretentious. **2** (of a person) **2a** *Brit.* warm and domesticated. **2b** *Chiefly US & Canad.* plain.
► **'homeliness** *n*

home-made *adj* **1** (esp. of foods) made at home or on the premises, esp. of high quality ingredients. **2** crudely fashioned.

homeo-, homoeo-, *or* **homoio-** *combining form.* like or similar: *homeomorphism.* [from L *homoeo-,* from Gk *homoio-,* from *homos* same]

Home Office *n Brit. government.* the department responsible for the maintenance of law and order, and all other domestic affairs not assigned to another department.

homeopathy *or* **homoeopathy** (ˌhəʊmɪ'ɒpəθɪ) *n* a method of treating disease by the use of small amounts of a drug that, in healthy persons, produces symptoms similar to those of the disease being treated.
► **homeopathic** *or* **homoeopathic** (ˌhəʊmɪə'pæθɪk) *adj* ► **homeopathist, homoeopathist** (ˌhəʊmɪ'ɒpəθɪst) *or* **homeopath, homoeopath** ('həʊmɪəˌpæθ) *n*

homeostasis *or* **homoeostasis** (ˌhəʊmɪəʊ'steɪsɪs) *n* **1** the maintenance of metabolic equilibrium within an animal by a tendency to compensate for disrupting changes. **2** the maintenance of equilibrium within a social group, person, etc.

homeowner ('həʊmˌəʊnə) *n* a person who owns the house in which he or she lives.
► **ˌhome'ownership** *n*

home page *n Computing.* (on a website) the main document relating to an individual or an institution that provides introductory information about a website with links to the actual details of services or information provided.

homer ('həʊmə) *n* a homing pigeon.

Homeric (həʊ'merɪk) *adj* **1** of, relating to, or resembling Homer, Greek poet (circa 800 B.C.), to whom are attributed the *Iliad* and the *Odyssey,* or his poems. **2** imposing or heroic.

home rule *n* **1** self-government, esp. in domestic affairs. **2** the partial autonomy sometimes granted to a national minority or a colony.

Home Secretary *n Brit. government.* the head of the Home Office.

homesick ('həʊmˌsɪk) *adj* depressed or melancholy at being away from home and family.
► **'homeˌsickness** *n*

homespun Ⓣ ('həʊmˌspʌn) *adj* **1** having plain or unsophisticated character. **2** woven or spun at home. ◆ *n* **3** cloth made at home or made of yarn spun at home.

homestead ('həʊmˌsted, -stɪd) *n* **1** a house or estate and the adjoining land, buildings, etc., esp. a farm. **2** (in the US) a house and adjoining land designated by the owner as his fixed residence and exempt

THESAURUS

able, venerated **2** = **devout**, divine, faithful, god-fearing, godly, hallowed, pious, pure, religious, righteous, saintly, sublime, virtuous **4** **holier-than-thou** = **self-righteous**, goody-goody, pietistic, pietistical, priggish, religiose, sanctimonious, self-satisfied, smug, squeaky-clean, unctuous

Antonyms *adj* ≠ **sacred:** desecrated, unconsecrated, unhallowed, unholy, unsanctified ≠ **devout:** blasphemous, corrupt, earthly, evil, human, immoral, impious, irreligious, sacrilegious, secular, sinful, unholy, wicked, worldly

homage *n* **1** = **respect**, admiration, adoration, adulation, awe, deference, devotion, duty, esteem, honour, reverence, worship **2** = **allegiance**, devotion, faithfulness, fealty, fidelity, loyalty, obeisance, service, tribute, troth (*arch.*)

Antonyms *n* ≠ **respect:** condemnation, contempt, disdain, disregard, disrespect, irreverence, scorn

home *n* **1, 2** = **dwelling**, abode, domicile, dwelling place, habitation, house, pad (*sl.*), residence **4** = **birthplace**, family, fireside, hearth, homestead, home town, household **5** = **territory**, abode, element, environment, habitat, habitation, haunt, home ground, range, stamping ground **11 at home: a** = **having guests**, available, present **b** comfortable, familiar, relaxed **c** entertaining, giving a party, receiving **12 at home in, on,** *or* **with** = **familiar with**, conversant with, knowledgeable, proficient, skilled, well-versed ◆ *adj* **15** = **domestic**, central, familiar, family, household, inland, internal, local, national, native ◆ *n* **22a bring home to** = **make clear**, drive home, emphasize, impress upon, press home

homeland *n* **1** = **native land**, country of origin, fatherland, mother country, motherland

homeless *adj* **a** = **destitute**, abandoned, displaced, dispossessed, down-and-out, exiled, forlorn, forsaken, outcast, unsettled ◆ *n* **b the homeless** = **vagrants**, dossers (*Brit. sl.*), squatters

homely *adj* **1** = **comfortable**, comfy (*inf.*), cosy, domestic, downhome (*sl., chiefly US*), down-to-earth, everyday, familiar, friendly, homelike, homespun, homy, informal, modest, natural, ordinary, plain, simple, unaffected, unassuming, unfussy, unpretentious, welcoming

Antonyms *adj* affected, elaborate, elegant, grand, ostentatious, pretentious, refined, regal, sophisticated, splendid

homespun *adj* **1** = **unsophisticated**, artless,

under the homestead laws from seizure and forced sale for debts. **3** (in western Canada) a piece of land granted to a settler by the federal government. **4** *Austral. & NZ.* (on a sheep or cattle station) the owner's or manager's residence; in New Zealand, the term includes all outbuildings.

Homestead Act *n* **1** an act passed by the US Congress in 1862 making available to settlers 160-acre tracts of public land for cultivation. **2** (in Canada) a similar act passed by the Canadian Parliament in 1872.

homesteader ('həʊm,stɛdə) *n US and Canad.* a person who possesses land under a homestead law.

homestead law *n* (in the US and Canada) any of various laws conferring privileges on owners of homesteads.

home straight *n* **1** *Horse racing.* the section of a racecourse forming the approach to the finish. **2** the final stage of an undertaking. ◆ Also (chiefly US): **home stretch.**

home truth *n* (*often pl*) an unpleasant fact told to a person about himself.

home unit *n Austral. & NZ.* a self-contained residence which is part of a series of similar residences. Often shortened to **unit.**

homeward ('həʊmwəd) *adj* **1** going home. **2** (of a voyage, etc.) returning to the home port. ◆ *adv also* **homewards. 3** towards home.

homework ('həʊm,wɜːk) *n* **1** school work done at home. **2** any preparatory study. **3** work done at home for pay.

homey ('həʊmɪ) *adj* **homier, homiest.** a variant spelling (esp. US) of **homy.**
▸**'homeyness** *n*

homicide ❶ ('hɒmɪ,saɪd) *n* **1** the killing of a human being by another person. **2** a person who kills another. [C14: from OF, from L *homo* man + *caedere* to slay]
▸**,homi'cidal** *adj*

homiletics (,hɒmɪ'lɛtɪks) *n* (*functioning as sing*) the art of preaching or writing sermons. [C17: from Gk *homilētikos* cordial, from *homilein;* see HOMILY]

homily ❶ ('hɒmɪlɪ) *n, pl* **homilies. 1** a sermon. **2** moralizing talk or writing. [C14: from Church L *homīlia,* from Gk: discourse, from *homilein* to converse with, from *homilos* crowd, from *homou* together + *ilē* crowd]
▸**,homi'letic** *adj* ▸**'homilist** *n*

homing ('həʊmɪŋ) *n* (*modifier*) **1** *Zool.* relating to the ability to return home after travelling great distances. **2** (of an aircraft, missile, etc.) capable of guiding itself onto a target.

homing pigeon *n* any breed of pigeon developed for its homing instinct, used for racing. Also called: **homer.**

hominid ('hɒmɪnɪd) *n* **1** any primate of the family Hominidae, which includes modern man (*Homo sapiens*) and the extinct precursors of man. ◆ *adj* **2** of or belonging to the Hominidae. [C19: via NL from L *homo* man + -ID[1]]

hominoid ('hɒmɪ,nɔɪd) *adj* **1** of or like man; manlike. **2** of or belonging to the primate family, which includes the anthropoid apes and man. ◆ *n* **3** a hominoid animal. [C20: from L *homin-, homo* man + -OID]

hominy ('hɒmɪnɪ) *n Chiefly US.* coarsely ground maize prepared as a food by boiling in milk or water. [C17: prob. of Algonquian origin]

hominy grits *pl n US.* finely ground hominy.

homo ('həʊməʊ) *n, pl* **homos.** *Inf., derog.* short for **homosexual.**

Homo ('həʊməʊ) *n* a genus of hominids including modern man (see ***Homo sapiens***) and several extinct species of primitive man. [L: man]

homo- *combining form.* same or like: *homologous; homosexual.* [via L from Gk *homos* same]

homocyclic (,həʊməʊ'saɪklɪk) *adj* (of a chemical compound) containing a closed ring of atoms of the same kind, esp. carbon atoms.

homoeo- *combining form.* a variant of **homeo-.**

homogamy (hɒ'mɒgəmɪ) *n* **1** a condition in which all the flowers of an inflorescence are either of the same sex or hermaphrodite. **2** the maturation of the anthers and stigmas at the same time, ensuring self-pollination.
▸**ho'mogamous** *adj*

homogeneous ❶ (,həʊmə'dʒiːnɪəs, ,hɒm-) *adj* **1** composed of similar or identical parts or elements. **2** of uniform nature. **3** similar in kind or nature. **4** *Maths.* containing terms of the same degree with respect to all the variables, as in $x^2 + 2xy + y^2$.
▸**homogeneity** (,həʊməʊdʒɪ'niːɪtɪ, ,hɒm-) *n* ▸**,homo'geneousness** *n*

homogenize *or* **homogenise** (hɒ'mɒdʒɪ,naɪz) *vb* **homogenizes, homogenizing, homogenized** *or* **homogenises, homogenising, homogenised. 1** (*tr*) to break up the fat globules in (milk or cream) so that they are evenly distributed. **2** to make or become homogeneous.
▸**ho,mogeni'zation** *or* **ho,mogeni'sation** *n* ▸**ho'moge,nizer** *or* **ho'moge,niser** *n*

homogenous (hə'mɒdʒɪnəs) *adj* of, relating to, or exhibiting homogeny.

homogeny (hɒ'mɒdʒɪnɪ) *n Biol.* similarity in structure because of common ancestry. [C19: from Gk *homogeneia* community of origin, from *homogenēs* of the same kind]

homograph ('hɒmə,grɑːf) *n* one of a group of words spelt in the same way but having different meanings.
▸**,homo'graphic** *adj*

homoiothermic (həʊ,mɔɪə'θɜːmɪk) *or* **homothermal** (,həʊməʊ'θɜːməl, ,hɒm-) *adj* having a constant body temperature, usually higher than the temperature of the surroundings; warm-blooded.
▸**ho'moio,thermy** *or* **'homo,thermy** *n*

homologize *or* **homologise** (hɒ'mɒlə,dʒaɪz) *vb* **homologizes, homologizing, homologized** *or* **homologises, homologising, homologised.** to be, show to be, or make homologous.

homologous ❶ (həʊ'mɒləgəs, hɒ-), **homological** (,həʊ-mə'lɒdʒɪk[ə]l, ,hɒm-), *or* **homologic** *adj* **1** having a related or similar position, structure, etc. **2** *Biol.* (of organs and parts) having the same evolutionary origin but different functions: *the wing of a bat and the paddle of a whale are homologous.*
▸**,homo'logically** *adv* ▸**'homo,logue** *or US* (*sometimes*) **'homolog** *n*

homology (həʊ'mɒlədʒɪ) *n, pl* **homologies.** the condition of being homologous. [C17: from Gk *homologia* agreement, from *homologos* agreeing, from HOMO- + *legein* to speak]

homolosine projection (hɒ'mɒlə,saɪn) *n* a map projection of the world on which the oceans are distorted to allow for greater accuracy in representing the continents. [C20: from Gk *homologos* agreeing + SINE[1]]

homomorphism (,həʊməʊ'mɔːfɪzəm, ,hɒm-) *or* **homomorphy** *n Biol.* similarity in form.
▸**,homo'morphic** *or* **,homo'morphous** *adj*

homonym ('hɒmənɪm) *n* **1** one of a group of words spelt in the same way but having different meanings. Cf. **homograph, homophone. 2** *Biol.* a specific or generic name that has been used for two or more different organisms. [C17: from L *homōnymum,* from Gk, from *homōnumos* of the same name; see HOMO-, -ONYM]
▸**,homo'nymic** *or* **ho'monymous** *adj*

homophobia (,həʊməʊ'fəʊbɪə) *n* intense hatred or fear of homosexuals or homosexuality. [C20: from HOMO(SEXUAL) + -PHOBIA]
▸**'homo,phobe** *n* ▸**,homo'phobic** *adj*

homophone ('hɒmə,fəʊn) *n* **1** one of a group of words pronounced in the same way but differing in meaning or spelling or both, as *bear* and *bare.* **2** a written letter or combination of letters that represents the same speech sound as another: *"ph" is a homophone of "f".*

homophonic (,hɒmə'fɒnɪk) *adj* of or relating to music in which the parts move together rather than exhibit individual rhythmic independence.

homopterous (həʊ'mɒptərəs) *or* **homopteran** *adj* of or belonging to a suborder of hemipterous insects having wings of a uniform texture held over the back at rest. [C19: from Gk *homopteros,* from HOMO- + *pteron* wing]

Homo sapiens ('sæpɪ,ɛnz) *n* the specific name of modern man; the only extant species of the genus *Homo.* This species also includes some extinct types of primitive man, such as Cro-Magnon man. [NL, from L *homo* man + *sapiens* wise]

homosexual ❶ (,həʊməʊ'sɛksjʊəl, ,hɒm-) *n* **1** a person who is sexually attracted to members of the same sex. ◆ *adj* **2** of or relating to homosexuals or homosexuality. **3** of or relating to the same sex.

homosexuality (,həʊməʊ,sɛksjʊ'ælɪtɪ, ,hɒm-) *n* sexual attraction to or sexual relations with members of the same sex.

homozygote (,həʊməʊ'zaɪgəʊt) *n* an animal or plant that is homozygous and breeds true to type.
▸**homozygotic** (,həʊməʊzaɪ'gɒtɪk) *adj*

homozygous (,həʊməʊ'zaɪgəs) *adj Genetics.* (of an organism) having identical alleles for any one gene: *these two fruit flies are homozygous for red eye colour.*

homunculus (hɒ'mʌŋkjʊləs) *n, pl* **homunculi** (-,laɪ). a miniature man; midget. Also called: **homuncule** (həʊ'mʌŋkjuːl). [C17: from L, dim. of *homo* man]
▸**ho'muncular** *adj*

homy ❶ *or esp. US* **homey** ('həʊmɪ) *adj* **homier, homiest.** like a home; cosy.
▸**'hominess** *or esp. US* **'homeyness** *n*

hon. *abbrev. for:* **1** honorary. **2** honourable.

Hon. *abbrev. for* Honourable (title).

honcho ('hɒntʃəʊ) *n, pl* **honchos.** *Inf., chiefly US.* the person in charge; the boss. [C20: from Japanese *han'chō* group leader]

THESAURUS

homely, home-made, inelegant, plain, rough, rude, rustic, unpolished

homicidal *adj* **1, 2** = **murderous,** deadly, death-dealing, lethal, maniacal, mortal

homicide *n* **1** = **murder,** bloodshed, killing, manslaughter, slaying **2** = **murderer,** killer, slayer

homily *n* **1** = **sermon,** address, discourse, lecture, preaching, preachment

homogeneity *n* **1-3** = **uniformity,** analogousness, comparability, consistency, correspondence, identicalness, oneness, sameness, similarity

homogeneous *adj* **1-3** = **uniform,** akin, alike, analogous, cognate, comparable, consistent, identical, kindred, similar, unvarying
Antonyms *adj* different, disparate, dissimilar, divergent, diverse, heterogeneous, manifold, mixed, unlike, unrelated, varied, various, varying

homologous *adj* **1** = **similar,** analogous, comparable, correspondent, corresponding, like, parallel, related

homosexual *adj* **2** = **gay,** bent (*sl.*), camp (*inf.*), dykey (*sl.*), homoerotic, lesbian, pink (*inf.*), queer (*inf., derogatory*), sapphic

homy *adj* = **cosy,** comfortable, comfy (*inf.*), congenial, domestic, familiar, friendly, informal, intimate, pleasant, warm

hone ⓣ (həʊn) *n* **1** a fine whetstone for sharpening. ◆ *vb* **hones, honing, honed. 2** (*tr*) to sharpen or polish with or as if with a hone. [OE *hān* stone]

> **USAGE NOTE** *Hone* is sometimes wrongly used where *home* is meant: *this device makes it easier to home in on* (not *hone in on*) *the target.*

honest ⓣ ('ɒnɪst) *adj* **1** not given to lying, cheating, stealing, etc.; trustworthy. **2** not false or misleading; genuine. **3** just or fair: *honest wages.* **4** characterized by sincerity: *an honest appraisal.* **5** without pretensions: *honest farmers.* **6** *Arch.* (of a woman) respectable. **7 honest broker.** a mediator in disputes, esp. international ones. **8 make an honest woman of.** to marry (a woman, esp. one who is pregnant) to prevent scandal. [C13: from OF *honeste,* from L *honestus* distinguished, from *honōs* HONOUR]

honestly ⓣ ('ɒnɪstlɪ) *adv* **1** in an honest manner. **2** (intensifier): *I honestly don't believe it.*

honesty ⓣ ('ɒnɪstɪ) *n, pl* **honesties. 1** the condition of being honest. **2** *Arch.* virtue or respect. **3** Also called: **moonwort, satinpod.** a purple-flowered European plant cultivated for its flattened silvery pods, which are used for indoor decoration.

honey ('hʌnɪ) *n* **1** a sweet viscid substance made by bees from nectar and stored in their nests or hives as food. **2** anything that is sweet or delightful. **3** (*often cap.*) *Chiefly US & Canad.* a term of endearment. **4** *Inf., chiefly US & Canad.* something very good of its kind. ◆ *vb* **honeys, honeying, honeyed. 5** (*tr*) to sweeten with or as if with honey. **6** (often foll. by *up*) to talk to (someone) in a flattering way. [OE *huneg*]
▸**'honey-ˌlike** *adj*

honey badger *n* another name for **ratel.**

honeybee ('hʌnɪˌbiː) *n* any of various social bees widely domesticated as a source of honey and beeswax. Also called: **hive bee.**

honey buzzard *n* a common European bird of prey having broad wings and a typically dull brown plumage with white-streaked underparts.

honeycomb ('hʌnɪˌkəʊm) *n* **1** a waxy structure, constructed by bees in a hive, that consists of adjacent hexagonal cells in which honey is stored, eggs are laid, and larvae develop. **2** something resembling this in structure. **3** *Zool.* another name for **reticulum** (sense 2). ◆ *vb* (*tr*) **4** to pierce with holes, cavities, etc. **5** to permeate: *honeycombed with spies.*

honey creeper *n* a small tropical American songbird having a slender downward-curving bill and feeding on nectar.

honeydew ('hʌnɪˌdjuː) *n* **1** a sugary substance excreted by aphids and similar insects. **2** a similar substance exuded by certain plants.

honeydew melon *n* a variety of muskmelon with a smooth greenish-white rind and sweet greenish flesh.

honey-eater ('hʌnɪˌiːtə) *n* a small Australasian songbird having a downward-curving bill and a brushlike tongue specialized for extracting nectar from flowers.

honeyed ⓣ *or* **honied** ('hʌnɪd) *adj Poetic.* **1** flattering or soothing. **2** made sweet or agreeable: *honeyed words.* **3** full of honey.

honey guide *n* a small bird inhabiting tropical forests of Africa and Asia and feeding on beeswax, honey, and insects.

honeymoon ('hʌnɪˌmuːn) *n* **1** a holiday taken by a newly married couple. **2** a holiday considered to resemble a honeymoon: *a second honeymoon.* **3** the early, usually calm period of a relationship or enterprise. ◆ *vb* **4** (*intr*) to take a honeymoon. [C16: traditionally explained as an allusion to the feelings of married couples as changing with the phases of the moon]
▸**'honeyˌmooner** *n*

honeysuckle ('hʌnɪˌsʌkᵊl) *n* **1** a temperate climbing shrub with fragrant white, yellow, or pink tubular flowers. **2** any of various Australian trees or shrubs of the genus *Banksia,* having flowers in dense spikes. [OE *hunigsūce,* from HONEY + SUCK]

honeytrap ('hʌnɪˌtræp) *n Inf.* a scheme in which a victim is lured into a compromising sexual situation that provides the opportunity for blackmail.

honk (hɒŋk) *n* **1** a representation of the sound made by a goose. **2** any sound resembling this, esp. a motor horn. **3** *Brit. & Austral. sl.* a bad smell. ◆ *vb* **4** to make or cause (something) to make such a sound. **5** (*intr*) *Brit. sl.* to vomit. **6** (*intr*) *Brit. & Austral. sl.* to have a bad smell.

honky ('hɒnkɪ) *n, pl* **honkies.** *Derog. sl., chiefly US.* a White man or White men collectively. [C20: from ?]

honky-tonk ('hɒŋkɪˌtɒŋk) *n* **1** *US & Canad. sl.* a cheap disreputable nightclub, bar, etc. **2a** a style of ragtime piano-playing, esp. on a tinny-sounding piano. **2b** (*as modifier*): *honky-tonk music.* [C19: rhyming compound based on HONK]

honorarium (ˌɒnə'rɛərɪəm) *n, pl* **honorariums** *or* **honoraria** (-rɪə). a fee paid for a nominally free service. [C17: from L: something presented on being admitted to a post of HONOUR]

honorary ⓣ ('ɒnərərɪ) *adj* (*usually prenominal*) **1a** held or given only as an honour, without the normal privileges or duties: *an honorary degree.* **1b** (of a secretary, treasurer, etc.) unpaid. **2** having such a position or title. **3** depending on honour rather than legal agreement.

honorific (ˌɒnə'rɪfɪk) *adj* **1** showing respect. **2a** (of a pronoun, verb inflection, etc.) indicating the speaker's respect for the addressee. **2b** (*as n*): *a Japanese honorific.*
▸ˌ**honor'ifically** *adv*

honour ⓣ *or US* **honor** ('ɒnə) *n* **1** personal integrity; allegiance to moral principles. **2a** fame or glory. **2b** a person who wins this for his country, school, etc. **3** (*often pl*) great respect, esteem, etc., or an outward sign of this. **4** (*often pl*) high or noble rank. **5** a privilege or pleasure: *it is an honour to serve you.* **6** a woman's chastity. **7a** *Bridge, etc.* any of the top five cards in a suit or any of the four aces at no trumps. **7b** *Whist.* any of the top four cards. **8** *Golf.* the right to tee off first. **9 in honour bound.** under a moral obligation. **10 in honour of.** out of respect for. **11 on one's honour.** on the pledge of one's word or good name. ◆ *vb* (*tr*) **12** to hold in respect. **13** to show courteous behaviour towards. **14** to worship. **15** to confer a distinction upon. **16** to accept and then pay when due (a cheque, draft, etc.). **17** to keep (one's promise); fulfil (a previous agreement). **18** to bow or curtsy to (one's dancing partner). [C12: from OF *onor,* from L *honor* esteem]

Honour ('ɒnə) *n* (preceded by *Your, His,* or *Her*) a title used to or of certain judges.

honourable ⓣ *or US* **honorable** ('ɒnərəbᵊl) *adj* **1** possessing or characterized by high principles. **2** worthy of honour or esteem. **3** consistent with or bestowing honour.
▸**'honourably** *or US* **'honorably** *adv*

Honourable *or US* **Honorable** ('ɒnərəbᵊl) *adj* (*prenominal*) **the.** a title of respect placed before a name: used of various officials in the English-speaking world, as a courtesy title in Britain for the children of certain peers, and in Parliament by one member speaking of another. Abbrev.: **Hon.**

honours ⓣ *or US* **honors** ('ɒnəz) *pl n* **1** observances of respect. **2** (*often cap.*) **2a** (in a university degree course) a rank of the highest academic standard. **2b** (*as modifier*): *an honours degree.* Abbrev.: **Hons. 3** a high mark awarded for an examination; distinction. **4 do the honours.** to serve as host or hostess. **5 last** (*or* **funeral**) **honours.** observances of respect at a funeral. **6 military honours.** ceremonies performed by troops in honour of royalty, at the burial of an officer, etc.

honours of war *pl n Mil.* the honours granted by the victorious to the defeated, esp. as of marching out with all arms and flags flying.

hooch *or* **hootch** (huːtʃ) *n Inf., chiefly US & Canad.* alcoholic drink, esp. illicitly distilled spirits. [C20: of Amerind origin, *Hootchinoo,* name of a tribe that distilled a type of liquor]

THESAURUS

hone *vb* **2** = **sharpen,** edge, file, grind, point, polish, strop, whet

honest *adj* **1** = **trustworthy,** conscientious, decent, ethical, high-minded, honourable, law-abiding, reliable, reputable, scrupulous, trusty, truthful, upright, veracious, virtuous **2** = **genuine,** above board, authentic, bona fide, honest to goodness, on the level (*inf.*), on the up and up, proper, real, straight, true **3** = **fair,** equitable, fair and square, impartial, just **4** = **open,** candid, direct, forthright, frank, ingenuous, outright, plain, round, sincere, straightforward, undisguised, unfeigned, upfront (*inf.*)
Antonyms *adj* ≠ **trustworthy:** bad, corrupt, crooked, deceitful, dishonest, guilty, immoral, treacherous, unethical, unfair, unfaithful, unlawful, unprincipled, unreliable, unrighteous, unscrupulous, untrustworthy, untruthful ≠ **genuine:** counterfeit, false, fraudulent, illegitimate ≠ **open:** disguised, false, insincere, secretive

honestly *adv* **1** = **ethically,** by fair means, cleanly, honourably, in good faith, lawfully, legally, legitimately, on the level (*inf.*), with clean hands ◆ *intensifier* **2** = **frankly,** candidly, in all sincerity, truthfully

honesty *n* **1** = **integrity,** bluntness, candour, equity, even-handedness, fairness, faithfulness, fidelity, frankness, genuineness, honour, incorruptibility, morality, openness, outspokenness, plainness, probity, rectitude, reputability, scrupulousness, sincerity, straightforwardness, straightness, trustworthiness, truthfulness, uprightness, veracity, virtue

honeyed *adj Poetic* **1, 2** = **flattering,** agreeable, alluring, cajoling, dulcet, enticing, mellow, melodious, seductive, soothing, sweet, sweetened, unctuous

honorary *adj* **1a** = **nominal,** complimentary, ex officio, formal, *honoris causa,* in name *or* title only, titular, unofficial **1b** = **unpaid**

honour *n* **1** = **integrity,** decency, fairness, goodness, honesty, morality, principles, probity, rectitude, righteousness, trustworthiness, uprightness **2a, 4** = **prestige,** credit, dignity, distinction, elevation, eminence, esteem, fame, glory, high standing, rank, renown, reputation, repute **3** = **tribute,** acclaim, accolade, adoration, Brownie points, commendation, deference, homage, kudos, praise, recognition, regard, respect, reverence, veneration **5** = **privilege,** compliment, credit, favour, pleasure, source of pride *or* satisfaction **6** = **virginity,** chastity, innocence, modesty, purity, virtue ◆ *vb* **12–14** = **respect,** admire, adore, appreciate, esteem, exalt, glorify, hallow, prize, revere, reverence, value, venerate, worship **15** = **acclaim,** celebrate, commemorate, commend, compliment, crack up (*inf.*), decorate, dignify, exalt, glorify, laud, lionize, praise **16** = **pay,** accept, acknowledge, cash, clear, credit, pass, take **17** = **fulfil,** be as good as (*inf.*), be faithful to, be true to, carry out, discharge, keep, live up to, observe
Antonyms *n* ≠ **integrity:** degradation, dishonesty, dishonour, insincerity, lowness, meanness, unscrupulousness ≠ **prestige:** disgrace, dishonour, disrepute, disrespect, infamy, shame ≠ **tribute:** condemnation, contempt, disfavour, insult, scorn, slight ◆ *vb* ≠ **respect, acclaim:** condemn, defame, degrade, dishonour, insult, offend, scorn, slight ≠ **pay:** refuse

honourable *adj* **1** = **principled,** ethical, fair, high-minded, honest, just, moral, true, trustworthy, trusty, upright, upstanding, virtuous **2** = **respected,** creditable, estimable, proper, reputable, respectable, right, righteous, virtuous **3** = **prestigious,** distinguished, eminent, great, illustrious, noble, notable, noted, renowned, venerable

honours *pl n* **1** = **titles,** adornments, awards, decorations, dignities, distinctions, laurels

hood[1] (hʊd) *n* **1** a loose head covering either attached to a cloak or coat or made as a separate garment. **2** something resembling this in shape or use. **3** the US and Canad. name for **bonnet** (of a car). **4** the folding roof of a convertible car. **5** a hoodlike garment worn over an academic gown, indicating its wearer's degree and university. **6** *Biol.* a hoodlike structure, such as the fold of skin on the head of a cobra. ◆ *vb* **7** (*tr*) to cover with or as if with a hood. [OE *hōd*]
▸**'hood,like** *adj*

hood[2] (hʊd) *n Sl.* short for **hoodlum.**

-hood *suffix forming nouns.* **1** indicating state or condition: *manhood.* **2** indicating a body of persons: *knighthood; priesthood.* [OE *-hād*]

hooded ('hʊdɪd) *adj* **1** covered with, having, or shaped like a hood. **2** (of eyes) having heavy eyelids that appear to be half closed.

hooded crow *n* a crow that has a grey body and black head, wings, and tail. Also called (Scot.): **hoodie** ('hʊdɪ), **hoodie crow.**

hoodlum ('huːdləm) *n* **1** a petty gangster. **2** a lawless youth. [C19: ?from Southern G *Haderlump* ragged good-for-nothing]

hoodman-blind (ˌhʊdmən'blaɪnd) *n Brit., arch.* blind man's buff.

hoodoo Ⓣ ('huːduː) *n, pl* **hoodoos. 1** a variant of **voodoo. 2** *Inf.* a person or thing that brings bad luck. **3** *Inf.* bad luck. ◆ *vb* **hoodoos, hoodooing, hoodooed. 4** (*tr*) *Inf.* to bring bad luck to.

hoodwink Ⓣ ('hʊdˌwɪŋk) *vb* (*tr*) **1** to dupe; trick. **2** *Obs.* to cover or hide. [C16: orig., to cover the eyes with a hood, blindfold]

hooey ('huːɪ) *n, interj Sl.* nonsense. [C20: from ?]

hoof (huːf) *n, pl* **hooves** *or* **hoofs. 1a** the horny covering of the end of the foot in the horse, deer, and all other ungulate mammals. **1b** (*in combination*): *a hoofbeat.* Related adj: **ungular. 2** the foot of an ungulate mammal. **3** a hoofed animal. **4** *Facetious.* a person's foot. **5 on the hoof. 5a** (of livestock) alive. **5b** in an impromptu manner: *he did his thinking on the hoof.* ◆ *vb* **6 hoof it.** *Sl.* **6a** to walk. **6b** to dance. [OE *hōf*]
▸**hoofed** *adj*

hoofer ('huːfə) *n Sl.* a professional dancer.

hoo-ha ('huːˌhɑː) *n* a noisy commotion or fuss. [C20: from ?]

hook Ⓣ (hʊk) *n* **1** a curved piece of material, usually metal, used to suspend, hold, or pull something. **2** short for **fish-hook. 3** a trap or snare. **4** something resembling a hook in design or use. **5a** a sharp bend, esp. in a river. **5b** a sharply curved spit of land. **6** *Boxing.* a short swinging blow delivered with the elbow bent. **7** *Cricket.* a shot in which the ball is hit square on the leg side with the bat held horizontally. **8** *Golf.* a shot that causes the ball to go to the player's left. **9** a hook-shaped stroke used in writing, such as a part of a letter extending above or below the line. **10** *Music.* a stroke added to the stem of a note to indicate time values shorter than a crotchet. **11** a sickle. **12** *Naut.* an anchor. **13 by hook or (by) crook.** by any means. **14 hook, line, and sinker.** *Inf.* completely: *he fell for it hook, line, and sinker.* **15 off the hook.** *Sl.* free from obligation or guilt. **16 sling one's hook.** *Brit. sl.* to leave. ◆ *vb* **17** (often foll. by *up*) to fasten or be fastened with or as if with a hook or hooks. **18** (*tr*) to catch (something, such as a fish) on a hook. **19** to curve like or into the shape of a hook. **20** (*tr*) to make (a rug) by hooking yarn through a stiff fabric backing with a special instrument. **21** *Boxing.* to hit (an opponent) with a hook. **22** *Cricket, etc.* to play (a ball) with a hook. **23** *Rugby.* to obtain and pass (the ball) backwards from a scrum, using the feet. **24** (*tr*) *Sl.* to steal. [OE *hōc*]
▸**'hook,like** *adj*

hookah *or* **hooka** ('hʊkə) *n* an oriental pipe for smoking marijuana, tobacco, etc., consisting of one or more long flexible stems connected to a container of water or other liquid through which smoke is drawn and cooled. Also called: **hubble-bubble, water pipe.** [C18: from Ar. *huqqah*]

hooked Ⓣ (hʊkt) *adj* **1** bent like a hook. **2** having a hook or hooks. **3** caught or trapped. **4** a slang word for **married. 5** *Sl.* addicted to a drug. **6** (often foll. by *on*) obsessed (with).

hooker ('hʊkə) *n* **1** a person or thing that hooks. **2** *Sl.* a prostitute. **3** *Rugby.* the central forward in the front row of a scrum.

Hooke's law (hʊks) *n* the principle that the stress imposed on a solid is directly proportional to the strain produced, within the elastic limit. [C18: after R. *Hooke* (1635–1703), E scientist]

hook-up *n* **1** the contact of an aircraft in flight with the refuelling hose of a tanker aircraft. **2** an alliance or relationship. **3** the linking of broadcasting equipment or stations to transmit a special programme. ◆ *vb* **hook up** (*adv*). **4** to connect (two or more people or things).

hookworm ('hʊkˌwɜːm) *n* any of various parasitic bloodsucking worms which cause disease. They have hooked mouthparts and enter their hosts by boring through the skin. Cf. **ancylostomiasis.**

hooky *or* **hookey** ('hʊkɪ) *n Inf., chiefly US, Canad., & NZ.* truancy, usually from school (esp. in **play hooky**). [C20: ?from *hook it* to escape]

hooligan Ⓣ ('huːlɪgən) *n Sl.* a rough lawless young person. [C19: ? var. of *Houlihan,* Irish surname]
▸**'hooliganism** *n*

hoop[1] Ⓣ (huːp) *n* **1** a rigid circular band of metal or wood. **2** something resembling this. **3** a band of iron that holds the staves of a barrel together. **4** a child's toy shaped like a hoop and rolled on the ground or whirled around the body. **5** *Croquet.* any of the iron arches through which the ball is driven. **6a** a light curved frame to spread out a skirt. **6b** (*as modifier*): *a hoop skirt.* **7** *Basketball.* the round metal frame to which the net is attached to form the basket. **8** a large ring through which performers or animals jump. **9 go** *or* **be put through the hoop.** to be subjected to an ordeal. ◆ *vb* **10** (*tr*) to surround with or as if with a hoop. [OE *hōp*]
▸**hooped** *adj*

hoop[2] (huːp) *n, vb* a variant spelling of **whoop.**

hoopla ('huːplɑː) *n* **1** *Brit.* a fairground game in which a player tries to throw a hoop over an object and so win it. **2** *US & Canad. sl.* **2a** noise; bustle. **2b** nonsense; ballyhoo. [C20: see WHOOP, LA[2]]

hoopoe ('huːpuː) *n* an Old World bird having a pinkish-brown plumage with black-and-white wings and an erectile crest. [C17: from earlier *hoopoop,* imit.]

hoop pine *n* a fast-growing timber tree of Australia having rough bark with hooplike cracks around the trunk and branches.

hooray (huː'reɪ) *interj, n, vb* **1** a variant spelling of **hurrah.** ◆ *sentence substitute.* **2** Also: **hooroo** (huː'ruː). *Austral. & NZ.* cheerio.

Hooray Henry ('huːˌreɪ 'hɛnrɪ) *n, pl* **Hooray Henries** *or* **Hooray Henrys.** a young upper-class man, often with affectedly hearty voice and manners. Sometimes shortened to **Hooray.**

hoosegow *or* **hoosgow** ('huːsgaʊ) *n US.* a slang word for **jail.** [C20: from Mexican Sp. *jusgado* prison, from Sp.: court of justice, ult. from L *judex* a JUDGE]

hoot[1] Ⓣ (huːt) *n* **1** the mournful wavering cry of some owls. **2** a similar sound, such as that of a train whistle. **3** a jeer of derision. **4** *Inf.* an amusing person or thing. ◆ *vb* **5** (often foll. by *at*) to jeer or yell (something) contemptuously (at someone). **6** (*tr*) to drive (speakers, actors on stage, etc.) off by hooting. **7** (*intr*) to make a hoot. **8** (*intr*) *Brit.* to blow a horn. [C13 *hoten,* imit.]

hoot[2] (huːt) *n Austral. & NZ.* a slang word for **money.** [from Maori *utu* price]

hootenanny ('huːtᵊˌnænɪ) *or* **hootnanny** ('huːtˌnænɪ) *n, pl* **hootenannies** *or* **hootnannies.** *US & Canad.* an informal performance by folk singers. [C20: from ?]

hooter ('huːtə) *n Chiefly Brit.* **1** a person or thing that hoots, esp. a car horn. **2** *Sl.* a nose.

Hoover ('huːvə) *n* **1** *Trademark.* a type of vacuum cleaner. ◆ *vb* (*usually not cap.*) **2** to vacuum-clean (a carpet, etc.). **3** (*tr;* often foll. by *up*) to consume or dispose of (something) quickly and completely: *he hoovered up his grilled fish.*

hooves (huːvz) *n* a plural of **hoof.**

hop[1] Ⓣ (hɒp) *vb* **hops, hopping, hopped. 1** (*intr*) to jump forwards or upwards on one foot. **2** (*intr*) (esp. of frogs, birds, etc.) to move forwards in short jumps. **3** (*tr*) to jump over. **4** (*intr*) *Inf.* to move quickly (in, on, out of, etc.): *hop on a bus.* **5** (*tr*) *Inf.* to cross (an ocean) in an aircraft. **6** (*tr*) *US & Canad. inf.* to travel by means of: *he hopped a train to Chicago.* **7** (*intr*) another word for **limp**[1] (senses 1 and 2). **8 hop it** (*or* **off**). *Brit. sl.* to go away. ◆ *n* **9** the act or an instance of hopping. **10** *Inf.* an informal dance. **11** *Inf.* a trip, esp. in an aircraft. **12 on the hop.** *Inf.* **12a** active or busy. **12b** *Brit.* unawares or unprepared. [OE *hoppian*]

hop[2] (hɒp) *n* **1** a climbing plant which has green conelike female flowers and clusters of small male flowers. **2 hop garden.** a field of hops. **3** *Obs. sl.* opium or any other narcotic drug. ◆ See also **hops.** [C15: from MDu. *hoppe*]

hope Ⓣ (həʊp) *n* **1** (*sometimes pl*) a feeling of desire for something and confidence in the possibility of its fulfilment: *his hope for peace was justified.* **2** a reasonable ground for this feeling: *there is still hope.* **3** a person or thing that gives cause for hope. **4** a thing, situation, or event that is desired: *my hope is that prices will fall.* **5 not a hope** *or* **some hope.** used ironically to express little confidence that expectations will be

THESAURUS

hoodoo *n* **1** = **voodoo 2, 3** *Informal* = **jinx,** bad luck, curse, evil eye, evil star, hex (*US & Canad. inf.*)

hoodwink *vb* **1** = **deceive,** bamboozle (*inf.*), befool, cheat, con (*inf.*), cozen, delude, dupe, fool, gull (*arch.*), hoax, impose, kid (*inf.*), lead up the garden path (*inf.*), mislead, pull a fast one on (*inf.*), rook (*sl.*), sell a pup, swindle, take (someone) for a ride (*inf.*), trick

hook *n* **1** = **fastener,** catch, clasp, hasp, holder, link, lock, peg **3** = **trap,** noose, snare, springe **13 by hook or by crook** = **by any means,** by fair means or foul, somehow, somehow or other, someway **14 hook, line, and sinker** *Informal* = **completely,** entirely, lock, stock and barrel, thoroughly, through and through, totally, utterly, wholly **15 off the hook** *Slang* = **let off,** acquitted, cleared, exonerated, in the clear, under no obligation, vindicated ◆ *vb* **17** = **fasten,** catch, clasp, fix, hasp, secure **18** = **catch,** enmesh, ensnare, entrap, snare, trap

hooked *adj* **1** = **bent,** aquiline, beaked, beaky, curved, hooklike, hook-shaped, uncinate (*Biology*) **5** *Slang* = **addicted 6** *often foll. by* **on** = **obsessed,** devoted, enamoured, taken

hooligan *n Slang* = **delinquent,** casual, hoodlum (*chiefly US*), lager lout, rowdy, ruffian, tough, vandal, yob *or* yobbo (*Brit. sl.*)

hooliganism *n* = **delinquency,** disorder, loutishness, rowdiness, vandalism, violence, yobbishness

hoop[1] *n* **1, 2** = **ring,** band, circlet, girdle, loop, round, wheel

hoot[1] *n* **1** = **cry,** call **2** = **toot 3** = **catcall,** boo, hiss, jeer, yell **4** *Informal* = **laugh,** card (*inf.*), caution (*inf.*), scream (*inf.*) ◆ *vb* **5, 6** = **jeer,** boo, catcall, condemn, decry, denounce, hiss, howl down, yell at **7** = **cry,** scream, shout, shriek, whoop, yell **8** *Brit.* = **toot**

hop[1] *vb* **2, 3** = **jump,** bound, caper, dance, leap, skip, spring, trip, vault ◆ *n* **9** = **jump,** bounce, bound, leap, skip, spring, step, vault

hope *n* **1** = **belief,** ambition, anticipation, assumption, confidence, desire, dream, expectancy, expectation, faith, longing ◆ *vb* **6** = **desire,** anticipate, aspire, await, believe, contemplate, count on, cross one's fingers, expect, foresee, keep one's fingers crossed, long, look forward to, rely, set one's heart on, trust
Antonyms *n* ≠ **belief:** despair, distrust, doubt, dread, hopelessness

fulfilled. ◆ *vb* **hopes, hoping, hoped. 6** (*tr; takes a clause as object or an infinitive*) to desire (something) with some possibility of fulfilment: *I hope to tell you.* **7** (*intr;* often foll. by *for*) to have a wish. **8** (*tr; takes a clause as object*) to trust or believe: *we hope that this is satisfactory.* [OE *hopa*]

hope chest *n* the US, Canad., and NZ name for **bottom drawer.**

hopeful ➊ ('həʊpfʊl) *adj* **1** having or expressing hope. **2** inspiring hope; promising. ◆ *n* **3** a person considered to be on the brink of success (esp. in **a young hopeful**).
▸ **'hopefulness** *n*

hopefully ➊ ('həʊpfʊlɪ) *adv* **1** in a hopeful manner. **2** *Inf.* it is hoped: *hopefully they will be married soon.*

> **USAGE NOTE** The use of *hopefully* to mean *it is hoped* used to be considered incorrect by some people but has now become acceptable in informal contexts.

hopeless ➊ ('həʊplɪs) *adj* **1** having or offering no hope. **2** impossible to solve. **3** unable to learn, function, etc. **4** *Inf.* without skill or ability.
▸ **'hopelessly** *adv* ▸ **'hopelessness** *n*

Hopi ('həʊpɪ) *n* **1** (*pl* **Hopis** *or* **Hopi**) a member of a North American Indian people of NE Arizona. **2** the language of this people. [from Hopi *Hópi* peaceful]

hoplite ('hɒplaɪt) *n* (in ancient Greece) a heavily armed infantryman. [C18: from Gk *hoplitēs*, from *hoplon* weapon, from *hepein* to prepare]

hopper ('hɒpə) *n* **1** a person or thing that hops. **2** a funnel-shaped reservoir from which solid materials can be discharged into a receptacle below, esp. for feeding fuel to a furnace, loading a truck, etc. **3** a machine used for picking hops. **4** any of various long-legged hopping insects. **5** an open-topped railway truck for loose minerals, etc., unloaded through doors on the underside. **6** *S. African.* another name for **cocopan. 7** *Computing.* a device for holding punched cards and feeding them to a card reader.

hopping ('hɒpɪŋ) *adv* **hopping mad.** in a terrible rage.

hops (hɒps) *pl n* the dried flowers of the hop plant, used to give a bitter taste to beer.

hopsack ('hɒp,sæk) *n* **1** a roughly woven fabric of wool, cotton, etc., used for clothing. **2** Also called: **hopsacking.** a coarse fabric used for bags, etc., made generally of hemp or jute.

hopscotch ('hɒp,skɒtʃ) *n* a children's game in which a player throws a small stone or other object to land in one of a pattern of squares marked on the ground and then hops over to it to pick it up. [C19: HOP[1] + SCOTCH[1]]

horary ('hɔːrərɪ) *adj Arch.* **1** relating to the hours. **2** hourly. [C17: from Med. L *hōrārius*, from L *hora*]

horde ➊ (hɔːd) *n* **1** a vast crowd; throng; mob. **2** a nomadic group of people, esp. an Asiatic group. **3** a large moving mass of animals, esp. insects. [C16: from Polish *horda*, from Turkish *ordū* camp]

> **USAGE NOTE** *Horde* is sometimes wrongly written where *hoard* is meant: *a hoard* (not *horde*) *of gold coins.*

horehound *or* **hoarhound** ('hɔː,haʊnd) *n* a downy herbaceous Old World plant with small white flowers that contain a bitter juice formerly used as a cough medicine and flavouring. [OE *hārhūne*, from *hār* grey + *hūne* horehound, from ?]

horizon ➊ (hə'raɪzᵊn) *n* **1** Also called: **visible horizon, apparent horizon.** the apparent line that divides the earth and the sky. **2** *Astron.* **2a** Also called: **sensible horizon.** the circular intersection with the celestial sphere of the plane tangential to the earth at the position of the observer. **2b** Also called: **celestial horizon.** the great circle on the celestial sphere, the plane of which passes through the centre of the earth and is parallel to the sensible horizon. **3** the range or limit of scope, interest, knowledge, etc. **4** a layer of rock within a stratum that has a particular composition by which the stratum may be dated. [C14: from L, from Gk *horizōn kuklos* limiting circle, from *horizein* to limit]

horizontal ➊ (,hɒrɪ'zɒntᵊl) *adj* **1** parallel to the plane of the horizon; level; flat. **2** of or relating to the horizon. **3** in a plane parallel to that of the horizon. **4** applied uniformly to all members of a group. **5** *Econ.* relating to identical stages of commercial activity: *horizontal integration.* ◆ *n* **6** a horizontal plane, position, line, etc.
▸ **,horizon'tality** *n* ▸ **,hori'zontally** *adv*

horizontal bar *n Gymnastics.* a raised bar on which swinging and vaulting exercises are performed.

hormone ('hɔːməʊn) *n* **1** a chemical substance produced in an endocrine gland and transported in the blood to a certain tissue, on which it exerts a specific effect. **2** an organic compound produced by a plant that is essential for growth. **3** any synthetic substance having the same effects. [C20: from Gk *hormōn*, from *horman* to stir up, from *hormē* impulse]
▸ **hor'monal** *adj*

hormone replacement therapy *n* a form of oestrogen treatment used to control menopausal symptoms and in the prevention of osteoporosis. Abbrev.: **HRT.**

horn (hɔːn) *n* **1** either of a pair of permanent bony outgrowths on the heads of cattle, antelopes, etc. **2** the outgrowth from the nasal bone of a rhinoceros, consisting of a mass of fused hairs. **3** any hornlike projection, such as the eyestalk of a snail. **4** the antler of a deer. **5a** the constituent substance, mainly keratin, of horns, hooves, etc. **5b** (*in combination*): *horn-rimmed spectacles.* **6** a container or device made from this substance or an artificial substitute: *a drinking horn.* **7** an object resembling a horn in shape, such as a cornucopia. **8** a primitive musical wind instrument made from horn. **9** any musical instrument consisting of a pipe or tube of brass fitted with a mouthpiece. See **French horn, cor anglais. 10** *Jazz sl.* any wind instrument. **11a** a device for producing a warning or signalling noise. **11b** (*in combination*): *a foghorn.* **12** (*usually pl*) the imaginary hornlike parts formerly supposed to appear on the forehead of a cuckold. **13a** a hollow conical device coupled to a gramophone to control the direction and quality of the sound. **13b** a similar device attached to an electrical loudspeaker, esp. in a public-address system. **14** a stretch of land or water shaped like a horn. **15** *Brit. taboo sl.* an erection of the penis. ◆ *vb* (*tr*) **16** to provide with a horn or horns. **17** to gore or butt with a horn. **18** to remove or shorten the horns of (cattle, etc.). ◆ See also **horn in.** [OE]
▸ **horned** *adj* ▸ **'hornless** *adj*

hornbeam ('hɔːn,biːm) *n* **1** a tree of Europe and Asia having smooth grey bark and hard white wood. **2** its wood. ◆ Also called: **ironwood.** [C14: from HORN + BEAM, referring to its tough wood]

hornbill ('hɔːn,bɪl) *n* a bird of tropical Africa and Asia, having a very large bill with a basal bony protuberance.

hornblende ('hɔːn,blɛnd) *n* a mineral of the amphibole group consisting of the aluminium silicates of calcium, sodium, magnesium, and iron: varies in colour from green to black. [C18: from G *Horn* horn + BLENDE]

hornbook ('hɔːn,bʊk) *n* a page bearing a religious text or the alphabet, held in a frame with a thin window of horn over it.

horned toad *or* **lizard** *n* a small insectivorous burrowing lizard inhabiting desert regions of America, having a flattened toadlike body covered with spines.

horned viper *n* a venomous snake that occurs in desert regions of N Africa and SW Asia and has a small horny spine above each eye.

hornet ('hɔːnɪt) *n* **1** any of various large social wasps that can inflict a severe sting. **2 hornet's nest.** a strongly unfavourable reaction (often in **stir up a hornet's nest**). [OE *hyrnetu*]

horn in *vb* (*intr, adv;* often foll. by *on*) *Sl.* to interrupt or intrude.

horn of plenty *n* another term for **cornucopia.**

hornpipe ('hɔːn,paɪp) *n* **1** an obsolete reed instrument with a mouthpiece made of horn. **2** an old British solo dance to a hornpipe accompaniment, traditionally performed by sailors. **3** a piece of music for such a dance.

hornswoggle ('hɔːn,swɒgᵊl) *vb* **hornswoggles, hornswoggling, hornswoggled.** (*tr*) *Sl.* to cheat or trick; bamboozle. [C19: from ?]

horny ➊ ('hɔːnɪ) *adj* **hornier, horniest. 1** of, like, or hard as horn. **2** having a horn or horns. **3** *Sl.* **3a** sexually aroused. **3b** provoking or intended to provoke sexual arousal. **3c** sexually eager or lustful.
▸ **'horniness** *n*

horologe ('hɒrə,lɒdʒ) *n* a rare word for **timepiece.** [C14: from L *hōrologium*, from Gk *hōrologion*, from *hōra* HOUR + *-logos* from *legein* to tell]

horologist (hɒ'rɒlədʒɪst) *or* **horologer** *n* a person skilled in horology.

horology (hɒ'rɒlədʒɪ) *n* the art or science of making timepieces or of measuring time.
▸ **horologic** (,hɒrə'lɒdʒɪk) *or* **,horo'logical** *adj*

horoscope ('hɒrə,skəʊp) *n* **1** the prediction of a person's future based on zodiacal data for the time of birth. **2** the configuration of the planets, sun, and moon in the sky at a particular moment. **3** a diagram showing the positions of the planets, sun, moon, etc., at a particular time and place. [OE *horoscopus*, from L, from Gk *hōroskopos*, from *hōra* HOUR + -SCOPE]
▸ **horoscopic** (,hɒrə'skɒpɪk) *adj* ▸ **horoscopy** (hɒ'rɒskəpɪ) *n*

THESAURUS

hopeful *adj* **1** = **optimistic**, anticipating, assured, buoyant, confident, expectant, looking forward to, sanguine **2** = **promising**, auspicious, bright, cheerful, encouraging, heartening, propitious, reassuring, rosy
Antonyms *adj* ≠ **optimistic:** cheerless, dejected, despairing, hopeless, pessimistic ≠ **promising:** depressing, discouraging, disheartening, unpromising

hopefully *adv* **1** = **optimistically**, confidently, expectantly, sanguinely **2** *Informal* = **it is hoped**, all being well, conceivably, expectedly, feasibly, probably

hopeless *adj* **1** = **pessimistic**, abject, defeatist, dejected, demoralized, despairing, desperate, despondent, disconsolate, downhearted, forlorn, in despair, woebegone **2** = **impossible**, forlorn, futile, impracticable, not having a prayer, no-win, pointless, unachievable, unattainable, useless, vain **4** *Informal* = **no good**, inadequate, incompetent, ineffectual, inferior, pathetic, poor, useless (*inf.*)
Antonyms *adj* ≠ **pessimistic:** assured, cheerful, confident, expectant, happy, heartened, hopeful, optimistic, uplifted

hopelessly *adv* **1** = **without hope**, beyond all hope, despairingly, in despair, irredeemably, irremediably

horde *n* **1** = **crowd**, band, crew, drove, gang, host, mob, multitude, pack, press, swarm, throng, troop

horizon *n* **1** = **skyline**, field of vision, vista **3** = **scope**, ambit, compass, ken, perspective, prospect, purview, range, realm, sphere, stretch

horizontal *adj* **1** = **level**, flat, parallel, plane, supine

horny *adj* **3a, 3c** = **aroused**, amorous, excited, lustful, randy (*inf., chiefly Brit.*), raunchy (*sl.*), turned on (*sl.*)

horrendous (hɒ'rɛndəs) *adj* another word for **horrific**. [C17: from L *horrendus* fearful, from *horrēre* to bristle, shudder, tremble; see HORROR]
▸**hor'rendously** *adv*

horrible Ⓣ ('hɒrɪbᵊl) *adj* **1** causing horror; dreadful. **2** disagreeable. **3** *Inf.* cruel or unkind. [C14: via OF from L *horribilis*, from *horrēre* to tremble]
▸**'horribleness** *n* ▸**'horribly** *adv*

horrid Ⓣ ('hɒrɪd) *adj* **1** disagreeable; unpleasant: *a horrid meal.* **2** repulsive or frightening. **3** *Inf.* unkind. [C16 (in the sense: bristling, shaggy): from L *horridus* prickly, from *horrēre* to bristle]
▸**'horridly** *adv* ▸**'horridness** *n*

horrific Ⓣ (hɒ'rɪfɪk, hə-) *adj* provoking horror; horrible.
▸**hor'rifically** *adv*

horrify Ⓣ ('hɒrɪˌfaɪ) *vb* **horrifies, horrifying, horrified.** (*tr*) **1** to cause feelings of horror in; terrify. **2** to shock greatly.
▸**ˌhorrifi'cation** *n* ▸**'horriˌfied** *adj* ▸**'horriˌfying** *adj* ▸**'horriˌfyingly** *adv*

horripilation (hɒˌrɪpɪ'leɪʃən) *n Physiol.* a technical name for **goose flesh.** [C17: from LL *horripilātiō* a bristling, from L *horrēre* to stand on end + *pilus* hair]

horror Ⓣ ('hɒrə) *n* **1** extreme fear; terror; dread. **2** intense hatred. **3** (*often pl*) a thing or person causing fear, loathing, etc. **4** (*modifier*) having a frightening subject: *a horror film.* [C14: from L: a trembling with fear]

horrors ('hɒrəz) *pl n* **1** *Sl.* a fit of depression or anxiety. **2** *Inf.* See **delirium tremens.** ◆ *interj* **3** an expression of dismay, sometimes facetious.

hors de combat *French.* (ɔr də kɔ̃ba) *adj* (*postpositive*), *adv* disabled or injured. [lit.: out of (the) fight]

hors d'oeuvre (ɔː 'dɜːvr) *n, pl* **hors d'oeuvre** *or* **hors d'oeuvres** ('dɜːvr). an appetizer, usually served before the main meal. [C18: from F, lit.: outside the work]

horse Ⓣ (hɔːs) *n* **1** a solid-hoofed, herbivorous, domesticated mammal used for draught work and riding. Related adj: **equine. 2** the adult male of this species; stallion. **3 wild horse.** another name for **Przewalski's horse. 4** (*functioning as pl*) horsemen, esp. cavalry: *a regiment of horse.* **5** Also called: **buck.** *Gymnastics.* a padded apparatus on legs, used for vaulting, etc. **6** a narrow board supported by a pair of legs at each end, used as a frame for sawing or as a trestle, barrier, etc. **7** a contrivance on which a person may ride and exercise. **8** a slang word for **heroin. 9** *Mining.* a mass of rock within a vein of ore. **10** *Naut.* a rod, rope, or cable, fixed at the ends, along which something may slide; traveller. **11** *Inf.* short for **horsepower. 12** (*modifier*) drawn by a horse or horses: *a horse cart.* **13 a horse of another** *or* **a different colour.** a completely different topic, argument, etc. **14 be** (*or* **get**) **on one's high horse.** *Inf.* to act disdainfully aloof. **15 hold one's horses.** to restrain oneself. **16 horses for courses.** a policy, course of action, etc. modified slightly to take account of special circumstances without departing in essentials from the original. **17 the horse's mouth.** the most reliable source. ◆ *vb* **horses, horsing, horsed. 18** (*tr*) to provide with a horse or horses. **19** to put or be put on horseback. [OE *hors*]
▸**'horseˌlike** *adj*

horse around Ⓣ *or* **about** *vb* (*intr, adv*) *Inf.* to indulge in horseplay.

horseback ('hɔːsˌbæk) *n* **a** a horse's back (esp. in **on horseback**). **b** *Chiefly US.* (*as modifier*): *horseback riding.*

horsebox ('hɔːsˌbɒks) *n Brit.* a van or trailer used for carrying horses.

horse brass *n* a decorative brass ornament, originally attached to a horse's harness.

horse chestnut *n* **1** a tree having palmate leaves, erect clusters of white, pink, or red flowers, and brown shiny inedible nuts enclosed in a spiky bur. **2** Also called: **conker.** the nut of this tree. [C16: from its having been used in the treatment of respiratory disease in horses]

horseflesh ('hɔːsˌflɛʃ) *n* **1** horses collectively. **2** the flesh of a horse, esp. edible horse meat.

horsefly ('hɔːsˌflaɪ) *n, pl* **horseflies.** a large stout-bodied dipterous fly, the female of which sucks the blood of mammals, esp. horses, cattle, and man. Also called: **gadfly, cleg.**

horsehair ('hɔːsˌhɛə) *n* hair taken chiefly from the tail or mane of a horse, used in upholstery and for fabric, etc.

horsehide ('hɔːsˌhaɪd) *n* **1** the hide of a horse. **2** leather made from this hide.

horse latitudes *pl n Naut.* the latitudes near 30°N or 30°S at sea, characterized by baffling winds, calms, and high barometric pressure. [C18: referring either to the high mortality of horses on board ship in these latitudes or to *dead horse* (nautical slang: advance pay), which sailors expected to work off by this stage of a voyage]

horse laugh *n* a coarse or raucous laugh.

horseleech ('hɔːsˌliːtʃ) *n* **1** any of several large carnivorous freshwater leeches. **2** an archaic name for a **veterinary surgeon.**

horse mackerel *n* **1** Also called: **scad.** a mackerel-like fish of European Atlantic waters, with a row of bony scales along the lateral line. Sometimes called (US): **saurel. 2** any of various large tunnies or related fishes.

horseman ('hɔːsmən) *n, pl* **horsemen. 1** a person skilled in riding. **2** a person who rides a horse.
▸**'horsemanˌship** *n* ▸**'horseˌwoman** *fem n*

horse mushroom *n* a large edible mushroom, with a white cap and greyish gills.

horse pistol *n* a large holstered pistol formerly carried by horsemen.

horseplay Ⓣ ('hɔːsˌpleɪ) *n* rough or rowdy play.

horsepower ('hɔːsˌpaʊə) *n* an fps unit of power, equal to 550 foot-pounds per second (equivalent to 745.7 watts). Abbrev.: **HP, h.p.**

horseradish ('hɔːsˌrædɪʃ) *n* a coarse Eurasian plant cultivated for its thick white pungent root, which is ground and combined with vinegar, etc., to make a sauce.

horse sense *n* another term for **common sense.**

horseshoe ('hɔːsˌʃuː) *n* **1** a piece of iron shaped like a U nailed to the underside of the hoof of a horse to protect the soft part of the foot: commonly thought to be a token of good luck. **2** an object of similar shape.

horseshoe bat *n* any of numerous large-eared Old World bats with a fleshy growth around the nostrils, used in echolocation.

horseshoe crab *n* a marine arthropod of North America and Asia, having a rounded heavily armoured body with a long pointed tail. Also called: **king crab.**

horsetail ('hɔːsˌteɪl) *n* **1** a plant having jointed stems with whorls of small dark toothlike leaves and producing spores within conelike structures at the tips of the stems. **2** a stylized horse's tail formerly used as the emblem of a pasha.

horse trading *n* shrewd bargaining.

horsewhip ('hɔːsˌwɪp) *n* **1** a whip, usually with a long thong, used for managing horses. ◆ *vb* **horsewhips, horsewhipping, horsewhipped. 2** (*tr*) to flog with such a whip.
▸**'horseˌwhipper** *n*

horsey *or* **horsy** ('hɔːsɪ) *adj* **horsier, horsiest. 1** of or relating to horses: *a horsey smell.* **2** dealing with or devoted to horses. **3** like a horse: *a horsey face.*
▸**'horsily** *adv* ▸**'horsiness** *n*

horst (hɔːst) *n* a ridge of land that has been forced upwards between two parallel faults. [C20: from G *Horst* thicket]

hortatory ('hɔːtətərɪ) *or* **hortative** ('hɔːtətɪv) *adj* tending to exhort; encouraging. [C16: from LL *hortātōrius*, from L *hortārī* to EXHORT]
▸**hor'tation** *n* ▸**'hortatorily** *or* **'hortatively** *adv*

horticulture ('hɔːtɪˌkʌltʃə) *n* the art or science of cultivating gardens. [C17: from L *hortus* garden + CULTURE; cf. AGRICULTURE]
▸**ˌhorti'cultural** *adj* ▸**ˌhorti'culturalist** *or* **ˌhorti'culturist** *n*

Hos. *Bible. abbrev. for* Hosea.

hosanna (həʊ'zænə) *interj* an exclamation of praise, esp. one to God. [OE *osanna*, via LL from Gk, from Heb. *hōshī 'āh nnā* save now, we pray]

hose[1] (həʊz) *n* **1** a flexible pipe, for conveying a liquid or gas. ◆ *vb* **hoses, hosing, hosed. 2** (sometimes foll. by *down*) to wash, water, or sprinkle (a person or thing) with or as if with a hose. [C15: later use of HOSE[2]]

hose[2] (həʊz) *n, pl* **hose** *or* **hosen** ('həʊzᵊn). **1** stockings, socks, and tights collectively. **2** *History.* a man's garment covering the legs and reaching up to the waist. **3 half-hose.** socks. [OE *hosa*]

hosier ('həʊzɪə) *n* a person who sells stockings, etc.

hosiery ('həʊzɪərɪ) *n* stockings, socks, and knitted underclothing collectively.

hospice ('hɒspɪs) *n* **1** a nursing home that specializes in caring for the terminally ill. **2** *Arch.* a place of shelter for travellers, esp. one kept by a monastic order. [C19: from F, from L *hospitium* hospitality, from *hospes* guest]

hospitable Ⓣ ('hɒspɪtəbᵊl, hɒ'spɪt-) *adj* **1** welcoming to guests or

THESAURUS

horrible *adj* **1 = terrifying**, abhorrent, abominable, appalling, awful, dreadful, fearful, frightful, from hell (*inf.*), ghastly, grim, grisly, gruesome, heinous, hellacious (*US sl.*), hideous, horrid, loathsome, obscene, repulsive, revolting, shameful, shocking, terrible **2, 3 = dreadful**, awful, beastly (*inf.*), cruel, disagreeable, ghastly (*inf.*), horrid, mean, nasty, terrible, unkind, unpleasant
Antonyms *adj* agreeable, appealing, attractive, charming, cute, delightful, enchanting, fetching, lovely, pleasant, wonderful

horrid *adj* **1 = unpleasant**, awful, disagreeable, disgusting, dreadful, horrible, nasty, obscene, offensive, terrible, yucky *or* yukky (*sl.*) **2 = repulsive**, abominable, alarming, appalling, formidable, frightening, from hell (*inf.*), hair-raising, harrowing, hideous, horrific, odious, revolting, shocking, terrifying, terrorizing **3** *Informal* **= unkind**, beastly (*inf.*), cruel, mean, nasty

horrific *adj* **= horrifying**, appalling, awful, dreadful, frightening, frightful, from hell, ghastly, grim, grisly, hellacious (*US sl.*), horrendous, shocking, terrifying

horrify *vb* **1 = terrify**, affright, alarm, frighten, gross out (*US sl.*), intimidate, make one's hair stand on end, petrify, put the wind up (*inf.*), scare, terrorize **2 = shock**, appal, disgust, dismay, outrage, sicken
Antonyms *vb* comfort, delight, enchant, encourage, gladden, hearten, please, reassure, soothe

horror *n* **1 = terror**, alarm, apprehension, awe, consternation, dismay, dread, fear, fright, panic **2 = hatred**, abhorrence, abomination, antipathy, aversion, detestation, disgust, loathing, odium, repugnance, revulsion
Antonyms *n* ≠ **hatred:** affinity, approval, attraction, delight, liking, love

horse *n* **1 = nag**, colt, cuddy *or* cuddie (*dialect, chiefly Scot.*), filly, gee-gee (*sl.*), gelding, jade, mare, moke (*Austral. sl.*), mount, stallion, steed (*arch. or literary*), studhorse *or* stud, yarraman (*Austral.*), yearling

horse around *vb Informal* **= play around**, clown, fool about *or* around, misbehave, play the fool, play the goat, roughhouse (*sl.*)

horseplay *n* **= rough-and-tumble**, buffoonery, clowning, fooling around, high jinks, pranks, romping, roughhousing (*sl.*), skylarking (*inf.*)

hospitable *adj* **1, 2 = welcoming**, amicable, bountiful, cordial, friendly, generous, genial, gracious, kind, liberal, sociable
Antonyms *adj* ≠ **welcoming:** inhospitable, parsimonious

strangers. **2** fond of entertaining. [C16: from Med. L *hospitāre* to receive as a guest, from L *hospes* guest]
▸'**hospitableness** *n* ▸'**hospitably** *adv*

hospital ('hɒspɪtᵊl) *n* **1** an institution for the medical or psychiatric care and treatment of patients. **2** (*modifier*) having the function of a hospital: *a hospital ship.* **3** a repair shop for something specified: *a dolls' hospital.* **4** *Arch.* a charitable home, hospice, or school. [C13: from Med. L *hospitāle* hospice, from L, from *hospes* guest]

hospitality 🅣 (ˌhɒspɪ'tælɪtɪ) *n, pl* **hospitalities.** kindness in welcoming strangers or guests.

hospitality suite *n* a room or suite, as at a conference, where free drinks are offered.

hospitalize *or* **hospitalise** ('hɒspɪtəˌlaɪz) *vb* **hospitalizes, hospitalizing, hospitalized** *or* **hospitalises, hospitalising, hospitalised.** (*tr*) to admit or send (a person) into a hospital.
▸ˌ**hospitali'zation** *or* ˌ**hospitali'sation** *n*

hospitaller *or US* **hospitaler** ('hɒspɪtələ) *n* a person, esp. a member of certain religious orders, dedicated to hospital work, ambulance services, etc. [C14: from OF *hospitalier,* from Med. L, from *hospitāle* hospice; see HOSPITAL]

Hospitaller *or US* **Hospitaler** ('hɒspɪtələ) *n* a member of the order of the Knights Hospitallers.

host[1] 🅣 (həʊst) *n* **1** a person who receives or entertains guests, esp. in his own home. **2a** a country or organization which provides facilities for and receives visitors to an event. **2b** (*as modifier*): *the host nation.* **3** the compere of a show or television programme. **4** *Biol.* **4a** an animal or plant that supports a parasite. **4b** an animal into which tissue is experimentally grafted. **5** *Computing.* a computer that is connected to others on a network. **6** the owner or manager of an inn. ◆ *vb* **7** to be the host of (a party, programme, etc.): *to host one's own show.* [C13: from F *hoste,* from L *hospes* guest]

host[2] 🅣 (həʊst) *n* **1** a great number; multitude. **2** an archaic word for **army.** [C13: from OF *hoste,* from L *hostis* stranger]

Host (həʊst) *n Christianity.* the wafer of unleavened bread consecrated in the Eucharist. [C14: from OF *oiste,* from L *hostia* victim]

hosta ('hɒstə) *n* a plant cultivated esp. for its ornamental foliage. [C19: NL, after N. T. *Host* (1761–1834), Austrian physician]

hostage 🅣 ('hɒstɪdʒ) *n* **1** a person held as a security or pledge or to be ransomed, exchanged for prisoners, etc. **2** the state of being held as a hostage. **3** any security or pledge. **4 give hostages to fortune.** to place oneself in a position in which misfortune may strike through the loss of what one values most. [C13: from OF, from *hoste* guest]

hostel ('hɒstᵊl) *n* **1** a building providing overnight accommodation, as for homeless people. **2** See **youth hostel. 3** *Brit.* a supervised lodging house for nurses, workers, etc. **4** *Arch.* another word for **hostelry.** [C13: from OF, from Med. L *hospitāle* hospice; see HOSPITAL]

hosteller *or US* **hosteler** ('hɒstələ) *n* **1** a person who stays at youth hostels. **2** an archaic word for **innkeeper.**

hostelling *or US* **hosteling** ('hɒstəlɪŋ) *n* the practice of staying at youth hostels when travelling.

hostelry ('hɒstəlrɪ) *n, pl* **hostelries.** *Arch. or facetious.* an inn.

hostess ('həʊstɪs) *n* **1** a woman acting as host. **2** a woman who receives and entertains patrons of a club, restaurant, etc. **3** See **air hostess.**

hostile 🅣 ('hɒstaɪl) *adj* **1** antagonistic; opposed. **2** of or relating to an enemy. **3** unfriendly. [C16: from L *hostīlis,* from *hostis* enemy]
▸'**hostilely** *adv*

hostility 🅣 (hɒ'stɪlɪtɪ) *n, pl* **hostilities. 1** enmity. **2** an act expressing enmity. **3** (*pl*) fighting; warfare.

hostler ('ɒslə) *n* a variant (esp. Brit.) of **ostler.**

hot 🅣 (hɒt) *adj* **hotter, hottest. 1** having a relatively high temperature. **2** having a temperature higher than desirable. **3** causing a sensation of bodily heat. **4** causing a burning sensation on the tongue: *a hot curry.* **5** expressing or feeling intense emotion, such as anger or lust. **6** intense or vehement. **7** recent; new: *hot from the press.* **8** *Ball games.* (of a ball) thrown or struck hard, and so difficult to respond to. **9** much favoured: *a hot favourite.* **10** *Inf.* having a dangerously high level of radioactivity. **11** *Sl.* stolen or otherwise illegally obtained. **12** *Sl.* (of people) being sought by the police. **13** (of a colour) intense; striking: *hot pink.* **14** following closely: *hot on the scent.* **15** *Inf.* at a dangerously high electric potential. **16** *Sl.* good (esp. in **not so hot**). **17** *Jazz sl.* arousing great excitement by inspired improvisation, strong rhythms, etc. **18** *Inf.* dangerous or unpleasant (esp. in **make it hot for someone**). **19** (in various games) very near the answer. **20** *Metallurgy.* (of a process) at a sufficiently high temperature for metal to be in a soft workable state. **21** *Austral. & NZ inf.* (of a price, etc.) excessive. **22 hot on.** *Inf.* **22a** very severe: *the police are hot on drunk drivers.* **22b** particularly knowledgeable about. **23 hot under the collar.** *Inf.* aroused with anger, annoyance, etc. **24 in hot water.** *Inf.* in trouble. ◆ *adv* **25** in a hot manner; hotly. ◆ See also **hots, hot up.** [OE *hāt*]
▸'**hotly** *adv* ▸'**hotness** *n* ▸'**hottish** *adj*

hot air 🅣 *n Inf.* empty and usually boastful talk.

hotbed 🅣 ('hɒtˌbɛd) *n* **1** a glass-covered bed of soil, usually heated, for propagating plants, forcing early vegetables, etc. **2** a place offering ideal conditions for the growth of an idea, activity, etc., esp. one considered bad.

hot-blooded 🅣 *adj* **1** passionate or excitable. **2** (of a horse) being of thoroughbred stock.

hotchpotch 🅣 ('hɒtʃˌpɒtʃ) *or esp. US & Canad.* **hodgepodge** *n* **1** a jumbled mixture. **2** a thick soup or stew. [C15: var. of *hotchpot* from OF, from *hocher* to shake + POT[1]]

hot cross bun *n* a yeast bun marked with a cross and traditionally eaten on Good Friday.

hot desking ('dɛskɪŋ) *n* the practice of not assigning permanent desks in a workplace, so that employees may work at any available desk.

hot dog[1] *n* a sausage, esp. a frankfurter, usually served hot in a long roll split lengthways. [C20: from the supposed resemblance of the sausage to a dachshund]

hot dog[2] *n* **1** *Chiefly US.* a person who performs showy acrobatic manoeuvres when skiing or surfing. ◆ *vb* **hot-dog, hot-dogs, hot-dogging, hot-dogged. 2** (*intr*) to perform a series of manoeuvres in skiing, surfing, etc.

hotel (həʊ'tɛl) *n* a commercially run establishment providing lodging and usually meals for guests and often containing a public bar. [C17: from F *hôtel,* from OF *hostel;* see HOSTEL]

hotelier (hɒ'tɛljeɪ) *n* an owner or manager of one or more hotels.

hotel ship *n* an accommodation barge anchored near an oil production rig.

hot flush *or US* **hot flash** *n* a sudden unpleasant hot feeling experienced by menopausal women.

hotfoot 🅣 ('hɒtˌfʊt) *adv* with all possible speed.

hothead 🅣 ('hɒtˌhɛd) *n* an excitable person.

hot-headed 🅣 *adj* impetuous, rash, or hot-tempered.
▸ˌ**hot-'headedness** *n*

hothouse 🅣 ('hɒtˌhaʊs) *n* **1a** a greenhouse in which the temperature is maintained at a fixed level. **1b** (*as modifier*): *a hothouse plant.* **2a** an environment that encourages rapid development. **2b** (*as modifier*): *a hothouse atmosphere.* **3** (*modifier*) *Inf., often disparaging.* sensitive or delicate: *a hothouse temperament.*

hot key *n Computing.* a single key on the keyboard of a computer which carries out a series of commands.

hotline ('hɒtˌlaɪn) *n* **1** a direct telephone, teletype, or other communications link between heads of government, etc., for emergency use. **2** any such direct line kept for urgent use.

hot link *n Computing.* a word or phrase in a hypertext document that can be selected to access additional information.

THESAURUS

hospitality *n* = **welcome,** cheer, conviviality, cordiality, friendliness, geniality, heartiness, hospitableness, neighbourliness, sociability, warmth

host[1] *n* **1** = **master of ceremonies,** entertainer, innkeeper, landlord *or* landlady, proprietor **3** = **presenter,** anchorman *or* anchorwoman, compere (*Brit.*) ◆ *vb* **7** = **present,** compere (*Brit.*), front (*inf.*), introduce

host[2] *n* **1** = **multitude,** array, drove, horde, legion, myriad, swarm, throng **2** = **army**

hostage *n* = **prisoner,** captive, gage, pawn, pledge, security, surety

hostile *adj* **1, 3** = **unfriendly,** antagonistic, anti (*inf.*), bellicose, belligerent, contrary, ill-disposed, inimical, malevolent, opposed, opposite, rancorous, unkind, warlike
Antonyms *adj* affable, agreeable, amiable, approving, cordial, friendly, kind, peaceful, sympathetic, warm

hostility *n* **1** = **unfriendliness,** abhorrence, animosity, animus, antagonism, antipathy, aversion, bad blood, detestation, enmity, hatred, ill will, malevolence, malice, opposition, resentment **3** *plural* = **warfare,** conflict, fighting, state of war, war
Antonyms *n* ≠ **unfriendliness:** agreement, amity, approval, congeniality, cordiality, friendliness, goodwill, sympathy ≠ **warfare:** alliance, ceasefire, peace, treaty, truce

hot *adj* **1-3** = **burning,** blistering, boiling, fiery, flaming, heated, piping hot, roasting, scalding, scorching, searing, steaming, sultry, sweltering, torrid, warm **4** = **spicy,** acrid, biting, peppery, piquant, pungent, sharp **5, 6** = **passionate,** ablaze, animated, ardent, excited, fervent, fervid, fierce, fiery, flaming, impetuous, inflamed, intense, irascible, lustful, raging, stormy, touchy, vehement, violent **7** = **new,** fresh, just out, latest, recent, up to the minute **9** = **popular,** approved, favoured, in demand, in vogue, sought-after **14** = **following closely,** close, in hot pursuit, near
Antonyms *adj* ≠ **heated:** chilly, cold, cool, freezing, frigid, frosty, icy, parky (*Brit. inf.*) ≠ **spicy:** mild ≠ **passionate:** apathetic, calm, dispassionate, half-hearted, indifferent, mild, moderate ≠ **new:** old, stale, trite ≠ **popular:** out of favour, unpopular ≠ **following closely:** cold

hot air *n Informal* = **empty talk,** blether, bombast, bosh (*inf.*), bunkum *or* buncombe (*chiefly US*), claptrap (*inf.*), rant, verbiage, wind

hotbed *n* **1** = **nursery,** forcing house, seedbed **2** = **breeding ground,** den, nest

hot-blooded *adj* **1** = **passionate,** ardent, excitable, fervent, fiery, heated, impulsive, rash, spirited, temperamental, wild
Antonyms *adj* apathetic, calm, cold, cool, frigid, impassive, restrained, unenthusiastic

hotchpotch *n* **1** = **mixture,** conglomeration, farrago, gallimaufry, hash, hodgepodge (*US*), jumble, medley, *mélange,* mess, miscellany, mishmash, olio, olla podrida, potpourri

hotfoot *adv* = **speedily,** hastily, helter-skelter, hurriedly, pell-mell, posthaste, quickly

hothead *n* = **tearaway,** adrenalin junky (*sl.*), daredevil, desperado, hotspur, madcap

hot-headed *adj* = **rash,** fiery, foolhardy, hasty, hot-tempered, impetuous, precipitate, quick-tempered, reckless, unruly, volatile

hothouse *n* **1** = **greenhouse,** conservatory, glasshouse ◆ *modifier* **3** = **delicate,** coddled, dainty, exotic, fragile, frail, overprotected, pampered, sensitive

hotly *adv* **5, 6** = **passionately,** angrily, fiercely, heatedly, impetuously, indignantly, vehemently, with indignation **14** = **enthusiastically,** closely, eagerly, hotfoot, with enthusiasm

hot money *n* capital that is transferred from one financial centre to another seeking the best opportunity for short-term gain.

hotplate ('hɒtˌpleɪt) *n* **1** an electrically heated plate on a cooker or one set into a working surface. **2** a portable device on which food can be kept warm.

hotpot ('hɒtˌpɒt) *n* **1** *Brit.* a casserole covered with a layer of potatoes. **2** *Austral. sl.* a heavily backed horse.

hot potato *n Sl.* a delicate or awkward matter.

hot-press *n* **1** a machine for applying a combination of heat and pressure to give a smooth surface to paper, to express oil from it, etc. ◆ *vb* **2** (*tr*) to subject (paper, cloth, etc.) to such a process.

hot rod *n* a car with an engine that has been radically modified to produce increased power.

hots (hɒts) *pl n* **the.** *Sl.* intense sexual desire; lust (esp. in the phrase **have the hots for (someone)**).

hot seat *n* **1** *Inf.* a difficult or dangerous position. **2** *US.* a slang term for **electric chair.**

hot spot *n* **1** an area of potential violence. **2** a lively nightclub. **3** any local area of high temperature in a part of an engine, etc. **4** *Med.* **4a** a small area on the surface or within a body with an exceptionally high level of radioactivity or of some chemical or mineral considered harmful. **4b** a similar area that generates an abnormal amount of heat, as revealed by thermography.

hot spring *n* a natural spring of mineral water at 21°C (70°F) or above, found in areas of volcanic activity. Also called: **thermal spring.**

hotspur ('hɒtˌspɜː) *n* an impetuous or fiery person. [C15: from *Hotspur*, nickname of Sir Henry Percy (1364–1403)]

hot stuff *n Inf.* **1** a person, object, etc., considered important, attractive, etc. **2** a pornographic or erotic book, play, film, etc.

Hottentot ('hɒtᵊnˌtɒt) *n* another name for **Khoikhoi.**

hotting ('hɒtɪŋ) *n Inf.* the practice of stealing from cars and putting on a show of skilful but dangerous driving.
▸**'hotter** *n*

hot up *vb* **hots, hotting, hotted.** (*adv*) *Inf.* **1** to make or become more exciting, active, or intense. **2** (*tr*) another term for **soup up.**

hot-water bottle *n* a receptacle now usually made of rubber, designed to be filled with hot water and used for warming a bed.

hot-wire *vb* **hot-wires, hot-wiring, hot-wired.** (*tr*) *Sl.* to start the engine of (a motor vehicle) by bypassing the ignition switch.

hough (hɒk) *Brit.* ◆ *n* **1** a variant of **hock**[1]. ◆ *vb* (*tr*) **2** to hamstring (cattle, horses, etc.). [C14: from OE *hōh* heel]

hound ❶ (haʊnd) *n* **1a** any of several breeds of dog used for hunting. **1b** (*in combination*): *a deerhound.* **2** a dog, esp. one regarded as annoying. **3** a despicable person. **4** (in hare and hounds) a runner who pursues a hare. **5** *Sl., chiefly US & Canad.* an enthusiast. **6 ride to hounds** *or* **follow the hounds.** to take part in a fox hunt. **7 the hounds.** a pack of foxhounds, etc. ◆ *vb* (*tr*) **8** to pursue relentlessly. **9** to urge on. [OE *hund*]
▸**'hounder** *n*

hound's-tongue *n* a plant which has small reddish-purple flowers and spiny fruits. Also called: **dog's-tongue.** [OE *hundestunge,* translation of L *cynoglōssos,* from Gk, from *kuōn* dog + *glōssa* tongue; referring to the shape of its leaves]

hound's-tooth check *n* a pattern of broken or jagged checks, esp. on cloth. Also called: **dog's-tooth check, dogtooth check.**

hour ('aʊə) *n* **1** a period of time equal to 3600 seconds; 1/24th of a calendar day. Related adj: **horary.** **2** any of the points on the face of a timepiece that indicate intervals of 60 minutes. **3** the time. **4** the time allowed for or used for something: *lunch hour.* **5** a special moment: *our finest hour.* **6** the distance covered in an hour: *we live an hour away.* **7** *Astron.* an angular measurement of right ascension equal to 15° or a 24th part of the celestial equator. **8 one's last hour.** the time of one's death. **9 the hour.** an exact number of complete hours: *the bus leaves on the hour.* ◆ See also **hours.** [C13: from OF *hore,* from L *hōra,* from Gk: season]

hour circle *n* a great circle on the celestial sphere passing through the celestial poles and a specified point, such as a star.

hourglass ('aʊəˌglɑːs) *n* **1** a device consisting of two transparent chambers linked by a narrow channel, containing a quantity of sand that takes a specified time to trickle from one chamber to the other. **2** (*modifier*) well-proportioned with a small waist: *an hourglass figure.*

hour hand *n* the pointer on a timepiece that indicates the hour.

houri ('hʊərɪ) *n, pl* **houris.** **1** (in Muslim belief) any of the nymphs of Paradise. **2** any alluring woman. [C18: from F, from Persian, from Ar. *hūr,* pl. of *haurā'* woman with dark eyes]

hourly ('aʊəlɪ) *adj* **1** of, occurring, or done every hour. **2** done in or measured by the hour: *an hourly rate.* **3** continual or frequent. ◆ *adv* **4** every hour. **5** at any moment.

hours ('aʊəz) *pl n* **1** a period regularly appointed for work, etc. **2** one's times of rising and going to bed: *he keeps late hours.* **3 till all hours.** until very late. **4** an indefinite time. **5** *RC Church.* Also called: **canonical hours.** **5a** the seven times of the day laid down for the recitation of the prayers of the divine office. **5b** the prayers recited at these times.

house ❶ *n* (haʊs), *pl* **houses** ('haʊzɪz). **1a** a building used as a home; dwelling. **1b** (*as modifier*): *house dog.* **2** the people present in a house. **3a** a building for some specific purpose. **3b** (*in combination*): *a schoolhouse.* **4** (*often cap.*) a family or dynasty: *the House of York.* **5a** a commercial company: *a publishing house.* **5b** (*as modifier*): *a house journal.* **6** a legislative body. **7** a quorum in such a body (esp. in **make a house**). **8** a dwelling for a religious community. **9** *Astrol.* any of the 12 divisions of the zodiac. **10** any of several divisions of a large school. **11** a hotel, restaurant, club, etc., or the management of such an establishment. **12** (*modifier*) (of wine) sold unnamed by a restaurant, at a lower price than wines specified on the wine list: *the house red.* **13** the audience in a theatre or cinema. **14** an informal word for **brothel.** **15** a hall in which a legislative body meets. **16** See **full house.** **17** *Naut.* any structure or shelter on the weather deck of a vessel. **18 bring the house down.** *Theatre.* to win great applause. **19 like a house on fire.** *Inf.* very well. **20 on the house.** (usually of drinks) paid for by the management of the hotel, bar, etc. **21 put one's house in order.** to settle or organize one's affairs. **22 safe as houses.** *Brit.* very secure. ◆ *vb* (haʊz), **houses, housing, housed.** **23** (*tr*) to provide with or serve as accommodation. **24** to give or receive lodging. **25** (*tr*) to contain or cover; protect. **26** (*tr*) to fit (a piece of wood) into a mortise, etc. [OE *hūs*]
▸**'houseless** *adj*

house agent *n Brit.* another name for **estate agent.**

house arrest *n* confinement to one's own home rather than in prison.

houseboat ('haʊsˌbəʊt) *n* a stationary boat or barge used as a home.

housebound ('haʊsˌbaʊnd) *adj* unable to leave one's house because of illness, injury, etc.

housebreaking ('haʊsˌbreɪkɪŋ) *n Criminal law.* the act of entering a building as a trespasser for an unlawful purpose. Assimilated with burglary (1968).
▸**'houseˌbreaker** *n*

housecoat ('haʊsˌkəʊt) *n* a woman's loose robelike informal garment.

house-craft *n* skill in domestic management.

housefly ('haʊsˌflaɪ) *n, pl* **houseflies.** a common dipterous fly that frequents human habitations, spreads disease, and lays its eggs in carrion, decaying vegetables, etc.

household ❶ ('haʊsˌhəʊld) *n* **1** the people living together in one house. **2** (*modifier*) relating to the running of a household: *household management.*

householder ❶ ('haʊsˌhəʊldə) *n* a person who owns or rents a house.
▸**'houseˌholderˌship** *n*

household name *or* **word** *n* a person or thing that is very well known.

housekeeper ('haʊsˌkiːpə) *n* a person, esp. a woman, employed to run a household.

housekeeping ❶ ('haʊsˌkiːpɪŋ) *n* **1** the running of a household. **2** money allotted for this. **3** general maintenance as of records, data, etc., in an organization.

houseleek ('haʊsˌliːk) *n* an Old World plant which has a rosette of succulent leaves and pinkish flowers: grows on walls.

house lights *pl n* the lights in the auditorium of a theatre, cinema, etc.

housemaid ('haʊsˌmeɪd) *n* a girl or woman employed to do housework, esp. one who is resident in the household.

housemaid's knee *n* inflammation and swelling of the bursa in front of the kneecap, caused esp. by constant kneeling on a hard surface. Technical name: **prepatellar bursitis.**

houseman ('haʊsmən) *n, pl* **housemen.** *Med.* a junior doctor who is a member of the medical staff of a hospital. US and Canad. equivalent: **intern.**

house martin *n* a Eurasian swallow with a forked tail.

house mouse *n* any of various greyish mice, a common household pest in most parts of the world.

House music *or* **House** *n* a type of disco music of the late 1980s, based on funk, with fragments of other recordings edited in electronically.

House of Assembly *n* a legislative assembly or the lower chamber of such an assembly.

house of cards *n* **1** a tiered structure created by balancing playing cards on their edges. **2** an unstable situation, etc.

House of Commons *n* (in Britain, Canada, etc.) the lower chamber of Parliament.

house of correction *n* (formerly) a place of confinement for persons convicted of minor offences.

house of ill repute *or* **ill fame** *n* a euphemistic name for **brothel.**

House of Keys *n* the lower chamber of the legislature of the Isle of Man.

House of Lords *n* (in Britain) the upper chamber of Parliament, composed of the peers of the realm.

THESAURUS

hound *vb* **8** = **pursue**, chase, drive, give chase, hunt, hunt down **9** = **harass**, badger, goad, harry, impel, persecute, pester, prod, provoke

house *n* **1a** = **home**, abode, building, domicile, dwelling, edifice, habitation, homestead, pad (*sl.*), residence **2** = **household**, family, ménage **4** = **dynasty**, ancestry, clan, family tree, kindred, line, lineage, race, tribe **5a** = **firm**, business, company, concern, establishment, organization, outfit (*inf.*), partnership **6** = **assembly**, Commons, legislative body, parliament **11** = **inn**, hotel, public house, tavern **20 on the house** = **free**, for nothing, gratis, without expense ◆ *vb* **23, 24** = **accommodate**, billet, board, domicile, harbour, lodge, put up, quarter, take in **25** = **contain**, cover, keep, protect, sheathe, shelter, store

household *n* **1** = **family**, home, house, ménage ◆ *modifier* **2** = **domestic**, domiciliary, family

householder *n* = **occupant**, homeowner, resident, tenant

housekeeping *n* **1** = **household management**, home economy, homemaking, housecraft, housewifery

House of Representatives *n* **1** (in the US) the lower chamber of Congress, or of many state legislatures. **2** (in Australia) the lower chamber of Parliament. **3** the sole chamber of New Zealand's Parliament.

houseparent ('haʊsˌpɛərənt) *n* a person in charge of the welfare of a group of children in an institution.

house party *n* **1** a party, usually in a country house, at which guests are invited to stay for several days. **2** the guests who are invited.

house plant *n* a plant that can be grown indoors.

house-proud *adj* proud of the appearance, cleanliness, etc., of one's house, sometimes excessively so.

houseroom ('haʊsˌrʊm, -ˌruːm) *n* **1** room for storage or lodging. **2 give (something) houseroom.** (*used with a negative*) to have or keep (something) in one's house.

Houses of Parliament *n* (in Britain) **1** the building in which the House of Commons and the House of Lords assemble. **2** these two chambers considered together.

house sparrow *n* a small Eurasian bird, now established in North America and Australia. It has a brown plumage with grey underparts. Also called (US): **English sparrow.**

housetop ('haʊsˌtɒp) *n* **1** the roof of a house. **2 proclaim from the housetops.** to announce (something) publicly.

house-train *vb* (*tr*) *Brit.* to train (pets) to urinate and defecate outside the house.
▸ **'house-ˌtrained** *adj*

house-warming *n* a party given after moving into a new home.

housewife *n, pl* **housewives. 1** ('haʊsˌwaɪf). a woman who keeps house. **2** ('hʌzɪf). Also called: **hussy, huswife.** *Chiefly Brit.* a small sewing kit.
▸ **housewifery** ('haʊsˌwɪfərɪ) *n* ▸ **'housewifely** *adj*

housework ('haʊsˌwɜːk) *n* the work of running a home, such as cleaning, cooking, etc.

housey-housey ('haʊsɪ'haʊsɪ) *n* another name for **bingo** or **lotto.** [C20: from the cry of "house!" shouted by the winner, prob. from FULL HOUSE]

housing[1] ❶ ('haʊzɪŋ) *n* **1a** houses collectively. **1b** (*as modifier*): *a housing problem.* **2** the act of providing with accommodation. **3** a hole or slot made in one wooden member to receive another. **4** a part designed to contain or support a component or mechanism: *a wheel housing.*

housing[2] ('haʊzɪŋ) *n* (*often pl*) *Arch.* another word for **trappings** (sense 2). [C14: from OF *houce* covering, of Gmc origin]

housing estate *n* a planned area of housing, often with its own shops and other amenities.

housing scheme *n* a local-authority housing estate. Often shortened to **scheme.**

hove (həʊv) *vb Chiefly naut.* a past tense and past participle of **heave.**

hovel ❶ ('hɒvᵊl) *n* **1** a ramshackle dwelling place. **2** an open shed for livestock, carts, etc. **3** the conical building enclosing a kiln. [C15: from ?]

hover ❶ ('hɒvə) *vb* (*intr*) **1** to remain suspended in one place. **2** (of certain birds, esp. hawks) to remain in one place in the air by rapidly beating the wings. **3** to linger uncertainly. **4** to be in a state of indecision. ◆ *n* **5** the act of hovering. [C14: *hoveren*, var. of *hoven*, from ?]
▸ **'hoverer** *n*

hovercraft ('hɒvəˌkrɑːft) *n* a vehicle that is able to travel across both land and water on a cushion of air.

hover fly *n* a dipterous fly with a hovering flight.

hoverport ('hɒvəˌpɔːt) *n* a port for hovercraft.

hovertrain ('hɒvəˌtreɪn) *n* a train that moves over a concrete track and is supported by a cushion of air supplied by powerful fans.

how (haʊ) *adv* **1** in what way? by what means?: *how did it happen?* Also used in indirect questions: *tell me how he did it.* **2** to what extent?: *how tall is he?* **3** how good? how well? what...like?: *how did she sing?* **4 and how!** (intensifier) very much so! **5 how about?** used to suggest something: *how about a cup of tea?* **6 how are you?** what is your state of health? **7 how come?** *Inf.* what is the reason (that)?: *how come you told him?* **8 how's that? 8a** what is your opinion? **8b** *Cricket.* Also written: **howzat** (haʊ'zæt). (an appeal to the umpire) is the batsman out? **9 how now?** *or* **how so?** *Arch.* what is the meaning of this? **10** in whatever way: *do it how you wish.* ◆ *n* **11** the way a thing is done: *the how of it.* [OE *hu*]

howbeit (haʊ'biːɪt) *Arch.* ◆ *sentence connector.* **1** however. ◆ *conj* **2** (*subordinating*) though; although.

howdah ('haʊdə) *n* a seat for riding on an elephant's back, esp. one with a canopy. [C18: from Hindi *haudah*, from Ar. *haudaj* load carried by elephant or camel]

how do you do *sentence substitute.* **1** a formal greeting said by people who are being introduced to each other. ◆ *n* **how-do-you-do. 2** *Inf.* a difficult situation.

howdy ('haʊdɪ) *sentence substitute. Chiefly US.* an informal word for **hello.** [C16: from *how d'ye do*]

however ❶ (haʊ'ɛvə) *sentence connector.* **1** still; nevertheless. **2** on the other hand; yet. ◆ *adv* **3** by whatever means. **4** (*used with adjectives of quantity or degree*) no matter how: *however long it takes, finish it.* **5** an emphatic form of **how** (sense 1).

howitzer ('haʊɪtsə) *n* a cannon having a short barrel with a low muzzle velocity and a steep angle of fire. [C16: from Du. *houwitser*, from G, from Czech *houfnice* stone-sling]

howl ❶ (haʊl) *n* **1** a long plaintive cry characteristic of a wolf or hound. **2** a similar cry of pain or sorrow. **3** a prolonged outburst of laughter. **4** *Electronics.* an unwanted high-pitched sound produced by a sound-producing system as a result of feedback. ◆ *vb* **5** to express in a howl or utter such cries. **6** (*intr*) (of the wind, etc.) to make a wailing noise. **7** (*intr*) *Inf.* to shout or laugh. [C14: *houlen*]

howl down *vb* (*tr, adv*) to prevent (a speaker) from being heard by shouting disapprovingly.

howler ❶ ('haʊlə) *n* **1** Also called: **howler monkey.** a large New World monkey inhabiting tropical forests in South America and having a loud howling cry. **2** *Inf.* a glaring mistake. **3** a person or thing that howls.

howling ('haʊlɪŋ) *adj* (*prenominal*) *Inf.* (intensifier): *a howling success; a howling error.*

howsoever (ˌhaʊsəʊ'ɛvə) *sentence connector, adv* a less common word for **however.**

how-to *adj* (of a book or guide) giving basic instructions to the lay person on how to do or make something: *a how-to book on carpentry.*

hoy[1] (hɔɪ) *n Naut.* **1** a freight barge. **2** a coastal fishing and trading vessel used during the 17th and 18th centuries. [C15: from MDu. *hoei*]

hoy[2] (hɔɪ) *interj* a cry used to attract attention or drive animals. [C14: var. of HEY]

hoya ('hɔɪə) *n* any plant of the genus *Hoya*, of E Asia and Australia, esp. the waxplant. [C19: after Thomas *Hoy* (died 1821), E gardener]

hoyden *or* **hoiden** ('hɔɪdᵊn) *n* a wild boisterous girl; tomboy. [C16: ?from MDu. *heidijn* heathen]
▸ **'hoydenish** *or* **'hoidenish** *adj*

Hoyle (hɔɪl) *n* an authoritative book of rules for card games. [after Sir Edmund *Hoyle*, 18th-cent. E authority on games, its compiler]

HP *abbrev. for:* **1** *Brit.* hire-purchase. **2** horsepower. **3** high pressure. **4** (in Britain) Houses of Parliament. ◆ Also (for senses 1–3): **h.p.**

HPV *abbrev. for* human papilloma virus.

HQ *or* **h.q.** *abbrev. for* headquarters.

hr *abbrev. for* hour.

HRH *abbrev. for* His (*or* Her) Royal Highness.

HRT *abbrev. for* hormone replacement therapy.

HS (in Britain) *abbrev. for* Home Secretary.

HSH *abbrev. for* His (*or* Her) Serene Highness.

ht *abbrev. for* height.

HT *Physics. abbrev. for* high tension.

HTLV *abbrev. for* human T-cell lymphotropic virus: any one of a family of viruses that cause certain rare human diseases in the T-cells. HTLV-III was an early name for the AIDS virus.

HTML *abbrev. for* hypertext markup language: a text description language that is used for electronic publishing, esp. on the World Wide Web.

HTTP *abbrev. for* hypertext transfer protocol, used esp. on the World Wide Web. See also **hypertext.**

hub ❶ (hʌb) *n* **1** the central portion of a wheel, propeller, fan, etc., through which the axle passes. **2** the focal point. [C17: prob. var. of HOB[1]]

hubble-bubble ('hʌbᵊl'bʌbᵊl) *n* **1** another name for **hookah. 2** turmoil. **3** a gargling sound. [C17: rhyming jingle based on BUBBLE]

Hubble's law *n Astron.* a law stating that the velocity of recession of a galaxy is proportional to its distance from the observer. [C20: after E. P. *Hubble* (1889–1953), US astronomer]

Hubble telescope *n* a telescope launched into orbit around the earth in 1990 to provide information about the universe.

hubbub ❶ ('hʌbʌb) *n* **1** a confused noise of many voices. **2** tumult; uproar. [C16: prob. from Irish *hooboobbes*]

hubby ('hʌbɪ) *n, pl* **hubbies.** an informal word for **husband.** [C17: by shortening and altering]

hubcap ('hʌbˌkæp) *n* a cap fitting over the hub of a wheel.

hubris ❶ ('hjuːbrɪs) *n* **1** pride or arrogance. **2** (in Greek tragedy) ambition, arrogance, etc., ultimately causing the transgressor's ruin. [C19: from Gk]
▸ **hu'bristic** *adj*

THESAURUS

housing[1] *n* **1a = accommodation**, dwellings, homes, houses **4 = case**, casing, container, cover, covering, enclosure, sheath

hovel *n* **1 = hut**, cabin, den, hole, shack, shanty, shed

hover *vb* **1, 2 = float**, be suspended, drift, flutter, fly, hang, poise **3 = linger**, hang about, wait nearby **4 = waver**, alternate, dither, falter, fluctuate, haver (*Brit.*), oscillate, pause, seesaw, swither (*Scot. dialect*), vacillate

however *sentence connector* **1 = nevertheless**, after all, anyhow, be that as it may, but, even though, nonetheless, notwithstanding, still, though **2 = on the other hand**, yet

howl *n* **1, 2 = cry**, bawl, bay, bell, bellow, clamour, groan, hoot, outcry, roar, scream, shriek, ululation, wail, yelp, yowl ◆ *vb* **5 = cry**, bawl, bell, bellow, cry out, lament, quest (*used of hounds*), roar, scream, shout, shriek, ululate, wail, weep, yell, yelp

howler *n* **2** *Informal* **= mistake**, bloomer (*Brit. inf.*), blunder, boner, boob (*Brit. sl.*), bull (*sl.*), clanger (*inf.*), error, malapropism, schoolboy howler

hub *n* **2 = centre**, core, focal point, focus, heart, middle, nerve centre, pivot

hubbub *n* **1, 2 = noise**, babel, bedlam, brouhaha, clamour, confusion, din, disorder, disturbance, hue and cry, hullabaloo, hurly-burly, pandemonium, racket, riot, ruckus (*inf.*), ruction (*inf.*), rumpus, tumult, uproar

hubris *n* **1 = pride**, arrogance **2 = nemesis**

DICTIONARY

huckaback (ˈhʌkəˌbæk) *n* a coarse absorbent linen or cotton fabric used for towels, etc. Also: **huck** (hʌk). [C17: from ?]

huckleberry (ˈhʌkəlˌbərɪ) *n, pl* **huckleberries. 1** an American shrub having edible dark blue berries. **2** the fruit of this shrub. **3** a Brit. name for **whortleberry** (sense 1,2). [C17: prob. var. of *hurtleberry,* from ?]

huckster Ⓣ (ˈhʌkstə) *n* **1** a person who uses aggressive or questionable methods of selling. **2** *Now rare.* a person who sells small articles or fruit in the street. **3** *US.* a person who writes for radio or television advertisements. ◆ *vb* **4** (*tr*) to peddle. **5** (*tr*) to sell or advertise aggressively or questionably. **6** to haggle (over). [C12: ?from MDu. *hoekster,* from *hoeken* to carry on the back]

huddle Ⓣ (ˈhʌdəl) *n* **1** a heaped or crowded mass of people or things. **2** *Inf.* a private or impromptu conference (esp. in **go into a huddle**). ◆ *vb* **huddles, huddling, huddled. 3** to crowd or nestle closely together. **4** (often foll. by *up*) to hunch (oneself), as through cold. **5** (*intr*) *Inf.* to confer privately. **6** (*tr*) *Chiefly Brit.* to do (something) in a careless way. **7** (*tr*) *Rare.* to put on (clothes) hurriedly. [C16: from ?; cf. ME *hoderen* to wrap up]
▸ **ˈhuddler** *n*

hue Ⓣ (hjuː) *n* **1** the attribute of colour that enables an observer to classify it as red, blue, etc., and excludes white, black, and grey. **2** a shade of a colour. **3** aspect: *a different hue on matters.* [OE *hīw* beauty]
▸ **hued** *adj*

hue and cry Ⓣ *n* **1** (formerly) the pursuit of a suspected criminal with loud cries in order to raise the alarm. **2** any loud public outcry. [C16: from Anglo-F *hu et cri,* from OF *hue* outcry, from *hu!* shout of warning + *cri* CRY]

huff Ⓣ (hʌf) *n* **1** a passing mood of anger or pique (esp. in **in a huff**). ◆ *vb* **2** to make or become angry or resentful. **3** (*intr*) to blow or puff heavily. **4** Also: **blow.** *Draughts.* to remove (an opponent's draught) from the board for failure to make a capture. **5** (*tr*) *Obs.* to bully. **6 huffing and puffing.** empty threats or objections: bluster. [C16: imit.; cf. PUFF]
▸ **ˈhuffish** *or* **ˈhuffy** *adj* ▸ **ˈhuffily** *or* **ˈhuffishly** *adv*

hug Ⓣ (hʌg) *vb* **hugs, hugging, hugged.** (*mainly tr*) **1** (*also intr*) to clasp tightly, usually with affection; embrace. **2** to keep close to a shore, kerb, etc. **3** to cling to (beliefs, etc.); cherish. **4** to congratulate (oneself). ◆ *n* **5** a tight or fond embrace. [C16: prob. of Scand. origin]
▸ **ˈhuggable** *adj*

huge Ⓣ (hjuːdʒ) *adj* extremely large. [C13: from OF *ahuge,* from ?]
▸ **ˈhugely** *adv* ▸ **ˈhugeness** *n*

hugger-mugger (ˈhʌgəˌmʌgə) *n* **1** confusion. **2** *Rare.* secrecy. ◆ *adj, adv Arch.* **3** with secrecy. **4** in confusion. ◆ *vb Obs.* **5** (*tr*) to keep secret. **6** (*intr*) to act secretly. [C16: from ?]

Huguenot (ˈhjuːgəˌnəʊ, -ˌnɒt) *n* **1** a French Calvinist, esp. of the 16th or 17th centuries. ◆ *adj* **2** designating the French Protestant Church. [C16: from F, from Genevan dialect *eyguenot* one who opposed annexation by Savoy, ult. from Swiss G *Eidgenoss* confederate]

huh (*spelling pron* hʌ) *interj* an exclamation of derision, bewilderment, inquiry, etc.

huhu (ˈhuːhuː) *n* a New Zealand beetle with a hairy body. [from Maori]

hui (ˈhuːɪ) *n NZ.* **1** a Maori social gathering. **2** *Inf.* any party. [from Maori]

huia (ˈhuɪjə) *n* an extinct New Zealand bird, prized by early Maoris for its distinctive tail feathers. [from Maori]

hula (ˈhuːlə) *or* **hula-hula** *n* a Hawaiian dance performed by a woman. [from Hawaiian]

Hula Hoop *n Trademark.* a light hoop that is whirled around the body by movements of the waist and hips.

hulk Ⓣ (hʌlk) *n* **1** the body of an abandoned vessel. **2** *Disparaging.* a large or unwieldy vessel. **3** *Disparaging.* a large ungainly person or thing. **4** (*often pl*) the hull of a ship, used as a storehouse, etc., or (esp. in 19th-century Britain) as a prison. [OE *hulc,* from Med. L *hulca,* from Gk *holkas* barge, from *helkein* to tow]

hulking Ⓣ (ˈhʌlkɪŋ) *adj* big and ungainly.

hull Ⓣ (hʌl) *n* **1** the main body of a vessel, tank, etc. **2** the outer covering of a fruit or seed. **3** the calyx at the base of a strawberry, raspberry, or similar fruit. **4** the outer casing of a missile, rocket, etc. ◆ *vb* **5** to remove the hulls from (fruit or seeds). **6** (*tr*) to pierce the hull of (a vessel, tank, etc.). [OE *hulu*]

hullabaloo Ⓣ *or* **hullaballoo** (ˌhʌləbəˈluː) *n, pl* **hullabaloos** *or* **hullaballoos.** loud confused noise; commotion. [C18: ?from HALLO + Scot. *baloo* lullaby]

hullo (hʌˈləʊ) *sentence substitute, n* a variant spelling of **hello.**

hum Ⓣ (hʌm) *vb* **hums, humming, hummed.** (*intr*) **1** to make a low continuous vibrating sound. **2** (of a person) to sing with the lips closed. **3** to utter an indistinct sound, as in hesitation; hem. **4** *Inf.* to be in a state of feverish activity. **5** *Brit. & Irish sl.* to smell unpleasant. **6 hum and haw.** See **hem**[2] (sense 3). ◆ *n* **7** a low continuous murmuring sound. **8** *Electronics.* an undesired low-frequency noise in the output of an amplifier or receiver. ◆ *interj, n* **9** an indistinct sound of hesitation, embarrassment, etc.; hem. [C14: imit.]

human Ⓣ (ˈhjuːmən) *adj* **1** of or relating to mankind: *human nature.* **2** consisting of people: *a human chain.* **3** having the attributes of man as opposed to animals, divine beings, or machines: *human failings.* **4a** kind or considerate. **4b** natural. ◆ *n* **5** a human being; person. [C14: from L *hūmānus;* rel. to L *homō* man]
▸ **ˈhumanness** *n*

human being *n* a member of any of the races of *Homo sapiens;* person; man, woman, or child.

humane Ⓣ (hjuːˈmeɪn) *adj* **1** characterized by kindness, sympathy, etc. **2** inflicting as little pain as possible: *a humane killing.* **3** civilizing or liberal: *humane studies.* [C16: var. of HUMAN]
▸ **huˈmanely** *adv* ▸ **huˈmaneness** *n*

human interest *n* (in a newspaper story, etc.) reference to individuals and their emotions, sometimes from exploitative motives.

humanism (ˈhjuːməˌnɪzəm) *n* **1** the rejection of religion in favour of a belief in the advancement of humanity by its own efforts. **2** (*often cap.*) a cultural movement of the Renaissance, based on classical studies. **3** interest in the welfare of people.
▸ **ˈhumanist** *n* ▸ **ˌhumanˈistic** *adj*

humanitarian Ⓣ (hjuːˌmænɪˈtɛərɪən) *adj* **1** having the interests of mankind at heart. ◆ *n* **2** a philanthropist.
▸ **huˌmaniˈtarianism** *n*

humanity Ⓣ (hjuːˈmænɪtɪ) *n, pl* **humanities. 1** the human race. **2** the quality of being human. **3** kindness or mercy. **4** (*pl; usually preceded by the*) the study of literature, philosophy, and the arts, esp. study of Ancient Greece and Rome.

humanize Ⓣ *or* **humanise** (ˈhjuːməˌnaɪz) *vb* **humanizes, humanizing, hu-**

THESAURUS

huckster *n* **1, 2** = **pedlar**, barker, hawker, pitchman (*US*), salesman, vendor

huddle *n* **1** = **crowd**, confusion, disorder, heap, jumble, mass, mess, muddle **2** *Informal* = **conference**, confab (*inf.*), discussion, meeting, powwow ◆ *vb* **3** = **crowd**, cluster, converge, flock, gather, press, throng **4** = **curl up**, crouch, cuddle, hunch up, make oneself small, nestle, snuggle

hue *n* **1, 2** = **colour**, dye, shade, tincture, tinge, tint, tone **3** = **aspect**, cast, complexion, light

hue and cry *n* **2** = **outcry**, brouhaha, clamour, furore, hullabaloo, much ado, ruction (*inf.*), rumpus, uproar

huff *n* **1** = **sulk**, anger, bad mood, bate (*Brit. sl.*), passion, pet, pique, rage, temper, wax (*inf., chiefly Brit.*) ◆ *vb* **3** = **puff**, blow, exhale

huffy *adj* **1** = **resentful**, angry, cross, crotchety, curt, disgruntled, edgy, grumpy, irritable, moody, moping, offended, peevish, pettish, petulant, querulous, ratty (*Brit. & NZ inf.*), shirty (*sl., chiefly Brit.*), snappy, sulky, sullen, surly, testy, tetchy
Antonyms *adj* amiable, calm, cheerful, friendly, gay, good-humoured, happy, pleasant, sunny

hug *vb* **1** = **clasp**, cuddle, embrace, enfold, hold close, squeeze, take in one's arms **2** = **follow closely**, cling to, keep close, stay near **3** = **cherish**, cling, hold onto, nurse, retain ◆ *n* **5** = **embrace**, bear hug, clasp, clinch (*sl.*), squeeze

huge *adj* = **enormous**, Brobdingnagian, bulky, colossal, elephantine, extensive, gargantuan, giant, gigantic, ginormous (*inf.*), great, humongous *or* humungous (*US sl.*), immense, jumbo (*inf.*), large, mammoth, massive, mega (*sl.*), monumental, mountainous, prodigious, stupendous, titanic, tremendous, vast
Antonyms *adj* insignificant, little, microscopic, minute, petty, puny, small, tiny

hugely *adv* = **immensely**, by leaps and bounds, enormously, massively, monumentally, on a grand scale, prodigiously, stupendously

hulk *n* **1** = **wreck**, derelict, frame, hull, shell, shipwreck **3** *Disparaging* = **oaf**, lout, lubber, lump (*inf.*)

hulking *adj* = **ungainly**, awkward, bulky, clumsy, clunky (*inf.*), cumbersome, gross, lubberly, lumbering, lumpish, massive, oafish, overgrown, ponderous, unwieldy

hull *n* **1** = **frame**, body, casing, covering, framework, skeleton **2** = **husk**, peel, pod, rind, shell, shuck, skin ◆ *vb* **5** = **peel**, husk, shell, shuck, skin, trim

hullabaloo *n* = **commotion**, babel, bedlam, brouhaha, clamour, confusion, din, disturbance, furore, hubbub, hue and cry, hurly-burly, noise, outcry, pandemonium, racket, ruckus (*inf.*), ruction (*inf.*), rumpus, to-do, tumult, turmoil, upheaval, uproar

hum *vb* **1** = **drone**, bombinate *or* bombilate (*literary*), buzz, croon, mumble, murmur, purr, sing, throb, thrum, vibrate, whir **4** *Informal* = **be busy**, be active, bustle, buzz, move, pulsate, pulse, stir, vibrate

human *adj* **1, 3** = **mortal**, anthropoid, fleshly, manlike **4a** = **kind**, approachable, compassionate, considerate, humane, kindly, understanding ◆ *n* **5** = **human being**, body, child, creature, individual, man *or* woman, mortal, person, soul, wight (*arch.*)
Antonyms *adj* ≠ **mortal:** animal, nonhuman ≠ **kind:** beastly, brutish, cruel, inhuman, unsympathetic ◆ *n* ≠ **human being:** animal, god, nonhuman

humane *adj* **1** = **kind**, benevolent, benign, charitable, clement, compassionate, forbearing, forgiving, gentle, good, good-natured, kind-hearted, kindly, lenient, merciful, mild, sympathetic, tender, understanding
Antonyms *adj* barbarous, brutal, cruel, inhuman, inhumane, ruthless, uncivilized, unkind, unmerciful, unsympathetic

humanitarian *adj* **1** = **philanthropic**, altruistic, beneficent, benevolent, charitable, compassionate, humane, public-spirited ◆ *n* **2** = **philanthropist**, altruist, benefactor, Good Samaritan

humanitarianism *n* **1** = **philanthropy**, beneficence, benevolence, charity, generosity, goodwill, humanism

humanity *n* **1** = **human race**, flesh, Homo sapiens, humankind, man, mankind, men, mortality, people **2** = **human nature**, humanness, mortality **3** = **kindness**, benevolence, benignity, brotherly love, charity, compassion, fellow feeling, kind-heartedness, mercy, philanthropy, sympathy, tenderness, tolerance, understanding **4** *plural* = **classical studies**, classics, liberal arts, literae humaniores

humanize *vb* **2** = **civilize**, cultivate, educate, enlighten, improve, mellow, polish, reclaim, refine, soften, tame

manized *or* **humanises, humanising, humanised. 1** to make or become human. **2** to make or become humane.
▸ **ˌhumaniˈzation** *or* **ˌhumaniˈsation** *n*
humankind (ˌhjuːmənˈkaɪnd) *n* the human race; humanity.

USAGE NOTE See at **mankind.**

humanly (ˈhjuːmənlɪ) *adv* **1** by human powers or means. **2** in a human or humane manner.
human nature *n* the qualities common to humanity, esp. with reference to human weakness.
humanoid (ˈhjuːməˌnɔɪd) *adj* **1** like a human being in appearance. ◆ *n* **2** a being with human rather than anthropoid characteristics. **3** (in science fiction) a robot or creature resembling a human being.
human papilloma virus *n* any of a class of viruses that cause tumours, including warts, in humans. Certain strains have been implicated as a cause of cervical cancer. Abbrev.: **HPV.**
human rights *pl n* the rights of individuals to liberty, justice, etc.
humble ➊ (ˈhʌmbᵊl) *adj* **1** conscious of one's failings. **2** unpretentious; lowly: *a humble cottage; my humble opinion.* **3** deferential or servile. ◆ *vb* **humbles, humbling, humbled.** (*tr*) **4** to cause to become humble; humiliate. **5** to lower in status. [C13: from OF, from L *humilis* low, from *humus* the ground]
▸ **ˈhumbleness** *n* ▸ **ˈhumbly** *adv*
humblebee (ˈhʌmbᵊlˌbiː) *n* another name for the **bumblebee.** [C15: rel. to MDu. *hommel* bumblebee, OHG *humbal*]
humble pie *n* **1** (formerly) a pie made from the heart, entrails, etc., of a deer. **2 eat humble pie.** to be forced to behave humbly; be humiliated. [C17: earlier *an umble pie,* by mistaken word division from *a numble pie,* from *numbles* offal of a deer, ult. from L *lumbulus* a little loin]
humbug ➊ (ˈhʌmˌbʌg) *n* **1** a person or thing that deceives. **2** nonsense. **3** *Brit.* a hard boiled sweet, usually having a striped pattern. ◆ *vb* **humbugs, humbugging, humbugged. 4** to cheat or deceive (someone). [C18: from ?]
▸ **ˈhumˌbugger** *n* ▸ **ˈhumˌbuggery** *n*
humdinger (ˈhʌmˌdɪŋə) *n Sl.* an excellent person or thing. [C20: from ?]
humdrum ➊ (ˈhʌmˌdrʌm) *adj* **1** ordinary; dull. ◆ *n* **2** a monotonous routine, task, or person. [C16: rhyming compound, prob. based on HUM]
humectant (hjuːˈmɛktənt) *adj* **1** producing moisture. ◆ *n* **2** a substance added to another to keep it moist. [C17: from L *ūmectāre* to wet, from *ūmēre* to be moist]
humerus (ˈhjuːmərəs) *n, pl* **humeri** (-məˌraɪ). **1** the bone that extends from the shoulder to the elbow in man. **2** the corresponding bone in other vertebrates. [C17: from L *umerus;* rel. to Gothic *ams* shoulder, Gk *ōmos*]
▸ **ˈhumeral** *adj*
humid ➊ (ˈhjuːmɪd) *adj* moist; damp. [C16: from L *ūmidus,* from *ūmēre* to be wet]
▸ **ˈhumidly** *adv* ▸ **ˈhumidness** *n*
humidex (ˈhjuːmɪˌdɛks) *n Canad.* an index of discomfort showing the combined effect of humidity and temperature.
humidify (hjuːˈmɪdɪˌfaɪ) *vb* **humidifies, humidifying, humidified.** (*tr*) to make (air, etc.) humid or damp.
▸ **huˌmidifiˈcation** *n* ▸ **huˈmidiˌfier** *n*
humidity ➊ (hjuːˈmɪdɪtɪ) *n* **1** dampness. **2** a measure of the amount of moisture in the air.
humidor (ˈhjuːmɪˌdɔː) *n* a humid place or container for storing cigars, tobacco, etc.
humify (ˈhjuːmɪˌfaɪ) *vb* **humifies, humifying, humified.** to convert or be converted into humus.
▸ **ˌhumifiˈcation** *n*
humiliate ➊ (hjuːˈmɪlɪˌeɪt) *vb* **humiliates, humiliating, humiliated.** (*tr*) to lower or hurt the dignity or pride of. [C16: from LL *humiliāre,* from L *humilis* HUMBLE]
▸ **huˈmiliˌatingly** *adv* ▸ **huˌmiliˈation** *n* ▸ **huˈmiliˌator** *n*
humility ➊ (hjuːˈmɪlɪtɪ) *n, pl* **humilities.** the state or quality of being humble.
hummingbird (ˈhʌmɪŋˌbɜːd) *n* a very small American bird having a brilliant iridescent plumage, long slender bill, and wings specialized for very powerful vibrating flight.
hummock (ˈhʌmək) *n* **1** a hillock; knoll. **2** a ridge or mound of ice in an ice field. **3** *Chiefly southern US.* a wooded area lying above the level of an adjacent marsh. [C16: from ?; cf. HUMP]
▸ **ˈhummocky** *adj*
hummus *or* **houmous** (ˈhʊməs) *n* a creamy dip originating in the Middle East, made from puréed chickpeas. [from Turkish *humus*]

USAGE NOTE Avoid confusion with **humus.**

humoral (ˈhjuːmərəl) *adj* **1** *Immunol.* denoting or relating to a type of immunity caused by free antibodies circulating in the blood. **2** *Obs.* of or relating to the four bodily fluids (humours).
humoresque (ˌhjuːməˈrɛsk) *n* a short lively piece of music. [C19: from G *Humoreske,* ult. from E HUMOUR]
humorist ➊ (ˈhjuːmərɪst) *n* a person who acts, speaks, or writes in a humorous way.
humorous ➊ (ˈhjuːmərəs) *adj* **1** funny; comical; amusing. **2** displaying or creating humour.
▸ **ˈhumorously** *adv* ▸ **ˈhumorousness** *n*
humour ➊ *or US* **humor** (ˈhjuːmə) *n* **1** the quality of being funny. **2** Also called: **sense of humour.** the ability to appreciate or express that which is humorous. **3** situations, speech, or writings that are humorous. **4a** a state of mind; mood. **4b** (*in combination*): *good humour.* **5** temperament or disposition. **6** a caprice or whim. **7** any of various fluids in the body: *aqueous humour.* **8** Also called: **cardinal humour.** *Arch.* any of the four bodily fluids (blood, phlegm, choler or yellow bile, melancholy or black bile) formerly thought to determine emotional and physical disposition. **9 out of humour.** in a bad mood. ◆ *vb* (*tr*) **10** to gratify; indulge: *he humoured the boy's whims.* **11** to adapt oneself to: *to humour someone's fantasies.* [C14: from L *humor* liquid; rel. to L *ūmēre* to be wet]
▸ **ˈhumourless** *or US* **ˈhumorless** *adj*
hump ➊ (hʌmp) *n* **1** a rounded protuberance or projection. **2** a

THESAURUS

humble *adj* **1 = modest,** meek, self-effacing, submissive, unassuming, unostentatious, unpretentious **2 = lowly,** common, commonplace, insignificant, low, low-born, mean, modest, obscure, ordinary, plebeian, poor, simple, undistinguished, unimportant, unpretentious **3 = servile,** courteous, deferential, obliging, obsequious, polite, respectful, subservient ◆ *vb* **4, 5 = humiliate,** abase, abash, break, bring down, chagrin, chasten, crush, debase, degrade, demean, disgrace, lower, mortify, put down (*sl.*), put (someone) in their place, reduce, shame, sink, subdue, take down a peg (*inf.*)
Antonyms *adj* ≠ **modest:** arrogant, assuming, conceited, haughty, immodest, lordly, ostentatious, overbearing, pompous, presumptuous, pretentious, proud, snobbish, superior, vain ≠ **lowly:** aristocratic, distinguished, elegant, famous, glorious, high, important, rich, significant, superior, wealthy ◆ *vb* ≠ **humiliate:** elevate, exalt, magnify, raise
humbly *adv* **1, 3 = meekly,** cap in hand, deferentially, diffidently, modestly, obsequiously, on bended knee, respectfully, servilely, submissively, subserviently, unassumingly
humbug *n* **1 = fraud,** charlatan, cheat, con man (*inf.*), faker, fraudster, impostor, phoney *or* phony (*inf.*), quack, swindler, trickster **1 = deception,** bluff, canard, cheat, deceit, dodge, feint, fraud, hoax, imposition, imposture, ruse, sham, swindle, trick, trickery, wile **2 = nonsense,** baloney (*inf.*), cant, charlatanry, claptrap, eyewash (*inf.*), gammon (*Brit. inf.*), hypocrisy, rubbish, trash ◆ *vb* **4 = deceive,** bamboozle (*inf.*), befool, beguile, cheat, con (*inf.*), cozen, delude, dupe, fool, gull (*arch.*), hoax, hoodwink, impose, mislead, swindle, take in (*inf.*), trick
humdrum *adj* **1 = dull,** banal, boring, commonplace, dreary, ho-hum (*inf.*), mind-numbing, monotonous, mundane, ordinary, repetitious, routine, tedious, tiresome, uneventful, uninteresting, unvaried, wearisome
Antonyms *adj* dramatic, entertaining, exciting, extraordinary, interesting, lively, sexy (*inf.*), stimulating
humid *adj* **= damp,** clammy, dank, moist, muggy, steamy, sticky, sultry, watery, wet
Antonyms *adj* arid, dry, sunny, torrid
humidity *n* **1 = damp,** clamminess, dampness, dankness, dew, humidness, moistness, moisture, mugginess, sogginess, wetness
humiliate *vb* **= embarrass,** abase, abash, bring low, chagrin, chasten, crush, debase, degrade, discomfit, disgrace, humble, make (someone) eat humble pie, mortify, put down, put (someone) in their place, shame, subdue, take down a peg (*inf.*), take the wind out of someone's sails
Antonyms *vb* elevate, honour, magnify, make proud
humiliating *adj* **= embarrassing,** cringe-making (*Brit. inf.*), cringeworthy (*Brit. inf.*), crushing, degrading, disgracing, humbling, ignominious, mortifying, shaming
humiliation *n* **= embarrassment,** abasement, affront, chagrin, condescension, degradation, disgrace, dishonour, humbling, ignominy, indignity, loss of face, mortification, put-down, resignation, self-abasement, shame, submission, submissiveness
humility *n* **= modesty,** diffidence, humbleness, lack of pride, lowliness, meekness, self-abasement, servility, submissiveness, unpretentiousness
Antonyms *n* arrogance, conceit, disdain, haughtiness, pomposity, presumption, pretentiousness, pride, snobbishness, superciliousness, superiority, vanity
humorist *n* **= comedian,** card (*inf.*), comic, eccentric, funny man, jester, joker, wag, wit
humorous *adj* **1, 2 = funny,** amusing, comic, comical, droll, entertaining, facetious, farcical, hilarious, jocose, jocular, laughable, ludicrous, merry, playful, pleasant, side-splitting, waggish, whimsical, witty
Antonyms *adj* earnest, grave, sad, serious, sober, solemn
humour *n* **1 = funniness,** amusement, comedy, drollery, facetiousness, fun, jocularity, ludicrousness **3 = joking,** comedy, farce, gags (*inf.*), jesting, jests, jokes, pleasantry, wisecracks (*inf.*), wit, witticisms, wittiness **4 = mood,** disposition, frame of mind, spirits, temper **5 = whim,** bent, bias, fancy, freak, mood, propensity, quirk, vagary ◆ *vb* **10 = indulge,** accommodate, cosset, favour, fawn on, feed, flatter, go along with, gratify, mollify, pamper, pander to, spoil
Antonyms *n* ≠ **funniness:** gravity, grief, melancholy, sadness, seriousness, sobriety, solemnity, sorrow ◆ *vb* ≠ **indulge:** aggravate, excite, oppose, rouse, stand up to
humourless *adj* **1, 2 = serious,** dour, dry, heavy-going, intense, po-faced, solemn, straight, unamused, unamusing, unfunny, unsmiling
hump *n* **1 = lump,** bulge, bump, hunch, knob, mound, projection, protrusion, protuberance, swelling **4 the hump** *Brit. informal* **= sulks,** blues,

rounded deformity of the back, consisting of a spinal curvature. **3** a rounded protuberance on the back of a camel or related animal. **4 the hump.** *Brit. inf.* a fit of sulking. ◆ *vb* **5** to form or become a hump; hunch; arch. **6** (*tr*) *Sl.* to carry or heave. **7** *Taboo sl.* to have sexual intercourse with (someone). [C18: prob. from earlier *humpbacked*]
▸ **'humpy** *adj*

humpback ('hʌmp,bæk) *n* **1** another word for **hunchback. 2** Also called: **humpback whale.** a large whalebone whale with a humped back and long flippers. **3** a Pacific salmon, the male of which has a humped back. **4** Also: **humpback bridge.** *Brit.* a road bridge having a sharp incline and decline and usually a narrow roadway. [C17: alteration of earlier *crumpbacked,* ? infl. by HUNCHBACK]
▸ **'hump,backed** *adj*

humph (*spelling pron* hʌmf) *interj* an exclamation of annoyance, indecision, etc.

humpty dumpty ('hʌmptɪ 'dʌmptɪ) *n, pl* **humpty dumpties.** *Chiefly Brit.* **1** a short fat person. **2** a person or thing that once broken cannot be mended. [C18: from the nursery rhyme *Humpty Dumpty*]

humpy ('hʌmpɪ) *n, pl* **humpies.** *Austral.* a primitive hut. [C19: from Abor.]

humus ('hju:məs) *n* a dark brown or black colloidal mass of partially decomposed organic matter in the soil. It improves the fertility and water retention of the soil. [C18: from L: soil]

> **USAGE NOTE** Avoid confusion with **hummus.**

Hun (hʌn) *n, pl* **Huns** *or* **Hun. 1** a member of any of several Asiatic nomadic peoples who dominated much of Asia and E Europe from before 300 B.C., invading the Roman Empire in the 4th and 5th centuries A.D. **2** *Inf.* (esp. in World War I) a derogatory name for a **German. 3** *Inf.* a vandal. [OE *Hūnas,* from LL *Hūnī,* from Turkish *Hun-yū*]
▸ **'Hunnish** *adj* ▸ **'Hun,like** *adj*

hunch ⓣ (hʌntʃ) *n* **1** an intuitive guess or feeling. **2** another word for **hump. 3** a lump or large piece. ◆ *vb* **4** to draw (oneself or a part of the body) up or together. **5** (*intr; usually foll. by up*) to sit in a hunched position. [C16: from ?]

hunchback ⓣ ('hʌntʃ,bæk) *n* **1** a person having an abnormal curvature of the spine. **2** such a curvature. ◆ Also called: **humpback.** [C18: from earlier *hunchbacked*]
▸ **'hunch,backed** *adj*

hundred ('hʌndrəd) *n, pl* **hundreds** *or* **hundred. 1** the cardinal number that is the product of ten and ten; five score. **2** a numeral, 100, C, etc., representing this number. **3** (*often pl*) a large but unspecified number, amount, or quantity. **4** (*pl*) the 100 years of a specified century: *in the sixteen hundreds.* **5** something representing, represented by, or consisting of 100 units. **6** *Maths.* the position containing a digit representing that number followed by two zeros: *in 4376, 3 is in the hundred's place.* **7** an ancient division of a county. ◆ *determiner* **8** amounting to or approximately a hundred: *a hundred reasons for that.* [OE]
▸ **'hundredth** *adj, n*

hundreds and thousands *pl n* tiny beads of coloured sugar, used in decorating cakes, etc.

hundredweight ('hʌndrəd,weɪt) *n, pl* **hundredweights** *or* **hundredweight. 1** Also called: **long hundredweight.** *Brit.* a unit of weight equal to 112 pounds (50.802 kg). **2** Also called: **short hundredweight.** *US & Canad.* a unit of weight equal to 100 pounds (45.359 kg). **3** Also called: **metric hundredweight.** a metric unit of weight equal to 50 kilograms. ◆ Abbrev. (for senses 1, 2): **cwt.**

hung (hʌŋ) *vb* **1** the past tense and past participle of **hang** (except in the sense of *to execute*). ◆ *adj* **2** (of a political party, jury, etc.) not having a majority: *a hung parliament.* **3 hung over.** *Inf.* suffering from the effects of a hangover. **4 hung up.** *Sl.* **4a** impeded by some difficulty or delay. **4b** emotionally disturbed. **5 hung up on.** *Sl.* obsessively interested in.

Hungarian (hʌŋ'gɛərɪən) *n* **1** the official language of Hungary, also spoken in Romania and elsewhere, belonging to the Finno-Ugric family. **2** a native, inhabitant, or citizen of Hungary. ◆ *adj* **3** of or relating to Hungary, its people, or their language. ◆ Cf. **Magyar.**

hunger ⓣ ('hʌŋgə) *n* **1** a feeling of emptiness or weakness induced by lack of food. **2** desire or craving: *hunger for a woman.* ◆ *vb* **3** (*intr; usually foll. by for or after*) to have a great appetite or desire (for). [OE]

hunger march *n* a procession of protest or demonstration, esp. by the unemployed.

hunger strike *n* a voluntary fast undertaken, usually by a prisoner, as a means of protest.
▸ **hunger striker** *n*

hungry ⓣ ('hʌŋgrɪ) *adj* **hungrier, hungriest. 1** desiring food. **2** (*postpositive; foll. by for*) having a craving, desire, or need (for). **3** expressing or appearing to express greed, craving, or desire. **4** lacking fertility; poor. **5** *Austral. & NZ.* greedy; mean. **6** *NZ.* (of timber) dry and bare.
▸ **'hungrily** *adv* ▸ **'hungriness** *n*

hunk ⓣ (hʌŋk) *n* **1** a large piece. **2** *Sl.* a sexually attractive man. [C19: prob. rel. to Flemish *hunke*]

hunkers ('hʌŋkəz) *pl n* haunches. [C18: from ?]

hunky-dory (,hʌŋkɪ'dɔ:rɪ) *adj Inf.* very satisfactory; fine. [C20: from ?]

hunt ⓣ (hʌnt) *vb* **1** to seek out and kill (animals) for food or sport. **2** (*intr; often foll. by for*) to search (for): *to hunt for a book.* **3** (*tr*) to use (hounds, horses, etc.) in the pursuit of wild animals, game, etc.: *to hunt a pack of hounds.* **4** (*tr*) to search (country) to hunt game, etc.: *to hunt the parkland.* **5** (*tr; often foll. by down*) to track diligently so as to capture: *to hunt down a criminal.* **6** (*tr; usually passive*) to persecute; hound. **7** (*intr*) (of a gauge indicator, etc.) to oscillate about a mean value or position. **8** (*intr*) (of an aircraft, rocket, etc.) to oscillate about a flight path or its course axis. ◆ *n* **9** the act or an instance of hunting. **10** chase or search, esp. of animals. **11** the area of a hunt. **12** a party or institution organized for the pursuit of wild animals, esp. for sport. **13** the members of such a party or institution. [OE *huntian*]

huntaway ('hʌntə,weɪ) *n NZ.* a dog trained to drive sheep at a long distance from the shepherd.

hunted ⓣ ('hʌntɪd) *adj* harassed: *a hunted look.*

hunter ⓣ ('hʌntə) *n* **1** a person or animal that seeks out and kills or captures game. Fem.: **huntress** ('hʌntrɪs). **2a** a person who looks diligently for something. **2b** (*in combination*): *a fortune-hunter.* **3** a specially bred horse used in hunting, characterized by strength and stamina. **4** a watch with a hinged metal lid or case (**hunting case**) to protect the crystal.

hunter-killer *adj* denoting a type of submarine designed and equipped to pursue and destroy enemy craft.

hunter's moon *n* the full moon following the harvest moon.

hunting ('hʌntɪŋ) *n* **a** the pursuit and killing or capture of wild animals, regarded as a sport. **b** (*as modifier*): *hunting lodge.*

hunting horn *n* a long straight metal tube with a flared end, used in giving signals in hunting.

Huntington's disease ('hʌntɪŋtənz) *n* a hereditary form of chorea associated with progressive dementia. Former name: **Huntington's chorea.** [after G. *Huntington* (1850–1916), US physician]

huntsman ('hʌntsmən) *n, pl* **huntsmen. 1** a person who hunts. **2** a person who trains hounds, beagles, etc., and manages them during a hunt.

Huon pine ('hju:ɒn) *n* a tree of Australasia, SE Asia, and Chile, with scalelike leaves and cup-shaped berry-like fruits. [after the *Huon* River, Tasmania]

hurdle ⓣ ('hɜ:dᵊl) *n* **1a** *Athletics.* one of a number of light barriers over which runners leap in certain events. **1b** a low barrier used in certain horse races. **2** an obstacle: *the next hurdle in his career.* **3** a light framework of interlaced osiers, etc., used as a temporary fence. **4** a sledge on which criminals were dragged to their executions. ◆ *vb* **hurdles, hurdling, hurdled. 5** to jump (a hurdle). **6** (*tr*) to surround with hurdles. **7** (*tr*) to overcome. [OE *hyrdel*]
▸ **'hurdler** *n*

hurdy-gurdy ('hɜ:dɪ'gɜ:dɪ) *n, pl* **hurdy-gurdies.** any mechanical musical instrument, such as a barrel organ. [C18: rhyming compound, prob. imit.]

hurl ⓣ (hɜ:l) *vb* (*tr*) **1** to throw with great force. **2** to utter with force; yell: *to hurl insults.* ◆ *n* **3** the act of hurling. [C13: prob. imit.]

hurling ('hɜ:lɪŋ) *or* **hurley** *n* a traditional Irish game resembling hockey, played with sticks and a ball between two teams of 15 players.

hurly-burly ⓣ ('hɜ:lɪ'bɜ:lɪ) *n, pl* **hurly-burlies.** confusion or commotion. [C16: from earlier *hurling and burling,* rhyming phrase based on *hurling* in obs. sense of uproar]

Huron ('hjʊərən) *n* **1** (*pl* **Hurons** *or* **Huron**) a member of a North American Indian people formerly living in the region east of Lake Huron. **2** the Iroquoian language of this people.

hurrah (hʊ'rɑ:), **hooray** (hu:'reɪ), *or* **hurray** (hʊ'reɪ) *interj, n* **1** a cheer of

THESAURUS

doldrums, dumps (*inf.*), grumps, megrims (*rare*), mopes ◆ *vb* **5** = **hunch**, arch, curve, form a hump, lift, tense **6** *Slang* = **carry**, heave, hoist, lug, shoulder

hunch *n* **1** = **feeling**, idea, impression, inkling, intuition, premonition, presentiment, suspicion ◆ *vb* **4, 5** = **draw in**, arch, bend, crouch, curve, huddle, hump, squat, stoop, tense

hunchback *n* **1** = **Quasimodo**, humpback **2** = **humpback**, crookback (*rare*), crouch-back (*arch.*), kyphosis (*Pathology*)

hunchbacked *adj* **2** = **humpbacked**, deformed, humped, malformed, misshapen, stooped

hunger *n* **1** = **appetite**, emptiness, esurience, hungriness, ravenousness, voracity **2** = **desire**, ache, appetence, appetite, craving, greediness, itch, lust, thirst, yearning, yen (*inf.*) ◆ *vb* **3** = **want**, ache, crave, desire, hanker, hope, itch, long, pine, starve, thirst, wish, yearn

hungry *adj* **1** = **empty**, esurient, famished, famishing, hollow, peckish (*inf., chiefly Brit.*), ravenous, sharp-set, starved, starving, voracious **2** = **eager**, athirst, avid, covetous, craving, desirous, greedy, keen, yearning

hunk *n* **1** = **lump**, block, chunk, gobbet, mass, nugget, piece, slab, wedge, wodge (*Brit. inf.*)

hunt *vb* **1** = **stalk**, chase, gun for, hound, pursue, track, trail **2** = **search**, ferret about, forage, go in quest of, look, look high and low, rummage through, scour, seek, try to find ◆ *n* **9** = **search**, chase, hunting, investigation, pursuit, quest

hunted *adj* = **harassed**, careworn, desperate, distraught, gaunt, haggard, harried, persecuted, stricken, terror-stricken, tormented, worn

hunter *n* **1** = **huntsman** *or* **huntress**, sportsman *or* sportswoman

hurdle *n* **1b** = **fence**, barricade, barrier, block, hedge, wall **2** = **obstacle**, barrier, block, complication, difficulty, handicap, hazard, hindrance, impediment, obstruction, snag, stumbling block

hurl *vb* **1** = **throw**, cast, chuck (*inf.*), fire, fling, heave, launch, let fly, pitch, project, propel, send, shy, sling, toss

hurly-burly *n* = **commotion**, bedlam, brouhaha, chaos, confusion, disorder, furore, hubbub, pandemonium, tumult, turbulence, turmoil, upheaval, uproar
Antonyms *n* composure, order, organization, tidiness

joy, victory, etc. ◆ *vb* **2** to shout "hurrah". [C17: prob. from G *hurra;* cf. HUZZAH]

hurricane Ⓣ (ˈhʌrɪkən) *n* **1** a severe, often destructive storm, esp. a tropical cyclone. **2** a wind of force 12 on the Beaufort scale, with speeds over 72 mph. [C16: from Sp. *huracán,* of Amerind origin, from *hura* wind]

hurricane deck *n* a ship's deck that is covered by a light deck as a sunshade.

hurricane lamp *n* a paraffin lamp with a glass covering. Also called: **storm lantern.**

hurried Ⓣ (ˈhʌrɪd) *adj* performed with great or excessive haste.
▸**ˈhurriedly** *adv* ▸**ˈhurriedness** *n*

hurry Ⓣ (ˈhʌrɪ) *vb* **hurries, hurrying, hurried. 1** (*intr;* often foll. by *up*) to hasten; rush. **2** (*tr;* often foll. by *along*) to speed up the completion, progress, etc., of. ◆ *n* **3** haste. **4** urgency or eagerness. **5 in a hurry.** *Inf.* **5a** easily: *you won't beat him in a hurry.* **5b** willingly: *we won't go there again in a hurry.* [C16 *horyen,* prob. imit.]

hurst (hɜːst) *n Arch.* **1** a wood. **2** a sandbank. [OE *hyrst*]

hurt Ⓣ (hɜːt) *vb* **hurts, hurting, hurt. 1** (*tr*) to cause physical pain to (someone or something). **2** (*tr*) to cause emotional pain or distress to (someone). **3** to produce a painful sensation in (someone): *the bruise hurts.* **4** (*intr*) *Inf.* to feel pain. ◆ *n* **5** physical or mental pain or suffering. **6** a wound, cut, or sore. **7** damage or injury; harm. ◆ *adj* **8** injured or pained: *a hurt knee; a hurt look.* [C12 *hurten* to hit, from OF *hurter* to knock against, prob. of Gmc origin]

hurtful Ⓣ (ˈhɜːtful) *adj* causing distress or injury: *to say hurtful things.*
▸**ˈhurtfully** *adv*

hurtle Ⓣ (ˈhɜːtəl) *vb* **hurtles, hurtling, hurtled.** to project or be projected very quickly, noisily, or violently. [C13 *hurtlen,* from *hurten* to strike; see HURT]

husband Ⓣ (ˈhʌzbənd) *n* **1** a woman's partner in marriage. **2** *Arch.* a manager of an estate. ◆ *vb* **3** to manage or use (resources, finances, etc.) thriftily. **4** (*tr*) *Arch.* to find a husband for. **5** (*tr*) *Obs.* to till (the soil). [OE *hūsbonda,* from ON *hūsbōndi,* from *hūs* house + *bōndi* one who has a household]
▸**ˈhusbander** *n*

husbandman (ˈhʌzbəndmən) *n, pl* **husbandmen.** *Arch.* a farmer.

husbandry Ⓣ (ˈhʌzbəndrɪ) *n* **1** farming, esp. when regarded as a science, skill, or art. **2** management of affairs and resources.

hush Ⓣ (hʌʃ) *vb* **1** to make or become silent; quieten; soothe. ◆ *n* **2** stillness; silence. ◆ *interj* **3** a plea or demand for silence. [C16: prob. from earlier *husht* quiet!, the *-t* being thought to indicate a past participle]
▸**hushed** *adj*

hushaby (ˈhʌʃəˌbaɪ) *interj* **1** used in quietening a baby or child to sleep. ◆ *n, pl* **hushabies. 2** a lullaby. [C18: from HUSH + *by,* as in BYE-BYES]

hush-hush Ⓣ *adj Inf.* (esp. of official work, documents, etc.) secret; confidential.

hush money *n Sl.* money given to a person to ensure that something is kept secret.

hush up Ⓣ *vb* (*tr, adv*) to suppress information or rumours about.

husk Ⓣ (hʌsk) *n* **1** the external green or membranous covering of certain fruits and seeds. **2** any worthless outer covering. ◆ *vb* **3** (*tr*) to remove the husk from. [C14: prob. based on MDu. *huusken* little house, from *hūs* house]

husky[1] Ⓣ (ˈhʌskɪ) *adj* **huskier, huskiest. 1** (of a voice, utterance, etc.) slightly hoarse or rasping. **2** of or containing husks. **3** *Inf.* big and strong. [C19: prob. from HUSK, from the toughness of a corn husk]
▸**ˈhuskily** *adv* ▸**ˈhuskiness** *n*

husky[2] (ˈhʌskɪ) *n, pl* **huskies. 1** a breed of Arctic sled dog with a thick dense coat, pricked ears, and a curled tail. **2** *Canad. sl.* **2a** a member of the Inuit people. **2b** their language. [C19: prob. based on ESKIMO]

hussar (hʊˈzɑː) *n* **1** a member of any of various light cavalry regiments, renowned for their elegant dress. **2** a Hungarian horseman of the 15th century. [C15: from Hungarian *huszár* hussar, formerly freebooter, ult. from OIt. *corsaro* CORSAIR]

Hussite (ˈhʌsaɪt) *n* **1** an adherent of the ideas of John Huss, 14th-century Bohemian religious reformer, or a member of the movement initiated by him. ◆ *adj* **2** of or relating to John Huss, his teachings, followers, etc.
▸**ˈHussitism** *n*

hussy Ⓣ (ˈhʌsɪ, -zɪ) *n, pl* **hussies.** *Contemptuous.* a shameless or promiscuous woman. [C16 (in the sense: housewife): from *hussif* HOUSEWIFE]

hustings (ˈhʌstɪŋz) *n* (*functioning as pl or sing*) **1** *Brit.* (before 1872) the platform on which candidates were nominated for Parliament and from which they addressed the electors. **2** the proceedings at a parliamentary election. [C11: from ON *hūsthing,* from *hūs* HOUSE + *thing* assembly]

hustle Ⓣ (ˈhʌsəl) *vb* **hustles, hustling, hustled. 1** to shove or crowd (someone) roughly. **2** to move hurriedly or furtively: *he hustled her out of sight.* **3** (*tr*) to deal with hurriedly: *to hustle legislation through.* **4** *Sl.* to obtain (something) forcefully. **5** *US & Canad. sl.* (of procurers and prostitutes) to solicit. ◆ *n* **6** an instance of hustling. [C17: from Du. *husselen* to shake, from MDu. *hutsen*]
▸**ˈhustler** *n*

hut Ⓣ (hʌt) *n* **1** a small house or shelter. ◆ *vb* **huts, hutting, hutted. 2** to furnish with or live in a hut. [C17: from F *hutte,* of Gmc origin]
▸**ˈhutˌlike** *adj*

hutch (hʌtʃ) *n* **1** a cage, usually of wood and wire mesh, for small animals. **2** *Inf., derog.* a small house. **3** a cart for carrying ore. [C14 *hucche,* from OF *huche,* from Med. L *hutica,* from ?]

hutment (ˈhʌtmənt) *n Chiefly mil.* a number or group of huts.

huzzah (həˈzɑː) *interj, n, vb* an archaic word for **hurrah.** [C16: from ?]

HV *or* **h.v.** *abbrev. for* high voltage.

HWM *abbrev. for* high-water mark.

hwyl (ˈhuːɪl) *n* emotional fervour, as in the recitation of poetry. [C19: Welsh]

hyacinth (ˈhaɪəsɪnθ) *n* **1** any plant of the Mediterranean genus *Hyacinthus,* esp. a cultivated variety having a thick flower stalk bearing bell-shaped fragrant flowers. **2** the flower or bulb of such a plant. **3** any similar plant, such as the grape hyacinth. **4** Also called: **jacinth.** a reddish transparent variety of the mineral zircon, used as a gemstone. **5a** any of the varying colours of the hyancinth flower or stone. **5b** (*as adj*): *hyacinth eyes.* [C16: from L *hyacinthus,* from Gk *huakinthos*]
▸**ˌhyaˈcinthine** *adj*

Hyades[1] (ˈhaɪəˌdiːz) *pl n* an open cluster of stars in the constellation Taurus, formerly believed to bring rain when they rose with the sun. [C16: via L from Gk *huades,* ?from *huein* to rain]

hyaena (haɪˈiːnə) *n* a variant spelling of **hyena.**

hyaline (ˈhaɪəlɪn) *adj Biol.* clear and translucent, as a common type of cartilage. [C17: from LL *hyalinus,* from Gk, from *hualos* glass]

hyalite (ˈhaɪəˌlaɪt) *n* a clear and colourless variety of opal in globular form.

hyaloid (ˈhaɪəˌlɔɪd) *adj Anat., zool.* clear and transparent; hyaline. [C19: from Gk *hualoeidēs*]

THESAURUS

hurricane *n* **1, 2** = **storm**, cyclone, gale, tempest, tornado, twister (*US inf.*), typhoon, willy-willy (*Austral.*), windstorm

hurried *adj* = **hasty**, breakneck, brief, cursory, hectic, perfunctory, precipitate, quick, quickie (*inf.*), rushed, short, slapdash, speedy, superficial, swift

hurriedly *adv* = **hastily**, hurry-scurry, in a rush, perfunctorily, quickly

hurry *vb* **1** = **rush**, barrel (along), burn rubber (*inf.*), dash, fly, get a move on (*inf.*), get one's skates on (*inf.*), lose no time, make haste, scoot, scurry, step on it (*inf.*) **2** = **speed (up)**, accelerate, expedite, goad, hasten, hustle, push on, quicken, urge ◆ *n* **3** = **haste**, bustle, celerity, commotion, dispatch, expedition, flurry, precipitation, promptitude, quickness, rush, speed, urgency
Antonyms *vb* ≠ **rush:** crawl, creep, dawdle, drag one's feet, move slowly ≠ **speed (up):** delay, retard, slow, slow down ◆ *n* ≠ **haste:** calmness, slowness

hurt *vb* **1** = **harm**, bruise, damage, disable, impair, injure, lay a finger on, mar, spoil, wound **2** = **upset**, afflict, aggrieve, annoy, cut to the quick, distress, grieve, pain, sadden, sting, wound **3** = **ache**, be sore, be tender, burn, smart, sting, throb ◆ *n* **5** = **distress**, discomfort, pain, pang, soreness, suffering **6** = **wound**, bruise, sore **7** = **harm**, damage, detriment, disadvantage, injury, loss, mischief, wrong ◆ *adj* **8** = **injured**, bruised, cut, damaged, grazed, harmed, scarred, scraped, scratched, wounded **8** = **upset**, aggrieved, crushed, injured, miffed (*inf.*), offended, pained, piqued, rueful, sad, wounded
Antonyms *vb* ≠ **harm:** alleviate, cure, heal, relieve, repair, restore, soothe ◆ *n* ≠ **distress:** delight, happiness, joy, pleasure, pride, satisfaction ◆ *adj* ≠ **injured:** alleviated, assuaged, healed, relieved, repaired, restored, soothed ≠ **upset:** calmed, consoled, placated

hurtful *adj* = **unkind**, cruel, cutting, damaging, destructive, detrimental, disadvantageous, distressing, harmful, injurious, maleficent, malicious, mean, mischievous, nasty, pernicious, prejudicial, spiteful, upsetting, wounding

hurtle *vb* = **rush**, barrel (along) (*inf., chiefly US & Canad.*), burn rubber (*inf.*), charge, crash, fly, go hell for leather (*inf.*), plunge, race, rush headlong, scoot, scramble, shoot, speed, spurt, stampede, tear

husband *n* **1** = **partner**, better half (*humorous*), bridegroom, man (*inf.*), mate, old man (*inf.*), significant other (*US inf.*), spouse ◆ *vb* **3** = **economize**, budget, conserve, hoard, manage thriftily, save, store, use sparingly
Antonyms *vb* ≠ **economize:** be extravagant, fritter away, spend, splash out (*inf., chiefly Brit.*), squander

husbandry *n* **1** = **farming**, agriculture, agronomy, cultivation, land management, tillage **2** = **thrift**, careful management, economy, frugality, good housekeeping

hush *vb* **1** = **quieten**, allay, appease, calm, compose, mollify, mute, muzzle, shush, silence, soothe, still, suppress ◆ *n* **2** = **quiet**, calm, peace, peacefulness, silence, still (*poetic*), stillness, tranquillity

hush-hush *adj Informal* = **secret**, classified, confidential, restricted, top-secret, under wraps

hush up *vb* = **cover up**, conceal, draw a veil over, keep dark, keep secret, sit on (*inf.*), smother, squash, suppress, sweep under the carpet (*inf.*)

husk *n* **1** = **rind**, bark, chaff, covering, hull, shuck

huskiness *n* **1** = **hoarseness**, dryness, harshness, raspingness, roughness

husky[1] *adj* **1** = **hoarse**, croaking, croaky, gruff, guttural, harsh, rasping, raucous, rough, throaty **3** *Informal* = **muscular**, beefy (*inf.*), brawny, burly, hefty, powerful, rugged, stocky, strapping, thickset

hussy *n Contemptuous* = **slut**, baggage (*inf., old-fashioned*), floozy (*sl.*), jade, scrubber, slapper (*Brit. sl.*), strumpet, tart (*inf.*), tramp (*sl.*), trollop, wanton

hustle *vb* **1, 2** = **jostle**, bustle, crowd, elbow, force, haste, hasten, hurry, impel, jog, push, rush, shove, thrust

hut *n* **1** = **shed**, cabin, den, hovel, lean-to, refuge, shanty, shelter

hyaloid membrane *n* the delicate transparent membrane enclosing the vitreous humour of the eye.

hybrid Ⓣ (ˈhaɪbrɪd) *n* **1** an animal or plant resulting from a cross between genetically unlike individuals; usually sterile. **2** anything of mixed ancestry. **3** a word, part of which is derived from one language and part from another, such as *monolingual.* ◆ *adj* **4** denoting or being a hybrid; of mixed origin. [C17: from L *hibrida* offspring of a mixed union (human or animal)]
▸ˈ**hybridism** *n* ▸**hyˈbridity** *n*

hybrid computer *n* a computer that uses both analogue and digital techniques.

hybridize *or* **hybridise** (ˈhaɪbrɪˌdaɪz) *vb* **hybridizes, hybridizing, hybridized** *or* **hybridises, hybridising, hybridised.** to produce or cause to produce hybrids; crossbreed.
▸ˌ**hybridiˈzation** *or* ˌ**hybridiˈsation** *n*

hybridoma (ˌhaɪbrɪˈdəʊmə) *n* a hybrid cell formed by the fusion of two different types of cell, esp. one capable of producing antibodies fused with an immortal tumour cell. [C20: from HYBRID + -OMA]

hybrid vigour *n Biol.* the increased size, strength, etc., of a hybrid as compared to either of its parents. Also called: **heterosis.**

hydatid (ˈhaɪdətɪd) *n* **1** a large bladder containing encysted larvae of the tapeworm *Echinococcus:* causes serious disease in man. **2** Also called: **hydatid cyst.** a sterile fluid-filled cyst produced in man and animals during infestation by *Echinococcus* larval forms. [C17: from Gk *hudatis* watery vesicle, from *hudōr, hudat-* water]

hydr- *combining form.* a variant of **hydro-** before a vowel.

hydra (ˈhaɪdrə) *n, pl* **hydras** *or* **hydrae** (-driː). **1** a freshwater coelenterate in which the body is a slender polyp with tentacles around the mouth. **2** a persistent trouble or evil. [C16: from L, from Gk *hudra* water serpent]

hydracid (haɪˈdræsɪd) *n* an acid, such as hydrochloric acid, that does not contain oxygen.

hydrangea (haɪˈdreɪndʒə) *n* a shrub or tree of an Asian and American genus cultivated for their large clusters of white, pink, or blue flowers. [C18: from NL, from Gk *hudōr* water + *angeion* vessel: prob. from the cup-shaped fruit]

hydrant (ˈhaɪdrənt) *n* an outlet from a water main, usually an upright pipe with a valve attached, from which water can be tapped for fighting fires, etc. [C19: from HYDRO- + -ANT]

hydrate (ˈhaɪdreɪt) *n* **1** a chemical compound containing water that is chemically combined with a substance. **2** a crystalline chemical compound containing weakly bound water molecules. ◆ *vb* **hydrates, hydrating, hydrated. 3** to undergo or cause to undergo treatment or impregnation with water.
▸**hyˈdration** *n* ▸ˈ**hydrator** *n*

hydrated (ˈhaɪdreɪtɪd) *adj* (of a compound) chemically bonded to water molecules.

hydraulic (haɪˈdrɒlɪk) *adj* **1** operated by pressure transmitted through a pipe by a liquid, such as water or oil. **2** of or employing liquids in motion. **3** of hydraulics. **4** hardening under water: *hydraulic cement.* [C17: from L *hydraulicus,* from Gk *hudraulikos,* from *hudraulos* water organ, from HYDRO- + *aulos* pipe]
▸**hyˈdraulically** *adv*

hydraulic brake *n* a type of brake, used in motor vehicles, in which the braking force is transmitted from the brake pedal to the brakes by a liquid under pressure.

hydraulic coupling *n* another name for **torque converter.**

hydraulic press *n* a press that utilizes liquid pressure to enable a small force applied to a small piston to produce a large force on a larger piston.

hydraulic ram *n* **1** the larger or working piston of a hydraulic press. **2** a form of water pump utilizing the kinetic energy of running water to provide static pressure to raise water to a reservoir higher than the source.

hydraulics (haɪˈdrɒlɪks) *n* (*functioning as sing*) another name for **fluid mechanics.**

hydraulic suspension *n* a system of motor-vehicle suspension using hydraulic members, often with hydraulic compensation between front and rear systems (**hydroelastic suspension**).

hydrazine (ˈhaɪdrəˌziːn, -zɪn) *n* a colourless liquid made from sodium hypochlorite and ammonia: used as a rocket fuel. Formula: N_2H_4. [C19: from HYDRO- + AZO + -INE[2]]

hydric (ˈhaɪdrɪk) *adj* **1** of or containing hydrogen. **2** containing or using moisture.

hydride (ˈhaɪdraɪd) *n* any compound of hydrogen with another element.

hydrilla (haɪˈdrɪlə) *n* a type of underwater aquatic weed that was introduced from Asia into the south US, where it has become a serious problem, choking fish and hindering navigation. [C20: NL, prob. from L *hydra*: see HYDRA]

hydriodic acid (ˌhaɪdrɪˈɒdɪk) *n* a solution of hydrogen iodide in water: a strong acid. [C19: from HYDRO- + IODIC]

hydro[1] (ˈhaɪdrəʊ) *n, pl* **hydros.** *Brit.* (esp. formerly) a hotel or resort, often near a spa, offering facilities for hydropathic treatment.

hydro[2] (ˈhaɪdrəʊ) *adj* **1** short for **hydroelectric.** ◆ *n* **2** a Canadian name for **electricity.**

Hydro (ˈhaɪdrəʊ) *n* (esp. in Canada) a hydroelectric power company or board.

hydro- *or sometimes before a vowel* **hydr-** *combining form.* **1** indicating water or fluid: *hydrodynamics.* **2** indicating hydrogen in a chemical compound: *hydrochloric acid.* **3** indicating a hydroid: *hydrozoan.* [from Gk *hudōr* water]

hydrobromic acid (ˌhaɪdrəʊˈbrəʊmɪk) *n* a solution of hydrogen bromide in water: a strong acid.

hydrocarbon (ˌhaɪdrəʊˈkɑːbᵊn) *n* any organic compound containing only carbon and hydrogen.

hydrocele (ˈhaɪdrəʊˌsiːl) *n* an abnormal collection of fluid in any saclike space.

hydrocephalus (ˌhaɪdrəʊˈsɛfələs) *or* **hydrocephaly** (ˌhaɪdrəʊˈsɛfəlɪ) *n* accumulation of cerebrospinal fluid within the ventricles of the brain because its normal outlet has been blocked by congenital malformation or disease. Nontechnical name: **water on the brain.**
▸**hydrocephalic** (ˌhaɪdrəʊsɛˈfælɪk) *or* ˌ**hydroˈcephalous** *adj*

hydrochloric acid (ˌhaɪdrəˈklɒrɪk) *n* a solution of hydrogen chloride in water: a strong acid used in many industrial and laboratory processes.

hydrochloride (ˌhaɪdrəˈklɔːraɪd) *n* a quaternary salt formed by the addition of hydrochloric acid to an organic base.

hydrocyanic acid (ˌhaɪdrəʊsaɪˈænɪk) *n* another name for **hydrogen cyanide.**

hydrodynamics (ˌhaɪdrəʊdaɪˈnæmɪks, -dɪ-) *n* (*functioning as sing*) the branch of science concerned with the mechanical properties of fluids, esp. liquids. Also called: **hydromechanics.**

hydroelastic suspension (ˌhaɪdrəʊɪˈlæstɪk) *n* See **hydraulic suspension.**

hydroelectric (ˌhaɪdrəʊɪˈlɛktrɪk) *adj* **1** generated by the pressure of falling water: *hydroelectric power.* **2** of the generation of electricity by water pressure: *a hydroelectric scheme.*
▸**hydroelectricity** (ˌhaɪdrəʊɪlɛkˈtrɪsɪtɪ) *n*

hydrofluoric acid (ˌhaɪdrəʊfluːˈɒrɪk) *n* a solution of hydrogen fluoride in water: a strong acid that attacks glass.

hydrofoil (ˈhaɪdrəˌfɔɪl) *n* **1** a fast light vessel the hull of which is raised out of the water on one or more pairs of fixed vanes. **2** any of these vanes.

hydroforming (ˈhaɪdrəʊˌfɔːmɪŋ) *n* **1** *Chem.* the catalytic reforming of petroleum to increase the proportion of aromatic and branched-chain hydrocarbons. **2** *Engineering.* a forming process in which a metal is shaped by a punch forced against a die, consisting of a flexible bag containing a fluid.

hydrogen (ˈhaɪdrɪdʒən) *n* **a** a flammable colourless gas that is the lightest and most abundant element in the universe. It occurs in water and in most organic compounds. Symbol: H; atomic no.: 1; atomic wt.: 1.007 94. **b** (*as modifier*): *hydrogen bomb.* [C18: from F *hydrogène,* from HYDRO- + -GEN; because its combustion produces water]
▸**hydrogenous** (haɪˈdrɒdʒɪnəs) *adj*

hydrogenate (ˈhaɪdrədʒɪˌneɪt, haɪˈdrɒdʒɪˌneɪt) *vb* **hydrogenates, hydrogenating, hydrogenated.** to undergo or cause to undergo a reaction with hydrogen: *to hydrogenate ethylene.*
▸ˌ**hydrogenˈation** *n*

hydrogen bomb *n* a type of bomb in which energy is released by fusion of hydrogen nuclei to give helium nuclei. The energy required to initiate the fusion is provided by the detonation of an atomic bomb, which is surrounded by a hydrogen-containing substance. Also called: **H-bomb.**

hydrogen bond *n* a weak chemical bond between an electronegative atom, such as fluorine, oxygen, or nitrogen, and a hydrogen atom bound to another electronegative atom.

hydrogen bromide *n* **1** a colourless pungent gas used in organic synthesis. Formula: HBr. **2** an aqueous solution of hydrogen bromide; hydrobromic acid.

hydrogen carbonate *n* another name for **bicarbonate.**

hydrogen chloride *n* **1** a colourless pungent corrosive gas obtained by the action of sulphuric acid on sodium chloride: used in making vinyl chloride and other organic chemicals. Formula: HCl. **2** an aqueous solution of hydrogen chloride; hydrochloric acid.

hydrogen cyanide *n* a colourless poisonous liquid with a faint odour of bitter almonds. It forms prussic acid in aqueous solution and is used for making plastics and as a war gas. Formula: HCN. Also called: **hydrocyanic acid.**

hydrogen fluoride *n* **1** a colourless poisonous corrosive gas or liquid made by reaction between calcium fluoride and sulphuric acid: used as a fluorinating agent and catalyst. Formula: HF. **2** an aqueous solution of hydrogen fluoride; hydrofluoric acid.

hydrogen iodide *n* **1** a colourless poisonous corrosive gas obtained by a catalysed reaction between hydrogen and iodine vapour: used in making iodides. Formula HI. **2** an aqueous solution of this gas; hydriodic acid.

THESAURUS

hybrid *n* **1, 2** = **crossbreed**, amalgam, composite, compound, cross, half-blood, half-breed, mixture, mongrel, mule

hydrogen ion *n* an ionized hydrogen atom, occurring in aqueous solutions of acids; proton. Formula: H^+.

hydrogenize *or* **hydrogenise** ('haɪdrədʒɪˌnaɪz, haɪ'drɒdʒɪˌnaɪz) *vb* **hydrogenizes, hydrogenizing, hydrogenized** *or* **hydrogenises, hydrogenising, hydrogenised.** a variant of **hydrogenate.**

hydrogen peroxide *n* a colourless oily unstable liquid used as a bleach and as an oxidizer in rocket fuels. Formula: H_2O_2.

hydrogen sulphide *n* a colourless poisonous gas with an odour of rotten eggs. Formula: H_2S. Also called: **sulphuretted hydrogen.**

hydrography (haɪ'drɒgrəfɪ) *n* the study, surveying, and mapping of the oceans, seas, and rivers.
▸**hy'drographer** *n* ▸**hydrographic** (ˌhaɪdrə'græfɪk) *adj*

hydroid ('haɪdrɔɪd) *adj* **1** of or relating to the *Hydroida,* an order of hydrozoan coelenterates that have the polyp phase dominant. **2** having or consisting of hydra-like polyps. ◆ *n* **3** a hydroid colony or individual.

hydrokinetics (ˌhaɪdrəʊkɪ'nɛtɪks, -kaɪ-) *n* (*functioning as sing*) the branch of science concerned with the behaviour and properties of fluids in motion. Also called: **hydrodynamics.**

hydrolase ('haɪdrəˌleɪz) *n* an enzyme that controls hydrolysis.

hydrology (haɪ'drɒlədʒɪ) *n* the study of the distribution, conservation, use, etc., of the water of the earth and its atmosphere.
▸**hydrological** (ˌhaɪdrə'lɒdʒɪkᵊl) *adj* ▸**hy'drologist** *n*

hydrolyse *or US* **hydrolyze** ('haɪdrəˌlaɪz) *vb* **hydrolyses, hydrolysing, hydrolysed** *or US* **hydrolyzes, hydrolyzing, hydrolyzed.** to subject to or undergo hydrolysis.

hydrolysis (haɪ'drɒlɪsɪs) *n* a chemical reaction in which a compound reacts with water to produce other compounds.
▸**hydrolytic** (ˌhaɪdrə'lɪtɪk) *adj*

hydrolyte ('haɪdrəˌlaɪt) *n* a substance subjected to hydrolysis.

hydromel ('haɪdrəʊˌmɛl) *n Arch.* another word for **mead** (the drink). [C15: from L, from Gk *hudromeli,* from HYDRO- + *meli* honey]

hydrometer (haɪ'drɒmɪtə) *n* an instrument for measuring the relative density of a liquid.
▸**hydrometric** (ˌhaɪdrəʊ'mɛtrɪk) *or* ˌ**hydro'metrical** *adj*

hydronaut ('haɪdrəʊˌnɔːt) *n US Navy.* a person trained to operate deep submergence vessels. [C20: from Gk, from HYDRO- + *-naut,* as in *astronaut*]

hydropathy (haɪ'drɒpəθɪ) *n* a pseudoscientific method of treating disease by the use of large quantities of water both internally and externally.
▸**hydropathic** (ˌhaɪdrəʊ'pæθɪk) *adj*

hydrophilic (ˌhaɪdrəʊ'fɪlɪk) *adj Chem.* tending to dissolve in, mix with, or be wetted by water: *a hydrophilic colloid.*
▸**hydrophile** ('haɪdrəʊˌfaɪl) *n*

hydrophobia (ˌhaɪdrə'fəʊbɪə) *n* **1** another name for **rabies. 2** a fear of drinking fluids, esp. that of a person with rabies, because of painful spasms when trying to swallow.
▸ˌ**hydro'phobic** *adj*

hydrophone ('haɪdrəˌfəʊn) *n* an electroacoustic transducer that converts sound travelling through water into electrical oscillations.

hydrophyte ('haɪdrəʊˌfaɪt) *n* a plant that grows only in water or very moist soil.

hydroplane ('haɪdrəʊˌpleɪn) *n* **1** a motorboat equipped with hydrofoils or with a shaped bottom that raises its hull out of the water at high speeds. **2** an attachment to an aircraft to enable it to glide along the surface of the water. **3** another name for a **seaplane. 4** a horizontal vane on the hull of a submarine for controlling its vertical motion. ◆ *vb* **hydroplanes, hydroplaning, hydroplaned. 5** (*intr*) (of a boat) to rise out of the water in the manner of a hydroplane.

hydroponics (ˌhaɪdrəʊ'pɒnɪks) *n* (*functioning as sing*) a method of cultivating plants by growing them in gravel, etc., through which water containing dissolved inorganic nutrient salts is pumped. [C20: from HYDRO- + (*geo*)*ponics* science of agriculture]
▸ˌ**hydro'ponic** *adj* ▸ˌ**hydro'ponically** *adv*

hydropower ('haɪdrəʊˌpaʊə) *n* hydroelectric power.

hydroquinone (ˌhaɪdrəʊkwɪ'nəʊn) *or* **hydroquinol** (ˌhaɪdrəʊ'kwɪnɒl) *n* a white crystalline soluble phenol used as a photographic developer.

hydrosphere ('haɪdrəˌsfɪə) *n* the watery part of the earth's surface, including oceans, lakes, water vapour in the atmosphere, etc.

hydrostatics (ˌhaɪdrəʊ'stætɪks) *n* (*functioning as sing*) the branch of science concerned with the mechanical properties and behaviour of fluids that are not in motion.
▸ˌ**hydro'static** *adj*

hydrotherapeutics (ˌhaɪdrəʊˌθɛrə'pjuːtɪks) *n* (*functioning as sing*) the branch of medical science concerned with hydrotherapy.

hydrotherapy (ˌhaɪdrəʊ'θɛrəpɪ) *n Med.* the treatment of certain diseases by the application of water, esp. by exercising in water to mobilize stiff joints or strengthen weak muscles.

hydrothermal (ˌhaɪdrəʊ'θɜːməl) *adj* of or relating to the action of water under conditions of high temperature, esp. in forming rocks.

hydrotropism (haɪ'drɒtrəˌpɪzəm) *n* the directional growth of plants in response to the stimulus of water.

hydrous ('haɪdrəs) *adj* containing water.

hydrovane ('haɪdrəʊˌveɪn) *n* a vane on a seaplane conferring stability on water (a sponson) or facilitating takeoff (a hydrofoil).

hydroxide (haɪ'drɒksaɪd) *n* **1** a base or alkali containing the ion OH^-. **2** any compound containing an -OH group.

hydroxy (haɪ'drɒksɪ) *adj* (of a chemical compound) containing one or more hydroxyl groups. [C19: HYDRO- + OXY(GEN)]

hydroxyl (haɪ'drɒksɪl) *n* (*modifier*) of, consisting of, or containing the monovalent group -OH or the ion OH^-: *a hydroxyl group or radical.*

hydroxytryptamine (haɪˌdrɒksɪ'trɪptəˌmiːn) *n* 5-hydroxytryptamine: another name for **serotonin.** Abbrev.: **5HT.**

hydrozoan (ˌhaɪdrəʊ'zəʊən) *n* **1** any coelenterate of the class *Hydrozoa,* which includes the hydra and the Portuguese man-of-war. ◆ *adj* **2** of the *Hydrozoa.*

hyena *or* **hyaena** (haɪ'iːnə) *n* any of several long-legged carnivorous doglike mammals such as the spotted or laughing hyena, of Africa and S Asia. [C16: from Med. L, from L *hyaena,* from Gk, from *hus* hog]
▸**hy'enic** *or* **hy'aenic** *adj*

hygiene ⓣ ('haɪdʒiːn) *n* **1** Also called: **hygienics.** the science concerned with the maintenance of health. **2** clean or healthy practices or thinking: *personal hygiene.* [C18: from NL *hygiēna,* from Gk *hugieinē,* from *hugiēs* healthy]

hygienic ⓣ (haɪ'dʒiːnɪk) *adj* promoting health or cleanliness; sanitary.
▸**hy'gienically** *adv*

hygienics (haɪ'dʒiːnɪks) *n* (*functioning as sing*) another word for **hygiene** (sense 1).

hygienist ('haɪdʒiːnɪst) *n* a person skilled in the practice of hygiene.

hygro- *or before a vowel* **hygr-** *combining form.* indicating moisture: *hygrometer.* [from Gk *hugros* wet]

hygrometer (haɪ'grɒmɪtə) *n* any of various instruments for measuring humidity.
▸**hygrometric** (ˌhaɪgrə'mɛtrɪk) *adj*

hygrophyte ('haɪgrəˌfaɪt) *n* any plant that grows in wet or waterlogged soil.
▸**hygrophytic** (ˌhaɪgrə'fɪtɪk) *adj*

hygroscope ('haɪgrəˌskəʊp) *n* any device that indicates the humidity of the air without necessarily measuring it.

hygroscopic (ˌhaɪgrə'skɒpɪk) *adj* (of a substance) tending to absorb water from the air.
▸ˌ**hygro'scopically** *adv*

hying ('haɪɪŋ) *vb* a present participle of **hie.**

hyla ('haɪlə) *n* a tree frog of tropical America. [C19: from NL, from Gk *hulē* forest]

hylomorphism (ˌhaɪlə'mɔːfɪzəm) *n* the philosophical doctrine that identifies matter with the first cause of the universe.

hylozoism (ˌhaɪlə'zəʊɪzəm) *n* the philosophical doctrine that life is one of the properties of matter. [C17: from Gk *hulē* wood, matter + *zōē* life]

hymen ('haɪmɛn) *n Anat.* a fold of mucous membrane that partly covers the entrance to the vagina and is usually ruptured when sexual intercourse takes place for the first time. [C17: from Gk: membrane]
▸**'hymenal** *adj*

hymeneal (ˌhaɪmɛ'niːəl) *adj* **1** *Chiefly poetic.* of or relating to marriage. ◆ *n* **2** a wedding song or poem.

hymenopteran (ˌhaɪmɪ'nɒptərən) *or* **hymenopteron** *n, pl* **hymenopterans, hymenoptera** (-tərə), *or* **hymenopterons.** any hymenopterous insect.

hymenopterous (ˌhaɪmɪ'nɒptərəs) *adj* of or belonging to an order of insects, including bees, wasps, and ants, having two pairs of membranous wings. [C19: from Gk *humenopteros* membrane wing; see HYMEN, -PTEROUS]

hymn ⓣ (hɪm) *n* **1** a Christian song of praise sung to God or a saint. **2** a similar song praising other gods, a nation, etc. ◆ *vb* **3** to express (praises, thanks, etc.) by singing hymns. [C13: from L *hymnus,* from Gk *humnos*]
▸**hymnic** ('hɪmnɪk) *adj*

hymnal ('hɪmnᵊl) *n* **1** Also: **hymn book.** a book of hymns. ◆ *adj* **2** of, relating to, or characteristic of hymns.

hymnody ('hɪmnədɪ) *n* **1** the composition or singing of hymns. **2** hymns collectively. ◆ Also called: **hymnology.** [C18: from Med. L *hymnōdia,* from Gk, from *humnōidein,* from HYMN + *aeidein* to sing]

hymnology (hɪm'nɒlədʒɪ) *n* **1** the study of hymn composition. **2** another word for **hymnody.**
▸**hym'nologist** *n*

hyoid ('haɪɔɪd) *adj* of or relating to the **hyoid bone,** the horseshoe-shaped bone that lies at the base of the tongue. [C19: from NL *hȳoïdes,* from Gk *huoeidēs* having the shape of the letter UPSILON, from *hu* upsilon + -OID]

hyoscine ('haɪəˌsiːn) *n* another name for **scopolamine.** [C19: from *huosc(yamus)* a medicinal plant + -INE²; see HYOSCYAMINE]

hyoscyamine (ˌhaɪə'saɪəˌmiːn) *n* a poisonous alkaloid occurring in henbane and related plants: used in medicine. [C19: from NL, from Gk *huoskuamos* (from *hus* pig + *kuamos* bean) + AMINE]

hyp. *abbrev. for:* **1** hypotenuse. **2** hypothesis. **3** hypothetical.

THESAURUS

hygiene *n* **1, 2** = **cleanliness,** hygienics, sanitary measures, sanitation

hygienic *adj* = **clean,** aseptic, disinfected, germ-free, healthy, pure, salutary, sanitary, sterile

Antonyms *adj* dirty, filthy, germ-ridden, harmful, insanitary, polluted, unhealthy, unhygienic, unwholesome

hymn *n* **1, 2** = **song of praise,** anthem, canticle, carol, chant, doxology, paean, psalm

hypaethral *or US* **hypethral** (hɪˈpiːθrəl, haɪ-) *adj* (esp. of a classical temple) having no roof. [C18: from L *hypaethrus* uncovered, from Gk, from HYPO- + *aithros* clear sky]

hypallage (haɪˈpæləˌdʒiː) *n Rhetoric.* a figure of speech in which the natural relations of two words in a statement are interchanged, as in *the fire spread the wind.* [C16: via LL from Gk *hupallagē*, from HYPO- + *allassein* to exchange]

hype[1] ⓣ (haɪp) *Sl.* ◆ *n* **1** an intensive or exaggerated publicity or sales promotion. **2** a deception or racket. ◆ *vb* **hypes, hyping, hyped. 3** (*tr*) to market or promote (a product) using intensive or exaggerated publicity. [C20: from ?]

hype[2] (haɪp) *Sl.* ◆ *n* **1** a hypodermic needle or injection. ◆ *vb* **hypes, hyping, hyped. 2** (*intr;* usually foll. by *up*) to inject oneself with a drug. **3** (*tr*) to stimulate artificially or excite. [C20: shortened from HYPODERMIC]

hyped up *adj Sl.* stimulated or excited by or as if by the effect of a stimulating drug.

hyper (ˈhaɪpə) *adj Inf.* overactive; overexcited. [C20: prob. independent use of HYPER-]

hyper- *prefix* **1** above, over, or in excess: *hypercritical.* **2** denoting an abnormal excess: *hyperacidity.* **3** indicating that a chemical compound contains a greater than usual amount of an element: *hyperoxide.* [from Gk *huper* over]

hyperacidity (ˌhaɪpərəˈsɪdɪtɪ) *n* excess acidity of the gastrointestinal tract, esp. the stomach, producing a burning sensation.

hyperactive (ˌhaɪpərˈæktɪv) *adj* abnormally active.
▸**ˌhyperacˈtivity** *n*

hyperaemia *or US* **hyperemia** (ˌhaɪpərˈiːmɪə) *n Pathol.* an excessive amount of blood in an organ or part.

hyperaesthesia *or US* **hyperesthesia** (ˌhaɪpəriːsˈθiːzɪə) *n Pathol.* increased sensitivity of any of the sense organs.
▸**hyperaesthetic** *or US* **hyperesthetic** (ˌhaɪpəriːsˈθɛtɪk) *adj*

hyperbaton (haɪˈpɜːbəˌtɒn) *n Rhetoric.* a figure of speech in which the normal order of words is reversed, as in *cheese I love.* [C16: via L from Gk, lit.: an overstepping, from HYPER- + *bainein* to step]

hyperbola (haɪˈpɜːbələ) *n, pl* **hyperbolas** *or* **hyperbole** (-ˌliː). a conic section formed by a plane that cuts both bases of a cone: it consists of two branches asymptotic to two intersecting fixed lines. [C17: from Gk *huperbolē*, lit.: excess, extravagance, from HYPER- + *ballein* to throw]

hyperbole ⓣ (haɪˈpɜːbəlɪ) *n* a deliberate exaggeration used for effect: *he embraced her a thousand times.* [C16: from Gk, from HYPER- + *bolē*, from *ballein* to throw]
▸**hyˈperbolism** *n*

hyperbolic (ˌhaɪpəˈbɒlɪk) *or* **hyperbolical** *adj* **1** of a hyperbola. **2** *Rhetoric.* of a hyperbole.
▸**ˌhyperˈbolically** *adv*

hyperbolic function *n* any of a group of functions of an angle expressed as a relationship between the distances of a point on a hyperbola to the origin and to the coordinate axes.

hyperbolize *or* **hyperbolise** (haɪˈpɜːbəˌlaɪz) *vb* **hyperbolizes, hyperbolizing, hyperbolized** *or* **hyperbolises, hyperbolising, hyperbolised.** to express (something) by means of hyperbole.

hyperboloid (haɪˈpɜːbəˌlɔɪd) *n* a geometric surface consisting of one sheet, or of two sheets separated by a finite distance, whose sections parallel to the three coordinate planes are hyperbolas or ellipses.

Hyperborean (ˌhaɪpəˈbɔːrɪən) *n* **1** *Greek myth.* one of a people believed to have lived beyond the North Wind in a sunny land. **2** an inhabitant of the extreme north. ◆ *adj* **3** (*sometimes not cap.*) of or relating to the extreme north. [C16: from L *hyperboreus*, from Gk, from HYPER- + *Boreas* the north wind]

hypercharge (ˈhaɪpəˌtʃɑːdʒ) *n* a property of baryons that is used to account for the absence of certain strong interaction decays.

hypercholesterolaemia *or US* **hypercholesterolemia** (ˌhaɪpəkəˌlɛstərɒlˈiːmɪə) *n* the condition of having high levels of cholesterol in the blood, predisposing to atherosclerosis of the coronary arteries.

hypercorrect (ˌhaɪpəkəˈrɛkt) *adj* **1** excessively correct or fastidious. **2** resulting from or characterized by hypercorrection.

hypercorrection (ˌhaɪpəkəˈrɛkʃən) *n* a mistaken correction to text or speech made through a desire to avoid nonstandard pronunciation or grammar: *"between you and I" is a hypercorrection of "between you and me."*

hypercritical ⓣ (ˌhaɪpəˈkrɪtɪkᵊl) *adj* excessively or severely critical.
▸**ˌhyperˈcritically** *adv*

hyperfocal distance (ˌhaɪpəˈfəʊkᵊl) *n* the distance from a camera lens to the point beyond which all objects appear sharp and clearly defined.

hyperglycaemia *or US* **hyperglycemia** (ˌhaɪpəglaɪˈsiːmɪə) *n Pathol.* an abnormally large amount of sugar in the blood. [C20: from HYPER- + GLYCO- + -AEMIA]
▸**ˌhyperglyˈcaemic** *or US* **ˌhyperglyˈcemic** *adj*

hypergolic (ˌhaɪpəˈgɒlɪk) *adj* (of a rocket fuel) able to ignite spontaneously on contact with an oxidizer. [C20: from G *Hypergol* (?from HYP(ER-) + ERG[1] + -OL[2]) + -IC]

hypericum (haɪˈpɛrɪkəm) *n* any herbaceous plant or shrub of the temperate genus *Hypericum.* See **rose of Sharon, Saint John's wort.** [C16: via L from Gk *hupereikon*, from HYPER- + *ereikē* heath]

hyperinflation (ˌhaɪpəɪnˈfleɪʃən) *n* an extremely high level of inflation (with price rises of 50 percent per month), often involving social disorder.

hypermarket (ˈhaɪpəˌmɑːkɪt) *n Brit.* a huge self-service store, usually built on the outskirts of a town. [C20: translation of F *hypermarché*]

hypermedia (ˈhaɪpəˌmiːdɪə) *n* computer software and hardware that allows users to interact with text, graphics, sound, and video, each of which can be accessed from within any of the others. Cf. **hypertext.**

hypermetropia (ˌhaɪpəmɪˈtrəʊpɪə) *or* **hypermetropy** (ˌhaɪpəˈmɛtrəpɪ) *n Pathol.* a variant of **hyperopia.** [C19: from Gk *hupermetros* beyond measure (from HYPER- + *metron* measure) + -OPIA]

hyperon (ˈhaɪpəˌrɒn) *n Physics.* any baryon that is not a nucleon. [C20: from HYPER- + -ON]

hyperopia (ˌhaɪpəˈrəʊpɪə) *n* inability to see near objects clearly because the images received by the eye are focused behind the retina; long-sightedness.
▸**hyperopic** (ˌhaɪpəˈrɒpɪk) *adj*

hyperphysical (ˌhaɪpəˈfɪzɪkᵊl) *adj* beyond the physical; supernatural or immaterial.

hyperpyrexia (ˌhaɪpəpaɪˈrɛksɪə) *n Pathol.* an extremely high fever, with a temperature of 41°C (106°F) or above.

hypersensitive (ˌhaɪpəˈsɛnsɪtɪv) *adj* **1** having unduly vulnerable feelings. **2** abnormally sensitive to an allergen, a drug, or other agent.
▸**ˌhyperˈsensitiveness** *or* **ˌhyperˌsensiˈtivity** *n*

hypersonic (ˌhaɪpəˈsɒnɪk) *adj* concerned with or having a velocity of at least five times that of sound in the same medium under the same conditions.
▸**ˌhyperˈsonics** *n*

hyperspace (ˌhaɪpəˈspeɪs) *n* **1** *Maths.* space having more than three dimensions. **2** (in science fiction) a theoretical dimension within which conventional space-time relationship does not apply.

hypersthene (ˈhaɪpəˌsθiːn) *n* a green, brown, or black pyroxene mineral. [C19: from HYPER- + Gk *sthenos* strength]

hypertension (ˌhaɪpəˈtɛnʃən) *n Pathol.* abnormally high blood pressure.
▸**hypertensive** (ˌhaɪpəˈtɛnsɪv) *adj, n*

hypertext (ˈhaɪpəˌtɛkst) *n* computer software and hardware that allows users to create, store, and view text and move between related items easily and in a nonsequential way.

hyperthermia (ˌhaɪpəˈθɜːmɪə) *or* **hyperthermy** (ˌhaɪpəˈθɜːmɪ) *n Pathol.* a variant of **hyperpyrexia.**
▸**ˌhyperˈthermal** *adj*

hyperthyroidism (ˌhaɪpəˈθaɪrɔɪˌdɪzəm) *n* overproduction of thyroid hormone by the thyroid gland, causing nervousness, insomnia, and sensitivity to heat.
▸**ˌhyperˈthyroid** *adj, n*

hypertonic (ˌhaɪpəˈtɒnɪk) *adj* **1** (esp. of muscles) being in a state of abnormally high tension. **2** (of a solution) having a higher osmotic pressure than that of a specified solution.

hypertrophy (haɪˈpɜːtrəfɪ) *n, pl* **hypertrophies. 1** enlargement of an organ or part resulting from an increase in the size of the cells. ◆ *vb* **hypertrophies, hypertrophying, hypertrophied. 2** to undergo or cause to undergo this condition.

hyperventilation (ˌhaɪpəˌvɛntɪˈleɪʃən) *n* an increase in the rate of breathing, sometimes resulting in cramp and dizziness.
▸**ˌhyperˈventiˌlate** *vb*

hypha (ˈhaɪfə) *n, pl* **hyphae** (-fiː). any of the filaments that constitute the body (mycelium) of a fungus. [C19: from NL, from Gk *huphē* web]
▸**ˈhyphal** *adj*

hyphen (ˈhaɪfᵊn) *n* **1** the punctuation mark **hyphen**, used to separate parts of compound words, to link the words of a phrase, and between syllables of a word split between two consecutive lines. ◆ *vb* **2** (*tr*) another word for **hyphenate.** [C17: from LL (meaning: the combining of two words), from Gk *huphen* (adv) together, from HYPO- + *heis* one]

hyphenate (ˈhaɪfᵊˌneɪt) *vb* **hyphenates, hyphenating, hyphenated.** (*tr*) to separate (words, etc.) with a hyphen.
▸**ˌhyphenˈation** *n*

hyphenated (ˈhaɪfᵊˌneɪtɪd) *adj* **1** containing or linked with a hyphen. **2** *Chiefly US.* having a nationality denoted by a hyphenated word: *Irish-American.*

hypno- *or before a vowel* **hypn-** *combining form.* **1** indicating sleep: *hypnopaedia.* **2** relating to hypnosis: *hypnotherapy.* [from Gk *hupnos* sleep]

hypnoid (ˈhɪpˌnɔɪd) *or* **hypnoidal** (hɪpˈnɔɪdᵊl) *adj Psychol.* of or relating to a state resembling sleep or hypnosis.

hypnology (hɪpˈnɒlədʒɪ) *n Psychol.* the study of sleep and hypnosis.
▸**hypˈnologist** *n*

hypnopaedia (ˌhɪpnəʊˈpiːdɪə) *n* the learning of lessons heard during sleep. [C20: from HYPNO- + Gk *paideia* education]

hypnopompic (ˌhɪpnəʊˈpɒmpɪk) *adj Psychol.* relating to the state existing between sleep and full waking, characterized by the persistence of

THESAURUS

hype[1] *Slang n* **1 = publicity**, ballyhoo (*inf.*), brouhaha, build-up, plugging (*inf.*), promotion, puffing, racket, razzmatazz (*sl.*)

hyperbole *n* = **exaggeration**, amplification, enlargement, magnification, overstatement

hypercritical *adj* = **fault-finding**, captious, carping, cavilling, censorious, finicky, fussy, hairsplitting, niggling, overcritical, over- exacting, overscrupulous, pernickety (*inf.*), strict

dreamlike imagery. [C20: from HYPNO- + Gk *pompē* a sending forth, escort + -IC]

hypnosis (hɪp'nəʊsɪs) *n, pl* **hypnoses** (-siːz). an artificially induced state of relaxation and concentration in which deeper parts of the mind become more accessible.

hypnotherapy (ˌhɪpnəʊ'θɛrəpɪ) *n* the use of hypnosis in the treatment of emotional and psychogenic problems.
▸ **ˌhypno'therapist** *n*

hypnotic ❶ (hɪp'nɒtɪk) *adj* **1** of or producing hypnosis or sleep. **2** (of a person) susceptible to hypnotism. ◆ *n* **3** a drug that induces sleep. **4** a person susceptible to hypnosis. [C17: from LL *hypnōticus*, from Gk, from *hupnoun* to put to sleep, from *hupnos* sleep]
▸ **hyp'notically** *adv*

hypnotism ('hɪpnəˌtɪzəm) *n* **1** the scientific study and practice of hypnosis. **2** the process of inducing hypnosis.
▸ **'hypnotist** *n*

hypnotize ❶ *or* **hypnotise** ('hɪpnəˌtaɪz) *vb* **hypnotizes, hypnotizing, hypnotized** *or* **hypnotises, hypnotising, hypnotised.** (*tr*) **1** to induce hypnosis in (a person). **2** to charm or beguile; fascinate.
▸ **ˌhypnoti'zation** *or* **ˌhypnoti'sation** *n* ▸ **'hypnoˌtizer** *or* **'hypnoˌtiser** *n*

hypo[1] ('haɪpəʊ) *n* short for **hyposulphite.** [C19]

hypo[2] ('haɪpəʊ) *n, pl* **hypos.** *Inf.* short for **hypodermic syringe.**

hypo- *or before a vowel* **hyp-** *prefix* **1** beneath or below: *hypodermic.* **2** lower: *hypogastrium.* **3** less than; denoting a deficiency: *hypothyroid.* **4** indicating that a chemical compound contains an element in a lower oxidation state than usual: *hypochlorous acid.* [from Gk, from *hupo* under]

hypoallergenic (ˌhaɪpəʊˌælə'dʒɛnɪk) *adj* (of cosmetics, earrings, etc.) not likely to cause an allergic reaction.

hypoblast ('haɪpəˌblæst) *n Embryol.* the inner layer of an embryo at an early stage of development that becomes the endoderm.

hypocaust ('haɪpəˌkɔːst) *n* an ancient Roman heating system in which hot air circulated under the floor and between double walls. [C17: from L *hypocaustum*, from Gk, from *hupokaiein* to light a fire beneath, from HYPO- + *kaiein* to burn]

hypocentre ('haɪpəʊˌsɛntə) *n* the point immediately below the centre of explosion of a nuclear bomb. Also called: **ground zero.**

hypochlorite (ˌhaɪpə'klɔːraɪt) *n* any salt or ester of hypochlorous acid.

hypochlorous acid (ˌhaɪpə'klɔːrəs) *n* an unstable acid known only in solution and in the form of its salts: a strong oxidizing and bleaching agent. Formula: HOCl.

hypochondria (ˌhaɪpə'kɒndrɪə) *n* chronic abnormal anxiety concerning the state of one's health. Also called: **hypochondriasis** (ˌhaɪpəkɒn'draɪəsɪs). [C18: from LL: abdomen, supposedly the seat of melancholy, from Gk, from *hupokhondrios*, from HYPO- + *khondros* cartilage]

hypochondriac (ˌhaɪpə'kɒndrɪˌæk) *n* **1** a person suffering from hypochondria. ◆ *adj also* **hypochondriacal** (ˌhaɪpəkɒn'draɪək^əl). **2** relating to or suffering from hypochondria.

hypocorism (haɪ'pɒkəˌrɪzəm) *n* a pet name, esp. one using a diminutive affix: *"Sally" is a hypocorism for "Sarah".* [C19: from Gk *hupo-korisma*, from *hupokorizesthai* to use pet names, from *hypo-* beneath + *korizesthai*, from *korē* girl, *koros* boy]
▸ **hypocoristic** (ˌhaɪpəkɔː'rɪstɪk) *adj*

hypocotyl (ˌhaɪpə'kɒtɪl) *n* the part of an embryo plant between the cotyledons and the radicle. [C19: from HYPO- + COTYL(EDON)]

hypocrisy ❶ (hɪ'pɒkrəsɪ) *n, pl* **hypocrisies. 1** the practice of professing standards, beliefs, etc., contrary to one's real character or actual behaviour. **2** an act or instance of this.

hypocrite ❶ ('hɪpəkrɪt) *n* a person who pretends to be what he is not. [C13: from OF *ipocrite*, via LL from Gk *hupokritēs* one who plays a part, from *hupokrinein* to feign, from *krinein* to judge]
▸ **ˌhypo'critical** *adj* ▸ **ˌhypo'critically** *adv*

hypocycloid (ˌhaɪpə'saɪklɔɪd) *n* a curve described by a point on the circumference of a circle as the circle rolls around the inside of a fixed coplanar circle.
▸ **ˌhypocy'cloidal** *adj*

hypodermic ❶ (ˌhaɪpə'dɜːmɪk) *adj* **1** of or relating to the region of the skin beneath the epidermis. **2** injected beneath the skin. ◆ *n* **3** a hypodermic syringe or needle. **4** a hypodermic injection.
▸ **ˌhypo'dermically** *adv*

hypodermic syringe *n Med.* a type of syringe consisting of a hollow cylinder, usually of glass or plastic, a tightly fitting piston, and a hollow needle (**hypodermic needle**), used for withdrawing blood samples, etc.

hypodermis (ˌhaɪpə'dɜːmɪs) *or* **hypoderm** *n* **1** *Bot.* a layer of thick-walled supportive or water-storing cells beneath the epidermis in some plants. **2** *Zool.* the epidermis of arthropods, annelids, etc. [C19: from HYPO- + EPIDERMIS]

hypogastrium (ˌhaɪpə'gæstrɪəm) *n, pl* **hypogastria** (-trɪə). *Anat.* the lower front central region of the abdomen. [C17: from NL, from Gk *hupogastrion*, from HYPO- + *gastrion*, dim. of *gastēr* stomach]

hypogeal (ˌhaɪpə'dʒiːəl) *or* **hypogeous** *adj* occurring or living below the surface of the ground. [C19: from L *hypogēus*, from Gk, from HYPO- + *gē* earth]

hypogene ('haɪpəˌdʒiːn) *adj* formed or originating beneath the surface of the earth.

hypogeum (ˌhaɪpə'dʒiːəm) *n, pl* **hypogea** (-'dʒiːə). an underground vault, esp. one used for burials. [C18: from L, from Gk *hupogeion*; see HYPOGEAL]

hypoid gear ('haɪpɔɪd) *n* a gear having a tooth form generated by a hypocycloidal curve. [C20: *hypoid*, shortened from HYPOCYCLOID]

hyponasty ('haɪpəˌnæstɪ) *n* increased growth of the lower surface of a plant part, resulting in an upward bending of the part.
▸ **ˌhypo'nastic** *adj*

hypophosphate (ˌhaɪpə'fɒsfeɪt) *n* any salt or ester of hypophosphoric acid.

hypophosphite (ˌhaɪpə'fɒsfaɪt) *n* any salt of hypophosphorous acid.

hypophosphoric acid (ˌhaɪpəfɒs'fɒrɪk) *n* a tetrabasic acid produced by the slow oxidation of phosphorus in moist air. Formula: $H_4P_2O_6$.

hypophosphorous acid (ˌhaɪpə'fɒsfərəs) *n* a monobasic acid and a reducing agent. Formula: H_3PO_2.

hypophysis (haɪ'pɒfɪsɪs) *n, pl* **hypophyses** (-ˌsiːz). the technical name for **pituitary gland.** [C18: from Gk: outgrowth, from HYPO- + *phuein* to grow]
▸ **hypophyseal** *or* **hypophysial** (ˌhaɪpə'fɪzɪəl, haɪˌpɒfɪ'sɪəl) *adj*

hypostasis (haɪ'pɒstəsɪs) *n, pl* **hypostases** (-ˌsiːz). **1** *Metaphysics.* the essential nature of a substance. **2** *Christianity.* **2a** any of the three persons of the Godhead. **2b** the one person of Christ in which the divine and human natures are united. **3** the accumulation of blood in an organ or part as the result of poor circulation. [C16: from LL: substance, from Gk *hupostasis* foundation, from *huphistasthai*, from HYPO- + *histanai* to cause to stand]
▸ **hypostatic** (ˌhaɪpə'stætɪk) *or* **ˌhypo'statical** *adj*

hypostyle ('haɪpəʊˌstaɪl) *adj* **1** having a roof supported by columns. ◆ *n* **2** a building constructed in this way.

hyposulphite (ˌhaɪpə'sʌlfaɪt) *n* another name for **sodium thiosulphate,** esp. when used as a photographic fixer. Often shortened to **hypo.**

hyposulphurous acid (ˌhaɪpə'sʌlfərəs) *n* an unstable acid known only in solution: a powerful reducing agent. Formula $H_2S_2O_4$.

hypotension (ˌhaɪpəʊ'tɛnʃən) *n Pathol.* abnormally low blood pressure.
▸ **hypotensive** (ˌhaɪpəʊ'tɛnsɪv) *adj*

hypotenuse (haɪ'pɒtɪˌnjuːz) *n* the side in a right-angled triangle that is opposite the right angle. Abbrev.: **hyp.** [C16: from L *hypotēnūsa*, from Gk *hupoteinousa grammē* subtending line, from HYPO- + *teinein* to stretch]

hypothalamus (ˌhaɪpə'θæləməs) *n, pl* **hypothalami** (-ˌmaɪ). a neural control centre at the base of the brain, concerned with hunger, thirst, satiety, and other autonomic functions.
▸ **hypothalamic** (ˌhaɪpəθə'læmɪk) *adj*

hypothec (haɪ'pɒθɪk) *n Roman & Scots Law.* a charge on property in favour of a creditor. [C16: from LL *hypotheca*, from Gk *hupothēkē* pledge, from *hupotithenai* to deposit as a security, from HYPO- + *tithenai* to place]

hypothecate (haɪ'pɒθɪˌkeɪt) *vb* **hypothecates, hypothecating, hypothecated.** (*tr*) *Law.* to pledge (personal property or a ship) as security for a debt without transferring possession or title.
▸ **hyˌpothe'cation** *n* ▸ **hy'potheˌcator** *n*

hypothermia (ˌhaɪpəʊ'θɜːmɪə) *n* **1** *Pathol.* an abnormally low body temperature, as induced in the elderly by exposure to cold weather. **2** *Med.* the intentional reduction of normal body temperature to reduce the patient's metabolic rate.

hypothesis ❶ (haɪ'pɒθɪsɪs) *n, pl* **hypotheses** (-ˌsiːz). **1** a suggested explanation for a group of facts or phenomena, either accepted as a basis for further verification (**working hypothesis**) or accepted as likely to be true. **2** an assumption used in an argument; supposition. [C16: from Gk, from *hupotithenai* to propose, lit.: put under; see HYPO-, THESIS]
▸ **hy'pothesist** *n*

hypothesize *or* **hypothesise** (haɪ'pɒθɪˌsaɪz) *vb* **hypothesizes, hypothesizing, hypothesized** *or* **hypothesises, hypothesising, hypothesised.** to form or assume as a hypothesis.
▸ **hy'potheˌsizer** *or* **hy'potheˌsiser** *n*

hypothetical ❶ (ˌhaɪpə'θɛtɪk^əl) *or* **hypothetic** *adj* **1** having the nature

THESAURUS

hypnotic *adj* **1** = **mesmerizing**, mesmeric, narcotic, opiate, sleep-inducing, somniferous, soothing, soporific, spellbinding

hypnotize *vb* **1** = **mesmerize**, put in a trance, put to sleep **2** = **fascinate**, absorb, entrance, magnetize, spellbind

hypocrisy *n* **1, 2** = **insincerity**, cant, deceit, deceitfulness, deception, dissembling, duplicity, falsity, imposture, pharisaism, phariseeism, phoneyness *or* phoniness (*inf.*), pretence, sanctimoniousness, speciousness, two-facedness
Antonyms *n* honesty, sincerity, truthfulness

hypocrite *n* = **fraud**, charlatan, deceiver, dissembler, impostor, pharisee, phoney *or* phony (*inf.*), pretender, whited sepulchre

hypocritical *adj* = **insincere**, canting, deceitful, deceptive, dissembling, duplicitous, false, fraudulent, hollow, pharisaical, phoney *or* phony (*inf.*), sanctimonious, specious, spurious, two-faced

hypodermic *n* **3** = **syringe**, needle

hypothesis *n* **1, 2** = **assumption**, postulate, premise *or* premiss, proposition, supposition, theory, thesis

hypothetical *adj* **1, 2** = **theoretical**, academic, assumed, conjectural, imaginary, putative, speculative, supposed
Antonyms *adj* actual, confirmed, established, known, proven, real, true

of a hypothesis. **2** assumed or thought to exist. **3** *Logic.* another word for **conditional** (sense 3).
▸ˌ**hypo'thetically** *adv*

hypothyroidism (ˌhaɪpəʊ'θaɪrɔɪˌdɪzəm) *n Pathol.* **1** insufficient production of thyroid hormones by the thyroid gland. **2** any disorder, such as cretinism or myxoedema, resulting from this.
▸ˌ**hypo'thyroid** *n, adj*

hypotonic (ˌhaɪpə'tɒnɪk) *adj* **1** *Pathol.* (of muscles) lacking normal tone or tension. **2** (of a solution) having a lower osmotic pressure than that of a specified solution.

hypoxia (haɪ'pɒksɪə) *n* deficiency in the amount of oxygen delivered to the body tissues. [C20: from HYPO- + OXY-[2] + -IA]
▸**hypoxic** (haɪ'pɒksɪk) *adj*

hypso- *or before a vowel* **hyps-** *combining form.* indicating height: *hypsometry.* [from Gk *hupsos*]

hypsography (hɪp'sɒgrəfɪ) *n* the scientific study and mapping of the earth's topography above sea level.

hypsometer (hɪp'sɒmɪtə) *n* **1** an instrument for measuring altitudes by determining the boiling point of water at a given altitude. **2** any instrument used to calculate the heights of trees by triangulation.

hypsometry (hɪp'sɒmɪtrɪ) *n* (in mapping) the establishment of height above sea level.

hyrax ('haɪræks) *n, pl* **hyraxes** *or* **hyraces** ('haɪrəˌsiːz). any of various agile herbivorous mammals of Africa and SW Asia. They resemble rodents but have feet with hooflike toes. Also called: **dassie.** [C19: from NL, from Gk *hurax* shrewmouse]

hyssop ('hɪsəp) *n* **1** a widely cultivated Asian plant with spikes of small blue flowers and aromatic leaves, used as a condiment and in perfumery and folk medicine. **2** a Biblical plant, used for sprinkling in the ritual practices of the Hebrews. [OE *ysope,* from L *hyssōpus,* from Gk *hussōpos,* of Semitic origin]

hysterectomy (ˌhɪstə'rɛktəmɪ) *n, pl* **hysterectomies.** surgical removal of the uterus.

hysteresis (ˌhɪstə'riːsɪs) *n Physics.* the lag in a variable property of a system with respect to the effect producing it as this effect varies, esp. the phenomenon in which the magnetic induction of a ferromagnetic material lags behind the changing external field. [from Gk *husterēsis,* from *husteros* coming after]
▸**hysteretic** (ˌhɪstə'rɛtɪk) *adj*

hysteresis loop *n* a closed curve showing the variation of the magnetic induction of a ferromagnetic material with the external magnetic field producing it, when this field is changed through a complete cycle.

hysteria Ⓣ (hɪ'stɪərɪə) *n* **1** a mental disorder characterized by emotional outbursts and, often, symptoms such as paralysis. **2** any frenzied emotional state, esp. of laughter or crying. [C19: from NL, from L *hystericus* HYSTERIC]

hysteric (hɪ'stɛrɪk) *n* **1** a hysterical person. ◆ *adj* **2** hysterical. [C17: from L *hystericus,* lit.: of the womb, from Gk, from *hustera* womb; from the belief that hysteria in women originated in disorders of the womb]

hysterical Ⓣ (hɪ'stɛrɪkᵊl) *adj* **1** suggesting hysteria: *hysterical cries.* **2** suffering from hysteria. **3** *Inf.* wildly funny.
▸**hys'terically** *adv*

hysterics (hɪ'stɛrɪks) *n* (*functioning as pl or sing*) **1** an attack of hysteria. **2** *Inf.* wild uncontrollable bursts of laughter.

hystero- *or before a vowel* **hyster-** *combining form.* the uterus: *hysterectomy.* [from Gk *hustera* womb]

hysteron proteron ('hɪstəˌrɒn 'prɒtəˌrɒn) *n* **1** *Logic.* a fallacious argument in which the proposition to be proved is assumed as a premise. **2** *Rhetoric.* a figure of speech in which the normal order of two sentences, clauses, etc., is reversed: *bred and born* (for *born and bred*). [C16: from LL, from Gk *husteron proteron* the latter (placed as) former]

hystricomorph (hɪ'straɪkəʊˌmɔːf) *n* **1** any rodent of the suborder *Hystricomorpha,* which includes porcupines, cavies, agoutis, and chinchillas. ◆ *adj* also: **hystricomorphic** (hɪˌstraɪkəʊ'mɔːfɪk). **2** of the *Hystricomorpha.* [C19: from L *hystrix* porcupine, from Gk *hustrix*]

Hz *symbol for* hertz.

THESAURUS

hysteria *n* **2** = **frenzy,** agitation, delirium, hysterics, madness, panic, unreason

hysterical *adj* **1, 2** = **frenzied,** berserk, beside oneself, convulsive, crazed, distracted, distraught, frantic, mad, overwrought, raving, uncontrollable **3** *Informal* = **hilarious,** comical, farcical, screaming, side-splitting, uproarious, wildly funny

Antonyms *adj* ≠ **frenzied:** calm, composed, poised, self-possessed, unfazed (*inf.*) ≠ **hilarious:** grave, melancholy, sad, serious

Ii

i *or* **I** (aɪ) *n, pl* **i's, I's,** *or* **Is. 1** the ninth letter and third vowel of the English alphabet. **2** any of several speech sounds represented by this letter. **3a** something shaped like an I. **3b** *(in combination)*: *an I-beam.*
i *symbol for* the imaginary number $\sqrt{-1}$.
I[1] (aɪ) *pron (subjective)* refers to the speaker or writer. [C12: from OE *ic;* cf. OSaxon *ik,* OHG *ih,* Sansk. *ahám*]
I[2] *symbol for:* **1** *Chem.* iodine. **2** *Physics.* current. **3** *Physics.* isospin. ◆ **4** *the Roman numeral for* one. See **Roman numerals.**
I. *abbrev. for:* **1** Independence. **2** Independent. **3** Institute. **4** International. **5** Island; Isle.
-ia *suffix forming nouns.* **1** in place names: *Columbia.* **2** in names of diseases: *pneumonia.* **3** in words denoting condition or quality: *utopia.* **4** in names of botanical genera and zoological classes: *Reptilia.* **5** in collective nouns borrowed from Latin: *regalia.* [(for senses 1–4) NL, from L & Gk, suffix of fem nouns; (for sense 5) from L, neuter pl suffix]
IAA *abbrev. for* indoleacetic acid.
IAEA *abbrev. for* International Atomic Energy Agency.
-ial *suffix forming adjectives.* of or relating to: *managerial.* [from L *-iālis,* adj. suffix; cf. -AL[1]]
iamb ('aɪæm, 'aɪæmb) *or* **iambus** (aɪ'æmbəs) *n, pl* **iambs, iambi** (aɪ'æmbaɪ), *or* **iambuses.** *Prosody.* **1** a metrical foot of two syllables, a short one followed by a long one. **2** a line of verse of such feet. [C19 *iamb,* from C16 *iambus,* from L, from Gk *iambos*]
iambic (aɪ'æmbɪk) *Prosody.* ◆ *adj* **1** of, relating to, or using an iamb. **2** (in Greek literature) denoting a satirical verse written in iambs. ◆ *n* **3** a metrical foot, line, or stanza consisting of iambs. **4** an ancient Greek satirical verse written in iambs.
-ian *suffix.* a variant of **-an:** *Etonian.* [from L *-iānus*]
-iana *suffix forming nouns.* a variant of **-ana.**
IAP *abbrev. for* Internet access provider.
-iasis *or* **-asis** *n combining form.* (in medicine) indicating a diseased condition: *psoriasis.* Cf. **-osis** (sense 2). [from NL, from Gk, suffix of action]
IATA (aɪ'ɑːtə, iː'ɑːtə) *n acronym for* International Air Transport Association.
-iatrics *n combining form.* indicating medical care or treatment: *paediatrics.* [C19: from Gk, from *iasthai* to heal]
iatrogenic (aɪˌætrəʊ'dʒenɪk) *adj Med.* (of an illness) induced in a patient as the result of a physician's action.
▸**iatrogenicity** (aɪˌætrəʊdʒɪ'nɪsɪtɪ) *n*
-iatry *n combining form.* indicating healing or medical treatment: *psychiatry.* Cf. **-iatrics.** [from NL *-iatria,* from Gk *iatreia* the healing art, from *iatros* healer, physician]
▸**-iatric** *adj combining form.*
IBA (in Britain) *abbrev. for* Independent Broadcasting Authority.
I-beam *n* a rolled steel joist or a girder with a cross section in the form of a capital *I.*
Iberian (aɪ'bɪərɪən) *n* **1** a member of a group of ancient Caucasoid peoples who inhabited the Iberian Peninsula, in classical times. **2** a native or inhabitant of the Iberian Peninsula; a Spaniard or Portuguese. **3** a native or inhabitant of ancient Iberia. ◆ *adj* **4** relating to the pre-Roman peoples of the Iberian Peninsula or of Caucasian Iberia. **5** of or relating to the Iberian Peninsula, its inhabitants, or any of their languages.
iberis (aɪ'bɪərɪs) *n* any of various Mediterranean plants with white, lilac, or purple flowers. Also called: **candytuft.** [from Gk *ibēris* pepperwort]
ibex ('aɪbeks) *n, pl* **ibexes, ibices** ('ɪbɪˌsiːz, 'aɪ-), *or* **ibex.** any of three species of wild goat of mountainous regions of Europe, Asia, and North Africa, having large backward-curving horns. [C17: from L: chamois]
ibid. *or* **ib.** (referring to a book, etc., previously cited) *abbrev. for* ibidem. [L: in the same place]
ibis ('aɪbɪs) *n, pl* **ibises** *or* **ibis.** any of various wading birds such as the sacred ibis, that occur in warm regions and have a long thin down-curved bill. [C14: via L from Gk, from Egyptian *hby*]
-ible *suffix forming adjectives.* a variant of **-able.**
▸**-ibly** *suffix forming adverbs.* ▸**-ibility** *suffix forming nouns.*
Ibo *or* **Igbo** ('iːbəʊ) *n* **1** *(pl* **Ibos** *or* **Ibo)** a member of a Negroid people of W Africa, living in S Nigeria. **2** their language, belonging to the Niger-Congo family.
IBRD *abbrev. for* International Bank for Reconstruction and Development (the World Bank).
ibuprofen (aɪ'bjuːˌprəʊfen) *n* a drug that relieves pain and reduces inflammation: used to treat arthritis and muscular strains.
i/c *abbrev. for:* **1** in charge (of). **2** internal combustion.
-ic *suffix forming adjectives.* **1** of, relating to, or resembling: *periodic.* See also **-ical. 2** (in chemistry) indicating that an element is chemically combined in the higher of two possible valence states: *ferric.* Cf. **-ous** (sense 2). [from L *-icus* or Gk *-ikos; -ic* also occurs in nouns that represent a substantive use of adjectives (*magic*) and in nouns borrowed directly from L or Gk (*critic, music*)]
ICA *abbrev. for:* **1** (in Britain) Institute of Contemporary Arts. **2** Institute of Chartered Accountants.
-ical *suffix forming adjectives.* a variant of **-ic,** but having a less literal application than corresponding adjectives ending in *-ic: economical.* [from L *-icālis*]
▸**-ically** *suffix forming adverbs.*
ICAO *abbrev. for* International Civil Aviation Organization.
ICBM *abbrev. for* intercontinental ballistic missile: a missile with a range greater than 5550 km.
ice ❶ (aɪs) *n* **1** water in the solid state, formed by freezing liquid water. Related adj: **glacial. 2** a portion of ice cream. **3** *Sl.* a diamond or diamonds. **4** *Sl.* a concentrated and highly potent form of methamphetamine with dangerous side effects. **5 break the ice. 5a** to relieve shyness, etc., esp. between strangers. **5b** to be the first of a group to do something. **6 on ice.** in abeyance; pending. **7 on thin ice.** unsafe; vulnerable. ◆ *vb* **ices, icing, iced. 8** (often foll. by *up, over,* etc.) to form ice; freeze. **9** *(tr)* to mix with ice or chill (a drink, etc.). **10** *(tr)* to cover (a cake, etc.) with icing. [OE *īs*]
▸**iced** *adj*
ICE (in Britain) *abbrev. for* Institution of Civil Engineers.
ice age *n* another name for **glacial period.**
ice axe *n* a light axe used by mountaineers for cutting footholds in ice.
ice bag *n* a waterproof bag used as an ice pack.
iceberg ('aɪsbɜːg) *n* **1** a large mass of ice floating in the sea. **2 tip of the iceberg.** the small visible part of something, esp. a problem, that is much larger. **3** *Sl., chiefly US.* a person considered to have a cold or reserved manner. [C18: prob. part translation of MDu. *ijsberg* ice mountain; cf. Norwegian *isberg*]
iceberg lettuce *n* a type of lettuce with very crisp pale leaves tightly enfolded.
iceblink ('aɪsˌblɪŋk) *n* a reflected glare in the sky over an ice field. Also called: **blink.**
icebound ('aɪsˌbaʊnd) *adj* covered or made immobile by ice; frozen in: *an icebound ship.*
icebox ('aɪsˌbɒks) *n* **1** a compartment in a refrigerator for storing or making ice. **2** an insulated cabinet packed with ice for storing food. **3** a US and Canad. name for **refrigerator.**
icebreaker ('aɪsˌbreɪkə) *n* **1** Also called: **iceboat.** a vessel with a reinforced bow for breaking up the ice in bodies of water. **2** a device for breaking ice into smaller pieces. **3** something intended to relieve shyness between strangers.
icecap ('aɪsˌkæp) *n* a thick mass of glacial ice that permanently covers an area, such as the polar regions or the peak of a mountain.
ice cream *n* a sweetened frozen liquid, made from cream, milk, or a custard base, flavoured in various ways.
ice dance *n* any of a number of dances, mostly based on ballroom dancing, performed by a couple skating on ice.
▸**ice dancer** *n* ▸**ice dancing** *n*
icefall ('aɪsˌfɔːl) *n* a steep part of a glacier that resembles a frozen waterfall.
ice field *n* **1** a large ice floe. **2** a large mass of ice permanently covering an extensive area of land.
ice floe *n* a sheet of ice, of variable size, floating in the sea. See also **ice field** (sense 1).
ice hockey *n* a game played on ice by two teams wearing skates, who try to propel a flat puck into their opponents' goal with long sticks.
ice house *n* a building for storing ice.
Icelander ('aɪslændə, 'aɪsləndə) *n* a native or inhabitant of Iceland.
Icelandic (aɪs'lændɪk) *adj* **1** of or relating to Iceland, its people, or their language. ◆ *n* **2** the official language of Iceland.
Iceland poppy (ˌaɪslənd) *n* any of various arctic poppies with white or yellow nodding flowers.
Iceland spar *n* a pure transparent variety of calcite with double-refracting crystals.
ice lolly *n Brit. inf.* a water ice or an ice cream on a stick. Also called: **lolly.**
ice pack *n* **1** a bag or folded cloth containing ice, applied to a part of the body to reduce swelling, etc. **2** another name for **pack ice. 3** a sachet containing a gel that retains its temperature for an extended period of time, used esp. in cool bags.
ice pick *n* a pointed tool used for breaking ice.
ice plant *n* a low-growing plant of southern Africa, with fleshy leaves covered with icelike hairs and pink or white rayed flowers.
ice point *n* the temperature at which a mixture of ice and water are in

THESAURUS

ice *n* **5 break the ice = begin,** initiate the proceedings, kick off (*inf.*), lead the way, make a start, start *or* set the ball rolling (*inf.*), take the plunge (*inf.*) **7 on thin ice = unsafe,** at risk, in jeopardy, open to attack, out on a limb, sticking one's neck out (*inf.*), vulnerable

equilibrium at a pressure of one atmosphere. It is 0° on the Celsius scale and 32° on the Fahrenheit scale. Cf. **steam point.**

ice sheet *n* a thick layer of ice covering a large area of land for a long time, esp. the layer that covered much of the N hemisphere during the last glacial period.

ice shelf *n* a thick mass of ice that is permanently attached to the land but projects into and floats on the sea.

ice skate *n* **1** a boot having a steel blade fitted to the sole to enable the wearer to glide over ice. **2** the steel blade on such a boot. ◆ *vb* **ice-skate, ice-skates, ice-skating, ice-skated. 3** (*intr*) to glide over ice on ice skates.
▸**'ice-ˌskater** *n*

ice station *n* a scientific research station in polar regions, where ice movement, weather, and environmental conditions are monitored.

IChemE *abbrev. for* Institution of Chemical Engineers.

I Ching ('iː 'tʃɪŋ) *n* an ancient Chinese book of divination and a source of Confucian and Taoist philosophy.

ichneumon (ɪk'njuːmən) *n* a mongoose of Africa and S Europe, having greyish-brown speckled fur. **[**C16: via L from Gk, lit.: tracker, hunter, from *ikhneuein* to track, from *ikhnos* a footprint; so named from the animal's alleged ability to locate the eggs of crocodiles**]**

ichneumon fly *or* **wasp** *n* any hymenopterous insect whose larvae are parasitic in caterpillars and other insect larvae.

ichnography (ɪk'nɒgrəfɪ) *n* **1** the art of drawing ground plans. **2** the ground plan of a building. **[**C16: from L, from Gk, from *ikhnos* trace, track**]**
▸**ichnographic** (ˌɪknə'græfɪk) *or* ˌ**ichno'graphical** *adj*

ichor ('aɪkɔː) *n* **1** *Greek myth.* the fluid said to flow in the veins of the gods. **2** *Pathol.* a foul-smelling watery discharge from a wound or ulcer. **[**C17: from Gk *ikhōr*, from ?**]**
▸**'ichorous** *adj*

ichthyo- *or before a vowel* **ichthy-** *combining form.* indicating or relating to fishes: *ichthyology.* **[**from L, from Gk *ikhthus* fish**]**

ichthyoid ('ɪkθɪˌɔɪd) *adj also* **ichthyoidal. 1** resembling a fish. ◆ *n* **2** a fishlike vertebrate.

ichthyology (ˌɪkθɪ'ɒlədʒɪ) *n* the study of fishes.
▸**ichthyologic** (ˌɪkθɪə'lɒdʒɪk) *or* ˌ**ichthyo'logical** *adj* ▸ˌ**ichthy'ologist** *n*

ichthyosaur ('ɪkθɪəˌsɔː) *or* **ichthyosaurus** (ˌɪkθɪə'sɔːrəs) *n, pl* **ichthyosaurs, ichthyosauruses,** *or* **ichthyosauri** (-'sɔːraɪ). an extinct marine Mesozoic reptile which had a porpoise-like body with dorsal and tail fins and paddle-like limbs. See also **plesiosaur.**

ichthyosis (ˌɪkθɪ'əʊsɪs) *n* a congenital disease in which the skin is coarse, dry, and scaly.
▸**ichthyotic** (ˌɪkθɪ'ɒtɪk) *adj*

ICI *abbrev. for* Imperial Chemical Industries.

-ician *suffix forming nouns.* indicating a person skilled or involved in a subject or activity: *physician; beautician.* **[**from F *-icien*; see -IC, -IAN**]**

icicle ('aɪsɪkəl) *n* a hanging spike of ice formed by the freezing of dripping water. **[**C14: from ICE + *ickel*, from OE *gicel* icicle, rel. to ON *jökull* glacier**]**

icing ('aɪsɪŋ) *n* **1** Also (esp. US and Canad.): **frosting.** a sugar preparation, variously flavoured and coloured, for coating and decorating cakes, etc. **2 icing on the cake** any unexpected extra or bonus. **3** the formation of ice, as on a ship, due to the freezing of moisture in the atmosphere.

icing sugar *n Brit.* a very finely ground sugar used for icings, confections, etc. US term: **confectioners' sugar.**

icon *or* **ikon** ('aɪkɒn) *n* **1** a representation of Christ or a saint, esp. one painted in oil on a wooden panel in a traditional Byzantine style and venerated in the Eastern Church. **2** an image, picture, etc. **3** a symbol resembling or analogous to the thing it represents. **4** a person regarded as a sex symbol or as a symbol of a belief or cultural movement. **5** a pictorial representation of a facility available on a computer that can be implemented by a cursor rather than by a textual instruction. **[**C16: from L, from Gk *eikōn* image, from *eikenai* to be like**]**

icono- *or before a vowel* **icon-** *combining form.* indicating an image or likeness: *iconology.*

iconoclast (aɪ'kɒnəˌklæst) *n* **1** a person who attacks established or traditional concepts, principles, etc. **2a** a destroyer of religious images or objects. **2b** an adherent of a heretical iconoclastic movement within the Greek Orthodox Church from 725 to 842 A.D. **[**C16: from LL, from LGk *eikonoklastes*, from *eikōn* icon + *klastes* breaker**]**
▸**iˌcono'clastic** *adj* ▸**i'conoˌclasm** *n*

iconography (ˌaɪkɒ'nɒgrəfɪ) *n, pl* **iconographies. 1a** the symbols used in a work of art. **1b** the conventional significance attached to such symbols. **2** a collection of pictures of a particular subject. **3** the representation of the subjects of icons or portraits, esp. on coins.
▸ˌ**ico'nographer** *n* ▸**iconographic** (aɪˌkɒnə'græfɪk) *or* **iˌcono'graphical** *adj*

iconolatry (ˌaɪkɒ'nɒlətrɪ) *n* the worship of icons as idols.
▸ˌ**ico'nolater** *n* ▸ˌ**ico'nolatrous** *adj*

iconology (ˌaɪkɒ'nɒlədʒɪ) *n* **1** the study of icons. **2** icons collectively. **3** the symbolic representation of icons.
▸**iconological** (aɪˌkɒnə'lɒdʒɪkəl) *adj* ▸ˌ**ico'nologist** *n*

iconoscope (aɪ'kɒnəˌskəʊp) *n* a television camera tube in which an electron beam scans a surface, converting an optical image into electrical pulses.

iconostasis (ˌaɪkəʊ'nɒstəsɪs) *or* **iconostas** (aɪ'kɒnəˌstæs) *n, pl* **iconostases** (ˌaɪkəʊ'nɒstəˌsiːz *or* aɪ'kɒnəˌstæsɪz). *Eastern Church.* a screen with doors and with icons set in tiers, which separates the sanctuary from the nave. **[**C19: Church L, from LGk *eikonostasion* shrine, lit.: area where images are placed, from *icono-* + *histanai* to stand**]**

icosahedron (ˌaɪkəsə'hiːdrən) *n, pl* **icosahedrons** *or* **icosahedra** (-drə). a solid figure having 20 faces. **[**C16: from Gk, from *eikosi* twenty + *-edron* -HEDRON**]**
▸ˌ**icosa'hedral** *adj*

-ics *suffix forming nouns; functioning as sing* **1** indicating a science, art, or matters relating to a particular subject: *politics.* **2** indicating certain activities: *acrobatics.* **[**pl. of *-ic*, representing L *-ica*, from Gk *-ika***]**

ictus ('ɪktəs) *n, pl* **ictuses** *or* **ictus. 1** *Prosody.* metrical or rhythmic stress in verse feet, as contrasted with the stress accent on words. **2** *Med.* a sudden attack or stroke. **[**C18: from L *icere* to strike**]**
▸**'ictal** *adj*

ICU *abbrev. for* intensive care unit.

icy Ⓣ ('aɪsɪ) *adj* **icier, iciest. 1** made of, covered with, or containing ice. **2** resembling ice. **3** freezing or very cold. **4** cold or reserved in manner; aloof.
▸**'icily** *adv* ▸**'iciness** *n*

id (ɪd) *n Psychoanal.* the primitive instincts and energies in the unconscious mind that, modified by the ego and the superego, underlie all psychic activity. **[**C20: NL, from L: it; used to render G *Es***]**

ID *abbrev. for:* **1.** identification. **2** Also **i.d.** intradermal(ly).

id. *abbrev. for* idem.

I'd (aɪd) *contraction of* I had *or* I would.

-id[1] *suffix forming nouns and adjectives.* indicating members of a zoological family: *cyprinid.* **[**from NL *-idae* or *-ida*, from Gk *-idēs* suffix indicating offspring**]**

-id[2] *suffix forming nouns.* a variant of **-ide.**

IDA *abbrev. for* International Development Association.

-idae *suffix forming plural proper nouns.* indicating names of zoological families: *Felidae.* **[**NL, from L, from Gk *-idai*, suffix indicating offspring**]**

-ide *or* **-id** *suffix forming nouns.* **1** (*added to the combining form of the nonmetallic or electronegative elements*) indicating a binary compound: *sodium chloride.* **2** indicating an organic compound derived from another: *acetanilide.* **3** indicating one of a class of compounds or elements: *peptide.* **[**from G *-id*, from F *oxide* OXIDE, based on the suffix of *acide* ACID**]**

idea Ⓣ (aɪ'dɪə) *n* **1** any product of mental activity; thought. **2** the thought of something: *the idea appals me.* **3** a belief; opinion. **4** a scheme, intention, plan, etc. **5** a vague notion; inkling: *he had no idea of the truth.* **6** a person's conception of something: *her idea of honesty is not the same as mine.* **7** significance or purpose: *the idea of the game is to discover the murderer.* **8** *Philosophy.* **8a** an immediate object of thought or perception. **8b** (*sometimes cap.*) (in Plato) the universal essence or archetype of any class of things or concepts. **9 get ideas.** to become ambitious, restless, etc. **10 not one's idea of.** not what one regards as (hard work, a holiday, etc.). **11 that's an idea.** that is worth considering. **12 the very idea!** that is preposterous, unreasonable, etc. **[**C16: via LL from Gk: model, notion, from *idein* to see**]**

> **USAGE NOTE** It is usually considered correct to say that someone has the *idea of doing* something, rather than *the idea to do it: he had the idea of taking* (not *the idea to take*) *a short holiday.*

ideal Ⓣ (aɪ'dɪəl) *n* **1** a conception of something that is perfect. **2** a person or thing considered to represent perfection. **3** something existing only as an idea. **4** a pattern or model, esp. of ethical behaviour. ◆ *adj* **5** conforming to an ideal. **6** of, involving, or existing in the form of an idea. **7** *Philosophy.* **7a** of or relating to a highly desirable and possible state of affairs. **7b** of or relating to idealism.
▸**i'deally** *adv* ▸**i'dealness** *n*

ideal element *n* any element added to a mathematical theory in order

THESAURUS

icy *adj* **2 = slippery,** glacial, glassy, like a sheet of glass, rimy, slippy (*inf. or dialect*) **3 = cold,** arctic, biting, bitter, chill, chilling, chilly, freezing, frost-bound, frosty, frozen over, ice-cold, parky (*Brit. inf.*), raw **4 = unfriendly,** aloof, cold, distant, forbidding, frigid, frosty, glacial, hostile, indifferent, steely, stony, unwelcoming
Antonyms *adj* ≠ **cold:** blistering, boiling, hot, sizzling, warm ≠ **unfriendly:** cordial, friendly, gracious, warm

idea *n* **1 = thought,** abstraction, concept, conception, conclusion, fancy, impression, judgment, perception, understanding **3 = belief,** conviction, doctrine, interpretation, notion, opinion, teaching, view, viewpoint **4 = plan,** design, hypothesis, recommendation, scheme, solution, suggestion, theory **5 = impression,** approximation, ballpark figure, clue, estimate, guess, hint, inkling, intimation, notion, suspicion **7 = intention,** aim, end, import, meaning, object, objective, plan, purpose, *raison d'être*, reason, sense, significance **8b** *Philosophy* **= pattern,** archetype, essence, form

ideal *n* **1, 2 = model,** archetype, criterion, epitome, example, exemplar, last word, nonpareil, paradigm, paragon, pattern, perfection, prototype, standard, standard of perfection **4 = principle,** moral value, standard ◆ *adj* **5 = perfect,** archetypal, classic, complete, consummate, model, optimal, quintessential, supreme **6 = hypothetical,** abstract, conceptual, intellectual, mental, notional, theoretical, transcendental
Antonyms *adj* ≠ **perfect:** deficient, flawed, impaired, imperfect, unsuitable ≠ **hypothetical:** actual, factual, literal, mundane, ordinary, real

to eliminate special cases. The ideal element i = √–1 allows all algebraic equations to be solved.

ideal gas *n* a hypothetical gas which obeys Boyle's law exactly at all temperatures and pressures, and which has internal energy that depends only upon the temperature.

idealism ❶ (aɪˈdɪəˌlɪzəm) *n* **1** belief in or pursuance of ideals. **2** the tendency to represent things in their ideal forms, rather than as they are. **3** *Philosophy*. the doctrine that material objects and the external world do not exist in reality, but are creations of the mind. Cf. **materialism.** ▸**iˈdealist** *n* ▸**iˌdealˈistic** *adj* ▸**iˌdealˈistically** *adv*

idealize ❶ *or* **idealise** (aɪˈdɪəˌlaɪz) *vb* **idealizes, idealizing, idealized** *or* **idealises, idealising, idealised. 1** to consider or represent (something) as ideal. **2** (*tr*) to portray as ideal; glorify. **3** (*intr*) to form an ideal or ideals. ▸**iˌdealiˈzation** *or* **iˌdealiˈsation** *n* ▸**iˈdealˌizer** *or* **iˈdealˌiser** *n*

idée fixe ❶ *French*. (ide fiks) *n, pl* ***idées fixes*** (ide fiks). a fixed idea; obsession.

idem *Latin*. (ˈaɪdɛm, ˈɪdɛm) *pron, adj* the same: used to refer to an article, chapter, etc., previously cited.

identic (aɪˈdɛntɪk) *adj Diplomacy*. (esp. of opinions expressed by two or more governments) having the same wording or intention regarding another power.

identical ❶ (aɪˈdɛntɪkᵊl) *adj* **1** being the same: *we got the identical hotel room as last year*. **2** exactly alike or equal. **3** designating either or both of a pair of twins of the same sex who developed from a single fertilized ovum that split into two. Cf. **fraternal** (sense 3). [C17: from Med. L *identicus*, from L *idem* the same] ▸**iˈdentically** *adv*

identification ❶ (aɪˌdɛntɪfɪˈkeɪʃən) *n* **1** the act of identifying or the state of being identified. **2a** something that identifies a person or thing. **2b** (*as modifier*): *an identification card*. **3** *Psychol*. **3a** the process of recognizing specific objects as the result of remembering. **3b** the process by which one incorporates aspects of another person's personality. **3c** the transferring of a response from one situation to another because the two bear similar features.

identification parade *n* a group of persons, including one suspected of a crime, assembled for the purpose of discovering whether a witness can identify the suspect.

identify ❶ (aɪˈdɛntɪˌfaɪ) *vb* **identifies, identifying, identified.** (*mainly tr*) **1** to prove or recognize as being a certain person or thing; determine the identity of. **2** to consider as the same or equivalent. **3** (*also intr; often foll. by with*) to consider (oneself) as similar to another. **4** to determine the taxonomic classification of (a plant or animal). **5** (*intr; usually foll. by with*) *Psychol*. to engage in identification. ▸**iˈdentiˌfiable** *adj* ▸**iˈdentiˌfiableness** *n* ▸**iˈdentiˌfier** *n*

Identikit (aɪˈdɛntɪˌkɪt) *n Trademark*. **1a** a set of transparencies of typical facial characteristics that can be superimposed on one another to build up a picture of a person sought by the police. **1b** (*as modifier*): *an Identikit picture*. **2** (*modifier*) artificially created by copying different elements in an attempt to form a whole: *an Identikit pop group*.

identity ❶ (aɪˈdɛntɪtɪ) *n, pl* **identities. 1** the state of having unique identifying characteristics. **2** the individual characteristics by which a person or thing is recognized. **3** the state of being the same in nature, quality, etc.: *linked by the identity of their tastes*. **4** the state of being the same as a person or thing described or known: *the identity of the stolen goods was soon established*. **5** *Maths*. **5a** an equation that is valid for all values of its variables, as in $(x - y)(x + y) = x^2 - y^2$. Often denoted by the symbol ≡. **5b** Also called: **identity element.** a member of a set that when operating on another member, *x*, produces that member *x*: the identity for multiplication of numbers is 1 since $x.1 = 1.x = x$. **6** *Logic*. the relationship between an object and itself. **7** *Austral. inf*. a well-known local person; figure: *a Barwidgee identity*. **8** *Austral. & NZ inf*. an eccentric; character: *an old identity in the town*. [C16: from LL *identitās*, from L *idem* the same]

identity card *n* a card that establishes a person's identity, esp. one issued to all members of the population in wartime, to the staff of an organization, etc.

ideo- *combining form*. of or indicating idea or ideas: *ideology*. [from F *idéo-*, from Gk *idea* IDEA]

ideogram (ˈɪdɪəʊˌgræm) *or* **ideograph** (ˈɪdɪəʊˌgrɑːf) *n* **1** a sign or symbol, used in a writing system such as that of China, that directly represents a concept or thing, rather than a word for it. **2** any graphic sign or symbol, such as % or &.

ideography (ˌɪdɪˈɒgrəfɪ) *n* the use of ideograms to communicate ideas.

ideology ❶ (ˌaɪdɪˈɒlədʒɪ) *n, pl* **ideologies. 1** a body of ideas that reflects the beliefs of a nation, political system, class, etc. **2** speculation that is imaginary or visionary. **3** the study of the nature and origin of ideas. ▸**ideological** (ˌaɪdɪəˈlɒdʒɪkᵊl) *or* **ˌideoˈlogic** *adj* ▸**ˌideoˈlogically** *adv* ▸**ˌideˈologist** *or* **ˈideoˌlogue** *n*

ides (aɪdz) *n* (*functioning as sing*) (in the Roman calendar) the 15th day in March, May, July, and October and the 13th day of each other month. [C15: from OF, from L *īdūs* (pl), from ?]

id est *Latin*. (ˈɪd ˈɛst) the full form of **i.e.**

idiocy ❶ (ˈɪdɪəsɪ) *n, pl* **idiocies. 1** (*not in technical usage*) severe mental retardation. **2** foolishness; stupidity. **3** a foolish act or remark.

idiom ❶ (ˈɪdɪəm) *n* **1** a group of words whose meaning cannot be predicted from the constituent words: (*It was raining*) *cats and dogs*. **2** linguistic usage that is grammatical and natural to native speakers. **3** the characteristic vocabulary or usage of a specific human group or subject. **4** the characteristic artistic style of an individual, school, etc. [C16: from L *idiōma* peculiarity of language, from Gk *idios* private, separate] ▸**idiomatic** (ˌɪdɪəˈmætɪk) *adj* ▸**ˌidioˈmatically** *adv*

idiosyncrasy ❶ (ˌɪdɪəʊˈsɪŋkrəsɪ) *n, pl* **idiosyncrasies. 1** a tendency, type of behaviour, etc., of a person; quirk. **2** the composite physical or psychological make-up of a person. **3** an abnormal reaction of an individual to specific foods, drugs, etc. [C17: from Gk, from *idios* private, separate + *sunkrasis* mixture, temperament] ▸**idiosyncratic** (ˌɪdɪəʊsɪŋˈkrætɪk) *adj* ▸**ˌidiosynˈcratically** *adv*

idiot ❶ (ˈɪdɪət) *n* **1** a person with severe mental retardation. **2** a foolish or senseless person. [C13: from L *idiōta* ignorant person, from Gk *idiōtēs* private person, ignoramus]

idiot board *n* a slang name for **Autocue.**

idiot box *n Sl*. a television set.

idiotic ❶ (ˌɪdɪˈɒtɪk) *adj* of or resembling an idiot; foolish; senseless. ▸**ˌidiˈotically** *adv*

idiot savant (ˈiːdjəʊ sæˈvɑ̃, ˈɪdɪət ˈsævənt) *n, pl* **idiots savants** (ˈiːdjəʊ sæˈvɑ̃) *or* **idiot savants.** a person of subnormal intelligence who performs brilliantly at some specialized intellectual task.

idiot tape *n Computing*. a tape that prints out information in a continuous stream, with no line breaks.

idle ❶ (ˈaɪdᵊl) *adj* **1** unemployed or unoccupied; inactive. **2** not operating or being used. **3** (of money) not used to earn interest, etc. **4** not wanting to work; lazy. **5** (*usually prenominal*) frivolous or trivial: *idle pleasures*. **6** ineffective or powerless; vain. **7** without basis; unfounded. ◆ *vb* **idles, idling, idled. 8** (when *tr*, often foll. by *away*) to waste or pass

THESAURUS

idealist *n* **1** = **romantic**, dreamer, Utopian, visionary

idealistic *adj* **1** = **perfectionist**, impracticable, optimistic, quixotic, romantic, starry-eyed, Utopian, visionary
Antonyms *adj* down-to-earth, practical, pragmatic, realistic, sensible

idealization *n* **2** = **glorification**, ennoblement, exaltation, magnification, worship

idealize *vb* **2** = **romanticize**, apotheosize, deify, ennoble, exalt, glorify, magnify, put on a pedestal, worship

ideally *adv* **5** = **in a perfect world**, all things being equal, if one had one's way, under the best of circumstances

idée fixe *n* = **obsession**, bee in one's bonnet, fixation, fixed idea, hobbyhorse, monomania, one-track mind (*inf.*), preoccupation, thing (*inf.*)

identical *adj* **1, 2** = **alike**, a dead ringer (*sl.*), corresponding, duplicate, equal, equivalent, indistinguishable, interchangeable, like, like two peas in a pod, matching, selfsame, the same, twin
Antonyms *adj* different, disparate, distinct, diverse, separate, unlike

identifiable *adj* **1** = **noticeable**, ascertainable, detectable, discernible, distinguishable, known, recognizable, unmistakable

identification *n* **1** = **recognition**, cataloguing, classifying, establishment of identity, labelling, naming, pinpointing **2** = **identity card**, credentials, ID, letters of introduction, papers **3** = **sympathy**, association, connection, empathy, fellow feeling, involvement, rapport, relationship

identify *vb* **1** = **recognize**, catalogue, classify, diagnose, flag, label, make out, name, pick out, pinpoint, place, put one's finger on (*inf.*), single out, spot, tag **3** *with* **with** = **relate to**, ally with, associate with, empathize with, feel for, put in the same category as, put oneself in the place *or* shoes of, respond to, see through another's eyes, think of in connection with

identity *n* **2** = **existence**, distinctiveness, individuality, oneness, particularity, personality, self, selfhood, singularity, uniqueness **3** = **sameness**, accord, correspondence, empathy, rapport, unanimity, unity

ideology *n* **1** = **philosophy**, articles of faith, belief(s), creed, dogma, ideas, principles, tenets, *Weltanschauung*, world view

idiocy *n* **2** = **foolishness**, abject stupidity, asininity, cretinism, fatuity, fatuousness, imbecility, inanity, insanity, lunacy, senselessness, tomfoolery
Antonyms *n* acumen, sagacity, sanity, sense, soundness, wisdom

idiom *n* **1** = **phrase**, expression, locution, set phrase, turn of phrase **2, 3** = **language**, jargon, mode of expression, parlance, style, talk, usage, vernacular

idiomatic *adj* **2** = **vernacular**, dialectal, native

idiosyncrasy *n* **1** = **peculiarity**, affectation, characteristic, eccentricity, habit, mannerism, oddity, personal trait, quirk, singularity, trick

idiosyncratic *adj* **1** = **distinctive**, individual, individualistic, peculiar

idiot *n* **2** = **fool**, ass, berk (*Brit. sl.*), blockhead, booby, charlie (*Brit. inf.*), chump, coot, cretin, dimwit (*inf.*), dork (*sl.*), dunderhead, geek (*sl.*), halfwit, imbecile, jerk (*sl., chiefly US & Canad.*), lamebrain (*inf.*), mooncalf, moron, nerd *or* nurd (*sl.*), nincompoop, nitwit (*inf.*), numbskull *or* numskull, oaf, prat (*sl.*), schmuck (*US sl.*), simpleton, twit (*inf., chiefly Brit.*)

idiotic *adj* = **foolish**, asinine, braindead (*inf.*), crackpot (*inf.*), crazy, daft (*inf.*), dumb (*inf.*), dumb-ass (*sl.*), fatuous, foolhardy, halfwitted, harebrained, imbecile, imbecilic, inane, insane, loopy (*inf.*), lunatic, moronic, senseless, stupid, unintelligent
Antonyms *adj* brilliant, commonsensical, intelligent, sensible, thoughtful, wise

idle *adj* **1** = **inactive**, dead, empty, gathering dust, jobless, mothballed, out of action *or* operation, out of work, redundant, stationary, ticking over, unemployed, unoccupied, unused, vacant **4** = **lazy**, good-for-nothing, indolent, lackadaisical, shiftless, slothful, sluggish **5** = **trivial**, frivolous, insignificant, irrelevant, nugatory, superficial, unhelpful, unnecessary **6** = **useless**, abortive, bootless, fruitless, futile, groundless,

(time) fruitlessly or inactively. **9** (*intr*) (of a shaft, etc.) to turn without doing useful work. **10** (*intr*) (of an engine) to run at low speed with the transmission disengaged. [OE *īdel*]
▸**'idleness** *n* ▸**'idly** *adv*

idle pulley *or* **idler pulley** *n* a freely rotating pulley used to control the tension or direction of a belt. Also called: **idler.**

idler 🅣 ('aɪdlə) *n* **1** a person who idles. **2** another name for **idle pulley** or **idle wheel.**

idle wheel *n* a gearwheel interposed between two others to transmit torque without changing the direction of rotation or the velocity ratio. Also called: **idler.**

idol 🅣 ('aɪdᵊl) *n* **1** a material object that is worshipped as a god. **2** *Christianity, Judaism.* any being (other than the one God) to which divine honour is paid. **3** a person who is revered, admired, or highly loved. [C13: from LL, from L: image, from Gk, from *eidos* shape, form]

idolatry 🅣 (aɪ'dɒlətrɪ) *n* **1** the worship of idols. **2** great devotion or reverence.
▸**i'dolater** *n or* **i'dolatress** *fem n* ▸**i'dolatrous** *adj*

idolize 🅣 *or* **idolise** ('aɪdəˌlaɪz) *vb* **idolizes, idolizing, idolized** *or* **idolises, idolising, idolised. 1** (*tr*) to admire or revere greatly. **2** (*tr*) to worship as an idol. **3** (*intr*) to worship idols.
▸**ˌidoli'zation** *or* **ˌidoli'sation** *n* ▸**'idolˌizer** *or* **'idolˌiser** *n*

idolum (ɪ'dəʊləm) *n* **1** a mental picture; idea. **2** a false idea; fallacy. [C17: from L: IDOL]

IDP *abbrev. for* integrated data processing.

idyll 🅣 *or US (sometimes)* **idyl** ('ɪdɪl) *n* **1** a poem or prose work describing an idealized rural life, pastoral scenes, etc. **2** a charming or picturesque scene or event. **3** a piece of music with a pastoral character. [C17: from L, from Gk *eidullion*, from *eidos* shape, (literary) form]
▸**i'dyllic** *adj* ▸**i'dyllically** *adv*

IE *abbrev. for* Indo-European (languages).

i.e. *abbrev. for* id est. [L: that is (to say); in other words]

-ie *suffix forming nouns.* a variant of **-y**[2]: *groupie.*

IEE *abbrev. for* Institution of Electrical Engineers.

-ier *suffix forming nouns.* a variant of **-eer:** *brigadier.* [from OE *-ere* -ER[1] or (in some words) from OF *-ier*, from L *-ārius* -ARY]

if 🅣 (ɪf) *conj* (*subordinating*) **1** in case that, or on condition that: *if you try hard it might work.* **2** used to introduce an indirect question. In this sense, *if* approaches the meaning of *whether.* **3** even though: *an attractive if awkward girl.* **4a** used to introduce expressions of desire, with *only: if I had only known.* **4b** used to introduce exclamations of surprise, dismay, etc.: *if this doesn't top everything!* ◆ *n* **5** an uncertainty or doubt: *the big if is whether our plan will work.* **6** a condition or stipulation: *I won't have any ifs or buts.* [OE *gif*]

IF *or* **i.f.** *Electronics. abbrev. for* intermediate frequency.

IFA *abbrev. for* independent financial adviser.

IFC *abbrev. for* International Finance Corporation.

-iferous *suffix forming adjectives.* containing or yielding: *carboniferous.*

iffy 🅣 ('ɪfɪ) *adj* **iffier, iffiest.** *Inf.* uncertain or subject to contingency. [C20: from IF + -Y[1]]

-ify *suffix forming verbs.* a variant of **-fy:** *intensify.*
▸**-ification** *suffix forming nouns.*

Igbo ('iːbəʊ) *n, pl* **Igbo** *or* **Igbos.** a variant spelling of **Ibo.**

igloo *or* **iglu** ('ɪgluː) *n, pl* **igloos** *or* **iglus. 1** a dome-shaped Eskimo house, built of blocks of solid snow. **2** a hollow made by a seal in the snow over its breathing hole in the ice. [C19: from Eskimo *igdlu* house]

igneous ('ɪgnɪəs) *adj* **1** (of rocks) derived from magma or lava that has solidified on or below the earth's surface. **2** of or relating to fire. [C17: from L *igneus* fiery, from *ignis* fire]

ignis fatuus ('ɪgnɪs 'fætjʊəs) *n, pl* **ignes fatui** ('ɪgniːz 'fætjʊˌaɪ). another name for **will-o'-the-wisp.** [C16: from Med. L, lit.: foolish fire]

ignite 🅣 (ɪg'naɪt) *vb* **ignites, igniting, ignited. 1** to catch fire or set fire to; burn or cause to burn. **2** (*tr*) *Chem.* to heat strongly. [C17: from L, from *ignis* fire]
▸**ig'nitable** *or* **ig'nitible** *adj* ▸**igˌnita'bility** *or* **igˌniti'bility** *n* ▸**ig'niter** *n*

ignition (ɪg'nɪʃən) *n* **1** the act or process of initiating combustion. **2** the process of igniting the fuel in an internal-combustion engine. **3** (preceded by *the*) the devices used to ignite the fuel in an internal-combustion engine.

ignition coil *n* an induction coil that supplies the high voltage to the sparking plugs on an internal-combustion engine.

ignition key *n* the key used in a motor vehicle to turn the switch that connects the battery to the ignition system.

ignitron (ɪg'naɪtrɒn, 'ɪgnɪˌtrɒn) *n* a rectifier controlled by a subsidiary electrode, the igniter, partially immersed in a mercury cathode. A current passed between igniter and cathode forms a hot spot sufficient to strike an arc between cathode and anode. [C20: from *igniter* + ELECTRON]

ignoble 🅣 (ɪg'nəʊbᵊl) *adj* **1** dishonourable; base; despicable. **2** of low birth or origins; humble; common. **3** of low quality; inferior. [C16: from L, from IN-[1] + OL *gnōbilis* NOBLE]
▸**ˌigno'bility** *or* **ig'nobleness** *n* ▸**ig'nobly** *adv*

ignominy 🅣 ('ɪgnəˌmɪnɪ) *n, pl* **ignominies. 1** disgrace or public shame; dishonour. **2** a cause of disgrace; a shameful act. [C16: from L *ignōminia* disgrace, from *ig-* (see IN-[2]) + *nōmen* name, reputation]
▸**ˌigno'minious** *adj* ▸**ˌigno'miniously** *adv* ▸**ˌigno'miniousness** *n*

ignoramus 🅣 (ˌɪgnə'reɪməs) *n, pl* **ignoramuses.** an ignorant person; fool. [C16: from legal L, lit.: we have no knowledge of, from L *ignōrāre* to be ignorant of; see IGNORE; modern usage originated from use of *Ignoramus* as the name of an unlettered lawyer in a play by G. Ruggle, 17th-century E dramatist]

ignorance 🅣 ('ɪgnərəns) *n* lack of knowledge, information, or education; the state of being ignorant.

ignorant 🅣 ('ɪgnərənt) *adj* **1** lacking in knowledge or education; unenlightened. **2** (*postpositive;* often foll. by *of*) lacking in awareness or knowledge (of): *ignorant of the law.* **3** resulting from or showing lack of knowledge or awareness: *an ignorant remark.*
▸**'ignorantly** *adv*

ignore 🅣 (ɪg'nɔː) *vb* **ignores, ignoring, ignored.** (*tr*) to fail or refuse to notice; disregard. [C17: from L *ignōrāre* not to know, from *ignārus* ignorant of]
▸**ig'norer** *n*

THESAURUS

ineffective, of no avail, otiose, pointless, unavailing, unproductive, unsuccessful, vain, worthless ◆ *vb* **8** *often with* **away** = **laze**, dally, dawdle, fool, fritter, hang out (*inf.*), kill time, loaf, loiter, lounge, potter, take it easy, vegetate, waste, while
Antonyms *adj* ≠ **inactive, lazy:** active, busy, employed, energetic, functional, industrious, occupied, operative, working ≠ **trivial:** important, meaningful ≠ **useless:** advantageous, effective, fruitful, profitable, useful, worthwhile

idleness *n* **1** = **inactivity**, inaction, leisure, time on one's hands, unemployment **4** = **laziness**, hibernation, inertia, shiftlessness, sloth, sluggishness, torpor, vegetating **8** = **loafing**, dilly-dallying (*inf.*), lazing, pottering, skiving (*Brit. sl.*), time-wasting, trifling

idler *n* **1** = **loafer**, clock-watcher, couch potato (*sl.*), dawdler, deadbeat (*inf., chiefly US & Canad.*), dodger, drone, laggard, layabout, lazybones, lounger, malingerer, shirker, skiver (*Brit. sl.*), slacker, sloth, slouch (*inf.*), sluggard, time-waster

idly *adv* **4** = **lazily**, apathetically, casually, inactively, indolently, inertly, lackadaisically, languidly, languorously, lethargically, passively, shiftlessly, slothfully, sluggishly, unthinkingly
Antonyms *adv* actively, animatedly, busily, dynamically, energetically, industriously

idol *n* **1, 2** = **graven image**, deity, god, image, pagan symbol **3** = **hero**, beloved, darling, fave (*inf.*), favourite, pet, pin-up (*sl.*), superstar

idolater *n* **1** = **heathen**, idol-worshipper, pagan **2** = **admirer**, adorer, devotee, idolizer, votary, worshipper

idolatrous *adj* **2** = **adoring**, adulatory, reverential, uncritical, worshipful

idolatry *n* **2** = **adoration**, adulation, apotheosis, deification, exaltation, glorification, hero worship, idolizing

idolize *vb* **1** = **worship**, admire, adore, apotheosize, bow down before, deify, dote upon, exalt, glorify, hero-worship, look up to, love, revere, reverence, venerate, worship to excess

idyllic *adj* **2** = **idealized**, arcadian, charming, halcyon, heavenly, ideal, out of this world, pastoral, peaceful, picturesque, rustic, unspoiled

if *conj* **1** = **provided**, admitting, allowing, assuming, granting, in case, on condition that, on the assumption that, providing, supposing, though, whenever, wherever **2** = **whether** ◆ *n* **5** = **doubt**, condition, hesitation, stipulation, uncertainty

iffy *adj* = **uncertain**, chancy (*inf.*), conditional, doubtful, in the lap of the gods, problematical, undecided, unpredictable, up in the air

ignite *vb* **1** = **set fire to**, burn, burst into flames, fire, flare up, inflame, kindle, light, put a match to (*inf.*), set alight, take fire, torch, touch off

ignoble *adj* **1** = **dishonourable**, abject, base, contemptible, craven, dastardly, degenerate, degraded, despicable, disgraceful, heinous, infamous, low, mean, petty, shabby, shameless, unworthy, vile, wretched **2** = **lowly**, baseborn (*arch.*), common, humble, lowborn (*rare*), mean, of humble birth, peasant, plebeian, vulgar

ignominious *adj* **1** = **humiliating**, abject, despicable, discreditable, disgraceful, dishonourable, disreputable, indecorous, inglorious, mortifying, scandalous, shameful, sorry, undignified
Antonyms *adj* creditable, honourable, reputable, worthy

ignominy *n* **1** = **disgrace**, bad odour, contempt, discredit, dishonour, disrepute, humiliation, infamy, mortification, obloquy, odium, opprobrium, reproach, shame, stigma
Antonyms *n* credit, honour, repute

ignoramus *n* = **dunce**, ass, blockhead, bonehead (*sl.*), dolt, donkey, duffer (*inf.*), dullard, fathead (*inf.*), fool, illiterate, lowbrow, numbskull *or* numskull, simpleton

ignorance *n* = **lack of education**, benightedness, greenness, inexperience, innocence, nescience (*literary*), oblivion, unawareness, unconsciousness, unfamiliarity
Antonyms *n* comprehension, enlightenment, insight, intelligence, knowledge, understanding, wisdom

ignorant *adj* **1** = **uneducated**, as green as grass, green, illiterate, naive, unaware, uncultivated, unknowledgeable, unlearned, unlettered, unread, untaught, untrained, untutored, wet behind the ears (*inf.*) **2** = **uninformed**, benighted, blind to, inexperienced, innocent, in the dark about, oblivious, out of the loop, unaware, unconscious, unenlightened, uninitiated, unknowing, unschooled, unwitting **3** = **insensitive**, crass, crude, gross, half-baked (*inf.*), rude, shallow, superficial, uncomprehending, unscholarly
Antonyms *adj* ≠ **uneducated:** astute, brilliant, cultured, educated, knowledgeable, learned, literate, sagacious, sophisticated, wise ≠ **uninformed:** aware, conscious, informed, in the loop

ignore *vb* = **overlook**, be oblivious to, blank (*sl.*), bury one's head in the sand, cold-shoulder, cut, discount, disregard, give the cold shoulder to, neglect, pass over, pay no attention to, reject, send (someone) to Coventry, shut one's eyes to, take no notice of, turn a

iguana (ɪˈgwɑːnə) *n* either of two large tropical American arboreal herbivorous lizards, esp. the common iguana, having a greyish-green body with a row of spines along the back. [C16: from Sp., from S Amerind *iwana*]
▸**iˈguanian** *n, adj*

iguanodon (ɪˈgwɑːnəˌdɒn) *n* a massive herbivorous long-tailed bipedal dinosaur common in Europe and N Africa in Jurassic and Cretaceous times. [C19: NL, from IGUANA + Gk *odōn* tooth]

IHC (in New Zealand) *abbrev. for* intellectually handicapped child.

IHS the first three letters of the name Jesus in Greek (ΙΗΣΟΥΣ), often used as a Christian emblem.

ikat (ˈiːkæt) *n* a method of creating patterns in fabric by tie-dyeing the yarn before weaving. [C20: from Malay, lit.: to tie, bind]

ikebana (ˌiːkəˈbɑːnə) *n* the Japanese decorative art of flower arrangement.

ikon (ˈaɪkɒn) *n* a variant spelling of **icon**.

il- *prefix* a variant of **in-**[1] and **in-**[2] before *l*.

-ile *or* **-il** *suffix forming adjectives and nouns.* indicating capability, liability, or a relationship with something: *agile; juvenile.* [via F from L or directly from L *-ilis*]
▸**-ility** *suffix forming nouns.*

ileitis (ˌɪlɪˈaɪtɪs) *n* inflammation of the ileum.

ileostomy (ˌɪlɪˈɒstəmɪ) *n, pl* **ileostomies.** the surgical formation of a permanent opening through the abdominal wall into the ileum.

ileum (ˈɪlɪəm) *n* the part of the small intestine between the jejunum and the caecum. [C17: NL, from L *īlium, īleum* flank, groin, from ?]
▸**ˈileˌac** *adj*

ilex (ˈaɪlɛks) *n* **1** any of a genus of trees or shrubs such as the holly and inkberry. **2** another name for the **holm oak.** [C16: from L]

ilium (ˈɪlɪəm) *n, pl* **ilia** (-ɪə). the uppermost and widest of the three sections of the hipbone.

ilk ❶ (ɪlk) *n* **1** a type; class; sort (esp. in **of that, his,** etc., **ilk**): *people of that ilk should not be allowed here.* **2 of that ilk.** *Scot.* of the place of the same name: to indicate that the person is laird of the place named: *Moncrieff of that ilk.* [OE *ilca* the same family, same kind]

USAGE NOTE Although the use of *ilk* in sense 1 is sometimes condemned as being the result of a misunderstanding of the original Scottish expression *of that ilk,* it is nevertheless well established and generally acceptable.

ill ❶ (ɪl) *adj* **worse, worst. 1** (*usually postpositive*) not in good health; sick. **2** characterized by or intending harm, etc.; hostile: *ill deeds.* **3** causing pain, harm, adversity, etc. **4** ascribing or imputing evil to something referred to: *ill repute.* **5** promising an unfavourable outcome; unpropitious: *an ill omen.* **6** harsh; lacking kindness: *ill will.* **7** not up to an acceptable standard; faulty: *ill manners.* **8 ill at ease.** unable to relax; uncomfortable. ◆ *n* **9** evil or harm; misfortune; trouble. **10** a mild disease. ◆ *adv* **11** badly: *the title ill befits him.* **12** with difficulty; hardly: *he can ill afford the money.* **13** not rightly: *he ill deserves such good fortune.* [C11 (in the sense: evil): from ON *illr* bad]

ill. *abbrev. for:* **1** illustrated. **2** illustration.

I'll (aɪl) *contraction of* I will *or* I shall.

ill-advised ❶ *adj* **1** acting without reasonable care or thought: *you would be ill-advised to sell your house now.* **2** badly thought out; not or insufficiently considered: *an ill-advised plan of action.*
▸**ill-advisedly** (ˌɪlədˈvaɪzɪdlɪ) *adv*

ill-affected *adj* (often foll. by *towards*) not well disposed; disaffected.

ill-assorted ❶ *adj* badly matched; incompatible.

illative (ɪˈleɪtɪv) *adj* **1** relating to inference; inferential. **2** *Grammar.* denoting a word or morpheme used to signal inference, for example *so* or *therefore.* **3** (esp. in Finnish grammar) denoting a case of nouns expressing a relation of motion or direction, usually translated by *into* or *towards.* ◆ *n* **4** *Grammar.* **4a** the illative case. **4b** an illative word or speech element. [C16: from LL *illātīvus* inferring, concluding]
▸**ilˈlatively** *adv*

ill-bred ❶ *adj* badly brought up; lacking good manners.
▸**ˌill-ˈbreeding** *n*

ill-considered ❶ *adj* done without due consideration; not thought out: *an ill-considered decision.*

ill-defined ❶ *adj* imperfectly defined; having no clear outline.

ill-disposed ❶ *adj* (often foll. by *towards*) not kindly disposed.

illegal ❶ (ɪˈliːgᵊl) *adj* **1** forbidden by law; unlawful; illicit. **2** unauthorized or prohibited by a code of official or accepted rules. ◆ *n* **3** a person who has entered or attempted to enter a country illegally.
▸**ilˈlegally** *adv* ▸**ˌilleˈgality** *n*

illegible ❶ (ɪˈlɛdʒɪbᵊl) *adj* unable to be read or deciphered.
▸**ilˌlegiˈbility** *or* **ilˈlegibleness** *n* ▸**ilˈlegibly** *adv*

illegitimate ❶ (ˌɪlɪˈdʒɪtɪmɪt) *adj* **1a** born of parents who were not married to each other at the time of birth; bastard. **1b** occurring outside marriage: *of illegitimate birth.* **2** illegal; unlawful. **3** contrary to logic; incorrectly reasoned. ◆ *n* **4** an illegitimate person; bastard.
▸**ˌilleˈgitimacy** *or* **ˌilleˈgitimateness** *n* ▸**ˌilleˈgitimately** *adv*

ill-fated ❶ *adj* doomed or unlucky.

ill-favoured ❶ *adj* **1** unattractive or repulsive in appearance; ugly. **2** disagreeable or objectionable.
▸**ˌill-ˈfavouredly** *adv* ▸**ˌill-ˈfavouredness** *n*

ill feeling ❶ *n* hostile feeling; animosity.

ill-founded ❶ *adj* not founded on true or reliable premises; unsubstantiated.

ill-gotten *adj* obtained dishonestly or illegally (esp. in **ill-gotten gains**).

ill humour ❶ *n* a disagreeable or sullen mood; bad temper.
▸**ˌill-ˈhumoured** *adj* ▸**ˌill-ˈhumouredly** *adv*

THESAURUS

blind eye to, turn a deaf ear to, turn one's back on
Antonyms *vb* acknowledge, heed, note, pay attention to, recognize, regard

ilk *n* **1 = type**, brand, breed, character, class, description, disposition, kidney, kind, sort, stamp, style, variety

ill *adj* **1 = unwell**, ailing, at death's door, dicky (*Brit. inf.*), diseased, funny (*inf.*), green about the gills, indisposed, infirm, laid up (*inf.*), off-colour, out of sorts (*inf.*), poorly (*inf.*), queasy, queer, seedy (*inf.*), sick, under the weather (*inf.*), unhealthy, valetudinarian **2 = harmful**, bad, damaging, deleterious, detrimental, evil, foul, iniquitous, injurious, ruinous, unfortunate, unlucky, vile, wicked, wrong **5 = ominous**, disturbing, foreboding, inauspicious, sinister, threatening, unfavourable, unhealthy, unlucky, unpromising, unpropitious, unwholesome **6 = hostile**, acrimonious, adverse, antagonistic, cantankerous, cross, harsh, hateful, hurtful, inimical, malevolent, malicious, sullen, surly, unfriendly, unkind **8 ill at ease = uncomfortable**, anxious, awkward, disquieted, disturbed, edgy, faltering, fidgety, hesitant, like a fish out of water, nervous, neurotic, on edge, on pins and needles (*inf.*), on tenterhooks, out of place, restless, self-conscious, strange, tense, twitchy (*inf.*), uneasy, unquiet, unrelaxed, unsettled, unsure ◆ *n* **9 = harm**, affliction, evil, hardship, hurt, injury, misery, misfortune, pain, trial, tribulation, trouble, unpleasantness, wickedness, woe ◆ *adv* **11 = badly**, hard, inauspiciously, poorly, unfavourably, unfortunately, unluckily **12 = hardly**, barely, by no means, insufficiently, scantily
Antonyms *adj* ≠ **unwell:** hale, healthy, strong, well ≠ **harmful:** favourable, good ≠ **hostile:** generous, kind ◆ *n* ≠ **harm:** good, kindness ◆ *adv* ≠ **hardly:** easily, well

ill-advised *adj* **1, 2 = misguided**, foolhardy, foolish, ill-considered, ill-judged, impolitic, imprudent, inappropriate, incautious, indiscreet, injudicious, overhasty, rash, reckless, short-sighted, thoughtless, unseemly, unwise, wrong-headed
Antonyms *adj* appropriate, cautious, discreet, judicious, politic, prudent, seemly, sensible, wise

ill-assorted *adj* **= incompatible**, incongruous, inharmonious, mismatched, uncongenial, unsuited

ill-bred *adj* **= bad-mannered**, boorish, churlish, coarse, crass, discourteous, ill-mannered, impolite, indelicate, rude, uncivil, uncivilized, uncouth, ungallant, ungentlemanly, unladylike, unmannerly, unrefined, vulgar
Antonyms *adj* civil, courteous, delicate, mannerly, refined, urbane, well-bred

ill-considered *adj* **= unwise**, careless, hasty, heedless, improvident, imprudent, injudicious, overhasty, precipitate, rash

ill-defined *adj* **= unclear**, blurred, dim, fuzzy, indistinct, nebulous, shadowy, vague, woolly
Antonyms *adj* apparent, bold, clear, conspicuous, cut-and-dried, distinct, evident, manifest, obvious, plain

ill-disposed *adj* **= unfriendly**, against, antagonistic, anti (*inf.*), antipathetic, averse, disobliging, down on (*inf.*), hostile, inimical, opposed, uncooperative, unwelcoming
Antonyms *adj* amicable, cooperative, friendly, obliging, welcoming, well-disposed

illegal *adj* **1 = unlawful**, actionable (*Law*), banned, black-market, bootleg, criminal, felonious, forbidden, illicit, lawless, off limits, outlawed, prohibited, proscribed, unauthorized, unconstitutional, under-the-counter, under-the-table, unlicensed, unofficial, wrongful
Antonyms *adj* lawful, legal, licit, permissible

illegality *n* **1 = crime**, criminality, felony, illegitimacy, illicitness, lawlessness, unlawfulness, wrong, wrongness

illegible *adj* **= indecipherable**, crabbed, faint, hard to make out, hieroglyphic, obscure, scrawled, undecipherable, unreadable
Antonyms *adj* clear, decipherable, legible, plain, readable

illegitimacy *n* **1 = bastardy**, bastardism **2 = illegality**, illicitness, irregularity, unconstitutionality, unlawfulness

illegitimate *adj* **1 = born out of wedlock**, baseborn, bastard, born on the wrong side of the blanket, fatherless, misbegotten (*literary*), natural, spurious (*rare*) **2 = unlawful**, illegal, illicit, improper, unauthorized, unconstitutional, under-the-table, unsanctioned **3 = invalid**, illogical, incorrect, spurious, unsound
Antonyms *adj* ≠ **unlawful:** authorized, constitutional, lawful, legal, legitimate, proper, sanctioned

ill-fated *adj* **= doomed**, blighted, hapless, ill-omened, ill-starred, luckless, star-crossed, unfortunate, unhappy, unlucky

ill-favoured *adj* **1 = ugly**, hideous, no oil painting, plain, repulsive, unattractive, unlovely, unprepossessing, unsightly

ill feeling *n* **= hostility**, animosity, animus, antagonism, bad blood, bitterness, chip on one's shoulder, disgruntlement, dissatisfaction, dudgeon (*arch.*), enmity, frustration, hard feelings, ill will, indignation, offence, rancour, resentment
Antonyms *n* amity, benevolence, favour, friendship, goodwill, satisfaction

ill-founded *adj* **= groundless**, baseless, empty, idle, unjustified, unproven, unreliable, unsubstantiated, unsupported

ill humour *n* **= irascibility**, (bad) mood, (bad) temper, bate, crabbiness, crossness, disagreeableness, grumpiness, irritability, moodiness, moroseness, petulance, pique, sharpness, spleen, sulkiness, sulks, tartness, testiness

ill-humoured *adj* **= bad-tempered**, acrimonious, crabbed, crabby, cross, disagreeable, grumpy, impatient, irascible, irritable, liverish,

illiberal ➊ (ɪˈlɪbərəl) *adj* **1** narrow-minded; prejudiced; bigoted; intolerant. **2** not generous; mean. **3** lacking in culture or refinement.
▸**il,liber'ality** *n* ▸**il'liberally** *adv*

illicit ➊ (ɪˈlɪsɪt) *adj* **1** another word for **illegal. 2** not allowed or approved by common custom, rule, or standard: *illicit sexual relations.*
▸**il'licitly** *adv* ▸**il'licitness** *n*

illimitable ➊ (ɪˈlɪmɪtəbᵊl) *adj* limitless; boundless.
▸**il,limita'bility** *or* **il'limitableness** *n*

illiterate ➊ (ɪˈlɪtərɪt) *adj* **1** unable to read and write. **2** violating accepted standards in reading and writing: *an illiterate scrawl.* **3** uneducated, ignorant, or uncultured: *scientifically illiterate.* ◆ *n* **4** an illiterate person.
▸**il'literacy** *or* **il'literateness** *n* ▸**il'literately** *adv*

ill-judged ➊ *adj* rash; ill-advised.

ill-mannered ➊ *adj* having bad manners; rude; impolite.
▸**,ill-'manneredly** *adv*

ill-natured ➊ *adj* naturally unpleasant and mean.
▸**,ill-'naturedly** *adv* ▸**,ill-'naturedness** *n*

illness ➊ (ˈɪlnɪs) *n* **1** a disease or indisposition; sickness. **2** a state of ill health.

illogical ➊ (ɪˈlɒdʒɪkᵊl) *adj* **1** characterized by lack of logic; senseless or unreasonable. **2** disregarding logical principles.
▸**illogicality** (ɪ,lɒdʒɪˈkælɪtɪ) *or* **il'logicalness** *n* ▸**il'logically** *adv*

ill-starred ➊ *adj* unlucky; unfortunate; ill-fated.

ill temper ➊ *n* bad temper; irritability.
▸**,ill-'tempered** *adj* ▸**,ill-'temperedly** *adv*

ill-timed ➊ *adj* occurring at or planned for an unsuitable time.

ill-treat ➊ *vb* (*tr*) to behave cruelly or harshly towards; misuse; maltreat.
▸**,ill-'treatment** *n*

illuminance (ɪˈluːmɪnəns) *n* the luminous flux incident on unit area of a surface. Sometimes called: **illumination.** Cf. **irradiance.**

illuminant (ɪˈluːmɪnənt) *n* **1** something that provides or gives off light. ◆ *adj* **2** giving off light; illuminating.

illuminate ➊ *vb* (ɪˈluːmɪ,neɪt), **illuminates, illuminating, illuminated. 1** (*tr*) to throw light in or into; light up. **2** (*tr*) to make easily understood; clarify. **3** to adorn, decorate, or be decorated with lights. **4** (*tr*) to decorate (a letter, etc.) by the application of colours, gold, or silver. **5** (*intr*) to become lighted up. ◆ *adj* (ɪˈluːmɪnɪt, -,neɪt). **6** *Arch.* made clear or bright with light. ◆ *n* (ɪˈluːmɪnɪt, -,neɪt). **7** a person who claims to have special enlightenment. [C16: from L *illūmināre* to light up, from *lūmen* light]
▸**il'lumi,nating** *adj* ▸**il'luminative** *adj* ▸**il'lumi,nator** *n*

illuminati (ɪ,luːmɪˈnɑːtiː) *pl n, sing* **illuminato** (-təʊ). **1** a group of persons claiming exceptional enlightenment on some subject, esp. religion. **2** (*cap.*) any of several groups of illuminati, esp. in 18th-century France and Bavaria or 16th-century Spain. [C16: from L, lit.: the enlightened ones, from *illūmināre* to ILLUMINATE]

illumination ➊ (ɪ,luːmɪˈneɪʃən) *n* **1** the act of illuminating or the state of being illuminated. **2** a source of light. **3** (*often pl*) *Chiefly Brit.* a light or lights used as decoration in streets, parks, etc. **4** spiritual or intellectual enlightenment; insight or understanding. **5** the act of making understood; clarification. **6** decoration in colours, gold, or silver used on some manuscripts. **7** *Physics.* another name (not in technical usage) for **illuminance.**

illumine (ɪˈluːmɪn) *vb* **illumines, illumining, illumined.** a literary word for **illuminate.** [C14: from L *illūmināre* to make light]
▸**il'luminable** *adj*

ill-use *vb* (ˈɪlˈjuːz), **ill-uses, ill-using, ill-used. 1** to use badly or cruelly; abuse; maltreat. ◆ *n* (ˈɪlˈjuːs), *also* **ill-usage. 2** harsh or cruel treatment; abuse.

illusion ➊ (ɪˈluːʒən) *n* **1** a false appearance or deceptive impression of reality: *the mirror gives an illusion of depth.* **2** a false or misleading perception or belief; delusion. **3** *Psychol.* a perception that is not true to reality, having been altered subjectively in the mind of the perceiver. See also **hallucination.** [C14: from L *illūsiō* deceit, from *illūdere* to sport with, from *ludus* game]
▸**il'lusionary** *or* **il'lusional** *adj* ▸**il'lusioned** *adj*

illusionism (ɪˈluːʒə,nɪzəm) *n* **1** *Philosophy.* the doctrine that the external world exists only in illusory sense perceptions. **2** the use of highly illusory effects in art.

illusionist (ɪˈluːʒənɪst) *n* **1** a person given to illusions; visionary; dreamer. **2** *Philosophy.* a person who believes in illusionism. **3** an artist who practises illusionism. **4** a conjuror; magician.
▸**il,lusion'istic** *adj*

illusory ➊ (ɪˈluːsərɪ) *or* **illusive** (ɪˈluːsɪv) *adj* producing or based on illusion; deceptive or unreal.
▸**il'lusorily** *adv* ▸**il'lusoriness** *n*

> **USAGE NOTE** *Illusive* is sometimes wrongly used where *elusive* is meant: *they fought hard, but victory remained elusive* (not *illusive*).

illust. *or* **illus.** *abbrev. for:* **1** illustrated. **2** illustration.

illustrate ➊ (ˈɪlə,streɪt) *vb* **illustrates, illustrating, illustrated. 1** to clarify or explain by use of examples, analogy, etc. **2** (*tr*) to be an example of. **3** (*tr*) to explain or decorate (a book, text, etc.) with pictures. [C16: from L, from *lustrāre* to purify, brighten; see LUSTRUM]
▸**'illus,trative** *adj* ▸**'illus,trator** *n*

THESAURUS

moody, morose, out of sorts, out of temper, petulant, sharp, snappish, snappy, sulky, sullen, tart, testy, tetchy, thin-skinned, touchy, unpleasant, waspish
Antonyms *adj* affable, agreeable, amiable, charming, congenial, delightful, genial, good-humoured, good-natured, pleasant

illiberal *adj* **1** = **intolerant**, bigoted, hidebound, narrow-minded, prejudiced, reactionary, small-minded, uncharitable, ungenerous **2** = **mean**, close-fisted, miserly, niggardly, parsimonious, selfish, sordid, stingy, tight, tight-arsed (*taboo sl.*), tight as a duck's arse (*taboo sl.*), tight-assed (*US taboo sl.*), tightfisted, ungenerous
Antonyms *adj* ≠ **intolerant:** broad-minded, charitable, generous, liberal, open-minded, politically correct *or* PC, right-on (*inf.*), tolerant

illicit *adj* **1** = **illegal**, black-market, bootleg, contraband, criminal, felonious, illegitimate, off limits, prohibited, unauthorized, unlawful, unlicensed **2** = **forbidden**, clandestine, furtive, guilty, immoral, improper, wrong
Antonyms *adj* ≠ **illegal:** above-board, lawful, legal, legitimate, licit, permissible

illimitable *adj* **1** = **unlimited**, boundless, eternal, immeasurable, immense, infinite, limitless, unbounded, unending, vast, without end

illiteracy *n* **1** = **lack of education**, benightedness, ignorance, illiterateness

illiterate *adj* **1** = **uneducated**, benighted, ignorant, uncultured, unlettered, untaught, untutored
Antonyms *adj* cultured, educated, lettered, literate, taught, tutored

ill-judged *adj* = **misguided**, foolish, ill-advised, ill-considered, injudicious, overhasty, rash, short-sighted, unwise, wrong-headed

ill-mannered *adj* = **rude**, badly behaved, boorish, churlish, coarse, discourteous, ill-behaved, ill-bred, impolite, insolent, loutish, uncivil, uncouth, unmannerly
Antonyms *adj* civil, courteous, cultivated, mannerly, polished, polite, refined, well mannered

ill-natured *adj* = **unkind**, bad-tempered, catty (*inf.*), churlish, crabbed, cross, cross-grained, disagreeable, disobliging, malevolent, malicious, mean, nasty, perverse, petulant, shrewish, spiteful, sulky, sullen, surly, unfriendly, unpleasant
Antonyms *adj* agreeable, amiable, cheerful, congenial, friendly, good-natured, kind, obliging, pleasant

illness *n* **1, 2** = **sickness**, affliction, ailment, attack, complaint, disability, disease, disorder, ill health, indisposition, infirmity, lurgy (*inf.*), malady, malaise, poor health

illogical *adj* **1** = **irrational**, absurd, fallacious, faulty, inconclusive, inconsistent, incorrect, invalid, meaningless, senseless, sophistical, specious, spurious, unreasonable, unscientific, unsound
Antonyms *adj* coherent, consistent, correct, logical, rational, reasonable, scientific, sound, valid

ill-starred *adj* = **doomed**, hapless, ill-fated, ill-omened, inauspicious, star-crossed, unfortunate, unhappy, unlucky

ill temper *n* = **irascibility**, annoyance, bad temper, crossness, curtness, impatience, irritability, petulance, sharpness, spitefulness, tetchiness

ill-tempered *adj* = **irascible**, annoyed, bad-tempered, choleric, cross, curt, grumpy, ill-humoured, impatient, irritable, liverish, ratty (*Brit. & NZ inf.*), sharp, spiteful, testy, tetchy, touchy
Antonyms *adj* benign, cheerful, good-natured, mild-mannered, patient, pleasant, sweet-tempered

ill-timed *adj* = **inopportune**, awkward, inappropriate, inconvenient, inept, unseasonable, untimely, unwelcome
Antonyms *adj* appropriate, convenient, opportune, seasonable, timely, well-timed

ill-treat *vb* = **abuse**, damage, dump on (*sl., chiefly US*), handle roughly, harass, harm, harry, ill-use, injure, knock about *or* around, maltreat, mishandle, misuse, oppress, shit on (*taboo sl.*), wrong

ill-treatment *n* = **abuse**, damage, harm, ill-use, injury, mistreatment, misuse, rough handling

illuminate *vb* **1** = **light up**, brighten, illumine (*literary*), irradiate, light **2** = **clarify**, clear up, elucidate, enlighten, explain, explicate, give insight into, instruct, interpret, make clear, shed light on **3** = **decorate**, adorn, illustrate, ornament
Antonyms *vb* ≠ **light up:** black out, darken, dim, obscure, overshadow ≠ **clarify:** befog, cloud, dull, obfuscate, overcast, shade, veil

illuminating *adj* **2** = **informative**, enlightening, explanatory, helpful, instructive, revealing
Antonyms *adj* confusing, obscuring, puzzling, unhelpful

illumination *n* **1, 2** = **light**, beam, brightening, brightness, lighting, lighting up, lights, radiance, ray **3** *plural* = **lights**, decorations, fairy lights **4** = **enlightenment**, awareness, clarification, edification, insight, inspiration, instruction, perception, revelation, understanding

illusion *n* **1** = **fantasy**, chimera, daydream, figment of the imagination, hallucination, ignis fatuus, mirage, mockery, phantasm, semblance, will-o'-the-wisp **2** = **misconception**, deception, delusion, error, fallacy, false impression, fancy, misapprehension
Antonyms *n* actuality, fact, reality, truth

illusory *adj* = **unreal**, apparent, Barmecide, beguiling, chimerical, deceitful, deceptive, delusive, fallacious, false, hallucinatory, misleading, mistaken, seeming, sham, untrue
Antonyms *adj* authentic, down-to-earth, factual, genuine, real, reliable, solid, true

illustrate *vb* **1** = **demonstrate**, bring home, clarify, elucidate, emphasize, exemplify, exhibit, explain, explicate, instance, interpret, make clear, make plain, point up, show **3** = **draw**, adorn, decorate, depict, ornament, picture, sketch

illustrated *adj* **3** = **pictorial**, decorated, em-

illustration ➊ (ˌɪləˈstreɪʃən) *n* **1** pictorial matter used to explain or decorate a text. **2** an example: *an illustration of his ability.* **3** the act of illustrating or the state of being illustrated.
▸ˌ**illusˈtrational** *adj*

illustrious ➊ (ɪˈlʌstrɪəs) *adj* **1** of great renown; famous and distinguished. **2** glorious or great: *illustrious deeds.* [C16: from L *illustris* bright, famous, from *illustrāre* to make light; see ILLUSTRATE]
▸**ilˈlustriously** *adv* ▸**ilˈlustriousness** *n*

ill will ➊ *n* hostile feeling; enmity; antagonism.

ILO *abbrev. for* International Labour Organisation.

IM *or* **i.m.** *abbrev. for* intramuscular(ly).

I'm (aɪm) *contraction of* I am.

im- *prefix* a variant of **in-**[1] and **in-**[2] before *b, m,* and *p.*

image ➊ (ˈɪmɪdʒ) *n* **1** a representation or likeness of a person or thing, esp. in sculpture. **2** an optically formed reproduction of an object, such as one formed by a lens or mirror. **3** a person or thing that resembles another closely; double or copy. **4** a mental picture; idea produced by the imagination. **5** the personality presented to the public by a person, organization, etc.: *a politician's image.* **6** the pattern of light that is focused onto the retina. **7** *Psychol.* the mental experience of something that is not immediately present to the senses, often involving memory. See also **imagery. 8** a personification of a specified quality; epitome: *the image of good breeding.* **9** a mental picture or association of ideas evoked in a literary work. **10** a figure of speech such as a simile or metaphor. ◆ *vb* **images, imaging, imaged.** (*tr*) **11** to picture in the mind; imagine. **12** to make or reflect an image of. **13** to project or display on a screen, etc. **14** to portray or describe. **15** to be an example or epitome of; typify. [C13: from OF *imagene,* from L *imāgō* copy, representation; rel. to L *imitārī* to IMITATE]
▸ˈ**imageable** *adj* ▸ˈ**imageless** *adj*

image converter *or* **tube** *n* an electronic device that converts an invisible image, esp. one formed by X-rays, into an image that is visible on a fluorescent screen.

image enhancement *n* a method of improving the definition of a video picture by a computer program which reduces the lowest grey values to black and the highest to white: used for pictures from microscopes, surveillance cameras, and scanners.

image intensifier *or* **tube** *n* any of various devices for amplifying the intensity of an optical image, sometimes used in conjunction with an image converter.

image orthicon *n* a television camera tube in which electrons, emitted from a surface in proportion to the intensity of the incident light, are focused onto the target causing secondary emission of electrons.

imagery (ˈɪmɪdʒrɪ, -dʒərɪ) *n, pl* **imageries. 1** figurative or descriptive language in a literary work. **2** images collectively. **3** *Psychol.* **3a** the materials or general processes of the imagination. **3b** the characteristic kind of mental images formed by a particular individual. See also **image** (sense 7), **imagination** (sense 1).

image tube *n* another name for **image converter** or **image intensifier.**

imaginary ➊ (ɪˈmædʒɪnərɪ, -dʒɪnrɪ) *adj* **1** existing in the imagination; unreal; illusory. **2** *Maths.* involving or containing imaginary numbers.
▸**imˈaginarily** *adv*

imaginary number *n* any complex number of the form $a + ib$, where b is not zero and $i = \sqrt{-1}$.

imagination ➊ (ɪˌmædʒɪˈneɪʃən) *n* **1** the faculty or action of producing ideas, esp. mental images of what is not present or has not been experienced. **2** mental creative ability. **3** the ability to deal resourcefully with unexpected or unusual problems, circumstances, etc.

imaginative ➊ (ɪˈmædʒɪnətɪv) *adj* **1** produced by or indicative of a creative imagination. **2** having a vivid imagination.
▸**imˈaginatively** *adv* ▸**imˈaginativeness** *n*

imagine ➊ (ɪˈmædʒɪn) *vb* **imagines, imagining, imagined. 1** (when *tr, may take a clause as object*) to form a mental image of. **2** (when *tr, may take a clause as object*) to think, believe, or guess. **3** (*tr; takes a clause as object*) to suppose; assume: *I imagine he'll come.* **4** (*tr; takes a clause as object*) to believe without foundation: *he imagines he knows the whole story.* [C14: from L *imāginārī* to fancy, picture mentally, from *imāgō* likeness; see IMAGE]
▸**imˈaginable** *adj* ▸**imˈaginably** *adv* ▸**imˈaginer** *n*

imagism (ˈɪmɪˌdʒɪzəm) *n* an early 20th-century poetic movement, advocating the use of ordinary speech and the precise presentation of images.
▸ˈ**imagist** *n, adj* ▸ˌ**imagˈistic** *adj*

imago (ɪˈmeɪgəʊ) *n, pl* **imagoes** *or* **imagines** (ɪˈmædʒəˌniːz). **1** an adult sexually mature insect. **2** *Psychoanal.* an idealized image of another person, usually a parent, carried in the unconscious. [C18: NL, from L: likeness]

imam (ɪˈmɑːm) *or* **imaum** (ɪˈmɑːm, ɪˈmɔːm) *n Islam.* **1** a leader of congregational prayer in a mosque. **2** a caliph, as leader of a Muslim community. **3** any of a succession of Muslim religious leaders regarded by their followers as divinely inspired. [C17: from Ar.: leader]

imamate (ɪˈmɑːmeɪt) *n Islam.* **1** the region or territory governed by an imam. **2** the office, rank, or period of office of an imam.

imbalance ➊ (ɪmˈbæləns) *n* a lack of balance, as in emphasis, proportion, etc.: *the political imbalance of the programme.*

imbecile ➊ (ˈɪmbɪˌsiːl, -ˌsaɪl) *n* **1** *Psychol.* a person of very low intelligence (IQ of 25 to 50). **2** *Inf.* an extremely stupid person; dolt. ◆ *adj also* **imbecilic** (ˌɪmbɪˈsɪlɪk). **3** of or like an imbecile; mentally deficient; feeble-minded. **4** stupid or senseless: *an imbecile thing to do.* [C16: from L *imbēcillus* feeble (physically or mentally)]
▸ˈ**imbeˌcilely** *or* ˌ**imbeˈcilically** *adv* ▸ˌ**imbeˈcility** *n*

imbed (ɪmˈbɛd) *vb* **imbeds, imbedding, imbedded.** a less common spelling of **embed.**

imbibe ➊ (ɪmˈbaɪb) *vb* **imbibes, imbibing, imbibed. 1** to drink (esp. alcoholic drinks). **2** *Literary.* to take in or assimilate (ideas, etc.): *to imbibe the spirit of the Renaissance.* **3** (*tr*) to take in as if by drinking: *to imbibe fresh air.* **4** to absorb or cause to absorb liquid or moisture; assimilate or saturate. [C14: from L *imbibere,* from *bibere* to drink]
▸**imˈbiber** *n*

imbricate *adj* (ˈɪmbrɪkɪt, -ˌkeɪt), *also* **imbricated. 1** *Archit.* relating to or having tiles, shingles, or slates that overlap. **2** (of leaves, scales, etc.) overlapping each other. ◆ *vb* (ˈɪmbrɪˌkeɪt), **imbricates, imbricating, imbricated. 3** (*tr*) to decorate with a repeating pattern resembling scales or overlapping tiles. [C17: from L *imbricāre* to cover with overlapping tiles, from *imbrex* pantile]
▸ˈ**imbricately** *adv* ▸ˌ**imbriˈcation** *n*

imbroglio ➊ (ɪmˈbrəʊlɪˌəʊ) *n, pl* **imbroglios. 1** a confused or perplexing political or interpersonal situation. **2** *Obs.* a confused heap; jumble. [C18: from It., from *imbrogliare* to confuse, EMBROIL]

imbrue (ɪmˈbruː) *vb* **imbrues, imbruing, imbrued.** (*tr*) *Rare.* **1** to stain, esp.

THESAURUS

bellished, graphic, illuminated, picture, pictured, with illustrations

illustration *n* **1 = picture**, adornment, decoration, figure, plate, sketch **2 = example**, analogy, case, case in point, clarification, demonstration, elucidation, exemplification, explanation, instance, interpretation, specimen

illustrative *adj* **1 = explanatory**, descriptive, explicatory, expository, illustrational, interpretive, representative, sample, typical **3 = pictorial**, delineative, diagrammatic, graphic

illustrious *adj* **1 = famous**, brilliant, celebrated, distinguished, eminent, exalted, famed, glorious, great, noble, notable, noted, prominent, remarkable, renowned, resplendent, signal, splendid
Antonyms *adj* humble, ignoble, infamous, lowly, meek, notorious, obscure, unassuming

ill will *n* **= hostility**, acrimony, animosity, animus, antagonism, antipathy, aversion, bad blood, dislike, enmity, envy, grudge, hard feelings, hatred, malevolence, malice, no love lost, rancour, resentment, spite, unfriendliness, venom
Antonyms *n* amiability, amity, charity, congeniality, cordiality, friendship, goodwill

image *n* **1 = representation**, appearance, effigy, figure, icon, idol, likeness, picture, portrait, reflection, statue **3 = replica**, chip off the old block (*inf.*), counterpart, (dead) ringer (*sl.*), Doppelgänger, double, facsimile, similitude, spit (*inf., chiefly Brit.*), spitting image (*inf.*) **4 = concept**, conception, idea, impression, mental picture, perception **10 = figure**, conceit, trope

imaginable *adj* **2 = possible**, believable, comprehensible, conceivable, credible, likely, plausible, supposable, thinkable, under the sun, within the bounds of possibility
Antonyms *adj* impossible, incomprehensible, inconceivable, incredible, unbelievable, unimaginable, unlikely, unthinkable

imaginary *adj* **1 = fictional**, assumed, chimerical, dreamlike, fancied, fanciful, fictitious, hallucinatory, hypothetical, ideal, illusive, illusory, imagined, invented, legendary, made-up, mythological, nonexistent, phantasmal, shadowy, supposed, unreal, unsubstantial, visionary
Antonyms *adj* actual, factual, genuine, known, proven, real, substantial, tangible, true

imagination *n* **1 = unreality**, chimera, conception, idea, ideality, illusion, image, invention, notion, supposition **2, 3 = creativity**, enterprise, fancy, ingenuity, insight, inspiration, invention, inventiveness, originality, resourcefulness, vision, wit, wittiness

imaginative *adj* **1 = creative**, clever, dreamy, enterprising, fanciful, fantastic, ingenious, inspired, inventive, original, poetical, visionary, vivid, whimsical
Antonyms *adj* literal, mundane, ordinary, uncreative, unimaginative, uninspired, unoriginal, unpoetical, unromantic

imagine *vb* **1 = envisage**, conceive, conceptualize, conjure up, create, devise, dream up (*inf.*), fantasize, form a mental picture of, frame, invent, picture, plan, project, scheme, see in the mind's eye, think of, think up, visualize **2, 3 = believe**, apprehend, assume, conjecture, deduce, deem, fancy, gather, guess (*inf., chiefly US & Canad.*), infer, realize, suppose, surmise, suspect, take for granted, take it, think

imbalance *n* **= unevenness**, bias, disproportion, inequality, lack of proportion, lopsidedness, partiality, top-heaviness, unfairness

imbecile *n* **2 = idiot**, berk (*Brit. sl.*), chump, coot, cretin, dolt, dork (*sl.*), fool, halfwit, jerk (*sl., chiefly US & Canad.*), moron, nerd *or* nurd (*sl.*), numbskull *or* numskull, pillock (*Brit. sl.*), prat (*sl.*), schmuck (*US sl.*), thickhead, twit (*inf., chiefly Brit.*) ◆ *adj* **4 = stupid**, asinine, braindead (*inf.*), dead from the neck up, dumb-ass (*sl.*), fatuous, feeble-minded, foolish, idiotic, imbecilic, inane, ludicrous, moronic, simple, simple-minded, thick, witless

imbecility *n* **2 = stupidity**, asininity, childishness, cretinism, fatuity, foolishness, idiocy, inanity, incompetency
Antonyms *n* comprehension, intelligence, perspicacity, reasonableness, sagacity, sense, soundness, wisdom

imbibe *vb* **1 = drink**, consume, knock back (*inf.*), quaff, sink (*inf.*), suck, swallow, swig (*inf.*) **2 = absorb**, acquire, assimilate, gain, gather, ingest, receive, take in

imbroglio *n* **1 = complication**, complexity, embarrassment, entanglement, involvement, misunderstanding, quandary

DICTIONARY

with blood. **2** to permeate or impregnate. [C15: from OF *embreuver,* from L *imbibere* to IMBIBE]
▸**im'bruement** *n*

imbue ❶ (ɪm'bjuː) *vb* **imbues, imbuing, imbued.** (*tr;* usually foll. by *with*) **1** to instil or inspire (with ideals, principles, etc.). **2** *Rare.* to soak, esp. with dye, etc. [C16: from L *imbuere* to stain, accustom]
▸**im'buement** *n*

IMechE *abbrev. for* Institution of Mechanical Engineers.

IMF *abbrev. for* International Monetary Fund.

imit. *abbrev. for:* **1** imitation. **2** imitative.

imitate ❶ ('ɪmɪˌteɪt) *vb* **imitates, imitating, imitated.** (*tr*) **1** to try to follow the manner, style, etc., of or take as a model: *many writers imitated the language of Shakespeare.* **2** to pretend to be or to impersonate, esp. for humour; mimic. **3** to make a copy or reproduction of; duplicate. [C16: from L *imitārī;* see IMAGE]
▸**imitable** ('ɪmɪtəbᵊl) *adj* ▸ˌ**imita'bility** *n* ▸'**imiˌtator** *n*

imitation ❶ (ˌɪmɪ'teɪʃən) *n* **1** the act or practice of imitating; mimicry. **2** an instance or product of imitating, such as a copy of the manner of a person; impression. **3a** a copy of a genuine article; counterfeit. **3b** (*as modifier*): *imitation jewellery.* **4** *Music.* the repetition of a phrase or figure in one part after its appearance in another, as in a fugue.
▸ˌ**imi'tational** *adj*

imitative ❶ ('ɪmɪtətɪv) *adj* **1** imitating or tending to copy. **2** characterized by imitation. **3** copying or reproducing an original, esp. in an inferior manner: *imitative painting.* **4** another word for **onomatopoeic.**
▸'**imitatively** *adv* ▸'**imitativeness** *n*

immaculate ❶ (ɪ'mækjʊlɪt) *adj* **1** completely clean; extremely tidy: *his clothes were immaculate.* **2** completely flawless, etc.: *an immaculate rendering of the symphony.* **3** morally pure; free from sin or corruption. **4** *Biol.* with no spots or markings. [C15: from L, from IM- (not) + *macula* blemish]
▸**im'maculacy** *or* **im'maculateness** *n* ▸**im'maculately** *adv*

Immaculate Conception *n Christian theol., RC Church.* the doctrine that the Virgin Mary was conceived without any stain of original sin.

immanent ('ɪmənənt) *adj* **1** existing, operating, or remaining within; inherent. **2** (of God) present throughout the universe. [C16: from L *immanēre* to remain in]
▸'**immanence** *or* '**immanency** *n* ▸'**immanently** *adv* ▸'**immanenˌtism** *n*

immaterial ❶ (ˌɪmə'tɪərɪəl) *adj* **1** of no real importance; inconsequential. **2** not formed of matter; incorporeal; spiritual.
▸ˌ**immaˌteri'ality** *n* ▸ˌ**imma'terially** *adv*

immaterialism (ˌɪmə'tɪərɪəˌlɪzəm) *n Philosophy.* the doctrine that the material world exists only in the mind.
▸ˌ**imma'terialist** *n*

immature ❶ (ˌɪmə'tjʊə, -'tʃʊə) *adj* **1** not fully grown or developed. **2** deficient in maturity; lacking wisdom, insight, emotional stability, etc.
▸ˌ**imma'turely** *adv* ▸ˌ**imma'turity** *or* ˌ**imma'tureness** *n*

immeasurable ❶ (ɪ'mɛʒərəbᵊl) *adj* incapable of being measured, esp. by virtue of great size; limitless.
▸**imˌmeasura'bility** *or* **im'measurableness** *n* ▸**im'measurably** *adv*

immediate ❶ (ɪ'miːdɪət) *adj* (*usually prenominal*) **1** taking place or accomplished without delay: *an immediate reaction.* **2** closest or most direct in effect or relationship: *the immediate cause of his downfall.* **3** having no intervening medium; direct in effect: *an immediate influence.* **4** contiguous in space, time, or relationship: *our immediate neighbour.* **5** present; current: *the immediate problem is food.* **6** *Philosophy.* of or relating to a concept that is directly known or intuited. [C16: from Med. L, from L IM- (not) + *mediāre* to be in the middle; see MEDIATE]
▸**im'mediacy** *or* **im'mediateness** *n*

immediately ❶ (ɪ'miːdɪətlɪ) *adv* **1** without delay or intervention; at once; instantly. **2** very closely or directly: *this immediately concerns you.* **3** near or close by: *somewhere immediately in this area.* ◆ *conj* **4** (*subordinating*) *Chiefly Brit.* as; as soon as: *immediately he opened the door, there was a gust of wind.*

immemorial ❶ (ˌɪmɪ'mɔːrɪəl) *adj* originating in the distant past; ancient (postpositive in **time immemorial**). [C17: from Med. L, from L IM- (not) + *memoria* MEMORY]
▸ˌ**imme'morially** *adv*

immense ❶ (ɪ'mɛns) *adj* **1** unusually large; huge; vast. **2** without limits; immeasurable. **3** *Inf.* very good; excellent. [C15: from L *immensus,* lit.: unmeasured, from IM- (not) + *mētīrī* to measure]
▸**im'mensely** *adv* ▸**im'menseness** *n*

immensity ❶ (ɪ'mɛnsɪtɪ) *n, pl* **immensities. 1** the state of being immense; vastness; enormity. **2** enormous expanse, distance, or volume. **3** *Inf.* a huge amount: *an immensity of wealth.*

immerse ❶ (ɪ'mɜːs) *vb* **immerses, immersing, immersed.** (*tr*) **1** (often foll. by *in*) to plunge or dip into liquid. **2** (*often passive;* often foll. by *in*) to involve deeply; engross: *to immerse oneself in a problem.* **3** to baptize by dipping the whole body into water. [C17: from L *immergere,* from IM- (in) + *mergere* to dip]
▸**im'mersible** *adj* ▸**im'mersion** *n*

immerser (ɪ'mɜːsə) *n* an informal term for **immersion heater.**

immersion heater *n* an electrical device, usually thermostatically controlled, for heating the liquid in which it is immersed, esp. as a fixture in a domestic hot-water tank.

immigrant ❶ ('ɪmɪgrənt) *n* **1a** a person who immigrates. **1b** (*as modifier*): *an immigrant community.* **2** *Brit.* a person who has been settled in a country of which he is not a native for less than ten years.

immigrate ('ɪmɪˌgreɪt) *vb* **immigrates, immigrating, immigrated. 1** (*intr*) to come to a place or country of which one is not a native in order to settle there. **2** (*tr*) to introduce or bring in as an immigrant. [C17: from L *immigrāre* to go into]
▸ˌ**immi'gration** *n* ▸'**immiˌgrator** *n* ▸'**immiˌgratory** *adj*

imminent ❶ ('ɪmɪnənt) *adj* **1** liable to happen soon; impending. **2** *Obs.*

THESAURUS

imbue *vb* **1** = **instil,** bathe, impregnate, inculcate, infuse, permeate, pervade, saturate, steep

imitate *vb* **1-3** = **copy,** affect, ape, burlesque, caricature, counterfeit, do (*inf.*), do an impression of, duplicate, echo, emulate, follow, follow in the footsteps of, follow suit, impersonate, mimic, mirror, mock, parody, personate, repeat, send up (*Brit. inf.*), simulate, spoof (*inf.*), take a leaf out of (someone's) book, take off (*inf.*), travesty

imitation *n* **1** = **mimicry,** aping, copy, counterfeit, counterfeiting, duplication, echoing, likeness, resemblance, simulation **2, 3a** = **replica,** carbon copy (*inf.*), fake, forgery, impersonation, impression, mockery, parody, reflection, reproduction, sham, substitution, takeoff (*inf.*), travesty ◆ *modifier* **3b** = **artificial,** dummy, ersatz, man-made, mock, phoney *or* phony (*inf.*), pseudo (*inf.*), repro, reproduction, sham, simulated, synthetic
Antonyms *modifier* ≠ **artificial:** authentic, genuine, original, real, true, valid

imitative *adj* **1-4** = **derivative,** copied, copycat (*inf.*), copying, echoic, mimetic, mimicking, mock, onomatopoeic, parrot-like, plagiarized, pseudo (*inf.*), put-on, second-hand, simulated, unoriginal

imitator *n* **1** = **copier,** carbon copy (*inf.*), copycat (*inf.*), echo, epigone (*rare*), follower, parrot, shadow **2** = **impersonator,** impressionist, mimic

immaculate *adj* **1** = **clean,** impeccable, neat, neat as a new pin, spick-and-span, spotless, spruce, squeaky-clean, trim **3** = **pure,** above reproach, faultless, flawless, guiltless, impeccable, incorrupt, innocent, perfect, sinless, squeaky-clean, stainless, unblemished, uncontaminated, undefiled, unexceptionable, unpolluted, unsullied, untarnished, virtuous
Antonyms *adj* ≠ **clean:** dirty, filthy, unclean ≠ **pure:** contaminated, corrupt, impeachable, impure, polluted, stained, tainted

immaterial *adj* **1** = **irrelevant,** a matter of indifference, extraneous, impertinent, inapposite, inconsequential, inconsiderable, inessential, insignificant, of little account, of no consequence, of no importance, trifling, trivial, unimportant, unnecessary **2** = **spiritual,** airy, disembodied, ethereal, ghostly, incorporeal, metaphysical, unembodied, unsubstantial
Antonyms *adj* ≠ **irrelevant:** crucial, essential, germane, important, material, relevant, significant, substantial ≠ **spiritual:** earthly, physical, real, tangible

immature *adj* **1** = **young,** adolescent, crude, green, imperfect, premature, raw, undeveloped, unfinished, unfledged, unformed, unripe, unseasonable, untimely **2** = **childish,** babyish, callow, inexperienced, infantile, jejune, juvenile, puerile, wet behind the ears (*inf.*)
Antonyms *adj* adult, developed, fully-fledged, mature, mellow, ripe

immaturity *n* **1** = **unripeness,** crudeness, crudity, greenness, imperfection, rawness, unpreparedness **2** = **childishness,** babyishness, callowness, inexperience, juvenility, puerility

immeasurable *adj* = **incalculable,** bottomless, boundless, endless, illimitable, immense, inestimable, inexhaustible, infinite, limitless, measureless, unbounded, unfathomable, unlimited, vast
Antonyms *adj* bounded, calculable, estimable, exhaustible, fathomable, finite, limited, measurable

immediate *adj* **1** = **instant,** instantaneous **4** = **nearest,** adjacent, close, contiguous, direct, near, next, primary, proximate, recent **5** = **current,** actual, existing, extant, on hand, present, pressing, up to date, urgent
Antonyms *adj* ≠ **instant:** delayed, late, later, leisurely, postponed, slow, tardy ≠ **nearest:** distant, far, remote

immediately *adv* **1** = **at once,** before you could say Jack Robinson (*inf.*), directly, forthwith, instantly, now, on the nail, posthaste, promptly, pronto (*inf.*), right away, right now, straight away, this instant, this very minute, *tout de suite,* unhesitatingly, without delay, without hesitation **2** = **closely,** at first hand, directly, nearly

immemorial *adj* = **age-old,** ancient, archaic, fixed, long-standing, of yore, olden (*arch.*), rooted, time-honoured, traditional

immense *adj* **1** = **huge,** colossal, elephantine, enormous, extensive, giant, gigantic, ginormous (*inf.*), great, humongous *or* humungous (*US sl.*), jumbo (*inf.*), large, mammoth, massive, mega (*sl.*), monstrous, monumental, prodigious, stellar (*inf.*), stupendous, titanic, tremendous, vast **2** = **immeasurable,** illimitable, infinite, interminable
Antonyms *adj* ≠ **huge:** infinitesimal, little, microscopic, minuscule, minute, puny, small, tiny

immensity *n* **1-3** = **size,** bulk, enormity, expanse, extent, greatness, hugeness, infinity, magnitude, massiveness, scope, sweep, vastness

immerse *vb* **1** = **plunge,** bathe, dip, douse, duck, dunk, sink, submerge, submerse **2** = **engross,** absorb, busy, engage, involve, occupy, take up

immersed *adj* **2** = **engrossed,** absorbed, bound up, buried, busy, consumed, deep, in a brown study, involved, mesmerized, occupied, rapt, spellbound, taken up, wrapped up

immersion *n* **1, 3** = **dipping,** baptism, bathe, dip, dousing, ducking, dunking, plunging, submerging **2** = **involvement,** absorption, concentration, preoccupation

immigrant *n* **1** = **settler,** incomer, newcomer

imminent *adj* **1** = **near,** at hand, brewing, close, coming, fast-approaching, forthcoming, gathering, impending, in the air, in the offing, in the pipeline, just round the corner, looming,

overhanging. [C16: from L *imminēre* to project over; rel. to *mons* mountain]
▸'**imminence** *n* ▸'**imminently** *adv*

immiscible (ɪ'mɪsɪbᵊl) *adj* (of liquids) incapable of being mixed: *oil and water are immiscible.*
▸**im,misci'bility** *n* ▸**im'miscibly** *adv*

immitigable (ɪ'mɪtɪgəbᵊl) *adj Rare.* unable to be mitigated.
▸**im,mitiga'bility** *n* ▸**im'mitigably** *adv*

immobile ⓣ (ɪ'məʊbaɪl) *adj* **1** not moving; motionless. **2** not able to move or be moved; fixed.
▸**immobility** (,ɪməʊ'bɪlɪtɪ) *n*

immobilize ⓣ *or* **immobilise** (ɪ'məʊbɪ,laɪz) *vb* **immobilizes, immobilizing, immobilized** *or* **immobilises, immobilising, immobilised.** (*tr*) **1** to make immobile: *to immobilize a car.* **2** *Finance.* to convert (circulating capital) into fixed capital.
▸**im,mobili'zation** *or* **im,mobili'sation** *n* ▸**im'mobi,lizer** *or* **im'mobi,liser** *n*

immoderate ⓣ (ɪ'mɒdərɪt, ɪ'mɒdrɪt) *adj* lacking in moderation; excessive: *immoderate demands.*
▸**im'moderately** *adv* ▸**im,moder'ation** *or* **im'moderateness** *n*

immodest ⓣ (ɪ'mɒdɪst) *adj* **1** indecent, esp. with regard to sexual propriety; improper. **2** bold, impudent, or shameless.
▸**im'modestly** *adv* ▸**im'modesty** *n*

immolate ('ɪməʊ,leɪt) *vb* **immolates, immolating, immolated.** (*tr*) **1** to kill or offer as a sacrifice, esp. by fire. **2** *Literary.* to sacrifice (something highly valued). [C16: from L *immolāre* to sprinkle an offering with sacrificial meal, sacrifice; see MILL]
▸**,immo'lation** *n* ▸'**immo,lator** *n*

immoral ⓣ (ɪ'mɒrəl) *adj* **1** transgressing accepted moral rules; corrupt. **2** sexually dissolute; profligate or promiscuous. **3** unscrupulous or unethical: *immoral trading.* **4** tending to corrupt or resulting from corruption: *immoral earnings.*
▸**im'morally** *adv*

immorality ⓣ (,ɪmə'rælɪtɪ) *n, pl* **immoralities. 1** the quality or state of being immoral. **2** immoral behaviour, esp. in sexual matters; licentiousness; promiscuity. **3** an immoral act.

immortal ⓣ (ɪ'mɔːtᵊl) *adj* **1** not subject to death or decay; having perpetual life. **2** having everlasting fame; remembered throughout time. **3** everlasting; perpetual; constant. **4** of or relating to immortal beings or concepts. ◆ *n* **5** an immortal being. **6** (*often pl*) a person who is remembered enduringly, esp. an author.
▸**,immor'tality** *n* ▸**im'mortally** *adv*

immortalize ⓣ *or* **immortalise** (ɪ'mɔːtə,laɪz) *vb* **immortalizes, immortalizing, immortalized** *or* **immortalises, immortalising, immortalised.** (*tr*) **1** to give everlasting fame to, as by treating in a literary work: *Macbeth was immortalized by Shakespeare.* **2** to give immortality to.
▸**im,mortali'zation** *or* **im,mortali'sation** *n* ▸**im'mortal,izer** *or* **im'mortal,iser** *n*

immortelle (,ɪmɔː'tel) *n* any of various composite plants that retain their colour when dried. Also called: **everlasting.** [C19: from F (*fleur*) *immortelle* everlasting (flower)]

immovable ⓣ *or* **immoveable** (ɪ'muːvəbᵊl) *adj* **1** unable to move or be moved; immobile. **2** unable to be diverted from one's intentions; steadfast. **3** unaffected by feeling; impassive. **4** unchanging; unalterable. **5** (of feasts, etc.) on the same date every year. **6** *Law.* **6a** (of property) not liable to be removed; fixed. **6b** of or relating to immovable property.
▸**im,mova'bility, im,movea'bility** *or* **im'movableness, im'moveableness** *n*
▸**im'movably** *or* **im'moveably** *adv*

immune ⓣ (ɪ'mjuːn) *adj* **1** protected against a specific disease by inoculation or as the result of innate or acquired resistance. **2** relating to or conferring immunity: *an immune body* (see **antibody**). **3** (*usually postpositive;* foll. by *to*) unsusceptible (to) or secure (against): *immune to inflation.* **4** exempt from obligation, penalty, etc. ◆ *n* **5** an immune person or animal. [C15: from L *immūnis* exempt from a public service]

immune response *n* the reaction of an organism's body to foreign materials (antigens), including the production of antibodies.

immunity ⓣ (ɪ'mjuːnɪtɪ) *n, pl* **immunities. 1** the ability of an organism to resist disease, either through the activities of specialized blood cells or antibodies produced by them in response to natural exposure or inoculation (**active immunity**) or by the injection of antiserum or the transfer of antibodies from a mother to her baby via the placenta or breast milk (**passive immunity**). See also **acquired immunity, natural immunity. 2** freedom from obligation or duty, esp. exemption from tax, legal liability, etc.

immunize ⓣ *or* **immunise** ('ɪmjʊ,naɪz) *vb* **immunizes, immunizing, immunized** *or* **immunises, immunising, immunised.** (*tr*) to make immune, esp. by inoculation.
▸**,immuni'zation** *or* **,immuni'sation** *n* ▸'**immu,nizer** *or* '**immu,niser** *n*

immuno- *or before a vowel* **immun-** *combining form.* indicating immunity or immune: *immunology.*

immunoassay (,ɪmjʊnəʊ'æseɪ) *n Immunol.* a technique of identifying a substance, esp. a protein, through its action as an antigen.

immunocompromised (,ɪmjʊnəʊ'kɒmprəmaɪzd) *adj* having an impaired immune system and therefore incapable of an effective immune response, usually as a result of disease, such as AIDS, that damages the immune system.

immunodeficiency (,ɪmjʊnəʊdɪ'fɪʃənsɪ) *n* a deficiency in or breakdown of a person's immune system.

immunogenic (,ɪmjʊnəʊ'dʒenɪk) *adj* causing or producing immunity or an immune response.
▸**,immuno'genically** *adv*

immunoglobulin (,ɪmjʊnəʊ'glɒbjʊlɪn) *n* any of five classes of proteins, all of which show antibody activity.

immunology (,ɪmjʊ'nɒlədʒɪ) *n* the branch of biological science concerned with the study of immunity.
▸**immunologic** (,ɪmjʊnə'lɒdʒɪk) *or* **,immuno'logical** *adj* ▸**,immuno'logically** *adv* ▸**,immu'nologist** *n*

immunoreaction (ɪ,mjuːnəʊrɪ'ækʃən) *n* the reaction between an antigen and its antibody.

immunosuppression (,ɪmjʊnəʊsə'preʃən) *n* medical suppression of the body's immune system, esp. in order to reduce the likelihood of rejection of a transplanted organ.
▸**,immunosup'pressant** *n, adj*

immunosuppressive (,ɪmjʊnəʊsə'presɪv) *n* **1** any drug that lessens the body's rejection, esp. of a transplanted organ. ◆ *adj* **2** of or relating to such a drug.

THESAURUS

menacing, nigh (*arch.*), on the cards, on the horizon, on the way, threatening, upcoming
Antonyms *adj* delayed, distant, far-off, remote

immobile *adj* **1, 2** = **stationary**, at a standstill, at rest, fixed, frozen, immobilized, immotile, immovable, like a statue, motionless, rigid, riveted, rooted, stable, static, stiff, still, stock-still, stolid, unmoving
Antonyms *adj* active, mobile, movable, on the move, pliant, portable, vigorous

immobility *n* **1, 2** = **stillness**, absence of movement, firmness, fixity, immovability, inertness, motionlessness, stability, steadiness

immobilize *vb* **1** = **paralyse**, bring to a standstill, cripple, disable, freeze, halt, lay up (*inf.*), put out of action, render inoperative, stop, transfix

immoderate *adj* = **excessive**, egregious, enormous, exaggerated, exorbitant, extravagant, extreme, inordinate, intemperate, over the odds (*inf.*), over the top (*sl.*), profligate, steep (*inf.*), uncalled-for, unconscionable, uncontrolled, undue, unjustified, unreasonable, unrestrained, unwarranted, wanton
Antonyms *adj* controlled, judicious, mild, moderate, reasonable, restrained, temperate

immoderation *n* = **excess**, exorbitance, extravagance, intemperance, lack of restraint *or* balance, overindulgence, prodigality, unrestraint

immodest *adj* **1** = **indecent**, bawdy, coarse, depraved, flirtatious, gross, immoral, improper, impure, indecorous, indelicate, lewd, obscene, revealing, titillating, unchaste **2** = **shameless**, bold, bold as brass, brass-necked (*Brit. inf.*), brazen, forward, fresh (*inf.*), impudent, pushy (*inf.*), unblushing

immodesty *n* **1** = **lewdness**, bawdiness, coarseness, impurity, indecorousness, indelicacy, obscenity **2** = **shamelessness**, audacity, boldness, brass neck (*Brit. inf.*), forwardness, gall, impudence, temerity
Antonyms *n* ≠ **lewdness:** decency, decorousness, delicacy, modesty, restraint, sobriety

immoral *adj* **1** = **wicked**, abandoned, bad, corrupt, debauched, degenerate, depraved, dishonest, dissolute, evil, impure, indecent, iniquitous, lewd, licentious, nefarious, obscene, profligate, reprobate, sinful, sink, unchaste, unethical, unprincipled, vicious, vile, wrong
Antonyms *adj* conscientious, good, honourable, inoffensive, law-abiding, moral, pure, upright, virtuous

immorality *n* **1, 2** = **wickedness**, badness, corruption, debauchery, depravity, dissoluteness, evil, iniquity, licentiousness, profligacy, sin, turpitude, vice, wrong
Antonyms *n* goodness, honesty, lawfulness, morality, purity

immorally *adv* **1** = **wickedly**, corruptly, degenerately, dishonestly, dissolutely, evilly, sinfully, unethically, unrighteously

immortal *adj* **1, 3** = **eternal**, abiding, constant, death-defying, deathless, endless, enduring, everlasting, imperishable, incorruptible, indestructible, lasting, perennial, perpetual, sempiternal (*literary*), timeless, undying, unfading ◆ *n* **5** = **god**, goddess, Olympian **6** = **great**, genius, hero, paragon
Antonyms *adj* ≠ **eternal:** ephemeral, fading, fleeting, mortal, passing, perishable, temporary, transitory

immortality *n* **1** = **eternity**, deathlessness, endlessness, everlasting life, incorruptibility, indestructibility, perpetuity, timelessness **2** = **fame**, celebrity, glorification, gloriousness, glory, greatness, renown

immortalize *vb* **1** = **commemorate**, apotheosize, celebrate, enshrine, eternalize, eternize, exalt, glorify, memorialize, perpetuate, solemnize

immovable *adj* **1** = **fixed**, fast, firm, immutable, jammed, rooted, secure, set, stable, stationary, stuck, unbudgeable **2** = **inflexible**, adamant, constant, impassive, obdurate, resolute, steadfast, stony-hearted, unchangeable, unimpressionable, unshakable, unshaken, unwavering, unyielding
Antonyms *adj* ≠ **inflexible:** changeable, flexible, impressionable, movable, shakable, wavering, yielding

immune *adj* **1, 3, 4** = **exempt**, clear, free, insusceptible, invulnerable, let off (*inf.*), not affected, not liable, not subject, proof (against), protected, resistant, safe, unaffected
Antonyms *adj* exposed, liable, prone, susceptible, unprotected, vulnerable

immunity *n* **1** = **resistance**, immunization, protection **2** = **exemption**, amnesty, charter, exoneration, franchise, freedom, indemnity, invulnerability, liberty, licence, prerogative, privilege, release, right
Antonyms *n* ≠ **resistance:** exposure, liability, openness, proneness, susceptibility, vulnerability

immunize *vb* = **vaccinate**, inoculate, protect, safeguard

immunotherapy (ˌɪmjʊnəʊˈθɛrəpɪ) *n* the treatment of disease by stimulating or modifying the immune response.
▸**immunotherapeutic** (ˌɪmjʊnəʊˌθɛrəˈpjuːtɪk) *adj*

immure (ɪˈmjʊə) *vb* **immures, immuring, immured.** (*tr*) **1** *Arch. or literary.* to enclose within or as if within walls; imprison. **2** to shut (oneself) away from society. [C16: from Med. L, from L IM- (in) + *mūrus* wall]
▸**imˈmurement** *n*

immutable 🅣 (ɪˈmjuːtəbᵊl) *adj* unchanging through time; unalterable; ageless: *immutable laws.*
▸**imˌmutaˈbility** *or* **imˈmutableness** *n*

imp 🅣 (ɪmp) *n* **1** a small demon or devil; mischievous sprite. **2** a mischievous child. ◆ *vb* **3** (*tr*) *Falconry.* to insert new feathers in order to repair (the wing of a falcon). [OE *impa* bud, graft, hence offspring, child, from *impian* to graft]

imp. *abbrev. for:* **1** imperative. **2** imperfect. **3** imperial. **4** impersonal. **5** import. **6** importer.

impact 🅣 *n* (ˈɪmpækt). **1** the act of one body, etc., striking another; collision. **2** the force with which one thing hits another. **3** the impression made by an idea, social group, etc. ◆ *vb* (ɪmˈpækt). **4** to drive or press (an object) firmly into (another object, thing, etc.) or (of two objects) to be driven or pressed firmly together. **5** to have an impact or strong effect (on). [C18: from L *impactus* pushed against, fastened on, from *impingere* to thrust at, from *pangere* to drive in]
▸**imˈpaction** *n*

impacted (ɪmˈpæktɪd) *adj* **1** (of a tooth) unable to erupt, esp. because of being wedged against another tooth below the gum. **2** (of a fracture) having the jagged broken ends wedged into each other.

impair 🅣 (ɪmˈpɛə) *vb* (*tr*) to reduce or weaken in strength, quality, etc.: *his hearing was impaired by an accident.* [C14: from OF *empeirer* to make worse, from LL, from L *pēior* worse; see PEJORATIVE]
▸**imˈpairable** *adj* ▸**imˈpairer** *n* ▸**imˈpairment** *n*

impala (ɪmˈpɑːlə) *n, pl* **impalas** *or* **impala.** an antelope of southern and eastern Africa, having lyre-shaped horns and able to move with enormous leaps. [from Zulu]

impale 🅣 *or* **empale** (ɪmˈpeɪl) *vb* **impales, impaling, impaled** *or* **empales, empaling, empaled.** (*tr*) **1** (often foll. by *on, upon,* or *with*) to pierce with a sharp instrument: *they impaled his severed head on a spear.* **2** *Heraldry.* to charge (a shield) with two coats of arms placed side by side. [C16: from Med. L, from L IM- (in) + *pālus* PALE[2]]
▸**imˈpalement** *or* **emˈpalement** *n*

impalpable 🅣 (ɪmˈpælpəbᵊl) *adj* **1** imperceptible, esp. to the touch: *impalpable shadows.* **2** difficult to understand; abstruse.
▸**imˌpalpaˈbility** *n* ▸**imˈpalpably** *adv*

impanel (ɪmˈpænᵊl) *vb* **impanels, impanelling, impanelled** *or US* **impanels, impaneling, impaneled.** a variant spelling (esp. US) of **empanel.**
▸**imˈpanelment** *n*

impart 🅣 (ɪmˈpɑːt) *vb* (*tr*) **1** to communicate (information, etc.); relate. **2** to give or bestow (an abstract quality): *to impart wisdom.* [C15: from OF, from L, from IM- (in) + *partīre* to share, from *pars* part]
▸**imˈpartable** *adj* ▸ˌ**imparˈtation** *or* **imˈpartment** *n*

impartial 🅣 (ɪmˈpɑːʃəl) *adj* not prejudiced towards or against any particular side; fair; unbiased.
▸**imˌpartiˈality** *or* **imˈpartialness** *n* ▸**imˈpartially** *adv*

impartible (ɪmˈpɑːtəbᵊl) *adj Law.* (of land, an estate, etc.) incapable of partition; indivisible.
▸**imˌpartiˈbility** *n* ▸**imˈpartibly** *adv*

impassable 🅣 (ɪmˈpɑːsəbᵊl) *adj* (of terrain, roads, etc.) not able to be travelled through or over.
▸**imˌpassaˈbility** *or* **imˈpassableness** *n* ▸**imˈpassably** *adv*

impasse 🅣 (æmˈpɑːs, ˈæmpɑːs) *n* a situation in which progress is blocked; an insurmountable difficulty; stalemate. [C19: from F; see IM-, PASS]

impassible (ɪmˈpæsəbᵊl) *adj Rare.* **1** not susceptible to pain or injury. **2** impassive or unmoved.
▸**imˌpassiˈbility** *or* **imˈpassibleness** *n* ▸**imˈpassibly** *adv*

impassion (ɪmˈpæʃən) *vb* (*tr*) to arouse the passions of; inflame.

impassioned 🅣 (ɪmˈpæʃənd) *adj* filled with passion; fiery; inflamed: *an impassioned appeal.*
▸**imˈpassionedly** *adv* ▸**imˈpassionedness** *n*

impassive 🅣 (ɪmˈpæsɪv) *adj* **1** not revealing or affected by emotion; reserved. **2** calm; serene; imperturbable.
▸**imˈpassively** *adv* ▸**imˈpassiveness** *or* **impassivity** (ˌɪmpæˈsɪvɪtɪ) *n*

impasto (ɪmˈpæstəʊ) *n* **1** paint applied thickly, so that brush marks are evident. **2** the technique of painting in this way. [C18: from It., from *impastare*, from *pasta* PASTE]

impatience 🅣 (ɪmˈpeɪʃəns) *n* **1** lack of patience; intolerance of or irritability with anything that impedes or delays. **2** restless desire for change and excitement.

impatiens (ɪmˈpeɪʃɪˌɛnz) *n, pl* **impatiens.** a plant with explosive pods, such as balsam, touch-me-not, and busy Lizzie. [C18: NL from L: impatient; from the fact that the ripe pods burst open when touched]

impatient 🅣 (ɪmˈpeɪʃənt) *adj* **1** lacking patience; easily irritated at delay, etc. **2** exhibiting lack of patience. **3** (*postpositive;* foll. by *of*) intolerant (of) or indignant (at): *impatient of indecision.* **4** (*postpositive;* often foll. by *for*) restlessly eager (for *or* to do something).
▸**imˈpatiently** *adv*

impeach 🅣 (ɪmˈpiːtʃ) *vb* (*tr*) **1** *Criminal law.* to bring a charge or accusation against. **2** *Brit. criminal law.* to accuse of a crime against the state. **3** *Chiefly US.* to charge (a public official) with an offence committed in office. **4** to challenge or question (a person's honesty, etc.). [C14: from OF, from LL *impedicāre* to entangle, catch, from L IM- (in) + *pedica* a fetter, from *pēs* foot]
▸**imˈpeachable** *adj* ▸**imˈpeachment** *n*

impeccable 🅣 (ɪmˈpɛkəbᵊl) *adj* **1** without flaw or error; faultless: *an impeccable record.* **2** *Rare.* incapable of sinning. [C16: from LL *impeccābilis* sinless, from L IM- (not) + *peccāre* to sin]
▸**imˌpeccaˈbility** *n* ▸**imˈpeccably** *adv*

impecunious 🅣 (ˌɪmpɪˈkjuːnɪəs) *adj* without money; penniless. [C16: from IM- (not) + from L *pecūniōsus* wealthy, from *pecūnia* money]
▸ˌ**impeˈcuniously** *adv* ▸ˌ**impeˈcuniousness** *or* **impecuniosity** (ˌɪmpɪkjuːnɪˈɒsɪtɪ) *n*

THESAURUS

immutability *n* = **permanence**, agelessness, changelessness, constancy, durability, invariability, stability, unalterableness, unchangeableness

immutable *adj* = **unchanging**, abiding, ageless, changeless, constant, enduring, fixed, immovable, inflexible, invariable, permanent, perpetual, sacrosanct, stable, steadfast, unalterable, unchangeable

imp *n* **1** = **demon**, devil, sprite **2** = **rascal**, brat, gamin, minx, pickle (*Brit. inf.*), rogue, scamp, urchin

impact *n* **1** = **collision**, bang, blow, bump, concussion, contact, crash, force, jolt, knock, shock, smash, stroke, thump **3** = **effect**, brunt, burden, consequences, full force, impression, influence, meaning, power, repercussions, significance, thrust, weight ◆ *vb* **4** = **hit**, clash, collide, crash, crush, strike

impair *vb* = **worsen**, blunt, damage, debilitate, decrease, deteriorate, diminish, enervate, enfeeble, harm, hinder, injure, lessen, mar, reduce, spoil, undermine, vitiate, weaken
Antonyms *vb* ameliorate, amend, better, enhance, facilitate, improve, strengthen

impaired *adj* = **damaged**, defective, faulty, flawed, imperfect, unsound

impale *vb* **1** = **pierce**, lance, run through, skewer, spear, spike, spit, stick, transfix

impalpable *adj* **1** = **intangible**, airy, delicate, disembodied, fine, imperceptible, incorporeal, indistinct, insubstantial, shadowy, tenuous, thin, unsubstantial

impart *vb* **1** = **communicate**, convey, disclose, discover, divulge, make known, pass on, relate, reveal, tell **2** = **give**, accord, afford, bestow, confer, contribute, grant, lend, offer, yield

impartial *adj* = **neutral**, detached, disinterested, equal, equitable, even-handed, fair, just, nondiscriminating, nonpartisan, objective, open-minded, unbiased, unprejudiced, without fear or favour
Antonyms *adj* biased, bigoted, influenced, partial, prejudiced, swayed, unfair, unjust

impartiality *n* = **neutrality**, detachment, disinterest, disinterestedness, dispassion, equality, equity, even-handedness, fairness, lack of bias, nonpartisanship, objectivity, open-mindedness
Antonyms *n* bias, favouritism, partiality, partisanship, subjectivity, unfairness

impassable *adj* = **blocked**, closed, impenetrable, obstructed, pathless, trackless, unnavigable

impasse *n* = **deadlock**, blind alley, dead end, stalemate, standoff, standstill

impassioned *adj* = **intense**, ablaze, animated, ardent, blazing, excited, fervent, fervid, fiery, flaming, furious, glowing, heated, inflamed, inspired, passionate, rousing, stirring, vehement, violent, vivid, warm, worked up
Antonyms *adj* apathetic, cool, impassive, indifferent, objective, reasoned

impassive *adj* **1, 2** = **unemotional**, aloof, apathetic, callous, calm, composed, cool, dispassionate, emotionless, impassible (*rare*), imperturbable, indifferent, inscrutable, insensible, insusceptible, phlegmatic, poker-faced (*inf.*), reserved, self-contained, serene, stoical, stolid, unconcerned, unexcitable, unfazed (*inf.*), unfeeling, unimpressible, unmoved, unruffled

impassiveness *n* **1, 2** = **inscrutability**, aloofness, calmness, composure, dispassion, imperturbability, indifference, insensibility, nonchalance, phlegm, stoicism, stolidity

impatience *n* **1** = **irritability**, intolerance, irritableness, quick temper, shortness, snappiness **2** = **restlessness**, agitation, anxiety, avidity, disquietude, eagerness, edginess, fretfulness, nervousness, restiveness, uneasiness
Antonyms *n* ≠ **irritability:** control, forbearance, patience, restraint, tolerance ≠ **restlessness:** calm, composure, serenity

impatient *adj* **1** = **irritable**, demanding, hot-tempered, intolerant, quick-tempered, snappy, testy **2** = **hasty**, abrupt, brusque, curt, headlong, impetuous, indignant, sudden, vehement, violent **4** = **restless**, agog, athirst, chafing, eager, edgy, fretful, like a cat on hot bricks (*inf.*), straining at the leash
Antonyms *adj* ≠ **irritable:** easy-going, tolerant ≠ **restless:** calm, composed, cool, imperturbable, patient, quiet, serene

impeach *vb* **1** = **charge**, accuse, arraign, blame, censure, criminate (*rare*), denounce, indict, tax **4** = **challenge**, call into question, cast aspersions on, cast doubt on, disparage, impugn, question

impeachment *n* **1** = **accusation**, arraignment, indictment

impeccable *adj* **1** = **faultless**, above suspicion, blameless, exact, exquisite, flawless, immaculate, incorrupt, innocent, irreproachable, perfect, precise, pure, sinless, squeaky-clean, stainless, unblemished, unerring, unimpeachable
Antonyms *adj* blameworthy, corrupt, defective, deficient, faulty, flawed, shallow, sinful

impecunious *adj* = **poor**, broke (*inf.*), cleaned out (*sl.*), destitute, dirt-poor (*inf.*), down and out, flat broke (*inf.*), indigent, in queer street, insolvent, penniless, poverty-stricken, short, skint (*Brit. sl.*), stony (*Brit. sl.*), strapped (*sl.*), without two pennies to rub together (*inf.*)

impedance (ɪm'piːdᵊns) *n* **1** a measure of the opposition to the flow of an alternating current equal to the square root of the sum of the squares of the resistance and the reactance, expressed in ohms. **2** the ratio of the sound pressure in a medium to the rate of alternating flow through a specified surface due to the sound wave. **3** the ratio of the mechanical force to the velocity of the resulting vibration.

impede ⓘ (ɪm'piːd) *vb* **impedes, impeding, impeded.** *(tr)* to restrict or retard in action, progress, etc.; obstruct. [C17: from L *impedīre* to hinder, lit.: shackle the feet, from *pēs* foot]
▸**im'peder** *n* ▸**im'pedingly** *adv*

impediment ⓘ (ɪm'pɛdɪmənt) *n* **1** a hindrance or obstruction. **2** a physical defect, esp. one of speech, such as a stammer. **3** (*pl* **impediments** *or* **impedimenta** (-'mɛntə)) *Law.* an obstruction to the making of a contract, esp. one of marriage.
▸**imˌpedi'mental** *or* **imˌpedi'mentary** *adj*

impedimenta ⓘ (ɪmˌpɛdɪ'mɛntə) *pl n* **1** any objects that impede progress, esp. the baggage and equipment carried by an army. **2** a plural of **impediment** (sense 3). [C16: from L, pl of *impedīmentum* hindrance; see IMPEDE]

impel ⓘ (ɪm'pɛl) *vb* **impels, impelling, impelled.** *(tr)* **1** to urge or force (a person) to an action; constrain or motivate. **2** to push, drive, or force into motion. [C15: from L *impellere* to push against, drive forward]
▸**im'pellent** *n, adj*

impeller (ɪm'pɛlə) *n* the vaned rotating disc of a centrifugal pump, compressor, etc.

impend ⓘ (ɪm'pɛnd) *vb (intr)* **1** (esp. of something threatening) to be imminent. **2** (foll. by *over*) *Rare.* to be suspended; hang. [C16: from L *impendēre* to overhang, from *pendēre* to hang]
▸**im'pendence** *or* **im'pendency** *n* ▸**im'pending** *adj*

impenetrable ⓘ (ɪm'pɛnɪtrəbᵊl) *adj* **1** incapable of being pierced through or penetrated: *an impenetrable forest.* **2** incapable of being understood; incomprehensible. **3** incapable of being seen through: *impenetrable gloom.* **4** not susceptible to ideas, influence, etc.: *impenetrable ignorance.* **5** *Physics.* (of a body) incapable of occupying the same space as another body.
▸**imˌpenetra'bility** *n* ▸**im'penetrableness** *n* ▸**im'penetrably** *adv*

impenitent ⓘ (ɪm'pɛnɪtənt) *adj* not sorry or penitent; unrepentant.
▸**im'penitence, im'penitency,** *or* **im'penitentness** *n* ▸**im'penitently** *adv*

imper. *abbrev. for* imperative.

imperative ⓘ (ɪm'pɛrətɪv) *adj* **1** extremely urgent or important; essential. **2** peremptory or authoritative: *an imperative tone of voice.* **3** Also: **imperatival** (ɪmˌpɛrə'taɪvᵊl). *Grammar.* denoting a mood of verbs used in giving orders, making requests, etc. ◆ *n* **4** something that is urgent or essential. **5** an order or command. **6** *Grammar.* **6a** the imperative mood. **6b** a verb in this mood. [C16: from LL, from L *imperāre* to command]
▸**im'peratively** *adv* ▸**im'perativeness** *n*

imperator (ˌɪmpə'rɑːtɔː) *n* (in ancient Rome) a title bestowed upon generals and, later, emperors. [C16: from L: commander, from *imperāre* to command]
▸**imperatorial** (ɪmˌpɛrə'tɔːrɪəl) *adj* ▸**ˌimpe'ratorˌship** *n*

imperceptible ⓘ (ˌɪmpə'sɛptɪbᵊl) *adj* too slight, subtle, gradual, etc., to be perceived.
▸**ˌimperˌcepti'bility** *or* **ˌimper'ceptibleness** *n* ▸**ˌimper'ceptibly** *adv*

imperceptive ⓘ (ˌɪmpə'sɛptɪv) *adj, also* **impercipient** (ˌɪmpə'sɪpɪənt). lacking in perception; obtuse.
▸**ˌimper'ception** *n* ▸**ˌimper'ceptively** *adv* ▸**ˌimper'ceptiveness** *or* **ˌimper'cipience** *n*

imperf. *abbrev. for:* **1** Also: **impf.** imperfect. **2** (of stamps) imperforate.

imperfect ⓘ (ɪm'pɜːfɪkt) *adj* **1** exhibiting or characterized by faults, mistakes, etc.; defective. **2** not complete or finished; deficient. **3** *Grammar.* denoting a tense of verbs used most commonly in describing continuous or repeated past actions or events. **4** *Law.* legally unenforceable. **5** *Music.* **5a** proceeding to the dominant from the tonic, subdominant, or any chord other than the dominant. **5b** of or relating to all intervals other than the fourth, fifth, and octave. Cf. **perfect** (sense 9). ◆ *n* **6** *Grammar.* **6a** the imperfect tense. **6b** a verb in this tense.
▸**im'perfectly** *adv* ▸**im'perfectness** *n*

imperfection ⓘ (ˌɪmpə'fɛkʃən) *n* **1** the condition or quality of being imperfect. **2** a fault or defect.

imperfective (ˌɪmpə'fɛktɪv) *Grammar.* ◆ *adj* **1** denoting an aspect of the verb to indicate that the action is in progress without regard to its completion. Cf. **perfective.** ◆ *n* **2a** the imperfective aspect of a verb. **2b** a verb in this aspect.
▸**ˌimper'fectively** *adv*

imperforate (ɪm'pɜːfərɪt, -ˌreɪt) *adj* **1** not perforated. **2** (of a postage stamp) not provided with perforation or any other means of separation. **3** *Anat.* without the normal opening.
▸**imˌperfo'ration** *n*

imperial ⓘ (ɪm'pɪərɪəl) *adj* **1** of or relating to an empire, emperor, or empress. **2** characteristic of an emperor; majestic; commanding. **3** exercising supreme authority; imperious. **4** (esp. of products) of a superior size or quality. **5** (*usually prenominal*) (of weights, measures, etc.) conforming to standards legally established in Great Britain. ◆ *n* **6** a book size, esp. 7½ by 11 inches or 11 by 15 inches. **7** a size of writing paper, 23 by 31 inches (US and Canad.) or 22 by 30 inches (Brit.). **8** *US.* **8a** the top of a carriage. **8b** a luggage case carried there. **9** a small tufted beard popularized by the French emperor Napoleon III. **10** a wine bottle holding the equivalent of eight normal bottles. [C14: from LL, from L *imperium* command, authority, empire]
▸**im'perially** *adv* ▸**im'perialness** *n*

imperialism (ɪm'pɪərɪəˌlɪzəm) *n* **1** the policy or practice of extending a state's rule over other territories. **2** the extension or attempted extension of authority, influence, power, etc., by any person, country, institution, etc.: *cultural imperialism.* **3** a system of imperial government or rule by an emperor. **4** the spirit, character, authority, etc., of an empire.
▸**im'perialist** *adj, n* ▸**imˌperial'istic** *adj* ▸**imˌperial'istically** *adv*

imperil ⓘ (ɪm'pɛrɪl) *vb* **imperils, imperilling, imperilled** *or US* **imperils, imperiling, imperiled.** *(tr)* to place in danger or jeopardy; endanger.
▸**im'perilment** *n*

imperious ⓘ (ɪm'pɪərɪəs) *adj* **1** domineering; overbearing. **2** *Rare.* urgent. [C16: from L, from *imperium* command, power]
▸**im'periously** *adv* ▸**im'periousness** *n*

imperishable ⓘ (ɪm'pɛrɪʃəbᵊl) *adj* **1** not subject to decay or deterioration. **2** not likely to be forgotten: *imperishable truths.*
▸**imˌperisha'bility** *or* **im'perishableness** *n* ▸**im'perishably** *adv*

THESAURUS

Antonyms *adj* affluent, prosperous, rich, wealthy, well-off, well-to-do

impede *vb* = **hinder**, bar, block, brake, check, clog, cumber, curb, delay, disrupt, encumber, hamper, hold up, obstruct, restrain, retard, slow (down), stop, throw a spanner in the works (*Brit. inf.*), thwart
Antonyms *vb* advance, aid, assist, further, help, promote

impediment *n* **1** = **obstacle**, bar, barrier, block, check, clog, curb, defect, difficulty, encumbrance, fly in the ointment, hazard, hindrance, millstone around one's neck, obstruction, snag, stumbling block
Antonyms *n* advantage, aid, assistance, benefit, encouragement, relief, support

impedimenta *pl n* **1** = **baggage**, accoutrements, belongings, effects, equipment, gear, junk (*inf.*), luggage, movables, odds and ends, paraphernalia, possessions, stuff, things, trappings, traps

impel *vb* **1** = **force**, actuate, chivy, compel, constrain, drive, goad, incite, induce, influence, inspire, instigate, motivate, move, oblige, power, prod, prompt, propel, push, require, spur, stimulate, urge
Antonyms *vb* check, discourage, dissuade, rebuff, repulse, restrain

impending *adj* **1** = **looming**, approaching, brewing, coming, forthcoming, gathering, hovering, imminent, in the offing, in the pipeline, menacing, near, nearing, on the horizon, threatening, upcoming

impenetrable *adj* **1** = **impassable**, dense, hermetic, impermeable, impervious, inviolable, solid, thick, unpierceable **2** = **incomprehensible**, arcane, baffling, cabbalistic, dark, enigmatic, enigmatical, hidden, indiscernible, inexplicable, inscrutable, mysterious, obscure, unfathomable, unintelligible
Antonyms *adj* ≠ **impassable:** accessible, enterable, passable, penetrable, pierceable, vulnerable ≠ **incomprehensible:** clear, explicable, obvious, soluble, understandable

impenitence *n* = **hardheartedness**, impenitency, incorrigibility, obduracy, stubbornness

impenitent *adj* = **unrepentant**, defiant, hardened, hardhearted, incorrigible, obdurate, recidivistic, relentless, remorseless, unabashed, unashamed, uncontrite, unreformed

imperative *adj* **1** = **urgent**, compulsory, crucial, essential, exigent, indispensable, insistent, obligatory, pressing, vital **2** = **commanding**, authoritative, autocratic, dictatorial, domineering, high-handed, imperious, lordly, magisterial, peremptory
Antonyms *adj* ≠ **urgent:** avoidable, discretional, nonessential, optional, unimportant, unnecessary

imperceptible *adj* = **undetectable**, faint, fine, gradual, impalpable, inappreciable, inaudible, indiscernible, indistinguishable, infinitesimal, insensible, invisible, microscopic, minute, shadowy, slight, small, subtle, teensy-weensy, teeny-weeny, tiny, unnoticeable
Antonyms *adj* audible, detectable, discernible, distinguishable, noticeable, perceptible, visible

imperceptibly *adv* = **invisibly**, by a hair's-breadth, inappreciably, indiscernibly, little by little, slowly, subtly, unnoticeably, unobtrusively, unseen

imperceptive *adj* = **unobservant**, impercipient, insensitive, obtuse, superficial, unappreciative, unaware, undiscerning, unseeing

imperfect *adj* **1, 2** = **flawed**, broken, damaged, defective, deficient, faulty, immature, impaired, incomplete, inexact, limited, partial, patchy, rudimentary, sketchy, undeveloped, unfinished
Antonyms *adj* complete, developed, exact, finished, flawless, perfect

imperfection *n* **1, 2** = **fault**, blemish, defect, deficiency, failing, fallibility, flaw, foible, frailty, inadequacy, incompleteness, infirmity, insufficiency, peccadillo, scar, shortcoming, stain, taint, weakness, weak point
Antonyms *n* adequacy, completeness, consummation, excellence, faultlessness, flawlessness, perfection, sufficiency

imperial *adj* **1** = **royal**, kingly, majestic, princely, queenly, regal, sovereign **3** = **supreme**, august, exalted, grand, great, high, imperious, lofty, magnificent, noble, superior

imperil *vb* = **endanger**, expose, hazard, jeopardize, risk
Antonyms *vb* care for, guard, protect, safeguard, secure

imperious *adj* **1** = **domineering**, arrogant, authoritative, autocratic, bossy (*inf.*), commanding, despotic, dictatorial, exacting, haughty, high-handed, imperative, lordly, magisterial, overbearing, overweening, tyrannical, tyrannous

imperishable *adj* **1** = **indestructible**, abiding,

impermanent Ⓣ (ɪmˈpɜːmənənt) *adj* not permanent; fleeting.
▸**imˈpermanence** *or* **imˈpermanency** *n* ▸**imˈpermanently** *adv*

impermeable Ⓣ (ɪmˈpɜːmɪəbᵊl) *adj* (of a substance) not allowing the passage of a fluid through interstices; not permeable.
▸**imˌpermeaˈbility** *or* **imˈpermeableness** *n* ▸**imˈpermeably** *adv*

impermissible (ˌɪmpəˈmɪsɪbᵊl) *adj* not permissible; not allowed.
▸**ˌimperˌmissiˈbility** *n*

impersonal Ⓣ (ɪmˈpɜːsənᵊl) *adj* **1** without reference to any individual person; objective: *an impersonal assessment.* **2** devoid of human warmth or sympathy; cold: *an impersonal manner.* **3** not having human characteristics: *an impersonal God.* **4** *Grammar.* (of a verb) having no logical subject: *it is raining.* **5** *Grammar.* (of a pronoun) not denoting a person.
▸**imˌpersonˈality** *n* ▸**imˈpersonally** *adv*

impersonalize *or* **impersonalise** (ɪmˈpɜːsənəˌlaɪz) *vb* **impersonalizes, impersonalizing, impersonalized** *or* **impersonalises, impersonalising, impersonalised.** (*tr*) to make impersonal, esp. to rid of such human characteristics as sympathy, etc.; dehumanize.
▸**imˌpersonaliˈzation** *or* **imˌpersonaliˈsation** *n*

impersonate Ⓣ (ɪmˈpɜːsəˌneɪt) *vb* **impersonates, impersonating, impersonated.** (*tr*) **1** to pretend to be (another person). **2** to imitate the character, mannerisms, etc., of (another person). **3** *Rare.* to play the part or character of. **4** an archaic word for **personify.**
▸**imˌpersonˈation** *n* ▸**imˈpersonˌator** *n*

impertinence Ⓣ (ɪmˈpɜːtɪnəns) *or* **impertinency** *n* **1** disrespectful behaviour or language; rudeness; insolence. **2** an impertinent act, gesture, etc. **3** *Rare.* lack of pertinence; irrelevance; inappropriateness.

impertinent Ⓣ (ɪmˈpɜːtɪnənt) *adj* **1** rude; insolent; impudent. **2** irrelevant or inappropriate. [C14: from L *impertinēns* not belonging, from L IM- (not) + *pertinēre* to be relevant; see PERTAIN]
▸**imˈpertinently** *adv*

imperturbable Ⓣ (ˌɪmpɜːˈtɜːbəbᵊl) *adj* not easily perturbed; calm; unruffled.
▸**ˌimperˌturbaˈbility** *or* **ˌimperˈturbableness** *n* ▸**ˌimperˈturbably** *adv*

impervious Ⓣ (ɪmˈpɜːvɪəs) *or* **imperviable** *adj* **1** not able to be penetrated, as by water, light, etc.; impermeable. **2** (*often postpositive;* foll. by *to*) not able to be influenced (by) or not receptive (to): *impervious to argument.*
▸**imˈperviously** *adv* ▸**imˈperviousness** *n*

impetigo (ˌɪmpɪˈtaɪgəʊ) *n* a contagious pustular skin disease. [C16: from L: scabby eruption, from *impetere* to assail; see IMPETUS; for form, cf. VERTIGO]
▸**impetiginous** (ˌɪmpɪˈtɪdʒɪnəs) *adj*

impetuous Ⓣ (ɪmˈpɛtjʊəs) *adj* **1** liable to act without consideration; rash; impulsive. **2** resulting from or characterized by rashness or haste. **3** *Poetic.* moving with great force or violence; rushing: *the impetuous stream hurtled down the valley.* [C14: from LL *impetuōsus* violent; see IMPETUS]
▸**imˈpetuously** *adv* ▸**imˈpetuousness** *or* **impetuosity** (ɪmˌpɛtjʊˈɒsɪtɪ) *n*

impetus Ⓣ (ˈɪmpɪtəs) *n, pl* **impetuses. 1** an impelling movement or force; incentive or impulse; stimulus. **2** *Physics.* the force that sets a body in motion or that tends to resist changes in a body's motion. [C17: from L: attack, from *impetere* to assail, from IM- (in) + *petere* to make for, seek out]

impf. *or* **imperf.** *abbrev. for* imperfect.

impi (ˈɪmpɪ) *n, pl* **impi** *or* **impies.** a group of Bantu warriors. [C19: from Zulu]

impiety Ⓣ (ɪmˈpaɪɪtɪ) *n, pl* **impieties. 1** lack of reverence or proper respect for a god. **2** any lack of proper respect. **3** an impious act.

impinge Ⓣ (ɪmˈpɪndʒ) *vb* **impinges, impinging, impinged. 1** (*intr;* usually foll. by *on* or *upon*) to encroach or infringe; trespass: *to impinge on someone's time.* **2** (*intr;* usually foll. by *on, against,* or *upon*) to collide (with); strike. [C16: from L *impingere* to drive at, dash against, from *pangere* to fasten, drive in]
▸**imˈpingement** *n* ▸**imˈpinger** *n*

impious Ⓣ (ˈɪmpɪəs) *adj* **1** lacking piety or reverence for a god. **2** lacking respect; undutiful.
▸**ˈimpiously** *adv* ▸**ˈimpiousness** *n*

impish Ⓣ (ˈɪmpɪʃ) *adj* of or like an imp; mischievous.
▸**ˈimpishly** *adv* ▸**ˈimpishness** *n*

implacable Ⓣ (ɪmˈplækəbᵊl) *adj* **1** incapable of being placated or pacified; unappeasable. **2** inflexible; intractable.
▸**imˌplacaˈbility** *n* ▸**imˈplacably** *adv*

implant Ⓣ *vb* (ɪmˈplɑːnt). (*tr*) **1** to inculcate; instil: *to implant sound moral principles.* **2** to plant or embed; infix; entrench. **3** *Surgery.* to graft or insert (a tissue, hormone, etc.) into the body. ◆ *n* (ˈɪmplɑːnt). **4** anything implanted, esp. surgically, such as a tissue graft or hormone.
▸**ˌimplanˈtation** *n*

implausible Ⓣ (ɪmˈplɔːzəbᵊl) *adj* not plausible; provoking disbelief; unlikely.
▸**imˌplausiˈbility** *or* **imˈplausibleness** *n* ▸**imˈplausibly** *adv*

implement Ⓣ *n* (ˈɪmplɪmənt). **1** a piece of equipment; tool or utensil: *gardening implements.* **2** a means to achieve a purpose; agent. ◆ *vb* (ˈɪmplɪˌmɛnt). (*tr*) **3** to carry out; put into action: *to implement a plan.* **4** *Rare.* to supply with tools. [C17: from LL *implēmentum,* lit.: a filling up, from L *implēre* to fill up, satisfy, fulfil]
▸**ˌimpleˈmental** *adj* ▸**ˌimplemenˈtation** *n*

implicate Ⓣ (ˈɪmplɪˌkeɪt) *vb* **implicates, implicating, implicated.** (*tr*) **1** to show to be involved, esp. in a crime. **2** to imply: *his protest implicated censure by the authorities.* **3** *Rare.* to entangle. [C16: from L *implicāre* to involve, from *plicāre* to fold]
▸**implicative** (ɪmˈplɪkətɪv) *adj* ▸**imˈplicatively** *adv*

THESAURUS

enduring, eternal, everlasting, immortal, perennial, permanent, perpetual, undying, unfading, unforgettable
Antonyms *adj* destructible, dying, fading, forgettable, mortal, perishable

impermanent *adj* = **temporary,** brief, elusive, ephemeral, evanescent, fleeting, fly-by-night, flying, fugacious, fugitive, here today, gone tomorrow (*inf.*), inconstant, momentary, mortal, passing, perishable, short-lived, transient, transitory

impermeable *adj* = **impenetrable,** hermetic, impassable, impervious, nonporous, proof, resistant

impersonal *adj* **2** = **detached,** aloof, bureaucratic, businesslike, cold, dispassionate, formal, inhuman, neutral, remote
Antonyms *adj* friendly, intimate, outgoing, personal, warm

impersonate *vb* **1** = **pass oneself off as,** masquerade as, personate, pose as (*inf.*) **2** = **imitate,** act, ape, caricature, do (*inf.*), do an impression of, enact, mimic, parody, take off (*inf.*)

impersonation *n* **2** = **imitation,** caricature, impression, mimicry, parody, takeoff (*inf.*)

impertinence *n* **1** = **rudeness,** assurance, audacity, backchat (*inf.*), boldness, brass neck (*Brit. inf.*), brazenness, cheek (*inf.*), chutzpah (*US & Canad. inf.*), disrespect, effrontery, face (*inf.*), forwardness, front, impudence, incivility, insolence, neck (*inf.*), nerve (*inf.*), pertness, presumption, sauce (*inf.*)

impertinent *adj* **1** = **rude,** bold, brazen, cheeky (*inf.*), discourteous, disrespectful, flip (*inf.*), forward, fresh (*inf.*), impolite, impudent, insolent, interfering, lippy (*US & Canad. sl.*), pert, presumptuous, sassy (*US inf.*), saucy (*inf.*), uncivil, unmannerly **2** = **inappropriate,** inapplicable, incongruous, irrelevant
Antonyms *adj* ≠ **rude:** mannerly, polite, respectful ≠ **inappropriate:** appropriate, germane, important, pertinent, relevant, vital

imperturbable *adj* = **calm,** collected, complacent, composed, cool, equanimous, nerveless, sedate, self-possessed, serene, stoic, stoical, tranquil, undisturbed, unexcitable, unfazed (*inf.*), unflappable (*inf.*), unmoved, unruffled
Antonyms *adj* agitated, excitable, frantic, jittery (*inf.*), nervous, panicky, ruffled, touchy, upset

impervious *adj* **1** = **sealed,** hermetic, impassable, impenetrable, impermeable, imperviable, invulnerable, resistant **2** = **unaffected,** closed, immune, invulnerable, proof against, unmoved, unreceptive, unswayable, untouched

impetuous *adj* **1** = **rash,** ardent, eager, fierce, furious, hasty, headlong, impassioned, impulsive, passionate, precipitate, spontaneous, spur-of-the-moment, unbridled, unplanned, unpremeditated, unreflecting, unrestrained, unthinking, vehement, violent
Antonyms *adj* cautious, leisurely, mild, slow, wary

impetuously *adv* **1** = **rashly,** helter-skelter, impulsively, in the heat of the moment, on the spur of the moment, passionately, recklessly, spontaneously, unthinkingly, vehemently, without thinking

impetuousness *n* **1** = **haste,** hastiness, impulsiveness, precipitancy, precipitateness, rashness, vehemence, violence

impetus *n* **1** = **incentive,** catalyst, goad, impulse, impulsion, motivation, push, spur, stimulus **2** = **force,** energy, momentum, power

impiety *n* **1** = **sacrilege,** godlessness, iniquity, irreligion, irreverence, profaneness, profanity, sinfulness, ungodliness, unholiness, unrighteousness, wickedness
Antonyms *n* devoutness, godliness, holiness, piety, respect, reverence, righteousness

impinge *vb* **1** = **encroach,** infringe, invade, make inroads, obtrude, trespass, violate

impious *adj* **1** = **sacrilegious,** blasphemous, godless, iniquitous, irreligious, irreverent, profane, sinful, ungodly, unholy, unrighteous, wicked
Antonyms *adj* devout, godly, holy, pious, religious, reverent, righteous

impish *adj* = **mischievous,** devilish, elfin, prankish, puckish, rascally, roguish, sportive, waggish

implacability *n* **1, 2** = **pitilessness,** implacableness, inexorability, inflexibility, intractability, mercilessness, relentlessness, ruthlessness, unforgivingness, vengefulness

implacable *adj* **1, 2** = **unyielding,** cruel, inexorable, inflexible, intractable, merciless, pitiless, rancorous, relentless, remorseless, ruthless, unappeasable, unbending, uncompromising, unforgiving, unrelenting
Antonyms *adj* appeasable, flexible, lenient, merciful, relenting, tolerant, yielding

implant *vb* **1** = **instil,** inculcate, infix, infuse, inseminate, sow **2** = **insert,** embed, fix, graft, ingraft, place, plant, root, sow

implausible *adj* = **improbable,** cock-and-bull (*inf.*), dubious, far-fetched, flimsy, incredible, suspect, unbelievable, unconvincing, unlikely, unreasonable, weak

implement *n* **1** = **tool,** apparatus, appliance, device, gadget, instrument, utensil ◆ *vb* **3** = **carry out,** bring about, complete, effect, enforce, execute, fulfil, perform, put into action *or* effect, realize
Antonyms *vb* ≠ **carry out:** delay, hamper, hinder, impede, weaken

implementation *n* **3** = **carrying out,** accomplishment, discharge, effecting, enforcement, execution, fulfilment, performance, performing, realization

implicate *vb* **1** = **incriminate,** associate, compromise, concern, embroil, entangle, include, inculpate, involve, mire, stitch up (*sl.*), tie up with
Antonyms *vb* acquit, disentangle, dissociate, eliminate, exclude, exculpate, rule out

implicated *adj* **1** = **involved,** incriminated, suspected, under suspicion

implication Ⓣ (ˌɪmplɪˈkeɪʃən) *n* **1** the act of implicating. **2** something that is implied. **3** *Logic.* a relation between two propositions, such that the second can be logically deduced from the first.

implicit Ⓣ (ɪmˈplɪsɪt) *adj* **1** not explicit; implied; indirect. **2** absolute and unreserved; unquestioning: *implicit trust.* **3** (when *postpositive,* foll. by *in*) contained or inherent: *to bring out the anger implicit in the argument.* [C16: from L *implicitus,* var. of *implicātus* interwoven; see IMPLICATE]
▸**imˈplicitly** *adv* ▸**imˈplicitness** *n*

implied Ⓣ (ɪmˈplaɪd) *adj* hinted at or suggested; not directly expressed: *an implied criticism.*

implode (ɪmˈpləʊd) *vb* **implodes, imploding, imploded.** to collapse inwards. Cf. **explode.** [C19: from IM- + (EX)PLODE]

implore Ⓣ (ɪmˈplɔː) *vb* **implores, imploring, implored.** (*tr*) to beg or ask (someone) earnestly (to do something); plead with; beseech; supplicate. [C16: from L *implōrāre,* from IM- + *plōrāre* to bewail]
▸ˌ**imploˈration** *n* ▸**imˈploratory** *adj* ▸**imˈploringly** *adv*

imply Ⓣ (ɪmˈplaɪ) *vb* **implies, implying, implied.** (*tr; may take a clause as object*) **1** to express or indicate by a hint; suggest. **2** to suggest or involve as a necessary consequence. [C14: from OF *emplier,* from L; see IMPLICATE]

> **USAGE NOTE** See at **infer.**

impolder (ɪmˈpəʊldə) *or* **empolder** *vb* to make into a polder; reclaim (land) from the sea. [C19: from Du. *inpolderen,* see IN-[2], POLDER]

impolite Ⓣ (ˌɪmpəˈlaɪt) *adj* discourteous; rude.
▸ˌ**impoˈlitely** *adv* ▸ˌ**impoˈliteness** *n*

impolitic Ⓣ (ɪmˈpɒlɪtɪk) *adj* not politic or expedient; unwise.
▸**imˈpoliticly** *adv*

imponderable (ɪmˈpɒndərəbᵊl, -drəbᵊl) *adj* **1** unable to be weighed or assessed. ◆ *n* **2** something difficult or impossible to assess.
▸**imˌponderaˈbility** *or* **imˈponderableness** *n* ▸**imˈponderably** *adv*

import Ⓣ *vb* (ɪmˈpɔːt, ˈɪmpɔːt). **1** to buy or bring in (goods or services) from a foreign country. **2** (*tr*) to bring in from an outside source: *to import foreign words into the language.* **3** *Rare.* to signify; mean: *to import doom.* ◆ *n* (ˈɪmpɔːt). **4** (*often pl*) **4a** goods or services that are bought from foreign countries. **4b** (*as modifier*): *an import licence.* **5** importance: *a man of great import.* **6** meaning. **7** *Inf.* a sportsman or -woman who is not native to the country in which he or she plays. [C15: from L *importāre* to carry in]
▸**imˈportable** *adj* ▸**imˈporter** *n*

importance Ⓣ (ɪmˈpɔːtᵊns) *n* **1** the state of being important; significance. **2** social status; standing; esteem: *a man of importance.* **3** *Obs.* **3a** meaning or signification. **3b** an important matter. **3c** importunity.

important Ⓣ (ɪmˈpɔːtᵊnt) *adj* **1** of great significance or value; outstanding. **2** of social significance; notable; eminent; esteemed: *an important man in the town.* **3** (when postpositive, usually foll. by *to*) of great concern (to); valued highly (by): *your wishes are important to me.* [C16: from OIt., from Med. L *importāre* to signify, be of consequence, from L: to carry in]
▸**imˈportantly** *adv*

> **USAGE NOTE** The use of *more importantly* as in *more importantly, the local council is opposed to this proposal* has become very common, but many people still prefer to use *more important.*

importation (ˌɪmpɔːˈteɪʃən) *n* **1** the act, business, or process of importing goods or services. **2** an imported product or service.

importunate Ⓣ (ɪmˈpɔːtjʊnɪt) *adj* **1** persistent or demanding; insistent. **2** *Rare.* troublesome; annoying.
▸**imˈportunately** *adv* ▸**imˈportunateness** *n*

importune Ⓣ (ɪmˈpɔːtjuːn, ˌɪmpɔːˈtjuːn) *vb* **importunes, importuning, importuned.** (*tr*) **1** to harass with persistent requests; demand of (someone) insistently. **2** to beg for persistently; request with insistence. [C16: from L *importūnus* tiresome, from *im-* IN-[1] + *-portūnus* as in *opportūnus* OPPORTUNE]
▸**imˈportunely** *adv* ▸**imˈportuner** *n* ▸ˌ**imporˈtunity** *or* **imˈportunacy** *n*

impose Ⓣ (ɪmˈpəʊz) *vb* **imposes, imposing, imposed.** (usually foll. by *on* or *upon*) **1** (*tr*) to establish as something to be obeyed or complied with; enforce. **2** to force (oneself, one's presence, etc.) on others; obtrude. **3** (*intr*) to take advantage, as of a person or quality: *to impose on someone's kindness.* **4** (*tr*) *Printing.* to arrange (pages, type, etc.) in a chase so that the pages will be in the correct order. **5** (*tr*) to pass off deceptively; foist. [C15: from OF, from L *impōnere* to place upon, from *pōnere* to place, set]
▸**imˈposable** *adj* ▸**imˈposer** *n*

imposing Ⓣ (ɪmˈpəʊzɪŋ) *adj* grand or impressive: *an imposing building.*
▸**imˈposingly** *adv* ▸**imˈposingness** *n*

imposition Ⓣ (ˌɪmpəˈzɪʃən) *n* **1** the act of imposing. **2** something imposed unfairly on someone. **3** a task set as a school punishment. **4** the arrangement of pages for printing.

impossibility Ⓣ (ɪmˌpɒsəˈbɪlɪtɪ, ˌɪmpɒs-) *n, pl* **impossibilities. 1** the state or quality of being impossible. **2** something that is impossible.

impossible Ⓣ (ɪmˈpɒsəbᵊl) *adj* **1** incapable of being done, undertaken, or experienced. **2** incapable of occurring or happening. **3** absurd or inconceivable; unreasonable. **4** *Inf.* intolerable; outrageous: *those children are impossible.*
▸**imˈpossibleness** *n* ▸**imˈpossibly** *adv*

impossible figure *n* a picture of an object that at first sight looks three-dimensional but cannot be a two-dimensional projection of a real three-dimensional object, for example a picture of a staircase that re-enters itself while appearing to ascend continuously.

impost[1] (ˈɪmpəʊst) *n* **1** a tax, esp. a customs duty. **2** the weight that a horse must carry in a handicap race. ◆ *vb* **3** (*tr*) *US.* to classify (imported goods) according to the duty payable on them. [C16: from Med. L *impostus* tax, from L *impositus* imposed; see IMPOSE]
▸ˈ**imposter** *n*

impost[2] (ˈɪmpəʊst) *n Archit.* a member at the top of a column that sup-

THESAURUS

implication *n* **1 = involvement**, association, connection, entanglement, incrimination **2 = suggestion**, conclusion, inference, innuendo, meaning, overtone, presumption, ramification, significance, signification

implicit *adj* **1, 3 = implied**, contained, inferred, inherent, latent, tacit, taken for granted, undeclared, understood, unspoken **2 = absolute**, constant, entire, firm, fixed, full, steadfast, total, unhesitating, unqualified, unreserved, unshakable, unshaken, wholehearted
Antonyms *adj* ≠ **implied:** declared, explicit, expressed, obvious, patent, spoken, stated

implicitly *adv* **2 = absolutely**, completely, firmly, unconditionally, unhesitatingly, unreservedly, utterly, without reservation

implied *adj* **= unspoken**, hinted at, implicit, indirect, inherent, insinuated, suggested, tacit, undeclared, unexpressed, unstated

implore *vb* **= beg**, beseech, conjure, crave, entreat, go on bended knee to, importune, plead with, pray, solicit, supplicate

imply *vb* **1 = hint**, connote, give (someone) to understand, insinuate, intimate, signify, suggest **2 = entail**, betoken, denote, evidence, import, include, indicate, involve, mean, point to, presuppose

impolite *adj* **= bad-mannered**, boorish, churlish, discourteous, disrespectful, ill-bred, ill-mannered, indecorous, indelicate, insolent, loutish, rough, rude, uncivil, uncouth, ungallant, ungentlemanly, ungracious, unladylike, unmannerly, unrefined
Antonyms *adj* courteous, decorous, gallant, gracious, mannerly, polite, refined, respectful, well-bred

impoliteness *n* **= bad manners**, boorishness, churlishness, discourtesy, disrespect, incivility, indelicacy, insolence, rudeness, unmannerliness
Antonyms *n* civility, courtesy, delicacy, mannerliness, politeness, respect

impolitic *adj* **= unwise**, ill-advised, ill-judged, imprudent, indiscreet, inexpedient, injudicious, maladroit, misguided, undiplomatic, untimely
Antonyms *adj* diplomatic, discreet, expedient, judicious, politic, prudent, timely, wise

import *vb* **1 = bring in**, introduce, land ◆ *n* **5 = importance**, bottom, consequence, magnitude, moment, significance, substance, weight **6 = meaning**, bearing, drift, gist, implication, intention, message, purport, sense, significance, thrust

importance *n* **1 = significance**, concern, consequence, import, interest, moment, momentousness, substance, usefulness, value, weight, worth **2 = prestige**, bottom, distinction, eminence, esteem, influence, mark, pre-eminence, prominence, standing, status

important *adj* **1 = significant**, far-reaching, grave, large, material, meaningful, momentous, of substance, primary, salient, seminal, serious, signal, substantial, urgent, weighty **2 = powerful**, big-time (*inf.*), eminent, foremost, high-level, high-ranking, influential, leading, major league (*inf.*), notable, noteworthy, of note, outstanding, pre-eminent, prominent **3** *usually with* **to = of concern**, basic, essential, of interest, relevant, valuable, valued
Antonyms *adj* ≠ **significant:** inconsequential, insignificant, minor, needless, negligible, secondary, trivial, undistinctive, unimportant, unnecessary

importunate *adj* **1 = persistent**, burning, clamant, clamorous, demanding, dogged, earnest, exigent, insistent, pertinacious, pressing, solicitous, troublesome, urgent

importune *vb* **1 = pester**, badger, beset, besiege, dun, entreat, harass, hound, lay siege to, plague, press, solicit

importunity *n* **1 = persistence**, cajolery, dunning, entreaties, insistence, pressing, solicitations, urging

impose *vb* **1 = establish**, decree, enforce, exact, fix, institute, introduce, lay, levy, ordain, place, prescribe, promulgate, put, set **2 = intrude**, butt in, encroach, foist, force oneself, gate-crash (*inf.*), inflict, obtrude, presume, take liberties, trespass **3 = take advantage of**, abuse, exploit, play on, use

imposing *adj* **= impressive**, august, commanding, dignified, effective, grand, majestic, stately, striking
Antonyms *adj* insignificant, mean, modest, ordinary, petty, poor, unimposing

imposition *n* **1 = application**, decree, introduction, laying on, levying, promulgation **2 = intrusion**, cheek, encroachment, liberty, presumption

impossibility *n* **1 = hopelessness**, impracticability, inability, inconceivability

impossible *adj* **2 = inconceivable**, beyond one, beyond the bounds of possibility, hopeless, impracticable, not to be thought of, out of the question, unachievable, unattainable, unobtainable, unthinkable **3 = absurd**, inadmissible, insoluble, intolerable, ludicrous, outrageous, preposterous, unacceptable, unanswerable, ungovernable, unreasonable, unsuitable, unworkable
Antonyms *adj* ≠ **inconceivable:** conceivable, imaginable, likely, plausible, possible, reasonable

DICTIONARY

ports an arch. [C17: from F *imposte*, from L *impositus* placed upon; see IMPOSE]

impostor Ⓣ *or* **imposter** (ɪmˈpɒstə) *n* a person who deceives others, esp. by assuming a false identity; charlatan. [C16: from LL: deceiver; see IMPOSE]

imposture Ⓣ (ɪmˈpɒstʃə) *n* the act or an instance of deceiving others, esp. by assuming a false identity. [C16: from F, from LL, from L *impōnere*; see IMPOSE]
▸**impostrous** (ɪmˈpɒstrəs) *or* **impostorous** (ɪmˈpɒstərəs) *adj*

impotent Ⓣ (ˈɪmpətənt) *adj* **1** (when *postpositive*, often takes an infinitive) lacking sufficient strength; powerless. **2** (esp. of males) unable to perform sexual intercourse.
▸ˈ**impotence** *or* ˈ**impotency** *n* ▸ˈ**impotently** *adv*

impound (ɪmˈpaʊnd) *vb (tr)* **1** to confine (animals, etc.) in a pound. **2** to take legal possession of (a document, evidence, etc.). **3** to collect (water) in a reservoir or dam.
▸**imˈpoundable** *adj* ▸**imˈpoundage** *or* **imˈpoundment** *n* ▸**imˈpounder** *n*

impoverish Ⓣ (ɪmˈpɒvərɪʃ) *vb (tr)* **1** to make poor or diminish the quality of: *to impoverish society by cutting the grant to the arts.* **2** to deprive (soil, etc.) of fertility. [C15: from OF *empovrir*, from *povre* POOR]
▸**imˈpoverishment** *n*

impracticable Ⓣ (ɪmˈpræktɪkəbəl) *adj* **1** incapable of being put into practice or accomplished; not feasible. **2** unsuitable for a desired use; unfit.
▸**imˌpracticaˈbility** *or* **imˈpracticableness** *n* ▸**imˈpracticably** *adv*

impractical Ⓣ (ɪmˈpræktɪkəl) *adj* **1** not practical or workable: *an impractical solution.* **2** not given to practical matters or gifted with practical skills.
▸**imˌpractiˈcality** *or* **imˈpracticalness** *n* ▸**imˈpractically** *adv*

imprecate Ⓣ (ˈɪmprɪˌkeɪt) *vb* **imprecates, imprecating, imprecated. 1** (*intr*) to swear or curse. **2** (*tr*) to invoke or bring down (evil, a curse, etc.). [C17: from L *imprecārī* to invoke, from *im-* IN-[2] + *precārī* to PRAY]
▸ˌ**impreˈcation** *n* ▸ˈ**impreˌcatory** *adj*

imprecise Ⓣ (ˌɪmprɪˈsaɪs) *adj* not precise; inexact or inaccurate.
▸ˌ**impreˈcisely** *adv* ▸**imprecision** (ˌɪmprɪˈsɪʒən) *or* ˌ**impreˈciseness** *n*

impregnable[1] Ⓣ (ɪmˈprɛɡnəbəl) *adj* **1** unable to be broken into or taken by force: *an impregnable castle.* **2** unshakable: *impregnable self-confidence.* **3** incapable of being refuted: *an impregnable argument.* [C15 *imprenable*, from OF, from IM- (not) + *prenable* able to be taken, from *prendre* to take]
▸**imˌpregnaˈbility** *n* ▸**imˈpregnably** *adv*

impregnable[2] (ɪmˈprɛɡnəbəl) *or* **impregnatable** (ˌɪmprɛɡˈneɪtəbəl) *adj* able to be impregnated; fertile.

impregnate Ⓣ *vb* (ˈɪmprɛɡˌneɪt), **impregnates, impregnating, impregnated.** (*tr*) **1** to saturate, soak, or infuse. **2** to imbue or permeate; pervade. **3** to cause to conceive; make pregnant; fertilize. **4** to make (land, soil, etc.) fruitful. ◆ *adj* (ɪmˈprɛɡnɪt, -ˌneɪt). **5** pregnant or fertilized. [C17: from LL, from L *im-* IN-[2] + *praegnans* PREGNANT]
▸ˌ**impregˈnation** *n* ▸**imˈpregnator** *n*

impresario (ˌɪmprəˈsɑːrɪˌəʊ) *n, pl* **impresarios.** the director or manager of an opera, ballet, etc. [C18: from It., lit.: one who undertakes]

imprescriptible (ˌɪmprɪˈskrɪptəbəl) *adj Law.* immune or exempt from prescription.
▸ˌ**impreˌscriptiˈbility** *n* ▸ˌ**impreˈscriptibly** *adv*

impress[1] Ⓣ *vb* (ɪmˈprɛs). (*tr*) **1** to make an impression on; have a strong, lasting, or favourable effect on: *I am impressed by your work.* **2** to produce (an imprint, etc.) by pressure in or on (something): *to impress a seal in wax.* **3** (often foll. by *on*) to stress (something to a person); urge; emphasize. **4** to exert pressure on; press. ◆ *n* (ˈɪmprɛs). **5** the act or an instance of impressing. **6** a mark, imprint, or effect produced by impressing. [C14: from L *imprimere* to press into, imprint]
▸**imˈpresser** *n* ▸**imˈpressible** *adj*

impress[2] *vb* (ɪmˈprɛs). **1** to commandeer or coerce (men or things) into government service; press-gang. ◆ *n* (ˈɪmprɛs). **2** the act of commandeering or coercing into government service. [C16: see *im-* IN-[2], PRESS[2]]

impression Ⓣ (ɪmˈprɛʃən) *n* **1** an effect produced in the mind by a stimulus; sensation: *he gave the impression of wanting to help.* **2** an imprint or mark produced by pressing. **3** a vague idea, consciousness, or belief: *I had the impression we had met before.* **4** a strong, favourable, or remarkable effect. **5** the act of impressing or the state of being impressed. **6** *Printing.* **6a** the act, process, or result of printing from type, plates, etc. **6b** the total number of copies of a publication printed at one time. **7** an imprint of the teeth and gums for preparing crowns, dentures, etc. **8** an imitation or impersonation.
▸**imˈpressional** *adj* ▸**imˈpressionally** *adv*

impressionable Ⓣ (ɪmˈprɛʃənəbəl, -ˈprɛʃnə-) *adj* easily influenced or characterized by susceptibility to influence: *an impressionable age.*
▸**imˌpressionaˈbility** *or* **imˈpressionableness** *n*

impressionism (ɪmˈprɛʃəˌnɪzəm) *n* (*often cap.*) a 19th-century movement in French painting, having the aim of objectively recording experience by a system of fleeting impressions, esp. of natural light.
▸**imˈpressionist** *n*

impressive Ⓣ (ɪmˈprɛsɪv) *adj* capable of impressing, esp. by size, magnificence, etc.; awe-inspiring; commanding.
▸**imˈpressively** *adv* ▸**imˈpressiveness** *n*

imprest (ɪmˈprɛst) *n* **1** a fund of cash from which a department, etc., pays incidental expenses, topped up periodically from central funds. **2** *Chiefly Brit.* an advance from government funds for some public business or service. [C16: prob. from It. *imprestare* to lend, from L *in-* towards + *praestāre* to pay, from *praestō* at hand; see PRESTO]

imprimatur (ˌɪmprɪˈmeɪtə, -ˈmɑː-) *n* **1** sanction or approval for something to be printed. **2** *RC Church.* a licence certifying the Church's approval. [C17: NL, lit.: let it be printed]

imprint Ⓣ *n* (ˈɪmprɪnt). **1** a mark or impression produced by pressure, printing, or stamping. **2** a characteristic mark or indication; stamp: *the imprint of great sadness on his face.* **3a** the publisher's name and address, often with the date of publication, printed in a book, usually on the title page or the verso title page. **3b** the printer's name and address on any printed matter. ◆ *vb* (ɪmˈprɪnt). (*tr*) **4** to produce (a mark, impression, etc.) on (a surface) by pressure, printing, or stamping: *to imprint a seal on wax.* **5** to establish firmly; impress: *to imprint the details on one's mind.* **6** to cause (a young animal) to undergo the process of imprinting: *chicks can be imprinted on human beings.*

THESAURUS

impostor *n* = **impersonator**, charlatan, cheat, deceiver, fake, fraud, hypocrite, knave (*arch.*), phoney *or* phony (*inf.*), pretender, quack, rogue, sham, trickster

imposture *n* = **deception**, artifice, canard, cheat, con trick (*inf.*), counterfeit, fraud, hoax, impersonation, imposition, quackery, swindle, trick

impotence *n* **1** = **powerlessness**, disability, enervation, feebleness, frailty, helplessness, inability, inadequacy, incapacity, incompetence, ineffectiveness, inefficacy, inefficiency, infirmity, paralysis, uselessness, weakness
Antonyms *n* ability, adequacy, competence, effectiveness, efficacy, efficiency, powerfulness, strength, usefulness

impotent *adj* **1** = **powerless**, disabled, emasculate, enervated, feeble, frail, helpless, incapable, incapacitated, incompetent, ineffective, infirm, nerveless, paralysed, unable, unmanned, weak
Antonyms *adj* able, capable, competent, effective, manned, potent, powerful, strong

impoverish *vb* **1** = **bankrupt**, beggar, break, pauperize, ruin **2** = **diminish**, deplete, drain, exhaust, reduce, sap, use up, wear out

impoverished *adj* **1** = **poor**, bankrupt, destitute, distressed, impecunious, indigent, in reduced *or* straitened circumstances, necessitous, needy, on one's uppers, penurious, poverty-stricken, ruined, straitened **2** = **depleted**, barren, denuded, drained, empty, exhausted, played out, reduced, spent, sterile, worn out
Antonyms *adj* ≠ **poor:** affluent, rich, wealthy, well-off ≠ **depleted:** fecund, fertile, productive

impracticability *n* **1, 2** = **impracticality**, futility, hopelessness, impossibility, unsuitableness, unworkability, uselessness

impracticable *adj* **1** = **unfeasible**, impossible, out of the question, unachievable, unattainable, unworkable **2** = **unsuitable**, awkward, impractical, inapplicable, inconvenient, unserviceable, useless
Antonyms *adj* ≠ **unfeasible:** feasible, possible, practicable ≠ **unsuitable:** practical, serviceable, suitable

impractical *adj* **1** = **unworkable**, impossible, impracticable, inoperable, nonviable, unrealistic, unserviceable, visionary, wild **2** = **idealistic**, romantic, starry-eyed, unbusinesslike, unrealistic, visionary
Antonyms *adj* ≠ **unworkable:** possible, practical, serviceable, viable, workable ≠ **idealistic:** down-to-earth, realistic, sensible

impracticality *n* **1** = **unworkability**, hopelessness, impossibility, inapplicability

imprecation *n* **2** = **curse**, anathema, blasphemy, denunciation, execration, malediction, profanity, vilification

imprecise *adj* = **indefinite**, ambiguous, blurred round the edges, careless, equivocal, estimated, fluctuating, hazy, ill-defined, inaccurate, indeterminate, inexact, inexplicit, loose, rough, sloppy (*inf.*), vague, wide of the mark, woolly
Antonyms *adj* accurate, careful, definite, determinate, exact, explicit, precise

impregnable[1] *adj* **1-3** = **invulnerable**, immovable, impenetrable, indestructible, invincible, secure, strong, unassailable, unbeatable, unconquerable, unshakable
Antonyms *adj* destructible, exposed, insecure, open, pregnable, shakable, vulnerable

impregnate *vb* **1, 2** = **saturate**, fill, imbrue (*rare*), imbue, infuse, percolate, permeate, pervade, seep, soak, steep, suffuse **3** = **fertilize**, get with child, inseminate, make pregnant **4** = **fecundate**, fructify

impress[1] *vb* **1** = **excite**, affect, grab (*inf.*), influence, inspire, make an impression, move, stir, strike, sway, touch **2** = **imprint**, emboss, engrave, indent, mark, print, stamp **3** = **stress**, bring home to, emphasize, fix, inculcate, instil into

impression *n* **2** = **mark**, brand, dent, hollow, impress, imprint, indentation, outline, stamp, stamping **3** = **idea**, belief, concept, conviction, fancy, feeling, funny feeling (*inf.*), hunch, memory, notion, opinion, recollection, sense, suspicion **4** = **effect**, feeling, impact, influence, reaction, sway **6** = **edition**, imprinting, issue, printing **8** = **imitation**, impersonation, parody, send-up (*Brit. inf.*), takeoff (*inf.*)

impressionability *n* = **suggestibility**, ingenuousness, receptiveness, receptivity, sensitivity, susceptibility, vulnerability

impressionable *adj* = **suggestible**, feeling, gullible, ingenuous, open, receptive, responsive, sensitive, susceptible, vulnerable
Antonyms *adj* blasé, hardened, insensitive, jaded, unresponsive

impressive *adj* = **grand**, affecting, awesome, dramatic, exciting, forcible, moving, powerful, stirring, striking, touching
Antonyms *adj* ordinary, unimposing, unimpressive, uninspiring, unmemorable, weak

imprint *n* **1** = **mark**, impression, indentation, print, sign, stamp ◆ *vb* **4, 5** = **fix**, engrave, establish, etch, impress, print, stamp

imprinting (ɪmˈprɪntɪŋ) *n* the development in young animals of recognition of and attraction to members of their own species or surrogates.

imprison ◐ (ɪmˈprɪzən) *vb (tr)* to confine in or as if in prison.
▸**imˈprisonment** *n*

improbable ◐ (ɪmˈprɒbəbᵊl) *adj* not likely or probable; doubtful; unlikely.
▸**imˌprobaˈbility** *or* **imˈprobableness** *n* ▸**imˈprobably** *adv*

improbity ◐ (ɪmˈprəubɪtɪ) *n, pl* **improbities.** dishonesty, wickedness, or unscrupulousness.

impromptu ◐ (ɪmˈprɒmptjuː) *adj* **1** unrehearsed; spontaneous. **2** produced or done without care or planning; improvised. ◆ *adv* **3** in a spontaneous or improvised way: *he spoke impromptu.* ◆ *n* **4** something that is impromptu. **5** a short piece of instrumental music, sometimes improvisatory in character. [C17: from F, from L *in promptū* in readiness, from *promptus* (adj) ready, PROMPT]

improper ◐ (ɪmˈprɒpə) *adj* **1** lacking propriety; not seemly. **2** unsuitable for a certain use or occasion; inappropriate. **3** irregular or abnormal.
▸**imˈproperly** *adv* ▸**imˈproperness** *n*

improper fraction *n* a fraction in which the numerator is greater than the denominator, as 7/6.

impropriate *vb* (ɪmˈprəuprɪˌeɪt), **impropriates, impropriating, impropriated. 1** *(tr)* to transfer (property, rights, etc.) from the Church into lay hands. ◆ *adj* (ɪmˈprəuprɪɪt, -ˌeɪt). **2** transferred in this way. [C16: from Med. L *impropriāre* to make one's own, from L *im-* IN-[2] + *propriāre* to APPROPRIATE]
▸**imˌpropriˈation** *n* ▸**imˈpropriˌator** *n*

impropriety ◐ (ˌɪmprəˈpraɪɪtɪ) *n, pl* **improprieties. 1** lack of propriety; indecency; indecorum. **2** an improper act or use. **3** the state of being improper.

improve ◐ (ɪmˈpruːv) *vb* **improves, improving, improved. 1** to make or become better in quality; ameliorate. **2** *(tr)* to make (buildings, land, etc.) more valuable by additions or betterment. **3** *(intr; usually foll. by on or upon)* to achieve a better standard or quality in comparison (with): *to improve on last year's crop.* [C16: from Anglo-F *emprouer* to turn to profit, from LL *prōde* beneficial, from L *prōdesse* to be advantageous]
▸**imˈprovable** *adj* ▸**imˌprovaˈbility** *or* **imˈprovableness** *n* ▸**imˈprover** *n*

improvement ◐ (ɪmˈpruːvmənt) *n* **1** the act of improving or the state of being improved. **2** something that improves, esp. an addition or alteration. **3** *(usually pl) Austral. & NZ.* a building, etc., on a piece of land, adding to its value.

improvident ◐ (ɪmˈprɒvɪdənt) *adj* **1** not provident; thriftless, imprudent, or prodigal. **2** heedless or incautious; rash.
▸**imˈprovidence** *n* ▸**imˈprovidently** *adv*

improvise ◐ (ˈɪmprəˌvaɪz) *vb* **improvises, improvising, improvised. 1** to perform or make quickly from materials and sources available, without previous planning. **2** to perform (a poem, play, piece of music, etc.), composing as one goes along. [C19: from F, from It., from L *imprōvīsus* unforeseen, from *prōvidēre* to foresee; see PROVIDE]
▸**ˈimproˌviser** *n* ▸**ˌimproviˈsation** *n* ▸**improvisatory** (ˌɪmprəˈvaɪzətərɪ, -ˈvɪz-, ˌɪmprəvaɪzˈeɪtərɪ) *adj*

imprudent ◐ (ɪmˈpruːdᵊnt) *adj* not prudent; rash, heedless, or indiscreet.
▸**imˈprudence** *n* ▸**imˈprudently** *adv*

impudence ◐ (ˈɪmpjudəns) *or* **impudency** *n* **1** the quality of being impudent. **2** an impudent act or statement. [C14: from L *impudēns* shameless]

impudent ◐ (ˈɪmpjudənt) *adj* **1** mischievous, impertinent, or disrespectful. **2** *Obs.* immodest.
▸**ˈimpudently** *adv* ▸**ˈimpudentness** *n*

impugn ◐ (ɪmˈpjuːn) *vb (tr)* to challenge or attack as false; criticize. [C14: from OF, from L *impugnāre* to fight against, attack]
▸**imˈpugnable** *adj* ▸**imˈpugnment** *n* ▸**imˈpugner** *n*

impulse ◐ (ˈɪmpʌls) *n* **1** an impelling force or motion; thrust; impetus. **2** a sudden desire, whim, or inclination. **3** an instinctive drive; urge. **4** tendency; current; trend. **5** *Physics.* **5a** the product of the average magnitude of a force acting on a body and the time for which it acts. **5b** the change in the momentum of a body as a result of a force acting upon it. **6** *Physiol.* See **nerve impulse. 7 on impulse.** spontaneously or impulsively. [C17: from L *impulsus* a pushing against, incitement, from *impellere* to strike against; see IMPEL]

impulse buying *n* the buying of merchandise prompted by a whim.
▸**impulse buyer** *n*

impulsion (ɪmˈpʌlʃən) *n* **1** the act of impelling or the state of being impelled. **2** motion produced by an impulse; propulsion. **3** a driving force; compulsion.

impulsive ◐ (ɪmˈpʌlsɪv) *adj* **1** characterized by actions based on sudden desires, whims, or inclinations: *an impulsive man.* **2** based on emotional impulses or whims; spontaneous. **3** forceful, inciting, or impelling. **4** (of physical forces) acting for a short time; not continuous. **5** (of a sound) brief, loud, and having a wide frequency range.
▸**imˈpulsively** *adv* ▸**imˈpulsiveness** *n*

impundulu (ˈɪmpunˌdulu) *n S. African.* a mythical bird often associated with witchcraft. [from Bantu]

impunity ◐ (ɪmˈpjuːnɪtɪ) *n, pl* **impunities. 1** exemption or immunity from punishment, recrimination, or other unpleasant consequences. **2 with impunity.** with no care or heed for such consequences. [C16:

THESAURUS

imprison *vb* = **jail**, confine, constrain, detain, immure, incarcerate, intern, lock up, put away, put under lock and key, send down *(inf.)*, send to prison
Antonyms *vb* discharge, emancipate, free, liberate, release

imprisoned *adj* = **jailed**, behind bars, captive, confined, immured, incarcerated, in irons, in jail, inside *(sl.)*, interned, locked up, put away, under lock and key

imprisonment *n* = **custody**, confinement, detention, durance *(arch.)*, duress, incarceration, internment, porridge *(sl.)*

improbability *n* = **doubt**, doubtfulness, dubiety, uncertainty, unlikelihood

improbable *adj* = **doubtful**, cock-and-bull, dubious, fanciful, far-fetched, implausible, questionable, unbelievable, uncertain, unconvincing, unlikely, weak
Antonyms *adj* certain, convincing, doubtless, likely, plausible, probable, reasonable

improbity *n* = **dishonesty**, chicanery, crookedness *(inf.)*, faithlessness, fraud, knavery, unfairness, unscrupulousness, villainy

impromptu *adj* **1, 2** = **unprepared**, ad-lib, extemporaneous, extempore, extemporized, improvised, offhand, off the cuff *(inf.)*, spontaneous, unpremeditated, unrehearsed, unscripted, unstudied ◆ *adv* **3** = **spontaneously**, ad lib, off the cuff *(inf.)*, off the top of one's head *(inf.)*, on the spur of the moment, without preparation
Antonyms *adj* ≠ **unprepared:** considered, planned, premeditated, prepared, rehearsed

improper *adj* **1** = **indecent**, impolite, indecorous, indelicate, off-colour, risqué, smutty, suggestive, unbecoming, unfitting, unseemly, untoward, vulgar **2** = **inappropriate**, ill-timed, inapplicable, inapposite, inapt, incongruous, infelicitous, inopportune, malapropos, out of place, uncalled-for, unfit, unseasonable, unsuitable, unsuited, unwarranted **3** = **incorrect**, abnormal, erroneous, false, inaccurate, irregular, wrong
Antonyms *adj* ≠ **indecent:** becoming, decent, decorous, delicate, fitting, proper, seemly ≠ **inappropriate:** apposite, appropriate, apt, felicitous, opportune, seasoned, suitable

impropriety *n* **1** = **indecency**, bad taste, immodesty, incongruity, indecorum, unsuitability, vulgarity **2** = **lapse**, bloomer *(Brit. inf.)*, blunder, faux pas, gaffe, gaucherie, mistake, slip, solecism
Antonyms *n* ≠ **indecency:** decency, decorum, delicacy, modesty, propriety, suitability

improve *vb* **1** = **enhance**, ameliorate, amend, augment, better, correct, help, increase, mend, polish, rectify, touch up, upgrade
Antonyms *vb* damage, harm, impair, injure, mar, worsen

improvement *n* **1** = **enhancement**, advancement, amelioration, amendment, augmentation, betterment, correction, development, face-lift, furtherance, gain, increase, progress, rectification, rise, upswing

improvidence *n* **1** = **imprudence**, carelessness, extravagance, heedlessness, lavishness, negligence, prodigality, profligacy, shortsightedness, thriftlessness, wastefulness

improvident *adj* **1** = **imprudent**, careless, heedless, inconsiderate, negligent, prodigal, profligate, reckless, shiftless, short-sighted, spendthrift, thoughtless, thriftless, uneconomical, unthrifty, wasteful
Antonyms *adj* careful, considerate, economical, heedful, provident, prudent, thrifty

improvisation *n* **2** = **spontaneity**, ad-libbing, extemporizing, invention

improvise *vb* **1** = **concoct**, contrive, devise, make do, throw together **2** = **extemporize**, ad-lib, busk, coin, invent, play it by ear *(inf.)*, speak off the cuff *(inf.)*, vamp, wing it *(inf.)*

improvised *adj* **2** = **unprepared**, ad-lib, extemporaneous, extempore, extemporized, makeshift, off the cuff *(inf.)*, spontaneous, spur-of-the-moment, unrehearsed

imprudence *n* = **rashness**, carelessness, folly, foolhardiness, foolishness, heedlessness, improvidence, inadvisability, incaution, incautiousness, inconsideration, indiscretion, irresponsibility, recklessness, temerity

imprudent *adj* = **unwise**, careless, foolhardy, foolish, heedless, ill-advised, ill-considered, ill-judged, impolitic, improvident, incautious, inconsiderate, indiscreet, injudicious, irresponsible, overhasty, rash, reckless, temerarious, unthinking
Antonyms *adj* careful, cautious, considerate, discreet, judicious, politic, provident, prudent, responsible, wise

impudence *n* **1** = **boldness**, assurance, audacity, backchat *(inf.)*, brazenness, bumptiousness, cheek *(inf.)*, chutzpah *(US & Canad. inf.)*, effrontery, face *(inf.)*, front, impertinence, insolence, lip *(sl.)*, nerve *(inf.)*, pertness, presumption, rudeness, shamelessness

impudent *adj* **1** = **bold**, audacious, bold-faced, brazen, bumptious, cheeky *(inf.)*, cocky *(inf.)*, forward, fresh *(inf.)*, immodest, impertinent, insolent, lippy *(US & Canad. sl.)*, pert, presumptuous, rude, sassy *(US inf.)*, saucy *(inf.)*, shameless
Antonyms *adj* courteous, modest, polite, respectful, retiring, self-effacing, timid, well-behaved

impugn *vb* = **challenge**, assail, attack, call into question, cast aspersions upon, cast doubt upon, criticize, dispute, gainsay *(arch. or literary)*, oppose, question, resist, traduce

impulse *n* **1** = **force**, catalyst, impetus, momentum, movement, pressure, push, stimulus, surge, thrust **2, 3** = **urge**, caprice, drive, feeling, incitement, inclination, influence, instinct, motive, notion, passion, resolve, whim, wish

impulsive *adj* **1, 2** = **instinctive**, devil-may-care, emotional, hasty, headlong, impetuous, intuitive, passionate, precipitate, quick, rash, spontaneous, unconsidered, unpredictable, unpremeditated
Antonyms *adj* calculating, cautious, considered, cool, deliberate, halting, planned, premeditated, rehearsed, restrained

impunity *n* **1** = **security**, dispensation, exemp-

from L, from *impūnis* unpunished, from IM- (not) + *poena* punishment]

impure ⓘ (ɪmˈpjʊə) *adj* **1** not pure; combined with something else; tainted or sullied. **2** (in certain religions) ritually unclean. **3** (of a colour) mixed with another colour. **4** of more than one origin or style, as of architecture.
▸**imˈpurely** *adv* ▸**imˈpureness** *n*

impurity ⓘ (ɪmˈpjʊərɪtɪ) *n, pl* **impurities. 1** the quality of being impure. **2** an impure thing, constituent, or element: *impurities in the water.* **3** *Electronics.* a small quantity of an element added to a pure semiconductor crystal to control its electrical conductivity.

impute ⓘ (ɪmˈpjuːt) *vb* **imputes, imputing, imputed.** (*tr*) **1** to attribute or ascribe (something dishonest or dishonourable) to a person. **2** to attribute to a source or cause: *I impute your success to nepotism.* **3** *Commerce.* to give (a notional value) to goods, etc., when the real value is unknown. [C14: from L, from IM- + *putāre* to think, calculate]
▸ˌ**impuˈtation** *n* ▸**imˈputative** *adj* ▸**imˈputer** *n* ▸**imˈputable** *adj*

IMunE *abbrev. for* Institution of Municipal Engineers.

in (ɪn) *prep* **1** inside; within: *no smoking in the auditorium.* **2** at a place where there is: *in the shade.* **3** indicating a state, situation, or condition: *in silence.* **4** when (a period of time) has elapsed: *return in one year.* **5** using: *written in code.* **6** concerned with, esp. as an occupation: *in journalism.* **7** while or by performing the action of: *in crossing the street he was run over.* **8** used to indicate purpose: *in honour of the king.* **9** (of certain animals) pregnant with: *in calf.* **10** a variant of **into:** *she fell in the water.* **11 have it in one.** (often foll. by an infinitive) to have the ability (to do something). **12 in that** *or* **in so far as.** (*conj*) because or to the extent that: *I regret my remark in that it upset you.* **13 nothing in it.** no difference or interval between two things. ◆ *adv* (*particle*) **14** in or into a particular place; inward or indoors: *come in.* **15** so as to achieve office or power: *Labour got in at the last election.* **16** so as to enclose: *block in.* **17** (in certain games) so as to take one's turn of the play: *you have to get the other side out before you go in.* **18** *NZ.* competing: *you've got to be in to win.* **19** *Brit.* (of a fire) alight. **20** (*in combination*) indicating an activity or gathering: *teach-in; work-in.* **21 in at.** present at (the beginning, end, etc.). **22 in for.** about to be affected by (something, esp. something unpleasant): *you're in for a shock.* **23 in on.** acquainted with or sharing in: *I was in on all his plans.* **24 in with.** associated with; friendly with; regarded highly by. **25 have (got) it in for.** to wish or intend harm towards. ◆ *adj* **26** (*stressed*) fashionable; modish: *the in thing to do.* ◆ *n* **27 ins and outs.** intricacies or complications; details. [OE]

In *the chemical symbol for* indium.

in. *abbrev. for* inch(es).

in-[1], **il-, im-,** *or* **ir-** *prefix* **a** not; non-: *incredible; illegal; imperfect; irregular.* **b** lack of: *inexperience.* Cf. **un-**. [from L *in-;* rel. to *ne-, nōn* not]

in-[2], **il-, im-,** *or* **ir-** *prefix* **1** in; into; towards; within; on: *infiltrate; immigrate.* **2** having an intensive or causative function: *inflame; imperil.* [from IN (prep, adv)]

-in *suffix forming nouns.* **1** indicating a neutral organic compound, including proteins, glucosides, and glycerides: *insulin; tripalmitin.* **2** indicating an enzyme in certain nonsystematic names: *pepsin.* **3** indicating a pharmaceutical substance: *penicillin; aspirin.* **4** indicating a chemical substance in certain nonsystematic names: *coumarin.* [from NL *-ina;* cf. -INE[2]]

in absentia *Latin.* (ɪn æbˈsɛntɪə) *adv* in the absence of (someone indicated).

inaccessible ⓘ (ˌɪnækˈsɛsəbᵊl) *adj* not accessible; unapproachable.
▸ˌ**inacˌcessiˈbility** *or* ˌ**inacˈcessibleness** *n* ▸ˌ**inacˈcessibly** *adv*

inaccuracy ⓘ (ɪnˈækjʊrəsɪ) *n, pl* **inaccuracies. 1** lack of accuracy; imprecision. **2** an error, mistake, or slip.
▸**inˈaccurate** *adj*

inaction ⓘ (ɪnˈækʃən) *n* lack of action; idleness; inertia.

inactivate (ɪnˈæktɪˌveɪt) *vb* **inactivates, inactivating, inactivated.** (*tr*) to render inactive.
▸**inˌactiˈvation** *n*

inactive ⓘ (ɪnˈæktɪv) *adj* **1** idle or inert; not active. **2** sluggish or indolent. **3** *Mil.* of or relating to persons or equipment not in active service. **4** *Chem.* (of a substance) having little or no reactivity.
▸**inˈactively** *adv* ▸ˌ**inacˈtivity** *n*

inadequate ⓘ (ɪnˈædɪkwɪt) *adj* **1** not adequate; insufficient. **2** not capable; lacking.
▸**inˈadequacy** *n* ▸**inˈadequately** *adv*

inadvertence (ˌɪnədˈvɜːtᵊns) *or* **inadvertency** *n* **1** lack of attention; heedlessness. **2** an oversight; slip.

inadvertent ⓘ (ˌɪnədˈvɜːtᵊnt) *adj* **1** failing to act carefully or considerately; inattentive. **2** resulting from heedless action; unintentional.
▸ˌ**inadˈvertently** *adv*

-inae *suffix forming plural proper nouns.* occurring in names of zoological subfamilies: *Felinae.* [NL, from L, fem pl of *-īnus* -INE[1]]

inalienable ⓘ (ɪnˈeɪljənəbᵊl) *adj* not able to be transferred to another; not alienable: *the inalienable rights of the citizen.*
▸**inˌalienaˈbility** *or* **inˈalienableness** *n* ▸**inˈalienably** *adv*

inalterable (ɪnˈɔːltərəbᵊl) *adj* not alterable; unalterable.
▸**inˌalteraˈbility** *or* **inˈalterableness** *n* ▸**inˈalterably** *adv*

inamorata (ɪnˌæməˈrɑːtə, ˌɪnæmə-) *or* (*masc*) **inamorato** (ɪnˌæməˈrɑːtəʊ, ˌɪnæmə-) *n, pl* **inamoratas** *or* (*masc*) **inamoratos.** a person with whom one is in love; lover. [C17: from It., from *innamorare* to cause to fall in love, from *amore* love, from L *amor*]

inane ⓘ (ɪˈneɪn) *adj* **1** senseless, unimaginative, or empty; unintelligent: *inane remarks.* ◆ *n* **2** *Arch.* something empty or vacant, esp. the void of space. [C17: from L *inānis* empty]
▸**inˈanely** *adv*

inanimate ⓘ (ɪnˈænɪmɪt) *adj* **1** lacking the qualities of living beings; not animate: *inanimate objects.* **2** lacking any sign of life or consciousness; appearing dead. **3** lacking vitality; dull.
▸**inˈanimately** *adv* ▸**inˈanimateness** *or* **inanimation** (ɪnˌænɪˈmeɪʃən) *n*

inanition (ˌɪnəˈnɪʃən) *n* **1** exhaustion resulting from lack of food. **2** mental, social, or spiritual weakness or lassitude. [C14: from LL *inānītio* emptiness, from L *inānis* empty; see INANE]

inanity ⓘ (ɪˈnænɪtɪ) *n, pl* **inanities. 1** lack of intelligence or imagination; senselessness; silliness. **2** a senseless action, remark, etc. **3** an archaic word for **emptiness.**

THESAURUS

tion, freedom, immunity, liberty, licence, nonliability, permission

impure *adj* **1** = **unrefined**, admixed, adulterated, alloyed, debased, mixed **2** = **unclean**, contaminated, defiled, dirty, filthy, foul, infected, polluted, sullied, tainted, unwholesome, vitiated
Antonyms *adj* ≠ **unclean:** clean, immaculate, spotless, squeaky-clean, undefiled, unsullied

impurity *n* **1** = **contamination**, befoulment, defilement, dirtiness, filth, foulness, infection, pollution, taint, uncleanness **2** = **dirt**, bits, contaminant, dross, foreign body, foreign matter, grime, marks, pollutant, scum, spots, stains

imputable *adj* **2** = **attributable**, accreditable, ascribable, chargeable, referable, traceable

imputation *n* **1** = **blame**, accusation, ascription, aspersion, attribution, censure, charge, insinuation, reproach, slander, slur

impute *vb* **2** = **attribute**, accredit, ascribe, assign, credit, lay at the door of, refer, set down to

inaccessible *adj* = **out of reach**, impassable, out of the way, remote, unapproachable, unattainable, un-get-at-able (*inf.*), unreachable
Antonyms *adj* accessible, approachable, attainable, reachable

inaccuracy *n* **1** = **imprecision**, erroneousness, incorrectness, inexactness, unfaithfulness, unreliability **2** = **error**, blunder, boob, corrigendum, defect, erratum, fault, howler (*inf.*), lapse, miscalculation, mistake, slip

inaccurate *adj* **1** = **incorrect**, careless, defective, discrepant, erroneous, faulty, imprecise, in error, inexact, mistaken, off base (*US & Canad. inf.*), off beam (*inf.*), out, unfaithful, unreliable, unsound, way off beam (*inf.*), wide of the mark, wild, wrong

Antonyms *adj* accurate, correct, exact, precise, reliable, sound

inaction *n* = **inactivity**, dormancy, idleness, immobility, inertia, rest, torpidity, torpor

inactive *adj* **1** = **unused**, abeyant, dormant, idle, immobile, inert, inoperative, jobless, kicking one's heels, latent, mothballed, out of service, out of work, unemployed, unoccupied **2** = **slothful**, dull, indolent, lazy, lethargic, low-key (*inf.*), passive, quiet, sedentary, slow, sluggish, somnolent, torpid
Antonyms *adj* ≠ **unused:** employed, mobile, occupied, operative, running, used, working ≠ **slothful:** active, busy, diligent, energetic, industrious, vibrant

inactivity *n* **1** = **immobility**, dormancy, hibernation, inaction, passivity, unemployment **2** = **sloth**, dilatoriness, *dolce far niente,* dullness, heaviness, indolence, inertia, inertness, lassitude, laziness, lethargy, quiescence, sluggishness, stagnation, torpor, vegetation
Antonyms *n* action, activeness, bustle, employment, exertion, mobility, movement

inadequacy *n* **1** = **shortage**, dearth, inadequateness, incompleteness, insufficiency, meagreness, paucity, poverty, scantiness, skimpiness **2** = **incompetence**, defectiveness, deficiency, faultiness, inability, inaptness, incapacity, incompetency, ineffectiveness, inefficacy, unfitness, unsuitableness

inadequate *adj* **1** = **insufficient**, incommensurate, incomplete, insubstantial, meagre, niggardly, scant, scanty, short, sketchy, skimpy, sparse **2** = **incapable**, defective, deficient, faulty, found wanting, imperfect, inapt, incompetent, not up to scratch (*inf.*), pathetic, unequal, unfitted, unqualified
Antonyms *adj* ≠ **insufficient:** adequate, ample, complete, perfect, satisfactory, substantial, sufficient ≠ **incapable:** apt, capable, competent, equal, fit, qualified

inadequately *adv* **1** = **insufficiently**, imperfectly, meagrely, poorly, scantily, sketchily, skimpily, sparsely, thinly

inadvertent *adj* **2** = **unintentional**, accidental, careless, chance, heedless, negligent, thoughtless, unheeding, unintended, unplanned, unpremeditated, unthinking, unwitting

inadvertently *adv* **1** = **carelessly**, heedlessly, in an unguarded moment, negligently, thoughtlessly, unguardedly, unthinkingly **2** = **unintentionally**, accidentally, by accident, by mistake, involuntarily, mistakenly, unwittingly
Antonyms *adv* carefully, consciously, deliberately, heedfully, intentionally

inalienable *adj* = **sacrosanct**, absolute, entailed (*Law*), inherent, inviolable, non-negotiable, nontransferable, unassailable, untransferable

inane *adj* **1** = **senseless**, asinine, daft (*inf.*), devoid of intelligence, empty, fatuous, frivolous, futile, idiotic, imbecilic, mindless, puerile, silly, stupid, trifling, unintelligent, vacuous, vain, vapid, worthless
Antonyms *adj* meaningful, profound, sensible, serious, significant, weighty, worthwhile

inanimate *adj* **1, 2** = **lifeless**, cold, dead, defunct, extinct, inactive, inert, insensate, insentient, quiescent, soulless, spiritless
Antonyms *adj* active, alive, alive and kicking, animate, full of beans (*inf.*), lively, living, moving

inanity *n* **1** = **senselessness**, asininity, daftness (*inf.*), fatuity, folly, frivolity, imbecility, puerility, silliness, vacuity, vapidity, worthlessness

inapposite Ⓣ (ɪnˈæpəzɪt) *adj* not appropriate or pertinent; unsuitable. ▸**inˈappositely** *adv* ▸**inˈappositeness** *n*

inapt Ⓣ (ɪnˈæpt) *adj* **1** not apt or fitting; inappropriate. **2** lacking skill; inept. ▸**inˈaptiˌtude** *or* **inˈaptness** *n* ▸**inˈaptly** *adv*

inarch (ɪnˈɑːtʃ) *vb* (*tr*) to graft (a plant) by uniting stock and scion while both are still growing independently.

inasmuch as (ˌɪnəzˈmʌtʃ) *conj* (*subordinating*) **1** in view of the fact that; seeing that; since. **2** to the extent or degree that; in so far as.

inaugural Ⓣ (ɪnˈɔːgjʊrəl) *adj* **1** characterizing or relating to an inauguration. ◆ *n* **2** a speech made at an inauguration, esp. by a president of the US.

inaugurate Ⓣ (ɪnˈɔːgjʊˌreɪt) *vb* **inaugurates, inaugurating, inaugurated.** (*tr*) **1** to commence officially or formally; initiate. **2** to place in office formally and ceremonially; induct. **3** to open ceremonially; dedicate formally: *to inaugurate a factory.* [C17: from L *inaugurāre*, lit.: to take omens, practise augury, hence to install in office after taking auguries; see IN-[2], AUGUR] ▸**inˌauguˈration** *n* ▸**inˈauguˌrator** *n* ▸**inauguratory** (ɪnˈɔːgjʊrətərɪ, -trɪ) *adj*

in-between *adj* intermediate: *he's at the in-between stage, neither a child nor an adult.*

inboard (ˈɪnˌbɔːd) *adj* **1** (esp. of a boat's motor or engine) situated within the hull. **2** situated between the wing tip of an aircraft and its fuselage: *an inboard engine.* ◆ *adv* **3** towards the centre line of or within a vessel, aircraft, etc.

inborn Ⓣ (ˈɪnˈbɔːn) *adj* existing from birth; congenital; innate.

inbred Ⓣ (ˈɪnˈbrɛd) *adj* **1** produced as a result of inbreeding. **2** deeply ingrained; innate: *inbred good manners.*

inbreed (ˈɪnˈbriːd) *vb* **inbreeds, inbreeding, inbred. 1** to breed from unions between closely related individuals, esp. over several generations. **2** (*tr*) to develop within; engender. ▸**ˈinˈbreeding** *n, adj*

in-built Ⓣ *adj* built-in, integral.

inc. *abbrev. for:* **1** including. **2** inclusive. **3** income. **4** increase.

Inc. (esp. US) *abbrev. for* incorporated.

incalculable Ⓣ (ɪnˈkælkjʊləbᵊl) *adj* beyond calculation; unable to be predicted or determined. ▸**inˌcalculaˈbility** *n* ▸**inˈcalculably** *adv*

incandesce (ˌɪnkænˈdɛs) *vb* **incandesces, incandescing, incandesced.** (*intr*) to make or become incandescent.

incandescent Ⓣ (ˌɪnkænˈdɛsᵊnt) *adj* **1** emitting light as a result of being heated; red-hot or white-hot. **2** *Inf.* extremely angry. [C18: from L *incandescere* to become hot, glow, from *candēre* to be white; see CANDID] ▸**ˌincanˈdescently** *adv* ▸**ˌincanˈdescence** *n*

incandescent lamp *n* a source of light that contains a heated solid, such as an electrically heated filament.

incantation Ⓣ (ˌɪnkænˈteɪʃən) *n* **1** ritual recitation of magic words or sounds. **2** the formulaic words or sounds used; a magic spell. [C14: from LL *incantātiō* an enchanting, from *incantāre* to repeat magic formulas, from L, from IN-[2] + *cantāre* to sing; see ENCHANT] ▸**ˌincanˈtational** *or* **inˈcantatory** *adj*

incapacitate Ⓣ (ˌɪnkəˈpæsɪˌteɪt) *vb* **incapacitates, incapacitating, incapacitated.** (*tr*) **1** to deprive of power, strength, or capacity; disable. **2** to deprive of legal capacity or eligibility. ▸**ˌincaˌpaciˈtation** *n*

incapacity Ⓣ (ˌɪnkəˈpæsɪtɪ) *n, pl* **incapacities. 1** lack of power, strength, or capacity; inability. **2** *Law.* legal disqualification or ineligibility.

in-car *adj* (of hi-fi equipment, etc.) installed inside a car.

incarcerate Ⓣ (ɪnˈkɑːsəˌreɪt) *vb* **incarcerates, incarcerating, incarcerated.** (*tr*) to confine or imprison. [C16: from Med. L, from L IN-[2] + *carcer* prison] ▸**inˌcarcerˈation** *n* ▸**inˈcarcerˌator** *n*

incarnadine (ɪnˈkɑːnəˌdaɪn) *Arch. or literary.* ◆ *vb* **incarnadines, incarnadining, incarnadined. 1** (*tr*) to tinge or stain with red. ◆ *adj* **2** of a pinkish or reddish colour similar to that of flesh or blood. [C16: from F *incarnadin* flesh-coloured, from It., from LL *incarnātus* made flesh, INCARNATE]

incarnate Ⓣ *adj* (ɪnˈkɑːnɪt, -neɪt). (*usually immediately postpositive*) **1** possessing bodily form, esp. the human form: *a devil incarnate.* **2** personified or typified: *stupidity incarnate.* ◆ *vb* (ɪnˈkɑːneɪt), **incarnates, incarnating, incarnated.** (*tr*) **3** to give a bodily or concrete form to. **4** to be representative or typical of. [C14: from LL *incarnāre* to make flesh, from L IN-[2] + *carō* flesh]

incarnation Ⓣ (ˌɪnkɑːˈneɪʃən) *n* **1** the act of manifesting or state of being manifested in bodily form, esp. human form. **2** a bodily form assumed by a god, etc. **3** a person or thing that typifies or represents some quality, idea, etc.

Incarnation (ˌɪnkɑːˈneɪʃən) *n Christian theol.* the assuming of a human body by the Son of God.

incarvillea (ˌɪnkɑːˈvɪlɪə) *n* any of various perennials with pink flowers and pinnate leaves. Also called: **Chinese trumpet flower.** [C18: after Pierre d'*Incarville*, F missionary in China]

incase (ɪnˈkeɪs) *vb* **incases, incasing, incased.** a variant spelling of **encase.** ▸**inˈcasement** *n*

incautious Ⓣ (ɪnˈkɔːʃəs) *adj* not careful or cautious. ▸**inˈcautiously** *adv* ▸**inˈcautiousness** *or* **inˈcaution** *n*

incendiary Ⓣ (ɪnˈsɛndɪərɪ) *adj* **1** of or relating to the illegal burning of property, goods, etc. **2** tending to create strife, violence, etc. **3** (of a substance) capable of catching fire or burning readily. ◆ *n, pl* **incendiaries. 4** a person who illegally sets fire to property, goods, etc.; arsonist. **5** (esp. formerly) a person who stirs up civil strife, violence, etc.; agitator. **6** Also called: **incendiary bomb.** a bomb that is designed to start fires. **7** an incendiary substance, such as phosphorus. [C17: from L, from *incendium* fire, from *incendere* to kindle] ▸**inˈcendiaˌrism** *n*

incense[1] Ⓣ (ˈɪnsɛns) *n* **1** any of various aromatic substances burnt for their fragrant odour, esp. in religious ceremonies. **2** the odour or smoke so produced. **3** any pleasant fragrant odour; aroma. ◆ *vb* **incenses, incensing, incensed. 4** to burn incense in honour of (a deity). **5** (*tr*) to perfume or fumigate with incense. [C13: from OF *encens*, from Church L *incensum*, from L *incendere* to kindle]

incense[2] Ⓣ (ɪnˈsɛns) *vb* **incenses, incensing, incensed.** (*tr*) to enrage greatly. [C15: from L *incensus* set on fire, from *incendere* to kindle] ▸**inˈcensement** *n*

incensory (ˈɪnsɛnsərɪ) *n, pl* **incensories.** a less common name for **censer.** [C17: from Med. L *incensorium*]

incentive Ⓣ (ɪnˈsɛntɪv) *n* **1** a motivating influence; stimulus. **2a** an additional payment made to employees to increase production. **2b** (*as modifier*): *an incentive scheme.* ◆ *adj* **3** serving to incite to action. [C15: from LL, from L: striking up, setting the tune, from *incinere* to sing]

incept (ɪnˈsɛpt) *vb* (*tr*) **1** (of organisms) to ingest (food). **2** *Brit.* (formerly) to take a master's or doctor's degree at a university. [C19:

THESAURUS

inapposite *adj* = **inappropriate**, impertinent, inapplicable, infelicitous, irrelevant, out of place, unfit, unsuitable

inapt *adj* **1** = **inappropriate**, ill-fitted, ill-suited, inapposite, infelicitous, unsuitable, unsuited **2** = **incompetent**, awkward, clumsy, dull, gauche, inept, inexpert, maladroit, slow, stupid
Antonyms *adj* ≠ **inappropriate**: apposite, appropriate, apt, felicitous, fitting, suitable, suited

inaptitude *n* **2** = **incompetence**, awkwardness, clumsiness, maladroitness, unfitness, unreadiness, unsuitableness

inaugural *adj* **1** = **first**, dedicatory, initial, introductory, maiden, opening

inaugurate *vb* **1** = **launch**, begin, commence, get under way, initiate, institute, introduce, kick off (*inf.*), originate, set in motion, set up, usher in **2** = **invest**, induct, install, instate **3** = **open**, commission, dedicate, ordain

inauguration *n* **1** = **launch**, initiation, institution, launching, opening, setting up **2** = **investiture**, induction, installation

inborn *adj* = **natural**, congenital, connate, hereditary, immanent, inbred, ingrained, inherent, inherited, innate, in one's blood, instinctive, intuitive, native

inbred *adj* **2** = **innate**, constitutional, deep-seated, immanent, ingrained, inherent, native, natural

in-built *adj* = **integral**, built-in, component, incorporated

incalculable *adj* = **countless**, boundless, enormous, immense, incomputable, inestimable, infinite, innumerable, limitless, measureless, numberless, uncountable, untold, vast, without number

incandescent *adj* **1** = **glowing**, brilliant, Day-Glo, luminous, phosphorescent, radiant, red-hot, shining, white-hot

incantation *n* **2** = **chant**, abracadabra, charm, conjuration, formula, hex (*US & Canad. inf.*), invocation, spell

incapacitate *vb* **1** = **disable**, cripple, disqualify, immobilize, lay up (*inf.*), paralyse, prostrate, put out of action (*inf.*), scupper (*Brit. sl.*), unfit (*rare*)

incapacitated *adj* **1** = **indisposed**, disqualified, *hors de combat*, immobilized, laid up (*inf.*), out of action (*inf.*), unfit

incapacity *n* **1** = **inability**, disqualification, feebleness, impotence, inadequacy, incapability, incompetency, ineffectiveness, powerlessness, unfitness, weakness

incarcerate *vb* = **imprison**, commit, confine, coop up, detain, immure, impound, intern, jail *or* gaol, lock up, put under lock and key, restrain, restrict, send down (*Brit.*), throw in jail

incarceration *n* = **imprisonment**, bondage, captivity, confinement, detention, internment, porridge (*sl.*), restraint

incarnate *adj* **1** = **made flesh**, in bodily form, in human form, in the flesh **2** = **personified**, embodied, typified

incarnation *n* **2, 3** = **embodiment**, avatar, bodily form, epitome, exemplification, impersonation, manifestation, personification, type

incautious *adj* = **careless**, hasty, heedless, ill-advised, ill-judged, improvident, imprudent, impulsive, inconsiderate, indiscreet, injudicious, negligent, precipitate, rash, reckless, thoughtless, unguarded, unthinking, unwary
Antonyms *adj* careful, cautious, considerate, discreet, guarded, heedful, judicious, prudent, thoughtful, wary

incautiously *adv* = **rashly**, imprudently, impulsively, indiscreetly, precipitately, recklessly, thoughtlessly, unthinkingly

incendiary *adj* **2** = **inflammatory**, dissentious, provocative, rabble-rousing, seditious, subversive ◆ *n* **4** = **arsonist**, firebug (*inf.*), fire raiser, pyromaniac **5** = **agitator**, demagogue, firebrand, insurgent, rabble-rouser, revolutionary

incense[1] *n* **2, 3** = **perfume**, aroma, balm, bouquet, fragrance, redolence, scent

incense[2] *vb* = **anger**, enrage, exasperate, excite, gall, inflame, infuriate, irritate, madden, make one's blood boil (*inf.*), make one see red (*inf.*), make one's hackles rise, nark (*Brit., Austral., & NZ sl.*), provoke, rile (*inf.*), rub one up the wrong way

incentive *n* **1** = **encouragement**, bait, carrot (*inf.*), carrot and stick, enticement, goad, impetus, impulse, inducement, lure, motivation, motive, spur, stimulant, stimulus
Antonyms *n* deterrent, discouragement, disincentive, dissuasion, warning

from L *inceptus* begun, attempted, from *incipere* to begin, take in hand]
▸**in'ceptor** *n*

inception ⊕ (ɪn'sɛpʃən) *n* the beginning, as of a project or undertaking.

inceptive (ɪn'sɛptɪv) *adj* **1** beginning; incipient; initial. **2** Also called: **inchoative.** *Grammar.* denoting a verb used to indicate the beginning of an action. ◆ *n* **3** *Grammar.* an inceptive verb.
▸**in'ceptively** *adv*

incertitude (ɪn'sɜːtɪˌtjuːd) *n* **1** uncertainty; doubt. **2** a state of mental or emotional insecurity.

incessant ⊕ (ɪn'sɛsᵊnt) *adj* not ceasing; continual. [C16: from LL, from L IN-[1] + *cessāre* to CEASE]
▸**in'cessancy** *n* ▸**in'cessantly** *adv*

incest ('ɪnsɛst) *n* sexual intercourse between two persons who are too closely related to marry. [C13: from L, from IN-[1] + *castus* CHASTE]

incestuous (ɪn'sɛstjʊəs) *adj* **1** relating to or involving incest: *an incestuous union.* **2** guilty of incest. **3** resembling incest in excessive or claustrophobic intimacy.
▸**in'cestuously** *adv* ▸**in'cestuousness** *n*

inch[1] (ɪntʃ) *n* **1** a unit of length equal to one twelfth of a foot or 0.0254 metre. **2** *Meteorol.* **2a** an amount of precipitation that would cover a surface with water one inch deep. **2b** a unit of pressure equal to a mercury column one inch high in a barometer. **3** a very small distance, degree, or amount. **4 every inch.** in every way; completely: *every inch an aristocrat.* **5 inch by inch.** gradually; little by little. **6 within an inch of one's life.** almost to death. ◆ *vb* **7** to move or be moved very slowly or in very small steps: *the car inched forward.* **8** (*tr*; foll. by *out*) to defeat (someone) by a very small margin. [OE *ynce*; see OUNCE[1]]

inch[2] (ɪntʃ) *n Scot. & Irish.* a small island. [C15: from Gaelic *innis* island; cf. Welsh *ynys*]

inchoate *adj* (ɪn'kəʊeɪt, -'kəʊɪt). **1** just beginning; incipient. **2** undeveloped; immature; rudimentary. ◆ *vb* (ɪn'kəʊeɪt), **inchoates, inchoating, inchoated.** (*tr*) **3** to begin. [C16: from L *incohāre* to make a beginning, lit.: to hitch up, from IN-[2] + *cohum* yokestrap]
▸**in'choately** *adv* ▸**in'choateness** *n* ▸ˌ**incho'ation** *n* ▸**inchoative** (ɪn'kəʊətɪv) *adj*

inchworm ('ɪntʃˌwɜːm) *n* another name for **measuring worm.**

incidence ⊕ ('ɪnsɪdəns) *n* **1** degree, extent, or frequency of occurrence; amount: *a high incidence of death from pneumonia.* **2** the act or manner of impinging on or affecting by proximity or influence. **3** *Physics.* the arrival of a beam of light or particles at a surface. See also **angle of incidence. 4** *Geom.* the partial coincidence of two configurations, such as a point on a circle.

incident ⊕ ('ɪnsɪdənt) *n* **1** a definite occurrence; event. **2** a minor, subsidiary, or related event. **3** a relatively insignificant event that might have serious consequences. **4** a public disturbance. ◆ *adj* **5** (*postpositive;* foll. by *to*) related (to) or dependent (on). **6** (when *postpositive,* often foll. by *to*) having a subsidiary or minor relationship (with). **7** (esp. of a beam of light or particles) arriving at or striking a surface. [C15: from Med. L, from L *incidere*, lit.: to fall into, hence befall, happen]

incidental ⊕ (ˌɪnsɪ'dɛntᵊl) *adj* **1** happening in connection with or resulting from something more important; casual or fortuitous. **2** (*postpositive;* foll. by *to*) found in connection (with); related (to). **3** (*postpositive;* foll. by *upon*) caused (by). **4** occasional or minor: *incidental expenses.* ◆ *n* **5** (*often pl*) a minor expense, event, or action.
▸ˌ**inci'dentalness** *n*

incidentally ⊕ (ˌɪnsɪ'dɛntəlɪ) *adv* **1** as a subordinate or chance occurrence. **2** (*sentence modifier*) by the way.

incidental music *n* background music for a film, etc.

incinerate ⊕ (ɪn'sɪnəˌreɪt) *vb* **incinerates, incinerating, incinerated.** to burn up completely; reduce to ashes. [C16: from Med. L, from L IN-[2] + *cinis* ashes]
▸**inˌciner'ation** *n*

incinerator (ɪn'sɪnəˌreɪtə) *n* a furnace or apparatus for incinerating something, esp. refuse.

incipient ⊕ (ɪn'sɪpɪənt) *adj* just starting to be or happen; beginning. [C17: from L, from *incipere* to begin, take in hand]
▸**in'cipience** *or* **in'cipiency** *n* ▸**in'cipiently** *adv*

incise ⊕ (ɪn'saɪz) *vb* **incises, incising, incised.** (*tr*) to produce (lines, a design, etc.) by cutting into the surface of (something) with a sharp tool. [C16: from L *incīdere* to cut into]

incision ⊕ (ɪn'sɪʒən) *n* **1** the act of incising. **2** a cut, gash, or notch. **3** a cut made with a knife during a surgical operation.

incisive ⊕ (ɪn'saɪsɪv) *adj* **1** keen, penetrating, or acute. **2** biting or sarcastic; mordant: *an incisive remark.* **3** having a sharp cutting edge: *incisive teeth.*
▸**in'cisively** *adv* ▸**in'cisiveness** *n*

incisor (ɪn'saɪzə) *n* a chisel-edged tooth at the front of the mouth.

incite ⊕ (ɪn'saɪt) *vb* **incites, inciting, incited.** (*tr*) to stir up or provoke to action. [C15: from L, from IN-[2] + *citāre* to excite]
▸ˌ**inci'tation** *n* ▸**in'citement** *n* ▸**in'citer** *n* ▸**in'citingly** *adv*

incivility ⊕ (ˌɪnsɪ'vɪlɪtɪ) *n, pl* **incivilities. 1** lack of civility or courtesy; rudeness. **2** an impolite or uncivil act or remark.

incl. *abbrev. for:* **1** including. **2** inclusive.

inclement ⊕ (ɪn'klɛmənt) *adj* **1** (of weather) stormy, severe, or tempestuous. **2** severe or merciless.
▸**in'clemency** *n* ▸**in'clemently** *adv*

inclination ⊕ (ˌɪnklɪ'neɪʃən) *n* **1** (often foll. by *for, to, towards,* or an infinitive) a particular disposition, esp. a liking; tendency: *I've no inclination for such dull work.* **2** the degree of deviation from a particular plane, esp. a horizontal or vertical plane. **3** a sloping or slanting surface; incline. **4** the act of inclining or the state of being inclined. **5** the act of bowing or nodding the head. **6** another name for **dip** (sense 24).
▸ˌ**incli'national** *adj*

incline ⊕ *vb* (ɪn'klaɪn), **inclines, inclining, inclined. 1** to deviate from a particular plane, esp. a vertical or horizontal plane; slope or slant. **2** (when *tr,* may take an infinitive) to be disposed or cause to be disposed (towards some attitude or to do something). **3** to bend or lower (part of the body, esp. the head), as in a bow or in order to listen. **4 incline one's ear.** to listen favourably (to). ◆ *n* ('ɪnklaɪn, ɪn'klaɪn). **5** an inclined surface or slope; gradient. [C13: from L *inclīnāre* to cause to lean, from *clīnāre* to bend; see LEAN[1]]
▸**in'clined** *adj* ▸**in'cliner** *n*

inclined plane *n* a plane whose angle to the horizontal is less than a right angle.

inclinometer (ˌɪnklɪ'nɒmɪtə) *n* an aircraft instrument that indicates the angle an aircraft makes with the horizontal.

THESAURUS

inception *n* = **beginning**, birth, commencement, dawn, inauguration, initiation, kickoff (*inf.*), origin, outset, rise, start
Antonyms *n* completion, conclusion, end, ending, finish, termination

incessant *adj* = **endless**, ceaseless, constant, continual, continuous, eternal, everlasting, interminable, never-ending, nonstop, perpetual, persistent, relentless, unbroken, unceasing, unending, unrelenting, unremitting
Antonyms *adj* infrequent, intermittent, occasional, periodic, rare, sporadic

incessantly *adv* = **endlessly**, all the time, ceaselessly, constantly, continually, eternally, everlastingly, interminably, nonstop, perpetually, persistently, without a break

incidence *n* **1** = **prevalence**, amount, degree, extent, frequency, occurrence, rate

incident *n* **1** = **happening**, adventure, circumstance, episode, event, fact, matter, occasion, occurrence **4** = **disturbance**, brush, clash, commotion, confrontation, contretemps, mishap, scene, skirmish

incidental *adj* **1** = **accidental**, casual, chance, fortuitous, odd, random **2** = **accompanying**, attendant, by-the-way, concomitant, contingent, contributory, related **4** = **secondary**, ancillary, minor, nonessential, occasional, subordinate, subsidiary ◆ *n* **5** *plural* = **odds and ends**, contingencies, extras, minutiae
Antonyms *adj* ≠ **secondary:** crucial, essential, important, necessary, vital

incidentally *adv* **1** = **accidentally**, by chance, casually, fortuitously **2** = **parenthetically**, by the bye, by the way, in passing

incinerate *vb* = **burn up**, carbonize, char, consume by fire, cremate, reduce to ashes

incipient *adj* = **beginning**, commencing, developing, embryonic, inceptive, inchoate, nascent, originating, starting

incise *vb* = **cut into**, carve, chisel, engrave, etch, inscribe

incision *n* **2** = **cut**, gash, notch, opening, slash, slit

incisive *adj* **1** = **penetrating**, acute, keen, perspicacious, piercing, sharp, trenchant
Antonyms *adj* dense, dull, superficial, vague, woolly

incisiveness *n* **1** = **perspicacity**, keenness, penetration, sharpness, trenchancy

incite *vb* = **provoke**, agitate for *or* against, animate, drive, egg on, encourage, excite, foment, goad, impel, inflame, instigate, prod, prompt, put up to, rouse, set on, spur, stimulate, stir up, urge, whip up
Antonyms *vb* dampen, deter, discourage, dishearten, dissuade, restrain

incitement *n* = **provocation**, agitation, clarion call, encouragement, goad, impetus, impulse, inducement, instigation, motivation, motive, prompting, spur, stimulus

incivility *n* **1** = **rudeness**, bad manners, boorishness, discourteousness, discourtesy, disrespect, ill-breeding, impoliteness, unmannerliness
Antonyms *n* civility, courteousness, courtesy, good manners, mannerliness, politeness, respect

inclemency *n* **1** = **storminess**, bitterness, boisterousness, rawness, rigour, roughness, severity **2** = **harshness**, callousness, cruelty, mercilessness, severity, tyranny, unfeelingness

inclement *adj* **1** = **stormy**, bitter, boisterous, foul, harsh, intemperate, rigorous, rough, severe, tempestuous **2** = **cruel**, callous, draconian, harsh, intemperate, merciless, pitiless, rigorous, severe, tyrannical, unfeeling, unmerciful
Antonyms *adj* ≠ **stormy:** balmy, calm, clement, fine, mild, pleasant, temperate ≠ **cruel:** compassionate, gentle, humane, kind, merciful, tender

inclination *n* **1** = **tendency**, affection, aptitude, bent, bias, desire, disposition, fancy, fondness, leaning, liking, partiality, penchant, predilection, predisposition, prejudice, proclivity, proneness, propensity, stomach, taste, thirst, turn, turn of mind, wish **2, 3** = **slope**, angle, bend, bending, deviation, gradient, incline, leaning, pitch, slant, tilt **5** = **bow**, bending, bowing, nod
Antonyms *n* ≠ **tendency:** antipathy, aversion, disinclination, dislike, revulsion

incline *vb* **1** = **slope**, bend, bevel, cant, deviate, diverge, heel, lean, slant, tend, tilt, tip, veer **2** = **predispose**, be disposed *or* predisposed, bias, influence, persuade, prejudice, sway, tend, turn **3** = **bend**, bow, lower, nod, stoop ◆ *n* **5** = **slope**, acclivity, ascent, declivity, descent, dip, grade, gradient, ramp, rise

inclined *adj* **2** = **disposed**, apt, given, liable, likely, minded, of a mind (*inf.*), predisposed, prone, willing

inclose ➊ (ɪn'kləʊz) *vb* **incloses, inclosing, inclosed.** a less common spelling of **enclose.**
▸**in'closure** *n*

include ➊ (ɪn'klu:d) *vb* **includes, including, included.** (*tr*) **1** to have as contents or part of the contents; be made up of or contain. **2** to add as part of something else; put in as part of a set, group, or category. **3** to contain as a secondary or minor ingredient or element. [C15 (in the sense: to enclose): from L, from IN-[2] + *claudere* to close]
▸**in'cludable** *or* **in'cludible** *adj*

include out *vb* (*tr, adv*) *Inf.* to exclude: *you can include me out of that deal.*

inclusion ➊ (ɪn'klu:ʒən) *n* **1** the act of including or the state of being included. **2** something included.

inclusion body *n Pathol.* any of the small particles found in cells infected with certain viruses.

inclusive ➊ (ɪn'klu:sɪv) *adj* **1** (*postpositive;* foll. by *of*) considered together (with): *capital inclusive of profit.* **2** (*postpositive*) including the limits specified: *Monday to Friday inclusive.* **3** comprehensive. **4** *Logic.* (of a disjunction) true if at least one of its component propositions is true.
▸**in'clusively** *adv* ▸**in'clusiveness** *n*

incognito ➊ (,ɪnkɒg'ni:təʊ, ɪn'kɒgnɪtəʊ) *or* (*fem*) **incognita** *adv, adj* (*postpositive*) **1** under an assumed name or appearance; in disguise. ◆ *n, pl* **incognitos** *or* (*fem*) **incognitas. 2** a person who is incognito. **3** the assumed name or disguise of such a person. [C17: from It., from L *incognitus* unknown]

incognizant (ɪn'kɒgnɪzənt) *adj* (when *postpositive,* often foll. by *of*) unaware (of).
▸**in'cognizance** *n*

incoherent ➊ (,ɪnkəʊ'hɪərənt) *adj* **1** lacking in clarity or organization; disordered. **2** unable to express oneself clearly; inarticulate. **3** *Physics.* (of two or more waves) having the same frequency but not the same phase: *incoherent light.*
▸**,inco'herently** *adv* ▸**,inco'herence** *or* **,inco'herency** *n*

income ➊ ('ɪnkʌm, 'ɪnkəm) *n* **1** the amount of monetary or other returns, either earned or unearned, accruing over a given period of time. **2** receipts; revenue. [C13 (in the sense: arrival, entrance): from OE *incumen* a coming in]

incomer ➊ ('ɪnkʌmə) *n* a person who comes to live in a place in which he was not born.

incomes policy *n* an economic policy that attempts to reduce or control inflation by limiting incomes.

income support *n* (in Britain, formerly) a social security payment for people on very low incomes.

income tax *n* a personal tax levied on annual income subject to certain deductions.

incoming ➊ ('ɪn,kʌmɪŋ) *adj* **1** coming in; entering. **2** about to come into office; succeeding. **3** (of interest, dividends, etc.) being received; accruing. ◆ *n* **4** the act of coming in; entrance. **5** (*usually pl*) income or revenue.

incommensurable (,ɪnkə'mɛnʃərəb^əl) *adj* **1** incapable of being judged, measured, or considered comparatively. **2** (*postpositive;* foll. by *with*) not in accordance; incommensurate. **3** *Maths.* not having a common factor other than 1, such as 2 and $\sqrt{-5}$. ◆ *n* **4** something incommensurable.
▸**,incom,mensura'bility** *n* ▸**,incom'mensurably** *adv*

incommensurate ➊ (,ɪnkə'mɛnʃərɪt) *adj* **1** (when *postpositive,* often foll. by *with*) not commensurate; disproportionate. **2** incommensurable.
▸**,incom'mensurately** *adv* ▸**,incom'mensurateness** *n*

incommode ➊ (,ɪnkə'məʊd) *vb* **incommodes, incommoding, incommoded.** (*tr*) to bother, disturb, or inconvenience. [C16: from L *incommodāre* to be troublesome, from *incommodus* inconvenient; see COMMODE]

incommodious (,ɪnkə'məʊdɪəs) *adj* **1** insufficiently spacious; cramped. **2** troublesome or inconvenient.
▸**,incom'modiously** *adv*

incommodity (,ɪnkə'mɒdɪtɪ) *n, pl* **incommodities.** anything that causes inconvenience.

incommunicado ➊ (,ɪnkə,mju:nɪ'kɑ:dəʊ) *adv, adj* (*postpositive*) deprived of communication with other people, as while in solitary confinement. [C19: from Sp., from *incomunicar* to deprive of communication; see IN-[1], COMMUNICATE]

incomparable ➊ (ɪn'kɒmpərəb^əl, -prəb^əl) *adj* **1** beyond or above comparison; matchless; unequalled. **2** lacking a basis for comparison; not having qualities or features that can be compared.
▸**in,compara'bility** *or* **in'comparableness** *n* ▸**in'comparably** *adv*

incompatible ➊ (,ɪnkəm'pætəb^əl) *adj* **1** incapable of living or existing together in harmony; conflicting. **2** opposed in nature or quality; inconsistent. **3** *Med.* (esp. of two drugs or two types of blood) incapable of being combined or used together; antagonistic. **4** *Logic.* (of two propositions) unable to be both true at the same time. **5** (of plants) incapable of self-fertilization. ◆ *n* **6** (*often pl*) a person or thing that is incompatible with another.
▸**,incom,pati'bility** *or* **,incom'patibleness** *n* ▸**,incom'patibly** *adv*

incompetent ➊ (ɪn'kɒmpɪtənt) *adj* **1** not possessing the necessary ability, skill, etc., to do or carry out a task; incapable. **2** marked by lack of ability, skill, etc. **3** *Law.* not legally qualified: *an incompetent witness.* ◆ *n* **4** an incompetent person.
▸**in'competence** *or* **in'competency** *n* ▸**in'competently** *adv*

incomplete ➊ (,ɪnkəm'pli:t) *adj* **1** not complete or finished. **2** not completely developed; imperfect.
▸**,incom'pletely** *adv* ▸**,incom'pleteness** *or* **,incom'pletion** *n*

incomprehensible ➊ (,ɪnkɒmprɪ'hensəb^əl, ɪn'kɒm-) *adj* **1** incapable of being understood; unintelligible. **2** *Archaic.* limitless; boundless.
▸**,incompre,hensi'bility** *or* **,incompre'hensibleness** *n* ▸**,incompre'hensibly** *adv*

inconceivable ➊ (,ɪnkən'si:vəb^əl) *adj* incapable of being conceived, imagined, or considered.
▸**,incon,ceiva'bility** *or* **,incon'ceivableness** *n* ▸**,incon'ceivably** *adv*

inconclusive ➊ (,ɪnkən'klu:sɪv) *adj* not conclusive or decisive; not finally settled; indeterminate.
▸**,incon'clusively** *adv* ▸**,incon'clusiveness** *n*

incongruous ➊ (ɪn'kɒŋgrʊəs) *or* **incongruent** *adj* **1** (when *postpositive,*

THESAURUS

inclose *see* **enclose**

include *vb* **1** = **contain**, comprehend, comprise, cover, embody, embrace, encompass, incorporate, involve, subsume, take in, take into account **2** = **introduce**, add, allow for, build in, count, enter, insert, number among
Antonyms *vb* eliminate, exclude, leave out, omit, rule out

inclusion *n* **1** = **addition**, incorporation, insertion
Antonyms *n* exception, exclusion, omission, rejection

inclusive *adj* **3** = **comprehensive**, across-the-board, all-embracing, all in, all together, blanket, catch-all (*chiefly US*), full, general, global, *in toto*, overall, overarching, sweeping, umbrella, without exception
Antonyms *adj* confined, exclusive, limited, narrow, restricted, unique

incognito *adj* **1** = **in disguise**, disguised, under an assumed name, unknown, unrecognized

incoherence *n* **1** = **disjointedness**, disconnectedness **2** = **unintelligibility**, inarticulateness

incoherent *adj* **1** = **disordered**, confused, disconnected, disjointed, inconsistent, jumbled, loose, muddled, unconnected, uncoordinated, wild **2** = **unintelligible**, inarticulate, rambling, stammering, stuttering, wandering
Antonyms *adj* coherent, connected, intelligible, logical, rational

income *n* **1, 2** = **revenue**, earnings, gains, interest, means, pay, proceeds, profits, receipts, salary, takings, wages

incomer *n* = **immigrant**

incoming *adj* **1** = **arriving**, approaching, entering, homeward, landing, returning **2** = **succeeding**, new
Antonyms *adj* ≠ **arriving**: departing, exiting, leaving, outgoing

incommensurate *adj* **1** = **disproportionate**, inadequate, inequitable, insufficient, unequal

incommode *vb* = **inconvenience**, annoy, be a trouble to, bother, disturb, embarrass, get in one's hair (*inf.*), give (someone) bother *or* trouble, hassle (*inf.*), hinder, impede, irk, put out, put (someone) to trouble, trouble, upset, vex

incommunicado *adv* = **in purdah**, under house arrest

incomparable *adj* **1** = **unequalled**, beyond compare, inimitable, matchless, paramount, peerless, superlative, supreme, transcendent, unmatched, unparalleled, unrivalled

incomparably *adv* **1** = **immeasurably**, beyond compare, by far, easily, eminently, far and away

incompatibility *n* **1, 2** = **inconsistency**, antagonism, conflict, discrepancy, disparateness, incongruity, irreconcilability, uncongeniality

incompatible *adj* **1, 2** = **inconsistent**, antagonistic, antipathetic, conflicting, contradictory, discordant, discrepant, disparate, ill-assorted, incongruous, inconsonant, irreconcilable, mismatched, uncongenial, unsuitable, unsuited
Antonyms *adj* alike, appropriate, compatible, congenial, consistent, harmonious, reconcilable, suitable, suited

incompetence *n* **2** = **ineptitude**, inability, inadequacy, incapability, incapacity, incompetency, ineffectiveness, ineptness, insufficiency, unfitness, uselessness

incompetent *adj* **2** = **inept**, bungling, cowboy (*inf.*), floundering, incapable, incapacitated, ineffectual, inexpert, insufficient, unable, unfit, unfitted, unskilful, useless
Antonyms *adj* able, capable, competent, expert, fit, proficient, skilful

incomplete *adj* **1** = **unfinished**, broken, defective, deficient, fragmentary, imperfect, insufficient, lacking, partial, short, unaccomplished, undeveloped, undone, unexecuted, wanting
Antonyms *adj* accomplished, complete, developed, finished, perfect, unified, whole

incomprehensible *adj* **1** = **unintelligible**, above one's head, all Greek to one (*inf.*), baffling, beyond comprehension, beyond one's grasp, enigmatic, impenetrable, inconceivable, inscrutable, mysterious, obscure, opaque, perplexing, puzzling, unfathomable, unimaginable, unthinkable
Antonyms *adj* apparent, clear, comprehensible, conceivable, evident, intelligible, manifest, obvious, understandable

inconceivable *adj* = **unimaginable**, beyond belief, impossible, incomprehensible, incredible, mind-boggling (*inf.*), not to be thought of, out of the question, staggering (*inf.*), unbelievable, unheard-of, unknowable, unthinkable
Antonyms *adj* believable, comprehensible, conceivable, credible, imaginable, likely, plausible, possible, reasonable

inconclusive *adj* = **indecisive**, ambiguous, indeterminate, open, uncertain, unconvincing, undecided, unsettled, up in the air (*inf.*), vague

incongruous *adj* **1** = **inappropriate**, absurd, conflicting, contradictory, contrary, disconsonant, discordant, extraneous, improper, inapt, incoherent, incompatible, inconsistent, out of keeping, out of place, unbecoming, unsuitable, unsuited
Antonyms *adj* appropriate, becoming, compatible, consistent, harmonious, suitable, suited

incongruousness *n* **1** = **inappropriateness**, conflict, discrepancy, disparity, inaptness, in-

foll. by *with* or *to*) incompatible with (what is suitable); inappropriate. **2** containing disparate or discordant elements or parts.
▸**in'congruously** *adv* ▸**in'congruousness** *or* **incongruity** (ˌɪnkɒŋ'gruːɪtɪ) *n*

inconnu ('ɪnkənjuː, 'ɪnkənuː) *n Canad.* a whitefish of Far Northern waters. [C19: from F, lit: unknown]

inconsequential ⓣ (ˌɪnkɒnsɪ'kwɛnʃəl, ɪnˌkɒn-) *or* **inconsequent** (ɪn'kɒnsɪkwənt) *adj* **1** not following logically as a consequence. **2** trivial or insignificant. **3** not in a logical sequence; haphazard.
▸ˌ**inconseˌquenti'ality,** ˌ**inconse'quentialness,** *or* **in'consequence** *n* ▸ˌ**inconse'quentially** *or* **in'consequently** *adv*

inconsiderable ⓣ (ˌɪnkən'sɪdərəbᵊl) *adj* **1** relatively small. **2** not worthy of consideration; insignificant.
▸ˌ**incon'siderableness** *n* ▸ˌ**incon'siderably** *adv*

inconsiderate ⓣ (ˌɪnkən'sɪdərɪt) *adj* lacking in care or thought for others; thoughtless.
▸ˌ**incon'siderately** *adv* ▸ˌ**incon'siderateness** *or* ˌ**inconˌsider'ation** *n*

inconsistency ⓣ (ˌɪnkən'sɪstənsɪ) *n, pl* **inconsistencies. 1** lack of consistency or agreement; incompatibility. **2** an inconsistent feature or quality.

inconsistent ⓣ (ˌɪnkən'sɪstənt) *adj* **1** lacking in consistency, agreement, or compatibility; at variance. **2** containing contradictory elements. **3** irregular or fickle in behaviour or mood. **4** *Logic.* (of a set of propositions) enabling an explicit contradiction to be validly derived.
▸ˌ**incon'sistently** *adv*

inconsolable ⓣ (ˌɪnkən'səʊləbᵊl) *adj* incapable of being consoled or comforted; disconsolate.
▸ˌ**inconˌsola'bility** *or* ˌ**incon'solableness** *n* ▸ˌ**incon'solably** *adv*

inconsonant (ɪn'kɒnsənənt) *adj* lacking in harmony or compatibility; discordant.
▸**in'consonance** *n* ▸**in'consonantly** *adv*

inconspicuous ⓣ (ˌɪnkən'spɪkjʊəs) *adj* not easily noticed or seen; not prominent or striking.
▸ˌ**incon'spicuously** *adv* ▸ˌ**incon'spicuousness** *n*

incontinent[1] ⓣ (ɪn'kɒntɪnənt) *adj* **1** relating to or exhibiting involuntary urination or defecation. **2** lacking in restraint or control, esp. sexually. **3** (foll. by *of*) having little or no control (over). **4** unrestrained; uncontrolled. [C14: from OF, from L, from IN-[1] + *continere* to hold, restrain]
▸**in'continence** *n* ▸**in'continently** *adv*

incontinent[2] (ɪn'kɒntɪnənt) *or* **incontinently** *adv* obsolete words for **immediately.** [C15: from LL *in continentī tempore,* lit.: in continuous time, that is, with no interval]

incontrovertible ⓣ (ˌɪnkɒntrə'vɜːtəbᵊl, ɪnˌkɒn-) *adj* incapable of being contradicted or disputed; undeniable.
▸ˌ**incontroˌverti'bility** *n* ▸ˌ**incontro'vertibly** *adv*

inconvenience ⓣ (ˌɪnkən'viːnjəns, -'viːnɪəns) *n* **1** the state or quality of being inconvenient. **2** something inconvenient; a hindrance, trouble, or difficulty. ◆ *vb* **3** (*tr*) to cause inconvenience to; trouble or harass.

inconvenient ⓣ (ˌɪnkən'viːnjənt, -'viːnɪənt) *adj* not convenient; troublesome, awkward, or difficult.
▸ˌ**incon'veniently** *adv*

incorporate ⓣ *vb* (ɪn'kɔːpəˌreɪt), **incorporates, incorporating, incorporated. 1** to include or be included as a part or member of a united whole. **2** to form a united whole or mass; merge or blend. **3** to form into a corporation or other organization with a separate legal identity. ◆ *adj* (ɪn'kɔːpərɪt, -prɪt). **4** combined into a whole; incorporated. **5** formed into or constituted as a corporation. [C14 (in the sense: put into the body of something else): from LL *incorporāre* to embody, from L IN-[2] + *corpus* body]
▸**in'corpoˌrated** *adj* ▸**inˌcorpo'ration** *n* ▸**in'corporative** *adj*

incorporeal (ˌɪnkɔː'pɔːrɪəl) *adj* **1** without material form, body, or substance. **2** spiritual or metaphysical. **3** *Law.* having no material existence but existing by reason of its annexation of something material: *an incorporeal hereditament.*
▸ˌ**incor'poreally** *adv* ▸**incorporeity** (ɪnˌkɔːpə'riːɪtɪ) *or* ˌ**incorpore'ality** *n*

incorrect ⓣ (ˌɪnkə'rekt) *adj* **1** false; wrong: *an incorrect calculation.* **2** not fitting or proper: *incorrect behaviour.*
▸ˌ**incor'rectly** *adv* ▸ˌ**incor'rectness** *n*

incorrigible ⓣ (ɪn'kɒrɪdʒəbᵊl) *adj* **1** beyond correction, reform, or alteration. **2** firmly rooted; ineradicable. ◆ *n* **3** a person or animal that is incorrigible.
▸**inˌcorrigi'bility** *or* **in'corrigibleness** *n* ▸**in'corrigibly** *adv*

incorruptible ⓣ (ˌɪnkə'rʌptəbᵊl) *adj* **1** incapable of being corrupted; honest; just. **2** not subject to decay or decomposition.
▸ˌ**incorˌrupti'bility** *n* ▸ˌ**incor'ruptibly** *adv*

incr. *abbrev. for:* **1** increase. **2** increased. **3** increasing.

incrassate *adj* (ɪn'kræsɪt, -eɪt), *also* **incrassated. 1** *Biol.* thickened or swollen. ◆ *vb* (ɪn'kræseɪt), **incrassates, incrassating, incrassated. 2** *Obs.* to make or become thicker. [C17: from LL, from L *crassus* thick, dense]
▸ˌ**incras'sation** *n*

increase ⓣ *vb* (ɪn'kriːs), **increases, increasing, increased. 1** to make or become greater in size, degree, frequency, etc.; grow or expand. ◆ *n* ('ɪnkriːs). **2** the act of increasing; augmentation. **3** the amount by which something increases. **4 on the increase.** increasing, esp. becoming more frequent. [C14: from OF *encreistre,* from L, from IN-[2] + *crēscere* to grow]
▸**in'creasable** *adj* ▸**increasedly** (ɪn'kriːsɪdlɪ) *or* **in'creasingly** *adv* ▸**in'creaser** *n*

incredible ⓣ (ɪn'krɛdəbᵊl) *adj* **1** beyond belief or understanding; unbelievable. **2** *Inf.* marvellous; amazing.
▸**inˌcredi'bility** *or* **in'credibleness** *n* ▸**in'credibly** *adv*

THESAURUS

compatibility, inconsistency, inharmoniousness, unsuitability

inconsequential *adj* **2** = **unimportant**, immaterial, inconsiderable, insignificant, measly, minor, negligible, nickel-and-dime (*US sl.*), of no significance, paltry, petty, trifling, trivial

inconsiderable *adj* **2** = **insignificant**, exiguous, inconsequential, light, minor, negligible, petty, slight, small, small-time (*inf.*), trifling, trivial, unimportant

inconsiderate *adj* = **selfish**, careless, indelicate, insensitive, intolerant, rude, self-centred, tactless, thoughtless, uncharitable, ungracious, unkind, unthinking
Antonyms *adj* attentive, careful, considerate, gracious, kind, sensitive, tactful, thoughtful, tolerant

inconsistency *n* **1** = **incompatibility**, contrariety, disagreement, discrepancy, disparity, divergence, incongruity, inconsonance, paradox, variance

inconsistent *adj* **1** = **incompatible**, at odds, at variance, conflicting, contradictory, contrary, discordant, discrepant, incoherent, in conflict, incongruous, inconstant, irreconcilable, out of step **3** = **changeable**, capricious, erratic, fickle, inconstant, irregular, uneven, unpredictable, unstable, unsteady, vagarious (*rare*), variable
Antonyms *adj* ≠ **incompatible:** coherent, compatible, homogeneous, orderly, reconcilable, uniform ≠ **changeable:** consistent, constant, predictable, reliable, stable, steady, unchanging

inconsistently *adv* **1** = **unpredictably**, contradictorily, differently, eccentrically, erratically, inequably, randomly, unequally, unfairly, variably

inconsolable *adj* = **heartbroken**, brokenhearted, desolate, despairing, heartsick, prostrate with grief, sick at heart

inconspicuous *adj* = **unobtrusive**, camouflaged, hidden, insignificant, modest, muted, ordinary, plain, quiet, retiring, unassuming, unnoticeable, unostentatious
Antonyms *adj* bold, conspicuous, noticeable, obtrusive, obvious, salient, significant, visible

incontinent[1] *adj* **2** = **promiscuous**, debauched, lascivious, lecherous, lewd, loose, lustful, profligate, unchaste, wanton **4** = **unrestrained**, unbridled, unchecked, uncontrollable, uncontrolled, ungovernable, ungoverned

incontrovertible *adj* = **indisputable**, beyond dispute, certain, established, incontestable, indubitable, irrefutable, positive, sure, undeniable, unquestionable, unshakable

inconvenience *n* **1** = **awkwardness**, cumbersomeness, unfitness, unhandiness, unsuitableness, untimeliness, unwieldiness **2** = **trouble**, annoyance, awkwardness, bother, difficulty, disadvantage, disruption, disturbance, downside, drawback, fuss, hassle (*inf.*), hindrance, nuisance, uneasiness, upset, vexation ◆ *vb* **3** = **trouble**, bother, discommode, disrupt, disturb, give (someone) bother *or* trouble, hassle (*inf.*), irk, make (someone) go out of his way, put out, put to trouble, upset

inconvenient *adj* = **troublesome**, annoying, awkward, bothersome, cumbersome, difficult, disadvantageous, disturbing, embarrassing, inopportune, tiresome, unhandy, unmanageable, unseasonable, unsuitable, untimely, unwieldy, vexatious
Antonyms *adj* convenient, handy, opportune, seasonable, suitable, timely

incorporate *vb* **1, 2** = **include**, absorb, amalgamate, assimilate, blend, coalesce, combine, consolidate, embody, fuse, integrate, meld, merge, mix, subsume, unite

incorporation *n* **1, 2** = **inclusion**, absorption, amalgamation, assimilation, blend, coalescence, federation, fusion, integration, merger, unifying

incorrect *adj* **1** = **false**, erroneous, faulty, flawed, inaccurate, inexact, mistaken, off base (*US & Canad. inf.*), off beam (*inf.*), out, specious, untrue, wide of the mark (*inf.*), wrong **2** = **inappropriate**, improper, unfitting, unsuitable, wrong
Antonyms *adj* ≠ **false:** accurate, correct, exact, faultless, right, true ≠ **inappropriate:** fitting, flawless, suitable

incorrectness *n* **1** = **inaccuracy**, erroneousness, error, fallacy, faultiness, impreciseness, imprecision, inexactness, speciousness, unsoundness **2** = **impropriety**, unsuitability, wrongness

incorrigible *adj* **1** = **incurable**, hardened, hopeless, intractable, inveterate, irredeemable, unreformed

incorruptibility *n* **1** = **integrity**, honesty, honour, justness, uprightness

incorruptible *adj* **1** = **honest**, above suspicion, honourable, just, straight, trustworthy, unbribable, upright **2** = **imperishable**, everlasting, undecaying

increase *vb* **1** = **grow**, add to, advance, aggrandize, amplify, augment, boost, build up, develop, dilate, enhance, enlarge, escalate, expand, extend, heighten, inflate, intensify, magnify, mount, multiply, proliferate, prolong, raise, snowball, spread, step up (*inf.*), strengthen, swell, wax ◆ *n* **2** = **growth**, addition, augmentation, boost, development, enlargement, escalation, expansion, extension, gain, increment, intensification, rise, upsurge, upturn **4 on the increase** = **growing**, developing, escalating, expanding, increasing, multiplying, on the rise, proliferating, spreading
Antonyms *vb* ≠ **grow:** abate, abbreviate, abridge, condense, curtail, decline, decrease, deflate, diminish, dwindle, lessen, reduce, shorten, shrink

increasingly *adv* **1** = **progressively**, more and more, to an increasing extent

incredible *adj* **1** = **implausible**, absurd, beyond belief, cock-and-bull (*inf.*), far-fetched, impossible, improbable, inconceivable, not able to hold water, preposterous, unbelievable, unimaginable, unthinkable **2** *Informal* = **amaz-**

incredulity ⓣ (ˌɪnkrɪˈdjuːlɪtɪ) *n* lack of belief; scepticism.

incredulous ⓣ (ɪnˈkrɛdjʊləs) *adj* (often foll. by *of*) not prepared or willing to believe (something); unbelieving.
▸**inˈcredulously** *adv* ▸**inˈcredulousness** *n*

increment ⓣ (ˈɪnkrɪmənt) *n* **1** an increase or addition, esp. one of a series. **2** the act of increasing; augmentation. **3** *Maths.* a small positive or negative change in a variable or function. [C15: from L *incrēmentum* growth, INCREASE]
▸**incremental** (ˌɪnkrɪˈmɛntᵊl) *adj*

incremental plotter *n* a device that plots graphs on paper from computer-generated instructions.

incriminate ⓣ (ɪnˈkrɪmɪˌneɪt) *vb* **incriminates, incriminating, incriminated.** (*tr*) **1** to imply or suggest the guilt or error of (someone). **2** to charge with a crime or fault. [C18: from LL *incrīmināre* to accuse, from L *crīmen* accusation; see CRIME]
▸**inˌcrimiˈnation** *n* ▸**inˈcrimiˌnator** *n* ▸**inˈcriminatory** *adj*

incrust (ɪnˈkrʌst) *vb* a variant spelling of **encrust.**
▸**inˈcrustant** *n, adj* ▸ˌ**incrusˈtation** *n*

incubate (ˈɪnkjʊˌbeɪt) *vb* **incubates, incubating, incubated. 1** (of birds) to supply (eggs) with heat for their development, esp. by sitting on them. **2** to cause (bacteria, etc.) to develop, esp. in an incubator or culture medium. **3** (*intr*) (of embryos, etc.) to develop in favourable conditions, esp. in an incubator. **4** (*intr*) (of disease germs) to remain inactive in an animal or human before causing disease. **5** to develop gradually; foment or be fomented. [C18: from L *incubāre* to lie upon, hatch, from IN-[2] + *cubāre* to lie down]
▸ˌ**incuˈbation** *n* ▸ˌ**incuˈbational** *adj* ▸ˈ**incuˌbative** *or* ˈ**incuˌbatory** *adj*

incubation period *n Med.* the time between exposure to an infectious disease and the appearance of the first signs or symptoms.

incubator (ˈɪnkjʊˌbeɪtə) *n* **1** *Med.* an apparatus for housing prematurely born babies until they are strong enough to survive. **2** a container in which birds' eggs can be artificially hatched or bacterial cultures grown. **3** a person, animal, or thing that incubates.

incubus (ˈɪnkjʊbəs) *n, pl* **incubi** (-ˌbaɪ) *or* **incubuses. 1** a demon believed in folklore to have sexual intercourse with sleeping women. Cf. **succubus. 2** something that oppresses or disturbs greatly, esp. a nightmare or obsession. [C14: from LL, from L *incubāre* to lie upon; see INCUBATE]

inculcate (ˈɪnkʌlˌkeɪt, ɪnˈkʌlkeɪt) *vb* **inculcates, inculcating, inculcated.** (*tr*) to instil by insistent repetition. [C16: from L *inculcāre* to tread upon, ram down, from IN-[2] + *calcāre* to trample, from *calx* heel]
▸ˌ**inculˈcation** *n* ▸ˈ**inculˌcator** *n*

inculpate (ˈɪnkʌlˌpeɪt, ɪnˈkʌlpeɪt) *vb* **inculpates, inculpating, inculpated.** (*tr*) to incriminate; cause blame to be imputed to. [C18: from LL, from L *culpāre* to blame, from *culpa* fault, blame]
▸ˌ**inculˈpation** *n* ▸**inculpative** (ɪnˈkʌlpətɪv) *or* **inculpatory** (ɪnˈkʌlpətərɪ, -trɪ) *adj*

incumbency (ɪnˈkʌmbənsɪ) *n, pl* **incumbencies. 1** the state or quality of being incumbent. **2** the office, duty, or tenure of an incumbent.

incumbent ⓣ (ɪnˈkʌmbənt) *adj* **1** *Formal.* (often *postpositive* and foll. by *on* or *upon* and an infinitive) morally binding; obligatory: *it is incumbent on me to attend.* **2** (usually *postpositive* and foll. by *on*) resting or lying (on). **3** (usually *prenominal*) occupying or holding an office. ◆ *n* **4** a person who holds an office, esp. a clergyman holding a benefice. [C16: from L *incumbere* to lie upon, devote one's attention to]

incunabula (ˌɪnkjʊˈnæbjʊlə) *pl n, sing* **incunabulum** (-ləm). **1** any book printed before 1500. **2** the earliest stages of something; beginnings. [C19: from L, orig.: swaddling clothes, hence beginnings, from IN-[2] + *cūnābula* cradle]
▸ˌ**incuˈnabular** *adj*

incur ⓣ (ɪnˈkɜː) *vb* **incurs, incurring, incurred.** (*tr*) **1** to make oneself subject to (something undesirable); bring upon oneself. **2** to run into or encounter. [C16: from L *incurrere* to run into, from *currere* to run]
▸**inˈcurrable** *adj*

incurable ⓣ (ɪnˈkjʊərəbᵊl) *adj* **1** (esp. of a disease) not curable; unresponsive to treatment. ◆ *n* **2** a person having an incurable disease.
▸**inˌcuraˈbility** *or* **inˈcurableness** *n* ▸**inˈcurably** *adv*

incurious ⓣ (ɪnˈkjʊərɪəs) *adj* not curious; indifferent or uninterested.
▸**incuriosity** (ɪnˌkjʊərɪˈɒsɪtɪ) *or* **inˈcuriousness** *n* ▸**inˈcuriously** *adv*

incursion ⓣ (ɪnˈkɜːʃən) *n* **1** a sudden invasion, attack, or raid. **2** the act of running or leaking into; penetration. [C15: from L *incursiō* onset, attack, from *incurrere* to run into; see INCUR]
▸**incursive** (ɪnˈkɜːsɪv) *adj*

incus (ˈɪŋkəs) *n, pl* **incudes** (ɪnˈkjuːdiːz). the central of the three small bones in the middle ear of mammals. Cf. **malleus, stapes.** [C17: from L: anvil, from *incūdere* to forge]

incuse (ɪnˈkjuːz) *n* **1** a design stamped or hammered onto a coin. ◆ *vb* **incuses, incusing, incused. 2** to impress (a coin) with a design by hammering or stamping. ◆ *adj* **3** stamped or hammered onto a coin. [C19: from L *incūsus* hammered; see INCUS]

ind. *abbrev. for:* **1** independence. **2** independent. **3** index. **4** indicative. **5** indirect. **6** industrial. **7** industry.

Ind. *abbrev. for:* **1** Independent. **2** India. **3** Indian. **4** Indies.

indaba (ɪnˈdɑːbə) *n* **1** (among Bantu peoples of southern Africa) a meeting to discuss a serious topic. **2** *S. African inf.* a matter of concern or for discussion. [C19: from Zulu: topic]

indebted ⓣ (ɪnˈdɛtɪd) *adj* (*postpositive*) **1** owing gratitude for help, favours, etc.; obligated. **2** owing money.

indebtedness (ɪnˈdɛtɪdnɪs) *n* **1** the state of being indebted. **2** the total of a person's debts.

indecency ⓣ (ɪnˈdiːsənsɪ) *n, pl* **indecencies. 1** the state or quality of being indecent. **2** an indecent act, etc.

indecent ⓣ (ɪnˈdiːsᵊnt) *adj* **1** offensive to standards of decency, esp. in sexual matters. **2** unseemly or improper (esp. in **indecent haste**).
▸**inˈdecently** *adv*

indecent assault *n* the offence of subjecting a person to a form of sexual activity, other than rape, against his or her will.

indecent exposure *n* the offence of indecently exposing one's body in public, esp. the genitals.

indecisive ⓣ (ˌɪndɪˈsaɪsɪv) *adj* **1** (of a person) vacillating; irresolute. **2** not decisive or conclusive.
▸ˌ**indeˈcision** *or* ˌ**indeˈcisiveness** *n* ▸ˌ**indeˈcisively** *adv*

indecorum ⓣ (ˌɪndɪˈkɔːrəm) *n* lack of decorum; unseemliness.
▸**inˈdecorous** *adj*

indeed ⓣ (ɪnˈdiːd) (*sentence connector*). **1** certainly; actually: *indeed, it may never happen.* ◆ *adv* **2** (intensifier): *that is indeed amazing.* **3** or rather; what is more: *a comfortable, indeed wealthy family.* ◆ *interj* **4** an expression of doubt, surprise, etc.

indef. *abbrev. for* indefinite.

indefatigable ⓣ (ˌɪndɪˈfætɪgəbᵊl) *adj* unable to be tired out; unflagging. [C16: from L, from *fatigāre* to tire]
▸ˌ**indeˌfatigaˈbility** *n* ▸ˌ**indeˈfatigably** *adv*

indefeasible (ˌɪndɪˈfiːzəbᵊl) *adj Law.* not liable to be annulled or forfeited.
▸ˌ**indeˌfeasiˈbility** *n* ▸ˌ**indeˈfeasibly** *adv*

indefensible ⓣ (ˌɪndɪˈfɛnsəbᵊl) *adj* **1** not justifiable or excusable. **2** capable of being disagreed with; untenable. **3** incapable of defence against attack.
▸ˌ**indeˌfensiˈbility** *n* ▸ˌ**indeˈfensibly** *adv*

indefinite ⓣ (ɪnˈdɛfɪnɪt) *adj* **1** not certain or determined; unsettled. **2**

THESAURUS

ing, astonishing, astounding, awe-inspiring, brilliant, extraordinary, far-out (*sl.*), great, marvellous, prodigious, sensational (*inf.*), superhuman, wonderful

incredulity *n* = **disbelief**, distrust, doubt, scepticism, unbelief

incredulous *adj* = **disbelieving**, distrustful, doubtful, doubting, dubious, mistrustful, sceptical, suspicious, unbelieving, unconvinced
Antonyms *adj* believing, credulous, gullible, naive, trusting, unsuspecting, wet behind the ears (*inf.*)

increment *n* **1, 2** = **increase**, accretion, accrual, accruement, addition, advancement, augmentation, enlargement, gain, step up, supplement

incriminate *vb* **1, 2** = **implicate**, accuse, arraign, blacken the name of, blame, charge, impeach, inculpate, indict, involve, point the finger at (*inf.*), stigmatize

incumbent *adj Formal* **1** = **obligatory**, binding, compulsory, mandatory, necessary

incur *vb* **1** = **earn**, arouse, bring (upon oneself), contract, draw, expose oneself to, gain, induce, lay oneself open to, meet with, provoke

incurable *adj* **1** = **fatal**, inoperable, irrecoverable, irremediable, remediless, terminal

incurious *adj* = **indifferent**, apathetic, pococurante, unconcerned, uninquiring, uninterested

incursion *n* **1** = **foray**, infiltration, inroad, invasion, irruption, penetration, raid

indebted *adj* **1** = **grateful**, beholden, in debt, obligated, obliged, under an obligation

indecency *n* **1** = **obscenity**, bawdiness, coarseness, crudity, foulness, grossness, immodesty, impropriety, impurity, indecorum, indelicacy, lewdness, licentiousness, outrageousness, pornography, smut, smuttiness, unseemliness, vileness, vulgarity
Antonyms *n* decency, decorum, delicacy, modesty, propriety, purity, seemliness

indecent *adj* **1** = **lewd**, blue, coarse, crude, dirty, filthy, foul, gross, immodest, improper, impure, indelicate, licentious, pornographic, salacious, scatological, smutty, vile **2** = **unbecoming**, ill-bred, improper, in bad taste, indecorous, offensive, outrageous, tasteless, unseemly, vulgar
Antonyms *adj* decent, decorous, delicate, modest, proper, pure, respectable, seemly, tasteful

indecision *n* **1** = **hesitation**, ambivalence, dithering (*chiefly Brit.*), doubt, hesitancy, indecisiveness, irresolution, shilly-shallying (*inf.*), uncertainty, vacillation, wavering

indecisive *adj* **1** = **hesitating**, dithering (*chiefly Brit.*), doubtful, faltering, in two minds (*inf.*), irresolute, pussyfooting (*inf.*), tentative, uncertain, undecided, undetermined, vacillating, wavering **2** = **inconclusive**, indefinite, indeterminate, unclear, undecided
Antonyms *adj* ≠ **hesitating:** certain, decided, determined, positive, resolute, unhesitating ≠ **inconclusive:** clear, conclusive, decisive, definite, determinate, final

indecorous *adj* = **improper**, boorish, churlish, coarse, ill-bred, immodest, impolite, indecent, rude, tasteless, uncivil, uncouth, undignified, unmannerly, unseemly, untoward

indeed *adv* **2** = **really**, actually, certainly, doubtlessly, in point of fact, in truth, positively, strictly, to be sure, truly, undeniably, undoubtedly, verily (*arch.*), veritably

indefatigable *adj* = **tireless**, assiduous, diligent, dogged, inexhaustible, patient, persevering, pertinacious, relentless, sedulous, unflagging, unremitting, untiring, unwearied, unwearying

indefensible *adj* **1** = **unforgivable**, faulty, inexcusable, insupportable, unjustifiable, unpardonable, untenable, unwarrantable, wrong
Antonyms *adj* defensible, excusable, forgivable, justifiable, legitimate, pardonable, supportable, tenable, warrantable

indefinite *adj* **1-3** = **unclear**, ambiguous, confused, doubtful, equivocal, evasive, general, ill-

without exact limits; indeterminate: *an indefinite number.* **3** vague or unclear. **4** in traditional logic, a proposition in which it is not stated whether the subject is universal or particular, as in *men are mortal.*
▸**in'definitely** *adv* ▸**in'definiteness** *n*

indefinite article *n Grammar.* a determiner that expresses nonspecificity of reference, such as *a, an,* or *some.*

indehiscent (ˌɪndɪˈhɪsᵊnt) *adj* (of fruits, etc.) not dehiscent; not opening to release seeds, etc.
▸**ˌinde'hiscence** *n*

indelible ❶ (ɪnˈdɛlɪbᵊl) *adj* **1** incapable of being erased or obliterated. **2** making indelible marks: *indelible ink.* [C16: from L, from IN-[1] + *delēre* to destroy]
▸**inˌdeli'bility** *or* **in'delibleness** *n* ▸**in'delibly** *adv*

indelicate ❶ (ɪnˈdɛlɪkɪt) *adj* **1** coarse, crude, or rough. **2** offensive, embarrassing, or tasteless.
▸**in'delicacy** *or* **in'delicateness** *n* ▸**in'delicately** *adv*

indemnify ❶ (ɪnˈdɛmnɪˌfaɪ) *vb* **indemnifies, indemnifying, indemnified.** (*tr*) **1** to secure against future loss, damage, or liability; give security for; insure. **2** to compensate for loss, etc.; reimburse.
▸**inˌdemnifi'cation** *n* ▸**in'demniˌfier** *n*

indemnity ❶ (ɪnˈdɛmnɪtɪ) *n, pl* **indemnities. 1** compensation for loss or damage; reimbursement. **2** protection or insurance against future loss or damage. **3** legal exemption from penalties incurred through one's acts or defaults. **4** *Canad.* the annual salary paid by the government to a member of Parliament or of a provincial legislature. [C15: from LL, from *indemnis* uninjured, from L IN-[1] + *damnum* damage]

indene (ˈɪndiːn) *n* a colourless liquid hydrocarbon obtained from coal tar and used in making synthetic resins. Formula: C_9H_8. [C20: from INDOLE + -ENE]

indent[1] ❶ *vb* (ɪnˈdɛnt). (*mainly tr*) **1** to place (written matter, etc.) in from the margin. **2** to cut (a document in duplicate) so that the irregular lines may be matched. **3** *Chiefly Brit.* (in foreign trade) to place an order for (foreign goods). **4** (when *intr,* foll. by *for, on,* or *upon*) *Chiefly Brit.* to make an order on (a source or supply) or for (something). **5** to notch (an edge, border, etc.); make jagged. **6** to bind (an apprentice, etc.) by indenture. ◆ *n* (ˈɪnˌdɛnt). *Chiefly Brit.* **7** (in foreign trade) an order for foreign merchandise. **8** an official order for goods. [C14: from OF *endenter,* from EN-[1] + *dent* tooth, from L *dēns*]
▸**in'denter** *or* **in'dentor** *n*

indent[2] *vb* (ɪnˈdɛnt). **1** (*tr*) to make a dent or depression in. ◆ *n* (ˈɪnˌdɛnt). **2** a dent or depression. [C15: from IN-[2] + DENT]

indentation ❶ (ˌɪndɛnˈteɪʃən) *n* **1** a hollowed, notched, or cut place, as on an edge or on a coastline. **2** a series of hollows, notches, or cuts. **3** the act of indenting or the condition of being indented. **4** Also: **indention, indent.** the leaving of space or the amount of space left between a margin and the start of an indented line.

indention (ɪnˈdɛnʃən) *n* another word for **indentation** (sense 4).

indenture (ɪnˈdɛntʃə) *n* **1** any deed, contract, or sealed agreement between two or more parties. **2** (formerly) a deed drawn up in duplicate, each part having correspondingly indented edges for identification and security. **3** (*often pl*) a contract between an apprentice and his master. **4** a less common word for **indentation.** ◆ *vb* **indentures, indenturing, indentured. 5** (*intr*) to enter into an agreement by indenture. **6** (*tr*) to bind (an apprentice, servant, etc.) by indenture.
▸**in'dentureˌship** *n*

independence ❶ (ˌɪndɪˈpɛndəns) *n* the state or quality of being independent. Also: **independency.**

independency (ˌɪndɪˈpɛndənsɪ) *n, pl* **independencies. 1** a territory or state free from the control of any other power. **2** another word for **independence.**

independent ❶ (ˌɪndɪˈpɛndənt) *adj* **1** free from control in action, judgment, etc.; autonomous. **2** not dependent on anything else for function, validity, etc.; separate. **3** not reliant on the support, esp. financial support, of others. **4** capable of acting for oneself or on one's own: *a very independent little girl.* **5** providing a large unearned sum towards one's support (esp. in **independent income, independent means**). **6** living on an unearned income. **7** *Maths.* (of a system of equations) not linearly dependent. See also **independent variable. 8** *Logic.* (of two or more propositions) unrelated. ◆ *n* **9** an independent person or thing. **10** a person who is not affiliated to or who acts independently of a political party.
▸**ˌinde'pendently** *adv*

Independent (ˌɪndɪˈpɛndənt) *Christianity.* ◆ *n* **1** (in England) a member of the Congregational Church. ◆ *adj* **2** of or relating to the Congregational Church.

independent clause *n Grammar.* a main or coordinate clause.

independent school *n* **1** (in Britain) a school that is neither financed nor controlled by the government or local authorities. **2** (in Australia) a school that is not part of the state system.

independent variable *n* a variable in a mathematical equation or statement whose value determines that of the dependent variable: in $y = f(x)$, x is the independent variable.

in-depth ❶ *adj* detailed and thorough: *an in-depth study.*

indescribable ❶ (ˌɪndɪˈskraɪbəbᵊl) *adj* beyond description; too intense, extreme, etc., for words.
▸**ˌindeˌscriba'bility** *n* ▸**ˌinde'scribably** *adv*

indestructible ❶ (ˌɪndɪˈstrʌktəbᵊl) *adj* incapable of being destroyed; very durable.
▸**ˌindeˌstructi'bility** *or* **ˌinde'structibleness** *n* ▸**ˌinde'structibly** *adv*

indeterminate ❶ (ˌɪndɪˈtɜːmɪnɪt) *adj* **1** uncertain in extent, amount, or nature. **2** not definite; inconclusive: *an indeterminate reply.* **3** unable to be predicted, calculated, or deduced. **4** *Maths.* **4a** having no numerical meaning, as 0/0. **4b** (of an equation) having more than one variable and an unlimited number of solutions.
▸**ˌinde'terminacy** *or* **ˌinde'terminateness** *n* ▸**ˌinde'terminately** *adv*

indeterminism (ˌɪndɪˈtɜːmɪˌnɪzəm) *n* the philosophical doctrine that behaviour is not entirely determined by motives.
▸**ˌinde'terminist** *n, adj* ▸**ˌindeˌtermin'istic** *adj*

index ❶ (ˈɪndɛks) *n, pl* **indexes** *or* **indices** (-dɪˌsiːz). **1** an alphabetical list of persons, subjects, etc., mentioned in a printed work, usually at the back, and indicating where they are referred to. **2** See **thumb index. 3** *Library science.* a systematic list of book titles or authors' names, giving cross-references and the location of each book; catalogue. **4** an indication, sign, or token. **5** a pointer, needle, or other indicator, as on an instrument. **6** *Maths.* **6a** another name for **exponent** (sense 4). **6b** a number or variable placed as a superscript to the left of a radical sign indicating the root to be extracted, as in $\sqrt[3]{8} = 2$. **7** a numerical scale by means of which levels of the cost of living can be compared with some base number. **8** a number or ratio indicating a specific characteristic, property, etc.: *refractive index.* **9** Also called: **fist.** a printer's mark, * used to indicate notes, paragraphs, etc. ◆ *vb* (*tr*) **10** to put an index in (a book). **11** to enter (a word, item, etc.) in an index. **12** to point out; indicate. **13** to make index-linked. **14** to move (a machine, etc.) so that an operation will be repeated at certain defined intervals. [C16: from L: pointer, hence forefinger, title, index, from *indicāre* to disclose, show; see INDICATE]
▸**'indexer** *n*

indexation (ˌɪndɛkˈseɪʃən) *or* **index-linking** *n* the act of making wages, interest rates, etc., index-linked.

index case *n Med.* the first case of a disease.

index finger *n* the finger next to the thumb. Also called: **forefinger.**

THESAURUS

defined, imprecise, indeterminate, indistinct, inexact, loose, obscure, oracular, uncertain, undefined, undetermined, unfixed, unknown, unlimited, unsettled, vague
Antonyms *adj* certain, clear, definite, determinate, distinct, exact, fixed, settled, specific

indefinitely *adv* **2** = **endlessly,** ad infinitum, continually, for ever, *sine die,* till the cows come home (*inf.*)

indelible *adj* **1** = **permanent,** enduring, indestructible, ineffaceable, ineradicable, inexpungible, inextirpable, ingrained, lasting
Antonyms *adj* eradicable, erasable, impermanent, removable, short-lived, temporary, washable

indelicacy *n* **1, 2** = **vulgarity,** bad taste, coarseness, crudity, grossness, immodesty, impropriety, indecency, obscenity, offensiveness, rudeness, smuttiness, suggestiveness, tastelessness

indelicate *adj* **1, 2** = **offensive,** blue, coarse, crude, embarrassing, gross, immodest, improper, indecent, indecorous, low, near the knuckle (*inf.*), obscene, off-colour, risqué, rude, suggestive, tasteless, unbecoming, unseemly, untoward, vulgar, X-rated (*inf.*)
Antonyms *adj* becoming, decent, decorous, delicate, modest, proper, refined, seemly

indemnify *vb* **1** = **insure,** endorse, guarantee, protect, secure, underwrite **2** = **compensate,** pay, reimburse, remunerate, repair, repay, requite, satisfy

indemnity *n* **1** = **compensation,** redress, reimbursement, remuneration, reparation, requital, restitution, satisfaction **2** = **insurance,** guarantee, protection, security **3** = **exemption,** immunity, impunity, privilege

indent[1] *vb* **3** = **order,** ask for, request, requisition **5** = **notch,** cut, dint, mark, nick, pink, scallop, score, serrate

indentation *n* **1** = **notch,** cut, dent, depression, dimple, dip, hollow, jag, nick, pit

independence *n* = **freedom,** autarchy, autonomy, home rule, liberty, self-determination, self-government, self-reliance, self-rule, self-sufficiency, separation, sovereignty
Antonyms *n* bondage, dependence, subjection, subjugation, subordination, subservience

independent *adj* **1** = **self-governing,** autarchic, autarchical, autonomous, decontrolled, nonaligned, self-determining, separated, sovereign **2** = **free,** absolute, liberated, separate, unconnected, unconstrained, uncontrolled, unrelated **3, 4** = **self-sufficient,** bold, individualistic, liberated, self-contained, self-reliant, self-supporting, unaided, unconventional
Antonyms *adj* ≠ **self-governing:** aligned, controlled, dependent, subject, submissive, subordinate, subservient, subsidiary ≠ **free:** controlled, dependent, restrained, subject

independently *adv* **3** = **separately,** alone, autonomously, by oneself, individually, on one's own, solo, unaided, under one's own steam

in-depth *adj* = **thorough,** comprehensive, extensive, intensive

indescribable *adj* = **unutterable,** beggaring description, beyond description, beyond words, incommunicable, indefinable, ineffable, inexpressible

indestructible *adj* = **permanent,** abiding, durable, enduring, everlasting, immortal, imperishable, incorruptible, indelible, indissoluble, lasting, nonperishable, unbreakable, unfading
Antonyms *adj* breakable, corruptible, destructible, fading, impermanent, mortal, perishable

indeterminate *adj* **1, 2** = **uncertain,** imprecise, inconclusive, indefinite, inexact, undefined, undetermined, unfixed, unspecified, unstipulated, vague
Antonyms *adj* certain, clear, conclusive, definite, determinate, exact, fixed, precise, specified, stipulated

index *n* **4** = **indication,** clue, guide, mark, sign, symptom, token

index fossil *n* a fossil species that characterizes and is used to delimit a geological zone. Also called: **zone fossil.**

index futures *pl n* a form of financial futures based on projected movements of a share price index, such as the Financial Times Stock Exchange 100 Share Index.

indexical (ɪnˈdɛksɪkəl) *adj* **1** arranged as or relating to an index or indexes. ◆ *n* **2** Also called: **deictic.** *Logic, linguistics.* a term whose reference depends on the context of utterance, such as *I, you, here, now,* or *tomorrow.*

Index Librorum Prohibitorum *Latin.* (ˈɪndɛks laɪˈbrɔːrʊm prəʊˌhɪbɪˈtɔːrʊm) *n RC Church.* (formerly) an official list of proscribed books. Often called: **the Index.** [C17, lit.: list of forbidden books]

index-linked *adj* (of wages, interest rates, etc.) directly related to the cost-of-living index and rising or falling accordingly.

index number *n Statistics.* a statistic indicating the relative change occurring in the price or value of a commodity or in a general economic variable, with reference to a previous base period conventionally given the number 100.

Indiaman (ˈɪndɪəmən) *n, pl* **Indiamen.** (formerly) a merchant ship engaged in trade with India.

Indian (ˈɪndɪən) *n* **1** a native or inhabitant of the Republic of India, in S Asia, or a descendant of one. **2** an American Indian. **3** (*not in scholarly usage*) any of the languages of the American Indians. ◆ *adj* **4** of or relating to India, its inhabitants, or any of their languages. **5** of or relating to the American Indians or any of their languages.

Indian club *n* a bottle-shaped club, usually used in pairs by gymnasts, jugglers, etc.

Indian corn *n* another name for **maize** (sense 1).

Indian file *n* another term for **single file.**

Indian hemp *n* another name for **hemp,** esp. the variety *Cannabis indica,* from which several narcotic drugs are obtained.

Indian ink *or esp. US & Canad.* **India ink** (ˈɪndɪə) *n* **1** a black pigment made from a mixture of lampblack and a binding agent such as gelatine or glue: usually formed into solid cakes and sticks. **2** a black liquid ink made from this pigment. ◆ Also called: **China ink, Chinese ink.**

Indian list *n Inf.* (in Canada) a list of persons to whom spirits may not be sold.

Indian meal *n* another name for **corn meal.**

Indian rope-trick *n* the supposed Indian feat of climbing an unsupported rope.

Indian summer *n* **1** a period of unusually warm weather in the late autumn. **2** a period of tranquillity or of renewed productivity towards the end of something, esp. a person's life. [orig. US: prob. so named because it was first noted in Amerind regions]

Indian tobacco *n* a poisonous North American plant with small pale bell-shaped blue flowers and rounded inflated seed capsules.

India paper *n* a thin soft opaque printing paper originally made in the Orient.

India rubber *n* another name for **rubber**[1] (sense 1).

Indic (ˈɪndɪk) *adj* **1** denoting, belonging to, or relating to a branch of Indo-European consisting of certain languages of India, including Sanskrit, Hindi and Urdu. ◆ *n* **2** this group of languages. ◆ Also: **Indo-Aryan.**

indicate ❶ (ˈɪndɪˌkeɪt) *vb* **indicates, indicating, indicated.** (*tr*) **1** (*may take a clause as object*) to be or give a sign or symptom of; imply: *cold hands indicate a warm heart.* **2** to point out or show. **3** (*may take a clause as object*) to state briefly; suggest. **4** (of instruments) to show a reading of. **5** (*usually passive*) to recommend or require: *surgery seems to be indicated for this patient.* [C17: from L *indicāre* to point out, from IN-² + *dicāre* to proclaim; cf. INDEX]
▸ˈ**indiˌcatable** *adj* ▸**indicatory** (ɪnˈdɪkətərɪ, -trɪ) *adj*

indication ❶ (ˌɪndɪˈkeɪʃən) *n* **1** something that serves to indicate or suggest; sign: *an indication of foul play.* **2** the degree or quantity represented on a measuring instrument or device. **3** the action of indicating. **4** something that is indicated as advisable, necessary, or expedient.

indicative ❶ (ɪnˈdɪkətɪv) *adj* **1** (*usually postpositive;* foll. by *of*) serving as a sign; suggestive: *indicative of trouble ahead.* **2** *Grammar.* denoting a mood of verbs used chiefly to make statements. ◆ *n* **3** *Grammar.* **3a** the indicative mood. **3b** a verb in the indicative mood. ◆ Abbrev.: **indic.**
▸**inˈdicatively** *adv*

indicator ❶ (ˈɪndɪˌkeɪtə) *n* **1** something that provides an indication, esp. of trends. See **economic indicator. 2** a device to attract attention, such as the pointer of a gauge or a warning lamp. **3** an instrument that displays certain operating conditions in a machine, such as a gauge showing temperature, etc. **4** a device that registers something, such as the movements of a lift, or that shows information, such as train departure times. **5** Also called: **blinker.** a device for indicating that a motor vehicle is about to turn left or right, esp. two pairs of lights that flash. **6** a delicate measuring instrument used to determine small differences in the height of mechanical components. **7** *Chem.* a substance used to indicate the completion of a chemical reaction, usually by a change of colour. **8** Also called: **indicator species.** *Ecology.* a plant or animal species that thrives only under particular environmental conditions and therefore indicates these conditions where it is found.

indices (ˈɪndɪˌsiːz) *n* a plural of **index.**

indicia (ɪnˈdɪʃɪə) *pl n, sing* **indicium** (-ʃɪəm). distinguishing markings or signs; indications. [C17: from L, pl of *indicium* a notice, from INDEX]
▸**inˈdicial** *adj*

indict ❶ (ɪnˈdaɪt) *vb* (*tr*) to charge (a person) with crime, esp. formally in writing; accuse. [C14: alteration of *enditen* to INDITE]
▸ˌ**indictˈee** *n* ▸**inˈdicter** *or* **inˈdictor** *n* ▸**inˈdictable** *adj*

> **USAGE NOTE** See at **indite.**

indictment ❶ (ɪnˈdaɪtmənt) *n Criminal law.* **1** a formal written charge of crime formerly referred to and presented on oath by a grand jury. **2** any formal accusation of crime. **3** the act of indicting or the state of being indicted.

indie (ˈɪndɪ) *n Inf.* **a** an independent record company. **b** (*as modifier*): *the indie charts.*

indifference ❶ (ɪnˈdɪfrəns, -fərəns) *n* **1** the fact or state of being indifferent; lack of care or concern. **2** lack of quality; mediocrity. **3** lack of importance; insignificance.

indifferent ❶ (ɪnˈdɪfrənt, -fərənt) *adj* **1** (often foll. by *to*) showing no care or concern; uninterested: *he was indifferent to my pleas.* **2** unimportant; immaterial. **3a** of only average or moderate size, extent, quality, etc. **3b** not at all good; poor. **4** showing or having no preferences; impartial. [C14: from L *indifferēns* making no distinction]
▸**inˈdifferently** *adv*

indifferentism (ɪnˈdɪfrənˌtɪzəm, -fərən-) *n* systematic indifference, esp. in matters of religion.
▸**inˈdifferentist** *n*

indigenous ❶ (ɪnˈdɪdʒɪnəs) *adj* (when *postpositive,* foll. by *to*) **1** originating or occurring naturally (in a country, etc.); native. **2** innate (to); inherent (in). [C17: from L *indigenus,* from *indi-* in + *gignere* to beget]
▸**inˈdigenously** *adv* ▸**inˈdigenousness** *n*

indigent ❶ (ˈɪndɪdʒənt) *adj* **1** so poor as to lack even necessities; very needy. **2** (usually foll. by *of*) *Arch.* lacking (in) or destitute (of). ◆ *n* **3** an impoverished person. [C14: from L *indigēre* to need, from *egēre* to lack]
▸ˈ**indigence** *n* ▸ˈ**indigently** *adv*

indigestible (ˌɪndɪˈdʒɛstəbəl) *adj* **1** incapable of being digested or difficult to digest. **2** difficult to understand or absorb mentally: *an indigestible book.*
▸ˌ**indiˌgestiˈbility** *n* ▸ˌ**indiˈgestibly** *adv*

indigestion ❶ (ˌɪndɪˈdʒɛstʃən) *n* difficulty in digesting food, accompanied by abdominal pain, heartburn, and belching.

indignant ❶ (ɪnˈdɪgnənt) *adj* feeling or showing indignation. [C16: from L *indignārī* to be displeased with]
▸**inˈdignantly** *adv*

THESAURUS

indicate *vb* **1** = **signify**, add up to (*inf.*), bespeak, be symptomatic of, betoken, denote, evince, imply, manifest, point to, reveal, show, signal, suggest **2** = **point out**, designate, point to, specify **4** = **show**, display, express, mark, read, record, register

indicated *adj* **5** = **recommended**, advisable, called-for, desirable, necessary, needed, suggested

indication *n* **1** = **sign**, clue, evidence, explanation, forewarning, hint, index, inkling, intimation, manifestation, mark, note, omen, portent, signal, suggestion, symptom, warning

indicative *adj* **1** = **suggestive**, exhibitive, indicatory, indicial, pointing to, significant, symptomatic

indicator *n* **1-3** = **sign**, display, gauge, guide, index, mark, marker, meter, pointer, signal, signpost, symbol

indict *vb* = **charge**, accuse, arraign, impeach, prosecute, serve with a summons, summon, summons, tax

indictment *n* **1-3** = **charge**, accusation, allegation, impeachment, prosecution, summons

indifference *n* **1** = **disregard**, absence of feeling, aloofness, apathy, callousness, carelessness, coldness, coolness, detachment, disinterestedness, dispassion, heedlessness, inattention, lack of interest, negligence, nonchalance, stoicalness, unconcern **3** = **irrelevance**, insignificance, triviality, unimportance
Antonyms *n* ≠ **disregard:** attention, care, commitment, concern, enthusiasm, heed, interest, regard

indifferent *adj* **1** = **unconcerned**, aloof, apathetic, callous, careless, cold, cool, detached, distant, heedless, impervious, inattentive, regardless, uncaring, unimpressed, uninterested, unmoved, unresponsive, unsympathetic **2** = **unimportant**, immaterial, insignificant, of no consequence **3a** = **mediocre**, average, fair, middling, moderate, no great shakes (*inf.*), ordinary, passable, perfunctory, so-so (*inf.*), undistinguished, uninspired **4** = **impartial**, disinterested, dispassionate, equitable, neutral, nonaligned, nonpartisan, objective, unbiased, uninvolved, unprejudiced
Antonyms *adj* ≠ **unconcerned:** avid, compassionate, concerned, eager, enthusiastic, interested, keen, responsive, sensitive, susceptible, sympathetic ≠ **mediocre:** excellent, exceptional, fine, first-class, notable, remarkable

indigenous *adj* **1** = **native**, aboriginal, autochthonous, home-grown, original

indigent *adj* **1** = **destitute**, dirt-poor, down and out, down at heel (*inf.*), flat broke (*inf.*), impecunious, impoverished, in want, necessitous, needy, on one's uppers (*inf.*), on the breadline, penniless, penurious, poor, poverty-stricken, short, straitened, without two pennies to rub together (*inf.*)
Antonyms *adj* affluent, prosperous, rich, wealthy, well-off, well-to-do

indigestion *n* = **heartburn**, dyspepsia, dyspepsy, upset stomach

indignant *adj* = **resentful**, angry, annoyed, choked, disgruntled, exasperated, fuming (*inf.*), furious, heated, hot under the collar (*inf.*),

indignation ◐ (ˌɪndɪɡˈneɪʃən) *n* anger aroused by something felt to be unfair, unworthy, or wrong.

indignity ◐ (ɪnˈdɪɡnɪtɪ) *n, pl* **indignities.** injury to one's self-esteem or dignity; humiliation.

indigo (ˈɪndɪˌɡəʊ) *n, pl* **indigos** *or* **indigoes. 1** a blue vat dye originally obtained from plants but now made synthetically. **2** any of various leguminous tropical plants, such as the anil, that yield this dye. **3a** any of a group of colours that have the same blue-violet hue; a spectral colour. **3b** (*as adj*): *an indigo rug.* [C16: from Sp. *indico,* via L from Gk *Indikos* of India]
▸**indigotic** (ˌɪndɪˈɡɒtɪk) *adj*

indigo blue *n, adj* (**indigo-blue** *when prenominal*). the full name for **indigo** (the colour and the dye).

indirect ◐ (ˌɪndɪˈrɛkt) *adj* **1** deviating from a direct course or line; roundabout; circuitous. **2** not coming as a direct effect or consequence; secondary: *indirect benefits.* **3** not straightforward, open, or fair; devious or evasive.
▸ˌ**indiˈrectly** *adv* ▸ˌ**indiˈrectness** *n*

indirect costs *pl n* another name for **overheads.**

indirection (ˌɪndɪˈrɛkʃən) *n* **1** indirect procedure, courses, or methods. **2** lack of direction or purpose; aimlessness. **3** indirect dealing; deceit.

indirect lighting *n* reflected or diffused light from a concealed source.

indirect object *n Grammar.* a noun, pronoun, or noun phrase indicating the recipient or beneficiary of the action of a verb and its direct object, as *John* in the sentence *I bought John a newspaper.*

indirect proof *n Logic, maths.* proof of a conclusion by showing its negation to be self-contradictory. Cf. **direct** (sense 17).

indirect question *n* a question reported in indirect speech, as in *She asked why you came.*

indirect speech *or esp. US* **indirect discourse** *n* the reporting of something said or written by conveying what was meant rather than repeating the exact words, as in the sentence *He said I looked happy* as opposed to *He said to me, "You look happy."* Also called: **reported speech.**

indirect tax *n* a tax levied on goods or services rather than on individuals or companies.

indiscreet ◐ (ˌɪndɪˈskriːt) *adj* not discreet; imprudent or tactless.
▸ˌ**indisˈcreetly** *adv* ▸ˌ**indisˈcreetness** *n*

indiscrete (ˌɪndɪˈskriːt) *adj* not divisible or divided into parts.

indiscretion ◐ (ˌɪndɪˈskrɛʃən) *n* **1** the characteristic or state of being indiscreet. **2** an indiscreet act, remark, etc.

indiscriminate ◐ (ˌɪndɪˈskrɪmɪnɪt) *adj* **1** lacking discrimination or careful choice; random or promiscuous. **2** jumbled; confused.
▸ˌ**indisˈcriminately** *adv* ▸ˌ**indisˈcriminateness** *n* ▸ˌ**indisˌcrimiˈnation** *n*

indispensable ◐ (ˌɪndɪˈspɛnsəbᵊl) *adj* **1** absolutely necessary; essential. **2** not to be disregarded or escaped: *an indispensable role.* ◆ *n* **3** an indispensable person or thing.
▸ˌ**indisˌpensaˈbility** *or* ˌ**indisˈpensableness** *n* ▸ˌ**indisˈpensably** *adv*

indispose (ˌɪndɪˈspəʊz) *vb* **indisposes, indisposing, indisposed.** (*tr*) **1** to make unwilling or opposed; disincline. **2** to cause to feel ill. **3** to make unfit (for something or to do something).

indisposed ◐ (ˌɪndɪˈspəʊzd) *adj* **1** sick or ill. **2** unwilling. [C15: from L *indispositus* disordered]
▸**indisposition** (ˌɪndɪspəˈzɪʃən) *n*

indisputable ◐ (ˌɪndɪˈspjuːtəbᵊl) *adj* beyond doubt; not open to question.
▸ˌ**indisˌputaˈbility** *or* ˌ**indisˈputableness** *n* ▸ˌ**indisˈputably** *adv*

indissoluble ◐ (ˌɪndɪˈsɒljʊbᵊl) *adj* incapable of being dissolved or broken; permanent.
▸ˌ**indisˈsolubly** *adv*

indistinct ◐ (ˌɪndɪˈstɪŋkt) *adj* incapable of being clearly distinguished, as by the eyes, ears, or mind; not distinct.
▸ˌ**indisˈtinctly** *adv* ▸ˌ**indisˈtinctness** *n*

indistinguishable ◐ (ˌɪndɪˈstɪŋɡwɪʃəbᵊl) *adj* **1** (*often postpositive;* foll. by *from*) identical or very similar (to): *twins indistinguishable from one another.* **2** not easily perceptible; indiscernible.
▸ˌ**indisˌtinguishaˈbility** *or* ˌ**indisˈtinguishableness** *n* ▸ˌ**indisˈtinguishably** *adv*

indite (ɪnˈdaɪt) *vb* **indites, inditing, indited.** (*tr*) *Arch.* to write. [C14: from OF *enditer,* from L *indīcere* to declare, from IN-[2] + *dīcere* to say]
▸**inˈditement** *n* ▸**inˈditer** *n*

> **USAGE NOTE** *Indite* and *inditement* are sometimes wrongly used where *indict* and *indictment* are meant: *he was indicted* (not *indited*) *for fraud.*

indium (ˈɪndɪəm) *n* a rare soft silvery metallic element associated with zinc ores: used in alloys, electronics, and electroplating. Symbol: In; atomic no.: 49; atomic wt.: 114.82. [C19: NL, from INDIGO + -IUM]

individual ◐ (ˌɪndɪˈvɪdjʊəl) *adj* **1** of, relating to, characteristic of, or meant for a single person or thing. **2** separate or distinct, esp. from others of its kind; particular: *please mark the individual pages.* **3** characterized by unusual and striking qualities; distinctive. **4** *Obs.* indivisible; inseparable. ◆ *n* **5** a single person, esp. when regarded as distinct from others. **6** *Biol.* a single animal or plant, esp. as distinct from a species. **7** *Inf.* a person: *a most obnoxious individual.* [C15: from Med. L, from L *indīviduus* indivisible, from IN-[1] + *dīvidere* to DIVIDE]
▸ˌ**indiˈvidually** *adv*

individualism ◐ (ˌɪndɪˈvɪdjʊəˌlɪzəm) *n* **1** the principle of asserting one's independence and individuality; egoism. **2** an individual quirk. **3** another word for **laissez faire** (sense 1). **4** *Philosophy.* the doctrine that only individual things exist.
▸ˌ**indiˈvidualist** *n*

individuality ◐ (ˌɪndɪˌvɪdjʊˈælɪtɪ) *n, pl* **individualities. 1** distinctive or unique character or personality: *a work of great individuality.* **2** the qualities that distinguish one person or thing from another; identity. **3** the state or quality of being a separate entity; discreteness.

individualize *or* **individualise** (ˌɪndɪˈvɪdjʊəˌlaɪz) *vb* **individualizes, individualizing, individualized** *or* **individualises, individualising, individualised.** (*tr*) **1** to make or mark as individual or distinctive in character. **2** to consider or treat individually; particularize. **3** to make or modify so as to meet the special requirements of a person.
▸ˌ**indiˌvidualiˈzation** *or* ˌ**indiˌvidualiˈsation** *n* ▸ˌ**indiˈvidualˌizer** *or* ˌ**indiˈvidualˌiser** *n*

individuate (ˌɪndɪˈvɪdjʊˌeɪt) *vb* **individuates, individuating, individuated.** (*tr*) **1** to give individuality or an individual form to. **2** to distinguish from others of the same species or group; individualize.
▸ˌ**indiˈviduˌator** *n*

THESAURUS

in a huff, incensed, in high dudgeon, irate, livid (*inf.*), mad (*inf.*), miffed (*inf.*), peeved (*inf.*), provoked, riled, scornful, sore (*inf.*), up in arms (*inf.*), wrathful

indignation *n* = **resentment**, anger, exasperation, fury, ire (*literary*), pique, rage, righteous anger, scorn, umbrage, wrath

indignity *n* = **humiliation**, abuse, affront, contumely, dishonour, disrespect, injury, insult, obloquy, opprobrium, outrage, reproach, slap in the face (*inf.*), slight, snub

indirect *adj* **1** = **circuitous**, backhanded, circumlocutory, crooked, devious, long-drawn-out, meandering, oblique, periphrastic, rambling, roundabout, tortuous, wandering, winding, zigzag **2** = **incidental**, ancillary, collateral, contingent, secondary, subsidiary, unintended
Antonyms *adj* ≠ **circuitous:** direct, straight, straightforward, undeviating, uninterrupted

indiscreet *adj* = **tactless**, foolish, hasty, heedless, ill-advised, ill-considered, ill-judged, impolitic, imprudent, incautious, injudicious, naive, rash, reckless, undiplomatic, unthinking, unwise
Antonyms *adj* cautious, diplomatic, discreet, judicious, politic, prudent, tactful, wise

indiscretion *n* **2** = **mistake**, bloomer (*Brit. inf.*), boob (*Brit. sl.*), error, faux pas, folly, foolishness, gaffe, gaucherie, imprudence, lapse, rashness, recklessness, slip, slip of the tongue, tactlessness

indiscriminate *adj* **1** = **random**, aimless, careless, desultory, general, hit or miss (*inf.*), sweeping, uncritical, undiscriminating, unmethodical, unselective, unsystematic, wholesale **2** = **jumbled**, chaotic, confused, haphazard, higgledy-piggledy (*inf.*), mingled, miscellaneous, mixed, mongrel, motley, promiscuous, undistinguishable
Antonyms *adj* ≠ **random:** deliberate, discriminating, exclusive, methodical, selective, systematic

indispensable *adj* **1** = **essential**, crucial, imperative, key, necessary, needed, needful, requisite, vital
Antonyms *adj* dispensable, disposable, nonessential, superfluous, unimportant, unnecessary

indisposed *adj* **1** = **ill**, ailing, confined to bed, laid up (*inf.*), on the sick list (*inf.*), poorly (*inf.*), sick, under the weather, unwell **2** = **unwilling**, averse, disinclined, loath, reluctant
Antonyms *adj* ≠ **ill:** fine, fit, hardy, healthy, sound, well

indisposition *n* **1** = **illness**, ailment, ill health, sickness **2** = **reluctance**, aversion, disinclination, dislike, distaste, hesitancy, unwillingness

indisputable *adj* = **undeniable**, absolute, beyond doubt, certain, evident, incontestable, incontrovertible, indubitable, irrefutable, positive, sure, unassailable, unquestionable
Antonyms *adj* assailable, disputable, doubtful, indefinite, questionable, refutable, uncertain, vague

indissoluble *adj* = **permanent**, abiding, binding, enduring, eternal, fixed, imperishable, incorruptible, indestructible, inseparable, lasting, solid, unbreakable

indistinct *adj* = **unclear**, ambiguous, bleary, blurred, confused, dim, doubtful, faint, fuzzy, hazy, ill-defined, indefinite, indeterminate, indiscernible, indistinguishable, misty, muffled, obscure, out of focus, shadowy, undefined, unintelligible, vague, weak
Antonyms *adj* clear, defined, determinate, discernible, distinct, distinguishable, evident, intelligible

indistinguishable *adj* **1** = **identical**, alike, cut from the same cloth, like as two peas in a pod (*inf.*), (the) same, twin **2** = **imperceptible**, indiscernible, invisible, obscure

individual *adj* **1-3** = **personal**, characteristic, discrete, distinct, distinctive, exclusive, identical, idiosyncratic, own, particular, peculiar, personalized, proper, respective, separate, several, single, singular, special, specific, unique ◆ *n* **5** = **person**, being, body (*inf.*), character, creature, mortal, party, personage, soul, type, unit
Antonyms *adj* ≠ **personal:** collective, common, conventional, general, indistinct, ordinary, universal

individualism *n* **1** = **self-interest**, egocentricity, egoism, freethinking, independence, originality, self-direction, self-reliance

individualist *n* **1** = **maverick**, freethinker, independent, loner, lone wolf, nonconformist, original

individuality *n* **1** = **distinctiveness**, character, discreteness, distinction, originality, peculiarity, personality, separateness, singularity, uniqueness

individually *adv* **2** = **separately**, apart, independently, one at a time, one by one, personally, severally, singly

indivisible (ˌɪndɪˈvɪzəbᵊl) *adj* **1** unable to be divided. **2** *Maths.* leaving a remainder when divided by a given number.
▸ˌ**indiˌvisiˈbility** *n* ▸ˌ**indiˈvisibly** *adv*

Indo- (ˈɪndəʊ) *combining form.* denoting India or Indian: *Indo-European.*

indoctrinate Ⓣ (ɪnˈdɒktrɪˌneɪt) *vb* **indoctrinates, indoctrinating, indoctrinated.** *(tr)* **1** to teach (a person or group of people) systematically to accept doctrines, esp. uncritically. **2** *Rare.* to instruct.
▸**inˌdoctriˈnation** *n* ▸**inˈdoctriˌnator** *n*

Indo-European *adj* **1** denoting, belonging to, or relating to a family of languages that includes English: characteristically marked, esp. in the older languages, such as Latin, by inflection showing gender, number, and case. **2** denoting or relating to the hypothetical parent language of this family, primitive Indo-European. **3** denoting, belonging to, or relating to any of the peoples speaking these languages. ◆ *n* **4** the Indo-European family of languages. **5** the reconstructed hypothetical parent language of this family. ◆ Also (*obs.*): **Indo-Germanic.**

Indo-Iranian *adj* **1** of or relating to the Indic and Iranian branches of the Indo-European family of languages. ◆ *n* **2** this group of languages, sometimes considered as forming a single branch of Indo-European.

indole (ˈɪndəʊl) *or* **indol** (ˈɪndəʊl, -dɒl) *n* a white or yellowish crystalline heterocyclic compound extracted from coal tar and used in perfumery, medicine, and as a flavouring agent. [C19: from IND(IGO) + -OLE[1]]

indolent Ⓣ (ˈɪndələnt) *adj* **1** disliking work or effort; lazy; idle. **2** *Pathol.* causing little pain: *an indolent tumour.* **3** (esp. of a painless ulcer) slow to heal. [C17: from L *indolēns* not feeling pain, from IN-[1] + *dolēre* to grieve, cause distress]
▸ˈ**indolence** *n* ▸ˈ**indolently** *adv*

indomitable Ⓣ (ɪnˈdɒmɪtəbᵊl) *adj* (of courage, pride, etc.) difficult or impossible to defeat or subdue. [C17: from LL, from L *indomitus* untameable, from *domāre* to tame]
▸**inˌdomitaˈbility** *or* **inˈdomitableness** *n* ▸**inˈdomitably** *adv*

Indonesian (ˌɪndəʊˈniːzɪən) *adj* **1** of or relating to Indonesia, its people, or their language. ◆ *n* **2** a native or inhabitant of Indonesia.

indoor (ˈɪnˌdɔː) *adj (prenominal)* of, situated in, or appropriate to the inside of a house or other building: *an indoor pool; indoor amusements.*

indoors (ˌɪnˈdɔːz) *adv, adj (postpositive)* inside or into a house or other building.

indorse Ⓣ (ɪnˈdɔːs) *vb* **indorses, indorsing, indorsed.** a variant spelling of **endorse.**

indraught *or US* **indraft** (ˈɪnˌdrɑːft) *n* **1** the act of drawing or pulling in. **2** an inward flow, esp. of air.

indrawn (ˌɪnˈdrɔːn) *adj* **1** drawn or pulled in. **2** inward-looking or introspective.

indris (ˈɪndrɪs) *or* **indri** (ˈɪndrɪ) *n, pl* **indris. 1** a large Madagascan arboreal lemuroid primate with thick silky fur patterned in black, white, and fawn. **2 woolly indris.** a related nocturnal Madagascan animal with thick grey-brown fur and a long tail. [C19: from F: lemur, from native word *indry!* look! mistaken for the animal's name]

indubitable Ⓣ (ɪnˈdjuːbɪtəbᵊl) *adj* incapable of being doubted; unquestionable. [C18: from L, from IN-[1] + *dubitāre* to doubt]
▸**inˈdubitably** *adv*

induce Ⓣ (ɪnˈdjuːs) *vb* **induces, inducing, induced.** *(tr)* **1** (often foll. by an infinitive) to persuade or use influence on. **2** to cause or bring about. **3** *Med.* to initiate or hasten (labour), as by administering a drug to stimulate uterine contractions. **4** *Logic, obs.* to assert or establish (a general proposition, etc.) by induction. **5** to produce (an electromotive force or electrical current) by induction. **6** to transmit (magnetism) by induction. [C14: from L *indūcere* to lead in]
▸**inˈducer** *n* ▸**inˈducible** *adj*

inducement Ⓣ (ɪnˈdjuːsmənt) *n* **1** the act of inducing. **2** a means of inducing; persuasion; incentive. **3** *Law.* the introductory part that leads up to and explains the matter in dispute.

induct Ⓣ (ɪnˈdʌkt) *vb (tr)* **1** to bring in formally or install in an office, place, etc.; invest. **2** (foll. by *to* or *into*) to initiate in knowledge (of). **3** *US.* to enlist for military service. **4** *Physics.* another word for **induce** (senses 5, 6). [C14: from L *inductus* led in, p.p. of *indūcere* to introduce; see INDUCE]

inductance (ɪnˈdʌktəns) *n* **1** the property of an electric circuit as a result of which an electromotive force is created by a change of current in the same or in a neighbouring circuit. **2** a component, such as a coil, in an electrical circuit, the main function of which is to produce inductance.

induction Ⓣ (ɪnˈdʌkʃən) *n* **1** the act of inducting or state of being inducted. **2** the act of inducing. **3** (in an internal-combustion engine) the drawing in of mixed air and fuel from the carburettor to the cylinder. **4** *Logic.* **4a** a process of reasoning by which a general conclusion is drawn from a set of premises, based mainly on experience or experimental evidence. **4b** a conclusion reached by this process of reasoning. **5** the process by which electrical or magnetic properties are transferred, without physical contact, from one circuit or body to another. See also **inductance. 6** *Maths.* a method of proving a proposition P(*n*) by showing that it is true for all preceding values of *n* and for *n* + 1. **7a** a formal introduction or entry into an office or position. **7b** (*as modifier*): *induction course.* **8** *US.* the enlistment of a civilian into military service.
▸**inˈductional** *adj*

induction coil *n* **1** any coil of wire used to introduce inductance into a circuit. **2** another name for **ignition coil.**

induction heating *n* the heating of a conducting material as a result of the electric currents induced in it by an externally applied alternating magnetic field.

induction loop system *n* an electronic system enabling partially deaf people to hear dialogue and sound in theatres, cinemas, etc. Often shortened to **induction loop.**

induction motor *n* a type of electric motor in which an alternating supply fed to the windings of the stator creates a magnetic field that induces a current in the windings of the rotor. Rotation of the rotor results from the interaction of the magnetic field created by the rotor current with the field of the stator.

inductive (ɪnˈdʌktɪv) *adj* **1** relating to or operated by electrical or magnetic induction: *an inductive reactance.* **2** *Logic, maths.* of, relating to, or using induction: *inductive reasoning.* **3** serving to induce or cause.
▸**inˈductively** *adv* ▸**inˈductiveness** *n*

inductor (ɪnˈdʌktə) *n* **1** a person or thing that inducts. **2** another name for an **inductance** (sense 2).

indue (ɪnˈdjuː) *vb* **indues, induing, indued.** a variant spelling of **endue.**

indulge Ⓣ (ɪnˈdʌldʒ) *vb* **indulges, indulging, indulged. 1** (when *intr,* often foll. by *in*) to yield to or gratify (a whim or desire for): *to indulge in new clothes.* **2** *(tr)* to yield to the wishes of; pamper: *to indulge a child.* **3** *(tr)* to allow (oneself) the pleasure of something: *he indulged himself.* **4** *(intr) Inf.* to take alcoholic drink, esp. to excess. [C17: from L *indulgēre* to concede]
▸**inˈdulger** *n* ▸**inˈdulgingly** *adv*

indulgence Ⓣ (ɪnˈdʌldʒəns) *n* **1** the act of indulging or state of being indulgent. **2** a pleasure, habit, etc., indulged in; extravagance. **3** liberal or tolerant treatment. **4** something granted as a favour or privilege. **5** *RC Church.* a remission of the temporal punishment for sin after its guilt has been forgiven. **6** Also called: **Declaration of Indulgence.** a royal grant during the reigns of Charles II and James II of England giving Nonconformists and Roman Catholics a measure of religious freedom.

indulgent Ⓣ (ɪnˈdʌldʒənt) *adj* showing or characterized by indulgence.
▸**inˈdulgently** *adv*

induna (ɪnˈduːnə) *n* (in South Africa) a Black African overseer in a factory, mine, etc. [C20: from Zulu *nduna* an official]

indurate *vb* (ˈɪndjʊˌreɪt), **indurates, indurating, indurated. 1** to make or become hard or callous. **2** to make or become hardy. ◆ *adj* (ˈɪndjʊrɪt). **3** hardened, callous, or unfeeling. [C16: from L *indūrāre* to make hard; see ENDURE]
▸ˌ**induˈration** *n* ▸ˈ**induˌrative** *adj*

indusium (ɪnˈdjuːzɪəm) *n, pl* **indusia** (-zɪə). **1** a membranous outgrowth on the undersurface of fern leaves that protects the developing

THESAURUS

indoctrinate *vb* **1** = **train**, brainwash, drill, ground, imbue, initiate, instruct, school, teach

indoctrination *n* **1** = **training**, brainwashing, drilling, grounding, inculcation, instruction, schooling

indolence *n* **1** = **idleness**, heaviness, inactivity, inertia, inertness, languidness, languor, laziness, lethargy, shirking, skiving (*Brit. sl.*), slacking, sloth, sluggishness, torpidity, torpor

indolent *adj* **1** = **lazy**, good-for-nothing, idle, inactive, inert, lackadaisical, languid, lethargic, listless, lumpish, slack, slothful, slow, sluggish, torpid, workshy
Antonyms *adj* active, assiduous, busy, conscientious, diligent, energetic, industrious, vigorous

indomitable *adj* = **invincible**, bold, resolute, set, staunch, steadfast, unbeatable, unconquerable, unflinching, untameable, unyielding
Antonyms *adj* cowardly, faltering, feeble, shrinking, wavering, weak, yielding

indorse *see* **endorse**

indubitable *adj* = **certain**, evident, incontestable, incontrovertible, indisputable, irrefutable, obvious, open-and-shut, sure, unarguable, undeniable, undoubted, unquestionable, veritable

induce *vb* **1** = **persuade**, actuate, convince, draw, encourage, get, impel, incite, influence, instigate, move, press, prevail upon, prompt, talk into **2** = **cause**, bring about, effect, engender, generate, give rise to, lead to, occasion, produce, set in motion, set off
Antonyms *vb* curb, deter, discourage, dissuade, hinder, prevent, restrain, stop, suppress

inducement *n* **2** = **incentive**, attraction, bait, carrot (*inf.*), cause, clarion call, come-on (*inf.*), consideration, encouragement, impulse, incitement, influence, lure, motive, reward, spur, stimulus, urge

induct *vb* **1** = **install**, inaugurate, initiate, introduce, invest, swear in

induction *n* **1** = **installation**, inauguration, initiation, institution, introduction, investiture **4b** = **inference**, conclusion, generalization

indulge *vb* **1** = **gratify**, cater to, feed, give way to, pander to, regale, satiate, satisfy, treat oneself to, yield to **2** = **spoil**, baby, coddle, cosset, favour, fawn on, foster, give in to, go along with, humour, mollycoddle, pamper, pet

indulgence *n* **1** = **intemperance**, excess, fondness, immoderation, intemperateness, kindness, leniency, pampering, partiality, permissiveness, profligacy, profligateness, spoiling **2** = **luxury**, extravagance, favour, privilege, treat **3** = **tolerance**, courtesy, forbearance, goodwill, patience, understanding
Antonyms *n* ≠ **intemperance:** moderation, strictness, temperance, temperateness

indulgent *adj* = **lenient**, compliant, easygoing, favourable, fond, forbearing, gentle, gratifying, kind, kindly, liberal, mild, permissive, tender, tolerant, understanding
Antonyms *adj* austere, demanding, harsh, intolerant, rigorous, stern, strict, stringent, unmerciful

spores. **2** an enveloping membrane, such as the amnion. [C18: NL, from L: tunic, from *induere* to put on]
▸**in'dusial** *adj*

industrial (ɪn'dʌstrɪəl) *adj* **1** of, relating to, or derived from industry. **2** employed in industry: *the industrial workforce.* **3** relating to or concerned with workers in industry: *industrial conditions.* **4** used in industry: *industrial chemicals.*
▸**in'dustrially** *adv*

industrial action *n Brit.* any action, such as a strike or go-slow, taken by employees in industry to protest against working conditions, etc.

industrial archaeology *n* the study of industrial machines, works, etc. of the past.

industrial design *n* the art or practice of designing any object for manufacture.
▸**industrial designer** *n*

industrial diamond *n* a small often synthetic diamond, valueless as a gemstone, used in cutting tools, abrasives, etc.

industrial disease *n* any disease to which workers in a particular industry are prone.

industrial espionage *n* attempting to obtain trade secrets by dishonest means, as by telephone- or computer-tapping, infiltration of a competitor's workforce, etc.

industrial estate *n Brit.* another name for **trading estate.** US equivalent: **industrial park.**

industrialism (ɪn'dʌstrɪəˌlɪzəm) *n* an organization of society characterized by large-scale mechanized manufacturing industry rather than trade, farming, etc.

industrialist ❶ (ɪn'dʌstrɪəlɪst) *n* a person who has a substantial interest in the ownership or control of industrial enterprise.

industrialize *or* **industrialise** (ɪn'dʌstrɪəˌlaɪz) *vb* **industrializes, industrializing, industrialized** *or* **industrialises, industrialising, industrialised. 1** (*tr*) to develop industry on an extensive scale in (a country, region, etc.). **2** (*intr*) (of a country, region, etc.) to undergo the development of industry on an extensive scale.
▸**inˌdustriali'zation** *or* **inˌdustriali'sation** *n*

industrial medicine *n* the study and practice of the health care of employees of large organizations.

industrial relations *n* **1** (*functioning as pl*) relations between the employers and employees in an industrial enterprise. **2** (*functioning as sing*) the management of such relations.

Industrial Revolution *n* **the.** the transformation in the 18th and 19th centuries of Britain and other countries into industrial nations.

industrial tribunal *n* a tribunal that rules on disputes between employers and employees regarding unfair dismissal, redundancy, etc.

industrious ❶ (ɪn'dʌstrɪəs) *adj* hard-working, diligent, or assiduous.
▸**in'dustriously** *adv* ▸**in'dustriousness** *n*

industry ❶ ('ɪndəstrɪ) *n, pl* **industries. 1** organized economic activity concerned with manufacture, processing of raw materials, or construction. **2** a branch of commercial enterprise concerned with the output of a specified product: *the steel industry.* **3a** industrial ownership and management interests collectively. **3b** manufacturing enterprise collectively, as opposed to agriculture. **4** diligence; assiduity. [C15: from L *industria* diligence, from *industrius* active, from ?]

indwell (ɪn'dwɛl) *vb* **indwells, indwelling, indwelt. 1** (*tr*) (of a spirit, principle, etc.) to inhabit; suffuse. **2** (*intr*) to dwell; exist.
▸**in'dweller** *n*

-ine[1] *suffix forming adjectives.* **1** of, relating to, or belonging to: *saturnine.* **2** consisting of or resembling: *crystalline.* [from L *-īnus,* from Gk *-inos*]

-ine[2] *suffix forming nouns.* **1** indicating a halogen: *chlorine.* **2** indicating a nitrogenous organic compound, including amino acids, alkaloids, and certain other bases: *nicotine.* **3** Also: **-in.** indicating a chemical substance in certain nonsystematic names: *glycerine.* **4** indicating a mixture of hydrocarbons: *benzine.* **5** indicating feminine form: *heroine.* [via F from L *-ina* (from *-inus*) and Gk *-inē*]

inebriate ❶ *vb* (ɪn'iːbrɪˌeɪt), **inebriates, inebriating, inebriated.** (*tr*) **1** to make drunk; intoxicate. **2** to arouse emotionally; make excited. ◆ *n* (ɪn'iːbrɪɪt). **3** a person who is drunk, esp. habitually. ◆ *adj* (ɪn'iːbrɪɪt), *also* **inebriated. 4** drunk, esp. habitually. [C15: from L, from IN-[2] + *ēbriāre* to intoxicate, from *ēbrius* drunk]
▸**inˌebri'ation** *n* ▸**inebriety** (ˌɪnɪ'braɪɪtɪ) *n*

inedible (ɪn'ɛdɪbᵊl) *adj* not fit to be eaten.
▸**inˌedi'bility** *n*

ineducable (ɪn'ɛdjʊkəbᵊl) *adj* incapable of being educated, esp. on account of mental retardation.
▸**inˌeduca'bility** *n*

ineffable ❶ (ɪn'ɛfəbᵊl) *adj* **1** too great or intense to be expressed in words; unutterable. **2** too sacred to be uttered. **3** indescribable; indefinable. [C15: from L, from IN-[1] + *effābilis,* from *fārī* to speak]
▸**inˌeffa'bility** *or* **in'effableness** *n* ▸**in'effably** *adv*

ineffective ❶ (ˌɪnɪ'fɛktɪv) *adj* **1** having no effect. **2** incompetent or inefficient.
▸ˌ**inef'fectively** *adv* ▸ˌ**inef'fectiveness** *n*

ineffectual ❶ (ˌɪnɪ'fɛktʃʊəl) *adj* **1** having no effect or an inadequate effect. **2** lacking in power or forcefulness; impotent: *an ineffectual ruler.*
▸ˌ**ineffectu'ality** *or* ˌ**inef'fectualness** *n* ▸ˌ**inef'fectually** *adv*

inefficacious ❶ (ˌɪnɛfɪ'keɪʃəs) *adj* failing to produce the desired effect.
▸ˌ**ineffi'caciously** *adv* ▸**inefficacy** (ɪn'ɛfɪkəsɪ), ˌ**ineffi'caciousness,** *or* **inefficacity** (ˌɪnɛfɪ'kæsɪtɪ) *n*

inefficient ❶ (ˌɪnɪ'fɪʃənt) *adj* **1** unable to perform a task or function to the best advantage; wasteful or incompetent. **2** unable to produce the desired result.
▸ˌ**inef'ficiency** *n* ▸ˌ**inef'ficiently** *adv*

ineligible ❶ (ɪn'ɛlɪdʒəbᵊl) *adj* **1** (often foll. by *for* or an infinitive) not fit or qualified: *ineligible for a grant; ineligible to vote.* ◆ *n* **2** an ineligible person.
▸**inˌeligi'bility** *or* **in'eligibleness** *n* ▸**in'eligibly** *adv*

ineluctable (ˌɪnɪ'lʌktəbᵊl) *adj* (esp. of fate) incapable of being avoided; inescapable. [C17: from L, from IN-[1] + *ēluctārī* to escape, from *luctārī* to struggle]
▸ˌ**ineˌlucta'bility** *n* ▸ˌ**ine'luctably** *adv*

inept ❶ (ɪn'ɛpt) *adj* **1** awkward, clumsy, or incompetent. **2** not suitable, appropriate, or fitting; out of place. [C17: from L *ineptus,* from IN-[1] + *aptus* fitting]
▸**in'eptiˌtude** *n* ▸**in'eptly** *adv* ▸**in'eptness** *n*

inequable (ɪn'ɛkwəbᵊl) *adj* **1** uneven. **2** not uniform. **3** changeable.

inequality ❶ (ˌɪnɪ'kwɒlɪtɪ) *n, pl* **inequalities. 1** the state or quality of being unequal; disparity. **2** an instance of disparity. **3** lack of smoothness or regularity. **4** social or economic disparity. **5** *Maths.* **5a** a statement indicating that the value of one quantity or expression is not equal to another. **5b** the relation of being unequal. **6** *Astron.* a departure from uniform orbital motion.

inert ❶ (ɪn'ɜːt) *adj* **1** having no inherent ability to move or to resist motion. **2** inactive, lazy, or sluggish. **3** having only a limited ability to react chemically; unreactive. [C17: from L *iners* unskilled, from IN-[1] + *ars* skill; see ART[1]]
▸**in'ertly** *adv* ▸**in'ertness** *n*

THESAURUS

industrialist *n* = **capitalist,** baron, big businessman, boss, captain of industry, financier, magnate, manufacturer, producer, tycoon

industrious *adj* = **hard-working,** active, assiduous, busy, conscientious, diligent, energetic, laborious, persevering, persistent, productive, purposeful, sedulous, steady, tireless, zealous
Antonyms *adj* good-for-nothing, idle, indolent, lackadaisical, lazy, shiftless, slothful

industriously *adv* = **diligently,** assiduously, conscientiously, doggedly, hard, like a Trojan, nose to the grindstone (*inf.*), perseveringly, sedulously, steadily, without slacking

industry *n* **1** = **business,** commerce, commercial enterprise, manufacturing, production, trade **4** = **effort,** activity, application, assiduity, determination, diligence, labour, perseverance, persistence, tirelessness, toil, vigour, zeal

inebriate *vb* **1** = **intoxicate,** make drunk, stupefy **2** = **arouse,** animate, carry away, excite, exhilarate, fire, stimulate ◆ *n* **3** = **drunkard,** alcoholic, boozer, dipsomaniac, drunk, heavy drinker, lush (*sl.*), soak (*sl.*), sot, toper

inebriated *adj* **1** = **drunk,** blotto (*sl.*), half-cut (*inf.*), inebriate, in one's cups, intoxicated, legless (*inf.*), merry (*Brit. inf.*), paralytic (*inf.*), pissed (*taboo sl.*), plastered (*sl.*), rat-arsed (*taboo sl.*), smashed (*sl.*), tight (*inf.*), tipsy, under the influence (*inf.*)

inebriation *n* **1** = **drunkenness,** crapulence, inebriety, insobriety, intemperance, intoxication, sottishness

ineffable *adj* **1, 3** = **indescribable,** beyond words, incommunicable, indefinable, inexpressible, unspeakable, unutterable

ineffective *adj* **1** = **useless,** barren, bootless, feeble, fruitless, futile, idle, impotent, inadequate, ineffectual, inefficacious, inefficient, pathetic, unavailing, unproductive, vain, weak, worthless
Antonyms *adj* effective, efficacious, efficient, fruitful, potent, productive, useful, worthwhile

ineffectual *adj* **2** = **weak,** abortive, bootless, emasculate, feeble, fruitless, futile, idle, impotent, inadequate, incompetent, ineffective, inefficacious, inefficient, inept, lame, pathetic, powerless, unavailing, useless, vain

inefficacious *adj* = **ineffective,** abortive, futile, ineffectual, unavailing, unproductive, unsuccessful

inefficacy *n* = **ineffectiveness,** futility, inadequacy, ineffectuality, nonsuccess, unproductiveness, uselessness

inefficiency *n* **1** = **incompetence,** carelessness, disorganization, muddle, slackness, sloppiness

inefficient *adj* **1** = **incompetent,** cowboy (*inf.*), disorganized, feeble, incapable, ineffectual, inefficacious, inept, inexpert, slipshod, sloppy, wasteful, weak
Antonyms *adj* able, capable, competent, effective, efficient, expert, organized, skilled

ineligible *adj* **1** = **unqualified,** disqualified, incompetent (*Law*), objectionable, ruled out, unacceptable, undesirable, unequipped, unfit, unfitted, unsuitable

inept *adj* **1** = **incompetent,** awkward, bumbling, bungling, cack-handed (*inf.*), clumsy, cowboy (*inf.*), gauche, inexpert, maladroit, unhandy, unskilful, unworkmanlike **2** = **unsuitable,** absurd, improper, inappropriate, inapt, infelicitous, malapropos, meaningless, out of place, pointless, ridiculous, unfit
Antonyms *adj* ≠ **incompetent:** able, adroit, competent, dexterous, efficient, qualified, skilful, talented ≠ **unsuitable:** appropriate, apt, effectual, germane, sensible, suitable

ineptitude *n* **1** = **incompetence,** clumsiness, gaucheness, incapacity, inexpertness, unfitness, unhandiness **2** = **inappropriateness,** absurdity, pointlessness, uselessness

inequality *n* **1** = **disparity,** bias, difference, disproportion, diversity, imparity, irregularity, lack of balance, preferentiality, prejudice, unevenness

inert *adj* **2** = **inactive,** dead, dormant, dull, idle, immobile, inanimate, indolent, lazy, leaden, lifeless, motionless, passive, quiescent, slack, slothful, sluggish, slumberous (*chiefly poetic*), static, still, torpid, unmoving, unreactive, unresponsive

inert gas *n* **1** any of the unreactive gaseous elements helium, neon, argon, krypton, xenon, and radon. **2** (loosely) any gas, such as carbon dioxide, that is nonoxidizing.

inertia ❶ (ɪnˈɜːʃə, -ʃɪə) *n* **1** the state of being inert; disinclination to move or act. **2** *Physics.* **2a** the tendency of a body to preserve its state of rest or uniform motion unless acted upon by an external force. **2b** an analogous property of other physical quantities that resist change: *thermal inertia.*
▸**inˈertial** *adj*

inertial guidance *or* **navigation** *n* a method of controlling the flight path of a missile by instruments contained within it.

inertial mass *n* the mass of a body as determined by its momentum, as opposed to the extent to which it responds to the force of gravity. Cf. **gravitational mass.**

inertia-reel seat belt *n* a type of car seat belt in which the belt is free to unwind from a metal drum except when the drum locks as a result of rapid change of velocity.

inertia selling *n* the illegal practice of sending unrequested goods to householders, followed by a bill for the goods if they do not return them.

inescapable ❶ (ˌɪnɪˈskeɪpəbᵊl) *adj* incapable of being escaped or avoided.
▸**ˌinesˈcapably** *adv*

inestimable ❶ (ɪnˈɛstɪməbᵊl) *adj* **1** not able to be estimated; immeasurable. **2** of immeasurable value.
▸**inˌestimaˈbility** *or* **inˈestimableness** *n* ▸**inˈestimably** *adv*

inevitable ❶ (ɪnˈɛvɪtəbᵊl) *adj* **1** unavoidable. **2** sure to happen; certain. ◆ *n* **3** (often preceded by *the*) something that is unavoidable. [C15: from L, from IN-[1] + *ēvītāre* to shun, from *vītāre* to avoid]
▸**inˌevitaˈbility** *or* **inˈevitableness** *n* ▸**inˈevitably** *adv*

inexcusable ❶ (ˌɪnɪkˈskjuːzəbᵊl) *adj* not able to be excused or justified.
▸**ˌinexˌcusaˈbility** *or* **ˌinexˈcusableness** *n* ▸**ˌinexˈcusably** *adv*

inexhaustible ❶ (ˌɪnɪgˈzɔːstəbᵊl) *adj* **1** incapable of being used up; endless. **2** incapable or apparently incapable of becoming tired; tireless.
▸**ˌinexˌhaustiˈbility** *n* ▸**ˌinexˈhaustibly** *adv*

inexorable ❶ (ɪnˈɛksərəbᵊl) *adj* **1** not able to be moved by entreaty or persuasion. **2** relentless. [C16: from L, from IN-[1] + *exōrāre* to prevail upon, from *ōrāre* to pray]
▸**inˌexoraˈbility** *n* ▸**inˈexorably** *adv*

inexpensive ❶ (ˌɪnɪkˈspɛnsɪv) *adj* not expensive; cheap.
▸**ˌinexˈpensively** *adv* ▸**ˌinexˈpensiveness** *n*

inexperience ❶ (ˌɪnɪkˈspɪərɪəns) *n* lack of experience or of the knowledge and understanding derived from experience.
▸**ˌinexˈperienced** *adj*

inexpiable (ɪnˈɛkspɪəbᵊl) *adj* **1** incapable of being expiated; unpardonable. **2** *Arch.* implacable.
▸**inˈexpiableness** *n*

inexplicable ❶ (ˌɪnɪkˈsplɪkəbᵊl, ɪnˈɛksplɪkəbᵊl) *adj* not capable of explanation; unexplained.
▸**ˌinexplicaˈbility** *n* ▸**ˌinexˈplicably** *adv*

in extenso *Latin.* (ɪn ɪkˈstɛnsəʊ) *adv* at full length.

in extremis *Latin.* (ɪn ɪkˈstriːmɪs) *adv* **1** in extremity; in dire straits. **2** at the point of death. [lit.: in the furthest reaches]

inextricable ❶ (ˌɪnɛksˈtrɪkəbᵊl) *adj* **1** not able to be escaped from: *an inextricable dilemma.* **2** not able to be disentangled, etc.: *an inextricable knot.* **3** extremely involved or intricate.
▸**ˌinextricaˈbility** *or* **ˌinexˈtricableness** *n* ▸**ˌinexˈtricably** *adv*

inf. *abbrev. for:* **1** Also: **Inf.** infantry. **2** inferior. **3** infinitive. **4** informal. **5** information.

infallible ❶ (ɪnˈfæləbᵊl) *adj* **1** not fallible; not liable to error. **2** not liable to failure; certain; sure: *an infallible cure.* ◆ *n* **3** a person or thing that is incapable of error or failure.
▸**inˌfalliˈbility** *or* **inˈfallibleness** *n* ▸**inˈfallibly** *adv*

infamous ❶ (ˈɪnfəməs) *adj* **1** having a bad reputation; notorious. **2** causing or deserving a bad reputation; shocking: *infamous conduct.*
▸**ˈinfamously** *adv* ▸**ˈinfamousness** *n*

infamy ❶ (ˈɪnfəmɪ) *n, pl* **infamies. 1** the state or condition of being infamous. **2** an infamous act or event. [C15: from L *infāmis* of evil repute, from IN-[1] + *fāma* FAME]

infancy ❶ (ˈɪnfənsɪ) *n, pl* **infancies. 1** the state or period of being an infant; childhood. **2** an early stage of growth or development. **3** infants collectively. **4** the period of life prior to attaining legal majority; minority nonage.

infant ❶ (ˈɪnfənt) *n* **1** a child at the earliest stage of its life; baby. **2** *Law.* another word for **minor** (sense 9). **3** *Brit.* a young schoolchild. **4** a person who is beginning or inexperienced in an activity. **5** (*modifier*) **5a** of or relating to young children or infancy. **5b** designed or intended for young children. ◆ *adj* **6** in an early stage of development; nascent: *an infant science.* **7** *Law.* of or relating to the legal status of infancy. [C14: from L *infāns,* lit.: speechless, from IN-[1] + *fārī* to speak]
▸**ˈinfantˌhood** *n*

infanta (ɪnˈfæntə) *n* (formerly) **1** a daughter of a king of Spain or Portugal. **2** the wife of an infante. [C17: from Sp. or Port., fem of INFANTE]

infante (ɪnˈfæntɪ) *n* (formerly) a son of a king of Spain or Portugal, esp. one not heir to the throne. [C16: from Sp. or Port., lit.: INFANT]

infanticide (ɪnˈfæntɪˌsaɪd) *n* **1** the killing of an infant. **2** the practice of killing newborn infants, still prevalent in some primitive tribes. **3** a person who kills an infant.
▸**inˌfantiˈcidal** *adj*

infantile ❶ (ˈɪnfənˌtaɪl) *adj* **1** like a child in action or behaviour; childishly immature; puerile. **2** of, relating to, or characteristic of infants or infancy. **3** in an early stage of development.
▸**infantility** (ˌɪnfənˈtɪlɪtɪ) *n*

infantile paralysis *n* a former name for **poliomyelitis.**

THESAURUS

Antonyms *adj* active, alive, alive and kicking, animated, energetic, full of beans (*inf.*), living, mobile, moving, reactive, responsive, vital

inertia *n* **1** = **inactivity**, apathy, deadness, disinclination to move, drowsiness, dullness, idleness, immobility, indolence, languor, lassitude, laziness, lethargy, listlessness, passivity, sloth, sluggishness, stillness, stupor, torpor, unresponsiveness
Antonyms *n* action, activity, animation, brio, energy, liveliness, vigour, vitality

inescapable *adj* = **unavoidable**, certain, destined, fated, ineluctable, ineludible (*rare*), inevitable, inexorable, sure

inestimable *adj* **1, 2** = **incalculable**, beyond price, immeasurable, invaluable, precious, priceless, prodigious

inevitability *n* **1, 2** = **certainty**, fate, ineluctability, inexorability *or* inexorableness, sureness, unavoidability *or* unavoidableness

inevitable *adj* **1, 2** = **unavoidable**, assured, certain, decreed, destined, fixed, ineluctable, inescapable, inexorable, necessary, ordained, settled, sure, unpreventable
Antonyms *adj* avoidable, escapable, evadable, preventable, uncertain

inevitably *adv* **1, 2** = **unavoidably**, as a necessary consequence, as a result, automatically, certainly, necessarily, of necessity, perforce, surely, willy-nilly

inexcusable *adj* = **unforgivable**, indefensible, inexpiable, outrageous, unjustifiable, unpardonable, unwarrantable
Antonyms *adj* defensible, excusable, forgivable, justifiable, pardonable

inexhaustible *adj* **1** = **endless**, bottomless, boundless, illimitable, infinite, limitless, measureless, never-ending, unbounded **2** = **tireless**, indefatigable, undaunted, unfailing, unflagging, untiring, unwearied, unwearying
Antonyms *adj* ≠ **endless:** bounded, exhaustible, finite, limitable, limited, measurable ≠ **tireless:** daunted, enervated, failing, flagging, tiring, wearied

inexorable *adj* **1** = **unrelenting**, adamant, cruel, hard, harsh, immovable, implacable, ineluctable, inescapable, inflexible, merciless, obdurate, pitiless, relentless, remorseless, severe, unappeasable, unbending, unyielding
Antonyms *adj* bending, flexible, lenient, movable, relenting, yielding

inexorably *adv* **1** = **relentlessly**, implacably, inevitably, irresistibly, remorselessly, unrelentingly

inexpensive *adj* = **cheap**, bargain, budget, economical, low-cost, low-priced, modest, reasonable
Antonyms *adj* costly, dear, exorbitant, expensive, high-priced, pricey, uneconomical

inexperience *n* = **unfamiliarity**, callowness, greenness, ignorance, newness, rawness, unexpertness

inexperienced *adj* = **immature**, amateur, callow, fresh, green, new, raw, unaccustomed, unacquainted, unfamiliar, unfledged, unpractised, unschooled, unseasoned, unskilled, untrained, untried, unused, unversed, wet behind the ears (*inf.*)
Antonyms *adj* experienced, familiar, knowledgeable, practised, seasoned, skilled, trained, versed

inexplicable *adj* = **unaccountable**, baffling, beyond comprehension, enigmatic, incomprehensible, inscrutable, insoluble, mysterious, mystifying, strange, unfathomable, unintelligible
Antonyms *adj* comprehensible, explainable, explicable, fathomable, intelligible, soluble, understandable

inextricably *adv* = **inseparably**, indissolubly, indistinguishably, intricately, irretrievably, totally

infallibility *n* **1** = **perfection**, faultlessness, impeccability, irrefutability, omniscience, supremacy, unerringness **2** = **reliability**, dependability, safety, sureness, trustworthiness

infallible *adj* **1** = **perfect**, faultless, impeccable, omniscient, unerring, unimpeachable **2** = **sure**, certain, dependable, foolproof, reliable, sure- fire (*inf.*), trustworthy, unbeatable, unfailing
Antonyms *adj* ≠ **perfect:** errant, fallible, human, imperfect, mortal ≠ **sure:** doubtful, dubious, uncertain, undependable, unreliable, unsure

infamous *adj* **1** = **notorious**, disreputable, ill-famed **2** = **shocking**, abominable, atrocious, base, detestable, disgraceful, dishonourable, egregious, flagitious, hateful, heinous, ignominious, iniquitous, loathsome, monstrous, nefarious, odious, opprobrious, outrageous, scandalous, scurvy, shameful, vile, villainous, wicked
Antonyms *adj* ≠ **notorious:** esteemed, glorious, honourable, noble, reputable, virtuous

infamy *n* **1** = **notoriety**, abomination, atrocity, discredit, disgrace, dishonour, disrepute, ignominy, obloquy, odium, opprobrium, outrageousness, scandal, shame, stigma, villainy

infancy *n* **1** = **early childhood**, babyhood **2** = **beginnings**, cradle, dawn, early stages, emergence, inception, origins, outset, start
Antonyms *n* ≠ **beginnings:** close, conclusion, death, end, expiration, finish, termination

infant *n* **1** = **baby**, ankle-biter, babe, babe in arms, bairn (*Scot.*), child, little one, neonate, newborn child, rug rat (*sl.*), sprog (*sl.*), suckling, toddler, tot, wean (*Scot.*) ◆ *adj* **6** = **early**, baby, dawning, developing, emergent, growing, immature, initial, nascent, newborn, unfledged, young

infantile *adj* **1** = **childish**, babyish, immature, puerile, tender, weak, young
Antonyms *adj* adult, developed, mature

infantilism (ɪnˈfæntɪˌlɪzəm) *n* **1** *Psychol.* a condition in which an older child or adult is mentally or physically undeveloped. **2** childish speech; baby talk.

infantry (ˈɪnfəntrɪ) *n, pl* **infantries. a** soldiers or units of soldiers who fight on foot with small arms. **b** (*as modifier*): *an infantry unit.* [C16: from It. *infanteria,* from *infante* boy, foot soldier; see INFANT]

infantryman (ˈɪnfəntrɪmən) *n, pl* **infantrymen.** a soldier belonging to the infantry.

infant school *n* (in England and Wales) a school for children aged between 5 and 7.

infarct (ɪnˈfɑːkt) *n* a localized area of dead tissue resulting from obstruction of the blood supply to that part. Also called: **infarction.** [C19: via NL from L *infarctus* stuffed into, from *farcīre* to stuff]
▸**inˈfarcted** *adj*

infatuate Ⓣ *vb* (ɪnˈfætjʊˌeɪt), **infatuates, infatuating, infatuated.** (*tr*) **1** to inspire or fill with foolish, shallow, or extravagant passion. **2** to cause to act foolishly. ◆ *n* (ɪnˈfætjʊɪt, -ˌeɪt). **3** *Literary.* a person who is infatuated. [C16: from L *infatuāre,* from IN-[2] + *fatuus* FATUOUS]
▸**inˌfatuˈation** *n*

infatuated Ⓣ (ɪnˈfætjʊˌeɪtɪd) *adj* (often foll. by *with*) possessed by a foolish or extravagant passion, esp. for another person.

infect Ⓣ (ɪnˈfɛkt) *vb* (*mainly tr*) **1** to cause infection in; contaminate (an organism, wound, etc.) with pathogenic microorganisms. **2** (*also intr*) to affect or become affected with a communicable disease. **3** to taint, pollute, or contaminate. **4** to affect, esp. adversely, as if by contagion. **5** (*also intr*) *Computing.* to affect or become affected with a computer virus. ◆ *adj* **6** *Arch.* contaminated or polluted with or as if with a disease; infected. [C14: from L *inficere* to dip into, stain, from *facere* to make]
▸**inˈfector** *or* **inˈfecter** *n*

infection Ⓣ (ɪnˈfɛkʃən) *n* **1** invasion of the body by pathogenic microorganisms. **2** the resulting condition in the tissues. **3** an infectious disease. **4** the act of infecting or state of being infected. **5** an agent or influence that infects. **6** persuasion or corruption, as by ideas, perverse influences, etc.

infectious Ⓣ (ɪnˈfɛkʃəs) *adj* **1** (of a disease) capable of being transmitted. **2** (of a disease) caused by microorganisms, such as bacteria, viruses, or protozoa. **3** causing or transmitting infection. **4** tending or apt to spread, as from one person to another: *infectious mirth.*
▸**inˈfectiously** *adv* ▸**inˈfectiousness** *n*

infectious hepatitis *n* any form of hepatitis caused by viruses. See **hepatitis A, hepatitis B, non-A, non-B hepatitis.**

infectious mononucleosis *n* an acute infectious disease, caused by a virus (**Epstein-Barr virus**), characterized by fever, sore throat, swollen and painful lymph nodes, and abnormal lymphocytes in the blood. Also called: **glandular fever.**

infective (ɪnˈfɛktɪv) *adj* **1** capable of causing infection. **2** a less common word for **infectious.**
▸**inˈfectively** *adv* ▸**inˈfectiveness** *n*

infelicity Ⓣ (ˌɪnfɪˈlɪsɪtɪ) *n, pl* **infelicities. 1** unhappiness; misfortune. **2** an instance of bad luck or mischance. **3** something, esp. a remark or expression, that is inapt or inappropriate.
▸**ˌinfeˈlicitous** *adj*

infer Ⓣ (ɪnˈfɜː) *vb* **infers, inferring, inferred.** (when *tr, may take a clause as object*) **1** to conclude (a state of affairs, supposition, etc.) by reasoning from evidence; deduce. **2** (*tr*) to have or lead to as a necessary or logical consequence; indicate. **3** (*tr*) to hint or imply. [C16: from L *inferre* to bring into, from *ferre* to bear, carry]
▸**inˈferable** *or* **inˈferrable** *adj* ▸**inˈferrer** *n*

> **USAGE NOTE** The use of *infer* to mean *imply* is common in both speech and writing, but is regarded by many people as incorrect.

inference Ⓣ (ˈɪnfərəns, -frəns) *n* **1** the act or process of inferring. **2** an inferred conclusion, deduction, etc. **3** any process of reasoning from premises to a conclusion. **4** *Logic.* the specific mode of reasoning used.

inferential (ˌɪnfəˈrɛnʃəl) *adj* of, relating to, or derived from inference.
▸**ˌinferˈentially** *adv*

inferior Ⓣ (ɪnˈfɪərɪə) *adj* **1** lower in value or quality. **2** lower in rank, position, or status; subordinate. **3** not of the best; mediocre; commonplace. **4** lower in position; situated beneath. **5** (of a plant ovary) situated below the other floral parts. **6** *Astron.* **6a** orbiting between the sun and the earth: *an inferior planet.* **6b** lying below the horizon. **7** *Printing.* (of a character) printed at the foot of an ordinary character. ◆ *n* **8** an inferior person. **9** *Printing.* an inferior character. [C15: from L: lower, from *inferus* low]
▸**inferiority** (ɪnˌfɪərɪˈɒrɪtɪ) *n* ▸**inˈferiorly** *adv*

inferiority complex *n Psychiatry.* a disorder arising from the conflict between the desire to be noticed and the fear of being humiliated, characterized by aggressiveness or withdrawal into oneself.

infernal Ⓣ (ɪnˈfɜːnᵊl) *adj* **1** of or relating to an underworld of the dead. **2** deserving or befitting hell; diabolic; fiendish. **3** *Inf.* irritating; confounded. [C14: from LL, from *infernus* hell, from L (adj): lower, hellish; rel. to L *inferus* low]
▸**ˌinferˈnality** *n* ▸**inˈfernally** *adv*

infernal machine *n Arch.* an explosive device (usually disguised) or booby trap.

inferno (ɪnˈfɜːnəʊ) *n, pl* **infernos. 1** (*sometimes cap.;* usually preceded by *the*) hell; the infernal region. **2** any place or state resembling hell, esp. a conflagration. [C19: from It., from LL *infernus* hell]

infertile Ⓣ (ɪnˈfɜːtaɪl) *adj* **1** not capable of producing offspring; sterile. **2** (of land) not productive; barren.
▸**inˈfertilely** *adv* ▸**infertility** (ˌɪnfəˈtɪlɪtɪ) *n*

infest Ⓣ (ɪnˈfɛst) *vb* (*tr*) **1** to inhabit or overrun in unpleasantly large numbers. **2** (of parasites such as lice) to invade and live on or in (a host). [C15: from L *infestāre* to molest, from *infestus* hostile]
▸**ˌinfesˈtation** *n* ▸**inˈfester** *n*

infeudation (ˌɪnfjʊˈdeɪʃən) *n History.* **1** (in feudal society) the act of putting a vassal in possession of a fief. **2** the granting of tithes to laymen.

infidel Ⓣ (ˈɪnfɪdᵊl) *n* **1** a person who has no religious belief; unbeliever. ◆ *adj* **2** rejecting a specific religion, esp. Christianity or Islam. **3** of or relating to unbelievers or unbelief. [C15: from Med. L, from L (adj): unfaithful, from IN-[1] + *fidēlis* faithful; see FEALTY]

infidelity Ⓣ (ˌɪnfɪˈdɛlɪtɪ) *n, pl* **infidelities. 1** lack of faith or constancy, esp. sexual faithfulness. **2** lack of religious faith; disbelief. **3** an act or instance of disloyalty.

infield (ˈɪnˌfiːld) *n* **1** *Cricket.* the area of the field near the pitch. Cf. **outfield** (sense 1). **2** *Baseball.* the area of the playing field enclosed by the base lines. **3** *Agriculture.* the part of a farm nearest to the farm buildings.
▸**ˈinˌfielder** *n*

infighting (ˈɪnˌfaɪtɪŋ) *n* **1** *Boxing.* combat at close quarters in which proper blows are inhibited. **2** intense competition, as between members of an organization.
▸**ˈinˌfighter** *n*

infill (ˈɪnfɪl) *or* **infilling** (ˈɪnfɪlɪŋ) *n* **1** the act of filling or closing gaps, etc., in something, such as a row of buildings. **2** material used to fill a cavity, gap, hole, etc.

infiltrate Ⓣ (ˈɪnfɪlˌtreɪt) *vb* **infiltrates, infiltrating, infiltrated. 1** to undergo the process in which a fluid passes into the pores or interstices of a

THESAURUS

infatuate *vb* **1 = obsess,** befool, beguile, bewitch, captivate, delude, enchant, enrapture, fascinate, make a fool of, mislead, stupefy, sweep one off one's feet, turn (someone's) head

infatuated *adj* **= obsessed,** beguiled, besotted, bewitched, captivated, carried away, crazy about (*inf.*), enamoured, enraptured, fascinated, head over heels in love with, inflamed, intoxicated, possessed, smitten (*inf.*), spellbound, swept off one's feet, under the spell of

infatuation *n* **1 = obsession,** crush (*inf.*), fixation, folly, foolishness, madness, passion, thing (*inf.*)

infect *vb* **3 = contaminate,** affect, blight, corrupt, defile, influence, poison, pollute, spread to *or* among, taint, touch, vitiate

infection *n* **1-4 = contamination,** contagion, corruption, defilement, poison, pollution, septicity, virus

infectious *adj* **1, 3 = catching,** communicable, contagious, contaminating, corrupting, defiling, infective, pestilential, poisoning, polluting, spreading, transmittable, virulent, vitiating

infelicity *n* **1 = misfortune,** bad luck, misery, sadness, unhappiness, woe, wretchedness

infer *vb* **1 = deduce,** conclude, conjecture, derive, gather, presume, put two and two together, read between the lines, surmise, understand

inference *n* **2 = deduction,** assumption, conclusion, conjecture, consequence, corollary, illation (*rare*), presumption, reading, surmise

inferior *adj* **2 = lower,** junior, lesser, menial, minor, secondary, subordinate, subsidiary, under, underneath **3 = substandard,** bad, duff (*Brit. inf.*), imperfect, indifferent, low-grade, low-rent (*inf., chiefly US*), mean, mediocre, no great shakes (*inf.*), not a patch on, not much cop (*Brit. sl.*), of a sort *or* of sorts, poor, poorer, second-class, second-rate, shoddy, worse ◆ *n* **8 = underling,** junior, menial, subordinate
Antonyms *adj* ≠ **lower:** greater, higher, senior, superior, top ≠ **substandard:** excellent, fine, first-class

inferiority *n* **2 = subservience,** abasement, inferior status *or* standing, lowliness, subordination **3 = inadequacy,** badness, deficiency, imperfection, insignificance, meanness, mediocrity, shoddiness, unimportance, worthlessness
Antonyms *n* ≠ **subservience:** advantage, ascendancy, dominance, superiority ≠ **inadequacy:** eminence, excellence, superiority

infernal *adj* **1 = hellish,** chthonian, Hadean, lower, nether, Plutonian, Stygian, Tartarean (*literary*), underworld **2 = devilish,** accursed, damnable, damned, demonic, diabolical, fiendish, hellish, malevolent, malicious, satanic
Antonyms *adj* ≠ **hellish:** celestial, heavenly ≠ **devilish:** angelic, glorious, godlike, seraphic

infertile *adj* **1, 2 = barren,** infecund, nonproductive, sterile, unfruitful, unproductive
Antonyms *adj* fecund, fertile, fruitful, generative, productive

infertility *n* **1, 2 = sterility,** barrenness, infecundity, unfruitfulness, unproductiveness

infest *vb* **1 = overrun,** beset, flood, invade, penetrate, permeate, ravage, swarm, throng

infested *adj* **1 = overrun,** alive, beset, crawling, lousy, pervaded, plagued, ravaged, ridden, swarming, teeming

infidel *n* **1 = pagan,** atheist, freethinker, Gentile, giaour (*Turkish*), heathen, heretic, sceptic, unbeliever

infidelity *n* **1 = unfaithfulness,** adultery, bad faith, betrayal, cheating (*inf.*), disloyalty, duplicity, faithlessness, false-heartedness, falseness, perfidy

infiltrate *vb* **3 = penetrate,** creep in, filter through, insinuate oneself, make inroads (into), percolate, permeate, pervade, sneak in (*inf.*), work *or* worm one's way into

solid; permeate. **2** *Mil.* to pass undetected through (an enemy-held line or position). **3** to gain or cause to gain entrance or access surreptitiously: *they infiltrated the party structure.* ◆ *n* **4** something that infiltrates. [C18: from IN-[2] + FILTRATE]
▸ˌ**infil'tration** *n* ▸'**infilˌtrative** *adj* ▸'**infilˌtrator** *n*

infin. *abbrev. for* infinitive.

infinite Ⓣ ('ɪnfɪnɪt) *adj* **1a** having no limits or boundaries in time, space, extent, or magnitude. **1b** (*as n; preceded by the*): *the infinite.* **2** extremely or immeasurably great or numerous: *infinite wealth.* **3** all-embracing, absolute, or total: *God's infinite wisdom.* **4** *Maths.* having an unlimited or uncountable number of digits, factors, terms, etc.
▸'**infinitely** *adv* ▸'**infiniteness** *n*

infinitesimal Ⓣ (ˌɪnfɪnɪ'tɛsɪməl) *adj* **1** infinitely or immeasurably small. **2** *Maths.* of, relating to, or involving a small change in the value of a variable that approaches zero as a limit. ◆ *n* **3** *Maths.* an infinitesimal quantity.
▸ˌ**infini'tesimally** *adv*

infinitesimal calculus *n* another name for **calculus** (sense 1).

infinitive (ɪn'fɪnɪtɪv) *n Grammar.* a form of the verb not inflected for grammatical categories such as tense and person and used without an overt subject. In English, the infinitive usually consists of the word *to* followed by the verb.
▸**infinitival** (ˌɪnfɪnɪ'taɪvᵊl) *adj* ▸**in'finitively** *or* ˌ**infini'tivally** *adv*

infinitude (ɪn'fɪnɪˌtjuːd) *n* **1** the state or quality of being infinite. **2** an infinite extent, quantity, degree, etc.

infinity Ⓣ (ɪn'fɪnɪtɪ) *n, pl* **infinities. 1** the state or quality of being infinite. **2** endless time, space, or quantity. **3** an infinitely or indefinitely great number or amount. **4** *Maths.* **4a** the concept of a value greater than any finite numerical value. **4b** the reciprocal of zero. **4c** the limit of an infinite sequence of numbers.

infirm Ⓣ (ɪn'fɜːm) *adj* **1a** weak in health or body, esp. from old age. **1b** (*as collective n; preceded by the*): *the infirm.* **2** lacking moral certainty; indecisive or irresolute. **3** not stable, sound, or secure: *an infirm structure.* **4** *Law.* (of a law, etc.) lacking legal force; invalid.
▸**in'firmly** *adv* ▸**in'firmness** *n*

infirmary (ɪn'fɜːmərɪ) *n, pl* **infirmaries.** a place for the treatment of the sick or injured; hospital.

infirmity Ⓣ (ɪn'fɜːmɪtɪ) *n, pl* **infirmities. 1** the state or quality of being infirm. **2** physical weakness or debility; frailty. **3** a moral flaw or failing.

infix *vb* (ɪn'fɪks, 'ɪnˌfɪks). **1** (*tr*) to fix firmly in. **2** (*tr*) to instil or inculcate. **3** *Grammar.* to insert (an affix) into the middle of a word. ◆ *n* ('ɪnˌfɪks). **4** *Grammar.* an affix inserted into the middle of a word.
▸ˌ**infix'ation** *or* **infixion** (ɪn'fɪkʃən) *n*

in flagrante delicto (ɪn flə'græntɪ dɪ'lɪktəʊ) *adv Chiefly law.* while committing the offence; red-handed. Also: **flagrante delicto.** [L, lit.: with the crime still blazing]

inflame Ⓣ (ɪn'fleɪm) *vb* **inflames, inflaming, inflamed. 1** to arouse or become aroused to violent emotion. **2** (*tr*) to increase or intensify; aggravate. **3** to produce inflammation in (a tissue, organ, or part) or (of a tissue, etc.) to become inflamed. **4** to set or be set on fire. **5** (*tr*) to cause to redden.
▸**in'flamer** *n*

inflammable Ⓣ (ɪn'flæməbᵊl) *adj* **1** liable to catch fire; flammable. **2** readily aroused to anger or passion. ◆ *n* **3** something that is liable to catch fire.
▸**inˌflamma'bility** *or* **in'flammableness** *n* ▸**in'flammably** *adv*

USAGE NOTE See at **flammable.**

inflammation Ⓣ (ˌɪnflə'meɪʃən) *n* **1** the reaction of living tissue to injury or infection, characterized by heat, redness, swelling, and pain. **2** the act of inflaming or the state of being inflamed.

inflammatory Ⓣ (ɪn'flæmətərɪ, -trɪ) *adj* **1** characterized by or caused by inflammation. **2** tending to arouse violence, strong emotion, etc.
▸**in'flammatorily** *adv*

inflatable (ɪn'fleɪtəbᵊl) *n* **1** any of various large air-filled objects made of strong plastic or rubber. ◆ *adj* **2** capable of being inflated.

inflate Ⓣ (ɪn'fleɪt) *vb* **inflates, inflating, inflated. 1** to expand or cause to expand by filling with gas or air. **2** (*tr*) to cause to increase excessively; puff up; swell: *to inflate one's opinion of oneself.* **3** (*tr*) to cause inflation of (prices, money, etc.). **4** (*tr*) to raise in spirits; elate. **5** (*intr*) to undergo economic inflation. [C16: from L *inflāre* to blow into, from *flāre* to blow]
▸**in'flatedly** *adv* ▸**in'flatedness** *n* ▸**in'flater** *or* **in'flator** *n*

inflation Ⓣ (ɪn'fleɪʃən) *n* **1** the act of inflating or state of being inflated. **2** *Econ.* a progressive increase in the general level of prices brought about by an expansion in demand or the money supply or by autonomous increases in costs. Cf. **reflation. 3** *Inf.* the rate of increase of prices. **4** *Astron.* a very fast expansion of the universe occurring immediately after the big bang, postulated in certain models of the universe (**inflationary universes**) to account for the present distribution of matter.
▸**in'flationary** *adj*

inflationary spiral *n* a self-sustaining form of inflation in which a rise in prices generates a wage demand, causing a further price rise and a further wage demand.

inflationism (ɪn'fleɪʃəˌnɪzəm) *n* the policy of inflation through expansion of the supply of money and credit.
▸**in'flationist** *n, adj*

inflect (ɪn'flɛkt) *vb* **1** *Grammar.* to change (the form of a word) by inflection. **2** (*tr*) to change (the voice) in tone or pitch; modulate. **3** (*tr*) to cause to deviate from a straight or normal line or course; bend. [C15: from L *inflectere* to curve round, alter, from *flectere* to bend]
▸**in'flectedness** *n* ▸**in'flective** *adj* ▸**in'flector** *n*

inflection Ⓣ *or* **inflexion** (ɪn'flɛkʃən) *n* **1** modulation of the voice. **2** *Grammar.* a change in the form of a word, signalling change in such grammatical functions as tense, person, gender, number, or case. **3** an angle or bend. **4** the act of inflecting or the state of being inflected. **5** *Maths.* a change in curvature from concave to convex or vice versa.
▸**in'flectional** *or* **in'flexional** *adj* ▸**in'flectionally** *or* **in'flexionally** *adv*
▸**in'flectionless** *or* **in'flexionless** *adj*

inflexible Ⓣ (ɪn'flɛksəbᵊl) *adj* **1** not flexible; rigid; stiff. **2** obstinate; unyielding. **3** without variation; unalterable; fixed. [C14: from L *inflexibilis*; see INFLECT]
▸**inˌflexi'bility** *or* **in'flexibleness** *n* ▸**in'flexibly** *adv*

inflict Ⓣ (ɪn'flɪkt) *vb* (*tr*) **1** (often foll. by *on* or *upon*) to impose (something unwelcome, such as pain, oneself, etc.). **2** to deal out (blows, lashes, etc.). [C16: from L *inflīgere* to strike (something) against, dash against, from *flīgere* to strike]
▸**in'flictable** *adj* ▸**in'flicter** *or* **in'flictor** *n* ▸**in'fliction** *n*

in-flight *adj* provided during flight in an aircraft: *in-flight entertainment.*

inflorescence (ˌɪnflɔː'rɛsəns) *n* **1** the part of a plant that consists of the flower-bearing stalks. **2** the arrangement of the flowers on the stalks.

THESAURUS

infinite *adj* **1-3** = **never-ending**, absolute, all-embracing, bottomless, boundless, enormous, eternal, everlasting, illimitable, immeasurable, immense, inestimable, inexhaustible, interminable, limitless, measureless, numberless, perpetual, stupendous, total, unbounded, uncounted, untold, vast, wide, without end, without number
Antonyms *adj* bounded, circumscribed, finite, limited, measurable, restricted

infinitesimal *adj* **1** = **microscopic**, atomic, inappreciable, insignificant, minuscule, minute, negligible, teeny, teeny-weeny, tiny, unnoticeable, wee
Antonyms *adj* enormous, great, huge, infinite, large, vast

infinity *n* **1, 2** = **eternity**, boundlessness, endlessness, immensity, infinitude, perpetuity, vastness

infirm *adj* **1** = **frail**, ailing, debilitated, decrepit, doddering, doddery, enfeebled, failing, feeble, lame, weak **2** = **irresolute**, faltering, indecisive, insecure, shaky, unsound, unstable, vacillating, wavering, weak, wobbly
Antonyms *adj* ≠ **frail:** healthy, hearty, robust, sound, strong, sturdy, vigorous

infirmity *n* **1, 2** = **frailty**, debility, decrepitude, deficiency, feebleness, ill health, imperfection, sickliness, vulnerability **3** = **ailment**, defect, disorder, failing, fault, malady, sickness, weakness
Antonyms *n* ≠ **frailty:** health, soundness, stability, strength, vigour, wellness

inflame *vb* **1** = **enrage**, agitate, anger, arouse, embitter, exasperate, excite, fire, foment, heat, ignite, impassion, incense, infuriate, intoxicate, kindle, madden, make one's blood boil, provoke, rile, rouse, stimulate **2** = **aggravate**, exacerbate, exasperate, fan, increase, intensify, worsen
Antonyms *vb* allay, calm, cool, discourage, extinguish, pacify, quench, quiet, soothe, suppress

inflamed *adj* **3** = **sore**, angry, chafing, festering, fevered, heated, hot, infected, red, septic, swollen

inflammable *adj* **1** = **flammable**, combustible, incendiary

inflammation *n* **1** = **soreness**, burning, heat, painfulness, rash, redness, sore, tenderness

inflammatory *adj* **2** = **provocative**, anarchic, demagogic, explosive, fiery, incendiary, inflaming, instigative, insurgent, intemperate, like a red rag to a bull, rabble-rousing, rabid, riotous, seditious

inflate *vb* **1, 2** = **expand**, aerate, aggrandize, amplify, balloon, bloat, blow up, boost, dilate, distend, enlarge, escalate, exaggerate, increase, puff up *or* out, pump up, swell
Antonyms *vb* collapse, compress, contract, deflate, diminish, lessen, shrink

inflated *adj* **2** = **exaggerated**, bombastic, grandiloquent, ostentatious, overblown, swollen

inflation *n* **1** = **expansion**, aggrandizement, blowing up, distension, enhancement, enlargement, escalation, extension, increase, intensification, puffiness, rise, spread, swelling, tumefaction

inflection *n* **1** = **intonation**, accentuation, modulation **2** *Grammar* = **conjugation**, declension **3** = **bend**, angle, arc, arch, bow, crook, curvature

inflexibility *n* **1** = **rigidity**, hardness, immovability, inelasticity, stiffness, stringency **2** = **obstinacy**, fixity, intransigence, obduracy, steeliness

inflexible *adj* **1** = **inelastic**, hard, hardened, nonflexible, rigid, stiff, taut **2** = **obstinate**, adamant, brassbound, dyed-in-the-wool, firm, fixed, hard and fast, immovable, immutable, implacable, inexorable, intractable, iron, obdurate, relentless, resolute, rigorous, set, set in one's ways, steadfast, steely, stiff-necked, strict, stringent, stubborn, unadaptable, unbending, unchangeable, uncompromising, unyielding
Antonyms *adj* ≠ **inelastic:** elastic, flexible, lissom(e), pliable, pliant, supple, yielding ≠ **obstinate:** flexible, irresolute, movable, variable, yielding

inflict *vb* **1** = **impose**, administer, apply, deliver, exact, levy, mete *or* deal out, visit, wreak

infliction *n* **1** = **imposition**, administration, exaction, perpetration, wreaking

DICTIONARY

3 the process of flowering; blossoming. [C16: from NL, from LL, from *flōrescere* to bloom]
▸ **ˌinfloˈrescent** *adj*

inflow (ˈɪnˌfləʊ) *n* **1** something, such as a liquid or gas, that flows in. **2** Also called: **inflowing.** the act of flowing in; influx.

influence Ⓣ (ˈɪnflʊəns) *n* **1** an effect of one person or thing on another. **2** the power of a person or thing to have such an effect. **3** power resulting from ability, wealth, position, etc. **4** a person or thing having influence. **5** *Astrol.* an ethereal fluid regarded as emanating from the stars and affecting a person's future. **6 under the influence.** *Inf.* drunk. ◆ *vb* **influences, influencing, influenced.** *(tr)* **7** to persuade or induce. **8** to have an effect upon (actions, events, etc.); affect. [C14: from Med. L *influentia* emanation of power from the stars, from L *influere* to flow into, from *fluere* to flow]
▸ **ˈinfluenceable** *adj* ▸ **ˈinfluencer** *n*

influent (ˈɪnflʊənt) *adj also* **inflowing. 1** flowing in. ◆ *n* **2** something flowing in, esp. a tributary. **3** *Ecology.* an organism that has a major effect on its community.

influential Ⓣ (ˌɪnflʊˈɛnʃəl) *adj* having or exerting influence.
▸ **ˌinfluˈentially** *adv*

influenza (ˌɪnflʊˈɛnzə) *n* a highly contagious viral disease characterized by fever, muscular aches and pains, and inflammation of the respiratory passages. [C18: from It., lit.: INFLUENCE, hence, incursion, epidemic (first applied to influenza in 1743)]
▸ **ˌinfluˈenzal** *adj*

influx Ⓣ (ˈɪnˌflʌks) *n* **1** the arrival or entry of many people or things. **2** the act of flowing in; inflow. **3** the mouth of a stream or river. [C17: from LL *influxus,* from *influere;* see INFLUENCE]

info (ˈɪnfəʊ) *n Inf.* short for **information.**

infold Ⓣ (ɪnˈfəʊld) *vb (tr)* a variant of **enfold.**

inform Ⓣ (ɪnˈfɔːm) *vb* **1** *(tr;* often foll. by *of* or *about)* to give information to; tell. **2** *(tr;* often foll. by *of* or *about)* to make conversant (with). **3** *(intr;* often foll. by *against* or *on)* to give information regarding criminals, to the police, etc. **4** *(tr)* to give form to. **5** *(tr)* to impart some essential or formative characteristic to. **6** *(tr)* to animate or inspire. [C14: from L *informāre* to give form to, describe, from *formāre* to FORM]
▸ **inˈformable** *adj*

informal Ⓣ (ɪnˈfɔːməl) *adj* **1** not of a formal, official, or stiffly conventional nature. **2** appropriate to everyday life or use. **3** denoting or characterized by idiom, vocabulary, etc., appropriate to conversational language rather than to formal written language. **4** denoting a second-person pronoun in some languages used when the addressee is regarded as a friend or social inferior.
▸ **inˈformally** *adv*

informality Ⓣ (ˌɪnfɔːˈmælɪtɪ) *n, pl* **informalities. 1** the condition or quality of being informal. **2** an informal act.

informal vote *n Austral. & NZ.* an invalid vote or ballot.

informant (ɪnˈfɔːmənt) *n* a person who gives information.

information Ⓣ (ˌɪnfəˈmeɪʃən) *n* **1** knowledge acquired through experience or study. **2** knowledge of specific and timely events or situations; news. **3** the act of informing or the condition of being informed. **4a** an office, agency, etc., providing information. **4b** *(as modifier): information service.* **5** a charge or complaint made before justices of the peace, usually on oath, to institute summary criminal proceedings. **6** *Computing.* **6a** the meaning given to data by the way it is interpreted. **6b** another word for **data** (sense 2).
▸ **ˌinforˈmational** *adj*

information retrieval *n Computing.* the process of recovering information from stored data.

information superhighway *n* **1** the concept of a worldwide network of computers capable of transferring all types of digital information at high speed. **2** another name for the **Internet.** ◆ Also called: **information highway.**

information technology *n* the production, storage, and communication of information using computers, etc.

information theory *n* a collection of mathematical theories concerned with coding, transmitting, storing, retrieving, and decoding information.

informative Ⓣ (ɪnˈfɔːmətɪv) *or* **informatory** *adj* providing information; instructive.
▸ **inˈformatively** *adv* ▸ **inˈformativeness** *n*

informed Ⓣ (ɪnˈfɔːmd) *adj* **1** having much knowledge or education; learned or cultured. **2** based on information: an informed judgment.

informer Ⓣ (ɪnˈfɔːmə) *n* **1** a person who informs against someone, esp. a criminal. **2** a person who provides information.

infotainment (ˌɪnfəʊˈteɪnmənt) *n* (in television) the practice of presenting serious or instructive subjects in a style designed primarily to be entertaining. [C20: from INFO + (ENTER)TAINMENT]

infra- *prefix* below; beneath; after: *infrasonic.* [from L *infrā*]

infract Ⓣ (ɪnˈfrækt) *vb (tr)* to violate or break (a law, etc.). [C18: from L *infractus* broken off; see INFRINGE]
▸ **inˈfraction** *n* ▸ **inˈfractor** *n*

infra dig (ˈɪnfrə ˈdɪg) *adj (postpositive) Inf.* beneath one's dignity. [C19: from L *infrā dignitātem*]

infrangible (ɪnˈfrændʒɪbᵊl) *adj* **1** incapable of being broken. **2** not capable of being violated or infringed. [C16: from LL, from L IN-[1] + *frangere* to break]
▸ **inˌfrangiˈbility** *or* **inˈfrangibleness** *n* ▸ **inˈfrangibly** *adv*

infrared (ˌɪnfrəˈrɛd) *n* **1** the part of the electromagnetic spectrum with a longer wavelength than light but a shorter wavelength than radio waves. ◆ *adj* **2** of, relating to, using, or consisting of radiation lying within the infrared.

infrared astronomy *n* the study of radiations from space in the infrared region of the electromagnetic spectrum.

infrared photography *n* photography using film with an emulsion that is sensitive to infrared light, enabling it to be used in dark or misty conditions.

infrasound (ˈɪnfrəˌsaʊnd) *n* soundlike waves having a frequency below the audible range, i.e. below about 16 Hz.
▸ **infrasonic** (ˌɪnfrəˈsɒnɪk) *adj*

infrastructure (ˈɪnfrəˌstrʌktʃə) *n* **1** the basic structure of an organization, system, etc. **2** the stock of fixed capital equipment in a country, including factories, roads, schools, etc., considered as a determinant of economic growth.

infrequent Ⓣ (ɪnˈfriːkwənt) *adj* rarely happening or present; only occasional.
▸ **inˈfrequency** *or* **inˈfrequence** *n* ▸ **inˈfrequently** *adv*

infringe Ⓣ (ɪnˈfrɪndʒ) *vb* **infringes, infringing, infringed. 1** *(tr)* to violate or break (a law, agreement, etc.). **2** *(intr;* foll. by *on* or *upon)* to encroach or trespass. [C16: from L *infringere* to break off, from *frangere* to break]
▸ **inˈfringement** *n* ▸ **inˈfringer** *n*

infundibular (ˌɪnfʌnˈdɪbjʊlə) *adj* funnel-shaped. [C18: from L *infundibulum* funnel]

infuriate Ⓣ *vb* (ɪnˈfjʊərɪˌeɪt), **infuriates, infuriating, infuriated. 1** *(tr)* to anger; annoy. ◆ *adj* (ɪnˈfjʊərɪɪt). **2** *Arch.* furious. [C17: from Med. L *infuriāre* (vb); see IN-[2], FURY]
▸ **inˈfuriˌating** *adj* ▸ **inˈfuriˌatingly** *adv*

infuse Ⓣ (ɪnˈfjuːz) *vb* **infuses, infusing, infused. 1** *(tr;* often foll. by *into)* to

THESAURUS

influence *n* **1** = **effect**, hold, magnetism, power, rule, spell, sway, weight **2** = **control**, ascendancy, authority, direction, domination, mastery **3** = **power**, bottom, clout (*inf.*), connections, good offices, importance, leverage, prestige, pull (*inf.*), weight ◆ *vb* **7** = **persuade**, arouse, dispose, incite, incline, induce, instigate, move, predispose, prompt, rouse **8** = **affect**, act *or* work upon, control, direct, guide, impact on, manipulate, modify, sway

influential *adj* = **important**, authoritative, controlling, effective, efficacious, forcible, guiding, instrumental, leading, meaningful, momentous, moving, persuasive, potent, powerful, significant, telling, weighty
Antonyms *adj* impotent, ineffective, ineffectual, powerless, unimportant, uninfluential, unpersuasive, weak

influx *n* = **arrival**, convergence, flow, incursion, inflow, inrush, inundation, invasion, rush

infold *see* **enfold**

inform *vb* **1** = **tell**, acquaint, advise, apprise, clue in (*inf.*), communicate, enlighten, give (someone) to understand, instruct, keep (someone) posted, leak to, let know, make conversant (with), notify, put (someone) in the picture (*inf.*), send word to, teach, tip off **3** = **betray**, blab, blow the whistle on (*inf.*), denounce, grass (*Brit. sl.*), incriminate, inculpate, let the cat out of the bag, rat (*inf.*), shop (*sl., chiefly Brit.*), sing (*sl., chiefly US*), snitch (*sl.*), spill the beans (*inf.*), squeal (*sl.*), tell all, tell on (*inf.*) **6** = **inspire**, animate, characterize, illuminate, imbue, permeate, suffuse, typify

informal *adj* **1-3** = **relaxed**, casual, colloquial, cosy, easy, familiar, natural, simple, unceremonious, unconstrained, unofficial
Antonyms *adj* ceremonious, constrained, conventional, formal, official, stiff

informality *n* **1** = **familiarity**, casualness, ease, lack of ceremony, naturalness, relaxation, simplicity

information *n* **1, 2** = **facts**, advice, blurb, counsel, data, dope (*inf.*), gen (*Brit. inf.*), info (*inf.*), inside story, instruction, intelligence, knowledge, latest (*inf.*), lowdown (*inf.*), material, message, news, notice, report, tidings, word

informative *adj* = **instructive**, chatty, communicative, edifying, educational, enlightening, forthcoming, gossipy, illuminating, newsy, revealing

informed *adj* **1** = **knowledgeable**, abreast, acquainted, *au courant, au fait,* briefed, conversant, enlightened, erudite, expert, familiar, genned up (*Brit. inf.*), in the know (*inf.*), in the loop, in the picture, keeping one's finger on the pulse, learned, posted, primed, reliable, up, up to date, versed, well-read

informer *n* **1** = **betrayer**, accuser, grass (*Brit. sl.*), Judas, nark (*Brit., Austral., & NZ sl.*), sneak, squealer (*sl.*), stool pigeon

infraction *n* = **violation**, breach, breaking, contravention, infringement, nonfulfilment, transgression, trespass

infrequent *adj* = **occasional**, few and far between, once in a blue moon, rare, sporadic, uncommon, unusual
Antonyms *adj* common, customary, frequent, habitual, often, regular, usual

infringe *vb* **1** = **break**, contravene, disobey, transgress, violate **2** *with* **on** *or* **upon** = **intrude on**, encroach on, trespass on

infringement *n* **1** = **contravention**, breach, infraction, noncompliance, nonobservance, transgression, trespass, violation

infuriate *vb* **1** = **enrage**, anger, be like a red rag to a bull, exasperate, gall, get one's back up, incense, irritate, madden, make one's blood boil, make one see red (*inf.*), make one's hackles rise, nark (*Brit., Austral., & NZ sl.*), provoke, put one's back up, rile
Antonyms *vb* appease, calm, mollify, pacify, placate, propitiate, soothe

infuriating *adj* **1** = **annoying**, exasperating, galling, irritating, maddening, mortifying, pestilential, provoking, vexatious

infuse *vb* **1** = **instil**, breathe into, engraft, impart to, implant, inculcate, inspire, introduce **3** = **soak**, brew, macerate, steep

instil or inculcate. 2 (*tr; foll. by with*) to inspire; emotionally charge. 3 to soak or be soaked so as to extract flavour or other properties. 4 *Rare.* (foll. by *into*) to pour. [C15: from L *infundere* to pour into]
▸**in'fuser** *n*

infusible[1] (ɪn'fjuːzəbᵊl) *adj* not fusible; not easily melted; having a high melting point. [C16: from IN-[1] + FUSIBLE]
▸**in,fusi'bility** *or* **in'fusibleness** *n*

infusible[2] (ɪn'fjuːzəbᵊl) *adj* capable of being infused. [C17: from INFUSE + -IBLE]
▸**in,fusi'bility** *or* **in'fusibleness** *n*

infusion (ɪn'fjuːʒən) *n* 1 the act of infusing. 2 something infused. 3 an extract obtained by soaking.
▸**infusive** (ɪn'fjuːsɪv) *adj*

infusorian (,ɪnfju'zɔːrɪən) *Obs.* ◆ *n* 1 any of the microscopic organisms, such as protozoans, found in infusions of organic material. ◆ *adj* 2 of or relating to infusorians. [C18: from NL *Infusoria* former class name; see INFUSE]
▸**,infu'sorial** *adj*

-ing[1] *suffix forming nouns.* 1 (*from verbs*) the action of, process of, result of, or something connected with the verb: *meeting; winnings.* 2 (*from other nouns*) something used in, consisting of, involving, etc.: *tubing; soldiering.* 3 (*from other parts of speech*): *an outing.* [OE *-ing, -ung*]

-ing[2] *suffix.* 1 forming the present participle of verbs: *walking; believing.* 2 forming participial adjectives: *a sinking ship.* 3 forming adjectives not derived from verbs: *swashbuckling.* [ME *-ing, -inde,* from OE *-ende*]

-ing[3] *suffix forming nouns.* a person or thing having a certain quality or being of a certain kind: *sweeting; whiting.* [OE *-ing;* rel. to ON *-ingr*]

ingather (ɪn'gæðə) *vb* (*tr*) to gather together or in (a harvest, etc.).
▸**in'gatherer** *n*

ingeminate (ɪn'dʒɛmɪ,neɪt) *vb* **ingeminates, ingeminating, ingeminated.** (*tr*) *Rare.* to repeat; reiterate. [C16: from L *ingemināre* to redouble, from IN-[2] + *gemināre* to GEMINATE]

ingenious ⓣ (ɪn'dʒiːnjəs, -nɪəs) *adj* possessing or done with ingenuity; skilful or clever. [C15: from L, from *ingenium* natural ability; see ENGINE]
▸**in'geniously** *adv* ▸**in'geniousness** *n*

ingénue (,ænʒeɪ'njuː) *n* an artless, innocent, or inexperienced girl or young woman. [C19: from F, fem of *ingénu* INGENUOUS]

ingenuity ⓣ (,ɪndʒɪ'njuːɪtɪ) *n, pl* **ingenuities.** 1 inventive talent; cleverness. 2 an ingenious device, act, etc. 3 *Arch.* frankness; candour. [C16: from L *ingenuitās* a freeborn condition, outlook consistent with such a condition, from *ingenuus* native, freeborn (see INGENUOUS); meaning infl. by INGENIOUS]

ingenuous ⓣ (ɪn'dʒɛnjuəs) *adj* 1 naive, artless, or innocent. 2 candid; frank; straightforward. [C16: from L *ingenuus* freeborn, virtuous, from IN-[2] + *gignere* to beget]
▸**in'genuously** *adv* ▸**in'genuousness** *n*

ingest (ɪn'dʒɛst) *vb* (*tr*) to take (food or liquid) into the body. [C17: from L *ingerere* to put into, from IN-[2] + *gerere* to carry; see GEST]
▸**in'gestible** *adj* ▸**in'gestion** *n* ▸**in'gestive** *adj*

ingle ('ɪŋgᵊl) *n Arch. or dialect.* a fire in a room or a fireplace. [C16: prob. from Scot. Gaelic *aingeal* fire]

inglenook ('ɪŋgᵊl,nʊk) *n Brit.* a corner by a fireplace; chimney corner.

ingoing ('ɪn,gəʊɪŋ) *adj* going in; entering.

ingot ('ɪŋgət) *n* a piece of cast metal obtained from a mould in a form suitable for storage, etc. [C14: ?from IN-[2] + OE *goten,* p.p. of *geotan* to pour]

ingraft ⓣ (ɪn'grɑːft) *vb* a variant spelling of **engraft.**
▸**in'graftment** *or* **,ingraf'tation** *n*

ingrain ⓣ *or* **engrain** *vb* (ɪn'greɪn). (*tr*) 1 to impress deeply on the mind or nature; instil. 2 *Arch.* to dye into the fibre of (a fabric). ◆ *adj* ('ɪn,greɪn). 3 (of woven or knitted articles) made of dyed yarn or of fibre that is dyed before being spun into yarn. ◆ *n* ('ɪn,greɪn). 4 a carpet made from ingrained yarn. [C18: from *dyed in grain* dyed with kermes through the fibre]

ingrained ⓣ *or* **engrained** (ɪn'greɪnd) *adj* 1 deeply impressed or instilled. 2 (*prenominal*) complete or inveterate; utter. 3 (esp. of dirt) worked into or through the fibre, pores, etc.
▸**ingrainedly** *or* **engrainedly** (ɪn'greɪnɪdlɪ) *adv* ▸**in'grainedness** *or* **en'grainedness** *n*

ingrate ('ɪngreɪt, ɪn'greɪt) *Arch.* ◆ *n* 1 an ungrateful person. ◆ *adj* 2 ungrateful. [C14: from L *ingrātus* (adj), from IN-[1] + *grātus* GRATEFUL]
▸**'ingrately** *adv*

ingratiate ⓣ (ɪn'greɪʃɪ,eɪt) *vb* **ingratiates, ingratiating, ingratiated.** (*tr; often foll. by with*) to place (oneself) purposely in the favour (of another). [C17: from L, from IN-[2] + *grātia* grace, favour]
▸**in'grati,ating** *or* **in'gratiatory** *adj* ▸**in'grati,atingly** *adv* ▸**in,grati'ation** *n*

ingredient ⓣ (ɪn'griːdɪənt) *n* a component of a mixture, compound, etc., esp. in cooking. [C15: from L *ingrediēns* going into, from *ingredī* to enter; see INGRESS]

ingress ⓣ ('ɪngrɛs) *n* 1 the act of going or coming in; an entering. 2 a way in; entrance. 3 the right or permission to enter. [C15: from L *ingressus,* from *ingredī* to go in, from *gradī* to step, go]
▸**ingression** (ɪn'grɛʃən) *n*

in-group *n Sociol.* a highly cohesive and relatively closed social group characterized by the preferential treatment reserved for its members.

ingrowing ('ɪn,grəʊɪŋ) *adj* 1 (esp. of a toenail) growing abnormally into the flesh. 2 growing within or into.
▸**'in,growth** *n*

ingrown ('ɪn,grəʊn, ɪn'grəʊn) *adj* 1 (esp. of a toenail) grown abnormally into the flesh; covered by adjacent tissues. 2 grown within; native; innate.

inguinal ('ɪŋgwɪnᵊl) *adj Anat.* of or relating to the groin. [C17: from L *inguinālis,* from *inguen* groin]

ingulf ⓣ (ɪn'gʌlf) *vb* (*tr*) a variant of **engulf.**

ingurgitate (ɪn'gɜːdʒɪ,teɪt) *vb* **ingurgitates, ingurgitating, ingurgitated.** to swallow (food, etc.) greedily or in excess. [C16: from L *ingurgitāre* to flood, from IN-[2] + *gurges* abyss]
▸**in,gurgi'tation** *n*

inhabit ⓣ (ɪn'hæbɪt) *vb* **inhabits, inhabiting, inhabited.** (*tr*) to live or dwell in; occupy. [C14: from L *inhabitāre,* from *habitāre* to dwell]
▸**in'habitable** *adj* ▸**in,habita'bility** *n* ▸**in,habi'tation** *n*

inhabitant ⓣ (ɪn'hæbɪtənt) *n* a person or animal that is a permanent resident of a particular place or region.
▸**in'habitancy** *or* **in'habitance** *n*

inhalant (ɪn'heɪlənt) *adj* 1 (esp. of a medicinal preparation) inhaled for its therapeutic effect. 2 inhaling. ◆ *n* 3 an inhalant medicinal preparation.

inhale ⓣ (ɪn'heɪl) *vb* **inhales, inhaling, inhaled.** to draw (breath, etc.) into the lungs; breathe in. [C18: from IN-[2] + L *halāre* to breathe]
▸**,inha'lation** *n*

inhaler (ɪn'heɪlə) *n* 1 a device for breathing in therapeutic vapours, esp. one for relieving nasal congestion. 2 a person who inhales.

inhere (ɪn'hɪə) *vb* **inheres, inhering, inhered.** (*intr; foll. by in*) to be an inseparable part (of). [C16: from L *inhaerēre* to stick in, from *haerēre* to stick]

inherent ⓣ (ɪn'hɪərənt, -'hɛr-) *adj* existing as an inseparable part; intrinsic.
▸**in'herently** *adv*

inherit ⓣ (ɪn'hɛrɪt) *vb* **inherits, inheriting, inherited.** 1 to receive (property, etc.) by succession or under a will. 2 (*intr*) to succeed as heir. 3 (*tr*) to possess (a characteristic) through genetic transmission. 4 (*tr*) to receive (a position, etc.) from a predecessor. [C14: from OF *enheriter,* from LL *inhērēditāre* to appoint an heir, from L *hērēs* HEIR]
▸**in'herited** *adj* ▸**in'heritor** *n* ▸**in'heritress** *or* **in'heritrix** *fem n*

inheritable (ɪn'hɛrɪtəbᵊl) *adj* 1 capable of being transmitted by hered-

THESAURUS

ingenious *adj* = **creative**, adroit, bright, brilliant, clever, crafty, dexterous, fertile, inventive, masterly, original, ready, resourceful, shrewd, skilful, subtle
Antonyms *adj* artless, clumsy, unimaginative, uninventive, unoriginal, unresourceful, unskilful

ingenuity *n* 1 = **originality**, adroitness, cleverness, faculty, flair, genius, gift, ingeniousness, inventiveness, knack, resourcefulness, sharpness, shrewdness, skill, turn
Antonyms *n* clumsiness, dullness, incompetence, ineptitude, ineptness

ingenuous *adj* 1, 2 = **naive**, artless, candid, childlike, frank, guileless, honest, innocent, open, plain, simple, sincere, trustful, trusting, unreserved, unsophisticated, unstudied
Antonyms *adj* artful, crafty, devious, insincere, reserved, sly, sophisticated, subtle, wily

ingenuousness *n* 1, 2 = **naivety**, artlessness, candour, frankness, guilelessness, innocence, openness, trustingness, unsuspiciousness
Antonyms *n* artfulness, craftiness, insincerity, slyness, sophistication, subterfuge, subtlety

ingraft *see* **engraft**

ingrain *vb* 1 = **fix**, embed, entrench, imbue, implant, impress, imprint, instil, root, sow the seeds

ingrained *adj* 1 = **fixed**, brassbound, constitutional, deep-rooted, deep-seated, fundamental, hereditary, inborn, inbred, inbuilt, indelible, ineradicable, inherent, in the blood, intrinsic, inveterate, rooted

ingratiate *vb* = **pander to**, be a yes man, blandish, crawl, curry favour, fawn, flatter, get in with, get on the right side of, grovel, insinuate oneself, keep (someone) sweet, lick (someone's) boots, play up to, rub (someone) up the right way (*inf.*), seek the favour (of someone), suck up to (*inf.*), toady, worm oneself into (someone's) favour

ingratiating *adj* = **sycophantic**, bootlicking (*inf.*), crawling, fawning, flattering, humble, obsequious, servile, timeserving, toadying, unctuous

ingredient *n* = **component**, constituent, element, part

ingress *n* 1-3 = **entrance**, access, admission, admittance, door, entrée, entry, right of entry, way in

ingulf *see* **engulf**

inhabit *vb* = **live**, abide, dwell, lodge, make one's home, occupy, people, populate, possess, reside, take up residence in, tenant

inhabitant *n* = **dweller**, aborigine, citizen, denizen, indigene, indweller, inmate, native, occupant, occupier, resident, tenant

inhabited *adj* = **populated**, colonized, developed, held, occupied, peopled, settled, tenanted

inhalation *n* = **breathing**, breath, inhaling, inspiration

inhale *vb* = **breathe in**, draw in, gasp, respire, suck in
Antonyms *vb* blow, breathe out, exhale, expire

inherent *adj* = **innate**, basic, congenital, connate, essential, hereditary, immanent, inborn, inbred, inbuilt, ingrained, inherited, in one's blood, instinctive, intrinsic, native, natural
Antonyms *adj* alien, extraneous, extrinsic, imposed, superficial, supplementary

inherit *vb* 1-4 = **be left**, accede to, be bequeathed, come into, fall heir to, succeed to

ity from one generation to a later one. **2** capable of being inherited. **3** *Rare.* having the right to inherit.
▸**in,herita'bility** *or* **in'heritableness** *n* ▸**in'heritably** *adv*

inheritance Ⓣ (ɪn'hɛrɪtəns) *n* **1** *Law.* **1a** hereditary succession to an estate, title, etc. **1b** the right of an heir to succeed on the death of an ancestor. **1c** something that may legally be transmitted to an heir. **2** the act of inheriting. **3** something inherited; heritage. **4** the derivation of characteristics of one generation from an earlier one by heredity.

inheritance tax *n* **1** (in Britain) a tax introduced in 1986 to replace capital transfer tax, consisting of a percentage levied on that part of an inheritance exceeding a specified allowance. **2** (in the US) a state tax imposed on an inheritance according to its size and the relationship of the beneficiary to the deceased.

inhibit Ⓣ (ɪn'hɪbɪt) *vb* **inhibits, inhibiting, inhibited.** (*tr*) **1** to restrain or hinder (an impulse, desire, etc.). **2** to prohibit, forbid, or prevent. **3** to stop, prevent, or decrease the rate of (a chemical reaction). [C15: from L *inhibēre* to restrain, from IN-^{2} + *habēre* to have]
▸**in'hibitable** *adj* ▸**in'hibitive** *or* **in'hibitory** *adj*

inhibition Ⓣ (,ɪnɪ'bɪʃən, ,ɪnhɪ-) *n* **1** the act of inhibiting or the condition of being inhibited. **2** *Psychol.* a mental state or condition in which the varieties of expression and behaviour of an individual become restricted. **3** the process of stopping or retarding a chemical reaction. **4** *Physiol.* the suppression of the function or action of an organ or part, as by stimulation of its nerve supply.

inhibitor (ɪn'hɪbɪtə) *n* **1** Also: **inhibiter.** a person or thing that inhibits. **2** a substance that retards or stops a chemical reaction. **3** *Biochem.* **3a** a substance that inhibits the action of an enzyme. **3b** a substance that inhibits a metabolic or physiological process: *a plant growth inhibitor.*

inhospitable Ⓣ (ɪn'hɒspɪtəbᵊl, ,ɪnhɒ'spɪt-) *adj* **1** not hospitable; unfriendly. **2** (of a region, an environment, etc.) lacking a favourable climate, terrain, etc.
▸**in'hospitableness** *n* ▸**in'hospitably** *adv*

in-house *adj, adv* within an organization or group: *an in-house job; the job was done in-house.*

inhuman Ⓣ (ɪn'hjuːmən) *adj* **1** Also: **inhumane** (,ɪnhjuː'meɪn). lacking humane feelings, such as sympathy, understanding, etc.; cruel; brutal. **2** not human.
▸**,inhu'manely** *adv* ▸**in'humanly** *adv* ▸**in'humanness** *n*

inhumanity Ⓣ (,ɪnhjuː'mænɪtɪ) *n, pl* **inhumanities.** **1** lack of humane qualities. **2** an inhumane act, decision, etc.

inhume Ⓣ (ɪn'hjuːm) *vb* **inhumes, inhuming, inhumed.** (*tr*) to inter; bury. [C17: from L, from IN-^{2} + *humus* ground]
▸**,inhu'mation** *n* ▸**in'humer** *n*

inimical Ⓣ (ɪ'nɪmɪkᵊl) *adj* **1** adverse or unfavourable. **2** not friendly; hostile. [C17: from LL, from *inimīcus,* from IN-^{1} + *amīcus* friendly; see ENEMY]
▸**in'imically** *adv* ▸**in'imicalness** *or* **in,imi'cality** *n*

inimitable Ⓣ (ɪ'nɪmɪtəbᵊl) *adj* incapable of being duplicated or imitated; unique.
▸**in,imita'bility** *or* **in'imitableness** *n* ▸**in'imitably** *adv*

iniquity Ⓣ (ɪ'nɪkwɪtɪ) *n, pl* **iniquities.** **1** lack of justice or righteousness; wickedness; injustice. **2** a wicked act; sin. [C14: from L, from *inīquus* unfair, from IN-^{1} + *aequus* even, level; see EQUAL]
▸**in'iquitous** *adj* ▸**in'iquitously** *adv* ▸**in'iquitousness** *n*

initial Ⓣ (ɪ'nɪʃəl) *adj* **1** of, at, or concerning the beginning. ◆ *n* **2** the first letter of a word, esp. a person's name. **3** *Printing.* a large letter set at the beginning of a chapter or work. **4** *Bot.* a cell from which tissues and organs develop by division and differentiation. ◆ *vb* **initials, initialling, initialled** *or US* **initials, initialing, initialed. 5** (*tr*) to sign with one's initials, esp. to indicate approval; endorse. [C16: from L *initiālis* of the beginning, from *initium* beginning, lit.: an entering upon, from *inīre* to go in]
▸**in'itialer** *or* **in'itialler** *n* ▸**in'itially** *adv*

initialize *or* **initialise** (ɪ'nɪʃə,laɪz) *vb* **initializes, initializing, initialized** *or* **initialises, initialising, initialised.** (*tr*) to assign an initial value to (a variable or storage location) in a computer program.
▸**in,itiali'zation** *or* **in,itiali'sation** *n*

initiate Ⓣ *vb* (ɪ'nɪʃɪ,eɪt), **initiates, initiating, initiated.** (*tr*) **1** to begin or originate. **2** to accept (new members) into an organization such as a club, through often secret ceremonies. **3** to teach fundamentals to. ◆ *adj* (ɪ'nɪʃɪɪt, -,eɪt). **4** initiated; begun. ◆ *n* (ɪ'nɪʃɪɪt, -,eɪt). **5** a person who has been initiated, esp. recently. **6** a beginner; novice. [C17: from L *initiāre* (vb), from *initium;* see INITIAL]
▸**in'itiatory** *adj*

initiation Ⓣ (ɪ,nɪʃɪ'eɪʃən) *n* **1** the act of initiating or the condition of being initiated. **2** the ceremony, often secret, initiating new members into an organization.

initiative Ⓣ (ɪ'nɪʃɪətɪv, -'nɪʃətɪv) *n* **1** the first step or action of a matter; commencing move: *a peace initiative.* **2** the right or power to begin or initiate something: *he has the initiative.* **3** the ability or attitude required to begin or initiate something. **4** *Government.* the right of citizens to introduce legislation, etc., in a legislative body, as in Switzerland. **5 on one's own initiative.** without being prompted. ◆ *adj* **6** of or concerning initiation or serving to initiate; initiatory.
▸**in'itiatively** *adv*

initiator (ɪ'nɪʃɪ,eɪtə) *n* **1** a person or thing that initiates. **2** *Chem.* a substance that starts a chain reaction. **3** *Chem.* a very sensitive explosive used in detonators.

inject Ⓣ (ɪn'dʒɛkt) *vb* (*tr*) **1** *Med.* to introduce (a fluid) into the body (of a person or animal) by means of a syringe. **2** (foll. by *into*) to introduce (a new aspect or element): *to inject humour into a scene.* **3** to interject (a comment, idea, etc.). [C17: from *injicere* to throw in, from *jacere* to throw]
▸**in'jectable** *adj* ▸**in'jector** *n*

injection Ⓣ (ɪn'dʒɛkʃən) *n* **1** fluid injected into the body, esp. for medicinal purposes. **2** something injected. **3** the act of injecting. **4a** the act or process of introducing fluid under pressure, such as fuel into the combustion chamber of an engine. **4b** (*as modifier*): *injection moulding.*
▸**in'jective** *adj*

injunction Ⓣ (ɪn'dʒʌŋkʃən) *n* **1** *Law.* an instruction or order issued by a court to a party to an action, esp. to refrain from some act. **2** a command, admonition, etc. **3** the act of enjoining. [C16: from LL, from L *injungere* to ENJOIN]
▸**in'junctive** *adj* ▸**in'junctively** *adv*

injure Ⓣ ('ɪndʒə) *vb* **injures, injuring, injured.** (*tr*) **1** to cause physical or

THESAURUS

inheritance *n* **3** = **legacy**, bequest, birthright, heritage, patrimony

inheritor *n* **1** = **heir**, beneficiary, legatee, recipient, successor

inhibit *vb* **1** = **restrain**, arrest, bar, bridle, check, constrain, cramp (someone's) style (*inf.*), curb, debar, discourage, forbid, frustrate, hinder, hold back *or* in, impede, obstruct, prevent, prohibit, stem the flow, stop, throw a spanner in the works
Antonyms *vb* abet, allow, enable, encourage, further, let, permit, support

inhibited *adj* **1** = **shy**, constrained, frustrated, guarded, repressed, reserved, reticent, self-conscious, subdued, uptight (*inf.*), withdrawn
Antonyms *adj* free, natural, outgoing, relaxed, spontaneous, uninhibited, unreserved

inhibition *n* **1** = **shyness**, bar, block, check, embargo, hang-up (*inf.*), hindrance, interdict, mental blockage, obstacle, prohibition, reserve, restraint, restriction, reticence, self-consciousness

inhospitable *adj* **1** = **unfriendly**, cool, uncongenial, ungenerous, unkind, unreceptive, unsociable, unwelcoming, xenophobic **2** = **bleak**, bare, barren, desolate, empty, forbidding, godforsaken, hostile, lonely, sterile, unfavourable, uninhabitable
Antonyms *adj* ≠ **unfriendly:** amicable, friendly, generous, genial, gracious, hospitable, sociable, welcoming

inhuman *adj* **1** = **cruel**, animal, barbaric, barbarous, bestial, brutal, cold-blooded, diabolical, fiendish, heartless, inhumane, merciless, pitiless, remorseless, ruthless, savage, unfeeling, vicious
Antonyms *adj* charitable, compassionate, feeling, humane, merciful, sensitive, tender, warm-hearted

inhumanity *n* **1** = **cruelty**, atrocity, barbarism, brutality, brutishness, cold-bloodedness, cold-heartedness, hardheartedness, heartlessness, pitilessness, ruthlessness, unkindness, viciousness

inhumation *n* = **burial**, entombment, interment, sepulture

inimical *adj* **1, 2** = **hostile**, adverse, antagonistic, antipathetic, contrary, destructive, disaffected, harmful, hurtful, ill-disposed, injurious, noxious, opposed, oppugnant (*rare*), pernicious, repugnant, unfavourable, unfriendly, unwelcoming
Antonyms *adj* affable, amicable, congenial, favourable, friendly, good, helpful, kindly, sympathetic, welcoming

inimitable *adj* = **unique**, consummate, incomparable, matchless, nonpareil, peerless, supreme, unequalled, unexampled, unmatched, unparalleled, unrivalled, unsurpassable

iniquitous *adj* **1** = **wicked**, abominable, accursed, atrocious, base, criminal, evil, heinous, immoral, infamous, nefarious, reprehensible, reprobate, sinful, unjust, unrighteous, vicious

iniquity *n* **1, 2** = **wickedness**, abomination, baseness, crime, evil, evildoing, heinousness, infamy, injustice, misdeed, offence, sin, sinfulness, unrighteousness, wrong, wrongdoing
Antonyms *n* fairness, goodness, honesty, integrity, justice, morality, righteousness, uprightness, virtue

initial *adj* **1** = **first**, beginning, commencing, early, inaugural, inceptive, inchoate, incipient, introductory, opening, primary
Antonyms *adj* closing, concluding, ending, final, last, terminal, ultimate

initially *adv* **1** = **at first**, at *or* in the beginning, at the outset, at the start, first, firstly, in the early stages, originally, primarily, to begin with

initiate *vb* **1** = **begin**, break the ice, commence, get under way, inaugurate, institute, kick off (*inf.*), kick-start, launch, lay the foundations of, open, originate, pioneer, set going, set in motion, set the ball rolling, start **2** = **induct**, indoctrinate, instate, introduce, invest **3** = **instruct**, acquaint with, coach, familiarize with, teach, train ◆ *n* **6** = **novice**, beginner, convert, entrant, learner, member, probationer, proselyte, tyro

initiation *n* **1** = **introduction**, admission, baptism of fire, commencement, debut, enrolment, entrance, inauguration, inception, induction, installation, instatement, investiture

initiative *n* **1** = **first step**, advantage, beginning, commencement, first move, lead **3** = **resourcefulness**, ambition, drive, dynamism, enterprise, get-up-and-go, inventiveness, leadership, originality, push (*inf.*), resource

inject *vb* **1** = **vaccinate**, inoculate, jab (*inf.*), shoot (*inf.*) **2** = **introduce**, bring in, infuse, insert, instil, interject

injection *n* **1** = **vaccination**, inoculation, jab (*inf.*), shot (*inf.*), vaccine **2** = **introduction**, dose, infusion, insertion, interjection

injunction *n* **2** = **order**, admonition, command, dictate, exhortation, instruction, mandate, precept, ruling

injure *vb* **1** = **hurt**, abuse, blemish, blight, break, damage, deface, disable, harm, impair, mal-

mental harm or suffering to; hurt or wound. **2** to offend, esp. by an injustice. [C16: back formation from INJURY]
▸ **'injurable** *adj* ▸ **'injured** *adj* ▸ **'injurer** *n*

injurious Ⓣ (ɪn'dʒʊərɪəs) *adj* **1** causing damage or harm; deleterious; hurtful. **2** abusive, slanderous, or libellous.
▸ **in'juriously** *adv* ▸ **in'juriousness** *n*

injury Ⓣ ('ɪndʒərɪ) *n, pl* **injuries. 1** physical damage or hurt. **2** a specific instance of this: *a leg injury.* **3** harm done to a reputation. **4** *Law.* a violation or infringement of another person's rights that causes him harm and is actionable at law. [C14: from L *injūria* injustice, wrong, from *injūriōsus* acting unfairly, wrongful, from IN-[1] + *jūs* right]

injury time *n Soccer, rugby, etc.* extra playing time added on to compensate for time spent attending to injured players during the match. Also called: **stoppage time.**

injustice Ⓣ (ɪn'dʒʌstɪs) *n* **1** the condition or practice of being unjust or unfair. **2** an unjust act.

ink (ɪŋk) *n* **1** a fluid or paste used for printing, writing, and drawing. **2** a dark brown fluid ejected into the water for self-concealment by an octopus or related mollusc. ◆ *vb (tr)* **3** to mark with ink. **4** to coat (a printing surface) with ink. [C13: from OF *enque,* from LL *encaustum* a purplish-red ink, from Gk *enkauston* purple ink, from *enkaustos* burnt in, from *enkaiein* to burn in; see EN-[2], CAUSTIC]
▸ **'inker** *n*

Inkatha (ɪn'kɑːtə) *n* a South African political party; originally a Zulu organization founded in 1975 as a paramilitary group seeking nonracial democracy; won four seats in democratic multiracial elections in 1994. [C20: Zulu name for the grass coil used by Zulu women carrying loads on their heads]

inkblot ('ɪŋkˌblɒt) *n* a patch of ink accidentally or deliberately spilled. Ten such patches, of different shapes, are used in the Rorschach test.

ink-cap *n* any of several saprotrophic fungi whose caps disintegrate into a black inky fluid after the spores mature.

inkhorn ('ɪŋkˌhɔːn) *n* (formerly) a small portable container for ink, usually made from horn.

ink in *vb (adv)* **1** *(tr)* to use ink to go over pencil lines in (a drawing). **2** to apply ink to (a printing surface) in preparing to print from it. **3** to arrange or confirm definitely.

inkling Ⓣ ('ɪŋklɪŋ) *n* a slight intimation or suggestion; suspicion. [C14: prob. from *inclen* to hint at]

inkstand ('ɪŋkˌstænd) *n* a stand or tray on which are kept writing implements and containers for ink.

inkwell ('ɪŋkˌwɛl) *n* a small container for pen ink, often let into the surface of a desk.

inky ('ɪŋkɪ) *adj* **inkier, inkiest. 1** resembling ink, esp. in colour; dark or black. **2** of, containing, or stained with ink.
▸ **'inkiness** *n*

INLA *abbrev. for* Irish National Liberation Army.

inlaid ('ɪnˌleɪd, ɪn'leɪd) *adj* **1** set in the surface, as a design in wood. **2** having such a design or inlay: *an inlaid table.*

inland Ⓣ *adj* ('ɪnlənd). **1** of or located in the interior of a country or region away from a sea or border. **2** *Chiefly Brit.* operating within a country or region; domestic; not foreign. ◆ *n* ('ɪnˌlænd, -lənd). **3** the interior of a country or region. ◆ *adv* ('ɪnˌlænd, -lənd). **4** towards or into the interior of a country or region.
▸ **'inlander** *n*

Inland Revenue *n* (in Britain and New Zealand) a government board that administers and collects major direct taxes, such as income tax.

in-law *n* **1** a relative by marriage. ◆ *adj* **2** *(postpositive; in combination)* related by marriage: *a father-in-law.* [C19: back formation from *father-in-law,* etc.]

inlay *vb* (ɪn'leɪ), **inlays, inlaying, inlaid.** *(tr)* **1** to decorate (an article, esp. of furniture) by inserting pieces of wood, ivory, etc., into slots in the surface. ◆ *n* ('ɪnˌleɪ). **2** *Dentistry.* a filling inserted into a cavity and held in position by cement. **3** decoration made by inlaying. **4** an inlaid article, surface, etc.
▸ **'inˌlayer** *n*

inlet Ⓣ *n* ('ɪnˌlɛt). **1** a narrow inland opening of the coastline. **2** an entrance or opening. **3** the act of letting someone or something in. **4** something let in or inserted. **5a** a passage or valve through which a substance, esp. a fluid, enters a machine. **5b** *(as modifier): an inlet valve.* ◆ *vb* (ɪn'lɛt), **inlets, inletting, inlet. 6** *(tr)* to insert or inlay.

inlier ('ɪnˌlaɪə) *n* an outcrop of rocks that is entirely surrounded by younger rocks.

in loco parentis *Latin.* (ɪn 'ləʊkəʊ pə'rɛntɪs) in place of a parent: said of a person acting in a parental capacity.

inly ('ɪnlɪ) *adv Poetic.* inwardly; intimately.

inmate ('ɪnˌmeɪt) *n* a person who is confined to an institution such as a prison or hospital.

in medias res *Latin.* (ɪn 'miːdɪˌæs 'reɪs) in or into the middle of events or a narrative. [lit.: into the midst of things, taken from a passage in Horace's *Ars Poetica*]

in memoriam (ɪn mɪ'mɔːrɪəm) in memory of: used in obituaries, epitaphs, etc. [L]

inmost ('ɪnˌməʊst) *adj* another word for **innermost.**

inn (ɪn) *n* a pub or small hotel providing food and accommodation.

innards Ⓣ ('ɪnədz) *pl n Inf.* **1** the internal organs of the body, esp. the viscera. **2** the interior parts of anything, esp. the working parts. [C19: colloquial var. of *inwards*]

innate Ⓣ (ɪ'neɪt, 'ɪneɪt) *adj* **1** existing from birth; congenital; inborn. **2** being an essential part of the character of a person or thing. **3** instinctive; not learned: *innate capacities.* **4** *Philosophy.* (of ideas) present in the mind before any experience and knowable by pure reason. [C15: from L, from *innascī* to be born in, from *nascī* to be born]
▸ **in'nately** *adv* ▸ **in'nateness** *n*

inner Ⓣ ('ɪnə) *adj (prenominal)* **1** being or located further inside: *an inner room.* **2** happening or occurring inside. **3** relating to the soul, mind, spirit, etc. **4** more profound or obscure; less apparent: *the inner meaning.* **5** exclusive or private: *inner regions of the party.* ◆ *n* **6** *Archery.* **6a** the red innermost ring on a target. **6b** a shot which hits this ring.
▸ **'innerly** *adv* ▸ **'innerness** *n*

inner bar *n* **the.** *Brit.* all Queen's or King's Counsel collectively.

inner child *n Psychol.* the part of the psyche that retains feelings as they were experienced in childhood.

inner city *n* **a** the parts of a city in or near its centre, esp. when associated with poverty, substandard housing, etc. **b** *(as modifier): inner-city schools.*

inner man *or (fem)* **inner woman** *n* **1** the mind or soul. **2** *Jocular.* the stomach or appetite.

innermost Ⓣ ('ɪnəˌməʊst) *adj* **1** being or located furthest within; central. **2** intimate; private.

inner tube *n* an inflatable rubber tube that fits inside a pneumatic tyre casing.

innervate ('ɪnɜːˌveɪt) *vb* **innervates, innervating, innervated.** *(tr)* **1** to supply nerves to (a bodily organ or part). **2** to stimulate (a bodily organ or part) with nerve impulses.
▸ **ˌinner'vation** *n*

innings ('ɪnɪŋz) *n* **1** *(functioning as sing) Cricket, etc.* **1a** the batting turn of a player or team. **1b** the runs scored during such a turn. **2** *(sometimes sing)* a period of opportunity or action.

innkeeper Ⓣ ('ɪnˌkiːpə) *n* an owner or manager of an inn.

innocence Ⓣ ('ɪnəsəns) *n* the quality or state of being innocent. Archaic word: **innocency** ('ɪnəsənsɪ). [C14: from L *innocentia* harmlessness, from *innocēns* blameless, from IN-[1] + *nocēre* to hurt]

innocent Ⓣ ('ɪnəsənt) *adj* **1** not corrupted or tainted with evil; sinless; pure. **2** not guilty of a particular crime; blameless. **3** *(postpositive;* foll.

THESAURUS

treat, mar, ruin, spoil, tarnish, undermine, vitiate, weaken, wound, wrong

injured *adj* **1** = **hurt,** broken, damaged, disabled, lamed, undermined, weakened, wounded **2** = **wronged,** abused, blackened, blemished, defamed, ill-treated, maligned, maltreated, offended, tarnished, vilified

injurious *adj* **1** = **harmful,** adverse, bad, baneful (*arch.*), corrupting, damaging, deleterious, destructive, detrimental, disadvantageous, hurtful, iniquitous, maleficent, mischievous, noxious, pernicious, ruinous, unconducive, unhealthy, unjust, wrongful

injury *n* **1** = **harm,** abuse, damage, detriment, disservice, evil, grievance, hurt, ill, injustice, mischief, ruin, trauma (*Pathology*), wound, wrong

injustice *n* **1** = **unfairness,** bias, discrimination, favouritism, inequality, inequity, iniquity, one-sidedness, oppression, partiality, partisanship, prejudice, unjustness, unlawfulness, wrong
Antonyms *n* equality, equity, fairness, impartiality, justice, lawfulness, rectitude, right

inkling *n* = **suspicion,** clue, conception, faintest *or* foggiest idea, glimmering, hint, idea, indication, intimation, notion, suggestion, whisper

inland *adj* **1** = **interior,** domestic, internal, upcountry

inlet *n* **1** = **bay,** arm (of the sea), bight, cove, creek, firth *or* frith (*Scot.*), fjord, sea loch (*Scot.*) **2** = **bay,** entrance, ingress, passage

innards *pl n* **1** = **intestines,** entrails, guts, insides (*inf.*), inwards, viscera, vitals **2** = **works,** guts (*inf.*), mechanism

innate *adj* **1-3** = **inborn,** congenital, connate, constitutional, essential, immanent, inbred, indigenous, ingrained, inherent, inherited, in one's blood, instinctive, intrinsic, intuitive, native, natural
Antonyms *adj* accidental, acquired, affected, assumed, cultivated, fostered, incidental, learned, nurtured, unnatural

inner *adj* **1, 2** = **inside,** central, essential, interior, internal, intestinal, inward, middle **3** = **mental,** emotional, psychological, spiritual **4** = **hidden,** esoteric, intimate, personal, private, repressed, secret, unrevealed
Antonyms *adj* ≠ **inside:** exterior, external, outer, outside, outward ≠ **hidden:** exposed, obvious, overt, revealed, surface, unconcealed, unrepressed, visible

innermost *adj* **2** = **deepest,** basic, buried, central, deep, essential, intimate, personal, private, secret

innkeeper *n* = **publican,** host *or* hostess, hotelier, landlord *or* landlady, mine host

innocence *n* = **guiltlessness,** blamelessness, chastity, clean hands, incorruptibility, inexperience, ingenuousness, inoffensiveness, naïveté, purity, righteousness, sinlessness, stainlessness, uprightness, virginity, virtue
Antonyms *n* ≠ **guiltlessness:** corruption, guilt, impurity, offensiveness, sinfulness, wrongness

innocent *adj* **1** = **pure,** chaste, immaculate, impeccable, incorrupt, pristine, righteous, sinless, spotless, stainless, unblemished, unsullied, upright, virgin, virginal **2** = **not guilty,** blameless, clear, faultless, guiltless, honest, in the clear, squeaky-clean, uninvolved, unoffending **3** *with* **of** = **lacking,** clear of, empty of, free from, ignorant, nescient, unacquainted with, unaware, unfamiliar with, untouched by **4** = **harmless,** innocuous, inoffensive, unmalicious, unobjectionable, well-intentioned, well-meant **5** =

by *of*) free (of); lacking: *innocent of all knowledge of history.* **4a** harmless or innocuous: *an innocent game.* **4b** not cancerous: *an innocent tumour.* **5** credulous, naive, or artless. **6** simple-minded; slow-witted. ◆ *n* **7** an innocent person, esp. a young child or an ingenuous adult. **8** a simple-minded person; simpleton.
▸**'innocently** *adv*

innocuous ❶ (ɪ'nɒkjʊəs) *adj* having little or no adverse or harmful effect; harmless. [C16: from L *innocuus* harmless, from IN-[1] + *nocēre* to harm]
▸**in'nocuously** *adv* ▸**in'nocuousness** *or* **innocuity** (ˌɪnə'kjuːɪtɪ) *n*

innominate bone (ɪ'nɒmɪnɪt) *n* either of the two bones that form the sides of the pelvis, consisting of the ilium, ischium, and pubis. Nontechnical name: **hipbone.**

innovate ❶ ('ɪnəˌveɪt) *vb* **innovates, innovating, innovated.** to invent or begin to apply (methods, ideas, etc.). [C16: from L *innovāre* to renew, from IN-[2] + *novāre* to make new, from *novus* new]
▸**'innoˌvative** *or* **'innoˌvatory** *adj* ▸**'innoˌvator** *n*

innovation ❶ (ˌɪnə'veɪʃən) *n* **1** something newly introduced, such as a new method or device. **2** the act of innovating.
▸**ˌinno'vational** *adj* ▸**ˌinno'vationist** *n*

innuendo ❶ (ˌɪnjʊ'ɛndəʊ) *n, pl* **innuendos** *or* **innuendoes. 1** an indirect or subtle reference, esp. one made maliciously or indicating criticism or disapproval; insinuation. **2** *Law.* (in an action for defamation) an explanation of the construction put upon words alleged to be defamatory where this meaning is not apparent. [C17: from L, lit.: by hinting, from *innuere* to convey by a nod, from IN-[2] + *nuere* to nod]

Innuit ('ɪnjuːɪt) *n* a variant spelling of **Inuit.**

innumerable ❶ (ɪ'njuːmərəbᵊl, ɪ'njuːmrəbᵊl) *or* **innumerous** *adj* so many as to be uncountable; extremely numerous.
▸**inˌnumera'bility** *or* **in'numerableness** *n* ▸**in'numerably** *adv*

innumerate (ɪ'njuːmərɪt) *adj* **1** having neither knowledge nor understanding of mathematics or science. ◆ *n* **2** an innumerate person.
▸**in'numeracy** *n*

inoculate (ɪ'nɒkjʊˌleɪt) *vb* **inoculates, inoculating, inoculated. 1** to introduce (the causative agent of a disease) into the body in order to induce immunity. **2** (*tr*) to introduce (microorganisms, esp. bacteria) into (a culture medium). **3** (*tr*) to cause to be influenced or imbued, as with ideas. [C15: from L *inoculāre* to implant, from IN-[2] + *oculus* eye, bud]
▸**inˌocu'lation** *n* ▸**in'oculative** *adj* ▸**in'ocuˌlator** *n*

inoculum (ɪ'nɒkjʊləm) *or* **inoculant** *n, pl* **inocula** (-lə) *or* **inoculants.** *Med.* the substance used in giving an inoculation. [C20: NL; see INOCULATE]

in-off *n Billiards.* a shot that goes into a pocket after striking another ball.

inoperable ❶ (ɪn'ɒpərəbᵊl, -'ɒprə-) *adj* **1** incapable of being implemented or operated. **2** *Surgery.* not suitable for operation without risk, esp. because of metastasis.
▸**inˌopera'bility** *or* **in'operableness** *n* ▸**in'operably** *adv*

inordinate ❶ (ɪn'ɔːdɪnɪt) *adj* **1** exceeding normal limits; immoderate. **2** unrestrained, as in behaviour or emotion; intemperate. **3** irregular or disordered. [C14: from L *inordinātus* disordered, from IN-[1] + *ordināre* to put in order]
▸**in'ordinacy** *or* **in'ordinateness** *n* ▸**in'ordinately** *adv*

inorganic ❶ (ˌɪnɔː'gænɪk) *adj* **1** not having the structure or characteristics of living organisms; not organic. **2** relating to or denoting chemical compounds that do not contain carbon. **3** not having a system, structure, or ordered relation of parts; amorphous. **4** not resulting from or produced by growth; artificial.
▸**ˌinor'ganically** *adv*

inorganic chemistry *n* the branch of chemistry concerned with the elements and all their compounds except those containing carbon.

inosculate (ɪn'ɒskjʊˌleɪt) *vb* **inosculates, inosculating, inosculated. 1** *Physiol.* (of small blood vessels) to communicate by anastomosis. **2** to unite or be united so as to be continuous; blend. **3** to intertwine or cause to intertwine. [C17: from IN-[2] + L *ōsculāre* to equip with an opening, from *ōsculum*, dim. of *ōs* mouth]
▸**inˌoscu'lation** *n*

inositol (ɪ'nəʊsɪˌtɒl) *n* a cyclic alcohol, one isomer of which (*i*-inositol) is present in yeast and is a growth factor for some organisms. [C19: from Gk *in-*, *is* sinew + -OSE[2] + -ITE[1] + -OL[1]]

inpatient ('ɪnˌpeɪʃənt) *n* a patient living in the hospital where he is being treated.

in perpetuum *Latin.* (ɪn pɜː'pɛtjʊəm) forever.

input ('ɪnˌpʊt) *n* **1** the act of putting in. **2** that which is put in. **3** (*often pl*) a resource required for industrial production, such as capital goods, etc. **4** *Electronics.* the signal or current fed into a component or circuit. **5** *Computing.* the data fed into a computer from a peripheral device. **6** (*modifier*) of or relating to electronic, computer, or other input: *input program.* ◆ *vb* **inputs, inputting, input. 7** (*tr*) to insert (data) into a computer.

input/output *n Computing.* **1** the data or information passed into or out of a computer. **2** (*modifier*) concerned with or relating to such passage of data or information.

inquest ❶ ('ɪnˌkwɛst) *n* **1** an inquiry, esp. into the cause of an unexplained, sudden, or violent death, held by a coroner, in certain cases with a jury. **2** *Inf.* any inquiry or investigation. [C13: from Med. L, from L IN-[2] + *quaesītus* investigation, from *quaerere* to examine]

inquietude (ɪn'kwaɪɪˌtjuːd) *n* restlessness, uneasiness, or anxiety.
▸**inquiet** (ɪn'kwaɪət) *adj* ▸**in'quietly** *adv*

inquiline ('ɪnkwɪˌlaɪn) *n* **1** an animal that lives in close association with another animal without harming it. See also **commensal** (sense 1). ◆ *adj* **2** of or living as an inquiline. [C17: from L *inquilīnus* lodger, from IN-[2] + *colere* to dwell]
▸**inquilinous** (ˌɪnkwɪ'laɪnəs) *adj*

inquire ❶ *or* **enquire** (ɪn'kwaɪə) *vb* **inquires, inquiring, inquired** *or* **enquires, enquiring, enquired. 1a** to seek information (about); ask: *she inquired his age; she inquired about rates of pay.* **1b** (*intr*; foll. by *of*) to ask (a person) for information: *I'll inquire of my aunt when she is coming.* **2** (*intr*; often foll. by *into*) to make a search or investigation. [C13: from L *inquīrere*, from IN-[2] + *quaerere* to seek]
▸**in'quirer** *or* **en'quirer** *n* ▸**in'quiry** *or* **en'quiry** *n*

inquisition ❶ (ˌɪnkwɪ'zɪʃən) *n* **1** the act of inquiring deeply or searchingly; investigation. **2** a deep or searching inquiry, esp. a ruthless official investigation in order to suppress revolt or root out the unorthodox. **3** an official inquiry, esp. one held by a jury before an officer of the Crown. [C14: from legal L *inquīsītiō*, from *inquīrere* to seek for; see INQUIRE]
▸**ˌinqui'sitional** *adj* ▸**ˌinqui'sitionist** *n*

Inquisition (ˌɪnkwɪ'zɪʃən) *n History.* a judicial institution of the Roman Catholic Church (1232–1820) founded to suppress heresy.

inquisitive ❶ (ɪn'kwɪzɪtɪv) *adj* **1** excessively curious, esp. about the affairs of others; prying. **2** eager to learn; inquiring.
▸**in'quisitively** *adv* ▸**in'quisitiveness** *n*

inquisitor (ɪn'kwɪzɪtə) *n* **1** a person who inquires, esp. deeply, searchingly, or ruthlessly. **2** (*often cap.*) an official of the ecclesiastical court of the Inquisition.

inquisitorial (ɪnˌkwɪzɪ'tɔːrɪəl) *adj* **1** of, relating to, or resembling inquisition or an inquisitor. **2** offensively curious; prying. **3** *Law.* denoting criminal procedure in which one party is both prosecutor and judge, or in which the trial is held in secret. Cf. **accusatorial** (sense 2).
▸**inˌquisi'torially** *adv* ▸**inˌquisi'torialness** *n*

inquorate (ɪn'kwɔːˌreɪt) *adj Brit.* not consisting of or being a quorum: *this meeting is inquorate.*

in re (ɪn 'reɪ) *prep* in the matter of: used esp. in bankruptcy proceedings. [C17: from L]

INRI *abbrev. for* Iesus Nazarenus Rex Iudaeorum (the inscription placed over Christ's head during the Crucifixion). [L: Jesus of Nazareth, King of the Jews]

inro ('ɪnrəʊ) *n, pl* **inro.** a set of small lacquer boxes formerly worn hung from the belt by Japanese men and used to carry medicines, seals, etc.

inroad ❶ ('ɪnˌrəʊd) *n* **1** an invasion or hostile attack; raid or incursion. **2** an encroachment or intrusion.

inrush ('ɪnˌrʌʃ) *n* a sudden usually overwhelming inward flow or rush; influx.
▸**'inˌrushing** *n, adj*

ins. *abbrev. for:* **1** inches. **2** insulated. **3** insurance.

THESAURUS

naive, artless, childlike, credulous, frank, guileless, gullible, ingenuous, open, simple, unsuspicious, unworldly, wet behind the ears (*inf.*) ◆ *n* **7** = **child**, babe (in arms) (*inf.*), greenhorn (*inf.*), ingénue *or (masc.)* ingénu
Antonyms *adj* ≠ **pure:** corrupt, dishonest, immoral, impure, sinful, wrong ≠ **not guilty:** blameworthy, culpable, guilty, responsible ≠ **harmless:** evil, harmful, iniquitous, malicious, offensive, wicked ≠ **naive:** artful, disingenuous, sophisticated, worldly

innocuous *adj* = **harmless**, innocent, innoxious, inoffensive, safe, unobjectionable

innovation *n* **2** = **modernization**, alteration, change, departure, introduction, modernism, newness, novelty, variation

innovative *adj* = **novel**, inventive, new, transformational, variational

innovator *n* = **modernizer**, changer, introducer, inventor, transformer

innuendo *n* **1** = **insinuation**, aspersion, hint, implication, imputation, intimation, overtone, suggestion, whisper

innumerable *adj* = **countless**, beyond number, incalculable, infinite, many, multitudinous, myriad, numberless, numerous, unnumbered, untold
Antonyms *adj* calculable, computable, finite, limited, measurable, numbered

inoperable *adj* **1** = **unworkable**, impracticable, impractical, nonviable, unrealistic

inordinate *adj* **1** = **excessive**, disproportionate, exorbitant, extravagant, immoderate, intemperate, preposterous, unconscionable, undue, unreasonable, unrestrained, unwarranted
Antonyms *adj* inhibited, moderate, reasonable, restrained, rightful, sensible, temperate

inorganic *adj* **1** = **artificial**, chemical, man-made, mineral

inquest *n* **2** = **inquiry**, inquisition, investigation, probe

inquire *vb* **1** = **ask**, query, question, request information, seek information **2** = **investigate**, examine, explore, inspect, look into, make inquiries, probe, research, scrutinize, search

inquiry *n* **1** = **question**, query **2** = **investigation**, examination, exploration, inquest, interrogation, probe, research, scrutiny, search, study, survey

inquisition *n* **1, 2** = **investigation**, cross-examination, examination, grilling (*inf.*), inquest, inquiry, questioning, quizzing, third degree (*inf.*)

inquisitive *adj* **1** = **curious**, inquiring, intrusive, nosy (*inf.*), nosy-parkering (*inf.*), peering, probing, prying, questioning, scrutinizing, snooping (*inf.*), snoopy (*inf.*)
Antonyms *adj* apathetic, incurious, indifferent, unconcerned, uninterested, unquestioning

inroad *n* **1** = **incursion**, advance, encroachment, foray, intrusion, invasion, irruption, onslaught, raid

insane Ⓣ (ɪnˈseɪn) *adj* **1a** mentally deranged; crazy; of unsound mind. **1b** (*as collective n; preceded by the*): *the insane.* **2** characteristic of a person of unsound mind: *an insane stare.* **3** irresponsible; very foolish; stupid.
▸**inˈsanely** *adv* ▸**inˈsaneness** *n*

insanitary Ⓣ (ɪnˈsænɪtərɪ, -trɪ) *adj* not sanitary; dirty or infected.

insanity Ⓣ (ɪnˈsænɪtɪ) *n, pl* **insanities. 1** relatively permanent disorder of the mind; state or condition of being insane. **2** utter folly; stupidity.

insatiable Ⓣ (ɪnˈseɪʃəbᵊl, -ʃɪə-) *or* **insatiate** (ɪnˈseɪʃɪɪt) *adj* not able to be satisfied; greedy or unappeasable.
▸**inˌsatiaˈbility** *or* **inˈsatiateness** *n* ▸**inˈsatiably** *or* **inˈsatiately** *adv*

inscape (ˈɪnskeɪp) *n* the essential inner nature of a person, object, etc. [C19: from IN-[2] + *-scape*, as in LANDSCAPE; coined by Gerard Manley *Hopkins* (1844–89), E poet]

inscribe Ⓣ (ɪnˈskraɪb) *vb* **inscribes, inscribing, inscribed.** (*tr*) **1** to make, carve, or engrave (writing, letters, etc.) on (a surface such as wood, stone, or paper). **2** to enter (a name) on a list or in a register. **3** to sign one's name on (a book, etc.) before presentation to another person. **4** to draw (a geometric construction) inside another construction so that the two are in contact but do not intersect. [C16: from L *inscrībere;* see INSCRIPTION]
▸**inˈscribable** *adj* ▸**inˈscribableness** *n* ▸**inˈscriber** *n*

inscription Ⓣ (ɪnˈskrɪpʃən) *n* **1** something inscribed, esp. words carved or engraved on a coin, tomb, etc. **2** a signature or brief dedication in a book or on a work of art. **3** the act of inscribing. [C14: from L *inscriptiō* a writing upon, from *inscrībere* to write upon, from IN-[2] + *scrībere* to write]
▸**inˈscriptional** *or* **inˈscriptive** *adj* ▸**inˈscriptively** *adv*

inscrutable Ⓣ (ɪnˈskruːtəbᵊl) *adj* mysterious or enigmatic; incomprehensible. [C15: from LL, from L IN-[1] + *scrūtārī* to examine]
▸**inˌscrutaˈbility** *or* **inˈscrutableness** *n* ▸**inˈscrutably** *adv*

insect (ˈɪnsɛkt) *n* **1** any of a class of small air-breathing arthropods, having a body divided into head, thorax, and abdomen, three pairs of legs, and (in most species) two pairs of wings. **2** (loosely) any similar invertebrate, such as a spider, tick, or centipede. **3** a contemptible, loathsome, or insignificant person. [C17: from L *insectum* (animal that has been) cut into, insect, from *insecāre,* from IN-[2] + *secāre* to cut]
▸**inˈsectile** *adj* ▸**ˈinsect-ˌlike** *adj*

insectarium (ˌɪnsɛkˈtɛərɪəm) *or* **insectary** (ɪnˈsɛktərɪ) *n, pl* **insectariums, insectaria** (-ˈtɛərɪə), *or* **insectaries.** a place where living insects are kept, bred, and studied.

insecticide (ɪnˈsɛktɪˌsaɪd) *n* a substance used to destroy insect pests.
▸**inˌsectiˈcidal** *adj*

insectivore (ɪnˈsɛktɪˌvɔː) *n* **1** any of an order of placental mammals, being typically small, with simple teeth, and feeding on invertebrates. The group includes shrews, moles, and hedgehogs. **2** any animal or plant that derives nourishment from insects.
▸**ˌinsecˈtivorous** *adj*

insecure Ⓣ (ˌɪnsɪˈkjʊə) *adj* **1** anxious or afraid; not confident or certain. **2** not adequately protected: *an insecure fortress.* **3** unstable or shaky.
▸**ˌinseˈcurely** *adv* ▸**ˌinseˈcureness** *n* ▸**ˌinseˈcurity** *n*

inselberg (ˈɪnzᵊlˌbɜːg) *n* an isolated rocky hill rising abruptly from a flat plain. [from G, from *Insel* island + *Berg* mountain]

inseminate (ɪnˈsɛmɪˌneɪt) *vb* **inseminates, inseminating, inseminated.** (*tr*) **1** to impregnate (a female) with semen. **2** to introduce (ideas or attitudes) into the mind of (a person or group). [C17: from L *insēmināre,* from IN-[2] + *sēmināre* to sow, from *sēmen* seed]
▸**inˌsemiˈnation** *n* ▸**inˈsemiˌnator** *n*

insensate Ⓣ (ɪnˈsɛnseɪt, -sɪt) *adj* **1** lacking sensation or consciousness. **2** insensitive; unfeeling. **3** foolish; senseless.
▸**inˈsensately** *adv* ▸**inˈsensateness** *n*

insensible Ⓣ (ɪnˈsɛnsəbᵊl) *adj* **1** lacking sensation or consciousness. **2** (foll. by *of* or *to*) unaware (of) or indifferent (to): *insensible to suffering.* **3** thoughtless or callous. **4** a less common word for **imperceptible.**
▸**inˌsensiˈbility** *or* **inˈsensibleness** *n* ▸**inˈsensibly** *adv*

insensitive Ⓣ (ɪnˈsɛnsɪtɪv) *adj* **1** lacking sensitivity; unfeeling. **2** lacking physical sensation. **3** (*postpositive;* foll. by *to*) not sensitive (to) or affected (by): *insensitive to radiation.*
▸**inˈsensitively** *adv* ▸**inˈsensitiveness** *or* **inˌsensiˈtivity** *n*

insentient (ɪnˈsɛnʃɪənt) *adj* lacking consciousness or senses; inanimate.
▸**inˈsentience** *n*

inseparable Ⓣ (ɪnˈsɛpərəbᵊl, -ˈsɛprə-) *adj* incapable of being separated or divided.
▸**inˌseparaˈbility** *or* **inˈseparableness** *n* ▸**inˈseparably** *adv*

insert Ⓣ *vb* (ɪnˈsɜːt). (*tr*) **1** to put in or between; introduce. **2** to introduce into text, as in a newspaper; interpolate. ◆ *n* (ˈɪnsɜːt). **3** something inserted. **4** Also called: **inset. 4a** a folded section placed in another for binding in with a book. **4b** a printed sheet, esp. one bearing advertising, placed loose between the leaves of a book, periodical, etc. [C16: from L *inserere* to plant in, from IN-[2] + *serere* to join]
▸**inˈsertable** *adj* ▸**inˈserter** *n*

insertion Ⓣ (ɪnˈsɜːʃən) *n* **1** the act of inserting or something that is inserted. **2** a word, sentence, correction, etc., inserted into text, such as a newspaper. **3** a strip of lace, embroidery, etc., between two pieces of material. **4** *Anat.* the point or manner of attachment of a muscle to the bone that it moves.
▸**inˈsertional** *adj*

in-service *adj* denoting training that is given to employees during the course of employment: *an in-service course.*

insessorial (ˌɪnsɛˈsɔːrɪəl) *adj* **1** (of feet or claws) adapted for perching. **2** (of birds) having insessorial feet. [C19: from NL *Insessōrēs* birds that perch, from L: perchers, from *insidēre* to sit upon]

inset *vb* (ɪnˈsɛt), **insets, insetting, inset. 1** (*tr*) to set or place in or within; insert. ◆ *n* (ˈɪnˌsɛt). **2** something inserted. **3** *Printing.* **3a** a small map or diagram set within the borders of a larger one. **3b** another name for **insert** (sense 4). **4** a piece of fabric inserted into a garment, as to shape it or for decoration.
▸**ˈinˌsetter** *n*

inshallah (ɪnˈʃælə) *sentence substitute. Islam.* if Allah wills it. [C19: from Ar.]

inshore (ˈɪnˈʃɔː) *adj* **1** in or on the water, but close to the shore: *inshore weather.* ◆ *adv, adj* **2** towards the shore from the water: *an inshore wind; we swam inshore.*

THESAURUS

insane *adj* **1** = **mad**, crackers (*Brit. sl.*), crazed, crazy, demented, deranged, mentally disordered, mentally ill, *non compos mentis,* nuts (*sl.*), off one's rocker (*sl.*), of unsound mind, out of one's mind, round the bend (*inf.*) **3** = **stupid**, bizarre, daft (*inf.*), fatuous, foolish, idiotic, impractical, inane, irrational, irresponsible, lunatic, preposterous, senseless
Antonyms *adj* logical, lucid, normal, practical, rational, reasonable, reasoned, sane, sensible, sound

insanitary *adj* = **unhealthy**, contaminated, dirtied, dirty, disease-ridden, feculent, filthy, impure, infected, infested, insalubrious, noxious, polluted, unclean, unhygienic
Antonyms *adj* clean, healthy, hygienic, pure, salubrious, unpolluted

insanity *n* **1** = **madness**, aberration, craziness, delirium, dementia, frenzy, mental derangement, mental disorder, mental illness **2** = **stupidity**, folly, irresponsibility, lunacy, preposterousness, senselessness
Antonyms *n* logic, lucidity, normality, rationality, reason, sanity, sense, soundness, wisdom

insatiable *adj* = **unquenchable**, edacious, gluttonous, greedy, insatiate, intemperate, quenchless, rapacious, ravenous, unappeasable, voracious
Antonyms *adj* appeasable, limited, quenchable, satiable, temperate

inscribe *vb* **1** = **carve**, cut, engrave, etch, impress, imprint **2** = **enrol**, engross, enlist, enter, record, register, write **3** = **dedicate**, address

inscription *n* **1** = **engraving**, label, legend, lettering, saying, words **2** = **dedication**

inscrutable *adj* = **enigmatic**, blank, deadpan, impenetrable, mysterious, poker-faced (*inf.*), sphinxlike, unfathomable, unreadable
Antonyms open, penetrable, readable, revealing, transparent

insecure *adj* **1** = **anxious**, afraid, uncertain, unconfident, unsure **2** = **unsafe**, dangerous, defenceless, exposed, hazardous, ill-protected, open to attack, perilous, unguarded, unprotected, unshielded, vulnerable, wide-open **3** = **unstable**, built upon sand, flimsy, frail, insubstantial, loose, on thin ice, precarious, rickety, rocky, shaky, unreliable, unsound, unsteady, weak, wobbly
Antonyms *adj* ≠ **anxious:** assured, certain, confident, decisive, secure ≠ **unsafe:** protected, safe, secure ≠ **unstable:** firm, reliable, secure, sound, stable, steady, substantial, sure

insecurity *n* **1** = **anxiety**, fear, uncertainty, unsureness, worry **2** = **vulnerability**, danger, defencelessness, hazard, peril, risk, uncertainty, weakness **3** = **unsteadiness**, dubiety, frailness, instability, precariousness, shakiness, uncertainty, unreliability, weakness
Antonyms *n* ≠ **anxiety:** assurance, certainty, confidence, security ≠ **vulnerability:** dependability, safety ≠ **unsteadiness:** firmness, reliability, security, stability, steadiness

insensate *adj* **1** = **lifeless**, anaesthetized, dead, inanimate, inert, insensible, insentient, numbed, out (*inf.*), unconscious **2** = **unfeeling**, hardened, imperceptive, impercipient, indifferent, insensitive, inured, obtuse, stolid, thick-skinned, thoughtless, unperceiving **3** = **foolish**, brainless, fatuous, mindless, senseless, stupid, thoughtless, unreasonable, witless

insensibility *n* **1** = **unconsciousness**, inertness, numbness **2** = **insensitivity**, apathy, callousness, dullness, indifference, inertia, lethargy, torpor

insensible *adj* **1** = **benumbed**, anaesthetized, dull, inert, insensate, numbed, torpid **2** = **unaware**, apathetic, callous, cold, deaf, hard-hearted, impassive, impervious, indifferent, oblivious, unaffected, unconscious, unfeeling, unmindful, unmoved, unresponsive, unsusceptible, untouched **4** = **imperceptible**, imperceivable, minuscule, negligible, unnoticeable
Antonyms *adj* ≠ **unaware:** affected, aware, conscious, feeling, mindful, responsive, sensible

insensibly *adv* **4** = **imperceptibly**, by degrees, gradually, invisibly, little by little, slightly, unnoticeably

insensitive *adj* **1** = **unfeeling**, callous, crass, hardened, imperceptive, indifferent, obtuse, tactless, thick-skinned, tough, uncaring, unconcerned, unresponsive, unsusceptible **3** *with* **to** = **unaffected by**, dead to, immune to, impervious to, proof against, unmoved by
Antonyms *adj* ≠ **unfeeling:** caring, concerned, perceptive, responsive, sensitive, sentient, susceptible, sympathetic, tactful, tender

inseparable *adj* = **indivisible**, conjoined, inalienable, indissoluble, inseverable

insert *vb* **1** = **enter**, embed, implant, infix, interject, interpolate, interpose, introduce, place, pop in (*inf.*), put, set, stick in, tuck in, work in
Antonyms *vb* delete, extract, pull out, remove, take out, withdraw

insertion *n* **1** = **inclusion**, addition, implant, insert, inset, interpolation, introduction, supplement

inside ⓣ *n* ('ɪn'saɪd). **1** the interior; inner or enclosed part or surface. **2** the side of a path away from the road or adjacent to a wall. **3** (*also pl*) *Inf.* the internal organs of the body, esp. the stomach and bowels. **4 inside of.** in a period of time less than; within. **5 inside out.** with the inside facing outwards. **6 know (something) inside out.** to know thoroughly or perfectly. ◆ *prep* (ˌɪn'saɪd). **7** in or to the interior of; within or to within; on the inside of. ◆ *adj* ('ɪnˌsaɪd). **8** on or of an interior; on the inside: *an inside door.* **9** (*prenominal*) arranged or provided by someone within an organization or building, esp. illicitly: *the raid was an inside job; inside information.* ◆ *adv* (ˌɪn'saɪd). **10** within or to within a thing or place; indoors. **11** *Sl.* in or into prison.

USAGE NOTE See at **outside.**

inside job *n Inf.* a crime committed with the assistance of someone associated with the victim.

inside lane *n Athletics.* the inside, and therefore the shortest, route around a circular or oval multi-lane running track.

insider (ˌɪn'saɪdə) *n* **1** a member of a specified group. **2** a person with access to exclusive information.

insider dealing *or* **trading** *n* the illegal practice of a person on the Stock Exchange or in some branches of the Civil Service taking advantage of early confidential information in order to deal in shares for personal profit.
▸**insider dealer** *or* **trader** *n*

insidious ⓣ (ɪn'sɪdɪəs) *adj* **1** stealthy, subtle, cunning, or treacherous. **2** working in a subtle or apparently innocuous way, but nevertheless deadly: *an insidious illness.* [C16: from L *insidiōsus* cunning, from *insidiae* an ambush, from *insidēre* to sit in]
▸**in'sidiously** *adv* ▸**in'sidiousness** *n*

insight ⓣ ('ɪnˌsaɪt) *n* **1** the ability to perceive clearly or deeply; penetration. **2** a penetrating and often sudden understanding, as of a complex situation or problem. **3** *Psychol.* the capacity for understanding one's own or another's mental processes. **4** *Psychiatry.* the ability to understand one's own problems.
▸**'inˌsightful** *adj*

insignia ⓣ (ɪn'sɪgnɪə) *n, pl* **insignias** *or* **insignia. 1** a badge or emblem of membership, office, or dignity. **2** a distinguishing sign or mark. [C17: from L: badges, from *insignis* distinguished by a mark, prominent, from IN-[2] + *signum* mark]

insignificant ⓣ (ˌɪnsɪg'nɪfɪkənt) *adj* **1** having little or no importance; trifling. **2** almost or relatively meaningless. **3** small or inadequate: *an insignificant wage.* **4** not distinctive in character, etc.
▸ˌ**insig'nificance** *or* ˌ**insig'nificancy** *n* ▸ˌ**insig'nificantly** *adv*

insincere ⓣ (ˌɪnsɪn'sɪə) *adj* lacking sincerity; hypocritical.
▸ˌ**insin'cerely** *adv* ▸**insincerity** (ˌɪnsɪn'sɛrɪtɪ) *n*

insinuate ⓣ (ɪn'sɪnjʊˌeɪt) *vb* **insinuates, insinuating, insinuated. 1** (*may take a clause as object*) to suggest by indirect allusion, hints, innuendo, etc. **2** (*tr*) to introduce subtly or deviously. **3** (*tr*) to cause (someone, esp. oneself) to be accepted by gradual approaches or manoeuvres. [C16: from L *insinuāre* to wind one's way into, from IN-[2] + *sinus* curve]
▸**in'sinuative** *or* **in'sinuatory** *adj* ▸**in'sinuˌator** *n*

insinuation ⓣ (ɪnˌsɪnjʊ'eɪʃən) *n* **1** an indirect or devious hint or suggestion. **2** the act or practice of insinuating.

insipid ⓣ (ɪn'sɪpɪd) *adj* **1** lacking spirit or interest; boring. **2** lacking taste; unpalatable. [C17: from L, from IN-[1] + *sapidus* full of flavour, SAPID]
▸ˌ**insi'pidity** *or* **in'sipidness** *n* ▸**in'sipidly** *adv*

insist ⓣ (ɪn'sɪst) *vb* (when *tr, takes a clause as object;* when *intr,* usually foll. by *on* or *upon*) **1** to make a determined demand (for): *he insisted on his rights.* **2** to express a convinced belief (in) or assertion (of). [C16: from L *insistere* to stand upon, urge, from IN-[2] + *sistere* to stand]
▸**in'sister** *n* ▸**in'sistingly** *adv*

insistent ⓣ (ɪn'sɪstənt) *adj* **1** making continual and persistent demands. **2** demanding notice or attention; compelling: *the insistent cry of a bird.*
▸**in'sistence** *or* **in'sistency** *n* ▸**in'sistently** *adv*

in situ *Latin.* (ɪn 'sɪtjuː) *adv, adj* (*postpositive*) in the natural, original, or appropriate position.

in so far as *or* **insofar as** (ˌɪnsəʊ'fɑː) *adv* to the degree or extent that.

insolation (ˌɪnsəʊ'leɪʃən) *n* **1** the quantity of solar radiation falling upon a body or planet, esp. per unit area. **2** exposure to the sun's rays. **3** another name for **sunstroke.**

insole ('ɪnˌsəʊl) *n* **1** the inner sole of a shoe or boot. **2** a loose additional inner sole used to give extra warmth or to make a shoe fit.

insolent ⓣ ('ɪnsələnt) *adj* impudent or disrespectful. [C14: from L, from IN-[1] + *solēre* to be accustomed]
▸**'insolence** *n* ▸**'insolently** *adv*

insoluble ⓣ (ɪn'sɒljʊbᵊl) *adj* **1** incapable of being dissolved; incapable of forming a solution, esp. in water. **2** incapable of being solved.
▸**inˌsolu'bility** *or* **in'solubleness** *n* ▸**in'solubly** *adv*

insolvent ⓣ (ɪn'sɒlvənt) *adj* **1** having insufficient assets to meet debts and liabilities; bankrupt. **2** of or relating to bankrupts or bankruptcy. ◆ *n* **3** a person who is insolvent; bankrupt.
▸**in'solvency** *n*

insomnia ⓣ (ɪn'sɒmnɪə) *n* chronic inability to fall asleep or to enjoy uninterrupted sleep. [C18: from L, from *insomnis* sleepless, from *somnus* sleep]
▸**in'somniˌac** *n, adj* ▸**in'somnious** *adj*

THESAURUS

inside *n* **1** = **interior**, contents, inner part **3** *plural Informal* = **stomach**, belly, bowels, entrails, gut, guts, innards (*inf.*), internal organs, viscera, vitals ◆ *adj* **8** = **inner**, innermost, interior, internal, intramural, inward **9** = **confidential**, classified, esoteric, exclusive, internal, limited, private, restricted, secret ◆ *adv* **10** = **indoors**, under cover, within
Antonyms *adj* ≠ **inner**: exterior, external, extramural, outer, outermost, outside, outward

insidious *adj* **1** = **stealthy**, artful, crafty, crooked, cunning, deceitful, deceptive, designing, disingenuous, duplicitous, guileful, intriguing, Machiavellian, slick, sly, smooth, sneaking, subtle, surreptitious, treacherous, tricky, wily
Antonyms *adj* artless, conspicuous, forthright, harmless, honest, ingenuous, obvious, open, sincere, straightforward, upright

insight *n* **1** = **understanding**, acumen, awareness, comprehension, discernment, intuition, intuitiveness, judgment, observation, penetration, perception, perspicacity, vision

insightful *adj* **1** = **perceptive**, astute, discerning, knowledgeable, observant, penetrating, perspicacious, sagacious, shrewd, understanding, wise

insignia *n* **1, 2** = **badge**, crest, decoration, distinguishing mark, earmark, emblem, ensign, symbol

insignificance *n* **1** = **unimportance**, immateriality, inconsequence, irrelevance, meaninglessness, negligibility, paltriness, pettiness, triviality, worthlessness
Antonyms *n* consequence, importance, matter, meaningfulness, relevance, significance, weight, worth

insignificant *adj* **1** = **unimportant**, flimsy, immaterial, inconsequential, inconsiderable, irrelevant, meagre, meaningless, measly, minor, negligible, nickel-and-dime (*US sl.*), nondescript, nonessential, not worth mentioning, nugatory, of no account, of no consequence, of no moment, paltry, petty, scanty, small potatoes, trifling, trivial
Antonyms *adj* consequential, considerable, essential, important, meaningful, momentous, relevant, significant, substantial, vital, weighty

insincere *adj* = **deceitful**, deceptive, devious, dishonest, disingenuous, dissembling, dissimulating, double-dealing, duplicitous, evasive, faithless, false, hollow, hypocritical, Janus-faced, lying, mendacious, perfidious, pretended, two-faced, unfaithful, untrue, untruthful, with tongue in cheek
Antonyms *adj* direct, earnest, faithful, genuine, honest, sincere, straightforward, true, truthful

insincerity *n* = **deceitfulness**, deviousness, dishonesty, disingenuousness, dissimulation, duplicity, faithlessness, hypocrisy, lip service, mendacity, perfidy, pretence, untruthfulness
Antonyms *n* directness, faithfulness, honesty, sincerity, truthfulness

insinuate *vb* **1** = **imply**, allude, hint, indicate, intimate, suggest **3** = **ingratiate**, curry favour, get in with, worm *or* work one's way in

insinuation *n* **1** = **implication**, allusion, aspersion, hint, innuendo, slur, suggestion

insipid *adj* **1** = **bland**, anaemic, banal, characterless, colourless, drab, dry, dull, flat, jejune, lifeless, limp, pointless, prosaic, spiritless, stale, stupid, tame, tedious, tiresome, trite, unimaginative, uninteresting, vapid, weak, wearisome, wishy-washy (*inf.*) **2** = **tasteless**, bland, flavourless, savourless, unappetizing, watered down, watery, wishy-washy (*inf.*)
Antonyms *adj* ≠ **bland**: colourful, engaging, exciting, interesting, lively, provocative, spirited, stimulating ≠ **tasteless**: appetizing, fiery, palatable, piquant, pungent, savoury, tasty

insipidity *n* **1** = **dullness**, banality, colourlessness, flatness, lack of imagination, pointlessness, staleness, tameness, tediousness, triteness, uninterestingness, vapidity **2** = **tastelessness**, blandness, flavourlessness, lack of flavour
Antonyms *n* ≠ **dullness**: animation, character, dynamism, gaiety, liveliness, spirit, vitality, vivacity

insist *vb* **1** = **demand**, be firm, brook no refusal, lay down the law, not take no for an answer, persist, press (someone), put one's foot down (*inf.*), require, stand firm, stand one's ground, take *or* make a stand, urge **2** = **assert**, asseverate, aver, claim, contend, hold, maintain, reiterate, repeat, swear, urge, vow

insistence *n* **1** = **persistence**, assertion, contention, demands, emphasis, importunity, insistency, pressing, reiteration, stress, urging

insistent *adj* **1** = **persistent**, demanding, dogged, emphatic, exigent, forceful, importunate, incessant, peremptory, persevering, pressing, unrelenting, urgent

insolence *n* = **rudeness**, abuse, audacity, backchat (*inf.*), boldness, cheek (*inf.*), chutzpah (*US & Canad. inf.*), contemptuousness, contumely, disrespect, effrontery, front, gall (*inf.*), impertinence, impudence, incivility, insubordination, offensiveness, pertness, uncivility
Antonyms *n* civility, courtesy, deference, esteem, mannerliness, politeness, respect, submission

insolent *adj* = **rude**, abusive, bold, brazen-faced, contemptuous, fresh (*inf.*), impertinent, impudent, insubordinate, insulting, pert, saucy, uncivil
Antonyms *adj* civil, courteous, deferential, mannerly, polite, respectful, submissive

insoluble *adj* **2** = **inexplicable**, baffling, impenetrable, indecipherable, mysterious, mystifying, obscure, unaccountable, unfathomable, unsolvable
Antonyms *adj* accountable, comprehensible, explicable, fathomable, penetrable, soluble, solvable

insolvency *n* **1** = **bankruptcy**, failure, liquidation, ruin

insolvent *adj* **1** = **bankrupt**, broke (*inf.*), failed, gone bust (*inf.*), gone to the wall, in queer street (*inf.*), in receivership, in the hands of the receivers, on the rocks (*inf.*), ruined

insomnia *n* = **sleeplessness**, wakefulness

insomuch (ˌɪnsəʊˈmʌtʃ) *adv* **1** (foll. by *as* or *that*) to such an extent or degree. **2** (foll. by *as*) because of the fact (that); inasmuch (as).

insouciant ❶ (ɪnˈsuːsɪənt) *adj* carefree or unconcerned; light-hearted. [C19: from F, from IN-[1] + *souciant* worrying, from *soucier* to trouble, from L *sollicitāre*]
▸**inˈsouciance** *n* ▸**inˈsouciantly** *adv*

inspan (ɪnˈspæn) *vb* **inspans, inspanning, inspanned.** (*tr*) *Chiefly S. African.* **1** to harness (animals) to (a vehicle); yoke. **2** to press (people) into service. [C19: from Afrik., from MDu. *inspannen,* from *spannen* to stretch]

inspect ❶ (ɪnˈspɛkt) *vb* (*tr*) **1** to examine closely, esp. for faults or errors. **2** to scrutinize officially (a document, military personnel on ceremonial parade, etc.). [C17: from L *inspicere,* from *specere* to look]
▸**inˈspectable** *adj* ▸**inˈspection** *n* ▸**inˈspective** *adj*

inspector ❶ (ɪnˈspɛktə) *n* **1** a person who inspects, esp. an official who examines for compliance with regulations, standards, etc. **2** a police officer ranking below a superintendent and above a sergeant.
▸**inˈspectoral** *or* **inspectorial** (ˌɪnspɛkˈtɔːrɪəl) *adj* ▸**inˈspectorˌship** *n*

inspectorate (ɪnˈspɛktərɪt) *n* **1** the office, rank, or duties of an inspector. **2** a body of inspectors. **3** a district under an inspector.

inspiration ❶ (ˌɪnspɪˈreɪʃən) *n* **1** stimulation or arousal of the mind, feelings, etc., to special activity or creativity. **2** the state or quality of being so stimulated or aroused. **3** someone or something that causes this state. **4** an idea or action resulting from such a state. **5** the act or process of inhaling; breathing in.

inspiratory (ɪnˈspaɪərətərɪ, -trɪ) *adj* of or relating to inhalation or the drawing in of air.

inspire ❶ (ɪnˈspaɪə) *vb* **inspires, inspiring, inspired. 1** to exert a stimulating or beneficial effect upon (a person, etc.); animate or invigorate. **2** (*tr*; foll. by *with* or *to*; *may take an infinitive*) to arouse (with a particular emotion or to a particular action); stir. **3** (*tr*) to prompt or instigate; give rise to. **4** (*tr*; *often passive*) to guide or arouse by divine influence or inspiration. **5** to take or draw (air, gas, etc.) into the lungs; inhale. **6** (*tr*) *Arch.* to breathe into or upon. [C14 (in the sense: to breathe upon, blow into): from L *inspīrāre,* from *spīrāre* to breathe]
▸**inˈspirable** *adj* ▸**inˈspirative** *adj* ▸**inˈspirer** *n* ▸**inˈspiringly** *adv*

inspirit (ɪnˈspɪrɪt) *vb* (*tr*) to fill with vigour; inspire.
▸**inˈspiriter** *n* ▸**inˈspiriting** *adj* ▸**inˈspiritment** *n*

inspissate (ɪnˈspɪseɪt) *vb* **inspissates, inspissating, inspissated.** *Arch.* to thicken, as by evaporation. [C17: from LL *inspissātus* thickened, from L, from *spissus* thick]
▸ˌ**inspisˈsation** *n* ▸ˈ**inspisˌsator** *n*

inst. *abbrev. for:* **1** instant (this month). **2** instantaneous. **3** instrumental.

Inst. *abbrev. for:* **1** Institute. **2** Institution.

instability ❶ (ˌɪnstəˈbɪlɪtɪ) *n, pl* **instabilities. 1** lack of stability or steadiness. **2** tendency to variable or unpredictable behaviour.

install ❶ *or* **instal** (ɪnˈstɔːl) *vb* **installs** *or* **instals, installing, installed.** (*tr*) **1** to place (equipment) in position and connect and adjust for use. **2** to transfer (computer software) from a distribution file to a permanent location on disk, and prepare it for its particular environment and application. **3** to put in a position, rank, etc. **4** to settle (a person, esp. oneself) in a position or state: *she installed herself in an armchair.* [C16: from Med. L *installāre,* from IN-[2] + *stallum* STALL[1]]
▸**inˈstaller** *n*

installation ❶ (ˌɪnstəˈleɪʃən) *n* **1** the act of installing or the state of being installed. **2** a large device, system, or piece of equipment that has been installed.

installment plan *or esp. Canad.* **instalment plan** *n* the US and Canad. name for **hire-purchase.**

instalment ❶ *or US* **installment** (ɪnˈstɔːlmənt) *n* **1** one of the portions into which a debt is divided for payment at specified intervals over a fixed period. **2** a portion of something that is issued, broadcast, or published in parts. [C18: from obs. *estallment,* prob. from OF *estaler* to fix, from *estal* something fixed, from OHG *stal* STALL[1]]

instance ❶ (ˈɪnstəns) *n* **1** a case or particular example. **2 for instance.** for or as an example. **3** a specified stage in proceedings; step (in **in the first, second,** etc., **instance**). **4** urgent request or demand (esp. in **at the instance of**). ◆ *vb* **instances, instancing, instanced.** (*tr*) **5** to cite as an example. [C14 (in the sense: case, example): from Med. L *instantia* example, (in the sense: urgency) from L: a being close upon, from *instāns* urgent; see INSTANT]

instant ❶ (ˈɪnstənt) *n* **1** a very brief time; moment. **2** a particular moment or point in time: *at the same instant.* **3 on the instant.** immediately; without delay. ◆ *adj* **4** immediate; instantaneous. **5** (esp. of foods) prepared or designed for preparation with very little time and effort: *instant coffee.* **6** urgent or imperative. **7** (*postpositive*) of the present month: *a letter of the 7th instant.* Abbrev.: **inst.** [C15: from L *instāns,* from *instāre* to be present, press closely, from IN-[2] + *stāre* to stand]

instantaneous ❶ (ˌɪnstənˈteɪnɪəs) *adj* **1** occurring with almost no delay; immediate. **2** happening or completed within a moment: *instantaneous death.*
▸ˌ**instanˈtaneously** *adv* ▸ˌ**instanˈtaneousness** *or* **instantaneity** (ɪnˌstæntəˈniːɪtɪ) *n*

instanter (ɪnˈstæntə) *adv Law.* without delay; the same day or within 24 hours. [C17: from L: urgently, from *instans* INSTANT]

instantly ❶ (ˈɪnstəntlɪ) *adv* **1** immediately; at once. **2** *Arch.* urgently or insistently.

instar (ˈɪnstɑː) *n* the stage in the development of an insect between any two moults. [C19: NL from L: image]

instate (ɪnˈsteɪt) *vb* **instates, instating, instated.** (*tr*) to place in a position or office; install.
▸**inˈstatement** *n*

instead ❶ (ɪnˈstɛd) *adv* **1** as a replacement, substitute, or alternative. **2 instead of.** (*prep*) in place of or as an alternative to. [C13: from *in stead* in place]

instep (ˈɪnˌstɛp) *n* **1** the middle section of the human foot, forming the arch between the ankle and toes. **2** the part of a shoe, stocking, etc., covering this. [C16: prob. from IN-[2] + STEP]

instigate ❶ (ˈɪnstɪˌgeɪt) *vb* **instigates, instigating, instigated.** (*tr*) **1** to bring about, as by incitement: *to instigate rebellion.* **2** to urge on to some drastic or unadvisable action. [C16: from L *instīgāre* to incite]
▸ˌ**instiˈgation** *n* ▸ˈ**instiˌgative** *adj* ▸ˈ**instiˌgator** *n*

THESAURUS

insouciance *n* = **nonchalance,** airiness, breeziness, carefreeness, jauntiness, light-heartedness

insouciant *adj* = **nonchalant,** airy, breezy, buoyant, carefree, casual, free and easy, gay, happy-go-lucky, jaunty, light-hearted, sunny, unconcerned, untroubled, unworried

inspect *vb* **1** = **examine,** audit, check, check out (*inf.*), eye, eyeball (*sl.*), give (something *or* someone) the once-over (*inf.*), go over *or* through, investigate, look over, oversee, recce (*sl.*), research, scan, scrutinize, search, superintend, supervise, survey, take a dekko at (*Brit. sl.*), vet, work over

inspection *n* **1** = **examination,** check, checkup, investigation, look-over, once-over (*inf.*), recce (*sl.*), review, scan, scrutiny, search, superintendence, supervision, surveillance, survey

inspector *n* **1** = **examiner,** auditor, censor, checker, critic, investigator, overseer, scrutineer, scrutinizer, superintendent, supervisor

inspiration *n* **1** = **revelation,** afflatus, arousal, awakening, creativity, elevation, encouragement, enthusiasm, exaltation, genius, illumination, insight, stimulation **3** = **influence,** muse, spur, stimulus
Antonyms *n* depressant, deterrent, discouragement, disenchantment

inspire *vb* **1** = **stimulate,** animate, be responsible for, encourage, enliven, fire *or* touch the imagination of, galvanize, gee up, hearten, imbue, influence, infuse, inspirit, instil, rouse, spark off, spur **2** = **arouse,** enkindle, excite, give rise to, produce, quicken, rouse, stir
Antonyms *vb* ≠ **stimulate:** daunt, deflate, depress, discourage, disenchant, dishearten, dispirit

inspiring *adj* **1** = **uplifting,** affecting, encouraging, exciting, exhilarating, heartening, moving, rousing, stimulating, stirring
Antonyms *adj* boring, depressing, discouraging, disheartening, dispiriting, dull, uninspiring

instability *n* **1, 2** = **unpredictability,** capriciousness, changeableness, disequilibrium, fickleness, fitfulness, fluctuation, fluidity, frailty, imbalance, impermanence, inconstancy, insecurity, irresolution, mutability, oscillation, precariousness, restlessness, shakiness, transience, unsteadiness, vacillation, variability, volatility, wavering, weakness
Antonyms *n* balance, constancy, equilibrium, permanence, predictability, resolution, security, stability, steadiness, strength

install *vb* **1** = **set up,** fix, lay, lodge, place, position, put in, station **3** = **induct,** establish, inaugurate, instate, institute, introduce, invest, set up **4** = **settle,** ensconce, position

installation *n* **1** = **setting up,** establishment, fitting, inauguration, instalment, placing, positioning **2** = **equipment,** machinery, plant, system

instalment *n* **1, 2** = **portion,** chapter, division, episode, part, repayment, section

instance *n* **1** = **example,** case, case in point, illustration, occasion, occurrence, precedent, situation, time **4** = **insistence,** application, behest, demand, entreaty, importunity, impulse, incitement, instigation, pressure, prompting, request, solicitation, urging ◆ *vb* **5** = **quote,** adduce, cite, mention, name, specify

instant *n* **1** = **second,** bat of an eye (*inf.*), flash, jiffy (*inf.*), moment, shake (*inf.*), split second, tick (*Brit. inf.*), trice, twinkling, twinkling of an eye (*inf.*), two shakes of a lamb's tail (*inf.*) **2** = **juncture,** moment, occasion, point, time ◆ *adj* **4** = **immediate,** direct, instantaneous, on-the-spot, prompt, quick, quickie (*inf.*), split-second, urgent **5** = **precooked,** convenience, fast, ready-mixed **6** = **urgent,** burning, exigent, imperative, importunate, pressing

instantaneous *adj* **1** = **immediate,** direct, instant, on-the-spot, prompt

instantaneously *adv* **1** = **immediately,** at once, forthwith, in a fraction of a second, instantly, in the same breath, in the twinkling of an eye (*inf.*), like a bat out of hell (*sl.*), like greased lightning (*inf.*), on the instant, on the spot, posthaste, promptly, pronto (*inf.*), straight away, then and there

instantly *adv* **1** = **immediately,** at once, directly, forthwith, instantaneously, instanter (*Law*), now, on the spot, posthaste, pronto (*inf.*), right away, right now, straight away, there and then, this minute, *tout de suite,* without delay

instead *adv* **1** = **rather,** alternatively, in lieu, in preference, on second thoughts, preferably **2 instead of** = **in place of,** as an alternative *or* equivalent to, in lieu of, rather than

instigate *vb* **1** = **provoke,** actuate, bring about, encourage, foment, get going, impel, incite, influence, initiate, kick-start, kindle, move, persuade, prod, prompt, rouse, set off, set on, spur, start, stimulate, stir up, trigger, urge, whip up
Antonyms *vb* discourage, repress, restrain, stop, suppress

instigation *n* **1** = **prompting,** behest, bidding, encouragement, incentive, incitement, urging

instigator *n* **2** = **ringleader,** agitator, firebrand, fomenter, goad, incendiary, inciter, leader, mischief-maker, motivator, prime mover, spur, stirrer (*inf.*), troublemaker

instil ⊙ *or US* **instill** (ɪn'stɪl) *vb* **instils** *or US* **instills, instilling, instilled.** (*tr*) **1** to introduce gradually; implant or infuse. **2** *Rare.* to pour in or inject in drops. [C16: from L *instillāre* to pour in a drop at a time, from *stillāre* to drip]
▸**in'stiller** *n* ▸**in'stilment**, *US* **in'stillment**, *or* **ˌinstil'lation** *n*

instinct ⊙ *n* ('ɪnstɪŋkt). **1** the innate capacity of an animal to respond to a given stimulus in a relatively fixed way. **2** inborn intuitive power. ◆ *adj* (ɪn'stɪŋkt). **3** (*postpositive; often foll. by with*) *Rare.* **3a** animated or impelled (by). **3b** imbued or infused (with). [C15: from L *instinctus* roused, from *instinguere* to incite]

instinctive ⊙ (ɪn'stɪŋktɪv) *adj* **1** of, relating to, or resulting from instinct. **2** conditioned so as to appear innate: *an instinctive movement in driving.*
▸**in'stinctively** *adv*

instinctual (ɪn'stɪŋktjʊəl) *adj* of or pertaining to instinct.
▸**in'stinctually** *adv*

institute ⊙ ('ɪnstɪˌtjuːt) *vb* **institutes, instituting, instituted.** (*tr*) **1** to organize; establish. **2** to initiate: *to institute a practice.* **3** to establish in a position or office; induct. ◆ *n* **4** an organization founded for particular work, such as education, promotion of the arts, or scientific research. **5** the building where such an organization is situated. **6** something instituted, esp. a rule, custom, or precedent. [C16: from L *instituere*, from *statuere* to place]
▸**'instiˌtutor** *or* **'instiˌtuter** *n*

institutes ('ɪnstɪˌtjuːts) *pl n* a digest or summary, esp. of laws.

institution ⊙ (ˌɪnstɪ'tjuːʃən) *n* **1** the act of instituting. **2** an organization or establishment founded for a specific purpose, such as a hospital or college. **3** the building where such an organization is situated. **4** an established custom, law, or relationship in a society or community. **5** Also called: **institutional investor.** a large organization, such as an insurance company or pension fund, that has substantial sums to invest on a stock exchange. **6** *Inf.* a constant feature or practice: *Jones's drink at the bar was an institution.* **7** the appointment of an incumbent to an ecclesiastical office or pastoral charge.
▸**ˌinsti'tutionary** *adj*

institutional ⊙ (ˌɪnstɪ'tjuːʃənᵊl) *adj* **1** of, relating to, or characteristic of institutions. **2** dull, routine, and uniform: *institutional meals.* **3** relating to principles or institutes, esp. of law.
▸**ˌinsti'tutionally** *adv* ▸**ˌinsti'tutionaˌlism** *n*

institutionalize *or* **institutionalise** (ˌɪnstɪ'tjuːʃənəˌlaɪz) *vb* **institutionalizes, institutionalizing, institutionalized** *or* **institutionalises, institutionalising, institutionalised. 1** (*tr; often passive*) to subject to the deleterious effects of confinement in an institution. **2** (*tr*) to place in an institution. **3** to make or become an institution.
▸**ˌinstiˌtutionali'zation** *or* **ˌinstiˌtutionali'sation** *n*

in-store *adj* available within a department store: *in-store banking facilities.*

instruct ⊙ (ɪn'strʌkt) *vb* (*tr*) **1** to direct to do something; order. **2** to teach (someone) how to do (something). **3** to furnish with information; apprise. **4** *Law, chiefly Brit.* (esp. of a client to his solicitor or a solicitor to a barrister) to give relevant facts or information to. [C15: from L *instruere* to construct, equip, teach, from *struere* to build]
▸**in'structible** *adj*

instruction ⊙ (ɪn'strʌkʃən) *n* **1** a direction; order. **2** the process or act of imparting knowledge; teaching; education. **3** *Computing.* a part of a program consisting of a coded command to the computer to perform a specified function.
▸**in'structional** *adj*

instructions ⊙ (ɪn'strʌkʃənz) *pl n* **1** directions, orders, or recommended rules for guidance, use, etc. **2** *Law.* the facts and details relating to a case given by a client to his solicitor or by a solicitor to a barrister.

instructive ⊙ (ɪn'strʌktɪv) *adj* serving to instruct or enlighten; conveying information.
▸**in'structively** *adv* ▸**in'structiveness** *n*

instructor ⊙ (ɪn'strʌktə) *n* **1** someone who instructs; teacher. **2** *US & Canad.* a university teacher ranking below assistant professor.
▸**in'structorship** *n* ▸**instructress** (ɪn'strʌktrɪs) *fem n*

instrument ⊙ *n* ('ɪnstrəmənt). **1** a mechanical implement or tool, esp. one used for precision work. **2** *Music.* any of various contrivances or mechanisms that can be played to produce musical tones or sounds. **3** an important factor or agency in something: *her evidence was an instrument in his arrest.* **4** *Inf.* a person used by another to gain an end; dupe. **5** a measuring device, such as a pressure gauge. **6a** a device or system for use in navigation or control, esp. of aircraft. **6b** (*as modifier*): *instrument landing.* **7** a formal legal document. ◆ *vb* ('ɪnstrəˌmɛnt). (*tr*) **8** another word for **orchestrate** (sense 1). **9** to equip with instruments. [C13: from L *instrūmentum* tool, from *instruere* to erect, furnish; see INSTRUCT]

instrumental ⊙ (ˌɪnstrə'mɛntᵊl) *adj* **1** serving as a means or influence; helpful. **2** of, relating to, or characterized by an instrument. **3** played by or composed for musical instruments. **4** *Grammar.* denoting a case of nouns, etc. indicating the instrument used in performing an action, usually using the prepositions *with* or *by means of.* ◆ *n* **5** a piece of music composed for instruments rather than for voices. **6** *Grammar.* the instrumental case.
▸**ˌinstrumen'tality** *n* ▸**ˌinstru'mentally** *adv*

instrumentalist (ˌɪnstrə'mɛntəlɪst) *n* a person who plays a musical instrument.

instrumentation (ˌɪnstrəmɛn'teɪʃən) *n* **1** the instruments specified in a musical score or arrangement. **2** another word for **orchestration. 3** the study of the characteristics of musical instruments. **4** the use of instruments or tools.

instrument panel *or* **board** *n* **1** a panel on which instruments are mounted, as on a car. See also **dashboard. 2** an array of instruments, gauges, etc., mounted to display the condition or performance of a machine.

insubordinate ⊙ (ˌɪnsə'bɔːdɪnɪt) *adj* **1** not submissive to authority; disobedient or rebellious. **2** not in a subordinate position or rank. ◆ *n* **3** an insubordinate person.
▸**ˌinsub'ordinately** *adv* ▸**ˌinsubˌordi'nation** *n*

insubstantial ⊙ (ˌɪnsəb'stænʃəl) *adj* **1** not substantial; flimsy, tenuous, or slight. **2** imaginary; unreal.
▸**ˌinsubˌstanti'ality** *n* ▸**ˌinsub'stantially** *adv*

insufferable ⊙ (ɪn'sʌfərəbᵊl) *adj* intolerable; unendurable.
▸**in'sufferableness** *n* ▸**in'sufferably** *adv*

THESAURUS

instil *vb* **1** = **introduce**, engender, engraft, imbue, implant, impress, inculcate, infix, infuse, insinuate, sow the seeds

instinct *n* **2** = **intuition**, aptitude, faculty, feeling, gift, gut feeling (*inf.*), gut reaction (*inf.*), impulse, knack, natural inclination, predisposition, proclivity, sixth sense, talent, tendency, urge

instinctive *adj* **1** = **inborn**, automatic, inherent, innate, instinctual, intuitional, intuitive, involuntary, mechanical, native, natural, reflex, spontaneous, unlearned, unpremeditated, unthinking, visceral
Antonyms *adj* acquired, calculated, considered, learned, mindful, premeditated, thinking, voluntary, willed

instinctively *adv* **1** = **intuitively**, automatically, by instinct, in one's bones, involuntarily, naturally, without thinking

institute *vb* **1-3** = **establish**, appoint, begin, bring into being, commence, constitute, enact, fix, found, induct, initiate, install, introduce, invest, launch, ordain, organize, originate, pioneer, put into operation, set in motion, settle, set up, start ◆ *n* **4, 5** = **society**, academy, association, college, conservatory, foundation, guild, institution, school, seat of learning, seminary **6** = **custom**, decree, doctrine, dogma, edict, law, maxim, precedent, precept, principle, regulation, rule, tenet
Antonyms *vb* ≠ **establish:** abandon, abolish, cancel, cease, discontinue, end, stop, suspend, terminate

institution *n* **1** = **creation**, constitution, enactment, establishment, formation, foundation, initiation, introduction, investiture, investment, organization **2, 3** = **establishment**, academy, college, foundation, hospital, institute, school, seminary, society, university **4** = **custom**, convention, fixture, law, practice, ritual, rule, tradition

institutional *adj* **2** = **routine**, cheerless, clinical, cold, drab, dreary, dull, forbidding, formal, impersonal, monotonous, regimented, uniform, unwelcoming **3** = **conventional**, accepted, bureaucratic, established, establishment (*inf.*), formal, organized, orthodox, societal

instruct *vb* **1** = **order**, bid, canon, charge, command, direct, enjoin, tell **2** = **teach**, coach, discipline, drill, educate, enlighten, ground, guide, inform, school, train, tutor **3** = **brief**, acquaint, advise, apprise, counsel, inform, notify, tell

instruction *n* **1** = **order**, briefing, command, demand, direction, directive, injunction, mandate, ruling **2** = **teaching**, apprenticeship, coaching, discipline, drilling, education, enlightenment, grounding, guidance, information, lesson(s), preparation, schooling, training, tuition, tutelage

instructions *pl n* **1** = **orders**, advice, directions, guidance, information, key, recommendations, rules

instructive *adj* = **informative**, cautionary, didactic, edifying, educational, enlightening, helpful, illuminating, instructional, revealing, useful

instructor *n* **1** = **teacher**, adviser, coach, demonstrator, exponent, guide, guru, handler, master *or* mistress, mentor, pedagogue, preceptor (*rare*), schoolmaster *or* schoolmistress, trainer, tutor

instrument *n* **1** = **tool**, apparatus, appliance, contraption (*inf.*), contrivance, device, gadget, implement, mechanism, utensil, waldo **3** = **means**, agency, agent, channel, factor, force, mechanism, medium, organ, vehicle **4** *Informal* = **puppet**, cat's-paw, dupe, pawn, tool

instrumental *adj* **1** = **active**, assisting, auxiliary, conducive, contributory, helpful, helping, influential, involved, of help *or* service, subsidiary, useful

insubordinate *adj* **1** = **disobedient**, contumacious, defiant, disorderly, fractious, insurgent, mutinous, rebellious, recalcitrant, refractory, riotous, seditious, turbulent, undisciplined, ungovernable, unruly
Antonyms *adj* compliant, deferential, disciplined, docile, obedient, orderly, submissive, subservient

insubordination *n* **1** = **disobedience**, defiance, indiscipline, insurrection, mutinousness, mutiny, rebellion, recalcitrance, revolt, riotousness, sedition, ungovernability
Antonyms *n* acquiescence, compliance, deference, discipline, docility, obedience, submission, subordination

insubstantial *adj* **1** = **flimsy**, feeble, frail, poor, slight, tenuous, thin, weak **2** = **imaginary**, chimerical, ephemeral, false, fanciful, idle, illusory, immaterial, incorporeal, unreal
Antonyms *adj* ≠ **flimsy:** firm, solid, strong, substantial, weighty

insufferable *adj* = **unbearable**, detestable, dreadful, impossible, insupportable, intolerable, more than flesh and blood can stand, outrageous, past bearing, too much, unendurable, unspeakable

insufficiency ⓘ (ˌɪnsəˈfɪʃənsɪ) *n* **1** Also: **ˌinsufˈficience.** the state of being insufficient. **2** *Pathol.* failure in the functioning of an organ, tissue, etc.: *cardiac insufficiency.*

insufficient ⓘ (ˌɪnsəˈfɪʃənt) *adj* not sufficient; inadequate or deficient.
▸**ˌinsufˈficiently** *adv*

insufflate (ˈɪnsʌˌfleɪt) *vb* **insufflates, insufflating, insufflated. 1** (*tr*) to breathe or blow (something) into (a room, area, etc.). **2** *Med.* to blow (air, medicated powder, etc.) into a body cavity. **3** (*tr*) to breathe or blow upon (someone or something) as a ritual or sacramental act.
▸**ˌinsufˈflation** *n* ▸**ˈinsufˌflator** *n*

insular ⓘ (ˈɪnsjʊlə) *adj* **1** of, relating to, or resembling an island. **2** remote, detached, or aloof. **3** illiberal or narrow-minded. **4** isolated or separated. [C17: from LL, from L *insula* island]
▸**ˈinsularism** *or* **insularity** (ˌɪnsjʊˈlærɪtɪ) *n* ▸**ˈinsularly** *adv*

insulate ⓘ (ˈɪnsjʊˌleɪt) *vb* **insulates, insulating, insulated.** (*tr*) **1** to prevent the transmission of electricity, heat, or sound to or from (a body or device) by surrounding with a nonconducting material. **2** to isolate or detach. [C16: from LL *insulātus* made into an island]

insulation (ˌɪnsjʊˈleɪʃən) *n* **1** Also: **insulant.** material used to insulate a body or device. **2** the act or process of insulating.

insulator (ˈɪnsjʊˌleɪtə) *n* any material or device that insulates, esp. a material with a very low electrical conductivity or thermal conductivity.

insulin (ˈɪnsjʊlɪn) *n* a protein hormone, secreted in the pancreas by the islets of Langerhans, that controls the concentration of glucose in the blood. [C20: from NL *insula* islet (of the pancreas) + -IN]

insult ⓘ *vb* (ɪnˈsʌlt). (*tr*) **1** to treat, mention, or speak to rudely; offend; affront. ◆ *n* (ˈɪnsʌlt). **2** an offensive or contemptuous remark or action; affront; slight. **3** a person or thing producing the effect of an affront: *some television is an insult to intelligence.* **4** *Med.* an injury or trauma. [C16: from L *insultāre* to jump upon]
▸**inˈsulter** *n*

insuperable ⓘ (ɪnˈsuːpərəbᵊl, -prəbᵊl, -ˈsjuː-) *adj* incapable of being overcome; insurmountable.
▸**inˌsuperaˈbility** *n* ▸**inˈsuperably** *adv*

insupportable ⓘ (ˌɪnsəˈpɔːtəbᵊl) *adj* **1** incapable of being endured; intolerable; insufferable. **2** incapable of being supported or justified; indefensible.
▸**ˌinsupˈportableness** *n* ▸**ˌinsupˈportably** *adv*

insurance ⓘ (ɪnˈʃʊərəns, -ˈʃɔː-) *n* **1a** the act, system, or business of providing financial protection against specified contingencies, such as death, loss, or damage. **1b** the state of having such protection. **1c** Also called: **insurance policy.** the policy providing such protection. **1d** the pecuniary amount of such protection. **1e** the premium payable in return for such protection. **f.** (*as modifier*): *insurance agent; insurance broker; insurance company.* **2** a means of protecting or safeguarding against risk or injury.

insure ⓘ (ɪnˈʃʊə, -ˈʃɔː) *vb* **insures, insuring, insured. 1** (often foll. by *against*) to guarantee or protect (against risk, loss, etc.). **2** (often foll. by *against*) to issue (a person) with an insurance policy or take out an insurance policy (on): *his house was heavily insured against fire.* **3** a variant spelling (esp. US) of **ensure.** ◆ Also (rare) (for senses 1, 2): **ensure.**
▸**inˈsurable** *adj* ▸**inˌsuraˈbility** *n*

insured (ɪnˈʃʊəd, -ˈʃɔːd) *adj* **1** covered by insurance: *an insured risk.* ◆ *n* **2** the person, persons, or organization covered by an insurance policy.

insurer (ɪnˈʃʊərə, -ˈʃɔː-) *n* **1** a person or company offering insurance policies in return for premiums. **2** a person or thing that insures.

insurgence (ɪnˈsɜːdʒəns) *n* rebellion, uprising, or riot.

insurgent ⓘ (ɪnˈsɜːdʒənt) *adj* **1** rebellious or in revolt, as against a government in power or the civil authorities. ◆ *n* **2** a person who takes part in an uprising or rebellion; insurrectionist. [C18: from L *insurgēns* rising upon or against, from *surgere* to rise]
▸**inˈsurgency** *n*

insurmountable ⓘ (ˌɪnsəˈmaʊntəbᵊl) *adj* incapable of being overcome; insuperable.
▸**ˌinsurˌmountaˈbility** *or* **ˌinsurˈmountableness** *n* ▸**ˌinsurˈmountably** *adv*

insurrection ⓘ (ˌɪnsəˈrɛkʃən) *n* the act or an instance of rebelling against a government in power or the civil authorities; insurgency. [C15: from LL *insurrectiō*, from *insurgere* to rise up]
▸**ˌinsurˈrectional** *adj* ▸**ˌinsurˈrectionary** *n, adj* ▸**ˌinsurˈrectionist** *n, adj*

int. *abbrev. for:* **1** interest. **2** interior. **3** internal. **4** Also: **Int.** international.

intact ⓘ (ɪnˈtækt) *adj* untouched or unimpaired; left complete or perfect. [C15: from L *intactus* not touched, from *tangere* to touch]
▸**inˈtactness** *n*

intaglio (ɪnˈtɑːlɪˌəʊ) *n, pl* **intaglios** *or* **intagli** (-ljiː). **1** a seal, gem, etc., ornamented with a sunken or incised design. **2** the art or process of incised carving. **3** a design, figure, or ornamentation carved, engraved, or etched into the surface of the material used. **4** any of various printing techniques using an etched or engraved plate. **5** an incised die used to make a design in relief. [C17: from It., from *intagliare* to engrave, from *tagliare* to cut, from LL *tāliāre;* see TAILOR]
▸**intagliated** (ɪnˈtɑːlɪˌeɪtɪd) *adj*

intake (ˈɪnˌteɪk) *n* **1** a thing or a quantity taken in: *an intake of students.* **2** the act of taking in. **3** the opening through which fluid enters a duct or channel, esp. the air inlet of a jet engine. **4** a ventilation shaft in a mine. **5** a contraction or narrowing: *an intake in a garment.*

intangible ⓘ (ɪnˈtændʒɪbᵊl) *adj* **1** incapable of being perceived by touch; impalpable. **2** imprecise or unclear to the mind: *intangible ideas.* **3** (of property or a business asset) saleable though not possessing intrinsic productive value. ◆ *n* **4** something that is intangible.
▸**inˌtangiˈbility** *n* ▸**inˈtangibly** *adv*

intarsia (ɪnˈtɑːsɪə) *or* **tarsia** *n* **1** a decorative mosaic of inlaid wood of a style developed in the Italian Renaissance. **2** (in knitting) **2a** an individually worked motif. **2b** the method of knitting blocks of colour in place to create such a pattern. [C19: changed from It. *intarsio*]

integer (ˈɪntɪdʒə) *n* **1** any rational number that can be expressed as the sum or difference of a finite number of units, as 1, 2, 3, etc. **2** an individual entity or whole unit. [C16: from L: untouched, from *tangere* to touch]

integral ⓘ (ˈɪntɪgrəl, ɪnˈtɛgrəl) *adj* **1** (often foll. by *to*) being an essential part (of); intrinsic (to). **2** intact; entire. **3** formed of constituent parts; united. **4** *Maths.* **4a** of or involving an integral. **4b** involving or being an integer. ◆ *n* **5** *Maths.* the sum of a large number of infinitesimally small quantities, summed either between stated limits (**definite integral**) or in the absence of limits (**indefinite integral**). **6** a complete thing; whole.
▸**integrality** (ˌɪntɪˈgrælɪtɪ) *n* ▸**ˈintegrally** *adv*

integral calculus *n* the branch of calculus concerned with the determination of integrals (**integration**) and their application to the solution of differential equations.

integrand (ˈɪntɪˌgrænd) *n* a mathematical function to be integrated. [C19: from L: to be integrated]

integrant (ˈɪntəgrənt) *adj* **1** part of a whole; integral; constituent. ◆ *n* **2** an integrant part.

integrate ⓘ *vb* (ˈɪntɪˌgreɪt), **integrates, integrating, integrated. 1** to make or be made into a whole; incorporate or be incorporated. **2** (*tr*) to designate (a school, park, etc.) for use by all races or groups; desegregate. **3** to amalgamate or mix (a racial or religious group) with an existing community. **4** *Maths.* to determine the integral of a function or variable. ◆ *adj* (ˈɪntɪgrɪt). **5** made up of parts; integrated. [C17: from L *integrāre;* see INTEGER]
▸**integrable** (ˈɪntəgrəbᵊl) *adj* ▸**ˌintegraˈbility** *n* ▸**ˌinteˈgration** *n* ▸**ˈinteˌgrative** *adj*

THESAURUS

Antonyms *adj* appealing, attractive, bearable, charming, disarming, pleasant

insufficiency *n* **1 = shortage**, dearth, deficiency, inadequacy, inadequateness, lack, paucity, poverty, scantiness, scarcity, short supply, want

insufficient *adj* **= inadequate**, deficient, incapable, incommensurate, incompetent, lacking, scant, short, unfitted, unqualified
Antonyms *adj* adequate, ample, commensurate, competent, enough, plentiful, qualified, sufficient

insular *adj* **3 = narrow-minded**, blinkered, circumscribed, closed, contracted, cut off, illiberal, inward-looking, isolated, limited, narrow, parish-pump, parochial, petty, prejudiced, provincial
Antonyms *adj* broad-minded, cosmopolitan, experienced, liberal, open-minded, tolerant, worldly

insulate *vb* **2 = isolate**, close off, cocoon, cushion, cut off, protect, sequester, shield, wrap up in cotton wool

insult *vb* **1 = offend**, abuse, affront, call names, give offence to, injure, miscall (*dialect*), outrage, put down, revile, slag (off) (*sl.*), slander, slight, snub ◆ *n* **2 = abuse**, affront, aspersion, contumely, indignity, insolence, offence, outrage, put-down, rudeness, slap in the face (*inf.*), slight, snub
Antonyms *vb* ≠ **offend:** flatter, please, praise ◆ *n* ≠ **abuse:** compliment, flattery, honour

insulting *adj* **1 = offensive**, abusive, affronting, contemptuous, degrading, disparaging, insolent, rude, scurrilous, slighting
Antonyms *adj* complimentary, deferential, flattering, laudatory, respectful

insuperable *adj* **= insurmountable**, impassable, invincible, unconquerable
Antonyms *adj* conquerable, possible, surmountable

insupportable *adj* **1 = intolerable**, insufferable, past bearing, unbearable, unendurable **2 = unjustifiable**, indefensible, untenable

insurance *n* **2 = protection**, assurance, cover, coverage, guarantee, indemnification, indemnity, provision, safeguard, security, something to fall back on (*inf.*), warranty

insure *vb* **1 = protect**, assure, cover, guarantee, indemnify, underwrite, warrant

insurgent *adj* **1 = rebellious**, disobedient, insubordinate, insurrectionary, mutinous, revolting, revolutionary, riotous, seditious ◆ *n* **2 = rebel**, insurrectionist, mutineer, resister, revolter, revolutionary, revolutionist, rioter

insurmountable *adj* **= insuperable**, hopeless, impassable, impossible, invincible, overwhelming, unconquerable

insurrection *n* **= rebellion**, coup, insurgency, mutiny, putsch, revolt, revolution, riot, rising, sedition, uprising

intact *adj* **= undamaged**, all in one piece, complete, entire, perfect, scatheless, sound, together, unbroken, undefiled, unharmed, unhurt, unimpaired, uninjured, unscathed, untouched, unviolated, virgin, whole
Antonyms *adj* broken, damaged, harmed, impaired, injured

intangible *adj* **1, 2 = elusive**, airy, dim, ethereal, evanescent, impalpable, imperceptible, incorporeal, indefinite, invisible, shadowy, unreal, unsubstantial, vague

integral *adj* **1 = essential**, basic, component, constituent, elemental, fundamental, indispensable, intrinsic, necessary, requisite **2 = whole**, complete, entire, full, intact, undivided
Antonyms *adj* ≠ **essential:** inessential, unimportant, unnecessary ≠ **whole:** fractional

integrate *vb* **1 = join**, accommodate, amalgamate, assimilate, blend, coalesce, combine,

integrated circuit *n* a very small electronic circuit consisting of an assembly of elements made from a chip of semiconducting material.

integrity ⊤ (ɪnˈtɛɡrɪtɪ) *n* **1** adherence to moral principles; honesty. **2** the quality of being unimpaired; soundness. **3** unity; wholeness. [C15: from L *integritās*; see INTEGER]

integument (ɪnˈtɛɡjʊmənt) *n* any outer protective layer or covering, such as a cuticle, seed coat, rind, or shell. [C17: from L *integumentum*, from *tegere* to cover]
▸**inˌteguˈmental** *or* **inˌteguˈmentary** *adj*

intellect ⊤ (ˈɪntɪˌlɛkt) *n* **1** the capacity for understanding, thinking, and reasoning. **2** a mind or intelligence, esp. a brilliant one: *his intellect is wasted on that job.* **3** *Inf.* a person possessing a brilliant mind; brain. [C14: from L *intellectus* comprehension, from *intellegere* to understand; see INTELLIGENCE]
▸ˌ**intelˈlective** *adj* ▸ˌ**intelˈlectively** *adv*

intellection (ˌɪntɪˈlɛkʃən) *n* **1** mental activity; thought. **2** an idea or thought.

intellectual ⊤ (ˌɪntɪˈlɛktʃʊəl) *adj* **1** of or relating to the intellect. **2** appealing to or characteristic of people with a developed intellect: *intellectual literature.* **3** expressing or enjoying mental activity. ◆ *n* **4** a person who enjoys mental activity and has highly developed tastes in art, etc. **5** a person who uses his intellect. **6** a highly intelligent person.
▸ˌ**intelˌlectuˈality** *or* ˌ**intelˈlectualness** *n* ▸ˌ**intelˈlectualˌize** *or* ˌ**intelˈlectualˌise** *vb* ▸ˌ**intelˈlectually** *adv*

intellectualism (ˌɪntɪˈlɛktʃʊəˌlɪzəm) *n* **1** development and exercise of the intellect. **2** *Philosophy.* the doctrine that reason is the ultimate criterion of knowledge.
▸ˌ**intelˈlectualist** *n, adj* ▸ˌ**intelˌlectualˈistic** *adj*

intellectual property *n* an intangible asset, such as a copyright or patent.

intelligence ⊤ (ɪnˈtɛlɪdʒəns) *n* **1** the capacity for understanding; ability to perceive and comprehend meaning. **2** *Old-fashioned.* news; information. **3** military information about enemies, spies, etc. **4** a group or department that gathers or deals with such information. **5** (*often cap.*) an intelligent being, esp. one that is not embodied. **6** (*modifier*) of or relating to intelligence: *an intelligence network.* [C14: from L *intellegentia*, from *intellegere* to discern, lit.: to choose between, from INTER- + *legere* to choose]
▸**inˌtelliˈgential** *adj*

intelligence quotient *n* a measure of the intelligence of an individual. The quotient is derived by dividing an individual's mental age by his chronological age and multiplying the result by 100. Abbrev.: **IQ**.

intelligence test *n* any of a number of tests designed to measure a person's mental skills.

intelligent ⊤ (ɪnˈtɛlɪdʒənt) *adj* **1** having or indicating intelligence; clever. **2** indicating high intelligence; perceptive: *an intelligent guess.* **3** (of computerized functions, weapons, etc.) able to initiate or modify action in the light of ongoing events. **4** (*postpositive*; foll. by *of*) *Arch.* having knowledge or information.
▸**inˈtelligently** *adv*

intelligent card *n* another name for **smart card.**

intelligentsia ⊤ (ɪnˌtɛlɪˈdʒɛntsɪə) *n* (usually preceded by *the*) the educated or intellectual people in a society or community. [C20: from Russian *intelligentsiya*, from L *intellegentia* INTELLIGENCE]

intelligible ⊤ (ɪnˈtɛlɪdʒəbᵊl) *adj* **1** able to be understood; comprehensible. **2** *Philosophy.* capable of being apprehended by the mind or intellect alone. [C14: from L *intellegibilis*; see INTELLECT]
▸**inˌtelligiˈbility** *n* ▸**inˈtelligibly** *adv*

intemperate ⊤ (ɪnˈtɛmpərɪt, -prɪt) *adj* **1** consuming alcoholic drink habitually or to excess; immoderate. **2** unrestrained: *intemperate rage.* **3** extreme or severe: *an intemperate climate.*
▸**inˈtemperance** *or* **inˈtemperateness** *n* ▸**inˈtemperately** *adv*

intend ⊤ (ɪnˈtɛnd) *vb* **1** (*may take a clause as object*) to propose or plan (something or to do something); have in mind; mean. **2** (*tr*; often foll. by *for*) to design or destine (for a certain purpose, person, etc.). **3** (*tr*) to mean to express or indicate: *what do his words intend?* **4** (*intr*) to have a purpose as specified; mean: *he intends well.* [C14: from L *intendere* to stretch forth, give one's attention to, from *tendere* to stretch]
▸**inˈtender** *n*

intendancy (ɪnˈtɛndənsɪ) *n* **1** the position or work of an intendant. **2** intendants collectively.

intendant (ɪnˈtɛndənt) *n* a senior administrator; superintendent or manager.

intended ⊤ (ɪnˈtɛndɪd) *adj* **1** planned or future. ◆ *n* **2** *Inf.* a person whom one is to marry; fiancé or fiancée.

intense ⊤ (ɪnˈtɛns) *adj* **1** of extreme force, strength, degree, or amount: *intense heat.* **2** characterized by deep or forceful feelings: *an intense person.* [C14: from L *intensus* stretched, from *intendere* to stretch out]
▸**inˈtensely** *adv* ▸**inˈtenseness** *n*

> **USAGE NOTE** *Intense* is sometimes wrongly used where *intensive* is meant: *the land is under intensive* (not *intense*) *cultivation. Intensely* is sometimes wrongly used where *intently* is meant: *he listened intently* (not *intensely*).

intensifier (ɪnˈtɛnsɪˌfaɪə) *n* **1** a person or thing that intensifies. **2** a word, esp. an adjective or adverb, that serves to intensify the meaning of the word or phrase that it modifies. **3** a substance, esp. one containing silver or uranium, used to increase the density of a photographic film or plate.

intensify ⊤ (ɪnˈtɛnsɪˌfaɪ) *vb* **intensifies, intensifying, intensified. 1** to make or become intense or more intense. **2** (*tr*) to increase the density of (a photographic film or plate).
▸**inˌtensifiˈcation** *n*

intension (ɪnˈtɛnʃən) *n Logic.* the set of characteristics or properties that distinguish the referent or referents of a given word.
▸**inˈtensional** *adj*

intensity ⊤ (ɪnˈtɛnsɪtɪ) *n, pl* **intensities. 1** the state or quality of being intense. **2** extreme force, degree, or amount. **3** *Physics.* **3a** a measure of field strength or of the energy transmitted by radiation. **3b** (of sound in a specified direction) the average rate of flow of sound energy for

THESAURUS

fuse, harmonize, incorporate, intermix, knit, meld, merge, mesh, unite
Antonyms *vb* disperse, divide, segregate, separate

integration *n* **1** = **assimilation**, amalgamation, blending, combining, commingling, fusing, harmony, incorporation, mixing, unification

integrity *n* **1** = **honesty**, candour, goodness, honour, incorruptibility, principle, probity, purity, rectitude, righteousness, uprightness, virtue **2, 3** = **soundness**, coherence, cohesion, completeness, unity, wholeness
Antonyms *n* ≠ **honesty:** corruption, deceit, dishonesty, disrepute, duplicity, immorality ≠ **soundness:** faultiness, flimsiness, fragility, uncertainty, unsoundness

intellect *n* **1** = **intelligence**, brains (*inf.*), judgment, mind, reason, sense, understanding **3** *Informal* = **thinker**, brain (*inf.*), egghead, genius, intellectual, intelligence, mind

intellectual *adj* **3** = **scholarly**, bookish, cerebral, highbrow, intelligent, mental, rational, studious, thoughtful ◆ *n* **4** = **academic**, bluestocking (*usually disparaging*), egghead (*inf.*), highbrow, thinker
Antonyms *adj* ≠ **scholarly:** ignorant, illiterate, material, physical, stupid, unintellectual, unlearned ◆ *n* ≠ **academic:** idiot, moron

intelligence *n* **1** = **understanding**, acumen, alertness, aptitude, brain power, brains (*inf.*), brightness, capacity, cleverness, comprehension, discernment, grey matter (*inf.*), intellect, mind, nous (*Brit. sl.*), penetration, perception, quickness, reason, sense, smarts (*sl., chiefly US*) **2** = **information**, advice, data, disclosure, facts, findings, gen (*Brit. inf.*), knowledge, low-down (*inf.*), news, notice, notification, report, rumour, tidings, tip-off, word
Antonyms *n* ≠ **understanding:** dullness, ignorance, stupidity ≠ **information:** concealment, misinformation

intelligent *adj* **1** = **clever**, acute, alert, apt, brainy (*inf.*), bright, discerning, enlightened, instructed, knowing, penetrating, perspicacious, quick, quick-witted, rational, sharp, smart, thinking, well-informed
Antonyms *adj* dim-witted, dull, foolish, ignorant, obtuse, stupid, unintelligent

intelligentsia *n* = **intellectuals**, eggheads (*inf.*), highbrows, illuminati, literati, masterminds, the learned

intelligibility *n* **1** = **clarity**, clearness, comprehensibility, distinctness, explicitness, lucidity, plainness, precision, simplicity

intelligible *adj* **1** = **understandable**, clear, comprehensible, distinct, lucid, open, plain
Antonyms *adj* confused, garbled, incomprehensible, puzzling, unclear, unintelligible

intemperance *n* **1** = **overindulgence**, crapulence, excess, extravagance, immoderation, inebriation, insobriety, intoxication, unrestraint

intemperate *adj* **1** = **excessive**, immoderate, incontinent, intoxicated, prodigal, profligate, self-indulgent **2** = **excessive**, extravagant, inordinate, over the top (*sl.*), passionate, unbridled, uncontrollable, ungovernable, unrestrained, violent **3** = **excessive**, extreme, severe, tempestuous, wild
Antonyms *adj* ≠ **excessive:** continent, disciplined, moderate, restrained, self-controlled, temperate

intend *vb* **1** = **plan**, aim, be resolved *or* determined, contemplate, determine, have in mind *or* view, mean, meditate, propose, purpose, scheme **2** *often with* **for** = **destine**, aim, consign, design, earmark, mark out, mean, set apart

intended *adj* **1** = **planned**, betrothed, destined, future, proposed ◆ *n* **2** *Informal* = **betrothed**, fiancé, fiancée, future wife *or* husband, husband- *or* wife-to-be

intense *adj* **1** = **extreme**, acute, agonizing, close, concentrated, deep, drastic, excessive, exquisite, fierce, forceful, great, harsh, intensive, powerful, profound, protracted, severe, strained, unqualified **2** = **passionate**, ardent, burning, consuming, eager, earnest, energetic, fanatical, fervent, fervid, fierce, flaming, forcible, heightened, impassioned, keen, speaking, vehement
Antonyms *adj* ≠ **extreme:** easy, gentle, mild, moderate, relaxed, slight ≠ **passionate:** casual, cool, indifferent, subdued, weak

intensely *adv* **1** = **strongly**, deeply, extremely, fiercely, passionately, profoundly, seriously (*inf.*)

intensify *vb* **1** = **increase**, add fuel to the flames (*inf.*), add to, aggravate, augment, boost, concentrate, deepen, emphasize, enhance, escalate, exacerbate, fan the flames of, heighten, magnify, quicken, redouble, reinforce, set off, sharpen, step up (*inf.*), strengthen, whet
Antonyms *vb* damp down, decrease, dilute, diminish, dull, lessen, minimize, weaken

intensity *n* **1** = **force**, ardour, concentration, depth, earnestness, emotion, energy, excess, extremity, fanaticism, fervency, fervour, fierceness, fire, intenseness, keenness, passion, potency, power, severity, strain, strength, tension, vehemence, vigour

one period through unit area at right angles to the specified direction.

intensive ➊ (ɪn'tensɪv) *adj* **1** of, relating to, or characterized by intensity: *intensive training.* **2** (*usually in combination*) using one factor of production proportionately more than others, as specified: *capital-intensive; labour-intensive.* **3** *Agriculture.* involving or farmed using large amounts of capital or labour to increase production from a particular area. Cf. **extensive** (sense 3). **4** denoting or relating to a grammatical intensifier. **5** denoting or belonging to a class of pronouns used to emphasize a noun or personal pronoun. **6** of or relating to intension. ◆ *n* **7** an intensifier or intensive pronoun or grammatical construction.
▸**in'tensively** *adv* ▸**in'tensiveness** *n*

intensive care *n* **1** extensive and continuous care provided for an acutely ill patient in a hospital. **2** the unit in which this care is provided; intensive-care unit.

intent ➊ (ɪn'tɛnt) *n* **1** something that is intended; aim; purpose; design. **2** the act of intending. **3** *Law.* the will or purpose with which one does an act. **4** implicit meaning; connotation. **5 to all intents and purposes.** for all practical purposes; virtually. ◆ *adj* **6** firmly fixed; determined; concentrated: *an intent look.* **7** (*postpositive;* usually foll. by *on* or *upon*) having the fixed intention (of); directing one's mind or energy (to): *intent on committing a crime.* [C13 (in the sense: intention): from LL *intentus* aim, from L: a stretching out; see INTEND]
▸**in'tently** *adv* ▸**in'tentness** *n*

intention ➊ (ɪn'tɛnʃən) *n* **1** a purpose or goal; aim: *it is his intention to reform.* **2** *Med.* a natural healing process in which the edges of a wound cling together with no tissue between (**first intention**), or in which the edges adhere with tissue between (**second intention**). **3** (*usually pl*) design or purpose with respect to a proposal of marriage (esp. in **honourable intentions**).

intentional ➊ (ɪn'tɛnʃənᵊl) *adj* **1** performed by or expressing intention; deliberate. **2** of or relating to intention or purpose.
▸**in,tention'ality** *n* ▸**in'tentionally** *adv*

inter ➊ (ɪn'tɜː) *vb* **inters, interring, interred.** (*tr*) to place (a body, etc.) in the earth; bury, esp. with funeral rites. [C14: from OF *enterrer,* from L IN-² + *terra* earth]

inter- *prefix* **1** between or among: *international.* **2** together, mutually, or reciprocally: *interdependent; interchange.* [from L]

interact (,ɪntər'ækt) *vb* (*intr*) to act on or in close relation with each other.

interaction (,ɪntə'ækʃən) *n* **1** a mutual or reciprocal action. **2** *Physics.* the transfer of energy between elementary particles, between a particle and a field, or between fields. See **fundamental interaction.**

interactive (,ɪntər'æktɪv) *adj* **1** allowing or relating to continuous two-way transfer of information between a user and the central point of a communication system, such as a computer or television. **2** (of two or more persons, forces, etc.) acting upon or in close relation with each other; interacting.

inter alia *Latin.* ('ɪntər 'eɪlɪə) *adv* among other things.

interbreed (,ɪntə'briːd) *vb* **interbreeds, interbreeding, interbred. 1** to breed within a single family or strain so as to produce particular characteristics in the offspring. **2** another term for **crossbreed** (sense 1).

interbroker dealer (,ɪntə'brəʊkə) *n Stock Exchange.* a specialist who matches the needs of different market makers and facilitates dealings between them.

intercalary (ɪn'tɜːkələrɪ) *adj* **1** (of a day, month, year, etc.) inserted in the calendar. **2** (of a particular year) having one or more days inserted. **3** inserted, introduced, or interpolated. [C17: from L *intercalārius;* see INTERCALATE]

intercalate (ɪn'tɜːkə,leɪt) *vb* **intercalates, intercalating, intercalated.** (*tr*) **1** to insert (one or more days) into the calendar. **2** to interpolate or insert. [C17: from L *intercalāre* to insert, proclaim that a day has been inserted, from INTER- + *calāre* to proclaim]
▸**in,terca'lation** *n* ▸**in'tercalative** *adj*

intercede ➊ (,ɪntə'siːd) *vb* **intercedes, interceding, interceded.** (*intr;* often foll. by *in*) to come between parties or act as mediator or advocate: *to intercede in the strike.* [C16: from L *intercēdere,* from INTER- + *cēdere* to move]
▸**,inter'ceder** *n*

intercensal (,ɪntə'sɛnsəl) *adj* (of population figures, etc.) estimated at a time between official censuses. [C19: from INTER- + *censal,* irregularly formed from CENSUS]

intercept ➊ *vb* (,ɪntə'sɛpt). (*tr*) **1** to stop, deflect, or seize on the way from one place to another; prevent from arriving or proceeding. **2** *Sport.* to seize or cut off (a pass) on its way from one opponent to another. **3** *Maths.* to cut off, mark off, or bound (some part of a line, curve, plane, or surface). ◆ *n* ('ɪntə,sɛpt). **4** *Maths.* **4a** a point at which two figures intersect. **4b** the distance from the origin to the point at which a line, curve, or surface cuts a coordinate axis. **5** *Sport, US & Canad.* the act of intercepting an opponent's pass. [C16: from L *intercipere* to seize before arrival, from INTER- + *capere* to take]
▸**,inter'ception** *n* ▸**,inter'ceptive** *adj*

interceptor *or* **intercepter** (,ɪntə'sɛptə) *n* **1** a person or thing that intercepts. **2** a fast highly manoeuvrable fighter aircraft used to intercept enemy aircraft.

intercession ➊ (,ɪntə'sɛʃən) *n* **1** the act or an instance of interceding. **2** the act of interceding or offering petitionary prayer to God on behalf of others. **3** such petitionary prayer. [C16: from L *intercessio;* see INTERCEDE]
▸**,inter'cessional** *or* **,inter'cessory** *adj* ▸**,inter'cessor** *n* ▸**,interces'sorial** *adj*

interchange ➊ *vb* (,ɪntə'tʃeɪndʒ), **interchanges, interchanging, interchanged. 1** to change places or cause to change places; alternate; exchange; switch. ◆ *n* ('ɪntə,tʃeɪndʒ). **2** the act of interchanging; exchange or alternation. **3** a motorway junction of interconnecting roads and bridges designed to prevent streams of traffic crossing one another.
▸**,inter'changeable** *adj* ▸**,inter,changea'bility** *or* **,inter'changeableness** *n* ▸**,inter'changeably** *adv*

Intercity (,ɪntə'sɪtɪ) *adj* (in Britain) *Trademark.* denoting a fast train or passenger rail service, esp. between main towns.

intercom ('ɪntə,kɒm) *n Inf.* an internal telephone system for communicating within a building, aircraft, etc. [C20: short for INTERCOMMUNICATION]

intercommunicate (,ɪntəkə'mjuːnɪ,keɪt) *vb* **intercommunicates, intercommunicating, intercommunicated.** (*intr*) **1** to communicate mutually. **2** to interconnect, as two rooms, etc.
▸**,intercom'municable** *adj* ▸**,intercom,muni'cation** *n* ▸**,intercom'municative** *adj*

intercommunion (,ɪntəkə'mjuːnjən) *n* association between Churches, involving esp. mutual reception of Holy Communion.

intercontinental (,ɪntə,kɒntɪ'nɛntᵊl) *adj* travelling between or linking continents.

interconvertible (,ɪntəkən'vɜːtɪbᵊl) *adj* (of two or more things) capable of being converted into each other.

intercostal (,ɪntə'kɒstᵊl) *adj Anat.* between the ribs: *intercostal muscles.* [C16: via NL from L INTER- + *costa* rib]

intercourse ➊ ('ɪntə,kɔːs) *n* **1** See **sexual intercourse. 2** communication or exchange between individuals; mutual dealings. [C15: from Med. L *intercursus* business, from L *intercurrere* to run between]

intercurrent (,ɪntə'kʌrənt) *adj* **1** occurring during or in between; intervening. **2** *Pathol.* (of a disease) occurring during the course of another disease.
▸**,inter'currence** *n*

interdependent (,ɪntədɪ'pɛndənt) *adj* (of two or more things) dependent on each other.

interdict ➊ *n* ('ɪntə,dɪkt). **1** *RC Church.* the exclusion of a person in a particular place from certain sacraments, although not from communion. **2** *Civil law.* any order made by a court or official prohibiting an act. **3** *Scots Law.* an order having the effect of an injunction. ◆ *vb* (,ɪntə'dɪkt). (*tr*) **4** to place under legal or ecclesiastical sanction; prohibit; forbid. **5** *Mil.* to destroy (an enemy's lines of communication) by firepower. [C13: from L *interdictum* prohibition, from *interdīcere* to forbid, from INTER- + *dīcere* to say]
▸**,inter'diction** *n* ▸**,inter'dictive** *or* **,inter'dictory** *adj* ▸**,inter'dictively** *adv* ▸**,inter'dictor** *n*

THESAURUS

intensive *adj* **1 = concentrated,** all-out, comprehensive, demanding, exhaustive, in-depth, thorough, thoroughgoing

intent *n* **1 = intention,** aim, design, end, goal, meaning, object, objective, plan, purpose **5 to all intents and purposes = virtually,** as good as, practically ◆ *adj* **6 = intense,** absorbed, alert, attentive, committed, concentrated, earnest, engrossed, fixed, industrious, occupied, piercing, preoccupied, rapt, steadfast, steady, watchful, wrapped up **7 = resolved,** bent, determined, eager, hellbent (*inf.*), resolute, set
Antonyms *n* ≠ **intention:** chance, fortune ◆ *adj* ≠ **intense:** casual, indifferent ≠ **resolved:** irresolute, unsteady, wavering

intention *n* **1 = purpose,** aim, design, end, end in view, goal, idea, intent, meaning, object, objective, point, scope, target, view

intentional *adj* **1 = deliberate,** calculated, designed, done on purpose, intended, meant, planned, prearranged, preconcerted, premeditated, purposed, studied, wilful
Antonyms *adj* accidental, inadvertent, unintentional, unplanned

intentionally *adv* **1 = deliberately,** by design, designedly, on purpose, wilfully

intently *adv* **6 = attentively,** closely, fixedly, hard, keenly, searchingly, steadily, watchfully

inter *vb* **= bury,** entomb, inhume, inurn, lay to rest, sepulchre

intercede *vb* **= mediate,** advocate, arbitrate, interpose, intervene, plead, speak

intercept *vb* **1 = seize,** arrest, block, catch, check, cut off, deflect, head off, interrupt, obstruct, stop, take

intercession *n* **1 = pleading,** advocacy, entreaty, good offices, intervention, mediation, plea, prayer, solicitation, supplication

intercessor *n* **1 = mediator,** advocate, arbitrator, go-between, interceder, intermediary, middleman, negotiator, pleader

interchange *vb* **1 = switch,** alternate, bandy, barter, exchange, reciprocate, swap, trade ◆ *n* **2 = junction,** alternation, crossfire, exchange, give and take, intersection, reciprocation

interchangeable *adj* **1 = identical,** commutable, equivalent, exchangeable, reciprocal, synonymous, the same, transposable

intercourse *n* **1 = sexual intercourse,** carnal knowledge, coition, coitus, congress, copulation, intimacy, sex (*inf.*), sexual relations **2 = communication,** association, commerce, communion, connection, contact, converse, correspondence, dealings, intercommunication, trade, traffic, truck

interdict *n* **2 = ban,** disallowance, disqualification, interdiction, prohibition, taboo, veto ◆ *vb* **4 = prohibit,** ban, bar, debar, disallow, forbid, outlaw, prevent, proscribe, veto

interdigitate (ˌɪntəˈdɪdʒɪˌteɪt) *vb* **interdigitates, interdigitating, interdigitated.** (*intr*) to interlock like the fingers of clasped hands. [C19: from INTER- + L *digitus* (see DIGIT) + -ATE[1]]

interdisciplinary (ˌɪntəˈdɪsɪˌplɪnərɪ) *adj* involving two or more academic disciplines.

interest ➊ (ˈɪntrɪst, -tərɪst) *n* **1** the sense of curiosity about or concern with something or someone. **2** the power of stimulating such a sense: *to have great interest.* **3** the quality of such stimulation. **4** something in which one is interested; a hobby or pursuit. **5** (*often pl*) benefit; advantage: *in one's own interest.* **6** (*often pl*) a right, share, or claim, esp. in a business or property. **7a** a charge for the use of credit or borrowed money. **7b** such a charge expressed as a percentage per time unit of the sum borrowed or used. **8** (*often pl*) a section of a community, etc., whose members have common aims: *the landed interest.* **9 declare an interest.** to make known one's connection, esp. a prejudicial connection, with an affair. ◆ *vb* (*tr*) **10** to arouse or excite the curiosity or concern of. **11** to cause to become involved in something; concern. [C15: from L: it concerns, from *interesse,* from INTER- + *esse* to be]

interested ➊ (ˈɪntrɪstɪd, -tərɪs-) *adj* **1** showing or having interest. **2** (*usually prenominal*) personally involved or implicated: *the interested parties met to discuss the business.*
▸**ˈinterestedly** *adv* ▸**ˈinterestedness** *n*

interesting ➊ (ˈɪntrɪstɪŋ, -tərɪs-) *adj* inspiring interest; absorbing.
▸**ˈinterestingly** *adv* ▸**ˈinterestingness** *n*

interest-rate futures *pl n* financial futures based on projected movements of interest rates.

interface ➊ *n* (ˈɪntəˌfeɪs). **1** *Physical chem.* a surface that forms the boundary between two liquids or chemical phases. **2** a common point or boundary between two things. **3** an electrical circuit linking one device, esp. a computer, with another. ◆ *vb* (ˌɪntəˈfeɪs), **interfaces, interfacing, interfaced. 4** (*tr*) to design or adapt the input and output configurations of (two electronic devices) so that they may work together compatibly. **5** to be an interface (with). **6** to be interactive (with).
▸**interfacial** (ˌɪntəˈfeɪʃəl) *adj* ▸**ˌinterˈfacially** *adv*

interfacing (ˈɪntəˌfeɪsɪŋ) *n* **1** a piece of fabric sewn beneath the facing of a garment, usually at the inside of the neck, armholes, etc., to give shape and firmness. **2** another name for **interlining.**

interfere ➊ (ˌɪntəˈfɪə) *vb* **interferes, interfering, interfered.** (*intr*) **1** (often foll. by *in*) to interpose, esp. meddlesomely or unwarrantedly; intervene. **2** (often foll. by *with*) to come between or into opposition; hinder. **3** (foll. by *with*) *Euphemistic.* to assault sexually. **4** to strike one against the other, as a horse's legs. **5** *Physics.* to cause or produce interference. [C16: from OF *s'entreferir* to collide, from *entre-* INTER- + *ferir* to strike, from L *ferīre*]
▸**ˌinterˈfering** *adj*

interference ➊ (ˌɪntəˈfɪərəns) *n* **1** the act or an instance of interfering. **2** *Physics.* the process in which two or more coherent waves combine to form a resultant wave in which the displacement at any point is the vector sum of the displacements of the individual waves. **3** any undesired signal that tends to interfere with the reception of radio waves.
▸**interferential** (ˌɪntəfəˈrenʃəl) *adj*

interferometer (ˌɪntəfəˈrɒmɪtə) *n Physics.* any acoustic, optical, or microwave instrument that uses interference patterns to make accurate measurements of wavelength, distance, etc.
▸**interferometric** (ˌɪntəˌfɛrəˈmɛtrɪk) *adj* ▸**ˌinterˌferoˈmetrically** *adv* ▸**ˌinterferˈometry** *n*

interferon (ˌɪntəˈfɪərɒn) *n Biochem.* any of a family of proteins made by cells in response to virus infection that prevent the growth of the virus. [C20: from INTERFERE + -ON]

interfuse (ˌɪntəˈfjuːz) *vb* **interfuses, interfusing, interfused. 1** to diffuse or mix throughout or become so diffused or mixed; intermingle. **2** to blend or fuse or become blended or fused.
▸**ˌinterˈfusion** *n*

intergovernmental (ˌɪntəˌgʌvənˈmɛntᵊl) *adj* conducted between or involving two or more governments.

interim ➊ (ˈɪntərɪm) *adj* **1** (*prenominal*) temporary, provisional, or intervening: *interim measures to deal with the emergency.* ◆ *n* **2** (usually preceded by *the*) the intervening time; the meantime (esp. in **in the interim**). ◆ *adv* **3** *Rare.* meantime. [C16: from L: meanwhile]

interior ➊ (ɪnˈtɪərɪə) *n* **1** a part, surface, or region that is inside or on the inside: *the interior of Africa.* **2** inner character or nature. **3** a film or scene shot inside a building, studio, etc. **4** a picture of the inside of a room or building, as in a painting or stage design. **5** the inside of a building or room, with respect to design and decoration. ◆ *adj* **6** of, situated on, or suitable for the inside; inner. **7** coming or acting from within; internal. **8** of or involving a nation's domestic affairs; internal. **9** (esp. of one's spiritual or mental life) secret or private; not observable. [C15: from L (adj), comp. of *inter* within]
▸**inˈteriorly** *adv*

interior angle *n* an angle of a polygon contained between two adjacent sides.

interior decoration *n* **1** the colours, furniture, etc., of the interior of a house, etc. **2** Also called: **interior design.** the art or business of planning the interiors of houses, etc.
▸**interior decorator** *n*

interiorize *or* **interiorise** (ɪnˈtɪərɪəˌraɪz) *vb* **interiorizes, interiorizing, interiorized** *or* **interiorises, interiorising, interiorised.** (*tr*) another word for **internalize.**

interj. *abbrev. for* interjection.

interject ➊ (ˌɪntəˈdʒɛkt) *vb* (*tr*) to interpose abruptly or sharply; interrupt with; throw in: *she interjected clever remarks.* [C16: from L *interjicere* to place between, from *jacere* to throw]
▸**ˌinterˈjector** *n*

interjection ➊ (ˌɪntəˈdʒɛkʃən) *n* **1** the act of interjecting. **2** a word or phrase that is used in syntactic isolation and that expresses sudden emotion; expletive. Abbrev.: **interj.**
▸**ˌinterˈjectional** *or* **ˌinterˈjectory** *adj* ▸**ˌinterˈjectionally** *adv*

interlard (ˌɪntəˈlɑːd) *vb* (*tr*) **1** to scatter thickly in or between; intersperse: *to interlard one's writing with foreign phrases.* **2** to occur frequently in; be scattered in or through: *foreign phrases interlard his writings.*

interlay (ˌɪntəˈleɪ) *vb* **interlays, interlaying, interlaid.** (*tr*) to insert (layers) between; interpose.

interleaf (ˈɪntəˌliːf) *n, pl* **interleaves.** a blank leaf inserted between the leaves of a book.

interleave (ˌɪntəˈliːv) *vb* **interleaves, interleaving, interleaved.** (*tr*) **1** (often foll. by *with*) to intersperse (with), esp. alternately, as the illustrations in a book (with protective leaves). **2** to provide (a book) with blank leaves for notes, etc., or to protect illustrations.

interleukin (ˌɪntəˈluːkɪn) *n* a substance extracted from white blood cells that stimulates their activity against infection and may be used to combat some forms of cancer.

interline[1] (ˌɪntəˈlaɪn) *or* **interlineate** (ˌɪntəˈlɪnɪˌeɪt) *vb* **interlines, interlining, interlined** *or* **interlineates, interlineating, interlineated.** (*tr*) to write or print (matter) between the lines of (a text, book, etc.).
▸**ˈinterˌlining** *or* **ˌinterˌlineˈation** *n*

interline[2] (ˌɪntəˈlaɪn) *vb* **interlines, interlining, interlined.** (*tr*) to provide (a part of a garment) with a second lining, esp. of stiffened material.
▸**ˈinterˌliner** *n*

interlinear (ˌɪntəˈlɪnɪə) *or* **interlineal** *adj* **1** written or printed between lines of text. **2** written or printed with the text in different languages or versions on alternate lines.
▸**ˌinterˈlinearly** *or* **ˌinterˈlineally** *adv*

interlining (ˈɪntəˌlaɪnɪŋ) *n* the material used to interline parts of garments, now often made of reinforced paper.

interlock *vb* (ˌɪntəˈlɒk). **1** to join or be joined firmly, as by a mutual interconnection of parts. ◆ *n* (ˈɪntəˌlɒk). **2** the act of interlocking or the state of being interlocked. **3** a device, esp. one operated electromechanically, used in a logic circuit to prevent an activity being initiated unless preceded by certain events. **4** a closely knitted fabric. ◆ *adj* **5** closely knitted.
▸**ˈinterˌlocker** *n*

interlocutor (ˌɪntəˈlɒkjʊtə) *n* **1** a person who takes part in a conversa-

THESAURUS

interest *n* **1** = **curiosity,** affection, attention, attentiveness, attraction, concern, notice, regard, suspicion, sympathy **2** = **importance,** concern, consequence, moment, note, relevance, significance, weight **4** = **hobby,** activity, diversion, leisure activity, pastime, preoccupation, pursuit, relaxation **5** *often plural* = **advantage,** benefit, boot (*dialect*), gain, good, profit **6** = **stake,** authority, claim, commitment, influence, investment, involvement, participation, portion, right, share ◆ *vb* **10** = **arouse one's curiosity,** amuse, attract, catch one's eye, divert, engross, fascinate, hold the attention of, intrigue, move, touch **11** = **engage,** affect, concern, involve
Antonyms *n* ≠ **curiosity:** boredom, coolness, disinterest, dispassion, disregard, unconcern ≠ **importance:** inconsequence, insignificance, irrelevance, worthlessness ◆ *vb* ≠ **arouse one's curiosity:** bore, burden, irk, repel, tire, weary

interested *adj* **1** = **curious,** affected, attentive, attracted, drawn, excited, fascinated, intent, into (*inf.*), keen, moved, responsive, stimulated **2** = **involved,** biased, concerned, implicated, partial, partisan, predisposed, prejudiced
Antonyms *adj* ≠ **curious:** apathetic, bored, detached, inattentive, indifferent, unconcerned, uninterested, wearied

interesting *adj* = **intriguing,** absorbing, amusing, appealing, attractive, compelling, curious, engaging, engrossing, entertaining, gripping, pleasing, provocative, stimulating, stirring, suspicious, thought-provoking, unusual
Antonyms *adj* boring, dull, mind-numbing, tedious, tiresome, uninteresting

interface *n* **2** = **connection,** border, boundary, frontier, link ◆ *vb* **5** = **connect,** combine, couple, join together, link

interfere *vb* **1** = **intrude,** butt in, get involved, intermeddle, intervene, meddle, poke one's nose in (*inf.*), put one's two cents in (*US sl.*), stick one's oar in (*inf.*), tamper **2** *often with* **with** = **conflict,** be a drag upon (*inf.*), block, clash, collide, cramp, frustrate, get in the way of, hamper, handicap, hinder, impede, inhibit, obstruct, trammel

interference *n* **1** = **intrusion,** clashing, collision, intervention, meddlesomeness, meddling, obstruction, opposition, prying

interfering *adj* **1** = **meddling,** interruptive, intrusive, meddlesome, obtrusive, prying

interim *adj* **1** = **temporary,** acting, caretaker, improvised, intervening, makeshift, pro tem, provisional, stopgap ◆ *n* **2** = **interval,** entr'acte, interregnum, meantime, meanwhile, respite

interior *n* **1** = **inside,** bosom, centre, contents, core, heart, innards (*inf.*) ◆ *adj* **6, 7** = **inside,** inner, internal, inward **8** = **domestic,** home **9** = **mental,** hidden, inner, intimate, personal, private, secret, spiritual
Antonyms *adj* ≠ **inside:** exterior, external, outer, outside, outward

interject *vb* = **interrupt with,** interpolate, interpose, introduce, put in, throw in

interjection *n* **1** = **exclamation,** cry, ejaculation, interpolation, interposition

tion. **2** the man in the centre of a troupe of minstrels who engages the others in talk or acts as announcer. **3** *Scots Law.* a decree by a judge.
► **ˌinterˈlocutress, ˌinterˈlocutrice,** *or* **ˌinterˈlocutrix** *fem n*

interlocutory (ˌɪntəˈlɒkjʊtərɪ, -trɪ) *adj* **1** *Law.* pronounced during the course of proceedings; provisional: *an interlocutory injunction.* **2** interposed, as into a conversation, narrative, etc. **3** of, relating to, or characteristic of dialogue.
► **ˌinterˈlocutorily** *adv*

interloper ➊ (ˈɪntəˌləʊpə) *n* **1** an intruder. **2** a person who introduces himself into professional or social circles where he does not belong. **3** a person who interferes in matters that are not his concern. [C17: from INTER- + *loper,* from MDu. *loopen* to leap]
► **ˌinterˈlope** *vb (intr)*

interlude ➊ (ˈɪntəˌluːd) *n* **1** a period of time or different activity between longer periods, processes, or events; episode or interval. **2** *Theatre.* a short dramatic piece played separately or as part of a longer entertainment, common in 16th-century England. **3** a brief piece of music, dance, etc., given between the sections of another performance. [C14: from Med. L, from L INTER- + *lūdus* play]

intermarry (ˌɪntəˈmærɪ) *vb* **intermarries, intermarrying, intermarried.** *(intr)* **1** (of different races, religions, etc.) to become connected by marriage. **2** to marry within one's own family, clan, group, etc.
► **ˌinterˈmarriage** *n*

intermediary ➊ (ˌɪntəˈmiːdɪərɪ) *n, pl* **intermediaries. 1** a person who acts as a mediator or agent between parties. **2** something that acts as a medium or means. ◆ *adj* **3** acting as an intermediary. **4** situated, acting, or coming between.

intermediate ➊ *adj* (ˌɪntəˈmiːdɪɪt). **1** occurring or situated between two points, extremes, places, etc.; in between. **2** (of a class, course, etc.) suitable for learners with some degree of skill or competence. ◆ *n* (ˌɪntəˈmiːdɪɪt). **3** something intermediate. **4** a substance formed during one of the stages of a chemical process before the desired product is obtained. ◆ *vb* (ˌɪntəˈmiːdɪˌeɪt), **intermediates, intermediating, intermediated. 5** *(intr)* to act as an intermediary or mediator. [C17: from Med. L *intermediāre* to intervene, from L INTER- + *medius* middle]
► **ˌinterˈmediacy** *or* **ˌinterˈmediateness** *n* ► **ˌinterˈmediately** *adv* ► **ˌinterˌmediˈation** *n* ► **ˌinterˈmediˌator** *n*

intermediate-acting *adj* (of a drug) intermediate in its effects between long- and short-acting drugs. Cf. **long-acting, short-acting.**

intermediate frequency *n Electronics.* the frequency to which the signal carrier frequency is changed in a superheterodyne receiver and at which most of the amplification takes place.

intermediate-level waste *n* radioactive waste material, such as reactor components, that can be mixed with concrete and safely stored in steel drums in deep mines or beneath the seabed in concrete chambers. Cf. **high-level waste, low-level waste.**

intermediate vector boson *n Physics.* a hypothetical particle believed to mediate the weak interaction between elementary particles.

interment ➊ (ɪnˈtɜːmənt) *n* burial, esp. with ceremonial rites.

intermezzo (ˌɪntəˈmɛtsəʊ) *n, pl* **intermezzos** *or* **intermezzi** (-tsiː). **1** a short piece of instrumental music composed for performance between the acts or scenes of an opera, drama, etc. **2** an instrumental piece either inserted between two longer movements in an extended composition or intended for independent performance. [C19: from It., from LL *intermedium* interval; see INTERMEDIATE]

interminable ➊ (ɪnˈtɜːmɪnəbᵊl) *adj* endless or seemingly endless because of monotony or tiresome length.
► **inˈterminableness** *n* ► **inˈterminably** *adv*

intermission ➊ (ˌɪntəˈmɪʃən) *n* **1** an interval, as between parts of a film, etc. **2** a period between events or activities; pause. **3** the act of intermitting or the state of being intermitted. [C16: from L, from *intermittere* to INTERMIT]
► **ˌinterˈmissive** *adj*

intermit (ˌɪntəˈmɪt) *vb* **intermits, intermitting, intermitted.** to suspend (activity) or (of activity) to be suspended temporarily or at intervals. [C16: from L *intermittere* to leave off, from INTER- + *mittere* to send]
► **ˌinterˈmittor** *n*

intermittent ➊ (ˌɪntəˈmɪtᵊnt) *adj* occurring occasionally or at regular or irregular intervals; periodic.
► **ˌinterˈmittence** *or* **ˌinterˈmittency** *n* ► **ˌinterˈmittently** *adv*

intermix (ˌɪntəˈmɪks) *vb* **1** *(tr)* to mix (ingredients, liquids, etc.) together. **2** *(intr)* to become or have the capacity to become combined, joined, etc.

intermixture (ˌɪntəˈmɪkstʃə) *n* **1** the act of intermixing or state of being intermixed. **2** an additional ingredient.

intern ➊ *vb* **1** (ɪnˈtɜːn). *(tr)* to detain or confine within a country or a limited area, esp. during wartime. **2** (ˈɪntɜːn). *(intr) Chiefly US.* to serve or train as an intern. ◆ *n* (ˈɪntɜːn). **3** another word for **internee. 4** Also: **interne.** the approximate US and Canad. equivalent of **houseman. 5** Also: **interne.** *Chiefly US.* a student teacher. **6** Also: **interne.** *Chiefly US.* a student or recent graduate undergoing practical training in a working environment. [C19: from L *internus* internal]
► **inˈternment** *n* ► **ˈinternship** *or* **ˈinterneship** *n*

internal ➊ (ɪnˈtɜːnᵊl) *adj* **1** of, situated on, or suitable for the inside; inner. **2** coming or acting from within; interior. **3** involving the spiritual or mental life; subjective. **4** of or involving a nation's domestic as opposed to foreign affairs. **5** situated within, affecting, or relating to the inside of the body. ◆ *n* **6** *Euphemistic.* a medical examination of the vagina or uterus. [C16: from Med. L, from LL *internus* inward]
► **ˌinterˈnality** *or* **inˈternalness** *n* ► **inˈternally** *adv*

internal-combustion engine *n* a heat engine in which heat is supplied by burning the fuel in the working fluid (usually air).

internal energy *n* the thermodynamic property of a system that changes by an amount equal to the work done on the system when it suffers an adiabatic change.

internalize *or* **internalise** (ɪnˈtɜːnəˌlaɪz) *vb* **internalizes, internalizing, internalized** *or* **internalises, internalising, internalised.** *(tr) Psychol., sociol.* to make internal, esp. to incorporate within oneself (values, attitudes, etc.) through learning or socialization. Also: **interiorize.**
► **inˌternaliˈzation** *or* **inˌternaliˈsation** *n*

internal medicine *n* the branch of medical science concerned with the diagnosis and nonsurgical treatment of disorders of the internal structures of the body.

international ➊ (ˌɪntəˈnæʃənᵊl) *adj* **1** of, concerning, or involving two or more nations or nationalities. **2** established by, controlling, or legislating for several nations: *an international court.* **3** available for use by all nations: *international waters.* ◆ *n* **4** *Sport.* **4a** a contest between two national teams. **4b** a member of a national team.
► **ˌinterˌnationˈality** *n* ► **ˌinterˈnationally** *adv*

International (ˌɪntəˈnæʃənᵊl) *n* **1** any of several international socialist organizations, esp. **First International** (1864–76) and **Second International** (1889 until World War I). **2** a member of any of these organizations.

International Atomic Time *n* the scientific standard of time based on the SI unit, the second, used to synchronize the time standards of the major nations. Abbrev.: **TAI.**

International Bank for Reconstruction and Development *n* the official name for the **World Bank.**

International Court of Justice *n* a court established in the Hague, in the Netherlands, to settle disputes brought by nations that are parties to the Statute of the Court. Also called: **World Court.**

International Date Line *n* the line approximately following the 180° meridian from Greenwich on the east side of which the date is one day earlier than on the west.

internationalism (ˌɪntəˈnæʃənəˌlɪzəm) *n* **1** the ideal or practice of cooperation and understanding between nations. **2** the state or quality of being international.
► **ˌinterˈnationalist** *n*

internationalize *or* **internationalise** (ˌɪntəˈnæʃənəˌlaɪz) *vb* **internationalizes, internationalizing, internationalized** *or* **internationalises, internationalising, internationalised.** *(tr)* **1** to make international. **2** to put under international control.
► **ˌinterˌnationaliˈzation** *or* **ˌinterˌnationaliˈsation** *n*

international law *n* the body of rules generally recognized by civilized nations as governing their conduct towards each other.

International Modernism *n* See **International Style.**

International Phonetic Alphabet *n* a series of signs and letters for the representation of human speech sounds. It is based on the Roman alphabet but supplemented by modified signs or symbols from other writing systems.

International Practical Temperature Scale *n* a temperature scale adopted by international agreement in 1968 based on thermodynamic temperature and using experimental values to define 11 fixed points.

International Style *or* **Modernism** *n* an architectural style of the 1920s that used cubic forms, large windows, and modern materials.

International Telecommunications Union *n* a special agency of the United Nations, founded in 1947, that is responsible for the international allocation and registration of frequencies for communications and the regulation of telegraph, telephone, and radio services.

interne (ˈɪntɜːn) *n* a variant spelling of **intern** (senses 4, 5, 6).

THESAURUS

interloper *n* **1** = **trespasser**, gate-crasher (*inf.*), intruder, meddler, uninvited guest, unwanted visitor

interlude *n* **1** = **interval**, break, breathing space, delay, entr'acte, episode, halt, hiatus, intermission, pause, respite, rest, spell, stop, stoppage, wait

intermediary *n* **1** = **mediator**, agent, broker, entrepreneur, go-between, middleman

intermediate *adj* **1** = **middle**, halfway, in-between (*inf.*), intermediary, interposed, intervening, mean, mid, midway, transitional

interment *n* = **burial**, burying, funeral, inhumation, sepulture

interminable *adj* = **endless**, boundless, ceaseless, dragging, everlasting, immeasurable, infinite, limitless, long, long-drawn-out, long-winded, never-ending, perpetual, protracted, unbounded, unlimited, wearisome
Antonyms *adj* bounded, finite, limited, measurable, restricted, temporary

intermission *n* **1-3** = **interval**, break, breathing space, cessation, entr'acte, interlude, interruption, let-up (*inf.*), lull, pause, recess, respite, rest, stop, stoppage, suspense, suspension

intermittent *adj* = **periodic**, broken, discontinuous, fitful, irregular, occasional, punctuated, recurrent, recurring, spasmodic, sporadic, stop-go (*inf.*)
Antonyms *adj* continuous, steady, unceasing

intern *vb* **1** = **imprison**, confine, detain, hold, hold in custody

internal *adj* **1, 2** = **inner**, inside, interior **3** = **private**, intimate, subjective **4** = **domestic**, civic, home, in-house, intramural
Antonyms *adj* ≠ **inner:** exterior, external, outer, outermost, outside ≠ **private:** exposed, revealed, unconcealed

international *adj* **1-3** = **universal**, cosmopolitan, ecumenical, global, intercontinental, worldwide

internecine (ˌɪntəˈniːsaɪn) *adj* **1** mutually destructive or ruinous; maiming both or all sides: *internecine war.* **2** of or relating to slaughter or carnage; bloody. **3** of or involving conflict within a group or organization. [C17: from L, from *internecāre* to destroy, from *necāre* to kill]

internee (ˌɪntɜːˈniː) *n* a person who is interned, esp. an enemy citizen in wartime or a terrorism suspect.

Internet ❶ (ˈɪntəˌnɛt) *n* **the.** the single worldwide computer network that interconnects other computer networks, on which end-user services, such as World Wide Web sites or data archives, are located, enabling data and other information to be exchanged. Also called: the **Net.**

internist (ˈɪntɜːnɪst, ɪnˈtɜːnɪst) *n* a physician who specializes in internal medicine.

interpellate (ɪnˈtɜːpɛˌleɪt) *vb* **interpellates, interpellating, interpellated.** (*tr*) *Parliamentary procedure.* (in European legislatures) to question (a member of the government) on a point of government policy, often interrupting the business of the day. [C16: from L *interpellāre* to disturb, from INTER- + *pellere* to push]
▸**inˌterpelˈlation** *n* ▸**inˈterpelˌlator** *n*

interpenetrate (ˌɪntəˈpɛnɪˌtreɪt) *vb* **interpenetrates, interpenetrating, interpenetrated. 1** to penetrate (something) thoroughly; pervade. **2** to penetrate each other or one another mutually.
▸**ˌinterˈpenetrable** *adj* ▸**ˌinterˈpenetrant** *adj* ▸**ˌinterˌpeneˈtration** *n* ▸**ˌinterˈpenetrative** *adj* ▸**ˌinterˈpenetratively** *adv*

interplay ❶ (ˈɪntəˌpleɪ) *n* reciprocal and mutual action and reaction, as in circumstances, events, or personal relations.

interpleader (ˌɪntəˈpliːdə) *n Law.* **1** a process by which a person holding money claimed by two or more parties and having no interest in it himself can require the claimants to litigate with each other. **2** a person who interpleads.

Interpol (ˈɪntəˌpɒl) *n acronym for* International Criminal Police Organization, an association of over 100 national police forces, devoted to fighting international crime.

interpolate ❶ (ɪnˈtɜːpəˌleɪt) *vb* **interpolates, interpolating, interpolated. 1** to insert or introduce (a comment, passage, etc.) into (a conversation, text, etc.). **2** to falsify or alter (a text, manuscript, etc.) by the later addition of (material, esp. spurious passages). **3** (*intr*) to make additions, interruptions, or insertions. **4** *Maths.* to estimate (a value of a function) between the values already known or determined. Cf. **extrapolate** (sense 1). [C17: from L *interpolāre* to give a new appearance to]
▸**inˈterpoˌlater** *or* **inˈterpoˌlator** *n* ▸**inˈterpolative** *adj*

interpose ❶ (ˌɪntəˈpəʊz) *vb* **interposes, interposing, interposed. 1** to put or place between or among other things. **2** to introduce (comments, questions, etc.) into a speech or conversation; interject. **3** to exert or use influence or action in order to alter or intervene in (a situation). [C16: from OF, from L *interpōnere,* from INTER- + *pōnere* to put]
▸**ˌinterˈposal** *n* ▸**ˌinterˈposer** *n* ▸**ˌinterpoˈsition** *n*

interpret ❶ (ɪnˈtɜːprɪt) *vb* **1** (*tr*) to clarify or explain the meaning of; elucidate. **2** (*tr*) to construe the significance or intention of. **3** (*tr*) to convey the spirit or meaning of (a poem, song, etc.) in performance. **4** (*intr*) to act as an interpreter; translate orally. [C14: from L *interpretārī,* from *interpres* negotiator, one who explains]
▸**inˈterpretable** *adj* ▸**inˌterpretaˈbility** *or* **inˈterpretableness** *n* ▸**inˈterpretably** *adv* ▸**inˈterpretive** *adj*

interpretation ❶ (ɪnˌtɜːprɪˈteɪʃən) *n* **1** the act or process of interpreting or explaining; elucidation. **2** the result of interpreting; an explanation. **3** a particular view of an artistic work, esp. as expressed by stylistic individuality in its performance. **4** explanation, as of a historical site, provided by the use of original objects, visual display material, etc.
▸**inˌterpreˈtational** *adj*

interpreter ❶ (ɪnˈtɜːprɪtə) *n* **1** a person who translates orally from one language into another. **2** a person who interprets the work of others. **3** *Computing.* a program that translates a statement in a source program to machine code and executes it before translating and executing the next statement.
▸**inˈterpretership** *n* ▸**inˈterpretress** *fem n*

interpretive centre *n* (at a historical site, etc.) a building that provides interpretation of the site through a variety of media, such as video displays and exhibitions, and, often, includes facilities such as refreshment rooms.

interregnum (ˌɪntəˈrɛgnəm) *n, pl* **interregnums** *or* **interregna** (-nə). **1** an interval between two reigns, governments, etc. **2** any period in which a state lacks a ruler, government, etc. **3** a period of absence of some control, authority, etc. **4** a gap in a continuity. [C16: from L, from INTER- + *regnum* REIGN]
▸**ˌinterˈregnal** *adj*

interrelate (ˌɪntərɪˈleɪt) *vb* **interrelates, interrelating, interrelated.** to place in or come into a mutual or reciprocal relationship.
▸**ˌinterreˈlation** *n* ▸**ˌinterreˈlationˌship** *n*

interrogate ❶ (ɪnˈtɛrəˌgeɪt) *vb* **interrogates, interrogating, interrogated.** to ask questions (of), esp. to question (a witness in court, spy, etc.) closely. [C15: from L *interrogāre,* from *rogāre* to ask]
▸**inˈterroˌgator** *n*

interrogation ❶ (ɪnˌtɛrəˈgeɪʃən) *n* **1** the technique, practice, or an instance of interrogating. **2** a question or query. **3** *Telecomm.* the transmission of one or more triggering pulses to a transponder.
▸**inˌterroˈgational** *adj*

interrogation mark *n* a less common term for **question mark.**

interrogative ❶ (ˌɪntəˈrɒgətɪv) *adj* **1** asking or having the nature of a question. **2** denoting a form or construction used in asking a question. **3** denoting or belonging to a class of words, such as *which* and *whom,* that serve to question which individual referent is intended. ◆ *n* **4** an interrogative word, phrase, sentence, or construction. **5** a question mark.
▸**ˌinterˈrogatively** *adv*

interrogatory (ˌɪntəˈrɒgətərɪ, -trɪ) *adj* **1** expressing or involving a question. ◆ *n, pl* **interrogatories. 2** a question or interrogation.

interrupt ❶ (ˌɪntəˈrʌpt) *vb* **1** to break the continuity of (an action, event, etc.) or hinder (a person) by intrusion. **2** (*tr*) to cease to perform (some action). **3** (*tr*) to obstruct (a view, etc.). **4** to prevent or disturb (a conversation, discussion, etc.) by questions, interjections, or comment. [C15: from L *interrumpere,* from INTER- + *rumpere* to break]
▸**ˌinterˈruptible** *adj* ▸**ˌinterˈruptive** *adj* ▸**ˌinterˈruptively** *adv* ▸**ˌinterˈrupted** *adj*

interrupted screw *n* a screw with a slot cut into the thread, esp. one used in the breech of some guns permitting both engagement and release of the block by a partial turn of the screw.

interrupter *or* **interruptor** (ˌɪntəˈrʌptə) *n* **1** a person or thing that interrupts. **2** an electromechanical device for opening and closing an electric circuit.

interruption ❶ (ˌɪntəˈrʌpʃən) *n* **1** something that interrupts, such as a comment, question, or action. **2** an interval or intermission. **3** the act of interrupting or the state of being interrupted.

interscholastic (ˌɪntəskəˈlæstɪk) *adj* **1** (of sports events, competitions, etc.) occurring between two or more schools. **2** representative of various schools.

intersect ❶ (ˌɪntəˈsɛkt) *vb* **1** to divide, cut, or mark off by passing through or across. **2** (esp. of roads) to cross (each other). **3** *Maths.* (often foll. by *with*) to have one or more points in common (with another configuration). [C17: from L *intersecāre* to divide, from INTER- + *secāre* to cut]

intersection ❶ (ˌɪntəˈsɛkʃən, ˈɪntəˌsɛk-) *n* **1** a point at which things intersect, esp. a road junction. **2** the act of intersecting or the state of being intersected. **3** *Maths.* **3a** a point or set of points common to two or more geometric configurations. **3b** Also called: **product.** the set of elements that are common to two sets. **3c** the operation that yields that set from a pair of given sets.
▸**ˌinterˈsectional** *adj*

intersex (ˈɪntəˌsɛks) *n Zool.* an individual with characteristics intermediate between those of a male and a female.

intersexual (ˌɪntəˈsɛksjʊəl) *adj* **1** occurring or existing between the sexes. **2** relating to or being an intersex.
▸**ˌinterˌsexuˈality** *n* ▸**ˌinterˈsexually** *adv*

interspace *vb* (ˌɪntəˈspeɪs), **interspaces, interspacing, interspaced. 1** (*tr*) to make or occupy a space between. ◆ *n* (ˈɪntəˌspeɪs). **2** space between or among things.
▸**interspatial** (ˌɪntəˈspeɪʃəl) *adj* ▸**ˌinterˈspatially** *adv*

intersperse ❶ (ˌɪntəˈspɜːs) *vb* **intersperses, interspersing, interspersed.** (*tr*) **1** to scatter or distribute among, between, or on. **2** to diversify (some-

THESAURUS

Internet *n* = **information superhighway**, cyberspace, the net (*inf.*), the web (*inf.*), World Wide Web

interplay *n* = **interaction**, give-and-take, meshing, reciprocation, reciprocity

interpolate *vb* **1, 3** = **insert**, add, intercalate, introduce

interpose *vb* **2** = **interrupt**, insert, interject, introduce, put forth, put one's oar in **3** = **intervene**, come *or* place between, intercede, interfere, intermediate, intrude, mediate, step in

interpret *vb* **1, 2** = **explain**, adapt, clarify, construe, decipher, decode, define, elucidate, explicate, expound, make sense of, paraphrase, read, render, solve, spell out, take, throw light on, translate, understand

interpretation *n* **1, 2** = **explanation**, analysis, clarification, construction, diagnosis, elucidation, exegesis, explication, exposition, meaning, performance, portrayal, reading, rendering, rendition, sense, signification, translation, understanding, version

interpreter *n* **2** = **translator**, annotator, commentator, exponent, scholiast

interrogate *vb* = **question**, ask, catechize, cross-examine, cross-question, enquire, examine, give (someone) the third degree (*inf.*), grill (*inf.*), inquire, investigate, pump, put the screws on (*inf.*), quiz

interrogation *n* **1** = **questioning**, cross-examination, cross-questioning, examination, grilling (*inf.*), inquiry, inquisition, probing, third degree (*inf.*)

interrogative *adj* **1** = **questioning**, curious, inquiring, inquisitive, inquisitorial, quizzical

interrupt *vb* **1** = **intrude**, barge in (*inf.*), break in, break (someone's) train of thought, butt in, disturb, heckle, hinder, interfere (with), obstruct, punctuate, separate, sever **2** = **suspend**, break, break off, check, cut, cut off, cut short, delay, disconnect, discontinue, disjoin, disunite, divide, hold up, lay aside, stay, stop

interrupted *adj* **1, 2** = **disturbed**, broken, cut off, disconnected, discontinuous, incomplete, intermittent, uneven

interruption *n* **3** = **stoppage**, break, cessation, disconnection, discontinuance, disruption, dissolution, disturbance, disuniting, division, halt, hiatus, hindrance, hitch, impediment, intrusion, obstacle, obstruction, pause, separation, severance, stop, suspension

intersect *vb* **1** = **cross**, bisect, crisscross, cut, cut across, divide, meet

intersection *n* **1** = **junction**, crossing, crossroads, interchange

intersperse *vb* **1** = **scatter**, bestrew, interlard, intermix, pepper, sprinkle

thing) with other things scattered here and there. [C16: from L *interspargere*, from INTER- + *spargere* to sprinkle]
▸**interspersedly** (ˌɪntəˈspɜːsɪdlɪ) *adv* ▸**interspersion** (ˌɪntəˈspɜːʃən) *or* **ˌinterˈspersal** *n*

interstate (ˈɪntəˌsteɪt) *n US.* a motorway crossing between states.

interstellar (ˌɪntəˈstɛlə) *adj* between or among stars.

interstice (ɪnˈtɜːstɪs) *n* (*usually pl*) **1** a minute opening or crevice between things. **2** *Physics.* the space between adjacent atoms in a crystal lattice. [C17: from L *interstitium* interval, from *intersistere*, from INTER- + *sistere* to stand]

interstitial (ˌɪntəˈstɪʃəl) *adj* **1** of or relating to an interstice or interstices. **2** *Physics.* forming or occurring in an interstice: *an interstitial atom.* **3** *Anat., zool.* occurring in the spaces between organs, tissues, etc.: *interstitial cells.* ◆ *n* **4** *Chem.* an atom or ion situated in the interstices of a crystal lattice.
▸**ˌinterˈstitially** *adv*

intertrigo (ˌɪntəˈtraɪgəʊ) *n* chafing between two skin surfaces, as at the armpit. [C18: from INTER- + *-trigo*, from L *terere* to rub]

interval Ⓣ (ˈɪntəvəl) *n* **1** the period of time between two events, instants, etc. **2** the distance between two points, objects, etc. **3** a pause or interlude, as between periods of intense activity. **4** *Brit.* a short period between parts of a play, etc.; intermission. **5** *Music.* the difference of pitch between two notes, either sounded simultaneously or in succession as in a musical part. **6** the ratio of the frequencies of two sounds. **7 at intervals. 7a** occasionally or intermittently. **7b** with spaces between. [C13: from L *intervallum*, lit.: space between two palisades, from INTER- + *vallum* palisade]
▸**intervallic** (ˌɪntəˈvælɪk) *adj*

intervene Ⓣ (ˌɪntəˈviːn) *vb* **intervenes, intervening, intervened.** (*intr*) **1** (often foll. by *in*) to take a decisive or intrusive role (in) in order to determine events. **2** (foll. by *in* or *between*) to come or be (among or between). **3** (of a period of time) to occur between events or points in time. **4** (of an event) to disturb or hinder a course of action. **5** *Econ.* to take action to affect the market forces of an economy, esp. to maintain the stability of a currency. **6** *Law.* to interpose and become a party to a legal action between others, esp. in order to protect one's interests. [C16: from L *intervenīre* to come between]
▸**ˌinterˈvener** *or* **ˌinterˈvenor** *n*

intervention Ⓣ (ˌɪntəˈvɛnʃən) *n* **1** an act of intervening. **2** any interference in the affairs of others, esp. by one state in the affairs of another. **3** *Econ.* the action of a central bank in supporting the international value of a currency by buying large quantities of the currency to keep the price up. **4** *Commerce.* the action of the EU in buying up surplus produce when the market price drops to a certain value.

interventionist (ˌɪntəˈvɛnʃənɪst) *adj* **1** of, relating to, or advocating intervention, esp. in order to achieve a policy objective. ◆ *n* **2** a person or state that pursues a policy of intervention.

intervertebral disc (ˌɪntəˈvɜːtɪbrəl) *n* any of the cartilaginous discs between individual vertebrae, acting as shock absorbers.

interview Ⓣ (ˈɪntəˌvjuː) *n* **1** a conversation with or questioning of a person, usually conducted for television or a newspaper. **2** a formal discussion, esp. one in which an employer assesses a job applicant. ◆ *vb* **3** to conduct an interview with (someone). [C16: from OF *entrevue*]
▸**ˌinterviewˈee** *n* ▸**ˈinterˌviewer** *n*

inter vivos *Latin.* (ˈɪntə ˈviːvɒs) *adj Law.* between living people: *an inter vivos gift.*

interwar (ˌɪntəˈwɔː) *adj* of or happening in the period between World War I and World War II.

intestate (ɪnˈtɛsteɪt, -tɪt) *adj* **1a** (of a person) not having made a will. **1b** (of property) not disposed of by will. ◆ *n* **2** a person who dies without having made a will. [C14: from L *intestātus*, from IN-[1] + *testārī* to bear witness, make a will, from *testis* a witness]
▸**inˈtestacy** *n*

intestine Ⓣ (ɪnˈtɛstɪn) *n* the part of the alimentary canal between the stomach and the anus. See **large intestine, small intestine.** [C16: from L *intestīnum* gut, from *intestīnus* internal, from *intus* within]
▸**intestinal** (ɪnˈtɛstɪnˀl, ˌɪntɛsˈtaɪnˀl) *adj*

inti (ˈɪntɪ) *n* a former monetary unit of Peru. [C20: from Quechua]

intifada (ˌɪntɪˈfɑːdə) *n* the Palestinian uprising against Israel in the West Bank and Gaza Strip that started at the end of 1987. [C20: Ar., lit.: uprising]

intimacy Ⓣ (ˈɪntɪməsɪ) *n, pl* **intimacies. 1** close or warm friendship or understanding; personal relationship. **2** (*often pl*) *Euphemistic.* sexual relations.

intimate[1] Ⓣ (ˈɪntɪmɪt) *adj* **1** characterized by a close or warm personal relationship: *an intimate friend.* **2** deeply personal, private, or secret. **3** (*often postpositive; foll. by with*) *Euphemistic.* having sexual relations (with). **4** (*postpositive; foll. by with*) having a deep or unusual knowledge (of). **5** having a friendly, warm, or informal atmosphere: *an intimate nightclub.* **6** of or relating to the essential part or nature of something; intrinsic. ◆ *n* **7** a close friend. [C17: from L *intimus* very close friend, from (adj): innermost, from *intus* within]
▸**ˈintimately** *adv* ▸**ˈintimateness** *n*

intimate[2] Ⓣ (ˈɪntɪˌmeɪt) *vb* **intimates, intimating, intimated.** (*tr; may take a clause as object*) **1** to hint; suggest. **2** to proclaim; make known. [C16: from LL *intimāre* to proclaim, from L *intimus* innermost]
▸**ˈintiˌmater** *n* ▸**ˌintiˈmation** *n*

intimidate Ⓣ (ɪnˈtɪmɪˌdeɪt) *vb* **intimidates, intimidating, intimidated.** (*tr*) **1** to make timid or frightened; scare. **2** to discourage, restrain, or silence unscrupulously, as by threats. [C17: from Med. L *intimidāre*, from L IN-[2] + *timidus* fearful, from *timor* fear]
▸**ˌinˈtimiˌdating** *adj* ▸**inˌtimiˈdation** *n* ▸**inˈtimiˌdator** *n*

intinction (ɪnˈtɪŋkʃən) *n Christianity.* the practice of dipping the Eucharistic bread into the wine at Holy Communion. [C16: from LL *intinctiō* a dipping in, from L *intingere*, from *tingere* to dip]

intitule (ɪnˈtɪtjuːl) *vb* **intitules, intituling, intituled.** (*tr*) *Parliamentary procedure.* (in Britain) to entitle (an Act). [C15: from OF *intituler*, from L *titulus* TITLE]

intl *abbrev. for* international.

into (ˈɪntuː; *unstressed* ˈɪntə) *prep* **1** to the interior or inner parts of: *to look into a case.* **2** to the middle or midst of so as to be surrounded by: *into the bushes.* **3** against; up against: *he drove into a wall.* **4** used to indicate the result of a change: *he changed into a monster.* **5** *Maths.* used to indicate a dividend: *three into six is two.* **6** *Inf.* interested or enthusiastically involved in: *I'm really into Freud.*

intonation Ⓣ (ˌɪntəʊˈneɪʃən) *n* **1** the sound pattern of phrases and sentences produced by pitch variation in the voice. **2** the act or manner of intoning. **3** an intoned, chanted, or monotonous utterance; incantation. **4** *Music.* the opening of a piece of plainsong, sung by a soloist. **5** *Music.* the capacity to play or sing in tune.
▸**ˌintoˈnational** *adj*

intone Ⓣ (ɪnˈtəʊn) *or* **intonate** *vb* **intones, intoning, intoned** *or* **intonates, intonating, intonated. 1** to utter, recite, or sing (a chant, prayer, etc.) in a monotonous or incantatory tone. **2** (*intr*) to speak with a particular or characteristic intonation or tone. **3** to sing (the opening phrase of a psalm, etc.) in plainsong. [C15: from Med. L *intonare*, from IN-[2] + TONE]
▸**inˈtoner** *n*

in toto Ⓣ *Latin.* (ɪn ˈtəʊtəʊ) *adv* totally; entirely.

intoxicant (ɪnˈtɒksɪkənt) *n* **1** anything that causes intoxication. ◆ *adj* **2** causing intoxication.

intoxicate Ⓣ (ɪnˈtɒksɪˌkeɪt) *vb* **intoxicates, intoxicating, intoxicated.** (*tr*) **1**

THESAURUS

interval *n* **1-4** = **break**, delay, distance, entr'acte, gap, hiatus, interim, interlude, intermission, meantime, meanwhile, opening, pause, period, playtime, respite, rest, season, space, spell, term, time, wait

intervene *vb* **1** = **step in** (*inf.*), arbitrate, intercede, interfere, interpose oneself, intrude, involve oneself, mediate, put one's oar in, put one's two cents in (*US sl.*), take a hand (*inf.*)

intervention *n* **1** = **mediation**, agency, intercession, interference, interposition, intrusion

interview *n* **1** = **meeting**, audience, conference, consultation, dialogue, evaluation, oral (examination), press conference, talk ◆ *vb* **3** = **question**, examine, interrogate, sound out, talk to

interviewer *n* **3** = **questioner**, examiner, interlocutor, interrogator, investigator, reporter

intestinal *adj* = **abdominal**, coeliac, duodenal, gut (*inf.*), inner, stomachic, visceral

intestine *n* = **gut**, bowel

intimacy *n* **1** = **familiarity**, closeness, confidence, confidentiality, fraternization, understanding
Antonyms *n* alienation, aloofness, coldness, detachment, distance, estrangement, remoteness, separation

intimate[1] *adj* **1** = **close**, bosom, cherished, confidential, dear, friendly, near, nearest and dearest, thick (*inf.*), warm **2** = **private**, confidential, personal, privy, secret **4** = **detailed**, deep, exhaustive, experienced, first-hand, immediate, in-depth, penetrating, personal, profound, thorough **5** = **snug**, comfy (*inf.*), cosy, friendly, tête-à-tête, warm ◆ *n* **7** = **friend**, bosom friend, buddy (*inf.*), chum (*inf.*), close friend, comrade, confidant *or* confidante, (constant) companion, crony, homeboy (*sl., chiefly US*), mate (*inf.*), pal
Antonyms *adj* ≠ **close:** distant, remote, superficial ≠ **private:** known, open, public ◆ *n* ≠ **friend:** enemy, foe, stranger

intimate[2] *vb* **1** = **suggest**, allude, drop a hint, give (someone) to understand, hint, imply, indicate, insinuate, let it be known, tip (someone) the wink (*Brit. inf.*), warn **2** = **announce**, communicate, declare, impart, make known, remind, state

intimately[1] *adv* **1, 2** = **confidingly**, affectionately, closely, confidentially, familiarly, personally, tenderly, very well, warmly **4** = **in detail**, fully, inside out, thoroughly, through and through, to the core, very well

intimation[2] *n* **1** = **hint**, allusion, indication, inkling, insinuation, reminder, suggestion, warning **2** = **announcement**, communication, declaration, notice

intimidate *vb* **1** = **frighten**, alarm, appal, daunt, dishearten, dismay, dispirit, overawe, scare, subdue, terrify **2** = **threaten**, browbeat, bully, coerce, cow, lean on (*inf.*), scare off, terrorize, twist someone's arm (*inf.*)

intimidation *n* **2** = **bullying**, arm-twisting (*inf.*), browbeating, coercion, fear, menaces, pressure, terror, terrorization, threat(s)

intonation *n* **1** = **tone**, accentuation, cadence, inflection, modulation **3** = **incantation**, chant

intone *vb* **1** = **recite**, chant, croon, intonate, sing

in toto *adv* = **totally**, as a whole, completely, entirely, in its entirety, unabridged, uncut, wholly

intoxicate *vb* **1** = **go to one's head**, addle, befuddle, fuddle, inebriate, put (someone) under the table (*inf.*), stupefy **2** = **exhilarate**, elate, excite, go to one's head, inflame, make one's head spin, stimulate

intoxicated *adj* **1** = **drunk**, drunken, inebriated, in one's cups (*inf.*), legless (*inf.*), out of it (*sl.*), paralytic (*inf.*), pissed (*taboo sl.*), plastered (*sl.*), smashed (*sl.*), sozzled (*inf.*), three sheets in the wind (*inf.*), tight (*inf.*), tipsy, under the influence **2** = **euphoric**, dizzy, ecstatic, elated, en-

(of an alcoholic drink) to produce in (a person) a state ranging from euphoria to stupor; make drunk; inebriate. **2** to stimulate, excite, or elate so as to overwhelm. **3** (of a drug, etc.) to poison. [C16: from Med. L, from *intoxicāre* to poison, from L *toxicum* poison; see TOXIC]
▸**in'toxicable** *adj* ▸**in'toxi,cating** *adj* ▸**in'toxi,catingly** *adv*

intoxication ⓘ (ɪn,tɒksɪ'keɪʃən) *n* **1** drunkenness; inebriation. **2** great elation. **3** the act of intoxicating. **4** poisoning.

intr. *abbrev. for* intransitive.

intra- *prefix* within; inside: *intrastate; intravenous.* [from L *intrā* within; see INTERIOR]

intractable ⓘ (ɪn'træktəbᵊl) *adj* **1** difficult to influence or direct: *an intractable disposition.* **2** (of a problem, illness, etc.) difficult to solve, alleviate, or cure.
▸**in,tracta'bility** *or* **in'tractableness** *n* ▸**in'tractably** *adv*

intradermal (,ɪntrə'dɜ:məl) *adj* within the skin: *an intradermal injection.* Abbrevs. (esp. of an injection): **ID, i.d.**
▸**,intra'dermally** *adv*

intrados (ɪn'treɪdɒs) *n, pl* **intrados** *or* **intradoses.** *Archit.* the inner curve or surface of an arch. [C18: from F, from INTRA- + *dos* back, from L *dorsum*]

intramural (,ɪntrə'mjʊərəl) *adj Education, chiefly US & Canad.* operating within or involving those in a single establishment.
▸**,intra'murally** *adv*

intramuscular (,ɪntrə'mʌskjʊlə) *adj* within a muscle: *an intramuscular injection.* Abbrevs. (esp. of an injection): **IM, i.m.**
▸**,intra'muscularly** *adv*

intranet ('ɪntrə,nɛt) *n Computing.* an internal network that makes use of Internet technology. [C20: INTRA- + NET (sense 8), modelled on INTERNET]

intrans. *abbrev. for* intransitive.

intransigent ⓘ (ɪn'trænsɪdʒənt) *adj* **1** not willing to compromise; obstinately maintaining an attitude. ◆ *n* **2** an intransigent person, esp. in politics. [C19: from Sp. *los intransigentes* the uncompromising (ones), a name adopted by certain political extremists, from IN-[1] + *transigir* to compromise, from L *transigere* to settle; see TRANSACT]
▸**in'transigence** *or* **in'transigency** *n* ▸**in'transigently** *adv*

intransitive (ɪn'trænsɪtɪv) *adj* **1a** denoting a verb that does not require a direct object: *"to faint" is an intransitive verb.* **1b** (*as n*) such a verb. **2** denoting an adjective or noun that does not require any particular noun phrase as a referent. **3** having the property that if it holds between one argument and a second, and between the second and a third, it must fail to hold between the first and third: *"being the mother of" is an intransitive relation.* ◆ Cf. **transitive.**
▸**in'transitively** *adv* ▸**in,transi'tivity** *or* **in'transitiveness** *n*

intrapreneur (,ɪntrəprə'nɜ:) *n* a person who while remaining within a larger organization uses entrepreneurial skills to develop a new product or line of business as a subsidiary of the organization. [C20: from INTRA- + (ENTRE)PRENEUR]

intrauterine (,ɪntrə'ju:tərаɪn) *adj* within the womb.

intrauterine device *n* a metal or plastic device, in the shape of a loop, coil, or ring, inserted into the uterus to prevent conception. Abbrev.: **IUD.**

intravenous (,ɪntrə'vi:nəs) *adj Anat.* within a vein: *an intravenous injection.* Abbrevs. (esp. of an injection): **IV, i.v.**
▸**,intra'venously** *adv*

in-tray *n* a tray for incoming papers, etc., requiring attention.

intrench ⓘ (ɪn'trɛntʃ) *vb* a less common spelling of **entrench.**
▸**in'trencher** *n* ▸**in'trenchment** *n*

intrepid ⓘ (ɪn'trɛpɪd) *adj* fearless; daring; bold. [C17: from L *intrepidus,* from IN-[1] + *trepidus* fearful]
▸**,intre'pidity** *n* ▸**in'trepidly** *adv*

intricate ⓘ ('ɪntrɪkɪt) *adj* **1** difficult to understand; obscure; complex; puzzling. **2** entangled or involved: *intricate patterns.* [C15: from L *intrīcāre* to entangle, perplex, from IN-[2] + *trīcae* trifles, perplexities]
▸**'intricacy** *or* **'intricateness** *n* ▸**'intricately** *adv*

intrigue ⓘ *vb* (ɪn'tri:g), **intrigues, intriguing, intrigued. 1** (*tr*) to make interested or curious. **2** (*intr*) to make secret plots or employ underhand methods; conspire. **3** (*intr;* often foll. by *with*) to carry on a clandestine love affair. ◆ *n* (ɪn'tri:g, 'ɪntri:g). **4** the act or an instance of secret plotting, etc. **5** a clandestine love affair. **6** the quality of arousing interest or curiosity; beguilement. [C17: from F *intriguer,* from It., from L *intrīcāre;* see INTRICATE]
▸**in'triguer** *n* ▸**in'triguingly** *adv*

intrinsic ⓘ (ɪn'trɪnsɪk) *or* **intrinsical** *adj* **1** of or relating to the essential nature of a thing; inherent. **2** *Anat.* situated within or peculiar to a part: *intrinsic muscles.* [C15: from LL *intrinsecus* from L, inwardly, from *intrā* within + *secus* alongside]
▸**in'trinsically** *adv*

intro ('ɪntrəʊ) *n, pl* **intros.** *Inf.* short for **introduction.**

intro. *or* **introd.** *abbrev. for:* **1** introduction. **2** introductory.

intro- *prefix* in, into, or inward: *introvert.* [from L *intrō* inwardly, within]

introduce ⓘ (,ɪntrə'dju:s) *vb* **introduces, introducing, introduced.** (*tr*) **1** (often foll. by *to*) to present (someone) by name (to another person). **2** (foll. by *to*) to cause to experience for the first time: *to introduce a visitor to beer.* **3** to present for consideration or approval, esp. before a legislative body: *to introduce a bill in parliament.* **4** to bring in; establish: *to introduce decimal currency.* **5** to present (a radio or television programme, etc.) verbally. **6** (foll. by *with*) to start: *he introduced his talk with some music.* **7** (often foll. by *into*) to insert or inject: *he introduced the needle into his arm.* **8** to place (members of a plant or animal species) in a new environment with the intention of producing a resident breeding population. [C16: from L *intrōdūcere* to bring inside]
▸**,intro'ducer** *n* ▸**,intro'ducible** *adj*

introduction ⓘ (,ɪntrə'dʌkʃən) *n* **1** the act of introducing or fact of being introduced. **2** a presentation of one person to another or others. **3** a means of presenting a person to another person, such as a letter of introduction or reference. **4** a preliminary part, as of a book. **5** *Music.* an opening passage in a movement or composition that precedes the main material. **6** a basic or elementary work of instruction, reference, etc.

introductory ⓘ (,ɪntrə'dʌktərɪ, -trɪ) *adj* serving as an introduction; preliminary; prefatory.

introit ('ɪntrɔɪt) *n RC Church, Church of England.* a short prayer said or sung as the celebrant is entering the sanctuary to celebrate Mass or Holy Communion. [C15: from Church L *introitus* introit, from L: entrance, from *introīre* to go in]
▸**in'troital** *adj*

THESAURUS

raptured, excited, exhilarated, high (*inf.*), infatuated, sent (*sl.*), stimulated

intoxicating *adj* **1 = alcoholic,** inebriant, intoxicant, spirituous, strong **2 = exciting,** exhilarating, heady, sexy (*inf.*), stimulating, thrilling

intoxication *n* **1 = drunkenness,** inebriation, inebriety, insobriety, tipsiness **2 = excitement,** delirium, elation, euphoria, exaltation, exhilaration, infatuation

intractability *n* **1 = obstinacy,** awkwardness, cantankerousness, contrariness, incorrigibility, indiscipline, indocility, mulishness, obduracy, perverseness, perversity, pig-headedness, stubbornness, uncooperativeness, ungovernability, waywardness

intractable *adj* **1 = difficult,** awkward, bullheaded, cantankerous, contrary, fractious, headstrong, intransigent, obdurate, obstinate, perverse, pig-headed, refractory, self-willed, stiff-necked, stubborn, unbending, uncooperative, undisciplined, ungovernable, unmanageable, unruly, unyielding, wayward, wild, wilful **2 = incurable,** insoluble

intransigent *adj* **1 = uncompromising,** hardline, immovable, intractable, obdurate, obstinate, stiff-necked, stubborn, tenacious, tough, unbending, unbudgeable, unyielding
Antonyms *adj* acquiescent, compliant, compromising, flexible, open-minded

intrenched *see* **entrenched**

intrepid *adj* **= fearless,** audacious, bold, brave, courageous, daring, dauntless, doughty, gallant, game (*inf.*), have-a-go (*inf.*), heroic, lion-hearted, nerveless, plucky, resolute, stalwart, stouthearted, unafraid, undaunted, unflinching, valiant, valorous
Antonyms *adj* afraid, cautious, cowardly, craven, daunted, faint-hearted, fearful, flinching, irresolute, timid

intrepidity *n* **= fearlessness,** audacity, boldness, bravery, courage, daring, dauntlessness, doughtiness, fortitude, gallantry, grit, guts (*inf.*), heroism, lion-heartedness, nerve, pluck, prowess, spirit, stoutheartedness, valour

intricacy *n* **1, 2 = complexity,** complication, convolutions, elaborateness, entanglement, intricateness, involution, involvement, knottiness, obscurity

intricate *adj* **1, 2 = complicated,** baroque, Byzantine, complex, convoluted, difficult, elaborate, fancy, involved, knotty, labyrinthine, obscure, perplexing, rococo, sophisticated, tangled, tortuous
Antonyms *adj* clear, easy, obvious, plain, simple, straightforward

intrigue *vb* **1 = interest,** arouse the curiosity of, attract, charm, fascinate, pique, rivet, tickle one's fancy, titillate **2 = plot,** connive, conspire, machinate, manoeuvre, scheme ◆ *n* **4 = plot,** cabal, chicanery, collusion, conspiracy, double-dealing, knavery, machination, manipulation, manoeuvre, ruse, scheme, sharp practice, stratagem, trickery, wile **5 = affair,** amour, intimacy, liaison, romance

intriguing *adj* **1 = interesting,** beguiling, compelling, diverting, exciting, fascinating, tantalizing, titillating

intrinsic *adj* **1 = inborn,** basic, built-in, central, congenital, constitutional, elemental, essential, fundamental, genuine, inbred, inherent, native, natural, radical, real, true, underlying
Antonyms *adj* acquired, added, appended, artificial, extraneous, extrinsic, incidental

intrinsically *adv* **1 = essentially,** as such, at heart, basically, by definition, constitutionally, fundamentally, in itself, per se

introduce *vb* **1 = present,** acquaint, do the honours, familiarize, make known, make the introduction **3 = bring up,** advance, air, broach, moot, offer, propose, put forward, recommend, set forth, submit, suggest, ventilate **4 = bring in,** begin, commence, establish, found, inaugurate, initiate, institute, launch, organize, pioneer, set up, start, usher in **6 = lead into,** announce, lead off, open, preface **7 = insert,** add, inject, interpolate, interpose, put in, throw in (*inf.*)

introduction *n* **1 = launch,** baptism, debut, establishment, first acquaintance, inauguration, induction, initiation, institution, pioneering, presentation **4, 5 = opening,** commencement, exordium, foreword, intro (*inf.*), lead-in, opening passage, opening remarks, overture, preamble, preface, preliminaries, prelude, proem, prolegomena, prolegomenon, prologue
Antonyms *n* ≠ **launch:** completion, elimination, termination ≠ **opening:** conclusion, end, epilogue

introductory *adj* **= preliminary,** early, elementary, first, inaugural, initial, initiatory, opening, precursory, prefatory, preparatory, starting
Antonyms *adj* closing, concluding, final, last, terminating

intromit (ˌɪntrəˈmɪt) *vb* **intromits, intromitting, intromitted.** (*tr*) *Rare.* to enter or insert. [C15: from L *intrōmittere* to send in]
▸ˌ**introˈmissible** *adj* ▸ˌ**introˈmission** *n* ▸ˌ**introˈmittent** *adj*

introspection ❶ (ˌɪntrəˈspɛkʃən) *n* the examination of one's own thoughts, impressions, and feelings. [C17: from L *intrōspicere* to look within]
▸ˌ**introˈspective** *adj* ▸ˌ**introˈspectively** *adv*

introversion (ˌɪntrəˈvɜːʃən) *n Psychol.* the directing of interest inwards towards one's own thoughts and feelings rather than towards the external world or making social contacts.
▸ˌ**introˈversive** *or* ˌ**introˈvertive** *adj*

introvert ❶ *n* (ˈɪntrəˌvɜːt). **1** *Psychol.* a person prone to introversion. ◆ *adj* (ˈɪntrəˌvɜːt). **2** Also: **introverted.** characterized by introversion. ◆ *vb* (ˌɪntrəˈvɜːt). **3** (*tr*) *Pathol.* to turn (a hollow organ or part) inside out. [C17: see INTRO-, INVERT]

intrude ❶ (ɪnˈtruːd) *vb* **intrudes, intruding, intruded. 1** (often foll. by *into, on,* or *upon*) to put forward or interpose (oneself, one's views, something) abruptly or without invitation. **2** *Geol.* to force or thrust (molten magma) between solid rocks. [C16: from L *intrūdere* to thrust in]
▸**inˈtruder** *n* ▸**inˈtrudingly** *adv*

intrusion ❶ (ɪnˈtruːʒən) *n* **1** the act or an instance of intruding; an unwelcome visit, etc.: *an intrusion on one's privacy.* **2a** the movement of magma into spaces in the overlying strata to form igneous rock. **2b** any igneous rock formed in this way. **3** *Property law.* an unlawful entry onto land by a stranger after determination of a particular estate of freehold.
▸**inˈtrusional** *adj*

intrusive ❶ (ɪnˈtruːsɪv) *adj* **1** characterized by intrusion or tending to intrude. **2** (of igneous rocks) formed by intrusion. **3** *Phonetics.* relating to or denoting a speech sound that is introduced into a word or piece of connected speech for a phonetic reason.
▸**inˈtrusively** *adv* ▸**inˈtrusiveness** *n*

intrust ❶ (ɪnˈtrʌst) *vb* a less common spelling of **entrust.**

intubate (ˈɪntjʊˌbeɪt) *vb* **intubates, intubating, intubated.** (*tr*) *Med.* to insert a tube into (a hollow organ).
▸ˌ**intuˈbation** *n*

intuit (ɪnˈtjuːɪt) *vb* **intuits, intuiting, intuited.** to know or discover by intuition.
▸**inˈtuitable** *adj*

intuition ❶ (ˌɪntjʊˈɪʃən) *n* **1** knowledge or belief obtained neither by reason nor perception. **2** instinctive knowledge or belief. **3** a hunch or unjustified belief. [C15: from LL *intuitiō* a contemplation, from L *intuērī* to gaze upon, from *tuērī* to look at]
▸ˌ**intuˈitional** *adj* ▸ˌ**intuˈitionally** *adv*

intuitionism (ˌɪntjʊˈɪʃəˌnɪzəm) *or* **intuitionalism** *n Philosophy.* **1** the doctrine that knowledge is acquired primarily by intuition. **2** the theory that the solution to moral problems can be discovered by intuition. **3** the doctrine that external objects are known to be real by intuition.
▸ˌ**intuˈitionist** *or* ˌ**intuˈitionalist** *n*

intuitive ❶ (ɪnˈtjuːɪtɪv) *adj* **1** resulting from intuition: *an intuitive awareness.* **2** of, characterized by, or involving intuition.
▸**inˈtuitively** *adv* ▸**inˈtuitiveness** *n*

intumesce (ˌɪntjʊˈmɛs) *vb* **intumesces, intumescing, intumesced.** (*intr*) to swell. [C18: from L *intumescere,* from *tumescere* to begin to swell, from *tumēre* to swell]
▸ˌ**intuˈmescence** *n*

intussusception (ˌɪntəssəˈsɛpʃən) *n* **1** *Pathol.* the telescoping of one section of the intestinal tract into a lower section. **2** *Biol.* growth in the surface area of a cell by the deposition of new particles between the existing particles of the cell wall. [C18: from L *intus* within + *susceptiō* a taking up]

Inuit *or* **Innuit** (ˈɪnjuːɪt) *n, pl* **Inuit, Inuits** *or* **Innuit, Innuits.** an Eskimo of North America or Greenland, as distinguished from one from Asia or the Aleutian Islands. [from Eskimo *inuit* people, pl of *inuk* a man]

Inuktitut (ɪˈnʊktɪˌtʊt) *n Canad.* the language of the Inuit; Eskimo. [from Eskimo *inuk* man + *titut* speech]

inunction (ɪnˈʌŋkʃən) *n* **1** the application of an ointment to the skin, esp. by rubbing. **2** the ointment so used. **3** the act of anointing; anointment. [C15: from L *inunguere* to anoint, from *unguere;* see UNCTION]

inundate ❶ (ˈɪnʌnˌdeɪt) *vb* **inundates, inundating, inundated.** (*tr*) **1** to cover completely with water; overflow; flood; swamp. **2** to overwhelm, as if with a flood: *to be inundated with requests.* [C17: from L *inundāre,* from *unda* wave]
▸ˈ**inundant** *or* **inˈundatory** *adj* ▸ˌ**inunˈdation** *n* ▸ˈ**inunˌdator** *n*

inure ❶ *or* **enure** (ɪˈnjʊə) *vb* **inures, inuring, inured** *or* **enures, enuring, enured. 1** (*tr; often passive;* often foll. by *to*) to cause to accept or become hardened to; habituate. **2** (*intr*) (esp. of a law, etc.) to come into operation; take effect. [C15 *enuren* to accustom, from *ure* use, from OF *euvre* custom, work, from L *opera* works]
▸**inˈurement** *or* **enˈurement** *n*

in utero *Latin.* (ɪn ˈjuːtərəʊ) *adv, adj* in the uterus.

inv. *abbrev. for:* **1** invented. **2** inventor. **3** invoice.

in vacuo *Latin.* (ɪn ˈvækjʊˌəʊ) *adv* in a vacuum.

invade ❶ (ɪnˈveɪd) *vb* **invades, invading, invaded. 1** to enter (a country, territory, etc.) by military force. **2** (*tr*) to occupy in large numbers; overrun; infest. **3** (*tr*) to trespass or encroach upon (privacy, etc.). **4** (*tr*) to enter and spread throughout, esp. harmfully; pervade. [C15: from L *invādere,* from *vādere* to go]
▸**inˈvadable** *adj* ▸**inˈvader** *n*

invaginate *vb* (ɪnˈvædʒɪˌneɪt), **invaginates, invaginating, invaginated. 1** *Pathol.* to push one section of (a tubular organ or part) back into itself so that it becomes ensheathed. **2** (*intr*) (of the outer layer of an organism or part) to undergo this process. ◆ *adj* (ɪnˈvædʒɪnɪt, -ˌneɪt). **3** (of an organ or part) folded back upon itself. [C19: from Med. L *invāgīnāre,* from L IN-[2] + *vāgīna* sheath]
▸**inˈvaginable** *adj* ▸**inˌvagiˈnation** *n*

invalid[1] ❶ (ˈɪnvəˌliːd, -lɪd) *n* **1a** a person suffering from disablement or chronic ill health. **1b** (*as modifier*): *an invalid chair.* ◆ *adj* **2** suffering from or disabled by injury, sickness, etc. ◆ *vb* (*tr*) **3** to cause to become an invalid; disable. **4** (*often passive;* usually foll. by *out*) *Chiefly Brit.* to require (a member of the armed forces) to retire from active service through wounds or illness. [C17: from L *invalidus* infirm, from IN-[1] + *validus* strong]
▸**invalidity** (ˌɪnvəˈlɪdɪtɪ) *n*

invalid[2] ❶ (ɪnˈvælɪd) *adj* **1** not valid; having no cogency or legal force. **2** *Logic.* (of an argument) having a conclusion that does not follow from the premises. [C16: from Med. L *invalidus* without legal force; see INVALID[1]]
▸ˌ**invaˈlidity** *or* **inˈvalidness** *n* ▸**inˈvalidly** *adv*

invalidate ❶ (ɪnˈvælɪˌdeɪt) *vb* **invalidates, invalidating, invalidated.** (*tr*) **1** to render weak or ineffective (an argument). **2** to take away the legal force or effectiveness of; annul (a contract).
▸**inˌvaliˈdation** *n* ▸**inˈvaliˌdator** *n*

invaluable ❶ (ɪnˈvæljʊəbᵊl) *adj* having great value that is impossible to calculate; priceless.
▸**inˈvaluableness** *n* ▸**inˈvaluably** *adv*

Invar (ɪnˈvɑː) *n Trademark.* an alloy containing iron, nickel, and carbon. It has a very low coefficient of expansion and is used for the balance springs of watches, etc. [C20: shortened from INVARIABLE]

invariable ❶ (ɪnˈvɛərɪəbᵊl) *adj* **1** not subject to alteration; unchanging. ◆ *n* **2** a mathematical quantity having an unchanging value; a constant.
▸**inˌvariaˈbility** *or* **inˈvariableness** *n* ▸**inˈvariably** *adv*

THESAURUS

introspection *n* = **self-examination**, brooding, heart-searching, introversion, navel-gazing (*sl.*), self-analysis

introspective *adj* = **inward-looking**, brooding, contemplative, inner-directed, introverted, meditative, pensive, subjective

introvert *adj* **2** = **introspective**, indrawn, inner-directed, introverted, inward-looking, self-centred, self-contained, withdrawn

intrude *vb* **1** = **interfere**, butt in, encroach, infringe, interrupt, meddle, obtrude, push in, put one's two cents in (*US sl.*), thrust oneself in *or* forward, trespass, violate

intruder *n* **1** = **trespasser**, burglar, gate-crasher (*inf.*), infiltrator, interloper, invader, prowler, raider, snooper (*inf.*), squatter, thief

intrusion *n* **1** = **invasion**, encroachment, infringement, interference, interruption, trespass, violation

intrusive *adj* **1** = **interfering**, disturbing, forward, impertinent, importunate, invasive, meddlesome, nosy (*inf.*), officious, presumptuous, pushy (*inf.*), uncalled-for, unwanted

intrust *see* **entrust**

intuition *n* **1-3** = **instinct**, discernment, hunch, insight, perception, presentiment, sixth sense

intuitive *adj* **1, 2** = **instinctive**, innate, instinctual, involuntary, spontaneous, unreflecting, untaught

intuitively *adv* **1, 2** = **instinctively**, automatically, innately, instinctually, involuntarily, spontaneously

inundate *vb* **1, 2** = **flood**, deluge, drown, engulf, glut, immerse, overflow, overrun, overwhelm, submerge, swamp

inundation *n* **1, 2** = **flood**, deluge, overflow, tidal wave, torrent

inured *adj* **1** = **accustomed**, annealed, case-hardened, desensitized, familiarized, habituated, hardened, strengthened, tempered, toughened, trained

invade *vb* **1** = **attack**, assail, assault, burst in, descend upon, encroach, infringe, make inroads, occupy, raid, violate **2** = **infest**, infect, overrun, overspread, penetrate, permeate, pervade, swarm over

invader *n* **1** = **attacker**, aggressor, alien, looter, plunderer, raider, trespasser

invalid[1] *n* **1** = **patient**, convalescent, valetudinarian ◆ *adj* **2** = **disabled**, ailing, bedridden, feeble, frail, ill, infirm, poorly (*inf.*), sick, sickly, valetudinarian, weak

invalid[2] *adj* **1, 2** = **null and void**, baseless, fallacious, false, ill-founded, illogical, inoperative, irrational, not binding, nugatory, null, unfounded, unscientific, unsound, untrue, void, worthless
Antonyms *adj* logical, operative, rational, solid, sound, true, valid, viable

invalidate *vb* **2** = **nullify**, abrogate, annul, cancel, overrule, overthrow, quash, render null and void, rescind, undermine, undo, weaken
Antonyms *vb* authorize, empower, ratify, sanction, strengthen, validate

invalidity[2] *n* **1, 2** = **falsity**, fallaciousness, fallacy, illogicality, inconsistency, irrationality, sophism, speciousness, unsoundness

invaluable *adj* = **precious**, beyond price, costly, inestimable, priceless, valuable, worth one's *or* its weight in gold
Antonyms *adj* cheap, rubbishy, valueless, worthless

invariable *adj* **1** = **regular**, changeless, consistent, constant, fixed, immutable, inflexible, rigid, set, unalterable, unchangeable, unchanging, unfailing, uniform, unvarying, unwavering
Antonyms *adj* alterable, changeable, changing, differing, flexible, inconsistent, irregular, uneven, variable, varying

invariably *adv* **1** = **consistently**, always, cus-

invariant (ɪnˈvɛərɪənt) *Maths.* ◆ *n* **1** an entity, quantity, etc., that is unaltered by a particular transformation of coordinates. ◆ *adj* **2** (of a relationship or a property of a function, configuration, or equation) unaltered by a particular transformation of coordinates.
▸**inˈvariance** *or* **inˈvariancy** *n*

invasion ⓘ (ɪnˈveɪʒən) *n* **1** the act of invading with armed forces. **2** any encroachment or intrusion: *an invasion of rats.* **3** the onset or advent of something harmful, esp. of a disease. **4** *Pathol.* the spread of cancer from its point of origin into surrounding tissues. **5** the movement of plants to an area to which they are not native.

invasive (ɪnˈveɪsɪv) *adj* **1** of or relating to an invasion, intrusion, etc. **2** (of surgery) involving making a relatively large incision in the body to gain access to the target of the surgery.

invective ⓘ (ɪnˈvɛktɪv) *n* **1** vehement accusation or denunciation, esp. of a bitterly abusive or sarcastic kind. ◆ *adj* **2** characterized by or using abusive language, bitter sarcasm, etc. [C15: from LL *invectīvus* reproachful, from L *invectus* carried in; see INVEIGH]
▸**inˈvectively** *adv* ▸**inˈvectiveness** *n*

inveigh (ɪnˈveɪ) *vb* (*intr;* foll. by *against*) to speak with violent or invective language; rail. [C15: from L *invehī*, lit.: to be carried in, hence, assail physically or verbally]
▸**inˈveigher** *n*

inveigle ⓘ (ɪnˈviːgᵊl, -ˈveɪ-) *vb* **inveigles, inveigling, inveigled.** (*tr;* often foll. by *into* or an infinitive) to lead (someone into a situation) or persuade (to do something) by cleverness or trickery; cajole. [C15: from OF *avogler* to blind, deceive, from *avogle* blind, from Med. L *ab oculis* without eyes]
▸**inˈveiglement** *n* ▸**inˈveigler** *n*

invent ⓘ (ɪnˈvɛnt) *vb* **1** to create or devise (new ideas, machines, etc.). **2** to make up (falsehoods, etc.); fabricate. [C15: from L *invenīre* to find, come upon]
▸**inˈventable** *adj*

invention ⓘ (ɪnˈvɛnʃən) *n* **1** the act or process of inventing. **2** something that is invented. **3** *Patent law.* the discovery or production of some new or improved process or machine. **4** creative power or ability; inventive skill. **5** *Euphemistic.* a fabrication; lie. **6** *Music.* a short piece consisting of two or three parts usually in imitative counterpoint.
▸**inˈventional** *adj* ▸**inˈventionless** *adj*

inventive ⓘ (ɪnˈvɛntɪv) *adj* **1** skilled or quick at contriving; ingenious; resourceful. **2** characterized by inventive skill: *an inventive programme of work.* **3** of or relating to invention.
▸**inˈventively** *adv* ▸**inˈventiveness** *n*

inventor ⓘ (ɪnˈvɛntə) *n* a person who invents, esp. as a profession.
▸**inˈventress** *fem n*

inventory ⓘ (ˈɪnvəntərɪ, -trɪ) *n, pl* **inventories. 1** a detailed list of articles, goods, property, etc. **2** (*often pl*) *Accounting, chiefly US.* **2a** the amount or value of a firm's current assets that consist of raw materials, work in progress, and finished goods; stock. **2b** such assets individually. ◆ *vb* **inventories, inventorying, inventoried. 3** (*tr*) to enter (items) in an inventory; make a list of. [C16: from Med. L *inventōrium;* see INVENT]
▸**ˈinventoriable** *adj* ▸**ˌinvenˈtorial** *adj* ▸**ˌinvenˈtorially** *adv*

Inverness (ˌɪnvəˈnɛs) *n* (*sometimes not cap.*) an overcoat with a removable cape. [C19: after *Inverness*, town in N Scotland]

inverse ⓘ (ɪnˈvɜːs, ˈɪnvɜːs) *adj* **1** opposite or contrary in effect, sequence, direction, etc. **2** *Maths.* **2a** (of a relationship) containing two variables such that an increase in one results in a decrease in the other. **2b** (of an element) operating on a specified member of a set to produce the identity of the set: *the additive inverse element of x is –x.* **3** (*usually prenominal*) upside-down; inverted: *in an inverse position.* ◆ *n* **4** *Maths.* an inverse element. [C17: from L *inversus*, from *invertere* to INVERT]
▸**inˈversely** *adv*

inverse function *n* a function whose independent variable is the dependent variable of a given trigonometric or hyperbolic function: *the inverse function of* sin *x is* arcsin *y* (*also written* $\sin^{-1}y$).

inversion ⓘ (ɪnˈvɜːʃən) *n* **1** the act of inverting or state of being inverted. **2** something inverted, esp. a reversal of order, mutual functions, etc.: *an inversion of their previous relationship.* **3** Also: **anastrophe.** *Rhetoric.* the reversal of a normal order of words, as in the phrase *weeping left she sorrowfully.* **4** *Chem.* **4a** the conversion of a dextrorotatory solution of sucrose into a laevorotatory solution of glucose and fructose by hydrolysis. **4b** any similar reaction in which the optical properties of the reactants are opposite to those of the products. **5** *Music.* **5a** the process or result of transposing the notes of a chord such that the root, originally in the bass, is placed in an upper part. **5b** the modification of an interval in which the higher note becomes the lower or the lower one the higher. **6** *Pathol.* abnormal positioning of an organ or part, as in being upside down or turned inside out. **7** *Psychiatry.* **7a** the adoption of the role or characteristics of the opposite sex. **7b** another word for **homosexuality. 8** *Meteorol.* an abnormal condition in which the layer of air next to the earth's surface is cooler than an overlying layer. **9** *Computing.* an operation by which each digit of a binary number is changed to the alternative digit, as *10110* to *01001.*
▸**inˈversive** *adj*

invert ⓘ *vb* (ɪnˈvɜːt). **1** to turn or cause to turn upside down or inside out. **2** (*tr*) to reverse in effect, sequence, direction, etc. **3** (*tr*) *Phonetics.* to turn (the tip of the tongue) up and back to pronounce (a speech sound). ◆ *n* (ˈɪnvɜːt). **4** *Psychiatry.* **4a** a person who adopts the role of the opposite sex. **4b** another word for **homosexual. 5** *Archit.* **5a** the lower inner surface of a drain, sewer, etc. **5b** an arch that is concave upwards, esp. one used in foundations. [C16: from L *invertere*, from IN-[2] + *vertere* to turn]
▸**inˈvertible** *adj* ▸**inˌvertiˈbility** *n*

invertase (ɪnˈvɜːteɪz) *n* an enzyme, occurring in the intestinal juice of animals and in yeasts, that hydrolyses sucrose to glucose and fructose.

invertebrate (ɪnˈvɜːtɪbrɪt, -ˌbreɪt) *n* **1** any animal lacking a backbone, including all species not classified as vertebrates. ◆ *adj also* **invertebral. 2** of, relating to, or designating invertebrates.

inverted comma *n* another term for **quotation mark.**

inverted mordent *n Music.* a melodic ornament consisting of the rapid alternation of a principal note with a note one degree higher.

inverter *or* **invertor** (ɪnˈvɜːtə) *n* any device for converting a direct current into an alternating current.

invert sugar *n* a mixture of fructose and glucose obtained by the inversion of sucrose.

invest ⓘ (ɪnˈvɛst) *vb* **1** (often foll. by *in*) to lay out (money or capital in an enterprise) with the expectation of profit. **2** (*tr;* often foll. by *in*) to devote (effort, resources, etc., to a project). **3** (*tr;* often foll. by *in* or *with*) *Arch. or ceremonial.* to clothe or adorn (in some garment, esp. the robes of an office). **4** (*tr;* often foll. by *in*) to install formally or ceremoniously (in an official position, rank, etc.). **5** (*tr;* foll. by *in* or *with*) to place (power, authority, etc., in) or provide (with power or authority): *to invest new rights in the monarchy.* **6** (*tr; usually passive;* foll. by *in* or *with*) to provide or endow (a person with qualities, characteristics, etc.). **7** (*tr;* foll. by *with*) *Usually poetic.* to cover or adorn, as if with a coat or garment: *when spring invests the trees with leaves.* **8** (*tr*) *Rare.* to surround with military forces; besiege. **9** (*intr;* foll. by *in*) *Inf.* to purchase; buy. [C16: from Med. L *investīre* to clothe, from L, from *vestīre*, from *vestis* a garment]
▸**inˈvestable** *or* **inˈvestible** *adj* ▸**inˈvestor** *n*

investigate ⓘ (ɪnˈvɛstɪˌgeɪt) *vb* **investigates, investigating, investigated.** to inquire into (a situation or problem, esp. a crime or death) thoroughly; examine systematically, esp. in order to discover the truth. [C16: from L *investīgāre* to search after, from IN-[2] + *vestīgium* track; see VESTIGE]
▸**inˈvestiˌgative** *or* **inˈvestigatory** *adj* ▸**inˈvestiˌgator** *n*

THESAURUS

tomarily, day in, day out, ever, every time, habitually, inevitably, on every occasion, perpetually, regularly, unfailingly, without exception

invasion *n* **1** = **attack**, aggression, assault, campaign, foray, incursion, inroad, irruption, offensive, onslaught, raid **2** = **intrusion**, breach, encroachment, infiltration, infraction, infringement, overstepping, usurpation, violation

invective *n* **1** = **abuse**, berating, billingsgate, castigation, censure, contumely, denunciation, diatribe, obloquy, philippic(s), reproach, revilement, sarcasm, tirade, tongue-lashing, vilification, vituperation

inveigle *n* = **coax**, allure, bamboozle (*inf.*), beguile, cajole, con (*sl.*), decoy, ensnare, entice, entrap, lead on, lure, manipulate, manoeuvre, persuade, seduce, sweet-talk (*inf.*), wheedle

invent *vb* **1** = **create**, coin, come up with (*inf.*), conceive, contrive, design, devise, discover, dream up (*inf.*), formulate, imagine, improvise, originate, think up **2** = **make up**, concoct, cook up (*inf.*), fabricate, feign, forge, manufacture, trump up

invention *n* **2** = **creation**, brainchild (*inf.*), contraption, contrivance, design, development, device, discovery, gadget, instrument, waldo **4** = **creativity**, coinage, creativeness, genius, imagination, ingenuity, inspiration, inventiveness, originality, resourcefulness **5** = **fiction**, deceit, fabrication, fake, falsehood, fantasy, fib (*inf.*), figment *or* product of (someone's) imagination, forgery, lie, prevarication, sham, story, tall story (*inf.*), untruth, urban legend, urban myth, yarn

inventive *adj* **1** = **creative**, fertile, gifted, ground-breaking, imaginative, ingenious, innovative, inspired, original, resourceful
Antonyms *adj* imitative, pedestrian, trite, unimaginative, uninspired, uninventive

inventor *n* = **creator**, architect, author, coiner, designer, father, framer, maker, originator

inventory *n* **1** = **list**, account, catalogue, file, record, register, roll, roster, schedule, stock book

inverse *adj* **1** = **opposite**, contrary, converse, inverted, reverse, reversed, transposed

inversion *n* **1** = **reversal**, contraposition, contrariety, transposal, transposition **2** = **opposite**, antipode, antithesis, contrary

invert *vb* **1, 2** = **overturn**, capsize, introvert, intussuscept (*Pathology*), invaginate (*Pathology*), overset, reverse, transpose, turn inside out, turn turtle, turn upside down, upset, upturn

invest *vb* **1** = **spend**, advance, devote, lay out, put in, sink **3** *Archaic* = **clothe**, array, bedeck, bedizen (*arch.*), deck, drape, dress, robe **4** = **install**, adopt, consecrate, enthrone, establish, inaugurate, induct, ordain **5** = **empower**, authorize, charge, license, sanction, vest **6** = **provide**, endow, endue, supply **8** = **besiege**, beleaguer, beset, enclose, lay siege to, surround

investigate *vb* = **examine**, consider, explore, go into, inquire into, inspect, look into, make inquiries, probe, put to the test, recce (*sl.*), research, scrutinize, search, sift, study, work over

investigation *n* = **examination**, analysis, exploration, fact finding, hearing, inquest, inquiry, inspection, probe, recce (*sl.*), research, review, scrutiny, search, study, survey

investigative *adj* = **fact-finding**, inspecting, investigating, research, researching

investigator *n* = **examiner**, gumshoe (*US sl.*),

investigation Ⓣ (ɪnˌvɛstɪˈgeɪʃən) *n* the act or process of investigating; a careful search or examination in order to discover facts, etc.

investiture Ⓣ (ɪnˈvɛstɪtʃə) *n* **1** the act of presenting with a title or with the robes and insignia of an office or rank. **2** (in feudal society) the formal bestowal of the possessory right to a fief.
▸**inˈvestitive** *adj*

investment Ⓣ (ɪnˈvɛstmənt) *n* **1a** the act of investing money. **1b** the amount invested. **1c** an enterprise, asset, etc., in which money is or can be invested. **2a** the act of investing effort, resources, etc. **2b** the amount invested. **3** *Biol.* the outer layer or covering of an organ, part, or organism. **4** a less common word for **investiture** (sense 1). **5** the act of investing or state of being invested, as with an official robe, specific quality, etc. **6** *Rare.* the act of besieging with military forces, works, etc.

investment analyst *n* a specialist in forecasting the prices of stocks and shares.

investment bond *n* a single-premium life-assurance policy in which a fixed sum is invested in an asset-backed fund.

investment trust *n* a financial enterprise that invests its subscribed capital in securities for its investors' benefit.

inveterate Ⓣ (ɪnˈvɛtərɪt) *adj* **1** long established, esp. so as to be deep-rooted or ingrained: *an inveterate feeling of hostility.* **2** (*prenominal*) confirmed in a habit or practice, esp. a bad one; hardened. [C16: from L *inveterātus* of long standing, from *inveterāre* to make old, from IN-[2] + *vetus* old]
▸**inˈveteracy** *n* ▸**inˈveterately** *adv*

invidious Ⓣ (ɪnˈvɪdɪəs) *adj* **1** incurring or tending to arouse resentment, unpopularity, etc.: *an invidious task.* **2** (of comparisons or distinctions) unfairly or offensively discriminating. [C17: from L *invidiōsus* full of envy, from *invidia* ENVY]
▸**inˈvidiously** *adv* ▸**inˈvidiousness** *n*

invigilate Ⓣ (ɪnˈvɪdʒɪˌleɪt) *vb* **invigilates, invigilating, invigilated.** (*intr*) **1** *Brit.* to watch examination candidates, esp. to prevent cheating. US word: **proctor. 2** *Arch.* to keep watch. [C16: from L *invigilāre* to watch over; see VIGIL]
▸**inˌvigiˈlation** *n* ▸**inˈvigiˌlator** *n*

invigorate Ⓣ (ɪnˈvɪgəˌreɪt) *vb* **invigorates, invigorating, invigorated.** (*tr*) to give vitality and vigour to; animate; brace; refresh: *to be invigorated by fresh air.* [C17: from IN-[2] + L *vigor* VIGOUR]
▸**inˈvigorˌating** *adj* ▸**inˌvigorˈation** *n* ▸**inˈvigorative** *adj* ▸**inˈvigorˌator** *n*

invincible Ⓣ (ɪnˈvɪnsəbᵊl) *adj* incapable of being defeated; unconquerable. [C15: from LL *invincibilis,* from L IN-[1] + *vincere* to conquer]
▸**inˌvinciˈbility** *or* **inˈvincibleness** *n* ▸**inˈvincibly** *adv*

inviolable Ⓣ (ɪnˈvaɪələbᵊl) *adj* that must not or cannot be transgressed, dishonoured, or broken; to be kept sacred: *an inviolable oath.*
▸**inˌviolaˈbility** *n* ▸**inˈviolably** *adv*

inviolate Ⓣ (ɪnˈvaɪəlɪt, -ˌleɪt) *adj* **1** free from violation, injury, disturbance, etc. **2** a less common word for **inviolable.**
▸**inˈviolacy** *or* **inˈviolateness** *n* ▸**inˈviolately** *adv*

invisible Ⓣ (ɪnˈvɪzəbᵊl) *adj* **1** not visible; not able to be perceived by the eye: *invisible rays.* **2** concealed from sight; hidden. **3** not easily seen or noticed: *invisible mending.* **4** kept hidden from public view; secret. **5** *Econ.* of or relating to services, such as insurance and freight, rather than goods: *invisible earnings.* ◆ *n* **6** *Econ.* an invisible item of trade; service.
▸**inˌvisiˈbility** *or* **inˈvisibleness** *n* ▸**inˈvisibly** *adv*

invitation Ⓣ (ˌɪnvɪˈteɪʃən) *n* **1a** the act of inviting, such as an offer of entertainment or hospitality. **1b** (*as modifier*): *an invitation race.* **2** the act of enticing or attracting; allurement.

invite Ⓣ *vb* (ɪnˈvaɪt), **invites, inviting, invited.** (*tr*) **1** to ask (a person) in a friendly or polite way (to do something, attend an event, etc.). **2** to make a request for, esp. publicly or formally: *to invite applications.* **3** to bring on or provoke; give occasion for: *you invite disaster by your actions.* **4** to welcome or tempt. ◆ *n* (ˈɪnvaɪt). **5** *Inf.* an invitation. [C16: from L *invītāre* to invite, entertain]
▸**inˈviter** *n*

inviting Ⓣ (ɪnˈvaɪtɪŋ) *adj* tempting; alluring; attractive.
▸**inˈvitingness** *n*

in vitro (ɪn ˈviːtrəʊ) *adv, adj* (of biological processes or reactions) made to occur outside the body of the organism in an artificial environment. [NL, lit.: in glass]

in vitro fertilization *n* a technique enabling some women who are unable to conceive to bear children. Egg cells removed from a woman's ovary are fertilized by sperm in vitro; some of the resulting fertilized egg cells are then implanted into her uterus. Abbrev.: **IVF.**

in vivo (ɪn ˈviːvəʊ) *adv, adj* (of biological processes or experiments) occurring or carried out in the living organism. [NL, lit.: in a living (thing)]

invocation Ⓣ (ˌɪnvəˈkeɪʃən) *n* **1** the act of invoking or calling upon some agent for assistance. **2** a prayer asking God for help, forgiveness, etc. **3** an appeal for inspiration from a Muse or deity at the beginning of a poem. **4a** the act of summoning a spirit from another world by ritual incantation or magic. **4b** the incantation used in this act.
▸ˌ**invoˈcational** *adj* ▸**invocatory** (ɪnˈvɒkətərɪ, -trɪ) *adj*

invoice (ˈɪnvɔɪs) *n* **1** a document issued by a seller to a buyer listing the goods or services supplied and stating the sum of money due. **2** *Rare.* a consignment of invoiced merchandise. ◆ *vb* **invoices, invoicing, invoiced. 3** (*tr*) **3a** to present (a customer, etc.) with an invoice. **3b** to list (merchandise sold) on an invoice. [C16: from earlier *invoyes,* from OF *envois,* pl. of *envoi* message; see ENVOY[1]]

invoke Ⓣ (ɪnˈvəʊk) *vb* **invokes, invoking, invoked.** (*tr*) **1** to call upon (an agent, esp. God or another deity) for help, inspiration, etc. **2** to put (a law, penalty, etc.) into use: *the union invoked the dispute procedure.* **3** to appeal to (an outside authority) for confirmation, corroboration, etc. **4** to implore or beg (help, etc.). **5** to summon (a spirit, etc.); conjure up. [C15: from L *invocāre* to appeal to, from *vocāre* to call]
▸**inˈvocable** *adj* ▸**inˈvoker** *n*

> **USAGE NOTE** *Invoke* is sometimes wrongly used where *evoke* is meant: *this proposal evoked* (not *invoked*) *a strong reaction.*

involucre (ˈɪnvəˌluːkə) *or* **involucrum** (ˌɪnvəˈluːkrəm) *n, pl* **involucres** *or* **involucra** (-krə). a ring of bracts at the base of an inflorescence. [C16 (in the sense: envelope): from NL *involucrum,* from L: wrapper, from *involvere* to wrap]
▸ˌ**invoˈlucral** *adj* ▸ˌ**invoˈlucrate** *adj*

involuntary Ⓣ (ɪnˈvɒləntərɪ, -trɪ) *adj* **1** carried out without one's conscious wishes; not voluntary; unintentional. **2** *Physiol.* (esp. of a movement or muscle) performed or acting without conscious control.
▸**inˈvoluntarily** *adv* ▸**inˈvoluntariness** *n*

involute *adj* (ˈɪnvəˌluːt), *also* **involuted. 1** complex, intricate, or involved. **2** *Bot.* (esp. of petals, leaves, etc., in bud) having margins that are rolled inwards. **3** (of certain shells) closely coiled so that the axis is obscured. ◆ *n* (ˈɪnvəˌluːt). **4** *Geom.* the curve described by the free end of a thread as it is wound around another curve, the **evolute,** such that its normals are tangential to the evolute. ◆ *vb* (ˌɪnvəˈluːt), **involutes, involuting, involuted. 5** (*intr*) to become involute. [C17: from L *involūtus,* from *involvere;* see INVOLVE]
▸ˈ**invoˌlutely** *adv* ▸ˌ**invoˈlutedly** *adv*

THESAURUS

inquirer, (private) detective, private eye (*inf.*), researcher, reviewer, sleuth

investiture *n* **1** = **installation,** admission, enthronement, inauguration, induction, instatement, investing, investment, ordination

investment *n* **1a** = **transaction,** investing, speculation, venture **1b** = **stake,** ante (*inf.*), contribution **6** = **siege,** beleaguering, besieging, blockading, surrounding

inveterate *adj* **1, 2** = **long-standing,** chronic, confirmed, deep-dyed (*usually derogatory*), deep-rooted, deep-seated, dyed-in-the-wool, entrenched, established, habitual, hard-core, hardened, incorrigible, incurable, ineradicable, ingrained, obstinate

invidious *adj* **1** = **undesirable,** hateful, thankless, unpleasant
Antonyms *adj* desirable, pleasant, pleasing

invigilate *vb* **1** = **watch over,** conduct, keep an eye on, oversee, preside over, run, superintend, supervise

invigorate *vb* = **refresh,** animate, brace, buck up (*inf.*), energize, enliven, exhilarate, fortify, freshen (up), galvanize, harden, liven up, nerve, pep up, perk up, put new heart into, quicken, rejuvenate, revitalize, stimulate, strengthen

invigorating *adj* = **refreshing,** bracing, energizing, exhilarating, fresh, healthful, rejuvenating, rejuvenative, restorative, salubrious, stimulating, tonic, uplifting

invincible *adj* = **unbeatable,** impregnable, indestructible, indomitable, inseparable, insuperable, invulnerable, unassailable, unconquerable, unsurmountable, unyielding
Antonyms *adj* assailable, beatable, conquerable, defenceless, fallible, powerless, unprotected, vulnerable, weak, yielding

inviolability *n* = **sanctity,** holiness, inalienability, inviolacy, invulnerability, sacredness

inviolable *adj* = **sacrosanct,** hallowed, holy, inalienable, sacred, unalterable

inviolate *adj* **1** = **intact,** entire, pure, sacred, stainless, unbroken, undefiled, undisturbed, unhurt, unpolluted, unstained, unsullied, untouched, virgin, whole
Antonyms *adj* abused, broken, defiled, polluted, stained, sullied, touched, violated

invisible *adj* **1** = **unseen,** imperceptible, indiscernible, out of sight, unperceivable **2** = **hidden,** concealed, disguised, inappreciable, inconspicuous, infinitesimal, microscopic
Antonyms *adj* ≠ **unseen:** discernible, distinct, obvious, perceptible, seen, visible

invitation *n* **1** = **request,** asking, begging, bidding, call, invite (*inf.*), solicitation, summons, supplication **2** = **inducement,** allurement, challenge, come-on (*inf.*), coquetry, enticement, glad eye, incitement, open door, overture, provocation, temptation

invite *vb* **1, 2** = **request,** ask, beg, bid, call, request the pleasure of (someone's) company, solicit, summon **3, 4** = **encourage,** allure, ask for (*inf.*), attract, bring on, court, draw, entice, lead, leave the door open to, provoke, solicit, tempt, welcome

inviting *adj* = **tempting,** alluring, appealing, attractive, beguiling, captivating, delightful, engaging, enticing, fascinating, intriguing, magnetic, mouthwatering, pleasing, seductive, warm, welcoming, winning
Antonyms *adj* disagreeable, offensive, off-putting (*Brit. inf.*), repellent, unappealing, unattractive, undesirable, uninviting, unpleasant

invocation *n* **1, 2** = **appeal,** beseeching, entreaty, petition, prayer, supplication

invoke *vb* **1, 3, 4** = **call upon,** adjure, appeal to, beg, beseech, conjure, entreat, implore, petition, pray, solicit, supplicate **2** = **apply,** call in, have recourse to, implement, initiate, put into effect, resort to, use

involuntary *adj* **1** = **unintentional,** automatic, blind, conditioned, instinctive, instinctual, reflex, spontaneous, unconscious, uncontrolled, unthinking
Antonyms *adj* calculated, deliberate, intentional, planned, purposed, volitional, voluntary, wilful

involution (ˌɪnvəˈluːʃən) *n* **1** the act of involving or complicating or the state of being involved or complicated. **2** something involved or complicated. **3** *Zool.* degeneration or structural deformation. **4** *Biol.* an involute formation or structure. **5** *Physiol.* reduction in size of an organ or part, as of the uterus following childbirth or as a result of ageing. **6** an algebraic operation in which a number, expression, etc., is raised to a specified power.
▸ˌ**invoˈlutional** *adj*

involve ❶ (ɪnˈvɒlv) *vb* **involves, involving, involved.** (*tr*) **1** to include or contain as a necessary part. **2** to have an effect on; spread to: *the investigation involved many innocent people.* **3** (*often passive; usually foll. by in* or *with*) to concern or associate significantly: *many people were involved in the crime.* **4** (*often passive*) to make complicated; tangle. **5** *Rare, often poetic.* to wrap or surround. **6** *Maths, obs.* to raise to a specified power. [C14: from L *involvere* to surround, from IN-[2] + *volvere* to roll]
▸**inˈvolvement** *n* ▸**inˈvolver** *n*

invulnerable ❶ (ɪnˈvʌlnərəbᵊl, -ˈvʌlnrəbᵊl) *adj* **1** incapable of being wounded, hurt, damaged, etc. **2** incapable of being damaged or captured: *an invulnerable fortress.*
▸**inˌvulneraˈbility** *or* **inˈvulnerableness** *n* ▸**inˈvulnerably** *adv*

inward ❶ (ˈɪnwəd) *adj* **1** going or directed towards the middle of or into something. **2** situated within; inside. **3** of, relating to, or existing in the mind or spirit: *inward meditation.* **4** of one's own country or a specific country: *inward investment.* ◆ *adv* **5** a variant of **inwards.** ◆ *n* **6** the inward part; inside.
▸**ˈinwardness** *n*

inwardly ❶ (ˈɪnwədlɪ) *adv* **1** within the private thoughts or feelings; secretly. **2** not aloud: *to laugh inwardly.* **3** with reference to the inside or inner part; internally.

inwards *adv* (ˈɪnwədz), *also* **inward. 1** towards the interior or middle of something. **2** in, into, or towards the mind or spirit. ◆ *pl n* (ˈɪnədz). **3** a variant of **innards** (sense 1).

inweave (ɪnˈwiːv) *vb* **inweaves, inweaving, inwove** *or* **inweaved; inwoven** *or* **inweaved.** (*tr*) to weave together into or as if into a design, fabric, etc.

inwrap (ɪnˈræp) *vb* **inwraps, inwrapping, inwrapped.** a less common spelling of **enwrap.**

inwrought (ˌɪnˈrɔːt) *adj* **1** worked or woven into material, esp. decoratively. **2** *Rare.* blended with other things.

in-your-face *adj Sl.* aggressive and confrontational: *provocative in-your-face activism.*

Io *the chemical symbol for* ionium.

IOC *abbrev. for* International Olympic Committee.

iodic (aɪˈɒdɪk) *adj* of or containing iodine, esp. in the pentavalent state.

iodide (ˈaɪəˌdaɪd) *n* **1** a salt of hydriodic acid, containing the iodide ion, I^-. **2** a compound containing an iodine atom, such as methyl iodide (iodomethane).

iodine (ˈaɪəˌdiːn) *n* a bluish-black element of the halogen group that sublimates into a violet irritating gas. Its compounds are used in medicine and photography and in dyes. The radioisotope **iodine-131** is used in the treatment of thyroid disease. Symbol: I; atomic no.: 53; atomic wt.: 126.90. [C19: from F *iode,* from Gk *iōdēs* rust-coloured, but mistaken as violet-coloured, from *ion* violet]

iodize *or* **iodise** (ˈaɪəˌdaɪz) *vb* **iodizes, iodizing, iodized** *or* **iodises, iodising, iodised.** (*tr*) to treat or react with iodine or an iodine compound. Also: **iodate.**
▸ˌ**iodiˈzation** *or* ˌ**iodiˈsation** *n* ▸**ˈioˌdizer** *or* **ˈioˌdiser** *n*

iodoform (aɪˈɒdəˌfɔːm) *n* a yellow crystalline solid made by heating alcohol with iodine and an alkali: used as an antiseptic. Formula: CHI_3. Systematic name: **triiodomethane.**

iodopsin (ˌaɪəˈdɒpsɪn) *n* a violet light-sensitive pigment in the cones of the retina of the eye. See also **rhodopsin.**

IOM *abbrev. for* Isle of Man.

ion (ˈaɪən, -ɒn) *n* an electrically charged atom or group of atoms formed by the loss or gain of one or more electrons. See also **cation, anion.** [C19: from Gk, lit.: going, from *ienai* to go]

-ion *suffix forming nouns.* indicating an action, process, or state: *creation; objection.* Cf. **-ation, -tion.** [from L *-iōn-, -io*]

ion exchange *n* the process in which ions are exchanged between a solution and an insoluble solid, usually a resin. It is used to soften water.

ionic (aɪˈɒnɪk) *adj* of, relating to, or occurring in the form of ions.

Ionic (aɪˈɒnɪk) *adj* **1** of, denoting, or relating to one of the five classical orders of architecture, characterized by fluted columns and capitals with scroll-like ornaments. **2** of or relating to Ionia, on the coast of Asia Minor, its inhabitants or their dialect of Ancient Greek. ◆ *n* **3** one of four chief dialects of Ancient Greek; the dialect spoken in Ionia.

ionium (aɪˈəʊnɪəm) *n Obs.* a naturally occurring radioisotope of thorium with a mass number of 230. Symbol: Io [C20: from NL]

ionization *or* **ionisation** (ˌaɪənaɪˈzeɪʃən) *n* **a** the formation of ions as a result of a chemical reaction, high temperature, electrical discharge, or radiation. **b** (*as modifier*): *ionization temperature.*

ionize *or* **ionise** (ˈaɪəˌnaɪz) *vb* **ionizes, ionizing, ionized** *or* **ionises, ionising, ionised.** to change or become changed into ions.
▸**ˈionˌizable** *or* **ˈionˌisable** *adj* ▸**ˈionˌizer** *or* **ˈionˌiser** *n*

ionosphere (aɪˈɒnəˌsfɪə) *n* a region of the earth's atmosphere, extending from about 60 to 1000 km above the earth's surface, in which there is a high concentration of free electrons formed as a result of ionizing radiation entering the atmosphere from space.
▸**ionospheric** (aɪˌɒnəˈsfɛrɪk) *adj*

iota ❶ (aɪˈəʊtə) *n* **1** the ninth letter in the Greek alphabet (Ι, ι), a vowel or semivowel. **2** (*usually used with a negative*) a very small amount; jot (esp. in **not one** *or* **an iota**). [C16: via L from Gk, of Semitic origin]

IOU *n* a written promise or reminder to pay a debt. [C17: representing *I owe you*]

-ious *suffix forming adjectives from nouns.* characterized by or full of: *suspicious.* [from L *-ius* & *-iōsus* full of]

IOW *abbrev. for* Isle of Wight.

IPA *abbrev. for* International Phonetic Alphabet.

ipecacuanha (ˌɪpɪˌkækjʊˈænə) *or* **ipecac** (ˈɪpɪˌkæk) *n* **1** a low-growing South American shrub. **2** a drug prepared from the dried roots of this plant, used as a purgative and emetic. [C18: from Port., from Amerind *ipekaaguéne,* from *ipeh* low + *kaa* leaves + *guéne* vomit]

ipomoea (ˌɪpəˈmɪə, ˌaɪ-) *n* **1** any tropical or subtropical plant, such as the morning-glory, sweet potato, and jalap, having trumpet-shaped flowers. **2** the dried root of a Mexican species which yields a cathartic resin. [C18: NL, from Gk *ips* worm + *homoios* like]

ippon (ˈɪpɒn) *n Judo & karate.* a winning point awarded in a sparring competition for a perfectly executed technique. [C20: Japanese, lit.: one point]

ipse dixit *Latin.* (ˈɪpseɪ ˈdɪksɪt) *n* an arbitrary and unsupported assertion. [C16, lit.: he himself said it]

ipso facto (ˈɪpsəʊ ˈfæktəʊ) *adv* by that very fact or act. [from L]

IQ *abbrev. for* intelligence quotient.

Ir *the chemical symbol for* iridium.

Ir. *abbrev. for:* **1** Ireland. **2** Irish.

ir- *prefix* a variant of **in-**[1] and **in-**[2] before *r.*

IRA *abbrev. for* Irish Republican Army.

irade (ɪˈrɑːdɛ) *n* a written edict of a Muslim ruler. [C19: from Turkish: will, from Ar. *irādah*]

Iranian (ɪˈreɪnɪən) *n* **1** a native or inhabitant of Iran. **2** a branch of the Indo-European family of languages, including Persian. **3** the modern Persian language. ◆ *adj* **4** relating to or characteristic of Iran, its inhabitants, or their language; Persian. **5** belonging to or relating to the Iranian branch of Indo-European.

Iran-Iraq War *n* the indecisive war (1980–88) fought by Iran and Iraq, following the Iraqi invasion of disputed border territory in Iran. Also called: **Gulf War.**

Iraqi (ɪˈrɑːkɪ) *adj* **1** of or characteristic of Iraq, in SW Asia, its inhabitants, or their language. ◆ *n, pl* **Iraqis. 2** a native or inhabitant of Iraq.

irascible ❶ (ɪˈræsɪbᵊl) *adj* **1** easily angered; irritable. **2** showing irritability: *an irascible action.* [C16: from LL *īrascibilis,* from L *īra* anger]
▸**iˌrasciˈbility** *or* **iˈrascibleness** *n* ▸**iˈrascibly** *adv*

irate ❶ (aɪˈreɪt) *adj* **1** incensed with anger; furious. **2** marked by ex-

THESAURUS

involve *vb* **1 = include,** comprehend, comprise, contain, cover, embrace, incorporate, number among, take in **3 = concern,** affect, associate, compromise, connect, draw in, implicate, incriminate, inculpate, mix up (*inf.*), stitch up (*sl.*), touch **4 = complicate,** embroil, enmesh, entangle, link, mire, mix up, snarl up, tangle

involved *adj* **3 = concerned,** caught (up), implicated, in on (*inf.*), mixed up in *or* with, occupied, participating, taking part, up to one's ears in **4 = complicated,** Byzantine, complex, confusing, convoluted, difficult, elaborate, intricate, knotty, labyrinthine, sophisticated, tangled, tortuous
Antonyms *adj* ≠ **complicated:** easy, easy-peasy (*sl.*), elementary, simple, simplified, straightforward, uncomplicated, unsophisticated

involvement *n* **3 = connection,** association, commitment, concern, dedication, interest, participation, responsibility **4 = complication,** complexity, difficulty, embarrassment, entanglement, imbroglio, intricacy, problem, ramification

invulnerability *n* **1, 2 = safety,** impenetrability, inviolability, security, strength, unassailability, untouchability

invulnerable *adj* **1, 2 = safe,** impenetrable, indestructible, insusceptible, invincible, proof against, secure, unassailable
Antonyms *adj* assailable, defenceless, insecure, susceptible, unprotected, vulnerable, weak

inward *adj* **1 = incoming,** entering, inbound, inflowing, ingoing, inpouring, penetrating **2 = internal,** inner, inside, interior **3 = private,** confidential, hidden, inmost, innermost, personal, privy, secret
Antonyms *adj* ≠ **internal:** exterior, external, outer, outermost, outside, outward ≠ **private:** open, public

inwardly *adv* **1, 2 = privately,** at heart, deep down, in one's head, in one's inmost heart, inside, secretly, to oneself, within

iota *n* **2 = bit,** atom, grain, hint, jot, mite, particle, scintilla (*rare*), scrap, speck, tittle, trace, whit

irascibility *n* **1 = bad temper,** asperity, cantankerousness, choler, crossness, edginess, fieriness, ill temper, impatience, irritability, irritation, petulance, shortness, snappishness, testiness, touchiness, uncertain temper

irascible *adj* **1 = bad-tempered,** cantankerous, choleric, crabbed, cross, hasty, hot-tempered, irritable, peppery, petulant, quick-tempered, ratty (*Brit. & NZ inf.*), short-tempered, testy, tetchy, touchy

irate *adj* **1 = angry,** angered, annoyed, choked, cross, enraged, exasperated, fuming (*inf.*), furious, hacked (off) (*US sl.*), hot under the collar (*inf.*), incandescent, incensed, indignant, in-

treme anger: *an irate letter.* [C19: from L *īrātus* enraged, from *īrascī* to be angry]
▸**iˈrately** *adv*

IRBM *abbrev. for* intermediate-range ballistic missile.

ire Ⓣ (ˈaɪə) *n Literary.* anger; wrath. [C13: from OF, from L *īra*]
▸**ˈireful** *adj* ▸**ˈirefulness** *n*

Ire. *abbrev. for* Ireland.

irenic, eirenic (aɪˈriːnɪk, -ˈrɛn-) *or* **irenical, eirenical** *adj* tending to conciliate or spromote peace. [C19: from Gk *eirēnikos,* from *eirēnē* peace]
▸**iˈrenically** *or* **eiˈrenically** *adv*

iridaceous (ˌɪrɪˈdeɪʃəs, ˌaɪ-) *adj* of, relating to, or belonging to the family of monocotyledonous plants, including the iris, having swordlike leaves and showy flowers.

iridescent Ⓣ (ˌɪrɪˈdɛsᵊnt) *adj* displaying a spectrum of colours that shimmer and change due to interference and scattering as the observer's position changes. [C18: from L *irid-* iris + -ESCENT]
▸**ˌiriˈdescence** *n* ▸**ˌiriˈdescently** *adv*

iridium (aɪˈrɪdɪəm, ɪˈrɪd-) *n* a very hard yellowish-white transition element that is the most corrosion-resistant metal known. It occurs in platinum ores and is used as an alloy with platinum. Symbol: Ir; atomic no.: 77; atomic wt.: 192.2. [C19: NL, from L *irid-* iris + -IUM; from its colourful appearance when dissolving in certain acids]

iris (ˈaɪrɪs) *n, pl* **irises** *or* **irides** (ˈaɪrɪˌdiːz, ˈɪrɪ-). **1** the coloured muscular diaphragm that surrounds and controls the size of the pupil of the eye. **2** Also called: **fleur-de-lys.** any iridaceous plant having brightly coloured flowers composed of three petals and three drooping sepals. **3** a poetic word for **rainbow. 4** short for **iris diaphragm.** [C14: from L: rainbow, iris (flower), crystal, from Gk]

iris diaphragm *n* an adjustable diaphragm that regulates the amount of light entering an optical instrument, esp. a camera.

Irish Ⓣ (ˈaɪrɪʃ) *adj* **1** of, relating to, or characteristic of Ireland, its people, their Celtic language, or their dialect of English. **2** *Inf. offens.* ludicrous or illogical. ◆ *n* **3 the Irish.** (*functioning as pl*) the natives or inhabitants of Ireland. **4** another name for **Irish Gaelic. 5** the dialect of English spoken in Ireland.

Irish coffee *n* hot coffee mixed with Irish whiskey and topped with double cream.

Irish Gaelic *n* the Goidelic language of the Celts of Ireland, now spoken mainly along the west coast; an official language of the Republic of Ireland since 1921.

Irishman (ˈaɪrɪʃmən) *or* (*fem*) **Irishwoman** *n, pl* **Irishmen** *or* **Irishwomen.** a native or inhabitant of Ireland.

Irish pipes *pl n* another name for **uillean pipes.**

Irish Republican Army *n* a militant organization of Irish nationalists founded with the aim of striving for a united independent Ireland by means of guerrilla warfare. Abbrev.: **IRA.**

Irish stew *n* a stew made of mutton, lamb, or beef, with potatoes, onions, etc.

Irish wolfhound *n* a large breed of hound with a rough thick coat.

iritis (aɪˈraɪtɪs) *n* inflammation of the iris of the eye.
▸**iritic** (aɪˈrɪtɪk) *adj*

irk Ⓣ (ɜːk) *vb* (*tr*) to irritate, vex, or annoy. [C13 *irken* to grow weary]

irksome Ⓣ (ˈɜːksəm) *adj* causing vexation, annoyance, or boredom; troublesome or tedious.
▸**ˈirksomely** *adv* ▸**ˈirksomeness** *n*

IRO *abbrev. for:* **1** (in Britain) Inland Revenue Office. **2** International Refugee Organization.

iron Ⓣ (ˈaɪən) *n* **1a** a malleable ductile silvery-white ferromagnetic metallic element. It is widely used for structural and engineering purposes. Symbol: Fe; atomic no.: 26; atomic wt.: 55.847. Related adjs.: **ferric, ferrous.** Related prefix: **ferro-. 1b** (*as modifier*): *iron railings.* **2** any of certain tools or implements made of iron or steel, esp. for use when hot: *a grappling iron; a soldering iron.* **3** an appliance for pressing fabrics using dry heat or steam, esp. a small electrically heated device with a handle and a weighted flat bottom. **4** any of various golf clubs with metal heads, numbered from 1 to 10 according to the slant of the face. **5** a splintlike support for a malformed leg. **6** great hardness, strength, or resolve: *a will of iron.* **7 strike while the iron is hot.** to act at an opportune moment. ◆ *adj* **8** very hard, immovable, or implacable: *iron determination.* **9** very strong; extremely robust: *an iron constitution.* **10** cruel or unyielding: *he ruled with an iron hand.* ◆ *vb* **11** to smooth (clothes or fabric) by removing (creases or wrinkles) using a heated iron; press. **12** (*tr*) to furnish or clothe with iron. **13** (*tr*) *Rare.* to place (a prisoner) in irons. ◆ See also **iron out, irons.** [OE *īren*]
▸**ˈironer** *n* ▸**ˈironless** *adj* ▸**ˈironˌlike** *adj*

Iron Age *n* **a** the period following the Bronze Age characterized by the extremely rapid spread of iron tools and weapons. **b** (*as modifier*): *an Iron-Age weapon.*

ironbark (ˈaɪənˌbɑːk) *n* any of several Australian eucalyptus trees that have hard rough bark.

ironbound (ˈaɪənˌbaʊnd) *adj* **1** bound with iron. **2** unyielding; inflexible. **3** (of a coast) rocky; rugged.

ironclad *adj* (ˌaɪənˈklæd). **1** covered or protected with iron: *an ironclad warship.* **2** inflexible; rigid: *an ironclad rule.* ◆ *n* (ˈaɪənˌklæd). **3** a large wooden 19th-century warship with armoured plating.

Iron Curtain *n* **1** (formerly) **1a** the guarded border between the countries of the Soviet bloc and the rest of Europe. **1b** (*as modifier*): *Iron Curtain countries.* **2** (*sometimes not caps.*) any barrier that separates communities or ideologies.

iron hand *n* harsh or rigorous control; overbearing or autocratic force.

iron horse *n Arch.* a steam-driven railway locomotive.

ironic Ⓣ (aɪˈrɒnɪk) *or* **ironical** *adj* of, characterized by, or using irony.
▸**iˈronically** *adv* ▸**iˈronicalness** *n*

ironing (ˈaɪənɪŋ) *n* **1** the act of ironing washed clothes. **2** clothes, etc., that are to be or that have been ironed.

ironing board *n* a board, usually on legs, with a suitable covering on which to iron clothes.

iron lung *n* an airtight metal cylinder enclosing the entire body up to the neck and providing artificial respiration.

iron maiden *n* a medieval instrument of torture, consisting of a hinged case (often shaped in the form of a woman) lined with iron spikes, which was forcibly closed on the victim.

iron man *n Austral.* **1** an event at a surf carnival in which contestants compete at swimming, surfing, running, etc. **2** a participant in such an event.

ironmaster (ˈaɪənˌmɑːstə) *n Brit.* a manufacturer of iron.

ironmonger (ˈaɪənˌmʌŋgə) *n Brit.* a dealer in metal utensils, hardware, locks, etc. US and Canad. equivalent: **hardware dealer.**
▸**ˈironˌmongery** *n*

iron out Ⓣ *vb* (*tr, adv*) **1** to smooth, using a heated iron. **2** to put right or settle (a problem or difficulty) as a result of negotiations or discussions. **3** *Austral. inf.* to knock unconscious.

iron pyrites (ˈpaɪraɪts) *n* another name for **pyrite.**

iron rations *pl n* emergency food supplies, esp. for military personnel in action.

irons Ⓣ (ˈaɪənz) *pl n* **1** fetters or chains (often in **in** *or* **into irons**). **2 have several irons in the fire.** to be involved in many projects, etc.

ironsides (ˈaɪənˌsaɪdz) *n* **1** a person with great stamina or resistance. **2** an ironclad ship. **3** (*often cap.*) (in the English Civil War) **3a** the cavalry regiment trained and commanded by Oliver Cromwell. **3b** Cromwell's entire army.

ironstone (ˈaɪənˌstəʊn) *n* **1** any rock consisting mainly of an iron-bearing ore. **2** a tough durable earthenware.

ironware (ˈaɪənˌwɛə) *n* domestic articles made of iron.

ironwood (ˈaɪənˌwʊd) *n* **1** any of various trees, such as hornbeam, that have very hard wood. **2** a Californian rosaceous tree with very hard wood. **3** any of various other trees with hard wood, such as the mopani. **4** the wood of any of these trees.

ironwork (ˈaɪənˌwɜːk) *n* **1** work done in iron, esp. decorative work. **2** the craft or practice of working in iron.

ironworks (ˈaɪənˌwɜːks) *n* (*sometimes functioning as sing*) a building in which iron is smelted, cast, or wrought.

irony[1] Ⓣ (ˈaɪrənɪ) *n, pl* **ironies. 1** the humorous or mildly sarcastic use of words to imply the opposite of what they normally mean. **2** an instance of this, used to draw attention to some incongruity or irrationality. **3** incongruity between what is expected to be and what actually is, or a situation or result showing such incongruity. **4** See **dramatic irony. 5** *Philosophy.* See **Socratic irony.** [C16: from L, from Gk *eirōneia,* from *eirōn* dissembler, from *eirein* to speak]

irony[2] (ˈaɪənɪ) *adj* of, resembling, or containing iron.

Iroquois (ˈɪrəˌkwɔɪ) *n* **1** (*pl* **Iroquois**) a member of a confederacy of North American Indian tribes formerly living in and around New York State. **2** any of the languages of these people.
▸**ˌIroˈquoian** *adj*

irradiance (ɪˈreɪdɪəns) *n* the radiant flux incident on unit area of a surface. Also: **irradiation.** Cf. **illuminance.**

THESAURUS

furiated, irritated, livid, mad (*inf.*), piqued, provoked, riled, up in arms, worked up, wrathful

ire *n* = **anger,** annoyance, choler, displeasure, exasperation, fury, indignation, passion, rage, wrath

iridescent *adj* = **shimmering,** nacreous, opalescent, opaline, pearly, polychromatic, prismatic, rainbow-coloured, shot

Irish *adj* **1** = **Hibernian,** green

irk *vb* = **irritate,** aggravate (*inf.*), annoy, bug (*inf.*), gall, get one's back up, get on one's nerves (*inf.*), miff (*inf.*), nettle, peeve (*inf.*), provoke, put one's back up, put one's nose out of joint (*inf.*), put out (*inf.*), rile, rub one up the wrong way (*inf.*), ruffle, vex

irksome *adj* = **irritating,** aggravating, annoying, boring, bothersome, burdensome, disagreeable, exasperating, tedious, tiresome, troublesome, trying, uninteresting, unwelcome, vexatious, vexing, wearisome
Antonyms *adj* agreeable, enjoyable, gratifying, interesting, pleasant, pleasing, welcome

iron *modifier* **1b** = **ferrous,** chalybeate, ferric, irony ◆ *adj* **8-10** = **inflexible,** adamant, cruel, hard, heavy, immovable, implacable, indomitable, obdurate, rigid, robust, steel, steely, strong, tough, unbending, unyielding
Antonyms *adj* ≠ **inflexible:** bending, easy, flexible, light, malleable, pliable, soft, weak, yielding

ironic *adj* = **sarcastic,** double-edged, incongruous, mocking, mordacious, paradoxical, sardonic, satirical, scoffing, sneering, with tongue in cheek, wry

iron out *vb* **2** = **settle,** clear up, eliminate, eradicate, erase, expedite, get rid of, harmonize, put right, reconcile, resolve, simplify, smooth over, sort out, straighten out, unravel

irons *pl n* **1** = **chains,** bonds, fetters, gyves (*arch.*), manacles, shackles

irony[1] *n* **1, 2** = **sarcasm,** mockery, satire **3** = **paradox,** contrariness, incongruity

irradiate ❶ (ɪ'reɪdɪˌeɪt) *vb* **irradiates, irradiating, irradiated. 1** (*tr*) *Physics.* to subject to or treat with light or other electromagnetic radiation or with beams of particles. **2** (*tr*) to expose (food) to electromagnetic radiation to kill bacteria and retard deterioration. **3** (*tr*) to make clear or bright intellectually or spiritually; illumine. **4** a less common word for **radiate** (sense 1). **5** (*intr*) *Obs.* to become radiant.
▸**irˌradi'ation** *n* ▸**ir'radiative** *adj* ▸**ir'radiˌator** *n*

irrational ❶ (ɪ'ræʃən^əl) *adj* **1** inconsistent with reason or logic; illogical; absurd. **2** incapable of reasoning. **3a** *Maths.* (of an equation, etc.) containing one or more variables in irreducible radical form or raised to a fractional power: $\sqrt{(x^2 + 1)} = x^{5/3}$. **3b** (*as n*): *an irrational.*
▸**irˌration'ality** *n* ▸**ir'rationally** *adv*

irrational number *n* any real number that cannot be expressed as the ratio of two integers, such as π.

irreclaimable (ˌɪrɪ'kleɪməb^əl) *adj* not able to be reclaimed.
▸**ˌirreˌclaima'bility** *or* **ˌirre'claimableness** *n* ▸**ˌirre'claimably** *adv*

irreconcilable ❶ (ɪ'rɛk^ənˌsaɪləb^əl, ɪˌrɛk^ən'saɪ-) *adj* **1** not able to be reconciled; uncompromisingly conflicting; incompatible. ◆ *n* **2** a person or thing that is implacably hostile or uncompromisingly opposed. **3** (*usually pl*) one of various principles, ideas, etc., that are incapable of being brought into agreement.
▸**irˌreconˌcila'bility** *or* **ir'reconˌcilableness** *n* ▸**ir'reconˌcilably** *adv*

irrecoverable ❶ (ˌɪrɪ'kʌvərəb^əl, -'kʌvrə-) *adj* **1** not able to be recovered or regained. **2** not able to be remedied or rectified.
▸**ˌirre'coverableness** *n* ▸**ˌirre'coverably** *adv*

irrecusable (ˌɪrɪ'kju:zəb^əl) *adj* not able to be rejected or challenged, as evidence, etc.

irredeemable (ˌɪrɪ'di:məb^əl) *adj* **1** (of bonds, shares, etc.) without a date of redemption of capital; incapable of being bought back directly or paid off. **2** (of paper money) not convertible into specie. **3** (of a loss) not able to be recovered; irretrievable. **4** not able to be improved or rectified; irreparable.
▸**ˌirreˌdeema'bility** *or* **ˌirre'deemableness** *n* ▸**ˌirre'deemably** *adv*

irredentist (ˌɪrɪ'dɛntɪst) *n* **1** (*sometimes cap.*) a person, esp. a member of a 19th-century Italian association, who favours the acquisition of territory that was once part of his country or is considered to have been. ◆ *adj* **2** of or relating to irredentists or their policies. [C19: from It. *irredentista,* from *ir-* IN-[1] + *redento* redeemed, from L *redemptus* bought back; see REDEEM]
▸**ˌirre'dentism** *n*

irreducible (ˌɪrɪ'dju:sɪb^əl) *adj* **1** not able to be reduced or lessened. **2** not able to be brought to a simpler or reduced form. **3** *Maths.* (of a polynomial) unable to be factorized into polynomials of lower degree, as $(x^2 + 1)$.
▸**ˌirreˌduci'bility** *n* ▸**ˌirre'ducibly** *adv*

irrefragable (ɪ'rɛfrəgəb^əl) *adj* not able to be denied or refuted. [C16: from LL *irrefrāgābilis,* from L *ir-* + *refrāgārī* to resist]
▸**irˌrefraga'bility** *or* **ir'refragableness** *n* ▸**ir'refragably** *adv*

irrefrangible (ˌɪrɪ'frændʒəb^əl) *adj* **1** not to be broken or transgressed; inviolable. **2** *Physics.* incapable of being refracted.
▸**ˌirreˌfrangi'bility** *or* **ˌirre'frangibleness** *n* ▸**ˌirre'frangibly** *adv*

irrefutable ❶ (ɪ'rɛfjʊtəb^əl, ˌɪrɪ'fju:təb^əl) *adj* impossible to deny or disprove; incontrovertible.
▸**irˌrefuta'bility** *n* ▸**ir'refutably** *adv*

irreg. *abbrev. for* irregular(ly).

irregular ❶ (ɪ'rɛgjʊlə) *adj* **1** lacking uniformity or symmetry; uneven in shape, position, arrangement, etc. **2** not occurring at expected or equal intervals: *an irregular pulse.* **3** differing from the normal or accepted practice or routine; unconventional. **4** (of the formation, inflections, or derivations of a word) not following the usual pattern of formation in a language. **5** of or relating to guerrillas or volunteers not belonging to regular forces: *irregular troops.* **6** (of flowers) having any of their petals differing in size, shape, etc. **7** *US.* (of merchandise) not up to the manufacturer's standards or specifications; imperfect. ◆ *n* **8** a soldier not in a regular army. **9** (*often pl*) *US.* imperfect or flawed merchandise.
▸**irˌregu'larity** *n* ▸**ir'regularly** *adv*

irrelevant ❶ (ɪ'rɛləvənt) *adj* not relating or pertinent to the matter at hand.
▸**ir'relevance** *or* **ir'relevancy** *n* ▸**ir'relevantly** *adv*

irreligion ❶ (ˌɪrɪ'lɪdʒən) *n* **1** lack of religious faith. **2** indifference or opposition to religion.
▸**ˌirre'ligionist** *n* ▸**ˌirre'ligious** *adj* ▸**ˌirre'ligiously** *adv* ▸**ˌirre'ligiousness** *n*

irremediable ❶ (ˌɪrɪ'mi:dɪəb^əl) *adj* not able to be remedied; incurable or irreparable.
▸**ˌirre'mediableness** *n* ▸**ˌirre'mediably** *adv*

irremissible (ˌɪrɪ'mɪsəb^əl) *adj* **1** unpardonable; inexcusable. **2** that must be done, as through duty or obligation.
▸**ˌirreˌmissi'bility** *or* **ˌirre'missibleness** *n* ▸**ˌirre'missibly** *adv*

irremovable (ˌɪrɪ'mu:vəb^əl) *adj* not able to be removed.
▸**ˌirreˌmova'bility** *n* ▸**ˌirre'movably** *adv*

irreparable ❶ (ɪ'rɛpərəb^əl, ɪ'rɛprəb^əl) *adj* not able to be repaired or remedied; beyond repair.
▸**irˌrepara'bility** *or* **ir'reparableness** *n* ▸**ir'reparably** *adv*

irreplaceable ❶ (ˌɪrɪ'pleɪsəb^əl) *adj* not able to be replaced: *an irreplaceable antique.*
▸**ˌirre'placeably** *adv*

irrepressible ❶ (ˌɪrɪ'prɛsəb^əl) *adj* not capable of being repressed, controlled, or restrained.
▸**ˌirreˌpressi'bility** *or* **ˌirre'pressibleness** *n* ▸**ˌirre'pressibly** *adv*

irreproachable ❶ (ˌɪrɪ'prəʊtʃəb^əl) *adj* not deserving reproach; blameless.
▸**ˌirreˌproacha'bility** *or* **ˌirre'proachableness** *n* ▸**ˌirre'proachably** *adv*

irresistible ❶ (ˌɪrɪ'zɪstəb^əl) *adj* **1** not able to be resisted or refused; overpowering: *an irresistible impulse.* **2** very fascinating or alluring: *an irresistible woman.*
▸**ˌirreˌsisti'bility** *or* **ˌirre'sistibleness** *n* ▸**ˌirre'sistibly** *adv*

irresolute ❶ (ɪ'rɛzəˌlu:t) *adj* lacking resolution; wavering; hesitating.
▸**ir'resoˌlutely** *adv* ▸**ir'resoˌluteness** *or* **irˌreso'lution** *n*

THESAURUS

irradiate *vb* **3** = **light up**, brighten, cast light upon, enlighten, illume (*poetic*), illuminate, illumine, lighten, shine upon

irrational *adj* **1** = **illogical**, absurd, crackpot (*inf.*), crazy, foolish, injudicious, nonsensical, preposterous, silly, unreasonable, unreasoning, unsound, unthinking, unwise **2** = **senseless**, aberrant, brainless, crazy, demented, insane, mindless, muddle-headed, raving, unstable, wild
Antonyms *adj* ≠ **illogical:** circumspect, judicious, logical, rational, reasonable, sensible, sound, wise

irrationality *n* **1** = **senselessness**, absurdity, brainlessness, illogicality, insanity, lack of judgment, lunacy, madness, preposterousness, unreasonableness, unsoundness

irreconcilable *adj* **1** = **incompatible**, clashing, conflicting, diametrically opposed, incongruous, inconsistent, opposed

irrecoverable *adj* **1, 2** = **lost**, gone for ever, irreclaimable, irredeemable, irremediable, irreparable, irretrievable, unregainable, unsalvageable, unsavable

irrefutable *adj* = **undeniable**, apodeictic, apodictic, beyond question, certain, incontestable, incontrovertible, indisputable, indubitable, invincible, irrefragable, irresistible, sure, unanswerable, unassailable, unquestionable

irregular *adj* **1** = **uneven**, asymmetrical, broken, bumpy, craggy, crooked, elliptic, elliptical, holey, jagged, lopsided, lumpy, pitted, ragged, rough, serrated, unequal, unsymmetrical **2** = **variable**, desultory, disconnected, eccentric, erratic, fitful, fluctuating, fragmentary, haphazard, inconstant, intermittent, nonuniform, occasional, out of order, patchy, random, shifting, spasmodic, sporadic, uncertain, uneven, unmethodical, unpunctual, unsteady, unsystematic, wavering **3** = **unconventional**, abnormal, anomalous, capricious, disorderly, eccentric, exceptional, extraordinary, immoderate, improper, inappropriate, inordinate, odd, peculiar, queer, quirky, rum (*Brit. sl.*), unofficial, unorthodox, unsuitable, unusual ◆ *n* **8** = **guerrilla**, partisan, volunteer
Antonyms *adj* ≠ **uneven:** balanced, equal, even, regular, smooth, symmetrical ≠ **variable:** certain, invariable, methodical, punctual, reliable, steady, systematic ≠ **unconventional:** appropriate, conventional, normal, orthodox, proper, regular, standard, usual

irregularity *n* **1** = **unevenness**, asymmetry, bumpiness, crookedness, jaggedness, lack of symmetry, lopsidedness, lumpiness, patchiness, raggedness, roughness, spottiness **2** = **uncertainty**, confusion, desultoriness, disorderliness, disorganization, haphazardness, lack of method, randomness, unpunctuality, unsteadiness **3** = **abnormality**, aberration, anomaly, breach, deviation, eccentricity, freak, malfunction, malpractice, oddity, peculiarity, singularity, unconventionality, unorthodoxy

irregularly *adv* **2** = **erratically**, anyhow, by fits and starts, disconnectedly, eccentrically, fitfully, haphazardly, in snatches, intermittently, jerkily, now and again, occasionally, off and on, out of sequence, spasmodically, unevenly, unmethodically, unpunctually

irrelevance *n* = **inappropriateness**, inappositeness, inaptness, inconsequence, non sequitur
Antonyms *n* appositeness, appropriateness, aptness, consequence, pertinence, point, relevance, suitability

irrelevant *adj* = **unconnected**, beside the point, extraneous, immaterial, impertinent, inapplicable, inapposite, inappropriate, inapt, inconsequent, neither here nor there, unrelated
Antonyms *adj* applicable, apposite, appropriate, apt, connected, fitting, pertinent, related, relevant, suitable

irreligious *adj* **1** = **atheistic**, agnostic, freethinking, godless, pagan, sceptical, unbelieving **2** = **sacrilegious**, blasphemous, iconoclastic, impious, irreverent, profane, sinful, undevout, ungodly, unholy, unrighteous, wicked

irremediable *adj* = **incurable**, beyond redress, deadly, fatal, final, hopeless, irrecoverable, irredeemable, irreparable, irreversible, mortal, remediless, terminal

irreparable *adj* = **beyond repair**, incurable, irrecoverable, irremediable, irreplaceable, irretrievable, irreversible

irreplaceable *adj* = **indispensable**, invaluable, priceless, unique, vital

irrepressible *adj* = **ebullient**, boisterous, bubbling over, buoyant, effervescent, insuppressible, uncontainable, uncontrollable, unmanageable, unquenchable, unrestrainable, unstoppable

irreproachable *adj* = **blameless**, beyond reproach, faultless, guiltless, impeccable, inculpable, innocent, irreprehensible, irreprovable, perfect, pure, squeaky-clean, unblemished, unimpeachable

irresistible *adj* **1** = **overwhelming**, compelling, compulsive, imperative, overmastering, overpowering, potent, urgent **2** = **seductive**, alluring, beckoning, enchanting, fascinating, ravishing, tempting

irresolute *adj* = **indecisive**, doubtful, fickle, half-hearted, hesitant, hesitating, infirm, in two minds, tentative, undecided, undetermined,

irrespective ❶ (ˌɪrɪˈspɛktɪv) *adj* **1 irrespective of.** without taking account of; regardless of. ◆ *adv* **2** *Inf.* regardless; without due consideration: *he carried on with his plan irrespective.*
▸ˌ**irreˈspectively** *adv*

irresponsible ❶ (ˌɪrɪˈspɒnsəbᵊl) *adj* **1** not showing or done with due care for the consequences of one's actions or attitudes; reckless. **2** not capable of bearing responsibility.
▸ˌ**irreˌsponsiˈbility** *or* ˌ**irreˈsponsibleness** *n* ▸ˌ**irreˈsponsibly** *adv*

irresponsive (ˌɪrɪˈspɒnsɪv) *adj* not responsive.
▸ˌ**irreˈsponsively** *adv* ▸ˌ**irreˈsponsiveness** *n*

irretrievable (ˌɪrɪˈtriːvəbᵊl) *adj* not able to be retrieved, recovered, or repaired.
▸ˌ**irreˌtrievaˈbility** *n* ▸ˌ**irreˈtrievably** *adv*

irreverence ❶ (ɪˈrɛvərəns, ɪˈrɛvrəns) *n* **1** lack of due respect or veneration; disrespect. **2** a disrespectful remark or act.
▸**irˈreverent** *or* **irˌreveˈrential** *adj* ▸**irˈreverently** *adv*

irreversible ❶ (ˌɪrɪˈvɜːsəbᵊl) *adj* **1** not able to be reversed: *the irreversible flow of time.* **2** not able to be revoked or repealed; irrevocable. **3** *Chem., physics.* capable of changing or producing a change in one direction only: *an irreversible reaction.*
▸ˌ**irreˌversiˈbility** *or* ˌ**irreˈversibleness** *n* ▸ˌ**irreˈversibly** *adv*

irrevocable ❶ (ɪˈrɛvəkəbᵊl) *adj* not able to be revoked, changed, or undone.
▸**irˌrevocaˈbility** *or* **irˈrevocableness** *n* ▸**irˈrevocably** *adv*

irrigate ❶ (ˈɪrɪˌgeɪt) *vb* **irrigates, irrigating, irrigated. 1** to supply (land) with water by means of artificial canals, etc., esp. to promote the growth of food crops. **2** *Med.* to bathe or wash out (a bodily part, cavity, or wound). **3** (*tr*) to make fertile, fresh, or vital by or as if by watering. [C17: from L *irrigāre,* from *rigāre* to moisten, conduct water]
▸ˈ**irrigable** *adj* ▸ˌ**irriˈgation** *n* ▸ˈ**irriˌgative** *adj* ▸ˈ**irriˌgator** *n*

irritable ❶ (ˈɪrɪtəbᵊl) *adj* **1** quickly irritated; easily annoyed; peevish. **2** (of all living organisms) capable of responding to such stimuli as heat, light, and touch. **3** *Pathol.* abnormally sensitive.
▸ˌ**irritaˈbility** *n* ▸ˈ**irritableness** *n* ▸ˈ**irritably** *adv*

irritable bowel syndrome *n Med.* a chronic condition of recurring abdominal pain with constipation or diarrhoea or both.

irritant (ˈɪrɪtənt) *adj* **1** causing irritation; irritating. ◆ *n* **2** something irritant.
▸ˈ**irritancy** *n*

irritate ❶ (ˈɪrɪˌteɪt) *vb* **irritates, irritating, irritated. 1** to annoy or anger (someone). **2** (*tr*) *Biol.* to stimulate (an organism or part) to respond in a characteristic manner. **3** (*tr*) *Pathol.* to cause (a bodily organ or part) to become excessively stimulated, resulting in inflammation, tenderness, etc. [C16: from L *irrītāre* to provoke]
▸ˈ**irriˌtator** *n*

irritation ❶ (ˌɪrɪˈteɪʃən) *n* **1** something that irritates. **2** the act of irritating or the condition of being irritated.
▸ˈ**irriˌtative** *adj*

irrupt (ɪˈrʌpt) *vb* (*intr*) **1** to enter forcibly or suddenly. **2** (of a plant or animal population) to enter a region suddenly and in very large numbers. **3** (of a population) to increase suddenly and greatly. [C19: from L *irrumpere* to rush into, invade, from *rumpere* to break, burst]
▸**irˈruption** *n* ▸**irˈruptive** *adj*

is (ɪz) *vb* (used with *he, she, it,* and with singular nouns) a form of the present tense (indicative mood) of **be.** [OE]

Is. *abbrev. for:* **1** Also: **Isa.** *Bible.* Isaiah. **2** Island(s) *or* Isle(s).

is- *combining form.* a variant of **iso-** before a vowel: *isentropic.*

ISA (ˈaɪsə) *n acronym for* individual savings account: a tax-free savings scheme introduced in the UK in 1999.

isagogics (ˌaɪsəˈgɒdʒɪks) *n* introductory studies, esp. in the history of the Bible. [C19: from L, from Gk, from *eisagein* to introduce, from *eis-* into + *agein* to lead]

isallobar (aɪˈsæləˌbɑː) *n* a line on a map connecting places with equal pressure changes.

isatin (ˈaɪsətɪn) *or* **isatine** (ˈaɪsəˌtiːn) *n* a yellowish-red crystalline compound soluble in hot water, used for the preparation of vat dyes. [C19: from L *isatis* woad + -IN]
▸ˌ**isaˈtinic** *adj*

ISBN *abbrev. for* International Standard Book Number.

ischaemia *or* **ischemia** (ɪˈskiːmɪə) *n Pathol.* an inadequate supply of blood to an organ or part, as from an obstructed blood flow. [C19: from Gk *iskhein* to restrict, + -AEMIA]
▸**ischaemic** *or* **ischemic** (ɪˈskemɪk) *adj*

ischium (ˈɪskɪəm) *n, pl* **ischia** (-kɪə). one of the three sections of the hipbone, situated below the ilium. [C17: from L: hip joint, from Gk *iskhion*]
▸ˈ**ischial** *adj*

-ise *suffix forming verbs.* a variant of **-ize.**

> **USAGE NOTE** See at **-ize.**

isentropic (ˌaɪsɛnˈtrɒpɪk) *adj* having or taking place at constant entropy.

-ish *suffix forming adjectives.* **1** of or belonging to a nationality: *Scottish.* **2** *Often derog.* having the manner or qualities of; resembling: *slavish; boyish.* **3** somewhat; approximately: *yellowish; sevenish.* **4** concerned or preoccupied with: *bookish.* [OE *-isc*]

isinglass (ˈaɪzɪŋˌglɑːs) *n* **1** a gelatine made from the air bladders of freshwater fish, used as a clarifying agent and adhesive. **2** another name for **mica.** [C16: from MDu. *huysenblase,* lit.: sturgeon bladder; infl. by E GLASS]

Isl. *abbrev. for:* **1** Island. **2** Isle.

Islam (ˈɪzlɑːm) *n* **1** Also called: **Islamism.** the religion of Muslims, teaching that there is only one God and that Mohammed is his prophet; Mohammedanism. **2a** Muslims collectively and their civilization. **2b** the countries where the Muslim religion is predominant. [C19: from Ar.: surrender (to God), from *aslama* to surrender]
▸**Isˈlamic** *adj*

Islamist (ˈɪzˌləmɪst) *adj* **1** supporting or advocating Islamic fundamentalism. ◆ *n* **2** a supporter or advocate of Islamic fundamentalism.

Islamize *or* **Islamise** (ˈɪzləˌmaɪz) *vb* **Islamizes, Islamizing, Islamized** *or* **Islamises, Islamising, Islamised.** (*tr*) to convert or subject to the influence of Islam.
▸ˌ**Islamiˈzation** *or* ˌ**Islamiˈsation** *n*

island ❶ (ˈaɪlənd) *n* **1** a mass of land that is surrounded by water and is smaller than a continent. **2** something isolated, detached, or surrounded: *a traffic island.* **3** *Anat.* a part, structure, or group of cells distinct in constitution from its immediate surroundings. ◆ Related adj: **insular.** ◆ *vb* (*tr*) *Rare.* **4** to cause to become an island. **5** to intersperse with islands. **6** to place on an island; insulate; isolate. [OE *īgland*]
▸ˈ**island-ˌlike** *adj*

islander (ˈaɪləndə) *n* a native or inhabitant of an island.

THESAURUS

unsettled, unstable, unsteady, vacillating, wavering, weak
Antonyms *adj* decisive, determined, firm, fixed, resolute, resolved, settled, stable, stalwart, steadfast, steady, strong

irresoluteness *n* = **indecisiveness,** dithering (*chiefly Brit.*), faint-heartedness, half-heartedness, hesitancy, hesitation, infirmity (of purpose), shillyshallying (*inf.*), uncertainty, vacillation, wavering

irrespective *adj* **1 irrespective of** = **despite,** apart from, discounting, in spite of, notwithstanding, regardless of, without reference to, without regard to

irresponsible *adj* **1, 2** = **thoughtless,** careless, featherbrained, flighty, giddy, good-for-nothing, harebrained, harum-scarum, ill-considered, immature, reckless, scatterbrained, shiftless, undependable, unreliable, untrustworthy, wild
Antonyms *adj* careful, dependable, level-headed, mature, reliable, responsible, sensible, trustworthy

irreverence *n* **1** = **disrespect,** cheek (*inf.*), cheekiness (*inf.*), chutzpah (*US & Canad. inf.*), derision, flippancy, impertinence, impudence, lack of respect, mockery, sauce (*inf.*)

irreverent *adj* **1** = **disrespectful,** cheeky (*inf.*), contemptuous, derisive, flip (*inf.*), flippant, fresh (*inf.*), iconoclastic, impertinent, impious, impudent, mocking, sassy (*US inf.*), saucy, tongue-in-cheek
Antonyms *adj* awed, deferential, meek, pious, respectful, reverent, submissive

irreversible *adj* **1, 2** = **irrevocable,** final, incurable, irreparable, unalterable

irrevocable *adj* = **fixed,** changeless, fated, immutable, invariable, irremediable, irretrievable, irreversible, predestined, predetermined, settled, unalterable, unchangeable, unreversible

irrigate *vb* **1** = **water,** flood, inundate, moisten, wet

irritability *n* **1** = **bad temper,** ill humour, impatience, irascibility, peevishness, petulance, prickliness, testiness, tetchiness, touchiness
Antonyms *n* bonhomie, cheerfulness, complacence, good humour, patience

irritable *adj* = **bad-tempered,** cantankerous, choleric, crabbed, crabby, cross, crotchety (*inf.*), dyspeptic, edgy, exasperated, fiery, fretful, hasty, hot, ill-humoured, ill-tempered, irascible, out of humour, oversensitive, peevish, petulant, prickly, snappish, snappy, snarling, tense, testy, tetchy, touchy
Antonyms *adj* agreeable, calm, cheerful, complacent, composed, even-tempered, good-natured, imperturbable, patient, unexcitable

irritate *vb* **1** = **annoy,** anger, bother, enrage, exasperate, gall, get one's back up, get one's dander up (*inf.*), get on one's nerves (*inf.*), get under one's skin (*inf.*), harass, incense, inflame, infuriate, nark (*Brit., Austral., & NZ sl.*), needle (*inf.*), nettle, offend, pester, provoke, put one's back up, raise one's hackles, rankle with, rub up the wrong way (*inf.*), ruffle, try one's patience, vex **3** = **rub,** aggravate, chafe, fret, inflame, intensify, pain
Antonyms *vb* ≠ **annoy:** calm, comfort, gratify, mollify, placate, please, soothe

irritated *adj* **1** = **annoyed,** angry, bothered, cross, displeased, exasperated, flustered, harassed, impatient, irritable, nettled, out of humour, peeved (*inf.*), piqued, put out, ruffled, vexed

irritating *adj* **1** = **annoying,** displeasing, disquieting, disturbing, galling, infuriating, irksome, maddening, nagging, pestilential, provoking, thorny, troublesome, trying, upsetting, vexatious, worrisome
Antonyms *adj* agreeable, assuaging, calming, comforting, mollifying, pleasant, pleasing, quieting, soothing

irritation *n* **1** = **nuisance,** annoyance, drag (*inf.*), gall, goad, irritant, pain (*inf.*), pain in the neck (*inf.*), pest, provocation, tease, thorn in one's flesh **2** = **annoyance,** anger, crossness, displeasure, exasperation, ill humour, ill temper, impatience, indignation, irritability, resentment, shortness, snappiness, testiness, vexation, wrath
Antonyms *n* ≠ **annoyance:** calm, composure, ease, pleasure, quietude, satisfaction, serenity, tranquillity

island *n* **1** = **isle,** ait *or* eyot (*dialect*), atoll, cay *or* key, holm (*dialect*), inch (*Scot. & Irish*), islet

island universe *n* a former name for **galaxy.**

isle (aɪl) *n Poetic except when cap. and part of place name.* an island, esp. a small one. [C13: from OF, from L *insula* island]

islet ('aɪlɪt) *n* a small island. [C16: from OF *islette;* see ISLE]

islets *or* **islands of Langerhans** ('læŋəˌhæns) *pl n* small groups of endocrine cells in the pancreas that secrete insulin. [C19: after Paul *Langerhans* (1847–88), G physician]

ism ('ɪzəm) *n Inf., often derog.* an unspecified doctrine, system, or practice.

-ism *suffix forming nouns.* **1** indicating an action, process, or result: *criticism.* **2** indicating a state or condition: *paganism.* **3** indicating a doctrine, system, or body of principles and practices: *Leninism; spiritualism.* **4** indicating behaviour or a characteristic quality: *heroism.* **5** indicating a characteristic usage, esp. of a language: *Scotticism.* **6** indicating prejudice on the basis specified: *sexism; ageism.* [from OF *-isme,* from L *-ismus,* from Gk *-ismos*]

Ismaili *or* **Isma'ili** (ˌɪzmɑː'iːlɪ) *n Islam.* **1** a Shiah sect whose adherents believe that Ismail, son of the sixth imam, was the rightful seventh imam. **2** a member of this sect.

isn't ('ɪzᵊnt) *contraction of* is not.

ISO *abbrev. for:* **1** International Standards Organization. **2** Imperial Service Order (a Brit. decoration).

iso- *or before a vowel* **is-** *combining form.* **1** equal or identical: *isomagnetic.* **2** indicating that a chemical compound is an isomer of a specified compound: *isobutane.* [from Gk *isos* equal]

isobar ('aɪsəʊˌbɑː) *n* **1** a line on a map connecting places of equal atmospheric pressure, usually reduced to sea level for purposes of comparison, at a given time or period. **2** *Physics.* any of two or more atoms that have the same mass number but different atomic numbers. Cf. **isotope.** [C19: from Gk *isobarēs* of equal weight]
▸ˌ**iso'baric** *adj* ▸'**isobarˌism** *n*

isobutene (ˌaɪsəʊ'bjuːtiːn) *n* a colourless gas used in the manufacture of synthetic rubber.

isocheim *or* **isochime** ('aɪsəʊˌkaɪm) *n* a line on a map connecting places with the same mean winter temperature. Cf. **isothere.** [C19: from ISO- + Gk *kheima* winter weather]
▸ˌ**iso'cheimal** *or* ˌ**iso'chimal** *adj*

isochronal (aɪ'sɒkrənᵊl) *or* **isochronous** *adj* **1** having the same duration; equal in time. **2** occurring at equal time intervals; having a uniform period of vibration. [C17: from NL, from Gk *isokhronos,* from ISO- + *khronos* time]
▸**i'sochronally** *or* **i'sochronously** *adv* ▸**i'sochroˌnism** *n*

isoclinal (ˌaɪsəʊ'klaɪnᵊl) *or* **isoclinic** (ˌaɪsəʊ'klɪnɪk) *adj* **1** sloping in the same direction and at the same angle. **2** *Geol.* (of folds) having limbs that are parallel to each other. ◆ *n* **3** Also: **isocline, isoclinal line.** an imaginary line connecting points on the earth's surface having equal angles of magnetic dip.

isocline ('aɪsəʊˌklaɪn) *n* **1** a series of rock strata with isoclinal folds. **2** another name for **isoclinal** (sense 3).

isodynamic (ˌaɪsəʊdaɪ'næmɪk) *adj Physics.* **1** having equal force or strength. **2** of or relating to an imaginary line on the earth's surface connecting points of equal magnetic intensity.

isogeotherm (ˌaɪsəʊ'dʒiːəʊˌθɜːm) *n* an imaginary line below the surface of the earth connecting points of equal temperature.
▸ˌ**isoˌgeo'thermal** *or* ˌ**isoˌgeo'thermic** *adj*

isogloss ('aɪsəʊˌglɒs) *n* a line drawn on a map around the area in which a linguistic feature is to be found.
▸ˌ**iso'glossal** *or* ˌ**iso'glottic** *adj*

isogonic (ˌaɪsəʊ'gɒnɪk) *or* **isogonal** (aɪ'sɒgənᵊl) *adj* **1** *Maths.* having, making, or involving equal angles. ◆ *n* **2** Also called: **isogonic line, isogonal line, isogone.** *Physics.* an imaginary line connecting points on the earth's surface having equal magnetic declination.

isohel ('aɪsəʊˌhɛl) *n* a line on a map connecting places with an equal period of sunshine. [C20: from ISO- + Gk *hēlios* sun]

isohyet (ˌaɪsəʊ'haɪɪt) *n* a line on a map connecting places having equal rainfall. [C19: from ISO- + *-hyet,* from Gk *huetos* rain]

isolate ❶ *vb* ('aɪsəˌleɪt), **isolates, isolating, isolated.** (*tr*) **1** to place apart; cause to be alone. **2** *Med.* to quarantine (a person or animal) having a contagious disease. **3** to obtain (a compound) in an uncombined form. **4** to obtain pure cultures of (bacteria, esp. those causing a particular disease). **5** *Electronics.* to prevent interaction between (circuits, components, etc.); insulate. ◆ *n* ('aɪsəlɪt). **6** an isolated person or group. [C19: back formation from *isolated,* via It. from L *insulātus,* lit.: made into an island]
▸'**isolable** *adj* ▸ˌ**isola'bility** *n* ▸'**isoˌlator** *n* ▸ˌ**iso'lation** *n*

isolationism (ˌaɪsə'leɪʃəˌnɪzəm) *n* **1** a policy of nonparticipation in or withdrawal from international affairs. **2** an attitude favouring such a policy.
▸ˌ**iso'lationist** *n, adj*

isomer ('aɪsəmə) *n* **1** *Chem.* a compound that exhibits isomerism with one or more other compounds. **2** *Physics.* a nuclide that exhibits isomerism with one or more other nuclides.
▸**isomeric** (ˌaɪsə'mɛrɪk) *adj*

isomerism (aɪ'sɒməˌrɪzəm) *n* **1** the existence of two or more compounds having the same molecular formula but a different arrangement of atoms. **2** the existence of two or more nuclides having the same atomic numbers and mass numbers but different energy states.

isomerous (aɪ'sɒmərəs) *adj* (of flowers) having floral whorls with the same number of parts.

isometric (ˌaɪsəʊ'mɛtrɪk) *adj also* **isometrical. 1** having equal dimensions or measurements. **2** *Physiol.* of or relating to muscular contraction that does not produce shortening of the muscle. **3** (of a crystal or system of crystallization) having three mutually perpendicular equal axes. **4** (of a method of projecting a drawing in three dimensions) having the three axes equally inclined and all lines drawn to scale. ◆ *n* **5** Also called: **isometric drawing.** a drawing made in this way. [C19: from Gk *isometria*]
▸ˌ**iso'metrically** *adv*

isometrics (ˌaɪsəʊ'mɛtrɪks) *n* (*functioning as sing*) physical exercise involving isometric contraction of muscles.

isomorphism (ˌaɪsəʊ'mɔːˌfɪzəm) *n* **1** *Biol.* similarity of form, as in different generations of the same life cycle. **2** *Chem.* the existence of two or more substances of different composition in a similar crystalline form. **3** *Maths.* a one-to-one correspondence between the elements of two or more sets, such as those of Arabic and Roman numerals.
▸'**isoˌmorph** *n* ▸ˌ**iso'morphic** *or* ˌ**iso'morphous** *adj*

isopleth ('aɪsəʊˌplɛθ) *n* a line on a map connecting places registering the same amount or ratio of some geographical, etc. phenomenon. [C20: from Gk *isoplēthēs* equal in number, from ISO- + *plēthos* multitude]

isopod ('aɪsəʊˌpɒd) *n* a crustacean, such as the woodlouse, in which the body is flattened.
▸**isopodan** (aɪ'sɒpədən) *or* **i'sopodous** *adj*

isoprene ('aɪsəʊˌpriːn) *n* a colourless volatile liquid with a penetrating odour: used in making synthetic rubbers. Formula: CH_2:C(CH_3)CH:CH_2. Systematic name: **methylbuta-1,3-diene.** [C20: from ISO- + PR(OPYL) + -ENE]

isopteran (aɪ'sɒptərən) *n, pl* **isopterans** *or* **isoptera** (-tərə). **1** any of an order of insects having two pairs of wings equal in size: comprises the termites. ◆ *adj also* **isopterous. 2** of, relating to, or belonging to this order. [C19: from NL, from ISO- + Gk *pteron* wing]

ISO rating *n Photog.* a classification of film speed in which a doubling of the ISO number represents a doubling in sensitivity; for example, ISO 400 film requires half the exposure of ISO 200 under the same conditions. The system uses identical numbers to the obsolete ASA rating. [C20: from *I*nternational *S*tandards *O*rganization]

isosceles (aɪ'sɒsɪˌliːz) *adj* (of a triangle) having two sides of equal length. [C16: from LL, from Gk, from ISO- + *skelos* leg]

isoseismal (ˌaɪsəʊ'saɪzməl) *adj* **1** of or relating to equal intensity of earthquake shock. ◆ *n* **2** a line on a map connecting points at which earthquake shocks are of equal intensity. ◆ Also: **isoseismic.**

isostasy (aɪ'sɒstəsɪ) *n* the state of balance which sections of the earth's lithosphere are thought ultimately to achieve when the vertical forces upon them remain unchanged. If a section is loaded as by ice, it slowly subsides. If a section is reduced in mass, as by erosion, it slowly rises. [C19: ISO- + *-stasy,* from Gk *stasis* a standing]
▸**isostatic** (ˌaɪsəʊ'stætɪk) *adj*

isothere ('aɪsəʊˌθɪə) *n* a line on a map linking places of equal mean summer temperature. Cf. **isocheim.** [C19: from ISO- + Gk *theros* summer]
▸**isotheral** (aɪ'sɒθərəl) *adj*

isotherm ('aɪsəʊˌθɜːm) *n* **1** a line on a map linking places of equal temperature. **2** *Physics.* a curve on a graph that connects points of equal temperature. ◆ Also called: **isothermal, isothermal line.**

isothermal (ˌaɪsəʊ'θɜːməl) *adj* **1** (of a process or change) taking place at constant temperature. **2** of or relating to an isotherm. ◆ *n* **3** another word for **isotherm.**
▸ˌ**iso'thermally** *adv*

isotonic (ˌaɪsəʊ'tɒnɪk) *adj* **1** *Physiol.* (of two or more muscles) having equal tension. **2** (of a drink) designed to replace the fluid and salts lost from the body during strenuous exercise. **3** Also: **isosmotic.** (of two solutions) having the same osmotic pressure, commonly having physiological osmotic pressure. Cf. **hypertonic, hypotonic.**
▸**isotonicity** (ˌaɪsəʊtəʊ'nɪsɪtɪ) *n*

isotope ('aɪsəˌtəʊp) *n* one of two or more atoms with the same atomic number that contain different numbers of neutrons. [C20: from ISO- + Gk *topos* place]
▸**isotopic** (ˌaɪsə'tɒpɪk) *adj* ▸ˌ**iso'topically** *adv* ▸**isotopy** (aɪ'sɒtəpɪ) *n*

isotropic (ˌaɪsəʊ'trɒpɪk) *or* **isotropous** (aɪ'sɒtrəpəs) *adj* **1** having uniform physical properties in all directions. **2** *Biol.* not having predetermined axes: *isotropic eggs.*
▸ˌ**iso'tropically** *adv* ▸**i'sotropy** *n*

ISP *abbrev. for* Internet service provider.

I-spy *n* a game in which one player specifies the initial letter of the name of an object that he can see, which the other players then try to guess.

Israeli (ɪz'reɪlɪ) *n, pl* **Israelis** *or* **Israeli. 1** a citizen or inhabitant of the

THESAURUS

isolate *vb* **1 = separate,** cut off, detach, disconnect, divorce, insulate, quarantine, segregate, sequester, set apart

isolated *adj* **1 = remote,** backwoods, hidden, incommunicado, in the middle of nowhere, lonely, off the beaten track, outlying, out-of-the-way, retired, secluded, solitary, unfrequented

isolation *n* **1 = separation,** aloofness, detachment, disconnection, exile, insularity, insulation, ivory tower, loneliness, quarantine, remoteness, retirement, seclusion, segregation, self-sufficiency, solitude, withdrawal

state of Israel, in SW Asia. ◆ *adj* **2** of or relating to the state of Israel or its inhabitants.

Israelite ('ɪzrɪəˌlaɪt, -rə-) *n* **1** *Bible.* a member of the ethnic group claiming descent from Jacob; a Hebrew. **2** a member of any of various Christian sects who regard themselves as God's chosen people. **3** an archaic word for a **Jew**. [from *Israel*, the ancient kingdom of the Jews, at the SE end of the Mediterranean + -ITE[1]]

issuance ('ɪʃjuəns) *n* the act of issuing.

issue ❶ ('ɪʃjuː) *n* **1** the act of sending or giving out something; supply; delivery. **2** something issued; an edition of stamps, a magazine, etc. **3** the number of identical items, such as banknotes or shares in a company, that become available at a particular time. **4** the act of emerging; outflow; discharge. **5** something flowing out, such as a river. **6** a place of outflow; outlet. **7** the descendants of a person; offspring; progeny. **8** a topic of interest or discussion. **9** an important subject requiring a decision. **10** an outcome or consequence; result. **11** *Pathol.* discharge from a wound. **12** *Law.* the matter remaining in dispute between the parties to an action after the pleadings. **13** the yield from or profits arising out of land or other property. **14 at issue. 14a** under discussion. **14b** in disagreement. **15 force the issue.** to compel decision on some matter. **16 join issue.** to join in controversy. **17 take issue.** to disagree. ◆ *vb* **issues, issuing, issued. 18** to come forth or emerge or cause to come forth or emerge. **19** to publish or deliver (a newspaper, magazine, etc.). **20** (*tr*) to make known or announce. **21** (*intr*) to originate or proceed. **22** (*intr*) to be a consequence; result. **23** (*intr*; foll. by *in*) to end or terminate. **24** (*tr*) (foll. by *with*) to supply officially (with). [C13: from OF *eissue* way out, from *eissir* to go out, from L *exīre*]
▸ **'issuable** *adj* ▸ **'issuer** *n*

issue price *n Stock Exchange.* the price at which a new issue of shares is offered to the public.

-ist *suffix.* **1** (*forming nouns*) a person who performs a certain action or is concerned with something specified: *motorist; soloist.* **2** (*forming nouns*) a person who practises in a specific field: *physicist.* **3** (*forming nouns and adjectives*) a person who advocates a particular doctrine, system, etc., or relating to such a person or the doctrine advocated: *socialist.* **4** (*forming nouns and adjectives*) a person characterized by a specified trait, tendency, etc., or relating to such a person or trait: *purist.* **5** (*forming nouns and adjectives*) a person who is prejudiced on the basis specified: *sexist; ageist.* [via OF from L *-ista, -istēs*, from Gk *-istēs*]

isthmian ('ɪsθmɪən) *adj* relating to or situated in an isthmus.

isthmus ❶ ('ɪsməs) *n, pl* **isthmuses** *or* **isthmi** (-maɪ). **1** a narrow strip of land connecting two relatively large land areas. **2** *Anat.* **2a** a narrow band of tissue connecting two larger parts of a structure. **2b** a narrow passage connecting two cavities. [C16: from L, from Gk *isthmos*]
▸ **'isthmoid** *adj*

-istic *suffix forming adjectives.* equivalent to a combination of **-ist** and **-ic** but in some words having a less specific or literal application and sometimes a mildly pejorative force, as compared with corresponding adjectives ending in **-ist**: *communistic; impressionistic.* [from L *-isticus*, from Gk *istikos*]

istle ('ɪstlɪ) *or* **ixtle** *n* a fibre obtained from various tropical American agave and yucca trees used in making carpets, cord, etc. [C19: from Mexican Sp. *ixtle*, from Amerind *ichtli*]

it (ɪt) *pron* (*subjective or objective*) **1** refers to a nonhuman, animal, plant, or inanimate thing, or sometimes to a small baby: *it looks dangerous; give it a bone.* **2** refers to an unspecified or implied antecedent or to a previous or understood clause, phrase, etc.: *it is impossible; I knew it.* **3** used to represent human life or experience in respect of the present situation: *how's it going? I've had it; to brazen it out.* **4** used as a formal subject (or object), referring to a following clause, phrase, or word: *it helps to know the truth; I consider it dangerous to go on.* **5** used in the nominative as the formal grammatical subject of impersonal verbs: *it is raining; it hurts.* **6** (used as complement with *be*) *Inf.* the crucial or ultimate point: *the steering failed and I thought that was it.* ◆ *n* **7** (in children's games) the player whose turn it is to try to touch another. **8** *Inf.* **8a** sexual intercourse. **8b** sex appeal. **9** *Inf.* a desirable quality or ability: *he's really got it.* [OE *hit*]

IT *abbrev. for* information technology.

It. *abbrev. for:* **1** Italian. **2** Italy.

i.t.a. *or* **ITA** *abbrev. for* initial teaching alphabet, a partly phonetic alphabet used to teach reading.

ital. *abbrev. for* italic.

Ital. *abbrev. for:* **1** Italian. **2** Italy.

Italian (ɪ'tæljən) *n* **1** the official language of Italy and one of the official languages of Switzerland. **2** a native or inhabitant of Italy or a descendant of one. ◆ *adj* **3** relating to, denoting, or characteristic of Italy, its inhabitants, or their language.

Italianate (ɪ'tæljənɪt, -ˌneɪt) *or* **Italianesque** *adj* Italian in style or character.

italic (ɪ'tælɪk) *adj* **1** Also: **Italian.** of, relating to, or denoting a style of handwriting with the letters slanting to the right. **2** of, relating to, or denoting a style of printing type modelled on this, chiefly used to indicate emphasis, a foreign word, etc. Cf. **roman.** ◆ *n* **3** (*often pl*) italic type or print. [C16 (after an edition of Virgil (1501) printed in Venice and dedicated to Italy): from L *Italicus* of Italy, from Gk *Italikos*]

Italic (ɪ'tælɪk) *n* **1** a branch of the Indo-European family of languages that includes many of the ancient languages of Italy. ◆ *adj* **2** denoting, relating to, or belonging to this group of languages, esp. the extinct ones.

italicize *or* **italicise** (ɪ'tælɪˌsaɪz) *vb* **italicizes, italicizing, italicized** *or* **italicises, italicising, italicised. 1** to print (textual matter) in italic type. **2** (*tr*) to underline (words, etc.) with a single line to indicate italics.
▸ **iˌtalici'zation** *or* **iˌtalici'sation** *n*

ITC (in Britain) *abbrev. for* Independent Television Commission.

itch ❶ (ɪtʃ) *n* **1** an irritation or tickling sensation of the skin causing a desire to scratch. **2** a restless desire. **3** any skin disorder, such as scabies, characterized by intense itching. ◆ *vb* (*intr*) **4** to feel or produce an irritating or tickling sensation. **5** to have a restless desire (to do something). **6 have itchy feet.** to be restless; have a desire to travel. **7 itching palm.** a grasping nature; avarice. [OE *gīccean*]
▸ **'itchy** *adj* ▸ **'itchiness** *n*

-ite[1] *suffix forming nouns.* **1** a native or inhabitant of: *Israelite.* **2** a follower or advocate of; a supporter of a group: *Luddite; labourite.* **3** (in biology) indicating a division of a body or organ: *somite.* **4** indicating a mineral or rock: *nephrite; peridotite.* **5** indicating a commercial product: *vulcanite.* [via L *-ita* from Gk *-itēs* or directly from Gk]

-ite[2] *suffix forming nouns.* indicating a salt or ester of an acid having a name ending in *-ous: a nitrite is a salt of nitrous acid.* [from F, arbitrary alteration of -ATE[1]]

item ❶ *n* ('aɪtəm). **1** a thing or unit, esp. included in a list or collection. **2** *Book-keeping.* an entry in an account. **3** a piece of information, detail, or note: *a news item.* **4** *Inf.* two people having a romantic or sexual relationship. ◆ *vb* ('aɪtəm). **5** (*tr*) *Arch.* to itemize. ◆ *adv* ('aɪtɛm). **6** likewise; also. [C14 (adv) from L: in like manner]

itemize ❶ *or* **itemise** ('aɪtəˌmaɪz) *vb* **itemizes, itemizing, itemized** *or* **itemises, itemising, itemised.** (*tr*) to put on a list or make a list of.
▸ **ˌitemi'zation** *or* **ˌitemi'sation** *n* ▸ **'itemˌizer** *or* **'itemˌiser** *n*

iterate ('ɪtəˌreɪt) *vb* **iterates, iterating, iterated.** (*tr*) to say or do again. [C16: from L *iterāre*, from *iterum* again]
▸ **'iterant** *adj* ▸ **ˌiter'ation** *n* ▸ **'iterative** *adj*

itinerancy (ɪ'tɪnərənsɪ, aɪ-) *or* **itineracy** *n* **1** the act of itinerating. **2** *Chiefly Methodist Church.* the system of appointing a minister to a circuit of churches or chapels. **3** itinerants collectively.

itinerant ❶ (ɪ'tɪnərənt, aɪ-) *adj* **1** itinerating. **2** working for a short time in various places, esp. as a casual labourer. ◆ *n* **3** an itinerant worker or other person. [C16: from LL *itinerārī* to travel, from L *iter* a journey]
▸ **i'tinerantly** *adv*

itinerary ❶ (aɪ'tɪnərərɪ, ɪ-) *n, pl* **itineraries. 1** a plan or line of travel; route. **2** a record of a journey. **3** a guidebook for travellers. ◆ *adj* **4** of or relating to travel or routes of travel.

itinerate (aɪ'tɪnəˌreɪt, ɪ-) *vb* **itinerates, itinerating, itinerated.** (*intr*) to travel from place to place.
▸ **iˌtiner'ation** *n*

-itis *suffix forming nouns.* **1** indicating inflammation of a specified part: *tonsillitis.* **2** *Inf.* indicating a preoccupation with or imaginary condition of illness caused by: *computeritis; telephonitis.* [NL, from Gk, fem of *-itēs* belonging to]

it'll ('ɪtᵊl) *contraction of* it will *or* it shall.

ITO *abbrev. for* International Trade Organization.

-itol *suffix forming nouns.* indicating that certain chemical compounds

THESAURUS

issue *n* **1** = **distribution**, circulation, delivery, dispersal, dissemination, granting, issuance, issuing, publication, sending out, supply, supplying **2** = **edition**, copy, impression, instalment, number, printing **7** = **children**, descendants, heirs, offspring, progeny, scions, seed (*chiefly Biblical*) **8, 9** = **topic**, affair, argument, bone of contention, can of worms (*inf.*), concern, controversy, matter, matter of contention, point, point in question, problem, question, subject **10** = **outcome**, conclusion, consequence, culmination, effect, end, end result, finale, pay-off (*inf.*), result, termination, upshot **14 at issue** = **under discussion**, at variance, controversial, in disagreement, in dispute, to be decided, unsettled **17 take issue** = **disagree**, challenge, dispute, object, oppose, raise an objection, take exception ◆ *vb* **18** = **emerge**, arise, be a consequence of, come forth, emanate, flow, originate, proceed, rise, spring, stem **19** = **give out**, circulate, deliver, distribute, emit, promulgate, publish, put in circulation, put out, release **20** = **make known**, announce, broadcast
Antonyms *n* ≠ **distribution:** cancellation, recall ≠ **children:** parent, sire ≠ **outcome:** beginning, cause, inception, start ◆ *vb* ≠ **give out:** revoke, withdraw ≠ **emerge:** cause

isthmus *n* **1** = **strip**, spit

itch *n* **1** = **irritation**, itchiness, prickling, tingling **2** = **desire**, craving, hankering, hunger, longing, lust, passion, restlessness, yearning, yen (*inf.*) ◆ *vb* **4** = **prickle**, crawl, irritate, tickle, tingle **5** = **long**, ache, burn, crave, hanker, hunger, lust, pant, pine, yearn

itching *adj* **5** = **longing**, agog, aquiver, atremble, avid, burning, consumed with curiosity, eager, impatient, inquisitive, mad keen (*inf.*), raring, spoiling for

itchy *adj* **2** = **impatient**, eager, edgy, fidgety, restive, restless, unsettled

item *n* **1** = **detail**, article, aspect, component, consideration, entry, matter, particular, point, thing **3** = **report**, account, article, bulletin, dispatch, feature, note, notice, paragraph, piece

itemize *vb* = **list**, count, detail, document, enumerate, instance, inventory, number, particularize, record, set out, specify

itinerant *adj* **1** = **wandering**, ambulatory, Gypsy, journeying, migratory, nomadic, peripatetic, roaming, roving, travelling, unsettled, vagabond, vagrant, wayfaring
Antonyms *adj* established, fixed, resident, rooted, settled, stable

itinerary *n* **1** = **schedule**, circuit, journey, line, programme, route, timetable, tour **3** = **guidebook**, Baedeker, guide

are alcohols containing two or more hydroxyl groups: *inisitol; sorbitol.* [from -ITE[2] + -OL[1]]

its (ɪts) *determiner* **a** of, belonging to, or associated in some way with it: *its left rear wheel; I can see its logical consequence.* **b** (*as pronoun*): *each town claims its is the best.*

it's (ɪts) *contraction of* it is *or* it has.

itself (ɪt'sɛlf) *pron* **1a** the reflexive form of **it**. **1b** (intensifier)*: even the money itself won't convince me.* **2** (*preceded by a copula*) its normal or usual self: *my cat doesn't seem itself these days.*

itsy-bitsy ('ɪtsɪ'bɪtsɪ) *or* **itty-bitty** ('ɪtɪ'bɪtɪ) *adj Inf.* very small; tiny. [C20: baby talk alteration of *little bit*]

ITU *abbrev. for:* **1** Intensive Therapy Unit. **2** International Telecommunications Union.

ITV (in Britain) *abbrev. for* Independent Television.

-ity *suffix forming nouns.* indicating state or condition: *technicality.* [from OF *-ite*, from L *-itās*]

IU *abbrev. for:* **1** immunizing unit. **2** international unit.

IU(C)D *abbrev. for* intrauterine (contraceptive) device.

-ium *or sometimes* **-um** *suffix forming nouns.* **1** indicating a metallic element: *platinum; barium.* **2** (in chemistry) indicating groups forming positive ions: *ammonium chloride; hydroxonium ion.* **3** indicating a biological structure: *syncytium.* [NL, from L, from Gk *-ion*, dim. suffix]

i.v. *abbrev. for:* **1** initial velocity. **2** Also: **IV**. intravenous(ly).

I've (aɪv) *contraction of* I have.

-ive *suffix.* **1** (*forming adjectives*) indicating a tendency, inclination, character, or quality: *divisive; festive; massive.* **2** (*forming nouns of adjectival origin*): *detective; expletive.* [from L *-īvus*]

IVF *abbrev. for* in vitro fertilization.

ivied ('aɪvɪd) *adj* covered with ivy.

Ivorian (aɪ'vɔːrɪən) *n* **1** a native or inhabitant of the Côte d'Ivoire. ◆ *adj* **2** of or relating to the Côte d'Ivoire or its inhabitants.

ivories ('aɪvərɪz, -vrɪz) *pl n Sl.* **1** the keys of a piano. **2** billiard balls. **3** another word for **teeth.** **4** another word for **dice.**

ivory ('aɪvərɪ, -vrɪ) *n, pl* **ivories. 1a** a hard smooth creamy white variety of dentine that makes up a major part of the tusks of elephants and walruses. **1b** (*as modifier*)*: ivory ornaments.* **2** a tusk made of ivory. **3a** a yellowish-white colour; cream. **3b** (*as adj*)*: ivory shoes.* **4** a substance resembling elephant tusk. **5** an ornament, etc., made of ivory. **6 black ivory.** *Obs.* Black slaves collectively. [C13: from OF, from L *evoreus* made of ivory, from *ebur* ivory]
▸'**ivory-ˌlike** *adj*

ivory black *n* a black pigment obtained by grinding charred scraps of ivory in oil.

ivory nut *n* **1** the seed of the ivory palm, which contains an ivory-like substance used to make buttons, etc. **2** any similar seed from other palms. ◆ Also called: **vegetable ivory.**

ivory tower ❶ ('taʊə) *n* **a** seclusion or remoteness of attitude regarding problems, everyday life, etc. **b** (*as modifier*): *ivory-tower aestheticism.*
▸ˌ**ivory-'towered** *adj*

ivorywood ('aɪvərɪˌwʊd) *n* **1** the yellowish-white wood of an Australian tree, used for engraving, inlaying, and turnery. **2** the tree itself.

IVR *abbrev. for* International Vehicle Registration.

ivy ('aɪvɪ) *n, pl* **ivies. 1** a woody climbing or trailing plant having lobed evergreen leaves and black berry-like fruits. **2** any of various other climbing or creeping plants, such as poison ivy and ground ivy. [OE *īfig*]
▸'**ivy-ˌlike** *adj*

IWW *abbrev. for* Industrial Workers of the World.

ixia ('ɪksɪə) *n* an iridaceous plant of southern Africa, having showy ornamental funnel-shaped flowers. [C18: NL from Gk *ixos* mistletoe]

ixtle ('ɪkstlɪ, 'ɪst-) *n* a variant spelling of **istle.**

izard ('ɪzəd) *n* (esp. in the Pyrenees) another name for **chamois.**

-ize *or* **-ise** *suffix forming verbs.* **1** to cause to become, resemble, or agree with: *legalize.* **2** to become; change into: *crystallize.* **3** to affect in a specified way; subject to: *hypnotize.* **4** to act according to some practice, principle, policy, etc.: *economize.* [from OF *-iser*, from LL *-izāre*, from Gk *-izein*]

USAGE NOTE In Britain and the US *-ize* is the preferred ending for many verbs, but *-ise* is equally acceptable in British English. Certain words (chiefly those not formed by adding the suffix to an existing word) are, however, always spelt with *-ise* in both Britain and the US: *advertise, revise.*

THESAURUS

ivory tower *n* = **seclusion**, cloister, refuge, remoteness, retreat, sanctum, splendid isolation, unreality, world of one's own

ivory-towered *adj* = **withdrawn**, cloistered, far from the madding crowd, remote, retired, sequestered, sheltered

Jj

j *or* **J** (dʒeɪ) *n, pl* **j's, J's,** *or* **Js. 1** the tenth letter of the English alphabet. **2** a speech sound represented by this letter.

j *symbol for:* **1** *Maths.* the unit vector along the *y*-axis. **2** the imaginary number √–1.

J *symbol for:* **1** current density. **2** *Cards.* jack. **3** joule(s).

J. *abbrev. for:* **1** Journal. **2** (*pl* **JJ.**) Judge. **3** (*pl* **JJ.**) Justice.

jab ❶ (dʒæb) *vb* **jabs, jabbing, jabbed. 1** to poke or thrust sharply. **2** to strike with a quick short blow or blows. ◆ *n* **3** a sharp poke or stab. **4** a quick short blow. **5** *Inf.* an injection: *polio jabs.* [C19: orig. Scot. var. of JOB]
▸ **'jabbing** *adj*

jabber ❶ ('dʒæbə) *vb* **1** to speak or say rapidly, incoherently, and without making sense; chatter. ◆ *n* **2** such talk. [C15: imit.]

jabberwocky ('dʒæbə,wɒkɪ) *n* nonsensical writing or speech. [C19: coined by Lewis Carroll as the title of a poem in *Through the Looking Glass* (1871)]

jabiru ('dʒæbɪ,ruː) *n* **1** a large white tropical American stork with a dark naked head and a dark bill. **2** Also called: **black-necked stork, policeman bird.** a large Australian stork, having a white plumage, dark green back and tail, and red legs. **3** another name for **saddlebill.** [C18: via Port., of Amerind origin]

jabot ('ʒæbəʊ) *n* a frill or ruffle on the breast or throat of a garment. [C19: from F: bird's crop, jabot]

jaçana (,ʒɑːsə'nɑː, ,dʒæ-) *n* a bird of tropical and subtropical marshy regions, having long legs and very long toes that enable walking on floating plants. [C18: from Port., of Amerind origin, from *jasaná*]

jacaranda (,dʒækə'rændə) *n* **1** a tropical American tree having fernlike leaves and pale purple flowers and widely cultivated in temperate areas of Australia. **2** the fragrant ornamental wood of this tree. **3** any of several related or similar trees or their wood. [C18: from Port., of Amerind origin, from *yacarandá*]

jacaré ('dʒækə,reɪ) *n* another name for **cayman.** [C18: from Port., of Amerind origin]

jacinth ('dʒæsɪnθ) *n* another name for **hyacinth** (sense 4). [C13: from Med. L *jacinthus,* from L *hyacinthus* plant, precious stone; see HYACINTH]

jack (dʒæk) *n* **1** a man or fellow. **2** a sailor. **3** the male of certain animals, esp. of the ass or donkey. **4** a mechanical or hydraulic device for exerting a large force, esp. to raise a heavy weight such as a motor vehicle. **5** any of several mechanical devices that replace manpower, such as a contrivance for rotating meat on a spit. **6** one of four playing cards in a pack, one for each suit; knave. **7** *Bowls.* a small usually white bowl at which the players aim with their own bowls. **8** *Electrical engineering.* a female socket with two or more terminals designed to receive a male plug (**jack plug**) that either makes or breaks the circuit or circuits. **9** a flag, esp. a small flag flown at the bow of a ship indicating the ship's nationality. **10** a part of the action of a harpsichord, consisting of a fork-shaped device on the end of a pivoted lever on which a plectrum is mounted. **11a** any of various tropical and subtropical fishes. **11b** an immature pike. **12** Also called: **jackstone.** one of the pieces used in the game of jacks. **13** *US.* a slang word for **money. 14 every man jack.** everyone without exception. **15 the jack.** *Austral. sl.* syphilis. ◆ *adj* **16** *Austral. sl.* tired or fed up (esp. in **be jack of something**). ◆ *vb* **17** (*tr*) to lift or push (an object) with a jack. ◆ See also **jack in, jack up.** [C16 *jakke,* var. of *Jankin,* dim. of *John*]

Jack (dʒæk) *n* **I'm all right, Jack.** *Brit. inf.* a remark indicating smug and complacent selfishness.

jackal ('dʒækɔːl) *n* **1** any of several African or S Asian mammals closely related to the dog, having long legs and pointed ears and muzzle: they are predators and carrion-eaters. **2** a person who does menial tasks for another. [C17: from Turkish, from Persian, from Sansk. *srgāla*]

jackanapes ('dʒækə,neɪps) *n* (*functioning as sing*) **1** a conceited impertinent person. **2** a mischievous child. **3** *Arch.* a monkey. [C16: var. of *Jakken-apes,* lit.: Jack of the ape, nickname of William de la Pole (1396–1450), first Duke of Suffolk, whose badge showed an ape's ball and chain]

jackass ❶ ('dʒæk,æs) *n* **1** a male donkey. **2** a fool. [C18: from JACK (male) + ASS[1]]

jackboot ('dʒæk,buːt) *n* **1** an all-leather military boot, extending up to or above the knee. **2** authoritarian rule or behaviour.
▸ **'jack,booted** *adj*

jackdaw ('dʒæk,dɔː) *n* a large Eurasian bird, related to the crow, having a black and dark grey plumage: noted for its thieving habits. [C16: from JACK + *daw,* obs. name for jackdaw]

jackeroo *or* **jackaroo** (,dʒækə'ruː) *n, pl* **jackeroos** *or* **jackaroos.** *Austral. inf.* a novice on a sheep or cattle station. [C19: from JACK + (KANG)AROO]

jacket ❶ ('dʒækɪt) *n* **1** a short coat, esp. one that is hip-length and has a front opening and sleeves. **2** something that resembles this: *a life jacket.* **3** any exterior covering or casing, such as the insulating cover of a boiler. **4** See **dust jacket. 5a** the skin of a baked potato. **5b** (*as modifier*): *jacket potatoes.* **6** *Oil industry.* the support structure, esp. the legs, of an oil platform. ◆ *vb* **7** (*tr*) to put a jacket on (someone or something). [C15: from OF *jaquet* short jacket, from *jacque* peasant, from *Jacques* James]
▸ **'jacketed** *adj*

Jack Frost *n* a personification of frost.

Jackie *or* **Jacky** ('dʒækɪ) *n, pl* **Jackies.** *Austral. offens. sl.* **1** a native Australian. **2** native Australians collectively. **3 sit up like Jackie.** to sit bolt upright, esp. cheekily.

jack in *vb* (*tr, adv*) *Sl.* to abandon or leave (an attempt or enterprise).

jack-in-office *n* a self-important petty official.

jack-in-the-box *n, pl* **jack-in-the-boxes** *or* **jacks-in-the-box.** a toy consisting of a figure on a compressed spring in a box, which springs out when the lid is opened.

Jack Ketch (kɛtʃ) *n Brit. arch.* a hangman. [C18: after *John Ketch* (died 1686), public executioner in England]

jackknife ('dʒæk,naɪf) *n, pl* **jackknives. 1** a knife with the blade pivoted to fold into a recess in the handle. **2** a former name for a type of dive in which the diver bends at the waist in midair; forward pike dive. ◆ *vb* **jackknifes, jackknifing, jackknifed.** (*intr*) **3** (of an articulated lorry) to go out of control in such a way that the trailer swings round at an angle to the tractor.

jack of all trades *n, pl* **jacks of all trades.** a person who undertakes many different kinds of work.

jack-o'-lantern *n* **1** a lantern made from a hollowed pumpkin, which has holes cut in it to represent a human face. **2** a will-o'-the-wisp.

jack plane *n* a carpenter's plane, usually with a wooden body, used for rough planing of timber.

jack plug *n* See **jack** (sense 8).

jackpot ❶ ('dʒæk,pɒt) *n* **1** any large prize, kitty, or accumulated stake that may be won in gambling. **2 hit the jackpot. 2a** to win a jackpot. **2b** *Inf.* to achieve great success, esp. through luck. [C20: prob. from JACK (playing card) + POT[1]]

jack rabbit *n* any of various W North American hares having long hind legs and large ears. [C19: shortened from *jackass-rabbit,* referring to its long ears]

Jack Robinson ('rɒbɪnsən) *n* **before you could** (*or* **can**) **say Jack Robinson.** extremely quickly or suddenly.

Jack Russell ('rʌsᵊl) *n* a small short-legged terrier having a white coat with tan, black, or lemon markings. [after John *Russell* (1795-1883), E clergyman who developed the breed]

jacks (dʒæks) *n* (*functioning as sing*) a game in which bone, metal, or plastic pieces (**jackstones**) are thrown and then picked up between bounces of a small ball or throws of another piece (the **jack**). [C19: shortened from *jackstones,* var. of *checkstones* pebbles]

jacksie *or* **jacksy** ('dʒæksɪ) *n, pl* **jacksies.** *Brit. sl.* the buttocks or anus. Also: **jaxie, jaxy.** [C19: ? from JACK]

jacksnipe ('dʒæk,snaɪp) *n, pl* **jacksnipe** *or* **jacksnipes.** a small Eurasian short-billed snipe.

jackstraws ('dʒæk,strɔːz) *n* (*functioning as sing*) another name for **spillikins.**

Jack Tar *n Now chiefly literary.* a sailor.

jack up ❶ *vb* (*adv*) **1** (*tr*) to increase (prices, salaries, etc.). **2** (*tr*) to raise an object, such as a car, with or as with a jack. **3** (*intr*) *Sl.* to inject oneself with a drug. **4** (*intr*) *Austral. inf.* to refuse to comply.

Jacobean (,dʒækə'bɪən) *adj* **1** *History.* relating to James I of England or to the period of his rule (1603–25). **2** of or relating to the style of furniture current at this time, characterized by the use of dark brown carved oak. **3** relating to or having the style of architecture used in England during this period. [C18: from NL, from *Jacōbus* James]

Jacobin ('dʒækəbɪn) *n* **1** a member of the most radical club founded during the French Revolution, which instituted the Reign of Terror. **2** an extreme political radical. **3** a French Dominican friar. ◆ *adj* **4** of or relating to the Jacobins or their policies. [C14: from OF, from Med. L

THESAURUS

jab *vb, n* **1, 3 = poke,** dig, lunge, nudge, prod, punch, stab, tap, thrust

jabber *vb* **1 = chatter,** babble, blather, blether, drivel, gabble, mumble, prate, rabbit (on) (*Brit. inf.*), ramble, run off at the mouth (*sl.*), tattle, waffle (*inf., chiefly Brit.*), yap (*inf.*)

jackass *n* **2 = fool,** blockhead, chump, coot, dolt, dork (*sl.*), idiot, imbecile, jerk (*sl., chiefly US & Canad.*), lamebrain (*inf.*), nerd *or* nurd (*sl.*), nincompoop, ninny, nitwit (*inf.*), numbskull *or* numskull, oaf (*sl.*), schmuck (*US sl.*), simpleton, twit (*inf., chiefly Brit.*), wally (*sl.*)

jacket *n* **3, 4 = covering,** case, casing, coat, envelope, folder, sheath, skin, wrapper, wrapping

jackpot *n* **1 = prize,** award, bonanza, kitty, pool, pot, pot of gold at the end of the rainbow, reward, winnings

jack up *vb* **1 = increase,** accelerate, augment, boost, escalate, inflate, put up, raise **2 = lift,** elevate, heave, hoist, lift up, raise, rear

Jacōbīnus, from LL *Jacōbus* James; the political club orig. met in the convent near the church of *St Jacques* in 1789]
▸ˌ**Jacoˈbinic** *or* ˌ**Jacoˈbinical** *adj* ▸ˈ**Jacobinism** *n*

Jacobite (ˈdʒækəˌbaɪt) *n Brit. history.* an adherent of James II after his overthrow in 1688, or of his descendants in their attempts to regain the throne. [C17: from LL *Jacōbus* James + -ITE[1]]
▸**Jacobitic** (ˌdʒækəˈbɪtɪk) *adj*

Jacob's ladder *n* **1** *Old Testament.* the ladder reaching up to heaven that Jacob saw in a dream (Genesis 28:12–17). **2** a ladder made of wooden or metal steps supported by ropes or chains. **3** a North American plant with blue flowers and a ladder-like arrangement of leaves.

Jacob's staff *n* a medieval instrument for measuring heights and distances.

jaconet (ˈdʒækənɪt) *n* a light cotton fabric used for clothing, etc. [C18: from Urdu *jagannāthī*, from *Jagannāthpūrī*, India, where orig. made]

Jacquard (ˈdʒækɑːd, dʒəˈkɑːd) *n* **1** Also called: **Jacquard weave.** a fabric in which the design is incorporated into the weave. **2** Also called: **Jacquard loom.** the loom that produces this fabric. [C19: after Joseph M. *Jacquard* (1752–1834), F inventor]

jactation (dʒækˈteɪʃən) *n* **1** *Rare.* the act of boasting. **2** *Pathol.* another word for **jactitation.** [C16: from L *jactātiō* bragging, from *jactāre* to flourish, from *jacere* to throw]

jactitation (ˌdʒæktɪˈteɪʃən) *n* **1** the act of boasting. **2** a false assertion that one is married to another, formerly actionable at law. **3** *Pathol.* restless tossing in bed, characteristic of severe fevers. [C17: from Med. L, from L *jacitāre* to utter publicly, from *jactitāre* to toss about; see JACTATION]

Jacuzzi (dʒəˈkuːzɪ) *n Trademark.* **1** a device which swirls water in a bath. **2** a bath containing such a device. [C20: from *Candido* and *Roy Jacuzzi*, who developed and marketed it]

jade[1] (dʒeɪd) *n* **1** a semiprecious stone which varies in colour from white to green and is used for making ornaments and jewellery. **2a** the green colour of jade. **2b** (*as adj*): *a jade skirt.* [C18: from F, from It. *giada*, from obs. Sp. *piedra de ijada* colic stone (lit.: stone of the flank, because it was believed to cure renal colic)]

jade[2] Ⓣ (dʒeɪd) *n* **1** an old overworked horse. **2** *Derog., facetious.* a woman considered to be disreputable. ◆ *vb* **jades, jading, jaded. 3** to exhaust or make exhausted from work or use. [C14: from ?]
▸ˈ**jadish** *adj*

jaded Ⓣ (ˈdʒeɪdɪd) *adj* **1** exhausted or dissipated. **2** satiated.
▸ˈ**jadedly** *adv* ▸ˈ**jadedness** *n*

jadeite (ˈdʒeɪdaɪt) *n* a green or white mineral, a variety of jade, consisting of sodium aluminium silicate in monoclinic crystalline form.

j'adoube *French.* (ʒadub) *interj Chess.* an expression of an intention to touch a piece in order to adjust its placement rather than to make a move. [lit.: I adjust]

Jaffa (ˈdʒæfə, ˈdʒɑː-) *n* a large variety of orange, grown esp. in Israel, having a thick skin. [after *Jaffa*, port in W Israel (now part of Tel Aviv) where orig. cultivated]

jag[1] Ⓣ (dʒæg) *vb* **jags, jagging, jagged. 1** (*tr*) to cut unevenly. **2** *Austral.* to catch (fish) by impaling them on an unbaited hook. ◆ *n* **3** *Scot.* an informal word for **jab** (senses 3, 5). **4** a jagged notch or projection. [C14: from ?]

jag[2] Ⓣ (dʒæg) *n Sl.* **1a** intoxication from drugs or alcohol. **1b** a bout of drinking or drug taking. **2** a period of uncontrolled activity: *a crying jag.* [of unknown origin]

jagged Ⓣ (ˈdʒægɪd) *adj* having sharp projecting notches.
▸ˈ**jaggedly** *adv*

jaggy (ˈdʒægɪ) *adj* **jaggier, jaggiest. 1** a less common word for **jagged. 2** *Scot.* prickly.

jaguar (ˈdʒægjuə) *n* a large feline mammal of S North America, Central America, and N South America, similar to the leopard but with larger spots on its coat. [C17: from Port., from Guarani *yaguara*]

jai alai (ˈhaɪ ˈlaɪ, ˈhaɪ əˌlaɪ) *n* a version of pelota played by two or four players. [via Sp. from Basque, from *jai* game + *alai* merry]

jail Ⓣ *or* **gaol** (dʒeɪl) *n* **1** a place for the confinement of persons convicted and sentenced to imprisonment or of persons awaiting trial. ◆ *vb* **2** (*tr*) to confine in prison. [C13: from OF *jaiole* cage, from Vulgar L *caveola* (unattested), from L *cavea* enclosure]

jailbird Ⓣ *or* **gaolbird** (ˈdʒeɪlˌbɜːd) *n* a person who is or has been confined to jail, esp. repeatedly; convict.

jailbreak *or* **gaolbreak** (ˈdʒeɪlˌbreɪk) *n* an escape from jail.

jailer Ⓣ**, jailor,** *or* **gaoler** (ˈdʒeɪlə) *n* a person in charge of prisoners in a jail.

Jain (dʒaɪn) *or* **Jaina** (ˈdʒaɪnə) *n* **1** an adherent of Jainism. ◆ *adj* **2** of or relating to Jainism. [C19: from Hindi *jaina* saint, lit.: overcomer, from Sansk.]

Jainism (ˈdʒaɪˌnɪzəm) *n* an ancient Hindu religion, characterized by the belief that the material world is progressing endlessly in a series of cycles.
▸ˈ**Jainist** *n, adj*

jake (dʒeɪk) *adj Austral. & NZ sl.* all right; fine: *she's jake.* [from ?]

jalap *or* **jalop** (ˈdʒæləp) *n* **1** a Mexican climbing plant. **2** the dried and powdered root of any of these plants, used as a purgative. [C17: from F, from Mexican Sp. *jalapa*]
▸**jalapic** (dʒəˈlæpɪk) *adj*

jalapeño (dʒæləˈpiːnəʊ; *Spanish* xalaˈpeɲo) *n, pl* **jalapeñoños.** a type of red capsicum with a hot taste used in Mexican cookery. [Mexican Sp.]

jalopy *or* **jaloppy** (dʒəˈlɒpɪ) *n, pl* **jalopies** *or* **jaloppies.** *Inf.* a dilapidated old car. [C20: from ?]

jalousie (ˈʒæluˌziː) *n* **1** a window blind or shutter constructed from angled slats of wood, etc. **2** a window made of angled slats of glass. [C19: from OF *gelosie* latticework screen]

jam[1] Ⓣ (dʒæm) *vb* **jams, jamming, jammed. 1** (*tr*) to cram or wedge into or against something: *to jam paper into an incinerator.* **2** (*tr*) to crowd or pack: *cars jammed the roads.* **3** to make or become stuck or locked. **4** (*tr;* often foll. by *on*) to activate suddenly (esp. in **jam on the brakes**). **5** (*tr*) to block; congest. **6** (*tr*) to crush or squeeze. **7** *Radio.* to prevent the clear reception of (radio communications) by transmitting other signals on the same frequency. **8** (*intr*) *Sl.* to play in a jam session. ◆ *n* **9** a crowd or congestion in a confined space: *a traffic jam.* **10** the act of jamming or the state of being jammed. **11** *Inf.* a predicament: *to help a friend out of a jam.* **12** See **jam session.** [C18: prob. imit.]
▸ˈ**jammer** *n*

jam[2] (dʒæm) *n* **1** a preserve containing fruit, which has been boiled with sugar until the mixture sets. **2** *Sl.* something desirable: *you want jam on it.* [C18: ?from JAM[1] (the act of squeezing)]

Jam. *Bible. abbrev. for* James.

Jamaican (dʒəˈmeɪkən) *adj* **1** of Jamaica, an island in the West Indies in the Caribbean Sea. ◆ *n* **2** a native or inhabitant of Jamaica or a descendant of one.

jamb *or* **jambe** (dʒæm) *n* a vertical side member of a doorframe, window frame, or lining. [C14: from OF *jambe* leg, jamb, from LL *gamba* hoof, from Gk *kampē* joint]

jamboree Ⓣ (ˌdʒæmbəˈriː) *n* **1** a large and often international gathering of Scouts. **2** a party or celebration. [C19: from ?]

jammy Ⓣ (ˈdʒæmɪ) *adj* **jammier, jammiest.** *Brit. sl.* **1** pleasant; desirable. **2** lucky.

jam-packed *adj* packed or filled to capacity.

jam session *n Sl.* an unrehearsed or improvised performance by jazz or rock musicians. [C20: prob. from JAM[1]]

Jan. *abbrev. for* January.

Jandal (ˈdʒændᵊl) *n NZ trademark.* a kind of sandal with a strip of material between the big toe and the other toes and over the foot.

jangle Ⓣ (ˈdʒæŋgᵊl) *vb* **jangles, jangling, jangled. 1** to sound or cause to sound discordantly, harshly, or unpleasantly. **2** (*tr*) to produce a jarring effect on: *the accident jangled his nerves.* **3** *Arch.* to wrangle. ◆ *n* **4** a harsh unpleasant ringing noise. **5** an argument or quarrel. [C13: from OF *jangler*, of Gmc origin]
▸ˈ**jangler** *n*

janissary (ˈdʒænɪsərɪ) *or* **janizary** (ˈdʒænɪzərɪ) *n, pl* **janissaries** *or* **janizaries.** an infantryman in the Turkish army, originally a member of the sovereign's guard, from the 14th to the 19th century. [C16: from F, from It., from Turkish *yeniçeri*, from *yeni* new + *çeri* soldiery]

janitor Ⓣ (ˈdʒænɪtə) *n* **1** *Scot., US, & Canad.* the caretaker of a building, esp. a school. **2** *Chiefly US & Canad.* a person employed to clean and maintain a building. [C17: L: doorkeeper, from *jānua* door, from *jānus* covered way]
▸**janitorial** (ˌdʒænɪˈtɔːrɪəl) *adj*

THESAURUS

jade[2] *n* **2** *Derogatory, facetious* = **slut**, harridan, hussy, nag, shrew, slattern, trollop, vixen, wench

jaded *adj* **1** = **tired**, clapped out (*Austral. & NZ inf.*), exhausted, fagged (out) (*inf.*), fatigued, spent, tired-out, weary, zonked (*sl.*) **2** = **bored**, cloyed, dulled, glutted, gorged, sated, satiated, surfeited, tired
Antonyms *adj* ≠ **tired:** bright-eyed and bushy-tailed (*inf.*), fresh, refreshed ≠ **bored:** eager, enthusiastic, keen, life-loving, naive

jag[1] *n* **4** = **notch**, point, projection, protuberance, snag, spur, tooth

jag[2] *n* **1b** = **spree**, binge, bout, carousal, carouse, fit, orgy, period, spell

jagged *adj* = **uneven**, barbed, broken, cleft, craggy, denticulate, indented, notched, pointed, ragged, ridged, rough, serrated, snaggy, spiked, toothed
Antonyms *adj* glassy, level, regular, rounded, smooth

jail *n* **1** = **prison**, borstal, brig (*chiefly US*), calaboose (*US inf.*), can (*sl.*), clink (*sl.*), cooler (*sl.*), inside (*sl.*), jailhouse (*Southern US*), jug, lockup, nick (*Brit. sl.*), penitentiary (*US*), poky *or* pokey (*US & Canad. sl.*), quod (*sl.*), reformatory, slammer (*sl.*), stir (*sl.*) ◆ *vb* **2** = **imprison**, confine, detain, immure, impound, incarcerate, lock up, send down

jailbird *n* = **prisoner**, con (*sl.*), convict, felon, lag, malefactor, trusty

jailer *n* = **guard**, captor, keeper, screw (*sl.*), turnkey (*arch.*), warden, warder

jam[1] *vb* **1** = **pack**, cram, force, press, ram, squeeze, stuff, wedge **2** = **crowd**, crush, throng **5** = **congest**, block, cease, clog, halt, obstruct, stall, stick ◆ *n* **9** = **crush**, crowd, horde, mass, mob, multitude, pack, press, swarm, throng **11** *Informal* = **predicament**, bind, deep water, dilemma, fix (*inf.*), hole (*sl.*), hot water, pickle (*inf.*), plight, quandary, scrape (*inf.*), spot (*inf.*), strait, tight spot, trouble

jamboree *n* **2** = **festival**, beano (*Brit. sl.*), blast (*US sl.*), carnival, carousal, carouse, celebration, festivity, fête, frolic, hooley *or* hoolie (*chiefly Irish & NZ*), jubilee, merriment, party, rave (*Brit. sl.*), rave-up (*Brit. sl.*), revelry, spree

jammy *adj* **2** *Brit. slang* = **lucky**, favoured, fortunate

jangle *vb* **1** = **rattle**, chime, clank, clash, clatter, jingle, vibrate ◆ *n* **4** = **clash**, cacophony, clang, clangour, din, dissonance, jar, racket, rattle, reverberation
Antonyms *n* ≠ **clash:** harmoniousness, mellifluousness, quiet, silence

janitor *n* **1** = **caretaker**, concierge, custodian, doorkeeper, porter

Jansenism ('dʒænsəˌnɪzəm) *n RC Church.* the doctrine of Cornelis Jansen and his disciples, who believed in predestination and denied free will.
▸'**Jansenist** *n, adj* ▸ˌ**Jansen'istic** *adj*

jansky ('dʒænskɪ) *n, pl* **janskys.** (in radio astronomy) a unit used to measure the intensity of radio waves. Also called: **flux unit.** [C20: after Karl G. *Jansky* (1905–50), US electrical engineer]

January ('dʒænjʊərɪ) *n, pl* **Januaries.** the first month of the year, consisting of 31 days. [C14: from L *Jānuārius*]

japan (dʒə'pæn) *n* **1** a glossy black lacquer originally from the Orient, used on wood, metal, etc. **2** work decorated and varnished in the Japanese manner. ◆ *vb* **japans, japanning, japanned. 3** (*tr*) to lacquer with japan or any similar varnish.

Japanese (ˌdʒæpə'ni:z) *adj* **1** of or characteristic of Japan, its people, or their language. ◆ *n* **2** (*pl* **Japanese**) a native or inhabitant of Japan. **3** the official language of Japan.

Japanese stranglehold *n* a wrestling hold in which an opponent's arms exert pressure on his own windpipe.

jape (dʒeɪp) *n* **1** a jest or joke. ◆ *vb* **japes, japing, japed. 2** to joke or jest (about). [C14: ?from OF *japper* to yap, imit.]
▸'**japer** *n* ▸'**japery** *n*

Japlish ('dʒæplɪʃ) *n* the adoption and adaptation of English words into the Japanese language. [C20: from a blend of JAPANESE + ENGLISH]

japonica (dʒə'pɒnɪkə) *n* **1** Also called: **Japanese quince.** a Japanese shrub cultivated for its red flowers and yellowish fruit. **2** another name for the **camellia.** [C19: from NL, fem of *japonicus* Japanese, from *Japonia* Japan]

jar[1] ❶ (dʒɑ:) *n* **1** a wide-mouthed container that is usually cylindrical, made of glass or earthenware, and without handles. **2** Also: **jarful.** the contents or quantity contained in a jar. **3** *Brit. inf.* a glass of beer. [C16: from OF *jarre, jarra,* from Ar. *jarrah* large earthen vessel]

jar[2] ❶ (dʒɑ:) *vb* **jars, jarring, jarred. 1** to vibrate or cause to vibrate. **2** to make or cause to make a harsh discordant sound. **3** (often foll. by *on*) to have a disturbing or painful effect (on the nerves, mind, etc.). **4** (*intr*) to disagree; clash. ◆ *n* **5** a jolt or shock. **6** a harsh discordant sound. [C16: prob. imit.]
▸'**jarring** *adj* ▸'**jarringly** *adv*

jar[3] (dʒɑ:) *n* **on a** (*or* **the**) **jar.** (of a door) slightly open; ajar. [C17 (in the sense: turn): from earlier *char,* from OE *cierran* to turn]

jardinière (ˌʒɑ:dɪ'njɛə) *n* **1** an ornamental pot or trough for plants. **2** a garnish of fresh vegetables for a dish of meat. [C19: from F, fem of *jardinier* gardener, from *jardin* GARDEN]

jargon ❶ ('dʒɑ:gən) *n* **1** specialized language concerned with a particular subject, culture, or profession. **2** language characterized by pretentious vocabulary or meaning. **3** gibberish. [C14: from OF, ? imit.]

jarl (jɑ:l) *n Medieval history.* a Scandinavian chieftain or noble. [C19: from ON]
▸'**jarldom** *n*

jarrah ('dʒærə) *n* an Australian eucalyptus tree that yields a valuable timber. [from Abor.]

jasmine ('dʒæsmɪn, 'dʒæz-) *n* **1** Also called: **jessamine.** any tropical or subtropical oleaceous shrub or climbing plant widely cultivated for their white, yellow, or red fragrant flowers. **2** any of several other shrubs with fragrant flowers, such as the Cape jasmine, yellow jasmine, and frangipani (**red jasmine**). [C16: from OF *jasmin,* from Ar., from Persian *yāsmīn*]

jaspé ('dʒæspeɪ) *adj* resembling jasper; variegated. [C19: from F, from *jasper* to marble]

jasper ('dʒæspə) *n* **1** an opaque impure form of quartz, red, yellow, brown, or dark green in colour, used as a gemstone and for ornamental decoration. **2** Also called: **jasper ware.** a dense hard stoneware. [C14: from OF *jaspe,* from L *jaspis,* from Gk *iaspis,* of Semitic origin]

jato ('dʒeɪtəʊ) *n, pl* **jatos.** *Aeronautics.* jet-assisted takeoff. [C20: from *j(et-)a(ssisted) t(ake)o(ff)*]

jaundice ('dʒɔ:ndɪs) *n* **1** Also called: **icterus.** yellowing of the skin due to the abnormal presence of bile pigments in the blood, as in hepatitis. **2** jealousy, envy, and ill humour. ◆ *vb* **jaundices, jaundicing, jaundiced. 3** to distort (the judgment, etc.) adversely: *jealousy had jaundiced his mind.* **4** (*tr*) to affect with or as if with jaundice. [C14: from OF *jaunisse,* from *jaune* yellow, from L *galbinus* yellowish]

jaunt ❶ (dʒɔ:nt) *n* **1** a short pleasurable excursion; outing. ◆ *vb* **2** (*intr*) to go on such an excursion. [C16: from ?]

jaunting car *n* a light two-wheeled one-horse car, formerly widely used in Ireland.

jaunty ❶ ('dʒɔ:ntɪ) *adj* **jauntier, jauntiest. 1** sprightly and cheerful: *a jaunty step.* **2** smart; trim: *a jaunty hat.* [C17: from F *gentil* noble; see GENTEEL]
▸'**jauntily** *adv* ▸'**jauntiness** *n*

Java ('dʒɑ:və) *n Trademark.* a programming language especially applicable to the World Wide Web. [C20: named after *Java* coffee, said to have been consumed in large quantities by the language's creators]

Java man ('dʒɑ:və) *n* a type of primitive man, *Homo erectus,* that lived in the middle Palaeolithic Age in Java.

Javanese (ˌdʒɑ:və'ni:z) *adj* **1** of or relating to the island of Java, in Indonesia. ◆ *n* **2** (*pl* **Javanese**) a native or inhabitant of Java. **3** the Malayo-Polynesian language of Java.

javelin ('dʒævlɪn) *n* **1** a long pointed spear thrown as a weapon or in competitive field events. **2 the javelin.** the event or sport of throwing the javelin. [C16: from OF *javeline,* var. of *javelot,* of Celtic origin]

jaw ❶ (dʒɔ:) *n* **1** the part of the skull of a vertebrate that frames the mouth and holds the teeth. **2** the corresponding part of an invertebrate, esp. an insect. **3** a pair or either of a pair of hinged or sliding components of a machine or tool designed to grip an object. **4** *Sl.* **4a** impudent talk. **4b** idle conversation. **4c** a lecture. ◆ *vb* **5** (*intr*) *Sl.* **5a** to chat; gossip. **5b** to lecture. [C14: prob. from OF *joue* cheek]

jawbone ('dʒɔ:ˌbəʊn) *n* a nontechnical name for **mandible** or (less commonly) **maxilla.**

jawbreaker ('dʒɔ:ˌbreɪkə) *n* **1** a device having hinged jaws for crushing rocks and ores. **2** *Inf.* a word that is hard to pronounce.
▸'**jawˌbreaking** *adj*

jaws ❶ (dʒɔ:z) *pl n* **1** the narrow opening of some confined place such as a gorge. **2 the jaws.** a dangerously close position: *the jaws of death.*

jay (dʒeɪ) *n* **1** a passerine bird related to the crow having a pinkish-brown body, blue-and-black wings, and a black-and-white crest. **2** a foolish or gullible person. [C13: from OF *jai,* from LL *gāius,* ?from name *Gāius*]

Jaycee ('dʒeɪ'si:) *n US, Canad., Austral., & NZ.* a young person who belongs to a junior chamber of commerce. [C20: from *J(unior) C(hamber)*]

jaywalk ('dʒeɪˌwɔ:k) *vb* (*intr*) to cross or walk in a street recklessly or illegally. [C20: from JAY (sense 2)]
▸'**jayˌwalker** *n* ▸'**jayˌwalking** *n*

jazz (dʒæz) *n* **1a** music of US Black origin, characterized by syncopated rhythms, solo and group improvisation, and a variety of harmonic idioms and instrumental techniques. **1b** (*as modifier*): *a jazz band.* **1c** (*in combination*): *a jazzman.* **2** *Sl.* rigmarole: *legal papers and all that jazz.* ◆ *vb* **3** (*intr*) to play or dance to jazz music. [C20: from ?]
▸'**jazzy** *adj* ▸'**jazzily** *adv* ▸'**jazziness** *n*

jazz up ❶ *vb* (*tr, adv*) *Inf.* **1** to imbue (a piece of music) with jazz qualities, esp. by playing at a quicker tempo. **2** to make more lively or appealing.

JCB *n Trademark.* a type of construction machine with a hydraulically operated shovel on the front and an excavator arm on the back. [from the initials of *J*(oseph) *C*(yril) *B*(amford) (born 1916), its Brit. manufacturer]

jealous ❶ ('dʒɛləs) *adj* **1** suspicious or fearful of being displaced by a rival. **2** (often *postpositive* and foll. by *of*) resentful (of) or vindictive (towards). **3** (often *postpositive* and foll. by *of*) possessive and watchful in the protection (of): *jealous of one's reputation.* **4** characterized by or resulting from jealousy. **5** *Obsolete except in Biblical use.* demanding exclusive loyalty: *a jealous God.* [C13: from OF *gelos,* from Med. L, from LL *zēlus* emulation, from Gk *zēlos* ZEAL]
▸'**jealously** *adv*

jealousy ❶ ('dʒɛləsɪ) *n, pl* **jealousies.** the state or quality of being jealous.

jean (dʒi:n) *n* a tough twill-weave cotton fabric used for hard-wearing trousers, overalls, etc. [C16: short for *jean fustian,* from *Gene* Genoa]

Jean Baptiste (*French* ʒɑ̃bɑtist) *n Canad. sl.* a French Canadian. [F: John the Baptist, traditional patron saint of French Canada]

jeans ❶ (dʒi:nz) *pl n* trousers for casual wear, made esp. of denim or corduroy. [pl. of JEAN]

THESAURUS

jar[1] *n* **1** = **pot**, amphora, carafe, container, crock, flagon, jug, pitcher, receptacle, urn, vase, vessel

jar[2] *vb* **1** = **jolt**, agitate, bump, convulse, disturb, grate, rasp, rattle, rock, shake, vibrate **3** = **irritate**, annoy, clash, discompose, gall, get on one's nerves (*inf.*), grate, grind, irk, nark (*Brit., Austral., & NZ sl.*), nettle, offend **4** = **clash**, bicker, contend, disagree, interfere, oppose, quarrel, wrangle ◆ *n* **5** = **jolt**, bump, convulsion, shock, vibration

jargon *n* **1** = **parlance**, argot, cant, dialect, idiom, lingo (*inf.*), patois, patter, slang, tongue, usage **3** = **gobbledegook**, balderdash, bunkum *or* buncombe (*chiefly US*), drivel, gabble, gibberish, Greek (*inf.*), mumbo jumbo, nonsense, palaver, rigmarole, twaddle

jaundiced *adj* **3** = **cynical**, preconceived, sceptical **3** = **bitter**, biased, bigoted, distorted, envious, hostile, jealous, partial, prejudiced, resentful, spiteful, suspicious
Antonyms *adj* ≠ **cynical:** credulous, ingenuous, naive, optimistic ≠ **bitter:** open-minded, trusting, unbiased

jaunt *n* **1** = **outing**, airing, excursion, expedition, promenade, ramble, stroll, tour, trip

jaunty *adj* **1, 2** = **sprightly**, airy, breezy, buoyant, carefree, dapper, gay, high-spirited, lively, perky, self-confident, showy, smart, sparky, spruce, trim
Antonyms *adj* dignified, dull, lifeless, sedate, serious, staid

jaw *Slang n* **4b** = **chat**, chinwag (*Brit. inf.*), conversation, gabfest (*inf., chiefly US & Canad.*), gossip, natter, talk ◆ *vb* **5** = **talk**, babble, chat, chatter, chew the fat *or* rag (*sl.*), gossip, lecture, run off at the mouth (*sl.*), spout

jaws *pl n* **1** = **opening**, abyss, aperture, entrance, gates, ingress, maw, mouth, orifice

jazz up *vb* = **enliven**, animate, enhance, heighten, improve

jazzy *adj* = **flashy**, animated, fancy, gaudy, lively, smart, snazzy (*inf.*), spirited, vivacious, wild, zestful

jealous *adj* **1, 3** = **suspicious**, anxious, apprehensive, attentive, guarded, mistrustful, possessive, protective, solicitous, vigilant, wary, watchful, zealous **2, 4** = **envious**, covetous, desirous, emulous, green, green-eyed, grudging, intolerant, invidious, resentful, rival
Antonyms *adj* ≠ **suspicious:** carefree, indifferent, trusting ≠ **envious:** satisfied

jealousy *n* = **envy**, covetousness, distrust, heart-burning, ill-will, mistrust, possessiveness, resentment, spite, suspicion

jeans *pl n* = **denims**, Levis (*Trademark*)

Jeep (dʒi:p) *n Trademark.* a small road vehicle with four-wheel drive. [C20: ?from *GP*, for *general-purpose (vehicle)*, infl. by Eugene the *Jeep*, creature in a comic strip by E. C. Segar]

jeepers *or* **jeepers creepers** (ˈdʒi:pəz ˈkri:pəz) *interj US sl.* a mild exclamation of surprise. [C20: euphemism for *Jesus*]

jeer ⓣ (dʒɪə) *vb* **1** (often foll. by *at*) to laugh or scoff (at a person or thing). ◆ *n* **2** a remark or cry of derision. [C16: from ?]
▸ˈ**jeerer** *n* ▸ˈ**jeering** *adj, n* ▸ˈ**jeeringly** *adv*

jehad (dʒɪˈhæd) *n* a variant spelling of **jihad.**

Jehovah (dʒɪˈhəʊvə) *n Old Testament.* the personal name of God, revealed to Moses on Mount Horeb (Exodus 3). [C16: from Med. L, from Heb. YHVH YAHWEH]

Jehovah's Witness *n* a member of a Christian Church of American origin, the followers of which believe that the end of the present world system of government is near.

Jehu (ˈdʒi:hju:) *n* **1** *Old Testament.* the successor to Ahab as king of Israel. **2** *Humorous.* a reckless driver.

jejune (dʒɪˈdʒu:n) *adj* **1** naive; unsophisticated. **2** insipid; dull. **3** lacking nourishment. [C17: from L *jējūnus* hungry, empty]
▸**jeˈjunely** *adv* ▸**jeˈjuneness** *n*

jejunum (dʒɪˈdʒu:nəm) *n* the part of the small intestine between the duodenum and the ileum. [C16: from L, from *jējūnus* empty; from the belief that the jejunum is empty after death]

Jekyll and Hyde (ˈdʒɛkᵊl; haɪd) *n* **a** a person with two distinct personalities, one good, the other evil. **b** (*as modifier*): *a Jekyll-and-Hyde personality.* [C19: after the principal character of Robert Louis Stevenson's novel *The Strange Case of Dr Jekyll and Mr Hyde* (1886)]

jell ⓣ *or* **gel** (dʒɛl) *vb* **1** to make or become gelatinous; congeal. **2** (*intr*) to assume definite form: *his ideas have jelled.* [C19: back formation from JELLY[1]]

jellaba *or* **jellabah** (ˈdʒɛləbə) *n* a variant spelling of **djellaba.**

jellies (ˈdʒɛlɪz) *pl n Brit. sl.* gelatine capsules of temazepam, dissolved and injected as a recreational drug. [C20: shortened from GELATINE]

jellify (ˈdʒɛlɪˌfaɪ) *vb* **jellifies, jellifying, jellified.** to make into or become jelly.
▸ˌ**jellifiˈcation** *n*

jelly[1] (ˈdʒɛlɪ) *n, pl* **jellies. 1** a fruit-flavoured clear dessert set with gelatine. **2** a preserve made from the juice of fruit boiled with sugar and used as jam. **3** a savoury food preparation set with gelatine or with gelatinous stock: *calf's-foot jelly.* ◆ *vb* **jellies, jellying, jellied. 4** to jellify. [C14: from OF *gelee* frost, jelly, from *geler* to set hard, from L, from *gelu* frost]
▸ˈ**jellied** *adj* ▸ˈ**jelly-ˌlike** *adj*

jelly[2] (ˈdʒɛlɪ) *n Brit.* a slang name for **gelignite.**

jelly baby *n Brit.* a small sweet made from a gelatinous substance formed to resemble a baby.

jellyfish (ˈdʒɛlɪˌfɪʃ) *n, pl* **jellyfish** *or* **jellyfishes. 1** any marine coelenterate having a gelatinous umbrella-shaped body with trailing tentacles. **2** *Inf.* a weak indecisive person.

jelly fungus *n* a fungus that grows on trees and has a jelly-like consistency when wet.

jemmy (ˈdʒɛmɪ) *or US* **jimmy** *n, pl* **jemmies** *or US* **jimmies. 1** a short steel crowbar used, esp. by burglars, for forcing doors and windows. ◆ *vb* **jemmies, jemmying, jemmied** *or US* **jimmies, jimmying, jimmied. 2** (*tr*) to prise (something) open with a jemmy. [C19: from the pet name for *James*]

jennet, genet, *or* **gennet** (ˈdʒɛnɪt) *n* a small Spanish riding horse. [C15: from OF *genet*, from Catalan *ginet*, horse used by the *Zenete*, from Ar. *Zanātah* the Zenete, a Moorish people renowned for their horsemanship]

jenny (ˈdʒɛnɪ) *n, pl* **jennies. 1** a machine for turning up the edge of a piece of sheet metal in preparation for making a joint. **2** the female of certain animals or birds, esp. a donkey, ass, or wren. **3** short for **spinning jenny. 4** *Billiards, etc.* an in-off. [C17: from name *Jenny*, dim. of *Jane*]

jeopardize ⓣ *or* **jeopardise** (ˈdʒɛpəˌdaɪz) *vb* **jeopardizes, jeopardizing, jeopardized** *or* **jeopardises, jeopardising, jeopardised.** (*tr*) **1** to risk; hazard: *he jeopardized his job by being persistently unpunctual.* **2** to put in danger.

jeopardy ⓣ (ˈdʒɛpədɪ) *n* (usually preceded by *in*) **1** danger of injury, loss, death, etc.: *his health was in jeopardy.* **2** *Law.* danger of being convicted and punished for a criminal offence. [C14: from OF *jeu parti*, lit.: divided game, hence uncertain issue, from *jeu* game, from L *jocus* joke, game + *partir* to divide]

jequirity (dʒɪˈkwɪrɪtɪ) *n, pl* **jequirities.** a tropical climbing plant with scarlet black-spotted seeds used as beads, and roots used as a substitute for liquorice. Also called: **Indian liquorice.** [C19: from Port. *jequiritì*, of Amerind origin, from *jekiritì*]

Jer. *Bible. abbrev. for* Jeremiah.

jerbil (ˈdʒɜ:bɪl) *n* a variant spelling of **gerbil.**

jerboa (dʒɜ:ˈbəʊə) *n* any small nocturnal burrowing rodent inhabiting dry regions of Asia and N Africa, having long hind legs specialized for jumping. [C17: from NL, from Ar. *yarbū'*]

jeremiad (ˌdʒɛrɪˈmaɪəd) *n* a long mournful lamentation or complaint. [C18: from F *jérémiade*, referring to the Lamentations of Jeremiah in the Old Testament]

jerepigo (ˌdʒɛrɪˈpɪgəʊ) *n S. African.* a sweet white or red sherry-type wine. [from Port. *cheripiga* an adulterant of port wine]

jerk[1] ⓣ (dʒɜ:k) *vb* **1** to move or cause to move with an irregular or spasmodic motion. **2** to throw, twist, pull, or push (something) abruptly or spasmodically. **3** (*tr;* often foll. by *out*) to utter (words, etc.) in a spasmodic or breathless manner. ◆ *n* **4** an abrupt or spasmodic movement. **5** an irregular jolting motion: *the car moved with a jerk.* **6** (*pl*) Also called: **physical jerks.** *Brit. inf.* physical exercises. **7** *Sl., chiefly US & Canad.* a stupid or ignorant person. [C16: prob. var. of *yerk* to pull stitches tight]
▸ˈ**jerker** *n*

jerk[2] (dʒɜ:k) *vb* (*tr*) **1** to preserve beef, etc., by cutting into thin strips and drying in the sun. ◆ *n* **2** Also called: **jerky.** jerked meat. [C18: back formation from *jerky*, from Sp. *charqui*, from Quechuan]

jerkin (ˈdʒɜ:kɪn) *n* **1** a sleeveless short jacket worn by men or women. **2** a man's sleeveless fitted jacket, often made of leather, worn in the 16th and 17th centuries. [C16: from ?]

jerk off *or US* **jack off** *vb* (*adv often reflexive*) *Taboo sl.* (of a male) to masturbate.

jerky ⓣ (ˈdʒɜ:kɪ) *adj* **jerkier, jerkiest.** characterized by jerks.
▸ˈ**jerkily** *adv* ▸ˈ**jerkiness** *n*

jeroboam (ˌdʒɛrəˈbəʊəm) *n* a wine bottle holding the equivalent of four normal bottles. [C19: allusion to *Jeroboam*, a "mighty man of valour" (I Kings 11:28) who "made Israel to sin" (I Kings 14:16)]

jerry (ˈdʒɛrɪ) *n, pl* **jerries.** *Brit.* an informal word for **chamber pot.**

Jerry (ˈdʒɛrɪ) *n, pl* **Jerries.** *Brit. sl.* **1** a German, esp. a German soldier. **2** the Germans collectively.

jerry-build *vb* **jerry-builds, jerry-building, jerry-built.** (*tr*) to build (houses, flats, etc.) badly using cheap materials.
▸ˈ**jerry-ˌbuilder** *n*

jerry can *n* a flat-sided can with a capacity of between 4.5 and 5 gallons used for storing or transporting liquids, esp. motor fuel. [C20: from JERRY]

jersey (ˈdʒɜ:zɪ) *n* **1** a knitted garment covering the upper part of the body. **2a** a machine-knitted slightly elastic cloth of wool, silk, nylon, etc., used for clothing. **2b** (*as modifier*): *a jersey suit.* **3** a football shirt. [C16: from *Jersey*, from the woollen sweaters worn by the fishermen]

Jersey (ˈdʒɜ:zɪ) *n* a breed of dairy cattle producing milk with a high butterfat content, originating from the island of Jersey. [after *Jersey*, island in the English Channel]

Jerusalem artichoke (dʒəˈru:sələm) *n* **1** a North American sunflower widely cultivated for its underground edible tubers. **2** the tuber of this plant, which is eaten as a vegetable. [C17: by folk etymology from It. *girasole articiocco;* see GIRASOL]

jess (dʒɛs) *n Falconry.* a short leather strap, one end of which is permanently attached to the leg of a hawk or falcon. [C14: from OF *ges*, from L *jactus* a throw, from *jacere* to throw]
▸**jessed** *adj*

jessamine (ˈdʒɛsəmɪn) *n* another name for **jasmine** (sense 1).

jessie (ˈdʒɛsɪ) *n Sl.* an effeminate, weak, or cowardly boy or man.

jest ⓣ (dʒɛst) *n* **1** something done or said for amusement; joke. **2** playfulness; fun: *to act in jest.* **3** a jeer or taunt. **4** an object of derision. ◆ *vb* **5** to act or speak in an amusing or frivolous way. **6** to make fun of (a person or thing). [C13: var. of GEST]
▸ˈ**jesting** *adj, n* ▸ˈ**jestingly** *adv*

jester ⓣ (ˈdʒɛstə) *n* a professional clown employed by a king or nobleman during the Middle Ages. [C17: from LL, vocative of JESUS]

Jesuit (ˈdʒɛzjʊɪt) *n* **1** a member of a Roman Catholic religious order (the **Society of Jesus**) founded by Ignatius Loyola in 1534 with the aim of defending Catholicism against the Reformation. **2** (*sometimes not cap.*) *Inf., offens.* a person given to subtle and equivocating arguments. [C16: from NL *Jēsuita*, from LL *Jēsus* + *-ita* -ITE[1]]
▸ˌ**Jesuˈitical** *adj*

Jesus (ˈdʒi:zəs) *n* **1** Also called: **Jesus Christ, Jesus of Nazareth.** ?4 B.C.–?29 A.D., founder of Christianity and believed by Christians to be the Son

THESAURUS

jeer *vb* **1** = **mock**, banter, barrack, cock a snook at (*Brit.*), contemn (*formal*), deride, flout, gibe, heckle, hector, knock (*inf.*), ridicule, scoff, sneer, taunt ◆ *n* **2** = **mockery**, abuse, aspersion, boo, catcall, derision, gibe, hiss, hoot, obloquy, ridicule, scoff, sneer, taunt
Antonyms *vb* ≠ **mock**: acclaim, applaud, cheer, clap, praise ◆ *n* ≠ **mockery**: adulation, applause, cheers, encouragement, praise

jell *vb* **1** = **solidify**, congeal, harden, set, thicken **2** = **take shape**, come together, crystallize, finalize, form, materialize

jeopardize *vb* **1, 2** = **endanger**, chance, expose, gamble, hazard, imperil, risk, stake, venture

jeopardy *n* **1** = **danger**, endangerment, exposure, hazard, insecurity, liability, peril, pitfall, precariousness, risk, venture, vulnerability

jerk[1] *vb, n* **1, 2, 4, 5** = **tug**, jolt, lurch, pull, throw, thrust, tweak, twitch, wrench, yank

jerky *adj* = **bumpy**, bouncy, convulsive, fitful, jolting, jumpy, rough, shaky, spasmodic, tremulous, twitchy, uncontrolled
Antonyms *adj* flowing, frictionless, gliding, smooth

jerry-built *adj* = **ramshackle**, cheap, defective, faulty, flimsy, rickety, shabby, slipshod, thrown together, unsubstantial
Antonyms *adj* sturdy, substantial, well-built, well-constructed

jest *n* **1, 2** = **joke**, banter, bon mot, crack (*sl.*), fun, gag (*inf.*), hoax, jape, josh (*sl., chiefly US & Canad.*), play, pleasantry, prank, quip, sally, sport, wisecrack (*inf.*), witticism ◆ *vb* **5, 6** = **joke**, banter, chaff, deride, gibe, jeer, josh (*sl., chiefly US & Canad.*), kid (*inf.*), mock, quip, scoff, sneer, tease

jester *n* **1** = **clown**, buffoon, fool, harlequin, madcap, mummer, pantaloon, prankster, zany

of God. ◆ *interj also* **Jesus wept.** **2** used to express intense surprise, dismay, etc. [via L from Gk *Iēsous,* from Heb. *Yeshūa',* shortened from *Yehōshūa'* God is help]

Jesus freak *n Inf.* a vociferous Christian, esp. one who is evangelical and belongs to a community.

jet[1] Ⓣ (dʒɛt) *n* **1** a thin stream of liquid or gas forced out of a small aperture. **2** an outlet or nozzle for emitting such a stream. **3** a jet-propelled aircraft. ◆ *vb* **jets, jetting, jetted.** **4** to issue or cause to issue in a jet: *water jetted from the hose.* **5** to transport or be transported by jet aircraft. [C16: from OF *jeter* to throw, from L *jactāre* to toss about]

jet[2] Ⓣ (dʒɛt) *n* **a** a hard black variety of lignite that takes a brilliant polish and is used for jewellery, etc. **b** (*as modifier*): *jet earrings.* [C14: from OF *jaiet,* from L, from Gk *lithos gagatēs* stone of *Gagai,* a town in Lycia, Asia Minor]

jet black *n* **a** a deep black colour. **b** (*as adj*): *jet-black hair.*

jeté (ʒə'teɪ) *n Ballet.* a step in which the dancer springs from one leg and lands on the other. [F, lit.: thrown, from *jeter;* see JET[1]]

jet engine *n* a gas turbine, esp. one fitted to an aircraft.

jet lag *n* a general feeling of fatigue, disorientation, or nausea often experienced by air travellers after long journeys.

jet-propelled *adj* **1** driven by jet propulsion. **2** *Inf.* very fast.

jet propulsion *n* **1** propulsion by means of a jet of fluid. **2** propulsion by means of a gas turbine, esp. when the exhaust gases provide the propulsive thrust.

jetsam ('dʒɛtsəm) *n* **1** that portion of the cargo of a vessel thrown overboard to lighten her, as during a storm. Cf. **flotsam** (sense 1). **2** another word for **flotsam** (sense 2). [C16: shortened from JETTISON]

jet set *n* **a** a rich and fashionable social set, the members of which travel widely for pleasure. **b** (*as modifier*): *jet-set travellers.*
▸ **'jet-ˌsetter** *n* ▸ **'jet-ˌsetting** *n, adj*

jet ski *Trademark. n* **1** a small self-propelled vehicle for one person resembling a scooter, which skims across water on a flat keel, and is steered by means of handlebars. ◆ *vb* **jet-ski, jet-skis, jet-skiing, jet-skied** *or* **jet ski'd.** (*intr*) **2** to ride a jet ski.
▸ **jet skier** *n* ▸ **jet skiing** *n*

jet stream *n* **1** *Meteorol.* a narrow belt of high-altitude winds moving east at high speeds. **2** the jet of exhaust gases produced by a gas turbine, etc.

jettison Ⓣ ('dʒɛtɪs^{ə}n, -z^{ə}n) *vb* **jettisons, jettisoning, jettisoned.** (*tr*) **1** to abandon: *to jettison old clothes.* **2** to throw overboard. ◆ *n* **3** another word for **jetsam** (sense 1). [C15: from OF, ult. from L *jactātiō* a tossing about]

jetton ('dʒɛt^{ə}n) *n* a counter or token, esp. a chip used in such gambling games as roulette. [C18: from F *jeton,* from *jeter* to cast up (accounts); see JET[1]]

jetty Ⓣ ('dʒɛtɪ) *n, pl* **jetties.** **1** a structure built from a shore out into the water to direct currents or protect a harbour. **2** a landing pier; dock. [C15: from OF *jetee* projecting part, lit.: something thrown out, from *jeter* to throw]

jeu d'esprit (*French* ʒø dɛspri) *n, pl* ***jeux d'esprit*** (ʒø dɛspri). a light-hearted display of wit or cleverness, esp. in literature. [lit.: play of spirit]

Jew (dʒuː) *n* **1** a member of the Semitic people who are descended from the ancient Israelites. **2** a person whose religion is Judaism. [C12: from OF *juiu,* from L *jūdaeus,* from Gk *ioudaios,* from Heb., from *yehūdāh* Judah]

jewel Ⓣ ('dʒuːəl) *n* **1** a precious or semiprecious stone; gem. **2** a person or thing resembling a jewel in preciousness, brilliance, etc. **3** a gemstone used as a bearing in a watch. **4** a piece of jewellery. ◆ *vb* **jewels, jewelling, jewelled** *or US* **jewels, jeweling, jeweled.** **5** (*tr*) to fit or decorate with a jewel or jewels. [C13: from OF *jouel,* ?from *jeu* game, from L *jocus*]

jewelfish ('dʒuːəlˌfɪʃ) *n, pl* **jewelfish** *or* **jewelfishes.** a beautifully coloured and popular aquarium fish native to Africa.

jeweller *or US* **jeweler** ('dʒuːələ) *n* a person whose business is the cutting or setting of gemstones or the making or selling of jewellery.

jeweller's rouge *n* a finely powdered form of ferric oxide used as a metal polish.

jewellery Ⓣ *or US* **jewelry** ('dʒuːəlrɪ) *n* objects that are worn for personal adornment, such as rings, necklaces, etc., considered collectively.

Jewess ('dʒuːɪs) *n* a Jewish girl or woman.

jewfish ('dʒuːˌfɪʃ) *n, pl* **jewfish** *or* **jewfishes.** **1** any of various large dark fishes of warm or tropical seas. **2** *Austral.* a freshwater catfish. [C17: from ?]

Jewish ('dʒuːɪʃ) *adj* of or characteristic of Jews.
▸ **'Jewishly** *adv* ▸ **'Jewishness** *n*

Jew lizard *n* a large Australian lizard with spiny scales round its neck.

Jewry ('dʒʊərɪ) *n, pl* **Jewries.** **1a** Jews collectively. **1b** the Jewish religion or culture. **2** a quarter of a town inhabited by Jews.

jew's-ear *n* a pinky-red fungus.

jew's-harp *n* a musical instrument consisting of a small lyre-shaped metal frame held between the teeth, with a steel tongue plucked with the finger.

Jezebel ('dʒɛzəˌbɛl) *n* **1** *Old Testament.* the wife of Ahab, king of Israel. **2** (*sometimes not cap.*) a shameless or scheming woman.

jib[1] (dʒɪb) *n* **1** *Naut.* any triangular sail set forward of the foremast of a vessel. **2 cut of someone's jib.** someone's manner, style, etc. [C17: from ?]

jib[2] Ⓣ (dʒɪb) *vb* **jibs, jibbing, jibbed.** (*intr*) *Chiefly Brit.* **1** (often foll. by *at*) to be reluctant (to). **2** (of an animal) to stop short and refuse to go forwards. **3** *Naut.* a variant of **gybe.** [C19: from ?]
▸ **'jibber** *n*

jib[3] (dʒɪb) *n* the projecting arm of a crane or the boom of a derrick. [C18: prob. based on GIBBET]

jib boom *n Naut.* a spar forming an extension of the bowsprit.

jibe[1] (dʒaɪb) *or* **jib** (dʒɪb) *vb* **jibes, jibing, jibed** *or* **jibs, jibbing, jibbed.** *n Naut.* a variant of **gybe.**

jibe[2] Ⓣ (dʒaɪb) *vb* **jibes, jibing, jibed.** a variant spelling of **gibe**[1].

jibe[3] (dʒaɪb) *vb* **jibes, jibing, jibed.** (*intr*) *Inf.* to agree; accord; harmonize. [C19: from ?]

jiffy Ⓣ ('dʒɪfɪ) *or* **jiff** *n, pl* **jiffies** *or* **jiffs.** *Inf.* a very short time: *wait a jiffy.* [C18: from ?]

Jiffy bag *n Trademark.* a large padded envelope.

jig Ⓣ (dʒɪg) *n* **1** any of several old rustic kicking and leaping dances. **2** a piece of music composed for or in the rhythm of this dance. **3** a mechanical device designed to hold and locate a component during machining. **4** *Angling.* any of various spinning lures that wobble when drawn through the water. **5** Also called: **jigger.** *Mining.* a device for separating ore or coal from waste material by agitation in water. ◆ *vb* **jigs, jigging, jigged.** **6** to dance (a jig). **7** to jerk or cause to jerk up and down rapidly. **8** (often foll. by *up*) to fit or be fitted in a jig. **9** (*tr*) to drill or cut (a workpiece) in a jig. **10** (*tr*) *Mining.* to separate ore or coal from waste material using a jig. [C16: from ?]

jigger[1] ('dʒɪgə) *n* **1** a person or thing that jigs. **2** *Golf.* (formerly) a club, an iron, usually No. 4. **3** any of a number of mechanical devices having a vibratory motion. **4** a light lifting tackle used on ships. **5** a small glass, esp. for whisky. **6** *Billiards.* another word for **bridge**[1] (sense 11). **7** *NZ.* a light hand- or power-propelled vehicle used on railway lines.

jigger[2] *or* **jigger flea** ('dʒɪgə) *n* another name for the **chigoe** (sense 1).

jiggered ('dʒɪgəd) *adj* (*postpositive*) *Inf.* damned; blowed: *I'm jiggered if he'll get away with it.* [C19: prob. euphemism for *buggered;* see BUGGER]

jiggermast ('dʒɪgəˌmɑːst) *n Naut.* any small mast on a sailing vessel.

jiggery-pokery ('dʒɪgərɪ'pəʊkərɪ) *n Inf., chiefly Brit.* dishonest or deceitful behaviour. [C19: from Scot. dialect *joukery-pawkery*]

jiggle Ⓣ ('dʒɪg^{ə}l) *vb* **jiggles, jiggling, jiggled.** **1** to move or cause to move up and down or to and fro with a short jerky motion. ◆ *n* **2** a short jerky motion. [C19: frequentative of JIG]
▸ **'jiggly** *adj*

jigsaw ('dʒɪgˌsɔː) *n* **1** a mechanical saw with a fine steel blade for cutting intricate curves in sheets of material. **2** See **jigsaw puzzle.** [C19: from JIG (to jerk up and down rapidly) + SAW[1]]

jigsaw puzzle *n* a puzzle in which the player has to reassemble a picture that has been cut into irregularly shaped interlocking pieces.

jihad *or* **jehad** (dʒɪ'hæd) *n Islam.* a holy war against infidels undertaken by Muslims. [C19: from Ar. *jihād* a conflict]

jilt Ⓣ (dʒɪlt) *vb* **1** (*tr*) to leave or reject (a lover), esp. without previous warning. ◆ *n* **2** a woman who jilts a lover. [C17: from dialect *jillet* flighty girl, dim. of name *Gill*]

jim crow ('dʒɪm 'krəʊ) *n (often caps.) US.* **1a** the policy or practice of segregating Blacks. **1b** (*as modifier*): *jim-crow laws.* **2** a derogatory term for **Negro.** **3** an implement for bending iron bars or rails. [C19: from *Jim Crow,* name of song used as the basis of an act by Thomas Rice (1808–60), US entertainer]
▸ **'jim-'crowism** *n*

jimjams ('dʒɪmˌdʒæmz) *pl n* **1** *Sl.* delirium tremens. **2** a state of nervous tension or anxiety. **3** *Inf.* pyjamas. [C19: whimsical formation based on JAM[1]]

jimmy ('dʒɪmɪ) *n, pl* **jimmies,** *vb* **jimmies, jimmying, jimmied.** a US variant of **jemmy.**

jingle Ⓣ ('dʒɪŋg^{ə}l) *vb* **jingles, jingling, jingled.** **1** to ring or cause to ring lightly and repeatedly. **2** (*intr*) to sound in a manner suggestive of jin-

THESAURUS

jet[1] *n* **1** = **stream**, flow, fountain, gush, spout, spray, spring **2** = **nozzle**, atomizer, nose, rose, spout, sprayer, sprinkler ◆ *vb* **4** = **stream**, flow, gush, issue, rush, shoot, spew, spout, squirt, surge **5** = **fly**, soar, zoom

jet[2] *modifier* **b** = **black**, coal-black, ebony, inky, pitch-black, raven, sable

jet-setting *adj* = **fashionable**, cosmopolitan, high-society, rich, ritzy (*sl.*), sophisticated, trendsetting, trendy (*Brit. inf.*), well-off

jettison *vb* **1, 2** = **abandon**, discard, dump, eject, expel, heave, scrap, throw overboard, unload

jetty *n* **1, 2** = **pier**, breakwater, dock, groyne, mole, quay, wharf

jewel *n* **1** = **gemstone**, brilliant, ornament, precious stone, rock (*sl.*), sparkler (*inf.*), trinket **2** = **rarity**, charm, collector's item, find, gem, humdinger (*sl.*), masterpiece, paragon, pearl, prize, treasure, wonder

jewellery *n* = **jewels**, finery, gems, ornaments, precious stones, regalia, treasure, trinkets

jib[2] *vb* **1, 2** = **refuse**, balk, recoil, retreat, shrink, stop short

jibe[2] *see* **gibe**[1]

jiffy *n Informal* = **moment**, bat of an eye (*inf.*), flash, instant, second, split second, trice, twinkling

jig *vb* **6, 7** = **skip**, bob, bounce, caper, jiggle, jounce, prance, shake, twitch, wiggle, wobble

jiggle *vb* **1** = **jerk**, agitate, bounce, fidget, jig, jog, joggle, shake, shimmy, twitch, wiggle

jilt *vb* **1** = **reject**, abandon, betray, break with, coquette, deceive, desert, disappoint, discard, ditch (*sl.*), drop, forsake, leave (someone) in the lurch, throw over

jingle *vb* **1** = **ring**, chime, clatter, clink, jangle, rattle, tinkle ◆ *n* **3** = **rattle**, clang, clangour,

gling: *a jingling verse.* ◆ *n* **3** a sound of metal jingling. **4** a rhythmic verse, etc., esp. one used in advertising. [C16: prob. imit.]
▸ **'jingly** *adj*

jingo ('dʒɪŋgəʊ) *n, pl* **jingoes. 1** a loud and bellicose patriot. **2** jingoism. **3 by jingo.** an exclamation of surprise. [C17: orig. ? euphemism for *Jesus;* applied to bellicose patriots after the use of *by Jingo!* in a 19th-cent. song]

jingoism ❶ ('dʒɪŋgəʊˌɪzəm) *n* the belligerent spirit or foreign policy of jingoes.
▸ **'jingoist** *n, adj* ▸ **ˌjingo'istic** *adj*

jink (dʒɪŋk) *vb* **1** (*intr*) to move swiftly or turn in order to dodge. ◆ *n* **2** a jinking movement. [C18: of Scot. origin, imit. of swift movement]

jinker ('dʒɪŋkə) *n Austral.* a vehicle for transporting timber, consisting of a tractor and two sets of wheels for supporting the logs. [from ?]

jinks (dʒɪŋks) *pl n* boisterous or mischievous play (esp. in **high jinks**). [C18: from ?]

jinn (dʒɪn) *n* (*often functioning as sing*) the plural of **jinni.**

jinni, jinnee, *or* **djinni** (dʒɪ'niː) *n, pl* **jinn** *or* **djinn** (dʒɪn). a being or spirit in Muslim belief who could assume human or animal form and influence man by supernatural powers. [C17: from Ar.]

jinrikisha, jinricksha, *or* **jinrickshaw** (dʒɪn'rɪkʃɔː) *n* another name for **rickshaw.** [C19: from Japanese, from *jin* man + *riki* power + *sha* carriage]

jinx ❶ (dʒɪŋks) *n* **1** an unlucky force, person, or thing. ◆ *vb* **2** (*tr*) to be or put a jinx on. [C20: ?from NL *Jynx,* genus name of the wryneck, from Gk *iunx* wryneck, a bird used in magic]

JIT *abbrev. for* just-in-time.

jitter ❶ ('dʒɪtə) *Inf.* ◆ *vb* **1** (*intr*) to be anxious or nervous. ◆ *n* **2 the jitters.** nervousness and anxiety. [C20: from ?]
▸ **'jittery** *adj* ▸ **'jitteriness** *n*

jitterbug ('dʒɪtəˌbʌg) *n* **1** a fast jerky American dance, usually to a jazz accompaniment, that was popular in the 1940s. **2** a person who dances the jitterbug. ◆ *vb* **jitterbugs, jitterbugging, jitterbugged. 3** (*intr*) to perform such a dance.

jiujitsu *or* **jiujutsu** (dʒuː'dʒɪtsuː) *n* a variant spelling of **jujitsu.**

jive (dʒaɪv) *n* **1** a style of lively and jerky dance, popular esp. in the 1940s and 1950s. **2** *Sl., chiefly US.* **2a** misleading or deceptive talk. **2b** (*as modifier*): *jive talk.* ◆ *vb* **jives, jiving, jived. 3** (*intr*) to dance the jive. **4** *Sl., chiefly US.* to mislead; tell lies (to). [C20: from ?]
▸ **'jiver** *n*

job ❶ (dʒɒb) *n* **1** an individual piece of work or task. **2** an occupation. **3** an object worked on or a result produced from working. **4** a duty or responsibility: *her job was to cook the dinner.* **5** *Inf.* a difficult task or problem: *I had a job to contact him.* **6** a state of affairs: *make the best of a bad job.* **7** *Inf.* a particular type of something: *a four-wheel drive job.* **8** *Inf.* a crime, esp. a robbery. **9** *Computing.* a unit of work for a computer. **10 jobs for the boys.** jobs given to or created for allies or favourites. **11 just the job.** exactly what was required. **12 on the job.** actively engaged in one's employment. ◆ *vb* **jobs, jobbing, jobbed. 13** (*intr*) to work by the piece or at casual jobs. **14** to make a private profit out of (a public office, etc.). **15** (*intr;* usually foll. by *in*) **15a** to buy and sell (goods or services) as a middleman: *he jobs in government surplus.* **15b** *Brit.* to buy and sell stocks and shares as a stockjobber. **16** *Austral. sl.* to punch. [C16: from ?]
▸ **'jobless** *adj*

jobber ('dʒɒbə) *n* **1** *Brit.* short for **stockjobber** (sense 1). See also **market maker. 2** a person who jobs.

jobbery ('dʒɒbərɪ) *n* the practice of making private profit out of a public office.

jobbing ('dʒɒbɪŋ) *adj* working by the piece, not regularly employed: *a jobbing gardener.*

Jobcentre ('dʒɒbˌsentə) *n Brit.* any of a number of government offices usually having premises situated in or near the main shopping area of a town in which people seeking jobs can consult displayed advertisements.

Jobclub ('dʒɒbˌklʌb) *n* a group of unemployed people organized through a Jobcentre, which meets every weekday and is given advice on job seeking to increase its members' chances of finding employment.

job description *n* a formal description of the duties and responsibilities involved in a job, esp. as given to applicants for the job.

job lot *n* **1** a miscellaneous collection of articles sold as a lot. **2** a collection of cheap or trivial items.

job satisfaction *n* the extent to which the desires and hopes of a worker are fulfilled as a result of his work.

Job's comforter (dʒəʊbz) *n* a person who, while purporting to give sympathy, succeeds only in adding to distress. [from *Job* in the Old Testament (Job 16:1–5)]

jobseeker's allowance ('dʒɒbˌsiːkəz) *n* (in Britain) a National Insurance or social security payment for unemployed people; replaced unemployment benefit in 1996. Abbrev.: **JSA.**

job sharing *n* the division of a job between two or more people such that each covers the same job for complementary parts of the day or week.
▸ **job share** *n*

jobsworth ('dʒɒbzˌwɜːθ) *n Inf.* a person in a position of minor authority who invokes the letter of the law in order to avoid any action requiring initiative, cooperation, etc. [C20: from *it's more than my job's worth to...*]

jock (dʒɒk) *n Inf.* **1** short for **disc jockey. 2** short for **jockey. 3** short for **jockstrap.**

Jock (dʒɒk) *n* a slang word or term of address for a **Scot.**

jockey ❶ ('dʒɒkɪ) *n* **1** a person who rides horses in races, esp. as a profession. ◆ *vb* **2a** (*tr*) to ride (a horse) in a race. **2b** (*intr*) to ride as a jockey. **3** (*intr:* often foll. by *for*) to try to obtain an advantage by manoeuvring (esp. in **jockey for position**). **4** to trick or cheat (a person). [C16 (in the sense: lad): from name *Jock* + -EY]

jockstrap ('dʒɒkˌstræp) *n* an elasticated belt with a pouch worn by men, esp. athletes, to support the genitals. Also called: **athletic support.** [C20: from sl. *jock* penis + STRAP]

jocose ❶ (dʒə'kəʊs) *adj* characterized by humour. [C17: from L *jocōsus* given to jesting, from *jocus* joke]
▸ **jo'cosely** *adv* ▸ **jocosity** (dʒə'kɒsɪtɪ) *n*

jocular ❶ ('dʒɒkjʊlə) *adj* **1** characterized by joking and good humour. **2** meant lightly or humorously. [C17: from L *joculāris,* from *joculus* little JOKE]
▸ **jocularity** (ˌdʒɒkjʊ'lærɪtɪ) *n* ▸ **'jocularly** *adv*

jocund ('dʒɒkənd) *adj* of a humorous temperament; merry. [C14: from LL *jocundus,* from L *jūcundus* pleasant, from *juvāre* to please]
▸ **jocundity** (dʒəʊ'kʌndɪtɪ) *n* ▸ **'jocundly** *adv*

jodhpurs ('dʒɒdpəz) *pl n* riding breeches, loose-fitting around the thighs and tight-fitting from the knees to the ankles. [C19: from *Jodhpur,* town in NW India]

Joe Blake (ˌdʒəʊ 'bleɪk) *n Austral. sl.* **1** a snake. **2 the Joe Blakes.** the DT's.

Joe Bloggs ('blɒgz) *n Brit. sl.* an average or typical man. US, Canad., and Austral. equivalent: **Joe Blow.** See also **Joe Six-Pack.**

Joe Public *n Sl.* the general public.

joes (dʒəʊz) *pl n* **the.** *Austral. inf.* a fit of depression. [short for *the Joe Blakes*]

Joe Six-Pack *n US sl.* an average or typical man.

joey ('dʒəʊɪ) *n Austral. inf.* **1** a young kangaroo. **2** a young animal or child. [C19: from Abor.]

jog ❶ (dʒɒg) *vb* **jogs, jogging, jogged. 1** (*intr*) to run or move slowly or at a jog trot, esp. for physical exercise. **2** (*intr;* foll. by *on* or *along*) to continue in a plodding way. **3** (*tr*) to jar or nudge slightly. **4** (*tr*) to remind: *jog my memory.* ◆ *n* **5** the act of jogging. **6** a slight jar or nudge. **7** a jogging motion; trot. [C14: prob. var. of *shog* to shake]

jogger ('dʒɒgə) *n* **1** a person who runs at a jog trot over some distance for exercise. **2** *NZ.* a cart with rubber tyres used on farms.

jogger's nipple *n Inf.* painful inflammation of the nipple, caused by friction with a garment when running for long distances.

jogging ('dʒɒgɪŋ) *n* a slow run or trot, esp. as a keep-fit exercise.

joggle ('dʒɒgᵊl) *vb* **joggles, joggling, joggled. 1** to shake or move (someone or something) with a slightly jolting motion. **2** (*tr*) to join or fasten (two pieces of building material) by means of a joggle. ◆ *n* **3** the act of joggling. **4** a slight irregular shake. **5** a joint between two pieces of building material by means of a projection on one piece that fits into a notch in the other. [C16: frequentative of JOG]
▸ **'joggler** *n*

jog trot *n* **1** an easy bouncy gait, esp. of a horse, midway between a walk and a trot. **2** a regular way of living or doing something.

john (dʒɒn) *n Chiefly US & Canad.* a slang word for **lavatory.** [C20: special use of the name]

THESAURUS

clink, reverberation, ringing, tinkle **4** = **song,** chorus, ditty, doggerel, limerick, melody, tune

jingoism *n* = **chauvinism,** belligerence, bigotry, flag-waving (*inf.*), hawkishness, insularity, xenophobia

jinx *n* **1** = **curse,** black magic, evil eye, hex (*US & Canad. inf.*), hoodoo (*inf.*), nemesis, plague, voodoo ◆ *vb* **2** = **curse,** bewitch, hex (*US & Canad. inf.*)

jitter *n* **2 the jitters** = **nerves,** anxiety, butterflies (in one's stomach), cold feet (*inf.*), fidgets, heebie-jeebies (*sl.*), nervousness, tenseness, the shakes (*inf.*), the willies (*inf.*)

jittery *adj* = **nervous,** agitated, anxious, fidgety, hyper (*inf.*), jumpy, neurotic, quivering, shaky, trembling, twitchy (*inf.*), wired (*sl.*)

Antonyms *adj* calm, composed, laid-back (*inf.*), relaxed, together (*sl.*), unfazed (*inf.*), unflustered

job *n* **1** = **task,** affair, assignment, charge, chore, concern, contribution, duty, enterprise, errand, function, pursuit, responsibility, role, stint, undertaking, venture, work **2** = **occupation,** activity, bread and butter (*inf.*), business, calling, capacity, career, craft, employment, function, livelihood, métier, office, position, post, profession, situation, trade, vocation **3** = **consignment,** allotment, assignment, batch, commission, contract, lot, output, piece, portion, product, share

jobless *adj* **2** = **unemployed,** idle, inactive, out of work, unoccupied

jockey *vb* **3** = **manoeuvre,** cajole, engineer, finagle (*inf.*), ingratiate, insinuate, manage, manipulate, negotiate, trim, wheedle

jocose *adj* = **humorous,** blithe, comical, droll, facetious, funny, jesting, jocular, jovial, joyous, merry, mischievous, playful, pleasant, sportive, teasing, waggish, witty

jocular *adj* **1, 2** = **humorous,** amusing, comical, droll, facetious, frolicsome, funny, jesting, jocose, jocund, joking, jolly, jovial, playful, roguish, sportive, teasing, waggish, whimsical, witty

Antonyms *adj* earnest, humourless, serious, solemn

jog *vb* **1** = **run,** canter, dogtrot, lope, trot **2** = **plod,** lumber, traipse (*inf.*), tramp, trudge **4** =

John Barleycorn *n Usually humorous.* the personification of alcoholic drink.
John Bull *n* **1** a personification of England or the English people. **2** a typical Englishman. [C18: name of a character intended to be representative of the English nation in *The History of John Bull* (1712) by John Arbuthnot]
John Doe *n* See **Doe.**
John Dory ('dɔːrɪ) *n* a European dory (the fish), having a deep compressed body and massive mobile jaws. [C18: from name *John* + DORY[1]; on the model of DOE]
John Hop *n Austral. sl.* a policeman. [rhyming sl. for COP[1]]
johnny ('dʒɒnɪ) *n, pl* **johnnies.** *Brit. inf. (often cap.)* a man or boy; chap.
Johnny Canuck ('dʒɒnɪ kə'nʌk) *n Canad.* **1** an informal name for a **Canadian. 2** a personification of Canada.
Johnny-come-lately *n, pl* **Johnny-come-latelies** *or* **Johnnies-come-lately.** *Sl.* a brash newcomer, novice, or recruit.
Johnsonian (dʒɒn'səʊnɪən) *adj* of, relating to, or characteristic of Samuel Johnson, 18th-cent. English lexicographer, his works, or his style of writing.
John Thomas *n Sl.* a euphemistic name for **penis.**
joie de vivre 🅣 *French.* (ʒwa də vivrə) *n* joy of living; enjoyment of life; ebullience.
join 🅣 (dʒɔɪn) *vb* **1** to come or bring together. **2** to become a member of (a club, etc.). **3** *(intr;* often foll. by *with)* to become associated or allied. **4** *(intr;* usually foll. by *in)* to take part. **5** *(tr)* to meet (someone) as a companion. **6** *(tr)* to become part of. **7** *(tr)* to unite (two people) in marriage. **8** *(tr) Geom.* to connect with a straight line or a curve. **9 join hands. 9a** to hold one's own hands together. **9b** (of two people) to hold each other's hands. **9c** (usually foll. by *with*) to work together in an enterprise. ◆ *n* **10** a joint; seam. **11** the act of joining. ◆ See also **join up.** [C13: from OF, from L *jungere* to yoke]
joinder ('dʒɔɪndə) *n* **1** the act of joining, esp. in legal contexts. **2** *Law.* **2a** (in pleading) the stage at which the parties join issue (**joinder of issue**). **2b** the joining of two or more persons as coplaintiffs or codefendants (**joinder of parties**). [C17: from F *joindre* to JOIN]
joiner ('dʒɔɪnə) *n* **1** *Chiefly Brit.* a person skilled in making finished woodwork, such as windows and stairs. **2** a person or thing that joins. **3** *Inf.* a person who joins many clubs, etc.
joinery ('dʒɔɪnərɪ) *n* **1** the skill or craft of a joiner. **2** work made by a joiner.
joint 🅣 (dʒɔɪnt) *n* **1** a junction of two or more parts or objects. **2** *Anat.* the junction between two or more bones. **3** the point of connection between movable parts in invertebrates. **4** the part of a plant stem from which a branch or leaf grows. **5** one of the parts into which a carcass of meat is cut by the butcher, esp. for roasting. **6** *Geol.* a crack in a rock along which no displacement has occurred. **7** *Sl.* **7a** a bar or nightclub. **7b** *Often facetious.* a dwelling or meeting place. **8** *Sl.* a cannabis cigarette. **9 out of joint. 9a** dislocated. **9b** out of order. ◆ *adj* **10** shared by or belonging to two or more: *joint property.* **11** created by combined effort. **12** sharing with others or with one another: *joint rulers.* ◆ *vb (tr)* **13** to provide with or fasten by a joint or joints. **14** to plane the edge of (a board, etc.) into the correct shape for a joint. **15** to cut or divide (meat, etc.) into joints.
▸ **'jointed** *adj* ▸ **'jointly** *adv*
joint account *n* a bank account registered in the name of two or more persons, any of whom may make deposits and withdrawals.
joint stock *n* capital funds held in common and usually divided into shares.
joint-stock company *n* **1** *Brit.* a business enterprise characterized by the sharing of ownership between shareholders, whose liability is limited. **2** *US.* a business enterprise whose owners are issued shares of transferable stock but do not enjoy limited liability.
jointure ('dʒɔɪntʃə) *n Law.* **a** a provision made by a husband for his wife by settling property upon her at marriage for her use after his death. **b** the property so settled. [C14: from OF, from L *junctūra* a joining]
join up *vb (adv)* **1** *(intr)* to become a member of a military or other organization; enlist. **2** (often foll. by *with*) to unite or connect.
joist (dʒɔɪst) *n* a beam made of timber, steel, or reinforced concrete, used in the construction of floors, roofs, etc. [C14: from OF *giste* beam supporting a bridge, from Vulgar L *jacitum* (unattested) support, from *jacēre* to lie]
jojoba (həʊ'həʊbə) *n* a shrub or small tree of SW North America having edible seeds containing a valuable oil that is used in cosmetics.
joke 🅣 (dʒəʊk) *n* **1** a humorous anecdote. **2** something that is said or done for fun. **3** a ridiculous or humorous circumstance. **4** a person or thing inspiring ridicule or amusement. **5 no joke.** something very serious. ◆ *vb* **jokes, joking, joked. 6** *(intr)* to tell jokes. **7** *(intr)* to speak or act facetiously. **8** to make fun of (someone). **9 joking apart.** seriously: said after there has been joking in a discussion. [C17: from L *jocus* a jest]
▸ **'jokey** *or* **'joky** *adj* ▸ **'jokingly** *adv*
joker 🅣 ('dʒəʊkə) *n* **1** a person who jokes, esp. in an obnoxious manner. **2** *Sl., often derog.* a person: *who does that joker think he is?* **3** an extra playing card in a pack, which in many card games can rank above any other card.
jollify 🅣 ('dʒɒlɪˌfaɪ) *vb* **jollifies, jollifying, jollified.** to be or cause to be jolly.
▸ **ˌjollifi'cation** *n*
jollity 🅣 ('dʒɒlɪtɪ) *n, pl* **jollities.** the condition of being jolly.
jolly 🅣 ('dʒɒlɪ) *adj* **jollier, jolliest. 1** full of good humour. **2** having or provoking gaiety and merrymaking. **3** pleasing. ◆ *adv* **4** *Brit.* (intensifier): *you're jolly nice.* ◆ *vb* **jollies, jollying, jollied.** *(tr) Inf.* **5** (often foll. by *up* or *along*) to try to make or keep (someone) cheerful. **6** to make good-natured fun of. [C14: from OF *jolif,* prob. from ON *jōl* YULE]
▸ **'jolliness** *n*
jolly boat *n* a small boat used as a utility tender for a vessel. [C18 *jolly* prob. from Danish *jolle* YAWL]
Jolly Roger *n* the traditional pirate flag, consisting of a white skull and crossbones on a black field.
jolt 🅣 (dʒəʊlt) *vb* **1** *(tr)* to bump against with a jarring blow. **2** to move in a jolting manner. **3** *(tr)* to surprise or shock. ◆ *n* **4** a sudden jar or blow. **5** an emotional shock. [C16: prob. blend of dialect *jot* to jerk & dialect *joll* to bump]
Jon. *Bible. abbrev. for* Jonah.
Jonah ('dʒəʊnə) *or* **Jonas** ('dʒəʊnəs) *n* **1** *Old Testament.* a Hebrew prophet who, having been thrown overboard from a ship was swallowed by a great fish and vomited onto dry land. **2** a person believed to bring bad luck to those around him.
jongleur (*French* ʒɔ̃glœr) *n* (in medieval France) an itinerant minstrel. [C18: from OF *jogleour,* from L *joculātor* jester]
jonquil ('dʒɒŋkwɪl) *n* a Eurasian variety of narcissus with long fragrant yellow or white short-tubed flowers. [C17: from F *jonquille,* from Sp. *junquillo,* dim. of *junco* reed]
jorum ('dʒɔːrəm) *n* a large drinking bowl or vessel or its contents. [C18: prob. after *Jorum,* who brought vessels of silver, gold, and brass to King David (II Samuel 8:10)]
josh (dʒɒʃ) *Sl., chiefly US & Canad.* ◆ *vb* **1** to tease (someone) in a bantering way. ◆ *n* **2** a teasing joke. [C19: ?from JOKE, infl. by BOSH]
▸ **'josher** *n*
Josh. *Bible. abbrev. for* Joshua.
joss (dʒɒs) *n* a Chinese deity worshipped in the form of an idol. [C18: from pidgin E, from Port. *deos* god, from L *deus*]
joss house *n* a Chinese temple or shrine where an idol or idols are worshipped.
joss stick *n* a stick of dried perfumed paste, giving off a fragrant odour when burnt as incense.
jostle 🅣 ('dʒɒsᵊl) *vb* **jostles, jostling, jostled. 1** to bump or push (someone) roughly. **2** to come or bring into contact. **3** to force (one's way) by pushing. ◆ *n* **4** the act of jostling. **5** a rough bump or push. [C14: see JOUST]
jot 🅣 (dʒɒt) *vb* **jots, jotting, jotted. 1** *(tr;* usually foll. by *down)* to write a

THESAURUS

nudge, activate, arouse, prod, prompt, push, remind, shake, stimulate, stir, suggest
joie de vivre *n* = **enthusiasm,** ebullience, enjoyment, gaiety, gusto, joy, joyfulness, pleasure, relish, zest
Antonyms *n* apathy, depression, distaste
join *vb* **1, 7** = **connect,** accompany, add, adhere, annex, append, attach, cement, combine, couple, fasten, knit, link, marry, splice, tie, unite, yoke **2, 3** = **enrol,** affiliate with, associate with, enlist, enter, sign up **8** = **meet,** adjoin, border, border on, butt, conjoin, extend, reach, touch, verge on
Antonyms *vb* ≠ **connect:** detach, disconnect, disengage, disentangle, divide, separate, sever, unfasten ≠ **enrol:** leave, part, quit, resign
joint *n* **1** = **junction,** articulation, connection, hinge, intersection, juncture, knot, nexus, node, seam, union ◆ *adj* **10** = **shared,** collective, combined, communal, concerted, consolidated, cooperative, joined, mutual, united ◆ *vb* **13** = **join,** connect, couple, fasten, fit, unite **15** = **divide,** carve, cut up, dismember, dissect, segment, sever, sunder
jointly *adv* **10** = **collectively,** as one, in common, in conjunction, in league, in partnership, mutually, together, unitedly
Antonyms *adv* individually, separately, singly
joke *n* **1, 2** = **jest,** frolic, fun, gag *(inf.)*, jape, josh *(sl., chiefly US & Canad.)*, lark, play, prank, pun, quip, quirk, sally, sport, whimsy, wisecrack *(inf.)*, witticism, yarn **4** = **laughing stock,** buffoon, butt, clown, simpleton, target ◆ *vb* **6-8** = **jest,** banter, chaff, deride, frolic, gambol, josh *(sl., chiefly US & Canad.)*, kid *(inf.)*, mock, play the fool, quip, ridicule, taunt, tease, wind up *(Brit. sl.)*
joker *n* **1** = **comedian,** buffoon, clown, comic, humorist, jester, kidder *(inf.)*, prankster, trickster, wag, wit
jokey *adj* **1, 2** = **playful,** amusing, droll, facetious, funny, humorous, jesting, mischievous, nonserious, prankish, teasing, waggish, wisecracking
Antonyms *adj* dry, grave, humourless, solemn, straight-faced, unsmiling
jollification *n* = **festivity,** beano *(Brit. sl.)*, carousal, celebration, jolly *(inf., chiefly Brit.)*, knees-up *(Brit. inf.)*, merrymaking, party, reception, shindig *(inf.)*
jollity *n* = **fun,** conviviality, gaiety, liveliness, merriment, merrymaking, mirth, revelry
jolly *adj* **1, 2** = **happy,** blithesome, carefree, cheerful, chirpy *(inf.)*, convivial, festive, frolicsome, funny, gay, genial, gladsome *(arch.)*, hilarious, jocund, jovial, joyful, joyous, jubilant, merry, mirthful, playful, sportive, sprightly
Antonyms *adj* doleful, down in the dumps *(inf.)*, gaunt, grave, lugubrious, miserable, morose, saturnine, serious, solemn
jolt *vb* **1** = **jerk,** jar, jog, jostle, knock, push, shake, shove **3** = **surprise,** astonish, discompose, disturb, perturb, stagger, startle, stun, upset ◆ *n* **4** = **jerk,** bump, jar, jog, jump, lurch, quiver, shake, start **5** = **surprise,** blow, bolt from the blue, bombshell, reversal, setback, shock, thunderbolt, whammy *(inf., chiefly US)*
jostle *vb* **1, 3** = **push,** bump, butt, crowd, elbow, hustle, jog, joggle, jolt, press, scramble, shake, shove, squeeze, throng, thrust
jot *vb* **1** = **note down,** list, note, record, register, scribble, tally ◆ *n* **2** = **bit,** ace, atom, detail, frac-

brief note of. ◆ *n* **2** (*used with a negative*) a little bit (in **not care** (*or* **give**) **a jot**). [C16: from L *jota*, from Gk *iōta*, of Semitic origin]

jota (*Spanish* 'xota) *n* a Spanish dance in fast triple time. [Sp., prob. from OSp. *sota*, from *sotar* to dance, from L *saltāre*]

jotter Ⓣ ('dʒɒtə) *n* a small notebook.

jotting ('dʒɒtɪŋ) *n* something jotted down. [from ON, from *jötunn* giant + *heimr* world, HOME]

joual (ʒwɑːl) *n* nonstandard Canadian French dialect, esp. as associated with ill-educated speakers. [from the pronunciation in this dialect of F *cheval* horse]

joule (dʒuːl) *n* the derived SI unit of work or energy; the work done when the point of application of a force of 1 newton is displaced through a distance of 1 metre in the direction of the force. Symbol: J [C19: after J. P. *Joule* (1818–89), E physicist]

jounce (dʒaʊns) *vb* **jounces, jouncing, jounced. 1** to shake or jolt or cause to shake or jolt. ◆ *n* **2** a shake; bump. [C15: prob. from dialect *joll* to bump + BOUNCE]

journal Ⓣ ('dʒɜːnᵊl) *n* **1** a newspaper or periodical. **2** a book in which a daily record of happenings, etc., is kept. **3** an official record of the proceedings of a legislative body. **4** *Book-keeping.* one of several books in which transactions are initially recorded to facilitate subsequent entry in the ledger. **5** *Machinery.* the part of a shaft or axle in contact with or enclosed by a bearing. [C14: from OF: daily, from L *diurnālis*; see DIURNAL]

journal box *n Machinery.* a case enclosing or supporting a journal.

journalese (ˌdʒɜːnᵊ'liːz) *n Derog.* a superficial style of writing regarded as typical of newspapers, etc.

journalism ('dʒɜːnᵊˌlɪzəm) *n* **1** the profession or practice of reporting about, photographing, or editing news stories for one of the mass media. **2** newspapers and magazines collectively.

journalist Ⓣ ('dʒɜːnᵊlɪst) *n* **1** a person whose occupation is journalism. **2** a person who keeps a journal.
▸ˌ**journa'listic** *adj* ▸ˌ**journa'listically** *adv*

journalize *or* **journalise** ('dʒɜːnᵊˌlaɪz) *vb* **journalizes, journalizing, journalized** *or* **journalises, journalising, journalised.** to record (daily events) in a journal.
▸ˌ**journali'zation** *or* ˌ**journali'sation** *n*

journey Ⓣ ('dʒɜːnɪ) *n* **1** a travelling from one place to another. **2a** the distance travelled in a journey. **2b** the time taken to make a journey. ◆ *vb* **3** (*intr*) to make a journey. [C13: from OF *journee* a day, a day's travelling, from L *diurnum* day's portion]
▸'**journeyer** *n*

journeyman ('dʒɜːnɪmən) *n, pl* **journeymen. 1** a craftsman, artisan, etc., who is qualified to work at his trade in the employment of another. **2** a competent workman. [C15: from JOURNEY (in obs. sense: a day's work) + MAN]

joust Ⓣ (dʒaʊst) *History.* ◆ *n* **1** a combat between two mounted knights tilting against each other with lances. ◆ *vb* **2** (*intr*; often foll. by *against* or *with*) to encounter or engage in such a tournament: *he jousted with five opponents.* [C13: from OF, from *jouster* to fight on horseback, from Vulgar L *juxtāre* (unattested) to come together, from L *juxtā* close]
▸'**jouster** *n*

Jove (dʒəʊv) *n* **1** another name for **Jupiter**[1]. **2 by Jove.** an exclamation of surprise or excitement. [C14: from OL *Jovis* Jupiter]
▸'**Jovian** *n*

jovial Ⓣ ('dʒəʊvɪəl) *adj* having or expressing convivial humour. [C16: from L *joviālis* of (the planet) Jupiter, considered by astrologers to foster good humour]
▸**joviality** (ˌdʒəʊvɪ'ælɪtɪ) *n* ▸'**jovially** *adv*

jowl[1] (dʒaʊl) *n* **1** the jaw, esp. the lower one. **2** (*often pl*) a cheek. **3 cheek by jowl.** See **cheek**. [OE *ceafl* jaw]
▸**jowled** *adj*

jowl[2] (dʒaʊl) *n* **1** fatty flesh hanging from the lower jaw. **2** a similar fleshy part in animals, such as the dewlap of a bull. [OE *ceole* throat]

joy Ⓣ (dʒɔɪ) *n* **1** a deep feeling or condition of happiness or contentment. **2** something causing such a feeling. **3** an outward show of pleasure or delight. **4** *Brit. inf.* success; satisfaction: *I went for a loan, but got no joy.* ◆ *vb Chiefly poetic.* **5** (*intr*) to feel joy. **6** (*tr*) to gladden. [C13: from OF, from L *gaudium* joy, from *gaudēre* to be glad]

Joycean ('dʒɔɪsɪən) *adj* **1** of, relating to, or like, James Joyce (1882–1941), Irish writer, or his works. ◆ *n* **2** a student or admirer of Joyce or his works.

joyful Ⓣ ('dʒɔɪfʊl) *adj* **1** full of joy; elated. **2** expressing or producing joy: *a joyful look; a joyful occasion.*
▸'**joyfully** *adv* ▸'**joyfulness** *n*

joyless Ⓣ ('dʒɔɪlɪs) *adj* having or producing no joy or pleasure.
▸'**joylessly** *adv* ▸'**joylessness** *n*

joyous Ⓣ ('dʒɔɪəs) *adj* **1** having a happy nature or mood. **2** joyful.
▸'**joyously** *adv*

joyride ('dʒɔɪˌraɪd) *n* **1** a ride taken for pleasure in a car, esp. in a stolen car driven recklessly. ◆ *vb* **joy-ride, joy-rides, joy-riding, joy-rode, joy-ridden. 2** (*intr*) to take such a ride.
▸'**joyˌrider** *n* ▸'**joyriding** *n*

joystick ('dʒɔɪˌstɪk) *n* **1** *Inf.* the control stick of an aircraft, machine, etc. **2** *Computing.* a lever for controlling the movement of a cursor on a screen.

JP *abbrev. for* Justice of the Peace.

J/psi particle *n* a type of elementary particle thought to be formed from charmed quarks.

Jr *or* **jr** *abbrev. for* junior.

JSA (in Britain) *abbrev. for* jobseeker's allowance.

jubbah ('dʒʊbə) *n* a long loose outer garment with wide sleeves, worn by Muslim men and women, esp. in India. [C16: from Ar.]

jube (dʒuːb) *n Austral. & NZ inf.* any jelly-like sweet. [C20: shortened from JUJUBE]

jubilant Ⓣ ('dʒuːbɪlənt) *adj* feeling or expressing great joy. [C17: from L, from *jūbilāre* to give a joyful cry, from *jūbilum* a shout]
▸'**jubilance** *n* ▸'**jubilantly** *adv*

jubilate ('dʒuːbɪˌleɪt) *vb* **jubilates, jubilating, jubilated.** (*intr*) **1** to have or express great joy; rejoice. **2** to celebrate a jubilee. [C17: from L *jūbilāre*; see JUBILANT]

jubilation Ⓣ (ˌdʒuːbɪ'leɪʃən) *n* a feeling of great joy and celebration.

jubilee Ⓣ ('dʒuːbɪˌliː) *n* **1** a time or season for rejoicing. **2** a special anniversary, esp. a 25th or 50th one. **3** *RC Church.* a specially appointed period in which special indulgences are granted. **4** *Old Testament.* a year that was to be observed every 50th year, during which Hebrew slaves were to be liberated, etc. **5** a less common word for **jubilation.** [C14: from OF *jubile*, from LL *jubilaeus*, from LGk, from Heb. *yōbhēl* ram's horn, used for the proclamation of the year of jubilee]

Jud. *Bible. abbrev. for:* **1** Also: **Judg.** Judges. **2** Judith.

Judaic (dʒuː'deɪɪk) *adj* of or relating to the Jews or Judaism.
▸**Ju'daically** *adv*

Judaism ('dʒuːdeɪˌɪzəm) *n* **1** the religion of the Jews, based on the Old Testament and the Talmud and having as its central point a belief in one God. **2** the religious and cultural traditions of the Jews.
▸ˌ**Juda'istic** *adj*

Judaize *or* **Judaise** ('dʒʊdeɪˌaɪz) *vb* **Judaizes, Judaizing, Judaized** *or* **Judaises, Judaising, Judaised. 1** to conform or bring into conformity with Judaism. **2** (*tr*) to convert to Judaism.
▸ˌ**Judai'zation** *or* ˌ**Judai'sation** *n*

Judas ('dʒuːdəs) *n* **1** *New Testament.* the apostle who betrayed Jesus to his enemies for 30 pieces of silver (Luke 22:3–6, 47–48). **2** a person who betrays a friend; traitor.

Judas tree *n* small Eurasian leguminous tree with pinkish-purple flowers that bloom before the leaves appear.

judder ('dʒʌdə) *Inf., chiefly Brit.* ◆ *vb* **1** (*intr*) to shake or vibrate. ◆ *n* **2** abnormal vibration in a mechanical system. **3** a juddering motion. [prob. blend of JAR[2] + SHUDDER]

judge Ⓣ (dʒʌdʒ) *n* **1** a public official with authority to hear cases in a court of law and pronounce judgment upon them. **2** a person who is appointed to determine the result of contests or competitions. **3** a

THESAURUS

tion, grain, iota, mite, morsel, particle, scintilla, scrap, speck, tad (*inf., chiefly US*), tittle, trifle, whit

jotter *n* = **notebook**, Filofax (*Trademark*), notepad, pad

journal *n* **1** = **newspaper**, chronicle, daily, gazette, magazine, monthly, paper, periodical, record, register, review, tabloid, weekly, zine (*inf.*) **2** = **diary**, chronicle, commonplace book, daybook, log, record

journalist *n* **1** = **reporter**, broadcaster, columnist, commentator, contributor, correspondent, hack, journo (*sl.*), newsman *or* newswoman, newspaperman *or* newspaperwoman, pressman, scribe (*inf.*), stringer

journey *n* **1** = **trip**, excursion, expedition, jaunt, odyssey, outing, passage, peregrination, pilgrimage, progress, ramble, tour, travel, trek, voyage ◆ *vb* **3** = **travel**, fare, fly, go, peregrinate, proceed, ramble, range, roam, rove, tour, traverse, trek, voyage, wander, wend

joust *n* **1** = **duel**, combat, encounter, engagement, lists, match, passage of arms, set-to, tilt, tournament, tourney ◆ *vb* **2** = **cross swords**, break a lance, engage, enter the lists, fight, tilt, trade blows

jovial *adj* = **cheerful**, airy, animated, blithe, buoyant, cheery, convivial, cordial, gay, glad, happy, hilarious, jocose, jocund, jolly, jubilant, merry, mirthful
Antonyms *adj* antisocial, doleful, grumpy, morose, solemn, unfriendly

joviality *n* = **mirth**, fun, gaiety, glee, hilarity, jollity, merriment

joy *n* **1** = **delight**, bliss, ecstasy, elation, exaltation, exultation, felicity, festivity, gaiety, gladness, glee, hilarity, pleasure, rapture, ravishment, satisfaction, transport **2** = **treasure**, charm, delight, gem, jewel, pride, prize, treat, wonder
Antonyms *n* ≠ **delight:** despair, grief, misery, sorrow, tribulation, unhappiness ≠ **treasure:** bane

joyful *adj* **1** = **delighted**, blithesome, cock-a-hoop, elated, enraptured, floating on air, glad, gladsome (*arch.*), gratified, happy, jocund, jolly, jovial, jubilant, light-hearted, merry, on cloud nine (*inf.*), over the moon (*inf.*), pleased, rapt, satisfied

joyless *adj* = **unhappy**, cheerless, dejected, depressed, dismal, dispirited, downcast, down in the dumps (*inf.*), dreary, gloomy, miserable, sad

joyous *adj* **1, 2** = **joyful**, blithe, cheerful, festive, heartening, merry, rapturous

jubilant *adj* = **overjoyed**, cock-a-hoop, elated, enraptured, euphoric, excited, exuberant, exultant, glad, joyous, rejoicing, rhapsodic, thrilled, triumphal, triumphant
Antonyms *adj* despondent, doleful, downcast, melancholy, sad, sorrowful

jubilation *n* = **joy**, celebration, ecstasy, elation, excitement, exultation, festivity, jamboree, jubilee, triumph

jubilee *n* **1** = **celebration**, carnival, festival, festivity, fête, gala, holiday

judge *n* **1** = **magistrate**, beak (*Brit. sl.*), justice **2** = **referee**, adjudicator, arbiter, arbitrator, moder-

person qualified to comment critically: *a good judge of antiques.* **4** a leader of the peoples of Israel from Joshua's death to the accession of Saul. ◆ *vb* **judges, judging, judged. 5** to hear and decide upon (a case at law). **6** (*tr*) to pass judgment on. **7** (when *tr, may take a clause as object or an infinitive*) to decide (something) after inquiry. **8** to determine the result of (a contest or competition). **9** to appraise (something) critically. **10** (*tr; takes a clause as object*) to believe something to be the case. [C14: from OF, from L *jūdicāre* to pass judgment, from *jūdex* a judge]
▸ **'judge,like** *adj* ▸ **'judger** *n* ▸ **'judgeship** *n*

judge advocate *n, pl* **judge advocates.** an officer who superintends proceedings at a military court martial.

judges' rules *pl n* (in English law) a set of rules, not legally binding, governing the behaviour of police towards suspects.

judgment ❶ *or* **judgement** ('dʒʌdʒmənt) *n* **1** the faculty of being able to make critical distinctions and achieve a balanced viewpoint. **2a** the verdict pronounced by a court of law. **2b** an obligation arising as a result of such a verdict, such as a debt. **2c** (*as modifier*): *a judgment debtor.* **3** the formal decision of one or more judges at a contest or competition. **4** a particular decision formed in a case in dispute or doubt. **5** an estimation: *a good judgment of distance.* **6** criticism or censure. **7 against one's better judgment.** contrary to a preferred course of action. **8 in someone's judgment.** in someone's opinion. **9 sit in judgment. 9a** to preside as judge. **9b** to assume the position of critic.

Judgment ('dʒʌdʒmənt) *n* **1** the estimate by God of the ultimate worthiness or unworthiness of the individual or of all mankind. **2** God's subsequent decision determining the final destinies of all individuals.

judgmental ❶ *or* **judgemental** (dʒʌdʒ'mɛntᵊl) *adj* of or denoting an attitude in which judgments about other people's conduct are made.

Judgment Day *n* the occasion of the Last Judgment by God at the end of the world. Also called: **Day of Judgment.** See **Last Judgment.**

judicatory ('dʒuːdɪkətərɪ) *adj* **1** of or relating to the administration of justice. ◆ *n* **2** a court of law. **3** the administration of justice.

judicature ('dʒuːdɪkətʃə) *n* **1** the administration of justice. **2** the office, function, or power of a judge. **3** the extent of authority of a court or judge. **4** a body of judges; judiciary. **5** a court of justice or such courts collectively.

judicial ❶ (dʒuː'dɪʃəl) *adj* **1** of or relating to the administration of justice. **2** of or relating to judgment in a court of law or to a judge exercising this function. **3** allowed or enforced by a court of law: *judicial separation.* **4** having qualities appropriate to a judge. **5** giving or seeking judgment. [C14: from L *jūdiciālis* belonging to the law courts, from *jūdicium* judgment, from *jūdex* a judge]
▸ **ju'dicially** *adv*

judiciary (dʒuː'dɪʃɪərɪ) *adj* **1** of or relating to courts of law, judgment, or judges. ◆ *n, pl* **judiciaries. 2** the branch of the central authority in a state concerned with the administration of justice. **3** the system of courts in a country. **4** the judges collectively.

judicious ❶ (dʒuː'dɪʃəs) *adj* having or proceeding from good judgment.
▸ **ju'diciously** *adv* ▸ **ju'diciousness** *n*

judo ('dʒuːdəʊ) *n* **a** the modern sport derived from jujitsu, in which the object is to force an opponent to submit using the minimum of physical effort. **b** (*as modifier*): *a judo throw.* [Japanese, from *jū* gentleness + *dō* way]
▸ **'judoist** *n*

Judy ('dʒuːdɪ) *n, pl* **Judies. 1** the wife of Punch in the children's puppet show *Punch and Judy.* See **Punch. 2** (*often not cap.*) *Brit. sl.* a girl.

jug ❶ (dʒʌg) *n* **1** a vessel for holding or pouring liquids, usually having a handle and a lip. US equivalent: **pitcher. 2** *Austral. & NZ.* a container in which water is boiled, esp. an electric kettle. **3** *US.* a large vessel with a narrow mouth. **4** Also called: **jugful.** the amount of liquid held by a jug. **5** *Brit. inf.* a glass of beer. **6** *Sl.* jail. ◆ *vb* **jugs, jugging, jugged. 7** to stew or boil (meat, esp. hare) in an earthenware container. **8** (*tr*) *Sl.* to put in jail. [C16: prob. from *Jug,* nickname from name *Joan*]

jugate ('dʒuːgeɪt, -gɪt) *adj* (esp. of compound leaves) having parts arranged in pairs. [C19: from NL *jugātus* (unattested), from L *jugum* a yoke]

juggernaut ('dʒʌgə,nɔːt) *n* **1** any terrible force, esp. one that demands complete self-sacrifice. **2** *Brit.* a very large heavy lorry. [C17: from Hindi, from Sansk. *Jagannātha* lord of the world: devotees supposedly threw themselves under a cart carrying *Juggernaut,* an idol of Krishna]

juggins ('dʒʌgɪnz) *n* (*functioning as sing*) *Brit. inf.* a silly person. [C19: special use of the surname *Juggins*]

juggle ❶ ('dʒʌgᵊl) *vb* **juggles, juggling, juggled. 1** to throw and catch (several objects) continuously so that most are in the air all the time. **2** to manipulate (facts, etc.) so as to give a false picture. **3** (*tr*) to keep (several activities) in progress, esp. with difficulty. ◆ *n* **4** an act of juggling. [C14: from OF *jogler* to perform as a jester, from L, from *jocus* a jest]
▸ **'juggler** *n*

Jugoslav ('juːgəʊ,slɑːv) *n, adj* a variant spelling of **Yugoslav.**

jugular ('dʒʌgjʊlə) *adj* **1** of, relating to, or situated near the throat or neck. ◆ *n* **2** Also called: **jugular vein.** any of the large veins in the neck carrying blood to the heart from the head. [C16: from LL, from L *jugulum* throat]

juice ❶ (dʒuːs) *n* **1** any liquid that occurs naturally in or is secreted by plant or animal tissue: *the juice of an orange.* **2** *Inf.* **2a** petrol. **2b** electricity. **2c** alcoholic drink. **3** vigour or vitality. [C13: from OF *jus,* from L]
▸ **'juiceless** *adj*

juice up *vb* (*tr, adv*) *US sl.* to make lively: *to juice up a party.*

juicy ❶ ('dʒuːsɪ) *adj* **juicier, juiciest. 1** full of juice. **2** provocatively interesting; spicy: *juicy gossip.* **3** profitable: *a juicy contract.*
▸ **'juicily** *adv* ▸ **'juiciness** *n*

jujitsu, jujutsu, *or* **jiujutsu** (dʒuː'dʒɪtsuː) *n* the traditional Japanese system of unarmed self-defence perfected by the samurai. See also **judo.** [C19: from Japanese, from *jū* gentleness + *jutsu* art]

juju ('dʒuːdʒuː) *n* **1** an object superstitiously revered by certain West African peoples and used as a charm or fetish. **2** the power associated with a juju. [C19: prob. from Hausa *djudju* evil spirit, fetish]

jujube ('dʒuːdʒuːb) *n* **1** any of several Old World spiny trees that have small yellowish flowers and dark red edible fruits. **2** the fruit of any of these trees. **3** a chewy sweet made of flavoured gelatine and sometimes medicated to soothe sore throats. [C14: from Med. L *jujuba,* modification of L *zīzyphum,* from Gk *zizuphon*]

jukebox ('dʒuːk,bɒks) *n* a coin-operated machine, usually found in pubs, clubs, etc., that contains records, CDs, or videos, which are played when selected by a customer. [C20: from Gullah (an African-American language) *juke* bawdy (as in *juke house* brothel) + BOX[1]]

jukskei ('jʊk,skeɪ) *n* a South African game in which a peg is thrown over a fixed distance at a stake driven into the ground. [from Afrik. *juk* yoke + *skei* pin]

julep ('dʒuːlɪp) *n* **1** a sweet drink, variously prepared and sometimes medicated. **2** *Chiefly US.* short for **mint julep.** [C14: from OF, from Ar. *julāb,* from Persian, from *gul* rose + *āb* water]

Julian calendar ('dʒuːljən, -lɪən) *n* the calendar introduced by Julius Caesar in 46 B.C., in which leap years occurred every fourth year and in every centenary year. Cf. **Gregorian calendar.**

julienne (,dʒuːlɪ'ɛn) *adj* **1** (of vegetables) cut into thin shreds. ◆ *n* **2** a clear consommé to which such vegetables have been added. [F, from name *Jules, Julien,* or *Julienne*]

July (dʒuː'laɪ) *n, pl* **Julies.** the seventh month of the year, consisting of 31 days. [C13: from Anglo-F *julie,* from L *Jūlius,* after Gaius *Julius* Caesar, in whose honour it was named]

jumble ❶ ('dʒʌmbᵊl) *vb* **jumbles, jumbling, jumbled. 1** to mingle (objects, etc.) in a state of disorder. **2** (*tr; usually passive*) to remember in a confused form. ◆ *n* **3** a disordered mass, state, etc. **4** *Brit.* articles donated for a jumble sale. [C16: from ?]
▸ **'jumbly** *adj*

jumble sale *n* a sale of miscellaneous articles, usually second-hand, in aid of charity. US and Canad. equivalent: **rummage sale.**

jumbo ❶ ('dʒʌmbəʊ) *n, pl* **jumbos. 1** *Inf.* **1a** a very large person or thing. **1b** (*as modifier*): *a jumbo box of detergent.* **2** See **jumbo jet.** [C19: after a famous elephant exhibited by P. T. Barnum, from Swahili *jumbe* chief]

jumbo jet *n Inf.* a type of large jet-propelled airliner that carries several hundred passengers.

jumbo pack *n* **1** the promotion of bulk sales of small unit items, such

THESAURUS

ator, umpire **3** = **critic**, appraiser, arbiter, assessor, authority, connoisseur, evaluator, expert ◆ *vb* **5** = **try**, adjudge, condemn, decree, doom, find, pass sentence, pronounce sentence, rule, sentence, sit **7, 8** = **adjudicate**, adjudge, arbitrate, ascertain, conclude, decide, determine, discern, distinguish, mediate, referee, umpire **9** = **consider**, appraise, appreciate, assess, criticize, esteem, estimate, evaluate, examine, rate, review, value

judgment *n* **1** = **sense**, acumen, common sense, discernment, discrimination, intelligence, penetration, percipience, perspicacity, prudence, sagacity, shrewdness, smarts (*sl., chiefly US*), taste, understanding, wisdom **2a** = **verdict**, arbitration, award, conclusion, decision, decree, determination, finding, order, result, ruling, sentence **5** = **opinion**, appraisal, assessment, belief, conviction, deduction, diagnosis, estimate, finding, valuation, view

judgmental *adj* = **condemnatory**, censorious, pharisaic, self-righteous

judicial *adj* **1-3** = **legal**, judiciary, juridical, official **4** = **discriminating**, distinguished, impartial, judgelike, magisterial, magistral

judicious *adj* = **sensible**, acute, astute, careful, cautious, circumspect, considered, diplomatic, discerning, discreet, discriminating, enlightened, expedient, informed, politic, prudent, rational, reasonable, sagacious, sage, sane, sapient, shrewd, skilful, sober, sound, thoughtful, well-advised, well-judged, wise
Antonyms *adj* imprudent, indiscreet, injudicious, tactless, thoughtless

jug *n* **1** = **container**, carafe, crock, ewer, jar, pitcher, urn, vessel

juggle *vb* **2** = **manipulate**, alter, change, disguise, doctor (*inf.*), falsify, fix (*inf.*), manoeuvre, misrepresent, modify, tamper with

juice *n* **1** = **liquid**, extract, fluid, liquor, nectar, sap, secretion, serum

juicy *adj* **1** = **moist**, lush, sappy, succulent, watery **2** = **interesting**, colourful, provocative, racy, risqué, sensational, spicy (*inf.*), suggestive, vivid

jumble *vb* **1** = **mix**, confound, confuse, disarrange, dishevel, disorder, disorganize, entangle, mistake, muddle, ravel, shuffle, tangle ◆ *n* **3** = **muddle**, chaos, clutter, confusion, disarrangement, disarray, disorder, farrago, gallimaufry, hodgepodge, hotchpotch (*US*), litter, medley, *mélange,* mess, miscellany, mishmash, mixture, pig's breakfast (*inf.*)

jumbo *modifier* **1b** = **giant**, elephantine, gigantic, ginormous (*inf.*), huge, humongous *or* humungous (*US sl.*), immense, large, mega (*inf.*), oversized
Antonyms *adj* baby, dwarf, micro, mini, pocket, tiny, wee

as confectionery, by packing several in one wrapping, usually with a unit price reduction. **2** such a package of items.

jumbuck ('dʒʌmˌbʌk) *n Austral.* an informal word for **sheep.** [C19: from Abor.]

jump (dʒʌmp) *vb* **1** (*intr*) to leap or spring clear of the ground or other surface by using the muscles in the legs and feet. **2** (*tr*) to leap over or clear (an obstacle): *to jump a gap.* **3** (*tr*) to cause to leap over an obstacle: *to jump a horse over a hedge.* **4** (*intr*) to move or proceed hastily (into, onto, out of, etc.): *she jumped into a taxi.* **5** (*tr*) *Inf.* to board so as to travel illegally on: *he jumped the train as it was leaving.* **6** (*intr*) to parachute from an aircraft. **7** (*intr*) to jerk or start, as with astonishment, surprise, etc. **8** to rise or cause to rise suddenly or abruptly. **9** to pass or skip over (intervening objects or matter): *she jumped a few lines and then continued reading.* **10** (*intr*) to change from one thing to another, esp. from one subject to another. **11** *Draughts.* to capture (an opponent's piece) by moving one of one's own pieces over it to an unoccupied square. **12** (*intr*) *Bridge.* to bid in response to one's partner at a higher level than is necessary, to indicate a strong hand. **13** (*tr*) to come off (a track, etc.): *the locomotive jumped the rails.* **14** (*intr*) (of the stylus of a record player) to be jerked out of the groove. **15** (*intr*) *Sl.* to be lively: *the party was jumping.* **16** (*tr*) *Inf.* to attack without warning: *thieves jumped the old man.* **17** (*tr*) *Inf.* (of a driver or a motor vehicle) to pass through (a red traffic light) or move away from (traffic lights) before they change to green. **18 jump down someone's throat.** *Inf.* to address or reply to someone sharply. **19 jump ship.** to desert, esp. to leave a ship in which one is legally bound to serve. **20 jump the queue.** *Inf.* to obtain some advantage out of turn or unfairly. **21 jump to it.** *Inf.* to begin something quickly and efficiently. ◆ *n* **22** an act or instance of jumping. **23** a space, distance, or obstacle to be jumped or that has been jumped. **24** a descent by parachute from an aircraft. **25** *Sport.* any of several contests involving a jump: *the high jump.* **26** a sudden rise: *the jump in prices last month.* **27** a sudden or abrupt transition. **28** a sudden jerk or involuntary muscular spasm, esp. as a reaction of surprise. **29** a step or degree: *one jump ahead.* **30** *Draughts.* a move that captures an opponent's piece by jumping over it. **31** *Films.* **31a** a break in continuity in the normal sequence of shots. **31b** (*as modifier*): *a jump cut.* **32 on the jump.** *Inf., chiefly US & Canad.* **32a** in a hurry. **32b** busy. **33 take a running jump.** *Brit. inf.* a contemptuous expression of dismissal. ◆ See also **jump at, jump-off,** etc. [C16: prob. imit.]

jump at *vb* (*intr, prep*) to be glad to accept: *I would jump at the chance of going.*

jumped-up *adj Inf.* suddenly risen in significance, esp. when appearing arrogant.

jumper[1] ('dʒʌmpə) *n* **1** *Chiefly Brit.* a knitted or crocheted garment covering the upper part of the body. **2** the US and Canad. term for **pinafore dress.** [C19: from obs. *jump* man's loose jacket, var. of *jupe,* from OF, from Ar. *jubbah* long cloth coat]

jumper[2] ('dʒʌmpə) *n* **1** a boring tool that works by repeated impact, such as a steel bit in a drill used in boring rock. **2** Also called: **jumper cable, jumper lead.** a short length of wire used to make a connection, usually temporarily. **3** a person or animal that jumps.

jumping bean *n* a seed of any of several Mexican plants that contains a moth caterpillar whose movements cause it to jerk about.

jumping jack *n* a toy figure of a man with jointed limbs that can be moved by pulling attached strings.

jump jet *n Inf.* a fixed-wing jet aircraft that is capable of landing and taking off vertically.

jump jockey *n Brit. inf.* a jockey riding in a steeplechase, as opposed to racing on the flat.

jump leads (li:dz) *pl n* two heavy cables fitted with crocodile clips used to start a motor vehicle with a discharged battery by connecting the battery to an external battery.

jump-off *n* **1** an extra round in a showjumping contest when two or more horses are equal first, deciding the winner. ◆ *vb* **jump off. 2** (*intr, adv*) to engage in a jump-off.

jump on *vb* (*intr, prep*) *Inf.* to reprimand or attack suddenly and forcefully.

jump seat *n* **1** a folding seat on some aircraft for an additional crew member. **2** *Brit.* a folding seat in a motor vehicle.

jump-start *vb* **1** to start the engine of (a car) by pushing or rolling it and then engaging the gears or (of a car) to start in this way. ◆ *n* **2** the act of starting a car in this way. ◆ Also called (Brit.): **bump-start.**

jump suit *n* a one-piece garment of combined trousers and jacket or shirt.

jumpy ('dʒʌmpɪ) *adj* **jumpier, jumpiest. 1** nervous or apprehensive. **2** moving jerkily or fitfully.
▸**'jumpily** *adv* ▸**'jumpiness** *n*

Jun. *abbrev. for:* **1** June. **2** Also: **jun.** junior.

junco ('dʒʌŋkəʊ) *n, pl* **juncos** *or* **juncoes.** a North American bunting having a greyish plumage. [C18: from Sp.: a rush, from L *juncus* rush]

junction ('dʒʌŋkʃən) *n* **1** a place where several routes, lines, or roads meet, link, or cross each other: *a railway junction.* **2** a point on a motorway where traffic may leave or join it. **3** *Electronics.* **3a** a contact between two different metals or other materials: *a thermocouple junction.* **3b** a transition region in a semiconductor. **4** the act of joining or the state of being joined. [C18: from L *junctiō* a joining, from *jungere* to join]

junction box *n* an earthed enclosure within which wires or cables can be safely connected.

junction transistor *n* a bipolar transistor consisting of two p-n junctions combined to form either an n-p-n or a p-n-p transistor.

juncture ('dʒʌŋktʃə) *n* **1** a point in time, esp. a critical one (often in **at this juncture**). **2** *Linguistics.* the set of phonological features signalling a division between words, such as those that distinguish *a name* from *an aim.* **3** a less common word for **junction.**

June (dʒu:n) *n* the sixth month of the year, consisting of 30 days. [OE *iunius,* from L *junius,* prob. from *Junius* name of Roman gens]

jungle ('dʒʌŋgᵊl) *n* **1** an equatorial forest area with luxuriant vegetation. **2** any dense or tangled thicket or growth. **3** a place of intense or ruthless struggle for survival: *the concrete jungle.* **4** a type of fast electronic dance music, originating in the early 1990s, which combines elements of techno and ragga. [C18: from Hindi, from Sansk. *jāngala* wilderness]
▸**'jungly** *adj*

jungle fever *n* a serious malarial fever occurring in the East Indies.

jungle fowl *n* **1** any small gallinaceous bird of S and SE Asia, the males of which (**junglecock**) have an arched tail and a combed and wattled head. **2** *Austral.* any of several megapodes.

jungle juice *n Sl.* alcoholic liquor.

junior ('dʒu:njə) *adj* **1** lower in rank or length of service; subordinate. **2** younger in years. **3** of or relating to youth or childhood. **4** *Brit.* of schoolchildren between the ages of 7 and 11 approximately. **5** *US.* of or designating the third year of a four-year course at college or high school. ◆ *n* **6** *Law.* (in England) any barrister below the rank of Queen's Counsel. **7** a junior person. **8** *Brit.* a junior schoolchild. **9** *US.* a junior student. [C17: from L: younger, from *juvenis* young]

Junior ('dʒu:njə) *adj* being the younger: usually used after a name to distinguish the son from the father: *Charles Parker, Junior.* Abbrev.: **Jnr, Jr, Jun., Junr.**

junior common room *n* (in certain universities and colleges) a common room for the use of students.

junior lightweight *n* **a** a professional boxer weighing 126–130 pounds (57–59 kg). **b** (*as modifier*): *a junior-lightweight bout.*

junior middleweight *n* **a** a professional boxer weighing 147–154 pounds (66.5–70 kg). **b** (*as modifier*): *the junior-middleweight championship.*

junior school *n* (in England and Wales) a school for children aged between 7 and 11.

junior technician *n* a rank in the Royal Air Force comparable to that of private in the army.

junior welterweight *n* **a** a professional boxer weighing 135–140 pounds (61–63.5 kg). **b** (*as modifier*): *a junior-welterweight fight.*

juniper ('dʒu:nɪpə) *n* a coniferous shrub or small tree of the N hemisphere having purple berry-like cones. The cones of the **common** or **dwarf juniper** are used as a flavouring in making gin. [C14: from L *jūniperus,* from ?]

junk[1] (dʒʌŋk) *n* **1** discarded objects, etc., collectively. **2** *Inf.* **2a** rubbish generally. **2b** nonsense: *the play was absolute junk.* **3** *Sl.* any narcotic drug, esp. heroin. ◆ *vb* **4** (*tr*) *Inf.* to discard as junk. [C15 *jonke* old useless rope]

junk[2] (dʒʌŋk) *n* a sailing vessel used in Chinese waters and characterized by a very high poop, flat bottom, and square sails supported by battens. [C17: from Port. *junco,* from Javanese *jon*]

junk bond *n Finance.* a security that offers a high yield but often involves a high risk of default.

Junker ('jʊŋkə) *n* **1** *History.* any of the aristocratic landowners of Prussia. **2** an arrogant German army officer or official. **3** (formerly) a young German nobleman. [C16: from G, from OHG *junchērro* young lord]
▸**'Junkerdom** *n*

junket ('dʒʌŋkɪt) *n* **1** a sweet dessert made of flavoured milk set to a curd with rennet. **2** a feast. **3** an excursion, esp. one made for pleasure at public expense. ◆ *vb* **4** to have or entertain with a feast. **5** (*intr*) (of

THESAURUS

jump *vb* **1, 2** = **leap**, bounce, bound, caper, clear, gambol, hop, hurdle, skip, spring, vault **7** = **recoil**, flinch, jerk, start, wince **8** = **increase**, advance, ascend, boost, escalate, gain, hike, mount, rise, surge **9** = **miss**, avoid, digress, evade, omit, overshoot, skip, switch ◆ *n* **22** = **leap**, bound, buck, caper, hop, skip, spring, vault **23** = **hurdle**, barricade, barrier, fence, impediment, obstacle, rail **26** = **rise**, advance, augmentation, boost, increase, increment, upsurge, upturn **28** = **jolt**, jar, jerk, lurch, shock, start, swerve, twitch, wrench

jumped-up *adj Informal* = **conceited**, arrogant, cocky, immodest, insolent, overbearing, pompous, presumptuous, puffed up, self-opinionated, stuck-up, toffee-nosed, too big for one's boots *or* breeches

jumper[1] *n* **1** = **sweater**, jersey, pullover, woolly

jumpy *adj* **1** = **nervous**, agitated, anxious, apprehensive, fidgety, hyper (*inf.*), jittery (*inf.*), neurotic, on edge, restless, shaky, tense, timorous, twitchy (*inf.*), wired (*sl.*)
Antonyms *adj* calm, composed, laid-back (*inf.*), nerveless, together (*sl.*), unfazed (*inf.*), unflustered

junction *n* **1, 4** = **connection**, alliance, combination, coupling, joint, juncture, linking, seam, union

juncture *n* **1** = **moment**, conjuncture, contingency, crisis, crux, emergency, exigency, occasion, point, predicament, strait, time **3** = **junction**, bond, connection, convergence, edge, intersection, link, seam, weld

junior *adj* **1, 2** = **minor**, inferior, lesser, lower, secondary, subordinate, younger
Antonyms *adj* elder, higher-ranking, older, senior, superior

junk[1] *n* **1, 2a** = **rubbish**, clutter, debris, dreck (*sl.,*

a public official, etc.) to go on a junket. [C14 (in the sense: rush basket, hence custard served on rushes): from OF (dialect) *jonquette,* from *jonc* rush, from L *juncus* reed]
▸ 'junketing *n*

junk food *n* food which is eaten in addition to or instead of regular meals, and which often has a low nutritional value.

junkie ❶ *or* **junky** ('dʒʌŋkɪ) *n, pl* **junkies.** an informal word for **drug addict.**

junk mail *n* unsolicited mail advertising goods or services.

junk shop *n* a shop selling miscellaneous second-hand goods and sometimes antiques.

junta ❶ ('dʒʌntə, 'hʊntə) *n (functioning as sing or pl)* **1** a group of military officers holding the power in a country, esp. after a coup d'état. **2** Also called: **junto.** a small group of men. **3** a legislative or executive council in some parts of Latin America. [C17: from Sp.: council, from L, from *jungere* to join]

junto ('dʒʊntəʊ) *n, pl* **juntos.** a variant of **junta** (sense 2). [C17]

Jupiter[1] ('dʒu:pɪtə) *n* (in Roman tradition) the king and ruler of the Olympian gods. Also called: **Jove.**

Jupiter[2] ('dʒu:pɪtə) *n* the largest of the planets and the fifth from the sun.

Jurassic (dʒʊ'ræsɪk) *adj* **1** of or formed in the second period of the Mesozoic era, during which dinosaurs and ammonites flourished. ◆ *n* **2 the.** the Jurassic period or rock system. [C19: from F *jurassique,* after the *Jura* (Mountains) in W central Europe]

jurat ('dʒʊəræt) *n* **1** *Law.* a statement at the foot of an affidavit, naming the parties, stating when, where, and before whom it was sworn, etc. **2** (in England) a municipal officer of the Cinque Ports. **3** (in France and the Channel Islands) a magistrate. [C16: from Med. L *jūrātus* one who has been sworn, from L *jūrāre* to swear]

juridical (dʒʊ'rɪdɪk°l) *adj* of or relating to law or to the administration of justice; legal. [C16: from L, from *iūs* law + *dicere* to say]
▸ ju'ridically *adv*

jurisdiction ❶ (ˌdʒʊərɪs'dɪkʃən) *n* **1** the right or power to administer justice and to apply laws. **2** the exercise or extent of such right or power. **3** authority in general. [C13: from L *jūrisdictiō* administration of justice, from *jus* law + DICTION]
▸ ˌjuris'dictional *adj*

jurisprudence (ˌdʒʊərɪs'pru:d°ns) *n* **1** the science or philosophy of law. **2** a system or body of law. **3** a branch of law: *medical jurisprudence.* [C17: from L *jūris prūdentia,* from *jus* law + PRUDENCE]
▸ jurisprudential (ˌdʒʊərɪspru:'denʃəl) *adj*

jurist ('dʒʊərɪst) *n* a person versed in the science of law, esp. Roman or civil law. [C15: from F *juriste,* from Med. L *jūrista*]

juristic (dʒʊ'rɪstɪk) *or* **juristical** *adj* **1** of or relating to jurists. **2** of or characteristic of the study of law or the legal profession.

juror ('dʒʊərə) *n* **1** a member of a jury. **2** a person who takes an oath. [C14: from Anglo-F *jurour,* from OF *jurer* to take an oath, from L *jūrāre*]

jury[1] ('dʒʊərɪ) *n, pl* **juries. 1** a group of, usually, twelve people sworn to deliver a true verdict according to the evidence upon a case presented in a court of law. **2** a body of persons appointed to judge a competition and award prizes. [C14: from OF *juree,* from *jurer* to swear]

jury[2] ('dʒʊərɪ) *adj Chiefly naut.* (*in combination*) makeshift: *jury-rigged.* [C17: from ?]

jury box *n* an enclosure where the jury sits in court.

juryman ('dʒʊərɪmən) *or (fem)* **jurywoman** *n, pl* **jurymen** *or* **jurywomen.** a member of a jury.

jury-rigged *adj Chiefly naut.* set up in a makeshift manner.

just ❶ *adj* (dʒʌst). **1a** fair or impartial in action or judgment. **1b** (*as collective n; preceded by the*): *the just.* **2** conforming to high moral standards; honest. **3** consistent with justice: *a just action.* **4** rightly applied or given: *a just reward.* **5** legally valid; lawful: *a just inheritance.* **6** well-founded: *just criticism.* **7** correct or true: *a just account.* ◆ *adv* (dʒʌst; *unstressed* dʒəst). **8** used with forms of *have* to indicate an action performed in the very recent past: *I have just closed the door.* **9** at this very instant: *he's just coming in to land.* **10** no more than; only: *just an ordinary car.* **11** exactly: *that's just what I mean.* **12** barely: *he just got there in time.* **13 just about. 13a** at the point of starting (to do something). **13b** almost: *I've just about had enough.* **14 just a moment, second,** *or* **minute.** an expression requesting the hearer to wait or pause for a brief period of time. **15 just so.** arranged with precision. [C14: from L *jūstus* righteous, from *jūs* justice]
▸ 'justly *adv* ▸ 'justness *n*

> **USAGE NOTE** The use of *just* with *exactly* (*it's just exactly what they want*) is redundant and should be avoided: *it's exactly what they want.*

justice ❶ ('dʒʌstɪs) *n* **1** the quality or fact of being just. **2** *Ethics.* the principle of fairness that like cases should be treated alike. **3** the administration of law according to prescribed and accepted principles. **4** conformity to the law. **5** a judge of the Supreme Court of Judicature. **6** short for **justice of the peace. 7** good reason (esp. in **with justice**). **8 bring to justice.** to capture, try, and usually punish (a criminal, etc.). **9 do justice to. 9a** to show to full advantage. **9b** to show full appreciation of by action. **9c** to treat or judge fairly. **10 do oneself justice.** to make full use of one's abilities. [C12: from OF, from L *jūstitia,* from *justus* JUST]
▸ 'justiceˌship *n*

justice of the peace *n* a lay magistrate whose function is to preserve the peace in his area and try summarily such cases as are within his jurisdiction.

justiciar (dʒʌ'stɪʃɪˌɑ:) *n English legal history.* the chief political and legal officer from the time of William I to that of Henry III, who deputized for the king in his absence. Also called: **justiciary.**
▸ jus'ticiarˌship *n*

justiciary (dʒʌ'stɪʃɪərɪ) *adj* **1** of or relating to the administration of justice. ◆ *n, pl* **justiciaries. 2** an officer or administrator of justice; judge.

justifiable ❶ ('dʒʌstɪˌfaɪəb°l) *adj* capable of being justified.
▸ ˌjustiˌfia'bility *n* ▸ 'justiˌfiably *adv*

justifiable homicide *n* lawful killing, as in the execution of a death sentence.

justification ❶ (ˌdʒʌstɪfɪ'keɪʃən) *n* **1** reasonable grounds for complaint, defence, etc. **2** proof, vindication, or exculpation. **3** *Christian theol.* **3a** the act of justifying. **3b** the process of being justified or the condition of having been justified.
▸ 'justifiˌcatory *adj*

justify ❶ ('dʒʌstɪˌfaɪ) *vb* **justifies, justifying, justified.** (*mainly tr*) **1** (*often passive*) to prove or see to be just or valid; vindicate. **2** to show to be reasonable: *his behaviour justifies our suspicion.* **3** to declare or show to be free from blame or guilt. **4** *Law.* to show good reason in court for (some action taken). **5** (*also intr*) *Printing, computing.* to adjust the spaces between words in (a line of type or data) so that it is of the required length or (of a line of type or data) to fit exactly. **6a** *Protestant theol.* to declare righteous by the imputation of Christ's merits to the sinner. **6b** *RC theol.* to change from sinfulness to righteousness by the transforming effects of grace. **7** (*also intr*) *Law.* to prove (a person) to have sufficient means to act as surety, etc., or (of a person) to qualify to provide bail or surety. [C14: from OF *justifier,* from L *justificāre,* from *jūstus* JUST + *facere* to make]
▸ 'justiˌfier *n*

Justinian Code (dʒʌ'stɪnɪən) *n* a compilation of Roman imperial law made by order of Justinian I (483–565 A.D.), Byzantine emperor.

just-in-time *adj* denoting or relating to an industrial method in which waste, queues, bottlenecks, etc., are eliminated or reduced by producing production-line components, etc., and by delivering materials just before they are needed. Abbrev.: **JIT.**

justle ('dʒʌs°l) *vb* **justles, justling, justled.** a less common word for **jostle.**

jut ❶ (dʒʌt) *vb* **juts, jutting, jutted. 1** (*intr;* often foll. by *out*) to stick out or overhang beyond the surface or main part. ◆ *n* **2** something that juts out. [C16: var. of JET[1]]
▸ 'jutting *adj*

THESAURUS

chiefly US), leavings, litter, oddments, odds and ends, refuse, rummage, scrap, trash, waste

junkie *n* = **addict**, acidhead (*sl.*), cokehead (*sl.*), drug addict, druggie (*inf.*), head (*sl.*), mainliner (*sl.*), pill-popper (*sl.*), pothead (*sl.*), smackhead (*sl.*), user

junta *n* **2, 3** = **cabal**, assembly, camp, clique, combination, confederacy, convocation, coterie, council, crew, faction, gang, league, party, ring, schism, set

jurisdiction *n* **1** = **authority**, command, control, dominion, influence, power, prerogative, rule, say, sway **2** = **range**, area, bounds, circuit, compass, district, dominion, field, orbit, province, scope, sphere, zone

just *adj* **1, 2** = **fair**, blameless, conscientious, decent, equitable, fair-minded, good, honest, honourable, impartial, lawful, pure, right, righteous, unbiased, upright, virtuous **4, 6** = **fitting**, appropriate, apt, condign, deserved, due, justified, legitimate, merited, proper, reasonable, rightful, sensible, suitable, well-deserved **7** = **correct**, accurate, exact, faithful, normal, precise, proper, regular, sound, true ◆ *adv* **8** = **recently**, hardly, lately, only now, scarcely **10** = **merely**, at a push, at most, but, by the skin of one's teeth, no more than, nothing but, only, simply, solely **11** = **exactly**, absolutely, completely, entirely, perfectly, precisely **13 just about** = **practically**, all but, almost, around, close to, nearly, not quite, virtually, well-nigh
Antonyms *adj* ≠ **fair:** corrupt, devious, dishonest, inequitable, prejudiced, unfair, unjust, unlawful ≠ **fitting:** inappropriate, undeserved, unfit, unreasonable ≠ **correct:** untrue

justice *n* **1, 2** = **fairness**, equity, honesty, impartiality, integrity, justness, law, legality, legitimacy, reasonableness, rectitude, right **6** = **judge**, magistrate
Antonyms *n* ≠ **fairness:** dishonesty, favouritism, inequity, injustice, partiality, unfairness, unlawfulness, unreasonableness, wrong

justifiable *adj* = **reasonable**, acceptable, defensible, excusable, fit, lawful, legitimate, proper, right, sensible, sound, tenable, understandable, valid, vindicable, warrantable, well-founded
Antonyms *adj* arbitrary, capricious, indefensible, inexcusable, unreasonable, unwarranted

justification *n* **1** = **reason**, basis, defence, grounds, plea, warrant **2** = **explanation**, absolution, apology, approval, defence, exculpation, excuse, exoneration, extenuation, plea, rationalization, vindication

justify *vb* **1-3** = **explain**, absolve, acquit, approve, confirm, defend, establish, exculpate, excuse, exonerate, legalize, legitimize, maintain, substantiate, support, sustain, uphold, validate, vindicate, warrant

justly *adv* **1, 3, 4, 7** = **properly**, accurately, correctly, equally, equitably, fairly, honestly, impartially, lawfully

jut *vb* **1** = **stick out**, bulge, extend, impend, overhang, poke, project, protrude

jute (dʒuːt) *n* **1** either of two Old World tropical yellow-flowered herbaceous plants, cultivated for their strong fibre. **2** this fibre, used in making sacks, rope, etc. [C18: from Bengali *jhuto,* from Sansk. *jūta* braid of hair]

juv. *abbrev. for* juvenile.

juvenescence (ˌdʒuːvɪˈnɛsəns) *n* **1** youth or immaturity. **2** the act or process of growing from childhood to youth.
▸ **ˌjuveˈnescent** *adj*

juvenile ❶ (ˈdʒuːvɪˌnaɪl) *adj* **1** young, youthful, or immature. **2** suitable or designed for young people: *juvenile pastimes.* ◆ *n* **3** a juvenile person, animal, or plant. **4** an actor who performs youthful roles. **5** a book intended for young readers. [C17: from L *juvenīlis* youthful, from *juvenis* young]
▸ **ˈjuveˌnilely** *adv*

juvenile court *n* a court that deals with juvenile offenders and children beyond parental control or in need of care.

juvenile delinquency *n* antisocial or criminal conduct by juvenile delinquents.

juvenile delinquent *n* a child or young person guilty of some offence, act of vandalism, or antisocial behaviour and who may be brought before a juvenile court.

juvenilia (ˌdʒuːvɪˈnɪlɪə) *n* works of art, literature, or music produced in youth, before the artist, author, or composer has formed a mature style. [C17: from L, lit.: youthful things]

juxtapose ❶ (ˌdʒʌkstəˈpəʊz) *vb* **juxtaposes, juxtaposing, juxtaposed.** (*tr*) to place close together or side by side. [C19: back formation from *juxtaposition,* from L *juxta* next to + POSITION]
▸ **ˌjuxtapoˈsition** *n* ▸ **ˌjuxtapoˈsitional** *adj*

THESAURUS

juvenile *adj* **1** = **young**, babyish, boyish, callow, childish, girlish, immature, inexperienced, infantile, jejune, puerile, undeveloped, unsophisticated, youthful ◆ *n* **3** = **child**, adolescent, boy, girl, infant, minor, youth

Antonyms *adj* ≠ **young:** adult, grown-up, mature, responsible ◆ *n* ≠ **child:** adult, grown-up

juxtaposition *n* = **proximity**, adjacency, closeness, contact, contiguity, nearness, propinquity, vicinity

Kk

k *or* **K** (keɪ) *n, pl* **k's, K's,** *or* **Ks. 1** the 11th letter and 8th consonant of the English alphabet. **2** a speech sound represented by this letter, usually a voiceless velar stop, as in *kitten.*

k *symbol for:* **1** kilo(s). **2** *Maths.* the unit vector along the *z*-axis.

K *symbol for:* **1** Kelvin(s). **2** *Chess.* king. **3** *Chem.* potassium. [from NL *kalium*] **4** *Physics.* kaon. **5** *Currency.* **5a** kina. **5b** kip. **5c** kopeck. **5d** kwacha. **5e** kyat. **6** one thousand. [from KILO-] **7** *Computing.* **7a** a unit of 1024 words, bits, or bytes. **7b** (not in technical usage) 1000.

K *or* **K.** *abbrev. for* Köchel: indicating the serial number in the catalogue of the works of Mozart made by Ludwig von Köchel, 1800–77.

k. *abbrev. for:* **1** karat. **2** Also: **K.** king.

Kaaba *or* **Caaba** (ˈkɑːbə) *n* a cube-shaped building in Mecca, the most sacred Muslim pilgrim shrine, into which is built the black stone believed to have been given by Gabriel to Abraham. [from Ar. *ka'bah,* from *ka'b* cube]

kabaddi (kəˈbɑːdɪ) *n* a game played between two teams of seven players, in which individuals take turns to chase and try to touch members of the opposing team without being captured by them. [Tamil]

kabbala *or* **kabala** (kəˈbɑːlə) *n* variant spellings of **cabbala.**

kabuki (kæˈbuːkɪ) *n* a form of Japanese drama based on legends and characterized by elaborate costumes and the use of male actors. [Japanese, from *ka* singing + *bu* dancing + *ki* art]

Kabyle (kəˈbaɪl) *n* **1** (*pl* **Kabyles** *or* **Kabyle**) a member of a Berber people in Tunisia and Algeria. **2** the dialect of Berber spoken by this people. [C19: from Ar. *qabā'il,* pl. of *qabīlah* tribe]

kadi (ˈkɑːdɪ, ˈkeɪdɪ) *n, pl* **kadis.** a variant spelling of **cadi.**

Kaffir *or* **Kafir** (ˈkæfə) *n, pl* **Kaffirs** *or* **Kaffir, Kafirs** *or* **Kafir. 1** *Offens.* **1a** (in southern Africa) any Black African. **1b** (*as modifier*): *Kaffir farming.* **2** a former name for the **Xhosa** language. [C19: from Ar. *kāfir* infidel, from *kafara* to deny]

kaffir beer *n S. African.* beer made from sorghum (kaffir corn) or millet.

kaffirboom (ˈkæfəˌbuəm) *n* a S. African deciduous flowering tree. [from KAFFIR + Afrik. *boom* tree]

kaffir corn *n* a southern African variety of sorghum, cultivated in dry regions for its grain and as fodder. Sometimes shortened to **kaffir.**

Kafir (ˈkæfə) *n, pl* **Kafirs** *or* **Kafir. 1** a member of a people inhabiting E Afghanistan. **2** a variant spelling of **Kaffir.** [C19: from Ar.; see KAFFIR]

Kafkaesque (ˌkæfkəˈɛsk) *adj* of or like the writings of Franz Kafka (1883–1924), Czech novelist, esp. in having a nightmarish and dehumanized quality.

kaftan *or* **caftan** (ˈkæftæn) *n* **1** a long coatlike garment, usually with a belt, worn in the East. **2** an imitation of this, worn esp. by women, consisting of a loose dress with long wide sleeves. [C16: from Turkish *qaftān*]

kagoul (kəˈguːl) *n* a variant spelling of **cagoule.**

kahawai (ˈkɑːhəwaɪ, ˈkɑːwaɪ) *n* a New Zealand food and game fish. [from Maori]

kai (kaɪ) *n NZ inf.* food. [from Maori]

kaiak (ˈkaɪæk) *n* a variant spelling of **kayak.**

kail (keɪl) *n* a variant spelling of **kale.**

kai moana (məʊˈænə) *n NZ.* seafood. [Maori]

kainite (ˈkaɪnaɪt) *n* a white mineral consisting of potassium chloride and magnesium sulphate: a fertilizer and source of potassium salts. [C19: from G *Kainit,* from Gk *kainos* new + -ITE[1]]

Kaiser (ˈkaɪzə) *n* (*sometimes not cap.*) *History.* **1** any of the three German emperors. **2** *Obs.* any Austro-Hungarian emperor. [C16: from G, ult. from L *Caesar* emperor]

kaizen *Japanese.* (kaɪˈzɛn) *n* a philosophy of continuous improvement of working practices that underlies total quality management and just-in-time business techniques. [lit.: improvement]

kaka (ˈkɑːkə) *n* a New Zealand parrot with a long compressed bill. [C18: from Maori, ? imit. of its call]

kaka beak *n* a New Zealand shrub with beaklike red flowers. [from KAKA]

kakapo (ˈkɑːkəˌpəʊ) *n, pl* **kakapos.** a ground-living nocturnal parrot of New Zealand, resembling an owl. [C19: from Maori, lit.: night kaka]

kakemono (ˌkækɪˈməʊnəʊ) *n, pl* **kakemonos.** a Japanese paper or silk wall hanging, usually long and narrow, with a picture or inscription on it. [C19: from Japanese, from *kake* hanging + *mono* thing]

kala-azar (ˌkɑːləəˈzɑː) *n* a tropical infectious disease caused by a protozoan in the liver, spleen, etc. [C19: from Assamese *kālā* black + *āzār* disease]

Kalashnikov (kəˈlæʃnɪˌkɒf) *n* a Russian-made automatic rifle. See also **AK-47.** [C20: after Mikhail *Kalashnikov* (born 1919), its designer]

kale *or* **kail** (keɪl) *n* **1** a cultivated variety of cabbage with crinkled leaves. **2** *Scot.* a cabbage. ◆ Cf. **sea kale.** [OE *cāl*]

kaleidoscope ⓣ (kəˈlaɪdəˌskəʊp) *n* **1** an optical toy for producing symmetrical patterns by multiple reflections in inclined mirrors enclosed in a tube. Loose pieces of coloured glass, paper, etc., are placed between transparent plates at the far end of the tube, which is rotated to change the pattern. **2** any complex pattern of frequently changing shapes and colours. [C19: from Gk *kalos* beautiful + *eidos* form + -SCOPE]
▸**kaleidoscopic** (kəˌlaɪdəˈskɒpɪk) *adj*

kalends (ˈkælɪndz) *pl n* a variant spelling of **calends.**

Kalevala (ˌkɑːləˈvɑːlə) *n Finnish legend.* **1** the land of the hero Kaleva, who performed legendary exploits. **2** the Finnish national epic in which these exploits are recounted. [Finnish, from *kaleva* of a hero + *-la* home]

kaleyard *or* **kailyard** (ˈkeɪlˌjɑːd; *Scot.* -ˌjard) *n Scot.* a vegetable garden. [C19: lit.: cabbage garden]

kaleyard school *or* **kailyard school** *n* a group of writers who depicted the homely aspects of life in the Scottish Lowlands. The best-known contributor was J. M. Barrie.

kalied (ˈkeɪlaɪd) *adj N English dialect.* drunk.

kalmia (ˈkælmɪə) *n* an evergreen North American ericaceous shrub having showy clusters of white or pink flowers. [C18: after Peter *Kalm* (1715–79), Swedish botanist and pupil of Linnaeus]

Kalmuck (ˈkælmʌk) *or* **Kalmyk** (ˈkælmɪk) *n* **1** (*pl* **Kalmucks, Kalmuck** *or* **Kalmyks, Kalmyk**) a member of a Mongoloid people of Buddhist tradition, who migrated from W China to Russia in the 17th century. **2** the language of this people.

kalong (ˈkɑːlɒŋ) *n* a fruit bat of the Malay Archipelago; a flying fox. [Javanese]

kalpa (ˈkælpə) *n* (in Hindu cosmology) a period in which the universe experiences a cycle of creation and destruction. [C18: Sansk.]

Kamasutra (ˌkɑːməˈsuːtrə) *n* **the.** an ancient Hindu text on erotic pleasure. [Sansk.: book on love, from *kāma* love + *sūtra* thread]

kame (keɪm) *n* an irregular mound or ridge of gravel, sand, etc., deposited by water derived from melting glaciers. [C19: Scot. & N English var. of COMB]

kamikaze ⓣ (ˌkæmɪˈkɑːzɪ) *n* **1** (*often cap.*) (in World War II) one of a group of Japanese pilots who performed suicidal missions. **2** (*modifier*) (of an action) undertaken or (of a person) undertaking an action in the knowledge that it will result in the death of the person performing it in order to inflict maximum damage on an enemy: *a kamikaze attack.* **3** (*modifier*) extremely foolhardy and possibly self-defeating: *kamikaze prices.* [C20: from Japanese, from *kami* divine + *kaze* wind]

kamilaroi (ˈkæmələˌrɔɪ) *n* an Australian Aboriginal language formerly used in NW New South Wales.

Kamloops trout (ˈkæmluːps) *n* a variety of rainbow trout common in British Columbia.

kampong (ˈkæmpɒŋ) *n* (in Malaysia) a village. [C19: from Malay]

Kampuchean (ˌkæmpuˈtʃɪən) *adj, n* a former word for **Cambodian.**

Kanak (kəˈnæk) *n* a native or inhabitant of New Caledonia who seeks independence from France. [C20: from Hawaiian: man]

Kanaka (kəˈnækə) *n* **1** a native Hawaiian. **2** (*often not cap.*) *Austral.* any native of the South Pacific islands, esp. (formerly) one abducted to work in Australia. [C19: from Hawaiian: man]

Kanarese *or* **Canarese** (ˌkænəˈriːz) *n* **1** (*pl* **Kanarese** *or* **Canarese**) a member of a people of S India living chiefly in Kanara. **2** the language of this people.

kanban *Japanese.* (ˈkænbæn) *n* **1** a just-in-time manufacturing process in which the movements of materials through a process are recorded on specially designed cards. **2** any of the cards used for ordering materials in such a system. [lit.: advertisement hoarding]

kanga *or* **khanga** (ˈkæŋgə) *n* a piece of gaily decorated thin cotton cloth used as a woman's garment, originally in E Africa. [from Swahili]

kangaroo (ˌkæŋgəˈruː) *n, pl* **kangaroos. 1** a large herbivorous marsupial of Australia and New Guinea, having large powerful hind legs used for leaping, and a long thick tail. **2** (*usually pl*) *Stock Exchange.* an Australian share, esp. in mining, land, or a tobacco company. [C18: prob. from Abor.]
▸ˌ**kanga'roo-**ˌ**like** *adj*

kangaroo closure *n Parliamentary procedure.* a form of closure in which the chairman or speaker selects certain amendments for discussion and excludes others.

kangaroo court *n* an irregular court, esp. one set up by strikers to judge strikebreakers.

kangaroo paw *n* any of various Australian plants having green-and-red hairy flowers.

kangaroo rat *n* **1** a small leaping rodent related to the squirrels and inhabiting desert regions of North America, having a stocky body and very long hind legs and tail. **2** Also called: **kangaroo mouse.** any of several leaping Australian rodents.

THESAURUS

kaleidoscopic *adj* **2** = **changeable,** fluctuating, fluid, many-coloured, mobile, motley, mutable, unstable, variegated **2** = **complicated,** complex, confused, convoluted, disordered, intricate, jumbled, varied

kamikaze *modifier* **2, 3** = **self-destructive,** foolhardy, suicidal

kanji ('kændʒɪ) *n, pl* **kanji** *or* **kanjis. 1** a Japanese writing system using characters mainly derived from Chinese ideograms. **2** a character in this system. [Japanese, from Chinese *han* Chinese + *zi* character]

KANU ('kɑːnuː) *n acronym for* Kenya African National Union.

kaolin ('keɪəlɪn) *n* a fine white clay used for the manufacture of hard-paste porcelain and bone china and in medicine as a poultice. Also called: **china clay.** [C18: from F, from Chinese *Kaoling* Chinese mountain where supplies for Europe were first obtained]
▸ˌ**kao'linic** *adj* ▸**'kaolinˌize** *or* **'kaolinˌise** *vb*

kaon ('keɪɒn) *n* a meson that has a rest mass of about 996 or 964 electron masses. Also called: **K-meson.** [C20 *ka* representing the letter *k* + (MES)ON]

kapellmeister (kæ'pɛlˌmaɪstə) *n* a variant spelling of **capellmeister.**

kapok ('keɪpɒk) *n* a silky fibre obtained from the hairs covering the seeds of a tropical tree (**kapok tree**): used for stuffing pillows, etc. [C18: from Malay]

Kaposi's sarcoma (kæ'pəʊsɪz) *n* a form of skin cancer found in Africans and more recently in victims of AIDS. [C20: after Moritz Kohn *Kaposi* (1837–1902), Austrian dermatologist who first described the sores that characterize the disease]

kappa ('kæpə) *n* the tenth letter in the Greek alphabet (Κ, κ). [Gk, of Semitic origin]

kaput 🅣 (kæ'pʊt) *adj* (*postpositive*) *Inf.* ruined, broken, or not functioning. [C20: from G *kaputt* done for]

karabiner (ˌkærə'biːnə) *n Mountaineering.* a metal clip with a spring for attaching to a piton, belay, etc. Also called: **snaplink, krab.** [shortened from G *Karabinerhaken*, lit.: carbine hook]

karakul *or* **caracul** ('kærək^əl) *n* **1** a breed of sheep of central Asia having coarse black, grey, or brown hair: the lambs have soft curled hair. **2** the fur prepared from these lambs. ◆ See also **Persian lamb.** [C19: from Russian, from the name of a region in Bukhara where the sheep originated]

karaoke (ˌkɑːrə'əʊkɪ) *n* **a** an entertainment of Japanese origin in which people take it in turns to sing well-known songs over a prerecorded backing tape. **b** (*as modifier*): *a karaoke bar.* [from Japanese, from *kara* empty + *ōkesutora* orchestra]

karat ('kærət) *n* the usual US and Canad. spelling of **carat** (sense 2).

karate (kə'rɑːtɪ) *n* **a** a traditional Japanese system of unarmed combat, employing smashes, chops, kicks, etc., made with the hands, feet, elbows, or legs. **b** (*as modifier*): *karate chop.* [Japanese, lit.: empty hand]

karateka (kə'rɑːtɪˌkɑː) *n* a competitor or expert in karate. [Japanese; see KARATE]

Karitane (ˌkærɪ'tɑːnɛ) *n NZ.* a nurse for babies; nanny. [from former child-care hospital at *Karitane*, New Zealand]

karma ('kɑːmə) *n* **1** *Hinduism, Buddhism.* the principle of retributive justice determining a person's state of life and the state of his reincarnations as the effect of his past deeds. **2** destiny or fate. **3** *Inf.* an aura or quality that a person, place, or thing is felt to have. [C19: from Sansk.: action, effect, from *karoti* he does]
▸**'karmic** *adj*

kaross (kə'rɒs) *n* a garment of skins worn by indigenous peoples in southern Africa. [C18: from Afrik. *karos*, ?from Du., from F *cuirasse* CUIRASS]

karri ('kɑːrɪ) *n, pl* **karris. 1** an Australian eucalyptus tree. **2** the durable dark red wood of this tree, used for construction, etc. [from Abor.]

karst (kɑːst) *n* (*modifier*) denoting the characteristic scenery of a limestone region, including underground streams, gorges, etc. [C19: G, from *Karst*, limestone plateau near Trieste]

kart (kɑːt) *n* a light low-framed vehicle with small wheels and engine used for recreational racing (**karting**). Also called: **go-cart, go-kart.**

karyo- *or* **caryo-** *combining form.* indicating the nucleus of a cell. [from NL, from Gk *karuon* kernel]

karyotype ('kærɪəˌtaɪp) *n* **1** the appearance of the chromosomes in a somatic cell of an individual or species, with reference to their number, size, shape, etc. ◆ *vb* **karyotypes, karyotyping, karyotyped.** (*tr*) **2** to determine the karyotype of (a cell).
▸**karyotypic** (ˌkærɪə'tɪpɪk) *or* ˌ**karyo'typical** *adj*

kasbah *or* **casbah** ('kæzbɑː) *n* (*sometimes cap.*) **1** the citadel of any of various North African cities. **2** the quarter in which a kasbah is located. [from Ar. *kaṣbạ* citadel]

kashruth *or* ***kashrut*** *Hebrew.* (kaʃ'ruːt) *n* **1** the condition of being fit for ritual use in general. **2** the system of dietary laws that requires ritual slaughter, the complete separation of milk and meat, and the prohibition of such foods as pig meat and shell fish. ◆ See also **kosher** (sense 1). [lit.: appropriateness]

kata ('kætə) *n* an exercise consisting of a sequence of the specific movements of a martial art, used in training and designed to show skill in technique. [C20: Japanese, lit.: shape, pattern]

kata- *prefix* a variant spelling of **cata-.**

katabatic (ˌkætə'bætɪk) *adj* (of winds) blowing downhill through having become denser with cooling.

katydid ('keɪtɪˌdɪd) *n* a green long-horned grasshopper living on the foliage of trees in North America. [C18: imit.]

kaumatua (kaʊ'mɑːtuːə) *n NZ.* a senior member of a tribe; elder. [Maori]

kauri ('kaʊrɪ) *n, pl* **kauris. 1** a New Zealand coniferous tree with oval leaves and round cones. **2** the wood or resin of this tree. [C19: from Maori]

kauri gum *n* the fossil resin of the kauri tree.

kava ('kɑːvə) *n* **1** a Polynesian shrub. **2** a drink prepared from the aromatic roots of this shrub. [C18: from Polynesian: bitter]

Kawasaki's disease (ˌkæwə'sækɪz) *n* a disease of children that causes a rash, fever, and swelling of the lymph nodes and often damages the heart muscle. [C20: after T. *Kawasaki*, Japanese physician who first described it]

kayak *or* **kaiak** ('kaɪæk) *n* **1** a canoe-like boat used by Eskimos, consisting of a frame covered with animal skins. **2** a fibreglass or canvas-covered canoe of similar design. [C18: from Eskimo]

kayo *or* **KO** ('keɪ'əʊ) *n, pl* **kayos,** *vb* **kayos, kayoing, kayoed.** *Boxing, sl.* another term for **knockout** or **knock out.** [C20: from the initial letters of *knock out*]

kazoo (kə'zuː) *n, pl* **kazoos.** a cigar-shaped musical instrument of metal or plastic with a membranous diaphragm of thin paper that vibrates with a nasal sound when the player hums into it. [C20: prob. imit.]

KB (in Britain) *abbrev. for:* **1** King's Bench. **2** *Computing.* kilobyte.

KBE *abbrev. for* Knight (Commander of the Order) of the British Empire.

kbyte *Computing. abbrev. for* kilobyte.

kc *abbrev. for* kilocycle.

KC (in Britain) *abbrev. for:* **1** King's Counsel. **2** Kennel Club.

kcal *abbrev. for* kilocalorie.

KCB *abbrev. for* Knight Commander of the Bath (a Brit. title).

KCMG *abbrev. for* Knight Commander (of the Order) of St Michael and St George (a Brit. title).

KE *abbrev. for* kinetic energy.

kea ('kɛə) *n* a large New Zealand parrot with a brownish-green plumage. [C19: from Maori, imit. of its call]

kebab (kə'bæb) *n* a dish consisting of small pieces of meat, tomatoes, onions, etc., grilled on skewers. Also called: **shish kebab.** [C17: from Ar. *kabāb* roast meat]

kecks *or* **keks** (kɛks) *pl n N English dialect.* trousers. [C19: from obs. *kicks* breeches]

kedge (kɛdʒ) *Naut.* ◆ *vb* **kedges, kedging, kedged. 1** to draw (a vessel) along by hauling in on the cable of a light anchor, or (of a vessel) to be drawn in this fashion. ◆ *n* **2** a light anchor, used esp. for kedging. [C15: from *caggen* to fasten]

kedgeree (ˌkɛdʒə'riː) *n Chiefly Brit.* a dish consisting of rice, cooked flaked fish, and hard-boiled eggs. [C17: from Hindi, from Sansk. *khiccā*]

keek (kiːk) *n, vb* a Scot. word for **peep**[1]. [C18: prob. from MDu. *kīken* to look]

keel[1] (kiːl) *n* **1** one of the main longitudinal structural members of a vessel to which the frames are fastened. **2 on an even keel.** well-balanced; steady. **3** any structure corresponding to or resembling the keel of a ship. **4** *Biol.* a ridgelike part; carina. ◆ *vb* **5** to capsize. ◆ See also **keel over.** [C14: from ON *kjölr*]

keel[2] (kiːl) *n Eastern English dialect.* **1** a flat-bottomed vessel, esp. one used for carrying coal. **2** a measure of coal. [C14 *kele*, from MDu. *kiel*]

keelage ('kiːlɪdʒ) *n* a fee charged by certain ports to allow a ship to dock.

keelhaul ('kiːlˌhɔːl) *vb* (*tr*) **1** to drag (a person) by a rope from one side of a vessel to the other through the water under the keel. **2** to rebuke harshly. [C17: from Du. *kielhalen*; see KEEL[1], HAUL]

keel over 🅣 *vb* (*adv*) **1** to turn upside down; capsize. **2** (*intr*) *Inf.* to collapse suddenly.

keelson ('kɛlsən, 'kiːl-) *or* **kelson** *n* a longitudinal beam fastened to the keel of a vessel for strength and stiffness. [C17: prob. from Low G *kielswin* keel swine, ult. of Scand. origin]

keen[1] 🅣 (kiːn) *adj* **1** eager or enthusiastic. **2** (*postpositive*; foll. by *on*) fond (of); devoted (to): *keen on golf.* **3** intellectually acute: *a keen wit.* **4** (of sight, smell, hearing, etc.) capable of recognizing fine distinctions. **5** having a sharp cutting edge or point. **6** extremely cold and penetrating: *a keen wind.* **7** intense or strong: *a keen desire.* **8** *Chiefly Brit.* extremely low so as to be competitive: *keen prices.* [OE *cēne*]
▸**'keenly** *adv* ▸**'keenness** *n*

keen[2] 🅣 (kiːn) *vb* (*intr*) **1** to lament the dead. ◆ *n* **2** a dirge or lament for the dead. [C19: from Irish Gaelic *caoine*, from OIrish *coīnim* I wail]
▸**'keener** *n*

THESAURUS

kaput *adj Informal* = **broken**, dead, defunct, destroyed, extinct, finished, ruined, undone, wrecked

keel over *vb* **1, 2** = **collapse**, black out, capsize, faint, founder, overturn, pass out, swoon (*literary*), topple over, upset

keen[1] *adj* **1, 2** = **eager**, ardent, avid, bright-eyed and bushy-tailed (*inf.*), devoted to, earnest, ebullient, enthusiastic, fervid, fierce, fond of, impassioned, intense, into (*inf.*), zealous **3** = **astute**, brilliant, canny, clever, discerning, discriminating, perceptive, perspicacious, quick, sagacious, sapient, sensitive, shrewd, wise **5** = **sharp**, acid, acute, biting, caustic, cutting, edged, finely honed, incisive, penetrating, piercing, pointed, razor-like, sardonic, satirical, tart, trenchant, vitriolic

Antonyms *adj* ≠ **eager:** apathetic, half-hearted, indifferent, laodicean, lukewarm, unenthusiastic, uninterested ≠ **astute:** dull, obtuse, unperceptive ≠ **sharp:** blunt, dull

keen[2] *vb* **1** = **lament**, bewail, grieve, mourn, wail, weep ◆ *n* **2** = **lament**, coronach (*Scot. & Irish*), dirge, lamentation, mourning, wailing, weeping

keenness *n* **1, 2** = **eagerness**, ardour, avidity, avidness, diligence, earnestness, ebullience, enthusiasm, fervour, impatience, intensity, pas-

keep Ⓣ (kiːp) *vb* **keeps, keeping, kept. 1** (*tr*) to have or retain possession of. **2** (*tr*) to have temporary possession or charge of: *keep my watch for me.* **3** (*tr*) to store in a customary place: *I keep my books in the desk.* **4** to remain or cause to remain in a specified state or condition: *keep ready.* **5** to continue or cause to continue: *keep in step.* **6** (*tr*) to have or take charge or care of: *keep the shop for me till I return.* **7** (*tr*) to look after or maintain for use, pleasure, etc.: *to keep chickens.* **8** (*tr*) to provide for the upkeep or livelihood of. **9** (*tr*) to support financially, esp. in return for sexual favours. **10** to confine or detain or be confined or detained. **11** to withhold or reserve or admit of withholding or reserving: *your news will keep.* **12** (*tr*) to refrain from divulging or violating: *to keep a secret.* **13** to preserve or admit of preservation. **14** (*tr;* sometimes foll. by *up*) to observe with due rites or ceremonies. **15** (*tr*) to maintain by writing regular records in: *to keep a diary.* **16** (when *intr*, foll. by *in, on, to,* etc.) to stay in, on, or at (a place or position): *keep to the path.* **17** (*tr*) to associate with (esp. in **keep bad company**). **18** (*tr*) to maintain in existence: *to keep court in the palace.* **19** (*tr*) *Chiefly Brit.* to have habitually in stock: *this shop keeps all kinds of wool.* **20 how are you keeping?** how are you? ◆ *n* **21** living or support. **22** *Arch.* charge or care. **23** Also called: **dungeon, donjon.** the main tower within the walls of a medieval castle or fortress. **24 for keeps.** *Inf.* **24a** permanently. **24b** for the winner or possessor to keep permanently. ◆ See also **keep at, keep away,** etc. [OE *cēpan* to observe]

keep at Ⓣ *vb* (*prep*) **1** (*intr*) to persist in. **2** (*tr*) to constrain (a person) to continue doing (a task).

keep away *vb* (*adv;* often foll. by *from*) to refrain or prevent from coming (near).

keep back Ⓣ *vb* (*adv;* often foll. by *from*) **1** (*tr*) to refuse to reveal or disclose. **2** to prevent or be prevented from advancing, entering, etc.

keep down *vb* (*adv, mainly tr*) **1** to repress. **2** to restrain or control: *he had difficulty keeping his anger down.* **3** to cause not to increase or rise. **4** (*intr*) to lie low. **5** not to vomit.

keeper Ⓣ ('kiːpə) *n* **1** a person in charge of animals, esp. in a zoo. **2** a person in charge of a museum, collection, or section of a museum. **3** a person in charge of other people, such as a warder in a jail. **4** See **goalkeeper, wicketkeeper, gamekeeper, park keeper. 5** a person who keeps something. **6** a bar placed across the poles of a permanent magnet to close the magnetic circuit when it is not in use.

keep fit *n* exercises designed to promote physical fitness if performed regularly.

keep from *vb* (*prep*) **1** (foll. by a gerund) to prevent or restrain (oneself or another); refrain or cause to refrain. **2** (*tr*) to protect or preserve from.

keeping Ⓣ ('kiːpɪŋ) *n* **1** conformity or harmony (esp. in **in** *or* **out of keeping**). **2** charge or care: *valuables in the keeping of a bank.*

keepnet ('kiːpˌnɛt) *n* a net strung on wire hoops and sealed at one end, suspended in water by anglers to keep alive the fish they have caught.

keep off *vb* **1** to stay or cause to stay at a distance (from). **2** (*prep*) not to eat or drink or to prevent from eating or drinking. **3** (*prep*) to avoid or cause to avoid (a topic).

keep on Ⓣ *vb* (*adv*) **1** to continue or persist in (doing something): *keep on running.* **2** (*tr*) to continue to wear. **3** (*tr*) to continue to employ: *the firm kept on only ten men.* **4** (*intr;* foll. by *about*) to persist in talking (about). **5** (*intr;* foll. by *at*) to nag (a person).

keep out *vb* (*adv*) **1** to remain or cause to remain outside. **2 keep out of. 2a** to remain or cause to remain unexposed to. **2b** to avoid or cause to avoid: *keep out of his way.*

keepsake Ⓣ ('kiːpˌseɪk) *n* a gift that evokes memories of a person or event.

keep to *vb* (*prep*) **1** to adhere to or stand by or cause to adhere to or stand by. **2** to confine or be confined to. **3 keep oneself to oneself.** to avoid the society of others. **4 keep to oneself. 4a** (*intr*) to avoid the society of others. **4b** (*tr*) to refrain from sharing or disclosing.

keep up Ⓣ *vb* (*adv*) **1** (*tr*) to maintain (prices, one's morale) at the present level. **2** (*intr;* often foll. by *with*) to maintain a pace or rate set by another. **3** (*intr;* often foll. by *with*) to remain informed: *to keep up with developments.* **4** (*tr*) to maintain in good condition. **5** (*tr*) to hinder (a person) from going to bed at night. **6 keep it up.** to continue a good performance. **7 keep up with.** to remain in contact with, esp. by letter. **8 keep up with (the Joneses).** *Inf.* to compete with (one's neighbours) in material possessions, etc.

kef (kɛf) *n* a variant spelling of **kif.**

keffiyeh (kɛ'fiːjə), **kaffiyeh,** *or* **kufiyah** *n* a cotton headdress worn by Arabs. [C19: from Ar., ?from LL *cofea* COIF]

keg Ⓣ (kɛg) *n* **1** a small barrel with a capacity of between five and ten gallons. **2** *Brit., Austral., & NZ.* an aluminium container in which beer is transported and stored. [C17: var. of ME *kag,* of Scand. origin]

keks (kɛks) *pl n* a variant spelling of **kecks.**

keloid ('kiːlɔɪd) *n Pathol.* a hard raised growth of scar tissue at the site of an injury. [C19: from Gk *khēlē* claw]

kelp (kɛlp) *n* **1** any large brown seaweed. **2** the ash of such seaweed, used as a source of iodine and potash. [C14: from ?]

kelpie[1] *or* **kelpy** ('kɛlpɪ) *n, pl* **kelpies.** an Australian breed of sheepdog having a coat of various colours and erect ears. [named after a particular specimen of the breed, c 1870]

kelpie[2] ('kɛlpɪ) *n* (in Scottish folklore) a water spirit in the form of a horse. [C18: prob. rel. to Scot. Gaelic *cailpeach* heifer, from ?]

kelson ('kɛlsən) *n* a variant spelling of **keelson.**

kelt (kɛlt) *n* a salmon that has recently spawned. [C14: from ?]

Kelt (kɛlt) *n* a variant spelling of **Celt.**

kelter ('kɛltə) *n* a variant of **kilter.**

kelvin ('kɛlvɪn) *n* the basic SI unit of thermodynamic temperature; the fraction 1/273.16 of the thermodynamic temperature of the triple point of water. Symbol: K [C20: after William Thomson *Kelvin,* 1st Baron Kelvin (1824–1907), Brit. physicist]

Kelvin scale *n* a thermodynamic temperature scale in which the zero is absolute zero. Originally the degree was equal to that on the Celsius scale but it is now defined so that the triple point of water is exactly 273.16 kelvins.

kempt (kɛmpt) *adj* (of hair) tidy; combed. See also **unkempt.** [C20: back formation from *unkempt;* orig. p.p. of dialect *kemb* to COMB]

ken Ⓣ (kɛn) *n* **1** range of knowledge (esp. in **beyond** *or* **in one's ken**). ◆ *vb* **kens, kenning, kenned** *or* **kent. 2** *Scot. & northern English dialect.* to know. **3** *Scot. & northern English dialect.* to understand. [OE *cennan*]

kendo ('kɛndəʊ) *n* the Japanese art of fencing with pliable bamboo staves or, sometimes, real swords. [Japanese, lit.: way of the sword, from *ken* sword + *do* way]

kennel ('kenᵊl) *n* **1** a hutlike shelter for a dog. US name: **doghouse. 2** (*usually pl*) an establishment where dogs are bred, trained, boarded, etc. **3** a hovel. **4** a pack of hounds. ◆ *vb* **kennels, kennelling, kennelled** *or US* **kennels, kenneling, kenneled. 5** to keep or stay in a kennel. [C14: from OF, from Vulgar L *canīle* (unattested), from L *canis* dog]

kenning ('kɛnɪŋ) *n* a conventional metaphoric name for something, esp. in Old Norse and Old English poetry. [C14: from ON, from *kenna;* see KEN]

kenspeckle ('kɛnˌspɛkᵊl) *adj Scot.* easily seen or recognized. [C18: from dialect *kenspeck,* of Scand. origin]

kepi ('keɪpiː) *n, pl* **kepis.** a military cap with a circular top and a horizontal peak. [C19: from F *képi,* from G (Swiss dialect) *käppi* a little cap, from *kappe* CAP]

Kepler's laws ('kɛpləz) *pl n* three laws of planetary motion published by Johannes Kepler (1571–1630), German astronomer, between 1609 and 1619. They deal with the shape of a planet's orbit, the constant velocity of the planet in orbit, and the relationship between the length of a planetary year and the distance from the sun.

kept (kɛpt) *vb* **1** the past tense and past participle of **keep. 2 kept woman.** *Censorious.* a woman maintained by a man as his mistress.

keratin ('kɛrətɪn) *n* a fibrous protein that occurs in the outer layer of the skin and in hair, nails, hooves, etc.

keratose ('kɛrəˌtəʊs, -ˌtəʊz) *adj* (esp. of certain sponges) having a horny skeleton. [C19: from Gk *keras* horn + -OSE[1]]

kerb *or US & Canad.* **curb** (kɜːb) *n* a line of stone or concrete forming an

THESAURUS

sion, zeal, zest **3** = **astuteness,** canniness, cleverness, discernment, insight, sagacity, sapience, sensitivity, shrewdness, wisdom **5** = **sharpness,** acerbity, harshness, incisiveness, mordancy, penetration, pungency, rigour, severity, sternness, trenchancy, unkindness, virulence

keep *vb* **1** = **retain,** conserve, control, hold, maintain, possess, preserve **2, 6** = **look after,** care for, defend, guard, maintain, manage, mind, operate, protect, safeguard, shelter, shield, tend, watch over **8** = **support,** board, feed, foster, maintain, nourish, nurture, provide for, provision, subsidize, sustain, victual **10** = **detain,** arrest, block, check, constrain, control, curb, delay, deter, hamper, hamstring, hinder, hold, hold back, impede, inhibit, keep back, limit, obstruct, prevent, restrain, retard, shackle, stall, withhold **14** = **comply with,** adhere to, celebrate, commemorate, fulfil, hold, honour, obey, observe, perform, respect, ritualize, solemnize **17** = **associate with,** accompany, consort with, fraternize with **19** = **store,** accumulate, amass, carry, deal in, deposit, furnish, garner, heap, hold, pile, place, stack, stock, trade in ◆ *n* **21** = **board,** food, livelihood, living, maintenance, means, nourishment, subsistence, support **23** = **tower,** castle, citadel, donjon, dungeon, fastness, stronghold

Antonyms *vb* ≠ **retain:** abandon, discard, give up, lose ≠ **detain:** free, liberate, release ≠ **comply with:** disregard, ignore

keep at *vb* **1** = **persist,** be steadfast, carry on, complete, continue, drudge, endure, finish, grind, labour, last, maintain, persevere, remain, slave, stay, stick, toil

keep back *vb* **1** = **suppress,** censor, conceal, hide, keep dark, keep under one's hat, reserve, withhold **2** = **restrain,** check, constrain, control, curb, delay, hold back, keep a tight rein on, limit, prohibit, restrict, retard, withhold

keeper *n* **2, 3** = **guardian,** attendant, caretaker, curator, custodian, defender, governor, guard, jailer *or* gaoler, overseer, preserver, steward, superintendent, warden, warder

keeping *n* **1** *As in* **in keeping with** = **agreement,** accord, balance, compliance, conformity, congruity, consistency, correspondence, harmony, observance, proportion **2** = **care,** aegis, auspices, charge, custody, guardianship, keep, maintenance, patronage, possession, protection, safekeeping, trust

keep on *vb* **1** = **continue,** carry on, endure, last, persevere, persist, prolong, remain

keepsake *n* = **souvenir,** emblem, favour, memento, relic, remembrance, reminder, symbol, token

keep up *vb* **1, 2** = **maintain,** balance, compete, contend, continue, emulate, keep pace, match, persevere, preserve, rival, sustain, vie

keg *n* **1** = **barrel,** cask, drum, firkin, hogshead, tun, vat

ken *n* **1** = **knowledge,** acquaintance, awareness, cognizance, comprehension, notice, understanding

edge between a pavement and a roadway. [C17: from OF *courbe* bent, from L *curvus;* see CURVE]
▸ 'kerbing *n*

kerb crawling *n* the act of driving slowly beside the pavement seeking to entice someone into the car for sexual purposes.
▸ **kerb crawler** *n*

kerb drill *n* a pedestrian's procedure for crossing a road safely, esp. as taught to children.

kerbstone *or US & Canad.* **curbstone** ('kɜːbˌstəʊn) *n* one of a series of stones that form a kerb.

kerchief ● ('kɜːtʃɪf) *n* a piece of cloth worn over the head. [C13: from OF, from *covrir* to COVER + *chef* head]
▸ 'kerchiefed *adj*

kerel ('kɛərəl) *n S. African.* a young man. [from Afrik. *kêrel;* cf. OE *ceorl*]

kerf (kɜːf) *n* the cut made by a saw, an axe, etc. [OE *cyrf* a cutting]

kerfuffle (kə'fʌfəl) *n Inf., chiefly Brit.* commotion; disorder. [from Scot. *curfuffle, carfuffle,* from Scot. Gaelic *car* twist, turn + *fuffle* to disarrange]

kermes ('kɜːmɪz) *n* **1** the dried bodies of female scale insects used as a red dyestuff. **2** a small evergreen Eurasian oak tree: the host plant of kermes scale insects. [C16: from F, from Ar. *qirmiz,* from Sansk. *krmija-* red dye, lit.: produced by a worm]

kermis *or* **kirmess** ('kɜːmɪs) *n* **1** (formerly, esp. in Holland and northern Germany) an annual country festival. **2** *US & Canad.* a similar event held to collect money for charity. [C16: from MDu., from *kerc* church + *misse* MASS; orig. a festival held to celebrate the dedication of a church]

kern[1] *or* **kerne** (kɜːn) *n* the part of the character on a piece of printer's type that projects beyond the body. [C17: from F *carne* corner of type, ult. from L *cardō* hinge]

kern[2] (kɜːn) *n* **1** a lightly armed foot soldier in medieval Ireland or Scotland. **2** *Arch.* a loutish peasant. [C14: from MIrish *cethern* band of foot soldiers, from *cath* battle]

kernel ● ('kɜːnəl) *n* **1** the edible seed of a nut or fruit within the shell or stone. **2** the grain of a cereal, esp. wheat, consisting of the seed in a hard husk. **3** the central or essential part of something. [OE *cyrnel* a little seed, from *corn* seed]
▸ 'kernel-less *adj*

kerosene *or* **kerosine** ('kɛrəˌsiːn) *n* **1** another name (esp. US, Canad., Austral., & NZ) for **paraffin** (sense 1). **2** the general name for paraffin as a fuel for jet aircraft. [C19: from Gk *kēros* wax + -ENE]

> **USAGE NOTE** The spelling *kerosine* is now the preferred form in technical and industrial usage.

kersey ('kɜːzɪ) *n* a twilled woollen cloth with a cotton warp. [C14: prob. from *Kersey,* village in Suffolk]

kerseymere ('kɜːzɪˌmɪə) *n* a fine soft woollen cloth of twill weave. [C18: from KERSEY + *(cassi)mere,* var. of CASHMERE]

kestrel ('kɛstrəl) *n* any of several small falcons that feed on small mammals and tend to hover against the wind. [C15: changed from OF *cresserele,* from *cressele* rattle, from Vulgar L *crepicella* (unattested), from L, from *crepāre* to rustle]

ketch (kɛtʃ) *n* a two-masted sailing vessel, fore-and-aft rigged, with a tall mainmast. [C15 *cache,* prob. from *cacchen* to hunt; see CATCH]

ketchup ('kɛtʃəp), **catchup,** *or* **catsup** *n* any of various sauces containing vinegar: *tomato ketchup.* [C18: from Chinese *kōetsiap* brine of pickled fish, from *kōe* seafood + *tsiap* sauce]

ketone ('kiːtəʊn) *n* any of a class of compounds with the general formula R'COR, where R and R' are alkyl or aryl groups. [C19: from G, from *Aketon* ACETONE]
▸ **ketonic** (kɪ'tɒnɪk) *adj*

ketone body *n Biochem.* any of three compounds produced when fatty acids are broken down in the liver to provide a source of energy. Excess ketone bodies are present in the blood and urine of people unable to use glucose as an energy source, as in diabetes.

kettle ('kɛtəl) *n* **1** a metal container with a handle and spout for boiling water. **2** any of various metal containers for heating liquids, cooking fish, etc. **3** a large metal vessel designed to withstand high temperatures, used in various industrial processes such as refining and brewing. [C13: from ON *ketill,* ult. from L *catillus* a little pot, from *catīnus* pot]

kettledrum ('kɛtəlˌdrʌm) *n* a percussion instrument of definite pitch, consisting of a hollow bowl-like hemisphere covered with a skin or membrane, supported on a tripod. The pitch may be adjusted by means of screws, which alter the tension of the skin.
▸ 'kettle,drummer *n*

kettle hole *n* a round hollow formed by the melting of a mass of buried ice.

kettle of fish *n* **1** a situation; state of affairs (often used ironically in **a pretty** *or* **fine kettle of fish**). **2** case; matter for consideration: *that's quite a different kettle of fish.*

key[1] ● (kiː) *n* **1** a metal instrument, usually of a specifically contoured shape, that is made to fit a lock and, when rotated, operates the lock's mechanism. **2** any instrument that is rotated to operate a valve, clock winding mechanism, etc. **3** a small metal peg or wedge inserted to prevent relative motion. **4** any of a set of buttons operating a typewriter, computer, etc. **5** any of the visible parts of the lever mechanism of a musical keyboard instrument that when depressed cause the instrument to sound. **6a** Also called: **tonality.** any of the 24 major and minor diatonic scales considered as a corpus of notes upon which a piece of music draws for its tonal framework. **6b** the main tonal centre in an extended composition: *a symphony in the key of F major.* **7** something that is crucial in providing an explanation or interpretation. **8** (*modifier*) of great importance: *a key issue.* **9** a means of achieving a desired end: *the key to happiness.* **10** a means of access or control: *Gibraltar is the key to the Mediterranean.* **11** a list of explanations of symbols, codes, etc. **12** a text that explains or gives information about a work of literature, art, or music. **13** *Electrical engineering.* a hand-operated switch that is pressed to transmit coded signals, esp. Morse code. **14** the grooving or scratching of a surface or the application of a rough coat of plaster, etc., to provide a bond for a subsequent finish. **15** pitch: *he spoke in a low key.* **16** a mood or style: *a poem in a melancholic key.* **17** short for **keystone** (sense 1). **18** *Bot.* any dry winged fruit, esp. that of the ash. ◆ *vb* (*mainly tr*) **19** (foll. by *to*) to harmonize (with): *to key one's actions to the prevailing mood.* **20** to adjust or fasten with a key or some similar device. **21** to provide with a key or keys. **22** (*also intr*) another word for **keyboard** (sense 3). **23** to include a distinguishing device in (an advertisement, etc.), so that responses to it can be identified. **24** (*also intr*) to groove, scratch, or apply a rough coat of plaster, etc., to (a surface) to provide a bond for a subsequent finish. ◆ See also **key in, key up.** [OE *cǣg*]
▸ 'keyless *adj*

key[2] (kiː) *n* a variant spelling of **cay.**

keyboard ('kiːˌbɔːd) *n* **1a** a set of keys, usually hand-operated, as on a piano, typewriter, or typesetting machine. **1b** (*as modifier*): *a keyboard instrument.* **2** (*pl*) electronic keyboard instruments: *John plays keyboards for the band.* ◆ *vb* **3** (*tr*) to set (a text) in type by using a keyboard machine.
▸ 'key,boarder *n*

key grip *n* the person in charge of moving and setting up camera tracks and scenery in a film or television studio.

keyhole ('kiːˌhəʊl) *n* an aperture in a door or a lock case through which a key may be passed to engage the lock mechanism.

keyhole surgery *n* surgery carried out through a very small incision.

key in ● *vb* (*tr, adv*) to enter (information or instructions) in a computer or other device by means of a keyboard or keypad.

key-man assurance *n* an assurance policy taken out, esp. by a small company, on the life of a senior executive whose death would create a serious loss.

key money *n* a fee payment required from a new tenant of a house or flat before he moves in.

keynote ● ('kiːˌnəʊt) *n* **1a** a central or determining principle in a speech, literary work, etc. **1b** (*as modifier*): *a keynote speech.* **2** the note upon which a scale or key is based; tonic. ◆ *vb* **keynotes, keynoting, keynoted.** (*tr*) **3** to deliver a keynote address to (a political convention, etc.).

keypad ('kiːˌpæd) *n* a small panel with a set of buttons for operating a teletext system, electronic calculator, etc.

key punch *n* **1** Also called: **card punch.** a device having a keyboard that is operated manually to transfer data onto punched cards, paper tape, etc. ◆ *vb* **key-punch. 2** to transfer (data) by using a key punch.

key signature *n Music.* a group of sharps or flats appearing at the beginning of each stave line to indicate the key in which a piece, section, etc., is to be performed.

key stage *n Brit. education.* any one of four broad age-group divisions (5–7; 7–11; 11–14; 14–16) to which each level of the National Curriculum applies.

keystone ● ('kiːˌstəʊn) *n* **1** the central stone at the top of an arch or the top stone of a dome or vault. **2** something that is necessary to connect other related things.

key up *vb* (*tr, adv*) to raise the intensity, excitement, tension, etc., of.

kg 1 *abbrev. for* keg. ◆ **2.** *symbol for* kilogram.

KG *abbrev. for* Knight of the Order of the Garter (a Brit. title).

KGB *abbrev. for* the former Soviet secret police, founded in 1954. [from Russian *Komitet gosudarstvennoi bezopasnosti* State Security Committee]

khaddar ('kɑːdə) *or* **khadi** ('kɑːdɪ) *n* a cotton cloth of plain weave, produced in India. [from Hindi *khādar*]

khaki ('kɑːkɪ) *n, pl* **khakis. 1** a dull yellowish-brown colour. **2a** a hard-wearing fabric of this colour, used esp. for military uniforms. **2b** (*as modifier*): *a khaki jacket.* [C19: from Urdu, from Persian: dusty, from *khāk* dust]

khalif ('keɪlɪf) *n* a variant spelling of **caliph.**

THESAURUS

kerchief *n* = **scarf,** babushka, headscarf, headsquare, square

kernel *n* **3** = **essence,** core, germ, gist, grain, marrow, nub, pith, seed, substance

key[1] *n* **1** = **opener,** latchkey **7** = **answer,** clue, cue, explanation, guide, indicator, interpretation, lead, means, pointer, sign, solution, translation ◆ *modifier* **8** = **essential,** basic, chief, crucial, decisive, fundamental, important, leading, main, major, pivotal, principal
Antonyms *adj* ≠ **essential:** minor, secondary, subsidiary, superficial

key in *vb* = **type,** enter, input, keyboard

keynote *n* **1** = **heart,** centre, core, essence, gist, kernel, marrow, pith, substance, theme

keystone *n* **2** = **basis,** core, cornerstone, crux, fundament, ground, linchpin, mainspring, motive, principle, quoin, root, source, spring

Khalsa ('kælsə) *n* an order of the Sikh religion, founded (1699) by Guru Gobind Singh.

khan[1] (kɑːn) *n* **1a** (formerly) a title borne by medieval Chinese emperors and Mongol and Turkic rulers. **1b** such a ruler. **2** a title of respect borne by important personages in Afghanistan and central Asia. [C14: from OF, from Med. L, from Turkish *khān*, contraction of *khāqān* ruler]
▸ **'khanate** *n*

khan[2] (kɑːn) *n* an inn in Turkey, etc.; caravanserai. [C14: via Ar. from Persian]

khedive (kɪ'diːv) *n* the viceroy of Egypt under Ottoman suzerainty (1867–1914). [C19: from F, from Turkish, from Persian *khidīw* prince]
▸ **khe'dival** *or* **khe'divial** *adj*

Khmer (kmɛə) *n* **1** a member of a people of Cambodia, noted for a civilization that flourished from about 800 A.D. to about 1370. **2** the language of this people: the official language of Cambodia. ◆ *adj* **3** of or relating to this people or their language.
▸ **'Khmerian** *adj*

Khoikhoi (kɔɪ'kɔɪ *or* xɔɪ'xɔɪ) *n* **1** a member of a Southern African people who formerly occupied the region around the Cape of Good Hope and are now almost extinct. **2** any of the languages of this people.

kHz *symbol for* kilohertz.

kiang (kɪ'æŋ) *n* a variety of the wild ass that occurs in Tibet and surrounding regions. [C19: from Tibetan *rkyan*]

kia ora (ˌkɪə 'ɔːrə) *sentence substitute. NZ.* greetings! good luck! [Maori, lit.: be well!]

kibble[1] ('kɪbᵊl) *n Brit.* a bucket used in wells or in mining for hoisting. [C17: from G *kübel*, ult. from Med. L *cuppa* CUP]

kibble[2] ('kɪbᵊl) *vb* **kibbles, kibbling, kibbled.** (*tr*) to grind into small pieces. [C18: from ?]

kibbutz (kɪ'bʊts) *n, pl* **kibbutzim** (ˌkɪbʊt'siːm). a collective agricultural settlement in modern Israel, owned and administered communally by its members. [C20: from Mod. Heb. *qibbūs* gathering, from Heb. *qibbūtz*]

kibe (kaɪb) *n* a chilblain, esp. an ulcerated one on the heel. [C14: prob. from Welsh *cibi*, from ?]

kiblah ('kɪblɑː) *n Islam.* the direction of Mecca, to which Muslims turn in prayer. [C18: from Ar. *qiblah* that which is placed opposite]

kibosh ('kaɪˌbɒʃ) *n* **put the kibosh on.** *Sl.* to put a stop to; prevent from continuing; halt. [C19: from ?]

kick ❶ (kɪk) *vb* **1** (*tr*) to drive or impel with the foot. **2** (*tr*) to hit with the foot or feet. **3** (*intr*) to strike out or thrash about with the feet, as in fighting or swimming. **4** (*intr*) to raise a leg high, as in dancing. **5** (of a gun, etc.) to recoil or strike in recoiling when fired. **6** (*tr*) *Rugby.* to make (a conversion or a drop goal) by means of a kick. **7** (*tr*) *Soccer.* to score (a goal) by a kick. **8** (*intr*) *Athletics.* to put on a sudden spurt. **9** (*intr*) to make a sudden violent movement. **10** (*intr;* sometimes foll. by *against*) *Inf.* to object or resist. **11** (*intr*) *Inf.* to be active and in good health (esp. in **alive and kicking**). **12** *Inf.* to change gear in (a car): *he kicked into third.* **13** (*tr*) *Inf.* to free oneself of (an addiction, etc.): *he tried to kick the habit.* **14 kick up one's heels.** *Inf.* to enjoy oneself without inhibition. ◆ *n* **15** a thrust or blow with the foot. **16** any of certain rhythmic leg movements used in swimming. **17** the recoil of a gun or other firearm. **18** *Inf.* exciting quality or effect (esp. in **get a kick out of, for kicks**). **19** *Athletics.* a sudden spurt, acceleration, or boost. **20** a sudden violent movement. **21** *Inf.* the sudden stimulating effect of strong alcoholic drink or certain drugs. **22** *Inf.* power or force. **23 kick in the teeth.** *Sl.* a humiliating rebuff. ◆ See also **kick about, kickback,** etc. [C14 *kiken*, ?from ON]
▸ **'kickable** *adj*

kick about *or* **around** *vb* (*mainly adv*) *Inf.* **1** (*tr*) to treat harshly. **2** (*tr*) to discuss (ideas, etc.) informally. **3** (*intr*) to wander aimlessly. **4** (*intr*) to lie neglected or forgotten.

kickback ❶ ('kɪkˌbæk) *n* **1** a strong reaction. **2** part of an income paid to a person in return for an opportunity to make a profit, often by some illegal arrangement. ◆ *vb* **kick back.** (*adv*) **3** (*intr*) to have a strong reaction. **4** (*intr*) (esp. of a gun) to recoil. **5** to pay a kickback to (someone).

kick boxing *n* a martial art that resembles boxing but permits blows with the feet as well as punches.

kickdown ('kɪkˌdaʊn) *n* a method of changing gear in a car with automatic transmission, by fully depressing the accelerator.

kicker ('kɪkə) *n* **1** a person or thing that kicks. **2** *US & Canad. sl.* a hidden and disadvantageous factor.

kick in *vb* (*adv*) **1** (*intr*) to start or become activated. **2** (*tr*) *Chiefly Austral. & NZ inf.* to contribute.

kick off ❶ *vb* (*intr, adv*) **1** to start play in a game of football by kicking the ball from the centre of the field. **2** *Inf.* to commence (a discussion, job, etc.). ◆ *n* **kickoff. 3a** a place kick from the centre of the field in a game of football. **3b** the time at which the first such kick is due to take place.

kick on *vb* (*adv*) *Inf.* to continue.

kick out ❶ *vb* (*tr, adv*) *Inf.* to eject or dismiss.

kickshaw ('kɪkˌʃɔː) *or* **kickshaws** *n* **1** a valueless trinket. **2** *Arch.* a small exotic delicacy. [C16: back formation from *kickshaws*, by folk etymology from F *quelque chose* something]

kickstand ('kɪkˌstænd) *n* a short metal bar attached to the frame of a motorcycle or bicycle, which when kicked into a vertical position holds the stationary vehicle upright.

kick-start ('kɪkˌstɑːt) *vb* (*tr*) **1** to start (an engine, esp. of a motorcycle) by means of a pedal that is kicked downwards. **2** *Inf.* to make (something) active, functional, or productive again. ◆ *n* **3** an action or event resulting in the reactivation of something.
▸ **'kick-ˌstarter** *n*

kick up *vb* (*adv*) *Inf.* to cause (trouble, etc.).

kick upstairs *vb* (*tr, adv*) *Inf.* to promote to a higher but effectively powerless position.

kid[1] ❶ (kɪd) *n* **1** the young of a goat or of a related animal, such as an antelope. **2** soft smooth leather made from the hide of a kid. **3** *Inf.* **3a** a young person; child. **3b** (*modifier*) younger or being still a child: *kid brother.* ◆ *vb* **kids, kidding, kidded. 4** (of a goat) to give birth to (young). [C12: from ON]
▸ **'kiddishness** *n* ▸ **'kidˌlike** *adj*

kid[2] ❶ (kɪd) *vb* **kids, kidding, kidded.** *Inf.* (sometimes foll. by *on* or *along*) **1** (*tr*) to tease or deceive for fun. **2** (*intr*) to behave or speak deceptively for fun. **3** (*tr*) to fool (oneself) into believing (something): *don't kid yourself that no-one else knows.* [C19: prob. from KID[1]]
▸ **'kidder** *n* ▸ **'kiddingly** *adv*

Kidderminister ('kɪdəˌmɪnstə) *n* a type of ingrain reversible carpet originally made at Kidderminister. [after *Kidderminster*, town in W central England]

kiddy *or* **kiddie** ('kɪdɪ) *n, pl* **kiddies.** *Inf.* an affectionate word for **child.**

kid glove *n* **1** a glove made of kidskin. **2 handle with kid gloves.** to treat with great tact or caution. ◆ *adj* **kidglove. 3** overdelicate. **4** diplomatic; tactful: *a kidglove approach.*

kidnap ❶ ('kɪdnæp) *vb* **kidnaps, kidnapping, kidnapped** *or US* **kidnaps, kidnaping, kidnaped.** (*tr*) to carry off and hold (a person), usually for ransom. [C17: KID[1] + obs. *nap* to steal; see NAB]
▸ **'kidnapper** *n*

kidney ('kɪdnɪ) *n* **1** either of two bean-shaped organs at the back of the abdominal cavity in man. They filter waste products from the blood, which are excreted as urine. Related adj: **renal. 2** the corresponding organ in other animals. **3** the kidneys of certain animals used as food. **4** class, type, or disposition (esp. in **of the same** *or* **a different kidney**). [C14: from ?]

kidney bean *n* **1** any of certain bean plants having kidney-shaped seeds, esp. the scarlet runner. **2** the seed of any of these beans.

kidney machine *n* a machine carrying out the functions of a kidney, esp. used in haemodialysis.

kidney stone *n* **1** *Pathol.* a hard mass formed in the kidney, usually composed of oxalates, phosphates, and carbonates. **2** *Mineralogy.* another name for **nephrite.**

kidology (kɪ'dɒlədʒɪ) *n Brit. inf.* the practice of bluffing or deception. [C20: from KID[2] + *ology* a science]

kidskin ('kɪdˌskɪn) *n* a soft smooth leather made from the hide of a young goat. Often shortened to **kid.**

kids' stuff *n Sl.* **1** something considered fit only for children. **2** something considered easy.

kidstakes ('kɪdˌsteɪks) *pl n Austral. inf.* pretence; nonsense: *cut the kidstakes!*

kie kie ('kiːɛ kiːɛ) *n* a New Zealand climbing plant with edible bracts. [from Maori]

kieselguhr ('kiːzᵊlˌgʊə) *n* an unconsolidated form of diatomite. [C19: from G *Kieselgur*, from *Kiesel* flint + *Gur* loose earthy deposit]

kif (kɪf, kiːf), **kef,** *or* **kief** (kiːf) *n* **1** another name for **marijuana. 2** any drug that when smoked is capable of producing a euphoric condition. **3** the euphoric condition produced by smoking marijuana. [C20: from Ar. *kayf* pleasure]

kike (kaɪk) *n US & Canad. sl.* an offensive word for **Jew.** [C20: prob. var. of *kiki*, reduplication of *-ki*, common name-ending among Jews from Slavic countries]

kilderkin ('kɪldəkɪn) *n* **1** an obsolete unit of liquid capacity equal to 16 or 18 Imperial gallons or of dry capacity equal to 16 or 18 wine gallons. **2** a cask capable of holding a kilderkin. [C14: from MDu. *kindekijn*, from *kintal* hundredweight, from Med. L *quintale*]

THESAURUS

kick *vb* **1, 2** = **boot**, punt, put the boot in(to) (*sl.*) **10** *Informal* = **resist**, complain, gripe (*inf.*), grumble, object, oppose, protest, rebel, spurn **13** *Informal* = **give up**, abandon, desist from, leave off, quit, stop ◆ *n* **18** *Informal* = **thrill**, buzz (*sl.*), enjoyment, excitement, fun, gratification, jollies (*sl.*), pleasure, stimulation **22** *Informal* = **pungency**, force, intensity, pep, power, punch, snap (*inf.*), sparkle, strength, tang, verve, vitality, zest

kickback *adj* **2** = **bribe**, cut (*inf.*), gift, graft (*inf.*), payment, payoff, recompense, reward, share, sop, sweetener (*sl.*)

kick off *vb* **2** *Informal* = **begin**, commence, get the show on the road, get under way, initiate, kick-start, open, start

kick out *vb Informal* = **dismiss**, discharge, eject, evict, expel, get rid of, give (someone) their marching orders, give the boot (*sl.*), oust, reject, remove, sack (*inf.*), show one the door, throw out on one's ear (*inf.*), toss out

kid[1] *n* **3a** *Informal* = **child**, ankle-biter (*Austral. sl.*), baby, bairn, boy, girl, infant, lad, lass, little one, rug rat (*US & Canad. inf.*), sprog (*sl.*), stripling, teenager, tot, youngster, youth

kid[2] *vb* **1, 2** *Informal* = **tease**, bamboozle, beguile, cozen, delude, fool, gull, hoax, hoodwink, jest, joke, mock, plague, pretend, rag (*Brit.*), ridicule, trick, wind up (*Brit. sl.*)

kidnap *vb* = **abduct**, capture, hijack, hold to ransom, remove, seize, steal

DICTIONARY

kilim (kɪˈliːm, ˈkiːlɪm) *n* a pileless woven rug of intricate design made in the Middle East. [C19: from Turkish, from Persian *kilīm*]

kill Ⓣ (kɪl) *vb (mainly tr)* **1** *(also intr;* when *tr,* sometimes foll. by *off)* to cause the death of (a person or animal). **2** to put an end to: *to kill someone's interest.* **3** to occupy (time) by doing something unimportant, esp. while waiting for something. **4** to deaden (sound). **5** *Inf.* to tire out: *the effort killed him.* **6** *Inf.* to cause to suffer pain or discomfort: *my shoes are killing me.* **7** *Inf.* to quash or veto: *the bill was killed in the House of Lords.* **8** *Inf.* to switch off; stop. **9** *(also intr) Inf.* to overcome with attraction, laughter, surprise, etc.: *she was dressed to kill.* **10** *Tennis, squash, etc.* to hit (a ball) so hard or so accurately that the opponent cannot return it. **11** *Soccer.* to bring (a moving ball) under control. **12 kill oneself.** *Inf.* to overexert oneself: *don't kill yourself.* **13 kill two birds with one stone.** to achieve two results with one action. ◆ *n* **14** the act of causing death, esp. at the end of a hunt, bullfight, etc. **15** the animal or animals killed during a hunt. **16** *NZ.* a seasonal tally of the number of stock killed at a meatworks. **17** the destruction of a battleship, tank, etc. **18 in at the kill.** present at the end of some undertaking. [C13 *cullen;* see QUELL]

killdeer (ˈkɪlˌdɪə) *n, pl* **killdeer** *or* **killdeers.** a large brown-and-white North American plover with two black breast bands. [C18: imit.]

killer Ⓣ (ˈkɪlə) *n* **1a** a person or animal that kills, esp. habitually. **1b** *(as modifier): a killer shark.* **2** something, esp. a task or activity, that is particularly taxing or exhausting. **3** *Austral. & NZ.* a farm animal selected to be killed for food.

killer bee *n* an African honeybee, or one of its hybrids originating in Brazil, that is extremely aggressive when disturbed.

killer cell *n* a type of white blood cell that is able to kill cells, such as cancer cells and cells infected with viruses.

killer whale *n* a predatory black-and-white toothed whale most common in cold seas.

killick (ˈkɪlɪk) *or* **killock** (ˈkɪlək) *n Naut.* a small anchor, esp. one made of a heavy stone. [C17: from ?]

killifish (ˈkɪlɪˌfɪʃ) *n, pl* **killifish** *or* **killifishes.** any of various chiefly American minnow-like fishes of fresh and brackish waters: used to control mosquitoes and as anglers' bait. [C19: from MDu. *kille* river + FISH]

killing Ⓣ (ˈkɪlɪŋ) *Inf.* ◆ *adj* **1** very tiring: *a killing pace.* **2** extremely funny. **3** causing death; fatal. ◆ *n* **4** the act of causing death; slaying. **5** a sudden stroke of success, usually financial, as in speculations on the stock market (esp. in **make a killing**).

killjoy Ⓣ (ˈkɪlˌdʒɔɪ) *n* a person who spoils other people's pleasure.

kiln (kɪln) *n* a large oven for burning, drying, or processing something, such as porcelain or bricks. [OE *cylen,* from LL *culīna* kitchen, from L *coquere* to COOK]

kilo (ˈkiːləʊ) *n, pl* **kilos.** short for **kilogram** or **kilometre.**

kilo- *prefix* **1** denoting 10^3 (1000): *kilometre.* Symbol: k **2** (in computers) denoting 2^{10} (1024): *kilobyte:* in computer usage, *kilo-* is restricted to sizes of storage (e.g. *kilobit*) when it means 1024; in other computer contexts it retains its usual meaning of 1000. [from F, from Gk *khilioi* thousand]

kilobyte (ˈkɪləˌbaɪt) *n Computing.* 1024 bytes. Abbrev.: **KB, kbyte.** See also **kilo-** (sense 2).

kilocalorie (ˈkɪləʊˌkælərɪ) *n* another name for **Calorie.**

kilocycle (ˈkɪləʊˌsaɪkᵊl) *n* short for kilocycle per second: a former unit of frequency equal to 1 kilohertz.

kilogram (ˈkɪləʊˌgræm) *n* **1** one thousand grams. **2** the basic SI unit of mass, equal to the mass of the international prototype held by the *Bureau International des Poids et Mesures.* Symbol: kg

kilohertz (ˈkɪləʊˌhɜːts) *n* one thousand hertz; one thousand cycles per second. Symbol: kHz

kilolitre (ˈkɪləˌliːtə) *n* one thousand litres. Symbol: kl

kilometre *or US* **kilometer** (ˈkɪləˌmiːtə, kɪˈlɒmɪtə) *n* one thousand metres. Symbol: km
▸**kilometric** (ˌkɪləʊˈmɛtrɪk) *adj*

kiloton (ˈkɪləʊˌtʌn) *n* **1** one thousand tons. **2** an explosive power, esp. of a nuclear weapon, equal to the power of 1000 tons of TNT. Abbrev.: **kt.**

kilovolt (ˈkɪləʊˌvəʊlt) *n* one thousand volts. Symbol: kV

kilowatt (ˈkɪləʊˌwɒt) *n* one thousand watts. Symbol: kW

kilowatt-hour *n* a unit of energy equal to the work done by a power of 1000 watts in one hour. Symbol: kWh

kilt (kɪlt) *n* **1** a knee-length pleated skirt, esp. one in tartan, as worn by men in Highland dress. ◆ *vb (tr)* **2** to tuck (the skirt) up around one's body. **3** to put pleats in (cloth, etc.). [C18: of Scand. origin]
▸ˈ**kilted** *adj*

kilter (ˈkɪltə) *or* **kelter** *n* working order (esp. in **out of kilter**). [C17: from ?]

kimberlite (ˈkɪmbəˌlaɪt) *n* an intrusive igneous rock consisting largely of peridotite and often containing diamonds. [C19: from *Kimberley,* city in South Africa, + -ITE[1]]

kimono (kɪˈməʊnəʊ) *n, pl* **kimonos.** a loose sashed ankle-length garment with wide sleeves, worn in Japan. [C19: from Japanese: clothing, from *kiru* to wear + *mono* thing]
▸**kiˈmonoed** *adj*

kin Ⓣ (kɪn) *n* **1** a person's relatives collectively. **2** a class or group with similar characteristics. **3** See **next of kin.** ◆ *adj* **4** *(postpositive)* related by blood. [OE *cyn*]

-kin *suffix forming nouns.* small: *lambkin.* [from MDu., of West Gmc origin]

kinaesthesia (ˌkɪnɪsˈθiːzɪə) *or US* **kinesthesia** *n* the sensation by which bodily position, weight, muscle tension, and movement are perceived. [C19: from NL, from Gk *kinein* to move + AESTHESIA]
▸**kinaesthetic** *or US* **kinesthetic** (ˌkɪnɪsˈθɛtɪk) *adj*

kincob (ˈkɪŋkɒb) *n* a fine silk fabric embroidered with threads of gold or silver, of a kind made in India. [C18: from Urdu *kimkhāb*]

kind[1] Ⓣ (kaɪnd) *adj* **1** having a friendly nature or attitude. **2** helpful to others or to another: *a kind deed.* **3** considerate or humane. **4** cordial; courteous (esp. in **kind regards**). **5** pleasant; mild: *a kind climate.* **6** *Inf.* beneficial or not harmful. [OE *gecynde* natural, native]

kind[2] Ⓣ (kaɪnd) *n* **1** a class or group having characteristics in common; sort; type: *two of a kind.* **2** an instance or example of a class or group, esp. a rudimentary one: *heating of a kind.* **3** essential nature or character: *the difference is one of kind rather than degree.* **4** *Arch.* nature; the natural order. **5 in kind. 5a** (of payment) in goods or produce rather than in money. **5b** with something of the same sort: *to return an insult in kind.* [OE *gecynd* nature]

> **USAGE NOTE** The mixture of plural and singular constructions, although often used informally with *kind* and *sort,* should be avoided in serious writing: *children enjoy those kinds* (not *those kind*) *of stories; these sorts* (not *these sort*) *of distinctions are becoming blurred.*

kindergarten (ˈkɪndəˌgɑːtᵊn) *n* a class or small school for young children, usually between the ages of four and six. [C19: from G, lit.: children's garden]

kind-hearted Ⓣ *adj* kindly, readily sympathetic.
▸ˌ**kind-ˈheartedly** *adv* ▸ˌ**kind-ˈheartedness** *n*

kindle Ⓣ (ˈkɪndᵊl) *vb* **kindles, kindling, kindled. 1** to set alight or start to burn. **2** to arouse or be aroused: *the project kindled his interest.* **3** to make or become bright. [C12: from ON *kynda,* infl. by ON *kyndill* candle]
▸ˈ**kindler** *n*

kindling (ˈkɪndlɪŋ) *n* material for starting a fire, such as dry wood, straw, etc.

kindly Ⓣ (ˈkaɪndlɪ) *adj* **kindlier, kindliest. 1** having a sympathetic or warm-hearted nature. **2** motivated by warm and sympathetic feelings. **3** pleasant: *a kindly climate.* **4** *Arch.* natural; normal. ◆ *adv* **5** in a considerate or humane way. **6** with tolerance: *he kindly forgave my rudeness.* **7** cordially: *he greeted us kindly.* **8** please (often used to express

THESAURUS

kill *vb* **1 = slay,** annihilate, assassinate, blow away *(sl., chiefly US),* bump off *(sl.),* butcher, destroy, dispatch, do away with, do in *(sl.),* eradicate, execute, exterminate, extirpate, knock off *(sl.),* liquidate, massacre, murder, neutralize, obliterate, slaughter, take out *(sl.),* take (someone's) life, waste *(inf.)* **7** *Informal* **= suppress,** cancel, cease, deaden, defeat, extinguish, halt, quash, quell, ruin, scotch, smother, stifle, still, stop, veto

killer *n* **1 = assassin,** butcher, cut-throat, destroyer, executioner, exterminator, gunman, hit man *(sl.),* liquidator, murderer, slaughterer, slayer

killing *Informal adj* **1 = tiring,** debilitating, enervating, exhausting, fatiguing, punishing **2 = hilarious,** absurd, amusing, comical, ludicrous, uproarious **3 = deadly,** death-dealing, deathly, fatal, lethal, mortal, murderous ◆ *n* **4 = slaughter,** bloodshed, carnage, execution, extermination, fatality, homicide, manslaughter, massacre, murder, necktie party *(inf.),* slaying **5 = bonanza,** bomb *(sl.),* cleanup *(inf.),* coup, gain, profit, success, windfall

killjoy *n* **= spoilsport,** dampener, damper, wet blanket *(inf.)*

kin *n* **1 = family,** connections, kindred, kinsfolk, kinsmen, kith, people, relations, relatives

kind[1] *adj* **1, 3, 4 = considerate,** affectionate, amiable, amicable, beneficent, benevolent, benign, bounteous, charitable, clement, compassionate, congenial, cordial, courteous, friendly, generous, gentle, good, gracious, humane, indulgent, kind-hearted, kindly, lenient, loving, mild, neighbourly, obliging, philanthropic, propitious, sympathetic, tender-hearted, thoughtful, understanding
Antonyms *adj* cruel, hard-hearted, harsh, heartless, merciless, severe, unkind, unsympathetic, vicious

kind[2] *n* **1 = class,** brand, breed, family, genus, ilk, race, set, sort, species, stamp, type, variety **3 = nature,** character, description, essence, habit, manner, mould, persuasion, sort, style, temperament, type

kind-hearted *adj* **= sympathetic,** altruistic, amicable, compassionate, considerate, generous, good-natured, gracious, helpful, humane, kind, tender, tender-hearted
Antonyms *adj* cold, cold-hearted, cruel, hard-hearted, harsh, heartless, selfish, severe, unkind, unsympathetic

kindle *vb* **1 = set fire to,** fire, ignite, inflame, light **2 = arouse,** agitate, animate, awaken, bestir, enkindle, exasperate, excite, foment, incite, induce, inflame, inspire, provoke, rouse, sharpen, stimulate, stir, thrill
Antonyms *vb* douse, extinguish, quell, quench

kindliness *n* **1, 2 = kindness,** amiability, beneficence, benevolence, benignity, charity, compassion, friendliness, gentleness, humanity, kind-heartedness, sympathy

kindly *adj* **1, 2 = benevolent,** affable, beneficial, benign, compassionate, cordial, favourable, genial, gentle, good-natured, hearty, helpful, kind, mild, pleasant, polite, sympathetic, warm ◆ *adv* **5, 7 = benevolently,** agreeably, cordially, graciously, politely, tenderly, thoughtfully

impatience or formality): *will you kindly behave yourself!* **9** *Arch.* appropriately. **10 not take kindly to.** to react unfavourably towards.
▸ **'kindliness** *n*

kindness ❶ ('kaɪndnɪs) *n* **1** the practice or quality of being kind. **2** a kind or helpful act.

kindred ❶ ('kɪndrɪd) *adj* **1** having similar or common qualities, origin, etc. **2** related by blood or marriage. **3 kindred spirit.** a person with whom one has something in common. ◆ *n* **4** relationship by blood. **5** similarity in character. **6** a person's relatives collectively. [C12 *kinred,* from KIN + *-red,* from OE *rǣden* rule, from *rǣdan* to rule]

kine (kaɪn) *n* (*functioning as pl*) an archaic word for cows or cattle. [OE *cȳna* of cows, from *cū* COW[1]]

kinematics (ˌkɪnɪ'mætɪks) *n* (*functioning as sing*) the study of the motion of bodies without reference to mass or force. [C19: from Gk *kinēma* movement; see CINEMA, -ICS]
▸ **ˌkine'matic** *adj* ▸ **ˌkine'matically** *adv*

kinematograph (ˌkɪnɪ'mætəˌgrɑːf) *n* a variant spelling of **cinematograph.**

kinesics (kɪ'niːsɪks) *n* (*functioning as sing*) the study of the role of body movements, such as winking, shrugging, etc., in communication.

kinesis (kɪ'niːsɪs, kaɪ-) *n Biol.* the nondirectional movement of an organism or cell in response to a stimulus, the rate of movement being dependent on the strength of the stimulus.

kinesthesia (ˌkɪnɪs'θiːzɪə) *n* the usual US spelling of **kinaesthesia.**

kinetic (kɪ'nɛtɪk) *adj* relating to or caused by motion. [C19: from Gk *kinētikos,* from *kinein* to move]
▸ **ki'netically** *adv*

kinetic art *n* art, esp. sculpture, that moves or has moving parts.

kinetic energy *n* the energy of motion of a body equal to the work it would do if it were brought to rest. It is equal to the product of the increase of mass caused by motion times the square of the speed of light.

kinetics (kɪ'nɛtɪks, kaɪ-) *n* (*functioning as sing*) **1** another name for **dynamics** (sense 2). **2** the branch of mechanics, including both dynamics and kinematics, concerned with the study of bodies in motion. **3** the branch of dynamics that excludes the study of bodies at rest.

kinetic theory (of gases) *n* **the.** a theory of gases postulating that they consist of particles moving at random and undergoing elastic collisions.

kinfolk ('kɪnˌfəʊk) *pl n Chiefly US & Canad.* another word for **kinsfolk.**

king ❶ (kɪŋ) *n* **1** a male sovereign prince who is the official ruler of an independent state; monarch. Related adjs.: **royal, regal. 2a** a ruler or chief: *king of the fairies.* **2b** (*in combination*): *the pirate king.* **3** a person, animal, or thing considered as the best or most important of its kind. **4** any of four playing cards in a pack, one for each suit, bearing the picture of a king. **5** the most important chess piece. **6** *Draughts.* a piece that has moved entirely across the board and has been crowned, after which it may move backwards as well as forwards. **7 king of kings. 7a** God. **7b** a title of any of various oriental monarchs. ◆ *vb* (*tr*) **8** to make (someone) a king. **9 king it.** to act in a superior fashion. [OE *cyning*]
▸ **'kingˌhood** *n* ▸ **'kingˌlike** *adj*

kingbird ('kɪŋˌbɜːd) *n* any of several large American flycatchers.

kingbolt ('kɪŋˌbəʊlt) *or* **king rod** *n* **a** the pivot bolt that connects the body of a horse-drawn carriage to the front axle and provides the steering joint. **b** a similar bolt placed between a railway carriage and the bogies.

King Charles spaniel *n* a toy breed of spaniel with a short turned-up nose and a domed skull. [C17: after *Charles* II of England, who popularized the breed]

king cobra *n* a very large venomous tropical Asian snake that extends its neck into a hood when alarmed. Also called: **hamadryad.**

king crab *n* another name for the **horseshoe crab.**

kingcup ('kɪŋˌkʌp) *n Brit.* any of several yellow-flowered plants, esp. the marsh marigold.

kingdom ❶ ('kɪŋdəm) *n* **1** a territory, state, people, or community ruled or reigned over by a king or queen. **2** any of the three groups into which natural objects may be divided: the animal, plant, and mineral kingdoms. **3** *Biol.* any of the major categories into which living organisms are classified. Modern systems recognize five kingdoms: *Prokaryotae* (bacteria), *Protoctista* (algae, protozoans, etc.), *Fungi, Plantae,* and *Animalia.* **4** *Theol.* the eternal sovereignty of God. **5** an area of activity: *the kingdom of the mind.*

kingdom come *n* **1** the next world. **2** *Inf.* the end of the world (esp. in **until kingdom come**). **3** *Inf.* unconsciousness.

kingfish ('kɪŋˌfɪʃ) *n, pl* **kingfish** *or* **kingfishes. 1** a marine food and game fish occurring in warm American Atlantic coastal waters. **2** *Austral.* any of various types of trevally, mulloway, and barracouta. **3** any of various other large food fishes, esp. the Spanish mackerel.

kingfisher ('kɪŋˌfɪʃə) *n* a bird which has a greenish-blue and orange plumage, a large head, short tail, and long sharp bill, and feeds on fish. [C15: orig. *king's fisher*]

King James Version *or* **Bible** *n* **the.** another name for the **Authorized Version.**

kingklip ('kɪŋˌklɪp) *n* an edible eel-like marine fish. [from Afrik., from Du. *koning* king + *klip* rock]

kinglet ('kɪŋlɪt) *n* **1** *Often derog.* the king of a small or insignificant territory. **2** *US & Canad.* any of various small warblers having a black-edged yellow crown.

kingly ❶ ('kɪŋlɪ) *adj* **kinglier, kingliest. 1** appropriate to a king. **2** royal. ◆ *adv* **3** *Poetic or arch.* in a manner appropriate to a king.
▸ **'kingliness** *n*

kingmaker ('kɪŋˌmeɪkə) *n* a person who has control over appointments to positions of authority.

king-of-arms *n, pl* **kings-of-arms. 1** the highest rank of heraldic officer. **2** a person holding this rank.

king of the castle *n Chiefly Brit.* a children's game in which each child attempts to stand alone on a mound by pushing other children off it.

king penguin *n* a large New Zealand subantarctic penguin.

kingpin ('kɪŋˌpɪn) *n* **1** the most important person in an organization. **2** Also called (Brit.): **swivel pin.** a pivot pin that provides a steering joint in a motor vehicle by securing the stub axle to the axle beam. **3** *Tenpin bowling.* the front pin in the triangular arrangement of the ten pins. **4** (in ninepins) the central pin in the diamond pattern of the nine pins.

king post *n* a vertical post connecting the apex of a triangular roof truss to the tie beam.

King's Bench *n* (when the sovereign is male) another name for **Queen's Bench.**

King's Counsel *n* (when the sovereign is male) another name for **Queen's Counsel.**

King's English *n* (esp. when the British sovereign is male) standard Southern British English.

king's evidence *n* (when the sovereign is male) another name for **queen's evidence.**

king's evil *n* **the.** *Pathol.* a former name for **scrofula.** [C14: from the belief that the king's touch would heal scrofula]

king's highway *n* (in Britain, esp. when the sovereign is male) any public road or right of way.

kingship ('kɪŋʃɪp) *n* **1** the position or authority of a king. **2** the skill of ruling as a king.

king-size *or* **king-sized** *adj* larger or longer than a standard size.

kinin ('kaɪnɪn) *n* **1** any of a group of polypeptides in the blood that cause dilation of the blood vessels. **2** *Bot.* another name for **cytokinin.** [C20: from Gk *kin(ēma)* motion + -IN]

kink ❶ (kɪŋk) *n* **1** a sharp twist or bend in a wire, rope, hair, etc. **2** a crick in the neck or similar muscular spasm. **3** a flaw or minor difficulty in some undertaking. **4** a flaw or idiosyncrasy of personality. [C17: from Du.: a curl in a rope]

kinkajou ('kɪŋkəˌdʒuː) *n* an arboreal fruit-eating mammal of Central and South America, with a long prehensile tail. Also called: **honey bear.** [C18: from F *quincajou,* from Algonquian]

kinky ❶ ('kɪŋkɪ) *adj* **kinkier, kinkiest. 1** *Sl.* given to unusual, abnormal, or deviant sexual practices. **2** *Inf.* exhibiting unusual idiosyncrasies of personality. **3** *Inf.* attractive or provocative in a bizarre way: *kinky clothes.* **4** tightly looped, as a wire or rope. **5** tightly curled, as hair.
▸ **'kinkily** *adv* ▸ **'kinkiness** *n*

kino ('kiːnəʊ) *n* a dark red resin obtained from various tropical plants, esp. an Indian leguminous tree, used as an astringent and in tanning. [C18: of West African origin]

kin selection *n Biol.* natural selection resulting from altruistic behaviour by animals towards members of the same species, esp. their offspring or other relatives.

kinsfolk ❶ ('kɪnzˌfəʊk) *pl n* one's family or relatives.

kinship ❶ ('kɪnʃɪp) *n* **1** blood relationship. **2** the state of having common characteristics.

THESAURUS

Antonyms *adj* ≠ **benevolent:** cruel, harsh, malevolent, malicious, mean, severe, spiteful, unkindly, unsympathetic ◆ *adv* ≠ **benevolently:** cruelly, harshly, malevolently, maliciously, meanly, spitefully, unkindly, unsympathetically

kindness *n* **1** = **goodwill,** affection, amiability, beneficence, benevolence, charity, clemency, compassion, decency, fellow-feeling, generosity, gentleness, goodness, grace, hospitality, humanity, indulgence, kindliness, magnanimity, patience, philanthropy, tenderness, tolerance, understanding **2** = **good deed,** aid, assistance, benefaction, bounty, favour, generosity, help, service
Antonyms *n* ≠ **goodwill:** animosity, callousness, cold-heartedness, cruelty, hard-heartedness, heartlessness, ill will, inhumanity, malevolence, malice, misanthropy, viciousness

kindred *adj* **1, 2** = **similar,** affiliated, akin, allied, cognate, congenial, corresponding, kin, like, matching, related ◆ *n* **4** = **relationship,** affinity, consanguinity **6** = **family,** connections, flesh, kin, kinsfolk, kinsmen, lineage, relations, relatives

king *n* **1, 2** = **ruler,** crowned head, emperor, majesty, monarch, overlord, prince, sovereign

kingdom *n* **1** = **country,** commonwealth, division, nation, province, realm, state, territory, tract **5** = **domain,** area, field, province, sphere, territory

kingly *adj* **2** = **royal,** imperial, monarchical, regal, sovereign

kink *n* **1** = **twist,** bend, coil, corkscrew, crimp, entanglement, frizz, knot, tangle, wrinkle **3** = **flaw,** complication, defect, difficulty, hitch, imperfection, knot, tangle **4** = **quirk,** crotchet, eccentricity, fetish, foible, idiosyncrasy, singularity, vagary, whim

kinky *adj* **1** *Slang* = **perverted,** degenerated, depraved, deviant, licentious, unnatural, warped **2** *Informal* = **weird,** bizarre, eccentric, odd, oddball (*inf.*), off-the-wall (*sl.*), outlandish, outré, peculiar, queer, quirky, strange, unconventional **4, 5** = **twisted,** coiled, crimped, curled, curly, frizzled, frizzy, tangled

kinsfolk *pl n* = **family,** connections, kin, kindred, kinsmen, relations, relatives

kinship *n* **1** = **relation,** blood relationship, con-

kinsman Ⓣ (ˈkɪnzmən) *n, pl* **kinsmen.** a blood relation or a relation by marriage.
▸ **ˈkins,woman** *fem n*

kiosk Ⓣ (ˈkiːɒsk) *n* **1** a small sometimes movable booth from which cigarettes, newspapers, sweets, etc., are sold. **2** *Chiefly Brit.* a telephone box. **3** (in Turkey, Iran, etc.) a light open-sided pavilion. [C17: from F *kiosque* bandstand, from Turkish, from Persian *kūshk* pavilion]

kip[1] (kɪp) *Brit. sl.* ◆ *n* **1** sleep or slumber: *to get some kip.* **2** a bed or lodging. ◆ *vb* **kips, kipping, kipped.** (*intr*) **3** to sleep or take a nap. **4** (foll. by *down*) to prepare for sleep. [C18: from ?]

kip[2] (kɪp) *or* **kipskin** *n* the hide of a young animal, esp. a calf or lamb. [C16: from MDu. *kipp*]

kip[3] (kɪp) *n Austral.* a small board used to spin the coins in two-up. [C19: from Brit. dialect *kep* to catch]

kipper (ˈkɪpə) *n* **1** a fish, esp. a herring, that has been cleaned, salted, and smoked. **2** a male salmon during the spawning season. ◆ *vb* **3** (*tr*) to cure (herrings or other fish) by salting and smoking. [OE *cypera*, ?from *coper* COPPER[1], referring to its colour]

kir (kɜː; *French* kir) *n* a drink made from dry white wine and cassis. [after Canon F. *Kir* (1876–1968), mayor of Dijon, who is said to have invented it]

kirby grip (ˈkɜːbɪ) *n Trademark.* a type of hairgrip with one straight and one wavy side.

kirk (kɜːk) *n* **1** a Scottish word for **church. 2** a Scottish church. [C12: from ON *kirkja*, from OE *cirice* CHURCH]

kirk session *n* the lowest court of the Presbyterian Church.

kirmess (ˈkɜːmɪs) *n* a variant spelling of **kermis.**

Kirsch (kɪəʃ) *or* **Kirschwasser** (ˈkɪəʃ,vɑːsə) *n* a brandy distilled from cherries, made chiefly in the Black Forest in Germany. [G *Kirschwasser* cherry water]

kirtle (ˈkɜːtᵊl) *n Arch.* **1** a woman's skirt or dress. **2** a man's coat. [OE *cyrtel*, prob. from *cyrtan* to shorten, ult. from L *curtus* cut short]

kismet Ⓣ (ˈkɪzmɛt, ˈkɪs-) *n* **1** *Islam.* the will of Allah. **2** fate or destiny. [C19: from Turkish, from Persian *qismat*, from Ar. *qasama* he divided]

kiss Ⓣ (kɪs) *vb* **1** (*tr*) to touch with the lips or press the lips against as an expression of love, greeting, respect, etc. **2** (*intr*) to join lips with another person in an act of love or desire. **3** to touch (each other) lightly. **4** *Billiards.* (of balls) to touch (each other) lightly while moving. ◆ *n* **5** a caress with the lips. **6** a light touch. [OE *cyssan*, from *coss*]
▸ **ˈkissable** *adj*

kissagram (ˈkɪsə,græm) *n* a greetings service in which a person is employed to present greetings by kissing the person celebrating. [C20: blend of *kiss* and *telegram*]

kiss-and-tell *n* (*modifier*) denoting the practice of publicizing one's former sexual relationship with a celebrity, esp. in the tabloid press: *a kiss-and-tell interview.*

kiss curl *n Brit.* a circular curl of hair pressed flat against the cheek or forehead.

kisser (ˈkɪsə) *n* **1** a person who kisses, esp. in a way specified. **2** a slang word for **mouth** or **face.**

kissing gate *n* a gate set in a U- or V-shaped enclosure, allowing only one person to pass through at a time.

kiss of life *n* **the.** mouth-to-mouth resuscitation in which a person blows gently into the mouth of an unconscious person, allowing the lungs to deflate after each blow.

kist (kɪst) *n S. African.* a large wooden chest in which linen is stored, esp. one used to store a bride's trousseau. [from Afrik., from Du.: CHEST]

kit[1] Ⓣ (kɪt) *n* **1** a set of tools, supplies, etc., for use together or for a purpose: *a first-aid kit.* **2** the case or container for such a set. **3** a set of pieces of equipment sold ready to be assembled. **4a** clothing and other personal effects, esp. those of a traveller or soldier: *safari kit.* **4b** *Inf.* clothing in general (esp. in the phrase **get one's kit off**). ◆ See also **kit out.** [C14: from MDu. *kitte* tankard]

kit[2] (kɪt) *n NZ.* a string bag for shopping. [from Maori *kete*]

kitbag (ˈkɪt,bæg) *n* a canvas or other bag for a serviceman's kit.

kitchen Ⓣ (ˈkɪtʃɪn) *n* **a** a room or part of a building equipped for preparing and cooking food. **b** (*as modifier*): *a kitchen table.* [OE *cycene*, ult. from LL *coquīna*, from L *coquere* to COOK]

kitchen cabinet *n* a group of unofficial advisers to a political leader, esp. when considered to be more influential than the offical cabinet.

kitchenette (,kɪtʃɪˈnɛt) *n* a small kitchen or part of a room equipped for use as a kitchen.

kitchen garden *n* a garden where vegetables and sometimes also fruit are grown.

kitchen midden *n Archaeol.* the site of a large mound of domestic refuse marking a prehistoric settlement.

kitchen sink *n* **1** a sink in a kitchen for washing dishes, vegetables, etc. **2** (*modifier*) denoting a type of drama or painting of the 1950s depicting sordid reality.

kitchen tea *n Austral. & NZ.* a party held before a wedding to which guests bring items of kitchen equipment as wedding presents.

kitchenware (ˈkɪtʃɪn,wɛə) *n* pots and pans, knives, forks, spoons, etc., used in the kitchen.

kite (kaɪt) *n* **1** a light frame covered with a thin material flown in the wind at the end of a length of string. **2** *Brit. sl.* an aeroplane. **3** (*pl*) *Naut.* any of various light sails set in addition to the working sails of a vessel. **4** a bird of prey having a long forked tail and long broad wings and usually preying on small mammals and insects. **5** *Arch.* a person who preys on others. **6** *Commerce.* a negotiable paper drawn without any actual transaction or assets and designed to obtain money on credit, give an impression of affluence, etc. ◆ *vb* **kites, kiting, kited. 7** to issue (fictitious papers) to obtain credit or money. **8** (*intr*) to soar and glide. [OE *cӯta*]

Kite mark *n Brit.* the official mark of quality and reliability, in the form of a kite, on articles approved by the British Standards Institution.

kith (kɪθ) *n* **kith and kin.** one's friends and relations. [OE *cӯthth*, from *cūth*; see UNCOUTH]

kit out Ⓣ *or* **up** *vb* **kits, kitting, kitted.** (*tr, adv*) *Chiefly Brit.* to provide with (a kit of personal effects and necessities).

kitsch (kɪtʃ) *n* tawdry, vulgarized, or pretentious art, literature, etc., usually with popular appeal. [C20: from G]
▸ **ˈkitschy** *adj*

kitten (ˈkɪtᵊn) *n* **1** a young cat. **2 have kittens.** *Brit. inf.* to react with disapproval, anxiety, etc.: *she had kittens when she got the bill.* ◆ *vb* **3** (of cats) to give birth to (young). [C14: from OF *caton*, from CAT; prob. infl. by ME *kiteling*]

kittenish (ˈkɪtᵊnɪʃ) *adj* **1** like a kitten; lively. **2** (of a woman) flirtatious, esp. coyly flirtatious.

kittiwake (ˈkɪtɪ,weɪk) *n* either of two oceanic gulls having pale grey black-tipped wings and a square-cut tail. [C17: imit.]

kitty[1] (ˈkɪtɪ) *n, pl* **kitties.** a diminutive or affectionate name for a **kitten** or **cat.** [C18]

kitty[2] (ˈkɪtɪ) *n, pl* **kitties. 1** the pool of bets in certain gambling games. **2** any shared fund of money. **3** (in bowls) the jack. [C19: see KIT[1]]

kitty-cornered *adj* a variant of **cater-cornered.**

Kiwano (kɪˈwɑːnəʊ) *n, pl* **Kiwanos.** *Trademark.* an edible oval fruit of the passionflower family, having a golden spiky skin, juicy green pulp and many seeds.

kiwi (ˈkiːwiː) *n, pl* **kiwis. 1** a nocturnal flightless New Zealand bird having a long beak, stout legs, and weakly barbed feathers. **2** *Inf. except in NZ.* a New Zealander. **3** *NZ inf.* a lottery. [C19: from Maori, imit.: NZ sense from the *Golden Kiwi Lottery*]

kiwi fruit *n* the fuzzy edible fruit of an Asian climbing plant. Also called: **Chinese gooseberry.**

KKK *abbrev. for* Ku Klux Klan.

Klan (klæn) *n* (usually preceded by *the*) short for **Ku Klux Klan.**
▸ **ˈKlanism** *n*

klaxon (ˈklæksᵊn) *n* a type of loud horn formerly used on motor vehicles. [C20: former trademark]

Kleenex (ˈkliːnɛks) *n, pl* **Kleenex** *or* **Kleenexes.** *Trademark.* a kind of soft paper tissue, used esp. as a handkerchief.

Klein bottle (klaɪn) *n Maths.* a three-dimensional surface formed by inserting the smaller end of an open tapered tube through the surface of the tube and making this end stretch to fit the other end. [after Felix *Klein* (1849–1925), G mathematician]

kleptomania (,klɛptəʊˈmeɪnɪə) *n Psychol.* a strong impulse to steal, esp. when there is no obvious motivation. [C19: *klepto-* from Gk, from *kleptein* to steal + -MANIA]
▸ **,kleptoˈmani,ac** *n*

klieg light (kliːg) *n* an intense carbon-arc light used in producing films. [C20: after John H. *Kliegl* (1869–1959) & his brother Anton (1872–1927), German-born American inventors]

klipspringer (ˈklɪp,sprɪŋə) *n* a small agile antelope inhabiting rocky regions of Africa south of the Sahara. [C18: from Afrik., from Du. *klip* rock + *springer*, from *springen* to SPRING]

kloof (kluːf) *n* a mountain pass or gorge in southern Africa. [C18: from Afrik., from MDu. *clove* a cleft]

klystron (ˈklɪstrɒn) *n* an electron tube for the amplification or generation of microwaves. [C20: *klys-*, from Gk *kluzein* to wash over + -TRON]

km *symbol for* kilometre.

K-meson *n* another name for **kaon.**

knack Ⓣ (næk) *n* **1** a skilful, ingenious, or resourceful way of doing something. **2** a particular talent or aptitude, esp. an intuitive one. [C14: prob. var. of *knak* sharp knock, imit.]

knacker Ⓣ (ˈnækə) *Brit.* ◆ *n* **1** a person who buys up old horses for slaughter. **2** a person who buys up old buildings and breaks them up

THESAURUS

sanguinity, kin, ties of blood **2** = **similarity**, affinity, alliance, association, bearing, connection, correspondence, relationship

kinsman *n* = **relative**, blood relative, fellow clansman, fellow tribesman, relation

kiosk *n* **1** = **booth**, bookstall, counter, newsstand, stall, stand

kismet *n* **2** = **fate**, destiny, fortune, karma, lot, portion, preordination, Providence

kiss *vb* **1, 2** = **osculate**, buss (*arch.*), canoodle (*sl.*), greet, neck (*inf.*), peck (*inf.*), salute, smooch (*inf.*) **3** = **brush**, caress, glance, graze, scrape, touch ◆ *n* **5** = **osculation**, buss, peck (*inf.*), smacker (*sl.*)

kit[1] *n* **1** = **equipment**, accoutrements, apparatus, effects, gear, impedimenta, implements, instruments, outfit, paraphernalia, provisions, rig, supplies, tackle, tools, trappings, utensils

kitchen *n* = **cookhouse**, galley, kitchenette

kit out *vb* = **equip**, accoutre, arm, deck out, fit out, fix up, furnish, outfit, provide with, supply

knack *n* **1, 2** = **skill**, ability, adroitness, aptitude, bent, capacity, dexterity, expertise, expertness, facility, flair, forte, genius, gift, handiness, ingenuity, propensity, quickness, skilfulness, talent, trick
Antonyms *n* awkwardness, clumsiness, disability, ineptitude

knackered *adj* **4** *Slang* = **exhausted**, all in (*sl.*),

for scrap. **3** *Irish sl.* a despicable person. ◆ *vb* **4** (*tr; usually passive*) *Sl.* to tire. [C16: prob. from *nacker* saddler, prob. of Scand. origin]
▸'**knackery** *n*

knacker's yard *n Brit.* **1** a slaughterhouse for horses. **2** *Inf.* destruction because of being beyond all usefulness (esp. in the phrase **ready for the knacker's yard**).

knag (næg) *n* **1** a knot in wood. **2** a wooden peg. [C15: ?from Low G *knagge*]

knap (næp) *vb* **knaps, knapping, knapped.** (*tr*) *Dialect.* to hit or chip. [C15 (in the sense: to strike with a sharp sound): imit.]
▸'**knapper** *n*

knapping hammer *n* a hammer used for breaking and shaping stones.

knapsack ('næpˌsæk) *n* a canvas or leather bag carried strapped on the back or shoulder. [C17: from Low G, prob. from *knappen* to bite + *sack* bag]

knapweed ('næpˌwiːd) *n* any of several plants having purplish thistle-like flowers. [C15 *knopwed,* from *knop* of Gmc origin + WEED]

knar (nɑː) *n* a variant of **knur.** [C14 *knarre* rough stone, knot on a tree]

knave Ⓣ (neɪv) *n* **1** *Arch.* a dishonest man. **2** another word for **jack** (the playing card). **3** *Obs.* a male servant. [OE *cnafa*]
▸'**knavish** *adj*

knavery Ⓣ ('neɪvərɪ) *n, pl* **knaveries. 1** a deceitful or dishonest act. **2** dishonest conduct; trickery.

knead Ⓣ (niːd) *vb* (*tr*) **1** to work and press (a soft substance, such as bread dough) into a uniform mixture with the hands. **2** to squeeze or press with the hands. **3** to make by kneading. [OE *cnedan*]
▸'**kneader** *n*

knee (niː) *n* **1** the joint of the human leg connecting the tibia and fibula with the femur and protected in front by the patella. Technical name: **genu. 2a** the area surrounding and above this joint. **2b** (*modifier*) reaching or covering the knee: *knee socks.* **3** the upper surface of a sitting person's thigh: *the child sat on her mother's knee.* **4** a corresponding or similar part in other vertebrates. **5** the part of a garment that covers the knee. **6** anything resembling a knee in action or shape. **7** any of the hollow rounded protuberances that project upwards from the roots of the swamp cypress. **8 bend** *or* **bow the knee.** to kneel or submit. **9 bring someone to his knees.** to force someone into submission. ◆ *vb* **knees, kneeing, kneed. 10** (*tr*) to strike, nudge, or push with the knee. [OE *cnēow*]

kneecap ('niːˌkæp) *n* **1** *Anat.* a nontechnical name for **patella.** ◆ *vb* **kneecaps, kneecapping, kneecapped.** (*tr*) **2** (esp. of certain terrorist groups) to shoot (a person) in the kneecap.

knee-deep *adj* **1** so deep as to reach or cover the knees. **2** (*postpositive;* often foll. by *in*) **2a** sunk or covered to the knees: *knee-deep in sand.* **2b** deeply involved: *knee-deep in work.*

knee-high *adj* another word for **knee-deep** (sense 1).

kneehole ('niːˌhəʊl) *n* a space for the knees, esp. under a desk.

knee jerk *n* **1** *Physiol.* an outward reflex kick of the lower leg caused by a sharp tap on the tendon just below the kneecap. ◆ *modifier.* **kneejerk. 2** made or occurring as a predictable and automatic response, without thought: *a kneejerk reaction.*

kneel Ⓣ (niːl) *vb* **kneels, kneeling, knelt** *or* **kneeled. 1** (*intr*) to rest, fall, or support oneself on one's knees. ◆ *n* **2** the act or position of kneeling. [OE *cnēowlian;* see KNEE]
▸'**kneeler** *n*

knees-up *n, pl* **knees-ups.** *Brit. inf.* a lively party. [C20: after popular song *Knees-up, Mother Brown!*]

knell Ⓣ (nɛl) *n* **1** the sound of a bell rung to announce a death or a funeral. **2** something that precipitates or indicates death or destruction. ◆ *vb* **3** (*intr*) to ring a knell. **4** (*tr*) to proclaim by or as if by a tolling bell. [OE *cnyll*]

knelt (nɛlt) *vb* a past tense and past participle of **kneel.**

Knesset ('knɛsɪt) *n* the representative assembly of Israel. [C20: Heb., lit.: gathering]

knew (njuː) *vb* the past tense of **know.**

knickerbocker glory ('nɪkəˌbɒkə) *n* a rich confection consisting of layers of ice cream, jelly, cream, and fruit, served in a tall glass.

knickerbockers ('nɪkəˌbɒkəz) *pl n* baggy breeches fastened with a band at the knee or above the ankle. Also called (US): **knickers.** [C19: regarded as the traditional dress of the Du. settlers in America; after Diedrich *Knickerbocker,* fictitious author of Washington Irving's *History of New York* (1809)]

knickers Ⓣ ('nɪkəz) *pl n* an undergarment for women covering the lower trunk and sometimes the thighs and having separate legs or leg-holes. [C19: contraction of KNICKERBOCKERS]

knick-knack Ⓣ *or* **nick-nack** ('nɪkˌnæk) *n* **1** a cheap ornament. **2** an ornamental article of furniture, dress, etc. [C17: by reduplication from *knack,* in obs. sense: toy]

knife Ⓣ (naɪf) *n, pl* **knives** (naɪvz). **1** a cutting instrument consisting of a sharp-edged blade of metal fitted into a handle or onto a machine. **2** a similar instrument used as a weapon. **3 have one's knife in someone.** to have a grudge against someone. **4 under the knife.** undergoing a surgical operation. ◆ *vb* **knifes, knifing, knifed.** (*tr*) **5** to stab or kill with a knife. **6** to betray or depose in an underhand way. [OE *cnīf*]
▸'**knifeˌlike** *adj*

knife edge *n* **1** the sharp cutting edge of a knife. **2** any sharp edge, esp. an arête. **3** a sharp-edged wedge of hard material on which the beam of a balance pivots. **4** a critical point.

knight (naɪt) *n* **1** (in medieval Europe) **1a** (originally) a person who served his lord as a mounted and heavily armed soldier. **1b** (later) a gentleman with the military and social standing of this rank. **2** (in modern times) a person invested by a sovereign with a nonhereditary rank and dignity usually in recognition of personal services, achievements, etc. **3** a chess piece, usually shaped like a horse's head. **4** a heroic champion of a lady or of a cause or principle. **5** a member of the Roman class below the senators. ◆ *vb* **6** (*tr*) to make (a person) a knight. [OE *cniht* servant]

knight errant *n, pl* **knights errant.** (esp. in medieval romance) a knight who wanders in search of deeds of courage, chivalry, etc.
▸**knight errantry** *n*

knighthood ('naɪthʊd) *n* **1** the order, dignity, or rank of a knight. **2** the qualities of a knight.

knightly Ⓣ ('naɪtlɪ) *adj* of, relating to, resembling, or befitting a knight.
▸'**knightliness** *n*

knight of the road *n Inf. or facetious.* **1** a tramp. **2** a commercial traveller. **3** a lorry driver.

Knights Hospitallers *pl n* a military Christian religious order founded about the time of the first crusade (1096–99).

Knight Templar *n, pl* **Knights Templars** *or* **Knights Templar.** another term for **Templar.**

kniphofia (nɪf'əʊfɪə) *n* the Latin name for **red-hot poker.** [C19: after Johann Hieronymus *Kniphof* (1704–63), G professor of medicine]

knit Ⓣ (nɪt) *vb* **knits, knitting, knitted** *or* **knit. 1** to make (a garment, etc.) by looping and entwining (wool) by hand by means of long eyeless needles (**knitting needles**) or by machine (**knitting machine**). **2** to join or be joined together closely. **3** to draw (the brows) together or (of the brows) to come together, as in frowning or concentrating. **4** (of a broken bone) to join together; heal. ◆ *n* **5a** a fabric made by knitting. **5b** (*in combination*): *a heavy knit.* [OE *cnyttan* to tie in]
▸'**knitter** *n*

knitting ('nɪtɪŋ) *n* knitted work or the process of producing it.

knitwear ('nɪtˌwɛə) *n* knitted clothes, esp. sweaters.

knives (naɪvz) *n* the plural of **knife.**

knob Ⓣ (nɒb) *n* **1** a rounded projection from a surface, such as a lump on a tree trunk. **2** a handle of a door, drawer, etc., esp. one that is rounded. **3** a round hill or knoll. ◆ *vb* **knobs, knobbing, knobbed. 4** (*tr*) to supply or ornament with knobs. **5** (*intr*) to bulge. [C14: from MLow G *knobbe* knot in wood]
▸'**knobbly** *adj* ▸'**knobby** *adj* ▸'**knobˌlike** *adj*

knobkerrie ('nɒbˌkɛrɪ), **knobkierie,** *or* **knobstick** *n* a stick with a round knob at the end, used as a club or missile by South African tribesmen. [C19: from Afrik., from *knop* knob, from MDu. *cnoppe* + *kierie* stick, from Khoikhoi *kīrri*]

knock Ⓣ (nɒk) *vb* **1** (*tr*) to give a blow or push to. **2** (*intr*) to rap sharply with the knuckles, a hard object, etc.: *to knock at the door.* **3** (*tr*) to make or force by striking: *to knock a hole in the wall.* **4** (*intr; usually* foll. by *against*) to collide (with). **5** (*tr*) to bring into a certain condition by hitting: *to knock someone unconscious.* **6** (*tr*) *Inf.* to criticize adversely. **7** (*intr*) Also: **pink.** (of an internal-combustion engine) to emit a metallic noise as a result of faulty combustion. **8** (*intr*) (of a bearing, esp. one in

THESAURUS

beat (*sl.*), buggered (*Brit. sl.*), dead beat (*sl.*), dead tired, debilitated, dog-tired (*inf.*), done in (*inf.*), drained, enervated, prostrated, ready to drop, tired out, worn out, zonked (*sl.*)

knave *n* **1** *Archaic* = **rogue**, blackguard, bounder (*old-fashioned Brit. sl.*), cheat, rapscallion, rascal, reprobate, rotter (*sl., chiefly Brit.*), scallywag (*inf.*), scamp, scapegrace, scoundrel, scumbag (*sl.*), swindler, varlet (*arch.*), villain

knavery *n* **1, 2** = **dishonesty**, chicanery, corruption, deceit, deception, double-dealing, duplicity, fraud, imposture, rascality, roguery, trickery, villainy

knavish *adj* **1** *Archaic* = **dishonest**, deceitful, deceptive, dishonourable, fraudulent, lying, rascally, roguish, scoundrelly, tricky, unprincipled, unscrupulous, villainous

Antonyms *adj* honest, honourable, noble, principled, trustworthy

knead *vb* **1, 2** = **squeeze**, blend, form, manipulate, massage, mould, press, rub, shape, stroke, work

kneel *vb* **1** = **genuflect**, bow, bow down, curtsey, curtsy, get down on one's knees, kowtow, make obeisance, stoop

knell *n* **1** = **ringing**, chime, peal, sound, toll ◆ *vb* **3, 4** = **ring**, announce, chime, herald, peal, resound, sound, toll

knickers *pl n* = **underwear**, bloomers, briefs, drawers, panties, smalls

knick-knack *n* **1** = **trinket**, bagatelle, bauble, bibelot, bric-a-brac, gewgaw, gimcrack, kickshaw, plaything, trifle

knife *n* **1** = **blade**, cutter, cutting tool ◆ *vb* **5** = **cut**, impale, lacerate, pierce, slash, stab, wound

knightly *adj* = **chivalrous**, courageous, courtly, gallant, gracious, heroic, noble, valiant

knit *vb* **1, 2, 4** = **join**, affix, ally, bind, connect, contract, fasten, heal, interlace, intertwine, link, loop, mend, secure, tie, unite, weave **3** = **wrinkle**, crease, furrow, knot, pucker

knob *n* **1** = **lump**, boss, bulk, bump, bunch, hump, knot, knurl, nub, projection, protrusion, protuberance, snag, stud, swell, swelling, tumour

knock *vb* **1, 2** = **hit**, belt (*inf.*), buffet, chin (*sl.*), clap, cuff, deck, lay one on (*sl.*), punch, rap, slap, smack, smite (*arch.*), strike, thump, thwack **6** *Informal* = **criticize**, abuse, asperse, belittle, carp, cavil, censure, condemn, denigrate, deprecate, disparage, find fault, have a

an engine) to emit a regular characteristic sound as a result of wear. **9** *Brit. sl.* to have sexual intercourse with (a person). **10 knock (a person) into the middle of next week.** *Inf.* to hit (a person) with a very heavy blow. **11 knock on the head. 11a** to daze or kill (a person) by striking on the head. **11b** to prevent the further development of (a plan). ◆ *n* **12a** a blow, push, or rap: *he gave the table a knock.* **12b** the sound so caused. **13** the sound of knocking in an engine or bearing. **14** *Inf.* a misfortune, rebuff, or setback. **15** *Inf.* criticism. ◆ See also **knock about, knock back,** etc. [OE *cnocian,* imit.]

knock about ❶ *or* **around** *vb* **1** (*intr, adv*) to wander about aimlessly. **2** (*intr, prep*) to travel about, esp. as resulting in varied experience: *he's knocked about the world.* **3** (*intr, adv;* foll. by *with*) to associate. **4** (*tr, adv*) to treat brutally: *he knocks his wife about.* **5** (*tr, adv*) to consider or discuss informally. ◆ *adj* **knockabout. 6** tough; boisterous: *knockabout farce.*

knock back *vb* (*tr, adv*) *Inf.* **1** to drink, esp. quickly. **2** to cost. **3** to reject or refuse. **4** to shock; disconcert. ◆ *n* **knock-back. 5** *Sl.* a refusal or rejection. **6** *Prison sl.* failure to obtain parole.

knock down ❶ *vb* (*tr, adv*) **1** to strike to the ground with a blow, as in boxing. **2** (in auctions) to declare (an article) sold. **3** to demolish. **4** to dismantle for ease of transport. **5** *Inf.* to reduce (a price, etc.). **6** *Austral. sl.* to spend (a cheque). **7** *Austral. sl.* to drink. ◆ *adj* **knockdown.** (*prenominal*) **8** powerful: *a knockdown blow.* **9** *Chiefly Brit.* cheap: *a knockdown price.* **10** easily dismantled: *knockdown furniture.*

knocker ('nɒkə) *n* **1** an object, usually made of metal, attached to a door by a hinge and used for knocking. **2** *Inf.* a person who finds fault or disparages. **3** (*usually pl*) *Sl.* a female breast. **4** a person or thing that knocks. **5 on the knocker.** *Inf.* promptly: *you pay on the knocker here.*

knocking copy *n* publicity material designed to denigrate a competing product.

knocking-shop *n Brit.* a slang word for **brothel.**

knock-knee *n* a condition in which the legs are bent inwards causing the knees to touch when standing.
▸ ,**knock-'kneed** *adj*

knock off ❶ *vb* (*mainly adv*) **1** (*intr, also prep*) *Inf.* to finish work: *we knocked off an hour early.* **2** (*tr*) *Inf.* to make or do hastily or easily: *to knock off a novel in a week.* **3** (*tr; also prep*) *Inf.* to reduce the price of (an article). **4** (*tr*) *Sl.* to kill. **5** (*tr*) *Sl.* to rob or steal: *to knock off a bank.* **6** (*tr*) *Sl.* to stop doing something, used as a command: *knock it off!*

knock-on *Rugby.* ◆ *n* **1** the infringement of playing the ball forward with the hand or arm. ◆ *vb* **knock on.** (*adv*) **2** to play (the ball) forward with the hand or arm.

knock-on effect *n* the indirect result of an action: *the number of redundancies was not great but there were as many again from the knock-on effect.*

knockout ❶ ('nɒk,aʊt) *n* **1** the act of rendering unconscious. **2** a blow that renders an opponent unconscious. **3a** a competition in which competitors are eliminated progressively. **3b** (*as modifier*): *a knockout contest.* **4** *Inf.* a person or thing that is overwhelmingly impressive or attractive: *she's a knockout.* ◆ *vb* **knock out.** (*tr, adv*) **5** to render unconscious, esp. by a blow. **6** *Boxing.* to defeat (an opponent) by a knockout. **7** to destroy or injure badly. **8** to eliminate, esp. in a knockout competition. **9** *Inf.* to overwhelm or amaze: *I was knocked out by that new song.* **10 knock the bottom out of.** *Inf.* to invalidate (an argument).

knockout drops *pl n Sl.* a drug secretly put into someone's drink to cause stupefaction. ◆ See also **Mickey Finn.**

knock up *vb* (*adv, mainly tr*) **1** Also: **knock together.** *Inf.* to assemble quickly: *to knock up a set of shelves.* **2** *Brit. inf.* to waken; rouse: *to knock someone up early.* **3** *Sl.* to make pregnant. **4** *Brit. inf.* to exhaust. **5** *Cricket.* to score (runs). **6** (*intr*) *Tennis, squash, etc.* to practise, esp. before a match. ◆ *n* **knock-up. 7** a practice session at tennis, squash, etc.

knoll ❶ (nəʊl) *n* a small rounded hill. [OE *cnoll*]
▸ '**knolly** *adj*

knot[1] ❶ (nɒt) *n* **1** any of various fastenings formed by looping and tying a piece of rope, cord, etc., in upon itself or to another piece of rope. **2** a prescribed method of tying a particular knot. **3** a tangle, as in hair or string. **4** a decorative bow, as of ribbon. **5** a small cluster or huddled group. **6** a tie or bond: *the marriage knot.* **7** a difficult problem. **8a** a hard mass of wood where a branch joins the trunk of a tree. **8b** a cross section of this visible on a piece of timber. **9** a sensation of constriction, caused by tension or nervousness: *his stomach was tying itself in knots.* **10** *Pathol.* a lump of vessels or fibres formed in a part, as in a muscle. **11** a unit of velocity used by ships and aircraft, being one nautical mile (about 1.15 statute miles or 1.85 km) per hour. **12 at a rate of knots.** very fast. **13 tie (someone) in knots.** to completely perplex (someone). ◆ *vb* **knots, knotting, knotted. 14** (*tr*) to tie or fasten in a knot. **15** to form or cause to form into a knot. **16** (*tr*) to entangle or become entangled. **17** (*tr*) to make (an article or design) by tying thread in ornamental knots. [OE *cnotta*]
▸ '**knotted** *adj* ▸ '**knotter** *n* ▸ '**knotless** *adj*

knot[2] (nɒt) *n* a small northern sandpiper with a short bill and grey plumage. [C15: from ?]

knot garden *n* (esp. formerly) a formal garden of intricate design.

knotgrass ('nɒt,grɑːs) *n* **1** Also called: **allseed.** a weed whose small green flowers produce numerous seeds. **2** any of several related plants.

knothole ('nɒt,həʊl) *n* a hole in a piece of wood where a knot has been.

knotty ❶ ('nɒtɪ) *adj* **knottier, knottiest. 1** (of wood, rope, etc.) full of or characterized by knots. **2** extremely difficult or intricate.

knout (naʊt) *n* a stout whip used formerly in Russia as an instrument of punishment. [C17: from Russian *knut,* of Scand. origin]

know ❶ (nəʊ) *vb* **knows, knowing, knew, known.** (*mainly tr*) **1** (*also intr; may take a clause as object*) to be or feel certain of the truth or accuracy of (a fact, etc.). **2** to be acquainted or familiar with: *she's known him five years.* **3** to have a familiarity or grasp of: *he knows French.* **4** (*also intr; may take a clause as object*) to understand, be aware of, or perceive (facts, etc.): *he knows the answer now.* **5** (foll. by *how*) to be sure or aware of (how to be or do something). **6** to experience, esp. deeply: *to know poverty.* **7** to be intelligent, informed, or sensible enough (to do something). **8** (*may take a clause as object*) to be able to distinguish or discriminate. **9** *Arch.* to have sexual intercourse with. **10 know what's what.** to know how one thing or things in general work. **11 you never know.** things are uncertain. ◆ *n* **12 in the know.** *Inf.* aware or informed. [OE *gecnāwan*]
▸ '**knowable** *adj* ▸ '**knower** *n*

know-all ❶ *n Inf., disparaging.* a person who pretends or appears to know a great deal.

know-how ❶ *n Inf.* **1** ingenuity, aptitude, or skill. **2** commercial and saleable knowledge of how to do a particular thing.

knowing ❶ ('nəʊɪŋ) *adj* **1** suggesting secret knowledge. **2** wise, shrewd, or clever. **3** deliberate. ◆ *n* **4 there is no knowing.** one cannot tell.
▸ '**knowingly** *adv* ▸ '**knowingness** *n*

knowledge ❶ ('nɒlɪdʒ) *n* **1** the facts or experiences known by a person or group of people. **2** the state of knowing. **3** consciousness or familiarity gained by experience or learning. **4** erudition or informed learning. **5** specific information about a subject. **6 to my knowledge. 6a** as I understand it. **6b** as I know.

knowledgeable ❶ *or* **knowledgable** ('nɒlɪdʒəbᵊl) *adj* possessing or indicating much knowledge.
▸ '**knowledgeably** *or* '**knowledgably** *adv*

THESAURUS

go (at) (*inf.*), lambast(e), run down, slag (off) (*sl.*), slam (*sl.*) ◆ *n* **12** = **blow**, belt (*inf.*), box, clip, clout (*inf.*), cuff, hammering, rap, slap, smack, thump **14** *Informal* = **setback**, defeat, failure, rebuff, rejection, reversal **15** *Informal* = **criticism**, blame, censure, condemnation, heat (*sl., chiefly US & Canad.*), slagging (off) (*sl.*), stick (*sl.*), stricture

knock about *vb* **1, 2** = **wander**, ramble, range, roam, rove, traipse, travel **4** = **hit**, abuse, batter, beat up (*inf.*), bruise, buffet, clobber, damage, hurt, lambast(e), maltreat, manhandle, maul, mistreat, strike, work over (*sl.*), wound ◆ *adj* **knockabout 6** = **boisterous**, farcical, harum-scarum, rambunctious (*inf.*), riotous, rollicking, rough-and-tumble, rumbustious, slapstick

knock down *vb* **1** = **demolish**, batter, clout (*inf.*), deck (*sl.*), destroy, fell, floor, level, pound, raze, smash, wallop (*inf.*), wreck

knock off *vb* **1** *Informal* = **stop work**, clock off, clock out, complete, conclude, finish, terminate **4** *Slang* = **kill**, assassinate, blow away (*sl., chiefly US*), bump off (*sl.*), do away with, do in (*sl.*), liquidate, murder, slay, take out (*sl.*), waste (*inf.*) **5** *Slang* = **steal**, blag (*sl.*), cabbage (*Brit. sl.*), filch, nick (*sl., chiefly Brit.*), pilfer, pinch, purloin, rob, thieve

knockout *n* **1, 2** = **killer blow**, *coup de grâce*, kayo (*sl.*), KO *or* K.O. (*sl.*) **4** *Informal* = **success**, hit, sensation, smash, stunner, triumph, winner

Antonyms *n* ≠ **success:** failure, flop (*inf.*), turkey (*inf.*)

knoll *n* = **hillock**, barrow, hill, hummock, mound, swell

knot[1] *n* **1** = **connection**, bond, bow, braid, joint, ligature, loop, rosette, tie **5** = **cluster**, aggregation, bunch, clump, collection, heap, mass, pile, tuft **5** = **group**, assemblage, band, circle, clique, company, crew (*inf.*), gang, pack, set, squad ◆ *vb* **14-16** = **tie**, bind, complicate, entangle, knit, loop, secure, tether, weave

knotty *adj* **1** = **knotted**, bumpy, gnarled, knobby, nodular, rough, rugged **2** = **puzzling**, baffling, complex, complicated, difficult, hard, intricate, mystifying, perplexing, problematical, thorny, tricky, troublesome

know *vb* **1, 4** = **understand**, apprehend, comprehend, experience, fathom, feel certain, ken (*Scot.*), learn, notice, perceive, realize, recognize, see, undergo **2, 3** = **be acquainted with**, associate with, be familiar with, fraternize with, have dealings with, have knowledge of, recognize **8** = **distinguish**, differentiate, discern, identify, make out, perceive, recognize, see, tell

Antonyms *vb* ≠ **understand:** misunderstand ≠ **be acquainted with:** be ignorant, be unfamiliar with

know-all *n Informal, disparaging* = **smart aleck** (*inf.*), clever-clogs (*inf.*), clever Dick, smarty (*inf.*), smarty-boots (*inf.*), smarty-pants (*inf.*), wiseacre, wise guy (*inf.*)

know-how *n* **1** *Informal* = **capability**, ability, adroitness, aptitude, craft, dexterity, experience, expertise, faculty, flair, ingenuity, knack, knowledge, proficiency, savoir-faire, skill, talent

knowing *adj* **1** = **meaningful**, eloquent, expressive, significant **2** = **cunning**, acute, astute, perceptive, sagacious, shrewd **2** = **well-informed**, clever, clued-up (*inf.*), competent, discerning, experienced, expert, intelligent, qualified, skilful **3** = **deliberate**, aware, conscious, intended, intentional

Antonyms *adj* ≠ **cunning:** ingenuous, naive, wet behind the ears (*inf.*) ≠ **well-informed:** ignorant, obtuse ≠ **deliberate:** accidental, unintentional

knowingly *adv* **3** = **deliberately**, consciously, intentionally, on purpose, purposely, wilfully, wittingly

knowledge *n* **3** = **understanding**, ability, apprehension, cognition, comprehension, consciousness, discernment, grasp, judgment, recognition **3** = **acquaintance**, cognizance, familiarity, information, intimacy, notice **4** = **learning**, education, enlightenment, erudition, instruction, intelligence, scholarship, schooling, science, tuition, wisdom

Antonyms ≠ **understanding:** misunderstanding, unawareness ≠ **acquaintance:** unfamiliarity *n* ≠ **learning:** ignorance, illiteracy

knowledgeable *adj* = **well-informed**, acquainted, *au courant*, *au fait*, aware, clued-up (*inf.*), cognizant, conscious, conversant, educated, erudite, experienced, familiar, intelli-

known ❶ (nəʊn) *vb* **1** the past participle of **know**. ◆ *adj* **2** identified: *a known criminal.*

knuckle ('nʌkᵊl) *n* **1** a joint of a finger, esp. that connecting a finger to the hand. **2** a joint of veal, pork, etc., consisting of the part of the leg below the knee joint. **3 near the knuckle.** *Inf.* approaching indecency. ◆ *vb* **knuckles, knuckling, knuckled. 4** (*tr*) to rub or press with the knuckles. **5** (*intr*) to keep the knuckles on the ground while shooting a marble. ◆ See also **knuckle down, knuckle under.** [C14]
▸'**knuckly** *adj*

knucklebones ('nʌkᵊl,bəʊnz) *n* (*functioning as sing*) a less common name for **jacks** (the game).

knuckle down *vb* (*intr, adv*) *Inf.* to apply oneself diligently: *to knuckle down to some work.*

knuckle-duster *n* (*often pl*) a metal bar fitted over the knuckles, often with holes for the fingers, for inflicting injury by a blow with the fist.

knucklehead ('nʌkᵊl,hɛd) *n Inf.* a fool; idiot.
▸'**knuckle,headed** *adj*

knuckle under ❶ *vb* (*intr, adv*) to give way under pressure or authority; yield.

knur, knurr (nɜː), *or* **knar** *n* a knot or protuberance in a tree trunk or in wood. [C16 *knor;* cf. KNAR]

knurl *or* **nurl** (nɜːl) *vb* (*tr*) **1** to impress with a series of fine ridges or serrations. ◆ *n* **2** a small ridge, esp. one of a series. [C17: prob. from KNUR]

KO *or* **k.o.** ('keɪ'əʊ) *vb* **KO's, KO'ing, KO'd** *or* **k.o.'s, k.o.'ing, k.o.'d,** *n, pl* **KO's** *or* **k.o.'s.** a slang term for **knockout** or **knock out.**

koala *or* **koala bear** (kəʊ'ɑːlə) *n* a slow-moving Australian arboreal marsupial, having dense greyish fur and feeding on eucalyptus leaves. Also called (Austral.): **native bear.** [from Abor.]

koan ('kəʊæn) *n* (in Zen Buddhism) a problem that admits no logical solution. [from Japanese]

kobold ('kɒbəʊld) *n German myth.* **1** a mischievous household sprite. **2** a spirit that haunts mines. [C19: from G; see COBALT]

kochia ('kɒ'fiːə) *n* an annual plant with ornamental foliage that turns purple-red in late summer. [C19: after W.D.J. *Koch,* G botanist]

Kodiak bear *or* **Kodiak** ('kəʊdɪ,æk) *n* a large variety of the brown bear inhabiting the W coast of Alaska and neighbouring islands, esp. Kodiak.

koeksister ('kʊk,sɪstə) *n S. African.* a plaited doughnut deep-fried and soaked in syrup. [Afrik. but possibly of Malay origin]

koel ('kəʊəl) *n* any of several parasitic cuckoos of S and SE Asia and Australia. [C19: from Hindi, from Sansk. *kokila*]

koha ('kəʊhə) *n NZ.* a gift or donation. [Maori]

kohl (kəʊl) *n* a cosmetic powder used, originally esp. in Muslim and Asian countries, to darken the area around the eyes. [C18: from Ar. *kohl;* see ALCOHOL]

kohlrabi (kəʊl'rɑːbɪ) *n, pl* **kohlrabies.** a cultivated variety of cabbage whose thickened stem is eaten as a vegetable. Also called: **turnip cabbage.** [C19: from G, from It. *cavoli rape* (pl), from *cavolo* cabbage (from L *caulis*) + *rapa* turnip (from L)]

koi (kɔɪ) *n* any of various ornamental forms of the common carp. [Japanese]

koine ('kɔɪniː) *n* a common language among speakers of different languages; lingua franca. [from Gk *koinē dialektos* common language]

Koine ('kɔɪniː) *n* (*sometimes not cap.*) **the.** the ancient Greek dialect that was the lingua franca of the empire of Alexander the Great and in Roman times.

kokanee (kəʊ'kænɪ) *n* a landlocked salmon of lakes in W North America: a variety of sockeye. [prob. from *Kokanee* Creek, in SE British Columbia]

kola ('kəʊlə) *n* a variant spelling of **cola.**

kola nut *n* a variant spelling of **cola nut.**

kolinsky (kə'lɪnskɪ) *n, pl* **kolinskies. 1** any of various Asian minks. **2** the rich tawny fur of this animal. [C19: from Russian *kolinsky* of *Kola,* in NW Russia]

kolkhoz (kɒl'hɔːz) *n* a Russian collective farm. [C20: from Russian, short for *kollektivnoe khozyaistvo* collective farm]

Kol Nidre (kɔːl 'nɪdreɪ) *n Judaism.* **1** the evening service with which Yom Kippur begins. **2** the opening prayer of that service. [Aramaic *kōl nidhrē* all the vows; the prayer's opening words]

komatik ('kəʊmætɪk) *n* a sledge having wooden runners and crossbars bound with rawhide, used by Eskimos. [C20: from Eskimo]

koodoo ('kuːduː) *n* a variant spelling of **kudu.**

kook (kuːk) *n US & Canad. inf.* an eccentric or foolish person. [C20: prob. from CUCKOO]
▸'**kooky** *or* '**kookie** *adj*

kookaburra ('kʊkə,bʌrə) *n* a large Australian kingfisher with a cackling cry. Also called: **laughing jackass.** [C19: from Abor.]

kopeck *or* **copeck** ('kəʊpɛk) *n* a monetary unit of Russia and Belarus worth one hundredth of a rouble: coins are still used as tokens for coin-operated machinery although the kopeck itself is virtually valueless. [Russian *kopeika,* from *kopye* lance]

koppie *or* **kopje** ('kɒpɪ) *n* (in southern Africa) a small isolated hill. [C19: from Afrik., from Du. *kopje,* lit.: a little head, from *kop* head]

kora ('kɔːrə) *n* a West African instrument with twenty-one strings, combining features of the harp and the lute.

Koran (kɔː'rɑːn) *n* the sacred book of Islam, believed by Muslims to be the infallible word of God dictated to Mohammed. Also: **Qur'an.** [C17: from Ar. *qur'ān* reading, book]
▸**Ko'ranic** *adj*

Korean (kə'riːən) *adj* **1** of or relating to Korea in SE Asia, its people, or their language. ◆ *n* **2** a native or inhabitant of Korea. **3** the official language of North and South Korea.

korfball ('kɔːf,bɔːl) *n* a game similar to basketball, in which each team consists of six men and six women. [C20: from Du. *korfbal* basketball]

korma ('kɔːmə) *n* an Indian dish consisting of meat or vegetables braised with stock, yogurt, or cream. [from Urdu]

Korsakoffian (,kɔːsə'kɒfɪən) *adj* **1** relating to or suffering from **Korsakoff's psychosis,** a mental illness involving severe confusion and inability to retain recent memories, usually caused by alcoholism. ◆ *n* **2** a person suffering from Korsakoff's psychosis. [C19: after Sergei *Korsakoff* (1854–1900), Russian neuropsychiatrist]

kosher ('kəʊʃə) *adj* **1** *Judaism.* conforming to religious law; fit for use: esp. (of food) prepared in accordance with the dietary laws. **2** *Inf.* **2a** genuine or authentic. **2b** legitimate. [C19: from Yiddish, from Heb. *kāshēr* proper]

koto ('kəʊtəʊ) *n, pl* **kotos.** a Japanese stringed instrument. [Japanese]

kotuku ('kəʊtʊkuː) *n, pl* **kotuku.** *NZ.* a white heron having brilliant white plumage, black legs and yellow eyes and bill. [Maori]

kouprey ('kuːpreɪ) *n* a large wild member of the cattle tribe, of SE Asia, having a blackish-brown body and white legs: an endangered species. [C20: from F, from Cambodian, from Pali *gō* cow + Khmer *brai* forest]

kowhai ('koːwaɪ) *n, pl* **kowhais.** *NZ.* a small leguminous tree of New Zealand and Chile with clusters of yellow flowers. [C19: from Maori]

kowtow ❶ (,kaʊ'taʊ) *vb* (*intr*) **1** to touch the forehead to the ground as a sign of deference: a former Chinese custom. **2** (often foll. by *to*) to be servile (towards). ◆ *n* **3** the act of kowtowing. [C19: from Chinese, from *k'o* to strike, knock + *t'ou* head]

Kr 1 *Currency. symbol for:* **1a** krona. **1b** krone. **2** *the chemical symbol for* krypton.

kr. *abbrev. for:* **1** krona. **2** krone.

kraal (krɑːl) *n S. African.* **1** a hut village in southern Africa, esp. one surrounded by a stockade. **2** an enclosure for livestock. [C18: from Afrik., from Port. *curral* pen]

kraft (krɑːft) *n* strong wrapping paper. [G: force]

krait (kraɪt) *n* any nonaggressive brightly coloured venomous snake of S and SE Asia. [C19: from Hindi *karait,* from ?]

kraken ('krɑːkən) *n* a legendary sea monster of gigantic size believed to dwell off the coast of Norway. [C18: from Norwegian, from ?]

krans (krɑːns) *n S. African.* a sheer rock face; precipice. [C18: from Afrik.]

kremlin ('krɛmlɪn) *n* the citadel of any Russian city. [C17: from obs. G *Kremelin,* from Russian *kreml*]

Kremlin ('krɛmlɪn) *n* **1** the 12th-century citadel in Moscow, containing the offices of the Russian government. **2** (formerly) the central government of the Soviet Union.

krill (krɪl) *n, pl* **krill.** any small shrimplike marine crustacean: the principal food of whalebone whales. [C20: from Norwegian *kril* young fish]

krimmer ('krɪmə) *n* a tightly curled light grey fur obtained from the skins of lambs from Crimea in the Ukraine. [C20: from G, from *Krim* Crimea]

Kriol ('kriːɒl) *n* a creole language used by Aboriginal communities in the northern regions of Australia, developed from Northern Territory pidgin.

kris (krɪs) *n* a Malayan and Indonesian stabbing or slashing knife with a scalloped edge. Also called: **crease, creese.** [C16: from Malay]

krona ('krəʊnə) *n, pl* **kronor** (-nə). the standard monetary unit of Sweden.

króna ('krəʊnə) *n, pl* **krónur** (-nə). the standard monetary unit of Iceland.

krone ('krəʊnə) *n, pl* **kroner** (-nə). **1** the standard monetary unit of Denmark. **2** the standard monetary unit of Norway. [C19: from Danish or Norwegian, ult. from L *corōna* CROWN]

Krugerrand ('kruːgə,rænd) *n* a one-ounce gold coin minted in South Africa for investment only. [C20: from Paul *Kruger* (1825–1904), Boer statesman, + RAND[1]]

krummhorn ('krʌm,hɔːn) *or* **crumhorn** *n* a medieval wind instrument consisting of an upward-curving tube blown through a double reed.

krypton ('krɪptɒn) *n* an inert gaseous element occurring in trace amounts in air and used in fluorescent lights and lasers. Symbol: Kr;

THESAURUS

gent, in the know (*inf.*), in the loop, learned, lettered, scholarly, understanding

known *adj* **2** = **famous**, acknowledged, admitted, avowed, celebrated, common, confessed, familiar, manifest, noted, obvious, patent, plain, popular, published, recognized, well-known

Antonyms *adj* closet (*inf.*), concealed, hidden, secret, unfamiliar, unknown, unrecognized, unrevealed

knuckle under *vb* = **give way**, accede, acquiesce, capitulate, cave in (*inf.*), give in, submit, succumb, surrender, yield

Antonyms *vb* be defiant, dig one's heels in (*inf.*), hold out (against), kick up (a fuss *or* stink), rebel, resist

kowtow *vb* **1** = **bow**, genuflect, kneel **2** = **grovel**, brown-nose, court, cringe, fawn, flatter, lick someone's boots, pander to, suck up to (*sl.*), toady, truckle

atomic no.: 36; atomic wt.: 83.80. [C19: from Gk, from *kruptos* hidden]

krytron ('kraɪtrɒn) *n Electronics.* a type of fast electronic gas-discharge switch, used as a trigger in nuclear weapons.

Kshatriya ('kʃætrɪə) *n* a member of the second of the four main Hindu castes, the warrior caste. [C18: from Sansk., from *kshatra* rule]

kt *abbrev. for:* **1** karat. **2** *Naut.* knot.

Kt **1** Also: **knt.** *abbrev. for* Knight. **2** Also: **N.** *Chess. symbol for* knight.

kudos ❶ ('kjuːdɒs) *n (functioning as sing)* acclaim, glory, or prestige. [C18: from Gk]

kudu *or* **koodoo** ('kuːduː) *n* either of two spiral-horned antelopes (**greater kudu** or **lesser kudu**), which inhabit the bush of Africa. [C18: from Afrik. *koedoe*, prob. from Khoi]

Ku Klux Klan (ˌkuː klʌks 'klæn) *n* **1** a secret organization of White Southerners formed after the US Civil War to fight Black emancipation. **2** a secret organization of White Protestant Americans, mainly in the South, who use violence against Blacks, Jews, etc. [C19 *Ku Klux*, prob. based on Gk *kuklos* CIRCLE + *Klan* CLAN]
▸**Ku Klux Klanner** ('klænə) *n*

kukri ('kʊkrɪ) *n, pl* **kukris.** a knife with a curved blade that broadens towards the point, esp. as used by Gurkhas. [from Hindi]

kulak ('kuːlæk) *n* (in Russia after 1906) a member of the class of peasants who became proprietors of their own farms. In 1929 Stalin initiated their liquidation. [C19: from Russian: fist, hence, tightfisted person]

kulfi ('kʊlfɪ) *n* an Indian dessert that resembles ice cream flavoured with nuts and cardamom seeds.

kumera *or* **kumara** ('kuːmərə) *n NZ.* the sweet potato. [from Maori]

kumiss *or* **koumiss** ('kuːmɪs) *n* a drink made from fermented mare's or other milk, drunk by certain Asian tribes. [C17: from Russian *kumys*]

kumite ('kuːmɪˌteɪ) *n Karate, etc.* freestyle sparring or fighting. [C20: Japanese, lit.: sparring]

kümmel ('kʊməl) *n* a German liqueur flavoured with aniseed and cumin. [C19: from G, from OHG *kumil*, prob. var. of *kumin* CUMIN]

kumquat *or* **cumquat** ('kʌmkwɒt) *n* **1** a small Chinese citrus tree. **2** the small round orange fruit of such a tree, with a sweet rind, used in preserves and confections. [C17: from Mandarin Chinese *chin chü* golden orange]

kung fu ('kʌŋ 'fuː) *n* a Chinese martial art combining principles of karate and judo. [from Chinese: martial art]

kurchatovium (ˌkɜːtʃə'təʊvɪəm) *n* another name for **rutherfordium,** esp. as used in the former Soviet Union. [C20: from Russian, after I. V. *Kurchatov* (1903–60), Soviet physicist]

Kurd (kɜːd) *n* a member of a nomadic people living chiefly in E Turkey, N Iraq, and W Iran.

Kurdish ('kɜːdɪʃ) *n* **1** the language of the Kurds. ◆ *adj* **2** of or relating to the Kurds or their language.

kuri ('kuːrɪ) *n, pl* **kuris.** *NZ.* a mongrel dog. Also called: **goorie.** [Maori]

kurrajong *or* **currajong** ('kʌrəˌdʒɒŋ) *n* any of various Australian trees or shrubs, esp. one that yields a tough durable fibre. [C19: from Abor.]

kursaal ('kɜːzəl) *n* a public room at a health resort. [from G, lit.: cure room]

kurtosis (kə'təʊsɪs) *n Statistics.* a measure of the concentration of a distribution around its mean. [from Gk, from *kurtos* arched]

kuru ('kʊruː) *n* a degenerative disease of the nervous system, restricted to certain tribes in New Guinea, marked by loss of muscular control and thought to be caused by a slow virus. [C20: from a native name]

kvass (kvɑːs) *n* an alcoholic drink of low strength made in Russia and E Europe from cereals and stale bread. [C16: from Russian *kvas*]

kvetch (kvɛtʃ) *vb (intr) Sl., chiefly US.* to complain or grumble, esp. incessantly. [C20: from Yiddish *kvetshn*, lit.: to squeeze, press]

kW *abbrev. for* kilowatt.

kwacha ('kwɑːtʃɑː) *n* **1** the standard monetary unit of Zambia. **2** the standard monetary unit of Malawi. [from a native word in Zambia]

kwashiorkor (ˌkwæʃɪ'ɔːkə) *n* severe malnutrition of infants and young children, resulting from dietary deficiency of protein. [C20: from native word in Ghana]

kWh *abbrev. for* kilowatt-hour.

KWIC (kwɪk) *n acronym for* key word in context (esp. in **KWIC index**).

KWOC (kwɒk) *n acronym for* key word out of context.

kyanite ('kaɪəˌnaɪt) *n* a variant spelling of **cyanite.**
▸**kyanitic** (ˌkaɪə'nɪtɪk) *adj*

kyanize *or* **kyanise** ('kaɪəˌnaɪz) *vb* **kyanizes, kyanizing, kyanized** *or* **kyanises, kyanising, kyanised.** *(tr)* to treat (timber) with corrosive sublimate to make it resistant to decay. [C19: after J.H. *Kyan* (died 1850), Brit. inventor of the process]
▸ˌ**kyani'zation** *or* ˌ**kyani'sation** *n*

kyle (kaɪl) *n Scot.* (esp. in place names) a narrow strait or channel: *Kyle of Lochalsh.* [C16: from Gaelic *caol* narrow]

kylie *or* **kiley** ('kaɪlɪ) *n Austral.* a boomerang that is flat on one side and convex on the other. [C19: from Abor.]

kyloe ('kaɪləʊ) *n* a breed of small long-horned long-haired beef cattle from NW Scotland. [C19: from ?]

kymograph ('kaɪməˌgrɑːf) *n* a rotatable drum for holding paper on which a tracking stylus continuously records variations in sound waves, blood pressure, respiratory movements, etc. [C20: from Gk *kuma* wave + -GRAPH]
▸ˌ**kymo'graphic** *adj*

Kymric ('kɪmrɪk) *n, adj* a variant spelling of **Cymric.**

Kymry ('kɪmrɪ) *pl n* a variant spelling of **Cymry.**

kyphosis (kaɪ'fəʊsɪs) *n Pathol.* backward curvature of the thoracic spine, of congenital origin or resulting from injury or disease. [C19: from NL, from Gk *kuphōsis*, from *kuphos* humpbacked]
▸**kyphotic** (kaɪ'fɒtɪk) *adj*

Kyrgyz ('kɪəgɪz) *n* **1** *(pl* **Kyrgyz)** a member of a Mongoloid people of central Asia, inhabiting Kyrgyzstan and a vast area of central Siberia. **2** the language of this people, belonging to the Turkic branch of the Altaic family. Also: **Kirghiz, Kirgiz.**

Kyrie eleison ('kɪrɪɪ ə'leɪsən) *n* **1** a formal invocation used in the liturgies of the Roman Catholic, Greek Orthodox, and Anglican Churches. **2** a musical setting of this. Often shortened to **Kyrie.** [C14: via LL from LGk *kurie, eleēson* Lord, have mercy]

kyu (kjuː) *n Judo.* one of the student grades for inexperienced competitors. [from Japanese]

THESAURUS

kudos *n* = **prestige**, acclaim, applause, distinction, esteem, fame, glory, honour, laudation, notability, plaudits, praise, regard, renown, repute

Ll

l *or* **L** (ɛl) *n, pl* **l's, L's,** *or* **Ls. 1** the 12th letter of the English alphabet. **2** a speech sound represented by this letter. **3a** something shaped like an L. **3b** *(in combination): an L-shaped room.*

l *symbol for* litre.

L *symbol for:* **1** lambert(s). **2** large. **3** Latin. **4** (on British motor vehicles) learner driver. **5** *Physics.* length. **6** live. **7** Usually written: £, pound. [L *libra*]. **8** lire. **9** *Electronics.* inductor (in circuit diagrams). **10** *Physics.* **10a** latent heat. **10b** self-inductance. **11** the Roman numeral for 50. See **Roman numerals.**

L. *or* **l.** *abbrev. for:* **1** lake. **2** law. **3** leaf. **4** league. **5** left. **6** length. **7** (*pl* **LL** *or* **ll.**) line. **8** link. **9** low.

L. *abbrev. for:* **1** *Politics.* Liberal. **2** (in titles) Licentiate. **3** Linnaeus.

la[1] (lɑː) *n Music.* the syllable used in the fixed system of solmization for the note A. [C14: see GAMUT]

la[2] (lɔː) *interj* an exclamation of surprise or emphasis. [OE *lā* lo]

La *the chemical symbol for* lanthanum.

laager (ˈlɑːgə) *n* **1** (in Africa) a camp, esp. one defended by a circular formation of wagons. **2** *Mil.* a place where armoured vehicles are parked. ◆ *vb* **3** to form (wagons) into a laager. **4** *(tr)* to park (armoured vehicles) in a laager. [C19: from Afrik. *lager,* via G from OHG *legar* bed, lair]

lab (læb) *n Inf.* short for **laboratory.**

lab. *abbrev. for:* **1** laboratory. **2** labour.

Lab. *abbrev. for:* **1** *Politics.* Labour. **2** Labrador.

label Ⓣ (ˈleɪbəl) *n* **1** a piece of paper, card, or other material attached to an object to identify it or give instructions or details concerning its ownership, use, nature, destination, etc.; tag. **2** a brief descriptive phrase or term given to a person, group, school of thought, etc.: *the label "Romantic" is applied to many different kinds of poetry.* **3** a word or phrase heading a piece of text to indicate or summarize its contents. **4** a trademark or company or brand name on certain goods, esp. on gramophone records. **5** *Computing.* a group of characters appended to a statement in a program to allow it to be identified. **6** *Chem.* a radioactive element used in a compound to trace the mechanism of a chemical reaction. ◆ *vb* **labels, labelling, labelled** *or US* **labels, labeling, labeled.** *(tr)* **7** to fasten a label to. **8** to mark with a label. **9** to describe or classify in a word or phrase: *to label someone a liar.* **10** to make (one or more atoms in a compound) radioactive, for use in determining the mechanism of a reaction. [C14: from OF, from Gmc]
▸ˈ**labeller** *n*

labia (ˈleɪbɪə) *n* the plural of **labium.**

labial (ˈleɪbɪəl) *adj* **1** of, relating to, or near lips or labia. **2** *Music.* producing sounds by the action of an air stream over a narrow liplike fissure, as in a flue pipe of an organ. **3** *Phonetics.* relating to a speech sound whose articulation involves movement or use of the lips. ◆ *n* **4** Also called: **labial pipe.** *Music.* an organ pipe with a liplike fissure. **5** *Phonetics.* a speech sound such as English *p* or *m,* whose articulation involves movement or use of the lips. [C16: from Med. L *labiālis,* from L *labium* lip]
▸ˈ**labially** *adv*

labiate (ˈleɪbɪˌeɪt, -ɪt) *n* **1** any plant of the family *Labiatae,* having square stems, aromatic leaves, and a two-lipped corolla: includes mint, thyme, sage, rosemary, etc. ◆ *adj* **2** of, relating to, or belonging to the family *Labiatae.* [C18: from NL *labiātus,* from L *labium* lip]

labile (ˈleɪbɪl) *adj Chem.* (of a compound) prone to chemical change. [C15: via LL *lābilis,* from L *lābī* to slide]
▸**lability** (ləˈbɪlɪtɪ) *n*

labiodental (ˌleɪbɪəʊˈdɛntəl) *Phonetics.* ◆ *adj* **1** pronounced by bringing the bottom lip into contact with the upper teeth, as for *f* in *fat, puff.* ◆ *n* **2** a labiodental consonant. [C17: from L LABIUM + DENTAL]

labium (ˈleɪbɪəm) *n, pl* **labia** (-bɪə). **1** a lip or liplike structure. **2** any one of the four lip-shaped folds of the female vulva, comprising an outer pair (**labia majora**) and an inner pair (**labia minora**). [C16: NL, from L.: lip]

laboratory (ləˈbɒrətərɪ, -trɪ; *US.* ˈlæbrəˌtɔːrɪ) *n, pl* **laboratories. 1a** a building or room equipped for conducting scientific research or for teaching practical science. **1b** *(as modifier): laboratory equipment.* **2** a place where chemicals or medicines are manufactured. ◆ Often shortened to **lab.** [C17: from Med. L *labōrātōrium* workshop, from L *labōrāre* to LABOUR]

Labor Day *n* **1** a public holiday in the US and Canada in honour of labour, held on the first Monday in September. **2** a public holiday in Australia, observed on different days in different states.

laborious Ⓣ (ləˈbɔːrɪəs) *adj* **1** involving great exertion or long effort. **2** given to working hard. **3** (of literary style, etc.) not fluent.
▸**laˈboriously** *adv* ▸**laˈboriousness** *n*

Labor Party *n* one of the chief political parties of Australia, generally supporting the interests of organized labour.

labour Ⓣ *or US & sometimes Canad.* **labor** (ˈleɪbə) *n* **1** productive work, esp. physical toil done for wages. **2a** the people, class, or workers involved in this, esp. in contrast to management, capital, etc. **2b** *(as modifier): labour relations.* **3a** difficult or arduous work or effort. **3b** *(in combination): labour-saving.* **4** a particular job or task, esp. of a difficult nature. **5a** the process or effort of childbirth or the time during which this takes place. **5b** *(as modifier): labour pain; labour ward.* ◆ *vb* **6** *(intr)* to perform labour; work. **7** *(intr;* foll. by *for,* etc.) to strive or work hard (for something). **8** *(intr;* usually foll. by *under)* to be burdened (by) or be at a disadvantage (because of): *to labour under a misapprehension.* **9** *(intr)* to make one's way with difficulty. **10** *(tr)* to deal with too persistently: *to labour a point.* **11** *(intr)* (of a woman) to be in labour. **12** *(intr)* (of a ship) to pitch and toss. [C13: via OF from L *labor*]

labour camp *n* **1** a penal colony involving forced labour. **2** a camp for migratory labourers.

Labour Day *n* a public holiday in many countries in honour of labour, usually held on May 1.

laboured Ⓣ *or US & sometimes Canad.* **labored** (ˈleɪbəd) *adj* **1** (of breathing) performed with difficulty. **2** showing effort; contrived; lacking grace or fluency.

labourer Ⓣ *or US & sometimes Canad.* **laborer** (ˈleɪbərə) *n* a person engaged in physical work, esp. unskilled work.

labour exchange *n Brit.* a former name for the **employment office.**

labour-intensive *adj* of or denoting a task, organization, industry, etc., in which a high proportion of the costs are due to wages, salaries, etc.

Labourite (ˈleɪbəˌraɪt) *n* an adherent of the Labour Party.

Labour Party *n* **1** a British political party, formed in 1900 as an amalgam of various trade unions and socialist groups, generally supporting the interests of organized labour and advocating democratic socialism and social equality. **2** any similar party in any of various other countries.

Labrador retriever (ˈlæbrəˌdɔː) *n* a powerfully-built variety of retriever with a short dense usually black or golden-brown coat. Often shortened to **Labrador.**

labret (ˈleɪbrɛt) *n* a piece of bone, shell, etc., inserted into the lip as an ornament by certain peoples. [C19: from L **labrum** lip]

labrum (ˈleɪbrəm, ˈlæb-) *n, pl* **labra** (-brə). a lip or liplike part, such as the cuticular plate forming the upper lip of insects. [C19: NL, from L]

laburnum (ləˈbɜːnəm) *n* any tree or shrub of a Eurasian genus having clusters of yellow drooping flowers: all parts of the plant are poisonous. [C16: NL, from L]

labyrinth Ⓣ (ˈlæbərɪnθ) *n* **1** a mazelike network of tunnels, chambers, or paths, either natural or man-made. **2** any complex or confusing system of streets, passages, etc. **3** a complex or intricate situation. **4** any system of interconnecting cavities, esp. those comprising the internal ear. **5** *Electronics.* an enclosure behind a high-performance loudspeaker, consisting of a series of air chambers designed to absorb unwanted sound waves. [C16: via L from Gk *laburinthos,* from ?]

THESAURUS

label *n* **1** = **tag,** docket (*chiefly Brit.*), flag, marker, sticker, tally, ticket **2** = **epithet,** characterization, classification, description **4** = **brand,** company, mark, trademark ◆ *vb* **7, 8** = **tag,** docket, flag, mark, stamp, sticker, tally **9** = **describe,** brand, call, characterize, class, classify, define, designate, identify, name

laborious *adj* **1** = **hard,** arduous, backbreaking, burdensome, difficult, exhausting, fatiguing, herculean, onerous, strenuous, tiresome, tiring, toilsome, tough, uphill, wearing, wearisome **2** = **industrious,** assiduous, diligent, hard-working, indefatigable, painstaking, persevering, sedulous, tireless, unflagging **3** = **forced,** laboured, not fluent, ponderous, strained

Antonyms *adj* ≠ **hard:** easy, easy-peasy (*sl.*), effortless, light ≠ **forced:** natural, simple

labour *n* **1** = **work,** industry, toil **2a** = **workers,** employees, hands, labourers, workforce, workmen **3a** = **toil,** donkey-work, drudgery, effort, exertion, grind (*inf.*), industry, pains, painstaking, sweat (*inf.*), travail **4** = **chore,** job, task, undertaking **5a** = **childbirth,** contractions, delivery, labour pains, pains, parturition, throes, travail ◆ *vb* **6, 7** = **work,** drudge, endeavour, grind (*inf.*), peg along *or* away (*chiefly Brit.*), plod, plug along *or* away (*inf.*), slave, strive, struggle, sweat (*inf.*), toil, travail **8** *usually with* **under** = **be disadvantaged,** be a victim of, be burdened by, suffer **10** = **overemphasize,** dwell on, elaborate, go on about, make a federal case of (*US inf.*), make a production (out) of (*inf.*), overdo, strain

Antonyms *n* ≠ **toil:** ease, idleness, leisure, relaxation, repose, respite, rest ◆ *vb* ≠ **work:** relax, rest

laboured *adj* **1** = **difficult,** awkward, forced, heavy, stiff, strained **2** = **contrived,** affected, overdone, overwrought, ponderous, studied, unnatural

labourer *n* = **worker,** blue-collar worker, drudge, hand, labouring man, manual worker, navvy (*Brit. inf.*), unskilled worker, working man, workman

labyrinth *n* **3** = **maze,** coil, complexity, complication, convolution, entanglement, intricacy, jungle, knotty problem, perplexity, puzzle, riddle, snarl, tangle, windings

labyrinthine ⓣ (ˌlæbəˈrɪnθaɪn) *adj* **1** of or relating to a labyrinth. **2** resembling a labyrinth in complexity.

lac[1] (læk) *n* a resinous substance secreted by certain insects (**lac insects**), used in the manufacture of shellac. [C16: from Du. *lak* or F *laque,* from Hindi *lākh* resin, ult. from Sansk. *lākshā*]

lac[2] (lɑːk) *n* a variant spelling of **lakh.**

laccolith (ˈlækəlɪθ) *or* **laccolite** (ˈlækəˌlaɪt) *n* a dome of igneous rock between two layers of older sedimentary rock. [C19: from Gk *lakkos* cistern + -LITH]

lace ⓣ (leɪs) *n* **1** a delicate decorative fabric made from cotton, silk, etc., woven in an open web of different symmetrical patterns and figures. **2** a cord or string drawn through eyelets or around hooks to fasten a shoe or garment. **3** ornamental braid often used on military uniforms, etc. ◆ *vb* **laces, lacing, laced.** (*tr*) **4** to fasten (shoes, etc.) with a lace. **5** to draw (a cord or thread) through holes, eyes, etc., as when tying shoes. **6** to compress the waist of (someone), as with a corset. **7** to add a small amount of alcohol or drugs to (food or drink). **8** (*usually passive* and foll. by *with*) to streak or mark with lines or colours: *the sky was laced with red.* **9** to intertwine; interlace. **10** *Inf.* to give a sound beating to. [C13 *las,* from OF *laz,* from L *laqueus* noose]

lacebark (ˈleɪsbɑːk) *n* another name for **ribbonwood.**

lacerate ⓣ *vb* (ˈlæsəˌreɪt), **lacerates, lacerating, lacerated.** (*tr*) **1** to tear (the flesh, etc.) jaggedly. **2** to hurt or harrow (the feelings, etc.). ◆ *adj* (ˈlæsəˌreɪt, -rɪt). **3** having edges that are jagged: *lacerate leaves.* [C16: from L *lacerāre* to tear, from *lacer* mangled]
▸ˌ**laceˈration** *n*

lace up *vb* **1** (*tr, adv*) to tighten or fasten (clothes or footwear) with laces. ◆ *adj* **lace-up. 2** (of footwear) to be fastened with laces. ◆ *n* **lace-up. 3** a lace-up shoe or boot.

lacewing (ˈleɪsˌwɪŋ) *n* any of various insects, esp. the green lacewings and brown lacewings, having lacy wings and preying on aphids and similar pests.

laches (ˈlætʃɪz) *n Law.* negligence or unreasonable delay in pursuing a legal remedy. [C14 *lachesse,* via OF *lasche* slack, from L *laxus* LAX]

Lachesis (ˈlækɪsɪs) *n Greek myth.* one of the three Fates. [via L from Gk, from *lakhesis* destiny, from *lakhein* to befall by lot]

lachrymal (ˈlækrɪməl) *adj* a variant spelling of **lacrimal.**

lachrymatory (ˈlækrɪmətərɪ, -trɪ) *n, pl* **lachrymatories. 1** a small vessel found in ancient tombs, formerly thought to hold the tears of mourners. ◆ *adj* **2** a variant spelling of **lacrimatory.**

lachrymose (ˈlækrɪˌməʊs) *adj* **1** given to weeping; tearful. **2** mournful; sad. [C17: from L, from *lacrima* a tear]
▸ˈ**lachryˌmosely** *adv*

lacing (ˈleɪsɪŋ) *n* **1** *Chiefly Brit.* a course of bricks, stone, etc., for strengthening a rubble or flint wall. **2** another word for **lace** (senses 2, 3). **3** *Inf.* a severe beating.

laciniate (ləˈsɪnɪˌeɪt, -ɪt) *or* **laciniated** *adj* **1** *Biol.* jagged: *a laciniate leaf.* **2** having a fringe. [C17: from L *lacinia* flap]
▸**laˌciniˈation** *n*

lack ⓣ (læk) *n* **1** an insufficiency, shortage, or absence of something required or desired. **2** something that is required but is absent or in short supply. ◆ *vb* **3** (when *intr,* often foll. by *in* or *for*) to be deficient (in) or have need (of). [C12: rel. to MDu. *laken* to be wanting]

lackadaisical ⓣ (ˌlækəˈdeɪzɪkəl) *adj* **1** lacking vitality and purpose. **2** lazy, esp. in a dreamy way. [C18: from earlier *lackadaisy*]
▸ˌ**lackaˈdaisically** *adv*

lackey ⓣ (ˈlækɪ) *n* **1** a servile follower; hanger-on. **2** a liveried male servant or valet. **3** a person who is treated like a servant. ◆ *vb* **4** (when *intr,* often foll. by *for*) to act as a lackey (to). [C16: via F *laquais,* from OF, ?from Catalan *lacayo, alacayo*]

lacklustre ⓣ *or US* **lackluster** (ˈlækˌlʌstə) *adj* lacking force, brilliance, or vitality.

laconic ⓣ (ləˈkɒnɪk) *adj* (of a person's speech) using few words; terse. [C16: via L from Gk *Lakōnikos,* from *Lakōn* Laconian, Spartan; referring to the Spartans' terseness of speech]
▸**laˈconically** *adv*

lacquer (ˈlækə) *n* **1** a hard glossy coating made by dissolving cellulose derivatives or natural resins in a volatile solvent. **2** a black resinous substance, obtained from certain trees (**lacquer trees**), used to give a hard glossy finish to wooden furniture. **3** Also called: **hair lacquer.** a mixture of shellac and alcohol for spraying onto the hair to hold a style in place. **4** *Art.* decorative objects coated with such lacquer, often inlaid. ◆ *vb* (*tr*) **5** to apply lacquer to. [C16: from obs. F *lacre* sealing wax, from Port. *laca* LAC[1]]
▸ˈ**lacquerer** *n*

lacrimal, lachrymal, *or* **lacrymal** (ˈlækrɪməl) *adj* of or relating to tears or to the glands that secrete tears. [C16: from Med. L, from L *lacrima* a tear]

lacrimation (ˌlækrɪˈmeɪʃən) *n* the secretion of tears.

lacrimatory, lachrymatory, *or* **lacrymatory** (ˈlækrɪmətərɪ, -trɪ) *adj* of, causing, or producing tears.

lacrosse (ləˈkrɒs) *n* a ball game invented by American Indians, now played by two teams who try to propel a ball into each other's goal by means of long-handled pouched sticks (**lacrosse sticks**). [C19: Canad. F: the hooked stick, crosier]

lactam (ˈlæktæm) *n Chem.* any of a group of cyclic amides, derived from amino acids, having the characteristic group -CONH-. [C20: from LACTO- + AM(IDE)]

lactate[1] (ˈlækteɪt) *n* an ester or salt of lactic acid. [C18]

lactate[2] (lækˈteɪt) *vb* **lactates, lactating, lactated.** (*intr*) (of mammals) to produce or secrete milk.

lactation (lækˈteɪʃən) *n* **1** the secretion of milk from the mammary glands after parturition. **2** the period during which milk is secreted.

lacteal (ˈlæktɪəl) *adj* **1** of, relating to, or resembling milk. **2** (of lymphatic vessels) conveying or containing chyle. ◆ *n* **3** any of the lymphatic vessels conveying chyle from the small intestine to the thoracic duct. [C17: from L *lacteus* of milk, from *lac* milk]

lactescent (lækˈtɛsᵊnt) *adj* **1** (of plants and certain insects) secreting a milky fluid. **2** milky or becoming milky. [C18: from L, from *lactescēre* to become milky, from *lact-, lac* milk]
▸**lacˈtescence** *n*

lactic (ˈlæktɪk) *adj* relating to or derived from milk. [C18: from L *lact-, lac* milk]

lactic acid *n* a colourless syrupy carboxylic acid found in sour milk and many fruits and used as a preservative (**E270**) for foodstuffs. Formula: $CH_3CH(OH)COOH$. Systematic name: **2-hydroxypropanoic acid.**

lactiferous (lækˈtɪfərəs) *adj* producing, conveying, or secreting milk or a milky fluid. [C17: from L *lactifer,* from *lact-, lac* milk]

lacto- (ˈlæktəʊ) *or before a vowel* **lact-** *combining form.* indicating milk: *lactobacillus.* [from L *lact-, lac* milk]

lactose (ˈlæktəʊs, -təʊz) *n* a white crystalline sugar occurring in milk and used in pharmaceuticals and baby foods. Formula: $C_{12}H_{22}O_{11}$.

lacto-vegetarian *n* a vegetarian whose diet includes dairy produce.

lacuna (ləˈkjuːnə) *n, pl* **lacunae** (-niː) *or* **lacunas. 1** a gap or space, esp. in a book or manuscript. **2** *Biol.* a cavity or depression, such as any of the spaces in the matrix of bone. [C17: from L *lacūna* pool, cavity, from *lacus* lake]
▸**laˈcunose, laˈcunal, laˈcunar,** *or* **laˈcunary** *adj*

lacustrine (ləˈkʌstraɪn) *adj* **1** of or relating to lakes. **2** living or growing in or on the shores of a lake. [C19: from It. *lacustre,* from L *lacus* lake]

lacy ⓣ (ˈleɪsɪ) *adj* **lacier, laciest.** made of or resembling lace.
▸ˈ**lacily** *adv* ▸ˈ**laciness** *n*

lad ⓣ (læd) *n* **1** a boy or young man. **2** *Inf.* a familiar form of address for any male. **3** a lively or dashing man or youth (esp. in **a bit of a lad**). **4** *Brit.* a boy or man who looks after horses. [C13 *ladde;* ?from ON]

ladanum (ˈlædənəm) *n* a dark resinous juice obtained from various rockroses: used in perfumery. [C16: L from Gk, from *lēdon* rockrose]

ladder (ˈlædə) *n* **1** a portable framework of wood, metal, rope, etc., in the form of two long parallel members connected by rungs or steps fixed to them at right angles, for climbing up or down. **2** any hierarchy conceived of as having a series of ascending stages, levels, etc.: *the social ladder.* **3** Also called: **run.** *Chiefly Brit.* a line of connected stitches that have come undone in knitted material, esp. stockings. ◆ *vb* **4** *Chiefly Brit.* to cause a line of interconnected stitches in (stockings, etc.) to undo, as by snagging, or (of a stocking) to come undone in this way. [OE *hlǣdder*]

ladder back *n* a type of chair in which the back is constructed of horizontal slats between two uprights.

laddie (ˈlædɪ) *n Chiefly Scot.* a familiar term for a male, esp. a boy; lad.

laddish (ˈlædɪʃ) *adj Inf., usually derog.* characteristic of male adolescents or young men, esp. by being rowdy, macho, or immature: *laddish behaviour.*

lade (leɪd) *vb* **lades, lading, laded; laden** *or* **laded. 1** to put cargo or freight on board (a ship, etc.) or (of a ship, etc.) to take on cargo or freight. **2**

THESAURUS

labyrinthine *adj* **2** = **complex,** Byzantine, confused, convoluted, intricate, involved, knotty, mazelike, mazy, perplexing, puzzling, tangled, tortuous, winding

lace *n* **1** = **netting,** filigree, openwork, tatting **2** = **cord,** bootlace, shoelace, string, thong, tie ◆ *vb* **4** = **fasten,** attach, bind, close, do up, thread, tie **7** = **mix in,** add to, fortify, spike **9** = **intertwine,** interweave, twine

lacerate *vb* **1** = **tear,** claw, cut, gash, jag, maim, mangle, rend, rip, slash, wound **2** = **hurt,** afflict, distress, harrow, rend, torment, torture, wound

laceration *n* **1** = **cut,** gash, injury, mutilation, rent, rip, slash, tear, trauma (*Pathology*), wound

lack *n* **1** = **shortage,** absence, dearth, deficiency, deprivation, destitution, insufficiency, need, privation, scantiness, scarcity, shortcoming, shortness, want ◆ *vb* **3** = **need,** be deficient in, be short of, be without, miss, require, want
Antonyms *n* ≠ **shortage:** abundance, adequacy, excess, plentifulness, sufficiency, surplus ◆ *vb* ≠ **need:** enjoy, have, own, possess

lackadaisical *adj* **1** = **lethargic,** apathetic, dull, enervated, half-hearted, indifferent, languid, languorous, limp, listless, spiritless **2** = **lazy,** abstracted, dreamy, idle, indolent, inert
Antonyms *adj* ambitious, diligent, excited, inspired, spirited

lackey *n* **1** = **hanger-on,** creature, fawner, flatterer, flunky, instrument, menial, minion, parasite, pawn, sycophant, toady, tool, yes man **2** = **manservant,** attendant, cohort (*chiefly US*), flunky, footman, valet, varlet (*arch.*)

lacking *adj* **3** = **without,** defective, deficient, flawed, impaired, inadequate, minus, missing, needing, sans (*arch.*), wanting

lacklustre *adj* = **flat,** boring, dim, drab, dry, dull, leaden, lifeless, lustreless, muted, prosaic, sombre, unimaginative, uninspired, vapid

laconic *adj* = **terse,** brief, clipped, compact, concise, crisp, curt, monosyllabic, pithy, sententious, short, succinct, to the point
Antonyms *adj* long-winded, loquacious, rambling, verbose, voluble, wordy

lacy *adj* = **filigree,** delicate, fine, frilly, gauzy, gossamer, lace-like, meshy, net-like, open, sheer

lad *n* **1** = **boy,** chap (*inf.*), fellow, guy (*inf.*), juvenile, kid (*inf.*), laddie (*Scot.*), schoolboy, stripling, youngster, youth

(*tr; usually passive* and foll. by *with*) to burden or oppress. **3** (*tr; usually passive* and foll. by *with*) to fill or load. **4** to remove (liquid) with or as if with a ladle. [OE *hladen* to load]

laden Ⓣ (ˈleɪdᵊn) *vb* **1** a past participle of **lade**. ◆ *adj* **2** weighed down with a load; loaded. **3** encumbered; burdened.

la-di-da Ⓣ, **lah-di-dah**, *or* **la-de-da** (ˌlɑːdiːˈdɑː) *adj Inf.* affecting exaggeratedly genteel manners or speech. [C19: mockingly imit. of affected speech]

ladies *or* **ladies' room** *n (functioning as sing) Inf.* a women's public lavatory.

lading (ˈleɪdɪŋ) *n* a load; cargo; freight.

ladle (ˈleɪdᵊl) *n* **1** a long-handled spoon having a deep bowl for serving or transferring liquids. **2** a large bucket-shaped container for transferring molten metal. ◆ *vb* **ladles, ladling, ladled. 3** (*tr*) to serve out as with a ladle. [OE *hlædel*, from *hladan* to draw out]
▸ **ˈladleful** *n*

ladle out *vb (tr, adv) Inf.* to distribute (money, gifts, etc.) generously.

lady Ⓣ (ˈleɪdɪ) *n, pl* **ladies. 1** a woman regarded as having the characteristics of a good family and high social position. **2a** a polite name for a woman. **2b** (*as modifier*): *a lady doctor.* **3** an informal name for **wife. 4 lady of the house.** the female head of the household. **5** *History.* a woman with proprietary rights and authority, as over a manor. [OE *hlǣfdīge*, from *hlāf* bread + *dīge* kneader, rel. to *dāh* dough]

Lady (ˈleɪdɪ) *n, pl* **Ladies. 1** (in Britain) a title of honour borne by various classes of women of the peerage. **2 my lady.** a term of address to holders of the title Lady. **3 Our Lady.** a title of the Virgin Mary.

ladybird (ˈleɪdɪˌbɜːd) *n* any of various small brightly coloured beetles, esp. one having red elytra with black spots. [C18: after Our *Lady*, the Virgin Mary]

lady bountiful *n* an ostentatiously charitable woman. [C19: after a character in George Farquhar's play *The Beaux' Stratagem* (1707)]

Lady Chapel *n* a chapel within a church or cathedral, dedicated to the Virgin Mary.

Lady Day *n* March 25, the feast of the Annunciation of the Virgin Mary. Also called: **Annunciation Day.**

lady-in-waiting *n, pl* **ladies-in-waiting.** a lady who attends a queen or princess.

lady-killer Ⓣ *n Inf.* a man who is, or believes he is, irresistibly fascinating to women.

ladylike Ⓣ (ˈleɪdɪˌlaɪk) *adj* like or befitting a lady in manners and bearing; refined and fastidious.

ladylove (ˈleɪdɪˌlʌv) *n Now rare.* a beloved woman.

Lady Macbeth strategy (məkˈbeθ) *n* a strategy in a takeover battle in which a third party makes a bid acceptable to the target company, appearing to act as a white knight but subsequently joining forces with the original (unwelcome) bidder. [C20: after *Lady Macbeth*, character in *Macbeth* (1605), a play by William Shakespeare]

lady mayoress *n Brit.* the wife of a lord mayor.

lady's bedstraw *n* a Eurasian plant with clusters of small yellow flowers.

lady's finger *n* another name for **bhindi.**

Ladyship (ˈleɪdɪʃɪp) *n* (preceded by *your* or *her*) a title used to address or refer to any peeress except a duchess.

lady's-slipper *n* any of various orchids having reddish or purple flowers.

lady's-smock *n* a N temperate plant with white or rose-pink flowers. Also called: **cuckooflower.**

laevo- *or US* **levo-** *combining form.* **1** on or towards the left: *laevorotatory.* **2** (in chemistry) denoting a laevorotatory compound. [from L *laevus* left]

laevorotation (ˌliːvəʊrəʊˈteɪʃən) *n* **1** a rotation to the left. **2** an anticlockwise rotation of the plane of polarization of plane-polarized light as a result of its passage through a crystal, liquid, or solution. ◆ Cf. **dextrorotation.**
▸ **laevorotatory** (ˌliːvəʊˈrəʊtətərɪ) *adj*

Laffer curve (ˈlæfə) *n Econ.* a graph showing government tax revenue plotted against percentage tax rates; it illustrates that a cut in a high tax rate can increase government revenue. [C20: after Arthur *Laffer* (born 1940), US economist]

LAFTA (ˈlæftə) *n acronym for* Latin American Free Trade Area, the name before 1981 of the Latin American Integration Association. See **LAIA.**

lag[1] Ⓣ (læg) *vb* **lags, lagging, lagged.** (*intr*) **1** (often foll. by *behind*) to hang (back) or fall (behind) in movement, progress, development, etc. **2** to fall away in strength or intensity. ◆ *n* **3** the act or state of slowing down or falling behind. **4** the interval of time between two events, esp. between an action and its effect. [C16: from ?]

lag[2] (læg) *Sl.* ◆ *n* **1** a convict or ex-convict (esp. in **old lag**). **2** a term of imprisonment. ◆ *vb* **lags, lagging, lagged. 3** (*tr*) to arrest or put in prison. [C19: from ?]

lag[3] (læg) *vb* **lags, lagging, lagged. 1** (*tr*) to cover (a pipe, cylinder, etc.) with lagging to prevent loss of heat. ◆ *n* **2** the insulating casing of a steam cylinder, boiler, etc. **3** a stave. [C17: of Scand. origin]

lagan (ˈlægᵊn) *n* goods or wreckage on the sea bed, sometimes attached to a buoy to permit recovery. [C16: from OF *lagan*, prob. of Gmc origin]

lager (ˈlɑːgə) *n* a light-bodied effervescent beer, fermented in a closed vessel using yeasts that sink to the bottom of the brew. [C19: from G *Lagerbier* beer for storing, from *Lager* storehouse]

lager lout *n* a rowdy or aggressive young drunk male.

laggard Ⓣ (ˈlægəd) *n* **1** a person who lags behind. ◆ *adj* **2** *Rare.* sluggish, slow, or dawdling.
▸ **ˈlaggardly** *adj, adv* ▸ **ˈlaggardness** *n*

lagging (ˈlægɪŋ) *n* **1** insulating material wrapped around pipes, boilers, etc., or laid in a roof loft, to prevent loss of heat. **2** the act or process of applying lagging.

lagomorph (ˈlægəʊˌmɔːf) *n* any placental mammal having two pairs of upper incisors specialized for gnawing, such as rabbits and hares. [C19: via NL from Gk *lagōs* hare; see -MORPH]

lagoon (ləˈguːn) *n* **1** a body of water cut off from the open sea by coral reefs or sand bars. **2** any small body of water, esp. one adjoining a larger one. [C17: from It. *laguna*, from L *lacūna* pool; see LACUNA]

Lagrangian point (ləˈgreɪndʒɪən) *n Astron.* one of five points in the plane of revolution of two bodies in orbit around their common centre of gravity, at which a third body of negligible mass can remain in equilibrium with respect to the other two bodies. [after J. L. *Lagrange* (1736–1813), F mathematician and astronomer]

lah (lɑː) *n Music.* (in tonic sol-fa) the sixth note of any major scale; submediant. [C14: later variant of *la*; see GAMUT]

lahar (ˈlɑːhɑː) *n* a landslide of volcanic debris mixed with water down the sides of a volcano, usually precipitated by heavy rainfall. [C20: from Javanese: lava]

lah-di-dah (ˌlɑːdiːˈdɑː) *adj, n Inf.* a variant spelling of **la-di-da.**

LAIA *abbrev. for* Latin American Integration Association (before 1981, known as the Latin American Free Trade Area). An economic group, its members are Argentina, Bolivia, Brazil, Chile, Colombia, Ecuador, Mexico, Paraguay, Peru, Uruguay, and Venezuela.

laic (ˈleɪɪk) *adj also* **laical. 1** of or involving the laity; secular. ◆ *n* **2** a rare word for **layman.** [C15: from LL *lāicus* LAY[3]]
▸ **ˈlaically** *adv*

laicize *or* **laicise** (ˈleɪɪˌsaɪz) *vb* **laicizes, laicizing, laicized** *or* **laicises, laicising, laicised.** (*tr*) to withdraw clerical or ecclesiastical character or status from (an institution, building, etc.).
▸ **ˌlaiciˈzation** *or* **ˌlaiciˈsation** *n*

laid (leɪd) *vb* the past tense and past participle of **lay**[1].

laid-back Ⓣ *adj* relaxed in style or character; easy-going and unhurried.

laid paper *n* paper with a regular mesh impressed upon it.

Lailat-ul-Qadr (ˌleɪlætʊlˈkɑːdə) *n* a night of study and prayer observed annually by Muslims to mark the communication of the Koran: it usually follows the 27th day of Ramadan. [from Ar.: night of determination]

lain (leɪn) *vb* the past participle of **lie**[2].

Laingian (ˈlæŋɪən) *adj* **1** of or based on the theory of R. D. Laing (1927–89), Scottish psychiatrist, that mental illnesses can be responses to stress in family and social situations. ◆ *n* **2** a follower or adherent of Laing's teaching.

lair[1] Ⓣ (lɛə) *n* **1** the resting place of a wild animal. **2** *Inf.* a place of seclusion or hiding. ◆ *vb* **3** (*intr*) (esp. of a wild animal) to retreat to or rest in a lair. **4** (*tr*) to drive or place (an animal) in a lair. [OE *leger*]

lair[2] (lɛə) *Austral. sl.* ◆ *n* **1** a flashy man who shows off. ◆ *vb* **2** (*intr;* foll. by *up* or *around*) to behave or dress like a lair. [?from LEER]

laird (lɛəd) *n Scot.* a landowner, esp. of a large estate. [C15: Scot. var. of LORD]

laissez faire Ⓣ *or* **laisser faire** *French.* (ˌlɛseɪ ˈfɛə) *n* **1a** Also called: **individualism.** the doctrine of unrestricted freedom in commerce, esp. for private interests. **1b** (*as modifier*): *a laissez-faire economy.* **2** indifference or noninterference, esp. in the affairs of others. [F, lit.: let (them) act]

THESAURUS

laden *adj* **2** = **loaded**, burdened, charged, encumbered, fraught, full, hampered, oppressed, taxed, weighed down, weighted

la-di-da *adj Informal* = **affected**, arty-farty (*inf.*), conceited, highfalutin (*inf.*), mannered, mincing, overrefined, posh (*inf., chiefly Brit.*), precious, pretentious, snobbish, snooty (*inf.*), stuck-up (*inf.*), toffee-nosed (*sl., chiefly Brit.*)

lady *n* **1** = **gentlewoman**, dame **2** = **woman**, female

lady-killer *n Informal* = **womanizer**, Casanova, Don Juan, heartbreaker, ladies' man, libertine, Lothario, philanderer, rake, roué, wolf (*inf.*)

ladylike *adj* = **refined**, courtly, cultured, decorous, elegant, genteel, modest, polite, proper, respectable, sophisticated, well-bred
Antonyms *adj* discourteous, ill-bred, ill-mannered, impolite, rude, uncultured, unladylike, unmannerly, unrefined

lag[1] *vb* **1** = **hang back**, be behind, dawdle, delay, drag (behind), drag one's feet (*inf.*), idle, linger, loiter, saunter, straggle, tarry, trail **2** = **flag**, decrease, diminish, ebb, fail, fall off, lose strength, slacken, wane

laggard *n* **1** = **straggler**, dawdler, idler, lingerer, loafer, loiterer, lounger, saunterer, skiver (*Brit. sl.*), slowcoach (*Brit. inf.*), slowpoke (*US & Canad. inf.*), sluggard, snail

laid-back *adj* = **relaxed**, at ease, casual, easy-going, easy-oasy (*sl.*), free and easy, together (*sl.*), unflappable (*inf.*), unhurried
Antonyms *adj* edgy, jittery (*inf.*), jumpy, keyed-up, nervous, on edge, tense, twitchy (*inf.*), uptight (*inf.*), wound-up (*inf.*)

lair[1] *n* **1** = **nest**, burrow, den, earth, form, hole, resting place **2** *Informal* = **hide-out**, den, refuge, retreat, sanctuary

laissez faire *n* **1a** = **nonintervention**, free enterprise, free trade, individualism, live and let live

laissez passer (ˌlɛseɪ ˈpæseɪ) *n* a permit allowing someone to pass, cross a frontier, etc. [F, lit.: let (them) pass]

laity (ˈleɪɪtɪ) *n* **1** laymen, as distinguished from clergymen. **2** all people not of a specific occupation. [C16: from LAY[3]]

lake[1] ❶ (leɪk) *n* **1** an expanse of water entirely surrounded by land and unconnected to the sea except by rivers or streams. Related adj: **lacustrine. 2** anything resembling this. **3** a surplus of a liquid commodity: *a wine lake.* [C13: *lac,* via OF from L *lacus* basin]

lake[2] (leɪk) *n* **1** a bright pigment produced by the combination of an organic colouring matter with an inorganic compound, usually a metallic salt, oxide, or hydroxide. **2** a red dye obtained by combining a metallic compound with cochineal. [C17: var. of LAC[1]]

Lake District *n* a region of lakes and mountains in NW England, in Cumbria. Also called: **Lakeland, the Lakes.**

lake dwelling *n* a dwelling, esp. in prehistoric villages, constructed on platforms supported by wooden piles driven into the bottom of a lake.
▸**lake dweller** *n*

Lakeland terrier (ˈleɪkˌlænd) *n* a wire-haired breed of terrier, originally from the Lake District.

Lake Poets *pl n* the English poets Wordsworth, Coleridge, and Southey, who lived in and drew inspiration from the Lake District at the beginning of the 19th century.

lake trout *n* a yellow-spotted char of the Great Lakes region of Canada.

lakh *or* **lac** (lɑːk) *n* (in India) the number 100 000, esp. referring to this sum of rupees. [C17: from Hindi *lākh,* ult. from Sansk. *lakshā* a sign]

-lalia *n combining form.* indicating a speech defect or abnormality: *echolalia.* [NL, from Gk *lalia* chatter, from *lalein* to babble]

Lallans (ˈlælənz) *or* **Lallan** (ˈlælən) *n* **1** a literary version of the variety of English spoken and written in the Lowlands of Scotland. **2** (*modifier*) of or relating to the Lowlands of Scotland or their dialects. [Scot. var. of *Lowlands*]

lallation (læˈleɪʃən) *n Phonetics.* a defect of speech consisting of the pronunciation of (r) as (l). [C17: from L *lallāre* to sing lullaby, imit.]

lam[1] ❶ (læm) *vb* **lams, lamming, lammed.** *Sl.* **1** (*tr*) to thrash or beat. **2** (*intr;* usually foll. by *into* or *out*) to make a sweeping stroke or blow. [C16: from Scand.]

lam[2] (læm) *n US & Canad. sl.* **1** a sudden flight or escape, esp. to avoid arrest. **2 on the lam.** making an escape. [C19: ? from LAM[1] (hence, to be off)]

Lam. *Bible. abbrev. for* Lamentations.

lama (ˈlɑːmə) *n* a priest or monk of Lamaism. [C17: from Tibetan *blama*]

Lamaism (ˈlɑːməˌɪzəm) *n* the Mahayana form of Buddhism of Tibet and Mongolia.
▸ˈ**Lamaist** *n, adj* ▸ˌ**Lamaˈistic** *adj*

Lamarckism (lɑːˈmɑːkɪzəm) *n* the theory of organic evolution proposed by Lamarck (1744–1829), French naturalist, based on the principle that characteristics of an organism modified during its lifetime are inheritable.

lamasery (ˈlɑːməsərɪ) *n, pl* **lamaseries.** a monastery of lamas. [C19: from F *lamaserie,* from LAMA + F *-serie,* from Persian *serāī* palace]

lamb ❶ (læm) *n* **1** the young of a sheep. **2** the meat of a young sheep. **3** a person, esp. a child, who is innocent, meek, good, etc. **4** a person easily deceived. ◆ *vb* **5** (*intr*) (of a ewe) to give birth. **6** (*intr*) (of a shepherd) to tend the ewes and newborn lambs at lambing time. [OE *lamb,* from Gmc]
▸ˈ**lambˌlike** *adj*

Lamb (læm) *n* **the.** a title given to Christ in the New Testament.

lambada (læmˈbɑːdə) *n* **1** an erotic dance, originating in Brazil, performed by two people who hold each other closely and gyrate their hips in synchronized movements. **2** the music that accompanies the lambada, combining salsa, calypso, and reggae. [C20: from Port., lit.: the snapping of a whip]

lambast ❶ (læmˈbæst) *or* **lambaste** (læmˈbeɪst) *vb* **lambasts, lambasting, lambasted** *or* **lambastes, lambasting, lambasted.** (*tr*) **1** to beat or whip severely. **2** to reprimand or scold. [C17: ?from LAM[1] + BASTE[3]]

lambda (ˈlæmdə) *n* the 11th letter of the Greek alphabet (Λ, λ). [C14: from Gk, from Semitic]

lambent (ˈlæmbənt) *adj* **1** (esp. of a flame) flickering softly over a surface. **2** glowing with soft radiance. **3** (of wit or humour) light or brilliant. [C17: from the present participle of L *lambere* to lick]
▸ˈ**lambency** *n* ▸ˈ**lambently** *adv*

lambert (ˈlæmbət) *n* the cgs unit of illumination, equal to 1 lumen per square centimetre. Symbol: L [C20: after J. H. *Lambert* (1728–77), G mathematician & physicist]

lambing (ˈlæmɪŋ) *n* **1** the birth of lambs. **2** the shepherd's work of tending the ewes and newborn lambs at this time.

lambkin (ˈlæmkɪn) *n* **1** a small lamb. **2** a term of affection for a small endearing child.

lambrequin (ˈlæmbrɪkɪn, ˈlæmbə-) *n* **1** an ornamental hanging covering the edge of a shelf or the upper part of a window or door. **2** (*often pl*) a scarf worn over a helmet. [C18: from F, from Du. *lamperkin* (unattested), dim. of *lamper* veil]

Lambrusco (læmˈbruskəʊ) *n* **1** a red grape grown in Italy. **2** a sparkling red wine made in Italy from this grape. **3** a much less common white variety of this grape or wine.

lambskin (ˈlæmˌskɪn) *n* **1** the skin of a lamb, esp. with the wool still on. **2** a material or garment prepared from this skin.

lamb's lettuce *n* another name for **corn salad.**

lamb's tails *pl n* the pendulous catkins of the hazel tree.

lame ❶ (leɪm) *adj* **1** disabled or crippled in the legs or feet. **2** painful or weak: *a lame back.* **3** weak; unconvincing: *a lame excuse.* **4** not effective or enthusiastic: *a lame try.* **5** *US sl.* conventional or uninspiring. ◆ *vb* **lames, laming, lamed. 6** (*tr*) to make lame. [OE *lama*]
▸ˈ**lamely** *adv* ▸ˈ**lameness** *n*

lamé (ˈlɑːmeɪ) *n* a fabric of silk, cotton, or wool interwoven with threads of metal. [C20: from F, from OF *lame* gold or silver thread, thin plate, from L *lāmina* thin plate]

lame duck *n* **1** a person or thing that is disabled or ineffectual. **2** *Stock Exchange.* a speculator who cannot discharge his liabilities. **3** *US.* an elected official or body of officials remaining in office in the interval between the election and inauguration of a successor.

lamella (ləˈmɛlə) *n, pl* **lamellae** (-liː) *or* **lamellas.** a thin layer, plate, or membrane, esp. any of the calcified layers of which bone is formed. [C17: NL, from L, dim. of *lāmina* thin plate]
▸**laˈmellar, lamellate** (ˈlæmɪˌleɪt, -lɪt), *or* **lamellose** (ləˈmɛləʊs, ˈlæmɪˌləʊs) *adj*

lamellibranch (ləˈmɛlɪˌbræŋk) *n, adj* another word for **bivalve.** [C19: from NL *lamellibranchia* plate-gilled (animals)]

lamellicorn (ləˈmɛlɪˌkɔːn) *n* **1** any beetle having flattened terminal plates to the antennae, such as the scarabs and stag beetles. ◆ *adj* **2** designating antennae with platelike terminal segments. [C19: from NL *Lamellicornia* plate-horned (animals)]

lament ❶ (ləˈmɛnt) *vb* **1** to feel or express sorrow, remorse, or regret (for or over). ◆ *n* **2** an expression of sorrow. **3** a poem or song in which a death is lamented. [C16: from L *lāmentum*]
▸**laˈmenter** *n* ▸**laˈmentingly** *adv*

lamentable ❶ (ˈlæməntəbᵊl) *adj* **1** wretched, deplorable, or distressing. **2** an archaic word for **mournful.**
▸ˈ**lamentably** *adv*

lamentation ❶ (ˌlæmɛnˈteɪʃən) *n* **1** a lament; expression of sorrow. **2** the act of lamenting.

lamented (ləˈmɛntɪd) *adj* grieved for or regretted (often in **late lamented**): *our late lamented employer.*
▸**laˈmentedly** *adv*

lamina (ˈlæmɪnə) *n, pl* **laminae** (-ˌniː) *or* **laminas. 1** a thin plate, esp. of bone or mineral. **2** *Bot.* the flat blade of a leaf. [C17: NL, from L: thin plate]
▸ˈ**laminar** *or* **laminose** (ˈlæmɪˌnəʊs, -ˌnəʊz) *adj*

laminar flow *n* nonturbulent motion of a fluid in which parallel layers have different velocities relative to each other.

laminate ❶ *vb* (ˈlæmɪˌneɪt), **laminates, laminating, laminated. 1** (*tr*) to make (material in sheet form) by bonding together two or more thin sheets. **2** to split or be split into thin sheets. **3** (*tr*) to beat, form, or press (material, esp. metal) into thin sheets. **4** (*tr*) to cover or overlay with a thin sheet of material. ◆ *n* (ˈlæmɪˌneɪt, -nɪt). **5** a material made by bonding together two or more sheets. ◆ *adj* (ˈlæmɪˌneɪt, -nɪt). **6** having or composed of lamina; laminated. [C17: from NL *lāminātus* plated]
▸ˈ**laminable** *adj* ▸ˌ**lamiˈnation** *n* ▸ˈ**lamiˌnator** *n*

laminated (ˈlæmɪˌneɪtɪd) *adj* **1** composed of many layers of plastic, wood, etc., bonded together. **2** covered with a thin protective layer of plastic, etc.

lamington (ˈlæmɪŋtən) *n Austral. & NZ.* a cube of sponge cake coated in chocolate and dried coconut. [C20 (in the earlier sense: a homburg hat): after Lady *Lamington,* wife of Baron Lamington, governor of Queensland (1896–1901)]

Lammas (ˈlæməs) *n* **1** *RC Church.* Aug. 1, held as a feast, commemorating St Peter's miraculous deliverance from prison. **2** Also called: **Lammas Day.** the same day formerly observed in England as a harvest festival. [OE *hlāfmæsse* loaf mass]

lammergeier *or* **lammergeyer** (ˈlæməˌgaɪə) *n* a rare vulture of S Eu-

THESAURUS

lake[1] *n* **1 = pond,** lagoon, loch (*Scot.*), lough (*Irish*), mere, reservoir, tarn

lam[1] *vb Slang* **1 = attack,** batter, beat, hit, knock, lambast(e), pelt, pound, strike, thrash

lambast *vb* **1 = beat,** bludgeon, cosh (*Brit.*), cudgel, drub, flog, strike, thrash, whip **2 = reprimand,** bawl out, berate, carpet (*inf.*), castigate, censure, chew out (*US & Canad. inf.*), excoriate, give a rocket (*Brit. & NZ inf.*), rap over the knuckles, read the riot act, rebuke, scold, slap on the wrist, tear into (*inf.*), tear (someone) off a strip (*Brit. inf.*), upbraid

lamblike *adj* **3 = meek,** gentle, mild, passive, peaceable, submissive **4 = innocent,** artless, childlike, guileless, naive, simple, trusting

lame *adj* **1 = disabled,** crippled, defective, game, halt (*arch.*), handicapped, hobbling, limping **3, 4 = unconvincing,** feeble, flimsy, inadequate, insufficient, pathetic, poor, thin, unsatisfactory, weak

lament *vb* **1 = bemoan,** bewail, complain, deplore, grieve, mourn, regret, sorrow, wail, weep ◆ *n* **2 = complaint,** keening, lamentation, moan, moaning, plaint, ululation, wail, wailing **3 = dirge,** coronach, elegy, monody, requiem, threnody

lamentable *adj* **1 = regrettable,** deplorable, distressing, grievous, gut-wrenching, harrowing, sorrowful, tragic, unfortunate, woeful, wretched

lamentation *n* **1, 2 = sorrow,** dirge, grief, grieving, keening, lament, moan, mourning, plaint, sobbing, ululation, wailing, weeping

laminate *vb* **2 = split,** exfoliate, flake, separate **4 = cover,** coat, face, foliate, layer, stratify, veneer

rope, Africa, and Asia, with dark wings, a pale breast, and black feathers around the bill. [C19: from G *Lämmergeier,* from *Lämmer* lambs + *Geier* vulture]

lamp (læmp) *n* **1a** any of a number of devices that produce illumination: *an electric lamp; a gas lamp; an oil lamp.* **1b** (*in combination*): *lampshade.* **2** a device for holding one or more electric light bulbs: *a table lamp.* **3** a vessel in which a liquid fuel is burned to supply illumination. **4** any of a variety of devices that produce radiation, esp. for therapeutic purposes: *an ultraviolet lamp.* [C13 *lampe,* via OF from L *lampas,* from Gk, from *lampein* to shine]

lampblack (ˈlæmpˌblæk) *n* a finely divided form of almost pure carbon produced by the incomplete combustion of organic compounds, such as natural gas, used in making carbon electrodes and dynamo brushes and as a pigment.

lamp chimney *n* a glass tube that surrounds the wick in an oil lamp.

lamplight (ˈlæmpˌlaɪt) *n* the light produced by a lamp or lamps.

lamplighter (ˈlæmpˌlaɪtə) *n* **1** (formerly) a person who lit and extinguished street lamps, esp. gas ones. **2** *Chiefly US & Canad.* any of various devices used to light lamps.

lampoon ❶ (læmˈpuːn) *n* **1** a satire in prose or verse ridiculing a person, literary work, etc. ◆ *vb* **2** (*tr*) to attack or satirize in a lampoon. [C17: from F *lampon,* ?from *lampons* let us drink (frequently used as a refrain in poems)]
▸**lamˈpooner** *or* **lamˈpoonist** *n* ▸**lamˈpoonery** *n*

lamppost (ˈlæmpˌpəʊst) *n* a post supporting a lamp, esp. in a street.

lamprey (ˈlæmprɪ) *n* any eel-like vertebrate having a round sucking mouth for clinging to and feeding on the blood of other animals. Also called: **lamper eel.** [C13: from OF *lamproie,* from LL *lamprēda,* from ?]

Lancashire (ˈlæŋkəˈʃɪə) *n* a mild whitish-coloured cheese with a crumbly texture. [after *Lancashire,* a county in England]

Lancastrian (læŋˈkæstrɪən) *n* **1** a native or resident of Lancashire or Lancaster. **2** an adherent of the house of Lancaster in the Wars of the Roses. ◆ *adj* **3** of or relating to Lancashire or Lancaster. **4** of or relating to the house of Lancaster.

lance (lɑːns) *n* **1** a long weapon with a pointed head used by horsemen. **2** a similar weapon used for hunting, whaling, etc. **3** *Surgery.* another name for **lancet.** ◆ *vb* **lances, lancing, lanced.** (*tr*) **4** to pierce (an abscess or boil) with a lancet. **5** to pierce with or as with a lance. [C13 *launce,* from OF *lance,* from L *lancea*]

lance corporal *n* a noncommissioned army officer of the lowest rank.

lancelet (ˈlɑːnslɪt) *n* any of several marine animals closely related to the vertebrates: they burrow in sand. Also called: **amphioxus.** [C19: referring to the slender shape]

lanceolate (ˈlɑːnsɪəˌleɪt, -lɪt) *adj* narrow and tapering to a point at each end: *lanceolate leaves.* [C18: from LL *lanceolātus,* from *lanceola* small LANCE]

lancer (ˈlɑːnsə) *n* **1** (formerly) a cavalryman armed with a lance. **2** a member of a regiment retaining such a title.

lancers (ˈlɑːnsəz) *n* (*functioning as sing*) **1** a quadrille for eight or sixteen couples. **2** a piece of music composed for or in the rhythm of this dance.

lancet (ˈlɑːnsɪt) *n* **1** Also called: **lance.** a pointed surgical knife with two sharp edges. **2** short for **lancet arch** or **lancet window.** [C15 *lancette,* from OF: small LANCE]

lancet arch *n* a narrow acutely pointed arch.

lancet window *n* a narrow window having a lancet arch.

lancewood (ˈlɑːnsˌwʊd) *n* a New Zealand tree with slender leaves showing different configurations in youth and maturity.

Lancs (læŋks) *abbrev. for* Lancashire.

land ❶ (lænd) *n* **1** the solid part of the surface of the earth as distinct from seas, lakes, etc. Related adj: **terrestrial.** **2** ground, esp. with reference to its use, quality, etc. **3** rural or agricultural areas as contrasted with urban ones. **4** farming as an occupation or way of life. **5** *Law.* any tract of ground capable of being owned as property. **6a** a country, region, or area. **6b** the people of a country, etc. **7** *Econ.* the factor of production consisting of all natural resources. ◆ *vb* **8** to transfer (something) or go from a ship or boat to the shore: *land the cargo.* **9** (*intr*) to come to or touch shore. **10** (*intr*) (in Canada) to be legally admitted to the country, as an immigrant or **landed immigrant.** **11** to come down or bring (something) down to earth after a flight or jump. **12** to come or bring to some point, condition, or state. **13** (*tr*) *Angling.* to retrieve (a hooked fish) from the water. **14** (*tr*) *Inf.* to win or obtain: *to land a job.* **15** (*tr*) *Inf.* to deliver (a blow). ◆ See also **land up.** [OE]
▸**ˈlandless** *adj*

Land (*German* lant) *n, pl* ***Länder*** (ˈlɛndər). **1** any of the federal states of Germany. **2** any of the provinces of Austria. [G]

land agent *n* **1** a person who administers a landed estate and its tenancies. **2** a person who acts as an agent for the sale of land.
▸**land agency** *n*

landau (ˈlændɔː) *n* a four-wheeled carriage, usually horse-drawn, with two folding hoods over the passenger compartment. [C18: after *Landau* (a town in Germany), where first made]

landaulet (ˌlændɔːˈlɛt) *n* **1** a small landau. **2** *US.* an early type of car with a folding hood over the passenger seats.

landed (ˈlændɪd) *adj* **1** owning land: *landed gentry.* **2** consisting of or including land: *a landed estate.*

landfall (ˈlændˌfɔːl) *n* **1** the act of sighting or nearing land, esp. from the sea. **2** the land sighted or neared.

landfill (ˈlændˌfɪl) *adj* of or denoting low-lying sites or tips being filled up with alternate layers of rubbish and earth.

landform (ˈlændˌfɔːm) *n Geol.* any natural feature of the earth's surface.

land girl *n* a girl or woman who does farm work, esp. in wartime.

landgrave (ˈlændˌgreɪv) *n German history.* **1** (from the 13th century to 1806) a count who ruled over a specified territory. **2** (after 1806) the title of any of various sovereign princes. [C16: via G, from MHG *lantgrāve,* from *lant* land + *grāve* count]

land-holder *n* a person who owns or occupies land.
▸**ˈland-ˌholding** *adj, n*

landing ❶ (ˈlændɪŋ) *n* **1a** the act of coming to land, esp. after a flight or a sea voyage. **1b** (*as modifier*): *landing place.* **2** a place of disembarkation. **3** the floor area at the top of a flight of stairs.

landing craft *n Mil.* any small vessel designed for the landing of troops and equipment on beaches.

landing field *n* an area of land on which aircraft land and from which they take off.

landing gear *n* another name for **undercarriage.**

landing net *n Angling.* a loose long-handled net for lifting hooked fish from the water.

landing stage *n* a platform used for landing goods and passengers from a vessel.

landing strip *n* another name for **airstrip.**

landlady (ˈlændˌleɪdɪ) *n, pl* **landladies.** **1** a woman who owns and leases property. **2** a woman who owns or runs a lodging house, pub, etc.

ländler (*German* ˈlɛntlər) *n* **1** an Austrian country dance in which couples spin and clap. **2** a piece of music composed for or in the rhythm of this dance, in three-four time. [G, from dialect *Landl* Upper Austria]

land line *n* a telecommunications wire or cable laid over land.

landlocked (ˈlændˌlɒkt) *adj* **1** (esp. of lakes) completely surrounded by land. **2** (esp. of certain salmon) living in fresh water that is permanently isolated from the sea.

landlord ❶ (ˈlændˌlɔːd) *n* **1** a man who owns and leases property. **2** a man who owns or runs a lodging house, pub, etc.

landlubber (ˈlændˌlʌbə) *n Naut.* any person having no experience at sea.

landmark ❶ (ˈlændˌmɑːk) *n* **1** a prominent or well-known object in or feature of a particular landscape. **2** an important or unique decision, event, fact, discovery, etc. **3** a boundary marker.

landmass (ˈlændˌmæs) *n* a large continuous area of land, as opposed to seas or islands.

land mine *n Mil.* an explosive charge placed in the ground, usually detonated by stepping or driving on it.

land of milk and honey *n* **1** *Old Testament.* the fertile land promised to the Israelites by God (Ezekiel 20:6). **2** any fertile land, state, etc.

land of Nod *n* **1** *Old Testament.* a region to the east of Eden to which Cain went after he had killed Abel (Genesis 4:14). **2** an imaginary land of sleep.

landowner (ˈlændˌəʊnə) *n* a person who owns land.
▸**ˈlandˌownerˌship** *n* ▸**ˈlandˌowning** *n, adj*

land rail *n* another name for **corncrake.**

land reform *n* the redistributing of large agricultural holdings among the landless.

landscape ❶ (ˈlændˌskeɪp) *n* **1** an extensive area of land regarded as being visually distinct. **2** a painting, drawing, photograph, etc., depicting natural scenery. **3** the genre including such pictures. **4** the distinctive features of a given area of intellectual activity, regarded as an integrated whole. ◆ *adj* **5** *Printing.* **5a** (of an illustration in a book, magazine, etc.) of greater width than depth. Cf. **portrait** (sense 3). **5b** (of a page) carrying an illustration or table printed at right angles to the normal text. ◆ *vb* **landscapes, landscaping, landscaped.** **6** (*tr*) to improve the natural features of (a garden, park, etc.), as by creating contoured features and planting trees. **7** (*intr*) to work as a landscape gardener. [C16 *landskip* (orig. a term in painting), from MDu. *lantscap* region]

landscape gardening *n* the art of laying out grounds in imitation of natural scenery. Also called: **landscape architecture.**
▸**landscape gardener** *n*

THESAURUS

lampoon *n* **1** = **satire**, burlesque, caricature, parody, pasquinade, send-up (*Brit. inf.*), skit, squib, takeoff (*inf.*) ◆ *vb* **2** = **ridicule**, burlesque, caricature, make fun of, mock, parody, pasquinade, satirize, send up (*Brit. inf.*), squib, take off (*inf.*)

land *n* **1** = **ground**, dry land, earth, terra firma **2** = **soil**, dirt, ground, loam **3** = **countryside**, farmland, rural districts **4** = **farming** **5** *Law* = **property**, acres, estate, grounds, real property, realty **6a** = **country**, district, fatherland, motherland, nation, province, region, territory, tract ◆ *vb* **8, 9** = **arrive**, alight, berth, come to rest, debark, disembark, dock **11** = **touch down**, alight **14** *Informal* = **obtain**, acquire, gain, get, score (*sl.*), secure, win

landing *n* **1a** = **coming in**, arrival, disembarkation, disembarkment, touchdown **2** = **platform**, jetty, landing stage, quayside

landlord *n* **1** = **owner**, freeholder, lessor, proprietor **2** = **innkeeper**, host, hotelier, hotel-keeper

landmark *n* **1** = **feature**, monument **2** = **milestone**, crisis, turning point, watershed **3** = **boundary marker**, benchmark, cairn, milepost, signpost

landscape *n* **1** = **scenery**, countryside, outlook, panorama, prospect, scene, view, vista

landscapist ('lænd,skeɪpɪst) *n* a painter of landscapes.

landside ('lænd,saɪd) *n* **1** the part of an airport farthest from the aircraft, the boundary of which is the security check, customs, passport control, etc. Cf. **airside. 2** the part of a plough that slides along the face of the furrow wall on the opposite side to the mouldboard.

landslide ⓣ ('lænd,slaɪd) *n* **1** Also called: **landslip. 1a** the sliding of a large mass of rock material, soil, etc., down the side of a mountain or cliff. **1b** the material dislodged in this way. **2** an overwhelming electoral victory.

landsman ('lændzmən) *n, pl* **landsmen.** a person who works or lives on land, as distinguished from a seaman.

land up ⓣ *vb (adv, usually intr)* to arrive or cause to arrive at a final point or condition.

landward ('lændwəd) *adj* **1** lying, facing, or moving towards land. **2** in the direction of the land. ◆ *adv* **3** a variant of **landwards.**

landwards ('lændwədz) *or* **landward** *adv* towards land.

lane ⓣ (leɪn) *n* **1** a narrow road or way between buildings, hedges, fences, etc. **2a** any of the parallel strips into which the carriageway of a major road or motorway is divided. **2b** any narrow well-defined route or course for ships or aircraft. **3** one of the parallel strips into which a running track or swimming bath is divided for races. **4** the long strip of wooden flooring down which balls are bowled in a bowling alley. [OE *lane, lanu*]

lang. *abbrev. for* language.

Langerhans islets *or* **islands** ('læŋə,hæns) *pl n Anat.* See **islets of Langerhans.**

langlauf ('læŋ,laʊf) *n* cross-country skiing. [G, lit.: long run]
▸**langläufer** ('læŋ,lɔɪfə) *n* ▸**langläufing** ('læŋ,lɔɪfɪŋ) *n*

langouste ('lɒŋguːst, lɒŋ'guːst) *n* another name for the **spiny lobster.** [F, from OProvençal *langosta*, ? from L *lōcusta* lobster, locust]

langoustine (,lɒŋguː'stiːn) *n* a large prawn or small lobster. [from F, dim. of LANGOUSTE]

langsam ('læŋzæm) *adj Music.* slow. [G]

langsyne (,læŋ'saɪn) *Scot.* ◆ *adv* **1** long ago; long since. ◆ *n* **2** times long past, esp. those fondly remembered. [C16: Scot.: long since]

language ⓣ ('læŋgwɪdʒ) *n* **1** a system for the expression of thoughts, feelings, etc., by the use of spoken sounds or conventional symbols. **2** the faculty for the use of such systems, which is a distinguishing characteristic of man as compared with other animals. **3** the language of a particular nation or people. **4** any other means of communicating, such as gesture or animal sounds: *the language of love.* **5** the specialized vocabulary used by a particular group: *medical language.* **6** a particular manner or style of verbal expression: *your language is disgusting.* **7** *Computing.* See **programming language.** [C13: from OF *language*, ult. from L *lingua* tongue]

language laboratory *n* a room equipped with tape recorders, etc., for learning foreign languages.

langue (lɑːŋg) *n Linguistics.* language considered as an abstract system or a social institution, being the common possession of a speech community. [C19: from F: language]

langue d'oc *French.* (lɑ̃g dɔk) *n* the group of medieval French dialects spoken in S France: often regarded as including Provençal. [lit.: language of *oc* (form for the Provençal *yes*), ult. from L *hoc* this]

languid ⓣ ('læŋgwɪd) *adj* **1** without energy or spirit. **2** without interest or enthusiasm. **3** sluggish; inactive. [C16: from L *languidus*, from *languēre* to languish]
▸'**languidly** *adv* ▸'**languidness** *n*

languish ⓣ ('læŋgwɪʃ) *vb (intr)* **1** to lose or diminish in strength or energy. **2** (often foll. by *for*) to be listless with desire; pine. **3** to suffer deprivation, hardship, or neglect: *to languish in prison.* **4** to put on a tender, nostalgic, or melancholic expression. [C14 *languishen*, from OF *languiss-*, stem of *languir*, ult. from L *languēre*]
▸'**languishing** *adj* ▸'**languishingly** *adv* ▸'**languishment** *n*

languor ⓣ ('læŋgə) *n* **1** physical or mental laziness or weariness. **2** a feeling of dreaminess and relaxation. **3** oppressive silence or stillness. [C14 *langour*, via OF from L *languor*, from *languēre* to languish; the modern spelling is directly from L]
▸'**languorous** *adj*

langur (lʌŋ'guə) *n* any of various agile arboreal Old World monkeys of S and SE Asia having a long tail and long hair surrounding the face. [Hindi]

laniard ('lænjəd) *n* a variant spelling of **lanyard.**

laniary ('lænɪərɪ) *adj* **1** (esp. of canine teeth) adapted for tearing. ◆ *n, pl* **laniaries. 2** a tooth adapted for tearing. [C19: from L *lanius* butcher, from *laniāre* to tear]

laniferous (lə'nɪfərəs) *or* **lanigerous** (lə'nɪdʒərəs) *adj Biol.* bearing wool or fleecy hairs resembling wool. [C17: from L *lānifer*, from *lāna* wool]

lank ⓣ (læŋk) *adj* **1** long and limp. **2** thin or gaunt. [OE *hlanc* loose]
▸'**lankly** *adv* ▸'**lankness** *n*

lanky ⓣ ('læŋkɪ) *adj* **lankier, lankiest.** tall, thin, and loose-jointed.
▸'**lankily** *adv* ▸'**lankiness** *n*

lanner ('lænə) *n* **1** a large falcon of Mediterranean regions, N Africa, and S Asia. **2** *Falconry.* the female of this falcon. The male is called **lanneret.** [C15: from OF *(faucon) lanier* cowardly (falcon), from L *lanārius* wool worker, coward; referring to its sluggish flight and timid nature]

lanolin ('lænəlɪn) *or* **lanoline** ('lænəlɪn, -,liːn) *n* a yellowish viscous substance extracted from wool: used in some ointments. [C19: via G from L *lāna* wool + *oleum* oil; see -IN]

lantern ('læntən) *n* **1** a light with a transparent protective case. **2** a structure on top of a dome or roof having openings or windows to admit light or air. **3** the upper part of a lighthouse that houses the light. [C13: from L *lanterna*, from Gk *lamptēr* lamp, from *lampein* to shine]

lantern jaw *n* (when *pl*, refers to upper and lower jaw; when *sing*, usually to lower jaw) a long hollow jaw that gives the face a drawn appearance.
▸'**lantern-,jawed** *adj*

lantern slide *n* (formerly) a photographic slide for projection, used in a magic lantern.

lanthanide ('lænθə,naɪd) *or* **lanthanoid** ('lænθə,nɔɪd) *n* any of a class of 15 chemically related elements with atomic numbers from 57 (lanthanum) to 71 (lutetium).

lanthanum ('lænθənəm) *n* a silvery-white ductile metallic element of the lanthanide series: used in pyrophoric alloys, electronic devices, and in glass manufacture. Symbol: La; atomic no.: 57; atomic wt.: 138.91. [C19: NL, from Gk *lanthanein* to lie unseen]

lanthorn ('lænt,hɔːn, 'læntən) *n* an archaic word for **lantern.**

lanugo (lə'njuːgəʊ) *n, pl* **lanugos.** a layer of fine hairs, esp. the covering of the human fetus before birth. [C17: from L: down, from *lāna* wool]

lanyard *or* **laniard** ('lænjəd) *n* **1** a cord, esp. one worn around the neck, to hold a whistle, knife, etc. **2** a cord used in firing certain types of cannon. **3** *Naut.* a line for extending or tightening standing rigging. [C15 *lanyer*, from F *lanière*, from *lasne* strap, prob. of Gmc origin]

laodicean (,leɪəʊdɪ'sɪən) *adj* **1** lukewarm and indifferent, esp. in religious matters. ◆ *n* **2** a person having a lukewarm attitude towards religious matters. [C17: referring to the early Christians of Laodicea (Revelation 3:14–16)]

lap[1] (læp) *n* **1** the area formed by the upper surface of the thighs of a seated person. **2** Also called: **lapful.** the amount held in one's lap. **3** a protected place or environment: *in the lap of luxury.* **4** the part of one's clothing that covers the lap. **5 drop in someone's lap.** give someone the responsibility of. [OE *læppa* flap]

lap[2] ⓣ (læp) *n* **1** one circuit of a racecourse or track. **2** a stage or part of a journey, race, etc. **3a** an overlapping part or projection. **3b** the extent of overlap. **4** the length of material needed to go around an object. **5** a rotating disc coated with fine abrasive for polishing gemstones. ◆ *vb* **laps, lapping, lapped. 6** *(tr)* to wrap or fold (around or over): *he lapped a bandage around his wrist.* **7** *(tr)* to enclose or envelop in: *he lapped his wrist in a bandage.* **8** to place or lie partly or completely over or project beyond. **9** *(tr; usually passive)* to envelop or surround with comfort, love, etc.: *lapped in luxury.* **10** *(intr)* to be folded. **11** *(tr)* to overtake (an opponent) in a race so as to be one or more circuits ahead. **12** *(tr)* to polish or cut (a workpiece, gemstone, etc.) with a fine abrasive. [C13 (in the sense: to wrap): prob. from LAP[1]]
▸'**lapper** *n*

THESAURUS

landslide *n* **1** = **landslip**, avalanche, rockfall

land up *vb* = **end up**, arrive, lead, turn up, wind up

lane *n* **1** = **road**, aisle, alley, corridor, footpath, passageway, path, pathway, street, strip, way

language *n* **2** = **speech**, communication, conversation, discourse, expression, interchange, parlance, talk, utterance, verbalization, vocalization **3, 5** = **tongue**, argot, cant, dialect, idiom, jargon, lingo (*inf.*), lingua franca, patois, patter, speech, terminology, vernacular, vocabulary **6** = **style**, diction, expression, phraseology, phrasing, wording

languid *adj* **1** = **feeble**, drooping, faint, languorous, limp, pining, sickly, weak, weary **2** = **lazy**, indifferent, lackadaisical, languorous, listless, spiritless, unenthusiastic, uninterested **3** = **lethargic**, dull, heavy, inactive, inert, sluggish, torpid

Antonyms *adj* active, alive and kicking, energetic, strong, tireless, vigorous

languish *vb* **1** = **decline**, droop, fade, fail, faint, flag, sicken, waste, weaken, wilt, wither **2** *often with* **for** = **pine**, desire, eat one's heart out over, hanker, hunger, long, sigh, suspire, want, yearn **3** = **waste away**, be abandoned, be disregarded, be neglected, rot, suffer

Antonyms *vb* ≠ **decline, waste away:** bloom, flourish, prosper, thrive

languishing *adj* **1** = **fading**, declining, deteriorating, drooping, droopy, failing, flagging, sickening, sinking, wasting away, weak, weakening, wilting, withering **2** = **lovesick**, dreamy, longing, lovelorn, melancholic, nostalgic, pensive, pining, soulful, tender, wistful, woebegone, yearning

languor *n* **1** = **lethargy**, apathy, debility, enervation, ennui, faintness, fatigue, feebleness, frailty, heaviness, inertia, lassitude, listlessness, torpor, weakness, weariness **2** = **relaxation**, dreaminess, drowsiness, indolence, laziness, lotus-eating, sleepiness, sloth **3** = **stillness**, calm, hush, lull, oppressiveness, silence

lank *adj* **1** = **limp**, dull, lifeless, long, lustreless, straggling **2** = **thin**, attenuated, emaciated, gaunt, lanky, lean, rawboned, scraggy, scrawny, skinny, slender, slim, spare

lanky *adj* = **gangling**, angular, bony, gaunt, loose-jointed, rangy, rawboned, scraggy, scrawny, spare, tall, thin, weedy (*inf.*)

Antonyms *adj* brawny, burly, chubby, fat, muscular, plump, portly, rotund, rounded, short, sinewy, stocky, stout

lap[2] *n* **1** = **circuit**, circle, course, distance, loop, orbit, round, tour ◆ *vb* **6, 7** = **wrap**, cover, enfold, envelop, fold, swaddle, swathe, turn, twist

lap[3] Ⓣ (læp) *vb* **laps, lapping, lapped. 1** (of small waves) to wash against (a shore, boat, etc.), usually with light splashing sounds. **2** (often foll. by *up*) (esp. of animals) to scoop (a liquid) into the mouth with the tongue. ◆ *n* **3** the act or sound of lapping. **4** a thin food for dogs or other animals. ◆ See also **lap up.** [OE *lapian*]
▸ **'lapper** *n*

laparoscope ('læpərəˌskəʊp) *n* a medical instrument consisting of a tube that is inserted through the abdominal wall and illuminated to enable a doctor to view the internal organs. [C19 (applied to various instruments used to examine the abdomen) and C20 (in the specific modern sense): from Gk *lapara* (see LAPAROTOMY) + -SCOPE]
▸ **ˌlapa'roscopy** *n*

laparotomy (ˌlæpə'rɒtəmɪ) *n, pl* **laparotomies.** surgical incision through the abdominal wall. [C19: from Gk *lapara* flank, from *laparos* soft + -TOMY]

lap dancing *n* a form of entertainment in which scantily dressed women dance erotically for individual members of the audience.

lap dissolve *n Films.* the technique of allowing the end of one scene to overlap the beginning of the next scene by fading out the former while fading in the latter.

lapdog ('læpˌdɒg) *n* a pet dog small and docile enough to be cuddled in the lap.

lapel (lə'pɛl) *n* the continuation of the turned or folded back collar on a suit, coat, jacket, etc. [C18: from LAP[1]]
▸ **la'pelled** *adj*

lapheld ('læpˌhɛld) *adj* (esp. of a personal computer) small enough to be used on one's lap; portable.

lapidary ('læpɪdərɪ) *n, pl* **lapidaries. 1** a person whose business is to cut, polish, set, or deal in gemstones. ◆ *adj* **2** of or relating to gemstones or the work of a lapidary. **3** Also: **lapidarian** (ˌlæpɪ'dɛərɪən). engraved, cut, or inscribed in a stone or gemstone. **4** of sufficiently high quality to be engraved on a stone: *a lapidary inscription.* [C14: from L *lapidārius,* from *lapid-, lapis* stone]

lapillus (lə'pɪləs) *n, pl* **lapilli** (-laɪ). a small piece of lava thrown from a volcano. [C18: L: little stone]

lapis lazuli ('læpɪs 'læzjʊˌlaɪ) *n* **1** a brilliant blue mineral used as a gemstone. **2** the deep blue colour of lapis lazuli. [C14: from L *lapis* stone + Med. L *lazulī,* from Ar. *lāzaward,* from Persian *lāzhuward,* from ?]

lap joint *n* a joint made by placing one member over another and fastening them together. Also called: **lapped joint.**
▸ **'lap-ˌjointed** *adj*

Laplace operator (læ'plæs; *French* laplas) *n Maths.* the operator $\partial^2/\partial x^2 + \partial^2/\partial y^2 + \partial^2/\partial z^2$, used in differential analysis. Symbol: ∇^2 [C19: after Pierre Simon *Laplace* (1749–1827), F mathematician]

lap of honour *n* a ceremonial circuit of a racing track, etc., by the winner of a race.

Lapp (læp) *n* **1** Also **Laplander.** a member of a nomadic people living chiefly in N Scandinavia and the Kola Peninsula of Russia. **2** the language of this people. ◆ *adj* **3** of or relating to this people or their language.
▸ **'Lappish** *adj, n*

lappet ('læpɪt) *n* **1** a small hanging flap or piece of lace, etc. **2** *Zool.* a lobelike hanging structure, such as the wattle on a bird's head. [C16: from LAP[1] + -ET]

lapse Ⓣ (læps) *n* **1** a drop in standard of an isolated or temporary nature: *a lapse of justice.* **2** a break in occurrence, usage, etc.: *a lapse of five weeks between letters.* **3** a gradual decline or a drop to a lower degree, condition, or state: *a lapse from high office.* **4** a moral fall. **5** *Law.* the termination of some right, interest, or privilege, as by neglecting to exercise it or through failure of some contingency. **6** *Insurance.* the termination of coverage following a failure to pay the premiums. ◆ *vb* **lapses, lapsing, lapsed.** (*intr*) **7** to drop in standard or fail to maintain a norm. **8** to decline gradually or fall in status, condition, etc. **9** to be discontinued, esp. through negligence or other failure. **10** (usually foll. by *into*) to drift or slide (into a condition): *to lapse into sleep.* **11** (often foll. by *from*) to turn away (from beliefs or norms). **12** (of time) to slip away. [C15: from L *lāpsus* error, from *lābī* to glide]
▸ **'lapsable** *or* **'lapsible** *adj* ▸ **lapsed** *adj* ▸ **'lapser** *n*

lapse rate *n* the rate of change of any meteorological factor with altitude, esp. atmospheric temperature.

laptop ('læpˌtɒp) *or* **laptop computer** *n* a personal computer that is small and light enough to be operated on the user's lap. Cf. **palmtop computer.**

lap up *vb* (*tr, adv*) **1** to eat or drink. **2** to relish or delight in: *he laps up horror films.* **3** to believe or accept eagerly and uncritically: *he laps up stories.*

lapwing ('læpˌwɪŋ) *n* any of several plovers, typically having a crested head, wattles, and spurs. Also called: **green plover, peewit.** [C17: altered form of OE *hlēapewince* plover]

larboard ('lɑːbəd) *n, adj Naut.* a former word for **port**[2]. [C14 *laddeborde* (changed to *larboard* by association with *starboard*), from *laden* to load + *borde* BOARD]

larceny Ⓣ ('lɑːsɪnɪ) *n, pl* **larcenies.** *Law.* (formerly) a technical word for **theft.** [C15: from OF *larcin,* from L *lātrocinium* robbery, from *latrō* robber]
▸ **'larcenist** *or* **'larcener** *n* ▸ **'larcenous** *adj*

larch (lɑːtʃ) *n* **1** any coniferous tree having deciduous needle-like leaves and egg-shaped cones. **2** the wood of any of these trees. [C16: from G *Lärche,* ult. from L *larix*]

lard (lɑːd) *n* **1** the rendered fat from a pig, used in cooking. ◆ *vb* (*tr*) **2** to prepare (lean meat, poultry, etc.) by inserting small strips of bacon or fat before cooking. **3** to cover or smear (foods) with lard. **4** to add extra material to (speech or writing); embellish. [C15: via OF from L *lāridum* bacon fat]
▸ **'lardy** *adj*

larder ('lɑːdə) *n* a room or cupboard, used as a store for food. [C14: from OF *lardier,* from LARD]

lardon ('lɑːdᵊn) *or* **lardoon** (lɑː'duːn) *n* a strip of fat used in larding meat. [C15: from OF, from LARD]

lardy cake ('lɑːdɪ) *n Brit.* a rich sweet cake made of bread dough, lard, sugar, and dried fruit.

lares and penates ('lɛəriːz, 'lɑː-) *pl n* **1** *Roman myth.* **1a** household gods. **1b** statues of these gods kept in the home. **2** the valued possessions of a household. [from L]

large Ⓣ (lɑːdʒ) *adj* **1** having a relatively great size, quantity, extent, etc.; big. **2** of wide or broad scope, capacity, or range; comprehensive. **3** having or showing great breadth of understanding. ◆ *n* **4 at large. 4a** (esp. of a dangerous criminal or wild animal) free; not confined. **4b** roaming freely, as in a foreign country. **4c** as a whole; in general. **4d** in full detail; exhaustively. **4e ambassador at large.** See **ambassador** (sense 4). [C12 (orig.: generous): via OF from L *largus* ample]
▸ **'largeness** *n*

large intestine *n* the part of the alimentary canal consisting of the caecum, colon, and rectum.

largely Ⓣ ('lɑːdʒlɪ) *adv* **1** principally; to a great extent. **2** on a large scale or in a large manner.

larger-than-life *adj* exceptionally striking or colourful.

large-scale Ⓣ *adj* **1** wide-ranging or extensive. **2** (of maps and models) constructed or drawn to a big scale.

largesse Ⓣ *or* **largess** (lɑː'dʒɛs) *n* **1** the generous bestowal of gifts, favours, or money. **2** the things so bestowed. **3** generosity of spirit or attitude. [C13: from OF, from LARGE]

larghetto (lɑː'gɛtəʊ) *Music.* ◆ *adj, adv* **1** to be performed moderately slowly. ◆ *n, pl* **larghettos. 2** a piece or passage to be performed in this way. [It.: dim. of LARGO]

largish ('lɑːdʒɪʃ) *adj* fairly large.

largo ('lɑːgəʊ) *Music.* ◆ *adj, adv* **1** to be performed slowly and broadly. ◆ *n, pl* **largos. 2** a piece or passage to be performed in this way. [C17: from It., from L *largus* large]

Lariam ('lærɪəm) *n Trademark.* a preparation of the drug mefloquine, used in the treatment and prevention of malaria.

lariat ('lærɪət) *n US & Canad.* **1** another word for **lasso. 2** a rope for tethering animals. [C19: from Sp. *la reata* the LASSO]

lark[1] (lɑːk) *n* **1** any brown bird of a predominantly Old World family of songbirds, esp. the skylark: noted for their singing. **2** short for **titlark.** [OE *lāwerce, lǣwerce,* of Gmc origin]

lark[2] Ⓣ (lɑːk) *Inf.* ◆ *n* **1** a carefree adventure or frolic. **2** a harmless piece of mischief. ◆ *vb* (*intr*) **3** (often foll. by *about*) to have a good time by frolicking. **4** to play a prank. [C19: orig. sl.]
▸ **'larkish** *or* **'larky** *adj*

larkspur ('lɑːkˌspɜː) *n* any of various plants related to the delphinium,

THESAURUS

lap[3] *vb* **1 = ripple,** gurgle, plash, purl, slap, splash, swish, wash **2 = drink,** lick, sip, sup

lapse *n* **1 = mistake,** error, failing, fault, indiscretion, negligence, omission, oversight, slip **2 = interval,** break, breathing space, gap, intermission, interruption, lull, passage, pause **3 = drop,** backsliding, decline, descent, deterioration, fall, relapse ◆ *vb* **7, 8 = drop,** decline, degenerate, deteriorate, fail, fall, sink, slide, slip **9 = end,** become obsolete, become void, expire, run out, stop, terminate

lapsed *adj* **9 = expired,** discontinued, ended, finished, invalid, out of date, run out, unrenewed **11 = backsliding,** lacking faith, nonpractising

larceny *n Law* **= theft,** burglary, misappropriation, pilfering, purloining, robbery, stealing

large *adj* **1 = big,** bulky, colossal, considerable, elephantine, enormous, giant, gigantic, ginormous (*inf.*), goodly, great, huge, humongous *or* humungous (*US sl.*), immense, jumbo (*inf.*), king-size, man-size, massive, mega (*sl.*), monumental, sizable *or* sizeable, substantial, tidy (*inf.*), vast **2 = comprehensive,** abundant, ample, broad, capacious, copious, extensive, full, generous, grand, grandiose, liberal, plentiful, roomy, spacious, sweeping, wide **4 at large: a = free,** at liberty, on the loose, on the run, roaming, unconfined **c = in general,** as a whole, chiefly, generally, in the main, mainly **d = at length,** considerably, exhaustively, greatly, in full detail

Antonyms *adj* ≠ **big:** inconsiderable, infinitesimal, little, minute, petty, short, slender, slight, slim, small, tiny, trivial ≠ **comprehensive:** brief, narrow, scanty, scarce, sparse, thin

largely *adv* **1 = mainly,** as a rule, by and large, chiefly, considerably, extensively, generally, mostly, predominantly, primarily, principally, to a great extent, widely

large-scale *adj* **1 = wide-ranging,** broad, extensive, far-reaching, global, sweeping, vast, wholesale, wide

largesse *n* **1 = generosity,** alms-giving, benefaction, bounty, charity, liberality, munificence, open-handedness, philanthropy **2 = gift,** bequest, bounty, donation, endowment, grant, present

lark[2] *Informal n* **1, 2 = prank,** antic, caper, escapade, fling, frolic, fun, gambol, game, jape, mischief, revel, rollick, romp, skylark, spree ◆

with spikes of blue, pink, or white irregular spurred flowers. [C16: LARK[1] + SPUR]

larn (lɑːn) *vb Not standard.* **1** *Facetious.* to learn. **2** (*tr*) to teach (someone) a lesson: *that'll larn you!* [C18: from a dialect form of LEARN]

larrigan ('lærɪɡən) *n* a knee-high oiled leather moccasin boot worn by trappers, etc. [C19: from ?]

larrikin ('lærɪkɪn) *Austral. & NZ sl.* ◆ *n* **1** a mischievous person. **2** a hooligan. ◆ *adj* **3** mischievous: *larrikin wit.* [C19: from E dialect: a mischievous youth]

larrup ('lærəp) *vb* (*tr*) *Dialect.* to beat or flog. [C19: from ?]
▸ **'larruper** *n*

Larry ('lærɪ) *n* **happy as Larry.** *Inf.* very happy.

larva ('lɑːvə) *n, pl* **larvae** (-viː). an immature free-living form of many animals that develops into a different adult form by metamorphosis. [C18: (C17 in the orig. L sense: ghost): NL]
▸ **'larval** *adj*

laryngeal (ˌlærɪn'dʒiːəl, lə'rɪndʒɪəl) *or* **laryngal** (lə'rɪŋɡəl) *adj* **1** of or relating to the larynx. **2** *Phonetics.* articulated at the larynx; glottal. [C18: from NL *laryngeus* of the LARYNX]

laryngitis (ˌlærɪn'dʒaɪtɪs) *n* inflammation of the larynx.
▸ **laryngitic** (ˌlærɪn'dʒɪtɪk) *adj*

laryngo- *or before a vowel* **laryng-** *combining form.* indicating the larynx: *laryngoscope.*

laryngoscope (lə'rɪŋɡəˌskəʊp) *n* a medical instrument for examining the larynx.
▸ **ˌlaryn'goscopy** *n*

laryngotomy (ˌlærɪŋ'ɡɒtəmɪ) *n, pl* **laryngotomies.** surgical incision into the larynx to facilitate breathing.

larynx ('lærɪŋks) *n, pl* **larynges** (lə'rɪndʒiːz) *or* **larynxes.** a cartilaginous and muscular hollow organ forming part of the air passage to the lungs: in higher vertebrates it contains the vocal cords. [C16: from NL, from Gk *larunx*]

lasagne *or* **lasagna** (lə'zænjə, -'sæn-) *n* **1** a form of pasta consisting of wide flat sheets. **2** any of several dishes made from layers of lasagne and meat, cheese, etc. [from It. *lasagna*, from L *lasanum* cooking pot]

La Scala (læ 'skɑːlə) *n* the chief opera house in Italy, in Milan (opened 1776).

lascar ('læskə) *n* a sailor from the East Indies. [C17: from Urdu *lashkar* soldier, from Persian: the army]

lascivious ❶ (lə'sɪvɪəs) *adj* **1** lustful; lecherous. **2** exciting sexual desire. [C15: from LL *lascīviōsus*, from L *lascīvia* wantonness, from *lascīvus*]
▸ **las'civiously** *adv* ▸ **las'civiousness** *n*

lase (leɪz) *vb* **lases, lasing, lased.** (*intr*) (of a substance, such as carbon dioxide or ruby) to be capable of acting as a laser.

laser ('leɪzə) *n* **1** a source of high-intensity optical, infrared, or ultraviolet radiation produced as a result of stimulated emission maintained within a solid, liquid, or gaseous medium. The photons involved in the emission process all have the same energy and phase so that the laser beam is monochromatic and coherent, allowing it to be brought to a fine focus. **2** any similar source producing a beam of any electromagnetic radiation, such as infrared or microwave radiation. [C20: from *l*ight *a*mplification by *s*timulated *e*mission of *r*adiation]

laser printer *n* a quiet high-quality computer printer that uses a laser beam shining on a photoconductive drum to produce characters, which are then transferred to paper.

lash[1] ❶ (læʃ) *n* **1** a sharp cutting blow from a whip or other flexible object. **2** the flexible end or ends of a whip. **3** a cutting or hurtful blow to the feelings, as one caused by ridicule or scolding. **4** a forceful beating or impact, as of wind, rain, or waves against something. **5 have a lash at.** *Austral. & NZ inf.* to make an attempt at or take part in (something). **6** See **eyelash.** ◆ *vb* (*tr*) **7** to hit (a person or thing) sharply with a whip, rope, etc., esp. as punishment. **8** (of rain, waves, etc.) to beat forcefully against. **9** to attack with words, ridicule, etc. **10** to flick or wave sharply to and fro: *the panther lashed his tail.* **11** to urge or drive as with a whip: *to lash the audience into a violent mood.* ◆ See also **lash out.** [C14: ? imit.]
▸ **'lasher** *n*

lash[2] ❶ (læʃ) *vb* (*tr*) to bind or secure with rope, string, etc. [C15: from OF *lachier*, ult. from L *laqueāre* to ensnare, from *laqueus* noose]

-lashed *adj* having eyelashes as specified: *long-lashed.*

lashing[1] ('læʃɪŋ) *n* **1** a whipping; flogging. **2** a scolding. **3** (*pl; usually foll. by of*) *Brit. inf.* large amounts; lots.

lashing[2] ('læʃɪŋ) *n* rope, cord, etc., used for binding or securing.

lash out *vb* (*intr, adv*) **1** to burst into or resort to verbal or physical attack. **2** *Brit. inf.* to be extravagant, as in spending.

lash-up *n* a temporary connection of equipment for experimental or emergency use.

lass ❶ (læs) *n* **1** a girl or young woman. **2** *Inf.* a familiar form of address for any female. [C13: from ?]

Lassa fever ('læsə) *n* a serious viral disease of Central West Africa, characterized by high fever and muscular pains. [from *Lassa*, the Nigerian village where it was first identified]

lassie ('læsɪ) *n Inf.* a little lass; girl.

lassitude ❶ ('læsɪˌtjuːd) *n* physical or mental weariness. [C16: from L *lassitūdō*, from *lassus* tired]

lasso (læ'suː, 'læsəʊ) *n, pl* **lassos** *or* **lassoes. 1** a long rope or thong with a running noose at one end, used (esp. in America) for roping horses, cattle, etc.; lariat. ◆ *vb* **lassos, lassoing, lassoed. 2** (*tr*) to catch as with a lasso. [C19: from Sp. *lazo*, ult. from L *laqueus* noose]
▸ **las'soer** *n*

last[1] ❶ (lɑːst) *adj* (*often prenominal*) **1** being, happening, or coming at the end or after all others: *the last horse in the race.* **2** being or occurring just before the present; most recent: *last Thursday.* **3** only remaining: *one's last cigarette.* **4** most extreme; utmost. **5** least suitable, appropriate, or likely: *he was the last person I would have chosen.* **6** (esp. relating to the end of a person's life or of the world) final or ultimate: *last rites.* ◆ *adv* **7** after all others; at or in the end: *he came last.* **8** most recently: *he was last seen in the mountains.* **9** (*sentence modifier*) as the last or latest item. ◆ *n* **10 the last. 10a** a person or thing that is last. **10b** the final moment; end. **11** one's last moments before death. **12** the final appearance, mention, or occurrence: *we've seen the last of him.* **13 at last.** in the end; finally. **14 at long last.** finally, after difficulty, delay, or irritation. [var. of OE *latest, lætest*, sup. of LATE]

> **USAGE NOTE** Since *last* can mean either *after all others* or *most recent*, it is better to avoid using this word where ambiguity might arise as in *her last novel. Final* or *latest* should be used in such contexts to avoid ambiguity.

last[2] ❶ (lɑːst) *vb* **1** (when *intr*, often foll. by *for*) to remain in being (for a length of time); continue: *his hatred lasted for several years.* **2** to be sufficient for the needs of (a person) for (a length of time): *it will last us until Friday.* **3** (when *intr*, often foll. by *for*) to remain fresh, uninjured, or unaltered (for a certain time). ◆ See also **last out.** [OE *lǣstan*]
▸ **'laster** *n*

last[3] (lɑːst) *n* **1** the wooden or metal form on which a shoe or boot is fashioned or repaired. ◆ *vb* **2** (*tr*) to fit (a shoe or boot) on a last. [OE *lǣste*, from *lāst* footprint]
▸ **'laster** *n*

last-ditch ❶ *n* **a** a last resort or place of last defence. **b** (*as modifier*): *a last-ditch effort.*

last-gasp *n* (*modifier*) done in desperation at the last minute: *a last-gasp attempt to save the talks.*

lasting ❶ ('lɑːstɪŋ) *adj* permanent or enduring.
▸ **'lastingly** *adv* ▸ **'lastingness** *n*

Last Judgment *n* **the.** the occasion, after the resurrection of the dead at the end of the world, when, according to biblical tradition, God will decree the final destinies of all men according to the good and evil in their earthly lives. Also called: **the Last Day, Doomsday, Judgment Day.**

lastly ❶ ('lɑːstlɪ) *adv* **1** at the end or at the last point. ◆ *sentence connector.* **2** finally.

last name *n* another term for **surname.**

last out *vb* (*intr, adv*) **1** to be sufficient for one's needs: *how long will our supplies last out?* **2** to endure or survive: *some old people don't last out the winter.*

THESAURUS

vb **3** *often foll. by* **about** = **play**, caper, cavort, cut capers, frolic, gambol, have fun, make mischief, rollick, romp, sport

lascivious *adj* **1** = **lustful**, horny (*sl.*), lecherous, lewd, libidinous, licentious, prurient, randy (*inf., chiefly Brit.*), salacious, sensual, unchaste, voluptuous, wanton **2** = **bawdy**, blue, coarse, crude, dirty, indecent, obscene, offensive, pornographic, ribald, scurrilous, smutty, suggestive, vulgar, X-rated (*inf.*)

lash[1] *n* **1** = **blow**, hit, stripe, stroke, swipe (*inf.*) ◆ *vb* **7** = **whip**, beat, birch, chastise, flagellate, flog, horsewhip, lam (*sl.*), lambast(e), scourge, thrash **8** = **pound**, beat, buffet, dash, drum, hammer, hit, knock, lambast(e), larrup (*dialect*), punch, smack, strike **9** = **censure**, attack, belabour, berate, blast, castigate, criticize, flay, lambast(e), put down, ridicule, satirize, scold, slate (*inf., chiefly Brit.*), tear into (*inf.*), upbraid

lash[2] *vb* = **fasten**, bind, join, make fast, rope, secure, strap, tie

lass *n* **1** = **girl**, bird (*sl.*), chick (*sl.*), colleen (*Irish*), damsel, lassie (*inf.*), maid, maiden, miss, schoolgirl, wench (*facetious*), young woman

lassitude *n* = **weariness**, apathy, drowsiness, dullness, enervation, ennui, exhaustion, fatigue, heaviness, inertia, languor, lethargy, listlessness, prostration, sluggardliness, sluggishness, tiredness, torpor

last[1] *adj* **1** = **hindmost**, aftermost, at the end, rearmost **2** = **most recent**, latest **4, 6** = **final**, closing, concluding, extreme, furthest, remotest, terminal, ultimate, utmost ◆ *adv* **7** = **in** *or* **at the end**, after, behind, bringing up the rear, in the rear ◆ *n* **10b** = **end**, close, completion, conclusion, ending, finale, finish, termination **13 at last** = **finally**, at length, at the end of the day, eventually, in conclusion, in the end, in the fullness of time, ultimately
Antonyms *adj* ≠ **hindmost:** first, foremost, leading ≠ **final:** earliest, first, initial, introductory, opening

last[2] *vb* **1** = **continue**, abide, carry on, endure, hold on, hold out, keep, keep on, persist, remain, stand up, survive, wear
Antonyms *vb* cease, depart, die, end, expire, fade, fail, stop, terminate

last-ditch *n* **b** *as modifier* = **final**, all-out (*inf.*), desperate, frantic, heroic, straining, struggling

lasting *adj* = **continuing**, abiding, deep-rooted, durable, enduring, eternal, indelible, lifelong, long-standing, long-term, perennial, permanent, perpetual, unceasing, undying, unending
Antonyms *adj* ephemeral, fleeting, momentary, passing, short-lived, transient, transitory

lastly *adv, sentence connector* **1, 2** = **finally**, after

last post *n* (in the British military services) **1** a bugle call that orders men to retire for sleep. **2** a similar call sounded at military funerals.
last rites *pl n Christianity.* religious rites prescribed for those close to death.
Last Supper *n* **the.** the meal eaten by Christ with his disciples on the night before his Crucifixion.
lat. *abbrev. for* latitude.
Lat. *abbrev. for* Latin.
latah ('lɑːtə) *n* a psychological condition, observed esp. in Malaysian cultures, in which an individual, after experiencing a shock, becomes anxious and suggestible, often imitating the actions of another person. [C19: from Malay]
latch ● (lætʃ) *n* **1** a fastening for a gate or door that consists of a bar that may be slid or lowered into a groove, hole, etc. **2** a spring-loaded door lock that can be opened by a key from outside. **3** Also called: **latch circuit.** *Electronics.* a logic circuit that transfers the input states to the output states when signalled. ◆ *vb* **4** to fasten, fit, or be fitted as with a latch. [OE *læccan* to seize, of Gmc origin]
latchkey ('lætʃˌkiː) *n* **1** a key for an outside door or gate, esp. one that lifts a latch. **2** a supposed freedom from restrictions.
latchkey child *n* a child who has to let himself in at home on returning from school, as his parents are out at work.
latch on *vb* (*intr, adv;* often foll. by *to*) *Inf.* **1** to attach oneself (to). **2** to understand.
latchstring ('lætʃˌstrɪŋ) *n* a length of string fastened to a latch and passed through a hole in the door so that it can be opened from the other side.
late ● (leɪt) *adj* **1** occurring or arriving after the correct or expected time: *the train was late.* **2** (*prenominal*) occurring at, scheduled for, or being at a relatively advanced time: *a late marriage.* **3** (*prenominal*) towards or near the end: *the late evening.* **4** at an advanced time in the evening or at night: *it was late.* **5** (*prenominal*) occurring or being just previous to the present time: *his late remarks on industry.* **6** (*prenominal*) having died, esp. recently: *my late grandfather.* **7** (*prenominal*) just preceding the present or existing person or thing; former: *the late manager of this firm.* **8 of late.** recently; lately. ◆ *adv* **9** after the correct or expected time: *he arrived late.* **10** at a relatively advanced age: *she married late.* **11** recently; lately: *as late as yesterday he was selling books.* **12 late in the day. 12a** at a late or advanced stage. **12b** too late. [OE *læt*]
▸ **'lateness** *n*

> **USAGE NOTE** Since *late* can mean *deceased*, many people think it is better to avoid using this word to refer to the person who held a post or position before its present holder: *the previous* (not *the late*) editor of *The Times.*

lateen (lə'tiːn) *adj Naut.* denoting a rig with a triangular sail (**lateen sail**) bent to a yard hoisted to the head of a low mast, used esp. in the Mediterranean. [C18: from F *voile latine* Latin sail]
Late Greek *n* the Greek language from about the 3rd to the 8th centuries A.D.
Late Latin *n* the form of written Latin used from the 3rd to the 7th centuries A.D.
lately ● ('leɪtlɪ) *adv* in recent times; of late.
La Tène (læ 'tɛn) *adj* of or relating to a Celtic culture in Europe from about the 5th to the 1st centuries B.C., characterized by a distinctive type of curvilinear decoration. [C20: from *La Tène*, a part of Lake Neuchâtel, Switzerland, where remains of this culture were first discovered]
latent ● ('leɪtᵊnt) *adj* **1** potential but not obvious or explicit. **2** (of buds, spores, etc.) dormant. **3** *Pathol.* (esp. of an infectious disease) not yet revealed or manifest. **4** (of a virus) inactive in the host cell. **5** *Psychoanal.* relating to that part of a dream expressive of repressed desires: *latent content.* Cf. **manifest** (sense 2). [C17: from L *latēnt-*, from *latēre* to lie hidden]
▸ **'latency** *n* ▸ **'latently** *adv*
latent heat *n* (*no longer in technical usage*) the heat evolved or absorbed by unit mass (**specific latent heat**) or unit amount of substance (**molar latent heat**) when it changes phase without change of temperature.
latent image *n Photog.* the invisible image produced by the action of light, etc., on silver halide crystals suspended in the emulsion of a photographic material. It becomes visible after development.
later ● ('leɪtə) *adj, adv* **1** the comparative of **late.** ◆ *adv* **2** afterwards; subsequently.
lateral ● ('lætərəl) *adj* **1** of or relating to the side or sides: *a lateral blow.* ◆ *n* **2** a lateral object, part, passage, or movement. [C17: from L *laterālis*, from *latus* side]
▸ **'laterally** *adv*
lateral thinking *n* a way of solving problems by employing unorthodox and apparently illogical means.
laterite ('lætəˌraɪt) *n* any of a group of residual insoluble deposits of ferric and aluminium oxides: formed by weathering of rocks in tropical regions. [C19: from L *later* brick]
latest ● ('leɪtɪst) *adj, adv* **1** the superlative of **late.** ◆ *adj* **2** most recent, modern, or new: *the latest fashions.* ◆ *n* **3 at the latest.** no later than the time specified. **4 the latest.** *Inf.* the most recent fashion or development.
latex ('leɪtɛks) *n, pl* **latexes** *or* **latices** ('lætɪˌsiːz). **1** a whitish milky fluid containing protein, starch, alkaloids, etc., that is produced by many plants. Latex from the rubber tree is used in the manufacture of rubber. **2** a suspension of synthetic rubber or plastic in water, used in the manufacture of synthetic rubber products, etc. [C19: NL, from L: liquid]
lath (lɑːθ) *n, pl* **laths** (lɑːðz, lɑːθs). **1** one of several thin narrow strips of wood used to provide a supporting framework for plaster, tiles, etc. **2** expanded sheet metal, wire mesh, etc., used to provide backing for plaster or rendering. **3** any thin strip of wood. ◆ *vb* **4** (*tr*) to attach laths to (a ceiling, roof, floor, etc.). [OE *lætt*]
lathe (leɪð) *n* **1** a machine for shaping or boring metal, wood, etc., in which the workpiece is turned about a horizontal axis against a fixed tool. ◆ *vb* **lathes, lathing, lathed. 2** (*tr*) to shape or bore (a workpiece) on a lathe. [? C15 *lath* a support, from ON]
lather ● ('lɑːðə) *n* **1** foam formed by the action of soap or a detergent in water. **2** foam formed by other liquid, such as the sweat of a horse. **3** *Inf.* a state of agitation. ◆ *vb* **4** to coat or become coated with lather. **5** (*intr*) to form a lather. [OE *lēathor* soap]
▸ **'lathery** *adj*
lathi ('lɑːtɪ) *n, pl* **lathis.** a long heavy wooden stick used as a weapon in India, esp. by the police. [Hindi]
Latin ('lætɪn) *n* **1** the language of ancient Rome and the Roman Empire and of the educated in medieval Europe. Having originally been the language of Latium in W central Italy, belonging to the Italic branch of the Indo-European family, it later formed the basis of the Romance group. **2** a member of any of those peoples whose languages are derived from Latin. **3** an inhabitant of ancient Latium. ◆ *adj* **4** of or relating to the Latin language, the ancient Latins, or Latium. **5** characteristic of or relating to those peoples in Europe and Latin America whose languages are derived from Latin. **6** of or relating to the Roman Catholic Church. [OE *latin* and *læden* Latin, language, from L *Latīnus* of Latium]
Latin America *n* those areas of America whose official languages are Spanish and Portuguese, derived from Latin: South America, Central America, Mexico, and certain islands in the Caribbean.
▸ **Latin American** *n, adj*
Latinate ('lætɪˌneɪt) *adj* (of writing, vocabulary, etc.) imitative of or derived from Latin.
Latinism ('lætɪˌnɪzəm) *n* a word, idiom, or phrase borrowed from Latin.
Latinist ('lætɪnɪst) *n* a person who studies or is proficient in Latin.
Latinize *or* **Latinise** ('lætɪˌnaɪz) *vb* **Latinizes, Latinizing, Latinized** *or* **Latinises, Latinising, Latinised.** (*tr*) **1** to translate into Latin or Latinisms. **2** to cause to acquire Latin style or customs. **3** to bring Roman Catholic influence to bear upon (the form of religious ceremonies, etc.).
▸ **ˌLatiniˈzation** *or* **ˌLatiniˈsation** *n* ▸ **'LatinˌIzer** *or* **'Latinˌiser** *n*
latish ('leɪtɪʃ) *adj, adv* rather late.
latitude ● ('lætɪˌtjuːd) *n* **1a** an angular distance measured in degrees north or south of the equator (latitude 0°). **1b** (*often pl*) a region considered with regard to its distance from the equator. **2** scope for freedom of action, thought, etc.; freedom from restriction: *his parents gave him a great deal of latitude.* [C14: from L *lātitūdō*, from *lātus* broad]
▸ **ˌlatiˈtudinal** *adj* ▸ **ˌlatiˈtudinally** *adv*
latitudinarian (ˌlætɪˌtjuːdɪ'nɛərɪən) *adj* **1** permitting or marked by freedom of attitude or behaviour, esp. in religious matters. ◆ *n* **2** a person with latitudinarian views. [C17: from L *lātitūdō* breadth, infl. in form by TRINITARIAN]

THESAURUS

all, all in all, at last, in conclusion, to conclude, to sum up, ultimately

latch *n* **1** = **fastening**, bar, bolt, catch, clamp, hasp, hook, lock, sneck (*dialect*) ◆ *vb* **4** = **fasten**, bar, bolt, lock, make fast, secure, sneck (*dialect*)

late *adj* **1** = **overdue**, behind, behindhand, belated, delayed, last-minute, slow, tardy, unpunctual **6** = **dead**, deceased, defunct, departed, ex-, former, old, past, preceding, previous ◆ *adv* **9** = **belatedly**, at the last minute, behindhand, behind time, dilatorily, slowly, tardily, unpunctually
Antonyms *adj* ≠ **overdue**: beforehand, early, prompt, punctual, seasoned, timely ≠ **dead**: alive, existing ◆ *adv* ≠ **belatedly**: beforehand, early, in advance

lately *adv* = **recently**, in recent times, just now, latterly, not long ago, of late

lateness *n* **1** = **delay**, advanced hour, belatedness, late date, retardation, tardiness, unpunctuality

latent *adj* **1** = **hidden**, concealed, dormant, immanent, inherent, invisible, lurking, potential, quiescent, secret, undeveloped, unexpressed, unrealized, unseen, veiled
Antonyms *adj* apparent, conspicuous, developed, evident, expressed, manifest, obvious, realized

later *adv* **2** = **afterwards**, after, by and by, in a while, in time, later on, next, subsequently, thereafter

lateral *adj* **1** = **sideways**, edgeways, flanking, side, sideward

latest *adj* **2** = **up-to-date**, current, fashionable, happening (*inf.*), in, modern, most recent, newest, now, up-to-the-minute, with it (*inf.*)

lather *n* **1** = **froth**, bubbles, foam, soap, soapsuds, suds **3** *Informal* = **fluster**, dither (*chiefly Brit.*), fever, flap (*inf.*), fuss, pother, state (*inf.*), stew (*inf.*), sweat, tizzy (*inf.*), twitter (*inf.*) ◆ *vb* **4** = **froth**, foam, soap

lathery *adj* **1** = **frothy**, bubbly, foamy, soapy, sudsy

latitude *n* **2** = **scope**, a free hand, elbowroom, freedom, indulgence, laxity, leeway, liberty, licence, play, room, space, unrestrictedness

▸ˌ**latiˌtudiˈnarianism** *n*

latria (ləˈtraɪə) *n RC Church, theol.* the adoration that may be offered to God alone. [C16: via L from Gk *latreia* worship]

latrine (ləˈtriːn) *n* a lavatory, as in a barracks, camp, etc. [C17: from F, from L *lātrīna,* shortened form of *lavātrīna* bath, from *lavāre* to wash]

-latry *n combining form.* indicating worship of or excessive veneration of: *idolatry; Mariolatry.* [from Gk *-latria,* from *latreia* worship]
▸**-latrous** *adj combining form.*

latter Ⓣ (ˈlætə) *adj (prenominal)* **1a** denoting the second or second mentioned of two: distinguished from *former.* **1b** *(as n; functioning as sing or pl): the latter is not important.* **2** near or nearer the end: *the latter part of a film.* **3** more advanced in time or sequence; later. [OE *lætra*]

> **USAGE NOTE** *The latter* should only be used to refer to the second of two items: *many people choose to go by hovercraft rather than use the ferry, but I prefer the latter.* The last of three or more items can be referred to as *the last-named.*

latter-day *adj* present-day; modern.

Latter-day Saint *n* a more formal name for a **Mormon.**

latterly Ⓣ (ˈlætəlɪ) *adv* recently; lately.

lattice Ⓣ (ˈlætɪs) *n* **1** Also called: **latticework.** an open framework of strips of wood, metal, etc., arranged to form an ornamental pattern. **2a** a gate, screen, etc., formed of such a framework. **2b** *(as modifier): a lattice window.* **3** something, such as a decorative or heraldic device, resembling such a framework. **4** an array of objects or points in a periodic pattern in two or three dimensions, esp. an array of atoms, ions, etc., in a crystal or an array of points indicating their positions in space. ◆ *vb* **lattices, latticing, latticed. 5** to make, adorn, or supply with a lattice or lattices. [C14: from OF *lattis,* from *latte* LATH]
▸ˈ**latticed** *adj*

Latvian (ˈlætvɪən) *adj* **1** of or relating to Latvia, a republic on the Gulf of Riga and the Baltic Sea. **2** of or relating to the people of Latvia or their language. ◆ *n* **3** a native or inhabitant of Latvia.

laud Ⓣ (lɔːd) *Literary.* ◆ *vb* **1** *(tr)* to praise or glorify. ◆ *n* **2** praise or glorification. [C14: vb from L *laudāre;* n from *laudēs,* pl. of L *laus* praise]

laudable Ⓣ (ˈlɔːdəbᵊl) *adj* deserving or worthy of praise; admirable; commendable.
▸ˈ**laudableness** *or* ˌ**laudaˈbility** *n* ▸ˈ**laudably** *adv*

laudanum (ˈlɔːdᵊnəm) *n* **1** a tincture of opium. **2** (formerly) any medicine of which opium was the main ingredient. [C16: NL, name chosen by Paracelsus (1493–1541), Swiss alchemist, for a preparation prob. containing opium]

laudation (lɔːˈdeɪʃən) *n* a formal word for **praise.**

laudatory Ⓣ (ˈlɔːdətərɪ, -trɪ) *or* **laudative** *adj* expressing or containing praise; eulogistic.

lauds (lɔːdz) *n (functioning as sing or pl) Chiefly RC Church.* the traditional morning prayer, constituting with matins the first of the seven canonical hours. [C14: see LAUD]

laugh Ⓣ (lɑːf) *vb* **1** *(intr)* to express or manifest emotion, esp. mirth or amusement, typically by expelling air from the lungs in short bursts to produce an inarticulate voiced noise, with the mouth open. **2** *(intr)* (esp. of certain mammals or birds) to make a noise resembling a laugh. **3** *(tr)* to utter or express with laughter: *he laughed his derision at the play.* **4** *(tr)* to bring or force (someone, esp. oneself) into a certain condition by laughter: *he laughed himself sick.* **5** *(intr;* foll. by *at)* to make fun (of); jeer (at). **6 laugh up one's sleeve.** to laugh or have grounds for amusement, self-satisfaction, etc., secretly. **7 laugh on the other side of one's face.** to show sudden disappointment or shame after appearing cheerful or confident. ◆ *n* **8** the act or an instance of laughing. **9** a manner of laughter. **10** *Inf.* a person or thing that causes laughter: *that holiday was a laugh.* **11 the last laugh.** the final success in an argument, situation, etc., after previous defeat. ◆ See also **laugh off.** [OE *læhan, hliehhen*]
▸ˈ**laugher** *n* ▸ˈ**laughing** *n, adj* ▸ˈ**laughingly** *adv*

laughable Ⓣ (ˈlɑːfəbᵊl) *adj* **1** producing scorn; ludicrous: *he offered me a laughable sum for the picture.* **2** arousing laughter.
▸ˈ**laughableness** *n* ▸ˈ**laughably** *adv*

laughing gas *n* another name for **nitrous oxide.**

laughing jackass *n* another name for the **kookaburra.**

laughing stock Ⓣ *n* an object of humiliating ridicule.

laugh off Ⓣ *vb (tr, adv)* to treat or dismiss lightly, esp. with stoicism.

laughter Ⓣ (ˈlɑːftə) *n* **1** the action of or noise produced by laughing. **2** the experience or manifestation of mirth, amusement, scorn, or joy. [OE *hleahtor*]

launch[1] Ⓣ (lɔːntʃ) *vb* **1** to move (a vessel) into the water. **2** to move (a newly built vessel) into the water for the first time. **3** *(tr)* **3a** to start off or set in motion: *to launch a scheme.* **3b** to put (a new product) on the market. **4** *(tr)* to propel with force. **5** to involve (oneself) totally and enthusiastically: *to launch oneself into work.* **6** *(tr)* to set (a missile, spacecraft, etc.) into motion. **7** *(intr;* foll. by *into)* to start talking or writing (about): *he launched into a story.* **8** *(intr;* usually foll. by *out)* to start (out) on a fresh course. ◆ *n* **9** an act or instance of launching. [C14: from Anglo-F *lancher,* from LL *lanceāre* to use a lance, hence, to set in motion. See LANCE]
▸ˈ**launcher** *n*

launch[2] (lɔːntʃ) *n* **1** a motor driven boat used chiefly as a transport boat. **2** the largest of the boats of a man-of-war. [C17: via Sp. *lancha* and Port. from Malay *lancharan* boat, from *lanchar* speed]

launch pad *or* **launching pad** *n* **1** a platform from which a spacecraft, rocket, etc., is launched. **2** an effective starting point for a career, enterprise, or campaign.

launch window *n* the limited period during which a spacecraft can be launched on a particular mission.

launder Ⓣ (ˈlɔːndə) *vb* **1** to wash and often also iron (clothes, linen, etc.). **2** *(intr)* to be capable of being laundered without shrinking, fading, etc. **3** *(tr)* to make (money illegally obtained) appear to be legally gained by passing it through foreign banks or legitimate enterprises. [C14 (n, meaning: a person who washes linen): changed from *lavender* washerwoman, from OF *lavandiere,* ult. from L *lavāre* to wash]
▸ˈ**launderer** *n*

Launderette (ˌlɔːndəˈrɛt, lɔːnˈdrɛt) *Brit. & NZ trademark.* a commercial establishment where clothes can be washed and dried, using coin-operated machines. Also called (US, Canad., and NZ): **Laundromat.**

laundress (ˈlɔːndrɪs) *n* a woman who launders clothes, sheets, etc., for a living.

laundry (ˈlɔːndrɪ) *n, pl* **laundries. 1** a place where clothes and linen are washed and ironed. **2** the clothes or linen washed and ironed. **3** the act of laundering. [C16: changed from C14 *lavendry;* see LAUNDER]

laundryman (ˈlɔːndrɪmən) *or (fem)* **laundrywoman** *n, pl* **laundrymen** *or* **laundrywomen. 1** a person who collects or delivers laundry. **2** a person who works in a laundry.

Laurasia (lɔːˈreɪʃə) *n* one of the two ancient supercontinents comprising what are now North America, Greenland, Europe, and Asia (excluding India). [C20: from NL *Laur(entia)* (referring to the ancient N American landmass, from *Laurentian* strata of the Canadian Shield) + *(Eur)asia*]

laureate (ˈlɔːrɪɪt) *adj (usually immediately postpositive)* **1** *Literary.* crowned with laurel leaves as a sign of honour. ◆ *n* **2** short for **poet laureate. 3** a person honoured with an award for art or science: *a Nobel laureate.* **4** *Rare.* a person honoured with the laurel crown or wreath. [C14: from L *laureātus,* from *laurea* LAUREL]
▸ˈ**laureateˌship** *n*

laurel Ⓣ (ˈlɒrəl) *n* **1** Also called: **bay, bay laurel, sweet bay, true laurel.** a small Mediterranean evergreen tree with glossy aromatic leaves, used for flavouring in cooking, and small blackish berries. **2** a similar and related tree of the Canary Islands and Azores. **3** short for **mountain laurel. 4 spurge laurel.** a European evergreen shrub, *Daphne laureola,* with glossy leaves and small green flowers. **5** *(pl)* a wreath of true laurel, worn on the head as an emblem of victory or honour in classical times. **6** *(pl)* honour, distinction, or fame. **7 look to one's laurels.** to be on guard against one's rivals. **8 rest on one's laurels.** to be satisfied with distinction won by past achievements and cease to strive for further achievements. ◆ *vb* **laurels, laurelling, laurelled** *or US* **laurels, laureling, laureled. 9** *(tr)* to crown with laurels. [C13 *lorer,* from OF *lorier* laurel tree, ult. from L *laurus*]

Laurentian (lɔːˈrɛnʃən) *adj* **1** Also: **Lawrentian.** of or resembling the style

THESAURUS

latter *adj* **1 = second,** last, last-mentioned **2 = concluding,** closing **3 = later**
Antonyms *adj* ≠ **second:** antecedent, earlier, foregoing, former, preceding, previous, prior

latterly *adv* **= recently,** hitherto, lately, of late

lattice *n* **1 = framework,** fretwork, grating, grid, grille, latticework, mesh, network, openwork, reticulation, tracery, trellis, web

laud *vb* **1** *Literary* **= praise,** acclaim, approve, celebrate, crack up *(inf.),* extol, glorify, honour, magnify *(arch.),* sing *or* sound the praises of

laudable *adj* **= praiseworthy,** admirable, commendable, creditable, estimable, excellent, meritorious, of note, worthy
Antonyms *adj* base, blameworthy, contemptible, ignoble, lowly, unworthy

laudatory *adj* **= eulogistic,** acclamatory, adulatory, approbatory, approving, commendatory, complimentary, panegyrical

laugh *vb* **1 = chuckle,** be convulsed *(inf.),* be in stitches, be rolling in the aisles *(inf.),* bust a gut *(inf.),* chortle, crack up *(inf.),* crease up *(inf.),* giggle, guffaw, roar with laughter, snigger, split one's sides, titter **5 laugh at = make fun of,** belittle, deride, jeer, lampoon, make a mock of, mock, ridicule, scoff at, take the mickey (out of) *(inf.),* taunt ◆ *n* **8 = chuckle,** belly laugh *(inf.),* chortle, giggle, guffaw, roar *or* shriek of laughter, snigger, titter **10** *Informal* **= joke,** card *(inf.),* caution *(inf.),* clown, comedian, comic, entertainer, hoot *(inf.),* humorist, lark, scream *(inf.),* wag, wit

laughable *adj* **1 = ridiculous,** absurd, derisive, derisory, farcical, ludicrous, nonsensical, preposterous, risible, worthy of scorn **2 = funny,** amusing, comical, diverting, droll, hilarious, humorous, mirthful

laughing stock *n* **= figure of fun,** Aunt Sally *(Brit.),* butt, everybody's fool, fair game, target, victim

laugh off *vb* **= disregard,** brush aside, dismiss, ignore, minimize, pooh-pooh, shrug off

laughter *n* **1 = laughing,** cachinnation, chortling, chuckling, giggling, guffawing, tittering **2 = amusement,** glee, hilarity, merriment, mirth

launch[1] *vb* **2, 6 = propel,** cast, discharge, dispatch, fire, project, send off, set afloat, set in motion, throw **3 = begin,** commence, embark upon, inaugurate, initiate, instigate, introduce, open, start ◆ *n* **9 = start,** beginning, commencement, inauguration, initiation, instigation, introduction, opening, projection, propelling, sendoff

launder *vb* **1 = wash,** clean, tub **3 = process,** cook *(sl.),* doctor, manipulate

laurel *n* **6** *plural* **= glory,** acclaim, awards, Brownie points, commendation, credit, distinc-

of D. H. or T. E. Lawrence. **2** of, relating to, or situated near the St Lawrence River.

Laurentian Shield *n* another name for the **Canadian Shield.** Also: **Laurentian Plateau.**

laurustinus (ˌlɔːrəˈstaɪnəs) *n* a Mediterranean shrub with glossy evergreen leaves and white or pink fragrant flowers. [C17: from NL, from L *laurus* laurel]

lav (læv) *n Brit. inf.* short for **lavatory.**

lava (ˈlɑːvə) *n* **1** magma emanating from volcanoes. **2** any extrusive igneous rock formed by the solidification of lava. [C18: from It., from L *lavāre* to wash]

lavabo (ləˈveɪbəʊ) *n, pl* **lavaboes** *or* **lavabos.** *Chiefly RC Church.* **1a** the ritual washing of the celebrant's hands after the offertory at Mass. **1b** (*as modifier*): *lavabo basin; lavabo towel.* **2** another name for **washbasin. 3** a trough for washing in a convent or monastery. [C19: from L: I shall wash, the opening of Psalm 26:6]

lavage (ˈlævɪdʒ, læˈvɑːʒ) *n Med.* the washing out of a hollow organ by flushing with water. [C19: via F, from L *lavāre* to wash]

lavatorial (ˌlævəˈtɔːrɪəl) *adj* characterized by excessive mention of the excretory functions; vulgar or scatological: *lavatorial humour.*

lavatory ❶ (ˈlævətərɪ, -trɪ) *n, pl* **lavatories. a** a sanitary installation for receiving and disposing of urine and faeces, consisting of a bowl fitted with a water-flushing device and connected to a drain. **b** a room containing such an installation. Also called: **toilet, water closet, WC.** [C14: from LL *lavātōrium,* from L *lavāre* to wash]

lavatory paper *n Brit.* another name for **toilet paper.**

lave (leɪv) *vb* **laves, laving, laved.** an archaic word for **wash.** [OE *lafian,* ?from L *lavāre* to wash]

lavender (ˈlævəndə) *n* **1** any of various perennial shrubs or herbaceous plants of the labiate family, esp. *Lavandula vera,* cultivated for its mauve or blue flowers and as the source of a fragrant oil (**oil of lavender**). **2** the dried parts of *L. vera,* used to perfume clothes. **3** a pale or light bluish-purple colour. **4** perfume scented with lavender. [C13 *lavendre,* via F from Med. L *lavendula,* from ?]

laver (ˈleɪvə) *n Old Testament.* a large basin of water used by the priests for ritual ablutions. [C14: from OF *laveoir,* from LL *lavātōrium* washing place]

lavish ❶ (ˈlævɪʃ) *adj* **1** prolific, abundant, or profuse. **2** generous; unstinting; liberal. **3** extravagant; prodigal; wasteful: *lavish expenditure.* ◆ *vb* **4** (*tr*) to give, expend, or apply abundantly, generously, or in profusion. [C15: adj use of *lavas* profusion, from OF *lavasse* torrent, from L *lavāre* to wash]
▸ **ˈlavisher** *n* ▸ **ˈlavishly** *adv* ▸ **ˈlavishness** *n*

law ❶ (lɔː) *n* **1** a rule or set of rules, enforceable by the courts regulating the relationship between the state and its subjects, and the conduct of subjects towards one another. **2a** a rule or body of rules made by the legislature. See **statute law. 2b** a rule or body of rules made by a municipal or other authority. See **bylaw. 3a** the condition and control enforced by such rules. **3b** (*in combination*): *lawcourt.* **4 law and order. 4a** the policy of strict enforcement of the law, esp. against crime and violence. **4b** (*as modifier*): *law-and-order candidate.* **5** a rule of conduct: *a law of etiquette.* **6** one of a set of rules governing a particular field of activity: *the laws of tennis.* **7 the law. 7a** the legal or judicial system. **7b** the profession or practice of law. **7c** *Inf.* the police or a policeman. **8** Also called: **law of nature.** a generalization based on a recurring fact or event. **9** the science or knowledge of law; jurisprudence. **10** the principles originating and formerly applied only in courts of common law. Cf. **equity** (sense 3). **11** a general principle, formula, or rule describing a phenomenon in mathematics, science, philosophy, etc.: *the laws of thermodynamics.* **12** Also called: **Law of Moses.** (*often cap.;* preceded by *the*) the body of laws contained in the first five books of the Old Testament. **13 go to law.** to resort to legal proceedings on some matter. **14 lay down the law.** to speak in an authoritative or dogmatic manner. ◆ Related adjs.: **judicial, juridical, legal.** [OE *lagu,* from ON]

law-abiding ❶ *adj* adhering more or less strictly to the laws: *a law-abiding citizen.*

law agent *n* (in Scotland) a solicitor entitled to appear for a client in any Sheriff Court.

lawbreaker ❶ (ˈlɔːˌbreɪkə) *n* a person who breaks the law.
▸ **ˈlawˌbreaking** *n, adj*

law centre *n Brit.* an independent service financed by a local authority, which provides free legal advice and information to the general public.

lawful ❶ (ˈlɔːfʊl) *adj* allowed, recognized, or sanctioned by law; legal.
▸ **ˈlawfully** *adv* ▸ **ˈlawfulness** *n*

lawgiver (ˈlɔːˌgɪvə) *n* **1** the giver of a code of laws. **2** Also called: **lawmaker.** a maker of laws.
▸ **ˈlawˌgiving** *n, adj*

lawks (lɔːks) *interj Brit.* an expression of surprise or dismay. [C18: var. of *Lord!,* prob. infl. in form by ALACK]

lawless ❶ (ˈlɔːlɪs) *adj* **1** without law. **2** disobedient to the law. **3** contrary to or heedless of the law. **4** uncontrolled; unbridled: *lawless rage.*
▸ **ˈlawlessly** *adv* ▸ **ˈlawlessness** *n*

Law Lords *pl n* (in Britain) members of the House of Lords who sit as the highest court of appeal.

lawn[1] (lɔːn) *n* a flat and usually level area of mown and cultivated grass. [C16: changed form of C14 *launde,* from OF *lande,* of Celtic origin]
▸ **ˈlawny** *adj*

lawn[2] (lɔːn) *n* a fine linen or cotton fabric, used for clothing. [C15: prob. from *Laon,* town in France where made]
▸ **ˈlawny** *adj*

lawn mower *n* a hand-operated or power-operated machine for cutting grass on lawns.

lawn tennis *n* **1** tennis played on a grass court. **2** the formal name for **tennis.**

law of averages *n* (popularly) the expectation that a possible event is bound to occur regularly with a frequency approximating to its probability.

law of supply and demand *n* the theory that the price of an article or service is determined by the interaction of supply and demand.

law of the jungle *n* a state of ruthless competition or self-interest.

law of thermodynamics *n* any of three principles governing the relationships between different forms of energy. The **first law** (conservation of energy) states that energy can be transformed but not destroyed. The **second law** states that in any irreversible process entropy always increases. The **third law** states that it is impossible to reduce the temperature of a system to absolute zero in a finite number of steps.

lawrencium (lɒˈrɛnsɪəm) *n* an element artificially produced from californium. Symbol: Lr; atomic no.: 103; half-life of most stable isotope, ^{256}Lr: 35 seconds. [C20: after Ernest O. *Lawrence* (1901–58), US physicist]

Lawrentian (lɔːˈrɛnʃən) *adj* a variant spelling of **Laurentian** (sense 1).

lawsuit ❶ (ˈlɔːˌsuːt) *n* a proceeding in a court of law brought by one party against another, esp. a civil action.

law term *n* **1** an expression or word used in law. **2** any of various periods of time appointed for the sitting of law courts.

lawyer ❶ (ˈlɔːjə, ˈlɔɪə) *n* a member of the legal profession, esp. a solicitor. [C14: from LAW]

lax ❶ (læks) *adj* **1** lacking firmness; not strict. **2** lacking precision or definition. **3** not taut. **4** *Phonetics.* (of a speech sound) pronounced with little muscular effort. [C14 (orig. used with reference to the bowels): from L *laxus* loose]
▸ **ˈlaxly** *adv* ▸ **ˈlaxity** *or* **ˈlaxness** *n*

laxative ❶ (ˈlæksətɪv) *n* **1** an agent stimulating evacuation of faeces. ◆ *adj* **2** stimulating evacuation of faeces. [C14 (orig.: relaxing): from Med. L *laxātīvus,* from L *laxāre* to loosen]

lay[1] ❶ (leɪ) *vb* **lays, laying, laid.** (*mainly tr*) **1** to put in a low or horizontal position; cause to lie: *to lay a cover on a bed.* **2** to place, put, or be in a

THESAURUS

tion, fame, honour, kudos, praise, prestige, recognition, renown, reward

lavatory *n* = **toilet**, bathroom, bog (*sl.*), can (*US & Canad. sl.*), cloakroom (*Brit.*), Gents *or* Ladies, head(s) (*Nautical sl.*), john (*sl., chiefly US & Canad.*), latrine, little boy's room *or* little girl's room (*inf.*), loo (*Brit. inf.*), powder room, privy, (public) convenience, washroom, water closet, W.C.

lavish *adj* **1** = **plentiful**, abundant, copious, exuberant, lush, luxuriant, opulent, profuse, prolific, sumptuous **2** = **generous**, bountiful, effusive, free, liberal, munificent, open-handed, unstinting **3** = **extravagant**, exaggerated, excessive, immoderate, improvident, intemperate, prodigal, thriftless, unreasonable, unrestrained, wasteful, wild ◆ *vb* **4** = **spend**, deluge, dissipate, expend, heap, pour, shower, squander, waste
Antonyms *adj* ≠ **plentiful:** frugal, meagre, miserly, scanty, stingy ≠ **generous:** cheap, miserly, parsimonious, stingy, tight-fisted ≠ **extravagant:** sparing, thrifty ◆ *vb* ≠ **spend:** begrudge, economize, stint, withhold

law *n* **1** = **constitution**, charter, code, jurisprudence **2** = **rule**, act, canon, code, command, commandment, covenant, decree, demand, edict, enactment, order, ordinance, regulation, statute **5, 6** = **principle**, axiom, canon, criterion, formula, precept, standard **14 lay down the law** = **dictate**, dogmatize, emphasize, pontificate

law-abiding *adj* = **obedient**, compliant, dutiful, good, honest, honourable, lawful, orderly, peaceable, peaceful

lawbreaker *n* = **criminal**, convict, crook (*inf.*), culprit, delinquent, felon (*formerly Criminal law*), miscreant, offender, sinner, transgressor, trespasser, villain, violater, wrongdoer

lawful *adj* = **legal**, allowable, authorized, constitutional, just, legalized, legitimate, licit, permissible, proper, rightful, valid, warranted
Antonyms *adj* banned, forbidden, illegal, illegitimate, illicit, prohibited, unauthorized, unlawful

lawless *adj* **1** = **anarchic**, chaotic, ungoverned **2, 3** = **disorderly**, insubordinate, insurgent, mutinous, rebellious, reckless, riotous, seditious, unruly **4** = **unrestrained**, wild
Antonyms *adj* ≠ **anarchic:** civilized, lawful, well-governed ≠ **disorderly:** compliant, disciplined, law-abiding, obedient, orderly ≠ **unrestrained:** restrained

lawlessness *n* **1** = **anarchy**, chaos, disorder, mobocracy, mob rule, ochlocracy, reign of terror

lawsuit *n* = **case**, action, argument, cause, contest, dispute, industrial tribunal, litigation, proceedings, prosecution, suit, trial

lawyer *n* = **legal adviser**, advocate, attorney, barrister, counsel, counsellor, solicitor

lax *adj* **1** = **slack**, careless, casual, easy-going, easy-oasy (*sl.*), lenient, neglectful, negligent, overindulgent, remiss, slapdash, slipshod **2** = **vague**, broad, general, imprecise, inaccurate, indefinite, inexact, nonspecific, shapeless **3** = **loose**, flabby, flaccid, slack, soft, yielding
Antonyms *adj* ≠ **slack:** conscientious, disciplined, firm, heedful, moral, rigid, scrupulous, severe, stern, strict, stringent ≠ **loose:** firm, rigid

laxative *n* **1** = **purgative**, aperient, cathartic, physic, purge, salts

lay[1] *vb* **1, 2** = **place**, deposit, establish, leave, plant, posit, put, set, set down, settle, spread **5** = **arrange**, dispose, locate, organize, position,

particular state or position: *he laid his finger on his lips.* **3** (*intr*) *Dialect or not standard.* to be in a horizontal position; lie: *he often lays in bed all the morning.* **4** (sometimes foll. by *down*) to establish as a basis: *to lay a foundation for discussion.* **5** to place or dispose in the proper position: *to lay a carpet.* **6** to arrange (a table) for eating a meal. **7** to prepare (a fire) for lighting by arranging fuel in the grate. **8** (*also intr*) (of birds, esp. the domestic hen) to produce (eggs). **9** to present or put forward: *he laid his case before the magistrate.* **10** to impute or attribute: *all the blame was laid on him.* **11** to arrange, devise, or prepare: *to lay a trap.* **12** to place, set, or locate: *the scene is laid in London.* **13** to make (a bet) with (someone): *I lay you five to one on Prince.* **14** to cause to settle: *to lay the dust.* **15** to allay; suppress: *to lay a rumour.* **16** to bring down forcefully: *to lay a whip on someone's back.* **17** *Taboo sl.* to have sexual intercourse with. **18** to press down or make smooth: *to lay the nap of cloth.* **19** (*intr*) *Naut.* to move or go, esp. into a specified position or direction: *to lay close to the wind.* **20 lay bare.** to reveal or explain: *he laid bare his plans.* **21 lay hold of.** to seize or grasp. **22 lay oneself open.** to make oneself vulnerable (to criticism, attack, etc.). **23 lay open.** to reveal or disclose. ◆ *n* **24** the manner or position in which something lies or is placed. **25** *Taboo sl.* **25a** an act of sexual intercourse. **25b** a sexual partner. ◆ See also **lay aside, lay-by,** etc. [OE *lecgan*]

> **USAGE NOTE** In careful English, the verb *lay* is used with an object and *lie* without one: *the soldier laid down his arms; the Queen laid a wreath; the book was lying on the table; he was lying on the floor.* In informal English, *lay* is frequently used for *lie*: *the book was laying on the table.* All careful writers and speakers observe the distinction even in informal contexts.

lay[2] (leɪ) *vb* the past tense of **lie**[2].

lay[3] Ⓣ (leɪ) *adj* **1** of, involving, or belonging to people who are not clergy. **2** nonprofessional or nonspecialist; amateur. [C14: from OF *lai,* from LL *lāicus,* ult. from Gk *laos* people]

lay[4] Ⓣ (leɪ) *n* **1** a ballad or short narrative poem, esp. one intended to be sung. **2** a song or melody. [C13: from OF *lai,* ? of Gmc origin]

layabout Ⓣ (ˈleɪəˌbaʊt) *n* a lazy person; loafer.

lay analyst *n* a person without medical qualifications who practises psychoanalysis.

lay aside Ⓣ *vb* (*tr, adv*) **1** to abandon or reject. **2** to store or reserve for future use.

lay brother *or (fem)* **lay sister** *n* a person who has taken the vows of a religious order but is not ordained and not bound to divine office.

lay-by Ⓣ *n* **1** *Brit.* a place for drivers to stop at the side of a main road. **2** *Naut.* an anchorage in a narrow waterway, away from the channel. **3** a small railway siding where rolling stock may be stored or parked. **4** *Austral. & NZ.* a system of payment whereby a buyer pays a deposit on an article, which is reserved for him until he has paid the full price. ◆ *vb* **lay by.** (*tr, adv*) **5** to set aside or save for future needs.

lay days *pl n* **1** *Commerce.* the number of days permitted for the loading or unloading of a ship without payment of demurrage. **2** *Naut.* the time during which a ship is kept from sailing because of loading, bad weather, etc.

lay down Ⓣ *vb* (*tr, adv*) **1** to place on the ground, etc. **2** to relinquish or discard: *to lay down one's life.* **3** to formulate (a rule, principle, etc.). **4** to build or begin to build: *the railway was laid down as far as Chester.* **5** to record (plans) on paper. **6** to convert (land) into pasture. **7** to store or stock: *to lay down wine.* **8** *Inf.* to wager or bet. **9** *Inf.* to record (tracks) in a studio.

layer Ⓣ (ˈleɪə) *n* **1** a thickness of some homogeneous substance, such as a stratum or a coating on a surface. **2** a laying hen. **3** *Horticulture.* a shoot or branch rooted during layering. ◆ *vb* **4** to form or make a layer of (something). **5** to take root or cause to take root by layering. [C14 *leyer, legger,* from LAY[1] + -ER[1]]

layering (ˈleɪərɪŋ) *n* **1** *Horticulture.* a method of propagation that induces a shoot to take root while it is still attached to the parent plant. **2** *Geol.* the banded appearance of certain igneous rocks, each band being of a different mineral composition.

layette (leɪˈɛt) *n* a complete set of articles, including clothing, bedclothes, and other accessories, for a newborn baby. [C19: from F, from OF, from *laie,* from MDu. *laege* box]

lay figure *n* **1** an artist's jointed dummy, used in place of a live model, esp. for studying effects of drapery. **2** a person considered to be subservient or unimportant. [C18: from obs. *layman,* from Du. *leeman,* lit.: joint-man]

lay in Ⓣ *vb* (*tr, adv*) to accumulate and store: *we must lay in food for the party.*

lay into Ⓣ *vb* (*intr, prep*) *Inf.* **1** to attack forcefully. **2** to berate severely.

layman Ⓣ (ˈleɪmən) *or (fem)* **laywoman** *n, pl* **laymen** *or* **laywomen. 1** a person who is not a clergyman. **2** a person who does not have specialized or professional knowledge of a subject: *science for the layman.*

lay off Ⓣ *vb* **1** (*tr, adv*) to suspend from work with the intention of re-employing later: *the firm had to lay off 100 men.* **2** (*intr*) *Inf.* to leave (a person, thing, or activity) alone: *lay off me, will you!* **3** (*tr, adv*) to mark off the boundaries of. ◆ *n* **lay-off. 4** the act of suspending employees. **5** a period of imposed unemployment.

lay on Ⓣ *vb* (*tr, adv*) **1** to provide or supply: *to lay on entertainment.* **2** *Brit.* to install: *to lay on electricity.* **3 lay it on.** *Sl.* **3a** to exaggerate, esp. when flattering. **3b** to charge an exorbitant price. **3c** to punish or strike harshly.

lay out Ⓣ *vb* (*tr, adv*) **1** to arrange or spread out. **2** to prepare (a corpse) for burial or cremation. **3** to plan or contrive. **4** *Inf.* to spend (money), esp. lavishly. **5** *Inf.* to knock unconscious. ◆ *n* **layout. 6** the arrangement or plan of something, such as a building. **7** the arrangement of written material, photographs, or other artwork on an advertisement or page in a book, newspaper, etc. **8** a preliminary plan indicating this. **9** a drawing showing the relative disposition of parts in a machine, etc. **10** the act of laying out. **11** something laid out.

lay over *US.* ◆ *vb* (*adv*) **1** (*tr*) to postpone for future action. **2** (*intr*) to make a temporary stop in a journey. ◆ *n* **layover. 3** a break in a journey, esp. in waiting for a connection.

lay reader *n* **1** *Church of England.* a person licensed by a bishop to conduct religious services other than the Eucharist. **2** *RC Church.* a layman chosen from among the congregation to read the epistle at Mass.

lay up Ⓣ *vb* (*tr, adv*) **1** to store or reserve for future use. **2** (*usually passive*) *Inf.* to incapacitate or confine through illness.

lazar (ˈlæzə) *n* an archaic word for **leper.** [C14: via OF and Med. L, after *Lazarus,* beggar in Jesus' parable (Luke 16:19–31)]

lazaretto (ˌlæzəˈrɛtəʊ), **lazaret,** *or* **lazarette** (ˌlæzəˈrɛt) *n, pl* **lazarettos, lazarets,** *or* **lazarettes. 1** Also called: **glory hole.** *Naut.* a small locker at the stern of a boat or a storeroom between decks of a ship. **2** Also called: **lazar house, pesthouse.** (formerly) a hospital for persons with infectious diseases, esp. leprosy. [C16: It., from *lazzaro* LAZAR]

laze Ⓣ (leɪz) *vb* **lazes, lazing, lazed. 1** (*intr*) to be indolent or lazy. **2** (*tr;* often foll. by *away*) to spend (time) in indolence. ◆ *n* **3** the act or an instance of idling. [C16: back formation from LAZY]

lazy Ⓣ (ˈleɪzɪ) *adj* **lazier, laziest. 1** not inclined to work or exertion. **2** conducive to or causing indolence. **3** moving in a languid or sluggish manner: *a lazy river.* [C16: from ?]
▸ˈ**lazily** *adv* ▸ˈ**laziness** *n*

lazybones Ⓣ (ˈleɪzɪˌbəʊnz) *n Inf.* a lazy person.

lazy Susan *n* a revolving tray, often divided into sections, for holding condiments, etc.

lb *abbrev. for:* **1** pound (weight). [L *libra*] **2** *Cricket.* leg bye.

THESAURUS

set out **8** = **produce**, bear, deposit **9** = **put forward**, advance, bring forward, lodge, offer, present, submit **10** = **attribute**, allocate, allot, ascribe, assign, charge, impute **11** = **devise**, concoct, contrive, design, hatch, plan, plot, prepare, work out **13** = **bet**, gamble, give odds, hazard, risk, stake, wager **15** = **allay**, alleviate, appease, assuage, calm, quiet, relieve, soothe, still, suppress **20 lay bare** = **reveal**, disclose, divulge, explain, expose, show, unveil **21 lay hold of** = **grasp**, get, get hold of, grab, grip, seize, snatch

lay[3] *adj* **1** = **nonclerical**, laic, laical, secular **2** = **nonspecialist**, amateur, inexpert, nonprofessional

lay[4] *n* **1, 2** = **poem**, ballad, lyric, ode, song

layabout *n* = **idler**, couch potato (*sl.*), good-for-nothing, laggard, loafer, lounger, ne'er-do-well, shirker, skiver (*Brit. sl.*), vagrant, wastrel

lay aside *vb* **1** = **abandon**, cast aside, dismiss, postpone, put aside, put off, reject, shelve

lay-by *vb* **lay by 5** = **keep**, accumulate, collect, hoard, lay aside, lay in, salt away, save, stash (*inf.*), stockpile, store

lay down *vb* **2** = **sacrifice**, give up, relinquish, surrender, yield **3** = **stipulate**, affirm, assume, establish, formulate, ordain, postulate, prescribe

layer *n* **1** = **thickness**, bed, blanket, coat, coating, cover, covering, film, mantle, ply, row, seam, sheet, stratum, tier

lay in *vb* = **store (up)**, accumulate, amass, build up, collect, hoard, stockpile, stock up

lay into *vb* **1** *Informal* = **attack**, assail, belabour, go for the jugular, hit out at, lambast(e), let fly at, pitch into (*inf.*), set about

layman *n* **2** = **nonprofessional**, amateur, lay person, outsider

lay off *vb* **1** = **dismiss**, discharge, drop, give the boot to (*sl.*), let go, make redundant, oust, pay off **2** *Informal* = **stop**, belay (*Nautical*), cease, desist, get off someone's back (*inf.*), give it a rest (*inf.*), give over (*inf.*), give up, leave alone, leave off, let up, quit ◆ *n* **lay-off 4** = **unemployment**, discharge, dismissal

lay on *vb* **1** = **provide**, cater (for), furnish, give, purvey, supply **3a lay it on** *Slang* = **exaggerate**, butter up, flatter, overdo it, overpraise, soft-soap (*inf.*)

lay out *vb* **1** = **arrange**, design, display, exhibit, plan, spread out **4** *Informal* = **spend**, disburse, expend, fork out (*sl.*), invest, pay, shell out (*inf.*) **5** *Informal* = **knock out**, kayo (*sl.*), knock for six (*inf.*), knock unconscious, KO *or* K.O. (*sl.*) ◆ *n* **layout 6** = **arrangement**, design, draft, format, formation, geography, outline, plan

lay up *vb* **1** = **store up**, accumulate, amass, garner, hoard, keep, preserve, put away, save, treasure **2** *Informal* = **confine (to bed)**, hospitalize, incapacitate

laze *vb* **1** = **idle**, hang around, loaf, loll, lounge, stand around **2** *often with* **away** = **kill time**, fool away, fritter away, pass time, veg out (*sl., chiefly US*), waste time, while away the hours

laziness *n* **1** = **idleness**, dilatoriness, do-nothingness, inactivity, indolence, lackadaisicalness, slackness, sloth, slothfulness, slowness, sluggishness, tardiness

lazy *adj* **1** = **idle**, good-for-nothing, inactive, indolent, inert, remiss, shiftless, slack, slothful, slow, workshy **3** = **lethargic**, drowsy, languid, languorous, sleepy, slow-moving, sluggish, somnolent, torpid

Antonyms *adj* active, assiduous, diligent, energetic, industrious, quick, stimulated

lazybones *n Informal* = **idler**, couch potato (*sl.*), loafer, lounger, shirker, skiver (*Brit. sl.*), sleepyhead, slugabed, sluggard

LBO *abbrev. for* leveraged buyout.
lbw *Cricket. abbrev. for* leg before wicket.
lc *abbrev. for:* **1** left centre (of a stage, etc.). **2** loco citato. [L: in the place cited] **3** *Printing.* lower case.
L/C, l/c, *or* **lc** *abbrev. for* letter of credit.
LCD *abbrev. for:* **1** liquid-crystal display. **2** Also: **lcd.** lowest common denominator.
LCJ (in Britain) *abbrev. for* Lord Chief Justice.
lcm *or* **LCM** *abbrev. for* lowest common multiple.
L/Cpl *abbrev. for* lance corporal.
LD *abbrev. for* lethal dose (esp. in $\mathbf{LD_{50}}$). See **median lethal dose.**
LDL *abbrev. for* low-density lipoprotein.
L-dopa (ˌɛlˈdəupə) *n* a substance occurring naturally in the body and used to treat Parkinson's disease. Also called: **levodopa.** [C20: from *L-d(ihydr)o(xy)p(henyl)a(lanine)*]
LDS *abbrev. for:* **1** Latter-day Saints. **2** laus Deo semper. [L: praise be to God forever] **3** (in Britain) Licentiate in Dental Surgery.
lea (li:) *n* **1** *Poetic.* a meadow or field. **2** land that has been sown with grass seed. [OE *lēah*]
LEA (in Britain) *abbrev. for* Local Education Authority.
leach Ⓣ (li:tʃ) *vb* **1** to remove or be removed from a substance by a percolating liquid. **2** to lose or cause to lose soluble substances by the action of a percolating liquid. ◆ *n* **3** the act or process of leaching. **4** a substance that is leached or the constituents removed by leaching. **5** a porous vessel for leaching. [C17: var. of obs. *letch* to wet, ?from OE *leccan* to water]
▸ˈ**leacher** *n*
lead[1] Ⓣ (li:d) *vb* **leads, leading, led. 1** to show the way to (an individual or a group) by going with or ahead: *lead the party into the garden.* **2** to guide or be guided by holding, pulling, etc.: *he led the horse by its reins.* **3** (*tr*) to cause to act, feel, think, or behave in a certain way; induce; influence: *he led me to believe that he would go.* **4** (when *intr,* foll. by *to*) (of a road, route, etc.) to serve as the means of reaching a place. **5** (*tr*) to go ahead so as to indicate (esp. in **lead the way**). **6** to guide, control, or direct: *to lead an army.* **7** (*tr*) to direct the course of or conduct (water, a rope, or wire, etc.) along or as if along a channel. **8** to initiate the action of (something); have the principal part in (something): *to lead a discussion.* **9** to go at the head of or have the top position in (something): *he leads his class in geography.* **10** (*intr;* foll. by *with*) to have as the first or principal item: *the newspaper led with the royal birth.* **11** *Music, Brit.* to play first violin in (an orchestra). **12** to direct and guide (one's partner) in a dance. **13** (*tr*) **13a** to pass or spend: *I lead a miserable life.* **13b** to cause to pass a life of a particular kind: *to lead a person a dog's life.* **14** (*intr;* foll. by *to*) to tend (to) or result (in): *this will only lead to misery.* **15** to initiate a round of cards by putting down (the first card) or to have the right to do this: *she led a diamond.* **16** (*intr*) *Boxing.* to make an offensive blow, esp. as one's habitual attacking punch. ◆ *n* **17a** the first, foremost, or most prominent place. **17b** (*as modifier*): *lead singer.* **18** example, precedence, or leadership: *the class followed the teacher's lead.* **19** an advance or advantage held over others: *the runner had a lead of twenty yards.* **20** anything that guides or directs; indication; clue. **21** another name for **leash. 22** the act or prerogative of playing the first card in a round of cards or the card so played. **23** the principal role in a play, film, etc., or the person playing such a role. **24a** the principal news story in a newspaper: *the scandal was the lead in the papers.* **24b** (*as modifier*): *lead story.* **25** *Music.* an important entry assigned to one part. **26** a wire, cable, or other conductor for making an electrical connection. **27** *Boxing.* **27a** one's habitual attacking punch. **27b** a blow made with this. **28** a deposit of metal or ore; lode. ◆ See also **lead off, lead on,** etc. [OE *lǣdan;* rel. to *līthan* to travel]
lead[2] (lɛd) *n* **1** a heavy toxic bluish-white metallic element that is highly malleable: used in alloys, accumulators, cable sheaths, paints, and as a radiation shield. Symbol: Pb; atomic no.: 82; atomic wt.: 207.2. **2** a lead weight suspended on a line used to take soundings of the depth of water. **3** lead weights or shot, as used in cartridges, fishing lines, etc. **4** a thin grooved strip of lead for holding small panes of glass or pieces of stained glass. **5** (*pl*) **5a** thin sheets or strips of lead used as a roof covering. **5b** a flat or low-pitched roof covered with such sheets. **6** Also called: **leading.** *Printing.* a thin strip of type metal used for spacing between lines. **7a** graphite used for drawing. **7b** a thin stick of this material, esp. the core of a pencil. **8** (*modifier*) of, consisting of, relating to, or containing lead. ◆ *vb* (*tr*) **9** to fill or treat with lead. **10** to surround, cover, or secure with lead or leads. **11** *Printing.* to space (type) by use of leads. [OE]
lead acetate (lɛd) *n* a white crystalline toxic solid used in dyeing cotton and in making varnishes and enamels. Formula: $Pb(CH_3COOH)_2$. Systematic name: **lead ethanoate.**
lead chromate (lɛd) *n Chem.* a yellow solid used as a pigment, as in chrome yellow. Formula: $PbCrO_4$.
leaded (ˈlɛdɪd) *adj* (of windows) composed of small panes of glass held in place by thin grooved strips of lead: *leaded lights.*
leaden Ⓣ (ˈlɛdᵊn) *adj* **1** heavy and inert. **2** laboured or sluggish: *leaden steps.* **3** gloomy, spiritless, or lifeless. **4** made partly or wholly of lead. **5** of a dull greyish colour: *a leaden sky.*
▸ˈ**leadenly** *adv* ▸ˈ**leadenness** *n*
leader Ⓣ (ˈli:də) *n* **1** a person who rules, guides, or inspires others; head. **2** *Music.* **2a** Also called (esp. US and Canad.): **concertmaster.** the principal first violinist of an orchestra, who plays solo parts, and acts as the conductor's deputy and spokesman for the orchestra. **2b** *US.* a conductor or director of an orchestra or chorus. **3a** the leading horse or dog in a team. **3b** the first man on a climbing rope. **4** *Chiefly Brit.* the leading editorial in a newspaper. Also: **leading article. 5** *Angling.* another word for **trace**[2] (sense 2). **6** a strip of blank film or tape used to facilitate threading a projector, developing machine, etc. **7** (*pl*) *Printing.* rows of dots or hyphens used to guide the reader's eye across a page, as in a table of contents. **8** *Bot.* any of the long slender shoots that grow from the stem or branch of a tree. **9** *Brit.* a member of the Government having primary authority in initiating legislative business (esp. in **Leader of the House of Commons** and **Leader of the House of Lords**).
▸ˈ**leaderless** *adj*
leadership Ⓣ (ˈli:dəʃɪp) *n* **1** the position or function of a leader. **2** the period during which a person occupies the position of leader: *during her leadership very little was achieved.* **3a** the ability to lead. **3b** (*as modifier*): *leadership qualities.* **4** the leaders as a group of a party, union, etc.: *the union leadership is now very reactionary.*
lead-free (ˌlɛdˈfri:) *adj* See **unleaded.**
lead glass (lɛd) *n* glass that contains lead oxide as a flux.
lead-in (ˈli:dˌɪn) *n* **1** an introduction to a subject. **2** the connection between a radio transmitter, receiver, etc., and the aerial or transmission line.
leading[1] Ⓣ (ˈli:dɪŋ) *adj* **1** guiding, directing, or influencing. **2** (*prenominal*) principal or primary. **3** in the first position.
leading[2] (ˈlɛdɪŋ) *n Printing.* **1** the spacing between lines of photocomposed or digitized type. **2** another name for **lead**[2] (sense 6). ◆ Also called: **interlinear spacing.**
leading aircraftman (ˈli:dɪŋ) *n Brit. airforce.* the rank above aircraftman.
▸**leading aircraftwoman** *fem n*
leading edge (ˈli:dɪŋ) *n* **1** the forward edge of a propeller blade, wing, or aerofoil. Cf. **trailing edge. 2** *Electrical engineering.* the part of a pulse signal that has an increasing amplitude. ◆ *modifier.* **leading-edge. 3** advanced; foremost: *leading-edge technology.*
leading light (ˈli:dɪŋ) *n* an important or outstanding person, esp. in an organization.
leading note (ˈli:dɪŋ) *n Music.* **1** another word for **subtonic. 2** (esp. in cadences) a note that tends most naturally to resolve to the note lying one semitone above it.
leading question (ˈli:dɪŋ) *n* a question phrased in a manner that tends to suggest the desired answer, such as *What do you think of the horrible effects of pollution?*
leading rating (ˈli:dɪŋ) *n* a rank in the Royal Navy comparable but junior to that of a corporal in the army.
leading reins *or US & Canad.* **leading strings** (ˈli:dɪŋ) *pl n* **1** straps or a harness and strap used to assist and control a child who is learning to walk. **2** excessive guidance or restraint.
lead monoxide (lɛd) *n* a poisonous insoluble oxide of lead existing in red and yellow forms: used in making glass, glazes, and cements, and as a pigment. Formula: PbO. Systematic name: **lead(II) oxide.**
lead off Ⓣ (li:d) *vb* (*adv*) **1** to initiate the action of (something); begin. ◆ *n* **lead-off. 2** an initial move or action.
lead on Ⓣ (li:d) *vb* (*tr, adv*) to lure or entice, esp. into trouble or wrongdoing.

THESAURUS

leach *vb* **1, 2** = **extract,** drain, filter, filtrate, lixiviate (*Chemistry*), percolate, seep, strain
lead[1] *vb* **1, 2** = **guide,** conduct, escort, pilot, precede, show the way, steer, usher **3** = **cause,** dispose, draw, incline, induce, influence, persuade, prevail, prompt **6** = **command,** direct, govern, head, manage, preside over, supervise **9** = **be ahead (of),** blaze a trail, come first, exceed, excel, outdo, outstrip, surpass, transcend **13a** = **live,** experience, have, pass, spend, undergo **14** = **result in,** bring on, cause, conduce, contribute, produce, serve, tend ◆ *n* **17a** = **first place,** cutting edge, precedence, primacy, priority, supremacy, van, vanguard **18** = **example,** direction, guidance, leadership, model **19** = **advantage,** advance, edge, margin, start **20** = **clue,** guide, hint, indication, suggestion, tip, trace **23** = **leading role,** principal, protagonist, star part, title role ◆ *modifier* **24b** = **main,** chief, first, foremost, head, leading, most important, premier, primary, prime, principal
leaden *adj* **1** = **heavy,** burdensome, crushing, cumbersome, inert, lead, onerous, oppressive **2** = **laboured,** humdrum, plodding, sluggish, stiff, stilted, wooden **3** = **lifeless,** dismal, dreary, dull, gloomy, languid, listless, spiritless **5** = **grey,** dingy, greyish, lacklustre, louring *or* lowering, lustreless, overcast, sombre
leader *n* **1** = **principal,** boss (*inf.*), captain, chief, chieftain, commander, conductor, counsellor, director, guide, head, number one, ringleader, ruler, superior, torchbearer
Antonyms *n* adherent, disciple, follower, hanger-on, henchman, sidekick (*sl.*), supporter
leadership *n* **1** = **management,** administration, authority, command, control, direction, directorship, domination, guidance, influence, initiative, pre-eminence, running, superintendency, supremacy, sway
leading[1] *adj* **1, 2** = **principal,** chief, dominant, first, foremost, governing, greatest, highest, main, number one, outstanding, pre-eminent, primary, ruling, superior
Antonyms *adj* following, hindmost, incidental, inferior, lesser, minor, secondary, subordinate, superficial
lead off *vb* **1** = **begin,** commence, get going, get under way, inaugurate, initiate, kick off (*inf.*), open, set out, start, start the ball rolling (*inf.*)
lead on *vb* = **entice,** beguile, deceive, draw on, inveigle, lure, seduce, string along (*inf.*), tempt

lead pencil (lɛd) *n* a pencil containing a thin stick of a graphite compound.

lead poisoning (lɛd) *n* **1** acute or chronic poisoning by lead, characterized by abdominal pain, vomiting, convulsions, and coma. **2** *US sl.* death or injury resulting from being shot with bullets.

lead screw (li:d) *n* a threaded rod that drives the tool carriage in a lathe.

lead tetraethyl (lɛd) *n* another name for **tetraethyl lead.**

lead time (li:d) *n* **1** *Manufacturing, chiefly US.* the time between the design of a product and its production. **2** *Commerce.* the time from the placing of an order to the delivery of the goods.

lead up to ❶ (li:d) *vb* (*intr, adv + prep*) **1** to act as a preliminary or introduction to. **2** to approach (a topic) gradually or cautiously.

leaf ❶ (li:f) *n, pl* **leaves** (li:vz). **1** the main organ of photosynthesis and transpiration in higher plants, usually consisting of a flat green blade attached to the stem directly or by a stalk. **2** foliage collectively. **3 in leaf.** (of shrubs, trees, etc.) having a full complement of foliage leaves. **4** one of the sheets of paper in a book. **5** a hinged, sliding, or detachable part, such as an extension to a table. **6** metal in the form of a very thin flexible sheet: *gold leaf.* **7 take a leaf out of** (*or* **from**) **someone's book.** to imitate someone, esp. in one particular course of action. **8 turn over a new leaf.** to begin a new and improved course of behaviour. ◆ *vb* **9** (when *intr*, usually foll. by *through*) to turn (through pages, sheets, etc.) cursorily. **10** (*intr*) (of plants) to produce leaves. [OE]
►**'leafless** *adj* ►**'leaf,like** *adj*

leafage ('li:fɪdʒ) *n* a less common word for **foliage.**

leaflet ❶ ('li:flɪt) *n* **1** a printed and usually folded sheet of paper for distribution, usually free, esp. for advertising, giving information about a charity, etc. **2** any of the subdivisions of a compound leaf such as a fern leaf. **3** any small leaf or leaflike part. ◆ *vb* **leaflets, leafleting, leafleted. 4** to distribute leaflets (to).

leaf miner *n* **1** any of various insect larvae that bore into and feed on leaf tissue. **2** the adult insect of any of these larvae.

leaf mould *n* **1** a nitrogen-rich material consisting of decayed leaves, etc., used as a fertilizer. **2** any of various fungus diseases affecting the leaves of certain plants.

leaf spring *n* **1** one of a number of metal strips bracketed together in length to form a spring. **2** the compound spring so formed.

leafstalk ('li:f,stɔ:k) *n* the stalk attaching a leaf to a stem or branch. Technical name: **petiole.**

leafy ❶ ('li:fɪ) *adj* **leafier, leafiest. 1** covered with or having leaves. **2** resembling a leaf or leaves.
►**'leafiness** *n*

league[1] **❶** (li:g) *n* **1** an association or union of persons, nations, etc., formed to promote the interests of its members. **2** an association of sporting clubs that organizes matches between member teams. **3** a class, category, or level: *he is not in the same league.* **4 in league** (**with**). working or planning together with. **5** (*modifier*) of, involving, or belonging to a league: *a league game; a league table.* ◆ *vb* **leagues, leaguing, leagued. 6** to form or be formed into a league. [C15: from OF *ligue*, from It. *liga*, ult. from L *ligāre* to bind]

league[2] (li:g) *n* an obsolete unit of distance of varying length. It is commonly equal to 3 miles. [C14 *leuge*, from LL *leuga, leuca*, of Celtic origin]

league football *n* **1** Also called: **league.** *Chiefly Austral.* rugby league football. Cf. **rugby union. 2** *Austral.* an Australian Rules competition conducted within a league.

leaguer ('li:gə) *n Chiefly US & Canad.* a member of a league.

league table *n* **1** a list of sports clubs ranked in order according to their performance. **2** a comparison of performance in any sphere.

leak ❶ (li:k) *n* **1a** a crack, hole, etc., that allows the accidental escape or entrance of fluid, light, etc. **1b** such escaping or entering fluid, light, etc. **2 spring a leak.** to develop a leak. **3** something resembling this in effect: *a leak in the defence system.* **4** the loss of current from an electrical conductor because of faulty insulation, etc. **5** a disclosure of secret information. **6** the act or an instance of leaking. **7** a slang word for **urination.** ◆ *vb* **8** to enter or escape or allow to enter or escape through a crack, hole, etc. **9** (when *intr*, often foll. by *out*) to disclose (secret information) or (of secret information) to be disclosed. **10** (*intr*) a slang word for **urinate.** [C15: from ON]
►**'leaker** *n*

leakage ('li:kɪdʒ) *n* **1** the act or an instance of leaking. **2** something that escapes or enters by a leak. **3** *Physics.* an undesired flow of electric current, neutrons, etc.

leaky ❶ ('li:kɪ) *adj* **leakier, leakiest.** leaking or tending to leak.
►**'leakiness** *n*

leal (li:l) *adj Arch. or Scot.* loyal; faithful. [C13: from OF *leial*, from L *lēgālis* LEGAL; rel. to LOYAL]
►**'leally** *adv* ►**lealty** ('li:əltɪ) *n*

lean[1] **❶** (li:n) *vb* **leans, leaning, leaned** *or* **leant. 1** (foll. by *against, on,* or *upon*) to rest or cause to rest against a support. **2** to incline or cause to incline from a vertical position. **3** (*intr;* foll. by *to* or *towards*) to have or express a tendency or leaning. ◆ *n* **4** the condition of inclining from a vertical position. [OE *hleonian, hlinian*]

lean[2] **❶** (li:n) *adj* **1** (esp. of a person or animal) having no surplus flesh or bulk; not fat. **2** not bulky or full. **3** (of meat) having little or no fat. **4** not rich, abundant, or satisfying. **5** (of mixture of fuel and air) containing insufficient fuel and too much air. ◆ *n* **6** the part of meat that contains little or no fat. [OE *hlǣne*, of Gmc origin]
►**'leanly** *adv* ►**'leanness** *n*

lean-burn *adj* (esp. of an internal-combustion engine) designed to use a lean mixture of fuel and air in order to reduce petrol consumption and exhaust emissions.

leaning ❶ ('li:nɪŋ) *n* a tendency or inclination.

leant (lɛnt) *vb* a past tense and past participle of **lean**[1].

lean-to *n, pl* **lean-tos. 1** a roof that has a single slope adjoining a wall or building. **2** a shed or outbuilding with such a roof.

leap ❶ (li:p) *vb* **leaps, leaping, leapt** *or* **leaped. 1** (*intr*) to jump suddenly from one place to another. **2** (*intr;* often foll. by *at*) to move or react quickly. **3** (*tr*) to jump over. **4** to come into prominence rapidly: *the thought leapt into his mind.* **5** (*tr*) to cause (an animal, esp. a horse) to jump a barrier. ◆ *n* **6** the act of jumping. **7** a spot from which a leap was or may be made. **8** an abrupt change or increase. **9 a leap in the dark.** an action performed without knowledge of the consequences. **10 by leaps and bounds.** with unexpectedly rapid progress. [OE *hlēapan*]
►**'leaper** *n*

leapfrog ('li:p,frɒg) *n* **1** a children's game in which each player in turn leaps over the others' bent backs. ◆ *vb* **leapfrogs, leapfrogging, leapfrogged. 2a** (*intr*) to play leapfrog. **2b** (*tr*) to leap in this way over (something). **3** to advance or cause to advance by jumps or stages.

leap second *n* a second added to or removed from a scale for reckoning time on one particular occasion, to synchronize it with another scale.

leapt (lɛpt, li:pt) *vb* a past tense and past participle of **leap.**

leap year *n* a calendar year of 366 days, February 29 (**leap day**) being the additional day, that occurs every four years (those whose number is divisible by four) except for century years whose number is not divisible by 400.

learn ❶ (lɜ:n) *vb* **learns, learning, learned** (lɜ:nd) *or* **learnt. 1** (when *tr, may take a clause as object*) to gain knowledge of (something) or acquire skill in (some art or practice). **2** (*tr*) to commit to memory. **3** (*tr*) to gain by experience, example, etc. **4** (*intr;* often foll. by *of* or *about*) to become informed; know. **5** *Not standard.* to teach. [OE *leornian*]
►**'learnable** *adj* ►**'learner** *n*

learned ❶ ('lɜ:nɪd) *adj* **1** having great knowledge or erudition. **2** involving or characterized by scholarship. **3** (*prenominal*) a title applied in re-

THESAURUS

lead up to *vb* **1, 2** = **introduce**, approach, intimate, make advances, make overtures, pave the way, prepare for, prepare the way, work round to

leaf *n* **1** = **frond**, blade, bract, flag, needle, pad **4** = **page**, folio, sheet **8 turn over a new leaf** = **reform**, amend, begin anew, change, change one's ways, improve ◆ *vb* **9** *usually foll. by* **through** = **skim**, browse, flip, glance, riffle, thumb (through) **10** = **put out leaves**, bud, green, turn green

leaflet *n* **1** = **booklet**, advert (*Brit. inf.*), bill, brochure, circular, handbill, mailshot, pamphlet

leafy *adj* **1** = **green**, bosky (*literary*), in foliage, leafed, leaved, shaded, shady, springlike, summery, verdant, wooded

league[1] *n* **1** = **association**, alliance, band, coalition, combination, combine, compact, confederacy, confederation, consortium, federation, fellowship, fraternity, group, guild, order, partnership, union **3** *Informal* = **class**, ability group, category, level **4 in league (with)** = **collaborating**, allied, hand in glove, in cahoots (*inf.*), leagued ◆ *vb* **6** = **unite**, ally, amalgamate, associate, band, collaborate, combine, confederate, join forces

leak *n* **1a** = **hole**, aperture, chink, crack, crevice, fissure, opening, puncture **1b** = **leakage**, drip, leaking, oozing, percolation, seepage **5** = **disclosure**, divulgence ◆ *vb* **8** = **escape**, discharge, drip, exude, ooze, pass, percolate, seep, spill, trickle **9** = **disclose**, blow wide open (*sl.*), divulge, give away, let slip, let the cat out of the bag, make known, make public, pass on, reveal, spill the beans (*inf.*), tell

leaky *adj* = **leaking**, cracked, holey, not watertight, perforated, porous, punctured, split, waterlogged

lean[1] *vb* **1** = **rest**, be supported, prop, recline, repose **2** = **bend**, heel, incline, slant, slope, tilt, tip **3** = **tend**, be disposed to, be prone to, favour, gravitate towards, have a propensity, prefer

lean[2] *adj* **1** = **trim**, angular, bony, emaciated, gaunt, lank, rangy, scraggy, scrawny, skinny, slender, slim, spare, thin, unfatty, wiry **4** = **poor**, bare, barren, inadequate, infertile, meagre, pathetic, pitiful, scanty, sparse, unfruitful, unproductive

Antonyms *adj* ≠ **trim:** ample, brawny, burly, fat, full, obese, plump, portly ≠ **poor:** abundant, fertile, plentiful, profuse, rich

leaning *n* = **tendency**, aptitude, bent, bias, disposition, inclination, liking, partiality, penchant, predilection, proclivity, proneness, propensity, taste

leap *vb* **1** = **jump**, bounce, bound, caper, cavort, frisk, gambol, hop, skip, spring **2** = **rush**, arrive at, come to, form hastily, hasten, hurry, jump, reach **3** = **jump over**, clear, vault **4** = **increase**, advance, become prominent, escalate, gain attention, rocket, soar, surge ◆ *n* **6** = **jump**, bound, caper, frisk, hop, skip, spring, vault **8** = **rise**, change, escalation, increase, surge, upsurge, upswing

learn *vb* **1** = **master**, acquire, attain, become able, grasp, imbibe, pick up **2** = **memorize**, commit to memory, con (*arch.*), get off pat, get (something) word-perfect, learn by heart **4** = **discover**, ascertain, detect, determine, discern, find out, gain, gather, hear, suss (out) (*sl.*), understand

learned *adj* **1, 2** = **scholarly**, academic, cultured, erudite, experienced, expert, highbrow, intellectual, lettered, literate, skilled, versed, well-informed, well-read

Antonyms *adj* ignorant, illiterate, uneducated, unlearned

learner *n* **1** = **pupil**, apprentice, beginner, disci-

ferring to a member of the legal profession, esp. to a barrister: *my learned friend.*
▶ **'learnedly** *adv* ▶ **'learnedness** *n*

learning Ⓣ ('lɜːnɪŋ) *n* **1** knowledge gained by study; instruction or scholarship. **2** the act of gaining knowledge.

learning curve *n* a graphical representation of progress in learning: *I'm still only halfway up the learning curve.*

learnt (lɜːnt) *vb* a past tense and past participle of **learn.**

lease Ⓣ (liːs) *n* **1** a contract by which property is conveyed to a person for a specified period, usually for rent. **2** the instrument by which such property is conveyed. **3** the period of time for which it is conveyed. **4** a prospect of renewed health, happiness, etc.: *a new lease of life.* ◆ *vb* **leases, leasing, leased.** (*tr*) **5** to grant possession of (land, buildings, etc.) by lease. **6** to take a lease of (property); hold under a lease. [C15: via Anglo-F from OF *lais* (n), from *laissier* to let go, from L *laxāre* to loosen]
▶ **'leasable** *adj* ▶ **'leaser** *n*

leaseback ('liːsˌbæk) *n* a transaction in which the buyer leases the property to the seller.

leasehold ('liːsˌhəʊld) *n* **1** land or property held under a lease. **2** the tenure by which such property is held. **3** (*modifier*) held under a lease.
▶ **'lease,holder** *n*

leash Ⓣ (liːʃ) *n* **1** a line or rope used to walk or control a dog or other animal; lead. **2** something resembling this in function: *he kept a tight leash on his emotions.* **3 straining at the leash.** eagerly impatient to begin something. ◆ *vb* **4** (*tr*) to control or secure as by a leash. [C13: from OF *laisse,* from *laissier* to loose (hence, to let a dog run on a leash), ult. from L *laxus* lax]

least Ⓣ (liːst) *determiner* **1a the.** the superlative of **little:** *you have the least talent of anyone.* **1b** (*as pronoun; functioning as sing*): *least isn't necessarily worst.* **2 at least. 2a** if nothing else: *you should at least try.* **2b** at the least. **3 at the least.** Also: **at least.** at the minimum: *at the least you should earn a hundred pounds.* **4 in the least.** (*usually used with a negative*) in the slightest degree; at all: *I don't mind in the least.* ◆ *adv* **5 the least.** superlative of **little:** *they travel the least.* ◆ *adj* **6** of very little importance. [OE *lǣst,* sup. of *lǣssa* less]

least common denominator *n* another name for **lowest common denominator.**

least common multiple *n* another name for **lowest common multiple.**

least squares *n* a method for determining the best value of an unknown quantity relating one or more sets of observations or measurements, esp. to find a curve that best fits a set of data.

leastways ('liːstˌweɪz) *or US & Canad.* **leastwise** *adv Inf.* at least; anyway; at any rate.

least-worst *adj Inf.* bad but better than any available alternative: *a least-worst scenario.*

leather ('lɛðə) *n* **1a** a material consisting of the skin of an animal made smooth and flexible by tanning, removing the hair, etc. **1b** (*as modifier*): *leather goods.* **2** (*pl*) leather clothes, esp. as worn by motorcyclists. ◆ *vb* (*tr*) **3** to cover with leather. **4** to whip as with a leather strap. [OE *lether-* (in compound words)]

leatherjacket ('lɛðəˌdʒækɪt) *n* **1** any of various tropical fishes having a leathery skin. **2** the greyish-brown tough-skinned larva of certain craneflies, which destroy the roots of grasses, etc.

leathern ('lɛðən) *adj Arch.* made of or resembling leather.

leatherneck ('lɛðəˌnɛk) *n Sl.* a member of the US Marine Corps. [from the custom of facing the neckband of their uniform with leather]

leathery Ⓣ ('lɛðərɪ) *adj* having the appearance or texture of leather, esp. in toughness.
▶ **'leatheriness** *n*

leave[1] Ⓣ (liːv) *vb* **leaves, leaving, left.** (*mainly tr*) **1** (*also intr*) to go or depart (from a person or place). **2** to cause to remain behind, often by mistake, in a place: *he often leaves his keys in his coat.* **3** to cause to be or remain in a specified state: *paying the bill left him penniless.* **4** to renounce or abandon: *to leave a political movement.* **5** to refrain from consuming or doing something: *the things we have left undone.* **6** to result in; cause: *childhood problems often leave emotional scars.* **7** to entrust or commit: *leave the shopping to her.* **8** to pass in a specified direction: *flying out of the country, we left the cliffs on our left.* **9** to be survived by (members of one's family): *he leaves a wife and two children.* **10** to bequeath: *he left his investments to his children.* **11** (*tr*) to have as a remainder: *37 – 14 leaves 23.* **12** *Not standard.* to permit; let. **13 leave (someone) alone. 13a** Also: **let alone.** See **let**[1] (sense 6). **13b** to permit to stay or be alone. [OE *lǣfan;* rel. to *belīfan* to be left as a remainder] ◆ See also **leave off, leave out.**
▶ **'leaver** *n*

leave[2] Ⓣ (liːv) *n* **1** permission to do something: *he was granted leave to speak.* **2 by** *or* **with your leave.** with your permission. **3** permission to be absent, as from a place of work: *leave of absence.* **4** the duration of such absence: *ten days' leave.* **5** a farewell or departure (esp. in **take (one's) leave**). **6 on leave.** officially excused from work or duty. **7 take leave (of).** to say farewell (to). [OE *lēaf;* rel. to *alȳfan* to permit]

leave[3] (liːv) *vb* **leaves, leaving, leaved.** (*intr*) to produce or grow leaves.

leaved (liːvd) *adj* **a** having a leaf or leaves; leafed. **b** (*in combination*): *a five-leaved stem.*

leaven Ⓣ ('lɛvᵊn) *n also* **leavening. 1** any substance that produces fermentation in dough or batter, such as yeast, and causes it to rise. **2** a piece of such a substance kept to ferment a new batch of dough. **3** an agency or influence that produces a gradual change. ◆ *vb* (*tr*) **4** to cause fermentation in (dough or batter). **5** to pervade, causing a gradual change, esp. with some moderating or enlivening influence. [C14: via OF ult. from L *levāmen* relief, (hence, raising agent), from *levāre* to raise]

leave off Ⓣ *vb* **1** (*intr*) to stop; cease. **2** (*tr, adv*) to stop wearing or using.

leave out Ⓣ *vb* (*tr, adv*) **1** to cause to remain in the open. **2** to omit or exclude.

leaves (liːvz) *n* the plural of **leaf.**

leave-taking Ⓣ *n* the act of departing; a farewell.

leavings Ⓣ ('liːvɪŋz) *pl n* something remaining, such as food on a plate, residue, refuse, etc.

Lebensraum ('leɪbənzˌraʊm) *n* territory claimed by a nation or state as necessary for survival or growth. [G, lit.: living space]

LEC (lɛk) *n acronym for* Local Enterprise Company. See **Training Agency.**

lech (lɛtʃ) *Inf.* ◆ *vb* **1** (*intr; usually foll. by after*) to behave lecherously (towards); lust (after). ◆ *n* **2** a lecherous act or indulgence. [C19: back formation from LECHER]

lecher Ⓣ ('lɛtʃə) *n* a promiscuous or lewd man. [C12: from OF *lecheor,* from *lechier* to lick, of Gmc origin]

lecherous Ⓣ ('lɛtʃərəs) *adj* characterized by or inciting lechery.
▶ **'lecherously** *adv*

lechery Ⓣ ('lɛtʃərɪ) *n, pl* **lecheries.** unrestrained and promiscuous sexuality.

lecithin ('lɛsɪθɪn) *n Biochem.* any of a group of phospholipids that are found in many plant and animal tissues, esp. egg yolk: used in making candles, cosmetics, and inks, and as an emulsifier and stabilizer (**E322**) in foods. Systematic name: **phosphatidycholine.** [C19: from Gk *lekithos* egg yolk]

lecky ('lɛkɪ) *n Brit. sl.* short for **electricity.**

Leclanché cell (ləˈklɑːnʃeɪ) *n Electrical engineering.* a primary cell with a carbon anode, surrounded by crushed carbon and manganese dioxide in a porous container in an electrolyte of aqueous ammonium chloride into which a zinc cathode dips. [C19: after Georges *Leclanché* (1839–82), F engineer]

lectern ('lɛktən) *n* **1** a reading desk in a church. **2** any similar desk or

THESAURUS

ple, neophyte, novice, scholar, student, trainee, tyro
Antonyms *n* adept, coach, expert, grandmaster, guru, instructor, master, maven, mentor, past master, teacher, tutor, virtuoso, wizard

learning *n* **1** = **knowledge**, acquirements, attainments, culture, education, erudition, information, letters, literature, lore, research, scholarship, schooling, wisdom **2** = **study**, education, schooling, tuition

lease *vb* **5, 6** = **hire**, charter, let, loan, rent

leash *n* **1** = **lead**, rein, tether **2** = **restraint**, check, control, curb, hold ◆ *vb* **4** = **restrain**, check, control, curb, fasten, hold back, secure, suppress

least *determiner* **1** = **smallest**, feeblest, fewest, last, lowest, meanest, minimum, minutest, poorest, slightest, tiniest

leathery *adj* = **tough**, coriaceous, durable, hard, hardened, leatherlike, leathern (*arch.*), rough, rugged, wrinkled

leave[1] *vb* **1** = **depart**, abandon, abscond, decamp, desert, disappear, do a bunk (*Brit. sl.*), exit, flit (*inf.*), forsake, go, go away, make tracks, move, pull out, quit, relinquish, retire, set out, take off (*inf.*), withdraw **2** = **forget**, lay down, leave behind, mislay **4** = **renounce**, abandon, desert **5** = **give up**, cease, desist, drop, forbear, refrain, relinquish, stop **6** = **cause**, generate, produce, result in **7** = **entrust**, allot, assign, cede, commit, consign, give over, refer **10** = **bequeath**, demise, devise (*Law*), hand down, transmit, will
Antonyms *vb* ≠ **depart:** appear, arrive, come, emerge, stay ≠ **give up:** assume, continue, hold, persist, remove, retain

leave[2] *n* **1** = **permission**, allowance, authorization, concession, consent, dispensation, freedom, liberty, sanction **3, 4** = **holiday**, furlough, leave of absence, sabbatical, time off, vacation **5** = **departure**, adieu, farewell, goodbye, leave-taking, parting, retirement, withdrawal
Antonyms *n* ≠ **permission:** denial, prohibition, refusal, rejection ≠ **holiday:** duty ≠ **departure:** arrival, stay

leaven *n* **1, 2** = **yeast**, barm, ferment, leavening **3** = **catalyst**, influence, inspiration ◆ *vb* **4** = **ferment**, lighten, raise, work **5** = **stimulate**, elevate, imbue, inspire, permeate, pervade, quicken, suffuse

leave off *vb* **1** = **stop**, abstain, belay (*Nautical*), break off, cease, desist, discontinue, end, give over (*inf.*), give up, halt, kick (*inf.*), knock off (*inf.*), refrain

leave out *vb* **2** = **omit**, bar, cast aside, count out, disregard, except, exclude, ignore, neglect, overlook, reject

leave-taking *n* = **departure**, farewell, going, goodbye, leaving, parting, sendoff (*inf.*), valediction

leavings *pl n* = **leftovers**, bits, dregs, fragments, pieces, refuse, remains, remnants, residue, scraps, spoil, sweepings, waste

lecher *n* = **womanizer**, adulterer, Casanova, debauchee, dirty old man, Don Juan, fornicator, goat (*inf.*), lech *or* letch (*inf.*), libertine, profligate, rake, roué, satyr, seducer, sensualist, wanton, wolf (*inf.*)

lecherous *adj* = **lustful**, carnal, concupiscent, lascivious, lewd, libidinous, licentious, prurient, randy (*inf., chiefly Brit.*), raunchy (*sl.*), ruttish, salacious, unchaste, wanton
Antonyms *adj* prim, proper, prudish, puritanical, strait-laced, virginal, virtuous

lechery *n* = **lustfulness**, carnality, concupiscence, debauchery, lasciviousness, lecherousness, leching (*inf.*), lewdness, libertinism, libidinousness, licentiousness, lust, profligacy, prurience, rakishness, randiness (*inf., chiefly Brit.*), salaciousness, sensuality, wantonness, womanizing

support. [C14: from OF *lettrun,* from LL *lectrum,* ult. from *legere* to read]

lectionary ('lɛkʃənərɪ) *n, pl* **lectionaries.** a book containing readings appointed to be read at divine services. [C15: from Church L *lectiōnārium,* from *lectio* a reading, from *legere* to read]

lector ('lɛktɔː) *n* **1** a lecturer or reader in certain universities. **2** *RC Church.* **2a** a person appointed to read lessons at certain services. **2b** (in convents or monastic establishments) a member of the community appointed to read aloud during meals. [C15: from L, from *legere* to read]

lecture ❶ ('lɛktʃə) *n* **1** a discourse on a particular subject given or read to an audience. **2** the text of such a discourse. **3** a method of teaching by formal discourse. **4** a lengthy reprimand or scolding. ◆ *vb* **lectures, lecturing, lectured. 5** to give or read a lecture (to an audience or class). **6** (*tr*) to reprimand at length. [C14: from Med. L *lectūra* reading, from *legere* to read]
▸ **'lecturer** *n* ▸ **'lectureship** *n*

led (lɛd) *vb* the past tense and past participle of **lead**[1].

LED *Electronics. abbrev. for* light-emitting diode.

lederhosen ('leɪdəˌhəuzᵊn) *pl n* leather shorts with H-shaped braces, worn by men in Austria, Bavaria, etc. [G]

ledge ❶ (lɛdʒ) *n* **1** a narrow horizontal surface resembling a shelf and projecting from a wall, window, etc. **2** a layer of rock that contains an ore; vein. **3** a ridge of rock that lies beneath the surface of the sea. **4** a narrow shelflike projection on a cliff or mountain. [C14 *legge,* ?from *leggen* to LAY[1]]
▸ **'ledgy** *or* **ledged** *adj*

ledger ('lɛdʒə) *n* **1** *Book-keeping.* the principal book in which the commercial transactions of a company are recorded. **2** *Angling.* a wire trace that allows the weight to rest on the bottom and the bait to float freely. ◆ *vb* **3** (*intr*) *Angling.* to fish using a ledger. [C15 *legger* book retained in a specific place, prob. from *leggen* to LAY[1]]

ledger line *n Music.* a short line placed above or below the staff to accommodate notes representing pitches above or below the staff.

lee ❶ (liː) *n* **1** a sheltered part or side; the side away from the direction from which the wind is blowing. ◆ *adj* **2** (*prenominal*) *Naut.* on, at, or towards the side or part away from the wind: *on a lee shore.* Cf. **weather** (sense 4). [OE *hlēow* shelter]

leech[1] ❶ (liːtʃ) *n* **1** an annelid worm which has a sucker at each end of the body and feeds on the blood or tissues of other animals. **2** a person who clings to or preys on another person. **3a** an archaic word for **physician. 3b** (*in combination*): *leechcraft.* ◆ *vb* (*tr*) **4** to use leeches to suck the blood of (a person), as a method of medical treatment. [OE *lǣce, lœce*]

leech[2] (liːtʃ) *n Naut.* the after edge of a fore-and-aft sail or either of the vertical edges of a squaresail. [C15: of Gmc origin]

leek (liːk) *n* **1** a vegetable with a slender white bulb, cylindrical stem, and broad flat overlapping leaves. **2** a leek, or a representation of one, as a national emblem of Wales. [OE *lēac*]

leer ❶ (lɪə) *vb* **1** (*intr*) to give an oblique, sneering, or suggestive look or grin. ◆ *n* **2** such a look. [C16: ? verbal use of obs. *leer* cheek, from OE *hlēor*]
▸ **'leering** *adj, n* ▸ **'leeringly** *adv*

leery ❶ ('lɪərɪ) *adj* **leerier, leeriest. 1** *Now chiefly dialect.* knowing or sly. **2** *Sl.* (foll. by *of*) suspicious or wary. [C18: ?from obs. sense (to look askance) of LEER]
▸ **'leeriness** *n*

lees ❶ (liːz) *pl n* the sediment from an alcoholic drink. [C14: pl of obs. *lee,* from OF, prob. from Celtic]

leet (liːt) *n Scot.* a list of candidates for an office. [C15: ?from Anglo-F *litte,* var. of LIST[1]]

leeward ('liːwəd; *Naut.* 'luːəd) *Chiefly naut.* ◆ *adj* **1** of, in, or moving to the quarter towards which the wind blows. ◆ *n* **2** the point or quarter towards which the wind blows. **3** the side towards the lee. ◆ *adv* **4** towards the lee. ◆ Cf. **windward.**

lee wave *n Meteorol.* a stationary wave sometimes formed in an air stream on the leeward side of a hill or mountain range.

leeway ❶ ('liːˌweɪ) *n* **1** room for free movement within limits, as in action or expenditure. **2** sideways drift of a boat or aircraft.

left[1] ❶ (lɛft) *adj* **1** (*usually prenominal*) of or designating the side of something or someone that faces west when the front is turned towards the north. **2** (*usually prenominal*) worn on a left hand, foot, etc. **3** (*sometimes cap.*) of or relating to the political left. **4** (*sometimes cap.*) radical or progressive. ◆ *adv* **5** on or in the direction of the left. ◆ *n* **6** a left side, direction, position, area, or part. Related adjs.: **sinister, sinistral. 7** (*often cap.*) the supporters or advocates of varying degrees of social, political, or economic change, reform, or revolution. **8** *Boxing.* **8a** a blow with the left hand. **8b** the left hand. [OE *left* idle, weak, var. of *lyft-* (in *lyftādl* palsy, lit.: left-disease)]

left[2] (lɛft) *vb* the past tense and past participle of **leave**[1].

left-hand *adj* (*prenominal*) **1** of, relating to, located on, or moving towards the left. **2** for use by the left hand; left-handed.

left-handed ❶ *adj* **1** using the left hand with greater ease than the right. **2** performed with the left hand. **3** designed or adapted for use by the left hand. **4** awkward or clumsy. **5** ironically ambiguous: *a left-handed compliment.* **6** turning from right to left; anticlockwise. ◆ *adv* **7** with the left hand.
▸ **ˌleft-'handedly** *adv* ▸ **ˌleft-'handedness** *n* ▸ **ˌleft-'hander** *n*

leftist ('lɛftɪst) *adj* **1** of, tending towards, or relating to the political left or its principles. ◆ *n* **2** a person who supports or belongs to the political left.
▸ **'leftism** *n*

left-luggage office *n Brit.* a place at a railway station, etc., where luggage may be left for a small charge. US and Canad. name: **checkroom.**

leftover ❶ ('lɛftˌəuvə) *n* **1** (*often pl*) an unused portion or remnant, as of material or of cooked food. ◆ *adj* **2** left as an unused portion.

leftward ('lɛftwəd) *adj* **1** on or towards the left. ◆ *adv* **2** a variant of **leftwards.**

leftwards ('lɛftwədz) *or* **leftward** *adv* towards or on the left.

left wing ❶ *n* **1** (*often cap.*) the leftist faction of an assembly, party, group, etc.; the radical or progressive wing. **2** *Sport.* **2a** the left-hand side of the field of play from the point of view of either team facing its opponents' goal. **2b** a player positioned in this area in certain games. ◆ *adj* **left-wing. 3** of, belonging to, or relating to the political left wing.
▸ **ˌleft-'winger** *n*

lefty ('lɛftɪ) *n, pl* **lefties.** *Inf.* **1** a left-winger. **2** *Chiefly US & Canad.* a left-handed person.

leg ❶ (lɛg) *n* **1** either of the two lower limbs in humans, or any similar or analogous structure in animals that is used for locomotion or support. **2** this part of an animal, esp. the thigh, used for food: *leg of lamb.* **3** something similar to a leg in appearance or function, such as one of the four supporting members of a chair. **4** a branch, limb, or part of a forked or jointed object. **5** the part of a garment that covers the leg. **6** a section or part of a journey or course. **7** a single stage, lap, length, etc., in a relay race. **8** either the opposite or adjacent side of a right-angled triangle. **9** one of a series of games, matches, or parts of games. **10** *Austral. & NZ.* either one of two races on which a cumulative bet has been placed. **11** *Cricket.* **11a** the side of the field to the left of a right-handed batsman as he faces the bowler. **11b** (*as modifier*): *a leg slip; leg stump.* **12 not have a leg to stand on.** *Inf.* to have no reasonable or logical basis for an opinion or argument. **13 on his, its,** etc., **last legs.** (of a person or thing) worn out; exhausted. **14 pull (someone's) leg.** *Inf.* to tease, fool, or make fun of (someone). **15 shake a leg.** *Inf.* to hurry up: usually used in the imperative. **16 stretch one's legs.** to stand up or walk around, esp. after sitting for some time. ◆ *vb* **legs, legging, legged. 17 leg it.** *Inf.* to walk, run, or hurry. [C13: from ON *leggr,* from ?]

leg. *abbrev. for:* **1** legal. **2** legate. **3** legato. **4** legislation. **5** legislative. **6** legislature.

legacy ❶ ('lɛgəsɪ) *n, pl* **legacies. 1** a gift by will, esp. of money or personal property. **2** something handed down or received from an ancestor or predecessor. [C14 (meaning: office of a legate), C15 (meaning: bequest): from Med. L *lēgātia* commission; see LEGATE]

legal ❶ ('liːgᵊl) *adj* **1** established by or founded upon law; lawful. **2** of or relating to law. **3** recognized, enforceable, or having a remedy at law

THESAURUS

lecture *n* **1** = **talk**, address, discourse, disquisition, harangue, instruction, lesson, speech **4** = **telling off** (*inf.*), castigation, censure, chiding, dressing-down (*inf.*), rebuke, reprimand, reproof, scolding, talking-to (*inf.*) ◆ *vb* **5** = **talk**, address, discourse, expound, give a talk, harangue, hold forth, speak, spout, teach **6** = **tell off** (*inf.*), admonish, bawl out (*inf.*), berate, carpet (*inf.*), castigate, censure, chew out, chide, give a rocket (*Brit. & NZ inf.*), read the riot act, reprimand, reprove, scold, tear into (*inf.*), tear (someone) off a strip (*Brit. inf.*)

ledge *n* **1, 3, 4** = **shelf**, mantle, projection, ridge, sill, step

lee *n* **1** = **shelter**, cover, protection, refuge, screen, shade, shadow, shield

leech[1] *n* **2** = **parasite**, bloodsucker (*inf.*), freeloader (*sl.*), hanger-on, ligger (*sl.*), sponger (*inf.*), sycophant

leer *vb, n* **1, 2** = **grin**, drool, eye, gloat, goggle, ogle, smirk, squint, stare, wink

leery *adj* **2** *Slang* = **wary**, careful, cautious, chary, distrustful, doubting, dubious, on one's guard, sceptical, shy, suspicious, uncertain, unsure

lees *pl n* = **sediment**, deposit, dregs, grounds, precipitate, refuse, settlings

leeway *n* **1** = **room**, elbowroom, latitude, margin, play, scope, space

left[1] *adj* **1** = **left-hand**, larboard (*Nautical*), port, sinistral **3, 4** = **socialist**, leftist, left-wing, liberal, progressive, radical

left-handed *adj* **4** = **awkward**, cack-handed (*inf.*), careless, clumsy, fumbling, gauche, maladroit **5** = **ambiguous**, backhanded, double-edged, enigmatic, equivocal, indirect, ironic, sardonic

leftover *n* **1** = **remnant**, leaving, oddment, remains, scrap ◆ *adj* **2** = **surplus**, excess, extra, remaining, uneaten, unused, unwanted

left wing *adj* **left-wing 3** = **socialist**, collectivist, communist, Marxist, radical, red (*inf.*)

leg *n* **1** = **limb**, lower limb, member, pin (*inf.*), stump (*inf.*) **3** = **support**, brace, prop, upright **6** = **stage**, lap, part, portion, section, segment, stretch **12 not have a leg to stand on** *Informal* = **have no basis**, be defenceless, be full of holes, be illogical, be invalid, be undermined, be vulnerable, lack support **13 on one's (its) last legs** = **worn out**, about to break down, about to collapse, at death's door, dying, exhausted, failing, giving up the ghost **14 pull someone's leg** *Informal* = **tease**, chaff, deceive, fool, have (someone) on, joke, kid (*inf.*), make fun of, poke fun at, rag, rib (*inf.*), trick, twit, wind up (*Brit. sl.*) **15 shake a leg** *Informal* = **hurry**, get a move on (*inf.*), get cracking (*inf.*), hasten, look lively (*inf.*), rush, stir one's stumps **16 stretch one's legs** = **take a walk**, exercise, go for a walk, move about, promenade, stroll, take the air ◆ *vb* **17 leg it** *Informal* = **run**, go on foot, hotfoot, hurry, skedaddle (*inf.*), walk

legacy *n* **1** = **bequest**, devise (*Law*), estate, gift, heirloom, inheritance **2** = **heritage**, birthright, endowment, inheritance, patrimony, throwback, tradition

legal *adj* **1** = **lawful**, allowable, allowed, authorized, constitutional, legalized, legitimate, licit,

rather than in equity. **4** relating to or characteristic of the profession of law. [C16: from L *lēgālis*, from *lēx* law]
▸ **'legally** *adv*

legal aid *n* financial assistance available to persons unable to meet the full cost of legal proceedings.

legalese (ˌliːgəˈliːz) *n* the conventional language in which legal documents are written.

legalism ⓣ (ˈliːgəˌlɪzəm) *n* strict adherence to the law, esp. the letter of the law rather than its spirit.
▸ **'legalist** *n, adj* ▸ **ˌlegal'istic** *adj*

legality ⓣ (lɪˈgælɪtɪ) *n, pl* **legalities. 1** the state or quality of being legal or lawful. **2** adherence to legal principles.

legalize ⓣ *or* **legalise** (ˈliːgəˌlaɪz) *vb* **legalizes, legalizing, legalized** *or* **legalises, legalising, legalised.** (*tr*) to make lawful or legal.
▸ **ˌlegali'zation** *or* **ˌlegali'sation** *n*

legal tender ⓣ *n* currency that a creditor must by law accept in redemption of a debt.

legate ⓣ (ˈlɛgɪt) *n* **1** a messenger, envoy, or delegate. **2** *RC Church.* an emissary representing the Pope. [OE, via OF from L *lēgātus* deputy, from *lēgāre* to delegate; rel. to *lēx* law]
▸ **'legateˌship** *n*

legatee ⓣ (ˌlɛgəˈtiː) *n* a person to whom a legacy is bequeathed.

legation ⓣ (lɪˈgeɪʃən) *n* **1** a diplomatic mission headed by a minister. **2** the official residence and office of a diplomatic minister. **3** the act of sending forth a diplomatic envoy. **4** the mission of a diplomatic envoy. **5** the rank or office of a legate. [C15: from L *lēgātiō*, from *lēgātus* LEGATE]

legato (lɪˈgɑːtəʊ) *Music.* ◆ *adj, adv* **1** to be performed smoothly and connectedly. ◆ *n, pl* **legatos. 2a** a style of playing with no perceptible gaps between notes. **2b** (*as modifier*): *a legato passage.* [C19: from It., lit.: bound]

leg before wicket *n Cricket.* a manner of dismissal on the grounds that a batsman has been struck on the leg by a bowled ball that otherwise would have hit the wicket. Abbrev.: **lbw.**

leg break *n Cricket.* a bowled ball that spins from leg to off on pitching.

legend ⓣ (ˈlɛdʒənd) *n* **1** a popular story handed down from earlier times whose truth has not been ascertained. **2** a group of such stories: *the Arthurian legend.* **3** a modern story that has the characteristics of a traditional tale. **4** a person whose fame or notoriety makes him a source of exaggerated or romanticized tales. **5** an inscription or title, as on a coin or beneath a coat of arms. **6** explanatory matter accompanying a table, map, chart, etc. [C14 (in the sense: a saint's life): from Med. L *legenda* passages to be read, from L *legere* to read]

legendary ⓣ (ˈlɛdʒəndərɪ, -drɪ) *adj* **1** of or relating to legend. **2** celebrated or described in a legend or legends. **3** very famous or notorious.

legerdemain ⓣ (ˌlɛdʒədəˈmeɪn) *n* **1** another name for **sleight of hand. 2** cunning deception or trickery. [C15: from OF: light of hand]

leger line (ˈlɛdʒə) *n* a variant spelling of **ledger line.**

legged (ˈlɛgɪd, lɛgd) *adj* **a** having a leg or legs. **b** (*in combination*): *three-legged; long-legged.*

leggiero (lɛdʒˈɛərəʊ) *adj, adv Music.* to be performed lightly and nimbly. [It.]

leggings (ˈlɛgɪŋz) *pl n* **1** an extra outer covering for the lower legs. **2** children's closefitting trousers, usually with a strap under the instep, worn for warmth in winter. **3** a fashion garment for women consiting of closefitting trousers.

leggy (ˈlɛgɪ) *adj* **leggier, leggiest. 1** having unusually long legs. **2** (of a woman) having long and shapely legs. **3** (of a plant) having an unusually long and weak stem.
▸ **'legginess** *n*

leghorn (ˈlɛgˌhɔːn) *n* **1** a type of Italian wheat straw that is woven into hats. **2** any hat made from this straw. [C19: after LEGHORN (Livorno), a port in W central Italy.]

Leghorn (lɛˈgɔːn) *n* a breed of domestic fowl.

legible ⓣ (ˈlɛdʒəbᵊl) *adj* (of handwriting, print, etc.) able to be read or deciphered. [C14: from LL *legibilis*, from L *legere* to read]
▸ **ˌlegi'bility** *n* ▸ **'legibly** *adv*

legion ⓣ (ˈliːdʒən) *n* **1** a unit in the ancient Roman army of infantry with supporting cavalry of three to six thousand men. **2** any large military force: *the French Foreign Legion.* **3** (*usually cap.*) an association of ex-servicemen: *the British Legion.* **4** (*often pl*) any very large number. ◆ *adj* **5** (*usually postpositive*) very numerous. [C13: from OF, from L *legio*, from *legere* to choose]

legionary (ˈliːdʒənərɪ) *adj* **1** of a legion. ◆ *n, pl* **legionaries. 2** a soldier belonging to a legion.

legionnaire (ˌliːdʒəˈnɛə) *n* (*often cap.*) a member of certain military forces or associations.

Legionnaire's disease (ˌliːdʒəˈnɛəz) *n* a serious, sometimes fatal, infection, caused by a bacterium (**legionella**), which has symptoms similar to those of pneumonia. [C20: after the outbreak at a meeting of the American Legion in Philadelphia in 1976]

legislate ⓣ (ˈlɛdʒɪsˌleɪt) *vb* **legislates, legislating, legislated. 1** (*intr*) to make or pass laws. **2** (*tr*) to bring into effect by legislation. [C18: back formation from LEGISLATOR]

legislation ⓣ (ˌlɛdʒɪsˈleɪʃən) *n* **1** the act or process of making laws. **2** the laws so made.

legislative ⓣ (ˈlɛdʒɪslətɪv) *adj* **1** of or relating to legislation. **2** having the power or function of legislating: *a legislative assembly.* **3** of or relating to a legislature.
▸ **'legislatively** *adv*

legislative assembly *n* (*often caps.*) **1** the bicameral legislature in 28 states of the US. **2** the chamber of the bicameral state legislatures in several Commonwealth countries, such as Australia. **3** the unicameral legislature in most Canadian provinces. **4** any assembly with legislative powers.

legislative council *n* (*often caps.*) **1** the upper chamber of certain bicameral legislatures, such as those of the Indian and Australian states (except Queensland). **2** the unicameral legislature of certain colonies or dependent territories. **3** (in the US) a committee of members of both chambers of a state legislature that discusses problems, constructs a legislative programme, etc.

legislator ⓣ (ˈlɛdʒɪsˌleɪtə) *n* **1** a person concerned with the making of laws. **2** a member of a legislature. [C17: from L *lēgis lātor*, from *lēx* law + *lātor* from *lātus*, p.p. of *ferre* to bring]

legislature ⓣ (ˈlɛdʒɪsˌleɪtʃə) *n* a body of persons vested with power to make and repeal laws.

legit (lɪˈdʒɪt) *Sl.* ◆ *adj* **1** short for **legitimate.** ◆ *n* **2** legitimate drama.

legitimate ⓣ *adj* (lɪˈdʒɪtɪmɪt). **1** born in lawful wedlock. **2** conforming to established standards of usage, behaviour, etc. **3** based on correct or acceptable principles of reasoning. **4** authorized by or in accordance with law. **5** of, relating to, or ruling by hereditary right: *a legitimate monarch.* **6** of or relating to a body of famous long-established plays as distinct from films, television, vaudeville, etc. ◆ *vb* (lɪˈdʒɪtɪˌmeɪt), **legitimates, legitimating, legitimated. 7** (*tr*) to make, pronounce, or show to be legitimate. [C15: from Med. L *lēgitimātus* made legal, from *lēx* law]
▸ **le'gitimacy** *n* ▸ **le'gitimately** *adv* ▸ **leˌgiti'mation** *n*

legitimist (lɪˈdʒɪtɪmɪst) *n* a monarchist who supports the rule of a legitimate dynasty or of its senior branch.
▸ **le'gitimism** *n*

legitimize ⓣ, **legitimise** (lɪˈdʒɪtɪˌmaɪz) *or* **legitimatize, legitimatise** (lɪˈdʒɪtɪməˌtaɪz) *vb* **legitimizes, legitimizing, legitimized; legitimises, le-**

THESAURUS

permissible, proper, rightful, sanctioned, valid **2, 4** = **judicial**, forensic, judiciary, juridical

legalistic *adj* = **hairsplitting**, contentious, disputatious, literal, litigious, narrow, narrow-minded, polemical, strict

legality *n* **1** = **lawfulness**, accordance with the law, admissibleness, legitimacy, permissibility, rightfulness, validity

legalize *vb* = **permit**, allow, approve, authorize, decriminalize, legitimate, legitimize, license, sanction, validate

legal tender *n* = **currency**, medium, money, payment, specie

legate *n* **1** = **messenger**, ambassador, delegate, depute (*Scot.*), deputy, emissary, envoy, nuncio

legatee *n* = **beneficiary**, heir, inheritor, recipient

legation *n* **1** = **delegation**, consulate, diplomatic mission, embassy, envoys, ministry, representation

legend *n* **1, 3** = **myth**, fable, fiction, folk tale, narrative, saga, story, tale, urban legend, urban myth **4** = **celebrity**, big name, celeb (*inf.*), luminary, marvel, megastar (*inf.*), phenomenon, prodigy, spectacle, wonder **5** = **inscription**, caption, device, motto **6** = **key**, cipher, code, table of symbols

legendary *adj* **1, 2** = **mythical**, apocryphal, fabled, fabulous, fanciful, fictitious, romantic, storied, traditional **3** = **famous**, celebrated, famed, illustrious, immortal, renowned, well-known
Antonyms *adj* ≠ **mythical:** factual, genuine, historical ≠ **famous:** unknown

legerdemain *n* **1** = **sleight of hand**, prestidigitation **2** = **deception**, artfulness, artifice, chicanery, contrivance, craftiness, cunning, feint, hocus-pocus, manipulation, manoeuvring, subterfuge, trickery

legibility *n* = **readability**, clarity, decipherability, ease of reading, legibleness, neatness, plainness, readableness

legible *adj* = **readable**, bold, clear, decipherable, distinct, easily read, easy to read, neat, plain

legion *n* **1, 2** = **army**, brigade, company, division, force, troop **4** = **multitude**, drove, horde, host, mass, myriad, number, throng ◆ *adj* **5** = **very many**, countless, multitudinous, myriad, numberless, numerous

legislate *vb* **1, 2** = **make laws**, codify, constitute, enact, establish, ordain, pass laws, prescribe, put in force

legislation *n* **1** = **lawmaking**, codification, enactment, prescription, regulation **2** = **law**, act, bill, charter, measure, regulation, ruling, statute

legislative *adj* **1-3** = **law-making**, congressional, judicial, juridical, jurisdictive, law-giving, ordaining, parliamentary

legislator *n* **1, 2** = **lawmaker**, lawgiver, parliamentarian

legislature *n* = **parliament**, assembly, chamber, congress, diet, house, law-making body, senate

legitimate *adj* **2, 4, 5** = **lawful**, acknowledged, authentic, authorized, genuine, kosher (*inf.*), legal, legit (*sl.*), licit, proper, real, rightful, sanctioned, statutory, true **4** = **reasonable**, admissible, correct, just, justifiable, logical, sensible, valid, warranted, well-founded ◆ *vb* **7** = **legitimize**, authorize, give the green light for, legalize, legitimatize, permit, pronounce lawful, sanction
Antonyms *adj* ≠ **lawful:** false, fraudulent, illegal, illegitimate, unlawful ≠ **reasonable:** unfair, unfounded, unjustified, unreasonable, unsound

legitimize *vb* = **legalize**, authorize, give the green light for, legitimate, permit, pronounce lawful, sanction

gitimising, legitimised *or* **legitimatizes, legitimatizing, legitimatized; legitimatises, legitimatising, legitimatised.** (*tr*) to make legitimate; legalize.
▸**le,gitimi'zation, le,gitimi'sation** *or* **le,gitimati,zation, le,gitimati'sation** *n*

legless ('lɛglɪs) *adj* **1** without legs. **2** *Inf.* very drunk.

Lego ('lɛgəʊ) *n Trademark.* a construction toy consisting of plastic bricks and other components that fit together. [C20: from Danish *leg godt* play well]

leg-of-mutton *or* **leg-o'-mutton** *n* (*modifier*) (of a sail, sleeve, etc.) tapering sharply.

leg-pull *n Brit. inf.* a practical joke or mild deception.

legroom ('lɛg,ruːm) *n* room to move one's legs comfortably, as in a car.

leg rope *n Austral. & NZ.* a rope used to secure an animal by its hind leg.

leguan ('lɛgʊ,ɑːn) *n* a large amphibious S African lizard. [C19: Du., from F *l'iguane* the iguana]

legume ('lɛgjuːm, lɪ'gjuːm) *n* **1** the long dry fruit produced by leguminous plants; a pod. **2** any of various table vegetables, esp. beans or peas. **3** any leguminous plant. [C17: from F *légume,* from L *legūmen* bean, from *legere* to pick (a crop)]

leguminous (lɪ'gjuːmɪnəs) *adj* of, relating to, or belonging to any family of flowering plants having pods (or legumes) as fruits and root nodules enabling storage of nitrogen-rich material. [C17: from L *legūmen;* see LEGUME]

legwarmer ('lɛg,wɔːmə) *n* one of a pair of garments resembling stockings without feet, often worn over jeans, tights, etc., or during exercise.

legwork ('lɛg,wɜːk) *n Inf.* work that involves travelling on foot or as if on foot.

lei (leɪ) *n* (in Hawaii) a garland of flowers, worn around the neck. [from Hawaiian]

Leibnitzian (laɪb'nɪtsɪən) *adj* of the philosophy of Gottfried Leibnitz (1646–1716), German mathematician and philosopher, in which matter was conceived as existing in the form of independent units or monads, synchronized by pre-established harmony.

Leicester ('lɛstə) *n* a mild dark orange cheese similar to Cheddar but looser and more moist. [after *Leicester,* a county in England]

leishmaniasis (,liːʃmə'naɪəsɪs) *or* **leishmaniosis** (liːʃ,meɪnɪ'əʊsɪs, -,mæn-) *n* any disease, such as kala-azar, caused by protozoa of the genus *Leishmania.* [C20: NL, after Sir W. B. *Leishman* (1865-1926), Scot. bacteriologist]

leister ('liːstə) *n* **1** a spear with three or more prongs for spearing fish, esp. salmon. ◆ *vb* **2** (*tr*) to spear (a fish) with a leister. [C16: from Scand.]

leisure ❶ ('lɛʒə) *n* **1a** time or opportunity for ease, relaxation, etc. **1b** (*as modifier*): *leisure activities.* **2** ease or leisureliness. **3 at leisure. 3a** having free time. **3b** not occupied or engaged. **3c** without hurrying. **4 at one's leisure.** when one has free time. [C14: from OF *leisir;* ult. from L *licēre* to be allowed]
▸**'leisured** *adj*

leisure centre *n* a building designed to provide such leisure facilities as a library, sports hall, café, and rooms for meetings.

leisurely ❶ ('lɛʒəlɪ) *adj* **1** unhurried; relaxed. ◆ *adv* **2** without haste; in a relaxed way.
▸**'leisureliness** *n*

leitmotif ❶ *or* **leitmotiv** ('laɪtməʊ,tiːf) *n* **1** *Music.* a recurring short melodic phrase used, esp. in Wagnerian music dramas, to suggest a character, thing, etc. **2** an often repeated image or theme in a literary work. [C19: from G: leading motif]

lek (lɛk) *n* a small area in which birds of certain species, notably the black grouse, gather for sexual display and courtship. [C19: ?from dialect *lake* (vb) from OE *lácan* to frolic, fight, or ?from Swedish *leka* to play]

lekker ('lɛkə) *adj S. African sl.* **1** pleasing, enjoyable, or likeable. **2** tasty. [from Afrik., from Du.]

LEM (lɛm) *n acronym for* lunar excursion module.

lemma ('lɛmə) *n, pl* **lemmas** *or* **lemmata** (-mətə). **1** a subsidiary proposition, assumed to be valid, that is used in the proof of another proposition. **2** an argument or theme, esp. when used as the subject or title of a composition. **3** *Linguistics.* a word considered as its citation form together with all the inflected forms. [C16 (meaning: proposition), C17 (meaning: title, theme): via L from Gk: premise, from *lambanein* to take (for granted)]

lemming ('lɛmɪŋ) *n* **1** any of various volelike rodents of northern and arctic regions of Europe, Asia, and North America. **2** a member of any group following an unthinking course towards destruction. [C17: from Norwegian]
▸**'lemming-,like** *adj*

lemon ('lɛmən) *n* **1** a small Asian evergreen tree widely cultivated in warm and tropical regions for its edible fruits. Related adjs.: **citric, citrine, citrous. 2a** the yellow oval fruit of this tree, having juicy acidic flesh. **2b** (*as modifier*): *a lemon jelly.* **3** Also called: **lemon yellow. 3a** a greenish-yellow or pale yellow colour. **3b** (*as adj*): *lemon wallpaper.* **4** a distinctive tart flavour made from or in imitation of the lemon. **5** *Sl.* a person or thing considered to be useless or defective. [C14: from Med. L *lemōn-,* from Ar. *laymūn*]
▸**'lemony** *adj*

lemonade (,lɛmə'neɪd) *n* a drink made from lemon juice, sugar, and water or from carbonated water, citric acid, etc.

lemon balm *n* the full name of **balm.**

lemon cheese *or* **curd** *n* a soft spread made from lemons, sugar, eggs, and butter.

lemon grass *n* a perennial grass with a large flower spike: used in cooking and grown in tropical regions as the source of an aromatic oil (**lemon grass oil**).

lemon sole *n* a European flatfish with a variegated brown body: highly valued as a food fish.

lemon squash *n Brit.* a drink made from a sweetened lemon concentrate and water.

lemur ('liːmə) *n* **1** any of a family of Madagascan prosimian primates such as the ring-tailed lemur. They are typically arboreal, having foxy faces and long tails. **2** any similar or closely related animal, such as a loris or indris. [C18: NL, adapted from L *lemurēs* ghosts; so named for its ghost-like face and nocturnal habits]
▸**lemuroid** ('lɛmjʊ,rɔɪd) *n, adj*

lend ❶ (lɛnd) *vb* **lends, lending, lent. 1** (*tr*) to permit the use of (something) with the expectation of its return. **2** to provide (money) temporarily, often at interest. **3** (*intr*) to provide loans, esp. as a profession. **4** (*tr*) to impart or contribute (something, esp. some abstract quality): *her presence lent beauty.* **5 lend an ear.** to listen. **6 lend oneself** *or* **itself.** to possess the right characteristics or qualities for: *the novel lends itself to serialization.* [C15 *lende* (orig. the past tense), from OE *lǣnan,* from *lǣn* loan]
▸**'lender** *n*

lending library *n* **1** Also called (esp. US): **circulating library.** the department of a public library providing books for use outside the building. **2** a small commercial library.

lend-lease *n* (during World War II) the system organized by the US in 1941 by which equipment and services were provided for countries fighting Germany.

length ❶ (lɛŋkθ, lɛŋθ) *n* **1** the linear extent or measurement of something from end to end, usually being the longest dimension. **2** the extent of something from beginning to end, measured in some more or less regular units or intervals: *the book was 600 pages in length.* **3** a specified distance, esp. between two positions: *the length of a race.* **4** a period of time, as between specified limits or moments. **5** a piece or section of something narrow and long: *a length of tubing.* **6** the quality, state, or fact of being long rather than short. **7** (*usually pl*) the amount of trouble taken in pursuing or achieving something (esp. in **to great lengths**). **8** (*often pl*) the extreme or limit of action (esp. in **to any length(s)**). **9** *Prosody, phonetics.* the metrical quantity or temporal duration of a vowel or syllable. **10** the distance from one end of a rectangular swimming bath to the other. **11** *NZ inf.* the general idea; the main purpose. **12 at length. 12a** in depth; fully. **12b** eventually. **12c** interminably. [OE *lengthu*]

lengthen ❶ ('lɛŋkθən, 'lɛŋθən) *vb* to make or become longer.
▸**'lengthener** *n*

lengthways ('lɛŋkθ,weɪz, 'lɛŋθ-) *or* **lengthwise** *adv, adj* in, according to, or along the direction of length.

lengthy ❶ ('lɛŋkθɪ, 'lɛŋθɪ) *adj* **lengthier, lengthiest.** of relatively great or tiresome extent or duration.
▸**'lengthily** *adv* ▸**'lengthiness** *n*

THESAURUS

leisure *n* **1a** = **spare time**, breathing space, ease, freedom, free time, holiday, liberty, opportunity, pause, quiet, recreation, relaxation, respite, rest, retirement, spare moments, time off, vacation **3b at leisure** = **free**, available, not booked up, unengaged, unoccupied **4 at one's leisure** = **in one's own (good) time**, at an unhurried pace, at one's convenience, deliberately, unhurriedly, when it suits one, when one gets round to it (*inf.*), without hurry
Antonyms *n* ≠ **spare time:** business, duty, employment, labour, obligation, occupation, work

leisurely *adj* **1** = **unhurried**, comfortable, easy, gentle, laid-back, lazy, relaxed, restful, slow ◆ *adv* **2** = **unhurriedly**, at one's convenience, at one's leisure, comfortably, deliberately, easily, indolently, lazily, lingeringly, slowly, without haste
Antonyms *adj* ≠ **unhurried:** brisk, fast, hasty, hectic, hurried, quick, rapid, rushed ◆ *adv* ≠ **unhurriedly:** briskly, hastily, hurriedly, quickly, rapidly

leitmotif *n* **1** = **melody**, air, strain, theme **2** = **theme**, convention, device, idea, motif, phrase

lend *vb* **1, 2** = **loan**, accommodate one with, advance **4** = **give**, add, afford, bestow, confer, contribute, furnish, grant, hand out, impart, present, provide, supply **5 lend an ear** = **listen**, give ear, hearken (*arch.*), heed, take notice **6 lend oneself** *or* **itself** = **be appropriate**, be adaptable, be serviceable, fit, present opportunities for, suit

length *n* **1-3** = **distance**, extent, longitude, measure, reach, span **4** = **duration**, period, space, span, stretch, term **5** = **piece**, measure, portion, section, segment **6** = **lengthiness**, extensiveness, protractedness **12 at length: a** = **in detail**, completely, fully, in depth, thoroughly, to the full **b** = **at last**, at long last, eventually, finally, in the end **c** = **for a long time**, for ages, for hours, interminably

lengthen *vb* = **extend**, continue, draw out, elongate, expand, increase, make longer, prolong, protract, spin out, stretch
Antonyms *vb* abbreviate, abridge, curtail, cut, cut down, diminish, shorten, trim

lengthy *adj* = **long**, diffuse, drawn-out, extended, interminable, lengthened, long-drawn-out, long-winded, overlong, prolix, prolonged, protracted, tedious, verbose, very long
Antonyms *adj* brief, concise, condensed, limited, short, succinct, terse, to the point

lenient Ⓣ ('li:nɪənt) *adj* showing or characterized by mercy or tolerance. [C17: from L *lēnīre* to soothe, from *lēnis* soft]
► **'leniency** *or* **'lenience** *n* ► **'leniently** *adv*

Leninism ('lɛnɪˌnɪzəm) *n* the political and economic theories of Lenin (1870–1924), Russian statesman and Marxist theorist.
► **'Leninist** *n, adj*

lenitive ('lɛnɪtɪv) *adj* **1** soothing or alleviating pain or distress. ◆ *n* **2** a lenitive drug. [C16: from Med. L *lēnītīvus,* from L *lēnīre* to soothe]

lenity ('lɛnɪtɪ) *n, pl* **lenities.** the state or quality of being lenient. [C16: from L *lēnitās* gentleness, from *lēnis* soft]

leno ('li:nəʊ) *n, pl* **lenos. 1** (in textiles) a weave in which the warp yarns are twisted together in pairs between the weft or filling yarns. **2** a fabric of this weave. [C19: prob. from F *linon* lawn, from *lin* flax, from L *līnum*]

lens (lɛnz) *n* **1** a piece of glass or other transparent material, used to converge or diverge transmitted light and form optical images. **2** Also called: **compound lens.** a combination of such lenses for forming images or concentrating a beam of light. **3** a device that diverges or converges a beam of electromagnetic radiation, sound, or particles. **4** *Anat.* See **crystalline lens.** [C17: from L *lēns* lentil, referring to the similarity of a lens to the shape of a lentil]

lent (lɛnt) *vb* the past tense and past participle of **lend.**

Lent (lɛnt) *n Christianity.* the period of forty weekdays lasting from Ash Wednesday to Holy Saturday, observed as a time of penance and fasting commemorating Jesus' fasting in the wilderness. [OE *lencten, lengten* spring, lit.: lengthening (of hours of daylight)]

lentamente (ˌlɛntə'mɛnteɪ) *adv Music.* slowly. [It.]

lenten ('lɛntən) *adj* **1** (*often cap.*) of or relating to Lent. **2** *Arch. or literary.* spare, plain, or meagre: *lenten fare.*

lenticel ('lɛntɪˌsɛl) *n* any of numerous pores in the stem of a woody plant allowing exchange of gases between the plant and the exterior. [C19: from NL *lenticella,* from L *lenticula* dim. of *lēns* lentil]

lenticular (lɛn'tɪkjʊlə) *adj* **1** shaped like a biconvex lens. **2** of or concerned with a lens or lenses. **3** shaped like a lentil seed. [C17: from L *lenticulāris* like a LENTIL]

lentil ('lɛntɪl) *n* **1** a small annual leguminous plant of the Mediterranean region and W Asia, having edible convex seeds. **2** any of the seeds of this plant, which are cooked and eaten in soups, etc. [C13: from OF *lentille,* from L *lenticula,* dim. of *lēns* lentil]

lentivirus ('lɛntɪˌvaɪrəs) *n* another name for **slow virus.** [C20: NL, from L *lentus* slow + VIRUS]

lent lily *n* another name for the **daffodil.**

lento ('lɛntəʊ) *Music.* ◆ *adj, adv* **1** to be performed slowly. ◆ *n, pl* **lentos. 2** a movement or passage performed in this way. [C18: It., from L *lentus* slow]

Lent term *n* the spring term at Cambridge University and some other educational establishments.

Leo ('li:əʊ) *n, Latin genitive* **Leonis** (li:'əʊnɪs). **1** *Astron.* a zodiacal constellation in the N hemisphere, lying between Cancer and Virgo. **2** *Astrol.* Also called: the **Lion.** the fifth sign of the zodiac. The sun is in this sign between about July 23 and Aug. 22.

Leonid ('li:ənɪd) *n, pl* **Leonids** *or* **Leonides** (lɪ'ɒnɪˌdi:z). any member of a meteor shower appearing to radiate from the constellation Leo. [C19: from NL *Leōnidēs,* from *leō* lion]

leonine ('li:əˌnaɪn) *adj* of, characteristic of, or resembling a lion. [C14: from L *leōnīnus,* from *leō* lion]

Leonine ('li:əˌnaɪn) *adj* **1** connected with one of the popes called Leo: an epithet applied to a district of Rome fortified by Pope Leo IV (**Leonine City**). **2 Leonine verse. 2a** a type of medieval hexameter or elegiac verse having internal rhyme. **2b** a type of English verse with internal rhyme.

leopard ('lɛpəd) *n* **1** Also called: **panther.** a large feline mammal of forests of Africa and Asia, usually having a tawny yellow coat with black rosette-like spots. **2** any of several similar felines, such as the snow leopard and cheetah. **3** *Heraldry.* a stylized leopard, painted as a lion with the face turned towards the front. [C13: from OF *lepart,* from LL, from LGk *leópardos,* from *leōn* lion + *pardos* PARD (the leopard was thought to be the result of cross-breeding)]
► **'leopardess** *fem n*

leotard ('lɪəˌtɑ:d) *n* **1** a tight-fitting garment covering the body from the shoulders down to the thighs and worn by acrobats, ballet dancers, etc. **2** (*pl*) *US & Canad.* another name for **tights** (sense 1b). [C19: after Jules *Léotard,* F acrobat]

leper Ⓣ ('lɛpə) *n* **1** a person who has leprosy. **2** a person who is ignored or despised. [C14: via LL from Gk *lepra,* n. use of *lepros* scaly, from *lepein* to peel]

lepido- *or before a vowel* **lepid-** *combining form.* scale or scaly: *lepidopterous.* [from Gk *lepis* scale; see LEPER]

lepidopteran (ˌlɛpɪ'dɒptərən) *n, pl* **lepidopterans** *or* **lepidoptera** (-tərə). **1** any of a large order of insects typically having two pairs of wings covered with fragile scales: comprises the butterflies and moths. ◆ *adj also* **lepidopterous. 2** of, relating to, or belonging to this order. [C19: from NL, from LEPIDO- + Gk *pteron* wing]

lepidopterist Ⓣ (ˌlɛpɪ'dɒptərɪst) *n* a person who studies or collects moths and butterflies.

leprechaun ('lɛprəˌkɔ:n) *n* (in Irish folklore) a mischievous elf, often believed to have a treasure hoard. [C17: from Irish Gaelic *leipreachān,* from MIrish *lūchorpān,* from *lū* small + *corp* body, from L *corpus* body]

leprosy ('lɛprəsɪ) *n Pathol.* a chronic infectious disease occurring mainly in tropical and subtropical regions, characterized by the formation of painful inflamed nodules beneath the skin and disfigurement and wasting of affected parts. [C16: from LEPROUS + -Y[3]]

leprous ('lɛprəs) *adj* **1** having leprosy. **2** relating to or resembling leprosy. [C13: from OF, from LL *leprosus,* from *lepra* LEPER]

-lepsy *or sometimes* **-lepsia** *n combining form.* indicating a seizure: *catalepsy.* [from NL *-lepsia,* from Gk, from *lēpsis* a seizure, from *lambanein* to seize]
► **-leptic** *adj combining form.*

leptodactylous (ˌlɛptəʊ'dæktɪləs) *adj Zool.* having slender digits.

lepton[1] ('lɛptɒn) *n, pl* **lepta** (-tə). **1** a Greek monetary unit worth one hundredth of a drachma. **2** a small coin of ancient Greece. [from Gk *lepton (nomisma)* small (coin)]

lepton[2] ('lɛptɒn) *n Physics.* any of a group of elementary particles and their antiparticles, such as an electron, muon, or neutrino, that participate in electromagnetic and weak interactions. [C20: from Gk *leptos* thin, from *lepein* to peel + -ON]

lepton number *n Physics.* a quantum number describing the behaviour of elementary particles, equal to the number of leptons present minus the number of antileptons. It is thought to be conserved in all processes.

leptospirosis (ˌlɛptəʊspaɪ'rəʊsɪs) *n* any of several infectious diseases caused by bacteria, transmitted to man by animals and characterized by jaundice, meningitis, and kidney failure. Also called: **Weil's disease.** [C20: from NL *Leptospira* (from Gk *leptos* thin + *speira* coil + -OSIS)]

lesbian Ⓣ ('lɛzbɪən) *n* **1** a female homosexual. ◆ *adj* **2** of or characteristic of lesbians. [C19: from the homosexuality attributed to Sappho (6th cent. B.C.), Gk poetess of *Lesbos*]
► **'lesbianism** *n*

lese-majesty ('li:z'mædʒɪstɪ) *n* **1** any of various offences committed against the sovereign power in a state; treason. **2** an attack on authority or position. [C16: from F *lèse majesté,* from L *laesa mājestās* wounded majesty]

lesion Ⓣ ('li:ʒən) *n* **1** any structural change in a bodily part resulting from injury or disease. **2** an injury or wound. [C15: via OF from LL *laesiō* injury, from L *laedere* to hurt]

less Ⓣ (lɛs) *determiner* **1a** the comparative of **little** (sense 1): *less sugar; less spirit than before.* **1b** (*as pronoun; functioning as sing or pl*): *she has less than she needs; the less you eat, the less you want.* **2** (usually preceded by *no*) lower in rank or importance: *no less a man than the president.* **3 less of.** to a smaller extent or degree: *we see less of John these days; less of a success than I'd hoped.* ◆ *adv* **4** the comparative of *a little: she walks less than she should; less quickly; less beautiful.* ◆ *prep* **5** subtracting; minus: *three weeks less a day.* [OE *lǣssa* (adj), *lǣs* (adv, n)]

> **USAGE NOTE** *Less* should not be confused with *fewer. Less* refers strictly only to quantity and not to number: *there is less water than before. Fewer* means smaller in number: *there are fewer people than before.*

-less *suffix forming adjectives.* **1** without; lacking: *speechless.* **2** not able to (do something) or not able to be (done, performed, etc.): *countless.* [OE *-lās,* from *lēas* lacking]

lessee (lɛ'si:) *n* a person to whom a lease is granted; a tenant under a lease. [C15: via Anglo-F from OF *lessé,* from *lesser* to LEASE]

lessen Ⓣ ('lɛsᵊn) *vb* **1** to make or become less. **2** (*tr*) to make little of.

lesser Ⓣ ('lɛsə) *adj* not as great in quantity, size, or worth.

lesser celandine *n* a Eurasian plant, related to the buttercup, having yellow flowers and heart-shaped leaves.

THESAURUS

leniency *n* = **mercy**, clemency, compassion, forbearance, gentleness, indulgence, lenity, mildness, moderation, pity, quarter, tenderness, tolerance

lenient *adj* = **merciful**, clement, compassionate, forbearing, forgiving, gentle, indulgent, kind, mild, sparing, tender, tolerant
Antonyms *adj* harsh, merciless, rigid, rigorous, severe, stern, strict, stringent

leper *n* **2** = **outcast**, pariah, untouchable

lepidopterist *n* = **butterfly collector**

lesbian *n* **1** = **dyke** (*sl.*), butch, tribade ◆ *adj* **2** = **homosexual**, butch (*sl.*), dykey, gay, sapphic, tribadic

lesion *n* **1, 2** = **injury**, abrasion, bruise, contusion, hurt, impairment, sore, trauma (*Pathology*), wound

less *determiner* **1** = **smaller**, shorter, slighter **2** = **inferior**, minor, secondary, subordinate ◆ *adv* **4** = **to a smaller extent**, barely, little, meagrely ◆ *prep* **5** = **minus**, excepting, lacking, subtracting, without

lessen *vb* **1** = **reduce**, abate, abridge, contract, curtail, decrease, de-escalate, degrade, die down, diminish, downsize, dwindle, ease, erode, grow less, lighten, lower, minimize, moderate, narrow, relax, shrink, slacken, slow down, weaken, wind down
Antonyms *vb* add to, augment, boost, enhance, enlarge, expand, increase, magnify, multiply, raise

lessening *n* **1** = **reduction**, abatement, contraction, curtailment, decline, decrease, de-escalation, diminution, dwindling, ebbing, erosion, let-up (*inf.*), minimization, moderation, petering out, shrinkage, slackening, slowing down, waning, weakening

lesser *adj* = **lower**, inferior, less important, minor, secondary, slighter, subordinate, under-
Antonyms *adj* greater, higher, major, primary, superior

DICTIONARY

lesser panda *n* See **panda** (sense 2).

lesson Ⓣ ('lɛsən) *n* **1a** a unit, or single period of instruction in a subject; class: *an hour-long music lesson.* **1b** the content of such a unit. **2** material assigned for individual study. **3** something from which useful knowledge or principles can be learned; example. **4** the principles, knowledge, etc., gained. **5** a reprimand or punishment intended to correct. **6** a portion of Scripture appointed to be read at divine service. [C13: from OF *leçon*, from L *lēctiō*, from *legere* to read]

lessor ('lɛsɔː, lɛ'sɔː) *n* a person who grants a lease of property.

lest (lɛst) *conj* (*subordinating; takes a subjunctive vb*) **1** so as to prevent any possibility that: *keep down lest anyone see us.* **2** (*after vbs. or phrases expressing fear, worry, anxiety, etc.*) for fear that; in case: *he was alarmed lest she should find out.* [OE *thē lǣste*, earlier *thȳ lǣs the*, lit.: whereby less that]

let[1] Ⓣ (lɛt) *vb* **lets, letting, let.** (*tr;* usually takes an infinitive without *to* or an implied infinitive) **1** to permit; allow: *she lets him roam around.* **2** (*imperative or dependent imperative*) **2a** used as an auxiliary to express a request, proposal, or command, or to convey a warning or threat: *let's get on; just let me catch you here again!* **2b** (in mathematical or philosophical discourse) used as an auxiliary to express an assumption or hypothesis: *let "a" equal "b".* **2c** used as an auxiliary to express resigned acceptance of the inevitable: *let the worst happen.* **3a** to allow the occupation of (accommodation) in return for rent. **3b** to assign (a contract for work). **4** to allow or cause the movement of (something) in a specified direction: *to let air out of a tyre.* **5 let alone.** (*conj*) much less; not to mention: *I can't afford wine, let alone champagne.* **6 let** *or* **leave alone** *or* **be.** refrain from annoying or interfering with: *let the poor cat alone.* **7 let go.** See **go** (sense 45). **8 let loose. 8a** to set free. **8b** *Inf.* to make (a sound or remark) suddenly: *he let loose a hollow laugh.* **8c** *Inf.* to discharge (rounds) from a gun or guns: *they let loose a couple of rounds of ammunition.* ◆ *n* **9** *Brit.* the act of letting property or accommodation. ◆ See also **let down, let off,** etc. [OE *lǣtan* to permit]

let[2] Ⓣ (lɛt) *n* **1** an impediment or obstruction (esp. in **without let or hindrance**). **2** *Tennis, squash, etc.* **2a** a minor infringement or obstruction of the ball, requiring a point to be replayed. **2b** the point so replayed. ◆ *vb* **lets, letting, letted** *or* **let. 3** (*tr*) *Arch.* to hinder; impede. [OE *lettan* to hinder, from *læt* late]

-let *suffix forming nouns.* **1** small or lesser: *booklet.* **2** an article of attire or ornament worn on a specified part of the body: *anklet.* [from OF *-elet*, from L *-āle*, from L *-ellus*, dim. suffix]

let down Ⓣ *vb* (*tr, mainly adv*) **1** (*also prep*) to lower. **2** to fail to fulfil the expectations of (a person); disappoint. **3** to undo, shorten, and resew (the hem) so as to lengthen (a dress, skirt, etc.). **4** to untie (long hair that is bound up) and allow to fall loose. **5** to deflate: *to let down a tyre.* ◆ *n* **letdown. 6** a disappointment.

lethal Ⓣ ('liːθəl) *adj* **1** able to cause or causing death. **2** of or suggestive of death. [C16: from L *lēthālis*, from *lētum* death]
▸**lethality** (liː'θælɪtɪ) *n* ▸**'lethally** *adv*

lethargy Ⓣ ('lɛθədʒɪ) *n, pl* **lethargies. 1** sluggishness, slowness, or dullness. **2** an abnormal lack of energy. [C14: from LL *lēthargia*, from Gk *lēthargos* drowsy, from *lēthē* forgetfulness]
▸**lethargic** (lɪ'θɑːdʒɪk) *adj* ▸**le'thargically** *adv*

Lethe ('liːθɪ) *n* **1** *Greek myth.* a river in Hades that caused forgetfulness in those who drank its waters. **2** forgetfulness. [C16: via L from Gk, from *lēthē* oblivion]
▸**Lethean** (lɪ'θiːən) *adj*

let off Ⓣ *vb* (*tr, mainly adv*) **1** (*also prep*) to allow to disembark or leave. **2** to explode or fire (a bomb, gun, etc.). **3** (*also prep*) to excuse from (work or other responsibilities): *I'll let you off for a week.* **4** *Inf.* to allow to get away without the expected punishment, work, etc. **5** to let (accommodation) in portions. **6** to release (liquid, air, etc.).

let on Ⓣ *vb* (*adv; when tr, takes a clause as object*) *Inf.* **1** to allow (something, such as a secret) to be known; reveal: *he never let on that he was married.* **2** (*tr*) to cause or encourage to be believed; pretend.

let out Ⓣ *vb* (*adv, mainly tr*) **1** to give vent to; emit: *to let out a howl.* **2** to allow to go or run free; release. **3** (*may take a clause as object*) to reveal (a secret). **4** to make available to tenants, hirers, or contractors. **5** to permit to flow out: *to let air out of the tyres.* **6** to make (a garment) larger, as by unpicking (the seams) and sewing nearer the outer edge. ◆ *n* **let-out. 7** a chance to escape.

let's (lɛts) *contraction of* let us: used to express a suggestion, command, etc., by the speaker to himself and his hearers.

Lett (lɛt) *n* a former name for a **Latvian.**

letter Ⓣ ('lɛtə) *n* **1** any of a set of conventional symbols used in writing or printing a language, each symbol being associated with a group of phonetic values; character of the alphabet. **2** a written or printed communication addressed to a person, company, etc., usually sent by post. **3** (often preceded by *the*) the strict legalistic or pedantic interpretation of the meaning of an agreement, document, etc.; exact wording as distinct from actual intention (esp. in **the letter of the law**). **4 to the letter. 4a** following the literal interpretation or wording exactly. **4b** attending to every detail. ◆ *vb* **5** to write or mark letters on (a sign, etc.), esp. by hand. **6** (*tr*) to set down or print using letters. [C13: from OF *lettre*, from L *littera* letter of the alphabet]
▸**'letterer** *n*

letter bomb *n* an explosive device in an envelope, detonated when the envelope is opened.

letter box *n Chiefly Brit.* **1a** a slot through which letters, etc., are delivered to a building. **1b** a private box into which letters, etc., are delivered. **2** Also: **postbox.** a public box into which letters, etc., are put for collection.

lettered Ⓣ ('lɛtəd) *adj* **1** well educated in literature, the arts, etc. **2** literate. **3** of or characterized by learning or culture. **4** printed or marked with letters.

letterhead ('lɛtəˌhɛd) *n* a sheet of writing paper printed with one's address, name, etc.

lettering ('lɛtərɪŋ) *n* **1** the act, art, or technique of inscribing letters on to something. **2** the letters so inscribed.

letter of credit *n* a letter issued by a bank entitling the bearer to draw funds up to a specified maximum from that bank or its agencies.

letter of intent *n* a letter indicating that the writer has the serious intention of doing something, such as signing a contract, in the circumstances specified. It does not constitute either a promise or a contract.

letter of marque *or* **letters of marque** *n* (formerly) a licence granted by a state to a private citizen to arm a ship and seize merchant vessels of another nation. Also called: **letter of marque and reprisal.**

letter-perfect *adj* another term (esp. US) for **word-perfect.**

letterpress ('lɛtəˌprɛs) *n* **1a** a method of printing in which ink is transferred from raised surfaces to paper by pressure. **1b** matter so printed. **2** text matter as distinct from illustrations.

letters Ⓣ ('lɛtəz) *n* (*functioning as sing or pl*) **1** literary knowledge, ability, or learning: *a man of letters.* **2** literary culture in general. **3** an official title, degree, etc., indicated by an abbreviation: *letters after one's name.*

letters patent *pl n* See **patent** (senses 1, 4).

Lettish ('lɛtɪʃ) *n* another name for **Latvian** (sense 2).

lettuce ('lɛtɪs) *n* **1** any of various plants of the composite family cultivated in many varieties for their large edible leaves. **2** the leaves of any of these varieties, which are eaten in salads. **3** any of various plants that resemble true lettuce, such as lamb's lettuce. [C13: prob. from OF *laitues*, from L *lactūca*, from *lac-* milk, because of its milky juice]

let up Ⓣ *vb* (*intr, adv*) **1** to diminish, slacken, or stop. **2** (foll. by *on*) *Inf.* to be less harsh (towards someone). ◆ *n* **let-up. 3** *Inf.* a lessening or abatement.

leuco-, leuko- *or before a vowel* **leuc-, leuk-** *combining form.* white or lacking colour: *leucocyte; leukaemia.* [from Gk *leukos* white]

leucoblast *or esp. US* **leukoblast** ('luːkəʊˌblæst) *n* an immature leucocyte.

leucocyte *or esp. US* **leukocyte** ('luːkəˌsaɪt) *n* any of the various large

THESAURUS

lesson *n* **1a** = **class**, coaching, instruction, period, schooling, teaching, tutoring **2** = **exercise**, assignment, drill, homework, lecture, practice, reading, recitation, task **3, 4** = **example**, deterrent, exemplar, message, model, moral, precept **5** = **punishment**, admonition, censure, chiding, rebuke, reprimand, reproof, scolding, warning

let[1] *vb* **1** = **allow**, authorize, entitle, give leave, give permission, give the go-ahead, give the green light, give the O.K. *or* okay (*inf.*), grant, permit, sanction, suffer (*arch.*), tolerate, warrant **2** = **enable**, allow, cause, grant, make, permit **3** = **lease**, hire, rent

let[2] *n* **1** = **hindrance**, constraint, impediment, interference, obstacle, obstruction, prohibition, restriction

let down *vb* **2** = **disappoint**, disenchant, disillusion, dissatisfy, fail, fall short, leave in the lurch, leave stranded ◆ *n* **letdown 6** = **disappointment**, anticlimax, blow, comedown (*inf.*), disillusionment, frustration, setback, washout (*inf.*), whammy (*inf., chiefly US*)

lethal *adj* **1** = **deadly**, baneful, dangerous, deathly, destructive, devastating, fatal, mortal, murderous, noxious, pernicious, poisonous, virulent
Antonyms *adj* harmless, healthy, innocuous, safe, wholesome

lethargic *adj* **1, 2** = **sluggish**, apathetic, comatose, debilitated, drowsy, dull, enervated, heavy, inactive, indifferent, inert, languid, lazy, listless, sleepy, slothful, slow, somnolent, stupefied, torpid
Antonyms *adj* active, alert, animated, energetic, responsive, spirited, stimulated, vigorous

lethargy *n* **1, 2** = **sluggishness**, apathy, drowsiness, dullness, inaction, indifference, inertia, languor, lassitude, listlessness, sleepiness, sloth, slowness, stupor, torpidity, torpor
Antonyms *n* animation, brio, energy, life, liveliness, spirit, verve, vigour, vim, vitality, vivacity, zeal, zest

let off *vb* **2** = **fire**, detonate, discharge, explode **3, 4** = **excuse**, absolve, discharge, dispense, exempt, exonerate, forgive, pardon, release, spare **6** = **emit**, exude, give off, leak, release

let on *vb Informal* **1** = **reveal**, admit, disclose, divulge, give away, let the cat out of the bag (*inf.*), make known, say **2** = **pretend**, act, counterfeit, dissemble, dissimulate, feign, make believe, make out, profess, simulate

let out *vb* **1** = **emit**, give vent to, produce **2** = **release**, discharge, free, let go, liberate **3** = **reveal**, betray, blow wide open (*sl.*), disclose, leak, let fall, let slip, make known, take the wraps off

letter *n* **1** = **character**, sign, symbol **2** = **message**, acknowledgment, answer, billet (*arch.*), communication, dispatch, epistle, line, missive, note, reply **4a to the letter** = **precisely**, accurately, exactly, literally, strictly, word for word

lettered *adj* **1, 3** = **educated**, accomplished, cultivated, cultured, erudite, informed, knowledgeable, learned, scholarly, versed, well-educated, well-read

letters *pl n* **1, 2** = **learning**, culture, erudition, humanities, literature, scholarship

let up *vb* **1** = **stop**, abate, decrease, diminish, ease (up), moderate, relax, slacken, subside ◆ *n* **let-up 3** *Informal* = **lessening**, abatement, break,

unpigmented cells in the blood of vertebrates. Also called: **white blood cell, white (blood) corpuscle.**
▸**leucocytic** *or esp. US* **leukocytic** (ˌluːkəˈsɪtɪk) *adj*

leucoma (luːˈkəʊmə) *n Pathol.* a white opaque scar of the cornea.

leucotomy (luːˈkɒtəmɪ) *n, pl* **leucotomies.** the surgical operation of cutting some of the nerve fibres in the frontal lobes of the brain for treating intractable mental disorders.

leukaemia *or esp. US* **leukemia** (luːˈkiːmɪə) *n* an acute or chronic disease characterized by a gross proliferation of leucocytes, which crowd into the bone marrow, spleen, lymph nodes, etc., and suppress the blood-forming apparatus. [C19: from LEUCO- + Gk *haima* blood]

Lev. *Bible. abbrev. for* Leviticus.

levant (lɪˈvænt) *n* a type of leather made from the skins of goats, sheep, or seals, having a pattern of irregular creases. [C19: shortened from *Levant morocco* (type of leather)]

Levant (lɪˈvænt) *n* **the.** a former name for the area of the E Mediterranean now occupied by Lebanon, Syria, and Israel. [C15: from OF, from *lever* to raise (referring to the rising of the sun in the east), from L *levāre*]
▸**Levantine** (ˈlɛvənˌtaɪn) *adj, n*

levanter (lɪˈvæntə) *n* (*sometimes cap.*) **1** an easterly wind in the W Mediterranean area. **2** an inhabitant of the Levant.

levator (lɪˈveɪtə, -tɔː) *n Anat.* any of various muscles that raise a part of the body. [C17: NL, from L *levāre* to raise]

levee[1] (ˈlɛvɪ) *n US.* **1** an embankment alongside a river, produced naturally by sedimentation or constructed by man to prevent flooding. **2** an embankment that surrounds a field that is to be irrigated. **3** a landing place on a river; quay. [C18: from F, from Med. L *levāta* from L *levāre* to raise]

levee[2] Ⓣ (ˈlɛvɪ, ˈlɛveɪ) *n* **1** a formal reception held by a sovereign just after rising from bed. **2** (in Britain) a public court reception for men. [C17: from F, var. of *lever* a rising, from L *levāre* to raise]

level Ⓣ (ˈlɛvᵊl) *adj* **1** on a horizontal plane. **2** having a surface of completely equal height. **3** being of the same height as something else. **4** (of quantities to be measured, as in recipes) even with the top of the cup, spoon, etc. **5** equal to or even with (something or someone else). **6** not having or showing inconsistency or irregularities. **7** Also: **level-headed.** even-tempered; steady. **8 one's level best.** the best one can do. ◆ *vb* **levels, levelling, levelled** *or US* **levels, leveling, leveled. 9** (*tr; sometimes foll. by off*) to make (a surface) horizontal, level, or even. **10** to make (two or more people or things) equal, as in position or status. **11** (*tr*) to raze to the ground. **12** (*tr*) to knock (a person) down as by a blow. **13** (*tr*) to direct (a gaze, criticism, etc.) emphatically at someone. **14** (*intr; often foll. by with*) *Inf.* to be straightforward and frank. **15** (*intr; foll. by off or out*) to manoeuvre an aircraft into a horizontal flight path after a dive, climb, or glide. **16** (often foll. by *at*) to aim (a weapon) horizontally. ◆ *n* **17** a horizontal datum line or plane. **18** a device, such as a spirit level, for determining whether a surface is horizontal. **19** a surveying instrument used for measuring relative heights of land. **20** position or status in a scale of values. **21** amount or degree of progress; stage. **22** a specified vertical position; altitude. **23** a horizontal line or plane with respect to which measurement of elevation is based: *sea level.* **24** a flat even surface or area of land. **25** *Physics.* the ratio of the magnitude of a physical quantity to an arbitrary magnitude: *sound-pressure level.* **26 on the level.** *Inf.* sincere or genuine. [C14: from OF *livel,* from Vulgar L *lībellum* (unattested), from L *lībella,* dim. of *lībra* scales]
▸**ˈleveller** *or US* **ˈleveler** *n* ▸**ˈlevelly** *adv* ▸**ˈlevelness** *n*

level crossing *n Brit., Austral., & NZ.* a point at which a railway and a road cross, esp. one with barriers that close the road when a train is due to pass.

level-headed Ⓣ *adj* even-tempered, balanced, and reliable; steady.
▸**ˌlevel-ˈheadedly** *adv* ▸**ˌlevel-ˈheadedness** *n*

level of attainment *n Brit. education.* one of ten groupings, each with its own attainment criteria based on pupil age and ability, within which a pupil is assessed.

level pegging *Brit. inf.* ◆ *n* **1** equality between two contestants. ◆ *adj* **2** (of two contestants) equal.

level playing field *n* a situation in which none of the competing parties has an advantage at the outset of a competitive activity.

lever Ⓣ (ˈliːvə) *n* **1** a rigid bar pivoted about a fulcrum, used to transfer a force to a load and usually to provide a mechanical advantage. **2** any of a number of mechanical devices employing this principle. **3** a means of exerting pressure in order to accomplish something. ◆ *vb* **4** to prise or move (an object) with a lever. [C13: from OF *leveour,* from *lever* to raise, from L *levāre* from *levis* light]

leverage Ⓣ (ˈliːvərɪdʒ, -vrɪdʒ) *n* **1** the action of a lever. **2** the mechanical advantage gained by employing a lever. **3** strategic advantage. **4** power or influence: *the supermarket chains have greater leverage than single-outlet enterprises.* **5** the US word for **gearing** (sense 3). **6** the use made by a company of its limited assets to guarantee the substantial loans required to finance its business.

leveraged buyout (ˈliːvərɪdʒd, -vrɪdʒd) *n* a takeover bid in which a small company makes use of its limited assets, and those of the usually larger target company, to raise the loans required to finance the takeover. Abbrev.: **LBO.**

leveret (ˈlɛvərɪt, -vrɪt) *n* a young hare, esp. one less than one year old. [C15: from Norman F *levrete,* dim. of *levre,* from L *lepus* hare]

leviable (ˈlɛvɪəbᵊl) *adj* **1** (of taxes, etc.) liable to be levied. **2** (of goods, etc.) liable to bear a levy; taxable.

leviathan Ⓣ (lɪˈvaɪəθən) *n* **1** *Bible.* a monstrous beast, esp. a sea monster. **2** any huge or powerful thing. [C14: from LL, ult. from Heb. *liwyāthān,* from ?]

levigate (ˈlɛvɪˌɡeɪt) *vb* **levigates, levigating, levigated.** *Chem.* **1** (*tr*) to grind into a fine powder or a smooth paste. **2** to form or cause to form a homogeneous mixture, as in the production of gels. **3** (*tr*) to suspend (fine particles) by grinding in a liquid, esp. as a method of separating fine from coarse particles. [C17: from L *lēvigāre,* from *lēvis* smooth]
▸**ˌleviˈgation** *n*

Levi's (ˈliːvaɪz) *pl n Trademark.* jeans, usually blue and made of denim.

levitate (ˈlɛvɪˌteɪt) *vb* **levitates, levitating, levitated.** to rise or cause to rise and float in the air, without visible agency, usually attributed, esp. formerly, to supernatural intervention. [C17: from L *levis* light + *-tate,* as in *gravitate*]
▸**ˌleviˈtation** *n* ▸**ˈleviˌtator** *n*

levity Ⓣ (ˈlɛvɪtɪ) *n, pl* **levities. 1** inappropriate lack of seriousness. **2** fickleness or instability. **3** *Arch.* lightness in weight. [C16: from L *levitās* lightness, from *levis* light]

levodopa (ˌliːvəʊˈdəʊpə) *n* another name for **L-dopa.**

levy Ⓣ (ˈlɛvɪ) *vb* **levies, levying, levied.** (*tr*) **1** to impose and collect (a tax, tariff, fine, etc.). **2** to conscript troops for service. **3** to seize or attach (property) in accordance with the judgment of a court. ◆ *n, pl* **levies. 4a** the act of imposing and collecting a tax, tariff, etc. **4b** the money so raised. **5a** the conscription of troops for service. **5b** a person conscripted in this way. [C15: from OF *levée* a raising, from *lever,* from L *levāre* to raise]

lewd Ⓣ (luːd) *adj* characterized by or intended to excite crude sexual desire; obscene. [C14: from OE *lǣwde* ignorant]
▸**ˈlewdly** *adv* ▸**ˈlewdness** *n*

lewis (ˈluːɪs) *n* a lifting device for heavy stone blocks consisting of a number of curved pieces of metal fitting into a dovetailed recess cut into the stone. [C18: ?from the name of the inventor]

Lewis acid *n* a substance capable of accepting a pair of electrons from a base to form a covalent bond. Cf. **Lewis base.** [C20: after G. N. *Lewis* (1875–1946), US chemist]

Lewis base *n* a substance capable of donating a pair of electrons to an acid to form a covalent bond. Cf. **Lewis acid.** [C20: after G. N. *Lewis;* see LEWIS ACID]

Lewis gun *n* a light air-cooled gas-operated machine gun used chiefly in World Wars I and II. [C20: after I. N. *Lewis* (1858–1931), US soldier]

lewisite (ˈluːɪˌsaɪt) *n* a colourless oily poisonous liquid having a power-

THESAURUS

breathing space, cessation, interval, lull, pause, recess, remission, respite, slackening

levee[2] *n* **2** = **reception**, ceremony, entertainment, gathering, party

level *adj* **1** = **horizontal**, as flat as a pancake, flat, plane **2** = **even**, consistent, plain, smooth, uniform **5** = **equal**, aligned, balanced, commensurate, comparable, equivalent, even, flush, in line, neck and neck, on a line, on a par, proportionate **7** = **calm**, equable, even, even-tempered, stable, steady ◆ *vb* **9** = **flatten**, even off *or* out, make flat, plane, smooth **10** = **equalize**, balance, even up **11** = **destroy**, bulldoze, demolish, devastate, flatten, knock down, lay low, pull down, raze, tear down, wreck **14** *often foll. by* **with** *Informal* = **be honest**, be above board, be frank, be open, be straightforward, be up front (*sl.*), come clean (*inf.*), keep nothing back **16** = **direct**, aim, beam, focus, point, train ◆ *n* **17** = **flat surface**, horizontal, plane **20, 21** = **position**, achievement, degree, grade, rank, stage, standard, standing, status **22** = **height**, altitude, elevation, vertical position **26 on the level** *Informal* = **honest**, above board, fair, genuine, open, sincere, square, straight, straightforward, up front (*sl.*)

Antonyms *adj* ≠ **horizontal:** slanted, tilted, vertical ≠ **even:** bumpy, hilly, uneven, warped ≠ **equal:** above, below ◆ *vb* ≠ **destroy:** build, erect, raise

level-headed *adj* = **calm**, balanced, collected, composed, cool, dependable, even-tempered, reasonable, sane, self-possessed, sensible, steady, together (*sl.*), unflappable (*inf.*)

lever *n* **1** = **handle**, bar, crowbar, handspike, jemmy ◆ *vb* **4** = **prise**, force, jemmy, move, pry (*US*), raise

leverage *n* **4** = **influence**, ascendancy, authority, clout (*inf.*), pull (*inf.*), purchasing power, rank, weight

leviathan *n* **2** = **monster**, behemoth, colossus, hulk, mammoth, Titan, whale

levity *n* **1** = **frivolity**, facetiousness, flippancy, light-heartedness, silliness, triviality **2** = **fickleness**, flightiness, giddiness, light-mindedness, skittishness

Antonyms *n* earnestness, gravity, seriousness, solemnity

levy *vb* **1** = **impose**, charge, collect, demand, exact, gather, tax **2** = **conscript**, call, call up, mobilize, muster, press, raise, summon ◆ *n* **4a** = **imposition**, assessment, collection, exaction, gathering **4b** = **tax**, assessment, duty, excise, fee, imposition, impost, tariff, toll

lewd *adj* = **indecent**, bawdy, blue, dirty, impure, lascivious, libidinous, licentious, loose, lustful, obscene, pornographic, salacious, smutty, unchaste, vile, vulgar, wanton, wicked, X-rated (*inf.*)

lewdness *n* = **indecency**, bawdiness, carnality, crudity, debauchery, depravity, impurity, lasciviousness, lechery, licentiousness, lubricity, obscenity, pornography, profligacy, salaciousness, smut, smuttiness, unchastity, vulgarity, wantonness

ful blistering action and used as a war gas. Formula: $ClCH:CHAsCl_2$. Systematic name: **1-chloro-2-dichloroarsinoethene.** [C20: after W. L. *Lewis* (1878–1943), US chemist]

lexeme ('lɛksiːm) *n Linguistics.* a minimal meaningful unit that cannot be understood from the meanings of its component morphemes. [C20: from LEX(ICON) + -EME]

lexical ('lɛksɪkᵊl) *adj* **1** of or relating to items of vocabulary in a language. **2** of or relating to a lexicon.
▸ **'lexically** *adv*

lexicography (ˌlɛksɪ'kɒgrəfɪ) *n* the process or profession of writing or compiling dictionaries.
▸ **ˌlexi'cographer** *n* ▸ **lexicographic** (ˌlɛksɪkə'græfɪk) *or* **ˌlexico'graphical** *adj*

lexicon ❶ ('lɛksɪkən) *n* **1** a dictionary, esp. one of an ancient language such as Greek or Hebrew. **2** a list of terms relating to a particular subject. **3** the vocabulary of a language or of an individual. **4** *Linguistics.* the set of all the morphemes of a language. [C17: NL, from Gk *lexikon*, n use of *lexikos* relating to words, from Gk *lexis* word, from *legein* to speak]

lexigraphy (lɛk'sɪgrəfɪ) *n* a system of writing in which each word is represented by a sign. [C19: from Gk *lexis* word + -GRAPHY]

lexis ('lɛksɪs) *n* the totality of vocabulary items in a language. [C20: from Gk *lexis* word]

ley (leɪ, liː) *n* **1** arable land temporarily under grass. **2** Also: **ley line.** a line joining two prominent points in the landscape, thought to be the line of a prehistoric track. [C14: var. of LEA]

Leyden jar ('laɪdᵊn) *n Physics.* an early type of capacitor consisting of a glass jar with the lower part of the inside and outside coated with tin foil. [C18: first made in Leiden (*Leyden*), city in the Netherlands]

lf *Printing. abbrev. for* light face.

LF *Radio. abbrev. for* low frequency.

LG *abbrev. for* Low German.

LGV (in Britain) *abbrev. for* large goods vehicle.

lh *or* **LH** *abbrev. for* left hand.

Li *the chemical symbol for* lithium.

liabilities (ˌlaɪə'bɪlɪtɪz) *pl n Accounting.* business obligations not discharged and shown as balanced against assets on the balance sheet.

liability ❶ (ˌlaɪə'bɪlɪtɪ) *n, pl* **liabilities. 1** the state of being liable. **2** a financial obligation. **3** a hindrance or disadvantage.

liable ❶ ('laɪəbᵊl) *adj* (*postpositive*) **1** legally obliged or responsible; answerable. **2** susceptible or exposed; subject. **3** probable or likely: *it's liable to happen soon.* [C15: ? via Anglo-F, from OF *lier* to bind, from L *ligāre*]

> **USAGE NOTE** The use of *liable to* to mean *likely to* was formerly considered incorrect, but is now acceptable.

liaise ❶ (lɪ'eɪz) *vb* **liaises, liaising, liaised.** (*intr;* usually foll. by *with*) to communicate and maintain contact (with). [C20: back formation from LIAISON]

liaison ❶ (lɪ'eɪzɒn) *n* **1** communication and contact between groups or units. **2** a secretive or adulterous sexual relationship. **3** the relationship between military units necessary to ensure unity of purpose. **4** (esp. in French) the pronunciation of a normally silent consonant at the end of a word immediately before another word commencing with a vowel, in such a way that the consonant is taken over as the initial sound of the following word, as in *ils ont* (ilzɔ̃). **5** any thickening for soups, sauces, etc., such as egg yolks or cream. [C17: via F from OF, from *lier* to bind, from L *ligāre*]

liana (lɪ'ɑːnə) *or* **liane** (lɪ'ɑːn) *n* any of various woody climbing plants of tropical forests. [C19: changed from earlier *liane* (through infl. of F *lier* to bind), from F, from ?]

liar ❶ ('laɪə) *n* a person who tells lies.

Lias ('laɪəs) *n* the lowest series of rocks of the Jurassic system. [C15 (referring to a kind of limestone), C19 (geological sense): from OF *liois*, ?from *lie* dregs, so called from its appearance]
▸ **Liassic** (laɪ'æsɪk) *adj*

lib (lɪb) *n Inf., sometimes derog.* short for **liberation.**

lib. *abbrev. for:* **1** liber. [L: book] **2** librarian. **3** library.

Lib. *abbrev. for* Liberal.

libation (laɪ'beɪʃən) *n* **1a** the pouring-out of wine, etc., in honour of a deity. **1b** the liquid so poured out. **2** *Usually facetious.* an alcoholic drink. [C14: from L *lībātiō*, from *lībāre* to pour an offering of drink]

libel ❶ ('laɪbᵊl) *n* **1** *Law.* **1a** the publication of defamatory matter in permanent form, as by a written or printed statement, picture, etc. **1b** the act of publishing such matter. **2** any defamatory or unflattering representation or statement. **3** *Scots Law.* the formal statement of a charge. ◆ *vb* **libels, libelling, libelled** *or US* **libels, libeling, libeled.** (*tr*) **4** *Law.* to make or publish a defamatory statement or representation about (a person). **5** to misrepresent injuriously. [C13 (in the sense: written statement), hence C14 legal sense: a plaintiff's statement, via OF from L *libellus* a little book]
▸ **'libeller** *or* **'libelist** *n* ▸ **'libellous** *or* **'libelous** *adj*

liberal ❶ ('lɪbərəl, 'lɪbrəl) *adj* **1** relating to or having social and political views that favour progress and reform. **2** relating to or having policies or views advocating individual freedom. **3** giving and generous in temperament or behaviour. **4** tolerant of other people. **5** abundant; lavish: *a liberal helping of cream.* **6** not strict; free: *a liberal translation.* **7** of or relating to an education that aims to develop general cultural interests and intellectual ability. ◆ *n* **8** a person who has liberal ideas or opinions. [C14: from L *līberālis* of freedom, from *līber* free]
▸ **'liberally** *adv* ▸ **'liberalness** *n*

Liberal ('lɪbərəl, 'lɪbrəl) *n* **1** a member or supporter of a Liberal Party or Liberal Democrat party. ◆ *adj* **2** of or relating to a Liberal Party.

liberal arts *pl n* the fine arts, humanities, sociology, languages, and literature. Often shortened to **arts.**

Liberal Democrat *n* a member or supporter of the Liberal Democrats.

Liberal Democrats *pl n* (in Britain) a political party with centrist policies; established in 1988 as the Social and Liberal Democrats when the Liberal Party merged with the Social Democratic Party; renamed Liberal Democrats in 1989.

liberalism ❶ ('lɪbərəˌlɪzəm, 'lɪbrə-) *n* liberal opinions, practices, or politics.

liberality ❶ (ˌlɪbə'rælɪtɪ) *n, pl* **liberalities. 1** generosity; bounty. **2** the quality or condition of being liberal.

liberalize ❶ *or* **liberalise** ('lɪbərəˌlaɪz, 'lɪbrə-) *vb* **liberalizes, liberalizing, liberalized** *or* **liberalises, liberalising, liberalised.** to make or become liberal.
▸ **ˌliberali'zation** *or* **ˌliberali'sation** *n* ▸ **'liberalˌizer** *or* **'liberalˌiser** *n*

Liberal Party *n* **1** one of the former major political parties in Britain; in 1988 it merged with the Social Democratic Party to form the Social and Liberal Democrats; renamed the Liberal Democrats in 1989. **2** one of the major political parties in Australia, a conservative party, generally opposed to the Labor Party. **3** any other party supporting liberal policies.

liberal studies *n* (*functioning as sing*) *Brit.* a supplementary arts course for those specializing in scientific, technical, or professional studies.

liberate ❶ ('lɪbəˌreɪt) *vb* **liberates, liberating, liberated.** (*tr*) **1** to give liberty to; make free. **2** to release (something, esp. a gas) from chemical combination. **3** to release from occupation or subjugation by a foreign power. **4** to free from social prejudices or injustices. **5** *Euphemistic or facetious.* to steal.
▸ **'liberˌator** *n*

liberated ('lɪbəˌreɪtɪd) *adj* **1** given liberty; freed; released. **2** released from occupation or subjugation by a foreign power. **3** (esp. in feminist theory) not bound by traditional sexual and social roles.

liberation ❶ (ˌlɪbə'reɪʃən) *n* **1** a liberating or being liberated. **2** the seek-

THESAURUS

lexicon *n* **1** = **dictionary,** wordbook **2** = **vocabulary,** glossary, word list

liability *n* **1** = **responsibility,** accountability, answerability, culpability, duty, obligation, onus **1** = **tendency,** likelihood, probability, proneness, susceptibility **2** = **debt,** arrear, debit, indebtedness, obligation **3** = **disadvantage,** albatross, burden, drag, drawback, encumbrance, handicap, hindrance, impediment, inconvenience, millstone, minus (*inf.*), nuisance

liable *adj* **1** = **responsible,** accountable, amenable, answerable, bound, chargeable, obligated **2** = **vulnerable,** exposed, open, subject, susceptible **3** = **likely,** apt, disposed, inclined, prone, tending

liaise *vb* = **communicate,** connect, hook up, interchange, intermediate, keep contact, link, mediate

liaison *n* **1** = **communication,** connection, contact, hook-up, interchange **2** = **affair,** amour, entanglement, fling, illicit romance, intrigue, love affair, romance

liar *n* = **falsifier,** fabricator, fibber, perjurer, prevaricator, storyteller (*inf.*)

libel *n* **2** = **defamation,** aspersion, calumny, denigration, obloquy, slander, smear, vituperation ◆ *vb* **5** = **defame,** blacken, calumniate, derogate, drag (someone's) name through the mud, malign, revile, slander, slur, smear, traduce, vilify

libellous *adj* **2** = **defamatory,** aspersive, calumniatory, calumnious, derogatory, false, injurious, malicious, maligning, scurrilous, slanderous, traducing, untrue, vilifying, vituperative

liberal *adj* **1, 2** = **progressive,** advanced, humanistic, latitudinarian, libertarian, politically correct *or* PC, radical, reformist, right-on (*inf.*) **3** = **generous,** altruistic, beneficent, bounteous, bountiful, charitable, free-handed, kind, openhanded, open-hearted, prodigal, unstinting **4** = **tolerant,** advanced, broad-minded, catholic, enlightened, high-minded, humanitarian, indulgent, magnanimous, permissive, politically correct *or* PC, right-on (*inf.*), unbiased, unbigoted, unprejudiced **5** = **abundant,** ample, bountiful, copious, handsome, lavish, munificent, plentiful, profuse, rich **6** = **flexible,** broad, free, general, inexact, lenient, loose, not close, not literal, not strict

Antonyms *adj* ≠ **progressive:** conservative, reactionary, right-wing ≠ **generous:** cheap, stingy ≠ **tolerant:** biased, bigoted, intolerant, prejudiced ≠ **abundant:** inadequate, limited, skimpy, small ≠ **flexible:** fixed, inflexible, literal, strict

liberalism *n* = **progressivism,** freethinking, humanitarianism, latitudinarianism, libertarianism, radicalism

liberality *n* **1** = **generosity,** altruism, beneficence, benevolence, bounty, charity, free-handedness, kindness, largesse *or* largess, munificence, open-handedness, philanthropy **2** = **broad-mindedness,** breadth, candour, catholicity, impartiality, latitude, liberalism, libertarianism, magnanimity, permissiveness, progressivism, toleration

liberalize *vb* = **relax,** ameliorate, broaden, ease, expand, extend, loosen, mitigate, moderate, modify, slacken, soften, stretch

liberate *vb* **1, 3** = **free,** deliver, discharge, disenthral, emancipate, let loose, let out, manumit, redeem, release, rescue, set free

Antonyms *vb* confine, detain, immure, imprison, incarcerate, intern, jail, lock up, put away

liberation *n* **1** = **freeing,** deliverance, emanci-

ing of equal status or just treatment for or on behalf of any group believed to be discriminated against: *women's liberation; animal liberation.* ▸ˌ**liber'ationist** *n, adj*

liberation theology *n* the belief that Christianity involves not only faith in the Church but a commitment to change social and political conditions where it is considered exploitation and oppression exist: applied esp. to South America.

libertarian (ˌlɪbəˈtɛərɪən) *n* **1** a believer in freedom of thought, expression, etc. **2** a believer in the doctrine of free will. Cf. **determinism.** ◆ *adj* **3** of, relating to, or characteristic of a libertarian. [C18: from LIBERTY] ▸ˌ**liber'tarianism** *n*

libertine Ⓣ (ˈlɪbəˌtiːn, -ˌtaɪn) *n* **1** a morally dissolute person. ◆ *adj* **2** morally dissolute. [C14 (in the sense: freedman, dissolute person): from L *lībertīnus* freedman, from *lībertus* freed, from *līber* free] ▸ˈ**liberˌtinage** *or* ˈ**libertinˌism** *n*

liberty Ⓣ (ˈlɪbətɪ) *n, pl* **liberties. 1** the power of choosing, thinking, and acting for oneself; freedom from control or restriction. **2** the right or privilege of access to a particular place; freedom. **3** (*often pl*) a social action regarded as being familiar, forward, or improper. **4** (*often pl*) an action that is unauthorized: *he took liberties with the translation.* **5a** authorized leave granted to a sailor. **5b** (*as modifier*): *liberty man; liberty boat.* **6 at liberty.** free, unoccupied, or unrestricted. **7 take liberties (with).** to be overfamiliar or overpresumptuous. [C14: from OF *liberté*, from L *lībertās*, from *līber* free]

liberty bodice *n* a sleeveless vestlike undergarment covering the upper part of the body, formerly worn esp. by young children.

liberty hall *n* (*sometimes caps.*) *Inf.* a place or condition of complete liberty.

libidinous Ⓣ (lɪˈbɪdɪnəs) *adj* characterized by excessive sexual desire. ▸**liˈbidinously** *adv* ▸**liˈbidinousness** *n*

libido (lɪˈbiːdəʊ) *n, pl* **libidos. 1** *Psychoanal.* psychic energy emanating from the id. **2** sexual urge or desire. [C20 (in psychoanalysis): from L: desire] ▸**libidinal** (lɪˈbɪdɪnᵊl) *adj* ▸**liˈbidinally** *adv*

libra (ˈlaɪbrə) *n, pl* **librae** (-briː). an ancient Roman unit of weight corresponding to 1 pound. [C14: from L, lit.: scales]

Libra (ˈliːbrə) *n, Latin genitive* **Librae** (ˈliːbriː). **1** *Astron.* a small faint zodiacal constellation in the S hemisphere, lying between Virgo and Scorpius. **2** Also called: the **Scales**, the **Balance.** *Astrol.* the seventh sign of the zodiac. The sun is in this sign between about Sept. 23 and Oct. 22.

librarian (laɪˈbrɛərɪən) *n* a person in charge of or assisting in a library. ▸**liˈbrarianˌship** *n*

library (ˈlaɪbrərɪ) *n, pl* **libraries. 1** a room or set of rooms where books and other literary materials are kept. **2** a collection of literary materials, films, CDs, etc., kept for borrowing or reference. **3** the building or institution that houses such a collection: *a public library.* **4** a set of books published as a series, often in a similar format. **5** *Computing.* a collection of standard programs and subroutines, usually stored on disk. **6** a collection of specific items for reference or checking against: *a library of genetic material.* [C14: from OF *librairie*, from Med. L *librāris*, n. use of L *librārius* relating to books, from *liber* book]

libration (laɪˈbreɪʃən) *n* **1** the act of oscillating. **2** a real or apparent oscillation of the moon enabling approximately nine per cent of the surface facing away from earth to be seen. [C17: from L, from *librāre* to balance]

librettist (lɪˈbrɛtɪst) *n* the author of a libretto.

libretto Ⓣ (lɪˈbrɛtəʊ) *n, pl* **librettos** *or* **libretti** (-tiː). a text written for and set to music in an opera, etc. [C18: from It., dim. of *libro* book]

Librium (ˈlɪbrɪəm) *n Trademark.* a preparation of the drug chlordiazepoxide used as a tranquillizer. See also **benzodiazepine.**

Libyan (ˈlɪbɪən) *adj* **1** of or relating to Libya, a republic in N Africa, on the Mediterranean, its people, or its language. ◆ *n* **2** a native or inhabitant of Libya. **3** the extinct Hamitic language of ancient Libya.

lice (laɪs) *n* the plural of **louse.**

licence Ⓣ *or US* **license** (ˈlaɪsəns) *n* **1** a certificate, tag, document, etc., giving official permission to do something. **2** formal permission or exemption. **3** liberty of action or thought; freedom. **4** intentional disregard of conventional rules to achieve a certain effect: *poetic licence.* **5** excessive freedom. [C14: via OF and Med. L *licentia* permission, from L: freedom, from *licet* it is allowed]

license Ⓣ (ˈlaɪsəns) *vb* **licenses, licensing, licensed.** (*tr*) **1** to grant or give a licence for (something, such as the sale of alcohol). **2** to give permission to or for. ▸ˈ**licensable** *adj* ▸ˈ**licenser** *or* ˈ**licensor** *n*

licensee (ˌlaɪsənˈsiː) *n* a person who holds a licence, esp. one to sell alcoholic drink.

licentiate (laɪˈsɛnʃɪɪt) *n* **1** a person who holds a formal attestation of competence to practise a certain profession. **2** a higher degree awarded by certain, chiefly European, universities. **3** a person who holds this degree. **4** *Chiefly Presbyterian Church.* a person holding a licence to preach. [C15: from Med. L *licentiātus*, from *licentiāre* to permit] ▸**liˈcentiateˌship** *n*

licentious Ⓣ (laɪˈsɛnʃəs) *adj* **1** sexually unrestrained or promiscuous. **2** *Now rare.* showing disregard for convention. [C16: from L *licentiōsus* capricious, from *licentia* LICENCE] ▸**liˈcentiously** *adv* ▸**liˈcentiousness** *n*

lichee (ˌlaɪˈtʃiː) *n* a variant spelling of **litchi.**

lichen (ˈlaɪkən, ˈlɪtʃən) *n* an organism that is formed by the symbiotic association of a fungus and an alga or cyanobacterium and occurs as crusty patches or bushy growths on tree trunks, bare ground, etc. Lichens are now classified as a phylum of fungi. [C17: via L from Gk *leikhēn*, from *leikhein* to lick] ▸ˈ**lichened** *adj* ▸ˈ**lichenous** *adj*

lich gate (lɪtʃ) *n* a variant spelling of **lych gate.**

licit (ˈlɪsɪt) *adj* a less common word for **lawful.** [C15: from L *licitus*, from *licēre* to be permitted] ▸ˈ**licitly** *adv* ▸ˈ**licitness** *n*

lick Ⓣ (lɪk) *vb* **1** (*tr*) to pass the tongue over, esp. in order to taste or consume. **2** to flicker or move lightly over or round (something): *the flames licked around the door.* **3** (*tr*) *Inf.* **3a** to defeat or vanquish. **3b** to flog or thrash. **3c** to be or do much better than. **4 lick into shape.** to put into a satisfactory condition. **5 lick one's wounds.** to retire after a defeat. ◆ *n* **6** an instance of passing the tongue over something. **7** a small amount: *a lick of paint.* **8** short for **salt lick. 9** *Inf.* a hit; blow. **10** *Sl.* a short musical phrase, usually on one instrument. **11** *Inf.* rate of movement; speed. **12 a lick and a promise.** something hastily done, esp. a hurried wash. [OE *liccian*] ▸ˈ**licker** *n*

lickerish *or* **liquorish** (ˈlɪkərɪʃ) *adj Arch.* **1** lecherous or lustful. **2** greedy; gluttonous. **3** appetizing or tempting. [C16: changed from C13 *lickerous*, from OF *lechereus* lecherous; see LECHER]

lickety-split (ˈlɪkɪtɪˈsplɪt) *adv US & Canad. inf.* very quickly; speedily. [C19: from LICK + SPLIT]

licking Ⓣ (ˈlɪkɪŋ) *n Inf.* **1** a beating. **2** a defeat.

lickspittle (ˈlɪkˌspɪtᵊl) *n* a flattering or servile person.

licorice (ˈlɪkərɪs) *n* the usual US and Canad. spelling of **liquorice.**

lictor (ˈlɪktə) *n* one of a group of ancient Roman officials, usually bearing fasces, who attended magistrates, etc. [C16 *lictor*, C14 *littour*, from L *ligāre* to bind]

lid (lɪd) *n* **1** a cover, usually removable or hinged, for a receptacle: *a*

THESAURUS

pation, enfranchisement, freedom, liberating, liberty, manumission, redemption, release, unfettering, unshackling

liberator *n* **1** = **deliverer**, emancipator, freer, manumitter, redeemer, rescuer, saviour

libertine *n* **1** = **reprobate**, debauchee, lech *or* letch (*inf.*), lecher, loose liver, profligate, rake, roué, seducer, sensualist, swinger (*sl.*), voluptuary, womanizer ◆ *adj* **2** = **promiscuous**, abandoned, corrupt, debauched, decadent, degenerate, depraved, dissolute, immoral, licentious, profligate, rakish, reprobate, voluptuous, wanton

liberty *n* **1** = **freedom**, autonomy, emancipation, immunity, independence, liberation, release, self-determination, sovereignty **2** = **permission**, authorization, blank cheque, carte blanche, dispensation, exemption, franchise, freedom, leave, licence, prerogative, privilege, right, sanction **3** = **impertinence**, disrespect, familiarity, forwardness, impropriety, impudence, insolence, overfamiliarity, presumption, presumptuousness **6 at liberty** = **free**, not confined, on the loose, unlimited, unoccupied, unrestricted

Antonyms *n* ≠ **freedom:** captivity, constraint, enslavement, imprisonment, restraint, slavery, tyranny ≠ **permission:** compulsion, duress, restriction

libidinous *adj* = **lustful**, carnal, concupiscent, debauched, impure, incontinent, lascivious, lecherous, lickerish (*arch.*), loose, prurient, randy (*inf., chiefly Brit.*), ruttish, salacious, sensual, unchaste, wanton, wicked

libretto *n* = **words**, book, lines, lyrics, script

licence *n* **1** = **certificate**, charter, permit, warrant **2, 3** = **permission**, a free hand, authority, authorization, blank cheque, carte blanche, dispensation, entitlement, exemption, immunity, leave, liberty, privilege, right **4** = **freedom**, independence, latitude, leeway, liberty **5** = **immoderation**, abandon, anarchy, disorder, excess, impropriety, indulgence, irresponsibility, lawlessness, laxity, profligacy, unruliness

Antonyms *n* ≠ **permission:** denial, prohibition, restriction ≠ **freedom:** constraint, restraint ≠ **immoderation:** moderation, strictness

license *vb* **1, 2** = **permit**, accredit, allow, authorize, certify, commission, empower, enable, entitle, give a blank cheque to, sanction, warrant

Antonyms *vb* ban, debar, disallow, forbid, outlaw, prohibit, proscribe, rule out, veto

licentious *adj* **1** = **promiscuous**, abandoned, debauched, disorderly, dissolute, immoral, impure, lascivious, lax, lewd, libertine, libidinous, lubricious (*literary*), lustful, profligate, sensual, uncontrollable, uncontrolled, uncurbed, unruly, wanton

Antonyms *adj* chaste, law-abiding, lawful, moral, principled, proper, scrupulous, virtuous

licentiousness *n* **1** = **promiscuity**, abandon, debauchery, dissipation, dissoluteness, lechery, lewdness, libertinism, libidinousness, lubricity, lust, lustfulness, profligacy, prurience, salaciousness, salacity, wantonness

lick *vb* **1** = **taste**, brush, lap, tongue, touch, wash **2** = **flicker**, dart, flick, ignite, kindle, play over, ripple, touch **3a** *Informal* = **beat**, best, blow out of the water (*sl.*), clobber (*sl.*), defeat, outdo, outstrip, overcome, rout, run rings around (*inf.*), surpass, tank (*sl.*), trounce, undo, vanquish, wipe the floor with (*inf.*) **3b** *Informal* = **thrash**, beat, clobber (*sl.*), flog, lambast(e), slap, spank, strike, wallop (*inf.*) ◆ *n* **7** = **dab**, bit, brush, little, sample, speck, stroke, taste, touch **11** *Informal* = **pace**, clip (*inf.*), rate, speed

licking *n Informal* **1** = **thrashing**, beating, drubbing, flogging, hiding (*inf.*), spanking, tanning (*sl.*), whipping **2** = **defeat**, beating, drubbing, pasting (*sl.*), trouncing

saucepan lid; a desk lid. **2** short for **eyelid. 3 put the lid on.** *Inf.* **3a** *Brit.* to be the final blow to. **3b** to curb, prevent, or discourage. [OE *hlid*]
►**'lidded** *adj* ►**'lidless** *adj*

lido ('liːdəʊ) *n, pl* **lidos.** *Brit.* a public place of recreation, including a swimming pool. [C20: after the *Lido,* island bathing beach near Venice, from L *litus* shore]

lie[1] Ⓣ (laɪ) *vb* **lies, lying, lied. 1** (*intr*) to speak untruthfully with intent to mislead or deceive. **2** (*intr*) to convey a false impression or practise deception: *the camera does not lie.* ◆ *n* **3** an untrue or deceptive statement deliberately used to mislead. **4** something that is deliberately intended to deceive. **5 give the lie to. 5a** to disprove. **5b** to accuse of lying. ◆ Related adj: **mendacious.** [OE *lyge* (n), *lēogan* (vb)]

lie[2] Ⓣ (laɪ) *vb* **lies, lying, lay, lain.** (*intr*) **1** (often foll. by *down*) to place oneself or be in a prostrate position, horizontal to the ground. **2** to be situated, esp. on a horizontal surface: *the pencil is lying on the desk; India lies to the south of Russia.* **3** to be buried: *here lies Jane Brown.* **4** (*copula*) to be and remain (in a particular state or condition): *to lie dormant.* **5** to stretch or extend: *the city lies before us.* **6** (usually foll. by *on* or *upon*) to rest or weigh: *my sins lie heavily on my mind.* **7** (usually foll. by *in*) to exist or consist inherently: *strength lies in unity.* **8** (foll. by *with*) **8a** to be or rest (with): *the ultimate decision lies with you.* **8b** *Arch.* to have sexual intercourse (with). **9** (of an action, claim, appeal, etc.) to subsist; be maintainable or admissible. **10** *Arch.* to stay temporarily. ◆ *n* **11** the manner, place, or style in which something is situated. **12** the hiding place or lair of an animal. **13 lie of the land. 13a** the topography of the land. **13b** the way in which a situation is developing. ◆ See also **lie down, lie in,** etc. [OE *licgan* akin to OHG *ligen* to lie, L *lectus* bed]

USAGE NOTE See at **lay**[1].

Liebig condenser ('liːbɪg) *n Chem.* a laboratory condenser consisting of a glass tube surrounded by a glass envelope through which cooling water flows. [C19: after Baron von *Liebig* (1803–73), G chemist]

lied (liːd; *German* liːt) *n, pl* **lieder** ('liːdə; *German* 'liːdər). *Music.* any of various musical settings for solo voice and piano of a romantic or lyrical poem. [from G: song]

lie detector *n Inf.* a polygraph used esp. by a police interrogator to detect false or devious answers to questions, a sudden change in one or more involuntary physiological responses being considered a manifestation of guilt, fear, etc.

lie down *vb* (*intr, adv*) **1** to place oneself or be in a prostrate position in order to rest. **2** to accept without protest or opposition (esp. in **take something lying down**). ◆ *n* **lie-down. 3** a rest.

lief (liːf) *adv* **1** *Now rare.* gladly; willingly: *I'd as lief go today as tomorrow.* ◆ *adj* **2** *Arch.* **2a** ready; glad. **2b** dear; beloved. [OE *leof;* rel. to *lufu* love]

liege Ⓣ (liːdʒ) *adj* **1** (of a lord) owed feudal allegiance (esp. in **liege lord**). **2** (of a vassal or servant) owing feudal allegiance: *a liege subject.* **3** faithful; loyal. ◆ *n* **4** a liege lord. **5** a liegeman or true subject. [C13: from OF *lige,* from Med. L *līticus,* from *lītus, laetus* serf, of Gmc origin]

liegeman ('liːdʒˌmæn) *n, pl* **liegemen. 1** (formerly) a vassal. **2** a loyal follower.

lie in *vb* (*intr, adv*) **1** to remain in bed late in the morning. **2** to be confined in childbirth. ◆ *n* **lie-in. 3** a long stay in bed in the morning.

lien ('liːən, liːn) *n Law.* a right to retain possession of another's property pending discharge of a debt. [C16: via OF from L *ligāmen* bond, from *ligāre* to bind]

lierne (lɪ'ɜːn) *n Archit.* a short rib that connects the intersections of the primary ribs, esp. in Gothic vaulting. [C19: from F, ? rel. to *lier* to bind]

lie to *vb* (*intr, adv*) *Naut.* (of a vessel) to be hove to with little or no swinging.

lieu (ljuː, luː) *n* stead; place (esp. in **in lieu, in lieu of**). [C13: from OF, ult. from L *locus* place]

lieutenant (lɛf'tɛnənt; *US* luː'tɛnənt) *n* **1** a military officer holding commissioned rank immediately junior to a captain. **2** a naval officer holding commissioned rank immediately junior to a lieutenant commander. **3** *US.* an officer in a police or fire department ranking immediately junior to a captain. **4** a person who holds an office in subordination to or in place of a superior. [C14: from OF, lit.: place-holding]
►**lieu'tenancy** *n*

lieutenant colonel *n* an officer holding commissioned rank immediately junior to a colonel in certain armies, air forces, and marine corps.

lieutenant commander *n* an officer holding commissioned rank in certain navies immediately junior to a commander.

lieutenant general *n* an officer holding commissioned rank in certain armies, air forces, and marine corps immediately junior to a general.

lieutenant governor *n* **1** a deputy governor. **2** (in the US) an elected official who acts as deputy to a state governor. **3** (in Canada) the representative of the Crown in a province: appointed by the federal government.

life Ⓣ (laɪf) *n, pl* **lives** (laɪvz). **1** the state or quality that distinguishes living beings or organisms from dead ones and from inorganic matter, characterized chiefly by metabolism, growth, and the ability to reproduce and respond to stimuli. Related adj: **animate. 2** the period between birth and death. **3** a living person or being: *to save a life.* **4** the time between birth and the present time. **5a** the remainder or extent of one's life. **5b** (*as modifier*): *a life sentence; life membership; life work.* **6** *Inf.* short for **life imprisonment. 7** the amount of time that something is active or functioning: *the life of a battery.* **8** a present condition, state, or mode of existence: *my life is very dull here.* **9a** a biography. **9b** (*as modifier*): *a life story.* **10** a characteristic state or mode of existence: *town life.* **11** the sum or course of human events and activities. **12** liveliness or high spirits: *full of life.* **13** a source of strength, animation, or vitality: *he was the life of the show.* **14** all living things, taken as a whole: *there is no life on Mars; plant life.* **15** (*modifier*) *Arts.* drawn or taken from a living model: *life drawing.* **16** (in certain games) one of a number of opportunities for participation. **17 a matter of life and death.** a matter of extreme urgency. **18 as large as life.** *Inf.* real and living. **19 for the life of me (him, her,** etc.) though trying desperately. **20 not on your life.** *Inf.* certainly not. **21 the life and soul.** *Inf.* a person regarded as the main source of merriment and liveliness: *the life and soul of the party.* **22 to the life.** (of a copy or image) resembling the original exactly. **23 true to life.** faithful to reality. [OE *līf*]

life assurance *n* a form of insurance providing for the payment of a specified sum to a named beneficiary on the death of the policy-holder. Also called: **life insurance.**

life belt *n* a buoyant ring used to keep a person afloat when in danger of drowning.

lifeblood Ⓣ ('laɪfˌblʌd) *n* **1** the blood, considered as vital to life. **2** the essential or animating force.

lifeboat ('laɪfˌbəʊt) *n* **1** a boat used for rescuing people at sea, escaping from a sinking ship, etc. **2** *Inf.* a fund set up by the dealers in a market to rescue any member who may become insolvent as a result of a collapse in market prices.

life buoy *n* any of various kinds of buoyant device for keeping people afloat in an emergency.

life cycle *n* the series of changes occurring in an animal or plant between one stage and the identical stage in the next generation.

life expectancy *n* the statistically determined average number of years of life remaining after a specified age.

lifeguard ('laɪfˌgɑːd) *n* a person at a beach or pool to guard people against the risk of drowning.

life imprisonment *n* an indeterminate sentence always given for murder and as a maximum sentence in several other crimes. There is no remission, although the Home Secretary may order the prisoner's release on licence.

life jacket *n* an inflatable sleeveless jacket worn to keep a person afloat when in danger of drowning.

lifeless Ⓣ ('laɪflɪs) *adj* **1** without life; inanimate; dead. **2** not sustaining living organisms. **3** having no vitality or animation. **4** unconscious.
►**'lifelessly** *adv* ►**'lifelessness** *n*

lifelike Ⓣ ('laɪfˌlaɪk) *adj* closely resembling or representing life.
►**'lifeˌlikeness** *n*

lifeline ('laɪfˌlaɪn) *n* **1** a line thrown or fired aboard a vessel for hauling in a hawser for a breeches buoy. **2** a line by which a deep-sea diver is raised or lowered. **3** a single means of contact, communication, or support on which a person or an area, etc., relies.

lifelong Ⓣ ('laɪfˌlɒŋ) *adj* lasting for or as if for a lifetime.

THESAURUS

lie[1] *vb* **1 = fib,** dissimulate, equivocate, fabricate, falsify, forswear oneself, invent, misrepresent, perjure, prevaricate, tell a lie, tell untruths ◆ *n* **3 = falsehood,** deceit, fabrication, falsification, falsity, fib, fiction, invention, mendacity, pork pie (*Brit. sl.*), porky (*Brit. sl.*), prevarication, untruth, white lie

lie[2] *vb* **1 = recline,** be prone, be prostrate, be recumbent, be supine, couch, loll, lounge, repose, rest, sprawl, stretch out **2 = be situated,** be, be found, be located, belong, be placed, exist, extend, remain **3 = be buried,** be interred **6** *usually with* **on** *or* **upon = weigh,** burden, oppress, press, rest **7** *usually with* **in = exist,** be present, consist, dwell, inhere, pertain

liege *n* **4 = feudal lord,** chieftain, master, overlord, seigneur, sovereign, superior, suzerain

life *n* **1 = being,** animation, breath, entity, growth, sentience, viability, vitality **2 = existence,** being, career, continuance, course, duration, lifetime, span, time **3 = person,** human, human being, individual, mortal, soul **9a = biography,** autobiography, career, confessions, history, life story, memoirs, story **10 = behaviour,** conduct, life style, way of life **11 = the human condition,** the school of hard knocks, the times, the world, this mortal coil, trials and tribulations, vicissitudes **12 = liveliness,** activity, animation, brio, energy, get-up-and-go (*inf.*), go (*inf.*), high spirits, oomph (*inf.*), pep, sparkle, spirit, verve, vigour, vitality, vivacity, zest **13 = spirit,** animating spirit, *élan vital,* essence, heart, lifeblood, soul, vital spark **14 = living things,** creatures, living beings, organisms, wildlife

lifeblood *n* **2 = animating force,** driving force, essence, guts (*inf.*), heart, inspiration, life, stimulus, vital spark

lifeless *adj* **1 = dead,** cold, deceased, defunct, extinct, inanimate, inert **2 = barren,** bare, desert, empty, sterile, uninhabited, unproductive, waste **3 = dull,** cold, colourless, flat, heavy, hollow, lacklustre, lethargic, listless, passive, pointless, slow, sluggish, spent, spiritless, static, stiff, torpid, wooden **4 = unconscious,** comatose, dead to the world (*inf.*), in a faint, inert, insensate, insensible, out cold, out for the count
Antonyms *adj* ≠ **dead:** alive, alive and kicking, animate, live, living, vital ≠ **dull:** active, animated, lively, spirited

lifelike *adj* **= realistic,** authentic, exact, faithful, graphic, natural, photographic, real, true-to-life, undistorted, vivid

lifelong *adj* **= long-lasting,** constant, deep-

life peer *n Brit.* a peer whose title lapses at his death.
life preserver *n* **1** *Brit.* a club or bludgeon, esp. one kept for self-defence. **2** *US & Canad.* a life belt or life jacket.
lifer ('laɪfə) *n Inf.* a prisoner sentenced to imprisonment for life.
life raft *n* a raft for emergency use at sea.
life-saver *n* **1** the saver of a person's life. **2** *Austral.* an expert swimmer, esp. a member of a surf life-saving club at a surfing beach, who rescues surfers or swimmers from drowning. **3** *Inf.* a person or thing that gives help in time of need.
▸'**life-,saving** *adj, n*
life science *n* any one of the branches of science concerned with the structure and behaviour of living organisms, such as biology, botany, zoology, physiology, or biochemistry.
life-size *or* **life-sized** *adj* representing actual size.
life span *n* the period of time during which a human being, animal, machine, etc., may be expected to live or function.
lifestyle ('laɪf,staɪl) *n* **1** a set of attitudes, habits, or possessions associated with a particular person or group. **2** such attitudes, etc., regarded as fashionable or desirable. **3** *NZ.* **3a** a luxurious semirural manner of living. **3b** (*as modifier*): *a lifestyle property.*
lifestyle business *n* a small business in which the owners are more anxious to pursue interests that reflect their lifestyle than to make more than a comfortable living.
life-support *adj* of, providing, or relating to the equipment or treatment necessary to keep a person alive.
lifetime ⓘ ('laɪf,taɪm) *n* **1a** the length of time a person or animal is alive. **1b** (*as modifier*): *a lifetime supply.* **2** the length of time that something functions, is useful, etc. **3** Also called: **life.** *Physics.* the average time of existence of an unstable or reactive entity.
LIFO ('laɪfəʊ) *n acronym for* last in, first out (as an accounting principle in sorting stock). Cf. **FIFO.**
lift ⓘ (lɪft) *vb* **1** to rise or cause to rise upwards from the ground or another support to a higher place: *to lift a sack.* **2** to move or cause to move upwards: *to lift one's eyes.* **3** (*tr*) to take hold of in order to carry or remove: *to lift something down from a shelf.* **4** (*tr*) to raise in status, spirituality, estimation, etc.: *his position lifted him from the common crowd.* **5** (*tr*) to revoke or rescind: *to lift tax restrictions.* **6** (*tr*) to take (plants or underground crops) out of the ground for transplanting or harvesting. **7** (*intr*) to disappear by lifting or as if by lifting: *the fog lifted.* **8** (*tr*) *Inf.* to take unlawfully or dishonourably; steal. **9** (*tr*) *Inf.* to plagiarize. **10** (*tr*) *Sl.* to arrest. **11** (*tr*) to perform a face-lift on. ◆ *n* **12** the act or an instance of lifting. **13** the power or force available or used for lifting. **14a** *Brit.* a platform, compartment, or cage raised or lowered in a vertical shaft to transport persons or goods in a building. US and Canad. word: **elevator. 14b** See **chairlift, ski lift. 15** the distance or degree to which something is lifted. **16** a ride in a car or other vehicle for part or all of a passenger's journey. **17** a rise in the height of the ground. **18** a rise in morale or feeling of cheerfulness usually caused by some specific thing or event. **19** the force required to lift an object. **20** a layer inserted in the heel of a shoe, etc., to give the wearer added height. **21** aid; help. **22** the component of the aerodynamic forces acting on a wing, etc., at right angles to the airflow and opposing gravity. [C13: from ON]
▸'**lifter** *n*
liftoff ('lɪft,ɒf) *n* **1** the initial movement of a rocket from its launch pad. **2** the instant at which this occurs. ◆ *vb* **lift off. 3** (*intr, adv*) (of a rocket) to leave its launch pad.
lift pump *n* a pump that raises a fluid to a higher level. Cf. **force pump.**
lig (lɪg) *Brit. sl.* ◆ *n* **1** (esp. in the media) a function at which free entertainment and refreshments are available. ◆ *vb* **ligs, ligging, ligged. 2** (*intr*) to attend such a function; freeload. [C20: from ?]
▸'**ligger** *n* ▸'**ligging** *n*
ligament ('lɪgəmənt) *n* **1** *Anat.* any one of the bands of tough fibrous connective tissue that restrict movement in joints, connect various bones or cartilages, support muscles, etc. **2** any physical or abstract bond. [C14: from Med. L *ligāmentum,* from L (in the sense: bandage), from *ligāre* to bind]
ligand ('lɪgənd, 'laɪ-) *n Chem.* an atom, molecule, radical, or ion forming a complex with a central atom. [C20: from L *ligandum,* from *ligāre* to bind]
ligate ('laɪgeɪt) *vb* **ligates, ligating, ligated.** (*tr*) to tie up or constrict (something) with a ligature. [C16: from L *ligātus,* from *ligāre* to bind]
▸**li'gation** *n*
ligature ⓘ ('lɪgətʃə, -,tʃʊə) *n* **1** the act of binding or tying up. **2** something used to bind. **3** a link, bond, or tie. **4** *Surgery.* a thread or wire for tying around a vessel, duct, etc., as for constricting the flow of blood. **5** *Printing.* a character of two or more joined letters, such as ff, fi, fl, ffi. **6** *Music.* a slur or the group of notes connected by it. ◆ *vb* **ligatures, ligaturing, ligatured. 7** (*tr*) to bind with a ligature; ligate. [C14: from LL *ligātūra,* ult. from L *ligāre* to bind]
liger ('laɪgə) *n* the hybrid offspring of a female tiger and a male lion.
light[1] ⓘ (laɪt) *n* **1** the medium of illumination that makes sight possible. **2** Also called: **visible radiation.** electromagnetic radiation that is capable of causing a visual sensation. See also **speed of light. 3** (*not in technical usage*) electromagnetic radiation that has a wavelength outside this range, esp. ultraviolet radiation: *ultraviolet light.* **4** the sensation experienced when electromagnetic radiation within the visible spectrum falls on the retina of the eye. **5** anything that illuminates, such as a lamp or candle. **6** See **traffic light. 7** a particular quality or type of light: *a good light for reading.* **8a** illumination from the sun during the day; daylight. **8b** the time this appears; daybreak; dawn. **9** anything that allows the entrance of light, such as a window or compartment of a window. **10** the condition of being visible or known (esp. in **bring** *or* **come to light**). **11** an aspect or view: *he saw it in a different light.* **12** mental understanding or spiritual insight. **13** a person considered to be an authority or leader. **14** brightness of countenance, esp. a sparkle in the eyes. **15a** the act of igniting or kindling something, such as a cigarette. **15b** something that ignites or kindles, esp. in a specified manner, such as a spark or flame. **15c** something used for igniting or kindling, such as a match. **16** See **lighthouse. 17 in (the) light of.** in view of; taking into account; considering. **18 see the light.** to acquire insight. **19 see the light (of day). 19a** to come into being. **19b** to come to public notice. **20 strike a light. 20a** (*vb*) to ignite something, esp. a match, by friction. **20b** (*interj*) *Brit.* an exclamation of surprise. ◆ *adj* **21** full of light; well-lighted. **22** (of a colour) reflecting or transmitting a large amount of light: *light yellow.* ◆ *vb* **lights, lighting, lighted** *or* **lit. 23** to ignite or cause to ignite. **24** (often foll. by *up*) to illuminate or cause to illuminate. **25** to make or become cheerful or animated. **26** (*tr*) to guide or lead by light. ◆ See also **lights**[1], **light up.** [OE *lēoht*]
▸'**lightish** *adj* ▸'**lightless** *adj*
light[2] ⓘ (laɪt) *adj* **1** not heavy; weighing relatively little. **2** having relatively low density: *magnesium is a light metal.* **3** lacking sufficient weight; not agreeing with standard or official weights. **4** not great in degree, intensity, or number: *light rain.* **5** without burdens, difficulties, or problems; easily borne or done: *a light heart; light work.* **6** graceful, agile, or deft: *light fingers.* **7** not bulky or clumsy. **8** not serious or profound; entertaining: *light music; light verse.* **9** without importance or consequence; insignificant: *no light matter.* **10** frivolous or capricious. **11** loose in morals. **12** dizzy or unclear: *a light head.* **13** (of bread, cake, etc.) spongy or well leavened. **14** easily digested: *a light meal.* **15** relatively low in alcoholic content: *a light wine.* **16** (of a soil) having a crumbly texture. **17** (of a vessel, lorry, etc.) **17a** designed to carry light loads. **17b** not loaded. **18** carrying light arms or equipment: *light infantry.* **19** (of an industry) engaged in the production of small consumer goods using light machinery. **20** *Aeronautics.* (of an aircraft) having a maximum take-off weight less than 5670 kilograms (12 500 pounds). **21** *Chem.* (of an oil fraction obtained from coal tar) having a boiling range between about 100° and 210°C. **22** (of a railway) having

THESAURUS

rooted, enduring, for all one's life, for life, lasting, lifetime, long-standing, perennial, permanent, persistent
lifetime *n* **1a** = **existence,** all one's born days, career, course, day(s), life span, one's natural life, period, span, time
lift *vb* **1, 2** = **raise,** bear aloft, buoy up, draw up, elevate, heft, hoist, pick up, raise high, rear, upheave, uplift, upraise **4** = **exalt,** advance, ameliorate, boost, dignify, elevate, enhance, improve, promote, raise, upgrade **5** = **revoke,** annul, cancel, countermand, end, relax, remove, rescind, stop, terminate **7** = **disappear,** be dispelled, disperse, dissipate, vanish **8** *Informal* = **steal,** appropriate, blag, copy, crib (*inf.*), nick (*sl., chiefly Brit.*), pilfer, pinch (*inf.*), pirate, plagiarize, pocket, purloin, take, thieve ◆ *n* **14a** = **elevator** (*chiefly US*) **16** = **ride,** car ride, drive, run, transport **18** = **boost,** encouragement, fillip, gee-up, pick-me-up, reassurance, shot in the arm (*inf.*), uplift
Antonyms *vb* ≠ **raise:** dash, descend, drop, fall, hang, lower ≠ **exalt:** depress ≠ **revoke:** establish, impose ◆ *n* ≠ **boost:** blow, letdown
ligature *n* **2, 3** = **link,** band, bandage, binding, bond, connection, ligament, tie
light[1] *n* **1, 2** = **brightness,** blaze, brilliance, effulgence, flash, glare, gleam, glint, glow, illumination, incandescence, lambency, luminescence, luminosity, lustre, phosphorescence, radiance, ray, refulgence, scintillation, shine, sparkle **5** = **lamp,** beacon, bulb, candle, flare, lantern, lighthouse, star, taper, torch **8** = **daybreak,** broad day, cockcrow, dawn, daylight, daytime, morn (*poetic*), morning, sun, sunbeam, sunrise, sunshine **11** = **aspect,** angle, approach, attitude, context, interpretation, point of view, slant, vantage point, viewpoint **12** = **understanding,** awareness, comprehension, elucidation, explanation, illustration, information, insight, knowledge **13** = **shining example,** example, exemplar, guiding light, model, paragon **15b, c** = **match,** flame, lighter **17 in (the) light of** = **considering,** bearing in mind, because of, in view of, taking into account, with knowledge of ◆ *adj* **21** = **bright,** aglow, brilliant, glowing, illuminated, luminous, lustrous, shining, sunny, well-lighted, well-lit **22** = **pale,** bleached, blond, blonde, faded, fair, light-hued, light-toned, pastel ◆ *vb* **23** = **ignite,** fire, inflame, kindle, set a match to, torch **24** = **illuminate,** brighten, clarify, floodlight, flood with light, illumine, irradiate, lighten, light up, put on, switch on, turn on **25** = **cheer,** animate, brighten, irradiate, lighten
Antonyms *n* ≠ **brightness:** cloud, dark, darkness, dusk, obscurity, shade, shadow ≠ **understanding:** mystery ◆ *adj* ≠ **bright:** dark, dim, dusky, gloomy ≠ **pale:** dark, deep ◆ *vb* ≠ **ignite:** douse, extinguish, put out, quench ≠ **illuminate:** cloud, darken, dull
light[2] *adj* **1** = **insubstantial,** buoyant, delicate, flimsy, imponderous, lightsome, lightweight, portable, slight **3** = **underweight 4** = **weak,** faint, gentle, indistinct, mild, moderate, slight, soft **5** = **undemanding,** cushy (*inf.*), easy, effortless, manageable, moderate, simple, unexacting, untaxing **6** = **nimble,** agile, airy, graceful, light-footed, lithe, sprightly, sylphlike **8, 10** = **light-hearted,** amusing, diverting, entertaining, frivolous, funny, gay, humorous, pleasing, superficial, trifling, trivial, witty **9** = **insignificant,** inconsequential, inconsiderable, minute, scanty, slight, small, thin, tiny, trifling, trivial, unsubstantial, wee **12** = **dizzy,** giddy, light-headed, reeling, unsteady, volatile **14** = **digestible,** frugal, modest, not heavy, not rich, restricted, small **16** = **crumbly,** friable, loose,

a narrow gauge, or in some cases a standard gauge with speed or load restrictions not applied to a main line. **23** *Phonetics, prosody.* (of a syllable, vowel, etc.) unaccented or weakly stressed; short. **24 light on.** *Inf.* lacking a sufficient quantity of (something). **25 make light of.** to treat as insignificant or trifling. ◆ *adv* **26** a less common word for lightly. **27** with little equipment, baggage, etc.: *to travel light.* ◆ *vb* **lights, lighting, lighted** *or* **lit.** (*intr*) **28** (esp. of birds) to settle or land after flight. **29** to get down from a horse, vehicle, etc. **30** (foll. by *on* or *upon*) to come upon unexpectedly. **31** to strike or fall on: *the choice lighted on me.* ◆ See also **light into, light out, lights**[2]. [OE *lēoht*]
▸ **'lightish** *adj* ▸ **'lightly** *adv* ▸ **'lightness** *n*

light air *n* very light air movement of force one (1–3 mph) on the Beaufort scale.

light box *n* a light source contained in a box and covered with a diffuser, used for viewing photographic transparencies, negatives, etc.

light breeze *n* a very light wind of force two (4–7 mph) on the Beaufort scale.

light bulb *n* a glass bulb containing a gas at low pressure and enclosing a thin metal filament that emits light when an electric current is passed through it. Sometimes shortened to **bulb.**

light-emitting diode *n* a semiconductor that emits light when an electric current is applied to it: used in electronic calculators, digital watches, etc.

lighten[1] 🅣 ('laɪtᵊn) *vb* **1** to become or make light. **2** (*intr*) to shine; glow. **3** (*intr*) (of lightning) to flash. **4** (*tr*) *Arch.* to cause to flash.

lighten[2] 🅣 ('laɪtᵊn) *vb* **1** to make or become less heavy. **2** to make or become less burdensome or oppressive; mitigate. **3** to make or become more cheerful or lively.

lightening ('laɪtᵊnɪŋ) *n Obstetrics.* the sensation, experienced by many women late in pregnancy when the head of the fetus enters the pelvis, of a reduction in pressure on the diaphragm.

lighter[1] ('laɪtə) *n* **1** a small portable device for providing a naked flame to light cigarettes, etc. **2** a person or thing that ignites something.

lighter[2] ('laɪtə) *n* a flat-bottomed barge used for transporting cargo, esp. in loading or unloading a ship. [C15: prob. from MDu.]

lighterage ('laɪtərɪdʒ) *n* **1** the conveyance or loading and unloading of cargo by means of a lighter. **2** the charge for this service.

light face *n* **1** *Printing.* a weight of type characterized by light thin lines. ◆ *adj also* **light-faced. 2** (of type) having this weight.

light-fingered 🅣 *adj* having nimble or agile fingers, esp. for thieving or picking pockets.

light flyweight *n* **1** an amateur boxer weighing not more than 48 kg (106 pounds). **2** an amateur wrestler weighing not more than 48 kg (106 pounds).

light-footed 🅣 *adj* having a light or nimble tread.
▸ **,light-'footedly** *adv*

light-headed 🅣 *adj* **1** frivolous. **2** giddy; feeling faint or slightly delirious.
▸ **,light-'headedly** *adv* ▸ **,light-'headedness** *n*

light-hearted 🅣 *adj* cheerful or carefree in mood or disposition.
▸ **,light-'heartedly** *adv* ▸ **,light-'heartedness** *n*

light heavyweight *n* **1** Also (in Britain): **cruiserweight. 1a** a professional boxer weighing 160–175 pounds (72.5–79.5 kg). **1b** an amateur boxer weighing 75–81 kg (165–179 pounds). **2a** a professional wrestler weighing not more than 198 pounds (90 kg). **2b** an amateur wrestler weighing not more than 90 kg (198 pounds).

lighthouse ('laɪt,haʊs) *n* a fixed structure in the form of a tower equipped with a light visible to mariners for warning them of obstructions, etc.

lighting ('laɪtɪŋ) *n* **1** the act or quality of illumination or ignition. **2** the apparatus for supplying artificial light effects to a stage, film, or television set. **3** the distribution of light on an object or figure, as in painting, photography, etc.

lighting cameraman *n Films.* the person who designs and supervises the lighting of scenes to be filmed.

lighting-up time *n* the time when vehicles are required by law to have their lights on.

light into 🅣 *vb* (*tr, prep*) *Inf.* to assail physically or verbally.

light middleweight *n* an amateur boxer weighing 67–71 kg (148–157 pounds).

lightness ('laɪtnɪs) *n* the attribute of an object or colour that enables an observer to judge the extent to which the object or colour reflects or transmits incident light.

lightning ('laɪtnɪŋ) *n* **1** a flash of light in the sky, occurring during a thunderstorm and caused by a discharge of electricity, either between clouds or between a cloud and the earth. **2** (*modifier*) fast and sudden: *a lightning raid.* [C14: var. of *lightening*]

lightning conductor *or* **rod** *n* a metal strip terminating in sharp points, attached to the highest part of a building, etc., to discharge the electric field before it can reach a dangerous level and cause a lightning strike.

light opera *n* another term for **operetta.**

light out 🅣 *vb* (*intr, adv*) *Inf.* to depart quickly, as if being chased.

light pen *n Computer technol.* **a** a rodlike device which, when applied to the screen of a cathode-ray tube, can detect the time of passage of the illuminated spot across that point thus enabling a computer to determine the position on the screen being pointed at. **b** a penlike device, used to read bar codes, that emits light and determines the intensity of that light as reflected from a small area of an adjacent surface.

light pollution *n* the glow from street and domestic lighting that obscures the night sky and hinders the observation of faint stars.

light rail *n* a transport system using small trains or trams, often serving parts of a large metropolitan area.

lights[1] (laɪts) *pl n* a person's ideas, knowledge, or understanding: *he did it according to his lights.*

lights[2] (laɪts) *pl n* the lungs, esp. of sheep, bullocks, and pigs, used esp. for feeding pets. [C13: pl n use of LIGHT[2], referring to the light weight of the lungs]

light-sensitive *adj Physics.* (of a surface) having a photoelectric property, such as the ability to generate a current, change its electrical resistance, etc., when exposed to light.

lightship ('laɪt,ʃɪp) *n* a ship equipped as a lighthouse and moored where a fixed structure would prove impracticable.

light show *n* a kaleidoscopic display of moving lights, etc., projected onto a screen, esp. during pop concerts.

lightsome ('laɪtsəm) *adj Arch. or poetic.* **1** light-hearted or gay. **2** airy or buoyant. **3** not serious; frivolous.

lights out *n* **1** the time when those resident at an institution, such as soldiers in barracks or children at a boarding school, are expected to retire to bed. **2** a signal indicating this.

light table *n Printing.* a translucent surface of ground glass or a similar substance, illuminated from below and used for the examination of film, pages, etc.

light trap *n* any mechanical arrangement that allows some form of movement to take place while excluding light, such as a light-proof door or the lips of a film cassette.

light up *vb* (*adv*) **1** to light a cigarette, pipe, etc. **2** to illuminate or cause to illuminate. **3** to make or become cheerful or animated.

lightweight 🅣 ('laɪt,weɪt) *adj* **1** of a relatively light weight. **2** not serious; trivial. ◆ *n* **3** a person or animal of a relatively light weight. **4a** a professional boxer weighing 130–135 pounds (59–61 kg). **4b** an amateur boxer weighing 57–60 kg (126–132 pounds). **5a** a professional wrestler weighing not more than 154 pounds (70 kg). **5b** an amateur wrestler weighing not more than 68 kg (150 pounds). **6** *Inf.* a person of little importance or influence.

light welterweight *n* an amateur boxer weighing 60–63.5 kg (132–140 pounds).

light year *n* a unit of distance used in astronomy, equal to the distance travelled by light in one year, i.e. 9.4607×10^{12} kilometres or 0.3066 parsecs.

THESAURUS

porous, sandy, spongy ◆ *vb* **28** = **settle**, alight, land, perch **30** *foll. by* **on** *or* **upon** = **come across**, chance upon, discover, encounter, find, happen upon, hit upon, stumble on

Antonyms *adj* ≠ **insubstantial:** heavy ≠ **weak:** forceful, strong ≠ **undemanding:** burdensome, strenuous ≠ **nimble:** clumsy ≠ **light-hearted:** serious, sombre ≠ **insignificant:** deep, profound, serious, weighty ≠ **digestible:** rich, substantial ≠ **crumbly:** hard, strong

lighten[1] *vb* **1, 2** = **brighten**, become light, gleam, illuminate, irradiate, light up, make bright, shine **3** = **flash**

lighten[2] *vb* **1** = **make lighter**, disburden, ease, reduce in weight, unload **2** = **ease**, allay, alleviate, ameliorate, assuage, facilitate, lessen, mitigate, reduce, relieve **3** = **cheer**, brighten, buoy up, elate, encourage, gladden, hearten, inspire, lift, perk up, revive

Antonyms *vb* ≠ **make lighter:** burden, encumber, handicap ≠ **ease:** aggravate, heighten, increase, intensify, make worse, worsen ≠ **cheer:** depress, oppress, sadden, weigh down

light-fingered *adj* = **thieving**, pilfering, pinching (*inf.*), stealing

light-footed *adj* = **nimble**, agile, graceful, sprightly, spry

light-headed *adj* **1** = **frivolous**, bird-brained (*inf.*), featherbrained, fickle, flighty, flippant, foolish, giddy, inane, shallow, silly, superficial, trifling **2** = **faint**, delirious, dizzy, giddy, hazy, vertiginous, woozy (*inf.*)

light-hearted *adj* = **carefree**, blithe, blithesome (*literary*), bright, cheerful, chirpy (*inf.*), effervescent, gay, genial, glad, gleeful, happy-go-lucky, insouciant, jocund, jolly, jovial, joyful, joyous, merry, playful, sunny, untroubled, upbeat (*inf.*)

Antonyms *adj* cheerless, dejected, depressed, despondent, gloomy, heavy-hearted, low, melancholy, morose, sad

light into *vb Informal* = **attack**, assail, belabour, clobber (*sl.*), lambast(e), lay into (*inf.*), let fly at, pitch into (*inf.*), sail into (*inf.*), set about, tear into (*inf.*)

lightless *adj* **1** = **dark**, dim, dusky, gloomy, inky, jet black, murky, pitch-black, pitch-dark, pitchy, Stygian, sunless, unilluminated, unlighted, unlit

lightly *adv* **4** = **moderately**, delicately, faintly, gently, slightly, softly, sparingly, sparsely, thinly **5** = **easily**, effortlessly, readily, simply **10** = **carelessly**, breezily, flippantly, frivolously, heedlessly, indifferently, slightingly, thoughtlessly

Antonyms *adv* ≠ **moderately:** abundantly, heavily, thickly ≠ **gently:** firmly, forcefully, heavily ≠ **easily:** arduously, awkwardly, slowly, with difficulty ≠ **carelessly:** carefully, earnestly, ponderously, seriously

light out *vb Informal* = **run away**, abscond, depart, do a bunk (*Brit. sl.*), do a runner (*sl.*), escape, fly the coop (*US & Canad. inf.*), make off, quit, scarper (*Brit. sl.*), skedaddle (*inf.*)

lightweight *adj* **2** = **unimportant**, inconsequential, insignificant, nickel-and-dime (*US sl.*), of no account, paltry, petty, slight, trifling, trivial, worthless

ligneous ('lɪgnɪəs) *adj* of or resembling wood. [C17: from L *ligneus*, from *lignum* wood]

lignin ('lɪgnɪn) *n* a complex polymer occurring in certain plant cell walls making the plant rigid. [C19: from L *lignum* wood + -IN]

lignite ('lɪgnaɪt) *n* a brown carbonaceous sedimentary rock with woody texture that consists of accumulated layers of partially decomposed vegetation: used as a fuel. Also called: **brown coal.**
▸**lignitic** (lɪg'nɪtɪk) *adj*

lignum vitae ('lɪgnəm 'vaɪtɪ) *n* **1** either of two tropical American trees having blue or purple flowers. **2** the heavy resinous wood of either of these trees. ◆ See also **guaiacum.** [NL, from LL, lit.: wood of life]

ligroin ('lɪgrəʊɪn) *n* a volatile fraction of petroleum: used as a solvent. [from ?]

likable ❶ *or* **likeable** ('laɪkəbᵊl) *adj* easy to like; pleasing.
▸'**likableness** *or* '**likeableness** *n*

like[1] ❶ (laɪk) *adj* **1** (*prenominal*) similar; resembling. ◆ *prep* **2** similar to; similarly to; in the manner of: *acting like a maniac; he's so like his father.* **3** used correlatively to express similarity: *like mother, like daughter.* **4** such as: *there are lots of games — like draughts, for instance.* ◆ *adv* **5** a dialect word for **likely.** ◆ *conj* **6** *Not standard.* as though; as if: *you look like you've just seen a ghost.* **7** in the same way as; in the same way that: *she doesn't dance like you do.* ◆ *n* **8** the equal or counterpart of a person or thing. **9 the like.** similar things: *dogs, foxes, and the like.* **10 the likes** (*or* **like**) **of.** people or things similar to (someone or something specified): *we don't want the likes of you around here.* [shortened from OE *gelīc*]

> **USAGE NOTE** The use of *like* to mean *such as* was formerly thought to be undesirable in formal writing, but has now become acceptable. It was also thought that *as* rather than *like* should be used to mean *in the same way that*, but now both *as* and *like* are acceptable: *they hunt and catch fish as/like their ancestors used to.* The use of *look like* and *seem like* before a clause, although very common, is thought by many people to be incorrect or non-standard: *it looks as though he won't come* (not *it looks like he won't come*).

like[2] ❶ (laɪk) *vb* **likes, liking, liked. 1** (*tr*) to find (something) enjoyable or agreeable or find it enjoyable or agreeable (to do something): *he likes boxing; he likes to hear music.* **2** (*tr*) to be fond of. **3** (*tr*) to prefer or wish (to do something): *we would like you to go.* **4** (*tr*) to feel towards; consider; regard: *how did she like it?* **5** (*intr*) to feel disposed or inclined; choose; wish. ◆ *n* **6** (*usually pl*) a favourable feeling, desire, preference, etc. (esp. in **likes and dislikes**). [OE *līcian*]

-like *suffix forming adjectives.* **1** resembling or similar to: *lifelike.* **2** having the characteristics of: *childlike.* [from LIKE[1] (prep)]

likelihood ❶ ('laɪklɪ,hʊd) *or* **likeliness** *n* **1** the condition of being likely or probable; probability. **2** something that is probable.

likely ❶ ('laɪklɪ) *adj* **1** (usually foll. by an infinitive) tending or inclined; apt: *likely to rain.* **2** probable: *a likely result.* **3** believable or feasible; plausible. **4** appropriate for a purpose or activity. **5** having good possibilities of success: *a likely candidate.* ◆ *adv* **6** probably or presumably. **7 as likely as not.** very probably. [C14: from ON *līkligr*]

> **USAGE NOTE** *Likely* as an adverb is preceded by another, intensifying adverb, as in *it will very likely rain* or *it will most likely rain.* Its use without an intensifier, as in *it will likely rain* is regarded as unacceptable by most users of British English, though it is common in colloquial US English.

like-minded ❶ *adj* agreeing in opinions, goals, etc.
▸,**like-'mindedly** *adv* ▸,**like-'mindedness** *n*

liken ❶ ('laɪkən) *vb* (*tr*) to see or represent as the same or similar; compare. [C14: from LIKE[1] (adj)]

likeness ❶ ('laɪknɪs) *n* **1** the condition of being alike; similarity. **2** a painted, carved, moulded, or graphic image of a person or thing. **3** an imitative appearance; semblance.

likewise ❶ ('laɪk,waɪz) *adv* **1** in addition; moreover; also. **2** in like manner; similarly.

liking ❶ ('laɪkɪŋ) *n* **1** the feeling of a person who likes; fondness. **2** a preference, inclination, or pleasure.

lilac ('laɪlək) *n* **1** any of various Eurasian shrubs or small trees of the olive family which have large sprays of purple or white fragrant flowers. **2a** a light or moderate purple colour. **2b** (*as adj*): *a lilac carpet.* [C17: via F from Sp., from Ar. *līlak*, changed from Persian *nīlak* bluish, from *nīl* blue]

liliaceous (,lɪlɪ'eɪʃəs) *adj* of, relating to, or belonging to a family of plants having showy flowers and a bulb or bulblike organ: includes the lily, tulip, bluebell, and onion. [C18: from LL *līliāceus*, from *līlium* lily]

Lilliputian ❶ (,lɪlɪ'pjuːʃɪən) *n* **1** a tiny person or being. ◆ *adj* **2** tiny; very small. **3** petty or trivial. [C18: from *Lilliput*, an imaginary country of tiny inhabitants in Swift's *Gulliver's Travels* (1726)]

Lilo ('laɪ,ləʊ) *n, pl* **Lilos.** *Trademark.* a type of inflatable plastic or rubber mattress.

lilt ❶ (lɪlt) *n* **1** (in music) a jaunty rhythm. **2** a buoyant motion. ◆ *vb* (*intr*) **3** (of a melody) to have a lilt. **4** to move in a buoyant manner. [C14 *lulten*, from ?]
▸'**lilting** *adj*

lily ('lɪlɪ) *n, pl* **lilies. 1** any perennial plant of a N temperate genus, such as the tiger lily, having scaly bulbs and showy typically pendulous flowers. **2** the bulb or flower of any of these plants. **3** any of various similar or related plants, such as the water lily. [OE, from L *līlium*; rel. to Gk *leirion* lily]
▸'**lily-,like** *adj*

lily-livered ❶ *adj* cowardly; timid.

lily of the valley *n, pl* **lilies of the valley.** a small liliaceous plant of Eurasia and North America cultivated for its spikes of fragrant white bell-shaped flowers.

lily-white ❶ *adj* **1** of a pure white: *lily-white skin.* **2** *Inf.* pure; irreproachable.

lima bean ('laɪmə, 'liː-) *n* **1** any of several varieties of the bean plant native to tropical America, cultivated for its flat pods containing pale green edible seeds. **2** the seed of such a plant. [C19: after *Lima*, Peru]

limb[1] ❶ (lɪm) *n* **1** an arm or leg, or the analogous part on an animal, such as a wing. **2** any of the main branches of a tree. **3** a branching or projecting section or member; extension. **4** a person or thing considered to be a member, part, or agent of a larger group or thing. **5** *Chiefly Brit.* a mischievous child (esp. in **limb of Satan,** etc.). **6 out on a limb. 6a** in a precarious or questionable position. **6b** *Brit.* isolated, esp. because of unpopular opinions. [OE *lim*]
▸'**limbless** *adj*

limb[2] (lɪm) *n* **1** the edge of the apparent disc of the sun, a moon, or a planet. **2** a graduated arc attached to instruments, such as the sextant, used for measuring angles. **3** *Bot.* the expanded part of a leaf, petal, or sepal. **4** Also called: **fold limb.** either of the sides of a geological fold. [C15: from L *limbus* edge]

limbed (lɪmd) *adj* **a** having limbs. **b** (*in combination*): *short-limbed; strong-limbed.*

limber[1] ❶ ('lɪmbə) *adj* **1** capable of being easily bent or flexed; pliant. **2** able to move or bend freely; agile. [C16: from ?]
▸'**limberness** *n*

limber[2] ('lɪmbə) *n* **1** part of a gun carriage, consisting of an axle, pole,

THESAURUS

Antonyms *adj* important, momentous, serious, significant, substantial, weighty

likable *adj* = **attractive,** agreeable, amiable, appealing, charming, engaging, friendly, genial, nice, pleasant, pleasing, sympathetic, winning, winsome

like[1] *adj* **1** = **similar,** akin, alike, allied, analogous, approximating, cognate, corresponding, equivalent, identical, parallel, relating, resembling, same ◆ *n* **8** = **equal,** counterpart, fellow, match, parallel, twin
Antonyms *adj* ≠ **similar:** contrasted, different, dissimilar, divergent, diverse, opposite, unlike ◆ *n* ≠ **equal:** opposite

like[2] *vb* **1, 2** = **enjoy,** admire, adore, appreciate, approve of, be fond of, be keen on, be partial to, cherish, delight in, dig (*sl.*), esteem, go for, hold dear, love, relish, revel in, take a shine to (*inf.*), take to **3, 5** = **wish,** care to, choose, choose to, desire, fancy, feel inclined, prefer, select, want ◆ *n* **6** *usually plural* = **preference,** cup of tea (*inf.*), favourite, liking, partiality, predilection
Antonyms *vb* ≠ **enjoy:** abominate, despise, detest, dislike, hate, loathe

likelihood *n* **1** = **probability,** chance, good chance, liability, likeliness, possibility, prospect, reasonableness, strong possibility

likely *adj* **1** = **inclined,** apt, disposed, liable, prone, tending **2** = **probable,** anticipated, expected, odds-on, on the cards, to be expected **3** = **plausible,** believable, credible, feasible, possible, reasonable, verisimilar **4** = **appropriate,** acceptable, agreeable, befitting, fit, pleasing, proper, qualified, suitable **5** = **promising,** fair, favourite, hopeful, up-and-coming ◆ *adv* **6** = **probably,** doubtlessly, in all probability, like as not (*inf.*), like enough (*inf.*), no doubt, presumably

like-minded *adj* = **agreeing,** compatible, *en rapport,* harmonious, in accord, in harmony, of one mind, of the same mind, unanimous

liken *vb* = **compare,** equate, juxtapose, match, mention in the same breath, parallel, relate, set beside

likeness *n* **1** = **resemblance,** affinity, correspondence, similarity, similitude **2** = **portrait,** copy, counterpart, delineation, depiction, effigy, facsimile, image, model, photograph, picture, replica, representation, reproduction, study **3** = **appearance,** form, guise, semblance

likewise *adv* **1** = **also,** besides, further, furthermore, in addition, moreover, too **2** = **similarly,** in like manner, in the same way

liking *n* **1** = **fondness,** affection, desire, love, soft spot **2** = **preference,** affinity, attraction, bent, bias, inclination, partiality, penchant, predilection, proneness, propensity, stomach, taste, tendency, thirst, weakness
Antonyms *n* abhorrence, aversion, dislike, hatred, loathing, repugnance

Lilliputian *n* **1** = **midget,** dwarf, homunculus, hop-o'-my-thumb, manikin, pygmy *or* pigmy, Tom Thumb ◆ *adj* **2** = **tiny,** baby, bantam, diminutive, dwarf, little, mini, miniature, minuscule, petite, pocket-sized, pygmy *or* pigmy, small, teensy-weensy, teeny, teeny-weeny, wee

lilt *n* **1** = **rhythm,** beat, cadence **2** = **swing,** sway

lily-livered *adj* = **cowardly,** abject, base, chicken (*sl.*), chicken-hearted, craven, faint-hearted, fearful, gutless (*inf.*), pusillanimous, scared, spineless, timid, timorous, yellow (*inf.*), yellow-bellied (*sl.*)

lily-white *adj* **1** = **pure white,** milk-white, white, white as snow, white-skinned **2** *Informal* = **innocent,** chaste, impeccable, irreproachable, pure, spotless, squeaky-clean, unsullied, untainted, untarnished, virgin, virtuous

limb[1] *n* **1** = **part,** appendage, arm, extension, extremity, leg, member, wing **2** = **branch,** bough, offshoot, projection, spur

limber[1] *adj* **1** = **pliant,** elastic, flexible, plas-

and two wheels. ◆ *vb* **2** (usually foll. by *up*) to attach the limber (to a gun, etc.). [C15 *lymour* shaft of a gun carriage, from ?]

limber up ⓘ *vb (intr, adv)* (esp. in sports) to exercise in order to be limber and agile.

limbic system (ˈlɪmbɪk) *n* the part of the brain concerned with basic emotion, hunger, and sex. [C19 *limbic*, from F, from *limbe*, from NL *limbus*, from L: border]

limbo[1] (ˈlɪmbəʊ) *n, pl* **limbos. 1** (*often cap.*) *Christianity*. the supposed abode of infants dying without baptism and the just who died before Christ. **2** an imaginary place for lost, forgotten, or unwanted persons or things. **3** an unknown intermediate place or condition between two extremes: *in limbo*. [C14: from Med. L *in limbo* on the border (of hell)]

limbo[2] (ˈlɪmbəʊ) *n, pl* **limbos.** a Caribbean dance in which dancers pass, while leaning backwards, under a bar. [C20: from ?]

Limburger (ˈlɪmˌbɜːgə) *n* a semihard white cheese of very strong smell and flavour. Also called: **Limburg cheese.**

lime[1] (laɪm) *n* **1** short for **quicklime, birdlime, slaked lime. 2** *Agriculture*. any of certain calcium compounds, esp. calcium hydroxide, spread as a dressing on lime-deficient land. ◆ *vb* **limes, liming, limed.** (*tr*) **3** to spread (twigs, etc.) with birdlime. **4** to spread a calcium compound upon (land) to improve plant growth. **5** to catch (animals, esp. birds) as with birdlime. **6** to whitewash (a wall, ceiling, etc.) with a mixture of lime and water (**limewash**). [OE *līm*]

lime[2] (laɪm) *n* **1** a small Asian citrus tree with stiff sharp spines and small round or oval greenish fruits. **2a** the fruit of this tree, having acid fleshy pulp rich in vitamin C. **2b** (*as modifier*): *lime juice*. ◆ *adj* **3** having the flavour of lime fruit. [C17: from F, from Ar. *līmah*]

lime[3] (laɪm) *n* a European linden tree planted in many varieties for ornament. [C17: changed from obs. *line*, from OE *lind* LINDEN]

limeade (ˌlaɪmˈeɪd) *n* a drink made from sweetened lime juice and plain or carbonated water.

lime green *n* **a** a moderate greenish-yellow colour. **b** (*as adj*): *a lime-green dress*.

limekiln (ˈlaɪmˌkɪln) *n* a kiln in which calcium carbonate is calcined to produce quicklime.

limelight ⓘ (ˈlaɪmˌlaɪt) *n* **1 the.** a position of public attention or notice (esp. in **in the limelight**). **2a** a type of lamp, formerly used in stage lighting, in which light is produced by heating lime to white heat. **2b** Also called: **calcium light.** brilliant white light produced in this way.

limerick (ˈlɪmərɪk) *n* a form of comic verse consisting of five anapaestic lines. [C19: allegedly from *will you come up to Limerick?*, a refrain sung between nonsense verses at a party]

limestone (ˈlaɪmˌstəʊn) *n* a sedimentary rock consisting mainly of calcium carbonate: used as a building stone and in making cement, lime, etc.

limewater (ˈlaɪmˌwɔːtə) *n* **1** a clear colourless solution of calcium hydroxide in water, sometimes used in medicine as an antacid. **2** water that contains dissolved lime or calcium salts, esp. calcium carbonate or calcium sulphate.

limey (ˈlaɪmɪ) *US, Canad., & Austral. sl.* ◆ *n* **1** a British person. **2** a British sailor or ship. ◆ *adj* **3** British. [abbrev. from C19 *lime-juicer*, because British sailors drank lime juice as a protection against scurvy]

limit ⓘ (ˈlɪmɪt) *n* **1** (*sometimes pl*) the ultimate extent, degree, or amount of something: *the limit of endurance*. **2** (*often pl*) the boundary or edge of a specific area: *the city limits*. **3** (*often pl*) the area of premises within specific boundaries. **4** the largest quantity or amount allowed. **5** *Maths*. **5a** a value to which a function approaches as the independent variable approaches a specified value or infinity. **5b** a value to which a sequence a_n approaches as n approaches infinity. **5c** the limit of a sequence of partial sums of a convergent infinite series. **6** *Maths*. one of the two specified values between which a definite integral is evaluated. **7 the limit.** *Inf.* a person or thing that is intolerably exasperating. ◆ *vb* **limits, limiting, limited.** (*tr*) **8** to restrict or confine, as to area, extent, time, etc. [C14: from L *līmes* boundary]
▸ˈ**limitable** *adj* ▸ˈ**limitless** *adj* ▸ˈ**limitlessly** *adv* ▸ˈ**limitlessness** *n*

limitary (ˈlɪmɪtərɪ, -trɪ) *adj* **1** of, involving, or serving as a limit. **2** restricted or limited.

limitation ⓘ (ˌlɪmɪˈteɪʃən) *n* **1** something that limits a quality or achievement. **2** the act of limiting or the condition of being limited. **3** *Law*. a certain period of time, legally defined, within which an action, claim, etc., must be commenced.

limited ⓘ (ˈlɪmɪtɪd) *adj* **1** having a limit; restricted; confined. **2** without fullness or scope; narrow. **3** (of governing powers, sovereignty, etc.) restricted or checked, by or as if by a constitution, laws, or an assembly: *limited government*. **4** *Chiefly Brit*. (of a business enterprise) owned by shareholders whose liability for the enterprise's debts is restricted.
▸ˈ**limitedly** *adv* ▸ˈ**limitedness** *n*

limited liability *n Brit.* liability restricted to the unpaid portion (if any) of the par value of the shares of a limited company.

limiter (ˈlɪmɪtə) *n* an electronic circuit that produces an output signal whose positive or negative amplitude, or both, is limited to some predetermined value above which the peaks become flattened. Also called: **clipper.**

limn (lɪm) *vb* (*tr*) **1** to represent in drawing or painting. **2** *Arch.* to describe in words. [C15: from OF *enluminer* to illumine (a manuscript) from L *inlūmināre* to brighten, from *lūmen* light]
▸**limner** (ˈlɪmnə) *n*

limnology (lɪmˈnɒlədʒɪ) *n* the study of bodies of fresh water with reference to their plant and animal life, physical properties, geographical features, etc. [C20: from Gk *limnē* lake]
▸**limnological** (ˌlɪmnəˈlɒdʒɪkᵊl) *adj* ▸**limˈnologist** *n*

limousine (ˈlɪməˌziːn, ˌlɪməˈziːn) *n* any large and luxurious car, esp. one that has a glass division between the driver and passengers. [C20: from F, lit.: cloak (orig. one worn by shepherds in *Limousin*), hence later applied to the car]

limp[1] ⓘ (lɪmp) *vb* (*intr*) **1** to walk with an uneven step, esp. with a weak or injured leg. **2** to advance in a labouring or faltering manner. ◆ *n* **3** an uneven walk or progress. [C16: prob. a back formation from obs. *limphalt* lame, from OE *lempheалt*]
▸ˈ**limper** *n* ▸ˈ**limping** *adj, n*

limp[2] ⓘ (lɪmp) *adj* **1** not firm or stiff. **2** not energetic or vital. **3** (of the binding of a book) not stiffened with boards. [C18: prob. of Scand. origin]
▸ˈ**limply** *adv* ▸ˈ**limpness** *n*

limpet (ˈlɪmpɪt) *n* **1** any of numerous marine gastropods, such as the common limpet and keyhole limpet, that have a conical shell and are found clinging to rocks. **2** (*modifier*) relating to or denoting certain weapons that are attached to their targets by magnetic or adhesive properties and resist removal: *limpet mines*. [OE *lempedu*, from L *lepas*, from Gk]

limpid ⓘ (ˈlɪmpɪd) *adj* **1** clear or transparent. **2** (esp. of writings, style, etc.) free from obscurity. **3** calm; peaceful. [C17: from F *limpide*, from L *limpidus* clear]
▸**limˈpidity** *or* ˈ**limpidness** *n* ▸ˈ**limpidly** *adv*

limp-wristed ⓘ *adj* ineffectual; effete.

limy[1] (ˈlaɪmɪ) *adj* **limier, limiest.** of, like, or smeared with birdlime.
▸ˈ**liminess** *n*

limy[2] (ˈlaɪmɪ) *adj* **limier, limiest.** of or tasting of lime (the fruit).

linage (ˈlaɪnɪdʒ) *n* **1** the number of lines in a piece of written or printed matter. **2** payment for written material calculated according to the number of lines.

linchpin ⓘ *or* **lynchpin** (ˈlɪntʃˌpɪn) *n* **1** a pin placed transversely through an axle to keep a wheel in position. **2** a person or thing regarded as an essential or coordinating element: *the linchpin of the company*. [C14 *lynspin*, from OE *lynis*]

Lincoln green (ˈlɪŋkən) *n* **1a** a yellowish-green or brownish-green colour. **1b** (*as adj*): *a Lincoln-green suit*. **2** a cloth of this colour. [C16: after a green fabric formerly made at *Lincoln*, in E central England]

Lincs (lɪŋks) *abbrev. for* Lincolnshire.

linctus (ˈlɪŋktəs) *n, pl* **linctuses.** a syrupy medicinal preparation, taken to relieve coughs and sore throats. [C17 (in the sense: medicine to be licked with the tongue): from L, p.p. of *lingere* to lick]

lindane (ˈlɪndeɪn) *n* a white poisonous crystalline powder: used as an insecticide and weedkiller. [C20: after T. van der *Linden*, Du. chemist]

linden (ˈlɪndən) *n* any of various deciduous trees of a N temperate genus having heart-shaped leaves and small fragrant yellowish flow-

THESAURUS

tic, pliable, supple **2** = **agile**, graceful, lissom(e), lithe, loose-jointed, loose-limbed, supple

limber up *vb* = **loosen up**, exercise, get ready, prepare, warm up

limelight *n* **1** = **publicity**, attention, celebrity, fame, glare of publicity, prominence, public eye, public notice, recognition, stardom, the spotlight

limit *n* **1** = **end**, bound, breaking point, cutoff point, deadline, end point, furthest bound, greatest extent, termination, the bitter end, ultimate, utmost **2** = **boundary**, border, confines, edge, end, extent, frontier, pale, perimeter, periphery, precinct **4** = **maximum**, ceiling, check, curb, limitation, obstruction, restraint, restriction **7 the limit** *Informal* = **the last straw**, enough, it (*inf.*), the end ◆ *vb* **8** = **restrict**, bound, check, circumscribe, confine, curb, delimit, demarcate, fix, hem in, hinder, ration, restrain, specify, straiten

limitation *n* **1** = **restriction**, block, check, condition, constraint, control, curb, disadvantage, drawback, impediment, obstruction, qualification, reservation, restraint, snag

limited *adj* **1** = **restricted**, bounded, checked, circumscribed, confined, constrained, controlled, curbed, defined, finite, fixed, hampered, hemmed in **2** = **narrow**, cramped, diminished, inadequate, insufficient, minimal, reduced, restricted, scant, short, unsatisfactory
Antonyms *adj* ≠ **restricted:** boundless, limitless, unlimited, unrestricted

limitless *adj* **1** = **infinite**, boundless, countless, endless, illimitable, immeasurable, immense, inexhaustible, measureless, never-ending, numberless, unbounded, uncalculable, undefined, unending, unlimited, untold, vast

limp[1] *vb* **1** = **hobble**, falter, halt (*arch.*), hirple (*Scot.*), hop, shamble, shuffle ◆ *n* **3** = **lameness**, hirple (*Scot.*), hobble

limp[2] *adj* **1** = **floppy**, drooping, flabby, flaccid, flexible, lax, limber, loose, pliable, relaxed, slack, soft **2** = **weak**, debilitated, enervated, exhausted, lethargic, spent, tired, worn out
Antonyms *adj* ≠ **floppy:** firm, hard, rigid, solid, stiff, taut, tense, unyielding ≠ **weak:** hardy, powerful, robust, strong, sturdy, tough

limpid *adj* **1** = **clear**, bright, crystal-clear, crystalline, pellucid, pure, translucent, transparent **2** = **understandable**, clear, comprehensible, intelligible, lucid, perspicuous, unambiguous **3** = **calm**, peaceful, placid, quiet, serene, still, tranquil, unruffled, untroubled

limp-wristed *adj* = **ineffectual**, effete, feeble, impotent, inadequate, ineffective, inept, useless, weak

linchpin *n* **2** = **driving force**, chief, coordinator, cornerstone, director, principal

ers: cultivated for timber and as shade trees. See also **lime**[3]. [C16: n use of obs. adj *linden*, from OE *linde* lime tree]

line[1] ❶ (laɪn) *n* **1** a narrow continuous mark, as one made by a pencil, pen, or brush across a surface. **2** such a mark cut into or raised from a surface. **3** a thin indented mark or wrinkle. **4** a straight or curved continuous trace having no breadth that is produced by a moving point. **5** *Maths.* **5a** any straight one-dimensional geometrical element whose identity is determined by two points. A **line segment** lies between any two points on a line. **5b** a set of points (x, y) that satisfies the equation $y = mx + c$, where m is the gradient and c is the intercept with the y-axis. **6** a border or boundary: *the county line.* **7** *Sport.* **7a** a white or coloured band indicating a boundary or division on a field, track, etc. **7b** a mark or imaginary mark at which a race begins or ends. **8** *American football.* **8a** See **line of scrimmage. 8b** the players arranged in a row on either side of the line of scrimmage at the start of each play. **9** a specified point of change or limit: *the dividing line between sanity and madness.* **10a** the edge or contour of a shape. **10b** the sum or type of such contours, characteristic of a style or design: *the line of a building.* **11** anything long, flexible, and thin, such as a wire or string: *a washing line; a fishing line.* **12** a telephone connection: *a direct line to New York.* **13** a conducting wire, cable, or circuit for making connections between pieces of electrical apparatus, such as a cable for electric-power transmission, telecommunications, etc. **14** a system of travel or transportation, esp. over agreed routes: *a shipping line.* **15** a company operating such a system. **16** a route between two points on a railway. **17** *Chiefly Brit.* a railway track, including the roadbed, sleepers, etc. **18** a course or direction of movement or advance: *the line of flight of a bullet.* **19** a course or method of action, behaviour, etc.: *take a new line with him.* **20** a policy or prescribed course of action or way of thinking (often in **bring** *or* **come into line**). **21** a field of study, interest, occupation, trade, or profession: *this book is in your line.* **22** alignment; true (esp. in **in line, out of line**). **23** one kind of product or article: *a nice line in hats.* **24** a row of persons or things: *a line of cakes on the conveyor belt.* **25** a chronological or ancestral series, esp. of people: *a line of prime ministers.* **26** a row of words printed or written across a page or column. **27** a unit of verse consisting of the number of feet appropriate to the metre being used and written or printed with the words in a single row. **28** a short letter; note: *just a line to say thank you.* **29** a piece of useful information or hint about something: *give me a line on his work.* **30** one of a number of narrow horizontal bands forming a television picture. **31** *Physics.* a narrow band in an electromagnetic spectrum, resulting from a transition in an atom of a gas. **32** *Music.* **32a** any of the five horizontal marks that make up the stave. **32b** the musical part or melody notated on one such set. **32c** a discernible shape formed by sequences of notes or musical sounds: *a meandering melodic line.* **32d** (in polyphonic music) a set of staves that are held together with a bracket or brace. **33** a defensive or fortified position, esp. one that marks the most forward position in war or a national boundary: *the front line.* **34** a formation adopted by a body or a number of military units when drawn up abreast. **35** the combatant forces of certain armies and navies, excluding supporting arms. **36a** the equator (esp. in **crossing the line**). **36b** any circle or arc on the terrestrial or celestial sphere. **37** a US and Canad. word for **queue. 38** *Sl.* a portion of a powdered drug for snorting. **39** *Sl.* something said for effect, esp. to solicit for money, sex, etc. **40 all along the line. 40a** at every stage in a series. **40b** in every detail. **41 draw the line (at).** to object (to) or set a limit (on): *her father draws the line at her coming in after midnight.* **42 get a line on.** *Inf.* to obtain information about. **43 hold the line. 43a** to keep a telephone line open. **43b** *Football.* to prevent the opponents from taking the ball forward. **43c** (of soldiers) to keep formation, as when under fire. **44 in line for.** in the running for; a candidate for: *he's in line for a directorship.* **45 in line with.** conforming to. **46 lay** *or* **put on the line. 46a** to pay money. **46b** to speak frankly and directly. **46c** to risk (one's career, reputation, etc.) on something. ◆ *vb* **lines, lining, lined. 47** *(tr)* to mark with a line or lines. **48** *(tr)* to draw or represent with a line or lines. **49** *(tr)* to be or put as a border to: *tulips lined the lawns.* **50** to place in or form a row, series, or alignment. ◆ See also **lines, line-up.** [C13: partly from OF *ligne,* ult. from L *līnea,* n. use of *līneus* flaxen, from *līnum* flax; partly from OE *līn,* ult. also from L *līnum* flax]
▸ **'linable** *or* **'lineable** *adj* ▸ **lined** *adj*

line[2] ❶ (laɪn) *vb* **lines, lining, lined.** *(tr)* **1** to attach an inside covering to (a garment, curtain, etc.), as for protection, to hide the seaming, or so that it should hang well. **2** to cover or fit the inside of: *to line the walls with books.* **3** to fill plentifully: *a purse lined with money.* [C14: ult. from L *līnum* flax, since linings were often of linen]

lineage[1] ❶ ('lɪnɪɪdʒ) *n* direct descent from an ancestor, esp. a line of descendants from one ancestor. [C14: from OF *lignage,* from L *līnea* LINE[1]]

lineage[2] ('laɪnɪdʒ) *n* a variant spelling of **linage.**

lineal ('lɪnɪəl) *adj* **1** being in a direct line of descent from an ancestor. **2** of, involving, or derived from direct descent. **3** a less common word for **linear.** [C14: via OF from LL *līneālis,* from L *līnea* LINE[1]]
▸ **'lineally** *adv*

lineament ❶ ('lɪnɪəmənt) *n* *(often pl)* **1** a facial outline or feature. **2** a distinctive feature. [C15: from L: line, from *līneāre* to draw a line]

linear ('lɪnɪə) *adj* **1** of, in, along, or relating to a line. **2** of or relating to length. **3** resembling, represented by, or consisting of a line or lines. **4** having one dimension. **5** designating a style in the arts, esp. painting, that obtains its effects through line rather than colour or light. **6** *Maths.* of or relating to the first degree: *a linear equation.* **7** narrow and having parallel edges: *a linear leaf.* **8** *Electronics.* **8a** (of a circuit, etc.) having an output that is directly proportional to input: *linear amplifier.* **8b** having components arranged in a line. [C17: from L *līneāris* of lines]
▸ **linearity** (ˌlɪnɪ'ærɪtɪ) *n* ▸ **'linearly** *adv*

linear accelerator *n* an accelerator in which charged particles are accelerated along a linear path by potential differences applied to a number of electrodes along their path.

Linear B *n* an ancient system of writing found on clay tablets and jars of the second millennium B.C. excavated in Crete and on the Greek mainland. The script is apparently a modified form of the earlier and hitherto undeciphered **Linear A** and is generally accepted as being an early representation of Mycenaean Greek.

linear measure *n* a unit or system of units for the measurement of length.

linear motor *n* a form of electric motor in which the stator and the rotor are linear and parallel. It can be used to drive a train, one part of the motor being in the locomotive, the other in the track.

linear programming *n* *Maths.* a technique used in economics, etc., for determining the maximum or minimum of a linear function of non-negative variables subject to constraints expressed as linear equalities or inequalities.

lineation (ˌlɪnɪ'eɪʃən) *n* **1** the act of marking with lines. **2** an arrangement of or division into lines.

line dancing *n* a form of dancing performed by rows of people to country and western music.

line drawing *n* a drawing made with lines only.

lineman ('laɪnmən) *n, pl* **linemen. 1** another name for **platelayer. 2** a person who does the chaining, taping, or marking of points for a surveyor. **3** *Austral. & NZ.* (formerly) the member of a beach life-saving team who controlled the line used to help drowning swimmers and surfers. **4** *American football.* a member of the row of players who start each down, positioned on either side of the line of scrimmage. **5** *US & Canad.* another word for **linesman** (sense 2).

line management *n* the managers in charge of specific functions and concerned in the day-to-day operations of a company.

linen ('lɪnɪn) *n* **1a** a hard-wearing fabric woven from the spun fibres of flax. **1b** *(as modifier): a linen tablecloth.* **2** yarn or thread spun from flax fibre. **3** clothes, sheets, tablecloths, etc., made from linen cloth or from cotton. [OE *linnen,* ult. from L *līnum* flax]

line of battle *n* a formation adopted by a military or naval force when preparing for action.

line of fire *n* the flight path of a missile discharged or to be discharged from a firearm.

line of force *n* a line in a field of force, such as an electric or magnetic field, for which the tangent at any point is the direction of the force at that point.

line of scrimmage *n American football.* an imaginary line, parallel to the goal lines, on which the ball is placed at the start of a down and on either side of which the offense and defense line up.

line-out *n Rugby Union.* the method of restarting play when the ball goes into touch, the forwards forming two parallel lines at right angles to the touchline and jumping for the ball when it is thrown in.

line printer *n* an electromechanical device that prints a line of characters at a time: used in printing and in computer systems.

liner[1] ('laɪnə) *n* **1** a passenger ship or aircraft, esp. one that is part of a commercial fleet. **2** See **freightliner. 3** Also called: **eyeliner.** a cosmetic

THESAURUS

line[1] *n* **1, 2** = **stroke**, band, bar, channel, dash, groove, mark, rule, score, scratch, streak, stripe, underline **3** = **wrinkle**, crease, crow's foot, furrow, mark **9** = **boundary**, border, borderline, demarcation, edge, frontier, limit, mark **10** = **outline**, configuration, contour, features, figure, profile, silhouette **11** = **string**, cable, cord, filament, rope, strand, thread, wire, wisp **18** = **trajectory**, axis, course, direction, path, route, track **19, 20** = **approach**, avenue, belief, course, course of action, ideology, method, policy, position, practice, procedure, scheme, system **21** = **occupation**, activity, area, bag (*sl.*), business, calling, department, employment, field, forte, interest, job, profession, province, pursuit, specialization, trade, vocation **24** = **row**, column, crocodile (*Brit.*), file, procession, queue, rank, sequence, series **25** = **lineage**, ancestry, breed, family, race, stock, strain, succession **28** = **note**, card, letter, message, postcard, report, word **29** = **clue**, hint, indication, information, lead **34** = **formation**, disposition, firing line, front, front line, position, trenches **41 draw the line** = **object**, lay down the law, prohibit, put one's foot down, restrict, set a limit **44 in line for** = **due for**, a candidate for, being considered for, in the running for, next in succession to, on the short list for **45 in line with** = **in accord**, in agreement, in conformity, in harmony, in step ◆ *vb* **47, 48** = **mark**, crease, cut, draw, furrow, inscribe, rule, score, trace, underline **49** = **border**, bound, edge, fringe, rank, rim, skirt, verge

line[2] *vb* **1, 2** = **cover**, ceil, face, interline **3** = **fill**

lineage[1] *n* = **descent**, ancestry, birth, breed, descendants, extraction, family, forebears, forefathers, genealogy, heredity, house, line, off- spring, pedigree, progeny, stock, succession

lineament *n, often plural* **1** = **features**, countenance, face, phiz *or* phizog (*sl., chiefly Brit.*), physiognomy, visage **2** = **configuration**, line, outline, trait

lined *adj* **1** = **ruled**, feint **3** = **wrinkled**, furrowed, wizened, worn

used to outline the eyes. **4** a person or thing that uses lines, esp. in drawing or copying.

liner[2] ('laɪnə) *n* **1** a material used as a lining. **2** a person who supplies or fits linings.

lines Ⓣ (laɪnz) *pl n* **1** general appearance or outline: *a car with fine lines.* **2** a plan of procedure or construction: *built on traditional lines.* **3a** the spoken words of a theatrical presentation. **3b** the words of a particular role: *he forgot his lines.* **4** *Inf., chiefly Brit.* a marriage certificate: *marriage lines.* **5** a defensive position, row of trenches, or other fortification: *we broke through the enemy lines.* **6** a school punishment of writing the same sentence or phrase out a specified number of times. **7 read between the lines.** to understand or find an implicit meaning in addition to the obvious one.

linesman ('laɪnzmən) *n, pl* **linesmen. 1** an official who helps the referee or umpire in various sports, esp. by indicating when the ball has gone out of play. **2** *Chiefly Brit.* a person who installs, maintains, or repairs telephone or electric-power lines. US and Canad. name: **lineman.**

line-up Ⓣ *n* **1** a row or arrangement of people or things assembled for a particular purpose: *the line-up for the football match.* **2** the members of such a row or arrangement. **3** *US.* an identity parade. ◆ *vb* **line up.** (*adv*) **4** to form, put into, or organize a line-up. **5** (*tr*) to produce, organize, and assemble: *they lined up some questions.* **6** (*tr*) to align.

ling[1] (lɪŋ) *n, pl* **ling** *or* **lings. 1** any of several northern coastal food fishes having an elongated body with long fins. **2** another name for **burbot** (a fish). [C13: prob. from Low G]

ling[2] (lɪŋ) *n* another name for **heather.** [C14: from ON *lyng*]

ling. *abbrev. for* linguistics.

-ling[1] *suffix forming nouns.* **1** *Often disparaging.* a person or thing belonging to or associated with the group, activity, or quality specified: *nestling; underling.* **2** used as a diminutive: *duckling.* [OE *-ling,* of Gmc origin]

-ling[2] *suffix forming adverbs.* in a specified condition, manner, or direction: *darkling.* [OE *-ling,* adv. suffix]

lingam ('lɪŋgəm) *or* **linga** ('lɪŋgə) *n* the Hindu phallic image of the god Siva. [C18: from Sansk.]

linger Ⓣ ('lɪŋgə) *vb* (*mainly intr*) **1** to delay or prolong departure. **2** to go in a slow or leisurely manner; saunter. **3** to remain just alive for some time prior to death. **4** to persist or continue, esp. in the mind. **5** to be slow to act; dither. [C13 (northern dialect) *lengeren* to dwell, from *lengen* to prolong, from OE *lengan*]
▸**'lingerer** *n* ▸**'lingering** *adj* ▸**'lingeringly** *adv*

lingerie ('lænʒərɪ) *n* women's underwear and nightwear. [C19: from F, from *linge,* from L *līneus* linen, from *līnum* flax]

lingo Ⓣ ('lɪŋgəʊ) *n, pl* **lingoes.** *Inf.* any foreign or unfamiliar language, jargon, etc. [C17: ?from LINGUA FRANCA]

lingua franca ('lɪŋgwə 'fræŋkə) *n, pl* **lingua francas** *or* **linguae francae** ('lɪŋgwi: 'frænsi:). **1** a language used for communication among people of different mother tongues. **2** a hybrid language containing elements from several different languages used in this way. **3** any system of communication providing mutual understanding. [C17: It., lit.: Frankish tongue]

Lingua Franca *n* a particular lingua franca spoken from the Crusades to the 18th century in the ports of the Mediterranean, based on Italian, Spanish, French, Arabic, Greek, and Turkish.

lingual ('lɪŋgwəl) *adj* **1** *Anat.* of or relating to the tongue. **2a** *Rare.* of or relating to language or languages. **2b** (*in combination*): *polylingual.* **3** articulated with the tongue. ◆ *n* **4** a lingual consonant, such as Scots (r).
▸**'lingually** *adv*

linguiform ('lɪŋgwɪˌfɔ:m) *adj* shaped like a tongue.

linguist ('lɪŋgwɪst) *n* **1** a person who is skilled in foreign languages. **2** a person who studies linguistics. [C16: from L *lingua* tongue]

linguistic (lɪŋ'gwɪstɪk) *adj* **1** of or relating to language. **2** of or relating to linguistics.
▸**lin'guistically** *adv*

linguistic atlas *n* an atlas showing the distribution of distinctive linguistic features.

linguistics (lɪŋ'gwɪstɪks) *n* (*functioning as sing*) the scientific study of language.

liniment Ⓣ ('lɪnɪmənt) *n* a medicated liquid, usually containing alcohol, camphor, and an oil, applied to the skin to relieve pain, stiffness, etc. [C15: from LL *linīmentum,* from *linere* to smear]

lining ('laɪnɪŋ) *n* **1** material used to line a garment, curtain, etc. **2** any material used as an interior covering.

link[1] Ⓣ (lɪŋk) *n* **1** any of the separate rings, loops, or pieces that connect or make up a chain. **2** something that resembles such a ring, loop, or piece. **3** a road, rail, air, or sea connection, as between two main routes. **4** a connecting part or episode. **5** a connecting piece in a mechanism. **6** Also called: **radio link.** a system of transmitters and receivers that connect two locations by means of radio and television signals. **7** a unit of length equal to one hundredth of a chain. 1 link of a Gunter's chain is equal to 7.92 inches, and of an engineer's chain to 1 foot. ◆ *vb* **8** (often foll. by *up*) to connect or be connected with or as if with links. **9** (*tr*) to connect by association, etc. [C14: from ON]

link[2] (lɪŋk) *n* (formerly) a torch used to light dark streets. [C16: ?from L *lychnus,* from Gk *lukhnos* lamp]

linkage ('lɪŋkɪdʒ) *n* **1** the act of linking or the state of being linked. **2** a system of interconnected levers or rods for transmitting or regulating the motion of a mechanism. **3** *Electronics.* the product of the total number of lines of magnetic flux and the number of turns in a coil or circuit through which they pass. **4** *Genetics.* the occurrence of two genes close together on the same chromosome so that they tend to be inherited as a single unit.

linkman ('lɪŋkmən) *n, pl* **linkmen.** a presenter of a television or radio programme, esp. a sports transmission, consisting of a number of outside broadcasts from different locations.

links (lɪŋks) *pl n* **1a** short for **golf links. 1b** (*as modifier*): *a links course.* See **golf course. 2** *Chiefly Scot.* undulating sandy ground near the shore. [OE *hlincas* pl. of *hlinc* ridge]

link-up *n* a joining or linking together of two factions, objects, etc.

linn (lɪn) *n Chiefly Scot.* **1** a waterfall or a pool at the foot of it. **2** a ravine or precipice. [C16: prob. from a confusion of two words, Scot. Gaelic *linne* pool and OE *hlynn* torrent]

Linnean *or* **Linnaean** (lɪ'ni:ən), -'neɪ-) *adj* **1** of or relating to Linnaeus (1707–78), Swedish botanist. **2** relating to the system of classification of plants and animals using binomial nomenclature.

linnet ('lɪnɪt) *n* a brownish Old World finch: the male has a red breast and forehead. [C16: from OF *linotte,* ult. from L *līnum* flax (because the bird feeds on flaxseeds)]

lino ('laɪnəʊ) *n* short for **linoleum.**

linocut ('laɪnəʊˌkʌt) *n* **1** a design cut in relief on linoleum mounted on a wooden block. **2** a print made from such a design.

linoleum (lɪ'nəʊlɪəm) *n* a sheet material made of hessian, jute, etc., coated with a mixture of powdered cork, linseed oil, rosin, and pigment, used as a floor covering. Often shortened to **lino.** [C19: from L *līnum* flax + *oleum* oil]

Linotype ('laɪnəʊˌtaɪp) *n* **1** *Trademark.* a typesetting machine, operated by a keyboard, that casts an entire line on one solid slug of metal. **2** type produced by such a machine.

linseed ('lɪnˌsi:d) *n* another name for **flaxseed.** [OE *līnsǣd,* from *līn* flax + *sǣd* seed]

linseed oil *n* a yellow oil extracted from seeds of the flax plant. It is used in making oil paints, printer's ink, linoleum, etc.

linsey-woolsey ('lɪnzɪ'wʊlzɪ) *n* **1** a thin rough fabric of linen warp and coarse wool or cotton filling. **2** a strange nonsensical mixture or confusion. [C15: prob. from *Lindsey,* village in Suffolk where first made + WOOL (with rhyming suffix *-sey*)]

lint (lɪnt) *n* **1** an absorbent cotton or linen fabric with the nap raised on one side, used to dress wounds, etc. **2** shreds of fibre, yarn, etc. [C14: prob. from L *linteus* made of linen, from *līnum* flax]
▸**'linty** *adj*

lintel ('lɪnt[ə]l) *n* a horizontal beam, as over a door or window. [C14: via OF prob. from LL *līmitāris* (unattested) of the boundary, infl. by *līminaris* of the threshold]

linter ('lɪntə) *n* **1** a machine for stripping the short fibres of ginned cotton seeds. **2** (*pl*) the fibres so removed.

lion Ⓣ ('laɪən) *n* **1** a large gregarious predatory feline mammal of open country in parts of Africa and India, having a tawny yellow coat and, in the male, a shaggy mane. Related adj: **leonine. 2** a conventionalized lion, the principal beast used as an emblem in heraldry. **3** a courageous, strong, or bellicose person. **4** a celebrity or idol who attracts much publicity and a large following. **5 the lion's share.** the largest portion. [OE *līo, lēo* (ME *lioun,* from Anglo-F *liun*), both from L *leo,* Gk *leōn*]
▸**'lioness** *fem n*

Lion ('laɪən) *n* **the.** the constellation Leo, the fifth sign of the zodiac.

lion-hearted Ⓣ *adj* very brave; courageous.

THESAURUS

lines *pl n* **1** = **outline**, appearance, configuration, contour, cut, shape, style **2** = **principle**, convention, example, model, pattern, plan, procedure **3** = **words**, part, script

line-up *n* **1, 2** = **arrangement**, array, row, selection, team ◆ *vb* **line up 4** = **queue up**, fall in, form ranks **5** = **produce**, assemble, come up with, lay on, obtain, organize, prepare, procure, secure **6** = **align**, arrange, array, marshal, order, range, regiment, sequence, straighten

linger *vb* **1** = **stay**, hang around, hang in the air, loiter, remain, stop, tarry, wait **3** = **hang on**, cling to life, die slowly, last, survive **4** = **continue**, abide, endure, persist, remain, stay **5** = **delay**, dally, dawdle, drag one's feet *or* heels, idle, lag, procrastinate, take one's time

lingering *adj* **3** = **slow**, dragging, long-drawn-out, protracted

lingo *n Informal* = **language**, argot, cant, dialect, idiom, jargon, patois, patter, speech, talk, tongue, vernacular

liniment *n* = **ointment**, balm, balsam, cream, embrocation, emollient, lotion, salve, unguent

link[1] *n* **1, 2** = **component**, constituent, division, element, member, part, piece **4** = **connection**, affiliation, affinity, association, attachment, bond, joint, knot, liaison, relationship, tie, tie-up ◆ *vb* **8** = **connect**, attach, bind, couple, fasten, join, tie, unite, yoke **9** = **associate**, bracket, connect, identify, relate
Antonyms *vb* ≠ **connect:** detach, disconnect, divide, separate, sever, split, sunder

lion *n* **3** = **hero**, brave person, champion, conqueror, fighter, warrior **4** = **celebrity**, big name, celeb (*inf.*), idol, luminary, megastar (*inf.*), notable, prodigy, star, superstar, V.I.P., wonder

lion-hearted *adj* = **brave**, bold, courageous, daring, dauntless, heroic, intrepid, resolute, stalwart, valiant, valorous
Antonyms *adj* abject, chicken-hearted, cowardly, craven, faint-hearted, gutless (*inf.*), lily-livered, pusillanimous, spineless, timorous, wimpish *or* wimpy (*inf.*), = **brave**, yellow (*inf.*)

lionize ❶ *or* **lionise** ('laɪəˌnaɪz) *vb* **lionizes, lionizing, lionized** *or* **lionises, lionising, lionised.** (*tr*) to treat as or make into a celebrity.
▸ˌ**lioni'zation** *or* ˌ**lioni'sation** *n* ▸'**lionˌizer** *or* '**lionˌiser** *n*

lip ❶ (lɪp) *n* **1** *Anat.* **1a** either of the two fleshy folds surrounding the mouth. Related adj: **labial. 1b** (*as modifier*): *lip salve.* **2** the corresponding part in animals, esp. mammals. **3** any structure resembling a lip, such as the rim of a crater, the margin of a gastropod shell, etc. **4** a nontechnical word for **labium. 5** *Sl.* impudent talk or backchat. **6 bite one's lip. 6a** to stifle one's feelings. **6b** to be annoyed or irritated. **7 keep a stiff upper lip.** to maintain one's courage or composure during a time of trouble. **8 lick** *or* **smack one's lips.** to anticipate or recall something with glee or relish. ◆ *vb* **lips, lipping, lipped. 9** (*tr*) to touch with the lip or lips. **10** (*tr*) to form or be a lip or lips for. **11** (*tr*) *Rare.* to murmur or whisper. **12** (*intr*) to use the lips in playing a wind instrument. [OE *lippa*]
▸'**lipless** *adj* ▸'**lipˌlike** *adj*

lipase ('laɪpeɪs, 'lɪpeɪs) *n* any of a group of fat-digesting enzymes produced in the stomach, pancreas, and liver. [C19: from Gk *lipos* fat + -ASE]

lip gloss *n* a cosmetic applied to the lips to give a sheen.

lipid *or* **lipide** ('laɪpɪd, 'lɪpɪd) *n Biochem.* any of a large group of organic compounds that are esters of fatty acids or closely related substances. They are important structural materials in living organisms. Former name: **lipoid.** [C20: from F *lipide,* from Gk *lipos* fat]

Lipizzaner *or* **Lippizaner** (ˌlɪpɪt'sɑːnə) *n* a breed of riding and carriage horse used by the Spanish Riding School in Vienna and nearly always grey in colour. [G, after *Lipizza,* near Trieste, where these horses were bred]

lipo- *or before a vowel* **lip-** *combining form.* fat or fatty: *lipoprotein.* [from Gk *lipos* fat]

lipogram ('lɪpəʊˌgræm) *n* a piece of writing from which all words containing a particular letter have been deliberately omitted.

lipography (lɪ'pɒgrəfɪ) *n* the accidental omission of words or letters in writing. [C19: from Gk *lip-,* stem of *leipein* to omit + -GRAPHY]

lipoid ('lɪpɔɪd, 'laɪ-) *adj also* **lipoidal. 1** resembling fat; fatty. ◆ *n* **2** a fatlike substance, such as wax. **3** *Biochem.* a former name for **lipid.**

lipoprotein (ˌlɪpəʊ'prəutiːn, ˌlaɪ-) *n* any of a group of proteins to which a lipid molecule is attached, important in the transport of lipids in the bloodstream. See also **low-density lipoprotein.**

liposuction ('lɪpəʊˌsʌkʃən) *n* a cosmetic surgical operation in which subcutaneous fat is removed from the body by suction.

-lipped *adj* having a lip or lips as specified: *tight-lipped.*

Lippizaner (ˌlɪpɪt'sɑːnə) *n* a variant spelling of **Lipizzaner.**

lip-read ('lɪpˌriːd) *vb* **lip-reads, lip-reading, lip-read** (-ˌrɛd). to interpret (words) by lip-reading.

lip-reading *n* a method used by the deaf to comprehend spoken words by interpreting movements of the speaker's lips. Also called: **speech-reading.**
▸'**lip-ˌreader** *n*

lip service *n* insincere support or respect expressed but not practised.

lipstick ('lɪpˌstɪk) *n* a cosmetic for colouring the lips, usually in the form of a stick.

lip-synch *or* **lip-sync** ('lɪpˌsɪŋk) *vb* to mouth (prerecorded words) on television or film.

liq. *abbrev. for:* **1** liquid. **2** liquor.

liquefacient (ˌlɪkwɪ'feɪʃənt) *n* **1** a substance that liquefies or that causes liquefaction. ◆ *adj* **2** becoming or causing to become liquid. [C19: from L *liquefacere* to make LIQUID]

liquefied natural gas *n* a mixture of various gases, esp. methane, liquefied under pressure for transportation and used as an engine fuel. Abbrev.: **LNG.**

liquefied petroleum gas *n* a mixture of various petroleum gases, esp. propane and butane, stored as a liquid under pressure and used as an engine fuel. Abbrev.: **LPG** *or* **LP gas.**

liquefy ❶ ('lɪkwɪˌfaɪ) *vb* **liquefies, liquefying, liquefied.** (esp. of a gas) to become or cause to become liquid. [C15: via OF from L *liquefacere* to make liquid]
▸**liquefaction** (ˌlɪkwɪ'fækʃən) *n* ▸'**liqueˌfiable** *adj* ▸'**liqueˌfier** *n*

liquescent (lɪ'kwɛsᵊnt) *adj* (of a solid or gas) becoming or tending to become liquid. [C18: from L *liquescere*]
▸**li'quescence** *or* **li'quescency** *n*

liqueur (lɪ'kjʊə; *French* likœr) *n* **1a** any of several highly flavoured sweetened spirits, such as Kirsch or Cointreau, intended to be drunk after a meal. **1b** (*as modifier*): *liqueur glass.* **2** a small hollow chocolate sweet containing liqueur. [C18: from F; see LIQUOR]

liquid ❶ ('lɪkwɪd) *n* **1** a substance in a physical state in which it does not resist change of shape but does resist change of size. Cf. **gas** (sense 1), **solid** (sense 1). **2** a substance that is a liquid at room temperature and atmospheric pressure. **3** *Phonetics.* a frictionless continuant, esp. (l) or (r). ◆ *adj* **4** of, concerned with, or being a liquid or having the characteristic state of liquids: *liquid wax.* **5** shining, transparent, or brilliant. **6** flowing, fluent, or smooth. **7** (of assets) in the form of money or easily convertible into money. [C14: via OF from L *liquidus,* from *liquēre* to be fluid]
▸**li'quidity** *or* '**liquidness** *n* ▸'**liquidly** *adv*

liquid air *n* air that has been liquefied by cooling: used in the production of pure oxygen, nitrogen, and as a refrigerant.

liquidambar (ˌlɪkwɪd'æmbə) *n* **1** a deciduous tree of Asia and North and Central America, with star-shaped leaves, and exuding a yellow aromatic balsam. **2** the balsam of this tree, used in medicine. [C16: NL, from L *liquidus* liquid + Med. L *ambar* AMBER]

liquidate ❶ ('lɪkwɪˌdeɪt) *vb* **liquidates, liquidating, liquidated. 1** to settle or pay off (a debt, claim, etc.). **2a** to terminate the operations of (a commercial firm, bankrupt estate, etc.) by assessment of liabilities and appropriation of assets for their settlement. **2b** (of a commercial firm, etc.) to terminate operations in this manner. **3** (*tr*) to convert (assets) into cash. **4** (*tr*) to eliminate or kill.
▸'**liquiˌdator** *n*

liquidation (ˌlɪkwɪ'deɪʃən) *n* **1a** the process of terminating the affairs of a business firm, etc., by realizing its assets to discharge its liabilities. **1b** the state of a business firm, etc., having its affairs so terminated (esp. in **to go into liquidation**). **2** destruction; elimination.

liquid-crystal display *n* a flat-screen display used, for example, in portable computers, digital watches, and calculators, in which an array of liquid-crystal elements can be selectively activated to generate an image, by means of an electric field, which when applied to an element alters its optical properties.

liquidize *or* **liquidise** ('lɪkwɪˌdaɪz) *vb* **liquidizes, liquidizing, liquidized** *or* **liquidises, liquidising, liquidised. 1** to make or become liquid; liquefy. **2** (*tr*) to pulverize (food) in a liquidizer so as to produce a fluid.

liquidizer *or* **liquidiser** ('lɪkwɪˌdaɪzə) *n* a kitchen appliance with blades for puréeing vegetables, blending liquids, etc. Also called: **blender.**

liquid measure *n* a unit or system of units for measuring volumes of liquids or their containers.

liquid oxygen *n* the clear pale blue liquid state of oxygen produced by liquefying air and allowing the nitrogen to evaporate: used in rocket fuels. Also called: **lox.**

liquid paraffin *n* an oily liquid obtained by petroleum distillation and used as a laxative. Also called (esp. US and Canad.): **mineral oil.**

liquor ❶ ('lɪkə) *n* **1** any alcoholic drink, esp. spirits, or such drinks collectively. **2** any liquid substance, esp. that in which food has been cooked. **3** *Pharmacol.* a solution of a pure substance in water. **4 in liquor.** drunk. [C13: via OF from L, from *liquēre* to be liquid]

liquorice *or US & Canad.* **licorice** ('lɪkərɪs, -ərɪʃ) *n* **1** a perennial Mediterranean leguminous shrub. **2** the dried root of this plant, used as a laxative and in confectionery. **3** a sweet having a liquorice flavour. [C13: via Anglo-Norman and OF from LL *liquirītia,* from L *glycyrrhīza,* from Gk *glukurrhiza,* from *glukus* sweet + *rhiza* root]

lira ('lɪərə; *Italian* 'liːra) *n, pl* **lire** ('lɪərɪ; *Italian* 'liːre) *or* **liras. 1** the standard monetary unit of Italy and San Marino. **2** Also called: **pound.** the standard monetary unit of Turkey. **3** the standard monetary unit of Malta. [It., from L *lībra* pound]

liriodendron (ˌlɪrɪəʊ'dɛndrən) *n, pl* **liriodendrons** *or* **liriodendra** (-drə). a deciduous tulip tree of North America or a similar Chinese tree. [C18: NL, from Gk *leiron* lily + *dendron* tree]

lisle (laɪl) *n* **a** a strong fine cotton thread or fabric. **b** (*as modifier*): *lisle stockings.* [C19: after *Lisle* (now Lille), town in France where this thread was orig. manufactured]

lisp (lɪsp) *n* **1** the articulation of *s* and *z* like or nearly like the *th* sounds in English *thin* and *then* respectively. **2** the habit or speech defect of pronouncing *s* and *z* in this manner. **3** the sound of a lisp in pronunciation. ◆ *vb* **4** to use a lisp in the pronunciation of (speech). **5** to speak or pronounce imperfectly or haltingly. [OE *āwlispian,* from *wlisp* lisping (adj), imit.]
▸'**lisper** *n* ▸'**lisping** *adj, n* ▸'**lispingly** *adv*

lissom ❶ *or* **lissome** ('lɪsəm) *adj* **1** supple in the limbs or body; lithe; flexible. **2** agile; nimble. [C19: var. of *lithesome,* LITHE + -SOME[1]]
▸'**lissomly** *or* '**lissomely** *adv* ▸'**lissomness** *or* '**lissomeness** *n*

list[1] ❶ (lɪst) *n* **1** an item-by-item record of names or things, usually written or printed one under the other. **2** *Computing.* a linearly ordered

THESAURUS

lionize *vb* = **idolize**, acclaim, adulate, aggrandize, celebrate, eulogize, exalt, fête, glorify, hero-worship, honour, make much of, mob

lip *n* **3** = **edge**, brim, brink, flange, margin, rim **5** *Slang* = **impudence**, backchat (*inf.*), cheek, effrontery, impertinence, insolence, rudeness, sauce (*inf.*) **8 lick** *or* **smack one's lips** = **relish**, anticipate, delight in, drool over, enjoy, gloat over, savour, slaver over

liquefaction *n* = **melting**, deliquescence, dissolution, dissolving, fusion, thawing

liquefy *vb* = **melt**, deliquesce, dissolve, flux, fuse, liquesce, liquidize, run, thaw

liquid *n* **1** = **fluid**, juice, liquor, solution ◆ *adj* **4** = **fluid**, aqueous, flowing, liquefied, melted, molten, running, runny, thawed, wet **5** = **clear**, bright, brilliant, limpid, shining, translucent, transparent **6** = **smooth**, dulcet, flowing, fluent, mellifluent, mellifluous, melting, soft, sweet **7** = **convertible**, negotiable

liquidate *vb* **1** = **pay**, clear, discharge, honour, pay off, settle, square **2** = **dissolve**, abolish, annul, cancel, terminate **3** = **convert to cash**, cash, realize, sell off, sell up **4** = **kill**, annihilate, blow away, bump off (*sl.*), destroy, dispatch, do away with, do in (*sl.*), eliminate, exterminate, finish off, get rid of, murder, remove, wipe out (*inf.*)

liquor *n* **1** = **alcohol**, booze (*inf.*), drink, Dutch courage (*inf.*), grog, hard stuff (*inf.*), hooch *or* hootch (*inf., chiefly US & Canad.*), intoxicant, juice (*inf.*), spirits, strong drink **2** = **juice**, broth, extract, gravy, infusion, liquid, stock

lissom *adj* **1** = **supple**, flexible, limber, lithe, loose-jointed, loose-limbed, pliable, pliant, willowy **2** = **agile**, graceful, light, nimble

list[1] *n* **1** = **inventory**, catalogue, directory, file, index, invoice, leet (*Scot.*), listing, record, register, roll, schedule, series, syllabus, tabulation, tally ◆ *vb* **3, 4** = **itemize**, bill, book, catalogue, enrol, enter, enumerate, file, index, note, record, register, schedule, set down, tabulate, write down

work. **8** *Med.* short for **local anaesthetic** (see **anaesthesia**). **9** *US & Canad.* an item of local interest in a newspaper. [C15: via OF from LL *locālis,* from L *locus* place]
▸'**locally** *adv* ▸'**localness** *n*

local anaesthetic *n Med.* See **anaesthesia.**

local authority *n Brit. & NZ.* the governing body of a county, district, etc. US equivalent: **local government.**

locale ➊ (ləʊ'kɑːl) *n* a place or area, esp. with reference to events connected with it. [C18: from F *local* (n use of adj); see LOCAL]

local government *n* **1** government of the affairs of counties, towns, etc., by locally elected political bodies. **2** the US equivalent of **local authority.**

Local Group *n Astron.* the cluster of galaxies to which the Galaxy and the Andromeda Galaxy belong.

localism ('ləʊkəˌlɪzəm) *n* **1** a pronunciation, phrase, etc., peculiar to a particular locality. **2** another word for **provincialism.**

locality ➊ (ləʊ'kælɪtɪ) *n, pl* **localities. 1** a neighbourhood or area. **2** the site or scene of an event. **3** the fact or condition of having a location or position in space.

localize ➊ *or* **localise** ('ləʊkəˌlaɪz) *vb* **localizes, localizing, localized** *or* **localises, localising, localised. 1** to make or become local in attitude, behaviour, etc. **2** (*tr*) to restrict or confine (something) to a particular area or part. **3** (*tr*) to assign or ascribe to a particular region.
▸'**localˌizable** *or* '**localˌisable** *adj* ▸ˌ**localiˈzation** *or* ˌ**localiˈsation** *n*

local loan *n* (in Britain) a loan issued by a local government authority.

local option *n* (esp. in Scotland, New Zealand, and the US) the privilege of a municipality, county, etc., to determine by referendum whether a particular activity, esp. the sale of liquor, shall be permitted there.

locate ➊ (ləʊ'keɪt) *vb* **locates, locating, located. 1** (*tr*) to discover the position, situation, or whereabouts of; find. **2** (*tr; often passive*) to situate or place: *located on the edge of the city.* **3** (*intr*) to become established or settled.
▸**lo'cater** *n*

location ➊ (ləʊ'keɪʃən) *n* **1** a site or position; situation. **2** the act or process of locating or the state of being located. **3** a place outside a studio where filming is done: *shot on location.* **4** (in South Africa) **4a** a Black African or Coloured township, usually located near a small town. **4b** (formerly) a Black African tribal reserve. **5** *Computing.* a position in a memory capable of holding a unit of information, such as a word, and identified by its address. [C16: from L *locatio,* from *locare* to place]

locative ('lɒkətɪv) *Grammar.* ◆ *adj* **1** (of a word or phrase) indicating place or direction. **2** denoting a case of nouns, etc., that refers to the place at which the action described by the verb occurs. ◆ *n* **3a** the locative case. **3b** a word or speech element in this case. [C19: LOCATE + -IVE, on the model of *vocative*]

loc. cit. (in textual annotation) *abbrev. for* loco citato. [L: in the place cited]

loch (lɒx, lɒk) *n* **1** a Scot. word for **lake**[1] (senses 1 and 2). **2** Also: **sea loch.** a long narrow bay or arm of the sea in Scotland. [C14: from Gaelic]

lochia ('lɒkɪə) *n* a vaginal discharge of cellular debris, mucus, and blood following childbirth. [C17: NL from Gk *lokhia,* from *lokhos* childbirth]
▸'**lochial** *adj*

loci ('ləʊsaɪ) *n* the plural of **locus.**

lock[1] ➊ (lɒk) *n* **1** a device fitted to a gate, door, drawer, lid, etc., to keep it firmly closed. **2** a similar device attached to a machine, vehicle, etc. **3a** a section of a canal or river that may be closed off by gates to control the water level and the raising and lowering of vessels that pass through it. **3b** (*as modifier*): *a lock gate; a lock keeper.* **4** the jamming, fastening, or locking together of parts. **5** *Brit.* the extent to which a vehicle's front wheels will turn to the right or left: *this car has a good lock.* **6** a mechanism that detonates the charge of a gun. **7 lock, stock, and barrel.** completely; entirely. **8** any wrestling hold in which a wrestler seizes a part of his opponent's body. **9** Also called: **lock forward.** *Rugby.* **9a** a player in the second row of the scrum. **9b** this position. **10** a gas bubble in a hydraulic system or a liquid bubble in a pneumatic system that stops the fluid flow in a pipe, capillary, etc.: *an air lock.* ◆ *vb* **11** to fasten (a door, gate, etc.) or (of a door, etc.) to become fastened with a lock, bolt, etc., so as to prevent entry or exit. **12** (*tr*) to secure (a building) by locking all doors, windows, etc. **13** to fix or become fixed together securely or inextricably. **14** to become or cause to become rigid or immovable: *the front wheels of the car locked.* **15** (when *tr, often passive*) to clasp or entangle (someone or each other) in a struggle or embrace. **16** (*tr*) to furnish (a canal) with locks. **17** (*tr*) to move (a vessel) through a system of locks. ◆ See also **lock out, lock up.** [OE *loc*]
▸'**lockable** *adj*

lock[2] ➊ (lɒk) *n* **1** a strand, curl, or cluster of hair. **2** a tuft or wisp of wool, cotton, etc. **3** (*pl*) *Chiefly literary.* hair, esp. when curly or fine. [OE *loc*]

locked-in syndrome *n* a condition in which a person is conscious but unable to move any part of the body except the eyes: results from damage to the brainstem.

locker ('lɒkə) *n* **1a** a small compartment or drawer that may be locked, as one of several in a gymnasium, etc., for clothes and valuables. **1b** (*as modifier*): *a locker room.* **2** a person or thing that locks.

locket ('lɒkɪt) *n* a small ornamental case, usually on a necklace or chain, that holds a picture, keepsake, etc. [C17: from F *loquet* latch, dim. of *loc* LOCK[1]]

lockjaw ('lɒkˌdʒɔː) *n Pathol.* a nontechnical name for **trismus** and (often) **tetanus.**

lock out ➊ *vb* (*tr, adv*) **1** to prevent from entering by locking a door. **2** to prevent (employees) from working during an industrial dispute, as by closing a factory. ◆ *n* **lockout. 3** the closing of a place of employment by an employer, in order to bring pressure on employees to agree to terms.

locksmith ('lɒkˌsmɪθ) *n* a person who makes or repairs locks.

lock step *n* a method of marching such that the men follow one another as closely as possible.

lock up ➊ *vb* (*adv*) **1** (*tr*) Also: **lock in, lock away.** to imprison or confine. **2** to lock or secure the doors, windows, etc., of (a building). **3** (*tr*) to keep or store securely: *secrets locked up in history.* **4** (*tr*) to invest (funds) so that conversion into cash is difficult. ◆ *n* **lockup. 5** the action or time of locking up. **6** a jail or block of cells. **7** *Brit.* a small shop with no attached quarters for the owner. **8** *Brit.* a garage or storage place separate from the main premises. **9** *Stock Exchange.* an investment that is intended to be held for a relatively long period. ◆ *adj* **lock-up. 10** *Brit. & NZ.* (of premises) without living quarters: *a lock-up shop.*

loco[1] ('ləʊkəʊ) *n, pl* **locos.** *Inf.* short for **locomotive.**

loco[2] ('ləʊkəʊ) *adj* **1** *Sl., chiefly US.* insane. **2** (of an animal) affected with loco disease. ◆ *n, pl* **locos. 3** *US.* short for **locoweed.** ◆ *vb* **locos, locoing, locoed.** (*tr*) **4** to poison with locoweed. **5** *US sl.* to make insane. [C19: via Mexican Sp. from Sp.: crazy]

loco[3] ('ləʊkəʊ) *adj* denoting a price for goods, esp. goods to be exported, that are in a place specified or known, the buyer being responsible for all transport charges from that place: *loco Bristol; a loco price.* [C20: from L *locō* from a place]

loco disease *n* a disease of cattle, sheep, and horses characterized by paralysis and faulty vision, caused by ingestion of locoweed.

locomotion ➊ (ˌləʊkə'məʊʃən) *n* the act, fact, ability, or power of moving. [C17: from L *locō* from a place, ablative of *locus* place + MOTION]

locomotive (ˌləʊkə'məʊtɪv) *n* **1a** Also called: **locomotive engine.** a self-propelled engine driven by steam, electricity, or diesel power and used for drawing trains along railway tracks. **1b** (*as modifier*): *a locomotive shed; a locomotive works.* ◆ *adj* **2** of or relating to locomotion. **3** moving or able to move, as by self-propulsion.

locomotor (ˌləʊkə'məʊtə) *adj* of or relating to locomotion. [C19: from L *locō* from a place + MOTOR (mover)]

locomotor ataxia *n Pathol.* another name for **tabes dorsalis.**

locoweed ('ləʊkəʊˌwiːd) *n* any of several perennial leguminous plants of W North America that cause loco disease in horses, cattle, and sheep.

loculus ('lɒkjʊləs) *n, pl* **loculi** ('lɒkjʊˌlaɪ). **1** *Bot.* any of the chambers of an ovary or anther. **2** *Biol.* any small cavity or chamber. [C19: NL, from L: compartment, from *locus* place]
▸'**locular** *adj*

locum tenens ('ləʊkəm 'tiːnɛnz) *n, pl* **locum tenentes** (tə'nɛntiːz). *Chiefly Brit.* a person who stands in temporarily for another member of the same profession, esp. for a physician, chemist, or clergyman. Often shortened to **locum.** [C17: Med. L: (someone) holding the place (of another)]

locus ('ləʊkəs) *n, pl* **loci. 1** (in many legal phrases) a place or area, esp. the place where something occurred. **2** *Maths.* a set of points or lines whose location satisfies or is determined by one or more specified conditions: *the locus of points equidistant from a given point is a circle.* **3** *Genetics.* the position of a particular gene on a chromosome. [C18: L]

locust ('ləʊkəst) *n* **1** any of numerous insects, related to the grasshopper, of warm and tropical regions of the Old World, which travel in vast swarms, stripping large areas of vegetation. **2** Also called: **locust tree.** a North American leguminous tree having prickly branches, hanging clusters of white fragrant flowers, and reddish-brown seed pods. **3** the yellowish durable wood of this tree. **4** any of several similar trees, such as the honey locust and carob. [C13 (the insect): from L *locusta;* applied to the tree (C17) because the pods resemble locusts]

locution ➊ (ləʊ'kjuːʃən) *n* **1** a word, phrase, or expression. **2** manner or style of speech. [C15: from L *locūtiō* an utterance, from *loquī* to speak]

THESAURUS

locale *n* = **site,** locality, location, locus, place, position, scene, setting, spot, venue

locality *n* **1** = **neighbourhood,** area, district, neck of the woods (*inf.*), region, vicinity **2** = **site,** locale, location, place, position, scene, setting, spot

localize *vb* **1, 2** = **restrict,** circumscribe, concentrate, confine, contain, delimit, delimitate, limit, restrain **3** = **ascribe,** assign, narrow down, pinpoint, specify

locate *vb* **1** = **find,** come across, detect, discover, lay one's hands on, pin down, pinpoint, run to earth *or* ground, track down, unearth **2, 3** = **place,** establish, fix, put, seat, set, settle, situate

location *n* **1** = **site,** bearings, locale, locus, place, point, position, situation, spot, venue, whereabouts

lock[1] *n* **1, 2** = **fastening,** bolt, clasp, padlock ◆ *vb* **11, 12** = **fasten,** bolt, close, latch, seal, secure, shut, sneck (*dialect*) **13** = **unite,** clench, engage, entangle, entwine, join, link, mesh **15** = **embrace,** clasp, clutch, encircle, enclose, grapple, grasp, hug, press

lock[2] *n* **1** = **strand,** curl, ringlet, tress, tuft

lock out *vb* **1** = **shut out,** ban, bar, debar, exclude, keep out, refuse admittance to

lock up *vb* **1** = **imprison,** cage, confine, detain, incarcerate, jail, put behind bars, shut up ◆ *n* **lockup 6** = **prison,** can (*sl.*), cell, cooler, jail *or* gaol, jug (*sl.*), police cell

locomotion *n* = **movement,** action, headway, motion, moving, progress, progression, travel, travelling

locution *n* **1** = **expression,** collocation, idiom, phrase, term, turn of speech, wording **2** = **man-**

lode (ləʊd) *n* **1** a deposit of valuable ore occurring between definite limits in the surrounding rock; vein. **2** a deposit of metallic ore filling a fissure in the surrounding rock. [OE *lād* course]

loden ('ləʊdᵊn) *n* **1** a thick heavy waterproof woollen cloth with a short pile, used for coats. **2** a dark bluish-green colour, in which the cloth is often made. [G, from OHG *lodo* thick cloth]

lodestar 🅣 *or* **loadstar** ('ləʊd,stɑː) *n* **1** a star, esp. the North Star, used in navigation or astronomy as a point of reference. **2** something that serves as a guide or model. [C14: lit.: guiding star]

lodestone 🅣 *or* **loadstone** ('ləʊd,stəʊn) *n* **1a** magnetite that is naturally magnetic. **1b** a piece of this, which can be used as a magnet. **2** a person or thing regarded as a focus of attraction. [C16: lit.: guiding stone]

lodge 🅣 (lɒdʒ) *n* **1** *Chiefly Brit.* a small house at the entrance to the grounds of a country mansion, usually occupied by a gatekeeper or gardener. **2** a house or cabin used occasionally, as for some seasonal activity. **3** (*cap. when part of a name*) a large house or hotel. **4** a room for the use of porters in a university, college, etc. **5** a local branch or chapter of certain societies. **6** the building used as the meeting place of such a society. **7** the dwelling place of certain animals, esp. beavers. **8** a hut or tent of certain North American Indian peoples. ◆ *vb* **lodges, lodging, lodged. 9** to provide or be provided with accommodation or shelter, esp. rented accommodation. **10** (*intr*) to live temporarily, esp. in rented accommodation. **11** to implant, embed, or fix or be implanted, embedded, or fixed. **12** (*tr*) to deposit or leave for safety, storage, etc. **13** (*tr*) to bring (a charge or accusation) against someone. **14** (*tr; often foll. by in or with*) to place (authority, power, etc.) in the control (of someone). [C15: from OF *loge*, ?from OHG *louba* porch]

lodger 🅣 ('lɒdʒə) *n* a person who pays rent in return for accommodation in someone else's house.

lodging ('lɒdʒɪŋ) *n* **1** a temporary residence. **2** (*sometimes pl*) sleeping accommodation.

lodging house *n* a private home providing accommodation and meals for lodgers.

lodgings 🅣 ('lɒdʒɪŋz) *pl n* a rented room or rooms, esp. in another person's house.

lodgment *or* **lodgement** ('lɒdʒmənt) *n* **1** the act of lodging or the state of being lodged. **2** a blockage or accumulation. **3** a small area gained and held in enemy territory.

loess ('ləʊɪs) *n* a light-coloured fine-grained accumulation of clay and silt deposited by the wind. [C19: from G *Löss*, from Swiss G dialect *lösch* loose]
▸**loessial** (ləʊ'ɛsɪəl) *adj*

loft (lɒft) *n* **1** the space inside a roof. **2** a gallery, esp. one for the choir in a church. **3** a room over a stable used to store hay. **4** *US.* an upper storey of a warehouse or factory. **5** a raised house or coop in which pigeons are kept. **6** *Sport.* **6a** (in golf) the angle from the vertical made by the club face to give elevation to a ball. **6b** elevation imparted to a ball. **6c** a lofting stroke or shot. ◆ *vb* (*tr*) **7** *Sport.* to strike or kick (a ball) high in the air. **8** to store or place in a loft. **9** *Golf.* to slant (the face of a golf club). [OE, from ON *lopt* air, ceiling]

lofty 🅣 ('lɒftɪ) *adj* **loftier, loftiest. 1** of majestic or imposing height. **2** exalted or noble in character or nature. **3** haughty or supercilious. **4** elevated, eminent, or superior.
▸**'loftily** *adv* ▸**'loftiness** *n*

log[1] 🅣 (lɒg) *n* **1a** a section of the trunk or a main branch of a tree, when stripped of branches. **1b** (*modifier*) constructed out of logs: *a log cabin.* **2a** a detailed record of a voyage of a ship or aircraft. **2b** a record of the hours flown by pilots and aircrews. **2c** a book in which these records are made; logbook. **3** a written record of information about transmissions kept by radio stations, amateur radio operators, etc. **4** Also called: **chip log.** a device consisting of a float with an attached line, formerly used to measure the speed of a ship. **5 like a log.** without stirring or being disturbed (in **sleep like a log**). ◆ *vb* **logs, logging, logged. 6** (*tr*) to fell the trees of (a forest, area, etc.) for timber. **7** (*tr*) to saw logs from (trees). **8** (*intr*) to work at the felling of timber. **9** (*tr*) to enter (a distance, event, etc.) in a logbook or log. **10** (*tr*) to travel (a specified distance or time) or move at (a specified speed). [C14: from ?]

log[2] (lɒg) *n* short for **logarithm.**

-log *n combining form.* a US variant of **-logue.**

logan ('ləʊgən) *n Canad.* another name for **bogan** (a backwater).

loganberry ('ləʊgənbərɪ, -brɪ) *n, pl* **loganberries. 1** a trailing prickly hybrid plant of the rose family, cultivated for its edible fruit. **2** the purplish-red acid fruit of this plant. [C19: after James H. *Logan* (1841–1928), American judge and horticulturalist who first grew it (1881)]

logarithm ('lɒgə,rɪðəm) *n* the exponent indicating the power to which a fixed number, the base, must be raised to obtain a given number or variable. It is used esp. to simplify multiplication and division. Often shortened to **log.** [C17: from NL *logarithmus*, coined 1614 by John Napier (1550–1617), Scot. mathematician, from Gk *logos* ratio + *arithmos* number]
▸**logarithmic** (,lɒgə'rɪðmɪk) *adj*

logarithmic function *n* **a** the mathematical function $y = \log x$. **b** a function that can be expressed in terms of this function.

logbook ('lɒg,bʊk) *n* **1** a book containing the official record of trips made by a ship or aircraft. **2** *Brit.* a former name for **registration document.**

log chip *n Naut.* the wooden chip or float of a chip log. See **log**[1] (sense 4).

loge (ləʊʒ) *n* a small enclosure or box in a theatre or opera house. [C18: F; see LODGE]

logger ('lɒgə) *n* another word for **lumberjack.**

loggerhead 🅣 ('lɒgə,hɛd) *n* **1** Also called: **loggerhead turtle.** a large-headed turtle occurring in most seas. **2** a tool consisting of a large metal sphere attached to a long handle, used for warming liquids, melting tar, etc. **3** *Arch. or dialect.* a blockhead; dunce. **4 at loggerheads.** engaged in dispute or confrontation. [C16: prob. from dialect *logger* wooden block + HEAD]

loggia ('lɒdʒə, 'lɒdʒɪə) *n, pl* **loggias** *or* **loggie** (-dʒɛ). a covered area on the side of a building. [C17: It., from F *loge*. See LODGE]

logging ('lɒgɪŋ) *n* the work of felling, trimming, and transporting timber.

logic 🅣 ('lɒdʒɪk) *n* **1** the branch of philosophy concerned with analysing the patterns of reasoning by which a conclusion is properly drawn from a set of premises, without reference to meaning or context. **2** any formal system in which are defined axioms and rules of inference. **3** the system and principles of reasoning used in a specific field of study. **4** a particular method of argument or reasoning. **5** force or effectiveness in argument or dispute. **6** reasoned thought or argument, as distinguished from irrationality. **7** the relationship and interdependence of a series of events, facts, etc. **8** *Electronics, computing.* the principles underlying the units in a computer system that perform arithmetical and logical operations. See also **logic circuit.** [C14: from OF *logique* from Med. L *logica*, from Gk *logikos* concerning speech or reasoning]

logical 🅣 ('lɒdʒɪkᵊl) *adj* **1** relating to, used in, or characteristic of logic: *logical connective.* **2** using, according to, or deduced from the principles of logic: *a logical conclusion.* **3** capable of or characterized by clear or valid reasoning. **4** reasonable or necessary because of facts, events, etc.: *the logical candidate.* **5** *Computing.* of, performed by, used in, or relating to the logic circuits in a computer.
▸**,logi'cality** *or* **'logicalness** *n* ▸**'logically** *adv*

logical form *n* the structure of an argument by virtue of which it can be shown to be formally valid.

logical positivism *or* **empiricism** *n* a philosophical theory holding that the only meaningful statements are those that are analytic or can be tested empirically. It therefore rejects theology, metaphysics, etc., as meaningless.

logic bomb *n Computing.* an unauthorized program that is inserted into a computer system; when activated it interferes with the operation of the computer.

logic circuit *n* an electronic circuit used in computers to perform a logical operation on its two or more input signals.

logician (lɒ'dʒɪʃən) *n* a person who specializes in or is skilled at logic.

logic programming *n* the study or implementation of computer programs capable of discovering or checking proofs of formal expressions or segments.

log in *Computing.* ◆ *vb* **1** Also: **log on.** to enter (an identification num-

THESAURUS

ner of speech, accent, articulation, diction, inflection, intonation, phrasing, style

lodestar *n* **2** = **guide**, beacon, model, par, pattern, signal, standard

lodestone *n* **2** = **focus**, beacon, focal point, lodestar, magnet

lodge *n* **1, 2** = **cabin**, chalet, cottage, gatehouse, house, hunting lodge, hut, shelter **5** = **society**, assemblage, association, branch, chapter, club, group **7** = **den**, haunt, lair, retreat ◆ *vb* **9** = **accommodate**, billet, entertain, harbour, put up, quarter, shelter **10** = **stay**, board, room, sojourn, stop **11** = **stick**, become fixed, catch, come to rest, imbed, implant **13** = **register**, file, lay, put on record, submit

lodger *n* = **tenant**, boarder, guest, paying guest, P.G., resident, roomer

lodgings *pl n* = **accommodation**, abode, apartments, boarding, digs (*Brit. inf.*), dwelling, habitation, quarters, residence, rooms, shelter

lofty *adj* **1** = **high**, elevated, raised, sky-high, soaring, tall, towering **2** = **noble**, dignified, distinguished, elevated, exalted, grand, illustrious, imposing, majestic, renowned, stately, sublime, superior **3** = **haughty**, arrogant, condescending, disdainful, high and mighty (*inf.*), lordly, patronizing, proud, snooty (*inf.*), supercilious, toffee-nosed (*sl., chiefly Brit.*)
Antonyms *adj* ≠ **high:** dwarfed, low, short, stunted ≠ **noble:** debased, degraded, humble, low, lowly, mean ≠ **haughty:** friendly, modest, unassuming, warm

log[1] *n* **1** = **stump**, block, bole, chunk, piece of timber, trunk **2** = **record**, account, chart, daybook, journal, listing, logbook, tally ◆ *vb* **6** = **chop**, cut, fell, hew **9** = **record**, book, chart, make a note of, note, register, report, set down, tally

loggerhead *n* **4 at loggerheads** = **quarrelling**, at daggers drawn, at each other's throats, at enmity, at odds, estranged, feuding, in dispute, opposed

logic *n* **1-3** = **science of reasoning**, argumentation, deduction, dialectics, ratiocination, syllogistic reasoning **6** = **reason**, good reason, good sense, sense, sound judgment **7** = **connection**, chain of thought, coherence, link, rationale, relationship

logical *adj* **1-3** = **rational**, clear, cogent, coherent, consistent, deducible, pertinent, reasonable, relevant, sound, valid, well-organized **4** = **reasonable**, judicious, most likely, necessary, obvious, plausible, sensible, wise
Antonyms *adj* ≠ **rational:** illogical, instinctive, irra-

ber, password, etc.) from a remote terminal to gain access to a multiaccess system. ◆ *n* **2** Also: **login.** the process by which a computer user logs in.

logistics ❶ (lɒ'dʒɪstɪks) *n (functioning as sing or pl)* **1** the science of the movement and maintenance of military forces. **2** the management of materials flow through an organization. **3** the detailed planning and organization of any large complex operation. [C19: from F *logistique*, from *loger* to LODGE]
▸**lo'gistical** *adj*

log jam *n Chiefly US & Canad.* **1** blockage caused by the crowding together of a number of logs floating in a river. **2** a deadlock; standstill.

loglog ('lɒglɒg) *n* the logarithm of a logarithm (in equations, etc.).

logo ('ləugəu, 'lɒg-) *n, pl* **logos.** short for **logotype** (sense 2).

logo- *combining form.* indicating word or speech: *logogram.* [from Gk *logos* word, from *legein* to speak]

logogram ('lɒgə,græm) *n* single symbol representing an entire morpheme, word, or phrase, as for example the symbol (%) meaning *per cent.*

logorrhoea *or esp. US* **logorrhea** (,lɒgə'rɪə) *n* uncontrollable or incoherent talkativeness.

logos (lɒgɒs) *n* **1** *Philosophy.* reason, regarded as the controlling principle of the universe. **2** *(cap.)* the divine Word; the second person of the Trinity. [C16: Gk: word, reason]

logotype ('lɒgəu,taɪp) *n* **1** *Printing.* a piece of type with several uncombined characters cast on it. **2** Also called: **logo.** a trademark, company emblem, or similar device.

log out *Computing.* ◆ *vb* **1** Also: **log off.** to disconnect a remote terminal from a multiaccess system by entering (an identification number, password, etc.). ◆ *n* **2** Also: **logout.** the process by which a computer user logs out.

logroll ('lɒg,rəul) *vb Chiefly US.* to use logrolling in order to procure the passage of (legislation).
▸**'log,roller** *n*

logrolling ('lɒg,rəulɪŋ) *n* **1** *US.* the practice of undemocratic agreements between politicians involving mutual favours, the trading of votes, etc. **2** another name for **birling.** See **birl.**

-logue *or US* **-log** *n combining form.* indicating speech or discourse of a particular kind: *travelogue; monologue.* [from F, from Gk *-logos*]

logwood ('lɒg,wud) *n* **1** a leguminous tree of the Caribbean and Central America. **2** the heavy reddish-brown wood of this tree, yielding a dye.

-logy *n combining form.* **1** indicating the science or study of: *musicology.* **2** indicating writing, discourse, or body of writings: *trilogy; phraseology; martyrology.* [from L *-logia*, from Gk, from *logos* word]
▸**-logical** *or* **-logic** *adj combining form.* ▸**-logist** *n combining form.*

loin (lɔɪn) *n* **1** *Anat.* the lower back and sides between the pelvis and the ribs. Related adj: **lumbar. 2** a cut of meat from this part of an animal. ◆ See also **loins.** [C14: from OF *loigne*, ?from Vulgar L *lumbra* (unattested), from L *lumbus* loin]

loincloth ('lɔɪn,klɒθ) *n* a piece of cloth worn round the loins. Also called: **breechcloth.**

loins (lɔɪnz) *pl n* **1** the hips and the inner surface of the legs where they join the trunk of the body; crotch. **2** *Euphemistic.* the reproductive organs.

loiter ❶ ('lɔɪtə) *vb (intr)* to stand or act aimlessly or idly. [C14: ?from MDu. *löteren* to wobble]
▸**'loiterer** *n* ▸**'loitering** *n, adj*

loll ❶ (lɒl) *vb* **1** *(intr)* to lie, lean, or lounge in a lazy or relaxed manner. **2** to hang or allow to hang loosely. ◆ *n* **3** an act or instance of lolling. [C14: ? imit.]
▸**'loller** *n* ▸**'lolling** *adj*

Lollard ('lɒləd) *n English history.* a follower of John Wycliffe (?1330–84), English religious reformer, during the 14th, 15th, and 16th centuries. [C14: from MDu.; mutterer, from *lollen* to mumble (prayers)]
▸**'Lollardism** *n*

lollipop ('lɒlɪ,pɒp) *n* **1** a boiled sweet or toffee stuck on a small wooden stick. **2** *Brit.* another word for **ice lolly.** [C18: ?from N. English dialect *lolly* the tongue + POP[1]]

lollipop man *or* **lady** *n Brit. inf.* a person who stops traffic by holding up a circular sign on a pole, to enable children to cross the road safely.

lollop ('lɒləp) *vb* **lollops, lolloping, lolloped.** *(intr) Chiefly Brit.* **1** to walk or run with a clumsy or relaxed bouncing movement. **2** a less common word for **lounge.** [C18: prob. from LOLL + *-op* as in GALLOP, to emphasize the contrast in meaning]

lollo rosso ('lɒləu 'rɒsəu) *n* a variety of lettuce originating in Italy, having curly red-tipped leaves and a slightly bitter taste.

lolly ('lɒlɪ) *n, pl* **lollies. 1** an informal word for **lollipop. 2** *Brit.* short for **ice lolly. 3** *Brit., Austral. & NZ.* a slang word for **money. 4** *Austral. & NZ inf.* a sweet, esp. a boiled one. **5 do the** *(or* **one's) lolly.** *Austral. inf.* to lose one's temper. [shortened from LOLLIPOP]

Lombard ('lɒmbəd, -bɑːd, 'lʌm-) *n* **1** a native or inhabitant of Lombardy, a region of N central Italy. **2** a member of an ancient Germanic people who settled in N Italy after 568 A.D. ◆ *adj* also **Lombardic. 3** of or relating to Lombardy or the Lombards.

Lombard Street *n* the British financial and banking world. [C16: from a street in London once occupied by Lombard bankers]

Lombardy poplar ('lɒmbədɪ, 'lʌm-) *n* an Italian poplar tree with upwardly pointing branches giving it a columnar shape.

London pride ('lʌndən) *n* a type of saxifrage plant having a basal rosette of leaves and pinkish-white flowers.

lone ❶ (ləun) *adj (prenominal)* **1** unaccompanied; solitary. **2** single or isolated: *a lone house.* **3** a literary word for **lonely. 4** unmarried or widowed. [C14: from the mistaken division of ALONE into *a lone*]
▸**'loneness** *n*

lonely ❶ ('ləunlɪ) *adj* **lonelier, loneliest. 1** unhappy as a result of being without companions. **2** causing or resulting from the state of being alone. **3** isolated, unfrequented, or desolate. **4** without companions; solitary.
▸**'loneliness** *n*

lonely hearts *adj (often caps.)* of or for people who wish to meet a congenial companion or marriage partner: *a lonely hearts advertisement.*

loner ❶ ('ləunə) *n Inf.* a person who avoids the company of others or prefers to be alone.

lonesome ❶ ('ləunsəm) *adj* **1** *Chiefly US & Canad.* another word for **lonely.** ◆ *n* **2 on** *or US* **by one's lonesome.** *Inf.* on one's own.
▸**'lonesomely** *adv* ▸**'lonesomeness** *n*

long[1] ❶ (lɒŋ) *adj* **1** having relatively great extent in space or duration in time. **2a** *(postpositive)* of a specified number of units in extent or duration: *three hours long.* **2b** *(in combination): a two-foot-long line.* **3** having or consisting of a relatively large number of items or parts: *a long list.* **4** having greater than the average or expected range, extent, or duration: *a long match.* **5** seeming to occupy a greater time than is really so: *she spent a long afternoon waiting.* **6** (of drinks) containing a large quantity of nonalcoholic beverage. **7** (of a garment) reaching to the wearer's ankles. **8** *Inf.* (foll. by *on*) plentifully supplied or endowed (with): *long on good ideas.* **9** *Phonetics.* (of a speech sound, esp. a vowel) **9a** of relatively considerable duration. **9b** (in popular usage) denoting the qualities of the five English vowels in such words as *mate, mete, mite, moat, moot,* and *mute.* **10** from end to end; lengthwise. **11** unlikely to win, happen, succeed, etc.: *a long chance.* **12** *Prosody.* **12a** denoting a vowel of relatively great duration. **12b** denoting a syllable containing such a vowel. **12c** carrying the emphasis. **13** *Finance.* having or characterized by large holdings of securities or commodities in anticipation of rising prices. **14** *Cricket.* (of a fielding position) near the boundary: *long leg.* **15 in the long run.** ultimately; after or over a period of time. ◆ *adv* **16** for a certain time or period: *how long will it last?* **17** for or during an extensive period of time: *long into the next year.* **18** at a distant time; quite a bit of time: *long before I met you; long ago.* **19** *Finance.* into a position with more security or commodity holdings than are required by sale contracts and therefore dependent on rising prices for profit: *to go long.* **20 as** *(or* **so) long as. 20a** for or during just the length of time that. **20b** inasmuch as; since. **20c** provided that; if. **21 no longer.** not any more; formerly but not now. ◆ *n* **22** a long time (esp. in **for long**). **23** a relatively long thing, such as a dash in Morse code. **24** *Phonetics.* a long vowel or syllable. **25** *Finance.* a person with large holdings of a security or commodity in expectation of a rise in its price; bull. **26 before long.** soon. **27 the long and the short of it.** the essential points or facts. ◆ See also **longs.** [OE *lang*]

long[2] ❶ (lɒŋ) *vb (intr; foll. by for or an infinitive)* to have a strong desire. [OE *langian*]

long. *abbrev. for* longitude.

long- *adv (in combination)* for or lasting a long time: *long-awaited; long-established; long-lasting.*

THESAURUS

tional, unorganized, unreasonable ≠ **reasonable:** illogical, implausible, unlikely, unreasonable

logistics *n* **3** = **organization**, coordination, engineering, management, masterminding, orchestration, plans, strategy

loiter *vb* = **linger**, dally, dawdle, delay, dilly-dally (*inf.*), hang about *or* around, idle, lag, loaf, loll, saunter, skulk, stroll

loll *vb* **1** = **lounge**, flop, lean, loaf, recline, relax, slouch, slump, sprawl **2** = **droop**, dangle, drop, flap, flop, hang, hang loosely, sag

lone *adj* **1** = **solitary**, by oneself, one, only, separate, separated, single, sole, unaccompanied **2** = **isolated**, deserted

loneliness *n* **1** = **solitude**, aloneness, forlornness, lonesomeness, solitariness **2** = **isolation**, desertedness, desolation, seclusion

lonely *adj* **1** = **abandoned**, destitute, estranged, forlorn, forsaken, friendless, lonesome, outcast **2, 4** = **solitary**, alone, apart, by oneself, companionless, isolated, lone, single, withdrawn **3** = **desolate**, deserted, godforsaken, isolated, off the beaten track (*inf.*), out-of-the-way, remote, secluded, sequestered, solitary, unfrequented, uninhabited
Antonyms *adj* ≠ **abandoned:** befriended, popular ≠ **solitary:** accompanied, together ≠ **desolate:** bustling, crowded, frequented, populous, teeming

loner *n Informal* = **individualist**, hermit, lone wolf, maverick, misanthrope, outsider, recluse, solitary

lonesome *adj* **1** *Chiefly U.S. & Canad.* = **lonely**, cheerless, companionless, deserted, desolate, dreary, forlorn, friendless, gloomy, isolated, lone

long[1] *adj* **1, 3, 4** = **elongated**, expanded, extended, extensive, far-reaching, lengthy, spread out, stretched **5** = **prolonged**, dragging, interminable, late, lengthy, lingering, long-drawn-out, protracted, slow, sustained, tardy
Antonyms *adj* ≠ **elongated:** compressed, contracted, little, short, small ≠ **prolonged:** abbreviated, abridged, brief, momentary, quick, short, short-lived

long[2] *vb* = **desire**, ache, covet, crave, dream of, eat one's heart out over, hanker, hunger, itch, lust, pine, set one's heart on, want, wish, yearn

long-acting *adj* (of a drug) slowly effective after initial dosage, but maintaining its effects over a long period of time. Cf. **intermediate-acting, short-acting.**

longboat ('lɒŋˌbəʊt) *n* the largest boat carried aboard a commercial sailing vessel.

longbow ('lɒŋˌbəʊ) *n* a large powerful hand-drawn bow, esp. as used in medieval England.

longcase clock ('lɒŋˌkeɪs) *n* another name for **grandfather clock.**

longcloth ('lɒŋˌklɒθ) *n* a fine plain-weave cotton cloth made in long strips.

long-dated *adj* (of a gilt-edged security) having more than 15 years to run before redemption. Cf. **medium-dated, short-dated.**

long-day *adj* (of certain plants) able to mature and flower only if exposed to long periods of daylight. Cf. **short-day.**

long-distance *n* **1** (*modifier*) covering relatively long distances: *a long-distance driver.* **2** (*modifier*) (of telephone calls, lines, etc.) connecting points a relatively long way apart. **3** *Chiefly US & Canad.* a long-distance telephone call. **4** a long-distance telephone system or its operator. ◆ *adv* **5** by a long-distance telephone line: *he phoned long-distance.*

long-drawn-out ❶ *adj* overprolonged or extended.

longeron ('lɒndʒərən) *n* a main longitudinal structural member of an aircraft. [C20: from F: side support, ult. from L *longus* LONG[1]]

longevity (lɒn'dʒɛvɪtɪ) *n* **1** long life. **2** relatively long duration of employment, service, etc. [C17: from LL *longaevitās*, from L *longaevus* long-lived, from *longus* LONG[1] + *aevum* age]

long face *n* a disappointed, solemn, or miserable facial expression.
▸ˌ**long-'faced** *adj*

longhand ('lɒŋˌhænd) *n* ordinary handwriting in which letters, words, etc., are set down in full, as opposed to typing or to shorthand.

long haul *n* **1** a journey over a long distance, esp. one involving the transport of goods. **2** a lengthy job.

long-headed *adj* astute; shrewd; sagacious.
▸ˌ**long-'headedly** *adv* ▸ˌ**long-'headedness** *n*

longhorn ('lɒŋˌhɔːn) *n* **1** a long-horned breed of beef cattle, formerly common in the southwestern US. **2** a British breed of beef cattle with long curved horns.

longing ❶ ('lɒŋɪŋ) *n* **1** a prolonged unfulfilled desire or need. ◆ *adj* **2** having or showing desire or need: *a longing look.*
▸'**longingly** *adv*

longish ('lɒŋɪʃ) *adj* rather long.

longitude ('lɒndʒɪˌtjuːd, 'lɒŋgɪ-) *n* distance in degrees east or west of the prime meridian at 0° measured by the angle between the plane of the prime meridian and that of the meridian through the point in question, or by the time difference. [C14: from L *longitūdō* length, from *longus* LONG[1]]

longitudinal (ˌlɒndʒɪ'tjuːdɪnᵊl, ˌlɒŋgɪ-) *adj* **1** of or relating to longitude or length. **2** placed or extended lengthways.
▸ˌ**longi'tudinally** *adv*

longitudinal wave *n* a wave that is propagated in the same direction as the displacement of the transmitting medium.

long johns *pl n Inf.* underpants with long legs.

long jump *n* an athletic contest in which competitors try to cover the farthest distance possible with a running jump from a fixed board or mark. US and Canad. equivalent: **broad jump.**

long leg *n Cricket.* **a** a fielding position on the leg side near the boundary almost directly behind the batsman's wicket. **b** a fielder in this position.

long-lived ❶ *adj* having long life, existence, or currency.
▸ˌ**long-'livedness** *n*

long-off *n Cricket.* **a** a fielding position on the off side near the boundary almost directly behind the bowler. **b** a fielder in this position.

long-on *n Cricket.* **a** a fielding position on the leg side near the boundary almost directly behind the bowler. **b** a fielder in this position.

long-playing *adj* of or relating to an LP (long player).

long-range *adj* **1** of or extending into the future: *a long-range weather forecast.* **2** (of vehicles, aircraft, etc.) capable of covering great distances without refuelling. **3** (of weapons) made to be fired at a distant target.

longs (lɒŋz) *pl n* **1** full-length trousers. **2** long-dated gilt-edged securities. **3** unsold securities or commodities held in anticipation of rising prices.

longship ('lɒŋˌʃɪp) *n* a narrow open vessel with oars and a square sail, used esp. by the Vikings.

longshore ('lɒŋˌʃɔː) *adj* situated on, relating to, or along the shore. [C19: short form of *alongshore*]

longshore drift *n* the process whereby beach material is gradually shifted laterally.

longshoreman ('lɒŋˌʃɔːmən) *n, pl* **longshoremen.** a US and Canad. word for **docker.**

long shot ❶ *n* **1** a competitor, as in a race, considered to be unlikely to win. **2** a bet against heavy odds. **3** an undertaking, guess, or possibility with little chance of success. **4** *Films, television.* a shot where the camera is or appears to be distant from the object to be photographed. **5 by a long shot.** by any means: *he still hasn't finished by a long shot.*

long-sighted *adj* **1** related to or suffering from hyperopia. **2** able to see distant objects in focus. **3** another term for **far-sighted.**
▸ˌ**long-'sightedly** *adv* ▸ˌ**long-'sightedness** *n*

long-standing ❶ *adj* existing for a long time.

long-suffering ❶ *adj* **1** enduring pain, unhappiness, etc., without complaint. ◆ *n* **2** long and patient endurance.
▸ˌ**long-'sufferingly** *adv*

long suit *n* **1a** the longest suit in a hand of cards. **1b** a holding of four or more cards of a suit. **2** *Inf.* an outstanding advantage, personal quality, or talent.

long-term *adj* **1** lasting or extending over a long time: *long-term prospects.* **2** *Finance.* maturing after a long period: *a long-term bond.*

longtime ('lɒŋˌtaɪm) *adj* of long standing.

long ton *n* the full name for **ton**[1] (sense 1).

longueur (*French* lɔ̃gœr) *n* a period of boredom or dullness. [lit.: length]

long vacation *n* the long period of holiday in the summer during which universities, law courts, etc., are closed.

long wave *n* **a** a radio wave with a wavelength greater than 1000 metres. **b** (*as modifier*): *a long-wave broadcast.*

longways ('lɒŋˌweɪz) *or US & Canad.* **longwise** *adv* another word for **lengthways.**

long weekend *n* a weekend holiday extended by a day or days on either side.

long-winded ❶ (ˌlɒŋ'wɪndɪd) *adj* **1** tiresomely long. **2** capable of energetic activity without becoming short of breath.
▸ˌ**long-'windedly** *adv* ▸ˌ**long-'windedness** *n*

lonicera (lɒ'nɪsərə) *n* See **honeysuckle.**

loo[1] (luː) *n, pl* **loos.** *Brit.* an informal word for **lavatory.** [C20: ?from F *lieux d'aisance* water closet]

loo[2] (luː) *n, pl* **loos. 1** a gambling card game. **2** a stake used in this game. [C17: shortened from *lanterloo*, via Du. from F *lanterelu*, orig. a nonsense word from the refrain of a popular song]

loofah ('luːfə) *n* the fibrous interior of the fruit of a type of gourd, which is dried and used as a bath sponge or for scrubbing. Also (esp. US): **loofa, luffa.** [C19: from NL *luffa*, from Ar. *lūf*]

look ❶ (lʊk) *vb* (*mainly intr*) **1** (often foll. by *at*) to direct the eyes (towards): *to look at the sea.* **2** (often foll. by *at*) to direct one's attention (towards): *let's look at the circumstances.* **3** (often foll. by *to*) to turn one's interests or expectations (towards): *to look to the future.* **4** (*copula*) to give the impression of being by appearance to the eye or mind; seem: *that looks interesting.* **5** to face in a particular direction: *the house looks north.* **6** to expect, hope, or plan (to do something): *I look to hear from you soon; he's looking to get rich.* **7** (foll. by *for*) **7a** to search or seek: *I looked for you everywhere.* **7b** to cherish the expectation (of); hope (for): *I look for success.* **8** (foll. by *to*) **8a** to be mindful (of): *to look to the promise one has made.* **8b** to have recourse (to): *look to your swords, men!* **9** (foll. by *into*) to carry out an investigation. **10** (*tr*) to direct a look at (someone) in a specified way: *she looked her rival up and down.* **11** (*tr*) to accord in appearance with (something): *to look one's age.* **12 look alive, lively, sharp,** *or* **smart.** to hurry up; get busy. **13 look here.** an expression used to attract someone's attention, add emphasis to a statement, etc. ◆ *n* **14** the act or an instance of looking: *a look of despair.* **15** a view or sight (of something): *let's have a look.* **16** (*often pl*) appearance to the eye or mind; aspect: *the look of innocence; I don't like the looks of this place.* **17**

THESAURUS

long-drawn-out *adj* = **prolonged**, dragged out, interminable, lengthy, marathon, overextended, overlong, protracted, spun out

longing *n* **1** = **desire**, ache, ambition, aspiration, coveting, craving, hankering, hope, hungering, itch, thirst, urge, wish, yearning, yen (*inf.*) ◆ *adj* **2** = **yearning**, anxious, ardent, avid, craving, desirous, eager, hungry, languishing, pining, wishful, wistful
Antonyms *n* ≠ **desire:** abhorrence, antipathy, apathy, disgust, disregard, indifference, loathing, revulsion, unconcern ◆ *adj* ≠ **yearning:** apathetic, cold, disgusted, hateful, indifferent, loathing, unconcerned, uninterested

long-lived *adj* = **long-lasting**, enduring, full of years, longevous, old as Methuselah

long shot *n* **1** = **outsider**, dark horse

long-standing *adj* = **established**, abiding, enduring, fixed, long-established, long-lasting, long-lived, time-honoured

long-suffering *adj* **1** = **uncomplaining**, easy-going, forbearing, forgiving, patient, resigned, stoical, tolerant

long-winded *adj* **1** = **rambling**, diffuse, discursive, garrulous, lengthy, long-drawn-out, overlong, prolix, prolonged, repetitious, tedious, tiresome, verbose, wordy
Antonyms *adj* brief, concise, crisp, curt, laconic, pithy, sententious, short, succinct, terse, to the point

look *vb* **1** = **see**, behold (*arch.*), check, check out (*inf.*), clock (*Brit. sl.*), examine, eye, eyeball (*sl.*), feast one's eyes upon, gaze, get a load of (*inf.*), glance, inspect, observe, peep, regard, scan, scrutinize, study, survey, take a dekko at (*Brit. sl.*), take a gander at (*inf.*), view, watch **2** = **consider**, contemplate **4** = **seem**, appear, display, evidence, exhibit, look like, make clear, manifest, present, seem to be, show, strike one as **5** = **face**, front, front on, give onto, overlook **7a** = **search**, forage, hunt, seek **7b** = **hope**, anticipate, await, expect, reckon on **9** *foll. by* **into** = **investigate**, check out, delve into, examine, explore, follow up, go into, inquire about, inspect, look over, make inquiries, probe, research, scrutinize, study ◆ *n* **14, 15** = **glimpse**, butcher's (*Brit. sl.*), examination, eyeful (*inf.*), gander (*inf.*), gaze, glance, inspection, look-see (*sl.*), observation, once-over (*inf.*), peek, review, shufti (*Brit. sl.*), sight, squint (*inf.*), survey, view **16** = **appearance**, air, aspect, bearing, cast, complexion, countenance, demeanour, effect, expression, face, fashion, guise, manner, mien (*literary*), semblance

style; fashion: *the new look for spring.* ♦ *sentence connector.* **18** an expression demanding attention or showing annoyance, determination, etc.: *look, I've had enough of this.* ♦ See also **look after, look back,** etc. [OE *lōcian*]
▸ **'looker** *n*

USAGE NOTE See at **like.**

look after ⓣ *vb (intr, prep)* **1** to take care of; be responsible for. **2** to follow with the eyes.
lookalike ⓣ ('lʊkə,laɪk) *n* **a** a person or thing that is the double of another, often well-known, person or thing. **b** *(as modifier)*: *a lookalike Minister; a lookalike newspaper.*
look back *vb (intr, adv)* **1** to cast one's mind to the past. **2 never look back**: to become increasingly successful: *after his first book was published, he never looked back.*
look down ⓣ *vb (intr, adv;* foll. by *on* or *upon)* to express or show contempt or disdain (for).
look forward to ⓣ *vb (intr, adv + prep)* to wait or hope for, esp. with pleasure.
look-in *Inf.* ♦ *n* **1** a chance to be chosen, participate, etc. **2** a short visit. ♦ *vb* **look in. 3** *(intr, adv;* often foll. by *on)* to pay a short visit.
looking glass *n* a mirror.
look on *vb (intr)* **1** *(adv)* to be a spectator at an event or incident. **2** *(prep)* Also: **look upon.** to consider or regard: *she looked on the whole affair as a joke.*
▸ **,looker-'on** *n*
lookout ⓣ ('lʊk,aʊt) *n* **1** the act of keeping watch against danger, etc. **2** a person or persons instructed or employed to keep such a watch, esp. on a ship. **3** a strategic point from which a watch is kept. **4** *Inf.* worry or concern: *that's his lookout.* **5** *Chiefly Brit.* outlook, chances, or view. ♦ *vb* **look out.** *(adv, mainly intr)* **6** to heed one's behaviour; be careful. **7** to be on the watch: *look out for my mother at the station.* **8** *(tr)* to search for and find. **9** (foll. by *on* or *over)* to face in a particular direction: *the house looks out over the moor.*
look over ⓣ *vb* **1** *(intr, prep)* to inspect by making a tour of (a factory, house, etc.). **2** *(tr, adv)* to examine (a document, letter, etc.). ♦ *n* **look-over. 3** an inspection.
look-see *n Sl.* a brief inspection or look.
look up ⓣ *vb (adv)* **1** *(tr)* to discover (something required to be known) by resorting to a work of reference, such as a dictionary. **2** *(intr)* to increase, as in quality or value: *things are looking up.* **3** *(intr;* foll. by *to)* to have respect (for): *I've always wanted a girlfriend I could look up to.* **4** *(tr)* to visit or make contact with (a person): *I'll look you up when I'm in town.*
loom[1] (lu:m) *n* an apparatus, worked by hand or mechanically (**power loom**), for weaving yarn into a textile. [C13 (meaning any kind of tool): var. of OE *gelōma* tool]
loom[2] ⓣ (lu:m) *vb (intr)* **1** to come into view indistinctly with an enlarged and often threatening aspect. **2** (of an event) to seem ominously close. **3** (often foll. by *over)* (of large objects) to dominate or overhang. ♦ *n* **4** a rising appearance, as of something far away. [C16: ?from East Frisian *lomen* to move slowly]
loon[1] (lu:n) *n* the US and Canad. name for **diver** (the bird). [C17: of Scand. origin]
loon[2] (lu:n) *n* **1** *Inf.* a simple-minded or stupid person. **2** *Arch.* a person of low rank or occupation. [C15: from ?]
loony *or* **looney** ('lu:nɪ) *Sl.* ♦ *adj* **loonier, looniest. 1** lunatic; insane. **2** foolish or ridiculous. ♦ *n, pl* **loonies** *or* **looneys. 3** a foolish or insane person. **4** *Canad.* a Canadian dollar coin with a loon bird on one of its faces.
▸ **'looniness** *n*
loony bin *n Sl.* a mental hospital or asylum.
loop ⓣ (lu:p) *n* **1** the round or oval shape formed by a line, string, etc., that curves around to cross itself. **2** any round or oval-shaped thing that is closed or nearly closed. **3** an intrauterine contraceptive device in the shape of a loop. **4** *Electronics.* a closed electric or magnetic circuit through which a signal can circulate, as in a feedback control system. **5** a flight manoeuvre in which an aircraft flies one complete circle in the vertical plane. **6** Also called: **loop line.** *Chiefly Brit.* a railway branch line which leaves the main line and rejoins it after a short distance. **7** *Maths, physics.* a closed curve on a graph: *hysteresis loop.* **8** a continuous strip of cinematographic film. **9** *Computing.* a series of instructions in a program, performed repeatedly until some specified condition is satisfied. **10** a group of people to whom information is circulated (esp. in **in** *or* **out of the loop**). ♦ *vb* **11** *(tr)* to make a loop in or of (a line, string, etc.). **12** *(tr)* to fasten or encircle with a loop or something like a loop. **13** Also: **loop the loop.** to cause (an aircraft) to perform a loop or (of an aircraft) to perform a loop. **14** *(intr)* to move in loops or in a path like a loop. [C14 *loupe,* from ?]
▸ **'looper** *n*
loophole ⓣ ('lu:p,həʊl) *n* **1** an ambiguity, omission, etc., as in a law, by which one can avoid a penalty or responsibility. **2** a small gap or hole in a wall, esp. one in a fortified wall. ♦ *vb* **loopholes, loopholing, loopholed. 3** *(tr)* to provide with loopholes.
loopy ('lu:pɪ) *adj* **loopier, loopiest. 1** full of loops; curly or twisted. **2** *Inf.* slightly mad, crazy.
loose ⓣ (lu:s) *adj* **1** free or released from confinement or restraint. **2** not close, compact, or tight in structure or arrangement. **3** not fitted or fitting closely: *loose clothing.* **4** not bundled, packaged, fastened, or put in a container: *loose nails.* **5** inexact; imprecise: *a loose translation.* **6** (of funds, cash, etc.) not allocated or locked away; readily available: *loose change.* **7a** (esp. of women) promiscuous or easy. **7b** (of attitudes, ways of life, etc.) immoral or dissolute. **8a** lacking a sense of responsibility or propriety: *loose talk.* **8b** *(in combination): loosetongued.* **9a** (of the bowels) emptying easily, esp. excessively. **9b** (of a cough) accompanied by phlegm, mucus, etc. **10** *Inf., chiefly US & Canad.* very relaxed; easy. ♦ *n* **11 the loose.** *Rugby.* the part of play when the forwards close round the ball in a ruck or loose scrum. **12 on the loose. 12a** free from confinement or restraint. **12b** *Inf.* on a spree. ♦ *adv* **13a** in a loose manner; loosely. **13b** *(in combination): loose-fitting.* ♦ *vb* **looses, loosing, loosed. 14** *(tr)* to set free or release, as from confinement, restraint, or obligation. **15** *(tr)* to unfasten or untie. **16** to make or become less strict, tight, firmly attached, compact, etc. **17** (when *intr,* often foll. by *off)* to let fly (a bullet, arrow, or other missile). [C13 (in the sense: not bound): from ON *lauss* free]
▸ **'loosely** *adv* ▸ **'looseness** *n*
loosebox ('lu:s,bɒks) *n* an enclosed stall with a door in which an animal can be confined.
loose cover *n* a fitted but easily removable cloth cover for a chair, sofa, etc.
loose end *n* **1** a detail that is left unsettled, unexplained, or incomplete. **2 at a loose end.** without purpose or occupation.
loose head *n Rugby.* the prop on the hooker's left in the front row of a scrum. Cf. **tight head.**
loose-jointed ⓣ *adj* **1** supple and easy in movement. **2** loosely built; with ill-fitting joints.
▸ **,loose-'jointedness** *n*
loose-leaf *adj* (of a binder, album, etc.) capable of being opened to allow removal and addition of pages.
loosen ⓣ ('lu:sᵊn) *vb* **1** to make or become less tight, fixed, etc. **2** (often foll. by *up)* to make or become less firm, compact, or rigid. **3** *(tr)* to untie. **4** *(tr)* to let loose; set free. **5** (often foll. by *up)* to make or be-

THESAURUS

look after *vb* **1** = **take care of,** attend to, care for, guard, keep an eye on, mind, nurse, protect, sit with, supervise, take charge of, tend, watch
lookalike *n* **a** = **double,** clone, dead ringer *(sl.)*, exact match, living image, replica, ringer *(sl.)*, spit *(inf., chiefly Brit.)*, spitting image *(inf.)*, twin
look down *vb, foll. by* **on** *or* **upon** = **disdain,** contemn, despise, hold in contempt, look down one's nose at *(inf.)*, scorn, sneer, spurn, treat with contempt, turn one's nose up (at) *(inf.)*
look forward to *vb* = **anticipate,** await, count on, count the days until, expect, hope for, long for, look for, set one's heart on, wait for
lookout *n* **1** = **watch,** guard, qui vive, readiness, vigil **2** = **watchman,** guard, sentinel, sentry, vedette *(Military)* **3** = **watchtower,** beacon, citadel, observation post, observatory, post, tower **4** *Informal* = **concern,** business, funeral *(inf.)*, pigeon *(Brit. inf.)*, worry **5** *Chiefly Brit.* = **prospect,** chances, future, likelihood, outlook, view ♦ *vb* **look out 6** = **be careful,** be alert, be on guard, be on the qui vive, be vigilant, beware, keep an eye out, keep one's eyes open, keep one's eyes peeled, keep one's eyes skinned, pay attention, watch out
look over *vb* **1** = **inspect,** cast an eye over, check, check out *(inf.)*, examine, eyeball *(sl.)*, monitor, take a dekko at *(Brit. sl.)*, view **2** = **look through,** cast an eye over, examine, flick through, peruse, scan
look up *vb* **1** = **research,** find, hunt for, search for, seek out, track down **2** = **improve,** ameliorate, come along, get better, perk up, pick up, progress, shape up *(inf.)*, show improvement **3** *foll. by* **to** = **respect,** admire, defer to, esteem, have a high opinion of, honour, regard highly, revere **4** = **visit,** call on, drop in on *(inf.)*, go to see, look in on, pay a visit to
loom[2] *vb* **1** = **appear,** become visible, bulk, emerge, hover, menace, take shape **2** = **be imminent,** impend, threaten **3** = **overhang,** dominate, hang over, mount, overshadow, overtop, rise, soar, tower
loop *n* **1, 2** = **curve,** bend, circle, coil, convolution, curl, eyelet, hoop, kink, loophole, noose, ring, spiral, twirl, twist, whorl ♦ *vb* **11, 12** = **twist,** bend, braid, circle, coil, connect, curl, curve round, encircle, fold, join, knot, roll, spiral, turn, wind round
loophole *n* **1** = **let-out,** avoidance, escape, evasion, excuse, means of escape, plea, pretence, pretext, subterfuge **2** = **opening,** aperture, knothole, slot
loose *adj* **1** = **free,** floating, insecure, movable, released, unattached, unbound, unconfined, unfastened, unfettered, unrestricted, unsecured, untied, wobbly **3** = **slack,** baggy, easy, hanging, loosened, not fitting, not tight, relaxed, slackened, sloppy **5** = **vague,** diffuse, disconnected, disordered, ill-defined, imprecise, inaccurate, indefinite, indistinct, inexact, rambling, random **7** = **promiscuous,** abandoned, debauched, disreputable, dissipated, dissolute, fast, immoral, lewd, libertine, licentious, profligate, unchaste, wanton **8** = **careless,** heedless, imprudent, lax, negligent, rash, thoughtless, unmindful ♦ *vb* **14, 16** = **free,** detach, disconnect, disengage, ease, let go, liberate, loosen, release, set free, slacken, unleash, unloose **15** = **unfasten,** unbind, unbridle, undo, untie
Antonyms *adj* ≠ **free:** bound, curbed, fastened, fettered, restrained, secured, tethered, tied ≠ **slack:** tight ≠ **vague:** accurate, clear, concise, exact, precise ≠ **promiscuous:** chaste, disciplined, moral, virtuous ♦ *vb* ≠ **free:** bind, cage, capture, fasten, fetter, imprison, tether
loose-jointed *adj* **1** = **supple,** agile, elastic, flexible, limber, lissom(e), lithe, pliable, pliant
loosen *vb* **1, 2** = **slacken,** detach, let out, sepa-

come less strict, severe, etc. **6** (*tr*) to rid or relieve (the bowels) of constipation. [C14: from LOOSE]
▸'**loosener** *n*

loosestrife ('luːsˌstraɪf) *n* **1** any of a genus of plants, esp. the yellow-flowered yellow loosestrife. **2 purple loosestrife.** a purple-flowered marsh plant. [C16: LOOSE + STRIFE, an erroneous translation of L *lysimachia,* as if from Gk *lusimakhos* ending strife, instead of from the name of the supposed discoverer, *Lusimakhos*]

loot Ⓣ (luːt) *n* **1** goods stolen during pillaging, as in wartime, during riots, etc. **2** goods, money, etc., obtained illegally. **3** *Inf.* money or wealth. ◆ *vb* **4** to pillage (a city, etc.) during war or riots. **5** to steal (money or goods), esp. during pillaging. [C19: from Hindi *lūṭ*]
▸'**looter** *n*

lop[1] Ⓣ (lɒp) *vb* **lops, lopping, lopped.** (*tr;* usually foll. by *off*) **1** to sever (parts) from a tree, body, etc., esp. with swift strokes. **2** to cut out or eliminate from as excessive. ◆ *n* **3** a part or parts lopped off, as from a tree. [C15 *loppe* branches cut off]
▸'**lopper** *n*

lop[2] (lɒp) *vb* **lops, lopping, lopped. 1** to hang or allow to hang loosely. **2** (*intr*) to slouch about or move awkwardly. [C16: ? rel. to LOP[1]]

lope Ⓣ (ləʊp) *vb* **lopes, loping, loped. 1** (*intr*) (of a person) to move or run with a long swinging stride. **2** (*intr*) (of four-legged animals) to run with a regular bounding movement. **3** to cause (a horse) to canter with a long easy stride or (of a horse) to canter in this manner. ◆ *n* **4** a long steady gait or stride. [C15: from ON *hlaupa* to LEAP]

lop-eared *adj* (of animals) having ears that droop.

lopsided Ⓣ (ˌlɒp'saɪdɪd) *adj* **1** leaning to one side. **2** greater in weight, height, or size on one side.
▸ˌ**lop'sidedly** *adv* ▸ˌ**lop'sidedness** *n*

loquacious Ⓣ (lɒ'kweɪʃəs) *adj* characterized by or showing a tendency to talk a great deal. [C17: from L *loquāx* from *loquī* to speak]
▸**lo'quaciously** *adv* ▸**loquacity** (lɒ'kwæsɪtɪ) *or* **lo'quaciousness** *n*

loquat ('ləʊkwɒt, -kwæt) *n* **1** an ornamental evergreen tree of China and Japan, having reddish woolly branches, white flowers, and small yellow edible plumlike fruits. **2** the fruit of this tree. [C19: from Chinese (Cantonese) *lō kwat,* lit.: rush orange]

lor (lɔː) *interj Not standard.* an exclamation of surprise or dismay. [from LORD (interj.)]

loran ('lɔːrən) *n* a radio navigation system operating over long distances. Synchronized pulses are transmitted from widely spaced radio stations to aircraft or shipping, the time of arrival of the pulses being used to determine position. [C20: *lo(ng-)ra(nge) n(avigation)*]

lord Ⓣ (lɔːd) *n* **1** a person who has power or authority over others, such as a monarch or master. **2** a male member of the nobility, esp. in Britain. **3** (in medieval Europe) a feudal superior, esp. the master of a manor. **4** a husband considered as head of the household (archaic except in the facetious phrase **lord and master**). **5 my lord.** a respectful form of address used to a judge, bishop, or nobleman. ◆ *vb* **6** (*tr*) *Now rare.* to make a lord of (a person). **7** to act in a superior manner towards (esp. in **lord it over**). [OE *hlāford* bread keeper]
▸'**lordless** *adj* ▸'**lord**ˌ**like** *adj*

Lord Ⓣ (lɔːd) *n* **1** a title given to God or Jesus Christ. **2** *Brit.* **2a** a title given to men of high birth, specifically to an earl, marquess, baron, or viscount. **2b** a courtesy title given to the younger sons of a duke or marquess. **2c** the ceremonial title of certain high officials or of a bishop or archbishop: *Lord Mayor.* ◆ *interj* **3** (*sometimes not cap.*) an exclamation of dismay, surprise, etc.: *Good Lord!*

Lord Chancellor *n Brit. government.* the cabinet minister who is head of the judiciary in England and Wales, and Speaker of the House of Lords.

Lord Chief Justice *n* the judge who is second only to the Lord Chancellor in the English legal hierarchy; president of one division of the High Court of Justice.

Lord High Chancellor *n* another name for the **Lord Chancellor.**

Lord Lieutenant *n* **1** (in Britain) the representative of the Crown in a county. **2** (formerly) the British viceroy in Ireland.

lordly Ⓣ ('lɔːdlɪ) *adj* **lordlier, lordliest. 1** haughty; arrogant; proud. **2** of or befitting a lord. ◆ *adv* **3** *Arch.* in the manner of a lord.
▸'**lordliness** *n*

Lord Mayor *n* the mayor in the City of London and in certain other important boroughs and large cities.

Lord of Misrule *n* (formerly, in England) a person appointed master of revels at a Christmas celebration. [translation of Hebrew: see BEELZEBUB]

lordosis (lɔː'dəʊsɪs) *n Pathol.* forward curvature of the lumbar spine. [C18: NL from Gk, from *lordos* bent backwards]
▸**lordotic** (lɔː'dɒtɪk) *adj*

Lord President of the Council *n* (in Britain) the cabinet minister who presides at meetings of the Privy Council.

Lord Privy Seal *n* (in Britain) the senior cabinet minister without official duties.

Lord Provost *n* the provost of one of the five major Scottish cities.

Lords (lɔːdz) *n* **the.** short for **House of Lords.**

Lord's (lɔːdz) *n* a cricket ground in N London; headquarters of the MCC.

lords-and-ladies *n* (*functioning as sing*) another name for **cuckoopint.**

Lord's Day *n* **the.** the Christian Sabbath; Sunday.

lordship ('lɔːdʃɪp) *n* the position or authority of a lord.

Lordship ('lɔːdʃɪp) *n* (preceded by *Your* or *His*) *Brit.* a title used to address or refer to a bishop, a judge of the high court, or any peer except a duke.

Lord's Prayer *n* **the.** the prayer taught by Jesus Christ to his disciples, as in Matthew 6:9–13, Luke 11:2–4. Also called: **Our Father, Paternoster** (esp. Latin version).

Lords Spiritual *pl n* the Anglican archbishops and senior bishops of England and Wales who are members of the House of Lords.

Lord's Supper *n* **the.** another term for **Holy Communion** (I Corinthians 11:20).

Lords Temporal *pl n* **the.** (in Britain) peers other than bishops in their capacity as members of the House of Lords.

lore Ⓣ (lɔː) *n* **1** collective knowledge or wisdom on a particular subject, esp. of a traditional nature. **2** knowledge or learning. [OE *lār;* rel. to *leornian* to LEARN]

lorgnette (lɔː'njɛt) *n* a pair of spectacles or opera glasses mounted on a handle. [C19: from F, from *lorgner* to squint, from OF *lorgne* squinting]

lorikeet ('lɒrɪˌkiːt, ˌlɒrɪ'kiːt) *n* any of various small lories, such as the varied lorikeet or rainbow lorikeet. [C18: from LORY + *-keet,* as in PARAKEET]

loris ('lɔːrɪs) *n, pl* **loris.** any of several omnivorous nocturnal slow-moving prosimian primates of S and SE Asia, esp. the slow loris and slender loris, having vestigial digits and no tails. [C18: from F; from ?]

lorn (lɔːn) *adj Poetic.* forsaken or wretched. [OE *loren,* p.p. of *-lēosan* to lose]

lorry ('lɒrɪ) *n, pl* **lorries. 1** a large motor vehicle designed to carry heavy loads, esp. one with a flat platform. US and Canad. name: **truck. 2 off the back of a lorry.** *Brit. inf.* a phrase used humorously to indicate that something has been dishonestly acquired. **3** any of various vehicles with a flat load-carrying surface, esp. one designed to run on rails. [C19: ? rel. to northern English dialect *lurry* to pull]

lory ('lɔːrɪ), **lowry,** *or* **lowrie** ('laʊrɪ) *n, pl* **lories** *or* **lowries.** any of various small brightly coloured parrots of Australia and Indonesia, having a brush-tipped tongue with which to feed on nectar and pollen. [C17: via Du. from Malay *lūrī,* var. of *nūrī*]

lose Ⓣ (luːz) *vb* **loses, losing, lost.** (*mainly tr*) **1** to part with or come to be without, as through theft, accident, negligence, etc. **2** to fail to keep or maintain: *to lose one's balance.* **3** to suffer the loss or deprivation of: *to lose a parent.* **4** to cease to have or possess. **5** to fail to get or make use of: *to lose a chance.* **6** (*also intr*) to fail to gain or win (a contest, game, etc.): *to lose the match.* **7** to fail to see, hear, perceive, or understand: *I lost the gist of his speech.* **8** to waste: *to lose money gambling.* **9** to wander from so as to be unable to find: *to lose one's way.* **10** to cause the loss of: *his delay lost him the battle.* **11** to allow to go astray or out of sight: *we lost him in the crowd.* **12** (*usually passive*) to absorb or engross: *he was lost in contemplation.* **13** (*usually passive*) to cause the death or destruction of: *two men were lost in the attack.* **14** to outdistance or elude: *he soon lost his pursuers.* **15** (*intr*) to decrease or depreciate in value or effectiveness: *poetry always loses in translation.* **16** (*also intr*) (of a timepiece) to run slow (by a specified amount). **17** (of a woman) to fail to give birth to (a viable baby), esp. as the result of a miscarriage.

THESAURUS

rate, work free, work loose **3** = **untie**, unbind, undo, unloose **4** = **free**, deliver, let go, liberate, release, set free **5** *often foll. by* **up** = **relax**, ease up *or* off, go easy, lessen, let up, lighten up (*sl.*), mitigate, moderate, soften, weaken

loot *n* **1, 2** = **plunder**, booty, goods, haul, prize, spoils, swag (*sl.*) ◆ *vb* **4** = **plunder**, despoil, pillage, raid, ransack, ravage, rifle, rob, sack

lop[1] *vb* **1, 2** = **cut**, chop, clip, crop, curtail, detach, dock, hack, prune, sever, shorten, trim, truncate

lope *vb* **1, 2** = **stride**, bound, canter, gallop, lollop, spring

lopsided *adj* **1** = **crooked**, askew, awry, cockeyed, out of true, skewwhiff (*Brit. inf.*), squint, tilting **2** = **unequal**, asymmetrical, disproportionate, off balance, one-sided, out of shape, unbalanced, uneven, warped

loquacious *adj* = **talkative**, babbling, blathering, chattering, chatty, gabby (*inf.*), garrulous, gossipy, voluble, wordy

loquacity *n* = **talkativeness**, babbling, chattering, chattiness, effusiveness, gabbling, garrulity, volubility

lord *n* **1** = **master**, commander, governor, king, leader, liege, monarch, overlord, potentate, prince, ruler, seigneur, sovereign, superior **2** = **nobleman**, earl, noble, peer, viscount ◆ *vb* **7** *As in* **lord it over** = **order around**, act big (*sl.*), be overbearing, boss around (*inf.*), domineer, play the lord, pull rank, put on airs, swagger

Lord *n* **1** = **Jesus Christ**, Christ, God, Jehovah, the Almighty, the Galilean, the Good Shepherd, the Nazarene

lordly *adj* **1** = **proud**, arrogant, condescending, despotic, dictatorial, disdainful, domineering, haughty, high and mighty (*inf.*), high-handed, hoity-toity (*inf.*), imperious, lofty, overbearing, patronizing, stuck-up (*inf.*), supercilious, toffee-nosed (*sl., chiefly Brit.*), tyrannical **2** = **noble**, aristocratic, dignified, exalted, gracious, grand, imperial, lofty, majestic, princely, regal, stately

lore *n* **1** = **traditions**, beliefs, doctrine, experience, folk-wisdom, mythos, saws, sayings, teaching, traditional wisdom, wisdom **2** = **learning**, erudition, know-how (*inf.*), knowledge, letters, scholarship

lose *vb* **1-4** = **mislay**, be deprived of, drop, fail to keep, forget, misplace, miss, suffer loss **5** = **forfeit**, fail, fall short, lose out on (*inf.*), miss, pass up (*inf.*), yield **6** = **be defeated**, be the loser, be worsted, come a cropper (*inf.*), come to grief, get the worst of, lose out, suffer defeat, take a licking (*inf.*) **7** = **stray from**, confuse, miss, wan-

18 lose it. *Sl.* to lose control of oneself or one's temper. [OE *losian* to perish]
▸**'losable** *adj*

lose out *vb Inf.* **1** (*intr, adv*) to be defeated or unsuccessful. **2 lose out on.** to fail to secure or make use of: *we lost out on the sale.*

loser ⓣ ('lu:zə) *n* **1** a person or thing that loses. **2** *Inf.* a person or thing that seems destined to be taken advantage of, fail, etc.: *a born loser.*

losing ('lu:zɪŋ) *adj* unprofitable; failing: *the business was a losing concern.*

losings ('lu:zɪŋz) *pl n* losses, esp. in gambling.

loss ⓣ (lɒs) *n* **1** the act or an instance of losing. **2** the disadvantage or deprivation resulting from losing: *a loss of reputation.* **3** the person, thing, or amount lost: *a large loss.* **4** (*pl*) military personnel lost by death or capture. **5** (*sometimes pl*) the amount by which the costs of a business transaction or operation exceed its revenue. **6** *Insurance.* **6a** an occurrence of something that has been insured against, thus giving rise to a claim by a policyholder. **6b** the amount of the resulting claim. **7 at a loss. 7a** uncertain what to do; bewildered. **7b** rendered helpless (for lack of something): *at a loss for words.* **7c** with income less than outlay: *the firm was running at a loss.* [C14: n prob. formed from *lost,* p.p. of *losen* to perish, from OE *lōsian* to be destroyed, from *los* destruction]

loss adjuster *n Insurance.* a person qualified to adjust losses incurred through fire, theft, natural disaster, etc., to agree the loss and the compensation to be paid.

loss leader *n* an article offered below cost to attract customers.

lost ⓣ (lɒst) *adj* **1** unable to be found or recovered. **2** unable to find one's way or ascertain one's whereabouts. **3** confused, bewildered, or helpless: *he is lost in discussions of theory.* **4** (sometimes foll. by *on*) not utilized, noticed, or taken advantage of (by): *rational arguments are lost on her.* **5** no longer possessed or existing because of defeat, misfortune, or the passage of time: *a lost art.* **6** destroyed physically: *the lost platoon.* **7** (foll. by *to*) no longer available or open (to). **8** (foll. by *to*) insensible or impervious (to a sense of shame, justice, etc.). **9** (foll. by *in*) engrossed (in): *he was lost in his book.* **10** morally fallen: *a lost woman.* **11** damned: *a lost soul.*

Lost Generation *n* (*sometimes not cap.*) **1** the large number of talented young men killed in World War I. **2** the generation of writers, esp. American authors, active after World War I.

lot ⓣ (lɒt) *pron* **1** (*functioning as sing or pl;* preceded by *a*) a great number or quantity: *a lot to do; a lot of people.* ◆ *n* **2** a collection of objects, items, or people: *a nice lot of youngsters.* **3** portion in life; destiny; fortune: *it falls to my lot to be poor.* **4** any object, such as a straw or slip of paper, drawn from others at random to make a selection or choice (esp. in **draw** *or* **cast lots**). **5** the use of lots in making a selection or choice (esp. in **by lot**). **6** an assigned or apportioned share. **7** an item or set of items for sale in an auction. **8** *Chiefly US & Canad.* an area of land: *a parking lot.* **9** *Chiefly US & Canad.* a film studio. **10 a bad lot.** an unpleasant or disreputable person. **11 cast** *or* **throw in one's lot with.** to join with voluntarily and share the fortunes of. **12 the lot.** the entire amount or number. ◆ *adv* (preceded by *a*) *Inf.* **13** to a considerable extent, degree, or amount; very much: *to delay a lot.* **14** a great deal of the time or often: *to sing madrigals a lot.* ◆ *vb* **lots, lotting, lotted. 15** to draw lots for (something). **16** (*tr*) to divide (land, etc.) into lots. **17** (*tr*) another word for **allot.** ◆ See also **lots.** [OE *hlot*]

loth ⓣ (ləʊθ) *adj* a variant spelling of **loath.**

Lothario (ləʊ'θɑ:rɪ,əʊ) *n, pl* **Lotharios.** (*sometimes not cap.*) a rake, libertine, or seducer. [C18: after a seducer in Nicholas Rowe's tragedy *The Fair Penitent* (1703)]

lotion ⓣ ('ləʊʃən) *n* a liquid preparation having a soothing, cleansing, or antiseptic action, applied to the skin, eyes, etc. [C14: via OF from L *lōtiō* a washing, from *lōtus* p.p. of *lavāre* to wash]

lots (lɒts) *Inf.* ◆ *pl n* **1** (often foll. by *of*) great numbers or quantities: *lots of people; to eat lots.* ◆ *adv* **2** a great deal. **3** (intensifier): *the journey is lots quicker by train.*

lottery ⓣ ('lɒtərɪ) *n, pl* **lotteries. 1** a game of chance in which tickets are sold, which may later qualify the holder for a prize. **2** an endeavour, the success of which is regarded as a matter of luck. [C16: from OF *loterie,* from MDu. *loterije*]

lotto ('lɒtəʊ) *n* **1** Also called: **housey-housey.** a children's game in which numbered discs are drawn at random and called out, while the players cover the corresponding numbers on cards, the winner being the first to cover all the numbers, a particular row, etc. Cf. **bingo. 2** *Austral.* a lottery with cash prizes based on this principle. [C18: from It., from OF *lot,* from Gmc]

lotus ('ləʊtəs) *n* **1** (in Greek mythology) a fruit that induces forgetfulness and a dreamy languor in those who eat it. **2** any of several water lilies of tropical Africa and Asia, esp. the **white lotus,** which was regarded as sacred in ancient Egypt. **3** a related plant which is the sacred lotus of India, China, and Tibet. **4** a representation of such a plant, common in Hindu, Buddhist, and ancient Egyptian art. **5** any of a genus of leguminous plants of the legume family of the Old World and North America, having yellow, pink, or white pealike flowers. ◆ Also (rare): **lotos.** [C16: via L from Gk *lōtos,* from Semitic]

lotus-eater *n Greek myth.* one of a people encountered by Odysseus in North Africa who lived in indolent forgetfulness, drugged by the fruit of the legendary lotus.

lotus position *n* a seated cross-legged position used in yoga, meditation, etc.

loud ⓣ (laʊd) *adj* **1** (of sound) relatively great in volume: *a loud shout.* **2** making or able to make sounds of relatively great volume: *a loud voice.* **3** clamorous, insistent, and emphatic: *loud protests.* **4** (of colours, designs, etc.) offensive or obtrusive to look at. **5** characterized by noisy, vulgar, and offensive behaviour. ◆ *adv* **6** in a loud manner. **7 out loud.** audibly, as distinct from silently. [OE *hlud*]
▸**'loudish** *adj* ▸**'loudly** *adv* ▸**'loudness** *n*

louden ('laʊdᵊn) *vb* to make or become louder.

loud-hailer *n* a portable loudspeaker having a built-in amplifier and microphone. Also (US and Canad.): **bullhorn.**

loudmouth ⓣ ('laʊd,maʊθ) *n Inf.* a person who brags or talks too loudly.
▸**loudmouthed** ('laʊd,maʊðd, -,maʊθt) *adj*

loudspeaker (,laʊd'spi:kə) *n* a device for converting audio-frequency signals into sound waves. Often shortened to **speaker.**

Lou Gehrig's disease (lu: 'gɛrɪg) *n* another name for **amyotrophic lateral sclerosis.** [C20: named after *Lou Gehrig* (1903–41), US baseball player who suffered from it]

lough (lɒx, lɒk) *n* **1** an Irish word for **lake**[1] (senses 1 and 2). **2** a long narrow bay or arm of the sea in Ireland. [C14: from Irish *loch* lake]

louis d'or (,lu:ɪ 'dɔ:) *n, pl* **louis d'or** (,lu:ɪz 'dɔ:). **1** a former French gold coin worth 20 francs. **2** an old French coin minted in the reign of Louis XIII. ◆ Often shortened to **louis.** [C17: from F: golden louis, after Louis XIII]

lounge ⓣ (laʊndʒ) *vb* **lounges, lounging, lounged. 1** (*intr;* often foll. by *about* or *around*) to sit, lie, walk, or stand in a relaxed manner. **2** to pass (time) lazily or idly. ◆ *n* **3** a communal room in a hotel, ship, etc., used for waiting or relaxing in. **4** *Chiefly Brit.* a living room in a private house. **5** Also called: **lounge bar, saloon.** *Brit.* a more expensive bar in a pub or hotel. **6** a sofa or couch. **7** the act or an instance of lounging. [C16: from ?]

lounger ('laʊndʒə) *n* **1** a comfortable couch or extending chair designed for someone to relax on. **2** a loose comfortable leisure garment. **3** a person who lounges.

THESAURUS

der from **8** = **waste**, consume, deplete, dissipate, drain, exhaust, expend, lavish, misspend, squander, use up **14** = **elude**, dodge, duck, escape, evade, give someone the slip, lap, leave behind, outdistance, outrun, outstrip, overtake, pass, shake off, slip away, throw off

loser *n* **1, 2** = **failure**, also-ran, clinker (*sl., chiefly US*), dud (*inf.*), flop (*inf.*), lemon (*sl.*), no-hoper (*Austral. sl.*), underdog, washout (*inf.*)

loss *n* **1, 2** = **losing**, bereavement, defeat, deprivation, disappearance, drain, failure, forfeiture, misfortune, mislaying, privation, squandering, waste **3** = **damage**, cost, destruction, detriment, disadvantage, harm, hurt, impairment, injury, ruin **4** *plural* = **casualties**, dead, death toll, fatalities, number killed, number wounded **5** *sometimes plural* = **deficit**, debit, debt, deficiency, depletion, losings, shrinkage **7a at a loss** = **confused**, at one's wits' end, baffled, bewildered, helpless, nonplussed, perplexed, puzzled, stuck (*inf.*), stumped
Antonyms *n* ≠ **losing**: acquisition, finding, gain, preservation, reimbursement, saving, winning ≠ **damage**: advantage, recovery, restoration ≠ **deficit**: gain

lost *adj* **1** = **missing**, disappeared, forfeited, mislaid, misplaced, missed, strayed, vanished, wayward **2** = **off-course**, adrift, astray, at sea, disoriented, off-track **3** = **bewildered**, baffled, clueless (*sl.*), confused, helpless, ignorant, mystified, perplexed, puzzled **4** = **wasted**, consumed, dissipated, frittered away, misapplied, misdirected, misspent, misused, squandered **5** = **past**, bygone, dead, extinct, forgotten, gone, lapsed, obsolete, out-of-date, unremembered **6** = **wiped out**, abolished, annihilated, demolished, destroyed, devastated, eradicated, exterminated, obliterated, perished, ruined, wasted, wrecked **9** = **engrossed**, absent, absorbed, abstracted, distracted, dreamy, entranced, preoccupied, rapt, spellbound, taken up **10** = **fallen**, abandoned, corrupt, damned, depraved, dissolute, irreclaimable, licentious, profligate, unchaste, wanton

lot *pron* **1** = **plenty**, abundance, a great deal, heap(s), large amount, load(s) (*inf.*), masses (*inf.*), numbers, ocean(s), oodles (*inf.*), piles (*inf.*), quantities, reams (*inf.*), scores, stack(s) ◆ *n* **2** = **collection**, assortment, batch, bunch (*inf.*), consignment, crowd, group, quantity, set **3** = **destiny**, accident, chance, doom, fate, fortune, hazard, plight, portion **6** = **share**, allowance, cut (*inf.*), parcel, part, percentage, piece, portion, quota, ration **11 cast** *or* **throw in one's lot with** = **join with**, ally *or* align oneself with, join forces with, join fortunes with, make common cause with, support

loth *see* **loath**

lotion *n* = **cream**, balm, embrocation, liniment, salve, solution

lottery *n* **1** = **raffle**, draw, sweepstake **2** = **gamble**, chance, hazard, risk, toss-up (*inf.*), venture

loud *adj* **1-3** = **noisy**, blaring, blatant, boisterous, booming, clamorous, deafening, ear-piercing, ear-splitting, forte (*Music*), obstreperous, piercing, resounding, rowdy, sonorous, stentorian, strident, strong, thundering, tumultuous, turbulent, vehement, vociferous **4** = **garish**, brash, brassy, flamboyant, flashy, gaudy, glaring, lurid, naff (*Brit. sl.*), ostentatious, showy, tacky (*inf.*), tasteless, tawdry, vulgar **5** = **loud-mouthed** (*inf.*), brash, brazen, coarse, crass, crude, offensive, raucous, vulgar
Antonyms *adj* ≠ **noisy**: gentle, inaudible, low, low-pitched, quiet, silent, soft, soundless, subdued ≠ **garish**: conservative, dull, sober, sombre ≠ **loud-mouthed**: quiet, reserved, retiring, shy, unassuming

loudly *adv* **1-3** = **noisily**, at full volume, at the top of one's voice, clamorously, deafeningly, fortissimo (*Music*), lustily, shrilly, uproariously, vehemently, vigorously, vociferously

loudmouth *n Informal* = **bigmouth** (*sl.*), blowhard (*inf.*), blusterer, braggart, gasbag (*inf.*), swaggerer, windbag (*sl.*)

lounge *vb* **1** = **relax**, laze, lie about, loaf, loiter, loll, make oneself at home, recline, saunter,

lounge suit *n* a man's suit of matching jacket and trousers worn for the normal business day.

loupe (luːp) *n* a small magnifying glass used by jewellers, horologists, etc., worn in the eye socket. [C20: from F (formerly an imperfect precious stone), from OF, from ?]

lour Ⓣ *or* **lower** ('laʊə) *vb* (*intr*) **1** (esp. of the sky, weather, etc.) to be overcast, dark, and menacing. **2** to scowl or frown. ◆ *n* **3** a menacing scowl or appearance. [C13 *louren* to scowl]
▸'**louring** *or* '**lowering** *adj*

lourie *or* **loerie** ('laʊrɪ) *n* a type of African bird with bright plumage. [from Malay *luri*]

louse (laʊs) *n, pl* **lice. 1** a wingless bloodsucking insect, such as the head louse, body louse, and crab louse, all of which infest man. **2 biting** *or* **bird louse.** a wingless insect, such as the chicken louse: external parasites of birds and mammals, with biting mouthparts. **3** any of various similar but unrelated insects. **4** (*pl* **louses**) *Sl.* an unpleasant or mean person. ◆ *vb* **louses, lousing, loused.** (*tr*) **5** to remove lice from. **6** (foll. by *up*) *Sl.* to ruin or spoil. [OE *lūs*]

lousewort ('laʊs,wɜːt) *n* any of various N temperate plants having spikes of white, yellow, or mauve flowers.

lousy Ⓣ ('laʊzɪ) *adj* **lousier, lousiest. 1** *Sl.* very mean or unpleasant. **2** *Sl.* inferior or bad. **3** infested with lice. **4** (foll. by *with*) *Sl.* provided with an excessive amount (of): *he's lousy with money.*
▸'**lousily** *adv* ▸'**lousiness** *n*

lout Ⓣ (laʊt) *n* a crude or oafish person; boor. [C16: ? from OE *lūtan* to stoop]
▸'**loutish** *adj*

louvre *or US* **louver** ('luːvə) *n* **1a** any of a set of horizontal parallel slats in a door or window, sloping outwards to throw off rain and admit air. **1b** Also called: **louvre boards.** the slats and frame supporting them. **2** *Archit.* a turret that allows smoke to escape. [C14: from OF *lovier,* from ?]
▸'**louvred** *or US* '**louvered** *adj*

lovable Ⓣ *or* **loveable** ('lʌvəb^{ə}l) *adj* attracting or deserving affection.
▸,**lova'bility,** ,**lovea'bility** *or* '**lovableness,** '**loveableness** *n* ▸'**lovably** *or* '**loveably** *adv*

lovage ('lʌvɪdʒ) *n* a European umbelliferous plant with greenish-white flowers and aromatic fruits, which are used for flavouring food. [C14 *loveache,* from OF *luvesche,* from LL *levisticum,* from L *ligusticum,* lit.: Ligurian (plant)]

love Ⓣ (lʌv) *vb* **loves, loving, loved. 1** (*tr*) to have a great attachment to and affection for. **2** (*tr*) to have passionate desire, longing, and feelings for. **3** (*tr*) to like or desire (to do something) very much. **4** (*tr*) to make love to. **5** (*intr*) to be in love. ◆ *n* **6a** an intense emotion of affection, warmth, fondness, and regard towards a person or thing. **6b** (*as modifier*): *love story.* **7** a deep feeling of sexual attraction and desire. **8** wholehearted liking for or pleasure in something. **9** *Christianity.* God's benevolent attitude towards man. **10** Also: **my love.** a beloved person: used esp. as an endearment. **11** *Brit. inf.* a term of address, not necessarily for a person regarded as likable. **12** (in tennis, squash, etc.) a score of zero. **13 fall in love.** to become in love. **14 for love.** without payment. **15 for love or money.** (*used with a negative*) in any circumstances: *I would not eat a snail for love or money.* **16 for the love of.** for the sake of. **17 in love.** in a state of strong emotional attachment and usually sexual attraction. **18 make love (to). 18a** to have sexual intercourse (with). **18b** *Now arch.* to court. [OE *lufu*]

love affair Ⓣ *n* a romantic or sexual relationship, esp. temporary, between two people.

love apple *n* an archaic name for **tomato.**

lovebird ('lʌv,bɜːd) *n* any of several small African parrots often kept as cagebirds.

lovebite ('lʌv,baɪt) *n* a temporary red mark left on a person's skin by a partner's biting or sucking it during lovemaking.

love child *n Euphemistic.* an illegitimate child; bastard.

love-in-a-mist *n* an erect S European plant, cultivated as a garden plant, having finely cut leaves and white or pale blue flowers.

loveless Ⓣ ('lʌvlɪs) *adj* **1** without love: *a loveless marriage.* **2** receiving or giving no love.
▸'**lovelessly** *adv* ▸'**lovelessness** *n*

love-lies-bleeding *n* any of several plants having drooping spikes of small red flowers.

lovelock ('lʌv,lɒk) *n* a long lock of hair worn on the forehead.

lovelorn Ⓣ ('lʌv,lɔːn) *adj* miserable because of unrequited love or unhappiness in love.

lovely Ⓣ ('lʌvlɪ) *adj* **lovelier, loveliest. 1** very attractive or beautiful. **2** highly pleasing or enjoyable: *a lovely time.* **3** inspiring love; lovable. ◆ *n, pl* **lovelies. 4** *Sl.* a lovely woman.
▸'**loveliness** *n*

lovemaking Ⓣ ('lʌv,meɪkɪŋ) *n* **1** sexual play and activity between lovers, esp. including sexual intercourse. **2** an archaic word for **courtship.**

love potion *n* any drink supposed to arouse sexual love in the one who drinks it.

lover Ⓣ ('lʌvə) *n* **1** a person, now esp. a man, who has an extramarital or premarital sexual relationship with another person. **2** (*often pl*) either of the two people involved in a love affair. **3a** someone who loves a specified person or thing: *a lover of music.* **3b** (*in combination*): *a music-lover; a cat-lover.*

love seat *n* a small upholstered sofa for two people.

lovesick Ⓣ ('lʌv,sɪk) *adj* pining or languishing because of love.
▸'**love,sickness** *n*

lovey-dovey (,lʌvɪ'dʌvɪ) *adj* making an excessive or ostentatious display of affection.

loving Ⓣ ('lʌvɪŋ) *adj* feeling or showing love and affection.
▸'**lovingly** *adv* ▸'**lovingness** *n*

loving cup *n* **1** a large vessel, usually two-handled, out of which people drink in turn at a banquet. **2** a similar cup awarded to the winner of a competition.

low[1] Ⓣ (ləʊ) *adj* **1** having a relatively small distance from base to top;

THESAURUS

sprawl, take it easy **2** = **pass time**, dawdle, fritter time away, hang out (*inf.*), idle, kill time, potter, veg out (*sl., chiefly US*), waste time

lour *vb* **1** = **darken**, be brewing, blacken, cloud up *or* over, loom, menace, threaten **2** = **glower**, frown, give a dirty look, glare, look daggers, look sullen, scowl

louring *adj* **1** = **darkening**, black, clouded, cloudy, dark, forbidding, foreboding, gloomy, grey, heavy, menacing, ominous, overcast, threatening **2** = **glowering**, brooding, forbidding, frowning, grim, scowling, sullen, surly

lousy *adj* **1** *Slang* = **mean**, base, contemptible, despicable, dirty, hateful, low, rotten (*inf.*), vicious, vile **2** *Slang* = **inferior**, awful, bad, bush-league (*Austral. & NZ inf.*), dime-a-dozen (*inf.*), low-rent (*inf., chiefly US*), miserable, no good, not much cop (*Brit. sl.*), of a sort *or* of sorts, poor, poxy (*sl.*), rotten (*inf.*), second-rate, shoddy, slovenly, strictly for the birds (*inf.*), terrible, tinhorn (*US sl.*), two-bit (*US & Canad. sl.*) **3** = **lice-infested**, lice-infected, lice-ridden, pedicular, pediculous **4** *foll. by* **with** *Slang* = **well-supplied with**, amply supplied with, not short of, rolling in (*sl.*)

lout *n* = **oaf**, bear, boor, bumpkin, churl, clod, dolt, gawk, lubber, lummox (*inf.*), yahoo, yob *or* yobbo (*Brit. sl.*)

loutish *adj* = **oafish**, boorish, bungling, clodhopping (*inf.*), coarse, doltish, gawky, gross, ill-bred, ill-mannered, lubberly, lumpen (*inf.*), lumpish, rough, stolid, swinish, uncouth, unmannerly

lovable *adj* = **endearing**, adorable, amiable, attractive, captivating, charming, cuddly, cute, delightful, enchanting, engaging, fetching (*inf.*), likable *or* likeable, lovely, pleasing, sweet, winning, winsome
Antonyms *adj* abhorrent, abominable, detestable, hateful, loathsome, obnoxious, odious, offensive, revolting

love *vb* **1, 2** = **adore**, adulate, be attached to, be in love with, cherish, dote on, have affection for, hold dear, idolize, prize, think the world of, treasure, worship **3** = **enjoy**, appreciate, delight in, desire, fancy, have a weakness for, like, relish, savour, take pleasure in **4** = **make love to**, canoodle (*sl.*), caress, cuddle, embrace, fondle, kiss, neck (*inf.*), pet ◆ *n* **6a, 7** = **passion**, adoration, adulation, affection, amity, ardour, attachment, devotion, fondness, friendship, infatuation, liking, rapture, regard, tenderness, warmth **8** = **liking**, delight, devotion, enjoyment, fondness, inclination, partiality, relish, soft spot, taste, weakness **10** = **beloved**, angel, darling, dear, dearest, dear one, inamorata *or* inamorato, leman (*arch.*), loved one, lover, sweet, sweetheart, truelove **13 fall in love (with)** = **lose one's heart (to)**, become attached (to), become enamoured (of), become fond (of), become infatuated (with), be smitten (by), be taken (with), conceive an affection (for), fall (for) **14 for love** = **without payment**, for nothing, freely, free of charge, gratis, pleasurably **15 for love or money** = **by any means**, ever, under any conditions **17 in love** = **enamoured**, besotted, charmed, enraptured, infatuated, smitten
Antonyms *vb* ≠ **adore, enjoy:** abhor, abominate, detest, dislike, hate, scorn ◆ *n* ≠ **passion, liking:** abhorrence, abomination, animosity, antagonism, antipathy, aversion, bad blood, bitterness, detestation, disgust, dislike, hate, hatred, hostility, ill will, incompatibility, loathing, malice, repugnance, resentment, scorn ≠ **beloved:** enemy, foe

love affair *n* = **romance**, affair, *affaire de coeur*, amour, intrigue, liaison, relationship

loveless *adj* **2** = **unloving**, cold, cold-hearted, frigid, hard, heartless, icy, insensitive, unfeeling, unfriendly, unresponsive

lovelorn *adj* = **lovesick**, crossed in love, jilted, languishing, mooning, moping, pining, slighted, spurned, unrequited, yearning

lovely *adj* **1** = **beautiful**, admirable, adorable, amiable, attractive, captivating, charming, comely, enchanting, exquisite, graceful, handsome, pretty, sweet, winning **2** = **enjoyable**, agreeable, delightful, engaging, gratifying, nice, pleasant, pleasing
Antonyms *adj* ≠ **beautiful:** hideous, ugly, unattractive ≠ **enjoyable:** abhorrent, detestable, hateful, loathsome, odious, repellent, repugnant, revolting

lovemaking *n* **1** = **sexual intercourse**, act of love, carnal knowledge, coition, coitus, copulation, intercourse, intimacy, mating, nookie (*sl.*), rumpy-pumpy (*sl.*), sexual relations, sexual union *or* congress, the other (*inf.*)

lover *n* **1, 2** = **sweetheart**, admirer, beau, beloved, boyfriend *or* girlfriend, fancy bit (*sl.*), fancy man *or* fancy woman (*sl.*), fiancé *or* fiancée, flame (*inf.*), inamorata *or* inamorato, mistress, paramour, suitor, swain (*arch.*), toy boy

lovesick *adj* = **lovelorn**, desiring, languishing, longing, pining, yearning

loving *adj* = **affectionate**, amorous, ardent, cordial, dear, demonstrative, devoted, doting, fond, friendly, kind, solicitous, tender, warm, warm-hearted
Antonyms *adj* aloof, cold, contemptuous, cruel, detached, distasteful, hateful, hostile, indifferent, mean, scornful, unconcerned, unloving

low[1] *adj* **1** = **small**, little, short, squat, stunted **2** = **low-lying**, deep, depressed, ground-level, shallow, subsided, sunken **5** = **meagre**, depleted, insignificant, little, measly, paltry, reduced,

not tall or high: *a low hill; a low building.* **2a** situated at a relatively short distance above the ground, sea level, the horizon, or other reference position: *low cloud.* **2b** (*in combination*): *low-lying.* **3** of less than usual height, depth, or degree: *low temperature.* **4a** (of numbers) small. **4b** (of measurements) expressed in small numbers. **5a** involving or containing a relatively small amount of something: *a low supply.* **5b** (*in combination*): *low-pressure.* **6a** having little value or quality. **6b** (*in combination*): *low-grade.* **7** coarse or vulgar: *a low conversation.* **8a** inferior in culture or status. **8b** (*in combination*): *low-class.* **9** in a physically or mentally depressed or weakened state. **10** low-necked: *a low dress.* **11** with a hushed tone; quiet or soft: *a low whisper.* **12** of relatively small price or monetary value: *low cost.* **13** *Music.* relating to or characterized by a relatively low pitch. **14** (of latitudes) situated not far north or south of the equator. **15** having little or no money. **16** abject or servile. **17** unfavourable: *a low opinion.* **18** not advanced in evolution: *a low form of plant life.* **19** deep: *a low bow.* **20** *Phonetics.* of, relating to, or denoting a vowel whose articulation is produced by moving the back of the tongue away from the soft palate, such as for the *a* in English *father.* **21** (of a gear) providing a relatively low forward speed for a given engine speed. **22** (*usually cap.*) of or relating to the Low Church. ◆ *adv* **23** in a low position, level, degree, intensity, etc.: *to bring someone low.* **24** at a low pitch; deep: *to sing low.* **25** at a low price; cheaply: *to buy low.* **26 lay low. 26a** to cause to fall by a blow. **26b** to overcome, defeat, or destroy. **27 lie low. 27a** to keep or be concealed or quiet. **27b** to wait for a favourable opportunity. ◆ *n* **28** a low position, level, or degree: *an all-time low.* **29** an area of relatively low atmospheric pressure, esp. a depression. [C12 *lāh,* from ON *lāgr*]
▸ **'lowness** *n*

low[2] ❶ (ləʊ) *n also* **lowing. 1** the sound uttered by cattle; moo. ◆ *vb* **2** to make or express by a low or moo. [OE *hlōwan*]

low-alcohol *adj* (of beer or wine) containing only a small amount of alcohol. Cf. **alcohol-free.**

lowan ('ləʊən) *n* another name for **mallee fowl.** [from Abor.]

lowborn (ˌləʊ'bɔːn) *or* **lowbred** (ˌləʊ'brɛd) *adj Now rare.* of ignoble or common parentage.

lowbrow ('ləʊˌbraʊ) *Disparaging.* ◆ *n* **1** a person who has uncultivated or nonintellectual tastes. ◆ *adj also* **lowbrowed. 2** of or characteristic of such a person.

Low Church *n* **1** the school of thought in the Church of England stressing evangelical beliefs and practices. ◆ *adj* **Low-Church. 2** of or relating to this school.

low comedy *n* comedy characterized by slapstick and physical action.

low-density lipoprotein *n* a lipoprotein that is the form in which cholesterol is transported in the bloodstream. High levels in the blood are associated with atheroma. Abbrev.: **LDL.**

low-down ❶ *Inf.* ◆ *adj* **1** mean, underhand, or despicable. ◆ *n* **low-down. 2 the.** information.

lower[1] ❶ ('ləʊə) *adj* **1** being below one or more other things: *the lower shelf.* **2** reduced in amount or value: *a lower price.* **3** *Maths.* (of a limit or bound) less than or equal to one or more numbers or variables. **4** (*sometimes cap.*) *Geol.* denoting the early part of a period, formation, etc.: *Lower Silurian.* ◆ *vb* **5** (*tr*) to cause to become low or on a lower level; bring, put, or cause to move down. **6** (*tr*) to reduce or bring down in estimation, dignity, value, etc.: *to lower oneself.* **7** to reduce or be reduced: *to lower one's confidence.* **8** (*tr*) to make quieter: *to lower the radio.* **9** (*tr*) to reduce the pitch of. **10** (*intr*) to diminish or become less. [C12 (comp. of LOW[1]); C17 (vb)]

lower[2] ❶ ('laʊə) *vb* a variant of **lour.**

lower case *n* **1** the bottom half of a compositor's type case, in which the small letters are kept. ◆ *adj* **lower-case. 2** of or relating to small letters. ◆ *vb* **lower-case, lower-cases, lower-casing, lower-cased. 3** (*tr*) to print with lower-case letters.

lower class *n* **1** the social stratum having the lowest position in the social hierarchy. ◆ *adj* **lower-class. 2** of or relating to the lower class. **3** inferior or vulgar.

lowerclassman (ˌləʊə'klɑːsmən) *n, pl* **lowerclassmen.** *US.* a freshman or sophomore. Also called: **underclassman.**

lower deck *n* **1** the deck of a ship situated immediately above the hold. **2** *Inf.* the petty officers and seamen of a ship collectively.

lower house *n* one of the houses of a bicameral legislature: usually the larger and more representative. Also called: **lower chamber.**

lowermost ('ləʊəˌməʊst) *adj* lowest.

lower regions *pl n* (usually preceded by *the*) hell.

lower world *n* **1** the earth as opposed to heaven. **2** another name for **hell.**

lowest common denominator *n* the smallest integer or polynomial that is exactly divisible by each denominator of a set of fractions. Abbrevs.: **lcd, LCD.** Also called: **least common denominator.**

lowest common multiple *n* the smallest number or quantity that is exactly divisible by each member of a set of numbers or quantities. Abbrevs.: **lcm, LCM.** Also called: **least common multiple.**

low frequency *n* a radio-frequency band or a frequency lying between 300 and 30 kilohertz.

Low German *n* a language of N Germany, spoken esp. in rural areas: more closely related to Dutch than to standard High German. Abbrev.: **LG.** Also called: **Plattdeutsch.**

low-key ❶ *or* **low-keyed** *adj* **1** having a low intensity or tone. **2** restrained or subdued. **3** (of a photograph, painting, etc.) having a predominance of dark grey tones or dark colours with few highlights. Cf. **high-key.**

lowland ('ləʊlənd) *n* **1** relatively low ground. **2** (*often pl*) a low generally flat region. ◆ *adj* **3** of or relating to a lowland or lowlands.
▸ **'lowlander** *n*

Lowland ('ləʊlənd) *adj* of or relating to the Lowlands of Scotland or the dialects of English spoken there.

Lowlands ('ləʊləndz) *pl n* **the.** a low generally flat region of central Scotland, around the Forth and Clyde valleys, separating the Southern Uplands from the Highlands.
▸ **'Lowlander** *n*

Low Latin *n* any form of Latin other than the classical, such as Medieval Latin.

low-level language *n* a computer programming language that is closer to machine language than to human language.

low-level waste *n* waste material contaminated by traces of radioactivity that can be disposed of in steel drums in concrete-lined trenches. Cf. **high-level waste, intermediate-level waste.**

lowlife ('ləʊˌlaɪf) *n, pl* **lowlifes.** *Sl.* a member or members of the criminal underworld.

low-loader *n* a road or rail vehicle with a low platform for ease of access.

lowly ❶ ('ləʊlɪ) *adj* **lowlier, lowliest. 1** humble or low in position, rank, status, etc. **2** full of humility; meek. **3** simple, unpretentious, or plain. ◆ *adv* **4** in a low or lowly manner.
▸ **'lowliness** *n*

Low Mass *n* a Mass that has a simplified ceremonial form and is spoken rather than sung.

low-minded ❶ *adj* having a vulgar or crude mind and character.
▸ **ˌlow-'mindedly** *adv* ▸ **ˌlow-'mindedness** *n*

low-pass filter *n Electronics.* a filter that transmits all frequencies below a specified value, attenuating frequencies above this value.

low-pitched *adj* **1** pitched low in tone. **2** (of a roof) having sides with a shallow slope.

low-pressure *adj* **1** having, using, or involving a pressure below normal: *a low-pressure gas.* **2** relaxed or calm.

low profile *n* **1** a position or attitude characterized by a deliberate avoidance of prominence or publicity. ◆ *adj* **low-profile. 2** (of a tyre) wide in relation to its height.

low-rise *adj* **1** of or relating to a building having only a few storeys. ◆ *n* **2** such a building.

lowry *or* **lowrie** ('laʊrɪ) *n* variant spellings of **lory.**

THESAURUS

scant, small, sparse, trifling **6 = inferior**, deficient, inadequate, low-grade, low-rent (*inf., chiefly US*), mediocre, pathetic, poor, puny, second-rate, shoddy, substandard, worthless **7 = coarse**, common, crude, disgraceful, dishonourable, disreputable, gross, ill-bred, obscene, rough, rude, unbecoming, undignified, unrefined, vulgar **8a = lowly**, humble, lowborn, meek, obscure, plain, plebeian, poor, simple, unpretentious **9 = dejected**, blue, brassed off (*Brit. sl.*), depressed, despondent, disheartened, dismal, down, downcast, down in the dumps (*inf.*), fed up, forlorn, gloomy, glum, miserable, morose, sad, sick as a parrot (*inf.*), unhappy **11 = quiet**, gentle, hushed, muffled, muted, soft, subdued, whispered **12 = inexpensive**, cheap, economical, moderate, modest, reasonable **16 = contemptible**, abject, base, cowardly, dastardly, degraded, depraved, despicable, ignoble, mean, menial, nasty, scurvy, servile, sordid, unworthy, vile, vulgar ◆ *adv* **27a lie low = hide**, conceal oneself, go to earth, go underground, hide away, hide out, hole up, keep a low profile, keep out of sight, lurk, skulk, take cover

Antonyms *adj* ≠ **small:** tall, towering ≠ **low-lying:** elevated ≠ **meagre:** important, significant ≠ **dejected:** cheerful, elated, happy, high ≠ **quiet:** loud, noisy ≠ **contemptible:** brave, eminent, exalted, fine, grand, high-ranking, honourable, laudable, lofty, praiseworthy, superior, worthy

low[2] *n* **1 = mooing**, bellow, bellowing, lowing, moo ◆ *vb* **2 = moo**, bellow

low-down *Informal adj* **1 = mean**, base, cheap, contemptible, despicable, low, nasty, reprehensible, scurvy, ugly, underhand ◆ *n* **lowdown 2 = information**, dope (*inf.*), gen (*Brit. inf.*), info (*inf.*), inside story, intelligence

lower[1] *adj* **1 = under**, inferior, junior, lesser, low-level, minor, secondary, second-class, smaller, subordinate **2 = reduced**, curtailed, decreased, diminished, lessened, pared down ◆ *vb* **5 = drop**, depress, fall, let down, make lower, sink, submerge, take down **6 = demean**, abase, belittle, condescend, debase, degrade, deign, devalue, disgrace, downgrade, humble, humiliate, stoop **7 = lessen**, abate, curtail, cut, decrease, diminish, minimize, moderate, reduce, slash **8 = quieten**, soften, tone down

Antonyms *adj* ≠ **reduced:** enlarged, higher, increased ◆ *vb* ≠ **drop:** elevate, hoist, lift, raise ≠ **lessen:** amplify, augment, boost, enlarge, extend, increase, inflate, magnify, raise

lower[2] *see* **lour**

low-key *adj* **1, 2 = subdued**, keeping a low profile, low-pitched, muffled, muted, played down, quiet, restrained, toned down, understated

lowly *adj* **1 = lowborn**, ignoble, inferior, mean, obscure, plebeian, proletarian, subordinate **2 = humble**, docile, dutiful, gentle, meek, mild, modest, submissive, unassuming **3 = unpretentious**, average, common, homespun, modest, ordinary, plain, poor, simple

low-minded *adj* **= vulgar**, coarse, crude, dirty, disgusting, filthy, foul, gross, indecent, obscene, rude, smutty, uncouth

DICTIONARY

low-spirited ❶ *adj* depressed or dejected.
▸ ˌ**low-ˈspiritedly** *adv* ▸ ˌ**low-ˈspiritedness** *n*

low tech ❶ *n* **1** short for **low technology**. **2** a style of interior design using items associated with low technology. ◆ *adj* **low-tech**. **3** of or using low technology. **4** of or in the interior design style. ◆ Cf. **hi tech**.

low technology *n* simple unsophisticated technology that is limited to the production of basic necessities.

low-tension *adj* subjected to, carrying, or operating at a low voltage. Abbrev.: **LT**.

low tide *n* **1** the tide when it is at its lowest level or the time at which it reaches this. **2** a lowest point.

lowveld (ˈləʊˌfɛlt) *n* (in South Africa) name for the grasslands of the Transvaal province. [from Afrik. *laeveld*]

low water *n* **1** another name for **low tide**. **2** the state of any stretch of water at its lowest level.

low-water mark *n* **1** the level reached at low tide. **2** the lowest point or level; nadir.

lox[1] (lɒks) *n* a kind of smoked salmon. [C19: from Yiddish *laks*, from MHG *lahs* salmon]

lox[2] (lɒks) *n* short for **liquid oxygen**, esp. when used as an oxidizer for rocket fuels.

loyal ❶ (ˈlɔɪəl) *adj* **1** showing allegiance. **2** faithful to one's country, government, etc. **3** of or expressing loyalty. [C16: from OF *loial, leial*, from L *lēgālis* LEGAL]
▸ ˈ**loyally** *adv*

loyalist (ˈlɔɪəlɪst) *n* a patriotic supporter of his sovereign or government.
▸ ˈ**loyalism** *n*

Loyalist (ˈlɔɪəlɪst) *n* **1** (in Northern Ireland) any of the Protestants wishing to retain Ulster's link with Britain. **2** (in North America) an American colonist who supported Britain during the War of American Independence. **3** (in Canada) short for **United Empire Loyalist**. **4** (during the Spanish Civil War) a supporter of the republican government.

loyalty ❶ (ˈlɔɪəltɪ) *n, pl* **loyalties**. **1** the state or quality of being loyal. **2** (*often pl*) allegiance.

loyalty card *n* a swipe card issued by a supermarket or chain store to a customer, used to record credit points awarded for money spent in the store.

lozenge ❶ (ˈlɒzɪndʒ) *n* **1** *Med.* a medicated tablet held in the mouth until it has dissolved. **2** *Geom.* another name for **rhombus**. **3** *Heraldry.* a diamond-shaped charge. [C14: from OF *losange* of Gaulish origin]
▸ ˈ**lozenged** *or* ˈ**lozengy** *adj*

LP[1] *n* **1a** a long-playing gramophone record, usually 12 inches (30 cm) in diameter, designed to rotate at 33⅓ revolutions per minute. **1b** (*as modifier*): *an LP sleeve*. **2** long play: a slow-recording facility on a VCR which allows twice the length of material to be recorded on a tape from that of standard play.

LP[2] *abbrev. for:* **1** (in Britain) Lord Provost. **2** Also: **lp.** low pressure.

L/P *Printing abbrev. for* letterpress.

LPG *or* **LP gas** *abbrev. for* liquefied petroleum gas.

L-plate *n Brit.* a white rectangle with an "L" sign fixed to the back and front of a motor vehicle; a red "L" sign shows that the driver has not passed the driving test; a green "L" sign may be displayed by new drivers for up to a year after passing the driving test.

L'pool *abbrev. for* Liverpool.

Lr *the chemical symbol for* lawrencium.

LSD *n* lysergic acid diethylamide; a crystalline compound prepared from lysergic acid, used in experimental medicine and taken illegally as a hallucinogenic drug. Informal name: **acid**.

L.S.D., £.s.d., *or* **l.s.d.** (in Britain, esp. formerly) *abbrev. for* librae, solidi, denarii. [L: pounds, shillings, pence]

LSE *abbrev. for* London School of Economics.

LSO *abbrev. for* London Symphony Orchestra.

Lt *abbrev. for* Lieutenant.

Ltd *or* **ltd** *abbrev. for* limited (liability). US equivalent: **Inc.**

Lu *the chemical symbol for* lutetium.

luau (luːˈaʊ, ˈluːaʊ) *n* a feast of Hawaiian food. [from Hawaiian *lu'au*]

lubber ❶ (ˈlʌbə) *n* **1** a big, awkward, or stupid person. **2** short for **landlubber**. [C14 *lobre*, prob. from ON]
▸ ˈ**lubberly** *adj, adv* ▸ ˈ**lubberliness** *n*

lubber line *n* a mark on a ship's compass that designates the fore-and-aft axis of the vessel. Also called: **lubber's line**.

lubra (ˈluːbrə) *n Austral.* an Aboriginal woman. [C19: from Abor.]

lubricant (ˈluːbrɪkənt) *n* **1** a lubricating substance, such as oil. ◆ *adj* **2** serving to lubricate. [C19: from L *lūbricāns*, present participle of *lūbricāre*]

lubricate ❶ (ˈluːbrɪˌkeɪt) *vb* **lubricates, lubricating, lubricated**. **1** (*tr*) to cover or treat with an oily substance so as to lessen friction. **2** (*tr*) to make greasy, slippery, or smooth. **3** (*intr*) to act as a lubricant. [C17: from L *lūbricāre*, from *lūbricus* slippery]
▸ ˌ**lubriˈcation** *n* ▸ ˈ**lubriˌcative** *adj* ▸ ˈ**lubriˌcator** *n*

lubricity (luːˈbrɪsɪtɪ) *n* **1** *Formal or literary.* lewdness or salaciousness. **2** *Rare.* smoothness or slipperiness. [C15 (lewdness), C17 (slipperiness): from OF *lubricité*, from Med. L *lubricitās*, from L, from *lūbricus* slippery]
▸ **lubricious** (luːˈbrɪʃəs) *or* **lubricous** (ˈluːbrɪkəs) *adj*

luce (luːs) *n* another name for the **pike** (the fish). [C14: from OF *lus*, from LL *lūcius* pike]

lucent (ˈluːsᵊnt) *adj* brilliant, shining, or translucent. [C16: from L *lūcēns*, present participle of *lūcēre* to shine]
▸ ˈ**lucency** *n* ▸ ˈ**lucently** *adv*

lucerne (luːˈsɜːn) *n Brit.* another name for **alfalfa**.

lucid ❶ (ˈluːsɪd) *adj* **1** readily understood; clear. **2** shining or glowing. **3** of or relating to a period of normality between periods of insane behaviour. [C16: from L *lūcidus* full of light, from *lūx* light]
▸ **luˈcidity** *or* ˈ**lucidness** *n* ▸ ˈ**lucidly** *adv*

lucifer (ˈluːsɪfə) *n* a friction match: originally a trade name.

Lucifer (ˈluːsɪfə) *n* **1** the leader of the rebellion of the angels; Satan. **2** the planet Venus when it rises as the morning star. [OE, from L *Lūcifer* light-bearer, from *lūx* light + *ferre* to bear]

luck ❶ (lʌk) *n* **1** events that are beyond control and seem subject to chance; fortune. **2** success or good fortune. **3** something considered to bring good luck. **4 down on one's luck.** having little or no good luck to the point of suffering hardships. **5 no such luck.** *Inf.* unfortunately not. **6 try one's luck.** to attempt something that is uncertain. [C15: from MDu. *luc*]

luckless ❶ (ˈlʌklɪs) *adj* having no luck; unlucky.
▸ ˈ**lucklessly** *adv* ▸ ˈ**lucklessness** *n*

lucky ❶ (ˈlʌkɪ) *adj* **luckier, luckiest**. **1** having or bringing good fortune. **2** happening by chance, esp. as desired.
▸ ˈ**luckily** *adv* ▸ ˈ**luckiness** *n*

lucky dip *n Brit., Austral., & NZ.* **1** a box filled with sawdust containing small prizes for which children search. **2** *Inf.* an undertaking of uncertain outcome.

lucrative ❶ (ˈluːkrətɪv) *adj* producing a profit; profitable. [C15: from OF *lucratif*; see LUCRE]
▸ ˈ**lucratively** *adv* ▸ ˈ**lucrativeness** *n*

lucre ❶ (ˈluːkə) *n Usually facetious.* money or wealth (esp. in **filthy lucre**). [C14: from L *lūcrum* gain]

lucubrate (ˈluːkjʊˌbreɪt) *vb* **lucubrates, lucubrating, lucubrated**. (*intr*) to write or study, esp. at night. [C17: from L *lūcubrāre* to work by lamplight]
▸ ˈ**lucuˌbrator** *n*

lucubration (ˌluːkjʊˈbreɪʃən) *n* **1** laborious study, esp. at night. **2** (*often pl*) a solemn literary work.

lud (lʌd) *n Brit.* lord (in **my lud, m'lud**): used when addressing a judge in court.

Luddite (ˈlʌdaɪt) *n Brit. history.* **1** any of the textile workers opposed to mechanization, believing that its use led to unemployment, who organized machine-breaking between 1811 and 1816. **2** any opponent

THESAURUS

low-spirited *adj* = **depressed**, apathetic, blue, brassed off (*Brit. sl.*), dejected, despondent, dismal, down, down-hearted, down in the dumps (*inf.*), down in the mouth, fed up, gloomy, heavy-hearted, low, miserable, moody, sad, unhappy

low tech *adj* **low-tech 3** = **unsophisticated**, basic, simple
Antonyms *adj* high-tech *or* hi-tech, scientific, technical, technological

loyal *adj* **1-3** = **faithful**, attached, constant, dependable, devoted, dutiful, immovable, patriotic, staunch, steadfast, tried and true, true, true-blue, true-hearted, trustworthy, trusty, unswerving, unwavering
Antonyms *adj* disloyal, false, perfidious, traitorous, treacherous, unfaithful, untrustworthy

loyalty *n* **1, 2** = **faithfulness**, allegiance, constancy, dependability, devotion, fealty, fidelity, patriotism, reliability, staunchness, steadfastness, troth (*arch.*), true-heartedness, trueness, trustiness, trustworthiness

lozenge *n* **1** = **tablet**, cough drop, jujube, pastille

lubberly *adj* **1** = **oafish**, awkward, blundering, bungling, churlish, clodhopping (*inf.*), clownish, clumsy, coarse, crude, doltish, gawky, heavy-handed, loutish, lumbering, lumpen (*inf.*), lumpish, uncouth, ungainly

lubricate *vb* **1-3** = **oil**, grease, make slippery, make smooth, oil the wheels, smear, smooth the way

lucid *adj* **1** = **clear**, clear-cut, comprehensible, crystal clear, distinct, evident, explicit, intelligible, limpid, obvious, pellucid, plain, transparent **2** = **bright**, beaming, brilliant, effulgent, gleaming, luminous, radiant, resplendent, shining **3** = **clear-headed**, all there, *compos mentis*, in one's right mind, rational, reasonable, sane, sensible, sober, sound
Antonyms *adj* ≠ **clear**: ambiguous, clear as mud (*inf.*), confused, equivocal, incomprehensible, indistinct, muddled, unclear, unintelligible, vague ≠ **bright**: dull ≠ **clear-headed**: confused, irrational, muddled, unclear, unperceptive, vague

luck *n* **1** = **fortune**, accident, chance, destiny, fate, fortuity, hap (*arch.*), hazard **2** = **good fortune**, advantage, blessing, break (*inf.*), fluke, godsend, good luck, prosperity, serendipity, stroke, success, windfall

luckily *adv* **1** = **fortunately**, favourably, happily, opportunely, propitiously, providentially **2** = **by chance**, as it chanced, as luck would have it, fortuitously

luckless *adj* = **unlucky**, calamitous, cursed, disastrous, doomed, hapless, hopeless, ill-fated, ill-starred, jinxed, star-crossed, unfortunate, unhappy, unpropitious, unsuccessful

lucky *adj* **1** = **fortunate**, advantageous, blessed, charmed, favoured, jammy (*Brit. sl.*), on a roll (*inf.*), prosperous, serendipitous, successful **2** = **fortuitous**, adventitious, auspicious, opportune, propitious, providential, timely
Antonyms *adj* ≠ **fortunate**: bad, detrimental, ominous, unfavourable, unfortunate, unhappy, unlucky, unpromising ≠ **fortuitous**: unlucky, untimely

lucrative *adj* = **profitable**, advantageous, fat, fruitful, gainful, high-income, money-making, paying, productive, remunerative, well-paid

lucre *n Usually facetious* = **money**, gain, mammon, pelf, profit, riches, spoils, wealth

of industrial change or innovation. ◆ *adj* **3** of or relating to the Luddites. [C19: alleged to be after Ned *Ludd,* an 18th-century Leicestershire workman, who destroyed industrial machinery]

ludicrous Ⓣ ('luːdɪkrəs) *adj* absurd or incongruous to the point of provoking laughter. [C17: from L *lūdicrus* done in sport, from *lūdus* game]
►'**ludicrously** *adv* ►'**ludicrousness** *n*

ludo ('luːdəʊ) *n Brit.* a simple board game in which players advance their counters by throwing dice. [C19: from L: I play]

luff (lʌf) *n* **1** *Naut.* the leading edge of a fore-and-aft sail. ◆ *vb* **2** *Naut.* to head (a sailing vessel) into the wind so that her sails flap. **3** (*intr*) *Naut.* (of a sail) to flap when the wind is blowing equally on both sides. **4** to move the jib of (a crane) in order to shift a load. [C13 (in the sense: steering gear): from OF *lof,* ?from MDu. *loef* peg of a tiller]

lug[1] Ⓣ (lʌg) *vb* **lugs, lugging, lugged. 1** to carry or drag (something heavy) with great effort. **2** (*tr*) to introduce (an irrelevant topic) into a conversation or discussion. ◆ *n* **3** the act or an instance of lugging. [C14: prob. from ON]

lug[2] (lʌg) *n* **1** a projecting piece by which something is connected, supported, or lifted. **2** a box or basket for vegetables or fruit. **3** *Inf. or Scot.* another word for **ear**[1]. **4** *Sl.* a man, esp. a stupid or awkward one. [C15 (Scots dialect) *lugge* ear]

lug[3] (lʌg) *n Naut.* short for **lugsail.**

luge (luːʒ) *n* **1** a racing toboggan on which riders lie on their backs, descending feet first. ◆ *vb* **luges, luging, luged. 2** (*intr*) to ride or race on a luge. [C20: from F]

Luger ('luːgə) *n Trademark.* a German 9 mm calibre automatic pistol.

luggage Ⓣ ('lʌgɪdʒ) *n* suitcases, trunks, etc. [C16: ? from LUG[1], infl. in form by BAGGAGE]

luggage van *n Brit.* a railway carriage used to transport passengers' luggage, bicycles, etc.

lugger ('lʌgə) *n Naut.* a small working boat rigged with a lugsail. [C18: from LUGSAIL]

lughole ('lʌg,həʊl) *n Brit.* an informal word for **ear**[1]. See also **lug**[2] (sense 3).

lugsail ('lʌgsəl) *n Naut.* a four-sided sail bent and hoisted on a yard. [C17: ?from ME (now dialect) *lugge* pole, or from *lugge* ear]

lug screw *n* a small screw without a head.

lugubrious Ⓣ (lʊ'guːbrɪəs) *adj* excessively mournful; doleful. [C17: from L *lūgubris* mournful, from *lūgēre* to grieve]
►**lu'gubriously** *adv* ►**lu'gubriousness** *n*

lugworm ('lʌg,wɜːm) *n* a worm living in burrows on sandy shores and having tufted gills: much used as bait. Sometimes shortened to **lug.** [C17: from ?]

lukewarm Ⓣ (,luːk'wɔːm) *adj* **1** (esp. of water) moderately warm; tepid. **2** having or expressing little enthusiasm or conviction. [C14 *luke* prob. from OE *hlēow* warm]
►,**luke'warmly** *adv* ►,**luke'warmness** *n*

lull Ⓣ (lʌl) *vb* (*tr*) **1** to soothe (a person or animal) by soft sounds or motions (esp. in **lull to sleep**). **2** to calm (someone or someone's fears, suspicions, etc.), esp. by deception. ◆ *n* **3** a short period of calm or diminished activity. [C14: ? imit. of crooning sounds; rel. to MLow G *lollen* to soothe, MDu. *lollen* to talk drowsily, mumble]

lullaby Ⓣ ('lʌlə,baɪ) *n, pl* **lullabies. 1** a quiet song to lull a child to sleep. ◆ *vb* **lullabies, lullabying, lullabied. 2** (*tr*) to quiet or soothe as with a lullaby. [C16: ? a blend of LULL + GOODBYE]

lumbago (lʌm'beɪgəʊ) *n* pain in the lower back; backache. [C17: from LL, from L *lumbus* loin]

lumbar ('lʌmbə) *adj* of, near, or relating to the part of the body between the lowest ribs and the hipbones. [C17: from NL *lumbāris,* from L *lumbus* loin]

lumbar puncture *n Med.* insertion of a hollow needle into the lower spinal cord to withdraw cerebrospinal fluid, introduce drugs, etc.

lumber[1] Ⓣ ('lʌmbə) *n* **1** *Chiefly US & Canad.* **1a** logs; sawn timber. **1b** (*as modifier*): *the lumber trade.* **2** *Brit.* **2a** useless household articles that are stored away. **2b** (*as modifier*): *lumber room.* ◆ *vb* **3** (*tr*) to pile together in a disorderly manner. **4** (*tr*) to fill up or encumber with useless household articles. **5** *Chiefly US & Canad.* to convert (the trees) of (a forest) into marketable timber. **6** (*tr*) *Brit. inf.* to burden with something unpleasant, tedious, etc. [C17: ?from a n use of LUMBER[2]]
►'**lumberer** *n* ►'**lumbering** *n*

lumber[2] Ⓣ ('lʌmbə) *vb* (*intr*) **1** to move or proceed in an awkward heavy manner. **2** an obsolete word for **rumble.** [C14 *lomeren*]
►'**lumbering** *adj*

lumberjack ('lʌmbə,dʒæk) *n* (esp. in North America) a person whose work involves felling trees, transporting the timber, etc. [C19: from LUMBER[1] + JACK (man)]

lumberjacket ('lʌmbə,dʒækɪt) *n* a boldly coloured, usually checked jacket in warm cloth.

lumberyard ('lʌmbə,jɑːd) *n* the US and Canad word for **timberyard.**

lumen ('luːmɪn) *n, pl* **lumens** *or* **lumina** (-mɪnə). **1** the derived SI unit of luminous flux; the flux emitted in a solid angle of 1 steradian by a point source having a uniform intensity of 1 candela. Symbol: lm **2** *Anat.* a passage, duct, or cavity in a tubular organ. **3** a cavity within a plant cell. [C19: NL, from L: light, aperture]
►'**luminal** *adj*

luminance ('luːmɪnəns) *n* **1** a state or quality of radiating or reflecting light. **2** a measure (in candelas per square metre) of the brightness of a point on a surface that is radiating or reflecting light. Symbol: *L* [C19: from L *lūmen* light]

luminary Ⓣ ('luːmɪnərɪ) *n, pl* **luminaries. 1** a person who enlightens or influences others. **2** a famous person. **3** *Literary.* something, such as the sun or moon, that gives off light. [C15: via OF, from L *lūmināre* lamp, from *lūmen* light]

luminesce (,luːmɪ'nɛs) *vb* **luminesces, luminescing, luminesced.** (*intr*) to exhibit luminescence. [back formation from LUMINESCENT]

luminescence Ⓣ (,luːmɪ'nɛsəns) *n Physics.* the emission of light at low temperatures by any process other than incandescence. [C19: from L *lūmen* light]
►,**lumi'nescent** *adj*

luminous Ⓣ ('luːmɪnəs) *adj* **1** radiating or reflecting light; shining; glowing: *luminous colours.* **2** (*not in technical use*) exhibiting luminescence: *luminous paint.* **3** full of light; well-lit. **4** (of a physical quantity in photometry) evaluated according to the visual sensation produced in an observer rather than by absolute energy measurements: *luminous intensity.* **5** easily understood; lucid; clear. **6** enlightening or wise. [C15: from L *lūminōsus* full of light, from *lūmen* light]
►**luminosity** (,luːmɪ'nɒsɪtɪ) *n* ►'**luminously** *adv* ►'**luminousness** *n*

luminous flux *n* a measure of the rate of flow of luminous energy, evaluated according to its ability to produce a visual sensation. It is measured in lumens.

luminous intensity *n* a measure of the amount of light that a point source radiates in a given direction.

lumme *or* **lummy** ('lʌmɪ) *interj Brit.* an exclamation of surprise or dismay. [C19: alteration of *Lord love me*]

lummox ('lʌməks) *n Inf.* a clumsy or stupid person. [C19: from ?]

lump[1] Ⓣ (lʌmp) *n* **1** a small solid mass without definite shape. **2** *Pathol.* any small swelling or tumour. **3** a collection of things; aggregate. **4** *Inf.* an awkward, heavy, or stupid person. **5 the lump.** *Brit.* self-employed workers in the building trade considered collectively. **6** (*modifier*) in the form of a lump or lumps: *lump sugar.* **7 a lump in one's throat.** a tight dry feeling in one's throat, usually caused by great emotion. **8 in the lump.** collectively; en masse. ◆ *vb* **9** (*tr; often foll. by together*) to collect into a mass or group. **10** (*intr*) to grow into lumps or become lumpy. **11** (*tr*) to consider as a single group, often without justification. **12** (*tr*) to make or cause lumps in or on. **13** (*intr; often foll. by along*) to move in a heavy manner. [C13: prob. rel. to early Du. *lompe* piece, Scand. dialect *lump* block, MHG *lumpe* rag]

lump[2] Ⓣ (lʌmp) *vb* (*tr*) *Inf.* to tolerate or put up with; endure (in **lump it**). [C16: from ?]

lumpectomy (lʌm'pɛktəmɪ) *n, pl* **lumpectomies.** the surgical removal of a tumour in a breast. [C20: from LUMP[1] + -ECTOMY]

lumpen ('lʌmpən) *adj Inf.* stupid or unthinking. [from G *Lump* vagabond, infl. by *Lumpen* rags, as in LUMPENPROLETARIAT]

lumpenproletariat (,lʌmpən,prəʊlɪ'tɛərɪət) *n* (esp. in Marxist theory) the urban social group below the proletariat, consisting of criminals, tramps, etc. [G, lit.: ragged proletariat]

THESAURUS

ludicrous *adj* = **ridiculous,** absurd, comic, comical, crazy, droll, farcical, funny, incongruous, laughable, nonsensical, odd, outlandish, preposterous, silly, zany
Antonyms *adj* grave, logical, sad, sensible, serious, solemn

lug[1] **1** *vb* **1** = **carry,** drag, haul, heave, hump (*Brit. sl.*), pull, tow, yank

luggage *n* = **baggage,** bags, cases, gear, impedimenta, paraphernalia, suitcases, things, trunks

lugubrious *adj* = **gloomy,** dirgelike, dismal, doleful, dreary, funereal, melancholy, morose, mournful, sad, serious, sombre, sorrowful, woebegone, woeful

lukewarm *adj* **1** = **tepid,** blood-warm, warm **2** = **half-hearted,** apathetic, cold, cool, indifferent, phlegmatic, unconcerned, unenthusiastic, uninterested, unresponsive

lull *vb* **1** = **calm,** allay, hush, lullaby, pacify, quell, quiet, rock to sleep, soothe, still, subdue, tranquillize ◆ *n* **3** = **respite,** calm, calmness, hush, let-up (*inf.*), pause, quiet, silence, stillness, tranquillity

lullaby *n* **1** = **cradlesong,** berceuse

lumber[1] *n* **2** *Brit.* = **junk,** castoffs, clutter, discards, jumble, refuse, rubbish, trash, white elephants ◆ *vb* **6** *Brit. informal* = **burden,** encumber, impose upon, land, load, saddle

lumber[2] *vb* **1** = **plod,** clump, lump along, shamble, shuffle, stump, trudge, trundle, waddle

lumbering *adj* **1** = **awkward,** blundering, bovine, bumbling, clumsy, elephantine, heavy, heavy-footed, hulking, lubberly, overgrown, ponderous, ungainly, unwieldy

luminary *n* **2** = **celebrity,** big name, celeb (*inf.*), dignitary, leading light, lion, megastar (*inf.*), notable, personage, somebody, star, V.I.P., worthy

luminescent *adj* = **glowing,** Day-Glo, effulgent, fluorescent, luminous, phosphorescent, radiant, shining

luminous *adj* **1, 3** = **bright,** brilliant, glowing, illuminated, lighted, lit, luminescent, lustrous, radiant, resplendent, shining, vivid **5** = **clear,** evident, intelligible, lucid, obvious, perspicuous, plain, transparent

lump[1] *n* **1** = **piece,** ball, bunch, cake, chunk, clod, cluster, dab, gob, gobbet, group, hunk, mass, nugget, spot, wedge **2** *Pathology* = **swelling,** bulge, bump, growth, hump, protrusion, protuberance, tumescence, tumour ◆ *vb* **9** = **group,** aggregate, bunch, coalesce, collect, combine, conglomerate, consolidate, mass, pool, unite

lump[2] *vb Informal* = **put up with,** bear, brook, en-

lumpfish (ˈlʌmpˌfɪʃ) *n, pl* **lumpfish** *or* **lumpfishes.** a North Atlantic fish having a globular body covered with tubercles, pelvic fins fused into a sucker, and an edible roe. Also called: **lumpsucker.** [C16 *lump* (now obs.) lumpfish, from MDu. *lumpe,* ? rel. to LUMP[1]]

lumpish Ⓣ (ˈlʌmpɪʃ) *adj* **1** resembling a lump. **2** stupid, clumsy, or heavy.
▸ **ˈlumpishly** *adv* ▸ **ˈlumpishness** *n*

lump sum *n* a relatively large sum of money, paid at one time, esp. in cash.

lumpy Ⓣ (ˈlʌmpɪ) *adj* **lumpier, lumpiest. 1** full of or having lumps. **2** (esp. of the sea) rough. **3** (of a person) heavy or bulky.
▸ **ˈlumpily** *adv* ▸ **ˈlumpiness** *n*

Luna (ˈluːnə) *n* the Roman goddess of the moon. [from L: moon]

lunacy Ⓣ (ˈluːnəsɪ) *n, pl* **lunacies. 1** (formerly) any severe mental illness. **2** foolishness.

luna moth *n* a large American moth having light green wings with a yellow crescent-shaped marking on each forewing. [C19: from the markings on its wings]

lunar (ˈluːnə) *adj* **1** of or relating to the moon. **2** occuring on or used on the moon: *lunar module.* **3** relating to, caused by, or measured by the position or orbital motion of the moon. [C17: from L *lūnāris,* from *lūna* the moon]

lunar eclipse *n* See **eclipse.**

lunar module *n* the module used to carry astronauts on a spacecraft to the surface of the moon and back to the spacecraft.

lunar month *n* See **month** (sense 6).

lunar year *n* See **year** (sense 6).

lunate (ˈluːneɪt) *or* **lunated** *adj Anat., bot.* shaped like a crescent. [C18: from L *lūnātus* crescent-shaped, from *lūna* moon]

lunatic Ⓣ (ˈluːnətɪk) *adj* **1** an archaic word for **insane. 2** foolish; eccentric. ◆ *n* **3** a person who is insane. [C13 (adj): via OF from LL *lūnāticus* crazy, moonstruck, from L *lūna* moon]

lunatic asylum *n Offens.* an institution for the mentally ill.

lunatic fringe *n* the members of a society who adopt views regarded as fanatical.

lunch (lʌntʃ) *n* **1** a meal eaten during the middle of the day. ◆ *vb* **2** (*intr*) to eat lunch. **3** (*tr*) to provide or buy lunch for. [C16: prob. short form of LUNCHEON]
▸ **ˈluncher** *n*

luncheon (ˈlʌntʃən) *n* a lunch, esp. a formal one. [C16: prob. var. of *nuncheon,* from ME *noneschench,* from *none* NOON + *schench* drink]

luncheon meat *n* a ground mixture of meat (often pork) and cereal, usually tinned.

luncheon voucher *n* a voucher worth a specified amount issued to employees and redeemable at a restaurant for food. Abbrev.: **LV.**

lunchroom (ˈlʌntʃˌruːm, -ˌrʊm) *n US & Canad.* a room where lunch is served or where students, employees, etc., may eat lunches they bring.

lunette (luːˈnɛt) *n* **1** anything that is shaped like a crescent. **2** an oval or circular opening to admit light in a dome. **3** a semicircular panel containing a window, mural, or sculpture. **4** a type of fortification like a detached bastion. **5** Also called: **lune.** *RC Church.* a case fitted with a bracket to hold the consecrated host. [C16: from F: crescent, from *lune* moon, from L *lūna*]

lung (lʌŋ) *n* **1** either one of a pair of spongy saclike respiratory organs within the thorax of higher vertebrates, which oxygenate the blood and remove its carbon dioxide. **2 at the top of one's lungs.** in one's loudest voice; yelling. [OE *lungen*]

lunge[1] Ⓣ (lʌndʒ) *n* **1** a sudden forward motion. **2** *Fencing.* a thrust made by advancing the front foot and straightening the back leg, extending the sword arm forwards. ◆ *vb* **lunges, lunging, lunged. 3** to move or cause to move with a lunge. **4** (*intr*) *Fencing.* to make a lunge. [C18: short form of obs. C17 *allonge,* from F *allonger* to stretch out (one's arm) from LL *ēlongāre* to lengthen]
▸ **ˈlunger** *n*

lunge[2] (lʌndʒ) *n* **1** a rope used in training or exercising a horse. ◆ *vb* **lunges, lunging, lunged. 2** to exercise or train (a horse) on a lunge. [C17: from OF *longe,* shortened from *allonge,* ult. from L *longus* long]

lungfish (ˈlʌŋˌfɪʃ) *n, pl* **lungfish** *or* **lungfishes.** a freshwater bony fish having an air-breathing lung, fleshy paired fins, and an elongated body.

lungwort (ˈlʌŋˌwɜːt) *n* **1** any of several Eurasian plants which have spotted leaves and clusters of blue or purple flowers: formerly used to treat lung diseases. **2** See **oyster plant.**

lunula (ˈluːnjʊlə) *n, pl* **lunulae** (-njʊˌliː). the white crescent-shaped area at the base of the human fingernail. Nontechnical name: **half-moon.** [C16: from L: small moon, from *lūna*]

Lupercalia (ˌluːpɜːˈkeɪlɪə) *n, pl* **Lupercalia** *or* **Lupercalias.** an ancient Roman festival of fertility, celebrated on Feb. 15. [L, from *Lupercālis* belonging to *Lupercus,* a Roman god of the flocks]
▸ **ˌLuperˈcalian** *adj*

lupin *or US* **lupine** (ˈluːpɪn) *n* a leguminous plant of North America, Europe, and Africa, with large spikes of brightly coloured flowers and flattened pods. [C14: from L *lupīnus* wolfish (see LUPINE); from the belief that the plant ravenously exhausted the soil]

lupine (ˈluːpaɪn) *adj* of, relating to, or resembling a wolf. [C17: from L *lupīnus,* from *lupus* wolf]

lupus (ˈluːpəs) *n* any of various ulcerative skin diseases. [C16: via Med. L from L: wolf; so called because it rapidly eats away the affected part]

lupus vulgaris (vʌlˈgɛərɪs) *n* tuberculosis of the skin, esp. of the face. Sometimes shortened to **lupus.**

lurch[1] Ⓣ (lɜːtʃ) *vb* (*intr*) **1** to lean or pitch suddenly to one side. **2** to stagger. ◆ *n* **3** the act or an instance of lurching. [C19: from ?]

lurch[2] (lɜːtʃ) *n* **1 leave (someone) in the lurch.** to desert (someone) in trouble. **2** *Cribbage.* the state of a losing player with less than 30 points at the end of a game. [C16: from F *lourche* a game similar to backgammon, from *lourche* (adj) deceived, prob. of Gmc origin]

lurch[3] (lɜːtʃ) *vb* (*intr*) *Arch. or dialect.* to prowl suspiciously. [C15: ? a var. of LURK]

lurcher (ˈlɜːtʃə) *n* **1** a crossbred hunting dog, esp. one trained to hunt silently. **2** *Arch.* a person who prowls or lurks. [C16: from LURCH[3]]

lure Ⓣ (lʊə) *vb* **lures, luring, lured.** (*tr*) **1** (sometimes foll. by *away* or *into*) to tempt or attract by the promise of some type of reward. **2** *Falconry.* to entice (a hawk or falcon) from the air to the falconer by a lure. ◆ *n* **3** a person or thing that lures. **4** *Angling.* any of various types of brightly coloured artificial spinning baits. **5** *Falconry.* a feathered decoy to which small pieces of meat can be attached. [C14: from OF *loirre* falconer's lure, from Gmc]
▸ **ˈlurer** *n*

Lurex (ˈlʊərɛks) *n* **1** *Trademark.* a thin metallic thread coated with plastic. **2** fabric containing such thread, which makes it glitter.

lurgy (ˈlɜːgɪ) *n, pl* **lurgies.** *Facetious.* any undetermined illness. [C20: from ?]

lurid Ⓣ (ˈlʊərɪd) *adj* **1** vivid in shocking detail; sensational. **2** horrible in savagery or violence. **3** pallid in colour; wan. **4** glowing with an unnatural glare. [C17: from L *lūridus* pale yellow]
▸ **ˈluridly** *adv* ▸ **ˈluridness** *n*

lurk Ⓣ (lɜːk) *vb* (*intr*) **1** to move stealthily or be concealed, esp. for evil purposes. **2** to be present in an unobtrusive way; be latent. ◆ *n* **3** *Austral. & NZ sl.* a scheme for success. [C13: prob. frequentative of LOUR]
▸ **ˈlurker** *n*

lurking (ˈlɜːkɪŋ) *adj* lingering but almost unacknowledged: *a lurking suspicion.*

luscious Ⓣ (ˈlʌʃəs) *adj* **1** extremely pleasurable, esp. to the taste or smell. **2** very attractive. **3** *Arch.* cloying. [C15 *lucius, licius,* ? short for DELICIOUS]
▸ **ˈlusciously** *adv* ▸ **ˈlusciousness** *n*

lush[1] Ⓣ (lʌʃ) *adj* **1** (of vegetation) abounding in lavish growth. **2** (esp. of fruits) succulent and fleshy. **3** luxurious, elaborate, or opulent. [C15: prob. from OF *lasche* lazy, from L *laxus* loose]
▸ **ˈlushly** *adv* ▸ **ˈlushness** *n*

lush[2] (lʌʃ) *Sl.* ◆ *n* **1** a heavy drinker, esp. an alcoholic. **2** alcoholic drink. ◆ *vb* **3** *US & Canad.* to drink (alcohol) to excess. [C19: from ?]

lust Ⓣ (lʌst) *n* **1** a strong desire for sexual gratification. **2** a strong desire

THESAURUS

dure, hack (*sl.*), stand, suffer, take, thole (*N English dialect*), tolerate

lumpish *adj* **2** = **clumsy**, awkward, bungling, doltish, elephantine, gawky, heavy, lethargic, lumbering, oafish, obtuse, puddingy, stolid, stupid, ungainly

lumpy *adj* **1** = **bumpy**, clotted, curdled, full of lumps, grainy, granular, knobbly, uneven

lunacy *n* **1** = **insanity**, dementia, derangement, idiocy, madness, mania, psychosis **2** = **foolishness**, aberration, absurdity, craziness, folly, foolhardiness, idiocy, imbecility, madness, senselessness, stupidity, tomfoolery
Antonyms *n* ≠ **insanity:** reason, sanity ≠ **foolishness:** prudence, reason, sense

lunatic *adj* **1, 2** = **irrational**, as daft as a brush (*inf., chiefly Brit.*), barking (*sl.*), barking mad (*sl.*), barmy (*sl.*), bonkers (*sl., chiefly Brit.*), crack-brained, crackpot (*inf.*), crazy, daft, demented, deranged, insane, loopy (*inf.*), mad, maniacal, not the full shilling (*inf.*), nuts (*sl.*), off one's trolley (*sl.*), out to lunch (*inf.*), psychotic, unhinged, up the pole (*inf.*) ◆ *n* **3** = **madman**, headbanger (*inf.*), headcase (*inf.*), loony (*sl.*), maniac, nut (*sl.*), nutcase (*sl.*), nutter (*Brit. sl.*), psychopath

lunge[1] **1** *n* **1** = **spring**, charge, pounce, swing, swipe (*inf.*) **2** *Fencing* = **thrust**, cut, jab, pass, stab ◆ *vb* **3** = **spring**, bound, charge, dash, dive, fall upon, hit at, leap, pitch into (*inf.*), plunge, pounce, set upon, strike at **4** *Fencing* = **thrust**, cut, jab, stab

lurch[1] *vb* **1** = **tilt**, heave, heel, lean, list, pitch, rock, roll, wallow **2** = **stagger**, reel, stumble, sway, totter, weave

lure *vb* **1** = **tempt**, allure, attract, beckon, decoy, draw, ensnare, entice, inveigle, invite, lead on, seduce ◆ *n* **3** = **temptation**, allurement, attraction, bait, carrot (*inf.*), come-on (*inf.*), decoy, enticement, incentive, inducement, magnet, siren song

lurid *adj* **1** = **sensational**, exaggerated, graphic, melodramatic, shock-horror (*facetious*), shocking, startling, unrestrained, vivid, yellow (*of journalism*) **2** = **gruesome**, disgusting, ghastly, gory, grim, grisly, macabre, revolting, savage, violent **3** = **pallid**, ashen, ghastly, pale, sallow, wan **4** = **glaring**, bloody, fiery, flaming, glowering, intense, livid, overbright, sanguine
Antonyms *adj* ≠ **sensational:** breezy, carefree, controlled, factual, jaunty, light-hearted, mild ≠ **glaring:** pale, pastel, watery

lurk *vb* **1** = **hide**, conceal oneself, crouch, go furtively, lie in wait, move with stealth, prowl, skulk, slink, sneak, snoop

luscious *adj* **1** = **delicious**, appetizing, delectable, honeyed, juicy, mouth-watering, palatable, rich, savoury, scrumptious (*inf.*), succulent, sweet, toothsome, yummy (*sl.*)

lush[1] *adj* **1** = **abundant**, dense, flourishing, green, lavish, overgrown, prolific, rank, teeming, verdant **2** = **succulent**, fresh, juicy, ripe, tender **3** = **luxurious**, elaborate, extravagant, grand, lavish, opulent, ornate, palatial, plush (*inf.*), ritzy (*sl.*), sumptuous

lust *n* **1** = **lechery**, carnality, concupiscence, las-

or drive. ◆ *vb* **3** (*intr; often foll. by after or for*) to have a lust (for). [OE]
▸ **'lustful** *adj* ▸ **'lustfully** *adv* ▸ **'lustfulness** *n*

lustral ('lʌstrəl) *adj* of or relating to a ceremony of purification. [C16: from L *lūstrālis* (adj) from LUSTRUM]

lustrate ('lʌstreɪt) *vb* **lustrates, lustrating, lustrated.** (*tr*) to purify by means of religious rituals or ceremonies. [C17: from L *lūstrāre* to brighten]
▸ **lus'tration** *n*

lustre ⓣ *or US* **luster** ('lʌstə) *n* **1** reflected light; sheen; gloss. **2** radiance or brilliance of light. **3** great splendour of accomplishment, beauty, etc. **4** a dress fabric of cotton and wool with a glossy surface. **5** a vase or chandelier from which hang cut-glass drops. **6** a drop-shaped piece of cut glass or crystal used as such a decoration. **7** a shiny metallic surface on some pottery and porcelain. **8** *Mineralogy.* the way in which light is reflected from the surface of a mineral. ◆ *vb* **lustres, lustring, lustred** *or US* **lusters, lustering, lustered. 9** to make, be, or become lustrous. [C16: from OF, from OIt. *lustro*, from L *lustrāre* to make bright]
▸ **'lustreless** *or US* **'lusterless** *adj* ▸ **'lustrous** *adj*

lustreware *or US* **lusterware** ('lʌstə,wɛə) *n* pottery with lustre decoration.

lustrum ('lʌstrəm) *or* **lustre** *n, pl* **lustrums, lustra** (-trə), *or* **lustres.** *Rare.* a period of five years. [C16: from L: ceremony of purification, from *lustrāre* to brighten, purify]

lusty ⓣ ('lʌstɪ) *adj* **lustier, lustiest. 1** having or characterized by robust health. **2** strong or invigorating.
▸ **'lustily** *adv* ▸ **'lustiness** *n*

lute[1] (lu:t) *n* an ancient plucked stringed instrument with a long fretted fingerboard and a body shaped like a sliced pear. [C14: from OF *lut*, from Ar. *al 'ūd*, lit.: the wood]

lute[2] (lu:t) *n* **1** a mixture of cement and clay used to seal the joints between pipes, etc. **2** *Dentistry.* a thin layer of cement used to fix a crown or inlay in place on a tooth. ◆ *vb* **lutes, luting, luted. 3** (*tr*) to seal (a joint or surface) with lute. [C14: via OF ult. from L *lutum* clay]

lutein ('lu:tɪɪn) *n* a xanthophyll pigment, occurring in plants, that has a light-absorbing function in photosynthesis. [C20: from L *lūteus* yellow + -IN]

luteinizing hormone ('lu:tɪɪ,naɪzɪŋ) *n* a hormone secreted by the anterior lobe of the pituitary gland. In female vertebrates it stimulates ovulation, and in mammals it also induces corpus luteum formation. In male vertebrates it promotes maturation of the interstitial cells of the testes and stimulates androgen secretion. [C19: from L *lūteum* egg yolk, from *lūteus* yellow]

lutenist, lutanist, ('lu:tənɪst) *or US & Canad.* (*sometimes*) **lutist** ('lu:tɪst) *n* a person who plays the lute. [C17: from Med. L *lūtānista*, from *lūtāna*, apparently from OF *lut* LUTE[1]]

lutetium *or* **lutecium** (lu'ti:ʃɪəm) *n* a silvery-white metallic element of the lanthanide series. Symbol: Lu; atomic no.: 71; atomic wt.: 174.97. [C19: NL, from L *Lūtētia* ancient name of Paris, home of G. Urbain (1872–1938), F chemist, who discovered it]

Lutheran ('lu:θərən) *n* **1** a follower of Martin Luther (1483–1546), German leader of the Protestant Reformation, or a member of the Lutheran Church. ◆ *adj* **2** of or relating to Luther or his doctrines. **3** of or denoting any of the Churches that follow Luther's doctrines.
▸ **'Lutheranism** *n*

Lutine bell ('lu:ti:n, lu:'ti:n) *n* a bell, taken from the ship *Lutine*, kept at Lloyd's in London and rung before important announcements, esp. the loss of a vessel.

lux (lʌks) *n, pl* **lux.** the derived SI unit of illumination equal to a luminous flux of 1 lumen per square metre. [C19: from L: light]

luxate ('lʌkseɪt) *vb* **luxates, luxating, luxated.** (*tr*) *Pathol.* to dislocate (a shoulder, knee, etc.). [C17: from L *luxāre* to displace, from *luxus* dislocated]
▸ **lux'ation** *n*

luxe (lʌks, luks; *French* lyks) *n* See **de luxe.** [C16: from F from L *luxus* extravagance]

luxuriant ⓣ (lʌg'zjuərɪənt) *adj* **1** rich and abundant; lush. **2** very elaborate or ornate. **3** extremely productive or fertile. [C16: from L *luxuriāns*, present participle of *luxuriāre* to abound to excess]
▸ **lux'uriance** *n* ▸ **lux'uriantly** *adv*

> **USAGE NOTE** See at **luxurious.**

luxuriate ⓣ (lʌg'zjuərɪ,eɪt) *vb* **luxuriates, luxuriating, luxuriated.** (*intr*) **1** (foll. by *in*) to take voluptuous pleasure; revel. **2** to flourish profusely. **3** to live in a sumptuous way. [C17: from L *luxuriāre*]
▸ **lux,uri'ation** *n*

luxurious ⓣ (lʌg'zjuərɪəs) *adj* **1** characterized by luxury. **2** enjoying or devoted to luxury. [C14: via OF from L *luxuriōsus* excessive]
▸ **lux'uriously** *adv* ▸ **lux'uriousness** *n*

> **USAGE NOTE** *Luxurious* is sometimes wrongly used where *luxuriant* is meant: *he had a luxuriant* (not *luxurious*) *moustache; the walls were covered with a luxuriant growth of wisteria.*

luxury ⓣ ('lʌkʃərɪ) *n, pl* **luxuries. 1** indulgence in and enjoyment of rich and sumptuous living. **2** (*sometimes pl*) something considered an indulgence rather than a necessity. **3** something pleasant and satisfying: *the luxury of independence.* **4** (*modifier*) relating to, indicating, or supplying luxury: *a luxury liner.* [C14 (in the sense: lechery): via OF from L *luxuria* excess, from *luxus* extravagance]

LV *abbrev. for* luncheon voucher.

LW *abbrev. for:* **1** *Radio.* long wave. **2** low water.

lx *Physics. symbol for* lux.

LXX *symbol for* Septuagint.

-ly[1] *suffix forming adjectives.* **1** having the nature or qualities of: *godly.* **2** occurring at certain intervals; every: *daily.* [OE *-lic*]

-ly[2] *suffix forming adverbs.* in a certain manner; to a certain degree: *quickly; recently; chiefly.* [OE *-lice*, from *-lic* -LY[1]]

lyase ('laɪeɪz) *n* any enzyme that catalyses the separation of two parts of a molecule by the formation of a double bond between them. [C20: from Gk *lusis* a loosening + -ASE]

lycanthropy (laɪ'kænθrəpɪ) *n* **1** the supposed magical transformation of a human being into a wolf. **2** *Psychiatry.* a delusion in which a person believes that he is a wolf. [C16: from Gk *lukanthrōpia*, from *lukos* wolf + *anthrōpos* man]
▸ **lycanthrope** ('laɪkən,θrəup) *n* ▸ **lycanthropic** (,laɪkən'θrɒpɪk) *adj*

lycée ('li:seɪ) *n, pl* **lycées** (-seɪz). *Chiefly French.* a secondary school. [C19: F, from L: *Lyceum* a school in ancient Athens]

lyceum (laɪ'sɪəm) *n* (now chiefly in the names of buildings) **1** a public building for concerts, lectures, etc. **2** *US.* a cultural organization responsible for presenting concerts, lectures, etc.

lychee (,laɪ'tʃi:) *n* a variant spelling of **litchi.**

lych gate *or* **lich gate** (lɪtʃ) *n* a roofed gate to a churchyard, formerly used as a temporary shelter for the bier. [C15: *lich*, from OE *līc* corpse]

lychnis ('lɪknɪs) *n* any of a genus of plants having red, pink, or white five-petalled flowers: includes ragged robin. [C17: NL, via L, from Gk *lukhnis* a red flower]

lycopodium (,laɪkə'pəudɪəm) *n* **1** any of a genus of club moss resembling moss but having woody tissue and spore-bearing cones. **2** a flammable yellow powder from the spores of this plant, used in medicine and in making fireworks. [C18: NL, from Gk, from *lukos* wolf + *pous* foot]

Lycra ('laɪkrə) *n Trademark.* a type of synthetic elastic fabric and fibre used for tight-fitting garments, such as swimming costumes.

lyddite ('lɪdaɪt) *n* an explosive consisting chiefly of fused picric acid. [C19: after *Lydd*, town in Kent near which the first tests were made]

lye (laɪ) *n* **1** any solution obtained by leaching, such as the caustic solution obtained by leaching wood ash. **2** a concentrated solution of sodium hydroxide or potassium hydroxide. [OE *lēag*]

lying[1] ⓣ ('laɪɪŋ) *vb* the present participle and gerund of **lie**[1].

THESAURUS

civiousness, lewdness, libido, licentiousness, pruriency, randiness (*inf., chiefly Brit.*), salaciousness, sensuality, the hots (*sl.*), wantonness **2** = **desire**, appetence, appetite, avidity, covetousness, craving, cupidity, greed, longing, passion, thirst ◆ *vb* **3** *often foll. by* **after** *or* **for** = **desire**, be consumed with desire for, covet, crave, hunger for *or* after, lech after (*inf.*), need, slaver over, want, yearn

lustful *adj* **1** = **lascivious**, carnal, concupiscent, craving, hankering, horny (*sl.*), hot-blooded, lecherous, lewd, libidinous, licentious, passionate, prurient, randy (*inf., chiefly Brit.*), raunchy (*sl.*), sensual, sexy (*inf.*), unchaste, wanton

lustily *adv* **2** = **vigorously**, forcefully, hard, loudly, powerfully, strongly, with all one's might, with might and main

lustre *n* **1** = **sparkle**, burnish, gleam, glint, glitter, gloss, glow, sheen, shimmer, shine **2** = **radiance**, brightness, brilliance, dazzle, lambency, luminousness, resplendence **3** = **glory**, distinction, fame, honour, illustriousness, prestige, renown

lustreless *adj* **1, 2** = **dull**, colourless, dingy, drab, faded, flat, lacklustre, lifeless, matt, pale, tarnished, unpolished, washed out

lustrous *adj* **1, 2** = **shining**, bright, burnished, dazzling, gleaming, glistening, glossy, glowing, luminous, radiant, shimmering, shiny, sparkling

lusty *adj* **1** = **vigorous**, brawny, energetic, hale, healthy, hearty, in fine fettle, powerful, red-blooded (*inf.*), robust, rugged, stalwart, stout, strapping, strong, sturdy, virile

luxuriant *adj* **1** = **abundant**, ample, copious, excessive, lavish, plenteous, plentiful, prodigal, profuse, superabundant **2** = **elaborate**, baroque, corinthian, decorated, extravagant, fancy, festooned, flamboyant, florid, flowery, ornate, rococo, sumptuous **3** = **fertile**, dense, exuberant, fecund, flourishing, fruitful, lush, overflowing, productive, prolific, rank, rich, riotous, teeming, thriving
Antonyms *adj* ≠ **abundant:** meagre, scanty, sparse, thin ≠ **elaborate:** plain, simple, unadorned

luxuriate *vb* **1** = **enjoy**, bask, delight, flourish, indulge, relish, revel, wallow **2** = **flourish**, abound, bloom, burgeon, grow, prosper, thrive **3** = **live in luxury**, be in clover, have the time of one's life, live the life of Riley, take it easy

luxurious *adj* **1** = **sumptuous**, comfortable, costly, de luxe, expensive, lavish, magnificent, opulent, plush (*inf.*), rich, ritzy (*sl.*), splendid, well-appointed **2** = **pleasure-loving**, epicurean, pampered, self-indulgent, sensual, sybaritic, voluptuous
Antonyms *adj* ascetic, austere, deprived, economical, plain, poor, sparing, Spartan, thrifty

luxury *n* **1, 3** = **pleasure**, bliss, comfort, delight, enjoyment, gratification, hedonism, indulgence, opulence, richness, satisfaction, voluptuousness, wellbeing **2** = **extravagance**, extra, frill, indulgence, nonessential, treat
Antonyms *n* ≠ **pleasure:** austerity, deprivation, destitution, difficulty, discomfort, hardship, misery, poverty, privation, want ≠ **extravagance:** necessity, need

lying[1] *n* **1** = **dishonesty**, deceit, dissimulation,

lying[2] ('laɪɪŋ) *vb* the present participle and gerund of **lie**[2].

lying-in *n, pl* **lyings-in.** confinement in childbirth.

lyke-wake ('laɪk,weɪk) *n Brit.* a watch held over a dead person, often with festivities. [C16: ?from ON]

Lyme disease (laɪm) *n* a disease of domestic animals and humans, caused by a spirochaete and transmitted by ticks, and affecting the joints, heart, and brain. [C20: after *Lyme*, Connecticut, the town where it was first identified in humans]

lymph (lɪmf) *n* the almost colourless fluid, containing chiefly white blood cells, that is collected from the tissues of the body and transported in the lymphatic system. [C17: from L *lympha* water, from earlier *limpa,* infl. in form by Gk *numphē* nymph]

lymphatic (lɪm'fætɪk) *adj* **1** of, relating to, or containing lymph. **2** of or relating to the lymphatic system. **3** sluggish or lacking vigour. ◆ *n* **4** a lymphatic vessel. [C17 (meaning: mad): from L *lymphāticus.* Original meaning ?from a confusion between *nymph* and LYMPH]

lymphatic system *n* an extensive network of capillary vessels that transports the interstitial fluid of the body as lymph to the venous blood circulation.

lymphatic tissue *n* tissue, such as the lymph nodes, tonsils, spleen, and thymus, that produces lymphocytes.

lymph gland *n* a former name for **lymph node.**

lymph node *n* any of numerous bean-shaped masses of tissue, situated along the course of lymphatic vessels, that help to protect against infection and are a source of lymphocytes.

lympho- *or before a vowel* **lymph-** *combining form.* indicating lymph or the lymphatic system: *lymphocyte.*

lymphocyte ('lɪmfəʊ,saɪt) *n* a type of white blood cell formed in lymphatic tissue.
▸**lymphocytic** (,lɪmfəʊ'sɪtɪk) *adj*

lymphoid ('lɪmfɔɪd) *adj* of or resembling lymph, or relating to the lymphatic system.

lymphoma (lɪm,fəʊmə) *n* cancer of the lymph nodes. Also called: **lymphosarcoma** (,lɪmfəʊsɑː'kəʊmə).

lynch (lɪntʃ) *vb* (*tr*) (of a mob) to punish (a person) for some supposed offence by hanging without a trial. [orig. *Lynch's law;* ? after Capt. William *Lynch* (1742–1820) of Virginia, USA]
▸'**lyncher** *n* ▸'**lynching** *n*

lynchet ('lɪntʃɪt) *n* a terrace or ridge formed in prehistoric or medieval times by ploughing a hillside. [OE *hlinc* ridge]

lynch law *n* the practice of punishing a person by mob action without a proper trial.

lynchpin ('lɪntʃ,pɪn) *n* a variant spelling of **linchpin.**

lynx (lɪŋks) *n, pl* **lynxes** *or* **lynx. 1** a feline mammal of Europe and North America, with grey-brown mottled fur, tufted ears, and a short tail. **2** the fur of this animal. **3 bay lynx.** another name for **bobcat. 4 desert lynx.** another name for **caracal.** [C14: via L from Gk *lunx*]
▸'**lynx,like** *adj*

lynx-eyed *adj* having keen sight.

Lyon King of Arms ('laɪən) *n* the chief herald of Scotland. Also called: **Lord Lyon.** [C14: archaic spelling of LION, referring to the figure on the royal shield]

lyrate ('laɪərɪt) *adj* **1** shaped like a lyre. **2** (of leaves) having a large terminal lobe and smaller lateral lobes. [C18: from NL *lyrātus, from* L *lyra* LYRE]

lyre ('laɪə) *n* an ancient Greek stringed instrument consisting of a resonating tortoise shell to which a crossbar was attached by two projecting arms. It was plucked with a plectrum and used for accompanying songs. [C13: via OF from L *lyra,* from Gk *lura*]

lyrebird ('laɪə,bɜːd) *n* either of two pheasant-like Australian birds: during courtship displays, the male spreads its tail into the shape of a lyre.

lyric ⓣ ('lɪrɪk) *adj* **1** (of poetry) **1a** expressing the writer's personal feelings and thoughts. **1b** having the form and manner of a song. **2** of or relating to such poetry. **3** (of music) having songlike qualities. **4** (of a singing voice) having a light quality and tone. **5** intended for singing, esp. (in classical Greece) to the accompaniment of the lyre. ◆ *n* **6** a short poem of songlike quality. **7** (*pl*) the words of a popular song. ◆ Also (for senses 1–4): **lyrical.** [C16: from L *lyricus,* from Gk *lurikos,* from *lura* lyre]
▸'**lyrically** *adv* ▸'**lyricalness** *n*

lyrical ⓣ ('lɪrɪk[ə]l) *adj* **1** another word for **lyric** (senses 1–4). **2** enthusiastic; effusive.

lyricism ('lɪrɪ,sɪzəm) *n* **1** the quality or style of lyric poetry. **2** emotional outpouring.

lyricist ('lɪrɪsɪst) *n* **1** a person who writes the words for a song, opera, or musical play. **2** Also called: **lyrist.** a lyric poet.

lyse (laɪs, laɪz) *vb* **lyses, lysing, lysed.** to undergo or cause to undergo lysis.

lysergic acid diethylamide (lɪ'sɜːdʒɪk; daɪ,ɛθɪl'eɪmaɪd) *n* See **LSD.**

lysin ('laɪsɪn) *n* any of a group of antibodies that cause dissolution of cells.

lysis ('laɪsɪs) *n, pl* **lyses** (-siːz). **1** the destruction of cells by the action of a particular lysin. **2** *Med.* the gradual reduction in the symptoms of a disease. [C19: NL, from Gk, from *luein* to release]

-lysis *n combining form.* indicating a loosening, decomposition, or breaking down: *electrolysis; paralysis.* [from Gk, from *lusis* a loosening; see LYSIS]

Lysol ('laɪsɒl) *n Trademark.* a solution containing a mixture of cresols in water, used as an antiseptic and disinfectant.

-lyte *n combining form.* indicating a substance that can be decomposed or broken down: *electrolyte.* [from Gk *lutos* soluble, from *luein* to loose]

-lytic *adj combining form.* indicating a loosening or dissolving: *paralytic.* [from Gk, from *lusis;* see -LYSIS]

THESAURUS

double-dealing, duplicity, fabrication, falsity, fibbing, guile, mendacity, perjury, prevarication, untruthfulness ◆ *adj* **2** = **deceitful,** dishonest, dissembling, double-dealing, false, guileful, mendacious, perfidious, treacherous, two-faced, untruthful

Antonyms *adj* ≠ **deceitful:** candid, forthright, frank, honest, reliable, sincere, straight, straightforward, truthful, veracious

lyric *adj* **1** = **songlike,** expressive, lyrical, melodic, musical **3, 4** = **melodic,** clear, dulcet, flowing, graceful, light ◆ *n* **7** *plural* = **words,** book, libretto, text, words of a song

lyrical *adj* **2** = **enthusiastic,** carried away, ecstatic, effusive, emotional, expressive, impassioned, inspired, rapturous, rhapsodic

Mm

m *or* **M** (ɛm) *n, pl* **m's, M's,** *or* **Ms. 1** the 13th letter of the English alphabet. **2** a speech sound represented by this letter, as in *mat.*

m *symbol for:* **1** metre(s). **2** mile(s). **3** milli-. **4** minute(s).

M *symbol for:* **1** mach. **2** *Currency.* mark(s). **3** medium. **4** mega-. **5** million. **6** (in Britain) motorway. **7** *the Roman numeral for* 1000.

m. *abbrev. for:* **1** *Cricket.* maiden (over). **2** male. **3** mare. **4** married. **5** masculine. **6** meridian. **7** month.

M. *abbrev. for:* **1** Majesty. **2** Manitoba. **3** Master. **4** Medieval. **5** (in titles) Member. **6** million. **7** (*pl* **MM.** *or* **MM**) Also: **M** *French.* Monsieur. [F equivalent of *Mr*]

m- *prefix* short for **meta-** (sense 4).

M'- *prefix* a variant of **Mac-**.

ma (mɑː) *n* an informal word for **mother.**

MA *abbrev. for:* **1** Massachusetts. **2** Master of Arts. **3** Military Academy.

ma'am (mæm, mɑːm; *unstressed* məm) *n* short for **madam:** used as a title of respect, esp. for female royalty.

mac *or* **mack** (mæk) *n Brit. inf.* short for **mackintosh.**

Mac (mæk) *n Chiefly US & Canad.* an informal term of address to a man. [C20: abstracted from MAC-]

Mac-, Mc-, *or* **M'-** *prefix* (in surnames of Scottish or Irish Gaelic origin) son of: *MacDonald.* [from Goidelic *mac* son of]

macabre ❶ (mə'kɑːbə, -brə) *adj* gruesome; ghastly; grim. [C15: from OF *danse macabre* dance of death, prob. from *macabé* relating to the Maccabees, who were associated with death because of the doctrines and prayers for the dead in II Macc. (12:43–46)]

macadam (mə'kædəm) *n* a road surface made of compressed layers of small broken stones, esp. one that is bound together with tar or asphalt. [C19: after John *McAdam* (1756–1836), Scot. engineer, the inventor]

macadamia (ˌmækə'deɪmɪə) *n* **1** an Australian tree having clusters of small white flowers and edible nutlike seeds. **2 macadamia nut.** the seed. [C19: NL, after John *Macadam* (died 1865), Australian chemist]

macadamize *or* **macadamise** (mə'kædəˌmaɪz) *vb* **macadamizes, macadamizing, macadamized** *or* **macadamises, macadamising, macadamised.** (*tr*) to construct or surface (a road) with macadam.
▸**macˌadami'zation** *or* **macˌadami'sation** *n* ▸**mac'adamˌizer** *or* **mac'adamˌiser** *n*

macaque (mə'kɑːk) *n* any of various Old World monkeys of Asia and Africa. Typically the tail is short or absent and cheek pouches are present. [C17: from F, from Port. *macaco,* from W African *makaku,* from *kaku* monkey]

macaroni *or* **maccaroni** (ˌmækə'rəʊnɪ) *n, pl* **macaronis, macaronies** *or* **maccaronis, maccaronies. 1** pasta tubes made from wheat flour. **2** (in 18th-century Britain) a dandy who affected foreign manners and style. [C16: from It. (dialect) *maccarone,* prob. from Gk *makaria* food made from barley]

macaroon (ˌmækə'ruːn) *n* a kind of sweet biscuit made of ground almonds, sugar, and egg whites. [C17: via F *macaron* from It. *maccarone* MACARONI]

Macassar oil (mə'kæsə) *n* an oily preparation formerly put on the hair to make it smooth and shiny. [C19: from *Makasar,* town in Indonesia]

macaw (mə'kɔː) *n* a large tropical American parrot having a long tail and brilliant plumage. [C17: from Port. *macau,* from ?]

Macc. *abbrev. for* Maccabees (books of the Apocrypha).

McCarthyism (mə'kɑːθɪˌɪzəm) *n Chiefly US.* **1** the practice of making unsubstantiated accusations of disloyalty or Communist leanings. **2** the use of unsupported accusations for any purpose. [C20: after Joseph *McCarthy* (1908–57), US senator]
▸**Mc'Carthyist** *n, adj*

McCoy (mə'kɔɪ) *n Sl.* the genuine person or thing (esp. in **the real McCoy**). [C20: ? after Kid *McCoy,* professional name of Norman Selby (1873–1940), American boxer, who was called "the real McCoy" to distinguish him from another boxer of that name]

mace[1] (meɪs) *n* **1** a club, usually having a spiked metal head, used esp. in the Middle Ages. **2** a ceremonial staff carried by certain officials. **3** See **macebearer. 4** an early form of billiard cue. [C13: from OF, prob. from Vulgar L *mattea* (unattested); apparently rel. to L *mateola* mallet]

mace[2] (meɪs) *n* a spice made from the dried aril round the nutmeg seed. [C14: formed as a singular from OF *macis* (wrongly assumed to be pl), from L *macir* a spice]

macebearer ('meɪsˌbɛərə) *n* a person who carries a mace in processions or ceremonies.

macedoine (ˌmæsɪ'dwɑːn) *n* **1** a mixture of diced vegetables. **2** a mixture of fruit in a syrup or in jelly. **3** any mixture; medley. [C19: from F, lit.: Macedonian, alluding to the mixture of nationalities in Macedonia]

macerate ('mæsəˌreɪt) *vb* **macerates, macerating, macerated. 1** to soften or separate or be softened or separated as a result of soaking. **2** to become or cause to become thin. [C16: from L *mācerāre* to soften]
▸ˌ**macer'ation** *n* ▸'**macerˌator** *n*

MacGuffin (mə'gʌfɪn) *n* an object or event in a book or a film that serves as the impetus for the plot. [C20: coined (c. 1935) by Sir Alfred Hitchcock (1899–1980), Brit. film director]

Mach (mæk) *n* short for **Mach number.**

mach. *abbrev. for:* **1** machine. **2** machinery. **3** machinist.

machair ('mæxər) *n Scot.* (in the western Highlands and islands of Scotland) a strip of sandy grassy land just above the shore: used for grazing, etc. [C17: from Scot. Gaelic]

machete (mə'ʃɛtɪ, -'tʃeɪ-) *n* a broad heavy knife used for cutting or as a weapon, esp. in parts of Central and South America. [C16 *macheto,* from Sp. *machete,* from *macho* club, ?from Vulgar L *mattea* (unattested) club]

Machiavellian ❶ (ˌmækɪə'vɛlɪən) *adj* **1** of or relating to the alleged political principles of the Florentine statesman Machiavelli (1469–1527); cunning, amoral, and opportunist. ◆ *n* **2** a cunning, amoral, and opportunist person, esp. a politician.
▸ˌ**Machia'vellianˌism** *n*

machicolate (mə'tʃɪkəʊˌleɪt) *vb* **machicolates, machicolating, machicolated.** (*tr*) to construct machicolations at the top of (a wall). [C18: from OF *machicoller,* ult. from Provençal *machacol,* from *macar* to crush + *col* neck]

machicolation (məˌtʃɪkəʊ'leɪʃən) *n* **1** (esp. in medieval castles) a projecting gallery or parapet having openings through which missiles could be dropped. **2** any such opening.

machinate ('mækɪˌneɪt) *vb* **machinates, machinating, machinated.** (*usually tr*) to contrive, plan, or devise (schemes, plots, etc.). [C17: from L *māchinārī* to plan, from *māchina* MACHINE]
▸'**machiˌnator** *n*

machination ❶ (ˌmækɪ'neɪʃən) *n* **1** a plot or scheme. **2** the act of devising plots or schemes.

machine ❶ (mə'ʃiːn) *n* **1** an assembly of interconnected components arranged to transmit or modify force in order to perform useful work. **2** a device for altering the magnitude or direction of a force, such as a lever or screw. **3** a mechanically operated device or means of transport, such as a car or aircraft. **4** any mechanical or electrical device that automatically performs tasks or assists in performing tasks. **5** any intricate structure or agency. **6** a mechanically efficient, rigid, or obedient person. **7** an organized body of people that controls activities, policies, etc. ◆ *vb* **machines, machining, machined. 8** (*tr*) to shape, cut, or remove (excess material) from (a workpiece) using a machine tool. **9** to use a machine to carry out a process on (something). [C16: via F from L *māchina* machine, from Doric Gk *makhana* pulley]
▸**ma'chinable** *or* **ma'chineable** *adj* ▸**maˌchina'bility** *n*

machine code *or* **language** *n* instructions for the processing of data in a binary, octal, or hexadecimal code that can be understood and executed by a computer.

machine-down time *n* a period during which a machine, computer, etc., is out of service, because it is out of order or being serviced.

machine gun *n* **1a** a rapid-firing automatic gun, using small-arms ammunition. **1b** (*as modifier*): *machine-gun fire.* ◆ *vb* **machine-gun, machine-guns, machine-gunning, machine-gunned. 2** (*tr*) to shoot or fire at with a machine gun.
▸**machine gunner** *n*

machine learning *n* a branch of artificial intelligence in which a computer generates rules underlying or based on raw data that has been fed into it.

machinery ❶ (mə'ʃiːnərɪ) *n, pl* **machineries. 1** machines, machine parts, or machine systems collectively. **2** a particular machine system or set of machines. **3** a system similar to a machine.

machine shop *n* a workshop in which machine tools are operated.

machine tool *n* a power-driven machine, such as a lathe, for cutting, shaping, and finishing metals, etc.
▸**ma'chine-ˌtooled** *adj*

machinist (mə'ʃiːnɪst) *n* **1** a person who operates machines to cut or process materials. **2** a maker or repairer of machines.

THESAURUS

macabre *adj* = **gruesome,** cadaverous, deathlike, deathly, dreadful, eerie, frightening, frightful, ghastly, ghostly, ghoulish, grim, grisly, hideous, horrid, morbid, unearthly, weird
Antonyms *adj* appealing, beautiful, charming, delightful, lovely, pleasant

Machiavellian *adj* **1** = **scheming,** amoral, artful, astute, crafty, cunning, cynical, deceitful, designing, double-dealing, foxy, intriguing, opportunist, perfidious, shrewd, sly, underhand, unscrupulous, wily

machination *n* **1** = **plot,** artifice, cabal, conspiracy, design, device, dodge, intrigue, manoeuvre, ploy, ruse, scheme, stratagem, trick

machine *n* **1-4** = **appliance,** apparatus, contraption, contrivance, device, engine, instrument, mechanism, tool **5** = **system,** agency, machinery, organization, party, setup (*inf.*), structure

machinery *n* **1, 2** = **equipment,** apparatus, gear, instruments, mechanism, tackle, tools, works **3** = **procedure,** agency, channels, machine, organization, structure, system

machismo (mæ'kɪzməʊ, -'tʃɪz-) *n* strong or exaggerated masculinity. [Mexican Sp., from Sp. *macho* male, from L *masculus* MASCULINE]

Mach number *n* (*often not cap.*) the ratio of the speed of a body in a particular medium to the speed of sound in that medium. Mach number 1 corresponds to the speed of sound. [C19: after Ernst *Mach* (1838–1916), Austrian physicist & philosopher]

macho ❶ ('mætʃəʊ) *adj* **1** strongly or exaggeratedly masculine. ◆ *n, pl* **machos. 2** a strong virile man. [see MACHISMO]

mack (mæk) *n Brit. inf.* short for **mackintosh.**

mackerel ('mækrəl) *n, pl* **mackerel** *or* **mackerels. 1** a spiny-finned food fish occurring in northern coastal regions of the Atlantic and in the Mediterranean. It has a deeply forked tail and a greenish-blue body marked with wavy dark bands on the back. **2** any of various related fishes. [C13: from Anglo-F, from OF *maquerel,* from ?]

mackerel sky *n* a sky patterned with cirrocumulus or small altocumulus clouds. [from similarity to pattern on mackerel's back]

mackintosh *or* **macintosh** ('mækɪn,tɒʃ) *n* **1** a waterproof raincoat made of rubberized cloth. **2** such cloth. **3** any raincoat. [C19: after Charles *Macintosh* (1760–1843), who invented it]

McNaughten Rules *or* **McNaghten Rules** (mək'nɔːtᵊn) *pl n* (in English law) a set of rules established by the case of Regina v. McNaughten (1843) by which legal proof of criminal insanity depends on the accused being shown to be incapable of understanding what he has done.

macramé (mə'krɑːmɪ) *n* a type of ornamental work made by knotting and weaving coarse thread. [C19: via F & It. from Turkish *makrama* towel, from Ar. *migramah* striped cloth]

macro ('mækrəʊ) *n, pl* **macros. 1** *Photog.* a camera lens used for close-up photography. Also called: **macro lens. 2** *Computing.* a single computer instruction that initiates a set of instructions. Also called: **macro instruction.** [C20: from Gk *makros* large]

macro- *or before a vowel* **macr-** *combining form.* **1** large, long, or great in size or duration: *macroscopic.* **2** *Pathol.* indicating abnormal enlargement or overdevelopment: *macrocephaly.* [from Gk *makros* large]

macrobiotics (,mækrəʊbaɪ'ɒtɪks) *n* (*functioning as sing*) a dietary system which advocates whole grains and vegetables grown without chemical additives. [C20: from MACRO- + Gk *biotos* life + -ICS]
▸ **,macrobi'otic** *adj*

macrocarpa (,mækrəʊ'kɑːpə) *n* a large Californian coniferous tree, used in New Zealand and elsewhere to form shelter belts on farms and for rough timber. [C19: from NL, from MACRO- + Gk *karpos* fruit]

macrocephaly (,mækrəʊ'sɛfəlɪ) *n* the condition of having an abnormally large head or skull.
▸ **macrocephalic** (,mækrəʊsɪ'fælɪk) *or* **,macro'cephalous** *adj*

macroclimate ('mækrəʊ,klaɪmɪt) *n* the predominant climate over a large area.

macrocosm ('mækrə,kɒzəm) *n* a complex structure, such as the universe or society, regarded as an entirety. Cf. **microcosm.** [C16: via F & L from Gk *makros kosmos* great world]
▸ **,macro'cosmic** *adj* ▸ **,macro'cosmically** *adv*

macroeconomics (,mækrəʊ,iːkə'nɒmɪks, -,ɛk-) *n* (*functioning as sing*) the branch of economics concerned with aggregates, such as national income, consumption, and investment.
▸ **,macro,eco'nomic** *adj*

macromolecule (,mækrəʊ'mɒlɪ,kjuːl) *n* any very large molecule, such as a protein or synthetic polymer.

macron ('mækrɒn) *n* a diacritical mark (¯) placed over a letter to represent a long vowel. [C19: from Gk *makron* something long, from *makros* long]

macropod ('mækrəʊ,pɒd) *n* any member of a family of marsupials consisting of the kangaroos and related animals.

macroscopic (,mækrəʊ'skɒpɪk) *adj* **1** large enough to be visible to the naked eye. **2** comprehensive; concerned with large units. [C19: see MACRO-, -SCOPIC]
▸ **,macro'scopically** *adv*

macula ('mækjʊlə) *or* **macule** ('mækjuːl) *n, pl* **maculae** (-jʊ,liː) *or* **macules.** *Anat.* **1** a small spot or area of distinct colour, esp. the macula lutea. **2** any small discoloured spot or blemish on the skin, such as a freckle. [C14: from L]
▸ **'macular** *adj* ▸ **,macu'lation** *n*

macula lutea ('luːtɪə) *n, pl* **maculae luteae** ('luːtɪ,iː). a small yellowish oval-shaped spot on the retina of the eye, where vision is especially sharp. [NL, lit.: yellow spot]

macular degeneration *n* pathological changes in the macula lutea, resulting in loss of central vision: a common cause of blindness in the elderly.

mad ❶ (mæd) *adj* **madder, maddest. 1** mentally deranged; insane. **2** senseless; foolish. **3** (often foll. by *at*) *Inf.* angry; resentful. **4** (foll. by *about, on,* or *over;* often *postpositive*) wildly enthusiastic (about) or fond (of). **5** extremely excited or confused; frantic: *a mad rush.* **6** temporarily overpowered by violent reactions, emotions, etc.: *mad with grief.* **7** (of animals) **7a** unusually ferocious: *a mad buffalo.* **7b** afflicted with rabies. **8 like mad.** *Inf.* with great energy, enthusiasm, or haste. ◆ *vb* **mads, madding, madded. 9** *US or arch.* to make or become mad; act or cause to act as if mad. [OE *gemǣded,* p.p. of *gemǣdan* to render insane]

madam ('mædəm) *n, pl* **madams** *or* (for sense 1) **mesdames. 1** a polite term of address for a woman, esp. one of relatively high social status. **2** a woman who runs a brothel. **3** *Brit. inf.* a precocious or pompous little girl. [C13: from OF *ma dame* my lady]

madame ('mædəm) *n, pl* **mesdames.** a married Frenchwoman: used as a title equivalent to *Mrs,* and sometimes extended to older unmarried women to show respect. [C17: from F; see MADAM]

madcap ❶ ('mæd,kæp) *adj* **1** impulsive, reckless, or lively. ◆ *n* **2** an impulsive, reckless, or lively person.

mad cow disease *n* an informal name for **BSE.**

madden ❶ ('mædᵊn) *vb* to make or become mad or angry.
▸ **'maddening** *adj* ▸ **'maddeningly** *adv*

madder ('mædə) *n* **1** a plant having small yellow flowers and a red fleshy root. **2** this root. **3** a dark reddish-purple dye formerly obtained from this root. **4** a red lake obtained from alizarin and an inorganic base; used as a pigment in inks and paints. [OE *mædere*]

madding ('mædɪŋ) *adj Arch.* **1** acting or behaving as if mad: *the madding crowd.* **2** making mad; maddening.
▸ **'maddingly** *adv*

made (meɪd) *vb* **1** the past tense and past participle of **make.** ◆ *adj* **2** artificially produced. **3** (*in combination*) produced or shaped as specified: *handmade.* **4 get** *or* **have it made.** *Inf.* to be assured of success.

Madeira (mə'dɪərə) *n* a rich strong fortified white wine made on Madeira, a Portuguese island in the N Atlantic.

madeleine ('mædəlɪn, -,leɪn) *n* a small fancy sponge cake. [C19: ? after *Madeleine* Paulmier, F pastry cook]

mademoiselle (,mædmwə'zel) *n, pl* **mesdemoiselles. 1** a young unmarried French girl or woman: used as a title equivalent to *Miss.* **2** a French teacher or governess. [C15: F, from *ma* my + *demoiselle* DAMSEL]

made-up ❶ *adj* **1** invented; fictional. **2** wearing make-up. **3** put together. **4** (of a road) surfaced with tarmac, concrete, etc.

madhouse ❶ ('mæd,haʊs) *n Inf.* **1** a mental hospital or asylum. **2** a state of uproar or confusion.

madly ❶ ('mædlɪ) *adv* **1** in an insane or foolish manner. **2** with great speed and energy. **3** *Inf.* extremely or excessively: *I love you madly.*

madman ❶ ('mædmən) *or* (*fem*) **madwoman** *n, pl* **madmen** *or* **madwomen.** a person who is insane.

THESAURUS

macho *adj* **1** = **manly,** butch (*sl.*), chauvinist, he-man, masculine, virile

mad *adj* **1** = **insane,** aberrant, bananas (*sl.*), barking mad (*sl.*), barmy (*sl.*), batty (*sl.*), bonkers (*sl., chiefly Brit.*), crackers (*Brit. sl.*), crackpot (*inf.*), crazed, crazy (*inf.*), demented, deranged, distracted, doolally (*sl.*), frantic, frenzied, loony (*sl.*), loopy (*inf.*), lunatic, mental (*sl.*), *non compos mentis,* not right in the head, nuts (*sl.*), nutty (*sl.*), of unsound mind, out of one's mind, out to lunch (*inf.*), psychotic, rabid, raving, round the bend (*Brit. sl.*), round the twist (*Brit. sl.*), screwy (*inf.*), unbalanced, unhinged, unstable, up the pole (*inf.*) **2** = **foolish,** absurd, as daft as a brush (*inf., chiefly Brit.*), asinine, daft (*inf.*), foolhardy, imprudent, inane, irrational, ludicrous, nonsensical, preposterous, senseless, unreasonable, unsafe, unsound, wild **3** *Informal* = **angry,** ape (*sl.*), berserk, choked, cross, enraged, exasperated, fit to be tied (*sl.*), fuming, furious, incandescent, incensed, infuriated, irate, irritated, livid (*inf.*), raging, resentful, seeing red (*inf.*), wild, wrathful **4** = **enthusiastic,** ardent, avid, crazy (*inf.*), daft (*inf.*), devoted, dotty (*sl., chiefly Brit.*), enamoured, fanatical, fond, hooked, impassioned, infatuated, in love with, keen, nuts (*sl.*), wild, zealous **5** = **frenzied,** abandoned, agitated, boisterous, ebullient, energetic, excited, frenetic, full-on (*inf.*), gay, riotous, uncontrolled, unrestrained, wild **8 like mad** *Informal* = **energetically,** enthusiastically, excitedly, furiously, hell for leather, like greased lightning (*inf.*), like lightning, like nobody's business (*inf.*), like the clappers (*Brit. inf.*), madly, quickly, rapidly, speedily, unrestrainedly, violently, wildly, with might and main
Antonyms *adj* ≠ **insane:** rational, sane ≠ **foolish:** sensible, sound ≠ **angry:** appeased, calm, composed, cool, mollified ≠ **enthusiastic:** nonchalant, uncaring

madcap *adj* **1** = **reckless,** crackpot, crazy, foolhardy, hare-brained, heedless, hot-headed, ill-advised, imprudent, impulsive, lively, rash, thoughtless, wild ◆ *n* **2** = **daredevil,** hothead, tearaway, wild man

madden *vb* = **infuriate,** aggravate, annoy, craze, dement, derange, drive one crazy, enrage, exasperate, gall, get one's back up, get one's dander up (*inf.*), get one's goat (*sl.*), get one's hackles up, incense, inflame, irritate, make one's blood boil, make one see red (*inf.*), make one's hackles rise, provoke, put one's back up, raise one's hackles, unhinge, upset, vex
Antonyms *vb* appease, calm, mollify, pacify, soothe

made-up *adj* **1** = **false,** fabricated, fictional, imaginary, invented, make-believe, mythical, specious, trumped-up, unreal, untrue

madhouse *Informal n* **1** = **mental hospital,** funny farm (*facetious*), insane asylum, laughing academy (*US sl.*), loony bin (*sl.*), lunatic asylum, mental institution, nuthouse (*sl.*), psychiatric hospital, rubber room (*US sl.*) **2** = **chaos,** Babel, bedlam, pandemonium, turmoil, uproar

madly *adv* **1** = **insanely,** crazily, deliriously, dementedly, distractedly, frantically, frenziedly, hysterically, rabidly **1** = **foolishly,** absurdly, irrationally, ludicrously, nonsensically, senselessly, unreasonably, wildly **2** = **energetically,** excitedly, furiously, hastily, hell for leather, hotfoot, hurriedly, like greased lightning (*inf.*), like lightning, like mad (*inf.*), like nobody's business (*inf.*), like the clappers (*Brit. inf.*), quickly, rapidly, recklessly, speedily, violently, wildly **3** *Informal* = **passionately,** desperately, devotedly, exceedingly, excessively, extremely, intensely, to distraction

madman *n* = **lunatic,** headbanger (*inf.*), headcase (*inf.*), loony (*sl.*), maniac, mental case

madness ❶ (ˈmædnɪs) *n* **1** insanity; lunacy. **2** extreme anger, excitement, or foolishness. **3** a nontechnical word for **rabies.**

Madonna (məˈdɒnə) *n* **1** *Chiefly RC Church.* a designation of the Virgin Mary. **2** (*sometimes not cap.*) a picture or statue of the Virgin Mary. [C16: It., from *ma* my + *donna* lady]

Madonna lily *n* a perennial widely cultivated Mediterranean lily plant with white trumpet-shaped flowers.

madras (ˈmædrəs, məˈdræs) *n* **1** a strong fine cotton or silk fabric, usually with a woven stripe. **2** a medium-hot curry: *chicken madras.* [from *Madras,* city in S India]

madrepore (ˌmædrɪˈpɔː) *n* any coral of the genus *Madrepora,* many of which occur in tropical seas and form large coral reefs. [C18: via F from It. *madrepora* mother-stone]
▸ **ˌmadreˈporal, madreporic** (ˌmædrɪˈpɒrɪk), *or* **ˌmadreˈporian** *adj*

madrigal (ˈmædrɪgᵊl) *n* **1** *Music.* a type of 16th- or 17th-century part song for unaccompanied voices, with an amatory or pastoral text. **2** a short love poem. [C16: from It., from Med. L *mātricāle* primitive, apparently from L *mātrīcālis,* from *matrīx* womb]
▸ **ˈmadrigalˌesque** *adj* ▸ **madrigalian** (ˌmædrɪˈgælɪən, -ˈgeɪ-) *adj* ▸ **ˈmadrigalist** *n*

Maecenas (miːˈsiːnæs) *n* a wealthy patron of the arts. [after Gaius *Maecenas* (?70–8 B.C.), Roman statesman and patron of Horace and Virgil]

maelstrom ❶ (ˈmeɪlstrəʊm) *n* **1** a large powerful whirlpool. **2** any turbulent confusion. [C17: from obs. Du. *maelstroom,* from *malen* to whirl round + *stroom* STREAM]

maenad (ˈmiːnæd) *n* **1** *Classical history.* a woman participant in the orgiastic rites of Dionysus, Greek god of wine. **2** a frenzied woman. [C16: from L *Maenas,* from Gk *mainas* madwoman]
▸ **maeˈnadic** *adj*

maestoso (maɪˈstəʊsəʊ) *Music.* ◆ *adj, adv* **1** to be performed majestically. ◆ *n, pl* **maestosos. 2** a piece or passage directed to be played in this way. [C18: It.: majestic, from L *māiestās* MAJESTY]

maestro ❶ (ˈmaɪstrəʊ) *n, pl* **maestri** (-trɪ) *or* **maestros. 1** a distinguished music teacher, conductor, or musician. **2** any master of an art: often used as a term of address. [C18: It.: master]

mae west (meɪ) *n Sl.* an inflatable life jacket, esp. as issued to the US armed forces. [C20: after *Mae West* (1892–1980), US actress, renowned for her large bust]

MAFF (in Britain) *abbrev. for* Ministry of Agriculture, Fisheries, and Food.

Mafia (ˈmæfɪə) *n* **1 the.** an international secret criminal organization founded in Sicily, and carried to the US by Italian immigrants. **2** any group considered to resemble the Mafia. [C19: from Sicilian dialect of It., lit.: hostility to the law, ?from Ar. *mahyah* bragging]

mafioso (ˌmæfɪˈəʊsəʊ) *n, pl* **mafiosos** *or* **mafiosi** (-sɪ). a person belonging to the Mafia.

mag. *abbrev. for:* **1** magazine. **2** magnesium. **3** magnetic. **4** magnetism. **5** magnitude.

magainin (məˈgeɪnɪn) *n* any of a series of related substances with antibiotic properties, derived from the skins of frogs. [C20: from Heb. *magain* a shield]

magazine ❶ (ˌmægəˈziːn) *n* **1** a periodical paperback publication containing articles, fiction, photographs, etc. **2** a metal case holding several cartridges used in some firearms; it is removed and replaced when empty. **3** a building or compartment for storing weapons, explosives, military provisions, etc. **4** a stock of ammunition. **5** *Photog.* another name for **cartridge** (sense 3). **6** a rack for automatically feeding slides through a projector. **7** a TV or radio programme made up of a series of short nonfiction items. [C16: via F *magasin* from It. *magazzino,* from Ar. *makhāzin,* pl. of *makhzan* storehouse, from *khazana* to store away]

magdalen (ˈmægdəlɪn) *or* **magdalene** (ˈmægdəˌliːn) *n* **1** *Literary.* a reformed prostitute. **2** *Rare.* a reformatory for prostitutes. [from Mary *Magdalene* (New Testament), a woman from Magdala in Israel, often identified with the sinful woman of Luke 7:36–50]

Magdalenian (ˌmægdəˈliːnɪən) *adj* **1** of or relating to the latest Palaeolithic culture in Europe, which ended about 10 000 years ago. ◆ *n* **2 the.** the Magdalenian culture. [C19: from F *magdalénien,* after *La Madeleine,* village in Dordogne, France, near which artefacts of the culture were found]

Magellanic cloud (ˌmægɪˈlænɪk) *n* either of two small irregular galaxies near the S celestial pole. Distances: 163 000 light years (Large Magellanic Cloud), 196 000 light years (Small Magellanic Cloud).

magenta (məˈdʒɛntə) *n* **1a** a deep purplish red. **1b** (*as adj*): *a magenta filter.* **2** another name for **fuchsin.** [C19: after *Magenta,* Italy, alluding to the blood shed in a battle there (1859)]

maggot (ˈmægət) *n* **1** the limbless larva of dipterous insects, esp. the housefly and blowfly. **2** *Rare.* a fancy or whim. [C14: from earlier *mathek;* rel. to ON *mathkr* worm, OE *matha,* OHG *mado* grub]

maggoty (ˈmægətɪ) *adj* **1** of, like, or ridden with maggots. **2** *Austral. sl.* angry.

magi (ˈmeɪdʒaɪ) *pl n, sing* **magus** (ˈmeɪgəs). **1** See **magus. 2 the three Magi.** the wise men from the East who came to do homage to the infant Jesus (Matthew 2:1–12). [see MAGUS]
▸ **magian** (ˈmeɪdʒɪən) *adj*

magic ❶ (ˈmædʒɪk) *n* **1** the art that, by use of spells, supposedly invokes supernatural powers to influence events; sorcery. **2** the practice of this art. **3** the practice of illusory tricks to entertain; conjuring. **4** any mysterious or extraordinary quality or power. **5 like magic.** very quickly. ◆ *adj also* **magical. 6** of or relating to magic. **7** possessing or considered to possess mysterious powers. **8** unaccountably enchanting. **9** *Inf.* wonderful; marvellous. ◆ *vb* **magics, magicking, magicked.** (*tr*) **10** to transform or produce by or as if by magic. **11** (foll. by *away*) to cause to disappear as if by magic. [C14: via OF *magique,* from Gk *magikē* witchcraft, from *magos* MAGUS]
▸ **ˈmagically** *adv*

magic bullet *n Inf.* any therapeutic agent, esp. one in the early stages of development, reputed to be very effective in treating a condition, such as a malignant tumour, by specifically targeting the diseased tissue.

magic eye *n* a miniature cathode-ray tube in some radio receivers, on the screen of which a pattern is displayed to assist tuning. Also called: **electric eye.**

magician ❶ (məˈdʒɪʃən) *n* **1** another term for **conjuror. 2** a person who practises magic. **3** a person with extraordinary skill, influence, etc.

magic lantern *n* an early type of slide projector.

magic mushroom *n Inf.* any of various types of fungi that contain a hallucinogenic substance.

magic realism *or* **magical realism** *n* a style of painting or writing that depicts images or scenes of surreal fantasy in a representational or realistic way.
▸ **magic realist** *or* **magical realist** *n*

magic square *n* a square array of rows of integers arranged so that the sum of the integers is the same when taken vertically, horizontally, or diagonally.

Maginot line (ˈmæʒɪˌnəʊ) *n* **1** a line of fortifications built by France to defend its border with Germany prior to World War II; it proved ineffective. **2** any line of defence in which blind confidence is placed. [after André *Maginot* (1877–1932), F minister of war when the fortifications were begun in 1929]

magisterial ❶ (ˌmædʒɪˈstɪərɪəl) *adj* **1** commanding; authoritative. **2** domineering; dictatorial. **3** of or relating to a teacher or person of similar status. **4** of or relating to a magistrate. [C17: from LL *magisteriālis,* from *magister* master]
▸ **ˌmagisˈterially** *adv*

magistracy (ˈmædʒɪstrəsɪ) *or* **magistrature** (ˈmædʒɪstrəˌtjʊə) *n, pl* **magistracies** *or* **magistratures. 1** the office or function of a magistrate. **2** magistrates collectively. **3** the district under the jurisdiction of a magistrate.

magistral (məˈdʒɪstrəl) *adj* **1** *Pharmacol.* made up according to a special prescription. **2** of a master; masterly. [C16: from L *magistrālis,* from *magister* master]
▸ **magistrality** (ˌmædʒɪˈstrælɪtɪ) *n*

magistrate ❶ (ˈmædʒɪˌstreɪt, -strɪt) *n* **1** a public officer concerned with the administration of law. **2** another name for **justice of the peace.** [C17: from L *magistrātus,* from *magister* master]
▸ **ˈmagisˌtrateship** *n*

magistrates' court *n* (in England) a court held before two or more justices of the peace or a stipendiary magistrate to deal with minor crimes, certain civil actions, and preliminary hearings.

Maglemosian *or* **Maglemosean** (ˌmægləˈməʊzɪən) *n* **1** the first Mesolithic culture of N Europe, dating from 8000 B.C. to about 5000 B.C. ◆ *adj* **2** designating or relating to this culture. [C20: after the site at *Maglemose,* Denmark, where the culture was first classified]

magma (ˈmægmə) *n, pl* **magmas** *or* **magmata** (-mətə). **1** a paste or suspension consisting of a finely divided solid dispersed in a liquid. **2** hot molten rock within the earth's crust which sometimes finds its way to the surface where it solidifies to form igneous rock. [C15: from L:

THESAURUS

(*sl.*), nut (*sl.*), nutcase (*sl.*), nutter (*Brit. sl.*), psycho (*sl.*), psychopath, psychotic

madness *n* **1** = **insanity,** aberration, craziness, delusion, dementia, derangement, distraction, lunacy, mania, mental illness, psychopathy, psychosis **2** = **anger,** exasperation, frenzy, fury, ire, rage, raving, wildness, wrath **2** = **frenzy,** abandon, agitation, excitement, furore, intoxication, riot, unrestraint, uproar **2** = **foolishness,** absurdity, daftness (*inf.*), folly, foolhardiness, idiocy, nonsense, preposterousness, wildness

maelstrom *n* **1** = **whirlpool,** vortex **2** = **turmoil,** bedlam, chaos, confusion, disorder, pandemonium, tumult, upheaval, uproar

maestro *n* **2** = **master,** expert, genius, virtuoso

magazine *n* **1** = **journal,** pamphlet, paper, periodical **3** = **storehouse,** ammunition dump, arsenal, depot, powder room (*obs.*), store, warehouse

magic *n* **1, 2** = **sorcery,** black art, enchantment, necromancy, occultism, sortilege, spell, theurgy, witchcraft, wizardry **3** = **conjuring,** hocus-pocus, illusion, jiggery-pokery (*inf., chiefly Brit.*), jugglery, legerdemain, prestidigitation, sleight of hand, trickery **4** = **charm,** allurement, enchantment, fascination, glamour, magnetism, power ◆ *adj* **8** = **miraculous,** bewitching, charismatic, charming, enchanting, entrancing, fascinating, magnetic, marvellous, spellbinding

magician *n* **1, 2** = **sorcerer,** archimage (*rare*), conjuror *or* conjuror, enchanter *or* enchantress, illusionist, necromancer, thaumaturge (*rare*), theurgist, warlock, witch, wizard **3** = **miracle-worker,** genius, marvel, spellbinder, virtuoso, wizard, wonder-worker

magisterial *adj* **1** = **authoritative,** commanding, imperious, lordly, masterful
Antonyms *adj* deferential, diffident, humble, servile, shy, submissive, subservient, wimpish *or* wimpy (*inf.*)

magistrate *n* **1, 2** = **judge,** bailie, J.P., justice, justice of the peace, provost (*Scot.*)

dregs (of an ointment), from Gk: salve made by kneading, from *massein* to knead]
▸**magmatic** (mæg'mætɪk) *adj*

Magna Carta *or* **Magna Charta** ('mægnə 'kɑːtə) *n English history.* the charter granted by King John at Runnymede in 1215, recognizing the rights and privileges of the barons, church, and freemen. [Med. L: great charter]

magnanimity ⓣ (ˌmægnə'nɪmɪtɪ) *n, pl* **magnanimities.** generosity. [C14: via OF from L *magnanimitās,* from *magnus* great + *animus* soul]

magnanimous ⓣ (mæg'nænɪməs) *adj* generous and noble. [C16: from L *magnanimus* great-souled]
▸**mag'nanimously** *adv*

magnate ⓣ ('mægneɪt, -nɪt) *n* **1** a person of power and rank, esp. in industry. **2** *History.* a great nobleman. [C15: back formation from earlier *magnates,* from LL: great men, from L *magnus* great]
▸**'magnateˌship** *n*

magnesia (mæg'niːʃə) *n* another name for **magnesium oxide.** [C14: via Med. L from Gk *Magnēsia,* of *Magnēs,* ancient mineral-rich region]
▸**mag'nesian** *or* **magnesic** (mæg'niːsɪk) *adj*

magnesium (mæg'niːzɪəm) *n* a light silvery-white metallic element of the alkaline earth series that burns with an intense white flame: used in light structural alloys, flashbulbs, flares, and fireworks. Symbol: Mg; atomic no.: 12; atomic wt.: 24.305. [C19: NL, from MAGNESIA]

magnesium oxide *n* a white tasteless substance used as an antacid and laxative and in refractory materials. Formula: MgO. Also called: **magnesia.**

magnet ('mægnɪt) *n* **1** a body that can attract certain substances, such as iron or steel, as a result of a magnetic field; a piece of ferromagnetic substance. See also **electromagnet. 2** a person or thing that exerts a great attraction. [C15: via L from Gk *magnēs,* shortened from *ho Magnēs lithos* the Magnesian stone. See MAGNESIA]

magnetic ⓣ (mæg'nɛtɪk) *adj* **1** of, producing, or operated by means of magnetism. **2** of or concerned with a magnet. **3** of or concerned with the magnetism of the earth: *the magnetic equator.* **4** capable of being magnetized. **5** exerting a powerful attraction: *a magnetic personality.*
▸**mag'netically** *adv*

magnetic constant *n* the magnetic permeability of free space; it has the value $4\pi \times 10^{-7}$ H m^{-1}.

magnetic declination *n* the angle that a compass needle makes with the direction of the geographical north pole at any given point on the earth's surface.

magnetic dip *or* **inclination** *n* another name for **dip** (sense 24).

magnetic dipole moment *n* a measure of the magnetic strength of a magnet or current-carrying coil, expressed as the torque produced when the magnet or coil is set with its axis perpendicular to unit magnetic field.

magnetic disk *n* another name for **disk** (sense 2).

magnetic equator *n* an imaginary line on the earth's surface, near the equator, at all points on which there is no magnetic dip.

magnetic field *n* a field of force surrounding a permanent magnet or a moving charged particle, in which another permanent magnet or moving charge experiences a force.

magnetic flux *n* a measure of the strength of a magnetic field over a given area, equal to the product of the area and the magnetic flux density through it. Symbol: ϕ

magnetic mine *n* a mine designed to explode when a magnetic field such as that generated by the metal of a ship's hull is detected.

magnetic needle *n* a slender magnetized rod used in certain instruments, such as the magnetic compass, for indicating the direction of a magnetic field.

magnetic north *n* the direction in which a compass needle points, at an angle (the declination) from the direction of true (geographic) north.

magnetic pick-up *n* a type of record-player pick-up in which the stylus moves an iron core in a coil, causing a changing magnetic field that produces the current.

magnetic pole *n* **1** either of two regions in a magnet where the magnetic induction is concentrated. **2** either of two variable points on the earth's surface towards which a magnetic needle points, where the lines of force of the earth's magnetic field are vertical.

magnetic resonance *n* the response by atoms, molecules, or nuclei subjected to a magnetic field to radio waves or other forms of energy: used in medicine for scanning (**magnetic resonance imaging**; abbrev.: **MRI**).

magnetic storm *n* a sudden severe disturbance of the earth's magnetic field, caused by emission of charged particles from the sun.

magnetic stripe *n* (across the back of various types of bank card, credit card, etc.) a dark stripe of magnetic material consisting of several tracks onto which information may be coded and which may be read or written to electronically.

magnetic tape *n* a long narrow plastic or metal strip coated or impregnated with iron oxide, chrome dioxide, etc., used to record sound or video signals or to store information in computing.

magnetism ⓣ ('mægnɪˌtɪzəm) *n* **1** the property of attraction displayed by magnets. **2** any of a class of phenomena in which a field of force is caused by a moving electric charge. **3** the branch of physics concerned with magnetic phenomena. **4** powerful attraction.

magnetite ('mægnɪˌtaɪt) *n* a black magnetizable mineral that is an important source of iron.

magnetize *or* **magnetise** ('mægnɪˌtaɪz) *vb* **magnetizes, magnetizing, magnetized** *or* **magnetises, magnetising, magnetised.** (*tr*) **1** to make (a substance or object) magnetic. **2** to attract strongly.
▸**'magnetˌizable** *or* **'magnetˌisable** *adj* ▸**ˌmagneti'zation** *or* **ˌmagneti'sation** *n* ▸**'magnetˌizer** *or* **'magnetˌiser** *n*

magneto (mæg'niːtəʊ) *n, pl* **magnetos.** a small electric generator in which the magnetic field is produced by a permanent magnet, esp. one for providing the spark in an internal-combustion engine. [C19: short for *magnetoelectric generator*]

magneto- *combining form.* indicating magnetism or magnetic properties: *magnetosphere.*

magnetoelectricity (mægˌniːtəʊɪlɛk'trɪsɪtɪ) *n* electricity produced by the action of magnetic fields.
▸**magˌnetoe'lectric** *or* **magˌnetoe'lectrical** *adj*

magnetometer (ˌmægnɪ'tɒmɪtə) *n* any instrument for measuring the intensity or direction of a magnetic field, esp. the earth's field.
▸**ˌmagne'tometry** *n*

magnetomotive (mægˌniːtəʊ'məʊtɪv) *adj* causing a magnetic flux.

magnetosphere (mæg'niːtəʊˌsfɪə) *n* the region surrounding a planet, such as the earth, in which the behaviour of charged particles is controlled by the planet's magnetic field.

magnetron ('mægnɪˌtrɒn) *n* a two-electrode electronic valve used with an applied magnetic field to generate high-power microwave oscillations, esp. for use in radar. [C20: from MAGNET + ELECTRON]

magnet school *n* a school that provides a focus on one subject area throughout its curriculum in order to attract, often from an early age, pupils who wish to specialize in this subject.

Magnificat (mæg'nɪfɪˌkæt) *n Christianity.* the hymn of the Virgin Mary (Luke 1:46-55), used as a canticle. [from the opening phrase, *Magnificat anima mea Dominum* (my soul doth magnify the Lord)]

magnification ⓣ (ˌmægnɪfɪ'keɪʃən) *n* **1** the act of magnifying or the state of being magnified. **2** the degree to which something is magnified. **3** a magnified copy, photograph, drawing, etc., of something. **4** a measure of the ability of a lens or other optical instrument to magnify.

magnificence ⓣ (mæg'nɪfɪsəns) *n* the quality of being magnificent. [C14: via F from L *magnificentia*]

magnificent ⓣ (mæg'nɪfɪsᵊnt) *adj* **1** splendid or impressive in appearance. **2** superb or very fine. **3** (esp. of ideas) noble or elevated. [C16: from L *magnificentior,* irregular comp. of *magnificus* great in deeds, from *magnus* great + *facere* to do]
▸**mag'nificently** *adv*

magnifico (mæg'nɪfɪkəʊ) *n, pl* **magnificoes.** a magnate; grandee. [C16: It. from L *magnificus;* see MAGNIFICENT]

magnify ⓣ ('mægnɪˌfaɪ) *vb* **magnifies, magnifying, magnified. 1** to increase, cause to increase, or be increased in apparent size, as through the action of a lens, microscope, etc. **2** to exaggerate or become exaggerated

THESAURUS

magnanimity *n* = **generosity**, beneficence, benevolence, big-heartedness, bountifulness, charitableness, high-mindedness, largesse *or* largess, munificence, nobility, open-handedness, selflessness, unselfishness

magnanimous *adj* = **generous**, beneficent, big, big-hearted, bountiful, charitable, free, great-hearted, handsome, high-minded, kind, kindly, munificent, noble, open-handed, selfless, ungrudging, unselfish, unstinting
Antonyms *adj* miserly, petty, resentful, selfish, small, unforgiving, vindictive

magnate *n* **1** = **tycoon**, baron, big cheese (*sl., old-fashioned*), big hitter (*inf.*), big noise (*inf.*), big shot (*inf.*), big wheel (*sl.*), bigwig (*inf.*), captain of industry, chief, fat cat (*sl., chiefly US*), heavy hitter (*inf.*), leader, Mister Big (*sl., chiefly US*), mogul, nabob (*inf.*), notable, plutocrat, V.I.P. **2** *History* = **aristocrat**, aristo (*inf.*), baron, bashaw, grandee, magnifico, nob (*sl., chiefly Brit.*), noble, notable, personage, prince

magnetic *adj* **5** = **attractive**, alluring, captivating, charismatic, charming, enchanting, entrancing, fascinating, hypnotic, irresistible, mesmerizing, seductive
Antonyms *adj* disagreeable, offensive, repellent, repulsive, unappealing, unattractive, unlikable *or* unlikeable, unpleasant

magnetism *n* **4** = **charm**, allure, appeal, attraction, attractiveness, captivatingness, charisma, draw, drawing power, enchantment, fascination, hypnotism, magic, mesmerism, power, pull, seductiveness, spell

magnification *n* **1, 3** = **increase**, aggrandizement, amplification, augmentation, blow-up (*inf.*), boost, build-up, deepening, dilation, enhancement, enlargement, exaggeration, expansion, heightening, inflation, intensification

magnificence *n* = **splendour**, brilliance, éclat, glory, gorgeousness, grandeur, luxuriousness, luxury, majesty, nobility, opulence, pomp, resplendence, stateliness, sublimity, sumptuousness

magnificent *adj* **1** = **splendid**, august, elegant, elevated, exalted, glorious, gorgeous, grand, grandiose, imposing, impressive, lavish, luxurious, majestic, noble, opulent, princely, regal, resplendent, rich, splendiferous (*facetious*), stately, striking, sublime, sumptuous, transcendent **2** = **excellent**, brilliant, divine (*inf.*), fine, outstanding, splendid, superb, superior
Antonyms *adj* bad, humble, ignoble, lowly, mean, modest, ordinary, petty, poor, trivial, undistinguished, unimposing

magnify *vb* **1** = **enlarge**, aggrandize, amplify, augment, blow up, boost, build up, deepen, dilate, expand, heighten, increase, intensify **2** = **overstate**, aggravate, blow up, blow up out of

in importance: *don't magnify your troubles.* **3** (*tr*) *Arch.* to glorify. [C14: via OF from L *magnificāre* to praise]
▸ **'magni,fiable** *adj*

magnifying glass *or* **magnifier** *n* a convex lens used to produce an enlarged image of an object.

magniloquent ❶ (mæg'nɪləkwənt) *adj* (of speech) lofty in style; grandiloquent. [C17: from L *magnus* great + *loquī* to speak]
▸ **mag'niloquence** *n* ▸ **mag'niloquently** *adv*

magnitude ❶ ('mægnɪ,tjuːd) *n* **1** relative importance or significance: *a problem of the first magnitude.* **2** relative size or extent. **3** *Maths.* a number assigned to a quantity as a basis of comparison for the measurement of similar quantities. **4** Also called: **apparent magnitude.** *Astron.* the apparent brightness of a celestial body expressed on a numerical scale on which bright stars have a low value. **5** Also called: **earthquake magnitude.** *Geol.* a measure of the size of an earthquake based on the quantity of energy released. [C14: from L *magnitūdō* size, from *magnus* great]

magnolia (mæg'nəʊlɪə) *n* **1** any tree or shrub of the genus *Magnolia* of Asia and North America: cultivated for their white, pink, purple, or yellow showy flowers. **2** the flower of any of these plants. **3a** a very pale pinkish-white colour. **3b** (*as adj*): *magnolia walls.* [C18: NL, after Pierre *Magnol* (1638–1715), F botanist]

magnox ('mægnɒks) *n* an alloy consisting mostly of magnesium with small amounts of aluminium, used in fuel elements of nuclear reactors. [C20: from *mag(nesium) n(o) ox(idation)*]

magnox reactor *n* a nuclear reactor using carbon dioxide as the coolant, graphite as the moderator, and uranium cased in magnox as the fuel.

magnum ('mægnəm) *n, pl* **magnums.** a wine bottle holding the equivalent of two normal bottles (approximately 52 fluid ounces). [C18: from L: a big thing, from *magnus* large]

magnum opus *n* a great work of art or literature, esp. the greatest single work of an artist. [L]

magpie ('mæg,paɪ) *n* **1** any of various birds having a black-and-white plumage, long tail, and a chattering call. **2** any of various similar birds of Australia. **3** *Brit.* a person who hoards small objects. **4** a person who chatters. **5a** the outermost ring but one on a target. **5b** a shot that hits this ring. [C17: from *Mag,* dim. of *Margaret,* used to signify a chatterbox + PIE[2]]

maguey ('mægweɪ) *n* **1** any of various tropical American agave plants, esp. one that yields a fibre or is used in making an alcoholic beverage. **2** the fibre from any of these plants, used esp. for rope. [C16: Sp., of Amerind origin]

magus ('meɪgəs) *n, pl* **magi. 1** a Zoroastrian priest. **2** an astrologer, sorcerer, or magician of ancient times. [C14: from L, from Gk *magos,* from OPersian *magus* magician]

Magyar ('mægjɑː) *n* **1** (*pl* **Magyars**) a member of the predominant ethnic group of Hungary. **2** the Hungarian language. ◆ *adj* **3** of or relating to the Magyars or their language. **4** *Sewing.* of or relating to a style of sleeve cut in one piece with the bodice.

Mahabharata (,mɑːhə'bɑːrətə), **Mahabharatam,** *or* **Mahabharatum** (,mɑːhə'bɑːrətəm) *n* an epic Sanskrit poem of India of which the *Bhagavad-Gita* forms a part. [Sansk., from *mahā* great + *bhārata* story]

maharajah *or* **maharaja** (,mɑːhə'rɑːdʒə) *n* any of various Indian princes, esp. any of the rulers of the former native states. [C17: Hindi, from *mahā* great + RAJAH]

maharani *or* **maharanee** (,mɑːhə'rɑːniː) *n* **1** the wife of a maharajah. **2** a woman holding the rank of maharajah. [C19: from Hindi, from *mahā* great + RANI]

maharishi (,mɑːhə'riːʃɪ, mə'hɑːriːʃɪ) *n Hinduism.* a Hindu teacher of religious and mystical knowledge. [from Hindi, from *mahā* great + *rishi* sage]

mahatma (mə'hɑːtmə) *n* (*sometimes cap.*) **1** *Hinduism.* a Brahman sage. **2** *Theosophy.* an adept or sage. [C19: from Sansk. *mahātman,* from *mahā* great + *ātman* soul]

Mahayana (,mɑːhə'jɑːnə) *n* **a** a liberal Buddhist school of Tibet, China, and Japan, whose adherents seek enlightenment for all sentient beings. **b** (*as modifier*): *Mahayana Buddhism.* [from Sansk., from *mahā* great + *yāna* vehicle]

Mahdi ('mɑːdɪ) *n Islam.* any of a number of Muslim messiahs expected to convert all mankind to Islam by force. [Ar. *mahdīy* one who is guided, from *madā* to guide aright]
▸ **'Mahdism** *n* ▸ **'Mahdist** *n, adj*

mah jong *or* **mah-jongg** (,mɑː'dʒɒŋ) *n* a game of Chinese origin, usually played by four people, using tiles bearing various designs. [from Chinese, lit.: sparrows]

mahlstick ('mɔːl,stɪk) *n* a variant spelling of **maulstick.**

mahogany (mə'hɒgənɪ) *n, pl* **mahoganies. 1** any of various tropical American trees valued for their hard reddish-brown wood. **2** any of several trees with similar wood, such as African mahogany and Philippine mahogany. **3a** the wood of any of these trees. **3b** (*as modifier*): *a mahogany table.* **4a** a reddish-brown colour. **4b** (*as adj*): *mahogany skin.* [C17: from ?]

Mahometan (mə'hɒmɪtᵊn) *n, adj* a former word for **Muslim.**

mahonia (mə'həʊnɪə) *n* any evergreen shrub of the Asian and American genus *Mahonia:* cultivated for their ornamental spiny divided leaves and clusters of small yellow flowers. [C19: NL, after Bernard *McMahon* (died 1816), American botanist]

mahout (mə'haʊt) *n* (in India and the East Indies) an elephant driver or keeper. [C17: Hindi *mahāut,* from Sansk. *mahāmātra* of great measure, orig. a title]

mahseer ('mɑːsɪə) *n* any of various large freshwater Indian cyprinid fishes. [from Hindi]

maid ❶ (meɪd) *n* **1** *Arch. or literary.* a young unmarried girl; maiden. **2a** a female servant. **2b** (*in combination*): *a housemaid.* **3** a spinster. [C12: form of MAIDEN]

maiden ❶ ('meɪdᵊn) *n* **1** *Arch. or literary.* **1a** a young unmarried girl, esp. a virgin. **1b** (*as modifier*): *a maiden blush.* **2** *Horse racing.* **2a** a horse that has never won a race. **2b** (*as modifier*): *a maiden race.* **3** *Cricket.* See **maiden over. 4** (*modifier*) of or relating to an older unmarried woman: *a maiden aunt.* **5** (*modifier*) of or involving an initial experience or attempt: *a maiden voyage.* **6** (*modifier*) (of a person or thing) untried; unused. **7** (*modifier*) (of a place) never trodden, penetrated, or captured. [OE *mægden*]
▸ **'maidenish** *adj* ▸ **'maiden,like** *adj*

maidenhair fern *or* **maidenhair** ('meɪdᵊn,hɛə) *n* any of various ferns of tropical and warm regions, having delicate fan-shaped fronds with small pale green leaflets. [C15: from the hairlike appearance of its fronds]

maidenhair tree *n* another name for **ginkgo.**

maidenhead ('meɪdᵊn,hɛd) *n* **1** a nontechnical word for the **hymen. 2** virginity; maidenhood. [C13: from *maiden* + *-hed,* var. of -HOOD]

maidenhood ('meɪdᵊn,hʊd) *n* **1** the time during which a woman is a maiden or virgin. **2** the condition of being a maiden or virgin.

maidenly ❶ ('meɪdᵊnlɪ) *adj* of or befitting a maiden.
▸ **'maidenliness** *n*

maiden name *n* a woman's surname before marriage.

maiden over *n Cricket.* an over in which no runs are scored.

maid of honour *n* **1** *US & Canad.* the principal unmarried attendant of a bride. **2** *Brit.* a small tart with an almond-flavoured filling. **3** an unmarried lady attending a queen or princess.

maidservant ('meɪd,sɜːvənt) *n* a female servant.

maihem ('meɪhɛm) *n* a variant spelling of **mayhem.**

mail[1] ❶ (meɪl) *n* **1** Also called (esp. Brit.): **post.** letters, packages, etc., that are transported and delivered by the post office. **2** the postal system. **3** a single collection or delivery of mail. **4** a train, ship, or aircraft that carries mail. **5** short for **electronic mail. 6** (*modifier*) of, involving, or used to convey mail: *a mail train.* ◆ *vb* (*tr*) **7** *Chiefly US & Canad.* to send by mail. **8** to contact (a person) by electronic mail. **9** to send (a message, document, etc.) by electronic mail. [C13: from OF *male* bag, prob. from OHG *malha* wallet]
▸ **'mailable** *adj*

mail[2] (meɪl) *n* **1** a type of flexible armour consisting of riveted metal rings or links. **2** the hard protective shell of such animals as the turtle and lobster. ◆ *vb* **3** (*tr*) to clothe or arm with mail. [C14: from OF *maille* mesh, from L *macula* spot]

mailbag ('meɪl,bæg) *or* **mailsack** *n* a large bag for transporting or delivering mail.

mailbox ('meɪl,bɒks) *n* another name (esp. US and Canad.) for **letter box.**

mailing list *n* a register of names and addresses to which advertising matter, etc., is sent by post or electronic mail.

maillot (mæ'jəʊ) *n* **1** tights worn for ballet, gymnastics, etc. **2** a woman's swimsuit. **3** a jersey. [from F]

mailman ('meɪl,mæn) *n, pl* **mailmen.** *Chiefly US & Canad.* another name for **postman.**

mail merging *n Computing.* a software facility that can produce a large

THESAURUS

all proportion, dramatize, enhance, exaggerate, inflate, make a mountain out of a molehill, make a production (out) of (*inf.*), overdo, overemphasize, overestimate, overplay, overrate
Antonyms *vb* ≠ **enlarge:** decrease, diminish, lessen, lower, minimize, reduce, shrink ≠ **overstate:** belittle, deflate, denigrate, deprecate, disparage, understate

magniloquence *n* = **pomposity,** bombast, fustian, grandiloquence, loftiness, pretentiousness, turgidity

magniloquent *adj* = **pompous,** arty-farty (*inf.*), bombastic, declamatory, elevated, exalted, grandiloquent, high-flown, high-sounding, lofty, orotund, overblown, pretentious, rhetorical, sonorous, stilted, turgid

magnitude *n* **1** = **importance,** consequence, eminence, grandeur, greatness, mark, moment, note, significance, weight **2** = **size,** amount, amplitude, bigness, bulk, capacity, dimensions, enormity, expanse, extent, hugeness, immensity, intensity, largeness, mass, measure, proportions, quantity, space, strength, vastness, volume
Antonyms *n* ≠ **importance:** insignificance, triviality, unimportance ≠ **size:** meanness, smallness

maid *n* **1** *Archaic or literary* = **girl,** damsel, lass, lassie (*inf.*), maiden, miss, nymph (*poetic*), wench **2** = **servant,** abigail (*arch.*), handmaiden (*arch.*), housemaid, maidservant, serving-maid

maiden *n* **1** *Archaic or literary* = **girl,** damsel, lass, lassie (*inf.*), maid, miss, nymph (*poetic*), virgin, wench ◆ *adj* **5** = **first,** inaugural, initial, initiatory, introductory

maidenly *adj* = **modest,** chaste, decent, decorous, demure, gentle, girlish, pure, reserved, undefiled, unsullied, vestal, virginal, virtuous
Antonyms *adj* brazen, corrupt, defiled, depraved, dirty, immodest, immoral, impure, indecent, loose, promiscuous, shameless, sinful, unchaste, wanton, wicked

mail[1] *n* **1** = **letters,** correspondence, packages, parcels, post **2** = **postal service,** post, postal sys-

number of personalized letters by combining a file containing a list of names and addresses with one containing a single standard document.

mail order *n* **1** an order for merchandise sent by post. **2a** a system of buying and selling merchandise through the post. **2b** (*as modifier*): *a mail-order firm.*

mailshot ('meɪl,ʃɒt) *n* a circular, leaflet, or other advertising material sent by post, or the posting of such material to a large group of people at one time.

maim ❶ (meɪm) *vb* (*tr*) **1** to mutilate, cripple, or disable a part of the body of (a person or animal). **2** to make defective. [C14: from OF *mahaignier* to wound, prob. of Gmc origin]

mai mai (maɪ maɪ) *n NZ.* a duck shooter's shelter; hide. [probably from Australian Aboriginal *mia-mia* shelter]

main[1] ❶ (meɪn) *adj* (*prenominal*) **1** chief or principal. **2** sheer or utmost (esp. in **by main force**). **3** *Naut.* of, relating to, or denoting any gear, such as a stay or sail, belonging to the mainmast. ◆ *n* **4** a principal pipe, conduit, duct, or line in a system used to distribute water, electricity, etc. **5** (*pl*) **5a** the main distribution network for water, gas, or electricity. **5b** (*as modifier*): *mains voltage.* **6** the chief or most important part or consideration. **7** great strength or force (now esp. in **might and main**). **8** *Literary.* the open ocean. **9** *Arch.* short for **Spanish Main. 10** *Arch.* short for **mainland. 11 in** (*or* **for**) **the main.** on the whole; for the most part. [C13: from OE *mægen* strength]

main[2] (meɪn) *n* **1** a throw of the dice in dice games. **2** a cockfighting contest. **3** a match in archery, boxing, etc. [C16: from ?]

mainbrace ('meɪn,breɪs) *n Naut.* **1** a brace attached to the main yard. **2 splice the mainbrace.** See **splice.**

main clause *n Grammar.* a clause that can stand alone as a sentence.

mainframe ('meɪn,freɪm) *Computing.* ◆ *adj* **1** denoting a high-speed general-purpose computer, usually with a large store capacity. ◆ *n* **2** such a computer. **3** the central processing unit of a computer.

mainland ('meɪnlənd) *n* the main part of a landmass as opposed to an island or peninsula.
▸**'mainlander** *n*

main line *n* **1** *Railways.* **1a** the trunk route between two points, usually fed by branch lines. **1b** (*as modifier*): *a main-line station.* **2** *US.* a main road. ◆ *vb* **mainline, mainlines, mainlining, mainlined. 3** (*intr*) *Sl.* to inject a drug into a vein. ◆ *adj* **mainline. 4** having an important position.
▸**'main,liner** *n*

mainly ❶ ('meɪnlɪ) *adv* for the most part; to the greatest extent; principally.

main market *n* the market for trading in the listed securities of companies on the London stock exchange. Cf. **Third Market, Unlisted Securities Market.**

mainmast ('meɪn,mɑːst) *n Naut.* the chief mast of a sailing vessel with two or more masts.

mainsail ('meɪn,seɪl; *Naut.* 'meɪnsᵊl) *n Naut.* the largest and lowermost sail on the mainmast.

mainsheet ('meɪn,ʃiːt) *n Naut.* the line used to control the angle of the mainsail to the wind.

mainspring ❶ ('meɪn,sprɪŋ) *n* **1** the principal spring of a mechanism, esp. in a watch or clock. **2** the chief cause or motive of something.

mainstay ❶ ('meɪn,steɪ) *n* **1** *Naut.* the forestay that braces the mainmast. **2** a chief support.

mainstream ❶ ('meɪn,striːm) *n* **1** the main current (of a river, cultural trend, etc.). ◆ *adj* **2** of or relating to the style of jazz that lies between the traditional and the modern.

mainstream corporation tax *n* (in Britain) the balance of the corporation tax paid by a company for an accounting period after the advance corporation tax has been deducted.

mainstreeting ('meɪn,striːtɪŋ) *n Canad.* the practice of a politician walking about the streets of a town or city to gain votes and greet supporters.

maintain ❶ (meɪn'teɪn) *vb* (*tr*) **1** to continue or retain; keep in existence. **2** to keep in proper or good condition. **3** to enable (a person) to support a style of living: *the money maintained us for a month.* **4** (*takes a clause as object*) to state or assert. **5** to defend against contradiction; uphold: *she maintained her innocence.* **6** to defend against physical attack. [C13: from OF *maintenir,* ult. from L *manū tenēre* to hold in the hand]
▸**main'tainable** *adj* ▸**main'tainer** *n*

maintenance ❶ ('meɪntɪnəns) *n* **1** the act of maintaining or the state of being maintained. **2** a means of support; livelihood. **3** (*modifier*) of or relating to the maintaining of buildings, machinery, etc.: *maintenance man.* **4** *Law.* the interference in a legal action by a person having no interest in it, as by providing funds to continue the action. **5** *Law.* a provision ordered to be made by way of periodical payments or a lump sum, as for a spouse after a divorce. [C14: from OF; see MAINTAIN]

maintop ('meɪn,tɒp) *n* a top or platform at the head of the mainmast.

main-topmast *n Naut.* the mast immediately above the mainmast.

maintopsail (,meɪn'tɒpseɪl; *Naut.* ,meɪn'tɒpsᵊl) *n Naut.* a topsail on the mainmast.

main yard *n Naut.* a yard for a square mainsail.

maiolica (mə'jɒlɪkə) *n* a variant of **majolica.**

maisonette *or* **maisonnette** (,meɪzə'nɛt) *n* self-contained living accommodation often occupying two floors of a larger house and having its own outside entrance. [C19: from F, dim. of *maison* house]

mai tai ('maɪ ,taɪ) *n* a mixed drink consisting of rum, Curaçao, fruit juice, and grenadine. [C20: from ?]

maître d'hôtel (,mɛtrə dəʊ'tɛl) *n, pl* **maîtres d'hôtel. 1** a head waiter or steward. **2** the manager or owner of a hotel. [C16: from F: master of (the) hotel]

maize (meɪz) *n* **1** Also called: **sweet corn, Indian corn. 1a** a tall annual grass cultivated for its yellow edible grains, which develop on a spike. **1b** the grain of this plant, used for food, for fodder, and as a source of oil. **2a** a yellow colour. **2b** (*as adj*): *a maize gown.* [C16: from Sp. *maíz,* from Taino *mahiz*]

Maj. *abbrev. for* Major.

majestic ❶ (mə'dʒɛstɪk) *adj* having or displaying majesty or great dignity; grand; lofty.
▸**ma'jestically** *adv*

majesty ❶ ('mædʒɪstɪ) *n* **1** great dignity of bearing; loftiness; grandeur. **2** supreme power or authority. [C13: from OF, from L *mājestās;* rel. to L *major,* comp. of *magnus* great]

Majesty ('mædʒɪstɪ) *n, pl* **Majesties.** (preceded by *Your, His, Her,* or *Their*) a title used to address or refer to a sovereign or the wife or widow of a sovereign.

majolica (mə'dʒɒlɪkə, mə'jɒl-) *or* **maiolica** *n* a type of porous pottery glazed with bright metallic oxides. It was originally imported into Italy via Majorca and was extensively made in Renaissance Italy. [C16: from It., from LL *Mājorica* Majorca]

major ❶ ('meɪdʒə) *n* **1** *Mil.* an officer immediately junior to a lieutenant colonel. **2** a person who is superior in a group or class. **3** (often preceded by *the*) *Music.* a major key, chord, mode, or scale. **4** *US, Canad., Austral., & NZ.* **4a** the principal field of study of a student. **4b** a student who is studying a particular subject as his principal field: *a sociology major.* **5** a person who has reached the age of legal majority. **6** a principal or important record company, film company, etc. **7** *Logic.* a major term or premise. ◆ *adj* **8** larger in extent, number, etc. **9** of greater importance or priority. **10** very serious or significant. **11** main, chief, or principal. **12** of, involving, or making up a majority. **13** *Music.* **13a** (of a scale or mode) having notes separated by a whole tone, except for the third and fourth degrees, and seventh and eighth degrees, which are separated by a semitone. **13b** relating to or employing notes from the major scale: *a major key.* **13c** (*postpositive*) denoting a specified key or scale as being major: *C major.* **13d** denoting a

THESAURUS

tem ◆ *vb* **7** = **post**, dispatch, forward, send, send by mail *or* post

maim *vb* **1** = **cripple**, disable, hamstring, hurt, impair, incapacitate, injure, lame, mangle, mar, mutilate, put out of action, wound

main[1] *adj* **1** = **chief**, capital, cardinal, central, critical, crucial, essential, foremost, head, leading, major, necessary, outstanding, paramount, particular, predominant, pre-eminent, premier, primary, prime, principal, special, supreme, vital **2** *As in* **by main force** = **sheer**, absolute, brute, direct, downright, entire, mere, pure, undisguised, utmost, utter ◆ *n* **4** = **conduit**, cable, channel, duct, line, pipe **7** = **force**, effort, might, potency, power, puissance, strength **11 in the main** = **on the whole**, for the most part, generally, in general, mainly, mostly
Antonyms *adj* ≠ **chief:** auxiliary, dependent, insignificant, least, lesser, minor, secondary, subordinate, trivial, unimportant

mainly *adv* = **chiefly**, above all, first and foremost, for the most part, generally, in general, in the main, largely, mostly, most of all, on the whole, overall, predominantly, primarily, principally, substantially, to the greatest extent, usually

mainspring *n* **2** = **cause**, driving force, generator, impulse, incentive, inspiration, motivation, motive, origin, prime mover, source

mainstay *n* **2** = **pillar**, anchor, backbone, bulwark, buttress, chief support, linchpin, prop

mainstream *adj* **2** = **conventional**, accepted, central, core, current, established, general, orthodox, prevailing, received
Antonyms *adj* fringe, marginal, peripheral, unconventional, unorthodox

maintain *vb* **1** = **continue**, carry on, conserve, keep, keep up, nurture, perpetuate, preserve, prolong, retain, sustain, uphold **3** = **look after**, care for, finance, provide for, supply, support, take care of **4** = **assert**, affirm, allege, asseverate, aver, avow, claim, contend, declare, hold, insist, profess, state **5** = **support**, advocate, argue for, back, champion, defend, fight for, justify, plead for, stand by, take up the cudgels for, uphold, vindicate
Antonyms *vb* ≠ **continue:** abolish, break off, conclude, discontinue, drop, end, finish, give up, relinquish, suspend, terminate ≠ **assert:** disavow ≠ **support:** abandon, desert

maintenance *n* **1** = **continuation**, carrying-on, continuance, perpetuation, prolongation, retainment, support, sustainment, sustention **1** = **upkeep**, care, conservation, keeping, nurture, preservation, provision, repairs, supply **2, 5** = **allowance**, aliment, alimony, food, keep, livelihood, living, subsistence, support, sustenance, upkeep

majestic *adj* = **grand**, august, awesome, dignified, elevated, exalted, grandiose, imperial, imposing, impressive, kingly, lofty, magnificent, monumental, noble, pompous, princely, regal, royal, splendid, splendiferous (*facetious*), stately, sublime, superb
Antonyms *adj* humble, ignoble, lowly, mean, modest, ordinary, unassuming, undistinguished, unimposing

majesty *n* **1** = **grandeur**, augustness, awesomeness, dignity, exaltedness, glory, imposingness, impressiveness, kingliness, loftiness, magnificence, nobility, pomp, queenliness, royalty, splendour, state, stateliness, sublimity
Antonyms *n* disgrace, meanness, shame, triviality

major *adj* **8, 11** = **main**, better, bigger, chief, elder, greater, head, higher, larger, lead, leading, most, senior, superior, supreme, uppermost **9, 10** = **important**, critical, crucial,

chord or triad having a major third above the root. **13e** (in jazz) denoting a major chord with a major seventh added above the root. **14** *Logic.* constituting the major term or major premise of a syllogism. **15** *Chiefly US, Canad., Austral., & NZ.* of or relating to a student's principal field of study at a university, etc. **16** *Brit.* the elder: used after a schoolboy's surname if he has one or more younger brothers in the same school: *Price major.* **17** of full legal age. ◆ *vb* **18** (*intr;* usually foll. by *in*) *US, Canad., Austral., & NZ.* to do one's principal study (in a particular subject): *to major in English literature.* **19** (*intr;* usually foll. by *on*) to take or deal with as the main area of interest: *the book majors on peasant dishes.* **[**C15 (adj): from L, comp. of *magnus* great; C17 (n, in military sense): from F, short for SERGEANT MAJOR**]**

▸ **'majorship** *n*

major-domo (-'dəʊməʊ) *n, pl* **major-domos. 1** the chief steward or butler of a great household. **2** *Facetious.* a steward or butler. **[**C16: from Sp. *mayordomo,* from Med. L *mājor domūs* head of the household**]**

majorette (ˌmeɪdʒə'rɛt) *n* **1** one of a group of girls who practise formation marching and baton twirling. **2** See **drum majorette.**

major general *n Mil.* an officer immediately junior to a lieutenant general.

▸ **ˌmajor-'generalship** *or* **major-'generalcy** *n*

majority Ⓣ (mə'dʒɒrɪtɪ) *n, pl* **majorities. 1** the greater number or part of something. **2** (in an election) the number of votes or seats by which the strongest party or candidate beats the combined opposition or the runner-up. **3** the largest party or group that votes together in a legislative or deliberative assembly. **4** the time of reaching or state of having reached full legal age. **5** the rank, office, or commission of major. **6** *Euphemistic.* the dead (esp. in **join the majority, go** *or* **pass over to the majority**). **7** (*modifier*) of, involving, or being a majority: *a majority decision.* **8 in the majority.** forming or part of the greater number of something. **[**C16: from Med. L *mājoritās,* from MAJOR (adj)**]**

> **USAGE NOTE** *The majority of* can only refer to a number of things or people. When talking about an amount, *most of* should be used: *most of* (not *the majority of*) *the harvest was saved.*

major league *n US & Canad.* a league of highest classification in baseball, football, hockey, etc.

majorly ('meɪdʒəlɪ) *adv Sl., chiefly US & Canad.* very; extremely: *it was majorly important for us to do that.*

major orders *pl n RC Church.* the three higher degrees of holy orders: bishop, priest, and deacon.

major premise *n Logic.* the premise of a syllogism containing the predicate of its conclusion.

major term *n Logic.* the predicate of the conclusion of a syllogism.

majuscule ('mædʒəˌskjuːl) *n* **1** a large letter, either capital or uncial, used in printing or writing. ◆ *adj* **2** relating to, printed, or written in such letters. ◆ Cf. **minuscule. [**C18: via F from L *mājusculus,* dim. of *mājor* bigger**]**

▸ **majuscular** (mə'dʒʌskjʊlə) *adj*

make Ⓣ (meɪk) *vb* **makes, making, made.** (*mainly tr*) **1** to bring into being by shaping, changing, or combining materials, ideas, etc.; form or fashion. **2** to draw up, establish, or form: *to make one's will.* **3** to cause to exist, bring about, or produce: *don't make a noise.* **4** to cause, compel, or induce: *please make him go away.* **5** to appoint or assign: *they made him chairman.* **6** to constitute: *one swallow doesn't make a summer.* **7** (*also intr*) to come or cause to come into a specified state or condition: *to make merry.* **8** (*copula*) to be or become through development: *he will make a good teacher.* **9** to cause or ensure the success of: *your news has made my day.* **10** to amount to: *twelve inches make a foot.* **11** to serve as or be suitable for: *that piece of cloth will make a coat.* **12** to prepare or put into a fit condition for use: *to make a bed.* **13** to be the essential element in or part of: *charm makes a good salesman.* **14** to carry out, effect, or do. **15** (*intr;* foll. by *to, as if to,* or *as though to*) to act with the intention or with a show of doing something: *he made as if to hit her.* **16** to use for a specified purpose: *I will make this town my base.* **17** to deliver or pronounce: *to make a speech.* **18** to give information or an opinion: *what time do you make it?* **19** to cause to seem or represent as being. **20** to earn, acquire, or win for oneself: *to make friends.* **21** to engage in: *to make war.* **22** to traverse or cover (distance) by travelling: *we can make a hundred miles by nightfall.* **23** to arrive in time for: *he didn't make the first act of the play.* **24** *Cards.* **24a** to win a trick with (a specified card). **24b** to shuffle (the cards). **24c** *Bridge.* to fulfil (a contract) by winning the necessary number of tricks. **25** *Cricket.* to score (runs). **26** *Electronics.* to close (a circuit) permitting a flow of current. **27** (*intr*) to increase in depth: *the water in the hold was making a foot a minute.* **28** *Inf.* to gain a place or position on or in: *to make the headlines.* **29** *Inf., chiefly US.* to achieve the rank of. **30** *Taboo sl.* to seduce. **31 make a book.** to take bets on a race or another contest. **32 make a day, night,** etc., **of it.** to cause an activity to last a day, night, etc. **33 make do.** See **do**[1] (sense 32). **34 make eyes at.** to flirt with or ogle. **35 make it. 35a** *Inf.* to be successful in doing something. **35b** (foll. by *with*) *Taboo sl.* to have sexual intercourse. **36 make like.** *Sl., chiefly US & Canad.* **36a** to imitate. **36b** to pretend. ◆ *n* **37** brand, type, or style. **38** the manner or way in which something is made. **39** disposition or character; make-up. **40** the act or process of making. **41** the amount or number made. **42** *Cards.* a player's turn to shuffle. **43 on the make.** *Sl.* **43a** out for profit or conquest. **43b** in search of a sexual partner. ◆ See also **make away, make for,** etc. **[**OE *macian***]**

▸ **'makable** *adj*

make away Ⓣ *vb* (*intr, adv*) **1** to depart in haste. **2 make away with. 2a** to steal or abduct. **2b** to kill, destroy, or get rid of.

make believe Ⓣ *vb* **makes believe, making believe, made believe. 1** to pretend or enact a fantasy. ◆ *n* **make-believe. 2a** a fantasy or pretence. **2b** (*as modifier*): *a make-believe world.*

make for Ⓣ *vb* (*intr, prep*) **1** to head towards. **2** to prepare to attack. **3** to help bring about.

make of *vb* (*tr, prep*) **1** to interpret as the meaning of. **2** to produce or construct from: *houses made of brick.* **3 make little, much,** etc., **of. 3a** to gain little, much, etc., benefit from. **3b** to attribute little, much, etc., significance to.

make off Ⓣ *vb* **1** (*intr, adv*) to go or run away in haste. **2 make off with.** to steal or abduct.

make out Ⓣ *vb* (*adv*) **1** (*tr*) to discern or perceive. **2** (*tr*) to understand or comprehend. **3** (*tr*) to write out: *he made out a cheque.* **4** (*tr*) to attempt to establish or prove: *he made me out to be a liar.* **5** (*intr*) to pretend: *he made out that he could cook.* **6** (*intr*) to manage or fare.

make over *vb* (*tr, adv*) **1** to transfer the title or possession of (property, etc.). **2** to renovate or remodel: *she made over the dress to fit her sister.* ◆ *n* **makeover. 3** a complete remodelling. **4** a series of alterations, including beauty treatments and new clothes, intended to make a significant improvement to a person's appearance.

maker Ⓣ ('meɪkə) *n* a person who executes a legal document, esp. one who signs a promissory note.

Maker Ⓣ ('meɪkə) *n* **1** a title given to God (as Creator). **2** (**go to**) **meet one's Maker.** to die.

THESAURUS

grave, great, mega (*sl.*), notable, outstanding, pre-eminent, radical, serious, significant, vital, weighty

Antonyms *adj* ≠ **main:** auxiliary, lesser, minor, secondary, smaller, subordinate ≠ **important:** inconsequential, insignificant, trivial, unimportant

majority *n* **1** = **most**, best part, bulk, greater number, mass, more, plurality, preponderance, superiority **4** = **adulthood**, manhood *or* womanhood, maturity, seniority

make *vb* **1** = **create**, assemble, build, compose, constitute, construct, fabricate, fashion, forge, form, frame, manufacture, mould, originate, produce, put together, shape, synthesize **2** = **enact**, draw up, establish, fix, form, frame, pass **3** = **produce**, accomplish, beget, bring about, cause, create, effect, engender, generate, give rise to, lead to, occasion **4** = **force**, cause, coerce, compel, constrain, dragoon, drive, impel, induce, oblige, press, pressurize, prevail upon, railroad (*inf.*), require **5** = **appoint**, assign, create, designate, elect, install, invest, nominate, ordain **6, 10** = **amount to**, add up to, compose, constitute, embody, form, represent **14** = **perform**, act, carry out, do, effect, engage in, execute, practise, prosecute **18** = **calculate**, estimate, gauge, judge, reckon, suppose, think **20** = **earn**, acquire, clear, gain, get, net, obtain, realize, secure, take in, win **23** = **get to**, arrive at, arrive in time for, attain, catch, meet, reach **35a** **make it** *Informal* = **succeed**, arrive (*inf.*), be successful, come through, crack it, cut it (*inf.*), get on, get somewhere, prosper, pull through, survive ◆ *n* **37, 38** = **brand**, build, character, composition, constitution, construction, cut, designation, form, kind, make-up, mark, model, shape, sort, structure, style, type, variety **39** = **nature**, cast of mind, character, disposition, frame of mind, humour, kidney, make-up, stamp, temper, temperament

make away *vb* **1** = **depart**, abscond, beat a hasty retreat, clear out (*inf.*), cut and run (*inf.*), decamp, do a runner (*sl.*), flee, fly, fly the coop (*US & Canad. inf.*), hook it (*sl.*), make off, run away *or* off, run for it (*inf.*), scoot, skedaddle (*inf.*), slope off **2a** *foll. by* **with** = **steal**, abduct, cabbage (*Brit. sl.*), carry off, cart off (*sl.*), filch, kidnap, knock off (*sl.*), make off with, nab (*inf.*), nick (*sl., chiefly Brit.*), pilfer, pinch (*inf.*), purloin, swipe (*sl.*) **2b** *foll. by* **with** = **kill**, blow away (*sl., chiefly US*), bump off (*sl.*), destroy, dispose of, do away with, do in (*sl.*), eliminate, get rid of, murder, rub out (*US sl.*)

make believe *vb* **1** = **pretend**, act as if *or* though, dream, enact, fantasize, imagine, play, play-act ◆ *n* **make-believe 2a** = **fantasy**, charade, dream, imagination, play-acting, pretence, unreality **2b** ◆ *modifier* = **imaginary**, dream, fantasized, fantasy, imagined, made-up, mock, pretend, pretended, sham, unreal

Antonyms *n* ≠ **fantasy:** actuality, fact, reality, truthfulness ◆ *adj* ≠ **imaginary:** authentic, genuine, real, unfeigned

make for *vb* **1** = **head for**, aim for, be bound for, head towards, proceed towards, steer (a course) for **2** = **attack**, assail, assault, fall on, fly at, go for, have a go at (*inf.*), lunge at, set upon **3** = **contribute to**, be conducive to, conduce to, facilitate, favour, promote

make off *vb* **1** = **flee**, abscond, beat a hasty retreat, bolt, clear out (*inf.*), cut and run (*inf.*), decamp, do a runner (*sl.*), fly, fly the coop (*US & Canad. inf.*), hook it (*sl.*), make away, run away *or* off, run for it (*inf.*), skedaddle (*inf.*), slope off **2 make off with** = **steal**, abduct, cabbage (*Brit. sl.*), carry off, cart off (*sl.*), filch, kidnap, knock off (*sl.*), make away with, nab (*inf.*), nick (*sl., chiefly Brit.*), pilfer, pinch (*inf.*), purloin, run away *or* off with, swipe (*sl.*)

make out *vb* **1** = **see**, descry, detect, discern, discover, distinguish, espy, perceive, recognize **2** = **understand**, comprehend, decipher, fathom, follow, grasp, perceive, realize, see, suss (out), work out **3** = **write out**, complete, draw up, fill in *or* out, inscribe **4** = **prove**, demonstrate, describe, represent, show **5** = **pretend**, assert, claim, let on, make as if *or* though **6** = **fare**, get on, manage, prosper, succeed, thrive

maker *n* = **manufacturer**, author, builder, constructor, director, fabricator, framer, producer

Maker *n* **1** = **God**, Creator

makeshift Ⓣ (ˈmeɪkˌʃɪft) *adj* **1** serving as a temporary or expedient means. ◆ *n* **2** something serving in this capacity.

make-up Ⓣ *n* **1** cosmetics, such as powder, lipstick, etc., applied to the face. **2a** the cosmetics, false hair, etc., used by an actor to adapt his appearance. **2b** the art or result of applying such cosmetics. **3** the manner of arrangement of the parts or qualities of someone or something. **4** the arrangement of type matter and illustrations on a page or in a book. **5** mental or physical constitution. ◆ *vb* **make up.** (*adv*) **6** (*tr*) to form or constitute: *these arguments make up the case for the defence.* **7** (*tr*) to devise, construct, or compose, sometimes with the intent to deceive: *to make up an excuse.* **8** (*tr*) to supply what is lacking or deficient in; complete: *these extra people will make up our total.* **9** (*tr*) to put in order, arrange, or prepare: *to make up a bed.* **10** (*intr*; foll. by *for*) to compensate or atone (for). **11** to settle (differences) amicably (often in **make it up**). **12** to apply cosmetics to (the face) to enhance one's appearance or for a theatrical role. **13** to assemble (type and illustrations) into (columns or pages). **14** (*tr*) to surface (a road) with tarmac, concrete, etc. **15 make up to.** *Inf.* **15a** to make friendly overtures to. **15b** to flirt with.

makeweight (ˈmeɪkˌweɪt) *n* **1** something put on a scale to make up a required weight. **2** an unimportant person or thing added to make up a lack.

making Ⓣ (ˈmeɪkɪŋ) *n* **1a** the act of a person or thing that makes or the process of being made. **1b** (*in combination*): *watchmaking.* **2 be the making of.** to cause the success of. **3 in the making.** in the process of becoming or being made. **4** something made or the quantity of something made at one time.

makings Ⓣ (ˈmeɪkɪŋz) *pl n* **1** potentials, qualities, or materials: *he had the makings of a leader.* **2** Also called: **rollings.** *Sl.* the tobacco and cigarette paper used for rolling a cigarette. **3** profits; earnings.

mako[1] (ˈmɑːkəʊ) *n, pl* **makos.** a blue-pointer game shark. [from Maori]

mako[2] (ˈmɑːkəʊ) *n, pl* **makos.** a small evergreen New Zealand tree. [from Maori]

Mal. *abbrev. for:* **1** *Bible.* Malachi. **2** Malay(an).

mal- *combining form.* bad or badly; wrong or wrongly; imperfect or defective: *maladjusted; malfunction.* [OF, from L *malus* bad, *male* badly]

malabsorption (mæləbˈsɔːpʃən) *n* a failure of absorption, esp. by the small intestine in coeliac disease, cystic fibrosis, etc.

malacca *or* **malacca cane** (məˈlækə) *n* **1** the stem of the rattan palm. **2** a walking stick made from this stem. [from *Malacca,* SW Peninsular Malaysia]

malachite (ˈmæləˌkaɪt) *n* a green mineral consisting of hydrated basic copper carbonate: a source of copper, also used for making ornaments. [C16: via OF from L *molochītēs,* from Gk *molokhitis* mallow-green stone, from *molokhē* mallow]

maladjustment Ⓣ (ˌmæləˈdʒʌstmənt) *n* **1** *Psychol.* a failure to meet the demands of society, such as coping with problems and social relationships. **2** faulty or bad adjustment.
▸ˌ**maladˈjusted** *adj*

maladminister Ⓣ (ˌmælədˈmɪnɪstə) *vb* (*tr*) to administer badly, inefficiently, or dishonestly.
▸ˌ**maladˌminisˈtration** *n*

maladroit Ⓣ (ˌmæləˈdrɔɪt) *adj* **1** clumsy; not dexterous. **2** tactless and insensitive. [C17: from F, from *mal* badly + ADROIT]
▸ˌ**malaˈdroitly** *adv* ▸ˌ**malaˈdroitness** *n*

malady Ⓣ (ˈmælədɪ) *n, pl* **maladies.** **1** any disease or illness. **2** any unhealthy, morbid, or desperate condition. [C13: from OF, from Vulgar L *male habitus* (unattested) in poor condition, from L *male* badly + *habitus,* from *habēre* to have]

Málaga (ˈmæləgə) *n* a sweet fortified dessert wine from Málaga, a port in S Spain.

Malagasy (ˌmæləˈgæsɪ) *n* **1** (*pl* **Malagasy** *or* **Malagasies**) a native or inhabitant of Madagascar. **2** the official language of Madagascar. ◆ *adj* **3** of or relating to Madagascar, its people, or their language.

malaise Ⓣ (mæˈleɪz) *n* **1** a feeling of unease or depression. **2** a mild sickness, not symptomatic of any disease or ailment. **3** a complex of problems affecting a country, economy, etc.: *Bulgaria's economic malaise.* [C18: from OF, from *mal* bad + *aise* EASE]

malamute *or* **malemute** (ˈmæləˌmuːt) *n* an Alaskan Eskimo dog of the spitz type. [from the name of an Eskimo tribe]

malapropism (ˈmæləprɒpˌɪzəm) *n* **1** the unintentional misuse of a word by confusion with one of similar sound, esp. when creating a ridiculous effect, as in *under the affluence of alcohol.* **2** the habit of misusing words in this manner. [C18: after Mrs *Malaprop* in Sheridan's play *The Rivals* (1775), a character who misused words, from MALAPROPOS]

malapropos (ˌmælæprəˈpəʊ) *adj* **1** inappropriate or misapplied. ◆ *adv* **2** in an inappropriate way or manner. ◆ *n* **3** something inopportune or inappropriate. [C17: from F *mal à propos* not to the purpose]

malaria (məˈlɛərɪə) *n* an infectious disease characterized by recurring attacks of chills and fever, caused by the bite of an anopheles mosquito infected with any of certain protozoans. [C18: from It. *mala aria* bad air, from the belief that the disease was caused by the unwholesome air in swampy districts]
▸**maˈlarial, maˈlarian,** *or* **maˈlarious** *adj*

malarkey *or* **malarky** (məˈlɑːkɪ) *n Sl.* nonsense; rubbish. [C20: from ?]

Malathion (ˌmæləˈθaɪɒn) *n Trademark.* an insecticide consisting of an organic phosphate. [C20: from (*diethyl*) MAL(EATE) + THIO- + -ON]

Malay (məˈleɪ) *n* **1** a member of a people living chiefly in Malaysia and Indonesia. **2** the language of this people. ◆ *adj* **3** of or relating to the Malays or their language.

Malayalam *or* **Malayalaam** (ˌmælɪˈɑːləm) *n* a language of SW India.

Malayan (məˈleɪən) *adj* **1** of or relating to Peninsular Malaysia in SE Asia. ◆ *n* **2** a native or inhabitant of Peninsular Malaysia.

Malayo-Polynesian *n* **1** Also called: **Austronesian.** a family of languages extending from Madagascar to the central Pacific. ◆ *adj* **2** of or relating to this family of languages.

Malaysian (məˈleɪzɪən) *adj* **1** of Malaysia in SE Asia. **2** a native or inhabitant of Malaysia.

malcontent Ⓣ (ˈmælkənˌtɛnt) *adj* **1** disgusted or discontented. ◆ *n* **2** a person who is malcontent. [C16: from OF]

mal de mer *French.* (mal də mɛr) *n* seasickness.

male Ⓣ (meɪl) *adj* **1** of, relating to, or designating the sex producing gametes (spermatozoa) that can fertilize female gametes (ova). **2** of, relating to, or characteristic of a man. **3** for or composed of men or boys: *a male choir.* **4** (of gametes) capable of fertilizing an egg cell. **5** (of reproductive organs) capable of producing male gametes. **6** (of flowers) bearing stamens but lacking a functional pistil. **7** *Electronics, engineering.* having a projecting part or parts that fit into a female counterpart: *a male plug.* ◆ *n* **8** a male person, animal, or plant. [C14: via OF from L *masculus* MASCULINE]
▸ˈ**maleness** *n*

maleate (ˈmælɪˌeɪt) *n* any salt or ester of maleic acid. [C19: from MALE(IC) ACID + -ATE[1]]

male chauvinism *n* the belief, held or alleged to be held by certain men, that men are superior to women.
▸**male chauvinist** *n, adj*

malediction Ⓣ (ˌmælɪˈdɪkʃən) *n* **1** the utterance of a curse against someone or something. **2** a slanderous accusation or comment. [C15: from L *maledictiō* a reviling, from *male* ill + *dīcere* to speak]
▸ˌ**maleˈdictive** *or* ˌ**maleˈdictory** *adj*

malefactor Ⓣ (ˈmælɪˌfæktə) *n* a criminal; wrongdoer. [C15: via OF from L, from *malefacere* to do evil]
▸ˈ**maleˌfaction** *n*

maleficent (məˈlɛfɪsənt) *adj* causing evil or mischief; harmful or baleful. [C17: from L, from *maleficus* wicked, from *malum* evil]
▸**maˈlefic** *adj* ▸**maˈleficence** *n*

maleic acid (məˈleɪɪk) *n* a colourless soluble crystalline substance used to synthesize other compounds, such as polyester resins. Formula: HOOCCH:CHCOOH. Systematic name: **cis-butenedioic acid.** [C19: from F *maléique,* altered form of *malique;* see MALIC ACID]

male menopause *n* a period in a man's later middle age in which he

THESAURUS

makeshift *adj* **1** = **temporary**, expedient, jury, make-do, provisional, rough and ready, stopgap, substitute ◆ *n* **2** = **stopgap**, expedient, shift, substitute

make-up *n* **1, 2a** = **cosmetics**, face (*inf.*), greasepaint (*Theatre*), *maquillage,* paint (*inf.*), powder, war paint (*inf., humorous*) **3** = **structure**, arrangement, assembly, composition, configuration, constitution, construction, form, format, formation, organization **5** = **nature**, build, cast of mind, character, constitution, disposition, figure, frame of mind, make, stamp, temper, temperament ◆ *vb* **make up 6** = **form**, compose, comprise, constitute **7** = **invent**, coin, compose, concoct, construct, cook up (*inf.*), create, devise, dream up, fabricate, formulate, frame, hatch, manufacture, originate, trump up, write **8** = **complete**, fill, meet, supply **10** *foll. by* **for** = **compensate for**, atone for, balance, make amends for, offset, recompense, redeem, redress, requite **11** = **settle**, bury the hatchet, call it quits, come to terms, compose, forgive and forget, make peace, mend, reconcile, shake hands **15 make up to** *Informal* = **court**, chat up (*inf.*), curry favour with, flirt with, make overtures to, woo

making *n* **1** = **creation**, assembly, building, composition, construction, fabrication, forging, manufacture, production **3 in the making** = **budding**, coming, emergent, growing, nascent, potential

makings *pl n* **1** = **beginnings**, capability, capacity, ingredients, materials, potential, potentiality, qualities

maladjusted *adj* **1** = **disturbed**, alienated, estranged, hung-up (*sl.*), neurotic, unstable

maladministration *n* = **mismanagement**, blundering, bungling, corruption, dishonesty, incompetence, inefficiency, malfeasance (*Law*), malpractice, misgovernment, misrule

maladroit *adj* **1** = **clumsy**, awkward, bungling, cack-handed (*inf.*), ham-fisted *or* ham-handed (*inf.*), inept, inexpert, unhandy, unskilful

malady *n* **1** = **disease**, affliction, ailment, complaint, disorder, ill, illness, indisposition, infirmity, lurgy (*inf.*), sickness

malaise *n* **1, 2** = **unease**, angst, anxiety, depression, discomfort, disquiet, doldrums, enervation, illness, lassitude, melancholy, sickness, weakness

malcontent *adj* **1** = **discontented**, disaffected, disgruntled, disgusted, dissatisfied, dissentious, factious, ill-disposed, rebellious, resentful, restive, unhappy, unsatisfied ◆ *n* **2** = **troublemaker**, agitator, complainer, fault-finder, grouch (*inf.*), grouser, grumbler, mischief-maker, rebel, stirrer (*inf.*)

male *adj* **1, 2** = **masculine**, manful, manlike, manly, virile
Antonyms *adj* camp (*inf.*), effeminate, female, feminine, girlie, unmanly, wimpish *or* wimpy (*inf.*), womanish, womanly

malediction *n* **1** = **curse**, anathema, damnation, damning, denunciation, execration, imprecation, malison (*arch.*)

malefactor *n* = **wrongdoer**, convict, criminal, crook (*inf.*), culprit, delinquent, evildoer, felon, lawbreaker, miscreant, offender, outlaw, transgressor, villain

may experience an identity crisis as he feels age overtake his sexual powers.

malevolent Ⓣ (mə'lɛvələnt) *adj* wishing or appearing to wish evil to others; malicious. [C16: from L *malevolens*, from *male* ill + *volens*, present participle of *velle* to wish]
▸**ma'levolence** *n* ▸**ma'levolently** *adv*

malfeasance (mæl'fi:zᵊns) *n Law.* the doing of a wrongful or illegal act, esp. by a public official. Cf. **misfeasance, nonfeasance.** [C17: from OF *mal faisant*, from *mal* evil + *faisant*, from *faire* to do, from L *facere*]
▸**mal'feasant** *n, adj*

malformation Ⓣ (ˌmælfɔ:'meɪʃən) *n* **1** the condition of being faulty or abnormal in form or shape. **2** *Pathol.* a deformity, esp. when congenital.
▸**mal'formed** *adj*

malfunction Ⓣ (mæl'fʌŋkʃən) *vb* **1** (*intr*) to function imperfectly or fail to function. ◆ *n* **2** failure to function or defective functioning.

malic acid ('mælɪk, 'meɪ-) *n* a colourless crystalline compound occurring in apples and other fruits. [C18 *malic*, via F *malique* from L *mālum* apple]

malice Ⓣ ('mælɪs) *n* **1** the desire to do harm or mischief. **2** evil intent. **3** *Law.* the state of mind with which an act is committed and from which the intent to do wrong may be inferred. [C13: via OF from L *malitia*, from *malus* evil]

malice aforethought *n Law.* **1** the predetermination to do an unlawful act, esp. to kill or seriously injure. **2** the intent with which an unlawful killing is effected, which must be proved for the crime to constitute murder.

malicious Ⓣ (mə'lɪʃəs) *adj* **1** characterized by malice. **2** motivated by wrongful, vicious, or mischievous purposes.
▸**ma'liciously** *adv* ▸**ma'liciousness** *n*

malign Ⓣ (mə'laɪn) *adj* **1** evil in influence, intention, or effect. ◆ *vb* **2** (*tr*) to slander or defame. [C14: via OF from L *malīgnus* spiteful, from *malus* evil]
▸**ma'ligner** *n* ▸**ma'lignly** *adv*

malignancy (mə'lɪgnənsɪ) *n, pl* **malignancies. 1** the state or quality of being malignant. **2** *Pathol.* a cancerous growth.

malignant Ⓣ (mə'lɪgnənt) *adj* **1** having or showing desire to harm others. **2** tending to cause great harm; injurious. **3** *Pathol.* (of a tumour) uncontrollable or resistant to therapy. [C16: from LL *malīgnāre* to behave spitefully, from L *malīgnus* MALIGN]
▸**ma'lignantly** *adv*

malignity Ⓣ (mə'lɪgnɪtɪ) *n, pl* **malignities. 1** the condition or quality of being malign or deadly. **2** (*often pl*) a malign or malicious act or feeling.

malines (mə'li:n) *n* **1** a type of silk net used in dressmaking. **2** another name for **Mechlin lace.** [C19: from F *Malines* (Mechelen), a Belgian city, where this lace was traditionally made]

malinger (mə'lɪŋgə) *vb* (*intr*) to pretend or exaggerate illness, esp. to avoid work. [C19: from F *malingre* sickly, ?from *mal* badly + OF *haingre* feeble]
▸**ma'lingerer** *n*

mall (mɔ:l, mæl) *n* **1** a shaded avenue, esp. one open to the public. **2** short for **shopping mall.** [C17: after *the Mall*, in St James's Park, London]

mallard ('mælɑ:d) *n, pl* **mallard** *or* **mallards.** a duck common over most of the N hemisphere, the male of which has a dark green head and reddish-brown breast: the ancestor of all domestic breeds of duck. [C14: from OF *mallart*, ?from *maslart* (unattested); see MALE, -ARD]

malleable Ⓣ ('mælɪəbᵊl) *adj* **1** (esp. of metal) able to be worked, hammered, or shaped under pressure or blows without breaking. **2** able to be influenced; pliable or tractable. [C14: via OF from Med. L *malleābilis*, from L *malleus* hammer]
▸ˌ**mallea'bility** *or* (*less commonly*) '**malleableness** *n* ▸'**malleably** *adv*

mallee ('mæli:) *n* **1** any of several low shrubby eucalyptus trees in desert regions of Australia. **2** (usually preceded by *the*) *Austral. inf.* another name for the **bush** (sense 4). [C19: Abor.]

Mallee ('mæli:) *n* a region in NW Victoria, Australia.

mallee fowl *n* an Australian megapode.

malleolus (mə'li:ələs) *n, pl* **malleoli** (-ˌlaɪ). either of two rounded bony projections, one on each side of the ankle. [C17: dim. of L *malleus* hammer]

mallet ('mælɪt) *n* **1** a tool resembling a hammer but having a large head of wood, copper, lead, leather, etc., used for driving chisels, beating sheet metal, etc. **2** a long stick with a head like a hammer used to strike the ball in croquet or polo. [C15: from OF *maillet* wooden hammer, dim. of *mail* MAUL (n)]

malleus ('mælɪəs) *n, pl* **mallei** (-lɪˌaɪ). the outermost and largest of the three small bones in the middle ear of mammals. See also **incus, stapes.** [C17: from L: hammer]

mallie ('mɔ:lɪ) *n Inf., chiefly US.* a teenage girl who spends most of her spare time loitering in shopping malls.

mallow ('mæləʊ) *n* **1** any of several malvaceous plants of Europe, having purple, pink, or white flowers. **2** any of various related plants, such as the marsh mallow. [OE *mealuwe*, from L *malva*]

malm (mɑ:m) *n* **1** a soft greyish limestone that crumbles easily. **2** a chalky soil formed from this. **3** an artificial mixture of clay and chalk used to make bricks. [OE *mealm-* (in compound words)]

malmsey ('mɑ:mzɪ) *n* a sweet Madeira wine. [C15: from Med. L *Malmasia*, corruption of Gk *Monembasia*, Gk port from which the wine was shipped]

malnutrition (ˌmælnju:'trɪʃən) *n* lack of adequate nutrition resulting from insufficient food, unbalanced diet, or defective assimilation.

malodorous Ⓣ (mæl'əʊdərəs) *adj* having a bad smell.

malpractice Ⓣ (mæl'præktɪs) *n* **1** immoral, illegal, or unethical professional conduct or neglect of professional duty. **2** any instance of improper professional conduct.

malt (mɔ:lt) *n* **1** cereal grain, such as barley, that is kiln-dried after it has germinated by soaking in water. **2** See **malt liquor, malt whisky.** ◆ *vb* **3** to make into or become malt. **4** to make (something, esp. liquor) with malt. [OE *mealt*]
▸'**malty** *adj*

malted milk *n* **1** a soluble powder made from dehydrated milk and malted cereals. **2** a drink made from this powder.

Maltese (mɔ:l'ti:z) *adj* **1** of or relating to Malta, an island in the Mediterranean, its inhabitants, or their language. ◆ *n* **2** (*pl* **Maltese**) a native or inhabitant of Malta or a descendant of one. **3** the official language of Malta, a form of Arabic with borrowings from Italian, etc.

Maltese cross *n* a cross with triangular arms that taper towards the centre, sometimes having indented outer sides.

malt extract *n* a sticky substance obtained from an infusion of malt.

Malthusian (mæl'θju:zɪən) *adj* **1** of or relating to the theory of T. R. Malthus (1766–1834), English economist, stating that increases in population tend to exceed increases in the means of subsistence and that therefore sexual restraint should be exercised. ◆ *n* **2** a supporter of this theory.
▸**Mal'thusianism** *n*

malting ('mɔ:ltɪŋ) *n* a building in which malt is made or stored. Also called: **malt house.**

malt liquor *n* any alcoholic drink brewed from malt.

maltose ('mɔ:ltəʊz) *n* a sugar formed by the enzymic hydrolysis of starch. [C19: from MALT + -OSE[2]]

maltreat Ⓣ (mæl'tri:t) *vb* (*tr*) to treat badly, cruelly, or inconsiderately. [C18: from F *maltraiter*]
▸**mal'treater** *n* ▸**mal'treatment** *n*

maltster ('mɔ:ltstə) *n* a person who makes or deals in malt.

malt whisky *n* whisky made from malted barley.

malvaceous (mæl'veɪʃəs) *adj* of, relating to, or belonging to a family of

THESAURUS

malevolence *n* = **malice**, hate, hatred, ill will, maliciousness, malignity, nastiness, rancour, spite, spitefulness, vengefulness, vindictiveness

malevolent *adj* = **spiteful**, baleful, evil-minded, hateful (*arch.*), hostile, ill-natured, maleficent, malicious, malign, malignant, pernicious, rancorous, vengeful, vicious, vindictive
Antonyms *adj* amiable, benevolent, benign, friendly, gracious, kind, warm-hearted

malformation *n* **1, 2** = **deformity**, crookedness, distortion, misshape, misshapenness

malformed *adj* **1, 2** = **misshapen**, abnormal, contorted, crooked, deformed, distorted, irregular, twisted

malfunction *vb* **1** = **break down**, develop a fault, fail, go wrong ◆ *n* **2** = **fault**, breakdown, defect, failure, flaw, glitch, impairment

malice *n* **1, 2** = **spite**, animosity, animus, bad blood, bitterness, enmity, evil intent, hate, hatred, ill will, malevolence, maliciousness, malignity, rancour, spitefulness, spleen, vengefulness, venom, vindictiveness

malicious *adj* **1, 2** = **spiteful**, baleful, bitchy (*inf.*), bitter, catty (*inf.*), evil-minded, hateful, ill-disposed, ill-natured, injurious, malevolent, malignant, mischievous, pernicious, rancorous, resentful, shrewish, vengeful, vicious
Antonyms *adj* amiable, benevolent, friendly, kind, warm-hearted

malign *adj* **1** = **evil**, bad, baleful, baneful, deleterious, destructive, harmful, hostile, hurtful, injurious, maleficent, malevolent, malignant, pernicious, vicious, wicked ◆ *vb* **2** = **disparage**, abuse, asperse, blacken (someone's name), calumniate, defame, denigrate, derogate, harm, injure, knock (*inf.*), libel, revile, rubbish (*inf.*), run down, slag (off) (*sl.*), slander, smear, speak ill of, traduce, vilify
Antonyms *adj* ≠ **evil**: agreeable, amiable, beneficial, benevolent, benign, friendly, good, harmless, honourable, innocuous, kind, moral, virtuous, warm-hearted, wholesome ◆ *vb* ≠ **disparage**: commend, compliment, extol, praise

malignant *adj* **1, 2** = **hostile**, baleful, bitter, destructive, harmful, hurtful, inimical, injurious, maleficent, malevolent, malicious, malign, of evil intent, pernicious, spiteful, vicious **3** *Pathol.* = **uncontrollable**, cancerous, dangerous, deadly, evil, fatal, irremediable, metastatic, virulent
Antonyms *adj* ≠ **hostile**: amicable, benevolent, benign, friendly, kind, warm-hearted

malignity *n* **1** = **deadliness**, balefulness, destructiveness, harmfulness, hurtfulness, perniciousness, virulence **2** = **malice**, animosity, animus, bad blood, bitterness, evil, hate, hatred, hostility, ill will, malevolence, maliciousness, rancour, spite, vengefulness, venom, viciousness, vindictiveness, wickedness

malleable *adj* **1** = **workable**, ductile, plastic, soft, tensile **2** = **manageable**, adaptable, biddable, compliant, governable, impressionable, pliable, tractable

malodorous *adj* = **smelly**, evil-smelling, fetid, foul-smelling, mephitic, nauseating, niffy, noisome, offensive, olid, putrid, rank, reeking, stinking

malpractice *n* **1** = **misconduct**, abuse, dereliction, misbehaviour, mismanagement, negligence

maltreat *vb* = **abuse**, bully, damage, handle roughly, harm, hurt, ill-treat, injure, mistreat

maltreatment *n* = **abuse**, bullying, harm, ill-treatment, ill-usage, injury, mistreatment, rough handling

plants that includes mallow, cotton, okra, althaea, and abutilon. [C17: from L *malvāceus,* from *malva* MALLOW]

malversation (ˌmælvɜːˈseɪʃən) *n Rare.* professional or public misconduct. [C16: from F, from *malverser* to behave badly, from L *male versārī*]

mam (mæm) *n Inf. or dialect.* another word for **mother.**

mama *or esp. US* **mamma** (məˈmɑː) *n Old-fashioned.* an informal word for **mother.** [C16: reduplication of childish syllable *ma*]

mamba (ˈmæmbə) *n* any of various partly arboreal tropical African venomous snakes, esp. the **green** and **black mambas.** [from Zulu *im-amba*]

mambo (ˈmæmbəʊ) *n, pl* **mambos. 1** a modern Latin American dance, resembling the rumba. ◆ *vb* **2** (*intr*) to perform this dance. [American Sp., prob. from Haitian Creole: voodoo priestess]

Mameluke *or* **Mamaluke** (ˈmæmɪˌluːk) *n* **1** a member of a military class, originally of Turkish slaves, ruling in Egypt from about 1250 to 1517 and remaining powerful until 1811. **2** (in Muslim countries) a slave. [C16: via F, ult. from Ar. *mamlūk* slave, from *malaka* to possess]

mamilla *or US* **mammilla** (mæˈmɪlə) *n, pl* **mamillae** (-liː) *or US* **mammillae. 1** a nipple or teat. **2** any nipple-shaped prominence. [C17: from L, dim. of *mamma* breast]
▸ **ˈmamillary** *or US* **ˈmammillary** *adj*

mamma (ˈmæmə) *n, pl* **mammae** (-miː). the milk-secreting organ of female mammals: the breast in women, the udder in cows, sheep, etc. [C17: from L: breast]
▸ **ˈmammary** *adj*

mammal (ˈmæməl) *n* any animal of the *Mammalia,* a large class of warm-blooded vertebrates having mammary glands in the female. [C19: via NL from L *mamma* breast]
▸ **mammalian** (mæˈmeɪlɪən) *adj, n*

mammary gland *n* any of the milk-producing glands in mammals.

mammogram (ˈmæməʊˌgræm) *n* an X-ray photograph of the breast.

mammography (mæˈmɒgrəfɪ) *n* examination of the breasts by X-ray, esp. to detect early signs of cancer.

mammon (ˈmæmən) *n* riches or wealth regarded as a source of evil and corruption. [C14: via LL from New Testament Gk *mammōnas,* from Aramaic *māmōnā* wealth]
▸ **ˈmammonish** *adj* ▸ **ˈmammonism** *n* ▸ **ˈmammonist** *or* **ˈmammonite** *n*

Mammon (ˈmæmən) *n Bible.* the personification of riches and greed in the form of a false god.

mammoth ➊ (ˈmæməθ) *n* **1** any large extinct elephant of the Pleistocene epoch, such as the **woolly mammoth,** having a hairy coat and long curved tusks. ◆ *adj* **2** of gigantic size or importance. [C18: from Russian *mamot,* from Tartar *mamont,* ?from *mamma* earth, because of a belief that the animal made burrows]

mammy *or* **mammie** (ˈmæmɪ) *n, pl* **mammies. 1** a child's word for **mother**[1] (senses 1–3). **2** *Chiefly southern US.* a Black woman employed as a nurse or servant to a White family.

man ➊ (mæn) *n, pl* **men. 1** an adult male human being, as distinguished from a woman. **2** (*modifier*) male; masculine: *a man child.* **3** a human being, considered as representative of mankind. **4** human beings collectively; mankind. **5** Also called: **modern man. 5a** a member of any of the living races of *Homo sapiens,* characterized by erect bipedal posture, a highly developed brain, and powers of articulate speech, abstract reasoning, and imagination. **5b** any extinct member of the species *Homo sapiens,* such as Cro-Magnon man. **6** a member of any of the extinct species of the genus *Homo,* such as Java man. **7** an adult male human being with qualities associated with the male, such as courage or virility: *be a man.* **8** manly qualities or virtues: *the man in him was outraged.* **9a** a subordinate, servant, or employee. **9b** (*in combination*): *the man-days required to complete a job.* **10** (*usually pl*) a member of the armed forces who does not hold commissioned, warrant, or noncommissioned rank (as in **officers and men**). **11** a member of a group, team, etc. **12** a husband, boyfriend, etc. **13** an expression used parenthetically to indicate an informal relationship between speaker and hearer. **14** a movable piece in various games, such as draughts. **15** a vassal of a feudal lord. **16** *S. African sl.* any person: used as a term of address. **17 as one man.** with unanimous action or response. **18 be one's own man.** to be independent or free. **19 he's your man.** he's the person needed. **20 man and boy.** from childhood. **21 sort out** *or* **separate the men from the boys.** to separate the experienced from the inexperienced. **22 to a man.** without exception. ◆ *interj* **23** *Inf.* an exclamation or expletive, often indicating surprise or pleasure. ◆ *vb* **mans, manning, manned.** (*tr*) **24** to provide with sufficient men for operation, defence, etc. **25** to take one's place at or near in readiness for action. [OE *mann*]

Man. *abbrev. for:* **1** Manila paper. **2** Manitoba.

-man *n combining form.* indicating a person who has a role, works in a place, or operates equipment as specified: *salesman; barman; cameraman.*

> **USAGE NOTE** The use of words ending in *-man* is avoided as implying a male in job advertisements, where sexual discrimination is illegal, and in many other contexts where a term that is not gender-specific is available, such as *salesperson, barperson, camera operator.*

mana (ˈmɑːnə) *n Anthropol.* **1** (in Polynesia, Melanesia, etc.) a concept of a life force associated with high social status and ritual power. **2** any power achieved by ritual means; prestige; authority. [of Polynesian origin]

man about town *n* a fashionable sophisticate, esp. one in a big city.

manacle ➊ (ˈmænəkᵊl) *n* **1** (*usually pl*) a shackle, handcuff, or fetter, used to secure the hands of a prisoner, convict, etc. ◆ *vb* **manacles, manacling, manacled.** (*tr*) **2** to put manacles on. **3** to confine or constrain. [C14: via OF from L *manicula,* dim. of *manus* hand]

manage ➊ (ˈmænɪdʒ) *vb* **manages, managing, managed.** (*mainly tr*) **1** (*also intr*) to be in charge (of); administer: *to manage a shop.* **2** to succeed in being able (to do something); contrive. **3** to have room, time, etc., for: *can you manage dinner tomorrow?* **4** to exercise control or domination over. **5** (*intr*) to contrive to carry on despite difficulties, esp. financial ones. **6** to wield or handle (a weapon). [C16: from It. *maneggiare* to train (esp. horses), ult. from L *manus* hand]

manageable ➊ (ˈmænɪdʒəbᵊl) *adj* able to be managed or controlled.
▸ **ˌmanageaˈbility** *or* **ˈmanageableness** *n* ▸ **ˈmanageably** *adv*

managed currency *n* a currency subject to governmental control with respect to the amount in circulation and rate of exchange.

managed fund *n* an investment managed by an insurance company to provide low-risk investments for the small investor.

management ➊ (ˈmænɪdʒmənt) *n* **1** the members of the executive or administration of an organization or business. **2** managers or employers collectively. **3** the technique, practice, or science of managing or controlling. **4** the skilful or resourceful use of materials, time, etc. **5** the specific treatment of a disease, etc.

management buyout *n* the purchase of a company by its managers, usually with outside backing from a bank or other institution.

management company *n* a company that manages a unit trust.

manager ➊ (ˈmænɪdʒə) *n* **1** a person who directs or manages an organization, industry, shop, etc. **2** a person who controls the business affairs of an actor, entertainer, etc. **3** a person who controls the training of a sportsman or team. **4** a person who has a talent for managing efficiently. **5** (in Britain) a member of either House of Parliament appointed to arrange a matter in which both Houses are concerned. **6** *Computing.* a computer program that organizes a resource, such as a set of files or a database.
▸ **ˈmanagership** *n*

manageress (ˌmænɪdʒəˈrɛs) *n* a woman who is in charge of a shop, department, etc.

managerial (ˌmænɪˈdʒɪərɪəl) *adj* of or relating to a manager or management.
▸ **ˌmanaˈgerially** *adv*

managing (ˈmænɪdʒɪŋ) *adj* having administrative control or authority: *a managing director.*

mañana *Spanish.* (məˈnjɑːnə) *n, adv* **a** tomorrow. **b** some other and later time.

man-at-arms *n, pl* **men-at-arms.** a soldier, esp. a heavily armed mounted soldier in medieval times.

manatee (ˌmænəˈtiː) *n* a sirenian mammal occurring in tropical

THESAURUS

mammoth *adj* **2** = **colossal,** Brobdingnagian, elephantine, enormous, gargantuan, giant, gigantic, ginormous (*inf.*), huge, humongous *or* humungous (*US sl.*), immense, jumbo (*inf.*), massive, mega (*sl.*), mighty, monumental, mountainous, prodigious, stellar (*inf.*), stupendous, titanic, vast
Antonyms *adj* diminutive, insignificant, little, miniature, minute, puny, small, tiny, trivial

man *n* **1** = **male,** bloke (*Brit. inf.*), chap (*inf.*), gentleman, guy (*inf.*) **3** = **human,** adult, being, body, human being, individual, one, person, personage, somebody, soul **5** = **mankind,** Homo sapiens, humanity, humankind, human race, mortals, people **9** = **manservant,** attendant, follower, retainer, servant, valet **12** = **boyfriend,** beau, husband, lover, partner, significant other (*US inf.*), spouse **15** = **employee,** hand, hireling, liegeman, soldier, subject, subordinate, vassal, worker, workman **22 to a man** = **without exception,** bar none, every one, one and all, unanimously ◆ *vb* **24** = **staff,** crew, fill, furnish with men, garrison, occupy, people

manacle *n* **1** = **handcuff,** bond, chain, fetter, gyve (*arch.*), iron, shackle, tie ◆ *vb* **2** = **handcuff,** bind, chain, check, clap *or* put in irons, confine, constrain, curb, fetter, hamper, inhibit, put in chains, restrain, shackle, tie one's hands

manage *vb* **1** = **administer,** be in charge (of), call the shots, call the tune, command, concert, conduct, direct, govern, handle, manipulate, oversee, preside over, rule, run, superintend, supervise **2** = **succeed,** accomplish, arrange, bring about *or* off, contrive, cope with, crack it (*inf.*), cut it (*inf.*), deal with, effect, engineer **4, 6** = **handle,** control, dominate, govern, guide, influence, manipulate, operate, pilot, ply, steer, train, use, wield **5** = **cope,** carry on, fare, get along, get by (*inf.*), get on, get through, make do, make out, muddle through, shift, survive
Antonyms *vb* ≠ **succeed:** bodge (*inf.*), botch, fail, make a mess of, make a nonsense of, mismanage, muff, spoil

manageable *adj* = **easy,** convenient, handy, user-friendly, wieldy = **docile,** amenable, compliant, controllable, governable, submissive, tamable, tractable
Antonyms *adj* ≠ **easy:** demanding, difficult, hard ≠ **docile:** disobedient, headstrong, obstinate, refractory, stubborn, ungovernable, unruly, unyielding, wild

management *n* **1, 2** = **directors,** administration, board, bosses (*inf.*), directorate, employers, executive(s) **3** = **administration,** care, charge, command, conduct, control, direction, governance, government, guidance, handling, manipulation, operation, rule, running, superintendence, supervision

manager *n* **1-3** = **supervisor,** administrator, boss (*inf.*), comptroller, conductor, controller,

coastal waters of America, the Caribbean, and Africa, having a prehensile upper lip and a broad flattened tail. [C16: via Sp. from Carib *Manattouï*]

manchester ('mæntʃɪstə) *n Austral. & NZ.* **1** goods, such as sheets and pillowcases, which are, or were originally, made of cotton. **2 manchester department.** a section of a store which sells such goods. [from *Manchester,* city of NW England, former centre of the textile trade]

manchineel (ˌmæntʃɪ'ni:l) *n* a tropical American tree having fruit and milky highly caustic poisonous sap, which causes skin blisters. [C17: via F from Sp. MANZANILLA]

Manchu (mæn'tʃu:) *n* **1** (*pl* **Manchus** *or* **Manchu**) a member of a Mongoloid people of Manchuria, a region of NE China, who conquered China in the 17th century, establishing a dynasty that lasted until 1912. **2** the language of this people. ◆ *adj* **3** Also: **Ching.** of or relating to the dynasty of the Manchus. [from Manchu, lit.: pure]

manciple ('mænsɪpᵊl) *n* a steward who buys provisions, esp. in an Inn of Court. [C13: via OF from L *mancipium* purchase, from *manceps* purchaser, from *manus* hand + *capere* to take]

Mancunian (mæŋ'kju:nɪən) *n* **1** a native or inhabitant of Manchester, a city in NW England. ◆ *adj* **2** of or relating to Manchester. [from Med. L *Mancunium* Manchester]

-mancy *n combining form.* indicating divination of a particular kind: *chiromancy.* [from OF *-mancie,* from L *-mantia,* from Gk *manteia* soothsaying]
▸**-mantic** *adj combining form.*

mandala ('mændələ, mæn'dɑ:lə) *n Hindu & Buddhist art.* any of various designs symbolizing the universe, usually circular. [Sansk.: circle]

mandamus (mæn'deɪməs) *n, pl* **mandamuses.** *Law.* (formerly) a writ from (now an order of) a superior court commanding an inferior tribunal, public official, etc., to carry out a public duty. [C16: L, lit.: we command, from *mandāre*]

mandarin ('mændərɪn) *n* **1** (in the Chinese Empire) a member of a senior grade of the bureaucracy. **2** a high-ranking official whose powers are extensive and thought to be outside political control. **3** a person of standing and influence, as in literary or intellectual circles, esp. one regarded as conservative or reactionary. **4a** a small citrus tree cultivated for its edible fruit. **4b** the fruit, resembling the tangerine. [C16: from Port. via Malay from Sansk. *mantrin* counsellor, from *mantra* counsel]
▸'**mandarinate** *n*

Mandarin Chinese *or* **Mandarin** *n* the official language of China since 1917.

Mandarin collar *n* a high stiff round collar.

mandarin duck *n* an Asian duck, the male of which has a distinctive brightly coloured and patterned plumage and crest.

mandate ❶ *n* ('mændeɪt, -dɪt). **1** an official or authoritative instruction or command. **2** *Politics.* the support or commission given to a government and its policies or an elected representative and his policies through an electoral victory. **3** (*often cap.*) Also called: **mandated territory.** (formerly) any of the territories under the trusteeship of the League of Nations administered by one of its member states. **4a** *Roman law.* a contract by which one person commissions another to act for him gratuitously. **4b** *Contract law.* a contract under which a party entrusted with goods undertakes to perform gratuitously some service in respect of such goods. **4c** *Scots Law.* a contract by which a person is engaged to act in the management of the affairs of another. ◆ *vb* ('mændeɪt), **mandates, mandating, mandated.** (*tr*) **5** to assign (territory) to a nation under a mandate. **6** to delegate authority to. [C16: from L *mandātum* something commanded, from *mandāre* to command, ?from *manus* hand + *dāre* to give]
▸'**mandator** *n*

mandatory ❶ ('mændətərɪ, -trɪ) *adj* **1** having the nature or powers of a mandate. **2** obligatory; compulsory. **3** (of a state) having received a mandate over some territory. ◆ *n, pl* **mandatories.** *also* **mandatary. 4** a person or state holding a mandate.
▸'**mandatorily** *adv*

mandible ('mændɪbᵊl) *n* **1** the lower jawbone in vertebrates. **2** either of a pair of mouthparts in insects and other arthropods that are usually used for biting and crushing food. **3** *Ornithol.* either part of the bill, esp. the lower part. [C16: via OF from LL *mandibula* jaw, from *mandere* to chew]
▸**mandibular** (mæn'dɪbjʊlə) *adj* ▸**mandibulate** (mæn'dɪbjʊlɪt, -ˌleɪt) *n, adj*

mandolin *or* **mandoline** (ˌmændə'lɪn) *n* a plucked stringed instrument having four pairs of strings stretched over a small light body with a fretted fingerboard: usually played with a plectrum. [C18: via F from It. *mandolino,* dim. of *mandora* lute, ult. from Gk *pandoura* musical instrument with three strings]
▸ˌ**mando'linist** *n*

mandrake ('mændreɪk) *or* **mandragora** (mæn'drægərə) *n* **1** a Eurasian plant with purplish flowers and a forked root. It was formerly thought to have magic powers and a narcotic was prepared from its root. **2** another name for the **May apple.** [C14: prob. via MDu. from L *mandragoras,* from Gk. The form *mandrake* was prob. adopted through folk etymology, because of the allegedly human appearance of the root and because *drake* (dragon) suggested magical powers]

mandrel *or* **mandril** ('mændrəl) *n* **1** a spindle on which a workpiece is supported during machining operations. **2** a shaft or arbor on which a machining tool is mounted. [C16: ? rel. to F *mandrin* lathe]

mandrill ('mændrɪl) *n* an Old World monkey of W Africa. It has a short tail and brown hair, and the ridged muzzle, nose, and hindquarters are red and blue. [C18: from MAN + DRILL⁴]

mane (meɪn) *n* **1** the long coarse hair that grows from the crest of the neck in such mammals as the lion and horse. **2** long thick human hair. [OE *manu*]
▸**maned** *adj*

manège *or* **manege** (mæ'neɪʒ) *n* **1** the art of training horses and riders. **2** a riding school. [C17: via F from It. *maneggio,* from *maneggiare* to MANAGE]

manes ('mɑ:neɪz) *pl n* (*sometimes cap.*) (in Roman legend) **1** the spirits of the dead, often revered as minor deities. **2** (*functioning as sing*) the shade of a dead person. [C14: from L, prob.: the good ones, from OL *mānus* good]

maneuver (mə'nu:və) *n, vb* the usual US spelling of **manoeuvre.**

man Friday *n* **1** a loyal male servant or assistant. **2** Also: **girl Friday, person Friday.** any factotum, esp. in an office. [after the native in Daniel Defoe's novel *Robinson Crusoe* (1719)]

manful ❶ ('mænfʊl) *adj* resolute, strong; manly.
▸'**manfully** *adv* ▸'**manfulness** *n*

mangabey ('mæŋgəˌbeɪ) *n* any of several large agile arboreal Old World monkeys of central Africa, having long limbs and tail. [C18: after a region in Madagascar]

manganese ('mæŋgəˌni:z) *n* a brittle greyish-white metallic element: used in making steel and ferromagnetic alloys. Symbol: Mn; atomic no.: 25; atomic wt.: 54.938. [C17: via F from It., prob. altered form of Med. L MAGNESIA]

mange (meɪndʒ) *n* an infectious disorder mainly affecting domestic animals, characterized by itching and loss of hair: caused by parasitic mites. [C14: from OF *mangeue* itch, from *mangier* to eat]

mangelwurzel ('mæŋgᵊlˌwɜ:zᵊl) *or* **mangoldwurzel** ('mæŋgəʊldˌwɜ:zᵊl) *n* a Eurasian variety of beet, cultivated as a cattle food, having a large yellowish root. [C18: from G *Mangoldwurzel,* from *Mangold* beet + *Wurzel* root]

manger ('meɪndʒə) *n* a trough or box in a stable, barn, etc., from which horses or cattle feed. [C14: from OF *maingeure* food trough, from *mangier* to eat, ult. from L *mandūcāre* to chew]

mangetout (ˌmɒnʒ'tu:) *n* a variety of garden pea in which the pod is also edible. Also called: **sugar pea.** [C20: from F lit.: eat all]

mangey ('meɪndʒɪ) *adj* **mangier, mangiest.** a variant spelling of **mangy.**

mangle[1] ❶ ('mæŋgᵊl) *vb* **mangles, mangling, mangled.** (*tr*) **1** to mutilate, disfigure, or destroy by cutting, crushing, or tearing. **2** to ruin, spoil, or mar. [C14: from Norman F *mangler,* prob. from OF *mahaignier* to maim]
▸'**mangled** *adj* ▸'**mangler** *n*

mangle[2] ('mæŋgᵊl) *n* **1** Also called: **wringer.** a machine for pressing or drying textiles, clothes, etc., consisting of two heavy rollers between which the cloth is passed. ◆ *vb* **mangles, mangling, mangled.** (*tr*) **2** to press or dry in a mangle. [C18: from Du. *mangel,* ult. from LL *manganum.* See MANGONEL]

mango ('mæŋgəʊ) *n, pl* **mangoes** *or* **mangos. 1** a tropical Asian evergreen tree, cultivated in the tropics for its fruit. **2** the ovoid edible fruit of this tree, having a smooth rind and sweet juicy flesh. [C16: via Port. from Malay *mangā,* from Tamil *mānkāy,* from *mān* mango tree + *kāy* fruit]

mangonel ('mæŋgəˌnɛl) *n History.* a war engine for hurling stones. [C13: via OF from Med. L *manganellus,* ult. from Gk *manganon*]

mangrove ('mæŋgrəʊv, 'mæn-) *n* any of various tropical evergreen trees or shrubs, having stiltlike intertwining aerial roots and forming dense thickets along coasts. [C17 *mangrow* (changed through infl. of *grove*), from Port. *mangue,* ult. from Taino]

mangy ❶ *or* **mangey** ('meɪndʒɪ) *adj* **mangier, mangiest. 1** having or caused by mange. **2** scruffy or shabby.
▸'**mangily** *adv* ▸'**manginess** *n*

THESAURUS

director, executive, gaffer (*inf., chiefly Brit.*), governor, head, organizer, overseer, proprietor, superintendent

mandate *n* **1, 2** = **command,** authority, authorization, bidding, canon, charge, commission, decree, directive, edict, fiat, injunction, instruction, order, precept, sanction, warrant

mandatory *adj* **2** = **compulsory,** binding, obligatory, required, requisite
Antonyms *adj* discretionary, nonbinding, noncompulsory, nonobligatory, optional, unnecessary, voluntary

manful *adj* = **brave,** bold, courageous, daring, determined, gallant, hardy, heroic, indomitable, intrepid, manly, noble, powerful, resolute, stalwart, stout, stout-hearted, strong, valiant, vigorous

manfully *adv* = **bravely,** boldly, courageously, desperately, determinedly, gallantly, hard, heroically, intrepidly, nobly, powerfully, resolutely, stalwartly, stoutly, strongly, valiantly, vigorously, with might and main

mangle[1] *vb* **1, 2** = **crush,** butcher, cripple, cut, deform, destroy, disfigure, distort, hack, lacerate, maim, mar, maul, mutilate, rend, ruin, spoil, tear, total (*sl.*), trash (*sl.*), wreck

mangy *adj* **2** = **scruffy,** dirty, grungy (*sl., chiefly US*), mean, moth-eaten, scabby (*inf.*), scuzzy (*sl., chiefly US*), seedy, shabby, shoddy, squalid
Antonyms *adj* attractive, choice, clean, de luxe, fine, splendid, spotless, superb, tidy, well-dressed, well-kempt, well-kept

manhandle ⓣ ('mæn,hænd°l, ,mæn'hænd°l) *vb* **manhandles, manhandling, manhandled.** (*tr*) **1** to handle or push (someone) about roughly. **2** to move or do by manpower rather than by machinery.

Manhattan (mæn'hæt°n, mən-) *n* a mixed drink consisting of four parts whisky, one part vermouth, and a dash of bitters. [after *Manhattan*, a borough of New York City, in the US]

manhole ('mæn,həʊl) *n* **1** Also called: **inspection chamber.** a shaft with a removable cover that leads down to a sewer or drain. **2** a hole, usually with a detachable cover, through which a man can enter a boiler, tank, etc.

manhood ⓣ ('mænhʊd) *n* **1** the state or quality of being a man or being manly. **2** men collectively. **3** the state of being human.

man-hour *n* a unit of work in industry, equal to the work done by one man in one hour.

manhunt ('mæn,hʌnt) *n* an organized search, usually by police, for a wanted man or fugitive.

mania ⓣ ('meɪnɪə) *n* **1** a mental disorder characterized by great excitement and occasionally violent behaviour. **2** obsessional enthusiasm or partiality. [C14: via LL from Gk: madness]

-mania *n combining form.* indicating extreme desire or pleasure of a specified kind or an abnormal excitement aroused by something: *kleptomania; nymphomania; pyromania.* [from MANIA]
▸**-maniac** *n and adj combining form.*

maniac ⓣ ('meɪnɪ,æk) *n* **1** a wild disorderly person. **2** a person who has a great craving or enthusiasm for something. **3** *Psychiatry, obs.* a person afflicted with mania. [C17: from LL *maniacus* belonging to madness, from Gk]

maniacal ⓣ (mə'naɪək°l) *or* **maniac** *adj* **1** affected with or characteristic of mania. **2** characteristic of or befitting a maniac: *maniacal laughter.*
▸**ma'niacally** *adv*

manic ('mænɪk) *adj* **1** characterizing, denoting, or affected by mania. ◆ *n* **2** a person afflicted with mania. [C19: from Gk, from MANIA]

manic-depressive *Psychiatry.* ◆ *adj* **1** denoting a mental disorder characterized by an alternation between extreme euphoria and deep depression. ◆ *n* **2** a person afflicted with this disorder.

Manichaeism *or* **Manicheism** ('mænɪki:,ɪzəm) *n* the system of religious doctrines taught by the Persian prophet Mani about the 3rd century A.D. It was based on a supposed primordial conflict between light and darkness or goodness and evil. [C14: from LL *Manichaeus*, from LGk *Manikhaios* of Mani]
▸**,Mani'chaean** *or* **,Mani'chean** *adj, n* ▸**'Manichee** *n*

manicure ('mænɪ,kjʊə) *n* **1** care of the hands and fingernails, involving shaping the nails, removing cuticles, etc. **2** Also called: **manicurist.** a person who gives manicures, esp. as a profession. ◆ *vb* **manicures, manicuring, manicured. 3** to care for (the hands and fingernails) in this way. [C19: from F, from L *manus* hand + *cūra* care]

manifest ⓣ ('mænɪ,fest) *adj* **1** easily noticed or perceived; obvious. **2** *Psychoanalysis.* of or relating to the ostensible elements of a dream: *manifest content.* Cf. **latent** (sense 5). ◆ *vb* **3** (*tr*) to show plainly; reveal or display. **4** (*tr*) to prove beyond doubt. **5** (*intr*) (of a disembodied spirit) to appear in visible form. ◆ *n* **6** a customs document containing particulars of a ship, its cargo, and its destination. **7a** a list of cargo, passengers, etc., on an aeroplane. **7b** a list of railway trucks or their cargo. [C14: from L *manifestus* plain, lit.: struck with the hand]
▸**'mani,festable** *adj* ▸**'mani,festly** *adv*

manifestation ⓣ (,mænɪfe'steɪʃən) *n* **1** the act of demonstrating; display. **2** the state of being manifested. **3** an indication or sign. **4** a public demonstration of feeling. **5** the materialization of a disembodied spirit.
▸**,mani'festative** *adj*

manifesto (,mænɪ'festəʊ) *n, pl* **manifestos** *or* **manifestoes.** a public declaration of intent, policy, aims, etc., as issued by a political party, government, or movement. [C17: from It., from *manifestare* to MANIFEST]

manifold ⓣ ('mænɪ,fəʊld) *adj Formal.* **1** of several different kinds; multiple. **2** having many different forms, features, or elements. ◆ *n* **3** something having many varied parts, forms, or features. **4** a chamber or pipe with a number of inlets or outlets used to collect or distribute a fluid. In an internal-combustion engine the **inlet manifold** carries the vaporized fuel from the carburettor to the inlet ports and the **exhaust manifold** carries the exhaust gases away. ◆ *vb* (*tr*) **5** to duplicate (a page, book, etc.). **6** to make manifold; multiply. [OE *manigfeald.* See MANY, -FOLD]
▸**'mani,foldly** *adv* ▸**'mani,foldness** *n*

manikin *or* **mannikin** ('mænɪkɪn) *n* **1** a little man; dwarf or child. **2** an anatomical model of the body or a part of the body, esp. for use in medical or art instruction. **3** a variant of **mannequin.** [C17: from Du. *manneken*, dim. of MAN]

Manila (mə'nɪlə) *n* **1** a type of cigar made in Manila, chief port of the Philippines. **2** short for **Manila hemp** *or* **Manila paper.**

Manila hemp *or* **Manilla hemp** *n* a fibre obtained from the abaca plant, used for rope, paper, etc.

Manila paper *or* **Manilla paper** *n* a strong usually brown paper made from Manila hemp or similar fibres.

manilla (mə'nɪlə) *n* an early form of currency in W Africa in the pattern of a small bracelet. [from Sp.: bracelet, dim. of *mano* hand, from L *manus*]

man in the street *n* the typical or ordinary person.

manioc ('mænɪ,ɒk) *or* **manioca** (,mænɪ'əʊkə) *n* another name for **cassava** (sense 1). [C16: from Tupi *mandioca*]

manipulate ⓣ (mə'nɪpjʊ,leɪt) *vb* **manipulates, manipulating, manipulated. 1** (*tr*) to handle or use, esp. with some skill. **2** to control or influence (something or someone) cleverly, deviously, or skilfully. **3** to falsify (a bill, accounts, etc.) for one's own advantage. **4** (in physiotherapy) to examine or treat manually, as in loosening a joint. [C19: back formation from *manipulation*, from L *manipulus* handful]
▸**manipulability** (mə,nɪpjʊlə'bɪlɪtɪ) *n* ▸**ma'nipu,latable** *or* **ma'nipulable** *adj* ▸**ma,nipu'lation** *n* ▸**ma'nipulative** *adj* ▸**ma'nipu,lator** *n* ▸**ma'nipulatory** *adj*

Manitoban (,mænɪ'təʊbən) *adj* **1** of or denoting Manitoba, a province of W Canada. ◆ *n* **2** a native or inhabitant of Manitoba.

manitou, manitu ('mænɪ,tu:), *or* **manito** ('mænɪ,təʊ) *n, pl* **manitous, manitus, manitos** *or* **manitou, manitu, manito.** (among the Algonquian Indians) a deified spirit or force. [C17: of Amerind origin]

man jack *n Inf.* a single individual (in **every man jack, no man jack**).

mankind ⓣ (,mæn'kaɪnd) *n* **1** human beings collectively; humanity. **2** men collectively, as opposed to womankind.

> **USAGE NOTE** Some people object to the use of *mankind* to refer to all human beings and prefer the term *humankind.*

manlike ('mæn,laɪk) *adj* resembling or befitting a man.

manly ⓣ ('mænlɪ) *adj* **manlier, manliest. 1** possessing qualities, such as vigour or courage, generally regarded as appropriate to or typical of a man; masculine. **2** characteristic of or befitting a man.
▸**'manliness** *n*

man-made ⓣ *adj* made by man; artificial.

manna ('mænə) *n* **1** *Old Testament.* the miraculous food which sustained the Israelites in the wilderness (Exodus 16:14–36). **2** any spiritual or divine nourishment. **3** a windfall (esp. in **manna from heaven**). **4** a sweet substance obtained from various plants, esp. from the **manna** or **flowering ash** of S Europe, used as a mild laxative. [OE via LL from Gk, from Heb. *mān*]

manned (mænd) *adj* **1** supplied or equipped with men, esp. soldiers. **2** (of spacecraft, etc.) having a human crew.

mannequin ('mænɪkɪn) *n* **1** a woman who wears the clothes displayed at a fashion show; model. **2** a life-size dummy of the human body used to fit or display clothes. [C18: via F from Du. *manneken* MANIKIN]

manner ⓣ ('mænə) *n* **1** a way of doing or being. **2** a person's bearing and behaviour. **3** the style or customary way of doing or accomplish-

THESAURUS

manhandle *vb* **1** = **rough up**, handle roughly, knock about *or* around, maul, paw (*inf.*), pull, push **2** = **haul**, carry, heave, hump (*Brit. sl.*), lift, manoeuvre, pull, push, shove, tug

manhood *n* **1** = **manliness**, bravery, courage, determination, firmness, fortitude, hardihood, manfulness, masculinity, maturity, mettle, resolution, spirit, strength, valour, virility

mania *n* **1** = **madness**, aberration, craziness, delirium, dementia, derangement, disorder, frenzy, insanity, lunacy **2** = **obsession**, craving, craze, desire, enthusiasm, fad (*inf.*), fetish, fixation, partiality, passion, preoccupation, rage, thing (*inf.*)

maniac *n* **1, 3** = **madman** *or* **madwoman**, headbanger (*inf.*), headcase (*inf.*), loony (*sl.*), lunatic, nutcase (*sl.*), nutter (*Brit. sl.*), psycho (*sl.*), psychopath **2** = **fanatic**, enthusiast, fan, fiend (*inf.*), freak (*inf.*)

maniacal *adj* **1, 2** = **crazed**, berserk, crazy, demented, deranged, frenzied, insane, lunatic, mad, neurotic, nutty (*sl.*), psychotic, raving, unbalanced, wild

manifest *adj* **1** = **obvious**, apparent, blatant, bold, clear, conspicuous, distinct, evident, glaring, noticeable, open, palpable, patent, plain, salient, unmistakable, visible ◆ *vb* **3, 4** = **display**, declare, demonstrate, establish, evince, exhibit, expose, express, make plain, prove, reveal, set forth, show
Antonyms *adj* ≠ **obvious:** concealed, disguised, hidden, inconspicuous, indistinct, masked, suppressed, unapparent, vague, veiled ◆ *vb* ≠ **display:** conceal, cover, cover up, deny, hide, mask, obscure, refute

manifestation *n* **1, 3** = **display**, appearance, demonstration, disclosure, exhibition, exposure, expression, indication, instance, mark, materialization, revelation, show, sign, symptom, token

manifold *adj* **1, 2** *Formal* = **numerous**, abundant, assorted, copious, diverse, diversified, many, multifarious, multifold, multiple, multiplied, multitudinous, varied, various

manipulate *vb* **1** = **work**, employ, handle, operate, ply, use, wield **2** = **influence**, conduct, control, direct, do a number on (*chiefly US*), engineer, guide, manoeuvre, negotiate, steer, twist around one's little finger

mankind *n* **1** = **people**, Homo sapiens, humanity, humankind, human race, man

manliness *n* **1** = **virility**, boldness, bravery, courage, fearlessness, firmness, hardihood, heroism, independence, intrepidity, machismo, manfulness, manhood, masculinity, mettle, resolution, stoutheartedness, valour, vigour

manly *adj* **1** = **virile**, bold, brave, butch (*sl.*), courageous, daring, dauntless, fearless, gallant, hardy, heroic, macho, male, manful, masculine, muscular, noble, powerful, red-blooded, resolute, robust, stout-hearted, strapping, strong, valiant, valorous, vigorous, well-built
Antonyms *adj* camp (*inf.*), cowardly, craven, delicate, effeminate, faint-hearted, feeble, feminine, frail, girlie, ignoble, irresolute, sickly, soft, timid, unmanly, weak, wimpish *or* wimpy (*inf.*), womanish

man-made *adj* = **artificial**, ersatz, manufactured, mock, plastic (*sl.*), synthetic

manner *n* **1, 3** = **style**, approach, custom, fashion, form, genre, habit, line, means, method,

ing something. **4** type or kind. **5** mannered style, as in art; mannerism. **6 in a manner of speaking.** in a way; so to speak. **7 to the manner born.** naturally fitted to a specified role or activity. [C12: via Norman F from OF *maniere,* from Vulgar L *manuāria* (unattested) a way of handling something, noun use of L *manuārius* belonging to the hand, from *manus* hand]

mannered Ⓣ ('mænəd) *adj* **1** having idiosyncrasies or mannerisms; affected. **2** (*in combination*) having manners as specified: *ill-mannered.*

mannerism Ⓣ ('mænə,rɪzəm) *n* **1** a distinctive and individual gesture or trait. **2** (*often cap.*) a principally Italian movement in art and architecture between the High Renaissance and Baroque periods (1520–1600), using distortion and exaggeration of human proportions, perspective, etc. **3** adherence to a distinctive or affected manner, esp. in art or literature.
▸**'mannerist** *n, adj* ▸**,manner'istic** *adj* ▸**,manner'istically** *adv*

mannerless ('mænəlɪs) *adj* having bad manners; boorish.
▸**'mannerlessness** *n*

mannerly Ⓣ ('mænəlɪ) *adj* **1** well-mannered; polite. ◆ *adv* **2** *Now rare.* with good manners; politely.
▸**'mannerliness** *n*

manners Ⓣ ('mænəz) *pl n* **1** social conduct. **2** a socially acceptable way of behaving.

mannikin ('mænɪkɪn) *n* a variant spelling of **manikin.**

mannish ('mænɪʃ) *adj* **1** (of a woman) displaying qualities regarded as typical of a man. **2** of or resembling a man.
▸**'mannishly** *adv* ▸**'mannishness** *n*

manoeuvre Ⓣ *or US* **maneuver** (mə'nuːvə) *n* **1** a contrived, complicated, and possibly deceptive plan or action. **2** a movement or action requiring dexterity and skill. **3a** a tactic or movement of a military or naval unit. **3b** (*pl*) tactical exercises, usually on a large scale. **4** a planned movement of an aircraft in flight. **5** any change from the straight steady course of a ship. ◆ *vb* **manoeuvres, manoeuvring, manoeuvred** *or US* **manoeuvers, manoeuvering, manoeuvered. 6** (*tr*) to contrive or accomplish with skill or cunning. **7** (*intr*) to manipulate situations, etc., in order to gain some end. **8** (*intr*) to perform a manoeuvre or manoeuvres. **9** to move or deploy or be moved or deployed, as military units, etc. [C15: from F, from Med. L *manuopera* manual work, from L *manū operāre* to work with the hand]
▸**ma'noeuvrable** *or US* **ma'neuverable** *adj* ▸**ma,noeuvra'bility** *or US* **ma,neuvera'bility** *n* ▸**ma'noeuvrer** *or US* **ma'neuverer** *n* ▸**ma'noeuvring** *or US* **ma'neuvering** *n*

man of God *n* **1** a saint or prophet. **2** a clergyman.

man of straw *n* **1** a man who cannot be relied upon to honour his financial commitments, esp. because of his limited resources. **2** any weak or vulnerable man.

man-of-war *or* **man o' war** *n, pl* **men-of-war** *or* **men o' war. 1** a warship. **2** See **Portuguese man-of-war.**

man-of-war bird *or* **man-o'-war bird** *n* another name for **frigate bird.**

manometer (mə'nɒmɪtə) *n* an instrument for comparing pressures. [C18: from F *manomètre,* from Gk *manos* sparse + *metron* measure]
▸**manometric** (,mænəʊ'mɛtrɪk) *or* **,mano'metrical** *adj*

manor ('mænə) *n* **1** (in medieval Europe) the manor house of a lord and the lands attached to it. **2** a manor house. **3** a landed estate. **4** *Brit. sl.* a geographical area of operation, esp. of a local police force. [C13: from OF *manoir* dwelling, from *maneir* to dwell, from L *manēre* to remain]
▸**manorial** (mə'nɔːrɪəl) *adj*

manor house *n* (esp. formerly) the house of the lord of a manor.

manpower ('mæn,paʊə) *n* **1** power supplied by men. **2** a unit of power based on the rate at which a man can work; roughly 75 watts. **3** the number of people needed or available for a job.

manqué *French.* ('mɒŋkeɪ) *adj* (*postpositive*) unfulfilled; potential; would-be: *the manager is an actor manqué.* [C19: lit.: having missed]

mansard ('mænsɑːd, -səd) *n* a roof having two slopes on both sides and both ends, the lower slopes being steeper than the upper. Also called: **mansard roof.** [C18: from F *mansarde,* after François *Mansart* (1598–1666), F architect]

manse (mæns) *n* (in certain religious denominations) the house provided for a minister. [C15: from Med. L *mansus* dwelling, from p.p. of L *manēre* to stay]

manservant ('mæn,sɜːvənt) *n, pl* **menservants.** a male servant, esp. a valet.

mansion Ⓣ ('mænʃən) *n* **1** Also called: **mansion house.** a large and imposing house. **2** a less common word for **manor house. 3** (*pl*) *Brit.* a block of flats. [C14: via OF from L *mansio* a remaining, from *mansus;* see MANSE]

Mansion House *n* **the. 1** the residence of the Lord Mayor of London. **2** the residence of the Lord Mayor of Dublin.

man-sized *adj* **1** of a size appropriate for or convenient for a man. **2** *Inf.* big; large.

manslaughter ('mæn,slɔːtə) *n* **1** *Law.* the unlawful killing of one human being by another without malice aforethought. Cf. **murder. 2** (loosely) the killing of a human being.

manta ('mæntə) *n* **1** Also called: **manta ray, devilfish, devil ray.** any large ray (fish), having very wide winglike pectoral fins and feeding on plankton. **2** a rough cotton cloth made in Spain and Spanish America. **3** a piece of this used as a blanket or shawl. [Sp.: cloak, from Vulgar L; see MANTLE]

manteau ('mæntəʊ) *n, pl* **manteaus** (-təʊz) *or* **manteaux** (-təʊ). a cloak or mantle. [C17: via F from L *mantellum* MANTLE]

mantel ('mænt^{ə}l) *n* **1** a wooden, stone, or iron frame around the opening of a fireplace, together with its decorative facing. **2** Also called: **mantel shelf.** a shelf above this frame. [C15: from F, var. of MANTLE]

mantelet ('mænt^{ə},lɛt) *or* **mantlet** *n* **1** a woman's short mantle, worn in the mid-19th century. **2** a portable bulletproof screen or shelter. [C14: from OF, dim. of *mantel* MANTLE]

mantelpiece ('mænt^{ə}l,piːs) *n* **1** Also called: **mantel shelf, chimneypiece.** a shelf above a fireplace often forming part of the mantel. **2** another word for **mantel** (sense 1).

mantic ('mæntɪk) *adj* **1** of or relating to divination and prophecy. **2** having divining or prophetic powers. [C19: from Gk *mantikos* prophetic, from *mantis* seer]
▸**'mantically** *adv*

-mantic *adj combining form.* forming adjectives from nouns ending in **-mancy.**

mantilla (mæn'tɪlə) *n* a woman's lace or silk scarf covering the shoulders and head, worn esp. in Spain. [C18: Sp., dim. of *manta* cloak]

mantis ('mæntɪs) *n, pl* **mantises** *or* **mantes** (-tiːz). any carnivorous typically green insect of warm and tropical regions, having a long body and large eyes and resting with the first pair of legs raised as if in prayer. Also called: **praying mantis.** [C17: NL, from Gk: prophet, alluding to its praying posture]

mantissa (mæn'tɪsə) *n* the fractional part of a common logarithm representing the digits of the associated number but not its magnitude: *the mantissa of 2.4771 is .4771.* [C17: from L: something added]

mantle Ⓣ ('mænt^{ə}l) *n* **1** *Arch.* a loose wrap or cloak. **2** such a garment regarded as a symbol of someone's power or authority. **3** anything that covers completely or envelops. **4** a small dome-shaped or cylindrical mesh, used to increase illumination in a gas or oil lamp by becoming incandescent. **5** *Zool.* a protective layer of epidermis in molluscs and brachiopods that secretes a substance forming the shell. **6** *Ornithol.* the feathers of the folded wings and back, esp. when of a different colour from the remaining feathers. **7** *Geol.* the part of the earth between the crust and the core. **8** a less common spelling of **mantel.** ◆ *vb* **mantles, mantling, mantled. 9** (*tr*) to envelop or supply with a mantle. **10** (*tr*) to spread over or become spread over. **11** (*intr*) to blush; flush. [C13: via OF from L *mantellum,* dim. of *mantum* cloak]

mantle rock *n* the loose rock material, including glacial drift, soils, etc., that covers the bedrock and forms the land surface.

mantra ('mæntrə, 'mʌn-) *n* **1** *Hinduism.* any of those parts of the Vedic literature which consist of the metrical psalms of praise. **2** *Hinduism, Buddhism.* any sacred word or syllable used as an object of concentration. [C19: from Sansk., lit.: speech, instrument of thought, from *man* to think]

mantua ('mæntjʊə) *n* a woman's loose gown of the 17th and 18th centuries. [C17: changed from MANTEAU, through the infl. of *Mantua,* city in N Italy]

manual Ⓣ ('mænjʊəl) *adj* **1** of or relating to a hand or hands. **2** operated or done by hand. **3** physical, as opposed to mental or mechanical: *manual labour.* **4** by human labour rather than automatic or computer-aided means. ◆ *n* **5** a book, esp. of instructions or information. **6** *Music.* one of the keyboards played by hand on an organ. **7** *Mil.* the prescribed drill with small arms. [C15: via OF from L *manuālis,* from *manus* hand]
▸**'manually** *adv*

THESAURUS

mode, practice, procedure, process, routine, tack, tenor, usage, way, wont **2** = **behaviour,** air, appearance, aspect, bearing, comportment, conduct, demeanour, deportment, look, mien (*literary*), presence, tone **4** = **type,** brand, breed, category, form, kind, nature, sort, variety

mannered *adj* **1** = **affected,** artificial, arty-farty (*inf.*), posed, pretentious, pseudo (*inf.*), put-on, stilted
Antonyms *adj* genuine, honest, natural, real, sincere, unaffected, unpretentious

mannerism *n* **1** = **habit,** characteristic, foible, idiosyncrasy, peculiarity, quirk, trait, trick

mannerly *adj* **1** = **polite,** civil, civilized, courteous, decorous, genteel, gentlemanly, gracious, ladylike, polished, refined, respectful, well-behaved, well-bred, well-mannered
Antonyms *adj* boorish, discourteous, disrespectful, ill-mannered, impertinent, impolite, impudent, insolent, rude, unmannerly

manners *pl n* **1** = **behaviour,** bearing, breeding, carriage, comportment, conduct, demeanour, deportment **2** = **politeness,** ceremony, courtesy, decorum, etiquette, formalities, good form, polish, politesse, proprieties, protocol, p's and q's, refinement, social graces, the done thing

manoeuvre *n* **1** = **stratagem,** action, artifice, dodge, intrigue, machination, move, movement, plan, plot, ploy, ruse, scheme, subterfuge, tactic, trick **3** = **movement,** deployment, evolution, exercise, operation ◆ *vb* **6** = **manipulate,** contrive, devise, engineer, intrigue, machinate, manage, plan, plot, pull strings, scheme, wangle (*inf.*) **8** = **steer,** direct, drive, guide, handle, navigate, negotiate, pilot **9** = **move,** deploy, exercise

mansion *n* **1, 2** = **residence,** abode, dwelling, habitation, hall, manor, seat, villa

mantle *n* **1** *Archaic* = **cloak,** cape, hood, shawl, wrap **3** = **covering,** blanket, canopy, cloud, cover, curtain, envelope, pall, screen, shroud, veil ◆ *vb* **9** = **cover,** blanket, cloak, cloud, disguise, envelop, hide, mask, overspread, screen, shroud, veil, wrap

manual *adj* **2-4** = **hand-operated,** done by hand, human, physical ◆ *n* **5** = **handbook,** bible, guide, guidebook, instructions, workbook

manufactory (ˌmænjuˈfæktərɪ, -trɪ) *n, pl* **manufactories.** an obsolete word for **factory.** [C17: from obs. *manufact;* see MANUFACTURE]

manufacture ❶ (ˌmænjuˈfæktʃə) *vb* **manufactures, manufacturing, manufactured. 1** to process or make (a product) from a raw material, esp. as a large-scale operation using machinery. **2** (*tr*) to invent or concoct. ◆ *n* **3** the production of goods, esp. by industrial processes. **4** a manufactured product. **5** the creation or production of anything. [C16: from obs. *manufact* handmade, from LL *manūfactus,* from L *manus* hand + *facere* to make]
▸ˌ**manuˈfacturing** *n, adj*

manufacturer ❶ (ˌmænjuˈfæktʃərə) *n* a person or business concern that manufactures goods or owns a factory.

manuka (ˈmɑːnukə) *n* a New Zealand tree with strong elastic wood and aromatic leaves. Also called: **tea tree.** [from Maori]

manumit ❶ (ˌmænjuˈmɪt) *vb* **manumits, manumitting, manumitted.** (*tr*) to free from slavery, servitude, etc.; emancipate. [C15: from L *manūmittere* to release, from *manū* from one's hand + *ēmittere* to send away]
▸**manumission** (ˌmænjuˈmɪʃən) *n*

manure ❶ (məˈnjʊə) *n* **1** animal excreta, usually with straw, etc., used to fertilize land. **2** *Chiefly Brit.* any material, esp. chemical fertilizer, used to fertilize land. ◆ *vb* **manures, manuring, manured. 3** (*tr*) to spread manure upon (fields or soil). [C14: from Med. L *manuopera* manual work; see MANOEUVRE]
▸**maˈnurer** *n*

manus (ˈmeɪnəs) *n, pl* **manus. 1** *Anat.* the wrist and hand. **2** the corresponding part in other vertebrates. [C19: L: hand]

manuscript (ˈmænjuˌskrɪpt) *n* **1** a book or other document written by hand. **2** the original handwritten or typed version of a book, article, etc., as submitted by an author for publication. **3** handwriting, as opposed to printing. [C16: from Med. L *manūscriptus,* from L *manus* hand + *scribere* to write]

Manx (mæŋks) *adj* **1** of or relating to the Isle of Man (an island in the Irish Sea), its inhabitants, their language, or their dialect of English. ◆ *n* **2** an almost extinct language of the Isle of Man, closely related to Scottish Gaelic. **3 the Manx.** (*functioning as pl*) the people of the Isle of Man. [C16: earlier *Maniske,* of Scand. origin, from *Mana* Isle of Man + *-iske* -ISH]

Manx cat *n* a short-haired tailless variety of cat, believed to originate on the Isle of Man.

Manxman (ˈmæŋksmən) *or* (*fem*) **Manxwoman** (ˈmæŋksˌwʊmən) *n, pl* **Manxmen** *or* **Manxwomen.** a native or inhabitant of the Isle of Man.

many ❶ (ˈmɛnɪ) *determiner* **1** (sometimes preceded by *a great* or *a good*) **1a** a large number of: *many times.* **1b** (*as pron; functioning as pl*): *many are seated already.* **2** (foll. by *a, an,* or *another,* and a sing noun) each of a considerable number of: *many a man.* **3** (preceded by *as, too, that,* etc.) **3a** a great number of: *as many apples as you like.* **3b** (*as pron; functioning as pl*): *I have as many as you.* ◆ *n* **4 the many.** the majority of mankind, esp. the common people. [OE *manig*]

many-sided *adj* having many sides, aspects, etc.
▸ˌ**many-ˈsidedness** *n*

many-valued logic *n* any of various logics in which the truth-values that a proposition may have are not restricted to truth and falsity.

manzanilla (ˌmænzəˈnɪlə) *n* a very dry pale sherry. [C19: from Sp.: camomile (referring to its bouquet)]

Maoism (ˈmaʊɪzəm) *n* Marxism-Leninism as interpreted by Mao Tse-tung (1893–1976), Chinese statesman: distinguished by its theory of guerrilla warfare and its emphasis on the revolutionary potential of the peasantry.
▸ˈ**Maoist** *n, adj*

Maori (ˈmaʊrɪ) *n* **1** (*pl* **Maoris** *or* **Maori**) a member of the people of Polynesian origin living in New Zealand and the Cook Islands since before the arrival of European settlers. **2** the language of this people, belonging to the Malayo-Polynesian family. ◆ *adj* **3** of or relating to this people or their language.
▸ˈ**Maoriˌland** *n*

map (mæp) *n* **1** a diagrammatic representation of the earth's surface or part of it, showing the geographical distributions, positions, etc., of features such as roads, towns, relief, rainfall, etc. **2** a diagrammatic representation of the stars or of the surface of a celestial body. **3** a maplike drawing of anything. **4** *Maths.* another name for **function** (sense 5). **5** a slang word for **face** (sense 1). **6 off the map.** no longer important; out of existence (esp. in **wipe off the map**). **7 put on the map.** to make (a town, company, etc.) well-known. ◆ *vb* **maps, mapping, mapped.** (*tr*) **8** to make a map of. **9** *Maths.* to represent or transform (a function, figure, set, etc.). ◆ See also **map out.** [C16: from Med. L *mappa (mundi)* map (of the world), from L *mappa* cloth]

maple (ˈmeɪpᵊl) *n* **1** any tree or shrub of a N temperate genus, having winged seeds borne in pairs and lobed leaves. **2** the hard wood of any of these trees, used for furniture and flooring. **3** the flavour of the sap of the sugar maple. ◆ See also **sugar maple.** [C14: from OE *mapel-,* as in *mapeltrēow* maple tree]

maple leaf *n* the leaf of the maple tree, the national emblem of Canada.

maple sugar *n US & Canad.* sugar made from the sap of the sugar maple.

maple syrup *n Chiefly US & Canad.* a very sweet syrup made from the sap of the sugar maple.

map out *vb* (*tr, adv*) to plan or design.

mapping (ˈmæpɪŋ) *n Maths.* another name for **function** (sense 5).

map projection *n* a means of representing or a representation of a globe or celestial sphere or part of it on a flat map.

maquette (mæˈkɛt) *n* a sculptor's small preliminary model or sketch. [C20: from F, from It. *macchietta* a little sketch, from *macchiare,* from L *macula* blemish]

maquis (mɑːˈkiː) *n, pl* **maquis** (-ˈkiː). **1** shrubby, mostly evergreen, vegetation found in coastal regions of the Mediterranean. **2** (*often cap.*) **2a** the French underground movement that fought against the German occupying forces in World War II. **2b** a member of this movement. [C20: from F, from It. *macchia* thicket, from L *macula* spot]

mar ❶ (mɑː) *vb* **mars, marring, marred.** (*tr*) to cause harm to; spoil or impair. [OE *merran*]
▸ˈ**marrer** *n*

mar. *abbrev. for:* **1** maritime. **2** married.

Mar. *abbrev. for* March.

marabou (ˈmærəˌbuː) *n* **1** a large black-and-white African carrion-eating stork. **2** a down feather of this bird, used to trim garments. [C19: from F, from Ar. *murābit* MARABOUT: the stork is considered a holy bird in Islam]

marabout (ˈmærəˌbuː) *n* **1** a Muslim holy man or hermit of North Africa. **2** a shrine of the grave of a marabout. [C17: via F & Port. *marabuto,* from Ar. *murābit*]

maraca (məˈrækə) *n* a percussion instrument, usually one of a pair, consisting of a gourd or plastic shell filled with dried seeds, pebbles, etc. [C20: Brazilian Port., of Amerind origin]

marae (məˈraɪ) *n* **1** *NZ.* a traditional Maori tribal meeting place, originally one in the open air, now frequently a purpose-built building. **2** (in Polynesia) an open-air place of worship. [from Maori]

maranta (mɑːˈræntə) *n* any of various tropical monocotyledons with ornamental leaves. [C19: after B. *Maranta* 16th-century Venetian botanist]

marasca (məˈræskə) *n* a European cherry tree with red acid-tasting fruit. [C19: from It., var. of *amarasca,* ult. from L *amārus* bitter]

maraschino (ˌmærəˈskiːnəʊ, -ˈʃiːnəʊ) *n* a liqueur made from marasca cherries, having a taste like bitter almonds. [C18: from It.; see MARASCA]

maraschino cherry *n* a cherry preserved in maraschino or an imitation of this liqueur.

marasmus (məˈræzməs) *n Pathol.* general emaciation, esp. of infants, thought to be associated with severe malnutrition or impaired utilization of nutrients. [C17: from NL, from Gk *marasmos,* from *marainein* to waste]
▸**maˈrasmic** *adj*

marathon (ˈmærəθən) *n* **1** a race on foot of 26 miles 385 yards (42.195 kilometres). **2a** any long or arduous task, etc. **2b** (*as modifier*): *a marathon effort.* [referring to the feat of the messenger who ran more than 20 miles from Marathon to Athens to bring the news of victory in 490 B.C.]

marathon group *n* (in psychotherapy) an encounter group that lasts for many hours or days.

maraud ❶ (məˈrɔːd) *vb* to wander or raid in search of plunder. [C18: from F *marauder* to prowl, from *maraud* vagabond]
▸**maˈrauder** *n* ▸**maˈrauding** *adj*

marble (ˈmɑːbᵊl) *n* **1a** a hard crystalline metamorphic rock resulting from the recrystallization of a limestone. **1b** (*as modifier*): *a marble bust.* **2** a block or work of art of marble. **3** a small round glass or stone ball used in playing marbles. ◆ *vb* **marbles, marbling, marbled. 4** (*tr*) to mottle with variegated streaks in imitation of marble. [C12: via OF from L *marmor,* from Gk *marmaros,* rel. to Gk *marmairein* to gleam]
▸ˈ**marbled** *adj*

marbles (ˈmɑːbᵊlz) *n* **1** (*functioning as sing*) a game in which marbles are rolled at one another, similar to bowls. **2** (*functioning as pl*) *Inf.* wits: *to lose one's marbles.*

marbling (ˈmɑːblɪŋ) *n* **1** a mottled effect or pattern resembling marble.

THESAURUS

manufacture *vb* **1** = **make**, assemble, build, compose, construct, create, fabricate, forge, form, mass-produce, mould, process, produce, put together, shape, turn out **2** = **concoct**, cook up (*inf.*), devise, fabricate, hatch, invent, make up, think up, trump up ◆ *n* **3, 5** = **making**, assembly, construction, creation, fabrication, mass-production, produce, production

manufacturer *n* = **maker**, builder, constructor, creator, fabricator, factory-owner, industrialist, producer

manumission *n* = **freeing**, deliverance, emancipation, enfranchisement, liberation, release, unchaining

manure *n* **1, 2** = **compost**, droppings, dung, excrement, fertilizer, muck, ordure

many *determiner* **1a** = **numerous**, abundant, copious, countless, divers (*arch.*), frequent, innumerable, manifold, multifarious, multifold, multitudinous, myriad, profuse, sundry, umpteen (*inf.*), varied, various ◆ *n* **4 the many** = **the masses**, the crowd, (the) hoi polloi, the majority, the multitude, the people, the rank and file

mar *vb* = **spoil**, blemish, blight, blot, damage, deface, detract from, disfigure, harm, hurt, impair, injure, maim, mangle, mutilate, ruin, scar, stain, sully, taint, tarnish, vitiate
Antonyms *vb* adorn, ameliorate, better, embellish, improve, ornament

maraud *vb* = **raid**, despoil, forage, foray, harry, loot, pillage, plunder, ransack, ravage, sack

marauder *n* = **raider**, bandit, brigand, buccaneer, corsair, freebooter, mosstrooper, outlaw, pillager, pirate, plunderer, ravager, robber, sea wolf

2 such an effect obtained by transferring floating colours from a gum solution. **3** the streaks of fat in lean meat.

Marburg disease (ˈmɑːbɜːg) *n* a severe, sometimes fatal, viral disease of vervet (green) monkeys, which may be transmitted to humans. Also called: **green monkey disease.** [C20: after *Marburg,* German city in which the first human cases were recorded]

marc (mɑːk) *n* **1** the remains of grapes or other fruit that have been pressed for wine-making. **2** a brandy distilled from these. [C17: from F, from OF *marchier* to trample (grapes)]

marcasite (ˈmɑːkəˌsaɪt) *n* **1** a metallic pale yellow mineral consisting of iron pyrites in crystalline form used in jewellery. **2** a cut and polished form of steel or any white metal used for making jewellery. [C15: from Med. L *marcasīta,* from Ar. *marqashītā,* ?from Persian]

marcato (mɑːˈkɑːtəʊ) *adj, adv Music.* with each note heavily accented. [from It.: marked]

march[1] **T** (mɑːtʃ) *vb* **1** (*intr*) to walk or proceed with stately or regular steps, usually in a procession or military formation. **2** (*tr*) to make (a person or group) proceed. **3** (*tr*) to traverse or cover by marching. ◆ *n* **4** the act or an instance of marching. **5** a regular stride. **6** a long or exhausting walk. **7** advance; progression (of time, etc.). **8** a distance or route covered by marching. **9** a piece of music, as for a march. **10 steal a march on.** to gain an advantage over, esp. by a secret enterprise or trick. [C16: from OF *marchier* to tread, prob. of Gmc origin]
▸ **ˈmarcher** *n*

march[2] **T** (mɑːtʃ) *n* **1** a frontier, border, or boundary or the land lying along it, often of disputed ownership. ◆ *vb* **2** (*intr;* often foll. by *upon* or *with*) to share a common border (with). [C13: from OF *marche,* of Gmc origin]

March (mɑːtʃ) *n* the third month of the year, consisting of 31 days. [from OF, from L *Martius* (month) of Mars]

Marches (ˈmɑːtʃɪz) *n* **the. 1** the border area between England and Wales or Scotland, both characterized by continual feuding (13th–16th centuries). **2** any of various other border regions.

March hare *n* a hare during its breeding season in March, noted for its wild and excitable behaviour (esp. in **mad as a March hare**).

marching orders *pl n* **1** military orders, esp. to infantry, giving instructions about a march, its destination, etc. **2** *Inf.* any dismissal, esp. notice of dismissal from employment.

marchioness (ˈmɑːʃənɪs, ˌmɑːʃəˈnɛs) *n* **1** the wife or widow of a marquis. **2** a woman who holds the rank of marquis. [C16: from Med. L *marchionissa,* fem. of *marchiō* MARQUIS]

marchpane (ˈmɑːtʃˌpeɪn) *n* an archaic word for **marzipan.** [C15: from F]

Mardi Gras (ˈmɑːdɪ ˈgrɑː) *n* the festival of Shrove Tuesday, celebrated in some cities with great revelry. [F: fat Tuesday]

Marduk (ˈmɑːdʊk) *n* the chief god of the Babylonian pantheon.

mare[1] (mɛə) *n* the adult female of a horse or zebra. [C12: from OE, of Gmc origin]

mare[2] (ˈmɑːreɪ, -rɪ) *n, pl* **maria. 1** (*cap. when part of a name*) any of a large number of huge dry plains on the surface of the moon, visible as dark markings and once thought to be seas. **2** a similar area on the surface of Mars. [from L: sea]

mare's-nest (ˈmɛəzˌnɛst) *n* **1** a discovery imagined to be important but proving worthless. **2** a disordered situation.

mare's-tail (ˈmɛəzˌteɪl) *n* **1** a wisp of trailing cirrus cloud, indicating strong winds at high levels. **2** an erect pond plant with minute flowers and crowded whorls of narrow leaves.

margaric (mɑːˈgærɪk) *or* **margaritic** *adj* of or resembling pearl. [C19: from Gk *margaron* pearl]

margarine (ˌmɑːdʒəˈriːn, ˌmɑːgə-) *n* a substitute for butter, prepared from vegetable and animal fats with added small amounts of milk, salt, vitamins, colouring matter, etc. [C19: from MARGARIC]

marge[1] (mɑːdʒ) *n Brit. inf.* short for **margarine.**

marge[2] (mɑːdʒ) *n Arch.* a margin. [C16: from F]

margin **T** (ˈmɑːdʒɪn) *n* **1** an edge or rim, and the area immediately adjacent to it; border. **2** the blank space surrounding the text on a page. **3** a vertical line on a page delineating this space. **4** an additional amount or one beyond the minimum necessary: *a margin of error.* **5** *Chiefly Austral.* a payment made in addition to a basic wage, esp. for special skill or responsibility. **6** a bound or limit. **7** the amount by which one thing differs from another. **8** *Commerce.* the profit on a transaction. **9** *Econ.* the minimum return below which an enterprise becomes unprofitable. **10** *Finance.* collateral deposited by a client with a broker as security. ◆ Also (archaic): **margent** (ˈmɑːdʒənt). ◆ *vb* (*tr*) **11** to provide with a margin; border. **12** *Finance.* to deposit a margin upon. [C14: from L *margō* border]

marginal **T** (ˈmɑːdʒɪnᵊl) *adj* **1** of, in, on, or constituting a margin. **2** close to a limit, esp. a lower limit: *marginal legal ability.* **3** not considered central or important; insignificant. **4** *Econ.* relating to goods or services produced and sold at the margin of profitability: *marginal cost.* **5** *Politics, chiefly Brit. & NZ.* of or designating a constituency in which elections tend to be won by small margins: *a marginal seat.* **6** designating agricultural land on the margin of cultivated zones. ◆ *n* **7** *Politics, chiefly Brit. & NZ.* a marginal constituency.
▸ **marginality** (ˌmɑːdʒɪˈnælɪtɪ) *n* ▸ **ˈmarginally** *adv*

marginalia (ˌmɑːdʒɪˈneɪlɪə) *pl n* notes in the margin of a book, manuscript, or letter. [C19: NL, noun (neuter pl) from *marginālis* marginal]

marginate (ˈmɑːdʒɪˌneɪt) *vb* **marginates, marginating, marginated. 1** (*tr*) to provide with a margin or margins. ◆ *adj* **2** *Biol.* having a margin of a distinct colour or form. [C18: from L *margināre*]
▸ **ˌmarginˈation** *n*

margrave (ˈmɑːˌgreɪv) *n* a German nobleman ranking above a count. Margraves were originally counts appointed to govern frontier provinces, but all eventually became princes of the Holy Roman Empire. [C16: from MDu. *markgrave,* lit.: count of the MARCH[2]]
▸ **margravate** (ˈmɑːgrəvɪt) *n*

margravine (ˈmɑːgrəˌviːn) *n* **1** the wife or widow of a margrave. **2** a woman who holds the rank of margrave. [C17: from MDu., fem of MARGRAVE]

marguerite (ˌmɑːgəˈriːt) *n* **1** a cultivated garden plant whose flower heads have white or pale yellow rays around a yellow disc. **2** any of various related plants with daisy-like flowers. [C19: from F: daisy, pearl, from L, from Gk, from *margaron*]

maria (ˈmɑːrɪə) *n* the plural of **mare**[2].

mariachi (ˌmɑːrɪˈɑːtʃɪ) *n* a small ensemble of street musicians in Mexico. [C20: from Mexican Sp.]

marigold (ˈmærɪˌgəʊld) *n* **1** any of various tropical American plants cultivated for their yellow or orange flower heads and strongly scented foliage. **2** any of various similar or related plants, such as the marsh marigold. [C14: from *Mary* (the Virgin) + GOLD]

marijuana **T** *or* **marihuana** (ˌmærɪˈhwɑːnə) *n* **1** the dried leaves and flowers of the hemp plant, used for its euphoric effects, esp. in cigarettes. See also **cannabis. 2** another name for **hemp** (the plant). [C19: from Mexican Sp.]

marimba (məˈrɪmbə) *n* a Latin American percussion instrument consisting of a set of hardwood plates placed over tuned metal resonators, played with two soft-headed sticks in each hand. [C18: of West African origin]

marina (məˈriːnə) *n* an elaborate docking facility for yachts and other pleasure boats. [C19: via It. & Sp. from L: MARINE]

marinade *n* (ˌmærɪˈneɪd). **1** a spiced liquid mixture of oil, wine, vinegar, etc., in which meat or fish is soaked before cooking. **2** meat or fish soaked in this. ◆ *vb* (ˈmærɪˌneɪd), **marinades, marinading, marinaded. 3** a variant of **marinate.** [C17: from F, from Sp., from *marinar* to MARINATE]

marinate (ˈmærɪˌneɪt) *vb* **marinates, marinating, marinated.** to soak in marinade. [C17: prob. from It. *marinato,* from *marinare* to pickle, ult. from L *marīnus* MARINE]
▸ **ˌmariˈnation** *n*

marine **T** (məˈriːn) *adj* (*usually prenominal*) **1** of, found in, or relating to the sea. **2** of or relating to shipping, navigation, etc. **3** of or relating to a body of seagoing troops: *marine corps.* **4** of or relating to a government department concerned with maritime affairs. **5** used or adapted for use at sea. ◆ *n* **6** shipping and navigation in general. **7** (*cap. when part of a name*) a member of a marine corps or similar body. **8** a picture of a ship, seascape, etc. **9 tell it to the marines.** *Inf.* an expression of disbelief. [C15: from OF *marin,* from L *marīnus,* from *mare* sea]

mariner **T** (ˈmærɪnə) *n* a formal or literary word for **seaman.** [C13: from Anglo-F, ult. from L *marīnus* MARINE]

Mariolatry (ˌmɛərɪˈɒlətrɪ) *n Derog.* devotion to the Virgin Mary, considered as excessive.
▸ **ˌMariˈolater** *n* ▸ **ˌMariˈolatrous** *adj*

marionette (ˌmærɪəˈnɛt) *n* a puppet or doll whose jointed limbs are moved by strings. [C17: from F, from *Marion,* dim. of *Marie* Mary + -ETTE]

Marist (ˈmɛərɪst) *n RC Church.* a member of the Society of Mary, a religious congregation founded in 1824. [C19: from F *Mariste,* from *Marie* Mary (the Virgin)]

marital **T** (ˈmærɪtᵊl) *adj* **1** of or relating to marriage. **2** of or relating to a husband. [C17: from L *marītālis,* from *marītus* married (adj), husband (n)]
▸ **ˈmaritally** *adv*

maritime **T** (ˈmærɪˌtaɪm) *adj* **1** of or relating to navigation, shipping, etc. **2** of, relating to, near, or living near the sea. **3** (of a climate) having small temperature differences between summer and winter. [C16: from L *maritimus,* from *mare* sea]

THESAURUS

march[1] *vb* **1 = walk**, file, footslog, pace, parade, stalk, stride, strut, tramp, tread ◆ *n* **5 = stride**, gait, pace, step **6 = walk**, hike, routemarch, tramp, trek **7 = progress**, advance, development, evolution, progression

march[2] *n* **1** *plural* **= borders**, borderland, boundaries, confines, frontiers, limits, march- lands

margin *n* **1, 6 = edge**, border, bound, boundary, brim, brink, confine, limit, perimeter, periphery, rim, side, verge **4 = room**, allowance, compass, elbowroom, extra, latitude, leeway, play, scope, space, surplus

marginal *adj* **1 = borderline**, bordering, on the edge, peripheral **3 = insignificant**, low, minimal, minor, negligible, slight, small

marijuana *n* **1 = cannabis**, bhang, blow (*sl.*), charas, chronic (*US sl.*), dope (*sl.*), ganja, grass (*sl.*), hash (*sl.*), hashish, hemp, kif, leaf (*sl.*), mary jane (*US sl.*), pot (*sl.*), sinsemilla, smoke (*inf.*), stuff (*sl.*), tea (*US sl.*), wacky baccy (*sl.*), weed (*sl.*)

marine *adj* **1, 2 = nautical**, maritime, naval, ocean-going, oceanic, pelagic, saltwater, sea, seafaring, seagoing, thalassic

mariner *n* **= sailor**, bluejacket, gob, hand, Jack Tar, matelot (*sl., chiefly Brit.*), navigator, salt, sea dog, seafarer, seafaring man, seaman, tar

marital *adj* **1 = matrimonial**, conjugal, connubial, married, nuptial, spousal, wedded

maritime *adj* **1 = nautical**, marine, naval, oceanic, sea, seafaring **2 = coastal**, littoral, seaside

Maritimer (ˈmærɪˌtaɪmə) *n* a native or inhabitant of the Maritime Provinces of Canada, consisting of the provinces of New Brunswick, Nova Scotia, Prince Edward Island, and usually Newfoundland.

marjoram (ˈmɑːdʒərəm) *n* **1** Also called: **sweet marjoram.** an aromatic Mediterranean plant with sweet-scented leaves, used for seasoning food and in salads. **2** Also called: **wild marjoram, pot marjoram, origan.** a similar and related European plant. See also **oregano.** [C14: via OF *majorane,* from Med. L *marjorana*]

mark[1] ❶ (mɑːk) *n* **1** a visible impression, stain, etc., on a surface, such as a spot or scratch. **2** a sign, symbol, or other indication that distinguishes something. **3** a cross or other symbol made instead of a signature. **4** a written or printed sign or symbol, as for punctuation. **5** a letter, number, or percentage used to grade academic work. **6** a thing that indicates position or directs; marker. **7** a desired or recognized standard: *up to the mark.* **8** an indication of some quality, feature, or prowess. **9** quality or importance: *a person of little mark.* **10** a target or goal. **11** impression or influence. **12** one of the temperature settings on a gas oven: *gas mark 5.* **13** *Sl.* a suitable victim, esp. for swindling. **14** (*often cap.*) (in trade names) a model, brand, or type. **15** *Naut.* one of the intervals distinctively marked on a sounding lead. **16** *Rugby.* an action in which a player within his own 22 m line catches a forward kick by an opponent and shouts "mark", which entitles him to a free kick. **17** *Australian Rules football.* **17a** a catch of the ball from a kick of at least 10 yards, after which a free kick is taken. **17b** the spot where this occurs. **18** (in medieval England and Germany) a piece of land held in common by the free men of a community. **19 the mark.** *Boxing.* the middle of the stomach. **20 make one's mark.** to succeed or achieve recognition. **21 on your mark** *or* **marks.** a command given to runners in a race to prepare themselves at the starting line. ◆ *vb* **22** to make or receive (a visible impression, trace, or stain) on (a surface). **23** (*tr*) to characterize or distinguish. **24** (often foll. by *off* or *out*) to set boundaries or limits (on). **25** (*tr*) to select, designate, or doom by or as if by a mark: *a marked man.* **26** (*tr*) to put identifying or designating labels, stamps, etc., on, esp. to indicate price. **27** (*tr*) to pay heed or attention to: *mark my words.* **28** to observe; notice. **29** to grade or evaluate (scholastic work). **30** *Football, etc.* to stay close to (an opponent) to hamper his play. **31** to keep (score) in some games. **32 mark time. 32a** to move the feet alternately as in marching but without advancing. **32b** to act in a mechanical and routine way. **32c** to halt progress temporarily. ◆ See also **markdown, mark-up.** [OE *mearc* mark]

▸ˈ**marker** *n*

mark[2] (mɑːk) *n* **1** See **Deutschmark, markka, Reichsmark, Ostmark. 2** a former monetary unit and coin in England and Scotland worth two thirds of a pound sterling. **3** a silver coin of Germany until 1924. [OE *marc* unit of weight of precious metal, ?from the marks on metal bars; apparently of Gmc origin and rel. to MARK[1]]

markdown (ˈmɑːkˌdaʊn) *n* **1** a price reduction. ◆ *vb* **mark down. 2** (*tr, adv*) to reduce in price.

marked ❶ (mɑːkt) *adj* **1** obvious, evident, or noticeable. **2** singled out, esp. as the target of attack: *a marked man.* **3** *Linguistics.* distinguished by a specific feature, as in phonology. For example, of the two phonemes /t/ and /d/, the /d/ is marked because it exhibits the feature of voice.

▸**markedly** (ˈmɑːkɪdlɪ) *adv* ▸ˈ**markedness** *n*

market ❶ (ˈmɑːkɪt) *n* **1a** an event or occasion, usually held at regular intervals, at which people meet to buy and sell merchandise. **1b** (*as modifier*): *market day.* **2** a place at which a market is held. **3** a shop that sells a particular merchandise: *an antique market.* **4** the trading or selling opportunities provided by a particular group of people: *the foreign market.* **5** demand for a particular product or commodity. **6** See **stock market. 7** See **market price, market value. 8 be in the market for.** to wish to buy or acquire. **9 on the market.** available for purchase. **10 seller's** (*or* **buyer's**) **market.** a market characterized by excess demand (or supply) and thus favourable to sellers (or buyers). **11 the market.** business or trade in a commodity as specified: *the sugar market.* ◆ *vb* **markets, marketing, marketed. 12** (*tr*) to offer or produce for sale. **13** (*intr*) to buy or deal in a market. [C12: from L *mercātus,* from *mercārī* to trade, from *merx* merchandise]

▸ˈ**marketable** *adj* ▸ˈ**marketer** *n*

marketeer (ˌmɑːkɪˈtɪə) *n* **1** *Brit.* a supporter of the EU and of Britain's membership of it. **2** a marketer.

market forces *pl n* the effect of supply and demand on trading within a free market.

market garden *n Chiefly Brit.* an establishment where fruit and vegetables are grown for sale.

▸**market gardener** *n* ▸**market gardening** *n*

marketing (ˈmɑːkɪtɪŋ) *n* the provision of goods or services to meet consumer needs.

market maker *n* a dealer in securities on the London stock exchange, who buys and sells as a principal and since 1986 can also deal directly with the public.

marketplace (ˈmɑːkɪtˌpleɪs) *n* **1** a place where a public market is held. **2** any centre where ideas, etc., are exchanged. **3** the commercial world of buying and selling.

market price *n* the prevailing price, as determined by supply and demand, at which goods, services, etc., may be bought or sold.

market research *n* the study of influences upon customer behaviour and the analysis of market characteristics and trends.

market-test *vb* (*tr*) to put (a section of a public-sector enterprise) out to tender, often as a prelude to full-scale privatization.

market town *n Chiefly Brit.* a town that holds a market, esp. an agricultural centre.

market value *n* the amount obtainable on the open market for the sale of property, financial assets, or goods and services.

markhor (ˈmɑːkɔː) *or* **markhoor** (ˈmɑːkʊə) *n, pl* **markhors, markhor** *or* **markhoors, markhoor.** a large wild Himalayan goat with large spiralled horns. [C19: from Persian, lit.: snake-eater]

marking (ˈmɑːkɪŋ) *n* **1** a mark or series of marks. **2** the arrangement of colours on an animal, plant, etc. **3** assessment and correction of pupils' or students' written work by teachers.

markka (ˈmɑːkɑː, -kə) *n, pl* **markkaa** (-kɑː). the standard monetary unit of Finland. [Finnish; see MARK[2]]

marksman ❶ (ˈmɑːksmən) *n, pl* **marksmen. 1** a person skilled in shooting. **2** a serviceman selected for his skill in shooting.

▸ˈ**marksmanship** *n*

mark-up *n* **1** an amount added to the cost of a commodity to provide the seller with a profit. **2a** an increase in the price of a commodity. **2b** the amount of this. ◆ *vb* **mark up.** (*tr, adv*) **3** to add a percentage for profit, etc., to the cost of (a commodity). **4** to increase the price of.

marl (mɑːl) *n* **1** a fine-grained sedimentary rock consisting of clay minerals, calcium carbonate, and silt: used as a fertilizer. ◆ *vb* **2** (*tr*) to fertilize (land) with marl. [C14: via OF, from LL *margila,* dim. of L *marga*]

▸ˈ**marly** *adj*

marlin (ˈmɑːlɪn) *n, pl* **marlin** *or* **marlins.** any of several large food and game fishes of warm and tropical seas, having a very long upper jaw. [C20: from MARLINESPIKE, from shape of the beak]

marline *or* **marlin** (ˈmɑːlɪn) *n Naut.* a light rope, usually tarred, made of two strands laid left-handed. [C15: from Du. *marlijn,* from *marren* to tie + *lijn* line]

marlinespike *or* **marlinspike** (ˈmɑːlɪnˌspaɪk) *n Naut.* a pointed metal tool used in separating strands of rope, etc.

marlite (ˈmɑːlaɪt) *or* **marlstone** (ˈmɑːlˌstəʊn) *n* a type of marl that is resistant to the decomposing action of air.

marmalade (ˈmɑːməˌleɪd) *n* a preserve made by boiling the pulp and rind of citrus fruits, esp. oranges, with sugar. [C16: via F from Port. *marmelada,* from *marmelo* quince, from L, from Gk *melimēlon,* from *meli* honey + *mēlon* apple]

marmite (ˈmɑːmaɪt) *n* a large cooking pot. [from F: pot]

Marmite (ˈmɑːmaɪt) *n Trademark.* a yeast and vegetable extract used as a spread, flavouring, etc.

marmoreal (mɑːˈmɔːrɪəl) *adj* of, relating to, or resembling marble. [C18: from L *marmoreus,* from *marmor* marble]

marmoset (ˈmɑːməˌzɛt) *n* **1** any of various small South American monkeys having long hairy tails. **2 pygmy marmoset.** a related form: the smallest monkey, inhabiting tropical forests of the Amazon. [C14: from OF *marmouset* grotesque figure, from ?]

marmot (ˈmɑːmət) *n* **1** any of various burrowing rodents of Europe, Asia, and North America. They are heavily built and have coarse fur. **2 prairie marmot.** another name for **prairie dog.** [C17: from F *marmotte,* ? ult. from L *mūr-* (stem of *mūs*) mouse + *montis* of the mountain]

marocain (ˈmærəˌkeɪn) *n* **1** a fabric of ribbed crepe. **2** a garment made from this fabric. [C20: from F *maroquin* Moroccan]

maroon[1] ❶ (məˈruːn) *vb* (*tr*) **1** to abandon ashore, esp. on an island. **2** to isolate without resources. ◆ *n* **3** a descendant of a group of runaway slaves living in the remoter areas of the Caribbean or Guyana.

THESAURUS

mark[1] *n* **1** = **spot**, blemish, blot, blotch, bruise, dent, impression, line, nick, pock, scar, scratch, smirch, smudge, splotch, stain, streak **2** = **sign**, badge, blaze, brand, characteristic, device, earmark, emblem, evidence, feature, flag, hallmark, impression, incision, index, indication, label, note, print, proof, seal, signet, stamp, symbol, symptom, token **7** = **criterion**, level, measure, norm, par, standard, yardstick **9** = **influence**, consequence, dignity, distinction, eminence, fame, importance, notability, note, notice, prestige, quality, regard, standing **10** = **target**, aim, end, goal, object, objective, purpose **20 make one's mark** = **succeed**, achieve recognition, be a success, find a place in the sun, get on in the world, make a success of oneself, make good, make it, make something of oneself, prosper ◆ *vb* **22** = **scar**, blemish, blot, blotch, brand, bruise, dent, impress, imprint, nick, scratch, smirch, smudge, splotch, stain, streak **23** = **distinguish**, betoken, denote, evince, exemplify, illustrate, show **26** = **characterize**, brand, flag, identify, label, stamp **27, 28** = **observe**, attend, hearken, mind, note, notice, pay attention, pay heed, regard, remark, watch **29** = **grade**, appraise, assess, correct, evaluate

marked *adj* **1** = **noticeable**, apparent, blatant, clear, considerable, conspicuous, decided, distinct, dramatic, evident, manifest, notable, noted, obvious, outstanding, patent, prominent, pronounced, remarkable, salient, signal, striking

Antonyms *adj* concealed, doubtful, dubious, hidden, imperceptible, inconspicuous, indistinct, insignificant, obscure, unclear, unnoticeable, vague

markedly *adv* **1** = **noticeably**, clearly, considerably, conspicuously, decidedly, distinctly, evidently, greatly, manifestly, notably, obviously, outstandingly, patently, remarkably, seriously (*inf.*), signally, strikingly, to a great extent

market *n* **1, 2** = **fair**, bazaar, mart ◆ *vb* **12** = **sell**, offer for sale, retail, vend

marksman *n* **1** = **sharpshooter**, crack shot (*inf.*), deadeye, dead shot (*inf.*), good shot

maroon[1] *vb* **1** = **abandon**, cast ashore, cast away, desert, leave, leave high and dry (*inf.*), strand

[C17 (applied to fugitive slaves): from American Sp. *cimarrón* wild, lit.: dwelling on peaks, from Sp. *cima* summit]

maroon[2] (mə'ru:n) *n* **1a** a dark red to purplish-red colour. **1b** (*as adj*): *a maroon carpet.* **2** an exploding firework, esp. one used as a warning signal. [C18: from F, lit.: chestnut]

Marq. *abbrev. for:* **1** Marquess. **2** Marquis.

marque (mɑ:k) *n* **1** a brand of product, esp. of a car. **2** See **letter of marque.** [from F, from *marquer* to MARK[1]]

marquee (mɑ:'ki:) *n* **1** a large tent used for entertainment, exhibition, etc. **2** Also called: **marquise.** *Chiefly US & Canad.* a canopy over the entrance to a theatre, hotel, etc. [C17 (orig. an officer's tent): invented sing form of MARQUISE, erroneously taken to be pl]

marquess ('mɑ:kwɪs) *n* **1** (in the British Isles) a nobleman ranking between a duke and an earl. **2** See **marquis.**

marquetry *or* **marqueterie** ('mɑ:kɪtrɪ) *n, pl* **marquetries** *or* **marqueteries.** a pattern of inlaid veneers of wood, brass, ivory, etc., used chiefly as ornamentation in furniture. [C16: from OF, from *marqueter* to inlay, from *marque* MARK[1]]

marquis ('mɑ:kwɪs, mɑ:'ki:) *n, pl* **marquises** *or* **marquis.** (in various countries) a nobleman ranking above a count, corresponding to a British marquess. The title of marquis is often used in place of that of marquess. [C14: from OF *marchis*, lit.: count of the march, from *marche* MARCH[2]]

marquise (mɑ:'ki:z) *n* **1** (in various countries) another word for **marchioness. 2a** a gemstone, esp. a diamond, cut in a pointed oval shape and usually faceted. **2b** a piece of jewellery, esp. a ring, set with such a stone or with an oval cluster of stones. **3** another name for **marquee** (sense 2). [C18: from F, fem of MARQUIS]

marquisette (ˌmɑ:kɪ'zɛt, -kwɪ-) *n* a leno-weave fabric of cotton, silk, etc. [C20: from F, dim. of MARQUISE]

marram grass ('mærəm) *n* any of several grasses that grow on sandy shores: often planted to stabilize sand dunes. [C17 *marram*, from ON *marálmr*, from *marr* sea + *hálmr* HAULM]

marri ('mærɪ) *n* a species of eucalyptus of Western Australia, widely cultivated for its coloured flowers. [C19: from Abor.]

marriage ⓣ ('mærɪdʒ) *n* **1** the state or relationship of being husband and wife. **2a** the legal union or contract made by a man and woman to live as husband and wife. **2b** (*as modifier*): *marriage certificate.* **3** the ceremony formalizing this union; wedding. **4** a close or intimate union, relationship, etc. [C13: from OF; see MARRY[1], -AGE]

marriageable ('mærɪdʒəbᵊl) *adj* (esp. of women) suitable for marriage, usually with reference to age.
▸ˌ**marriagea'bility** *n*

marriage guidance *n* advice given to couples who have problems in their married life.

married ⓣ ('mærɪd) *adj* **1** having a husband or wife. **2** joined in marriage. **3** of or involving marriage or married persons. **4** closely or intimately united. ◆ *n* **5** (*usually pl*) a married person (esp. in **young marrieds**).

marrons glacés *French.* (marɔ̃ glase) *pl n* chestnuts cooked in syrup and glazed.

marrow ⓣ ('mærəʊ) *n* **1** the fatty network of connective tissue that fills the cavities of bones. **2** the vital part; essence. **3** *Brit.* short for **vegetable marrow.** [OE *mærg*]
▸'**marrowy** *adj*

marrowbone ('mærəʊˌbəʊn) *n* **a** a bone containing edible marrow. **b** (*as modifier*): *marrowbone jelly.*

marrowfat ('mærəʊˌfæt) *or* **marrow pea** *n* **1** any of several varieties of pea plant that have large seeds. **2** the seed of such a plant.

marry[1] ⓣ ('mærɪ) *vb* **marries, marrying, married. 1** to take (someone as one's husband or wife) in marriage. **2** (*tr*) to join or give in marriage. **3** to unite closely or intimately. **4** (*tr;* sometimes foll. by *up*) to fit together or align (two things); join. **5** (*tr*) *Naut.* to match up (the strands of ropes) before splicing. [C13: from OF *marier*, from L *marītāre*, from *marītus* married (man), ?from *mās* male]

marry[2] ('mærɪ) *interj Arch.* an exclamation of surprise, anger, etc. [C14: euphemistic for the Virgin *Mary*]

marry off *vb* (*tr, adv*) to find a husband or wife for (a person, esp. one's son or daughter).

Mars[1] (mɑ:z) *n* the Roman god of war.

Mars[2] (mɑ:z) *n* the fourth planet from the sun.

Marsala (mɑ:'sɑ:lə) *n* a dark sweet dessert wine from Marsala, a port in Sicily.

Marseillaise (ˌmɑ:seɪ'jeɪz, -sə'leɪz) *n* **the.** the French national anthem. [C18: from F (*chanson*) *marseillaise* song of Marseilles (first sung in Paris by the battalion of Marseilles)]

marseille (mɑ:'seɪl) *or* **marseilles** (mɑ:'seɪlz) *n* a strong cotton fabric with a raised pattern, used for bedspreads, etc. [C18: from *Marseille quilting*, made in Marseilles]

marsh ⓣ (mɑ:ʃ) *n* low poorly drained land that is sometimes flooded and often lies at the edge of lakes, etc. Cf. **swamp** (sense 1). [OE *merisc*]

marshal ⓣ ('mɑ:ʃəl) *n* **1** (in some armies and air forces) an officer of the highest rank. **2** (in England) an officer who accompanies a judge on circuit and performs secretarial duties. **3** (in the US) **3a** a Federal court officer assigned to a judicial district whose functions are similar to those of a sheriff. **3b** (in some states) the chief police or fire officer. **4** an officer who organizes or conducts ceremonies, parades, etc. **5** Also called: **knight marshal.** (formerly in England) an officer of the royal family or court, esp. one in charge of protocol. ◆ *vb* **marshals, marshalling, marshalled** *or US* **marshals, marshaling, marshaled.** (*tr*) **6** to arrange in order: *to marshal the facts.* **7** to assemble and organize (troops, vehicles, etc.) prior to onward movement. **8** to guide or lead, esp. in a ceremonious way. **9** to combine (coats of arms) on one shield. [C13: from OF *mareschal;* rel. to OHG *marahscalc*, from *marah* horse + *scalc* servant]
▸'**marshalcy** *or* '**marshalship** *n*

marshalling yard *n Railways.* a place or depot where railway wagons are shunted and made up into trains.

Marshal of the Royal Air Force *n* a rank in the Royal Air Force comparable to that of a field marshal in the army.

marsh fever *n* another name for **malaria.**

marsh gas *n* a hydrocarbon gas largely composed of methane formed when organic material decays in the absence of air.

marshmallow (ˌmɑ:ʃ'mæləʊ) *n* **1** a spongy sweet containing gum arabic or gelatine, sugar, etc. **2** a sweetened paste or confection made from the root of the marsh mallow.

marsh mallow *n* a malvaceous plant that grows in salt marshes and has pale pink flowers. The roots yield a mucilage formerly used to make marshmallows.

marsh marigold *n* a yellow-flowered plant that grows in swampy places.

marshy ⓣ ('mɑ:ʃɪ) *adj* **marshier, marshiest.** of, involving, or like a marsh.
▸'**marshiness** *n*

marsupial (mɑ:'sju:pɪəl, -'su:-) *n* **1** any mammal of an order in which the young are born in an immature state and continue development in the marsupium. The order occurs mainly in Australia and South and Central America and includes the opossums and kangaroos. ◆ *adj* **2** of, relating to, or belonging to marsupials. **3** of or relating to a marsupium. [C17: see MARSUPIUM]

marsupium (mɑ:'sju:pɪəm, -'su:-) *n, pl* **marsupia** (-pɪə). an external pouch in most female marsupials within which the newly born offspring complete their development. [C17: NL, from L: purse, from Gk, dim. of *marsipos*]

mart (mɑ:t) *n* a market or trading centre. [C15: from MDu.: MARKET]

martagon *or* **martagon lily** ('mɑ:təgən) *n* a Eurasian lily plant cultivated for its mottled purplish-red flowers with reflexed petals. [C15: from F, from Turkish *martagān* a type of turban]

Martello tower (mɑ:'tɛləʊ) *n* a small circular tower for coastal defence. [C18: after Cape *Mortella* in Corsica, where the British navy captured a tower of this type in 1794]

marten ('mɑ:tɪn) *n, pl* **martens** *or* **marten. 1** any of several agile arboreal mammals of Europe, Asia, and North America, having bushy tails and golden-brown to blackish fur. See also **pine marten. 2** the highly valued fur of these animals. ◆ See also **sable** (sense 1). [C15: from MDu. *martren*, from OF (*peau*) *martrine* skin of a marten, from *martre*, prob. of Gmc origin]

martial ⓣ ('mɑ:ʃəl) *adj* of, relating to, or characteristic of war, soldiers, or the military life. [C14: from L *martiālis* of MARS[1]]
▸'**martialism** *n* ▸'**martialist** *n* ▸'**martially** *adv*

martial art *n* any of various philosophies of self-defence and techniques of single combat, such as judo or karate, originating in the Far East.

martial law *n* rule of law maintained by the military in the absence of civil law.

Martian ('mɑ:ʃən) *adj* **1** of, occurring on, or relating to the planet Mars. ◆ *n* **2** an inhabitant of Mars, esp. in science fiction.

martin ('mɑ:tɪn) *n* any of various birds of the swallow family, having a square or slightly forked tail. See also **house martin.** [C15: ?from St *Martin*, bishop of Tours & patron saint of France, because the birds were believed to migrate at the time of Martinmas]

martinet ⓣ (ˌmɑ:tɪ'nɛt) *n* a person who maintains strict discipline, esp. in a military force. [C17: from F, from General *Martinet*, drillmaster under Louis XIV]

martingale ('mɑ:tɪnˌgeɪl) *n* **1** a strap from the reins to the girth of a horse, preventing it from carrying its head too high. **2** any gambling system in which the stakes are raised, usually doubled, after each loss.

THESAURUS

marriage *n* **1, 3** = **wedding**, espousal, match, matrimony, nuptial rites, nuptials, wedding ceremony, wedlock **4** = **union**, alliance, amalgamation, association, confederation, coupling, link, merger

married *adj* **1, 2** = **wedded**, hitched (*sl.*), joined, one, spliced (*inf.*), united, wed **3** = **marital**, conjugal, connubial, husbandly, matrimonial, nuptial, spousal, wifely

marrow *n* **2** = **core**, cream, essence, gist, heart, kernel, pith, quick, quintessence, soul, spirit, substance

marry[1] *vb* **1** = **wed**, become man and wife, espouse, get hitched (*sl.*), get spliced (*inf.*), plight one's troth (*old-fashioned*), take the plunge (*inf.*), take to wife, tie the knot (*inf.*), walk down the aisle (*inf.*), wive (*arch.*) **3** = **unite**, ally, bond, join, knit, link, match, merge, splice, tie, unify, yoke

marsh *n* = **swamp**, bog, fen, morass, moss (*Scot. & N English dialect*), quagmire, slough

marshal *vb* **6, 7** = **arrange**, align, array, assemble, collect, deploy, dispose, draw up, gather, group, line up, muster, order, organize, rank, sequence **8** = **conduct**, escort, guide, lead, shepherd, usher

marshy *adj* = **swampy**, boggy, fenny, miry, paludal, quaggy, spongy, waterlogged, wet

martial *adj* = **military**, bellicose, belligerent, brave, heroic, soldierly, warlike

martinet *n* = **disciplinarian**, drillmaster, stickler

3 *Naut.* a chain or cable running from a jib boom to the stern or stem. [C16: from F, from ?]

martini (mɑːˈtiːnɪ) *n* **1** (*often cap.*) *Trademark.* an Italian vermouth. **2** a cocktail of gin and vermouth. [C19 (sense 2): ?from the name of the inventor]

Martinmas (ˈmɑːtɪnməs) *n* the feast of St Martin on Nov. 11; a quarter day in Scotland.

martyr ◐ (ˈmɑːtə) *n* **1** a person who suffers death rather than renounce his religious beliefs. **2** a person who suffers greatly or dies for a cause, belief, etc. **3** a person who suffers from poor health, misfortune, etc.: *a martyr to rheumatism.* ◆ *vb also* **ˈmartyrize** *or* **martyrise.** (*tr*) **4** to kill as a martyr. **5** to make a martyr of. [OE *martir,* from Church L *martyr,* from LGk *martur-, martus* witness]
▸**ˈmartyrdom** *n* ▸**ˌmartyriˈzation** *or* **ˌmartyriˈsation** *n*

martyrology (ˌmɑːtəˈrɒlədʒɪ) *n, pl* **martyrologies. 1** an official list of martyrs. **2** *Christianity.* the study of the lives of the martyrs. **3** a historical account of the lives of martyrs.
▸**ˌmartyrˈologist** *n*

marvel ◐ (ˈmɑːvᵊl) *vb* **marvels, marvelling, marvelled** *or US* **marvels, marveling, marveled. 1** (when *intr,* often foll. by *at* or *about;* when *tr, takes a clause as object*) to be filled with surprise or wonder. ◆ *n* **2** something that causes wonder. **3** *Arch.* astonishment. [C13: from OF *merveille,* from LL *mīrābilia,* from L *mīrābilis* from *mīrārī* to wonder at]

marvellous ◐ *or US* **marvelous** (ˈmɑːvᵊləs) *adj* **1** causing great wonder, surprise, etc.; extraordinary. **2** improbable or incredible. **3** excellent; splendid.
▸**ˈmarvellously** *or US* **ˈmarvelously** *adv* ▸**ˈmarvellousness** *or US* **ˈmarvelousness** *n*

marvel-of-Peru *n, pl* **marvels-of-Peru.** another name for **four-o'clock** (the plant). [C16: first found in Peru]

Marxism (ˈmɑːksɪzəm) *n* the economic and political theory and practice originated by Karl Marx (1818–83) and Friedrich Engels (1820–95), German political philosophers. It holds that actions and human institutions are economically determined, that the class struggle is the basic agency of historical change, and that capitalism will ultimately be superseded by communism.
▸**ˈMarxist** *n, adj*

Marxism-Leninism *n* the modification of Marxism by Lenin stressing that imperialism is the highest form of capitalism.
▸**ˈMarxist-ˈLeninist** *n, adj*

marzipan (ˈmɑːzɪˌpæn) *n* **1** a paste made from ground almonds, sugar, and egg whites, used to coat fruit cakes or moulded into sweets. **2** (*modifier*) *Inf.* of or relating to the stratum of middle managers in a financial institution or other business: *marzipan layer job losses.* [C19: via G from It. *marzapane*]

-mas *n combining form.* indicating a Christian festival: *Christmas; Michaelmas.* [from MASS]

Masai (ˈmɑːsaɪ, mɑːˈsaɪ) *n* **1** (*pl* **Masais** *or* **Masai**) a member of a Nilotic people, formerly noted as warriors, living chiefly in Kenya and Tanzania. **2** the language of this people.

masc. *abbrev. for* masculine.

mascara (mæˈskɑːrə) *n* a cosmetic for darkening the eyelashes. [C20: from Sp.: mask]

mascarpone (ˌmæskəˈpəʊnɪ) *n* an Italian soft cream cheese. [from It. from dialect *mascherpa* ricotta]

mascon (ˈmæskɒn) *n* any of several lunar regions of high gravity. [C20: from MAS(S) + CON(CENTRATION)]

mascot (ˈmæskət) *n* a person, animal, or thing considered to bring good luck. [C19: from F *mascotte,* from Provençal *mascotto* charm, from *masco* witch]

masculine ◐ (ˈmæskjʊlɪn) *adj* **1** possessing qualities or characteristics considered typical of or appropriate to a man; manly. **2** unwomanly. **3** *Grammar.* denoting a gender of nouns that includes all kinds of referents as well as some male animate referents. **4** *Prosody.* denoting an ending consisting of a single stressed syllable. **5** *Prosody.* denoting a rhyme between pairs of single final stressed syllables. [C14: via F from L *masculīnus,* from *masculus* male, from *mās* a male]
▸**ˈmasculinely** *adv* ▸**ˌmascuˈlinity** *n*

masculinize *or* **masculinise** (ˈmæskjʊlɪˌnaɪz) *vb* **masculinizes, masculinizing, masculinized** *or* **masculinises, masculinising, masculinised.** to make or become masculine, esp. to cause (a woman) to show male secondary characteristics as a result of taking steroids.
▸**ˌmasculiniˈzation** *or* **ˌmasculiniˈsation** *n*

maser (ˈmeɪzə) *n* a device for amplifying microwaves, working on the same principle as a laser. [C20: *m(icrowave) a(mplification by) s(timulated) e(mission of) r(adiation)*]

mash (mæʃ) *n* **1** a soft pulpy mass or consistency. **2** *Agriculture.* a feed of bran, meal, or malt mixed with water and fed to horses, cattle, or poultry. **3** (esp. in brewing) a mixture of mashed malt grains and hot water, from which malt is extracted. **4** *Brit. inf.* mashed potatoes. ◆ *vb* (*tr*) **5** to beat or crush into a mash. **6** to steep (malt grains) in hot water in order to extract malt. **7** *Scot. & N English dialect.* to brew (tea). [OE *mǣsc-* (in compound words)]
▸**mashed** *adj* ▸**ˈmasher** *n*

mashie *or* **mashy** (ˈmæʃɪ) *n, pl* **mashies.** *Golf.* (formerly) an iron for lofting shots, usually No. 5. [C19: ?from F *massue* club, ult. from L *mateola* mallet]

mask ◐ (mɑːsk) *n* **1** any covering for the whole or a part of the face worn for amusement, protection, disguise, etc. **2** a fact, action, etc., that conceals something. **3** another name for **masquerade. 4** a likeness of a face or head, either sculpted or moulded, such as a death mask. **5** an image of a face worn by an actor, esp. in classical drama, in order to symbolize a character. **6** a variant spelling of **masque. 7** *Surgery.* a sterile gauze covering for the nose and mouth worn to minimize the spread of germs. **8** *Sport.* a protective covering for the face worn for fencing, ice hockey, etc. **9** a carving in the form of a face or head, used as an ornament. **10** a device placed over the nose and mouth to facilitate or prevent inhalation of a gas. **11** *Photog.* a shield of paper, paint, etc., placed over an area of unexposed photographic surface to stop light falling on it. **12** the face or head of an animal, such as a fox. **13** *Rare.* a person wearing a mask. ◆ *vb* **14** to cover with or put on a mask. **15** (*tr*) to conceal; disguise: *to mask an odour.* **16** (*tr*) to cover; protect. **17** (*tr*) *Photog.* to shield a particular area of (an unexposed photographic surface) to prevent or reduce the action of light there. [C16: from It. *maschera,* ult. from Ar. *maskharah* clown, from *sakhira* mockery]
▸**masked** *adj* ▸**ˈmasker** *n*

masked ball *n* a ball at which masks are worn.

masking tape *n* an adhesive tape used to protect surfaces surrounding an area to be painted.

maskinonge (ˈmæskəˌnɒndʒ) *n* another name for **muskellunge.**

masochism (ˈmæsəˌkɪzəm) *n* **1** *Psychiatry.* an abnormal condition in which pleasure, esp. sexual pleasure, is derived from pain or from humiliation, domination, etc., by another person. **2** a tendency to take pleasure from one's own suffering. Cf. **sadism.** [C19: after Leopold von Sacher *Masoch* (1836–95), Austrian novelist, who described it]
▸**ˈmasochist** *n, adj* ▸**ˌmasoˈchistic** *adj* ▸**ˌmasoˈchistically** *adv*

mason (ˈmeɪsᵊn) *n* **1** a person skilled in building with stone. **2** a person who dresses stone. ◆ *vb* **3** (*tr*) to construct or strengthen with masonry. [C13: from OF *masson,* of Frankish origin; ? rel. to OE *macian* to make]

Mason (ˈmeɪsᵊn) *n* short for **Freemason.**

Mason-Dixon Line (-ˈdɪksən) *n* in the US, the state boundary between Maryland and Pennsylvania: surveyed between 1763 and 1767 by Charles Mason and Jeremiah Dixon; popularly regarded as the dividing line between North and South.

masonic (məˈsɒnɪk) *adj* **1** (*often cap.*) of or relating to Freemasons or Freemasonry. **2** of or relating to masons or masonry.
▸**maˈsonically** *adv*

Masonite (ˈmeɪsənaɪt) *n Austral. trademark.* a kind of dark brown hardboard.

masonry (ˈmeɪsənrɪ) *n, pl* **masonries. 1** the craft of a mason. **2** work that is built by a mason; stonework or brickwork. **3** (*often cap.*) short for **Freemasonry.**

masque *or* **mask** (mɑːsk) *n* **1** a dramatic entertainment of the 16th to 17th centuries, consisting of pantomime, dancing, dialogue, and song. **2** the words and music for this. **3** short for **masquerade.** [C16: var. of MASK]

masquerade ◐ (ˌmæskəˈreɪd) *n* **1** a party or other gathering at which the guests wear masks and costumes. **2** the disguise worn at such a function. **3** a pretence or disguise. ◆ *vb* **masquerades, masquerading, masqueraded.** (*intr*) **4** to participate in a masquerade; disguise oneself. **5** to dissemble. [C16: from Sp. *mascarada,* from *mascara* MASK]
▸**ˌmasquerˈader** *n*

mass ◐ (mæs) *n* **1** a large coherent body of matter without a definite shape. **2** a collection of the component parts of something. **3** a large

THESAURUS

martyrdom *n* **1, 2** = **persecution**, agony, anguish, ordeal, suffering, torment, torture
Antonyms *n* bliss, ecstasy, happiness, joy

marvel *vb* **1** = **wonder**, be amazed, be awed, be filled with surprise, gape, gaze, goggle ◆ *n* **2** = **wonder**, genius, miracle, phenomenon, portent, prodigy, whizz (*inf.*)

marvellous *adj* **1** = **amazing**, astonishing, astounding, breathtaking, brilliant, extraordinary, jaw-dropping, miraculous, phenomenal, prodigious, remarkable, sensational (*inf.*), singular, spectacular, stupendous, wondrous (*arch.* or *literary*) **3** = **excellent**, awesome, brill (*inf.*), cracking (*Brit. inf.*), divine (*inf.*), fabulous (*inf.*), fantastic (*inf.*), glorious, great (*inf.*), jim-dandy (*sl.*), magnificent, sensational (*inf.*), smashing (*inf.*), sovereign, splendid, stupendous, super (*inf.*), superb, terrific (*inf.*), topping (*Brit. sl.*), wonderful
Antonyms *adj* ≠ **amazing:** believable, commonplace, credible, everyday, ordinary ≠ **excellent:** awful, bad, terrible

masculine *adj* **1** = **male**, manful, manlike, manly, mannish, virile **1** = **strong**, bold, brave, butch (*sl.*), gallant, hardy, macho, muscular, powerful, red-blooded (*inf.*), resolute, robust, stout-hearted, strapping, vigorous, well-built

mask *n* **1** = **visor**, domino, false face, vizard (*arch.*) **2** = **disguise**, blind, camouflage, cloak, concealment, cover, cover-up, façade, front, guise, screen, semblance, show, veil, veneer ◆ *vb* **15** = **disguise**, camouflage, cloak, conceal, cover, hide, obscure, screen, veil

masquerade *n* **1** = **masked ball**, costume ball, fancy dress party, mask, masked party, mummery, revel **2, 3** = **pretence**, cloak, cover, cover-up, deception, disguise, dissimulation, front (*inf.*), guise, imposture, mask, pose, put-on (*sl.*), screen, subterfuge ◆ *vb* **4, 5** = **pose**, disguise, dissemble, dissimulate, impersonate, mask, pass oneself off, pretend (to be)

mass *n* **1** = **piece**, block, chunk, concretion, hunk, lump **2** = **collection**, aggregate, body, entirety, sum, sum total, totality, whole **2** = **lot**, accumulation, aggregation, assemblage, batch, bunch, collection, combination, conglomeration, heap, load, pile, quantity, rick, stack **3** =

amount or number, as of people. **4** the main part or majority. **5 in the mass.** in the main; collectively. **6** the size of a body; bulk. **7** *Physics.* a physical quantity expressing the amount of matter in a body. It is a measure of a body's resistance to changes in velocity (**inertial mass**) and also of the force experienced in a gravitational field (**gravitational mass**). **8** (in painting, drawing, etc.) an area of unified colour, shade, or intensity, usually denoting a solid form or plane. ◆ (*modifier*) **9** done or occurring on a large scale: *mass hysteria.* **10** consisting of a mass or large number, esp. of people: *a mass meeting.* ◆ *vb* **11** to form (people or things) or (of people or things) to join together into a mass. ◆ See also **masses.** [C14: from OF *masse,* from L *massa* that which forms a lump, from Gk *maza* barley cake]

Mass (mæs, mɑːs) *n* **1** (in the Roman Catholic Church and certain Protestant Churches) the celebration of the Eucharist. See also **High Mass, Low Mass. 2** a musical setting of those parts of the Eucharistic service sung by choir or congregation. [OE *mæsse,* from Church L *missa,* ult. from L *mittere* to send away; ?from the concluding dismissal in the Roman Mass, *Ite, missa est* Go, it is the dismissal]

massacre Ⓣ ('mæsəkə) *n* **1** the wanton or savage killing of large numbers of people, as in battle. **2** *Inf.* an overwhelming defeat, as in a game. ◆ *vb* **massacres, massacring, massacred.** (*tr*) **3** to kill indiscriminately or in large numbers. **4** *Inf.* to defeat overwhelmingly. [C16: from OF]

massage Ⓣ ('mæsɑːʒ, -sɑːdʒ) *n* **1** the act of kneading, rubbing, etc., parts of the body to promote circulation, suppleness, or relaxation. ◆ *vb* **massages, massaging, massaged.** (*tr*) **2** to give a massage to. **3** to treat (stiffness, etc.) by a massage. **4** to manipulate (statistics, etc.) to produce a desired result; doctor. **5 massage (someone's) ego.** to boost (someone's) sense of self-esteem by flattery. [C19: from F, from *masser* to rub]

massasauga (ˌmæsə'sɔːgə) *n* a North American venomous snake that has a horny rattle at the end of the tail. [C19: after the *Missisauga* River, Ontario, Canada, where it was first found]

mass defect *n Physics.* the amount by which the mass of a particular nucleus is less than the total mass of its constituent particles.

massé *or* **massé shot** ('mæsɪ) *n Billiards.* a stroke made by hitting the cue ball off centre with the cue held nearly vertically, esp. so as to make the ball move in a curve. [C19: from F, from *masser,* from *masse* sledgehammer, from OF *mace* MACE[1]]

masses Ⓣ ('mæsɪz) *pl n* **1** (preceded by *the*) the body of common people. **2** (often foll. by *of*) *Inf., chiefly Brit.* great numbers or quantities: *masses of food.*

masseur (mæ'sɜː) *or* (*fem*) **masseuse** (mæ'sɜːz) *n* a person who gives massages, esp. as a profession. [C19: from F *masser* to MASSAGE]

massif ('mæsiːf) *n* a mass of rock or a series of connected masses forming a mountain range. [C19: from F, noun use of *massif* MASSIVE]

massive Ⓣ ('mæsɪv) *adj* **1** (of objects) large in mass; bulky, heavy, and usually solid. **2** impressive or imposing. **3** relatively intensive or large; considerable: *a massive dose.* **4** *Geol.* **4a** (of igneous rocks) having no stratification, cleavage, etc.; homogeneous. **4b** (of sedimentary rocks) arranged in thick poorly defined strata. **5** *Mineralogy.* without obvious crystalline structure. [C15: from F *massif,* from *masse* MASS]
▸'**massively** *adv* ▸'**massiveness** *n*

mass-market *adj* of, for, or appealing to a large number of people; popular: *mass-market paperbacks.*

mass media *pl n* the means of communication that reach large numbers of people, such as television, newspapers, magazines, and radio.

mass noun *n* a noun that refers to an extended substance rather than to each of a set of objects, e.g., *water* as opposed to *lake.* In English when used indefinitely they are characteristically preceded by *some* rather than *a* or *an;* they do not have normal plural forms. Cf. **count noun.**

mass number *n* the total number of neutrons and protons in the nucleus of a particular atom.

mass observation *n* (*sometimes cap.*) *Chiefly Brit.* the study of the social habits of people through observation, interviews, etc.

mass-produce *vb* **mass-produces, mass-producing, mass-produced.** (*tr*) to manufacture (goods) to a standardized pattern on a large scale by means of extensive mechanization and division of labour.
▸ˌ**mass-pro'duced** *adj* ▸ˌ**mass-pro'ducer** *n* ▸**mass production** *n*

mass spectrometer *or* **spectroscope** *n* an instrument in which ions, produced from a sample, are separated by electric or magnetic fields according to their ratios of charge to mass. A record is produced (**mass spectrum**) of the types of ion present and their amounts.

mast[1] (mɑːst) *n* **1** *Naut.* any vertical spar for supporting sails, rigging, flags, etc., above the deck of a vessel. **2** any sturdy upright pole used as a support. **3 before the mast.** *Naut.* as an apprentice seaman. ◆ *vb* **4** (*tr*) *Naut.* to equip with a mast or masts. [OE *mæst;* rel. to MDu. *mast* & L *mālus* pole]

mast[2] (mɑːst) *n* the fruit of forest trees, such as beech, oak, etc., used as food for pigs. [OE *mæst;* rel. to OHG *mast* food]

mastaba *or* **mastabah** ('mæstəbə) *n* a mudbrick superstructure above tombs in ancient Egypt. [from Ar.: bench]

mast cell *n* any of a number of cells in connective tissue that release heparin, histamine, and serotonin during inflammation and allergic reactions.

mastectomy (mæ'stɛktəmɪ) *n, pl* **mastectomies.** the surgical removal of a breast.

master Ⓣ ('mɑːstə) *n* **1** the man in authority, such as the head of a household, the employer of servants, or the owner of slaves or animals. **2a** a person with exceptional skill at a certain thing. **2b** (*as modifier*): *a master thief.* **3** (*often cap.*) a great artist, esp. an anonymous but influential one. **4a** a person who has complete control of a situation, etc. **4b** an abstract thing regarded as having power or influence: *they regarded fate as the master of their lives.* **5a** a workman or craftsman fully qualified to practise his trade and to train others. **5b** (*as modifier*): *master carpenter.* **6a** an original copy, stencil, tape, etc., from which duplicates are made. **6b** (*as modifier*): *master copy.* **7** a player of a game, esp. chess or bridge, who has won a specified number of tournament games. **8** the principal of some colleges. **9** a highly regarded teacher or leader. **10** a graduate holding a master's degree. **11** the chief executive officer aboard a merchant ship. **12** a person presiding over a function, organization, or institution. **13** *Chiefly Brit.* a male teacher. **14** an officer of the Supreme Court of Judicature subordinate to a judge. **15** the superior person or side in a contest. **16** (*often cap.*) the heir apparent of a Scottish viscount or baron. ◆ (*modifier*) **17** overall or controlling: *master plan.* **18** designating a device or mechanism that controls others: *master switch.* **19** main; principal: *master bedroom.* ◆ *vb* (*tr*) **20** to become thoroughly proficient in. **21** to overcome; defeat. **22** to rule or control as master. [OE *magister* teacher, from L]

Master ('mɑːstə) *n* **1** a title of address for a boy. **2** a term of address, esp. as used by disciples addressing or referring to a religious teacher. **3** an archaic equivalent of **Mr.**

master aircrew *n* a warrant rank in the Royal Air Force, equal to but before a warrant officer.

master-at-arms *n, pl* **masters-at-arms.** the senior rating in a naval unit responsible for discipline and police duties.

master builder *n* **1** a person skilled in the design and construction of buildings, esp. before the foundation of the profession of architecture. **2** a self-employed builder who employs labour.

masterclass ('mɑːstəˌklɑːs) *n* a session of tuition by an expert, esp. a musician, for exceptional students, usually given in public or on television.

masterful Ⓣ ('mɑːstəfʊl) *adj* **1** having or showing mastery. **2** fond of playing the master; imperious.
▸'**masterfully** *adv* ▸'**masterfulness** *n*

> **USAGE NOTE** The use of *masterful* to mean *masterly* as in *a masterful performance,* although common, is considered incorrect by many people.

master key *n* a key that opens all the locks of a set. Also called: **passkey.**

THESAURUS

crowd, assemblage, band, body, bunch (*inf.*), group, horde, host, lot, mob, number, throng, troop **4** = **majority**, body, bulk, greater part, lion's share, preponderance **6** = **size**, bulk, dimension, greatness, magnitude ◆ *modifier* **9, 10** = **large-scale**, extensive, general, indiscriminate, pandemic, popular, wholesale, widespread ◆ *vb* **11** = **gather**, accumulate, amass, assemble, collect, congregate, foregather, mob, muster, rally, swarm, throng

massacre *n* **1** = **slaughter**, annihilation, blood bath, butchery, carnage, extermination, holocaust, killing, mass slaughter, murder ◆ *vb* **3** = **slaughter**, annihilate, blow away (*sl., chiefly US*), butcher, cut to pieces, exterminate, kill, mow down, murder, slay, take out (*sl.*), wipe out

massage *n* **1** = **rub-down**, acupressure, kneading, manipulation, reflexology, rubbing, shiatsu ◆ *vb* **2** = **rub down**, knead, manipulate, rub

masses *pl n* **1** *preceded by* **the** = **the multitude**, the commonalty, the common people, the crowd, (the) hoi polloi

massive *adj* **1, 2** = **huge**, big, bulky, colossal, elephantine, enormous, extensive, gargantuan, gigantic, ginormous (*inf.*), great, heavy, hefty, hulking, humongous *or* humungous (*US sl.*), immense, imposing, impressive, mammoth, mega (*sl.*), monster, monumental, ponderous, solid, stellar (*inf.*), substantial, titanic, vast, weighty, whacking (*inf.*), whopping (*inf.*)
Antonyms *adj* frail, light, little, minute, petty, slight, small, thin, tiny, trivial

master *n* **1** = **head**, boss (*inf.*), captain, chief, commander, controller, director, employer, governor, lord, manager, overlord, overseer, owner, principal, ruler, skipper (*inf.*), superintendent **2a** = **expert**, ace (*inf.*), adept, dab hand (*Brit. inf.*), doyen, genius, grandmaster, maestro, maven (*US*), past master, pro (*inf.*), virtuoso, wizard ◆ *modifier* **2b** = **expert**, adept, crack (*inf.*), masterly, proficient, skilful, skilled ◆ *n* **9** = **teacher**, guide, guru, instructor, pedagogue, preceptor, schoolmaster, spiritual leader, swami, torchbearer, tutor ◆ *modifier* **17, 19** = **main**, chief, controlling, foremost, grand, great, leading, predominant, prime, principal ◆ *vb* **20** = **learn**, acquire, become proficient in, get the hang of (*inf.*), grasp **21** = **overcome**, bridle, check, conquer, curb, defeat, lick, overpower, quash, quell, subdue, subjugate, suppress, tame, triumph over, vanquish **22** = **control**, command, direct, dominate, govern, manage, regulate, rule
Antonyms *n* ≠ **head:** crew, servant, slave, subject ≠ **expert:** amateur, novice ≠ **teacher:** student ◆ *modifier* ≠ **expert:** amateurish, clumsy, incompetent, inept, novice, unaccomplished, unskilled, untalented ≠ **main:** lesser, minor ◆ *vb* ≠ **overcome:** cave in (*inf.*), give in, surrender, yield

masterful *adj* **1** = **skilful**, adept, adroit, clever, consummate, crack (*inf.*), deft, dexterous, excellent, expert, exquisite, fine, finished, first-rate, masterly, skilled, superior, superlative, supreme, world-class **2** = **domineering**, arrogant, authoritative, bossy (*inf.*), despotic, dictatorial, high-handed, imperious, magisterial, overbearing, overweening, peremptory, self-willed, tyrannical

masterly ➊ ('mɑːstəlɪ) *adj* of the skill befitting a master.
▸**'masterliness** *n*

master mason *n* **1** see **master** (sense 5a). **2** a Freemason who has reached the rank of third degree.

mastermind ➊ ('mɑːstəˌmaɪnd) *vb* **1** (*tr*) to plan and direct (a complex undertaking). ◆ *n* **2** a person of great intelligence or executive talent, esp. one who directs an undertaking.

Master of Arts *n* a degree, usually postgraduate and in a nonscientific subject, or the holder of this degree. Abbrev.: **MA.**

master of ceremonies *n* a person who presides over a public ceremony, formal dinner, or entertainment, introducing the events, performers, etc.

Master of Science *n* a postgraduate degree, usually in science, or the holder of this degree. Abbrev.: **MSc.**

Master of the Rolls *n* (in England) a judge of the court of appeal: the senior civil judge in the country and the Keeper of the Records at the Public Record Office.

masterpiece ➊ ('mɑːstəˌpiːs) *or* (*less commonly*) **masterwork** ('mɑːstəˌwɜːk) *n* **1** an outstanding work or performance. **2** the most outstanding piece of work of a creative artist, craftsman, etc. [C17: cf. Du. *meesterstuk,* G *Meisterstück,* a sample of work submitted to a guild by a craftsman in order to qualify for the rank of master]

masterstroke ('mɑːstəˌstrəʊk) *n* an outstanding piece of strategy, skill, talent, etc.

mastery ➊ ('mɑːstərɪ) *n, pl* **masteries. 1** full command or understanding of a subject. **2** outstanding skill; expertise. **3** the power of command; control. **4** victory or superiority.

masthead ('mɑːstˌhɛd) *n* **1** *Naut.* the head of a mast. **2** the name of a newspaper or periodical, its proprietors, staff, etc., printed at the top of the front page. ◆ *vb* (*tr*) **3** to send (a sailor) to the masthead as a punishment. **4** to raise (a sail) to the masthead.

mastic ('mæstɪk) *n* **1** an aromatic resin obtained from the mastic tree and used as an astringent and to make varnishes and lacquers. **2 mastic tree.** a small Mediterranean evergreen tree that yields the resin mastic. **3** any of several putty-like substances used as a filler, adhesive, or seal in wood, plaster, or masonry. **4** a liquor flavoured with mastic gum. [C14: via OF from LL *mastichum,* from L from Gk *mastikhē* resin used as chewing gum]

masticate ➊ ('mæstɪˌkeɪt) *vb* **masticates, masticating, masticated. 1** to chew (food). **2** to reduce (materials such as rubber) to a pulp by crushing, grinding, or kneading. [C17: from LL *masticāre,* from Gk *mastikhan* to grind the teeth]
▸**ˌmastiˈcation** *n* ▸**'mastiˌcator** *n*

masticatory ('mæstɪkətərɪ, -trɪ) *adj* **1** of, relating to, or adapted to chewing. ◆ *n, pl* **masticatories. 2** a medicinal substance chewed to increase the secretion of saliva.

mastiff ('mæstɪf) *n* a breed of large powerful short-haired dog, usually fawn or brindled. [C14: from OF, ult. from L *mansuētus* tame]

mastitis (mæ'staɪtɪs) *n* inflammation of a breast or an udder.

masto- *or before a vowel* **mast-** *combining form.* indicating the breast, mammary glands, or something resembling a breast or nipple: *mastodon; mastoid.* [from Gk *mastos* breast]

mastodon ('mæstəˌdɒn) *n* an extinct elephant-like mammal common in Pliocene times. [C19: from NL, lit.: breast-tooth, referring to the nipple-shaped projections on the teeth]

mastoid ('mæstɔɪd) *adj* **1** shaped like a nipple or breast. **2** designating or relating to a nipple-like process of the temporal bone behind the ear. ◆ *n* **3** the mastoid process. **4** *Inf.* mastoiditis.

mastoiditis (ˌmæstɔɪ'daɪtɪs) *n* inflammation of the mastoid process.

masturbate ➊ ('mæstəˌbeɪt) *vb* **masturbates, masturbating, masturbated.** to stimulate the genital organs of (oneself or another) to achieve sexual pleasure. [C19: from L *masturbārī,* from ?; formerly thought to be derived from *manus* hand + *stuprāre* to defile]
▸**ˌmasturˈbation** *n* ▸**'masturˌbator** *n* ▸**masturbatory** ('mæstəˌbeɪtərɪ) *adj*

mat[1] (mæt) *n* **1** a thick flat piece of fabric used as a floor covering, a place to wipe one's shoes, etc. **2** a smaller pad of material used to protect a surface from the heat, scratches, etc., of an object placed upon it. **3** a large piece of thick padded material put on the floor as a surface for wrestling, judo, etc. **4** any surface or mass that is densely interwoven or tangled: *a mat of weeds.* ◆ *vb* **mats, matting, matted. 5** to tangle or weave or become tangled or woven into a dense mass. **6** (*tr*) to cover with a mat or mats. [OE *matte*]

mat[2] (mæt) *n* **1** a border of cardboard, cloth, etc., placed around a picture as a frame or between picture and frame. ◆ *adj* **2** having a dull, lustreless, or roughened surface. ◆ *vb* **mats, matting, matted.** (*tr*) **3** to furnish (a picture) with a mat. **4** to give (a surface) a mat finish. ◆ Also (for senses 2 & 4): **matt.** [C17: from F, lit.: dead]

mat[3] (mæt) *n Printing, inf.* short for **matrix** (senses 4 and 5).

mat. *abbrev. for* matinée.

matador ('mætəˌdɔː) *n* **1** the principal bullfighter who kills the bull. **2** (in some card games) one of the highest cards. **3** a game played with dominoes in which the dots on adjacent halves must total seven. [C17: from Sp., from *matar* to kill]

matagouri (ˌmætə'guːrɪ) *n* a New Zealand thorny bush which forms thickets in open country. Also called: **wild Irishman.** [from Maori *tumatakuru*]

matai ('mɑːtaɪ) *n* a New Zealand tree, the black pine, the wood of which is used as building timber. Also called: **black pine.** [from Maori]

match[1] ➊ (mætʃ) *n* **1** a formal game or sports event in which people, teams, etc., compete. **2** a person or thing able to provide competition for another: *she's met her match.* **3** a person or thing that resembles, harmonizes with, or is equivalent to another in a specified respect. **4** a person or thing that is an exact copy or equal of another. **5a** a partnership between a man and a woman, as in marriage. **5b** an arrangement for such a partnership. **6** a person regarded as a possible partner, as in marriage. ◆ *vb* (*mainly tr*) **7** to fit (parts) together. **8** (*also intr; sometimes* foll. by *up*) to resemble, harmonize with, or equal (one another or something else). **9** (sometimes foll. by *with* or *against*) to compare in order to determine which is the superior. **10** (often foll. by *to* or *with*) to adapt so as to correspond with: *to match hope with reality.* **11** (often foll. by *with* or *against*) to arrange a competition between. **12** to find a match for. **13** *Electronics.* to connect (two circuits) so that their impedances are equal, to produce a maximum transfer of energy. [OE *gemæcca* spouse]
▸**'matchable** *adj* ▸**'matching** *adj*

match[2] (mætʃ) *n* **1** a thin strip of wood or cardboard tipped with a chemical that ignites by friction on a rough surface or a surface coated with a suitable chemical (see **safety match**). **2** a length of cord or wick impregnated with a chemical so that it burns slowly. It is used to fire cannons, explosives, etc. [C14: from OF *meiche,* ?from L *myxa* wick, from Gk *muxa* lamp nozzle]

matchboard ('mætʃˌbɔːd) *n* a long flimsy board tongued and grooved for lining work.

matchbox ('mætʃˌbɒks) *n* a small box for holding matches.

match-fit *adj Sport.* in good physical condition for competing in a match.

matchless ➊ ('mætʃlɪs) *adj* unequalled; incomparable; peerless.
▸**'matchlessly** *adv*

matchlock ('mætʃˌlɒk) *n* **1** an obsolete type of gunlock igniting the powder by means of a slow match. **2** a gun having such a lock.

matchmaker ('mætʃˌmeɪkə) *n* **1** a person who brings together suitable partners for marriage. **2** a person who arranges competitive matches.
▸**'matchˌmaking** *n, adj*

match play *n Golf.* scoring according to the number of holes won and lost. Cf. **Stableford, stroke play.**
▸**match player** *n*

match point *n* **1** *Tennis, squash, etc.* the final point needed to win a match. **2** *Bridge.* the unit used for scoring in tournaments.

matchstick ('mætʃˌstɪk) *n* **1** the wooden part of a match. ◆ *adj* **2** made with or as if with matchsticks. **3** (esp. of drawn figures) thin and straight: *matchstick men.*

matchwood ('mætʃˌwʊd) *n* **1** wood suitable for making matches. **2** splinters or fragments.

mate[1] ➊ (meɪt) *n* **1** the sexual partner of an animal. **2** a marriage part-

THESAURUS

Antonyms *adj* ≠ **skilful:** amateurish, clumsy, incompetent, inept, unaccomplished, unskilled, untalented ≠ **domineering:** irresolute, meek, spineless, weak, wimpish *or* wimpy (*inf.*)

masterly *adj* = **skilful**, adept, adroit, clever, consummate, crack (*inf.*), dexterous, excellent, expert, exquisite, fine, finished, first-rate, masterful, skilled, superior, superlative, supreme, world-class

mastermind *vb* **1** = **plan**, be the brains behind (*inf.*), conceive, devise, direct, manage, organize ◆ *n* **2** = **organizer**, architect, authority, brain(s) (*inf.*), brainbox, director, engineer, genius, intellect, manager, planner, virtuoso

masterpiece *n* **1, 2** = **classic**, *chef-d'oeuvre,* jewel, magnum opus, master work, *pièce de résistance, tour de force*

mastery *n* **1** = **understanding**, command, comprehension, familiarity, grasp, grip, knowledge **2** = **expertise**, ability, acquirement, attainment, cleverness, deftness, dexterity, finesse, know-how (*inf.*), proficiency, prowess, skill, virtuosity **3, 4** = **control**, ascendancy, authority, command, conquest, domination, dominion, pre-eminence, rule, superiority, supremacy, sway, triumph, upper hand, victory, whip hand

masticate *vb* **1** = **chew**, champ, crunch, eat, munch

masturbation *n* = **self-abuse**, autoeroticism, onanism, playing with oneself (*sl.*), wanking (*taboo sl.*)

match[1] *n* **1** = **game**, bout, competition, contest, head-to-head, test, trial **2** = **equal**, competitor, counterpart, equivalent, peer, rival **3** = **companion**, complement, counterpart, equal, equivalent, fellow, mate, tally **4** = **replica**, copy, dead ringer (*sl.*), double, duplicate, equal, lookalike, ringer (*sl.*), spit (*inf., chiefly Brit.*), spit and image (*inf.*), spitting image (*inf.*), twin **5** = **marriage**, affiliation, alliance, combination, couple, duet, item (*inf.*), pair, pairing, partnership, union ◆ *vb* **7** = **pair**, ally, combine, couple, join, link, marry, mate, unite, yoke **8, 10** = **correspond**, accompany, accord, adapt, agree, blend, coordinate, fit, go with, harmonize, suit, tally, tone with **9** = **rival**, compare, compete, contend, emulate, equal, measure up to, oppose, pit against, vie

matching *adj* **8** = **identical**, analogous, comparable, coordinating, corresponding, double, duplicate, equal, equivalent, like, paired, parallel, same, toning, twin
Antonyms *adj* different, disparate, dissimilar, distinct, divergent, diverse, nonparallel, other, unequal, unlike

matchless *adj* = **unequalled**, consummate, exquisite, incomparable, inimitable, peerless, perfect, superlative, supreme, unique, unmatched, unparalleled, unrivalled, unsurpassed
Antonyms *adj* average, common, commonplace, comparable, equalled, everyday, excelled, inferior, lesser, mediocre, no great shakes (*inf.*), ordinary, second-class, surpassed

mate[1] *n* **2** = **partner**, better half (*humorous*), husband *or* wife, significant other (*US inf.*), spouse **3a** *Informal, chiefly Brit., Austral., & N.Z.* = **friend**,

ner. **3a** *Inf., chiefly Brit., Austral. & NZ.* a friend, usually of the same sex: often used to any male in direct address. **3b** (*in combination*) an associate, colleague, fellow sharer, etc.: *a classmate.* **4** one of a pair of matching items. **5** *Naut.* **5a** short for **first mate. 5b** any officer below the master on a commercial ship. **6** (in some trades) an assistant: *a plumber's mate.* ◆ *vb* **mates, mating, mated. 7** to pair (a male and female animal) or (of animals) to pair for reproduction. **8** to marry or join in marriage. **9** (*tr*) to join as a pair. [C14: from MLow G; rel. to OE *gemetta* table-guest, from *mete* MEAT]

mate[2] (meɪt) *n, vb* **mates, mating, mated.** *Chess.* See **checkmate.**

maté *or* **mate** ('mɑːteɪ) *n* **1** an evergreen tree cultivated in South America for its leaves, which contain caffeine. **2** a stimulating milky beverage made from the dried leaves of this tree. ◆ Also called: **Paraguay tea, yerba, yerba maté.** [C18: from American Sp. (orig. referring to the vessel in which the drink was brewed), from Quechua *máti* gourd]

matelot, matlo, *or* **matlow** ('mætləʊ) *n Sl., chiefly Brit.* a sailor. [C20: from F]

mater ('meɪtə) *n Brit. sl.* a word for **mother**[1]: often used facetiously. [C16: from L]

material ⓣ (mə'tɪərɪəl) *n* **1** the substance of which a thing is made or composed; component or constituent matter. **2** facts, notes, etc., that a finished work may be based on or derived from. **3** cloth or fabric. **4** a person who has qualities suitable for a given occupation, training, etc.: *that boy is university material.* ◆ *adj* **5** of, relating to, or composed of physical substance: *material possessions.* **6** of, relating to, or affecting economic or physical wellbeing: *material ease.* **7** of or concerned with physical rather than spiritual interests. **8** of great import or consequence: *material benefit.* **9** (often foll. by *to*) relevant. **10** *Philosophy.* of or relating to matter as opposed to form. ◆ See also **materials.** [C14: via F from LL *māteriālis,* from L *māteria* MATTER]
▸**ma,teri'ality** *n*

material implication *n Logic.* a form of implication in which the proposition "if A then B" is true except when A is true and B is false.

materialism (mə'tɪərɪə,lɪzəm) *n* **1** interest in and desire for money, possessions, etc., rather than spiritual or ethical values. **2** *Philosophy.* the doctrine that matter is the only reality and that the mind, the emotions, etc., are merely functions of it. Cf. **idealism, dualism. 3** *Ethics.* the rejection of any religious or supernatural account of things.
▸**ma'terialist** *n* ▸**ma,terial'istic** *adj* ▸**ma,terial'istically** *adv*

materialize ⓣ *or* **materialise** (mə'tɪərɪə,laɪz) *vb* **materializes, materializing, materialized** *or* **materialises, materialising, materialised. 1** (*intr*) to become fact; actually happen. **2** to invest or become invested with a physical shape or form. **3** to cause (a spirit, as of a dead person) to appear in material form or (of a spirit) to appear in such form. **4** (*intr*) to take shape; become tangible.
▸**ma,teriali'zation** *or* **ma,teriali'sation** *n* ▸**ma'terial,izer** *or* **ma'terial,iser** *n*

materially ⓣ (mə'tɪərɪəlɪ) *adv* **1** to a significant extent; considerably. **2** with respect to material objects. **3** *Philosophy.* with respect to substance as distinct from form.

materials (mə'tɪərɪəlz) *pl n* the equipment necessary for a particular activity.

materia medica (mə'tɪərɪə 'mɛdɪkə) *n* **1** the branch of medical science concerned with the study of drugs used in the treatment of disease. **2** the drugs used in the treatment of disease. [C17: from Med. L: medical matter]

materiel ⓣ *or* **matériel** (mə,tɪərɪ'ɛl) *n* the materials and equipment of an organization, esp. of a military force. [C19: from F: MATERIAL]

maternal ⓣ (mə'tɜːnᵊl) *adj* **1** of, relating to, or characteristic of a mother. **2** related through the mother's side of the family: *his maternal uncle.* [C15: from Med. L *māternālis,* from L *māternus,* from *māter* mother]
▸**ma'ternalism** *n* ▸**ma,ternal'istic** *adj* ▸**ma'ternally** *adv*

maternity ⓣ (mə'tɜːnɪtɪ) *n* **1** motherhood. **2** the characteristics associated with motherhood; motherliness. **3** (*modifier*) relating to pregnant women or women at the time of childbirth: *a maternity ward.*

mateship ('meɪtʃɪp) *n Austral.* friendly egalitarian comradeship.

mate's rates *pl n NZ inf.* discounted or preferential rates of payment offered to a friend or colleague: *he got the job done cheaply by a plumber friend at mate's rates.*

matey ⓣ *or* **maty** ('meɪtɪ) *Brit. inf.* ◆ *adj* **1** friendly or intimate. ◆ *n* **2** friend or fellow: usually used in direct address.
▸**'mateyness** *or* **'matiness** *n*

math (mæθ) *n US & Canad. inf.* short for **mathematics.** Brit. equivalent: **maths.**

mathematical (,mæθə'mætɪkᵊl) *or* **mathematic** *adj* **1** of, used in, or relating to mathematics. **2** characterized by or using the precision of mathematics. **3** using, determined by, or in accordance with the principles of mathematics.
▸**,mathe'matically** *adv*

mathematical logic *n* symbolic logic, esp. when concerned with the foundations of mathematics.

mathematician (,mæθəmə'tɪʃən) *n* an expert or specialist in mathematics.

mathematics (,mæθə'mætɪks) *n* **1** (*functioning as sing*) a group of related sciences, including algebra, geometry, and calculus, concerned with the study of number, quantity, shape, and space and their interrelationships by using a specialized notation. **2** (*functioning as sing or pl*) mathematical operations and processes involved in the solution of a problem or study of some scientific field. [C14 *mathematik* (n), via L from Gk (adj), from *mathēma* a science; rel. to *manthanein* to learn]

maths (mæθs) *n* (*functioning as sing*) *Brit. inf.* short for **mathematics.** US and Canad. equivalent: **math.**

Matilda (mə'tɪldə) *n Austral. inf.* **1** a bushman's swag. **2 waltz Matilda.** to travel as a bushman carrying one's swag. [C20: from the Christian name]

matin, mattin ('mætɪn), *or* **matinal** *adj* of or relating to matins. [C14: see MATINS]

matinée ('mætɪ,neɪ) *n* a daytime, esp. afternoon, performance of a play, concert, etc. [C19: from F; see MATINS]

matinée coat *or* **jacket** *n* a short coat for a baby.

matins *or* **mattins** ('mætɪnz) *n* (*functioning as sing or pl*) **1a** *Chiefly RC Church.* the first of the seven canonical hours of prayer. **1b** the service of morning prayer in the Church of England. **2** *Literary.* a morning song, esp. of birds. [C13: from OF, ult. from L *mātūtīnus* of the morning, from *Mātūta* goddess of dawn]

matlo *or* **matlow** ('mætləʊ) *n* variant spellings of **matelot.**

matrass ('mætrəs) *n Chem., obs.* a long-necked glass flask, used for distilling, dissolving substances, etc. [C17: from F, ? rel. to L *mētiri* to measure]

matri- *combining form.* mother or motherhood: *matriarchy.* [from L *māter* mother]

matriarch ('meɪtrɪ,ɑːk) *n* **1** a woman who dominates an organization, community, etc. **2** the female head of a tribe or family. **3** a very old or venerable woman. [C17: from MATRI- + -ARCH, by false analogy with PATRIARCH]
▸**'matri,archal** *or* **'matri,archic** *adj*

matriarchy ('meɪtrɪ,ɑːkɪ) *n, pl* **matriarchies. 1** a form of social organization in which a female is head of the family or society, and descent and kinship are traced through the female line. **2** any society dominated by women.

matric (mə'trɪk) *n Brit.* short for **matriculation** (see **matriculate**).

matrices ('meɪtrɪ,siːz, 'mæ-) *n* a plural of **matrix.**

matricide ('mætrɪ,saɪd, 'meɪ-) *n* **1** the act of killing one's own mother. **2** a person who kills his mother. [C16: from L *mātrīcīdium* (the act), *mātrīcīda* (the agent). See MATRI-, -CIDE]
▸**,matri'cidal** *adj*

matriculate (mə'trɪkjʊ,leɪt) *vb* **matriculates, matriculating, matriculated. 1** to enrol or be enrolled in an institution, esp. a college or university. **2** (*intr*) to attain the academic standard required for a course at such an institution. [C16: from Med. L *mātrīculāre* to register, from *mātrīcula,* dim. of *matrix* list]
▸**ma,tricu'lation** *n*

matrilineal (,mætrɪ'lɪnɪəl, ,meɪ-) *adj* relating to descent or kinship through the female line.

matrimony ⓣ ('mætrɪmənɪ) *n, pl* **matrimonies. 1** the state or condition of being married. **2** the ceremony of marriage. **3a** a card game in which the king and queen together are a winning combination. **3b** such a combination. [C14: via Norman F from L *mātrimōnium* wedlock, from *māter* mother]
▸**,matri'monial** *adj*

matrix ('meɪtrɪks, 'mæ-) *n, pl* **matrices** *or* **matrixes. 1** a substance, situation, or environment in which something has its origin, takes form, or is enclosed. **2** the intercellular substance of bone, cartilage, connective tissue, etc. **3** the rock in which fossils, pebbles, etc., are embedded. **4** *Printing.* **4a** a metal mould for casting type. **4b** a papier-mâché or plastic mould impressed from the forme and used for stereotyping. **5** a mould used in the production of gramophone records. **6** a bed of perforated material placed beneath a workpiece in a

THESAURUS

buddy (*inf.*), china (*Brit. sl.*), chum (*inf.*), cock (*Brit. inf.*), comrade, crony, homeboy (*sl., chiefly US*), pal (*inf.*) **3b** = **colleague,** associate, companion, compeer, co-worker, fellow-worker **4** = **double,** companion, fellow, match, twin **6** = **assistant,** helper, subordinate ◆ *vb* **7** = **pair,** breed, copulate, couple **8** = **marry,** match, wed **9** = **join,** couple, match, pair, yoke

material *n* **1** = **substance,** body, constituents, element, matter, stuff **2** = **information,** data, evidence, facts, notes, work **3** = **cloth,** fabric, stuff ◆ *adj* **5, 7** = **physical,** bodily, concrete, corporeal, fleshly, nonspiritual, palpable, substantial, tangible, worldly **8** = **important,** consequential, essential, grave, indispensable, key, meaningful, momentous, serious, significant, vital, weighty **9** = **relevant,** applicable, apposite, apropos, germane, pertinent

materialize *vb* **1, 4** = **occur,** appear, come about, come into being, come to pass, happen, take place, take shape, turn up

materially *adv* **1** = **significantly,** considerably, essentially, gravely, greatly, much, seriously, substantially
Antonyms *adv* barely, hardly, insignificantly, little, scarcely, superficially, unsubstantially

materiel *n* = **equipment,** accoutrements, apparatus, gear, hardware, machinery, materials, stores, supplies, tackle, tools

maternal *adj* **1** = **motherly**

maternity *n* **1, 2** = **motherhood,** motherliness

matey *adj* **1** *Brit. informal* = **friendly,** amiable, buddy-buddy (*sl., chiefly US & Canad.*), chummy (*inf.*), clubby, companionable, comradely, hail-fellow-well-met, intimate, pally (*inf.*), palsy-walsy (*inf.*), sociable, thick (*inf.*)

matrimonial *adj* **1, 2** = **marital,** conjugal, connubial, hymeneal, married, nuptial, spousal, wedded, wedding

matrimony *n* **1, 2** = **marriage,** marital rites, nuptials, wedding ceremony, wedlock

press or stamping machine against which the punch operates. **7** *Maths.* a rectangular array of elements set out in rows and columns, used to facilitate the solution of problems, such as transformation of coordinates. **8** *Obs.* the womb. [C16: from L: womb, female animal used for breeding, from *māter* mother]

matron ('meɪtrən) *n* **1** a married woman regarded as staid or dignified. **2** a woman in charge of the domestic or medical arrangements in an institution. **3** *US.* a wardress in a prison. **4** *Brit.* the administrative head of the nursing staff in a hospital. Official name: **nursing officer.** [C14: via OF from L *mātrōna,* from *māter* mother]
▸ **'matronal** *or* **'matronly** *adj* ▸ **'matron,hood** *or* **'matronship** *n*

matron of honour *n, pl* **matrons of honour.** a married woman serving as chief attendant to a bride.

matt *or* **matte** (mæt) *adj, vb* **matts, matting, matted** *or* **mattes, matting, matted.** variant spellings of **mat**^{2} (senses 2 & 4).

Matt. *Bible. abbrev. for* Matthew.

mattamore ('mætə,mɔː) *n* a subterranean storehouse or dwelling. [C17: from F, from Ar. *matmūra,* from *tamara* to store, bury]

matted Ⓣ ('mætɪd) *adj* **1** tangled into a thick mass. **2** covered with or formed of matting.

matter Ⓣ ('mætə) *n* **1** that which makes up something, esp. a physical object; material. **2** substance that occupies space and has mass, as distinguished from substance that is mental, spiritual, etc. **3** substance of a specified type: *vegetable matter.* **4** (sometimes foll. by *of* or *for*) thing; affair; concern; question: *a matter of taste.* **5** a quantity or amount: *a matter of a few pence.* **6** the content of written or verbal material as distinct from its style or form. **7** (*used with a negative*) importance; consequence. **8** *Philosophy.* (in the writings of Aristotle and the Scholastics) that which is itself formless but can receive form and become substance. **9** *Philosophy.* (in the Cartesian tradition) one of two basic modes of existence, the other being mind. **10** *Printing.* **10a** type set up. **10b** copy to be set in type. **11** a secretion or discharge, such as pus. **12** *Law.* **12a** something to be proved. **12b** statements or allegations to be considered by a court. **13 for that matter.** as regards that. **14 no matter. 14a** regardless of; irrespective of: *no matter what the excuse, you must not be late.* **14b** (*sentence substitute*) it is unimportant. **15 the matter.** wrong; the trouble: *there's nothing the matter.* ◆ *vb* (*intr*) **16** to be of consequence or importance. **17** to form and discharge pus. [C13 (n), C16 (vb): from L *māteria* cause, substance, esp. wood, or a substance that produces something else]

matter of course *n* **1** an event or result that is natural or inevitable. ◆ *adj* **matter-of-course. 2** (*usually postpositive*) occurring as a matter of course. **3** accepting things as inevitable or natural: *a matter-of-course attitude.*

matter of fact Ⓣ *n* **1** a fact that is undeniably true. **2** *Law.* a statement of facts the truth of which the court must determine on the basis of the evidence before it. **3 as a matter of fact.** actually; in fact. ◆ *adj* **matter-of-fact. 4** unimaginative or emotionless: *he gave a matter-of-fact account of the murder.*

matting^1 ('mætɪŋ) *n* **1** a coarsely woven fabric, usually made of a natural fibre such as straw or hemp and used as a floor covering, packing material, etc. **2** the act or process of making mats. **3** material for mats.

matting^2 ('mætɪŋ) *n* **1** another word for **mat**^{2} (sense 1). **2** the process of producing a mat finish.

mattins ('mætɪnz) *n* a variant spelling of **matins.**

mattock ('mætək) *n* a type of large pick that has one end of its blade shaped like an adze, used for loosening soil, cutting roots, etc. [OE *mattuc,* from ?; rel. to L *mateola* club, mallet]

mattress ('mætrɪs) *n* **1** a large flat pad with a strong cover, filled with straw, foam rubber, etc., and often incorporating coiled springs, used as a bed or as part of a bed. **2** a woven mat of brushwood, poles, etc., used to protect an embankment, dyke, etc., from scour. **3** a concrete or steel raft or slab used as a foundation or footing. [C13: via OF from It. *materasso,* from Ar. *almatrah* place where something is thrown]

maturate ('mætjʊ,reɪt, 'mætʃʊ-) *vb* **maturates, maturating, maturated. 1** to mature or bring to maturity. **2** a less common word for **suppurate.**
▸ **,matu'ration** *n* ▸ **maturative** (mə'tjʊərətɪv, mə'tʃʊə-) *adj*

mature Ⓣ (mə'tjʊə, -'tʃʊə) *adj* **1** relatively advanced physically, mentally, etc.; grown-up. **2** (of plans, theories, etc.) fully considered; perfected. **3** due or payable: *a mature debenture.* **4** *Biol.* **4a** fully developed or differentiated: *a mature cell.* **4b** fully grown; adult: *a mature animal.* **5** (of fruit, wine, cheese, etc.) ripe or fully aged. ◆ *vb* **matures, maturing, matured. 6** to make or become mature. **7** (*intr*) (of notes, bonds, etc.) to become due for payment or repayment. [C15: from L *mātūrus* early, developed]
▸ **ma'turely** *adv* ▸ **ma'tureness** *n*

mature student *n* a student at a college or university who has passed the usual age for formal education.

maturity Ⓣ (mə'tjʊərɪtɪ, -'tʃʊə-) *n* **1** the state or quality of being mature; full development. **2** *Finance.* **2a** the date upon which a bond, note, etc., becomes due for repayment. **2b** the state of a bill, note, etc., when due.

matutinal (,mætjʊ'taɪnᵊl) *adj* of, occurring in, or during the morning. [C17: from LL *mātūtīnālis,* from L, from *Mātūta* goddess of the dawn]

matzo, matzoh ('mætsəʊ) *or* **matza, matzah** ('mætsə) *n, pl* **matzos, matzohs, matzas, matzahs,** *or* **matzoth** (*Hebrew* ma'tsɔt). a large very thin biscuit of unleavened bread, traditionally eaten during Passover. [from Heb. *matsāh*]

maudlin Ⓣ ('mɔːdlɪn) *adj* foolishly tearful or sentimental, as when drunk. [C17: from ME *Maudelen* Mary Magdalene, typically portrayed as a tearful penitent]

maugre *or* **mauger** ('mɔːgə) *prep Obs.* in spite of. [C13 (meaning: ill will): from OF *maugre,* lit.: bad pleasure]

maul Ⓣ (mɔːl) *vb* (*tr*) **1** to handle clumsily; paw. **2** to batter or lacerate. ◆ *n* **3** a heavy two-handed hammer. **4** *Rugby.* a loose scrum. [C13: from OF *mail,* from L *malleus* hammer]
▸ **'mauler** *n*

maulstick *or* **mahlstick** ('mɔːl,stɪk) *n* a long stick used by artists to steady the hand holding the brush. [C17: partial translation of Du. *maalstok,* from obs. *malen* to paint + *stok* STICK^1]

maunder ('mɔːndə) *vb* (*intr*) to move, talk, or act aimlessly or idly. [C17: ?from obs. *maunder* to beg, from L *mendīcāre*]

maundy ('mɔːndɪ) *n, pl* **maundies.** *Christianity.* the ceremonial washing of the feet of poor persons in commemoration of Jesus' washing of his disciples' feet. [C13: from OF *mandé* something commanded, from L, ult. from Christ's words: *Mandātum novum dō vōbīs* A new commandment give I unto you]

Maundy money *n* specially minted coins distributed by the British sovereign on the Thursday before Easter (**Maundy Thursday**).

mausoleum (,mɔːsə'lɪəm) *n, pl* **mausoleums** *or* **mausolea** (-'lɪə). a large stately tomb. [C16: via L from Gk *mausōleion,* the tomb of *Mausolus,* king of Caria; built at Halicarnassus in the 4th cent. B.C.]

mauve (məʊv) *n* **1a** any of various pale to moderate pinkish-purple or bluish-purple colours. **1b** (*as adj*): *a mauve flower.* **2** a reddish-purple aniline dye. [C19: from F, from L *malva* MALLOW]

maven *or* **mavin** ('meɪvən) *n US.* an expert or connoisseur. [C20: from Yiddish, from Heb. *mevin* understanding]

maverick Ⓣ ('mævərɪk) *n* **1** (in the US and Canada) an unbranded animal, esp. a stray calf. **2a** a person of independent or unorthodox views. **2b** (*as modifier*): *a maverick politician.* [C19: after Samuel A. *Maverick* (1803–70), Texas rancher, who did not brand his cattle]

mavis ('meɪvɪs) *n* a popular name for the **song thrush.** [C14: from OF *mauvis* thrush; from ?]

maw Ⓣ (mɔː) *n* **1** the mouth, throat, crop, or stomach of an animal, esp. of a voracious animal. **2** *Inf.* the mouth or stomach of a greedy person. [OE *maga*]

mawkish Ⓣ ('mɔːkɪʃ) *adj* **1** falsely sentimental, esp. in a weak or maudlin way. **2** nauseating or insipid. [C17: from obs. *mawk* MAGGOT + -ISH]
▸ **'mawkishly** *adv* ▸ **'mawkishness** *n*

max (mæks) *n Inf.* **1** the most significant, highest, furthest, or greatest thing. **2 to the max.** to the ultimate extent.

max. *abbrev. for* maximum.

maxi ('mæksɪ) *adj* **1a** (of a garment) reaching the ankle. **1b** (*as n*): *she wore a maxi.* **1c** (*in combination*): *a maxidress.* **2** large or considerable. [C20: from MAXIMUM]

maxilla (mæk'sɪlə) *n, pl* **maxillae** (-liː). **1** the upper jawbone in vertebrates. **2** any member of one or two pairs of mouthparts in insects and other arthropods. [C17: NL, from L: jaw]

THESAURUS

matted *adj* **1** = **tangled**, knotted, tousled, uncombed

matter *n* **1-3** = **substance**, body, material, stuff **4** = **situation**, affair, business, concern, episode, event, incident, issue, occurrence, proceeding, question, subject, thing, topic, transaction **5** = **amount**, quantity, sum **6** = **content**, argument, purport, sense, subject, substance, text, thesis **7** = **importance**, consequence, import, moment, note, significance, weight **11** = **pus**, discharge, purulence, secretion **15 the matter** = **problem**, complication, difficulty, distress, trouble, upset, worry ◆ *vb* **16** = **be important**, be of consequence, carry weight, count, have influence, make a difference, mean something, signify

matter-of-fact *adj* **4** = **unsentimental**, deadpan, down-to-earth, dry, dull, emotionless, flat, lifeless, mundane, plain, prosaic, sober, unembellished, unimaginative, unvarnished

mature *adj* **1, 2, 5** = **grown-up**, adult, complete, fit, full-blown, full-grown, fully fledged, grown, matured, mellow, of age, perfect, prepared, ready, ripe, ripened, seasoned ◆ *vb* **6** = **develop**, age, become adult, bloom, blossom, come of age, grow up, maturate, mellow, perfect, reach adulthood, ripen, season
Antonyms *adj* ≠ **grown-up**: adolescent, childish, green, immature, incomplete, juvenile, puerile, undeveloped, unfinished, unperfected, unripe, young, youthful

maturity *n* **1** = **adulthood**, completion, experience, full bloom, full growth, fullness, majority, manhood *or* womanhood, maturation, matureness, perfection, ripeness, wisdom
Antonyms *n* childishness, excitability, immaturity, imperfection, incompletion, irresponsibility, juvenility, puerility, youthfulness

maudlin *adj* = **sentimental**, lachrymose, mawkish, mushy (*inf.*), overemotional, slushy (*inf.*), soppy (*Brit. inf.*), tearful, weepy (*inf.*)

maul *vb* **1** = **ill-treat**, abuse, batter, beat, beat up (*inf.*), handle roughly, knock about *or* around, manhandle, molest, pummel, rough up, thrash, work over (*sl.*) **2** = **tear**, claw, lacerate, mangle

maverick *n* **2a** = **rebel**, dissenter, dissentient, eccentric, heretic, iconoclast, individualist, nonconformist, protester, radical ◆ *modifier* **2b** = **rebel**, dissenting, eccentric, heretical, iconoclastic, individualistic, nonconformist, radical
Antonyms *n* ≠ **rebel**: Babbitt (*US*), conventionalist, stick-in-the-mud (*inf.*), traditionalist, yes man

maw *n* **1** = **stomach**, craw, crop, gullet, jaws, mouth, throat

mawkish *adj* **1** = **sentimental**, emotional, feeble, gushy (*inf.*), maudlin, mushy, schmaltzy (*sl.*), slushy (*inf.*), soppy (*Brit. inf.*), three-hankie (*inf.*)

►**max'illary** *adj*

maxim ➊ ('mæksɪm) *n* a brief expression of a general truth, principle, or rule of conduct. [C15: via F from Med. L, from *maxima,* in the phrase *maxima prōpositio* basic axiom (lit.: greatest proposition)]

maxima ('mæksɪmə) *n* a plural of **maximum.**

maximal ('mæksɪməl) *adj* of, relating to, or achieving a maximum; being the greatest or best possible.
►**'maximally** *adv*

maximin ('mæksɪˌmɪn) *n* **1** *Maths.* the highest of a set of minimum values. **2** (in game theory, etc.) the procedure of choosing the strategy that most benefits the least advantaged member of a group. Cf. **minimax.** [C20: from MAXI(MUM) + MIN(IMUM)]

maximize *or* **maximise** ('mæksɪˌmaɪz) *vb* **maximizes, maximizing, maximized** *or* **maximises, maximising, maximised.** (*tr*) to make as high or great as possible; increase to a maximum.
►**ˌmaximi'zation** *or* **ˌmaximi'sation** *n* ►**'maxiˌmizer** *or* **'maxiˌmiser** *n*

maximum ➊ ('mæksɪməm) *n, pl* **maximums** *or* **maxima. 1** the greatest possible amount, degree, etc. **2** the highest value of a variable quantity. ◆ *adj* **3** of, being, or showing a maximum or maximums. ◆ Abbrev.: **max.** [C18: from L: greatest (neuter form used as noun), from *magnus* great]

maxwell ('mækswəl) *n* the cgs unit of magnetic flux equal to the flux through one square centimetre normal to a field of one gauss. It is equivalent to 10^{-8} weber. Symbol: Mx [C20: after J. C. *Maxwell* (1831–79), Scot. physicist]

may[1] (meɪ) *vb past* **might.** (takes an infinitive without *to* or an implied infinitive) used as an auxiliary: **1** to indicate that permission is requested by or granted to someone: *he may go.* **2** (often foll. by *well*) to indicate possibility: *the rope may break.* **3** to indicate ability or capacity, esp. in questions: *may I help you?* **4** to express a strong wish: *long may she reign.* **5** to indicate result or purpose: used only in clauses introduced by *that* or *so that: he writes so that the average reader may understand.* **6** another word for **might**[1]. **7** to express courtesy in a question: *whose child may this little girl be?* **8 be that as it may.** in spite of that: a sentence connector conceding the possible truth of a previous statement and introducing an adversative clause: *be that as it may, I still think he should come.* **9 come what may.** whatever happens. **10 that's as may be.** (foll. by a clause introduced by *but*) that may be so. [OE *mæg,* from *magan*]

> **USAGE NOTE** It was formerly considered correct to use *may* rather than *can* when referring to permission, as in: *you may use the laboratory for your experiments,* but this use of *may* is now almost entirely restricted to polite questions such as: *may I open the window?* The use of *may* with *if* in constructions such as *your analysis may have been more credible if...*is generally regarded as incorrect, *might* being preferred: *your analysis might have been more credible if...*

may[2] *or* **may tree** (meɪ) *n* a Brit. name for **hawthorn.** [C16: from MAY]

May (meɪ) *n* the fifth month of the year, consisting of 31 days. [from OF, from L *Maius* (month) of *Maia,* Roman goddess]

Maya ('maɪə) *n* **1** (*pl* **Maya** *or* **Mayas**) Also called: **Mayan.** a member of an American Indian people of Yucatán, Belize, and N Guatemala, once having an advanced civilization. **2** the language of this people.

May apple *n* **1** an American plant with edible yellowish egg-shaped fruit. **2** the fruit.

maybe ➊ ('meɪˌbiː) *adv* **1** perhaps. ◆ *sentence substitute.* **2** possibly; neither yes nor no.

May beetle *or* **bug** *n* another name for **cockchafer.**

Mayday ('meɪˌdeɪ) *n* the international radiotelephone distress signal. [C20: phonetic spelling of F *m'aidez* help me]

May Day *n* the first day of May, traditionally a celebration of the coming of spring: in some countries now observed as a holiday in honour of workers.

mayest ('meɪɪst) *vb* a variant of **mayst.**

mayflower ('meɪˌflaʊə) *n* **1** any of various plants that bloom in May. **2** *Brit.* another name for **hawthorn, cowslip,** or **marsh marigold.**

Mayflower ('meɪˌflaʊə) *n* **the.** the ship in which the Pilgrim Fathers sailed from Plymouth to America in 1620.

mayfly ('meɪˌflaɪ) *n, pl* **mayflies.** any of an order of short-lived insects having large transparent wings.

mayhap ('meɪˌhæp) *adv* an archaic word for **perhaps.** [C16: shortened from *it may hap*]

mayhem ➊ *or* **maihem** ('meɪhɛm) *n* **1** *Law.* the wilful and unlawful infliction of injury upon a person, esp. (formerly) the injuring or removing of a limb rendering him less capable of defending himself against attack. **2** any violent destruction or confusion. [C15: from Anglo-F *mahem* injury, of Gmc origin]

Maying ('meɪɪŋ) *n* the traditional celebration of May Day.

mayn't ('meɪənt, meɪnt) *contraction of* may not.

mayonnaise (ˌmeɪə'neɪz) *n* a thick creamy sauce made from egg yolks, oil, and vinegar or lemon juice. [C19: from F, ? from *mahonnais* of Mahón, a port in Minorca]

mayor (mɛə) *n* the civic head of a municipal corporation in many countries. Scot. equivalent: **provost.** [C13: from OF *maire,* from L *maior* greater]
►**'mayoral** *adj* ►**'mayorship** *n*

mayoralty ('mɛərəltɪ) *n, pl* **mayoralties.** the office or term of office of a mayor. [C14: from OF *mairalté*]

mayoress ('mɛərɪs) *n* **1** *Chiefly Brit.* the wife of a mayor. **2** a female mayor.

maypole ('meɪˌpəʊl) *n* a tall pole around which people dance during May-Day celebrations.

May queen *n* a girl chosen, esp. for her beauty, to preside over May-Day celebrations.

mayst (meɪst) *or* **mayest** *vb Arch.* (used with *thou* or its relative equivalent) a singular form of the present tense of **may**[1].

mayweed ('meɪˌwiːd) *n* **1** Also called: **dog fennel, stinking mayweed.** a widespread Eurasian weedy plant having evil-smelling leaves and daisy-like flower heads. **2 scentless mayweed.** a similar and related plant, with scentless leaves. [C16: changed from OE *mægtha* mayweed + WEED]

maze ➊ (meɪz) *n* **1** a complex network of paths or passages, esp. one with high hedges in a garden, designed to puzzle those walking through it. **2** a similar system represented diagrammatically as a pattern of lines. **3** any confusing network of streets, paths, etc. **4** a state of confusion. ◆ *vb* **mazes, mazing, mazed. 5** an archaic or dialect word for **amaze.** [C13: see AMAZE]
►**'mazement** *n* ►**'mazy** *adj*

mazurka *or* **mazourka** (mə'zɜːkə) *n* **1** a Polish national dance in triple time. **2** a piece of music composed for this dance. [C19: from Polish: (dance) of *Mazur* (Mazovia) province in Poland]

Mb *Computing. abbrev. for* megabyte.

MB *abbrev. for* Bachelor of Medicine.

MBA *abbrev. for* Master of Business Administration.

mbaqanga (ᵊmbɑː'kæŋgə) *n* a style of Black popular music of urban South Africa. [C20: ? from Zulu *umbaqanga* mixture]

MBE *abbrev. for* Member of the Order of the British Empire (a Brit. title).

mbira (ᵊm'biːrə) *n* an African musical instrument consisting of tuned metal strips attached to a resonating box, which are plucked with the thumbs. Also called: **thumb piano.** [Bantu]

MC *abbrev. for:* **1** Master of Ceremonies. **2** (in the US) Member of Congress. **3** (in Britain) Military Cross.

Mc- *prefix* a variant of **Mac-.** For entries beginning with this prefix, see under **Mac-.**

MCC (in Britain) *abbrev. for* Marylebone Cricket Club.

MCh *abbrev. for* Master of Surgery. [L *Magister Chirurgiae*]

MCP *Inf. abbrev. for* male chauvinist pig.

Md *the chemical symbol for* mendelevium.

MD *abbrev. for:* **1** Doctor of Medicine. [from L *Medicinae Doctor*] **2** Managing Director. **3** mentally deficient.

MDMA *abbrev. for* 3,4-methylenedioxymethamphetamine. See **ecstasy** (sense 4).

MDS See **MMDS.**

MDT (in the US and Canada) *abbrev. for* Mountain Daylight Time.

me[1] (miː; *unstressed* mɪ) *pron* (*objective*) **1** refers to the speaker or writer: *that shocks me.* ◆ *n* **2** *Inf.* the personality of the speaker or writer or something that expresses it: *the real me.* [OE *mē* (dative)]

> **USAGE NOTE** It was formerly regarded as correct to use *I, he, she,* etc. rather than *me, him, her,* after the verb *to be,* as in: *it is I who told him.* Since both *I* and *me* can sound strange in a sentence like this, it is better to use a different construction: *I am the one who told him.* The use of a possessive before an *-ing* form of a verb was formerly thought to be preferable to using *me,* etc., but now both forms are acceptable: *he didn't like my/me having a job of my own.*

me[2] (miː) *n* a variant spelling of **mi** (sense 2).

ME *abbrev. for:* **1** Marine Engineer. **2** Mechanical Engineer. **3** Methodist Episcopal. **4** Middle English. **5** Mining Engineer. **6** (in titles) Most Excellent. **7** myalgic encephalomyelitis.

mea culpa *Latin.* ('meɪɑː 'kʊlpɑː) an acknowledgment of guilt. [lit.: my fault]

mead[1] (miːd) *n* an alcoholic drink made by fermenting a solution of honey, often with spices added. [OE *meodu*]

mead[2] (miːd) *n* an archaic or poetic word for **meadow.** [OE *mæd*]

meadow ➊ ('mɛdəʊ) *n* **1** an area of grassland, often used for hay or for

THESAURUS

maxim *n* = **saying,** adage, aphorism, apophthegm, axiom, byword, dictum, gnome, motto, proverb, rule, saw

maximum *n* **1, 2** = **top,** apogee, ceiling, crest, extremity, height, most, peak, pinnacle, summit, upper limit, utmost, uttermost, zenith ◆ *adj* **3** = **greatest,** highest, maximal, most, paramount, supreme, topmost, utmost

Antonyms *n* ≠ **top:** bottom, minimum ◆ *adj* ≠ **greatest:** least, lowest, minimal

maybe *adv* **1** = **perhaps,** it could be, mayhap (*arch.*), peradventure (*arch.*), perchance (*arch.*), possibly

mayhem *n* **2** = **chaos,** commotion, confusion, destruction, disorder, fracas, havoc, trouble, violence

maze *n* **1-3** = **labyrinth,** convolutions, intricacy, meander **4** = **web,** bewilderment, confusion, imbroglio, mesh, perplexity, puzzle, snarl, tangle, uncertainty

meadow *n* **1** = **field,** grassland, lea (*poetic*), ley, pasture

grazing of animals. **2** a low-lying piece of grassland, often boggy and near a river. [OE *mædwe,* from *mǣd* MEAD[2]]
▸ˈ**meadowy** *adj*

meadow grass *n* a perennial grass that grows in meadows and similar places in N temperate regions.

meadow saffron *n* another name for **autumn crocus.**

meadowsweet (ˈmɛdəʊˌswiːt) *n* **1** a Eurasian plant with dense heads of small fragrant cream-coloured flowers. **2** any of several related North American plants. See also **spiraea.**

meagre ⓘ *or US* **meager** (ˈmiːgə) *adj* **1** deficient in amount, quality, or extent. **2** thin or emaciated. **3** lacking in richness or strength. [C14: from OF *maigre,* from L *macer* lean, poor]
▸ˈ**meagrely** *adv* ▸ˈ**meagreness** *n*

meal[1] ⓘ (miːl) *n* **1a** any of the regular occasions, such as breakfast, lunch, dinner, etc., when food is served and eaten. **1b** (*in combination*): *mealtime.* **2** the food served and eaten. **3 make a meal of.** *Inf.* to perform (a task) with unnecessarily great effort. [OE *mǣl* measure, set time, meal]

meal[2] (miːl) *n* **1** the edible part of a grain or pulse (excluding wheat) ground to a coarse powder. **2** *Scot.* oatmeal. **3** *Chiefly US.* maize flour. [OE *melu*]

mealie *or* **mielie** (ˈmiːlɪ) *n* (*often pl*) a S. African word for **maize.** [C19: from Afrik. *milie,* from Port. *milho,* from L *milium* millet]

mealie-meal *n S. African.* meal made from finely ground maize.

meals-on-wheels *n* (*functioning as sing*) a service taking hot meals to the elderly, infirm, etc., in their own homes.

meal ticket *n Sl.* a person, situation, etc., providing a source of livelihood or income. [from orig. US sense of ticket entitling holder to a meal]

mealworm (ˈmiːlˌwɜːm) *n* the larva of various beetles feeding on stored foods, esp. meal and flour.

mealy (ˈmiːlɪ) *adj* **mealier, mealiest. 1** resembling meal; powdery. **2** containing or consisting of meal or grain. **3** sprinkled or covered with meal or similar granules. **4** (esp. of horses) spotted; mottled. **5** pale in complexion. **6** short for **mealy-mouthed.**
▸ˈ**mealiness** *n*

mealy bug *n* any of various plant-eating insects coated with a powdery waxy secretion: some species are pests of citrus fruits and greenhouse plants.

mealy-mouthed ⓘ *adj* hesitant or afraid to speak plainly; not outspoken. [C16: from MEALY (in the sense: soft, soft-spoken)]

mean[1] ⓘ (miːn) *vb* **means, meaning, meant.** (*mainly tr*) **1** (*may take a clause as object or an infinitive*) to intend to convey or express. **2** (*may take a clause as object or an infinitive*) to intend: *she didn't mean to hurt it.* **3** (*may take a clause as object*) to say or do in all seriousness: *the boss means what he says.* **4** (*often passive;* often foll. by *for*) to destine or design (for a certain person or purpose): *she was meant for greater things.* **5** (*may take a clause as object*) to denote or connote; signify; represent. **6** (*may take a clause as object*) to produce; cause: *the weather will mean long traffic delays.* **7** (*may take a clause as object*) to foretell; portend: *those dark clouds mean rain.* **8** to have the importance of: *money means nothing to him.* **9** (*intr*) to have the intention of behaving or acting (esp. in **mean well** *or* **mean ill**). [OE *mænan*]

> **USAGE NOTE** In standard English, *mean* should not be followed by *for* when expressing intention: *I didn't mean this to happen* (not *I didn't mean for this to happen*).

mean[2] ⓘ (miːn) *adj* **1** *Chiefly Brit.* miserly, ungenerous, or petty. **2** despicable, ignoble, or callous: *a mean action.* **3** poor or shabby: *a mean abode.* **4** *Inf., chiefly US & Canad.* bad-tempered; vicious. **5** *Inf.* ashamed: *he felt mean about not letting the children stay out late.* **6** *Sl.* excellent; skilful: *he plays a mean trombone.* **7 no mean. 7a** of high quality: *no mean performer.* **7b** difficult: *no mean feat.* [C12: from OE *gemǣne* common]
▸ˈ**meanly** *adv* ▸ˈ**meanness** *n*

mean[3] ⓘ (miːn) *n* **1** the middle point, state, or course between limits or extremes. **2** moderation. **3** *Maths.* **3a** the second and third terms of a proportion, as *b* and *c* in $a/b = c/d$. **3b** another name for **average** (sense 2). **4** *Statistics.* a statistic obtained by multiplying each possible value of a variable by its probability and then taking the sum or integral over the range of the variable. ◆ *adj* **5** intermediate or medium in size, quantity, etc. **6** occurring halfway between extremes or limits; average. [C14: via Anglo-Norman from OF *moien,* from LL *mediānus* MEDIAN]

meander ⓘ (mɪˈændə) *vb* (*intr*) **1** to follow a winding course. **2** to wander without definite aim or direction. ◆ *n* **3** (*often pl*) a curve or bend, as in a river. **4** (*often pl*) a winding course or movement. **5** an ornamental pattern, esp. as used in ancient Greek architecture. [C16: from L *maeander,* from Gk *Maiandros* the River Maeander, now the River Menderes in SW Turkey]
▸**meˈandering** *adj*

mean deviation *n Statistics.* **1** the difference between an observed value of a variable and its mean. **2** Also called: **mean deviation from the mean** (*or* **median**), **average deviation.** a measure of dispersion derived by computing the mean of the absolute values of the differences between observed values of a variable and the variable's mean.

meanie *or* **meany** (ˈmiːnɪ) *n Inf.* **1** *Chiefly Brit.* a miserly or stingy person. **2** *Chiefly US.* a nasty ill-tempered person.

meaning ⓘ (ˈmiːnɪŋ) *n* **1** the sense or significance of a word, sentence, symbol, etc.; import. **2** the purpose behind speech, action, etc. **3** the inner, symbolic, or true interpretation, value, or message. **4** valid content; efficacy. ◆ *adj* **5** expressive of some sense, intention, criticism, etc.: *a meaning look.* ◆ See also **well-meaning.**

meaningful ⓘ (ˈmiːnɪŋfʊl) *adj* **1** having great meaning or validity. **2** eloquent; expressive: *a meaningful silence.*
▸ˈ**meaningfully** *adv* ▸ˈ**meaningfulness** *n*

meaningless ⓘ (ˈmiːnɪŋlɪs) *adj* futile or empty of meaning.
▸ˈ**meaninglessly** *adv* ▸ˈ**meaninglessness** *n*

mean lethal dose *n* another term for **median lethal dose.**

mean life *n Physics.* the average time of existence of an unstable or reactive entity, such as a nucleus, elementary particle, etc.

means ⓘ (miːnz) *n* **1** (*functioning as sing or pl*) the medium, method, or instrument used to obtain a result or achieve an end: *a means of com-*

THESAURUS

meagre *adj* **1 = insubstantial**, deficient, exiguous, inadequate, little, measly, paltry, pathetic, poor, puny, scant, scanty, scrimpy, short, skimpy, slender, slight, small, spare, sparse **2 = thin**, bony, emaciated, gaunt, hungry, lank, lean, scraggy, scrawny, skinny, starved, underfed

meal[1] *n* **1, 2 = repast**, board, spread (*inf.*)

mealy-mouthed *adj* **= hesitant**, afraid, doubtful, equivocal, euphemistic, indirect, mincing, overdelicate, prim, reticent

mean[1] *vb* **1, 5 = signify**, betoken, connote, convey, denote, drive at, express, hint at, imply, indicate, purport, represent, say, spell, stand for, suggest, symbolize **2 = intend**, aim, aspire, contemplate, design, desire, have in mind, plan, propose, purpose, set out, want, wish **4 = destine**, design, fate, fit, make, match, predestine, preordain, suit **6 = result in**, bring about, cause, engender, entail, give rise to, involve, lead to, necessitate, produce **7 = foretell**, adumbrate, augur, betoken, foreshadow, herald, portend, presage, promise

mean[2] *adj* **1 = miserly**, beggarly, close (*inf.*), mercenary, mingy, near (*inf.*), niggardly, parsimonious, penny-pinching, penurious, selfish, skimpy, stingy, tight, tight-arsed (*taboo sl.*), tight as a duck's arse (*taboo sl.*), tight-assed (*US taboo sl.*), tight-fisted, ungenerous **2 = dishonourable**, abject, base, callous, contemptible, degenerate, degraded, despicable, disgraceful, hard-hearted, ignoble, low-minded, narrow-minded, petty, scurvy, shabby, shameful, sordid, vile, wretched **3 = shabby**, beggarly, contemptible, down-at-heel, grungy (*sl., chiefly US*), insignificant, low-rent (*inf., chiefly US*), miserable, paltry, poor, run-down, scruffy, scuzzy (*sl., chiefly US*), seedy, sordid, squalid, tawdry, wretched **4 = malicious**, bad-tempered, cantankerous, churlish, disagreeable, hostile, ill-tempered, nasty, rude, sour, unfriendly, unpleasant
Antonyms *adj* ≠ **miserly:** altruistic, big, bountiful, generous, munificent, prodigal, unselfish ≠ **dishonourable:** good, honourable, praiseworthy ≠ **shabby:** attractive, choice, de luxe, excellent, first-rate, pleasing, superb, superior ≠ **malicious:** compassionate, gentle, humane, kind, liberal, sympathetic, warm-hearted

mean[3] *n* **1 = average**, balance, compromise, happy medium, median, middle, middle course *or* way, midpoint, norm ◆ *adj* **5, 6 = average**, intermediate, medial, median, medium, middle, middling, normal, standard

meander *vb* **1 = wind**, snake, turn, zigzag **2 = wander**, ramble, stravaig (*Scot. & N English dialect*), stray, stroll ◆ *n* **3, 4 = curve**, bend, coil, loop, turn, twist, zigzag

meandering *adj* **1, 2 = winding**, anfractuous, circuitous, convoluted, indirect, roundabout, serpentine, snaking, tortuous, wandering
Antonyms *adj* direct, straight, straightforward, undeviating

meaning *n* **1 = sense**, connotation, denotation, drift, explanation, gist, implication, import, interpretation, message, purport, significance, signification, substance, upshot, value **2 = purpose**, aim, design, end, goal, idea, intention, object, plan, point, trend **4 = force**, effect, efficacy, point, thrust, use, usefulness, validity, value, worth ◆ *adj* **5 = expressive**, eloquent, meaningful, pointed, pregnant, speaking, suggestive

meaningful *adj* **1 = significant**, important, material, purposeful, relevant, serious, useful, valid, worthwhile **2 = expressive**, eloquent, meaning, pointed, pregnant, speaking, suggestive
Antonyms *adj* ≠ **significant:** inconsequential, insignificant, meaningless, senseless, superficial, trivial, unimportant, useless, worthless

meaningless *adj* **= pointless**, aimless, empty, futile, hollow, inane, inconsequential, insignificant, insubstantial, nonsensical, nugatory, purposeless, senseless, trifling, trivial, useless, vain, valueless, worthless
Antonyms *adj* consequential, deep, evident, important, meaningful, obvious, purposeful, sensible, significant, useful, valuable, worthwhile

meanness *n* **1 = miserliness**, minginess (*Brit. inf.*), niggardliness, parsimony, penuriousness, selfishness, stinginess, tight-fistedness **2 = pettiness**, abjectness, baseness, degeneracy, degradation, despicableness, disgracefulness, dishonourableness, ignobility, low-mindedness, narrow-mindedness, scurviness, shabbiness, shamefulness, sordidness, vileness, wretchedness **3 = shabbiness**, beggarliness, contemptibleness, insignificance, paltriness, pettiness, poorness, scruffiness, seediness, sordidness, squalor, tawdriness, wretchedness **4 = malice**, bad temper, cantankerousness, churlishness, disagreeableness, hostility, ill temper, maliciousness, nastiness, rudeness, sourness, unfriendliness, unpleasantness

means *n* **1 = method**, agency, avenue, channel, course, expedient, instrument, measure, medium, mode, process, way ◆ *pl n* **2 = money**, affluence, capital, estate, fortune, funds, income, property, resources, riches, substance, wealth, wherewithal **4 by all means = certainly**, abso-

munication. **2** (*functioning as pl*) resources or income. **3** (*functioning as pl*) considerable wealth or income: *a man of means.* **4 by all means.** without hesitation or doubt; certainly. **5 by means of.** with the use or help of. **6 by no manner of means.** definitely not. **7 by no** (*or* **not by any**) **means.** on no account; in no way.

means test *n* the checking of a person's income to determine whether he qualifies for financial or social aid from a government.

mean sun *n* an imaginary sun moving along the celestial equator at a constant speed and completing its annual course in the same time as the sun takes to move round the ecliptic at a varying speed. It is used in the measurement of mean solar time.

meant (mɛnt) *vb* the past tense and past participle of **mean**[1].

meantime ❶ ('miːn,taɪm) *or* **meanwhile** ('miːn,waɪl) *n* **1** the intervening time or period (esp. in **in the meantime**). ◆ *adv* **2** during the intervening time or period. **3** at the same time, esp. in another place.

mean time *or* **mean solar time** *n* the times, at a particular place, measured in terms of the passage of the mean sun, giving 24-hour days (mean solar days) throughout a year.

meany ('miːnɪ) *n, pl* **meanies.** a variant of **meanie.**

measles ('miːzəlz) *n* (*functioning as sing*) **1** a highly contagious viral disease common in children, characterized by fever, profuse nasal discharge of mucus, conjunctivitis, and a rash of small red spots. See also **German measles. 2** a disease of cattle, sheep, and pigs, caused by infestation with tapeworm larvae. [C14: from MLow G *masele* spot on the skin; infl. by ME *mesel* leper, from L *misellus,* dim. of *miser* wretched]

measly ❶ ('miːzlɪ) *adj* **measlier, measliest. 1** *Inf.* meagre in quality or quantity. **2** (of meat) infested with tapeworm larvae. **3** having or relating to measles. [C17: see MEASLES]

measurable ❶ ('mɛʒərəbᵊl) *adj* able to be measured; perceptible or significant.
▸**'measurably** *adv*

measure ❶ ('mɛʒə) *n* **1** the extent, quantity, amount, or degree of something, as determined by measurement or calculation. **2** a device for measuring distance, volume, etc., such as a graduated scale or container. **3** a system of measurement: *metric measure.* **4** a standard used in a system of measurements. **5** a specific or standard amount of something: *a measure of grain; full measure.* **6** a basis or standard for comparison. **7** reasonable or permissible limit or bounds: *within measure.* **8** degree or extent (often in **in some measure, in a measure,** etc.): *a measure of freedom.* **9** (*often pl*) a particular action intended to achieve an effect. **10** a legislative bill, act, or resolution. **11** *Music.* another word for **bar**[1] (sense 15). **12** *Prosody.* poetic rhythm or cadence; metre. **13** a metrical foot. **14** *Poetic.* a melody or tune. **15** the act of measuring; measurement. **16** *Arch.* a dance. **17** *Printing.* the width of a page or column of type. **18 for good measure.** as an extra precaution or beyond requirements. **19 made to measure.** (of clothes) made to fit an individual purchaser. ◆ *vb* **measures, measuring, measured. 20** (*tr;* often foll. by *up*) to determine the size, amount, etc., of by measurement. **21** (*intr*) to make a measurement. **22** (*tr*) to estimate or determine. **23** (*tr*) to function as a measurement of: *the ohm measures electrical resistance.* **24** (*tr*) to bring into competition or conflict with: *he measured his strength against that of his opponent.* **25** (*intr*) to be as specified in extent, amount, etc.: *the room measures six feet.* **26** (*tr*) to travel or move over as if measuring. ◆ See also **measure up.** [C13: from OF, from L *mēnsūra,* from *mēnsus,* p.p. of *mētīrī* to measure]

measured ❶ ('mɛʒəd) *adj* **1** determined by measurement. **2** slow or stately. **3** carefully considered; deliberate.
▸**'measuredly** *adv*

measureless ❶ ('mɛʒəlɪs) *adj* limitless, vast, or infinite.
▸**'measurelessly** *adv*

measurement ❶ ('mɛʒəmənt) *n* **1** the act or process of measuring. **2** an amount, extent, or size determined by measuring. **3** a system of measures based on a particular standard.

measures ('mɛʒəz) *pl n* rock strata that are characterized by a particular type of sediment or deposit: *coal measures.*

measure up ❶ *vb* **1** (*adv*) to determine the size of (something) by measurement. **2 measure up to.** to fulfil (expectations, standards, etc.).

measuring jug *n* a graduated jug used in cooking to measure ingredients.

measuring worm *n* the larva of a geometrid moth: it moves in a series of loops. Also called: **inchworm.**

meat ❶ (miːt) *n* **1** the flesh of mammals used as food. **2** anything edible, esp. flesh with the texture of meat: *crab meat.* **3** food, as opposed to drink. **4** the essence or gist. **5** an archaic word for **meal**[1] (senses 1 and 2). **6 meat and drink.** a source of pleasure. [OE *mete*]
▸**'meatless** *adj*

meatball ('miːt,bɔːl) *n* **1** minced beef, shaped into a ball before cooking. **2** *US & Canad. sl.* a stupid or boring person.

meatus (mɪ'eɪtəs) *n, pl* **meatuses** *or* **meatus.** *Anat.* a natural opening or channel, such as the canal leading from the outer ear to the eardrum. [C17: from L: passage, from *meāre* to pass]

meaty ❶ ('miːtɪ) *adj* **meatier, meatiest. 1** of, relating to, or full of meat. **2** heavily built; fleshy or brawny. **3** full of import or interest: *a meaty discussion.*
▸**'meatily** *adv* ▸**'meatiness** *n*

Mecca *or* **Mekka** ('mɛkə) *n* **1** a city in W Saudi Arabia: birthplace of Mohammed; the holiest city of Islam. **2** (*sometimes not cap.*) a place that attracts many visitors.

Meccano (mɪ'kɑːnəʊ) *n Trademark.* a construction set of miniature metal parts from which mechanical models can be made.

mech. *abbrev. for:* **1** mechanical. **2** mechanics. **3** mechanism.

mechanic (mɪ'kænɪk) *n* a person skilled in maintaining or operating machinery, motors, etc. [C14: from L *mēchanicus,* from Gk, from *mēkhanē* MACHINE]

mechanical ❶ (mɪ'kænɪkᵊl) *adj* **1** made, performed, or operated by or as if by a machine or machinery. **2** concerned with machines or machinery. **3** relating to or controlled or operated by physical forces. **4** of or concerned with mechanics. **5** (of a gesture, etc.) automatic; lacking thought, feeling, etc. **6** *Philosophy.* accounting for phenomena by physically determining forces.
▸**me'chanicalism** *n* ▸**me'chanically** *adv* ▸**me'chanicalness** *n*

mechanical advantage *n* the ratio of the working force exerted by a mechanism to the applied effort.

mechanical drawing *n* a drawing to scale of a machine, machine component, architectural plan, etc., from which dimensions can be taken.

mechanical engineering *n* the branch of engineering concerned with the design, construction, and operation of machines.

mechanical equivalent of heat *n Physics.* a factor for converting units of energy into heat units.

mechanician (,mɛkə'nɪʃən) *or* **mechanist** *n* a person skilled in making machinery and tools; technician.

mechanics (mɪ'kænɪks) *n* **1** (*functioning as sing*) the branch of science, divided into statics, dynamics, and kinematics, concerned with the equilibrium or motion of bodies in a particular frame of reference. **2** (*functioning as sing*) the science of designing, constructing, and operating machines. **3** the working parts of a machine. **4** the technical aspects of something.

mechanism ❶ ('mɛkə,nɪzəm) *n* **1** a system or structure of moving parts that performs some function, esp. in a machine. **2** something resem-

THESAURUS

lutely, definitely, doubtlessly, of course, positively, surely **5 by means of = by way of,** by dint of, through, using, utilizing, via, with the aid of **7 by no means = in no way,** absolutely not, definitely not, not at all, not in the least, not in the slightest, not the least bit, no way, on no account

meantime *adv* **2, 3 = at the same time,** concurrently, for now, for the duration, for the moment, for then, in the interim, in the interval, in the intervening time, in the meantime, in the meanwhile, simultaneously

measly *adj* **1** *Informal* **= meagre,** beggarly, contemptible, mean, mingy (*Brit. inf.*), miserable, miserly, niggardly, paltry, pathetic, petty, pitiful, poor, puny, scanty, skimpy, stingy, ungenerous

measurable *adj* **= quantifiable,** assessable, computable, determinable, gaugeable, material, mensurable, perceptible, quantitative, significant

measure *n* **1 = quantity,** allotment, allowance, amount, amplitude, capacity, degree, extent, magnitude, portion, proportion, quota, range, ration, reach, scope, share, size **2 = gauge,** metre, rule, scale, yardstick **6 = standard,** criterion, example, model, norm, par, test, touchstone, yardstick **7 = limit,** bounds, control, limitation, moderation, restraint **9** *often plural* **= action,** act, course, deed, expedient, manoeuvre, means, procedure, proceeding, step **10 = law,** act, bill, enactment, resolution, statute **12, 13 = rhythm,** beat, cadence, foot, metre, verse **18 for good measure = in addition,** as a bonus, besides, into the bargain, to boot ◆ *vb* **20-22 = quantify,** appraise, assess, calculate, calibrate, compute, determine, estimate, evaluate, gauge, judge, mark out, rate, size, sound, survey, value, weigh

measured *adj* **1 = quantified,** exact, gauged, modulated, precise, predetermined, regulated, standard, verified **2 = steady,** dignified, even, leisurely, regular, sedate, slow, solemn, stately, unhurried **3 = considered,** calculated, deliberate, grave, planned, premeditated, reasoned, sober, studied, well-thought-out

measureless *adj* **= infinite,** beyond measure, boundless, endless, immeasurable, immense, incalculable, inestimable, limitless, unbounded, vast

measurement *n* **1 = calculation,** appraisal, assessment, calibration, computation, estimation, evaluation, judgment, mensuration, metage, survey, valuation **2 = size,** amount, amplitude, area, capacity, depth, dimension, extent, height, length, magnitude, volume, weight, width

measure up *vb* **2 measure up to = fulfil the expectations,** be adequate, be capable, be equal to, be fit, be suitable, be suited, come up to scratch (*inf.*), come up to standard, compare, equal, fit *or* fill the bill, make the grade (*inf.*), match, meet, rival

meat *n* **1-3 = food,** aliment, cheer, chow (*inf.*), comestibles, eats (*sl.*), fare, flesh, grub (*sl.*), nosh (*sl.*), nourishment, nutriment, provender, provisions, rations, subsistence, sustenance, viands, victuals **4 = gist,** core, essence, heart, kernel, marrow, nub, nucleus, pith, point, substance

meaty *adj* **2 = brawny,** beefy (*inf.*), burly, fleshy, heavily built, heavy, husky (*inf.*), muscular, solid, strapping, sturdy **3 = interesting,** meaningful, pithy, profound, rich, significant, substantial

mechanical *adj* **1 = automatic,** automated, machine-driven **5 = unthinking,** automatic, cold, cursory, dead, emotionless, habitual, impersonal, instinctive, involuntary, lacklustre, lifeless, machine-like, matter-of-fact, perfunctory, routine, spiritless, unconscious, unfeeling

Antonyms *adj* ≠ **automatic:** manual ≠ **unthinking:** conscious, genuine, sincere, thinking, voluntary, warm, wholehearted

mechanism *n* **1 = workings,** action, components, gears, innards (*inf.*), machinery, motor,

bling a machine in the arrangement and working of its parts. **3** any mechanical device or part of such a device. **4** a process or technique: *the mechanism of novel writing*. **5** *Philosophy*. the doctrine that human action can be explained in purely physical terms. **6** *Psychoanal*. **6a** the ways in which psychological forces interact and operate. **6b** a structure having an influence on the behaviour of a person, such as a defence mechanism.

mechanistic (ˌmɛkəˈnɪstɪk) *adj* **1** *Philosophy*. of or relating to the theory of mechanism. **2** *Maths*. of or relating to mechanics.
▸ **ˈmechanist** *n* ▸ **ˌmechaˈnistically** *adv*

mechanize *or* **mechanise** (ˈmɛkəˌnaɪz) *vb* **mechanizes, mechanizing, mechanized** *or* **mechanises, mechanising, mechanised.** (*tr*) **1** to equip (a factory, industry, etc.) with machinery. **2** to make mechanical, automatic, or monotonous. **3** to equip (an army, etc.) with motorized or armoured vehicles.
▸ **ˌmechaniˈzation** *or* **ˌmechaniˈsation** *n* ▸ **ˈmechaˌnizer** *or* **ˈmechaˌniser** *n*

mechanoreceptor (ˌmɛkənəʊrɪˈsɛptə) *n Physiol*. a sensory receptor, as in the skin, that is sensitive to a mechanical stimulus, such as pressure.

mechanotherapy (ˌmɛkənəʊˈθɛrəpɪ) *n* the treatment of disorders or injuries by means of mechanical devices, esp. devices that provide exercise for bodily parts.

Mechlin lace (ˈmɛklɪn) *n* bobbin lace characterized by patterns outlined by heavier thread, made at Mechlin, English name for Mechelen, a city in N Belgium.

meconium (mɪˈkəʊnɪəm) *n* the first faeces of a newborn infant. [C17: from NL, from L: poppy juice, from Gk, from *mēkōn* poppy]

meconopsis (ˌmiːkənˈɒpsɪs) *n* any of various mainly Asiatic poppies. [C19: from Gk *mēkōn* poppy + -OPSIS]

Med (mɛd) *n Inf*. the Mediterranean region.

MEd *abbrev. for* Master of Education.

med. *abbrev. for:* **1** medical. **2** medicine. **3** medieval. **4** medium.

médaillons (*French* medajɔ̃) *pl n Cookery*. small round pieces of meat, fish, vegetables, etc. Also called: **medallions.**

medal (ˈmɛdᵊl) *n* a small flat piece of metal bearing an inscription or image, given as an award or commemoration of some outstanding event, etc. [C16: from F *médaille*, prob. from It. *medaglia*, ult. from L *metallum* METAL]

medallion (mɪˈdæljən) *n* **1** a large medal. **2** an oval or circular decorative device resembling a medal, usually bearing a portrait or relief moulding, used in architecture and textile design. [C17: from F, from It., from *medaglia* MEDAL]

medallist *or US* **medalist** (ˈmɛdᵊlɪst) *n* **1** a designer, maker, or collector of medals. **2** *Chiefly sport*. a recipient of a medal or medals.

medal play *n Golf*. another name for **stroke play.**

meddle ❶ (ˈmɛdᵊl) *vb* **meddles, meddling, meddled.** (*intr*) **1** (usually foll. by *with*) to interfere officiously or annoyingly. **2** (usually foll. by *in*) to involve oneself unwarrantedly. [C14: from OF *medler*, ult. from L *miscēre* to mix]
▸ **ˈmeddler** *n* ▸ **ˈmeddling** *adj*

meddlesome ❶ (ˈmɛdᵊlsəm) *adj* intrusive or meddling.
▸ **ˈmeddlesomely** *adv* ▸ **ˈmeddlesomeness** *n*

Mede (miːd) *n* a member of an Indo-European people who established an empire in SW Asia in the 7th and 6th centuries B.C.
▸ **ˈMedian** *n, adj*

media (ˈmiːdɪə) *n* **1** a plural of **medium. 2** the means of communication that reach large numbers of people, such as television, newspapers, and radio. ◆ *adj* **3** of or relating to the mass media: *media hype*.

> **USAGE NOTE** When *media* refers to the mass media, it is sometimes treated as a singular form, as in: *the media has shown great interest in these events*. Many people think this use is incorrect and that *media* should always be treated as a plural form: *the media have shown great interest in these events*.

mediaeval (ˌmɛdɪˈiːvᵊl) *adj* a variant spelling of **medieval.**

media event *n* an event that is staged for or exploited by the mass media.

medial (ˈmiːdɪəl) *adj* **1** of or situated in the middle. **2** ordinary or average in size. **3** *Maths*. relating to an average. **4** another word for **median** (senses 1, 2). [C16: from LL *mediālis*, from *medius* middle]
▸ **ˈmedially** *adv*

median (ˈmiːdɪən) *adj* **1** of, relating to, situated in, or directed towards the middle. **2** *Statistics*. of or relating to the median. ◆ *n* **3** a middle point, plane, or part. **4** *Geom*. **4a** a straight line joining one vertex of a triangle to the midpoint of the opposite side. **4b** a straight line joining the midpoints of the nonparallel sides of a trapezium. **5** *Statistics*. the middle value in a frequency distribution, below and above which lie values with equal total frequencies. **6** *Statistics*. the middle number or average of the two middle numbers in an ordered sequence of numbers. [C16: from L *mediānus*, from *medius* middle]
▸ **ˈmedianly** *adv*

median lethal dose *or* **mean lethal dose** *n* **1** the amount of a drug or other substance that, when administered to a group of experimental animals, will kill 50 per cent of the group in a specified time. **2** the amount of ionizing radiation that will kill 50 per cent of a population in a specified time. ◆ Abbrev.: **LD_{50}.**

mediant (ˈmiːdɪənt) *n Music*. **a** the third degree of a major or minor scale. **b** (*as modifier*): *a mediant chord*. [C18: from It. *mediante*, from LL *mediāre* to be in the middle]

mediastinum (ˌmiːdɪəˈstaɪnəm) *n, pl* **mediastina** (-nə). *Anat*. **1** a membrane between two parts of an organ or cavity such as the pleural tissue between the two lungs. **2** the part of the thoracic cavity that lies between the lungs, containing the heart, trachea, etc. [C16: from Medical L, neuter of Med. L *mediastīnus* median, from L: low grade of servant, from *medius* mean]
▸ **ˌmediasˈtinal** *adj*

mediate ❶ *vb* (ˈmiːdɪˌeɪt), **mediates, mediating, mediated. 1** (*intr*; usually foll. by *between* or *in*) to intervene (between parties or in a dispute) in order to bring about agreement. **2** to bring about (an agreement) between parties in a dispute. **3** to resolve (differences) by mediation. **4** (*intr*) to be in an intermediate position. **5** (*tr*) to serve as a medium for causing (a result) or transferring (objects, information, etc.). ◆ *adj* (ˈmiːdɪɪt). **6** occurring as a result of or dependent upon mediation. [C16: from LL *mediāre* to be in the middle]
▸ **ˈmediately** *adv* ▸ **ˈmediˌator** *n*

mediation ❶ (ˌmiːdɪˈeɪʃən) *n* the act of mediating; intercession between people, states, etc. in an attempt to reconcile disputed matters.

Medibank (ˈmɛdɪbæŋk) *n* (in Australia), a government-run health insurance scheme.

medic[1] (ˈmɛdɪk) *n Inf*. a doctor, medical orderly, or medical student. [C17: from MEDICAL]

medic[2] (ˈmɛdɪk) *n* the usual US spelling of **medick.**

medicable (ˈmɛdɪkəbᵊl) *adj* potentially able to be treated or cured medically.

medical (ˈmɛdɪkᵊl) *adj* **1** of or relating to the science of medicine or to the treatment of patients by drugs, etc., as opposed to surgery. ◆ *n* **2** *Inf*. a medical examination. [C17: from Med. L *medicālis*, from L *medicus* physician, surgeon, from *medērī* to heal]
▸ **ˈmedically** *adv*

medical certificate *n* **1** a document stating the result of a satisfactory medical examination. **2** a doctor's certificate giving evidence of a person's unfitness for work.

medical jurisprudence *n* another name for **forensic medicine.**

medicament (mɪˈdɪkəmənt, ˈmɛdɪ-) *n* a medicine or remedy. [C16: via F from L *medicāmentum*, from *medicāre* to cure]

medicate (ˈmɛdɪˌkeɪt) *vb* **medicates, medicating, medicated.** (*tr*) **1** to cover or impregnate (a wound, etc.) with an ointment, etc. **2** to treat (a patient) with a medicine. **3** to add a medication to (a bandage, shampoo, etc.). [C17: from L *medicāre* to heal]
▸ **ˈmedicative** *adj*

medication (ˌmɛdɪˈkeɪʃən) *n* **1** treatment with drugs or remedies. **2** a drug or remedy.

medicinal ❶ (mɛˈdɪsɪnᵊl) *adj* **1** relating to or having therapeutic properties. ◆ *n* **2** a medicinal substance.
▸ **meˈdicinally** *adv*

medicine ❶ (ˈmɛdɪsɪn, ˈmɛdsɪn) *n* **1** any drug or remedy for use in treating, preventing, or alleviating the symptoms of disease. **2** the science of preventing, diagnosing, alleviating, or curing disease. **3** any nonsurgical branch of medical science. **4** the practice or profession of medicine. **5** something regarded by primitive people as having magical or remedial properties. **6 a taste** (*or* **dose**) **of one's own medicine.** an unpleasant experience in retaliation for a similar unkind or aggressive act. **7 take one's medicine.** to accept a deserved punishment. [C13: via OF from L *medicīna* (*ars*) (art) of healing, from *medicus* doctor, from *medērī* to heal]

medicine ball *n* a heavy ball used for physical training.

medicine man *n* (among certain peoples, esp. North American Indians) a person believed to have supernatural powers of healing; a magician or sorcerer.

medick *or US* **medic** (ˈmɛdɪk) *n* any of various small plants having yellow or purple flowers and trifoliate leaves. [C15: from L *mēdica*, from Gk *mēdikē* (*poa*) Median (grass), a type of clover]

medico (ˈmɛdɪˌkəʊ) *n, pl* **medicos.** *Inf*. a doctor or medical student. [C17: via It. from L *medicus*]

THESAURUS

works **3** = **machine**, apparatus, appliance, contrivance, device, instrument, structure, system, tool **4** = **process**, agency, execution, functioning, means, medium, method, methodology, operation, performance, procedure, system, technique, way, workings

meddle *vb* **1, 2** = **interfere**, butt in, intermeddle, interpose, intervene, intrude, pry, put one's oar in, put one's two cents in (*US sl.*), stick one's nose in (*inf.*), tamper

meddlesome *adj* = **interfering**, intermeddling, intruding, intrusive, meddling, mischievous, officious, prying

mediate *vb* **1-3** = **intervene**, act as middleman, arbitrate, bring to an agreement, bring to terms, conciliate, intercede, interpose, make peace between, moderate, reconcile, referee, resolve, restore harmony, settle, step in (*inf.*), umpire

mediation *n* = **arbitration**, conciliation, good offices, intercession, interposition, intervention, reconciliation

mediator *n* **1-3** = **negotiator**, advocate, arbiter, arbitrator, go-between, honest broker, interceder, intermediary, judge, middleman, moderator, peacemaker, referee, umpire

medicinal *adj* **1** = **therapeutic**, analeptic, curative, healing, medical, remedial, restorative, roborant, sanative

medicine *n* **1** = **remedy**, cure, drug, medicament, medication, nostrum, physic

medieval Ⓣ *or* **mediaeval** (ˌmɛdɪˈiːvəl) *adj* **1** of, relating to, or in the style of the Middle Ages. **2** *Inf.* old-fashioned; primitive. [C19: from NL *medium aevum* the middle age]

Medieval Greek *n* the Greek language from the 7th century A.D. to shortly after the sacking of Constantinople in 1204. Also called: **Middle Greek, Byzantine Greek.**

medievalism *or* **mediaevalism** (ˌmɛdɪˈiːvəˌlɪzəm) *n* **1** the beliefs, life, or style of the Middle Ages or devotion to those. **2** a belief, custom, or point of style copied or surviving from the Middle Ages.

medievalist *or* **mediaevalist** (ˌmɛdɪˈiːvəlɪst) *n* a student or devotee of the Middle Ages.

Medieval Latin *n* the Latin language as used throughout Europe in the Middle Ages.

mediocre Ⓣ (ˌmiːdɪˈəʊkə) *adj Often derog.* average or ordinary in quality. [C16: via F from L *mediocris* moderate, lit.: halfway up the mountain, from *medius* middle + *ocris* stony mountain]

mediocrity Ⓣ (ˌmiːdɪˈɒkrɪtɪ, ˌmɛd-) *n, pl* **mediocrities. 1** the state or quality of being mediocre. **2** a mediocre person or thing.

Medit. *abbrev. for* Mediterranean.

meditate Ⓣ (ˈmɛdɪˌteɪt) *vb* **meditates, meditating meditated. 1** (*intr;* foll. by *on* or *upon*) to think about something deeply. **2** (*intr*) to reflect deeply on spiritual matters, esp. as a religious act. **3** (*tr*) to plan, consider, or think of doing (something). [C16: from L *meditārī* to reflect upon]
▸**ˈmeditative** *adj* ▸**ˈmeditatively** *adv* ▸**ˈmediˌtator** *n*

meditation Ⓣ (ˌmɛdɪˈteɪʃən) *n* **1** the act of meditating; reflection. **2** contemplation of spiritual matters, esp. as a religious practice.

Mediterranean (ˌmɛdɪtəˈreɪnɪən) *n* **1** short for the **Mediterranean Sea,** the sea between S Europe, N Africa, and SW Asia. **2** a native or inhabitant of a Mediterranean country. ◆ *adj* **3** of, relating to, situated or dwelling near the Mediterranean Sea. **4** denoting a postulated subdivision of the Caucasoid race, characterized by slender build and dark complexion. **5** *Meteorol.* (of a climate) characterized by hot summers and relatively warm winters when most of the annual rainfall occurs. **6** (*often not cap.*) *Obs.* situated in the middle of a landmass; inland. [C16: from L *mediterrāneus,* from *medius* middle + *-terrāneus,* from *terra* land]

medium Ⓣ (ˈmiːdɪəm) *adj* **1** midway between extremes; average. ◆ *n, pl* **media** *or* **mediums. 2** an intermediate or middle state, degree, or condition; mean: *the happy medium.* **3** an intervening substance or agency for transmitting or producing an effect; vehicle. **4** a means or agency for communicating or diffusing information, news, etc., to the public. **5** a person supposedly used as a spiritual intermediary between the dead and the living. **6** the substance in which specimens of animals and plants are preserved or displayed. **7** *Biol.* Also called: **culture medium.** a nutritive substance in which cultures of bacteria or fungi are grown. **8** the substance or surroundings in which an organism naturally lives or grows. **9** *Art.* **9a** the category of a work of art, as determined by its materials and methods of production. **9b** the materials used in a work of art. **10** any solvent in which pigments are mixed and thinned. [C16: from L: neuter sing of *medius* middle]

USAGE NOTE See at **media.**

medium-dated *adj* (of a gilt-edged security) having between five and fifteen years to run before redemption. Cf. **long-dated, short-dated.**

medium frequency *n* a radio-frequency band or radio frequency lying between 3000 and 300 kilohertz. Abbrev: **MF.**

medium wave *n* **a** a radio wave with a wavelength between 100 and 1000 metres. **b** (*as modifier*): *a medium-wave broadcast.*

medlar (ˈmɛdlə) *n* **1** a small Eurasian tree. **2** its fruit, which resembles the crab apple and is not edible until it has begun to decay. [C14: from OF *medlier,* from L *mespilum* medlar fruit, from Gk *mespilon*]

medley Ⓣ (ˈmɛdlɪ) *n* **1** a mixture of various types or elements. **2** a musical composition consisting of various tunes arranged as a continuous whole. **3** Also called: **medley relay. 3a** *Swimming.* a race in which a different stroke is used for each length. **3b** *Athletics.* a relay race in which each leg has a different distance. [C14: from OF *medlee,* from *medler* to mix, quarrel]

medulla (mɪˈdʌlə) *n, pl* **medullas** *or* **medullae** (-liː). **1** *Anat.* **1a** the innermost part of an organ or structure. **1b** short for **medulla oblongata. 2** *Bot.* another name for **pith** (sense 4). [C17: from L: marrow, prob. from *medius* middle]
▸**meˈdullary** *or* **meˈdullar** *adj*

medulla oblongata (ˌɒblɒŋˈgɑːtə) *n, pl* **medulla oblongatas** *or* **medullae oblongatae** (mɪˈdʌliː ˌɒblɒŋˈgɑːtiː). the lower stalklike section of the brain, continuous with the spinal cord, containing control centres for the heart and lungs. [C17: NL: oblong-shaped medulla]

medusa (mɪˈdjuːzə) *n, pl* **medusas** *or* **medusae** (-ziː). another name for **jellyfish** (sense 1). [C18: from the likeness of its tentacles to the snaky locks of *Medusa,* the Gorgon]
▸**meˈdusoid** *adj, n*

meed (miːd) *n Arch.* a recompense; reward. [OE: wages]

meek Ⓣ (miːk) *adj* **1** patient, long-suffering, or submissive; humble. **2** spineless or spiritless; compliant. [C12: rel. to ON *mjūkr* amenable]
▸**ˈmeekly** *adv* ▸**ˈmeekness** *n*

meerkat (ˈmɪəˌkæt) *n* any of several South African mongooses, esp. the slender-tailed meerkat or suricate, which has a lemur-like face and four-toed feet. [C19: from Du.: sea-cat]

meerschaum (ˈmɪəʃəm) *n* **1** a white, yellowish, or pink compact earthy mineral consisting of hydrated magnesium silicate: used to make tobacco pipes and as a building stone. **2** a tobacco pipe having a bowl made of this mineral. [C18: from G *Meerschaum* lit.: sea foam]

meet[1] Ⓣ (miːt) *vb* **meets, meeting, met. 1** (sometimes foll. by *up* or (US) *with*) to come together (with), either by design or by accident; encounter. **2** to come into or be in conjunction or contact with (something or each other). **3** (*tr*) to come to or be at the place of arrival of: *to meet a train.* **4** to make the acquaintance of or be introduced to (someone or each other). **5** to gather in the company of (someone or each other). **6** to come into the presence of (someone or each other) as opponents. **7** (*tr*) to cope with effectively; satisfy: *to meet someone's demands.* **8** (*tr*) to be apparent to (esp. in **meet the eye**). **9** (*tr*) to return or counter: *to meet a blow with another.* **10** to agree with (someone or each other): *we met him on the price he suggested.* **11** (*tr;* sometimes foll. by *with*) to experience; suffer: *he met his death in a road accident.* **12** (*intr*) to occur together: *courage and kindliness met in him.* ◆ *n* **13** the assembly of hounds, huntsmen, etc., prior to a hunt. **14** a meeting, esp. a sports meeting. [OE *mētan*]
▸**ˈmeeter** *n*

meet[2] (miːt) *adj Arch.* proper, fitting, or correct. [C13: from var. of OE *gemǣte*]
▸**ˈmeetly** *adv*

meeting Ⓣ (ˈmiːtɪŋ) *n* **1** an act of coming together; encounter. **2** an assembly or gathering. **3** a conjunction or union. **4** a sporting competition, as of athletes, or of horse racing.

meeting house *n* the place in which certain religious groups, esp. Quakers, hold their meetings for worship.

mefloquine (ˈmɛfləʊˌkwiːn) *n* a synthetic drug administered orally to prevent or treat malaria. [C20]

mega (ˈmɛgə) *adj Sl.* extremely good, great, or successful. [C20: prob. independent use of MEGA-]

mega- *combining form.* **1** denoting 10^6: *megawatt.* Symbol: M **2** (in com-

THESAURUS

medieval *adj* **1** = **Gothic 2** *Informal* = **old-fashioned**, antediluvian, antiquated, antique, archaic, primitive, unenlightened

mediocre *adj* = **second-rate**, average, banal, bog-standard (*Brit. & Irish sl.*), commonplace, fair to middling (*inf.*), indifferent, inferior, insignificant, mean, medium, middling, no great shakes (*inf.*), ordinary, passable, pedestrian, run-of-the-mill, so-so (*inf.*), tolerable, undistinguished, uninspired, vanilla (*sl.*)
Antonyms *adj* distinctive, distinguished, excellent, extraordinary, fine, incomparable, superb, superior, unexcelled, unique, unrivalled, unsurpassed

mediocrity *n* **1** = **insignificance**, commonplaceness, indifference, inferiority, meanness, ordinariness, poorness, unimportance **2** = **nonentity**, cipher, lightweight (*inf.*), nobody, second-rater

meditate *vb* **1, 2** = **reflect**, be in a brown study, cogitate, consider, contemplate, deliberate, muse, ponder, ruminate, study, think **3** = **plan**, consider, contemplate, design, devise, have in mind, intend, mull over, purpose, scheme, think over

meditation *n* **1** = **reflection**, brown study, cerebration, cogitation, concentration, contemplation, musing, pondering, reverie, ruminating, rumination, study, thought

meditative *adj* **1** = **reflective**, cogitative, contemplative, deliberative, pensive, ruminative, studious, thoughtful

medium *adj* **1** = **average**, fair, intermediate, mean, medial, median, mediocre, middle, middling, midway ◆ *n* **2** = **middle**, average, centre, compromise, mean, middle course, middle ground, middle path, middle way, midpoint **2** = **means**, agency, avenue, channel, form, instrument, instrumentality, mode, organ, vehicle, way **5** = **spiritualist**, channeller, spiritist **8** = **environment**, atmosphere, conditions, element, habitat, influences, milieu, setting, surroundings
Antonyms *adj* ≠ **average:** curious, distinctive, extraordinary, extreme, uncommon, unique, unusual, utmost

medley *n* **1** = **mixture**, assortment, confusion, farrago, gallimaufry, hodgepodge, hotchpotch, jumble, *mélange*, miscellany, mishmash, mixed bag (*inf.*), olio, omnium-gatherum, pastiche, patchwork, potpourri, salmagundi

meek *adj* **1** = **submissive**, acquiescent, compliant, deferential, docile, forbearing, gentle, humble, long-suffering, mild, modest, patient, peaceful, soft, timid, unassuming, unpretentious, yielding **2** = **spineless**, boneless, resigned, spiritless, tame, unresisting, weak, weak-kneed (*inf.*), wimpish *or* wimpy (*inf.*)
Antonyms *adj* arrogant, bold, bossy, domineering, feisty (*inf., chiefly US & Canad.*), forward, immodest, overbearing, presumptuous, pretentious, proud, self-assertive, spirited, wilful

meekness *n* **1** = **submissiveness**, acquiescence, compliance, deference, docility, forbearance, gentleness, humbleness, humility, long-suffering, lowliness, mildness, modesty, patience, peacefulness, resignation, softness, submission, timidity **2** = **spinelessness**, resignation, spiritlessness, tameness, weakness

meet[1] *vb* **1** = **encounter**, bump into, chance on, come across, confront, contact, find, happen on, run across, run into **1** = **gather**, assemble, collect, come together, congregate, convene, foregather, muster, rally **2** = **converge**, abut, adjoin, come together, connect, cross, intersect, join, link up, touch, unite **7** = **fulfil**, answer, carry out, come up to, comply with, cope with, discharge, equal, gratify, handle, match, measure up to, perform, satisfy **11** = **experience**, bear, encounter, endure, face, go through, suffer, undergo
Antonyms *vb* ≠ **encounter:** avoid, elude, escape, miss ≠ **gather:** adjourn, disperse, scatter ≠ **converge:** diverge ≠ **fulfil:** fail, fall short, renege

meeting *n* **1** = **encounter**, assignation, confron-

puter technology) denoting 2^{20} (1 048 576): *megabyte*. **3** large or great: *megalith*. **4** *Inf*. greatest: *megastar*. [from Gk *megas* huge, powerful]

megabit ('mɛgəˌbɪt) *n Computing*. **1** one million bits. **2** 2^{20} bits.

megabuck ('mɛgəˌbʌk) *n US & Canad. sl.* a million dollars.

megacephaly (ˌmɛgə'sɛfəlɪ) *or* **megalocephaly** *n* the condition of having an unusually large head or cranial capacity.
▸**megacephalic** (ˌmɛgəsɪ'fælɪk), ˌ**mega'cephalous**, ˌ**megaloce'phalic**, *or* ˌ**megalo'cephalous** *adj*

megacycle ('mɛgəˌsaɪk°l) *n* a former unit of frequency equal to one million cycles per second; megahertz.

megadeath ('mɛgəˌdɛθ) *n* the death of a million people, esp. in a nuclear war or attack.

megafauna ('mɛgəˌfɔːnə) *n* the component of the fauna of a region or period that comprises the larger terrestrial animals.

megaflop ('mɛgəˌflɒp) *n Computing*. a measure of processing speed, consisting of a million floating-point operations a second. [C20: from MEGA- + *flo(ating) p(oint)*]

megahertz ('mɛgəˌhɜːts) *n, pl* **megahertz**. one million hertz. Former name: **megacycle**.

megalith ('mɛgəlɪθ) *n* a stone of great size, esp. one forming part of a prehistoric monument.
▸ˌ**mega'lithic** *adj*

megalo- *or before a vowel* **megal-** *combining form*. indicating greatness or abnormal size: *megalopolis*. [from Gk *megas* great]

megalomania (ˌmɛgələʊ'meɪnɪə) *n* **1** a mental illness characterized by delusions of grandeur, power, wealth, etc. **2** *Inf*. a lust or craving for power.
▸ˌ**megalo'maniac** *adj, n* ▸**megalomaniacal** (ˌmɛgələʊmə'naɪək°l) *adj*

megalopolis (ˌmɛgə'lɒpəlɪs) *n* an urban complex, usually comprising several large towns. [C20: MEGALO- + Gk *polis* city]
▸**megalopolitan** (ˌmɛgələ'pɒlɪt°n) *adj, n*

megalosaur ('mɛgələʊˌsɔː) *n* any very large Jurassic or Cretaceous bipedal carnivorous dinosaur. [C19: from NL *megalosaurus*, from MEGALO- + Gk *sauros* lizard]

megaphone ('mɛgəˌfəʊn) *n* a funnel-shaped instrument used to amplify the voice. See also **loud-hailer**.
▸**megaphonic** (ˌmɛgə'fɒnɪk) *adj*

megapode ('mɛgəˌpəʊd) *n* any of various ground-living gallinaceous birds of Australia, New Guinea, and adjacent islands. Their eggs incubate in mounds of sand, rotting vegetation, etc., by natural heat.

megathere ('mɛgəˌθɪə) *n* any of various gigantic extinct American sloths, common in late Cenozoic times. [C19: from NL *megathērium*, from MEGA- + *-there*, from Gk *thērion* wild beast]

megaton ('mɛgəˌtʌn) *n* **1** one million tons. **2** an explosive power, esp. of a nuclear weapon, equal to the power of one million tons of TNT.

Me generation *n* **the**. the generation, originally in the 1970s, characterized by self-absorption; in the 1980s, characterized by material greed.

Megger ('mɛgə) *n Trademark*. an instrument that generates a high voltage in order to test the resistance of insulation, etc.

megilp *or* **magilp** (mə'gɪlp) *n* an oil-painting medium of linseed oil mixed with mastic varnish or turpentine. [C18: from ?]

megohm ('mɛgˌəʊm) *n* one million ohms.

megrim ('miːgrɪm) *n Arch*. **1** a caprice. **2** a migraine. **3** *(pl) Rare*. a fit of depression. **4** *(pl)* a disease of horses and cattle; staggers. [C14: see MIGRAINE]

meibomian gland (maɪ'bəʊmɪən) *n* any of the small sebaceous glands in the eyelid, beneath the conjunctiva. [C19: after H. *Meibom* (1638–1700), G anatomist]

meiosis (maɪ'əʊsɪs) *n, pl* **meioses** (-ˌsiːz). **1** a type of cell division in which a nucleus divides into four daughter nuclei, each containing half the chromosome number of the parent nucleus. **2** *Rhetoric*. another word for **litotes**. [C16: via NL from Gk, from *meioun* to diminish, from *meiōn* less]
▸**meiotic** (maɪ'ɒtɪk) *adj* ▸**mei'otically** *adv*

Meistersinger ('maɪstəˌsɪŋə) *n, pl* **Meistersinger** *or* **Meistersingers**. a member of one of the German guilds organized to compose and perform poetry and music, esp. in the 15th and 16th centuries. [C19: from G *Meistersinger* master singer]

meitnerium (ˌmaɪt'nɛərɪəm) *n* a synthetic element produced in small quantities by high-energy ion bombardment. Symbol: Mt; atomic no.: 109. [C20: from Lise *Meitner* (1878–1968), Austrian physicist]

Mekka ('mɛkə) *n* a variant spelling of **Mecca**.

melaleuca (ˌmɛlə'luːkə) *n* any shrub or tree of the mostly Australian genus *Melaleuca*, found in sandy or swampy regions. [C19: NL from Gk *melas* black + *leukos* white, from its black trunk and white branches]

melamine ('mɛləˌmiːn) *n* **1** a colourless crystalline compound used in making synthetic resins. Formula: $C_3N_6H_6$. **2** a resin produced from melamine (**melamine resin**) or a material made from this resin. [C19: from G *Melamin*, from *Melam* distillate of ammonium thiocyanate, with *-am* representing *ammonia*]

melancholia (ˌmɛlən'kəʊlɪə) *n* a former name for **depression** (sense 3).
▸ˌ**melan'choliˌac** *adj, n*

melancholy ➊ ('mɛlənkəlɪ) *n, pl* **melancholies**. **1** a tendency to gloominess or depression. **2** a sad thoughtful state of mind. **3** *Arch*. **3a** a gloomy character. **3b** one of the four bodily humours; black bile. ◆ *adj* **4** characterized by, causing, or expressing sadness, dejection, etc. [C14: via OF from LL *melancholia*, from Gk, from *melas* black + *kholē* bile]
▸'**melanˌcholic** *adj, n*

Melanesian (ˌmɛlə'niːʒən, -ʒɪən) *adj* **1** of or relating to Melanesia (a division of islands in the Pacific), its people, or their languages. ◆ *n* **2** a native or inhabitant of Melanesia: generally Negroid with frizzy hair and small stature. **3** a group or branch of languages spoken in Melanesia.

melange ➊ *or* **mélange** (meɪ'lɑːnʒ) *n* a mixture; confusion. [C17: from F *mêler* to mix]

melanin ('mɛlənɪn) *n* any of a group of black or dark brown pigments present in the hair, skin, and eyes of man and animals: produced in excess in certain skin diseases and in melanomas.

melanism ('mɛləˌnɪzəm) *n* **1** the condition in man and animals of having dark-coloured or black skin, feathers, etc. **2** another name for **melanosis**.
▸ˌ**mela'nistic** *adj*

melano- *or before a vowel* **melan-** *combining form*. black or dark: *melanin; melanism; melanoma*. [from Gk *melas* black]

melanoma (ˌmɛlə'nəʊmə) *n, pl* **melanomas** *or* **melanomata** (-mətə). *Pathol*. a malignant tumour composed of melanin-containing cells, occurring esp. in the skin, often as a result of excessive exposure to sunlight.

melanosis (ˌmɛlə'nəʊsɪs) *or* **melanism** ('mɛləˌnɪzəm) *n Pathol*. a skin condition characterized by excessive deposits of melanin.
▸**melanotic** (ˌmɛlə'nɒtɪk) *adj*

Melba ('mɛlbə) *n* **do a Melba**. *Austral. sl*. to make repeated farewell appearances. [C20: after Dame Nellie *Melba* (1861–1931), Austral. operatic soprano]

Melba toast *n* very thin crisp toast. [C20: after Dame Nellie *Melba*]

meld[1] (mɛld) *vb* to blend or become blended; combine. [C20: blend of MELT + WELD[1]]

meld[2] (mɛld) *vb* **1** (in some card games) to declare or lay down (cards), which then score points. ◆ *n* **2** the act of melding. **3** a set of cards for melding. [C19: from G *melden* to announce]

melee ➊ *or* **mêlée** ('mɛleɪ) *n* a noisy riotous fight or brawl. [C17: from F *mêlée*, from *mêler* to mix]

meliorate ('miːlɪəˌreɪt) *vb* **meliorates, meliorating, meliorated**. a variant of **ameliorate**.
▸ˌ**melio'ration** *n* ▸**meliorative** ('miːlɪərətɪv) *adj, n*

melisma (mɪ'lɪzmə) *n, pl* **melismata** (-mətə) *or* **melismas**. *Music*. an expressive vocal phrase or passage consisting of several notes sung to one syllable. [C19: from Gk: melody]

melliferous (mɪ'lɪfərəs) *or* **mellific** (mɪ'lɪfɪk) *adj* forming or producing honey. [C17: from L *mellifer*, from *mel* honey + *ferre* to bear]

mellifluous ➊ (mɪ'lɪfluəs) *or* **mellifluent** *adj* (of sounds or utterances) smooth or honeyed; sweet. [C15: from LL *mellifluus*, from L *mel* honey + *fluere* to flow]
▸**mel'lifluously** *adv* ▸**mel'lifluousness** *or* **mel'lifluence** *n*

mellow ➊ ('mɛləʊ) *adj* **1** (esp. of fruits) full-flavoured; sweet; ripe. **2** (esp. of wines) well-matured. **3** (esp. of colours or sounds) soft or rich. **4** kind-hearted, esp. through maturity or old age. **5** genial, as through the effects of alcohol. **6** (of soil) soft and loamy. ◆ *vb* **7** to make or become mellow. **8** (foll. by *out*) to become calm and relaxed or (esp. of a drug) to have a calming and relaxing effect on (someone). [C15: ?from OE *meru* soft (as through ripeness)]
▸'**mellowness** *n*

melodeon *or* **melodion** (mɪ'ləʊdɪən) *n Music*. **1** a type of small accordion. **2** a type of keyboard instrument similar to the harmonium. [C19: from G, from *Melodie* melody]

melodic (mɪ'lɒdɪk) *adj* **1** of or relating to melody. **2** of or relating to a part in a piece of music. **3** melodious.
▸**me'lodically** *adv*

THESAURUS

tation, engagement, introduction, rendezvous, tryst **2** = **conference**, assembly, audience, company, conclave, congregation, congress, convention, convocation, gathering, get-together (*inf.*), meet, powwow, rally, reunion, session **3** = **convergence**, concourse, confluence, conjunction, crossing, intersection, junction, union

melancholy *n* **1, 2** = **sadness**, blues, dejection, depression, despondency, gloom, gloominess, low spirits, misery, pensiveness, sorrow, the hump (*Brit. inf.*), unhappiness, woe ◆ *adj* **4** = **sad**, blue, dejected, depressed, despondent, disconsolate, dismal, dispirited, doleful, down, downcast, downhearted, gloomy, glum, heavy-hearted, joyless, low, low-spirited, lugubrious, melancholic, miserable, moody, mournful, pensive, sombre, sorrowful, unhappy, woebegone, woeful
Antonyms *n* ≠ **sadness**: delight, gladness, happiness, joy, pleasure ◆ *adj* ≠ **sad**: blithe, bright, cheerful, gay, glad, happy, jolly, joyful, joyous, light-hearted, lively, merry, sunny

melange *n* = **mixture**, assortment, confusion, farrago, gallimaufry, hodge-podge, hotchpotch, jumble, medley, miscellany, mishmash, mix, mixed bag (*inf.*), pastiche, potpourri, salmagundi

melee *n* = **fight**, affray (*Law*), battle royal, brawl, broil, donnybrook, fracas, fray, free-for-all (*inf.*), ruckus (*inf.*), ruction (*inf.*), rumpus, scrimmage, scuffle, set-to (*inf.*), shindig (*inf.*), shindy (*inf.*), skirmish, stramash (*Scot.*), tussle

mellifluous *adj* = **sweet**, dulcet, euphonious, honeyed, mellow, silvery, smooth, soft, soothing, sweet-sounding

mellow *adj* **1, 2** = **ripe**, delicate, full-flavoured, juicy, mature, perfect, rich, soft, sweet, well-matured **3** = **tuneful**, dulcet, euphonic, full, mellifluous, melodious, rich, rounded, smooth, sweet, well-tuned **5** = **relaxed**, cheerful, cordial, elevated, expansive, genial, half-tipsy, happy,

melodic minor scale *n Music.* a minor scale modified from the natural by the sharpening of the sixth and seventh when taken in ascending order and the restoration of their original pitches when taken in descending order.

melodious Ⓣ (mɪ'ləʊdɪəs) *adj* **1** having a tune that is pleasant to the ear. **2** of or relating to melody; melodic.
▸**me'lodiously** *adv* ▸**me'lodiousness** *n*

melodist ('mɛlədɪst) *n* **1** a composer of melodies. **2** a singer.

melodize *or* **melodise** ('mɛlə,daɪz) *vb* **melodizes, melodizing, melodized** *or* **melodises, melodising, melodised. 1** (*tr*) to provide with a melody. **2** (*tr*) to make melodious. **3** (*intr*) to sing or play melodies.
▸**'melo,dizer** *or* **'melo,diser** *n*

melodrama Ⓣ ('mɛlə,drɑːmə) *n* **1** a play, film, etc., characterized by extravagant action and emotion. **2** (formerly) a romantic drama characterized by sensational incident, music, and song. **3** overdramatic emotion or behaviour. [C19: from F *mélodrame*, from Gk *melos* song + *drame* DRAMA]
▸**melodramatist** (,mɛlə'dræmətɪst) *n* ▸**melodramatic** (,mɛlədrə'mætɪk) *adj* ▸**,melodra'matics** *pl n* ▸**,melodra'matically** *adv*

melody Ⓣ ('mɛlədɪ) *n, pl* **melodies. 1** *Music.* **1a** a succession of notes forming a distinctive sequence; tune. **1b** the horizontally represented aspect of the structure of a piece of music. Cf. **harmony** (sense 4b). **2** sounds that are pleasant because of tone or arrangement, esp. words of poetry. [C13: from OF, from LL *melōdia*, from Gk *melōidia*, from *melos* song + *aoidein* to sing]

melon ('mɛlən) *n* **1** any of several varieties of trailing plants (see **muskmelon, watermelon**), cultivated for their edible fruit. **2** the fruit of any of these plants, which has a hard rind and juicy flesh. [C14: via OF from LL *mēlo*, form of *mēlopepō*, from Gk, from *mēlon* apple + *pepōn* gourd]

Melpomene (mel'pɒmɪnɪ) *n Greek myth.* the Muse of tragedy.

melt Ⓣ (mɛlt) *vb* **melts, melting, melted; melted** *or* **molten. 1** to liquefy (a solid) or (of a solid) to become liquefied, as a result of the action of heat. **2** to become or make liquid; dissolve. **3** (often foll. by *away*) to disappear; fade. **4** (foll. by *down*) to melt (metal scrap) for reuse. **5** (often foll. by *into*) to blend or cause to blend gradually. **6** to make or become emotional or sentimental; soften. ◆ *n* **7** the act or process of melting. **8** something melted or an amount melted. [OE *meltan* to digest]
▸**'meltable** *adj* ▸**'melter** *n* ▸**'meltingly** *adv*

meltdown ('mɛlt,daʊn) *n* **1** (in a nuclear reactor) the melting of the fuel rods as a result of a defect in the cooling system, with the possible escape of radiation. **2** *Inf.* a sudden disastrous failure with potential for widespread harm, as a stock-exchange crash. **3** *Inf.* the process or state of irreversible breakdown or decline: *the community is slowly going into meltdown.*

melting point *n* the temperature at which a solid turns into a liquid.

melting pot *n* **1** a pot in which metals or other substances are melted, esp. in order to mix them. **2** an area in which many races, ideas, etc., are mixed.

melton ('mɛltən) *n* a heavy smooth woollen fabric with a short nap. Also called: **melton cloth.** [C19: from *Melton Mowbray*, Leicestershire, a former centre for making this]

meltwater ('mɛlt,wɔːtə) *n* melted snow or ice.

mem. *abbrev. for:* **1** member. **2** memoir. **3** memorandum. **4** memorial.

member Ⓣ ('mɛmbə) *n* **1** a person who belongs to a club, political party, etc. **2** any individual plant or animal in a taxonomic group. **3** any part of an animal body, such as a limb. **4** any part of a plant, such as a petal, root, etc. **5** *Maths, logic.* any individual object belonging to a set or logical class. **6** a component part of a building or construction. [C13: from L *membrum* limb, part]
▸**'memberless** *adj*

Member ('mɛmbə) *n* (*sometimes not cap.*) **1** short for **Member of Parliament. 2** short for **Member of Congress. 3** a member of some other legislative body.

Member of Congress *n* a member of the US Congress, esp. of the House of Representatives.

Member of Parliament *n* a member of the House of Commons or similar legislative body, as in many Commonwealth countries.

membership Ⓣ ('mɛmbəʃɪp) *n* **1** the members of an organization collectively. **2** the state of being a member.

membrane ('mɛmbreɪn) *n* **1** any thin pliable sheet of material. **2** a pliable sheetlike usually fibrous tissue that covers, lines, or connects plant and animal organs or cells. [C16: from L *membrāna* skin covering a part of the body, from *membrum* MEMBER]
▸**membranous** ('mɛmbrənəs) *or* **membraneous** (mɛm'breɪnɪəs) *adj*

memento Ⓣ (mɪ'mɛntəʊ) *n, pl* **mementos** *or* **mementoes.** something that reminds one of past events; a souvenir. [C15: from L, imperative of *meminisse* to remember]

memento mori ('mɔːriː) *n, pl* **memento mori.** an object, such as a skull, intended to remind people of death. [C16: L: remember you must die]

memo ('mɛməʊ, 'miːməʊ) *n, pl* **memos.** short for **memorandum.**

memoir Ⓣ ('mɛmwɑː) *n* **1** a biography or historical account, esp. one based on personal knowledge. **2** an essay, as on a specialized topic. [C16: from F, from L *memoria* MEMORY]
▸**'memoirist** *n*

memoirs Ⓣ ('mɛmwɑːz) *pl n* **1** a collection of reminiscences about a period, series of events, etc., written from personal experience or special sources. **2** an autobiographical record. **3** a record, as of transactions of a society, etc.

memorabilia (,mɛmərə'bɪlɪə) *pl n, sing* **memorabile** (-'ræbɪlɪ). **1** memorable events or things. **2** objects connected with famous people or events. [C17: from L, from *memorābilis* MEMORABLE]

memorable Ⓣ ('mɛmərəb^{ə}l) *adj* worth remembering or easily remembered. [C15: from L *memorābilis*, from *memorāre* to recall, from *memor* mindful]
▸**,memora'bility** *n* ▸**'memorably** *adv*

memorandum Ⓣ (,mɛmə'rændəm) *n, pl* **memorandums** *or* **memoranda** (-də). **1** a written statement, record, or communication. **2** a note of things to be remembered. **3** an informal diplomatic communication. **4** *Law.* a short written summary of the terms of a transaction. ◆ Often (esp. for senses 1, 2) shortened to **memo.** [C15: from L: (something) to be remembered]

memorial Ⓣ (mɪ'mɔːrɪəl) *adj* **1** serving to preserve the memory of the dead or a past event. **2** of or involving memory. ◆ *n* **3** something serving as a remembrance. **4** a written statement of facts submitted to a government, authority, etc., in conjunction with a petition. **5** an informal diplomatic paper. [C14: from LL *memoriāle* a reminder, neuter of *memoriālis*]
▸**me'morially** *adv*

memorialize *or* **memorialise** (mɪ'mɔːrɪə,laɪz) *vb* **memorializes, memorializing, memorialized** *or* **memorialises, memorialising, memorialised.** (*tr*) **1** to honour or commemorate. **2** to present or address a memorial to.

memorize Ⓣ *or* **memorise** ('mɛmə,raɪz) *vb* **memorizes, memorizing, memorized** *or* **memorises, memorising, memorised.** (*tr*) to commit to memory; learn so as to remember.

memory Ⓣ ('mɛmərɪ) *n, pl* **memories. 1a** the ability of the mind to store and recall past sensations, thoughts, knowledge, etc.: *he can do it from memory.* **1b** the part of the brain that appears to have this function. **2** the sum of everything retained by the mind. **3** a particular recollection of an event, person, etc. **4** the time over which recollection extends: *within his memory.* **5** commemoration or remembrance: *in memory of our leader.* **6** the state of being remembered, as after death. **7** a part of a computer in which information is stored for immediate use by the central processing unit. Cf. **RAM**[1]. [C14: from OF *memorie*, from L *memoria*, from *memor* mindful]

memsahib ('mɛm,sɑːɪb, -hɪb) *n* (formerly, in India) a term of respect used for a European married woman. [C19: from MA'AM + SAHIB]

men (mɛn) *n* the plural of **man.**

menace Ⓣ ('mɛnɪs) *vb* **menaces, menacing, menaced. 1** to threaten with

THESAURUS

jolly, jovial, merry ◆ *vb* **7** = **mature**, develop, improve, perfect, ripen, season, soften, sweeten
Antonyms *adj* ≠ **ripe:** green, immature, raw, sour, unripe

melodious *adj* **1, 2** = **musical**, concordant, dulcet, euphonic, euphonious, harmonious, melodic, silvery, sweet-sounding, sweet-toned, tuneful
Antonyms *adj* cacophonous, discordant, grating, harsh, unharmonious, unmelodic, unmelodious, unmusical, untuneful

melodramatic *adj* **1, 3** = **theatrical**, actorly, actressy, blood-and-thunder, extravagant, hammy (*inf.*), histrionic, overdramatic, overemotional, sensational, stagy

melody *n* **1** = **tune**, air, descant, music, refrain, song, strain, theme **2** = **tunefulness**, euphony, harmony, melodiousness, music, musicality

melt *vb* **1, 2** = **dissolve**, deliquesce, diffuse, flux, fuse, liquefy, soften, thaw **3** *often foll. by* **away** = **disappear**, disperse, dissolve, evanesce, evaporate, fade, vanish **6** = **soften**, disarm, mollify, relax, touch

member *n* **1** = **representative**, associate, fellow **3** = **limb**, appendage, arm, component, constituent, element, extremity, leg, organ, part, portion

membership *n* **1** = **members**, associates, body, fellows **2** = **participation**, belonging, enrolment, fellowship

memento *n* = **souvenir**, keepsake, memorial, relic, remembrance, reminder, token, trophy

memoir *n* **1, 2** = **account**, biography, essay, journal, life, monograph, narrative, record, register

memoirs *pl n* **1, 2** = **autobiography**, diary, experiences, journals, life, life story, memories, recollections, reminiscences

memorable *adj* = **noteworthy**, catchy, celebrated, distinguished, extraordinary, famous, historic, illustrious, important, impressive, momentous, notable, remarkable, signal, significant, striking, unforgettable
Antonyms *adj* commonplace, forgettable, insignificant, ordinary, trivial, undistinguished, unimportant, unimpressive, unmemorable

memorandum *n* **1, 2** = **note**, communication, jotting, memo, message, minute, reminder

memorial *adj* **1** = **commemorative**, monumental ◆ *n* **3** = **monument**, cairn, memento, plaque, record, remembrance, souvenir **4** = **petition**, address, memorandum, statement

memorize *vb* = **remember**, commit to memory, con (*arch.*), get by heart, learn, learn by heart, learn by rote

memory *n* **1** = **recall**, recollection, remembrance, reminiscence, retention **5** = **commemoration**, honour, remembrance **6** = **reputation**, celebrity, fame, glory, name, renown, repute

menace *vb* **1** = **threaten**, alarm, bode ill, browbeat, bully, frighten, impend, intimidate, loom, lour *or* lower, terrorize, utter threats to ◆ *n* **2** *Literary* = **threat**, commination, intimidation, scare, warning **3** = **danger**, hazard, jeopardy, peril **4** *Informal* = **nuisance**, annoyance, pest, plague, troublemaker

menacing *adj* **1** = **threatening**, alarming, baleful, dangerous, forbidding, frightening, intimi-

violence, danger, etc. ◆ *n* **2** *Literary.* a threat. **3** something menacing; a source of danger. **4** *Inf.* a nuisance. [C13: ult. rel. to L *minax* threatening, from *minārī* to threaten]
▶'**menacer** *n* ▶'**menacing** *adj* ▶'**menacingly** *adv*

ménage (meɪ'nɑːʒ) *n* the persons of a household. [C17: from F, from Vulgar L (unattested) *mansiōnāticum* household]

ménage à trois *French.* (menaʒ a trwɑ) *n, pl* ***ménages à trois*** (menaʒ a trwɑ). a sexual arrangement involving a married couple and the lover of one of them. [lit.: household of three]

menagerie (mɪ'nædʒərɪ) *n* **1** a collection of wild animals kept for exhibition. **2** the place where such animals are housed. [C18: from F: household management, which formerly included care of domestic animals]

mend Ⓣ (mɛnd) *vb* **1** (*tr*) to repair (something broken or unserviceable). **2** to improve or undergo improvement; reform (often in **mend one's ways**). **3** (*intr*) to heal or recover. **4** (*intr*) (of conditions) to improve; become better. ◆ *n* **5** the act of repairing. **6** a mended area, esp. on a garment. **7 on the mend.** becoming better, esp. in health. [C12: from AMEND]
▶'**mendable** *adj* ▶'**mender** *n*

mendacity Ⓣ (mɛn'dæsɪtɪ) *n, pl* **mendacities. 1** the tendency to be untruthful. **2** a falsehood. [C17: from LL *mendācitās*, from L *mendāx* untruthful]
▶**mendacious** (mɛn'deɪʃəs) *adj* ▶**men'daciously** *adv*

mendelevium (ˌmɛndɪ'liːvɪəm) *n* a transuranic element artificially produced by bombardment of einsteinium. Symbol: Md; atomic no.: 101; half-life of most stable isotope, ^{258}Md: 60 days (approx.). [C20: after D. I. *Mendeleyev* (1843–1907), Russian chemist who devised the first form of periodic table]

Mendel's laws *pl n* the principles of heredity proposed by Gregor Mendel (1822–84), Austrian monk and botanist. The **Law of Segregation** states that each hereditary character is determined by a pair of units in the reproductive cells: the pairs separate during meiosis so that each gamete carries only one unit of each pair. The **Law of Independent Assortment** states that the separation of the units of each pair is not influenced by that of any other pair.

mendicant ('mɛndɪkənt) *adj* **1** begging. **2** (of a member of a religious order) dependent on alms for sustenance. ◆ *n* **3** a mendicant friar. **4** a less common word for **beggar.** [C16: from L *mendīcāre*, from *mendīcus* beggar, from *mendus* flaw]
▶'**mendicancy** *or* **mendicity** (mɛn'dɪsɪtɪ) *n*

meneer (mə'nɪə) *n* a S. African title of address equivalent to *sir* when used alone or *Mr* when placed before a name. [Afrik.]

menfolk ('mɛnˌfəʊk) *pl n* men collectively, esp. the men of a particular family.

menhaden (mɛn'heɪdᵊn) *n, pl* **menhaden.** a marine North American fish: source of fishmeal, fertilizer, and oil. [C18: from Algonquian; prob. rel. to another Amerind word, *munnawhatteaúg* fertilizer]

menhir ('mɛnhɪə) *n* a single standing stone, dating from prehistoric times. [C19: from Breton *men* stone + *hir* long]

menial Ⓣ ('miːnɪəl) *adj* **1** consisting of or occupied with work requiring little skill, esp. domestic duties. **2** of, involving, or befitting servants. **3** servile. ◆ *n* **4** a domestic servant. **5** a servile person. [C14: from Anglo-Norman *meignial*, from OF *meinie* household]

meninges (mɪ'nɪndʒiːz) *pl n, sing* **meninx** ('miːnɪŋks). the three membranes (**dura mater, arachnoid, pia mater**) that envelop the brain and spinal cord. [C17: from Gk, pl of *meninx* membrane]
▶**meningeal** (mɪ'nɪndʒɪəl) *adj*

meningitis (ˌmɛnɪn'dʒaɪtɪs) *n* inflammation of the membranes that surround the brain or spinal cord, caused by infection.
▶**meningitic** (ˌmɛnɪn'dʒɪtɪk) *adj*

meningococcus (mɛˌnɪŋgəʊ'kɒkəs) *n, pl* **meningococci** (-'kɒksaɪ). the bacterium that causes cerebrospinal meningitis.
▶**meˌningo'coccal** *adj*

meniscus (mɪ'nɪskəs) *n, pl* **menisci** (-'nɪsaɪ) *or* **meniscuses. 1** the curved upper surface of a liquid standing in a tube, produced by the surface tension. **2** a crescent-shaped lens; a concavo-convex or convexo-concave lens. [C17: from NL, from Gk *mēniskos* crescent, dim. of *mēnē* moon]
▶**me'niscoid** *adj*

Mennonite ('mɛnəˌnaɪt) *n* a member of a Protestant sect that rejects infant baptism and Church organization, and in most cases refuses military service, public office, and the taking of oaths. [C16: from G *Mennonit*, after *Menno* Simons (1496–1561), Frisian religious leader]
▶'**Mennonitism** *n*

meno ('mɛnəʊ) *adv Music.* to be played less quickly, less softly, etc. [from It., from L *minus* less]

meno- *combining form.* menstruation. [from Gk *mēn* month]

menopause ('mɛnəʊˌpɔːz) *n* the period during which a woman's menstrual cycle ceases, normally at an age of 45 to 50. [C19: from F, from Gk *mēn* month + *pausis* halt]
▶ˌ**meno'pausal** *adj*

menorah (mɪ'nɔːrə) *n Judaism.* **1** a seven-branched candelabrum used in the Temple and now an emblem of Judaism and the badge of the state of Israel. **2** a similar lamp lit during the Chanukah festival. [from Heb.: candlestick]

menorrhagia (ˌmɛnɔː'reɪdʒɪə) *n* excessive bleeding during menstruation.

menorrhoea (ˌmɛnə'rɪə) *n* normal bleeding in menstruation.

menses ('mɛnsiːz) *n* (*functioning as sing or pl*) **1** another name for **menstruation. 2** the period of time during which one menstruation occurs. **3** the matter discharged during menstruation. [C16: from L, pl of *mensis* month]

Menshevik ('mɛnʃɪvɪk) *or* **Menshevist** *n* a member of the moderate wing of the Russian Social Democratic Party. Cf. **Bolshevik.** [C20: from Russian, lit.: minority, from *menshe* less, from *malo* few]
▶'**Mensheˌvism** *n*

menstruate ('mɛnstrʊˌeɪt) *vb* **menstruates, menstruating, menstruated.** (*intr*) to undergo menstruation. [C17: from L *menstruāre*, from *mensis* month]

menstruation Ⓣ (ˌmɛnstrʊ'eɪʃən) *n* the approximately monthly discharge of blood and cellular debris from the uterus by nonpregnant women from puberty to the menopause.
▶'**menstrual** *or* '**menstruous** *adj*

menstruum ('mɛnstrʊəm) *n, pl* **menstruums** *or* **menstrua** (-strʊə). a solvent, esp. one used in the preparation of a drug. [C17 (meaning: solvent), C14 (menstrual discharge): from Med. L, from L *mēnstruus* monthly, from *mēnsis* month; from alchemical comparison between a base metal being transmuted into gold and the supposed action of the menses]

mensurable ('mɛnsjʊrəbᵊl, -ʃə-) *adj* a less common word for **measurable.** [C17: from LL *mēnsūrābilis*, from *mēnsūra* MEASURE]
▶ˌ**mensura'bility** *n*

mensural ('mɛnʃərəl) *adj* **1** of or involving measure. **2** *Music.* of or relating to music in which notes have fixed values. [C17: from LL *mēnsūrālis*, from *mēnsūra* MEASURE]

mensuration (ˌmɛnʃə'reɪʃən) *n* **1** the study of the measurement of geometric magnitudes such as length. **2** the act or process of measuring.
▶**mensurative** ('mɛnʃərətɪv) *adj*

-ment *suffix forming nouns, esp. from verbs.* **1** indicating state, condition, or quality: *enjoyment.* **2** indicating the result or product of an action: *embankment.* **3** indicating process or action: *management.* [from F, from L *-mentum*]

mental Ⓣ ('mɛntᵊl) *adj* **1** of or involving the mind. **2** occurring only in the mind: *mental arithmetic.* **3** affected by mental illness: *a mental patient.* **4** concerned with mental illness: *a mental hospital.* **5** *Sl.* insane. [C15: from LL *mentālis*, from L *mēns* mind]
▶'**mentally** *adv*

mental deficiency *n Psychiatry.* a less common term for **mental retardation.**

mental handicap *n* any intellectual disability resulting from injury to the brain or from abnormal neurological development.
▶**mentally handicapped** *adj*

mental healing *n* the healing of a disorder by mental concentration or suggestion.

mental illness *n* any of various disorders in which a person's thoughts, emotions, or behaviour are so abnormal as to cause suffering to himself, herself, or other people.

mentalism ('mɛntᵊˌlɪzəm) *n Philosophy.* the doctrine that mind is the fundamental reality and that objects of knowledge exist only as aspects of the subject's consciousness.
▶ˌ**mental'istic** *adj*

mentality Ⓣ (mɛn'tælɪtɪ) *n, pl* **mentalities. 1** the state or quality of men-

THESAURUS

dating, intimidatory, looming, louring *or* lowering, minacious, minatory, ominous
Antonyms *adj* auspicious, encouraging, favourable, promising

mend *vb* **1** = **repair**, cure, darn, fix, heal, patch, rectify, refit, reform, remedy, renew, renovate, restore, retouch **2** = **improve**, ameliorate, amend, better, correct, emend, rectify, reform, revise **3** = **heal**, convalesce, get better, recover, recuperate ◆ *n* **6** = **repair**, darn, patch, stitch **7 on the mend** = **convalescent**, convalescing, getting better, improving, recovering, recuperating

mendacious *adj* **1** = **lying**, deceitful, deceptive, dishonest, duplicitous, fallacious, false, fraudulent, insincere, perfidious, perjured, untrue, untruthful
Antonyms *adj* genuine, honest, true, truthful

mendacity *n* **1, 2** = **lying**, deceit, deceitfulness, dishonesty, distortion, duplicity, falsehood, falsification, fraudulence, insincerity, inveracity, lie, mendaciousness, misrepresentation, perfidy, perjury, untruth, untruthfulness

menial *adj* **1** = **unskilled**, boring, dull, humdrum, low-status, routine **3** = **humble**, abject, base, degrading, demeaning, fawning, grovelling, ignoble, ignominious, low, lowly, mean, obsequious, servile, slavish, sorry, subservient, sycophantic, vile ◆ *n* **4** = **servant**, attendant, dogsbody (*inf.*), domestic, drudge, flunky, labourer, lackey, serf, skivvy (*chiefly Brit.*), slave, underling, varlet (*arch.*), vassal
Antonyms *adj* ≠ **humble**: aristocratic, autocratic, bossy, dignified, domineering, elevated, haughty, high, noble, overbearing, proud ◆ *n* ≠ **servant**: boss, chief, commander, lord, master, superior

menstruation *n* = **period**, catamenia (*Physiology*), courses (*Physiology*), the curse (*inf.*), flow (*inf.*), menses, menstrual cycle, monthly (*inf.*)

mental *adj* **1** = **intellectual**, cerebral **5** *Slang* = **insane**, deranged, disturbed, lunatic, mad, mentally ill, not right in the head, psychiatric, psychotic, round the bend (*Brit. sl.*), unbalanced, unstable

mentality *n* **2** = **attitude**, cast of mind, character, disposition, frame of mind, make-up, outlook, personality, psychology, turn of mind, way of thinking

mentally *adv* **1** = **in the mind**, in one's head,

tal or intellectual ability. **2** a way of thinking; mental inclination or character.

mental lexicon *n* the store of words in a person's mind.

mental reservation *n* a tacit withholding of full assent or an unexpressed qualification made when taking an oath, making a statement, etc.

mental retardation *n Psychiatry.* the condition of having a low intelligence quotient (below 70).

menthol ('mɛnθɒl) *n* an organic compound found in peppermint oil and used as an antiseptic, in inhalants, and as an analgesic. Formula: $C_{10}H_{19}OH$. **[**C19: from G, from L *mentha* MINT[1]**]**

mentholated ('mɛnθə,leɪtɪd) *adj* containing, treated with, or impregnated with menthol.

mention ⓣ ('mɛnʃən) *vb* (*tr*) **1** to refer to or speak about briefly or incidentally. **2** to acknowledge or honour. **3 not to mention (something).** to say nothing of (something too obvious to mention). ◆ *n* **4** a recognition or acknowledgment. **5** a slight reference or allusion. **6** the act of mentioning. **[**C14: via OF from L *mentiō* a calling to mind, from *mēns* mind**]**
▸ **'mentionable** *adj*

mentor ⓣ ('mɛntɔː) *n* a wise or trusted adviser or guide. **[**C18: from *Mentor,* adviser of Telemachus in the Odyssey**]**

mentoring ('mɛntərɪŋ) *n* (in business) the practice of assigning a junior member of staff to the care of a more experienced person who assists him in his career.

menu ⓣ ('mɛnjuː) *n* **1** a list of dishes served at a meal or that can be ordered in a restaurant. **2** a list of options displayed on a visual display unit from which the operator selects an action to be carried out. **[**C19: from F *menu* small, detailed (list), from L *minūtus* MINUTE[2]**]**

menuetto (mɛnju'ɛtəʊ) *n, pl* **menuettos.** *Music.* another term for **minuet.** **[**from It.**]**

meow, miaou, miaow (mɪ'aʊ, mjaʊ), *or* **miaul** (mɪ'aʊl, mjaʊl) *vb* **1** (*intr*) (of a cat) to make a characteristic crying sound. ◆ *interj* **2** an imitation of this sound.

MEP (in Britain) *abbrev. for* Member of the European Parliament.

mepacrine ('mɛpəkrɪn) *n Brit.* a drug formerly widely used to treat malaria. **[**C20: from ME(THYL) + PA(LUDISM + A)CR(ID)INE**]**

meperidine (mə'pɛrɪ,diːn, -dɪn) *n* the US name for **pethidine.** **[**C20: from METHYL + PIPERIDINE**]**

Mephistopheles (,mɛfɪ'stɒfɪ,liːz) *or* **Mephisto** (mə'fɪstəʊ) *n* a devil in medieval mythology and the one to whom Faust sold his soul in German legend.
▸ **Mephistophelean** *or* **Mephistophelian** (,mɛfɪstə'fiːlɪən) *adj*

mephitic (mɪ'fɪtɪk) *or* **mephitical** *adj* **1** poisonous; foul. **2** foul-smelling; putrid. **[**C17: from LL *mephīticus* pestilential**]**

meprobamate (mə'prəʊbə,meɪt, ,mɛprəʊ'bæmeɪt) *n* a white bitter powder used as a tranquillizer. **[**C20: from ME(THYL) + PRO(PYL + *car*)*bamate* a salt or ester of an amide of carbonic acid**]**

-mer *suffix forming nouns. Chem.* denoting a substance of a particular class: *monomer; polymer.* **[**from Gk *meros* part**]**

mercantile ⓣ ('mɜːkən,taɪl) *adj* **1** of, relating to, or characteristic of trade or traders; commercial. **2** of or relating to mercantilism. **[**C17: from F, from It., from *mercante* MERCHANT**]**

mercantilism ('mɜːkəntɪ,lɪzəm) *n Econ.* a theory prevalent in Europe during the 17th and 18th centuries asserting that the wealth of a nation depends on possession of precious metals and therefore that a government must maximize foreign trade surplus and foster national commercial interests, a merchant marine, the establishment of colonies, etc.
▸ **'mercantilist** *n, adj*

mercaptan (mɜː'kæptæn) *n* another name (not in technical use) for **thiol.** **[**C19: from G, from Med. L *mercurium captans,* lit.: seizing quicksilver**]**

Mercator projection *n* a conformal map projection on which parallels and meridians form a rectangular grid, scale being exaggerated with increasing distance from the equator. Also called: **Mercator's projection.** **[**C17: after G. *Mercator,* Latinized name of G. Kremer (1512–94), Flemish cartographer**]**

mercenary ⓣ ('mɜːsɪnərɪ, -sɪnrɪ) *adj* **1** influenced by greed or desire for gain. **2** of or relating to a mercenary or mercenaries. ◆ *n, pl* **mercenaries. 3** a man hired to fight for a foreign army, etc. **4** *Rare.* any person who works solely for pay. **[**C16: from L *mercēnārius,* from *mercēs* wages**]**

mercer ('mɜːsə) *n Brit.* a dealer in textile fabrics and fine cloth. **[**C13: from OF *mercier* dealer, from Vulgar L, from L *merx* wares**]**
▸ **'mercery** *n*

mercerize *or* **mercerise** ('mɜːsə,raɪz) *vb* **mercerizes, mercerizing, mercerized** *or* **mercerises, mercerising, mercerised.** (*tr*) to treat (cotton yarn) with an alkali to increase its strength and reception to dye and impart a lustrous silky appearance. **[**C19: after John *Mercer* (1791–1866), E maker of textiles**]**

merchandise ⓣ *n* ('mɜːtʃən,daɪs, -,daɪz). **1** commercial goods; commodities. ◆ *vb* ('mɜːtʃən,daɪz), **merchandises, merchandising, merchandised. 2** to engage in the commercial purchase and sale of (goods or services); trade. **[**C13: from OF; see MERCHANT**]**

merchandising ('mɜːtʃən,daɪzɪŋ) *n* **1** the selection and display of goods in a retail outlet. **2** commercial goods, esp. ones issued to exploit the popularity of a pop group, sporting event, etc.

merchant ⓣ ('mɜːtʃənt) *n* **1** a person engaged in the purchase and sale of commodities for profit; trader. **2** *Chiefly Scot., US, & Canad.* a person engaged in retail trade. **3** (esp. in historical contexts) any trader. **4** *Derog.* a person dealing or involved in something undesirable: *a gossip merchant.* **5** (*modifier*) **5a** of the merchant navy: *a merchant sailor.* **5b** of or concerned with trade: *a merchant ship.* ◆ *vb* **6** (*tr*) to conduct trade in; deal in. **[**C13: from OF, prob. from Vulgar L, from L *mercārī* to trade, from *merx* wares**]**

merchantable ⓣ ('mɜːtʃəntəbᵊl) *adj* suitable for trading.

merchant bank *n Brit.* a financial institution engaged primarily in accepting foreign bills, advising companies on flotations and takeovers, underwriting new issues, hire-purchase finance, making long-term loans to companies, and managing investment portfolios, funds, and trusts.
▸ **merchant banker** *n*

merchantman ('mɜːtʃəntmən) *n, pl* **merchantmen.** a merchant ship.

merchant navy *or* **marine** *n* the ships or crew engaged in a nation's commercial shipping.

Mercian ('mɜːʃɪən) *adj* **1** of or relating to Mercia, an Anglo-Saxon kingdom in England, or its dialect. ◆ *n* **2** the dialect of Old and Middle English spoken in Mercia. **3** a native or inhabitant of Mercia.

merciful ⓣ ('mɜːsɪfʊl) *adj* showing or giving mercy; compassionate.
▸ **'mercifully** *adv* ▸ **'mercifulness** *n*

merciless ⓣ ('mɜːsɪlɪs) *adj* without mercy; pitiless, cruel, or heartless.
▸ **'mercilessly** *adv* ▸ **'mercilessness** *n*

mercurial ⓣ (mɜː'kjʊərɪəl) *adj* **1** of, like, containing, or relating to mercury. **2** volatile; lively: *a mercurial temperament.* **3** (*sometimes cap.*) of, like, or relating to the god or the planet Mercury. ◆ *n* **4** *Med.* any salt of mercury for use as a medicine. **[**C14: from L *mercuriālis*]**
▸ **mer,curi'ality** *n* ▸ **mer'curially** *adv*

mercuric (mɜː'kjʊərɪk) *adj* of or containing mercury in the divalent state; denoting a mercury(II) compound.

mercuric chloride *n* a white poisonous crystalline substance used as a pesticide, antiseptic, and preservative for wood. Formula: $HgCl_2$. Systematic name: **mercury(II) chloride.**

Mercurochrome (mə'kjʊərə,krəʊm) *n Trademark.* a solution of a crystalline compound, used as topical antibacterial agent.

mercurous ('mɜːkjʊrəs) *adj* of or containing mercury in the monovalent state; denoting a mercury(I) compound.

mercury ('mɜːkjʊrɪ) *n, pl* **mercuries. 1** Also called: **quicksilver.** a heavy silvery-white toxic liquid metallic element: used in thermometers, barometers, mercury-vapour lamps, and dental amalgams. Symbol: Hg; atomic no.: 80; atomic wt.: 200.59. **2** any plant of the genus *Mercurialis.* **3** *Arch.* a messenger or courier. **[**C14: from L *Mercurius,* messenger of Jupiter, god of commerce; rel. to *merx* merchandise**]**

Mercury[1] ('mɜːkjʊrɪ) *n Roman myth.* the messenger of the gods.

Mercury[2] ('mɜːkjʊrɪ) *n* the second smallest planet and the nearest to the sun.

mercury-vapour lamp *n* a lamp in which an electric discharge through mercury vapour is used to produce a greenish-blue light.

THESAURUS

intellectually, inwardly, psychologically, rationally, subjectively

mention *vb* **1 = refer to**, acknowledge, adduce, allude to, bring up, broach, call attention to, cite, communicate, declare, disclose, divulge, hint at, impart, intimate, make known, name, point out, recount, report, reveal, speak about *or* of, state, tell, touch upon **3 not to mention = to say nothing of**, as well as, besides, not counting ◆ *n* **4 = acknowledgment**, citation, recognition, tribute **5 = reference**, allusion, announcement, indication, notification, observation, remark

mentor *n* **= guide**, adviser, coach, counsellor, guru, instructor, teacher, tutor

menu *n* **1 = bill of fare**, *carte du jour,* tariff (*chiefly Brit.*)

mercantile *adj* **1 = commercial**, marketable, trade, trading

mercenary *adj* **1 = greedy**, acquisitive, avaricious, bribable, covetous, grasping, money-grubbing (*inf.*), sordid, venal **2 = hired**, bought, paid, venal ◆ *n* **3 = hireling**, condottiere (*History*), free companion (*History*), freelance (*History*), soldier of fortune

Antonyms *adj* ≠ **greedy:** altruistic, benevolent, generous, idealistic, liberal, munificent, philanthropic, unselfish

merchandise *n* **1 = goods**, commodities, produce, products, staples, stock, stock in trade, truck, vendibles, wares ◆ *vb* **2 = trade**, buy and sell, deal in, distribute, do business in, market, retail, sell, traffic in, vend

merchant *n* **1 = tradesman**, broker, dealer, purveyor, retailer, salesman, seller, shopkeeper, supplier, trader, trafficker, vendor, wholesaler

merchantable *adj* **= saleable**, marketable, tradable, vendible

merciful *adj* **= compassionate**, beneficent, benignant, clement, forbearing, forgiving, generous, gracious, humane, kind, lenient, liberal, mild, pitying, soft, sparing, sympathetic, tender-hearted

Antonyms *adj* cruel, hard-hearted, inhumane, merciless, pitiless, uncompassionate, unfeeling

merciless *adj* **= cruel**, barbarous, callous, fell (*arch.*), hard, hard-hearted, harsh, heartless, implacable, inexorable, inhumane, pitiless, relentless, ruthless, severe, unappeasable, unfeeling, unforgiving, unmerciful, unpitying, unsparing, unsympathetic

mercurial *adj* **2 = lively**, active, capricious, changeable, erratic, fickle, flighty, gay, impulsive, inconstant, irrepressible, light-hearted, mobile, quicksilver, spirited, sprightly, temperamental, unpredictable, unstable, variable, volatile

Antonyms *adj* consistent, constant, dependable, predictable, reliable, stable, steady, unchanging

mercy ➊ ('mɜːsɪ) *n, pl* **mercies. 1** compassionate treatment of or attitude towards an offender, adversary, etc., who is in one's power or care; clemency; pity. **2** the power to show mercy. **3** a relieving or welcome occurrence or state of affairs. **4 at the mercy of.** in the power of. [C12: from OF, from L *mercēs* recompense, from *merx* goods]

mercy flight *n* an aircraft flight to bring a seriously ill or injured person to hospital from an isolated community.

mercy killing *n* another term for **euthanasia.**

mere[1] ➊ (mɪə) *adj* being nothing more than something specified: *a mere child.* [C15: from L *merus* pure]
▸ **'merely** *adv*

mere[2] (mɪə) *n* **1** *Dialect or arch.* a lake or marsh. **2** *Obs.* the sea or an inlet of it. [OE *mere* sea, lake]

mere[3] ('mɛrɪ) *n* a short flat Maori striking weapon. [from Maori]

-mere *n combining form.* indicating a part or division. [from Gk *meros* part]
▸**meric** *adj combining form.*

meretricious ➊ (ˌmɛrɪ'trɪʃəs) *adj* **1** superficially or garishly attractive. **2** insincere. **3** *Arch.* of, like, or relating to a prostitute. [C17: from L *meretrīcius,* from *meretrix* prostitute, from *merēre* to earn money]
▸ **ˌmere'triciously** *adv* ▸ **ˌmere'triciousness** *n*

merganser (mɜː'gænsə) *n, pl* **mergansers** *or* **merganser.** any of several typically crested large marine diving ducks, having a long slender hooked bill with serrated edges. [C18: from NL, from L *mergus* waterfowl, from *mergere* to plunge + *anser* goose]

merge ➊ (mɜːdʒ) *vb* **merges, merging, merged. 1** to meet and join or cause to meet and join. **2** to blend or cause to blend; fuse. [C17: from L *mergere* to plunge]
▸ **'mergence** *n*

merger ➊ ('mɜːdʒə) *n* **1** *Commerce.* the combination of two or more companies. **2** *Law.* the absorption of an estate, interest, offence, etc., into a greater one. **3** the act of merging or the state of being merged.

meridian ➊ (mə'rɪdɪən) *n* **1a** one of the imaginary lines joining the north and south poles at right angles to the equator, designated by degrees of longitude from 0° at Greenwich to 180°. **1b** the great circle running through both poles. **2** *Astron.* the great circle on the celestial sphere passing through the north and south celestial poles and the zenith and nadir of the observer. **3** the peak; zenith: *the meridian of his achievements.* **4** (in acupuncture, etc.) any of the channels through which vital energy is believed to circulate round the body. **5** *Obs.* noon. ◆ *adj* **6** along or relating to a meridian. **7** of or happening at noon. **8** relating to the peak of something. [C14: from L *merīdiānus* of midday, from *merīdiēs* midday, from *medius* MID[1] + *diēs* day]

meridional (mə'rɪdɪənᵊl) *adj* **1** along, relating to, or resembling a meridian. **2** characteristic of or located in the south, esp. of Europe. ◆ *n* **3** an inhabitant of the south, esp. of France. [C14: from LL *merīdiōnālis* southern; see MERIDIAN]

meringue (mə'ræŋ) *n* **1** stiffly beaten egg whites mixed with sugar and baked. **2** a small cake or shell of this mixture, often filled with cream. [C18: from F, from ?]

merino (mə'riːnəʊ) *n, pl* **merinos. 1** a breed of sheep originating in Spain. **2** the long fine wool of this sheep. **3** the yarn made from this wool, often mixed with cotton. ◆ *adj* **4** made from merino wool. [C18: from Sp., from ?]

meristem ('mɛrɪˌstɛm) *n* a plant tissue responsible for growth, whose cells divide and differentiate to form the tissues and organs of the plant. [C19: from Gk *meristos* divided, from *merizein,* from *meris* portion]
▸**meristematic** (ˌmɛrɪstɪ'mætɪk) *adj*

merit ➊ ('mɛrɪt) *n* **1** worth or superior quality; excellence. **2** (*often pl*) a deserving or commendable quality or act. **3** *Christianity.* spiritual credit granted or received for good works. **4** the fact or state of deserving; desert. ◆ *vb* **merits, meriting, merited. 5** (*tr*) to be worthy of; deserve. [C13: via OF from L *meritum* reward, from *merēre* to deserve]
▸ **'merited** *adj* ▸ **'meritless** *adj*

meritocracy (ˌmɛrɪ'tɒkrəsɪ) *n, pl* **meritocracies. 1** rule by persons chosen for their superior talents or intellect. **2** the persons constituting such a group. **3** a social system formed on such a basis.
▸**meritocratic** (ˌmɛrɪtə'krætɪk) *adj*

meritorious ➊ (ˌmɛrɪ'tɔːrɪəs) *adj* praiseworthy; showing merit. [C15: from L *meritōrius* earning money]
▸ **ˌmeri'toriously** *adv* ▸ **ˌmeri'toriousness** *n*

merits ('mɛrɪts) *pl n* **1** the actual and intrinsic rights and wrongs of an issue, esp. in a law case. **2 on its (his, her,** etc.**) merits.** on the intrinsic qualities or virtues.

merle *or* **merl** (mɜːl) *n Scot.* another name for the (European) **blackbird.** [C15: via OF from L *merula*]

merlin ('mɜːlɪn) *n* a small falcon that has a dark plumage with a black-barred tail. [C14: from OF *esmerillon,* from *esmeril,* of Gmc origin]

mermaid ('mɜːˌmeɪd) *n* an imaginary sea creature fabled to have a woman's head and upper body and a fish's tail. [C14: from MERE[2] + MAID]

merman ('mɜːˌmæn) *n, pl* **mermen.** a male counterpart of the mermaid. [C17: see MERMAID]

-merous *adj combining form.* (in biology) having a certain number or kind of parts. [from Gk *meros* part]

Merovingian (ˌmɛrəʊ'vɪndʒɪən) *adj* **1** of or relating to a Frankish dynasty which ruled Gaul and W Germany from about 500 to 751 A.D. ◆ *n* **2** a member or supporter of this dynasty. [C17: from F, from Med. L *Merovingi* offspring of *Merovaeus,* L form of *Merowig,* traditional founder of the line]

merriment ➊ ('mɛrɪmənt) *n* gaiety, fun, or mirth.

merry ➊ ('mɛrɪ) *adj* **merrier, merriest. 1** cheerful; jolly. **2** very funny; hilarious. **3** *Brit. inf.* slightly drunk. **4 make merry.** to revel; be festive. **5 play merry hell with.** *Inf.* to disturb greatly; disrupt. [OE *merige* agreeable]
▸ **'merrily** *adv* ▸ **'merriness** *n*

merry-andrew (-'ændruː) *n* a joker, clown, or buffoon. [C17: from ?]

merry-go-round *n* **1** another name for **roundabout** (sense 1). **2** a whirl of activity.

merrymaking ➊ ('mɛrɪˌmeɪkɪŋ) *n* fun, revelry, or festivity.
▸ **'merryˌmaker** *n*

merrythought ('mɛrɪˌθɔːt) *n Brit.* a less common word for **wishbone.**

mesa ('meɪsə) *n* a flat tableland with steep edges, common in the southwestern US. [from Sp.: table]

mésalliance (me'zælɪəns) *n* a marriage with a person of lower social status. [C18: from F: MISALLIANCE]

mescal (me'skæl) *n* **1** Also called: **peyote.** a spineless globe-shaped cactus of Mexico and the southwestern US. Its button-like tubercles (**mescal buttons**) are chewed by certain Indian tribes for their hallucinogenic effects. **2** a colourless alcoholic spirit distilled from the fermented juice of certain agave plants. [C19: from American Sp., from Nahuatl *mexcalli* the liquor, from *metl* MAGUEY + *ixcalli* stew]

mescaline *or* **mescalin** ('mɛskəˌliːn, -lɪn) *n* a hallucinogenic drug derived from mescal buttons.

mesdames ('meɪˌdæm) *n* the plural of **madame** and **madam** (sense 1).

mesdemoiselles (ˌmeɪdmwə'zɛl) *n* the plural of **mademoiselle.**

meseems (mɪ'siːmz) *vb* (*tr; takes a clause as object*) *Arch.* it seems to me.

mesembryanthemum (mɪzˌɛmbrɪ'ænθɪməm) *n* any of a genus of plants with succulent leaves and bright flowers with rayed petals which typically open at midday. [C18: NL, from Gk *mesēmbria* noon + *anthemon* flower]

mesencephalon (ˌmɛsɛn'sɛfəˌlɒn) *n* the part of the brain that develops from the middle portion of the embryonic neural tube. Nontechnical name: **midbrain.**

mesentery ('mɛsəntərɪ, 'mɛz-) *n, pl* **mesenteries.** the double layer of peritoneum that is attached to the back wall of the abdominal cavity

THESAURUS

mercy *n* **1** = **compassion**, benevolence, charity, clemency, favour, forbearance, forgiveness, grace, kindness, leniency, pity, quarter **3** = **blessing**, benison (*arch.*), boon, godsend, piece of luck, relief **4 at the mercy of** = **in the power of**, defenceless against, exposed to, in the clutches of, naked before, open to, prey to, subject to, threatened by, unprotected against, vulnerable to
Antonyms *n* ≠ **compassion:** brutality, cruelty, harshness, inhumanity, pitilessness, severity

mere[1] *adj* = **simple**, absolute, bare, common, complete, entire, nothing more than, plain, pure, pure and simple, sheer, stark, unadulterated, unmitigated, unmixed, utter

meretricious *adj* **1** = **trashy**, flashy, garish, gaudy, gimcrack, plastic (*sl.*), showy, tawdry, tinsel **2** = **false**, bogus, counterfeit, deceitful, hollow, insincere, mock, phoney *or* phony (*inf.*), pseudo (*inf.*), put-on, sham, specious, spurious

merge *vb* **1, 2** = **combine**, amalgamate, become lost in, be swallowed up by, blend, coalesce, consolidate, converge, fuse, incorporate, intermix, join, meet, meld, melt into, mingle, mix, tone with, unite
Antonyms *vb* detach, diverge, divide, part, separate, sever

merger *n* **1, 3** = **union**, amalgamation, coalition, combination, consolidation, fusion, incorporation

meridian *n* **3, 5** = **peak**, acme, apex, apogee, climax, crest, culmination, high noon, high-water mark, pinnacle, summit, zenith

merit *n* **1** = **worth**, advantage, asset, excellence, good, goodness, integrity, quality, strong point, talent, value, virtue, worthiness **4** = **claim**, credit, desert, due, right ◆ *vb* **5** = **deserve**, be entitled to, be worthy of, earn, have a claim to, have a right to, have coming to one, incur, rate, warrant

merited *adj* **5** = **deserved**, appropriate, condign, earned, entitled, just, justified, rightful, rightly due, warranted

meritorious *adj* = **praiseworthy**, admirable, commendable, creditable, deserving, excellent, exemplary, good, honourable, laudable, right, righteous, virtuous, worthy
Antonyms *adj* discreditable, dishonourable, ignoble, unchivalrous, undeserving, unexceptional, ungenerous, unpraiseworthy

merriment *n* = **fun**, amusement, conviviality, festivity, frolic, gaiety, glee, hilarity, jocularity, jollity, joviality, laughter, levity, liveliness, merrymaking, mirth, revelry, sport

merry *adj* **1** = **cheerful**, blithe, blithesome, carefree, chirpy (*inf.*), convivial, festive, frolicsome, fun-loving, gay, genial, glad, gleeful, happy, jocund, jolly, joyful, joyous, light-hearted, mirthful, rollicking, sportive, upbeat (*inf.*), vivacious **2** = **comical**, amusing, comic, facetious, funny, hilarious, humorous, jocular, mirthful **3** *Brit. informal* = **tipsy**, elevated (*inf.*), happy, mellow, squiffy (*Brit. inf.*), tiddly (*sl., chiefly Brit.*) **4 make merry** = **have fun**, carouse, celebrate, enjoy oneself, feast, frolic, have a good time, make whoopee (*inf.*), revel
Antonyms *adj* ≠ **cheerful:** dejected, dismal, down in the dumps (*inf.*), gloomy, miserable, sad, unhappy

merrymaking *n* = **festivity**, carousal, carouse, celebration, conviviality, fun, gaiety, hooley *or* hoolie (*chiefly Irish & NZ*), jollification, merriment, party, revelry

and supports most of the small intestine. [C16: from NL *mesenterium, from* MESO- + Gk *enteron* intestine]
▶ˌ**mesen'teric** *adj* ▶**mesenteritis** (mɛsˌɛntə'raɪtɪs) *n*

mesh ⓘ (mɛʃ) *n* **1** a network; net. **2** an open space between the strands of a network. **3** (*often pl*) the strands surrounding these spaces. **4** anything that ensnares, or holds like a net. **5** the engagement of teeth on interacting gearwheels: *the gears are in mesh.* ◆ *vb* **6** to entangle or become entangled. **7** (of gear teeth) to engage or cause to engage. **8** (*intr;* often foll. by *with*) to coordinate (with). **9** to work or cause to work in harmony. [C16: prob. from Du. *maesche*]

mesial ('miːzɪəl) *adj Anat.* another word for **medial** (sense 1). [C19: from MESO- + -IAL]

mesmerism ('mɛzməˌrɪzəm) *n Psychol.* **1** a hypnotic state induced by the operator's imposition of his will on that of the patient. **2** an early doctrine concerning this. [C19: after F. A. *Mesmer* (1734–1815), Austrian physician]
▶**mesmeric** (mɛz'mɛrɪk) *adj* ▶'**mesmerist** *n*

mesmerize ⓘ *or* **mesmerise** ('mɛzməˌraɪz) *vb* **mesmerizes, mesmerizing, mesmerized** *or* **mesmerises, mesmerising, mesmerised.** (*tr*) **1** to hold (someone) as if spellbound. **2** a former word for **hypnotize.**
▶ˌ**mesmeri'zation** *or* ˌ**mesmeri'sation** *n* ▶'**mesmerˌizer** *or* '**mesmerˌiser** *n*

mesne (miːn) *adj Law.* **1** intermediate or intervening: *a mesne assignment of property.* **2 mesne profits.** rents or profits accruing during the rightful owner's exclusion from his land. [C15: from legal F *meien* in the middle]

meso- *or before a vowel* **mes-** *combining form.* middle or intermediate: *mesomorph.* [from Gk *misos* middle]

mesoblast ('mɛsəʊˌblæst) *n* another name for **mesoderm.**
▶ˌ**meso'blastic** *adj*

mesocarp ('mɛsəʊˌkɑːp) *n* the middle layer of the pericarp of a fruit, such as the flesh of a peach.

mesocephalic (ˌmɛsəʊsɪ'fælɪk) *Anat.* ◆ *adj* **1** having a medium-sized head. ◆ *n* **2** an individual with such a head.
▶**mesocephaly** (ˌmɛsəʊ'sɛfəlɪ) *n*

mesoderm ('mɛsəʊˌdɜːm) *n* the middle germ layer of an animal embryo, giving rise to muscle, blood, bone, connective tissue, etc.
▶ˌ**meso'dermal** *or* ˌ**meso'dermic** *adj*

Mesolithic (ˌmɛsəʊ'lɪθɪk) *n* **1** the period between the Palaeolithic and the Neolithic, in Europe from about 12 000 to 3000 B.C. ◆ *adj* **2** of or relating to the Mesolithic.

mesomorph ('mɛsəʊˌmɔːf) *n* a type of person having a muscular body build with a relatively prominent underlying bone structure.

mesomorphic (ˌmɛsəʊ'mɔːfɪk) *adj* **1** *Chem.* existing in or concerned with an intermediate state of matter between a true liquid and a true solid. **2** relating to or being a mesomorph. ◆ Also: **mesomorphous.**
▶ˌ**meso'morphism** *n*

meson ('miːzɒn) *n* any of a group of elementary particles that has a rest mass between those of an electron and a proton, and an integral spin. [C20: from MESO- + -ON]
▶**me'sonic** *or* '**mesic** *adj*

mesophyte ('mɛsəʊˌfaɪt) *n* any plant that grows in surroundings receiving an average supply of water.

mesosphere ('mɛsəʊˌsfɪə) *n* the atmospheric layer lying between the stratosphere and the thermosphere.

Mesozoic (ˌmɛsəʊ'zəʊɪk) *adj* **1** of, denoting, or relating to an era of geological time that began 225 000 000 years ago and lasted about 155 000 000 years. ◆ *n* **2 the.** the Mesozoic era.

mesquite *or* **mesquit** (mɛ'skiːt, 'mɛskiːt) *n* any of various small trees, esp. a tropical American variety, whose sugary pods (**mesquite beans**) are used as animal fodder. [C19: from Mexican Sp., from Nahautl *mizquitl*]

mess ⓘ (mɛs) *n* **1** a state of confusion or untidiness, esp. if dirty or unpleasant. **2** a chaotic or troublesome state of affairs; muddle. **3** *Inf.* a dirty or untidy person or thing. **4** *Arch.* a portion of food, esp. soft or semiliquid food. **5** a place where service personnel eat or take recreation. **6** a group of people, usually servicemen, who eat together. **7** the meal so taken. ◆ *vb* **8** (*tr;* often foll. by *up*) to muddle or dirty. **9** (*intr*) to make a mess. **10** (*intr;* often foll. by *with*) to interfere; meddle. **11** (*intr;* often foll. by *with* or *together*) *Mil.* to group together, esp. for eating. [C13: from OF *mes* dish of food, from LL *missus* course (at table), from L *mittere* to send forth]

mess about ⓘ *or* **around** *vb* (*adv*) **1** (*intr*) to occupy oneself trivially; potter. **2** (when *intr,* often foll. by *with*) to interfere or meddle (with). **3** (*intr;* sometimes foll. by *with*) *Chiefly US.* to engage in adultery.

message ⓘ ('mɛsɪdʒ) *n* **1** a communication, usually brief, from one person or group to another. **2** an implicit meaning, as in a work of art. **3** a formal communiqué. **4** an inspired communication of a prophet or religious leader. **5** a mission; errand. **6 get the message.** *Inf.* to understand. ◆ *vb* **messages, messaging, messaged. 7** (*tr*) to send as a message. [C13: from OF, from Vulgar L *missāticum* (unattested) something sent, from L *missus,* p.p. of *mittere*]

messages ('mɛsɪdʒɪz) *pl n Scot. & NE English dialect.* household shopping.

message stick *n* a stick bearing carved symbols, carried by a native Australian as identification.

messenger ⓘ ('mɛsɪndʒə) *n* **1** a person who takes messages from one person or group to another. **2** a person who runs errands. **3** a carrier of official dispatches; courier. [C13: from OF *messagier,* from MESSAGE]

messenger RNA *n Biochem.* a form of RNA, transcribed from a single strand of DNA, that carries genetic information required for protein synthesis from DNA to the ribosomes.

mess hall *n* a military dining room.

Messiah (mɪ'saɪə) *n* **1** *Judaism.* the awaited king of the Jews, to be sent by God to free them. **2** Jesus Christ, when regarded in this role. **3** an exceptional or hoped-for liberator of a country or people. [C14: from OF *Messie,* ult. from Heb. *māshīah* anointed]
▶**Mes'siahship** *n* ▶**Messianic** *or* **messianic** (ˌmɛsɪ'ænɪk) *adj*

Messier catalogue ('mɛsɪˌeɪ) *n Astronomy.* a catalogue of 103 nonstellar objects, such as nebulae and galaxies, prepared in 1781–86. An object is referred to by its number in this catalogue, for example the Andromeda Galaxy is referred to as *M31.* [C18: after Charles *Messier* (1730–1817), F astronomer]

messieurs ('mɛsəz) *n* the plural of **monsieur.**

mess jacket *n* a waist-length jacket, worn by officers in the mess for formal dinners.

mess kit *n Mil.* **1** *Brit.* formal evening wear for officers. **2** Also called: **mess gear.** eating utensils used esp. in the field.

messmate ('mɛsˌmeɪt) *n* a person with whom one shares meals in a mess, esp. in the army.

Messrs ('mɛsəz) *n* the plural of **Mr.** [C18: abbrev. from F *messieurs,* pl. of MONSIEUR]

messy ⓘ ('mɛsɪ) *adj* **messier, messiest.** dirty, confused, or untidy.
▶'**messily** *adv* ▶'**messiness** *n*

mestizo (mɛ'stiːzəʊ, mɪ-) *n, pl* **mestizos** *or* **mestizoes.** a person of mixed parentage, esp. the offspring of a Spanish American and an American Indian. [C16: from Sp., ult. from L *miscēre* to mix]
▶**mestiza** (mɛ'stiːzə) *fem n*

mestranol ('mɛstrəˌnɒl, -ˌnəʊl) *n* a synthetic oestrogen used in combination with progesterones as an oral contraceptive. [C20: from M(ETHYL) + (O)ESTR(OGEN) + (*pregn*)*an*(*e*) + -OL]

met (mɛt) *vb* the past tense and past participle of **meet**[1].

met. *abbrev. for:* **1** meteorological. **2** meteorology. **3** metropolitan.

meta- *or sometimes before a vowel* **met-** *prefix* **1** indicating change or alternation: *metabolism; metamorphosis.* **2** (of an academic discipline) concerned with the concepts and results of that discipline: *metamathematics.* **3** occurring or situated behind or after: *metaphysics.* **4** (*often in italics*) denoting that an organic compound contains a benzene ring with substituents in the 1,3-positions: *meta-cresol.* Abbrev.: *m-.* **5** denoting an isomer, polymer, or compound related to a specified compound: *metaldehyde.* **6** denoting an oxyacid that is the least hydrated form of the anhydride or a salt of such an acid: *metaphosphoric acid.* [from Gk (prep)]

metabolism (mɪ'tæbəˌlɪzəm) *n* **1** the sum total of the chemical processes that occur in living organisms, resulting in growth, production of energy, elimination of waste, etc. **2** the sum total of the chemical processes affecting a particular substance in the body: *carbohydrate metabolism.* [C19: from Gk *metabolē* change, from *metaballein,* from META- + *ballein* to throw]
▶**metabolic** (ˌmɛtə'bɒlɪk) *adj* ▶ˌ**meta'bolically** *adv*

metabolize *or* **metabolise** (mɪ'tæbəˌlaɪz) *vb* **metabolizes, metabolizing, metabolized** *or* **metabolises, metabolising, metabolised.** to produce or be produced by metabolism.

metacarpus (ˌmɛtə'kɑːpəs) *n, pl* **metacarpi** (-paɪ). **1** the skeleton of the hand between the wrist and the fingers, consisting of five long bones. **2** the corresponding bones in other vertebrates.
▶ˌ**meta'carpal** *adj, n*

metacentre *or US* **metacenter** ('mɛtəˌsɛntə) *n* the intersection of a vertical line through the centre of buoyancy of a floating body at

THESAURUS

mesh *n* **1** = **net**, netting, network, plexus, reticulation, tracery, web **4** = **trap**, entanglement, snare, tangle, toils, web ◆ *vb* **6** = **entangle**, catch, enmesh, ensnare, net, snare, tangle, trap **8, 9** = **engage**, combine, come together, connect, coordinate, dovetail, fit together, harmonize, interlock, knit

mesmerize *vb* **1, 2** = **entrance**, absorb, captivate, enthral, fascinate, grip, hold spellbound, hypnotize, magnetize, spellbind

mess *n* **1** = **disorder**, bodge (*inf.*), botch, chaos, clutter, confusion, dirtiness, disarray, disorganization, grot (*sl.*), hash, hodgepodge (*US*), hotchpotch, jumble, litter, mishmash, shambles, state, turmoil, untidiness **2** = **difficulty**, deep water, dilemma, fine kettle of fish (*inf.*), fix (*inf.*), hole (*inf.*), hot water (*inf.*), imbroglio, jam (*inf.*), mix-up, muddle, perplexity, pickle (*inf.*), plight, predicament, spot (*inf.*), stew (*inf.*), tight spot ◆ *vb* **8, 9** *often with* **up** = **dirty**, befoul, besmirch, botch, bungle, clutter, disarrange, dishevel, foul, litter, make a hash of (*inf.*), make a nonsense of, muck up (*Brit. sl.*), muddle, pollute, scramble **10** *often with* **with** = **interfere**, fiddle (*inf.*), meddle, play, tamper, tinker

mess about *vb* **1** = **potter**, amuse oneself, dabble, fool (about *or* around), footle (*inf.*), muck about (*inf.*), play about *or* around, trifle **2** = **meddle**, fiddle (*inf.*), fool (about *or* around), interfere, play, tamper, tinker, toy

message *n* **1, 3** = **communication**, bulletin, communiqué, dispatch, intimation, letter, memorandum, missive, note, notice, tidings, word **2** = **point**, idea, import, meaning, moral, purport, theme **5** = **errand**, commission, job, mission, task **6 get the message** = **understand**, catch on (*inf.*), comprehend, get it, get the point, see, take the hint, twig (*Brit. inf.*)

messenger *n* **1-3** = **courier**, agent, bearer, carrier, delivery boy, emissary, envoy, errand-boy, go-between, harbinger, herald, runner

messy *adj* = **untidy**, chaotic, cluttered, confused, dirty, dishevelled, disordered, disorganized, grubby, littered, muddled, shambolic, sloppy (*inf.*), slovenly, unkempt

equilibrium with a vertical line through the centre of buoyancy when the body is tilted.
▸ ˌ**meta'centric** *adj*

metage ('miːtɪdʒ) *n* **1** the official measuring of weight or contents. **2** a charge for this. [C16: from METE[1]]

metal ('mɛtᵊl) *n* **1a** any of a number of chemical elements, such as iron or copper, that are often lustrous ductile solids, have basic oxides, form positive ions, and are good conductors of heat and electricity. **1b** an alloy, such as brass or steel, containing one or more of these elements. **2** the substance of glass in a molten state or as the finished product. **3** short for **road metal**. **4** *Inf.* short for **heavy metal**. **5** *Heraldry.* gold or silver. **6** the basic quality of a person or thing; stuff. **7** (*pl*) the rails of a railway. ◆ *adj* **8** made of metal. ◆ *vb* **metals, metalling, metalled** *or US* **metals, metaling, metaled.** (*tr*) **9** to fit or cover with metal. **10** to make or mend (a road) with road metal. [C13: from L *metallum* mine, product of a mine, from Gk *metallon*]
▸ '**metalled** *adj*

metal. *or* **metall.** *abbrev. for:* **1** metallurgical. **2** metallurgy.

metalanguage ('mɛtəˌlæŋgwɪdʒ) *n* a language or system of symbols used to discuss another language or system. Cf. **object language.**

metal detector *n* a device that gives an audible or visual signal when its search head comes close to a metallic object embedded in food, buried in the ground, etc.

metallic (mɪ'tælɪk) *adj* **1** of, concerned with, or consisting of metal or a metal. **2** suggestive of a metal: *a metallic click; metallic lustre.* **3** *Chem.* (of a metal element) existing in the free state rather than in combination: *metallic copper.*

metallic soap *n* any one of a number of salts or esters containing a metal, such as aluminium, calcium, magnesium, iron, and zinc. They are used as bases for ointments, fungicides, fireproofing and waterproofing agents, and dryers for paints and varnishes.

metalliferous (ˌmɛtᵊ'lɪfərəs) *adj* containing a metallic element. [C17: from L *metallifer* yielding metal, from *metallum* metal + *ferre* to bear]

metallize, metallise, *or US* **metalize** ('mɛtəˌlaɪz) *vb* **metallizes, metallizing, metallized; metallises, metallising, metallised** *or US* **metalizes, metalizing, metalized.** (*tr*) to make metallic or to coat or treat with metal.
▸ ˌ**metalli'zation, metalli'sation,** *or US* ˌ**metali'zation** *n*

metallography (ˌmɛtə'lɒgrəfɪ) *n* the branch of metallurgy concerned with the composition and structure of metals and alloys.
▸**metallographic** (mɪˌtælə'græfɪk) *adj*

metalloid ('mɛtəˌlɔɪd) *n* **1** a nonmetallic element, such as arsenic or silicon, that has some of the properties of a metal. ◆ *adj also* ˌ**metal'loidal. 2** of or being a metalloid. **3** resembling a metal.

metallurgy (mɛ'tælədʒɪ) *n* the scientific study of the extraction, refining, alloying, and fabrication of metals and of their structure and properties.
▸**metallurgic** (ˌmɛtə'lɜːdʒɪk) *or* ˌ**metal'lurgical** *adj* ▸**metallurgist** (mɛ'tælədʒɪst, 'mɛtəˌlɜːdʒɪst) *n*

metal tape *n* a magnetic recording tape coated with pure iron: it gives enhanced recording quality.

metalwork ('mɛtᵊlˌwɜːk) *n* **1** the craft of working in metal. **2** work in metal or articles made from metal.

metalworking ('mɛtᵊlˌwɜːkɪŋ) *n* the processing of metal to change its shape, size, etc.
▸ '**metalˌworker** *n*

metamere ('mɛtəˌmɪə) *n* one of the similar body segments into which earthworms, crayfish, and similar animals are divided longitudinally.
▸**metameral** (mɪ'tæmərəl) *adj*

metamerism (mɪ'tæməˌrɪzəm) *n* **1** Also called: (**metameric**) **segmentation.** the division of an animal into metameres. **2** *Chem.* a type of isomerism in which molecular structures differ by the attachment of different groups to the same atom.
▸**metameric** (ˌmɛtə'mɛrɪk) *adj*

metamict ('mɛtəˌmɪkt) *adj* of or denoting the amorphous state of a substance that has lost its crystalline structure as a result of the radioactivity of uranium or thorium within it.
▸ ˌ**metaˌmicti'zation** *or* ˌ**metaˌmicti'sation** *n*

metamorphic (ˌmɛtə'mɔːfɪk) *or* **metamorphous** *adj* **1** relating to or resulting from metamorphosis or metamorphism. **2** (of rocks) altered considerably from the original structure and composition by pressure and heat.

metamorphism (ˌmɛtə'mɔːfɪzəm) *n* **1** the process by which metamorphic rocks are formed. **2** a variant of **metamorphosis.**

metamorphose ❶ (ˌmɛtə'mɔːfəʊz) *vb* **metamorphoses, metamorphosing, metamorphosed.** to undergo or cause to undergo metamorphosis or metamorphism.

metamorphosis ❶ (ˌmɛtə'mɔːfəsɪs) *n, pl* **metamorphoses** (-ˌsiːz). **1** a complete change of physical form or substance. **2** a complete change of character, appearance, etc. **3** a person or thing that has undergone metamorphosis. **4** *Zool.* the rapid transformation of a larva into an adult that occurs in certain animals, for example the stage between chrysalis and butterfly. [C16: via L from Gk: transformation, from META- + *morphē* form]

metaphor ❶ ('mɛtəfə, -ˌfɔː) *n* a figure of speech in which a word or phrase is applied to an object or action that it does not literally denote in order to imply a resemblance, for example *he is a lion in battle.* Cf. **simile.** [C16: from L, from Gk *metaphora,* from *metapherein* to transfer, from META- + *pherein* to bear]
▸**metaphoric** (ˌmɛtə'fɒrɪk) *or* ˌ**meta'phorical** *adj* ▸ˌ**meta'phorically** *adv*

metaphrase ('mɛtəˌfreɪz) *n* **1** a literal translation. ◆ *vb* **metaphrases, metaphrasing, metaphrased.** (*tr*) **2** to alter or manipulate the wording of. **3** to translate literally. [C17: from Gk *metaphrazein* to translate]

metaphrast ('mɛtəˌfræst) *n* a person who metaphrases, esp. one who changes the form of a text, as by rendering verse into prose. [C17: from Med. Gk *metaphrastēs* translator]
▸ ˌ**meta'phrastic** *or* ˌ**meta'phrastical** *adj* ▸ˌ**meta'phrastically** *adv*

metaphysic (ˌmɛtə'fɪzɪk) *n* the system of first principles and assumptions underlying an inquiry or philosophical theory.

metaphysical ❶ (ˌmɛtə'fɪzɪkᵊl) *adj* **1** of or relating to metaphysics. **2** (of a statement or theory) having an empirical form but in fact immune from empirical testing. **3** (popularly) abstract, abstruse, or unduly theoretical. **4** incorporeal; supernatural.
▸ ˌ**meta'physically** *adv*

Metaphysical (ˌmɛtə'fɪzɪkᵊl) *adj* **1** denoting or relating to certain 17th-century poets who combined intense feeling with elaborate imagery. ◆ *n* **2** a poet of this group.

metaphysics (ˌmɛtə'fɪzɪks) *n* (*functioning as sing*) **1** the branch of philosophy that deals with first principles, esp. of being and knowing. **2** the philosophical study of the nature of reality. **3** (popularly) abstract or subtle discussion or reasoning. [C16: from Med. L, from Gk *ta meta ta phusika* the things after the physics, from the arrangement of subjects treated in the works of Aristotle]
▸**metaphysician** (ˌmɛtəfɪ'zɪʃən) *or* **metaphysicist** (ˌmɛtə'fɪzɪsɪst) *n*

metapsychology (ˌmɛtəsaɪ'kɒlədʒɪ) *n Psychol.* **1** the study of philosophical questions, such as the relation between mind and body, that go beyond the laws of experimental psychology. **2** any attempt to state the general laws of psychology. **3** another word for **parapsychology.**
▸**metapsychological** (ˌmɛtəˌsaɪkə'lɒdʒɪkᵊl) *adj*

metastable (ˌmɛtə'steɪbᵊl) *adj Physics.* (of a body or system) having a state of apparent equilibrium although capable of changing to a more stable state.
▸ ˌ**metasta'bility** *n*

metastasis (mɪ'tæstəsɪs) *n, pl* **metastases** (-ˌsiːz). *Pathol.* the spreading of a disease organism, esp. cancer cells, from one part of the body to another. [C16: via L from Gk: transition]
▸**metastatic** (ˌmɛtə'stætɪk) *adj* ▸ˌ**meta'statically** *adv*

metastasize *or* **metastasise** (mɪ'tæstəˌsaɪz) *vb* **metastasizes, metastasizing, metastasized** *or* **metastasises, metastasising, metastasised.** (*intr*) *Pathol.* (esp. of cancer cells) to spread to a new site in the body via blood or lymph vessels.

metatarsus (ˌmɛtə'tɑːsəs) *n, pl* **metatarsi** (-saɪ). **1** the skeleton of the human foot between the toes and the tarsus, consisting of five long bones. **2** the corresponding skeletal part in other vertebrates.
▸ ˌ**meta'tarsal** *adj, n*

metathesis (mɪ'tæθəsɪs) *n, pl* **metatheses** (-ˌsiːz). the transposition of two sounds or letters in a word. [C16: from LL, from Gk, from *metatithenai* to transpose]
▸**metathetic** (ˌmɛtə'θɛtɪk) *or* ˌ**meta'thetical** *adj*

metazoan (ˌmɛtə'zəʊən) *n* **1** any multicellular animal: includes all animals except sponges. ◆ *adj also* **metazoic. 2** of or relating to the metazoans. [C19: from NL *Metazoa;* see META-, -ZOA]

mete[1] ❶ (miːt) *vb* **metes, meting, meted.** (*tr*) **1** (usually foll. by *out*) *Formal.* to distribute or allot (something, often unpleasant). **2** *Poetic, dialect.* to measure. [OE *metan*]

mete[2] (miːt) *n Rare.* a mark, limit, or boundary (esp. in **metes and bounds**). [C15: from OF, from L *mēta* goal, turning post (in race)]

metempsychosis (ˌmɛtəmsaɪ'kəʊsɪs) *n, pl* **metempsychoses** (-siːz). the migration of a soul from one body to another. [C16: via LL from Gk, from *metempsukhousthai,* from META- + *-em-* in + *psukhē* soul]
▸ ˌ**metempsy'chosist** *n*

meteor ('miːtɪə) *n* **1** a very small meteoroid that has entered the earth's atmosphere. **2** Also called: **shooting star, falling star.** the bright streak of light appearing in the sky due to the incandescence of such a body heated by friction at its surface. [C15: from Med. L *meteōrum,* from Gk *meteōron,* from *meteōros* lofty, from *meta-* (intensifier) + *aeirein* to raise]

meteoric ❶ (ˌmiːtɪ'ɒrɪk) *adj* **1** of, formed by, or relating to meteors. **2**

THESAURUS

Antonyms *adj* clean, meticulous, neat, ordered, orderly, shipshape, smart, squeaky-clean, tidy

metamorphose *vb* = **transform,** alter, be reborn, change, convert, mutate, remake, remodel, reshape, transfigure, translate, transmogrify (*jocular*), transmute, transubstantiate

metamorphosis *n* **1, 2** = **transformation,** alteration, change, changeover, conversion, mutation, rebirth, transfiguration, translation, transmogrification (*jocular*), transmutation, transubstantiation

metaphor *n* = **figure of speech,** allegory, analogy, emblem, image, symbol, trope

metaphorical *adj* = **figurative,** allegorical, emblematic, emblematical, symbolic, tropical (*Rhetoric*)

metaphysical *adj* **1** = **philosophical,** basic, esoteric, essential, eternal, fundamental, general, ideal, intellectual, profound, speculative, spiritual, subjective, universal **3** = **abstract,** abstruse, deep, high-flown, oversubtle, recondite, theoretical, transcendental **4** = **supernatural,** immaterial, impalpable, incorporeal, intangible, spiritual, unreal, unsubstantial

mete[1] *vb* **1, 2** = **distribute,** administer, allot, apportion, assign, deal, dispense, divide, dole, measure, parcel, portion, ration, share

meteoric *adj* **2** = **spectacular,** brief, brilliant, dazzling, ephemeral, fast, flashing, fleeting,

like a meteor in brilliance, speed, or transience. **3** *Rare.* of weather; meteorological.
▸ˌ**mete'orically** *adv*
meteorism ('miːtɪəˌrɪzəm) *n Med.* another name for **tympanites.**
meteorite ('miːtɪəˌraɪt) *n* a rocklike object consisting of the remains of a meteoroid that has fallen on earth.
▸**meteoritic** (ˌmiːtɪə'rɪtɪk) *adj*
meteoroid ('miːtɪəˌrɔɪd) *n* any of the small celestial bodies that are thought to orbit the sun. When they enter the earth's atmosphere, they become visible as meteors.
▸ˌ**meteor'oidal** *adj*
meteorol. *or* **meteor.** *abbrev for:* **1** meteorological. **2** meteorology.
meteorology (ˌmiːtɪə'rɒlədʒɪ) *n* the study of the earth's atmosphere, esp. of weather-forming processes and weather forecasting. [C17: from Gk; see METEOR, -LOGY]
▸**meteorological** (ˌmiːtɪərə'lɒdʒɪkᵊl) *or* ˌ**meteoro'logic** *adj* ▸ˌ**meteoro'logically** *adv* ▸ˌ**meteor'ologist** *n*
meteor shower *n* a transient rain of meteors occurring at regular intervals and coming from a particular region in the sky.
meter[1] ('miːtə) *n* **1** any device that measures and records a quantity, such as of gas, current, voltage, etc., that has passed through it during a specified period. **2** See **parking meter.** ◆ *vb* (*tr*) **3** to measure (a rate of flow) with a meter. [C19: see METE[1]]
meter[2] ('miːtə) *n* the US spelling of **metre**[1].
meter[3] ('miːtə) *n* the US spelling of **metre**[2].
-meter *n combining form.* **1** indicating an instrument for measuring: *barometer.* **2** *Prosody.* indicating a verse having a specified number of feet: *pentameter.* [from Gk *metron* measure]
Meth. *abbrev. for* Methodist.
meth- *combining form.* indicating a chemical compound derived from methane or containing methyl groups: *methacrylic acid.*
methacrylic acid (ˌmɛθə'krɪlɪk) *n* a colourless crystalline water-soluble substance used in the manufacture of acrylic resins.
methadone ('mɛθəˌdəʊn) *or* **methadon** ('mɛθəˌdɒn) *n* a narcotic analgesic drug similar to morphine and formerly thought to be less habit-forming. [C20: from *(di)meth(yl)* + A(MINO) + *d(iphenyl)* + -ONE]
methamphetamine (ˌmɛθæm'fɛtəmiːn, -mɪn) *n* a variety of amphetamine used for its stimulant action. [C20: from METH- + AMPHETAMINE]
methanal ('mɛθəˌnæl) *n* the systematic name for **formaldehyde.**
methane ('miːθeɪn) *n* a colourless odourless flammable gas, the main constituent of natural gas: used as a fuel. Formula: CH_4.
methane series *n* another name for **alkane series.**
methanoic acid ('mɛθəˌnəʊɪk) *n* the systematic name for **formic acid.**
methanol ('mɛθəˌnɒl) *n* a colourless volatile poisonous liquid compound used as a solvent and fuel. Formula: CH_3OH. Also called: **methyl alcohol, wood alcohol.** [C20: from METHANE + -OL[1]]
methinks (mɪ'θɪŋks) *vb past* **methought.** (*tr; takes a clause as object*) *Arch.* it seems to me.
metho ('mɛθəʊ) *n Austral. inf.* **1** another name for **methylated spirits. 2** (*pl* **methos**) a drinker of methylated spirits.
method ➊ ('mɛθəd) *n* **1** a way of proceeding or doing something, esp. a systematic or regular one. **2** orderliness of thought, action, etc. **3** (*often pl*) the techniques or arrangement of work for a particular field or subject. [C16: via F from L, from Gk *methodos,* lit.: a going after, from *meta-* after + *hodos* way]
Method ('mɛθəd) *n* (*sometimes not cap.*) **a** a technique of acting in which the actor bases his role on the inner motivation of the character played. **b** (*as modifier*): *a Method actor.*
methodical ➊ (mɪ'θɒdɪkᵊl) *or* (*less commonly*) **methodic** *adj* characterized by method or orderliness; systematic.
▸**me'thodically** *adv*
Methodism ('mɛθəˌdɪzəm) *n* the system and practices of the Methodist Church.
Methodist ('mɛθədɪst) *n* **1** a member of any of the Nonconformist denominations that derive from the system of faith and practice initiated by John Wesley and his followers. ◆ *adj also* ˌ**Method'istic** *or* ˌ**Method'istical. 2** of or relating to Methodism or the Church embodying it (the **Methodist Church**).
methodize *or* **methodise** ('mɛθəˌdaɪz) *vb* **methodizes, methodizing, methodized** *or* **methodises, methodising, methodised.** (*tr*) to organize according to a method; systematize
▸'**methodˌizer** *or* '**methodˌiser** *n*
methodology (ˌmɛθə'dɒlədʒɪ) *n, pl* **methodologies. 1** the system of methods and principles used in a particular discipline. **2** the branch of philosophy concerned with the science of method.
▸**methodological** (ˌmɛθədə'lɒdʒɪkᵊl) *adj* ▸ˌ**methodo'logically** *adv* ▸ˌ**method'ologist** *n*
methought (mɪ'θɔːt) *vb Arch.* the past tense of **methinks.**
meths (mɛθs) *n Chiefly Brit., Austral., & NZ.* an informal name for **methylated spirits.**
methyl ('miːθaɪl, 'mɛθɪl) *n* **1** (*modifier*) of, consisting of, or containing the monovalent group of atoms CH_3. **2** a compound in which methyl groups are bound directly to a metal atom. [C19: from F *méthyle,* back formation from METHYLENE]
▸**methylic** (mə'θɪlɪk) *adj*
methyl acetate *n* a colourless volatile flammable liquid ester used as a solvent, esp. in paint removers. Formula: CH_3COOCH_3. Systematic name: **methyl ethanoate.**
methyl alcohol *n* another name for **methanol.**
methylate ('mɛθɪˌleɪt) *vb* **methylates, methylating, methylated.** (*tr*) to mix with methanol.
methylated spirits *n* (*functioning as sing or pl*) alcohol that has been denatured by the addition of methanol and pyridine and a violet dye. Also: **methylated spirit.**
methyl chloride *n* a colourless gas with an ether-like odour, used as a refrigerant and anaesthetic. Formula: CH_3Cl. Systematic name: **chloromethane.**
methylene ('mɛθɪˌliːn) *n* (*modifier*) of, consisting of, or containing the divalent group of atoms $=CH_2$: *a methylene group or radical.* [C19: from F *méthylène,* from Gk *methu* wine + *hulē* wood + -ENE: orig. referring to a substance distilled from wood]
methylene dichloride *n* the traditional name for **dichloromethane.**
methylphenol (ˌmiːθaɪl'fiːnɒl) *n* the systematic name for **cresol.**
meticulous ➊ (mɪ'tɪkjʊləs) *adj* very precise about details; painstaking. [C16 (meaning: timid): from L *meticulōsus* fearful, from *metus* fear]
▸**me'ticulously** *adv* ▸**me'ticulousness** *n*
métier ➊ ('mɛtɪeɪ) *n* **1** a profession or trade. **2** a person's strong point or speciality. [C18: from F, ult. from L *ministerium* service]
Métis (me'tiːs) *n, pl* **Métis** (-'tiːs, -'tiːz). a person of mixed parentage, esp. the offspring of a French Canadian and a North American Indian. [C19: from F, from Vulgar L *mixtīcius* (unattested) of mixed race]
▸**Métisse** (mɛ'tiːs) *fem n*
metol ('miːtɒl) *n* a colourless soluble organic substance used, in the form of its sulphate, as a photographic developer. [C20: from G, arbitrary coinage]
Metonic cycle (mɪ'tɒnɪk) *n* a cycle of 235 synodic months after which the phases of the moon recur on the same day of the month. [C17: after *Meton,* 5th-cent. B.C. Athenian astronomer]
metonymy (mɪ'tɒnɪmɪ) *n, pl* **metonymies.** the substitution of a word referring to an attribute for the thing that is meant, e.g. *the crown,* used to refer to a monarch. Cf. **synecdoche.** [C16: from LL, from Gk, from *meta-* (indicating change) + *onoma* name]
▸**metonymical** (ˌmɛtə'nɪmɪkᵊl) *or* ˌ**meto'nymic** *adj*
metope ('mɛtəʊp, 'mɛtəpɪ) *n Archit.* a square space between triglyphs in a Doric frieze. [C16: via L from Gk, from *meta* between + *opē* one of the holes for the beam-ends]
metre[1] *or US* **meter** ('miːtə) *n* **1** a metric unit of length equal to approximately 1.094 yards. **2** the basic SI unit of length; the length of the path travelled by light in free space during a time interval of 1/299 792 458 of a second. Symbol: m [C18: from F; see METRE[2]]
metre[2] *or US* **meter** ('miːtə) *n* **1** *Prosody.* the rhythmic arrangement of syllables in verse, usually according to the number and kind of feet in a line. **2** *Music.* another word (esp. US) for **time** (sense 22). [C14: from L *metrum,* from Gk *metron* measure]
metre-kilogram-second *n* See **mks units.**
metric ('mɛtrɪk) *adj* of or relating to the metre or metric system.
metrical ('mɛtrɪkᵊl) *or* **metric** *adj* **1** of or relating to measurement. **2** of or in poetic metre.
▸'**metrically** *adv*
metricate ('mɛtrɪˌkeɪt) *vb* **metricates, metricating, metricated.** to convert (a measuring system, instrument, etc.) from nonmetric to metric units.
▸ˌ**metri'cation** *n*
metric system *n* any decimal system of units based on the metre. For scientific purposes SI units are used.
metric ton *n* another name (not in technical use) for **tonne.**
metro ('mɛtrəʊ) *or* **métro** *French.* (metro) *n, pl* **metros.** an underground, or largely underground, railway system in certain cities, such as that in Paris. [C20: from F, *chemin de fer métropolitain* metropolitan railway]
Metro ('mɛtrəʊ) *n Canad.* a metropolitan city administration, esp. Metropolitan Toronto.
metronome ('mɛtrəˌnəʊm) *n* a device which indicates the tempo of music by producing a clicking sound from a pendulum with an adjustable period of swing. [C19: from Gk *metron* measure + *nomos* law]
▸**metronomic** (ˌmɛtrə'nɒmɪk) *adj*
metronymic (ˌmɛtrəʊ'nɪmɪk) *adj* **1** (of a name) derived from the name

THESAURUS

momentary, overnight, rapid, speedy, sudden, swift, transient
Antonyms *adj* gradual, lengthy, long, prolonged, slow, steady, unhurried
method *n* **1** = **manner,** approach, arrangement, course, fashion, form, mode, modus operandi, plan, practice, procedure, process, programme, routine, rule, scheme, style, system, technique, way **2** = **orderliness,** design, form, order, organization, pattern, planning, purpose, regularity, structure, system
methodical *adj* = **orderly,** businesslike, deliberate, disciplined, efficient, meticulous, neat, ordered, organized, painstaking, planned, precise, regular, structured, systematic, tidy, well-regulated
Antonyms *adj* casual, chaotic, confused, disordered, disorderly, haphazard, irregular, random, unmethodical
meticulous *adj* = **thorough,** detailed, exact, fastidious, fussy, microscopic, painstaking, particular, perfectionist, precise, punctilious, scrupulous, strict
Antonyms *adj* careless, haphazard, imprecise, inexact, loose, negligent, slapdash, sloppy
métier *n* **1** = **profession,** calling, craft, line, occupation, pursuit, trade, vocation **2** = **strong point,** forte, long suit (*inf.*), speciality, specialty, strong suit

of the mother or other female ancestor. ◆ *n* **2** a metronymic name. [C19: from Gk *mētronumikos*, from *mētēr* mother + *onoma* name]

metropolis ❶ (mɪˈtrɒpəlɪs) *n, pl* **metropolises. 1** the main city, esp. of a country or region. **2** a centre of activity. **3** the chief see in an ecclesiastical province. [C16: from LL from Gk, from *mētēr* mother + *polis* city]

metropolitan (ˌmɛtrəˈpɒlɪtən) *adj* **1** of or characteristic of a metropolis. **2** constituting a city and its suburbs. **3** of, relating to, or designating an ecclesiastical metropolis. **4** of or belonging to the home territories of a country, as opposed to overseas territories: *metropolitan France*. ◆ *n* **5a** *Eastern Churches.* the head of an ecclesiastical province, ranking between archbishop and patriarch. **5b** *Church of England.* an archbishop. **5c** *RC Church.* an archbishop or bishop having authority over the dioceses in his province.
▸ˌ**metroˈpolitanism** *n*

metropolitan county *n* (in England) any of the six conurbations established as units in the new local government system in 1974; the metropolitan county councils were abolished in 1986.

metropolitan district *n* (in England since 1974) any of the districts that make up the metropolitan counties of England: since 1986 they have functioned as unitary authorities.

metrorrhagia (ˌmiːtrɔːˈreɪdʒɪə, ˌmɛt-) *n* abnormal bleeding from the uterus. [C19: NL, from Gk *mētra* womb + *-rrhagia* a breaking forth]

-metry *n combining form.* indicating the process or science of measuring: *geometry*. [from OF *-metrie*, from L, ult. from Gk *metron* measure]
▸**-metric** *adj combining form.*

mettle ❶ (ˈmɛtəl) *n* **1** courage; spirit. **2** character. **3 on one's mettle.** roused to making one's best efforts. [C16: orig. var. of METAL]

mettled (ˈmɛtəld) *or* **mettlesome** (ˈmɛtəlsəm) *adj* courageous, spirited, or valiant.

MeV *symbol for* million electronvolts (10^6 electronvolts).

mevrou (məˈfrəʊ) *n* a S. African title of address equivalent to *Mrs* when placed before a surname or *madam* when used alone. [Afrik.]

mew[1] (mjuː) *vb* **1** (*intr*) (esp. of a cat) to make a characteristic high-pitched cry. ◆ *n* **2** such a sound. [C14: imit.]

mew[2] (mjuː) *n* any seagull, esp. the common gull. [OE *mǣw*]

mew[3] (mjuː) *n* **1** a room or cage for hawks, esp. while moulting. ◆ *vb* (*tr*) **2** (often foll. by *up*) to confine (hawks or falcons) in a shelter, cage, etc. **3** to confine; conceal. [C14: from OF *mue*, from *muer* to moult, from L *mūtāre* to change]

mewl ❶ (mjuːl) *vb* **1** (*intr*) (esp. of a baby) to cry weakly; whimper. ◆ *n* **2** such a cry. [C17: imit.]

mews (mjuːz) *n* (*functioning as sing or pl*) *Chiefly Brit.* **1** a yard or street lined by buildings originally used as stables but now often converted into dwellings. **2** the buildings around a mews. [C14: pl of MEW[3], orig. referring to royal stables built on the site of hawks' mews at Charing Cross in London]

Mex. *abbrev. for:* **1** Mexican. **2** Mexico.

Mexican (ˈmɛksɪkən) *adj* **1** of or relating to Mexico, in Central America. ◆ *n* **2** a native or inhabitant of Mexico or a descendant of one.

Mexican wave *n* the rippling effect produced when the spectators in successive sections of a sports stadium stand up while raising their arms and then sit down. [C20: first seen at the World Cup in Mexico in 1986]

MEZ *abbrev. for* Central European Time. [from G *Mitteleuropäische Zeit*]

mezcal (mɛˈskæl) *n* a variant spelling of **mescal.**

mezcaline (ˈmɛskəˌliːn) *n* a variant spelling of **mescaline.**

mezuzah (məˈzuːzə) *n, pl* **mezuzahs** *or* **mezuzoth** (*Hebrew* məzuˈzɔt). *Judaism.* **1** a piece of parchment inscribed with biblical passages and fixed to the doorpost of a Jewish house. **2** a metal case for such a parchment, sometimes worn as an ornament. [from Heb., lit.: doorpost]

mezzanine (ˈmɛzəˌniːn, ˈmɛtsəˌniːn) *n* **1** Also called: **mezzanine floor.** an intermediate storey, esp. a low one between the ground and first floor of a building. **2** *Theatre, US & Canad.* the first balcony. **3** *Theatre, Brit.* a room or floor beneath the stage. ◆ *adj* **4** often shortened to **mezz.** of or relating to an intermediate stage in a financial process: *mezzanine funding*. [C18: from F, from It., dim. of *mezzano* middle, from L *mediānus* MEDIAN]

mezzo (ˈmɛtsəʊ) *adv Music.* moderately; quite: *mezzo piano*. [C19: from It., lit.: half, from L *medius* middle]

mezzo-soprano *n, pl* **mezzo-sopranos. 1** a female voice intermediate between a soprano and contralto. **2** a singer with such a voice.

mezzotint (ˈmɛtsəʊˌtɪnt) *n* **1** a method of engraving a copper plate by scraping and burnishing the roughened surface. **2** a print made from a plate so treated. ◆ *vb* **3** (*tr*) to engrave (a copper plate) in this fashion. [C18: from It. *mezzotinto* half tint]

mf *Music. symbol for* mezzo forte. [It.: moderately loud]

MF *abbrev. for:* **1** *Radio.* medium frequency. **2** Middle French.

mfd *abbrev. for* manufactured.

mfg *abbrev. for* manufacturing.

MFH *Hunting. abbrev. for* Master of Foxhounds.

mfr *abbrev. for:* **1** manufacture. **2** manufacturer.

mg *symbol for* milligram.

Mg *the chemical symbol for* magnesium.

M. Glam *abbrev. for* Mid Glamorgan.

Mgr *abbrev. for:* **1** manager. **2** Monseigneur. **3** Monsignor.

MHA (in Australia) *abbrev. for* Member of the House of Assembly.

MHG *abbrev. for* Middle High German.

mho (məʊ) *n, pl* **mhos.** the former name for **siemens.** [C19: formed by reversing the letters of OHM (first used by Lord Kelvin)]

MHR (in the US and Australia) *abbrev. for* Member of the House of Representatives.

MHz *symbol for* megahertz.

mi (miː) *n Music.* **1** the syllable used in the fixed system of solmization for the note E. **2** Also: **me.** (in tonic sol-fa) the third degree of any major scale; a mediant. [C14: see GAMUT]

MI *abbrev. for:* **1** Michigan. **2** Military Intelligence.

mi. *abbrev. for* mile.

MI5 *abbrev. for* Military Intelligence, section five; a former official and current popular name for the counterintelligence agency of the British Government.

MI6 *abbrev. for* Military Intelligence, section six; a former official and current popular name for the intelligence and espionage agency of the British Government.

miaou *or* **miaow** (mɪˈaʊ, mjaʊ) *vb, interj* variant spellings of **meow.**

miasma (mɪˈæzmə) *n, pl* **miasmata** (-mətə) *or* **miasmas. 1** an unwholesome or foreboding atmosphere. **2** pollution in the atmosphere, esp. noxious vapours from decomposing organic matter. [C17: NL, from Gk: defilement, from *miainein* to defile]
▸**miˈasmal** *or* **miasmatic** (ˌmiːəzˈmætɪk) *adj*

Mic. *Bible. abbrev. for* Micah.

mica (ˈmaɪkə) *n* any of a group of minerals consisting of hydrous silicates of aluminium, potassium, etc., in monoclinic crystalline form, occurring in igneous and metamorphic rock. Because of their resistance to electricity and heat they are used as dielectrics, in heating elements, etc. Also called: **isinglass.** [C18: from L: crumb]
▸**micaceous** (maɪˈkeɪʃəs) *adj*

mice (maɪs) *n* the plural of **mouse.**

micelle, micell (mɪˈsɛl), *or* **micella** (mɪˈsɛlə) *n Chem.* **a** a charged aggregate of molecules of colloidal size in a solution. **b** any molecular aggregate of colloidal size. [C19: from NL *micella*, dim. of L *mīca* crumb]

Mich. *abbrev. for:* **1** Michaelmas. **2** Michigan.

Michaelmas (ˈmɪkəlməs) *n* Sept. 29, the feast of St Michael the archangel; in England, Ireland, and Wales, one of the four quarter days.

Michaelmas daisy *n Brit.* any of various composite plants that have small autumn-blooming purple, pink, or white flowers.

Michaelmas term *n* the autumn term at Oxford and Cambridge Universities, the Inns of Court, and some other educational establishments.

Mick (mɪk) *n* (*sometimes not cap.*) **1** Also: **Mickey.** *Derog.* a slang name for an **Irishman** or a **Roman Catholic. 2** *Austral.* the tails side of a coin. [C19: from nickname for *Michael*]

mickey *or* **micky** (ˈmɪkɪ) *n Inf.* **take the mickey (out of).** to tease. [C20: from ?]

Mickey Finn *n Sl.* **a** a drink containing a drug to make the drinker unconscious. **b** the drug itself. ◆ Often shortened to **Mickey.** [C20: from ?]

mickle (ˈmɪkəl) *or* **muckle** (ˈmʌkəl) *Arch. or Scot. & N English dialect.* ◆ *adj* **1** great or abundant. ◆ *adv* **2** much; greatly. ◆ *n* **3** a great amount, esp. in the proverb, *many a little makes a mickle*. **4** *Scot.* a small amount, esp. in the proverb *mony a mickle makes a muckle*. [C13 *mikel*, from ON *mikell*, replacing OE *micel* MUCH]

micro (ˈmaɪkrəʊ) *adj* **1** very small. ◆ *n, pl* **micros. 2** short for **microcomputer, microprocessor, microwave oven.**

micro- *or* **micr-** *combining form.* **1** small or minute: *microdot*. **2** involving the use of a microscope: *microscopy*. **3** indicating a method or instrument for dealing with small quantities: *micrometer*. **4** (in pathology) indicating abnormal smallness or underdevelopment: *microcephaly*. **5** denoting 10^{-6}: *microsecond*. Symbol: μ [from Gk *mikros* small]

microbe ❶ (ˈmaɪkrəʊb) *n* any microscopic organism, esp. a disease-causing bacterium. [C19: from F, from MICRO- + Gk *bios* life]
▸**miˈcrobial** *or* **miˈcrobic** *adj*

microbiology (ˌmaɪkrəʊbaɪˈɒlədʒɪ) *n* the branch of biology involving the study of microorganisms.
▸**microbiological** (ˌmaɪkrəʊˌbaɪəˈlɒdʒɪkəl) *or* ˌ**microˌbioˈlogic** *adj*
▸ˌ**microˌbioˈlogically** *adv* ▸ˌ**microbiˈologist** *n*

microcephaly (ˌmaɪkrəʊˈsɛfəlɪ) *n* the condition of having an abnormally small head or cranial capacity.
▸**microcephalic** (ˌmaɪkrəʊsɪˈfælɪk) *adj, n* ▸ˌ**microˈcephalous** *adj*

microchemistry (ˌmaɪkrəʊˈkɛmɪstrɪ) *n* chemical experimentation with minute quantities of material.
▸ˌ**microˈchemical** *adj*

microchip (ˈmaɪkrəʊˌtʃɪp) *n* another word for **chip** (sense 7).

microcircuit (ˈmaɪkrəʊˌsɜːkɪt) *n* a miniature electronic circuit, esp. one in which a number of permanently connected components are contained in one small chip of semiconducting material. See **integrated circuit.**
▸ˌ**microˈcircuitry** *n*

microclimate (ˈmaɪkrəʊˌklaɪmɪt) *n Ecology.* the atmospheric conditions affecting an individual or a small group of organisms, esp. when they differ from the climate of the rest of the community.

THESAURUS

metropolis *n* **1** = **city**, capital

mettle *n* **1** = **courage**, ardour, boldness, bravery, daring, fire, fortitude, gallantry, gameness, grit, guts (*inf.*), hardihood, heart, indomitability, life, nerve, pluck, resolution, resolve, spirit, spunk (*inf.*), valour, vigour **2** = **character**, calibre, disposition, kidney, make-up, nature, quality, stamp, temper, temperament

mewl *vb* **1** = **whimper**, blubber, cry, grizzle (*inf., chiefly Brit.*), pule, snivel, whine, whinge (*inf.*)

microbe *n* = **microorganism**, bacillus, bacterium, bug (*inf.*), germ, virus

▸**microclimatic** (ˌmaɪkrəʊklaɪˈmætɪk) *adj* ▸ˌ**microˌclimaˈtology** *n*

microcomputer (ˌmaɪkrəʊkəmˈpjuːtə) *n* a computer in which the central processing unit is contained in one or more silicon chips.

microcosm (ˈmaɪkrəʊˌkɒzəm) *or* **microcosmos** (ˌmaɪkrəʊˈkɒzmɒs) *n* **1** a miniature representation of something. **2** man regarded as epitomizing the universe. ◆ Cf. **macrocosm.** [C15: via Med. L from Gk *mikros kosmos* little world]
▸ˌ**microˈcosmic** *or* ˌ**microˈcosmical** *adj*

microdot (ˈmaɪkrəʊˌdɒt) *n* **1** a greatly reduced photographic copy (about the size of a pinhead) of a document, etc., used esp. in espionage. **2** a tiny tablet containing LSD.

microeconomics (ˌmaɪkrəʊˌiːkəˈnɒmɪks, -ˌɛkə-) *n* (*functioning as sing*) the branch of economics concerned with particular commodities, firms, or individuals and the economic relationships between them.
▸ˌ**microˌecoˈnomic** *adj*

microelectronics (ˌmaɪkrəʊɪlɛkˈtrɒnɪks) *n* (*functioning as sing*) the branch of electronics concerned with microcircuits.

microfiche (ˈmaɪkrəʊˌfiːʃ) *n* a sheet of film, usually the size of a filing card, on which books, newspapers, documents, etc., can be recorded in miniaturized form. [C20: from F, from MICRO- + *fiche* small card]

microfilm (ˈmaɪkrəʊˌfɪlm) *n* **1** a strip of film on which books, documents, etc., can be recorded in miniaturized form. ◆ *vb* **2** to photograph (a page, document, etc.) on microfilm.

microgravity (ˈmaɪkrəʊˌɡrævɪtɪ) *n* gravitational effects operating, or apparently operating, in a localized region, as in a spacecraft under conditions of weightlessness.

microhabitat (ˌmaɪkrəʊˈhæbɪtæt) *n Ecology.* the smallest part of the environment that supports a distinct flora and fauna, such as a fallen log in a forest.

microlight *or* **microlite** (ˈmaɪkrəʊˌlaɪt) *n* a small private aircraft carrying no more than two people, with a wing area not less than 10 square metres: used in pleasure flying and racing.

microlith (ˈmaɪkrəʊˌlɪθ) *n Archaeol.* a small Mesolithic flint tool which formed part of a hafted tool.
▸ˌ**microˈlithic** *adj*

micrometer (maɪˈkrɒmɪtə) *n* **1** any of various instruments or devices for the accurate measurement of distances or angles. **2** Also called: **micrometer gauge, micrometer calliper.** a type of gauge for the accurate measurement of small distances, thicknesses, etc. The gap between its measuring faces is adjusted by a fine screw (**micrometer screw**).
▸**micrometric** (ˌmaɪkrəʊˈmɛtrɪk) *or* ˌ**microˈmetrical** *adj* ▸**miˈcrometry** *n*

microminiaturization *or* **microminiaturisation** (ˌmaɪkrəʊˌmɪnɪtʃəraɪˈzeɪʃən) *n* the production and application of very small components and the circuits and equipment in which they are used.

micron (ˈmaɪkrɒn) *n, pl* **microns** *or* **micra** (-krə). a unit of length equal to 10^{-6} metre. It is being replaced by the micrometre, the equivalent SI unit. [C19: NL, from Gk *mikros* small]

Micronesian (ˌmaɪkrəʊˈniːʒən, -ʒɪən) *adj* **1** of or relating to Micronesia (a division of islands in the Pacific), its inhabitants, or their languages. ◆ *n* **2** a native or inhabitant of Micronesia or a descendant of one. **3** a group of languages spoken in Micronesia.

microorganism (ˌmaɪkrəʊˈɔːɡəˌnɪzəm) *n* any organism, such as a bacterium, of microscopic size.

microphone (ˈmaɪkrəˌfəʊn) *n* a device used in sound-reproduction systems for converting sound into electrical energy.
▸**microphonic** (ˌmaɪkrəˈfɒnɪk) *adj*

microprint (ˈmaɪkrəʊˌprɪnt) *n* a greatly reduced photographic copy of print, read by a magnifying device. It is used in order to reduce the size of large books, etc.

microprocessor (ˌmaɪkrəʊˈprəʊsɛsə) *n Computing.* a single integrated circuit performing the basic functions of the central processing unit in a small computer.

microscope (ˈmaɪkrəˌskəʊp) *n* **1** an optical instrument that uses a lens or combination of lenses to produce a magnified image of a small, close object. **2** any instrument, such as the electron microscope, for producing a magnified visual image of a small object.

microscopic ❶ (ˌmaɪkrəˈskɒpɪk) *or* (*less commonly*) **microscopical** *adj* **1** not large enough to be seen with the naked eye but visible under a microscope. **2** very small; minute. **3** of, concerned with, or using a microscope.
▸ˌ**microˈscopically** *adv*

microscopy (maɪˈkrɒskəpɪ) *n* **1** the study, design, and manufacture of microscopes. **2** investigation by use of a microscope.
▸**microscopist** (maɪˈkrɒskəpɪst) *n*

microsecond (ˈmaɪkrəʊˌsɛkənd) *n* one millionth of a second.

microstructure (ˈmaɪkrəʊˌstrʌktʃə) *n* structure on a microscopic scale, esp. the structure of an alloy as observed by etching, polishing, and observation under a microscope.

microsurgery (ˌmaɪkrəʊˈsɜːdʒərɪ) *n* intricate surgery performed on cells, tissues, etc., using a specially designed operating microscope and miniature precision instruments.

microswitch (ˈmaɪkrəʊˌswɪtʃ) *n Electrical engineering.* a switch that operates by small movements of a lever.

microtome (ˈmaɪkrəʊˌtəʊm) *n* an instrument used for cutting thin sections for microscopical examination.
▸**microtomy** (maɪˈkrɒtəmɪ) *n*

microwave (ˈmaɪkrəʊˌweɪv) *n* **1a** electromagnetic radiation in the wavelength range 0.3 to 0.001 metres: used in radar, cooking, etc. **1b** (*as modifier*): *microwave oven.* **2** short for **microwave oven.** ◆ *vb* **microwaves, microwaving, microwaved.** (*tr*) **3** to cook in a microwave oven.

microwave background *n* a background of microwave electromagnetic radiation discovered in space in 1965, believed to have emanated from the big bang with which the universe began.

microwave detector *n NZ.* a device for recording the speed of a motorist.

microwave oven *n* an oven in which food is cooked by microwaves. Often shortened to **micro, microwave.**

microwave spectroscopy *n* a type of spectroscopy in which information is obtained on the structure and chemical bonding of molecules and crystals by measurements of the wavelengths of microwaves emitted or absorbed by the sample.
▸**microwave spectroscope** *n*

micturate (ˈmɪktjʊˌreɪt) *vb* **micturates, micturating, micturated.** (*intr*) a less common word for **urinate.** [C19: from L *micturīre* to desire to urinate, from *mingere* to urinate]
▸**micturition** (ˌmɪktjʊˈrɪʃən) *n*

mid[1] (mɪd) *adj* **1** *Phonetics.* of, relating to, or denoting a vowel whose articulation lies approximately halfway between high and low, such as *e* in English *bet.* ◆ *n* **2** an archaic word for **middle.** [C12 *midre* (inflected form of *midd,* unattested)]

mid[2] *or* **'mid** (mɪd) *prep* a poetic word for **amid.**

mid- *combining form.* indicating a middle part, point, time, or position: *midday; mid-April; mid-Victorian.* [OE; see MIDDLE, MID[1]]

midair (ˌmɪdˈɛə) *n* **a** some point above ground level, in the air. **b** (*as modifier*): *a midair collision of aircraft.*

mid-Atlantic *adj* characterized by a blend of British and American styles, elements, etc.: *a mid-Atlantic accent.*

midbrain (ˈmɪdˌbreɪn) *n* the nontechnical name for **mesencephalon.**

midday ❶ (ˈmɪdˈdeɪ) *n* **a** the middle of the day; noon. **b** (*as modifier*): *a midday meal.*

middelskot (ˈmɪdəlˌskɒt) *n* (in South Africa) an intermediate payment to a farmers' cooperative for a crop or wool clip. [from Afrik. *middel* middle + *skot* payment]

midden (ˈmɪdən) *n* **1a** *Arch. or dialect.* a dunghill or pile of refuse. **1b** *Dialect.* a dustbin. **2** See **kitchen midden.** [C14: from ON]

middle ❶ (ˈmɪdəl) *adj* **1** equally distant from the ends or periphery of something; central. **2** intermediate in status, situation, etc. **3** located between the early and late parts of a series, time sequence, etc. **4** not extreme, esp. in size; medium. **5** (esp. in Greek and Sanskrit grammar) denoting a voice of verbs expressing reciprocal or reflexive action. **6** (*usually cap.*) (of a language) intermediate between the earliest and the modern forms. ◆ *n* **7** an area or point equal in distance from the ends or periphery or in time between the early and late parts. **8** an intermediate part or section, such as the waist. **9** *Grammar.* the middle voice. **10** *Logic.* See **middle term. 11** *Cricket.* a position on the batting crease in alignment with the middle stumps on which a batsman may take guard. ◆ *vb* **middles, middling, middled.** (*tr*) **12** to place in the middle. **13** *Naut.* to fold in two. **14** *Cricket.* to hit (the ball) with the middle of the bat. [OE *middel*]

middle age *n* the period of life between youth and old age, usually (in man) considered to occur approximately between the ages of 40 and 60.
▸ˌ**middle-ˈaged** *adj*

Middle Ages *n* **the.** *European history.* **1** (broadly) the period from the deposition of the last W Roman emperor in 476 A.D. to the Italian Renaissance (or the fall of Constantinople in 1453). **2** (narrowly) the period from about 1000 A.D. to the 15th century. Cf. **Dark Ages.**

Middle America *n* **1** the territories between the US and South America: Mexico, Central America, and the Antilles. **2** the US middle class, esp. those groups that are politically conservative.
▸**Middle American** *adj, n*

middle-and-leg *n Cricket.* a position on the batting crease in alignment with the middle and leg stumps on which a batsman may take guard.

middle-and-off *n Cricket.* a position on the batting crease in alignment with the middle and off stumps on which a batsman may take guard.

middlebrow (ˈmɪdəlˌbraʊ) *Disparaging.* ◆ *n* **1** a person with conventional tastes and limited cultural appreciation. ◆ *adj also* **middlebrowed. 2** of or appealing to middlebrows.

middle C *n Music.* the note written on the first ledger line below the treble staff or the first ledger line above the bass staff.

middle class ❶ *n* **1** Also called: **bourgeoisie.** a social stratum between the lower and upper classes. It consists of businessmen, professional people, etc., along with their families, and is marked by bourgeois values. ◆ *adj* **middle-class. 2** of, relating to, or characteristic of the middle class.

THESAURUS

microscopic *adj* **2** = **tiny,** imperceptible, infinitesimal, invisible, minuscule, minute, negligible, teensy-weensy, teeny-weeny
Antonyms *adj* enormous, gigantic, ginormous (*inf.*), great, huge, immense, large, vast

midday *n* = **noon,** noonday, noontide, noontime, twelve noon, twelve o'clock

middle *adj* **1-4** = **central,** halfway, inner, inside, intermediate, intervening, mean, medial, median, medium, mid ◆ *n* **7** = **centre,** focus, halfway point, heart, mean, midpoint, mid-section, midst, thick **8** = **waist,** midriff, midsection

middle class *adj* **middle-class 2** = **bourgeois,** conventional, petit-bourgeois, suburban, traditional

middle ear *n* the sound-conducting part of the ear, containing the malleus, incus, and stapes.

Middle East *n* **1** (loosely) the area around the E Mediterranean, esp. Israel and the Arab countries from Turkey to North Africa and eastwards to Iran. **2** (formerly) the area extending from the Tigris and Euphrates to Myanmar.
▸**Middle Eastern** *adj*

Middle England *n* a characterization of a predominantly middle-class, middle-income section of British society living mainly in suburban and rural England.

Middle English *n* the English language from about 1100 to about 1450.

middle game *n Chess.* the central phase between the opening and the endgame.

Middle High German *n* High German from about 1200 to about 1500.

Middle Low German *n* Low German from about 1200 to about 1500.

middleman ❶ (ˈmɪdᵊlˌmæn) *n, pl* **middlemen. 1** a trader engaged in the distribution of goods from producer to consumer. **2** an intermediary.

middlemost (ˈmɪdᵊlˌməʊst) *adj* another word for **midmost.**

middle name *n* **1** a name between a person's first name and surname. **2** a characteristic quality for which a person is known: *caution is my middle name.*

middle-of-the-road *adj* **1** not extreme, esp. in political views; moderate. **2** of, denoting, or relating to popular music having a wide general appeal.

middle passage *n* **the.** *History.* the journey across the Atlantic Ocean from the W coast of Africa to the Caribbean: the longest part of the journey of the slave ships.

middle school *n* (in England and Wales) a school for children aged between 8 or 9 and 12 or 13.

middle term *n Logic.* the term that appears in both minor and major premises but not in the conclusion of a syllogism.

middle watch *n Naut.* the watch between midnight and 4 a.m.

middleweight (ˈmɪdᵊlˌweɪt) *n* **1a** a professional boxer weighing 154–160 pounds (70–72.5 kg). **1b** an amateur boxer weighing 71–75 kg (157–165 pounds). **2a** a professional wrestler weighing 166–176 pounds (76–80 kg). **2b** an amateur wrestler weighing 75–82 kg (162–180 pounds).

Middle West *n* another name for the **Midwest.**
▸**Middle Western** *adj* ▸**Middle Westerner** *n*

middling ❶ (ˈmɪdlɪŋ) *adj* **1** mediocre in quality, size, etc.; neither good nor bad, esp. in health (often in **fair to middling**). ◆ *adv* **2** *Inf.* moderately: *middling well.* [C15 (N English & Scot.): from MID[1] + -LING[2]]
▸ˈ**middlingly** *adv*

Middx. *abbrev. for* Middlesex.

middy (ˈmɪdɪ) *n, pl* **middies. 1** *Inf.* short for **midshipman. 2** *Austral.* **2a** a glass of middling size, used for beer. **2b** the measure of beer it contains.

midfield (ˌmɪdˈfiːld) *n Soccer.* **a** the general area between the two opposing defences. **b** (*as modifier*): *a midfield player.*

midge (mɪdʒ) *n* **1** a mosquito-like dipterous insect occurring in dancing swarms, esp. near water. **2** a small or diminutive person or animal. [OE *mycge*]
▸ˈ**midgy** *adj*

midget ❶ (ˈmɪdʒɪt) *n* **1** a dwarf whose skeleton and features are of normal proportions. **2a** something small of its kind. **2b** (*as modifier*): *a midget car.* [C19: from MIDGE + -ET]

midgut (ˈmɪdˌgʌt) *n* **1** the middle part of the digestive tract of vertebrates, including the small intestine. **2** the middle part of the digestive tract of arthropods.

mid-heavyweight *n* **a** a professional wrestler weighing 199–209 pounds (91–95 kg). **b** an amateur wrestler weighing 91–100 kg (199–220 pounds).

midi (ˈmɪdɪ) *adj* (formerly) **a** (of a skirt, coat, etc.) reaching to below the knee or midcalf. **b** (*as n*): *she wore her new midi.* [C20: from MID-, on the model of MINI]

MIDI (ˈmɪdɪ) *n* (*modifier*) a generally accepted specification for the external control of electronic musical instruments: *a MIDI synthesizer; a MIDI system.* [C20: from *m(usical) i(nstrument) d(igital) i(nterface)*]

midi- *combining form.* of medium or middle size, length, etc.: *midibus; midi system.*

midinette (ˌmɪdɪˈnɛt) *n* a Parisian seamstress or salesgirl in a clothes shop. [C20: from F, from *midi* noon + *dinette* light meal; the girls had time for only a snack at midday]

midiron (ˈmɪdˌaɪən) *n Golf.* a club, usually a No. 5, 6, or 7 iron, used for medium-length approach shots.

midi system *n* a complete set of hi-fi sound equipment designed as a single unit that is more compact than the standard equipment.

midland (ˈmɪdlənd) *n* **a** the central or inland part of a country. **b** (*as modifier*): *a midland region.*

Midlands (ˈmɪdləndz) *n* (*functioning as pl or sing*) **the.** the central counties of England: characterized by manufacturing industries.
▸ˈ**Midlander** *n*

midlife crisis *n* a crisis that may be experienced in middle age involving frustration, panic, and feelings of pointlessness, sometimes resulting in radical and often ill-advised changes of lifestyle.

midmost (ˈmɪdˌməʊst) *adj, adv* in the middle or midst.

midnight ❶ (ˈmɪdˌnaɪt) *n* **1a** the middle of the night; 12 o'clock at night. **1b** (*as modifier*): *the midnight hour.* **2 burn the midnight oil.** to work or study late into the night.

midnight sun *n* the sun visible at midnight during the summer inside the Arctic and Antarctic circles.

mid-off *n Cricket.* the fielding position on the off side closest to the bowler.

mid-on *n Cricket.* the fielding position on the on side closest to the bowler.

midpoint (ˈmɪdˌpɔɪnt) *n* **1** the point on a line that is at an equal distance from either end. **2** a point in time halfway between the beginning and end of an event.

midrib (ˈmɪdˌrɪb) *n* the main vein of a leaf, running down the centre of the blade.

midriff (ˈmɪdrɪf) *n* **1a** the middle part of the human body, esp. between waist and bust. **1b** (*as modifier*): *midriff bulge.* **2** *Anat.* another name for the **diaphragm** (sense 1). **3** the part of a woman's garment covering the midriff. [OE *midhrif,* from MID[1] + *hrif* belly]

midship (ˈmɪdˌʃɪp) *Naut.* ◆ *adj* **1** in, of, or relating to the middle of a vessel. ◆ *n* **2** the middle of a vessel.

midshipman (ˈmɪdˌʃɪpmən) *n, pl* **midshipmen.** a probationary rank held by young naval officers under training, or an officer holding such a rank.

midships (ˈmɪdˌʃɪps) *adv, adj Naut.* See **amidships.**

midst[1] ❶ (mɪdst) *n* **1 in our midst.** among us. **2 in the midst of.** surrounded or enveloped by; at a point during. [C14: back formation from *amiddes* AMID]

midst[2] (mɪdst) *prep Poetic.* See **amid.**

midsummer (ˈmɪdˈsʌmə) *n* **1a** the middle or height of the summer. **1b** (*as modifier*): *a midsummer carnival.* **2** another name for **summer solstice.**

Midsummer's Day *or* **Midsummer Day** *n* June 24, the feast of St John the Baptist; in England, Ireland, and Wales, one of the four quarter days. See also **summer solstice.**

midterm (ˈmɪdˈtɜːm) *n* **1a** the middle of a term in a school, university, etc. **1b** (*as modifier*): *midterm exam.* **2** *US politics.* **2a** the middle of a term of office, esp. of a presidential term, when congressional and local elections are held. **2b** (*as modifier*): *midterm elections.* **3a** the middle of the gestation period. **3b** (*as modifier*): *midterm pregnancy.* See **term** (sense 6).

mid-Victorian *adj* **1** *Brit. history.* of or relating to the middle period of the reign of Queen Victoria (1837–1901). ◆ *n* **2** a person of the mid-Victorian era.

midway ❶ (ˈmɪdˌweɪ *or, for adv, n* ˌmɪdˈweɪ) *adj* **1** in or at the middle of the distance; halfway. ◆ *adv* **2** to the middle of the distance. ◆ *n* **3** *Obs.* a middle place, way, etc.

midweek (ˈmɪdˈwiːk) *n* **a** the middle of the week. **b** (*as modifier*): *a midweek holiday.*

Midwest (ˈmɪdˈwɛst) *or* **Middle West** *n* the N central part of the US; the states from Ohio westwards that border on the Great Lakes, and often the upper Mississippi and Missouri valleys.
▸ˈ**Midˈwestern** *adj* ▸ˈ**Midˈwesterner** *n*

mid-wicket *n Cricket.* the fielding position on the on side, midway between square leg and mid-on.

midwife (ˈmɪdˌwaɪf) *n, pl* **midwives** (-ˌwaɪvz). a person qualified to deliver babies and to care for women before, during, and after childbirth. [C14: from OE *mid* with + *wif* woman]

midwifery (ˈmɪdˌwɪfərɪ) *n* the training, art, or practice of a midwife; obstetrics.

midwinter (ˈmɪdˈwɪntə) *n* **1a** the middle or depth of the winter. **1b** (*as modifier*): *a midwinter festival.* **2** another name for **winter solstice.**

midyear (ˈmɪdˈjɪə) *n* the middle of the year.

mien ❶ (miːn) *n Literary.* a person's manner, bearing, or appearance. [C16: prob. var. of obs. *demean* appearance; rel. to F *mine* aspect]

mifepristone (mɪˈfɛprɪˌstəʊn) *n* See **abortion pill.**

miff ❶ (mɪf) *Inf.* ◆ *vb* **1** to take offence or to offend. ◆ *n* **2** a petulant mood. **3** a petty quarrel. [C17: ? an imitative expression of bad temper]
▸ˈ**miffy** *adj*

might[1] (maɪt) *vb* (takes an implied infinitive or an infinitive without *to*) used as an auxiliary: **1** making the past tense or subjunctive mood

THESAURUS

middleman *n* **1, 2** = **intermediary**, broker, distributor, entrepreneur, go-between

middling *adj* **1** = **mediocre**, indifferent, run-of-the-mill, so-so (*inf.*), tolerable, unexceptional, unremarkable **1** = **moderate**, adequate, all right, average, bog-standard (*Brit. & Irish sl.*), fair, medium, modest, O.K. *or* okay (*inf.*), ordinary, passable, serviceable

midget *n* **1** = **dwarf**, gnome, homuncule, homunculus, manikin, pygmy *or* pigmy, shrimp (*inf.*), Tom Thumb ◆ *modifier* **2b** = **tiny**, baby, dwarf, Lilliputian, little, miniature, pocket, pygmy *or* pigmy, small, teensy-weensy, teeny-weeny

midnight *n* **1** = **twelve o'clock**, dead of night, middle of the night, the witching hour, twelve o'clock at night

midst[1] *n* **2 in the midst of** = **among**, amidst, during, enveloped by, in the middle of, in the thick of, surrounded by

midway *adj, adv* **1, 2** = **halfway**, betwixt and between, in the middle

mien *n Literary* = **demeanour**, air, appearance, aspect, aura, bearing, carriage, countenance, deportment, look, manner, presence

miffed *adj* **1** *Informal* = **upset**, aggrieved, annoyed, displeased, hacked (off) (*US sl.*), hurt, in

of **may**[1]: *he might have come.* **2** (often foll. by *well*) expressing possibility: *he might well come.* In this sense *might* looks to the future and functions as a weak form of *may.* See **may**[1] (sense 2). [OE *miht*]

USAGE NOTE See at **may**[1].

might[2] ❶ (maɪt) *n* **1** power, force, or vigour, esp. of a great or supreme kind. **2** physical strength. **3** (**with**) **might and main.** See **main**[1] (sense 7). [OE *miht*]

mighty ❶ ('maɪtɪ) *adj* **mightier, mightiest. 1a** having or indicating might; powerful or strong. **1b** (*as collective n;* preceded by *the*): *the mighty.* **2** very large; vast. **3** very great in extent, importance, etc. ◆ *adv* **4** *Inf., chiefly US & Canad.* (intensifier): *mighty tired.*
▸**'mightily** *adv* ▸**'mightiness** *n*

mignon ('mɪnjɒn) *adj* small and pretty; dainty. [C16: from F, from OF *mignot* dainty]
▸**mignonne** ('mɪnjɒn) *fem n*

mignonette (ˌmɪnjə'nɛt) *n* **1** any of various mainly Mediterranean plants, such as **garden mignonette**, that have spikes of small greenish-white flowers. **2** a type of fine pillow lace. **3a** a greyish-green colour. **3b** (*as adj*): *mignonette ribbons.* [C18: from F, dim. of MIGNON]

migraine ('miːgreɪn, 'maɪ-) *n* a throbbing headache usually affecting only one side of the head and commonly accompanied by nausea and visual disturbances. [C18: (earlier form, C14 *mygrame* MEGRIM): from F, from LL *hēmicrānia* pain in half of the head, from Gk, from HEMI- + *kranion* CRANIUM]
▸**'migrainous** *adj*

migrant ❶ ('maɪgrənt) *n* **1** a person or animal that moves from one region, place, or country to another. **2** an itinerant agricultural worker. ◆ *adj* **3** moving from one region, place, or country to another; migratory.

migrate ❶ (maɪ'greɪt) *vb* **migrates, migrating, migrated.** (*intr*) **1** to go from one place to settle in another, esp. in a foreign country. **2** (of birds, fishes, etc.) to journey between different habitats at specific times of the year. [C17: from L *migrāre* to change one's abode]
▸**mi'grator** *n*

migration ❶ (maɪ'greɪʃən) *n* **1** the act or an instance of migrating. **2** a group of people, birds, etc., migrating in a body. **3** *Chem.* a movement of atoms, ions, or molecules, such as the motion of ions in solution under the influence of electric fields.
▸**mi'grational** *adj*

migratory ❶ ('maɪgrətərɪ, -trɪ) *adj* **1** of or characterized by migration. **2** nomadic; itinerant.

mihrab ('miːræb, -rəb) *n Islam.* the niche in a mosque showing the direction of Mecca. [from Ar.]

mikado (mɪ'kɑːdəʊ) *n, pl* **mikados.** (*often cap.*) *Arch.* the Japanese emperor. [C18: from Japanese, from *mi-* honourable + *kado* gate]

mike (maɪk) *n Inf.* short for **microphone.**

mil (mɪl) *n* **1** a unit of length equal to one thousandth of an inch. **2** a unit of angular measure, used in gunnery, equal to one six-thousand-four-hundredth of a circumference. **3** *Photog.* short for millimetre: *35-mil film.* [C18: from L *millēsimus* thousandth]

mil. *abbrev. for:* **1** military. **2** militia.

milady *or* **miladi** (mɪ'leɪdɪ) *n, pl* **miladies.** (formerly) a continental title used for an English gentlewoman.

milch (mɪltʃ) *n* **1** (*modifier*) (esp. of cattle) yielding milk. **2 milch cow.** *Inf.* a source of easy income, esp. a person. [C13: from OE *-milce* (in compounds); rel. to OE *melcan* to milk]

mild ❶ (maɪld) *adj* **1** (of a taste, sensation, etc.) not powerful or strong; bland. **2** gentle or temperate in character, climate, behaviour, etc. **3** not extreme; moderate. **4** feeble; unassertive. ◆ *n* **5** *Brit.* draught beer, of darker colour than bitter and flavoured with fewer hops. [OE *milde*]
▸**'mildly** *adv* ▸**'mildness** *n*

mildew ('mɪlˌdjuː) *n* **1** any of various diseases of plants that affect mainly the leaves and are caused by parasitic fungi. **2** any fungus causing this. **3** another name for **mould**[2]. ◆ *vb* **4** to affect or become affected with mildew. [OE *mildēaw,* from *mil-* honey + *dēaw* DEW]
▸**'milˌdewy** *adj*

mild steel *n* any of a class of strong tough steels that contain a low quantity of carbon.

mile (maɪl) *n* **1** Also called: **statute mile.** a unit of length used in the UK, the US, and certain other countries, equal to 1760 yards. 1 mile is equivalent to 1.60934 kilometres. **2** See **nautical mile. 3** the Roman mile, equivalent to 1620 yards. **4** (*often pl*) *Inf.* a great distance; great deal: *he missed by a mile.* **5** a race extending over a mile. ◆ *adv* **6 miles.** (intensifier): *that's miles better.* [OE *mīl,* from L *mīlia* (*passuum*) a thousand (paces)]

mileage *or* **milage** ('maɪlɪdʒ) *n* **1** a distance expressed in miles. **2** the total number of miles that a motor vehicle has travelled. **3** allowance for travelling expenses, esp. as a fixed rate per mile. **4** the number of miles a motor vehicle will travel on one gallon of fuel. **5** *Inf.* use, benefit, or service provided by something. **6** *Inf.* grounds, substance, or weight: *some mileage in their arguments.*

mileometer *or* **milometer** (maɪ'lɒmɪtə) *n* a device that records the number of miles that a bicycle or motor vehicle has travelled.

milepost ('maɪlˌpəʊst) *n* **1** *Horse racing.* a marking post on a racecourse a mile before the finishing line. **2** *Chiefly US & Canad.* a signpost that shows the distance in miles to or from a place.

miler ('maɪlə) *n* an athlete, horse, etc., that runs or specializes in races of one mile.

milestone ('maɪlˌstəʊn) *n* **1** a stone pillar that shows the distance in miles to or from a place. **2** a significant event in life, history, etc.

milfoil ('mɪlˌfɔɪl) *n* **1** another name for **yarrow. 2** See **water milfoil.** [C13: from OF, from L *milifolium,* from *mille* thousand + *folium* leaf]

miliaria (ˌmɪlɪ'ɛərɪə) *n* an acute itching eruption of the skin, caused by blockage of the sweat glands. [C19: from NL, from L *miliārius* MILIARY]

miliary ('mɪljərɪ) *adj* **1** resembling or relating to millet seeds. **2** (of a disease or skin eruption) characterized by small lesions resembling millet seeds: *miliary fever.* [C17: from L *miliārius,* from *milium* MILLET]

milieu ❶ ('miːljɜː; *French* miljø) *n, pl* **milieux** (-ljɜː, -ljɜːz; *French* -ljø) *or* **milieus.** (miljø). surroundings, location, or setting. [C19: from F, from *mi-* MID[1] + *lieu* place]

militant ❶ ('mɪlɪtənt) *adj* **1** aggressive or vigorous, esp. in the support of a cause. **2** warring; engaged in warfare. ◆ *n* **3** a militant person. [C15: from L *mīlitāre* to be a soldier, from *mīles* soldier]
▸**'militancy** *n* ▸**'militantly** *adv*

militarism ('mɪlɪtəˌrɪzəm) *n* **1** military spirit; pursuit of military ideals. **2** domination by the military, esp. on a political level. **3** a policy of maintaining a strong military organization in aggressive preparedness for war.
▸**'militarist** *n*

militarize *or* **militarise** ('mɪlɪtəˌraɪz) *vb* **militarizes, militarizing, militarized** *or* **militarises, militarising, militarised.** (*tr*) **1** to convert to military use. **2** to imbue with militarism.
▸**ˌmilitari'zation** *or* **ˌmilitari'sation** *n*

military ❶ ('mɪlɪtərɪ, -trɪ) *adj* **1** of or relating to the armed forces, warlike matters, etc. **2** of or characteristic of soldiers. ◆ *n, pl* **militaries** *or* **military. 3** (preceded by *the*) the armed services, esp. the army. [C16: via F from L *mīlitāris,* from *mīles* soldier]
▸**mili'tarily** *adv*

military police *n* a corps within an army that performs police and disciplinary duties.
▸**military policeman** *n*

militate ❶ ('mɪlɪˌteɪt) *vb* **militates, militating, militated.** (*intr;* usually foll. by *against* or *for*) (of facts, etc.) to have influence or effect: *the evidence militated against his release.* [C17: from L *mīlitātus,* from *mīlitāre* to be a soldier]

USAGE NOTE See at **mitigate.**

THESAURUS

a huff, irked, irritated, narked (*Brit., Austral., & NZ sl.*), nettled, offended, piqued, put out, resentful, vexed

might[2] *n* **1, 2 = power,** ability, capability, capacity, clout (*inf.*), efficacy, efficiency, energy, force, potency, prowess, puissance, strength, sway, valour, vigour

mighty *adj* **1 = powerful,** doughty, forceful, hardy, indomitable, lusty, manful, potent, puissant, robust, stalwart, stout, strapping, strong, sturdy, vigorous **2 = great,** bulky, colossal, elephantine, enormous, gigantic, ginormous (*inf.*), grand, huge, humongous *or* humungous (*US sl.*), immense, large, massive, mega (*sl.*), monumental, prodigious, stellar (*inf.*), stupendous, titanic, towering, tremendous, vast
Antonyms *adj* ≠ **powerful:** feeble, impotent, weak, weedy (*inf.*), wimpish *or* wimpy (*inf.*) ≠ **great:** small, tiny, unimposing, unimpressive

migrant *n* **1, 2 = wanderer,** drifter, emigrant, gypsy, immigrant, itinerant, nomad, rover, tinker, transient, traveller, vagrant ◆ *adj* **3 = travelling,** drifting, gypsy, immigrant, itinerant, migratory, nomadic, roving, shifting, transient, vagrant, wandering

migrate *vb* **1 = move,** drift, emigrate, journey, roam, rove, shift, travel, trek, voyage, wander

migration *n* **1 = wandering,** emigration, journey, movement, roving, shift, travel, trek, voyage

migratory *adj* **2 = nomadic,** gypsy, itinerant, migrant, peripatetic, roving, shifting, transient, travelling, unsettled, vagrant, wandering

mild *adj* **1 = bland,** smooth **2 = gentle,** amiable, calm, compassionate, docile, easy, easy-going, easy-oasy (*sl.*), equable, forbearing, forgiving, indulgent, kind, meek, mellow, merciful, moderate, pacific, peaceable, placid, pleasant, serene, soft, tender **2 = temperate,** balmy, calm, clement, moderate, tranquil, warm
Antonyms *adj* ≠ **gentle:** harsh, powerful, severe, sharp, strong, unkind, unpleasant, violent ≠ **temperate:** bitter, cold, fierce, harsh, rough, stormy, violent, wild

mildness *n* **1, 2 = gentleness,** blandness, calmness, clemency, docility, forbearance, indulgence, kindness, leniency, lenity, meekness, mellowness, moderation, placidity, smoothness, softness, temperateness, tenderness, tranquillity, warmth

milieu *n* **= surroundings,** background, element, environment, locale, location, *mise en scène,* scene, setting, sphere

militant *adj* **1 = aggressive,** active, assertive, combative, vigorous **2 = warring,** belligerent, combating, contending, embattled, fighting, in arms ◆ *n* **3 = activist,** partisan **3 = warrior,** belligerent, combatant, fighter, gladiator
Antonyms *adj* ≠ **aggressive, warring:** concessive, pacific, pacifist, peaceful

military *adj* **1, 2 = warlike,** armed, martial, soldierlike, soldierly ◆ *n* **3 = armed forces,** army, forces, services

militate *vb, foll. by* **against = counteract,** be detrimental to, conflict with, contend with, count against, counter, oppose, resist, tell against,

militia ⓘ (mɪˈlɪʃə) *n* **1** a body of citizen (as opposed to professional) soldiers. **2** an organization containing men enlisted for service in emergency only. [C16: from L: soldiery, from *mīles* soldier]
▸**miˈlitiaman** *n*

milk ⓘ (mɪlk) *n* **1a** a whitish fluid secreted by the mammary glands of mature female mammals and used for feeding their young until weaned. **1b** the milk of cows, goats, etc., used by man as a food or in the production of butter, cheese, etc. **2** any similar fluid in plants, such as the juice of a coconut. **3** a milklike pharmaceutical preparation, such as milk of magnesia. **4 cry over spilt milk.** to lament something that cannot be altered. ◆ *vb* **5** to draw milk from the udder of (an animal). **6** (*intr*) (of animals) to yield milk. **7** (*tr*) to draw off or tap in small quantities: *to milk the petty cash.* **8** (*tr*) to extract as much money, help, etc., as possible from: *to milk a situation of its news value.* **9** (*tr*) to extract venom, sap, etc., from. [OE *milc*]
▸**ˈmilker** *n*

milk-and-water ⓘ *adj* (**milk and water** *when postpositive*). weak, feeble, or insipid.

milk bar *n* **1** a snack bar at which milk drinks and light refreshments are served. **2** (in Australia) a shop selling, in addition to milk, basic provisions and other items.

milk chocolate *n* chocolate that has been made with milk, having a creamy taste.

milk float *n Brit.* a small motor vehicle used to deliver milk to houses.

milk leg *n* inflammation and thrombosis of the femoral vein following childbirth, characterized by painful swelling of the leg.

milkmaid (ˈmɪlkˌmeɪd) *n* a girl or woman who milks cows.

milkman (ˈmɪlkmən) *n, pl* **milkmen.** a man who delivers or sells milk.

milk of magnesia *n* a suspension of magnesium hydroxide in water, used as an antacid and laxative.

milk pudding *n Chiefly Brit.* a pudding made by boiling or baking milk with a grain, esp. rice.

milk round *n Brit.* **1** a route along which a milkman regularly delivers milk. **2** a regular series of visits, esp. as made by recruitment officers from industry to universities.

milk run *n Aeronautics, inf.* a routine and uneventful flight. [C20: from a milkman's safe and regular routine]

milk shake *n* a cold frothy drink made of milk, flavouring, and sometimes ice cream, whisked or beaten together.

milksop ⓘ (ˈmɪlkˌsɒp) *n* a feeble or ineffectual man or youth.

milk sugar *n* another name for **lactose.**

milk tooth *n* any of the first teeth to erupt; a deciduous tooth. Also called: **baby tooth.**

milkwort (ˈmɪlkˌwɜːt) *n* any of several plants having small blue, pink, or white flowers. They were formerly believed to increase milk production in nursing women.

milky ⓘ (ˈmɪlkɪ) *adj* **milkier, milkiest. 1** resembling milk, esp. in colour or cloudiness. **2** of or containing milk. **3** spiritless or spineless.
▸**ˈmilkily** *adv* ▸**ˈmilkiness** *n*

Milky Way *n* **the.** the diffuse band of light stretching across the night sky that consists of millions of faint stars, nebulae, etc., and forms part of the Galaxy. [C14: translation of L *via lactea*]

mill ⓘ (mɪl) *n* **1** a building in which grain is crushed and ground to make flour. **2** a building fitted with machinery for processing materials, manufacturing goods, etc.; factory. **3** a machine that processes materials, manufactures goods, etc., by performing a continuous or repetitive operation, such as a machine to grind flour, pulverize solids, or press fruit. **4** a machine that tools or polishes metal. **5** a small machine for grinding solids: *a pepper mill.* **6** a system, institution, etc., that influences people or things in the manner of a factory: *the educational mill.* **7** an unpleasant experience; ordeal (esp. in **go** *or* **be put through the mill**). **8** a fist fight. ◆ *vb* **9** (*tr*) to grind, press, or pulverize in or as if in a mill. **10** (*tr*) to process or produce in or with a mill. **11** to cut or roll (metal) with or as if with a milling machine. **12** (*tr*) to groove or flute the edge of (a coin). **13** (*intr;* often foll. by *about* or *around*) to move about in a confused manner. **14** *Arch. sl.* to fight, esp. with the fists. [OE *mylen* from LL *molīna* a mill, from L *mola* mill, from *molere* to grind]
▸**ˈmillable** *adj* ▸**milled** *adj*

millboard (ˈmɪlˌbɔːd) *n* strong pasteboard, used esp. in book covers. [C18: from *milled board*]

milldam (ˈmɪlˌdæm) *n* a dam built in a stream to raise the water level sufficiently for it to turn a millwheel.

millefeuille *French.* (milfœj) *n Brit.* a small iced cake made of puff pastry filled with jam and cream. [lit.: thousand leaves]

millefleurs (ˈmiːlˌflɜː) *n* (*functioning as sing*) a design of stylized floral patterns, used in textiles, paperweights, etc. [F: thousand flowers]

millenarian (ˌmɪlɪˈnɛərɪən) *adj* **1** of or relating to a thousand or to a thousand years. **2** of or relating to the millennium or millenarianism. ◆ *n* **3** an adherent of millenarianism.

millenarianism (ˌmɪlɪˈnɛərɪəˌnɪzəm) *n* **1** *Christianity.* the belief in a future millennium during which Christ will reign on earth: based on Revelation 20:1–5. **2** any belief in a future period of ideal peace and happiness.

millenary (mɪˈlenərɪ) *n, pl* **millenaries. 1** a sum or aggregate of one thousand. **2** another word for a **millennium.** ◆ *adj, n* **3** another word for **millenarian.** [C16: from LL *millēnārius* containing a thousand, from L *mille* thousand]

millennium (mɪˈlenɪəm) *n, pl* **millennia** (-nɪə) *or* **millenniums. 1 the.** *Christianity.* the period of a thousand years of Christ's awaited reign upon earth. **2** a period or cycle of one thousand years. **3** a time of peace and happiness, esp. in the distant future. [C17: from NL, from L *mille* thousand + *annus* year]
▸**milˈlennial** *adj* ▸**milˈlennialist** *n*

millennium bug *n Computing.* any software problem arising from the change in date at the start of the 21st century.

millepede (ˈmɪlɪˌpiːd) *or* **milleped** *n* variants of **millipede.**

millepore (ˈmɪlɪˌpɔː) *n* any of a genus of tropical colonial coral-like hydrozoans, having a calcareous skeleton. [C18: from NL, from L *mille* thousand + *porus* hole]

miller (ˈmɪlə) *n* **1** a person who keeps, operates, or works in a mill, esp. a corn mill. **2** another name for **milling machine. 3** a person who operates a milling machine.

miller's thumb *n* any of several small freshwater European fishes having a flattened body. [C15: from the alleged likeness of the fish's head to a thumb]

millesimal (mɪˈlesɪməl) *adj* **1a** denoting a thousandth. **1b** (*as n*): *a millesimal.* **2** of, consisting of, or relating to a thousandth. [C18: from L *millēsimus*]

millet (ˈmɪlɪt) *n* **1** a cereal grass cultivated for grain and animal fodder. **2a** an Indian annual grass cultivated for grain and forage, having pale round shiny seeds. **2b** the seed of this plant. **3** any of various similar or related grasses. [C14: via OF from L *milium*]

milli- *prefix* denoting 10^{-3}: *millimetre.* Symbol: m [from F, from L *mille* thousand]

milliard (ˈmɪlɪˌɑːd, ˈmɪljɑːd) *n Brit.* (no longer in technical use) a thousand million. US & Canad. equivalent: **billion.** [C19: from F]

millibar (ˈmɪlɪˌbɑː) *n* a cgs unit of atmospheric pressure equal to 10^{-3} bar, 100 newtons per square metre or 0.7500617 millimetre of mercury.

milligram *or* **milligramme** (ˈmɪlɪˌɡræm) *n* one thousandth of a gram. [C19: from F]

millilitre *or US* **milliliter** (ˈmɪlɪˌliːtə) *n* one thousandth of a litre.

millimetre *or US* **millimeter** (ˈmɪlɪˌmiːtə) *n* one thousandth of a metre.

millimicron (ˈmɪlɪˌmaɪkrɒn) *n Obs.* one thousand-millionth of a metre; nanometre.

milliner (ˈmɪlɪnə) *n* a person who makes or sells women's hats. [C16: orig. *Milaner,* a native of *Milan,* at that time famous for its fancy goods]

millinery (ˈmɪlɪnərɪ, -nrɪ) *n* **1** hats, trimmings, etc., sold by a milliner. **2** the business or shop of a milliner.

milling (ˈmɪlɪŋ) *n* **1** the act or process of grinding, pressing, or crushing in a mill. **2** the grooves or fluting on the edge of a coin, etc.

milling machine *n* a machine tool in which a horizontal arbor or vertical spindle rotates a cutting tool above a horizontal table.

million (ˈmɪljən) *n, pl* **millions** *or* **million. 1** the cardinal number that is the product of 1000 multiplied by 1000. **2** a numeral, 1 000 000, 10^6, M̄, etc., representing this number. **3** (*often pl*) *Inf.* an extremely large but unspecified number or amount: *I have millions of things to do.* ◆ *determiner* **4** (preceded by *a* or by a numeral) **4a** amounting to a million: *a million light years.* **4b** (*as pron*): *I can see a million.* [C17: via OF from early It. *millione,* from *mille* thousand, from L]

millionaire (ˌmɪljəˈnɛə) *n* a person whose assets are worth at least a million of the standard monetary units of his or her country.
▸**ˌmillionˈairess** *fem n*

millionth (ˈmɪljənθ) *n* **1a** one of 1 000 000 equal parts of something. **1b** (*as modifier*): *a millionth part.* **2** one of 1 000 000 equal divisions of a scientific quantity. **3** the fraction one divided by 1 000 000. ◆ *adj* **4** (*usually prenominal*) **4a** being the ordinal number of 1 000 000 in numbering or counting order, etc. **4b** (*as n*): *the millionth to be manufactured.*

millipede, millepede (ˈmɪlɪˌpiːd), *or* **milleped** (ˈmɪlɪˌped) *n* any of various terrestrial herbivorous arthropods, having a cylindrical segmented body, each segment of which bears two pairs of legs. [C17: from L, from *mille* thousand + *pēs* foot]

millisecond (ˈmɪlɪˌsekənd) *n* one thousandth of a second.

millpond (ˈmɪlˌpɒnd) *n* **1** a pool formed by damming a stream to provide water to turn a mill-wheel. **2** any expanse of calm water.

millrace (ˈmɪlˌreɪs) *or* **millrun** *n* **1** the current of water that turns a millwheel. **2** the channel for this water.

THESAURUS

weigh against *foll. by* **for** = **promote**, advance, aid, further, help

militia *n* **1, 2** = **reserve(s)**, fencibles (*History*), National Guard (*US*), Territorial Army (*Brit.*), trainband (*History*), yeomanry (*History*)

milk *vb* **5, 9** = **siphon**, drain, draw off, express, extract, let out, press, tap **8** = **exploit**, bleed, drain, extract, impose on, pump, take advantage of, use, wring

milk-and-water *adj* = **weak**, feeble, innocuous, insipid, jejune, nerdy *or* nurdy (*sl.*), vapid, weedy (*inf.*), wimpish *or* wimpy (*inf.*), wishy-washy (*inf.*)
Antonyms *adj* effective, energetic, forceful, healthy, strong

milksop *n* = **weakling**, chinless wonder (*Brit. inf.*), coward, dastard (*arch.*), jessie (*Scot. sl.*), namby-pamby, sissy, wimp (*inf.*)

milky *n* **1** = **white**, alabaster, clouded, cloudy, milk-white, opaque, whitish

mill *n* **2** = **factory**, foundry, plant, shop, works **3** = **grinder**, crusher ◆ *vb* **9** = **grind**, comminute, crush, granulate, grate, pound, powder, press, pulverize **13** = **swarm**, crowd, seethe, throng

Mills bomb (mɪlz) *n* a type of high-explosive hand grenade. [C20: after Sir William *Mills* (1856–1932), Brit. inventor]

millstone ➊ ('mɪlˌstəʊn) *n* **1** one of a pair of heavy flat disc-shaped stones that are rotated one against the other to grind grain. **2** a heavy burden, such as a responsibility or obligation.

millstream ('mɪlˌstri:m) *n* a stream of water used to turn a millwheel.

millwheel ('mɪlˌwi:l) *n* a wheel, esp. a waterwheel, that drives a mill.

millwork ('mɪlˌwɜ:k) *n* work done in a mill.

millwright ('mɪlˌraɪt) *n* a person who designs, builds, or repairs grain mills or mill machinery.

milometer (maɪ'lɒmɪtə) *n* a variant spelling of **mileometer.**

milord (mɪ'lɔ:d) *n* (formerly) a continental title used for an English gentleman. [C19: via F from E *my lord*]

milt (mɪlt) *n* **1** the testis of a fish. **2** the spermatozoa and seminal fluid produced by a fish. **3** *Rare.* the spleen, esp. of fowls and pigs. ◆ *vb* **4** to fertilize (fish roe) with milt, esp. artificially. [OE *milte* spleen; in the sense: fish sperm, prob. from MDu. *milte*]
▸'**milter** *n*

mim (mɪm) *adj Dialect.* prim, modest, or demure. [C17: ? imit. of lip-pursing]

mime ➊ (maɪm) *n* **1** the theatrical technique of expressing an idea or mood or portraying a character entirely by gesture and bodily movement without the use of words. **2** Also called: **mime artist.** a performer specializing in this. **3** a dramatic presentation using such a technique. **4** (in the classical theatre) **4a** a comic performance with exaggerated gesture and physical action. **4b** an actor in such a performance. ◆ *vb* **mimes, miming, mimed. 5** to express (an idea, etc.) in actions or gestures without speech. **6** (of singers or musicians) to perform as if singing a song or playing a piece of music that is actually prerecorded. [OE *mīma,* from L *mīmus* mimic actor, from Gk *mimos* imitator]
▸'**mimer** *n*

Mimeograph ('mɪmɪəˌgrɑ:f) *n* **1** *Trademark.* an office machine for printing multiple copies of text or line drawings from a stencil. **2** a copy produced by this. ◆ *vb* **3** to print copies from (a prepared stencil) using this machine.

mimesis (mɪ'mi:sɪs) *n* **1** *Art, literature.* the imitative representation of nature or human behaviour. **2** *Biol.* another name for **mimicry** (sense 2). **3** *Rhetoric.* representation of another person's alleged words in a speech. [C16: from Gk, from *mimeisthai* to imitate]

mimetic (mɪ'mɛtɪk) *adj* **1** of, resembling, or relating to mimesis or imitation, as in art, etc. **2** *Biol.* of or exhibiting mimicry.
▸**mi'metically** *adv*

mimic ➊ ('mɪmɪk) *vb* **mimics, mimicking, mimicked.** (*tr*) **1** to imitate (a person, a manner, etc.), esp. for satirical effect; ape. **2** to take on the appearance of: *certain flies mimic wasps.* **3** to copy closely or in a servile manner. ◆ *n* **4** a person or an animal, such as a parrot, that is clever at mimicking. **5** an animal that displays mimicry. ◆ *adj* **6** of, relating to, or using mimicry. **7** simulated, make-believe, or mock. [C16: from L *mīmicus,* from Gk *mimikos,* from *mimos* MIME]
▸'**mimicker** *n*

mimicry ➊ ('mɪmɪkrɪ) *n, pl* **mimicries. 1** the act or art of copying or imitating closely; mimicking. **2** the resemblance shown by one animal species to another, which protects it from predators.

MIMinE *abbrev. for* Member of the Institute of Mining Engineers.

mimosa (mɪ'məʊsə, -zə) *n* any of various tropical shrubs or trees having ball-like clusters of typically yellow flowers and leaves that are often sensitive to touch or light. See also **sensitive plant.** [C18: from NL, prob. from L *mīmus* MIME, because the plant's sensitivity to touch imitates the similar reaction of animals]

mimulus ('mɪmjʊləs) *n* any of a genus of flowering plants of temperate regions. See **monkey flower.** [C19: Med. L, from L *mimus* MIME, alluding to masklike flowers]

min. *abbrev. for:* **1** mineralogy. **2** minimum. **3** mining. **4** minute *or* minutes.

Min. *abbrev. for:* **1** Minister. **2** Ministry.

minaret (ˌmɪnə'rɛt, 'mɪnəˌrɛt) *n* a slender tower of a mosque having one or more balconies. [C17: from F, from Turkish, from Ar. *manārat* lamp, from *nār* fire]
▸ˌ**mina'reted** *adj*

minatory ('mɪnətərɪ, -trɪ) *or* **minatorial** *adj* threatening or menacing. [C16: from LL *minātōrius,* from L *minārī* to threaten]

mince ➊ (mɪns) *vb* **minces, mincing, minced. 1** (*tr*) to chop, grind, or cut into very small pieces. **2** (*tr*) to soften or moderate: *I didn't mince my words.* **3** (*intr*) to walk or speak in an affected dainty manner. ◆ *n* **4** *Chiefly Brit.* minced meat. [C14: from OF *mincier,* ult. from LL *minūtia;* see MINUTIAE]
▸'**mincer** *n*

mincemeat ('mɪnsˌmi:t) *n* **1** a mixture of dried fruit, spices, etc., used esp. for filling pies. **2 make mincemeat of.** *Inf.* to defeat completely.

mince pie *n* a small round pastry tart filled with mincemeat.

mincing ➊ ('mɪnsɪŋ) *adj* (of a person) affectedly elegant in gait, manner, or speech.
▸'**mincingly** *adv*

mind ➊ (maɪnd) *n* **1** the human faculty to which are ascribed thought, feelings, intention, etc. **2** intelligence or the intellect, esp. as opposed to feelings or wishes. **3** recollection or remembrance: *it comes to mind.* **4** the faculty of original or creative thought; imagination: *it's all in the mind.* **5** a person considered as an intellectual being: *great minds.* **6** condition, state, or manner of feeling or thought: *his state of mind.* **7** an inclination, desire, or purpose: *I have a mind to go.* **8** attention or thoughts: *keep your mind on your work.* **9** a sound mental state; sanity (esp. in **out of one's mind**). **10** (in Cartesian philosophy) one of two basic modes of existence, the other being matter. **11 blow someone's mind.** *Sl.* **11a** (of a drug) to alter someone's mental state. **11b** to astound or surprise someone. **12 change one's mind.** to alter one's decision or opinion. **13 in** *or* **of two minds.** undecided; wavering. **14 give** (**someone**) **a piece of one's mind.** to criticize or censure (someone) frankly or vehemently. **15 make up one's mind.** to decide (something or to do something). **16 on one's mind.** in one's thoughts. ◆ *vb* **17** (when *tr, may take a clause as object*) to take offence at: *do you mind if I smoke?* **18** to pay attention to (something); heed; notice: *to mind one's own business.* **19** (*tr; takes a clause as object*) to make certain; ensure: *mind you tell her.* **20** (*tr*) to take care of; have charge of: *to mind the shop.* **21** (when *tr, may take a clause as object*) to be cautious or careful about (something): *mind how you go.* **22** (*tr*) to obey (someone or something); heed: *mind your father!* **23** to be concerned (about); be troubled (about): *never mind about your hat.* **24** (*tr; passive; takes an infinitive*) to be intending or inclined (to do something): *clearly he was not minded to finish the story.* **25 mind you.** an expression qualifying a previous statement: *Dogs are nice. Mind you, I don't like all dogs.* ◆ Related adj: **mental.** ◆ See also **mind out.** [OE *gemynd* mind]

mind-bending *adj Inf.* **1** Also: **mind-blowing.** altering one's state of consciousness, esp. as a result of taking drugs. **2** reaching the limit of credibility: *they offered a mind-bending salary.* ◆ *n* **3** the process of brainwashing.

mind-boggling *adj Inf.* astonishing; bewildering.

minded ('maɪndɪd) *adj* **1** having a mind, inclination, intention, etc., as specified: *politically minded.* **2** (*in combination*): *money-minded.*

minder ('maɪndə) *n* **1** someone who looks after someone or something. **2** short for **childminder. 3** *Sl.* an aide to someone in public life who keeps control of press and public relations. **4** *Sl.* someone acting as a bodyguard or assistant, esp. in the criminal underworld.

mindful ➊ ('maɪndfʊl) *adj* (usually *postpositive* and foll. by *of*) keeping aware; heedful: *mindful of your duty.*
▸'**mindfully** *adv* ▸'**mindfulness** *n*

mindless ➊ ('maɪndlɪs) *adj* **1** stupid or careless. **2** requiring little or no intellectual effort.
▸'**mindlessly** *adv* ▸'**mindlessness** *n*

mind-numbing *adj* extremely boring and uninspiring.
▸'**mind-**ˌ**numbingly** *adv*

mind out ➊ *vb* (*intr, adv*) *Brit.* to be careful or pay attention.

THESAURUS

millstone *n* **1** = **grindstone**, quernstone **2** = **burden**, affliction, albatross, dead weight, drag, encumbrance, load, weight

mime *n* **1** = **dumb show**, gesture, mummery, pantomime ◆ *vb* **5** = **act out**, gesture, pantomime, represent, simulate

mimic *vb* **1** = **imitate**, ape, caricature, do (*inf.*), impersonate, parody, take off (*inf.*) **2** = **resemble**, echo, look like, mirror, simulate, take on the appearance of ◆ *n* **4** = **imitator**, caricaturist, copycat (*inf.*), impersonator, impressionist, parodist, parrot ◆ *adj* **6, 7** = **imitative**, echoic, imitation, make-believe, mimetic, mock, sham, simulated

mimicry *n* **1** = **imitation**, apery, burlesque, caricature, copying, imitating, impersonation, impression, mimicking, mockery, parody, take-off (*inf.*)

mince *vb* **1** = **cut**, chop, crumble, grind, hash **2** *As in* **mince one's words** = **tone down**, diminish, euphemize, extenuate, hold back, moderate, palliate, soften, spare, weaken **3** = **posture**, attitudinize, give oneself airs, ponce (*sl.*), pose

mincing *adj* = **affected**, arty-farty (*inf.*), camp (*inf.*), dainty, effeminate, foppish, lah-di-dah (*inf.*), nice, niminy-piminy, poncy (*sl.*), precious, pretentious, sissy

mind *n* **1** = **brain**, head, imagination, psyche **2** = **intelligence**, brain(s), grey matter (*inf.*), intellect, mentality, ratiocination, reason, sense, spirit, understanding, wits **3** = **memory**, recollection, remembrance **5** = **thinker**, brain, brainbox, genius, intellect, intellectual **6** = **attitude**, belief, feeling, judgment, opinion, outlook, point of view, sentiment, thoughts, view, way of thinking **7** = **intention**, bent, desire, disposition, fancy, inclination, leaning, notion, purpose, tendency, urge, will, wish **8** = **attention**, concentration, thinking, thoughts **9** = **sanity**, judgment, marbles (*inf.*), mental balance, rationality, reason, senses, wits **13 in** *or* of two minds = **undecided**, dithering (*chiefly Brit.*), hesitant, shillyshallying (*inf.*), swithering (*Scot.*), uncertain, unsure, vacillating, wavering **15 make up one's mind** = **decide**, choose, come to a decision, determine, make a decision, reach a decision, resolve, settle ◆ *vb* **17** = **take offence**, be affronted, be bothered, care, disapprove, dislike, look askance at, object, resent **18, 22** = **pay attention**, adhere to, attend, comply with, follow, heed, listen to, mark, note, notice, obey, observe, pay heed to, regard, respect, take heed, watch **19** = **be sure**, ensure, make certain **20** = **guard**, attend to, have charge of, keep an eye on, look after, take care of, tend, watch **21** = **be careful**, be cautious, be on (one's) guard, be wary, take care, watch

mindful *adj* = **aware**, alert, alive to, attentive, careful, chary, cognizant, conscious, heedful, regardful, respectful, sensible, thoughtful, wary, watchful
Antonyms *adj* heedless, inattentive, incautious, mindless, oblivious, thoughtless, unaware

mindless *adj* **1** = **unthinking**, asinine, braindead (*inf.*), brutish, careless, foolish, forgetful, gratuitous, heedless, idiotic, imbecilic, inane, inattentive, moronic, neglectful, negligent, oblivious, obtuse, stupid, thoughtless, unintel-

mind-reader *n* a person seemingly able to discern the thoughts of another.
▸ **'mind-ˌreading** *n*

mind-set *n* the ideas and attitudes with which a person approaches a situation, esp. when these are seen as being difficult to alter.

mind's eye *n* the visual memory or the imagination.

mine[1] (maɪn) *pron* **1** something or someone belonging to or associated with me: *mine is best.* **2 of mine.** belonging to or associated with me. ◆ *determiner* **3** (*preceding a vowel*) an archaic word for **my:** *mine eyes; mine host.* [OE *mīn*]

mine[2] (maɪn) *n* **1** a system of excavations made for the extraction of minerals, esp. coal, ores, or precious stones. **2** any deposit of ore or minerals. **3** a lucrative source or abundant supply: *a mine of information.* **4** a device containing explosive designed to destroy ships, vehicles, or personnel, usually laid beneath the ground or in water. **5** a tunnel dug to undermine a fortification, etc. ◆ *vb* **mines, mining, mined. 6** to dig into (the earth) for (minerals). **7** to make (a hole, tunnel, etc.) by digging or boring. **8** to place explosive mines in position below the surface of (the sea or land). **9** to undermine (a fortification, etc.) by digging mines. **10** another word for **undermine.** [C13: from OF, prob. of Celtic origin]

mine detector *n* an instrument designed to detect explosive mines.
▸ **mine detection** *n*

mine dump *n S. African.* a large mound of residue esp. from gold-mining operations.

minefield ('maɪnˌfiːld) *n* **1** an area of ground or water containing explosive mines. **2** a subject, situation, etc., beset with hidden problems.

minelayer ('maɪnˌleɪə) *n* a warship or aircraft designed for the carrying and laying of mines.

miner ('maɪnə) *n* **1** a person who works in a mine. **2** any of various insects or insect larvae that bore into and feed on plant tissues. See also **leaf miner. 3** *Austral.* any of several honeyeaters.

mineral ('mɪnərəl, 'mɪnrəl) *n* **1** any of a class of naturally occurring solid inorganic substances with a characteristic crystalline form and a homogeneous chemical composition. **2** any inorganic matter. **3** any substance obtained by mining, esp. a metal ore. **4** (*often pl*) *Brit.* short for **mineral water. 5** *Brit.* a soft drink containing carbonated water and flavourings. ◆ *adj* **6** of, relating to, containing, or resembling minerals. [C15: from Med. L *minerāle* (n), from *minerālis* (adj); rel. to *minera* mine, ore, from ?]

mineral. *abbrev. for* mineralogy *or* mineralogical.

mineralize *or* **mineralise** ('mɪnərəˌlaɪz) *vb* **mineralizes, mineralizing, mineralized** *or* **mineralises, mineralising, mineralised.** (*tr*) **1a** to impregnate (organic matter, water, etc.) with a mineral substance. **1b** to convert (such matter) into a mineral; petrify. **2** (of gases, vapours, etc., in magma) to transform (a metal) into an ore.
▸ **ˌminerali'zation** *or* **ˌminerali'sation** *n* ▸ **'mineralˌizer** *or* **'mineralˌiser** *n*

mineralogy (ˌmɪnə'rælədʒɪ) *n* the branch of geology concerned with the study of minerals.
▸ **mineralogical** (ˌmɪnərə'lɒdʒɪkᵊl) *or* **ˌminera'logic** *adj* ▸ **ˌminer'alogist** *n*

mineral oil *n Brit.* any oil of mineral origin, esp. petroleum.

mineral water *n* water containing dissolved mineral salts or gases, usually having medicinal properties.

mineral wool *n* a fibrous material made by blowing steam or air through molten slag and used for packing and insulation.

miner's right *n Austral.* a licence to prospect for and mine gold, etc.

minestrone (ˌmɪnɪ'strəʊnɪ) *n* a soup made from a variety of vegetables and pasta. [from It., from *minestrare* to serve]

minesweeper ('maɪnˌswiːpə) *n* a naval vessel equipped to clear mines.
▸ **'mineˌsweeping** *n*

Ming (mɪŋ) *n* **1** the imperial dynasty of China from 1368 to 1644. ◆ *adj* **2** of or relating to Chinese porcelain from the Ming dynasty.

mingle ('mɪŋgᵊl) *vb* **mingles, mingling, mingled. 1** to mix or cause to mix. **2** (*intr; often foll. by with*) to come into close association. [C15: from OE *mengan* to mix]
▸ **'mingler** *n*

mingy ('mɪndʒɪ) *adj* **mingier, mingiest.** *Brit. inf.* miserly, stingy, or niggardly. [C20: prob. a blend of MEAN[2] + STINGY[1]]

mini ('mɪnɪ) *adj* **1** (of a woman's dress, skirt, etc.) very short; thigh-length. **2** (*prenominal*) small; miniature. ◆ *n, pl* **minis. 3** something very small of its kind, esp. a small car or a miniskirt.

mini- *combining form.* smaller or shorter than the standard size: *minibus; miniskirt.* [C20: from MINIATURE & MINIMUM]

miniature ('mɪnɪtʃə) *n* **1** a model, copy, or representation on a very small scale. **2** anything that is very small of its kind. **3** a very small painting, esp. a portrait. **4** an illuminated decoration in a manuscript. **5 in miniature.** on a small scale. ◆ *adj* **6** greatly reduced in size, etc. **7** on a small scale; minute. [C16: from It., from Med. L, from *miniāre* to paint red (in illuminating manuscripts), from *minium* red lead]
▸ **'miniaturist** *n*

miniaturize *or* **miniaturise** ('mɪnɪtʃəˌraɪz) *vb* **miniaturizes, miniaturizing, miniaturized** *or* **miniaturises, miniaturising, miniaturised.** (*tr*) to make or construct (something, esp. electronic equipment) on a very small scale; reduce in size.
▸ **ˌminiaturi'zation** *or* **ˌminiaturi'sation** *n*

minibar ('mɪnɪˌbɑː) *n* a selection of drinks and confectionery provided in a hotel room and charged to the guest's bill if used.

minibus ('mɪnɪˌbʌs) *n* a small bus able to carry approximately ten passengers.

minicab ('mɪnɪˌkæb) *n Brit.* a small saloon car used as a taxi.

minicomputer (ˌmɪnɪkəm'pjuːtə) *n* a small comparatively cheap digital computer.

minim ('mɪnɪm) *n* **1** a unit of fluid measure equal to one sixtieth of a drachm. It is approximately equal to one drop. Symbol: **M 2.** *Music.* a note having the time value of half a semibreve. **3** a small or insignificant thing. **4** a downward stroke in calligraphy. [C15 (*Music.*): from L *minimus* smallest]

minimal art *n* abstract painting or sculpture in which expressiveness and illusion are minimized by the use of simple geometric shapes, flat colour, and arrangements of ordinary objects.
▸ **minimal artist** *n*

minimalism ('mɪnɪməˌlɪzəm) *n* **1** another name for **minimal art. 2** a type of music based on simple elements and avoiding elaboration or embellishment. **3** design or style in which the simplest and fewest elements are used to create the maximum effect.
▸ **'minimalist** *adj, n*

minimax ('mɪnɪˌmæks) *n* **1** *Maths.* the lowest of a set of maximum values. **2** (in game theory, etc.) the procedure of choosing the strategy that least benefits the most advantaged member of a group. Cf. **maximin.** [C20: from MINI(MUM) + MAX(IMUM)]

minimize *or* **minimise** ('mɪnɪˌmaɪz) *vb* **minimizes, minimizing, minimized** *or* **minimises, minimising, minimised.** (*tr*) **1** to reduce to or estimate at the least possible degree or amount. **2** to rank or treat at less than the true worth; belittle.
▸ **ˌminimi'zation** *or* **ˌminimi'sation** *n* ▸ **'miniˌmizer** *or* **'miniˌmiser** *n*

minimum ('mɪnɪməm) *n, pl* **minimums** *or* **minima** (-mə). **1** the least possible amount, degree, or quantity. **2** the least amount recorded, allowed, or reached. **3** (*modifier*) being the least possible, recorded, allowed, etc.: *minimum age.* ◆ *adj* **4** of or relating to a minimum or minimums. [C17: from L: smallest thing, from *minimus* least]
▸ **'minimal** *adj* ▸ **'minimally** *adv*

minimum lending rate *n* (in Britain) the minimum rate at which the Bank of England would lend to discount houses between 1971 and 1981, after which it was replaced by the less formal base rate.

minimum wage *n* the lowest wage that an employer is permitted to pay by law or union contract.

mining ('maɪnɪŋ) *n* **1** the act, process, or industry of extracting coal, ores, etc., from the earth. **2** *Mil.* the process of laying mines.

minion ('mɪnjən) *n* **1** a favourite or dependant, esp. a servile or fawning one. **2** a servile agent. [C16: from F *mignon,* from OF *mignot,* of Gaulish origin]

minipill ('mɪnɪˌpɪl) *n* a low-dose oral contraceptive containing progesterone only.

miniseries ('mɪnɪˌsɪəriːz) *n, pl* **miniseries.** a television programme in several parts that is shown on consecutive days for a short period.

miniskirt ('mɪnɪˌskɜːt) *n* a very short skirt, originally in the 1960s, one at least four inches above the knee. Often shortened to **mini.**

THESAURUS

ligent, unmindful, witless **2** = **mechanical**, automatic, brainless
Antonyms *adj* ≠ **unthinking:** attentive, aware, considerate, intelligent, mindful, reasonable, reasoning, sane, sensitive, thinking

mind out *vb Brit* = **be careful**, be on one's guard, beware, keep one's eyes open, look out, pay attention, take care, watch

mind's eye *n* = **imagination**, head, memory, mind, recollection, remembrance

mine[2] *n* **1, 2** = **pit**, coalfield, colliery, deposit, excavation, lode, shaft, vein **3** = **source**, abundance, fund, hoard, reserve, stock, store, supply, treasury, wealth ◆ *vb* **6, 7** = **dig up**, delve, dig for, excavate, extract, hew, quarry, unearth **8** = **lay mines in** *or* **under**, sow with mines **10** = **tunnel**, sap, subvert, undermine, weaken

miner *n* **1** = **coalminer**, collier (*Brit.*), pitman (*Brit.*)

mingle *vb* **1** = **mix**, admix, alloy, blend, coalesce, combine, commingle, compound, intermingle, intermix, interweave, join, marry, meld, merge, unite **2** = **associate**, circulate, consort, fraternize, hang about *or* around, hang out (*inf.*), hobnob, rub shoulders (*inf.*), socialize
Antonyms *vb* ≠ **mix:** detach, dissolve, divide, part, separate ≠ **associate:** avoid, dissociate, estrange

miniature *adj* **6, 7** = **small**, baby, diminutive, dwarf, Lilliputian, little, midget, mini, minuscule, minute, pocket, pygmy *or* pigmy, reduced, scaled-down, teensy-weensy, teeny-weeny, tiny, toy, wee
Antonyms *adj* big, enlarged, enormous, giant, gigantic, ginormous (*inf.*), great, huge, immense, large, mega (*sl.*), oversize

minimal *adj* **1, 2** = **minimum**, least, least possible, littlest, nominal, slightest, smallest, token

minimize *vb* **1** = **reduce**, abbreviate, attenuate, curtail, decrease, diminish, downsize, miniaturize, prune, shrink **2** = **play down**, belittle, decry, deprecate, depreciate, discount, disparage, make light *or* little of, underestimate, underrate
Antonyms *vb* ≠ **reduce:** augment, enlarge, expand, extend, heighten, increase, magnify ≠ **play down:** boast about, elevate, enhance, exalt, praise, vaunt

minimum *n* **1, 2** = **least**, bottom, depth, lowest, nadir, slightest ◆ *adj* **4** = **least**, least possible, littlest, lowest, minimal, slightest, smallest
Antonyms *adj* ≠ **least:** greatest, highest, largest, maximum, most

minion *n* **1, 2** = **follower**, bootlicker, cohort (*chiefly US*), creature, darling, dependant, favourite, flatterer, flunky, hanger-on, henchman, hireling, lackey, lickspittle, myrmidon, parasite, pet, sycophant, toady, underling, yes man

minister ❶ (ˈmɪnɪstə) *n* **1** (esp. in Presbyterian and some Nonconformist Churches) a member of the clergy. **2** a head of a government department. **3** any diplomatic agent accredited to a foreign government or head of state. **4** Also called: **minister plenipotentiary.** another term for **envoy**[1] (sense 1). **5** Also called: **minister resident.** a diplomat ranking after an envoy. **6** a person who attends to the needs of others, esp. in religious matters. **7** a person who acts as the agent or servant of a person or thing. ◆ *vb* **8** (*intr;* often foll. by *to*) to attend to the needs (of); take care (of). **9** (*tr*) *Arch.* to provide; supply. [C13: via OF from L: servant; rel. to *minus* less]

ministerial (ˌmɪnɪˈstɪərɪəl) *adj* **1** of or relating to a minister of religion or his office. **2** of or relating to a government minister or ministry. **3** (*often cap.*) of or supporting the ministry against the opposition. **4** *Law.* relating to or possessing delegated executive authority. **5** acting as an agent or cause; instrumental.
▸ˌ**minisˈterially** *adv*

minister of state *n* **1** (in the British Parliament) a minister, usually below cabinet rank, appointed to assist a senior minister. **2** any government minister.

Minister of the Crown *n Brit.* any Government minister of cabinet rank.

minister plenipotentiary *n, pl* **ministers plenipotentiary.** another term for **envoy**[1] (sense 1).

ministrant (ˈmɪnɪstrənt) *adj* **1** ministering or serving as a minister. ◆ *n* **2** a person who ministers. [C17: from L *ministrans,* from *ministrāre* to wait upon]

ministration ❶ (ˌmɪnɪˈstreɪʃən) *n* **1** the act or an instance of serving or giving aid. **2** the act or an instance of ministering religiously. [C14: from L *ministrātiō,* from *ministrāre* to wait upon]
▸**ministrative** (ˈmɪnɪstrətɪv) *adj*

ministry ❶ (ˈmɪnɪstrɪ) *n, pl* **ministries. 1a** the profession or duties of a minister of religion. **1b** the performance of these duties. **2** ministers of religion or government ministers considered collectively. **3** the tenure of a minister. **4a** a government department headed by a minister. **4b** the buildings of such a department. [C14: from L *ministerium* service; see MINISTER]

miniver (ˈmɪnɪvə) *n* white fur, used in ceremonial costumes. [C13: from OF *menu vair,* from *menu* small + *vair* variegated fur]

mink (mɪŋk) *n, pl* **mink** *or* **minks. 1** any of several mammals of Europe, Asia, and North America, having slightly webbed feet. **2** their highly valued fur, esp. that of the American mink. **3** a garment made of this, esp. a woman's coat or stole. [C15: from ON]

minneola (ˌmɪnɪˈəʊlə) *n* a juicy citrus fruit that is a cross between a tangerine and a grapefruit. [C20: ?from *Mineola,* Texas]

minnesinger (ˈmɪnɪˌsɪŋə) *n* one of the German lyric poets and musicians of the 12th to 14th centuries. [C19: from G *Minnesinger* love-singer]

minnow (ˈmɪnəʊ) *n, pl* **minnows** *or* **minnow. 1** a small slender European freshwater cyprinid fish. **2** a small or insignificant person. [C15: rel. to OE *myne* minnow]

Minoan (mɪˈnəʊən) *adj* **1** of or denoting the Bronze Age culture of Crete from about 3000 B.C. to about 1100 B.C. ◆ *n* **2** a Cretan belonging to the Minoan culture. [C19: after *Minos* in Gk myth, king of Crete, from the excavations of his supposed palace at Knossos]

minor ❶ (ˈmaɪnə) *adj* **1** lesser or secondary in amount, importance, etc. **2** of or relating to the minority. **3** below the age of legal majority. **4** *Music.* **4a** (of a scale) having a semitone between the second and third and fifth and sixth degrees (**natural minor**). **4b** (of a key) based on the minor scale. **4c** (*postpositive*) denoting a specified key based on the minor scale: *C minor.* **4d** (of an interval) reduced by a semitone from the major. **4e** (of a chord, esp. a triad) having a minor third above the root. **f.** (esp. in jazz) of or relating to a chord built upon a minor triad and containing a minor seventh: *a minor ninth.* **5** *Logic.* (of a term or premise) having less generality or scope than another term or proposition. **6** *US education.* of or relating to an additional secondary subject taken by a student. **7** (*immediately postpositive*) *Brit.* the younger or junior: sometimes used after the surname of a schoolboy if he has an older brother in the same school. ◆ *n* **8** a person or thing that is lesser or secondary. **9** a person below the age of legal majority. **10** *US & Canad. education.* a subsidiary subject. **11** *Music.* a minor key, chord, mode, or scale. **12** *Logic.* a minor term or premise. ◆ *vb* **13** (*intr;* usually foll. by *in*) *US education.* to take a minor. [C13: from L: less, smaller]

minor axis *n* the shorter or shortest axis of an ellipse or ellipsoid.

minority (maɪˈnɒrɪtɪ, mɪ-) *n, pl* **minorities. 1** the smaller of two parts, factions, or groups. **2** a group that is different racially, politically, etc., from a larger group of which it is a part. **3a** the state of being a minor. **3b** the period during which a person is below legal age. **4** (*modifier*) relating to or being a minority: *a minority opinion.* [C16: from Med. L *minōritās,* from L MINOR]

minor league *n US & Canad.* any professional league in baseball other than a major league.

minor orders *pl n RC Church.* the four lower degrees of holy orders, namely porter, exorcist, lector, and acolyte.

minor premise *n Logic.* the premise of a syllogism containing the subject of its conclusion.

minor term *n Logic.* the subject of the conclusion of a syllogism.

minster (ˈmɪnstə) *n Brit.* any of certain cathedrals and large churches, usually originally connected to a monastery. [OE *mynster,* prob. from Vulgar L *monisterium* (unattested), var. of Church L *monastērium* MONASTERY]

minstrel ❶ (ˈmɪnstrəl) *n* **1** a medieval musician who performed songs or recited poetry with instrumental accompaniment. **2** a performer in a minstrel show. **3** *Arch. or poetic.* any poet, musician, or singer. [C13: from OF *menestral,* from LL *ministeriālis* an official, from L MINISTER]

minstrel show *n* a theatrical entertainment consisting of songs, dances, etc., performed by actors wearing black face make-up.

minstrelsy (ˈmɪnstrəlsɪ) *n, pl* **minstrelsies. 1** the art of a minstrel. **2** the poems, music, or songs of a minstrel. **3** a troupe of minstrels.

mint[1] (mɪnt) *n* **1** any N temperate plant of a genus having aromatic leaves. The leaves of some species are used for seasoning and flavouring. See also **peppermint, spearmint. 2** a sweet flavoured with mint. [OE *minte,* from L *mentha,* from Gk *minthē*]
▸ˈ**minty** *adj*

mint[2] ❶ (mɪnt) *n* **1** a place where money is coined by governmental authority. **2** a very large amount of money. ◆ *adj* **3** (of coins, postage stamps, etc.) in perfect condition as issued. **4 in mint condition.** in perfect condition; as if new. ◆ *vb* **5** to make (coins) by stamping metal. **6** (*tr*) to invent (esp. phrases or words). [OE *mynet* coin, from L *monēta* money, mint, from the temple of Juno *Monēta,* used as a mint in ancient Rome]
▸ˈ**minter** *n*

mintage (ˈmɪntɪdʒ) *n* **1** the process of minting. **2** the money minted. **3** a fee paid for minting a coin. **4** an official impression stamped on a coin.

mint julep *n Chiefly US.* a long drink consisting of bourbon whiskey, crushed ice, sugar, and sprigs of mint.

minuend (ˈmɪnjuˌend) *n* the number from which another number, the **subtrahend,** is to be subtracted. [C18: from L *minuendus* (*numerus*) (the number) to be diminished]

minuet (ˌmɪnjuˈet) *n* **1** a stately court dance of the 17th and 18th centuries in triple time. **2** a piece of music composed for or in the rhythm of this dance. [C17: from F *menuet* dainty, from *menu* small]

minus (ˈmaɪnəs) *prep* **1** reduced by the subtraction of: *four minus two* (written 4 – 2). **2** *Inf.* deprived of; lacking: *minus the trimmings.* ◆ *adj* **3a** indicating or involving subtraction: *a minus sign.* **3b** Also: **negative.** having a value or designating a quantity less than zero: *a minus number.* **4** involving a disadvantage, harm, etc.: *a minus factor.* **5** (*postpositive*) *Education.* slightly below the standard of a particular grade: *a B minus.* **6** denoting a negative electric charge. ◆ *n* **7** short for **minus sign. 8** a negative quantity. **9** a disadvantage, loss, or deficit. **10** *Inf.* something detrimental or negative. ◆ Mathematical symbol: – [C15: from L, neuter of MINOR]

minuscule ❶ (ˈmɪnəˌskjuːl) *n* **1** a lower-case letter. **2** writing using such letters. **3** a small cursive 7th-century style of lettering. ◆ *adj* **4** relating to, printed in, or written in small letters. Cf. **majuscule. 5** very small. **6** (of letters) lower-case. [C18: from F, from L (*littera*) *minuscula* very small (letter), dim. of MINOR]
▸**minuscular** (mɪˈnʌskjulə) *adj*

minus sign *n* the symbol –, indicating subtraction or a negative quantity.

minute[1] ❶ (ˈmɪnɪt) *n* **1** a period of time equal to 60 seconds; one sixtieth of an hour. **2** Also called: **minute of arc.** a unit of angular measure equal to one sixtieth of a degree. Symbol: ′. **3** any very short period of time; moment. **4** a short note or memorandum. **5** the distance that can be travelled in a minute: *it's only two minutes away.* **6 up to the minute** (**up-to-the-minute** *when prenominal*). the very latest or newest. ◆ *vb* **minutes, minuting, minuted.** (*tr*) **7** to record in minutes: *to minute a meeting.* **8**

THESAURUS

minister *n* **1 = clergyman,** chaplain, churchman, cleric, divine, ecclesiastic, padre (*inf.*), parson, pastor, preacher, priest, rector, vicar **2, 3 = official,** administrator, ambassador, cabinet member, delegate, diplomat, envoy, executive, office-holder, plenipotentiary **7 = assistant,** agent, aide, lieutenant, servant, subordinate, underling ◆ *vb* **8 = attend,** accommodate, administer, answer, be solicitous of, cater to, pander to, serve, take care of, tend

ministration *n* **1 = help,** aid, assistance, favour, patronage, relief, service, succour, support

ministry *n* **1 = the priesthood,** holy orders, the church, the pulpit **4a = department,** administration, bureau, cabinet, council, government, office, quango

minor *adj* **1, 7 = small,** inconsequential, inconsiderable, inferior, insignificant, junior, lesser, light, negligible, nickel-and-dime (*US sl.*), paltry, petty, secondary, slight, smaller, subordinate, trifling, trivial, unimportant, younger
Antonyms *adj* appreciable, consequential, considerable, essential, grand, great, heavy, important, major, profound, serious, significant, substantial, superior, vital, weighty

minstrel *n* **1-3 = musician,** bard, harper, jongleur, singer, songstress, troubadour

mint[2] *n* **2 = fortune,** bomb (*Brit. sl.*), bundle (*sl.*), heap (*inf.*), King's ransom, million, packet (*sl.*), pile (*inf.*) ◆ *adj* **3 = perfect,** brand-new, excellent, first-class, fresh, unblemished, undamaged, untarnished ◆ *vb* **5 = make,** cast, coin, produce, punch, stamp, strike **6 = invent,** coin, construct, devise, fabricate, fashion, forge, make up, produce, think up

minuscule *adj* **6 = tiny,** diminutive, fine, infinitesimal, Lilliputian, little, microscopic, miniature, minute, teensy-weensy, teeny-weeny, very small

minute[1] *n* **1 = sixty seconds,** sixtieth of an hour **3 = moment,** flash, instant, jiffy (*inf.*), second, shake (*inf.*), tick (*Brit. inf.*), trice **6 up to the minute = latest,** all the rage, in, modish, (most) fashionable, newest, now (*inf.*), smart, stylish,

to time in terms of minutes. ◆ See also **minutes**. [C14: from OF, from Med. L *minūta*, n. use of L *minūtus* MINUTE[2]]
▸**minutely** ('mɪnɪtlɪ) *adv*

minute[2] ❶ (maɪ'nju:t) *adj* **1** very small; diminutive; tiny. **2** unimportant; petty. **3** precise or detailed. [C15: from L *minūtus*, p.p. of *minuere* to diminish]
▸**mi'nuteness** *n* ▸**mi'nutely** *adv*

minute gun ('mɪnɪt) *n* a gun fired at one-minute intervals as a sign of distress or mourning.

minute hand ('mɪnɪt) *n* the pointer on a timepiece that indicates minutes.

Minuteman ('mɪnɪt,mæn) *n, pl* **Minutemen. 1** (*sometimes not cap.*) (in the War of American Independence) a colonial militiaman who promised to be ready to fight at one minute's notice. **2** a US three-stage intercontinental ballistic missile.

minutes ❶ ('mɪnɪts) *pl n* an official record of the proceedings of a meeting, conference, etc.

minute steak ('mɪnɪt) *n* a small piece of steak that can be cooked quickly.

minutiae ❶ (mɪ'nju:ʃɪ,i:) *pl n, sing* **minutia** (-ʃɪə). small, precise, or trifling details. [C18: pl of LL *minūtia* smallness, from L *minūtus* MINUTE[2]]

minx ❶ (mɪŋks) *n* a bold, flirtatious, or scheming woman. [C16: from ?]

Miocene ('maɪə,si:n) *adj* **1** of or denoting the fourth epoch of the Tertiary period. ◆ *n* **2 the.** this epoch or rock series. [C19: Gk *meiōn* less + -CENE]

miosis *or* **myosis** (maɪ'əʊsɪs) *n, pl* **mioses** (-si:z) *or* **myoses. 1** excessive contraction of the pupil of the eye. **2** a variant spelling of **meiosis** (sense 1). [C20: from Gk *muein* to shut the eyes + -OSIS]
▸**miotic** *or* **myotic** (maɪ'ɒtɪk) *adj, n*

MIP *abbrev. for:* **1** monthly investment plan. **2** maximum investment plan: an endowment assurance policy designed to produce maximum profits.

Mir (mɪə) *n* the Russian (formerly Soviet) orbiting space station. [Russian]

miracle ❶ ('mɪrək[ə]l) *n* **1** an event contrary to the laws of nature and attributed to a supernatural cause. **2** any amazing or wonderful event. **3** a marvellous example of something: *a miracle of engineering*. **4** short for **miracle play. 5** (*modifier*) being or seeming a miracle: *a miracle cure.* [C12: from L *mīrāculum*, from *mīrārī* to wonder at]

miracle play *n* a medieval play based on a biblical story or the life of a saint. Cf. **mystery play.**

miraculous ❶ (mɪ'rækjʊləs) *adj* **1** of, like, or caused by a miracle; marvellous. **2** surprising. **3** having the power to work miracles.
▸**mi'raculously** *adv* ▸**mi'raculousness** *n*

mirage ❶ (mɪ'rɑ:ʒ) *n* **1** an image of a distant object or sheet of water, often inverted or distorted, caused by atmospheric refraction by hot air. **2** something illusory. [C19: from F, from (*se*) *mirer* to be reflected]

mire ❶ ('maɪə) *n* **1** a boggy or marshy area. **2** mud, muck, or dirt. ◆ *vb* **mires, miring, mired. 3** to sink or cause to sink in a mire. **4** (*tr*) to make dirty or muddy. **5** (*tr*) to involve, esp. in difficulties. [C14: from ON *mȳrr*]

mirepoix (mɪə'pwɑ:) *n* a mixture of sautéed root vegetables used as a base for braising meat or for various sauces. [F, prob. after Duke of *Mirepoix*, 18th-cent. F general]

mirk (mɜ:k) *n* a variant spelling of **murk.**
▸**'mirky** *adj* ▸**'mirkily** *adv* ▸**'mirkiness** *n*

mirror ❶ ('mɪrə) *n* **1** a surface, such as polished metal or glass coated with a metal film, that reflects an image of an object placed in front of it. **2** such a reflecting surface mounted in a frame. **3** any reflecting surface. **4** a thing that reflects or depicts something else. ◆ *vb* **5** (*tr*) to reflect, represent, or depict faithfully: *he mirrors his teacher's ideals.* [C13: from OF from *mirer* to look at, from L *mīrārī* to wonder at]

mirror ball *n* a large revolving ball covered with small pieces of mirror glass so that it reflects light in changing patterns: used in discos and ballrooms.

mirror carp *n* a variety of carp with a smooth shiny body surface.

mirror image *n* **1** an image as observed in a mirror. **2** an object that corresponds to another but has left and right reversed as if seen in a mirror.

mirror writing *n* backward writing that forms a mirror image of normal writing.

mirth ❶ (mɜ:θ) *n* laughter, gaiety, or merriment. [OE *myrgth*]
▸**'mirthful** *adj* ▸**'mirthfulness** *n* ▸**'mirthless** *adj* ▸**'mirthlessness** *n*

MIRV (mɜ:v) *n acronym for* multiple independently targeted re-entry vehicle: a missile that has several warheads, each one being directed to a different enemy target.

mis- *prefix* **1** wrong or bad; wrongly or badly: *misunderstanding; misfortune; mistreat; mislead.* **2** lack of; not: *mistrust.* [OE *mis(se)*-]

misadventure ❶ (,mɪsəd'ventʃə) *n* **1** an unlucky event; misfortune. **2** *Law.* accidental death not due to crime or negligence.

misalliance (,mɪsə'laɪəns) *n* an unsuitable alliance or marriage.
▸**,misal'ly** *vb*

misanthrope ❶ ('mɪzən,θrəʊp) *or* **misanthropist** (mɪ'zænθrəpɪst) *n* a person who dislikes or distrusts other people or mankind in general. [C17: from Gk *mīsanthrōpos*, from *misos* hatred + *anthrōpos* man]
▸**misanthropic** (,mɪzən'θrɒpɪk) *or* **,misan'thropical** *adj* ▸**misanthropy** (mɪ'zænθrəpɪ) *n*

misapply ❶ (,mɪsə'plaɪ) *vb* **misapplies, misapplying, misapplied.** (*tr*) **1** to apply wrongly or badly. **2** another word for **misappropriate.**
▸**misapplication** (,mɪsæplɪ'keɪʃən) *n*

misapprehend ❶ (,mɪsæprɪ'hend) *vb* (*tr*) to misunderstand.
▸**misapprehension** (,mɪsæprɪ'henʃən) *n* ▸**,misappre'hensive** *adj* ▸**,misappre'hensiveness** *n*

misappropriate ❶ (,mɪsə'prəʊprɪ,eɪt) *vb* **misappropriates, misappropriating, misappropriated.** (*tr*) to appropriate for a wrong or dishonest use; embezzle or steal.
▸**,misap,propri'ation** *n*

misbecome (,mɪsbɪ'kʌm) *vb* **misbecomes, misbecoming, misbecame, misbecome.** (*tr*) to be unbecoming to or unsuitable for.

misbegotten ❶ (,mɪsbɪ'gɒt[ə]n) *adj* **1** unlawfully obtained. **2** badly conceived, planned, or designed. **3** *Literary and dialect.* illegitimate; bastard.

misbehave ❶ (,mɪsbɪ'heɪv) *vb* **misbehaves, misbehaving, misbehaved.** to behave (oneself) badly.
▸**,misbe'haver** *n* ▸**misbehaviour** *or US* **misbehavior** (,mɪsbɪ'heɪvjə) *n*

THESAURUS

trendiest, trendy (*Brit. inf.*), up to date, vogue, with it (*inf.*)

minute[2] *adj* **1** = **small**, diminutive, fine, infinitesimal, Lilliputian, little, microscopic, miniature, minuscule, slender, teensy-weensy, teeny-weeny, tiny **2** = **negligible**, inconsiderable, paltry, petty, picayune (*US*), piddling (*inf.*), puny, slight, trifling, trivial, unimportant **3** = **precise**, close, critical, detailed, exact, exhaustive, meticulous, painstaking, punctilious
Antonyms *adj* ≠ **small:** enormous, generous, gigantic, ginormous (*inf.*), grand, great, huge, immense, mega (*sl.*), monstrous ≠ **negligible:** important, major, significant, vital ≠ **precise:** careless, haphazard, imprecise, inexact, loose, quick, rough, superficial

minutely *adv* **3** = **precisely**, closely, critically, exactly, exhaustively, in detail, meticulously, painstakingly, with a fine-tooth comb

minutes *pl n* = **record**, memorandum, notes, proceedings, transactions, transcript

minutiae *pl n* = **details**, finer points, ins and outs, niceties, particulars, subtleties, trifles, trivia

minx *n* = **flirt**, baggage, coquette, hoyden, hussy, jade, tomboy, wanton

miracle *n* **1** = **wonder**, marvel, phenomenon, prodigy, thaumaturgy

miraculous *adj* **1, 3** = **wonderful**, amazing, astonishing, astounding, extraordinary, incredible, inexplicable, magical, marvellous, phenomenal, preternatural, prodigious, superhuman, supernatural, thaumaturgic, unaccountable, unbelievable, wondrous (*arch. or literary*)
Antonyms *adj* awful, bad, banal, common, commonplace, everyday, normal, ordinary, run-of-the-mill, terrible, unexceptional, unremarkable, usual

mirage *n* **1, 2** = **illusion**, hallucination, optical illusion, phantasm

mire *n* **1** = **swamp**, bog, marsh, morass, quagmire **2** = **mud**, dirt, gloop (*inf.*), grot (*sl.*), muck, ooze, slime, slob (*Irish*) ◆ *vb* **3** = **bog down**, flounder, sink, stick in the mud **4** = **begrime**, besmirch, bespatter, cake, dirty, muddy, soil **5** = **entangle**, catch up, enmesh, involve

mirror *n* **1, 2** = **looking-glass**, glass, reflector, speculum ◆ *vb* **5** = **reflect**, copy, depict, echo, emulate, follow, represent, show

mirth *n* = **merriment**, amusement, cheerfulness, festivity, frolic, fun, gaiety, gladness, glee, hilarity, jocularity, jollity, joviality, joyousness, laughter, levity, merrymaking, pleasure, rejoicing, revelry, sport

mirthful *adj* = **merry**, amused, amusing, blithe, cheerful, cheery, festive, frolicsome, funny, gay, glad, gladsome (*arch.*), happy, hilarious, jocund, jolly, jovial, laughable, light-hearted, playful, sportive, uproarious, vivacious
Antonyms *adj* dejected, depressed, despondent, dismal, down in the dumps (*inf.*), gloomy, grave, lugubrious, melancholy, miserable, morose, sad, saturnine, sedate, serious, solemn, sombre, sorrowful, unhappy

misadventure *n* **1** = **misfortune**, accident, bad break (*inf.*), bad luck, bummer (*sl.*), calamity, catastrophe, debacle, disaster, failure, ill fortune, ill luck, mischance, mishap, reverse, setback

misanthrope *n* = **cynic**, egoist, egotist, mankind-hater, misanthropist

misanthropic *adj* = **antisocial**, cynical, egoistic, inhumane, malevolent, unfriendly, unsociable

misanthropy *n* = **cynicism**, egoism, hatred of mankind, inhumanity, malevolence

misapply *vb* **1, 2** = **misuse**, abuse, misappropriate, misemploy, pervert

misapprehend *vb* = **misunderstand**, get hold of the wrong end of the stick, get one's lines crossed, get the wrong idea *or* impression, misconceive, misconstrue, misinterpret, misread, mistake

misapprehension *n* = **misunderstanding**, delusion, error, fallacy, false belief, false impression, misconception, misconstruction, misinterpretation, misreading, mistake, wrong idea *or* impression

misappropriate *vb* = **steal**, defalcate (*Law*), embezzle, misapply, misspend, misuse, peculate, pocket, swindle

misbegotten *adj* **1** = **ill-gotten**, dishonest, disreputable, illicit, purloined, shady (*inf.*), stolen, unlawful, unrespectable **2** = **ill-conceived**, abortive, hare-brained, ill-advised, poorly thought-out **3** *Literary and dialect* = **illegitimate**, bastard, born out of wedlock, natural, spurious (*rare*)

misbehave *vb* = **be naughty**, act up (*inf.*), be bad, be insubordinate, carry on (*inf.*), get up to mischief (*inf.*), muck about (*Brit. sl.*)
Antonyms *vb* act correctly, be good, behave, conduct oneself properly, mind one's manners, mind one's p's and q's, toe the line

misbehaviour *n* = **misconduct**, acting up (*inf.*), bad behaviour, impropriety, incivility, in-

misbelief ➊ (ˌmɪsbɪˈliːf) *n* a false or unorthodox belief.
▸ˌ**misbeˈliever** *n*

misc. *abbrev. for:* **1** miscellaneous. **2** miscellany.

miscalculate ➊ (ˌmɪsˈkælkjʊˌleɪt) *vb* **miscalculates, miscalculating, miscalculated.** (*tr*) to calculate wrongly.
▸ˌ**miscalcuˈlation** *n*

miscall (ˌmɪsˈkɔːl) *vb* (*tr*) **1** to call by the wrong name. **2** *Dialect.* to abuse or malign.
▸ˌ**misˈcaller** *n*

miscarriage ➊ (mɪsˈkærɪdʒ) *n* **1** (*also* ˈmɪskær-). spontaneous expulsion of a fetus from the womb, esp. prior to the 20th week of pregnancy. **2** an act of mismanagement or failure: *a miscarriage of justice.* **3** *Brit.* the failure of freight to reach its destination.

miscarry ➊ (mɪsˈkærɪ) *vb* **miscarries, miscarrying, miscarried.** (*intr*) **1** to expel a fetus prematurely from the womb; abort. **2** to fail. **3** *Brit.* (of freight, mail, etc.) to fail to reach a destination.

miscast (ˌmɪsˈkɑːst) *vb* **miscasts, miscasting, miscast.** (*tr*) **1** to cast badly. **2** (*often passive*) **2a** to cast (a role) in (a play, film, etc.) inappropriately: *Falstaff was miscast.* **2b** to assign an inappropriate role to: *he was miscast as Othello.*

miscegenation (ˌmɪsɪdʒɪˈneɪʃən) *n* interbreeding of races, esp. where differences of pigmentation are involved. [C19: from L *miscēre* to mingle + *genus* race]

miscellanea (ˌmɪsəˈleɪnɪə) *pl n* a collection of miscellaneous items, esp. literary works. [C16: from L: neuter pl of *miscellāneus* MISCELLANEOUS]

miscellaneous ➊ (ˌmɪsəˈleɪnɪəs) *adj* **1** composed of or containing a variety of things; mixed. **2** having varied capabilities, sides, etc. [C17: from L *miscellāneus,* from *miscellus* mixed, from *miscēre* to mix]
▸ˌ**miscelˈlaneously** *adv* ▸ˌ**miscelˈlaneousness** *n*

miscellany ➊ (mɪˈsɛlənɪ; *US* ˈmɪsəˌleɪnɪ) *n, pl* **miscellanies. 1** a mixed assortment of items. **2** (*sometimes pl*) a miscellaneous collection of items, esp. essays, poems, etc. [C16: from F *miscellanées* (pl) MISCELLANEA]
▸**miscellanist** (mɪˈsɛlənɪst) *n*

mischance ➊ (mɪsˈtʃɑːns) *n* **1** bad luck. **2** a stroke of bad luck.

mischief ➊ (ˈmɪstʃɪf) *n* **1** wayward but not malicious behaviour, usually of children, that causes trouble, irritation, etc. **2** a playful inclination to behave in this way or to tease or disturb. **3** injury or harm caused by a person or thing. **4** a person, esp. a child, who is mischievous. **5** a source of trouble, difficulty, etc. [C13: from OF *meschief,* from *meschever* to meet with calamity; from *mes-* MIS- + *chever,* from *chef* end]

mischievous ➊ (ˈmɪstʃɪvəs) *adj* **1** inclined to acts of mischief. **2** teasing; slightly malicious. **3** causing or intended to cause harm.
▸ˈ**mischievously** *adv* ▸ˈ**mischievousness** *n*

miscible (ˈmɪsɪbᵊl) *adj* capable of mixing: *miscible with water.* [C16: from Med. L *miscibilis,* from L *miscēre* to mix]
▸ˌ**misciˈbility** *n*

misconceive ➊ (ˌmɪskənˈsiːv) *vb* **misconceives, misconceiving, misconceived.** to have the wrong idea; fail to understand.
▸ˌ**misconˈceiver** *n*

misconception ➊ (ˌmɪskənˈsɛpʃən) *n* a false or mistaken view, opinion, or attitude.

misconduct ➊ *n* (mɪsˈkɒndʌkt). **1** behaviour, such as adultery or professional negligence, that is regarded as immoral or unethical. ◆ *vb* (ˌmɪskənˈdʌkt). (*tr*) **2** to conduct (oneself) in such a way. **3** to manage (something) badly.

misconstrue ➊ (ˌmɪskənˈstruː) *vb* **misconstrues, misconstruing, misconstrued.** (*tr*) to interpret mistakenly.
▸ˌ**misconˈstruction** *n*

miscreant ➊ (ˈmɪskrɪənt) *n* **1** a wrongdoer or villain. **2** *Arch.* an unbeliever or heretic. ◆ *adj* **3** evil or villainous. **4** *Arch.* unbelieving or heretical. [C14: from OF *mescreant* unbelieving, from *mes-* MIS- + *creant,* ult. from L *credere* to believe]

miscue (ˌmɪsˈkjuː) *n* **1** *Billiards, etc.* a faulty stroke in which the cue tip slips off the cue ball or misses it. **2** *Inf.* a blunder or mistake. ◆ *vb* **miscues, miscuing, miscued.** (*intr*) **3** *Billiards.* to make a miscue. **4** *Theatre.* to fail to answer one's cue.

miscue analysis *n Brit. education.* analysis of the errors a pupil makes while reading.

misdate (mɪsˈdeɪt) *vb* **misdates, misdating, misdated.** (*tr*) to date (a letter, event, etc.) wrongly.

misdeal (ˌmɪsˈdiːl) *vb* **misdeals, misdealing, misdealt. 1** (*intr*) to deal out cards incorrectly. ◆ *n* **2** a faulty deal.
▸ˌ**misˈdealer** *n*

misdeed ➊ (ˌmɪsˈdiːd) *n* an evil or illegal action.

misdemean (ˌmɪsdɪˈmiːn) *vb* a rare word for **misbehave.**

misdemeanour ➊ *or US* **misdemeanor** (ˌmɪsdɪˈmiːnə) *n* **1** *Criminal law.* (formerly) an offence generally less heinous than a felony. **2** any minor offence or transgression.

misdirect (ˌmɪsdɪˈrɛkt) *vb* (*tr*) **1** to give (a person) wrong directions or instructions. **2** to address (a letter, parcel, etc.) wrongly.
▸ˌ**misdiˈrection** *n*

misdoubt (mɪsˈdaʊt) *vb* an archaic word for **doubt** or **suspect.**

mise en scène *French.* (miz ɑ̃ sɛn) *n* **1a** the arrangement of properties, scenery, etc., in a play. **1b** the objects so arranged; stage setting. **2** the environment of an event.

miser ➊ (ˈmaɪzə) *n* **1** a person who hoards money or possessions, often living miserably. **2** a selfish person. [C16: from L: wretched]

miserable ➊ (ˈmɪzərəbᵊl) *adj* **1** unhappy or depressed; wretched. **2** causing misery, discomfort, etc.: *a miserable life.* **3** contemptible: *a miserable villain.* **4** sordid or squalid: *miserable living conditions.* **5** mean; stingy. [C16: from OF, from L *miserābilis,* from *miserārī* to pity, from *miser* wretched]
▸ˈ**miserableness** *n* ▸ˈ**miserably** *adv*

misère (mɪˈzɛə) *n* **1** a call in solo whist, etc. declaring a hand that will win no tricks. **2** a hand that will win no tricks. [C19: from F: misery]

Miserere (ˌmɪzəˈrɛərɪ, -ˈrɪərɪ) *n* the 51st psalm, the Latin version of which begins "Miserere mei, Deus" ("Have mercy on me, O God").

misericord *or* **misericorde** (mɪˈzɛrɪˌkɔːd) *n* **1** a ledge projecting from the underside of the hinged seat of a choir stall in a church, on which the occupant can support himself while standing. **2** *Christianity.* **2a** a relaxation of certain monastic rules for infirm or aged monks or nuns. **2b** a monastery or room where this can be enjoyed. **3** a medieval dagger used to give the death stroke to a wounded foe. [C14: from OF, from L *misericordia* compassion, from *miserēre* to pity + *cor* heart]

THESAURUS

discipline, insubordination, mischief, misdeeds, misdemeanour, monkey business (*inf.*), naughtiness, rudeness, shenanigans (*inf.*)

misbelief *n* = **delusion**, error, fallacy, false belief, heresy, unorthodoxy

miscalculate *vb* = **misjudge**, blunder, calculate wrongly, err, get (it) wrong, go wrong, make a mistake, overestimate, overrate, slip up, underestimate, underrate

miscarriage *n* **1** = **spontaneous abortion**, miss (*inf.*) **2** = **failure**, botch (*inf.*), breakdown, error, misadventure, mischance, misfire, mishap, mismanagement, nonsuccess, perversion, thwarting, undoing

miscarry *vb* **1** = **abort 2** = **fail**, come to grief, come to nothing, fall through, gang agley (*Scot.*), go amiss, go astray, go awry, go pear-shaped (*inf.*), go wrong, misfire

miscellaneous *adj* **1** = **mixed**, assorted, confused, diverse, diversified, farraginous, heterogeneous, indiscriminate, jumbled, manifold, many, mingled, motley, multifarious, multiform, promiscuous, sundry, varied, various

miscellany *n* **1, 2** = **assortment**, anthology, collection, diversity, farrago, gallimaufry, hotchpotch, jumble, medley, *mélange,* mixed bag, mixture, omnium-gatherum, potpourri, salmagundi, variety

mischance *n* **1, 2** = **misfortune**, accident, bad break, bad luck, bummer (*sl.*), calamity, contretemps, disaster, ill chance, ill fortune, ill luck, infelicity, misadventure, mishap

mischief *n* **1** = **misbehaviour**, devilment, impishness, monkey business (*inf.*), naughtiness, pranks, roguery, roguishness, shenanigans (*inf.*), trouble, waywardness **3** = **harm**, damage, detriment, disadvantage, disruption, evil, hurt, injury, misfortune, trouble **4** = **rogue**, devil, imp, monkey, nuisance, pest, rascal, scallywag (*inf.*), scamp, tyke (*inf.*), villain

mischievous *adj* **1, 2** = **naughty**, arch, bad, badly behaved, exasperating, frolicsome, impish, playful, puckish, rascally, roguish, sportive, teasing, troublesome, vexatious, wayward **3** = **malicious**, bad, damaging, deleterious, destructive, detrimental, evil, harmful, hurtful, injurious, malignant, pernicious, sinful, spiteful, troublesome, vicious, wicked

misconceive *vb* = **misunderstand**, fail to understand, get one's lines crossed, get the wrong idea (about), misapprehend, misconstrue, misjudge, mistake

misconception *n* = **delusion**, error, fallacy, misapprehension, misconstruction, mistaken belief, misunderstanding, wrong end of the stick, wrong idea

misconduct *n* **1** = **immorality**, delinquency, dereliction, impropriety, malfeasance (*Law*), malpractice, malversation (*rare*), misbehaviour, misdemeanour, mismanagement, naughtiness, rudeness, transgression, unethical behaviour, wrongdoing ◆ *vb* **2, 3** = **mismanage**, behave badly, botch (up), bungle, err, make a mess of, misdirect, sin

misconstruction *n* = **misinterpretation**, false interpretation, misapprehension, misreading, mistake, mistaken *or* false impression, misunderstanding, wrong idea

misconstrue *vb* = **misinterpret**, get a false impression, get one's lines crossed, make a wrong interpretation, misapprehend, misconceive, misjudge, misread, mistake, mistranslate, misunderstand, take the wrong way (*inf.*)

miscreant *n* **1** = **wrongdoer**, blackguard, caitiff (*arch.*), criminal, evildoer, knave, malefactor, rascal, reprobate, rogue, scoundrel, sinner, vagabond, villain ◆ *adj* **3** = **wicked**, corrupt, criminal, depraved, evil, iniquitous, nefarious, rascally, reprehensible, reprobate, scoundrelly, unprincipled, vicious, villainous

misdeed *n* = **offence**, crime, fault, misconduct, misdemeanour, sin, transgression, trespass, villainy, wrong

misdemeanour *n* **2** = **offence**, fault, infringement, misbehaviour, misconduct, misdeed, peccadillo, transgression, trespass

miser *n* **1** = **hoarder**, cheapskate (*inf.*), churl (*arch.*), curmudgeon, hunks (*rare*), niggard, penny-pincher (*inf.*), screw (*sl.*), Scrooge, skinflint

miserable *adj* **1** = **unhappy**, afflicted, broken-hearted, crestfallen, dejected, depressed, desolate, despondent, disconsolate, dismal, distressed, doleful, down, downcast, down in the dumps (*inf.*), down in the mouth (*inf.*), forlorn, gloomy, heartbroken, low, melancholy, mournful, sorrowful, woebegone, wretched **3** = **despicable**, abject, bad, contemptible, deplorable, detestable, disgraceful, lamentable, low, mean, pathetic, piteous, pitiable, scurvy, shabby, shameful, sordid, sorry, squalid, vile, worthless, wretched

miserly Ⓣ ('maɪzəlɪ) *adj* of or resembling a miser; avaricious.
▸'**miserliness** *n*

misery Ⓣ ('mɪzərɪ) *n, pl* **miseries. 1** intense unhappiness, suffering, etc. **2** a cause of such unhappiness, etc. **3** squalid or poverty-stricken conditions. **4** *Brit. inf.* a person who is habitually depressed: *he is such a misery.* [C14: via Anglo-Norman from L *miseria,* from *miser* wretched]

misfeasance (mɪs'fiːzəns) *n Law.* the improper performance of an act that is lawful in itself. Cf. **malfeasance, nonfeasance.** [C16: from OF *mesfaisance,* from *mesfaire* to perform misdeeds]

misfile (ˌmɪs'faɪl) *vb* **misfiles, misfiling, misfiled.** to file (papers, records, etc.) wrongly.

misfire Ⓣ (ˌmɪs'faɪə) *vb* **misfires, misfiring, misfired.** (*intr*) **1** (of a firearm or its projectile) to fail to fire or explode as expected. **2** (of a motor engine or vehicle, etc.) to fail to fire at the appropriate time. **3** to fail to operate or occur as intended. ◆ *n* **4** the act or an instance of misfiring.

misfit Ⓣ *n* ('mɪsˌfɪt). **1** a person not suited to a particular social environment. **2** something that does not fit or fits badly. ◆ *vb* (ˌmɪs'fɪt), **misfits, misfitting, misfitted.** (*intr*) **3** to fail to fit or be fitted.

misfortune Ⓣ (mɪs'fɔːtʃən) *n* **1** evil fortune; bad luck. **2** an unfortunate or disastrous event.

misgive (mɪs'gɪv) *vb* **misgives, misgiving, misgave, misgiven.** to make or be apprehensive or suspicious.

misgiving Ⓣ (mɪs'gɪvɪŋ) *n* (*often pl*) a feeling of uncertainty, apprehension, or doubt.

misguide (ˌmɪs'gaɪd) *vb* **misguides, misguiding, misguided.** (*tr*) to guide or direct wrongly or badly.

misguided Ⓣ (ˌmɪs'gaɪdɪd) *adj* foolish or unreasonable, esp. in action or behaviour.
▸ˌ**mis'guidedly** *adv*

mishandle Ⓣ (ˌmɪs'hænd[ə]l) *vb* **mishandles, mishandling, mishandled.** (*tr*) to handle or treat badly or inefficiently.

mishap Ⓣ ('mɪshæp) *n* **1** an unfortunate accident. **2** bad luck.

mishit *Sport.* ◆ *n* ('mɪsˌhɪt). **1** a faulty shot or stroke. ◆ *vb* (ˌmɪs'hɪt), **mishits, mishitting, mishit. 2** to hit (a ball) with a faulty stroke.

mishmash Ⓣ ('mɪʃˌmæʃ) *n* a confused collection or mixture. [C15: reduplication of MASH]

Mishna ('mɪʃnə) *n, pl* **Mishnayoth** (mɪʃ'nɑːjəʊt). *Judaism.* a compilation of precepts collected in the late second century A.D. It forms the earlier part of the Talmud. [C17: from Heb., from *shānāh* to repeat]
▸**Mishnaic** (mɪʃ'neɪɪk) *or* '**Mishnic** *adj*

misinform Ⓣ (ˌmɪsɪn'fɔːm) *vb* (*tr*) to give incorrect information to.
▸**misinformation** (ˌmɪsɪnfə'meɪʃən) *n*

misinterpret Ⓣ (ˌmɪsɪn'tɜːprɪt) *vb* (*tr*) to interpret badly, misleadingly, or incorrectly.
▸ˌ**misinˌterpre'tation** *n* ▸ˌ**misin'terpreter** *n*

misjudge Ⓣ (mɪs'dʒʌdʒ) *vb* **misjudges, misjudging, misjudged.** to judge (a person or persons) wrongly or unfairly.
▸**mis'judger** *n* ▸**mis'judgment** *or* **mis'judgement** *n*

mislay Ⓣ (mɪs'leɪ) *vb* **mislays, mislaying, mislaid.** (*tr*) **1** to lose (something) temporarily, esp. by forgetting where it is. **2** to lay (something) badly.

mislead Ⓣ (mɪs'liːd) *vb* **misleads, misleading, misled.** (*tr*) **1** to give false or confusing information to. **2** to lead or guide in the wrong direction.
▸**mis'leader** *n* ▸**mis'leading** *adj*

mismarriage (mɪs'mærɪdʒ) *n* a marriage to an unsuitable partner.

mismatch Ⓣ (ˌmɪs'mætʃ) *vb* **1** to match badly, esp. in marriage. ◆ *n* **2** a bad match.

misname (mɪs'neɪm) *vb* **misnames, misnaming, misnamed.** (*tr*) to call by a wrong or inappropriate name.

misnomer (ˌmɪs'nəʊmə) *n* **1** an incorrect or unsuitable name for a person or thing. **2** the act of referring to a person by the wrong name. [C15: via Anglo-Norman from OF *mesnommer* to misname, from L *nōmināre* to call by name]

miso- *or before a vowel* **mis-** *combining form.* indicating hatred: *misogyny.* [from Gk *misos* hatred]

misogamy (mɪ'sɒgəmɪ, maɪ-) *n* hatred of marriage.
▸**mi'sogamist** *n*

misogyny (mɪ'sɒdʒɪnɪ, maɪ-) *n* hatred of women. [C17: from Gk, from MISO- + *gunē* woman]
▸**mi'sogynist** *n* ▸**mi'sogynous** *or* **miˌsogy'nistic** *adj*

misplace Ⓣ (ˌmɪs'pleɪs) *vb* **misplaces, misplacing, misplaced.** (*tr*) **1** to put (something) in the wrong place, esp. to lose (something) temporarily by forgetting where it was placed. **2** (*often passive*) to bestow (trust, affection, etc.) unadvisedly.
▸ˌ**mis'placement** *n*

misplaced modifier *n Grammar.* a participle intended to modify a noun but having the wrong grammatical relationship to it, for example *having left* in the sentence *Having left Europe for good, Peter's future seemed bleak.*

misplay (ˌmɪs'pleɪ) *vb* **1** (*tr*) to play badly or wrongly in games or sports. ◆ *n* **2** a wrong or unskilful play.

misprint Ⓣ *n* ('mɪsˌprɪnt). **1** an error in printing, made through damaged type, careless reading, etc. ◆ *vb* (ˌmɪs'prɪnt). **2** (*tr*) to print (a letter) incorrectly.

misprision[1] (mɪs'prɪʒən) *n* **a** a failure to inform the authorities of the commission of an act of treason. **b** the deliberate concealment of the commission of a felony. [C15: via Anglo-F from OF *mesprision* error, from *mesprendre* to mistake, from *mes-* MIS- + *prendre* to take]

misprision[2] (mɪs'prɪʒən) *n Arch.* **1** contempt. **2** failure to appreciate the value of something. [C16: from MISPRIZE]

misprize *or* **misprise** (mɪs'praɪz) *vb* **misprizes, misprizing, misprized** *or* **misprises, misprising, misprised.** to fail to appreciate the value of; disparage. [C15: from OF *mesprisier,* from *mes-* MIS- + *prisier* to PRIZE[2]]

mispronounce (ˌmɪsprə'naʊns) *vb* **mispronounces, mispronouncing, mispronounced.** to pronounce (a word) wrongly.
▸**mispronunciation** (ˌmɪsprəˌnʌnsɪ'eɪʃən) *n*

misproportion (ˌmɪsprə'pɔːʃən) *n* a lack of due proportion.

misquote Ⓣ (ˌmɪs'kwəʊt) *vb* **misquotes, misquoting, misquoted.** to quote (a text, speech, etc.) inaccurately.
▸ˌ**misquo'tation** *n*

misread (ˌmɪs'riːd) *vb* **misreads, misreading, misread** (-'rɛd). (*tr*) **1** to read incorrectly. **2** to misinterpret.

THESAURUS

Antonyms *adj* ≠ **unhappy:** cheerful, happy ≠ **despicable:** admirable, good, respectable

miserliness *n* = **meanness,** avarice, cheeseparing, churlishness, close- *or* tightfistedness, covetousness, graspingness, minginess (*Brit. inf.*), nearness, niggardliness, parsimony, penny-pinching (*inf.*), penuriousness, stinginess

miserly *adj* = **mean,** avaricious, beggarly, close, close-fisted, covetous, grasping, illiberal, mingy (*Brit. inf.*), near, niggardly, parsimonious, penny-pinching (*inf.*), penurious, sordid, stingy, tightfisted, ungenerous
Antonyms *adj* charitable, extravagant, generous, prodigal, unselfish

misery *n* **1** = **unhappiness,** agony, anguish, depression, desolation, despair, discomfort, distress, gloom, grief, hardship, melancholy, sadness, sorrow, suffering, torment, torture, woe, wretchedness **2** = **misfortune,** affliction, bitter pill (*inf.*), burden, calamity, catastrophe, curse, disaster, hardship, load, ordeal, sorrow, trial, tribulation, trouble, woe **3** = **poverty,** destitution, indigence, need, penury, privation, sordidness, squalor, want, wretchedness **4** *Brit. informal* = **moaner,** grouch (*inf.*), killjoy, pessimist, prophet of doom, sourpuss (*inf.*), spoilsport, wet blanket (*inf.*), wowser (*Austral. & NZ sl.*)
Antonyms *n* ≠ **unhappiness:** comfort, contentment, ease, enjoyment, happiness, joy, pleasure ≠ **poverty:** luxury

misfire *vb* **1, 3** = **fail,** fail to go off, fall through, go pear-shaped (*inf.*), go phut (*inf.*), go wrong, miscarry

misfit *n* **1** = **nonconformist,** eccentric, fish out of water (*inf.*), oddball (*inf.*), square peg (in a round hole) (*inf.*)

misfortune *n* **1** = **bad luck,** adversity, evil fortune, hard luck, ill luck, infelicity **2** = **mishap,** accident, affliction, blow, bummer (*sl.*), calamity, disaster, evil chance, failure, hardship, harm, loss, misadventure, mischance, misery, reverse, setback, stroke of bad luck, tragedy, trial, tribulation, trouble, whammy (*inf., chiefly US*)
Antonyms *n* fortune, good luck, relief

misgiving *n* = **unease,** anxiety, apprehension, distrust, doubt, dubiety, hesitation, qualm, reservation, scruple, suspicion, trepidation, uncertainty, worry

misguided *adj* = **unwise,** deluded, erroneous, foolish, ill-advised, imprudent, injudicious, misled, misplaced, mistaken, uncalled-for, unreasonable, unwarranted

mishandle *vb* = **mismanage,** bodge (*inf.*), botch, bungle, make a hash of (*inf.*), make a mess of, make a nonsense of, mess up (*inf.*), muff, screw (up) (*inf.*)

mishap *n* **1, 2** = **accident,** adversity, bad luck, calamity, contretemps, disaster, evil chance, evil fortune, hard luck, ill fortune, ill luck, infelicity, misadventure, mischance, misfortune

mishmash *n* = **jumble,** farrago, gallimaufry, hash, hotchpotch, medley, potpourri, salmagundi

misinform *vb* = **mislead,** deceive, give (someone) a bum steer (*inf., chiefly US*), give (someone) duff gen (*Brit. inf.*), misdirect, misguide

misinterpret *vb* = **misunderstand,** distort, falsify, get wrong, misapprehend, misconceive, misconstrue, misjudge, misread, misrepresent, mistake, pervert

misjudge *vb* = **miscalculate,** be wrong about, get the wrong idea about, overestimate, overrate, underestimate, underrate

mislay *vb* **1** = **lose,** be unable to find, be unable to put *or* lay one's hand on, forget the whereabouts of, lose track of, misplace, miss

mislead *vb* **1** = **deceive,** beguile, bluff, delude, fool, give (someone) a bum steer (*inf., chiefly US*), hoodwink, lead astray, misdirect, misguide, misinform, pull the wool over (someone's) eyes (*inf.*), take for a ride (*inf.*), take in (*inf.*)

misleading *adj* **1** = **confusing,** ambiguous, casuistical, deceitful, deceptive, delusive, delusory, disingenuous, evasive, false, sophistical, specious, spurious, tricky (*inf.*), unstraightforward
Antonyms *adj* candid, clear, correct, direct, explicit, frank, genuine, honest, obvious, open, plain, simple, sincere, straightforward, true, truthful

mismatched *adj* **1** = **incompatible,** clashing, discordant, disparate, ill-assorted, incongruous, irregular, misallied, unreconcilable, unsuited

misplace *vb* **1** = **lose,** be unable to find, be unable to put *or* lay one's hand on, forget the whereabouts of, lose track of, misfile, mislay, miss, put in the wrong place **2** = **place wrongly,** place unwisely

misprint *n* **1** = **mistake,** corrigendum, erratum, literal, printing error, typo (*inf.*), typographical error

misquote *vb* = **misrepresent,** distort, falsify, garble, mangle, misreport, misstate, muddle, pervert, quote *or* take out of context, twist

misrepresent ❶ (ˌmɪsreprɪˈzɛnt) *vb (tr)* to represent wrongly or inaccurately.
▸ˌ**misrepresenˈtation** *n* ▸ˌ**misrepreˈsentative** *adj*

misrule ❶ (ˌmɪsˈruːl) *vb* **misrules, misruling, misruled. 1** *(tr)* to govern inefficiently or without justice. ◆ *n* **2** inefficient or unjust government. **3** disorder.

miss[1] ❶ (mɪs) *vb* **1** to fail to reach, hit, meet, find, or attain (some aim, target, etc.). **2** *(tr)* to fail to attend or be present for: *to miss an appointment.* **3** *(tr)* to fail to see, hear, understand, or perceive. **4** *(tr)* to lose, overlook, or fail to take advantage of: *to miss an opportunity.* **5** *(tr)* to leave out; omit: *to miss an entry in a list.* **6** *(tr)* to discover or regret the loss or absence of: *she missed him.* **7** *(tr)* to escape or avoid (something, esp. a danger), usually narrowly: *he missed death by inches.* ◆ *n* **8** a failure to reach, hit, etc. **9 give (something) a miss.** *Inf.* to avoid (something): *give the pudding a miss.* ◆ See also **miss out.** [OE *missan* (meaning: to fail to hit)]

miss[2] ❶ (mɪs) *n Inf.* an unmarried woman or girl. [C17: from MISTRESS]

Miss (mɪs) *n* a title of an unmarried woman or girl, usually used before the surname or sometimes alone in direct address. [C17: shortened from MISTRESS]

missal (ˈmɪsᵊl) *n RC Church.* a book containing the prayers, rites, etc., of the Masses for a complete year. [C14: from Church L *missale* (n), from *missālis* concerning the MASS]

misshape *vb* (ˌmɪsˈʃeɪp), **misshapes, misshaping, misshaped; misshaped** *or* **misshapen. 1** *(tr)* to shape badly; deform. ◆ *n* (ˈmɪsˌʃeɪp). **2** something that is badly shaped.

misshapen ❶ (ˌmɪsˈʃeɪpᵊn) *adj* badly shaped; deformed.
▸ˌ**misˈshapenness** *n*

missile ❶ (ˈmɪsaɪl) *n* **1** any object or weapon that is thrown at a target or shot from an engine, gun, etc. **2** a rocket-propelled weapon that flies either in a fixed trajectory (**ballistic missile**) or in a trajectory controlled during flight (**guided missile**). [C17: from L *missilis,* from *mittere* to send]

missilery *or* **missilry** (ˈmɪsaɪlrɪ) *n* **1** missiles collectively. **2** the design, operation, or study of missiles.

missing ❶ (ˈmɪsɪŋ) *adj* **1** not present; absent or lost. **2** not able to be traced and not known to be dead: *nine men were missing after the attack.* **3 go missing.** to become lost or disappear.

missing link *n* **1** *(sometimes cap.;* usually preceded by *the)* a hypothetical extinct animal, formerly thought to be intermediate between the anthropoid apes and man. **2** any missing section or part in a series.

mission ❶ (ˈmɪʃən) *n* **1** a specific task or duty assigned to a person or group of people. **2** a person's vocation (often in **mission in life**). **3** a group of persons representing or working for a particular country, business, etc., in a foreign country. **4** a special embassy sent to a foreign country for a specific purpose. **5a** a group of people sent by a religious body, esp. a Christian church, to a foreign country to do religious and social work. **5b** the campaign undertaken by such a group. **6a** a building in which missionary work is performed. **6b** the area assigned to a particular missionary. **7** the dispatch of aircraft or spacecraft to achieve a particular task. **8** a charitable centre that offers shelter or aid to the destitute or underprivileged. **9** *(modifier)* of or relating to an ecclesiastical mission: *a mission station.* ◆ *vb* **10** *(tr)* to direct a mission to or establish a mission in (a given region). [C16: from L *missiō,* from *mittere* to send]

missionary ❶ (ˈmɪʃənərɪ) *n, pl* **missionaries. 1** a member of a religious mission. ◆ *adj* **2** of or relating to missionaries: *missionary work.* **3** resulting from a desire to convert people to one's own beliefs: *missionary zeal.*

missionary position *n Inf.* a position for sexual intercourse in which the man lies on top of the woman and they are face to face. [C20: from the belief that missionaries advocated this as the proper position to primitive peoples among whom it was unknown]

Mississippian (ˌmɪsɪˈsɪpɪən) *adj* **1** of or relating to the state of Mississippi in the US, or the Mississippi river. **2** (in North America) of or denoting the lower of two subdivisions of the Carboniferous period (see also **Pennsylvanian** (sense 2)). ◆ *n* **3** an inhabitant or native of the state of Mississippi. **4 the.** the Mississippian period or rock system.

missive ❶ (ˈmɪsɪv) *n* **1** a formal or official letter. **2** a formal word for **letter.** [C15: from Med. L *missivus,* from *mittere* to send]

miss out *vb (adv)* **1** *(tr)* to leave out; overlook. **2** *(intr;* often foll. by *on)* to fail to experience: *you missed out on the celebrations.*

misspell (ˌmɪsˈspɛl) *vb* **misspells, misspelling, misspelt** *or* **misspelled.** to spell (a word or words) wrongly.

misspelling (ˌmɪsˈspɛlɪŋ) *n* a wrong spelling.

misspend ❶ (ˌmɪsˈspɛnd) *vb* **misspends, misspending, misspent.** to spend thoughtlessly or wastefully.

misstep ❶ (ˌmɪsˈstɛp) *n* **1** a false step. **2** an error.

missus *or* **missis** (ˈmɪsɪz, -ɪs) *n* **1** (usually preceded by *the) Inf.* one's wife or the wife of the person addressed or referred to. **2** an informal term of address for a woman. [C19: spoken version of MISTRESS]

missy (ˈmɪsɪ) *n, pl* **missies.** *Inf.* an affectionate or disparaging form of address to a young girl.

mist ❶ (mɪst) *n* **1** a thin fog resulting from condensation in the air near the earth's surface. **2** *Meteorol.* such an atmospheric condition with a horizontal visibility of 1–2 kilometres. **3** a fine spray of liquid, such as that produced by an aerosol container. **4** condensed water vapour on a surface. **5** something that causes haziness or lack of clarity, such as a film of tears. ◆ *vb* **6** to cover or be covered with or as if with mist. [OE]

mistake ❶ (mɪˈsteɪk) *n* **1** an error or blunder in action, opinion, or judgment. **2** a misconception or misunderstanding. ◆ *vb* **mistakes, mistaking, mistook, mistaken. 3** *(tr)* to misunderstand; misinterpret: *she mistook his meaning.* **4** *(tr;* foll. by *for)* to take (for), interpret (as), or confuse (with): *she mistook his directness for honesty.* **5** *(tr)* to choose badly or incorrectly: *he mistook his path.* **6** *(intr)* to make a mistake. [C13 (meaning: to do wrong, err): from ON *mistaka* to take erroneously]
▸**misˈtakable** *adj*

mistaken ❶ (mɪˈsteɪkən) *adj* **1** *(usually predicative)* wrong in opinion, judgment, etc.: *a mistaken viewpoint.* **2** arising from error in opinion, judgment, etc.
▸**misˈtakenly** *adv* ▸**misˈtakenness** *n*

mister (ˈmɪstə) *(sometimes cap.)* ◆ *n* **1** an informal form of address for a man. **2** *Mil.* the official form of address for subordinate or senior warrant officers. **3** *Naval.* the official form of address for all officers in a merchant ship, other than the captain. **4** *Brit.* the form of address for a surgeon. **5** the form of address for officials holding certain positions: *mister chairman.* ◆ *vb* **6** *(tr) Inf.* to call (someone) mister. [C16: var. of MASTER]

Mister (ˈmɪstə) *n* the full form of **Mr.**

misterioso (mɪˌstɛrɪˈəʊsəʊ) *adv Music.* in a mysterious manner; mysteriously. [It.]

mistigris (ˈmɪstɪgriː) *n* **1** the joker or a blank card used as a wild card in a variety of draw poker. **2** the game. [C19: from F: jack of clubs, game in which this card was wild]

mistime ❶ (ˌmɪsˈtaɪm) *vb* **mistimes, mistiming, mistimed.** *(tr)* to time (an action, utterance, etc.) wrongly.

mistle thrush *or* **missel thrush** (ˈmɪsᵊl) *n* a large European thrush with a brown back and spotted breast, noted for feeding on mistletoe berries. [C18: from OE *mistel* MISTLETOE]

mistletoe (ˈmɪsᵊlˌtəʊ) *n* **1** a Eurasian evergreen shrub with waxy white

THESAURUS

misrepresent *vb* = **distort**, belie, disguise, falsify, garble, misinterpret, misstate, pervert, twist

misrule *n* **2** = **mismanagement**, bad government, maladministration, misgovernment **3** = **disorder**, anarchy, chaos, confusion, lawlessness, tumult, turmoil

miss[1] *vb* **1-5** = **omit**, be late for, blunder, err, fail, fail to grasp, fail to notice, forego, lack, leave out, let go, let slip, lose, miscarry, mistake, overlook, pass over, pass up, skip, slip, trip **6** = **long for**, feel the loss of, hunger for, need, pine for, want, wish, yearn for **7** = **avoid**, escape, evade ◆ *n* **8** = **mistake**, blunder, error, failure, fault, loss, omission, oversight, want

miss[2] *n Informal* = **girl**, damsel, lass, lassie *(inf.)*, maid, maiden, schoolgirl, spinster, young lady

misshapen *adj* **1** = **deformed**, contorted, crippled, crooked, distorted, grotesque, ill-made, ill-proportioned, malformed, twisted, ugly, ungainly, unshapely, unsightly, warped, wry

missile *n* **1, 2** = **rocket**, projectile, weapon

missing *adj* **1, 2** = **absent**, astray, gone, lacking, left behind, left out, lost, mislaid, misplaced, not present, nowhere to be found, unaccounted-for, wanting
Antonyms *adj* accounted for, at hand, available, here, in attendance, on hand, present, there, to hand

mission *n* **1, 2** = **task**, aim, assignment, business, calling, charge, commission, duty, errand, goal, job, office, operation, purpose, pursuit, quest, trust, undertaking, vocation, work **3-5** = **delegation**, commission, deputation, embassy, legation, ministry, task force

missionary *n* **1** = **evangelist**, apostle, converter, preacher, propagandist, proselytizer

missive *n* **1** = **letter**, communication, dispatch, epistle, memorandum, message, note, report

misspent *adj* = **wasted**, dissipated, idle, imprudent, misapplied, prodigal, profitless, squandered, thrown away
Antonyms *adj* active, fruitful, industrious, meaningful, profitable, unwasted, useful, worthwhile

misstep *n* **1, 2** = **slip**, bad move, blunder, error, false step, faux pas, gaffe, indiscretion, lapse, mistake, slip-up *(inf.)*, stumble, trip, wrong move

mist *n* **1** = **fog**, cloud, condensation, dew, drizzle, film, haar *(Eastern Brit.)*, haze, smog, smur *or* smir *(Scot.)*, spray, steam, vapour ◆ *vb* **6** = **steam (up)**, becloud, befog, blear, blur, cloud, film, fog, obscure

mistake *n* **1, 2** = **error**, bloomer *(Brit. inf.)*, blunder, boob *(Brit. sl.)*, boo-boo *(inf.)*, clanger *(inf.)*, erratum, error of judgment, false move, fault, faux pas, gaffe, goof *(inf.)*, howler *(inf.)*, inaccuracy, miscalculation, misconception, misstep, misunderstanding, oversight, slip, slip-up *(inf.)*, solecism ◆ *vb* **4** = **misunderstand**, get wrong, misapprehend, misconceive, misconstrue, misinterpret, misjudge, misread **5** = **confuse with**, accept as, confound, misinterpret as, mix up with, take for **6** = **miscalculate**, be wide of *or* be off the mark, be wrong, blunder, boob *(Brit. sl.)*, drop a clanger *(inf.)*, err, goof *(inf.)*, misjudge, put one's foot in it *(inf.)*, slip up *(inf.)*

mistaken *adj* **1, 2** = **wrong**, barking up the wrong tree *(inf.)*, erroneous, fallacious, false, faulty *(inf.)*, inaccurate, inappropriate, incorrect, in the wrong, misguided, misinformed, misled, off base *(US & Canad. inf.)*, off beam *(inf.)*, off target, off the mark, unfounded, unsound, way off beam *(inf.)*, wide of the mark
Antonyms *adj* accurate, correct, logical, right, sound, true

mistakenly *adv* **1, 2** = **incorrectly**, by mistake, erroneously, fallaciously, falsely, inaccurately, inappropriately, in error, misguidedly, wrongly

mistimed *adj* = **inopportune**, badly timed, ill-timed, inconvenient, unseasonable, unsynchronized, untimely

berries: grows as a partial parasite on various trees: used as a Christmas decoration. **2** any of several similar and related American plants. [OE *misteltān*, from *mistel* mistletoe + *tān* twig; rel. to ON *mistilteinn*]

mistook (mɪˈstʊk) *vb* the past tense of **mistake.**

mistral (ˈmɪstrəl, mɪˈstrɑːl) *n* a strong cold dry wind that blows through the Rhône valley and S France to the Mediterranean coast, mainly in the winter. [C17: via F from Provençal, from L *magistrālis* MAGISTRAL]

mistreat Ⓣ (ˌmɪsˈtriːt) *vb* (*tr*) to treat badly.
▸ **ˌmisˈtreatment** *n*

mistress Ⓣ (ˈmɪstrɪs) *n* **1** a woman who has a continuing extramarital sexual relationship with a man, esp. a married man. **2** a woman in a position of authority, ownership, or control. **3** a woman having control over something specified: *mistress of her own destiny.* **4** *Chiefly Brit.* short for **schoolmistress. 5** an archaic or dialect word for **sweetheart.** [C14: from OF; see MASTER, -ESS]

Mistress (ˈmɪstrɪs) *n* an archaic or dialect title equivalent to **Mrs.**

Mistress of the Robes *n* (in Britain) a lady of high rank in charge of the Queen's wardrobe.

mistrial (mɪsˈtraɪəl) *n* **1** a trial made void because of some error. **2** *US.* an inconclusive trial, as when a jury cannot agree on a verdict.

mistrust Ⓣ (ˌmɪsˈtrʌst) *vb* **1** to have doubts or suspicions about (someone or something). ◆ *n* **2** distrust.
▸ **ˌmisˈtrustful** *adj* ▸ **ˌmisˈtrustfully** *adv* ▸ **ˌmisˈtrustfulness** *n*

misty Ⓣ (ˈmɪstɪ) *adj* **mistier, mistiest. 1** consisting of or resembling mist. **2** obscured as by mist. **3** indistinct; blurred.
▸ **ˈmistily** *adv* ▸ **ˈmistiness** *n*

misunderstand Ⓣ (ˌmɪsʌndəˈstænd) *vb* **misunderstands, misunderstanding, misunderstood.** to fail to understand properly.

misunderstanding Ⓣ (ˌmɪsʌndəˈstændɪŋ) *n* **1** a failure to understand properly. **2** a disagreement.

misunderstood Ⓣ (ˌmɪsʌndəˈstʊd) *adj* not properly or sympathetically understood: *a misunderstood adolescent.*

misuse Ⓣ *n* (ˌmɪsˈjuːs), *also* **misusage. 1** erroneous, improper, or unorthodox use: *misuse of words.* **2** cruel or inhumane treatment. ◆ *vb* (ˌmɪsˈjuːz), **misuses, misusing, misused.** (*tr*) **3** to use wrongly. **4** to treat badly or harshly.
▸ **ˌmisˈuser** *n*

mite[1] (maɪt) *n* any of numerous small terrestrial or aquatic free-living or parasitic arachnids. [OE *mīte*]

mite[2] (maɪt) *n* **1** a very small particle, creature, or object. **2** a very small contribution or sum of money. See also **widow's mite. 3** a former Flemish coin of small value. **4 a mite.** *Inf.* somewhat: *he's a mite foolish.* [C14: from MLow G, MDu. *mīte*]

Mithraism (ˈmɪθreɪˌɪzəm) *or* **Mithraicism** (mɪθˈreɪɪˌsɪzəm) *n* the ancient religion of Mithras, the Persian god of light.
▸ **Mithraic** (mɪθˈreɪɪk) *adj* ▸ **ˈMithraist** *n, adj*

mithridatism (ˈmɪθrɪdeɪˌtɪzəm) *n* immunity to large doses of poison by prior ingestion of gradually increased doses.
▸ **mithridatic** (ˌmɪθrɪˈdætɪk, -ˈdeɪ-) *adj*

mitigate Ⓣ (ˈmɪtɪˌgeɪt) *vb* **mitigates, mitigating, mitigated.** to make or become less severe or harsh; moderate. [C15: from L *mītigāre*, from *mītis* mild + *agere* to make]
▸ **ˈmitigable** *adj* ▸ **ˌmitiˈgation** *n* ▸ **ˈmitiˌgative** *or* **ˈmitiˌgatory** *adj* ▸ **ˈmitiˌgator** *n*

> **USAGE NOTE** *Mitigate* is sometimes wrongly used where *militate* is meant: *his behaviour militates* (not *mitigates*) *against his chances of promotion.*

mitochondrion (ˌmaɪtəʊˈkɒndrɪən) *n, pl* **mitochondria** (-drɪə). a small spherical or rodlike body, in the cytoplasm of most cells: contains enzymes responsible for energy production. [C19: NL, from Gk *mitos* thread + *khondrion* small grain]

mitosis (maɪˈtəʊsɪs, mɪ-) *n* a method of cell division, in which the nucleus divides into daughter nuclei, each containing the same number of chromosomes as the parent nucleus. [C19: from NL, from Gk *mitos* thread]
▸ **mitotic** (maɪˈtɒtɪk, mɪ-) *adj*

mitral (ˈmaɪtrəl) *adj* **1** of or like a mitre. **2** *Anat.* of or relating to the mitral valve.

mitral valve *n* the valve between the left atrium and the left ventricle of the heart.

mitre *or US* **miter** (ˈmaɪtə) *n* **1** *Christianity.* the liturgical headdress of a bishop or abbot, consisting of a tall pointed cleft cap with two bands hanging down at the back. **2** Also called: **mitre joint.** a corner joint formed by cutting bevels of equal angles at the ends of each piece of material. **3** a bevelled surface of a mitre joint. ◆ *vb* **mitres, mitring, mitred** *or US* **miters, mitering, mitered.** (*tr*) **4** to make a mitre joint between (two pieces of material). **5** to confer a mitre upon: *a mitred abbot.* [C14: from OF, from L *mitra*, from Gk: turban]

mitre box *n* an open-ended box with sides slotted to guide a saw in cutting mitre joints.

mitt (mɪt) *n* **1** any of various glovelike hand coverings, such as one that does not cover the fingers. **2** short for **mitten** (sense 1). **3** *Baseball.* a large round thickly padded leather mitten worn by the catcher. **4** (*often pl*) a slang word for **hand. 5** *Sl.* a boxing glove. [C18: from MITTEN]

mitten (ˈmɪtᵊn) *n* **1** a glove having one section for the thumb and a single section for the other fingers. Sometimes shortened to **mitt. 2** *Sl.* a boxing glove. [C14: from OF *mitaine*, from ?]

mittimus (ˈmɪtɪməs) *n, pl* **mittimuses.** *Law.* a warrant of commitment to prison or a command to a jailer to hold someone in prison. [C15: from L: we send, the first word of such a command]

mix Ⓣ (mɪks) *vb* **1** (*tr*) to combine or blend (ingredients, liquids, objects, etc.) together into one mass. **2** (*intr*) to become or have the capacity to become combined, joined, etc.: *some chemicals do not mix.* **3** (*tr*) to form (something) by combining constituents: *to mix cement.* **4** (*tr;* often foll. by *in* or *into*) to add as an additional element (to a mass or compound): *to mix flour into a batter.* **5** (*tr*) to do at the same time: *to mix study and pleasure.* **6** (*tr*) to consume (different alcoholic drinks) in close succession. **7** to come or cause to come into association socially: *Pauline mixed well.* **8** (*intr;* often foll. by *with*) to go together; complement. **9** (*tr*) to crossbreed (differing strains of plants or breeds of livestock), esp. more or less at random. **10** *Music.* to balance and adjust (individual performers' parts) to make an overall sound by electronic means. **11 mix it.** *Inf.* to cause mischief or trouble, often for a person named: *she tried to mix it for John.* ◆ *n* **12** the act or an instance of mixing. **13** the result of mixing; mixture. **14** a mixture of ingredients, esp. one commercially prepared for making a cake, bread, etc. **15** *Inf.* a state of confusion. **16** *Music.* the sound produced by mixing. ◆ See also **mix-up.** [C15: back formation from *mixt* mixed, via OF from L *mixtus*, from *miscēre* to mix]
▸ **ˈmixable** *adj*

mixed Ⓣ (mɪkst) *adj* **1** formed or blend together by mixing. **2** composed of different elements, races, sexes, etc.: *a mixed school.* **3** consisting of conflicting elements, thoughts, attitudes, etc.: *mixed feelings.* **4** *Maths.* (of a number) consisting of the sum of an integer and a fraction or a decimal fraction, as 5½ or 17.43.
▸ **mixedness** (ˈmɪksɪdnɪs) *n*

THESAURUS

mistreat *vb* = **abuse**, brutalize, handle roughly, harm, ill-treat, ill-use, injure, knock about *or* around, maltreat, manhandle, maul, misuse, molest, rough up, wrong

mistreatment *n* = **abuse**, brutalization, harm, ill-treatment, ill-usage, injury, maltreatment, manhandling, mauling, misuse, molestation, rough handling, roughing up, unkindness

mistress *n* **1** = **lover**, concubine, doxy (*arch.*), fancy bit (*sl.*), fancy woman (*sl.*), floozy (*sl.*), girlfriend, inamorata, kept woman, ladylove (*rare*), paramour

mistrust *vb* **1** = **doubt**, apprehend, beware, be wary of, distrust, fear, have doubts about, suspect ◆ *n* **2** = **suspicion**, apprehension, distrust, doubt, dubiety, fear, misgiving, scepticism, uncertainty, wariness

mistrustful *adj* **2** = **suspicious**, apprehensive, cautious, chary, cynical, distrustful, doubtful, dubious, fearful, hesitant, leery (*sl.*), nervous, sceptical, uncertain, wary
Antonyms *adj* certain, definite, positive, sure, unafraid

misty *adj* **1-3** = **foggy**, bleary, blurred, cloudy, dark, dim, fuzzy, hazy, indistinct, murky, nebulous, obscure, opaque, overcast, unclear, vague
Antonyms *adj* bright, clear, distinct, lucid, obvious, plain, sunny, well-defined

misunderstand *vb* = **misinterpret**, be at cross-purposes, get (it) wrong, get one's lines crossed, get one's wires crossed, get the wrong end of the stick, get the wrong idea (about), misapprehend, misconceive, misconstrue, mishear, misjudge, misread, miss the point (of), mistake

misunderstanding *n* **1** = **mistake**, error, false impression, misapprehension, misconception, misconstruction, misinterpretation, misjudgment, misreading, mix-up, wrong idea **2** = **disagreement**, argument, breach, conflict, difference, difficulty, discord, dissension, falling-out (*inf.*), quarrel, rift, rupture, squabble, variance

misunderstood *adj* = **misjudged**, misconstrued, misheard, misinterpreted, misread, unappreciated, unrecognized

misuse *n* **1** = **waste**, abuse, barbarism, catachresis, corruption, desecration, dissipation, malapropism, misapplication, misemployment, misusage, perversion, profanation, solecism, squandering **2** = **mistreatment**, abuse, cruel treatment, exploitation, harm, ill-treatment, ill-usage, inhumane treatment, injury, maltreatment, manhandling, rough handling ◆ *vb* **3** = **waste**, abuse, corrupt, desecrate, dissipate, misapply, misemploy, pervert, profane, prostitute, squander **4** = **mistreat**, abuse, brutalize, exploit, handle roughly, harm, ill-treat, ill-use, injure, maltreat, manhandle, maul, molest, wrong
Antonyms *vb* ≠ **waste:** appreciate, prize, treasure, use ≠ **mistreat:** cherish, honour, respect

mitigate *vb* = **ease**, abate, allay, appease, assuage, blunt, calm, check, diminish, dull, extenuate, lessen, lighten, moderate, modify, mollify, pacify, palliate, placate, quiet, reduce the force of, remit, soften, soothe, subdue, take the edge off, temper, tone down, tranquillize, weaken
Antonyms *vb* aggravate, augment, enhance, heighten, increase, intensify, strengthen

mitigation *n* = **relief**, abatement, allaying, alleviation, assuagement, diminution, easement, extenuation, moderation, mollification, palliation, remission

mix *vb* **1-3** = **combine**, alloy, amalgamate, associate, blend, coalesce, commingle, commix, compound, cross, fuse, incorporate, intermingle, interweave, join, jumble, meld, merge, mingle, put together, unite **7** = **socialize**, associate, come together, consort, fraternize, hang out (*inf.*), hobnob, join, mingle ◆ *n* **13** = **mixture**, alloy, amalgam, assortment, blend, combination, compound, fusion, medley, meld, mixed bag

mixed *adj* **1** = **combined**, alloyed, amalgamated, blended, composite, compound, fused, incorporated, joint, mingled, united **2** = **varied**, assorted, cosmopolitan, diverse, diversified, heterogeneous, manifold, miscellaneous, mot-

mixed bag *n Inf.* something composed of diverse elements, characteristics, people, etc.
mixed blessing *n* an event, situation, etc., having both advantages and disadvantages.
mixed doubles *pl n Tennis.* a doubles game with a man and a woman as partners on each side.
mixed economy *n* an economic system in which the public and private sectors coexist.
mixed farming *n* combined arable and livestock farming (on **mixed farms**).
mixed marriage *n* a marriage between persons of different races or religions.
mixed metaphor *n* a combination of incongruous metaphors, as *when the Nazi jackboots sing their swan song.*
mixed-up ➊ *adj* in a state of mental confusion.
mixer ('mɪksə) *n* **1** a person or thing that mixes. **2** *Inf.* **2a** a person considered in relation to his ability to mix socially. **2b** a person who creates trouble for others. **3** a kitchen appliance, usually electrical, used for mixing foods, etc. **4** a drink such as ginger ale, fruit juice, etc., used in preparing cocktails. **5** *Electronics.* a device in which two or more input signals are combined to give a single output signal.
mixer tap *n* a tap in which hot and cold water supplies have a joint outlet but are controlled separately.
mixture ➊ ('mɪkstʃə) *n* **1** the act of mixing or state of being mixed. **2** something mixed; a result of mixing. **3** *Chem.* a substance consisting of two or more substances mixed together without any chemical bonding between them. **4** *Pharmacol.* a liquid medicine in which an insoluble compound is suspended in the liquid. **5** *Music.* an organ stop that controls several ranks of pipes. **6** the mixture of petrol vapour and air in an internal-combustion engine. [C16: from L *mixtūra,* from *mixtus,* p.p. of *miscere* to mix]
mix-up ➊ *n* **1** a confused condition or situation. **2** *Inf.* a fight. ◆ *vb* **mix up.** (*tr, adv*) **3** to make into a mixture. **4** to confuse or confound: *Tom mixes John up with Bill.* **5** (*often passive*) to put (someone) into a state of confusion: *I'm all mixed up.* **6** (foll. by *in* or *with; usually passive*) to involve (in an activity or group, esp. one that is illegal): *mixed up in the drugs racket.*
mizzen *or* **mizen** ('mɪzᵊn) *Naut.* ◆ *n* **1** a sail set on a mizzenmast. **2** short for **mizzenmast.** ◆ *adj* **3** of or relating to a mizzenmast: *a mizzen staysail.* [C15: from F *misaine,* from It. *mezzana, mezzano* middle]
mizzenmast *or* **mizenmast** ('mɪzᵊn,mɑːst; *Naut.* 'mɪzᵊnməst) *n Naut.* (on a vessel with three or more masts) the third mast from the bow.
mizzle[1] ('mɪzᵊl) *vb* **mizzles, mizzling, mizzled,** *n* a dialect word for **drizzle.** [C15: ?from Low G *miseln* to drizzle]
▸**'mizzly** *adj*
mizzle[2] ('mɪzᵊl) *vb* **mizzles, mizzling, mizzled.** (*intr*) *Brit. sl.* to decamp. [C18: from ?]
mk *Currency. symbol for:* **1** mark. **2** markka.
mks units *pl n* a metric system of units based on the metre, kilogram, and second as the units of length, mass, and time; it forms the basis of the SI units.
mkt *abbrev. for* market.
ml *symbol for:* **1** mile. **2** millilitre.
ML *abbrev. for* Medieval Latin.
MLA *abbrev. for:* **1** Member of the Legislative Assembly. **2** Modern Language Association (of America).
MLC (in Australia and India) *abbrev. for* Member of the Legislative Council.
MLitt *abbrev. for* Master of Letters. [L *Magister Litterarum*]
Mlle *or* **Mlle.** *pl* **Mlles** *or* **Mlles.** the French equivalent of **Miss.** [from F *Mademoiselle*]
MLR *abbrev. for* minimum lending rate.
mm *symbol for* millimetre.
MM **1** the French equivalent of **Messrs.** [from F *Messieurs*] **2** *abbrev. for* Military Medal.
MMC (formerly in Britain) *abbrev. for* Monopolies and Mergers Commission.
MMDS *abbrev. for* multipoint microwave distribution system: a radio alternative to cable television. Sometimes shortened to **MDS.**
Mme *pl* **Mmes** the French equivalent of **Mrs.** [from F *Madame, Mesdames*]
MMP *abbrev. for* mixed member proportional: a system of proportional representation, used in Germany and New Zealand.
MMR *n* a combined vaccine against measles, mumps, and rubella, given to very young children.
MMus *abbrev. for* Master of Music.
Mn *the chemical symbol for* manganese.
MNA (in Canada) *abbrev. for* Member of the National Assembly (of Quebec).
mnemonic (nɪ'mɒnɪk) *adj* **1** aiding or meant to aid one's memory. **2** of or relating to memory or mnemonics. ◆ *n* **3** something, such as a verse, to assist memory. [C18: from Gk *mnēmonikos,* from *mnēmōn* mindful, from *mnasthai* to remember]
▸**mne'monically** *adv*
mnemonics (nɪ'mɒnɪks) *n* (*usually functioning as sing*) **1** the art or practice of improving or of aiding the memory. **2** a system of rules to aid the memory.
mo (məʊ) *n Inf.* **1** *Chiefly Brit.* short for **moment** (sense 1) (esp. in **half a mo**). **2** *Austral.* short for **moustache** (sense 1).
Mo *the chemical symbol for* molybdenum.
MO *abbrev. for:* **1** Missouri. **2** Medical Officer.
m.o. *or* **MO** *abbrev. for:* **1** mail order. **2** money order.
-mo *suffix forming nouns.* (in bookbinding) indicating book size by specifying the number of leaves formed by folding one sheet of paper: *16mo* or *sixteenmo.* [abstracted from DUODECIMO]
moa ('məʊə) *n* any of various recently extinct large flightless birds of New Zealand (see **ratite**). [C19: from Maori]
moa hunter *n NZ.* an anthropologists' term for an early Maori.
moan ➊ (məʊn) *n* **1** a low prolonged mournful sound expressive of suffering or pleading. **2** any similar mournful sound, esp. that made by the wind. **3** *Inf.* a grumble or complaint. ◆ *vb* **4** to utter (words, etc.) in a low mournful manner. **5** (*intr*) to make a sound like a moan. **6** (*usually intr*) *Inf.* to grumble or complain. [C13: rel. to OE *mǣnan* to grieve over]
▸**'moaner** *n* ▸**'moanful** *adj* ▸**'moaning** *n, adj*
moat (məʊt) *n* **1** a wide water-filled ditch surrounding a fortified place, such as a castle. ◆ *vb* **2** (*tr*) to surround with or as if with a moat. [C14: from OF *motte* mound]
mob ➊ (mɒb) *n* **1a** a riotous or disorderly crowd of people; rabble. **1b** (*as modifier*): *mob law.* **2** *Often derog.* a group or class of people, animals, or things. **3** *Often derog.* the masses. **4** *Sl.* a gang of criminals. **5** *Austral. & NZ.* a large number of anything. **6** *Austral. & NZ.* a flock or herd of animals. **7** **mobs of.** *Austral. & NZ inf.* lots of. ◆ *vb* **mobs, mobbing, mobbed.** (*tr*) **8** to attack in a group resembling a mob. **9** (of a group of animals of a prey species) to harass (a predator). **10** to surround, esp. in order to acclaim. **11** to crowd into (a building, etc.). [C17: shortened from L *mōbile vulgus* the fickle populace]
mobcap ('mɒb,kæp) *n* a woman's large cotton cap with a pouched crown, worn esp. during the 18th century. [C18: from obs. *mob* woman, esp. loose-living, + CAP]
mobile ➊ ('məʊbaɪl) *adj* **1** having freedom of movement; movable. **2** changing quickly in expression: *a mobile face.* **3** *Sociol.* (of individuals or social groups) moving within and between classes, occupations, and localities. **4** (of military forces) able to move freely and quickly. **5** (*postpositive*) *Inf.* having transport available: *are you mobile?* ◆ *n* **6a** a sculpture suspended in midair with delicately balanced parts that are set in motion by air currents. **6b** (*as modifier*): *mobile sculpture.* **7** short for **mobile phone.** [C15: via OF from L *mōbilis,* from *movēre* to move]
▸**mobility** (məʊ'bɪlɪtɪ) *n*
-mobile (məʊ,biːl) *suffix forming nouns.* indicating a vehicle designed for a particular person or purpose: *Popemobile.*
mobile home *n* living quarters mounted on wheels and capable of being towed by a motor vehicle.
mobile phone *n* a portable telephone that works by means of a cellular radio system.
mobilize ➊ *or* **mobilise** ('məʊbɪ,laɪz) *vb* **mobilizes, mobilizing, mobilized** *or* **mobilises, mobilising, mobilised.** **1** to prepare for war or another emergency by organizing (national resources, the armed services, etc.). **2** (*tr*) to organize for a purpose. **3** (*tr*) to put into motion or use.
▸**'mobi,lizable** *or* **'mobi,lisable** *adj* ▸**,mobili'zation** *or* **,mobili'sation** *n*

THESAURUS

ley **2** = **crossbred**, hybrid, interbred, interdenominational, mongrel **3** = **uncertain**, ambivalent, equivocal, indecisive
Antonyms *adj* ≠ **combined:** isolated, pure, straight, unmixed ≠ **varied:** homogeneous, unmixed ≠ **crossbred:** pure

mixed-up *adj* = **confused**, at sea, bewildered, distraught, disturbed, maladjusted, muddled, perplexed, puzzled, upset

mixture *n* **2** = **blend**, admixture, alloy, amalgam, amalgamation, association, assortment, brew, combine, composite, compound, concoction, conglomeration, cross, fusion, hotchpotch, jumble, medley, *mélange,* meld, miscellany, mix, mixed bag (*inf.*), potpourri, salmagundi, union, variety

mix-up *n* **1** = **confusion**, disorder, fankle (*Scot.*), jumble, mess, mistake, misunderstanding, muddle, snarl-up (*inf., chiefly Brit.*), tangle ◆ *vb* **mix up 3** = **combine**, blend, commix, mix **4** = **confuse**, confound, muddle **5** = **bewilder**, confuse, disturb, fluster, muddle, perplex, puzzle, throw into confusion, unnerve, upset **6** = **entangle**, embroil, implicate, involve, rope in

moan *n* **1, 2** = **groan**, lament, lamentation, sigh, sob, sough, wail, whine **3** *Informal* = **grumble**, beef, bitch (*sl.*), complaint, gripe (*inf.*), grouch (*inf.*), grouse, kvetch (*US sl.*), protest, whine ◆ *vb* **4, 5** = **groan**, bemoan, bewail, deplore, grieve, keen, lament, mourn, sigh, sob, sough, whine **6** *Informal* = **grumble**, beef (*sl.*), bitch (*sl.*), bleat, carp, complain, gripe (*inf.*), groan, grouch (*inf.*), grouse, moan and groan, whine, whinge (*inf.*)

mob *n* **1** = **crowd**, assemblage, body, collection, drove, flock, gang, gathering, herd, horde, host, mass, multitude, pack, press, swarm, throng **2** *Often derogatory* = **gang**, class, company, crew (*inf.*), group, lot, set, troop **3** *Often derogatory* = **masses**, *canaille,* commonalty, great unwashed (*inf. & derogatory*), hoi polloi, rabble, riffraff, scum ◆ *vb* **8, 10** = **surround**, crowd around, jostle, overrun, set upon, swarm around **11** = **crowd into**, cram into, crowd, fill, fill to overflowing, jam, pack

mobile *adj* **1** = **movable**, ambulatory, itinerant, locomotive, migrant, motile, moving, peripatetic, portable, travelling, wandering **2** = **changeable**, animated, ever-changing, expressive

mobilize *vb* **1, 2** = **prepare**, activate, animate, call to arms, call up, get *or* make ready, marshal, muster, organize, put in motion, rally, ready

Möbius strip ('mɜːbɪəs) *n Maths.* a one-sided continuous surface, formed by twisting a long narrow rectangular strip of material through 180° and joining the ends. [C19: after August *Möbius* (1790–1868), G mathematician]

mobocracy (mɒ'bɒkrəsɪ) *n, pl* **mobocracies. 1** rule or domination by a mob. **2** the mob that rules.

mobster ('mɒbstə) *n* a US slang word for **gangster.**

moccasin ('mɒkəsɪn) *n* **1** a shoe of soft leather, esp. deerskin, worn by North American Indians. **2** any soft shoe resembling this. **3** short for **water moccasin.** [C17: of Amerind origin]

moccasin flower *n* any of several North American orchids with a pink solitary flower. See also **lady's-slipper, cypripedium.**

mocha ('mɒkə) *n* **1** a dark brown coffee originally imported from the port of Mocha in Arabia. **2** a flavouring made from coffee and chocolate. **3** a soft glove leather, made from goatskin or sheepskin. **4a** a dark brown colour. **4b** (*as adj*): *mocha shoes.*

mock ➊ (mɒk) *vb* **1** (when *intr*, often foll. by *at*) to behave with scorn or contempt (towards); show ridicule (for). **2** (*tr*) to imitate, esp. in fun; mimic. **3** (*tr*) to deceive, disappoint, or delude. **4** (*tr*) to defy or frustrate. ◆ *n* **5** the act of mocking. **6** a person or thing mocked. **7** a counterfeit; imitation. **8** (*often pl*) *Inf.* (in England and Wales) school examinations taken as practice before public exams. ◆ *adj* (*prenominal*) **9** sham or counterfeit. **10** serving as an imitation or substitute, esp. for practice purposes: *a mock battle.* ◆ See also **mock-up.** [C15: from OF *mocquer*]
▸**'mocker** *n* ▸**'mocking** *n, adj* ▸**'mockingly** *adv*

mockers ('mɒkəz) *pl n Inf.* **put the mockers on.** to ruin the chances of success of. [C20: ?from MOCK]

mockery ➊ ('mɒkərɪ) *n, pl* **mockeries. 1** ridicule, contempt, or derision. **2** a derisive action or comment. **3** an imitation or pretence, esp. a derisive one. **4** a person or thing that is mocked. **5** a person, thing, or action that is inadequate.

mock-heroic *adj* **1** (of a literary work, esp. a poem) imitating the style of heroic poetry in order to satirize an unheroic subject. ◆ *n* **2** burlesque imitation of the heroic style.

mockingbird ('mɒkɪŋˌbɜːd) *n* any of various American songbirds, noted for their ability to mimic the song of other birds.

mock orange *n* **1** Also called: **syringa, philadelphus.** a shrub with white fragrant flowers resembling those of the orange. **2** an Australian shrub with white flowers and dark shiny leaves.

mock turtle soup *n* an imitation turtle soup made from a calf's head.

mock-up *n* **1** a working full-scale model of a machine, apparatus, etc., for testing, research, etc. **2** a layout of printed matter. ◆ *vb* **mock up. 3** (*tr, adv*) to build or make a mock-up of.

mod[1] (mɒd) *n Brit.* **a** a member of a group of teenagers, originally in the mid-1960s, noted for their clothes-consciousness. **b** a member of a revived group of this type in the late 1970s and early 1980s. [C20: from MODERNIST]

mod[2] (mɒd) *n* an annual Highland Gaelic meeting with musical and literary competitions. [C19: from Gaelic *mōd* assembly, from ON]

MOD (in Britain) *abbrev. for* Ministry of Defence.

mod. *abbrev. for:* **1** moderate. **2** moderato. **3** modern.

modal ('məʊdᵊl) *adj* **1** of or relating to mode or manner. **2** *Grammar.* (of a verb form or auxiliary verb) expressing a distinction of mood, such as that between possibility and actuality. **3** qualifying, or expressing a qualification of, the truth of some statement. **4** *Metaphysics.* of or relating to the form of a thing as opposed to its attributes, substance, etc. **5** *Music.* of or relating to a mode. **6** of or relating to a statistical mode.
▸**mo'dality** *n* ▸**'modally** *adv*

modal logic *n* **1** the logical study of such philosophical concepts as necessity, possibility, contingency, etc. **2** the logical study of concepts whose formal properties resemble certain moral, epistemological, and psychological concepts.

mod cons *pl n Inf.* modern conveniences; the usual installations of a modern house, such as hot water, heating, etc.

mode ➊ (məʊd) *n* **1** a manner or way of doing, acting, or existing. **2** the current fashion or style. **3** *Music.* **3a** any of the various scales of notes within one octave, esp. any of the twelve natural diatonic scales taken in ascending order used in plainsong, folk song, and art music until 1600. **3b** (in the music of classical Greece) any of the descending diatonic scales from which the liturgical modes evolved. **3c** either of the two main scale systems in music since 1600: *major mode; minor mode.* **4** *Logic, linguistics.* another name for **mood**[2]. **5** *Philosophy.* a complex combination of ideas which is not simply the sum of its component ideas. **6** that one of a range of values that has the highest frequency as determined statistically. [C14: from L *modus* manner]

model ➊ ('mɒdᵊl) *n* **1a** a representation, usually on a smaller scale, of a device, structure, etc. **1b** (*as modifier*): *a model train.* **2a** a standard to be imitated. **2b** (*as modifier*): *a model wife.* **3** a representative form, style, or pattern. **4** a person who poses for a sculptor, painter, or photographer. **5** a person who wears clothes to display them to prospective buyers; mannequin. **6** a preparatory sculpture in clay, wax, etc., from which the finished work is copied. **7** a design or style of a particular product. ◆ *vb* **models, modelling, modelled** *or US* **models, modeling, modeled. 8** to make a model of (something or someone). **9** to form in clay, wax, etc.; mould. **10** to display (clothing and accessories) as a mannequin. **11** to plan or create according to a model or models. [C16: from OF *modelle,* from It., from L *modulus,* dim. of *modus* MODE]
▸**'modeller** *or US* **'modeler** *n*

modelling *or US* **modeling** ('mɒdᵊlɪŋ) *n* **1** the act or an instance of making a model. **2** the practice or occupation of a person who models clothes. **3** a technique in psychotherapy in which the therapist encourages the patient to model his behaviour on his own.

modem ('məʊdɛm) *n Computing.* a device for connecting two computers by a telephone line, consisting of a modulator that converts computer signals into audio signals and a corresponding demodulator. [C20: from *mo(dulator) dem(odulator)*]

moderate ➊ *adj* ('mɒdərɪt). **1** not extreme or excessive. **2** not violent; mild or temperate. **3** of average quality or extent: *moderate success.* ◆ *n* ('mɒdərɪt). **4** a person who holds moderate views, esp. in politics. ◆ *vb* ('mɒdəˌreɪt). **moderates, moderating, moderated. 5** to become or cause to become less extreme or violent. **6** (when *intr,* often foll. by *over*) to preside over a meeting, discussion, etc. **7** *Physics.* to slow down (neutrons), esp. by using a moderator. [C14: from L *moderātus,* from *moderārī* to restrain]

moderate breeze *n* a wind of force 4 on the Beaufort scale, reaching speeds of 13 to 18 mph.

moderation ➊ (ˌmɒdə'reɪʃən) *n* **1** the state or an instance of being moderate. **2** the act of moderating. **3 in moderation.** within moderate or reasonable limits.

moderato (ˌmɒdə'rɑːtəʊ) *adv Music.* **1** at a moderate tempo. **2** a direction indicating that the tempo specified is to be used with restraint: *allegro moderato.* [It.]

moderator ('mɒdəˌreɪtə) *n* **1** a person or thing that moderates. **2** *Presbyterian Church.* a minister appointed to preside over a Church court, synod, or general assembly. **3** a presiding officer at a public or legislative assembly. **4** a material, such as heavy water, used for slowing down neutrons in nuclear reactors. **5** an examiner at Oxford or Cambridge Universities in first public examinations. **6** (in Britain and New Zealand) one who is responsible for consistency of standards in the grading of some public examinations.
▸**'moderˌatorship** *n*

modern ➊ ('mɒdən) *adj* **1** of, involving, or befitting the present or a re-

THESAURUS

mock *vb* **1 = laugh at,** chaff, deride, flout, insult, jeer, laugh to scorn, make a monkey out of, make fun of, poke fun at, ridicule, scoff, scorn, show contempt for, sneer, take the mickey (out of) (*inf.*), taunt, tease, wind up (*Brit. sl.*) **2 = mimic,** ape, burlesque, caricature, counterfeit, do (*inf.*), imitate, lampoon, parody, satirize, send up (*Brit. inf.*), take off (*inf.*), travesty **3 = deceive,** belie, cheat, delude, disappoint, dupe, elude, fool, let down, mislead **4 = foil,** defeat, defy, disappoint, frustrate, thwart ◆ *n* **6 = laughing stock,** Aunt Sally (*Brit.*), butt, dupe, fool, jest, sport, travesty ◆ *adj* **9 = imitation,** artificial, bogus, counterfeit, dummy, ersatz, fake, faked, false, feigned, forged, fraudulent, phoney *or* phony (*inf.*), pretended, pseudo (*inf.*), sham, spurious
Antonyms *vb* ≠ **laugh at:** encourage, praise, respect, revere ◆ *adj* ≠ **imitation:** authentic, genuine, natural, real, sincere, true, unfeigned

mockery *n* **1 = derision,** contempt, contumely, disdain, disrespect, gibes, insults, jeering, ridicule, scoffing, scorn **2, 3 = parody,** burlesque, caricature, deception, farce, imitation, lampoon, mimicry, pretence, send-up (*Brit. inf.*), sham, spoof (*inf.*), take-off (*inf.*), travesty **5 = farce,** apology (*inf.*), disappointment, joke, laughing stock, letdown

mocking *adj* **1 = scornful,** contemptuous, contumelious, derisive, derisory, disdainful, disrespectful, insulting, irreverent, sarcastic, sardonic, satiric, satirical, scoffing, taunting

mode *n* **1 = method,** approach, condition, course, custom, fashion, form, manner, plan, practice, procedure, process, quality, rule, state, style, system, technique, vein, way **2 = fashion,** craze, look, rage, style, trend, vogue

model *n* **1a = representation,** copy, dummy, facsimile, image, imitation, miniature, mock-up, replica ◆ *modifier* **1b = imitation,** copy, dummy, facsimile, miniature ◆ *n* **2a = pattern,** archetype, design, epitome, example, exemplar, gauge, ideal, lodestar, mould, norm, original, par, paradigm, paragon, prototype, standard, type ◆ *modifier* **2b = ideal,** archetypal, exemplary, illustrative, paradigmatic, perfect, standard, typical ◆ *n* **4 = sitter,** poser, subject **5 = mannequin,** supermodel **7 = version,** configuration, design, form, kind, mark, mode, stamp, style, type, variety ◆ *vb* **8, 9 = shape,** carve, cast, design, fashion, form, mould, sculpt, stamp **10 = show off,** display, sport (*inf.*), wear **11 = base,** pattern, plan
Antonyms *modifier* ≠ **ideal:** deficient, flawed, impaired, imperfect

moderate *adj* **1, 2 = mild,** calm, controlled, cool, deliberate, equable, gentle, judicious, limited, middle-of-the-road, modest, peaceable, reasonable, restrained, sober, steady, temperate **3 = average,** fair, fairish, fair to middling (*inf.*), indifferent, mediocre, medium, middling, ordinary, passable, so-so (*inf.*), unexceptional ◆ *vb* **5 = lessen,** abate, allay, appease, assuage, calm, clear the air, control, curb, decrease, diminish, ease, mitigate, modulate, pacify, play down, quiet, regulate, relax, repress, restrain, soften, soft-pedal (*inf.*), subdue, tame, temper, tone down **6 = arbitrate,** chair, judge, mediate, preside, referee, take the chair
Antonyms *adj* ≠ **mild:** extreme, intemperate, ruffled, unreasonable, wild ≠ **average:** excessive, extreme, immoderate, inordinate, unusual ◆ *vb* ≠ **lessen:** heighten, increase, intensify

moderation *n* **1 = restraint,** calmness, composure, coolness, equanimity, fairness, judiciousness, justice, justness, mildness, moderateness, reasonableness, sedateness, temperance **3 in moderation = moderately,** within limits, within reason

modern *adj* **1 = current,** contemporary, fresh,

cent time; contemporary. **2** of, relating to, or characteristic of contemporary styles or schools of art, literature, music, etc., esp. those of an experimental kind. **3** belonging or relating to the period in history from the end of the Middle Ages to the present. ◆ *n* **4** a contemporary person. [C16: from OF, from LL *modernus*, from *modō* (adv) just recently, from *modus* MODE]
▸**mo'dernity** *or* **'modernness** *n*

modern apprenticeship *n* an arrangement that allows a school-leaver to gain vocational qualifications while being trained in a job.

Modern English *n* the English language since about 1450.

Modern Hebrew *n* the official language of Israel; a revived form of ancient Hebrew.

modernism ('mɒdə,nɪzəm) *n* **1** modern tendencies, thoughts, etc., or the support of these. **2** something typical of contemporary life or thought. **3** a 20th-century divergence in the arts from previous traditions, esp. in architecture. See **International Style**. **4** (*cap.*) *RC Church.* the movement at the end of the 19th and beginning of the 20th centuries that sought to adapt doctrine to modern thought.
▸**'modernist** *n, adj* ▸**,modern'istic** *adj* ▸**,modern'istically** *adv*

modernize ⓣ *or* **modernise** ('mɒdə,naɪz) *vb* **modernizes, modernizing, modernized** *or* **modernises, modernising, modernised. 1** (*tr*) to make modern in appearance or style. **2** (*intr*) to adopt modern ways, ideas, etc.
▸**,moderni'zation** *or* **,moderni'sation** *n* ▸**'modern,izer** *or* **'modern,iser** *n*

modern pentathlon *n* an athletic contest consisting of five different events: horse riding with jumps, fencing with electric épée, freestyle swimming, pistol shooting, and cross-country running.

modest ⓣ ('mɒdɪst) *adj* **1** having or expressing a humble opinion of oneself or one's accomplishments or abilities. **2** reserved or shy. **3** not ostentatious or pretentious. **4** not extreme or excessive. **5** decorous or decent. [C16: via OF from L *modestus* moderate, from *modus* MODE]
▸**'modestly** *adv*

modesty ⓣ ('mɒdɪstɪ) *n, pl* **modesties.** the quality or condition of being modest.

modicum ⓣ ('mɒdɪkəm) *n* a small amount or portion. [C15: from L: a little way, from *modicus* moderate]

modification ⓣ (,mɒdɪfɪ'keɪʃən) *n* **1** the act of modifying or the condition of being modified. **2** something modified. **3** a small change or adjustment. **4** *Grammar.* the relation between a modifier and the word or phrase that it modifies.
▸**'modifi,catory** *or* **'modifi,cative** *adj*

modifier ('mɒdɪ,faɪə) *n* **1** Also called: **qualifier.** *Grammar.* a word or phrase that qualifies the sense of another word; for example, the noun *alarm* is a modifier of *clock* in *alarm clock* and the phrase *every day* is an adverbial modifier of *walks* in *he walks every day*. **2** a person or thing that modifies.

modify ⓣ ('mɒdɪ,faɪ) *vb* **modifies, modifying, modified.** (*mainly tr*) **1** to change the structure, character, intent, etc., of. **2** to make less extreme or uncompromising. **3** *Grammar.* (of a word or phrase) to bear the relation of modifier to (another word or phrase). **4** *Linguistics.* to change (a vowel) by umlaut. **5** (*intr*) to be or become modified. [C14: from OF *modifier*, from L *modificāre* to limit, from *modus* measure + *facere* to make]
▸**'modi,fiable** *adj*

modish ⓣ ('məʊdɪʃ) *adj* in the current fashion or style.
▸**'modishly** *adv* ▸**'modishness** *n*

modiste (məʊ'di:st) *n* a fashionable dressmaker or milliner. [C19: from F, from *mode* fashion]

modular ('mɒdjʊlə) *adj* of, consisting of, or resembling a module or modulus.

modulate ⓣ ('mɒdjʊ,leɪt) *vb* **modulates, modulating, modulated. 1** (*tr*) to change the tone, pitch, or volume of. **2** (*tr*) to adjust or regulate the degree of. **3** *Music.* **3a** to change or cause to change from one key to another. **3b** (often foll. by *to*) to make or become in tune (with a pitch, key, etc.). **4** *Physics, electronics.* to superimpose the amplitude, frequency, phase, etc., of a wave or signal onto another wave or signal or onto an electron beam. [C16: from L *modulātus* in due measure, melodious, from *modulārī*, from *modus* measure]
▸**,modu'lation** *n* ▸**'modu,lator** *n*

module ('mɒdju:l) *n* **1** a standard unit of measure, esp. one used to coordinate the dimensions of buildings and components. **2** a standard self-contained unit or item, such as an assembly of electronic components, or a standardized piece of furniture, that can be used in combination with other units. **3** *Astronautics.* any of several self-contained separable units making up a spacecraft or launch vehicle, each of which has one or more specified tasks. **4** *Education.* a short course of study that together with other such courses counts towards a qualification. [C16: from L *modulus*, dim. of *modus* MODE]

modulus ('mɒdjʊləs) *n, pl* **moduli** (-,laɪ). **1** *Physics.* a coefficient expressing a specified property of a specified substance. See **modulus of elasticity. 2** *Maths.* another name for the **absolute value** of a complex number. **3** *Maths.* the number by which a logarithm to one base is multiplied to give the corresponding logarithm to another base. **4** *Maths.* an integer that can be divided exactly into the difference between two other integers: *7 is a modulus of 25 and 11.* [C16: from L, dim. of *modus* measure]

modulus of elasticity *n* the ratio of the stress applied to a body or substance to the resulting strain within the elastic limit. Also called: **elastic modulus.**

modus operandi ⓣ ('məʊdəs ,ɒpə'rændi:, -'rændaɪ) *n, pl* **modi operandi** ('məʊdi: ,ɒpə'rændi:, 'məʊdaɪ ,ɒpə'rændaɪ). procedure; method of operating. [C17: from L]

modus vivendi ('məʊdəs vɪ'vɛndi:, -'vɛndaɪ) *n, pl* **modi vivendi** ('məʊdi: vɪ'vɛndi:, 'məʊdaɪ vɪ'vɛndaɪ). a working arrangement between conflicting interests; practical compromise. [C19: from L: way of living]

mog (mɒg) *or* **moggy** *n, pl* **mogs** *or* **moggies.** *Brit.* a slang name for **cat**[1]. [C20: dialect, orig. a pet name for a cow]

Mogadon ('mɒgə,dɒn) *n Trademark.* a minor tranquillizer used to treat insomnia.

mogul ⓣ ('məʊgʌl, məʊ'gʌl) *n* an important or powerful person. [C18: from MOGUL]

Mogul ('məʊgʌl, məʊ'gʌl) *n* **1** a member of the Muslim dynasty of Indian emperors established in 1526. **2** a Muslim Indian, Mongol, or Mongolian. ◆ *adj* **3** of or relating to the Moguls or their empire. [C16: from Persian *mughul* Mongolian]

mogul skiing *n* an event in which skiers descend a slope covered in mounds of snow, making two jumps during their descent. [C20: *mogul* ? from G dialect *Mugl* hillock or hummock]

MOH (in Britain) *abbrev. for* Medical Officer of Health.

mohair ('məʊ,hɛə) *n* **1** Also called: **angora.** the long soft silky hair of the Angora goat. **2a** a fabric made from the yarn of this hair and cotton or wool. **2b** (*as modifier*): *a mohair suit.* [C16: (infl. by *hair*), ult. from Ar. *mukhayyar*, lit.: choice]

Moham. *abbrev. for* Mohammedan.

Mohammedan (məʊ'hæmɪdᵊn) *n, adj* another word (not in Muslim use) for **Muslim.**

Mohammedanism (məʊ'hæmɪdᵊ,nɪzəm) *n* another word (not in Muslim use) for **Islam.**

Mohawk ('məʊhɔ:k) *n* **1** (*pl* **Mohawks** *or* **Mohawk**) a member of a North American Indian people formerly living along the Mohawk River. **2** the Iroquoian language of this people.

mohican (məʊ'hi:kən) *n* a punk hairstyle in which the head is shaved at the sides and the remaining strip of hair is worn stiffly erect and sometimes brightly coloured.

moidore ('mɔɪdɔ:) *n* a former Portuguese gold coin. [C18: from Port. *moeda de ouro* money of gold]

moiety ('mɔɪɪtɪ) *n, pl* **moieties. 1** a half. **2** one of two parts or divisions of something. [C15: from OF *moitié*, from L *mediētās* middle, from *medius*]

moil (mɔɪl) *Arch. or dialect.* ◆ *vb* **1** to moisten or soil or become moist, soiled, etc. **2** (*intr*) to toil or drudge (esp. in **toil and moil**). ◆ *n* **3** toil; drudgery. **4** confusion. [C14 (to moisten; later: to work hard in unpleasantly wet conditions) from OF *moillier*, ult. from L *mollis* soft]

moire (mwɑ:) *n* a fabric, usually silk, having a watered effect. [C17: from F, earlier *mouaire*, from MOHAIR]

moiré ('mwɑ:reɪ) *adj* **1** having a watered or wavelike pattern. ◆ *n* **2** such a pattern, impressed on fabrics by means of engraved rollers. **3** any fabric having such a pattern; moire. **4** Also: **moiré pattern.** a pattern

THESAURUS

late, latest, neoteric (*rare*), new, newfangled, novel, present, present-day, recent, up-to-date, up-to-the-minute, with it (*inf.*)
Antonyms *adj* ancient, antiquated, archaic, former, obsolete, old, old-fashioned, old hat, outmoded, passé, past, square (*inf.*), uncool (*sl.*)

modernity *n* **1** = **novelty**, contemporaneity, currency, freshness, innovation, newness, recentness

modernize *vb* **1, 2** = **update**, bring up to date, face-lift, make over, rebrand, rejuvenate, remake, remodel, renew, renovate, revamp

modest *adj* **1-3** = **unpretentious**, bashful, blushing, coy, demure, diffident, discreet, humble, meek, quiet, reserved, reticent, retiring, self-conscious, self-effacing, shy, simple, unassuming **4** = **moderate**, fair, limited, middling, ordinary, small, unexceptional

modesty *n* = **reserve**, bashfulness, coyness, decency, demureness, diffidence, discreetness, humbleness, humility, lack of pretension, meekness, propriety, quietness, reticence, self-effacement, shyness, simplicity, timidity, unobtrusiveness, unpretentiousness
Antonyms *n* arrogance, assurance, boastfulness, boldness, conceit, confidence, egotism, extravagance, forwardness, haughtiness, immodesty, indecency, ostentation, presumption, pretentiousness, pride, showiness, vanity

modicum *n* = **little**, atom, bit, crumb, dash, drop, fragment, grain, inch, iota, mite, ounce, particle, pinch, scrap, shred, small amount, speck, tad (*inf., chiefly US*), tinge, touch

modification *n* **1, 3** = **change**, adjustment, alteration, modulation, mutation, qualification, refinement, reformation, restriction, revision, variation

modify *vb* **1** = **change**, adapt, adjust, alter, convert, recast, redo, refashion, reform, remodel, reorganize, reshape, revise, rework, transform, tweak (*inf.*), vary **2** = **tone down**, abate, ease, lessen, limit, lower, moderate, qualify, reduce, relax, restrain, restrict, soften, temper

modish *adj* = **fashionable**, à la mode, all the rage, chic, contemporary, current, hip (*sl.*), in, now (*inf.*), smart, stylish, trendy (*Brit. inf.*), up-to-the-minute, vogue, voguish, with it (*inf.*)

modulate *vb* **2** = **adjust**, attune, balance, harmonize, inflect, regulate, tone, tune, vary

modus operandi *n* = **procedure**, method, operation, practice, praxis, process, system, technique, way

mogul *n* = **tycoon**, baron, bashaw, big gun (*inf.*), big hitter, big noise (*inf.*), big shot (*inf.*), big wheel (*sl.*), heavy hitter (*inf.*), lord, magnate, nabob (*inf.*), notable, personage, potentate, V.I.P.

seen when two geometrical patterns, such as grids, are visually superimposed. [C17: from F, from *moire* MOHAIR]

Moism ('məʊ,ɪzəm) *n* the religious and ethical teaching of Mo-Zi (?470–?391 B.C.), Chinese philosopher, and his followers, emphasizing universal love, ascetic self-discipline, and obedience to the will of Heaven.

moist ❶ (mɔɪst) *adj* **1** slightly damp or wet. **2** saturated with or suggestive of moisture. [C14: from OF, ult. rel. to L *mūcidus* musty]
▸ **'moistly** *adv* ▸ **'moistness** *n*

moisten ❶ ('mɔɪsᵊn) *vb* to make or become moist.

moisture ❶ ('mɔɪstʃə) *n* water or other liquid diffused as vapour or condensed on or in objects.

moisturize *or* **moisturise** ('mɔɪstʃə,raɪz) *vb* **moisturizes, moisturizing, moisturized** *or* **moisturises, moisturising, moisturised.** (*tr*) to add moisture to (the air, the skin, etc.).
▸ **'moistur,izer** *or* **'moistur,iser** *n*

mojo ('məʊdʒəʊ) *n, pl* **mojos** *or* **mojoes.** *US sl.* **1** an amulet, charm, or magic spell. **2** the art of casting magic spells. [C20: of W African origin]

moke (məʊk) *n Brit. sl.* a donkey. [C19: from ?]

mol *Chem. symbol for* mole[3].

mol. *abbrev. for:* **1** molecular. **2** molecule.

molal ('məʊləl) *adj Chem.* of or consisting of a solution containing one mole of solute per thousand grams of solvent. [C20: from MOLE[3] + -AL[1]]

molar[1] ('məʊlə) *n* **1** any of the 12 grinding teeth in man. **2** a corresponding tooth in other mammals. ◆ *adj* **3** of or relating to any of these teeth. **4** used for or capable of grinding. [C16: from L *molāris*, from *mola* millstone]

molar[2] ('məʊlə) *adj* **1** (of a physical quantity) per unit amount of substance: *molar volume.* **2** (not recommended in technical usage) (of a solution) containing one mole of solute per litre of solution. [C19: from L *mōlēs* a mass]

molasses (mə'læsɪz) *n* (*functioning as sing*) **1** the thick brown uncrystallized bitter syrup obtained from sugar during refining. **2** the US and Canad. name for **treacle** (sense 1). [C16: from Port. *melaço*, from LL *mellāceum* must, from L *mel* honey]

mold (məʊld) *n, vb* the US spelling of **mould.**

moldboard ('məʊld,bɔːd) *n* the US spelling of **mouldboard.**

molder ('məʊldə) *vb* the US spelling of **moulder.**

molding ('məʊldɪŋ) *n* the US spelling of **moulding.**

moldy ('məʊldɪ) *adj* the US spelling of **mouldy.**

mole[1] (məʊl) *n Pathol.* a nontechnical name for **naevus.** [OE *māl*]

mole[2] (məʊl) *n* **1** any small burrowing mammal of a family of Europe, Asia, and North and Central America. They have velvety, typically dark fur and forearms specialized for digging. **2** *Inf.* a spy who has infiltrated an organization and become a trusted member of it. [C14: from MDu. *mol*, of Gmc origin]

mole[3] (məʊl) *n* the basic SI unit of amount of substance; the amount that contains as many elementary entities as there are atoms in 0.012 kilogram of carbon-12. The entity may be an atom, a molecule, an ion, a radical, etc. Symbol: mol. See **gram molecule.** [C20: from G *Mol*, short for *Molekül* MOLECULE]

mole[4] ❶ (məʊl) *n* **1** a breakwater. **2** a harbour protected by a breakwater. [C16: from F *môle*, from L *mōlēs* mass]

Molech ('məʊlɛk) *n Old Testament.* a variant of **Moloch.**

molecular (məʊ'lɛkjʊlə, mə-) *adj* of or relating to molecules.
▸ **mo'lecularly** *adv*

molecular biology *n* the study of the structure and function of biological molecules, esp. nucleic acids and proteins.

molecular formula *n* a chemical formula indicating the numbers and types of atoms in a molecule: *H_2SO_4 is the molecular formula of sulphuric acid.*

molecular genetics *n* (*functioning as sing*) the study of the molecular constitution of genes and chromosomes.

molecular weight *n* the former name for **relative molecular mass.**

molecule ❶ ('mɒlɪ,kjuːl) *n* **1** the simplest unit of a chemical compound that can exist, consisting of two or more atoms held together by chemical bonds. **2** a very small particle. [C18: via F from NL *mōlēcula*, dim. of L *mōlēs* mass]

molehill ('məʊl,hɪl) *n* **1** the small mound of earth thrown up by a burrowing mole. **2 make a mountain out of a molehill.** to exaggerate an unimportant matter out of all proportion.

moleskin ('məʊl,skɪn) *n* **1** the dark grey dense velvety pelt of a mole, used as a fur. **2** a hard-wearing cotton fabric of twill weave. **3** (*modifier*): *a moleskin waistcoat.*

molest ❶ (mə'lɛst) *vb* (*tr*) **1** to disturb or annoy by malevolent interference. **2** to accost or attack, esp. with the intention of assaulting sexually. [C14: from L *molestāre* to annoy, from *molestus* troublesome, from *mōlēs* mass]
▸ **molestation** (,məʊlɛ'steɪʃən) *n* ▸ **mo'lester** *n*

moll (mɒl) *n Sl.* **1** the female accomplice of a gangster. **2** a prostitute. [C17: from *Moll*, familiar form of *Mary*]

mollify ❶ ('mɒlɪ,faɪ) *vb* **mollifies, mollifying, mollified.** (*tr*) **1** to pacify; soothe. **2** to lessen the harshness or severity of. [C15: from OF *mollifier*, via LL, from L *mollis* soft + *facere* to make]
▸ **'molli,fiable** *adj* ▸ **,mollifi'cation** *n* ▸ **'molli,fier** *n*

mollusc *or US* **mollusk** ('mɒləsk) *n* any of various invertebrates having a soft unsegmented body and often a shell, secreted by a fold of skin (the mantle). The group includes the gastropods (snails, slugs, etc.), bivalves (clams, mussels, etc.), and cephalopods (squid, octopuses, etc.). [C18: via NL from L *molluscus*, from *mollis* soft]
▸ **molluscan** *or US* **molluskan** (mɒ'lʌskən) *adj, n* ▸ **mollusc-like** *or US* **mollusk-like** *adj*

molly[1] ('mɒlɪ) *n, pl* **mollies.** any of various brightly coloured tropical or subtropical American freshwater fishes. [C19: from NL *Mollienisia*, from Comte F. N. *Mollien* (1758–1850), F statesman]

molly[2] ('mɒlɪ) *n, pl* **mollies.** *Irish inf.* an effeminate, weak, or cowardly boy or man. [C18: perhaps from *Molly*, pet name for *Mary*]

mollycoddle ❶ ('mɒlɪ,kɒdᵊl) *vb* **mollycoddles, mollycoddling, mollycoddled. 1** (*tr*) to treat with indulgent care; pamper. ◆ *n* **2** a pampered person. [C19: from MOLLY[2] + CODDLE]

Moloch ('məʊlɒk) *or* **Molech** ('məʊlɛk) *n Old Testament.* a Semitic deity to whom parents sacrificed their children.

Molotov cocktail ('mɒlə,tɒf) *n* an elementary incendiary weapon, usually a bottle of petrol with a short delay fuse or wick; petrol bomb. [C20: after V. M. *Molotov* (1890–1986), Soviet statesman]

molt (məʊlt) *vb, n* the usual US spelling of **moult.**
▸ **'molter** *n*

molten ('məʊltən) *adj* **1** liquefied; melted. **2** made by having been melted: *molten casts.* ◆ *vb* **3** the past participle of **melt.**

molto ('mɒltəʊ) *adv Music.* very: *allegro molto; molto adagio.* [from It., from L *multum* (adv) much]

mol. wt. *abbrev. for* molecular weight.

moly ('məʊlɪ) *n, pl* **molies. 1** *Greek myth.* a magic herb given by Hermes to Odysseus to nullify the spells of Circe. **2** a variety of wild garlic of S Europe having yellow flowers. [C16: from L *mōly*, from Gk *mōlu*]

molybdenite (mɒ'lɪbdɪ,naɪt) *n* a soft grey mineral consisting of molybdenum sulphide in hexagonal crystalline form with rhenium as an impurity. Formula: MoS_2.

molybdenum (mɒ'lɪbdɪnəm) *n* a very hard silvery-white metallic element occurring principally in molybdenite: used in alloys, esp. to harden and strengthen steels. Symbol: Mo; atomic no.: 42; atomic wt.: 95.94. [C19: from NL, from L *molybdaena* galena, from Gk, from *molubdos* lead]

mom (mɒm) *n Chiefly US & Canad.* an informal word for **mother**[1].

moment ❶ ('məʊmənt) *n* **1** a short indefinite period of time. **2** a specific instant or point in time: *at that moment the phone rang.* **3 the moment.** the present point of time: *at the moment it's fine.* **4** import, significance, or value: *a man of moment.* **5** *Physics.* **5a** a tendency to produce motion, esp. rotation about a point or axis. **5b** the product of a physical quantity, such as force or mass, and its distance from a fixed reference point. See also **moment of inertia.** [C14: from OF, from L *mōmentum*, from *movēre* to move]

momentarily ❶ ('məʊməntərɪlɪ, -trɪlɪ, ,məʊmən'tærɪlɪ) *adv* **1** for an instant; temporarily. **2** from moment to moment; every instant. **3** *US & Canad.* very soon. ◆ Also (for senses 1, 2): **momently.**

momentary ❶ ('məʊməntərɪ, -trɪ) *adj* **1** lasting for only a moment; temporary. **2** *Rare.* occurring or present at each moment.
▸ **'momentariness** *n*

moment of inertia *n* the tendency of a body to resist angular acceleration, expressed as the sum of the products of the mass of each particle in the body and the square of its perpendicular distance from the axis of rotation.

moment of truth *n* **1** a moment when a person or thing is put to the test. **2** the point in a bullfight when the matador is about to kill the bull.

THESAURUS

moist *adj* **1, 2 = damp**, clammy, dampish, dank, dewy, dripping, drizzly, humid, not dry, rainy, soggy, wet, wettish

moisten *vb* **= dampen**, bedew, damp, humidify, lick, moisturize, soak, water, wet

moisture *n* **= damp**, dampness, dankness, dew, humidity, liquid, perspiration, sweat, water, wateriness, wetness

mole[4] *n* **1 = breakwater**, dike, dyke, embankment, groyne, jetty, pier, sea wall

molecule *n* **2 = particle**, atom, iota, jot, mite, mote, speck

molest *vb* **1 = annoy**, abuse, afflict, badger, beset, bother, bug (*inf.*), disturb, harass, harry, hector, irritate, persecute, pester, plague, tease, torment, upset, vex, worry **2 = abuse**, accost, assail, attack, harm, hurt, ill-treat, injure, interfere with, maltreat, manhandle

mollify *vb* **1 = pacify**, appease, calm, compose, conciliate, placate, pour oil on troubled waters, propitiate, quell, quiet, soothe, sweeten **2 = soften**, abate, allay, assuage, blunt, curb, cushion, ease, lessen, lull, mitigate, moderate, modify, relieve, temper, tone down, tranquillize

mollycoddle *vb* **1 = pamper**, baby, coddle, cosset, indulge, pet, ruin, spoil

moment *n* **1 = instant**, bat of an eye (*inf.*), flash, jiffy (*inf.*), minute, no time, second, shake (*inf.*), split second, tick (*Brit. inf.*), trice, twinkling, two shakes (*inf.*), two shakes of a lamb's tail (*inf.*) **2 = time**, hour, instant, juncture, point, point in time, stage **4 = importance**, concern, consequence, gravity, import, seriousness, significance, substance, value, weight, weightiness, worth

momentarily *adv* **1 = briefly**, for a little while, for a minute, for a moment, for an instant, for a second, for a short time, for a short while, for the nonce, temporarily

momentary *adj* **1 = short-lived**, brief, ephemeral, evanescent, fleeting, flying, fugitive, hasty, passing, quick, short, temporary, transitory

Antonyms *adj* lasting, lengthy, long-lived, permanent

momentous ❶ (məʊ'mɛntəs) *adj* of great significance.
▸**mo'mentously** *adv* ▸**mo'mentousness** *n*

momentum ❶ (məʊ'mɛntəm) *n, pl* **momenta** (-tə) *or* **momentums. 1** *Physics.* the product of a body's mass and its velocity. **2** the impetus of a body resulting from its motion. **3** driving power or strength. [C17: from L: movement; see MOMENT]

momma ('mɒmə) *n Chiefly US.* **1** an informal or childish word for **mother**[1]. **2** *Inf.* a buxom and voluptuous woman.

mon. *abbrev. for* monetary.

Mon. *abbrev. for* Monday.

mon- *combining form.* a variant of **mono-** before a vowel.

monad ('mɒnæd, 'məʊ-) *n* **1** (*pl* **monads** *or* **monades** (-ə,di:z)). *Philosophy.* any fundamental singular metaphysical entity, esp. if autonomous. **2** a single-celled organism. **3** an atom, ion, or radical with a valency of one. ◆ Also (for senses 1, 2): **monas.** [C17: from LL *monas,* from Gk: unit, from *monos* alone]
▸**monadic** (mɒ'nædɪk) *adj*

monadelphous (,mɒnə'dɛlfəs) *adj* **1** (of stamens) having united filaments forming a tube around the style. **2** (of flowers) having monadelphous stamens. [C19: from MONO- + Gk *adelphos* brother]

monadnock (mə'nædnɒk) *n* a residual hill of hard rock in an otherwise eroded area. [C19: after Mount *Monadnock,* New Hampshire, US]

monandrous (mɒ'nændrəs) *adj* **1** having only one male sexual partner over a period of time. **2** (of plants) having flowers with only one stamen. **3** (of flowers) having only one stamen. [C19: from MONO- + -ANDROUS]
▸**mo'nandry** *n*

monarch ❶ ('mɒnək) *n* **1** a sovereign head of state, esp. a king, queen, or emperor, who rules usually by hereditary right. **2** a supremely powerful or pre-eminent person or thing. **3** Also called: **milkweed.** a large migratory orange-and-black butterfly that feeds on the milkweed plant. [C15: from LL *monarcha,* from Gk; see MONO-, -ARCH]
▸**monarchal** (mɒ'nɑ:kᵊl) *or* **mo'narchial** *adj* ▸**mo'narchical** *or* **mo'narchic** *adj* ▸**'monarchism** *n* ▸**'monarchist** *n, adj* ▸**,monar'chistic** *adj*

monarchy ❶ ('mɒnəkɪ) *n, pl* **monarchies. 1** a form of government in which supreme authority is vested in a single and usually hereditary figure, such as a king. **2** a country reigned over by a monarch.

monarda (mɒ'nɑ:də) *n* any of various mintlike North American plants. [C19: from NL, after N. *Monardés* (1493–1588), Sp. botanist]

monastery ❶ ('mɒnəstərɪ) *n, pl* **monasteries.** the residence of a religious community, esp. of monks, living in seclusion from secular society and bound by religious vows. [C15: from Church L *monastērium,* ult. from Gk *monazein* to live alone, from *monos* alone]
▸**monasterial** (,mɒnə'stɪərɪəl) *adj*

monastic ❶ (mə'næstɪk) *adj* **1** of or relating to monasteries or monks, nuns, etc. **2** resembling this sort of life. ◆ *n* **3** a person committed to this way of life, esp. a monk.

monasticism (mə'næstɪ,sɪzəm) *n* the monastic system, movement, or way of life.

monatomic (,mɒnə'tɒmɪk) *or* **monoatomic** (,mɒnəʊə'tɒmɪk) *adj Chem.* **1** (of an element) having or consisting of single atoms. **2** (of a compound or molecule) having only one atom or group that can be replaced in a chemical reaction.

monaural (mɒ'nɔ:rəl) *adj* **1** relating to, having, or hearing with only one ear. **2** another word for **monophonic.**
▸**mon'aurally** *adv*

monazite ('mɒnə,zaɪt) *n* a yellow to reddish-brown mineral consisting of a phosphate of thorium, cerium, and lanthanum in monoclinic crystalline form. [C19: from G, from Gk *monazein* to live alone, so called because of its rarity]

Monday ('mʌndɪ) *n* the second day of the week; first day of the working week. [OE *mōnandæg* moon's day, translation of LL *lūnae diēs*]

monecious (mɒ'ni:ʃəs) *adj* a variant spelling of **monoecious.**

Monel metal *or* **Monell metal** (mɒ'nɛl) *n Trademark.* any of various silvery corrosion-resistant alloys. [C20: after A. *Monell* (died 1921), president of the International Nickel Co., New York, which introduced the alloys]

monetarism ('mʌnɪtə,rɪzəm) *n* **1** the theory that inflation is caused by an excess quantity of money in an economy. **2** an economic policy based on this theory and on a belief in the efficiency of free market forces.
▸**'monetarist** *n, adj*

monetary ❶ ('mʌnɪtərɪ, -trɪ) *adj* **1** of or relating to money or currency. **2** of or relating to monetarism. [C19: from LL *monētārius,* from L *monēta* MONEY]
▸**'monetarily** *adv*

monetize *or* **monetise** ('mʌnɪ,taɪz) *vb* **monetizes, monetizing, monetized** *or* **monetises, monetising, monetised.** (*tr*) **1** to establish as legal tender. **2** to give a legal value to (a coin).
▸**,moneti'zation** *or* **,moneti'sation** *n*

money ❶ ('mʌnɪ) *n* **1** a medium of exchange that functions as legal tender. **2** the official currency, in the form of banknotes, coins, etc., issued by a government or other authority. **3** a particular denomination or form of currency: *silver money.* **4** (*Law or arch. pl* **moneys** *or* **monies**) a pecuniary sum or income. **5** an unspecified amount of paper currency or coins: *money to lend.* **6 for one's money.** in one's opinion. **7 in the money.** *Inf.* well-off; rich. **8 one's money's worth.** full value for the money one has paid for something. **9 put money on.** to place a bet on. ◆ Related adj: **pecuniary.** [C13: from OF *moneie,* from L *monēta;* see MINT[2]]

moneybags ('mʌnɪ,bægz) *n (functioning as sing) Inf.* a very rich person.

moneychanger ('mʌnɪ,tʃeɪndʒə) *n* **1** a person engaged in the business of exchanging currencies or money. **2** *Chiefly US.* a machine for dispensing coins.

moneyed ❶ *or* **monied** ('mʌnɪd) *adj* **1** having a great deal of money; rich. **2** arising from or characterized by money.

money-grubbing *adj Inf.* seeking greedily to obtain money.
▸**'money-,grubber** *n*

moneylender ('mʌnɪ,lɛndə) *n* a person who lends money at interest as a living.
▸**'money,lending** *adj, n*

moneymaker ❶ ('mʌnɪ,meɪkə) *n* **1** a person who is intent on accumulating money. **2** a person or thing that is or might be profitable.
▸**'money,making** *adj, n*

money of account *n* another name (esp. US and Canad.) for **unit of account.**

money-spinner *n Inf.* an enterprise, idea, person, or thing that is a source of wealth.

money supply *n* the total amount of money in a country's economy at a given time, which can be calculated in various ways.

monger ('mʌŋgə) *n* **1** (*in combination except in archaic use*) a trader or dealer: *ironmonger.* **2** (*in combination*) a promoter of something: *warmonger.* [OE *mangere,* ult. from L *mangō* dealer]
▸**'mongering** *n, adj*

mongol ('mɒŋgᵊl) *n* (not in technical use) a person affected by Down's syndrome.

Mongol ('mɒŋgɒl, -gᵊl) *n* another word for **Mongolian.**

mongolian (mɒŋ'gəʊlɪən) *adj* (not in technical use) of, relating to, or affected by Down's syndrome.

Mongolian (mɒŋ'gəʊlɪən) *adj* **1** of or relating to Mongolia, a country in Central Asia, its people, or their language. ◆ *n* **2** a native or inhabitant of Mongolia. **3** the language of Mongolia.

Mongolic (mɒŋ'gɒlɪk) *n* **1** a branch or subfamily of the Altaic family of languages, including Mongolian and Kalmuck. **2** another word for **Mongoloid.**

mongolism ('mɒŋgə,lɪzəm) *n Pathol.* a former name (not in technical use) for **Down's syndrome.** [C20: the condition produces facial features similar to those of the Mongoloid peoples]

mongoloid ('mɒŋgə,lɔɪd) *adj* (not in technical use) **1** relating to or characterized by Down's syndrome. ◆ *n* **2** a person affected by Down's syndrome.

Mongoloid ('mɒŋgə,lɔɪd) *adj* **1** of or relating to a major racial group of mankind, characterized by yellowish complexion, straight black hair, slanting eyes, short nose, and scanty facial hair, including most of the peoples of Asia, the Eskimos, and the North American Indians. ◆ *n* **2** a member of this group.

mongoose ('mɒŋ,gu:s) *n, pl* **mongooses.** any of various small predatory mammals occurring in Africa and from S Europe to SE Asia, typically having a long tail and brindled coat. [C17: from Marathi (a language of India) *mangūs*]

mongrel ❶ ('mʌŋgrəl) *n* **1** a plant or animal, esp. a dog, of mixed or unknown breeding. **2** *Derog.* a person of mixed race. ◆ *adj* **3** of mixed origin, breeding, character, etc. [C15: from obs. *mong* mixture]
▸**'mongrelism** *n* ▸**'mongre,lize** *or* **'mongre,lise** *vb* ▸**,mongreli'zation** *or* **,mongreli'sation** *n* ▸**'mongrelly** *adj*

THESAURUS

momentous *adj* = **significant**, consequential, critical, crucial, decisive, earth-shaking (*inf.*), fateful, grave, historic, important, of moment, pivotal, serious, vital, weighty
Antonyms *adj* inconsequential, insignificant, trifling, trivial, unimportant

momentum *n* **2, 3** = **impetus**, drive, energy, force, power, propulsion, push, strength, thrust

monarch *n* **1** = **ruler**, crowned head, emperor *or* empress, king, potentate, prince *or* princess, queen, sovereign

monarchy *n* **1** = **sovereignty**, absolutism, autocracy, despotism, kingship, monocracy, royalism **2** = **kingdom**, empire, principality, realm

monastery *n* = **abbey**, cloister, convent, friary, house, nunnery, priory, religious community

monastic *adj* **1, 2** = **monkish**, ascetic, austere, celibate, cenobitic, cloistered, cloistral, coenobitic, contemplative, conventual, eremitic, hermit-like, monachal, recluse, reclusive, secluded, sequestered, withdrawn

monetary *adj* **1** = **financial**, budgetary, capital, cash, fiscal, pecuniary

money *n* **1, 2** = **cash**, banknotes, brass (*N English dialect*), bread, capital, coin, currency, dibs (*sl.*), dosh (*Brit. & Austral. sl.*), dough (*sl.*), filthy lucre (*facetious*), funds, hard cash, legal tender, lolly (*Brit. sl.*), loot (*inf.*), moolah (*sl.*), necessary (*inf.*), needful (*inf.*), pelf (*contemptuous*), readies (*inf.*), rhino (*Brit. sl.*), riches, shekels (*inf.*), silver, specie, spondulicks (*sl.*), tin (*sl.*), wealth **7 in the money** *Informal* = **rich**, affluent, flush (*inf.*), in clover (*inf.*), loaded (*sl.*), on Easy Street (*inf.*), prosperous, rolling (*sl.*), wealthy, well-heeled (*inf.*), well-off, well-to-do

moneyed *adj* **1** = **rich**, affluent, flush (*inf.*), loaded (*sl.*), prosperous, wealthy, well-heeled (*inf.*), well-off, well-to-do

moneymaking *adj* **1, 2** = **profitable**, gainful, going, lucrative, paying, remunerative, successful, thriving

mongrel *n* **1** = **hybrid**, bigener (*Biology*), cross, crossbreed, half-breed, mixed breed ◆ *adj* **3** =

'mongst (mʌŋst) *prep Poetic.* short for **amongst.**
monied ('mʌnɪd) *adj* a less common spelling of **moneyed.**
monies ('mʌnɪz) *n Law, arch.* a plural of **money.**
moniker *or* **monicker** ('mɒnɪkə) *n Sl.* a person's name or nickname. [C19: from Shelta *munnik,* altered from Irish Gaelic *ainm* name]
monism ('mɒnɪzəm) *n* **1** *Philosophy.* the doctrine that reality consists of only one basic substance or element, such as mind or matter. Cf. **dualism** (sense 2), **pluralism** (sense 4). **2** the attempt to explain anything in terms of one principle only.
▸**'monist** *n, adj* ▸**mo'nistic** *adj*
monition (məʊ'nɪʃən) *n* **1** a warning or caution; admonition. **2** *Christianity.* a formal notice from a bishop or ecclesiastical court requiring a person to refrain from committing a specific offence. [C14: via OF from L *monitiō,* from *monēre* to warn]
monitor ❶ ('mɒnɪtə) *n* **1** a person or piece of equipment that warns, checks, controls, or keeps a continuous record of something. **2** *Education.* **2a** a senior pupil with various supervisory duties, etc. **2b** a pupil assisting a teacher in classroom organization, etc. **3** a television set used to display certain kinds of information in a television studio, airport, etc. **4a** a loudspeaker used in a recording studio to determine quality or balance. **4b** a loudspeaker used on stage to enable musicians to hear themselves. **5** any of various large predatory lizards inhabiting warm regions of Africa, Asia, and Australia. **6** (formerly) a small heavily armoured warship used for coastal assault. ◆ *vb* **7** to act as a monitor of. **8** (*tr*) to observe or record (the activity or performance of) (an engine or other device). **9** (*tr*) to check (the technical quality of) (a radio or television broadcast). [C16: from L, from *monēre* to advise]
▸**monitorial** (ˌmɒnɪ'tɔːrɪəl) *adj* ▸**'monitorship** *n* ▸**'monitress** *fem n*
monitory ('mɒnɪtərɪ, -trɪ) *adj also* **monitorial. 1** warning or admonishing. ◆ *n, pl* **monitories. 2** *Rare.* a letter containing a monition.
monk ❶ (mʌŋk) *n* a male member of a religious community bound by vows of poverty, chastity, and obedience. Related adj: **monastic.** [OE *munuc,* from LL *monachus,* from LGk: solitary (man), from Gk *monos* alone]
▸**'monkish** *adj*
monkey ❶ ('mʌŋkɪ) *n* **1** any of numerous long-tailed primates excluding lemurs, tarsiers, etc.: see **Old World monkey, New World monkey. 2** any primate except man. **3** a naughty or mischievous person, esp. a child. **4** the head of a pile-driver (**monkey engine**) or of some similar mechanical device. **5** *US & Canad. sl.* an addict's dependence on a drug (esp. in **have a monkey on one's back**). **6** *Sl.* a butt of derision; someone made to look a fool (esp. in **make a monkey of**). **7** *Sl.* (esp. in bookmaking) £500. **8** *US & Canad. sl.* $500. ◆ *vb* **9** (*intr;* usually foll. by *around, with,* etc.) to meddle, fool, or tinker. **10** (*tr*) *Rare.* to imitate; ape. [C16: ?from Low G; cf. MLow G *Moneke,* name of the ape's son in the tale of Reynard the Fox]
monkey business ❶ *n Inf.* mischievous, suspect, or dishonest behaviour or acts.
monkey flower *n* any of various plants of the genus *Mimulus,* cultivated for their yellow or red flowers.
monkey jacket *n* a short close-fitting jacket, esp. a waist-length jacket similar to a mess jacket.
monkey nut *n Brit.* another name for a **peanut.**
monkey puzzle *n* a South American coniferous tree having branches shaped like a candelabrum and stiff sharp leaves. Also called: **Chile pine.**
monkey's wedding *n S. African inf.* a combination of rain and sunshine. [from ?]
monkey tricks *or US* **monkey shines** *pl n Inf.* mischievous behaviour or acts.
monkey wrench *n* a wrench with adjustable jaws.
monkfish ('mʌŋkˌfɪʃ) *n, pl* **monkfish** *or* **monkfishes. 1** any of various angler fishes. **2** another name for **angelfish** (sense 3).
monk's cloth *n* a heavy cotton fabric of basket weave, used mainly for bedspreads.
monkshood ('mʌŋkshʊd) *n* any of several poisonous N temperate plants that have hooded blue-purple flowers.
mono ('mɒnəʊ) *adj* **1** short for **monophonic.** ◆ *n* **2** monophonic sound.
mono- *or before a vowel* **mon-** *combining form.* **1** one; single: *monorail.* **2** indicating that a chemical compound contains a single specified atom or group: *monoxide.* [from Gk *monos*]
monoacid (ˌmɒnəʊ'æsɪd), **monacid, monoacidic** (ˌmɒnəʊə'sɪdɪk), *or* **monacidic** *adj Chem.* (of a base) capable of reacting with only one molecule of a monobasic acid; having only one hydroxide ion per molecule.
monobasic (ˌmɒnəʊ'beɪsɪk) *adj Chem.* (of an acid, such as hydrogen chloride) having only one replaceable hydrogen atom per molecule.
monocarpic (ˌmɒnəʊ'kɑːpɪk) *or* **monocarpous** *adj* (of some flowering plants) producing fruit only once before dying.
monochromatic (ˌmɒnəʊkrəʊ'mætɪk) *or* **monochroic** (ˌmɒnəʊ'krəʊɪk) *adj* (of light or other electromagnetic radiation) having only one wavelength.
monochromator (ˌmɒnəʊ'krəʊmˌeɪtə) *n Physics.* a device that isolates a single wavelength of radiation.
monochrome ('mɒnəˌkrəʊm) *n* **1** a black-and-white photograph or transparency. **2** *Photog.* black-and-white. **3a** a painting, drawing, etc., done in a range of tones of a single colour. **3b** the technique or art of this. **4** (*modifier*) executed in or resembling monochrome: *a monochrome print.* ◆ *adj* **5** devoid of any distinctive or stimulating characteristics. ◆ Also called (for senses 3, 4): **monotint.** [C17: via Med. L from Gk *monokhrōmos* of one colour]
▸ˌ**mono'chromic** *adj* ▸**'monoˌchromist** *n*
monocle ('mɒnəkᵊl) *n* a lens for correcting defective vision of one eye, held in position by the facial muscles. [C19: from F, from LL, from MONO- + *oculus* eye]
▸**'monocled** *adj*
monocline ('mɒnəʊˌklaɪn) *n* a fold in stratified rocks in which the strata are inclined in the same direction from the horizontal. [C19: from MONO- + Gk *klīnein* to lean]
▸ˌ**mono'clinal** *adj, n*
monoclinic (ˌmɒnəʊ'klɪnɪk) *adj Crystallog.* relating to or belonging to the crystal system characterized by three unequal axes, one pair of which are not at right angles to each other. [C19: from MONO- + Gk *klīnein* to lean]
monoclinous (ˌmɒnəʊ'klaɪnəs, 'mɒnəʊˌklaɪnəs) *adj* (of flowering plants) having the male and female reproductive organs on the same flower. Cf. **diclinous.** [C19: from MONO- + Gk *klīne* bed]
▸**'monoˌclinism** *n*
monoclonal antibody (ˌmɒnəʊ'kləʊnᵊl) *n* an antibody, produced by a single clone of cells grown in culture, that is both pure and specific and capable of proliferating indefinitely: used in diagnosis, therapy, and biotechnology.
monocotyledon (ˌmɒnəʊˌkɒtɪ'liːdᵊn) *n* any of various flowering plants having a single embryonic seed leaf, leaves with parallel veins, and flowers with parts in threes: includes grasses, lilies, palms, and orchids. Cf. **dicotyledon.**
▸ˌ**monoˌcoty'ledonous** *adj*
monocracy (mɒ'nɒkrəsɪ) *n, pl* **monocracies.** government by one person.
▸**monocrat** ('mɒnəˌkræt) *n* ▸ˌ**mono'cratic** *adj*
monocular (mɒ'nɒkjʊlə) *adj* having or intended for the use of only one eye. [C17: from LL *monoculus* one-eyed]
▸**mo'nocularly** *adv*
monoculture ('mɒnəʊˌkʌltʃə) *n* the continuous growing of one type of crop.
monocycle ('mɒnəˌsaɪkᵊl) *n* another name for **unicycle.**
monocyte ('mɒnəʊˌsaɪt) *n* the largest type of white blood cell that acts as part of the immune system by engulfing particles, such as invading microorganisms.
monody ('mɒnədɪ) *n, pl* **monodies. 1** (in Greek tragedy) an ode sung by a single actor. **2** any poem of lament for someone's death. **3** *Music.* a style of composition consisting of a single vocal part, usually with accompaniment. [C17: via LL from Gk *monōidia,* from MONO- + *aeidein* to sing]
▸**monodic** (mɒ'nɒdɪk) *adj* ▸**'monodist** *n*
monoecious (mɒ'niːʃəs) *adj* **1** (of some flowering plants) having the male and female reproductive organs in separate flowers on the same plant. **2** (of some animals and lower plants) hermaphrodite. [C18: from NL *monoecia,* from MONO- + Gk *oikos* house]
monofilament (ˌmɒnə'fɪləmənt) *or* **monofil** ('mɒnəfɪl) *n* synthetic thread or yarn composed of a single strand rather than twisted fibres.
monogamy (mɒ'nɒgəmɪ) *n* **1** the state or practice of having only one husband or wife over a period of time. **2** *Zool.* the practice of having only one mate. [C17: via F from LL *monogamia,* from Gk; see MONO- + -GAMY]
▸**mo'nogamist** *n* ▸**mo'nogamous** *adj*
monogenesis (ˌmɒnəʊ'dʒɛnɪsɪs) *or* **monogeny** (mɒ'nɒdʒɪnɪ) *n* **1** the hypothetical descent of all organisms from a single cell. **2** asexual reproduction in animals. **3** the direct development of an ovum into an organism resembling the adult. **4** the hypothetical descent of all human beings from a single pair of ancestors.
monogram ('mɒnəˌgræm) *n* a design of one or more letters, esp. initials, on clothing, stationery, etc. [C17: from LL *monogramma,* from Gk; see MONO-, -GRAM]
▸**monogrammatic** (ˌmɒnəgrə'mætɪk) *adj*
monograph ('mɒnəˌgrɑːf) *n* **1** a paper, book, or other work concerned with a single subject or aspect of a subject. ◆ *vb* **monographs, monographing, monographed.** (*tr*) **2** to write a monograph on.
▸**monographer** (mɒ'nɒgrəfə) *or* **mo'nographist** *n* ▸ˌ**mono'graphic** *adj*
monogyny (mɒ'nɒdʒɪnɪ) *n* the custom of having only one female sexual partner over a period of time.
▸**mo'nogynous** *adj*
monohull ('mɒnəʊˌhʌl) *n* a sailing vessel with a single hull.

THESAURUS

hybrid, bastard, crossbred, half-breed, of mixed breed

monitor *n* **1, 2** = **watchdog**, guide, invigilator, overseer, prefect, supervisor ◆ *vb* **7, 8** = **check**, follow, keep an eye on, keep tabs on, keep track of, observe, oversee, record, scan, supervise, survey, watch

monk *n* = **friar** (*loosely*), brother, monastic, religious

monkey *n* **1, 2** = **simian**, jackanapes (*arch.*), primate **3** = **rascal**, devil, imp, mischief maker, pickle, rogue, scamp ◆ *vb* **9** *with* **around** *or* **about with** = **fool**, fiddle (*inf.*), interfere, meddle, mess, play, tamper, tinker, trifle

monkey business *n Informal* = **mischief**, carry-on (*inf., chiefly Brit.*), clowning, horseplay, monkey tricks, pranks, shenanigans (*inf.*), skylarking (*inf.*), tomfoolery = **dishonesty**, chicanery, funny business, hanky-panky (*inf.*), skulduggery (*inf.*), trickery

monokini ('mɒnəʊˌkiːnɪ) *n* a woman's one-piece bathing garment usually equivalent to the bottom half of a bikini. [C20: from MONO- + BIKINI (as if *bikini* were from BI-)]
monolayer ('mɒnəʊˌleɪə) *n* a single layer of atoms or molecules adsorbed on a surface. Also called: **molecular film.**
monolingual (ˌmɒnəʊ'lɪŋgwəl) *adj* knowing or expressed in only one language.
monolith ('mɒnəlɪθ) *n* **1** a large block of stone or anything that resembles one in appearance, intractability, etc. **2** a statue, obelisk, column, etc., cut from one block of stone. **3** a large hollow foundation piece sunk as a caisson and filled with concrete. [C19: via F from Gk *monolithos* made from a single stone]
▸ˌ**mono'lithic** *adj*
monologue ('mɒnəˌlɒg) *n* **1** a long speech made by one actor in a play, film, etc., esp. when alone. **2** a dramatic piece for a single performer. **3** any long speech by one person, esp. when interfering with conversation. [C17: via F from Gk *monologos* speaking alone]
▸**monologic** (ˌmɒnə'lɒdʒɪk) *or* ˌ**mono'logical** *adj* ▸**monologist** ('mɒnəˌlɒgɪst) *n* ▸**monologize** *or* **monologise** (mɒ'nɒlədʒaɪz) *vb*

USAGE NOTE See at **soliloquy.**

monomania (ˌmɒnəʊ'meɪnɪə) *n* an excessive mental preoccupation with one thing, idea, etc.
▸ˌ**mono'maniˌac** *n, adj* ▸**monomaniacal** (ˌmɒnəʊmə'naɪək^əl) *adj*
monomark ('mɒnəmɑːk) *n Brit.* a series of letters or figures to identify goods, personal articles, etc.
monomer ('mɒnəmə) *n Chem.* a compound whose molecules can join together to form a polymer.
▸**monomeric** (ˌmɒnə'mɛrɪk) *adj*
monometallism (ˌmɒnəʊ'mɛt^əˌlɪzəm) *n* **1** the use of one metal, esp. gold or silver, as the sole standard of value and currency. **2** the economic policies supporting a monometallic standard.
▸**monometallic** (ˌmɒnəʊmɪ'tælɪk) *adj* ▸ˌ**mono'metallist** *n*
monomial (mɒ'nəʊmɪəl) *n* **1** *Maths.* an expression consisting of a single term, such as *5ax.* ◆ *adj* **2** consisting of a single algebraic term. [C18: MONO- + (BIN)OMIAL]
monomorphic (ˌmɒnəʊ'mɔːfɪk) *or* **monomorphous** *adj* **1** (of an individual organism) showing little or no change in structure during the entire life history. **2** (of a species) existing or having parts that exist in only one form. **3** (of a chemical compound) having only one crystalline form.
mononucleosis (ˌmɒnəʊˌnjuːklɪ'əʊsɪs) *n* **1** *Pathol.* the presence of a large number of monocytes in the blood. **2** See **infectious mononucleosis.**
monophonic (ˌmɒnəʊ'fɒnɪk) *adj* **1** Also: **monaural.** (of a system of broadcasting, recording, or reproducing sound) using only one channel between source and loudspeaker. Sometimes shortened to **mono.** Cf. **stereophonic. 2** *Music.* of or relating to a style of musical composition consisting of a single melodic line.
monophthong ('mɒnəfˌθɒŋ) *n* a simple or pure vowel. [C17: from Gk *monophthongos,* from MONO- + *thongos* sound]
Monophysite (mɒ'nɒfɪˌsaɪt) *n Christianity.* a person who holds that there is only one nature in the person of Christ, which is primarily divine with human attributes. [C17: via Church L from LGk, from MONO- + *phusis* nature]
▸**Monophysitic** (ˌmɒnəʊfɪ'sɪtɪk) *adj*
monoplane ('mɒnəʊˌpleɪn) *n* an aeroplane with only one pair of wings. Cf. **biplane.**
monopole ('mɒnəˌpəʊl) *n Physics.* **1** an electric charge or magnetic pole considered in isolation. **2** Also called: **magnetic monopole.** a hypothetical elementary particle postulated in certain theories of particle physics to exist as an isolated north or south magnetic pole.
monopolize *or* **monopolise** (mə'nɒpəˌlaɪz) *vb* **monopolizes, monopolizing, monopolized** *or* **monopolises, monopolising, monopolised.** (*tr*) **1** to have, control, or make use of fully, excluding others. **2** to obtain, maintain, or exploit a monopoly of (a market, commodity, etc.).
▸**moˌnopoli'zation** *or* **moˌnopoli'sation** *n* ▸**mo'nopoˌlizer** *or* **mo'nopoˌliser** *n*
monopoly (mə'nɒpəlɪ) *n, pl* **monopolies. 1** exclusive control of the market supply of a product or service. **2a** an enterprise exercising this control. **2b** the product or service so controlled. **3** *Law.* the exclusive right granted to a person, company, etc., by the state to purchase, manufacture, use, or sell some commodity or to trade in a specified area. **4** exclusive control, possession, or use of something. [C16: from LL, from Gk *monopōlion,* from MONO- + *pōlein* to sell]
▸**mo'nopolist** *n* ▸**moˌnopo'listic** *adj*
Monopoly (mə'nɒpəlɪ) *n Trademark.* a board game for two to six players who throw dice to advance their tokens, the object being to acquire the property on which their tokens land.
monorail ('mɒnəʊˌreɪl) *n* a single-rail railway, often elevated and with suspended cars.
monosaccharide (ˌmɒnəʊ'sækəˌraɪd) *n* a simple sugar, such as glucose or fructose, that does not hydrolyse to yield other sugars.
monoski ('mɒnəʊˌskiː) *n* a wide ski on which the skier stands with both feet.
▸'**monoˌskier** *n* ▸'**monoˌskiing** *n*
monosodium glutamate (ˌmɒnəʊ'səʊdɪəm 'gluːtəˌmeɪt) *n* a white crystalline substance that has little flavour itself but enhances protein flavours: used as a food additive.
monostable (ˌmɒnəʊ'steɪb^əl) *adj Physics.* (of an electronic circuit) having only one stable state but able to pass into a second state in response to an input pulse.
monosyllabic (ˌmɒnəsɪ'læbɪk) *adj* **1** (of a word) containing only one syllable. **2** characterized by monosyllables; curt.
▸ˌ**monosyl'labically** *adv*
monosyllable ('mɒnəˌsɪləb^əl) *n* a word of one syllable, esp. one used as a sentence.
monoterpene ('mɒnəˌtɜːpiːn) *n Chem.* an isoprene unit, C_5H_8, forming a terpene.
monotheism ('mɒnəʊθɪˌɪzəm) *n* the belief or doctrine that there is only one God.
▸'**monoˌtheist** *n, adj* ▸ˌ**monothe'istic** *adj* ▸ˌ**monothe'istically** *adv*
monotint ('mɒnəˌtɪnt) *n* another word for **monochrome** (senses 3, 4).
monotone ('mɒnəˌtəʊn) *n* **1** a single unvaried pitch level in speech, sound, etc. **2** utterance, etc., without change of pitch. **3** lack of variety in style, expression, etc. ◆ *adj* **4** unvarying.
monotonous (mə'nɒtənəs) *adj* **1** tedious, esp. because of repetition. **2** in unvarying tone.
▸**mo'notonously** *adv* ▸**mo'notonousness** *n*
monotony (mə'nɒtənɪ) *n, pl* **monotonies. 1** wearisome routine; dullness. **2** lack of variety in pitch or cadence.
monotreme ('mɒnəʊˌtriːm) *n* any mammal of a primitive order of Australia and New Guinea, having a single opening (cloaca) for the passage of eggs or sperm, faeces, and urine. The group contains only the echidnas and the platypus. [C19: via NL from MONO- + Gk *trēma* hole]
▸**monotrematous** (ˌmɒnəʊ'triːmətəs) *adj*
monotype ('mɒnəˌtaɪp) *n* **1** a single print made from a metal or glass plate on which a picture has been painted. **2** *Biol.* a monotypic genus or species.
Monotype ('mɒnəˌtaɪp) *n* **1** *Trademark.* any of various typesetting systems, esp. originally one in which each character was cast individually from hot metal. **2** type produced by such a system.
monotypic (ˌmɒnəʊ'tɪpɪk) *adj* **1** (of a genus or species) consisting of only one type of animal or plant. **2** of or relating to a monotype.
monounsaturated (ˌmɒnəʊʌn'sætʃəˌreɪtɪd) *adj* of or relating to a class of vegetable oils, such as olive oil, the molecules of which have long chains of carbon atoms containing only one double bond. See also **polyunsaturated.**
monovalent (ˌmɒnəʊ'veɪlənt) *adj Chem.* **a** having a valency of one. **b** having only one valency. ◆ Also: **univalent.**
▸ˌ**mono'valence** *or* ˌ**mono'valency** *n*
monoxide (mɒ'nɒksaɪd) *n* an oxide that contains one oxygen atom per molecule.
Monseigneur *French.* (mɔ̃sɛɲœr) *n, pl* ***Messeigneurs*** (mesɛɲœr). a title given to French bishops, prelates, and princes. [lit.: my lord]
monsieur (məs'jɜː) *n, pl* **messieurs.** a French title of address equivalent to *sir* when used alone or *Mr* before a name. [lit.: my lord]
Monsignor (mɒn'siːnjə) *n, pl* **Monsignors** *or* **Monsignori** (*Italian* monsiɲ'ɲoːri). *RC Church.* an ecclesiastical title attached to certain offices. [C17: from It., from F MONSEIGNEUR]
monsoon (mɒn'suːn) *n* **1** a seasonal wind of S Asia from the southwest in summer and from the northeast in winter. **2** the rainy season when the SW monsoon blows, from about April to October. **3** any wind that changes direction with the seasons. [C16: from obs. Du. *monssoen,* from Port., from Ar. *mawsim* season]
▸**mon'soonal** *adj*
mons pubis ('mɒnz 'pjuːbɪs) *n, pl* **montes pubis** ('mɒntiːz). the fatty flesh in human males over the junction of the pubic bones. Cf. **mons veneris.** [C17: NL: hill of the pubes]
monster ('mɒnstə) *n* **1** an imaginary beast, usually made up of various animal or human parts. **2** a person, animal, or plant with a marked deformity. **3** a cruel, wicked, or inhuman person. **4a** a very large person, animal, or thing. **4b** (*as modifier*): *a monster cake.* [C13: from OF *monstre,* from L *monstrum* portent, from *monēre* to warn]
monstera (mɒn'stɪərə) *n* any of various tropical evergreen climbing plants. [from ?]

THESAURUS

monolithic *adj* **1** = **huge,** colossal, giant, gigantic, immovable, impenetrable, imposing, intractable, massive, monumental, solid, substantial, undifferentiated, undivided, unitary
monologue *n* **1, 3** = **speech,** harangue, lecture, sermon, soliloquy
monopolize *vb* **1, 2** = **control,** corner, corner the market in, dominate, engross, exercise *or* have a monopoly of, hog (*sl.*), keep to oneself, take over, take up
monotonous *adj* **1, 2** = **tedious,** all the same, boring, colourless, droning, dull, flat, ho-hum (*inf.*), humdrum, mind-numbing, plodding, repetitious, repetitive, samey (*inf.*), soporific, tiresome, toneless, unchanging, uniform, uninflected, unvaried, wearisome
Antonyms *adj* animated, enjoyable, entertaining, enthralling, exciting, exhilarating, interesting, lively, sexy (*inf.*), stimulating
monotony *n* **1** = **tedium,** boredom, colourlessness, dullness, flatness, humdrumness, monotonousness, repetitiousness, repetitiveness, routine, sameness, tediousness, tiresomeness, uniformity, wearisomeness
monster *n* **2** = **freak,** abortion, lusus naturae, miscreation, monstrosity, mutant, teratism **3** = **brute,** barbarian, beast, bogeyman, demon, devil, fiend, ghoul, ogre, savage, villain **4a** = **giant,** behemoth, Brobdingnagian, colossus, leviathan, mammoth, titan ◆ *modifier* **4b** = **huge,**

monstrance ('mɒnstrəns) *n RC Church.* a receptacle in which the consecrated Host is exposed for adoration. [C16: from Med. L *mōnstrantia*, from L *mōnstrāre* to show]

monstrosity ❶ (mɒn'strɒsɪtɪ) *n, pl* **monstrosities.** **1** an outrageous or ugly person or thing; monster. **2** the state or quality of being monstrous.

monstrous ❶ ('mɒnstrəs) *adj* **1** abnormal, hideous, or unnatural in size, character, etc. **2** (of plants and animals) abnormal in structure. **3** outrageous, atrocious, or shocking. **4** huge. **5** of, relating to, or resembling a monster.
▸ **'monstrously** *adv* ▸ **'monstrousness** *n*

mons veneris ('mɒnz 'vɛnərɪs) *n, pl* **montes veneris** ('mɒnti:z). the fatty flesh in human females over the junction of the pubic bones. Cf. **mons pubis.** [C17: NL: hill of Venus]

montage (mɒn'tɑ:ʒ) *n* **1** the art or process of composing pictures of miscellaneous elements, such as other pictures or photographs. **2** such a composition. **3** a method of film editing by juxtaposition or partial superimposition of several shots to form a single image. **4** a film sequence of this kind. [C20: from F, from *monter* to MOUNT[1]]

montane ('mɒnteɪn) *adj* of or inhabiting mountainous regions. [C19: from L *montānus*, from *mons* MOUNTAIN]

montbretia (mɒn'bri:ʃə) *n* any plant of an African genus related to the iris with ornamental orange or yellow flowers. [C19: NL, after A. F. E. Coquebert de *Montbret* (1780–1801), F botanist]

monte ('mɒntɪ) *n* a gambling card game of Spanish origin. [C19: from Sp.: mountain, hence pile of cards]

Montessori method (ˌmɒntɪ'sɔ:rɪ) *n* a method of nursery education in which children are provided with facilities for practical play and allowed to develop at their own pace. [C20: after Maria *Montessori* (1870–1952), It. educationalist]

month ❶ (mʌnθ) *n* **1** one of the twelve divisions (**calendar months**) of the calendar year. **2** a period of time extending from one date to a corresponding date in the next calendar month. **3** a period of four weeks or of 30 days. **4** the period of time (**solar month**) taken by the moon to return to the same longitude after one complete revolution around the earth; 27.321 58 days (approximately 27 days, 7 hours, 43 minutes, 4.5 seconds). **5** the period of time (**sidereal month**) taken by the moon to make one complete revolution around the earth, measured between two successive conjunctions with a particular star; 27.321 66 days (approximately 27 days, 7 hours, 43 minutes, 11 seconds). **6** Also called: **lunation.** the period of time (**lunar** or **synodic month**) taken by the moon to make one complete revolution around the earth, measured between two successive new moons; 29.530 59 days (approximately 29 days, 12 hours, 44 minutes, 3 seconds). [OE *mōnath*]

monthly ('mʌnθlɪ) *adj* **1** occurring, done, appearing, payable, etc., once every month. **2** lasting or valid for a month. ◆ *adv* **3** once a month. ◆ *n, pl* **monthlies.** **4** a book, periodical, magazine, etc., published once a month. **5** *Inf.* a menstrual period.

monument ❶ ('mɒnjʊmənt) *n* **1** an obelisk, statue, building, etc., erected in commemoration of a person or event. **2** a notable building or site, esp. one preserved as public property. **3** a tomb or tombstone. **4** a literary or artistic work regarded as commemorative of its creator or a particular period. **5** *US.* a boundary marker. **6** an exceptional example: *his lecture was a monument of tedium.* [C13: from L *monumentum*, from *monēre* to remind]

monumental ❶ (ˌmɒnjʊ'mɛntᵊl) *adj* **1** like a monument, esp. in large size, endurance, or importance. **2** of, relating to, or being a monument. **3** *Inf.* (intensifier): *monumental stupidity.*
▸ **ˌmonu'mentally** *adv*

moo (mu:) *vb* **1** (*intr*) (of a cow, bull, etc.) to make a characteristic deep long sound; low. ◆ *interj* **2** an instance or imitation of this sound.

mooch (mu:tʃ) *vb Sl.* **1** (*intr;* often with *around*) to loiter or walk aimlessly. **2** (*intr*) to lurk; skulk. **3** (*tr*) to cadge. **4** (*tr*) *Chiefly US & Canad.* to steal. [C17: ?from OF *muchier* to skulk]
▸ **'moocher** *n*

mood[1] ❶ (mu:d) *n* **1** a temporary state of mind or temper: *a cheerful mood.* **2** a sullen or gloomy state of mind, esp. when temporary: *she's in a mood.* **3** a prevailing atmosphere or feeling. **4 in the mood.** in a favourable state of mind. [OE *mōd* mind, feeling]

mood[2] (mu:d) *n* **1** *Grammar.* a category of the verb or verbal inflections that expresses semantic and grammatical differences, including such forms as the indicative, subjunctive, and imperative. **2** *Logic.* one of the possible arrangements of the syllogism, classified by whether the component propositions are universal or particular and affirmative or negative. ◆ Also called: **mode.** [C16: from MOOD[1], infl. in meaning by MODE]

moody ❶ ('mu:dɪ) *adj* **moodier, moodiest.** **1** sullen, sulky, or gloomy. **2** temperamental or changeable.
▸ **'moodily** *adv* ▸ **'moodiness** *n*

Moog (mu:g, məʊg) *n Music, trademark.* a type of synthesizer. [C20: after Robert *Moog* (born 1934), US engineer]

mooi (mɔɪ) *adj S. African sl.* pleasing; nice. [from Afrik.]

mooli ('mu:lɪ) *n* a type of large white radish. [E African native name]

moolvie *or* **moolvi** ('mu:lvi:) *n* (esp. in India) a Muslim doctor of the law, teacher, or learned man: also used as a title of respect. [C17: from Urdu, from Ar. *mawlawīy;* cf. MULLAH]

Moomba ('mu:mbə) *n* an annual carnival that takes place in Melbourne, Australia, in March. [from Abor. *moom* buttocks, anus; *moomba* orig. thought to be Abor. word meaning "Let's get together and have fun"]

moon ❶ (mu:n) *n* **1** the natural satellite of the earth. **2** the face of the moon as it is seen during its revolution around the earth, esp. at one of its phases: *new moon; full moon.* **3** any natural satellite of a planet. **4** moonlight. **5** something resembling a moon. **6** a month, esp. a lunar one. **7 over the moon.** *Inf.* extremely happy; ecstatic. ◆ *vb* **8** (when *tr,* often foll. by *away;* when *intr,* often foll. by *around*) to be idle in a listless way, as if in love, or to idle (time) away. **9** (*intr*) *Sl.* to expose one's buttocks to passers-by. [OE *mōna*]
▸ **'moonless** *adj*

moonbeam ('mu:nˌbi:m) *n* a ray of moonlight.

mooncalf ('mu:nˌkɑ:f) *n, pl* **mooncalves** (-ˌkɑ:vz). **1** a born fool; dolt. **2** a person who idles time away.

moon-faced *adj* having a round face.

moonlight ('mu:nˌlaɪt) *n* **1** light from the sun received on earth after reflection by the moon. **2** (*modifier*) illuminated by the moon: *a moonlight walk.* ◆ *vb* **moonlights, moonlighting, moonlighted.** **3** (*intr*) *Inf.* to work at a secondary job, esp. at night and illegally.
▸ **'moonˌlighter** *n*

moonlight flit *n Brit. inf.* a hurried departure at night, esp. from rented accommodation to avoid payments of rent owed. Often shortened to **moonlight.**

moonlit ('mu:nlɪt) *adj* illuminated by the moon.

moonquake ('mu:nˌkweɪk) *n* a light tremor of the moon, detected on the moon's surface.

moonscape ('mu:nˌskeɪp) *n* the general surface of the moon or a representation of it.

moonshine ❶ ('mu:nˌʃaɪn) *n* **1** another word for **moonlight** (sense 1). **2** *US & Canad.* illegally distilled or smuggled whisky. **3** foolish talk or thought.

moonshot ('mu:nˌʃɒt) *n* the launching of a spacecraft, rocket, etc., to the moon.

THESAURUS

Brobdingnagian, colossal, elephantine, enormous, gargantuan, giant, gigantic, ginormous (*inf.*), humongous *or* humungous (*US sl.*), immense, jumbo (*inf.*), mammoth, massive, mega (*sl.*), monstrous, stellar (*inf.*), stupendous, titanic, tremendous

monstrosity *n* **1** = **eyesore**, abortion, freak, horror, lusus naturae, miscreation, monster, mutant, ogre, teratism **2** = **hideousness**, abnormality, atrocity, dreadfulness, evil, frightfulness, heinousness, hellishness, horror, loathsomeness, obscenity

monstrous *adj* **1** = **unnatural**, abnormal, dreadful, enormous, fiendish, freakish, frightful, grotesque, gruesome, hellish, hideous, horrendous, horrible, miscreated, obscene, teratoid, terrible **3** = **outrageous**, atrocious, cruel, devilish, diabolical, disgraceful, egregious, evil, fiendish, foul, heinous, horrifying, infamous, inhuman, intolerable, loathsome, odious, satanic, scandalous, shocking, vicious, villainous **4** = **huge**, colossal, elephantine, enormous, gargantuan, giant, gigantic, ginormous (*inf.*), great, humongous *or* humungous (*US sl.*), immense, mammoth, massive, mega (*sl.*), prodigious, stellar (*inf.*), stupendous, titanic, towering, tremendous, vast
Antonyms *adj* ≠ **unnatural:** appealing, attractive, beautiful, delightful, lovely, natural, normal, ordinary, pleasant ≠ **outrageous:** admirable, decent, fine, good, honourable, humane, kind, merciful, mild ≠ **huge:** diminutive, insignificant, little, meagre, miniature, minute, puny, slight, small, tiny

month *n* **1, 3** = **four weeks**, moon, thirty days

monument *n* **1, 3** = **memorial**, cairn, cenotaph, commemoration, gravestone, headstone, marker, mausoleum, obelisk, pillar, shrine, statue, tombstone

monumental *adj* **1** = **important**, awe-inspiring, awesome, classic, enduring, enormous, epoch-making, historic, immortal, lasting, majestic, memorable, outstanding, prodigious, significant, stupendous, unforgettable **2** = **commemorative**, cyclopean, funerary, memorial, monolithic, statuary **3** *Informal* = **immense**, catastrophic, colossal, egregious, gigantic, great, horrible, indefensible, massive, staggering, terrible, tremendous, unforgivable, whopping (*inf.*)
Antonyms *adj* ≠ **important:** ephemeral, inconsequential, insignificant, modest, negligible, ordinary, trivial, undistinguished, unimportant, unimpressive, unremarkable ≠ **immense:** average, insignificant, mild, petty, slight, small, tiny, trivial

mood[1] *n* **1** = **state of mind**, disposition, frame of mind, humour, spirit, temper, tenor, vein **2** = **depression**, bad temper, bate (*Brit. sl.*), blues, doldrums, dumps (*inf.*), fit of pique, grumps (*inf.*), low spirits, melancholy, sulk, the hump (*Brit. inf.*), the sulks, wax (*inf., chiefly Brit.*) **4 in the mood** = **inclined**, disposed (towards), eager, favourable, interested, in the (right) frame of mind, keen, minded, willing

moody *adj* **1** = **gloomy**, broody, crestfallen, dismal, doleful, dour, downcast, down in the dumps (*inf.*), down in the mouth (*inf.*), frowning, glum, in the doldrums, introspective, lugubrious, melancholy, miserable, mopy, morose, out of sorts (*inf.*), pensive, sad, saturnine, sullen **2** = **changeable**, capricious, erratic, faddish, fickle, fitful, flighty, impulsive, inconstant, mercurial, temperamental, unpredictable, unstable, unsteady, volatile
Antonyms *adj* ≠ **gloomy:** amiable, cheerful, gay, happy, optimistic ≠ **changeable:** constant, stable, steady

moon *n* **1, 3** = **satellite** ◆ *vb* **8** = **idle**, daydream, languish, mooch (*sl.*), mope, waste time

moonshine *n* **1** = **moonlight**, moonbeams **2** *US & Canad.* = **bootleg**, hooch *or* hootch (*inf., chiefly US & Canad.*), poteen **3** = **nonsense**, blather, blether, bunk (*inf.*), bunkum *or* buncombe (*chiefly US*), claptrap (*inf.*), foolish talk, guff (*sl.*),

moonstone ('mu:nˌstəʊn) *n* a gem variety of orthoclase or albite that is white and translucent.

moonstruck ('mu:nˌstrʌk) *or* **moonstricken** ('mu:nˌstrɪkən) *adj* deranged or mad.

moony ('mu:nɪ) *adj* **moonier, mooniest. 1** *Inf.* dreamy or listless. **2** of or like the moon.

moor[1] ➊ (mʊə, mɔ:) *n* a tract of unenclosed ground, usually covered with heather, coarse grass, bracken, and moss. [OE *mōr*]

moor[2] ➊ (mʊə, mɔ:) *vb* **1** to secure (a ship, boat, etc.) with cables or ropes. **2** (of a ship, boat, etc.) to be secured in this way. **3** (not in technical usage) a less common word for **anchor** (senses 7 and 8). [C15: of Gmc origin; rel. to OE *mǣrelsrāp* rope for mooring]
▸**moorage** ('mʊərɪdʒ) *n*

Moor (mʊə, mɔ:) *n* a member of a Muslim people of North Africa, of mixed Arab and Berber descent. [C14: via OF from L *Maurus*, from Gk *Mauros*, ?from Berber]
▸**'Moorish** *adj*

moorcock ('mʊəˌkɒk, 'mɔ:-) *n* the male of the red grouse.

moorhen ('mʊəˌhɛn, 'mɔ:-) *n* **1** a bird of the rail family, inhabiting ponds, lakes, etc., having a black plumage, red bill, and a red shield above the bill. **2** the female of the red grouse.

mooring ('mʊərɪŋ, 'mɔ:-) *n* **1** a place for mooring a vessel. **2** a permanent anchor with a floating buoy, to which vessels can moor.

moorings ('mʊərɪŋz, 'mɔ:-) *pl n* **1** *Naut.* the ropes, anchors, etc., used in mooring a vessel. **2** (*sometimes sing*) something that provides security or stability.

Moorish idol *n* a tropical marine spiny-finned fish that is common around coral reefs. It has a deeply compressed body with yellow and black stripes.

moorland ('mʊələnd) *n Brit.* an area of moor.

moose (mu:s) *n, pl* **moose.** a large North American deer having large flattened palmate antlers: also occurs in Europe and Asia where it is called an elk. [C17: of Amerind origin]

moot ➊ (mu:t) *adj* **1** subject or open to debate: *a moot point.* ◆ *vb* **2** (*tr*) to suggest or bring up for debate. **3** (*intr*) to plead or argue hypothetical cases, as an academic exercise or as training for law students. ◆ *n* **4** a discussion or debate of a hypothetical case or point, held as an academic activity. **5** (in Anglo-Saxon England) an assembly dealing with local legal and administrative affairs. [OE *gemōt*]

moot court *n* a mock court trying hypothetical legal cases.

mop ➊ (mɒp) *n* **1** an implement with a wooden handle and a head made of twists of cotton or a piece of synthetic sponge, used for polishing or washing floors, or washing dishes. **2** something resembling this, such as a tangle of hair. ◆ *vb* **mops, mopping, mopped.** (*tr*) **3** (often foll. by *up*) to clean or soak up as with a mop. ◆ See also **mop up**. [C15 *mappe*, ult. from L *mappa* napkin]

mopani *or* **mopane** (mɒ'pɑ:nɪ) *n* **1** a leguminous tree, native to southern Africa, that is highly resistant to drought and produces very hard wood. **2** Also called: **mopani worm.** an edible caterpillar that feeds on mopani leaves. [C19: from Bantu]

mope ➊ (məʊp) *vb* **mopes, moping, moped.** (*intr*) **1** to be gloomy or apathetic. **2** to move or act in an aimless way. ◆ *n* **3** a gloomy person. [C16: ?from obs. *mope* fool & rel. to *mop* grimace]
▸**'moper** *n* ▸**'mopy** *adj*

moped ('məʊpɛd) *n* a light motorcycle not over 50cc. [C20: from MOTOR + PEDAL[1]]

mopes (məʊps) *pl n* **the.** low spirits.

mopoke ('məʊˌpəʊk) *n* **1** a small spotted owl of Australia and New Zealand. In Australia the tawny frogmouth is often wrongly identified as the mopoke. **2** *Austral. & NZ sl.* a slow or lugubrious person. ◆ Also called: **morepork.** [C19: imit. of the bird's cry]

moppet ('mɒpɪt) *n* a less common word for **poppet** (sense 1). [C17: from obs. *mop* rag doll; from ?]

mop up ➊ *vb* (*tr, adv*) **1** to clean with a mop. **2** *Inf.* to complete (a task, etc.). **3** *Mil.* to clear (remaining enemy forces) after a battle, as by killing, taking prisoner, etc.

moquette (mɒ'kɛt) *n* a thick velvety fabric used for carpets, upholstery, etc. [C18: from F; from ?]

MOR *abbrev. for* middle-of-the-road: used esp. in radio programming.

Mor. *abbrev. for* Morocco.

mora *or* **morra** ('mɔ:rə) *n* a guessing game played with the fingers, esp. in Italy and China. [C18: from It. *mora*]

moraine (mɒ'reɪn) *n* a mass of debris, carried by glaciers and forming ridges and mounds when deposited. [C18: from F, from Savoy dialect *morena*, from ?]
▸**mo'rainal** *or* **mo'rainic** *adj*

moral ➊ ('mɒrəl) *adj* **1** concerned with or relating to human behaviour, esp. the distinction between good and bad or right and wrong behaviour: *moral sense.* **2** adhering to conventionally accepted standards of conduct. **3** based on a sense of right and wrong according to conscience: *moral courage; moral law.* **4** having psychological rather than tangible effects: *moral support.* **5** having the effects but not the appearance of (victory or defeat): *a moral victory.* **6** having a strong probability: *a moral certainty.* ◆ *n* **7** the lesson to be obtained from a fable or event. **8** a concise truth; maxim. **9** (*pl*) principles of behaviour in accordance with standards of right and wrong. **10** *Austral. sl.* a certainty: *a moral to win.* [C14: from L *mōrālis* relating to morals or customs, from *mōs* custom]
▸**'morally** *adv*

morale ➊ (mɒ'rɑ:l) *n* the degree of mental or moral confidence of a person or group. [C18: morals, from F, n use of MORAL (adj)]

moralist ('mɒrəlɪst) *n* **1** a person who seeks to regulate the morals of others. **2** a person who lives in accordance with moral principles.
▸**ˌmoral'istic** *adj* ▸**ˌmoral'istically** *adv*

morality ➊ (mə'rælɪtɪ) *n, pl* **moralities. 1** the quality of being moral. **2** conformity, or degree of conformity, to conventional standards of moral conduct. **3** a system of moral principles. **4** an instruction or lesson in morals. **5** short for **morality play.**

morality play *n* a type of drama between the 14th and 16th centuries concerned with the conflict between personified virtues and vices.

moralize *or* **moralise** ('mɒrəˌlaɪz) *vb* **moralizes, moralizing, moralized** *or* **moralises, moralising, moralised. 1** (*intr*) to make moral pronouncements. **2** (*tr*) to interpret or explain in a moral sense. **3** (*tr*) to improve the morals of.
▸**ˌmorali'zation** *or* **ˌmorali'sation** *n* ▸**'moralˌizer** *or* **'moralˌiser** *n*

moral majority *n* a presumed majority of people believed to be in favour of a stricter code of public morals. [C20: after *Moral Majority*, a right-wing US religious organization, based on SILENT MAJORITY]

moral philosophy *n* the branch of philosophy dealing with ethics.

Moral Rearmament *n* a worldwide movement for moral and spiritual renewal founded by Frank Buchman in 1938. Also called: **Buchmanism.** Former name: **Oxford Group.**

moral theology *n* the branch of theology dealing with ethics.

morass ➊ (mə'ræs) *n* **1** a tract of swampy low-lying land. **2** a disordered or muddled situation or circumstance, esp. one that impedes progress. [C17: from Du. *moeras*, ult. from OF *marais* MARSH]

moratorium ➊ (ˌmɒrə'tɔ:rɪəm) *n, pl* **moratoria** (-rɪə) *or* **moratoriums. 1** a legally authorized postponement of the fulfilment of an obligation. **2** an agreed suspension of activity. [C19: NL, from LL *morātōrius* dilatory, from *mora* delay]

Moravian (mə'reɪvɪən, mɒ-) *adj* **1** of or relating to Moravia, a region of the Czech Republic, its people, or their dialect of Czech. **2** of or relating to the Moravian Church. ◆ *n* **3** the Moravian dialect. **4** a native or inhabitant of Moravia. **5** a member of the Moravian Church.
▸**Mo'ravianism** *n*

moray (mɒ'reɪ) *n, pl* **morays.** a voracious marine coastal eel marked with brilliant colours. [C17: from Port. *moréia*, from L *mūrēna*, from Gk *muraina*]

morbid ➊ ('mɔ:bɪd) *adj* **1** having an unusual interest in death or unpleasant events. **2** gruesome. **3** relating to or characterized by disease. [C17: from L *morbidus* sickly, from *morbus* illness]
▸**mor'bidity** *n* ▸**'morbidly** *adv* ▸**'morbidness** *n*

morbid anatomy *n* the branch of medical science concerned with the study of the structure of diseased organs and tissues.

morbific (mɔ:'bɪfɪk) *adj* causing disease.

THESAURUS

havers (*Scot.*), hogwash, hot air (*inf.*), rubbish, stuff and nonsense, tarradiddle, tosh (*sl., chiefly Brit.*), trash, tripe (*inf.*), twaddle

moor[1] *n* = **moorland**, fell (*Brit.*), heath, muir (*Scot.*)

moor[2] *vb* **1-3** = **tie up**, anchor, berth, dock, fasten, fix, lash, make fast, secure

moot *adj* **1** = **debatable**, arguable, at issue, contestable, controversial, disputable, doubtful, open, open to debate, undecided, unresolved, unsettled ◆ *vb* **2** = **bring up**, broach, introduce, propose, put forward, suggest, ventilate

mop *n* **1** = **squeegee**, sponge, swab **2** = **mane**, shock, tangle, thatch ◆ *vb* **3** = **clean**, soak up, sponge, swab, wash, wipe

mope *vb* **1** = **brood**, be apathetic, be dejected, be down in the mouth (*inf.*), be gloomy, eat one's heart out, fret, hang around, have a long face, idle, languish, moon, pine, pout, sulk, waste time, wear a long face

mop up *vb* **1** = **clean up**, mop, soak up, sponge, swab, wash, wipe **3** *Military* = **finish off**, account for, clean out, clear, eliminate, neutralize, pacify, round up, secure

moral *adj* **1** = **ethical 2, 3** = **good**, blameless, chaste, decent, ethical, high-minded, honest, honourable, incorruptible, innocent, just, meritorious, noble, principled, proper, pure, right, righteous, upright, upstanding, virtuous ◆ *n* **7** = **lesson**, meaning, message, point, significance **8** = **motto**, adage, aphorism, apophthegm, epigram, gnome, maxim, proverb, saw, saying **9** *plural* = **morality**, behaviour, conduct, ethics, habits, integrity, manners, mores, principles, scruples, standards
Antonyms *adj* ≠ **good:** amoral, dishonest, dishonourable, immoral, improper, sinful, unethical, unfair, unjust, wrong

morale *n* = **confidence**, esprit de corps, heart, mettle, self-esteem, spirit, temper

morality *n* **1** = **integrity**, chastity, decency, ethicality, ethicalness, goodness, honesty, justice, principle, rectitude, righteousness, rightness, uprightness, virtue **3** = **standards**, conduct, ethics, habits, ideals, manners, moral code, morals, mores, philosophy, principles

morass *n* **1** = **marsh**, bog, fen, marshland, moss (*Scot. & N English dialect*), quagmire, slough, swamp **2** = **mess**, chaos, confusion, jam, mix-up, muddle, quagmire, tangle

moratorium *n* **1, 2** = **postponement**, freeze, halt, respite, standstill, stay, suspension

morbid *adj* **1** = **unwholesome**, brooding, funereal, ghoulish, gloomy, grim, melancholy, pessimistic, sick, sombre, unhealthy **2** = **gruesome**, dreadful, ghastly, grisly, hideous, horrid, macabre **3** = **diseased**, ailing, deadly, infected, malignant, pathological, sick, sickly, unhealthy, unsound
Antonyms *adj* ≠ **unwholesome:** bright, cheerful, happy, healthy, wholesome ≠ **diseased:** healthy, salubrious

mordant Ⓣ ('mɔːdᵊnt) *adj* **1** sarcastic or caustic. **2** having the properties of a mordant. **3** pungent. ◆ *n* **4** a substance used before the application of a dye, possessing the ability to fix colours. **5** an acid or other corrosive fluid used to etch lines on a printing plate. [C15: from OF: biting, from *mordre* to bite, from L *mordēre*]
▸'**mordancy** *n* ▸'**mordantly** *adv*

mordent ('mɔːdᵊnt) *n Music.* a melodic ornament consisting of the rapid alternation of a note with a note one degree lower than it. [C19: from G, from It. *mordente,* from *mordere* to bite]

more Ⓣ (mɔː) *determiner* **1a** the comparative of **much** or **many:** *more joy than you know; more sausages.* **1b** (*as pron; functioning as sing or pl*): *he has more than she has; even more are dying.* **2a** additional; further: *no more bananas.* **2b** (*as pron; functioning as sing or pl*): *I can't take any more; more than expected.* **3 more of.** to a greater extent or degree: *we see more of Sue; more of a nuisance.* ◆ *adv* **4** used to form the comparative of some adjectives and adverbs: *a more believable story; more quickly.* **5** the comparative of **much:** *people listen to the radio more now.* **6 more or less. 6a** as an estimate; approximately. **6b** to an unspecified extent or degree: *the party was ruined, more or less.* [OE *māra*]

> **USAGE NOTE** See at **most.**

moreish *or* **morish** ('mɔːrɪʃ) *adj Inf.* (of food) causing a desire for more.

morel (mɒ'rɛl) *n* an edible fungus in which the mushroom has a pitted cap. [C17: from F *morille,* prob. of Gmc origin]

morello (mə'rɛləʊ) *n, pl* **morellos.** a variety of small very dark sour cherry. [C17: ?from Med. L *amārellum,* dim. of L *amārus* bitter, but also infl. by It. *morello* blackish]

morendo (mɒ'rɛndəʊ) *adv Music.* gradually dying away. [It.: dying]

moreover Ⓣ (mɔː'rəʊvə) *sentence connector.* in addition to what has already been said.

morepork ('mɔːˌpɔːk) *n* another name, esp. in New Zealand, for **mopoke.**

mores ('mɔːreɪz) *pl n* the customs and conventions embodying the fundamental values of a group or society. [C20: from L, pl of *mōs* custom]

morganatic (ˌmɔːgə'nætɪk) *adj* of or designating a marriage between a person of high rank and a person of low rank, by which the latter is not elevated to the higher rank and any issue have no rights to the succession of the higher party's titles, property, etc. [C18: from Med. L *mātrimōnium ad morganāticum* marriage based on the morning-gift (a token present after consummation representing the husband's only liability); *morganātica,* ult. from OHG *morgan* morning]
▸ˌ**morga'natically** *adv*

morgen ('mɔːgən) *n* **1** a South African unit of area, equal to about two acres or 0.8 hectare. **2** a unit of area, formerly used in Prussia and Scandinavia, equal to about two thirds of an acre. [C17: from Du.: morning, a morning's ploughing]

morgue Ⓣ (mɔːg) *n* **1** another word for **mortuary. 2** *Inf.* a room or file containing clippings, etc., used for reference in a newspaper. [C19: from F *le Morgue,* a Paris mortuary]

moribund Ⓣ ('mɒrɪˌbʌnd) *adj* **1** near death. **2** without force or vitality. [C18: from L, from *morī* to die]
▸ˌ**mori'bundity** *n* ▸'**moriˌbundly** *adv*

Morisco (mə'rɪskəʊ) *or* **Moresco** (mə'rɛskəʊ) *n, pl* **Moriscos, Moriscoes** *or* **Morescos, Morescoes. 1** a Spanish Moor. **2** a morris dance. ◆ *adj* **3** another word for **Moorish;** see **Moor.** [C16: from Sp., from *Moro* MOOR]

morish ('mɔːrɪʃ) *adj* a variant spelling of **moreish.**

Mormon ('mɔːmən) *n* **1** a member of the Church of Jesus Christ of Latter-day Saints, founded in 1830 in New York by Joseph Smith. **2** a prophet whose supposed revelations were recorded by Joseph Smith in the Book of Mormon. ◆ *adj* **3** of or relating to the Mormons, their Church, or their beliefs.
▸'**Mormonism** *n*

morn (mɔːn) *n* a poetic word for **morning.** [OE *morgen*]

mornay ('mɔːneɪ) *adj* (*often immediately postpositive*) denoting a cheese sauce: *eggs mornay.* [? after Philippe de *Mornay* (1549–1623), F Huguenot leader]

morning Ⓣ ('mɔːnɪŋ) *n* **1** the first part of the day, ending at noon. **2** sunrise; daybreak; dawn. **3** the beginning or early period. **4 the morning after.** *Inf.* the aftereffects of excess, esp. a hangover. **5** (*modifier*) of, used in, or occurring in the morning: *morning coffee.* [C13 *morwening,* from MORN, on the model of EVENING]

morning-after pill *n* an oral contraceptive that is effective if taken some hours after intercourse.

morning dress *n* formal day dress for men, comprising a cutaway frock coat (**morning coat**), usually with grey trousers and top hat.

morning-glory *n, pl* **morning-glories.** any of various mainly tropical plants of the convolvulus family, with trumpet-shaped blue, pink, or white flowers, which close in late afternoon.

mornings ('mɔːnɪŋz) *adv Inf.* in the morning, esp. regularly, or during every morning.

morning sickness *n* nausea occurring shortly after rising: a symptom of pregnancy.

morning star *n* a planet, usually Venus, seen just before sunrise. Also called: **daystar.**

Moro ('mɔːrəʊ) *n* **1** (*pl* **Moros** *or* **Moro**) a member of a group of predominantly Muslim peoples of the S Philippines. **2** the language of these peoples. [C19: via Sp. from L *Maurus* MOOR]

Moroccan (mə'rɒkən) *adj* **1** of or denoting Morocco, a kingdom in NW Africa, or its inhabitants, their customs, etc. ◆ *n* **2** a native or inhabitant of Morocco or a descendant of one.

morocco (mə'rɒkəʊ) *n* a fine soft leather made from goatskins, used for bookbinding, shoes, etc. [C17: after *Morocco,* kingdom in NW Africa, where it was orig. made]

moron Ⓣ ('mɔːrɒn) *n* **1** a foolish or stupid person. **2** a person having an intelligence quotient of between 50 and 70. [C20: from Gk *mōros* foolish]
▸**moronic** (mə'rɒnɪk) *adj* ▸**mo'ronically** *adv* ▸'**moronism** *or* **mo'ronity** *n*

morose Ⓣ (mə'rəʊs) *adj* ill-tempered or gloomy. [C16: from L *mōrōsus* peevish, from *mōs* custom, will]
▸**mo'rosely** *adv* ▸**mo'roseness** *n*

-morph *n combining form.* indicating shape, form, or structure of a specified kind: *ectomorph.* [from Gk *-morphos,* from *morphē* shape]
▸**-morphic** *or* **-morphous** *adj combining form.* ▸**-morphy** *n combining form.*

morpheme ('mɔːfiːm) *n Linguistics.* a speech element having a meaning or grammatical function that cannot be subdivided into further such elements. [C20: from F, from Gk *morphē* form, on the model of PHONEME]
▸**mor'phemic** *adj* ▸**mor'phemically** *adv*

morphine ('mɔːfiːn) *or* **morphia** ('mɔːfɪə) *n* an alkaloid extracted from opium: used in medicine as an anaesthetic and sedative. [C19: from F, from *Morpheus,* in Gk myth the god of sleep & dreams]

morphing ('mɔːfɪŋ) *n* a computer technique used for graphics and in films, in which one image is gradually transformed into another. [C20: from METAMORPHOSIS]

morphogenesis (ˌmɔːfəʊ'dʒɛnɪsɪs) *n* **1** the development of form in an organism during its growth. **2** the evolutionary development of form in an organism or part of an organism.
▸**morphogenetic** (ˌmɔːfəʊdʒɪ'nɛtɪk) *adj*

morphology (mɔː'fɒlədʒɪ) *n* **1** the branch of biology concerned with the form and structure of organisms. **2** the form and structure of words in a language. **3** the form and structure of anything.
▸**morphologic** (ˌmɔːfə'lɒdʒɪk) *or* ˌ**morpho'logical** *adj* ▸ˌ**morpho'logically** *adv* ▸**mor'phologist** *n*

Morris chair ('mɒrɪs) *n* an armchair with an adjustable back. [C19: after William *Morris* (1834–96), Brit. writer, painter, & craftsman]

morris dance *n* any of various old English folk dances usually performed by men (**morris men**) adorned with bells and often representing characters from folk tales. Often shortened to **morris.** [C15 *moreys daunce* Moorish dance]
▸**morris dancing** *n*

morro ('mɒrəʊ) *n, pl* **morros** (-rəʊz). a rounded hill or promontory. [from Sp.]

morrow ('mɒrəʊ) *n* (usually preceded by *the*) *Arch. or poetic.* **1** the next day. **2** the period following a specified event. **3** the morning. [C13 *morwe,* from OE *morgen* morning]

Morse code *n* (mɔːs) *n* a telegraph code used internationally for transmitting messages. Letters, numbers, etc., are represented by groups of shorter dots and longer dashes, or by groups of the corresponding sounds. [C19: after Samuel *Morse* (1791–1872), US inventor]

morsel Ⓣ ('mɔːsᵊl) *n* **1** a small slice or mouthful of food. **2** a small piece;

THESAURUS

mordant *adj* **1** = **sarcastic,** acerbic, acid, acrimonious, astringent, biting, caustic, cutting, edged, harsh, incisive, mordacious, pungent, scathing, sharp, stinging, trenchant, venomous, vitriolic, waspish **2, 3** = **corrosive,** acid, acidic, caustic, pungent, vitriolic

more *determiner* **1, 2** = **extra,** added, additional, fresh, further, new, new-found, other, spare, supplementary ◆ *adv* **4, 5** = **to a greater extent,** better, further, longer

moreover *sentence connector* = **furthermore,** additionally, also, as well, besides, further, in addition, into the bargain, likewise, to boot, too, what is more, withal (*literary*)

morgue *n* **1** = **mortuary**

moribund *adj* **1** = **dying,** at death's door, breathing one's last, doomed, fading fast, failing, (having) one foot in the grave, *in extremis,* near death, near the end, on one's deathbed, on one's last legs **2** = **declining,** at a standstill, forceless, obsolescent, on its last legs, on the way out, stagnant, stagnating, standing still, waning, weak

morning *n* **1, 2** = **dawn,** a.m., break of day, daybreak, forenoon, morn (*poetic*), morrow (*arch.*), sunrise

moron *n* **1** = **fool,** airhead (*sl.*), ass, berk (*Brit. sl.*), blockhead, bonehead (*sl.*), chump, coot, cretin, dolt, dope (*inf.*), dork (*sl.*), dummy (*sl.*), dunce, dunderhead, fathead (*inf.*), halfwit, idiot, imbecile, mental defective, muttonhead (*sl.*), nerd *or* nurd (*sl.*), nitwit (*inf.*), numbskull *or* numskull, oaf, pillock (*Brit. sl.*), schmuck (*US sl.*), simpleton, thickhead, twit (*inf., chiefly Brit.*), wally (*sl.*)

moronic *adj* **1** = **idiotic,** asinine, Boeotian, braindead (*inf.*), brainless, cretinous, dimwitted (*inf.*), doltish, foolish, gormless (*Brit. inf.*), half-witted, imbecilic, mentally defective, mindless, muttonheaded (*sl.*), retarded, simple, stupid, thick, unintelligent

morose *adj* = **sullen,** blue, churlish, crabbed, crabby, cross, crusty, depressed, dour, down, down in the dumps (*inf.*), gloomy, glum, grouchy, gruff, ill-tempered, in a bad mood, low, melancholy, miserable, moody, mournful, perverse, pessimistic, saturnine, sour, sulky, surly, taciturn
Antonyms *adj* amiable, blithe, cheerful, chirpy (*inf.*), friendly, gay, genial, good-humoured, good-natured, happy, pleasant, sweet

morsel *n* **1, 2** = **piece,** bit, bite, crumb, fraction, fragment, grain, mouthful, nibble, part, scrap,

bit. **3** *Irish inf.* a term of endearment for a child. [C13: from OF, from *mors* a bite, from L *morsus*, from *mordēre* to bite]

mortal ➊ ('mɔːtᵊl) *adj* **1** (of living beings, esp. human beings) subject to death. **2** of or involving life or the world. **3** ending in or causing death; fatal: *a mortal blow*. **4** deadly or unrelenting: *a mortal enemy*. **5** of or like the fear of death: *mortal terror*. **6** great or very intense: *mortal pain*. **7** conceivable or possible: *there was no mortal reason to go*. **8** *Sl.* long and tedious: *for three mortal hours*. ◆ *n* **9** a mortal being. **10** *Inf.* a person: *a mean mortal*. [C14: from L *mortālis*, from *mors* death]
▸ **'mortally** *adv*

mortality ➊ (mɔː'tælɪtɪ) *n, pl* **mortalities. 1** the condition of being mortal. **2** great loss of life, as in war or disaster. **3** the number of deaths in a given period. **4** mankind; humanity.

mortal sin *n Christianity.* a sin regarded as involving total loss of grace.

mortar ('mɔːtə) *n* **1** a mixture of cement or lime or both with sand and water, used as a bond between bricks or stones or as a covering on a wall. **2** a cannon having a short barrel and relatively wide bore that fires low-velocity shells in high trajectories. **3** a vessel, usually bowl-shaped, in which substances are pulverized with a pestle. ◆ *vb (tr)* **4** to join (bricks or stones) or cover (a wall) with mortar. **5** to fire on with mortars. [C13: from L *mortārium* basin in which mortar is mixed; in some senses, via OF *mortier* substance mixed inside such a vessel]

mortarboard ('mɔːtəˌbɔːd) *n* **1** a black tasselled academic cap with a flat square top. **2** a small square board with a handle on the underside for carrying mortar.

mortgage ('mɔːgɪdʒ) *n* **1** an agreement under which a person borrows money to buy property, esp. a house, and the lender may take possession of the property if the borrower fails to repay the money. **2** the deed affecting such an agreement. **3** the loan obtained under such an agreement: *a mortgage of £48000*. **4** a regular payment of money borrowed under such an agreement: *a mortgage of £347 per month*. ◆ *vb* **mortgages, mortgaging, mortgaged.** *(tr)* **4** to convey (property) by mortgage. **5** *Inf.* to pledge. [C14: from OF, lit.: dead pledge]
▸ **'mortgageable** *adj*

mortgagee (ˌmɔːgɪ'dʒiː) *n Law.* the party to a mortgage who makes the loan.

mortgagor (ˌmɔːgɪ'dʒɔː) *or* **mortgager** *n Property law.* a person who borrows money by mortgaging his property to the lender as security.

mortician (mɔː'tɪʃən) *n Chiefly US.* another word for **undertaker.** [C19: from MORTUARY + *-ician*, as in *physician*]

mortification ➊ (ˌmɔːtɪfɪ'keɪʃən) *n* **1** a feeling of humiliation. **2** something causing this. **3** *Christianity.* the practice of mortifying the senses. **4** another word for **gangrene.**

mortify ➊ ('mɔːtɪˌfaɪ) *vb* **mortifies, mortifying, mortified. 1** *(tr)* to humiliate or cause to feel shame. **2** *(tr) Christianity.* to subdue and bring under control by self-denial, disciplinary exercises, etc. **3** *(intr)* to undergo tissue death or become gangrenous. [C14: via OF from Church L *mortificāre* to put to death, from L *mors* death + *facere* to do]
▸ **'mortiˌfier** *n* ▸ **'mortiˌfying** *adj*

mortise *or* **mortice** ('mɔːtɪs) *n* **1** a slot or recess cut into a piece of wood, stone, etc., to receive a matching projection (tenon) of another piece, or a mortise lock. ◆ *vb* **mortises, mortising, mortised** *or* **mortices, morticing, morticed.** *(tr)* **2** to cut a slot or recess in (a piece of wood, stone, etc.). **3** to join (two pieces of wood, stone, etc.) by means of a mortise and tenon. [C14: from OF *mortoise*, ?from Ar. *murtazza* fastened in position]

mortise lock *n* a lock set into a mortise in a door so that the mechanism of the lock is enclosed by the door.

mortmain ('mɔːtˌmeɪn) *n Law.* the state or condition of lands, buildings, etc., held inalienably, as by an ecclesiastical or other corporation. [C15: from OF *mortemain*, from Med. L *mortua manus* dead hand, inalienable ownership]

mortuary ➊ ('mɔːtʃʊərɪ) *n, pl* **mortuaries. 1** Also called: **morgue.** a building where dead bodies are kept before cremation or burial. ◆ *adj* **2** of or relating to death or burial. [C14 (as n, a funeral gift to a parish priest): via Med. L *mortuārium* (n) from L *mortuārius* of the dead]

morwong ('mɔːˌwɒŋ) *n* a food fish of Australasian coastal waters. [from Abor.]

moryah (mɒr'jæ) *interj Irish.* an exclamation of annoyance, disbelief, etc. [from Irish Gaelic *Mar dhea* forsooth]

mosaic (mə'zeɪɪk) *n* **1** a design or decoration made up of small pieces of coloured glass, stone, etc. **2** the process of making a mosaic. **3a** a mottled yellowing that occurs in the leaves of plants affected with any of various virus diseases. **3b** Also called: **mosaic disease.** any of the diseases, such as **tobacco mosaic,** that produce this discoloration. **4** a light-sensitive surface on a television camera tube, consisting of a large number of granules of photoemissive material. [C16: via F & It. from Med. L, from LGk: mosaic work, from Gk: of the Muses, from *mousa* MUSE]
▸ **mosaicist** (mə'zeɪɪsɪst) *n*

Mosaic (məʊ'zeɪɪk) *adj* of or relating to Moses or the laws and traditions ascribed to him.

Mosaic law *n Bible.* the laws ascribed to Moses and contained in the Pentateuch.

moschatel (ˌmɒskə'tɛl) *n* a small N temperate plant with greenish-white musk-scented flowers. Also called: **townhall clock, five-faced bishop.** [C18: via F from It. *moscatella*, dim. of *moscato* MUSK]

Moselle (məʊ'zɛl) *n (sometimes not cap.)* a German white wine from the Moselle valley.

mosey ('məʊzɪ) *vb (intr) Inf.* (often foll. by *along* or *on*) to amble. [C19: from ?]

Moslem ('mɒzləm) *n, pl* **Moslems** *or* **Moslem.** *adj* a variant of **Muslim.**
▸ **Moslemic** (mɒz'lɛmɪk) *adj* ▸ **'Moslemism** *n*

mosque (mɒsk) *n* a Muslim place of worship. [C14: earlier *mosquee*, from OF via It. *moschea*, ult. from Ar. *masjid* temple]

mosquito (mə'skiːtəʊ) *n, pl* **mosquitoes** *or* **mosquitos.** any dipterous insect of the family Culicidae: the females have a long proboscis adapted for piercing the skin of man and animals to suck their blood. See also **aedes, anopheles, culex.** [C16: from Sp., dim. of *mosca* fly, from L *musca*]

mosquito net *or* **netting** *n* a fine curtain or net to keep mosquitoes out.

moss (mɒs) *n* **1** any of a class of plants, typically growing in dense mats on trees, rocks, moist ground, etc. **2** a clump or growth of any of these plants. **3** any of various similar but unrelated plants, such as Spanish moss and reindeer moss. **4** *Scot. & N English.* a peat bog or marsh. [OE *mos* swamp]
▸ **'mossˌlike** *adj* ▸ **'mossy** *adj* ▸ **'mossiness** *n*

moss agate *n* a variety of chalcedony with dark greenish mossy markings.

mossie ('mɒsɪ) *n* another name for the **Cape sparrow.** [Afrik.]

mosso ('mɒsəʊ) *adv Music.* to be performed with rapidity. [It., p.p. of *muovere* to MOVE]

moss rose *n* a variety of rose that has a mossy stem and calyx and fragrant pink flowers.

moss stitch *n* a knitting stitch made up of alternate plain and purl stitches.

mosstrooper ('mɒsˌtruːpə) *n* a raider in the Borders of England and Scotland in the mid-17th century. [C17 *moss*, in dialect sense: bog]

most (məʊst) *determiner* **1a** a great majority of; nearly all: *most people like eggs.* **1b** *(as pron; functioning as sing or pl): most of them don't know; most of it is finished.* **2 the most. 2a** the superlative of **many** and **much:** *you have the most money; the most apples.* **2b** *(as pron): the most he can afford is two pounds.* **3 at (the) most.** at the maximum: *that girl is four at the most.* **4 make the most of.** to use to the best advantage: *she makes the most of her accent.* ◆ *adv* **5 the most.** used to form the superlative of some adjectives and adverbs: *he suffered the most terribly of all.* **6** the superlative of **much:** *people welcome a drink most after work.* **7** (intensifier): *a most absurd story.* [OE *māst* or *mǣst*, whence ME *moste*, *mēst*]

> **USAGE NOTE** *More* and *most* should be distinguished when used in comparisons. *More* applies to cases involving two people, objects, etc., *most* to cases involving three or more: *John is the more intelligent of the two; he is the most intelligent of the students.*

-most *suffix. forming the superlative degree of some adjectives and adverbs: hindmost; uppermost.* [OE *-mǣst*, *-mest*, orig. a sup. suffix, later mistakenly taken as from *mǣst* (adv) most]

mostly ➊ ('məʊstlɪ) *adv* **1** almost entirely; chiefly. **2** on many or most occasions; usually.

Most Reverend *n* (in Britain) a courtesy title applied to Anglican and Roman Catholic archbishops.

THESAURUS

segment, slice, snack, *soupçon*, tad (*inf., chiefly US*), taste, titbit

mortal *adj* **1, 2** = **human**, corporeal, earthly, ephemeral, impermanent, passing, sublunary, temporal, transient, worldly **3** = **fatal**, deadly, death-dealing, destructive, killing, lethal, murderous, terminal **4** = **unrelenting**, bitter, deadly, implacable, irreconcilable, out-and-out, remorseless, sworn, to the death **6** = **great**, agonizing, awful, dire, enormous, extreme, grave, intense, serious, severe, terrible ◆ *n* **9, 10** = **human being**, being, body, earthling, human, individual, man, person, woman

mortality *n* **1** = **humanity**, ephemerality, impermanence, temporality, transience **2** = **killing**, bloodshed, carnage, death, destruction, fatality, loss of life

mortification *n* **1** = **humiliation**, abasement, annoyance, chagrin, discomfiture, dissatisfaction, embarrassment, loss of face, shame, vexation **3** *Christianity* = **discipline**, abasement, chastening, control, denial, subjugation **4** = **gangrene**, corruption, festering, necrosis, putrescence

mortified *adj* **1** = **humiliated**, abashed, affronted, annoyed, ashamed, chagrined, chastened, confounded, crushed, deflated, discomfited, displeased, embarrassed, given a showing-up (*inf.*), humbled, made to eat humble pie (*inf.*), pissed (*taboo sl.*), pissed off (*taboo sl.*), put down, put out (*inf.*), put to shame, rendered speechless, shamed, vexed **2** *Christianity* = **disciplined**, abased, chastened, conquered, controlled, crushed, subdued **3** = **gangrenous**, decayed, necrotic, rotted

mortify *vb* **1** = **humiliate**, abase, abash, affront, annoy, chagrin, chasten, confound, crush, deflate, disappoint, discomfit, displease, embarrass, humble, make (someone) eat humble pie (*inf.*), put down, put to shame, shame, take (someone) down a peg (*inf.*), vex **2** *Christianity* = **discipline**, abase, chasten, control, deny, subdue **3** = **putrefy**, become gangrenous, corrupt, deaden, die, fester, gangrene, necrose

mortuary *n* **1** = **morgue**, funeral home (*US*), funeral parlour

mostly *adv* **1, 2** = **generally**, above all, almost

mot (məʊ) *n* short for **bon mot.** [C16: via F from Vulgar L *mottum* (unattested) utterance, from L *muttum,* from *muttīre* to mutter]

MOT (in New Zealand and, formerly, in Britain) *abbrev. for:* **1** Ministry of Transport. **2** *Brit.* MOT test: a compulsory annual test for all road vehicles over a certain age, which require a valid **MOT certificate.**

mote ❶ (məʊt) *n* a tiny speck. [OE *mot*]

motel (məʊˈtɛl) *n* a roadside hotel for motorists. [C20: from *motor* + *hotel*]

motet (məʊˈtɛt) *n* a polyphonic choral composition used as an anthem in the Roman Catholic service. [C14: from OF, dim. of *mot* word; see MOT]

moth (mɒθ) *n* any of numerous insects that typically have stout bodies with antennae of various shapes (but not clubbed), including large brightly coloured species, such as hawk moths, and small inconspicuous types, such as the clothes moths. Cf. **butterfly** (sense 1). [OE *moththe*]

mothball (ˈmɒθˌbɔːl) *n* **1** a small ball of camphor or naphthalene used to repel clothes moths in stored clothing, etc. **2 put in mothballs.** to postpone work on (a project, activity, etc.). ◆ *vb* (*tr*) **3** to prepare (a ship) for a long period of storage by sealing with plastic. **4** to take (a factory, etc.) out of operation but maintain it for future use. **5** to postpone work on (a project, activity, etc.).

moth-eaten ❶ *adj* **1** decayed, decrepit, or outdated. **2** eaten away by or as if by moths.

mother[1] ❶ (ˈmʌðə) *n* **1a** a female who has given birth to offspring. **1b** (*as modifier*): *a mother bird.* **2** (*often cap., esp. as a term of address*) a person's own mother. **3** a female substituting in the function of a mother. **4** (*often cap.*) *Chiefly arch.* a term of address for an old woman. **5a** motherly qualities, such as maternal affection: *it appealed to the mother in her.* **5b** (*as modifier*): *mother love.* **5c** (*in combination*): *mothercraft.* **6a** a female or thing that creates, nurtures, protects, etc., something. **6b** (*as modifier*): *mother church; mother earth.* **7** a title given to certain members of female religious orders. **8** (*modifier*) native or innate: *mother wit.* **9 the mother of all...** *Inf.* the greatest example of its kind: *the mother of all parties.* ◆ *vb* (*tr*) **10** to give birth to or produce. **11** to nurture, protect, etc. as a mother. [OE *mōdor*]
▸ˈ**motherless** *adj*

mother[2] (ˈmʌðə) *n* a stringy slime containing various bacteria that forms on the surface of liquids undergoing fermentation. Also called: **mother of vinegar.** [C16: ?from MOTHER[1], but cf. Sp. *madre* scum, Du. *modder* dregs, MLow G *modder* decaying object, *mudde* sludge]

Mother Carey's chicken (ˈkɛərɪz) *n* another name for **stormy petrel.** [from ?]

mother country *n* **1** the original country of colonists or settlers. **2** a person's native country.

Mother Goose *n* the imaginary author of a collection of nursery rhymes. [C18: translated from F *Contes de ma mère l'Oye* (1697), a collection of tales by Charles Perrault (1628–1703)]

motherhood (ˈmʌðəˌhʊd) *n* **1** the state of being a mother. **2** the qualities characteristic of a mother.

Mothering Sunday (ˈmʌðərɪŋ) *n Brit.* the fourth Sunday in Lent, when mothers traditionally receive presents from their children. Also called: **Mother's Day.**

mother-in-law *n, pl* **mothers-in-law.** the mother of one's wife or husband.

motherland (ˈmʌðəˌlænd) *n* a person's native country.

mother lode *n Mining.* the principal lode in a system.

motherly ❶ (ˈmʌðəlɪ) *adj* of or resembling a mother, esp. in warmth or protectiveness.
▸ˈ**motherliness** *n*

mother-of-pearl *n* a hard iridescent substance that forms the inner layer of the shells of certain molluscs, such as the oyster. It is used to make buttons, etc. Also called: **nacre.**

Mother's Day *n* **1** *US & Canad.* the second Sunday in May, observed as a day in honour of mothers. **2** See **Mothering Sunday.**

mother ship *n* a ship providing facilities and supplies for a number of small vessels.

mother superior *n, pl* **mother superiors** *or* **mothers superior.** the head of a community of nuns.

mother tongue *n* **1** the language first learned by a child. **2** a language from which another has evolved.

mother wit ❶ *n* native practical intelligence; common sense.

mothproof (ˈmɒθˌpruːf) *adj* **1** (esp. of clothes) chemically treated so as to repel clothes moths. ◆ *vb* **2** (*tr*) to make (clothes, etc.) mothproof.

mothy (ˈmɒθɪ) *adj* **mothier, mothiest. 1** moth-eaten. **2** containing moths; full of moths.

motif ❶ (məʊˈtiːf) *n* **1** a distinctive idea, esp. a theme elaborated on in a piece of music, literature, etc. **2** Also called: **motive.** a recurring shape in a design. **3** a single decoration, such as a symbol or name on a jumper, sweatshirt, etc. [C19: from F; see MOTIVE]

motile (ˈməʊtaɪl) *adj* capable of moving spontaneously and independently. [C19: from L *mōtus* moved, from *movēre* to move]
▸**motility** (məʊˈtɪlɪtɪ) *n*

motion ❶ (ˈməʊʃən) *n* **1** the process of continual change in the physical position of an object; movement. **2** a movement or action, esp. of part of the human body; a gesture. **3a** the capacity for movement. **3b** a manner of movement, esp. walking; gait. **4** a mental impulse. **5** a formal proposal to be discussed and voted on in a debate, meeting, etc. **6** *Law.* an application made to a judge or court for an order or ruling necessary to the conduct of legal proceedings. **7** *Brit.* **7a** the evacuation of the bowels. **7b** excrement. **8a** part of a moving mechanism. **8b** the action of such a part. **9 go through the motions. 9a** to act or perform the task (of doing something) mechanically or without sincerity. **9b** to mimic the action (of something) by gesture. **10 in motion.** operational or functioning (often in **set in motion, set the wheels in motion**). ◆ *vb* **11** (when *tr, may take a clause as object or an infinitive*) to signal or direct (a person) by a movement or gesture. [C15: from L *mōtiō* a moving, from *movēre* to move]
▸ˈ**motionless** *adj*

motion picture *n* a US and Canad. term for **film** (sense 1).

motivate ❶ (ˈməʊtɪˌveɪt) *vb* **motivates, motivating, motivated.** (*tr*) to give incentive to.
▸ˌ**motiˈvation** *n*

motivational research (ˌməʊtɪˈveɪʃənᵊl) *n* the application of psychology to the study of consumer behaviour, esp. the planning of advertising and sales campaigns. Also called: **motivation research.**

motive ❶ (ˈməʊtɪv) *n* **1** the reason for a certain course of action, whether conscious or unconscious. **2** a variant of **motif** (sense 2). ◆ *adj* **3** of or causing motion: *a motive force.* **4** of or acting as a motive; motivating. ◆ *vb* **motives, motiving, motived.** (*tr*) **5** to motivate. [C14: from OF *motif,* from LL *mōtīvus* (adj) moving, from L *mōtus,* p.p. of *movēre* to move]
▸ˈ**motiveless** *adj*

motive power *n* **1** any source of energy used to produce motion. **2** the means of supplying power to an engine, vehicle, etc.

mot juste *French.* (mo ʒyst) *n, pl* ***mots justes*** (mo ʒyst). the appropriate word or expression.

motley ❶ (ˈmɒtlɪ) *adj* **1** made up of elements of varying type, quality, etc. **2** multicoloured. ◆ *n* **3** a motley collection. **4** the particoloured attire of a jester. [C14: ?from *mot* speck]

moto (ˈməʊtəʊ) *n Music.* movement. [It.]

motocross (ˈməʊtəˌkrɒs) *n* **1** cross-country motorcycle racing across rough ground. **2** another name for **rallycross.** [C20: from MOTO(R) + CROSS(-COUNTRY)]

motor (ˈməʊtə) *n* **1a** the engine, esp. an internal-combustion engine, of a vehicle. **1b** (*as modifier*): *a motor scooter.* **2** Also called: **electric motor.** a machine that converts electrical energy into mechanical energy. **3** any device that converts another form of energy into mechanical energy to produce motion. **4a** *Chiefly Brit.* a car. **4b** (*as modifier*): *motor spares.* ◆ *adj* **5** producing or causing motion. **6** *Physiol.* **6a** of or relating to nerves or neurons that carry impulses that cause muscles to

THESAURUS

entirely, as a rule, chiefly, customarily, for the most part, largely, mainly, most often, on the whole, particularly, predominantly, primarily, principally, usually

mote *n* = **speck**, atom, grain, mite, particle, spot

moth-eaten *adj* **1** = **decayed**, antiquated, decrepit, dilapidated, grungy (*sl., chiefly US*), obsolete, outdated, outworn, ragged, scuzzy (*sl., chiefly US*), seedy, shabby, stale, tattered, threadbare, worn-out

mother[1] *n* **1, 2** = **parent**, dam, ma, mater, mom (*US inf.*), mum (*Brit. inf.*), mummy (*Brit. inf.*), old lady (*inf.*), old woman (*inf.*) ◆ *modifier* **8** = **native**, connate, inborn, innate, natural ◆ *vb* **10** = **give birth to**, bear, bring forth, drop, produce **11** = **nurture**, care for, cherish, nurse, protect, raise, rear, tend

motherly *adj* = **maternal**, affectionate, caring, comforting, fond, gentle, kind, loving, protective, sheltering, tender, warm

mother wit *n* = **common sense**, brains, gumption (*Brit. inf.*), horse sense, judgment, native intelligence, nous (*Brit. sl.*), savvy (*sl.*), smarts (*sl., chiefly US*)

motif *n* **1** = **theme**, concept, idea, leitmotif, subject **2, 3** = **design**, decoration, form, ornament, shape

motion *n* **1** = **movement**, action, change, flow, kinesis, locomotion, mobility, motility, move, passage, passing, progress, travel **2** = **gesture**, gesticulation, sign, signal, wave **5** = **proposal**, proposition, recommendation, submission, suggestion **10 in motion** = **moving**, afoot, functioning, going, in progress, on the go (*inf.*), on the move (*inf.*), operational, travelling, under way, working ◆ *vb* **11** = **gesture**, beckon, direct, gesticulate, nod, signal, wave

motionless *adj* **1** = **still**, at a standstill, at rest, calm, fixed, frozen, halted, immobile, inanimate, inert, lifeless, paralysed, standing, static, stationary, stock-still, transfixed, unmoved, unmoving
Antonyms *adj* active, agitated, animated, frantic, lively, mobile, moving, restless, travelling

motivate *vb* = **inspire**, actuate, arouse, bring, cause, draw, drive, get going, give incentive to, impel, induce, inspirit, instigate, lead, move, persuade, prod, prompt, provoke, set off, set on, stimulate, stir, trigger

motivation *n* = **inspiration**, ambition, desire, drive, hunger, interest, wish = **incentive**, carrot and stick, impulse, incitement, inducement, inspiration, instigation, motive, persuasion, reason, spur, stimulus

motive *n* **1** = **reason**, cause, design, ground(s), incentive, incitement, inducement, influence, inspiration, intention, mainspring, motivation, object, occasion, purpose, rationale, spur, stimulus, the why and wherefore, thinking ◆ *adj* **3, 4** = **moving**, activating, driving, impelling, motivating, operative, prompting

motley *adj* **1** = **miscellaneous**, assorted, disparate, dissimilar, diversified, heterogeneous, mingled, mixed, unlike, varied **2** = **multicoloured**, chequered, parti-coloured, polychromatic, polychrome, polychromous, rainbow, variegated
Antonyms *adj* ≠ **miscellaneous:** homogeneous,

contract. **6b** of or relating to movement or to muscles that induce movement. ◆ *vb* **7** (*intr*) to travel by car. **8** (*tr*) *Brit.* to transport by car. **9** (*intr*) *Inf.* to move fast; make good progress. [C16: from L *mōtor* a mover, from *movēre* to move]

motorbicycle ('məʊtəˌbaɪsɪkᵊl) *n* **1** a motorcycle. **2** a moped.

motorbike ('məʊtəˌbaɪk) *n* a less formal name for **motorcycle.**

motorboat ('məʊtəˌbəʊt) *n* any boat powered by a motor.

motorbus ('məʊtəˌbʌs) *n* a bus driven by an internal-combustion engine.

motorcade ('məʊtəˌkeɪd) *n* a parade of cars. [C20: from MOTOR + CAVALCADE]

motorcar ('məʊtəˌkɑː) *n* **1** a more formal word for **car. 2** a self-propelled electric railway car.

motorcycle ('məʊtəˌsaɪkᵊl) *n* **1** Also called: **motorbike.** a two-wheeled vehicle that is driven by a petrol engine. ◆ *vb* **motorcycles, motorcycling, motorcycled.** (*intr*) **2** to ride on a motorcycle.
▸ **'motorˌcyclist** *n*

motorist ('məʊtərɪst) *n* a driver of a car.

motorize *or* **motorise** ('məʊtəˌraɪz) *vb* **motorizes, motorizing, motorized** *or* **motorises, motorising, motorised.** (*tr*) **1** to equip with a motor. **2** to provide (military units) with motor vehicles.
▸ **ˌmotori'zation** *or* **ˌmotori'sation** *n*

motorman ('məʊtəmən) *n, pl* **motormen. 1** the driver of an electric train. **2** the operator of a motor.

motormouth ('məʊtəˌmaʊθ) *n Sl.* a garrulous person.

motor scooter *n* a light motorcycle with small wheels and an enclosed engine. Often shortened to **scooter.**

motor vehicle *n* a road vehicle driven esp. by an internal-combustion engine.

motorway ('məʊtəˌweɪ) *n Brit., Austral., & NZ.* a main road for fast-moving traffic, having separate carriageways for vehicles travelling in opposite directions.

Motown ('məʊˌtaʊn) *n Trademark.* music combining rhythm and blues and pop, or gospel rhythms and modern ballad harmony. [C20: from *Motown Records* of Detroit, from *Mo(tor) Town,* nickname for Detroit, centre of the US car industry]

motte (mɒt) *n History.* a mound on which a castle was erected. [C14: see MOAT]

MOT test *n* (in Britain) See **MOT** (sense 2).

mottle Ⓣ ('mɒtᵊl) *vb* **mottles, mottling, mottled. 1** (*tr*) to colour with streaks or blotches of different shades. ◆ *n* **2** a mottled appearance, as of the surface of marble. [C17: back formation from MOTLEY]
▸ **'mottled** *adj*

motto Ⓣ ('mɒtəʊ) *n, pl* **mottoes** *or* **mottos. 1** a short saying expressing the guiding maxim or ideal of a family, organization, etc., esp. when part of a coat of arms. **2** a verse or maxim contained in a paper cracker. **3** a quotation prefacing a book or chapter of a book. [C16: via It. from L *muttum* utterance]

moue *French.* (mu) *n* a pouting look.

moufflon ('muːflɒn) *n* a wild short-fleeced mountain sheep of Corsica and Sardinia. [C18: via F from Romance *mufrone,* from LL *mufrō*]

mouillé ('mwiːeɪ) *adj Phonetics.* palatalized, as in the sounds represented by Spanish *ll* or *ñ,* (pronounced as (ʎ) and (ɲ)), or French *ll* (representing a (j) sound). [C19: from F, p.p. of *mouiller* to moisten, from L *mollis* soft]

moujik ('muːʒɪk) *n* a variant spelling of **muzhik.**

mould[1] Ⓣ *or US* **mold** (məʊld) *n* **1** a shaped cavity used to give a definite form to fluid or plastic material. **2** a frame on which something may be constructed. **3** something shaped in or made on a mould. **4** shape, form, design, or pattern. **5** specific nature, character, or type. ◆ *vb* (*tr*) **6** to make in a mould. **7** to shape or form, as by using a mould. **8** to influence or direct: *to mould opinion.* **9** to cling to: *the skirt moulds her figure.* **10** *Metallurgy.* to make (a material) into a mould used in casting. [C13 (n): from OF *modle,* from L *modulus* a small measure]
▸ **'mouldable** *or US* **'moldable** *adj* ▸ **'moulder** *or US* **'molder** *n*

mould[2] Ⓣ *or US* **mold** (məʊld) *n* **1** a coating or discoloration caused by various fungi that develop in a damp atmosphere on the surface of food, fabrics, etc. **2** any of the fungi that cause this growth. ◆ *vb* **3** to become or cause to become covered with this growth. ◆ Also called: **mildew.** [C15: dialect (N English) *mowlde* mouldy, from p.p. of *moulen* to become mouldy, prob. from ON]

mould[3] Ⓣ *or US* **mold** (məʊld) *n* loose soil, esp. when rich in organic matter. [OE *molde*]

mouldboard *or US* **moldboard** ('məʊldˌbɔːd) *n* the curved blade of a plough, which turns over the furrow.

moulder Ⓣ *or US* **molder** ('məʊldə) *vb* (often foll. by *away*) to crumble or cause to crumble, as through decay. [C16: verbal use of MOULD[3]]

moulding *or US* **molding** ('məʊldɪŋ) *n* **1** *Archit.* **1a** a shaped outline, esp. one used on cornices, etc. **1b** a shaped strip made of wood, stone, etc. **2** something moulded.

mouldy Ⓣ *or US* **moldy** ('məʊldɪ) *adj* **mouldier, mouldiest** *or US* **moldier, moldiest. 1** covered with mould. **2** stale or musty, esp. from age or lack of use. **3** *Sl.* boring; dull.
▸ **'mouldiness** *or US* **'moldiness** *n*

moult *or US* **molt** (məʊlt) *vb* **1** (of birds, mammals, arthropods, etc.) to shed (feathers, hair, or cuticle) in order that new growth can take place. ◆ *n* **2** the periodic process of moulting. [C14 *mouten,* from OE *mūtian,* as in *bimūtian* to exchange for, from L *mūtāre* to change]
▸ **'moulter** *or US* **'molter** *n*

mound Ⓣ (maʊnd) *n* **1** a raised mass of earth, debris, etc. **2** any heap or pile. **3** a small natural hill. **4** an artificial ridge of earth, stone, etc., as used for defence. ◆ *vb* **5** (often foll. by *up*) to gather into a mound; heap. **6** (*tr*) to cover or surround with a mound: *to mound a grave.* [C16: earthwork, ?from OE *mund* hand, hence defence]

Mound Builder *n* a member of a group of prehistoric inhabitants of the Mississippi region of the US, who built altar mounds, barrows, etc.

mound-builder *n* another name for **megapode.**

mount[1] Ⓣ (maʊnt) *vb* **1** to go up (a hill, stairs, etc.); climb. **2** to get up on (a horse, a platform, etc.). **3** (*intr;* often foll. by *up*) to increase; accumulate: *excitement mounted.* **4** (*tr*) to fix onto a backing, setting, or support: *to mount a photograph; to mount a slide.* **5** (*tr*) to provide with a horse for riding, or to place on a horse. **6** (of male animals) to climb onto (a female animal) for copulation. **7** (*tr*) to prepare (a play, etc.) for production. **8** (*tr*) to plan and organize (a campaign, etc.). **9** (*tr*) to prepare (a skeleton, etc.) for exhibition as a specimen. **10** (*tr*) to place or carry (weapons) in such a position that they can be fired. **11 mount guard.** See **guard.** ◆ *n* **12** a backing, setting, or support onto which something is fixed. **13** the act or manner of mounting. **14** a horse for riding. **15** a slide used in microscopy. [C16: from OF *munter,* from Vulgar L *montāre* (unattested) from L *mons* MOUNT[2]]
▸ **'mountable** *adj* ▸ **'mounter** *n*

mount[2] (maʊnt) *n* a mountain or hill: used in literature and (when cap.) in proper names: *Mount Everest.* [OE *munt,* from L *mons* mountain, but infl. in ME by OF *mont*]

mountain Ⓣ ('maʊntɪn) *n* **1a** a natural upward projection of the earth's surface, higher and steeper than a hill. **1b** (*as modifier*): *mountain scenery.* **1c** (*in combination*): *a mountaintop.* **2** a huge heap or mass: *a mountain of papers.* **3** anything of great quantity or size. **4** a surplus of a commodity, esp. in the European Union: *a butter mountain.* [C13: from OF *montaigne,* ult. from L *montānus,* from *mons* mountain]

mountain ash *n* **1** any of various trees, such as the European mountain ash or rowan, having clusters of small white flowers and bright red berries. **2** any of several Australian eucalyptus trees, such as *Eucalyptus regnans.*

mountain avens *n* See **avens** (sense 2).

mountain bike *n* a type of sturdy bicycle with at least 16 gears, straight handlebars, and heavy-duty tyres.

mountain cat *n* any of various wild feline mammals, such as the bobcat, lynx, or puma.

mountaineer (ˌmaʊntɪ'nɪə) *n* **1** a person who climbs mountains. **2** a person living in a mountainous area. ◆ *vb* **3** (*intr*) to climb mountains.
▸ **ˌmountain'eering** *n*

mountain goat *n* any wild goat inhabiting mountainous regions.

mountain laurel *n* any of various ericaceous shrubs or trees of E North America having leathery poisonous leaves and clusters of pink or white flowers. Also called: **calico bush.**

mountain lion *n* another name for **puma.**

THESAURUS

similar, uniform ≠ **multicoloured:** monochromatic, plain, self-coloured, solid

mottled *adj* **1** = **blotchy,** brindled, chequered, dappled, flecked, freckled, marbled, piebald, pied, speckled, spotted, stippled, streaked, tabby, variegated

motto *n* **1** = **saying,** adage, byword, cry, dictum, formula, gnome, maxim, precept, proverb, rule, saw, slogan, tag-line, watchword

mould[1] *n* **1** = **cast,** die, form, matrix, pattern, shape, stamp **2, 4** = **design,** brand, build, configuration, construction, cut, fashion, form, format, frame, kind, line, make, pattern, shape, stamp, structure, style **5** = **nature,** calibre, character, ilk, kidney, kind, quality, sort, stamp, type ◆ *vb* **6, 7** = **shape,** carve, cast, construct, create, fashion, forge, form, make, model, sculpt, stamp, work **8** = **influence,** affect, control, direct, form, make, shape

mould[2] *n* **1, 2** = **fungus,** blight, mildew, mouldiness, mustiness

mould[3] *n* = **soil,** dirt, earth, humus, loam

moulder *vb* = **decay,** break down, crumble, decompose, disintegrate, perish, rot, waste

mouldy *adj* **1, 2** = **stale,** bad, blighted, decaying, fusty, mildewed, musty, rotten, rotting, spoiled

mound *n* **1, 2** = **heap,** bing (*Scot.*), drift, pile, rick, stack **3** = **hill,** bank, dune, embankment, hillock, knoll, rise **4** = **earthwork,** bulwark, motte (*History*), rampart

mount[1] *vb* **1** = **ascend,** clamber up, climb, escalade, go up, make one's way up, scale **2** = **get (up) on,** bestride, climb onto, climb up on, get astride, jump on **3** = **increase,** accumulate, build, escalate, grow, intensify, multiply, pile up, swell **4** = **display,** frame, set, set off **4** = **fit,** emplace, install, place, position, put in place, set up **7** = **stage,** exhibit, get up, prepare, produce, put on **8** = **launch,** deliver, prepare, ready, set in motion, stage ◆ *n* **12** = **backing,** base, fixture, foil, frame, mounting, setting, stand, support **14** = **horse,** steed (*literary*)
Antonyms *vb* ≠ **ascend:** descend, drop, go down, make one's way down ≠ **get (up) on:** climb down from, climb off, dismount, get down from, get off, jump off ≠ **increase:** contract, decline, decrease, diminish, dwindle, fall, lessen, lower, reduce, shrink, wane

mountain *n* **1** = **peak,** alp, ben (*Scot.*), berg (*S. Afr.*), elevation, eminence, fell (*Brit.*), height, mount, Munro **2** = **heap,** abundance, mass, mound, pile, stack, ton

mountainous ⓣ ('maʊntɪnəs) *adj* **1** of or relating to mountains: *a mountainous region.* **2** like a mountain, esp. in size or impressiveness.

mountain sickness *n* nausea, headache, and shortness of breath caused by climbing to high altitudes. Also called: **altitude sickness.**

mountebank ⓣ ('maʊntɪˌbæŋk) *n* **1** (formerly) a person who sold quack medicines in public places. **2** a charlatan; fake. ◆ *vb* **3** (*intr*) to play the mountebank. [C16: from It. *montambanco* a climber on a bench, from *montare* to MOUNT[1] + *banco* BENCH]
▸ˌ**mounte'bankery** *n*

mounted ('maʊntɪd) *adj* **1** riding horses: *mounted police.* **2** provided with a support, backing, etc.

Mountie *or* **Mounty** ('maʊntɪ) *n, pl* **Mounties.** *Inf.* a member of the Royal Canadian Mounted Police. [from MOUNTED]

mounting ('maʊntɪŋ) *n* another word for **mount**[1] (sense 12).

mounting-block *n* a block of stone formerly used to aid a person when mounting a horse.

mourn ⓣ (mɔːn) *vb* **1** to feel or express sadness for the death or loss of (someone or something). **2** (*intr*) to observe the customs of mourning, as by wearing black. [OE *murnan*]
▸'**mourner** *n*

mournful ⓣ ('mɔːnful) *adj* **1** evoking grief; sorrowful. **2** gloomy; sad.
▸'**mournfully** *adv* ▸'**mournfulness** *n*

mourning ⓣ ('mɔːnɪŋ) *n* **1** the act or feelings of one who mourns; grief. **2** the conventional symbols of grief, such as the wearing of black. **3** the period of time during which a death is officially mourned. ◆ *adj* **4** of or relating to mourning.
▸'**mourningly** *adv*

mourning band *n* a piece of black material, esp. an armband, worn to indicate mourning.

mourning dove *n* a brown North American dove with a plaintive song.

mouse *n* (maʊs), *pl* **mice** (maɪs). **1** any of numerous small long-tailed rodents that are similar to but smaller than rats. See also **fieldmouse, harvest mouse, house mouse. 2** any of various related rodents, such as the jumping mouse. **3** a quiet, timid, or cowardly person. **4** *Computing.* a hand-held device used to control cursor movements and computing functions without keying. **5** *Sl.* a black eye. ◆ *vb* (maʊz), **mouses, mousing, moused. 6** to stalk and catch (mice, etc.). **7** (*intr*) to go about stealthily. [OE *mūs*]
▸'**mouseˌlike** *adj*

mouser ('maʊzə, 'maʊsə) *n* a cat or other animal that is used to catch mice.

mousetrap ('maʊsˌtræp) *n* **1** any trap for catching mice, esp. one with a spring-loaded metal bar that is released by the taking of the bait. **2** *Brit. inf.* cheese of indifferent quality.

moussaka *or* **mousaka** (mʊ'sɑːkə) *n* a dish originating in the Balkan States, consisting of meat, aubergines, and tomatoes, topped with cheese sauce. [C20: from Mod. Gk]

mousse (muːs) *n* **1** a light creamy dessert made with eggs, cream, fruit, etc., set with gelatine. **2** a similar dish made from fish or meat. **3** short for **styling mousse.** [C19: from F: froth]

mousseline (*French* muslin) *n* **1** a fine fabric made of rayon or silk. **2** a type of fine glass. [C17: F: MUSLIN]

moustache *or US* **mustache** (mə'stɑːʃ) *n* **1** the unshaved growth of hair on the upper lip. **2** a similar growth of hair or bristles (in animals). **3** a mark like a moustache. [C16: via F from It. *mostaccio,* ult. from Doric Gk *mustax* upper lip]
▸**mous'tached** *or US* **mus'tached** *adj*

moustache cup *n* a cup with a partial cover to protect a drinker's moustache.

Mousterian (muː'stɪərɪən) *n* **1** a culture characterized by flint flake tools and associated with Neanderthal man, dating from before 70 000–32 000 B.C. ◆ *adj* **2** of or relating to this culture. [C20: from F *moustérien,* from archaeological finds of the same period in the cave of *Le Moustier,* Dordogne, France]

mousy ⓣ *or* **mousey** ('maʊsɪ) *adj* **mousier, mousiest. 1** resembling a mouse, esp. in hair colour. **2** shy or ineffectual. **3** infested with mice.
▸'**mousily** *adv* ▸'**mousiness** *n*

mouth ⓣ *n* (maʊθ), *pl* **mouths** (maʊðz). **1** the opening through which many animals take in food and issue vocal sounds. **2** the system of organs surrounding this opening, including the lips, tongue, teeth, etc. **3** the visible part of the lips on the face. **4** a person regarded as a consumer of food: *four mouths to feed.* **5** a particular manner of speaking: *a foul mouth.* **6** *Inf.* boastful, rude, or excessive talk: *he is all mouth.* **7** the point where a river issues into a sea or lake. **8** the opening of a container, such as a jar. **9** the opening of a cave, tunnel, volcano, etc. **10** that part of the inner lip of a horse on which the bit acts. **11** a pout; grimace. **12 down in** *or* **at the mouth.** in low spirits. ◆ *vb* (maʊð). **13** to speak or say (something) insincerely, esp. in public. **14** (*tr*) to form (words) with movements of the lips but without speaking. **15** (*tr*) to take (something) into the mouth or to move (something) around inside the mouth. **16** (*intr;* usually foll. by *at*) to make a grimace. [OE *mūth*]
▸**mouther** ('maʊðə) *n*

mouthful ⓣ ('maʊθˌful) *n, pl* **mouthfuls. 1** as much as is held in the mouth at one time. **2** a small quantity, as of food. **3** a long word or phrase that is difficult to say. **4** *Brit. inf.* an abusive response.

mouth organ *n* another name for **harmonica.**

mouthpart ('maʊθˌpɑːt) *n* any of the paired appendages in arthropods that surround the mouth and are specialized for feeding.

mouthpiece ⓣ ('maʊθˌpiːs) *n* **1** the part of a wind instrument into which the player blows. **2** the part of a telephone receiver into which a person speaks. **3** the part of a container forming its mouth. **4** a person who acts as a spokesman, as for an organization. **5** a publication expressing the official views of an organization.

mouthwash ('maʊθˌwɒʃ) *n* a medicated solution for gargling and cleansing the mouth.

mouthy ('maʊðɪ) *adj* **mouthier, mouthiest.** bombastic; excessively talkative.

mouton ('muːtɒn) *n* sheepskin processed to resemble the fur of another animal, esp. beaver or seal. [from F: sheep]

movable ⓣ *or* **moveable** ('muːvəb[ə]l) *adj* **1** able to be moved; not fixed. **2** (esp. of Easter) varying in date from year to year. **3** (usually spelt **moveable**) *Law.* denoting or relating to personal property as opposed to realty. ◆ *n* **4** (*often pl*) a movable article, esp. a piece of furniture.
▸ˌ**mova'bility** *or* '**movableness** *n* ▸'**movably** *adv*

move ⓣ (muːv) *vb* **moves, moving, moved. 1** to go or take from one place to another; change in position. **2** (*usually intr*) to change (one's dwelling, place of business, etc.). **3** to be or cause to be in motion; stir. **4** (*intr*) (of machines, etc.) to work or operate. **5** (*tr*) to cause (to do something); prompt. **6** (*intr*) to begin to act: *move soon or we'll lose the order.* **7** (*intr*) to associate oneself with a specified social circle: *to move in exalted spheres.* **8** (*intr*) to make progress. **9** (*tr*) to arouse affection, pity, or compassion in; touch. **10** (in board games) to change the position of (a piece) or (of a piece) to change position. **11** (*intr*) (of merchandise) to be disposed of by being bought. **12** (when *tr, often takes a clause as object;* when *intr,* often foll. by *for*) to suggest (a proposal) formally, as in debating or parliamentary procedure. **13** (*intr;* usually foll. by *on* or *along*) to go away or to another place; leave. **14** to cause (the bowels) to evacuate or (of the bowels) to be evacuated. ◆ *n* **15** the act of moving; movement. **16** one of a sequence of actions, usually part of a plan; manoeuvre. **17** the act of moving one's residence, place of business, etc. **18** (in board games) **18a** a player's turn to move his piece. **18b** a manoeuvre of a piece. **19 get a move on.** *Inf.* **19a** to get started. **19b** to hurry up. **20 on the move. 20a** travelling from place to

THESAURUS

mountainous *adj* **1** = **high**, alpine, highland, rocky, soaring, steep, towering, upland **2** = **huge**, daunting, enormous, gigantic, great, hulking, immense, mammoth, mighty, monumental, ponderous, prodigious
Antonyms *adj* ≠ **huge:** diminutive, insignificant, little, minute, petty, puny, small, tiny, trivial, weak

mountebank *n* **1, 2** = **charlatan**, cheat, chiseller (*inf.*), confidence trickster, con man (*inf.*), fake, fraud, fraudster, hustler (*US inf.*), impostor, phoney *or* phony (*inf.*), pretender, quack, rogue, swindler

mourn *vb* **1, 2** = **grieve**, bemoan, bewail, deplore, keen, lament, miss, rue, sorrow, wail, wear black, weep

mournful *adj* **1** = **sad**, afflicting, calamitous, deplorable, distressing, grievous, harrowing, lamentable, melancholy, painful, piteous, plaintive, sorrowful, tragic, unhappy, woeful **2** = **dismal**, brokenhearted, cheerless, desolate, disconsolate, downcast, down in the dumps (*inf.*), funereal, gloomy, grief-stricken, grieving, heartbroken, heavy, heavy-hearted, joyless, lugubrious, melancholy, miserable, rueful, sad, sombre, unhappy, woeful
Antonyms *adj* ≠ **sad:** agreeable, cheerful, fortunate, happy, lucky, pleasant, satisfying ≠ **dismal:** bright, cheerful, chirpy (*inf.*), genial, happy, jolly, joyful, light-hearted, sunny, upbeat (*inf.*)

mourning *n* **1** = **grieving**, bereavement, grief, keening, lamentation, weeping, woe **2** = **black**, sackcloth and ashes, weeds, widow's weeds

mousy *adj* **1** = **brownish**, colourless, drab, dull, indeterminate, plain **2** = **shy**, diffident, ineffectual, quiet, self-effacing, timid, timorous, unassertive

mouth *n* **1, 3** = **lips**, chops (*sl.*), gob (*sl., especially Brit.*), jaws, maw, trap (*sl.*), yap (*sl.*) **6** *Informal* = **boasting**, braggadocio, bragging, empty talk, gas (*inf.*), hot air (*sl.*), idle talk **6** *Informal* = **insolence**, backchat, cheek (*inf.*), impudence, lip (*sl.*), rudeness, sauce (*inf.*) **8, 9** = **opening**, aperture, cavity, crevice, door, entrance, gateway, inlet, lips, orifice, rim **12 down in** *or* **at the mouth** = **depressed**, blue, crestfallen, dejected, disheartened, dispirited, down, downcast, down in the dumps (*inf.*), in low spirits, melancholy, miserable, sad, sick as a parrot (*inf.*), unhappy

mouthful *n* **2** = **taste**, bit, bite, drop, forkful, little, morsel, sample, sip, spoonful, sup, swallow

mouthpiece *n* **4** = **spokesperson**, agent, delegate, representative, spokesman *or* spokeswoman **5** = **publication**, journal, organ, periodical

movable *adj* **1** = **portable**, detachable, mobile, not fixed, portative, transferable, transportable ◆ *n* **4** *often plural* = **furniture**, belongings, chattels, effects, gear, goods, possessions, property, stuff (*inf.*), things (*inf.*)

move *vb* **1** = **go**, advance, budge, change position, drift, march, proceed, progress, shift, stir, walk **1** = **change**, carry, shift, switch, transfer, transport, transpose **2** = **relocate**, change residence, flit, go away, leave, migrate, move house, pack one's bags (*inf.*), quit, remove **3** = **drive**, activate, impel, motivate, operate, prod, propel, push, set going, shift, shove, start, turn **5** = **prompt**, actuate, cause, give rise to, impel, incite, induce, influence, inspire, instigate, lead, motivate, persuade, rouse, stimulate, urge **9** = **touch**, affect, agitate, excite, impress, make an impression on, tug at (someone's) heartstrings (*often facetious*) **12** = **propose**, advocate, put forward, recommend, suggest, urge ◆ *n* **15, 16, 18** = **action**, act, deed, manoeuvre, measure, motion, movement, ploy,

place. **20b** advancing; succeeding. **20c** very active; busy. [C13: from Anglo-F *mover*, from L *movēre*]

move in *vb* (*mainly adv*) **1** (*also prep*) Also (when *prep*): **move into.** to occupy or take possession of (a new residence, place of business, etc.). **2** (*intr; often foll. by on*) *Inf.* to creep close (to), as in preparing to capture. **3** (*intr; often foll. by on*) *Inf.* to try to gain power or influence (over).

movement ❶ ('mu:vmənt) *n* **1a** the act, process, or result of moving. **1b** an instance of moving. **2** the manner of moving. **3a** a group of people with a common ideology. **3b** the organized action of such a group. **4** a trend or tendency. **5** the driving and regulating mechanism of a watch or clock. **6** (*often pl*) a person's location and activities during a specific time. **7a** the evacuation of the bowels. **7b** the matter evacuated. **8** *Music.* a principal self-contained section of a symphony, sonata, etc. **9** tempo or pace, as in music or literature. **10** *Fine arts.* the appearance of motion in painting, sculpture, etc. **11** *Prosody.* the rhythmic structure of verse. **12** a positional change by one or a number of military units. **13** a change in the market price of a security or commodity.

mover ('mu:və) *n* **1** *Inf.* a person, business, idea, etc., that is advancing or progressing. **2** a person or thing that moves. **3** a person who moves a proposal, as in a debate. **4** *US & Canad.* a removal firm or a person who works for one.

movers and shakers *pl n Inf.* the people with power and influence in a particular field of activity. [C20: ? from the line "We are the movers and shakers of the world for ever" in 'Ode' by Arthur O'Shaughnessy (1844–81), Brit. poet]

movie ❶ ('mu:vɪ) *n* **a** an informal word for **film** (sense 1). **b** (*as modifier*): *movie ticket.*

moving ❶ ('mu:vɪŋ) *adj* **1** arousing or touching the emotions. **2** changing or capable of changing position. **3** causing motion.
▸**'movingly** *adv*

moving staircase *or* **stairway** *n* less common terms for **escalator** (sense 1).

mow ❶ (məʊ) *vb* **mows, mowing, mowed; mowed** *or* **mown. 1** to cut down (grass, crops, etc.), with a hand implement or machine. **2** (*tr*) to cut the growing vegetation of (a field, lawn, etc.). [OE *māwan*]
▸**'mower** *n*

mow down ❶ *vb* (*tr, adv*) to kill in large numbers, esp. by gunfire.

mown (məʊn) *vb* a past participle of **mow.**

mozzarella (ˌmɒtsə'relə) *n* a moist white curd cheese originally made in Italy from buffalo milk. [from It., dim. of *mozza* a type of cheese, from *mozzare* to cut off]

mp 1 *abbrev. for* melting point. **2** *Music. symbol for* mezzo piano. [It.: moderately soft]

MP *abbrev. for:* **1** (in Britain, Canada, etc.) Member of Parliament. **2** (in Britain) Metropolitan Police. **3** Military Police. **4** Mounted Police.

mpg *abbrev. for* miles per gallon.

mph *abbrev. for* miles per hour.

MPhil *or* **MPh** *abbrev. for* Master of Philosophy.

MPP (in Canada) *abbrev. for* Member of Provincial Parliament.

Mr ('mɪstə) *n, pl* **Messrs.** a title used before a man's name or before some office that he holds: *Mr Jones; Mr President.* [C17: abbrev. of MISTER]

MR *abbrev. for:* **1** (in Britain) Master of the Rolls. **2** motivation(al) research.

MRC (in Britain) *abbrev. for* Medical Research Council.

MRI *abbrev. for* magnetic resonance imaging.

m-RNA *abbrev. for* messenger RNA.

MRP *abbrev. for* manufacturers' recommended price.

Mrs ('mɪsɪz) *n, pl* **Mrs** *or* **Mesdames.** a title used before the name or names of a married woman. [C17: orig. abbrev. of MISTRESS]

MRSA *abbrev. for* methicillin-resistant *Staphylococcus aureus*: a bacterium that enters the skin through open wounds to cause septicaemia and is extremely resistant to most antibiotics. It has been responsible for outbreaks of untreatable infections among patients in hospitals.

Ms (mɪz, məs) *n* a title substituted for **Mrs** or **Miss** to avoid making a distinction between married and unmarried women.

MS *abbrev. for:* **1** Master of Surgery. **2** (on gravestones, etc.) memoriae sacrum. [L: sacred to the memory of] **3** multiple sclerosis.

MS. *or* **ms.** *pl* **MSS.** *or* **mss.** *abbrev. for* manuscript.

MSc *abbrev. for* Master of Science.

MS-DOS (ɛm'ɛs'dɒs) *n Trademark, computing.* a type of disk operating system. [C20: from *M(icro)s(oft)*, the company that developed it, + DOS]

MSF (in Britain) *abbrev. for* Manufacturing, Science, and Finance Union.

MSG *abbrev. for* monosodium glutamate.

Msgr *abbrev. for* Monsignor.

MST *abbrev. for* Mountain Standard Time.

Mt *or* **mt** *abbrev. for:* **1** mount: *Mt Everest.* **2** Also: **mtn.** mountain.

MTech *abbrev. for* Master of Technology.

mtg *abbrev. for:* **1** meeting. **2** Also: **mtge.** mortgage.

MTV *abbrev. for* music television: a US music channel that operates 24 hours a day.

mu (mju:) *n* the 12th letter in the Greek alphabet (M, μ).

much ❶ (mʌtʃ) *determiner* **1a** (*usually used with a negative*) a great quantity or degree of: *there isn't much honey left.* **1b** (*as pron*): *much has been learned from this.* **2 a bit much.** *Inf.* rather excessive. **3 make much of. 3a** (*used with a negative*) to make sense of: *he couldn't make much of her babble.* **3b** to give importance to: *she made much of this fact.* **3c** to pay flattering attention to: *the reporters made much of the film star.* **4 not much of.** not to any appreciable degree or extent: *he's not much of an actor really.* **5 not up to much.** *Inf.* of a low standard: *this beer is not up to much.* ◆ *adv* **6** considerably: *they're much better now.* **7** practically; nearly (esp. in **much the same**). **8** (*usually used with a negative*) often; a great deal: *it doesn't happen much in this country.* **9 (as) much as.** even though; although: *much as I'd like to, I can't come.* ◆ See also **more, most.** [OE *mycel*]

muchness ('mʌtʃnɪs) *n* **1** *Arch. or inf.* magnitude. **2 much of a muchness.** *Brit.* very similar.

mucilage ('mju:sɪlɪdʒ) *n* **1** a sticky preparation, such as gum or glue, used as an adhesive. **2** a complex glutinous carbohydrate secreted by certain plants. [C14: via OF from LL *mūcilāgo* mouldy juice, from L, from *mucēre* to be mouldy]
▸**mucilaginous** (ˌmju:sɪ'lædʒɪnəs) *adj*

muck ❶ (mʌk) *n* **1** farmyard dung or decaying vegetable matter. **2** an organic soil rich in humus and used as a fertilizer. **3** dirt or filth. **4** *Sl., chiefly Brit.* rubbish. **5 make a muck of.** *Sl., chiefly Brit.* to ruin or spoil. ◆ *vb* (*tr*) **6** to spread manure upon (fields, etc.). **7** to soil or pollute. **8** (usually foll. by *up*) *Brit. sl.* to ruin or spoil. **9** (often foll. by *out*) to clear muck from. [C13: prob. from ON]
▸**'mucky** *adj*

muck about *vb Brit. sl.* **1** (*intr*) to waste time; misbehave. **2** (when *intr,* foll. by *with*) to interfere (with), annoy, or waste the time (of).

mucker ('mʌkə) *n Brit. sl.* **a** a friend; mate. **b** a coarse person.
▸**'muckerish** *adj*

muck in *vb* (*intr, adv*) *Brit. sl.* to share duties, work, etc. (with other people).

muckrake ('mʌkˌreɪk) *vb* **muckrakes, muckraking, muckraked.** (*intr*) to seek out and expose scandal, esp. concerning public figures.
▸**'muckˌraker** *n* ▸**'muckˌraking** *n*

mucksweat ('mʌkˌswɛt) *n Brit. inf.* profuse sweat or a state of profuse sweating.

mucous ❶ ('mju:kəs) *adj* of, resembling, or secreting mucus. [C17: from L *mūcōsus* slimy, from MUCUS]
▸**mucosity** (mju:'kɒsɪtɪ) *n*

> **USAGE NOTE** The noun *mucus* is often misspelled as *mucous*. *Mucous* can only be correctly used as an adjective.

THESAURUS

shift, step, stratagem, stroke, turn **17** = **transfer**, change of address, flit, flitting (*Scot. & N English dialect*), migration, relocation, removal, shift **19 get a move on** = **speed up**, get cracking (*inf.*), get going, hurry (up), make haste, shake a leg (*inf.*), step on it (*inf.*), stir oneself **20 on the move: a** = **in transit**, journeying, moving, on the road (*inf.*), on the run, on the wing, travelling, under way, voyaging **b, c** = **active**, advancing, astir, going forward, moving, progressing, stirring, succeeding

Antonyms *vb* ≠ **prompt**: deter, discourage, dissuade, prevent, stop

movement *n* **1, 2** = **motion**, act, action, activity, advance, agitation, change, development, displacement, exercise, flow, gesture, manoeuvre, move, moving, operation, progress, progression, shift, steps, stir, stirring, transfer **3** = **group**, camp, campaign, crusade, drive, faction, front, grouping, organization, party **4** = **trend**, current, drift, flow, swing, tendency **5** = **workings**, action, innards (*inf.*), machinery, mechanism, works **8** *Music* = **section**, division, part, passage **9, 11** = **rhythm**, beat, cadence, measure (*Prosody*), metre, pace, swing, tempo

movie *n* **1** = **film**, feature, flick (*sl.*), motion picture, moving picture (*US*), picture

moving *adj* **1** = **emotional**, affecting, arousing, emotive, exciting, impelling, impressive, inspiring, pathetic, persuasive, poignant, stirring, touching **2** = **mobile**, motile, movable, portable, running, unfixed

Antonyms *adj* ≠ **emotional**: unemotional, unexciting, unimpressive, uninspiring ≠ **mobile**: fixed, immobile, immovable, stationary, still, unmoving

mow *vb* **1, 2** = **cut**, crop, scythe, shear, trim

mow down *vb* = **massacre**, blow away (*sl., chiefly US*), butcher, cut down, cut to pieces, shoot down, slaughter

much *determiner* **1a** = **great**, abundant, a lot of, ample, considerable, copious, plenteous, plenty of, sizable *or* sizeable, substantial ◆ *pron* **1b** = **a lot**, a good deal, a great deal, an appreciable amount, heaps (*inf.*), loads (*inf.*), lots (*inf.*), plenty ◆ *adv* **6, 8** = **greatly**, a great deal, a lot, considerably, decidedly, exceedingly, frequently, indeed, often, regularly

Antonyms *determiner* ≠ **great**: inadequate, insufficient, little, scant ◆ *pron* ≠ **a lot**: hardly anything, little, next to nothing, not a lot, not much, practically nothing, very little ◆ *adv* ≠ **greatly**: barely, hardly, infrequently, irregularly, not a lot, not much, occasionally, only just, rarely, scarcely, seldom, slightly

muck *n* **1** = **manure**, dung, ordure **3** = **dirt**, crap (*sl.*), crud (*sl.*), filth, grot (*sl.*), gunge (*inf.*), gunk (*inf.*), mire, mud, ooze, scum, sewage, shit (*taboo sl.*), slime, slob (*Irish*), sludge **5 make a muck of** *Slang, chiefly Brit.* = **spoil**, blow (*sl.*), botch, bungle, make a mess of, make a nonsense of, make a pig's ear of (*inf.*), mar, mess up, muff, ruin ◆ *vb* **8** *usually foll. by* **up** *Brit. slang* = **ruin**, blow (*sl.*), bodge (*inf.*), botch, bungle, make a mess of, make a muck of (*sl.*), make a nonsense of, make a pig's ear of (*inf.*), mar, mess up, muff, spoil

mucky *adj* **3** = **dirty**, begrimed, bespattered, filthy, grimy, messy, mud-caked, muddy, soiled, sticky

mucous *adj* = **slimy**, glutinous, gummy, mucilaginous, viscid, viscous

mucous membrane *n* a mucus-secreting membrane that lines body cavities or passages that are open to the external environment.

mucus (ˈmjuːkəs) *n* the slimy protective secretion of the mucous membranes. [C17: from L: nasal secretions; cf. *mungere* to blow the nose]

> **USAGE NOTE** See at **mucous.**

mud Ⓣ (mʌd) *n* **1** a fine-grained soft wet deposit that occurs on the ground after rain, at the bottom of ponds, etc. **2** *Inf.* slander or defamation. **3 clear as mud.** *Inf.* not at all clear. **4 here's mud in your eye.** *Inf.* a humorous drinking toast. **5 (someone's) name is mud.** *Inf.* (someone) is disgraced. **6 throw** (*or* **sling**) **mud at.** *Inf.* to slander; vilify. ◆ *vb* **muds, mudding, mudded. 7** (*tr*) to soil or cover with mud. [C14: prob. from MLow G *mudde*]

mud bath *n* **1** a medicinal bath in heated mud. **2** a dirty or muddy occasion, state, etc.

mudbrick (ˈmʌdˌbrɪk) *n* a brick made with mud.

muddle Ⓣ (ˈmʌdᵊl) *vb* **muddles, muddling, muddled.** (*tr*) **1** (often foll. by *up*) to mix up (objects, items, etc.). **2** to confuse. **3** *US.* to mix or stir (alcoholic drinks, etc.). ◆ *n* **4** a state of physical or mental confusion. [C16: ?from MDu. *moddelen* to make muddy]
▸**ˈmuddled** *adj* ▸**ˈmuddler** *n* ▸**ˈmuddling** *adj, n*

muddleheaded (ˌmʌdᵊlˈhɛdɪd) *adj* mentally confused or vague.
▸**ˌmuddleˈheadedness** *n*

muddle through Ⓣ *vb* (*intr, adv*) *Chiefly Brit.* to succeed in spite of lack of organization.

muddy Ⓣ (ˈmʌdɪ) *adj* **muddier, muddiest. 1** covered or filled with mud. **2** not clear or bright: *muddy colours.* **3** cloudy: *a muddy liquid.* **4** (esp. of thoughts) confused or vague. ◆ *vb* **muddies, muddying, muddied. 5** to become or cause to become muddy.
▸**ˈmuddily** *adv* ▸**ˈmuddiness** *n*

mudfish (ˈmʌdˌfɪʃ) *n, pl* **mudfish** *or* **mudfishes.** any of various fishes, such as the bowfin, that live at the muddy bottoms of rivers, lakes, etc.

mud flat *n* a tract of low muddy land that is covered at high tide and exposed at low tide.

mudflow (ˈmʌdˌfləʊ) *n Geol.* a flow of soil mixed with water down a steep unstable slope.

mudguard (ˈmʌdˌgɑːd) *n* a curved part of a motorcycle, bicycle, etc., attached above the wheels to reduce the amount of water or mud thrown up by them. US and Canad. name: **fender.**

mud hen *n* any of various birds that frequent marshes, esp. the coots, rails, etc.

mudlark (ˈmʌdˌlɑːk) *n* **1** (formerly) a person who made a living by picking up odds and ends in the mud of tidal rivers. **2** *Sl., now rare.* a street urchin. **3** *Austral. sl.* a racehorse that runs well on a wet or muddy course.

mud map *n Austral.* **1** a rough map drawn on the ground with a stick. **2** any rough sketch map.

mudpack (ˈmʌdˌpæk) *n* a cosmetic astringent paste containing fuller's earth.

mud puppy *n* an aquatic North American salamander having persistent larval features.

mudskipper (ˈmʌdˌskɪpə) *n* any of various gobies that occur in tropical coastal regions of Africa and Asia and can move on land by means of their strong pectoral fins.

mudslinging (ˈmʌdˌslɪŋɪŋ) *n* casting malicious slurs on an opponent, esp. in politics.
▸**ˈmudˌslinger** *n*

mudstone (ˈmʌdˌstəʊn) *n* a dark grey clay rock similar to shale.

mud turtle *n* any of various small turtles that inhabit muddy rivers in North and Central America.

muesli (ˈmjuːzlɪ) *n* a mixture of rolled oats, nuts, fruit, etc., usually eaten with milk. [Swiss G, from G *Mus* mush, purée + *-li*, dim. suffix]

muezzin (muːˈɛzɪn) *n Islam.* the official of a mosque who calls the faithful to prayer from the minaret. [C16: from Ar. *mu'adhdhin*]

muff[1] (mʌf) *n* an open-ended cylinder of fur or cloth into which the hands are placed for warmth. [C16: prob. from Du. *mof,* ult. from F *mouffle* MUFFLE[1]]

muff[2] Ⓣ (mʌf) *vb* **1** to perform (an action) awkwardly. **2** (*tr*) to bungle (a shot, catch, etc.). ◆ *n* **3** any unskilful play, esp. a dropped catch. **4** any bungled action. **5** a bungler. [C19: from ?]

muffin (ˈmʌfɪn) *n* **1** *Brit.* a thick round baked yeast roll, usually toasted and served with butter. **2** *US & Canad.* a small cup-shaped sweet bread roll, usually eaten hot with butter. [C18: ?from Low G *muffen* cakes]

muffin man *n Brit.* (formerly) an itinerant seller of muffins.

muffle[1] Ⓣ (ˈmʌfᵊl) *vb* **muffles, muffling, muffled.** (*mainly tr*) **1** (*also intr;* often foll. by *up*) to wrap up (the head) in a scarf, cloak, etc., esp. for warmth. **2** (*also intr*) to deaden (a sound or noise), esp. by wrapping. **3** to prevent (the expression of something) by (someone). ◆ *n* **4** something that muffles. **5** a kiln with an inner chamber for firing porcelain, enamel, etc. [C15: prob. from OF; cf. OF *moufle* mitten, *emmouflé* wrapped up]

muffle[2] (ˈmʌfᵊl) *n* the fleshy hairless part of the upper lip and nose in ruminants and some rodents. [C17: from F *mufle,* from ?]

muffler (ˈmʌflə) *n* **1** a thick scarf, collar, etc. **2** the US and Canad. name for **silencer** (sense 1).

mufti (ˈmʌftɪ) *n* civilian dress, esp. as worn by a person who normally wears a military uniform. [C19: ?from MUFTI]

Mufti (ˈmʌftɪ) *n, pl* **Muftis.** a Muslim legal expert and adviser on the law of the Koran. [C16: from Ar. *muftī,* from *aftā* to give a (legal) decision]

mug[1] Ⓣ (mʌg) *n* **1** a drinking vessel with a handle, usually cylindrical and made of earthenware. **2** Also called: **mugful.** the quantity held by a mug or its contents. [C16: prob. of Scand. origin]

mug[2] Ⓣ (mʌg) *n* **1** *Sl.* a person's face or mouth. **2** *Brit. sl.* a gullible person, esp. one who is swindled easily. **3 a mug's game.** a worthless activity. ◆ *vb* **mugs, mugging, mugged. 4** (*tr*) *Inf.* to attack or rob (someone) violently. [C18: ?from MUG[1], since drinking vessels were sometimes modelled into the likeness of a face]
▸**ˈmugger** *n*

muggins (ˈmʌgɪnz) *n* (*functioning as sing*) **1** *Brit. sl.* **1a** a simpleton. **1b** a title used humorously to refer to oneself as a dupe or victim. **2** a card game. [C19: prob. from the surname *Muggins*]

muggy Ⓣ (ˈmʌgɪ) *adj* **muggier, muggiest.** (of weather, air, etc.) unpleasantly warm and humid. [C18: dialect *mug* drizzle, prob. of Scand. origin]
▸**ˈmugginess** *n*

mug shot *n Inf.* a photograph of a person's face, esp. one resembling a police-file picture.

mug up Ⓣ *vb* (*adv*) *Brit. sl.* to study (a subject) hard, esp. for an exam. [C19: from ?]

Muhammadan *or* **Muhammedan** (mʊˈhæmədᵊn) *n, adj* another word (not in Muslim use) for **Muslim.**

mujaheddin *or* **mujahedeen** (ˌmuːdʒəhəˈdiːn) *pl n* (preceded by *the; sometimes cap.*) (in Afghanistan and Iran) fundamentalist Muslim guerrillas. In Afghanistan in 1992 the mujaheddin overthrew the government but were unable to agree on a new constitution and were themselves overthrown by the Taliban militia in 1996. [C20: from Ar. *mujāhidīn* fighters, ult. from JIHAD]

mukluk (ˈmʌklʌk) *n* a soft boot, usually of sealskin, worn by Eskimos. [from Eskimo *muklok* large seal]

mulatto (mjuːˈlætəʊ) *n, pl* **mulattos** *or* **mulattoes. 1** a person having one Black and one White parent. ◆ *adj* **2** of a light brown colour; tawny. [C16: from Sp. *mulato* young mule, var. of *mulo* MULE[1]]

mulberry (ˈmʌlbərɪ, -brɪ) *n, pl* **mulberries. 1** a tree having edible blackberry-like fruit, such as the white mulberry, the leaves of which are used to feed silkworms. **2** the fruit of any of these trees. **3** any of several similar or related trees. **4a** a dark purple colour. **4b** (*as adj*): *a mulberry dress.* [C14: from L *mōrum,* from Gk *moron;* rel. to OE *mōrberie*]

mulch (mʌltʃ) *n* **1** half-rotten vegetable matter, peat, etc., used to prevent soil erosion or enrich the soil. ◆ *vb* **2** (*tr*) to cover (the surface of land) with mulch. [C17: from obs. *mulch* soft; rel. to OE *mylisc* mellow]

mulct (mʌlkt) *vb* (*tr*) **1** to cheat or defraud. **2** to fine (a person). ◆ *n* **3** a fine or penalty. [C15: via F from L *multa* a fine]

mule[1] (mjuːl) *n* **1** the sterile offspring of a male donkey and a female

THESAURUS

mud *n* **1 = dirt,** clay, gloop (*inf.*), mire, ooze, silt, slime, slob (*Irish*), sludge

muddle *vb* **1 = jumble,** confuse, disarrange, disorder, disorganize, make a mess of, mess, mix up, ravel, scramble, spoil, tangle **2 = confuse,** befuddle, bewilder, confound, daze, disorient, perplex, stupefy ◆ *n* **4 = confusion,** chaos, clutter, daze, disarray, disorder, disorganization, fankle (*Scot.*), hodgepodge (*US*), hotchpotch, jumble, mess, mix-up, perplexity, pig's breakfast (*inf.*), plight, predicament, ravel, tangle

muddled *adj* **1 = jumbled,** chaotic, confused, disarrayed, disordered, disorganized, higgledy-piggledy (*inf.*), messy, mixed-up, scrambled, tangled **2 = bewildered,** at sea, befuddled, confused, dazed, disoriented, perplexed, stupefied, vague
Antonyms *adj* ≠ **jumbled:** cut-and-dried (*inf.*), orderly, organized

muddle through *vb Chiefly Brit.* **= scrape by,** cope, get along, get by, make it, manage, manage somehow

muddy *adj* **1 = dirty,** bespattered, clarty (*Scot. & N English dialect*), grimy, mucky, mud-caked, soiled **1 = boggy,** marshy, miry, quaggy, swampy **2 = dull,** blurred, dingy, flat, lustreless, smoky, unclear, washed-out **3 = cloudy,** dirty, foul, impure, opaque, turbid **4 = confused,** fuzzy, hazy, indistinct, muddled, unclear, vague, woolly ◆ *vb* **5 = smear,** begrime, bespatter, cloud, dirty, smirch, soil

muff[2] *vb* **1, 2 = botch,** bodge (*inf.*), bungle, fluff (*inf.*), make a mess of, make a muck of (*inf.*), make a nonsense of, make a pig's ear of (*inf.*), mess up, mismanage, spoil

muffle[1] *vb* **1 = wrap up,** cloak, conceal, cover, disguise, envelop, hood, mask, shroud, swaddle, swathe **2 = deaden,** dull, gag, hush, muzzle, quieten, silence, soften, stifle, suppress

muffled *adj* **2 = indistinct,** dim, dull, faint, muted, stifled, strangled, subdued, suppressed

mug[1] *n* **1 = cup,** beaker, flagon, jug, pot, stein, tankard, toby jug

mug[2] *n* **1** *Slang* **= face,** clock (*Brit. sl.*), countenance, dial (*sl.*), features, kisser (*sl.*), mush (*Brit. sl.*), phiz *or* phizog (*Brit. sl.*), puss (*sl.*), visage **2** *Brit. slang* **= fool,** charlie (*Brit. inf.*), chump (*inf.*), easy *or* soft touch (*sl.*), gull (*arch.*), innocent, mark (*sl.*), muggins (*Brit. sl.*), simpleton, sucker (*sl.*) ◆ *vb* **4** *Informal* **= attack,** assail, assault, beat up, do over (*Brit., Austral., & NZ sl.*), duff up (*Brit. sl.*), hold up, lay into (*inf.*), put the boot in (*sl.*), rob, set about *or* upon, steam (*inf.*), work over (*sl.*)

muggy *adj* **= humid,** clammy, close, damp, moist, oppressive, sticky, stuffy, sultry

mug up *vb Brit. slang* **= study,** bone up on (*inf.*), burn the midnight oil (*inf.*), cram (*inf.*), get up (*inf.*), swot (*Brit. inf.*)

horse, used as a beast of burden. **2** any hybrid animal: *a mule canary.* **3** Also called: **spinning mule.** a machine that spins cotton into yarn and winds the yarn on spindles. **4** *Inf.* an obstinate or stubborn person. [C13: from OF *mul,* from L *mūlus* ass, mule]

mule[2] (mju:l) *n* a backless shoe or slipper. [C16: from OF from L *mulleus* a magistrate's shoe]

muleta (mju:ˈlɛtə) *n* the small cape attached to a stick used by the matador during a bullfight. [Sp.: small mule, crutch, from *mula* MULE[1]]

muleteer (ˌmju:lɪˈtɪə) *n* a person who drives mules.

mulga (ˈmʌlgə) *n Austral.* **1** any of various Australian acacia shrubs. **2** scrub comprised of a dense growth of acacia. **3** *Inf.* the outback; bush. [from Abor.]

muliebrity (ˌmju:lɪˈɛbrɪtɪ) *n* **1** the condition of being a woman. **2** femininity. [C16: via LL from L *muliēbris* womanly, from *mulier* woman]

mulish Ⓣ (ˈmju:lɪʃ) *adj* stubborn; obstinate.
▸ **ˈmulishly** *adv* ▸ **ˈmulishness** *n*

mull[1] Ⓣ (mʌl) *vb* (*tr*) (often foll. by *over*) to study or ponder. [C19: prob. from MUDDLE]

mull[2] (mʌl) *vb* (*tr*) to heat (wine, ale, etc.) with sugar and spices. [C17: from ?]
▸ **mulled** *adj*

mull[3] (mʌl) *n* a light muslin fabric of soft texture. [C18: earlier *mulmull,* from Hindi *malmal*]

mull[4] (mʌl) *n Scot.* a promontory. [C14: rel. to Gaelic *maol,* Icelandic *múli*]

mullah *or* **mulla** (ˈmʌlə, ˈmʊlə) *n* (formerly) a Muslim scholar, teacher, or religious leader: also used as a title of respect. [C17: from Turkish *molla,* Persian & Hindi *mulla,* from Ar. *mawlā* master]

mullein (ˈmʌlɪn) *n* any of various Mediterranean herbaceous plants such as the common mullein or Aaron's rod, typically having tall spikes of yellow flowers and broad hairy leaves. [C15: from OF *moleine,* prob. from OF *mol* soft, from L *mollis*]

muller (ˈmʌlə) *n* a flat heavy implement of stone or iron used to grind material against a slab of stone, etc. [C15: prob. from *mullen* to grind to powder]

mullet (ˈmʌlɪt) *n* any of various teleost food fishes such as the grey mullet or red mullet. [C15: via OF from L *mullus,* from Gk *mullos*]

mulligatawny (ˌmʌlɪgəˈtɔ:nɪ) *n* a curry-flavoured soup of Anglo-Indian origin, made with meat stock. [C18: from Tamil *milakutanni,* from *milaku* pepper + *tanni* water]

mullion (ˈmʌlɪən) *n* **1** a vertical member between the casements or panes of a window. ◆ *vb* **2** (*tr*) to furnish (a window, screen, etc.) with mullions. [C16: var. of ME *munial,* from OF *moinel,* from ?]

mullock (ˈmʌlək) *n Austral.* **1** waste material from a mine. **2 poke mullock at.** *Inf.* to ridicule. [C14: rel. to OE *myl* dust, ON *mylja* to crush]

mulloway (ˈmʌləˌweɪ) *n* a large Australian marine food fish. [C19: from ?]

multangular (mʌlˈtæŋgjʊlə) *or* **multiangular** *adj* having many angles.

multi- *combining form.* **1** many or much: *multimillion.* **2** more than one: *multistorey.* [from L *multus* much, many]

multicultural (ˌmʌltɪˈkʌltʃərəl) *adj* consisting of, relating to, or designed for the cultures of several different races.
▸ **ˌmultiˈculturalˌism** *n*

multifactorial (ˌmʌltɪfækˈtɔ:rɪəl) *adj* having many separate factors, causes, components, etc.: *multifactorial disease; multifactorial inheritance.*

multifarious Ⓣ (ˌmʌltɪˈfɛərɪəs) *adj* having many parts of great variety. [C16: from LL *multifārius* manifold, from L *multifāriam* on many sides]
▸ **ˌmultiˈfariously** *adv* ▸ **ˌmultiˈfariousness** *n*

multiflora rose (ˌmʌltɪˈflɔ:rə) *n* an Asian climbing shrubby rose having clusters of small fragrant flowers.

multiform (ˈmʌltɪˌfɔ:m) *adj* having many forms.
▸ **ˌmultiˈformity** *n*

multigym (ˈmʌltɪˌdʒɪm) *n* an exercise apparatus incorporating a variety of weights, used for toning the muscles.

multilateral (ˌmʌltɪˈlætərəl, -ˈlætrəl) *adj* **1** of or involving more than two nations or parties: *a multilateral pact.* **2** having many sides.
▸ **ˌmultiˈlaterally** *adv*

multilingual (ˌmʌltɪˈlɪŋgwəl) *adj* **1** able to speak more than two languages. **2** written or expressed in more than two languages.

multimedia (ˌmʌltɪˈmi:dɪə) *adj* **1** of or relating to the combined use of such media as television, slides, etc. **2** *Computing.* of or relating to any of various systems that can manipulate data in a variety of forms, such as sound, graphics, or text.

multimillionaire (ˌmʌltɪˌmɪljəˈnɛə) *n* a person with a fortune of several million pounds, dollars, etc.

multinational (ˌmʌltɪˈnæʃənᵊl) *adj* **1** (of a large business company) operating in several countries. ◆ *n* **2** such a company.

multipack (ˈmʌltɪˌpæk) *n* a form of packaging of foodstuffs, etc., that contains several units and is offered at a price below that of the equivalent number of units.

multiparous (mʌlˈtɪpərəs) *adj* (of certain species of mammal) producing many offspring at one birth. [C17: from NL *multiparus*]

multipartite (ˌmʌltɪˈpɑ:taɪt) *adj* **1** divided into many parts or sections. **2** *Government.* a less common word for **multilateral.**

multiparty (ˌmʌltɪˈpɑ:tɪ) *adj* of or relating to a state, political system, etc., in which more than one political party is permitted: *multiparty democracy.*

multiple Ⓣ (ˈmʌltɪpᵊl) *adj* **1** having or involving more than one part, individual, etc. **2** *Electronics, US & Canad.* (of a circuit) having a number of conductors in parallel. ◆ *n* **3** the product of a given number or polynomial and any other one: *6 is a multiple of 2.* **4** short for **multiple store.** [C17: via F from LL *multiplus,* from L MULTIPLEX]
▸ **ˈmultiply** *adv*

multiple-choice *adj* having a number of possible given answers out of which the correct one must be chosen.

multiple personality *n Psychiatry.* a mental disorder in which an individual's personality appears to have become separated into two or more distinct personalities. Nontechnical name: **split personality.**

multiple sclerosis *n* a chronic progressive disease of the central nervous system, resulting in speech and visual disorders, tremor, muscular incoordination, partial paralysis, etc.

multiple store *n* one of several retail enterprises under the same ownership and management. Also called: **multiple shop.**

multiplex (ˈmʌltɪˌplɛks) *n* **1** *Telecomm.* **1a** the use of a common communications channel for sending two or more messages or signals. **1b** (*as modifier*): *a multiplex transmitter.* **2a** a purpose-built complex containing a number of cinemas and usually a restaurant or bar. **2b** (*as modifier*): *a multiplex cinema.* ◆ *adj* **3** a less common word for **multiple.** ◆ *vb* **4** to send (messages or signals) or (of messages and signals) to be sent by multiplex. [C16: from L: having many folds, from MULTI- + *plicāre* to fold]

multiplicand (ˌmʌltɪplɪˈkænd) *n* a number to be multiplied by another number, the **multiplier.** [C16: from L *multiplicandus,* gerund of *multiplicāre* to MULTIPLY]

multiplication (ˌmʌltɪplɪˈkeɪʃən) *n* **1** a mathematical operation, the inverse of division, in which the product of two or more numbers or quantities is calculated. Usually written $a \times b$, $a.b$, ab. **2** the act of multiplying or state of being multiplied. **3** the act or process in animals, plants, or people, of reproducing or breeding.

multiplication sign *n* the symbol ×, placed between numbers to be multiplied.

multiplication table *n* one of a group of tables giving the results of multiplying two numbers together.

multiplicity Ⓣ (ˌmʌltɪˈplɪsɪtɪ) *n, pl* **multiplicities. 1** a large number or great variety. **2** the state of being multiple.

multiplier (ˈmʌltɪˌplaɪə) *n* **1** a person or thing that multiplies. **2** the number by which another number, the **multiplicand,** is multiplied. **3** *Physics.* any instrument, such as a photomultiplier, for increasing an effect. **4** *Econ.* the ratio of the total change in income (resulting from successive rounds of spending) to an initial autonomous change in expenditure.

multiply Ⓣ (ˈmʌltɪˌplaɪ) *vb* **multiplies, multiplying, multiplied. 1** to increase or cause to increase in number, quantity, or degree. **2** (*tr*) to combine (two numbers or quantities) by multiplication. **3** (*intr*) to increase in number by reproduction. [C13: from OF *multiplier,* from L *multiplicāre* to multiply, from *multus* much, many + *plicāre* to fold]
▸ **ˈmultiˌpliable** *or* **multiplicable** (ˈmʌltɪˌplɪkəbᵊl) *adj*

multiprocessor (ˌmʌltɪˈprəʊsɛsə) *n Computing.* a number of central processing units linked together to enable parallel processing to take place.

multipurpose vehicle *n* a large car, similar to a van, designed to carry up to eight passengers. Abbrev.: **MPV.**

multiskilling (ˈmʌltɪˌskɪlɪŋ) *n* the practice of training employees to do a number of different tasks.

multistage (ˈmʌltɪˌsteɪdʒ) *adj* **1** (of a rocket or missile) having several stages, each of which can be jettisoned after it has burnt out. **2** (of a turbine, compressor, or supercharger) having more than one rotor. **3** (of any process or device) having more than one stage.

multistorey (ˌmʌltɪˈstɔ:rɪ) *adj* **1** (of a building) having many storeys. ◆ *n* **2** a multistorey car park.

multitrack (ˈmʌltɪˌtræk) *adj* (in sound recording) using tape containing two or more tracks, usually four to twenty-four.

multitude Ⓣ (ˈmʌltɪˌtju:d) *n* **1** a large gathering of people. **2 the.** the common people. **3** a large number. **4** the state or quality of being numerous. [C14: via OF from L *multitūdō*]

THESAURUS

mulish *adj* = **stubborn,** bull-headed, cross-grained, difficult, headstrong, inflexible, intractable, intransigent, obstinate, perverse, pig-headed, recalcitrant, refractory, rigid, self-willed, stiff-necked, unreasonable, wilful

mull[1] *vb* = **ponder,** consider, contemplate, deliberate, examine, meditate, muse on, reflect on, review, ruminate, study, think about, think over, turn over in one's mind, weigh

multifarious *adj* = **diverse,** different, diversified, legion, manifold, many, miscellaneous, multiform, multiple, multitudinous, numerous, sundry, varied, variegated

multiple *adj* **1** = **many,** collective, manifold, multitudinous, numerous, several, sundry, various

multiplicity *n* **1** = **number,** abundance, array, diversity, heaps (*inf.*), host, loads (*inf.*), lot, lots (*inf.*), mass, myriad, oodles (*inf.*), piles (*inf.*), profusion, scores, stacks, tons, variety

multiply *vb* **1** = **increase,** accumulate, augment, build up, expand, extend, proliferate, spread **3** = **reproduce,** breed, propagate
Antonyms *vb* ≠ **increase:** abate, decline, decrease, diminish, lessen, reduce

multitude *n* **1, 3** = **mass,** army, assemblage, assembly, collection, concourse, congregation,

multitudinous ➊ (ˌmʌltɪˈtjuːdɪnəs) *adj* **1** very numerous. **2** *Rare.* great in extent, variety, etc. **3** *Poetic.* crowded.
▸ˌ**multiˈtudinously** *adv* ▸ˌ**multiˈtudinousness** *n*

multi-user *adj* (of a computer) capable of being used by several people at once.

multivalent (ˌmʌltɪˈveɪlənt) *adj* another word for **polyvalent**.
▸ˌ**multiˈvalency** *n*

mum[1] (mʌm) *n Chiefly Brit.* an informal word for **mother**. [C19: a child's word]

mum[2] ➊ (mʌm) *adj* **1** keeping information, etc., to oneself; silent. ◆ *n* **2 mum's the word.** (*interj*) silence or secrecy is to be observed. [C14: suggestive of closed lips]

mum[3] (mʌm) *vb* **mums, mumming, mummed.** (*intr*) to act in a mummer's play. [C16: verbal use of MUM[2]]

mumble (ˈmʌmbᵊl) *vb* **mumbles, mumbling, mumbled. 1** to utter indistinctly, as with the mouth partly closed. **2** *Rare.* to chew (food) ineffectually. ◆ *n* **3** an indistinct or low utterance or sound. [C14 *momelen*, from MUM[2]]
▸ˈ**mumbler** *n* ▸ˈ**mumbling** *adj* ▸ˈ**mumblingly** *adv*

mumbo jumbo ➊ (ˈmʌmbəʊ) *n, pl* **mumbo jumbos. 1** foolish religious reverence, ritual, or incantation. **2** meaningless or unnecessarily complicated language. **3** an object of superstitious awe or reverence. [C18: prob. from W African *mama dyumbo*, name of a tribal god]

mu meson (mjuː) *n* a former name for **muon**.

mummer (ˈmʌmə) *n* **1** one of a group of masked performers in a folk play or mime. **2** *Humorous or derog.* an actor. [C15: from OF *momeur*, from *momer* to mime]

Mummerset (ˈmʌməsɪt, -ˌsɛt) *n* an imitation West Country accent used in drama. [C20: from *mummer* + (*Somer*)*set*, county in SW England]

mummery (ˈmʌmərɪ) *n, pl* **mummeries. 1** a performance by mummers. **2** hypocritical or ostentatious ceremony.

mummify (ˈmʌmɪˌfaɪ) *vb* **mummifies, mummifying, mummified. 1** (*tr*) to preserve (a body) as a mummy. **2** (*intr*) to dry up; shrivel.
▸ˌ**mummifiˈcation** *n*

mummy[1] (ˈmʌmɪ) *n, pl* **mummies. 1** an embalmed or preserved body, esp. as prepared for burial in ancient Egypt. **2** a mass of pulp. **3** a dark brown pigment. [C14: from OF *momie*, from Med. L, from Ar.: asphalt, from Persian *mūm* wax]

mummy[2] (ˈmʌmɪ) *n, pl* **mummies.** *Chiefly Brit.* a child's word for **mother**[1] (senses 1–3). [C19: var. of MUM[1]]

mumps (mʌmps) *n* (*functioning as sing or pl*) **1** an acute contagious viral disease of the parotid salivary glands, characterized by swelling of the affected parts, fever, and pain beneath the ear. **2** sulks. [C16: from *mump* to grimace]
▸ˈ**mumpish** *adj*

mumsy ➊ (ˈmʌmzɪ) *adj* **mumsier, mumsiest.** homely or drab.
▸ˈ**mumsiness** *n*

mun. *abbrev. for* municipal.

munch ➊ (mʌntʃ) *vb* to chew (food) steadily, esp. with a crunching noise. [C14 *monche*, imit.]

mundane ➊ (mʌnˈdeɪn, ˈmʌndeɪn) *adj* **1** everyday, ordinary, or banal. **2** relating to the world or worldly matters. [C15: from F *mondain*, via LL, from L *mundus* world]
▸**munˈdanely** *adv* ▸**munˈdaneness** *n*

mung bean (mʌŋ) *n* **1** an E Asian bean plant grown for forage and as the source of bean sprouts for cookery. **2** the seed of this plant. [C20: from *mung*, changed from *mungo*, from Tamil *mūngu*, from Sansk. *mudga*]

municipal ➊ (mjuːˈnɪsɪpᵊl) *adj* of or relating to a town, city, or borough or its local government. [C16: from L *mūnicipium* a free town, from *mūniceps* citizen, from *mūnia* responsibilities + *capere* to take]
▸**muˈnicipally** *adv*

municipality ➊ (mjuːˌnɪsɪˈpælɪtɪ) *n, pl* **municipalities. 1** a city, town, or district enjoying local self-government. **2** the governing body of such a unit.

municipalize *or* **municipalise** (mjuːˈnɪsɪpəˌlaɪz) *vb* **municipalizes, municipalizing, municipalized** *or* **municipalises, municipalising, municipalised.** (*tr*) **1** to bring under municipal ownership or control. **2** to make a municipality of.
▸**muˌnicipaliˈzation** *or* **muˌnicipaliˈsation** *n*

munificent ➊ (mjuːˈnɪfɪsənt) *adj* **1** (of a person) generous; bountiful. **2** (of a gift) liberal. [C16: back formation from L *mūnificentia* liberality, from *mūnificus*, from *mūnus* gift + *facere* to make]
▸**muˈnificence** *n* ▸**muˈnificently** *adv*

muniments (ˈmjuːnɪmənts) *pl n Law.* the title deeds and other documentary evidence relating to the title to land. [C15: via OF from L *munire* to defend]

munition (mjuːˈnɪʃən) *vb* (*tr*) to supply with munitions. [C16: via F from L *mūnītiō* fortification, from *mūnīre* to fortify]

munitions (mjuːˈnɪʃənz) *pl n* (*sometimes sing*) military equipment and stores, esp. ammunition.

Munro (mʌnˈrəʊ) *n, pl* **Munros.** *Mountaineering.* any separate mountain peak over 3000 feet high: originally used of Scotland only but now sometimes extended to other parts of the British Isles. [C20: after Hugh Thomas *Munro* (1856–1919), who listed these in 1891]

muntjac *or* **muntjak** (ˈmʌntˌdʒæk) *n* any small Asian deer typically having a chestnut-brown coat and small antlers. [C18: prob. from Javanese *mindjangan* deer]

muon (ˈmjuːɒn) *n* a positive or negative elementary particle with a mass 207 times that of an electron. It was originally called the **mu meson.** [C20: short for MU MESON]
▸**muˈonic** *adj*

mural (ˈmjʊərəl) *n* **1** a large painting on a wall. ◆ *adj* **2** of or relating to a wall. [C15: from L *mūrālis*, from *mūrus* wall]
▸ˈ**muralist** *n*

murder ➊ (ˈmɜːdə) *n* **1** the unlawful premeditated killing of one human being by another. Cf. **manslaughter. 2** *Inf.* something dangerous, difficult, or unpleasant: *driving around London is murder.* **3 cry blue murder.** *Inf.* to make an outcry. **4 get away with murder.** *Inf.* to escape censure; do as one pleases. ◆ *vb* (*mainly tr*) **5** (*also intr*) to kill (someone) unlawfully with premeditation or during the commission of a crime. **6** to kill brutally. **7** *Inf.* to destroy; ruin. **8** *Inf.* to defeat completely; beat decisively: *the home team murdered their opponents.* [OE *morthor*]
▸ˈ**murderer** *n* ▸ˈ**murderess** *fem n*

murderous ➊ (ˈmɜːdərəs) *adj* **1** intending, capable of, or guilty of murder. **2** *Inf.* very dangerous or difficult: *a murderous road.*
▸ˈ**murderously** *adv* ▸ˈ**murderousness** *n*

murex (ˈmjʊərɛks) *n, pl* **murices** (ˈmjʊərɪˌsiːz). any of a genus of spiny-shelled marine gastropods: formerly used as a source of the dye Tyrian purple. [C16: from L *mūrex* purple fish]

muriatic acid (ˌmjʊərɪˈætɪk) *n* a former name for **hydrochloric acid.** [C17: from L *muriāticus* pickled, from *muria* brine]

murk *or* **mirk** (mɜːk) *n* **1** gloomy darkness. ◆ *adj* **2** an archaic variant of **murky.** [C13: prob. from ON *myrkr* darkness]

murky ➊ *or* **mirky** (ˈmɜːkɪ) *adj* **murkier, murkiest** *or* **mirkier, mirkiest. 1** gloomy or dark. **2** cloudy or impenetrable, as with smoke or fog. **3** *Inf.* obscure and suspicious; shady: *she had a murky past.*
▸ˈ**murkily** *or* ˈ**mirkily** *adv* ▸ˈ**murkiness** *or* ˈ**mirkiness** *n*

THESAURUS

crowd, great number, horde, host, legion, lot, lots (*inf.*), mob, myriad, sea, swarm, throng **2 the multitude** = **public**, commonalty, common people, herd, hoi polloi, mob, populace, proletariat, rabble

multitudinous *adj* **1** = **numerous**, abounding, abundant, considerable, copious, countless, great, infinite, innumerable, legion, manifold, many, myriad, profuse, teeming, very numerous

mum[2] *adj* **1** = **silent**, closemouthed, dumb, mute, quiet, secretive, tight-lipped, uncommunicative, unforthcoming ◆ *n* **2 mum's the word** = **keep silent**, don't let on, don't tell a soul, keep quiet, keep (something) secret, keep (something) to oneself, keep (something) under one's hat, play dumb, say nothing, tell no-one

mumbo jumbo *n* **1** = **superstition**, abracadabra, chant, charm, conjuration, hocus-pocus, incantation, magic, rite, ritual, spell **2** = **gibberish**, cant, claptrap (*inf.*), double talk, gobbledegook (*inf.*), Greek (*inf.*), humbug, jargon, nonsense, rigmarole

mumsy *adj* = **homely**, dowdy, drab, fogeyish, frumpy *or* frumpish, old-fashioned, plain, square (*inf.*), unfashionable, unglamorous, unsophisticated
Antonyms *adj* attractive, beautiful, chic, elegant, fashionable, glamorous, modern, modish, smart, sophisticated, well-dressed

munch *vb* = **chew**, champ, chomp, crunch, masticate, scrunch

mundane *adj* **1** = **ordinary**, banal, commonplace, day-to-day, everyday, humdrum, prosaic, routine, vanilla (*sl.*), workaday **2** = **earthly**, fleshly, human, material, mortal, secular, sublunary, temporal, terrestrial, worldly
Antonyms *adj* ≠ **ordinary**: dramatic, exciting, extraordinary, ground-breaking, imaginative, interesting, left-field (*inf.*), novel, original, special, uncommon, unusual ≠ **earthly**: ethereal, heavenly, spiritual, unworldly

municipal *adj* = **civic**, borough, city, community, public, town, urban

municipality *n* **1** = **town**, borough, burgh (*Scot.*), city, district, township, urban community

munificence *n* **1, 2** = **generosity**, beneficence, benevolence, big-heartedness, bounteousness, bounty, generousness, largesse *or* largess, liberality, magnanimousness, open-handedness, philanthropy

munificent *adj* **1, 2** = **generous**, beneficent, benevolent, big-hearted, bounteous, bountiful, free-handed, lavish, liberal, magnanimous, open-handed, philanthropic, princely, rich, unstinting
Antonyms *adj* cheap, mean, miserly, parsimonious, small, stingy

murder *n* **1** = **killing**, assassination, bloodshed, butchery, carnage, homicide, manslaughter, massacre, slaying **2** *Informal* = **agony**, an ordeal, a trial, danger, difficulty, hell (*inf.*), misery, trouble ◆ *vb* **5, 6** = **kill**, assassinate, blow away (*sl., chiefly US*), bump off (*sl.*), butcher, destroy, dispatch, do in (*inf.*), do to death, eliminate (*sl.*), hit (*sl.*), massacre, rub out (*US sl.*), slaughter, slay, take out (*sl.*), take the life of, waste (*inf.*) **7** *Informal* = **ruin**, abuse, destroy, mangle, mar, misuse, spoil **8** *Informal* = **beat decisively**, blow out of the water (*sl.*), cream (*sl., chiefly US*), defeat utterly, drub, hammer (*inf.*), lick (*inf.*), make mincemeat of (*inf.*), slaughter, stuff (*sl.*), tank (*sl.*), thrash, wipe the floor with (*inf.*)

murderer *n* **1** = **killer**, assassin, butcher, cut-throat, hit man (*sl.*), homicide, slaughterer, slayer

murderous *adj* **1** = **deadly**, barbarous, bloodthirsty, bloody, brutal, cruel, cut-throat, death-dealing, destructive, devastating, fatal, fell (*arch.*), ferocious, internecine, lethal, sanguinary, savage, slaughterous, withering **2** *Informal* = **unpleasant**, arduous, dangerous, difficult, exhausting, harrowing, hellish (*inf.*), killing (*inf.*), sapping, strenuous

murky *adj* **1, 2** = **dark**, cheerless, cloudy, dim,

murmur ❶ ('mɜ:mə) *n* **1** a continuous low indistinct sound, as of distant voices. **2** an indistinct utterance: *a murmur of satisfaction.* **3** a complaint; grumble: *he made no murmur at my suggestion.* **4** *Med.* any abnormal soft blowing sound heard usually over the chest (**heart murmur**). ◆ *vb* **murmurs, murmuring, murmured. 5** to utter (something) in a murmur. **6** (*intr*) to complain. [C14: as n, from L *murmur;* vb. via OF *murmurer* from L *murmurāre* to rumble]
▸**'murmurer** *n* ▸**'murmuring** *n, adj* ▸**'murmuringly** *adv* ▸**'murmurous** *adj*

murphy ('mɜ:fɪ) *n, pl* **murphies.** a dialect or informal word for **potato.** [C19: from the common Irish surname *Murphy*]

murrain ('mʌrɪn) *n* **1** any plaguelike disease in cattle. **2** *Arch.* a plague. [C14: from OF *morine,* from *morir* to die, from L *morī*]

Murray cod *n* ('mʌrɪ) a large greenish Australian freshwater food fish. [after *Murray* River in SE Australia]

murther ('mɜ:ðə) *n, vb* an archaic word for **murder.**
▸**'murtherer** *n*

mus. *abbrev. for:* **1** museum. **2** music. **3** musical.

MusB *or* **MusBac** *abbrev. for* Bachelor of Music.

muscadine ('mʌskədɪn, -ˌdaɪn) *n* **1** a woody climbing plant of the southeastern US. **2** the musk-scented purple grape produced by this plant: used to make wine. [C16: from MUSCATEL]

muscae volitantes ('mʌsi: vɒlɪ'tænti:z) *pl n Pathol.* moving black specks or threads seen before the eyes, caused by opaque fragments floating in the vitreous humour or a defect in the lens. [C18: NL: flying flies]

muscat ('mʌskət, -kæt) *n* **1** any of various grapevines that produce sweet white grapes used for making wine or raisins. **2** another name for **muscatel** (sense 1). [C16: via OF from Provençal, from *musc* MUSK]

muscatel (ˌmʌskə'tɛl) *or* **muscadel** *n* **1** Also called: **muscat.** a rich sweet wine made from muscat grapes. **2** the grape or raisin from a muscat vine. [C14: from OF *muscadel,* from OProvençal, from *moscadel,* from *muscat* musky]

muscle ❶ ('mʌsᵊl) *n* **1** a tissue composed of bundles of elongated cells capable of contraction and relaxation to produce movement in an organ or part. **2** an organ composed of muscle tissue. **3** strength or force. ◆ *vb* **muscles, muscling, muscled. 4** (*intr;* often foll. by *in, on,* etc.) *Inf.* to force one's way (in). [C16: from Medical L *musculus* little mouse, from the imagined resemblance of some muscles to mice]
▸**'muscly** *adj*

muscle-bound *adj* **1** having overdeveloped and inelastic muscles. **2** lacking flexibility.

muscleman ('mʌsᵊlˌmæn) *n, pl* **musclemen. 1** a man with highly developed muscles. **2** a henchman employed by a gangster to intimidate or use violence upon victims.

Muscovite ('mʌskəˌvaɪt) *n* **1** a native or inhabitant of Moscow. ◆ *adj* **2** an archaic word for **Russian.**

Muscovy duck ('mʌskəvɪ) *or* **musk duck** *n* a large crested widely domesticated South American duck, having a greenish-black plumage with white markings and a large red caruncle on the bill. [C17: orig. *musk duck,* a name later mistakenly associated with *Muscovy,* an arch. name for Russia]

muscular ❶ ('mʌskjʊlə) *adj* **1** having well-developed muscles; brawny. **2** of, relating to, or consisting of muscle. [C17: from NL *muscularis,* from *musculus* MUSCLE]
▸**muscularity** (ˌmʌskjʊ'lærɪtɪ) *n* ▸**'muscularly** *adv*

muscular dystrophy *n* a genetic disease characterized by progressive deterioration and wasting of muscle fibres.

musculature ('mʌskjʊlətʃə) *n* **1** the arrangement of muscles in an organ or part. **2** the total muscular system of an organism.

MusD *or* **MusDoc** *abbrev. for* Doctor of Music.

muse[1] ❶ (mju:z) *vb* **muses, musing, mused. 1** (when *intr,* often foll. by *on* or *about*) to reflect (about) or ponder (on), usually in silence. **2** (*intr*) to gaze thoughtfully. ◆ *n* **3** a state of abstraction. [C14: from OF *muser,* ?from *mus* snout, from Med. L *mūsus*]

muse[2] (mju:z) *n* (often preceded by *the*) a goddess that inspires a creative artist, esp. a poet. [C14: from OF, from L *Mūsa,* from Gk *Mousa* a Muse]

Muse (mju:z) *n Greek myth.* any of nine sister goddesses, each of whom was regarded as the protectress of a different art or science.

musette (mju:'zɛt) *n* **1** a type of bagpipe popular in France during the 17th and 18th centuries. **2** a dance, originally accompanied by a musette. [C14: from OF, dim. of *muse* bagpipe]

museum (mju:'zɪəm) *n* a building where objects of historical, artistic, or scientific interest are exhibited and preserved. [C17: via L from Gk *Mouseion* home of the Muses, from *Mousa* MUSE]

museum piece *n* **1** an object of sufficient age or interest to be kept in a museum. **2** *Inf.* a person or thing regarded as antiquated.

mush[1] ❶ (mʌʃ) *n* **1** a soft pulpy mass or consistency. **2** *US.* a thick porridge made from corn meal. **3** *Inf.* cloying sentimentality. [C17: from obs. *moose* porridge; prob. rel. to MASH]

mush[2] (mʌʃ) *Canad.* ◆ *interj* **1** an order to dogs in a sled team to start up or go faster. ◆ *vb* **2** to travel by or drive a dogsled. ◆ *n* **3** a journey with a dogsled. [C19: ?from imperative of F *marcher* to advance]

mushroom ❶ ('mʌʃru:m, -rʊm) *n* **1a** the fleshy spore-producing body of any of various fungi, typically consisting of a cap at the end of a stem. Some species, such as the field mushroom, are edible. Cf. **toadstool. 1b** (*as modifier*): *mushroom soup.* **2a** something resembling a mushroom in shape or rapid growth. **2b** (*as modifier*): *mushroom expansion.* ◆ *vb* (*intr*) **3** to grow rapidly: *demand mushroomed overnight.* **4** to assume a mushroom-like shape. [C15: from OF *mousseron,* from LL *mussiriō,* from ?]

mushroom cloud *n* the large mushroom-shaped cloud produced by a nuclear explosion.

mushy ❶ ('mʌʃɪ) *adj* **mushier, mushiest. 1** soft and pulpy. **2** *Inf.* excessively sentimental or emotional.
▸**'mushily** *adv* ▸**'mushiness** *n*

music ('mju:zɪk) *n* **1** an art form consisting of sequences of sounds in time, esp. tones of definite pitch organized melodically, harmonically and rhythmically. **2** the sounds so produced, esp. by singing or musical instruments. **3** written or printed music, such as a score or set of parts. **4** any sequence of sounds perceived as pleasing or harmonious. **5 face the music.** *Inf.* to confront the consequences of one's actions. [C13: via OF from L *mūsica,* from Gk *mousikē* (*tekhnē*) (art) belonging to the Muses, from *Mousa* MUSE]

musical ❶ ('mju:zɪkᵊl) *adj* **1** of, relating to, or used in music. **2** harmonious; melodious: *musical laughter.* **3** talented in or fond of music. **4** involving or set to music. ◆ *n* **5** Also called: **musical comedy.** a light romantic play or film having dialogue interspersed with songs and dances.
▸ˌ**musi'cality** *n* ▸**'musically** *adv*

musical box *or* **music box** *n* a mechanical instrument that plays tunes by means of pins on a revolving cylinder striking the tuned teeth of a comblike metal plate, contained in a box.

musical chairs *n* (*functioning as sing*) **1** a party game in which players walk around chairs while music is played, there being one more player than chairs. Whenever the music stops, the player who fails to find a chair is eliminated. **2** any situation involving several people in a series of interrelated changes.

music centre *n* a single hi-fi unit containing a turntable, amplifier, radio, cassette player, and compact disc player.

music drama *n* **1** an opera in which the musical and dramatic elements are of equal importance and strongly interfused. **2** the genre of such operas. [C19: from G *Musikdrama,* coined by Wagner to describe his later operas]

music hall *n Chiefly Brit.* **1** a variety entertainment consisting of songs, comic turns, etc. US and Canad. name: **vaudeville. 2** a theatre at which such entertainments are staged.

musician (mju:'zɪʃən) *n* a person who plays or composes music, esp. as a profession.
▸**mu'sicianly** *adj* ▸**mu'sicianship** *n*

musicology (ˌmju:zɪ'kɒlədʒɪ) *n* the scholarly study of music.
▸**musicological** (ˌmju:zɪkə'lɒdʒɪkᵊl) *adj* ▸ˌ**musi'cologist** *n*

music paper *n* paper ruled or printed with a stave for writing music.

musique concrète *French.* (myzik kɔ̃krɛt) *n* another term for **concrete music.**

musk (mʌsk) *n* **1** a strong-smelling glandular secretion of the male musk deer, used in perfumery. **2** a similar substance produced by certain other animals, such as the civet and otter, or manufactured synthetically. **3** a North American plant which has yellow flowers and was formerly cultivated for its musky scent. **4** the smell of musk or a similar heady smell. **5** (*modifier*) containing or resembling musk: *musk oil.* [C14: from LL *muscus,* from Gk, from Persian, prob. from Sansk. *mushká* scrotum (from the appearance of the musk deer's musk bag), dim. of *mūsh* MOUSE]

THESAURUS

dismal, dreary, dull, dusky, foggy, gloomy, grey, impenetrable, misty, nebulous, obscure, overcast
Antonyms *adj* bright, cheerful, clear, distinct, sunny

murmur *n* **1, 2** = **drone**, babble, buzzing, humming, mumble, muttering, purr, rumble, susurrus (*literary*), undertone, whisper, whispering **3** = **complaint**, beef (*sl.*), gripe (*inf.*), grouse, grumble, moan (*inf.*), word ◆ *vb* **5** = **mumble**, babble, buzz, drone, hum, mutter, purr, rumble, speak in an undertone, whisper **6** = **grumble**, beef (*sl.*), carp, cavil, complain, gripe (*inf.*), grouse, moan (*inf.*)

muscle *n* **1** = **tendon**, muscle tissue, sinew, thew **3** = **strength**, brawn, clout (*inf.*), force, forcefulness, might, potency, power, stamina, sturdiness, weight ◆ *vb* **4** *often foll. by* **in** *Informal* = **impose oneself**, butt in, elbow one's way in, force one's way in

muscular *adj* **1** = **strong**, athletic, beefy (*inf.*), brawny, husky (*inf.*), lusty, powerful, powerfully built, robust, sinewy, stalwart, strapping, sturdy, thickset, vigorous, well-knit

muse[1] *vb* **1** = **ponder**, be in a brown study, be lost in thought, brood, cogitate, consider, contemplate, deliberate, dream, meditate, mull over, reflect, ruminate, speculate, think, think over, weigh

mush[1] *n* **1** = **pulp**, dough, mash, pap, paste **3** *Informal* = **sentimentality**, corn (*inf.*), mawkishness, schmaltz (*sl.*), slush (*inf.*)

mushroom *vb* **3** = **expand**, boom, burgeon, flourish, grow rapidly, increase, luxuriate, proliferate, shoot up, spread, spring up, sprout

mushy *adj* **1** = **soft**, doughy, pappy, paste-like, pulpy, semi-liquid, semi-solid, slushy, squashy, squelchy, squidgy (*inf.*) **2** *Informal* = **sentimental**, corny (*sl.*), maudlin, mawkish, saccharine, schmaltzy (*sl.*), sloppy (*inf.*), slushy (*inf.*), sugary, syrupy, three-hankie (*inf.*), weepy, wet (*Brit. inf.*)

musical *adj* **1, 2** = **melodious**, dulcet, euphonic, euphonious, harmonious, lilting, lyrical, melodic, sweet-sounding, tuneful
Antonyms *adj* discordant, grating, harsh, unmelodious, unmusical

musing *n* **1** = **thinking**, absent-mindedness, abstraction, brown study, cerebration, cogitation, contemplation, day-dreaming, dreaming, in-

musk deer *n* a small central Asian mountain deer. The male secretes musk.
musk duck *n* **1** another name for **Muscovy duck. 2** a duck inhabiting swamps, lakes, and streams in Australia. The male emits a musky odour.
muskeg ('mʌsˌkɛg) *n Chiefly Canad.* **1** undrained boggy land. **2** a bog or swamp of this nature. [C19: of Amerind origin: grassy swamp]
muskellunge ('mʌskəˌlʌndʒ) *or* **maskinonge** ('mæskɪˌnɒndʒ) *n, pl* **muskellunges** *or* **muskellunge, maskinonges** *or* **maskinonge.** a large North American freshwater game fish, related to the pike. Often shortened (informally) to **musky** or **muskie.** [C18 *maskinunga,* of Amerind origin]
musket ('mʌskɪt) *n* a long-barrelled muzzle-loading shoulder gun used between the 16th and 18th centuries by infantry soldiers. [C16: from F *mousquet,* from It. *moschetto* arrow, earlier: sparrow hawk, from *moscha* a fly, from L *musca*]
musketeer (ˌmʌskɪ'tɪə) *n* (formerly) a soldier armed with a musket.
musketry ('mʌskɪtrɪ) *n* **1** muskets or musketeers collectively. **2** the technique of using small arms.
muskmelon ('mʌskˌmɛlən) *n* **1** any of several varieties of the melon, such as the cantaloupe and honeydew. **2** the fruit of any of these melons, having ribbed or warty rind and sweet yellow, white, orange, or green flesh with a musky aroma.
musk ox *n* a large bovid mammal, which has a dark shaggy coat, short legs, and widely spaced downward-curving horns, and emits a musky smell: now confined to the tundras of Canada and Greenland.
muskrat ('mʌskˌræt) *n, pl* **muskrats** *or* **muskrat. 1** a North American beaver-like amphibious rodent, closely related to but larger than the voles. **2** the brown fur of this animal. ◆ Also called: **musquash.**
musk rose *n* a Mediterranean rose, cultivated for its white musk-scented flowers.
musky ('mʌskɪ) *adj* **muskier, muskiest.** resembling the smell of musk; having a heady or pungent sweet aroma.
▸**'muskiness** *n*
Muslim ('mʊzlɪm, 'mʌz-) *or* **Moslem** *n, pl* **Muslims** *or* **Muslim, Moslems** *or* **Moslem. 1** a follower of the religion of Islam. ◆ *adj* **2** of or relating to Islam, its doctrines, culture, etc. ◆ Also (but not in Muslim use): **Mohammedan, Muhammadan.** [C17: from Ar., lit.: one who surrenders]
▸**'Muslimism** *or* **'Moslemism** *n*
muslin ('mʌzlɪn) *n* a fine plain-weave cotton fabric. [C17: from F *mousseline,* from It., from Ar. *mawṣilīy* of Mosul (Iraq), where it was first produced]
muso ('mjuːzəʊ) *n, pl* **musos.** *Sl.* **1** *Brit. derog.* a musician, esp. a pop musician, regarded as being overconcerned with technique rather than musical content or expression. **2** *Austral.* any musician, esp. a professional one.
musquash ('mʌskwɒʃ) *n* another name for **muskrat,** esp. the fur. [C17: of Amerind origin]
muss (mʌs) *US & Canad. inf.* ◆ *vb* **1** (*tr;* often foll. by *up*) to make untidy; rumple. ◆ *n* **2** a state of disorder; muddle. [C19: prob. a blend of MESS + FUSS]
▸**'mussy** *adj*
mussel ('mʌsᵊl) *n* **1** any of various marine bivalves, esp. the edible mussel, having a dark slightly elongated shell and living attached to rocks, etc. **2** any of various freshwater bivalves, attached to rocks, sand, etc., having a flattened oval shell (a source of mother-of-pearl). [OE *muscle,* from Vulgar L *muscula* (unattested), from L *musculus,* dim. of *mūs* mouse]
Mussulman ('mʌsᵊlmən) *n pl* **Mussulmans.** an archaic word for **Muslim.** [C16: from Persian *Musulmān* (pl) from Ar. *Muslimūn,* pl. of MUSLIM]
must[1] ⓣ (mʌst; *unstressed* məst, məs) *vb* (takes an infinitive without *to* or an implied infinitive) used as an auxiliary: **1** to express obligation or compulsion: *you must pay your dues.* In this sense, *must* does not form a negative. If used with a negative infinitive it indicates obligatory prohibition. **2** to indicate necessity: *I must go to the bank tomorrow.* **3** to indicate the probable correctness of a statement: *he must be there by now.* **4** to indicate inevitability: *all good things must come to an end.* **5** to express resolution: **5a** on the part of the speaker: *I must finish this.* **5b** on the part of another or others: *let him get drunk if he must.* **6** (used emphatically) to express conviction or certainty on the part of the speaker: *you must be joking.* **7** (foll. by *away*) used with an implied verb of motion to express compelling haste: *I must away.* ◆ *n* **8** an essential or necessary thing: *strong shoes are a must for hill walking.* [OE *mōste,* p.t. of *mōtan* to be allowed, be obliged to]
must[2] (mʌst) *n* the pressed juice of grapes or other fruit ready for fermentation. [OE, from L *mustum* new wine, from *mustus* newborn]
must[3] ⓣ (mʌst) *n* mustiness or mould. [C17: back formation from MUSTY]
mustache (mə'stɑːʃ) *n* the US spelling of **moustache.**
▸**mus'tached** *adj*
mustachio (mə'stɑːʃɪˌəʊ) *n, pl* **mustachios.** (*often pl*) *Often humorous.* a moustache, esp. when bushy or elaborately shaped. [C16: from Sp. *mostacho* & It. *mostaccio*]
▸**mus'tachioed** *adj*
mustang ('mʌstæŋ) *n* a small breed of horse, often wild or half wild, found in the southwestern US. [C19: from Mexican Sp. *mestengo,* from *mesta* a group of stray animals]
mustard ('mʌstəd) *n* **1** any of several Eurasian plants, esp. black mustard and white mustard, having yellow flowers and slender pods: cultivated for their pungent seeds. **2** a paste made from the powdered seeds of any of these plants and used as a condiment. **3a** a brownish-yellow colour. **3b** (*as adj*): *a mustard carpet.* **4** *Sl., chiefly US.* zest or enthusiasm. [C13: from OF *moustarde,* from L *mustum* MUST[2], since the original was made by adding must]
mustard and cress *n* seedlings of white mustard and garden cress, used in salads, etc.
mustard gas *n* an oily liquid vesicant compound used in chemical warfare. Its vapour causes blindness and burns.
mustard plaster *n Med.* a mixture of powdered black mustard seeds applied to the skin for its counterirritant effects.
musteline ('mʌstɪˌlaɪn, -lɪn) *adj* of or belonging to a family of typically predatory mammals, including weasels, ferrets, badgers, skunks, and otters. [C17: from L *mustēlīnus,* from *mustēla* weasel]
muster ⓣ ('mʌstə) *vb* **1** to call together (numbers of men) for duty, inspection, etc., or (of men) to assemble in this way. **2 muster in** *or* **out.** *US.* to enlist into or discharge from military service. **3** (*tr;* sometimes foll. by *up*) to summon or gather: *to muster one's arguments; to muster up courage.* **4** (*tr*) *Austral. & NZ.* to round up (stock). ◆ *n* **5** an assembly of military personnel for duty, etc. **6** a collection, assembly, or gathering. **7** *Austral. & NZ.* the act of rounding up stock. **8 pass muster.** to be acceptable. [C14: from OF *moustrer,* from L *monstrāre* to show, from *monstrum* portent]
musth *or* **must** (mʌst) *n* (often preceded by *in*) a state of frenzied sexual excitement in the males of certain large mammals, esp. elephants. [C19: from Urdu *mast,* from Persian: drunk]
musty ⓣ ('mʌstɪ) *adj* **mustier, mustiest. 1** smelling or tasting old, stale, or mouldy. **2** old-fashioned, dull, or hackneyed: *musty ideas.* [C16: ? var. of obs. *moisty*]
▸**'mustily** *adv* ▸**'mustiness** *n*
mutable ⓣ ('mjuːtəbᵊl) *adj* able to or tending to change. [C14: from L *mūtābilis* fickle, from *mūtāre* to change]
▸**ˌmuta'bility** *or* (*less commonly*) **'mutableness** *n* ▸**'mutably** *adv*
mutagen ('mjuːtədʒən) *n* a substance that can induce genetic mutation. [C20: from MUTATION + -GEN]
▸**mutagenic** (ˌmjuːtə'dʒɛnɪk) *adj*
mutagenesis (ˌmjuːtə'dʒɛnɪsɪs) *n Genetics.* the origin and development of a mutation. [C20: from MUTA(TION) + -GENESIS]
mutant ('mjuːtᵊnt) *n* **1** Also called: **mutation.** an animal, organism, or gene that has undergone mutation. ◆ *adj* **2** of, undergoing, or resulting from mutation. [C20: from L *mutāre* to change]
mutate (mjuː'teɪt) *vb* **mutates, mutating, mutated.** to undergo or cause to undergo mutation. [C19: from L *mūtātus,* p.p. of *mūtāre* to change]
mutation ⓣ (mjuː'teɪʃən) *n* **1** the act or process of mutating; change; alteration. **2** a change or alteration. **3** a change in the chromosomes or genes of a cell which may affect the structure and development of the resultant offspring. **4** another word for **mutant** (sense 1). **5** a physical characteristic of an individual resulting from this type of chromosomal change. **6** *Phonetics.* **6a** (in Germanic languages) another name for **umlaut. 6b** (in Celtic languages) a phonetic change in certain initial consonants caused by a preceding word.
▸**mu'tational** *adj* ▸**mu'tationally** *adv*
mutatis mutandis *Latin.* (muː'tɑːtɪs muː'tændɪs) the necessary changes having been made.
mutch (mʌtʃ) *n* a close-fitting linen cap formerly worn by women and children in Scotland. [C15: from MDu. *mutse* cap, from Med. L *almucia* AMICE]
mute ⓣ (mjuːt) *adj* **1** not giving out sound or speech; silent. **2** unable to speak; dumb. **3** unspoken or unexpressed. **4** *Law.* (of a person arraigned on indictment) refusing to answer a charge. **5** *Phonetics.* another word for **plosive. 6** (of a letter in a word) silent. ◆ *n* **7** a person who is unable to speak. **8** *Law.* a person who refuses to plead. **9** any of various devices used to soften the tone of stringed or brass instru-

THESAURUS

trospection, meditation, navel gazing (*sl.*), reflection, reverie, rumination, woolgathering
must[1] *n* **8 = necessity,** duty, essential, fundamental, imperative, necessary thing, obligation, prerequisite, requirement, requisite, *sine qua non*
must[3] *n* **= mould,** decay, fetor, fustiness, mildew, mouldiness, mustiness, rot
muster *vb* **1, 3 = assemble,** call together, call up, collect, come together, congregate, convene, convoke, enrol, gather, group, marshal, meet, mobilize, rally, round up, summon ◆ *n* **6 = assembly,** assemblage, collection, concourse, congregation, convention, convocation, gathering, meeting, mobilization, rally, roundup **8 pass muster = be acceptable,** be *or* come up to scratch, fill the bill (*inf.*), make the grade, measure up, qualify
musty *adj* **1 = stale,** airless, dank, decayed, frowsty, fusty, mildewed, mildewy, mouldy, old, smelly, stuffy **2 = old-fashioned,** ancient, antediluvian, antiquated, banal, clichéd, dull, hackneyed, hoary, moth-eaten, obsolete, stale, threadbare, trite, worn-out
Antonyms *adj* ≠ **old-fashioned:** current, exciting, fashionable, fresh, imaginative, interesting, lively, modern, modish, new, novel, original, unusual, up-to-date, with it (*inf.*)
mutability *n* **= change,** alteration, evolution, metamorphosis, transition, variation, vicissitude
mutable *adj* **= changeable,** adaptable, alterable, changing, fickle, flexible, inconsistent, inconstant, irresolute, uncertain, undependable, unreliable, unsettled, unstable, unsteady, vacillating, variable, volatile, wavering
mutation *n* **1, 2 = change,** alteration, deviation, evolution, metamorphosis, modification, transfiguration, transformation, variation **4 = mutant,** anomaly, deviant
mute *adj* **1-3 = silent,** aphasiac, aphasic, aphonic, dumb, mum, speechless, unex-

ments. **10** *Phonetics.* a plosive consonant. **11** a silent letter. **12** an actor in a dumb show. **13** a hired mourner. ◆ *vb* **mutes, muting, muted.** (*tr*) **14** to reduce the volume of (a musical instrument) by means of a mute, soft pedal, etc. **15** to subdue the strength of (a colour, tone, lighting, etc.). [C14 *muwet* from OF *mu,* from L *mūtus* silent]
▸**'mutely** *adv* ▸**'muteness** *n*

mute swan *n* a Eurasian swan with a pure white plumage and an orange-red bill.

muti ('mu:tɪ) *n S. African inf.* medicine, esp. herbal. [from Zulu *umuthi* tree, medicine]

mutilate Ⓣ ('mju:tɪˌleɪt) *vb* **mutilates, mutilating, mutilated.** (*tr*) **1** to deprive of a limb, essential part, etc.; maim. **2** to expurgate, damage, etc. (a text, book, etc.). [C16: from L *mutilāre* to cut off; rel. to *mutilus* maimed]
▸**ˌmuti'lation** *n* ▸**'mutiˌlative** *adj* ▸**'mutiˌlator** *n*

mutineer (ˌmju:tɪ'nɪə) *n* a person who mutinies.

mutinous Ⓣ ('mju:tɪnəs) *adj* **1** openly rebellious. **2** characteristic or indicative of mutiny.
▸**'mutinously** *adv* ▸**'mutinousness** *n*

mutiny Ⓣ ('mju:tɪnɪ) *n, pl* **mutinies. 1** open rebellion against constituted authority, esp. by seamen or soldiers against their officers. ◆ *vb* **mutinies, mutinying, mutinied. 2** (*intr*) to engage in mutiny. [C16: from obs. *mutine,* from OF *mutin* rebellious, from *meute* mutiny, ult. from L *movēre* to move]

mutism ('mju:ˌtɪzəm) *n* **1** the state of being mute. **2** *Psychiatry.* **2a** a refusal to speak. **2b** the lack of development of speech.

mutt Ⓣ (mʌt) *n Sl.* **1** an inept, ignorant, or stupid person. **2** a mongrel dog; cur. [C20: from MUTTONHEAD]

mutter Ⓣ ('mʌtə) *vb* **1** to utter (something) in a low and indistinct tone. **2** (*intr*) to grumble or complain. **3** (*intr*) to make a low continuous murmuring sound. ◆ *n* **4** a muttered sound or complaint. [C14 *moteren*]
▸**'muttering** *n, adj*

mutton ('mʌtᵊn) *n* **1** the flesh of sheep, esp. of mature sheep, used as food. **2 mutton dressed as lamb.** an older woman dressed up to look young. [C13 *moton* sheep, from OF, from Med. L *multō,* of Celtic origin]
▸**'muttony** *adj*

mutton bird *n* any of several shearwaters, having a dark plumage with greyish underparts. In New Zealand, applied to one collected for food, esp. by Maoris. [C19: from the taste of its flesh]

mutton chop *n* a piece of mutton from the loin.

muttonchops ('mʌtᵊnˌtʃɒps) *pl n* side whiskers trimmed in the shape of chops.

muttonhead ('mʌtᵊnˌhɛd) *n Sl.* a stupid or ignorant person; fool.
▸**'muttonˌheaded** *adj*

mutual Ⓣ ('mju:tʃʊəl) *adj* **1** experienced or expressed by each of two or more people about the other; reciprocal: *mutual distrust.* **2** *Inf.* common to or shared by both: *a mutual friend.* **3** denoting an insurance company, etc., in which the policyholders share the profits and expenses and there are no shareholders. See also **mutual insurance.** [C15: from OF *mutuel,* from L *mūtuus* reciprocal (orig.: borrowed); rel. to *mūtāre* to change]
▸**mutuality** (ˌmju:tʃʊ'ælɪtɪ) *n* ▸**'mutually** *adv*

> **USAGE NOTE** The use of *mutual* to mean *common to or shared by two or more parties* was formerly considered incorrect, but is now acceptable. Tautologous use of *mutual* should be avoided: *cooperation* (not *mutual cooperation*) *between the two countries.*

mutual induction *n* the production of an electromotive force in a circuit by a current change in a second circuit magnetically linked to the first.

mutual insurance *n* a system of insurance by which all policyholders become company members under contract to pay premiums into a common fund out of which claims are paid. See also **mutual** (sense 3).

mutuel ('mju:tʃʊəl) *n* short for **pari-mutuel.**

muu-muu ('mu:ˌmu:) *n* a loose brightly coloured dress worn by women in Hawaii. [from Hawaiian]

Muzak ('mju:zæk) *n Trademark.* recorded light music played in shops, restaurants, factories, etc.

muzhik *or* **moujik** ('mu:ʒɪk) *n* a Russian peasant, esp. under the tsars. [C16: from Russian: peasant]

muzzle Ⓣ ('mʌzᵊl) *n* **1** the projecting part of the face, usually the jaws and nose, of animals such as the dog and horse. **2** a guard or strap fitted over an animal's nose and jaws to prevent it biting or eating. **3** the front end of a gun barrel. ◆ *vb* **muzzles, muzzling, muzzled.** (*tr*) **4** to prevent from being heard or noticed. **5** to put a muzzle on (an animal). [C15 *mosel,* from OF *musel,* dim. of *muse* snout, from Med. L *mūsus,* from ?]
▸**'muzzler** *n*

muzzle-loader *n* a firearm receiving its ammunition through the muzzle.
▸**'muzzle-ˌloading** *adj*

muzzle velocity *n* the velocity of a projectile as it leaves a firearm's muzzle.

muzzy ('mʌzɪ) *adj* **muzzier, muzziest. 1** blurred or hazy. **2** confused or befuddled. [C18: from ?]
▸**'muzzily** *adv* ▸**'muzziness** *n*

MVO (in Britain) *abbrev. for* Member of the Royal Victorian Order.

MW 1 *symbol for* megawatt. **2** *Radio. abbrev. for* medium wave.

Mx *Physics. symbol for* maxwell.

my (maɪ) *determiner* **1** of, belonging to, or associated with the speaker or writer (me): *my own ideas.* **2** used in various forms of address: *my lord.* ◆ *interj* **3** an exclamation of surprise, awe, etc.: *my, how you've grown!* [C12 *mī,* var. of OE *mīn* when preceding a word beginning with a consonant]

> **USAGE NOTE** See at **me**[1].

myalgia (maɪ'ældʒɪə) *n* pain in a muscle or a group of muscles. [C19: from MYO- + -ALGIA]

myalgic encephalomyelitis (maɪ'ældʒɪk ɛnˌsɛfələʊˌmaɪɪ'laɪtɪs) *n* a former name for **chronic fatigue syndrome.** Abbrev.: **ME.**

myalism ('maɪəˌlɪzəm) *n* a kind of witchcraft practised esp. in the Caribbean. [C19: from *myal,* prob. West African]

myall ('maɪəl) *n* **1** any of several Australian acacias having hard scented wood. **2** a native Australian living independently of society. [C19: Abor. name]

mycelium (maɪ'si:lɪəm) *n, pl* **mycelia** (-lɪə). the vegetative body of fungi: a mass of branching filaments (hyphae). [C19 (lit.: nail of fungus): from MYCO- + Gk *hēlos* nail]
▸**my'celial** *adj*

Mycenaean (ˌmaɪsɪ'ni:ən) *adj* **1** of or relating to ancient Mycenae, a city in S Greece, or its inhabitants. **2** of or relating to the Aegean civilization of Mycenae (1400 to 1100 B.C.).

-mycete *n combining form.* indicating a member of a class of fungi: *myxomycete.* [from NL *-mycetes,* from Gk *mukētes,* pl. of *mukēs* fungus]

myco- *or before a vowel* **myc-** *combining form.* indicating fungus: *mycology.* [from Gk *mukēs* fungus]

mycology (maɪ'kɒlədʒɪ) *n* the branch of biology concerned with the study of fungi.
▸**mycological** (ˌmaɪkə'lɒdʒɪkᵊl) *or* **ˌmyco'logic** *adj* ▸**my'cologist** *n*

mycoplasma (ˌmaɪkəʊ'plæzmə) *n* any one of a genus of prokaryotic microorganisms some species of which cause disease (**mycoplasmosis**) in animals and humans.

mycorrhiza *or* **mycorhiza** (ˌmaɪkə'raɪzə) *n, pl* **mycorrhizae** (-zi:) *or* **mycorrhizas, mycorhizae** *or* **mycorhizas.** an association of a fungus and a plant in which the fungus lives within or on the outside of the plant's roots forming a symbiotic or parasitic relationship. [C19: from MYCO- + Gk *rhiza* root]
▸**ˌmycor'rhizal** *or* **ˌmyco'rhizal** *adj*

mycosis (maɪ'kəʊsɪs) *n* any infection or disease caused by fungus.
▸**mycotic** (maɪ'kɒtɪk) *adj*

mycotoxin (ˌmaɪkə'tɒksɪn) *n* any of various toxic substances produced by fungi, some of which may affect food.
▸**ˌmycotox'ology** *n*

mycotrophic (ˌmaɪkəʊ'trɒfɪk) *adj Bot.* (of a plant) symbiotic with a fungus, esp. a mycorrhizal fungus.
▸**mycotrophy** (maɪ'kɒtrəfɪ) *n*

myelin ('maɪəlɪn) *or* **myeline** ('maɪɪˌli:n) *n* a white tissue forming an insulating sheath (**myelin sheath**) around certain nerve fibres. Damage to the myelin sheath causes neurological disease, as in multiple sclerosis.

myelitis (ˌmaɪɪ'laɪtɪs) *n* inflammation of the spinal cord or of the bone marrow.

myeloma (ˌmaɪə'ləʊmə) *n, pl* **myelomas** *or* **myelomata** (-mətə). a usually malignant tumour of the bone marrow.

mynah *or* **myna** ('maɪnə) *n* any of various tropical Asian starlings,

THESAURUS

pressed, unspeaking, unspoken, voiceless, wordless ◆ *vb* **14, 15** = **muffle**, dampen, deaden, lower, moderate, soften, soft-pedal, subdue, tone down, turn down

mutilate *vb* **1** = **maim**, amputate, butcher, cripple, cut to pieces, cut up, damage, disable, disfigure, dismember, hack, injure, lacerate, lame, mangle **2** = **distort**, adulterate, bowdlerize, butcher, censor, cut, damage, expurgate, hack, mar, spoil

mutinous *adj* **1** = **rebellious**, bolshie (*Brit. inf.*), contumacious, disobedient, insubordinate, insurgent, refractory, revolutionary, riotous, seditious, subversive, turbulent, ungovernable, unmanageable, unruly

mutiny *n* **1** = **rebellion**, defiance, disobedience, insubordination, insurrection, refusal to obey orders, resistance, revolt, revolution, riot, rising, strike, uprising ◆ *vb* **2** = **rebel**, be insubordinate, defy authority, disobey, refuse to obey orders, resist, revolt, rise up, strike

mutt *n Slang* **1** = **fool**, berk (*Brit. sl.*), coot, dolt, dunderhead, idiot, ignoramus, imbecile (*inf.*), jerk (*sl., chiefly US & Canad.*), moron, nerd *or* nurd (*sl.*), numbskull *or* numskull, prat (*sl.*), thickhead, twit (*inf., chiefly Brit.*), wally (*sl.*) **2** = **mongrel**, cur, dog

mutter *vb* **1, 2** = **grumble**, complain, grouch (*inf.*), grouse, mumble, murmur, rumble

mutual *adj* **1, 2** = **shared**, common, communal, correlative, interactive, interchangeable, interchanged, joint, reciprocal, reciprocated, requited, returned

muzzle *n* **1** = **jaws**, mouth, nose, snout **2** = **gag**, guard ◆ *vb* **4, 5** = **suppress**, censor, choke, curb, gag, restrain, silence, stifle

some of which can mimic human speech. [C18: from Hindi *mainā*, from Sansk. *madana*]

Mynheer (mə'nɪə) *n* a Dutch title of address equivalent to *Sir* when used alone or to *Mr* before a name. [C17: from Du. *mijnheer* my lord]

myo- *or before a vowel* **my-** *combining form.* muscle: *myocardium.* [from Gk *mus* MUSCLE]

myocardium (ˌmaɪəʊ'kɑːdɪəm) *n, pl* **myocardia** (-dɪə). the muscular tissue of the heart. [C19: *myo-* + *cardium,* from Gk *kardia* heart]
▸ˌ**myo'cardial** *adj*

myology (maɪ'ɒlədʒɪ) *n* the branch of medical science concerned with muscles.

myope ('maɪəʊp) *n* any person afflicted with myopia. [C18: via F from Gk *muōps;* see MYOPIA]

myopia ⓣ (maɪ'əʊpɪə) *n* inability to see distant objects clearly because the images are focused in front of the retina; short-sightedness. [C18: via NL from Gk *muōps* short-sighted, from *mūein* to close (the eyes), + *ōps* eye]
▸**myopic** (maɪ'ɒpɪk) *adj* ▸**my'opically** *adv*

myosin ('maɪəsɪn) *n* the chief protein of muscle. [C19: from MYO- + -OSE[2] + -IN]

myosotis (ˌmaɪə'səʊtɪs) *n* any plant of the genus *Myosotis.* See **forget-me-not.** [C18: NL from Gk *muosōtis* mouse-ear (referring to its furry leaves), from *mus* mouse + *ous* ear]

myriad ⓣ ('mɪrɪəd) *adj* **1** innumerable. ◆ *n (also used in pl)* **2** a large indefinite number. **3** *Arch.* ten thousand. [C16: via LL from Gk *murias* ten thousand]

myriapod ('mɪrɪəˌpɒd) *n* **1** any of a group of terrestrial arthropods having a long segmented body and many walking limbs, such as the centipedes and millipedes. ◆ *adj* **2** of, relating to, or belonging to this group. [C19: from NL *Myriapoda.* See MYRIAD, -POD]

Myrmidon ('mɜːmɪˌdɒn, -d^{ə}n) *n* **1** *Greek myth.* one of a race of people who were led against Troy by Achilles. **2** *(often not cap.)* a follower or henchman.

myrobalan (maɪ'rɒbələn, mɪ-) *n* **1** the dried plumlike fruit of various tropical trees used in dyeing, tanning, ink, and medicine. **2** a dye extracted from this fruit. [C16: via L from Gk *murobalanos,* from *muron* ointment + *balanos* acorn]

myrrh (mɜː) *n* **1** any of several trees and shrubs of Africa and S Asia that exude an aromatic resin. **2** the resin obtained from such a plant, used in perfume, incense, and medicine. [OE *myrre,* via L from Gk *murrha,* ult. from Akkadian *murrū*]

myrtle ('mɜːt^{ə}l) *n* an evergreen shrub or tree, esp. a S European shrub with pink or white flowers and aromatic blue-black berries. [C16: from Med. L *myrtilla,* from L *myrtus,* from Gk *murtos*]

myself (maɪ'sɛlf) *pron* **1a** the reflexive form of *I* or *me.* **1b** (intensifier): *I myself know of no answer.* **2** *(preceded by a copula)* my usual self: *I'm not myself today.* **3** *Not standard.* used instead of *I* or *me* in compound noun phrases: *John and myself are voting together.*

mysterious ⓣ (mɪ'stɪərɪəs) *adj* **1** characterized by or indicative of mystery. **2** puzzling, curious.
▸**mys'teriously** *adv* ▸**mys'teriousness** *n*

mystery[1] ⓣ ('mɪstərɪ, -trɪ) *n, pl* **mysteries. 1** an unexplained or inexplicable event, phenomenon, etc. **2** a person or thing that arouses curiosity or suspense because of an unknown, obscure, or enigmatic quality. **3** the state or quality of being obscure, inexplicable, or enigmatic. **4** a story, film, etc., which arouses suspense and curiosity because of facts concealed. **5** *Christianity.* any truth that is divinely revealed but otherwise unknowable. **6** *Christianity.* a sacramental rite, such as the Eucharist, or *(when pl)* the consecrated elements of the Eucharist. **7** *(often pl)* any rites of certain ancient Mediterranean religions. **8** short for **mystery play.** [C14: via L from Gk *mustērion* secret rites]

mystery[2] ('mɪstərɪ) *n, pl* **mysteries.** *Arch.* **1** a trade, occupation, or craft. **2** a guild of craftsmen. [C14: from Med. L *mistērium,* from L *ministerium* occupation, from *minister* official]

mystery play *n* (in the Middle Ages) a type of drama based on the life of Christ. Cf. **miracle play.**

mystery tour *n* an excursion to an unspecified destination.

mystic ⓣ ('mɪstɪk) *n* **1** a person who achieves mystical experience or an apprehension of divine mysteries. ◆ *adj* **2** another word for **mystical.** [C14: via L from Gk *mustikos,* from *mustēs* mystery initiate; rel. to *muein* to initiate into sacred rites]

mystical ('mɪstɪk^{ə}l) *adj* **1** relating to or characteristic of mysticism. **2** *Christianity.* having a divine or sacred significance that surpasses human apprehension. **3** having occult or metaphysical significance.
▸**'mystically** *adv*

mysticism ('mɪstɪˌsɪzəm) *n* **1** belief in or experience of a reality surpassing normal human understanding or experience. **2** a system of contemplative prayer and spirituality aimed at achieving direct intuitive experience of the divine. **3** obscure or confused belief or thought.

mystify ⓣ ('mɪstɪˌfaɪ) *vb* **mystifies, mystifying, mystified.** *(tr)* **1** to confuse, bewilder, or puzzle. **2** to make obscure. [C19: from F *mystifier,* from *mystère* MYSTERY[1] or *mystique* MYSTIC]
▸ˌ**mystifi'cation** *n* ▸**'mystiˌfying** *adj*

mystique ⓣ (mɪ'stiːk) *n* an aura of mystery, power, and awe that surrounds a person or thing. [C20: from F (adj): MYSTIC]

myth ⓣ (mɪθ) *n* **1a** a story about superhuman beings of an earlier age, usually of how natural phenomena, social customs, etc., came into existence. **1b** another word for **mythology** (senses 1, 3). **2** a person or thing whose existence is fictional or unproven. [C19: via LL from Gk *muthos* fable]

myth. *abbrev. for:* **1** mythological. **2** mythology.

mythical ⓣ ('mɪθɪk^{ə}l) *or* **mythic** *adj* **1** of or relating to myth. **2** imaginary or fictitious.
▸**'mythically** *adv*

mythicize *or* **mythicise** ('mɪθɪˌsaɪz) *vb* **mythicizes, mythicizing, mythicized** *or* **mythicises, mythicising, mythicised.** *(tr)* to make into or treat as a myth.
▸**'mythicist** *n*

mytho- *combining form.* myth: *mythopoeia.*

mythologize *or* **mythologise** (mɪ'θɒləˌdʒaɪz) *vb* **mythologizes, mythologizing, mythologized** *or* **mythologises, mythologising, mythologised. 1** to tell, study, or explain (myths). **2** *(intr)* to create or make up myths. **3** *(tr)* to convert into a myth.
▸**my'tholoˌgizer** *or* **my'tholoˌgiser** *n*

mythology ⓣ (mɪ'θɒlədʒɪ) *n, pl* **mythologies. 1** a body of myths, esp. one associated with a particular culture, person, etc. **2** a body of stories about a person, institution, etc. **3** myths collectively. **4** the study of myths.
▸**mythological** (ˌmɪθə'lɒdʒɪk^{ə}l) *adj* ▸**my'thologist** *n*

mythomania (ˌmɪθəʊ'meɪnɪə) *n Psychiatry.* the tendency to lie or exaggerate, occurring in some mental disorders.
▸ˌ**mytho'maniˌac** *n, adj*

mythopoeia (ˌmɪθəʊ'piːə) *n* the composition or making of myths. [C19: from Gk, ult. from *muthos* myth + *poiein* to make]
▸ˌ**mytho'poeic** *adj*

mythos ('maɪθɒs, 'mɪθɒs) *n, pl* **mythoi** (-θɔɪ). **1** the complex of beliefs, values, attitudes, etc., characteristic of a specific group or society. **2** another word for **myth** or **mythology.**

myxo ('mɪksəʊ) *n Austral. sl.* myxomatosis.

myxo- *or before a vowel* **myx-** *combining form.* mucus or slime: *myxomatosis.* [from Gk *muxa*]

myxoedema *or US* **myxedema** (ˌmɪksɪ'diːmə) *n* a disease resulting from underactivity of the thyroid gland characterized by puffy eyes, face, and hands and mental sluggishness. See also **cretinism.**

myxoma (mɪk'səʊmə) *n, pl* **myxomas** *or* **myxomata** (-mətə). a tumour composed of mucous connective tissue, usually situated in subcutaneous tissue.
▸**myxomatous** (mɪk'sɒmətəs) *adj*

myxomatosis (ˌmɪksəmə'təʊsɪs) *n* an infectious and usually fatal viral disease of rabbits characterized by swelling of the mucous membranes and formation of skin tumours.

myxomycete (ˌmɪksəʊmaɪ'siːt) *n* a slime mould, esp. a slime mould of the phylum *Myxomycota* (division *Myxomycetes* in traditional classifications).

myxovirus ('mɪksəʊˌvaɪrəs) *n* any of a group of viruses that cause influenza, mumps, etc.

THESAURUS

myopic *adj* = **short-sighted,** near-sighted

myriad *adj* **1** = **innumerable,** a thousand and one, countless, immeasurable, incalculable, multitudinous, untold ◆ *n* **2** = **multitude,** a million, army, flood, horde, host, millions, mountain, scores, sea, swarm, thousands

mysterious *adj* **1** = **secretive,** cloak-and-dagger, covert, furtive **2** = **strange,** abstruse, arcane, baffling, concealed, cryptic, curious, Delphic, enigmatic, hidden, impenetrable, incomprehensible, inexplicable, inscrutable, insoluble, mystical, mystifying, obscure, perplexing, puzzling, recondite, secret, sphinxlike, uncanny, unfathomable, unknown, veiled, weird

Antonyms *adj* apparent, clear, manifest, open, plain

mystery[1] *n* **1** = **puzzle,** cloak and dagger, closed book, conundrum, enigma, problem, question, riddle, secrecy, secret, teaser

mystic *adj* **2** = **supernatural,** abstruse, arcane, cabalistic, cryptic, enigmatical, esoteric, hidden, inscrutable, metaphysical, mysterious, nonrational, occult, otherworldly, paranormal, preternatural, transcendental

mystify *vb* **1** = **puzzle,** baffle, bamboozle (*inf.*), be all Greek to (*inf.*), beat (*sl.*), befog, bewilder, confound, confuse, elude, escape, flummox, nonplus, perplex, stump

mystique *n* = **fascination,** awe, charisma, charm, glamour, magic, spell

myth *n* **1a** = **legend,** allegory, fable, fairy story, fiction, folk tale, parable, saga, story, tradition, urban legend, urban myth

mythical *adj* **1** = **legendary,** allegorical, chimerical, fabled, fabulous, fairy-tale, mythological, storied **2** = **imaginary,** fabricated, fanciful, fantasy, fictitious, invented, made-up, make-believe, nonexistent, pretended, unreal, untrue

mythological *adj* **1** = **legendary,** fabulous, folkloric, heroic, mythic, mythical, traditional

mythology *n* **1-3** = **legend,** folklore, folk tales, lore, mythos, myths, stories, tradition

Nn

n *or* **N** (ɛn) *n, pl* **n's, N's,** *or* **Ns. 1** the 14th letter of the English alphabet. **2** a speech sound represented by this letter.

n[1] *symbol for:* **1** neutron. **2** *Optics.* index of refraction. **3** nano-.

n[2] (ɛn) *determiner* an indefinite number (of): *there are n objects in a box.*

N *symbol for:* **1** Also: **kt.** *Chess.* knight. **2** newton(s). **3** *Chem.* nitrogen. **4** North. **5** noun. **6** (*in combination*) nuclear: *N-power; N-plant.*

n. *abbrev. for:* **1** neuter. **2** new. **3** nominative. **4** noon. **5** note. **6** noun. **7** number.

N. *abbrev. for:* **1** National(ist). **2** Navy. **3** New. **4** Norse.

Na *the chemical symbol for* sodium. [L *natrium*]

NA *abbrev. for* North America.

NAAFI *or* **Naafi** ('næfɪ) *n* **1** *acronym for* Navy, Army, and Air Force Institutes: an organization providing canteens, shops, etc., for British military personnel at home or overseas. **2** a canteen, shop, etc., run by this organization.

naartjie ('nɑːtʃɪ) *n S. African.* a tangerine. [from Afrik., from Tamil]

nab ❶ (næb) *vb* **nabs, nabbing, nabbed.** (*tr*) *Inf.* **1** to arrest (a criminal, etc.). **2** to seize suddenly; snatch. [C17: ? of Scand. origin]

nabla ('næblə) *n Maths.* another name for **del.** [C19: from Gk: stringed instrument, because it is shaped like a harp]

nabob ('neɪbɒb) *n* **1** *Inf.* a rich or important man. **2** (formerly) a European who made a fortune in India. **3** another name for a **nawab.** [C17: from Port. *nababo,* from Hindi *nawwāb;* see NAWAB]

NAC *abbrev. for* National Advisory Council.

nacelle (nə'sɛl) *n* a streamlined enclosure on an aircraft, not part of the fuselage, to accommodate an engine, passengers, crew, etc. [C20: from F: small boat, from LL *nāvicella,* a dim. of L *nāvis* ship]

nacho ('nɑːtʃəʊ) *n, pl* **nachos.** a Mexican snack consisting of a piece of tortilla topped with melted cheese.

NACODS ('neɪkɒdz) *n* (in Britain) *acronym for* National Association of Colliery Overmen, Deputies, and Shotfirers.

nacre ('neɪkə) *n* the technical name for **mother-of-pearl.** [C16: via F from OIt. *naccara,* from Ar. *naqqārah* shell, drum]
▸'**nacred** *adj*

nacreous ('neɪkrɪəs) *adj* relating to, consisting of, or having the lustre of mother-of-pearl.

NACRO *or* **Nacro** ('nækrəʊ) *n* (in Britain) *acronym for* National Association for the Care and Resettlement of Offenders.

nadir ❶ ('neɪdɪə, 'næ-) *n* **1** the point on the celestial sphere directly below an observer and diametrically opposite the zenith. **2** the lowest point; depths. [C14: from OF, from Ar. *nazīr as-samt,* lit.: opposite the zenith]

nae (neɪ) *or* **na** (nɑː) a Scot. word for **no**[2] or **not.**

naevus ❶ *or US* **nevus** ('niːvəs) *n, pl* **naevi** *or US* **nevi** (-vaɪ). any pigmented blemish on the skin; birthmark or mole. [C19: from L; rel. to (*g*)*natus* born, produced by nature]
▸'**naevoid** *or US* '**nevoid** *adj*

naff ❶ (næf) *adj Brit. sl.* inferior; in poor taste. [C19: ?from back slang on *fan,* short for FANNY]
▸'**naffness** *n*

naff off *sentence substitute. Brit sl.* a forceful expression of dismissal or contempt.

nag[1] ❶ (næg) *vb* **nags, nagging, nagged. 1** to scold or annoy constantly. **2** (when *intr,* often foll. by *at*) to be a constant source of discomfort or worry (to). ◆ *n* **3** a person, esp. a woman, who nags. [C19: of Scand. origin]
▸'**nagger** *n*

nag[2] ❶ (næg) *n* **1** *Often derog.* a horse. **2** a small riding horse. [C14: of Gmc origin]

nagana (nə'gɑːnə) *n* a disease of hoofed animals of central and southern Africa, transmitted by tsetse flies. [from Zulu *u-nakane*]

Nah. *Bible. abbrev. for* Nahum.

NAHT (in Britain) *abbrev. for* National Association of Head Teachers.

Nahuatl ('nɑːwɑːtᵊl, nɑː'wɑːtᵊl) *n* **1** (*pl* **Nahuatl** *or* **Nahuatls**) a member of one of a group of Central American and Mexican Indian peoples including the Aztecs. **2** the language of these peoples.

naiad ❶ ('naɪæd) *n, pl* **naiads** *or* **naiades** (-əˌdiːz). **1** *Greek myth.* a nymph dwelling in a lake, river, or spring. **2** the aquatic larva of the dragonfly, mayfly, and related insects. **3** Also called: **water nymph.** a submerged aquatic plant, having narrow leaves and small flowers. [C17: via L from Gk *nāias* water nymph; rel. to *náein* to flow]

naïf (nɑː'iːf) *adj, n* a less common word for **naive.**

nail ❶ (neɪl) *n* **1** a fastening device, usually made of metal, having a point at one end and a head at the other. **2** anything resembling such a device in function or shape. **3** the horny plate covering part of the dorsal surface of the fingers or toes. Related adj: **ungual. 4** the claw of a mammal, bird, or reptile. **5** a unit of length, formerly used for measuring cloth, equal to two and a quarter inches. **6 hit the nail on the head.** to do or say something correct or telling. **7 on the nail.** (of payments) at once. ◆ *vb* (*tr*) **8** to attach with or as if with nails. **9** *Inf.* to arrest, catch, or seize. **10** *Inf.* to hit or bring down, as with a shot. **11** *Inf.* to expose or detect (a lie or liar). **12** to fix (one's eyes, attention, etc.) on. **13** to stud with nails. [OE *nægl*]
▸'**nailer** *n*

nail-biting *n* **1** the act or habit of biting one's fingernails. **2a** anxiety or tension. **2b** (*as modifier*): *nail-biting suspense.*

nail bomb *n* an explosive device containing nails, used by terrorists to cause serious injuries in crowded situations.

nailbrush ('neɪlˌbrʌʃ) *n* a small stiff-bristled brush for cleaning the fingernails.

nailfile ('neɪlˌfaɪl) *n* a small file of metal or of board coated with emery, used to trim the nails.

nail polish *or* **varnish** *or esp. US* **enamel** *n* a quick-drying cosmetic lacquer applied to colour the nails or make them shiny or esp. both.

nail set *or* **punch** *n* a punch for driving the head of a nail below or flush with the surrounding surface.

nainsook ('neɪnsʊk, 'næn-) *n* a light soft plain-weave cotton fabric. [C19: from Hindi, from *nain* eye + *sukh* delight]

naira ('naɪrə) *n* the standard monetary unit of Nigeria. [C20: altered from *Nigeria*]

naive ❶**, naïve** (nɑː'iːv, naɪ'iːv), *or* **naïf** *adj* **1** having or expressing innocence and credulity; ingenuous. **2** lacking developed powers of reasoning or criticism: *a naive argument.* **3** another word for **primitive** (sense 5). ◆ *n* **4** a person who is naive, esp. in artistic style. See **primitive** (sense 10). [C17: from F fem of *naïf,* from OF: native, spontaneous, from L *nātīvus* NATIVE]
▸**na'ively, na'ïvely,** *or* **na'ïfly** *adv* ▸**na'iveness, na'ïveness,** *or* **na'ïfness** *n*

naivety ❶ (naɪ'iːvtɪ), **naiveté,** *or* **naïveté** (ˌnɑːiːv'teɪ) *n, pl* **naiveties, naivetés** *or* **naïvetés. 1** the state or quality of being naive. **2** a naive act or statement.

naked ❶ ('neɪkɪd) *adj* **1** having the body unclothed; undressed. **2** having no covering; exposed: *a naked flame.* **3** with no qualification or concealment: *the naked facts.* **4** unaided by any optical instrument (esp. in **the naked eye**). **5** (usually foll. by *of*) destitute: *naked of weapons.* **6** (of animals) lacking hair, feathers, scales, etc. **7** *Law.* **7a** unsupported by authority: *a naked contract.* **7b** lacking some essential condition to render valid; incomplete. [OE *nacod*]
▸'**nakedly** *adv* ▸'**nakedness** *n*

naked ladies *n* (*functioning as sing*) another name for **autumn crocus.**

THESAURUS

nab *vb* **1** = **arrest**, apprehend, capture, catch, catch in the act, collar (*inf.*), feel one's collar (*sl.*), lift (*sl.*), nail (*inf.*), nick (*sl., chiefly Brit.*) **2** = **seize**, grab, snatch

nadir *n* **2** = **bottom**, depths, lowest point, minimum, rock bottom, zero
Antonyms *n* acme, apex, climax, crest, height, high point, peak, pinnacle, summit, top, vertex, zenith

naevus *n* = **birthmark**, mole

naff *adj Brit. slang* = **bad**, crappy (*sl.*), duff (*Brit. inf.*), inferior, low-grade, low-quality, poor, poxy (*sl.*), rubbishy, second-rate, shabby, shoddy, substandard, trashy, twopenny-halfpenny, valueless, worthless
Antonyms *adj* excellent, exceptional, fine, first-class, first-rate, high-quality, superior

nag[1] *vb* **1** = **annoy**, badger, bend someone's ear (*inf.*), be on one's back (*sl.*), berate, breathe down someone's neck, chivvy, harass, harry, hassle (*inf.*), henpeck, irritate, nark (*Brit., Austral., & NZ sl.*), pester, plague, scold, torment, upbraid ◆ *n* **3** = **scold**, harpy, shrew, tartar, termagant, virago

nag[2] *n* **1** = **horse**, hack, jade, plug (*US*)

nagging *adj* **1** = **critical**, irritating, on someone's back (*inf.*), scolding, shrewish **2** = **distressing**, continuous, painful, persistent, worrying

naiad *n* **1** = **nymph**, Oceanid (*Greek myth*), sprite, undine, water nymph

nail *vb* **8** = **fasten**, attach, beat, fix, hammer, join, pin, secure, tack

naive *adj* **1** = **innocent**, artless, as green as grass, callow, candid, childlike, confiding, credulous, frank, green, guileless, gullible, ingenuous, jejune, natural, open, simple, trusting, unaffected, unpretentious, unsophisticated, unsuspicious, unworldly, wet behind the ears (*inf.*)
Antonyms *adj* ≠ **innocent**: artful, disingenuous, experienced, sly, sophisticated, urbane, worldly, worldly-wise

naivety *n* **1** = **innocence**, artlessness, callowness, candour, credulity, frankness, guilelessness, inexperience, ingenuousness, naturalness, openness, simplicity

naked *adj* **1** = **nude**, bare, buck naked (*sl.*), denuded, disrobed, divested, exposed, in one's birthday suit (*inf.*), in the altogether, in the buff (*inf.*), naked as the day one was born (*inf.*), starkers (*inf.*), stripped, unclothed, uncovered, undraped, undressed, without a stitch on (*inf.*) **3** = **undisguised**, blatant, evident, manifest, open, overt, patent, plain, simple, stark, unadorned, unconcealed, unexaggerated, unmistakable, unqualified, unvarnished
Antonyms *adj* ≠ **nude**: clothed, concealed, covered, dressed, wrapped up ≠ **undisguised**: concealed, disguised

nakedness *n* **1** = **nudity**, bareness, undress **3** = **openness**, plainness, simplicity, starkness

naked lady *n* a pink orchid found in Australia and New Zealand.

NALGO ('nælgəʊ) *n* (formerly, in Britain) *acronym for* National and Local Government Officers' Association.

Nam *or* **'Nam** (næm) *n US inf.* short for Vietnam (referring to the Vietnam War).

namby-pamby Ⓣ (ˌnæmbɪ'pæmbɪ) *adj* **1** sentimental or prim in a weak insipid way. **2** clinging, feeble, or spineless. ◆ *n, pl* **namby-pambies. 3** a person who is namby-pamby. [C18: a nickname of Ambrose Phillips (died 1749), whose pastoral verse was ridiculed for being insipid]

name Ⓣ (neɪm) *n* **1** a word or term by which a person or thing is commonly and distinctively known. **2** mere outward appearance as opposed to fact: *he was ruler in name only.* **3** a word or phrase descriptive of character, usually abusive: *to call a person names.* **4** reputation, esp., if unspecified, good reputation: *he's made quite a name for himself.* **5a** a famous person or thing: *a name in the advertising world.* **5b** *Chiefly US & Canad. (as modifier): a name product.* **6** a member of Lloyd's who provides part of the capital of a syndicate and shares in its profits or losses but does not arrange its business. **7 in the name of. 7a** for the sake of. **7b** by the authority of. **8 name of the game. 8a** anything that is significant or important. **8b** normal conditions, circumstances, etc.: *in gambling, losing money's the name of the game.* **9 to one's name.** belonging to one: *I haven't a penny to my name.* ◆ *vb* **names, naming, named.** *(tr)* **10** to give a name to. **11** to refer to by name; cite: *he named three French poets.* **12** to fix or specify: *they have named a date for the meeting.* **13** to appoint or nominate: *he was named Journalist of the Year.* **14** *(tr)* to ban (an MP) from the House of Commons by mentioning him formally by name as being guilty of disorderly conduct. **15 name names.** to cite people, esp. in order to blame or accuse them. **16 name the day.** to choose the day for an event, esp. one's wedding. [OE *nama,* rel. to L *nomen,* Gk *noma*]
▸**'namable** *or* **'nameable** *adj*

name-calling *n* verbal abuse.

namecheck ('neɪmˌtʃɛk) *vb (tr)* **1** to mention (someone) specifically by name. ◆ *n* **2** a specific mention of someone's name, for example on a radio programme.

name day *n* **1** *RC Church.* the feast day of a saint whose name one bears. **2** another name for **ticket day.**

name-dropping *n Inf.* the practice of referring frequently to famous people, esp. as though they were intimate friends, in order to impress others.
▸**'name-ˌdropper** *n*

nameless Ⓣ ('neɪmlɪs) *adj* **1** without a name. **2** indescribable: *a nameless horror seized him.* **3** too unpleasant or disturbing to be mentioned: *nameless atrocities.*
▸**'namelessness** *n*

namely Ⓣ ('neɪmlɪ) *adv* that is to say.

nameplate ('neɪmˌpleɪt) *n* a small panel on or next to the door of a room or building, bearing the occupant's name and profession.

namesake ('neɪmˌseɪk) *n* a person or thing named after another, or with the same name as another. [C17: prob. describing people connected *for the name's sake*]

nametape ('neɪmˌteɪp) *n* a tape bearing the owner's name and attached to an article.

nan (næn), **nana,** *or* **nanna** ('nænə) *n* a child's word for **grandmother.**

nana ('nɑːnə) *n* **1** *Sl.* a fool. **2 do one's nana.** *Austral. sl.* to become very angry. **3 off one's nana.** *Austral. sl.* mad; insane. [C19: prob. from BANANA]

nan bread *or* **naan** (nɑːn) *n* (in Indian cookery) a slightly leavened bread in a large flat leaf shape. [from Hindi]

nancy ('nænsɪ) *n, pl* **nancies.** an effeminate or homosexual boy or man. Also called: **nance, nancy boy.** [C20: from the girl's name *Nancy*]

NAND circuit *or* **gate** (nænd) *n Electronics.* a computer logic circuit having two or more input wires and one output wire that has an output signal if one or more of the input signals are at a low voltage. Cf. **OR circuit.** [C20: from *not* + AND; see NOT CIRCUIT, AND CIRCUIT]

nankeen (næŋ'kiːn) *or* **nankin** ('nænkɪn) *n* **1** a hard-wearing buff-coloured cotton fabric. **2a** a pale greyish-yellow colour. **2b** *(as adj): a nankeen carpet.* [C18: after *Nanking,* China, where it originated]

nanny ('nænɪ) *n, pl* **nannies. 1** a nurse or nursemaid for children. **2a** any person or thing regarded as treating people like children, esp. by being overprotective. **2b** *(as modifier): the nanny state.* **3** a child's word for **grandmother.** ◆ *vb* **nannies, nannying, nannied. 4** *(intr)* to nurse or look after someone else's children. **5** *(tr)* to be overprotective towards. [C19: child's name for a nurse]

nannygai ('nænɪˌgaɪ) *n, pl* **nannygais.** an edible red Australian sea fish. [from Abor.]

nanny goat *n* a female goat.

nano- *combining form.* denoting 10^{-9}: *nanometre; nanosecond.* Symbol: n [from L *nānus* dwarf, from Gk *nanos*]

nanotechnology (ˌnænəʊtɛk'nɒlədʒɪ) *n* a branch of technology dealing with the manufacture of objects with dimensions of less than 100 thousand-millionths of a metre and the manipulation of individual molecules and atoms.

Nansen bottle ('nænsən) *n* an instrument used by oceanographers for obtaining samples of sea water from a desired depth. [C19: after F. *Nansen* (1861–1930), Norwegian arctic explorer & statesman]

nap[1] Ⓣ (næp) *vb* **naps, napping, napped.** *(intr)* **1** to sleep for a short while; doze. **2** to be inattentive or off guard (esp. in **catch someone napping**). ◆ *n* **3** a short light sleep; doze. [OE *hnappian*]

nap[2] Ⓣ (næp) *n* **1a** the raised fibres of velvet or similar cloth. **1b** the direction in which these fibres lie. **2** any similar downy coating. **3** *Austral. inf.* blankets; bedding. ◆ *vb* **naps, napping, napped. 4** *(tr)* to raise the nap of (velvet, etc.) by brushing. [C15: prob. from MDu. *noppe*]

nap[3] (næp) *n* **1** Also called: **napoleon.** a card game similar to whist, usually played for stakes. **2** a call in this game, undertaking to win all five tricks. **3** *Horse racing.* a tipster's choice for a certain winner. **4 nap hand.** a position in which there is a very good chance of success if a risk is taken. ◆ *vb* **naps, napping, napped.** *(tr)* **5** *Horse racing.* to name (a horse) as likely to win a race. [C19: from NAPOLEON, the card game]

napalm ('neɪpɑːm, 'næ-) *n* **1** a thick and highly incendiary liquid, usually consisting of petrol gelled with aluminium soaps, used in firebombs, flame-throwers, etc. ◆ *vb* **2** *(tr)* to attack with napalm. [C20: from NA(PHTHENE) + *palm(itate)* salt of PALMITIC ACID]

nape (neɪp) *n* the back of the neck. [C13: from ?]

napery ('neɪpərɪ) *n Scot. & Arch.* household linen, esp. table linen. [C14: from OF *naperie,* from *nape* tablecloth, from L *mappa*]

naphtha ('næfθə, 'næp-) *n* a distillation product from coal tar or petroleum: used as a solvent and in petrol. [C16: via L from Gk, from Iranian]

naphthalene ('næfθəˌliːn, 'næp-) *n* a white crystalline hydrocarbon with a characteristic penetrating odour, used in mothballs and in dyes, explosives, etc. Formula: $C_{10}H_8$. [C19: from NAPHTHA + ALCOHOL + -ENE]
▸**naphthalic** (næf'θælɪk, næp-) *adj*

naphthene ('næfθiːn, 'næp-) *n* any of various cyclic methylene hydrocarbons found in petroleum. [C20: from NAPHTHA + -ENE]

naphthol ('næfθɒl, 'næp-) *n* a white crystalline solid having two isomeric forms, used in dyes and as an antioxidant. Formula: $C_{10}H_7OH$. [C19: from NAPHTHA + -OL[1]]

Napierian logarithm (nə'pɪərɪən, neɪ-) *n* another name for **natural logarithm.**

Napier's bones ('neɪpɪəz) *pl n* a set of graduated rods formerly used for multiplication and division. [C17: based on a method invented by John *Napier* (1550–1617), Scot. mathematician]

napkin Ⓣ ('næpkɪn) *n* **1** Also called: **table napkin.** a usually square piece of cloth or paper used while eating to protect the clothes, wipe the mouth, etc.; serviette. **2** *Rare.* a small piece of cloth. **3** a more formal name for **nappy**[1]. **4** a less common term for **sanitary towel.** [C15: from OF, from *nape* tablecloth, from L *mappa* cloth]

napoleon (nə'pəʊlɪən) *n* **1** a former French gold coin worth 20 francs. **2** *Cards.* the full name for **nap**[3] (sense 1). [C19: from F *napoléon,* after Napoleon I, Emperor of the French (1804–15)]

Napoleonic (nəˌpəʊlɪ'ɒnɪk) *adj* relating to or characteristic of Napoleon I (1769–1821), Emperor of the French (1804–15), or his era.

nappe (næp) *n* **1** a large sheet or mass of rock, originally a recumbent fold, that has been thrust from its original position by earth movements. **2** the sheet of water that flows over a dam or weir. **3** *Geom.* either of the two parts into which a cone is divided by the vertex. [C20: from F: tablecloth]

nappy[1] ('næpɪ) *n, pl* **nappies.** *Brit.* a piece of soft towelling or a disposable material wrapped around a baby in order to absorb its urine or excrement. Also called: **napkin.** US and Canad. name: **diaper.** [C20: changed from NAPKIN]

nappy[2] ('næpɪ) *adj* **nappier, nappiest. 1** having a nap; downy; fuzzy. **2** (of beer) **2a** having a head; frothy. **2b** strong or heady.

nappy rash *n Brit.* (in babies) any irritation to the skin around the genitals, anus, or buttocks, usually caused by contact with urine or excrement. Formal name: **napkin rash.** US and Canad. name: **diaper rash.**

narc (nɑːk) *n US sl.* a narcotics agent.

narcissism Ⓣ ('nɑːsɪˌsɪzəm) *or* **narcism** ('nɑːsɪzəm) *n* **1** an exceptional

THESAURUS

namby-pamby *adj* **1** = **prim,** mawkish, niminy-piminy, prissy *(inf.),* sentimental **2** = **feeble,** anaemic, colourless, insipid, spineless, vapid, weak, weedy *(inf.),* wimpish *or* wimpy *(inf.),* wishy-washy *(inf.)*

name *n* **1, 3** = **title,** appellation, cognomen, denomination, designation, epithet, handle *(sl.),* moniker *or* monicker *(sl.),* nickname, sobriquet, term **4** = **reputation,** character, credit ◆ *vb* **10** = **call,** baptize, christen, denominate, dub, entitle, label, style, term **11** = **mention,** cite, identify, specify **12** = **fix,** choose, specify **13** = **nominate,** appoint, choose, commission, designate, select

named *adj* **10** = **called,** baptized, christened, denominated, dubbed, entitled, known as, labelled, styled, termed **11** = **mentioned,** cited, identified, specified **13** = **nominated,** appointed, chosen, commissioned, designated, picked, selected, singled out

nameless *adj* **1** = **anonymous,** innominate, undesignated, unnamed, untitled **2** = **indescribable,** ineffable, inexpressible **3** = **unspeakable,** abominable, horrible, unmentionable, unutterable

namely *adv* = **specifically,** i.e., that is to say, to wit, viz.

nap[1] *vb* **1** = **sleep,** catnap, doze, drop off *(inf.),* drowse, kip *(Brit. sl.),* nod, nod off *(inf.),* rest, snooze *(inf.),* zizz *(Brit. inf.)* ◆ *n* **3** = **sleep,** catnap, forty winks *(inf.),* kip *(Brit. sl.),* rest, shuteye *(sl.),* siesta, zizz *(Brit. inf.)*

nap[2] *n* **1** = **weave,** down, fibre, grain, pile, shag

napkin *n* **1** = **serviette,** cloth

narcissism *n* **1** = **egotism,** self-admiration, self-love, vanity

interest in or admiration for oneself, esp. one's physical appearance. **2** sexual satisfaction derived from contemplation of one's own physical endowments. [C19: after *Narcissus*, a beautiful youth in Gk myth., who fell in love with his reflection in a pool]
▸ **'narcissist** *n* ▸ **ˌnarcis'sistic** *adj*

narcissus (nɑː'sɪsəs) *n, pl* **narcissuses** *or* **narcissi** (-'sɪsaɪ). a plant of a Eurasian genus whose yellow, orange, or white flowers have a crown surrounded by spreading segments. [C16: via L from Gk *nárkissos*, ?from *narkē* numbness, because of narcotic properties attributed to the plant]

narco- *or sometimes before a vowel* **narc-** *combining form.* **1** indicating numbness or torpor: *narcolepsy.* **2** connected with or derived from illicit drug production: *narcoeconomies.* [from Gk *narkē* numbness]

narcoanalysis (ˌnɑːkəʊə'nælɪsɪs) *n* psychoanalysis of a patient in a trance induced by a narcotic drug.

narcolepsy ('nɑːkəˌlɛpsɪ) *n Pathol.* a rare condition characterized by sudden episodes of deep sleep.
▸ **ˌnarco'leptic** *adj*

narcosis (nɑː'kəʊsɪs) *n* unconsciousness induced by narcotics or general anaesthetics.

narcosynthesis (ˌnɑːkəʊ'sɪnθɪsɪs) *n* a method of treating severe personality disorders by working with the patient while he is under the influence of a barbiturate drug.

narcotic Ⓣ (nɑː'kɒtɪk) *n* **1** any of a group of drugs, such as opium and morphine, that produce numbness and stupor. **2** anything that relieves pain or induces sleep, mental numbness, etc. **3** any illegal drug. ◆ *adj* **4** of or relating to narcotics or narcotics addicts. **5** of or relating to narcosis. [C14: via Med. L from Gk *narkōtikós*, from *narkoūn* to numb, from *narkē* numbness]
▸ **nar'cotically** *adv*

narcotism ('nɑːkəˌtɪzəm) *n* stupor or addiction induced by narcotic drugs.

narcotize *or* **narcotise** ('nɑːkəˌtaɪz) *vb* **narcotizes, narcotizing, narcotized** *or* **narcotises, narcotising, narcotised.** (*tr*) to place under the influence of a narcotic drug.
▸ **ˌnarcoti'zation** *or* **ˌnarcoti'sation** *n*

nard (nɑːd) *n* **1** another name for **spikenard. 2** any of several plants whose aromatic roots were formerly used in medicine. [C14: via L from Gk *nárdos*, ? ult. from Sansk. *nalada* Indian spikenard]

nardoo ('nɑːduː) *n* (in Australia) **1** any of certain cloverlike ferns that grow in swampy areas. **2** the spores of such a plant, used as food. [C19: from Abor.]

nares ('nɛəriːz) *pl n, sing* **naris** ('nɛərɪs). *Anat.* the technical name for the nostrils. [C17: from L; rel. to OE *nasu*, L *nāsus* nose]
▸ **'narial** *adj*

narghile, nargile, *or* **nargileh** ('nɑːgɪlɪ, -ˌleɪ) *n* another name for **hookah.** [C19: from F *narguilé*, from Persian *nārgīleh* a pipe having a bowl made of coconut shell, from *nārgīl* coconut]

nark Ⓣ (nɑːk) *Sl.* ◆ *n* **1** *Brit., Austral., & NZ.* an informer or spy: *copper's nark.* **2** *Brit.* someone who complains in an irritating or whining manner. ◆ *vb* **3** *Brit., Austral., & NZ.* to annoy, upset, or irritate. **4** (*intr*) *Brit., Austral., & NZ.* to inform or spy, esp. for the police. **5** (*intr*) *Brit.* to complain irritatingly. [C19: prob. from Romany *nāk* nose]

narky ('nɑːkɪ) *adj* **narkier, narkiest.** *Sl.* irritable, complaining, or sarcastic.

Narraganset (ˌnærə'gænsɪt) *n* **1** (*pl* **Narraganset** *or* **Narragansets**) a member of a North American Indian people formerly living in Rhode Island. **2** the language of this people, belonging to the Algonquian family.

narrate Ⓣ (nə'reɪt) *vb* **narrates, narrating, narrated. 1** to tell (a story); relate. **2** to speak in accompaniment of (a film, etc.). [C17: from L *narrāre* to recount, from *gnārus* knowing]
▸ **nar'ratable** *adj* ▸ **nar'rator** *n*

narration Ⓣ (nə'reɪʃən) *n* **1** the act or process of narrating. **2** a narrated account or story.

narrative Ⓣ ('nærətɪv) *n* **1** an account or story, as of events, experiences, etc. **2** the part of a literary work, etc., that relates events. **3** the process or technique of narrating. ◆ *adj* **4** telling a story: *a narrative poem.* **5** of or relating to narration: *narrative art.*

narrow Ⓣ ('nærəʊ) *adj* **1** small in breadth, esp. in comparison to length. **2** limited in range or extent. **3** limited in outlook. **4** limited in means or resources. **5** barely adequate or successful (esp. in **a narrow escape**). **6** painstakingly thorough: *a narrow scrutiny.* **7** *Finance.* denoting an assessment of liquidity as including notes and coins in circulation with the public, banks' till money, and banks' balances: *narrow money.* Cf. **broad** (sense 12). **8** *Phonetics.* another word for **tense**[1] (sense 4). ◆ *vb* **9** to make or become narrow. **10** (often foll. by *down*) to limit or restrict. ◆ *n* **11** a narrow place, esp. a pass or strait. ◆ See also **narrows.** [OE *nearu*]
▸ **'narrowly** *adv* ▸ **'narrowness** *n*

narrowboat ('nærəʊˌbəʊt) *n* a long bargelike boat with a beam of 2.1 metres (7 feet), used on canals.

narrow gauge *n* **1** a railway track with a smaller distance between the lines than the standard gauge of 56½ inches. ◆ *adj* **narrow-gauge. 2** of or denoting a railway with a narrow gauge.

narrow-minded Ⓣ *adj* having a biased or illiberal viewpoint; bigoted, intolerant, or prejudiced.
▸ **ˌnarrow-'mindedness** *n*

narrows Ⓣ ('nærəʊz) *pl n* a narrow part of a strait, river, current, etc.

narthex ('nɑːθɛks) *n* **1** a portico at the west end of a church, esp. one at right angles to the nave. **2** a rectangular entrance hall between the porch and nave of a church. [C17: via L from Med. Gk: enclosed porch (earlier: box), from Gk *narthēx* giant fennel, the stems of which were used to make boxes]

narwhal, narwal ('nɑːwəl), *or* **narwhale** ('nɑːˌweɪl) *n* an arctic toothed whale having a black-spotted whitish skin and, in the male, a long spiral tusk. [C17: of Scand. origin; cf. Danish, Norwegian *narhval*, from ON *nāhvalr*, from *nār* corpse + *hvalr* whale]

nary ('nɛərɪ) *adv Dialect or inf.* not; never: *nary a man was left.* [C19: var. of *ne'er a* never a]

NASA ('næsə) *n* (in the US) *acronym for* National Aeronautics and Space Administration.

nasal ('neɪzəl) *adj* **1** of the nose. **2** *Phonetics.* pronounced with the soft palate lowered allowing air to escape via the nasal cavity. ◆ *n* **3** a nasal speech sound, such as English *m, n,* or *ng.* [C17: from F from LL *nāsālis*, from L *nāsus* nose]
▸ **nasality** (neɪ'zælɪtɪ) *n* ▸ **'nasally** *adv*

nasalize *or* **nasalise** ('neɪzəˌlaɪz) *vb* **nasalizes, nasalizing, nasalized** *or* **nasalises, nasalising, nasalised.** (*tr*) to pronounce nasally.
▸ **ˌnasali'zation** *or* **ˌnasali'sation** *n*

nascent ('næsənt, 'neɪ-) *adj* starting to grow or develop; being born. [C17: from L *nascēns*, present participle of *nāscī* to be born]
▸ **'nascency** *n*

nascent hydrogen *n Chem.* hydrogen produced in a reactive form within the reaction mixture.

naso- *combining form.* nose: *nasopharynx.* [from L *nāsus* nose]

nasogastric (ˌneɪzəʊ'gæstrɪk) *adj Anat.* of or relating to the nose and stomach: *a nasogastric tube.*

nastic movement ('næstɪk) *n* a response of plant parts that is independent of the direction of the external stimulus, such as the opening of buds caused by an alteration in light intensity. [C19 *nastic*, from Gk *nastos* close-packed, from *nassein* to press down]

nasturtium (nə'stɜːʃəm) *n* a plant having round leaves and yellow, red, or orange trumpet-shaped spurred flowers. [C17: from L: kind of cress, from *nāsus* nose + *tortus* twisted; because the pungent smell causes one to wrinkle one's nose]

nasty Ⓣ ('nɑːstɪ) *adj* **nastier, nastiest. 1** unpleasant or repugnant. **2** dangerous or painful: *a nasty wound.* **3** spiteful or ill-natured. **4** obscene or indecent. ◆ *n, pl* **nasties. 5** an offensive or unpleasant person or thing:

THESAURUS

narcotic *n* **1 = drug,** anaesthetic, analgesic, anodyne, opiate, painkiller, sedative, tranquillizer ◆ *adj* **5 = sedative,** analgesic, calming, dulling, hypnotic, Lethean, numbing, painkilling, somnolent, soporific, stupefacient, stupefactive, stupefying

nark *vb* **3 = annoy,** aggravate (*inf.*), bother, bug, exasperate, gall, get on one's nerves (*inf.*), irk, irritate, miff (*inf.*), nettle, peeve, pique, provoke, rile

narrate *vb* **1 = tell,** chronicle, describe, detail, recite, recount, rehearse, relate, repeat, report, set forth, unfold

narration *n* **1 = telling,** description, explanation, reading, recital, rehearsal, relation, storytelling, voice-over (*in film*)

narrative *n* **1 = story,** account, chronicle, detail, history, report, statement, tale

narrator *n* **1 = storyteller,** annalist, author, bard, chronicler, commentator, raconteur, reciter, relater, reporter, writer

narrow *adj* **1 = thin,** attenuated, fine, slender, slim, spare, tapering **2 = limited,** circumscribed, close, confined, constricted, contracted, cramped, incapacious, meagre, near, pinched, restricted, scanty, straitened, tight **3 = insular,** biased, bigoted, dogmatic, illiberal, intolerant, narrow-minded, partial, prejudiced, puritan, reactionary, small-minded ◆ *vb* **9 = tighten,** circumscribe, constrict, diminish, limit, reduce, simplify, straiten
Antonyms *adj* ≠ **thin:** broad, wide ≠ **limited:** ample, big, broad, generous, open, spacious, wide ≠ **insular:** broad-minded, generous, liberal, receptive, tolerant

narrowly *adv* **5 = just,** barely, by a whisker *or* hair's-breadth, by the skin of one's teeth, only just, scarcely **6 = painstakingly,** carefully, closely, scrutinizingly

narrow-minded *adj* **= intolerant,** biased, bigoted, conservative, hidebound, illiberal, insular, opinionated, parochial, petty, prejudiced, provincial, reactionary, short-sighted, small-minded, strait-laced
Antonyms *adj* broad-minded, catholic, cosmopolitan, freethinking, indulgent, open-minded, permissive, tolerant, unprejudiced

narrows *pl n* **= channel,** gulf, passage, sound, straits

nastiness *n* **1 = squalor,** defilement, dirtiness, filth, filthiness, foulness, impurity, pollution, uncleanliness **3 = unpleasantness,** disagreeableness, malice, meanness, offensiveness, spitefulness **4 = obscenity,** indecency, licentiousness, pollution, porn (*inf.*), pornography, ribaldry, smuttiness

nasty *adj* **1 = objectionable,** dirty, disagreeable, disgusting, filthy, foul, grotty (*sl.*), horrible, loathsome, malodorous, mephitic, nauseating, noisome, obnoxious, odious, offensive, polluted, repellent, repugnant, sickening, unappetizing, unpleasant, vile, yucky *or* yukky (*sl.*) **2 = painful,** bad, critical, dangerous, serious, severe **3 = spiteful,** abusive, annoying, bad-tempered, despicable, disagreeable, distasteful, malicious, mean, unpleasant, vicious, vile **4 = obscene,** blue, foul, gross, impure, indecent, lascivious, lewd, licentious, pornographic, ribald, smutty
Antonyms *adj* ≠ **objectionable:** admirable, agreeable, enjoyable, nice, pleasant, sweet ≠ **spiteful:**

a video nasty. [C14: from ?; prob. rel. to Swedish dialect *nasket* & Du. *nestig* dirty]
▸**'nastily** *adv* ▸**'nastiness** *n*

NAS/UWT (in Britain) *abbrev. for* National Association of Schoolmasters/Union of Women Teachers.

nat. *abbrev. for:* **1** national. **2** native. **3** natural.

natal ('neɪtᵊl) *adj* of or relating to birth. [C14: from L *nātālis* of one's birth, from *nātus,* from *nascī* to be born]

natant ('neɪtᵊnt) *adj* floating or swimming. [C18: from L *natāns,* present participle of *natāre* to swim]

natation (nə'teɪʃən) *n* a literary word for **swimming.** [C16: from L *natātiō* a swimming, from *natāre* to swim]

natatory (nə'teɪtərɪ) *or* **natatorial** (ˌnætə'tɔːrɪəl) *adj* of or relating to swimming. [C18: from LL *natātōrius,* from L *natāre* to swim]

natch (nætʃ) *sentence substitute. Inf.* short for **naturally.**

nates ('neɪtiːz) *pl n, sing* **natis** (-tɪs). a technical word for the **buttocks.** [C17: from L]

NATFHE (in Britain) *abbrev. for* National Association of Teachers in Further and Higher Education.

natheless ('neɪθlɪs) *or* **nathless** ('næθlɪs) *Arch. sentence connector.* nonetheless. [OE *nāthylǣs,* from *nā* never + *thȳ* for that + *lǣs* less]

nation ❶ ('neɪʃən) *n* **1** an aggregation of people or peoples of one or more cultures, races, etc., organized into a single state: *the Australian nation.* **2** a community of persons not constituting a state but bound by common descent, language, history, etc.: *the French-Canadian nation.* [C13: via OF from L *nātiō* birth, tribe, from *nascī* to be born]
▸**'nationˌhood** *n*

national ❶ ('næʃənᵊl) *adj* **1** of or relating to a nation as a whole. **2** characteristic of a particular nation: *the national dress of Poland.* ◆ *n* **3** a citizen or subject. **4** a national newspaper.
▸**'nationally** *adv*

national anthem *n* a patriotic song adopted by a nation for use on public occasions.

national assistance *n* (formerly, in Britain) a weekly allowance paid to individuals of various groups by the state to bring their incomes up to minimum levels established by law. Now replaced by income support.

national bank *n* **1** (in the US) a commercial bank incorporated under a Federal charter and legally required to be a member of the Federal Reserve System. **2** a bank operated by a government.

national call *n Brit.* a telephone call made to a number within the country but outside the local area.

National Curriculum *n* (in England and Wales) the curriculum of subjects taught in state schools from 1989. The ten foundation subjects are: English, maths, and science (the core subjects); art, design and technology, geography, history, music, physical education, and a foreign language. Pupils are assessed at four stages. Abbrev.: **NC.**

national debt *n* the total outstanding borrowings of a nation's central government.

National Economic Development Council *n* a former advisory body on economic policy in Britain, composed of representatives of government, management, and trade unions: abolished in 1992. Abbrevs.: **NEDC,** (inf.) **Neddy.**

National Enterprise Board *n* a public corporation established in 1975 to help the economy of the UK. In 1981 it merged with the National Research and Development Council to form the British Technology Group. Abbrev.: **NEB.**

National Football *n* (in Australia) another name for **Australian Rules.**

National Front *n* an extreme right-wing British political party founded in 1967.

national grid *n Brit.* **1** a network of high-voltage electric power lines linking major electric power stations. **2** the metric coordinate system used in ordnance survey maps.

National Guard *n* **1** (*sometimes not cap.*) the armed force that was established in France in 1789 and existed intermittently until 1871. **2** (in the US) a state military force that can be called into federal service by the president.

National Health Service *n* (in Britain) the system of national medical services since 1948, financed mainly by taxation. Abbrev.: **NHS.**

national hunt *n Brit.* (*often caps.*) **a** the racing of horses on racecourses with jumps. **b** (*as modifier*): *a National Hunt jockey.*

national income *n Econ.* the total of all incomes accruing over a specified period to residents of a country.

national insurance *n* (in Britain) state insurance based on weekly contributions from employees and employers and providing payments to the unemployed, the sick, the retired, etc., as well as medical services.

nationalism ❶ ('næʃənəˌlɪzəm) *n* **1** a sentiment based on common cultural characteristics that binds a population and often produces a policy of national independence. **2** loyalty to one's country; patriotism. **3** exaggerated or fanatical devotion to a national community.
▸**'nationalist** *n, adj* ▸**ˌnational'istic** *adj*

nationality ❶ (ˌnæʃə'nælɪtɪ) *n, pl* **nationalities. 1** the fact of being a citizen of a particular nation. **2** a body of people sharing common descent, history, language, etc.; a nation. **3** a national group: *30 different nationalities are found in this city.* **4** national character. **5** the fact of being a nation; national status.

nationalize *or* **nationalise** ('næʃənəˌlaɪz) *vb* **nationalizes, nationalizing, nationalized** *or* **nationalises, nationalising, nationalised.** (*tr*) **1** to put (an industry, resources, etc.) under state control. **2** to make national in character or status. **3** a less common word for **naturalize.**
▸**ˌnationali'zation** *or* **ˌnationali'sation** *n*

national park *n* an area of countryside for public use designated by a national government as being of notable scenic, environmental, or historical importance.

National Party *n* **1** (in New Zealand) the more conservative of the two main political parties. **2** (in Australia) a political party drawing its main support from rural areas. Former name: **National Country Party. 3** (in South Africa) a political party composed mainly of centre-to-right-wing Afrikaners. It ruled from 1948 until 1994, when South Africa's first multiracial elections were won by the African National Congress.

National Savings Bank *n* (in Britain) a government savings bank, run through the Post Office.

national service *n Chiefly Brit.* compulsory military service.

National Socialism *n German history.* the doctrines and practices of the Nazis, involving the supremacy of Hitler as Führer, anti-Semitism, state control of the economy, and national expansion.
▸**National Socialist** *n, adj*

national superannuation *n NZ.* a government pension given on the attainment of a specified age; old age pension.

National Trust *n* **1** (in Britain) an organization concerned with the preservation of historic buildings and areas of the countryside of great beauty. **2** (in Australia) a similar organization in each of the states.

nationwide ❶ ('neɪʃənˌwaɪd) *adj* covering or available to the whole of a nation; national.

native ❶ ('neɪtɪv) *adj* **1** relating or belonging to a person by virtue of conditions existing at birth: *a native language.* **2** natural or innate: *a native strength.* **3** born in a specified place: *a native Indian.* **4** (when *postpositive,* foll. by *to*) originating in: *kangaroos are native to Australia.* **5** relating to the indigenous inhabitants of a country: *the native art of the New Guinea Highlands.* **6** (of metals) found naturally in the elemental form; not chemically combined as in an ore. **7** unadulterated by civilization, artifice, or adornment; natural. **8** *Arch.* related by birth or race. **9 go native.** (of a settler) to adopt the lifestyle of the local population, esp. when it appears less civilized. ◆ *n* **10** (usually foll. by *of*) a person born in a particular place: *a native of Geneva.* **11** (usually foll. by *of*) a species of animal or plant originating in a particular place. **12** a member of an indigenous people of a country, esp. a non-White people, as opposed to colonial immigrants. [C14: from L *nātīvus* innate, natural, from *nascī* to be born]
▸**'natively** *adv* ▸**'nativeness** *n*

Native American *n* another name for an **American Indian.**

native bear *n* an Australian name for **koala.**

native-born *adj* born in the country or area indicated.

native companion *n* (in Australia) another name for **brolga.**

native dog *n Austral.* a dingo.

nativity ❶ (nə'tɪvɪtɪ) *n, pl* **nativities.** birth or origin. [C14: from LL *nātīvitas* birth; see NATIVE]

Nativity ❶ (nə'tɪvɪtɪ) *n* **1** the birth of Christ. **2** the feast of Christmas as a commemoration of this. **3a** an artistic representation of the circumstances of the birth of Christ. **3b** (*as modifier*): *a Nativity play.*

NATO *or* **Nato** ('neɪtəʊ) *n acronym for* North Atlantic Treaty Organization: an international organization established (1949) for purposes of collective security.

natron ('neɪtrən) *n* a whitish or yellow mineral that consists of hydrated sodium carbonate and occurs in saline deposits and salt lakes. [C17: via F & Sp. from Ar. *natrūn,* from Gk *nitron* NITRE]

NATSOPA (næt'səʊpə) *n* (formerly, in Britain) *acronym for* National Society of Operative Printers, Graphical and Media Personnel.

natter ❶ ('nætə) *Chiefly Brit. inf.* ◆ *vb* **1** (*intr*) to talk idly and at length; chatter. ◆ *n* **2** prolonged idle chatter. [C19: from *gnatter* to grumble, imit.]

THESAURUS

decent, kind, nice, pleasant, sweet ≠ **obscene:** clean, decent

nation *n* **1** = **country,** commonwealth, community, people, population, race, realm, society, state, tribe

national *adj* **1** = **nationwide,** civil, countrywide, governmental, public, state, widespread **2** = **domestic,** internal, social ◆ *n* **3** = **citizen,** inhabitant, native, resident, subject

nationalism *n* **2, 3** = **patriotism,** allegiance, chauvinism, fealty, jingoism, loyalty, nationality

nationalistic *adj* **2, 3** = **patriotic,** chauvinistic, jingoistic, loyal, xenophobic

nationality *n* **2, 3** = **race,** ethnic group, nation

nationwide *adj* = **national,** countrywide, general, overall, widespread

native *adj* **1** = **local,** domestic, home, homegrown, home-made, indigenous, mother, vernacular **2** = **inborn,** built-in, congenital, endemic, hereditary, immanent, inbred, ingrained, inherent, inherited, innate, instinctive, intrinsic, inveterate, natal, natural **5** = **indigenous,** aboriginal, autochthonous ◆ *n* **10** = **inhabitant,** citizen, countryman, dweller, national, resident **12** = **aborigine,** autochthon

nativity *n* = **birth,** delivery, parturition
Antonyms *n* death, demise, dying, expiration

Nativity *n* **3** = **crèche,** manger scene

natter *vb* **1** = **gossip,** blather, blether, chatter, chew the fat *or* rag (*sl.*), gabble, jabber, jaw (*sl.*), prate, prattle, rabbit (on) (*Brit. inf.*), talk, talk idly, witter (*inf.*) ◆ *n* **2** = **gossip,** blather, blether, chat, chinwag (*Brit. inf.*), chitchat, confab-

natterjack ('nætəˌdʒæk) *n* a European toad having a greyish-brown body marked with reddish warty processes. [C18: from ?]

natty Ⓣ ('nætɪ) *adj* **nattier, nattiest.** *Inf.* smart; spruce; dapper. [C18: from obs. *netty,* from *net* NEAT[1]]
▸'**nattily** *adv* ▸'**nattiness** *n*

natural Ⓣ ('nætʃrəl) *adj* **1** of, existing in, or produced by nature: *natural science; natural cliffs.* **2** in accordance with human nature. **3** as is normal or to be expected: *the natural course of events.* **4** not acquired; innate: *a natural gift for sport.* **5** being so through innate qualities: *a natural leader.* **6** not supernatural or strange: *natural phenomena.* **7** genuine or spontaneous. **8** lifelike: *she looked more natural without make-up.* **9** not affected by man; wild: *in the natural state this animal is not ferocious.* **10** being or made from organic material; not synthetic: *a natural fibre like cotton.* **11** born out of wedlock. **12** not adopted but rather related by blood: *her natural parents.* **13** *Music.* **13a** not sharp or flat. **13b** (*postpositive*) denoting a note that is neither sharp nor flat. **13c** (of a key or scale) containing no sharps or flats. **14** based on the principles and findings of human reason rather than on revelation: *natural religion.* ◆ *n* **15** *Inf.* a person or thing regarded as certain to qualify for success, selection, etc.: *the horse was a natural for first place.* **16** *Music.* **16a** Also called (US): **cancel.** an accidental cancelling a previous sharp or flat. Usual symbol: ♮ **16b** a note affected by this accidental. **17** *Obs.* an imbecile; idiot.
▸'**naturalness** *n*

natural childbirth *n* a method of childbirth characterized by the absence of anaesthetics, in which the expectant mother is given special breathing and relaxing exercises.

natural gas *n* a gaseous mixture, consisting mainly of methane, trapped below ground; used extensively as a fuel.

natural history *n* **1** the study of animals and plants in the wild state. **2** the sum of these phenomena in a given place or at a given time.
▸**natural historian** *n*

natural immunity *n* immunity with which an individual is born, which has a genetic basis.

naturalism Ⓣ ('nætʃrəˌlɪzəm) *n* **1** a movement, esp. in art and literature, advocating detailed realistic and factual description. **2** the belief that all religious truth is based not on revelation but rather on the study of natural causes and processes. **3** *Philosophy.* a scientific account of the world in terms of causes and natural forces. **4** action or thought caused by natural instincts.

naturalist Ⓣ ('nætʃrəlɪst) *n* **1** a person who is versed in or interested in botany or zoology. **2** a person who advocates or practises naturalism.

naturalistic Ⓣ (ˌnætʃrə'lɪstɪk) *adj* **1** of or reproducing nature in effect or characteristics. **2** of or characteristic of naturalism. **3** of naturalists.
▸ˌ**natural'istically** *adv*

naturalize Ⓣ *or* **naturalise** ('nætʃrəˌlaɪz) *vb* **naturalizes, naturalizing, naturalized** *or* **naturalises, naturalising, naturalised. 1** (*tr*) to give citizenship to (a person of foreign birth). **2** to be or cause to be adopted in another place, as a word, custom, etc. **3** (*tr*) to introduce (a plant or animal from another region) and cause it to adapt to local conditions. **4** (*intr*) (of a plant or animal) to adapt successfully to a foreign environment. **5** (*tr*) to make natural or more lifelike.
▸ˌ**naturali'zation** *or* ˌ**naturali'sation** *n*

natural language *n* a language that has evolved naturally as a means of communication among people, as opposed to an invented language or a code.

natural logarithm *n* a logarithm to the base e. Usually written $\log_e$ or ln. Also called: **Napierian logarithm.**

naturally Ⓣ ('nætʃrəlɪ) *adv* **1** in a natural way. **2** instinctively. ◆ *adv, sentence substitute.* **3** of course; surely.

natural number *n* any of the numbers 0 ,1, 2, 3, 4,… that can be used to count the members of a set; the non-negative integers.

natural philosophy *n* physical science, esp. physics.
▸**natural philosopher** *n*

natural resources *pl n* naturally occurring materials such as coal, fertile land, etc.

natural science *n* the sciences that are involved in the study of the physical world and its phenomena, including biology, physics, chemistry, and geology.

natural selection *n* a process resulting in the survival of those individuals from a population of animals or plants that are best adapted to the prevailing environmental conditions.

natural theology *n* the attempt to derive theological truth, and esp. the existence of God, from empirical facts by reasoned argument. Cf. **revealed religion.**

natural wastage *n* the loss of employees, etc., through not replacing those who retire or resign rather than dismissal or redundancy.

nature Ⓣ ('neɪtʃə) *n* **1** fundamental qualities; identity or essential character. **2** (*often cap.*) the whole system of the existence, forces, and events of all physical life that are not controlled by man. **3** plant and animal life, as distinct from man. **4** a wild primitive state untouched by man. **5** natural unspoilt countryside. **6** disposition or temperament. **7** desires or instincts governing behaviour. **8** the normal biological needs of the body. **9** sort; character. **10 against nature.** unnatural or immoral. **11 by nature.** essentially or innately. **12 call of nature.** *Inf.* the need to urinate or defecate. **13 from nature.** using natural models in drawing, painting, etc. **14 in** (*or* **of**) **the nature of.** essentially the same as; by way of. [C13: via OF from L *nātūra,* from *nātus,* p.p. of *nascī* to be born]

nature reserve *n* an area of land that is protected and managed in order to preserve its flora and fauna.

nature study *n* the study of the natural world, esp. animals and plants, by direct observation at an elementary level.

nature trail *n* a path through countryside designed and usually signposted to draw attention to natural features of interest.

naturism Ⓣ ('neɪtʃəˌrɪzəm) *n* another name for **nudism.**
▸'**naturist** *n, adj*

naturopathy (ˌnætʃə'rɒpæθɪ) *n* the treatment of illness by stimulating natural healing, esp. by herbal remedies, manipulation, etc.
▸'**naturoˌpath** *n* ▸ˌ**naturo'pathic** *adj*

naught Ⓣ (nɔːt) *n* **1** *Arch. or literary.* nothing; ruin or failure. **2** a variant spelling (esp. US) of **nought. 3 set at naught.** to disregard or scorn; disdain. ◆ *adv* **4** *Arch. or literary.* not at all: *it matters naught.* ◆ *adj* **5** *Obs.* worthless, ruined, or wicked. [OE *nāwiht,* from *nā* NO[1] + *wiht* thing, person]

naughty Ⓣ ('nɔːtɪ) *adj* **naughtier, naughtiest. 1** (esp. of children) mischievous or disobedient. **2** mildly indecent; titillating. [C14: (orig.: needy, poor): from NAUGHT]
▸'**naughtily** *adv* ▸'**naughtiness** *n*

nauplius ('nɔːplɪəs) *n, pl* **nauplii** (-plɪˌaɪ). the larva of many crustaceans, having a rounded unsegmented body with three pairs of limbs. [C19: from L: type of shellfish, from Gk *Nauplios,* one of the sons of the Greek god Poseidon]

nausea Ⓣ ('nɔːzɪə, -sɪə) *n* **1** the sensation that precedes vomiting. **2** a feeling of revulsion. [C16: via L from Gk: seasickness, from *naus* ship]

nauseate Ⓣ ('nɔːzɪˌeɪt, -sɪ-) *vb* **nauseates, nauseating, nauseated. 1** (*tr*) to arouse feelings of disgust or revulsion in. **2** to feel or cause to feel sick.
▸'**nauseˌating** *adj*

nauseous Ⓣ ('nɔːzɪəs, -sɪəs) *adj* **1** causing nausea. **2** distasteful; repulsive.
▸'**nauseously** *adv* ▸'**nauseousness** *n*

nautch *or* **nauch** (nɔːtʃ) *n* an intricate traditional Indian dance performed by professional dancing girls. [C18: from Hindi *nāc,* from Sansk., from *nṛtyati* he acts or dances]

THESAURUS

ulation, conversation, gab (*inf.*), gabble, gabfest (*inf., chiefly US & Canad.*), jabber, jaw (*sl.*), prattle, talk

natty *adj Informal* = **smart**, chic, crucial (*sl.*), dapper, elegant, fashionable, neat, snazzy (*inf.*), spruce, stylish, trendy (*Brit. inf.*), trim, well-dressed, well-turned-out

natural *adj* **3** = **normal**, common, everyday, legitimate, logical, ordinary, regular, typical, usual **4** = **innate**, characteristic, congenital, essential, immanent, inborn, indigenous, inherent, in one's blood, instinctive, intuitive, natal, native **7** = **unaffected**, artless, candid, frank, genuine, ingenuous, open, real, simple, spontaneous, unpretentious, unsophisticated, unstudied **10** = **pure**, organic, plain, unbleached, unmixed, unpolished, unrefined, whole
Antonyms *adj* ≠ **normal:** abnormal, irregular, out of the ordinary, strange, untypical ≠ **unaffected:** affected, artificial, assumed, counterfeit, feigned, phoney *or* phony (*inf.*), unnatural ≠ **pure:** manufactured, processed, synthetic, unnatural

naturalism *n* **1** = **realism**, factualism, verisimilitude

naturalist *n* **1** = **biologist**, botanist, ecologist, zoologist **2** = **realist**, factualist

naturalistic *adj* **2** = **realistic**, factualistic, kitchen sink, lifelike, photographic, real-life, representational, true-to-life, vérité, warts and all (*inf.*)

naturalize *vb* **1** = **acclimatize**, enfranchise, grant citizenship **2** = **adopt**, adapt **3** = **acclimate**, accustom, adapt, domesticate, familiarize, habituate

naturally *adv* **1** = **genuinely**, as anticipated, customarily, informally, normally, simply, spontaneously, typically, unaffectedly, unpretentiously ◆ *sentence substitute* **3** = **of course**, absolutely, as a matter of course, certainly

naturalness *n* **7** = **spontaneousness**, artlessness, candidness, frankness, genuineness, ingenuousness, openness, realism, simpleness, simplicity, unaffectedness, unpretentiousness, unsophisticatedness, unstudiedness **10** = **purity**, plainness, pureness, wholeness

nature *n* **1** = **make-up**, attributes, character, complexion, constitution, essence, features, quality, traits **2** = **creation**, cosmos, earth, environment, universe, world **5** = **country**, countryside, landscape, scenery **6** = **temperament**, disposition, humour, mood, outlook, temper **9** = **kind**, category, description, sort, species, style, type, variety

naturist *n* = **nudist**

naught *n Archaic or literary* **1** = **nothing**, nil, nothingness, nought, zero

naughty *adj* **1** = **disobedient**, annoying, bad, exasperating, fractious, impish, misbehaved, mischievous, perverse, playful, refractory, roguish, sinful, teasing, wayward, wicked, worthless **2** = **obscene**, bawdy, blue, improper, lewd, off-colour, ribald, risqué, smutty, vulgar, X-rated (*inf.*)
Antonyms *adj* ≠ **disobedient:** good, obedient, polite, proper, seemly, well-behaved, well-mannered ≠ **obscene:** polite, proper

nausea *n* **1** = **sickness**, biliousness, qualm(s), queasiness, retching, squeamishness, vomiting **2** = **disgust**, abhorrence, aversion, loathing, odium, repugnance, revulsion

nauseate *vb* **1, 2** = **sicken**, disgust, gross out (*US sl.*), horrify, offend, repel, repulse, revolt, turn one's stomach

nauseous *adj* **1, 2** = **sickening**, abhorrent, detestable, disgusting, distasteful, loathsome, nauseating, offensive, repugnant, repulsive, revolting, yucky *or* yukky (*sl.*)

nautical ❶ (ˈnɔːtɪkᵊl) *adj* of or involving ships, navigation, or seamen. [C16: from L *nauticus*, from Gk *nautikos*, from *naus* ship]
▸ **ˈnautically** *adv*

nautical mile *n* **1** Also called **international nautical mile, air mile.** a unit of length, used esp. in navigation, equivalent to the average length of a minute of latitude, and corresponding to a latitude of 45°, i.e. 1852 m (6076.12 ft). **2** a former British unit of length equal to 1853.18 m (6080 ft), which was replaced by the international nautical mile in 1970. Former name: **geographical mile.** Cf. **sea mile.**

nautilus (ˈnɔːtɪləs) *n, pl* **nautiluses** *or* **nautili** (-ˌlaɪ). **1** any of a genus of cephalopod molluscs, esp. the pearly nautilus. **2** short for **paper nautilus.** [C17: via L from Gk *nautilos* sailor, from *naus* ship]

NAV *abbrev. for* net asset value.

Navaho *or* **Navajo** (ˈnævəˌhəʊ) *n* **1** (*pl* **Navaho, Navahos, Navahoes** *or* **Navajo, Navajos, Navajoes**) a member of a North American Indian people of Arizona, New Mexico, and Utah. **2** the language of this people. [C18: from Sp. *Navajó* pueblo, from Tena *Navahu* large planted field]

naval ❶ (ˈneɪvᵊl) *adj* **1** of, characteristic of, or having a navy. **2** of or relating to ships; nautical. [C16: from L *nāvālis*, from *nāvis* ship]

naval architecture *n* the designing of ships.
▸ **naval architect** *n*

Navaratri (ˌnævəˈrɑːtrɪ) *n* an annual Hindu festival celebrated over nine days in September–October. It commemorates the slaying of demons by Rama and the goddess Durga. Also called: **Durga Puja.** [from Sansk. *navaratri* nine nights]

navarin (ˈnævərɪn) *n* a stew of mutton or lamb with root vegetables. [from F]

nave[1] (neɪv) *n* the central space in a church, extending from the narthex to the chancel and often flanked by aisles. [C17: via Med. L from L *nāvis* ship, from the similarity of shape]

nave[2] (neɪv) *n* the central block or hub of a wheel. [OE *nafu, nafa*]

navel ❶ (ˈneɪvᵊl) *n* **1** the scar in the centre of the abdomen, usually forming a slight depression, where the umbilical cord was attached. Technical name: **umbilicus.** Related adj: **umbilical. 2** a central part or point. [OE *nafela*]

navel orange *n* a sweet orange that has at its apex a navel-like depression enclosing an underdeveloped secondary fruit.

navelwort (ˈneɪvᵊlˌwɜːt) *n* another name for **pennywort** (sense 1).

navicular (nəˈvɪkjʊlə) *Anat.* ◆ *adj* **1** shaped like a boat. ◆ *n* **2** a small boat-shaped bone of the wrist or foot. [C16: from LL *nāviculāris*, from L *nāvicula*, dim. of *nāvis* ship]

navigable ❶ (ˈnævɪgəbᵊl) *adj* **1** wide, deep, or safe enough to be sailed through: *a navigable channel.* **2** capable of being steered: *a navigable raft.*
▸ **ˌnavigaˈbility** *n* ▸ **ˈnavigably** *adv*

navigate ❶ (ˈnævɪˌgeɪt) *vb* **navigates, navigating, navigated. 1** to direct or plot the path or position of (a ship, an aircraft, etc.). **2** (*tr*) to travel over, through, or on in a boat, aircraft, etc. **3** *Inf.* to direct (oneself) carefully or safely: *he navigated his way to the bar.* **4** (*intr*) (of a passenger in a motor vehicle) to give directions to the driver; point out the route. [C16: from L *nāvigāre* to sail, from *nāvis* ship + *agere* to drive]

navigation ❶ (ˌnævɪˈgeɪʃən) *n* **1** the skill or process of plotting a route and directing a ship, aircraft, etc., along it. **2** the act or practice of navigating: *dredging made navigation of the river possible.*
▸ **ˌnaviˈgational** *adj*

navigator ❶ (ˈnævɪˌgeɪtə) *n* **1** a person who performs navigation. **2** (esp. formerly) a person who explores by ship. **3** an instrument for assisting a pilot to navigate an aircraft.

navvy ❶ (ˈnævɪ) *n, pl* **navvies.** *Brit. inf.* a labourer on a building site, etc. [C19: from *navigator* builder of a *navigation* (in the sense: canal)]

navy ❶ (ˈneɪvɪ) *n, pl* **navies. 1** the warships and auxiliary vessels of a nation or ruler. **2** (*often cap.*) the branch of a country's armed services comprising such ships, their crews, and all their supporting services. **3** short for **navy blue. 4** *Arch. or literary.* a fleet of ships. [C14: via OF from Vulgar L *nāvia* (unattested) ship, from L *nāvis* ship]

navy blue *n* **a** a dark greyish-blue colour. **b** (*as adj*): *a navy-blue suit.* [C19: from the colour of the British naval uniform]

Navy List *n* (in Britain) an official list of all commissioned officers of the Royal Navy.

navy yard *n* a naval shipyard, esp. in the US.

nawab (nəˈwɑːb) *n* (formerly) a Muslim ruling prince or powerful landowner in India. [C18: from Hindi *nawwāb*, from Ar. *nuwwāb*, pl. of *na'ib* viceroy]

nay (neɪ) *sentence substitute.* **1** a word for **no**[1]: archaic or dialectal except in voting by voice. ◆ *n* **2** a person who votes in the negative. ◆ *adv* **3** (*sentence modifier*) *Arch.* an emphatic form of **no**[1]. [C12: from ON *nei*, from *ne* not + *ei* ever]

Nazarene (ˌnæzəˈriːn) *n* **1** an early name for a **Christian** (Acts 24:5) or (when preceded by *the*) for **Jesus Christ. 2** a member of one of several groups of Jewish-Christians found principally in Syria. ◆ *adj* **3** of Nazareth in N Israel, or the Nazarenes.

Nazarite (ˈnæzəˌraɪt) *or* **Nazirite** *n* a religious ascetic of ancient Israel. [C16: from L *Nazaraeus*, from Heb. *nāzar* to consecrate + -ITE[1]]

Nazi (ˈnɑːtsɪ) *n, pl* **Nazis. 1** a member of the fascist National Socialist German Workers' Party, which seized political control in Germany in 1933. ◆ *adj* **2** characteristic of or relating to the Nazis. [C20: from G, phonetic spelling of the first two syllables of *Nationalsozialist* National Socialist]
▸ **Nazism** (ˈnɑːtˌsɪzəm) *or* **Naziism** (ˈnɑːtsɪˌɪzəm) *n*

Nb *the chemical symbol for* niobium.

NB *abbrev. for* New Brunswick.

NB, N.B., nb, *or* **n.b.** *abbrev. for* nota bene. [L: note well]

NBA *abbrev. for* Net Book Agreement.

NC *or* **N.C.** *abbrev. for:* **1** North Carolina. **2** *Brit. education.* National Curriculum.

NCB (in Britain) *abbrev. for* National Coal Board: now British Coal.

NCC (in Britain) *abbrev. for:* **1** Nature Conservancy Council. **2** *Brit. education.* National Curriculum Council: a statutory organization responsible for the content of the National Curriculum.

NCO *abbrev. for* noncommissioned officer.

NCU (in Britain) *abbrev. for* National Communications Union.

nd *abbrev. for* no date.

Nd *the chemical symbol for* neodymium.

NDP *abbrev. for:* **1** net domestic product. **2** (in Canada) New Democratic Party.

NDT (in Canada) *abbrev. for* Newfoundland Daylight Time.

Ne *the chemical symbol for* neon.

NE 1 *symbol for* northeast(ern). **2** *abbrev. for* Nebraska. **3** Also: **N.E.** *abbrev. for* New England.

ne- *combining form.* a variant of **neo-,** esp. before a vowel: *Nearctic.*

Neanderthal man (nɪˈændəˌtɑːl) *n* a type of primitive man occurring throughout much of Europe in late Palaeolithic times. They are not thought to be ancestors of modern humans. [C19: from the anthropological findings (1857) in the Neandertal, a valley near Düsseldorf, Germany]

neap (niːp) *adj* **1** of, relating to, or constituting a neap tide. ◆ *n* **2** short for **neap tide.** [OE, as in *nēpflōd* neap tide, from ?]

Neapolitan (ˌnɪəˈpɒlɪtᵊn) *n* **1** a native or inhabitant of Naples, a city in SW Italy. ◆ *adj* **2** of or relating to Naples. [C15: from L *Neāpolītānus*, ult. from Gk *Neapolis* new town]

Neapolitan ice cream *n* ice cream with several layers of different colours and flavours.

neap tide *n* either of the tides that occur at the first or last quarter of the moon when the tide-generating forces of the sun and moon oppose each other and produce the smallest rise and fall in tidal level. Cf. **spring tide** (sense 1).

near ❶ (nɪə) *prep* **1** at or to a place or time not far away from; close to. ◆ *adv* **2** at or to a place or time not far away; close by. **3** short for **nearly** (sense 1): *I was damn near killed.* ◆ *adj* **4** (*postpositive*) at or in a place not far away. **5** (*prenominal*) only just successful or only just failing: *a near thing.* **6** (*postpositive*) *Inf.* miserly, mean. **7** (*prenominal*) closely connected or intimate: *a near relation.* ◆ *vb* **8** to come or draw close (to). ◆ *n* **9** Also called: **nearside. 9a** the left side of a horse, vehicle, etc. **9b** (*as modifier*): *the near foreleg.* [OE *nēar* (adv), comp. of *nēah* close]
▸ **ˈnearness** *n*

nearby ❶ *adj* (ˈnɪəˌbaɪ), *adv* (ˌnɪəˈbaɪ). not far away; close at hand.

Nearctic (nɪˈɑːktɪk) *adj* of a zoogeographical region consisting of North America, north of the tropic of Cancer, and Greenland.

Near East *n* **1** another term for the **Middle East. 2** (formerly) the Balkan States and the area of the Ottoman Empire.

near gale *n Meteorol.* a wind of force seven on the Beaufort scale or from 32-38 mph.

nearly ❶ (ˈnɪəlɪ) *adv* **1** almost. **2 not nearly.** nowhere near: *not nearly enough.* **3** closely: *the person most nearly concerned.*

near-market *n* (*modifier*) (of scientific research, etc.) very close to being commercially exploitable.

near miss *n* **1** a bomb, shell, etc., that does not exactly hit the target. **2** any attempt or shot that just fails to be successful. **3** an incident in which two aircraft, etc., narrowly avoid collision.

THESAURUS

nautical *adj* = **maritime**, marine, naval, oceanic, seafaring, seagoing, yachting

naval *adj* **2** = **nautical**, marine, maritime, oceanic

navel *n* **1** = **umbilicus**, bellybutton (*inf.*), omphalos **2** = **centre**, central point, hub, middle

navigable *adj* **1** = **passable**, clear, negotiable, traversable, unobstructed **2** = **sailable**, controllable, dirigible, steerable

navigate *vb* **1** = **direct**, drive, guide, handle, manoeuvre, pilot, plan, plot, sail, skipper, steer **2** = **travel**, cross, cruise, journey, voyage

navigation *n* **1, 2** = **sailing**, cruising, helmsmanship, pilotage, seamanship, steering, voyaging

navigator *n* **1** = **pilot**, mariner, seaman

navvy *n Brit. informal* = **labourer**, ganger, worker, workman

navy *n* **1** = **fleet**, argosy (*arch.*), armada, flotilla, warships

near *adj* **4** = **close**, adjacent, adjoining, a hop, skip and a jump away (*inf.*), alongside, at close quarters, beside, bordering, close by, contiguous, just round the corner, nearby, neighbouring, proximate, touching, within sniffing distance (*inf.*) **6** *Informal* = **mean**, close-fisted, miserly, niggardly, parsimonious, stingy, tight-fisted, ungenerous **7** = **intimate**, akin, allied, attached, connected, dear, familiar, related
Antonyms *adj* ≠ **close:** distant, far, faraway, far-flung, far-off, far-removed, outlying, out-of-the-way, remote, removed ≠ **intimate:** distant, remote

nearby *adj* = **neighbouring**, adjacent, adjoining, convenient, handy ◆ *adv* = **close at hand**, at close quarters, just round the corner, not far away, proximate, within reach, within sniffing distance (*inf.*)

nearly *adv* **1** = **almost**, about, all but, approaching, approximately, as good as, just about, not quite, practically, roughly, virtually, well-nigh

near point *n Optics.* the nearest point to the eye at which an object remains in focus.
nearside ('nɪəˌsaɪd) *n* **1** (usually preceded by *the*) *Chiefly Brit.* **1a** the side of a vehicle, etc., nearer the kerb. **1b** (*as modifier*): *the nearside door.* **2a** the left side of an animal, etc. **2b** (*as modifier*): *the nearside flank.*
near-sighted ➊ (ˌnɪə'saɪtɪd) *adj* relating to or suffering from myopia.
▸ **ˌnear-'sightedly** *adv*
near thing ➊ *n Inf.* an event or action whose outcome is nearly a failure, success, disaster, etc.
neat[1] ➊ (ni:t) *adj* **1** clean, tidy, and orderly. **2** liking or insisting on order and cleanliness. **3** smoothly or competently done; efficient: *a neat job.* **4** pat or slick: *his excuse was suspiciously neat.* **5** (of alcoholic drinks, etc.) undiluted. **6** (of language) concise and well-phrased. **7** *Sl., chiefly US & Canad.* pleasing; admirable; excellent. [C16: from OF *net,* from L *nitidus* clean, from *nitēre* to shine]
▸ **'neatly** *adv* ▸ **'neatness** *n*
neat[2] (ni:t) *n, pl* **neat.** *Arch. or dialect.* a domestic bovine animal. [OE *neat*]
neaten ➊ ('ni:tᵊn) *vb* (*tr*) to make neat; tidy.
neath *or* **'neath** (ni:θ) *prep Arch.* short for **beneath.**
neat's-foot oil *n* a yellow oil obtained by boiling the feet and shinbones of cattle.
neb (nɛb) *n Arch. or dialect.* **1** the peak of a cap. **2** the beak of a bird or the nose or snout of an animal. **3** the projecting end of anything. [OE *nebb*]
NEB *abbrev. for:* **1** New English Bible. **2** National Enterprise Board.
nebula ('nɛbjʊlə) *n, pl* **nebulae** (-ˌli:) *or* **nebulas. 1** *Astron.* a diffuse cloud of particles and gases visible either as a hazy patch of light (either an **emission** or **reflection nebula**) or an irregular dark region (**dark nebula**). **2** *Pathol.* opacity of the cornea. [C17: from L: mist, cloud]
▸ **'nebular** *adj*
nebular hypothesis *n* the theory that the solar system evolved from nebular matter.
nebulize *or* **nebulise** ('nɛbjʊˌlaɪz) *vb* **nebulizes, nebulizing, nebulized** *or* **nebulises, nebulising, nebulized.** (*tr*) to convert (a liquid) into a fine mist or spray; atomize.
▸ **ˌnebuli'zation** *or* **ˌnebuli'sation** *n*
nebulizer *or* **nebuliser** ('nɛbjʊˌlaɪzə) *n* a device for converting a drug in liquid form into a mist or fine spray which is inhaled through a mask to provide medication for the respiratory system.
nebulosity (ˌnɛbjʊ'lɒsɪtɪ) *n, pl* **nebulosities. 1** the state of being nebulous. **2** *Astron.* a nebula.
nebulous ➊ ('nɛbjʊləs) *adj* **1** lacking definite form, shape, or content; vague or amorphous. **2** of a nebula. **3** *Rare.* misty or hazy.
▸ **'nebulousness** *n*
NEC *abbrev. for* National Executive Committee.
necessaries ('nɛsɪsərɪz) *pl n* (*sometimes sing*) what is needed; essential items: *the necessaries of life.*
necessarily ➊ ('nɛsɪsərɪlɪ, ˌnɛsɪ'sɛrɪlɪ) *adv* **1** as an inevitable or natural consequence. **2** as a certainty: *he won't necessarily come.*
necessary ➊ ('nɛsɪsərɪ) *adj* **1** needed to achieve a certain desired result; required. **2** inevitable: *the necessary consequences of your action.* **3** *Logic.* **3a** (of a statement, formula, etc.) true under all interpretations. **3b** (of a proposition) determined to be true by its meaning, so that its denial would be self-contradictory. Cf. **sufficient** (sense 2). **4** *Rare.* compelled, as by necessity or law; not free. ◆ *n* **5** (preceded by *the*) *Inf.* the money required for a particular purpose. **6 do the necessary.** *Inf.* to do something that is necessary in a particular situation. ◆ See also **necessaries.** [C14: from L *necessārius* indispensable, from *necesse* unavoidable]
necessitarianism (nɪˌsɛsɪ'tɛərɪəˌnɪzəm) *n Philosophy.* another word for **determinism.**
▸ **neˌcessi'tarian** *n, adj*
necessitate ➊ (nɪ'sɛsɪˌteɪt) *vb* **necessitates, necessitating, necessitated.** (*tr*) **1** to cause as an unavoidable result. **2** (*usually passive*) to compel or require (someone to do something).
necessitous ➊ (nɪ'sɛsɪtəs) *adj* very needy; destitute; poverty-stricken.
necessity ➊ (nɪ'sɛsɪtɪ) *n, pl* **necessities. 1** (*sometimes pl*) something needed; prerequisite: *necessities of life.* **2** a condition or set of circumstances that inevitably requires a certain result: *it is a matter of necessity to wear formal clothes when meeting the Queen.* **3** the state or quality of being obligatory or unavoidable. **4** urgent requirement, as in an emergency. **5** poverty or want. **6** *Rare.* compulsion through laws of nature; fate. **7** *Logic.* the property of being necessary. **8 of necessity.** inevitably.
neck (nɛk) *n* **1** the part of an organism connecting the head with the body. **2** the part of a garment around the neck. **3** something resembling a neck in shape or position: *the neck of a bottle.* **4** *Anat.* a constricted portion of an organ or part. **5** a narrow strip of land; peninsula or isthmus. **6** a strait or channel. **7** the part of a violin, cello, etc., that extends from the body to the tuning pegs and supports the fingerboard. **8** a solid block of lava from an extinct volcano, exposed after erosion of the surrounding rock. **9** the length of a horse's head and neck taken as an approximate distance by which one horse beats another in a race: *to win by a neck.* **10** *Archit.* the narrow band at the top of the shaft of a column. **11** *Inf.* impudence or cheek. **12 get it in the neck.** *Inf.* to be reprimanded or punished severely. **13 neck and neck.** absolutely level in a race or competition. **14 neck of the woods.** *Inf.* a particular area: *what brings you to this neck of the woods?* **15 neck or nothing.** at any cost. **16 save one's** *or* **someone's neck.** *Inf.* to escape from or help someone else to escape from a difficult or dangerous situation. **17 stick one's neck out.** *Inf.* to risk criticism, ridicule, etc., by speaking one's mind. ◆ *vb* **18** (*intr*) *Inf.* to kiss or fondle someone or one another passionately. [OE *hnecca*]
neckband ('nɛkˌbænd) *n* a band around the neck of a garment as finishing, decoration, or a base for a collar.
neckcloth ➊ ('nɛkˌklɒθ) *n* a large ornamental usually white cravat worn formerly by men.
neckerchief ('nɛkətʃɪf, -ˌtʃi:f) *n* a piece of ornamental cloth, often square, worn round the neck. [C14: from NECK + KERCHIEF]
necking ('nɛkɪŋ) *n Inf.* the activity of kissing and embracing lovingly.
necklace ('nɛklɪs) *n* **1** a chain, band, or cord, often bearing beads, pearls, jewels, etc., worn around the neck as an ornament, esp. by women. **2** (in South Africa) **2a** a tyre soaked in petrol, placed round a person's neck, and set on fire in order to burn the person to death. **2b** (*as modifier*): *necklace victims.* ◆ *vb* **necklaces, necklacing, necklaced.** (*tr*) **3** (in South Africa) to kill (a person) by means of a necklace.
neckline ('nɛkˌlaɪn) *n* the shape or position of the upper edge of a dress, blouse, etc.
necktie ('nɛkˌtaɪ) *n* the US name for **tie** (sense 10).
neckwear ('nɛkˌwɛə) *n* articles of clothing, such as ties, scarves, etc., worn round the neck.
necro- *or before a vowel* **necr-** *combining form.* indicating death, a dead body, or dead tissue: *necrosis.* [from Gk *nekros* corpse]
necrobiosis (ˌnɛkrəʊbaɪ'əʊsɪs) *n Physiol.* the normal degeneration and death of cells.
necrolatry (nɛ'krɒlətrɪ) *n* the worship of the dead.
necrology (nɛ'krɒlədʒɪ) *n, pl* **necrologies. 1** a list of people recently dead. **2** a less common word for **obituary.**
▸ **necrological** (ˌnɛkrə'lɒdʒɪkᵊl) *adj*
necromancy ➊ ('nɛkrəʊˌmænsɪ) *n* **1** the art of supposedly conjuring up the dead, esp. in order to obtain from them knowledge of the future. **2** black magic; sorcery. [C13: (sense 1) ult. from Gk

THESAURUS

nearness *n* **4** = **closeness**, accessibility, availability, contiguity, handiness, juxtaposition, propinquity, proximity, vicinity **6** *Informal* = **meanness**, niggardliness, parsimony, stinginess **7** = **intimacy**, dearness, familiarity
near-sighted *adj* = **short-sighted**, myopic
near thing *n Informal* = **narrow escape**, close shave (*inf.*), near miss
neat[1] *adj* **1, 2** = **tidy**, accurate, dainty, fastidious, methodical, nice, orderly, shipshape, smart, spick-and-span, spruce, straight, systematic, trim, uncluttered **3** = **efficient**, adept, adroit, agile, apt, clever, deft, dexterous, effortless, elegant, expert, graceful, handy, nimble, practised, precise, skilful, stylish, well-judged **5** = **undiluted**, pure, straight, unmixed
Antonyms *adj* ≠ **tidy:** clumsy, cluttered, disarrayed, disorderly, disorganized, messy, slobby (*inf.*), sloppy (*inf.*), untidy ≠ **efficient:** awful, bad, clumsy, incompetent, inefficient, inelegant, terrible
neaten *vb* = **tidy up**, arrange, clean up, groom, put to rights, straighten out *or* up, tidy, trim
neatly *adv* **1, 2** = **tidily**, accurately, daintily, fastidiously, methodically, nicely, smartly, sprucely, systematically **3** = **elegantly**, adeptly, adroitly, agilely, aptly, cleverly, deftly, dexterously, efficiently, effortlessly, expertly, gracefully, handily, nimbly, precisely, skilfully, stylishly
neatness *n* **1, 2** = **tidiness**, accuracy, daintiness, fastidiousness, methodicalness, niceness, nicety, orderliness, smartness, spruceness, straightness, trimness **3** = **elegance**, adeptness, adroitness, agility, aptness, cleverness, deftness, dexterity, efficiency, effortlessness, expertness, grace, gracefulness, handiness, nimbleness, preciseness, precision, skilfulness, skill, style, stylishness
nebulous *adj* **1** = **vague**, ambiguous, amorphous, cloudy, confused, dim, hazy, imprecise, indefinite, indeterminate, indistinct, misty, murky, obscure, shadowy, shapeless, uncertain, unclear, unformed
necessarily *adv* **1** = **inevitably**, accordingly, automatically, by definition, compulsorily, consequently, incontrovertibly, ineluctably, inexorably, irresistibly, naturally, *nolens volens,* of course, of necessity, perforce, willy-nilly **2** = **certainly**, undoubtedly
necessary *adj* **1** = **needed**, compulsory, *de rigueur,* essential, imperative, indispensable, mandatory, needful, obligatory, required, requisite, vital **2** = **certain**, fated, inescapable, inevitable, inexorable, unavoidable
Antonyms *adj* ≠ **needed:** dispensable, expendable, inessential, nonessential, superfluous, unnecessary ≠ **certain:** unnecessary
necessitate *vb* **1, 2** = **compel**, call for, coerce, constrain, demand, entail, force, impel, make necessary, oblige, require
necessitous *adj* = **needy**, destitute, distressed, impecunious, impoverished, indigent, penniless, penurious, poor, poverty-stricken
necessity *n* **1** *sometimes plural* = **essentials**, exigencies, fundamentals, indispensables, needs, requirements **2** = **essential**, desideratum, fundamental, necessary, need, prerequisite, requirement, requisite, *sine qua non,* want **3** = **inevitability**, compulsion, destiny, fate, inexorableness, obligation **4** = **needfulness**, demand, exigency, indispensability, need, requirement **5** = **poverty**, destitution, extremity, indigence, need, penury, privation
neckcloth *n* = **neckerchief**, cravat, kerchief, scarf
necromancer *n* **2** = **magician**, black magician, diviner, enchanter, enchantress, sorcerer, sorceress, warlock, witch, wizard
necromancy *n* **2** = **magic**, black art, black

nekromanteia, from *nekros* corpse; (sense 2) from Med. L *nigromantia,* from L *niger* black, which replaced *necro-* through folk etymology]
▸ **'necro,mancer** *n* ▸ **,necro'mantic** *adj*

necrophilia (,nɛkrəʊ'fɪlɪə) *n* sexual attraction for or sexual intercourse with dead bodies. Also called: **necromania, necrophilism.**
▸ **necrophile** ('nɛkrəʊ,faɪl) *n* ▸ **,necro'philic** *adj*

necropolis ⊕ (nɛ'krɒpəlɪs) *n, pl* **necropolises** *or* **necropoleis** (-,leɪs). a burial site or cemetery. [C19: from Gk, from *nekros* dead + *polis* city]

necropsy ('nɛkrɒpsɪ) *or* **necroscopy** (nɛ'krɒskəpɪ) *n, pl* **necropsies** *or* **necroscopies.** another name for **autopsy.** [C19: from Gk *nekros* dead body + *opsis* sight]

necrosis (nɛ'krəʊsɪs) *n* **1** the death of one or more cells in the body, usually within a localized area, as from an interruption of the blood supply. **2** death of plant tissue due to disease, frost, etc. [C17: NL, from Gk *nekrōsis,* from *nekroun* to kill, from *nekros* corpse]
▸ **necrotic** (nɛ'krɒtɪk) *adj*

nectar ('nɛktə) *n* **1** a sugary fluid produced in the nectaries of flowers and collected by bees. **2** *Classical myth.* the drink of the gods. Cf. **ambrosia** (sense 1). **3** any delicious drink. [C16: via L from Gk *nektar*]
▸ **'nectarous** *adj*

nectarine ('nɛktərɪn) *n* **1** a variety of peach tree. **2** the smooth-skinned fruit of this tree. [C17: apparently from NECTAR]

nectary ('nɛktərɪ) *n, pl* **nectaries.** any of various structures secreting nectar that occur in the flowers, leaves, stipules, etc., of a plant. [C18: from NL *nectarium,* from NECTAR]

ned (nɛd) *n Scot. sl.* a hooligan. [from ?]

NEDC *abbrev. for* National Economic Development Council. Also (inf.): **Neddy** ('nɛdɪ).

neddy ('nɛdɪ) *n, pl* **neddies.** a child's word for a **donkey.** [C18: from *Ned,* pet form of *Edward*]

née *or* **nee** (neɪ) *adj* indicating the maiden name of a married woman: *Mrs Bloggs née Blandish.* [C19: from F: p.p. (fem) of *naître* to be born, from L *nascī*]

need ⊕ (ni:d) *vb* **1** (*tr*) to be in want of: *to need money.* **2** (*tr*) to be obliged: *to need to do more work.* **3** (takes an infinitive without *to*) used as an auxiliary to express necessity or obligation and does not add *-s* when used with *he, she, it,* and singular nouns: *need he go?* **4** (*intr*) *Arch.* to be essential to: *there needs no reason for this.* ◆ *n* **5** the fact or an instance of feeling the lack of something: *he has need of a new coat.* **6** a requirement: *the need for vengeance.* **7** necessity or obligation: *no need to be frightened.* **8** distress: *a friend in need.* **9** poverty or destitution. ◆ See also **needs.** [OE *nēad, nied*]

needful ⊕ ('ni:dfʊl) *adj* **1** necessary; required. **2** *Arch.* poverty-stricken. ◆ *n* **3 the needful.** *Inf.* what is necessary, esp. money.
▸ **'needfulness** *n*

needle ⊕ ('ni:dəl) *n* **1** a pointed slender piece of metal with a hole in it through which thread is passed for sewing. **2** a somewhat larger rod with a point at one end, used in knitting. **3** a similar instrument with a hook at one end for crocheting. **4** a small thin pointed device, esp. one made of stainless steel, used to transmit the vibrations from a gramophone record to the pick-up. Cf. **stylus** (sense 3). **5** *Med.* the long hollow pointed part of a hypodermic syringe, which is inserted into the body. **6** *Surgery.* a pointed instrument, often curved, for suturing, puncturing, or ligating. **7** a long narrow stiff leaf in which water loss is greatly reduced: *pine needles.* **8** any slender sharp spine. **9** a pointer on the scale of a measuring instrument. **10** short for **magnetic needle.** **11** a sharp pointed instrument used in engraving. **12** anything long and pointed, such as an obelisk. **13** *Inf.* **13a** anger or intense rivalry, esp. in a sporting encounter. **13b** (*as modifier*): *a needle match.* **14 have** *or* **get the needle.** *Brit. inf.* to feel dislike, nervousness, or annoyance: *she got the needle after he had refused her invitation.* ◆ *vb* **needles, needling, needled.** (*tr*) **15** *Inf.* to goad or provoke, as by constant criticism. **16** to sew, embroider, or prick (fabric) with a needle. [OE *nǣdl*]

needlecord ('ni:dəl,kɔ:d) *n* a corduroy fabric with narrow ribs.

needlepoint ('ni:dəl,pɔɪnt) *n* **1** embroidery done on canvas with various stitches so as to resemble tapestry. **2** another name for **point lace.**

needless ⊕ ('ni:dlɪs) *adj* not required; unnecessary.
▸ **'needlessly** *adv* ▸ **'needlessness** *n*

needle time *n* the limited time allocated by a radio channel to the broadcasting of music from records.

needlewoman ('ni:dəl,wʊmən) *n, pl* **needlewomen.** a woman who does needlework; seamstress.

needlework ⊕ ('ni:dəl,wɜ:k) *n* sewing and embroidery.

needs (ni:dz) *adv* **1** (preceded or foll. by *must*) of necessity: *we must needs go.* ◆ *pl n* **2** what is required; necessities: *his needs are modest.*

needy ⊕ ('ni:dɪ) *adj* **needier, neediest. a** in need of practical or emotional support; distressed. **b** (*as collective n;* preceded by *the*): *the needy.*

ne'er (nɛə) *adv* a poetic contraction of **never.**

ne'er-do-well ⊕ *n* **1** an improvident, irresponsible, or lazy person. ◆ *adj* **2** useless; worthless: *your ne'er-do-well schemes.*

nefarious ⊕ (nɪ'fɛərɪəs) *adj* evil; wicked; sinful. [C17: from L *nefārius,* from *nefās* unlawful deed, from *nē* not + *fās* divine law]
▸ **ne'fariously** *adv* ▸ **ne'fariousness** *n*

neg. *abbrev. for* negative(ly).

negate ⊕ (nɪ'geɪt) *vb* **negates, negating, negated.** (*tr*) **1** to nullify; invalidate. **2** to contradict. [C17: from L *negāre,* from *neg-,* var. of *nec* not + *aio* I say]
▸ **ne'gator** *or* **ne'gater** *n*

negation ⊕ (nɪ'geɪʃən) *n* **1** the opposite or absence of something. **2** a negative thing or condition. **3** the act of negating. **4** *Logic.* a proposition that is the denial of another proposition and is true only if the original proposition is false.

negative ⊕ ('nɛgətɪv) *adj* **1** expressing a refusal or denial: *a negative answer.* **2** lacking positive qualities, such as enthusiasm or optimism. **3** showing opposition or resistance. **4** measured in a direction opposite to that regarded as positive. **5** *Biol.* indicating movement or growth away from a stimulus: *negative geotropism.* **6** *Med.* indicating absence of the disease or condition for which a test was made. **7** another word for **minus** (senses 3b, 4). **8** *Physics.* **8a** (of an electric charge) having the same polarity as the charge of an electron. **8b** (of a body, system, ion, etc.) having a negative electric charge; having an excess of electrons. **9** short for **electronegative.** **10** of or relating to a photographic negative. **11** *Logic.* (of a categorial proposition) denying the satisfaction by the subject of the predicate, as in *some men are irrational; no pigs have wings.* ◆ *n* **12** a statement or act of denial or refusal. **13** a negative thing. **14** *Photog.* a piece of photographic film or a plate, previously exposed and developed, showing an image that, in black-and-white photography, has a reversal of tones. **15** *Physics.* a negative object, such as a terminal or a plate in a voltaic cell. **16** a sentence or other linguistic element with a negative meaning, as the English word *not.* **17** a quantity less than zero. **18** *Logic.* a negative proposition. **19 in the negative.** indicating denial or refusal. ◆ *vb* **negatives, negativing, negatived.** (*tr*) **20** to deny; negate. **21** to show to be false; disprove. **22** to refuse consent to or approval of: *the proposal was negatived.*
▸ **'negatively** *adv* ▸ **'negativeness** *or* **,nega'tivity** *n*

negative equity *n* the state of holding a property the value of which is less than the amount of mortgage still unpaid.

negative feedback *n* See **feedback.**

negative resistance *n* a characteristic of certain electronic components in which an increase in the applied voltage increases the resistance, producing a proportional decrease in current.

negative sign *n* the symbol (–) used to indicate a negative quantity or a subtraction.

negativism ('nɛgətɪv,ɪzəm) *n* **1** a tendency to be unconstructively critical. **2** any sceptical or derisive system of thought.
▸ **'negativist** *n, adj*

neglect ⊕ (nɪ'glɛkt) *vb* (*tr*) **1** to fail to give due care, attention, or time to: *to neglect a child.* **2** to fail (to do something) through carelessness:

THESAURUS

magic, demonology, divination, enchantment, sorcery, voodoo, witchcraft, witchery, wizardry

necropolis *n* = **cemetery**, burial ground, churchyard, God's acre, graveyard

need *vb* **1** = **lack**, miss, want ◆ *n* **5** = **lack**, inadequacy, insufficiency, paucity, shortage **6, 7** = **requirement**, demand, necessity, obligation **9** = **poverty**, deprivation, destitution, distress, extremity, impecuniousness, indigence, neediness, penury, privation

needed *adj* **1** = **necessary**, called for, desired, lacked, required, wanted

needful *adj* **1** = **necessary**, essential, indispensable, needed, required, requisite, stipulated, vital

needle *vb* **15** *Informal* = **irritate**, aggravate (*inf.*), annoy, bait, be on one's back (*sl.*), gall, get in one's hair (*inf.*), get on one's nerves (*inf.*), get under one's skin (*inf.*), goad, harass, hassle (*inf.*), irk, nag, nark (*Brit., Austral., & NZ sl.*), nettle, pester, provoke, rile, ruffle, sting

needless *adj* = **unnecessary**, causeless, excessive, gratuitous, groundless, nonessential, pointless, redundant, superfluous, uncalled-for, undesired, unwanted, useless

Antonyms *adj* beneficial, essential, obligatory, required, useful

needlework *n* = **embroidery**, fancywork, needlecraft, sewing, stitching, tailoring

needy *adj* **a** = **poor**, deprived, destitute, dirt-poor, disadvantaged, down at heel (*inf.*), impecunious, impoverished, indigent, on the breadline (*inf.*), penniless, poverty-stricken, underprivileged

Antonyms *adj* affluent, comfortable, moneyed, prosperous, rich, wealthy, well-off, well-to-do

ne'er-do-well *n* **1** = **layabout**, black sheep, good-for-nothing, idler, loafer, loser, skiver (*Brit. sl.*), wastrel

nefarious *adj* = **wicked**, abominable, atrocious, base, criminal, depraved, detestable, dreadful, evil, execrable, foul, heinous, horrible, infamous, infernal, iniquitous, monstrous, odious, opprobrious, shameful, sinful, vicious, vile, villainous

Antonyms *adj* admirable, good, honest, honourable, just, noble, praiseworthy, upright, virtuous

negate *vb* **1** = **invalidate**, abrogate, annul, cancel, countermand, neutralize, nullify, obviate, repeal, rescind, retract, reverse, revoke, void, wipe out **2** = **deny**, contradict, disallow, disprove, gainsay (*arch. or literary*), oppose, rebut, refute

Antonyms *vb* ≠ **deny:** affirm, assert, attest, avouch, avow, certify, confirm, declare, maintain, pronounce, ratify, state, swear, testify

negation *n* **1** = **denial**, antithesis, antonym, contradiction, contrary, converse, counterpart, disavowal, disclaimer, inverse, opposite, rejection, renunciation, reverse **3** = **cancellation**, neutralization, nullification

negative *adj* **1** = **contradictory**, contrary, denying, dissenting, opposing, recusant, refusing, rejecting, resisting **2** = **pessimistic**, colourless, cynical, gloomy, jaundiced, neutral, unenthusiastic, uninterested, weak **3** = **antagonistic**, contrary, uncooperative, unwilling ◆ *n* **12** = **contradiction**, denial, refusal

Antonyms *adj* ≠ **contradictory:** affirmative, approving, assenting, concurring, positive ≠ **pessimistic:** cheerful, enthusiastic, optimistic, positive

neglect *vb* **2** = **forget**, be remiss, evade, let slide, omit, pass over, procrastinate, shirk, skimp **3** = **disregard**, contemn, discount, disdain, ignore, leave alone, overlook, pass by, re-

he neglected to tell her. **3** to disregard. ◆ *n* **4** lack of due care or attention; negligence: *the child starved through neglect.* **5** the act or an instance of neglecting or the state of being neglected. [C16: from L *neglegere,* from *nec* not + *legere* to select]

neglectful ⓣ (nɪ'glɛktfʊl) *adj* (when *postpositive,* foll. by *of*) careless; heedless.

negligee *or* **negligée** ('nɛglɪˌʒeɪ) *n* **1** a woman's light dressing gown, esp. one that is lace-trimmed. **2** a thin and revealing woman's nightdress. **3** (formerly) any informal women's attire. [C18: from F *négligée,* p.p. (fem) of *négliger* to NEGLECT]

negligence ⓣ ('nɛglɪdʒəns) *n* **1** the state of being negligent. **2** a negligent act. **3** *Law.* a civil wrong whereby the defendant is in breach of a legal duty of care, resulting in injury to the plaintiff.

negligent ⓣ ('nɛglɪdʒənt) *adj* **1** lacking attention, care, or concern; neglectful. **2** careless or nonchalant.
► **'negligently** *adv*

negligible ⓣ ('nɛglɪdʒəbəl) *adj* so small, unimportant, etc., as to be not worth considering.
► **'negligibly** *adv*

negotiable ⓣ (nɪ'gəʊʃəbəl) *adj* **1** able to be negotiated. **2** (of a bill of exchange, promissory note, etc.) legally transferable in title from one party to another.
► **neˌgotia'bility** *n*

negotiable instrument *n* a legal document, such as a cheque or bill of exchange, that is freely negotiable.

negotiate ⓣ (nɪ'gəʊʃɪˌeɪt) *vb* **negotiates, negotiating, negotiated. 1** to talk (with others) to achieve (an agreement, etc.). **2** (*tr*) to succeed in passing round or over. **3** (*tr*) *Finance.* **3a** to transfer (a negotiable commercial paper) to another in return for value received. **3b** to sell (financial assets). **3c** to arrange for (a loan). [C16: from L *negōtiārī* to do business, from *negōtium* business, from *nec* not + *ōtium* leisure]
► **neˌgoti'ation** *n* ► **ne'gotiˌator** *n*

Negress ('ni:grɪs) *n* a female Black person.

Negrillo (nɪ'grɪləʊ) *n, pl* **Negrillos** *or* **Negrilloes.** a member of a dwarfish Negroid race of central and southern Africa. [C19: from Sp., dim. of *negro* black]

Negrito (nɪ'gri:təʊ) *n, pl* **Negritos** *or* **Negritoes.** a member of any of various dwarfish Negroid peoples of SE Asia and Melanesia. [C19: from Sp., dim. of *negro* black]

negritude ('ni:grɪˌtju:d, 'nɛg-) *n* **1** the fact of being a Negro. **2** awareness and cultivation of the Negro heritage, values, and culture. [C20: from F, from *nègre* NEGRO]

Negro ('ni:grəʊ) *Old-fashioned.* ◆ *n, pl* **Negroes. 1** a member of any of the dark-skinned indigenous peoples of Africa and their descendants elsewhere. ◆ *adj* **2** relating to or characteristic of Negroes. [C16: from Sp. or Port.: black, from L *niger*]
► **'Negroˌism** *n*

Negroid ('ni:grɔɪd) *adj* **1** denoting, relating to, or belonging to one of the major racial groups of mankind, characterized by brown-black skin, tightly curled hair, a short nose, and full lips. ◆ *n* **2** a member of this racial group.

negus ('ni:gəs) *n, pl* **neguses.** a hot drink of port and lemon juice, usually spiced and sweetened. [C18: after Col. Francis *Negus* (died 1732), its E inventor]

Negus ('ni:gəs) *n, pl* **Neguses.** *History.* a title of the emperor of Ethiopia. [from Amharic: king]

Neh. *Bible. abbrev. for* Nehemiah.

neigh (neɪ) *n* **1** the high-pitched cry of a horse. ◆ *vb* **2** to make a neigh or utter with a sound like a neigh. [OE *hnǣgan*]

neighbour ⓣ *or US* **neighbor** ('neɪbə) *n* **1** a person who lives near or next to another. **2a** a person or thing near or next to another. **2b** (*as modifier*): *neighbour states.* ◆ *vb* **3** (when *intr,* often foll. by *on*) to be or live close to. [OE *nēahbūr,* from *nēah* NIGH + *būr, gebūr* dweller; see BOOR]
► **'neighbouring** *or US* **'neighboring** *adj*

neighbourhood ⓣ *or US* **neighborhood** ('neɪbəˌhʊd) *n* **1** the immediate environment; surroundings. **2** a district where people live. **3** the people in a particular area. **4** *Maths.* the set of all points whose distance from a given point is less than a specified value. **5** (*modifier*) living or situated in and serving the needs of a local area: *a neighbourhood community worker.* **6 in the neighbourhood of.** approximately.

neighbourhood watch *n* a scheme in which members of a community agree to take joint responsibility for keeping a watch on each other's property, as a way of preventing crime.

neighbourly ⓣ *or US* **neighborly** ('neɪbəlɪ) *adj* kind, friendly, or sociable, as befits a neighbour.
► **'neighbourliness** *or US* **'neighborliness** *n*

neither ('naɪðə, 'ni:ðə) *determiner* **1a** not one nor the other (of two). **1b** (*as pronoun*): *neither can win.* ◆ *conj* **2** (*coordinating*) **2a** (used preceding alternatives joined by *nor*) not: *neither John nor Mary nor Joe went.* **2b** another word for **nor** (sense 2). ◆ *adv* (*sentence modifier*) **3** *Not standard.* another word for **either** (sense 4). [C13 (lit.: *ne either* not either): changed from OE *nāwther,* from *nāhwæther,* from *nā* not + *hwæther* which of two]

> **USAGE NOTE** A verb following a compound subject that uses *neither...(nor)* should be in the singular if both subjects are in the singular: *neither Jack nor John has done the work.*

nekton ('nɛktɒn) *n* the population of free-swimming animals that inhabits the middle depths of a sea or lake. [C19: via G from Gk *nēkton* a swimming thing, from *nēkhein* to swim]

nelly ('nɛlɪ) *n* **not on your nelly.** (*sentence substitute*). *Brit. sl.* certainly not.

nelson ('nɛlsən) *n* any wrestling hold in which a wrestler places his arm or arms under his opponent's arm or arms from behind and exerts pressure with the palms of his hands on the back of his opponent's neck. [C19: from a proper name]

nematic (nɪ'mætɪk) *adj Chem.* (of a substance) existing in or having a mesomorphic state in which a linear orientation of the molecules causes anisotropic properties. [C20: NEMAT(O)- (referring to the threadlike chains of molecules in liquid) + -IC]

nemato- *or before a vowel* **nemat-** *combining form.* indicating a threadlike form: *nematocyst.* [from Gk *nēma* thread]

nematocyst ('nɛmətəˌsɪst, nɪ'mætə-) *n* a structure in coelenterates, such as jellyfish, consisting of a capsule containing a hollow coiled thread that can sting or paralyse.

nematode ('nɛməˌtəʊd) *n* any of a class of unsegmented worms having a tough outer cuticle, including the hookworm and filaria. Also called: **nematode worm, roundworm.**

Nembutal ('nɛmbjʊˌtɑ:l) *n* a trademark for **pentobarbitone sodium.**

nemertean (nɪ'mɜ:tɪən) *or* **nemertine** ('nɛməˌtaɪn) *n* **1** any of a class of soft flattened ribbon-like marine worms having an eversible threadlike proboscis. ◆ *adj* **2** of or belonging to the *Nemertea.* [C19: via NL from Gk *Nēmertēs* a NEREID]

nemesia (nɪ'mi:ʒə) *n* any plant of a southern African genus cultivated for their brightly coloured flowers. [C19: NL, from Gk *nemesion,* name of a plant resembling this]

Nemesis ⓣ ('nɛmɪsɪs) *n* **1** *Greek myth.* the goddess of retribution and vengeance. **2** (*pl* **Nemeses** (-ˌsi:z)). (*sometimes not cap.*) any agency of retribution and vengeance. [C16: via L from Gk: righteous wrath, from *nemein* to distribute what is due]

nemophila (nɛ'mɒfɪlə) *n* an annual trailing plant with blue flowers. [from Gk *nemos* grove + *philos* loving]

neo- *or sometimes before a vowel* **ne-** *combining form.* **1** (*sometimes cap.*) new, recent, or a modern form: *neoclassicism; neocolonialism.* **2** (*usually cap.*) the most recent subdivision of a geological period: *Neogene.* [from Gk *neos* new]

neoclassicism (ˌni:əʊ'klæsɪˌsɪzəm) *n* **1** a late 18th- and early 19th-century style in architecture and art, based on classical models. **2** *Music.* a movement of the 1920s that sought to avoid the emotionalism of late romantic music.
► **neoclassical** (ˌni:əʊ'klæsɪkəl) *or* ˌ**neo'classic** *adj*

neocolonialism (ˌni:əʊkə'ləʊnɪəˌlɪzəm) *n* (in the modern world) political control by an outside power of a country that is in theory independent, esp. through the domination of its economy.

THESAURUS

buff, scorn, slight, spurn, turn one's back on ◆ *n* **4** = **negligence**, carelessness, default, dereliction, failure, forgetfulness, laxity, laxness, neglectfulness, oversight, remissness, slackness, slovenliness
Antonyms *vb* ≠ **disregard:** appreciate, attend to, notice, observe, regard, remember, value ◆ *n* ≠ **negligence, disregard:** attention, care, consideration, notice, regard, respect

neglected *adj* **1** = **abandoned**, derelict, overgrown **3** = **disregarded**, unappreciated, underestimated, undervalued

neglectful *adj* = **careless**, disregardful, heedless, inattentive, indifferent, lax, negligent, remiss, thoughtless, uncaring, unmindful

negligence *n* **1, 2** = **carelessness**, default, dereliction, disregard, failure, forgetfulness, heedlessness, inadvertence, inattention, inattentiveness, indifference, laxity, laxness, neglect, omission, oversight, remissness, shortcoming, slackness, thoughtlessness

negligent *adj* **1, 2** = **careless**, cursory, disregardful, forgetful, heedless, inadvertent, inattentive, indifferent, neglectful, nonchalant, offhand, regardless, remiss, slack, slapdash, slipshod, thoughtless, unmindful, unthinking
Antonyms *adj* attentive, careful, considerate, mindful, painstaking, rigorous, thorough, thoughtful

negligible *adj* = **insignificant**, imperceptible, inconsequential, minor, minute, nickel-and-dime (*US sl.*), petty, small, trifling, trivial, unimportant
Antonyms *adj* important, noteworthy, significant, vital

negotiable *adj* **1** = **debatable**, discussable *or* discussible **2** = **transactional**, transferable

negotiate *vb* **1** = **deal**, adjudicate, arbitrate, arrange, bargain, conciliate, confer, consult, contract, cut a deal, debate, discuss, handle, manage, mediate, parley, settle, transact, work out **2** = **get round**, clear, cross, get over, get past, pass, pass through, surmount

negotiation *n* **1** = **bargaining**, arbitration, debate, diplomacy, discussion, mediation, transaction, wheeling and dealing (*inf.*)

negotiator *n* **1** = **mediator**, adjudicator, ambassador, arbitrator, delegate, diplomat, honest broker, intermediary, moderator

neighbourhood *n* **1, 2** = **district**, community, confines, environs, locale, locality, precincts, proximity, purlieus, quarter, region, surroundings, vicinity

neighbouring *adj* **3** = **nearby**, abutting, adjacent, adjoining, bordering, connecting, contiguous, near, nearest, next, surrounding
Antonyms *adj* distant, far, far-off, remote

neighbourly *adj* = **helpful**, amiable, civil, companionable, considerate, friendly, genial, harmonious, hospitable, kind, obliging, sociable, social, well-disposed

Nemesis *n* **2** *sometimes not cap.* = **retribution**, destiny, destruction, fate, vengeance

▸ˌ**neocoˈlonialist** *n, adj*

Neo-Darwinism (ˌniːəʊˈdɑːwɪnˌɪzəm) *n* a modern theory of evolution that relates Darwinism to the occurrence of inheritable variation by genetic mutation.

neodymium (ˌniːəʊˈdɪmɪəm) *n* a toxic silvery-white metallic element of the lanthanide series. Symbol: Nd; atomic no.: 60; atomic wt.: 144.24. [C19: NL; see NEO- + DIDYMIUM]

neogothic (ˌniːəʊˈgɒθɪk) *n* another name for **Gothic Revival.**

Neolithic (ˌniːəˈlɪθɪk) *n* **1** the cultural period that was characterized by primitive farming and the use of polished stone and flint tools and weapons. ◆ *adj* **2** relating to this period.

neologism Ⓣ (nɪˈɒləˌdʒɪzəm) *or* **neology** *n, pl* **neologisms** *or* **neologies. 1** a newly coined word, or a phrase or familiar word used in a new sense. **2** the practice of using or introducing neologisms. [C18: via F from NEO- + *-logism,* from Gk *logos* word]

▸**neˈologist** *n*

neologize *or* **neologise** (nɪˈɒləˌdʒaɪz) *vb* **neologizes, neologizing, neologized** *or* **neologises, neologising, neologised.** (*intr*) to invent or use neologisms.

neomycin (ˌniːəʊˈmaɪsɪn) *n* an antibiotic obtained from the bacterium *Streptomyces fradiae,* administered in the treatment of skin and eye infections. [C20: from NEO- + Gk *mukēs* fungus + -IN]

neon (ˈniːɒn) *n* **1** a colourless odourless rare gaseous element occurring in trace amounts in the atmosphere: used in illuminated signs and lights. Symbol: Ne; atomic no.: 10; atomic wt.: 20.179. **2** (*modifier*) of or illuminated by neon: *neon sign.* [C19: via NL from Gk *neon* new]

neonatal (ˌniːəʊˈneɪtəl) *adj* occurring in or relating to the first few weeks of life in human babies.

▸ˈ**neoˌnate** *n*

neon light *n* a glass bulb or tube containing neon at low pressure that gives a pink or red glow when a voltage is applied.

neophyte Ⓣ (ˈniːəʊˌfaɪt) *n* **1** a person newly converted to a religious faith. **2** a novice in a religious order. **3** a beginner. [C16: via Church L from New Testament Gk *neophutos* recently planted, from *neos* new + *phuton* a plant]

neoplasm (ˈniːəʊˌplæzəm) *n Pathol.* any abnormal new growth of tissue; tumour.

Neo-Platonism (ˌniːəʊˈpleɪtəˌnɪzəm) *n* a philosophical system which was developed in the 3rd century A.D. as a synthesis of Platonic, Pythagorean, and Aristotelian elements.

▸**Neo-Platonic** (ˌniːəʊpləˈtɒnɪk) *adj* ▸ˌ**Neo-ˈPlatonist** *n, adj*

neoprene (ˈniːəʊˌpriːn) *n* a synthetic rubber obtained by the polymerization of chloroprene, a colourless liquid derivative of butadiene, resistant to oil and ageing and used in waterproof products. [C20: from NEO- + PR(OPYL) + -ENE]

neoteny (nɪˈɒtənɪ) *n* the persistence of larval or fetal features in the adult form of an animal. [C19: from NL *neotenia,* from Gk NEO- + *teinein* to stretch]

neoteric (ˌniːəʊˈtɛrɪk) *Rare.* ◆ *adj* **1** belonging to a new fashion or trend; modern. ◆ *n* **2** a new writer or philosopher. [C16: via LL from Gk *neōterikos* young, fresh, from *neoteros* younger, more recent, from *neos* new, recent]

Nepali (nɪˈpɔːlɪ) *n* **1** the official language of Nepal, also spoken in Sikkim and parts of India. **2** (*pl* **Nepali** *or* **Nepalis**) a native or inhabitant of Nepal; a Nepalese. ◆ *adj* **3** of or relating to Nepal, its inhabitants, or their language; Nepalese.

nepenthe (nɪˈpɛnθɪ) *or* **nepenthes** (nɪˈpɛnθiːz) *n* a drug that ancient writers referred to as a means of forgetting grief or trouble. [C16: via L from Gk *nēpenthes* sedative made from a herb, from *nē-* not + *penthos* grief]

nepeta (ˈnɛpətə, nəˈpetə) *n* any of a genus of plants found in N temperate regions. It includes catmint. [from L]

nephew (ˈnɛvjuː, ˈnɛf-) *n* a son of one's sister or brother. [C13: from OF *neveu,* from L *nepōs*]

nephology (nɪˈfɒlədʒɪ) *n* the study of clouds. [C19: from Gk *nephos* cloud + -LOGY]

nephridium (nɪˈfrɪdɪəm) *n, pl* **nephridia** (-ɪə). a simple excretory organ of many invertebrates, consisting of a tube through which waste products pass to the exterior. [C19: NL: little kidney]

nephrite (ˈnɛfraɪt) *n* a tough fibrous mineral: a variety of jade. Also called: **kidney stone.** [C18: via G from Gk *nephros* kidney; it was thought to help in kidney disorders]

nephritic (nɪˈfrɪtɪk) *adj* **1** of or relating to the kidneys. **2** relating to or affected with nephritis.

nephritis (nɪˈfraɪtɪs) *n* inflammation of a kidney.

nephro- *or before a vowel* **nephr-** *combining form.* kidney or kidneys: *nephritis.* [from Gk *nephros*]

nephrology (nɪˈfrɒlədʒɪ) *n* the branch of medicine concerned with diseases of the kidney.

▸**neˈphrologist** *n*

nephron (ˈnɛfrɒn) *n* one of the units of the kidney that secretes urine, via ducts, into the ureter.

nephroscope (ˈnɛfrəˌskəʊp) *n* a tubular medical instrument inserted through an incision in the skin to enable examination of a kidney.

▸**nephroscopy** (nɪˈfrɒskəpɪ) *n*

ne plus ultra *Latin.* (ˈneɪ ˈplʊs ˈʊltrɑː) *n* the extreme or perfect point or state. [lit.: not more beyond (that is, go no further), allegedly a warning to sailors inscribed on the Pillars of Hercules at Gibraltar]

nepotism Ⓣ (ˈnɛpəˌtɪzəm) *n* favouritism shown to relatives or close friends by those with power. [C17: from It. *nepotismo,* from *nepote* NEPHEW, from the former papal practice of granting favours to nephews or other relatives]

▸ˈ**nepotist** *n*

Neptune[1] (ˈnɛptjuːn) *n* the Roman god of the sea. Greek counterpart: **Poseidon.**

Neptune[2] (ˈnɛptjuːn) *n* the eighth planet from the sun, having two satellites, Triton and Nereid.

neptunium (nɛpˈtjuːnɪəm) *n* a silvery metallic element synthesized in the production of plutonium and occurring in trace amounts in uranium ores. Symbol: Np; atomic no.: 93; half-life of most stable isotope, ^{237}Np: 2.14×10^6 years. [C20: from NEPTUNE[2], the planet beyond Uranus, because neptunium is beyond uranium in the periodic table]

NERC *abbrev. for* Natural Environment Research Council.

nerd Ⓣ *or* **nurd** (nɜːd) *n Sl.* **1** a boring or unpopular person, esp. one obsessed with something specified: *computer nerd.* **2** a stupid and feeble person. [C20: from ?]

▸ˈ**nerdish** *or* ˈ**nurdish** *adj* ▸ˈ**nerdy** *or* ˈ**nurdy** *adj*

Nereid (ˈnɪərɪɪd) *n, pl* **Nereides** (nəˈriːədiːz). *Greek myth.* any of 50 sea nymphs who were the daughters of the sea god Nereus. [C17: via L from Gk]

nerine (nɪˈraɪnɪ; *S. African* nəˈriːn) *n* any of a genus of bulbous plants native to South Africa and grown elsewhere as greenhouse plants for their pink, red, or orange flowers: includes the Guernsey lily. [after the water nymph *Nerine* in Roman myth]

neroli oil *or* **neroli** (ˈnɪərəlɪ) *n* a brown oil distilled from the flowers of various orange trees: used in perfumery. [C17: after Anne Marie de la Tremoïlle of *Neroli,* French-born It. princess believed to have discovered it]

nervate (ˈnɜːveɪt) *adj* (of leaves) having veins.

nervation (nɜːˈveɪʃən) *or* **nervature** (ˈnɜːvətʃə) *n* a less common word for **venation.**

nerve Ⓣ (nɜːv) *n* **1** any of the cordlike bundles of fibres that conduct impulses between the brain or spinal cord and another part of the body. **2** bravery or steadfastness. **3 lose one's nerve.** to become timid, esp. failing to perform some audacious act. **4** *Inf.* effrontery; impudence. **5** muscle or sinew (often in **strain every nerve**). **6** a vein in a leaf or an insect's wing. ◆ *vb* **nerves, nerving, nerved.** (*tr*) **7** to give courage to (oneself); steel (oneself). **8** to provide with nerve or nerves. ◆ See also **nerves.** [C16: from L *nervus;* rel. to Gk *neuron*]

nerve block *n* induction of anaesthesia in a specific part of the body by injecting a local anaesthetic close to the sensory nerves that supply it.

nerve cell *n* another name for **neurone.**

nerve centre *n* **1** a group of nerve cells associated with a specific function. **2** a principal source of control over any complex activity.

nerve fibre *n* a threadlike extension of a nerve cell; axon.

nerve gas *n* any of various poisonous gases that have a paralysing effect on the central nervous system that can be fatal.

nerve impulse *n* the electrical wave transmitted along a nerve fibre, usually following stimulation of the nerve-cell body.

nerveless Ⓣ (ˈnɜːvlɪs) *adj* **1** calm and collected. **2** listless or feeble.

▸ˈ**nervelessly** *adv*

nerve-racking Ⓣ *or* **nerve-wracking** *adj* very distressing, exhausting, or harrowing.

nerves Ⓣ (nɜːvz) *pl n Inf.* **1** the imagined source of emotional control: *my nerves won't stand it.* **2** anxiety, tension, or imbalance: *she's all nerves.* **3 get on one's nerves.** to irritate or upset one.

nervine (ˈnɜːviːn) *adj* **1** having a soothing effect upon the nerves. ◆ *n* **2** a nervine agent. [C17: from NL *nervīnus,* from L *nervus* NERVE]

THESAURUS

neologism *n* **1** = **new word,** buzz word (*inf.*), coinage, new phrase, nonce word, vogue word

neophyte *n* **1** = **catechumen,** proselyte **2** = **novitiate,** novice **3** = **beginner,** amateur, apprentice, disciple, learner, novice, probationer, pupil, recruit, student, trainee, tyro

nepotism *n* = **favouritism,** bias, partiality, patronage, preferential treatment

nerd *n* **1** *Slang* = **bore,** anorak (*inf.*), geek (*inf.*), obsessive, trainspotter (*inf.*) **2** = **fool,** booby, divvy (*Brit. sl.*), drip (*inf.*), plonker (*sl.*), prat (*sl.*), sap (*sl.*), schmuck (*US sl.*), simpleton, sucker (*sl.*), twit (*inf., chiefly Brit.*), wally (*sl.*), weed, wimp (*inf.*)

nerve *n* **2** = **bravery,** balls (*taboo sl.*), bottle (*Brit. sl.*), coolness, courage, daring, determination, endurance, energy, face (*inf.*), fearlessness, firmness, force, fortitude, gameness, grit, guts (*inf.*), hardihood, intrepidity, mettle, might, pluck, resolution, spirit, spunk (*inf.*), steadfastness, vigour, will **4** *Informal* = **impudence,** audacity, boldness, brass neck (*Brit. inf.*), brazenness, cheek (*inf.*), chutzpah (*US & Canad. inf.*), effrontery, front, gall, impertinence, insolence, neck (*inf.*), sassiness (*US sl.*), sauce (*inf.*), temerity ◆ *vb* **7** = **brace (oneself),** embolden (oneself), encourage (oneself), fortify (oneself), gee (oneself) up, hearten (oneself), invigorate (oneself), steel (oneself), strengthen (oneself)

nerveless *adj* **1** = **calm,** collected, composed, controlled; cool, impassive, imperturbable, self-possessed, unemotional **2** = **feeble,** debilitated, enervated, spineless, weak

nerve-racking *adj* = **tense,** annoying, difficult, distressing, frightening, gut-wrenching, harassing, harrowing, maddening, stressful, trying, worrying

nerves *pl n* **2** = **tension,** anxiety, butterflies (in one's stomach) (*inf.*), cold feet (*inf.*), fretfulness, heebie-jeebies (*sl.*), imbalance, nervousness, strain, stress, worry

nervous ⓣ ('nɜːvəs) *adj* **1** very excitable or sensitive; highly strung. **2** (often foll. by *of*) apprehensive or worried. **3** of or containing nerves: *nervous tissue.* **4** affecting the nerves or nervous tissue: *a nervous disease.* **5** *Arch.* vigorous or forceful.
▸'**nervously** *adv* ▸'**nervousness** *n*

nervous breakdown ⓣ *n* any mental illness not primarily of organic origin, in which the patient ceases to function properly, often accompanied by severely impaired concentration, anxiety, insomnia, and lack of self-esteem.

nervous system *n* the sensory and control apparatus of animals, consisting of a network of neurones.

nervure ('nɜːvjʊə) *n* **1** *Entomol.* any of the chitinous rods that form the framework of an insect's wing; vein. **2** *Bot.* any of the veins of a leaf. [C19: from F; see NERVE, -URE]

nervy ⓣ ('nɜːvɪ) *adj* **nervier, nerviest. 1** *Brit. inf.* tense or apprehensive. **2** having or needing bravery or endurance. **3** *US & Canad. inf.* brash or cheeky. **4** *Arch.* muscular; sinewy.

nescience ('nɛsɪəns) *n* a formal or literary word for **ignorance.** [C17: from LL *nescientia,* from L *nescīre* to be ignorant of, from *ne* not + *scīre* to know]
▸'**nescient** *adj*

ness (nɛs) *n Arch.* a promontory or headland. [OE *næs* headland]

-ness *suffix forming nouns chiefly from adjectives and participles.* indicating state, condition, or quality: *greatness; selfishness.* [OE *-nes,* of Gmc origin]

nest ⓣ (nɛst) *n* **1** a place or structure in which birds, fishes, etc., lay eggs or give birth to young. **2** a number of animals of the same species occupying a common habitat: *an ants' nest.* **3** a place fostering something undesirable: *a nest of thievery.* **4** a cosy or secluded place. **5** a set of things, usually of graduated sizes, designed to fit together: *a nest of tables.* ◆ *vb* **6** (*intr*) to make or inhabit a nest. **7** (*intr*) to hunt for birds' nests. **8** (*tr*) to place in a nest. **9** *Computing.* to position data within other data at different ranks or levels so that the different levels of data can be used or accessed recursively. [OE]

nest egg ⓣ *n* **1** a fund of money kept in reserve; savings. **2** a natural or artificial egg left in a nest to induce hens to lay their eggs in it.

nestle ⓣ ('nɛsᵊl) *vb* **nestles, nestling, nestled. 1** (*intr;* often foll. by *up* or *down*) to snuggle, settle, or cuddle closely. **2** (*intr*) to be in a sheltered position; lie snugly. **3** (*tr*) to shelter or place snugly or partly concealed, as in a nest. [OE *nestlian*]

nestling ⓣ ('nɛstlɪŋ, 'nɛslɪŋ) *n* **a** a young bird not yet fledged. **b** (*as modifier*): *a nestling thrush.* [C14: from NEST + -LING[1]]

net[1] ⓣ (nɛt) *n* **1** an openwork fabric of string, wire, etc.; mesh. **2** a device made of net, used to protect or enclose things or to trap animals. **3** a thin light mesh fabric used for curtains, etc. **4** a plan, strategy, etc., intended to trap or ensnare: *the murderer slipped through the police net.* **5** *Tennis, badminton, etc.* **5a** a strip of net that divides the playing area into two equal parts. **5b** a shot that hits the net. **6** the goal in soccer, hockey, etc. **7** (*often pl*) *Cricket.* **7a** a pitch surrounded by netting, used for practice. **7b** a practice session in a net. **8** *Inf.* (*often cap.*) short for **Internet. 9** another word for **network** (sense 2). ◆ *vb* **nets, netting, netted. 10** (*tr*) to ensnare. **11** (*tr*) to shelter or surround with a net. **12** (*intr*) *Tennis, badminton, etc.* to hit a shot into the net. **13** to make a net out of (rope, string, etc.). [OE *net;* rel. to Gothic *nati,* Du. *net*]

net[2] ⓣ *or* **nett** (nɛt) *adj* **1** remaining after all deductions, as for taxes, expenses, losses, etc.: *net profit.* Cf. **gross** (sense 2). **2** (of weight) after deducting tare. **3** final; conclusive (esp. in **net result**). ◆ *n* **4** net income, profits, weight, etc. ◆ *vb* **nets, netting, netted. 5** (*tr*) to yield or earn as clear profit. [C14: clean, neat, from F *net* NEAT[1]]

net asset value *n* the total value of the assets of an organization less its liabilities and capital charges. Abbrev.: **NAV.**

netball ('nɛt,bɔːl) *n* a game for two teams of seven players (usually women) played on a hard court. Points are scored by shooting the ball through a net hanging from a ring at the top of a pole.

Net Book Agreement *n* a former (until 1995) agreement between UK publishers and booksellers that prohibited booksellers from reducing the price of books. Abbrev.: **NBA.**

net domestic product *n Econ.* the gross domestic product minus an allowance for the depreciation of capital goods. Abbrev.: **NDP.**

nether ⓣ ('nɛðə) *adj* below, beneath, or underground: *nether regions.* [OE *niothera, nithera,* lit.: further down, from *nither* down]

nethermost ('nɛðə,məʊst) *adj* **the.** farthest down; lowest.

nether world ⓣ *n* **1** the underworld. **2** hell. ◆ Also called: **nether regions.**

netiquette ('nɛtɪ,kɛt) *n* the informal code of behaviour on the Internet. [C20: from NET(WORK) + (ET)IQUETTE]

net national product *n* gross national product minus an allowance for the depreciation of capital goods. Abbrev.: **NNP.**

net present value *n Accounting.* an assessment of the long-term profitability of a project made by adding together all the revenue it can be expected to achieve over its whole life and deducting all the costs involved. Abbrev.: **NPV.**

net profit *n* gross profit minus all operating costs not included in the calculation of gross profit, esp. wages, overheads, and depreciation.

net realizable value *n* the net value of an asset if it were to be sold. Abbrev.: **NRV.**

net statutory income *n* (in Britain) the total taxable income of a person for the tax assessment year, after the deduction of personal allowances.

netsuke ('nɛtsʊkɪ) *n* (in Japan) a carved toggle, esp. of wood or ivory, originally used to tether a medicine box, purse, etc., worn dangling from the waist. [C19: from Japanese]

nett (nɛt) *adj, n, vb* a variant spelling of **net**[2].

netting ('nɛtɪŋ) *n* any netted fabric or structure.

nettle ⓣ ('nɛtᵊl) *n* **1** a plant having serrated leaves with stinging hairs and greenish flowers. **2** any of various other plants with stinging hairs or spines. **3** any of various plants that resemble nettles, such as the dead-nettle. **4 grasp the nettle.** to attempt something with boldness and courage. ◆ *vb* **nettles, nettling, nettled.** (*tr*) **5** to bother; irritate. **6** to sting as a nettle does. [OE *netele*]

nettle rash *n* a nontechnical name for **urticaria.**

network ⓣ ('nɛt,wɜːk) *n* **1** an interconnected group or system: *a network of shops.* **2** a system of intersecting lines, roads, veins, etc. **3** another name for **net**[1] (sense 1) or **netting. 4** *Radio & TV.* a group of broadcasting stations that all transmit the same programme simultaneously. **5** *Computing.* a system of interconnected computer systems, terminals, and other equipment. **6** *Electronics.* a system of interconnected components or circuits. ◆ *vb* **7** *Radio & TV.* to broadcast over a network. **8** (of computers, terminals, etc.) to connect or be connected. **9** (*intr*) to form business contacts through informal social meetings.

neume *or* **neum** (njuːm) *n Music.* one of a series of notational symbols used before the 14th century. [C15: from Med. L *neuma* group of notes sung on one breath, from Gk *pneuma* breath]

neural ('njʊərəl) *adj* of or relating to a nerve or the nervous system.
▸'**neurally** *adv*

neural chip *n* another name for **neurochip.**

neural computer *n* another name for **neurocomputer.**

neuralgia (njʊ'rældʒə) *n* severe spasmodic pain caused by damage to or malfunctioning of a nerve and often following the course of the nerve.
▸**neu'ralgic** *adj*

neural tube *n* the embryonic brain and spinal cord in mammals. Incomplete development results in **neural-tube defects,** such as spina bifida, in a newborn baby.

neurasthenia (,njʊərəs'θiːnɪə) *n* (no longer in technical use) a neurosis characterized by extreme lassitude and inability to cope with any but the most trivial tasks.

neuritis (njʊ'raɪtɪs) *n* inflammation of a nerve or nerves, often accompanied by pain and loss of function in the affected part.
▸**neuritic** (njʊ'rɪtɪk) *adj*

neuro- *or before a vowel* **neur-** *combining form.* indicating a nerve or the nervous system: *neurology.* [from Gk *neuron* nerve; rel. to L *nervus*]

neurobiology (,njʊərəʊbaɪ'ɒlədʒɪ) *n* the study of the anatomy, physiology, and biochemistry of the nervous system.
▸,**neurobi'ologist** *n*

neurochip ('njʊərəʊ,tʃɪp) *n Computing.* a semiconductor chip designed for use in an electronic neural network. Also called: **neural chip.**

neurocomputer ('njʊərəʊkəm,pjuːtə) *n* a type of computer designed

THESAURUS

nervous *adj* **1, 2** = **apprehensive,** agitated, anxious, edgy, excitable, fearful, fidgety, flustered, hesitant, highly strung, hyper (*inf.*), hysterical, jittery (*inf.*), jumpy, nervy (*Brit. inf.*), neurotic, on edge, ruffled, shaky, tense, timid, timorous, twitchy (*inf.*), uneasy, uptight (*inf.*), weak, wired (*sl.*), worried
Antonyms *adj* bold, calm, confident, constant, cool, equable, even, laid-back (*inf.*), peaceful, relaxed, steady, together (*sl.*), unfazed (*inf.*)

nervous breakdown *n* = **collapse,** breakdown, crack-up (*inf.*), nervous disorder, neurasthenia (*obs.*)

nervousness *n* **1, 2** = **anxiety,** agitation, disquiet, excitability, fluster, perturbation, tension, timidity, touchiness, tremulousness, worry

nervy *adj* **1** *Brit. informal* = **anxious,** agitated, excitable, fidgety, jittery (*inf.*), jumpy, nervous, on edge, restless, tense, twitchy (*inf.*), wired (*sl.*)

nest *n* **3** = **hotbed,** breeding-ground, den **4** = **refuge,** den, haunt, hideaway, resort, retreat, snuggery

nest egg *n* **1** = **reserve,** cache, deposit, fall-back, fund(s), savings, store

nestle *vb* **1** = **snuggle,** cuddle, curl up, huddle, nuzzle

nestling *n* **a** = **chick,** fledgling

net[1] *n* **1** = **mesh,** lacework, lattice, netting, network, openwork, reticulum, tracery, web ◆ *vb* **10** = **catch,** bag, capture, enmesh, ensnare, entangle, nab (*inf.*), trap

net[2] *adj* **1** = **take-home,** after taxes, clear, final **2** = **conclusive,** closing, final ◆ *vb* **5** = **earn,** accumulate, bring in, clear, gain, make, realize, reap

nether *adj* = **lower,** basal, below, beneath, bottom, inferior, Stygian, under, underground

nether world *n* **1** = **underworld,** Hades, infernal regions, nether regions **2** = **hell**

nettle *vb* **5** = **irritate,** aggravate, annoy, exasperate, fret, gall, get on one's nerves (*inf.*), harass, hassle (*inf.*), incense, nark (*Brit., Austral., & NZ sl.*), pique, provoke, ruffle, sting, tease, vex

nettled *adj* **5** = **irritated,** aggrieved, angry, annoyed, chafed, choked, cross, exasperated, galled, hacked (off) (*US sl.*), harassed, huffy, incensed, irritable, peeved, peevish, piqued, provoked, put out, ratty (*Brit. & NZ inf.*), riled, ruffled, stung, teased, tetchy, touchy, vexed

network *n* **1, 2** = **system,** arrangement, channels, circuitry, complex, convolution, grid, grill, interconnections, labyrinth, lattice, maze, mesh, net, nexus, organization, plexus, structure, tracks, web

to mimic the action of the human brain by use of an electronic neural network. Also called: **neural computer.**

neuroendocrine (ˌnjʊərəʊˈɛndəʊˌkraɪn) *adj* of, relating to, or denoting the dual control of certain body functions by both nervous and hormonal stimulation: *neuroendocrine system.*

neuroglia (njʊˈrɒglɪə) *n* another name for **glia.**

neurohormone (ˈnjʊərəʊˌhɔːməʊn) *n* a hormone, such as noradrenaline, that is produced by specialized nervous tissue rather than by endocrine glands.

neurolemma (ˌnjʊərəʊˈlɛmə) *n* the thin membrane that forms a sheath around nerve fibres. [C19: NL, from NEURO- + Gk *eilēma* covering]

neurology (njʊˈrɒlədʒɪ) *n* the study of the anatomy, physiology, and diseases of the nervous system.
▸**neurological** (ˌnʊərəˈlɒdʒɪkᵊl) *adj*

neuromuscular (ˌnjʊərəʊˈmʌskjʊlə) *adj* of, relating to, or affecting nerves and muscles.

neurone (ˈnjʊərəʊn) *or* **neuron** (ˈnjʊərɒn) *n* a cell specialized to conduct nerve impulses: consists of a cell body, axon, and dendrites. Also called: **nerve cell.**
▸**neuˈronal** *adj* ▸**neuronic** (njʊˈrɒnɪk) *adj*

neuropathology (ˌnjʊərəʊpəˈθɒlədʒɪ) *n* the study of diseases of the nervous system.

neuropathy (njʊˈrɒpəθɪ) *n* any disease of the nervous system.
▸**neuropathic** (ˌnjʊərəʊˈpæθɪk) *adj* ▸ˌ**neuroˈpathically** *adv*

neurophysiology (ˌnjʊərəʊˌfɪzɪˈɒlədʒɪ) *n* the study of the functions of the nervous system.
▸**neurophysiological** (ˌnjʊərəʊˌfɪzɪəˈlɒdʒɪkᵊl) *adj*

neuropterous (njʊˈrɒptərəs) *or* **neuropteran** *adj* of or belonging to an order of insects having two pairs of large much-veined wings and biting mouthparts. [C18: from NL *Neuroptera,* from NEURO- + Gk *pteron* wing]

neuroscience (ˈnjʊərəʊsaɪəns) *n* the study of the anatomy, physiology, and biochemistry of the nervous system.

neurosis ⓣ (njʊˈrəʊsɪs) *n, pl* **neuroses** (-siːz). a relatively mild mental disorder, characterized by hysteria, anxiety, depression, or obsessive behaviour.

neurosurgery (ˌnjʊərəʊˈsɜːdʒərɪ) *n* the branch of surgery concerned with the nervous system.
▸ˌ**neuroˈsurgical** *adj*

neurotic ⓣ (njʊˈrɒtɪk) *adj* **1** of or afflicted by neurosis. ◆ *n* **2** a person who is afflicted with a neurosis or who tends to be emotionally unstable.
▸**neuˈrotically** *adv* ▸**neuˈrotiˌcism** *n*

neurotomy (njʊˈrɒtəmɪ) *n, pl* **neurotomies.** the surgical cutting of a nerve.

neurotransmitter (ˌnjʊərəʊtrænzˈmɪtə) *n* a chemical by which a nerve cell communicates with another nerve cell or with a muscle.

neuter ⓣ (ˈnjuːtə) *adj* **1** *Grammar.* **1a** denoting or belonging to a gender of nouns which do not specify the sex of their referents. **1b** (*as n*): *German "Mädchen" (meaning "girl") is a neuter.* **2** (of animals and plants) having nonfunctional, underdeveloped, or absent reproductive organs. **3** giving no indication of sex. ◆ *n* **4** a sexually underdeveloped female insect, such as a worker bee. **5** a castrated animal. ◆ *vb* **6** (*tr*) to castrate (an animal). [C14: from L, from *ne* not + *uter* either (of two)]

neutral ⓣ (ˈnjuːtrəl) *adj* **1** not siding with any party to a war or dispute. **2** of or belonging to a neutral party, country, etc. **3** of no distinctive quality or type. **4** (of a colour) **4a** having no hue; achromatic. **4b** dull, but harmonizing with most other colours. **5** a less common term for **neuter** (sense 2). **6** *Chem.* neither acidic nor alkaline. **7** *Physics.* having zero charge or potential. **8** *Phonetics.* (of a vowel) articulated with the tongue relaxed in mid-central position: *"about" begins with a neutral vowel.* ◆ *n* **9** a neutral person, nation, etc. **10** a citizen of a neutral state. **11** the position of the controls of a gearbox that leaves the transmission disengaged. [C16: from L *neutrālis;* see NEUTER]
▸ˈ**neutrally** *adv*

neutralism (ˈnjuːtrəˌlɪzəm) *n* (in international affairs) the policy of noninvolvement or nonalignment with power blocs.
▸ˈ**neutralist** *n*

neutrality ⓣ (njuːˈtrælɪtɪ) *n* **1** the state of being neutral. **2** the condition of being chemically or electrically neutral.

neutralize ⓣ *or* **neutralise** (ˈnjuːtrəˌlaɪz) *vb* **neutralizes, neutralizing, neutralized** *or* **neutralises, neutralising, neutralised.** (*mainly tr*) **1** (*also intr*) to render or become neutral by counteracting, mixing, etc. **2** (*also intr*) to make or become electrically or chemically neutral. **3** to exclude (a country) from warfare or alliances by international agreement: *the great powers neutralized Belgium in the 19th century.*
▸ˌ**neutraliˈzation** *or* ˌ**neutraliˈsation** *n* ▸ˈ**neutralˌizer** *or* ˈ**neutralˌiser** *n*

neutretto (njuːˈtrɛtəʊ) *n, pl* **neutrettos.** *Physics.* **1** the neutrino associated with the muon. **2** (formerly) any of various hypothetical neutral particles. [C20: from NEUTR(INO) + diminutive suffix *-etto*]

neutrino (njuːˈtriːnəʊ) *n, pl* **neutrinos.** *Physics.* a stable elementary particle with zero rest mass and spin ½ that travels at the speed of light. [C20: from It., dim. of *neutrone* NEUTRON]

neutron (ˈnjuːtrɒn) *n Physics.* a neutral elementary particle with approximately the same mass as a proton. In the nucleus of an atom it is stable but when free it decays. [C20: from NEUTRAL, on the model of ELECTRON]

neutron bomb *n* a type of nuclear weapon designed to cause little blast or long-lived radioactive contamination. The neutrons destroy all life in the target area. Technical name: **enhanced radiation weapon.**

neutron gun *n Physics.* a device used for producing a beam of fast neutrons.

neutron number *n* the number of neutrons in the nucleus of an atom. Symbol: *N*

neutron star *n* a star, composed solely of neutrons, that has collapsed under its own gravity.

névé (ˈnɛveɪ) *n* a mass of porous ice, formed from snow, that has not yet become frozen into glacier ice. [C19: from Swiss F *névé* glacier, from LL *nivātus* snow-cooled, from *nix* snow]

never ⓣ (ˈnɛvə) *adv, sentence substitute.* **1** at no time; not ever. **2** certainly not; by no means; in no case. ◆ *sentence substitute.* **3** Also: **well I never!** surely not! [OE *næfre,* from *ne* not + *æfre* EVER]

> **USAGE NOTE** In informal speech and writing, *never* can be used instead of *not* with the simple past tenses of certain verbs, for emphasis (*I never said that; I never realized how clever he was*), but this usage should be avoided in serious writing.

nevermore (ˌnɛvəˈmɔː) *adv Literary.* never again.

never-never ⓣ *Inf.* ◆ *n* **1** *Brit.* the hire-purchase system of buying. **2** *Austral.* remote desert country. ◆ *adj* **3** imaginary; idyllic (esp. in **never-never land**).

nevertheless ⓣ (ˌnɛvəðəˈlɛs) *sentence connector.* in spite of that; however; yet.

new ⓣ (njuː) *adj* **1a** recently made or brought into being. **1b** (*as collective n; preceded by the*): *the new.* **2** of a kind never before existing; novel: *a new concept in marketing.* **3** recently discovered: *a new comet.* **4** markedly different from what was before: *the new liberalism.* **5** (often foll. by *to* or *at*) recently introduced (to); inexperienced (in) or unaccustomed (to): *new to this neighbourhood.* **6** (*cap. in names or titles*) more or most recent of things with the same name: *the New Testament.* **7** (*prenominal*) fresh; additional: *send some new troops.* **8** (often foll. by *to*) unknown: *this is new to me.* **9** (of a cycle) beginning or occurring again: *a new year.* **10** (*prenominal*) (of crops) harvested early. **11** changed, esp. for the better: *she returned a new woman.* **12** up-to-date; fashionable. ◆ *adv* (*usually in combination*) **13** recently, freshly: *new-laid eggs.* **14** anew; again. ◆ See also **news.** [OE *nīowe*]
▸ˈ**newness** *n*

New Age *n* **1a** a philosophy, originating in the late 1980s, characterized by a belief in alternative medicine, astrology, spiritualism, etc. **1b** (*as modifier*): *New Age therapies.* **2** short for **New Age music.**

New Age music *or* **New Age** *n* a type of gentle melodic popular music originating in the US in the late 1980s, which takes in elements of jazz, folk, and classical music and is played largely on synthesizers and acoustic instruments.

New Australian *n* an Australian name for a recent immigrant, esp. one from Europe.

THESAURUS

neurosis *n* = **obsession**, abnormality, affliction, derangement, deviation, instability, maladjustment, mental disturbance, mental illness, phobia, psychological *or* emotional disorder

neurotic *adj* **1** = **unstable**, abnormal, anxious, compulsive, deviant, disordered, distraught, disturbed, hyper (*inf.*), maladjusted, manic, nervous, obsessive, overwrought, twitchy (*inf.*), unhealthy
Antonyms *adj* calm, laid-back (*inf.*), level-headed, normal, rational, sane, stable, together (*sl.*), well-adjusted, well-balanced

neuter *vb* **6** = **castrate**, doctor (*inf.*), dress, emasculate, fix (*inf.*), geld, spay

neutral *adj* **1** = **unbiased**, disinterested, dispassionate, even-handed, impartial, indifferent, nonaligned, nonbelligerent, noncombatant, noncommittal, nonpartisan, sitting on the fence, unaligned, uncommitted, undecided, uninvolved, unprejudiced **4** = **indeterminate**, achromatic, colourless, dull, indistinct, indistinguishable, intermediate, toneless, undefined
Antonyms *adj* ≠ **unbiased:** active, belligerent, biased, decided, interested, interfering, partial, participating, positive, prejudiced

neutrality *n* **1** = **impartiality**, detachment, disinterestedness, nonalignment, noninterference, noninterventionism, noninvolvement, nonpartisanship

neutralize *vb* **1** = **counteract**, cancel, compensate for, counterbalance, frustrate, invalidate, negate, nullify, offset, undo

never *adv* **1** = **at no time 2** = **not at all**, not for love nor money (*inf.*), not on your life (*inf.*), not on your nelly (*Brit. sl.*), no way, on no account, under no circumstances
Antonyms *adv* ≠ **at no time:** always, aye (*Scot.*), constantly, continually, every time, forever, perpetually, without exception

never-never *n Informal* **1** = **hire-purchase** (*Brit.*), H.P. (*Brit.*)

nevertheless *sentence connector* = **nonetheless**, but, even so, (even) though, however, notwithstanding, regardless, still, yet

new *adj* **2** = **modern**, advanced, all-singing, all-dancing, contemporary, current, fresh, ground-breaking, happening (*inf.*), latest, modernistic, modish, newfangled, novel, original, recent, state-of-the-art, topical, ultramodern, unknown, unused, unusual, up-to-date, virgin **4** = **changed**, altered, improved, modernized, rebranded, redesigned, renewed **7** = **extra**, added, more, supplementary
Antonyms *adj* ≠ **modern:** aged, ancient, antiquated, antique, hackneyed, old, old-fashioned, outmoded, passé, stale, trite

newborn ('njuː,bɔːn) *adj* **1** recently or just born. **2** (of hope, faith, etc.) reborn.
new brutalism *n* another name for **brutalism.**
New Canadian *n Canad.* a recent immigrant to Canada.
new chum *n* **1** *Austral.* a novice in any activity. **2** *Austral. & NZ inf.* (formerly) a recent British immigrant.
newcomer ● ('njuː,kʌmə) *n* a person who has recently arrived or started to participate in something.
New Country *n* a style of country music of the late 1980s characterized by down-to-earth lyrics.
newel ('njuːəl) *n* **1** the central pillar of a winding staircase, esp. one that is made of stone. **2** Also called: **newel post.** the post at the top or bottom of a flight of stairs that supports the handrail. **[**C14: from OF *nouel* knob, from Med. L *nōdellus,* dim. of *nōdus* NODE**]**
New English Bible *n* a new translation of the Bible made between 1962 and 1970.
newfangled ● ('njuː'fæŋgᵊld) *adj* newly come into existence or fashion, esp. excessively modern. **[**C14 *newefangel* liking new things, from *new* + *-fangel,* from OE *fōn* to take**]**
new-found *adj* newly or recently discovered: *new-found confidence.*
newish ('njuːɪʃ) *adj* fairly new.
new issue *n Stock Exchange.* an issue of shares being offered to the public for the first time.
New Jerusalem *n Christianity.* heaven.
New Journalism *n* a style of journalism using techniques borrowed from fiction to portray a situation or event as vividly as possible.
New Latin *n* the form of Latin used since the Renaissance, esp. for scientific nomenclature.
New Look *n* **the.** a fashion in women's clothes introduced in 1947, characterized by long full skirts.
newly ● ('njuːlɪ) *adv* **1** recently. **2** again; anew: *newly raised hopes.* **3** in a new manner; differently: *a newly arranged hairdo.*
newlywed ('njuːlɪ,wɛd) *n* (*often pl*) a recently married person.
New Man *n* **the.** a type of modern man who allows the caring side of his nature to show by being supportive and by sharing child care and housework.
new maths *n* (*functioning as sing*) *Brit.* an approach to mathematics in which the basic principles of set theory are introduced at an elementary level.
new moon *n* the moon when it appears as a narrow waxing crescent.
news ● (njuːz) *n* (*functioning as sing*) **1** important or interesting recent happenings. **2** information about such events, as in the mass media. **3 the news.** a presentation, such as a radio broadcast, of information of this type. **4** interesting or important information not previously known. **5** a person, fashion, etc., widely reported in the mass media: *she is news in the film world.* **[**C15: from ME *newes,* pl. of *newe* new (adj), a model of OF *noveles* or Med. L *nova* new things**]**
▸ **'newsless** *adj*
news agency *n* an organization that collects news reports for newspapers, etc. Also called: **press agency.**
newsagent ('njuːz,eɪdʒənt) *or US* **newsdealer** *n* a shopkeeper who sells newspapers, stationery, etc.
newscast ('njuːz,kɑːst) *n* a radio or television broadcast of the news. **[**C20: from NEWS + (BROAD)CAST**]**
▸ **'news,caster** *n*
news conference *n* another term for **press conference.**
newsflash ('njuːz,flæʃ) *n* a brief item of important news, often interrupting a radio or television programme.
newsgroup ('njuːz,gruːp) *n Computing.* a forum where subscribers exchange information about a specific subject by electronic mail.
newsletter ('njuːz,lɛtə) *n* **1** Also called: **news-sheet.** a printed periodical bulletin circulated to members of a group. **2** *History.* a written or printed account of the news.
newsmonger ('njuːz,mʌŋgə) *n Old-fashioned.* a gossip.
newspaper ('njuːz,peɪpə) *n* a weekly or daily publication consisting of folded sheets and containing articles on the news, features, reviews, and advertisements. Often shortened to **paper.**
newspaperman ('njuːz,peɪpə,mæn) *n, pl* **newspapermen. 1** a person who works for a newspaper as a reporter or editor. **2** the owner or proprietor of a newspaper. **3** a person who sells newspapers in the street.
newspeak ('njuː,spiːk) *n* the language of bureaucrats and politicians, regarded as deliberately ambiguous and misleading. **[**C20: from *1984,* a novel by George Orwell**]**
newsprint ('njuːz,prɪnt) *n* an inexpensive wood-pulp paper used for newspapers.
newsreader ('njuːz,riːdə) *n* a news announcer on radio or television.
newsreel ('njuːz,riːl) *n* a short film with a commentary presenting current events.
newsroom ('njuːz,ruːm, -,rʊm) *n* a room in a newspaper office, television station, etc., where news is received and prepared for publication or broadcasting.
newsstand ('njuːz,stænd) *n* a portable stand or stall from which newspapers are sold.
New Style *n* the present method of reckoning dates using the Gregorian calendar.
news vendor *n* a person who sells newspapers.
newsworthy ● ('njuːz,wɜːðɪ) *adj* sufficiently interesting to be reported in a news bulletin, etc.
newsy ('njuːzɪ) *adj* **newsier, newsiest.** full of news, esp. gossipy or personal news.
newt (njuːt) *n* any of various small semiaquatic amphibians having a long slender body and tail and short feeble legs. **[**C15: from *a newt,* a mistaken division of *an ewt; ewt,* from OE *eveta* EFT**]**
New Testament *n* a collection of writings composed soon after Christ's death and added to the Jewish writings of the Old Testament to make up the Christian Bible.
newton ('njuːtᵊn) *n* the derived SI unit of force that imparts an acceleration of 1 metre per second per second to a mass of 1 kilogram. Symbol: N **[**C20: after Sir Isaac *Newton* (1643–1727), E scientist**]**
Newtonian telescope (njuː'təʊnɪən) *n* a type of astronomical reflecting telescope in which light is reflected from a large concave mirror onto a plane mirror, and through a hole in the side of the body of the telescope to form an image.
Newton's law of gravitation *n* the principle that two particles attract each other with forces directly proportional to the product of their masses divided by the square of the distance between them.
Newton's laws of motion *pl n* three laws of mechanics describing the motion of a body. **The first law** states that a body remains at rest or in uniform motion unless acted upon by a force. **The second law** states that a body's rate of change of momentum is proportional to the force causing it. **The third law** states that when a force acts on a body an equal and opposite force acts simultaneously on another body.
new town *n* (in Britain) a town planned as a complete unit and built with government sponsorship, esp. to accommodate overspill population.
new wave *n* a movement in art, politics, etc., that consciously breaks with traditional ideas, esp. **the New Wave,** a movement in the French cinema of the 1960s, characterized by a fluid use of the camera.
New World *n* **the.** the Americas; the western hemisphere.
New World monkey *n* any of a family of monkeys of Central and South America, many of which are arboreal and have a prehensile tail.
New Year *n* the first day or days of the year in various calendars, usually a holiday.
New Year's Day *n* January 1, celebrated as a holiday in many countries. Often shortened to (US and Canad. inf.) **New Year's.**
New Year's Eve *n* the evening of Dec. 31. See also **Hogmanay.**
New Zealander ('ziːləndə) *n* **1** a native or inhabitant of New Zealand. **2** in earlier usage, a Maori.
next ● (nɛkst) *adj* **1** immediately following: *the next patient to be examined.* **2** immediately adjoining: *the next room.* **3** closest to in degree: *the next-best thing.* **4 the next (Sunday) but one.** the (Sunday) after the next. ◆ *adv* **5** at a time immediately to follow: *the patient to be examined next.* **6 next to. 6a** adjacent to: *the house next to ours.* **6b** following in degree: *next to your mother, who do you love most?* **6c** almost: *next to impossible.* ◆ *prep* **7** *Arch.* next to. **[**OE *nēhst,* sup. of *nēah* NIGH**]**
next door *adj* (**next-door** *when prenominal*), *adv* at or to the adjacent house, flat, etc.
next of kin *n* a person's closest relative.
nexus ● ('nɛksəs) *n, pl* **nexus. 1** a means of connection; link; bond. **2** a connected group or series. **[**C17: from L, from *nectere* to bind**]**
Nez Percé ('nez 'pɜːs) *n* **1** (*pl* **Nez Percés** ('pɜːsɪz) *or* **Nez Percé**) a member of a North American Indian people of the Pacific coast. **2** the language of this people. **[**F, lit. pierced nose**]**
NF (in Britain) *abbrev. for* National Front.
Nfld. *or* **NF.** *abbrev. for* Newfoundland.
NFU (in Britain) *abbrev. for* National Farmers' Union.
NG *abbrev. for:* **1** (in the US) National Guard. **2** New Guinea. **3** Also: **ng.** no good.
NGA (formerly, in Britain) *abbrev. for* National Graphical Association.
ngaio ('naɪəʊ) *n, pl* **ngaios.** a small evergreen New Zealand tree. **[**from Maori**]**
ngati ('nɑːtiː) *n, pl* **ngati.** *NZ.* a tribe or clan. **[**from Maori**]**
NHI (in Britain) *abbrev. for* National Health Insurance.
NHS (in Britain) *abbrev. for* National Health Service.
Ni *the chemical symbol for* nickel.

THESAURUS

newcomer *n* = **novice**, alien, arrival, beginner, foreigner, immigrant, incomer, Johnny-come-lately (*inf.*), outsider, parvenu, settler, stranger
newfangled *adj* = **new**, all-singing, all-dancing, contemporary, fashionable, gimmicky, modern, new-fashioned, novel, recent, state-of-the-art
Antonyms *adj* antiquated, dated, obsolete, old-fashioned, outmoded, out-of-date, passé
newly *adv* **1** = **recently**, just, lately, latterly **2** = **anew**, freshly
newness *n* **2** = **novelty**, freshness, innovation, originality
news *n* **1, 2, 4** = **information**, account, advice, bulletin, buzz, communiqué, dirt (*US sl.*), disclosure, dispatch, exposé, gen (*Brit. inf.*), gossip, hearsay, intelligence, latest (*inf.*), leak, news flash, release, report, revelation, rumour, scandal, scuttlebutt (*US sl.*), statement, story, tidings, word
newsworthy *adj* = **interesting**, arresting, important, notable, noteworthy, remarkable, significant, stimulating
next *adj* **1** = **following**, consequent, ensuing, later, subsequent, succeeding **2** = **nearest**, adjacent, adjoining, closest, neighbouring ◆ *adv* **5** = **afterwards**, closely, following, later, subsequently, thereafter
nexus *n* **1** = **connection**, bond, joining, junction, link, tie

NI *abbrev. for:* **1** (in Britain) National Insurance. **2** Northern Ireland. **3** (in New Zealand) North Island.

niacin ('naɪəsɪn) *n* another name for **nicotinic acid.** [C20: from NI(COTINIC) AC(ID) + -IN]

nib (nɪb) *n* **1** the writing point of a pen, esp. an insertable tapered metal part. **2** a point, tip, or beak. **3** (*pl*) crushed cocoa beans. ◆ *vb* **nibs, nibbing, nibbed.** (*tr*) **4** to provide with a nib. **5** to sharpen the nib of. [C16 (in the sense: beak): from ?]

nibble ❶ ('nɪbᵊl) *vb* **nibbles, nibbling, nibbled.** (when *intr*, often foll. by *at*) **1** (esp. of animals) to take small repeated bites (of). **2** to take dainty or tentative bites: *to nibble at a cake.* **3** to bite (at) gently. ◆ *n* **4** a small mouthful. **5** an instance of nibbling. [C15: rel. to Low G *nibbelen*]
▸**'nibbler** *n*

niblick ('nɪblɪk) *n Golf.* (formerly) a club giving a great deal of lift. [C19: from ?]

nibs (nɪbz) *n* **his nibs.** *Sl.* a mock title used of someone in authority. [C19: from ?]

NICAM ('naɪkæm) *n acronym for* near-instantaneous companded audio multiplex: a technique for coding audio signals into digital form.

nice ❶ (naɪs) *adj* **1** pleasant: *a nice day.* **2** kind or friendly: *a nice gesture of help.* **3** good or satisfactory: *they made a nice job of it.* **4** subtle or discriminating: *a nice point in the argument.* **5** precise; skilful: *a nice fit.* **6** *Now rare.* fastidious; respectable: *he was not too nice about his methods.* **7** *Obs.* **7a** foolish or ignorant. **7b** delicate. **7c** shy; modest. **7d** wanton. [C13 (orig.: foolish): from OF *nice* simple, silly, from L *nescius,* from *nescīre* to be ignorant]
▸**'nicely** *adv* ▸**'niceness** *n* ▸**'nicish** *adj*

nice-looking *adj Inf.* attractive in appearance; pretty or handsome.

nicety ❶ ('naɪsɪtɪ) *n, pl* **niceties. 1** a subtle point: *a nicety of etiquette.* **2** (*usually pl*) a refinement or delicacy: *the niceties of first-class travel.* **3** subtlety, delicacy, or precision. **4 to a nicety.** with precision.

niche ❶ (nɪtʃ, niːʃ) *n* **1** a recess in a wall, esp. one that contains a statue, etc. **2** a position particularly suitable for the person occupying it: *he found his niche in politics.* **3** (*modifier*) relating to or aimed at a small specialized group or market: *shampoo shops and other niche retailing ventures.* **4** *Ecology.* the status of a plant or animal within its community, which determines its activities, relationships with other organisms, etc. ◆ *vb* **niches, niching, niched. 5** (*tr*) to place (a statue) in a niche; ensconce (oneself). [C17: from F, from OF *nichier* to nest, from Vulgar L *nīdicāre* (unattested), from L *nīdus* NEST]

Nichrome ('naɪ,krəʊm) *n Trademark.* any of various alloys containing nickel, iron, and chromium, used in electrical heating elements, furnaces, etc.

nick ❶ (nɪk) *n* **1** a small notch or indentation. **2** *Brit. sl.* a prison or police station. **3 in good nick.** *Inf.* in good condition. **4 in the nick of time.** just in time. ◆ *vb* **5** (*tr*) to chip or cut. **6** *Sl., chiefly Brit.* **6a** to steal. **6b** to arrest. **7** (*intr;* often foll. by *off*) *Inf.* to depart rapidly. **8 nick (someone) for.** *US & Canad. sl.* to defraud (someone) to the extent of. **9** to divide and reset (the tail muscles of a horse) to give the tail a high carriage. **10** (*tr*) to guess, catch, etc., exactly. [C15: ? changed from C14 *nocke* NOCK]

nickel ('nɪkᵊl) *n* **1** a malleable silvery-white metallic element that is corrosion-resistant: used in alloys, in electroplating, and as a catalyst in organic synthesis. Symbol: Ni; atomic no.: 28; atomic wt.: 58.71. **2** a US or Canadian coin worth five cents. ◆ *vb* **nickels, nickelling, nickelled** *or US* **nickels, nickeling, nickeled. 3** (*tr*) to plate with nickel. [C18: from G *Kupfernickel* niccolite, lit.: copper demon; it was mistakenly thought to contain copper]

nickelodeon (,nɪkə'ləʊdɪən) *n US.* **1** an early form of jukebox. **2** (formerly) a Pianola, esp. one operated by inserting a five-cent piece. [C20: from NICKEL + (MEL)ODEON]

nickel plate *n* a thin layer of nickel deposited on a surface, usually by electrolysis.

nickel silver *n* any of various white alloys containing copper, zinc, and nickel: used in making tableware, etc. Also called: **German silver.**

nickel steel *n Engineering.* steel containing between 0.5 and 6.0 per cent nickel to increase its strength.

nicker[1] ('nɪkə) *vb* (*intr*) **1** (of a horse) to neigh softly. **2** to snigger. [C18: ?from NEIGH]

nicker[2] ('nɪkə) *n, pl* **nicker.** *Brit. sl.* a pound sterling. [C20: from ?]

nick-nack ('nɪk,næk) *n* a variant spelling of **knick-knack.**

nickname ❶ ('nɪk,neɪm) *n* **1** a familiar, pet, or derisory name given to a person, animal, or place. **2** a shortened or familiar form of a person's name: *Joe is a nickname for Joseph.* ◆ *vb* **nicknames, nicknaming, nicknamed. 3** (*tr*) to call by a nickname. [C15 *a nekename,* mistaken division of *an ekename* an additional name]

Nicol prism ('nɪkᵊl) *n* two prisms of Iceland spar or calcite cut at specified angles and cemented together, to produce plane-polarized light. [C19: after William *Nicol* (?1768–1851), Scot. physicist, its inventor]

nicotiana (nɪ,kəʊʃɪ'ɑːnə) *n* a plant of an American and Australian genus, having white, yellow, or purple fragrant flowers. Also called: **tobacco plant.** [C16: see NICOTINE]

nicotinamide (,nɪkə'tɪnə,maɪd) *n* the amide of nicotinic acid: a component of the vitamin B complex. Formula: $C_6H_6ON_2$.

nicotine ('nɪkə,tiːn) *n* a colourless oily acrid toxic liquid that turns yellowish-brown in air and light: the principal alkaloid in tobacco. [C19: from F, from NL *herba nicotiana* Nicot's plant, after J. *Nicot* (1530-1600), F diplomat who introduced tobacco into France]
▸**'nico,tined** *adj* ▸**nicotinic** (,nɪkə'tɪnɪk) *adj*

nicotinic acid *n* a vitamin of the B complex that occurs in milk, liver, yeast, etc. Lack of it in the diet leads to the disease pellagra.

nicotinism ('nɪkətiː,nɪzəm) *n Pathol.* a toxic condition of the body caused by nicotine.

nictitate ('nɪktɪ,teɪt) *or* **nictate** ('nɪkteɪt) *vb* **nictitates, nictitating, nictitated** *or* **nictates, nictating, nictated.** a technical word for **blink.** [C19: from Med. L *nictitāre* to wink repeatedly, from L *nictāre* to blink]
▸**,nicti'tation** *or* **nic'tation** *n*

nictitating membrane *n* (in reptiles, birds, and some mammals) a thin fold of skin beneath the eyelid that can be drawn across the eye.

nidicolous (nɪ'dɪkələs) *adj* (of young birds) remaining in the nest some time after hatching. [C19: from L *nīdus* nest + *colere* to inhabit]

nidifugous (nɪ'dɪfjʊgəs) *adj* (of young birds) leaving the nest very soon after hatching. [C19: from L *nīdus* nest + *fugere* to flee]

nidify ('nɪdɪ,faɪ) *or* **nidificate** ('nɪdɪfɪ,keɪt) *vb* **nidifies, nidifying, nidified** *or* **nidificates, nidificating, nidificated.** (*intr*) (of birds) to make or build a nest. [C17: from L *nīdificāre,* from *nīdus* a nest + *facere* to make]
▸**,nidifi'cation** *n*

niece (niːs) *n* a daughter of one's sister or brother. [C13: from OF: niece, granddaughter, ult. from L *neptis* granddaughter]

niello (nɪ'ɛləʊ) *n, pl* **nielli** (-lɪ) *or* **niellos. 1** a black compound of sulphur and silver, lead, or copper used to incise a design on a metal surface. **2** this process. **3** an object decorated with niello. [C19: from It. from L *nigellus* blackish, from *niger* black]

niff (nɪf) *Brit. sl.* ◆ *n* **1** a bad smell. ◆ *vb* (*intr*) **2** to stink. [C20: ?from SNIFF]
▸**'niffy** *adj*

nifty ❶ ('nɪftɪ) *adj* **niftier, niftiest.** *Inf.* **1** pleasing, apt, or stylish. **2** quick; agile. [C19: from ?]
▸**'niftily** *adv* ▸**'niftiness** *n*

nigella (naɪ'dʒɛlə) *n* another name for **love-in-a-mist.**

Nigerian (naɪ'dʒɪərɪən) *n* **1** a native or inhabitant of Nigeria, a country in West Africa. **2** of Nigeria, its people, culture, etc.

niggard ❶ ('nɪgəd) *n* **1** a stingy person. ◆ *adj* **2** *Arch.* miserly. [C14: ?from ON]

niggardly ❶ ('nɪgədlɪ) *adj* **1** stingy. **2** meagre: *a niggardly salary.* ◆ *adv* **3** stingily; grudgingly.
▸**'niggardliness** *n*

nigger ('nɪgə) *n Derog.* **1** another name for a Negro. **2** a member of any

THESAURUS

nibble *vb* **1-3 = bite,** eat, gnaw, munch, nip, peck, pick at ◆ *n* **4 = snack,** bite, crumb, morsel, peck, *soupçon,* taste, titbit

nice *adj* **1 = pleasant,** agreeable, attractive, charming, delightful, good, pleasurable **2 = kind,** amiable, commendable, courteous, friendly, likable *or* likeable, polite, prepossessing, refined, well-mannered **4 = subtle,** accurate, careful, delicate, discriminating, exact, exacting, fine, meticulous, precise, rigorous, scrupulous, strict **5 = neat,** exact, fine, precise, tidy, trim
Antonyms *adj* ≠ **pleasant:** awful, disagreeable, dreadful, miserable, unpleasant ≠ **kind:** disagreeable, mean, unfriendly, unkind, unpleasant, vulgar ≠ **subtle:** careless, rough, sloppy (*inf.*), vague ≠ **neat:** coarse, crude, rough, shabby, sloppy (*inf.*)

nicely *adv* **1 = pleasantly,** acceptably, agreeably, attractively, charmingly, delightfully, pleasingly, pleasurably, well **2 = kindly,** amiably, commendably, courteously, likably, politely, prepossessingly **4 = subtly,** accurately, carefully, delicately, exactingly, exactly, finely, meticulously, precisely, rigorously, scrupulously, strictly **5 = neatly,** finely, precisely, tidily, trimly
Antonyms *adv* ≠ **pleasantly:** unattractively, unpleasantly ≠ **subtly:** carelessly, sloppily (*inf.*) ≠ **neatly:** sloppily (*inf.*)

niceness *n* **1, 2 = kindness,** agreeableness, amiability, attractiveness, charm, courtesy, delightfulness, friendliness, good manners, goodness, likableness *or* likeableness, pleasantness, pleasurableness, politeness, refinement **4 = precision,** accuracy, care, carefulness, delicacy, discrimination, exactingness, exactitude, exactness, fineness, meticulosity, meticulousness, preciseness, rigorousness, rigour, scrupulousness, strictness, subtleness, subtlety **5 = neatness,** daintiness, fineness, tidiness

nicety *n* **1, 2 = subtlety,** delicacy, distinction, nuance, refinement **3 = precision,** accuracy, exactness, fastidiousness, finesse, meticulousness, minuteness

niche *n* **1 = alcove,** corner, hollow, nook, opening, recess **2 = position,** calling, pigeonhole (*inf.*), place, slot (*inf.*), vocation

nick *n* **1 = cut,** chip, dent, mark, notch, scar, score, scratch, snick ◆ *vb* **5 = cut,** chip, damage, dent, mark, notch, scar, score, scratch, snick **6a** *Slang* **= steal,** finger (*sl.*), knock off (*sl.*), pilfer, pinch (*inf.*), snitch (*sl.*), swipe (*sl.*)

nickname *n* **1 = pet name,** epithet, familiar name, handle (*sl.*), label, moniker *or* monicker (*sl.*), sobriquet **2 = diminutive**

nifty *adj Informal* **1 = pleasing,** apt, attractive, chic, clever, enjoyable, excellent, neat, sharp, smart, spruce, stylish **2 = quick,** agile, deft

niggard *n* **1 = miser,** cheapskate (*inf.*), meanie *or* meany, penny-pincher (*inf.*), screw (*sl.*), Scrooge, skinflint

niggardliness *n* **1 = miserliness,** avarice, avariciousness, closeness, covetousness, frugality, grudgingness, meanness, mercenariness, nearness (*inf.*), parsimony, penuriousness, sordidness, sparingness, stinginess, thrift, tightfistedness, ungenerousness **2 = paltriness,** beggarliness, inadequacy, insufficiency, meagreness, meanness, miserableness, scantiness, skimpiness, smallness, wretchedness

niggardly *adj* **1 = stingy,** avaricious, close, covetous, frugal, grudging, mean, mercenary, miserly, near (*inf.*), parsimonious, penurious,

dark-skinned race. **3 nigger in the woodpile.** a hidden cause of trouble. [C18: from C16 dialect *neeger*, from F *nègre*, from Sp. NEGRO]

niggle ('nɪgᵊl) *vb* **niggles, niggling, niggled. 1** (*intr*) to find fault continually. **2** (*intr*) to be preoccupied with details; fuss. **3** (*tr*) to irritate; worry. ◆ *n* **4** a trivial objection or complaint. **5** a slight feeling as of misgiving, uncertainty, etc. [C16: from Scand.]
▸**'niggler** *n* ▸**'niggly** *adj*

niggling ('nɪglɪŋ) *adj* **1** petty. **2** fussy. **3** irritating. **4** requiring painstaking work. **5** persistently troubling.

nigh (naɪ) *adj, adv, prep* an archaic, poetic, or dialect word for **near.** [OE *nēah, nēh*]

night (naɪt) *n* **1** the period of darkness that occurs each 24 hours, as distinct from day. **2** (*modifier*) of, occurring, working, etc., at night: *a night nurse.* **3** this period considered as a unit: *four nights later they left.* **4** the period between sunset and retiring to bed; evening. **5** the time between bedtime and morning. **6** the weather at night: *a clear night.* **7** the activity or experience of a person during a night. **8** (*sometimes cap.*) any evening designated for a special observance or function. **9** nightfall or dusk. **10** a state or period of gloom, ignorance, etc. **11 make a night of it.** to celebrate for most of the night. ◆ Related adj: **nocturnal.** ◆ See also **nights.** [OE *niht*]

night blindness *n Pathol.* a nontechnical term for **nyctalopia.**
▸**'night-ˌblind** *adj*

nightcap ('naɪtˌkæp) *n* **1** a bedtime drink. **2** a soft cap formerly worn in bed.

nightclothes ('naɪtˌkləʊðz) *pl n* clothes worn in bed.

nightclub ('naɪtˌklʌb) *n* a place of entertainment open until late at night, usually offering food, drink, a floor show, dancing, etc.

nightdress ('naɪtˌdrɛs) *n Brit.* a loose dress worn in bed by women. Also called: **nightgown, nightie.**

nightfall ('naɪtˌfɔːl) *n* the approach of darkness; dusk.

night fighter *n* an interceptor aircraft used for operations at night.

nightgown ('naɪtˌgaʊn) *n* **1** another name for **nightdress. 2** a man's nightshirt.

nighthawk ('naɪtˌhɔːk) *n* **1** any of various nocturnal American birds. **2** *Inf.* another name for **night owl.**

nightie *or* **nighty** ('naɪtɪ) *n, pl* **nighties.** *Inf.* short for **nightdress.**

nightingale ('naɪtɪŋˌgeɪl) *n* a brownish European songbird with a broad reddish-brown tail: well known for its musical song, usually heard at night. [OE *nihtegale*, from NIGHT + *galan* to sing]

nightjar ('naɪtˌdʒɑː) *n* any of a family of nocturnal birds which have large eyes and feed on insects. [C17: NIGHT + JAR², so called from its discordant cry]

night latch *n* a door lock operated by means of a knob on the inside and a key on the outside.

nightlife ('naɪtˌlaɪf) *n* social life or entertainment taking place at night.

night-light *n* a dim light burning at night, esp. for children.

nightlong ('naɪtˌlɒŋ) *adj, adv* throughout the night.

nightly ('naɪtlɪ) *adj* **1** happening or relating to each night. **2** happening at night. ◆ *adv* **3** at night or each night.

nightmare ('naɪtˌmɛə) *n* **1** a terrifying or deeply distressing dream. **2a** an event or condition resembling a terrifying dream. **2b** (*as modifier*): *a nightmare drive.* **3** a thing that is feared. **4** (formerly) an evil spirit supposed to suffocate sleeping people. [C13 (meaning: incubus; C16: bad dream): from NIGHT + OE *mare, mære* evil spirit, from Gmc]
▸**'nightˌmarish** *adj*

night owl *or* **nighthawk** *n Inf.* a person who is or prefers to be up and about late at night.

nights (naɪts) *adv Inf.* at night, esp. regularly: *he works nights.*

night safe *n* a safe built into the outside wall of a bank, in which customers can deposit money at times when the bank is closed.

night school *n* an educational institution that holds classes in the evening.

nightshade ('naɪtˌʃeɪd) *n* any of various solanaceous plants, such as deadly nightshade and black nightshade. [OE *nihtscada*, apparently NIGHT + SHADE, referring to the poisonous or soporific qualities of these plants]

night shift *n* **1** a group of workers who work a shift during the night. **2** the period worked.

nightshirt ('naɪtˌʃɜːt) *n* a loose knee-length or longer shirtlike garment worn in bed.

nightspot ('naɪtˌspɒt) *n* an informal word for **nightclub.**

night-time *n* the time from sunset to sunrise; night as distinct from day.

night watch *n* **1** a watch or guard kept at night, esp. for security. **2** the period of time the watch is kept. **3** a night watchman.

night watchman *n* **1** Also called: **night watch.** a person who keeps guard at night on a factory, public building, etc. **2** *Cricket.* a batsman sent in to bat to play out time when a wicket has fallen near the end of a day's play.

nightwear ('naɪtˌwɛə) *n* apparel worn in bed or before retiring to bed; pyjamas, etc.

nigrescent (naɪ'grɛsᵊnt) *adj* blackish; dark. [C18: from L *nigrescere* to grow black, from *niger* black]
▸**ni'grescence** *n*

nihilism ('naɪɪˌlɪzəm) *n* **1** a complete denial of all established authority and institutions. **2** *Philosophy.* an extreme form of scepticism that systematically rejects all values, belief in existence, etc. **3** a revolutionary doctrine of destruction for its own sake. **4** the practice of terrorism. [C19: from L *nihil* nothing]
▸**'nihilist** *n, adj* ▸**ˌnihil'istic** *adj* ▸**nihility** (naɪ'hɪlɪtɪ) *n*

nihil obstat ('naɪhɪl 'ɒbstæt) the phrase used by a Roman Catholic censor to declare publication inoffensive to faith or morals. [L, lit.: nothing hinders]

-nik *suffix forming nouns.* denoting a person associated with a specified state or quality: *beatnik.* [C20: from Russian *-nik*, as in SPUTNIK, and infl. by Yiddish *-nik* (agent suffix)]

Nikkei Stock Average ('nɪkeɪ) *n* an index of share prices based on an average of 225 equities quoted on the Tokyo Stock Exchange. [C20: from *Nik(on) Kei(zai Shimbun)*, a Japanese newspaper group]

nil (nɪl) *n* nothing: used esp. in the scoring of certain games. [C19: from L]

Nile green (naɪl) *n* **a** a pale bluish-green colour. **b** (*as adj*): *a Nile-green dress.*

nilgai ('nɪlgaɪ) *or* **nilghau** ('nɪlgɔː) *n, pl* **nilgai, nilgais** *or* **nilghau, nilghaus.** a large Indian antelope, the male of which has small horns. [C19: from Hindi *nīlgāw*, from Sansk. *nīla* blue + *go* bull]

Nilotic (naɪ'lɒtɪk) *adj* **1** of the Nile. **2** of or belonging to a Negroid pastoral people inhabiting the S Sudan, parts of Kenya and Uganda, and neighbouring countries. **3** relating to the group of languages spoken by the Nilotic peoples. [C17: via L from Gk *Neilotikós*, from *Neilos* the River Nile]

nimble ('nɪmbᵊl) *adj* **1** agile, quick, and neat in movement. **2** alert; acute. [OE *næmel* quick to grasp, & *numol* quick at seizing, both from *niman* to take]
▸**'nimbleness** *n* ▸**'nimbly** *adv*

nimbostratus (ˌnɪmbəʊ'streɪtəs, -'strɑːtəs) *n, pl* **nimbostrati** (-taɪ). a dark rain-bearing stratus cloud.

nimbus ('nɪmbəs) *n, pl* **nimbi** (-baɪ) *or* **nimbuses. 1a** a dark grey rain-bearing cloud. **1b** (*in combination*): *cumulonimbus clouds.* **2a** an emanation of light surrounding a saint or deity. **2b** a representation of this emanation. **3** a surrounding aura. [C17: from L: cloud]

NIMBY ('nɪmbɪ) *n acronym for* not in my back yard: a person who objects to the occurrence of something if it will affect them or take place in their locality.

Nimrod ('nɪmrɒd) *n* **1** a hunter famous for his prowess (Genesis 10:8–9). **2** a person dedicated to or skilled in hunting.

nincompoop ('nɪnkəmˌpuːp, 'nɪŋ-) *n* a stupid person; fool; idiot. [C17: from ?]

nine (naɪn) *n* **1** the cardinal number that is the sum of one and eight. **2** a numeral, 9, IX, etc., representing this number. **3** something repre-

THESAURUS

Scrooge-like, sordid, sparing, stinging, tight-fisted, ungenerous **2** = **paltry**, beggarly, inadequate, insufficient, meagre, mean, measly, miserable, pathetic, scant, scanty, skimpy, small, wretched
Antonyms *adj* ≠ **stingy:** bountiful, generous, lavish, liberal, munificent, prodigal ≠ **paltry:** abundant, ample, bountiful, copious, generous, handsome, liberal, plentiful, profuse

niggle *vb* **2** = **criticize**, carp, cavil, find fault, fuss **3** = **worry**, annoy, irritate, rankle

niggling *adj* **1, 2** = **petty**, cavilling, finicky, fussy, insignificant, minor, nit-picking (*inf.*), pettifogging, picky (*inf.*), piddling (*inf.*), quibbling, trifling, unimportant **3, 5** = **persistent**, gnawing, irritating, troubling, worrying

nigh *adj* = **near**, adjacent, adjoining, approximate, at hand, bordering, close, contiguous, imminent, impending, next, upcoming ◆ *adv* = **near**, about, almost, approximately, close, practically

night *n* **1** = **darkness**, dark, dead of night, hours of darkness, night-time, night watches

nightfall *n* = **evening**, dusk, eve, eventide, gloaming (*Scot. or poetic*), sundown, sunset, twilight, vespers
Antonyms *n* aurora (*poetic*), cockcrow, dawn, dawning, daybreak, daylight, morning, sunrise

nightly *adv* **1** = **every night**, each night, night after night, nights (*inf.*) ◆ *adj* **2** = **nocturnal**, night-time ◆ *adv* **3** = **by night**, after dark, at night, in the night, nights (*inf.*), nocturnally

nightmare *n* **1** = **bad dream**, hallucination, incubus, night terror, succubus **2** = **ordeal**, hell on earth, horror, torment, trial, tribulation

nightmarish *adj* **2** = **frightening**, agonizing, alarming, creepy, disturbing, harrowing, horrible, Kafkaesque, scaring, terrifying, unreal

nihilism *n* **1, 2** = **nonbelief**, abnegation, agnosticism, atheism, denial, disbelief, rejection, renunciation, repudiation, scepticism **3, 4** = **lawlessness**, anarchy, disorder, terrorism

nihilist *n* **1, 2** = **nonbeliever**, agnostic, atheist, cynic, disbeliever, pessimist, sceptic **3, 4** = **anarchist**, agitator, extremist, revolutionary, terrorist

nil *n* = **nothing**, duck, love, naught, *nihil*, none, zero, zilch (*sl.*)

nimble *adj* **1** = **agile**, active, brisk, deft, dexterous, lively, nippy (*Brit. inf.*), proficient, prompt, quick, ready, sprightly, spry, swift **2** = **alert**, bright (*inf.*), quick-witted, smart
Antonyms *adj* ≠ **agile:** awkward, clumsy, dull, heavy, inactive, indolent, lethargic, slow

nimbleness *n* **1** = **agility**, adroitness, alacrity, dexterity, finesse, grace, lightness, nippiness (*Brit. inf.*), skill, sprightliness, spryness **2** = **alertness**, smartness

nimbly *adv* **1** = **quickly**, actively, agilely, briskly, deftly, dexterously, easily, fast, fleetly, hotfoot, posthaste, proficiently, promptly, pronto (*inf.*), readily, sharply, smartly, speedily, spryly, swiftly **2** = **alertly**, acutely, quick-wittedly

nimbus *n* **1a** = **cloud 2** = **halo**, aura, aureole, corona, glow, irradiation **3** = **atmosphere**, ambience, aura

nincompoop *n* = **idiot**, berk (*Brit. sl.*), blockhead, charlie (*Brit. inf.*), chump, coot, dimwit (*inf.*), divvy (*sl.*), dolt, dork (*sl.*), dunce, fathead

senting, represented by, or consisting of nine units, such as a playing card with nine symbols on it. **4** Also: **nine o'clock.** nine hours after noon or midnight: *the play starts at nine.* **5 dressed (up) to the nines.** *Inf.* elaborately dressed. **6 999** (in Britain) the telephone number of the emergency services. **7 nine to five.** normal office hours: *a nine-to-five job.* ◆ *determiner* **8a** amounting to nine: *nine days.* **8b** (*as pronoun*): *nine are ready.* [OE *nigon*]

nine-days wonder *n* something that arouses great interest but only for a short period.

ninefold ('naɪn,fəʊld) *adj* **1** equal to or having nine times as many or as much. **2** composed of nine parts. ◆ *adv* **3** by nine times as much.

ninepins ('naɪn,pɪnz) *n* **1** (*functioning as sing*) another name for **skittles.** **2** (*sing*) one of the pins used in this game.

nineteen ('naɪn'tiːn) *n* **1** the cardinal number that is the sum of ten and nine. **2** a numeral, 19, XIX, etc., representing this number. **3** something represented by, representing, or consisting of 19 units. **4 talk nineteen to the dozen.** to talk incessantly. ◆ *determiner* **5a** amounting to nineteen: *nineteen pictures.* **5b** (*as pronoun*): *only nineteen voted.* [OE *nigontīne*]

nineteenth (,naɪn'tiːnθ) *adj* **1** (*usually prenominal*) **1a** coming after the eighteenth in numbering, position, etc.; being the ordinal number of *nineteen.* Often written: 19th. **1b** (*as n*): *the nineteenth was rainy.* ◆ *n* **2a** one of 19 equal parts of something. **2b** (*as modifier*): *a nineteenth part.* **3** the fraction equal to one divided by 19 (1/19).

nineteenth hole *n Golf, sl.* the bar in a golf clubhouse. [C20: from its being the next objective after a standard 18-hole round]

ninetieth ('naɪntɪɪθ) *adj* **1** (*usually prenominal*) **1a** being the ordinal number of *ninety* in numbering, position, etc. Often written: 90th. **1b** (*as n*): *ninetieth in succession.* ◆ *n* **2a** one of 90 equal parts of something. **2b** (*as modifier*): *a ninetieth part.* **3** the fraction one divided by 90 (1/90).

ninety ('naɪntɪ) *n, pl* **nineties. 1** the cardinal number that is the product of ten and nine. **2** a numeral, 90, XC, etc., representing this number. **3** something represented by, representing, or consisting of 90 units. ◆ *determiner* **4a** amounting to ninety: *ninety times.* **4b** (*as pronoun*): *at least ninety are missing.* [OE *nigontig*]
▸**'ninetieth** *adj, n*

ninja ('nɪndʒə) *n, pl* **ninja** *or* **ninjas.** (*sometimes cap.*) a person skilled in **ninjutsu,** a Japanese martial art characterized by stealthy movement and camouflage. [Japanese]

ninny ('nɪnɪ) *n, pl* **ninnies.** a dull-witted person. [C16: ?from *an innocent* simpleton]

ninth (naɪnθ) *adj* **1** (*usually prenominal*) **1a** coming after the eighth in order, position, etc.; being the ordinal number of *nine.* Often written: 9th. **1b** (*as n*): *ninth in line.* ◆ *n* **2a** one of nine equal parts. **2b** (*as modifier*): *a ninth part.* **3** the fraction one divided by nine (1/9). **4** *Music.* an interval of one octave plus a second. ◆ *adv* **5** Also: **ninthly.** after the eighth person, position, event, etc. [OE *nigotha*]

niobium (naɪ'əʊbɪəm) *n* a ductile white superconductive metallic element that occurs principally in the black mineral columbite and tantalite. Symbol: Nb; atomic no.: 41; atomic wt.: 92.906. Former name: **columbium.** [C19: from NL, from *Niobe* (daughter of Tantalus); because it occurred in TANTALITE]

nip[1] ❶ (nɪp) *vb* **nips, nipping, nipped.** (*mainly tr*) **1** to compress, as between a finger and the thumb; pinch. **2** (often foll. by *off*) to remove by clipping, biting, etc. **3** (when *intr,* often foll. by *at*) to give a small sharp bite (to): *the dog nipped at his heels.* **4** (esp. of the cold) to affect with a stinging sensation. **5** to harm through cold: *the frost nipped the young plants.* **6** to check or destroy the growth of (esp. in **nip in the bud**). **7** (*intr;* foll. by *along, up, out,* etc.) *Brit. inf.* to hurry; dart. **8** *Sl., chiefly US & Canad.* to snatch. ◆ *n* **9** a pinch, snip, etc. **10** severe frost or cold: *the first nip of winter.* **11 put the nips in.** *Austral. & NZ sl.* to exert pressure on someone, esp. in order to extort money. **12** *Arch.* a taunting remark. **13 nip and tuck.** *US & Canad.* neck and neck. [C14: from ON]

nip[2] ❶ (nɪp) *n* **1** a small drink of spirits; dram. ◆ *vb* **nips, nipping, nipped.** **2** to drink spirits, esp. habitually in small amounts. [C18: from *nipperkin* a vessel holding a half-pint or less, from ?]

nipper ❶ ('nɪpə) *n* **1** a person or thing that nips. **2** the large pincer-like claw of a lobster, crab, etc. **3** *Inf., chiefly Brit. & Austral.* a small child. **4** *Austral.* a type of small prawn used as bait.

nippers ('nɪpəz) *pl n* an instrument or tool, such as a pair of pliers, for snipping or squeezing.

nipple ❶ ('nɪpᵊl) *n* **1** the small conical projection in the centre of each breast, which in women contains the outlet of the milk ducts. **2** something resembling a nipple in shape or function. **3** Also called: **grease nipple.** a small drilled bush, usually screwed into a bearing, through which grease is introduced. [C16: from earlier *neble, nible,* ?from NEB, NIB]

nipplewort ('nɪpᵊl,wɜːt) *n* an annual Eurasian plant with pointed oval leaves and small yellow flower heads.

nippy ❶ ('nɪpɪ) *adj* **nippier, nippiest. 1** (of weather) frosty or chilly. **2** *Brit. inf.* **2a** quick; nimble; active. **2b** (of a motor vehicle) small and relatively powerful. **3** (of dogs) inclined to bite.
▸**'nippily** *adv*

NIREX ('naɪrɛks) *n acronym for* Nuclear Industry Radioactive Waste Executive.

nirvana ❶ (nɪə'vɑːnə, nɜː-) *n Buddhism & Hinduism.* final release from the cycle of reincarnation attained by extinction of all desires and individual existence, culminating (in Buddhism) in absolute blessedness, or (in Hinduism) in absorption into Brahman. [C19: from Sansk.: extinction, from *nir-* out + *vāti* it blows]

Nisei ('niːseɪ) *n* a native-born citizen of the United States or Canada whose parents were Japanese immigrants. [Japanese, lit.: second generation]

nisi ('naɪsaɪ) *adj* (*postpositive*) *Law.* (of a court order) coming into effect on a specified date unless cause is shown why it should not: *a decree nisi.* [C19: from: unless, if not]

Nissen hut ('nɪsᵊn) *n* a military shelter of semicircular cross section, made of corrugated steel sheet. [C20: after Lt Col. Peter *Nissen* (1871–1930), British mining engineer, its inventor]

nit[1] (nɪt) *n* **1** the egg of a louse, esp. adhering to human hair. **2** the larva of a louse. [OE *hnitu*]

nit[2] (nɪt) *n* a unit of luminance equal to 1 candela per square metre. [C20: from L *nitor* brightness]

nit[3] (nɪt) *n Inf., chiefly Brit.* short for **nitwit.**

nit[4] (nɪt) *n* a unit of information equal to 1.44 bits. Also called: **nepit.** [C20: from *N*(*apierian dig*)*it*]

nit[5] (nɪt) *n* **keep nit.** *Austral. inf.* to keep watch, esp. during illegal activity. [C19: from *nix!* a shout of warning]
▸**'nit-,keeper** *n*

nit-picking ❶ *Inf.* ◆ *n* **1** a concern with insignificant details, esp. with the intention of finding fault. ◆ *adj* **2** showing such a concern; fussy. [C20: from NIT[1] + PICK[1]]
▸**'nit-,picker** *n*

nitrate ('naɪtreɪt) *n* **1** any salt or ester of nitric acid. **2** a fertilizer containing nitrate salts. ◆ *vb* **nitrates, nitrating, nitrated. 3** (*tr*) to treat with nitric acid or a nitrate. **4** to convert or be converted into a nitrate.
▸**ni'tration** *n*

nitre *or US* **niter** ('naɪtə) *n* another name for **potassium nitrate** or **sodium nitrate.** [C14: via OF from L *nitrum,* prob. from Gk *nitron*]

nitric ('naɪtrɪk) *adj* of or containing nitrogen.

nitric acid *n* a colourless corrosive liquid important in the manufacture of fertilizers, explosives, and many other chemicals. Formula: HNO_3. Former name: **aqua fortis.**

nitric oxide *n* a colourless reactive gas. Formula: NO. Systematic name: **nitrogen monoxide.**

nitride ('naɪtraɪd) *n* a compound of nitrogen with a more electropositive element.

nitrification (,naɪtrɪfɪ'keɪʃən) *n* **1** the oxidation of the ammonium compounds in dead organic material into nitrites and nitrates by soil nitrobacteria, making nitrogen available to plants. **2** the addition of a nitro group to an organic compound.

nitrify ('naɪtrɪ,faɪ) *vb* **nitrifies, nitrifying, nitrified.** (*tr*) **1** to treat or cause to react with nitrogen. **2** to treat (soil) with nitrates. **3** (of nitrobacteria) to convert (ammonium compounds) into nitrates by oxidation.
▸**'nitri,fiable** *adj*

nitrite ('naɪtraɪt) *n* any salt or ester of nitrous acid.

nitro- *or before a vowel* **nitr-** *combining form.* **1** indicating that a chemical compound contains a nitro group, $-NO_2$: *nitrobenzene.* **2** indicating that a chemical compound is a nitrate ester: *nitrocellulose.* [from Gk *nitron* NATRON]

nitrobacteria (,naɪtrəʊbæk'tɪərɪə) *pl n, sing* **nitrobacterium** (-'tɪərɪəm). soil bacteria that are involved in nitrification.

nitrobenzene (,naɪtrəʊ'bɛnziːn) *n* a yellow oily liquid compound, used as a solvent and in the manufacture of aniline. Formula: $C_6H_5NO_2$.

nitrocellulose (,naɪtrəʊ'sɛljʊ,ləʊs) *n* another name (not in chemical usage) for **cellulose nitrate.**

nitrogen ('naɪtrədʒən) *n* a colourless odourless relatively unreactive gaseous element that forms 78 per cent of the air and is an essential constituent of proteins and nucleic acids. Symbol: N; atomic no.: 7; atomic wt.: 14.0067.

nitrogen cycle *n* the natural circulation of nitrogen by living organisms. Nitrates in the soil, derived from dead organic matter by bacterial action, are absorbed and synthesized into complex organic compounds by plants and reduced to nitrates again when the plants and the animals feeding on them die and decay.

nitrogen dioxide *n* a red-brown poisonous gas that is an intermediate in the manufacture of nitric acid, a nitrating agent, and an oxidizer for rocket fuels. Formula: NO_2.

nitrogen fixation *n* **1** the conversion of atmospheric nitrogen into nitrogen compounds by certain bacteria in the root nodules of le-

THESAURUS

(*inf.*), fool, jerk (*sl., chiefly US & Canad.*), lamebrain (*inf.*), nerd *or* nurd (*sl.*), ninny, nitwit (*inf.*), numbskull *or* numskull, oaf, pillock (*Brit. sl.*), prat (*sl.*), prick (*sl.*), schmuck (*US sl.*), simpleton, twit (*inf., chiefly Brit.*), wally (*sl.*)

nip[1] *vb* **1 = pinch,** catch, compress, grip, snag, squeeze, tweak, twitch **3 = bite,** nibble, snap **6 = thwart,** check, frustrate

nip[2] *n* **1 = dram,** draught, drop, finger, mouthful, peg (*Brit.*), portion, shot (*inf.*), sip, snifter (*inf.*), soupçon, sup, swallow, taste

nipper *n* **2 = pincer,** claw **3** *Informal* **= child,** ankle-biter (*Austral. sl.*), baby, boy, girl, infant, kid (*inf.*), little one, rug rat (*sl.*), sprog (*sl.*), tot

nipple *n* **1 = teat,** boob (*sl.*), breast, dug, mamilla, pap, papilla, tit, udder

nippy *adj* **1 = chilly,** biting, nipping, sharp, stinging **2a** *Brit. informal* **= quick,** active, agile, fast, nimble, spry

nirvana *n* **= paradise,** bliss, joy, peace, serenity, tranquillity

nit-picking *adj* **2 = fussy,** captious, carping, cavilling, finicky, hairsplitting, pedantic, pettifogging, quibbling

gumes. **2** a process in which atmospheric nitrogen is converted into a nitrogen compound, used esp. for fertilizer.

nitrogenize *or* **nitrogenise** (naɪˈtrɒdʒɪˌnaɪz) *vb* **nitrogenizes, nitrogenizing, nitrogenized** *or* **nitrogenises, nitrogenising, nitrogenised.** to combine or treat with nitrogen or a nitrogen compound. ▸**niˌtrogeniˈzation** *or* **niˌtrogeniˈsation** *n*

nitrogen monoxide *n* the systematic name for **nitric oxide.**

nitrogen mustard *n* any of a class of organic compounds resembling mustard gas in their molecular structure: important in the treatment of cancer.

nitrogenous (naɪˈtrɒdʒɪnəs) *adj* containing nitrogen or a nitrogen compound.

nitroglycerine (ˌnaɪtrəʊˈglɪsəriːn) *or* **nitroglycerin** (ˌnaɪtrəʊˈglɪsəˌrɪn) *n* a pale yellow viscous explosive liquid made from glycerol and nitric and sulphuric acids. Formula: $CH_2NO_3CHNO_3CH_2NO_3$. Also called: **trinitroglycerine.**

nitromethane (ˌnaɪtrəʊˈmiːθeɪn) *n* an oily colourless liquid obtained from methane and used as a solvent and rocket fuel.

nitrous (ˈnaɪtrəs) *adj* of, derived from, or containing nitrogen, esp. in a low valency state. [C17: from L *nitrōsus* full of natron]

nitrous acid *n* a weak monobasic acid known only in solution and in the form of nitrite salts. Formula: HNO_2. Systematic name: **dioxonitric(III) acid.**

nitrous oxide *n* a colourless gas with a sweet smell: used as an anaesthetic in dentistry. Formula: N_2O. Also called: **laughing gas.** Systematic name: **dinitrogen oxide.**

nitty (ˈnɪtɪ) *adj* **nittier, nittiest.** infested with nits.

nitty-gritty ❶ (ˈnɪtɪˈgrɪtɪ) *n* **the.** *Inf.* the basic facts of a matter, situation, etc.; the core. [C20: ? rhyming compound from GRIT]

nitwit ❶ (ˈnɪtˌwɪt) *n Inf.* a foolish or dull person. [C20: ?from NIT[1] + WIT[1]]

nix[1] (nɪks) *Inf.* ◆ *sentence substitute.* **1** another word for **no**[1]. ◆ *n* **2** a refusal. **3** nothing. [C18: from G, inf. form of *nichts* nothing]

nix[2] (nɪks) *or (fem)* **nixie** (ˈnɪksɪ) *n Germanic myth.* a water sprite, usually unfriendly to humans. [C19: from G *Nixe,* from OHG *nihhus*]

NMR *abbrev. for* nuclear magnetic resonance.

NNE *symbol for* north-northeast.

NNP *abbrev. for* net national product.

NNW *symbol for* north-northwest.

no[1] ❶ (nəʊ) *sentence substitute.* **1** used to express denial, disagreement, refusal, etc. ◆ *n, pl* **noes** *or* **nos. 2** an answer or vote of *no.* **3 not take no for an answer.** to continue in a course of action, etc., despite refusals. **4** *(often pl)* a person who votes in the negative. **5 the noes have it.** there is a majority of votes in the negative. [OE *nā,* from *ne* not, no + *ā* ever]

no[2] (nəʊ) *determiner* **1** not any, not a, or not one: *there's no money left; no card in the file.* **2** not at all: *she's no youngster.* **3** (foll. by comparative adjectives and adverbs) not: *no less than forty; no taller than a child.* [OE *nā,* from *nān* NONE]

No[1] *or* **Noh** (nəʊ) *n, pl* **No** *or* **Noh.** the stylized classic drama of Japan, developed in the 15th century or earlier, using music, dancing, and themes from religious stories or myths. [from Japanese *nō* talent, from Chinese *neng*]

No[2] *the chemical symbol for* nobelium.

no' (no, nəʊ) *adv Scot.* not.

No. *abbrev. for:* **1** north(ern). **2** Also: **no.** *(pl* **Nos.** *or* **nos.)** number. [from L *numero* the ablative of *numerus* number]

n.o. *Cricket. abbrev. for* not out.

no-account *adj* **1** worthless; good-for-nothing. ◆ *n* **2** a worthless person.

nob[1] (nɒb) *n Cribbage.* **1** the jack of the suit turned up. **2 one for his nob.** the call made with this jack, scoring one point. [C19: from ?]

nob[2] ❶ (nɒb) *n Sl., chiefly Brit.* a person of wealth or social distinction. [C19: from ?]

no-ball *n* **1** *Cricket.* an illegal ball, as for overstepping the crease, for which the batting side scores a run, and from which the batsman can only be out by being run out. **2** *Rounders.* an illegal ball, esp. one bowled too high or too low. ◆ *interj* **3** *Cricket, rounders.* a call by the umpire indicating a no-ball.

nobble ❶ (ˈnɒbᵊl) *vb* **nobbles, nobbling, nobbled.** *(tr) Brit. sl.* **1** to disable (a racehorse), esp. with drugs. **2** to win over or outwit (a person) by underhand means. **3** to suborn (a person, esp. a juror) by threats, bribery, etc. **4** to steal. **5** to grab. **6** to kidnap. [C19: from *nobbler,* from a false division of *an hobbler* (one who hobbles horses) as *a nobbler*]

nobelium (nəʊˈbiːlɪəm) *n* a transuranic element produced artificially from curium. Symbol: No; atomic no.: 102; half-life of most stable isotope, ^{255}No: 180 seconds (approx.). [C20: NL, after *Nobel* Institute, Stockholm, where it was discovered]

Nobel prize (nəʊˈbɛl) *n* a prize for outstanding contributions to chemistry, physics, physiology or medicine, literature, economics, and peace that may be awarded annually; established 1901. [C20: after Alfred *Nobel* (1833–96), Swedish chemist and philanthropist]

nobility ❶ (nəʊˈbɪlɪtɪ) *n, pl* **nobilities. 1** a privileged class whose titles are conferred by descent or royal decree. **2** the quality of being good; dignity: *nobility of mind.* **3** (in the British Isles) the class of people holding the title of dukes, marquesses, earls, viscounts, or barons and their feminine equivalents; peerage.

nobilmente (ˌnəʊbɪlˈmɛnteɪ) *adj, adv Music.* to be performed in a noble manner. [It.]

noble ❶ (ˈnəʊbᵊl) *adj* **1** of or relating to a hereditary class with special status, often derived from a feudal period. **2** of or characterized by high moral qualities; magnanimous: *a noble deed.* **3** having dignity or eminence; illustrious. **4** imposing; magnificent: *a noble avenue of trees.* **5** superior; excellent: *a noble strain of horses.* **6** *Chem.* **6a** (of certain elements) chemically unreactive. **6b** (of certain metals, esp. copper, silver, and gold) resisting oxidation. ◆ *n* **7** a person belonging to a privileged class whose status is usually indicated by a title. **8** (in the British Isles) a person holding the title of duke, marquess, earl, viscount, or baron, or a feminine equivalent. **9** a former British gold coin having the value of one third of a pound. [C13: via OF from L *nōbilis,* orig., capable of being known, hence well-known, from *noscere* to know] ▸**ˈnobleness** *n* ▸**ˈnobly** *adv*

nobleman (ˈnəʊbᵊlmən) *or (fem)* **noblewoman** *n, pl* **noblemen** *or* **noblewomen.** a person of noble rank, title, or status; peer; aristocrat.

noble savage *n* (in romanticism) an idealized view of primitive man.

noblesse oblige (nəʊˈblɛs əʊˈbliːʒ) *n Often ironic.* the supposed obligation of nobility to be honourable and generous. [F, lit.: nobility obliges]

nobody ❶ (ˈnəʊbədɪ) *pron* **1** no person; no-one. ◆ *n, pl* **nobodies. 2** an insignificant person.

> **USAGE NOTE** See at **everyone.**

nock (nɒk) *n* **1** a notch on an arrow that fits on the bowstring. **2** either of the grooves at each end of a bow that hold the bowstring. ◆ *vb (tr)* **3** to fit (an arrow) on a bowstring. [C14: rel. to Swedish *nock* tip]

no-claims bonus *n* a reduction on an insurance premium, esp. one covering a motor vehicle, if no claims have been made within a specified period. Also called: **no-claim bonus.**

noctambulism (nɒkˈtæmbjʊˌlɪzəm) *or* **noctambulation** *n* another word for **somnambulism.** [C19: from L *nox* night + *ambulāre* to walk]

noctilucent (ˌnɒktɪˈluːsᵊnt) *adj* shining at night, usually of very thin high altitude clouds observable in the summer twilight sky. [from L, from *nox* night + *lūcēre* to shine]

noctuid (ˈnɒktjʊɪd) *n* any of a large family of nocturnal moths that includes the underwings. [C19: via NL from L *noctua* night owl, from *nox* night]

noctule (ˈnɒktjuːl) *n* any of several large Old World insectivorous bats. [C18: prob. from LL *noctula* small owl, from L *noctua* night owl]

nocturnal ❶ (nɒkˈtɜːnᵊl) *adj* **1** of, used during, occurring in, or relating to the night. **2** (of animals) active at night. **3** (of plants) having flowers that open at night and close by day. [C15: from LL *nocturnālis,* from L *nox* night] ▸**ˌnocturˈnality** *n* ▸**nocˈturnally** *adv*

nocturne (ˈnɒktɜːn) *n* **1** a short, dreamy, and melodic piece of music, esp. one for the piano. **2** a painting of a night scene.

nod ❶ (nɒd) *vb* **nods, nodding, nodded. 1** to lower and raise (the head) briefly, as to indicate agreement, etc. **2** *(tr)* to express by nodding: *she nodded approval.* **3** *(intr)* (of flowers, trees, etc.) to sway or bend forwards and back. **4** *(intr)* to let the head fall forwards through drowsiness; be almost asleep. **5** *(intr)* to be momentarily careless: *even Homer*

THESAURUS

nitty-gritty *n Informal* = **basics,** bottom line, brass tacks *(inf.),* core, crux, essence, essentials, facts, fundamentals, gist, heart of the matter, ins and outs, nuts and bolts, reality, substance

nitwit *n Informal* = **fool,** dimwit, divvy *(sl.),* dork *(sl.),* dummy *(sl.),* halfwit, lamebrain *(inf.),* nincompoop, ninny, oaf, simpleton

no[1] *sentence substitute* **1** = **never,** nay, not at all, no way ◆ *n* **2** = **refusal,** denial, negation, rejection, veto **4** = **objector,** dissenter, dissident, protester
Antonyms *sentence substitute* ≠ **never:** certainly, of course, yes ◆ *n* ≠ **refusal:** acceptance, assent, consent

nob[2] *n Slang* = **aristocrat,** aristo *(inf.),* big hitter *(inf.),* big shot *(inf.),* bigwig *(inf.),* celeb *(inf.),* fat cat *(sl., chiefly US),* heavy hitter *(inf.),* nabob *(inf.),* toff *(Brit. sl.),* V.I.P.

nobble *vb* **1** *Brit. slang* = **disable,** handicap, incapacitate, weaken **2, 3** *Brit. slang* = **bribe,** get at, influence, intimidate, outwit, win over **4** *Brit. slang* = **steal,** filch, knock off *(sl.),* nick *(sl., chiefly Brit.),* pilfer, pinch *(inf.),* purloin, snitch *(sl.),* swipe *(sl.)* **5** *Brit. slang* = **grab,** get hold of, take

nobility *n* **1, 3** = **aristocracy,** elite, high society, lords, nobles, patricians, peerage, ruling class, upper class **2** = **integrity,** honour, incorruptibility, uprightness, virtue

noble *adj* **1** = **aristocratic,** blue-blooded, gentle *(arch.),* highborn, lordly, patrician, titled **2** = **worthy,** generous, honourable, magnanimous, upright, virtuous **3, 4, 5** = **impressive,** august, dignified, distinguished, elevated, eminent, excellent, grand, great, imposing, lofty, splendid, stately, superb ◆ *n* **7, 8** = **lord,** aristo *(inf.),* aristocrat, nobleman, peer
Antonyms *adj* ≠ **aristocratic:** base, humble, ignoble, lowborn, lowly, peasant, plebeian, vulgar *adj* ≠ **worthy:** contemptible, despicable, dishonest, selfish ≠ **impressive:** base, humble, ignoble, insignificant, lowly, mean, modest, plain ◆ *n* ≠ **lord:** commoner, peasant, serf

nobody *pron* **1** = **no-one** ◆ *n* **2** = **nonentity,** cipher, lightweight *(inf.),* menial, nothing *(inf.)*
Antonyms *n* ≠ **nonentity:** big name, big noise *(inf.),* big shot *(sl.),* celeb *(inf.),* celebrity, megastar *(inf.),* personage, star, superstar, V.I.P.

nocturnal *adj* **1** = **nightly,** night, night-time, of the night

nod *vb* **1** = **acknowledge,** bob, bow, dip, duck, gesture, indicate, salute, signal **2** = **agree,** assent, concur, show agreement **4** = **sleep,** be sleepy, doze, droop, drowse, kip *(Brit. sl.),* nap, slump, zizz *(Brit. inf.)* ◆ *n* **7** = **gesture,** acknowl-

sometimes nods. **6 nodding acquaintance.** a slight, casual, or superficial knowledge (of a subject or person). ◆ *n* **7** a quick down-and-up movement of the head, as in assent, command, etc. **8 on the nod.** *Inf.* agreed, as in committee, without formal procedure. **9** See **land of Nod.** ◆ See also **nod off.** [C14 *nodde,* from ?]
▸ **'nodding** *adj, n*

noddle[1] ('nɒdᵊl) *n Inf., chiefly Brit.* the head or brains: *use your noddle!* [C15: from ?]

noddle[2] ('nɒdᵊl) *vb* **noddles, noddling, noddled.** *Inf., chiefly Brit.* to nod (the head), as through drowsiness. [C18: from NOD]

noddy[1] ('nɒdɪ) *n, pl* **noddies. 1** any of several tropical terns, typically having a dark plumage. **2** a fool or dunce. [C16: ? n use of obs. *noddy* foolish, drowsy, ?from NOD (vb); the bird is so called because it allows itself to be caught by hand]

noddy[2] ('nɒdɪ) *n, pl* **noddies.** (*usually pl*) *Television.* film footage of an interviewer's reactions to comments made by an interviewee, used in editing the interview after it has been recorded. [C20: from NOD]

node ➊ (nəʊd) *n* **1** a knot, swelling, or knob. **2** the point on a plant stem from which the leaves or lateral branches grow. **3** *Physics.* a point at which the amplitude of one of the two kinds of displacement in a standing wave has zero or minimum value. **4** Also called: **crunode.** *Maths.* a point at which two branches of a curve intersect. **5** *Maths., linguistics.* one of the objects of which a graph or a tree consists. **6** *Astron.* either of the two points at which the orbit of a body intersects the plane of the ecliptic. **7** *Anat.* any natural bulge or swelling, such as those along the course of a lymphatic vessel (**lymph node**). **8** *Computing.* an interconnection point on a computer network. [C16: from L *nōdus* knot]
▸ **'nodal** *adj*

nod off *vb* (*intr, adv*) *Inf.* to fall asleep.

nodule ('nɒdju:l) *n* **1** a small knot, lump, or node. **2** any of the knoblike outgrowths on the roots of clover and other legumes that contain bacteria involved in nitrogen fixation. **3** a small rounded lump of rock or mineral substance, esp. in a matrix of different rock material. [C17: from L *nōdulus,* from *nōdus* knot]
▸ **'nodular, 'nodulose,** *or* **'nodulous** *adj*

Noel *or* **Noël** (nəʊ'ɛl) *n* (in carols, etc.) another word for **Christmas.** [C19: from F, from L *nātālis* a birthday]

noetic (nəʊ'ɛtɪk) *adj* of or relating to the mind. [C17: from Gk *noētikos,* from *noein* to think]

nog *or* **nogg** (nɒg) *n* **1** Also called: **flip.** a drink, esp. an alcoholic one, containing beaten egg. **2** *East Anglian dialect.* strong local beer. [C17 (orig.: a strong beer): from ?]

noggin ➊ ('nɒgɪn) *n* **1** a small quantity of spirits. **2** a small mug. **3** *Inf.* the head. [C17: from ?]

no-go area *n* a district in a town that is barricaded off, usually by a paramilitary organization, which the police, army, etc., can only enter by force.

Noh (nəʊ) *n* a variant spelling of **No**[1].

noir (nwɑ:) *adj* (of a film) showing characteristics of a *film noir,* in plot or style. [C20: from French, lit.: black]

noise ➊ (nɔɪz) *n* **1** a sound, esp. one that is loud or disturbing. **2** loud shouting; clamour; din. **3** any undesired electrical disturbance in a circuit, etc. **4** undesired or irrelevant elements in a visual image: *removing noise from pictures.* **5** (*pl*) conventional comments or sounds conveying a reaction: *sympathetic noises.* **6 make a noise.** to talk a great deal or complain (about). ◆ *vb* **noises, noising, noised. 7** (*tr;* usually foll. by *abroad* or *about*) to spread (news, gossip, etc.). [C13: from OF, from L: NAUSEA]

noiseless ➊ ('nɔɪzlɪs) *adj* making little or no sound.
▸ **'noiselessly** *adv* ▸ **'noiselessness** *n*

noise pollution *n* annoying or harmful noise in an environment.

noisette (nwɑ:'zɛt) *adj* **1** flavoured with hazelnuts. **2** nutbrown, as butter browned over heat. ◆ *n* **3** a small round or oval piece of meat. **4** a hazelnut chocolate. [from F: hazelnut]

noisome ➊ ('nɔɪsəm) *adj* **1** (esp. of smells) offensive. **2** harmful or noxious. [C14: from obs. *noy,* var. of ANNOY + -SOME[1]]
▸ **'noisomeness** *n*

noisy ➊ ('nɔɪzɪ) *adj* **noisier, noisiest. 1** making a loud or constant noise. **2** full of or characterized by noise.
▸ **'noisily** *adv* ▸ **'noisiness** *n*

nolens volens *Latin.* ('nəʊlɛnz 'vəʊlɛnz) *adv* whether willing or unwilling.

nolle prosequi ('nɒlɪ 'prɒsɪˌkwaɪ) *n Law.* an entry made on the court record when the plaintiff or prosecutor undertakes not to continue the action or prosecution. [L: do not pursue]

nomad ➊ ('nəʊmæd) *n* **1** a member of a people or tribe who move from place to place to find pasture and food. **2** a wanderer. [C16: via F from L *nomas* wandering shepherd, from Gk]
▸ **no'madic** *adj* ▸ **'nomadism** *n*

no-man's-land *n* **1** land between boundaries, esp. an unoccupied zone between opposing forces. **2** an unowned or unclaimed piece of land. **3** an ambiguous area of activity.

nom de guerre ('nɒm də 'gɛə) *n, pl* **noms de guerre** ('nɒm də 'gɛə). an assumed name. [F, lit.: war name]

nom de plume ➊ ('nɒm də 'plu:m) *n, pl* **noms de plume** ('nɒm də 'plu:m). another term for **pen name.** [F]

nomenclature ➊ (nəʊ'mɛnklətʃə; *US.* 'nəʊmənˌkleɪtʃər) *n* the terminology used in a particular science, art, activity, etc. [C17: from L *nōmenclātūra* list of names]

nominal ➊ ('nɒmɪnᵊl) *adj* **1** in name only; theoretical: *the nominal leader.* **2** minimal in comparison with real worth; token: *a nominal fee.* **3** of, constituting, or giving a name. **4** *Grammar.* of or relating to a noun or noun phrase. ◆ *n* **5** *Grammar.* a noun, noun phrase, or syntactically similar structure. [C15: from L *nōminālis,* from *nōmen* name]
▸ **'nominally** *adv*

nominalism ('nɒmɪnᵊˌlɪzəm) *n* the philosophical theory that the variety of objects to which a single general name, such as *dog,* applies have nothing in common other than that name.
▸ **'nominalist** *n*

nominal value *n* another name for **par value.**

nominate ➊ ('nɒmɪˌneɪt) *vb* **nominates, nominating, nominated.** (*mainly tr*) **1** to propose as a candidate, esp. for an elective office. **2** to appoint to an office or position. **3** to name (someone) to act on one's behalf, esp. to conceal one's identity. **4** (*intr*) *Austral.* to stand as a candidate in an election. [C16: from L *nōmināre* to call by name, from *nōmen* name]
▸ **ˌnomi'nation** *n* ▸ **'nomiˌnator** *n*

nominative ('nɒmɪnətɪv) *adj* **1** *Grammar.* denoting a case of nouns and pronouns in inflected languages that is used esp. to identify the subject of a finite verb. **2** appointed rather than elected to a position, office, etc. ◆ *n* **3** *Grammar.* **3a** the nominative case. **3b** a word or speech element in the nominative case. [C14: from L *nōminātīvus* belonging to naming, from *nōmen* name]
▸ **nominatival** (ˌnɒmɪnə'taɪvᵊl) *adj*

nominee ➊ (ˌnɒmɪ'ni:) *n* **1** a person who is nominated to an office or as a candidate. **2a** a person or organization named to act on behalf of someone else, esp. to conceal the identity of the nominator. **2b** (*as modifier*): *nominee shareholder.* [C17: from NOMINATE + -EE]

nomogram ('nɒməˌgræm, 'nəʊmə-) *or* **nomograph** *n* an arrangement of two linear or logarithmic scales such that an intersecting straight line enables intermediate values or values on a third scale to be read off. [C20: from Gk *nomos* law + -GRAM]

-nomy *n combining form.* indicating a science or the laws governing a certain field of knowledge: *agronomy; economy.* [from Gk *-nomia* law]
▸ **-nomic** *adj combining form.*

non- *prefix* **1** indicating negation: *nonexistent.* **2** indicating refusal or failure: *noncooperation.* **3** indicating exclusion from a specified class: *nonfiction.* **4** indicating lack or absence: *nonobjective; nonevent.* [from L *nōn* not]

nonaddictive (ˌnɒnə'dɪktɪv) *adj* (of a drug, etc.) not causing addiction.

nonage ('nəʊnɪdʒ) *n* **1** *Law.* the state of being under any of various ages at which a person may legally enter into certain transactions, such as marrying, etc. **2** any period of immaturity.

nonagenarian (ˌnəʊnədʒɪ'nɛərɪən) *n* **1** a person who is from 90 to 99 years old. ◆ *adj* **2** of, relating to, or denoting a nonagenarian. [C19: from L *nōnāgēnārius,* from *nōnāginta* ninety]

nonaggression (ˌnɒnə'grɛʃən) *n* **a** restraint of aggression, esp. between states. **b** (*as modifier*): *a nonaggression pact.*

nonagon ('nɒnəˌgɒn) *n* a polygon having nine sides.
▸ **nonagonal** (nɒn'ægənᵊl) *adj*

nonalcoholic (ˌnɒnˌælkə'hɒl'ɪk) *adj* (of a drink, etc.) not containing alcohol.

THESAURUS

edgment, beck, greeting, indication, salute, sign, signal

node *n* **1** = **nodule,** bud, bump, burl, growth, knob, knot, lump, protuberance, swelling

noggin *n* **1** = **dram,** nip, tot **2** = **mug,** cup **3** *Informal* = **head,** bean (*US & Canad. sl.*), block (*inf.*), bonce (*Brit. sl.*), conk (*sl.*), dome (*sl.*), noddle (*inf., chiefly Brit.*), nut (*sl.*)

noise *n* **1, 2** = **sound,** babble, blare, clamour, clatter, commotion, cry, din, fracas, hubbub, outcry, pandemonium, racket, row, rumpus, talk, tumult, uproar ◆ *vb* **7** = **report,** advertise, bruit, circulate, gossip, publicize, repeat, rumour

noiseless *adj* = **silent,** hushed, inaudible, mute, muted, quiet, soundless, still

noisome *adj* **1** = **offensive,** disgusting, fetid, foul, malodorous, mephitic, niffy, putrid, reeking, smelly, stinking **2** = **harmful,** bad, baneful (*arch.*), deleterious, hurtful, injurious, noxious, pernicious, pestiferous, pestilential, poisonous, unhealthy, unwholesome

noisy *adj* **1, 2** = **loud,** boisterous, cacophonous, chattering, clamorous, deafening, ear-splitting, obstreperous, piercing, riotous, strident, tumultuous, turbulent, uproarious, vociferous
Antonyms *adj* hushed, quiet, silent, still, subdued, tranquil, tuneful

nomad *n* **2** = **wanderer,** drifter, itinerant, rambler, rover, vagabond

nomadic *adj* **1** = **migratory,** migrant, pastoral **2** = **wandering,** itinerant, peripatetic, roaming, roving, travelling, vagrant

nom de plume *n* = **pseudonym,** alias, assumed name, nom de guerre, pen name

nomenclature *n* = **terminology,** classification, codification, locution, phraseology, taxonomy, vocabulary

nominal *adj* **1** = **so-called,** formal, ostensible, pretended, professed, purported, self-styled, *soi-disant,* supposed, theoretical, titular **2** = **small,** inconsiderable, insignificant, minimal, symbolic, token, trifling, trivial

nominate *vb* **1** = **propose,** present, recommend, submit, suggest **2** = **appoint,** assign, choose, commission, designate, elect, elevate, empower, name, select

nomination *n* **1** = **proposal,** recommendation, suggestion **2** = **appointment,** choice, designation, election, selection

nominee *n* **1** = **candidate,** aspirant, contestant, entrant, favourite, protégé, runner

nonaligned Ⓣ (ˌnɒnəˈlaɪnd) *adj* (of states, etc.) not part of a major alliance or power bloc.
▸ **ˌnonaˈlignment** *n*

non-A, non-B hepatitis *n* a form of viral hepatitis, not caused by the agents responsible for hepatitis A and hepatitis B, that is commonly transmitted by infected blood transfusions. The causative virus has been isolated. Also called: **hepatitis C**.

nonce (nɒns) *n* the present time or occasion (now only in **for the nonce**). [C12: from *for the nonce*, a mistaken division of *for then anes*, from *then* dative singular of *the* + *anes* ONCE]

nonce word *n* a word coined for a single occasion.

nonchalant Ⓣ (ˈnɒnʃələnt) *adj* casually unconcerned or indifferent; uninvolved. [C18: from F, from *nonchaloir* to lack warmth, from NON- + *chaloir* from L *calēre* to be warm]
▸ **ˈnonchalance** *n*

non-com (ˈnɒnˌkɒm) *n* short for **noncommissioned officer**.

noncombatant Ⓣ (nɒnˈkɒmbətənt) *n* **1** a civilian in time of war. **2** a member of the armed forces whose duties do not include fighting, such as a chaplain or surgeon.

noncommissioned officer (ˌnɒnkəˈmɪʃənd) *n* (in the armed forces) a person, such as a sergeant or corporal, who is appointed from the ranks as a subordinate officer.

noncommittal Ⓣ (ˌnɒnkəˈmɪtᵊl) *adj* not involving or revealing commitment to any particular opinion or action.

non compos mentis Ⓣ *Latin.* (ˈnɒn ˈkɒmpəs ˈmɛntɪs) *adj* mentally incapable of managing one's own affairs; of unsound mind. [L: not in control of one's mind]

nonconformist Ⓣ (ˌnɒnkənˈfɔːmɪst) *n* **1** a person who does not conform to generally accepted patterns of behaviour or thought. ◆ *adj* **2** of or characterized by behaviour that does not conform to accepted patterns.
▸ **ˌnonconˈformity** *or* **ˌnonconˈformism** *n*

Nonconformist (ˌnɒnkənˈfɔːmɪst) *n* **1** a member of a Protestant denomination that dissents from an Established Church, esp. the Church of England. ◆ *adj* **2** of, relating to, or denoting Nonconformists.
▸ **ˌNonconˈformity** *or* **ˌNonconˈformism** *n*

noncontributory (ˌnɒnkənˈtrɪbjʊtərɪ) *adj* **1** denoting an insurance or pension scheme for employees, the premiums of which are paid by the employer. **2** (of a state benefit) not dependent on national insurance contributions.

nondenominational (ˌnɒndɪˌnɒmɪˈneɪʃənᵊl) *adj* not restricted with regard to religious denomination.

nondescript Ⓣ (ˈnɒndɪˌskrɪpt) *adj* **1** having no outstanding features. ◆ *n* **2** a nondescript person or thing. [C17: from NON- + L *dēscriptus*, p.p. of *dēscribere* to copy]

nondomiciled (nɒnˈdɒmɪˌsaɪld) *adj* of, relating to, or denoting a person who is not domiciled in his country of origin.

none[1] Ⓣ (nʌn) *pron* **1** not any of a particular class: *none of my letters has arrived.* **2** no-one; nobody: *there was none to tell the tale.* **3** not any (of): *none of it looks edible.* **4 none other.** no other person: *none other than the Queen herself.* **5 none the.** (*foll. by a comparative adj*) in no degree: *she was none the worse for her ordeal.* **6 none too.** not very: *he was none too pleased.* [OE *nān*, lit.: not one]

> **USAGE NOTE** *None* is a singular pronoun and should be used with a singular form of a verb: *none of the students has* (not *have*) a car.

none[2] (nəʊn) *n* another word for **nones**.

nonentity Ⓣ (nɒnˈɛntɪtɪ) *n, pl* **nonentities. 1** an insignificant person or thing. **2** a nonexistent thing. **3** the state of not existing; nonexistence.

nones (nəʊnz) *n* (*functioning as sing or pl*) **1** (in the Roman calendar) the ninth day before the ides of each month: the seventh day of March, May, July, and October, and the fifth of each other month. **2** *Chiefly RC Church.* the fifth of the seven canonical hours of the divine office, originally fixed at the ninth hour of the day, about 3 p.m. [OE *nōn*, from L *nōna hora* ninth hour, from *nōnus* ninth]

nonesuch *or* **nonsuch** (ˈnʌnˌsʌtʃ) *n Arch.* a matchless person or thing; nonpareil.

nonet (nəʊˈnet) *n* **1** a piece of music for nine instruments or voices. **2** a group of nine singers or instrumentalists.

nonetheless Ⓣ (ˌnʌnðəˈles) *sentence connector.* despite that; however; nevertheless.

non-Euclidean geometry *n* the branch of modern geometry in which certain axioms of Euclidean geometry are denied.

nonevent Ⓣ (ˌnɒnɪˈvɛnt) *n* a disappointing or insignificant occurrence, esp. one predicted to be important.

nonexecutive director (ˌnɒnɪgˈzɛkjʊtɪv) *n* a director of a commercial company who is not a full-time employee of the company.

nonexistent Ⓣ (ˌnɒnɪgˈzɪstənt) *adj* **1** not having being or reality. **2** not present under specified conditions or in a specified place.
▸ **nonexˈistence** *n*

nonfeasance (nɒnˈfiːzᵊns) *n Law.* a failure to act when under an obligation to do so. Cf. **malfeasance, misfeasance.** [C16: from NON- + *feasance* (obs.) doing, from F *faisance*, from *faire* to do, L *facere*]

nonferrous (nɒnˈfɛrəs) *adj* **1** denoting any metal other than iron. **2** not containing iron.

nonflammable (nɒnˈflæməbᵊl) *adj* incapable of burning or not easily set on fire.

nonfunctional (ˌnɒnˈfʌŋkʃənᵊl) *adj* not having a function.

nong (nɒŋ) *n Austral. sl.* a stupid or incompetent person. [C19: ?from obs. E dialect *nigmenog* silly fellow, from ?]

nonillion (nəʊˈnɪljən) *n* **1** (in Britain, France, and Germany) the number represented as one followed by 54 zeros (10^{54}). **2** (in the US and Canada) the number represented as one followed by 30 zeros (10^{30}). Brit. word: **quintillion.** [C17: from F, from L *nōnus* ninth, on the model of MILLION]

nonintervention (ˌnɒnɪntəˈvɛnʃən) *n* refusal to intervene, esp. the abstention by a state from intervening in the affairs of other states or in its own internal disputes.

noninvasive (ˌnɒnɪnˈveɪsɪv) *adj* (of medical treatment) not involving the making of a relatively large incision in the body or the insertion of instruments, etc., into the patient.

nonjudgmental (ˌnɒndʒʌdʒˈmɛntᵊl) *adj* avoiding moral judgments, esp. relating to the conduct of others.

nonjuror (nɒnˈdʒʊərə) *n* a person who refuses to take an oath, as of allegiance.

Nonjuror (nɒnˈdʒʊərə) *n* any of a group of clergy in England and Scotland who declined to take the oath of allegiance to William and Mary in 1689.

nonlinear (ˌnɒnˈlɪnɪə) *adj* not linear, esp. with regard to dimension.

nonmetal (nɒnˈmɛtᵊl) *n* any of a number of chemical elements that have acidic oxides and are poor conductors of heat and electricity.
▸ **ˌnonmeˈtallic** *adj*

nonmoral (nɒnˈmɒrəl) *adj* not involving morality or ethics; neither moral nor immoral.

nonobjective (ˌnɒnəbˈdʒɛktɪv) *adj* of or designating an art movement in which things are depicted in an abstract or purely formalized way.

no-nonsense (ˌnəʊˈnɒnsəns) *adj* sensible, practical, and straightforward: *a severe no-nonsense look.*

nonpareil (ˈnɒnpərəl, ˌnɒnpəˈreɪl) *n* a person or thing that is unsurpassed; peerless example. [C15: from F, from NON- + *pareil* similar]

nonpersistent (ˌnɒnpəˈsɪstənt) *adj* (of pesticides) breaking down rapidly after application; not persisting in the environment.

non-person *n* a person regarded as nonexistent or unimportant; a nonentity.

nonplus Ⓣ (nɒnˈplʌs) *vb* **nonplusses, nonplussing, nonplussed** *or US* **nonpluses, nonplusing, nonplused. 1** (*tr*) to put at a loss; confound. ◆ *n, pl* **nonpluses. 2** a state of utter perplexity prohibiting action or speech. [C16: from L *nōn plūs* no further]

nonprofessional (ˌnɒnprəˈfɛʃənᵊl) *adj* **1** not professional in status. ◆ *n* **2** a person who is not a professional.

THESAURUS

nonaligned *adj* = **neutral**, impartial, uncommitted, undecided

nonchalance *n* = **indifference**, calm, composure, cool (*sl.*), equanimity, imperturbability, sang-froid, self-possession, unconcern

nonchalant *adj* = **casual**, airy, apathetic, blasé, calm, careless, collected, cool, detached, dispassionate, indifferent, insouciant, laid-back (*inf.*), offhand, unconcerned, unemotional, unfazed (*inf.*), unperturbed
Antonyms *adj* anxious, caring, concerned, involved, worried

noncombatant *n* **1** = **civilian**, neutral, nonbelligerent

noncommittal *adj* = **evasive**, ambiguous, careful, cautious, circumspect, discreet, equivocal, guarded, indefinite, neutral, politic, reserved, tactful, temporizing, tentative, unrevealing, vague, wary

non compos mentis *adj* = **insane**, crazy, deranged, mentally ill, of unsound mind, unbalanced, unhinged
Antonyms *adj* all there (*inf.*), *compos mentis*, in one's right mind, lucid, mentally sound, rational, sane

nonconformist *n* **1** = **maverick**, dissenter, dissentient, eccentric, heretic, iconoclast, individualist, protester, radical, rebel
Antonyms *n* Babbitt (*US*), conventionalist, stick-in-the-mud (*inf.*), traditionalist, yes man

nonconformity *n* = **dissent**, eccentricity, heresy, heterodoxy, unconventionality

nondescript *adj* **1** = **ordinary**, bog-standard, characterless, common or garden (*inf.*), commonplace, dull, featureless, indeterminate, mousy, run-of-the-mill, undistinguished, unexceptional, uninspiring, uninteresting, unmemorable, unremarkable, vague, vanilla (*inf.*)
Antonyms *adj* distinctive, extraordinary, memorable, remarkable, unique, unusual

none[1] **1** *pron* **1** = **not any**, not one **2** = **no-one**, nobody **3** = **no part**, bugger all (*sl.*), nil, not a bit, nothing, zero, zilch (*sl., chiefly US & Canad.*)

nonentity *n* **1** = **nobody**, cipher, lightweight (*inf.*), mediocrity, small fry, unimportant person

nonetheless *sentence connector* = **nevertheless**, despite that, even so, however, in spite of that, yet

nonevent *n* = **flop** (*inf.*), disappointment, dud (*inf.*), failure, fiasco, washout

nonexistent *adj* **1** = **imaginary**, chimerical, fancied, fictional, hallucinatory, hypothetical, illusory, imagined, insubstantial, legendary, mythical, unreal
Antonyms *adj* actual, existent, existing, genuine, real, true, veritable

nonplus *vb* **1** = **take aback**, astonish, astound, baffle, bewilder, confound, confuse, discomfit, disconcert, discountenance, dismay, dumb-

non-profit-making *adj* not yielding a profit, esp. because organized or established for some other reason: *a non-profit-making organization.*

nonproliferation (ˌnɒnprəˌlɪfəˈreɪʃən) *n* **a** limitation of the production or spread of something, esp. nuclear or chemical weapons. **b** (*as modifier*): *a nonproliferation treaty.*

non-pros (ˌnɒnˈprɒs) *n* **1** short for **non prosequitur.** ◆ *vb* **non-prosses, non-prossing, non-prossed. 2** (*tr*) to enter a judgment of non prosequitur against (a plaintiff).

non prosequitur (ˈnɒn prəʊˈsɛkwɪtə) *n Law.* (formerly) a judgment in favour of a defendant when the plaintiff failed to take the necessary steps in an action within the time allowed. [L, lit.: he does not prosecute]

nonracial (ˌnɒnˈreɪʃəl) *adj* not involving race or racial factors.

nonrepresentational (ˌnɒnrɛprɪzɛnˈteɪʃənᵊl) *adj Art.* another word for **abstract.**

nonresident (nɒnˈrɛzɪdənt) *n* **1** a person who is not residing in the place implied or specified. **2** a British person employed abroad for a minimum of one year, who is exempt from UK income tax provided that he does not spend more than 90 days in the UK during that tax year. ◆ *adj* **3** not residing in the place specified.
▸**non'residence** *or* **non'residency** *n* ▸**ˌnonresi'dential** *adj*

nonresistant (ˌnɒnrɪˈzɪstənt) *adj* **1** incapable of resisting something, such as a disease; susceptible. **2** *History.* (esp. in 17th-century England) practising passive obedience to royal authority even when its commands were unjust.

nonrestrictive (ˌnɒnrɪˈstrɪktɪv) *adj* **1** not limiting. **2** *Grammar.* denoting a relative clause that is not restrictive. Cf. **restrictive** (sense 2).

nonsense ❶ (ˈnɒnsəns) *n* **1** something that has or makes no sense; unintelligible language; drivel. **2** conduct or action that is absurd. **3** foolish behaviour: *she'll stand no nonsense.* **4** things of little or no value; trash. ◆ *interj* **5** an exclamation of disagreement.
▸**nonsensical** (nɒnˈsɛnsɪkᵊl) *adj* ▸**non'sensically** *adv* ▸**non'sensicalness** *or* **nonˌsensi'cality** *n*

nonsense verse *n* verse in which the sense is nonexistent or absurd.

non sequitur (ˈnɒn ˈsɛkwɪtə) *n* **1** a statement having little or no relevance to what preceded it. **2** *Logic.* a conclusion that does not follow from the premises. [L, lit.: it does not follow]

nonsmoker (nɒnˈsməʊkə) *n* **1** a person who does not smoke. **2** a train compartment in which smoking is forbidden.
▸**non'smoking** *adj*

nonspecific urethritis *n* inflammation of the urethra as a result of a sexually transmitted infection that cannot be traced to a specific cause. Abbrev.: **NSU.**

nonstandard (nɒnˈstændəd) *adj* **1** denoting or characterized by idiom, vocabulary, etc., that is not regarded as correct and acceptable by educated native speakers of a language; not standard. **2** deviating from a given standard.

nonstarter ❶ (nɒnˈstɑːtə) *n* **1** a horse that fails to run in a race for which it has been entered. **2** a person or thing that has little chance of success.

nonstick (ˈnɒnˈstɪk) *adj* (of saucepans, etc.) coated with a substance that prevents food sticking to them.

nonstop ❶ (ˈnɒnˈstɒp) *adj, adv* done without pause or interruption: *a nonstop flight.*

nonsuch (ˈnʌnˌsʌtʃ) *n* a variant spelling of **nonesuch.**

nonsuit (nɒnˈsuːt) *Law.* ◆ *n* **1** an order of a judge dismissing a suit when the plaintiff fails to show he has a good cause of action or fails to produce any evidence. ◆ *vb* **2** (*tr*) to order the dismissal of the suit of (a person).

nontechnical (ˌnɒnˈtɛknɪkᵊl) *adj* **1** not technical in nature. **2** (of a person) not having technical knowledge or aptitude.

non troppo (ˈnɒn ˈtrɒpəʊ) *adv Music.* (preceded by a direction, esp. a tempo marking) not to be observed too strictly (esp. in **allegro ma non troppo, adagio ma non troppo**). [It.]

non-U (nɒnˈjuː) *adj Brit. inf.* (esp. of language) not characteristic of or used by the upper class.

nonunion (nɒnˈjuːnjən) *adj* **1** not belonging or related to a trade union: *nonunion workers.* **2** not favouring or employing union labour: *a nonunion shop.* **3** not produced by union labour.

nonvoter (nɒnˈvəʊtə) *n* **1** a person who does not vote. **2** a person not eligible to vote.

nonvoting (nɒnˈvəʊtɪŋ) *adj* **1** of or relating to a nonvoter. **2** *Finance.* (of shares, etc.) not entitling the holder to vote at company meetings.

noodle[1] (ˈnuːdᵊl) *n* (*often pl*) pasta in the form of ribbons or fine strands. [C18: from G *Nudel* from ?]

noodle[2] (ˈnuːdᵊl) *n* **1** *US & Canad. sl.* the head. **2** a simpleton. [C18: ? a blend of NODDLE[1] & NOODLE[1]]

nook ❶ (nʊk) *n* **1** a corner or narrow recess. **2** a secluded or sheltered place. [C13: from ?]

nooky *or* **nookie** (ˈnʊkɪ) *n Sl.* lovemaking.

noon ❶ (nuːn) *n* **1** the middle of the day; 12 o'clock. **2** *Poetic.* the most important part; culmination. [OE *nōn,* from L *nōna* (*hōra*) ninth hour (orig. 3 p.m., the ninth hour from sunrise)]

noonday (ˈnuːnˌdeɪ) *n* the middle of the day; noon.

no-one *or* **no one** *pron* no person; nobody.

> **USAGE NOTE** See at **everyone.**

noontime (ˈnuːnˌtaɪm) *or* **noontide** *n* the middle of the day; noon.

noose (nuːs) *n* **1** a loop in the end of a rope, such as a lasso or hangman's halter, usually tied with a slipknot. **2** something that restrains or traps. **3 put one's head in a noose.** to bring about one's own downfall. ◆ *vb* **nooses, noosing, noosed.** (*tr*) **4** to secure as in a noose. **5** to make a noose of or in. [C15: ?from Provençal *nous,* from L *nōdus* NODE]

no-par *adj* (of securities) without a par value.

nor (nɔː; *unstressed* nə) *conj* (*coordinating*) **1** (used to join alternatives, the first of which is preceded by *neither*) and not: *neither measles nor mumps.* **2** (foll. by a verb) (and) not...either: *they weren't talented — nor were they particularly funny.* **3** *Poetic.* neither: *nor wind nor rain.* [C13: contraction of OE *nōther,* from *nāhwæther* NEITHER]

Nor. *abbrev. for:* **1** Norman. **2** north. **3** Norway. **4** Norwegian.

noradrenaline (ˌnɔːrəˈdrɛnəlɪn, -liːn) *or* **noradrenalin** *n* a hormone secreted by the adrenal medulla, increasing blood pressure and heart rate. US name: **norepinephrine.**

NOR circuit *or* **gate** (nɔː) *n Computing.* a logic circuit having two or more input wires and one output wire that has a high-voltage output signal only if all input signals are at a low voltage. Cf. **AND circuit.** [C20: from NOR; the action performed is similar to the operation of the conjunction *nor* in logic]

nordic (ˈnɔːdɪk) *adj Skiing.* of competitions in cross-country racing and ski-jumping. Cf. **alpine** (sense 4).

Nordic (ˈnɔːdɪk) *adj* of or belonging to a subdivision of the Caucasoid race typified by the tall blond blue-eyed long-headed inhabitants of Scandinavia. [C19: from F *nordique,* from *nord* NORTH]

norepinephrine (ˌnɔːrɛpɪˈnɛfrɪn, -riːn) *n* the US name for **noradrenaline.**

Norfolk jacket (ˈnɔːfək) *n* a man's single-breasted belted jacket with one or two chest pockets and a box pleat down the back. [C19: worn in *Norfolk* for duck shooting]

noria (ˈnɔːrɪə) *n* a water wheel with buckets attached to its rim for raising water from a stream into irrigation canals, etc. [C18: via Sp. from Ar. *nā'ūra,* from *na'ara* to creak]

nork (nɔːk) *n* (*usually pl*) *Austral. taboo sl.* a female breast. [C20: from ?]

norm ❶ (nɔːm) *n* **1** an average level of achievement or performance, as of a group. **2** a standard of achievement or behaviour that is required, desired, or designated as normal. [C19: from L *norma* carpenter's square]

normal ❶ (ˈnɔːmᵊl) *adj* **1** usual; regular; common; typical: *the normal level.* **2** constituting a standard: *if we take this as normal.* **3** *Psychol.* **3a** being within certain limits of intelligence, ability, etc. **3b** conforming to the conventions of one's group. **4** (of laboratory animals) maintained in a natural state for purposes of comparison with animals treated with drugs, etc. **5** *Chem.* (of a solution) containing a number of grams equal to the equivalent weight of the solute in each litre of solvent. **6** *Geom.* another word for **perpendicular** (sense 1). ◆ *n* **7** the usual, average, or typical state, degree, form, etc. **8** anything that is normal. **9** *Geom.* a perpendicular line or plane. [C16: from L *normālis* conforming to the carpenter's square, from *norma* NORM]
▸**normality** (nɔːˈmælɪtɪ) *or esp. US* **'normalcy** *n*

THESAURUS

found, embarrass, faze, flummox, mystify, perplex, puzzle, stump, stun

nonsense *n* **1** = **rubbish,** balderdash, bilge (*inf.*), bosh (*inf.*), bunk (*inf.*), bunkum *or* buncombe (*chiefly US*), claptrap (*inf.*), cobblers (*Brit. taboo sl.*), crap (*sl.*), double Dutch (*Brit. inf.*), drivel, garbage (*inf.*), gibberish, hogwash, hokum (*sl., chiefly US & Canad.*), hot air (*inf.*), jest, moonshine, piffle (*inf.*), poppycock (*inf.*), rot, tommyrot, tosh (*sl., chiefly Brit.*), trash, tripe (*inf.*), twaddle, waffle (*inf., chiefly Brit.*) **2, 3** = **foolishness,** absurdity, fatuity, folly, idiocy, inanity, ludicrousness, ridiculousness, senselessness, silliness, stupidity
Antonyms *n* ≠ **rubbish:** fact, reality, reason, sense, truth ≠ **foolishness:** seriousness, wisdom

nonsensical *adj* **1** = **senseless,** incomprehensible, meaningless **2** = **foolish,** absurd, asinine, crazy, inane, irrational, ludicrous, ridiculous, silly

nonstarter *n* **2** = **dead loss,** dud (*inf.*), lemon (*inf.*), loser, no-hoper (*inf.*), turkey (*inf.*), washout (*inf.*), waste of space *or* time

nonstop *adj* = **continuous,** ceaseless, constant, direct, endless, incessant, interminable, relentless, steady, unbroken, unending, unfaltering, uninterrupted, unremitting ◆ *adv* = **continuously,** ceaselessly, constantly, directly, endlessly, incessantly, interminably, perpetually, relentlessly, steadily, unbrokenly, unendingly, unfalteringly, uninterruptedly, unremittingly, without stopping
Antonyms *adj* ≠ **continuous:** broken, discontinuous, fitful, intermittent, irregular, occasional, periodic, punctuated, recurrent, spasmodic, sporadic, stop-go (*inf.*)

nook *n* **1** = **niche,** alcove, cavity, corner, cranny, crevice, cubbyhole, hide-out, inglenook (*Brit.*), opening, recess, retreat

noon *n* **1** = **midday,** high noon, noonday, noontide, noontime, twelve noon

norm *n* **2** = **standard,** average, benchmark, criterion, mean, measure, model, par, pattern, rule, type, yardstick

normal *adj* **1, 2** = **usual,** accustomed, acknowledged, average, bog-standard (*Brit. & Irish sl.*), common, conventional, habitual, natural, ordinary, popular, regular, routine, run-of-the-mill, standard, typical **3a** = **sane,** rational, reasonable, well-adjusted
Antonyms *adj* ≠ **usual:** abnormal, exceptional, irregular, peculiar, rare, remarkable, singular, uncommon, unnatural, unusual

normality *n* **1, 2** = **regularity,** accustomedness, averageness, commonness, commonplaceness, conventionality, habitualness, naturalness, ordinariness, popularity, routineness, typicality,

normal curve *n Statistics.* a symmetrical bell-shaped curve representing the probability density function of a normal distribution.

normal distribution *n Statistics.* a continuous distribution of a random variable with its mean, median, and mode equal.

normalize *or* **normalise** ('nɔːmə,laɪz) *vb* **normalizes, normalizing, normalized** *or* **normalises, normalising, normalised.** *(tr)* **1** to bring or make into the normal state. **2** to bring into conformity with a standard. **3** to heat (steel) above a critical temperature and allow it to cool in air to relieve internal stresses; anneal.
► **,normali'zation** *or* **,normali'sation** *n*

normally Ⓣ ('nɔːməlɪ) *adv* **1** as a rule; usually; ordinarily. **2** in a normal manner.

Norman ('nɔːmən) *n* **1** (in the Middle Ages) a member of the people of Normandy in N France, descended from the 10th-century Scandinavian conquerors of the country and the native French. **2** a native or inhabitant of Normandy. **3** another name for **Norman French.** ◆ *adj* **4** of or characteristic of the Normans, esp. the Norman kings of England and the Norman people living in England, or their dialect of French. **5** of or characteristic of Normandy. **6** denoting or having the style of Romanesque architecture used in Britain from the Norman Conquest until the 12th century, characterized by the rounded arch, massive masonry walls, etc.

Norman Conquest *n* the invasion and settlement of England by the Normans, following the Battle of Hastings (1066).

Norman French *n* the medieval Norman and English dialect of Old French.

normative Ⓣ ('nɔːmətɪv) *adj* **1** implying, creating, or prescribing a norm or standard, as in language: *normative grammar.* **2** expressing value judgments as contrasted with stating facts.

Norn[1] (nɔːn) *n Norse myth.* any of the three virgin goddesses of fate. [C18: ON]

Norn[2] (nɔːn) *n* the medieval Norse language of the Orkneys, Shetlands, and parts of N Scotland. [C17: from ON *norrœna* Norwegian, from *northr* north]

Norse (nɔːs) *adj* **1** of ancient and medieval Scandinavia or its inhabitants. **2** of or characteristic of Norway. ◆ *n* **3a** the N group of Germanic languages, spoken in Scandinavia. **3b** any one of these languages, esp. in their ancient or medieval forms. **4 the Norse.** *(functioning as pl)* **4a** the Norwegians. **4b** the Vikings.

Norseman ('nɔːsmən) *n, pl* **Norsemen.** another name for a **Viking.**

north Ⓣ (nɔːθ) *n* **1** one of the four cardinal points of the compass, at 0° or 360°, that is 90° from east and west and 180° from south. **2** the direction along a meridian towards the North Pole. **3** the direction in which a compass needle points; magnetic north. **4 the north.** *(often cap.)* any area lying in or towards the north. **5** *(usually cap.) Cards.* the player or position at the table corresponding to north on the compass. ◆ *adj* **6** in, towards, or facing the north. **7** (esp. of the wind) from the north. ◆ *adv* **8** in, to, or towards the north. [OE]

North (nɔːθ) *n* **the. 1** the northern area of England, generally regarded as reaching the southern boundaries of Yorkshire, Derbyshire, and Cheshire. **2** (in the US) the states north of the Mason-Dixon Line that were known as the Free States during the Civil War. **3** the northern part of North America, esp. Alaska, the Yukon and the Northwest Territories. **4** the countries of the world that are economically and technically advanced. ◆ *adj* **5** of or denoting the northern part of a specified country, area, etc.

Northants (nɔː'θænts) *abbrev. for* Northamptonshire.

northbound ('nɔːθ,baʊnd) *adj* going or leading towards the north.

north by east *n* one point on the compass east of north.

north by west *n* one point on the compass west of north.

North Country *n* (usually preceded by *the*) **1** another name for **North** (sense 1). **2** another name for **North** (sense 3).

Northd *abbrev. for* Northumberland.

northeast (,nɔːθ'iːst; *Naut.* ,nɔːr'iːst) *n* **1** the point of the compass or direction midway between north and east. **2** *(often cap.;* usually preceded by *the)* any area lying in or towards this direction. ◆ *adj also* **northeastern. 3** *(sometimes cap.)* of or denoting the northeastern part of a specified country, area, etc.: *northeast Lincolnshire.* **4** in, towards, or facing the northeast. **5** (esp. of the wind) from the northeast. ◆ *adv* **6** in, to, or towards the northeast.
► **,north'easternmost** *adj*

Northeast (,nɔːθ'iːst) *n* (usually preceded by *the*) the northeastern part of England, esp. Northumberland, Durham, and the Tyneside area.

northeast by east *n* one point on the compass east of northeast.

northeast by north *n* one point on the compass north of northeast.

northeaster (,nɔːθ'iːstə; *Naut.* ,nɔːr'iːstə) *n* a strong wind or storm from the northeast.

northeasterly (,nɔːθ'iːstəlɪ; *Naut.* ,nɔːr'iːstəlɪ) *adj, adv* **1** in, towards, or (esp. of a wind) from the northeast. ◆ *n, pl* **northeasterlies. 2** a wind or storm from the northeast.

northeastward (,nɔːθ'iːstwəd; *Naut.* ,nɔːr'iːstwəd) *adj* **1** towards or (esp. of a wind) from the northeast. ◆ *n* **2** a direction towards or area in the northeast.
► **,north'eastwardly** *adj, adv*

norther ('nɔːðə) *n Chiefly southern US.* a wind or storm from the north.

northerly ('nɔːðəlɪ) *adj* **1** of or situated in the north. ◆ *adv, adj* **2** towards the north. **3** from the north: *a northerly wind.* ◆ *n, pl* **northerlies. 4** a wind from the north.
► **'northerliness** *n*

northern ('nɔːðən) *adj* **1** in or towards the north. **2** (esp. of winds) proceeding from the north. **3** *(sometimes cap.)* of or characteristic of the north or North.

Northerner ('nɔːðənə) *n (sometimes not cap.)* a native or inhabitant of the north of any specified region, esp. England, the US, or the far north of Canada.

northern hemisphere *n (often caps.)* that half of the globe lying north of the equator.

northern lights *pl n* another name for **aurora borealis.**

northernmost ('nɔːðən,məʊst) *adj* situated or occurring farthest north.

northing ('nɔːθɪŋ, -ðɪŋ) *n* **1** *Navigation.* movement or distance covered in a northerly direction, esp. as expressed in the resulting difference in latitude. **2** *Astron.* a north or positive declination.

Northland ('nɔːθlənd) *n* **1** the peninsula containing Norway and Sweden. **2** (in Canada) the far north.
► **'Northlander** *n*

Northman ('nɔːθmən) *n, pl* **Northmen.** another name for a **Viking.**

north-northeast *n* **1** the point on the compass or the direction midway between north and northeast. ◆ *adj, adv* **2** in, from, or towards this direction.

north-northwest *n* **1** the point on the compass or the direction midway between northwest and north. ◆ *adj, adv* **2** in, from, or towards this direction.

North Pole *n* **1** the northernmost point on the earth's axis, at a latitude of 90°N, characterized by very low temperatures. **2** Also called: **north celestial pole.** *Astron.* the point of intersection of the earth's extended axis and the northern half of the celestial sphere. **3** *(usually not cap.)* the pole of a freely suspended magnet, which is attracted to the earth's magnetic North Pole.

North-Sea gas *n* (in Britain) natural gas obtained from deposits below the North Sea.

North Star Ⓣ *n* **the.** another name for **Polaris.**

northward ('nɔːθwəd; *Naut.* 'nɔːðəd) *adj* **1** moving, facing, or situated towards the north. ◆ *n* **2** the northward part, direction, etc. ◆ *adv also* **northwards. 3** towards the north.

northwest (,nɔːθ'west; *Naut.* ,nɔː'west) *n* **1** the point of the compass or direction midway between north and west. **2** *(often cap.;* usually preceded by *the)* any area lying in or towards this direction. ◆ *adj also* **northwestern. 3** *(sometimes cap.)* of or denoting the northwestern part of a specified country, area, etc.: *northwest Greenland.* ◆ *adj, adv* **4** in, to, or towards the northwest.
► **,north'westernmost** *adj*

Northwest (,nɔːθ'west) *n* (usually preceded by *the*) the northwestern part of England, esp. Lancashire and the Lake District.

northwest by north *n* one point on the compass north of northwest.

northwest by west *n* one point on the compass south of northwest.

northwester (,nɔːθ'westə; *Naut.* ,nɔː'westə) *n* a strong wind or storm from the northwest.

northwesterly (,nɔːθ'westəlɪ; *Naut.* ,nɔː'westəlɪ) *adj, adv* **1** in, towards, or (esp. of a wind) from the northwest. ◆ *n, pl* **northwesterlies. 2** a wind or storm from the northwest.

Northwest Territories *pl n* the part of Canada north of the provinces and east of the Yukon Territory.

northwestward (,nɔːθ'westwəd; *Naut.* ,nɔː'westwəd) *adj* **1** towards or (esp. of a wind) from the northwest. ◆ *n* **2** a direction towards or area in the northwest.
► **,north'westwardly** *adj, adv*

Norw. *abbrev. for:* **1** Norway. **2** Norwegian.

Norway lobster ('nɔː,weɪ) *n* a European lobster fished for food.

Norway rat *n* the common brown rat.

Norway spruce *n* a European spruce tree having drooping branches and dark green needle-like leaves.

Norwegian (nɔː'wiːdʒən) *adj* **1** of or characteristic of Norway, its language, or its people. ◆ *n* **2** any of the various North Germanic languages of Norway. **3** a native or inhabitant of Norway.

Nos. *or* **nos.** *abbrev. for* numbers.

nose Ⓣ (nəʊz) *n* **1** the organ of smell and entrance to the respiratory tract, consisting of a prominent structure divided into two hair-lined air passages. Related adj: **nasal. 2** the sense of smell itself: in animals, the ability to follow trails by scent (esp. in **a good nose**). **3** the scent, aroma, bouquet of something, esp. wine. **4** instinctive skill in discovering things (sometimes in **follow one's nose**): *he had a nose for good news stories.* **5** any part resembling a nose in form or function, such as a nozzle or spout. **6** the forward part of a vehicle, aircraft, etc. **7** narrow margin of victory (in **(win) by a nose**). **8 cut off one's nose to spite one's**

THESAURUS

usualness **3 = sanity,** adjustment, balance, rationality, reason

normally *adv* **1 = usually,** as a rule, commonly, generally, habitually, ordinarily, regularly, typically

normative *adj* **1 = standardizing,** controlling, normalizing, prescriptive, regularizing, regulating

north *adj* **6,7 = northern,** Arctic, boreal, northerly, polar ◆ *adv* **8 = northward(s),** northerly

North Star *n* **= Pole Star,** lodestar, Polaris

nose *n* **1 = snout,** beak, bill, conk, hooter *(sl.)*, neb *(arch. or dialect)*, proboscis, schnozzle *(sl., chiefly US)*, snitch *(sl.)* ◆ *vb* **23 = ease forward,** nudge, nuzzle, push, shove **24 = pry,** meddle, snoop *(inf.)*

face. to carry out a vengeful action that hurts oneself more than another. **9 get up (someone's) nose.** *Inf.* to annoy or irritate (someone). **10 keep one's nose clean.** to stay out of trouble. **11 lead by the nose.** to make (someone) do unquestioningly all one wishes; dominate. **12 look down one's nose at.** *Inf.* to be disdainful of. **13 nose to tail.** (of vehicles) moving or standing very close behind one another. **14 on the nose.** *Sl.* **14a** (in horse-race betting) to win only: *I bet twenty pounds on the nose on that horse.* **14b** *Chiefly US & Canad.* precisely; exactly. **14c** *Austral.* bad or bad-smelling. **15 pay through the nose.** *Inf.* to pay an exorbitant price. **16 put someone's nose out of joint.** *Inf.* to thwart or offend someone. **17 rub someone's nose in it.** *Inf.* to remind someone unkindly of a failing or error. **18 turn up one's nose (at).** *Inf.* to behave disdainfully (towards). **19 with one's nose in the air.** haughtily. ◆ *vb* **noses, nosing, nosed. 20** (*tr*) (esp. of horses, dogs, etc.) to rub, touch, or sniff with the nose; nuzzle. **21** to smell or sniff (wine, etc.). **22** (*intr;* usually foll. by *after* or *for*) to search (for) by or as if by scent. **23** to move or cause to move forwards slowly and carefully: *we nosed the car into the garage.* **24** (*intr;* foll. by *into, around, about,* etc.) to pry or snoop (into) or meddle (in). [OE *nosu*]
▸**'noseless** *adj* ▸**'nose,like** *adj*

nosebag ('nəʊz,bæg) *n* a bag, fastened around the head of a horse and covering the nose, in which feed is placed.

noseband ('nəʊz,bænd) *n* the detachable part of a horse's bridle that goes around the nose.

nosebleed ('nəʊz,bli:d) *n* bleeding from the nose as the result of injury, etc.

nose cone *n* the conical forward section of a missile, spacecraft, etc., designed to withstand high temperatures, esp. during re-entry into the earth's atmosphere.

nose dive Ⓣ *n* **1** a sudden plunge with the nose or front pointing downwards, esp. of an aircraft. **2** *Inf.* a sudden drop or sharp decline: *prices took a nose dive.* ◆ *vb* **nose-dive, nose-dives, nose-diving, nose-dived.** (*intr*) **3** to perform a nose dive.

nose flute *n* (esp. in the South Sea Islands) a type of flute blown through the nose.

nosegay Ⓣ ('nəʊz,geɪ) *n* a small bunch of flowers; posy. [C15: from NOSE + *gay* (arch.) toy]

nose job *n Sl.* a surgical remodelling of the nose for cosmetic reasons.

nosepiece ('nəʊz,pi:s) *n* **1** a piece of armour to protect the nose. **2** the connecting part of a pair of spectacles that rests on the nose; bridge. **3** the part of a microscope to which one or more objective lenses are attached. **4** a less common word for **noseband.**

nose rag *n Sl.* a handkerchief.

nose ring *n* a ring fixed through the nose, as for leading a bull.

nose wheel *n* a wheel fitted to the forward end of a vehicle, esp. the landing wheel under the nose of an aircraft.

nosey ('nəʊzɪ) *adj* a variant spelling of **nosy.**

nosh Ⓣ (nɒʃ) *Sl.* ◆ *n* **1** food or a meal. ◆ *vb* **2** to eat. [C20: from Yiddish; cf. G *naschen* to nibble]

no-show *n* a person who fails to take up a reserved seat, place, etc., without having cancelled it.

nosh-up *n Brit. sl.* a large and satisfying meal.

no-side *n Rugby.* the end of a match, signalled by the referee's whistle.

nosocomial (,nɒsə'kəʊmɪəl) *adj* of or denoting an infection that originates in a hospital. [C19: from Gk *nosokomos* one that tends the sick, from *nosos* disease + *komein* to tend]

nosology (nɒ'sɒlədʒɪ) *n* the branch of medicine concerned with the classification of diseases. [C18: from Gk *nosos* disease]
▸**nosological** (,nɒsə'lɒdʒɪkᵊl) *adj*

nostalgia Ⓣ (nɒ'stældʒə, -dʒɪə) *n* **1** a yearning for past circumstances, events, etc. **2** the evocation of this emotion, as in a book, film, etc. **3** homesickness. [C18: NL, from Gk *nostos a* return home + -ALGIA]
▸**nos'talgic** *adj* ▸**nos'talgically** *adv*

nostoc ('nɒstɒk) *n* a gelatinous cyanobacterium occurring in moist places. [C17: NL, coined by Paracelsus (1493–1541) Swiss physician]

nostril ('nɒstrɪl) *n* either of the two external openings of the nose. See **nares.** [OE *nosthyrl,* from *nosu* NOSE + *thyrel* hole]

nostro account ('nɒstrəʊ) *n* a bank account conducted by a British bank with a foreign bank, usually in the foreign currency. Cf. **vostro account.**

nostrum Ⓣ ('nɒstrəm) *n* **1** a patent or quack medicine. **2** a favourite remedy. [C17: from L: our own (make), from *noster* our]

nosy Ⓣ *or* **nosey** ('nəʊzɪ) *adj* **nosier, nosiest.** *Inf.* prying or inquisitive.
▸**'nosily** *adv* ▸**'nosiness** *n*

nosy parker *n Inf.* a prying person. [C20: arbitrary use of surname *Parker*]

not (nɒt) *adv* **1a** used to negate the sentence, phrase, or word that it modifies: *I will not stand for it.* **1b** (*in combination*): *they cannot go.* **2 not that.** (*conj*) Also (arch.): **not but what.** which is not to say or suppose that: *I expect to lose the game — not that I mind.* ◆ *sentence substitute.* **3** used to indicate denial or refusal: *certainly not.* [C14 *not,* var. of *nought* nothing, from OE *nāwiht,* from *nā* no + *wiht* creature, thing]

nota bene *Latin.* ('nəʊtə 'bi:nɪ) note well; take note. Abbrevs.: **NB, N.B., nb, n.b.**

notability Ⓣ (,nəʊtə'bɪlɪtɪ) *n, pl* **notabilities. 1** the quality of being notable. **2** a distinguished person.

notable Ⓣ ('nəʊtəbᵊl) *adj* **1** worthy of being noted or remembered; remarkable; distinguished. ◆ *n* **2** a notable person. [C14: via OF from L *notābilis,* from *notāre* to NOTE]
▸**'notably** *adv*

notarize *or* **notarise** ('nəʊtə,raɪz) *vb* **notarizes, notarizing, notarized** *or* **notarises, notarising, notarised.** (*tr*) *US.* to attest to (a document, etc.), as a notary.

notary ('nəʊtərɪ) *n, pl* **notaries. 1** a notary public. **2** (formerly) a clerk licensed to prepare legal documents. **3** *Arch.* a clerk or secretary. [C14: from L *notārius* clerk, from *nota* a mark, note]
▸**notarial** (nəʊ'tɛərɪəl) *adj* ▸**'notaryship** *n*

notary public *n, pl* **notaries public.** a public official, usually a solicitor, who is legally authorized to administer oaths, attest and certify certain documents, etc.

notation Ⓣ (nəʊ'teɪʃən) *n* **1** any series of signs or symbols used to represent quantities or elements in a specialized system, such as music or mathematics. **2** the act or process of notating. **3** a note or record. [C16: from L *notātiō,* from *notāre* to NOTE]
▸**no'tational** *adj*

notch Ⓣ (nɒtʃ) *n* **1** a V-shaped cut or indentation; nick. **2** a nick made in a tally stick. **3** *US & Canad.* a narrow gorge. **4** *Inf.* a step or level (esp. in **a notch above**). ◆ *vb* (*tr*) **5** to cut or make a notch in. **6** to record with or as if with a notch. **7** (usually foll. by *up*) *Inf.* to score or achieve: *the team notched up its fourth win.* [C16: from incorrect division of *an otch* (as *a notch*), from OF *oche* notch, from L *obsecāre,* from *secāre* to cut]

NOT circuit *or* **gate** (nɒt) *n Computing.* a logic circuit that has a high-voltage output signal if the input signal is low, and vice versa: used extensively in computing. Also called: **inverter, negator.** [C20: the action performed on electrical signals is similar to the operation of *not* in logical constructions]

note Ⓣ (nəʊt) *n* **1** a brief record in writing, esp. a jotting for future reference. **2** a brief informal letter. **3** a formal written communication, esp. from one government to another. **4** a short written statement giving any kind of information. **5** a critical comment, explanatory statement, or reference in a book. **6** short for **banknote. 7** a characteristic atmosphere: *a note of sarcasm.* **8** a distinctive vocal sound, as of a species of bird or animal. **9** any of a series of graphic signs representing the pitch and duration of a musical sound. **10** Also called (esp. US and Canad.): **tone.** a musical sound of definite fundamental frequency or pitch. **11** a key on a piano, organ, etc. **12** a sound used as a signal or warning: *the note to retreat was sounded.* **13** short for **promissory note. 14** *Arch. or poetic.* a melody. **15 of note. 15a** distinguished or famous. **15b** important: *nothing of note.* **16 strike the right** (*or* **a false**) **note.** to behave appropriately (or inappropriately). **17 take note.** (often foll. by *of*) to pay attention (to). ◆ *vb* **notes, noting, noted.** (*tr; may take a clause as object*) **18** to notice; perceive. **19** to pay close attention to: *they noted every movement.* **20** to make a written note of: *she noted the date in her diary.* **21** to remark upon: *I note that you do not wear shoes.* **22** to write down (music, a melody, etc.) in notes. **23** to take (an unpaid or dishonoured bill of exchange) to a notary public to re-present the bill and if it is still unaccepted or unpaid to note the circumstances in a register. See

THESAURUS

nose dive *vb* **nose-dive 3** = **drop,** dive, plummet, plunge

nosegay *n* = **posy,** bouquet

nosh *Slang n* **1** = **food,** aliment, chow (*inf.*), comestibles, eats (*sl.*), fare, feed, grub (*sl.*), meal, repast, sustenance, tack (*inf.*), viands, victuals, vittles (*obs. or dialect*) ◆ *vb* **2** = **eat,** consume, scoff (*sl.*)

nostalgia *n* **1** = **reminiscence,** longing, pining, regret, regretfulness, remembrance, wistfulness, yearning **3** = **homesickness**

nostalgic *adj* **1** = **sentimental,** emotional, longing, maudlin, regretful, wistful **2** = **homesick**

nostrum *n* **1** = **patent medicine,** cure-all, elixir, panacea, quack medicine, sovereign cure **2** = **remedy,** cure, drug, medicine, potion, specific, treatment

nosy *adj* = **inquisitive,** curious, eavesdropping, interfering, intrusive, meddlesome, prying, snooping (*inf.*)

notability *n* **1** = **fame,** celebrity, distinction, eminence, esteem, renown **2** = **celebrity,** big name, celeb (*inf.*), dignitary, megastar (*inf.*), notable, personage, V.I.P., worthy

notable *adj* **1** = **remarkable,** celebrated, conspicuous, distinguished, eminent, evident, extraordinary, famous, manifest, marked, memorable, noteworthy, noticeable, notorious, outstanding, pre-eminent, pronounced, rare, renowned, salient, striking, uncommon, unusual, well-known ◆ *n* **2** = **celebrity,** big name, celeb (*inf.*), dignitary, luminary, megastar (*inf.*), notability, personage, V.I.P., worthy

Antonyms *adj* ≠ **remarkable:** anonymous, concealed, hidden, imperceptible, obscure, unknown, vague

notably *adv* **1** = **particularly,** conspicuously, distinctly, especially, markedly, noticeably, outstandingly, remarkably, seriously (*inf.*), signally, strikingly, uncommonly

notation *n* **1** = **signs,** characters, code, script, symbols, system **2** = **noting,** jotting, notating **3** = **note,** record

notch *n* **1** = **cut,** cleft, incision, indentation, mark, nick, score **4** *Informal* = **level,** cut (*inf.*), degree, grade, step ◆ *vb* **5** = **cut,** indent, mark, nick, score, scratch **7** *usually with* **up** = **register,** achieve, gain, make, score

note *n* **1** = **record,** jotting, minute, remark, reminder **2** = **message,** communication, epistle, letter, memo, memorandum **5** = **annotation,** comment, gloss **15 of note** = **famous,** distinguished, eminent, prestigious, renowned **17 take note** = **notice,** heed, observe, regard ◆ *vb* **18** = **see,** notice, observe, perceive **20** = **mark,** denote, indicate, record, register **21** = **mention,** remark

protest (sense 9). **24** a less common word for **annotate.** [C13: via OF from L *nota* sign]
▸ **'noteless** *adj*

notebook ⓣ ('nəʊt,bʊk) *n* a book for recording notes or memoranda.

notebook computer *n* a portable computer smaller than a laptop model, often approximately the size of a sheet of A4 paper.

notecase ('nəʊt,keɪs) *n* a less common word for **wallet** (sense 1).

noted ⓣ ('nəʊtɪd) *adj* **1** celebrated; famous. **2** of special significance; noticeable.
▸ **'notedly** *adv*

notelet ('nəʊtlɪt) *n* a folded card with a printed design on the front, for writing a short letter.

notepaper ('nəʊt,peɪpə) *n* paper for writing letters; writing paper.

noteworthy ⓣ ('nəʊt,wɜːðɪ) *adj* worthy of notice; notable.
▸ **'note,worthiness** *n*

nothing ⓣ ('nʌθɪŋ) *pron* **1** (*indefinite*) no thing; not anything: *I can give you nothing.* **2** no part or share: *to have nothing to do with this crime.* **3** a matter of no importance: *it doesn't matter, it's nothing.* **4** indicating the absence of anything perceptible; nothingness. **5** indicating the absence of meaning, value, worth, etc.: *to amount to nothing.* **6** zero quantity; nought. **7 be nothing to. 7a** not to concern or be significant to (someone). **7b** to be not nearly as good, etc., as. **8 have** *or* **be nothing to do with.** to have no connection with. **9 nothing but.** not something other than; only. **10 nothing doing.** *Inf.* an expression of dismissal, refusal, etc. **11 nothing if not.** at the very least; certainly. **12 nothing less than** *or* **nothing short of.** downright; truly. **13 there's nothing to it.** it is very simple, easy, etc. **14 think nothing of. 14a** to regard as easy or natural. **14b** to have no compunction about. **14c** to have a very low opinion of. ◆ *adv* **15** in no way; not at all: *he looked nothing like his brother.* ◆ *n* **16** *Inf.* a person or thing of no importancee.**17 sweet nothings.** words of endearment or affection. [OE *nāthing, nān thing,* from *nān* NONE[1] + THING]

> **USAGE NOTE** *Nothing* normally takes a singular verb, but when *nothing but* is followed by a plural form of a noun, a plural verb is usually used: *it was a large room where nothing but souvenirs were sold.*

nothingness ⓣ ('nʌθɪŋnɪs) *n* **1** the state of being nothing; nonexistence. **2** absence of consciousness or life. **3** complete insignificance. **4** something that is worthless.

notice ⓣ ('nəʊtɪs) *n* **1** observation; attention: *to escape notice.* **2 take notice.** to pay attention. **3 take no notice of.** to ignore or disregard. **4** a warning; announcement. **5** a displayed placard or announcement giving information. **6** advance notification of intention to end an arrangement, contract, etc., as of employment (esp. in **give notice**). **7 at short notice.** with notification only a little in advance. **8** *Chiefly Brit.* dismissal from employment. **9** interested, or polite attention: *she was beneath his notice.* **10** a theatrical or literary review: *the play received very good notices.* ◆ *vb* **notices, noticing, noticed. 11** to become aware (of); perceive; note. **12** (*tr*) to point out or remark upon. **13** (*tr*) to pay polite or interested attention to. **14** (*tr*) to acknowledge (an acquaintance, etc.). [C15: via OF from L *notitia* fame, from *nōtus* known]

noticeable ⓣ ('nəʊtɪsəbᵊl) *adj* easily seen or detected; perceptible.
▸ **'noticeably** *adv*

notice board *n* a board on which notices, advertisements, bulletins, etc., are displayed. US and Canad. name: **bulletin board.**

notifiable ('nəʊtɪ,faɪəbᵊl) *adj* **1** denoting certain infectious diseases of humans, such as tuberculosis, outbreaks of which must be reported to the public health authorities. **2** denoting certain infectious diseases of animals, such as BSE and rabies, outbreaks of which must be reported to the appropriate veterinary authority.

notification ⓣ (,nəʊtɪfɪ'keɪʃən) *n* **1** the act of notifying. **2** a formal announcement. **3** something that notifies; a notice.

notify ⓣ ('nəʊtɪ,faɪ) *vb* **notifies, notifying, notified.** (*tr*) **1** to tell. **2** *Chiefly Brit.* to make known; announce. [C14: from OF *notifier,* from L *notificāre,* from *nōtus* known + *facere* to make]
▸ **'noti,fier** *n*

notion ⓣ ('nəʊʃən) *n* **1** a vague idea; impression. **2** an idea, concept, or opinion. **3** an inclination or whim. ◆ See also **notions.** [C16: from L *nōtiō* a becoming acquainted (with), examination (of), from *noscere* to know]

notional ⓣ ('nəʊʃənᵊl) *adj* **1** expressing or consisting of ideas. **2** not evident in reality; hypothetical or imaginary: *a notional tax credit.* **3** characteristic of a notion, esp. in being speculative or abstract. **4** *Grammar.* **4a** (of a word) having lexical meaning. **4b** another word for **semantic.**
▸ **'notionally** *adv*

notions ('nəʊʃənz) *pl n Chiefly US & Canad.* pins, cotton, ribbon, etc., used for sewing; haberdashery.

notochord ('nəʊtə,kɔːd) *n* a fibrous longitudinal rod in all embryo and some adult chordate animals, immediately above the gut, that supports the body. [C19: from Gk *nōton* the back + CHORD[1]]

notorious ⓣ (nəʊ'tɔːrɪəs) *adj* **1** well-known for some bad quality, deed, etc.; infamous. **2** *Rare.* generally known or widely acknowledged. [C16: from Med. L *notōrius* well-known, from *nōtus* known]
▸ **notoriety** (,nəʊtə'raɪɪtɪ) *n* ▸ **no'toriously** *adv*

notornis (nəʊ'tɔːnɪs) *n* a rare flightless rail of New Zealand. [C19: NL, from Gk *notos* south + *ornis* bird]

not proven ('prəuvᵊn) *adj* (*postpositive*) a third verdict available to Scottish courts, returned when there is insufficient evidence against the accused to convict.

no-trump *Cards.* ◆ *n also* **no-trumps. 1** a bid or contract to play without trumps. ◆ *adj also* **no-trumper. 2** (of a hand) suitable for playing without trumps.

Notts (nɒts) *abbrev. for* Nottinghamshire.

notwithstanding ⓣ (,nɒtwɪθ'stændɪŋ) *prep* **1** (*often immediately postpositive*) in spite of; despite. ◆ *conj* **2** (*subordinating*) although. ◆ *sentence connector.* **3** nevertheless.

nougat ('nuːgɑː) *n* a hard chewy pink or white sweet containing chopped nuts, cherries, etc. [C19: via F from Provençal *nogat,* from *noga* nut, from L *nux* nut]

nought ⓣ (nɔːt) *n also* **naught, ought, aught. 1** another name for **zero:** used esp. in numbering. ◆ *n, adj, adv* **2** a variant spelling of **naught.** [OE *nōwiht,* from *ne* not, no + *ōwiht* something]

noughts and crosses *n* (*functioning as sing*) a game in which two players, one using a nought, "O", the other a cross, "X", alternately mark squares formed by two pairs of crossed lines, the winner being the first to get three of his symbols in a row. US and Canad. term: **tick-tack-toe,** (US) **crisscross.**

noun (naʊn) *n* **a** a word or group of words that refers to a person, place, or thing. **b** (*as modifier*): *a noun phrase.* Abbrev.: **N, n.** Related adj: **nominal.** [C14: via Anglo-F from L *nōmen* NAME]
▸ **'nounal** *adj*

nourish ⓣ ('nʌrɪʃ) *vb* (*tr*) **1** to provide with the materials necessary for life and growth. **2** to encourage (an idea, etc.); foster: *to nourish resentment.* [C14: from OF *norir,* from L *nūtrīre* to feed]
▸ **'nourisher** *n* ▸ **'nourishing** *adj*

nourishment ⓣ ('nʌrɪʃmənt) *n* **1** the act or state of nourishing. **2** a substance that nourishes; food.

nous (naʊs) *n* **1** *Metaphysics.* mind or reason, esp. regarded as the principle governing all things. **2** *Brit. sl.* common sense. [C17: from Gk: mind]

nouveau *or before a plural noun* **nouveaux** ('nuːvəʊ) *adj* (*prenominal*) *Facetious or derog.* having recently become the thing specified: *a nouveau hippy.* [C20: F, lit.: new; on the model of NOUVEAU RICHE]

nouveau riche ⓣ (riːʃ) *n, pl* **nouveaux riches** (riːʃ). (often preceded by *the*)

THESAURUS

notebook *n* = **jotter,** diary, exercise book, Filofax (*Trademark*), journal, memorandum book, notepad, record book

noted *adj* **1** = **famous,** acclaimed, celebrated, conspicuous, distinguished, eminent, illustrious, notable, prominent, recognized, renowned, well-known
Antonyms *adj* infamous, obscure, undistinguished, unknown

noteworthy *adj* = **remarkable,** exceptional, extraordinary, important, notable, outstanding, significant, unusual
Antonyms *adj* commonplace, insignificant, normal, ordinary, pedestrian, run-of-the-mill, unexceptional, unremarkable

nothing *pron* **3** = **trifle,** bagatelle, **4** = **nothingness,** emptiness, nonexistence, nullity, void **6** = **nought,** naught, nil, zero ◆ *n* **14 think nothing of: a** = **consider unimportant,** regard as routine **b** have no hesitation about **c** set no store by

nothingness *n* **1** = **oblivion,** nihility, nonbeing, nonexistence, nullity **3** = **insignificance,** unimportance, worthlessness

notice *n* **1** = **interest,** cognizance, consideration, heed, note, observation, regard **4** = **announcement,** advice, communication, instruction, intelligence, intimation, news, notification, order, warning **5** = **advertisement,** announcement, poster, sign **9** = **attention,** civility, respect **10** = **review,** comment, criticism ◆ *vb* **11** = **observe,** behold (*arch. or literary*), detect, discern, distinguish, eyeball (*sl.*), heed, mark, mind, note, perceive, remark, see, spot
Antonyms *n* ≠ **interest:** disregard, ignorance, neglect, omission, oversight ◆ *vb* ≠ **observe:** disregard, ignore, neglect, overlook

noticeable *adj* = **obvious,** appreciable, blatant, bold, clear, conspicuous, distinct, evident, manifest, observable, perceptible, plain, salient, striking, unmistakable

notification *n* **1** = **notifying,** advice, alert, information, intelligence, telling, warning **2** = **announcement,** declaration, message, notice, publication, statement

notify *vb* **1** = **inform,** acquaint, advise, alert, apprise, tell, warn **2** = **announce,** declare, make known, publish

notion *n* **1, 2** = **idea,** apprehension, belief, concept, conception, impression, inkling, judgment, knowledge, opinion, sentiment, understanding, view **3** = **whim,** caprice, desire, fancy, impulse, inclination, wish

notional *adj* **1, 3** = **conceptual,** abstract, ideal, unreal, visionary **2** = **hypothetical,** fanciful, imaginary, speculative, theoretical
Antonyms *adj* actual, factual, genuine, real

notoriety *n* **1** = **scandal,** dishonour, disrepute, infamy, obloquy, opprobrium

notorious *adj* **1** = **infamous,** dishonourable, disreputable, opprobrious, scandalous

notoriously *adv* **1** = **infamously,** dishonourably, disreputably, opprobriously, scandalously

notwithstanding *prep* **1** = **despite,** in spite of ◆ *conj* **2** = **although,** (even) though, though ◆ *sentence connector* **3** = **nevertheless,** however, nonetheless, yet

nought *n* **1** = **zero,** naught, nil, nothing

nourish *vb* **1** = **feed,** furnish, nurse, nurture, supply, sustain **2** = **encourage,** comfort, cultivate, foster, maintain, promote, support

nourishing *adj* **1** = **nutritious,** beneficial, healthful, health-giving, nutritive, wholesome

nourishment *n* **2** = **food,** aliment, diet, nutriment, nutrition, sustenance, tack (*inf.*), viands, victuals, vittles (*obs. or dialect*)

nouveau riche *n* = **new-rich,** arriviste, parvenu, upstart

a person who has acquired wealth recently and is regarded as vulgarly ostentatious or lacking in social graces. [C19: from F lit.: new rich]

nouvelle cuisine ('nu:vel kwi:'zi:n; *French* nuvel kɥizin) *n* a style of cooking based on presenting small attractively arranged helpings of lightly cooked fresh ingredients. [C20: F, lit.: new cookery]

Nov. *abbrev. for* November.

nova ('nəʊvə) *n, pl* **novae** (-vi:) *or* **novas.** a variable star that undergoes a cataclysmic eruption, observed as a sudden large increase in brightness with a subsequent decline over months or years; it is a close binary system with one component a white dwarf. [C19: NL *nova (stella)* new (star), from L *novus* new]

novel[1] ❶ ('nɒvᵊl) *n* **1** an extended fictional work in prose dealing with character, action, thought, etc., esp. in the form of a story. **2 the novel.** the literary genre represented by novels. [C15: from OF *novelle*, from L *novella (narrātiō)* new (story); see NOVEL[2]]

novel[2] ❶ ('nɒvᵊl) *adj* of a kind not seen before; fresh; new; original: *a novel suggestion.* [C15: from L *novellus*, dim. of *novus* new]

novelette (ˌnɒvə'lɛt) *n* **1** an extended prose narrative or short novel. **2** a novel that is regarded as slight, trivial, or sentimental. **3** a short piece of lyrical music, esp. for piano.

novelettish (ˌnɒvə'lɛtɪʃ) *adj* characteristic of a novelette; trite or sentimental.

novelist ('nɒvəlɪst) *n* a writer of novels.

novelistic (ˌnɒvə'lɪstɪk) *adj* of or characteristic of novels, esp. in style or method of treatment.

novella (nəʊ'vɛlə) *n, pl* **novellas** *or* **novelle** (-leɪ). **1** a short narrative tale, esp. one having a satirical point, such as those in Boccaccio's *Decameron.* **2** a short novel. [C20: from It.; see NOVEL[1]]

novelty ❶ ('nɒvᵊltɪ) *n, pl* **novelties. 1a** the quality of being new and interesting. **1b** *(as modifier): novelty value.* **2** a new or unusual experience. **3** *(often pl)* a small usually cheap new ornament or trinket. [C14: from OF *novelté;* see NOVEL[2]]

November (nəʊ'vɛmbə) *n* the eleventh month of the year, consisting of 30 days. [C13: via OF from L: ninth month (the Roman year orig. began in March), from *novem* nine]

novena (nəʊ'vi:nə) *n, pl* **novenas** *or* **novenae** (-ni:). *RC Church.* a devotion consisting of prayers or services on nine consecutive days. [C19: from Med. L, from L *novem* nine]

novice ❶ ('nɒvɪs) *n* **1a** a person who is new to or inexperienced in a certain task, situation, etc.; beginner; tyro. **1b** *(as modifier): novice driver.* **2** a probationer in a religious order. **3** a racehorse that has not won a specified number of races. [C14: via OF from L *novīcius*, from *novus* new]

novitiate ❶ *or* **noviciate** (nəʊ'vɪʃɪɪt, -ˌeɪt) *n* **1** the state of being a novice, esp. in a religious order, or the period for which this lasts. **2** the part of a religious house where the novices live. [C17: from F *noviciat*, from L *novīcius* NOVICE]

Novocaine ('nəʊvəˌkeɪn) *n* a trademark for **procaine hydrochloride.** See **procaine.**

now ❶ (naʊ) *adv* **1** at or for the present time. **2** immediately. **3** in these times; nowadays. **4** given the present circumstances: *now we'll have to stay to the end.* **5** (preceded by *just*) very recently: *he left just now.* **6** (often preceded by *just*) very soon: *he is leaving just now.* **7 (every) now and again** *or* **then.** occasionally; on and off. **8 now now!** an exclamation used to rebuke or pacify someone. ◆ *conj* **9** *(subordinating;* often foll. by *that)* seeing that: *now you're in charge, things will be better.* ◆ *sentence connector.* **10a** used as a hesitation word: *now, I can't really say.* **10b** used for emphasis: *now listen to this.* **10c** used at the end of a command: *run along, now.* ◆ *n* **11** the present time: *now is the time to go.* ◆ *adj* **12** *Inf.* of the moment; fashionable: *the now look.* [OE *nū*]

nowadays ❶ ('naʊəˌdeɪz) *adv* in these times. [C14: from NOW + *adays* from OE *a* on + *daeges* genitive of DAY]

noway ('nəʊˌweɪ) *adv* **1** not at all. ◆ *sentence substitute.* **no way. 2** used to make an emphatic refusal, denial, etc.

Nowel *or* **Nowell** (nəʊ'ɛl) *n* archaic spellings of **Noel.**

nowhere ('nəʊwɛə) *adv* **1** in, at, or to no place; not anywhere. **2 get nowhere (fast).** *Inf.* to fail completely to make any progress. **3 nowhere near.** far from; not nearly. ◆ *n* **4** a nonexistent or insignificant place. **5 middle of nowhere.** a completely isolated place.

no-win *adj* offering no possibility of a favourable outcome (esp. in **a no-win situation**).

nowise ('nəʊˌwaɪz) *adv* in no manner; not at all.

nowt (naʊt) *n N English.* a dialect word for **nothing.** [from NAUGHT]

noxious ❶ ('nɒkʃəs) *adj* poisonous or harmful. [C17: from L *noxius* harmful, from *noxa* injury]
▸'**noxiously** *adv* ▸'**noxiousness** *n*

nozzle ('nɒzᵊl) *n* a projecting pipe or spout from which fluid is discharged. [C17 *nosle, nosel,* dim. of NOSE]

Np *the chemical symbol for* neptunium.

NP *or* **np.** *abbrev. for* Notary Public.

NPA *abbrev. for* Newspaper Publishers' Association.

NPD *Commerce. abbrev. for* new product development.

NPL *abbrev. for* National Physical Laboratory.

NPV *abbrev. for:* **1** net present value. **2** no par value.

NRV *abbrev. for* net realizable value.

NS *abbrev. for:* **1** New Style (method of reckoning dates). **2** Nova Scotia. **3** Nuclear Ship.

NSAID *abbrev. for* nonsteroidal anti-inflammatory drug: any of a class of drugs, including aspirin and ibuprofen, used for treating rheumatic diseases.

NSB (in Britain) *abbrev. for* National Savings Bank.

NSC (in Britain) *abbrev. for* National Safety Council.

NSG *Brit. education. abbrev. for* nonstatutory guidelines: practical nonmandatory advice and information on the implementation of the National Curriculum.

NSPCC (in Britain) *abbrev. for* National Society for the Prevention of Cruelty to Children.

NST (in Canada) abbrev. for Newfoundland Standard Time.

NSU *abbrev. for* nonspecific urethritis.

NSW *abbrev. for* New South Wales.

NT *abbrev. for:* **1** (in Britain) National Trust. **2** New Testament. **3** Northern Territory. **4** no-trump.

-n't *contraction of* not: used as an enclitic after *be* and *have* when they function as main verbs and after auxiliary verbs or verbs operating syntactically as auxiliaries: *can't; don't; isn't.*

nth (ɛnθ) *adj* **1** *Maths.* of or representing an unspecified ordinal number, usually the greatest in a series: *the nth power.* **2** *Inf.* being the last or most extreme of a long series: *for the nth time.* **3 to the nth degree.** *Inf.* to the utmost extreme.

NTP *abbrev. for* normal temperature and pressure. Also: **STP.**

nt. wt. *or* **nt wt** *abbrev. for* net weight.

n-type *adj* **1** (of a semiconductor) having more conduction electrons than mobile holes. **2** associated with or resulting from the movement of electrons in a semiconductor.

nu (nju:) *n* the 13th letter in the Greek alphabet (Ν, ν), a consonant. [from Gk, of Semitic origin]

nuance ❶ (nju:'ɑ:ns, 'nju:ɑ:ns) *n* a subtle difference in colour, meaning, tone, etc. [C18: from F, from *nuer* to show light and shade, ult. from L *nūbēs* a cloud]

nub ❶ (nʌb) *n* **1** a small lump or protuberance. **2** a small piece or chunk. **3** the point or gist: *the nub of a story.* [C16: var. of *knub*, from MLow G *knubbe* KNOB]
▸'**nubbly** *or* '**nubby** *adj*

nubble ('nʌbᵊl) *n* a small lump. [C19: dim. of NUB]

nubile ❶ ('nju:baɪl) *adj* (of a girl) **1** ready or suitable for marriage by virtue of age or maturity. **2** sexually attractive. [C17: from L *nūbilis*, from *nūbere* to marry]
▸**nubility** (nju:'bɪlɪtɪ) *n*

nucha ('nju:kə) *n, pl* **nuchae** (-ki:). *Zool., anat.* the back or nape of the neck. [C14: from Med. L, from Ar.: spinal marrow]
▸'**nuchal** *adj*

nuclear ('nju:klɪə) *adj* **1** of or involving the nucleus of an atom: *nuclear fission.* **2** *Biol.* of, relating to, or contained within the nucleus of a cell: *a nuclear membrane.* **3** of, forming, or resembling any other kind of nucleus. **4** of or operated by energy from fission or fusion of atomic nuclei: *a nuclear weapon.* **5** involving or possessing nuclear weapons: *nuclear war.*

nuclear bomb *n* a bomb whose force is due to uncontrolled nuclear fusion or nuclear fission.

nuclear chemistry *n* the branch of chemistry concerned with nuclear reactions.

nuclear energy *n* energy released during a nuclear reaction as a result of fission or fusion. Also called: **atomic energy.**

THESAURUS

novel[1] *n* **1** = **story**, fiction, narrative, romance, tale

novel[2] *adj* = **new**, different, fresh, groundbreaking, innovative, left-field (*inf.*), original, rare, singular, strange, uncommon, unfamiliar, unusual
Antonyms *adj* ancient, common, customary, familiar, habitual, old-fashioned, ordinary, run-of-the-mill, traditional, usual

novelty *n* **1** = **newness**, freshness, innovation, oddity, originality, strangeness, surprise, unfamiliarity, uniqueness **3** = **trinket**, bagatelle, bauble, curiosity, gadget, gewgaw, gimmick, knick-knack, memento, souvenir, trifle

novice *n* **1** = **beginner**, amateur, apprentice, convert, learner, neophyte, newcomer, proselyte, pupil, trainee, tyro **2** = **novitiate**, probationer
Antonyms *n* ≠ **beginner**: ace, doyen, expert, grandmaster, guru, master, maven, old hand, professional, teacher

novitiate *n* **1** = **probation**, apprenticeship, training

now *adv* **2** = **immediately**, at once, instanter (*Law*), instantly, presently (*Scot. & US*), promptly, straightaway **3** = **nowadays**, any more, at the moment, these days **7 (every) now and again** *or* **then** = **occasionally**, at times, from time to time, infrequently, intermittently, on and off, once in a while, on occasion, sometimes, sporadically

nowadays *adv* = **now**, any more, at the moment, in this day and age, these days, today

noxious *adj* = **harmful**, baneful (*arch.*), corrupting, deadly, deleterious, destructive, detrimental, foul, hurtful, injurious, insalubrious, noisome, pernicious, pestilential, poisonous, unhealthy, unwholesome
Antonyms *adj* innocuous, innoxious, inoffensive, nontoxic, not dangerous, safe, unobjectionable

nuance *n* = **subtlety**, degree, distinction, gradation, graduation, hint, nicety, refinement, shade, shadow, suggestion, suspicion, tinge, touch, trace

nub *n* **1** = **knob**, bulge, bump, knot, lump, node, protuberance, swelling **3** = **gist**, core, crux, essence, heart, kernel, nucleus, pith, point

nubile *adj* **1** = **marriageable**, ripe (*inf.*)

nuclear family *n Sociol., anthropol.* a primary social unit consisting of parents and their offspring.
nuclear fission *n* the splitting of an atomic nucleus into approximately equal parts, either spontaneously or as a result of the impact of a particle usually with an associated release of energy. Sometimes shortened to **fission.**
nuclear fuel *n* a fuel that provides nuclear energy, used in nuclear submarines, etc.
nuclear fusion *n* a reaction in which two nuclei combine to form a nucleus with the release of energy. Sometimes shortened to **fusion.**
nuclear magnetic resonance *n* a technique for determining the magnetic moments of nuclei by subjecting a substance to high-frequency radiation and a large magnetic field. It is used for determining structure, esp. in body scanning. Abbrev.: **NMR.**
nuclear medicine *n* the branch of medicine concerned with the use of radionuclides in the diagnosis and treatment of disease.
nuclear physics *n (functioning as sing)* the branch of physics concerned with the structure and behaviour of the nucleus and the particles of which it consists.
nuclear power *n* power, esp. electrical or motive, produced by a nuclear reactor. Also called: **atomic power.**
nuclear reaction *n* a process in which the structure and energy content of an atomic nucleus is changed by interaction with another nucleus or particle.
nuclear reactor *n* a device in which a nuclear reaction is maintained and controlled for the production of nuclear energy. Sometimes shortened to **reactor.**
nuclear waste *n* another name for **radioactive waste.**
nuclear winter *n* a period of low temperatures and little light that has been suggested would occur after a nuclear war.
nuclease ('nju:klɪˌeɪz) *n* any of a group of enzymes that hydrolyse nucleic acids to simple nucleotides.
nucleate *adj* ('nju:klɪɪt, -ˌeɪt). **1** having a nucleus. ◆ *vb* ('nju:klɪˌeɪt), **nucleates, nucleating, nucleated.** *(intr)* **2** to form a nucleus.
nuclei ('nju:klɪˌaɪ) *n* a plural of **nucleus.**
nucleic acid (nju:'kli:ɪk, -'kleɪ-) *n Biochem.* any of a group of complex compounds with a high molecular weight that are vital constituents of all living cells. See also **RNA, DNA.**
nucleo- *or before a vowel* **nucle-** *combining form.* **1** nucleus or nuclear. **2** nucleic acid. [from Latin *nucleus* kernel, from *nux* nut]
nucleolus (ˌnju:klɪ'əʊləs) *n, pl* **nucleoli** (-laɪ). a small rounded body within a resting cell nucleus that contains RNA and proteins and is involved in protein synthesis. Also called: **nucleole.** [C19: from L, dim. of NUCLEUS]
►ˌ**nucle'olar** *adj*
nucleon ('nju:klɪˌɒn) *n* a proton or neutron, esp. one present in an atomic nucleus.
nucleonics (ˌnju:klɪ'ɒnɪks) *n (functioning as sing)* the branch of physics concerned with the applications of nuclear energy.
►ˌ**nucle'onic** *adj* ►ˌ**nucle'onically** *adv*
nucleon number *n* the number of nucleons in an atomic nucleus; mass number.
nucleophile ('nju:klɪəˌfaɪl) *n* a molecule or ion that can donate electrons.
►**nucleophilic** (ˌnju:klɪə'fɪlɪk) *adj*
nucleoside ('nju:klɪəˌsaɪd) *n Biochem.* a compound containing a purine or pyrimidine base linked to a sugar (usually ribose or deoxyribose).
nucleotide ('nju:klɪəˌtaɪd) *n Biochem.* a compound consisting of a nucleoside linked to phosphoric acid.
nucleus Ⓣ ('nju:klɪəs) *n, pl* **nuclei** *or* **nucleuses. 1** a central or fundamental thing around which others are grouped; core. **2** a centre of growth or development; basis: *the nucleus of an idea.* **3** *Biol.* the spherical or ovoid compartment of a cell that contains the chromosomes and associated molecules that control the characteristics and growth of the cell. **4** *Astron.* the central portion in the head of a comet, consisting of small solid particles of ice and frozen gases. **5** *Physics.* the positively charged dense region at the centre of an atom, composed of protons and neutrons, about which electrons orbit. **6** *Chem.* a fundamental group of atoms in a molecule serving as the base structure for related compounds. [C18: from L: kernel, from *nux* nut]
nuclide ('nju:klaɪd) *n* a species of atom characterized by its atomic number and its mass number. [C20: from NUCLEO- + *-ide,* from Gk *eidos* shape]
nude Ⓣ (nju:d) *adj* **1** completely undressed. **2** having no covering; bare; exposed. **3** *Law.* **3a** lacking some essential legal requirement. **3b** (of a contract, etc.) made without consideration and void unless under seal. ◆ *n* **4** the state of being naked (esp. in **in the nude**). **5** a naked figure, esp. in painting, sculpture, etc. [C16: from L *nūdus*]
►'**nudely** *adv*
nudge Ⓣ (nʌdʒ) *vb* **nudges, nudging, nudged.** *(tr)* **1** to push (someone) gently, esp. with the elbow, to get attention; jog. **2** to push slowly or lightly: *as I drove out, I just nudged the gatepost.* ◆ *n* **3** a gentle poke or push. [C17: ?from Scand.]
►'**nudger** *n*
nudibranch ('nju:dɪˌbræŋk) *n* a marine gastropod of an order characterized by a shell-less, often beautifully coloured, body bearing external gills. Also called: **sea slug.** [C19: from L *nudus* naked + *branche,* from L *branchia* gills]
nudism ('nju:dɪzəm) *n* the practice of nudity, esp. for reasons of health, etc.
►'**nudist** *n, adj*
nudity Ⓣ ('nju:dɪtɪ) *n, pl* **nudities.** the state or fact of being nude; nakedness.
nugatory Ⓣ ('nju:gətərɪ, -trɪ) *adj* **1** of little value. **2** not valid: *a nugatory law.* [C17: from L *nūgātōrius,* from *nūgārī* to jest, from *nūgae* trifles]
nugget Ⓣ ('nʌgɪt) *n* **1** a small piece or lump, esp. of gold in its natural state. **2** something small but valuable or excellent. [C19: from ?]
nuggety ('nʌgɪtɪ) *adj* **1** of or resembling a nugget. **2** *Austral. & NZ inf.* (of a person) thickset; stocky.
nuisance Ⓣ ('nju:səns) *n* **1a** a person or thing that causes annoyance or bother. **1b** *(as modifier)*: *nuisance calls.* **2** *Law.* something unauthorized that is obnoxious or injurious to the community at large or to an individual, esp. in relation to his ownership of property. **3 nuisance value.** the usefulness of a person's or thing's capacity to cause difficulties or irritation. [C15: via OF from *nuire* to injure, from L *nocēre*]
NUJ (in Britain) *abbrev. for* National Union of Journalists.
nuke (nju:k) *Sl., chiefly US.* ◆ *vb* **nukes, nuking, nuked.** *(tr)* **1** to attack or destroy with nuclear weapons. ◆ *n* **2** a nuclear bomb.
null Ⓣ (nʌl) *adj* **1** without legal force; invalid; (esp. in **null and void**). **2** without value or consequence; useless. **3** lacking distinction; characterless. **4** nonexistent; amounting to nothing. **5** *Maths.* **5a** quantitatively zero. **5b** relating to zero. **5c** (of a set) having no members. **6** *Physics.* involving measurement in which conditions are adjusted so that an instrument has a zero reading, as with a Wheatstone bridge. [C16: from L *nullus* none, from *ne* not + *ullus* any]
nullah ('nʌlɑ:) *n* a stream or drain. [C18: from Hindi *nālā*]
null hypothesis *n Statistics.* the residual hypothesis if the alternative hypothesis tested against it fails to achieve a predetermined significance level.
nullify Ⓣ ('nʌlɪˌfaɪ) *vb* **nullifies, nullifying, nullified.** *(tr)* **1** to render legally void or of no effect. **2** to render ineffective or useless; cancel out. [C16: from LL *nullificāre* to despise, from L *nullus* of no account + *facere* to make]
►ˌ**nullifi'cation** *n*
nullity Ⓣ ('nʌlɪtɪ) *n, pl* **nullities. 1** the state of being null. **2** a null or legally invalid act or instrument. **3** something null, ineffective, characterless, etc. [C16: from Med. L *nullitās,* from L *nullus* no, not any]
NUM (in Britain) *abbrev. for* National Union of Mineworkers.
num. *abbrev. for:* **1** number. **2** numeral.
Num. *Bible. abbrev. for* Numbers.
numb Ⓣ (nʌm) *adj* **1** deprived of feeling through cold, shock, etc. **2** unable to move; paralysed. ◆ *vb* **3** *(tr)* to make numb; deaden, shock, or paralyse. [C15 *nomen,* lit.: taken (with paralysis), from OE *niman* to take]
►'**numbly** *adv* ►'**numbness** *n*
numbat ('nʌmˌbæt) *n* a small Australian marsupial having a long snout and tongue and strong claws for hunting and feeding on termites. [C20: from Abor.]
number Ⓣ ('nʌmbə) *n* **1** a concept of quantity that is or can be derived from a single unit, the sum of a collection of units, or zero. Every number occupies a unique position in a sequence, enabling it to be used in counting. See also **cardinal number, ordinal number. 2** the symbol used to represent a number; numeral. **3** a numeral or string of numerals used to identify a person or thing: *a telephone number.* **4** the person or thing so identified or designated: *she was number seven in the race.* **5** sum or quantity: *a large number of people.* **6** one of a series, as of a maga-

THESAURUS

nucleus *n* **1 = centre,** basis, core, focus, heart, kernel, nub, pivot
nude *adj* **1 = naked,** *au naturel,* bare, buck naked (*sl.*), disrobed, exposed, in one's birthday suit (*inf.*), in the altogether (*inf.*), in the buff (*inf.*), naked as the day one was born (*Inf.*), starkers (*inf.*), stark-naked, stripped, unclad, unclothed, uncovered, undraped, undressed, without a stitch on (*inf.*)
Antonyms *adj* attired, clothed, covered, dressed
nudge *vb, n* **1, 3 = push,** bump, dig, elbow, jog, poke, prod, shove, touch
nudity *n* **= nakedness,** bareness, deshabille, nudism, undress
nugatory *adj* **1 = trivial,** insignificant, trifling, valueless, worthless **2 = invalid,** bootless, futile, ineffectual, inoperative, null and void, unavailing, useless, vain
nugget *n* **1 = lump,** chunk, clump, hunk, mass, piece
nuisance *n* **1a = problem,** annoyance, bore, bother, drag, gall, hassle (*inf.*), inconvenience, infliction, irritation, offence, pain in the neck, pest, plague, trouble, vexation
Antonyms *n* benefit, blessing, delight, happiness, joy, pleasure, satisfaction
null *adj* **1 = invalid,** inoperative, void **2 = useless,** ineffectual, powerless, vain, valueless, worthless **3 = characterless 4 = nonexistent**
nullify *vb* **1 = invalidate,** abolish, abrogate, annul, countervail, render null and void, repeal, rescind, revoke, veto, void **2 = cancel out,** bring to naught, counteract, negate, neutralize, obviate
Antonyms *vb* ≠ **invalidate:** authorize, confirm, endorse, ratify, validate
nullity *n* **1 = worthlessness,** characterlessness, ineffectualness, invalidity, nonexistence, powerlessness, uselessness, valuelessness, voidness
numb *adj* **1 = unfeeling,** benumbed, dead, deadened, frozen, immobilized, insensible, insensitive, paralysed, stupefied, torpid ◆ *vb* **3 = deaden,** benumb, dull, freeze, immobilize, paralyse, stun, stupefy
Antonyms *adj* ≠ **unfeeling:** feeling, responsive, sensitive, sentient
number *n* **2 = numeral,** character, count, digit, figure, integer **5 = sum,** aggregate, amount,

zine; issue. **7a** a self-contained piece of pop or jazz music. **7b** a self-contained part of an opera or other musical score. **8** a group of people, esp. an exclusive group: *he was not one of our number.* **9** *Sl.* a person, esp. a sexually attractive girl: *who's that nice little number?* **10** *Inf.* an admired article: *that little number is by Dior.* **11** a grammatical category for the variation in form of nouns, pronouns, and any words agreeing with them, depending on how many persons or things are referred to. **12 any number of.** several or many. **13 by numbers.** *Mil.* (of a drill procedure, etc.) performed step by step, each move being made on the call of a number. **14 get** *or* **have someone's number.** *Inf.* to discover a person's true character or intentions. **15 one's number is up.** *Brit. inf.* one is finished; one is ruined or about to die. **16 without** *or* **beyond number.** innumerable. ◆ *vb (mainly tr)* **17** to assign a number to. **18** to add up to; total. **19** *(also intr)* to list (items) one by one; enumerate. **20** *(also intr)* to put or be put into a group, category, etc.: *they were numbered among the worst hit.* **21** to limit the number of: *his days were numbered.* [C13: from OF *nombre,* from L *numerus*]

number crunching *n Computing.* the large-scale processing of numerical data.

numbered account *n Banking.* an account identified only by a number, esp. one in a Swiss bank that could contain funds illegally obtained.

numberless ⓣ (ˈnʌmbəlɪs) *adj* **1** too many to be counted; countless. **2** not containing numbers.

number one *n* **1** the first in a series or sequence. **2** an informal phrase for **oneself, myself,** etc.: *to look after number one.* **3** *Inf.* the most important person; chief: *he's number one in the organization.* **4** *Inf.* the bestselling pop record in any one week. ◆ *adj* **5** first in importance, urgency, quality, etc.: *number one priority.*

numberplate (ˈnʌmbəˌpleɪt) *n* a plate mounted on the front and back of a motor vehicle bearing the registration number. Usual US term: **license plate,** (Canad.) **licence plate.**

numbers game *or* **racket** *n US.* an illegal lottery in which money is wagered on a certain combination of digits appearing at the beginning of a series of numbers published in a newspaper, as in share prices or sports results. Often shortened to **numbers.**

Number Ten *n* 10 Downing Street, the British prime minister's official London residence.

number theory *n* the study of integers, their properties, and the relationship between integers.

numbfish (ˈnʌmˌfɪʃ) *n, pl* **numbfish** *or* **numbfishes.** any of several electric rays. [C18: so called because it numbs its victims]

numbles (ˈnʌmbᵊlz) *pl n Arch.* the heart, lungs, liver, etc., of a deer or other animal. [C14: from OF *nombles,* pl. of *nomble* thigh muscle of a deer, changed from L *lumbulus,* dim. of *lumbus* loin]

numbskull ⓣ *or* **numskull** (ˈnʌmˌskʌl) *n* a stupid person; dolt.

numen (ˈnjuːmɛn) *n, pl* **numina** (-mɪnə). **1** (esp. in ancient Roman religion) a deity or spirit presiding over a thing or place. **2** a guiding principle, force, or spirit. [C17: from L: a nod (indicating a command), divine power]

numerable (ˈnjuːmərəbᵊl) *adj* able to be numbered or counted.
▸ˈ**numerably** *adv*

numeral ⓣ (ˈnjuːmərəl) *n* **1** a symbol or group of symbols used to express a number: for example, *6 (Arabic), VI (Roman), 110 (binary).* ◆ *adj* **2** of, consisting of, or denoting a number. [C16: from LL *numerālis* belonging to number, from L *numerus*]

numerate *adj* (ˈnjuːmərɪt). **1** able to use numbers, esp. in arithmetical operations. ◆ *vb* (ˈnjuːməˌreɪt), **numerates, numerating, numerated.** *(tr)* **2** to read (a numerical expression). **3** a less common word for **enumerate.** [C18 (vb): from L *numerus* number + -ATE[1], by analogy with *literate*]
▸**numeracy** (ˈnjuːmərəsɪ) *n*

numeration (ˌnjuːməˈreɪʃən) *n* **1** the writing, reading, or naming of numbers. **2** a system of numbering.
▸ˈ**numerative** *adj*

numerator (ˈnjuːməˌreɪtə) *n* **1** *Maths.* the dividend of a fraction: the numerator of 7/8 is 7. Cf. **denominator. 2** a person or thing that numbers; enumerator.

numerical (njuːˈmɛrɪkᵊl) *or* **numeric** *adj* **1** of, relating to, or denoting a number or numbers. **2** measured or expressed in numbers: *numerical value.*
▸**nuˈmerically** *adv*

numerology (ˌnjuːməˈrɒlədʒɪ) *n* the study of numbers and of their supposed influence on human affairs.
▸**numerological** (ˌnjuːmərəˈlɒdʒɪkᵊl) *adj*

numerous ⓣ (ˈnjuːmərəs) *adj* **1** being many. **2** consisting of many parts: *a numerous collection.*
▸ˈ**numerously** *adv* ▸ˈ**numerousness** *n*

numinous ⓣ (ˈnjuːmɪnəs) *adj* **1** denoting, being, or relating to a numen; divine. **2** arousing spiritual or religious emotions. **3** mysterious or awe-inspiring. [C17: from L *numin-,* NUMEN + -OUS]

numismatics (ˌnjuːmɪzˈmætɪks) *n (functioning as sing)* the study or collection of coins, medals, etc. Also called: ˌ**numismaˈtology.** [C18: from F *numismatique,* from L *nomisma,* from Gk: piece of currency, from *nomizein* to have in use, from *nomos* use]
▸ˌ**numisˈmatic** *adj* ▸ˌ**numisˈmatically** *adv*

nummulite (ˈnʌmjʊˌlaɪt) *n* any of a family of large fossil protozoans common in Tertiary times. [C19: from NL, from L *nummulus,* from *nummus* coin]

numpty (ˈnʌmptɪ) *n, pl* **numpties.** *Scot. inf.* a foolish or ignorant person.

numskull (ˈnʌmˌskʌl) *n* a variant spelling of **numbskull.**

nun (nʌn) *n* a female member of a religious order. [OE *nunne,* from Church L *nonna,* from LL: form of address used for an elderly woman]
▸ˈ**nunhood** *n* ▸ˈ**nunlike** *adj*

nun buoy *n Naut.* a buoy, conical at the top, marking the right side of a channel leading into a harbour: green in British waters but red in US waters. [C18: from obs. *nun* child's spinning top + BUOY]

Nunc Dimittis (ˈnʌŋk dɪˈmɪtɪs, ˈnʊŋk) *n* **1** the Latin name for the Canticle of Simeon (Luke 2:29–32). **2** a musical setting of this. [from the opening words (Vulgate): now let depart]

nunciature (ˈnʌnsɪətʃə) *n* the office or term of office of a nuncio. [C17: from It. *nunziatura;* see NUNCIO]

nuncio ⓣ (ˈnʌnʃɪˌəʊ, -sɪ-) *n, pl* **nuncios.** *RC Church.* a diplomatic representative of the Holy See. [C16: via It. from L *nuntius* messenger]

nunnery ⓣ (ˈnʌnərɪ) *n, pl* **nunneries.** the convent or religious house of a community of nuns.

NUPE (ˈnjuːpɪ) *n* (formerly, in Britain) *acronym for* National Union of Public Employees.

nuptial ⓣ (ˈnʌpʃəl, -tʃəl) *adj* **1** relating to marriage; conjugal: *nuptial vows.* **2** *Zool.* of or relating to mating: *the nuptial flight of a queen bee.* [C15: from L *nuptiālis,* from *nuptiae* marriage, from *nubere* to marry]
▸ˈ**nuptially** *adv*

nuptials ⓣ (ˈnʌpʃəlz, -tʃəlz) *pl n (sometimes sing)* a marriage ceremony; wedding.

NUR (formerly, in Britain) *abbrev. for* National Union of Railwaymen.

nurd a variant spelling of **nerd.**

nurse ⓣ (nɜːs) *n* **1** a person, often a woman, who is trained to tend the sick and infirm, assist doctors, etc. **2** short for **nursemaid. 3** a woman employed to breast-feed another woman's child; wet nurse. **4** a worker in a colony of social insects that takes care of the larvae. ◆ *vb* **nurses, nursing, nursed.** *(mainly tr)* **5** *(also intr)* to tend (the sick). **6** *(also intr)* to feed (a baby) at the breast. **7** to try to cure (an ailment). **8** to clasp fondly: *she nursed the child in her arms.* **9** to look after (a child) as one's employment. **10** to harbour; preserve: *to nurse a grudge.* **11** to give special attention to, esp. in order to promote goodwill: *to nurse a difficult constituency.* **12** *Billiards.* to keep (the balls) together for a series of cannons. [C16: from earlier *norice,* OF *nourice,* from LL *nūtrīcia,* from L *nūtrīcius* nourishing, from *nūtrīre* to nourish]

nursemaid (ˈnɜːsˌmeɪd) *or* **nurserymaid** *n* a woman employed to look after someone else's children. Often shortened to **nurse.**

nursery ⓣ (ˈnɜːsrɪ) *n, pl* **nurseries. 1** a room in a house set apart for children. **2** a place where plants, young trees, etc., are grown commercially. **3** an establishment providing daycare for babies and young children; crèche. **4** anywhere serving to foster or nourish new ideas, etc. **5** Also called: **nursery cannon.** *Billiards.* **5a** a series of cannons with the three balls adjacent to a cushion, esp. near a corner pocket. **5b** a cannon in such a series.

nurseryman (ˈnɜːsrɪmən) *n, pl* **nurserymen.** a person who owns or works in a nursery in which plants are grown.

nursery rhyme *n* a short traditional verse or song for children, such as *Little Jack Horner.*

nursery school *n* a school for young children, usually from three to five years old.

nursery slopes *pl n* gentle slopes used by beginners in skiing.

THESAURUS

total **6** = **issue**, copy, edition, imprint, printing **8** = **quantity**, collection, company, crowd, horde, many, multitude, throng ◆ *vb* **18** = **calculate**, account, add, compute, count, include, reckon, tell, total **19** = **list**, enumerate
Antonyms *n* ≠ **quantity:** insufficiency, lack, scantiness, scarcity, shortage, want ◆ *vb* ≠ **calculate:** conjecture, guess, theorize

numbered *adj* **20** = **included**, categorized, contained, counted, designated, fixed, specified **21** = **limited**, limited in number

numberless *adj* **1** = **infinite**, countless, endless, innumerable, multitudinous, myriad, unnumbered, untold

numbness *n* **1** = **deadness**, dullness, insensibility, insensitivity, stupefaction, torpor, unfeelingness

numbskull *n* = **fool**, berk, blockhead, bonehead (*sl.*), buffoon, clot (*Brit. inf.*), coot, dimwit (*inf.*), dipstick (*Brit. sl.*), divvy (*sl.*), dolt, dope (*inf.*), dork (*sl.*), dullard, dummy (*sl.*), dunce, dunderhead, fathead (*inf.*), jerk (*sl., chiefly US & Canad.*), lamebrain (*inf.*), nerd *or* nurd (*sl.*), nitwit (*inf.*), oaf, pillock (*Brit. sl.*), prat (*sl.*), prick (*sl.*), schmuck (*US sl.*), simpleton, thickhead, twit (*inf.*), wally (*sl.*)

numeral *n* **1** = **number**, character, cipher, digit, figure, integer, symbol

numerous *adj* **1** = **many**, abundant, copious, plentiful, profuse, several, thick on the ground
Antonyms *adj* few, not many, scarcely any

numinous *adj* **1-3** = **holy**, awe-inspiring, divine, heavenly, mysterious, religious, spiritual, supernatural

nuncio *n* = **ambassador**, envoy, legate, messenger

nunnery *n* = **convent**, abbey, cloister, house, monastery

nuptial *adj* **1** = **marital**, bridal, conjugal, connubial, hymeneal (*poetic*), matrimonial, wedded, wedding

nuptials *pl n* = **wedding**, espousal (*arch.*), marriage, matrimony

nurse *vb* **5** = **look after**, care for, minister to, tend, treat **6** = **breast-feed**, feed, nourish, nurture, suckle, wet-nurse **10** = **foster**, cherish, cultivate, harbour, keep alive, preserve

nursery *n* **3** = **crèche**, kindergarten, playgroup

nursery stakes *pl n* a race for two-year-old horses.
nurse shark *n* any of various sharks having an external groove on each side of the head between the mouth and nostril. [C15 *nusse fisshe* (later infl. in spelling by NURSE), ?from a division of obs. *an huss* shark, dogfish (from ?) as *a nuss*]
nursing ('nɜːsɪŋ) *n* **1a** the practice or profession of caring for the sick and injured. **1b** (*as modifier*): *a nursing home.*
nursing home *n* a private hospital or residence for aged or infirm persons.
nursing officer *n* (in Britain) the official name for **matron** (sense 4).
nursling *or* **nurseling** ('nɜːslɪŋ) *n* a child or young animal that is being suckled, nursed, or fostered.
nurture ('nɜːtʃə) *n* **1** the act or process of promoting the development, etc., of a child. **2** something that nourishes. ◆ *vb* **nurtures, nurturing, nurtured.** (*tr*) **3** to feed or support. **4** to educate or train. [C14: from OF *norriture,* from L *nūtrīre* to nourish]
▸'**nurtural** *adj* ▸'**nurturer** *n*
NUS (in Britain) *abbrev. for:* **1** (formerly) National Union of Seamen. **2** National Union of Students.
nut (nʌt) *n* **1** a dry one-seeded indehiscent fruit that usually possesses a woody wall. **2** (*not in technical use*) any similar fruit, such as the walnut, having a hard shell and an edible kernel. **3** the edible kernel of such a fruit. **4** *Sl.* an eccentric or mad person. **5** *Sl.* the head. **6 do one's nut.** *Brit. sl.* to be extremely angry. **7 off one's nut.** *Sl.* mad or foolish. **8** a person or thing that presents difficulties (esp. in **a tough nut to crack**). **9** a small square hexagonal block, usually metal, with a threaded hole through the middle for screwing on the end of a bolt. **10** Also called (US and Canad.): **frog.** *Music.* **10a** the ridge at the upper end of the fingerboard of a violin, cello, etc., over which the strings pass to the tuning pegs. **10b** the end of a violin bow that is held by the player. **11** a small usually gingery biscuit. **12** *Brit.* a small piece of coal. ◆ *vb* **nuts, nutting, nutted. 13** (*intr*) to gather nuts. ◆ See also **nuts.** [OE *hnutu*]
NUT (in Britain) *abbrev. for* National Union of Teachers.
nutant ('njuːtᵊnt) *adj Bot.* having the apex hanging down. [C18: from L *nūtāre* to nod]
nutation (njuː'teɪʃən) *n* **1** *Astron.* a periodic variation in the precession of the earth's axis causing the earth's poles to oscillate about their mean position. **2** the spiral growth of a shoot or similar plant organ, caused by variation in the growth rate in different parts. **3** the act of nodding. [C17: from L *nūtātiō,* from *nūtāre* to nod]
nutbrown ('nʌt'braʊn) *adj* reddish-brown.
nutcase ('nʌtˌkeɪs) *n Sl.* an insane or very foolish person.
nutcracker ('nʌtˌkrækə) *n* **1** (*often pl*) a device for cracking the shells of nuts. **2** either an Old World bird or a North American bird (**Clark's nutcracker**) having speckled plumage and feeding on nuts, seeds, etc.
nutgall ('nʌtˌgɔːl) *n* a nut-shaped gall caused by gall wasps on the oak and other trees.
nuthatch ('nʌtˌhætʃ) *n* a songbird having strong feet and bill, and feeding on insects, seeds, and nuts. [C14 *notehache,* from *note* nut + *hache* hatchet, from its habit of splitting nuts]
nuthouse ('nʌtˌhaʊs) *n Sl.* a mental hospital.
nutmeg ('nʌtˌmɛg) *n* **1** an East Indian evergreen tree cultivated in the tropics for its hard aromatic seed. See also **mace**[2]. **2** the seed of this tree, used as a spice. ◆ *vb* **nutmegs, nutmegging, nutmegged.** (*tr*) **3** *Brit. sport inf.* to kick or hit the ball between the legs of (an opposing player). [C13: from OF *nois muguede,* from OProvençal *noz muscada* musk-scented nut, from L *nux* NUT + *muscus* MUSK]
nutria ('njuːtrɪə) *n* another name for **coypu,** esp. the fur. [C19: from Sp., var. of *lutria,* ult. from L *lūtra* otter]
nutrient ('njuːtrɪənt) *n* **1** any of the mineral substances that are absorbed by the roots of plants. **2** any substance that nourishes an animal. ◆ *adj* **3** providing or contributing to nourishment. [C17: from L *nūtrīre* to nourish]
nutriment ('njuːtrɪmənt) *n* any material providing nourishment. [C16: from L *nūtrīmentum,* from *nūtrīre* to nourish]
▸**nutrimental** (ˌnjuːtrɪ'mɛntᵊl) *adj*
nutrition (njuː'trɪʃən) *n* **1** a process in animals and plants involving the intake and assimilation of nutrient materials. **2** the act or process of nourishing. **3** the study of nutrition, esp. in humans. [C16: from LL *nūtrītiō,* from *nūtrīre* to nourish]
▸**nu'tritional** *adj* ▸**nu'tritionist** *n*
nutritious (njuː'trɪʃəs) *adj* nourishing. [C17: from L *nūtrīcius,* from *nūtrix* NURSE]
▸**nu'tritiously** *adv* ▸**nu'tritiousness** *n*
nutritive ('njuːtrɪtɪv) *adj* **1** providing nourishment. **2** of, concerning, or promoting nutrition. ◆ *n* **3** a nutritious food.
nuts (nʌts) *adj* **1** a slang word for **insane. 2** (foll. by *about* or *on*) *Sl.* extremely fond (of) or enthusiastic (about). ◆ *interj* **3** *Sl.* an expression of contempt, refusal, or defiance.
nuts and bolts *pl n Inf.* the essential or practical details.
nutshell ('nʌtˌʃɛl) *n* **1** the shell around the kernel of a nut. **2 in a nutshell.** in essence; briefly.
nutter ('nʌtə) *n Brit. sl.* a mad or eccentric person.
nutty ('nʌtɪ) *adj* **nuttier, nuttiest. 1** containing nuts. **2** resembling nuts. **3** a slang word for **insane. 4** (foll. by *over* or *about*) *Inf.* extremely enthusiastic (about).
▸'**nuttiness** *n*
nux vomica ('nʌks 'vɒmɪkə) *n* **1** an Indian tree with orange-red berries containing poisonous seeds. **2** any of the seeds of this tree, which contain strychnine and other poisonous alkaloids. **3** a medicine manufactured from the seeds of this tree, formerly used as a heart stimulant. [C16: from Med. L: vomiting nut]
nuzzle ('nʌzᵊl) *vb* **nuzzles, nuzzling, nuzzled. 1** to push or rub gently with the nose or snout. **2** (*intr*) to nestle; lie close. **3** (*tr*) to dig out with the snout. [C15 *nosele,* from NOSE (n)]
NVQ *abbrev. for* National Vocational Qualification.
NW *symbol for* northwest(ern).
NWMP (in Canada) *abbrev. for* North West Mounted Police.
NWT *abbrev. for* Northwest Territories (of Canada).
NY *or* **N.Y.** *abbrev. for* New York (city or state).
nyala ('njɑːlə) *n, pl* **nyala** *or* **nyalas. 1** a spiral-horned southern African antelope with a fringe of white hairs along the length of the back and neck. **2 mountain nyala.** a similar Ethiopian animal lacking the white crest. [from Zulu]
NYC *abbrev. for* New York City.
nyctalopia (ˌnɪktə'ləʊpɪə) *n* inability to see normally in dim light. Nontechnical name: **night blindness.** [C17: via LL from Gk *nuktálōps,* from *nux* night + *alaos* blind + *ōps* eye]
nyctitropism (nɪk'tɪtrəˌpɪzəm) *n* a tendency of some plant parts to assume positions at night that are different from their daytime positions. [C19: *nyct-,* from Gk *nukt-, nux* night + -TROPISM]
nye (naɪ) *n* a flock of pheasants. Also called: **nide, eye.** [C15: from OF *ni,* from L *nīdus* nest]
nylon ('naɪlɒn) *n* **1** a class of synthetic polyamide materials of which monofilaments are used for bristles, etc., and fibres can be spun into yarn. **2** yarn or cloth made of nylon, used for clothing, stockings, etc. [C20: orig. a trademark]
nylons ('naɪlɒnz) *pl n* stockings made of nylon.
nymph (nɪmf) *n* **1** *Myth.* a spirit of nature envisaged as a beautiful maiden. **2** *Chiefly poetic.* a beautiful young woman. **3** the larva of insects such as the dragonfly. It resembles the adult, apart from having underdeveloped wings, and develops without a pupal stage. [C14: via OF from L, from Gk *numphē*]
▸'**nymphal** *or* **nymphean** ('nɪmfɪən)*adj* ▸'**nymphlike** *adj*
nympha ('nɪmfə) *n, pl* **nymphae** (-fiː). *Anat.* either one of the labia minora. [C17: from L: bride]
nymphet ('nɪmfɪt) *n* a young girl who is sexually precocious and desirable. [C17 (meaning: a young nymph): dim. of NYMPH]
nympho ('nɪmfəʊ) *n, pl* **nymphos.** *Inf.* short for **nymphomaniac.**
nympholepsy ('nɪmfəˌlɛpsɪ) *n, pl* **nympholepsies.** a state of violent emotion, esp. when associated with a desire for something that one cannot have. [C18: from Gk *numpholēptos* caught by nymphs, from *numphē* nymph + *lambanein* to seize]
▸'**nymphoˌlept** *n* ▸ˌ**nympho'leptic** *adj*
nymphomania (ˌnɪmfə'meɪnɪə) *n* a neurotic compulsion in women to have sexual intercourse with many men without being able to have lasting relationships with them. [C18: NL, from Gk *numphē* nymph + -MANIA]
▸ˌ**nympho'maniac** *n, adj*
nystagmus (nɪ'stægməs) *n* involuntary movement of the eye comprising a smooth drift followed by a flick back. [C19: NL, from Gk *nustagmos*]
▸**nys'tagmic** *adj*
NZ *or* **N. Zeal.** *abbrev. for* New Zealand.
NZBC (formerly) *abbrev. for* New Zealand Broadcasting Commission.
NZEF (in New Zealand) *abbrev. for* New Zealand Expeditionary Force, the New Zealand army that served 1914-18. **2NZEF** refers to the Second New Zealand Expeditionary Force, in World War II.

THESAURUS

nurture *n* **1** = **development**, discipline, education, instruction, rearing, training, upbringing **2** = **food**, diet, nourishment ◆ *vb* **3** = **nourish**, feed, nurse, support, sustain, tend **4** = **develop**, bring up, cultivate, discipline, educate, instruct, rear, school, train
Antonyms *vb* ≠ **develop, nourish:** deprive, disregard, ignore, neglect, overlook
nut *n* **1-3** = **kernel**, pip, seed, stone **4** *Slang* = **madman**, crackpot, crank (*inf.*), eccentric, headbanger (*inf.*), headcase (*inf.*), loony (*sl.*), lunatic, maniac, nutcase (*sl.*), nutter (*Brit. sl.*), oddball (*inf.*), psycho (*sl.*) **5** *Slang* = **head**, brain, mind, reason, senses
nutriment *n* = **food**, aliment, diet, foodstuff, nourishment, nutrition, subsistence, support, sustenance
nutrition *n* **1, 2** = **nourishment**, nutriment, sustenance
nutritious *adj* = **nourishing**, alimental, alimentative, beneficial, healthful, health-giving, invigorating, nutritive, strengthening, wholesome
nuts *adj* **1** *Slang* = **insane**, bananas (*sl.*), barking mad (*sl.*), batty (*sl.*), crazy, demented, deranged, doolally (*sl.*), eccentric, irrational, loony (*sl.*), loopy (*inf.*), mad, not the full shilling (*inf.*), nutty (*sl.*), off one's trolley (*sl.*), out to lunch (*inf.*), psycho (*sl.*), psychopathic, up the pole (*inf.*)
nuts and bolts *pl n Informal* = **essentials**, basics, details, fundamentals, ins and outs, nitty-gritty (*inf.*), practicalities
nuzzle *vb* **2** = **snuggle**, burrow, cuddle, fondle, nestle, nudge, pet
nymph *n* **1** = **sylph**, dryad, hamadryad, naiad, Oceanid (*Greek myth*), oread **2** *Chiefly poetic* = **girl**, damsel, lass, maid, maiden

Oo

o *or* **O** (əʊ) *n, pl* **o's, O's,** *or* **Os. 1** the 15th letter and fourth vowel of the English alphabet. **2** any of several speech sounds represented by this letter, as in *code, pot, cow,* or *form.* **3** another name for **nought.**

O[1] *symbol for:* **1** *Chem.* oxygen. **2** a human blood type of the ABO group. **3** Old.

O[2] (əʊ) *interj* **1** a variant of **oh. 2** an exclamation introducing an invocation, entreaty, wish, etc.: *O God! O for the wings of a dove!*

o. *abbrev. for:* **1** octavo. **2** old. **3** only. **4** order. **5** *Pharmacol.* pint. [from L *octarius*]

O. *abbrev. for:* **1** Ocean. **2** octavo. **3** old.

o' (ə) *prep Inf. or arch.* shortened form of **of:** *a cup o' tea.*

O'- *prefix* (in surnames of Irish Gaelic origin) descendant of: *O'Corrigan.* [from Irish Gaelic *ó, ua* descendant]

-o *suffix forming nouns.* indicating a diminutive or slang abbreviation: *wino.*

oaf 🅣 (əʊf) *n* a stupid or loutish person. [C17: var. of OE *ælf* ELF]
▸**'oafish** *adj* ▸**'oafishness** *n*

oak (əʊk) *n* **1** any deciduous or evergreen tree or shrub having acorns as fruits and lobed leaves. **2a** the wood of any of these trees, used esp. as building timber and for making furniture. **2b** (*as modifier*): *an oak table.* **3** any of various trees that resemble the oak, such as the poison oak. **4** the leaves of an oak tree, worn as a garland. [OE *āc*]

oak apple *or* **gall** *n* any of various brownish round galls on oak trees, containing the larvae of certain wasps.

oaken ('əʊkən) *adj* made of the wood of the oak.

Oaks (əʊks) *n* (*functioning as sing*) **the.** a horse race for fillies held annually at Epsom since 1779: one of the classics of English flat racing. [named after an estate near Epsom]

oakum ('əʊkəm) *n* loose fibre obtained by unravelling old rope, used esp. for caulking seams in wooden ships. [OE *ācuma,* var. of *ācumba,* lit.: off-combings, from *ā-* off + *-cumba,* from *cemban* to COMB]

O & M *abbrev. for* organization and method (in studies of working methods).

OAP (in Britain) *abbrev. for* old age pension *or* pensioner.

oar (ɔː) *n* **1** a long shaft of wood for propelling a boat by rowing, having a broad blade that is dipped into and pulled against the water. **2** short for **oarsman. 3 stick** *or* **put one's oar in.** to interfere or interrupt. ◆ *vb* **4** to row or propel with or as if with oars. [OE *ār,* of Gmc origin]
▸**'oarless** *adj* ▸**'oar,like** *adj*

oarfish ('ɔːˌfɪʃ) *n, pl* **oarfish** *or* **oarfishes.** a very long ribbonfish with long slender ventral fins. [C19: referring to the flattened oarlike body]

oarlock ('ɔːˌlɒk) *n* the usual US and Canad. word for **rowlock.**

oarsman ('ɔːzmən) *n, pl* **oarsmen.** a man who rows, esp. one who rows in a racing boat.
▸**'oarsmanship** *n*

OAS *abbrev. for:* **1** *Organisation de l'Armée Secrète;* an organization which opposed Algerian independence by acts of terrorism. **2** Organization of American States.

oasis 🅣 (əʊ'eɪsɪs) *n, pl* **oases** (-iːz). **1** a fertile patch in a desert occurring where the water table approaches or reaches the ground surface. **2** a place of peace, safety, or happiness. [C17: via L from Gk, prob. from Egyptian]

oast (əʊst) *n Chiefly Brit.* **1** a kiln for drying hops. **2** Also called: **oast house.** a building containing such kilns, usually having a conical or pyramidal roof. [OE *āst*]

oat (əʊt) *n* **1** an erect annual grass grown in temperate regions for its edible seed. **2** (*usually pl*) the seeds or fruits of this grass. **3** any of various other grasses such as the wild oat. **4** *Poetic.* a flute made from an oat straw. **5 feel one's oats.** *US & Canad. inf.* **5a** to feel exuberant. **5b** to feel self-important. **6 sow one's (wild) oats.** to indulge in adventure or promiscuity during youth. [OE *āte,* from ?]

oatcake ('əʊtˌkeɪk) *n* a crisp brittle unleavened biscuit made of oatmeal.

oaten ('əʊtᵊn) *adj* made of oats or oat straw.

oath 🅣 (əʊθ) *n, pl* **oaths** (əʊðz). **1** a solemn pronouncement to affirm the truth of a statement or to pledge a person to some course of action. **2** the form of such a pronouncement. **3** an irreverent or blasphemous expression, esp. one involving the name of a deity; curse. **4 my oath.** *Austral. sl.* certainly; yes indeed. **5 on, upon,** *or* **under oath. 5a** under the obligation of an oath. **5b** *Law.* having sworn to tell the truth, usually with one's hand on the Bible. **6 take an oath.** to declare formally with a pledge, esp. before giving evidence. [OE *āth*]

oatmeal ('əʊtˌmiːl) *n* **1** meal ground from oats, used for making porridge, oatcakes, etc. **2a** a greyish-yellow colour. **2b** (*as adj*): *an oatmeal coat.*

OAU *abbrev. for* Organization of African Unity.

OB *Brit. abbrev. for:* **1** Old Boy. **2** outside broadcast.

ob. *abbrev. for:* **1** (on tombstones, etc.) obiit. [L: he (or she) died] **2** obiter. [L: incidentally; in passing] **3** oboe.

ob- *prefix* inverse or inversely: *obovate.* [from OF, from L *ob.* In compound words from L, *ob-* (and *oc-, of-, op-*) indicates: to, towards (*object*); against (*oppose*); away from (*obsolete*); before (*obstetric*); and is used as an intensifier (*oblong*)]

Obad. *Bible. abbrev. for* Obadiah.

obbligato *or* **obligato** (ˌɒblɪ'gɑːtəʊ) *Music.* ◆ *adj* **1** not to be omitted in performance ◆ *n, pl* **obbligatos, obbligati** (-tiː) *or* **obligatos, obligati** (-tiː). **2** an essential part in a score: *with oboe obbligato.* [C18: from It., from *obbligare* to OBLIGE]

obconic (ɒb'kɒnɪk) *or* **obconical** *adj Bot.* (of a fruit) shaped like a cone and attached at the pointed end.

obcordate (ɒb'kɔːdeɪt) *adj Bot.* heart-shaped and attached at the pointed end: *obcordate leaves.*

obdurate 🅣 ('ɒbdjʊrɪt) *adj* **1** not easily moved by feelings or supplication; hardhearted. **2** impervious to persuasion. [C15: from L *obdūrāre* to make hard, from *ob-* (intensive) + *dūrus* hard]
▸**'obduracy** *or* **'obdurateness** *n* ▸**'obdurately** *adv*

OBE *abbrev. for* Officer of the Order of the British Empire (a Brit. title).

obeah ('əʊbɪə) *n* **1** a kind of witchcraft practised by some West Indians. **2** a charm used in this. [of W African origin]

obedience 🅣 (ə'biːdɪəns) *n* **1** the condition or quality of being obedient. **2** the act or an instance of obeying; dutiful or submissive behaviour. **3** the authority vested in a Church or similar body. **4** the collective group of persons submitting to this authority.

obedient 🅣 (ə'biːdɪənt) *adj* obeying or willing to obey. [C13: from OF, from L *oboediens,* present participle of *oboedīre* to OBEY]
▸**o'bediently** *adv*

obeisance 🅣 (əʊ'beɪsəns) *n* **1** an attitude of deference or homage. **2** a gesture expressing obeisance. [C14: from OF *obéissant,* present participle of *obéir* to OBEY]
▸**o'beisant** *adj*

obelisk 🅣 ('ɒbɪlɪsk) *n* **1** a stone pillar having a square or rectangular cross section and sides that taper towards a pyramidal top. **2** *Printing.* another name for **dagger** (sense 2). [C16: via L from Gk *obeliskos* a little spit, from *obelos* spit]
▸ˌ**obe'liscal** *adj* ▸ˌ**obe'liskoid** *adj*

obelus ('ɒbɪləs) *n, pl* **obeli** (-laɪ). **1** a mark (— or ÷) used in ancient documents to indicate spurious words or passages. **2** another name for **dagger** (sense 2). [C14: via LL from Gk *obelos* spit]

obese 🅣 (əʊ'biːs) *adj* excessively fat or fleshy; corpulent. [C17: from L *obēsus,* from *ob-* (intensive) + *edere* to eat]
▸**o'besity** *or* **o'beseness** *n*

THESAURUS

oaf *n* = **dolt,** blockhead, brute, dummy (*sl.*), dunce, fathead (*inf.*), fool, goon, halfwit, idiot, imbecile, jerk (*sl., chiefly US & Canad.*), lout, lummox (*inf.*), moron, nerd *or* nurd (*sl.*), nincompoop, nitwit (*inf.*), numbskull *or* numskull, sap (*sl.*), schmuck (*US sl.*), simpleton, twit (*inf., chiefly Brit.*)
Antonyms *n* brain (*inf.*), egghead (*inf.*), genius, intellect, smart aleck (*inf.*), wiseacre

oafish *adj* = **stupid,** bovine, brutish, dense, dim, dim-witted (*inf.*), doltish, dozy (*Brit. inf.*), dull, dumb (*inf.*), loutish, lubberly, lumbering, moronic, obtuse, slow on the uptake (*inf.*), thick
Antonyms *adj* acute, brainy (*inf.*), bright, clever, intelligent, quick-witted, sharp, smart

oasis *n* **2** = **haven,** island, refuge, resting place, retreat, sanctuary, sanctum

oath *n* **1** = **promise,** affirmation, avowal, bond, pledge, sworn statement, vow, word **3** = **swearword,** blasphemy, curse, cuss (*inf.*), expletive, imprecation, malediction, profanity, strong language

obdurate *adj* **1, 2** = **stubborn,** adamant, callous, dogged, firm, fixed, hard, hard-hearted, harsh, immovable, implacable, indurate (*rare*), inexorable, inflexible, iron, mulish, obstinate, perverse, pig-headed, relentless, stiff-necked, unbending, unfeeling, unimpressible, unrelenting, unshakable, unyielding
Antonyms *adj* amenable, biddable, compliant, flexible, malleable, pliant, soft-hearted, submissive, tender, tractable, yielding

obedience *n* **1** = **submissiveness,** accordance, acquiescence, agreement, assent, compliance, conformability, deference, docility, dutifulness, duty, observance, respect, reverence, submission, subservience, tractability
Antonyms *n* defiance, disobedience, insubordination, obstinacy, recalcitrance, stubbornness, wilfulness

obedient *adj* = **submissive,** acquiescent, amenable, biddable, compliant, deferential, docile, duteous, dutiful, law-abiding, observant, regardful, respectful, subservient, tractable, under control, well-trained, yielding
Antonyms *adj* arrogant, contrary, disobedient, disrespectful, intractable, obdurate, obstinate, rebellious, stubborn, undutiful, ungovernable, unmanageable, unruly, wayward

obeisance *n* **1** = **respect,** deference, homage, reverence, salutation **2** = **bow,** bending of the knee, curtsy *or* curtsey, genuflection, kowtow, salaam

obelisk *n* **1** = **column,** monolith, monument, needle, pillar, shaft

obese *adj* = **fat,** corpulent, Falstaffian, fleshy, gross, heavy, outsize, overweight, paunchy, plump, podgy, portly, roly-poly, rotund, stout, tubby, well-upholstered (*inf.*)

obey ➊ (ə'beɪ) *vb* **1** to carry out (instructions or orders); comply with (demands). **2** to behave or act in accordance with (one's feelings, whims, etc.). [C13: from OF *obéir*, from L *oboedīre*, from *ob-* towards + *audīre* to hear]
▸**o'beyer** *n*

obfuscate ➊ ('ɒbfʌsˌkeɪt) *vb* **obfuscates, obfuscating, obfuscated.** (*tr*) **1** to obscure or darken. **2** to perplex or bewilder. [C16: from L *ob-* (intensive) + *fuscāre* to blacken, from *fuscus* dark]
▸ˌ**obfus'cation** *n* ▸'**obfusˌcatory** *adj*

obi ('əʊbɪ) *n, pl* **obis** *or* **obi.** a broad sash tied in a large flat bow at the back, worn as part of the Japanese national costume. [C19: from Japanese]

obit ('ɒbɪt, 'əʊbɪt) *n Inf.* **1** short for **obituary. 2** a memorial service.

obiter dictum ('ɒbɪtə 'dɪktəm, 'əʊ-) *n, pl* **obiter dicta** ('dɪktə). **1** *Law.* an observation by a judge on some point of law not directly in issue in the case before him. **2** any comment or remark made in passing. [L: something said in passing]

obituary (ə'bɪtjʊərɪ) *n, pl* **obituaries.** a published announcement of a death, often accompanied by a short biography of the dead person. [C18: from Med. L *obituārius*, from L *obīre* to fall]
▸**o'bituarist** *n*

obj. *abbrev. for:* **1** objection. **2** *Grammar.* object(ive).

object[1] ➊ ('ɒbdʒɪkt) *n* **1** a tangible and visible thing. **2** a person or thing seen as a focus for feelings, thought, etc. **3** an aim or objective. **4** *Inf.* a ridiculous or pitiable person, spectacle, etc. **5** *Philosophy.* that towards which cognition is directed as contrasted with the thinking subject. **6** *Grammar.* a noun, pronoun, or noun phrase whose referent is the recipient of the action of a verb. See also **direct object, indirect object. 7** *Grammar.* a noun, pronoun, or noun phrase that is governed by a preposition. **8** *Computing.* a self-contained identifiable component of a software system or design. **9 no object.** not a hindrance or obstacle: *money is no object.* [C14: from LL *objectus* something thrown before (the mind), from L *obicere;* see OBJECT[2]]

object[2] ➊ (əb'dʒɛkt) *vb* **1** (*tr; takes a clause as object*) to state as an objection. **2** (*intr;* often foll. by *to*) to raise or state an objection (to); present an argument (against). [C15: from L *obicere*, from *ob-* against + *jacere* to throw]
▸**ob'jector** *n*

object glass *n Optics.* another name for **objective** (sense 10).

objectify (əb'dʒɛktɪˌfaɪ) *vb* **objectifies, objectifying, objectified.** (*tr*) to represent concretely; present as an object.
▸**obˌjectifi'cation** *n*

objection ➊ (əb'dʒɛkʃən) *n* **1** an expression or feeling of opposition or dislike. **2** a cause for such an expression or feeling. **3** the act of objecting.

objectionable ➊ (əb'dʒɛkʃənəb[ə]l) *adj* unpleasant, offensive, or repugnant.
▸**obˌjectiona'bility** *or* **ob'jectionableness** *n* ▸**ob'jectionably** *adv*

objective ➊ (əb'dʒɛktɪv) *adj* **1** existing independently of perception or an individual's conceptions. **2** undistorted by emotion or personal bias. **3** of or relating to actual and external phenomena as opposed to thoughts, feelings, etc. **4** *Med.* (of disease symptoms) perceptible to persons other than the individual affected. **5** *Grammar.* denoting a case of nouns and pronouns, esp. in languages having only two cases, that is used to identify the direct object of a finite verb or preposition. See also **accusative. 6** of or relating to a goal or aim. ◆ *n* **7** the object of one's endeavours; goal; aim. **8** an actual phenomenon; reality. **9** *Grammar.* the objective case. **10** Also called: **object glass.** *Optics.* the lens or combination of lenses nearest to the object in an optical instrument. ◆ Abbrev.: **obj.** Cf. **subjective.**
▸**objectival** (ˌɒbdʒɛk'taɪvəl) *adj* ▸**ob'jectively** *adv* ▸ˌ**objec'tivity** *or* (*less commonly*) **ob'jectiveness** *n*

objectivism (əb'dʒɛktɪˌvɪzəm) *n* **1** the tendency to stress what is objective. **2** the philosophical doctrine that reality is objective, and that sense data correspond with it.
▸**ob'jectivist** *n, adj* ▸**obˌjectiv'istic** *adj*

object language *n* a language described by another language. Cf. **metalanguage.**

object lesson *n* a convincing demonstration of some principle or ideal.

object program *n* a computer program translated from the equivalent source program into machine language by the compiler or assembler.

object relations theory *n* a form of psychoanalytic theory postulating that people relate to others in order to develop themselves.

objet d'art *French.* (ɔbʒɛ dar) *n, pl* ***objets d'art*** (ɔbʒɛ dar). a small object considered to be of artistic worth. [F: object of art]

objurgate ('ɒbdʒəˌgeɪt) *vb* **objurgates, objurgating, objurgated.** (*tr*) to scold or reprimand. [C17: from L *objurgāre*, from *ob-* against + *jurgāre* to scold]
▸ˌ**objur'gation** *n* ▸'**objurˌgator** *n* ▸**objurgatory** (ɒb'dʒɜːgətərɪ, -trɪ) *adj*

obl. *abbrev. for:* **1** oblique. **2** oblong.

oblate[1] ('ɒbleɪt) *adj* having an equatorial diameter of greater length than the polar diameter: *the earth is an oblate sphere.* Cf. **prolate.** [C18: from NL *oblātus* lengthened, from L *ob-* towards + *lātus*, p.p. of *ferre* to bring]

oblate[2] ('ɒbleɪt) *n* a person dedicated to a monastic or religious life. [C19: from F *oblat*, from Med. L *oblātus*, from L *offerre* to OFFER]

oblation (ɒ'bleɪʃən) *n* **1** *Christianity.* the offering of the Eucharist to God. **2** any offering made for religious or charitable purposes. [C15: from Church L *oblātiō;* see OBLATE[2]]
▸**oblatory** ('ɒblətərɪ, -trɪ) *or* **ob'lational** *adj*

obligate ('ɒblɪˌgeɪt) *vb* **obligates, obligating, obligated. 1** to compel, constrain, or oblige morally or legally. **2** (in the US) to bind (property, funds, etc.) as security. ◆ *adj* **3** compelled, bound, or restricted. **4** *Biol.* able to exist under only one set of environmental conditions. [C16: from L *obligāre* to OBLIGE]
▸'**obligable** *adj* ▸**ob'ligative** *adj* ▸'**obliˌgator** *n*

obligation ➊ (ˌɒblɪ'geɪʃən) *n* **1** a moral or legal requirement; duty. **2** the act of obligating or the state of being obligated. **3** *Law.* **3a** a written contract containing a penalty. **3b** an instrument acknowledging indebtedness to secure the repayment of money borrowed. **4** a person or thing to which one is bound morally or legally. **5** a service or favour for which one is indebted.

obligato (ˌɒblɪ'gɑːtəʊ) *adj, n Music.* a variant spelling of **obbligato.**

obligatory ➊ (ɒ'blɪgətərɪ, -trɪ) *adj* **1** required to be done, obtained, possessed, etc. **2** of the nature of or constituting an obligation.
▸**ob'ligatorily** *adv*

oblige ➊ (ə'blaɪdʒ) *vb* **obliges, obliging, obliged. 1** (*tr; often passive*) to bind or constrain (someone to do something) by legal, moral, or physical means. **2** (*tr; usually passive*) to make indebted or grateful (to someone) by doing a favour. **3** to do a service or favour to (someone): *she obliged the guests with a song.* [C13: from OF *obliger*, from L *obligāre*, from *ob-* towards + *ligāre* to bind]
▸**o'bliger** *n*

obligee (ˌɒblɪ'dʒiː) *n* a person in whose favour an obligation, contract, or bond is created; creditor.

THESAURUS

Antonyms *adj* emaciated, gaunt, lean, scraggy, skeletal, skinny, slender, thin

obesity *n* = **fatness**, beef (*inf.*), bulk, corpulence, *embonpoint*, fleshiness, grossness, overweight, portliness, stoutness, tubbiness, weight problem
Antonyms *n* emaciation, gauntness, leanness, skinniness, slenderness, thinness

obey *vb* **1** = **carry out**, abide by, act upon, adhere to, be ruled by, comply, conform, discharge, do what is expected, embrace, execute, follow, fulfil, heed, keep, mind, observe, perform, respond, serve
Antonyms *vb* ≠ **carry out:** contravene, defy, disobey, disregard, ignore, transgress, violate

obfuscate *vb* **2** = **confuse**, befog, bewilder, cloud, darken, muddy the waters, obscure, perplex

object[1] *n* **1** = **thing**, article, body, entity, fact, item, phenomenon, reality **2** = **target**, butt, focus, recipient, victim **3** = **purpose**, aim, design, end, end in view, end purpose, goal, idea, intent, intention, motive, objective, point, reason, the why and wherefore

object[2] *vb* **2** = **protest**, argue against, demur, draw the line (at something), expostulate, oppose, raise objections, take exception
Antonyms *vb* accept, acquiesce, agree, approve, assent, comply, concur, consent, like, take on board, welcome

objection *n* **1** = **protest**, cavil, censure, counter-argument, demur, doubt, exception, niggle (*inf.*), opposition, remonstrance, scruple
Antonyms *n* acceptance, affirmation, agreement, approbation, assent, endorsement, support

objectionable *adj* = **unpleasant**, abhorrent, beyond the pale, deplorable, disagreeable, dislikable *or* dislikeable, displeasing, distasteful, exceptionable, indecorous, insufferable, intolerable, noxious, obnoxious, offensive, regrettable, repugnant, unacceptable, undesirable, unseemly, unsociable
Antonyms *adj* acceptable, agreeable, desirable, likable *or* likeable, pleasant, pleasing, welcome

objective *adj* **2** = **unbiased**, detached, disinterested, dispassionate, equitable, even-handed, fair, impartial, impersonal, judicial, just, open-minded, uncoloured, unemotional, uninvolved, unprejudiced ◆ *n* **7** = **purpose**, aim, ambition, aspiration, design, end, end in view, goal, Holy Grail (*inf.*), intention, mark, object, target
Antonyms *adj* ≠ **unbiased:** biased, personal, prejudiced, subjective, unfair, unjust

objectively *adv* **2** = **impartially**, disinterestedly, dispassionately, even-handedly, with an open mind, with objectivity *or* impartiality, without fear or favour

objectivity *n* **2** = **impartiality**, detachment, disinterest, disinterestedness, dispassion, equitableness, impersonality
Antonyms *n* bent, bias, partiality, predisposition, prejudice, subjectivity

obligation *n* **1** = **duty**, accountability, accountableness, burden, charge, compulsion, culpability, liability, must, onus, pigeon (*inf.*), requirement, responsibility, trust **3** = **contract**, agreement, bond, commitment, debt, engagement, promise, understanding

obligatory *adj* **1, 2** = **compulsory**, binding, coercive, *de rigueur*, enforced, essential, imperative, mandatory, necessary, required, requisite, unavoidable
Antonyms *adj* discretionary, elective, noncompulsory, optional, voluntary

oblige *vb* **1** = **compel**, bind, coerce, constrain, dragoon, force, impel, make, necessitate, obligate, railroad (*inf.*), require **2, 3** = **do (someone) a favour** *or* **a kindness**, accommodate, benefit, favour, gratify, indulge, please, put oneself out for, serve
Antonyms *vb* ≠ **do (someone) a favour** *or* **a kindness:** bother, discommode, disoblige, disrupt, inconvenience, put out, trouble

obliged *adj* **1** = **bound**, compelled, forced, required, under an obligation, under compulsion, without any option **2** = **grateful**, appreciative, beholden, gratified, indebted, in (someone's) debt, thankful

obliging ⓣ (ə'blaɪdʒɪŋ) *adj* ready to do favours; agreeable; kindly. ▸**o'bligingly** *adv* ▸**o'bligingness** *n*

obligor (ˌɒblɪ'gɔː) *n* a person who binds himself by contract to perform some obligation; debtor.

oblique ⓣ (ə'bliːk) *adj* **1** at an angle; slanting; sloping. **2** *Geom.* **2a** (of lines, planes, etc.) neither perpendicular nor parallel to one another or to another line, plane, etc. **2b** not related to or containing a right angle. **3** indirect or evasive. **4** *Grammar.* denoting any case of nouns, pronouns, etc., other than the nominative and vocative. **5** *Biol.* having asymmetrical sides or planes: *an oblique leaf.* ◆ *n* **6** something oblique, esp. a line. **7** another name for **solidus** (sense 1). ◆ *vb* **obliques, obliquing, obliqued.** (*intr*) **8** to take or have an oblique direction. **9** (of a military formation) to move forward at an angle. [C15: from OF, from L *oblīquus*, from ?] ▸**o'bliquely** *adv* ▸**o'bliqueness** *n* ▸**obliquity** (ə'blɪkwɪtɪ) *n*

oblique angle *n* an angle that is not a right angle or any multiple of a right angle.

obliterate ⓣ (ə'blɪtəˌreɪt) *vb* **obliterates, obliterating, obliterated.** (*tr*) to destroy every trace of; wipe out completely. [C16: from L *oblitterāre* to erase, from *ob-* out + *littera* letter] ▸**oˌblite'ration** *n* ▸**o'bliterative** *adj* ▸**o'bliterˌator** *n*

oblivion ⓣ (ə'blɪvɪən) *n* **1** the condition of being forgotten or disregarded. **2** *Law.* amnesty; pardon. [C14: via OF from L *oblīviō* forgetfulness, from *oblīviscī* to forget]

oblivious ⓣ (ə'blɪvɪəs) *adj* (foll. by *of* or *to*) unaware or forgetful. ▸**ob'liviously** *adv* ▸**ob'liviousness** *n*

> **USAGE NOTE** It was formerly considered incorrect to use *oblivious* to mean *unaware*, but this use is now acceptable.

oblong ('ɒbˌlɒŋ) *adj* **1** having an elongated, esp. rectangular, shape. ◆ *n* **2** a figure or object having this shape. [C15: from L *oblongus*, from *ob-* (intensive) + *longus* LONG[1]]

obloquy ⓣ ('ɒbləkwɪ) *n, pl* **obloquies. 1** defamatory or censorious statements, esp. when directed against one person. **2** disgrace brought about by public abuse. [C15: from L *obloquium* contradiction, from *ob-* against + *loquī* to speak]

obnoxious ⓣ (əb'nɒkʃəs) *adj* **1** extremely unpleasant. **2** *Obs.* exposed to harm, injury, etc. [C16: from L *obnoxius*, from *ob-* to + *noxa* injury, from *nocēre* to harm] ▸**ob'noxiously** *adv* ▸**ob'noxiousness** *n*

oboe ('əʊbəʊ) *n* **1** a woodwind instrument consisting of a conical tube fitted with a mouthpiece having a double reed. It has a penetrating nasal tone. **2** a person who plays this instrument in an orchestra. ◆ Arch. form: **hautboy.** [C18: via It. *oboe*, phonetic approximation to F *haut bois*, lit.: high wood (referring to its pitch)] ▸**'oboist** *n*

oboe d'amore (dɑː'mɔːreɪ) *n* a type of oboe pitched a minor third lower than the oboe itself: used chiefly in baroque music.

obs. *abbrev. for:* **1** observation. **2** obsolete.

obscene ⓣ (əb'siːn) *adj* **1** offensive or outrageous to accepted standards of decency or modesty. **2** *Law.* (of publications, etc.) having a tendency to deprave or corrupt. **3** disgusting; repellent. [C16: from L *obscēnus* inauspicious] ▸**ob'scenely** *adv*

obscenity ⓣ (əb'sɛnɪtɪ) *n, pl* **obscenities. 1** the state or quality of being obscene. **2** an obscene act, statement, word, etc.

obscurant (əb'skjʊərənt) *n* an opposer of reform and enlightenment. ▸**obscurantism** (ˌɒbskjʊə'rænˌtɪzəm) *n* ▸**ˌobscu'rantist** *n, adj*

obscure ⓣ (əb'skjʊə) *adj* **1** unclear. **2** indistinct, vague, or indefinite. **3** inconspicuous or unimportant. **4** hidden, secret, or remote. **5** (of a vowel) reduced to a neutral vowel (ə). **6** gloomy, dark, clouded, or dim. ◆ *vb* **obscures, obscuring, obscured.** (*tr*) **7** to make unclear, vague, or hidden. **8** to cover or cloud over. **9** *Phonetics.* to pronounce (a vowel) so that it becomes a neutral sound represented by (ə). [C14: via OF from L *obscūrus* dark] ▸**obscuration** (ˌɒbskjʊ'reɪʃən) *n* ▸**ob'scurely** *adv* ▸**ob'scureness** *n*

obscurity ⓣ (əb'skjʊərɪtɪ) *n, pl* **obscurities. 1** the state or quality of being obscure. **2** an obscure person or thing.

obsequies ⓣ ('ɒbsɪkwɪz) *pl n, sing* **obsequy.** funeral rites. [C14: via Anglo-Norman from Med. L *obsequiae* (infl. by L *exsequiae*), from *obsequium* compliance]

obsequious ⓣ (əb'siːkwɪəs) *adj* **1** obedient or attentive in an ingratiating or servile manner. **2** *Now rare.* submissive or compliant. [C15: from L *obsequiōsus* compliant, from *obsequi* to follow] ▸**ob'sequiously** *adv* ▸**ob'sequiousness** *n*

observance ⓣ (əb'zɜːvəns) *n* **1** recognition of or compliance with a law, custom, practice, etc. **2** a ritual, ceremony, or practice, esp. of a religion. **3** observation or attention. **4** the degree of strictness of a religious order in following its rule. **5** *Arch.* respectful or deferential attention.

observant ⓣ (əb'zɜːvənt) *adj* **1** paying close attention to detail; watchful or heedful. **2** adhering strictly to rituals, ceremonies, laws, etc. ▸**ob'servantly** *adv*

THESAURUS

obliging *adj* = **cooperative**, accommodating, agreeable, amiable, civil, complaisant, considerate, courteous, eager to please, friendly, good-natured, helpful, kind, polite, willing
Antonyms *adj* discourteous, disobliging, inconsiderate, rude, sullen, surly, unaccommodating, uncooperative, unhelpful, unobliging

oblique *adj* **1** = **slanting**, angled, aslant, at an angle, atilt, inclined, slanted, sloped, sloping, tilted **3** = **indirect**, backhanded, circuitous, circumlocutory, evasive, implied, roundabout, sidelong
Antonyms *adj* ≠ **indirect**: blunt, candid, direct, downright, forthright, frank, open, straightforward

obliquely *adv* **1** = **at an angle**, aslant, aslope, diagonally, slantwise **3** = **indirectly**, circuitously, evasively, in a roundabout manner *or* way, not in so many words

obliterate *vb* = **destroy**, annihilate, blot out, blow sky-high, cancel, delete, destroy root and branch, efface, eradicate, erase, expunge, extirpate, root out, wipe from *or* off the face of the earth, wipe out
Antonyms *vb* build, construct, create, establish, form, formulate, generate, make

obliteration *n* = **annihilation**, blotting out, deletion, effacement, elimination, eradication, erasure, expunction, extirpation, rooting out, sponging out, wiping out
Antonyms *n* building, construction, creation, establishment, formation, generation, making

oblivion *n* **1** = **neglect**, abeyance, disregard, forgetfulness, (waters of) Lethe

oblivious *adj* = **unaware**, blind, careless, deaf, disregardful, forgetful, heedless, ignorant, inattentive, insensible, neglectful, negligent, regardless, unconcerned, unconscious, unmindful, unobservant
Antonyms *adj* alert, attentive, aware, conscious, heedful, mindful, observant, watchful

obloquy *n* **1** = **abuse**, animadversion, aspersion, attack, bad press, blame, calumny, censure, character assassination, contumely, criticism, defamation, detraction, invective, opprobrium, reproach, slander, stick (*sl.*), vilification **2** = **disgrace**, discredit, disfavour, dishonour, humiliation, ignominy, ill fame, ill repute, infamy, odium, shame, stigma

obnoxious *adj* **1** = **offensive**, abhorrent, abominable, detestable, disagreeable, disgusting, dislikable *or* dislikeable, foul, hateable, hateful, horrid, insufferable, loathsome, nasty, nauseating, objectionable, obscene, odious, repellent, reprehensible, repugnant, repulsive, revolting, sickening, unpleasant
Antonyms *adj* agreeable, amiable, charming, congenial, delightful, likable *or* likeable, pleasant, pleasing

obscene *adj* **1** = **indecent**, bawdy, blue, coarse, dirty, filthy, foul, gross, immodest, immoral, improper, impure, lewd, licentious, loose, offensive, pornographic, prurient, ribald, salacious, scabrous, shameless, smutty, suggestive, unchaste, unwholesome, X-rated (*inf.*) **3** = **disgusting**, atrocious, evil, heinous, loathsome, outrageous, shocking, sickening, vile, wicked
Antonyms *adj* ≠ **indecent**: chaste, decent, decorous, inoffensive, modest, proper, pure, refined, respectable, seemly

obscenity *n* **1** = **indecency**, bawdiness, blueness, coarseness, dirtiness, filthiness, foulness, grossness, immodesty, impropriety, impurity, indelicacy, lewdness, licentiousness, pornography, prurience, salacity, smut, smuttiness, suggestiveness, vileness **2** = **swearword**, four-letter word, profanity, vulgarism
Antonyms *n* ≠ **indecency**: chastity, decency, decorum, delicacy, innocence, modesty, propriety, purity

obscure *adj* **1, 2** = **vague**, abstruse, ambiguous, arcane, clear as mud (*inf.*), concealed, confusing, cryptic, deep, Delphic, doubtful, enigmatic, esoteric, hazy, hidden, incomprehensible, indefinite, intricate, involved, mysterious, occult, opaque, recondite, unclear **3** = **little-known**, humble, inconspicuous, inglorious, lowly, minor, nameless, out-of-the-way, remote, undistinguished, unheard-of, unhonoured, unimportant, unknown, unnoted, unseen, unsung **6** = **dark**, blurred, clouded, cloudy, dim, dusky, faint, gloomy, indistinct, murky, obfuscated, shadowy, shady, sombre, tenebrous, unlit, veiled ◆ *vb* **7** = **conceal**, cover, disguise, hide, muddy, obfuscate, screen, throw a veil over, veil **8** = **cover**, adumbrate, bedim, befog, block, block out, blur, cloak, cloud, darken, dim, dull, eclipse, mask, overshadow, shade, shroud
Antonyms *adj* ≠ **vague**: apparent, clear, definite, distinct, evident, explicit, intelligible, lucid, manifest, obvious, plain, prominent, straightforward, transparent, unmistakable ≠ **little-known**: celebrated, distinguished, eminent, familiar, famous, illustrious, important, major, prominent, renowned, significant, well-known, widely-known ≠ **dark**: bright, clear, sharp, transparent, well-defined ◆ *vb* ≠ **conceal**: clarify, disclose, explain, explicate, expose, interpret, reveal, show ≠ **cover**: expose, reveal, uncover, unmask, unveil

obscurity *n* **1** = **indistinctness**, dimness, haze, impenetrableness, incomprehensibility, inconspicuousness, insignificance, murkiness, shadows, unimportance, vagueness
Antonyms *n* ≠ **indistinctness**: clarity, clearness, comprehensibility, explicitness, lucidity, obviousness

obsequies *pl n* = **funeral rites**, burial, burial service, exequies, funeral, last offices

obsequious *adj* **1** = **sycophantic**, abject, cringing, deferential, fawning, flattering, grovelling, ingratiating, mealy-mouthed, menial, servile, slavish, smarmy (*Brit. inf.*), submissive, toadying, unctuous

obsequiously *adv* **1** = **ingratiatingly**, abjectly, cringingly, deferentially, fawningly, on one's knees, servilely, slavishly, smarmily (*Brit. inf.*), sycophantically, unctuously

observable *adj* **1** = **noticeable**, apparent, appreciable, blatant, clear, detectable, discernible, evident, obvious, open, patent, perceivable, perceptible, recognizable, visible

observance *n* **1** = **carrying out**, adherence to, celebration, compliance, discharge, fulfilment, heeding, honouring, notice, observation, performance **2** = **ritual**, ceremonial, ceremony, custom, fashion, form, formality, practice, rite, service, tradition
Antonyms *n* ≠ **carrying out**: disdain, disregard, evasion, heedlessness, inattention, neglect, nonobservance, omission, oversight

observant *adj* **1** = **attentive**, alert, eagle-eyed,

observation ⓣ (ˌɒbzəˈveɪʃən) *n* **1** the act of observing or the state of being observed. **2** a comment or remark. **3** detailed examination of phenomena prior to analysis, diagnosis, or interpretation: *the patient was under observation.* **4** the facts learned from observing. **5** *Navigation.* **5a** a sight taken with an instrument to determine the position of an observer relative to that of a given heavenly body. **5b** the data so taken.
▸ˌ**obserˈvational** *adj* ▸ˌ**obserˈvationally** *adv*

observatory (əbˈzɜːvətərɪ, -trɪ) *n, pl* **observatories. 1** an institution or building specially designed and equipped for observing meteorological and astronomical phenomena. **2** any building or structure providing an extensive view of its surroundings.

observe ⓣ (əbˈzɜːv) *vb* **observes, observing, observed. 1** (*tr; may take a clause as object*) to see; perceive; notice: *we have observed that you steal.* **2** (when *tr, may take a clause as object*) to watch (something) carefully; pay attention to (something). **3** to make observations of (something), esp. scientific ones. **4** (when *intr,* usually foll. by *on* or *upon;* when *tr, may take a clause as object*) to make a comment or remark: *the speaker observed that times had changed.* **5** (*tr*) to abide by, keep, or follow (a custom, tradition, etc.). **[**C14: via OF from L *observāre,* from *ob-* to + *servāre* to watch**]**
▸**obˈservable** *adj* ▸**obˈserver** *n*

obsess ⓣ (əbˈsɛs) *vb* **1** (*tr;* when passive, foll. by *with* or *by*) to preoccupy completely; haunt. **2** (*intr,* usually foll. by *on* or *over*) to brood obsessively. **[**C16: from L *obsessus* besieged, p.p. of *obsidēre,* from *ob-* in front of + *sedēre* to sit**]**
▸**obˈsessive** *adj, n* ▸**obˈsessively** *adv* ▸**obˈsessiveness** *n*

obsession ⓣ (əbˈsɛʃən) *n* **1** *Psychiatry.* a persistent idea or impulse, often associated with anxiety and mental illness. **2** a persistent preoccupation, idea, or feeling. **3** the act of obsessing or the state of being obsessed.
▸**obˈsessional** *adj* ▸**obˈsessionally** *adv*

obsidian (ɒbˈsɪdɪən) *n* a dark glassy volcanic rock formed by very rapid solidification of lava. Also called: **Iceland agate. [**C17: from L *obsidiānus,* erroneous transcription of *obsiānus* (*lapis*) (stone of) *Obsius,* (in Pliny) the discoverer of a stone resembling obsidian**]**

obsolesce (ˌɒbsəˈlɛs) *vb* **obsolesces, obsolescing, obsolesced.** (*intr*) to become obsolete.

obsolescent ⓣ (ˌɒbsəˈlɛsᵊnt) *adj* becoming obsolete or out of date. **[**C18: from L *obsolescere;* see OBSOLETE**]**
▸ˌ**obsoˈlescence** *n*

obsolete ⓣ (ˈɒbsəˌliːt, ˌɒbsəˈliːt) *adj* **1** out of use or practice; not current. **2** out of date; unfashionable or outmoded. **3** *Biol.* (of parts, organs, etc.) vestigial; rudimentary. **[**C16: from L *obsolētus* worn out, p.p. of *obsolēre* (unattested), from *ob-* opposite to + *solēre* to be used**]**
▸ˈ**obsoˌletely** *adv* ▸ˈ**obsoˌleteness** *n*

> **USAGE NOTE** The word *obsoleteness* is hardly ever used, *obsolescence* standing as the noun form for both *obsolete* and *obsolescent.*

obstacle ⓣ (ˈɒbstəkᵊl) *n* **1** a person or thing that opposes or hinders something. **2** *Brit.* a fence or hedge used in showjumping. **[**C14: via OF from L *obstāculum,* from *obstāre,* from *ob-* against + *stāre* to stand**]**

obstacle race *n* a race in which competitors have to negotiate various obstacles.

obstetric (ɒbˈstɛtrɪk) *or* **obstetrical** *adj* of or relating to childbirth or obstetrics. **[**C18: via NL from L *obstetrīcius,* from *obstetrix* a midwife, lit.: woman who stands opposite, from *obstāre* to stand in front of; see OBSTACLE**]**
▸**obˈstetrically** *adv*

obstetrician (ˌɒbstɪˈtrɪʃən) *n* a physician who specializes in obstetrics.

obstetrics (ɒbˈstɛtrɪks) *n* (*functioning as sing*) the branch of medicine concerned with childbirth and the treatment of women before and after childbirth.

obstinacy ⓣ (ˈɒbstɪnəsɪ) *n, pl* **obstinacies. 1** the state or quality of being obstinate. **2** an obstinate act, attitude, etc.

obstinate ⓣ (ˈɒbstɪnɪt) *adj* **1** adhering fixedly to a particular opinion, attitude, course of action, etc. **2** self-willed or headstrong. **3** difficult to subdue or alleviate; persistent: *an obstinate fever.* **[**C14: from L *obstinātus,* p.p. of *obstināre* to persist in, from *ob-* (intensive) + *stin-,* var. of *stare* to stand**]**
▸ˈ**obstinately** *adv*

obstreperous ⓣ (əbˈstrɛpərəs) *adj* noisy or rough, esp. in resisting restraint or control. **[**C16: from L, from *obstrepere,* from *ob-* against + *strepere* to roar**]**
▸**obˈstreperously** *adv* ▸**obˈstreperousness** *n*

obstruct ⓣ (əbˈstrʌkt) *vb* (*tr*) **1** to block (a road, passageway, etc.) with an obstacle. **2** to make (progress or activity) difficult. **3** to impede or block a clear view of. **[**C17: L *obstructus* built against, p.p. of *obstruere,* from *ob-* against + *struere* to build**]**
▸**obˈstructive** *adj, n* ▸**obˈstructively** *adv* ▸**obˈstructiveness** *n* ▸**obˈstructor** *n*

obstruction ⓣ (əbˈstrʌkʃən) *n* **1** a person or thing that obstructs. **2** the act or an instance of obstructing. **3** delay of business, esp. in a legislature by means of procedural devices. **4** *Sport.* the act of unfairly impeding an opposing player.
▸**obˈstructional** *adj*

obstructionist (əbˈstrʌkʃənɪst) *n* a person who deliberately obstructs business, etc., esp. in a legislature.
▸**obˈstructionism** *n*

obtain ⓣ (əbˈteɪn) *vb* **1** (*tr*) to gain possession of; acquire; get. **2** (*intr*) to

THESAURUS

heedful, mindful, obedient, perceptive, quick, sharp-eyed, submissive, vigilant, watchful, wide-awake
Antonyms *adj* distracted, dreamy, heedless, inattentive, indifferent, negligent, preoccupied, unobservant, vague

observation *n* **1** = **study**, attention, cognition, consideration, examination, experience, information, inspection, knowledge, monitoring, notice, review, scrutiny, surveillance, watching **2** = **comment**, annotation, finding, note, obiter dictum, opinion, pronouncement, reflection, remark, thought, utterance

observe *vb* **1** = **see**, detect, discern, discover, espy, note, notice, perceive, spot, witness **2** = **watch**, behold (*arch. or literary*), check, check out (*inf.*), contemplate, eye, get a load of, keep an eye on (*inf.*), keep tabs on (*inf.*), keep track of, keep under observation, look at, monitor, pay attention to, regard, scrutinize, study, survey, take a dekko at (*Brit. sl.*), view **4** = **remark**, animadvert, comment, declare, mention, note, opine, say, state **5** = **carry out**, abide by, adhere to, comply, conform to, follow, fulfil, heed, honour, keep, mind, obey, perform, respect
Antonyms *vb* ≠ **carry out:** disregard, ignore, miss, neglect, omit, overlook, violate

observer *n* **2** = **spectator**, beholder, bystander, commentator, eyewitness, fly on the wall, looker-on, onlooker, spotter, viewer, watcher, witness

obsess *vb* **1** = **preoccupy**, bedevil, be on one's mind, be uppermost in one's thoughts, consume, dominate, engross, grip, haunt, monopolize, plague, possess, prey on one's mind, rule, torment

obsessed *adj* **1** = **preoccupied**, beset, dominated, gripped, hag-ridden, haunted, having a one-track mind, hung up on (*sl.*), immersed in, infatuated, in the grip of, troubled
Antonyms *adj* aloof, apathetic, detached, disinterested, impassive, indifferent, uncaring, unconcerned

obsession *n* **1, 2** = **preoccupation**, addiction, bee in one's bonnet (*inf.*), complex, enthusiasm, fetish, fixation, hang-up (*inf.*), *idée fixe,* infatuation, mania, phobia, ruling passion, thing (*inf.*)

obsessive *adj* **1** = **compulsive**, besetting, consuming, fixed, gripping, haunting, tormenting, unforgettable

obsolescent *adj* = **becoming obsolete**, ageing, declining, dying out, not with it (*inf.*), on the decline, on the wane, on the way out, past its prime, waning

obsolete *adj* **2** = **out of date**, anachronistic, ancient, antediluvian, antiquated, antique, archaic, bygone, dated, *démodé,* discarded, disused, extinct, musty, old, old-fashioned, old hat, out, outmoded, out of fashion, out of the ark (*inf.*), outworn, passé, past it, superannuated, *vieux jeu*
Antonyms *adj* à la mode, contemporary, current, fashionable, in, in vogue, modern, new, present day, trendy (*Brit. inf.*), up-to-date

obstacle *n* **1** = **difficulty**, bar, barrier, block, check, hindrance, hitch, hurdle, impediment, interference, interruption, obstruction, snag, stumbling block
Antonyms *n* advantage, aid, asset, assistance, benefit, crutch, help, support

obstinacy *n* **1** = **stubbornness**, doggedness, firmness, inflexibility, intransigence, mulishness, obduracy, perseverance, persistence, pertinacity, pig-headedness, resoluteness, tenacity, wilfulness
Antonyms *n* compliance, cooperativeness, docility, flexibility, meekness, submissiveness, tractability

obstinate *adj* **1, 2** = **stubborn**, contumacious, cussed, determined, dogged, firm, headstrong, immovable, inflexible, intractable, intransigent, mulish, opinionated, persistent, pertinacious, perverse, pig-headed, recalcitrant, refractory, self-willed, steadfast, stiff-necked, strong-minded, tenacious, unyielding, wilful
Antonyms *adj* amenable, biddable, complaisant, compliant, docile, flexible, irresolute, manageable, obedient, submissive, tractable, undecided, wavering

obstreperous *adj* = **unruly**, boisterous, clamorous, disorderly, loud, noisy, out of control, out of hand, rackety, rampaging, raucous, restive, riotous, rip-roaring (*inf.*), roistering, roisterous, rough, rowdy, stroppy (*Brit. sl.*), tempestuous, tumultuous, turbulent, uncontrolled, undisciplined, unmanageable, uproarious, vociferous, wild
Antonyms *adj* calm, controlled, disciplined, docile, gentle, orderly, peaceful, placid, quiet

obstruct *vb* **1-3** = **block**, arrest, bar, barricade, bring to a standstill, bung, check, choke, clog, cumber, curb, cut off, frustrate, get in the way of, hamper, hamstring, hide, hinder, hold up, impede, inhibit, interfere with, interrupt, mask, obscure, prevent, restrict, retard, shield, shut off, slow down, stop, thwart, trammel
Antonyms *vb* abet, advance, aid, assist, encourage, favour, further, gee up, help, promote, support

obstruction *n* **1** = **obstacle**, bar, barricade, barrier, block, blockage, check, difficulty, hazard, hindrance, impediment, occlusion, snag, stop, stoppage, trammel
Antonyms *n* aid, assistance, cooperation, encouragement, favour, furtherance, geeing-up, help, support

obstructive *adj* **2** = **unhelpful**, awkward, blocking, delaying, difficult, hindering, inhibiting, preventative, restrictive, stalling, uncooperative
Antonyms *adj* cooperative, encouraging, favourable, helpful, obliging, supportive

obtain *vb* **1** = **get**, achieve, acquire, attain, come by, earn, gain, get hold of, get one's

be customary, valid, or accepted: *a new law obtains in this case.* [C15: via OF from L *obtinēre* to take hold of]
▸**ob'tainable** *adj* ▸**ob,taina'bility** *n* ▸**ob'tainer** *n* ▸**ob'tainment** *n*

obtrude (əb'tru:d) *vb* **obtrudes, obtruding, obtruded. 1** to push (oneself, one's opinions, etc.) on others in an unwelcome way. **2** (*tr*) to push out or forward. [C16: from L *obtrūdere,* from *ob-* against + *trūdere* to push forward]
▸**ob'truder** *n* ▸**obtrusion** (əb'tru:ʒən) *n*

obtrusive ❶ (əb'tru:sɪv) *adj* **1** obtruding or tending to obtrude. **2** sticking out; protruding; noticeable.
▸**ob'trusively** *adv* ▸**ob'trusiveness** *n*

obtuse ❶ (əb'tju:s) *adj* **1** mentally slow or emotionally insensitive. **2** *Maths.* (of an angle) lying between 90° and 180°. **3** not sharp or pointed. **4** indistinctly felt, heard, etc.; dull: *obtuse pain.* **5** (of a leaf or similar flat part) having a rounded or blunt tip. [C16: from L *obtūsus* dulled, p.p. of *obtundere* to beat down]
▸**ob'tusely** *adv* ▸**ob'tuseness** *n*

obverse ('ɒbvɜ:s) *adj* **1** facing or turned towards the observer. **2** forming or serving as a counterpart. **3** (of leaves) narrower at the base than at the top. ◆ *n* **4** a counterpart or complement. **5** *Logic.* a proposition derived from another by replacing the original predicate by its negation and changing the proposition from affirmative to negative or vice versa, as *no sum is correct* from *every sum is incorrect.* **6** the side of a coin that bears the main design or device. [C17: from L *obversus* turned towards, p.p. of *obvertere*]
▸**ob'versely** *adv*

obvert (ɒb'vɜ:t) *vb* (*tr*) **1** *Logic.* to deduce the obverse of (a proposition). **2** *Rare.* to turn so as to show the main or other side. [C17: from L *obvertere* to turn towards]
▸**ob'version** *n*

obviate ❶ ('ɒbvɪ,eɪt) *vb* **obviates, obviating, obviated.** (*tr*) to avoid or prevent (a need or difficulty). [C16: from LL *obviātus* prevented, p.p. of *obviāre;* see OBVIOUS]
▸**,obvi'ation** *n*

> **USAGE NOTE** Only things which have not yet occurred can be *obviated.* For example, one can *obviate* a possible future difficulty, but not one which already exists.

obvious ❶ ('ɒbvɪəs) *adj* **1** easy to see or understand; evident. **2** exhibiting motives, feelings, intentions, etc., clearly or without subtlety. **3** naive or unsubtle: *the play was rather obvious.* [C16: from L *obvius,* from *obviam* in the way]
▸**'obviously** *adv* ▸**'obviousness** *n*

OC *abbrev. for* Officer Commanding.

Oc. *abbrev. for* Ocean.

o/c *abbrev. for* overcharge.

ocarina (,ɒkə'ri:nə) *n* an egg-shaped wind instrument with a protruding mouthpiece and six to eight finger holes, producing an almost pure tone. [C19: from It.: little goose, from *oca* goose, ult. from L *avis* bird]

Occam's razor *n* a variant spelling of **Ockham's razor.**

occas. *abbrev. for* occasional(ly).

occasion ❶ (ə'keɪʒən) *n* **1** (sometimes foll. by *of*) the time of a particular happening or event. **2** (sometimes foll. by *for*) a reason or cause (to do or be something); grounds: *there was no occasion to complain.* **3** an opportunity (to do something); chance. **4** a special event, time, or celebration: *the party was quite an occasion.* **5 on occasion.** every so often. **6 rise to the occasion.** to have the courage, wit, etc., to meet the special demands of a situation. **7 take occasion.** to avail oneself of an opportunity (to do something). ◆ *vb* **8** (*tr*) to bring about, esp. incidentally or by chance. [C14: from L *occāsiō* a falling down, from *occidere* to fall]

occasional ❶ (ə'keɪʒənᵊl) *adj* **1** taking place from time to time; not frequent or regular. **2** of, for, or happening on special occasions. **3** serving as an occasion (for something).
▸**oc'casionally** *adv*

occasional table *n* a small table with no regular use.

occident ('ɒksɪdənt) *n* a literary or formal word for **west.** Cf. **orient.** [C14: via OF from L *occidere* to fall (with reference to the setting sun)]
▸**,occi'dental** *adj*

Occident ('ɒksɪdənt) *n* (usually preceded by *the*) **1** the countries of Europe and America. **2** the western hemisphere.
▸**,Occi'dental** *adj, n*

occipital (ɒk'sɪpɪtᵊl) *adj* **1** of or relating to the back of the head or skull. ◆ *n* **2** short for **occipital bone.** [See OCCIPUT]

occipital bone *n* the bone that forms the back part of the skull and part of its base.

occipital lobe *n* the posterior portion of each cerebral hemisphere, concerned with the interpretation of visual sensory impulses.

occiput ('ɒksɪ,pʌt) *n, pl* **occiputs** *or* **occipita** (ɒk'sɪpɪtə). the back part of the head or skull. [C14: from L, from *ob-* at the back of + *caput* head]

occlude ❶ (ə'klu:d) *vb* **occludes, occluding, occluded. 1** (*tr*) to block or stop up (a passage or opening); obstruct. **2** (*tr*) to prevent the passage of. **3** (*tr*) *Chem.* (of a solid) to incorporate (a substance) by absorption or adsorption. **4** *Meteorol.* to form or cause to form an occluded front. **5** *Dentistry.* to produce or cause to produce occlusion, as in chewing. [C16: from L *occlūdere,* from *ob-* (intensive) + *claudere* to close]
▸**oc'cludent** *adj*

occluded front *n Meteorol.* the line or plane occurring where the cold front of a depression has overtaken the warm front, raising the warm sector from ground level. Also called: **occlusion.**

occlusion (ə'klu:ʒən) *n* **1** the act of occluding or the state of being occluded. **2** *Meteorol.* another term for **occluded front. 3** *Dentistry.* the normal position of the teeth when the jaws are closed.
▸**oc'clusive** *adj*

occult ❶ *adj* (ɒ'kʌlt, 'ɒkʌlt). **1a** of or characteristic of mystical or supernatural phenomena or influences. **1b** (*as n*): *the occult.* **2** beyond ordinary human understanding. **3** secret or esoteric. ◆ *vb* (ɒ'kʌlt). **4** *Astron.* (of a celestial body) to hide (another celestial body) from view by occultation or (of a celestial body) to become hidden by occultation. **5** to hide or become hidden or shut off from view. **6** (*intr*) (of lights, esp. in lighthouses) to shut off at regular intervals. [C16: from L *occultus,* p.p. of *occulere,* from *ob-* over, up + *-culere,* rel. to *celāre* to conceal]
▸**'occul,tism** *n* ▸**'occultist** *n* ▸**oc'cultness** *n*

occultation (,ɒkʌl'teɪʃən) *n* the temporary disappearance of one celestial body as it moves out of sight behind another body.

occupancy ❶ ('ɒkjʊpənsɪ) *n, pl* **occupancies. 1** the act of occupying; possession of a property. **2** *Law.* the possession and use of property by or without agreement and without any claim to ownership. **3** *Law.* the act of taking possession of unowned property, esp. land, with the intent of thus acquiring ownership. **4** the condition or fact of being an occupant, esp. a tenant. **5** the period of time during which one is an occupant, esp. of property.

THESAURUS

hands on, land, procure, score (*sl.*), secure **2** = **exist**, be in force, be prevalent, be the case, hold, prevail, stand
Antonyms *vb* ≠ **get:** forfeit, forgo, give up, hand over, lose, relinquish, renounce, surrender

obtainable *adj* **1** = **available**, achievable, at hand, attainable, on tap (*inf.*), procurable, ready, realizable, to be had

obtrusive *adj* **1** = **pushy** (*inf.*), forward, importunate, interfering, intrusive, meddling, nosy, officious, prying **2** = **noticeable**, blatant, obvious, prominent, protruding, protuberant, sticking out
Antonyms *adj* ≠ **pushy:** bashful, decorous, diffident, modest, reserved, reticent, retiring, shy, unassuming ≠ **noticeable:** concealed, covert, hidden, inconspicuous, low-key, muted, unnoticeable, unobtrusive

obtrusively *adv* **1** = **pushily**, blatantly, bluntly, boldly, crassly, importunately, obviously, officiously

obtuse *adj* **1** = **stupid**, boneheaded (*sl.*), dense, dopey (*inf.*), dull, dull-witted, dumb, imperceptive, insensitive, retarded, slow, slow on the uptake (*inf.*), stolid, thick, thick-skinned, uncomprehending, unintelligent **3** = **blunt**, rounded
Antonyms *adj* ≠ **stupid:** astute, bright, clever, keen, quick, sensitive, sharp, shrewd, smart

obviate *vb* = **preclude**, anticipate, avert, counter, counteract, do away with, prevent, remove, render unnecessary

obvious *adj* **1** = **evident**, apparent, blatant, bold, clear, clear as a bell, conspicuous, cut-and-dried (*inf.*), distinct, indisputable, manifest, much in evidence, noticeable, open, open-and-shut, overt, palpable, patent, perceptible, plain, pronounced, recognizable, right under one's nose (*inf.*), salient, self-evident, self-explanatory, staring one in the face (*inf.*), sticking out a mile (*inf.*), straightforward, transparent, unconcealed, undeniable, undisguised, unmistakable, unsubtle, visible
Antonyms *adj* ambiguous, clear as mud (*inf.*), concealed, dark, hidden, imperceptible, inconspicuous, indistinct, invisible, obscure, unapparent, unclear, vague

obviously *adv* **1** = **clearly**, certainly, distinctly, manifestly, needless to say, of course, palpably, patently, plainly, undeniably, unmistakably, unquestionably, without doubt

occasion *n* **1, 3** = **time**, chance, convenience, incident, moment, occurrence, opening, opportunity, window **2** = **reason**, call, cause, excuse, ground(s), inducement, influence, justification, motive, prompting, provocation **4** = **event**, affair, celebration, experience, happening, occurrence ◆ *vb* **8** = **cause**, bring about, create, effect, elicit, engender, evoke, generate, give rise to, induce, influence, inspire, lead to, move, originate, persuade, produce, prompt, provoke

occasional *adj* **1** = **infrequent**, casual, desultory, incidental, intermittent, irregular, odd, rare, sporadic, uncommon
Antonyms *adj* constant, continual, customary, frequent, habitual, incessant, regular, routine, usual

occasionally *adv* **1** = **sometimes**, at intervals, at times, (every) now and then, every so often, from time to time, irregularly, now and again, off and on, on and off, once in a while, on occasion, periodically
Antonyms *adv* constantly, continually, continuously, frequently, habitually, often, regularly, routinely

occlude *vb* **1** = **block**, bung, choke, clog, close, fill, hinder, obstruct, plug, seal, shut, stop up

occult *adj* **1** = **supernatural**, abstruse, arcane, cabbalistic, esoteric, magical, mysterious, mystic, mystical, preternatural, recondite **3** = **secret**, concealed, hidden, invisible, obscure, unknown, unrevealed, veiled
Antonyms *adj* ≠ **secret:** apparent, blatant, evident, exposed, manifest, obvious, open, overt, plain, revealed, visible

occultism *n* **1** = **black magic**, diabolism, magic, sorcery, supernaturalism, the black arts, witchcraft

occupancy *n* **1** = **tenancy**, habitation, hold-

occupant ❶ ('ɒkjupənt) *n* **1** a person, thing, etc., holding a position or place. **2** *Law.* a person who has possession of something, esp. an estate, house, etc.; tenant. **3** *Law.* a person who acquires by occupancy the title to something previously without an owner.

occupation ❶ (ˌɒkju'peɪʃən) *n* **1** a person's regular work or profession; job. **2** any activity on which time is spent by a person. **3** the act of occupying or the state of being occupied. **4** the control of a country by a foreign military power. **5** the period of time that a nation, place, or position is occupied. **6** (*modifier*) for the use of the occupier of a particular property: *occupation road.*
▸**ˌoccu'pational** *adj*

occupational psychology *n* the scientific study of mental or emotional problems associated with the working environment.

occupational therapy *n Med.* treatment of people with physical, emotional, or social problems, using purposeful activity to help them overcome or learn to deal with their problems.

occupation groupings *pl n* a system of classifying people according to occupation, based originally on information obtained by government census and subsequently developed by market research. The classifications are used by the advertising industry to identify potential markets. The groups are **A, B, C1, C2, D,** and **E.**

occupier ('ɒkjuˌpaɪə) *n* **1** *Brit.* a person who is in possession or occupation of a house or land. **2** a person or thing that occupies.

occupy ❶ ('ɒkjuˌpaɪ) *vb* **occupies, occupying, occupied.** (*tr*) **1** to live or be established in (a house, flat, office, etc.). **2** (*often passive*) to keep (a person) busy or engrossed. **3** (*often passive*) to take up (time or space). **4** to take and hold possession of, esp. as a demonstration: *students occupied the college buildings.* **5** to fill or hold (a position or rank). [C14: from OF *occuper,* from L *occupāre* to seize hold of]

occur ❶ (ə'kɜː) *vb* **occurs, occurring, occurred.** (*intr*) **1** to happen; take place; come about. **2** to be found or be present; exist. **3** (foll. by *to*) to be realized or thought of (by); suggest itself (to). [C16: from L *occurrere* to run up to]

> **USAGE NOTE** It is usually regarded as incorrect to talk of pre-arranged events *occurring* or *happening*: *the wedding took place* (not *occurred* or *happened*) *in the afternoon.*

occurrence ❶ (ə'kʌrəns) *n* **1** something that occurs; a happening; event. **2** the act or an instance of occurring: *a crime of frequent occurrence.*
▸**oc'current** *adj*

ocean ('əʊʃən) *n* **1** a very large stretch of sea, esp. one of the five oceans of the world, the Atlantic, Pacific, Indian, Arctic, and Antarctic. **2** the body of salt water covering approximately 70 per cent of the earth's surface. **3** a huge quantity or expanse: *an ocean of replies.* **4** *Literary.* the sea. [C13: via OF from L *ōceanus,* from *Oceanus,* Gk god of the stream believed to flow round the earth]

oceanarium (ˌəʊʃə'nɛərɪəm) *n, pl* **oceanariums** *or* **oceanaria** (-ɪə). a large saltwater aquarium for marine life.

ocean-going *adj* (of a ship, boat, etc.) suited for travel on the open ocean.

oceanic (ˌəʊʃɪ'ænɪk) *adj* **1** of or relating to the ocean. **2** living in the depths of the ocean beyond the continental shelf at a depth exceeding 200 metres: *oceanic fauna.* **3** huge or overwhelming.

Oceanid (əʊ'sɪənɪd) *n, pl* **Oceanids** *or* **Oceanides** (ˌəʊsɪ'ænɪˌdiːz). *Greek myth.* an ocean nymph.

oceanography (ˌəʊʃə'nɒgrəfɪ, ˌəʊʃɪə-) *n* the branch of science dealing with the physical, chemical, geological, and biological features of the oceans.
▸**ˌocean'ographer** *n* ▸**oceanographic** (ˌəʊʃənə'græfɪk, ˌəʊʃɪə-) *or* **ˌoceano'graphical** *adj*

oceanology (ˌəʊʃə'nɒlədʒɪ, ˌəʊʃɪə-) *n* the study of the sea, esp. of its economic geography.

ocellus (ɒ'sɛləs) *n, pl* **ocelli** (-laɪ). **1** the simple eye of insects and some other invertebrates, consisting basically of light-sensitive cells. **2** any eyelike marking in animals, such as the eyespot on the tail feather of a peacock. [C19: via NL from L: small eye, from *oculus* eye]
▸**o'cellar** *adj* ▸**ocellate** ('ɒsɪˌleɪt) *or* **'ocelˌlated** *adj* ▸**ˌocel'lation** *n*

ocelot ('ɒsɪˌlɒt, 'əʊ-) *n* a feline mammal inhabiting Central and South America and having a dark-spotted buff-brown coat. [C18: via F from Nahuatl *ocelotl* jaguar]

och (ɒx) *interj Scot. & Irish.* an expression of surprise, contempt, disagreement, etc.

oche ('ɒkɪ) *n Darts.* the mark or ridge on the floor behind which a player must stand to throw. [from ?]

ochlocracy (ɒk'lɒkrəsɪ) *n, pl* **ochlocracies.** rule by the mob; mobocracy. [C16: via F, from Gk *okhlokratia,* from *okhlos* mob + *kratos* power]
▸**ochlocrat** ('ɒkləˌkræt) *n* ▸**ˌochlo'cratic** *adj*

ochone (ɒ'xəʊn) *interj Scot. & Irish.* an expression of sorrow or regret. [from Gaelic *ochóin*]

ochre *or US* **ocher** ('əʊkə) *n* **1** any of various natural earths containing ferric oxide, silica, and alumina: used as yellow or red pigments. **2a** a moderate yellow-orange to orange colour. **2b** (*as adj*): *an ochre dress.* ◆ *vb* **ochres, ochring, ochred** *or US* **ochers, ochering, ochered. 3** (*tr*) to colour with ochre. [C15: from OF *ocre,* from L *ōchra,* from Gk *ōkhros* pale yellow]
▸**ochreous** ('əʊkrɪəs, 'əʊkərəs), **ochrous** ('əʊkrəs), **ochry** ('əʊkərɪ, 'əʊkrɪ) *or US* **'ocherous, 'ochery** *adj*

-ock *suffix forming nouns.* indicating smallness: *hillock.* [OE *-oc, -uc*]

ocker ('ɒkə) *Austral. sl.* ◆ *n* **1** (*often cap.*) an uncultivated or boorish Australian. ◆ *adj* **2** typical of such a person. [C20: after an Australian TV character]

Ockham's *or* **Occam's razor** ('ɒkəmz) *n* a maxim, attributed to William of Occam, English nominalist philosopher (died ?1349), stating that in explaining something assumptions must not be needlessly multiplied.

o'clock (ə'klɒk) *adv* **1** used after a number from one to twelve to indicate the hour of the day or night. **2** used after a number to indicate direction or position relative to the observer, twelve o'clock being directly ahead and other positions being obtained by comparisons with a clock face. [C18: abbrev. for *of the clock*]

OCR *abbrev. for* optical character reader *or* recognition.

oct. *abbrev. for* octavo.

Oct. *abbrev. for* October.

oct- *combining form.* a variant of **octo-** before a vowel.

octa- *combining form.* a variant of **octo-**.

octad ('ɒktæd) *n* **1** a group or series of eight. **2** *Chem.* an element with a valency of eight. [C19: from Gk *oktas,* from *oktō* eight]
▸**oc'tadic** *adj*

octagon ('ɒktəgən) *n* a polygon having eight sides. [C17: via L from Gk *oktagōnos* having eight angles]
▸**octagonal** (ɒk'tægənᵊl) *adj*

octahedron (ˌɒktə'hiːdrən) *n, pl* **octahedrons** *or* **octahedra** (-drə). a solid figure having eight plane faces.

octal notation *or* **octal** ('ɒktəl) *n Computing.* a number system having a base 8, one octal digit being equivalent to a group of three bits.

octane ('ɒkteɪn) *n* a liquid hydrocarbon found in petroleum. Formula: C_8H_{18}.

octane number *or* **rating** *n* a measure of the antiknock quality of a petrol expressed as a percentage.

octant ('ɒktənt) *n* **1** *Maths.* **1a** any of the eight parts into which the three planes containing the Cartesian coordinate axes divide space. **1b** an eighth part of a circle. **2** *Astron.* the position of a celestial body when it is at an angular distance of 45° from another body. **3** an instrument used for measuring angles, similar to a sextant but having a graduated arc of 45°. [C17: from L *octans* half quadrant, from *octo* eight]

octavalent (ˌɒktə'veɪlənt) *adj Chem.* having a valency of eight.

octave ('ɒktɪv) *n* **1a** the interval between two musical notes one of which has twice the pitch of the other and lies eight notes away from it counting inclusively along the diatonic scale. **1b** one of these two notes, esp. the one of higher pitch. **1c** (*as modifier*): *an octave leap.* **2** *Prosody.* a rhythmic group of eight lines of verse. **3** ('ɒkteɪv). **3a** a feast day and the seven days following. **3b** the final day of this period. **4** the eighth of eight basic positions in fencing. **5** any set or series of eight. ◆ *adj* **6** consisting of eight parts. [C14: (orig.: eighth day) via OF from Med. L *octāva diēs* eighth day (after a festival), from L *octo* eight]

octavo (ɒk'teɪvəʊ) *n, pl* **octavos. 1** a book size resulting from folding a sheet of paper of a specified size to form eight leaves: *demi-octavo.* Often written: **8vo, 8°. 2** a book of this size. [C16: from NL *in octavo* in an eighth (of a sheet)]

octennial (ɒk'tɛnɪəl) *adj* **1** occurring every eight years. **2** lasting for eight years. [C17: from L *octennium,* from *octo* eight + *annus* year]
▸**oc'tennially** *adv*

octet (ɒk'tɛt) *n* **1** any group of eight, esp. singers or musicians. **2** a piece

THESAURUS

ing, inhabitancy, occupation, possession, residence, tenure, term, use

occupant *n* **1 = inhabitant,** addressee, denizen, holder, incumbent, indweller, inmate, lessee, occupier, resident, tenant, user

occupation *n* **1 = profession,** activity, business, calling, craft, employment, job, line (of work), post, pursuit, trade, vocation, walk of life, work **3 = possession,** control, holding, occupancy, residence, tenancy, tenure, use **4 = invasion,** conquest, foreign rule, seizure, subjugation

occupied *adj* **1 = inhabited,** full, lived-in, peopled, settled, tenanted **2 = busy,** employed, engaged, hard at it (*inf.*), tied up (*inf.*), working **3 = in use,** engaged, full, taken, unavailable
Antonyms *adj* ≠ **inhabited:** deserted, empty, tenantless, uninhabited, unoccupied, untenanted, vacant

occupy *vb* **1 = live in,** be established in, be in residence in, dwell in, ensconce oneself in, establish oneself in, inhabit, own, possess, reside in, stay in (*Scot.*), tenant **2** *often passive* **= take up,** absorb, amuse, busy, divert, employ, engage, engross, entertain, hold the attention of, immerse, interest, involve, keep busy *or* occupied, monopolize, preoccupy, tie up **3, 5 = fill,** cover, hold, permeate, pervade, take up, use, utilize **4 = invade,** capture, garrison, hold, keep, overrun, seize, take over, take possession of
Antonyms *vb* ≠ **live in:** abandon, depart, desert, evacuate, quit, vacate ≠ **invade:** retreat, withdraw

occur *vb* **1 = happen,** arise, befall, betide, chance, come about, come off (*inf.*), come to pass (*arch.*), crop up (*inf.*), eventuate, materialize, result, take place, turn up (*inf.*) **2 = exist,** appear, be found, be met with, be present, develop, manifest itself, obtain, show itself **3** *with* **to = come to mind,** come to one, cross one's mind, dawn on, enter one's head, offer itself, present itself, spring to mind, strike one, suggest itself

occurrence *n* **1 = incident,** adventure, affair, circumstance, episode, event, happening, instance, proceeding, transaction

of music composed for such a group. **3** *Prosody.* another word for **octave** (sense 2). **4** *Chem.* a stable group of eight electrons. ◆ Also (for senses 1, 2, 3): **octette.** [C19: from L *octo* eight, on the model of DUET]

octillion (ɒkˈtɪljən) *n* **1** (in Britain and Germany) the number represented as one followed by 48 zeros (10^{48}). **2** (in the US, Canada, and France) the number represented as one followed by 27 zeros (10^{27}). [C17: from F, on the model of MILLION]
▸**ocˈtillionth** *adj, n*

octo-, octa-, *or before a vowel* **oct-** *combining form.* eight: *octosyllabic; octagon.* [from L *octo,* Gk *okto*]

October (ɒkˈtəʊbə) *n* the tenth month of the year, consisting of 31 days. [OE, from L, from *octo* eight, since it was orig. the eighth month in Roman reckoning]

Octobrist (ɒkˈtəʊbrɪst) *n* a member of a Russian political party favouring the constitutional reforms granted in a manifesto issued by Nicholas II in Oct. 1905.

octocentenary (ˌɒktəʊsenˈtiːnərɪ) *n, pl* **octocentenaries.** an 800th anniversary.

octogenarian (ˌɒktəʊdʒɪˈnɛərɪən) *n* **1** a person who is from 80 to 89 years old. ◆ *adj* **2** of or relating to an octogenarian. [C19: from L *octōgēnārius* containing eighty, from *octōgēnī* eighty each]

octopus (ˈɒktəpəs) *n, pl* **octopuses. 1** a cephalopod mollusc having a soft oval body with eight long suckered tentacles and occurring at the sea bottom. **2** a powerful influential organization, etc., with far-reaching effects, esp. harmful ones. [C18: via NL from Gk *oktōpous* having eight feet]

octoroon *or* **octaroon** (ˌɒktəˈruːn) *n* a person having one quadroon and one White parent and therefore having one-eighth Black blood. Cf. **quadroon.** [C19: OCTO- + *-roon* as in QUADROON]

octosyllable (ˈɒktəˌsɪləbᵊl) *n* **1** a line of verse composed of eight syllables. **2** a word of eight syllables.
▸**octosyllabic** (ˌɒktəʊsɪˈlæbɪk) *adj*

octroi (ˈɒktrwɑː) *n* **1** (in some European countries, esp. France) a duty on goods brought into certain towns. **2** the place where it is collected. **3** the officers responsible for its collection. [C17: from F *octroyer* to concede, from Med. L *auctorizāre* to AUTHORIZE]

octuple (ˈɒktjʊpᵊl) *n* **1** a quantity or number eight times as great as another. ◆ *adj* **2** eight times as much or as many. **3** consisting of eight parts. ◆ *vb* **octuples, octupling, octupled. 4** (*tr*) to multiply by eight. [C17: from L *octuplus,* from *octo* eight + *-plus* as in *duplus* double]

ocular (ˈɒkjʊlə) *adj* **1** of or relating to the eye. ◆ *n* **2** another name for **eyepiece.** [C16: from L *ocularis* from *oculus* eye]
▸ˈ**ocularly** *adv*

ocularist (ˈɒkjʊlərɪst) *n* a person who makes artificial eyes.

oculate (ˈɒkjʊlɪt) *adj Zool.* **1** having eyes. **2** relating to or resembling eyes: *oculate markings.*

oculist (ˈɒkjʊlɪst) *n Med.* a former term for **ophthalmologist.** [C17: via F from L *oculus* eye]

od (ɒd, əʊd), **odyl,** *or* **odyle** (ˈɒdɪl) *n Arch.* a hypothetical force formerly thought to be responsible for many natural phenomena, such as magnetism, light, and hypnotism. [C19: coined by Baron Karl von Reichenbach (1788–1869), G scientist]
▸ˈ**odic** *adj*

OD[1] (ˌəʊˈdiː) *Inf.* ◆ *n* **1** an overdose of a drug. ◆ *vb* **OD's, OD'ing, OD'd.** (*intr*) **2** to take an overdose of a drug. [C20: from *o(ver)d(ose)*]

OD[2] *abbrev. for:* **1** Officer of the Day. **2** Also: **o.d.** *Mil.* olive drab. **3** Also: **O/D** *Banking.* **3a** on demand. **3b** overdrawn. **4** ordnance datum. **5** outside diameter.

ODA (in Britain) *abbrev. for* Overseas Development Administration.

odalisque *or* **odalisk** (ˈəʊdəlɪsk) *n* a female slave or concubine. [C17: via F, changed from Turkish *ōdalik,* from *ōdah* room + *-lik,* n. suffix]

odd ❶ (ɒd) *adj* **1** unusual or peculiar in appearance, character, etc. **2** occasional, incidental, or random: *odd jobs.* **3** leftover or additional: *odd bits of wool.* **4a** not divisible by two. **4b** represented or indicated by a number that is not divisible by two: *graphs are on odd pages.* Cf. **even**[1] (sense 7). **5** being part of a matched pair or set when the other or others are missing: *an odd sock.* **6** (*in combination*) used to designate an indefinite quantity more than the quantity specified in round numbers: *fifty-odd pounds.* **7** out-of-the-way or secluded: *odd corners.* **8** **odd man out.** a person or thing excluded from others forming a group, unit, etc. ◆ *n* **9** *Golf.* **9a** one stroke more than the score of one's opponent. **9b** a handicap of one stroke. **10** a thing or person that is odd in sequence or number. ◆ See also **odds.** [from ON *oddi* triangle, point]
▸ˈ**oddly** *adv* ▸ˈ**oddness** *n*

oddball (ˈɒdˌbɔːl) *Inf.* ◆ *n* **1** Also: **odd bod, odd fish.** a strange or eccentric person or thing. ◆ *adj* **2** strange or peculiar.

Oddfellow (ˈɒdˌfeləʊ) *n* a member of a secret benevolent and fraternal association founded in England in the 18th century.

oddity ❶ (ˈɒdɪtɪ) *n, pl* **oddities. 1** an odd person or thing. **2** an odd quality or characteristic. **3** the condition of being odd.

odd-jobman *or* **odd-jobber** *n* a person who does casual work, esp. domestic repairs.

oddment ❶ (ˈɒdmənt) *n* **1** (*often pl*) an odd piece or thing; leftover. **2** *Printing.* **2a** pages that do not make a complete signature. **2b** any individual part of a book excluding the main text.

odd pricing *n* pricing goods in such a way as to imply that a bargain is being offered, as £5.99 instead of £6.

odds ❶ (ɒdz) *pl n* **1** (foll. by *on* or *against*) the probability, expressed as a ratio, that a certain event will take place: *the odds against the outsider are a hundred to one.* **2** the amount, expressed as a ratio, by which the wager of one better is greater than that of another: *he was offering odds of five to one.* **3** the likelihood that a certain state of affairs will be so: *the odds are that he is drunk.* **4** an equalizing allowance, esp. one given to a weaker side in a contest. **5** the advantage that one contender is judged to have over another. **6** *Brit.* a significant difference (esp. in **it makes no odds**). **7 at odds.** on bad terms. **8 give** *or* **lay odds.** to offer a bet with favourable odds. **9 over the odds. 9a** more than is expected, necessary, etc. **9b** unfair or excessive. **10 take odds.** to accept a bet with favourable odds. **11 what's the odds?** *Brit. inf.* what difference does it make?

odds and ends ❶ *pl n* miscellaneous items or articles.

odds-on *adj* **1** (of a horse, etc.) rated at even money or less to win. **2** regarded as more or most likely to win, succeed, happen, etc.

ode (əʊd) *n* **1** a lyric poem, typically addressed to a particular subject, with lines of varying lengths and complex rhythms. **2** (formerly) a poem meant to be sung. [C16: via F from LL *ōda,* from Gk *ōidē,* from *aeidein* to sing]

-ode[1] *n combining form.* denoting resemblance: *nematode.* [from Gk *-ōdēs,* from *eidos* shape]

-ode[2] *n combining form.* denoting a path or way: *electrode.* [from Gk *-odos,* from *hodos* a way]

odeum (ˈəʊdɪəm) *n, pl* **odea** (ˈəʊdɪə). (esp. in ancient Greece and Rome) a building for musical performances. Also called: **odeon.** [C17: from L, from Gk *ōideion,* from *ōidē* ODE]

odious ❶ (ˈəʊdɪəs) *adj* offensive; repugnant. [C17: from L; see ODIUM]
▸ˈ**odiousness** *n*

odium ❶ (ˈəʊdɪəm) *n* **1** the dislike accorded to a hated person or thing. **2** hatred; repugnance. [C17: from L; rel. to *ōdī* I hate, Gk *odussasthai* to be angry]

odometer (ɒˈdɒmɪtə, əʊ-) *n* the usual US and Canad. name for **mileometer.** [C18 *hodometer,* from Gk *hodos* way + -METER]
▸**oˈdometry** *n*

-odont *adj and n combining form.* -toothed: *acrodont.* [from Gk *odōn* tooth]

odonto- *or before a vowel* **odont-** *combining form.* indicating a tooth or teeth: *odontology.* [from Gk *odōn* tooth]

odontoglossum (ɒˌdɒntəˈglɒsəm) *n* a tropical American epiphytic orchid having clusters of brightly coloured flowers.

odontology (ˌɒdɒnˈtɒlədʒɪ) *n* the branch of science concerned with the anatomy, development, and diseases of teeth.
▸**odontological** (ɒˌdɒntəˈlɒdʒɪkᵊl) *adj* ▸ˌ**odonˈtologist** *n*

odoriferous (ˌəʊdəˈrɪfərəs) *adj* having or emitting an odour, esp. a fragrant one.
▸ˌ**odorˈiferously** *adv* ▸ˌ**odorˈiferousness** *n*

odoriphore (əʊˈdɒrɪˌfɔː) *n Chem.* the group of atoms in an odorous molecule responsible for its odour.

odorous ❶ (ˈəʊdərəs) *adj* having or emitting a characteristic smell or odour.
▸ˈ**odorously** *adv* ▸ˈ**odorousness** *n*

THESAURUS

odd *adj* **1** = **unusual,** abnormal, atypical, bizarre, curious, deviant, different, eccentric, exceptional, extraordinary, fantastic, freak, freakish, funny, irregular, kinky (*inf.*), left-field (*inf.*), off-the-wall (*sl.*), outlandish, out of the ordinary, outré, peculiar, quaint, queer, rare, remarkable, singular, strange, uncanny, uncommon, unconventional, weird, whimsical **2** = **occasional,** casual, fragmentary, incidental, irregular, miscellaneous, periodic, random, seasonal, sundry, varied, various **3** = **spare,** leftover, lone, remaining, single, solitary, surplus, unconsumed, uneven, unmatched, unpaired ◆ *n* **8 odd man out** = **misfit,** exception, freak, maverick, nonconformist, outsider, square peg in a round hole (*inf.*)
Antonyms *adj* ≠ **unusual:** common, customary, familiar, natural, normal, ordinary, regular, typical, unexceptional, unremarkable, usual ≠ **occasional:** habitual, permanent, regular, steady ≠ **spare:** even, matched, paired

oddity *n* **1** = **misfit,** card (*inf.*), crank (*inf.*), fish out of water, loose cannon, maverick, nut (*sl.*), oddball (*inf.*), rara avis, screwball (*sl., chiefly US & Canad.*), weirdo *or* weirdie (*inf.*) **2** = **irregularity,** abnormality, anomaly, eccentricity, freak, idiosyncrasy, kink, peculiarity, phenomenon, quirk, rarity **3** = **strangeness,** abnormality, bizarreness, eccentricity, extraordinariness, freakishness, incongruity, oddness, outlandishness, peculiarity, queerness, singularity, unconventionality, unnaturalness

oddment *n* **1** = **leftover,** bit, butt, end, end of a line, fag end, fragment, off cut, remnant, scrap, shred, sliver, snippet, stub, tail end

odds *pl n* **1, 3** = **probability,** balance, chances, likelihood **5** = **advantage,** allowance, edge, lead, superiority **6** *Brit.* = **difference,** disparity, dissimilarity, distinction **7 at odds** = **in conflict,** at daggers drawn, at loggerheads, at sixes and sevens, at variance, in disagreement, in opposition to, not in keeping, on bad terms, out of line

odds and ends *pl n* = **scraps,** bits, bits and pieces, debris, leavings, litter, oddments, remnants, rubbish, sundry *or* miscellaneous items

odious *adj* = **offensive,** abhorrent, abominable, detestable, disgusting, execrable, foul, hateful, horrible, horrid, loathsome, obnoxious, obscene, repellent, repugnant, repulsive, revolting, unpleasant, vile, yucky *or* yukky (*sl.*)
Antonyms *adj* agreeable, charming, congenial, delightful, enchanting, enjoyable, pleasant, pleasing, winsome

odium *n* **1, 2** = **hatred,** abhorrence, antipathy, censure, condemnation, detestation, disapprobation, disapproval, discredit, disfavour, disgrace, dishonour, dislike, disrepute, execration, infamy, obloquy, opprobrium, reprobation, shame

odorous *adj* = **scented,** aromatic, balmy, fra-

odour *or US* **odor** ('əʊdə) *n* **1** the property of a substance that gives it a characteristic scent or smell. **2** a pervasive quality about something: *an odour of dishonesty.* **3** repute or regard (in **in good odour, in bad odour**). **4** *Arch.* a sweet-smelling fragrance. [C13: from OF *odur,* from L *odor*]
▸'**odourless** *or US* '**odorless** *adj*

Odyssey ('ɒdɪsɪ) *n* **1** a Greek epic poem, attributed to Homer, describing the ten-year homeward wanderings of Odysseus, a mythical Greek hero, after the fall of Troy. **2** (*often not cap.*) any long eventful journey.
▸**Odyssean** (ˌɒdɪ'siːən) *adj*

Oe *symbol for* oersted.

OE *abbrev. for* Old English (language).

OECD *abbrev. for* Organization for Economic Cooperation and Development.

OED *abbrev. for* Oxford English Dictionary.

oedema *or* **edema** (ɪ'diːmə) *n, pl* **oedemata** *or* **edemata** (-mətə). **1** *Pathol.* an excessive accumulation of serous fluid in the intercellular spaces of tissue. **2** *Bot.* an abnormal swelling in a plant caused by parenchyma or an accumulation of water in the tissues. [C16: via NL from Gk *oidēma,* from *oidein* to swell]
▸**oedematous, edematous** (ɪ'dɛmətəs) *or* **oe'dema,tose, e'dema,tose** *adj*

Oedipus complex ('iːdɪpəs) *n Psychoanal.* the repressed sexual feeling of a child, esp. a male child, for its parent of the opposite sex combined with a rivalry with the parent of the same sex. [C20: after *Oedipus,* a legendary king who unknowingly killed his father and married his mother]
▸'**oedipal** *or* ˌ**oedi'pean** *adj*

OEEC *abbrev. for* Organization for European Economic Cooperation. It was superseded by the OECD in 1961.

OEM *abbrev. for* original equipment manufacturer: a computer company whose products are made by combining basic parts supplied by others to meet a customer's needs.

oenology *or* **enology** (iː'nɒlədʒɪ) *n* the study of wine. [C19: from Gk *oinos* wine + -LOGY]
▸**oenological** *or* **enological** (ˌiːnə'lɒdʒɪkᵊl) *adj* ▸**oe'nologist** *or* **e'nologist** *n*

oenothera (iː'nɒθərə) *n* any of various hardy biennial or herbaceous perennial plants having yellow flowers. Also called: **evening primrose.** [from Gk *oinothēras,* ?from *onothēras* a plant whose roots smell of wine]

o'er (ɔː, əʊə) *prep, adv* a poetic contraction of **over.**

oersted ('ɜːsted) *n* the cgs unit of magnetic field strength; the field strength that would cause a unit magnetic pole to experience a force of 1 dyne in free space. It is equivalent to 79.58 amperes per metre. Symbol. Oe [C20: after H. C. *Oersted* (1777–1851), Danish physicist who discovered electromagnetism]

oesophagus *or US* **esophagus** (iː'sɒfəgəs) *n, pl* **oesophagi** *or US* **esophagi** (-ˌgaɪ). the part of the alimentary canal between the pharynx and the stomach; gullet. [C16: via NL from Gk *oisophagos,* from *oisein,* future infinitive of *pherein* to carry + *-phagos,* from *phagein* to eat]
▸**oesophageal** *or US* **esophageal** (iːˌsɒfə'dʒiːəl) *adj*

oestradiol (ˌiːstrə'daɪɒl, ˌestrə-) *or US* **estradiol** *n* the most potent oestrogenic horome secreted by the mammalian ovary: synthesized and used to treat oestrogen deficiency and cancer of the breast. [C20: from NL, from OESTRIN + DI-[1] + -OL[1]]

oestrin ('iːstrɪn) *n* an obsolete term for **oestrogen.** [C20: from OESTR(US) + -IN]

oestrogen ('iːstrədʒən, 'ɛstrə-) *or US* **estrogen** *n* any of several hormones that induce oestrus, stimulate changes in the female reproductive organs, and promote development of female secondary sexual characteristics. [C20: from OESTRUS + -GEN]
▸**oestrogenic** (ˌiːstrə'dʒɛnɪk, ˌɛstrə-) *or US* **estrogenic** (ˌɛstrə'dʒɛnɪk, ˌiːstrə-) *adj* ▸ˌ**oestro'genically** *or US* ˌ**estro'genically** *adv*

oestrous cycle ('iːstrəs) *n* a hormonally controlled cycle of activity of the reproductive organs in many female mammals.

oestrus ('iːstrəs, 'ɛstrəs) *or US* **estrus, estrum** ('ɛstrəm, 'iːstrəm) *n* a regularly occurring period of sexual receptivity in most female mammals, except humans, during which ovulation occurs and copulation can take place; heat. [C17: from L *oestrus* gadfly, hence frenzy, from Gk *oistros*]
▸'**oestrous,** '**oestral** *or US* '**estrous,** '**estral** *adj*

oeuvre *French.* (œvrə) *n* **1** a work of art, literature, music, etc. **2** the total output of a writer, painter, etc. [ult. from L *opera,* pl. of *opus* work]

of (ɒv; *unstressed* əv) *prep* **1** used with a verbal noun or gerund to link it with a following noun that is either the subject or the object of the verb embedded in the gerund: *the breathing of a fine swimmer* (subject); *the breathing of clean air* (object). **2** used to indicate possession, origin, or association: *the house of my sister; to die of hunger.* **3** used after words or phrases expressing quantities: *a pint of milk.* **4** constituted by, containing, or characterized by: *a family of idiots; a rod of iron; a man of some depth.* **5** used to indicate separation, as in time or space: *within a mile of the town; within ten minutes of the beginning of the concert.* **6** used to mark apposition: *the city of Naples; a speech on the subject of archaeology.* **7** about; concerning: *speak to me of love.* **8** used in passive constructions to indicate the agent: *he was beloved of all.* **9** *Inf.* used to indicate a day or part of a period of time when some activity habitually occurs: *I go to the pub of an evening.* **10** *US.* before the hour of: *a quarter of nine.* [OE (as prep & adv); rel. to L *ab*]

> **USAGE NOTE** See at **off.**

OF *abbrev. for* Old French (language).

off (ɒf) *prep* **1** used to indicate actions in which contact is absent, as between an object and a surface: *to lift a cup off the table.* **2** used to indicate the removal of something that is appended to or in association with something else: *to take the tax off potatoes.* **3** out of alignment with: *we are off course.* **4** situated near to or leading away from: *just off the High Street.* **5** not inclined towards: *I've gone off you.* ◆ *adv* **6** (*particle*) so as to be deactivated or disengaged: *turn off the radio.* **7** (*particle*) **7a** so as to get rid of: *sleep off a hangover.* **7b** so as to be removed from, esp. as a reduction: *he took ten per cent off.* **8** spent away from work or other duties: *take the afternoon off.* **9a** on a trip, journey, or race: *I saw her off at the station.* **9b** (*particle*) so as to be completely absent, used up, or exhausted: *this stuff kills off all vermin.* **10** out from the shore or land: *the ship stood off.* **11a** out of contact; at a distance: *the ship was 10 miles off.* **11b** out of the present location: *the girl ran off.* **12** away in the future: *August is less than a week off.* **13** (*particle*) so as to be no longer taking place: *the match has been rained off.* **14** (*particle*) removed from contact with something, as clothing from the body: *the girl took all her clothes off.* **15** offstage: *noises off.* **16 off and on.** intermittently; from time to time: *he comes here off and on.* **17 off with.** (*interj*) a command or an exhortation to remove or cut off (something specified): *off with his head; off with that coat.* ◆ *adj* **18** not on; no longer operative: *the off position on the dial.* **19** (*postpositive*) not taking place; cancelled or postponed: *the meeting is off.* **20** in a specified condition regarding money, provisions, etc.: *well off; how are you off for bread?* **21** unsatisfactory or disappointing: *his performance was rather off; an off year for good tennis.* **22** (*postpositive*) in a condition as specified: *I'd be better off without this job.* **23** (*postpositive*) no longer on the menu: *haddock is off.* **24** (*postpositive*) (of food or drink) having gone bad, sour, etc.: *this milk is off.* ◆ *n* **25** *Cricket.* **25a** the part of the field on that side of the pitch to which the batsman presents his bat when taking strike. **25b** (*in combination*) a fielding position in this part of the field: *mid-off.* **25c** (*as modifier*): *the off stump.* [orig. var. of OF; fully distinguished from it in the 17th cent.]

> **USAGE NOTE** In standard English, *off* is not followed by *of*: *he stepped off* (not *off of*) *the platform.*

off. *abbrev. for:* **1** offer. **2** office. **3** officer. **4** official.

offal ('ɒfᵊl) *n* **1** the edible internal parts of an animal, such as the heart, liver, and tongue. **2** dead or decomposing organic matter. **3** refuse; rubbish. [C14: from OFF + FALL, referring to parts fallen or cut off]

off-balance-sheet reserve *n Accounting.* a sum of money or an asset that should appear on a company's balance but does not; hidden reserve.

offbeat ('ɒfˌbiːt) *n* **1** *Music.* any of the normally unaccented beats in a bar, such as the second and fourth beats in a bar of four-four time. ◆ *adj* **2a** unusual, unconventional, or eccentric. **2b** (*as n*): *he liked the offbeat in fashion.*

off break *n Cricket.* a bowled ball that spins from off to leg on pitching.

off-Broadway *adj* **1** designating the kind of experimental, low-budget, or noncommercial productions associated with theatre outside the Broadway area in New York. **2** (of theatres) not located on Broadway.

off colour *adj* (**off-colour** *when prenominal*). **1** *Chiefly Brit.* slightly ill; unwell. **2** indecent or indelicate; risqué.

offcut ('ɒfˌkʌt) *n* a piece of paper, wood, fabric, etc., remaining after the main pieces have been cut; remnant.

offence *or US* **offense** (ə'fens) *n* **1** a violation or breach of a law, rule, etc. **2** any public wrong or crime. **3** annoyance, displeasure, or resentment. **4 give offence (to).** to cause annoyance or displeasure (to). **5 take offence.** to feel injured, humiliated, or offended. **6** a source of annoyance, displeasure, or anger. **7** attack; assault. **8** *Arch.* injury or harm.

THESAURUS

grant, odoriferous, perfumed, redolent, sweet-smelling

odour *n* **1** = **smell,** aroma, bouquet, essence, fragrance, niff (*Brit. sl.*), perfume, redolence, scent, stench, stink **2** = **quality,** air, atmosphere, aura, emanation, flavour, spirit

Odyssey *n* **2** *often not cap.* = **journey,** crusade, peregrination, pilgrimage, quest, trek, voyage

off *adv* **8-11** = **away,** apart, aside, elsewhere, out **16 off and on** = **occasionally,** (every) now and again, every once in a while, from time to time, intermittently, now and then, on and off, sometimes, sporadically ◆ *adj* **19** = **cancelled,** absent, finished, gone, inoperative, postponed, unavailable **21** = **substandard,** bad, below par, disappointing, disheartening, displeasing, low-quality, mortifying, poor, quiet, slack, unrewarding, unsatisfactory **24** = **bad,** decomposed, high, mouldy, rancid, rotten, sour, turned

offbeat *adj* **2** = **unusual,** bizarre, Bohemian, eccentric, far-out (*sl.*), idiosyncratic, left-field (*inf.*), novel, oddball (*inf.*), off-the-wall (*sl.*), outré, rum (*Brit. sl.*), strange, uncommon, unconventional, unorthodox, way-out (*inf.*), weird
Antonyms *adj* common, conventional, normal, ordinary, orthodox, run-of-the-mill, stereotyped, traditional, unoriginal, usual

off colour *adj* **1** = **ill,** green about the gills, not up to par, off form, out of sorts, peaky, peely-wally (*Scot.*), poorly (*inf.*), queasy, run down, sick, under par, under the weather (*inf.*), unwell, washed out

offence *n* **1, 2** = **crime,** breach of conduct, delinquency, fault, lapse, misdeed, misdemeanour, peccadillo, sin, transgression, trespass, wrong, wrongdoing **3** = **annoyance,** anger, displeasure, hard feelings, huff, indignation, ire (*literary*), needle (*inf.*), pique, resentment, um-

offend ⓣ (əˈfɛnd) *vb* **1** to hurt the feelings, sense of dignity, etc., of (a person, etc.). **2** (*tr*) to be disagreeable to; disgust: *the smell offended him.* **3** (*intr except in archaic uses*) to break (a law). [C14: via OF *offendre* to strike against, from L *offendere*]
▸**ofˈfender** *n* ▸**ofˈfending** *adj*

offensive ⓣ (əˈfɛnsɪv) *adj* **1** unpleasant or disgusting, as to the senses. **2** causing anger or annoyance; insulting. **3** for the purpose of attack rather than defence. ◆ *n* **4** (usually preceded by *the*) an attitude or position of aggression. **5** an assault, attack, or military initiative, esp. a strategic one.
▸**ofˈfensively** *adv* ▸**ofˈfensiveness** *n*

offer ⓣ (ˈɒfə) *vb* **1** to present (something, someone, oneself, etc.) for acceptance or rejection. **2** (*tr*) to present as part of a requirement: *she offered English as a second subject.* **3** (*tr*) to provide or make accessible: *this stream offers the best fishing.* **4** (*intr*) to present itself: *if an opportunity should offer.* **5** (*tr*) to show or express willingness or the intention (to do something). **6** (*tr*) to put forward (a proposal, opinion, etc.) for consideration. **7** (*tr*) to present for sale. **8** (*tr*) to propose as payment; bid or tender. **9** (when *tr*, often foll. by *up*) to present (a prayer, sacrifice, etc.) as or during an act of worship. **10** (*tr*) to show readiness for: *to offer battle.* **11** (*intr*) *Arch.* to make a proposal of marriage. ◆ *n* **12** something, such as a proposal or bid, that is offered. **13** the act of offering or the condition of being offered. **14** a proposal of marriage. **15 on offer.** for sale at a reduced price. [OE, from L *offerre* to present, from *ob-* to + *ferre* to bring]

offer document *n* a document sent by a person or firm making a takeover bid to the shareholders of the target company, giving details of the offer that has been made and, usually, reasons for accepting it.

offering ⓣ (ˈɒfərɪŋ) *n* **1** something that is offered. **2** a contribution to the funds of a religious organization. **3** a sacrifice, as of an animal, to a deity.

offertory (ˈɒfətərɪ) *n, pl* **offertories.** *Christianity.* **1** the oblation of the bread and wine at the Eucharist. **2** the offerings of the worshippers at this service. **3** the prayers said or sung while the worshippers' offerings are being brought to the altar during the **offertory procession.** [C14: from Church L *offertōrium* place appointed for offerings, from L *offerre* to OFFER]

offhand ⓣ (ˌɒfˈhænd) *adj also* **offhanded,** *adv* **1** without care, thought, attention, or consideration; sometimes, brusque or ungracious: *an offhand manner.* **2** without preparation or warning; impromptu.
▸ˌ**offˈhandedly** *adv* ▸ˌ**offˈhandedness** *n*

office ⓣ (ˈɒfɪs) *n* **1a** a room or rooms in which business, professional duties, clerical work, etc., are carried out. **1b** (*as modifier*): *office furniture; an office boy.* **2** (*often pl*) the building or buildings in which the work of an organization, such as a business, is carried out. **3** a commercial or professional business: *the architect's office approved the plans.* **4** the group of persons working in an office: *it was a happy office until she came.* **5** (*cap. when part of a name*) a department of the national government: *the Home Office.* **6** (*cap. when part of a name*) **6a** a governmental agency, esp. of the Federal government in the US. **6b** a subdivision of such an agency: *Office of Science and Technology.* **7a** a position of trust, responsibility, or duty, esp. in a government or organization: *to seek office.* **7b** (*in combination*): *an office-holder.* **8** duty or function: *the office of an administrator.* **9** (*often pl*) a minor task or service: *domestic offices.* **10** (*often pl*) an action performed for another, usually a beneficial action: *through his good offices.* **11** a place where tickets, information, etc., can be obtained: *a ticket office.* **12** *Christianity.* **12a** (*often pl*) a ceremony or service, prescribed by ecclesiastical authorities, esp. one for the dead. **12b** *RC Church.* the official daily service. **12c** short for **divine office.** **13** (*pl*) the parts of a house or estate where work is done, goods are stored, etc. **14** (*usually pl*) *Brit., euphemistic.* a lavatory (esp. in **usual offices**). **15 in** (*or* **out of**) **office.** (of a government) in (*or* out of) power. **16 the office.** a hint or signal. [C13: via OF from L *officium* service, duty, from *opus* work, service + *facere* to do]

office block *n* a large building designed to provide office accommodation.

office boy *n* a male office junior.

office junior *n* a young person, esp. a school-leaver, employed in an office for running errands and doing other minor jobs.

officer ⓣ (ˈɒfɪsə) *n* **1** a person in the armed services who holds a position of responsibility, authority, and duty. **2** See **police officer.** **3** (on a non-naval ship) any person, including the captain and mate, who holds a position of authority and responsibility: *radio officer; engineer officer.* **4** a person appointed or elected to a position of responsibility or authority in a government, society, etc. **5** a government official: *a customs officer.* **6** (in the Order of the British Empire) a member of the grade below commander. ◆ *vb* (*tr*) **7** to furnish with officers. **8** to act as an officer over (some section, group, organization, etc.).

officer of the day *n* a military officer whose duty is to take charge of the security of the unit or camp for a day. Also called: **orderly officer.**

official ⓣ (əˈfɪʃəl) *adj* **1** of or relating to an office, its administration, or its duration. **2** sanctioned by, recognized by, or derived from authority: *an official statement.* **3** having a formal ceremonial character: *an official dinner.* ◆ *n* **4** a person who holds a position in an organization, government department, etc., esp. a subordinate position.
▸**ofˈficially** *adv*

officialdom (əˈfɪʃəldəm) *n* **1** the outlook or behaviour of officials, esp. those rigidly adhering to regulations; bureaucracy. **2** officials or bureaucrats collectively.

officialese (əˌfɪʃəˈliːz) *n* language characteristic of official documents, esp. when verbose or pedantic.

Official Receiver *n* an officer appointed by the Department of Trade and Industry to receive the income and manage the estate of a bankrupt. See also **receiver** (sense 2).

officiant (əˈfɪʃɪənt) *n* a person who presides and officiates at a religious ceremony.

officiate ⓣ (əˈfɪʃɪˌeɪt) *vb* **officiates, officiating, officiated.** (*intr*) **1** to hold the position, responsibility, or function of an official. **2** to conduct a religious or other ceremony. [C17: from Med. L *officiāre,* from L *officium;* see OFFICE]
▸**ofˌficiˈation** *n* ▸**ofˈficiˌator** *n*

officious ⓣ (əˈfɪʃəs) *adj* **1** unnecessarily or obtrusively ready to offer advice or services. **2** *Diplomacy.* informal or unofficial. [C16: from L *officiōsus* kindly, from *officium* service; see OFFICE]
▸**ofˈficiously** *adv* ▸**ofˈficiousness** *n*

offing ⓣ (ˈɒfɪŋ) *n* **1** the part of the sea that can be seen from the shore. **2 in the offing.** likely to occur soon.

offish (ˈɒfɪʃ) *adj Inf.* aloof or distant in manner.
▸ˈ**offishly** *adv* ▸ˈ**offishness** *n*

THESAURUS

brage, wounded feelings, wrath **4** *As in* **give offence** = **insult**, affront, displeasure, harm, hurt, indignity, injury, injustice, outrage, put-down (*sl.*), slight, snub **5 take offence** = **be offended**, be disgruntled, get riled, go into a huff, resent, take the huff, take the needle (*inf.*), take umbrage

offend *vb* **1** = **insult**, affront, annoy, cut to the quick, disgruntle, displease, fret, gall, give offence, hurt (someone's) feelings, irritate, miff (*inf.*), outrage, pain, pique, provoke, put down, put (someone's) back up, rile, slight, snub, tread on (someone's) toes (*inf.*), upset, vex, wound **2** = **disgust**, be disagreeable to, gross out (*US sl.*), make (someone) sick, nauseate, repel, repulse, sicken, turn (someone) off (*inf.*)
Antonyms *vb* ≠ **insult:** appease, assuage, conciliate, delight, mollify, placate, please, soothe

offended *adj* **1** = **resentful**, affronted, disgruntled, displeased, huffy, in a huff, miffed (*inf.*), outraged, pained, piqued, put out (*inf.*), smarting, stung, upset

offender *n* **3** = **criminal**, crook, culprit, delinquent, lawbreaker, malefactor, miscreant, sinner, transgressor, villain, wrongdoer

offensive *adj* **1** = **disgusting**, abominable, detestable, disagreeable, grisly, loathsome, nasty, nauseating, noisome, obnoxious, odious, repellent, revolting, sickening, unpalatable, unpleasant, unsavoury, vile, yucky *or* yukky (*sl.*) **2** = **insulting**, abusive, annoying, detestable, discourteous, displeasing, disrespectful, embarrassing, impertinent, insolent, irritating, objectionable, rude, uncivil, unmannerly **3** = **attacking**, aggressive, invading ◆ *n* **4** *As in* **on the offensive** = **aggression**, advance, attack, invasion, the warpath (*inf.*) **5** = **attack**, campaign, drive, onslaught, push (*inf.*)
Antonyms *adj* ≠ **disgusting:** agreeable, attractive, captivating, charming, delightful, pleasant ≠ **insulting:** civil, conciliatory, courteous, deferential, polite, respectful ≠ **attacking:** defensive ◆ *n* ≠ **aggression:** defensive

offer *vb* **1, 7, 8** = **proffer**, bid, extend, give, hold out, put on the market, put under the hammer, put up for sale, tender **3** = **provide**, afford, furnish, make available, place at (someone's) disposal, present, purvey, show **5** = **volunteer**, be at (someone's) service, come forward, offer one's services **6** = **propose**, advance, extend, move, put forth, put forward, submit, suggest ◆ *n* **12** = **proposal**, attempt, bid, endeavour, essay, overture, proposition, submission, suggestion, tender
Antonyms *vb* ≠ **proffer:** refuse, retract, revoke, take back, withdraw, withhold

offering *n* **2** = **contribution**, donation, gift, hand-out, present, subscription, widow's mite **3** = **sacrifice**, oblation

offhand *adj* **1** = **casual**, abrupt, aloof, brusque, careless, cavalier, couldn't-care-less, curt, glib, informal, offhanded, perfunctory, take-it-or-leave-it (*inf.*), unceremonious, unconcerned, uninterested ◆ *adv* **2** = **impromptu**, ad lib, extempore, just like that (*inf.*), off the cuff (*inf.*), off the top of one's head (*inf.*), without preparation
Antonyms *adj* ≠ **casual:** attentive, careful, grave, intent, planned, premeditated, prepared, responsible, serious, thoughtful

office *n* **7, 8** = **post**, appointment, business, capacity, charge, commission, duty, employment, function, obligation, occupation, place, responsibility, role, service, situation, station, trust, work

officer *n* **4** = **official**, agent, appointee, bureaucrat, dignitary, executive, functionary, office-holder, public servant, representative

official *adj* **2** = **authorized**, accredited, authentic, authoritative, bona fide, certified, endorsed, ex cathedra, ex officio, formal, legitimate, licensed, proper, sanctioned, signed and sealed, straight from the horse's mouth (*inf.*) ◆ *n* **4** = **officer**, agent, bureaucrat, executive, functionary, office bearer, representative
Antonyms *adj* ≠ **authorized:** casual, doubtful, dubious, informal, unauthorized, unofficial, unreliable

officiate *vb* **1** = **preside**, chair, conduct, emcee (*inf.*), manage, oversee, serve, superintend

officious *adj* **1** = **interfering**, bustling, dictatorial, forward, impertinent, inquisitive, intrusive, meddlesome, meddling, mischievous, obtrusive, opinionated, overbusy, overzealous, pragmatical (*rare*), pushy (*inf.*), self-important
Antonyms *adj* aloof, detached, indifferent, reserved, reticent, retiring, shy, taciturn, unforthcoming, withdrawn

offing *n* **2 in the offing** = **imminent**, close at hand, coming up, hovering, in prospect, in the immediate future, in the wings, on the horizon, on the way, upcoming

off key *adj* (**off-key** *when prenominal*), *adv* **1** *Music*. **1a** not in the correct key. **1b** out of tune. **2** out of keeping; discordant.

off-licence *n Brit*. **1** a shop or a counter in a pub or hotel where alcoholic drinks are sold for consumption elsewhere. US equivalents: **package store, liquor store.** **2** a licence permitting such sales.

off limits *adj* (**off-limits** *when prenominal*). **1** *US, chiefly mil*. not to be entered; out of bounds. ◆ *adv* **2** in or into an area forbidden by regulations.

off line *adj* (**off-line** *when prenominal*). **1** of or concerned with a part of a computer system not connected to the central processing unit but controlled by a computer storage device. Cf. **on line.** **2** disconnected from a computer; switched off.

off-load *vb* (*tr*) to get rid of (something unpleasant), as by delegation to another.

off message *adj* (**off-message** *when prenominal*) (esp. of a politician) not following the official line of his or her party.

off-peak *adj* of or relating to services as used outside periods of intensive use.

off-piste *adj* of or relating to skiing on virgin snow off the regular runs.

off-putting *adj Brit. inf*. arousing reluctance or aversion.

off-road *adj* **1** denoting the use of a vehicle away from public roads, esp. on rough terrain: *off-road motorcycling*. **2** (of a vehicle) designed or built for off-road use.

off-roader *n* a motor vehicle designed for use away from public roads, esp. on rough terrain.

off-sales *pl n Brit*. sales of alcoholic drink for consumption off the premises by a pub or an off-licence attached to a pub.

off season *adj* (**off-season** *when prenominal*). **1** denoting or occurring during a period of little activity in a trade or business. ◆ *n* **2** such a period. ◆ *adv* **3** in an off-season period.

offset *n* ('ɒfˌset). **1** something that counterbalances or compensates for something else. **2a** a printing method in which the impression is made onto an intermediate surface, such as a rubber blanket, which transfers it to the paper. **2b** (*modifier*) relating to, involving, or printed by offset: *offset letterpress*. **3** another name for **set off.** **4** *Bot*. a short runner in certain plants that produces roots and shoots at the tip. **5** a ridge projecting from a range of hills or mountains. **6** a narrow horizontal or sloping surface formed where a wall is reduced in thickness towards the top. **7** *Surveying*. a measurement of distance to a point at right angles to a survey line. ◆ *vb* (ˌɒf'set), **offsets, offsetting, offset.** **8** (*tr*) to counterbalance or compensate for. **9** (*tr*) to print (text, etc.) using the offset process. **10** (*tr*) to construct an offset in (a wall). **11** (*intr*) to project or develop as an offset.

offshoot ('ɒfˌʃuːt) *n* **1** a shoot or branch growing from the main stem of a plant. **2** something that develops or derives from a principal source or origin.

offshore (ˌɒf'ʃɔː) *adj, adv* **1** from, away from, or at some distance from the shore. ◆ *adj* **2** sited or conducted at sea: *offshore industries*. **3** based or operating abroad: *offshore banking; offshore fund*.

offside *adj, adv* (ˌɒf'saɪd). **1** *Sport*. (in football, etc.) in a position illegally ahead of the ball when it is played. Cf. **onside.** ◆ *n* ('ɒfˌsaɪd). **2** (usually preceded by *the*) *Chiefly Brit*. **2a** the side of a vehicle, etc., nearest the centre of the road. **2b** (*as modifier*): *the offside passenger door*.

off-sider (ˌɒf'saɪdə) *n Austral. & NZ*. a partner or assistant.

offspring ('ɒfˌsprɪŋ) *n* **1** the immediate descendant or descendants of a person, animal, etc.; progeny. **2** a product, outcome, or result.

offstage ('ɒf'steɪdʒ) *adj, adv* out of the view of the audience; off the stage.

off-the-peg *adj* (of clothing) ready to wear; not produced especially for the person buying.

off the shelf *adv* **1** from stock and readily available: *you can have this model off the shelf*. ◆ *adj* (**off-the-shelf** *when prenominal*). **2** of or relating to a product that is readily available: *an off-the-shelf model*. **3** of or denoting a company that has been registered with the Registrar of Companies for the sole purpose of being sold.

off-the-wall *adj* (**off the wall** *when postpositive*). *Sl*. new or unexpected in an unconventional or eccentric way. [C20: ?from the use of the phrase in handball and squash to describe a shot that is unexpected]

off-white *n* **1** a colour consisting of white with a tinge of grey or yellow. ◆ *adj* **2** of such a colour: *an off-white coat*.

oft (ɒft) *adv* short for **often** (archaic or poetic except in combinations such as **oft-repeated** and **oft-recurring**). [OE *oft*; rel. to OHG *ofto*]

OFT (in Britain) *abbrev. for* Office of Fair Trading.

Oftel ('ɒfˌtɛl) *n* (in Britain) *acronym for* Office of Telecommunications: a government body set up in 1984 to supervise telecommunications activities in the UK, and to protect the interests of the consumers.

often ('ɒfᵊn) *adv* **1** frequently or repeatedly; much of the time. Arch. equivalents: **'oftenˌtimes, 'oftˌtimes.** **2 as often as not.** quite frequently. **3 every so often.** at intervals. **4 more often than not.** in more than half the instances. ◆ *adj* **5** *Arch*. repeated; frequent. [C14: var. of OFT before vowels and *h*]

ogee ('əʊdʒiː) *n Archit*. **1** Also called: **talon.** a moulding having a cross section in the form of a letter S. **2** short for **ogee arch.** [C15: prob. var. of OGIVE]

ogee arch *n Archit*. a pointed arch having an S-shaped curve on both sides. Sometimes shortened to **ogee.**

Ogen melon ('əʊgɛn) *n* a variety of small melon with sweet pale orange flesh. [C20: after a kibbutz in Israel where it was first developed]

ogham *or* **ogam** ('ɒgəm) *n* an ancient alphabetical writing system used by the Celts in Britain, consisting of straight lines drawn or carved perpendicular to or at an angle to another long straight line. [C17: from OIrish *ogom*, from ?, but associated with the name *Ogma*, legendary inventor of this alphabet]

ogive ('əʊdʒaɪv, əʊ'dʒaɪv) *n* **1** a diagonal rib or groin of a Gothic vault. **2** another name for **lancet arch.** [C17: from OF, from ?]
▸ **o'gival** *adj*

ogle ('əʊgᵊl) *vb* **ogles, ogling, ogled.** **1** to look at (someone) amorously or lustfully. **2** (*tr*) to stare or gape at. ◆ *n* **3** a flirtatious or lewd look. [C17: prob. from Low G *oegeln*, from *oegen* to look at]
▸ **'ogler** *n*

O grade *n* (formerly, in Scotland). **1a** the basic level of the Scottish Certificate of Education, now replaced by **Standard Grade.** **1b** (*as modifier*): *O-grade history*. **2** a pass in a subject at O grade: *she has ten O grades*.

ogre ('əʊgə) *n* **1** (in folklore) a giant, usually given to eating human flesh. **2** any monstrous or cruel person. [C18: from F, ?from L *Orcus*, god of the infernal regions]
▸ **'ogreish** *adj* ▸ **'ogress** *fem n*

oh (əʊ) *interj* an exclamation expressive of surprise, pain, pleasure, etc.

OHG *abbrev. for* Old High German.

ohm (əʊm) *n* the derived SI unit of electrical resistance; the resistance between two points on a conductor when a constant potential difference of 1 volt between them produces a current of 1 ampere. Symbol: Ω [C19: after Georg Simon *Ohm* (1787–1854), G physicist]
▸ **'ohmage** *n*

ohmmeter ('əʊmˌmiːtə) *n* an instrument for measuring electrical resistance.

OHMS (in Britain and the Commonwealth) *abbrev. for* On Her (*or* His) Majesty's Service.

Ohm's law (əʊmz) *n* the principle that the electric current passing through a conductor is directly proportional to the potential difference across it. The constant of proportionality is the resistance of the conductor.

oho (əʊ'həʊ) *interj* an exclamation expressing surprise, exultation, or derision.

-oic *suffix forming adjectives*. indicating that a chemical compound is a carboxylic acid: *ethanoic acid*.

-oid *suffix forming adjectives and associated nouns*. indicating likeness, resemblance, or similarity: *anthropoid*. [from Gk *-oeidēs* resembling, from *eidos* form]

-oidea *suffix forming plural proper nouns*. forming the names of zoological classes or superfamilies: *Canoidea*. [from NL, from L *-oīdēs* -OID]

oil (ɔɪl) *n* **1** any of a number of viscous liquids with a smooth sticky feel. They are usually flammable, insoluble in water, soluble in organic solvents, and are obtained from plants and animals, from mineral deposits, and by synthesis. See also **essential oil.** **2a** another name for **petroleum.** **2b** (*as modifier*): *an oil engine; an oil rig*. **3a** any of a number of substances usually derived from petroleum and used for lubrication. **3b** (*in combination*): *an oilcan*. **3c** (*as modifier*): *an oil pump*. **4** Also called: **fuel oil.** a petroleum product used as a fuel in domestic heating, marine engines, etc. **5** *Brit*. **5a** paraffin, esp. when used as a domestic fuel. **5b** (*as modifier*): *an oil lamp*. **6** any substance of a consistency resembling that of oil: *oil of vitriol*. **7** the solvent, usually linseed oil, with which pigments are mixed to make artists' paints. **8a** (*often pl*) oil colour or paint. **8b** (*as modifier*): *an oil painting*. **9** an oil painting. **10** *Austral. & NZ sl*. facts or news. **11 strike oil.** **11a** to discover petroleum while drilling for it. **11b** *Inf*. to become very rich or successful. ◆ *vb* (*tr*) **12** to lubricate, smear, polish, etc., with oil or an oily substance. **13 oil one's tongue.** *Inf*. to speak flatteringly or glibly. **14 oil someone's palm.**

THESAURUS

off key *adj* **1, 2** = **out of tune**, discordant, dissonant, inharmonious, jarring, out of keeping

off-load *vb* = **get rid of**, disburden, discharge, dump, jettison, lighten, shift, take off, transfer, unburden, unload, unship

off-putting *adj Brit. informal* = **discouraging**, daunting, discomfiting, disconcerting, dismaying, dispiriting, disturbing, formidable, frustrating, intimidating, unnerving, unsettling, upsetting

offset *n* **1** = **counterbalance**, balance, compensation, counterweight, equipoise ◆ *vb* **8** = **cancel out**, balance out, compensate for, counteract, counterbalance, counterpoise, countervail, make up for, neutralize

offshoot *n* **1** = **outgrowth**, branch, limb, scion, sprout **2** = **by-product**, adjunct, appendage, development, spin-off

offspring *n* **1** = **children**, brood, descendants, family, fry, heirs, issue, kids (*inf.*), progeny, scions, seed (*chiefly Biblical*), spawn, successors, young
Antonyms *n* ancestor, begetter, forebear, forefather, forerunner, parent, predecessor, procreator, progenitor

often *adv* **1** = **frequently**, again and again, generally, many a time, much, oft (*arch. or poetic*), oftentimes (*arch.*), ofttimes (*arch.*), over and over again, repeatedly, time after time, time and again
Antonyms *adv* hardly ever, infrequently, irregularly, never, now and then, occasionally, rarely, scarcely, seldom

ogle *vb* **1** = **leer**, eye up (*inf.*), gawp at (*Brit. sl.*), give the glad eye (*inf.*), give the once-over (*inf.*), lech *or* letch after (*inf.*), make sheep's eyes at (*inf.*)

ogre *n* **1, 2** = **monster**, bogey, bogeyman, bugbear, demon, devil, giant, spectre

oil *vb* **12** = **lubricate**, grease

Inf. to bribe someone. **15 oil the wheels.** to make things run smoothly. [C12: from OF *oile,* from L *oleum* (olive) oil, from *olea* olive tree, from Gk *elaia* OLIVE]
►'**oiler** *n* ►'**oil-,like** *adj*

oil cake *n* stock feed consisting of compressed cubes made from the residue of the crushed seeds of oil-bearing crops such as linseed.

oilcan ('ɔɪl,kæn) *n* a container with a long nozzle for applying lubricating oil to machinery.

oilcloth ('ɔɪl,klɒθ) *n* **1** waterproof material made by treating one side of a cotton fabric with a drying oil or a synthetic resin. **2** another name for **linoleum.**

oil drum *n* a metal drum used to contain or transport oil.

oilfield ('ɔɪl,fi:ld) *n* an area containing reserves of petroleum, esp. one that is already being exploited.

oilfired ('ɔɪl,faɪəd) *adj* (of central heating, etc.) using oil as fuel.

oilgas ('ɔɪl,gæs) *n* a gaseous mixture of hydrocarbons used as a fuel, obtained by the destructive distillation of mineral oils.

oilman ('ɔɪlmən) *n, pl* **oilmen. 1** a person who owns or operates oil wells. **2** a person who sells oil.

oil minister *n* a government official in charge of or representing the interests of an oil-producing country.

oil of cloves *n* another name for **clove oil.**

oil of vitriol *n* another name for **sulphuric acid.**

oil paint *n* paint made of pigment ground in oil, usually linseed oil.

oil painting *n* **1** a picture painted with oil paints. **2** the art or process of painting with oil paints. **3 he's** *or* **she's no oil painting.** *Inf.* he *or* she is not good-looking.

oil palm *n* a tropical African palm tree, the fruits of which yield palm oil.

oil rig *n* See **rig** (sense 6).

oil sand *n* a sandstone impregnated with hydrocarbons, esp. such deposits in Alberta, Canada.

oil-seed rape *n* another name for **rape**[2].

oil shale *n* a carbonaceous rock from which oil can be extracted.

oilskin ('ɔɪl,skɪn) *n* **1a** a cotton fabric treated with oil and pigment to make it waterproof. **1b** (*as modifier*): *an oilskin hat.* **2** (*often pl*) a protective outer garment of this fabric.

oil slick *n* a mass of floating oil covering an area of water.

oilstone ('ɔɪl,stəʊn) *n* a stone with a fine grain lubricated with oil and used for sharpening cutting tools. See also **whetstone.**

oil well *n* a boring into the earth or sea bed for the extraction of petroleum.

oily ➊ ('ɔɪlɪ) *adj* **oilier, oiliest. 1** soaked in or smeared with oil or grease. **2** consisting of, containing, or resembling oil. **3** flatteringly servile or obsequious.
►'**oilily** *adv* ►'**oiliness** *n*

oink (ɔɪŋk) *interj* an imitation or representation of the grunt of a pig.

ointment ➊ ('ɔɪntmənt) *n* **1** a fatty or oily medicated preparation applied to the skin to heal or protect. **2** a similar substance used as a cosmetic. [C14: from OF *oignement,* from L *unguentum* UNGUENT]

Oireachtas ('ɛrəkθəs) *n* the parliament of the Republic of Ireland. [Irish Gaelic: assembly, from OIrish *airech* nobleman]

Ojibwa (əʊ'dʒɪbwə) *n* **1** (*pl* **Ojibwas** *or* **Ojibwa**) a member of a North American Indian people living west of Lake Superior. **2** the language of this people.

O.K. ➊ (,əʊ'keɪ) *Inf.* ◆ *sentence substitute.* **1** an expression of approval or agreement. ◆ *adj* (*usually postpositive*), *adv* **2** in good or satisfactory condition. ◆ *vb* **O.K.s, O.K.ing** (,əʊ'keɪɪŋ), **O.K.ed** (,əʊ'keɪd). **3** (*tr*) to approve or endorse. ◆ *n, pl* **O.K.s. 4** approval or agreement. ◆ Also: **okay.** [C19: ?from *o(ll) k(orrect),* jocular alteration of *all correct*]

okapi (əʊ'kɑ:pɪ) *n, pl* **okapis** *or* **okapi.** a ruminant mammal of the forests of central Africa, having a reddish-brown coat with horizontal white stripes on the legs, and small horns. [C20: from a Central African word]

okay (,əʊ'keɪ) *sentence substitute, adj, adv, vb, n* a variant spelling of **O.K.**

okra ('əʊkrə) *n* **1** an annual plant of the Old World tropics, with yellow-and-red flowers and edible oblong green pods. **2** the pod of this plant, eaten in soups, stews, etc. See also **gumbo** (sense 1). [C18: of West African origin]

-ol[1] *suffix forming nouns.* denoting a chemical compound containing a hydroxyl group, esp. alcohols and phenols: *ethanol; quinol.* [from ALCOHOL]

-ol[2] *n combining form.* (not used systematically) a variant of **-ole**[1].

old ➊ (əʊld) *adj* **1** having lived or existed for a relatively long time: *an old man; an old tradition; an old house.* **2a** of or relating to advanced years or a long life: *old age.* **2b** (*as collective n;* preceded by *the*): *the old.* **2c old and young.** people of all ages. **3** decrepit or senile. **4** worn with age or use: *old clothes; an old car.* **5a** (*postpositive*) having lived or existed for a specified period: *a child who is six years old.* **5b** (*in combination*): *a six-year-old child.* **5c** (*as n in combination*): *a six-year-old.* **6** (*cap. when part of a name or title*) earlier or earliest of two or more things with the same name: *the old edition; the Old Testament.* **7** (*cap. when part of a name*) designating the form of a language in which the earliest known records are written: *Old English.* **8** (*prenominal*) familiar through long acquaintance or repetition: *an old friend; an old excuse.* **9** practised; hardened: *old in cunning.* **10** (*prenominal;* often preceded by *good*) cherished; dear: used as a term of affection or familiarity: *good old George.* **11** *Inf.* (with any of several nouns) used as a familiar form of address to a person: *old thing; old bean; old stick.* **12** skilled through long experience (esp. in **an old hand**). **13** out of date; unfashionable. **14** remote or distant in origin or time of origin: *an old culture.* **15** (*prenominal*) former; previous: *my old house was small.* **16a** (*prenominal*) established for a relatively long time: *an old member.* **16b** (*in combination*): *old-established.* **17** sensible, wise, or mature: *old beyond one's years.* **18** (intensifier) (esp. in **a high old time, any old thing, any old how,** etc.). **19 good old days.** an earlier period of time regarded as better than the present. **20 little old.** *Inf.* indicating affection, esp. humorous affection. **21 the old one** (*or* **gentleman**). *Inf.* a jocular name for **Satan.** ◆ *n* **22** an earlier or past time: *in days of old.* [OE *eald*]
►'**oldish** *adj* ►'**oldness** *n*

old age pension *n* a former name for **retirement pension.**
►**old age pensioner** *n*

Old Bailey ('beɪlɪ) *n* the Central Criminal Court of England.

Old Bill (bɪl) *n* (*functioning as pl,* preceded by *the*) *Brit. sl.* policemen collectively. [C20: ?from the World War I cartoon of a soldier with a drooping moustache]

old boy *n* **1** (*sometimes caps.*) *Brit.* a male ex-pupil of a school. **2** *Inf., chiefly Brit.* **2a** a familiar name used to refer to a man. **2b** an old man.

old boy network *n Brit. inf.* the appointment to power of former pupils of the same small group of public schools or universities.

Old Contemptibles *pl n* the British expeditionary force to France in 1914. [from the Kaiser's alleged reference to them as a "contemptible little army"]

old country *n* the country of origin of an immigrant or an immigrant's ancestors.

Old Dart *n* **the.** *Austral. sl.* Britain, esp. England. [C19: from ?]

olden ('əʊld[ə]n) *adj* an archaic or poetic word for **old** (often in **in olden days** and **in olden times**).

Old English *n* **1** Also called: **Anglo-Saxon.** the English language from the time of the earliest Saxon settlements in the fifth century A.D. to about 1100. Abbrev.: **OE. 2** *Printing.* a Gothic typeface commonly used in England up to the 18th century.

Old English sheepdog *n* a breed of large bobtailed sheepdog with a profuse shaggy coat.

older ('əʊldə) *adj* **1** the comparative of **old. 2** Also (of people): **elder.** of greater age.

old-fashioned ➊ *adj* **1** belonging to, characteristic of, or favoured by former times; outdated: *old-fashioned ideas.* **2** favouring or adopting the dress, manners, fashions, etc., of a former time. **3** *Scot. & N English dialect.* old for one's age: *an old-fashioned child.* ◆ *n* **4** a cocktail containing spirit, bitters, fruit, etc.

Old French *n* the French language in its earliest forms, from about the 9th century up to about 1400. Abbrev.: **OF.**

old girl *n* **1** (*sometimes caps.*) *Brit.* a female ex-pupil of a school. **2** *Inf., chiefly Brit.* **2a** a familiar name used to refer to a woman. **2b** an old woman.

Old Glory *n* a nickname for the flag of the United States of America.

THESAURUS

oily *adj* **1, 2 = greasy,** fatty, oiled, oleaginous, smeary, swimming **3 = obsequious,** flattering, fulsome, glib, hypocritical, plausible, servile, smarmy (*Brit. inf.*), smooth, unctuous

ointment *n* **1 = lotion,** balm, cerate, cream, embrocation, emollient, liniment, salve, unguent

O.K. *sentence substitute* **1 = all right,** agreed, right, roger, very good, very well, yes ◆ *adj* **2 = fine,** acceptable, accurate, adequate, all right, approved, convenient, correct, fair, good, in order, middling, not bad (*inf.*), passable, permitted, satisfactory, so-so (*inf.*), tolerable, up to scratch (*inf.*) ◆ *vb* **3 = approve,** agree to, authorize, consent to, endorse, entitle, give one's consent to, give the go-ahead, give the green light, give the thumbs up (*inf.*), pass, rubber-stamp (*inf.*), sanction, say yes to ◆ *n* **4 = approval,** agreement, approbation, assent, authorization, consent, endorsement, go-ahead (*inf.*), green light, permission, sanction, say-so (*inf.*), seal of approval
Antonyms *adj* ≠ **fine:** displeasing, inaccurate, inadequate, incorrect, not up to scratch (*inf.*), poor, unacceptable, unsatisfactory, unsuitable

old *adj* **1-3 = aged,** advanced in years, ancient, decrepit, elderly, full of years, getting on, grey, grey-haired, grizzled, hoary, mature, over the hill (*inf.*), past it, past one's prime, patriarchal, senescent, senile, venerable **4 = worn-out,** crumbling, done **8, 9, 12 = long-established,** age-old, experienced, familiar, hardened, of long standing, practised, skilled, time-honoured, traditional, versed, veteran, vintage **13 = out of date,** antediluvian, antiquated, antique, cast-off, cobwebby, dated, decayed, hackneyed, obsolete, old-fashioned, outdated, outmoded, out of the ark (*inf.*), passé, stale, superannuated, timeworn, unfashionable, unoriginal **14 = early,** aboriginal, antique, archaic, bygone, immemorial, of old, of yore, olden (*arch.*), original, primeval, primitive, primordial, pristine, remote **15 = former,** earlier, erstwhile, ex-, one-time, previous, quondam
Antonyms *adj* ≠ **aged:** immature, juvenile, young, youthful ≠ **out of date:** current, fashionable, modern, modish, new, novel, recent, up-to-date

old-fashioned *adj* **1 = out of date,** ancient, antiquated, archaic, behind the times, cobwebby, corny (*sl.*), dated, dead, *démodé,* fusty, musty, not with it (*inf.*), obsolescent, obsolete, oldfangled, (old-)fogeyish, old hat, old-time, outdated, outmoded, out of style, out of the ark (*inf.*), passé, past, square (*inf.*), superannuated, unfashionable
Antonyms *adj* chic, contemporary, current, fashionable, happening (*inf.*), modern, modish, trendy (*Brit. inf.*), up-to-date, voguish, with it (*inf.*)

old gold *n* **a** a dark yellow colour, sometimes with a brownish tinge. **b** *(as adj): an old-gold carpet.*

old guard *n* **1** a group that works for a long-established or old-fashioned cause or principle. **2** the conservative element in a political party or other group. [C19: after Napoleon's imperial guard]

old hat *adj (postpositive)* old-fashioned or trite.

Old High German *n* a group of West Germanic dialects that eventually developed into modern German; High German up to about 1200. Abbrev.: **OHG.**

oldie ('əʊldɪ) *n Inf.* an old joke, song, film, person, etc.

Old Irish *n* the Celtic language of Ireland up to about 900 A.D.

old lady *n* an informal term for **mother** or **wife.**

Old Latin *n* the Latin language before the classical period, up to about 100 B.C.

Old Low German *n* the Saxon and Low Franconian dialects of German up to about 1200; the old form of modern Low German and Dutch. Abbrev.: **OLG.**

old maid *n* **1** a woman regarded as unlikely ever to marry; spinster. **2** *Inf.* a prim, fastidious, or excessively cautious person. **3** a card game in which players try to avoid holding the unpaired card at the end of the game.
▸ **ˌold-'maidish** *adj*

old man *n* **1** an informal term for **father** or **husband. 2** *(sometimes caps.) Inf.* a man in command, such as an employer, foreman, or captain of a ship. **3** *Sometimes facetious.* an affectionate term used in addressing a man. **4** Also called: **southernwood.** an aromatic shrubby wormwood of S Europe, having drooping yellow flowers. **5** *Christianity.* the unregenerate aspect of human nature.

old man's beard *n* any of various plants having white feathery seed heads, esp. traveller's joy and Spanish moss.

old master *n* **1** one of the great European painters of the period 1500 to 1800. **2** a painting by one of these.

old moon *n* a phase of the moon lying between last quarter and new moon, when it appears as a waning crescent.

Old Nick (nɪk) *n Inf.* a jocular name for **Satan.**

Old Norse *n* the language or group of dialects of medieval Scandinavia and Iceland from about 700 to about 1350. Abbrev.: **ON.**

Old Pretender *n* **James Francis Edward Stewart,** 1688–1766, son of James II and pretender to the British throne.

Old Prussian *n* the former language of the non-German Prussians, belonging to the Baltic branch of the Indo-European family: extinct by 1700.

old rose *n* **a** a greyish-pink colour. **b** *(as adj): old-rose gloves.*

Old Saxon *n* the Saxon dialect of Low German up to about 1200, from which modern Low German is derived. Abbrev.: **OS.**

old school *n* **1** *Chiefly Brit.* one's former school. **2** a group of people favouring traditional ideas or conservative practices.

old school tie *n* **1** *Brit.* a distinctive tie that indicates which school the wearer attended. **2** the attitudes, loyalties, values, etc., associated with British public schools.

Old South *n* the American South before the Civil War.

oldster ('əʊldstə) *n Inf.* an older person.

old style *n Printing.* a type style reviving the characteristics of **old face,** a type style that originated in the 18th century and was characterized by having little contrast between thick and thin strokes.

Old Style *n* the former method of reckoning dates using the Julian calendar. Cf. **New Style.**

Old Testament *n* the collection of books comprising the sacred Scriptures of the Hebrews; the first part of the Christian Bible.

old-time ❶ *adj (prenominal)* of or relating to a former time; old-fashioned: *old-time dancing.*

old-timer *n* **1** a person who has been in a certain place, occupation, etc., for a long time. **2** *US.* an old man.

old wives' tale *n* a belief, usually superstitious or erroneous, passed on by word of mouth as a piece of traditional wisdom.

old woman ❶ *n* **1** an informal term for **mother** or **wife. 2** a timid, fussy, or cautious person.
▸ **ˌold-'womanish** *adj*

Old World *n* that part of the world that was known before the discovery of the Americas; the eastern hemisphere.

old-world ❶ *adj* of or characteristic of former times, esp., in Europe, quaint or traditional.

Old World monkey *n* any monkey such as a macaque, baboon, or mandrill, which has nostrils that are close together and a nonprehensile tail.

-ole[1] *or* **-ol** *n combining form.* **1** denoting an organic unsaturated compound containing a 5-membered ring: *thiazole.* **2** denoting an aromatic organic ether: *anisole.* [from L *oleum* oil, from Gk *elaion,* from *elaia* olive]

-ole[2] *suffix of nouns.* indicating something small: *arteriole.* [from L *-olus,* dim. suffix]

oleaceous (ˌəʊlɪ'eɪʃəs) *adj* of, relating to, or belonging to a family of trees and shrubs which includes the ash, jasmine, privet, lilac, and olive. [C19: via NL from L *olea* OLIVE; see also OIL]

oleaginous ❶ (ˌəʊlɪ'ædʒɪnəs) *adj* **1** resembling or having the properties of oil. **2** containing or producing oil. [C17: from L *oleāginus,* from *olea* OLIVE; see also OIL]

oleander (ˌəʊlɪ'ændə) *n* a poisonous evergreen Mediterranean shrub or tree with fragrant white, pink, or purple flowers. Also called: **rosebay.** [C16: from Med. L, var. of *arodandrum,* ?from L RHODODENDRON]

oleate ('əʊlɪˌeɪt) *n* any salt or ester of oleic acid.

oleic acid (əʊ'liːɪk) *n* a colourless oily liquid unsaturated acid occurring, as the glyceride, in almost all natural fats; used in making soaps, ointments, cosmetics, and lubricating oils. Formula: $CH_3(CH_2)_7CH{:}CH(CH_2)_7COOH$. Systematic name: ***cis*-9-octadecenoic acid.** [C19 *oleic,* from L *oleum* oil + -IC]

olein ('əʊlɪɪn) *n* another name for **triolein.** [C19: from F *oléine,* from L *oleum* oil + -IN]

oleo- *combining form.* oil: *oleomargarine.* [from L *oleum* OIL]

oleomargarine (ˌəʊlɪəʊˌmɑːdʒə'riːn) *or* **oleomargarin** (ˌəʊlɪəʊ'mɑːdʒərɪn) *n* another name (esp. US) for **margarine.**

oleoresin (ˌəʊlɪəʊ'rɛzɪn) *n* **1** a semisolid mixture of a resin and essential oil, obtained from certain plants. **2** *Pharmacol.* a liquid preparation of resins and oils, obtained by extraction from plants.
▸ **ˌoleo'resinous** *adj*

oleum ('əʊlɪəm) *n, pl* **olea** ('əʊlɪə) *or* **oleums.** another name for **fuming sulphuric acid.** [from L: oil, referring to its oily consistency]

O level *n Brit.* **1a** the former basic (ordinary) level of the General Certificate of Education. **1b** *(as modifier): O-level maths.* **2** a pass in a particular subject at O level: *he has eight O levels.*

olfaction (ɒl'fækʃən) *n* **1** the sense of smell. **2** the act or function of smelling.

olfactory (ɒl'fæktərɪ, -trɪ) *adj* **1** of or relating to the sense of smell. ◆ *n, pl* **olfactories. 2** *(usually pl)* an organ or nerve concerned with the sense of smell. [C17: from L *olfactus,* p.p. of *olfacere,* from *olere* to smell + *facere* to make]

OLG *abbrev. for* Old Low German.

oligarch ('ɒlɪˌgɑːk) *n* a member of an oligarchy.

oligarchy ('ɒlɪˌgɑːkɪ) *n, pl* **oligarchies. 1** government by a small group of people. **2** a state or organization so governed. **3** a small body of individuals ruling such a state. **4** *Chiefly US.* a small clique of private citizens who exert a strong influence on government. [C16: via Med. L from Gk *oligarkhia,* from *oligos* few + -ARCHY]
▸ **ˌoli'garchic** *or* **ˌoli'garchical** *adj*

oligo- *or before a vowel* **olig-** *combining form.* indicating a few or little: *oligopoly.* [from Gk *oligos* little, few]

Oligocene ('ɒlɪgəʊˌsiːn, ɒ'lɪg-) *adj* **1** of, denoting, or formed in the third epoch of the Tertiary period. ◆ *n* **2 the.** the Oligocene epoch or rock series. [C19: OLIGO- + -CENE]

oligochaete ('ɒlɪgəʊˌkiːt) *n* **1** any freshwater or terrestrial annelid worm having bristles borne singly along the length of the body: includes the earthworms. ◆ *adj* **2** of or relating to this type of worm. [C19: from NL from OLIGO- + Gk *khaitē* long hair]

oligopoly (ˌɒlɪ'gɒpəlɪ) *n, pl* **oligopolies.** *Econ.* a market situation in which control over the supply of a commodity is held by a small number of producers. [C20: from OLIGO- + Gk *pōlein* to sell]
▸ **ˌoliˌgopo'listic** *adj*

oligospermia (ˌɒlɪgəʊ'spɜːmɪə) *n* the condition of having less than the normal number of spermatozoa in the semen: a cause of infertility in men.

oligotrophic (ˌɒlɪgəʊ'trɒfɪk) *adj* (of lakes and similar habitats) poor in nutrients and plant life and rich in oxygen. [C20: from OLIGO- + Gk *trophein* to nourish + -IC]
▸ **oligotrophy** (ˌɒlɪ'gɒtrəfɪ) *n*

olio ('əʊlɪˌəʊ) *n, pl* **olios. 1** a dish of many different ingredients. **2** a miscellany or potpourri. [C17: from Sp. *olla* stew, from L: jar]

olivaceous (ˌɒlɪ'veɪʃəs) *adj* of an olive colour.

olive ('ɒlɪv) *n* **1** an evergreen oleaceous tree of the Mediterranean region having white fragrant flowers and edible fruits that are black when ripe. **2** the fruit of this plant, eaten as a relish and used as a source of olive oil. **3** the wood of the olive tree, used for ornamental work. **4a** a yellow-green colour like that of an unripe olive. **4b** *(as adj): an olive coat.* ◆ *adj* **5** of, relating to, or made of the olive tree, its wood, or its fruit. [C13: via OF from L *oliva,* rel. to Gk *elaia* olive tree]

olive branch *n* **1** a branch of an olive tree used to symbolize peace. **2** any offering of peace or conciliation.

olive crown *n* (esp. in ancient Greece and Rome) a garland of olive leaves awarded as a token of victory.

olive drab *n US.* **1a** a dull but fairly strong greyish-olive colour. **1b** *(as adj): an olive-drab jacket.* **2** cloth or clothes in this colour, esp. the uniform of the US Army.

olive green *n* **a** a colour that is greener, stronger, and brighter than olive; deep yellowish-green. **b** *(as adj): an olive-green coat.*

olive oil *n* a yellow to yellowish-green oil pressed from ripe olive fruits and used in cooking, medicines, etc.

olivine ('ɒlɪˌviːn, ˌɒlɪ'viːn) *n* any of a group of hard glassy olive-green

THESAURUS

old-time *adj* = **old-fashioned,** ancient, antique, bygone, former, past, vintage

old-womanish *adj* **2** = **fussy,** finicky, niggly, niminy-piminy, old-maidish *(inf.),* overcautious, overparticular, pernickety *(inf.),* prim, prudish, strait-laced, timid, timorous

old-world *adj* = **traditional,** archaic, ceremonious, chivalrous, courtly, gallant, old-fashioned, picturesque, quaint

oleaginous *adj* **1** = **oily,** adipose, fat, fatty, greasy, sebaceous, unguinous *(obs.)*

minerals consisting of magnesium iron silicate in crystalline form. [C18: from G, after its colour]

olla ('ɒlə) *n* **1** a cooking pot. **2** short for **olla podrida**. [Sp., from L *olla*, var. of *aulla* pot]

olla podrida ('ɒlə pɒ'dri:də) *n* **1** a Spanish dish, consisting of a stew with beans, sausages, etc. **2** an assortment; miscellany. [Sp., lit.: rotten pot]

Olmec ('ɒlmɛk) *n, pl* **Olmecs** *or* **Olmec**. **1** a member of an ancient Central American Indian people who inhabited the S Gulf Coast of Mexico. ◆ *adj* **2** of or relating to this people.

ology ('ɒlədʒɪ) *n, pl* **ologies**. *Inf.* a science or other branch of knowledge. [C19: abstracted from words such as *theology, biology*, etc.; see -LOGY]

-ology *n combining form*. See **-logy**.

oloroso (,ɒlə'rəʊsəʊ) *n, pl* **olorosos**. a full-bodied golden-coloured sweet sherry. [from Sp.: fragrant]

Olympiad (ə'lɪmpɪ,æd) *n* **1** a staging of the modern Olympic Games. **2** the four-year period between consecutive celebrations of the Olympic Games; a unit of ancient Greek chronology dating back to 776 B.C. **3** an international contest in chess, bridge, etc.

Olympian ❶ (ə'lɪmpɪən) *adj* **1** of or relating to Mount Olympus or to the classical Greek gods. **2** majestic or godlike in manner or bearing. **3** of or relating to ancient Olympia, a plain in Greece, or its inhabitants. ◆ *n* **4** a god of Mount Olympus. **5** an inhabitant of ancient Olympia. **6** *Chiefly US*. a competitor in the Olympic Games.

Olympic (ə'lɪmpɪk) *adj* **1** of or relating to the Olympic Games. **2** of or relating to ancient Olympia.

Olympic Games *n* (*functioning as sing or pl*) **1** the greatest Panhellenic festival, held every fourth year in honour of Zeus at ancient Olympia, consisting of games and festivities. **2** Also called: **the Olympics**. the modern revival of these games, consisting of international athletic and sporting contests held every four years in a selected country.

OM *abbrev. for* Order of Merit (a Brit. title).

-oma *n combining form*. indicating a tumour: *carcinoma*. [from Gk *-ōma*]

omasum (əʊ'meɪsəm) *n, pl* **omasa** (-sə). another name for **psalterium**. [C18: from L: bullock's tripe]

ombre *or US* **omber** ('ɒmbə) *n* an 18th-century card game. [C17: from Sp. *hombre* man, referring to the player who attempts to win the stakes]

ombudsman ('ɒmbʊdzmən) *n, pl* **ombudsmen**. an official who investigates citizens' complaints against the government or its servants. Also called (Brit.): **Parliamentary Commissioner**. See also **Financial Ombudsman**. [C20: from Swedish: commissioner]

-ome *n combining form*. denoting a mass or part of a specified kind: *rhizome*. [var. of -OMA]

omega ('əʊmɪgə) *n* **1** the 24th and last letter of the Greek alphabet (Ω, ω). **2** the ending or last of a series. [C16: from Gk *ō mega* big o]

omega minus *n* an unstable negatively charged elementary particle, classified as a baryon, that has a mass 3276 times that of the electron.

omelette *or esp. US* **omelet** ('ɒmlɪt) *n* a savoury or sweet dish of beaten eggs cooked in fat. [C17: from F *omelette*, changed from *alumette*, from *alumelle* sword blade, changed by mistaken division from *la lemelle*, from L (see LAMELLA); apparently from the flat shape of the omelette]

omen ❶ ('əʊmən) *n* **1** a phenomenon or occurrence regarded as a sign of future happiness or disaster. **2** prophetic significance. ◆ *vb* **3** (*tr*) to portend. [C16: from L]

omentum (əʊ'mɛntəm) *n, pl* **omenta** (-tə). *Anat.* a double fold of peritoneum connecting the stomach with other abdominal organs. [C16: from L: membrane, esp. a caul, from ?]

omertà *Italian*. (omer'ta) *n* a conspiracy of silence.

omicron (əʊ'maɪkrɒn, 'ɒmɪkrɒn) *n* the 15th letter in the Greek alphabet (Ο, ο). [from Gk *ō mikron* small o]

ominous ❶ ('ɒmɪnəs) *adj* **1** foreboding evil. **2** serving as or having significance as an omen. [C16: from L *ōminōsus*, from OMEN]
▸**'ominously** *adv* ▸**'ominousness** *n*

omission ❶ (əʊ'mɪʃən) *n* **1** something that has been omitted or neglected. **2** the act of omitting or the state of having been omitted. [C14: from L *omissiō*, from *omittere* to OMIT]
▸**o'missive** *adj*

omit ❶ (əʊ'mɪt) *vb* **omits, omitting, omitted**. (*tr*) **1** to neglect to do or include. **2** to fail (to do something). [C15: from L *omittere*, from *ob-* away + *mittere* to send]
▸**omissible** (əʊ'mɪsɪbᵊl) *adj* ▸**o'mitter** *n*

omni- *combining form*. all or everywhere: *omnipresent*. [from L *omnis* all]

omnibus ('ɒmnɪ,bʌs, -bəs) *n, pl* **omnibuses**. **1** a formal word for **bus** (sense 1). **2** Also called: **omnibus volume**. a collection of works by one author or several works on a similar topic, reprinted in one volume. **3** Also called: **omnibus edition**. a television or radio programme consisting of two or more episodes of a serial broadcast earlier in the week. ◆ *adj* **4** (*prenominal*) of, dealing with, or providing for many different things or cases. [C19: from L, lit.: for all, dative pl of *omnis* all]

omnicompetent (,ɒmnɪ'kɒmpɪtənt) *adj* able to judge or deal with all matters.
▸**,omni'competence** *n*

omnidirectional (,ɒmnɪdɪ'rɛkʃənᵊl, -daɪ-) *adj* (of an antenna) capable of transmitting and receiving radio signals equally in any direction of the horizontal plane.

omnifarious (,ɒmnɪ'fɛərɪəs) *adj* of many or all varieties or forms. [C17: from LL *omnifārius*, from L *omnis* all + *-farius* doing]
▸**,omni'fariously** *adv* ▸**,omni'fariousness** *n*

omnific (ɒm'nɪfɪk) *or* **omnificent** (ɒm'nɪfɪsənt) *adj Rare.* creating all things. [C17: via Med. L from L *omni-* + *-ficus*, from *facere* to do]
▸**om'nificence** *n*

omnipotent ❶ (ɒm'nɪpətənt) *adj* **1** having very great or unlimited power. ◆ *n* **2 the Omnipotent**. an epithet for God. [C14: via OF from L *omnipotens* all-powerful, from OMNI- + *potens*, from *posse* to be able]
▸**om'nipotence** *n* ▸**om'nipotently** *adv*

omnipresent (,ɒmnɪ'prɛzᵊnt) *adj* (esp. of a deity) present in all places at the same time.
▸**,omni'presence** *n*

omniscient ❶ (ɒm'nɪsɪənt) *adj* **1** having infinite knowledge or understanding. **2** having very great or seemingly unlimited knowledge. [C17: from Med. L *omnisciens*, from L OMNI- + *scīre* to know]
▸**om'niscience** *n* ▸**om'nisciently** *adv*

omnium-gatherum ('ɒmnɪəm'gæðərəm) *n Often facetious.* a miscellaneous collection. [C16: from L *omnium* of all, + Latinized form of E *gather*]

omnivorous (ɒm'nɪvərəs) *adj* **1** eating any type of food indiscriminately. **2** taking in or assimilating everything, esp. with the mind. [C17: from L *omnivorus* all-devouring, from OMNI- + *vorāre* to eat greedily]
▸**'omni,vore** *n* ▸**om'nivorously** *adv* ▸**om'nivorousness** *n*

omphalos ('ɒmfə,lɒs) *n* **1** (in the ancient world) a sacred conical object, esp. a stone. The famous omphalos at Delphi was assumed to mark the centre of the earth. **2** the central point. **3** *Literary.* another word for **navel**. [Gk: navel]

on ❶ (ɒn) *prep* **1** in contact or connection with the surface of; at the upper surface of: *an apple on the ground; a mark on the tablecloth*. **2** attached to: *a puppet on a string*. **3** carried with: *I've no money on me*. **4** in the immediate vicinity of; close to or along the side of: *a house on the sea*. **5** within the time limits of (a day or date): *he arrived on Thursday*. **6** being performed upon or relayed through the medium of: *what's on the television?* **7** at the occasion of: *on his retirement*. **8** used to indicate support, subsistence, contingency, etc.: *he lives on bread*. **9a** regularly taking (a drug): *she's on the pill*. **9b** addicted to: *he's on heroin*. **10** by means of (something considered as a mode of transport) (esp. in **on foot, on horseback**, etc.). **11** in the process or course of: *on a journey; on strike*. **12** concerned with or relating to: *a programme on archaeology*. **13** used to indicate the basis or grounds, as of a statement or action: *I have it on good authority*. **14** against: used to indicate opposition: *they marched on the city at dawn*. **15** used to indicate a meeting or encounter: *he crept up on her*. **16** (used with an adj preceded by *the*) indicating the manner or way in which an action is carried out: *on the sly; on the cheap*. **17** staked or wagered as a bet upon: *ten pounds on that horse*. **18** *Inf.* charged to: *the drinks are on me*. ◆ *adv* (*often used as a particle*) **19** in the position or state required for the commencement or sustained continuation, as of a mechanical operation: *the radio's been on all night*. **20** attached to, surrounding, or placed in contact with something: *the child had nothing on*. **21** arranged: *we've nothing on for tonight*. **22** in a manner indicating continuity, persistence, etc.: *don't keep on about it; the play went on all afternoon*. **23** in a direction towards something, esp. forward: *we drove on towards London; march on!* **24 on and off**. intermittently; from time to time. **25 on and on**. without ceasing; continually. ◆ *adj* **26** functioning; operating: *the on position on a radio*. **27** (*postpositive*) *Inf.* performing, as on stage, etc.: *I'm on in five minutes*. **28** definitely taking place: *the match is on for Friday*. **29** tolerable or practicable, acceptable, etc.: *your plan just isn't on*. **30** *Cricket.* (of a bowler) bowling. **31 on at**. *Inf.* nagging: *she was always on at her husband*. ◆ *n* **32**

THESAURUS

Olympian *adj* **2** = **majestic**, elevated, exalted, glorious, godlike, lofty, rarefied, splendid, sublime

omen *n* **1** = **sign**, augury, foreboding, foretoken, indication, portent, premonition, presage, prognostic, prognostication, straw in the wind, warning, writing on the wall

ominous *adj* **1** = **threatening**, baleful, dark, fateful, forbidding, foreboding, inauspicious, menacing, minatory, portentous, premonitory, sinister, unpromising, unpropitious
Antonyms *adj* auspicious, encouraging, favourable, promising, propitious

omission *n* **2** = **exclusion**, default, failure, forgetfulness, gap, lack, leaving out, neglect, noninclusion, oversight
Antonyms *n* addition, inclusion, incorporation, insertion

omit *vb* **1, 2** = **leave out**, disregard, drop, eliminate, exclude, fail, forget, give (something) a miss (*inf.*), leave (something) undone, let (something) slide, miss (out), neglect, overlook, pass over, skip
Antonyms *vb* add, enter, include, incorporate, insert, put in

omnipotence *n* **1** = **supremacy**, divine right, invincibility, mastery, sovereignty, supreme power, undisputed sway
Antonyms *n* frailty, impotence, inability, inferiority, powerlessness, vulnerability, weakness

omnipotent *adj* **1** = **almighty**, all-powerful, supreme
Antonyms *adj* feeble, frail, impotent, incapable, inferior, powerless, vulnerable, weak

omniscient *adj* **1** = **all-knowing**, all-seeing, all-wise

on *adv* **24 on and off** = **occasionally**, by fits and starts, discontinuously, (every) now and again, fitfully, from time to time, intermittently, now and then, off and on, sometimes, spasmodically

Cricket. **32a** (*modifier*) relating to or denoting the leg side of a cricket field or pitch: *an on drive.* **32b** (*in combination*) used to designate certain fielding positions on the leg side: *mid-on.* [OE *an, on*]

ON *abbrev. for:* **1** Old Norse. **2** Ontario.

-on *suffix forming nouns.* **1** indicating a chemical substance: *interferon.* **2** (in physics) indicating an elementary particle or quantum: *electron; photon.* **3** (in chemistry) indicating an inert gas: *neon; radon.* **4** (in biochemistry) a molecular unit: *codon; operon.* [from ION]

onager (ˈɒnədʒə) *n, pl* **onagri** (-ˌgraɪ) *or* **onagers. 1** a Persian variety of the wild ass. **2** an ancient war engine for hurling stones, etc. [C14: from LL: military engine for stone throwing, from L: wild ass, from Gk *onagros,* from *onos* ass + *agros* field]

onanism (ˈəʊnəˌnɪzəm) *n* **1** the withdrawal of the penis from the vagina before ejaculation. **2** masturbation. [C18: after *Onan,* son of Judah; see Genesis 38:9]
▸**ˈonanist** *n, adj* ▸**ˌonanˈistic** *adj*

ONC (in Britain) *abbrev. for* Ordinary National Certificate.

once ⓘ (wʌns) *adv* **1** one time; on one occasion or in one case. **2** at some past time: *I could speak French once.* **3** by one step or degree (of relationship): *a cousin once removed.* **4** (*in conditional clauses, negatives, etc.*) ever; at all: *if you once forget it.* **5** multiplied by one. **6 once and away. 6a** conclusively. **6b** occasionally. **7 once and for all.** conclusively; for the last time. **8 once in a while.** occasionally; now and then. **9 once or twice** *or* **once and again.** a few times. **10 once upon a time.** used to begin fairy tales and children's stories. ◆ *conj* **11** (*subordinating*) as soon as; if ever: *once you begin, you'll enjoy it.* ◆ *n* **12** one occasion or case: *you may do it, this once.* **13 all at once. 13a** suddenly. **13b** simultaneously. **14 at once. 14a** immediately. **14b** simultaneously. **15 for once.** this time, if (or but) at no other time. [C12 *ones, anes,* adverbial genitive of *on, an* ONE]

once-over *n Inf.* **1** a quick examination or appraisal. **2** a quick but comprehensive piece of work. **3** a violent beating or thrashing (esp. in **give (a person** or **thing) the** (or **a**) **once-over**).

oncer (ˈwʌnsə) *n* **1** *Brit. sl.* (formerly) a one-pound note. **2** *Austral. sl.* a person elected to Parliament who can only expect to serve one term. **3** *Austral. & NZ.* something which happens only once. [C20: from ONCE]

oncogene (ˈɒŋkəʊˌdʒiːn) *n* any of several genes, present in all cells, that when abnormally activated can cause cancer. [C20: from Gk *onkos* mass, tumour + GENE]
▸**oncogenic** (ˌɒŋkəʊˈdʒɛnɪk) *adj*

oncoming ⓘ (ˈɒnˌkʌmɪŋ) *adj* **1** coming nearer in space or time; approaching. ◆ *n* **2** the approach or onset: *the oncoming of winter.*

oncost (ˈɒnˌkɒst) *n Brit.* **1** another word for **overhead** (sense 5). **2** (*sometimes pl*) another word for **overheads.**

OND (in Britain) *abbrev. for* Ordinary National Diploma.

on dit *French* (ɔ̃ di) *n, pl* **on dits** (ɔ̃ di). a rumour; piece of gossip. [lit.: it is said, they say]

one (wʌn) *determiner* **1a** single; lone; not two or more. **1b** (*as pron*): *one is enough for now; one at a time.* **1c** (*in combination*): *one-eyed.* **2a** distinct from all others; only; unique: *one girl in a million.* **2b** (*as pron*): *one of a kind.* **3a** a specified (person, item, etc.) as distinct from another or others of its kind: *raise one hand and then the other.* **3b** (*as pron*): *which one is correct?* **4** a certain, indefinite, or unspecified (time); some: *one day you'll be sorry.* **5** *Inf.* an emphatic word for **a** or **an**[1]: *it was one hell of a fight.* **6** a certain (person): *one Miss Jones was named.* **7 (all) in one.** combined; united. **8 all one. 8a** all the same. **8b** of no consequence: *it's all one to me.* **9 at one.** (often foll. by *with*) in a state of agreement or harmony. **10 be made one.** to become married. **11 many a one.** many people. **12 neither one thing nor the other.** indefinite, undecided, or mixed. **13 never a one.** none. **14 one and all.** everyone, without exception. **15 one by one.** one at a time; individually. **16 one or two.** a few. **17 one way and another.** on balance. **18 one with another.** on average. ◆ *pron* **19** an indefinite person regarded as typical of every person: *one can't say any more than that.* **20** any indefinite person: used as the subject of a sentence to form an alternative grammatical construction to that of the passive voice: *one can catch fine trout in this stream.* **21** *Arch.* an unspecified person: *one came to him.* ◆ *n* **22** the smallest natural number and the first cardinal number; unity. **23** a numeral (1, I, i, etc.) representing this number. **24** *Inf.* a joke or story (esp. in **the one about**). **25** something representing, represented by, or consisting of one unit. **26** Also: **one o'clock.** one hour after noon or midnight. **27** a blow or setback (esp. in **one in the eye for**). **28 the Evil one.** Satan. **29 the Holy One** *or* **the One above.** God. ◆ Related prefixes: **mono-, uni-.** [OE *ān*]

-one *suffix forming nouns.* indicating that a chemical compound is a ketone: *acetone.* [arbitrarily from Gk *-ōnē,* fem. patronymic suffix, but ? infl. by *-one* in OZONE]

one another *pron* the reflexive form of plural pronouns when the action, attribution, etc., is reciprocal: *they kissed one another; knowing one another.* Also: **each other.**

one-armed bandit *n Inf.* a fruit machine operated by pulling down a lever at one side.

one-horse ⓘ *adj* **1** drawn by or using one horse. **2** (*prenominal*) *Inf.* small or obscure: *a one-horse town.*

one-liner *n Inf.* a short joke or witty remark.

one-man *adj* consisting of or done by or for one man: *a one-man band; a one-man show.*

oneness (ˈwʌnnɪs) *n* **1** the state or quality of being one; singleness. **2** the state of being united; agreement. **3** uniqueness. **4** sameness.

one-night stand *n* **1** a performance given only once at any one place. **2** *Inf.* a sexual encounter lasting only one evening or night.

one-off *n Brit.* **a** something that is carried out or made only once. **b** (*as modifier*): *a one-off job.*

one-on-one *adj* another term for **one-to-one** (sense 2).

one-parent family *n* another term for **single-parent family.**

one-piece *adj* **1** (of a garment, esp. a bathing costume) consisting of one piece. ◆ *n* **2** a garment, esp. a bathing costume, consisting of one piece.

onerous ⓘ (ˈɒnərəs, ˈəʊ-) *adj* **1** laborious or oppressive. **2** *Law.* (of a contract, etc.) having or involving burdens or obligations. [C14: from L *onerōsus* burdensome, from *onus* load]
▸**ˈonerously** *adv* ▸**ˈonerousness** *n*

oneself (wʌnˈsɛlf) *pron* **1a** the reflexive form of *one.* **1b** (intensifier): *one doesn't do that oneself.* **2** (*preceded by a copula*) one's normal or usual self: *one doesn't feel oneself after such an experience.*

one-sided ⓘ *adj* **1** considering or favouring only one side of a matter, problem, etc. **2** having all the advantage on one side: *a one-sided boxing match.* **3** larger or more developed on one side. **4** having, existing on, or occurring on one side only.
▸**ˌone-ˈsidedly** *adv* ▸**ˌone-ˈsidedness** *n*

one-step *n* an early 20th-century ballroom dance with long quick steps, the precursor of the foxtrot.

one-stop *adj* having or providing a range of related services or goods in one place: *a one-stop shop.*

One Thousand Guineas *n* See **Thousand Guineas.**

one-time ⓘ *adj* (*prenominal*) at some time in the past; former.

one-to-one *adj* **1** (of two or more things) corresponding exactly. **2** denoting a relationship or encounter in which someone is involved with only one other person: *one-to-one tuition.* **3** *Maths.* involving the pairing of each member of one set with only one member of another set, without remainder.

one-track ⓘ *adj* **1** *Inf.* obsessed with one idea, subject, etc. **2** having or consisting of a single track.

one-up *adj Inf.* having an advantage or lead over someone or something.
▸**ˌone-ˈupmanship** *n*

one-way *adj* **1** moving or allowing travel in one direction only: *one-way traffic; a one-way bus ticket.* **2** entailing no reciprocal obligation, action, etc.: *a one-way agreement.*

ongoing ⓘ (ˈɒnˌgəʊɪŋ) *adj* **1** actually in progress: *ongoing projects.* **2** continually moving forward; developing. **3** remaining in existence; continuing.

onion (ˈʌnjən) *n* **1** an alliaceous plant having greenish-white flowers: cultivated for its rounded edible bulb. **2** the bulb of this plant, consisting of concentric layers of white succulent leaf bases with a pungent odour and taste. **3 know one's onions.** *Brit. sl.* to be fully acquainted with a subject. [C14: via Anglo-Norman from OF *oignon,* from L *unio* onion]
▸**ˈoniony** *adj*

onionskin (ˈʌnjənˌskɪn) *n* a glazed translucent paper.

on line *adj* (**on-line** *when prenominal*). of or concerned with a peripheral device that is directly connected to and controlled by the central processing unit of a computer. Cf. **off line.**

onlooker ⓘ (ˈɒnˌlʊkə) *n* a person who observes without taking part.
▸**ˈonˌlooking** *adj*

only ⓘ (ˈəʊnlɪ) *adj* (*prenominal*) **1 the.** being single or very few in number: *the only men left in town were too old to bear arms.* **2** (of a child) having no siblings. **3** unique by virtue of being superior to anything else; peerless. **4 one and only. 4a** (*adj*) incomparable; unique. **4b** (*as n*) the ob-

THESAURUS

once *adv* **1 = at one time**, formerly, in the old days, in the past, in times gone by, in times past, long ago, once upon a time, previously **7 once and for all = for the last time**, conclusively, decisively, finally, for all time, for good, permanently, positively, with finality **8 once in a while = occasionally**, at intervals, at times, every now and then, from time to time, now and again, on occasion, sometimes ◆ *n* **14 at once: a = immediately**, directly, forthwith, instantly, now, right away, straight away, this (very) minute, without delay, without hesitation **b = simultaneously**, at *or* in one go (*inf.*), at the same time, together

oncoming *adj* **1 = approaching**, advancing, forthcoming, imminent, impending, looming, onrushing, upcoming

one-horse *adj* **2** *Informal* **= small**, backwoods, inferior, minor, obscure, petty, quiet, sleepy, slow, small-time (*inf.*), tinpot (*Brit. inf.*), unimportant

onerous *adj* **1 = difficult**, backbreaking, burdensome, crushing, demanding, exacting, exhausting, exigent, formidable, grave, hard, heavy, laborious, oppressive, responsible, taxing, weighty
Antonyms *adj* cushy (*inf.*), easy, effortless, facile, light, painless, simple, trifling, undemanding, unexacting, untaxing

one-sided *adj* **1 = biased**, coloured, discriminatory, inequitable, lopsided, partial, partisan, prejudiced, unequal, unfair, unjust
Antonyms *adj* equal, equitable, fair, impartial, just, unbiased, uncoloured, unprejudiced

one-time *adj* **= former**, erstwhile, ex-, late, previous, quondam, sometime

one-track *adj* **1** *Informal* **= obsessed**, fanatical, fixated, monomaniacal, single-track

ongoing *adj* **1-3 = in progress**, advancing, continuous, current, developing, evolving, extant, growing, progressing, successful, unfinished, unfolding

onlooker *n* **= observer**, bystander, eyewitness, looker-on, spectator, viewer, watcher, witness

only *adj* **1 = sole**, exclusive, individual, lone, one

ject of all one's love: *you are my one and only.* ◆ *adv* **5** without anyone or anything else being included; alone: *you have one choice only; only a genius can do that.* **6** merely or just: *it's only Henry.* **7** no more or no greater than: *we met only an hour ago.* **8** used in conditional clauses introduced by *if* to emphasize the impossibility of the condition ever being fulfilled: *if I had only known, this would never have happened.* **9** not earlier than; not...until: *I only found out yesterday.* **10 if only** *or* **if...only.** an expression used to introduce a wish, esp. one felt to be unrealizable. **11 only if.** never...except when. **12 only too. 12a** (intensifier): *he was only too pleased to help.* **12b** most regrettably (esp. in **only too true**). ◆ *sentence connector.* **13** but; however: used to introduce an exception or condition: *you may play outside: only don't go into the street.* [OE *ānlīc,* from *ān* ONE + *-līc* -LY[1]]

USAGE NOTE In informal English, *only* is often used as a sentence connector: *I would have phoned you, only I didn't know your number.* This use should be avoided in formal writing: *I would have phoned you if I'd known your number.* In formal speech and writing, *only* is placed directly before the word or words that it modifies: *she could interview only three applicants in the morning.* In all but the most formal contexts, however, it is generally regarded as acceptable to put *only* before the verb: *she could only interview three applicants in the morning.* Care must be taken not to create ambiguity, esp. in written English, in which intonation will not, as it does in speech, help to show to which item in the sentence *only* applies. A sentence such as *she only drinks tea in the afternoon* is capable of two interpretations and is therefore better rephrased either as *she drinks only tea in the afternoon* (i.e. no other drink) or *she drinks tea only in the afternoon* (i.e. at no other time).

o.n.o. *abbrev. for* or near(est) offer.

onomastics (ˌɒnəˈmæstɪks) *n (functioning as sing)* the study of proper names, esp. of their origins. [from Gk *onomastikos,* from *onomazein* to name, from *onoma* NAME]

onomatopoeia ❶ (ˌɒnəˌmætəˈpiːə) *n* **1** the formation of words whose sound is imitative of the sound of the noise or action designated, such as *hiss.* **2** the use of such words for poetic or rhetorical effect. [C16: via LL from Gk *onoma* name + *poiein* to make]
▸**ˌonoˌmatoˈpoeic** *or* **onomatopoetic** (ˌɒnəˌmætəpəʊˈɛtɪk) *adj* ▸**ˌonoˌmatoˈpoeically** *or* **ˌonoˌmatopoˈetically** *adv*

onrush ❶ (ˈɒnˌrʌʃ) *n* a forceful forward rush or flow.

onset ❶ (ˈɒnˌsɛt) *n* **1** an attack; assault. **2** a start; beginning.

onshore (ˈɒnˈʃɔː) *adj, adv* **1** towards the land: *an onshore gale.* **2** on land; not at sea.

onside (ˌɒnˈsaɪd) *adj, adv* **1** *Football, etc.* (of a player) in a legal position, as when behind the ball or with a required number of opponents between oneself and the opposing team's goal line. Cf. **offside.** ◆ *adj* **2** taking one's part or side; working towards the same goal (esp. in **get someone onside**).

onslaught ❶ (ˈɒnˌslɔːt) *n* a violent attack. [C17: from MDu. *aenslag,* from *aan* ON + *slag* a blow]

Ont. *abbrev. for* Ontario.

Ontarian (ɒnˈtɛərɪən) *or* **Ontarioan** (ɒnˈtɛərɪˌəʊən) *adj* **1** of or denoting Ontario, a province of central Canada. ◆ *n* **2** a native or inhabitant of Ontario.

onto *or* **on to** (ˈɒntu; *unstressed* ˈɒntə) *prep* **1** to a position that is on: *step onto the train.* **2** having become aware of (something illicit or secret): *the police are onto us.* **3** into contact with: *get onto the factory.*

USAGE NOTE *Onto* is now generally accepted as a word in its own right. *On to* is still used, however, where *on* is considered to be part of the verb: *he moved on to a different town* as contrasted with *he jumped onto the stage.*

onto- *combining form.* existence or being: *ontogeny; ontology.* [from LGk, from *ōn* (stem *ont-*) being, present participle of *einai* to be]

ontogeny (ɒnˈtɒdʒənɪ) *or* **ontogenesis** (ˌɒntəˈdʒɛnɪsɪs) *n* the entire sequence of events involved in the development of an individual organism. Cf. **phylogeny.**
▸**ontogenic** (ˌɒntəˈdʒɛnɪk) *or* **ontogenetic** (ˌɒntədʒɪˈnɛtɪk) *adj* ▸**ˌontoˈgenically** *or* **ˌontogeˈnetically** *adv*

ontology (ɒnˈtɒlədʒɪ) *n* **1** *Philosophy.* the branch of metaphysics that deals with the nature of being. **2** *Logic.* the set of entities presupposed by a theory.
▸**ˌontoˈlogical** *adj* ▸**ˌontoˈlogically** *adv*

onus ❶ (ˈəʊnəs) *n, pl* **onuses.** a responsibility, task, or burden. [C17: L: burden]

onward (ˈɒnwəd) *adj* **1** directed or moving forwards, onwards, etc. ◆ *adv* **2** a variant of **onwards.**

onwards ❶ (ˈɒnwədz) *or* **onward** *adv* at or towards a point or position ahead, in advance, etc.

onychophoran (ˌɒnɪˈkɒfərən) *n* a wormlike invertebrate having a segmented body and short unjointed limbs, and breathing by means of tracheae. [from NL *Onychophora,* from Gk *onukh-* claw + -PHORE]

-onym *n combining form.* indicating a name or word: *pseudonym.* [from Gk *-onumon,* from var. of *onoma* name]

onyx (ˈɒnɪks) *n* **1** a variety of chalcedony with alternating black-and-white parallel bands, used as a gemstone. **2** a variety of calcite used as an ornamental stone; onyx marble. [C13: from L, from Gk: fingernail (so called from its veined appearance)]

ONZ *abbrev. for* Order of New Zealand.

oo- *or* **oö-** *combining form.* egg or ovum: *oosperm.* [from Gk *ōion* EGG[1]]

oocyte (ˈəʊəˌsaɪt) *n* an immature female germ cell that gives rise to an ovum after two meiotic divisions.

oodles (ˈuːdᵊlz) *pl n Inf.* great quantities: *oodles of money.* [C20: from ?]

oogamy (əʊˈɒgəmɪ) *n* sexual reproduction involving a small motile male gamete and a large much less motile female gamete.
▸**oˈogamous** *adj*

Ookpik (ˈuːkpɪk) *n Canad. trademark.* a sealskin doll resembling an owl, first made in 1963 by an Inuit and used abroad as a symbol of Canadian handicrafts. [from Eskimo *ukpik* a snowy owl]

oolite (ˈəʊəˌlaɪt) *n* any sedimentary rock, esp. limestone, consisting of tiny spherical concentric grains within a fine matrix. [C18: from F, from NL *oolitēs,* lit.: egg stone; prob. a translation of G *Rogenstein* roe stone]
▸**oolitic** (ˌəʊəˈlɪtɪk) *adj*

oolith (ˈəʊəˌlɪθ) *n* any of the tiny spherical grains of sedimentary rock of which oolite is composed.

oology (əʊˈɒlədʒɪ) *n* the branch of ornithology concerned with the study of birds' eggs.
▸**oological** (ˌəʊəˈlɒdʒɪkᵊl) *adj* ▸**oˈologist** *n*

oolong (ˈuːˌlɒŋ) *n* a kind of dark tea, grown in China, that is partly fermented before being dried. [C19: from Chinese *wu lung,* from *wu* black + *lung* dragon]

oomiak *or* **oomiac** (ˈuːmɪˌæk) *n* a variant of **umiak.**

oompah (ˈuːmˌpɑː) *n* a representation of the sound made by a deep brass instrument, esp. in military band music.

oomph (ʊmf) *n Inf.* **1** enthusiasm, vigour, or energy. **2** sex appeal. [C20: from ?]

oops (ʊps, uːps) *interj* an exclamation of surprise or of apology as when someone drops something or makes a mistake.

ooze[1] ❶ (uːz) *vb* **oozes, oozing, oozed. 1** (*intr*) to flow or leak out slowly, as through small holes. **2** to emit (moisture, etc.). **3** (*tr*) to overflow with: *to ooze charm.* **4** (*intr;* often foll. by *away*) to disappear or escape gradually. ◆ *n* **5** a slow flowing or leaking. **6** an infusion of vegetable matter, such as oak bark, used in tanning. [OE *wōs* juice]

ooze[2] ❶ (uːz) *n* **1** a soft thin mud found at the bottom of lakes and rivers. **2** a fine-grained marine deposit consisting of the hard parts of planktonic organisms. **3** muddy ground, esp. of bogs. [OE *wāse* mud]

oozy[1] ❶ (ˈuːzɪ) *adj* **oozier, ooziest.** moist or dripping.

oozy[2] ❶ (ˈuːzɪ) *adj* **oozier, ooziest.** of, resembling, or containing mud; slimy.
▸**ˈoozily** *adv* ▸**ˈooziness** *n*

OP *abbrev. for:* **1** Ordo Praedictatorum (the Dominicans). [L: Order of Preachers] **2** organophosphate.

op. *abbrev. for:* **1** opera. **2** operation. **3** operator. **4** optical. **5** opposite. **6** opus.

o.p. *or* **O.P.** *abbrev. for* out of print.

opacity ❶ (əʊˈpæsɪtɪ) *n, pl* **opacities. 1** the state or quality of being opaque. **2** the degree to which something is opaque. **3** an opaque object or substance. **4** obscurity of meaning; unintelligibility.

opah (ˈəʊpə) *n* a large soft-finned deep-sea teleost fish having a deep, brilliantly coloured body. Also called: **moonfish, kingfish.** [C18: of West African origin]

opal (ˈəʊpᵊl) *n* an amorphous form of hydrated silicon dioxide that can be of almost any colour. It is used as a gemstone. [C16: from L *opalus,* from Gk *opallios,* from Sansk. *upala* precious stone]
▸**ˈopal-ˌlike** *adj*

opalescent ❶ (ˌəʊpəˈlɛsᵊnt) *adj* having or emitting an iridescence like that of an opal.
▸**ˌopaˈlesce** *vb* ▸**ˌopalˈescence** *n*

THESAURUS

and only, single, solitary, unique ◆ *adv* **5-7** = **merely,** at most, barely, exclusively, just, purely, simply

onomatopoeic *adj* **1** = **imitative,** echoic, onomatopoetic

onrush *n* = **surge,** charge, flood, flow, onset, onslaught, push, rush, stampede, stream

onset *n* **1** = **attack,** assault, charge, onrush, onslaught **2** = **beginning,** inception, kick-off (*inf.*), outbreak, start
Antonyms *n* ≠ **beginning:** conclusion, culmination, end, ending, finish, outcome, termination, wind-up

onslaught *n* = **attack,** assault, blitz, charge, offensive, onrush, onset
Antonyms *n* defensive, escape, flight, recession, retreat, rout, stampede, withdrawal

onus *n* = **burden,** liability, load, obligation, responsibility, task
Antonyms *n* easement, exemption, exoneration, liberation, pardon, release, relief, remission

onwards *adv* = **ahead,** beyond, forth, forward, in front, on

ooze[1] *vb* **1, 2** = **seep,** bleed, discharge, drain, dribble, drip, drop, emit, escape, exude, filter, leach, leak, overflow with, percolate, strain, sweat, weep

ooze[2] *n* **1** = **mud,** alluvium, gloop (*inf.*), mire, muck, silt, slime, slob (*Irish*), sludge

oozy[1] *adj* = **moist,** dripping, sweaty, weeping

oozy[2] *adj* = **slimy,** miry, mucky, sloppy, sludgy

opacity *n* **1** = **opaqueness,** cloudiness, density, dullness, filminess, impermeability, milkiness, murkiness, obscurity

opalescent *adj* = **iridescent,** lustrous, nacre-

opal glass *n* glass that is opalescent or white, made by the addition of fluorides.

opaline ('əupəˌlaɪn) *adj* **1** opalescent. ◆ *n* **2** an opaque or semiopaque whitish glass.

opaque Ⓣ (əu'peɪk) *adj* **1** not transmitting light; not transparent or translucent. **2** not reflecting light; lacking lustre or shine; dull. **3** hard to understand; unintelligible. **4** unintelligent; dense. ◆ *n* **5** *Photog.* an opaque pigment used to block out areas on a negative. ◆ *vb* **opaques, opaquing, opaqued.** (*tr*) **6** to make opaque. **7** *Photog.* to block out areas on (a negative), using an opaque. [C15: from L *opācus* shady]
▸**o'paquely** *adv* ▸**o'paqueness** *n*

op art (ɒp) *n* a style of abstract art chiefly concerned with the exploitation of optical effects such as the illusion of movement. [C20 *op*, short for *optical*]

op. cit. (in textual annotations) *abbrev. for* opere citato. [L: in the work cited]

ope (əup) *vb* **opes, oping, oped,** *adj* an archaic or poetic word for **open.**

OPEC ('əupɛk) *n acronym for* Organization of Petroleum-Exporting Countries.

open Ⓣ ('əupᵊn) *adj* **1** not closed or barred. **2** affording free passage, access, view, etc.; not blocked or obstructed. **3** not sealed, fastened, or wrapped. **4** having the interior part accessible: *an open drawer.* **5** extended, expanded, or unfolded: *an open flower.* **6** ready for business. **7** able to be obtained; available: *the position is no longer open.* **8** unobstructed by buildings, trees, etc.: *open countryside.* **9** free to all to join, enter, use, visit, etc.: *an open competition.* **10** unengaged or unoccupied: *the doctor has an hour open for you to call.* **11** See **open season. 12** not decided or finalized: *an open question.* **13** ready to entertain new ideas; not biased or prejudiced. **14** unreserved or candid. **15** liberal or generous: *an open hand.* **16** extended or eager to receive (esp. in **with open arms**). **17** exposed to view; blatant: *open disregard of the law.* **18** liable or susceptible: *you will leave yourself open to attack.* **19** (of climate or seasons) free from frost; mild. **20** free from navigational hazards, such as ice, sunken ships, etc. **21** having large or numerous spacing or apertures: *open ranks.* **22** full of small openings or gaps; porous: *an open texture.* **23** *Music.* **23a** (of a string) not stopped with the finger. **23b** (of a pipe, such as an organ pipe) not closed at either end. **23c** (of a note) played on such a string or pipe. **24** *Commerce.* **24a** in operation; active: *an open account.* **24b** unrestricted; unlimited: *open credit; open insurance cover.* **25** See **open cheque. 26** (of a return ticket) not specifying a date for travel. **27** *Sport.* (of a goal, court, etc.) unguarded or relatively unprotected. **28** (of a wound) exposed to the air. **29** (esp. of the large intestine) free from obstruction. **30** undefended and of no military significance: *an open city.* **31** *Phonetics.* **31a** denoting a vowel pronounced with the lips relatively wide apart. **31b** denoting a syllable that does not end in a consonant, as in *pa.* **32** *Maths.* (of a set) containing points whose neighbourhood consists of other points of the same set. **33** *Computing.* designed to an internationally agreed standard in order to allow communication between computers, irrespective of size, manufacturer, etc. ◆ *vb* **34** to move from a closed or fastened position: *to open a window.* **35** (when *intr*, foll. by *on* or *onto*) to render, be, or become accessible or unobstructed: *to open a road; to open a parcel.* **36** (*intr*) to come into or appear in view: *the lake opened before us.* **37** to extend or unfold or cause to extend or unfold: *to open a newspaper.* **38** to disclose or uncover or be disclosed or uncovered: *to open one's heart.* **39** to cause (the mind) to become receptive or (of the mind) to become receptive. **40** to operate or cause to operate: *to open a shop.* **41** (when *intr*, sometimes foll. by *out*) to make or become less compact or dense in structure: *to open ranks.* **42** to set or be set in action; start: *to open the batting.* **43** (*tr*) to arrange for (a bank account, etc.), usually by making an initial deposit. **44** to turn to a specified point in (a book, etc.): *open at page one.* **45** *Law.* to make the opening statement in (a case before a court of law). **46** (*intr*) *Cards.* to bet, bid, or lead first on a hand. ◆ *n* **47** (often preceded by *the*) any wide or unobstructed space or expanse, esp. of land or water. **48** See **open air. 49** *Sport.* a competition which anyone may enter. **50 bring** (*or* **come**) **into the open.** to make (*or* become) evident or public. ◆ See also **open up.** [OE]
▸**'openable** *adj* ▸**'opener** *n* ▸**'openly** *adv* ▸**'openness** *n*

open air Ⓣ *n* **a** the place or space where the air is unenclosed; the outdoors. **b** (*as modifier*): *an open-air concert.*

open-and-shut Ⓣ *adj* easily decided or solved; obvious: *an open-and-shut case.*

opencast mining ('əupᵊnˌkɑːst) *n Brit.* mining by excavating from the surface. Also called: (esp. US) **strip mining,** (Austral. and NZ) **open cut mining.** [C18: from OPEN + arch. *cast* ditch, cutting]

open chain *n* a chain of atoms in a molecule that is not joined at its ends into the form of a ring.

open cheque *n* an uncrossed cheque that can be cashed at the drawee bank.

open circuit *n* an incomplete electrical circuit in which no current flows.

Open College *n* **the.** (in Britain) a college of art founded in 1987 for mature students studying foundation courses in arts and crafts by television programmes, written material, and tutorials.

open day *n* an occasion on which an institution, such as a school, is open for inspection by the public.

open door *n* **1** a policy or practice by which a nation grants opportunities for trade to all other nations equally. **2** free and unrestricted admission. ◆ *adj* **open-door. 3** open to all; accessible.

open-ended *adj* **1** without definite limits, as of duration or amount: *an open-ended contract.* **2** denoting a question, esp. one on a questionnaire, that cannot be answered "yes", "no", or "don't know".

open-eyed *adj* **1** with the eyes wide open, as in amazement. **2** watchful; alert.

open-faced *adj* **1** having an ingenuous expression. **2** (of a watch) having no lid or cover other than the glass.

open-handed Ⓣ *adj* generous.
▸ˌ**open-'handedly** *adv* ▸ˌ**open-'handedness** *n*

open-hearted *adj* **1** kindly and warm. **2** disclosing intentions and thoughts clearly; candid.
▸ˌ**open-'heartedness** *n*

open-hearth furnace *n* (esp. formerly) a steel-making reverbatory furnace in which pig iron and scrap are contained in a shallow hearth and heated by producer gas.

open-heart surgery *n* surgical repair of the heart during which the blood circulation is often maintained mechanically.

open house *n* **1** a US and Canad. name for **at-home. 2 keep open house.** to be always ready to receive guests.

opening Ⓣ ('əupənɪŋ) *n* **1** the act of making or becoming open. **2** a vacant or unobstructed space, esp. one that will serve as a passageway; gap. **3** *Chiefly US.* a tract in a forest in which trees are scattered or absent. **4** the first part or stage of something. **5a** the first performance of something, esp. a theatrical production. **5b** (*as modifier*): *the opening night.* **6** a specific or formal sequence of moves at the start of any of certain games, esp. chess or draughts. **7** an opportunity or chance. **8** *Law.* the preliminary statement made by counsel to the court or jury.

opening batsman *n Cricket.* one of the two batsmen beginning an innings.

THESAURUS

ous, opaline, pearly, prismatic, rainbow-hued, shot

opaque *adj* **2** = **cloudy,** clouded, dim, dull, filmy, hazy, impenetrable, lustreless, muddied, muddy, murky, obfuscated, turbid **3** = **incomprehensible,** abstruse, baffling, cryptic, difficult, enigmatic, obscure, unclear, unfathomable, unintelligible
Antonyms *adj* ≠ **cloudy:** bright, clear, crystal clear, limpid, lucid, pellucid, transparent, transpicuous ≠ **incomprehensible:** clear, crystal clear, lucid

open *adj* **1-3** = **unclosed,** agape, ajar, gaping, revealed, unbarred, uncovered, unfastened, unlocked, unobstructed, unsealed, yawning **5** = **extended,** expanded, spread out, unfolded, unfurled **8** = **unenclosed,** airy, bare, clear, exposed, extensive, free, not built-up, rolling, spacious, sweeping, uncluttered, uncrowded, unfenced, unsheltered, wide, wide-open **9, 10** = **accessible,** available, free, free to all, general, nondiscriminatory, public, unconditional, unengaged, unoccupied, unqualified, unrestricted, up for grabs (*inf.*), vacant **12** = **unresolved,** arguable, debatable, moot, undecided, unsettled, up in the air, yet to be decided **13** = **objective,** disinterested, free, impartial, receptive, unbiased, uncommitted, unprejudiced **14** = **frank,** above board, artless, candid, fair, guileless, honest, ingenuous, innocent, natural, sincere, transparent, unreserved **15** = **generous,** bounteous, bountiful, liberal, munificent, prodigal **17** = **obvious,** apparent, avowed, barefaced, blatant, bold, clear, conspicuous, downright, evident, flagrant, frank, manifest, noticeable, overt, plain, unconcealed, undisguised, visible **18** = **unprotected,** an easy target, at the mercy of, defenceless, exposed, liable, susceptible, undefended, unfortified, vulnerable **22** = **gappy,** filigree, fretted, holey, honeycombed, lacy, loose, openwork, porous, spongy ◆ *vb* **34** = **unfasten,** clear, crack, throw wide, unbar, unblock, unclose, uncork, uncover, undo, unlock, unseal, untie, unwrap **37** = **unfold,** expand, spread (out), unfurl, unroll **38** = **disclose,** divulge, exhibit, explain, lay bare, pour out, show, uncover **42** = **start,** begin, begin business, commence, get *or* start the ball rolling, inaugurate, initiate, kick off (*inf.*), launch, set in motion, set up shop
Antonyms *adj* ≠ **unclosed:** closed, fastened, locked, sealed, shut ≠ **unenclosed:** bounded, confined, covered, crowded, enclosed, limited, obstructed, restricted ≠ **accessible:** inaccessible, private, protected, restricted ≠ **objective:** biased, partial, prejudiced ≠ **frank:** artful, cunning, introverted, reserved, secretive, sly, withdrawn ≠ **obvious:** covert, disguised, hidden, secret, veiled ≠ **unprotected:** defended, protected ◆ *vb* ≠ **unfasten:** block, close, fasten, lock, obstruct, seal, shut ≠ **unfold:** fold ≠ **start:** close, conclude, end, finish, terminate

open-air *modifier* = **outdoor,** alfresco

open-and-shut *adj* = **straightforward,** foregone, noncontroversial, obvious, simple

open-handed *adj* = **generous,** bountiful, free, lavish, liberal, munificent, prodigal, unstinting
Antonyms *adj* avaricious, close-fisted, grasping, grudging, mean, miserly, parsimonious, penny-pinching (*inf.*), penurious, stingy, tight-fisted

opening *n* **1, 4** = **beginning,** birth, commencement, dawn, inauguration, inception, initiation, kickoff (*inf.*), launch, launching, onset, opening move, outset, overture, start **2** = **hole,** aperture, breach, break, chink, cleft, crack, fissure, gap, interstice, orifice, perforation, rent, rupture, slot, space, split, vent **7** = **opportunity,** break (*inf.*), chance, look-in (*inf.*), occasion, place, vacancy, window
Antonyms *n* ≠ **beginning:** cessation, close, completion, conclusion, culmination, ending, finale, finish, termination, winding up (*inf.*) ≠ **hole:** blockage, closing, closure, obstruction, occlusion, plug, seal, stoppage

openly *adv* **14** = **candidly,** face to face, forthrightly, frankly, overtly, plainly, straight from the shoulder (*inf.*), unhesitatingly, unreservedly **17** = **blatantly,** brazenly, flagrantly, in full view, in public, publicly, shamelessly, unabashedly, unashamedly, wantonly, without pretence

opening time *n Brit.* the time at which public houses can legally start selling alcoholic drinks.
open learning *n* a system of further education on a flexible part-time basis.
open letter *n* a letter, esp. one of protest, addressed to a person but also made public, as through the press.
open market *n* **a** a market in which prices are determined by supply and demand, there are no barriers to entry, and trading is not restricted to a specific area. **b** *(as modifier): open-market value.*
open marriage *n* a marriage in which the partners agree to pursue separate social and sexual lives.
open-minded ❶ *adj* having a mind receptive to new ideas, arguments, etc.; unprejudiced.
▸ **ˌopen-ˈmindedness** *n*
open-mouthed *adj* **1** having an open mouth, esp. in surprise. **2** greedy or ravenous. **3** clamorous or vociferous.
open-plan *adj* having no or few dividing walls between areas: *an open-plan office floor.*
open position *n Commerce.* a situation in which a dealer in commodities, securities, or currencies has either unsold stock or uncovered sales.
open prison *n* a penal establishment in which the prisoners are trusted to serve their sentences and so do not need to be locked up.
open punctuation *n* punctuation which has relatively few semicolons, commas, etc. Cf. **close punctuation.**
open question *n* **1** a matter which is undecided. **2** a question that cannot be answered with "yes" or "no" but requires a developed answer.
open-reel *adj* another term for **reel-to-reel.**
open season *n* a specified period of time in the year when it is legal to hunt or kill game or fish protected at other times by law.
open secret *n* something that is supposed to be secret but is widely known.
open sesame *n* a very successful means of achieving a result. [from the magical words used in the *Arabian Nights' Entertainments* to open the robbers' den]
open shop *n* an establishment in which persons are employed irrespective of their membership or nonmembership of a trade union.
open slather *n* See **slather.**
Open University *n* **the.** (in Britain) a university founded in 1969 for mature students studying by television and radio lectures, correspondence courses, local counselling, and summer schools.
open up *vb (adv)* **1** *(intr)* to start firing a gun or guns. **2** *(intr)* to speak freely or without restraint. **3** *(intr) Inf.* (of a motor vehicle) to accelerate. **4** *(tr)* to render accessible: *the motorway opened up the remoter areas.* **5** *(intr)* to make or become more exciting or lively: *the game opened up after half-time.*
open verdict *n* a finding by a coroner's jury of death without stating the cause.
openwork (ˈəupᵊnˌwɜːk) *n* ornamental work, as of metal or embroidery, having a pattern of openings or holes.
opera[1] (ˈɒpərə, ˈɒprə) *n* **1** an extended dramatic work in which music constitutes a dominating feature. **2** the branch of music or drama represented by such works. **3** the score, libretto, etc., of an opera. **4** a theatre where opera is performed. [C17: via It. from L: work, a work, pl of *opus* work]
opera[2] (ˈɒpərə) *n* a plural of **opus.**
operable (ˈɒpərəbᵊl, ˈɒprə-) *adj* **1** capable of being treated by a surgical operation. **2** capable of being operated. **3** capable of being put into practice.
▸ **ˌoperaˈbility** *n* ▸ **ˈoperably** *adv*
opéra bouffe (ˈɒpərə ˈbuːf) *n, pl* **opéras bouffes** (ˈɒpərə ˈbuːf). a type of light or satirical opera common in France during the 19th century. [F: comic opera]
opera buffa (ˈbuːfə) *n, pl* **opera buffas.** comic opera, esp. that originating in Italy during the 18th century. [It.: comic opera]
opéra comique (kɒˈmiːk) *n, pl* **opéras comiques.** (ˈɒpərə kɒˈmiːk). a type of opera current in France during the 19th century and characterized by spoken dialogue. [F: comic opera: it originated in satirical parodies of grand opera]
opera glasses *pl n* small low-powered binoculars used by audiences in theatres, etc.
opera hat *n* a collapsible top hat operated by a spring.
opera house *n* a theatre designed for opera.
operand (ˈɒpəˌrænd) *n* a quantity or function upon which a mathematical or logical operation is performed. [C19: from L *operandum* (something) to be worked upon, from *operārī* to work]
operant (ˈɒpərənt) *adj* **1** producing effects; operating. ◆ *n* **2** a person or thing that operates. **3** *Psychol.* any response by an organism that is not directly caused by stimulus.
opera seria (ˈsɪərɪə) *n, pl* **opera serias.** a type of opera current in 18th-century Italy based on a serious plot, esp. a mythological tale. [It.: serious opera]
operate ❶ (ˈɒpəˌreɪt) *vb* **operates, operating, operated. 1** to function or cause to function. **2** *(tr)* to control the functioning of. **3** to manage, direct, run, or pursue (a business, system, etc.). **4** *(intr)* to perform a surgical operation (upon a person or animal). **5** *(intr)* to produce a desired effect. **6** *(tr; usually foll. by on)* to treat or process in a particular or specific way. **7** *(intr)* to conduct military or naval operations. **8** *(intr)* to deal in securities on a stock exchange. [C17: from L *operārī* to work]
operatic (ˌɒpəˈrætɪk) *adj* **1** of or relating to opera. **2** histrionic or exaggerated.
▸ **ˌoperˈatically** *adv*
operating budget *n Accounting.* a forecast of the sales revenue, production costs, overheads, cash flow, etc., of an organization, used to monitor its trading activities, usually for one year.
operating cycle *n* the time taken by a firm to convert its raw materials into finished goods and thereafter sell them and collect payment.
operating system *n* the set of software controlling a computer.
operating theatre *n* a room in which surgical operations are performed.
operation ❶ (ˌɒpəˈreɪʃən) *n* **1** the act, process, or manner of operating. **2** the state of being in effect, in action, or operative (esp. in **in** *or* **into operation**). **3** a process, method, or series of acts, esp. of a practical or mechanical nature. **4** *Surgery.* any manipulation of the body or one of its organs or parts to repair damage, arrest the progress of a disease, remove foreign matter, etc. **5a** a military or naval action, such as a campaign, manoeuvre, etc. **5b** *(cap. and prenominal when part of a name): Operation Crossbow.* **6** *Maths.* any procedure, such as addition, in which one or more numbers or quantities are operated upon according to specific rules. **7** a commercial or financial transaction.
operational ❶ (ˌɒpəˈreɪʃənᵊl) *adj* **1** of or relating to an operation. **2** in working order and ready for use. **3** *Mil.* capable of, needed in, or actually involved in operations.
▸ **ˌoperˈationally** *adv*
operationalism (ˌɒpəˈreɪʃənəˌlɪzəm) *or* **operationism** (ˌɒpəˈreɪʃəˌnɪzəm) *n Philosophy.* the theory that scientific terms are defined by the experimental operations which determine their applicability.
▸ **ˌoperˌationalˈistic** *adj*
operations research *n* the analysis of problems in business and industry involving quantitative techniques. Also called: **operational research.**
operative ❶ (ˈɒpərətɪv) *adj* **1** in force, effect, or operation. **2** exerting force or influence. **3** producing a desired effect; significant: *the operative word.* **4** of or relating to a surgical procedure. ◆ *n* **5** a worker, esp. one with a special skill. **6** *US.* a private detective.
▸ **ˈoperatively** *adv* ▸ **ˈoperativeness** *or* **ˌoperaˈtivity** *n*
operator ❶ (ˈɒpəˌreɪtə) *n* **1** a person who operates a machine, instrument, etc., esp. a telephone switchboard. **2** a person who owns or operates an industrial or commercial establishment. **3** a speculator, esp. one who operates on currency or stock markets. **4** *Inf.* a person who manipulates affairs and other people. **5** *Maths.* any symbol, term, letter, etc., used to indicate or express a specific operation or process, such as ∫ (the integral operator).
operculum (əuˈpɜːkjuləm) *n, pl* **opercula** (-lə) *or* **operculums. 1** *Zool.* **1a** the hard bony flap covering the gill slits in fishes. **1b** the bony plate in certain gastropods covering the opening of the shell when the body is withdrawn. **2** *Biol. & Bot.* any other covering or lid in various organisms. [C18: via NL from L: lid, from *operīre* to cover]
▸ **oˈpercular** *or* **operculate** (əuˈpɜːkjulɪt, -ˌleɪt) *adj*
operetta (ˌɒpəˈretə) *n* a type of comic or light-hearted opera. [C18: from It.: a small OPERA[1]]
▸ **ˌoperˈettist** *n*

THESAURUS

Antonyms *adv* covertly, furtively, in camera, privately, quietly, secretly, slyly, surreptitiously

open-minded *adj* = **unprejudiced**, broad, broad-minded, catholic, dispassionate, enlightened, free, impartial, liberal, reasonable, receptive, tolerant, unbiased, undogmatic
Antonyms *adj* assertive, biased, bigoted, dogmatic, intolerant, narrow-minded, opinionated, pig-headed, prejudiced, uncompromising

openness *n* **14** = **frankness**, artlessness, candidness, candour *or* (*US*) candor, freedom, freeness, guilelessness, honesty, ingenuousness, naturalness, open-heartedness, sincerity *or* sincereness, transparency, unreservedness

operate *vb* **1** = **work**, act, be in action, be in business, function, go, perform, run **2** = **handle**, be in charge of, manage, manoeuvre, use, work **4** = **perform surgery**
Antonyms *vb* ≠ **work:** break down, conk out (*inf.*), cut out (*inf.*), fail, falter, halt, seize up, stall, stop

operation *n* **1** = **procedure**, action, affair, course, exercise, motion, movement, performance, process, use, working **2 in operation** = **in action**, effective, functioning, going, in business, in force, operative **4** = **surgery 5** = **manoeuvre**, assault, campaign, exercise **7** = **undertaking**, affair, business, deal, enterprise, proceeding, transaction

operational *adj* **2** = **working**, functional, going, in working order, operative, prepared, ready, up and running, usable, viable, workable
Antonyms *adj* broken, ineffective, inoperative, kaput (*inf.*), nonfunctional, on the blink (*sl.*), out of order

operative *adj* **1** = **in force**, active, current, effective, efficient, functional, functioning, in business, in operation, operational, serviceable, standing, workable **2, 3** = **relevant**, crucial, important, indicative, influential, key, significant ◆ *n* **5** = **worker**, artisan, employee, hand, labourer, machinist, mechanic
Antonyms *adj* ≠ **in force:** ineffective, inefficient, inoperative, nonfunctional, powerless, unusable, unworkable

operator *n* **1** = **worker**, conductor, driver, handler, mechanic, operative, practitioner, skilled employee, technician **2** = **manager**, administrator, contractor, dealer, director, speculator, trader **4** *Informal* = **manipulator**, Machiavellian,

ophicleide ('ɒfɪ,klaɪd) *n Music.* an obsolete keyed wind instrument of bass pitch. [C19: from F *ophicléide*, from Gk *ophis* snake + *kleis* key]

ophidian (əʊ'fɪdɪən) *adj* **1** snakelike. **2** of, relating to, or belonging to the suborder of reptiles that comprises the snakes. ◆ *n* **3** any reptile of this suborder; a snake. [C19: from NL *Ophidia*, name of suborder, from Gk *ophidion*, from *ophis* snake]

ophthalmia (ɒf'θælmɪə) *n* inflammation of the eye, often including the conjunctiva. [C16: via LL from Gk, from *ophthalmos* eye; see OPTIC]

ophthalmic (ɒf'θælmɪk) *adj* of or relating to the eye.

ophthalmic optician *n* See **optician.**

ophthalmo- *or before a vowel* **ophthalm-** *combining form.* indicating the eye or the eyeball. [from Gk *ophthalmos* EYE]

ophthalmology (,ɒfθæl'mɒlədʒɪ) *n* the branch of medicine concerned with the eye and its diseases.
▸**ophthalmological** (ɒf,θælmə'lɒdʒɪkᵊl) *adj* ▸,**ophthal'mologist** *n*

ophthalmoscope (ɒf'θælmə,skəʊp) *n* an instrument for examining the interior of the eye.
▸**ophthalmoscopic** (ɒf,θælmə'skɒpɪk) *adj*

-opia *n combining form.* indicating a visual defect or condition: *myopia.* [from Gk, from *ōps* eye]
▸**-opic** *adj combining form.*

opiate ⓣ *n* ('əʊpɪɪt). **1** any of various narcotic drugs containing opium. **2** any other narcotic or sedative drug. **3** something that soothes, deadens, or induces sleep. ◆ *adj* ('əʊpɪɪt). **4** containing or consisting of opium. **5** inducing relaxation; soporific. ◆ *vb* ('əʊpɪ,eɪt), **opiates, opiating, opiated.** (*tr*) *Rare.* **6** to treat with an opiate. **7** to dull or deaden. [C16: from Med. L *opiātus*, from L *opium* OPIUM]

opine ⓣ (əʊ'paɪn) *vb* **opines, opining, opined.** (when *tr, usually takes a clause as object*) to hold or express an opinion: *he opined that it was a mistake.* [C16: from L *opīnārī*]

opinion ⓣ (ə'pɪnjən) *n* **1** judgment or belief not founded on certainty or proof. **2** the prevailing or popular feeling or view: *public opinion.* **3** evaluation, impression, or estimation of the value or worth of a person or thing. **4** an evaluation or judgment given by an expert: *a medical opinion.* **5** the advice given by counsel on a case submitted to him for his view on the legal points involved. **6 a matter of opinion.** a point open to question. **7 be of the opinion (that).** to believe (that). [C13: via OF from L *opīniō* belief, from *opīnārī* to think]

opinionated ⓣ (ə'pɪnjə,neɪtɪd) *adj* holding obstinately and unreasonably to one's own opinions; dogmatic.
▸**o'pinion,atedly** *adv* ▸**o'pinion,atedness** *n*

opinionative (ə'pɪnjənətɪv) *adj Rare.* **1** of or relating to opinion. **2** another word for **opinionated.**
▸**o'pinionatively** *adv* ▸**o'pinionativeness** *n*

opinion poll *n* another term for a **poll** (sense 3).

opioid ('əʊpɪ,ɔɪd) *n* any of a group of substances that resemble morphine in their physiological or pharmacological effects, esp. in their pain-relieving properties.

opium ('əʊpɪəm) *n* **1** an addictive narcotic drug extracted from the seed capsules of the opium poppy: used in medicine as an analgesic and hypnotic. **2** something having a tranquillizing or stupefying effect. [C14: from L: poppy juice, from Gk *opion*, dim. of *opos*, juice of a plant]

opium poppy *n* a poppy of SW Asia, with greyish-green leaves and typically white or reddish flowers: widely cultivated as a source of opium.

opossum (ə'pɒsəm) *n, pl* **opossums** *or* **opossum.** **1** a thick-furred marsupial, esp. the **common opossum** of North and South America, having an elongated snout and a hairless prehensile tail. **2** *Austral. & NZ.* any of various similar animals, esp. a phalanger. ◆ Often shortened to **possum.** [C17: from Algonquian *aposoum*]

opp. *abbrev. for:* **1** opposed. **2** opposite.

opponent ⓣ (ə'pəʊnənt) *n* **1** a person who opposes another in a contest, battle, etc. **2** *Anat.* an opponent muscle. ◆ *adj* **3** opposite, as in position. **4** *Anat.* (of a muscle) bringing two parts into opposition. **5** opposing; contrary. [C16: from L *oppōnere* to oppose]
▸**op'ponency** *n*

opportune ⓣ ('ɒpə,tjuːn) *adj* **1** occurring at a time that is suitable or advantageous. **2** fit or suitable for a particular purpose or occurrence. [C15: via OF from L *opportūnus*, from *ob-* to + *portus* harbour (orig.: coming to the harbour, obtaining timely protection)]
▸'**oppor,tunely** *adv* ▸'**oppor,tuneness** *n*

opportunist ⓣ (,ɒpə'tjuːnɪst) *n* **1** a person who adapts his actions, responses, etc., to take advantage of opportunities, circumstances, etc. ◆ *adj* **2** taking advantage of opportunities and circumstances in this way.
▸,**oppor'tunism** *n*

opportunistic (,ɒpətjʊ'nɪstɪk) *adj* **1** of or characterized by opportunism. **2** *Med.* (of an infection) caused by any microorganism that is harmless to a healthy person but debilitates a person whose immune system has been weakened.

opportunity ⓣ (,ɒpə'tjuːnɪtɪ) *n, pl* **opportunities.** **1** a favourable, appropriate, or advantageous combination of circumstances. **2** a chance or prospect.

opportunity shop *n Austral. & NZ.* a shop selling used goods for charitable funds.

opposable (ə'pəʊzəbᵊl) *adj* **1** capable of being opposed. **2** Also: **apposable.** (of the thumb of primates, esp. man) capable of being moved into a position facing the other digits so as to be able to touch the ends of each. **3** capable of being placed opposite something else.
▸**op,posa'bility** *n* ▸**op'posably** *adv*

oppose ⓣ (ə'pəʊz) *vb* **opposes, opposing, opposed.** **1** (*tr*) to fight against, counter, or resist strongly. **2** (*tr*) to be hostile or antagonistic to; be against. **3** (*tr*) to place or set in opposition; contrast or counterbalance. **4** (*tr*) to place opposite or facing. **5** (*intr*) to be or act in opposition. [C14: via OF from L *oppōnere*, from *ob-* against + *pōnere* to place]
▸**op'poser** *n* ▸**op'posing** *adj* ▸**oppositive** (ə'pɒzɪtɪv) *adj*

opposite ⓣ ('ɒpəzɪt, -sɪt) *adj* **1** situated or being on the other side or at each side of something between. **2** facing or going in contrary directions: *opposite ways.* **3** diametrically different in character, tendency, belief, etc. **4** *Bot.* **4a** (of leaves) arranged in pairs on either side of the stem. **4b** (of parts of a flower) arranged opposite the middle of another part. **5** *Maths.* (of a side in a triangle) facing a specified angle. Abbrev.: **opp.** ◆ *n* **6** a person or thing that is opposite; antithesis. ◆ *prep* **7** Also: **opposite to.** facing; corresponding to (something on the other side of a division). **8** as a co-star with: *she played opposite Olivier.* ◆ *adv* **9** on opposite sides: *she lives opposite.*
▸'**oppositely** *adv* ▸'**oppositeness** *n*

opposite number *n* a person holding an equivalent and corresponding position on another side or situation.

opposition ⓣ (,ɒpə'zɪʃən) *n* **1** the act of opposing or the state of being opposed. **2** hostility, unfriendliness, or antagonism. **3** a person or group antagonistic or opposite in aims to another. **4a** (usually preceded by *the*) a political party or group opposed to the ruling party or government. **4b** (*cap. as part of a name, esp. in Britain and Commonwealth countries*): *Her Majesty's Loyal Opposition.* **4c in opposition.** (of a political party) opposing the government. **5** a position facing or opposite another. **6** something that acts as an obstacle to some course or progress. **7** *Astron.* the position of an outer planet or the moon when it is in line with the earth as seen from the sun and is approximately at its nearest to the earth. **8** *Astrol.* an exact aspect of 180° be-

THESAURUS

machinator, mover, shyster (*sl., chiefly US*), smart aleck (*inf.*), wheeler-dealer (*inf.*), wire-puller, worker

opiate *n* **2, 3** = **narcotic**, anodyne, bromide, downer, drug, nepenthe, pacifier, sedative, soporific, tranquillizer

opine *vb* = **give as one's opinion**, believe, conceive, conclude, conjecture, declare, judge, presume, say, suggest, suppose, surmise, think, venture, volunteer, ween (*poetic*)

opinion *n* **1** = **belief**, assessment, conception, conjecture, estimation, feeling, idea, impression, judgment, mind, notion, persuasion, point of view, sentiment, theory, view **6 matter of opinion** = **debatable point**, matter of judgment, moot point, open question **7 be of the opinion** = **believe**, be convinced, be under the impression, conclude, consider, hold, judge, reckon, suppose, surmise, think

opinionated *adj* = **dogmatic**, adamant, biased, bigoted, bull-headed, cocksure, dictatorial, doctrinaire, inflexible, obdurate, obstinate, overbearing, pig-headed, prejudiced, self-assertive, single-minded, stubborn, uncompromising
Antonyms *adj* broad-minded, compliant, compromising, dispassionate, flexible, open-minded, receptive, tolerant, unbiased, unbigoted, unprejudiced

opponent *n* **1** = **adversary**, antagonist, challenger, competitor, contestant, disputant, dissentient, enemy, foe, opposer, rival, the opposition
Antonyms *n* accomplice, ally, associate, colleague, friend, helper, mate, supporter

opportune *adj* **1, 2** = **timely**, advantageous, appropriate, apt, auspicious, convenient, falling into one's lap, favourable, felicitous, fit, fitting, fortunate, happy, lucky, proper, propitious, seasonable, suitable, well-timed
Antonyms *adj* inappropriate, inconvenient, inopportune, unfavourable, unfortunate, unsuitable, untimely

opportunism *n* **2** = **expediency**, exploitation, Machiavellianism, making hay while the sun shines (*inf.*), pragmatism, realism, *Realpolitik*, striking while the iron is hot (*inf.*), trimming, unscrupulousness

opportunity *n* **1** = **chance**, break, convenience, hour, look-in (*inf.*), moment, occasion, opening, scope, time, window

oppose *vb* **1** = **fight**, bar, block, check, combat, confront, contradict, counter, counterattack, defy, face, fly in the face of, hinder, obstruct, prevent, resist, set one's face against, speak against, stand up to, take a stand against, take issue with, take on, thwart, withstand **3** = **counterbalance**, compare, contrast, match, pit *or* set against, play off
Antonyms *vb* ≠ **fight:** advance, advocate, aid, back, defend, espouse, help, promote, support

opposed *adj* **2** = **against**, antagonistic, anti (*inf.*), antipathetic, antithetical, at daggers drawn, averse, clashing, conflicting, contra (*inf.*), contrary, dissentient, hostile, incompatible, inimical, in opposition, opposing, opposite

opposing *adj* **2** = **conflicting**, antagonistic, antipathetic, clashing, combatant, contrary, enemy, hostile, incompatible, irreconcilable, opposed, opposite, rival, warring

opposite *adj* **1** = **facing**, corresponding, fronting **3** = **different**, adverse, antagonistic, antithetical, conflicting, contradictory, contrary, contrasted, diametrically opposed, differing, diverse, hostile, inconsistent, inimical, irreconcilable, opposed, poles apart, reverse, unlike ◆ *n* **6** = **reverse**, antithesis, contradiction, contrary, converse, inverse, the other extreme, the other side of the coin (*inf.*)
Antonyms *adj* ≠ **different:** alike, consistent, corresponding, identical, like, matching, same, similar, uniform

opposition *n* **2** = **hostility**, antagonism,

tween two planets, etc., an orb of 8° being allowed. **9** *Logic.* the relation between propositions having the same subject and predicate but differing in quality, quantity, or both, as with *all men are wicked; no men are wicked; some men are not wicked.*
▸ **ˌoppoˈsitional** *adj* ▸ **ˌoppoˈsitionist** *n* ▸ **ˌoppoˈsitionless** *adj*

oppress ❶ (əˈprɛs) *vb* (*tr*) **1** to subjugate by cruelty, force, etc. **2** to afflict or torment. **3** to lie heavy on (the mind, etc.). [C14: via OF from Med. L *oppressāre,* from L *opprimere,* from *ob-* against + *premere* to press]
▸ **opˈpressing** *adj* ▸ **opˈpression** *n* ▸ **opˈpressor** *n*

oppressive ❶ (əˈprɛsɪv) *adj* **1** cruel, harsh, or tyrannical. **2** heavy, constricting, or depressing.
▸ **opˈpressively** *adv* ▸ **opˈpressiveness** *n*

opprobrious ❶ (əˈprəʊbrɪəs) *adj* **1** expressing scorn, disgrace, or contempt. **2** shameful or infamous.
▸ **opˈprobriously** *adv* ▸ **opˈprobriousness** *n*

opprobrium ❶ (əˈprəʊbrɪəm) *n* **1** the state of being abused or scornfully criticized. **2** reproach or censure. **3** a cause of disgrace or ignominy. [C17: from L *ob-* against + *probrum* a shameful act]

oppugn ❶ (əˈpjuːn) *vb* (*tr*) to call into question; dispute. [C15: from L *oppugnāre,* from *ob-* against + *pugnāre* to fight, from *pugnus* clenched fist]
▸ **opˈpugner** *n*

opsin (ˈɒpsɪn) *n* the protein that together with retinene makes up the purple visual pigment rhodopsin. [C20: back formation from RHODOPSIN]

-opsis *n combining form.* indicating a specified appearance or resemblance: *meconopsis.* [from Gk *opsis* sight]

opsonin (ˈɒpsənɪn) *n* a constituent of blood serum that renders bacteria more susceptible to ingestion by phagocytes. [C20: from Gk *opsōnion* victuals]
▸ **opsonic** (ɒpˈsɒnɪk) *adj*

opt ❶ (ɒpt) *vb* (when *intr,* foll. by *for*) to show preference (for) or choose (to do something). See also **opt in, opt out.** [C19: from F *opter,* from L *optāre* to choose]

opt. *abbrev. for:* **1** *Grammar.* optative. **2** optical. **3** optician. **4** optimum. **5** optional.

optative (ˈɒptətɪv) *adj* **1** indicating or expressing choice or wish. **2** *Grammar.* denoting a mood of verbs in Greek and Sanskrit expressing a wish. ◆ *n* **3** *Grammar.* **3a** the optative mood. **3b** a verb in this mood. [C16: via F *optatif,* from LL *optātīvus,* from L *optāre* to desire]

optic (ˈɒptɪk) *adj* **1** of or relating to the eye or vision. **2** a less common word for **optical.** ◆ *n* **3** an informal word for **eye**[1]. **4** *Brit., trademark.* a device attached to an inverted bottle for dispensing measured quantities of liquid. [C16: from Med. L *opticus,* from Gk *optikos,* from *optos* visible; rel. to *ōps* eye]

optical (ˈɒptɪkᵊl) *adj* **1** of, relating to, producing, or involving light. **2** of or relating to the eye or to the sense of sight; optic. **3** (esp. of a lens) aiding vision or correcting a visual disorder.
▸ **ˈoptically** *adv*

optical activity *n* the ability of substances that are optical isomers to rotate the plane of polarization of a transmitted beam of plane-polarized light.

optical character reader *n* a computer peripheral device enabling letters, numbers, or other characters usually printed on paper to be optically scanned and input to a storage device, such as magnetic tape. The device uses the process of **optical character recognition.** Abbrev. (for both *reader* and *recognition*): **OCR.**

optical crown *n* an optical glass of low dispersion and relatively low refractive index.

optical disc *n Computing.* an inflexible disc on which information is stored in digital form by laser technology. Also called: **video disc.**

optical fibre *n* a communications cable consisting of a thin glass fibre in a protective sheath. Light transmitted along the fibre may be modulated with vision, sound, or data signals. See also **fibre optics.**

optical flint *n* an optical glass of high dispersion and high refractive index containing lead oxide, used in the manufacture of lenses, artificial gems, and cut glass.

optical glass *n* any of several types of clear homogeneous glass of known refractive index used in the construction of lenses, etc.

optical isomerism *n* isomerism of chemical compounds in which the two isomers differ only in that their molecules are mirror images of each other.
▸ **optical isomer** *n*

optical scanner *n* a computer peripheral device enabling printed material, including characters and diagrams, to be scanned and converted into a form that can be stored in a computer. See also **optical character reader.**

optician (ɒpˈtɪʃən) *n* a general name used to refer to: **a** an **ophthalmic optician.** one qualified to examine the eyes and prescribe and supply spectacles and contact lenses. **b** a **dispensing optician.** one who supplies and fits spectacle frames and lenses, but is not qualified to prescribe lenses.

optics (ˈɒptɪks) *n* (*functioning as sing*) the branch of science concerned with vision and the generation, nature, propagation, and behaviour of electromagnetic light.

optimal (ˈɒptɪməl) *adj* another word for **optimum** (sense 2).

optimism ❶ (ˈɒptɪˌmɪzəm) *n* **1** the tendency to expect the best in all things. **2** hopefulness; confidence. **3** the doctrine of the ultimate triumph of good over evil. **4** the philosophical doctrine that this is the best of all possible worlds. ◆ Cf. **pessimism.** [C18: from F *optimisme,* from L *optimus* best, sup. of *bonus* good]
▸ **ˈoptimist** *n* ▸ **ˌoptiˈmistic** *adj* ▸ **ˌoptiˈmistically** *adv*

optimize *or* **optimise** (ˈɒptɪˌmaɪz) *vb* **optimizes, optimizing, optimized** *or* **optimises, optimising, optimised. 1** (*tr*) to take full advantage of. **2** (*tr*) to plan or carry out (an economic activity) with maximum efficiency. **3** (*intr*) to be optimistic. **4** (*tr*) to write or modify (a computer program) to achieve maximum efficiency.
▸ **ˌoptimiˈzation** *or* **ˌoptimiˈsation** *n*

optimum ❶ (ˈɒptɪməm) *n, pl* **optima** (-mə) *or* **optimums. 1** a condition, degree, amount, or compromise that produces the best possible result. ◆ *adj* **2** most favourable or advantageous; best: *optimum conditions.* [C19: from L: the best (thing), from *optimus* best; see OPTIMISM]

optimum population *n Econ.* a population that is sufficiently large to provide an adequate workforce with minimal unemployment.

opt in *vb* (*intr, adv*) to choose to be involved in or part of a scheme, etc.

option ❶ (ˈɒpʃən) *n* **1** the act or an instance of choosing or deciding. **2** the power or liberty to choose. **3** an exclusive opportunity, usually for a limited period, to buy something at a future date: *a six-month option on the Canadian rights to this book.* **4** *Commerce.* the right to buy (**call option**) or sell (**put option**) a fixed quantity of a commodity, security, foreign exchange, etc., at a fixed price at a specified date in the future. See also **traded option. 5** something chosen; choice. **6 keep** (*or* **leave**) **one's options open.** not to commit oneself. **7 soft option.** an easy alternative. ◆ *vb* **8** (*tr*) to obtain or grant an option on: *the BBC have optioned her latest novel.* [C17: from L *optiō* free choice, from *optāre* to choose]

optional ❶ (ˈɒpʃənᵊl) *adj* possible but not compulsory; left to personal choice.
▸ **ˈoptionally** *adv*

option money *n Commerce.* the price paid for buying an option.

THESAURUS

competition, contrariety, counteraction, disapproval, obstruction, obstructiveness, prevention, resistance, unfriendliness **3** = **opponent**, antagonist, competition, foe, other side, rival
Antonyms *n* ≠ **hostility:** agreement, approval, assent, collaboration, concurrence, cooperation, friendliness, responsiveness

oppress *vb* **1** = **subjugate**, abuse, crush, harry, maltreat, overpower, overwhelm, persecute, rule with an iron hand, subdue, suppress, trample underfoot, tyrannize over, wrong **2, 3** = **depress**, afflict, burden, dispirit, harass, lie *or* weigh heavy upon, sadden, take the heart out of, torment, vex
Antonyms *vb* ≠ **subjugate:** deliver, emancipate, free, liberate, loose, release, set free ≠ **depress:** unburden

oppressed *adj* **1** = **downtrodden**, abused, browbeaten, burdened, disadvantaged, enslaved, harassed, henpecked, maltreated, misused, prostrate, slave, subject, tyrannized, underprivileged
Antonyms *adj* advantaged, exalted, favoured, honoured, liberated, privileged

oppression *n* **1** = **subjugation**, abuse, brutality, calamity, cruelty, hardship, harshness, injury, injustice, iron hand, maltreatment, misery, persecution, severity, subjection, suffering, tyranny
Antonyms *n* benevolence, clemency, compassion, goodness, humaneness, justice, kindness, mercy, sympathy, tenderness

oppressive *adj* **1** = **tyrannical**, brutal, burdensome, cruel, despotic, grinding, harsh, heavy, inhuman, onerous, overbearing, overwhelming, repressive, severe, unjust **2** = **stifling**, airless, close, heavy, muggy, overpowering, stuffy, suffocating, sultry, torrid
Antonyms *adj* ≠ **tyrannical:** encouraging, gentle, humane, just, lenient, merciful, propitious, soft

oppressor *n* **1** = **persecutor**, autocrat, bully, despot, harrier, intimidator, iron hand, scourge, slave-driver, taskmaster, tormentor, tyrant

opprobrious *adj* **1** = **contemptuous**, abusive, calumniatory, contumelious, damaging, defamatory, hateful, insolent, insulting, invective, offensive, scandalous, scurrilous, vitriolic, vituperative **2** = **shameful**, abominable, contemptible, despicable, dishonourable, disreputable, hateful, ignominious, infamous, notorious, reprehensible

opprobrium *n* **1, 2** = **disgrace**, calumny, censure, contumely, discredit, disfavour, dishonour, disrepute, ignominy, ill repute, infamy, obloquy, odium, reproach, scurrility, shame, slur, stigma

oppugn *vb* = **dispute**, argue, assail, attack, call into question, cast doubt on, combat, oppose, resist, withstand

opt *vb, often with* **for** = **choose**, decide (on), elect, exercise one's discretion (in favour of), go for, make a selection, plump for, prefer
Antonyms *vb* decide against, dismiss, eliminate, exclude, preclude, reject, rule out, turn down

optimistic *adj* **1** = **idealistic**, disposed to take a favourable view, seen through rose-coloured spectacles, Utopian **2** = **hopeful**, assured, bright, buoyant, buoyed up, can-do (*inf.*), cheerful, confident, encouraged, expectant, looking on the bright side, positive, rosy, sanguine
Antonyms *adj* ≠ **hopeful:** bleak, cynical, despairing, despondent, downhearted, fatalistic, gloomy, glum, hopeless, pessimistic, resigned

optimum *adj* **2** = **ideal**, A1 *or* A-one (*inf.*), best, choicest, flawless, highest, most favourable *or* advantageous, optimal, peak, perfect, superlative
Antonyms *adj* inferior, least, lowest, minimal, poorest, worst

option *n* **1, 5** = **choice**, alternative, election, preference, selection

optional *adj* = **voluntary**, discretionary, elective, extra, noncompulsory, open, possible, up to the individual

optometrist (ɒpˈtɒmɪtrɪst) *n* a person who is qualified to examine the eyes and prescribe and supply spectacles and contact lenses. Also called (esp. Brit.): **ophthalmic optician.**

optometry (ɒpˈtɒmɪtrɪ) *n* the science or practice of testing visual acuity and prescribing corrective lenses.
▸**optometric** (ˌɒptəˈmɛtrɪk) *adj*

optophone (ˈɒptəˌfəʊn) *n* a device for blind people that converts printed words into sounds.

opt out *vb* **1** (*intr, adv;* often foll. by *of*) to choose not to be involved (in) or part (of). ◆ *n* **opt-out. 2** the act of opting out, esp. of a local-authority administration: *opt-outs by hospitals and schools.*

opulent 🅣 (ˈɒpjʊlənt) *adj* **1** having or indicating wealth. **2** abundant or plentiful. [C17: from L *opulens,* from *opēs* (pl) wealth]
▸ˈ**opulence** *or* (*less commonly*) ˈ**opulency** *n* ▸ˈ**opulently** *adv*

opuntia (ɒˈpʌnʃɪə) *n* a cactus, esp. the prickly pear, having fleshy branched stems and green, red, or yellow flowers. [C17: NL, from L *Opuntia* (*herba*) the Opuntian (plant), from *Opus,* ancient town of Locris, Greece]

opus 🅣 (ˈəʊpəs) *n, pl* **opuses** *or* **opera. 1** an artistic composition, esp. a musical work. **2** (*often cap.*) (usually followed by a number) a musical composition by a particular composer, generally catalogued in order of publication: *Beethoven's opus 61.* Abbrev.: **op.** [C18: from L: a work]

Opus Dei (ˈəʊpəs ˈdeɪiː) *n* **1** another name for **divine office. 2** an international Roman Catholic organization founded in Spain in 1928 by Josemaria Escrivá de Balaguer (1902–75), to spread Christian principles.

or[1] (ɔː; *unstressed* ə) *conj* (*coordinating*) **1** used to join alternatives. **2** used to join rephrasings of the same thing: *twelve, or a dozen.* **3** used to join two alternatives when the first is preceded by *either* or *whether: either yes or no.* **4 one or two, four or five,** etc. a few. **5** a poetic word for **either** or **whether,** as the first element in correlatives, with *or* also preceding the second alternative. [C13: contraction of *other,* changed (through infl. of EITHER) from OE *oththe*]

or[2] (ɔː) *adj* (*usually postpositive*) *Heraldry.* of the metal gold. [C16: via F from L *aurum* gold]

OR *abbrev. for:* **1** operational research. **2** Oregon. **3** *Mil.* other ranks.

-or[1] *suffix forming nouns from verbs.* a person or thing that does what is expressed by the verb: *actor; conductor; generator; sailor.* [via OF *-eur, -eor,* from L *-or* or *-ātor*]

-or[2] *suffix forming nouns.* **1** indicating state, condition, or activity: *terror; error.* **2** the US spelling of **-our.**

ora (ˈɔːrə) *n* the plural of **os**[2].

orache *or esp. US* **orach** (ˈɒrɪtʃ) *n* any of several herbaceous plants or small shrubs of the goosefoot family, esp. **garden orache,** which is cultivated as a vegetable. They have typically greyish-green lobed leaves and inconspicuous flowers. [C15: from OF *arache,* from L *atriplex,* from Gk *atraphaxus,* from ?]

oracle 🅣 (ˈɒrəkᵊl) *n* **1** a prophecy revealed through the medium of a priest or priestess at the shrine of a god. **2** a shrine at which an oracular god is consulted. **3** an agency through which a prophecy is transmitted. **4** any person or thing believed to indicate future action with infallible authority. [C14: via OF from L *ōrāculum,* from *ōrāre* to request]

Oracle (ˈɒrəkᵊl) *n Trademark.* the Teletext system operated by ITV. See **Teletext.** [C20: acronym of *o*(*ptional*) *r*(*eception of*) *a*(*nnouncements by*) *c*(*oded*) *l*(*ine*) *e*(*lectronics*)]

oracular 🅣 (ɒˈrækjʊlə) *adj* **1** of or relating to an oracle. **2** wise and prophetic. **3** mysterious or ambiguous.
▸**oˈracularly** *adv*

oracy (ˈɔːrəsɪ) *n* the capacity to express oneself in and understand speech. [C20: from L *or-, os* mouth, by analogy with *literacy*]

oral 🅣 (ˈɔːrəl, ˈɒrəl) *adj* **1** spoken or verbal. **2** relating to, affecting, or for use in the mouth: *an oral thermometer.* **3** denoting a drug to be taken by mouth: *an oral contraceptive.* **4** of, relating to, or using spoken words. **5** *Psychoanal.* relating to a stage of psychosexual development during which the child's interest is concentrated on the mouth. ◆ *n* **6** an examination in which the questions and answers are spoken rather than written. [C17: from LL *ōrālis,* from L *ōs* face]
▸ˈ**orally** *adv*

oral history *n* the memories of living people about events or social conditions in their earlier lives taped and preserved as historical evidence.

oral hygiene *n* the maintenance of healthy teeth and gums by brushing, etc. Also called: **dental hygiene.**

oral society *n* a society that has not developed literacy.

orange (ˈɒrɪndʒ) *n* **1** any of several citrus trees, esp. **sweet orange** and the Seville orange, cultivated in warm regions for their round edible fruit. **2a** the fruit of any of these trees, having a yellowish-red bitter rind and segmented juicy flesh. **2b** (*as modifier*): *orange peel.* **3** the hard wood of any of these trees. **4** any of a group of colours, such as that of the skin of an orange, that lie between red and yellow in the visible spectrum. **5** a dye or pigment producing these colours. **6** orange cloth or clothing: *dressed in orange.* **7** any of several trees or herbaceous plants that resemble the orange, such as mock orange. ◆ *adj* **8** of the colour orange. [C14: via OF *auranja,* from Ar. *nāranj,* from Persian, from Sansk. *nāranga*]

orangeade (ˌɒrɪndʒˈeɪd) *n* an effervescent or still orange-flavoured drink.

orange blossom *n* the flowers of the orange tree, traditionally worn by brides.

Orangeman (ˈɒrɪndʒmən) *n, pl* **Orangemen.** a member of a society founded in Ireland (1795) to uphold Protestantism. [C18: after William, prince of *Orange,* later William III]

Orangeman's Day *n* the 12th of July, celebrated by Protestants in Northern Ireland and elsewhere, to commemorate the anniversary of the Battle of the Boyne (1690).

orange pekoe *n* a superior grade of black tea growing in India and Sri Lanka.

orange roughy (ˈrʌfɪ) *n* a marine food fish of S Pacific waters.

orangery (ˈɒrɪndʒərɪ, -dʒrɪ) *n, pl* **orangeries.** a building, such as a greenhouse, in which orange trees are grown.

orange stick *n* a small stick used to clean the fingernails and cuticles.

orangewood (ˈɒrɪndʒˌwʊd) *n* **a** the hard fine-grained yellowish wood of the orange tree. **b** (*as modifier*): *an orangewood table.*

orang-utan (ɔːˌræŋuːˈtæn, ˌɔːræŋˈuːtæn) *or* **orang-utang** (ɔːˌræŋuːˈtæŋ, ˌɔːræŋˈuːtæŋ) *n* a large anthropoid ape of the forests of Sumatra and Borneo, with shaggy reddish-brown hair and strong arms. Sometimes shortened to **orang.** [C17: from Malay *orang hutan,* from *ōrang* man + *hūtan* forest]

orate 🅣 (ɔːˈreɪt) *vb* **orates, orating, orated.** (*intr*) **1** to make or give an oration. **2** to speak pompously and lengthily.

oration 🅣 (ɔːˈreɪʃən) *n* **1** a formal public declaration or speech. **2** any rhetorical, lengthy, or pompous speech. [C14: from L *ōrātiō* speech, harangue, from *ōrāre* to plead, pray]

orator 🅣 (ˈɒrətə) *n* **1** a public speaker, esp. one versed in rhetoric. **2** a person given to lengthy or pompous speeches. **3** *Obs.* the plaintiff in a cause of action in chancery.

oratorio (ˌɒrəˈtɔːrɪəʊ) *n, pl* **oratorios.** a dramatic but unstaged musical composition for soloists, chorus, and orchestra, based on a religious theme. [C18: from It., lit.: ORATORY[2], referring to the Church of the Oratory at Rome where musical services were held]

oratory[1] 🅣 (ˈɒrətərɪ, -trɪ) *n* **1** the art of public speaking. **2** rhetorical skill or style. [C16: from L (*ars*) *ōrātōria* (the art of) public speaking]
▸ˌ**oraˈtorical** *adj* ▸ˌ**oraˈtorically** *adv*

oratory[2] (ˈɒrətərɪ, -trɪ) *n, pl* **oratories.** a small room or secluded place, set apart for private prayer. [C14: from Anglo-Norman, from Church L *ōrātōrium* place of prayer, from *ōrāre* to plead, pray]

orb 🅣 (ɔːb) *n* **1** (in regalia) an ornamental sphere surmounted by a cross. **2** a sphere; globe. **3** *Poetic.* another word for **eye**[1] (sense 1). **4** *Obs. or poetic.* **4a** a celestial body, esp. the earth or sun. **4b** the orbit of a celestial body. ◆ *vb* **5** to make or become circular or spherical. **6** (*tr*) an archaic word for **encircle.** [C16: from L *orbis* circle, disc]

orbicular (ɔːˈbɪkjʊlə), **orbiculate,** *or* **orbiculated** *adj* **1** circular or spherical. **2** (of a leaf or similar flat part) circular or nearly circular.
▸**orbicularity** (ɔːˌbɪkjʊˈlærɪtɪ) *n* ▸**orˈbicularly** *adv*

orbit 🅣 (ˈɔːbɪt) *n* **1** *Astron.* the curved path followed by a planet, satellite, etc., in its motion around another celestial body. **2** a range or field of action or influence; sphere. **3** the bony cavity containing the eyeball; eye socket. **4** *Zool.* **4a** the skin surrounding the eye of a bird. **4b** the hollow in which lies the eye or eyestalk of an insect. **5** *Physics.*

THESAURUS

Antonyms *adj* compulsory, *de rigueur,* mandatory, obligatory, required

opulence *n* **1 = wealth,** affluence, Easy Street (*inf.*), fortune, lavishness, luxuriance, luxury, prosperity, riches, richness, sumptuousness **2 = abundance,** copiousness, cornucopia, fullness, plenty, profusion, richness, superabundance
Antonyms *n* ≠ **wealth:** impecuniousness, indigence, lack, penury, poverty, privation, want ≠ **abundance:** dearth, lack, paucity, scantiness, scarcity, want

opulent *adj* **1 = rich,** affluent, lavish, luxurious, moneyed, prosperous, sumptuous, wealthy, well-heeled (*inf.*), well-off, well-to-do **2 = abundant,** copious, lavish, luxuriant, plentiful, profuse, prolific
Antonyms *adj* ≠ **rich:** broke (*inf.*), destitute, down and out, indigent, moneyless, needy, on the rocks, penurious, poor, poverty-stricken

opus *n* **1 = work,** brainchild, composition, creation, *oeuvre,* piece, production

oracle *n* **1 = prophecy,** answer, augury, divination, divine utterance, prediction, prognostication, revelation, vision **3 = prophet,** augur, Cassandra, seer, sibyl, soothsayer **4 = authority,** adviser, guru, high priest, horse's mouth, mastermind, mentor, pundit, source, wizard

oracular *adj* **1 = prophetic,** auspicious, foreboding, ominous, portentous, prescient, sibylline **2 = wise,** authoritative, dictatorial, dogmatic, grave, positive, sage, significant, venerable **3 = mysterious,** ambiguous, arcane, cryptic, Delphic, equivocal, obscure, two-edged

oral *adj* **1 = spoken,** verbal, viva voce, vocal

orate *vb* **1, 2 = make a speech,** declaim, discourse, hold forth, pontificate, speak, speechify, talk

oration *n* **1 = speech,** address, declamation, discourse, harangue, homily, lecture, spiel (*inf.*)

orator *n* **1 = public speaker,** Cicero, declaimer, lecturer, rhetorician, speaker, spellbinder

oratorical *adj* **2 = rhetorical,** bombastic, Ciceronian, declamatory, eloquent, grandiloquent, high-flown, magniloquent, silver-tongued, sonorous

oratory[1] *n* **1, 2 = eloquence,** declamation, elocution, grandiloquence, public speaking, rhetoric, speechifying, speech-making, spieling (*inf.*)

orb *n* **2 = sphere,** ball, circle, globe, ring, round

orbit *n* **1 = path,** circle, course, cycle, ellipse, revolution, rotation, track, trajectory **2 = sphere of influence,** ambit, compass, course, domain, influence, range, reach, scope, sphere, sweep ◆ *vb* **7 = circle,** circumnavigate, encircle, revolve around

the path of an electron around the nucleus of an atom. **6 go into orbit.** *Inf.* to reach an extreme and often uncontrolled state: *when he realized the price he nearly went into orbit.* ◆ *vb* **7** to move around (a body) in a curved path. **8** (*tr*) to send (a satellite, spacecraft, etc.) into orbit. **9** (*intr*) to move in or as if in an orbit. [C16: from L *orbita* course, from *orbis* circle]
▸ **'orbitally** *adv*

orbital ('ɔːbɪtəl) *adj* **1** of or denoting an orbit. **2** (of a motorway or major road) circling a large city. ◆ *n* **3** the region around an atomic nucleus, or around two nuclei in a molecule, within which an electron moves. **4** an orbital road.

orbital velocity *n* the velocity required by a spacecraft to enter and maintain a given orbit.

orc (ɔːk) *n* **1** any of various whales, such as the killer and grampus. **2** a mythical monster. [C16: via L *orca*, ?from Gk *orux* whale]

Orcadian (ɔː'keɪdɪən) *n* **1** a native or inhabitant of the Orkneys, a group of islands off the N coast of Scotland. ◆ *adj* **2** of or relating to the Orkneys. [from L *Orcades* the Orkney Islands]

orchard ('ɔːtʃəd) *n* **1** an area of land devoted to the cultivation of fruit trees. **2** a collection of fruit trees especially cultivated. [OE *orceard*, *ortigeard*, from *ort-*, from L *hortus* garden + *geard* YARD[2]]

orchestra ('ɔːkɪstrə) *n* **1** a large group of musicians, esp. one whose members play a variety of different instruments. **2** a group of musicians, each playing the same type of instrument. **3** Also called: **orchestra pit.** the space reserved for musicians in a theatre, immediately in front of or under the stage. **4** *Chiefly US & Canad.* the stalls in a theatre. **5** (in ancient Greek theatre) the semicircular space in front of the stage. [C17: via L from Gk: the space in the theatre for the chorus, from *orkheisthai* to dance]
▸ **orchestral** (ɔː'kɛstrəl) *adj* ▸ **or'chestrally** *adv*

orchestrate ⓣ ('ɔːkɪˌstreɪt) *vb* **orchestrates, orchestrating, orchestrated.** (*tr*) **1** to score or arrange (a piece of music) for orchestra. **2** to arrange, organize, or build up for special or maximum effect.
▸ **ˌorches'tration** *n* ▸ **'orchesˌtrator** *n*

orchid ('ɔːkɪd) *n* a terrestrial or epiphytic plant having flowers of unusual shapes and beautiful colours, usually with one petal larger than the other two. The flowers are specialized for pollination by certain insects. [C19: from NL *Orchideae*; see ORCHIS]

orchidectomy (ˌɔːkɪ'dɛktəmɪ) *n, pl* **orchidectomies.** the surgical removal of one or both testes. [C19: from Gk *orkhis* testicle + -ECTOMY]

orchil ('ɔːkɪl, -tʃɪl) *or* **archil** *n* **1** a purplish dye obtained by treating various lichens with aqueous ammonia. **2** the lichens yielding this dye. [C15: from OF *orcheil*, from ?]

orchis ('ɔːkɪs) *n* **1** a N temperate terrestrial orchid having fleshy tubers and spikes of typically pink flowers. **2** any of various temperate or tropical orchids such as the fringed orchis. [C16: via L from Gk *orkhis* testicle; so called from the shape of its roots]

OR circuit *or* **gate** (ɔː) *n Computing.* a logic circuit having two or more input wires and one output wire that gives a high-voltage output signal if one or more input signals are at a high voltage: used extensively as a basic circuit in computing. [C20: from its similarity to the function of *or* in logical constructions]

ord. *abbrev. for:* **1** order. **2** ordinal. **3** ordinance. **4** ordinary.

ordain ⓣ (ɔː'deɪn) *vb* (*tr*) **1** to consecrate (someone) as a priest; confer holy orders upon. **2** (*may take a clause as object*) to decree, appoint, or predestine irrevocably. **3** (*may take a clause as object*) to order, establish, or enact with authority. [C13: from Anglo-Norman *ordeiner*, from LL *ordināre*, from L *ordo* ORDER]
▸ **or'dainer** *n* ▸ **or'dainment** *n*

ordeal ⓣ (ɔː'diːl) *n* **1** a severe or trying experience. **2** *History.* a method of trial in which the innocence of an accused person was determined by subjecting him to physical danger, esp. by fire or water. [OE *ordāl*, *ordēl* verdict]

order ⓣ ('ɔːdə) *n* **1** a state in which all components or elements are arranged logically, comprehensibly, or naturally. **2** an arrangement or disposition of things in succession; sequence: *alphabetical order.* **3** an established or customary method or state, esp. of society. **4** a peaceful or harmonious condition of society: *order reigned in the streets.* **5** (*often pl*) a class, rank, or hierarchy: *the lower orders.* **6** *Biol.* any of the taxonomic groups into which a class is divided and which contains one or more families. **7** an instruction that must be obeyed; command. **8a** a commission or instruction to produce or supply something in return for payment. **8b** the commodity produced or supplied. **8c** (*as modifier*): *order form.* **9** a procedure followed by an assembly, meeting, etc. **10** (*cap. when part of a name*) a body of people united in a particular aim or purpose. **11** (*usually cap.*) Also called: **religious order.** a group of persons who bind themselves by vows in order to devote themselves to the pursuit of religious aims. **12** (*often pl*) another name for **holy orders, major orders,** or **minor orders. 13** *History.* a society of knights constituted as a fraternity, such as the Knights Templars. **14a** a group of people holding a specific honour for service or merit, conferred on them by a sovereign or state. **14b** the insignia of such a group. **15a** any of the five major classical styles of architecture classified by the style of columns and entablatures used. **15b** any style of architecture. **16** *Christianity.* **16a** the sacrament by which bishops, priests, etc., have their offices conferred upon them. **16b** any of the degrees into which the ministry is divided. **16c** the office of an ordained Christian minister. **17** *Maths.* **17a** the number of times a function must be differentiated to obtain a given derivative. **17b** the order of the highest derivative in a differential equation. **17c** the number of rows or columns in a determinant or square matrix. **17d** the number of members of a finite group. **18** *Mil.* (often preceded by *the*) the dress, equipment, or formation directed for a particular purpose or undertaking: *battle order.* **19 a tall order.** something difficult, demanding, or exacting. **20 in order. 20a** in sequence. **20b** properly arranged. **20c** appropriate or fitting. **21 in order that.** (*conj*) with the purpose that; so that. **22 in order to.** (*prep;* foll. by an infinitive) so that it is possible to: *to eat in order to live.* **23 keep order.** to maintain or enforce order. **24 of** *or* **in the order of.** having an approximately specified size or quantity. **25 on order.** having been ordered but not having been delivered. **26 out of order. 26a** not in sequence. **26b** not working. **26c** not following the rules or customary procedure. **27 to order. 27a** according to a buyer's specifications. **27b** on request or demand. ◆ *vb* **28** (*tr*) to give a command to (a person or animal to do or be something). **29** to request (something) to be supplied or made, esp. in return for payment. **30** (*tr*) to instruct or command to move, go, etc. (to a specified place): *they ordered her into the house.* **31** (*tr; may take a clause as object*) to authorize; prescribe: *the doctor ordered a strict diet.* **32** (*tr*) to arrange, regulate, or dispose (articles, etc.) in their proper places. **33** (*tr*) (of fate) to will; ordain. ◆ *interj* **34** an exclamation demanding that orderly behaviour be restored. [C13: from OF *ordre*, from L *ordō*]
▸ **'orderer** *n*

order-driven *adj* denoting an electronic market system, esp. for stock exchanges, in which prices are determined by the publication of orders to buy or sell. Cf. **quote-driven.**

order in council *n* (in Britain) a decree of the Cabinet, usually made under the authority of a statute: in theory a decree of the sovereign and Privy Council.

orderly ⓣ ('ɔːdəlɪ) *adj* **1** in order, properly arranged, or tidy. **2** obeying or appreciating method, system, and arrangement. **3** *Mil.* of or relating to orders: *an orderly book.* ◆ *n, pl* **orderlies. 4** *Med.* a male hospital attendant. **5** *Mil.* a junior rank detailed to carry orders or perform minor tasks for a more senior officer.
▸ **'orderliness** *n*

orderly room *n Mil.* a room in the barracks of a battalion or company used for general administrative purposes.

order of magnitude *n* a numerical value expressed to the nearest power of ten.

Order of Merit *n Brit.* an order conferred on civilians and servicemen for eminence in any field.

order of the day *n* **1** the general directive of a commander in chief or the specific instructions of a commanding officer. **2** *Inf.* the pre-

THESAURUS

orchestrate *vb* **1** = **score**, arrange **2** = **organize**, arrange, concert, coordinate, integrate, present, put together, set up, stage-manage

ordain *vb* **1** = **appoint**, anoint, call, consecrate, destine, elect, frock, invest, nominate **2** = **predestine**, fate, foreordain, intend, predetermine **3** = **order**, decree, demand, dictate, enact, enjoin, establish, fix, lay down, legislate, prescribe, pronounce, rule, set, will

ordeal *n* **1** = **hardship**, affliction, agony, anguish, baptism of fire, nightmare, suffering, test, torture, trial, tribulation(s), trouble(s)
Antonyms *n* bliss, delight, elation, enjoyment, gladness, happiness, joy, pleasure

order *n* **1** = **tidiness**, arrangement, harmony, method, neatness, orderliness, organization, pattern, plan, propriety, regularity, symmetry, system **2** = **sequence**, arrangement, array, categorization, classification, codification, disposal, disposition, grouping, layout, line, line-up, ordering, placement, progression, series, setup (*inf.*), structure, succession **4** = **peace**, calm, control, discipline, law, law and order, quiet, tranquillity **5** = **class**, caste, degree, grade, hierarchy, pecking order (*inf.*), position, rank, status **6** = **kind**, breed, sort, taxonomic group, type **7** = **instruction**, behest, canon, command, decree, dictate, direction, directive, injunction, law, mandate, ordinance, precept, regulation, rule, say-so (*inf.*), stipulation **8a** = **request**, application, booking, commission, requisition, reservation **10** = **society**, association, brotherhood, community, company, fraternity, guild, league, lodge, organization, sect, sisterhood, sodality, union **20 in order: b** = **arranged**, in sequence, neat, orderly, shipshape **c** = **appropriate**, acceptable, called for, correct, fitting, O.K. *or* okay (*inf.*), right, suitable **26 out of order: b** = **broken**, broken-down, bust (*inf.*), in disrepair, inoperative, kaput (*inf.*), nonfunctional, on the blink (*sl.*), out of commission, U.S. (*inf.*), wonky (*Brit. sl.*) **c** = **improper**, indecorous, not cricket (*inf.*), not done, not on (*inf.*), out of place, out of turn, uncalled-for, wrong ◆ *vb* **28** = **command**, adjure, bid, charge, decree, demand, direct, enact, enjoin, instruct, ordain, prescribe, require **29** = **request**, apply for, book, contract for, engage, reserve, send away for **31** = **prescribe**, authorize, call for, demand **32** = **arrange**, adjust, align, catalogue, class, classify, conduct, control, dispose, group, lay out, manage, marshal, neaten, organize, put to rights, regulate, sequence, set in order, sort out, systematize, tabulate, tidy
Antonyms *n* ≠ **tidiness:** chaos, clutter, confusion, disarray, disorder, jumble, mess, muddle, pandemonium, shambles ◆ *vb* ≠ **arrange:** clutter, confuse, disarrange, disorder, disturb, jumble up, mess up, mix up, muddle, scramble

orderly *adj* **1** = **well-organized**, businesslike, in apple-pie order (*inf.*), in order, methodical, neat, regular, scientific, shipshape, systematic, systematized, tidy, trim, well-regulated **2** = **well-behaved**, controlled, decorous, disciplined, law-abiding, nonviolent, peaceable, quiet, restrained
Antonyms *adj* ≠ **well-organized:** chaotic, disorderly, disorganized, higgledy-piggledy (*inf.*), messy, sloppy, unsystematic ≠ **well-behaved:** disorderly, riotous, uncontrolled, undisciplined

scribed or only thing offered or available. **3** (in Parliament) any item of public business ordered to be considered on a specific day. **4** an agenda or programme.

Order of the Garter *n* See **Garter.**

order paper *n* a list indicating the order in which business is to be conducted, esp. in Parliament.

ordinal (ˈɔːdɪnᵊl) *adj* **1** denoting a certain position in a sequence of numbers. **2** of, relating to, or characteristic of an order in biological classification. ◆ *n* **3** short for **ordinal number. 4** a book containing the forms of services for the ordination of ministers. **5** *RC Church.* a service book.

ordinal number *n* a number denoting relative position in a sequence, such as *first, second, third.* Sometimes shortened to **ordinal.**

ordinance ⓣ (ˈɔːdɪnəns) *n* an authoritative regulation, decree, law, or practice. [C14: from OF *ordenance,* from L *ordināre* to set in order]

ordinarily ⓣ (ˈɔːdᵊnrɪlɪ) *adv* in ordinary, normal, or usual practice; usually; normally.

ordinary ⓣ (ˈɔːdᵊnrɪ) *adj* **1** of common or established type or occurrence. **2** familiar, everyday, or unexceptional. **3** uninteresting or commonplace. **4** having regular or ex officio jurisdiction: *an ordinary judge.* **5** *Maths.* (of a differential equation) containing two variables only and derivatives of one of the variables with respect to the other. ◆ *n, pl* **ordinaries. 6** a common or average situation, amount, or degree (esp. in **out of the ordinary**). **7** a normal or commonplace person or thing. **8** *Civil law.* a judge who exercises jurisdiction in his own right. **9** (*usually cap.*) an ecclesiastic, esp. a bishop, holding an office to which certain jurisdictional powers are attached. **10** *RC Church.* **10a** the parts of the Mass that do not vary from day to day. **10b** a prescribed form of divine service, esp. the Mass. **11** the US name for **penny-farthing. 12** *Heraldry.* any of several conventional figures, such as the bend, and the cross, commonly charged upon shields. **13** *History.* a clergyman who visited condemned prisoners. **14** *Brit. obs.* **14a** a meal provided regularly at a fixed price. **14b** the inn, etc., providing such meals. **15 in ordinary.** *Brit.* (used esp. in titles) in regular service or attendance: *physician in ordinary to the sovereign.* [C16 (adj) & C13 (some n senses): ult. from L *ordinārius* orderly, from *ordō* order]

Ordinary level *n* a formal name for **O level.**

ordinary rating *n* a rank in the Royal Navy comparable to that of a private in the army.

ordinary seaman *n* a seaman of the lowest rank, being insufficiently experienced to be an able-bodied seaman.

ordinary shares *pl n Brit.* shares representing part of the capital issued by a company, entitling their holders to a share in the profits and the net assets. US equivalent: **common stock.** Cf. **preference shares.**

ordinate (ˈɔːdɪnɪt) *n* the vertical or *y*-coordinate of a point in a two-dimensional system of Cartesian coordinates. Cf. **abscissa.** [C16: from NL (*linea*) *ordināte* (*applicāta*) (line applied) in an orderly manner, from *ordināre* to arrange in order]

ordination (ˌɔːdɪˈneɪʃən) *n* **1a** the act of conferring holy orders. **1b** the reception of holy orders. **2** the condition of being ordained or regulated. **3** an arrangement or order.

ordnance ⓣ (ˈɔːdnəns) *n* **1** cannon or artillery. **2** military supplies; munitions. **3 the.** a department of an army or government dealing with military supplies. [C14: var. of ORDINANCE]

ordnance datum *n* mean sea level calculated from observation taken at Newlyn, Cornwall, and used as the official basis for height calculation on British maps. Abbrev.: **OD.**

Ordnance Survey *n* the official map-making body of the British or Irish government.

Ordovician (ˌɔːdəʊˈvɪʃɪən) *adj* **1** of, denoting, or formed in the second period of the Palaeozoic era, between the Cambrian and Silurian periods. ◆ *n* **2 the.** the Ordovician period or rock system. [C19: from L *Ordovices,* ancient Celtic tribe in N Wales]

ordure (ˈɔːdjʊə) *n* excrement; dung. [C14: via OF, from *ord* dirty, from L *horridus* shaggy]

ore (ɔː) *n* any naturally occurring mineral or aggregate of minerals from which economically important constituents, esp. metals, can be extracted. [OE *ār, ōra*]

öre (ˈøːrə) *n, pl* **öre.** a Scandinavian monetary unit worth one hundredth of a Swedish krona and (**øre**) one hundredth of a Danish and Norwegian krone.

oread (ˈɔːrɪˌæd) *n Greek myth.* a mountain nymph. [C16: via L from Gk *Oreias,* from *oros* mountain]

oregano (ˌɒrɪˈgɑːnəʊ) *n* **1** a Mediterranean variety of wild marjoram (*Origanum vulgare*), with pungent leaves. **2** the dried powdered leaves of this plant, used to season food. [C18: American Sp., from Sp., from L *orīganum,* from Gk *origanon* an aromatic herb, ? marjoram]

orfe (ɔːf) *n* a small slender European cyprinoid fish, occurring in two colour varieties, namely the **silver orfe** and the **golden orfe,** popular aquarium fishes. [C17: from G; rel. to L *orphus,* Gk *orphos* the sea perch]

organ ⓣ (ˈɔːgən) *n* **1a** Also called: **pipe organ.** a large complex musical keyboard instrument in which sound is produced by means of a number of pipes arranged in sets or stops, supplied with air from a bellows. **1b** (*as modifier*): *organ stop; organ loft.* **2** any instrument, such as a harmonium, in which sound is produced in this way. **3** a fully differentiated structural and functional unit, such as a kidney or a root, in an animal or plant. **4** an agency or medium of communication, esp. a periodical issued by a specialist group or party. **5** an instrument with which something is done or accomplished. **6** a euphemistic word for **penis.** [C13: from OF *organe,* from L *organum* implement, from Gk *organon* tool]

organdie *or esp. US* **organdy** (ˈɔːgəndɪ) *n, pl* **organdies.** a fine and slightly stiff cotton fabric used for dresses, etc. [C19: from F *organdi,* from ?]

organelle (ˌɔːgəˈnɛl) *n* a structural and functional unit in a cell or unicellular organism. [C20: from NL *organella,* from L *organum;* see ORGAN]

organ-grinder *n* a street musician playing a hand organ for money.

organic ⓣ (ɔːˈgænɪk) *adj* **1** of, relating to, or derived from living plants and animals. **2** of or relating to animal or plant constituents or products having a carbon basis. **3** of or relating to one or more organs of an animal or plant. **4** of, relating to, or belonging to the class of chemical compounds that are formed from carbon: *an organic compound.* **5** constitutional in the structure of something; fundamental; integral. **6** of or characterized by the coordination of integral parts; organized. **7** of or relating to the essential constitutional laws regulating the government of a state: *organic law.* **8** of, relating to, or grown with the use of fertilizers or pesticides deriving from animal or vegetable matter, rather than from chemicals. ◆ *n* **9** any substance, such as a fertilizer or pesticide, that is derived from animal or vegetable matter rather than from chemicals.
▸**orˈganically** *adv*

organic chemistry *n* the branch of chemistry concerned with the compounds of carbon.

organism ⓣ (ˈɔːgəˌnɪzəm) *n* **1** any living animal or plant, including any bacterium or virus. **2** anything resembling a living creature in structure, behaviour, etc.
▸ˌ**organˈismal** *or* ˌ**organˈismic** *adj* ▸ˌ**organˈismally** *adv*

organist (ˈɔːgənɪst) *n* a person who plays the organ.

organization ⓣ *or* **organisation** (ˌɔːgənaɪˈzeɪʃən) *n* **1** the act of organizing or the state of being organized. **2** an organized structure or whole. **3** a business or administrative concern united and constructed for a particular end. **4** a body of administrative officials, as of a government department, etc. **5** order, tidiness, or system; method.
▸ˌ**organiˈzational** *or* ˌ**organiˈsational** *adj*

organizational psychology *n* the study of the structure of an organization and of the ways in which the people in it interact, usually undertaken in order to improve the organization.

organize ⓣ *or* **organise** (ˈɔːgəˌnaɪz) *vb* **organizes, organizing, organized** *or* **organises, organising, organised. 1** to form (parts or elements of something) into a structured whole; coordinate. **2** (*tr*) to arrange methodically or in order. **3** (*tr*) to provide with an organic structure. **4** (*tr*) to

THESAURUS

ordinance *n* = **rule,** canon, command, decree, dictum, edict, enactment, fiat, law, order, precept, regulation, ruling, statute

ordinarily *adv* = **usually,** as a rule, commonly, customarily, generally, habitually, in general, in the general run (of things), in the usual way, normally
Antonyms *adv* hardly ever, infrequently, occasionally, rarely, scarcely, seldom, uncommonly

ordinary *adj* **1, 2** = **usual,** accustomed, common, conventional, customary, down-to-earth, established, everyday, familiar, habitual, household, normal, prevailing, quotidian, regular, routine, settled, simple, standard, stock, typical, unexceptional, unpretentious, wonted **3** = **commonplace,** banal, common or garden (*inf.*), homespun, humble, humdrum, modest, mundane, pedestrian, plain, prosaic, run-of-the-mill, stereotyped, unmemorable, unremarkable, workaday ◆ *n* **6 out of the ordinary** = **unusual,** atypical, distinguished, exceptional, exciting, extraordinary, high-calibre, imaginative, important, impressive, inspired, noteworthy, outstanding, rare, remarkable, significant, special, striking, superior, uncommon
Antonyms *adj* ≠ **commonplace, average:** distinguished, exceptional, extraordinary, important, impressive, inspired, notable, novel, outstanding, rare, significant, superior, uncommon, unconventional, unique, unusual

ordnance *n* **1, 2** = **weapons,** arms, artillery, big guns, cannon, guns, materiel, munitions

organ *n* **3** = **part,** element, member, process, structure, unit **4** = **medium,** agency, channel, forum, journal, means, mouthpiece, newspaper, paper, periodical, publication, vehicle, voice **5** = **instrument,** device, implement, tool

organic *adj* **1** = **natural,** animate, biological, biotic, live, living **5** = **integral,** anatomical, constitutional, fundamental, immanent, inherent, innate, structural **6** = **systematic,** integrated, methodical, ordered, organized, structured

organism *n* **1** = **creature,** animal, being, body, entity, living thing, structure

organization *n* **1** = **management,** assembling, assembly, construction, coordination, direction, disposal, formation, forming, formulation, making, methodology, organizing, planning, regulation, running, standardization, structuring **2** = **structure,** arrangement, chemistry, composition, configuration, conformation, constitution, design, format, framework, grouping, make-up, method, organism, pattern, plan, system, unity, whole **3** = **group,** association, body, combine, company, concern, confederation, consortium, corporation, federation, institution, league, outfit (*inf.*), syndicate

organize *vb* **1** = **plan,** arrange, be responsible for, constitute, construct, coordinate, establish, form, frame, get going, get together, lay the foundations of, lick into shape, look after, marshal, put together, run, see to (*inf.*), set up, shape, straighten out, take care of **2** = **put in order,** arrange, catalogue, classify, codify, dispose, group, pigeonhole, systematize, tabulate
Antonyms *vb* ≠ **plan:** confuse, derange, disrupt,

enlist (the workers) of (a factory, etc.) in a trade union. **5** (*intr*) to join or form an organization or trade union. **6** (*tr*) *Inf.* to put (oneself) in an alert and responsible frame of mind. [C15: from Med. L *organizare,* from L *organum* ORGAN]
▸ **'organ,izer** *or* **'organ,iser** *n*

organometallic (ɔːˌgænəʊmɪ'tælɪk) *adj* of, concerned with, or being an organic compound with one or more metal atoms in its molecules.

organon ('ɔːgəˌnɒn) *or* **organum** *n, pl* **organa** (-nə), **organons** *or* **organa, organums. 1** *Epistemology.* a system of logical or scientific rules, esp. that of Aristotle. **2** *Arch.* a sense organ, regarded as an instrument for acquiring knowledge. [C16: from Gk: implement; see ORGAN]

organophosphate (ɔːˌgænəʊ'fɒsfeɪt) *n* any of a group of organic compounds containing phosphorus and used as a pesticide.

organotin (ɔːgænəʊ'tɪn) *adj* **1** of, concerned with, or being an organic compound with one or more tin atoms in its molecules. ◆ *n* **2** such a compound used as a pesticide, formerly believed to decompose safely, now found to be toxic in the food chain.

organza (ɔː'gænzə) *n* a thin stiff fabric of silk, cotton, nylon, rayon, etc. [C20: from ?]

orgasm ➊ ('ɔːgæzəm) *n* **1** the most intense point during sexual excitement. **2** *Rare.* intense or violent excitement. [C17: from NL *orgasmus,* from Gk *orgasmos,* from *organ* to mature, swell]
▸ **or'gasmic** *or* **or'gastic** *adj*

orgeat ('ɔːʒɑː) *n* a drink made from barley or almonds, and orangeflower water. [C18: via F, from *orge* barley, from L *hordeum*]

orgy ➊ ('ɔːdʒɪ) *n, pl* **orgies. 1** a wild gathering marked by promiscuous sexual activity, excessive drinking, etc. **2** an act of immoderate or frenzied indulgence. **3** (*often pl*) secret religious rites of Dionysus, Bacchus, etc., marked by drinking, dancing, and songs. [C16: from F *orgies,* from L *orgia,* from Gk: nocturnal festival]
▸ **ˌorgi'astic** *adj*

oribi ('ɒrɪbɪ) *n, pl* **oribi** *or* **oribis.** a small African antelope of the grasslands and bush south of the Sahara, with fawn-coloured coat and, in the male, ridged spikelike horns. [C18: from Afrik., prob. from Khoikhoi *arab*]

oriel window ('ɔːrɪəl) *n* a bay window, esp. one that is supported by one or more brackets or corbels. Sometimes shortened to **oriel.** [C14: from OF *oriol* gallery, ?from Med. L *auleolum* niche]

orient ➊ *n* ('ɔːrɪənt). **1** *Poetic.* another word for **east.** Cf. **occident. 2** *Arch.* the eastern sky or the dawn. **3a** the iridescent lustre of a pearl. **3b** (*as modifier*): *orient pearls.* **4** a pearl of high quality. ◆ *adj* ('ɔːrɪənt). **5** *Now chiefly poetic.* oriental. **6** *Arch.* (of the sun, stars, etc.) rising. ◆ *vb* ('ɔːrɪˌɛnt). **7** to adjust or align (oneself or something else) according to surroundings or circumstances. **8** (*tr*) to position or set (a map, etc.) with reference to the compass or other specific directions. **9** (*tr*) to build (a church) with the chancel end facing in an easterly direction. [C18: via F from L *oriēns* rising (sun), from *orīrī* to rise]

Orient ('ɔːrɪənt) *n* (usually preceded by *the*) **1** the countries east of the Mediterranean. **2** the eastern hemisphere.

oriental (ˌɔːrɪ'ɛntᵊl) *adj* another word for **eastern.**

Oriental (ˌɔːrɪ'ɛntᵊl) *adj* **1** (*sometimes not cap.*) of or relating to the Orient. **2** of or denoting a region consisting of southeastern Asia from India to Borneo, Java, and the Philippines. ◆ *n* **3** (*sometimes not cap.*) an inhabitant, esp. a native, of the Orient.

Orientalism (ˌɔːrɪ'ɛntəˌlɪzəm) *n* **1** knowledge of or devotion to the Orient. **2** an Oriental quality, style, or trait.
▸ **ˌOri'entalist** *n* ▸ **ˌOriˌental'istic** *adj*

orientate ('ɔːrɪɛnˌteɪt) *vb* **orientates, orientating, orientated.** another word for **orient** (senses 7, 8, 9).

orientation ➊ (ˌɔːrɪɛn'teɪʃən) *n* **1** the act or process of orienting or the state of being oriented. **2** positioning with relation to the compass or other specific directions. **3** the adjustment or alignment of oneself or one's ideas to surroundings or circumstances. **4** Also called: **orientation course.** *Chiefly US & Canad.* **4a** a course, lecture, etc., introducing a new situation or environment. **4b** (*as modifier*): *an orientation talk.* **5** *Psychol.* the knowledge of one's own temporal, social, and practical circumstances. **6** the siting of a church on an east-west axis.
▸ **ˌorien'tational** *adj*

-oriented *suffix forming adjectives.* geared or directed towards: *sports-oriented.*

orienteer (ˌɔːrɪən'tɪə) *vb* (*intr*) **1** to take part in orienteering. ◆ *n* **2** a person who takes part in orienteering.

orienteering (ˌɔːrɪɛn'tɪərɪŋ) *n* a sport in which contestants race on foot over a course consisting of checkpoints found with the aid of a map and a compass. [C20: from Swedish *orientering*]

orifice ➊ ('ɒrɪfɪs) *n Chiefly technical.* an opening or mouth into a cavity; vent; aperture. [C16: via F from LL *ōrificium,* from L *ōs* mouth + *facere* to make]

oriflamme ('ɒrɪˌflæm) *n* a scarlet flag adopted as the national banner of France in the Middle Ages. [C15: via OF, from L *aurum* gold + *flamma* flame]

orig. *abbrev. for:* **1** origin. **2** original(ly).

origami (ˌɒrɪ'gɑːmɪ) *n* the art or process, originally Japanese, of paper folding. [from Japanese, from *ori* a fold + *kami* paper]

origan ('ɒrɪgən) *n* another name for **marjoram** (sense 2). [C16: from L *orīganum,* from Gk *origanon* an aromatic herb]

origanum (ˌɒrɪ'gɑːnəm) *n* See **oregano.**

origin ➊ ('ɒrɪdʒɪn) *n* **1** a primary source; derivation. **2** the beginning of something; first part. **3** (*often pl*) ancestry or parentage; birth; extraction. **4** *Anat.* **4a** the end of a muscle, opposite its point of insertion. **4b** the beginning of a nerve or blood vessel or the site where it first starts to branch out. **5** *Maths.* **5a** the point of intersection of coordinate axes or planes. **5b** the point whose coordinates are all zero. **6** *Commerce.* the country from which a commodity or product originates: *shipment from origin.* [C16: from F *origine,* from L *orīgō* beginning]

original ➊ (ə'rɪdʒɪnᵊl) *adj* **1** of or relating to an origin or beginning. **2** fresh and unusual; novel. **3** able to think of or carry out new ideas or concepts. **4** being that from which a copy, translation, etc., is made. ◆ *n* **5** the first and genuine form of something, from which others are derived. **6** a person or thing used as a model in art or literature. **7** a person whose way of thinking is unusual or creative. **8** the first form or occurrence of something.
▸ **o'riginally** *adv*

originality ➊ (əˌrɪdʒɪ'nælɪtɪ) *n, pl* **originalities. 1** the quality or condition of being original. **2** the ability to create or innovate.

original sin *n* a state of sin held to be innate in mankind as the descendants of Adam.

originate ➊ (ə'rɪdʒɪˌneɪt) *vb* **originates, originating, originated. 1** to come or bring into being. **2** (*intr*) *US & Canad.* (of a bus, train, etc.) to begin its journey at a specified point.
▸ **oˌrigi'nation** *n* ▸ **o'rigiˌnator** *n*

O-ring *n* a rubber ring used in machinery as a seal against oil, air, etc.

oriole ('ɔːrɪˌəʊl) *n* **1** a tropical Old World songbird, such as the **golden oriole,** having a long pointed bill and a mostly yellow-and-black plumage. **2** an American songbird, esp. the Baltimore oriole, with a typical male plumage of black with either orange or yellow. [C18: from Med. L *oryolus,* from L *aureolus,* dim. of *aureus,* from *aurum* gold]

Orion (ə'raɪən) *n* a conspicuous constellation containing two first-magnitude stars (Betelgeuse and Rigel) and a distant bright emission nebula (the **Orion Nebula**).

orison ('ɒrɪzᵊn) *n Literary.* another word for **prayer**[1] (senses 1 and 2). [C12: from OF *oreison,* from LL *ōrātiō,* from L: speech, from *ōrāre* to speak]

Oriya (ɒ'riːə) *n* **1** (*pl* **Oriya**) a member of a people of India living chiefly

THESAURUS

upset ≠ **put in order:** disorganize, jumble, mix up, muddle, scramble

orgasm *n* **1** = **climax**

orgiastic *adj* **1** = **wild,** abandoned, bacchanalian, bacchic, debauched, depraved, Dionysian, dissolute, frenetic, riotous, Saturnalian, wanton

orgy *n* **1** = **revel,** bacchanal, bacchanalia, carousal, carouse, debauch, revelry, Saturnalia **2** = **spree,** binge (*inf.*), bout, excess, indulgence, overindulgence, splurge, surfeit

orient *vb* **7** = **adjust,** acclimatize, adapt, align, familiarize, find one's feet (*inf.*), get one's bearings, get the lie of the land, orientate

orientation *n* **1** = **adjustment,** acclimatization, adaptation, assimilation, breaking in, familiarization, introduction, settling in **2** = **position,** bearings, coordination, direction, location, sense of direction

orifice *n* = **opening,** aperture, cleft, hole, mouth, perforation, pore, rent, vent

origin *n* **1** = **root,** base, basis, cause, derivation, *fons et origo,* font (*poetic*), fount, fountain, fountainhead, occasion, provenance, roots, source, spring, wellspring **2** = **beginning,** birth, commencement, creation, dawning, early stages, emergence, foundation, genesis, inauguration, inception, launch, origination, outset, start **3** = **ancestry,** beginnings, birth, descent, extraction, family, heritage, lineage, parentage, pedigree, stirps, stock
Antonyms *n* ≠ **beginning:** conclusion, culmination, death, end, expiry, finale, finish, outcome, termination

original *adj* **1** = **first,** aboriginal, autochthonous, commencing, earliest, early, embryonic, infant, initial, introductory, opening, primary, primitive, primordial, pristine, rudimentary, starting **2** = **new,** fresh, groundbreaking, innovative, innovatory, novel, seminal, unconventional, unprecedented, untried, unusual **3** = **creative,** fertile, imaginative, ingenious, inventive, resourceful **4** = **authentic,** archetypal, first, first-hand, genuine, master, primary, prototypical ◆ *n* **5** = **prototype,** archetype, master, model, paradigm, pattern, precedent, standard, type **7** = **character,** card (*inf.*), case (*inf.*), eccentric, nonconformist, nut (*sl.*), oddball (*inf.*), oddity, queer fish (*Brit. inf.*)
Antonyms *adj* ≠ **first:** final, last, latest ≠ **new:** antiquated, banal, commonplace, conventional, familiar, normal, old, old-fashioned, ordinary, stale, standard, stock, traditional, typical, unimaginative, unoriginal, usual ≠ **authentic:** borrowed, copied, secondary, unoriginal ◆ *n* ≠ **prototype:** copy, imitation, replica, reproduction

originality *n* **2** = **novelty,** boldness, break with tradition, cleverness, creativeness, creative spirit, creativity, daring, freshness, imagination, imaginativeness, individuality, ingenuity, innovation, innovativeness, inventiveness, new ideas, newness, resourcefulness, unconventionality, unorthodoxy
Antonyms *n* conformity, conventionality, imitativeness, normality, orthodoxy, regularity, staleness, traditionalism

originally *adv* **1** = **initially,** at first, at the outset, at the start, by birth, by derivation, by origin, first, in the beginning, in the first place, to begin with

originate *vb* **1** = **begin,** arise, be born, come, conceive, create, derive, develop, emanate, emerge, evolve, flow, generate, initiate, issue, proceed, result, rise, set in motion, set up, spring, start, stem
Antonyms *vb* cease, conclude, end, finish, terminate, wind up

originator *n* **1** = **creator,** architect, author, father *or* mother, founder, generator, innovator, inventor, maker, pioneer, prime mover

in Orissa. **2** the state language of Orissa, belonging to the Indo-European family.

Orlon ('ɔːlɒn) *n Trademark.* a crease-resistant acrylic fibre or fabric used for clothing, etc.

orlop *or* **orlop deck** ('ɔːlɒp) *n Naut.* (in a vessel with four or more decks) the lowest deck. [C15: from Du. *overloopen* to spill]

ormer ('ɔːmə) *n* **1** Also called: **sea-ear.** an edible marine gastropod mollusc that has an ear-shaped shell perforated with holes and occurs near the Channel Islands. **2** any other abalone. [C17: from F, apparently from L *auris* ear + *mare* sea]

ormolu ('ɔːməˌluː) *n* **1a** a gold-coloured alloy of copper, tin, or zinc used to decorate furniture, etc. **1b** (*as modifier*): *an ormolu clock.* **2** gold prepared for gilding. [C18: from F *or moulu* ground gold]

ornament ❶ *n* ('ɔːnəmənt). **1** anything that enhances the appearance of a person or thing. **2** decorations collectively: *she was totally without ornament.* **3** a small decorative object. **4** something regarded as a source of pride or beauty. **5** *Music.* any of several decorations, such as the trill, etc. ◆ *vb* ('ɔːnəˌmɛnt). (*tr*) **6** to decorate with or as if with ornaments. **7** to serve as an ornament to. [C14: from L *ornāmentum*, from *ornāre* to adorn]

▸ **ˌornamenˈtation** *n*

ornamental ❶ (ˌɔːnəˈmɛntᵊl) *adj* **1** of value as an ornament; decorative. **2** (of a plant) used to decorate houses, gardens, etc. ◆ *n* **3** a plant cultivated for show or decoration.

▸ **ˌornaˈmentally** *adv*

ornate ❶ (ɔːˈneɪt) *adj* **1** heavily or elaborately decorated. **2** (of style in writing, etc.) over-embellished; flowery. [C15: from L *ornāre* to decorate]

▸ **orˈnately** *adv* ▸ **orˈnateness** *n*

ornery ('ɔːnərɪ) *adj US & Canad. dialect or inf.* **1** stubborn or vile-tempered. **2** low; treacherous: *an ornery trick.* **3** ordinary. [C19: alteration of ORDINARY]

▸ **ˈorneriness** *n*

ornitho- *or before a vowel* **ornith-** *combining form.* bird or birds. [from Gk *ornis, ornith-* bird]

ornithology (ˌɔːnɪˈθɒlədʒɪ) *n* the study of birds.

▸ **ornithological** (ˌɔːnɪθəˈlɒdʒɪkᵊl) *adj* ▸ **ˌornithoˈlogically** *adv* ▸ **ˌorniˈthologist** *n*

ornithorhynchus (ˌɔːnɪθəʊˈrɪŋkəs) *n* the technical name for **duck-billed platypus.** [C19: NL, from ORNITHO- + Gk *rhunkhos* bill]

oro-[1] *combining form.* mountain: *orogeny.* [from Gk *oros*]

oro-[2] *combining form.* oral; mouth: *oromaxillary.* [from L, from *ōs*]

orogeny (ɒˈrɒdʒɪnɪ) *or* **orogenesis** (ˌɒrəʊˈdʒɛnɪsɪs) *n* the formation of mountain ranges.

▸ **orogenic** (ˌɒrəʊˈdʒɛnɪk) *or* **orogenetic** (ˌɒrəudʒɪˈnɛtɪk) *adj*

orotund ('ɒrəʊˌtʌnd) *adj* **1** (of the voice) resonant; booming. **2** (of speech or writing) bombastic; pompous. [C18: from L *ore rotundo* with rounded mouth]

orphan ('ɔːfən) *n* **1a** a child, one or both of whose parents are dead. **1b** (*as modifier*): *an orphan child.* ◆ *vb* **2** (*tr*) to deprive of one or both parents. [C15: from LL *orphanus*, from Gk *orphanos*]

orphanage ('ɔːfənɪdʒ) *n* **1** an institution for orphans and abandoned children. **2** the state of being an orphan.

Orphean ('ɔːfɪən) *adj* **1** of or relating to Orpheus, a poet and lyre-player in Greek mythology. **2** melodious or enchanting.

Orphic ('ɔːfɪk) *adj* **1** of or relating to Orpheus or Orphism, a mystery religion of ancient Greece. **2** (*sometimes not cap.*) mystical or occult.

▸ **ˈOrphically** *adv*

orpine ('ɔːpaɪn) *or* **orpin** ('ɔːpɪn) *n* a succulent perennial N temperate plant with toothed leaves and heads of small purplish-white flowers. [C14: from OF, apparently from *orpiment*, a yellow mineral (? referring to the yellow flowers of a related species)]

orrery ('ɒrərɪ) *n, pl* **orreries.** a mechanical model of the solar system in which the planets can be moved at the correct relative velocities around the sun. [C18: orig. made for Charles Boyle, Earl of *Orrery*]

orris[1] *or* **orrice** ('ɒrɪs) *n* **1** any of various irises that have fragrant rhizomes. **2** Also: **orrisroot.** the rhizome of such a plant, prepared and used as perfume. [C16: var. of IRIS]

orris[2] ('ɒrɪs) *n* a kind of lace made of gold or silver, used esp. in the 18th century. [from Old French *orfreis*, from L *auriphrygium* Phrygian gold]

orthicon ('ɔːθɪˌkɒn) *n* a television camera tube in which an optical image produces a corresponding electrical charge pattern on a mosaic surface that is scanned from behind by an electron beam. The resulting discharge of the mosaic provides the output signal current. See also **image orthicon.** [C20: from ORTHO- + ICON(OSCOPE)]

ortho- *or before a vowel* **orth-** *combining form.* **1** straight or upright: *orthorhombic.* **2** perpendicular or at right angles: *orthogonal.* **3** correct or right: *orthodontics.* **4** (*often in italics*) denoting an organic compound containing a benzene ring with substituents attached to adjacent carbon atoms (the 1,2- positions). **5** denoting an oxyacid regarded as the highest hydrated form of the anhydride or a salt of such an acid: *orthophosphoric acid.* **6** denoting a diatomic substance in which the spins of the two atoms are parallel: *orthohydrogen.* [from Gk *orthos* straight, upright]

orthochromatic (ˌɔːθəʊkrəʊˈmætɪk) *adj Photog.* of or relating to an emulsion giving a rendering of relative light intensities of different colours that corresponds approximately to the colour sensitivity of the eye, esp. one that is insensitive to red light. Sometimes shortened to **ortho.**

▸ **orthochromatism** (ˌɔːθəʊˈkrəʊməˌtɪzəm) *n*

orthoclase ('ɔːθəʊˌkleɪs, -ˌkleɪz) *n* a white or coloured feldspar mineral consisting of an aluminium silicate of potassium in monoclinic crystalline form.

orthodontics (ˌɔːθəʊˈdɒntɪks) *or* **orthodontia** (ˌɔːθəʊˈdɒntɪə) *n* (*functioning as sing*) the branch of dentistry concerned with preventing or correcting irregularities of the teeth.

▸ **ˌorthoˈdontic** *adj* ▸ **ˌorthoˈdontist** *n*

orthodox ❶ ('ɔːθəˌdɒks) *adj* **1** conforming with established standards, as in religion, behaviour, or attitudes. **2** conforming to the Christian faith as established by the early Church. [C16: via Church L from Gk *orthodoxos*, from *orthos* correct + *doxa* belief]

▸ **ˈorthoˌdoxy** *n*

Orthodox ('ɔːθəˌdɒks) *adj* **1** of or relating to the Orthodox Church of the East. **2** (*sometimes not cap.*) of or relating to Orthodox Judaism.

Orthodox Church *n* **1** the collective body of those Eastern Churches that were separated from the western Church in the 11th century and are in communion with the Greek patriarch of Constantinople. **2** any of these Churches.

Orthodox Judaism *n* a form of Judaism characterized by traditional interpretation and strict observance of the Mosaic Law.

orthoepy ('ɔːθəʊˌɛpɪ) *n* the study of correct or standard pronunciation. [C17: from Gk *orthoepeia*, from ORTHO- straight + *epos* word]

▸ **orthoepic** (ˌɔːθəʊˈɛpɪk) *adj* ▸ **ˌorthoˈepically** *adv*

orthogenesis (ˌɔːθəʊˈdʒɛnɪsɪs) *n* **1** *Biol.* **1a** evolution of a group of organisms in a particular direction, which is generally predetermined. **1b** the theory that proposes such a development. **2** the theory that there is a series of stages through which all cultures pass in the same order.

▸ **orthogenetic** (ˌɔːθəʊdʒɪˈnɛtɪk) *adj* ▸ **ˌorthogeˈnetically** *adv*

orthogonal (ɔːˈθɒgənᵊl) *adj* relating to, consisting of, or involving right angles; perpendicular.

▸ **orˈthogonally** *adv*

orthographic (ˌɔːθəˈgræfɪk) *or* **orthographical** *adj* of or relating to spelling.

▸ **ˌorthoˈgraphically** *adv*

orthography (ɔːˈθɒgrəfɪ) *n, pl* **orthographies.** **1** a writing system. **2a** spelling considered to be correct. **2b** the principles underlying spelling. **3** the study of spelling.

▸ **orˈthographer** *or* **orˈthographist** *n*

orthopaedics *or US* **orthopedics** (ˌɔːθəʊˈpiːdɪks) *n* (*functioning as sing*) **1** the branch of surgery concerned with disorders of the spine and joints and the repair of deformities of these parts. **2 dental orthopaedics.** another name for **orthodontics.**

▸ **ˌorthoˈpaedic** *or US* **ˌorthoˈpedic** *adj* ▸ **ˌorthoˈpaedist** *or US* **ˌorthoˈpedist** *n*

orthopteran (ɔːˈθɒptərən) *n, pl* **orthoptera** (-tərə). **1** Also: **orthopteron** (*pl* **orthoptera**). any orthopterous insect. ◆ *adj* **2** another word for **orthopterous.**

orthopterous (ɔːˈθɒptərəs) *adj* of, relating to, or belonging to a large order of insects, including crickets, locusts, and grasshoppers, having leathery forewings and membranous hind wings.

orthoptic (ɔːˈθɒptɪk) *adj* relating to normal binocular vision.

orthoptics (ɔːˈθɒptɪks) *n* (*functioning as sing*) the science or practice of correcting defective vision, as by exercises to strengthen weak eye muscles.

▸ **orˈthoptist** *n*

orthorhombic (ˌɔːθəʊˈrɒmbɪk) *adj Crystallog.* relating to the crystal system characterized by three mutually perpendicular unequal axes.

ortolan ('ɔːtələn) *n* **1** a brownish Old World bunting regarded as a delicacy. **2** any of various other small birds eaten as delicacies, esp. the bobolink. [C17: via F from L *hortulānus*, from *hortulus*, dim. of *hortus* garden]

THESAURUS

ornament *n* **3** = **decoration**, accessory, adornment, bauble, embellishment, festoon, frill, furbelow, garnish, gewgaw, knick-knack, trimming, trinket **4** = **leading light**, flower, honour, jewel, pride, treasure ◆ *vb* **6** = **decorate**, adorn, beautify, bedizen (*arch.*), brighten, deck, dress up, embellish, festoon, garnish, gild, grace, prettify, prink, trim

ornamental *adj* **1** = **decorative**, attractive, beautifying, embellishing, for show, showy

ornamentation *n* **6** = **decoration**, adornment, elaboration, embellishment, embroidery, frills, ornateness

ornate *adj* **1, 2** = **elaborate**, aureate, baroque, beautiful, bedecked, busy, convoluted, decorated, elegant, fancy, florid, flowery, fussy, high-wrought, ornamented, overelaborate, rococo

Antonyms *adj* austere, bare, basic, ordinary, plain, severe, simple, spartan, stark, subdued, unadorned, unfussy

orthodox *adj* **1** = **established**, accepted, approved, conformist, conventional, correct, customary, doctrinal, kosher (*inf.*), official, received, sound, traditional, true, well-established

Antonyms *adj* eccentric, heretical, left-field (*inf.*), liberal, nonconformist, novel, off-the-wall (*sl.*), original, radical, unconventional, unorthodox, unusual

orthodoxy *n* **1** = **conformity**, authenticity, authoritativeness, authority, conformism, conventionality, devotion, devoutness, faithfulness, inflexibility, received wisdom, soundness, traditionalism

Antonyms *n* flexibility, heresy, heterodoxy, impiety, nonconformism, nonconformity, unconventionality

-ory[1] *suffix forming nouns.* **1** indicating a place for: *observatory.* **2** something having a specified use: *directory.* [via OF *-orie,* from L *-ōrium, -ōria*]

-ory[2] *suffix forming adjectives.* of or relating to; characterized by; having the effect of: *contributory.* [via OF *-orie,* from L *-ōrius*]

oryx ('ɒrɪks) *n, pl* **oryxes** *or* **oryx.** any large African antelope of the genus *Oryx,* typically having long straight nearly upright horns. [C14: via L from Gk *orux* stonemason's axe, used also of the pointed horns of an antelope]

os[1] (ɒs) *n, pl* **ossa** ('ɒsə). *Anat.* the technical name for **bone.** [C16: from L: bone]

os[2] (ɒs) *n, pl* **ora.** *Anat., zool.* a mouth or mouthlike part or opening. [C18: from L]

Os *the chemical symbol for* osmium.

OS *abbrev. for:* **1** Old Saxon (language). **2** Old Style. **3** Ordinary Seaman. **4** (in Britain) Ordnance Survey. **5** outsize.

Osage orange (əʊ'seɪdʒ) *n* **1** a North American thorny tree, grown for hedges and ornament. **2** the warty orange-like fruit of this plant. [from *Osage* Amerind tribe]

Oscar ('ɒskə) *n* any of several small gold statuettes awarded annually in the US for outstanding achievements in films. Official name: **Academy Award.** [C20: said to have been named after a remark made by a secretary that it reminded her of her uncle Oscar]

oscillate ❶ ('ɒsɪˌleɪt) *vb* **oscillates, oscillating, oscillated. 1** (*intr*) to move or swing from side to side regularly. **2** (*intr*) to waver between opinions, courses of action, etc. **3** *Physics.* to undergo or produce or cause to undergo or produce oscillation. [C18: from L *oscillāre* to swing]

oscillating universe theory *n* the theory that the universe is oscillating between periods of expansion and contraction.

oscillation ❶ (ˌɒsɪ'leɪʃən) *n* **1** *Statistics, physics.* **1a** regular fluctuation in value, position, or state about a mean value, such as the variation in an alternating current. **1b** a single cycle of such a fluctuation. **2** the act or process of oscillating.
▸**oscillatory** ('ɒsɪlətərɪ, -trɪ) *adj*

oscillator ('ɒsɪˌleɪtə) *n* **1** a circuit or instrument for producing an alternating current or voltage of a required frequency. **2** any instrument for producing oscillations. **3** a person or thing that oscillates.

oscillogram (ɒ'sɪləˌgræm) *n* the recording obtained from an oscillograph or the trace on an oscilloscope screen.

oscillograph (ɒ'sɪləˌgrɑːf) *n* a device for producing a graphical record of the variation of an oscillating quantity, such as an electric current.
▸**oscillographic** (ɒˌsɪlə'græfɪk) *adj* ▸**oscillography** (ˌɒsɪ'lɒgrəfɪ) *n*

oscilloscope (ɒ'sɪləˌskəʊp) *n* an instrument for producing a representation of a rapidly changing quantity on the screen of a cathode-ray tube.

oscine ('ɒsaɪn, 'ɒsɪn) *adj* of, relating to, or belonging to the suborder of passerine birds that includes most of the songbirds. [C17: via NL from L *oscen* singing bird]

oscitancy ('ɒsɪtənsɪ) *or* **oscitance** *n, pl* **oscitancies** *or* **oscitances. 1** the state of being drowsy, lazy, or inattentive. **2** the act of yawning. ◆ Also called: **oscitation.** [C17: from L *oscitāre* to yawn]
▸**'oscitant** *adj*

oscular ('ɒskjʊlə) *adj* **1** *Zool.* of or relating to a mouthlike aperture, esp. of a sponge. **2** of or relating to the mouth or to kissing.

osculate ('ɒskjʊˌleɪt) *vb* **osculates, osculating, osculated. 1** *Usually humorous.* to kiss. **2** (*intr*) (of an organism) to be intermediate between two taxonomic groups. **3** *Geom.* to touch in osculation. [C17: from L *ōsculārī* to kiss]

osculation (ˌɒskjʊ'leɪʃən) *n* **1** *Maths.* Also called: **tacnode.** a point at which two branches of a curve have a common tangent, each branch extending in both directions of the tangent. **2** *Rare.* the act of kissing.
▸**osculatory** ('ɒskjʊlətərɪ, -trɪ) *adj*

-ose[1] *suffix forming adjectives.* possessing; resembling: *grandiose.* [from L *-ōsus;* see -OUS]

-ose[2] *suffix forming nouns.* **1** indicating a carbohydrate, esp. a sugar: *lactose.* **2** indicating a decomposition product of protein: *albumose.* [from GLUCOSE]

osier ('əʊzɪə) *n* **1** any of various willow trees, whose flexible branches or twigs are used for making baskets, etc. **2** a twig or branch from such a tree. **3** any of several North American dogwoods, esp. the red osier. [C14: from OF, prob. from Med. L *ausēria,* ? of Gaulish origin]

-osis *suffix forming nouns.* **1** indicating a process or state: *metamorphosis.* **2** indicating a diseased condition: *tuberculosis.* Cf. **-iasis. 3** indicating the formation or development of something: *fibrosis.* [from Gk, suffix used to form nouns from verbs with infinitives in *-oein* or *-oun*]

Osmanli (ɒz'mænlɪ) *adj* **1** of or relating to the Ottoman Empire. ◆ *n* **2** (formerly) a subject of the Ottoman Empire. [C19: from Turkish, from *Osman* I (1259–1326), Turkish Sultan]

osmiridium (ˌɒzmɪ'rɪdɪəm) *n* a very hard corrosion-resistant white or grey natural alloy of osmium and iridium: used in pen nibs, etc. [C19: from OSM(IUM) + IRIDIUM]

osmium ('ɒzmɪəm) *n* a very hard brittle bluish-white metal, the heaviest known element, occurring with platinum and alloyed with iridium in osmiridium. Symbol: Os; atomic no.: 76; atomic wt.: 190.2. [C19: from Gk *osmē* smell, from its penetrating odour]

osmoregulation (ˌɒzməʊˌregjʊ'leɪʃən) *n Zool.* the adjustment of the osmotic pressure of a cell or organism in relation to the surrounding fluid.

osmose ('ɒzməʊs, -məʊz, 'ɒs-) *vb* **osmoses, osmosing, osmosed.** to undergo or cause to undergo osmosis. [C19 (n): abstracted from the earlier terms *endosmose* and *exosmose;* rel. to Gk *ōsmos* push]

osmosis (ɒz'məʊsɪs, ɒs-) *n* **1** the tendency of the solvent of a less concentrated solution of dissolved molecules to pass through a semipermeable membrane into a more concentrated solution until both solutions are of the same concentration. **2** diffusion through any membrane or porous barrier, as in dialysis. **3** gradual or unconscious assimilation or adoption, as of ideas. [C19: Latinized form from OSMOSE, from Gk *ōsmos* push]
▸**osmotic** (ɒz'mɒtɪk, ɒs-) *adj* ▸**os'motically** *adv*

osmotic pressure *n* the pressure necessary to prevent osmosis into a given solution when the solution is separated from the pure solvent by a semipermeable membrane.

osmunda (ɒz'mʌndə) *or* **osmund** ('ɒzmənd) *n* any of a genus of ferns having large spreading fronds. [C13: from OF *osmonde,* from ?]

osprey ('ɒsprɪ, -preɪ) *n* **1** a large broad-winged fish-eating diurnal bird of prey, with a dark back and whitish head and underparts. Often called (US and Canad.): **fish hawk. 2** any of the feathers of various other birds, used esp. as trimming for hats. [C15: from OF *ospres,* apparently from L *ossifraga,* lit.: bone-breaker, from *os* bone + *frangere* to break]

ossein ('ɒsɪɪn) *n* a protein that forms the organic matrix of bone. [C19: from L *osseus* bony, from *os* bone]

osseous ('ɒsɪəs) *adj* consisting of or containing bone, bony. [C17: from L *osseus,* from *os* bone]
▸**'osseously** *adv*

ossify ❶ ('ɒsɪˌfaɪ) *vb* **ossifies, ossifying, ossified. 1** to convert or be converted into bone. **2** (*intr*) (of habits, attitudes, etc.) to become inflexible. [C18: from F *ossifier,* from L *os* bone + *facere* to make]
▸ˌ**ossifi'cation** *n* ▸**'ossiˌfier** *n*

ossuary ('ɒsjʊərɪ) *n, pl* **ossuaries.** any container for the burial of human bones, such as an urn or vault. [C17: from LL *ossuārium,* from L *os* bone]

osteal ('ɒstɪəl) *adj* **1** of or relating to bone or to the skeleton. **2** composed of bone; osseous. [C19: from Gk *osteon* bone]

osteitis (ˌɒstɪ'aɪtɪs) *n* inflammation of a bone.
▸**osteitic** (ˌɒstɪ'ɪtɪk) *adj*

ostensible ❶ (ɒ'stensɪbᵊl) *adj* **1** apparent; seeming. **2** pretended. [C18: via F from Med. L *ostensibilis,* from L *ostendere* to show, from *ob-* before + *tendere* to extend]
▸**osˌtensi'bility** *n* ▸**os'tensibly** *adv*

ostensive (ɒ'stensɪv) *adj* **1** obviously or manifestly demonstrative. **2** (of a definition) giving examples of objects to which a word or phrase is properly applied. **3** a less common word for **ostensible.** [C17: from LL *ostentīvus,* from L *ostendere* to show; see OSTENSIBLE]
▸**os'tensively** *adv*

ostentation ❶ (ˌɒsten'teɪʃən) *n* pretentious, showy, or vulgar display.
▸ˌ**osten'tatious** *adj* ▸ˌ**osten'tatiously** *adv* ▸ˌ**osten'tatiousness** *n*

osteo- *or before a vowel* **oste-** *combining form.* indicating bone or bones. [from Gk *osteon*]

osteoarthritis (ˌɒstɪəʊɑː'θraɪtɪs) *n* chronic inflammation of the joints, esp. those that bear weight, with pain and stiffness.
▸**osteoarthritic** (ˌɒstɪəʊɑː'θrɪtɪk) *adj, n*

osteology (ˌɒstɪ'ɒlədʒɪ) *n* the study of the structure and function of bones.
▸**osteological** (ˌɒstɪə'lɒdʒɪkᵊl) *adj* ▸ˌ**osteo'logically** *adv* ▸ˌ**oste'ologist** *n*

osteoma (ˌɒstɪ'əʊmə) *n, pl* **osteomata** (-mətə) *or* **osteomas.** a benign tumour composed of bone or bonelike tissue.

osteomalacia (ˌɒstɪəʊmə'leɪʃɪə) *n* a disease characterized by softening of the bones, resulting from a deficiency of vitamin D and of calcium and phosphorus. [C19: from NL, from OSTEO- + Gk *malakia* softness]
▸ˌ**osteoma'lacial** *or* **osteomalacic** (ˌɒstɪəʊmə'læsɪk) *adj*

THESAURUS

oscillate *vb* **1, 2** = **fluctuate,** seesaw, sway, swing, vacillate, vary, vibrate, waver
Antonyms *vb* commit oneself, decide, determine, purpose, resolve, settle

oscillation *n* **2** = **swing,** fluctuation, instability, seesawing, vacillation, variation, wavering

ossified *adj* **2** = **hardened,** fixed, fossilized, frozen, indurated (*rare*), inflexible, petrified, rigid, rigidified, solid

ossify *vb* **2** = **harden,** fossilize, freeze, indurate (*rare*), petrify, solidify, stiffen

ostensible *adj* **1, 2** = **apparent,** alleged, avowed, exhibited, manifest, outward, plausible, pretended, professed, purported, seeming, so-called, specious, superficial, supposed

ostensibly *adv* **1** = **apparently,** for the ostensible purpose of, on the face of it, on the surface, professedly, seemingly, supposedly, to all intents and purposes

ostentation *n* = **display,** affectation, boasting, exhibitionism, flamboyance, flashiness, flaunting, flourish, pageantry, parade, pomp, pretension, pretentiousness, show, showiness, showing off (*inf.*), swank (*inf.*), vaunting, window-dressing
Antonyms *n* humility, inconspicuousness, modesty, plainness, reserve, simplicity, unpretentiousness

ostentatious *adj* = **pretentious,** boastful, brash, conspicuous, crass, dashing, extravagant, flamboyant, flash (*inf.*), flashy, flaunted, gaudy, loud, obtrusive, pompous, showy, swanky (*inf.*), vain, vulgar
Antonyms *adj* conservative, inconspicuous, low-key, modest, plain, reserved, simple, sombre

DICTIONARY

osteomyelitis (ˌɒstɪəʊˌmaɪɪˈlaɪtɪs) *n* inflammation of bone marrow, caused by infection.

osteopathy (ˌɒstɪˈɒpəθɪ) *n* a system of healing based on the manipulation of bones or other parts of the body.
▸**ˈosteoˌpath** *n* ▸**osteopathic** (ˌɒstɪəˈpæθɪk) *adj* ▸**ˌosteoˈpathically** *adv*

osteoplasty (ˈɒstɪəˌplæstɪ) *n, pl* **osteoplasties.** the branch of surgery concerned with bone repair or bone grafting.

osteoporosis (ˌɒstɪəʊpɔːˈrəʊsɪs) *n* porosity and brittleness of the bones caused by loss of calcium from the bone matrix. [C19: from OSTEO- + PORE[2] + -OSIS]
▸**osteoporotic** (ˌɒstɪəʊpɔːˈrɒtɪk) *adj*

ostinato (ˌɒstɪˈnɑːtəʊ) *n, pl* **ostinatos. a** a continuously reiterated musical phrase. **b** (*as modifier*): *an ostinato passage.* [It.: from L *obstinātus* OBSTINATE]

ostler *or* **hostler** (ˈɒslə) *n Arch.* a stableman, esp. one at an inn. [C15: var. of *hostler,* from HOSTEL]

Ostmark (ˈɒstmɑːk; *German* ˈɔstmark) *n* (formerly) the standard monetary unit of East Germany, divided into 100 pfennigs. [G, lit.: east mark]

ostracize Ⓣ *or* **ostracise** (ˈɒstrəˌsaɪz) *vb* **ostracizes, ostracizing, ostracized** *or* **ostracises, ostracising, ostracised.** (*tr*) **1** to exclude or banish (a person) from a particular group, society, etc. **2** (in ancient Greece) to punish by temporary exile. [C17: from Gk *ostrakizein* to select someone for banishment by voting on potsherds, from *ostrakon* potsherd]
▸**ˈostracism** *n* ▸**ˈostraˌcizable** *or* **ˈostraˌcisable** *adj* ▸**ˈostraˌcizer** *or* **ˈostraˌciser** *n*

ostrich (ˈɒstrɪtʃ) *n, pl* **ostriches** *or* **ostrich. 1** a fast-running flightless African bird that is the largest living bird with stout two-toed feet and dark feathers, except on the naked head, neck, and legs. **2 American ostrich.** another name for **rhea. 3** a person who refuses to recognize the truth, reality, etc. [C13: from OF *ostrice,* from L *avis* bird + LL *struthio* ostrich, from Gk *strouthion*]

OT *abbrev. for:* **1** occupational therapy. **2** Old Testament. **3** overtime.

otalgia (əʊˈtældʒɪə, -dʒə) *n* the technical name for **earache.**

OTC (in Britain) *abbrev. for:* **1** Officers' Training Corps. **2** over-the-counter.

OTE *abbrev. for* on target earnings: referring to the salary a salesman should be able to achieve.

other Ⓣ (ˈʌðə) *determiner* **1a** (when used before a singular noun, usually preceded by *the*) the remaining (one or ones in a group of which one or some have been specified): *I'll read the other sections of the paper later.* **1b the other.** (*as pron; functioning as sing*): *one walks while the other rides.* **2** (a) different (one or ones from that or those already specified or understood): *no other man but you.* **3** additional; further: *there are no other possibilities.* **4** (preceded by *every*) alternate; two: *it buzzes every other minute.* **5 other than. 5a** apart from; besides: *a lady other than his wife.* **5b** different from: *he couldn't be other than what he is.* Archaic form: **other from. 6 no other.** *Arch.* nothing else: *I can do no other.* **7 or other.** (preceded by a phrase or word with *some*) used to add vagueness to the preceding pronoun, noun, or noun phrase: *he's somewhere or other.* **8 other things being equal.** conditions being the same or unchanged. **9 the other day, night,** etc. a few days, nights, etc., ago. **10 the other thing.** an unexpressed alternative. ◆ *pron* **11** another: *show me one other.* **12** (*pl*) additional or further ones. **13** (*pl*) other people or things. **14 the others.** the remaining ones (of a group). ◆ *adv* **15** (usually used with a negative and foll. by *than*) otherwise; differently: *they couldn't behave other than they do.* [OE *ōther*]
▸**ˈotherness** *n*

> **USAGE NOTE** See at **otherwise.**

other-directed *adj* guided by values derived from external influences.

other ranks *pl n* (*rarely sing*) *Chiefly Brit.* (in the armed forces) all those who do not hold a commissioned rank.

otherwise Ⓣ (ˈʌðəˌwaɪz) *sentence connector.* **1** or else; if not, then: *go home — otherwise your mother will worry.* ◆ *adv* **2** differently: *I wouldn't have thought otherwise.* **3** in other respects: *an otherwise hopeless situation.* ◆ *adj* **4** (*predicative*) of an unexpected nature; different: *the facts are otherwise.* ◆ *pron* **5** something different in outcome: *success or otherwise.* [C14: from OE *on ōthre wīsan* in other manner]

> **USAGE NOTE** The expression *otherwise than* means *in any other way than* and should not be followed by an adjective: *no-one taught by this method can be other than* (not *otherwise than*) *successful; you are not allowed to use the building otherwise than as a private dwelling.*

other world *n* the spirit world or afterlife.

otherworldly (ˌʌðəˈwɜːldlɪ) *adj* **1** of or relating to the spiritual or imaginative world. **2** impractical or unworldly.
▸**ˌotherˈworldliness** *n*

Othman (ˈɒθmən, ɒθˈmɑːn) *adj, n* a variant of **Ottoman.**

otic (ˈəʊtɪk, ˈɒtɪk) *adj* of or relating to the ear. [C17: from Gk *ōtikos,* from *ous* ear]

-otic *suffix forming adjectives.* **1** relating to or affected by: *sclerotic.* **2** causing: *narcotic.* [from Gk *-ōtikos*]

otiose (ˈəʊtɪˌəʊs, -ˌəʊz) *adj* **1** serving no useful purpose: *otiose language.* **2** *Rare.* indolent; lazy. [C18: from L *ōtiōsus* leisured, from *ōtium* leisure]
▸**otiosity** (ˌəʊtɪˈɒsɪtɪ) *or* **ˈotiˌoseness** *n*

otitis (əʊˈtaɪtɪs) *n* inflammation of the ear.

oto- *or before a vowel* **ot-** *combining form.* indicating the ear. [from Gk *ous, ōt-* ear]

otolaryngology (ˌəʊtəʊˌlærɪŋˈgɒlədʒɪ) *n* another name for **otorhinolaryngology.**
▸**otolaryngological** (ˌəʊtəʊləˌrɪŋgəˈlɒdʒɪkᵊl) *adj* ▸**ˌotoˌlarynˈgologist** *n*

otolith (ˈəʊtəʊˌlɪθ) *n* any of the granules of calcium carbonate in the inner ear of vertebrates. Movement of otoliths, caused by a change in the animal's position, stimulates sensory hair cells, which convey information to the brain.
▸**ˌotoˈlithic** *adj*

otology (əʊˈtɒlədʒɪ) *n* the branch of medicine concerned with the ear.
▸**otological** (ˌəʊtəˈlɒdʒɪkᵊl) *adj* ▸**oˈtologist** *n*

otorhinolaryngology (ˌəʊtəʊˌraɪnəʊˌlærɪŋˈgɒlədʒɪ) *n* the branch of medicine concerned with the ear, nose, and throat. Sometimes called **otolaryngology.**

otoscope (ˈəʊtəʊˌskəʊp) *n* a medical instrument for examining the external ear.
▸**otoscopic** (ˌəʊtəʊˈskɒpɪk) *adj*

OTT *Sl. abbrev. for* over the top: see **top**[1] (sense 16b).

ottava rima (əʊˈtɑːvə ˈriːmə) *n Prosody.* a stanza form consisting of eight iambic pentameter lines, rhyming a b a b a b c c. [It.: eighth rhyme]

otter (ˈɒtə) *n, pl* **otters** *or* **otter. 1** a freshwater carnivorous mammal, esp. the **Eurasian otter,** typically having smooth fur, a streamlined body, and webbed feet. **2** the fur of this animal. **3** a type of fishing tackle consisting of a weighted board to which hooked and baited lines are attached. [OE *otor*]

otter hound *n* a large rough-coated dog of a breed formerly used for otter hunting.

ottoman (ˈɒtəmən) *n, pl* **ottomans. 1a** a low padded seat, usually armless, sometimes in the form of a chest. **1b** a cushioned footstool. **2** a corded fabric. [C17: from F *ottomane,* fem. of OTTOMAN]

Ottoman (ˈɒtəmən) *or* **Othman** (ˈɒθmən) *adj* **1** *History.* of or relating to the Ottomans or the Ottoman Empire. **2** denoting or relating to the Turkish language. ◆ *n, pl* **Ottomans** *or* **Othmans. 3** a member of a Turkish people who invaded the Near East in the late 13th century. [C17: from F, via Med. L, from Ar. *Othmāni* Turkish, from Turkish *Othman* or *Osman* I (1259–1326), Turkish Sultan]

Ottoman Empire *n* the former Turkish empire in Europe, Asia, and Africa, which lasted from the late 13th century until the end of World War I.

ou (əʊ) *n S. African. sl.* a man, bloke, or chap. [from Afrik., ?from Du.]

OU *abbrev. for:* **1** the Open University. **2** Oxford University.

ouananiche (ˌwɑːnəˈniːʃ) *n* a landlocked variety of the Atlantic salmon found in lakes in SE Canada. [from Canad. F, of Amerind origin, from *wananish,* dim. of *wanans* salmon]

oubaas (ˈəʊˌbɑːs) *n S. African.* a man in authority. [from Afrik., from Du. *oud* old + *baas* boss]

oubliette (ˌuːblɪˈɛt) *n* a dungeon, the only entrance to which is through the top. [C19: from F, from *oublier* to forget]

ouch (aʊtʃ) *interj* an exclamation of sharp sudden pain.

ought[1] (ɔːt) *vb* (foll. by *to; takes an infinitive or implied infinitive*) used as an auxiliary: **1** to indicate duty or obligation: *you ought to pay.* **2** to express prudent expediency: *you ought to be more careful with your money.* **3** (usually with reference to future time) to express probability or expectation: *you ought to finish this by Friday.* **4** to express a desire or wish on the part of the speaker: *you ought to come next week.* [OE *āhte,* p.t. of *āgan* to OWE]

> **USAGE NOTE** In correct English, *ought* is not used with *did* or *had. I ought not to do it,* not *I didn't ought to do it; I ought not to have done it,* not *I hadn't ought to have done it.*

ought[2] (ɔːt) *pron, adv* a variant spelling of **aught.**

ought[3] (ɔːt) *n* a less common word for **nought** (zero). [C19: mistaken division of *a nought* as *an ought;* see NOUGHT]

Ouija board (ˈwiːdʒə) *n Trademark.* a board on which are marked the letters of the alphabet. Answers to questions are spelt out by a pointer and are supposedly formed by spirits. [C19: from F *oui* yes + G *ja* yes]

ouma (ˈəʊmɑː) *n S. African.* **1** grandmother, esp. in titular use with her surname. **2** *Sl.* any elderly woman. [from Afrik., from Du. *oma* grandmother]

THESAURUS

ostracism *n* **1 = exclusion,** avoidance, banishment, boycott, cold-shouldering, exile, expulsion, isolation, rejection
Antonyms *n* acceptance, admission, approval, inclusion, invitation, reception, welcome

ostracize *vb* **1 = exclude,** avoid, banish, blackball, blacklist, boycott, cast out, cold-shoulder, excommunicate, exile, expatriate, expel, give (someone) the cold shoulder, reject, send to Coventry, shun, snub
Antonyms *vb* accept, admit, approve, embrace, greet, include, invite, receive, welcome

other *determiner* **2 = different,** contrasting, dissimilar, distinct, diverse, remaining, separate, unrelated, variant **3 = additional,** added, alternative, auxiliary, extra, further, more, spare, supplementary

otherwise *sentence connector* **1 = or else,** if not, or then ◆ *adv* **2 = differently,** any other way, contrarily

ounce[1] Ⓣ (auns) *n* **1** a unit of weight equal to one sixteenth of a pound (avoirdupois). Abbrev.: **oz. 2** a unit of weight equal to one twelfth of a Troy or Apothecaries' pound; 1 ounce is equal to 480 grains. **3** short for **fluid ounce. 4** a small portion or amount. [C14: from OF *unce,* from L *uncia* a twelfth]

ounce[2] (auns) *n* another name for **snow leopard.** [C18: from OF *once,* by mistaken division of *lonce* as if *l'once,* from L LYNX]

oupa ('əupɑː) *n S. African.* **1** grandfather, esp. in titular use with surname. **2** *Sl.* any elderly man. [Afrik.]

our ('auə) *determiner* **1** of, belonging to, or associated in some way with us: *our best vodka; our parents are good to us.* **2** belonging to or associated with all people or people in general: *our nearest planet is Venus.* **3** a formal word for *my* used by editors or other writers, and monarchs. [OE *ūre* (genitive pl), from US]

-our *suffix forming nouns.* indicating state, condition, or activity: *behaviour; labour.* [in OF *-eur,* from L *-or,* n. suffix]

Our Father *n* another name for the **Lord's Prayer,** taken from its opening words.

ours ('auəz) *pron* **1** something or someone belonging to or associated with us: *ours have blue tags.* **2 of ours.** belonging to or associated with us.

ourself (auə'sɛlf) *pron Arch.* a variant of **myself,** formerly used by monarchs or editors.

ourselves (auə'sɛlvz) *pron* **1a** the reflexive form of *we* or *us.* **1b** (intensifier): *we ourselves will finish it.* **2** (*preceded by a copula*) our usual selves: *we are ourselves when we're together.* **3** *Not standard.* used instead of *we* or *us* in compound noun phrases: *other people and ourselves.*

-ous *suffix forming adjectives.* **1** having or full of: *dangerous; spacious.* **2** (in chemistry) indicating that an element is chemically combined in the lower of two possible valency states: *ferrous.* Cf. **-ic** (sense 2). [from OF, from L *-ōsus* or *-us,* Gk *-os,* adj. suffixes]

ousel ('uːzᵊl) *n* a variant spelling of **ouzel.**

oust Ⓣ (aust) *vb* (*tr*) **1** to force out of a position or place; supplant or expel. **2** *Property law.* to deprive (a person) of the possession of land, etc. [C16: from Anglo-Norman *ouster,* from L *obstāre* to withstand]

ouster ('austə) *n Property law.* the act of dispossessing of freehold property; eviction.

out Ⓣ (aut) *adv* (*when predicative, can in some senses be regarded as adj*) **1** (*often used as a particle*) at or to a point beyond the limits of some location; outside: *get out at once.* **2** (*particle*) used to indicate exhaustion or extinction: *the sugar's run out; put the light out.* **3** not in a particular place, esp., not at home. **4** public; revealed: *the secret is out.* **5** on sale or on view to the public: *the book is being brought out next May.* **6** (of the sun, stars, etc.) visible. **7** in flower: *the roses are out now.* **8** not in fashion, favour, or current usage. **9** not or not any longer worth considering: *that plan is out.* **10** not allowed: *smoking on duty is out.* **11** (of a fire or light) no longer burning or providing illumination. **12** not working: *the radio's out.* **13** Also: **out on strike.** on strike. **14** (of a jury) withdrawn to consider a verdict in private. **15** (*particle*) out of consciousness: *she passed out.* **16** (*particle*) used to indicate a burst of activity as indicated by the verb: *fever broke out.* **17** (*particle*) used to indicate obliteration of an object: *the graffiti was painted out.* **18** (*particle*) used to indicate an approximate drawing or description: *chalk out.* **19** at or to the fullest length or extent: *spread out.* **20** loudly; clearly: *calling out.* **21** desirous of or intent on (something or doing something): *I'm out for as much money as I can get.* **22** (*particle*) used to indicate a goal or object achieved at the end of the action specified by the verb: *he worked it out.* **23** (*preceded by a superlative*) existing: *the friendliest dog out.* **24** an expression in signalling, radio, etc., to indicate the end of a transmission. **25** used up; exhausted: *our supplies are completely out.* **26** worn into holes: *out at the elbows.* **27** inaccurate, deficient, or discrepant: *out by six pence.* **28** not in office or authority. **29** completed or concluded, as of time: *before the year is out.* **30** *Obs.* (of a young woman) in or into society: *Lucinda had a large party when she came out.* **31** *Sport.* denoting the state in which a player is caused to discontinue active participation, esp. in some specified role. **32 out of. 32a** at or to a point outside: *out of his reach.* **32b** away from; not in: *stepping out of line; out of focus.* **32c** because of; motivated by: *out of jealousy.* **32d** from (a material or source): *made out of plastic.* **32e** not or no longer having any of (a substance, material, etc.): *we're out of sugar.* **32f** no longer in a specified state or condition: *out of work; out of practice.* **32g** (of a horse) born of. ◆ *adj* **33** directed or indicating direction outwards: *the out tray.* **34** (of an island) remote from the mainland. **35** *Inf.* not concealing one's homosexuality. ◆ *prep* **36** *Nonstandard or US.* out of; out through: *he ran out the door.* ◆ *interj* **37a** an exclamation of dismissal, reproach, etc. **37b** (in wireless telegraphy) an expression used to signal that the speaker is signing off. **38 out with it.** a command to make something known immediately, without missing any details. ◆ *n* **39** *Chiefly US.* a method of escape from a place, difficult situation, etc. **40** *Baseball.* an instance of causing a batter to be out by fielding. ◆ *vb* **41** (*tr*) to put or throw out. **42** (*intr*) to be made known or effective despite efforts to the contrary (esp. in **the truth will out**). **43** (*tr*) *Inf.* (of homosexuals) to expose (a public figure) as being a fellow homosexual. **44** *Inf.* to expose something secret, embarrassing, or unknown about (a person): *he was eventually outed as a talented goal scorer.* [OE *ūt*]

> **USAGE NOTE** The use of *out* as a preposition, though common in American English, is regarded as incorrect in British English: *he climbed out of* (not *out*) *a window; he went out through the door.*

out- *prefix* **1** excelling or surpassing in a particular action: *outlast; outlive.* **2** indicating an external location or situation away from the centre: *outpost; outpatient.* **3** indicating emergence, an issuing forth, etc.: *outcrop; outgrowth.* **4** indicating the result of an action: *outcome.*

outage ('autɪdʒ) *n* **1** a quantity of goods missing or lost after storage or shipment. **2** a period of power failure, machine stoppage, etc.

out and away *adv* by far.

out-and-out Ⓣ *adj* (*prenominal*) thoroughgoing; complete.

outback ('aut,bæk) *n* **a** the remote bush country of Australia. **b** (*as modifier*): *outback life.*

outbalance (,aut'bæləns) *vb* **outbalances, outbalancing, outbalanced.** another word for **outweigh.**

outboard ('aut,bɔːd) *adj* **1** (of a boat's engine) portable, with its own propeller, and designed to be attached externally to the stern. **2** in a position away from, or further away from, the centre line of a vessel or aircraft, esp. outside the hull or fuselage. ◆ *adv* **3** away from the centre line of a vessel or aircraft, esp. outside the hull or fuselage. ◆ *n* **4** an outboard motor.

outbound ('aut,baund) *adj* going out; outward bound.

outbrave (,aut'breɪv) *vb* **outbraves, outbraving, outbraved.** (*tr*) **1** to surpass in bravery. **2** to confront defiantly.

outbreak Ⓣ ('aut,breɪk) *n* a sudden, violent, or spontaneous occurrence, esp. of disease or strife.

outbuilding ('aut,bɪldɪŋ) *n* a building separate from a main building; outhouse.

outburst Ⓣ ('aut,bɜːst) *n* **1** a sudden and violent expression of emotion. **2** an explosion or eruption.

outcast Ⓣ ('aut,kɑːst) *n* **1** a person who is rejected or excluded from a social group. **2** a vagabond or wanderer. **3** anything thrown out or rejected. ◆ *adj* **4** rejected, abandoned, or discarded; cast out.

outcaste ('aut,kɑːst) *n* **1** a person who has been expelled from a caste. **2** a person having no caste. ◆ *vb* **outcastes, outcasting, outcasted. 3** (*tr*) to cause (someone) to lose his caste.

outclass Ⓣ (,aut'klɑːs) *vb* (*tr*) **1** to surpass in class, quality, etc. **2** to defeat easily.

outcome Ⓣ ('aut,kʌm) *n* something that follows from an action or situation; result; consequence.

outcrop *n* ('aut,krɒp). **1** part of a rock formation or mineral vein that appears at the surface of the earth. **2** an emergence; appearance. ◆ *vb* (,aut'krɒp), **outcrops, outcropping, outcropped. 3** (*intr*) (of rock strata, mineral veins, etc.) to protrude through the surface of the earth.

outcry Ⓣ *n* ('aut,kraɪ), *pl* **outcries. 1** a widespread or vehement protest. **2** clamour; uproar. **3** *Commerce.* a method of trading in which dealers shout out bids and offers at a prearranged meeting: *sale by open outcry.* ◆ *vb* (,aut'kraɪ), **outcries, outcrying, outcried.** (*tr*) **4** to cry louder or make more noise than (someone or something).

outdated Ⓣ (,aut'deɪtɪd) *adj* old-fashioned or obsolete.

outdo Ⓣ (,aut'duː) *vb* **outdoes, outdoing, outdid, outdone.** (*tr*) to surpass or exceed in performance.

THESAURUS

ounce[1] *n* **4** = **shred**, atom, crumb, drop, grain, iota, particle, scrap, speck, trace, whit

oust *vb* **1** = **expel**, depose, disinherit, dislodge, displace, dispossess, eject, evict, relegate, throw out, topple, turn out, unseat

out *adj* **1, 3** = **away**, abroad, absent, elsewhere, gone, not at home, outside **2, 11** = **extinguished**, at an end, cold, dead, doused, ended, exhausted, expired, finished, used up **8** = **old-fashioned**, antiquated, behind the times, dated, dead, *démodé*, old hat, passé, square (*inf.*), unfashionable **10** = **not allowed**, impossible, not on (*inf.*), ruled out, unacceptable
Antonyms *adj* ≠ **old-fashioned:** à la mode, fashionable, in, in fashion, latest, modern, trendy (*Brit. inf.*), up-to-date, with it (*inf.*)

out-and-out *adj* = **absolute**, arrant, complete, consummate, deep-dyed (*usually derogatory*), downright, dyed-in-the-wool, outright, perfect, thorough, thoroughgoing, total, unmitigated, unqualified, utter

outbreak *n* = **eruption**, burst, epidemic, explosion, flare-up, flash, outburst, rash, spasm, upsurge

outburst *n* **1** = **outpouring**, access, attack, discharge, eruption, explosion, fit of temper, flare-up, gush, outbreak, paroxysm, spasm, storm, surge

outcast *n* **1** = **pariah**, castaway, derelict, displaced person, exile, leper, *persona non grata*, refugee, reprobate, untouchable, wretch

outclass *vb* **1** = **surpass**, be a cut above (*inf.*), beat, eclipse, exceed, excel, leave *or* put in the shade, leave standing (*inf.*), outdistance, outdo, outrank, outshine, outstrip, overshadow, run rings around (*inf.*)

outcome *n* = **result**, aftereffect, aftermath, conclusion, consequence, end, end result, issue, payoff (*inf.*), sequel, upshot

outcry *n* **1, 2** = **protest**, clamour, commotion, complaint, cry, exclamation, howl, hue and cry, hullaballoo, noise, outburst, scream, screech, uproar, yell

outdated *adj* = **old-fashioned**, antiquated, antique, archaic, behind the times, *démodé*, obsolete, outmoded, out of date, out of style, out of the ark (*inf.*), passé, unfashionable
Antonyms *adj* à la mode, all the rage, contemporary, current, fashionable, in vogue, modern, modish, stylish, trendy (*Brit. inf.*), up-to-date, with it (*inf.*)

outdo *vb* = **surpass**, beat, be one up on, best, eclipse, exceed, excel, get the better of, go one better than (*inf.*), outclass, outdistance, outfox, outjockey, outmanoeuvre, outshine, outsmart

outdoor 🅣 ('aʊtˈdɔː) *adj* (*prenominal*) taking place, existing, or intended for use in the open air: *outdoor games; outdoor clothes.* Also: **out-of-door.**

outdoors (ˌaʊtˈdɔːz) *adv* **1** Also: **out-of-doors.** in the open air; outside. ◆ *n* **2** the world outside or far away from human habitation.

outer 🅣 ('aʊtə) *adj* (*prenominal*) **1** being or located on the outside; external. **2** further from the middle or central part. ◆ *n* **3** *Archery.* **3a** the white outermost ring on a target. **3b** a shot that hits this ring. **4** *Austral.* & *NZ.* the unsheltered part of the spectator area at a sports ground. **5 on the outer.** *Austral.* & *NZ.* excluded or neglected.

outer bar *n* (in England) a collective name for junior barristers who plead from outside the bar of the court.

outermost ('aʊtəˌməʊst) *adj* furthest from the centre or middle; outmost.

outer space *n* any region of space beyond the atmosphere of the earth.

outfall ('aʊtˌfɔːl) *n* the end of a river, sewer, drain, etc., from which it discharges.

outfield ('aʊtˌfiːld) *n* **1** *Cricket.* the area of the field relatively far from the pitch; the deep. Cf. **infield** (sense 1). **2** *Baseball.* **2a** the area of the playing field beyond the lines connecting first, second, and third bases. **2b** the positions of the left fielder, centre fielder, and right fielder taken collectively. **3** *Agriculture.* farmland most distant from the farmstead.
▸ **'outˌfielder** *n*

outfit 🅣 ('aʊtˌfɪt) *n* **1** a set of articles or equipment for a particular task, etc. **2** a set of clothes, esp. a carefully selected one. **3** *Inf.* any group or association regarded as a cohesive unit, such as a military company, etc. ◆ *vb* **outfits, outfitting, outfitted. 4** to furnish or be furnished with an outfit, equipment, etc.
▸ **'outˌfitter** *n*

outflank (ˌaʊtˈflæŋk) *vb* (*tr*) **1** to go around the flank of (an opposing army, etc.). **2** to get the better of.

outflow 🅣 ('aʊtˌfləʊ) *n* **1** anything that flows out, such as liquid, money, etc. **2** the amount that flows out. **3** the act or process of flowing out.

outfox (ˌaʊtˈfɒks) *vb* (*tr*) to surpass in guile or cunning.

outgeneral (ˌaʊtˈdʒenərəl) *vb* **outgenerals, outgeneralling, outgeneralled** *or US* **outgenerals, outgeneraling, outgeneraled.** (*tr*) to surpass in generalship.

outgo *vb* (ˌaʊtˈgəʊ), **outgoes, outgoing, outwent, outgone. 1** (*tr*) to exceed or outstrip. ◆ *n* ('aʊtˌgəʊ). **2** cost; outgoings; outlay. **3** something that goes out; outflow.

outgoing 🅣 ('aʊtˌgəʊɪŋ) *adj* **1** departing; leaving. **2** retiring from office. **3** friendly and sociable. ◆ *n* **4** the act of going out.

outgoings 🅣 ('aʊtˌgəʊɪŋz) *pl n* expenditure.

outgrow (ˌaʊtˈgrəʊ) *vb* **outgrows, outgrowing, outgrew, outgrown.** (*tr*) **1** to grow too large for (clothes, shoes, etc.). **2** to lose (a habit, idea, reputation, etc.) in the course of development or time. **3** to grow larger or faster than.

outgrowth 🅣 ('aʊtˌgrəʊθ) *n* **1** a thing growing out of a main body. **2** a development, result, or consequence. **3** the act of growing out.

outgun (ˌaʊtˈgʌn) *vb* **outguns, outgunning, outgunned.** (*tr*) **1** to surpass in fire power. **2** to surpass in shooting. **3** *Inf.* to surpass or excel.

outhouse ('aʊtˌhaʊs) *n* a building near to, but separate from, a main building; outbuilding.

outing 🅣 ('aʊtɪŋ) *n* **1** a short outward and return journey; trip; excursion. **2** *Inf.* the naming by homosexuals of other prominent homosexuals, often against their will.

outjockey (ˌaʊtˈdʒɒkɪ) *vb* (*tr*) to outwit by deception.

outlandish 🅣 (aʊtˈlændɪʃ) *adj* **1** grotesquely unconventional in appearance, habits, etc. **2** *Arch.* foreign.
▸ **out'landishly** *adv* ▸ **out'landishness** *n*

outlast 🅣 (ˌaʊtˈlɑːst) *vb* (*tr*) to last longer than.

outlaw 🅣 ('aʊtˌlɔː) *n* **1** (formerly) a person excluded from the law and deprived of its protection. **2** any fugitive from the law, esp. a habitual transgressor. ◆ *vb* (*tr*) **3** to put (a person) outside the law and deprive of its protection. **4** to ban.
▸ **'outˌlawry** *n*

outlay 🅣 *n* ('aʊtˌleɪ). **1** an expenditure of money, effort, etc. ◆ *vb* (ˌaʊtˈleɪ), **outlays, outlaying, outlaid. 2** (*tr*) to spend (money, etc.).

outlet 🅣 ('aʊtlet, -lɪt) *n* **1** an opening or vent permitting escape or release. **2a** a market for a product or service. **2b** a commercial establishment retailing the goods of a particular producer or wholesaler. **3** a channel that drains a body of water. **4** a point in a wiring system from which current can be taken to supply electrical devices.

outlier ('aʊtˌlaɪə) *n* **1** an outcrop of rocks that is entirely surrounded by older rocks. **2** a person, thing, or part situated away from a main or related body. **3** a person who lives away from his place of work, duty, etc.

outline 🅣 ('aʊtˌlaɪn) *n* **1** a preliminary or schematic plan, draft, etc. **2** (*usually pl*) the important features of a theory, work, etc. **3** the line by which an object or figure is or appears to be bounded. **4a** a drawing or manner of drawing consisting only of external lines. **4b** (*as modifier*): *an outline map.* ◆ *vb* **outlines, outlining, outlined.** (*tr*) **5** to draw or display the outline of. **6** to give the main features or general idea of.

outlive 🅣 (ˌaʊtˈlɪv) *vb* **outlives, outliving, outlived.** (*tr*) **1** to live longer than (someone). **2** to live beyond (a date or period): *he outlived the century.* **3** to live through (an experience).

outlook 🅣 ('aʊtˌlʊk) *n* **1** a mental attitude or point of view. **2** the probable or expected condition or outcome of something: *the weather outlook.* **3** the view from a place. **4** view or prospect. **5** the act or state of looking out.

outlying 🅣 ('aʊtˌlaɪɪŋ) *adj* distant or remote from the main body or centre, as of a town or region.

outmanoeuvre 🅣 *or US* **outmaneuver** (ˌaʊtməˈnuːvə) *vb* **outmanoeuvres, outmanoeuvring, outmanoeuvred** *or US* **outmaneuvers, outmaneuvering, outmaneuvered.** (*tr*) to secure a strategic advantage over by skilful manoeuvre.

outmoded 🅣 (ˌaʊtˈməʊdɪd) *adj* no longer fashionable or widely accepted.
▸ **ˌout'modedly** *adv* ▸ **ˌout'modedness** *n*

outmost ('aʊtˌməʊst) *adj* another word for **outermost.**

out of bounds 🅣 *adj* (*postpositive*), *adv* **1** (often foll. by *to*) not to be entered (by); barred (to). **2** outside specified or prescribed limits.

out of date 🅣 *adj* (**out-of-date** *when prenominal*), *adv* no longer valid, current, or fashionable; outmoded.

out-of-door *adj* (*prenominal*) another term for **outdoor.**

out-of-doors *adv, adj* (*postpositive*) in the open air; outside. Also: **outdoors.**

THESAURUS

(*inf.*), overcome, run rings around (*inf.*), score points off, top, transcend

outdoor *adj* = **open-air**, alfresco, out-of-door(s), outside
Antonyms *adj* indoor, inside, interior, within

outer *adj* **1** = **external**, exposed, exterior, outlying, outside, outward, peripheral, remote, superficial, surface
Antonyms *adj* central, closer, inner, inside, interior, internal, inward, nearer

outfit *n* **2** = **costume**, accoutrements, clothes, ensemble, garb, gear (*inf.*), get-up (*inf.*), kit, rigout (*inf.*), suit, threads (*sl.*), togs (*inf.*), trappings **3** *Informal* = **group**, clique, company, corps, coterie, crew, firm, organization, set, setup (*inf.*), squad, team, unit ◆ *vb* **4** = **equip**, accoutre, appoint, fit out, furnish, kit out, provision, stock, supply, turn out

outfitter *n* **4** = **clothier**, costumier, couturier, dressmaker, haberdasher (*US*), modiste, tailor

outflow *n* **1** = **discharge**, drainage, ebb, effluence, efflux, effusion, emanation, emergence, gush, issue, jet, outfall, outpouring, rush, spout

outgoing *adj* **1, 2** = **leaving**, departing, ex-, former, last, past, retiring, withdrawing **3** = **sociable**, approachable, communicative, cordial, demonstrative, easy, expansive, extrovert, friendly, genial, gregarious, informal, open, sympathetic, unreserved, warm
Antonyms *adj* ≠ **leaving:** arriving, entering, incoming ≠ **sociable:** austere, cold, indifferent, reserved, retiring, withdrawn

outgoings *pl n* = **expenses**, costs, expenditure, outlay, overheads

outgrowth *n* **1** = **offshoot**, bulge, excrescence, node, outcrop, process, projection, protuberance, scion, shoot, sprout **2** = **product**, by-product, consequence, derivative, development, emergence, issue, result, spin-off, yield

outing *n* **1** = **trip**, excursion, expedition, jaunt, pleasure trip, spin (*inf.*)

outlandish *adj* **1** = **strange**, alien, barbarous, bizarre, eccentric, exotic, fantastic, far-out, foreign, freakish, grotesque, left-field (*inf.*), outré, preposterous, queer, unheard-of, weird
Antonyms *adj* banal, commonplace, everyday, familiar, humdrum, mundane, normal, ordinary, usual, well-known

outlast *vb* = **outlive**, endure beyond, outstay, outwear, survive

outlaw *n* **1** = **bandit**, brigand, desperado, footpad (*arch.*), fugitive, highwayman, marauder, outcast, pariah, robber ◆ *vb* **3** = **put a price on (someone's) head 4** = **forbid**, ban, banish, bar, condemn, disallow, embargo, exclude, interdict, make illegal, prohibit, proscribe
Antonyms *vb* ≠ **forbid:** allow, approve, authorize, consent, endorse, legalise, permit, sanction, support

outlay *n* **1** = **expenditure**, cost, disbursement, expenses, investment, outgoings, spending

outlet *n* **1** = **opening**, avenue, channel, duct, egress, exit, orifice, release, safety valve, vent, way out **2** = **shop**, market, store

outline *n* **1** = **draft**, drawing, frame, framework, layout, lineament(s), plan, rough, skeleton, sketch, tracing **2** = **summary**, bare facts, main features, recapitulation, résumé, rough idea, rundown, synopsis, thumbnail sketch **3** = **shape**, configuration, contour, delineation, figure, form, profile, silhouette ◆ *vb* **5** = **trace**, delineate, draft, plan, rough out, sketch in **6** = **summarize**, adumbrate, delineate, sketch

outlive *vb* **1-3** = **survive**, come through, endure beyond, live through, outlast

outlook *n* **1** = **attitude**, angle, frame of mind, perspective, point of view, slant, standpoint, viewpoint, views **2** = **prospect**, expectations, forecast, future **3** = **view**, aspect, panorama, prospect, scene, vista

outlying *adj* = **remote**, backwoods, distant, far-flung, in the middle of nowhere, outer, out-of-the-way, peripheral, provincial

outmanoeuvre *vb* = **outwit**, circumvent, get the better of, outdo, outflank, outfox, outgeneral, outjockey, outsmart (*inf.*), run rings round (*inf.*), steal a march on (*inf.*)

outmoded *adj* = **old-fashioned**, anachronistic, antediluvian, antiquated, antique, archaic, behind the times, bygone, dated, *démodé*, fossilized, obsolescent, obsolete, old-time, out, out-of-date, out of style, out of the ark (*inf.*), outworn, passé, square (*inf.*), superannuated, superseded, unfashionable, unusable
Antonyms *adj* all the rage, fashionable, fresh, in vogue, latest, modern, modish, new, recent, usable

out of bounds *adj, adv* **1, 2** = **forbidden** (*chiefly US military*), banned, barred, off-limits, prohibited, taboo

out of date *adj* = **old-fashioned**, antiquated, archaic, dated, discarded, elapsed, expired, extinct, invalid, lapsed, obsolete, outmoded, out of the ark (*inf.*), outworn, passé, stale, superannuated, superseded, unfashionable

out of pocket *adj* (**out-of-pocket** *when prenominal*). **1** (*postpositive*) having lost money, as in a commercial enterprise. **2** without money to spend. **3** (*prenominal*) (of expenses) unbudgeted and paid for in cash.

out of the way ⓣ *adj* (**out-of-the-way** *when prenominal*). **1** distant from more populous areas. **2** uncommon or unusual.

outpace (ˌaʊt'peɪs) *vb* **outpaces, outpacing, outpaced.** (*tr*) **1** to go faster than (someone). **2** to surpass or outdo (something or someone) in growth, development. etc.

outpatient ('aʊtˌpeɪʃənt) *n* a nonresident hospital patient. Cf. **inpatient.**

outperform (ˌaʊtpə'fɔːm) *vb* (*tr*) to outdo or surpass in a specified field or activity.

outplacement ('aʊtˌpleɪsmənt) *n* a service that offers counselling and careers advice, esp. to redundant executives, which is paid for by their previous employer.

outpoint (ˌaʊt'pɔɪnt) *vb* (*tr*) to score more points than.

outport ('aʊtˌpɔːt) *n* **1** *Chiefly Brit.* a subsidiary port built in deeper water than the original port. **2** *Canad.* a small fishing village of Newfoundland.

outpost ('aʊtˌpəʊst) *n* **1** *Mil.* **1a** a position stationed at a distance from the area occupied by a major formation. **1b** the troops assigned to such a position. **2** an outlying settlement or position.

outpour *n* ('aʊtˌpɔː). **1** the act of flowing or pouring out. **2** something that pours out. ◆ *vb* (ˌaʊt'pɔː). **3** to pour or cause to pour out freely or rapidly.

outpouring ⓣ ('aʊtˌpɔːrɪŋ) *n* **1** a passionate or exaggerated outburst; effusion. **2** another word for **outpour** (senses 1, 2).

output ⓣ ('aʊtˌpʊt) *n* **1** the act of production or manufacture. **2** the amount produced, as in a given period: *a weekly output.* **3** the material produced, manufactured, etc. **4** *Electronics.* **4a** the power, voltage, or current delivered by a circuit or component. **4b** the point at which the signal is delivered. **5** the power, energy, or work produced by an engine or a system. **6** *Computing.* **6a** the information produced by a computer. **6b** the operations and devices involved in producing this information. **7** (*modifier*) of or relating to electronic or computer output: *output signal.* ◆ *vb* **outputs, outputting, outputted** *or* **output. 8** (*tr*) *Computing.* to cause (data) to be emitted as output.

outrage ⓣ ('aʊtˌreɪdʒ) *n* **1** a wantonly vicious or cruel act. **2** a gross violation of decency, morality, honour, etc. **3** profound indignation, anger, or hurt, caused by such an act. ◆ *vb* **outrages, outraging, outraged.** (*tr*) **4** to cause profound indignation, anger, or resentment in. **5** to offend grossly. **6** to commit an act of wanton viciousness, cruelty, or indecency on. **7** a euphemistic word for **rape**[1]. [C13 (meaning: excess): via F from *outré* beyond, from L *ultrā*]

outrageous ⓣ (aʊt'reɪdʒəs) *adj* **1** being or having the nature of an outrage. **2** grossly offensive to decency, authority, etc. **3** violent or unrestrained in behaviour or temperament. **4** extravagant or immoderate. ▸**out'rageously** *adv* ▸**out'rageousness** *n*

outrank (ˌaʊt'ræŋk) *vb* (*tr*) **1** to be of higher rank than. **2** to take priority over.

outré ⓣ ('uːtreɪ) *adj* deviating from what is usual or proper. [C18: from F, p.p. of *outrer* to pass beyond]

outride (ˌaʊt'raɪd) *vb* **outrides, outriding, outrode, outridden.** (*tr*) **1** to outdo by riding faster, farther, or better than. **2** (of a vessel) to ride out (a storm).

outrider ⓣ ('aʊtˌraɪdə) *n* **1** a person who goes in advance to investigate, discover a way, etc.; scout. **2** a person who rides in front of or beside a carriage, esp. as an attendant or guard. **3** *US.* a mounted herdsman.

outrigger ('aʊtˌrɪgə) *n* **1** a framework for supporting a pontoon outside and parallel to the hull of a boat to provide stability. **2** a boat equipped with such a framework, esp. one of the canoes of the South Pacific. **3** any projecting framework attached to a boat, aircraft, building, etc., to act as a support. **4** *Rowing.* another name for **rigger** (sense 2). [C18: from OUT- + RIG + -ER[1]]

outright ⓣ *adj* ('aʊtˌraɪt). (*prenominal*) **1** without qualifications or limitations: *outright ownership.* **2** complete; total. **3** straightforward; direct. ◆ *adv* (ˌaʊt'raɪt). **4** without restrictions. **5** without reservation or concealment: *ask outright.* **6** instantly: *he was killed outright.*

outrush ('aʊtˌrʌʃ) *n* a flowing or rushing out.

outset ⓣ ('aʊtˌsɛt) *n* a start; beginning (esp. in **from** (*or* **at**) **the outset**).

outside ⓣ *prep* (ˌaʊt'saɪd). **1** (sometimes foll. by *of*) on or to the exterior of: *outside the house.* **2** beyond the limits of. **3** apart from; other than: *no-one knows outside you.* ◆ *adj* ('aʊtˌsaɪd). **4** (*prenominal*) situated on the exterior: *an outside lavatory.* **5** remote; unlikely. **6** not a member of. **7** the greatest possible or probable (prices, odds, etc.). **8** (of a road lane, esp. in a dual carriageway or motorway) situated nearer or nearest to the central reservation, for use by faster or overtaking vehicles. ◆ *adv* (ˌaʊt'saɪd). **9** outside a specified thing or place; out of doors. **10** *Sl.* not in prison. ◆ *n* ('aʊt'saɪd). **11** the external side or surface. **12** the external appearance or aspect. **13** (of a pavement, etc.) the side nearest the road or away from a wall. **14** *Sport.* an outside player, as in football. **15** (*pl*) the outer sheets of a ream of paper. **16** *Canad.* (in the north) the settled parts of Canada. **17 at the outside.** *Inf.* at the most or at the greatest extent: *two days at the outside.*

> **USAGE NOTE** The use of *outside of* and *inside of*, although fairly common, is generally thought to be incorrect or nonstandard: *she waits outside* (not *outside of*) *the school.*

outside broadcast *n Radio, television.* a broadcast not made from a studio.

outside director *n* a director of a company who is not employed by that company but is often employed by a holding or associated company.

outsider ⓣ (ˌaʊt'saɪdə) *n* **1** a person or thing excluded from or not a member of a set, group, etc. **2** a contestant, esp. a horse, thought unlikely to win in a race. **3** *Canad.* a person who does not live in the Arctic regions.

outsize ⓣ ('aʊtˌsaɪz) *adj* **1** Also: **outsized.** very large or larger than normal. ◆ *n* **2** something outsize, such as a garment or person. **3** (*modifier*) relating to or dealing in outsize clothes: *an outsize shop.*

outskirts ⓣ ('aʊtˌskɜːts) *pl n* (*sometimes sing*) outlying or bordering areas, districts, etc., as of a city.

outsmart ⓣ (ˌaʊt'smɑːt) *vb* (*tr*) *Inf.* to get the better of; outwit.

outspan *S. African.* ◆ *n* ('aʊtˌspæn). **1** an area on a farm kept available for travellers to rest and refresh animals, etc. **2** the act of unharnessing or unyoking. ◆ *vb* (ˌaʊt'spæn), **outspans, outspanning, outspanned. 3** to unharness or unyoke (animals). [C19: partial translation of Afrik. *uitspan*, from *uit* out + *spannen* to stretch]

outspoken ⓣ (ˌaʊt'spəʊkən) *adj* **1** candid or bold in speech. **2** said or expressed with candour or boldness.

THESAURUS

Antonyms *adj* contemporary, current, fashionable, in, new, now (*inf.*), trendy (*Brit. inf.*), up to date, valid

out of the way *adj* **1** = **remote**, distant, far-flung, inaccessible, isolated, lonely, obscure, off the beaten track, outlying, secluded, unfrequented **2** = **unusual**, abnormal, curious, exceptional, extraordinary, odd, outlandish, out of the ordinary, peculiar, strange, uncommon
Antonyms *adj* ≠ **remote:** accessible, close, convenient, frequented, handy, near, nearby, proximate, reachable, within sniffing distance (*inf.*)

outpouring *n* **1, 2** = **stream**, cascade, debouchment, deluge, effluence, efflux, effusion, emanation, flow, flux, issue, outflow, spate, spurt, torrent

output *n* **1** = **production**, achievement, manufacture, product, productivity, yield

outrage *n* **1** = **atrocity**, barbarism, enormity, evil, inhumanity **2** = **violation**, abuse, affront, desecration, indignity, injury, insult, offence, profanation, rape, ravishing, sacrilege, shock, violence **3** = **indignation**, anger, fury, hurt, resentment, shock, wrath ◆ *vb* **5** = **offend**, affront, incense, infuriate, madden, make one's blood boil, scandalize, shock **6** = **abuse**, defile, desecrate, injure, insult, maltreat **7** = **rape**, ravage, ravish, violate

outrageous *adj* **1-3** = **atrocious**, abominable, barbaric, beastly, disgraceful, egregious, flagrant, heinous, horrible, infamous, inhuman, iniquitous, nefarious, offensive, scandalous, shocking, unspeakable, villainous, violent, wicked **4** = **unreasonable**, excessive, exorbitant, extravagant, immoderate, over the top (*sl.*), preposterous, scandalous, shocking, steep (*inf.*)
Antonyms *adj* ≠ **atrocious:** just, mild, minor, tolerable, trivial ≠ **unreasonable:** equitable, fair, moderate, reasonable

outré *adj* = **eccentric**, bizarre, extravagant, fantastic, freakish, freaky (*sl.*), grotesque, indecorous, kinky (*inf.*), left-field (*inf.*), odd, off-the-wall (*sl.*), outlandish, rum (*Brit. sl.*), unconventional, way-out (*inf.*), weird

outrider *n* **1, 2** = **escort**, advance guard, advance man, attendant, bodyguard, guard, harbinger, herald, precursor, scout, squire

outright *adj* **1, 2** = **absolute**, arrant, complete, consummate, deep-dyed (*usually derogatory*), downright, out-and-out, perfect, pure, thorough, thoroughgoing, total, unconditional, undeniable, unmitigated, unqualified, utter, wholesale **3** = **direct**, definite, flat, straight-forward, unequivocal, unqualified ◆ *adv* **4** = **absolutely**, completely, straightforwardly, thoroughly, to the full, without hesitation, without restraint **5** = **openly**, explicitly, overtly **6** = **instantly**, at once, cleanly, immediately, instantaneously, on the spot, straight away, there and then, without more ado

outset *n* = **beginning**, commencement, early days, inauguration, inception, kickoff (*inf.*), onset, opening, start, starting point
Antonyms *n* closing, completion, conclusion, consummation, end, finale, finish, termination

outside *adj* **4** = **external**, exterior, extramural, extraneous, extreme, out, outdoor, outer, outermost, outward, surface **5** = **remote**, distant, faint, marginal, negligible, slight, slim, small, unlikely ◆ *n* **11** = **exterior**, façade, face, front, skin, surface, topside
Antonyms *adj* ≠ **external:** in, indoor, inner, innermost, inside, interior, internal, intramural, inward

outsider *n* **1** = **interloper**, alien, foreigner, incomer, intruder, newcomer, nonmember, odd one out, outlander, stranger

outsize *adj* **1** = **extra-large**, enormous, gargantuan, giant, gigantic, huge, immense, jumbo (*inf.*), large, mammoth, monster, oversized
Antonyms *adj* baby, dwarf, micro, mini, pocket, tiny, undersized

outskirts *pl n* = **edge**, borders, boundary, environs, faubourgs, periphery, purlieus, suburbia, suburbs, vicinity

outsmart *vb Informal* = **outwit**, deceive, dupe, get the better of, go one better than (*inf.*), make a fool of (*inf.*), outfox, outjockey, outmanoeuvre, outperform, outthink, pull a fast one on (*inf.*), put one over on (*inf.*), run rings round (*inf.*), trick

outspoken *adj* **1, 2** = **forthright**, abrupt, blunt, candid, direct, downright, explicit, frank, free, free-spoken, open, plain-spoken, round, unceremonious, undissembling, unequivocal, unreserved
Antonyms *adj* diplomatic, gracious, judicious, reserved, reticent, tactful

outspread ➊ *vb* (ˌaʊtˈsprɛd), **outspreads, outspreading, outspread. 1** to spread out. ◆ *adj* (ˈaʊtˈsprɛd). **2** spread or stretched out. **3** scattered or diffused widely. ◆ *n* (ˈaʊtˌsprɛd). **4** a spreading out.

outstanding ➊ (ˌaʊtˈstændɪŋ) *adj* **1** superior; excellent. **2** prominent, remarkable, or striking. **3** unsettled, unpaid, or unresolved. **4** (of shares, bonds, etc.) issued and sold. **5** projecting or jutting upwards or outwards.
▸ˌ**out'standingly** *adv*

outstare (ˌaʊtˈstɛə) *vb* **outstares, outstaring, outstared.** (*tr*) **1** to outdo in staring. **2** to disconcert by staring.

outstation (ˈaʊtˌsteɪʃən) *n* a station or post at a distance from the base station or in a remote region.

outstay (ˌaʊtˈsteɪ) *vb* (*tr*) **1** to stay longer than. **2** to stay beyond (a limit). **3 outstay one's welcome.** See **overstay** (sense 2).

outstretch (ˌaʊtˈstrɛtʃ) *vb* (*tr*) **1** to extend or expand; stretch out. **2** to stretch or extend beyond.

outstrip ➊ (ˌaʊtˈstrɪp) *vb* **outstrips, outstripping, outstripped.** (*tr*) **1** to surpass in a sphere of activity, competition, etc. **2** to be or grow greater than. **3** to go faster than and leave behind.

outtake (ˈaʊtˌteɪk) *n* an unreleased take from a recording session, film, or television programme.

out-tray *n* (in an office, etc.) a tray for outgoing correspondence, documents, etc.

outturn (ˈaʊtˌtɜːn) *n* another word for **output** (sense 2).

outvote (ˌaʊtˈvəʊt) *vb* **outvotes, outvoting, outvoted.** (*tr*) to defeat by a majority of votes.

outward ➊ (ˈaʊtwəd) *adj* **1** of or relating to what is apparent or superficial. **2** of or relating to the outside of the body. **3** belonging or relating to the external, as opposed to the mental, spiritual, or inherent. **4** of, relating to, or directed towards the outside or exterior. **5 the outward man. 5a** *Theol.* the body as opposed to the soul. **5b** *Facetious.* clothing. ◆ *adv* **6** (of a ship) away from port. **7** a variant of **outwards.** ◆ *n* **8** the outward part; exterior.
▸ˈ**outwardness** *n*

Outward Bound movement *n Trademark.* (in Britain) a scheme to provide adventure training for young people.

outwardly ➊ (ˈaʊtwədlɪ) *adv* **1** in outward appearance. **2** with reference to the outside or outer surface; externally.

outwards (ˈaʊtwədz) *or* **outward** *adv* towards the outside; out.

outwear (ˌaʊtˈwɛə) *vb* **outwears, outwearing, outwore, outworn.** (*tr*) **1** to use up or destroy by wearing. **2** to last or wear longer than. **3** to outlive, outgrow, or develop beyond. **4** to deplete or exhaust in strength, determination, etc.

outweigh ➊ (ˌaʊtˈweɪ) *vb* (*tr*) **1** to prevail over; overcome. **2** to be more important or significant than. **3** to be heavier than.

outwit ➊ (ˌaʊtˈwɪt) *vb* **outwits, outwitting, outwitted.** (*tr*) to get the better of by cunning or ingenuity.

outwith (ˌaʊtˈwɪθ) *prep Scot.* outside; beyond.

outwork *n* (ˈaʊtˌwɜːk). **1** (*often pl*) defences which lie outside main defensive works. **2** work done away from the factory, etc., by which it has been commissioned. ◆ *vb* (ˌaʊtˈwɜːk). (*tr*) **3** to work better, harder, etc., than. **4** to work out to completion.
▸ˈ**outˌworker** *n*

ouzel *or* **ousel** (ˈuːzᵊl) *n* **1** short for **water ouzel.** See **dipper** (sense 2). **2** an archaic name for the (European) **blackbird.** [OE *ōsle*]

ouzo (ˈuːzəʊ) *n, pl* **ouzos.** a strong aniseed-flavoured spirit from Greece. [Mod. Gk *ouzon,* from ?]

ova (ˈəʊvə) *n* the plural of **ovum.**

oval ➊ (ˈəʊvᵊl) *adj* **1** having the shape of an ellipse or ellipsoid. ◆ *n* **2** anything that is oval in shape, such as a sports ground. **3** *Austral.* **3a** an Australian Rules ground. **3b** any sports field. [C16: from Med. L *ōvālis,* from L *ōvum* egg]
▸ˈ**ovally** *adv* ▸ˈ**ovalness** *or* **ovality** (əʊˈvælɪtɪ) *n*

ovariectomy (əʊˌvɛərɪˈɛktəmɪ) *n, pl* **ovariectomies.** *Surgery.* surgical removal of an ovary or ovarian tumour.

ovary (ˈəʊvərɪ) *n, pl* **ovaries. 1** either of the two female reproductive organs, which produce ova and secrete oestrogen hormones. **2** the corresponding organ in vertebrate and invertebrate animals. **3** *Bot.* the hollow basal region of a carpel containing one or more ovules. [C17: from NL *ōvārium,* from L *ōvum* egg]
▸**ovarian** (əʊˈvɛərɪən) *adj*

ovate (ˈəʊveɪt) *adj* **1** shaped like an egg. **2** (esp. of a leaf) shaped like the longitudinal section of an egg, with the broader end at the base. [C18: from L *ōvātus* egg-shaped]
▸ˈ**ovately** *adv*

ovation ➊ (əʊˈveɪʃən) *n* **1** an enthusiastic reception, esp. one of prolonged applause. **2** a victory procession less glorious than a triumph awarded to a Roman general. [C16: from L *ovātiō* rejoicing, from *ovāre* to exult]
▸**o'vational** *adj*

oven (ˈʌvᵊn) *n* **1** an enclosed heated compartment or receptacle for baking or roasting food. **2** a similar device, usually lined with a refractory material, used for drying substances, firing ceramics, heat-treating, etc. ◆ *vb* **3** (*tr*) to cook in an oven. [OE *ofen*]
▸ˈ**oven-ˌlike** *adj*

ovenable (ˈʌvᵊnəbᵊl) *adj* suitable for cooking in or using in an oven.

ovenbird (ˈʌvᵊnˌbɜːd) *n* **1** any of numerous small brownish South American passerine birds that build oven-shaped clay nests. **2** a common North American warbler that has an olive-brown striped plumage with an orange crown and builds a cup-shaped nest on the ground.

oven-ready *adj* (of various foods) bought already prepared so that they are ready to be cooked in the oven.

ovenware (ˈʌvᵊnˌwɛə) *n* heat-resistant dishes in which food can be both cooked and served.

over ➊ (ˈəʊvə) *prep* **1** directly above; on the top of; via the top or upper surface of: *over one's head.* **2** on or to the other side of: *over the river.* **3** during; through or throughout (a period of time). **4** in or throughout all parts of: *to travel over England.* **5** throughout the whole extent of: *over the racecourse.* **6** above; in preference to. **7** by the agency of (an instrument of telecommunication): *over the radio.* **8** more than: *over a century ago.* **9** on the subject of; about: *an argument over nothing.* **10** while occupied in: *discussing business over golf.* **11** having recovered from the effects of. **12 over and above.** added to; in addition to. ◆ *adv* **13** in a state, condition, situation, or position that is placed or put over something: *to climb over.* **14** (*particle*) so as to cause to fall: *knocking over a policeman.* **15** at or to a point across intervening space, water, etc. **16** throughout a whole area: *the world over.* **17** (*particle*) from beginning to end, usually cursorily: *to read a document over.* **18** throughout a period of time: *stay over for this week.* **19** (esp. in signalling and radio) it is now your turn to speak, act, etc. **20** more than is expected or usual: *not over well.* **21 over again.** once more. **22 over against. 22a** opposite to. **22b** contrasting with. **23 over and over.** (often foll. by *again*) repeatedly. ◆ *adj* **24** (*postpositive*) finished; no longer in progress. ◆ *adv, adj* **25** remaining; surplus (often in **left over**). ◆ *n* **26** *Cricket.* **26a** a series of six balls bowled by a bowler from the same end of the pitch. **26b** the play during this. [OE *ofer*]

over- *prefix* **1** excessive or excessively; beyond an agreed or desirable limit: *overcharge; overdue.* **2** indicating superior rank: *overseer.* **3** indicating location or movement above: *overhang.* **4** indicating movement downwards: *overthrow.*

overage (ˌəʊvərˈeɪdʒ) *adj* beyond a specified age.

overall ➊ *adj* (ˈəʊvərˌɔːl). (*prenominal*) **1** from one end to the other. **2** including or covering everything: *the overall cost.* ◆ *adv* (ˌəʊvərˈɔːl). **3** in general; on the whole. ◆ *n* (ˈəʊvərˌɔːl). **4** *Brit.* a protective work garment usually worn over ordinary clothes. **5** (*pl*) hard-wearing work trousers with a bib and shoulder straps or jacket attached.

overarch (ˌəʊvərˈɑːtʃ) *vb* (*tr*) to form an arch over.

THESAURUS

outspread *vb* **1** = **outstretch**, expand, extend, fan out, open, open wide, spread out, unfold, unfurl ◆ *adj* **2** = **outstretched**, expanded, extended, fanlike, fanned out, flared, open, opened up, unfolded, unfurled, wide-open

outstanding *adj* **1** = **excellent**, celebrated, distinguished, eminent, exceptional, great, important, impressive, meritorious, pre-eminent, special, stellar (*inf.*), superior, superlative, well-known **2** = **conspicuous**, arresting, eye-catching, marked, memorable, notable, noteworthy, prominent, salient, signal, striking **3** = **unpaid**, due, ongoing, open, owing, payable, pending, remaining, uncollected, unresolved, unsettled
Antonyms *adj* ≠ **excellent:** dull, inferior, insignificant, mediocre, no great shakes (*inf.*), ordinary, pedestrian, run-of-the-mill, unexceptional, unimpressive

outstrip *vb* **1** = **surpass**, beat, better, eclipse, exceed, excel, get ahead of, knock spots off (*inf.*), leave behind, leave standing (*inf.*), lose, outclass, outdo, outperform, outshine, overtake, run rings around (*inf.*), top, transcend **3** = **outdistance**, outpace, outrun, shake off

outward *adj* **1** = **apparent**, evident, exterior, external, noticeable, observable, obvious, ostensible, outer, outside, perceptible, superficial, surface, visible
Antonyms *adj* inner, inside, interior, internal, invisible, inward, obscure, unnoticeable

outwardly *adv* **1** = **apparently**, as far as one can see, externally, officially, on the face of it, on the surface, ostensibly, professedly, seemingly, superficially, to all appearances, to all intents and purposes, to the eye

outweigh *vb* **1** = **override**, cancel (out), compensate for, eclipse, make up for, outbalance, overcome, predominate, preponderate, prevail over, take precedence over, tip the scales

outwit *vb* = **outsmart** (*inf.*), cheat, circumvent, deceive, defraud, dupe, get the better of, gull, make a fool *or* monkey of, outfox, outjockey, outmanoeuvre, outthink, put one over on (*inf.*), run rings round (*inf.*), swindle, take in (*inf.*)

oval *adj* **1** = **elliptical**, egg-shaped, ellipsoidal, ovate, oviform, ovoid

ovation *n* **1** = **applause**, acclaim, acclamation, big hand, cheering, cheers, clapping, laudation, plaudits, tribute
Antonyms *n* abuse, booing, catcalls, derision, heckling, jeers, jibes, mockery, ridicule

over *prep* **1** = **on top of**, above, on, superior to, upon **8** = **more than**, above, exceeding, in excess of **12 over and above** = **in addition to**, added to, as well as, besides, let alone, not to mention, on top of, plus ◆ *adv* **13** = **above**, aloft, on high, overhead **23 over and over (again)** = **repeatedly**, ad nauseam, again and again, frequently, often, time and again ◆ *adj* **24** = **finished**, accomplished, ancient history (*inf.*), at an end, by, bygone, closed, completed, concluded, done (with), ended, gone, past, settled, up (*inf.*) **25** = **extra**, remaining, superfluous, surplus, unused

overall *adj* **2** = **total**, all-embracing, blanket, complete, comprehensive, general, global, inclusive, long-range, long-term, overarching, umbrella ◆ *adv* **3** = **in general**, generally speaking, in (the) large, in the long term, on the whole

overarching (ˌəʊvərˈɑːtʃɪŋ) *adj* overall; all-encompassing: *an overarching concept.*

overarm (ˈəʊvərˌɑːm) *adj* **1** *Sport, esp. cricket.* bowled, thrown, or performed with the arm raised above the shoulder. ◆ *adv* **2** with the arm raised above the shoulder.

overawe Ⓣ (ˌəʊvərˈɔː) *vb* **overawes, overawing, overawed.** (*tr*) to subdue, restrain, or overcome by affecting with a feeling of awe.

overbalance Ⓣ *vb* (ˌəʊvəˈbæləns), **overbalances, overbalancing, overbalanced. 1** to lose or cause to lose balance. **2** (*tr*) another word for **outweigh.** ◆ *n* (ˈəʊvəˌbæləns). **3** excess of weight, value, etc.

overbear (ˌəʊvəˈbɛə) *vb* **overbears, overbearing, overbore, overborne. 1** (*tr*) to dominate or overcome. **2** (*tr*) to press or bear down with weight or physical force. **3** to produce (fruit, etc.) excessively.

overbearing Ⓣ (ˌəʊvəˈbɛərɪŋ) *adj* **1** domineering or dictatorial in manner or action. **2** of particular or overriding importance or significance.
▸ ˌ**overˈbearingly** *adv*

overblown Ⓣ (ˌəʊvəˈbləʊn) *adj* **1** overdone or excessive. **2** bombastic; turgid: *overblown prose.* **3** (of flowers) past the stage of full bloom.

overboard (ˈəʊvəˌbɔːd) *adv* **1** from on board a vessel into the water. **2 go overboard.** *Inf.* **2a** to be extremely enthusiastic. **2b** to go to extremes. **3 throw overboard.** to reject or abandon.

overbook (ˌəʊvəˈbʊk) *vb* (*tr, also absol.*) to make more reservations than there are places, tickets, etc., available.

overbuild (ˌəʊvəˈbɪld) *vb* **overbuilds, overbuilding, overbuilt.** (*tr*) **1** to build over or on top of. **2** to erect too many buildings in (an area). **3** to build too large or elaborately.

overburden *vb* (ˌəʊvəˈbɜːdᵊn). **1** (*tr*) to load with excessive weight, work, etc. ◆ *n* (ˈəʊvəˌbɜːdᵊn). **2** an excessive burden or load. **3** *Geol.* the sedimentary rock material that covers coal seams, mineral veins, etc.
▸ ˌ**overˈburdensome** *adj*

overcast Ⓣ *adj* (ˈəʊvəˌkɑːst). **1** covered over or obscured, esp. by clouds. **2** *Meteorol.* (of the sky) cloud-covered. **3** gloomy or melancholy. **4** sewn over by overcasting. ◆ *vb* (ˌəʊvəˈkɑːst), **overcasts, overcasting, overcast. 5** to sew (an edge, as of a hem) with long stitches passing successively over the edge. ◆ *n* (ˈəʊvəˌkɑːst). **6** *Meteorol.* the state of the sky when it is cloud-covered.

overcharge Ⓣ *vb* (ˌəʊvəˈtʃɑːdʒ), **overcharges, overcharging, overcharged. 1** to charge too much. **2** (*tr*) to fill or load beyond capacity. **3** *Literary.* another word for **exaggerate.** ◆ *n* (ˈəʊvəˌtʃɑːdʒ). **4** an excessive price or charge. **5** an excessive load.

overcloud (ˌəʊvəˈklaʊd) *vb* **1** to make or become covered with clouds. **2** to make or become dark or dim.

overcoat (ˈəʊvəˌkəʊt) *n* a warm heavy coat worn over the outer clothes in cold weather.

overcome Ⓣ (ˌəʊvəˈkʌm) *vb* **overcomes, overcoming, overcame, overcome. 1** (*tr*) to get the better of in a conflict. **2** (*tr; often passive*) to render incapable or powerless by laughter, sorrow, exhaustion, etc. **3** (*tr*) to surmount obstacles, objections, etc. **4** (*intr*) to be victorious.

overcrop (ˌəʊvəˈkrɒp) *vb* **overcrops, overcropping, overcropped.** (*tr*) to exhaust (land) by excessive cultivation.

overdo Ⓣ (ˌəʊvəˈduː) *vb* **overdoes, overdoing, overdid, overdone.** (*tr*) **1** to take or carry too far; do to excess. **2** to exaggerate, overelaborate, or overplay. **3** to cook or bake too long. **4 overdo it** *or* **things.** to overtax one's strength, capacity, etc.

overdose *n* (ˈəʊvəˌdəʊs). **1** (esp. of drugs) an excessive dose. ◆ *vb* (ˌəʊvəˈdəʊs), **overdoses, overdosing, overdosed. 2** to take an excessive dose or give an excessive dose to.
▸ ˌ**overˈdosage** *n*

overdraft (ˈəʊvəˌdrɑːft) *n* **1** a deficit in a bank or building-society cheque account caused by withdrawing more money than is credited to it. **2** the amount of this deficit.

overdraw (ˌəʊvəˈdrɔː) *vb* **overdraws, overdrawing, overdrew, overdrawn. 1** to draw on (a bank account) in excess of the credit balance. **2** (*tr*) to exaggerate in describing or telling.

overdress *vb* (ˌəʊvəˈdrɛs). **1** to dress (oneself or another) too elaborately or finely. ◆ *n* (ˈəʊvəˌdrɛs). **2** a dress that may be worn over a jumper, blouse, etc.

overdrive *n* (ˈəʊvəˌdraɪv). **1** a very high gear in a motor vehicle used at high speeds to reduce wear. ◆ *vb* (ˌəʊvəˈdraɪv), **overdrives, overdriving, overdrove, overdriven. 2** (*tr*) to drive too hard or too far; overwork or overuse.

overdub (in multitrack recording) ◆ *vb* (ˌəʊvəˈdʌb), **overdubs, overdubbing, overdubbed. 1** to add (new sound) on a spare track or tracks. ◆ *n* (ˈəʊvəˌdʌb). **2** the blending of various layers of sound in one recording by this method.

overdue Ⓣ (ˌəʊvəˈdjuː) *adj* past the time specified, required, or preferred for arrival, occurrence, payment, etc.

overestimate *vb* (ˌəʊvərˈɛstɪˌmeɪt), **overestimates, overestimating, overestimated. 1** (*tr*) to estimate too highly. ◆ *n* (ˌəʊvərˈɛstɪmɪt). **2** an estimate that is too high.
▸ ˌ**overˌestiˈmation** *n*

overexpose (ˌəʊvərɪksˈpəʊz) *vb* **overexposes, overexposing, overexposed.** (*tr*) **1** to expose too much or for too long. **2** *Photog.* to expose (a film, etc.) for too long or with too bright a light.
▸ ˌ**overexˈposure** *n*

overflow Ⓣ *vb* (ˌəʊvəˈfləʊ), **overflows, overflowing, overflowed** *or (formerly)* **overflown. 1** to flow or run over (a limit, brim, etc.). **2** to fill or be filled beyond capacity so as to spill or run over. **3** (*intr; usually foll. by with*) to be filled with happiness, tears, etc. **4** (*tr*) to spread or cover over; flood or inundate. ◆ *n* (ˈəʊvəˌfləʊ). **5** overflowing matter, esp. liquid. **6** any outlet that enables surplus liquid to be discharged or drained off. **7** the amount by which a limit, capacity, etc., is exceeded.

overfold (ˈəʊvəˌfəʊld) *n Geol.* a fold in the form of an anticline in which one limb is more steeply inclined than the other.

overfunding (ˈəʊvəˌfʌndɪŋ) *n* (in Britain) a government policy in which it sells more of its securities than would be required to finance public spending, with the object of absorbing surplus funds to curb inflation.

overgrow (ˌəʊvəˈgrəʊ) *vb* **overgrows, overgrowing, overgrew, overgrown. 1** (*tr*) to grow over or across (an area, path, etc.). **2** (*tr*) to choke or supplant by a stronger growth. **3** (*tr*) to grow too large for. **4** (*intr*) to grow beyond normal size.
▸ ˈ**overˌgrowth** *n*

overhand (ˈəʊvəˌhænd) *adj* **1** thrown or performed with the hand raised above the shoulder. **2** sewn with thread passing over two edges in one direction. ◆ *adv* **3** with the hand above the shoulder; overarm. **4** with shallow stitches passing over two edges. ◆ *vb* **5** to sew (two edges) overhand.

overhang Ⓣ *vb* (ˌəʊvəˈhæŋ), **overhangs, overhanging, overhung. 1** to project or extend beyond (a surface, building, etc.). **2** (*tr*) to hang or be suspended over. **3** (*tr*) to menace, threaten, or dominate. ◆ *n* (ˈəʊvəˌhæŋ). **4** a formation, object, etc., that extends beyond or hangs over something, such as an outcrop of rock overhanging a mountain face. **5** the amount or extent of projection.

overhaul Ⓣ *vb* (ˌəʊvəˈhɔːl). (*tr*) **1** to examine carefully for faults, necessary repairs, etc. **2** to make repairs or adjustments to (a car, machine, etc.). **3** to overtake. ◆ *n* (ˈəʊvəˌhɔːl). **4** a thorough examination and repair.

THESAURUS

overawe *vb* = **intimidate**, abash, alarm, browbeat, cow, daunt, frighten, scare, terrify
Antonyms *vb* bolster, buoy up, cheer up, comfort, console, hearten, reassure

overbalance *vb* **1** = **topple over**, capsize, keel over, lose one's balance, lose one's footing, overset, overturn, slip, take a tumble, tip over, tumble, turn turtle, upset

overbearing *adj* **1** = **dictatorial**, arrogant, autocratic, bossy (*inf.*), cavalier, despotic, dogmatic, domineering, haughty, high-handed, imperious, lordly, magisterial, officious, oppressive, overweening, peremptory, supercilious, superior, tyrannical
Antonyms *adj* deferential, humble, modest, self-effacing, submissive, unassertive, unassuming

overblown *adj* **1** = **excessive**, disproportionate, fulsome, immoderate, inflated, overdone, over the top, undue **2** = **grandiloquent**, aureate, bombastic, euphuistic, florid, flowery, fustian, magniloquent, pompous, turgid, windy

overcast *adj* **1** = **cloudy**, clouded, clouded over, darkened, dismal, dreary, dull, grey, hazy, leaden, louring *or* lowering, murky, sombre, sunless, threatening
Antonyms *adj* bright, brilliant, clear, cloudless, fine, sunny, unclouded

overcharge *vb* **1** = **cheat**, clip (*sl.*), diddle (*inf.*), do (*sl.*), fleece, rip off (*sl.*), rook (*sl.*), short-change, skin (*sl.*), sting (*inf.*), surcharge **2** = **overload**, burden, oppress, overburden, overtask, overtax, strain, surfeit **3** *Literary* = **exaggerate**, embellish, embroider, hyperbolize, lay it on thick (*inf.*), overstate

overcome *vb* **1** = **conquer**, beat, best, be victorious, blow out of the water (*sl.*), bring (someone) to their knees (*inf.*), clobber (*sl.*), come out on top (*inf.*), crush, defeat, get the better of, lick (*inf.*), make mincemeat of (*inf.*), master, overpower, overthrow, overwhelm, prevail, rise above, subdue, subjugate, surmount, survive, triumph over, undo, vanquish, weather, wipe the floor with (*inf.*), worst

overdo *vb* **1, 2** = **exaggerate**, be intemperate, belabour, carry too far, do to death (*inf.*), gild the lily, go overboard (*inf.*), go to extremes, lay it on thick (*inf.*), not know when to stop, overindulge, overplay, overreach, overstate, overuse, overwork, run riot **4 overdo it** = **overwork**, bite off more than one can chew, burn the candle at both ends (*inf.*), drive oneself, go too far, have too many irons in the fire, overburden oneself, overload oneself, overtax one's strength, overtire oneself, strain *or* overstrain oneself, wear oneself out
Antonyms *vb* ≠ **exaggerate:** belittle, disparage, minimize, play down, underplay, underrate, understate, underuse, undervalue

overdone *adj* **1, 2** = **excessive**, beyond all bounds, exaggerated, fulsome, hyped, immoderate, inordinate, overelaborate, preposterous, too much, undue, unnecessary **3** = **overcooked**, burnt, burnt to a cinder, charred, dried up, spoiled
Antonyms *adj* ≠ **excessive:** belittled, minimized, moderated, played down, underdone, underplayed, understated

overdue *adj* = **late**, behindhand, behind schedule, behind time, belated, late in the day, long delayed, not before time (*inf.*), owing, tardy, unpunctual
Antonyms *adj* ahead of time, beforehand, early, in advance, in good time, punctual

overflow *vb* **1, 2** = **spill**, brim over, bubble over, discharge, fall over, pour out, pour over, run over, run with, shower, slop over, spray, surge, teem, well over **4** = **flood**, cover, deluge, drown, inundate, soak, submerge, swamp ◆ *n* **5** = **surplus**, discharge, flash flood, flood, flooding, inundation, overabundance, spill, spilling over

overflowing *adj* **1** = **plentiful**, abounding, bountiful, brimful, copious, profuse, rife, superabundant, swarming, teeming, thronged
Antonyms *adj* deficient, inadequate, insufficient, lacking, missing, scarce, wanting

overhang *vb* **1** = **project**, beetle, bulge, cast a shadow, extend, impend, jut, loom, protrude, stick out, threaten

overhaul *vb* **1** = **check**, do up (*inf.*), examine,

overhead ⓣ *adj* ('əʊvəˌhɛd). **1** situated or operating above head height or some other reference level. **2** (*prenominal*) inclusive: *the overhead price included meals.* ◆ *adv* (ˌəʊvə'hɛd). **3** over or above head height, esp. in the sky. ◆ *n* ('əʊvəˌhɛd). **4a** a stroke in racket games played from above head height. **4b** (*as modifier*): *an overhead smash.* **5** (*modifier*) of, concerned with, or resulting from overheads: *overhead costs.*

overhead camshaft *n* a type of camshaft situated above the cylinder head in an internal-combustion engine.

overhead projector *n* a projector that throws an enlarged image of a transparency onto a surface above and behind the person using it.

overheads ⓣ ('əʊvəˌhɛdz) *pl n* business expenses, such as rent, that are not directly attributable to any department or product and can therefore be assigned only arbitrarily.

overhead-valve engine *n* a type of internal-combustion engine in which the inlet and exhaust valves are in the cylinder head above the pistons. US name: **valve-in-head engine.**

overhear (ˌəʊvə'hɪə) *vb* **overhears, overhearing, overheard.** (*tr*) to hear (a person, remark, etc.) without the knowledge of the speaker.

overheat (ˌəʊvə'hi:t) *vb* **1** to make or become excessively hot. **2** (*tr; often passive*) to make very agitated, irritated, etc. **3** (*intr*) (of an economy) to tend towards inflation, often as a result of excessive growth in demand. **4** (*tr*) to cause (an economy) to tend towards inflation. ◆ *n* **5** the condition of being overheated.

overjoy ⓣ (ˌəʊvə'dʒɔɪ) *vb* (*tr*) to give great delight to.
▸ **ˌover'joyed** *adj*

overkill ('əʊvəˌkɪl) *n* **1** the capability to deploy more weapons, esp. nuclear weapons, than is necessary to ensure military advantage. **2** any capacity or treatment that is greater than that required or appropriate.

overland ('əʊvəˌlænd) *adj* (*prenominal*), *adv* **1** over or across land. ◆ *vb* **2** *Austral.* (formerly) to drive (cattle or sheep) overland.
▸ **'overˌlander** *n*

overlap *vb* (ˌəʊvə'læp), **overlaps, overlapping, overlapped. 1** (of two things) to extend or lie partly over (each other). **2** to cover and extend beyond (something). **3** (*intr*) to coincide partly in time, subject, etc. ◆ *n* ('əʊvəˌlæp). **4** a part that overlaps or is overlapped. **5** the amount, length, etc., overlapping. **6** *Geol.* the horizontal extension of the lower beds in a series of rock strata beyond the upper beds.

overlay ⓣ *vb* (ˌəʊvə'leɪ), **overlays, overlaying, overlaid.** (*tr*) **1** to lay or place over or upon (something else). **2** (often foll. by *with*) to cover, overspread, or conceal (with). **3** (foll. by *with*) to cover (a surface) with an applied decoration: *ebony overlaid with silver.* **4** to achieve the correct printing pressure all over (a forme or plate) by adding to the appropriate areas of the packing. ◆ *n* ('əʊvəˌleɪ). **5** something that is laid over something else; covering. **6** an applied decoration or layer, as of gold leaf. **7** a transparent sheet giving extra details to a map or diagram over which it is designed to be placed. **8** *Printing.* material, such as paper, used to overlay a forme or plate.

overleaf (ˌəʊvə'li:f) *adv* on the other side of the page.

overlie (ˌəʊvə'laɪ) *vb* **overlies, overlying, overlay, overlain.** (*tr*) **1** to lie or rest upon. Cf. **overlay. 2** to kill (a baby or newborn animal) by lying upon it.

overlong (ˌəʊvə'lɒŋ) *adj, adv* too or excessively long.

overlook ⓣ *vb* (ˌəʊvə'lʊk). (*tr*) **1** to fail to notice or take into account. **2** to disregard deliberately or indulgently. **3** to afford a view of from above: *the house overlooks the bay.* **4** to rise above. **5** to look at carefully. **6** to cast the evil eye upon (someone). ◆ *n* ('əʊvəˌlʊk). *US.* **7** a high place affording a view. **8** an act of overlooking.

overlord ('əʊvəˌlɔ:d) *n* a supreme lord or master.
▸ **'overˌlordship** *n*

overly ⓣ ('əʊvəlɪ) *adv* too; excessively.

overman *vb* (ˌəʊvə'mæn), **overmans, overmanning, overmanned. 1** (*tr*) to supply with an excessive number of men. ◆ *n* ('əʊvəˌmæn), *pl* **overmen. 2** a man who oversees others. **3** a superman.

overmaster (ˌəʊvə'mɑ:stə) *vb* (*tr*) to overpower.

overmatch *Chiefly US.* ◆ *vb* (ˌəʊvə'mætʃ). (*tr*) **1** to be more than a match for. **2** to match with a superior opponent. ◆ *n* ('əʊvəˌmætʃ). **3** a person superior in ability. **4** a match in which one contestant is superior.

overmuch (ˌəʊvə'mʌtʃ) *adv, adj* **1** too much; very much. ◆ *n* **2** an excessive amount.

overnice (ˌəʊvə'naɪs) *adj* too fastidious, precise, etc.

overnight *adv* (ˌəʊvə'naɪt). **1** for the duration of the night. **2** in or as if in the course of one night; suddenly: *the situation changed overnight.* ◆ *adj* ('əʊvəˌnaɪt). (*usually prenominal*) **3** done in, occurring in, or lasting the night: *an overnight stop.* **4** staying for one night. **5** for use during a single night. **6** occurring in or as if in the course of one night; sudden: *an overnight victory.*

overpass *n* ('əʊvəˌpɑ:s). **1** another name for **flyover** (sense 1). ◆ *vb* (ˌəʊvə'pɑ:s). (*tr*) *Now rare.* **2** to pass over, through, or across. **3** to exceed. **4** to ignore.

overplay (ˌəʊvə'pleɪ) *vb* **1** (*tr*) to exaggerate the importance of. **2** to act or behave in an exaggerated manner. **3 overplay one's hand.** to overestimate the worth or strength of one's position.

overpower ⓣ (ˌəʊvə'paʊə) *vb* (*tr*) **1** to conquer or subdue by superior force. **2** to have such a strong effect on as to make helpless or ineffective. **3** to supply with more power than necessary.
▸ **ˌover'powering** *adj*

overprice (ˌəʊvə'praɪs) *vb* **overprices, overpricing, overpriced.** (*tr*) to ask too high a price for.

overprint *vb* (ˌəʊvə'prɪnt). **1** (*tr*) to print (additional matter or another colour) on a sheet of paper. ◆ *n* ('əʊvəˌprɪnt). **2** additional matter or another colour printed onto a previously printed sheet. **3** additional matter applied to a finished postage stamp by printing, stamping, etc.

overqualified (ˌəʊvə'kwɒlɪfaɪd) *adj* having more managerial experience or academic qualifications than required for a particular job.

overrate ⓣ (ˌəʊvə'reɪt) *vb* **overrates, overrating, overrated.** (*tr*) to assess too highly.

overreach ⓣ (ˌəʊvə'ri:tʃ) *vb* **1** (*tr*) to defeat or thwart (oneself) by attempting to do or gain too much. **2** (*tr*) to aim for but miss by going too far. **3** to get the better of (a person) by trickery. **4** (*tr*) to reach beyond or over. **5** (*intr*) to reach or go too far. **6** (*intr*) (of a horse) to strike the back of a forefoot with the edge of the opposite hind foot.

overreact (ˌəʊvərɪ'ækt) *vb* (*intr*) to react excessively to something.
▸ **ˌoverre'action** *n*

override ⓣ *vb* (ˌəʊvə'raɪd), **overrides, overriding, overrode, overridden.** (*tr*) **1** to set aside or disregard with superior authority or power. **2** to supersede or annul. **3** to dominate or vanquish by or as if by trampling down. **4** to take manual control of (a system that is usually under automatic control). **5** to extend or pass over, esp. to overlap. **6** to ride (a horse, etc.) too hard. **7** to ride over. ◆ *n* ('əʊvəˌraɪd). **8** a device that can override an automatic control.

overrider ('əʊvəˌraɪdə) *n* either of two attachments fitted to the bumper of a motor vehicle to prevent it interlocking with that of another vehicle.

overriding ⓣ (ˌəʊvə'raɪdɪŋ) *adj* taking precedence.

overrule ⓣ (ˌəʊvə'ru:l) *vb* **overrules, overruling, overruled.** (*tr*) **1** to disallow the arguments of (a person) by the use of authority. **2** to rule or decide against (an argument, decision, etc.). **3** to prevail over, dominate, or influence. **4** to exercise rule over.

overrun ⓣ *vb* (ˌəʊvə'rʌn), **overruns, overrunning, overran, overrun. 1** (*tr*) to swarm or spread over rapidly. **2** to run over (something); overflow. **3**

THESAURUS

inspect, recondition, re-examine, repair, restore, service, survey **3 = overtake**, catch up with, draw level with, get ahead of, pass ◆ *n* **4 = checkup**, check, examination, going-over (*inf.*), inspection, reconditioning, service

overhead *adj* **1 = aerial**, overhanging, roof, upper ◆ *adv* **3 = above**, aloft, atop, in the sky, on high, skyward, up above, upward
Antonyms *adv* ≠ **above:** below, beneath, downward, underfoot, underneath

overheads *pl n* **= running costs**, burden, oncosts, operating costs

overjoyed *adj* **= delighted**, cock-a-hoop, deliriously happy, elated, euphoric, floating on air, happy as a lark, in raptures, joyful, jubilant, on cloud nine (*inf.*), only too happy, over the moon (*inf.*), rapt, rapturous, thrilled, tickled pink (*inf.*), transported
Antonyms *adj* crestfallen, dejected, disappointed, downcast, down in the dumps (*inf.*), heartbroken, miserable, sad, unhappy, woebegone

overlay *vb* **2, 3 = cover**, adorn, blanket, inlay, laminate, ornament, overspread, superimpose, veneer ◆ *n* **5, 6 = covering**, adornment, appliqué, decoration, ornamentation, veneer

overlook *vb* **1 = miss**, disregard, fail to notice, forget, leave out of consideration, leave undone, neglect, omit, pass, slight, slip up on **2 = ignore**, blink at, condone, disregard, excuse, forgive, let bygones be bygones, let one off with, let pass, let ride, make allowances for, pardon, turn a blind eye to, wink at **3 = have a view of**, afford a view of, command a view of, front on to, give upon, look over *or* out on
Antonyms *vb* ≠ **miss:** discern, heed, mark, note, notice, observe, perceive, regard, spot

overly *adv* **= excessively**, exceedingly, immoderately, inordinately, over, too, unduly, very much

overpower *vb* **1 = overwhelm**, beat, clobber, conquer, crush, defeat, get the upper hand over, immobilize, knock out, lick (*inf.*), make mincemeat of (*inf.*), master, overcome, overthrow, quell, subdue, subjugate, vanquish

overpowering *adj* **2 = overwhelming**, compelling, compulsive, extreme, forceful, invincible, irrefutable, irresistible, nauseating, powerful, sickening, strong, suffocating, telling, unbearable, uncontrollable

overrate *vb* **= overestimate**, assess too highly, exaggerate, make too much of, overpraise, overprize, oversell, overvalue, rate too highly, think *or* expect too much of, think too highly of

overreach *vb* **1 overreach oneself = try to be too clever**, be hoist with one's own petard, bite off more than one can chew, defeat one's own ends, go too far **3 = trick**, cheat, circumvent, deceive, defraud, dupe, gull (*arch.*), outsmart (*inf.*), outwit, swindle, victimize

override *vb* **1, 2 = overrule**, annul, cancel, countermand, discount, disregard, ignore, nullify, outweigh, quash, reverse, ride roughshod over, set aside, supersede, take no account of, trample underfoot, upset

overriding *adj* **= predominant**, cardinal, compelling, determining, dominant, final, major, mother of all (*inf.*), number one, overruling, paramount, pivotal, prevailing, primary, prime, ruling, supreme, ultimate
Antonyms *adj* immaterial, inconsequential, insignificant, irrelevant, minor, negligible, paltry, petty, trifling, trivial, unimportant

overrule *vb* **1 = reverse**, alter, annul, cancel, countermand, disallow, invalidate, make null and void, outvote, override, overturn, recall, repeal, rescind, revoke, rule against, set aside, veto **3 = influence**, bend to one's will, control, direct, dominate, govern, prevail over, sway
Antonyms *vb* ≠ **reverse:** allow, approve, consent to, endorse, pass, permit, sanction

overrun *vb* **1 = spread over**, choke, infest, inundate, overflow, overgrow, permeate, ravage,

to extend or run beyond a limit. **4** (*intr*) (of an engine) to run with a closed throttle at a speed dictated by that of the vehicle it drives. **5** (*tr*) to print (a book, journal, etc.) in a greater quantity than ordered. **6** (*tr*) *Printing.* to transfer (set type) from one column, line, or page, to another. **7** (*tr*) *Arch.* to run faster than. ◆ *n* ('əʊvəˌrʌn). **8** the act or an instance of overrunning. **9** the amount or extent of overrunning. **10** the number of copies of a publication in excess of the quantity ordered.

overseas *adv* (ˌəʊvə'siːz). **1** beyond the sea; abroad. ◆ *adj* ('əʊvə'siːz). **2** of, to, in, from, or situated in countries beyond the sea. **3** Also: **oversea.** of or relating to passage over the sea. ◆ *n* (ˌəʊvə'siːz). **4** (*functioning as sing*) *Inf.* a foreign country or foreign countries collectively.

overseas territory *n* See **United Kingdom overseas territory.**

oversee (ˌəʊvə'siː) *vb* **oversees, overseeing, oversaw, overseen.** (*tr*) **1** to watch over and direct; supervise. **2** to watch secretly or accidentally. **3** *Arch.* to scrutinize; inspect.

overseer ⓣ ('əʊvəˌsiːə) *n* **1** a person who oversees others, esp. workmen. **2** *Brit. history.* a minor official of a parish attached to the poorhouse.

oversell (ˌəʊvə'sɛl) *vb* **oversells, overselling, oversold. 1** (*tr*) to sell more of (a commodity, etc.) than can be supplied. **2** to use excessively aggressive methods in selling (commodities). **3** (*tr*) to exaggerate the merits of.

overset (ˌəʊvə'sɛt) *vb* **oversets, oversetting, overset.** (*tr*) **1** to disturb or upset. **2** *Printing.* to set (type or copy) in excess of the space available.

oversew ('əʊvəˌsəʊ, ˌəʊvə'səʊ) *vb* **oversews, oversewing, oversewed; oversewn** *or* **oversewed.** to sew (two edges) with close stitches that pass over them both.

oversexed (ˌəʊvə'sɛkst) *adj* having an excessive preoccupation with sexual activity.

overshadow ⓣ (ˌəʊvə'ʃædəʊ) *vb* (*tr*) **1** to render insignificant or less important in comparison. **2** to cast a shadow or gloom over.

overshoe ('əʊvəˌʃuː) *n* a protective shoe worn over an ordinary shoe.

overshoot *vb* (ˌəʊvə'ʃuːt), **overshoots, overshooting, overshot. 1** to shoot or go beyond (a mark or target). **2** (of an aircraft) to fly or taxi too far along a runway. **3** (*tr*) to pass swiftly over or down over, as water over a wheel. ◆ *n* ('əʊvəˌʃuːt). **4** an act or instance of overshooting. **5** the extent of such overshooting.

overshot ('əʊvəˌʃɒt) *adj* **1** having or designating an upper jaw that projects beyond the lower jaw. **2** (of a water wheel) driven by a flow of water that passes over the wheel.

oversight ⓣ ('əʊvəˌsaɪt) *n* **1** an omission or mistake, esp. one made through failure to notice something. **2** supervision.

oversize *adj* (ˌəʊvə'saɪz). **1** Also: **oversized.** larger than the usual size. ◆ *n* ('əʊvəˌsaɪz). **2** a size larger than the usual or proper size. **3** something that is oversize.

overskirt ('əʊvəˌskɜːt) *n* an outer skirt, esp. one that reveals a decorative underskirt.

overspend *vb* (ˌəʊvə'spɛnd), **overspends, overspending, overspent. 1** to spend in excess of (one's desires or what one can afford or is allocated). **2** (*tr; usually passive*) to wear out; exhaust. ◆ *n* ('əʊvəˌspɛnd). **3** the amount by which someone or something is overspent.

overspill *n* ('əʊvəˌspɪl). **1a** something that spills over or is in excess. **1b** (*as modifier*): *overspill population.* ◆ *vb* (ˌəʊvə'spɪl), **overspills, overspilling, overspilt** *or* **overspilled. 2** (*intr*) to overflow.

overspread (ˌəʊvə'sprɛd) *vb* (*tr*) **overspreads, overspreading, overspread.** to extend or spread over.

overstate (ˌəʊvə'steɪt) *vb* **overstates, overstating, overstated.** (*tr*) to state too strongly; exaggerate or overemphasize.
▸ **ˌover'statement** *n*

overstay (ˌəʊvə'steɪ) *vb* (*tr*) **1** to stay beyond the time, limit, or duration of. **2 overstay** *or* **outstay one's welcome.** to stay (at a party, etc.), longer than pleases the host or hostess.

overstep (ˌəʊvə'stɛp) *vb* **oversteps, overstepping, overstepped.** (*tr*) to go beyond (a certain or proper limit).

overstrung (ˌəʊvə'strʌŋ) *adj* **1** too highly strung; tense. **2** (of a piano) having two sets of strings crossing each other at an oblique angle.

overstuff (ˌəʊvə'stʌf) *vb* (*tr*) **1** to force too much into. **2** to cover (furniture, etc.) entirely with upholstery.

oversubscribe (ˌəʊvəsəb'skraɪb) *vb* **oversubscribes, oversubscribing, oversubscribed.** (*tr; often passive*) to subscribe or apply for in excess of available supply.
▸ **ˌoversub'scription** *n*

overt ⓣ ('əʊvɜːt, əʊ'vɜːt) *adj* **1** open to view; observable. **2** *Law.* open; deliberate. [C14: via OF, from *ovrir* to open, from L *aperīre*]
▸ **'overtly** *adv*

overtake ⓣ (ˌəʊvə'teɪk) *vb* **overtakes, overtaking, overtook, overtaken. 1** *Chiefly Brit.* to move past (another vehicle or person) travelling in the same direction. **2** (*tr*) to pass or do better than, after catching up with. **3** (*tr*) to come upon suddenly or unexpectedly: *night overtook him.* **4** (*tr*) to catch up with; draw level with.

overtax (ˌəʊvə'tæks) *vb* (*tr*) **1** to tax too heavily. **2** to impose too great a strain on.

over-the-counter *adj* **1** (of a stock exchange dealing) conducted between brokers in areas for which no official market prices are quoted. **2** (of a medicinal drug) able to be sold without prescription. Cf. **POM.** ◆ Abbrev.: **OTC.**

overthrow ⓣ *vb* (ˌəʊvə'θrəʊ), **overthrows, overthrowing, overthrew, overthrown. 1** (*tr*) to effect the downfall or destruction of (a ruler, institution, etc.), esp. by force. **2** (*tr*) to throw or turn over. **3** to throw (something, esp. a ball) too far. ◆ *n* ('əʊvəˌθrəʊ). **4** downfall; destruction. **5** *Cricket.* **5a** a ball thrown back too far by a fielder. **5b** a run scored because of this.

overthrust ('əʊvəˌθrʌst) *n Geol.* a reverse fault in which the rocks on the upper surface of a fault plane have moved over the rocks on the lower surface.

overtime *n* ('əʊvəˌtaɪm). **1a** work at a regular job done in addition to regular working hours. **1b** (*as modifier*): *overtime pay.* **2** the rate of pay established for such work. **3** time in excess of a set period. **4** *Sport, US & Canad.* extra time. ◆ *adv* ('əʊvəˌtaɪm). **5** beyond the regular or stipulated time. ◆ *vb* (ˌəʊvə'taɪm), **overtimes, overtiming, overtimed. 6** (*tr*) to exceed the required time for (a photographic exposure, etc.).

overtone ⓣ ('əʊvəˌtəʊn) *n* **1** (*often pl*) additional meaning or nuance: *overtones of despair.* **2** *Music, acoustics.* any of the tones, with the exception of the fundamental, that constitute a musical sound and contribute to its quality.

overture ⓣ ('əʊvəˌtjʊə) *n* **1** *Music.* **1a** a piece of orchestral music that is played at the beginning of an opera or oratorio, often containing the main musical themes of the work. **1b** a one-movement orchestral piece, usually having a descriptive or evocative title. **2** (*often pl*) a proposal, act, or gesture initiating a relationship, negotiation, etc. **3** something that introduces what follows. ◆ *vb* **overtures, overturing, overtured.** (*tr*) **4** to make or present an overture to. **5** to introduce with an overture. [C14: via OF from LL *apertūra* opening, from L *aperīre* to open]

overturn ⓣ *vb* (ˌəʊvə'tɜːn). **1** to turn or cause to turn from an upright or normal position. **2** (*tr*) to overthrow or destroy. **3** (*tr*) to invalidate; reverse. ◆ *n* ('əʊvəˌtɜːn). **4** the act of overturning or the state of being overturned.

overuse ⓣ *vb* (ˌəʊvə'juːz), **overuses, overusing, overused. 1** (*tr*) to use excessively. ◆ *n* (ˌəʊvə'juːs) **2** excessive use.

overview ('əʊvəˌvjuː) *n* a general survey.

overweening ⓣ (ˌəʊvə'wiːnɪŋ) *adj* **1** (of a person) excessively arrogant or presumptuous. **2** (of opinions, appetites, etc.) excessive; immoderate. [C14: from OVER + *weening* from OE *wēnan* WEEN]
▸ **ˌover'weeningness** *n*

overweight ⓣ *adj* (ˌəʊvə'weɪt). **1** weighing more than is usual, allowed, or healthy. ◆ *n* ('əʊvəˌweɪt). **2** extra or excess weight. ◆ *vb*

THESAURUS

spread like wildfire, surge over, swarm over **3** = **exceed**, go beyond, overshoot, run over *or* on

overseer *n* **1** = **supervisor**, boss, chief, foreman, gaffer (*inf., chiefly Brit.*), manager, master, super (*inf.*), superintendent, superior

overshadow *vb* **1** = **outshine**, dominate, dwarf, eclipse, excel, leave *or* put in the shade, outweigh, rise above, steal the limelight from, surpass, take precedence over, throw into the shade, tower above **2** = **spoil**, blight, cast a gloom upon, cloud, darken, mar, put a damper on, ruin, take the edge off, take the pleasure *or* enjoyment out of, temper

oversight *n* **1** = **mistake**, blunder, carelessness, delinquency, error, fault, inattention, lapse, laxity, neglect, omission, slip **2** = **supervision**, administration, care, charge, control, custody, direction, handling, inspection, keeping, management, superintendence, surveillance

overt *adj* **1** = **open**, apparent, blatant, bold, manifest, observable, obvious, patent, plain, public, unconcealed, undisguised, visible
Antonyms *adj* concealed, covert, disguised, hidden, hush-hush (*inf.*), invisible, secret, surreptitious, underhand

overtake *vb* **1, 2** = **pass**, get past, leave behind, outdistance, outdo, outstrip, overhaul **3** = **befall**, catch unprepared, come upon, engulf, happen, hit, overwhelm, strike, take by surprise **4** = **catch up with**, draw level with

overthrow *vb* **1** = **defeat**, abolish, beat, bring down, conquer, crush, depose, dethrone, do away with, master, oust, overcome, overpower, overwhelm, subdue, subjugate, topple, unseat, vanquish ◆ *n* **4** = **downfall**, defeat, deposition, destruction, dethronement, discomfiture, disestablishment, displacement, dispossession, end, fall, ousting, prostration, rout, ruin, subjugation, subversion, suppression, undoing, unseating
Antonyms *vb* ≠ **defeat:** defend, guard, keep, maintain, preserve, protect, restore, support, uphold ◆ *n* ≠ **downfall:** defence, preservation, protection

overtone *n* **1** *often plural* = **hint**, association, connotation, flavour, implication, innuendo, intimation, nuance, sense, suggestion, undercurrent

overture *n* **1a** *Music* = **introduction**, opening, prelude **2** *often plural* = **approach**, advance, conciliatory move, invitation, offer, opening move, proposal, proposition, signal, tender
Antonyms *n* ≠ **introduction:** coda, finale ≠ **approach:** rebuke, rejection, withdrawal

overturn *vb* **1** = **tip over**, capsize, keel over, knock over *or* down, overbalance, reverse, spill, topple, tumble, upend, upset, upturn **2, 3** = **overthrow**, abolish, annul, bring down, countermand, depose, destroy, invalidate, obviate, repeal, rescind, reverse, set aside, unseat

overused *adj* **1** = **hackneyed**, cliché'd, platitudinous, played out, stale, stereotyped, threadbare, tired, unoriginal, worn (out)

overweening *adj* **1** = **arrogant**, cavalier, cocksure, cocky, conceited, egotistical, haughty, high and mighty (*inf.*), high-handed, insolent, lordly, opinionated, pompous, presumptuous, proud, self-confident, supercilious, uppish (*Brit. inf.*), vain, vainglorious **2** = **excessive**, blown up out of all proportion, extravagant, immoderate
Antonyms *adj* ≠ **arrogant:** deferential, diffident, hesitant, modest, self-conscious, self-effacing, timid, unassuming, unobtrusive

overweight *adj* **1** = **fat**, ample, bulky, buxom, chubby, chunky, corpulent, fleshy, gross,

(ˌəʊvəˈweɪt). (*tr*) **3** to give too much emphasis or consideration to. **4** to add too much weight to. **5** to weigh down.

overwhelm ❶ (ˌəʊvəˈwɛlm) *vb* (*tr*) **1** to overpower the thoughts, emotions, or senses of. **2** to overcome with irresistible force. **3** to cover over or bury completely. **4** to weigh or rest upon overpoweringly.
▸ **ˌoverˈwhelming** *adj*

overwind (ˌəʊvəˈwaɪnd) *vb* **overwinds, overwinding, overwound.** (*tr*) to wind (a watch, etc.) beyond the proper limit.

overwork ❶ *vb* (ˌəʊvəˈwɜːk). (*mainly tr*) **1** (*also intr*) to work too hard or too long. **2** to use too much: *to overwork an excuse.* **3** to decorate the surface of. ◆ *n* (ˈəʊvəˌwɜːk). **4** excessive or excessively tiring work.

overwrite (ˌəʊvəˈraɪt) *vb* **overwrites, overwriting, overwrote, overwritten. 1** to write (something) in an excessively ornate style. **2** to write too much about (someone or something). **3** to write on top of (other writing). **4** to record on a storage medium, such as a magnetic disk, thus destroying what was originally recorded there.

overwrought ❶ (ˌəʊvəˈrɔːt) *adj* **1** full of nervous tension; agitated. **2** too elaborate; fussy: *an overwrought style.* **3** (*often postpositive* and foll. by *with*) with the surface decorated or adorned.

ovi- *or* **ovo-** *combining form.* egg or ovum: *oviform; ovoviviparous.* [from L *ōvum*]

oviduct (ˈɒvɪˌdʌkt, ˈəʊ-) *n* the tube through which ova are conveyed from an ovary. Also called (in mammals): **Fallopian tube.**
▸ **oviducal** (ˌɒvɪˈdjuːkᵊl, ˌəʊ-) *or* **ˌoviˈductal** *adj*

oviform (ˈəʊvɪˌfɔːm) *adj Biol.* shaped like an egg.

ovine (ˈəʊvaɪn) *adj* of, relating to, or resembling a sheep. [C19: from LL *ovīnus*, from L *ovis* sheep]

oviparous (əʊˈvɪpərəs) *adj* (of fishes, reptiles, birds, etc.) producing eggs that hatch outside the body of the mother. Cf. **ovoviviparous, viviparous** (sense 1).
▸ **oviparity** (ˌəʊvɪˈpærɪtɪ) *n* ▸ **oˈviparously** *adv*

ovipositor (ˌəʊvɪˈpɒzɪtə) *n* **1** the egg-laying organ of most female insects, consisting of a pair of specialized appendages at the end of the abdomen. **2** a similar organ in certain female fishes, formed by an extension of the edges of the genital opening. [C19:from OVI- + L *positor*, from *ponere* to place]
▸ **ˌoviˈposit** *vb* (*intr*)

ovoid (ˈəʊvɔɪd) *adj* **1** egg-shaped. ◆ *n* **2** something that is ovoid.

ovoviviparous (ˌəʊvəʊvaɪˈvɪpərəs) *adj* (of certain reptiles, fishes, etc.) producing eggs that hatch within the body of the mother. Cf. **oviparous, viviparous** (sense 1).
▸ **ovoviviparity** (ˌəʊvəʊˌvaɪvɪˈpærɪtɪ) *n*

ovulate (ˈɒvjʊˌleɪt) *vb* **ovulates, ovulating, ovulated.** (*intr*) to produce or discharge eggs from an ovary. [C19: from OVULE]
▸ **ˌovuˈlation** *n*

ovulation method *n* another name for **Billings method.**

ovule (ˈɒvjuːl) *n* **1** a small body in seed-bearing plants that contains the egg cell and develops into the seed after fertilization. **2** *Zool.* an immature ovum. [C19: via F from Med. L *ōvulum* a little egg, from L *ōvum* egg]
▸ **ˈovular** *adj*

ovum (ˈəʊvəm) *n, pl* **ova.** an unfertilized female gamete; egg cell. [from L: egg]

ow (aʊ) *interj* an exclamation of pain.

owe ❶ (əʊ) *vb* **owes, owing, owed.** (*mainly tr*) **1** to be under an obligation to pay (someone) to the amount of. **2** (*intr*) to be in debt: *he still owes for his house.* **3** (often foll. by *to*) to have as a result (of). **4** to feel the need or obligation to do, give, etc. **5** to hold or maintain in the mind or heart (esp. in **owe a grudge**). [OE *āgan* to have (C12: to have to)]

Owen gun (ˈəʊɪn) *n* a type of simple recoil-operated sub-machine-gun first used by Australian forces in World War II. [after E. E. *Owen* (1915–49), its Austral. inventor]

owing ❶ (ˈəʊɪŋ) *adj* **1** (*postpositive*) owed; due. **2 owing to.** because of or on account of.

owl (aʊl) *n* **1** a nocturnal bird of prey having large front-facing eyes, a small hooked bill, soft feathers, and a short neck. **2** any of various breeds of owl-like fancy domestic pigeon. **3** a person who looks or behaves like an owl, esp. in having a solemn manner. [OE *ūle*]
▸ **ˈowlish** *adj* ▸ **ˈowl-ˌlike** *adj*

owlet (ˈaʊlɪt) *n* a young or nestling owl.

own ❶ (əʊn) *determiner* (*preceded by a possessive*) **1a** (intensifier): *John's own idea.* **1b** (*as pron*): *I'll use my own.* **2** on behalf of oneself or in relation to oneself: *he is his own worst enemy.* **3 come into one's own. 3a** to become fulfilled: *she really came into her own when she got divorced.* **3b** to receive what is due to one. **4 hold one's own.** to maintain one's situation or position, esp. in spite of opposition or difficulty. **5 on one's own. 5a** without help. **5b** by oneself; alone. ◆ *vb* **6** (*tr*) to have as one's possession. **7** (when *intr*, often foll. by *up, to,* or *up to*) to confess or admit; acknowledge. **8** (*tr; takes a clause as object*) *Now rare.* to concede: *I own that you are right.* [OE *āgen*, orig. p.p. of *āgan* to have. See OWE]
▸ **ˈowner** *n* ▸ **ˈownership** *n*

own brand *n* a product which displays the name of the retailer rather than the producer.

owner-occupier *n* someone who has bought or is buying the house in which he lives.

own goal *n* **1** *Soccer.* a goal scored by a player accidentally playing the ball into his own team's net. **2** *Inf.* any action that results in disadvantage to the person who took it or to his associates.

ox (ɒks) *n, pl* **oxen. 1** an adult castrated male of any domesticated species of cattle used for draught work and meat. **2** any bovine mammal, esp. any of the domestic cattle. [OE *oxa*]

oxalic acid (ɒkˈsælɪk) *n* a colourless poisonous crystalline acid found in many plants: used as a bleach and a cleansing agent for metals. Formula: $(COOH)_2$. Recommended name: **ethanedioic acid.** [C18: from F *oxalique*, from L *oxalis* garden sorrel; see OXALIS]

oxalis (ˈɒksəlɪs, ɒkˈsælɪs) *n* a plant having clover-like leaves which contain oxalic acid and white, pink, red, or yellow flowers. See also **wood sorrel.** [C18: via L from Gk: sorrel, sour wine, from *oxus* acid, sharp]

oxblood (ˈɒksˌblʌd) *or* **oxblood red** *adj* of a dark reddish-brown colour.

oxbow (ˈɒksˌbəʊ) *n* **1** a U-shaped piece of wood fitted under and around the neck of a harnessed ox and attached to the yoke. **2** Also called: **oxbow lake.** a small curved lake lying on the flood plain of a river and constituting the remnant of a former meander.

Oxbridge (ˈɒksˌbrɪdʒ) *n* **a** the British universities of Oxford and Cambridge, esp. considered as ancient and prestigious academic institutions, bastions of privilege and superiority, etc. **b** (*as modifier*): *Oxbridge graduates.*

oxen (ˈɒksən) *n* the plural of **ox.**

oxeye (ˈɒksˌaɪ) *n* **1** a Eurasian composite plant having daisy-like flower heads with yellow rays and dark centres. **2** any of various North American plants having daisy-like flowers. **3 oxeye daisy.** a type of hardy perennial chrysanthemum.

ox-eyed *adj* having large round eyes, like those of an ox.

Oxfam (ˈɒksˌfæm) *n acronym for* Oxford Committee for Famine Relief.

Oxford (ˈɒksfəd) *n* (*sometimes not cap.*) **1** a type of stout laced shoe with a low heel. **2** a lightweight fabric of plain or twill weave used for men's shirts, etc. [from *Oxford*, city in S England]

Oxford bags *pl n* trousers with very wide baggy legs.

Oxford blue *n* **1a** a dark blue colour. **1b** (*as adj*): *an Oxford-blue scarf.* **2** a person who has been awarded a blue from Oxford University.

Oxford Movement *n* a movement within the Church of England that began at Oxford in 1833. It affirmed the continuity of the Church with early Christianity and strove to restore the High-Church ideals of the 17th century. Also called: **Tractarianism.**

oxidant (ˈɒksɪdənt) *n* a substance that acts or is used as an oxidizing agent. Also called (esp. in rocketry): **oxidizer.**

oxidation (ˌɒksɪˈdeɪʃən) *n* **a** the act or process of oxidizing. **b** (*as modifier*): *an oxidation state.*
▸ **ˈoxiˌdate** *vb* ▸ **ˌoxiˈdational** *adj* ▸ **ˈoxiˌdative** *adj*

oxidation-reduction *n* **a** a reversible chemical process usually involving the transfer of electrons, in which one reaction is an oxidation

THESAURUS

heavy, hefty, huge, massive, obese, outsize, plump, podgy, portly, stout, tubby (*inf.*)
Antonyms *adj* emaciated, gaunt, lean, pinched, scraggy, scrawny, skinny, thin, underweight

overwhelm *vb* **1 = overcome,** bowl over (*inf.*), confuse, devastate, knock (someone) for six (*inf.*), make mincemeat of, overpower, prostrate, render speechless, stagger, sweep (someone) off his *or* her feet, take (someone's) breath away **2 = destroy,** crush, cut to pieces, massacre, overpower, overrun, rout **3 = submerge,** bury, crush, deluge, engulf, flood, inundate, snow under, swamp

overwhelming *adj* **1 = overpowering,** breathtaking, crushing, devastating, invincible, irresistible, shattering, stunning, towering, uncontrollable, vast, vastly superior
Antonyms *adj* commonplace, incidental, insignificant, negligible, paltry, resistible, trivial, unimportant

overwork *vb* **1 = strain (oneself),** burn the candle at both ends, burn the midnight oil, drive into the ground, exhaust (oneself), fatigue (oneself), overstrain (oneself), overtax (oneself), sweat (*inf.*), wear (oneself) out, weary (oneself), work one's fingers to the bone

overwrought *adj* **1 = agitated,** beside oneself, distracted, excited, frantic, in a state, keyed up, on edge, overexcited, overworked, strung out (*inf.*), tense, uptight (*inf.*), wired (*sl.*), worked up (*inf.*), wound up (*inf.*) **2 = overelaborate,** baroque, busy, contrived, florid, flowery, fussy, overdone, overembellished, overornate, rococo
Antonyms *adj* ≠ **agitated:** calm, collected, controlled, cool, dispassionate, emotionless, impassive, self-contained, unfazed (*inf.*), unmoved

owe *vb* **1, 2 = be in debt,** be beholden (to), be in arrears, be obligated *or* indebted, be under an obligation (to)

owing *adj* **1 = unpaid,** due, outstanding, overdue, owed, payable, unsettled **2 owing to = because of,** as a result of, on account of

own *determiner* **2 = personal,** individual, particular, private **4 hold one's own = keep up,** compete, do well, hold fast, hold out, keep one's end up, keep one's head above water, keep pace, maintain one's position, stand firm, stand one's ground, stay put, stick to one's guns (*inf.*) **5 on one's own: a = alone,** by one's own efforts, independently, off one's own bat, singly, (standing) on one's own two feet, unaided, unassisted, under one's own steam **b** by oneself, left to one's own devices, on one's tod (*Brit. sl.*) ◆ *vb* **6 = possess,** be in possession of, be responsible for, enjoy, have, hold, keep, retain **7 = acknowledge,** admit, allow, allow to be valid, avow, concede, confess, disclose, go along with, grant, recognize

owner *n* **6 = possessor,** holder, landlord *or* landlady, lord, master *or* mistress, proprietor, proprietress, proprietrix

ownership *n* **6 = possession,** dominion, proprietary rights, proprietorship, right of possession, title

and the reverse reaction is a reduction. **b** (*as modifier*): *an oxidation-reduction reaction.* ◆ Also: **redox.**

oxide ('ɒksaɪd) *n* **1** any compound of oxygen with another element. **2** any organic compound in which an oxygen atom is bound to two alkyl groups; an ether. [C18: from F, from *ox(ygène)* + *(ac)ide*]

oxidize *or* **oxidise** ('ɒksɪˌdaɪz) *vb* **oxidizes, oxidizing, oxidized** *or* **oxidises, oxidising, oxidised. 1** to undergo or cause to undergo a chemical reaction with oxygen, as in formation of an oxide. **2** to form or cause to form a layer of metal oxide, as in rusting. **3** to lose or cause to lose hydrogen atoms. **4** to undergo or cause to undergo a decrease in the number of electrons.
▸**ˌoxidiˈzation** *or* **ˌoxidiˈsation** *n*

oxidizing agent *n Chem.* a substance that oxidizes another substance, being itself reduced in the process.

oxlip ('ɒksˌlɪp) *n* **1** a Eurasian woodland plant, with small drooping pale yellow flowers. **2** a similar and related plant that is a natural hybrid between the cowslip and primrose. [OE *oxanslyppe,* lit.: ox's slippery dropping; see SLIP[3]]

oxo acid ('ɒksəʊ) *n* another name for **oxyacid.**

Oxon *abbrev. for* Oxfordshire. [from L *Oxonia*]

Oxon. *abbrev. for* (in degree titles, etc.) of Oxford. [from L *Oxoniensis*]

Oxonian (ɒk'səʊnɪən) *adj* **1** of or relating to Oxford or Oxford University. ◆ *n* **2** a member of Oxford University. **3** an inhabitant or native of Oxford.

oxpecker ('ɒksˌpɛkə) *n* either of two African starlings, having flattened bills with which they obtain food from the hides of cattle. Also called: **tick-bird.**

oxtail ('ɒksˌteɪl) *n* the skinned tail of an ox, used esp. in soups and stews.

oxter ('əʊkstə) *n Scot., Irish, & N English dialect.* the armpit. [C16: from OE *oxta*]

oxtongue ('ɒksˌtʌŋ) *n* **1** any of various Eurasian composite plants having oblong bristly leaves and clusters of dandelion-like flowers. **2** any of various other plants having bristly tongue-shaped leaves. **3** the tongue of an ox, braised or boiled as food.

oxy-[1] *combining form.* denoting something sharp; acute: *oxytone.* [from Gk, from *oxus*]

oxy-[2] *combining form.* containing or using oxygen: *oxyacetylene.*

oxyacetylene (ˌɒksɪə'sɛtɪˌliːn) *n* **a** a mixture of oxygen and acetylene; used in torches for cutting or welding metals at high temperatures. **b** (*as modifier*): *an oxyacetylene burner.*

oxyacid (ˌɒksɪ'æsɪd) *n* any acid that contains oxygen with the acidic hydrogen atoms bound to oxygen atoms. Also called: **oxo acid.**

oxygen ('ɒksɪdʒən) *n* **a** a colourless odourless highly reactive gaseous element: the most abundant element in the earth's crust. Symbol: O; atomic no.: 8; atomic wt.: 15.9994. **b** (*as modifier*): *an oxygen mask.*
▸**oxygenic** (ˌɒksɪ'dʒɛnɪk) *or* **oxygenous** (ɒk'sɪdʒɪnəs) *adj*

oxygenate ('ɒksɪdʒɪˌneɪt) *or* **oxygenize, oxygenise** *vb* **oxygenates, oxygenating, oxygenated** *or* **oxygenizes, oxygenizing, oxygenized; oxygenises, oxygenising, oxygenised.** to enrich or be enriched with oxygen: *to oxygenate blood.*
▸**ˌoxygenˈation** *n* ▸**ˈoxygenˌizer** *or* **ˈoxygenˌiser** *n*

oxygen tent *n Med.* a transparent enclosure covering a bedridden patient, into which oxygen is released to help maintain respiration.

oxyhaemoglobin (ˌɒksɪˌhiːməʊ'gləʊbɪn) *n Biochem.* the bright red product formed when oxygen from the lungs combines with haemoglobin in the blood.

oxyhydrogen (ˌɒksɪ'haɪdrɪdʒən) *n* **a** a mixture of hydrogen and oxygen used to provide an intense flame for welding. **b** (*as modifier*): *an oxyhydrogen blowpipe.*

oxymoron (ˌɒksɪ'mɔːrɒn) *n, pl* **oxymora** (-'mɔːrə). *Rhetoric.* an epigrammatic effect, by which contradictory terms are used in conjunction: *living death.* [C17: via NL from Gk *oxumōron,* from *oxus* sharp + *mōros* stupid]

oyer and terminer ('ɔɪə; 'tɜːmɪnə) *n* **1** *English law.* (formerly) a commission issued to judges to try cases on assize. **2** the court in which such a hearing was held. [C15: from Anglo-Norman, from *oyer* to hear + *terminer* to judge]

oyez *or* **oyes** ('əʊ'jɛs, -'jɛz) *sentence substitute.* **1** a cry, usually uttered three times, by a public crier or court official for silence and attention before making a proclamation. ◆ *n* **2** such a cry. [C15: via Anglo-Norman from OF *oiez!* hear!]

-oyl *suffix of nouns* (in chemistry) indicating an acyl group or radical: *ethanoyl, methanoyl.* [C20: from O(XYGEN) + -YL]

oyster ('ɔɪstə) *n* **1a** an edible marine bivalve mollusc having a rough irregularly shaped shell and occurring on the sea bed, mostly in coastal waters. **1b** (*as modifier*): *oyster farm; oyster knife.* **2** any of various similar and related molluscs, such as the pearl oyster and the saddle oyster. **3** the oyster-shaped piece of dark meat in the hollow of the pelvic bone of a fowl. **4** something from which advantage, delight, profit, etc., may be derived: *the world is his oyster.* **5** *Inf.* a very uncommunicative person. ◆ *vb* **6** (*intr*) to dredge for, gather, or raise oysters. [C14 *oistre,* from OF *uistre,* from L *ostrea,* from Gk *ostreon;* rel. to Gk *osteon* bone, *ostrakon* shell]

oyster bed *n* a place, esp. on the sea bed, where oysters breed and grow naturally or are cultivated for food or pearls. Also called: **oyster bank, oyster park.**

oystercatcher ('ɔɪstəˌkætʃə) *n* a shore bird having a black or black-and-white plumage and a long stout laterally compressed red bill.

oyster crab *n* any of several small soft-bodied crabs that live as commensals in the mantles of oysters.

oyster plant *n* **1** another name for **salsify** (sense 1). **2** Also called: **sea lungwort.** a prostrate coastal plant with clusters of blue flowers.

oz *or* **oz.** *abbrev. for* ounce. [from It. *onza*]

Oz (ɒz) *n Austral. sl.* Australia.

Ozalid ('ɒzəlɪd) *n* **1** *Trademark.* a method of duplicating type matter, illustrations, etc., when printed on translucent paper. **2** a reproduction produced by this method.

ozocerite *or* **ozokerite** (əʊ'zəʊkəˌraɪt) *n* a brown or greyish wax that occurs associated with petroleum and is used for making candles and waxed paper. [C19: from G *Ozokerit,* from Gk *ozein* odour + *kēros* beeswax]

ozone ('əʊzəʊn, əʊ'zəʊn) *n* **1** a colourless gas with a chlorine-like odour, formed by an electric discharge in oxygen: a strong oxidizing agent, used in bleaching, sterilizing water, purifying air, etc. Formula: O_3. Technical name: **trioxygen. 2** *Inf.* clean bracing air, as found at the seaside. [C19: from G *Ozon,* from Gk: smell]
▸**ozonic** (əʊ'zɒnɪk) *or* **ˈozonous** *adj*

ozone-friendly *adj* not harmful to the ozone layer; using substances that do not produce gases harmful to the ozone layer: *an ozone-friendly refrigerator.*

ozone layer *n* the region of the stratosphere with the highest concentration of ozone molecules, which by absorbing high-energy solar ultraviolet radiation protects organisms on earth. Also called: **ozonosphere.**

ozonize *or* **ozonise** ('əʊzəʊˌnaɪz) *vb* **ozonizes, ozonizing, ozonized** *or* **ozonises, ozonising, ozonised.** (*tr*) **1** to convert (oxygen) into ozone. **2** to treat (a substance) with ozone.
▸**ˌozoniˈzation** *or* **ˌozoniˈsation** *n* ▸**ˈozoˌnizer** *or* **ˈozoˌniser** *n*

ozonosphere (əʊ'zəʊnəˌsfɪə, -'zɒnə-) *n* another name for **ozone layer.**

Pp

p *or* **P** (piː) *n, pl* **p's, P's,** *or* **Ps. 1** the 16th letter of the English alphabet. **2** a speech sound represented by this letter. **3 mind one's p's and q's.** to be careful to behave correctly and use polite or suitable language.

p *symbol for:* **1** (in Britain) penny *or* pence. **2** *Music.* piano: an instruction to play quietly. **3** *Physics.* pico-. **4** *Physics.* **4a** momentum. **4b** proton. **4c** pressure.

P *symbol for:* **1** *Chem.* phosphorus. **2** *Physics.* **2a** parity. **2b** poise. **2c** power. **2d** pressure. **3** (on road signs) parking. **4** *Chess.* pawn. **5** *Currency.* **5a** peseta. **5b** peso. **6** (of a medicine or drug) available only from a chemist's shop, but not requiring a prescription to obtain it.

p. *abbrev. for:* **1** (*pl* **pp.**) page. **2** part. **3** participle. **4** past. **5** per. **6** pint. **7** pipe. **8** population. **9** post. [L: after] **10** pro. [L: in favour of; for]

p- *prefix* short for **para-**[1] (sense 6).

pa (pɑː) *n* an informal word for **father.**

Pa 1 *the chemical symbol for* protactinium. **2** *symbol for* pascal.

PA *abbrev. for:* **1** personal assistant. **2** *Mil.* Post Adjutant. **3** power of attorney. **4** press agent. **5** Press Association. **6** private account. **7** public-address system. **8** publicity agent. **9** Publishers Association. **10** purchasing agent. **11** *Insurance.* particular average.

p.a. *abbrev. for* per annum. [L: yearly]

pabulum (ˈpæbjʊləm) *n Rare.* **1** food. **2** food for thought, esp. when bland or dull. [C17: from L, from *pascere* to feed]

PABX (in Britain) *abbrev. for* private automatic branch exchange. See also **PBX.**

paca (ˈpɑːkə, ˈpækə) *n* a large burrowing rodent of Central and South America, having white-spotted brown fur. [C17: from Sp., from Amerind]

pace[1] ❶ (peɪs) *n* **1a** a single step in walking. **1b** the distance covered by a step. **2** a measure of length equal to the average length of a stride, approximately 3 feet. **3** speed of movement, esp. of walking or running. **4** rate or style of proceeding at some activity: *to live at a fast pace.* **5** manner or action of stepping, walking, etc.; gait. **6** any of the manners in which a horse or other quadruped walks or runs. **7** a manner of moving, sometimes developed in the horse, in which the two legs on the same side are moved at the same time. **8 keep pace with.** to proceed at the same speed as. **9 put (someone) through his paces.** to test the ability of (someone). **10 set the pace.** to determine the rate at which a group runs or walks or proceeds at some other activity. ◆ *vb* **paces, pacing, paced. 11** (*tr*) to set or determine the pace for, as in a race. **12** (often foll. by *about, up and down,* etc.) to walk with regular slow or fast paces, as in boredom, agitation, etc.: *to pace the room.* **13** (*tr;* often foll. by *out*) to measure by paces: *to pace out the distance.* **14** (*intr*) to walk with slow regular strides. **15** (*intr*) (of a horse) to move at the pace (the specially developed gait). [C13: via OF from L *passūs* step, from *pandere* to extend (the legs as in walking)]

pace[2] (ˈpeɪsɪ; *Latin* ˈpɑːkɛ) *prep* with due deference to: used to acknowledge politely someone who disagrees. [C19: from L, from *pāx* peace]

PACE (peɪs) *n* (in England and Wales) *acronym for* Police and Criminal Evidence Act.

pace bowler *n Cricket.* a bowler who characteristically delivers the ball rapidly.

pacemaker (ˈpeɪsˌmeɪkə) *n* **1** a person, horse, vehicle, etc., used in a race or speed trial to set the pace. **2** a person, organization, etc., regarded as being the leader in a particular activity. **3** Also called: **cardiac pacemaker.** a small area of specialized tissue within the wall of the heart whose spontaneous electrical activity initiates and controls the heartbeat. **4** Also called: **artificial pacemaker.** an electronic device to assume the functions of the natural cardiac pacemaker.

pacer (ˈpeɪsə) *n* **1** a horse trained to move at a special gait. **2** another word for **pacemaker** (sense 1).

pacesetter (ˈpeɪsˌsetə) *n* another word for **pacemaker** (senses 1, 2).

paceway (ˈpeɪsˌweɪ) *n Austral.* a racecourse for trotting and pacing.

pachisi (pəˈtʃiːzɪ) *n* an Indian game somewhat resembling backgammon, played on a cruciform board using six cowries as dice. [C18: from Hindi, from *pacīs* twenty-five (the highest throw)]

pachyderm (ˈpækɪˌdɜːm) *n* any very large thick-skinned mammal, such as an elephant, rhinoceros, or hippopotamus. [C19: from F *pachyderme,* from Gk *pakhudermos,* from *pakhus* thick + *derma* skin]
▸ˌ**pachyˈdermatous** *adj*

pacific ❶ (pəˈsɪfɪk) *adj* **1** tending or conducive to peace; conciliatory. **2** not aggressive. **3** free from conflict; peaceful. [C16: from OF, from L *pācificus,* from *pāx* peace + *facere* to make]
▸**paˈcifically** *adv*

Pacific (pəˈsɪfɪk) *n* **1 the.** short for **Pacific Ocean.** ◆ *adj* **2** of or relating to the Pacific Ocean or its islands.

Pacific Ocean *n* the world's largest and deepest ocean, lying between Asia and Australia and North and South America.

Pacific rim *n* the regions, countries, etc. that lie on the western shores of the Pacific Ocean, esp. in the context of their developing manufacturing capacity and consumer markets.

pacifier (ˈpæsɪˌfaɪə) *n* **1** a person or thing that pacifies. **2** *US & Canad.* a baby's dummy or teething ring.

pacifism ❶ (ˈpæsɪˌfɪzəm) *n* **1** the belief that violence of any kind is unjustifiable and that one should not participate in war, etc. **2** the belief that international disputes can be settled by arbitration rather than war.
▸ˈ**pacifist** *n, adj*

pacify ❶ (ˈpæsɪˌfaɪ) *vb* **pacifies, pacifying, pacified.** (*tr*) **1** to calm the anger or agitation of; mollify. **2** to restore to peace or order. [C15: from OF *pacifier;* see PACIFIC]
▸ˈ**paciˌfiable** *adj* ▸**pacification** (ˌpæsɪfɪˈkeɪʃən) *n*

pack[1] ❶ (pæk) *n* **1a** a bundle or load, esp. one carried on the back. **1b** (*as modifier*)*: a pack animal.* **2** a collected amount of anything. **3** a complete set of similar things, esp. a set of 52 playing cards. **4** a group of animals of the same kind, esp. hunting animals: *a pack of hounds.* **5** any group or band that associates together, esp. for criminal purposes. **6** any group or set regarded dismissively: *a pack of fools; a pack of lies.* **7** *Rugby.* the forwards of a team. **8** the basic organizational unit of Cub Scouts and Brownie Guides. **9** *US & Canad.* same as **packet** (sense 1). **10** short for **pack ice. 11** the quantity of something, such as food, packaged for preservation. **12** *Med.* a sheet or blanket, either damp or dry, for wrapping about the body, esp. for its soothing effect. **13** another name for **rucksack** *or* **backpack. 14** Also called: **face pack.** a cream treatment that cleanses and tones the skin. **15** a parachute folded and ready for use. **16 go to the pack.** *Austral. & NZ inf.* to fall into a worse state or condition. **17** *Computing.* another name for **deck** (sense 4). ◆ *vb* **18** to place or arrange (articles) in (a container), such as clothes in a suitcase. **19** (*tr*) to roll up into a bundle. **20** (when *passive,* often foll. by *out*) to press tightly together; cram: *the audience packed into the foyer; the hall was packed out.* **21** to form (snow, ice, etc.) into a hard compact mass or (of snow, etc.) to become compacted. **22** (*tr*) to press in or cover tightly. **23** (*tr*) to load (a horse, donkey, etc.) with a burden. **24** (often foll. by *off* or *away*) to send away or go away, esp. hastily. **25** (*tr*) to seal (a joint) by inserting a layer of compressible material between the faces. **26** (*tr*) *Med.* to treat with a pack. **27** (*tr*) *Sl.* to be capable of inflicting (a blow, etc.): *he packs a mean punch.* **28** (*tr*) *US inf.* to carry or wear habitually: *he packs a gun.* **29** (*tr;* often foll. by *in, into, to,* etc.) *US, Canad., & NZ.* to carry (goods, etc.), esp. on the back. **30 send packing.** *Inf.* to dismiss peremptorily. ◆ See also **pack in, pack up.** [C13: from ?]
▸ˈ**packable** *adj*

pack[2] (pæk) *vb* (*tr*) to fill (a legislative body, committee, etc.) with one's own supporters: *to pack a jury.* [C16: ? changed from PACT]

package ❶ (ˈpækɪdʒ) *n* **1** any wrapped or boxed object or group of objects. **2a** a proposition, offer, or thing for sale in which separate items are offered together as a unit. **2b** (*as modifier*)*: a package holiday; a package deal.* **3** the act or process of packing or packaging. **4** *Computing.* a set of programs designed for a specific type of problem. **5** the usual US and Canad. word for **packet** (sense 1). ◆ *vb* **packages, packaging, packaged.** (*tr*) **6** to wrap in or put into a package. **7** to design and produce a

THESAURUS

pace[1] *n* **1, 5 = step,** gait, measure, stride, tread, walk **3, 4 = speed,** clip (*inf.*), lick, momentum, motion, movement, progress, rate, tempo, time, velocity ◆ *vb* **12 = stride,** march, patrol, pound, walk back and forth, walk up and down **13** *often foll. by* **out = measure,** count, determine, mark out, step

pacific *adj* **1 = peacemaking,** appeasing, conciliatory, diplomatic, irenic, pacificatory, placatory, propitiatory **2 = nonaggressive,** dovelike, dovish, friendly, gentle, mild, nonbelligerent, nonviolent, pacifist, peaceable, peace-loving **3 = peaceful,** at peace, calm, halcyon, placid, quiet, serene, smooth, still, tranquil, unruffled
Antonyms *adj* ≠ **nonaggressive:** aggressive, antagonistic, belligerent, hostile, nonconciliatory, pugnacious, unforgiving, unfriendly, violent, warlike

pacifist *n* **1, 2 = peace lover,** conchie (*inf.*), conscientious objector, dove, passive resister, peacemonger, peacenik (*inf.*), satyagrahi

pacify *vb* **1 = calm,** allay, ameliorate, appease, assuage, clear the air, compose, conciliate, make peace, moderate, mollify, placate, pour oil on troubled waters, propitiate, quiet, restore harmony, smooth down *or* over, smooth one's ruffled feathers, soften, soothe, still, tranquillize **2 = quell,** chasten, crush, impose peace, put down, repress, silence, subdue, tame

pack[1] *n* **1 = bundle,** back pack, bale, burden, fardel (*arch.*), kit, kitbag, knapsack, load, parcel, rucksack, truss **4, 5 = group,** assemblage, band, bunch, collection, company, crew, crowd, deck, drove, flock, gang, herd, lot, mob, set, troop **9 = packet,** package ◆ *vb* **18, 19 = package,** batch, bundle, burden, load, store, stow **20, 22 = cram,** charge, compact, compress, crowd, fill, jam, mob, press, ram, stuff, tamp, throng, wedge **24** *often foll. by* **off** *or* **away = send away,** bundle out, dismiss, hustle out, send packing (*inf.*), send someone about his business **30** *Informal* **send packing = send away,** discharge, dismiss, give the bird (*inf.*), give the brushoff (*sl.*), send about his *or* her business, send away with a flea in his *or* her ear (*inf.*)

package *n* **1 = parcel,** box, carton, container, packet **2 = unit,** amalgamation, combination,

package for (retail goods). **8** to group (separate items) together as a single unit. **9** to compile (complete books) for a publisher to market.
► **'packager** *n*

packaging ❶ ('pækɪdʒɪŋ) *n* **1** the box or wrapping in which a product is offered for sale. **2** the presentation of a person, product, etc., to the public in a way designed to build up a favourable image.

pack drill *n* a military punishment of marching about carrying a full pack of equipment.

packer ('pækə) *n* **1** a person or company whose business is to pack goods, esp. food: *a meat packer.* **2** a person or machine that packs.

packet ❶ ('pækɪt) *n* **1** a small or medium-sized container of cardboard, paper, etc., often together with its contents: *a packet of biscuits.* Usual US and Canad. word: **package, pack. 2** a small package; parcel. **3** Also called: **packet boat.** a boat that transports mail, passengers, goods, etc., on a fixed short route. **4** *Sl.* a large sum of money: *to cost a packet.* **5** *Computing.* a unit into which a larger piece of data is broken down for more efficient transmission. ◆ *vb* **6** (*tr*) to wrap up in a packet or as a packet. [C16: from OF *pacquet,* from *pacquer* to pack, from ODu. *pak* a pack]

packhorse ('pæk,hɔːs) *n* a horse used to transport goods, equipment, etc.

pack ice *n* a large area of floating ice, consisting of pieces that have become massed together.

pack in ❶ *vb* (*tr, adv*) *Brit. & NZ inf.* to stop doing (something) (esp. in **pack it in**).

packing ('pækɪŋ) *n* **1a** material used to cushion packed goods. **1b** (*as modifier*): *a packing needle.* **2** the packaging of foodstuffs. **3** any substance or material used to make joints watertight or gastight.

pack rat *n* a rat of W North America, having a long tail that is furry in some species.

packsaddle ('pæk,sædᵊl) *n* a saddle hung with packs, equipment, etc., used on a pack animal.

packthread ('pæk,θrɛd) *n* a strong twine for sewing or tying up packages.

pack up ❶ *vb* (*adv*) **1** to put (things) away in a proper or suitable place. **2** *Inf.* to give up (an attempt) or stop doing (something). **3** (*intr*) (of an engine, etc.) to fail to operate; break down.

pact ❶ (pækt) *n* an agreement or compact between two or more parties, nations, etc. [C15: from OF *pacte,* from L *pactum,* from *pacīscī* to agree]

pad[1] ❶ (pæd) *n* **1** a thick piece of soft material used to make something comfortable, give it shape, or protect it. **2** Also called: **stamp pad, ink pad.** a block of firm absorbent material soaked with ink for transferring to a rubber stamp. **3** Also called: **notepad, writing pad.** a number of sheets of paper fastened together along one edge. **4** a flat piece of stiff material used to back a piece of blotting paper. **5a** the fleshy cushion-like underpart of the foot of a cat, dog, etc. **5b** any of the parts constituting such a structure. **6** any of various level surfaces or flat-topped structures, such as a launch pad. **7** the large flat floating leaf of the water lily. **8** *Sl.* a person's residence. ◆ *vb* **pads, padding, padded.** (*tr*) **9** to line, stuff, or fill out with soft material, esp. in order to protect or shape. **10** (often foll. by *out*) to inflate with irrelevant or false information: *to pad out a story.* [C16: from ?]

pad[2] ❶ (pæd) *vb* **pads, padding, padded. 1** (*intr;* often foll. by *along, up,* etc.) to walk with a soft or muffled tread. **2** (when *intr,* often foll. by *around*) to travel (a route, etc.) on foot, esp. at a slow pace; tramp: *to pad around the country.* ◆ *n* **3** a dull soft sound, esp. of footsteps. [C16: ?from MDu. *paden,* from *pad* PATH]

padded cell *n* a room, esp. one in a mental hospital, with padded surfaces in which violent inmates are placed.

padding ❶ ('pædɪŋ) *n* **1** any soft material used to pad clothes, etc. **2** superfluous material put into a speech or written work to pad it out; waffle. **3** inflated or false entries in a financial account, esp. an expense account.

paddle[1] ❶ ('pædᵊl) *n* **1** a short light oar with a flat blade at one or both ends, used without a rowlock. **2** Also called: **float.** a blade of a water wheel or paddle wheel. **3** a period of paddling: *to go for a paddle upstream.* **4a** a paddle wheel used to propel a boat. **4b** (*as modifier*): *a paddle steamer.* **5** any of various instruments shaped like a paddle and used for beating, mixing, etc. **6** a table-tennis bat. **7** the flattened limb of a seal, turtle, etc., specialized for swimming. ◆ *vb* **paddles, paddling, paddled. 8** to propel (a canoe, etc.) with a paddle. **9 paddle one's own canoe. 9a** to be self-sufficient. **9b** to mind one's own business. **10** (*tr*) to stir or mix with or as if with a paddle. **11** to row (a boat) steadily, but not at full pressure. **12** (*intr*) to swim with short rapid strokes, like a dog. **13** (*tr*) *US & Canad. inf.* to spank. [C15: from ?]
► **'paddler** *n*

paddle[2] ❶ ('pædᵊl) *vb* **paddles, paddling, paddled.** (*mainly intr*) **1** to walk or play barefoot in shallow water, mud, etc. **2** to dabble the fingers, hands, or feet in water. **3** to walk unsteadily, like a baby. **4** (*tr*) *Arch.* to fondle with the fingers. ◆ *n* **5** the act of paddling in water. [C16: from ?]
► **'paddler** *n*

paddle wheel *n* a large wheel fitted with paddles, turned by an engine to propel a vessel.

paddock ('pædək) *n* **1** a small enclosed field, often for grazing or training horses. **2** (in horse racing) the enclosure in which horses are paraded and mounted before a race. **3** *Austral. & NZ.* any area of fenced land. [C17: var. of dialect *parrock,* from OE *pearruc* enclosure, of Gmc origin. See PARK]

paddy[1] ('pædɪ) *n, pl* **paddies. 1** Also called: **paddy field.** a field planted with rice. **2** rice as a growing crop or when harvested but not yet milled. [from Malay *pādī*]

paddy[2] ❶ ('pædɪ) *n, pl* **paddies.** *Brit. inf.* a fit of temper. [C19: from *Paddy* inf. name for an Irishman]

pademelon *or* **paddymelon** ('pædɪ,mɛlən) *n* a small wallaby of coastal scrubby regions of Australia. [C19: of Abor. origin]

padlock ('pæd,lɒk) *n* **1** a detachable lock having a hinged or sliding shackle, which can be used to secure a door, lid, etc., by passing the shackle through rings or staples. ◆ *vb* **2** (*tr*) to fasten as with a padlock. [C15 *pad,* from ?]

padre ('pɑːdrɪ) *n Inf.* (*sometimes cap.*) **1** father: used to address or refer to a priest. **2** a chaplain to the armed forces. [via Sp. or It. from L *pater* father]

padsaw ('pæd,sɔː) *n* a small narrow saw used for cutting curves. [C19: from PAD[1] (in the sense: a handle that can be fitted to various tools) + SAW[1]]

paean ❶ *or US* (*sometimes*) **pean** ('piːən) *n* **1** a hymn sung in ancient Greece in thanksgiving to a deity. **2** any song of praise. **3** enthusiastic praise: *the film received a paean from the critics.* [C16: via L from Gk *paiān* hymn to Apollo, from his title *Paiān,* the physician of the gods]

paediatrician *or esp. US* **pediatrician** (,piːdɪə'trɪʃən) *n* a medical practitioner who specializes in paediatrics.

paediatrics *or esp. US* **pediatrics** (,piːdɪ'ætrɪks) *n* (*functioning as sing*) the branch of medical science concerned with children and their diseases.
► **,paedi'atric** *or esp. US* **,pedi'atric** *adj*

paedo-, *before a vowel* **paed-,** *or esp. US* **pedo-, ped-** *combining form.* indicating a child or children: *paedophilia.* [from Gk *pais, paid-* child]

paedomorphosis (,piːdə'mɔːfəsɪs) *n* the resemblance of adult animals to the young of their ancestors.

paedophilia *or esp. US* **pedophilia** (,piːdəʊ'fɪlɪə) *n* the condition of being sexually attracted to children.
►**paedophile** *or esp. US* **pedophile** ('piːdəʊ,faɪl) *or* **,paedo'phili,ac** *or esp. US* **,pedo'phili,ac** *n, adj*

paella (paɪ'ɛlə) *n, pl* **paellas** (-ləz). **1** a Spanish dish made from rice, shellfish, chicken, and vegetables. **2** the pan in which a paella is cooked. [from Catalan, from OF *paelle,* from L *patella* small pan]

paeony ('piːənɪ) *n, pl* **paeonies.** a variant spelling of **peony.**

pagan ❶ ('peɪgən) *n* **1** a member of a group professing any religion other than Christianity, Judaism, or Islam. **2** a person without any religion; heathen. ◆ *adj* **3** of or relating to pagans. **4** heathen; irreligious. [C14: from Church L *pāgānus* civilian (hence, not a soldier of Christ), from L: villager, from *pāgus* village]
► **'pagandom** *n* ► **'paganish** *adj* ► **'paganism** *n*

paganize *or* **paganise** ('peɪgə,naɪz) *vb* **paganizes, paganizing, paganized** *or*

THESAURUS

entity, whole ◆ *vb* **6** = **pack**, batch, box, parcel (up), wrap, wrap up

packaging *n* **1** = **wrapping**, box, casing, packing **2** = **outward** *or* **external appearance**, appearance, exterior, facade, image, PR (*inf.*), presentation, surface show, window dressing

packed *adj* **20, 22** = **full**, brimful, bursting at the seams, chock-a-block, chock-full, congested, cram-full, crammed, crowded, filled, hoatching (*Scot.*), jammed, jam-packed, loaded *or* full to the gunwales, overflowing, overloaded, packed like sardines, seething, swarming
Antonyms *adj* deserted, empty, uncongested, uncrowded

packet *n* **1, 2** = **package**, bag, carton, container, parcel, poke (*dialect*), wrapper, wrapping **4** *Slang* = **fortune**, big bucks (*inf., chiefly US*), big money, bomb, bundle (*sl.*), king's ransom (*inf.*), lot(s), megabucks (*US & Canad. sl.*), mint, pile (*inf.*), pot(s) (*inf.*), pretty penny (*inf.*), small fortune, tidy sum (*inf.*)

pack in *vb Brit. & N.Z. informal* = **stop**, cease, chuck (*inf.*), desist, give up *or* over, jack in, kick (*inf.*), leave off

pack up *vb* **1** = **put away**, store, tidy up **2** *Informal* = **stop**, call it a day, call it a night (*inf.*), finish, give up, pack in (*Brit. inf.*) **3** = **break down**, conk out (*inf.*), fail, give out, stall, stop

pact *n* = **agreement**, alliance, arrangement, bargain, bond, compact, concord, concordat, contract, convention, covenant, deal, league, protocol, treaty, understanding

pad[1] *n* **1** = **cushion**, buffer, protection, stiffening, stuffing, wad **3** = **notepad**, block, jotter, tablet, writing pad **5** = **paw**, foot, sole **8** *Slang* = **home**, apartment, flat, hang-out (*inf.*), place, quarters, room ◆ *vb* **9** = **pack**, cushion, fill, line, protect, shape, stuff **10** *often foll. by* **out** = **lengthen**, amplify, augment, eke, elaborate, fill out, flesh out, inflate, protract, spin out, stretch

pad[2] *vb* **1** = **sneak**, creep, go barefoot, pussyfoot (*inf.*), steal **2** = **walk**, hike, march, plod, traipse (*inf.*), tramp, trek, trudge

padding *n* **1** = **filling**, packing, stuffing, wadding **2** = **waffle** (*inf., chiefly Brit.*), hot air, prolixity, verbiage, verbosity, wordiness

paddle[1] *n* **1** = **oar**, scull, sweep ◆ *vb* **8** = **row**, oar, propel, pull, scull

paddle[2] *vb* **1** = **wade**, plash, slop, splash (about) **2** = **dabble**, stir

paddy[2] *n Brit. informal* = **temper**, bate, fit of temper, passion, rage, tantrum, tiff, wax (*inf., chiefly Brit.*)

paean *n* **1** = **hymn**, anthem, psalm, thanksgiving **2, 3** = **praise**, encomium, eulogy, hymn of praise, ovation, panegyric, rave review (*inf.*)

pagan *n* **1, 2** = **heathen**, Gentile, idolater, infidel, polytheist, unbeliever ◆ *adj* **3, 4** = **heathen**, Gentile, heathenish, idolatrous, infidel, irreligious, polytheistic

paganises, paganising, paganised. to become pagan or convert to paganism.

page[1] ➊ (peɪdʒ) *n* **1** one side of one of the leaves of a book, newspaper, etc., or the written or printed matter it bears. **2** such a leaf considered as a unit. **3** an episode, phase, or period: *a glorious page in the revolution.* **4** a screenful of information from a website, teletext service, etc., displayed on a television monitor or visual display unit. ◆ *vb* **pages, paging, paged. 5** another word for **paginate.** [C15: via OF from L *pāgina*]

page[2] ➊ (peɪdʒ) *n* **1** a boy employed to run errands, carry messages, etc., for the guests in a hotel, club, etc. **2** a youth in attendance at official functions or ceremonies, esp. weddings. **3** *Medieval history.* **3a** a boy in training for knighthood in personal attendance on a knight. **3b** a youth in the personal service of a person of rank. ◆ *vb* **pages, paging, paged.** (*tr*) **4** to call out the name of (a person), esp. by a loudspeaker system, so as to give him a message. **5** to call (a person) by an electronic device, such as a bleeper. **6** to act as a page to or attend as a page. [C13: via OF from It. *paggio,* prob. from Gk *paidion* boy, from *pais* child]

pageant ➊ ('pædʒənt) *n* **1** an elaborate colourful display portraying scenes from history, etc. **2** any magnificent or showy display, procession, etc. [C14: from Med. L *pāgina* scene of a play, from L: PAGE[1]]

pageantry ➊ ('pædʒəntrɪ) *n, pl* **pageantries. 1** spectacular display or ceremony. **2** *Arch.* pageants collectively.

pageboy ('peɪdʒˌbɔɪ) *n* **1** a smooth medium-length hairstyle with the ends of the hair curled under. **2** a less common word for **page**[2].

pager ('peɪdʒə) *n* an electronic device, capable of receiving short messages, used by people who need to be contacted urgently.

page-three *n modifier Brit.* denoting a scantily dressed attractive girl, as photographed on page three of some tabloid newspapers.

page-turner *n* a very exciting or interesting book. [C20: from the notion that a reader cannot stop turning the pages]

paginate ('pædʒɪˌneɪt) *vb* **paginates, paginating, paginated.** (*tr*) to number the pages of (a book, manuscript, etc.) in sequence. Cf. **foliate.**
▸ˌ**pagi'nation** *n*

pagoda (pə'gəʊdə) *n* an Indian or Far Eastern temple, esp. a tower, usually pyramidal and having many storeys. [C17: from Port. *pagode,* ult. from Sansk. *bhagavatī* divine]

pagoda tree *n* a Chinese leguminous tree with ornamental white flowers.

paid (peɪd) *vb* **1** the past tense and past participle of **pay**[1]. **2 put paid to.** *Chiefly Brit. & NZ.* to end or destroy: *breaking his leg put paid to his hopes of running in the Olympics.*

paid-up *adj* **1** having paid the required fee to be a member of an organization, etc. **2** denoting a security in which all the instalments have been paid; fully paid: *a paid-up share.* **3** denoting all the money that a company has received from its shareholders: *the paid-up capital.* **4** denoting an endowment assurance policy on which the payment of premiums has stopped and the surrender value has been used to purchase a new single-premium policy.

pail (peɪl) *n* **1** a bucket, esp. one made of wood or metal. **2** Also called: **pailful.** the quantity that fills a pail. [OE *pægel*]

paillasse ('pælɪˌæs, ˌpælɪ'æs) *n* a variant spelling (esp. US) of **palliasse.**

pain ➊ (peɪn) *n* **1** the sensation of acute physical hurt or discomfort caused by injury, illness, etc. **2** emotional suffering or mental distress. **3 on pain of.** subject to the penalty of. **4** Also called: **pain in the neck.** *Inf.* a person or thing that is a nuisance. ◆ *vb* (*tr*) **5** to cause (a person) hurt, grief, anxiety, etc. **6** *Inf.* to annoy; irritate. ◆ See also **pains.** [C13: from OF *peine,* from L *poena* punishment, grief, from Gk *poinē* penalty]
▸'**painless** *adj*

pained ➊ (peɪnd) *adj* having or expressing pain or distress, esp. mental or emotional distress.

painful ➊ ('peɪnfʊl) *adj* **1** causing pain; distressing: *a painful duty.* **2** affected with pain. **3** tedious or difficult. **4** *Inf.* extremely bad.
▸'**painfully** *adv* ▸'**painfulness** *n*

painkiller ➊ ('peɪnˌkɪlə) *n* **1** an analgesic drug or agent. **2** anything that relieves pain.

pains ➊ (peɪnz) *pl n* **1** care or trouble (esp. in **take pains, be at pains to**). **2** painful sensations experienced during contractions in childbirth; labour pains.

painstaking ➊ ('peɪnzˌteɪkɪŋ) *adj* extremely careful, esp. as to fine detail.
▸'**painsˌtakingly** *adv* ▸'**painsˌtakingness** *n*

paint ➊ (peɪnt) *n* **1** a substance used for decorating or protecting a surface, esp. a mixture consisting of a solid pigment suspended in a liquid that dries to form a hard coating. **2** a dry film of paint on a surface. **3** *Inf.* face make-up, such as rouge. **4** short for **greasepaint.** ◆ *vb* **5** to make (a picture) of (a figure, landscape, etc.) with paint applied to a surface such as canvas. **6** to coat (a surface, etc.) with paint, as in decorating. **7** (*tr*) to apply (liquid, etc.) onto (a surface): *she painted the cut with antiseptic.* **8** (*tr*) to apply make-up onto (the face, lips, etc.). **9** (*tr*) to describe vividly in words. **10 paint the town red.** *Inf.* to celebrate uninhibitedly. [C13: from OF *peint* painted, from *peindre* to paint, from L *pingere* to paint]
▸'**painty** *adj*

paintball game ('peɪntˌbɔːl) *n* a game in which teams of players simulate a military skirmish, shooting each other with paint pellets that explode on impact.

paintbox ('peɪntˌbɒks) *n* a box containing a tray of dry watercolour paints.

paintbrush ('peɪntˌbrʌʃ) *n* a brush used to apply paint.

painted lady *n* a migratory butterfly with pale brownish-red mottled wings.

painter[1] ('peɪntə) *n* **1** a person who paints surfaces as a trade. **2** an artist who paints pictures.
▸'**painterly** *adj*

painter[2] ('peɪntə) *n* a line attached to the bow of a boat for tying it up. [C15: prob. from OF *penteur* strong rope]

painting ('peɪntɪŋ) *n* **1** the art of applying paints to canvas, etc. **2** a picture made in this way. **3** the act of applying paint to a surface.

paint stripper *or* **remover** *n* a liquid, often caustic, used to remove paint from a surface.

paintwork ('peɪntˌwɜːk) *n* a surface, such as wood or a car body, that is painted.

pair ➊ (pɛə) *n, pl* **pairs** *or* (*functioning as sing or pl*) **pair. 1** two identical or similar things matched for use together: *a pair of socks.* **2** two persons, animals, things, etc., used or grouped together: *a pair of horses; a pair of scoundrels.* **3** an object considered to be two identical or similar things joined together: *a pair of trousers.* **4** two people joined in love or marriage. **5** a male and a female animal of the same species kept for breeding purposes. **6** *Parliament.* **6a** two opposed members who both agree not to vote on a specified motion. **6b** the agreement so made. **7** two playing cards of the same rank or denomination. **8** one member of a matching pair: *I can't find the pair to this glove.* ◆ *vb* **9** (often foll. by *off*) to arrange or fall into groups of twos. **10** to group or be grouped in matching pairs. **11** to join or be joined in marriage; mate or couple. **12** (when *tr, usually passive*) *Parliament.* to form or cause to form a pair. [C13: from OF *paire,* from L *paria* equal (things), from *pār* equal]

> **USAGE NOTE** Like other collective nouns, *pair* takes a singular or a plural verb according to whether it is seen as a unit or as a collection of two things: *the pair are said to dislike each other; a pair of good shoes is essential.*

THESAURUS

page[1] *n* **1** = **folio**, leaf, sheet, side **3** = **period**, chapter, episode, epoch, era, event, incident, phase, point, stage, time ◆ *vb* **5** = **paginate**, foliate, number

page[2] *n* **1, 3** = **attendant**, bellboy (*US*), footboy, pageboy, servant, squire ◆ *vb* **4, 5** = **call**, announce, call out, preconize, seek, send for, summon

pageant *n* **1, 2** = **show**, display, extravaganza, parade, procession, ritual, spectacle, tableau

pageantry *n* **1** = **spectacle**, display, drama, extravagance, glamour, glitter, grandeur, magnificence, parade, pomp, show, showiness, splash (*inf.*), splendour, state, theatricality

pain *n* **1** = **hurt**, ache, cramp, discomfort, irritation, pang, smarting, soreness, spasm, suffering, tenderness, throb, throe (*rare*), trouble, twinge **2** = **suffering**, affliction, agony, anguish, bitterness, distress, grief, hardship, heartache, misery, torment, torture, tribulation, woe, wretchedness **4** *Informal* = **nuisance**, aggravation, annoyance, bore, bother, drag (*inf.*), gall, headache (*inf.*), irritation, pain in the neck (*inf.*), pest, vexation ◆ *vb* **5** = **hurt**, ail, chafe, discomfort, harm, inflame, injure, smart, sting, throb **5** = **distress**, afflict, aggrieve, agonize, cut to the quick, disquiet, grieve, hurt, sadden, torment, torture, vex, worry, wound **6** *Informal* = **irritate**, annoy, exasperate, gall, harass, nark (*Brit., Austral., & NZ sl.*), rile, vex

pained *adj* = **distressed**, aggrieved, anguished, hurt, injured, miffed (*inf.*), offended, reproachful, stung, unhappy, upset, worried, wounded

painful *adj* **1** = **distressing**, afflictive, disagreeable, distasteful, grievous, saddening, unpleasant **1, 2** = **sore**, aching, agonizing, excruciating, harrowing, hurting, inflamed, raw, smarting, tender, throbbing **3** = **difficult**, arduous, hard, laborious, severe, tedious, troublesome, trying, vexatious **4** *Informal* = **terrible**, abysmal, awful, dire, dreadful, excruciating, extremely bad
Antonyms *adj* ≠ **distressing**: agreeable, enjoyable, pleasant, satisfying ≠ **sore**: comforting, painless, relieving, soothing ≠ **difficult**: a piece of cake (*inf.*), easy, effortless, interesting, short, simple, straightforward, undemanding

painfully *adv* **1-4** = **distressingly**, alarmingly, clearly, deplorably, dreadfully, excessively, markedly, sadly, unfortunately, woefully

painkiller *n* **1** = **analgesic**, anaesthetic, anodyne, drug, palliative, remedy, sedative

painless *adj* = **simple**, easy, effortless, fast, no trouble, pain-free, quick, trouble-free

pains *pl n* **1** = **trouble**, assiduousness, bother, care, diligence, effort, industry, labour, special attention **2** = **contractions**, birth-pangs, childbirth, labour

painstaking *adj* = **thorough**, assiduous, careful, conscientious, diligent, earnest, exacting, hard-working, industrious, meticulous, persevering, punctilious, scrupulous, sedulous, strenuous, thoroughgoing
Antonyms *adj* careless, half-hearted, haphazard, heedless, lazy, negligent, slapdash, slipshod, thoughtless

paint *n* **1** = **colouring**, colour, dye, emulsion, pigment, stain, tint **3, 4** *Informal* = **make-up**, cosmetics, face, greasepaint, *maquillage,* war paint (*inf.*) ◆ *vb* **5** = **depict**, catch a likeness, delineate, draw, figure, picture, portray, represent, sketch **6, 7** = **coat**, apply, colour, cover, daub, decorate, slap on (*inf.*) **9** = **describe**, bring to life, capture, conjure up a vision, depict, evoke, make one see, portray, put graphically, recount, tell vividly **10 paint the town red** *Informal* = **celebrate**, carouse, go on a binge (*inf.*), go on a spree, go on the town, live it up (*inf.*), make merry, make whoopee (*inf.*), revel

pair *n* **1, 2, 4, 5** = **couple**, brace, combination, doublet, duo, match, matched set, span, twins, two of a kind, twosome, yoke ◆ *vb* **9-11** = **cou-**

paisley ('peɪzlɪ) *n* **1** a pattern of small curving shapes with intricate detailing. **2** a soft fine wool fabric traditionally printed with this pattern. **3** a shawl made of this fabric, popular in the late 19th century. **4** (*modifier*) of or decorated with this pattern: *a paisley scarf.* [C19: after *Paisley*, town in Scotland]

pajamas (pəˈdʒɑːməz) *pl n* the US spelling of **pyjamas**.

pakeha ('pɑːkɪˌhɑː) *n NZ.* a European, as distinct from a Maori: *Maori and pakeha.* [from Maori]

Paki ('pækɪ) *Brit. sl., offens.* ◆ *n, pl* **Pakis. 1** a Pakistani or person of Pakistani descent. ◆ *adj* **2** Pakistani or of Pakistani descent.

Pakistani (ˌpɑːkɪˈstɑːnɪ) *adj* **1** of or relating to Pakistan, a country in the Indian subcontinent. ◆ *n, pl* **Pakistanis. 2** a native or inhabitant of Pakistan or a descendant of one.

pakora (pəˈkɔːrə) *n* an Indian dish consisting of pieces of vegetable, chicken, etc., dipped in spiced batter and deep-fried. [C20: from Hindi]

pal ❶ (pæl) *Inf.* ◆ *n* **1** a close friend; comrade. ◆ *vb* **pals, palling, palled. 2** (*intr;* usually foll. by *with*) to associate as friends. [C17: from E Gypsy: brother, ult. from Sansk. *bhrātar* BROTHER]

PAL (pæl) *n acronym for* phase alternation line: a colour-television broadcasting system used generally in Europe.

palace ('pælɪs) *n* (*cap. when part of a name*) **1** the official residence of a reigning monarch. **2** the official residence of various high-ranking people, as of an archbishop. **3** a large and richly furnished building resembling a royal palace. [C13: from OF *palais*, from L *Palātium* Palatine, the site of the palace of the emperors in Rome]

paladin ('pælədɪn) *n* **1** one of the legendary twelve peers of Charlemagne's court. **2** a knightly champion. [C16: via F from It. *paladino*, from L *palātīnus* imperial official]

palaeo-, *before a vowel* **palae-** *or esp. US* **paleo-, pale-** *combining form.* old, ancient, or prehistoric: *palaeography.* [from Gk *palaios* old]

palaeobotany *or US* **paleobotany** (ˌpælɪəʊˈbɒtənɪ) *n* the study of fossil plants.
▸ˌ**palaeo'botanist** *or US* ˌ**paleo'botanist** *n*

Palaeocene *or US* **Paleocene** ('pælɪəʊˌsiːn) *adj* **1** of, denoting, or formed in the first epoch of the Tertiary period. ◆ *n* **2 the.** the Palaeocene epoch or rock series. [C19: from F, from *paléo* PALAEO- + Gk *kainos* new]

palaeoclimatology *or US* **paleoclimatology** (ˌpælɪəʊˌklaɪməˈtɒlədʒɪ) *n* the study of climates of the geological past.
▸ˌ**palaeoˌclima'tologist** *or US* ˌ**paleoˌclima'tologist** *n*

palaeoecology *or US* **paleoecology** (ˌpælɪəʊɪˈkɒlədʒɪ) *n* the study of fossil animals and plants in order to deduce their ecology and the environment conditions in which they lived.
▸ˌ**palaeoˌeco'logical** *or US* ˌ**paleoˌeco'logical** *adj* ▸ˌ**palaeoe'cologist** *or US* ˌ**paleoe'cologist** *n*

palaeography *or US* **paleography** (ˌpælɪˈɒgrəfɪ) *n* **1** the study of the handwritings of the past, and often the manuscripts, etc., so that they may be dated, read, etc. **2** a handwriting of the past.
▸ˌ**palae'ographer** *or US* ˌ**pale'ographer** *n* ▸**palaeographic** (ˌpælɪəʊˈgræfɪk), ˌ**palaeo'graphical** *or US* ˌ**paleo'graphic**, ˌ**paleo'graphical** *adj*

Palaeolithic *or US* **Paleolithic** (ˌpælɪəʊˈlɪθɪk) *n* **1** the period of the emergence of primitive man and the manufacture of unpolished chipped stone tools, about 2.5 million to 3 million years ago. ◆ *adj* **2** (*sometimes not cap.*) of or relating to this period.

palaeomagnetism *or US* **paleomagnetism** (ˌpælɪəʊˈmægnɪtɪzəm) *n* the study of the fossil magnetism in rocks, used to determine the past configuration of the earth's constituents.

palaeontology *or US* **paleontology** (ˌpælɪɒnˈtɒlədʒɪ) *n* the study of fossils to determine the structure and evolution of extinct animals and plants and the age and conditions of deposition of the rock strata in which they are found. [C19: from PALAEO- + ONTO- + -LOGY]
▸**palaeontological** *or US* **paleontological** (ˌpælɪˌɒntəˈlɒdʒɪkᵊl) *adj* ▸ˌ**palaeon'tologist** *or US* ˌ**paleon'tologist** *n*

Palaeozoic (ˌpælɪəʊˈzəʊɪk) *adj* **1** of, denoting, or relating to an era of geological time that began 600 million years ago with the Cambrian period and lasted about 375 million years until the end of the Permian period. ◆ *n* **2 the.** the Palaeozoic era. [C19: from PALAEO- + Gk *zōē* life + -IC]

palanquin *or* **palankeen** (ˌpælənˈkiːn) *n* a covered litter, formerly used in the Orient, carried on the shoulders of four men. [C16: from Port. *palanquim*, from Prakrit *pallanka*, from Sansk. *paryanka* couch]

palatable ❶ ('pælətəbᵊl) *adj* **1** pleasant to taste. **2** acceptable or satisfactory.
▸ˌ**palata'bility** *or* '**palatableness** *n* ▸'**palatably** *adv*

palatal ('pælətᵊl) *adj* **1** Also: **palatine.** of or relating to the palate. **2** *Phonetics.* of, relating to, or denoting a speech sound articulated with the blade of the tongue touching the hard palate. ◆ *n* **3** Also called: **palatine.** the bony plate that forms the palate. **4** *Phonetics.* a palatal speech sound, such as (j).
▸'**palatally** *adv*

palatalize *or* **palatalise** ('pælətəˌlaɪz) *vb* **palatalizes, palatalizing, palatalized** *or* **palatalises, palatalising, palatalised.** (*tr*) to pronounce (a speech sound) with the blade of the tongue touching the palate.
▸ˌ**palatali'zation** *or* ˌ**palatali'sation** *n*

palate ❶ ('pælɪt) *n* **1** the roof of the mouth, separating the oral and nasal cavities. See **hard palate, soft palate. 2** the sense of taste: *she had no palate for the wine.* **3** relish or enjoyment. [C14: from L *palātum*, ? of Etruscan origin]

USAGE NOTE Avoid confusion with **palette** or **pallet.**

palatial ❶ (pəˈleɪʃəl) *adj* of, resembling, or suitable for a palace; sumptuous.
▸**pa'latially** *adv*

palatinate (pəˈlætɪnɪt) *n* a territory ruled by a palatine prince or noble or count palatine.

palatine[1] ('pæləˌtaɪn) *adj* **1** (of an individual) possessing royal prerogatives in a territory. **2** of or relating to a count palatine, county palatine, palatinate, or palatine. **3** of or relating to a palace. ◆ *n* **4** *Feudal history.* the lord of a palatinate. **5** any of various important officials at the late Roman, Merovingian, or Carolingian courts. [C15: via F from L *palātīnus* belonging to the palace, from *palātium;* see PALACE]

palatine[2] ('pæləˌtaɪn) *adj* **1** of the palate. ◆ *n* **2** either of two bones forming the hard palate. [C17: from F *palatin*, from L *palātum* palate]

palaver ❶ (pəˈlɑːvə) *n* **1** tedious or time-consuming business, esp. when of a formal nature: *all the palaver of filling in forms.* **2** confused talk and activity; hubbub. **3** (often used humorously) a conference. **4** *Now rare.* talk intended to flatter or persuade. ◆ *vb* **5** (*intr*) (often used humorously) to have a conference. **6** (*intr*) to talk confusedly. **7** (*tr*) to flatter or cajole. [C18: from Port. *palavra* talk, from L *parabola* PARABLE]

pale[1] ❶ (peɪl) *adj* **1** lacking brightness or colour: *pale morning light.* **2** (of a colour) whitish. **3** dim or wan: *the pale stars.* **4** feeble: *a pale effort.* ◆ *vb* **pales, paling, paled. 5** to make or become pale or paler; blanch. **6** (*intr;* often foll. by *before*) to lose superiority (in comparison to): *her beauty paled before that of her hostess.* [C13: from OF *palle*, from L *pallidus*, from *pallēre* to look wan]
▸'**palely** *adv* ▸'**paleness** *n* ▸'**palish** *adj*

pale[2] ❶ (peɪl) *n* **1** a wooden post or strip used as an upright member in a fence. **2** an enclosing barrier, esp. a fence made of pales. **3** an area enclosed by a pale. **4** *Heraldry.* a vertical stripe, usually in the centre of a shield. **5 beyond the pale.** outside the limits of social convention. [C14: from OF *pal*, from L *pālus* stake]

paleface ('peɪlˌfeɪs) *n* a derogatory term for a White person, said to have been used by North American Indians.

paleo- *or before a vowel* **pale-** *combining form.* variants (esp. US) of **palaeo-.**

Palestine Liberation Organization ('pælɪˌstaɪn) *n* an organization founded in 1964 with the aim of creating a state for Palestinian Arabs. In 1993 it signed a peace agreement with Israel, which granted Palestinian autonomy in the Gaza Strip and West Bank. Abbrev.: **PLO.**

Palestinian (ˌpælɪˈstɪnɪən) *adj* **1a** of or relating to Palestine, an area of the Middle East between the Jordan River and the Mediterranean, or to the former (1922–48) British mandatory territory in this region. **1b** of or relating to the native Arab population of Palestine or their descendants. ◆ *n* **2** a Palestinian Arab, esp. one now living in the Palestinian Administered Territories, Israel, Jordan, Lebanon, or as a refugee from Israeli-occupied territory.

Palestinian National Authority *n* the authority formed in 1994 to govern the Palestinian Administered Territories. Abbrev.: **PNA.**

palette ('pælɪt) *n* **1** Also: **pallet.** a flat piece of wood, plastic, etc., used by artists as a surface on which to mix their paints. **2** the range of colours characteristic of a particular artist, painting, or school of painting: *a*

THESAURUS

ple, bracket, join, marry, match (up), mate, pair off, put together, team, twin, wed, yoke

pal *n* **1** *Informal* = **friend**, boon companion, buddy, chum (*inf.*), cock (*Brit. inf.*), companion, comrade, crony, homeboy (*sl., chiefly US*), mate (*inf.*)

palatable *adj* **1** = **delicious**, appetizing, delectable, luscious, mouthwatering, savoury, tasty, toothsome **2** = **acceptable**, agreeable, attractive, enjoyable, fair, pleasant, satisfactory
Antonyms *adj* ≠ **delicious:** bland, flat, insipid, stale, tasteless, unappetizing, unpalatable

palate *n* **2** = **taste**, appetite, heart, stomach **3** = **enjoyment**, appreciation, gusto, liking, relish, zest

palatial *adj* = **magnificent**, de luxe, gorgeous, grand, grandiose, illustrious, imposing, luxurious, majestic, opulent, plush (*inf.*), regal, spacious, splendid, splendiferous (*facetious*), stately, sumptuous

palaver *n* **1** = **fuss**, business (*inf.*), carry-on (*inf., chiefly Brit.*), pantomime (*inf., chiefly Brit.*), performance (*inf.*), procedure, rigmarole, song and dance (*Brit. inf.*), to-do **2** = **prattle**, babble, blather, blether, chatter, hubbub, natter (*Brit.*), tongue-wagging, yak (*sl.*) **3** = **conference**, colloquy, confab (*inf.*), discussion, get-together (*inf.*), parley, powwow, session ◆ *vb* **5** = **confer**, confab (*inf.*), discuss, go into a huddle (*inf.*), parley, powwow, put heads together **6** = **prattle**, blather, blether, chatter, gabble, jabber, jaw (*sl.*), natter (*Brit.*), yak (*sl.*)

pale[1] *adj* **1, 2** = **white**, anaemic, ashen, ashy, bleached, bloodless, colourless, faded, light, like death warmed up (*inf.*), pallid, pasty, sallow, wan, washed-out, whitish **4** = **poor**, feeble, inadequate, pathetic, thin, weak ◆ *vb* **5** = **become pale**, blanch, go white, lose colour, whiten **6** = **fade**, decrease, dim, diminish, dull, grow dull, lessen, lose lustre
Antonyms *adj* ≠ **white:** blooming, florid, flushed, glowing, rosy-cheeked, rubicund, ruddy, sanguine

pale[2] *n* **1** = **post**, paling, palisade, picket, slat, stake, upright **2** = **barrier**, barricade, fence, palisade, railing **3** = **boundary**, border, bounds, confines, district, limits, region, territory **5 beyond the pale** = **unacceptable**, forbidden, improper, inadmissible, indecent, irregular, not done, out of line, unseemly, unspeakable, unsuitable

restricted palette. **3** the available range of colours or patterns that can be displayed by a computer on a visual display unit. [C17: from F, dim. of *pale* shovel, from L *pala* spade]

USAGE NOTE Avoid confusion with **palate** or **pallet**.

palette *or* **pallet knife** *n* a spatula with a thin flexible blade used in painting and cookery.

palfrey ('pɔːlfrɪ) *n Arch.* a light saddle horse, esp. ridden by women. [C12: from OF *palefrei,* from Med. L, from LL *paraverēdus,* from Gk *para* beside + L *verēdus* light fleet horse, of Celtic origin]

Pali ('pɑːlɪ) *n* an ancient language of India derived from Sanskrit; the language of the Buddhist scriptures. [C19: from Sansk. *pāli-bhāsa,* from *pāli* canon + *bhāsa* language, of Dravidian origin]

palimony ('pælɪmənɪ) *n US.* alimony awarded to a nonmarried partner after the break-up of a long-term relationship. [C20: from PAL + ALIMONY]

palimpsest ('pælɪmpˌsɛst) *n* **1** a manuscript on which two or more texts have been written, each one being erased to make room for the next. ◆ *adj* **2** (of a text) written on a palimpsest. **3** (of a document, etc.) used as a palimpsest. [C17: from L *palimpsestus,* from Gk *palimpsēstos,* from *palin* again + *psēstos* rubbed smooth]

palindrome ('pælɪnˌdrəʊm) *n* a word or phrase the letters of which, when taken in reverse order, read the same: *able was I ere I saw Elba.* [C17: from Gk *palindromos* running back again]
▸**palindromic** (ˌpælɪn'drɒmɪk) *adj*

paling ('peɪlɪŋ) *n* **1** a fence made of pales. **2** pales collectively. **3** a single pale. **4** the act of erecting pales.

palisade ➊ (ˌpælɪ'seɪd) *n* **1** a strong fence made of stakes driven into the ground, esp. for defence. **2** one of the stakes used in such a fence. ◆ *vb* **palisades, palisading, palisaded. 3** (*tr*) to enclose with a palisade. [C17: via F from OProvençal *palissada,* ult. from L *pālus* stake]

pall[1] ➊ (pɔːl) *n* **1** a cloth covering, usually black, spread over a coffin or tomb. **2** a coffin, esp. during the funeral ceremony. **3** a dark heavy covering; shroud: *the clouds formed a pall over the sky.* **4** a depressing or oppressive atmosphere: *her bereavement cast a pall on the party.* **5** *Heraldry.* a Y-shaped bearing. **6** *Christianity.* a small square linen cloth with which the chalice is covered at the Eucharist. ◆ *vb* **7** (*tr*) to cover or depress with a pall. [OE *pæll,* from L *pallium* cloak]

pall[2] ➊ (pɔːl) *vb* **1** (*intr;* often foll. by *on*) to become boring, insipid, or tiresome (to): *history classes palled on me.* **2** to cloy or satiate, or become cloyed or satiated. [C14: var. of APPAL]

Palladian (pə'leɪdɪən) *adj* denoting, relating to, or having the style of architecture created by Andrea Palladio. [C18: after Andrea *Palladio* (1508–80), It. architect]
▸**Pal'ladianˌism** *n*

palladium[1] (pə'leɪdɪəm) *n* a ductile malleable silvery-white element of the platinum metal group: used as a catalyst and, alloyed with gold, in jewellery, etc. Symbol: Pd; atomic no.: 46; atomic wt.: 106.4. [C19: after the asteroid *Pallas,* at the time (1803) a recent discovery]

palladium[2] (pə'leɪdɪəm) *n* something believed to ensure protection; safeguard. [C17: after the *Palladium,* a statue of Pallas Athena, Gk goddess of wisdom]

pallbearer ('pɔːlˌbɛərə) *n* a person who carries or escorts the coffin at a funeral.

pallet[1] ('pælɪt) *n* a straw-filled mattress or bed. [C14: from Anglo-Norman *paillet,* from OF *paille* straw, from L *palea* straw]

USAGE NOTE Avoid confusion with **palate** or **palette**.

pallet[2] ('pælɪt) *n* **1** an instrument with a handle and a flat, sometimes flexible, blade used by potters for shaping. **2** a portable platform for storing and moving goods. **3** *Horology.* the locking lever that engages and disengages to give impulses to the balance. **4** a variant spelling of **palette** (sense 1). **5** *Music.* a flap valve that opens to allow air from the wind chest to enter an organ pipe, causing it to sound. [C16: from OF *palette* a little shovel, from L *pala* spade]

palletize *or* **palletise** ('pælətaɪz) *vb* **palletizes, palletizing, palletized** *or* **palletises, palletising, palletised.** (*tr*) to store or transport (goods) on pallets.
▸ˌ**palleti'zation** *or* ˌ**palleti'sation** *n*

palliasse *or esp. US* **paillasse** ('pælɪˌæs, ˌpælɪ'æs) *n* a straw-filled mattress; pallet. [C18: from F *paillasse,* from It. *pagliaccio,* ult. from L *palea* PALLET[1]]

palliate ('pælɪˌeɪt) *vb* **palliates, palliating, palliated.** (*tr*) **1** to lessen the severity of (pain, disease, etc.) without curing; alleviate. **2** to cause (an offence, etc.) to seem less serious; extenuate. [C16: from LL *palliāre* to cover up, from L *pallium* a cloak]
▸ˌ**palli'ation** *n*

palliative ('pælɪətɪv) *adj* **1** relieving without curing. ◆ *n* **2** something that palliates, such as a sedative drug.
▸'**palliatively** *adv*

pallid ➊ ('pælɪd) *adj* lacking colour, brightness, or vigour: *a pallid complexion; a pallid performance.* [C17: from L *pallidus,* from *pallēre* to be PALE[1]]
▸'**pallidly** *adv* ▸'**pallidness** *or* **pal'lidity** *n*

pall-mall ('pæl'mæl) *n Obs.* **1** a game in which a ball is driven by a mallet along an alley and through an iron ring. **2** the alley itself. [C17: from obs. F, from It. *pallamaglio,* from *palla* ball + *maglio* mallet]

pallor ➊ ('pælə) *n* a pale condition, esp. when unnatural: *fear gave his face a deathly pallor.* [C17: from L: whiteness (of the skin), from *pallēre* to be PALE[1]]

pally ➊ ('pælɪ) *adj* **pallier, palliest.** *Inf.* on friendly terms.

palm[1] ➊ (pɑːm) *n* **1** the inner part of the hand from the wrist to the base of the fingers. **2** a linear measure based on the breadth or length of a hand, equal to three to four inches (7.5 to 10 centimetres) or seven to ten inches (17.5 to 25 centimetres) respectively. **3** the part of a glove that covers the palm. **4a** one side of the blade of an oar. **4b** the face of the fluke of an anchor. **5** a flattened part of the antlers of certain deer. **6 in the palm of one's hand.** at one's mercy or command. ◆ *vb* (*tr*) **7** to conceal in or about the hand, as in sleight-of-hand tricks, etc. ◆ See also **palm off.** [C14 *paume,* via OF from L *palma*]
▸**palmar** ('pælmə) *adj*

palm[2] ➊ (pɑːm) *n* **1** any treelike plant of a tropical and subtropical family having a straight unbranched trunk crowned with large pinnate or palmate leaves. **2** a leaf or branch of any of these trees, a symbol of victory, success, etc. **3** merit or victory. [OE, from L *palma,* from the likeness of its spreading fronds to a hand; see PALM[1]]
▸**palmaceous** (pæl'meɪʃəs) *adj*

palmate ('pælmeɪt, -mɪt) *or* **palmated** *adj* **1** shaped like an open hand: *palmate antlers.* **2** *Bot.* having five lobes that spread out from a common point: *palmate leaves.* **3** (of most water birds) having three toes connected by a web.

palmer ('pɑːmə) *n* (in medieval Europe) **1** a pilgrim bearing a palm branch as a sign of his visit to the Holy Land. **2** any pilgrim. [C13: from OF *palmier,* from Med. L, from L *palma* PALM[2]]

palmetto (pæl'mɛtəʊ) *n, pl* **palmettos** *or* **palmettoes.** any of several small chiefly tropical palms with fan-shaped leaves. [C16: from Sp. *palmito* a little PALM[2]]

palmistry ('pɑːmɪstrɪ) *n* the process or art of telling fortunes, etc., by the configuration of lines and bumps on a person's hand. Also called: **chiromancy.** [C15 *pawmestry,* from *paume* PALM[1]; the second element is unexplained]
▸'**palmist** *n*

palmitic acid (pæl'mɪtɪk) *n* a white crystalline solid that is a saturated fatty acid: used in the manufacture of soap and candles. Formula: $C_{15}H_{31}COOH$. Systematic name: **hexadecanoic acid.** [C19: from F]

palm off ➊ *vb* (*tr, adv;* often foll. by *on*) **1** to offer, sell, or spend fraudulently: *to palm off a counterfeit coin.* **2** to divert in order to be rid of: *I palmed the unwelcome visitor off on John.*

palm oil *n* an oil obtained from the fruit of certain palms, used as an edible fat and in soap, etc.

Palm Sunday *n* the Sunday before Easter commemorating Christ's triumphal entry into Jerusalem.

palmtop computer ('pɒːmˌtɒp) *n* a computer that is small enough to be held in the hand. Often shortened to **palmtop.** Cf. **laptop computer.**

palmy ➊ ('pɑːmɪ) *adj* **palmier, palmiest. 1** prosperous, flourishing, or luxurious: *a palmy life.* **2** covered with, relating to, or resembling palms.

palmyra (pæl'maɪrə) *n* a tall tropical Asian palm with large fan-shaped leaves used for thatching and weaving. [C17: from Port. *palmeira* palm tree; ? infl. by *Palmyra,* city in Syria]

palomino (ˌpælə'miːnəʊ) *n, pl* **palominos.** a golden horse with a white mane and tail. [American Sp., from Sp.: dovelike, from L, from *palumbēs* ring dove]

palp (pælp) *or* **palpus** ('pælpəs) *n, pl* **palps** *or* **palpi** ('pælpaɪ). either of a pair of sensory appendages that arise from the mouthparts of crustaceans and insects. [C19: from F, from L *palpus* a touching]

palpable ➊ ('pælpəbᵊl) *adj* **1** (*usually prenominal*) easily perceived by the senses or the mind; obvious: *a palpable lie.* **2** capable of being touched;

THESAURUS

palisade *n* **1 = fence,** bulwark, defence, enclosure, paling, stockade

pall[1] *n* **1, 3 = cloud,** mantle, shadow, shroud, veil **4 = gloom,** check, damp, damper, dismay, melancholy

pall[2] *vb* **1, 2 = become boring,** become dull, become tedious, cloy, glut, jade, satiate, sicken, surfeit, tire, weary

pallid *adj* **= pale,** anaemic, ashen, ashy, cadaverous, colourless, like death warmed up (*inf.*), pasty, sallow, wan, waxen, wheyfaced, whitish **= insipid,** anaemic, bloodless, colourless, lifeless, spiritless, sterile, tame, tired, uninspired, vapid

pallor *n* **= paleness,** ashen hue, bloodlessness, lack of colour, pallidness, wanness, whiteness

pally *adj Informal* **= friendly,** affectionate, buddy-buddy (*sl., chiefly US & Canad.*), chummy, close, familiar, intimate, palsy-walsy (*inf.*), thick as thieves (*inf.*)

palm[1] *n* **1 = hand,** hook, mitt (*sl.*), paw (*inf.*) **6 in the palm of one's hand = in one's power,** at one's mercy, in one's clutches, in one's control

palm[2] *n* **3 = victory,** bays, crown, fame, glory, honour, laurels, merit, prize, success, triumph, trophy

palm off *vb* **1 = fob off,** foist off, pass off **2** *often foll. by* **on = foist on,** force upon, impose upon, thrust upon, unload upon

palmy *adj* **1 = prosperous,** flourishing, fortunate, glorious, golden, halcyon, happy, joyous, luxurious, thriving, triumphant

palpable *adj* **1 = obvious,** apparent, blatant, clear, conspicuous, evident, manifest, open, patent, plain, salient, unmistakable, visible **2 =**

tangible. [C14: from LL *palpābilis* that may be touched, from L *palpāre* to touch]
▸ ˌpalpaˈbility *n* ▸ ˈpalpably *adv*

palpate (ˈpælpeɪt) *vb* **palpates, palpating, palpated.** (*tr*) *Med.* to examine (an area of the body) by the sense of touch. [C19: from L *palpāre* to stroke]
▸ palˈpation *n*

palpebral (ˈpælpɪbrəl) *adj* of or relating to the eyelid. [C19: from LL, from L *palpebra* eyelid]

palpitate ⓣ (ˈpælpɪˌteɪt) *vb* **palpitates, palpitating, palpitated.** (*intr*) **1** (of the heart) to beat rapidly. **2** to flutter or tremble. [C17: from L *palpitāre* to throb, from *palpāre* to stroke]
▸ ˈpalpitant *adj* ▸ ˌpalpiˈtation *n*

palsy ⓣ (ˈpɔːlzɪ) *Pathol.* ◆ *n, pl* **palsies. 1** paralysis, esp. of a specified type: *cerebral palsy.* ◆ *vb* **palsies, palsying, palsied.** (*tr*) **2** to paralyse. [C13 *palesi*, from OF *paralisie*, from L PARALYSIS]
▸ ˈpalsied *adj*

palter (ˈpɔːltə) *vb* (*intr*) **1** to act or talk insincerely. **2** to haggle. [C16: from ?]

paltry ⓣ (ˈpɔːltrɪ) *adj* **paltrier, paltriest. 1** insignificant; meagre. **2** worthless or petty. [C16: from Low Gmc *palter, paltrig* ragged]
▸ ˈpaltrily *adv* ▸ ˈpaltriness *n*

paludal (pəˈljuːdᵊl) *adj Rare.* **1** of or relating to marshes. **2** malarial. [C19: from L *palus* marsh]

paludism (ˈpæljuˌdɪzəm) *n* a less common word for **malaria.** [C19: from L *palus* marsh]

palynology (ˌpælɪˈnɒlədʒɪ) *n* the study of living and fossil pollen grains and plant spores. [C20: from Gk *palunein* to scatter + -LOGY]
▸ **palynological** (ˌpælɪnəˈlɒdʒɪkᵊl) *adj* ▸ ˌpalyˈnologist *n*

pampas (ˈpæmpəz) *n* (*functioning as sing or more often pl*) **a** the extensive grassy plains of temperate South America, esp. in Argentina. **b** (*as modifier*): *pampas dwellers.* [C18: from American Sp. *pampa* (sing), from Amerind *bamba* plain]
▸ **pampean** (ˈpæmpɪən, pæmˈpiːən) *adj*

pampas grass (ˈpæmpəs, -pəz) *n* any of various large South American grasses, widely cultivated for their large feathery silver-coloured flower branches.

pamper ⓣ (ˈpæmpə) *vb* (*tr*) **1** to treat with affectionate and usually excessive indulgence; coddle; spoil. **2** *Arch.* to feed to excess. [C14: of Gmc origin]
▸ ˈpamperer *n*

pamphlet ⓣ (ˈpæmflɪt) *n* **1** a brief publication generally having a paper cover; booklet. **2** a brief treatise, often on a subject of current interest, in pamphlet form. [C14 *pamflet*, from Med. L *Pamphilus* title of a 12th-century amatory poem from Gk *Pamphilos* proper name]

pamphleteer (ˌpæmflɪˈtɪə) *n* **1** a person who writes or issues pamphlets. ◆ *vb* **2** (*intr*) to write or issue pamphlets.

Pamphylia (pæmˈfɪlɪə) *n* an area on the S coast of ancient Asia Minor.

pan[1] ⓣ (pæn) *n* **1a** a wide metal vessel used in cooking. **1b** (*in combination*): *saucepan.* **2** Also called: **panful.** the amount such a vessel will hold. **3** any of various similar vessels used in industry, etc. **4** a dish used esp. by gold prospectors for separating gold from gravel by washing and agitating. **5** either of the two dishlike receptacles on a balance. **6** Also called: **lavatory pan.** *Brit.* the bowl of a lavatory. **7a** a natural or artificial depression in the ground where salt can be obtained by the evaporation of brine. **7b** a natural depression containing water or mud. **8** See **hardpan, brainpan. 9** a small cavity containing priming powder in the locks of old guns. **10** a hard substratum of soil. ◆ *vb* **pans, panning, panned. 11** (when *tr*, often foll. by *off* or *out*) to wash (gravel) in a pan to separate particles of (valuable minerals) from it. **12** (*intr*; often foll. by *out*) (of gravel, etc.) to yield valuable minerals by this process. **13** (*tr*) *Inf.* to criticize harshly: *the critics panned his new play.* ◆ See also **pan out.** [OE *panne*]

pan[2] ⓣ (pæn) *vb* **pans, panning, panned. 1** to move (a film camera) or (of a film camera) to be moved so as to follow a moving object or obtain a panoramic effect. ◆ *n* **2** the act of panning. [C20: shortened from PANORAMIC]

pan- *combining form.* **1** all or every: *panchromatic.* **2** including or relating to all parts or members: *Pan-American; pantheistic.* [from Gk *pan*, neuter of *pas* all]

panacea ⓣ (ˌpænəˈsɪə) *n* a remedy for all diseases or ills. [C16: via L from Gk *panakeia*, from *pan* all + *akēs* remedy]
▸ ˌpanaˈcean *adj*

panache ⓣ (pəˈnæʃ, -ˈnɑːʃ) *n* **1** a dashing manner; swagger: *he rides with panache.* **2** a plume on a helmet. [C16: via F from OIt. *pennacchio*, from LL *pinnāculum* feather, from L *pinna* feather]

panada (pəˈnɑːdə) *n* a mixture of flour, water, etc., or of breadcrumbs soaked in milk, used as a thickening. [C16: from Sp., from *pan* bread, from L *pānis*]

Panama hat (ˌpænəˈmɑː) *n* (*sometimes not cap.*) a hat made of the plaited leaves of a palmlike plant of Central and South America. Often shortened to **panama** or **Panama.**

Pan-American *adj* of, relating to, or concerning North, South, and Central America collectively or the advocacy of political or economic unity among American countries.
▸ ˈPan-AˈmericanˌIsm *n*

panatella (ˌpænəˈtɛlə) *n* a long slender cigar. [American Sp. *panetela* long slim biscuit, from It. *panatella* small loaf, from *pane* bread, from L *pānis*]

pancake (ˈpænˌkeɪk) *n* **1** a thin flat cake made from batter and fried on both sides. **2** a stick or flat cake of compressed make-up. **3** Also called: **pancake landing.** an aircraft landing made by levelling out a few feet from the ground and then dropping onto it. ◆ *vb* **pancakes, pancaking, pancaked. 4** to cause (an aircraft) to make a pancake landing or (of an aircraft) to make a pancake landing.

Pancake Day *n* another name for **Shrove Tuesday.** See **Shrovetide.**

panchromatic (ˌpænkrəʊˈmætɪk) *adj Photog.* (of an emulsion or film) made sensitive to all colours.
▸ **panchromatism** (pænˈkrəʊməˌtɪzəm) *n*

pancosmism (pænˈkɒzˌmɪzəm) *n* the philosophical doctrine that the material universe is all that exists.

pancreas (ˈpæŋkrɪəs) *n* a large elongated glandular organ, situated behind the stomach, that secretes insulin and pancreatic juice. [C16: via NL from Gk *pankreas*, from PAN- + *kreas* flesh]
▸ **pancreatic** (ˌpæŋkrɪˈætɪk) *adj*

pancreatic juice *n* the clear alkaline secretion of the pancreas that is released into the duodenum and contains digestive enzymes.

pancreatin (ˈpæŋkrɪətɪn) *n* the powdered extract of the pancreas of certain animals, used in medicine as an aid to the digestion.

panda (ˈpændə) *n* **1** Also called: **giant panda.** a large black-and-white herbivorous bearlike mammal, related to the raccoons and inhabiting the high mountain bamboo forests of China. **2 lesser** *or* **red panda.** a closely related smaller animal resembling a raccoon, of the mountain forests of S Asia, having a reddish-brown coat and ringed tail. [C19: via F from a native Nepalese word]

panda car *n Brit.* a police patrol car. [C20: so called because its blue-and-white markings resemble the black-and-white markings of the giant panda]

pandanus (pænˈdeɪnəs) *n, pl* **pandanuses.** any of various Old World tropical palmlike plants having leaves and roots yielding a fibre used for making mats, etc. [C19: via NL from Malay *pandan*]

pandect (ˈpændɛkt) *n* **1** a treatise covering all aspects of a particular subject. **2** (*often pl*) the complete body of laws of a country; legal code, esp. the digest of Roman civil law made in the 6th century by order of Justinian. [C16: via LL from Gk *pandektēs* containing everything, from PAN- + *dektēs* receiver]

pandemic (pænˈdɛmɪk) *adj* **1** (of a disease) affecting persons over a wide geographical area; extensively epidemic. ◆ *n* **2** a pandemic disease. [C17: from LL *pandēmus*, from Gk *pandēmos* general, from PAN- + *dēmos* the people]

pandemonium ⓣ (ˌpændɪˈməʊnɪəm) *n* **1** wild confusion; uproar. **2** a place of uproar and chaos. [C17: coined by Milton for the capital of hell in *Paradise Lost*, from PAN- + Gk *daimōn* DEMON]

pander ⓣ (ˈpændə) *vb* **1** (*intr*; foll. by *to*) to give gratification (to weaknesses or desires). **2** (*arch.* when tr) to act as a go-between in a sexual intrigue (for). ◆ *n also* **panderer. 3** a person who caters for vulgar desires. **4** a person who procures a sexual partner for another; pimp. [C16 (n): from *Pandare* Pandarus, in legend, the procurer of Cressida for Troilus]

pandit (ˈpʌndɪt; *spelling pron* ˈpændɪt) *n Hinduism.* a variant of **pundit** (sense 3).

P & L *abbrev. for* profit and loss.

THESAURUS

tangible, concrete, material, real, solid, substantial, touchable

palpitate *vb* **1, 2** = **beat**, flutter, pitapat, pitter-patter, pound, pulsate, pulse, quiver, shiver, throb, tremble, vibrate

palsied *adj* **2** = **paralysed**, arthritic, atonic (*Pathology*), crippled, debilitated, disabled, helpless, paralytic, rheumatic, sclerotic, shaking, shaky, spastic, trembling

paltry *adj* **1, 2** = **insignificant**, base, beggarly, contemptible, crappy (*sl.*), derisory, despicable, inconsiderable, low, meagre, mean, measly, Mickey Mouse (*sl.*), minor, miserable, petty, piddling (*inf.*), pitiful, poor, poxy (*sl.*), puny, slight, small, sorry, trifling, trivial, two-penny-halfpenny (*Brit. inf.*), unimportant, worthless, wretched

Antonyms *adj* consequential, considerable, essential, grand, important, major, mega (*sl.*), significant, valuable

pamper *vb* **1** = **spoil**, baby, cater to one's every whim, coddle, cosset, fondle, gratify, humour, indulge, mollycoddle, pander to, pet, wait on (someone) hand and foot

pamphlet *n* **1** = **booklet**, brochure, circular, folder, leaflet, tract

pan[1] *n* **1** = **pot**, container, saucepan, vessel ◆ *vb* **11** = **sift out**, look for, search for, separate, wash **13** *Informal* = **criticize**, blast, censure, flay, hammer (*Brit. inf.*), knock (*inf.*), lambast(e), put down, roast (*inf.*), rubbish (*inf.*), slag (off) (*sl.*), slam (*sl.*), slate (*inf.*), tear into (*inf.*)

pan[2] *vb* **1** = **move**, follow, scan, sweep, swing, track, traverse

panacea *n* = **cure-all**, catholicon, elixir, nostrum, sovereign remedy, universal cure

panache *n* **1** = **style**, a flourish, brio, dash, élan, flair, flamboyance, spirit, swagger, verve

pandemonium *n* **1** = **uproar**, babel, bedlam, chaos, clamour, commotion, confusion, din, hubbub, hue and cry, hullabaloo, racket, ruckus (*inf.*), ruction (*inf.*), rumpus, tumult, turmoil

Antonyms *n* arrangement, calm, hush, order, peace, peacefulness, quietude, repose, stillness, tranquillity

pander *vb* **1** *foll. by* **to** = **indulge**, cater to, fawn on, gratify, play up to (*inf.*), please, satisfy ◆ *n* **4** *Chiefly archaic* = **pimp**, go-between, mack (*sl.*), ponce (*sl.*), procurer, white-slaver, whoremaster (*arch.*)

DICTIONARY

P & O *abbrev. for* the Peninsular and Oriental Steam Navigation Company.

p & p *Brit. abbrev. for* postage and packing.

pane (peɪn) *n* **1** a sheet of glass in a window or door. **2** a panel of a window, door, wall, etc. **3** a flat section or face, as of a cut diamond. [C13: from OF *pan* portion, from L *pannus* rag]

panegyric (ˌpænɪˈdʒɪrɪk) *n* a formal public commendation; eulogy. [C17: via F & L from Gk, from *panēguris* public gathering] ▸ˌ**paneˈgyrical** *adj* ▸ˌ**paneˈgyrically** *adv* ▸ˌ**paneˈgyrist** *n* ▸**panegyrize** *or* **panegyrise** (ˈpænɪdʒɪˌraɪz) *vb*

panel (ˈpænəl) *n* **1** a flat section of a wall, door, etc. **2** any distinct section of something formed from a sheet of material, esp. of a car body. **3** a piece of material inserted in a skirt, etc. **4a** a group of persons selected to act as a team in a quiz, to discuss a topic before an audience, etc. **4b** (*as modifier*): *a panel game*. **5** *Law*. **5a** a list of persons summoned for jury service. **5b** the persons on a jury. **6** *Scots Law*. a person accused of a crime. **7a** a thin board used as a surface or backing for an oil painting. **7b** a painting done on such a surface. **8** any picture with a length much greater than its breadth. **9** See **instrument panel**. **10** *Brit*. (formerly) **10a** a list of patients insured under the National Health Insurance Scheme. **10b** a list of medical practitioners available for consultation by these patients. ◆ *vb* **panels, panelling, panelled** *or US* **panels, paneling, paneled**. (*tr*) **11** to furnish or decorate with panels. **12** *Law*. **12a** to empanel (a jury). **12b** (in Scotland) to bring (a person) to trial; indict. [C13: from OF: portion, from *pan* piece of cloth, from L *pannus*]

panel beater *n* a person who beats out the bodywork of motor vehicles, etc.

panelling *or US* **paneling** (ˈpænəlɪŋ) *n* **1** panels collectively, as on a wall or ceiling. **2** material used for making panels.

panellist *or US* **panelist** (ˈpænəlɪst) *n* a member of a panel, esp. on radio or television.

panel pin *n* a slender nail with a narrow head.

panel saw *n* a saw with a long narrow blade for cutting thin wood.

panel van *n Austral. & NZ*. a small van.

Pan-European *adj* of or relating to all European countries or the advocacy of political or economic unity among European countries.

pang Ⓣ (pæŋ) *n* a sudden brief sharp feeling, as of loneliness, physical pain, or hunger. [C16: var. of earlier *prange*, of Gmc origin]

panga (ˈpæŋgə) *n* a broad heavy knife of E Africa. [from a native E African word]

pangolin (pæŋˈgəʊlɪn) *n* a mammal of tropical Africa, S Asia, and Indonesia, having a scaly body and a long snout for feeding on ants and termites. Also called: **scaly anteater**. [C18: from Malay *peng-gōling*, from *gōling* to roll over; from its ability to roll into a ball]

Pan Gu (pænˈguː) *or* **P'an Ku** *n* 32–92 A.D., Chinese historian and court official, noted for his history of the Han dynasty: died in prison.

panhandle[1] (ˈpænˌhændəl) *n* (*sometimes cap*.) (in the US) a narrow strip of land that projects from one state into another.

panhandle[2] (ˈpænˌhændəl) *vb* **panhandles, panhandling, panhandled**. *US inf*. to beg from (passers-by). [C19: prob. a back formation from *panhandler* a person who begs with a pan] ▸ˈ**panˌhandler** *n*

Panhellenic (ˌpænheˈlenɪk) *adj* of or relating to all the Greeks or all Greece.

panic Ⓣ (ˈpænɪk) *n* **1** a sudden overwhelming feeling of terror or anxiety, esp. one affecting a whole group of people. **2** (*modifier*) of or resulting from such terror: *panic measures*. **3** (*modifier*) for use in an emergency: *panic stations; panic button*. ◆ *vb* **panics, panicking, panicked**. **4** to feel or cause to feel panic. [C17: from F *panique*, from NL, from Gk *panikos* emanating from *Pan*, Gk god of the fields, considered as the source of irrational fear] ▸ˈ**panicky** *adj*

panic attack *n* an episode of acute and disabling anxiety associated with such physical symptoms as hyperventilation and sweating.

panic button *n* a button or switch that operates a safety device or alarm, for use in an emergency.

panic disorder *n Psychiatry*. a condition in which a person experiences recurrent panic attacks.

panic grass *n* any of various grasses, such as millet, grown in warm and tropical regions for fodder and grain. [C15 *panic*, from L *pānicum*, prob. a back formation from *pānicula* PANICLE]

panicle (ˈpænɪkəl) *n* a compound raceme, as in the oat. [C16: from L *pānicula* tuft, dim. of *panus* thread, ult. from Gk *penos* web] ▸ˈ**panicled** *adj* ▸**paniculate** (pəˈnɪkjʊˌleɪt, -lɪt) *adj*

panic-stricken Ⓣ *or* **panic-struck** *adj* affected by panic.

panjandrum (pænˈdʒændrəm) *n* a pompous self-important official or person of rank. [C18: after a character in a nonsense work (1755) by S. Foote, E playwright]

pan loaf *n Scot*. a loaf of bread with a light crust all the way round. Often shortened to **pan**.

pannage (ˈpænɪdʒ) *n Arch*. **1** the right to pasture pigs in a forest. **2** payment for this. **3** acorns, beech mast, etc., on which pigs feed. [C13: from OF *pasnage*, ult. from L *pastion-*, *pastiō* feeding, from *pascere* to feed]

pannier (ˈpænɪə) *n* **1** a large basket, esp. one of a pair slung over a beast of burden. **2** one of a pair of bags slung either side of the back wheel of a motorcycle, etc. **3** (esp. in the 18th century) **3a** a hooped framework to distend a woman's skirt. **3b** one of two puffed-out loops of material worn drawn back onto the hips. [C13: from OF *panier*, from L *pānārium* basket for bread, from *pānis* bread]

pannikin (ˈpænɪkɪn) *n Chiefly Brit*. a small metal cup or pan. [C19: from PAN[1] + -KIN]

pannikin boss *n Austral. sl*. a minor overseer.

panoply Ⓣ (ˈpænəplɪ) *n, pl* **panoplies**. **1** a complete or magnificent array. **2** the entire equipment of a warrior. [C17: via F from Gk, from PAN- + *hopla* armour] ▸ˈ**panoplied** *adj*

panoptic (pænˈɒptɪk) *adj* taking in all parts, aspects, etc., in a single view; all-embracing. [C19: from Gk *panoptēs* seeing everything]

panorama Ⓣ (ˌpænəˈrɑːmə) *n* **1** an extensive unbroken view in all directions. **2** a wide or comprehensive survey of a subject. **3** a large extended picture of a scene, unrolled before spectators a part at a time so as to appear continuous. **4** another name for **cyclorama**. [C18: from PAN- + Gk *horāma* view] ▸**panoramic** (ˌpænəˈræmɪk) *adj* ▸ˌ**panoˈramically** *adv*

pan out Ⓣ *vb* (*intr, adv*) *Inf*. to work out; result.

panpipes (ˈpænˌpaɪps) *pl n* (*often sing; often cap*.) a number of reeds or whistles of graduated lengths bound together to form a musical wind instrument. Also called: **pipes of Pan, syrinx**.

pansy (ˈpænzɪ) *n, pl* **pansies**. **1** a garden plant having flowers with rounded velvety petals, white, yellow, or purple in colour. See also **wild pansy**. **2** *Sl*. an effeminate or homosexual man or boy. [C15: from OF *pensée* thought, from *penser* to think, from L *pensāre*]

pant Ⓣ (pænt) *vb* **1** to breathe with noisy deep gasps, as when out of breath from exertion. **2** to say (something) while breathing thus. **3** (*intr; often foll. by for*) to have a frantic desire (for). **4** (*intr*) to throb rapidly. ◆ *n* **5** the act or an instance of panting. **6** a short deep gasping noise. [C15: from OF *pantaisier*, from Gk *phantasioun* to have visions, from *phantasia* FANTASY]

pantalets *or* **pantalettes** (ˌpæntəˈlets) *pl n* **1** long drawers extending below the skirts: worn during the 19th century. **2** ruffles for the ends of such drawers. [C19: dim. of PANTALOONS]

pantaloon (ˌpæntəˈluːn) *n* **1** (in pantomime) an absurd old man, the butt of the clown's tricks. **2** (*usually cap*.) (in commedia dell'arte) a lecherous old merchant dressed in pantaloons. [C16: from F *Pantalon*, from It. *Pantalone*, prob. from *San Pantaleone*, a fourth-century Venetian saint]

pantaloons (ˌpæntəˈluːnz) *pl n* **1** *History*. **1a** men's tight-fitting trousers fastened below the calf or under the shoe. **1b** children's trousers resembling these. **2** *Inf*. any trousers, esp. baggy ones.

pantechnicon (pænˈteknɪkən) *n Brit*. **1** a large van, esp. one used for furniture removals. **2** a warehouse where furniture is stored. [C19: from PAN- + Gk *tekhnikon* relating to the arts, from *tekhnē* art; orig. a London bazaar, later used as a furniture warehouse]

pantheism (ˈpænθɪˌɪzəm) *n* **1** the doctrine that regards God as identical with the material universe or the forces of nature. **2** readiness to worship all gods. ▸ˈ**pantheist** *n* ▸ˌ**pantheˈistic** *or* ˌ**pantheˈistical** *adj* ▸ˌ**pantheˈistically** *adv*

pantheon (ˈpænθɪən) *n* **1** (esp. in ancient Greece or Rome) a temple to all the gods. **2** all the gods of a religion. **3** a building commemorating a nation's dead heroes. [C14: via L from Gk *Pantheion*, from PAN- + *-theios* divine, from *theos* god]

panther (ˈpænθə) *n, pl* **panthers** *or* **panther**. **1** another name for **leopard** (sense 1), esp. the black variety (**black panther**). **2** *US & Canad*. any of various related animals, esp. the puma. [C14: from OF *pantère*, from L *panthēra*, from Gk *panthēr*]

panties (ˈpæntɪz) *pl n* a pair of women's or children's underpants.

pantihose (ˈpæntɪˌhəʊz) *pl n* See **panty hose**.

pantile (ˈpænˌtaɪl) *n* a roofing tile, with an S-shaped cross section, so

THESAURUS

pang *n* = **twinge**, ache, agony, anguish, discomfort, distress, gripe, pain, prick, spasm, stab, sting, stitch, throe (*rare*), wrench

panic *n* **1** = **fear**, agitation, alarm, consternation, dismay, fright, horror, hysteria, scare, terror ◆ *vb* **4** = **go to pieces**, become hysterical, be terror-stricken, have kittens (*inf*.), lose one's bottle (*Brit. sl*.), lose one's nerve, overreact **4** = **alarm**, put the wind up (someone) (*inf*.), scare, startle, terrify, unnerve

panicky *adj* **1** = **frightened**, afraid, agitated, distressed, fearful, frantic, frenzied, hysterical, in a flap (*inf*.), in a tizzy (*inf*.), jittery (*inf*.), nervous, windy (*sl*.), worked up, worried

Antonyms *adj* calm, collected, composed, confident, cool, imperturbable, self-controlled, together (*sl*.), unexcitable, unfazed (*inf*.), unflappable, unruffled

panic-stricken *adj* = **frightened**, aghast, agitated, alarmed, appalled, fearful, frenzied, frightened to death, horrified, horror-stricken, hysterical, in a cold sweat (*inf*.), panicky, petrified, scared, scared stiff, startled, terrified, terror-stricken, unnerved

panoply *n* **1** = **array**, attire, dress, garb, get-up (*inf*.), insignia, raiment (*arch. or poetic*), regalia, show, trappings, turnout

panorama *n* **1** = **view**, bird's-eye view, prospect, scenery, scenic view, vista **2** = **survey**, overall picture, overview, perspective

panoramic *adj* **1, 2** = **wide**, all-embracing, bird's-eye, comprehensive, extensive, far-reaching, general, inclusive, overall, scenic, sweeping

pan out *vb Informal* = **work out**, come out, come to pass (*arch*.), culminate, eventuate, happen, result, turn out

pant *vb* **1** = **puff**, blow, breathe, gasp, heave, huff, palpitate, throb, wheeze **3** *with* **for** = **long**, ache, covet, crave, desire, eat one's heart out over, hanker after, hunger, pine, set one's heart

that the downward curve of one tile overlaps the upward curve of the next. [C17: from PAN[1] + TILE]

pantisocracy (ˌpæntɪˈsɒkrəsɪ) *n, pl* **pantisocracies.** a community, social group, etc., in which all have rule and everyone is equal. [C18: (coined by Robert Southey, E poet) from Gk, from PANTO- + *isos* equal + -CRACY]

panto (ˈpæntəʊ) *n, pl* **pantos.** *Brit. inf.* short for **pantomime** (sense 1).

panto- *or before a vowel* **pant-** *combining form.* all: *pantisocracy; pantograph; pantomime.* [from Gk *pant-, pas*]

pantograph (ˈpæntəˌgrɑːf) *n* **1** an instrument consisting of pivoted levers for copying drawings, maps, etc., to any scale. **2** a sliding type of current collector, esp. a diamond-shaped frame mounted on a train roof in contact with an overhead wire. **3** a device used to suspend a studio lamp so that its height can be adjusted.
▸**pantographic** (ˌpæntəˈgræfɪk) *adj*

pantomime (ˈpæntəˌmaɪm) *n* **1** (in Britain) a kind of play performed at Christmas time characterized by farce, music, lavish sets, stock roles, and topical jokes. **2** a theatrical entertainment in which words are replaced by gestures and bodily actions. **3** action without words as a means of expression. **4** *Inf., chiefly Brit.* a confused or farcical situation. ◆ *vb* **pantomimes, pantomiming, pantomimed. 5** another word for **mime.** [C17: via L from Gk *pantomīmos*]
▸**pantomimic** (ˌpæntəˈmɪmɪk) *adj* ▸**pantomimist** (ˈpæntəˌmaɪmɪst) *n*

pantothenic acid (ˌpæntəˈθenɪk) *n* an oily acid that is a vitamin of the B complex: occurs widely in animal and vegetable foods. [C20: from Gk *pantothen* from every side]

pantry (ˈpæntrɪ) *n, pl* **pantries.** a small room in which provisions, cooking utensils, etc., are kept; larder. [C13: via Anglo-Norman from OF *paneterie* store for bread, ult. from L *pānis* bread]

pants ❶ (pænts) *pl n* **1** *Brit.* an undergarment covering the body from the waist to the thighs or knees. **2** the usual US and Canad. name for **trousers. 3 bore, scare,** etc., **the pants off.** *Inf.* to bore, scare, etc., extremely. [C19: shortened from *pantaloons*]

panty girdle (ˈpæntɪ) *n* a foundation garment with a crotch, often of lighter material than a girdle.

panty hose *pl n* the US name for **tights** (sense 1). Also (Canad. and NZ) **pantyhose,** (Austral.) **pantihose.**

panzer (ˈpænzə; *German* ˈpantsər) *n* **1** (*modifier*) of or relating to the fast mechanized armoured units employed by the German army in World War II: *a panzer attack.* **2** a vehicle belonging to a panzer unit, esp. a tank. **3** (*pl*) armoured troops. [C20: from G, from MHG, from OF *panciere* coat of mail, from L *pantex* PAUNCH]

pap[1] ❶ (pæp) *n* **1** any soft or semiliquid food, esp. for babies or invalids; mash. **2** worthless or oversimplified ideas, etc.; drivel. **3** *S. African.* maize porridge. [C15: from MLow G *pappe,* via Med. L from L *pappāre* to eat]

pap[2] (pæp) *n* **1** *Arch. or Scot. & N English dialect.* a nipple or teat. **2** something resembling a breast, such as one of a pair of rounded hilltops. [C12: from ON, imit. of a sucking sound]

papa (pəˈpɑː) *n Old-fashioned.* an informal word for **father.** [C17: from F, a children's word for father]

papacy (ˈpeɪpəsɪ) *n, pl* **papacies. 1** the office or term of office of a pope. **2** the system of government in the Roman Catholic Church that has the pope as its head. [C14: from Med. L *pāpātia,* from *pāpa* POPE]

papain (pəˈpeɪɪn, -ˈpaɪɪn) *n* an enzyme occurring in the unripe fruit of the papaya tree: used as a meat tenderizer and in medicine as an aid to protein digestion. [C19: from PAPAYA]

papal (ˈpeɪpᵊl) *adj* of or relating to the pope or the papacy.
▸ˈ**papally** *adv*

paparazzo (ˌpæpəˈrætsəʊ) *n, pl* **paparazzi** (-ˈrætsiː). a freelance photographer who specializes in candid camera shots of famous people. [C20: from It.]

papaver (pæˈpɑːvə) *n* any of a genus of hardy annual or perennial plants with showy flowers; poppy. [L: poppy]

papaveraceous (pəˌpeɪvəˈreɪʃəs) *adj* of or relating to a family of plants having large showy flowers and a cylindrical seed capsule with pores beneath the lid: includes the poppies and greater celandine. [C19: from NL, from L *papāver* poppy]

papaverine (pəˈpeɪvəˌriːn, -rɪn) *n* a white crystalline alkaloid found in opium and used to treat coronary spasms and certain types of colic. [C19: from L *papāver* poppy]

papaw (pəˈpɔː) *or* **pawpaw** *n* **1** Also called: **custard apple. 1a** a bush or small tree of Central North America, having small fleshy edible fruit. **1b** the fruit of this tree. **2** another name for **papaya.** [C16: from Sp. PAPAYA]

papaya (pəˈpaɪə) *n* **1** a Caribbean evergreen tree with a crown of large dissected leaves and large green hanging fruit. **2** the fruit of this tree, having a yellow sweet edible pulp and small black seeds. ◆ Also called: **papaw, pawpaw.** [C15 *papaye,* from Sp. *papaya,* of Amerind origin]

paper ❶ (ˈpeɪpə) *n* **1** a substance made from cellulose fibres derived from rags, wood, etc., and formed into flat thin sheets suitable for writing on, decorating walls, wrapping, etc. **2** a single piece of such material, esp. if written or printed on. **3** (*usually pl*) documents for establishing the identity of the bearer. **4** (*pl*) Also called: **ship's papers.** official documents relating to a ship. **5** (*pl*) collected diaries, letters, etc. **6** See **newspaper, wallpaper. 7** *Government.* See **white paper, green paper. 8** a lecture or treatise on a specific subject. **9** a short essay. **10a** a set of examination questions. **10b** the student's answers. **11** *Commerce.* See **commercial paper. 12** *Theatre sl.* a free ticket. **13 on paper.** in theory, as opposed to fact. ◆ *adj* **14** made of paper: *paper cups do not last long.* **15** thin like paper: *paper walls.* **16** (*prenominal*) existing only as recorded on paper but not yet in practice: *paper expenditure.* **17** taking place in writing: *paper battles.* ◆ *vb* **18** to cover (walls) with wallpaper. **19** (*tr*) to cover or furnish with paper. **20** (*tr*) *Theatre sl.* to fill (a performance, etc.) by giving away free tickets (esp. in **paper the house**). ◆ See also **paper over.** [C14: from L PAPYRUS]
▸ˈ**paperer** *n* ▸ˈ**papery** *adj*

paperback (ˈpeɪpəˌbæk) *n* **1** a book or edition with covers made of flexible card. ◆ *adj* **2** of or denoting a paperback or publication of paperbacks. ◆ *vb* **3** (*tr*) to publish a paperback edition of a book.

paperbark (ˈpeɪpəˌbɑːk) *n* any of several Australian trees of swampy regions, having papery bark that can be peeled off in thin layers.

paperboy (ˈpeɪpəˌbɔɪ) *n* a boy employed to deliver newspapers, etc.
▸ˈ**paperˌgirl** *fem n*

paper chase *n* a former type of cross-country run in which a runner laid a trail of paper for others to follow.

paperclip (ˈpeɪpəˌklɪp) *n* a clip for holding sheets of paper together, esp. one of bent wire.

paper-cutter *n* a machine for cutting paper, usually a blade mounted over a table.

paperhanger (ˈpeɪpəˌhæŋə) *n* a person who hangs wallpaper as an occupation.

paperknife (ˈpeɪpəˌnaɪf) *n, pl* **paperknives.** a knife with a comparatively blunt blade for opening sealed envelopes, etc.

paper money *n* paper currency issued by the government or the central bank as legal tender and which circulates as a substitute for specie.

paper mulberry *n* a small E Asian tree, the inner bark of which was formerly used for making paper in Japan. See also **tapa.**

paper nautilus *n* a cephalopod mollusc of warm and tropical seas, having a papery external spiral shell. Also called: **argonaut.**

paper over *vb* (*tr, adv*) to conceal (something controversial or unpleasant) (esp. in **paper over the cracks**).

paper tape *n* a strip of paper for recording information in the form of rows of either six or eight holes, some or all of which are punched to produce a combination used as a discrete code symbol, formerly used in computers, telex machines, etc. US equivalent: **perforated tape.**

paper tiger *n* a nation, institution, etc., that appears powerful but is in fact weak or insignificant. [C20: translation of a Chinese phrase first applied to the US]

paperweight (ˈpeɪpəˌweɪt) *n* a small heavy object to prevent loose papers from scattering.

paperwork (ˈpeɪpəˌwɜːk) *n* clerical work, such as the writing of reports or letters.

Paphian (ˈpeɪfɪən) *adj* **1** of or relating to Paphos, a village in SW Cyprus. **2** of or relating to Aphrodite, who was worshipped at Paphos. **3** *Literary.* of sexual love.

papier-mâché (ˌpæpjeɪˈmæʃeɪ) *n* **1** a hard strong substance made of paper pulp or layers of paper mixed with paste, size, etc., and moulded when moist. ◆ *adj* **2** made of papier-mâché. [C18: from F, lit.: chewed paper]

papilionaceous (pəˌpɪlɪəˈneɪʃəs) *adj* of, relating to, or belonging to a family of leguminous plants having irregular flowers: includes peas, beans, clover, alfalfa, gorse, and broom. [C17: from NL, from L *pāpiliō* butterfly]

papilla (pəˈpɪlə) *n, pl* **papillae** (-liː). **1** the small projection of tissue at the base of a hair, tooth, or feather. **2** any similar protuberance. [C18: from L: nipple]
▸**paˈpillary** *or* ˈ**papillate** *adj*

papilloma (ˌpæpɪˈləʊmə) *n, pl* **papillomata** (-mətə) *or* **papillomas.** *Pathol.* a benign tumour forming a rounded mass. [C19: from PAPILLA + -OMA]

papillon (ˈpæpɪˌlɒn) *n* a breed of toy dog with large ears. [F: butterfly, from L *pāpiliō*]

papillote (ˈpæpɪˌləʊt) *n* **1** a paper frill around cutlets, etc. **2 en papillote** (ɑ̃ papijɔt). (of food) cooked in oiled greaseproof paper or foil. [C18: from F PAPILLON]

papist (ˈpeɪpɪst) *n, adj* (*often cap.*) *Usually disparaging.* another term for **Roman Catholic.** [C16: from F *papiste,* from Church L *pāpa* POPE]
▸**paˈpistical** *or* **paˈpistic** *adj* ▸ˈ**papistry** *n*

papoose (pəˈpuːs) *n* **1** an American Indian baby. **2** a pouchlike bag

THESAURUS

on, sigh, suspire (*arch. or poetic*), thirst, want, yearn ◆ *n* **6** = **puff,** gasp, huff, wheeze

pants *pl n* **1** *Brit.* = **underpants,** boxer shorts, briefs, drawers, knickers, panties, Y-fronts (*Trademark*) **2** *U.S. & Canad.* = **trousers,** slacks

pap[1] *n* **1** = **mush,** baby food, mash, pulp **2** = **rubbish,** drivel, trash, trivia

paper *n* **3** *usually plural* = **documents,** certificates, deeds, instruments, records **5** *usually plural* = **letters,** archive, diaries, documents, dossier, file, records **6** = **newspaper,** blat, daily, gazette, journal, news, organ, rag (*inf.*) **8** = **essay,** analysis, article, assignment, composition, critique, dissertation, examination, monograph, report, script, study, thesis, treatise **13 on paper** = **in theory,** ideally, in the abstract, theoretically ◆ *adj* **14, 15** = **disposable,** cardboard, flimsy, insubstantial, paper-thin, papery, thin ◆ *vb* **18, 19** = **wallpaper,** cover with paper, hang, line, paste up

papery *adj* **15** = **thin,** flimsy, fragile, frail, insubstantial, light, lightweight, paperlike, paper-thin, wafer-thin

used for carrying a baby, worn on the back. [C17: from Algonquian *papoos*]

pappus ('pæpəs) *n, pl* **pappi** ('pæpaɪ). a ring of fine feathery hairs surrounding the fruit in composite plants, such as the thistle. [C18: via NL from Gk *pappos* old man, old man's beard, hence: pappus, down]
▸**'pappose** *or* **'pappous** *adj*

paprika ('pæprɪkə, pæ'pri:-) *n* **1** a mild powdered seasoning made from a sweet variety of red pepper. **2** the fruit or plant from which this seasoning is obtained. [C19: via Hungarian from Serbian, from *papar* PEPPER]

Pap test *or* **smear** (pæp) *n Med.* **1** another name for **cervical smear. 2** a similar test for precancerous cells in organs other than the cervix. ◆ Also called: **Papanicolaou smear.** [C20: after George *Papanicolaou* (1883–1962), US anatomist, who devised it]

papule ('pæpju:l) *or* **papula** ('pæpjʊlə) *n, pl* **papules** *or* **papulae** (-jʊ,li:). *Pathol.* a small solid usually round elevation of the skin. [C19: from L *papula* pustule]
▸**'papular** *adj*

papyrology (,pæpɪ'rɒlədʒɪ) *n* the study of ancient papyri.
▸**,papy'rologist** *n*

papyrus (pə'paɪrəs) *n, pl* **papyri** (-raɪ) *or* **papyruses. 1** a tall aquatic plant of S Europe and N and central Africa. **2** a kind of paper made from the stem pith of this plant, used by the ancient Egyptians, Greeks, and Romans. **3** an ancient document written on this paper. [C14: via L from Gk *papūros* reed used in making paper]

par Ⓣ (pɑ:) *n* **1** an accepted standard, such as an average (esp. in **up to par**). **2** a state of equality (esp. in **on a par with**). **3** *Finance.* the established value of the unit of one national currency in terms of the unit of another. **4** *Commerce.* **4a** See **par value. 4b** equality between the current market value of a share, bond, etc., and its face value, indicated by **at par; above** (*or* **below**) **par** indicates that the market value is above (or below) face value. **5** *Golf.* a standard score for a hole or course that a good player should make: *par for the course was 72.* ◆ *adj* **6** average or normal. **7** (*usually prenominal*) of or relating to par: *par value.* [C17: from L *pār* equal]

par. *abbrev. for:* **1** paragraph. **2** parallel. **3** parenthesis. **4** parish.

Par. *abbrev. for* Paraguay.

para ('pærə) *n Inf.* **1a** a soldier in an airborne unit. **1b** an airborne unit. **2** a paragraph.

para-[1] *or before a vowel* **par-** *prefix* **1** beside; near: *parameter.* **2** beyond: *parapsychology.* **3** resembling: *paratyphoid fever.* **4** defective; abnormal: *paranoia.* **5** (*usually in italics*) denoting that an organic compound contains a benzene ring with substituents attached to atoms that are directly opposite (the 1,4- positions): *paracresol.* **6** denoting an isomer, polymer, or compound related to a specified compound: *paraldehyde.* **7** denoting the form of a diatomic substance in which the spins of the two constituent atoms are antiparallel: *parahydrogen.* [from Gk *para* (prep) alongside, beyond]

para-[2] *combining form.* indicating an object that acts as a protection against something: *parachute; parasol.* [via F from It. *para-*, from *parare* to defend, ult. from L *parāre* to prepare]

para-aminobenzoic acid (ə,maɪnəʊbɛn'zəʊɪk, -,mi:-) *n Biochem.* an acid present in yeast and liver: used in the manufacture of dyes and pharmaceuticals.

parabasis (pə'ræbəsɪs) *n, pl* **parabases** (-,si:z). (in classical Greek comedy) an address by the chorus. [C19: from Gk, from *parabanein* to step forward]

parabiosis (,pærəbaɪ'əʊsɪs) *n* **1** the natural union of two individuals, such as Siamese twins. **2** a similar union induced for experimental or therapeutic purposes. [C20: from PARA-[1] + Gk *biōsis* manner of life, from *bios* life]
▸**parabiotic** (,pærəbaɪ'ɒtɪk) *adj*

parable Ⓣ ('pærəb(ə)l) *n* **1** a short story that uses familiar events to illustrate a religious or ethical point. **2** any of the stories of this kind told by Jesus Christ. [C14: from OF *parabole*, from L *parabola* comparison, from Gk *parabolē* analogy, from *paraballein* to throw alongside]

parabola (pə'ræbələ) *n* a conic section formed by the intersection of a cone by a plane parallel to its side. [C16: via NL from Gk *parabolē* a setting alongside; see PARABLE]

parabolic[1] (,pærə'bɒlɪk) *adj* **1** of, relating to, or shaped like a parabola. **2** shaped like a paraboloid: *a parabolic mirror.*

parabolic[2] Ⓣ (,pærə'bɒlɪk) *or* **parabolical** *adj* of or like a parable.
▸**,para'bolically** *adv*

parabolic aerial *n* a formal name for **dish aerial.**

paraboloid (pə'ræbə,lɔɪd) *n* a geometric surface whose sections parallel to two coordinate planes are parabolic and whose sections parallel to the third plane are either elliptical or hyperbolic.
▸**pa,rabo'loidal** *adj*

paracetamol (,pærə'si:tə,mɒl, -'sɛtə-) *n* a mild analgesic drug. [C20: from *para-acetamidophenol*]

parachronism (pə'rækrə,nɪzəm) *n* an error in dating, esp. by giving too late a date. [C17: from PARA-[1] + *-chronism*, as in ANACHRONISM]

parachute ('pærə,ʃu:t) *n* **1** a device used to retard the fall of a person or package from an aircraft, consisting of a large fabric canopy connected to a harness. ◆ *vb* **parachutes, parachuting, parachuted. 2** (of troops, supplies, etc.) to land or cause to land by parachute from an aircraft. [C18: from F, from PARA-[2] + *chute* fall]
▸**'para,chutist** *n*

Paraclete ('pærə,kli:t) *n Christianity.* the Holy Ghost as comforter or advocate. [C15: via OF from Church L *Paraclētus*, from LGk *Paraklētos* advocate, from Gk *parakalein* to summon help]

parade Ⓣ (pə'reɪd) *n* **1** an ordered, esp. ceremonial, march or procession, as of troops being reviewed. **2** Also called: **parade ground.** a place where military formations regularly assemble. **3** a visible show or display: *to make a parade of one's grief.* **4** a public promenade or street of shops. **5** a successive display of things or people. **6 on parade. 6a** on display. **6b** showing oneself off. ◆ *vb* **parades, parading, paraded. 7** (when *intr*, often foll. by *through* or *along*) to walk or march, esp. in a procession. **8** (*tr*) to exhibit or flaunt: *he was parading his medals.* **9** (*tr*) to cause to assemble in formation, as for a military parade. **10** (*intr*) to walk about in a public place. [C17: from F: a making ready, a boasting display]
▸**pa'rader** *n*

paradiddle ('pærə,dɪd(ə)l) *n* a group of four drumbeats played with alternate sticks in the pattern right-left-right-right or left-right-left-left. [C20: imit.]

paradigm Ⓣ ('pærə,daɪm) *n* **1** the set of all the inflected forms of a word. **2** a pattern or model. **3** (in the philosophy of science) a general conception of the nature of scientific endeavour within which a given enquiry is undertaken. [C15: via F & L from Gk *paradeigma* pattern, from *paradeiknunai* to compare]
▸**paradigmatic** (,pærədɪg'mætɪk) *adj*

paradisal Ⓣ (,pærə'daɪs(ə)l), **paradisiacal** (,pærədɪ'saɪək(ə)l), *or* **paradisiac** (,pærə'dɪsɪ,æk) *adj* of, relating to, or resembling paradise.

paradise Ⓣ ('pærə,daɪs) *n* **1** heaven as the ultimate abode or state of the righteous. **2** *Islam.* the sensual garden of delights that the Koran promises the faithful after death. **3** Also called: **limbo.** (according to some theologians) the intermediate abode or state of the just prior to the Resurrection of Jesus. **4** the Garden of Eden. **5** any place or condition that fulfils all one's desires or aspirations. **6** a park in which foreign animals are kept. [OE, from Church L *paradīsus*, from Gk *paradeisos* garden, of Persian origin]

paradise duck *n* a New Zealand duck with bright plumage.

paradox Ⓣ ('pærə,dɒks) *n* **1** a seemingly absurd or self-contradictory statement that is or may be true: *religious truths are often expressed in paradox.* **2** a self-contradictory proposition, such as *I always tell lies.* **3** a person or thing exhibiting apparently contradictory characteristics. **4** an opinion that conflicts with common belief. [C16: from LL *paradoxum*, from Gk *paradoxos* opposed to existing notions]
▸**,para'doxical** *adj* ▸**,para'doxically** *adv*

paradoxical sleep *n Physiol.* sleep that appears deep but is characterized by a brain wave pattern similar to that of wakefulness, rapid eye movements, and heavier breathing.

paraffin ('pærəfɪn) *n* **1** Also called: **paraffin oil,** (esp. US, Canad., Austral., & NZ) **kerosene.** a liquid mixture consisting mainly of alkane hydrocarbons, used as an aircraft fuel, in domestic heaters, and as a solvent. **2** another name for **alkane. 3** See **paraffin wax. 4** See **liquid paraffin.** ◆ *vb* (*tr*) **5** to treat with paraffin. [C19: from G, from L *parum* too little + *affinis* adjacent; so called from its chemical inertia]

paraffin wax *n* a white insoluble odourless waxlike solid consisting mainly of alkane hydrocarbons, used in candles, waterproof paper, and as a sealant. Also called: **paraffin.**

paragliding ('pærə,glaɪdɪŋ) *n* the sport of cross-country gliding using a specially designed parachute shaped like flexible wings. The parachutist glides from an aeroplane to a predetermined landing area.

paragon Ⓣ ('pærəgən) *n* a model of excellence; pattern: *a paragon of virtue.* [C16: via F from OIt. *paragone* comparison, from Med. Gk *parakonē*, from PARA-[1] + *akonē* whetstone]

paragraph Ⓣ ('pærə,grɑ:f) *n* **1** (in a piece of writing) one of a series of subsections each usually devoted to one idea and each marked by the

THESAURUS

par *n* **1 = average,** level, mean, median, norm, standard, usual **2 = equivalence,** balance, equal footing, equality, equilibrium, parity

parable *n* **1 = lesson,** allegory, exemplum, fable, moral tale, story

parabolic[2] *adj* **= allegorical,** figurative, metaphoric, symbolic

parade *n* **1 = procession,** array, cavalcade, ceremony, column, march, pageant, review, spectacle, train **3 = show,** array, display, exhibition, flaunting, ostentation, pomp, spectacle, vaunting ◆ *vb* **7 = march,** defile, process **8 = flaunt,** air, brandish, display, exhibit, make a show of, show, show off (*inf.*), strut, swagger, vaunt

paradigm *n* **2 = model,** archetype, example, exemplar, ideal, norm, original, pattern, prototype

paradisal *adj* **= heavenly,** blessed, blissful, celestial, divine, Elysian, glorious, golden, out of this world (*inf.*), utopian

paradise *n* **1 = heaven,** City of God, divine abode, Elysian fields, garden of delights, Happy Valley (*Islam*), heavenly kingdom, Olympus (*poetic*), Promised Land, Zion (*Christianity*) **4 = Garden of Eden,** Eden **5 = bliss,** delight, felicity, heaven, seventh heaven, utopia

paradox *n* **1, 2 = contradiction,** absurdity, ambiguity, anomaly, enigma, inconsistency, mystery, oddity, puzzle

paradoxical *adj* **1, 2 = contradictory,** absurd, ambiguous, baffling, confounding, enigmatic, equivocal, illogical, impossible, improbable, inconsistent, oracular, puzzling, riddling

paragon *n* **= model,** apotheosis, archetype, criterion, cynosure, epitome, exemplar, ideal, jewel, masterpiece, nonesuch (*arch.*), nonpareil, norm, paradigm, pattern, prototype, quintessence, standard

paragraph *n* **1 = section,** clause, item, notice, part, passage, portion, subdivision

beginning of a new line, indention, etc. **2** *Printing.* the character ¶, used to indicate the beginning of a new paragraph. **3** a short article, etc., in a newspaper. ◆ *vb (tr)* **4** to form into paragraphs. **5** to express or report in a paragraph. [C16: from Med. L *paragraphus,* from Gk *paragraphos* line drawing attention to part of a text, from *paragraphein* to write beside]
▸**paragraphic** (ˌpærəˈgræfɪk) *adj*

paragraphia (ˌpærəˈgrɑːfɪə) *n Psychiatry.* the habitual writing of a different word or letter from the one intended, often the result of a mental disorder. [C20: from NL; see PARA-[1], -GRAPH]

Paraguayan (ˈpærəˌgwaɪən) *adj* **1** of or relating to Paraguay, a republic in South America. ◆ *n* **2** a native or inhabitant of Paraguay or a descendant of one.

Paraguay tea (ˈpærəˌgwaɪ) *n* another name for **maté**.

parahydrogen (ˌpærəˈhaɪdrədʒən) *n Chem.* the form of molecular hydrogen in which the nuclei of the two atoms in each molecule spin in opposite directions.

parakeet *or* **parrakeet** (ˈpærəˌkiːt) *n* any of numerous small long-tailed parrots. [C16: from Sp. *periquito* & OF *paroquet* parrot, from ?]

paraldehyde (pəˈrældɪˌhaɪd) *n* a colourless liquid that is a cyclic trimer of acetaldehyde: used as a hypnotic.

paralipsis (ˌpaerəˈlɪpsɪs) *or* **paraleipsis** (ˌpærəˈlaɪpsɪs) *n, pl* **paralipses** *or* **paraleipses** (-siːz). a rhetorical device in which an idea is emphasized by the pretence that it is too obvious to discuss, as in *there are many practical drawbacks, not to mention the cost.* [C16: via LL from Gk: neglect, from *paraleipein* to leave aside]

parallax (ˈpærəˌlæks) *n* **1** an apparent change in the position of an object resulting from a change in position of the observer. **2** *Astron.* the angle subtended at a celestial body, esp. a star, by the radius of the earth's orbit. [C17: via F from NL *parallaxis,* from Gk: change, from *parallassein* to change]
▸**parallactic** (ˌpærəˈlæktɪk) *adj*

parallel ⓣ (ˈpærəˌlɛl) *adj* (when *postpositive,* usually foll. by *to*) **1** separated by an equal distance at every point; never touching or intersecting: *parallel walls.* **2** corresponding; similar: *parallel situations.* **3** *Music.* Also: **consecutive.** (of two or more parts or melodies) moving in similar motion but keeping the same interval apart throughout: *parallel fifths.* **4** *Grammar.* denoting syntactic constructions in which the constituents of one construction correspond to those of the other. **5** *Computing.* operating on several items of information, instructions, etc., simultaneously. ◆ *n* **6** *Maths.* one of a set of parallel lines, planes, etc. **7** an exact likeness. **8** a comparison. **9** Also called: **parallel of latitude.** any of the imaginary lines around the earth parallel to the equator, designated by degrees of latitude. **10** *Electronics.* **10a** an arrangement of two or more electrical components connected between two points in a circuit so that the same voltage is applied to each (esp. in **in parallel**). Cf. **series** (sense 6). **10b** (*as modifier*): *a parallel circuit.* **11** *Printing.* the character (‖) used as a reference mark. ◆ *vb* **parallels, paralleling, paralleled.** (*tr*) **12** to make parallel. **13** to supply a parallel to. **14** to be a parallel to or correspond with: *your experience parallels mine.* [C16: via F & L from Gk *parallēlos* alongside one another, from PARA-[1] + *allēlos* one another]

parallel bars *pl n Gymnastics.* a pair of wooden bars on uprights used for various exercises.

parallelepiped (ˌpærəˌlɛlɪˈpaɪpɛd) *or* **parallelepipedon** (ˌpærəˌlɛlɪˈpaɪpɪdən) *n* a geometric solid whose six faces are parallelograms. [C16: from Gk, from *parallēlos* PARALLEL + *epipedon* plane surface, from EPI- + *pedon* ground]

paralleling (ˈpærəˌlɛlɪŋ) *n* a form of trading in which companies buy highly priced goods in a market in which the prices are low in order to be able to sell them in a market in which the prices are higher.

parallelism (ˈpærəˌlɛlɪzəm) *n* **1** the state of being parallel. **2** *Grammar.* the repetition of a syntactic construction in successive sentences for rhetorical effect. **3** *Philosophy.* the doctrine that mental and physical processes are regularly correlated but are not casually connected, so that, for example, pain always accompanies, but is not caused by, a pinprick.

parallelogram (ˌpærəˈlɛləˌgræm) *n* a quadrilateral whose opposite sides are parallel and equal in length. [C16: via F from LL, from Gk *parallēlogrammon,* from *parallēlos* PARALLEL + *grammē* line]

parallelogram rule *n Maths, physics.* a rule for finding the resultant of two vectors by constructing a parallelogram with two adjacent sides representing the magnitudes and directions of the vectors, the diagonal through the point of intersection of the vectors representing their resultant.

parallel processing *n* the performance by a computer system of two or more simultaneous operations.

parallel ruler *n Engineering.* a drawing instrument in which two parallel edges are connected so that they remain parallel, although the distance between them can be varied.

paralogism (pəˈræləˌdʒɪzəm) *n* **1** *Logic, psychol.* an argument that is unintentionally invalid. Cf. **sophism. 2** any invalid argument or conclusion. [C16: via LL from Gk *paralogismos,* from *paralogizesthai* to argue fallaciously, from PARA-[1] + *-logizesthai,* ult. from *logos* word]
▸**paˈralogist** *n*

Paralympian (ˌpærəˈlɪmpɪən) *n* a competitor in the Paralympics.

Paralympics (ˌpærəˈlɪmpɪks) *n* **the.** (*functioning as sing or pl*) a sporting event, modelled on the Olympic Games, held solely for disabled competitors. Also called: **the Parallel Olympics.** [C20: from PARALLEL + OLYMPICS]

paralyse ⓣ *or US* **paralyze** (ˈpærəˌlaɪz) *vb* **paralyses, paralysing, paralysed** *or US* **paralyzes, paralyzing, paralyzed.** (*tr*) **1** *Pathol.* to affect with paralysis. **2** *Med.* to render (a part of the body) insensitive to pain, touch, etc. **3** to make immobile; transfix. [C19: from F *paralyser,* from *paralysie* PARALYSIS]
▸ˌ**paralyˈsation** *or US* ˌ**paralyˈzation** *n* ▸ˈ**paraˌlyser** *or US* ˈ**paraˌlyzer** *n*

paralysis ⓣ (pəˈrælɪsɪs) *n, pl* **paralyses** (-ˌsiːz). **1** *Pathol.* **1a** impairment or loss of voluntary muscle function or of sensation (**sensory paralysis**) in a part or area of the body. **1b** a disease characterized by such impairment or loss; palsy. **2** cessation or impairment of activity: *paralysis of industry by strikes.* [C16: via L from Gk *paralusis;* see PARA-[1], -LYSIS]

paralytic ⓣ (ˌpærəˈlɪtɪk) *adj* **1** of, relating to, or of the nature of paralysis. **2** afflicted with or subject to paralysis. **3** *Brit. inf.* very drunk. ◆ *n* **4** a person afflicted with paralysis.

paramagnetism (ˌpærəˈmægnɪˌtɪzəm) *n Physics.* a weakly magnetic condition of substances with a relative permeability just greater than unity: used in some special low temperature techniques.
▸**paramagnetic** (ˌpærəmægˈnɛtɪk) *adj*

paramatta *or* **parramatta** (ˌpærəˈmætə) *n* a lightweight twill-weave dress fabric of wool with silk or cotton, now used esp. for rubber-proofed garments. [C19: after *Parramatta,* New South Wales, Australia, where orig. produced]

paramecium (ˌpærəˈmiːsɪəm) *n, pl* **paramecia** (-sɪə). any of a genus of freshwater protozoa having an oval body covered with cilia and a ventral groove for feeding. [C18: NL, from Gk *paramēkēs* elongated, from PARA-[1] + *mēkos* length]

paramedic (ˌpærəˈmɛdɪk) *n* **1** a person, such as a laboratory technician, who supplements the work of the medical profession. **2** a member of an ambulance crew trained in a number of life-saving skills, including infusion and cardiac care.
▸ˌ**paraˈmedical** *adj*

parameter ⓣ (pəˈræmɪtə) *n* **1** an arbitrary constant that determines the specific form of a mathematical expression, such as *a* and *b* in $y = ax^2 + b$. **2** a characteristic constant of a statistical population, such as its variance or mean. **3** *Inf.* any constant or limiting factor: *a designer must work within the parameters of budget and practicality.* [C17: from NL; see PARA-[1], -METER]
▸**parametric** (ˌpærəˈmɛtrɪk) *adj*

parametric amplifier *n* a type of high-frequency amplifier in which energy is transferred to the input signal through a circuit with a varying reactance.

paramilitary (ˌpærəˈmɪlɪtərɪ, -trɪ) *adj* **1** denoting or relating to a group of personnel with military structure functioning either as a civil force or in support of military forces. **2** denoting or relating to a force with military structure conducting armed operations against a ruling power.

paramount ⓣ (ˈpærəˌmaʊnt) *adj* of the greatest importance or significance. [C16: via Anglo-Norman from OF *paramont,* from *par* by + *-amont* above, from L *ad montem* to the mountain]
▸ˈ**paraˌmountcy** *n* ▸ˈ**paraˌmountly** *adv*

paramour ⓣ (ˈpærəˌmʊə) *n* **1** *Now usually derog.* a lover, esp. adulterous. **2** an archaic word for **beloved.** [C13: from OF, lit.: through love]

parang (ˈpɑːræŋ) *n* a Malay short stout straight-edged knife used in Borneo. [C19: from Malay]

paranoia ⓣ (ˌpærəˈnɔɪə) *n* **1** a mental disorder characterized by any of several types of delusions, as of grandeur or persecution. **2** *Inf.* intense

THESAURUS

parallel *adj* **1** = **equidistant,** aligned, alongside, coextensive, side by side **2** = **matching,** akin, analogous, complementary, correspondent, corresponding, like, resembling, similar, uniform ◆ *n* **7** = **equivalent,** analogue, complement, corollary, counterpart, duplicate, equal, likeness, match, twin **8** = **similarity,** analogy, comparison, correlation, correspondence, likeness, parallelism, resemblance ◆ *vb* **14** = **correspond,** agree, be alike, chime with, compare, complement, conform, correlate, equal, keep pace (with), match
Antonyms *adj* ≠ **matching:** different, dissimilar, divergent, non-parallel, unlike ◆ *n* ≠ **equivalent:** opposite, reverse ≠ **similarity:** difference, dissimilarity, divergence ◆ *vb* ≠ **correspond:** be unlike, differ, diverge

paralyse *vb* **1** = **disable,** cripple, debilitate, incapacitate, lame **2, 3** = **immobilize,** anaesthetize, arrest, benumb, freeze, halt, numb, petrify, stop dead, stun, stupefy, transfix

paralysis *n* **1** = **immobility,** palsy, paresis (*Pathology*) **2** = **standstill,** arrest, breakdown, halt, inactivity, shutdown, stagnation, stoppage

paralytic *adj* **2** = **paralysed,** crippled, disabled, immobile, immobilized, incapacitated, lame, numb, palsied **3** *Brit. informal* = **drunk,** bevvied (*dialect*), blitzed (*sl.*), blotto (*sl.*), flying (*sl.*), inebriated, intoxicated, legless (*inf.*), pie-eyed (*sl.*), plastered (*sl.*), sloshed (*sl.*), smashed (*sl.*), stoned (*sl.*), tired and emotional (*euphemistic*), wasted (*sl.*), wrecked (*sl.*)

parameter *n* **3** *Informal* = **limit,** constant, criterion, framework, guideline, limitation, restriction, specification

paramount *adj* = **principal,** capital, cardinal, chief, dominant, eminent, first, foremost, main, outstanding, predominant, pre-eminent, primary, prime, superior, supreme
Antonyms *adj* inferior, insignificant, least, minor, negligible, secondary, slight, subordinate, trifling, unimportant

paramour *n Now usually derogatory* = **lover,** beau, concubine, courtesan, fancy bit (*sl.*),

fear or suspicion, esp. when unfounded. [C19: via NL from Gk: frenzy, from *paranoos* distraught, from PARA-[1] + *noos* mind]
▸ **'para,noid, paranoiac** (,pærə'nɔɪɪk) *or* **paranoic** (,pærə'nəʊɪk) *adj, n*

paranormal (,pærə'nɔ:məl) *adj* **1** beyond normal explanation. ◆ *n* **2** **the.** paranormal happenings generally.

parapente ('pærə,pɒnt) *n* **1** another name for **paraskiing. 2** the form of parachute used in this sport. [C20: from PARA(CHUTE) + F *pente* slope]

parapet ('pærəpɪt, -,pɛt) *n* **1** a low wall or railing along the edge of a balcony, roof, etc. **2** *Mil.* a rampart, mound of sandbags, etc., in front of a trench giving protection from fire. [C16: from It. *parapetto,* lit.: chest-high wall, from L *pectus* breast]

paraph ('pærəf) *n* a flourish after a signature, originally to prevent forgery. [C14: via F from Med. L *paraphus,* var. of *paragraphus* PARAGRAPH]

paraphernalia ➊ (,pærəfə'neɪlɪə) *pl n* (*sometimes functioning as sing*) **1** miscellaneous articles or equipment. **2** *Law.* (formerly) articles of personal property given to a married woman by her husband and regarded in law as her possessions. [C17: via Med. L from L *parapherna* personal property of a married woman, apart from her dowry, from Gk, from PARA-[1] + *phernē* dowry, from *pherein* to carry]

paraphrase ➊ ('pærə,freɪz) *n* **1** an expression of a statement or text in other words. ◆ *vb* **paraphrases, paraphrasing, paraphrased. 2** to put into other words; restate. [C16: via F from L *paraphrasis,* from Gk, from *paraphrazein* to recount]
▸ **paraphrastic** (,pærə'fræstɪk) *adj*

paraplegia (,pærə'pli:dʒə) *n Pathol.* paralysis of the lower half of the body, usually as the result of disease or injury of the spine. [C17: via NL from Gk: a blow on one side, from PARA-[1] + *plēssein* to strike]
▸ **,para'plegic** *adj, n*

parapraxis (,pærə'præksɪs) *n, pl* **parapraxes** (-'præksi:z) *Psychoanal.* a minor error in action, such as a slip of the tongue. [C20: from PARA-[1] + Gk *praxis* a deed]

parapsychology (,pærəsaɪ'kɒlədʒɪ) *n* the study of mental phenomena, such as telepathy, which are beyond the scope of normal physical explanation.
▸ **,parapsy'chologist** *n*

Paraquat ('pærə,kwɒt) *n Trademark.* a yellow extremely poisonous weedkiller.

parascending ('pærə,sɛndɪŋ) *n* a sport in which a parachutist, starting from ground level, is towed by a vehicle until he is airborne and then descends in the normal way.

paraselene (,pærəsɪ'li:nɪ) *n, pl* **paraselenae** (-ni:). a bright image of the moon on a lunar halo. Also called: **mock moon.** [C17: NL, from PARA-[1] + Gk *selēnē* moon]

parasite ➊ ('pærə,saɪt) *n* **1** an animal or plant that lives in or on another (the host) from which it obtains nourishment. **2** a person who habitually lives at the expense of others; sponger. [C16: via L from Gk *parasitos* one who lives at another's expense, from PARA-[1] + *sitos* grain]
▸ **parasitic** (,pærə'sɪtɪk) *or* **,para'sitical** *adj* ▸ **,para'sitically** *adv*
▸ **'parasi,tism** *n*

parasitize *or* **parasitise** ('pærəsɪ,taɪz) *vb* **parasitizes, parasitizing, parasitized** *or* **parasitises, parasitising, parasitised.** (*tr*) **1** to infest with parasites. **2** to live on (another organism) as a parasite.
▸ **,parasiti'zation** *or* **,parasiti'sation** *n*

parasitoid ('pærəsɪ,tɔɪd) *n Zool.* an animal, esp. an insect, that is parasitic as a larva but becomes free-living when adult.

parasitology (,pærəsaɪ'tɒlədʒɪ) *n* the branch of biology that is concerned with the study of parasites.
▸ **,parasit'ologist** *n*

paraskiing ('pærə,ski:ɪŋ) *n* the sport of jumping off high mountains wearing skis and a light parachute composed of inflatable fabric tubes that form a semirigid wing. Also called: **parapente.**

parasol ('pærə,sɒl) *n* an umbrella used for protection against the sun; sunshade. [C17: via F from It. *parasole,* from PARA-[2] + *sole* sun, from L *sōl*]

parasuicide (,pærə'su:ɪ,saɪd) *n* an attempt to inflict an injury on oneself, not motivated by a desire to die.

parasympathetic (,pærə,sɪmpə'θɛtɪk) *adj Anat., Physiol.* of or relating to the division of the autonomic nervous system that acts by slowing the heartbeat, constricting the bronchi of the lungs, stimulating the smooth muscles of the digestive tract, etc. Cf. **sympathetic** (sense 4).

parasynthesis (,pærə'sɪnθɪsɪs) *n* formation of words by compounding a phrase and adding an affix, as *light-headed, light* + *head* with the affix *-ed.*
▸ **parasynthetic** (,pærəsɪn'θɛtɪk) *adj*

parataxis (,pærə'tæksɪs) *n* the juxtaposition of clauses without the use of a conjunction, as *None of my friends stayed —they all left early.* [C19: NL from Gk, from *paratassein,* lit.: to arrange side by side]
▸ **paratactic** (,pærə'tæktɪk) *adj*

parathion (,pærə'θaɪɒn) *n* a toxic oil used as an insecticide. [from PARA-[1] + Gk *theion* sulphur]

parathyroid gland (,pærə'θaɪrɔɪd) *n* any one of the small egg-shaped endocrine glands situated near or embedded within the thyroid gland.

paratroops ('pærə,tru:ps) *pl n* troops trained and equipped to be dropped by parachute into a battle area. Also called: **paratroopers.**

paratyphoid fever (,pærə'taɪfɔɪd) *n* a disease resembling but less severe than typhoid fever, caused by bacteria of the genus *Salmonella.*

paravane ('pærə,veɪn) *n* a torpedo-shaped device towed from the bow of a vessel so that the cables will cut the anchors of any moored mines. [C20: from PARA-[2] + VANE]

par avion *French.* (par avjɔ̃) *adv* by aeroplane: used in labelling mail sent by air.

parazoan (,pærə'zəʊən) *n, pl* **parazoa** (-'zəʊə). any multicellular invertebrate of a division of the animal kingdom, the sponges. [C19: from *parazoa,* on the model of *protozoa* & *metazoa,* from PARA-[1] + Gk *zōon* animal]

parboil ('pɑ:,bɔɪl) *vb* (*tr*) **1** to boil until partially cooked. **2** to subject to uncomfortable heat. [C15: from OF *parboillir,* from LL *perbullīre* to boil thoroughly (see PER-, BOIL[1]); modern meaning due to confusion of *par-* with *part*]

parbuckle ('pɑ:,bʌkᵊl) *n* **1** a rope sling for lifting or lowering a heavy cylindrical object, such as a cask. ◆ *vb* **parbuckles, parbuckling, parbuckled. 2** (*tr*) to raise or lower (an object) with such a sling. [C17 *parbunkel:* from ?]

parcel ➊ ('pɑ:sᵊl) *n* **1** something wrapped up; package. **2** a group of people or things having some common characteristic. **3** a quantity of some commodity offered for sale; lot. **4** a distinct portion of land. ◆ *vb* **parcels, parcelling, parcelled** *or US* **parcels, parceling, parceled.** (*tr*) **5** (often foll. by *up*) to make a parcel of; wrap up. **6** (often foll. by *out*) to divide (up) into portions. [C14: from OF *parcelle,* from L *particula* PARTICLE]

parch ➊ (pɑ:tʃ) *vb* **1** to deprive or be deprived of water; dry up: *the sun parches the fields.* **2** (*tr; usually passive*) to make very thirsty. **3** (*tr*) to roast (corn, etc.) lightly. [C14: from ?]

Parcheesi (pɑ:'tʃi:zɪ) *n Trademark.* a board game derived from the ancient game of pachisi.

parchment ('pɑ:tʃmənt) *n* **1** the skin of certain animals, such as sheep, treated to form a durable material, as for manuscripts. **2** a manuscript, etc., made of this material. **3** a type of stiff yellowish paper resembling parchment. [C13: from OF *parchemin,* via L from Gk *pergamēnē,* from *Pergamēnos* of Pergamum (where parchment was made); OF *parchemin* was infl. by *parche* leather, from L *Parthica* (*pellis*) Parthian (leather)]

pard (pɑ:d) *n Arch.* a leopard or panther. [C13: via OF from L *pardus,* from Gk *pardos*]

pardon ➊ ('pɑ:dᵊn) *vb* (*tr*) **1** to excuse or forgive (a person) for (an offence, mistake, etc.): *to pardon someone; to pardon a fault.* ◆ *n* **2** forgiveness. **3a** release from punishment for an offence. **3b** the warrant granting such release. **4** a Roman Catholic indulgence. ◆ *sentence substitute.* **5** Also: **pardon me, I beg your pardon. 5a** sorry; excuse me. **5b** what did you say? [C13: from OF, from Med. L *perdōnum,* from *perdōnāre* to forgive freely, from L *per* (intensive) + *dōnāre* to grant]
▸ **'pardonable** *adj* ▸ **'pardonably** *adv*

pardoner ('pɑ:dᵊnə) *n* (before the Reformation) a person licensed to sell ecclesiastical indulgences.

pare ➊ (pɛə) *vb* **pares, paring, pared.** (*tr*) **1** to peel (the outer layer) from (something). **2** to cut the edges from (the nails). **3** to decrease bit by bit. [C13: from OF *parer* to adorn, from L *parāre* to make ready]
▸ **'parer** *n*

paregoric (,pærə'gɒrɪk) *n* a medicine consisting of opium, benzoic

THESAURUS

fancy man (*sl.*), fancy woman (*sl.*), inamorata, inamorato, kept woman, mistress

paranoid *adj* **1** = **mentally ill**, deluded, disturbed, manic, neurotic, obsessive, paranoiac, psychotic, unstable **2** *Informal* = **suspicious**, apprehensive, fearful, nervous, worried

paraphernalia *n* **1** = **equipment**, accoutrements, apparatus, appurtenances, baggage, belongings, effects, equipage, gear, impedimenta, material, stuff, tackle, things, trappings

paraphrase *n* **1** = **rewording**, interpretation, rehash, rendering, rendition, rephrasing, restatement, translation, version ◆ *vb* **2** = **reword**, express in other words *or* one's own words, interpret, rehash, render, rephrase, restate

parasite *n* **2** = **sponger** (*inf.*), bloodsucker (*inf.*), cadger, drone (*Brit.*), hanger-on, leech, scrounger (*inf.*), sponge (*inf.*)

parasitic *adj* **2** = **scrounging** (*inf.*), bloodsucking (*inf.*), cadging, leechlike, sponging (*inf.*)

parcel *n* **1** = **package**, bundle, carton, pack, packet **2** = **group**, band, batch, bunch, collection, company, crew, crowd, gang, lot, pack **4** = **plot**, piece of land, property, tract ◆ *vb* **5** *often foll. by* **up** = **wrap**, do up, pack, package, tie up **6** *often foll. by* **out** = **distribute**, allocate, allot, apportion, carve up, deal out, dispense, divide, dole out, mete out, portion, share out, split up

parch *vb* **1, 2** = **dry up**, blister, burn, dehydrate, desiccate, evaporate, make thirsty, scorch, sear, shrivel, wither

parched *adj* **1, 2** = **dried out** *or* **up**, arid, dehydrated, drouthy (*Scot.*), dry, scorched, shrivelled, thirsty, torrid, waterless, withered

pardon *vb* **1** = **forgive**, absolve, acquit, amnesty, condone, exculpate, excuse, exonerate, free, let off (*inf.*), liberate, overlook, release, remit, reprieve ◆ *n* **2, 3** = **forgiveness**, absolution, acquittal, allowance, amnesty, condonation, discharge, excuse, exoneration, grace, indulgence, mercy, release, remission, reprieve
Antonyms *vb* ≠ **forgive:** admonish, blame, castigate, censure, chasten, chastise, condemn, discipline, excoriate, fine, penalize, punish, rebuke ◆ *n* ≠ **forgiveness:** condemnation, guilt, penalty, punishment, redress, retaliation, retribution, revenge, vengeance

pardonable *adj* **1** = **forgivable**, allowable, condonable, excusable, minor, not serious, permissible, understandable, venial

pare *vb* **1, 2** = **peel**, clip, cut, shave, skin, trim **3** = **cut back**, crop, cut, decrease, dock, lop, prune, reduce, retrench, shear

acid, and camphor, formerly widely used to relieve diarrhoea and coughing. [C17 (meaning: relieving pain): via LL from Gk *parēgoros* relating to soothing speech, from PARA-[1] (beside) + *agora* assembly]

pareira (pəˈrɛərə) *n* the root of a South American climbing plant, used as a diuretic, tonic, and as a source of curare. [C18: from Port. *pareira brava,* lit.: wild vine]

parenchyma (pəˈrɛŋkɪmə) *n* **1** a soft plant tissue consisting of simple thin-walled cells: constitutes the greater part of fruits, stems, roots, etc. **2** animal tissue that constitutes the essential part of an organ as distinct from the blood vessels, connective tissue, etc. [C17: via NL from Gk *parenkhuma* something poured in beside, from PARA-[1] + *enkhuma* infusion]
▸**parenchymatous** (ˌpærɛŋˈkɪmətəs) *adj*

parent ❶ (ˈpɛərənt) *n* **1** a father or mother. **2** a person acting as a father or mother; guardian. **3** *Rare.* an ancestor. **4** a source or cause. **5** an organism or organization that has produced one or more organisms similar to itself. **6** *Physics, chem.* a precursor, such as a nucleus or compound, of a derived entity. [C15: via OF from L *parens* parent, from *parere* to bring forth]
▸**paˈrental** *adj* ▸**ˈparenthood** *n*

parentage ❶ (ˈpɛərəntɪdʒ) *n* **1** ancestry. **2** derivation from a particular origin.

parent company *n* a company that owns a number of subsidiary companies.

parenteral (pæˈrɛntərəl) *adj Med.* **1** (esp. of the route by which a drug is administered) by means other than through the digestive tract, esp. by injection. **2** designating a drug to be injected. [C20: from PARA-[1] + ENTERO- + -AL[1]]

parenthesis ❶ (pəˈrɛnθɪsɪs) *n, pl* **parentheses** (-ˌsiːz). **1** a phrase, often explanatory or qualifying, inserted into a passage with which it is not grammatically connected, and marked off by brackets, dashes, etc. **2** Also called: **bracket.** either of a pair of characters, ( ), used to enclose such a phrase or as a sign of aggregation in mathematical or logical expressions. **3** an interlude; interval. **4 in parenthesis.** inserted as a parenthesis. [C16: via LL from Gk: something placed in besides, from *parentithenai,* from PARA-[1] + EN-[2] + *tithenai* to put]
▸**parenthetic** (ˌpærənˈθɛtɪk) *or* **ˌparenˈthetical** *adj* ▸**ˌparenˈthetically** *adv*

parenthesize *or* **parenthesise** (pəˈrɛnθɪˌsaɪz) *vb* **parenthesizes, parenthesizing, parenthesized** *or* **parenthesises, parenthesising, parenthesised.** (*tr*) **1** to place in parentheses. **2** to insert as a parenthesis. **3** to intersperse (a speech, writing, etc.) with parentheses.

parenting (ˈpɛərəntɪŋ) *n* all the skills and experience of bringing up children.

parent teacher association *n* a social group of the parents of children at a school and their teachers formed in order to foster better understanding between them and to organize fund-raising activities on behalf of the school.

parergon (pəˈrɛəgɒn) *n, pl* **parerga** (-gə). work that is not one's main employment. [C17: from L, from Gk, from PARA-[1] + *ergon* work]

paresis (pəˈriːsɪs, ˈpærɪsɪs) *n, pl* **pareses** (-ˌsiːz). *Pathol.* incomplete or slight paralysis of motor functions. [C17: via NL from Gk: a relaxation, from *parienai* to let go]
▸**paretic** (pəˈrɛtɪk) *adj*

par excellence *French.* (par ɛkselɑ̃s; *English* pɑːr ˈɛksələns) *adv* to a degree of excellence; beyond comparison. [F, lit.: by (way of) excellence]

parfait (pɑːˈfeɪ) *n* a rich frozen dessert made from eggs and cream, fruit, etc. [from F: PERFECT]

parget (ˈpɑːdʒɪt) *n* **1** Also called: **pargeting. 1a** plaster, mortar, etc., used to line chimney flues or cover walls. **1b** plasterwork that has incised ornamental patterns. ◆ *vb* (*tr*). **2** to cover or decorate with parget. [C14: from OF *pargeter* to throw over, from *par* PER- + *geter* to throw]

parhelic circle *n Meteorol.* a luminous band at the same altitude as the sun, parallel to the horizon, caused by reflection of the sun's rays by ice crystals in the atmosphere.

parhelion (pɑːˈhiːlɪən) *n, pl* **parhelia** (-lɪə). one of several bright spots on the parhelic circle or solar halo, caused by the diffraction of light by ice crystals in the atmosphere. Also called: **mock sun.** [C17: via L from Gk *parēlion, from* PARA-[1] (beside) + *hēlios* sun]
▸**parˈhelic** *or* **parheliacal** (ˌpɑːhɪˈlaɪəkᵊl) *adj*

pariah ❶ (pəˈraɪə, ˈpærɪə) *n* **1** a social outcast. **2** (formerly) a member of a low caste in South India. [C17: from Tamil *paraiyan* drummer, from *parai* drum: members were drummers at festivals]

pariah dog *n* another term for **pye-dog.**

parietal (pəˈraɪɪtᵊl) *adj* **1** *Anat., biol.* of or forming the walls of a bodily cavity: *the parietal bones of the skull.* **2** of or relating to the side of the skull. **3** (of plant ovaries) having ovules attached to the walls. **4** *US.* living or having authority within a college. ◆ *n* **5** a parietal bone. [C16: from LL *parietālis,* from L *pariēs* wall]

parietal lobe *n* the portion of each cerebral hemisphere concerned with the perception of sensations of touch, temperature, and taste and with muscular movements.

pari-mutuel (ˌpærɪˈmjuːtʃʊəl) *n, pl* **pari-mutuels** *or* **paris-mutuels** (ˌpærɪˈmjuːtʃʊəlz). a system of betting in which those who have bet on the winners of a race share in the total amount wagered less a percentage for the management. [C19: from F, lit.: mutual wager]

paring ❶ (ˈpɛərɪŋ) *n* (*often pl*) something pared or cut off.

pari passu *Latin.* (ˌpærɪ ˈpæsuː, ˈpɑːrɪ) *adv Usually legal.* with equal speed or progress.

Paris Club (ˈpærɪs) *n* another name for **Group of Ten.**

Paris Commune *n French history.* the council established in Paris in the spring of 1871 in opposition to the National Assembly and esp. to the peace negotiated with Prussia following the Franco-Prussian War.

Paris green *n* an emerald-green poisonous substance used as a pigment and insecticide.

parish ❶ (ˈpærɪʃ) *n* **1** a subdivision of a diocese, having its own church and a clergyman. **2** the churchgoers of such a subdivision. **3** (in England and, formerly, Wales) the smallest unit of local government. **4** (in Louisiana) a county. **5** (in Quebec and New Brunswick, Canada) a subdivision of a county. **6** the people living in a parish. **7 on the parish.** *History.* receiving parochial relief. [C13: from OF *paroisse,* from Church L, from LGk, from *paroikos* Christian, sojourner, from Gk: neighbour, from PARA-[1] (beside) + *oikos* house]

parish clerk *n* a person designated to assist in various church duties.

parish council *n* (in England and, formerly, Wales) the administrative body of a parish. See **parish** (sense 3).

parishioner (pəˈrɪʃənə) *n* a member of a particular parish.

parish pump *adj* of only local interest; parochial.

parish register *n* a book in which the births, baptisms, marriages, and deaths in a parish are recorded.

parity ❶ (ˈpærɪtɪ) *n, pl* **parities. 1** equality of rank, pay, etc. **2** close or exact analogy or equivalence. **3** *Finance.* the amount of a foreign currency equivalent to a specific sum of domestic currency. **4** equality between prices of commodities or securities in two separate markets. **5** *Physics.* **5a** a property of a physical system characterized by the behaviour of the sign of its wave function when reflected in space. The wave function either remains unchanged (**even parity**) or changes in sign (**odd parity**). **5b** a quantum number describing this property, equal to +1 for even parity systems and –1 for odd parity systems. Symbol: *P* **6** *Maths.* a relationship between two integers. If both are odd or both even they have the same parity; if one is odd and one even they have different parity. [C16: from LL *pāritās;* see PAR]

parity check *n* a check made of computer data to ensure that the total number of bits of value 1 (or 0) in each unit of information remains odd or even after transfer between a peripheral device and the memory or vice versa.

park ❶ (pɑːk) *n* **1** a large area of land preserved in a natural state for recreational use by the public. **2** a piece of open land for public recreation in a town. **3** a large area of land forming a private estate. **4** an area designed to accommodate a number of related enterprises: *a business park.* **5** *US & Canad.* a playing field or sports stadium. **6 the park.** *Brit. inf.* a soccer pitch. **7** a gear selector position on the automatic transmission of a motor vehicle that acts as a parking brake. **8** the area in which the equipment and supplies of a military formation are assembled. ◆ *vb* **9** to stop and leave (a vehicle) temporarily. **10** to manoeuvre (a motor vehicle) into a space for it to be left: *try to park without hitting the kerb.* **11** *Stock Exchange.* to register (securities) in the name of another or of nominees in order to conceal their real ownership. **12** (*tr*) *Inf.* to leave or put somewhere: *park yourself in front of the fire.* **13** (*intr*) *Mil.* to arrange equipment in a park. **14** (*tr*) to enclose in or as a park. [C13: from OF *parc,* from Med. L *parricus* enclosure, from Gmc]

parka (ˈpɑːkə) *n* a warm weatherproof coat with a hood, originally worn by Eskimos. [C19: from Aleutian: skin]

parkin (ˈpɑːkɪn) *n* (in Britain and New Zealand) moist spicy ginger cake usually containing oatmeal. [C19: from ?]

parking lot *n* the US and Canad. term for **car park.**

parking meter *n* a timing device, usually coin-operated, that indicates how long a vehicle may be left parked.

parking orbit *n* an orbit around the earth or moon in which a spacecraft can be placed temporarily in order to prepare for the next step in its programme.

parking ticket *n* a summons served for a parking offence.

Parkinson's disease (ˈpɑːkɪnsənz) *n* a progressive chronic disorder of the central nervous system characterized by impaired muscular coor-

THESAURUS

parent *n* **1** = **father** *or* **mother,** begetter, procreator, progenitor, sire **4** = **source,** architect, author, cause, creator, forerunner, origin, originator, prototype, root, wellspring

parentage *n* **1, 2** = **family,** ancestry, birth, derivation, descent, extraction, line, lineage, origin, paternity, pedigree, race, stirps, stock

parenthetical *adj* **1** = **interposed,** bracketed, by-the-way, explanatory, extraneous, extrinsic, incidental, in parenthesis, inserted, qualifying

parenthetically *adv* **1** = **incidentally,** by the bye, by the way, by way of explanation, in parenthesis, in passing

parenthood *n* **1** = **fatherhood** *or* **motherhood,** baby *or* child care, bringing up, child rearing, fathering *or* mothering, nurturing, parenting, rearing, upbringing

pariah *n* **1** = **outcast,** exile, leper, outlaw, undesirable, unperson, untouchable

paring *n* = **clipping,** flake, fragment, peel, peeling, rind, shaving, shred, skin, slice, sliver, snippet

parish *n* **1, 2** = **community,** church, churchgoers, congregation, flock, fold, parishioners

parity *n* **1, 2** = **equality,** consistency, equal terms, equivalence, par, parallelism, quits (*inf.*), uniformity, unity

park *n* **1-3** = **parkland,** estate, garden, grounds, pleasure garden, recreation ground, woodland ◆ *vb* **9, 10** = **leave,** manoeuvre, position, station

dination and tremor. Often shortened to **Parkinson's.** Also called: **Parkinsonism.** [C19: after James *Parkinson* (1755–1824), Brit. surgeon, who first described it]

Parkinson's law *n* the notion, expressed facetiously as a law of economics, that work expands to fill the time available for its completion. [C20: after C. N. *Parkinson* (1909–93), Brit. historian and writer, who formulated it]

park keeper *n* (in Britain) an official who patrols and supervises a public park.

parkland ('pɑːk,lænd) *n* grassland with scattered trees.

parky ('pɑːkɪ) *adj* **parkier, parkiest.** (*usually postpositive*) *Brit. inf.* (of the weather) chilly; cold. [C19: ?from PERKY]

Parl. *abbrev. for:* **1** Parliament. **2** Also: **parl.** parliamentary.

parlance ⓣ ('pɑːləns) *n* a particular manner of speaking, esp. when specialized; idiom: *political parlance.* [C16: from OF, from *parler* to talk, via Med. L from LL *parabola* speech]

parlando (pɑː'lændəʊ) *adj, adv Music.* to be performed as though speaking. [It.: speaking]

parley ⓣ ('pɑːlɪ) *n* **1** a discussion, esp. between enemies under a truce to decide terms of surrender, etc. ◆ *vb* **2** (*intr*) to discuss, esp. with an enemy. [C16: from F, from *parler* to talk, from Med. L *parabolāre,* from LL *parabola* speech]

parliament ⓣ ('pɑːləmənt) *n* **1** an assembly of the representatives of a political nation or people, often the supreme legislative authority. **2** any legislative or deliberative assembly, conference, etc. [C13: from Anglo-L *parliamentum,* from OF *parlement,* from *parler* to speak; see PARLEY]

Parliament ⓣ ('pɑːləmənt) *n* **1** the highest legislative authority in Britain, consisting of the House of Commons, which exercises effective power, the House of Lords, and the sovereign. **2** a similar legislature in another country or state. **3** any of the assemblies of such a body created by a general election and royal summons and dissolved before the next election.

parliamentarian (,pɑːləmɛn'tɛərɪən) *n* **1** an expert in parliamentary procedures. ◆ *adj* **2** of or relating to a parliament.

parliamentary ⓣ (,pɑːlə'mɛntərɪ) *adj* (*sometimes cap.*) **1** of or proceeding from a parliament or Parliament: *a parliamentary decree.* **2** conforming to the procedures of a parliament or Parliament: *parliamentary conduct.* **3** having a parliament or Parliament.

Parliamentary Commissioner *or in full* **Parliamentary Commissioner for Administration** *n* (in Britain) the official name for **ombudsman** (sense 2).

parliamentary private secretary *n* (in Britain) a backbencher in Parliament who assists a minister. Abbrev.: **PPS.**

parliamentary secretary *n* a member of Parliament appointed to assist a minister of the Crown with his departmental responsibilities.

parlour ⓣ *or US* **parlor** ('pɑːlə) *n* **1** *Old-fashioned.* a living room, esp. one kept tidy for the reception of visitors. **2** a small room for guests away from the public rooms in an inn, club, etc. **3** *Chiefly US, Canad., & NZ.* a room or shop equipped as a place of business: *a billiard parlor.* **4** a building equipped for the milking of cows. [C13: from Anglo-Norman *parlur,* from OF *parleur* room in convent for receiving guests, from *parler* to speak; see PARLEY]

parlous ⓣ ('pɑːləs) *Arch. or humorous.* ◆ *adj* **1** dangerous or difficult. **2** cunning. ◆ *adv* **3** extremely. [C14 *perlous,* var. of PERILOUS]
▸ **'parlously** *adv*

Parmesan cheese (,pɑːmɪ'zæn, 'pɑːmɪzən) *n* a hard dry cheese used grated, esp. on pasta dishes and soups. [C16: from F, from It. *parmegiano* of Parma, town in Italy]

Parnassus (pɑː'næsəs) *n* **1 Mount.** a mountain in central Greece: in ancient times sacred to Apollo and the Muses. **2a** the world of poetry. **2b** a centre of poetic or other creative activity.
▸ **Par'nassian** *adj*

parochial ⓣ (pə'rəʊkɪəl) *adj* **1** narrow in outlook or scope; provincial. **2** of or relating to a parish. [C14: via OF from Church L *parochiālis;* see PARISH]
▸ **pa'rochial,ism** *n* ▸ **pa'rochially** *adv*

parody ⓣ ('pærədɪ) *n, pl* **parodies. 1** a musical, literary, or other composition that mimics the style of another composer, author, etc., in a humorous or satirical way. **2** something so badly done as to seem an intentional mockery; travesty. ◆ *vb* **parodies, parodying, parodied. 3** (*tr*) to make a parody of. [C16: via L from Gk *paroidiā* satirical poem, from PARA-[1] + *ōidē* song]
▸ **parodic** (pə'rɒdɪk) *or* **pa'rodical** *adj* ▸ **'parodist** *n*

parol ('pærəl, pə'rəʊl) *Law.* ◆ *n* **1** an oral statement; word of mouth (now only in **by parol**). ◆ *adj* **2a** (of a contract, lease, etc.) made orally or in writing but not under seal. **2b** expressed or given by word of mouth: *parol evidence.* [C15: from OF *parole* speech; see PAROLE]

parole (pə'rəʊl) *n* **1a** the freeing of a prisoner before his sentence has expired, on the condition that he is of good behaviour. **1b** the duration of such conditional release. **2** a promise given by a prisoner, as to be of good behaviour if granted liberty or partial liberty. **3** *Linguistics.* language as manifested in the individual speech acts of particular speakers. **4 on parole.** conditionally released from detention. ◆ *vb* **paroles, paroling, paroled.** (*tr*) **5** to place (a person) on parole. [C17: from OF, from *parole d'honneur* word of honour; *parole* from LL *parabola* speech]
▸ **parolee** (pə,rəʊ'liː) *n*

paronomasia (,pærənəʊ'meɪzɪə) *n Rhetoric.* a play on words, esp. a pun. [C16: via L from Gk, from *paronomazein* to make a change in naming, from PARA-[1] (besides) + *onomazein* to name, from *onoma* a name]

parotid (pə'rɒtɪd) *adj* **1** relating to or situated near the parotid gland. ◆ *n* **2** See **parotid gland.** [C17: via F, via L from Gk *parōtis,* from PARA-[1] (near) + *-ōtis,* from *ous* ear]

parotid gland *n* a large salivary gland, in man situated in front of and below each ear.

parotitis (,pærə'taɪtɪs) *n* inflammation of the parotid gland. See also **mumps.**

-parous *adj combining form.* giving birth to: *oviparous.* [from L *-parus,* from *parere* to bring forth]

paroxysm ⓣ ('pærək,sɪzəm) *n* **1** an uncontrollable outburst: *a paroxysm of giggling.* **2** *Pathol.* **2a** a sudden attack or recurrence of a disease. **2b** any fit or convulsion. [C17: via F from Med. L *paroxysmus* annoyance, from Gk, from *paroxunein* to goad, from PARA-[1] (intensifier) + *oxunein* to sharpen, from *oxus* sharp]
▸ **,parox'ysmal** *adj*

parquet ('pɑːkeɪ, -kɪ) *n* **1** a floor covering of pieces of hardwood fitted in a decorative pattern; parquetry. **2** Also called: **parquet floor.** a floor so covered. **3** *US.* the stalls of a theatre. ◆ *vb* (*tr*) **4** to cover a floor with parquet. [C19: from OF: small enclosure, from *parc* enclosure; see PARK]

parquetry ('pɑːkɪtrɪ) *n* a geometric pattern of inlaid pieces of wood, esp. as used to cover a floor.

parr (pɑː) *n, pl* **parrs** *or* **parr.** a salmon up to two years of age. [C18: from ?]

parrakeet ('pærə,kiːt) *n* a variant spelling of **parakeet.**

parramatta (,pærə'mætə) *n* a variant spelling of **paramatta.**

parricide ('pærɪ,saɪd) *n* **1** the act of killing either of one's parents. **2** a person who kills his or her parent. [C16: from L *parricīdium* murder of a parent or relative, & from *parricīda* one who murders a relative, from *parri-* (rel. to Gk *pēos* kinsman) + -CIDE]
▸ **,parri'cidal** *adj*

parrot ⓣ ('pærət) *n* **1** any of several related tropical and subtropical birds having a short hooked bill, bright plumage, and an ability to mimic sounds. **2** a person who repeats or imitates the words or actions of another. **3 sick as a parrot.** *Usually facetious.* extremely disappointed. ◆ *vb* **parrots, parroting, parroted. 4** (*tr*) to repeat or imitate without understanding. [C16: prob. from F *paroquet,* from ?]

parrot-fashion ⓣ *adv Inf.* without regard for meaning; by rote: *she learned it parrot-fashion.*

parrot fever *or* **disease** *n* another name for **psittacosis.**

parrotfish ('pærət,fɪʃ) *n, pl* **parrotfish** *or* **parrotfishes.** a brightly coloured tropical marine percoid fish having parrot-like jaws.

parry ⓣ ('pærɪ) *vb* **parries, parrying, parried. 1** to ward off (an attack, etc.) by blocking or deflecting, as in fencing. **2** (*tr*) to evade (questions, etc.), esp. adroitly. ◆ *n, pl* **parries. 3** an act of parrying. **4** a skilful evasion, as of a question. [C17: from F *parer* to ward off, from L *parāre* to prepare]

parse (pɑːz) *vb* **parses, parsing, parsed.** *Grammar.* to assign constituent structure to (a sentence or the words in a sentence). [C16: from L *pars* (*ōrātionis*) part (of speech)]

parsec ('pɑː,sɛk) *n* a unit of astronomical distance equivalent to

THESAURUS

parlance *n* = **language,** idiom, jargon, lingo (*inf.*), manner of speaking, phraseology, -speak, speech, talk, tongue

parley *n* **1** = **discussion,** colloquy, confab (*inf.*), conference, congress, council, dialogue, meeting, palaver, powwow, seminar, talk(s) ◆ *vb* **2** = **discuss,** confabulate, confer, deliberate, negotiate, palaver, powwow, speak, talk

parliament *n* **1, 2** = **assembly,** congress, convention, convocation, council, diet, legislature, senate, talking shop (*inf.*)

Parliament *n* **1** = **Houses of Parliament,** Mother of Parliaments, the House, the House of Commons and the House of Lords, Westminster

parliamentary *adj* **1** = **governmental,** congressional, deliberative, law-giving, law-making, legislative

parlour *n* **1** *Old-fashioned* = **sitting room,** best room, drawing room, front room, living room, lounge, reception room

parlous *adj* **1** *Archaic or humorous* = **dangerous,** chancy (*inf.*), desperate, difficult, dire, hairy (*sl.*), hazardous, perilous, risky

parochial *adj* **1** = **provincial,** insular, inward-looking, limited, narrow, narrow-minded, parish-pump, petty, restricted, small-minded
Antonyms *adj* all-embracing, broad, broad-minded, cosmopolitan, international, liberal, national, universal, world-wide

parochialism *n* **1** = **provincialism,** insularity, limitedness, localism, narrow-mindedness, narrowness, restrictedness, small-mindedness

parody *n* **1** = **takeoff** (*inf.*), burlesque, caricature, imitation, lampoon, satire, send-up, skit, spoof (*inf.*) **2** = **travesty,** apology, caricature, farce, mockery ◆ *vb* **3** = **take off** (*inf.*), burlesque, caricature, do a takeoff of (*inf.*), lampoon, mimic, poke fun at, satirize, send up (*Brit. inf.*), spoof (*inf.*), travesty

paroxysm *n* **1, 2** = **outburst,** attack, convulsion, eruption, fit, flare-up (*inf.*), seizure, spasm

parrot *n* **2** = **mimic,** copycat (*inf.*), imitator, (little) echo ◆ *vb* **4** = **repeat,** copy, echo, imitate, mimic, reiterate

parrot-fashion *n Informal* = **by rote,** mechanically, mindlessly

parry *vb* **1** = **ward off,** block, deflect, fend off, hold at bay, rebuff, repel, repulse, stave off **2** = **evade,** avoid, circumvent, dodge, duck (*inf.*), fence, fight shy of, shun, sidestep

3.0857 × 10^{16} metres or 3.262 light years. [C20: from PARALLAX + SECOND[2]]

Parsee *or* **Parsi** (ˌpɑːˈsiː, ˈpɑːˌsiː) *n* an adherent of a Zoroastrian religion, the practitioners of which were driven out of Persia by the Muslims in the eighth century A.D. It is now found chiefly in western India. [C17: from Persian *Pārsī* a Persian, from OPersian *Pārsa* Persia]
▸**ˈParseeˌism** *or* **ˈParsiˌism** *n*

parser (ˈpɑːzə) *n Computing.* a program that interprets ordinary language typed into a computer by recognizing key words or analysing sentence structure and then translating it into the appropriate machine language.

parsimony ❶ (ˈpɑːsɪmənɪ) *n* extreme care in spending; niggardliness. [C15: from L *parcimōnia,* from *parcere* to spare]
▸**parsimonious** (ˌpɑːsɪˈməʊnɪəs) *adj* ▸ˌ**parsiˈmoniously** *adv*

parsley (ˈpɑːslɪ) *n* **1** a S European umbelliferous plant, widely cultivated for its curled aromatic leaves, which are used in cooking. **2** any of various similar and related plants, such as fool's-parsley and cow parsley. [C14 *persely,* from OE *petersilie* + OF *persil, peresil,* both ult. from L *petroselīnum* rock parsley, from Gk, from *petra* rock + *selinon* parsley]

parsnip (ˈpɑːsnɪp) *n* **1** an umbelliferous plant cultivated for its long whitish root. **2** the root of this plant, eaten as a vegetable. [C14: from OF *pasnaie,* from L *pastināca,* from *pastināre* to dig, from *pastinum* two-pronged tool for digging]

parson ❶ (ˈpɑːsᵊn) *n* **1** a parish priest in the Church of England. **2** any clergyman. [C13: from Med. L *persōna* parish priest, from L: personage; see PERSON]

parsonage (ˈpɑːsᵊnɪdʒ) *n* the residence of a parson, as provided by the parish.

parson bird *n* another name for **tui.**

parson's nose *n* the fatty extreme end portion of the tail of a fowl when cooked.

part ❶ (pɑːt) *n* **1** a piece or portion of a whole. **2** an integral constituent of something: *dancing is part of what we teach.* **3** an amount less than the whole; bit: *they only recovered part of the money.* **4** one of several equal divisions: *mix two parts flour to one part water.* **5** an actor's role in a play. **6** a person's proper role or duty: *everyone must do his part.* **7** (*often pl*) region; area: *you're well known in these parts.* **8** *Anat.* any portion of a larger structure. **9** a component that can be replaced in a machine, etc. **10** the US, Canad., and Austral. word for **parting** (sense 1). **11** *Music.* one of a number of separate melodic lines which is assigned to one or more instrumentalists or singers. **12 for one's part.** as far as one is concerned. **13 for the most part.** generally. **14 in part.** to some degree; partly. **15 of many parts.** having many different abilities. **16 on the part of.** on behalf of. **17 part and parcel.** an essential ingredient. **18 play a part. 18a** to pretend to be what one is not. **18b** to have something to do with; be instrumental. **19 take in good part.** to respond to (teasing, etc.) with good humour. **20 take part in.** to participate in. **21 take someone's part.** to support one person in an argument, etc. ◆ *vb* **22** to divide or separate from one another; take or come apart: *to part the curtains; the seams parted when I washed the dress.* **23** to go away or cause to go away from one another: *the couple parted amicably.* **24** (*intr;* foll. by *from*) to leave; say goodbye to. **25** (*intr;* foll. by *with*) to relinquish, esp. reluctantly: *I couldn't part with my teddy bear.* **26** (*tr;* foll. by *from*) to cause to relinquish, esp. reluctantly: *he's not easily parted from his cash.* **27** (*intr*) to split; separate: *the path parts here.* **28** (*tr*) to arrange (the hair) in such a way that a line of scalp is left showing. **29** (*intr*) *Euphemistic.* to die. **30** (*intr*) *Arch.* to depart. ◆ *adv* **31** to some extent; partly. ◆ See also **parts.** [C13: via OF from L *partīre* to divide, from *pars* a part]

part. *abbrev. for:* **1** participle. **2** particular.

partake ❶ (pɑːˈteɪk) *vb* **partakes, partaking, partook, partaken.** (*mainly intr*) **1** (foll. by *in*) to have a share; participate. **2** (foll. by *of*) to take or receive a portion, esp. of food or drink. **3** (foll. by *of*) to suggest or have some of the quality (of): *music partaking of sadness.* [C16: back formation from *partaker,* earlier *part taker,* based on L *particeps* participant]
▸**parˈtaker** *n*

> **USAGE NOTE** *Partake of* is sometimes wrongly used as if it were a synonym for *eat* or *drink.* Correctly, one can only *partake of* food or drink which is available for several people to share.

parterre (pɑːˈtɛə) *n* **1** a formally patterned flower garden. **2** the pit of a theatre. [C17: from F, from *par* along + *terre* ground]

parthenogenesis (ˌpɑːθɪnəʊˈdʒɛnɪsɪs) *n* a type of reproduction, occurring in some insects and flowers, in which the unfertilized ovum develops directly into a new individual. [C19: from Gk *parthenos* virgin + *genesis* birth]
▸**parthenogenetic** (ˌpɑːθɪˌnəʊdʒɪˈnɛtɪk) *adj*

Parthian shot (ˈpɑːθɪən) *n* a hostile remark or gesture delivered while departing. [from the custom of archers from Parthia, an ancient Asian empire, who shot their arrows backwards while retreating]

partial ❶ (ˈpɑːʃəl) *adj* **1** relating to only a part; not general or complete: *a partial eclipse.* **2** biased: *a partial judge.* **3** (*postpositive;* foll. by *to*) having a particular liking (for). **4** *Maths.* designating or relating to an operation in which only one of a set of independent variables is considered at a time. ◆ *n* **5** Also called: **partial tone.** *Music, acoustics.* any of the component tones of a single musical sound. **6** *Maths.* a partial derivative. [C15: from OF *parcial,* from LL *partiālis* incomplete, from L *pars* part]
▸**ˈpartially** *adv* ▸**ˈpartialness** *n*

> **USAGE NOTE** See at **partly.**

partial derivative *n* the derivative of a function of two or more variables with respect to one of the variables, the other or others being considered constant. Written $\partial f/\partial x$.

partiality ❶ (ˌpɑːʃɪˈælɪtɪ) *n, pl* **partialities. 1** favourable bias. **2** (usually foll. by *for*) liking or fondness. **3** the state of being partial.

partible (ˈpɑːtəbᵊl) *adj* (esp. of property or an inheritance) divisible; separable. [C16: from LL *partibilis,* from *part-, pars* part]

participate ❶ (pɑːˈtɪsɪˌpeɪt) *vb* **participates, participating, participated.** (*intr;* often foll. by *in*) to take part, be or become actively involved, or share (in). [C16: from L *participāre,* from *pars* part + *capere* to take]
▸**parˈticipant** *adj, n* ▸**parˌticiˈpation** *n* ▸**parˈticiˌpator** *n* ▸**parˈticipatory** *adj*

participle (ˈpɑːtɪsɪpᵊl) *n* a nonfinite form of verbs, in English and other languages, used adjectivally and in the formation of certain compound tenses. See also **present participle, past participle.** [C14: via OF from L *participium,* from *particeps,* from *pars* part + *capere* to take]
▸**participial** (ˌpɑːtɪˈsɪpɪəl) *adj* ▸ˌ**partiˈcipially** *adv*

particle ❶ (ˈpɑːtɪkᵊl) *n* **1** an extremely small piece of matter; speck. **2** a very tiny amount; iota: *it doesn't make a particle of difference.* **3** a function word, esp. (in certain languages) a word belonging to an uninflected class having grammatical function: *"up" is sometimes regarded as an adverbial particle.* **4** a common affix, such as *re-, un-,* or *-ness.* **5**

THESAURUS

parsimonious *adj* = **mean,** cheeseparing, close, close-fisted, frugal, grasping, miserable, miserly, near (*inf.*), niggardly, penny-pinching (*inf.*), penurious, saving, scrimpy, skinflinty, sparing, stingy, stinting, tightfisted
Antonyms *adj* extravagant, generous, lavish, munificent, open-handed, spendthrift, wasteful

parsimony *n Formal* = **meanness,** frugality, miserliness, nearness (*inf.*), niggardliness, penny-pinching (*inf.*), stinginess, tightness

parson *n* **1, 2** = **clergyman,** churchman, cleric, divine, ecclesiastic, incumbent, man of God, man of the cloth, minister, pastor, preacher, priest, rector, reverend (*inf.*), vicar

part *n* **1** = **piece,** bit, fraction, fragment, lot, particle, portion, scrap, section, sector, segment, share, slice **2** = **component,** branch, constituent, department, division, element, ingredient, limb, member, module, organ, piece, unit **5** = **role,** character, lines **6** = **duty,** bit, business, capacity, charge, function, involvement, office, place, responsibility, role, say, share, task, work **7** *often plural* = **region,** airt (*Scot.*), area, district, neck of the woods, neighbourhood, quarter, territory, vicinity **13 for the most part** = **mainly,** chiefly, generally, in the main, largely, mostly, on the whole, principally **14 in part** = **partly,** a little, in some measure, partially, slightly, somewhat, to a certain extent, to some degree **16 on the part of** = **on behalf of,** for the sake of, in support of, in the name of **20 take part in** = **participate in,** associate oneself with, be instrumental in, be involved in, have a hand in, join in, partake in, play a part in, put one's twopence-worth in, take a hand in ◆ *vb* **22** = **divide,** break, cleave, come apart, detach, disconnect, disjoin, dismantle, disunite, rend, separate, sever, split, tear **23, 24** = **leave,** break up, depart, go, go away, go (their) separate ways, part company, quit, say goodbye, separate, split up, take one's leave, withdraw **25** *foll. by* **with** = **give up,** abandon, discard, forgo, let go of, relinquish, renounce, sacrifice, surrender, yield
Antonyms *n* ≠ **piece:** bulk, entirety, mass, totality, whole ◆ *vb* ≠ **divide:** adhere, close, combine, hold, join, stick, unite ≠ **leave:** appear, arrive, come, gather, remain, show up (*inf.*), stay, turn up

partake *vb* **1** *foll. by* **in** = **participate in,** engage in, enter into, share in, take part in **2** *foll. by* **of** = **consume,** eat, receive, share, take

partial *adj* **1** = **incomplete,** fragmentary, imperfect, limited, uncompleted, unfinished **2** = **biased,** discriminatory, influenced, interested, one-sided, partisan, predisposed, prejudiced, tendentious, unfair, unjust **3 be partial to** = **have a liking for,** be fond of, be keen on, be taken with, care for, have a soft spot for, have a weakness for
Antonyms *adj* ≠ **incomplete:** complete, entire, finished, full, total, whole ≠ **biased:** impartial, objective, unbiased, unprejudiced

partiality *n* **2** = **bias,** favouritism, partisanship, predisposition, preference, prejudice **3** = **liking,** affinity, fondness, inclination, love, penchant, predilection, predisposition, preference, proclivity, taste, weakness
Antonyms *n* ≠ **bias:** disinterest, equity, fairness, impartiality, objectivity ≠ **liking:** abhorrence, antipathy, aversion, disgust, disinclination, dislike, distaste, loathing, revulsion

partially *adv* **1** = **partly,** fractionally, halfway, incompletely, in part, moderately, not wholly, piecemeal, somewhat, to a certain extent *or* degree

participant *n* = **participator,** associate, contributor, member, partaker, party, player, shareholder, stakeholder

participate *vb* = **take part,** be a participant, be a party to, be involved in, engage in, enter into, get in on the act, have a hand in, join in, partake, perform, share
Antonyms *vb* abstain, boycott, forgo, forsake, forswear, opt out, pass up, refrain from, take no part of

participation *n* = **taking part,** assistance, contribution, involvement, joining in, partaking, partnership, sharing in

particle *n* **1, 2** = **bit,** atom, crumb, grain, iota, jot, mite, molecule, mote, piece, scrap, shred, speck, tittle, whit

Physics. a body with finite mass that can be treated as having negligible size, and internal structure. **6** See **elementary particle.** [C14: from L *particula* a small part, from *pars* part]

particle accelerator *n* a machine for accelerating charged elementary particles to very high energies, used in nuclear physics.

particle physics *n* the study of fundamental particles and their properties. Also called: **high-energy physics.**

parti-coloured ('pɑːtɪˌkʌləd) *adj* having different colours in different parts; variegated. [C16 *parti,* from (obs.) *party* of more than one colour, from OF: striped, from L *partīre* to divide]

particular Ⓣ (pə'tɪkjʊlə) *adj* **1** (*prenominal*) of or belonging to a single or specific person, thing, category, etc.; specific; special: *the particular demands of the job.* **2** (*prenominal*) exceptional or marked: *a matter of particular importance.* **3** (*prenominal*) relating to or providing specific details or circumstances: *a particular account.* **4** exacting or difficult to please, esp. in details; fussy. **5** (of the solution of a differential equation) obtained by giving specific values to the arbitrary constants in a general equation. **6** *Logic.* (of a proposition) affirming or denying something about only some members of a class of objects, as in *some men are not wicked.* Cf. **universal** (sense 9). ◆ *n* **7** a separate distinct item that helps to form a generalization: opposed to *general.* **8** (*often pl*) an item of information; detail: *complete in every particular.* **9 in particular.** especially or exactly. [C14: from OF *particuler,* from LL *particulāris* concerning a part, from L *particula* PARTICLE]
▸**par'ticularly** *adv*

particular average *n Insurance.* partial damage to or loss of a ship or its cargo affecting only the shipowner or one cargo owner. Abbrev.: **PA.** Cf. **general average.**

particularism (pə'tɪkjʊləˌrɪzəm) *n* **1** exclusive attachment to the interests of one group, class, sect, etc. **2** the principle of permitting each state in a federation the right to further its own interests. **3** *Christian theol.* the doctrine that divine grace is restricted to the elect.
▸**par'ticularist** *n, adj*

particularity Ⓣ (pəˌtɪkjʊ'lærɪtɪ) *n, pl* **particularities. 1** (*often pl*) a specific circumstance: *the particularities of the affair.* **2** great attentiveness to detail; fastidiousness. **3** the quality of being precise: *a description of great particularity.* **4** the state or quality of being particular as opposed to general; individuality.

particularize Ⓣ *or* **particularise** (pə'tɪkjʊləˌraɪz) *vb* **particularizes, particularizing, particularized** *or* **particularises, particularising, particularised. 1** to treat in detail; give details (about). **2** (*intr*) to go into detail.
▸**parˌticulari'zation** *or* **parˌticulari'sation** *n*

particulate (pɑː'tɪkjʊlɪt, -ˌleɪt) *n* **1** a substance consisting of separate particles. ◆ *adj* **2** of or made up of separate particles.

parting Ⓣ ('pɑːtɪŋ) *n* **1** *Brit.* the line of scalp showing when sections of hair are combed in opposite directions. US, Canad., and Austral. equivalent: **part. 2** the act of separating or the state of being separated. **3a** a departure or leave-taking, esp. one causing a final separation. **3b** (*as modifier*): *a parting embrace.* **4** a place or line of separation or division. **5** a euphemism for **death.** ◆ *adj* (*prenominal*) **6** *Literary.* departing: *the parting day.* **7** serving to divide or separate.

partisan Ⓣ *or* **partizan** (ˌpɑːtɪ'zæn, 'pɑːtɪˌzæn) *n* **1** an adherent or devotee of a cause, party, etc. **2** a member of an armed resistance group within occupied territory. ◆ *adj* **3** of, relating to, or characteristic of a partisan. **4** excessively devoted to one party, faction, etc.; one-sided. [C16: via F from OIt. *partigiano,* from *parte* faction, from L *pars* part]
▸ˌ**parti'sanship** *or* ˌ**parti'zanship** *n*

partita (pɑː'tiːtə) *n, pl* **partite** (-teɪ) *or* **partitas** *Music.* a type of suite. [It.: divided (piece), from L *partīre* to divide]

partite ('pɑːtaɪt) *adj* **1** (*in combination*) composed of or divided into a specified number of parts: *bipartite.* **2** (esp. of plant leaves) divided almost to the base to form two or more parts. [C16: from L *partīre* to divide]

partition Ⓣ (pɑː'tɪʃən) *n* **1** a division into parts; separation. **2** something that separates, such as a large screen dividing a room in two. **3** a part or share. **4** *Property law.* a division of property, esp. realty, among joint owners. ◆ *vb* (*tr*) **5** (often foll. by *off*) to separate or apportion into sections: *to partition a room off with a large screen.* **6** *Property law.* to divide (property, esp. realty) among joint owners. [C15: via OF from L *partītiō,* from *partīre* to divide]
▸**par'titioner** *or* **par'titionist** *n*

partitive ('pɑːtɪtɪv) *adj* **1** *Grammar.* indicating that a noun involved in a construction refers only to a part of what it otherwise refers to. The phrase *some of the butter* is a partitive construction. **2** serving to separate or divide into parts. ◆ *n* **3** *Grammar.* a partitive linguistic element or feature. [C16: from Med. L *partītīvus* serving to divide, from L *partīre* to divide]
▸**'partitively** *adv*

partly Ⓣ ('pɑːtlɪ) *adv* not completely.

> **USAGE NOTE** *Partly* and *partially* are to some extent interchangeable, but *partly* should be used when referring to a part or parts of something: *the building is partly* (not *partially*) *of stone,* while *partially* is preferred for the meaning *to some extent: his mother is partially* (not *partly*) *sighted.*

partner Ⓣ ('pɑːtnə) *n* **1** an ally or companion: *a partner in crime.* **2** a member of a partnership. **3** one of a pair of dancers or players on the same side in a game: *my bridge partner.* **4** either member of a couple in a relationship. ◆ *vb* **5** to be or cause to be a partner (of). [C14: var. (infl. by PART) of *parcener* one who shares equally with another, from OF *parçonier,* ult. from L *partīre* to divide]

partnership Ⓣ ('pɑːtnəʃɪp) *n* **1a** a contractual relationship between two or more persons carrying on a joint business venture. **1b** the deed creating such a relationship. **1c** the persons associated in such a relationship. **2** the state or condition of being a partner.

part of speech *n* a class of words sharing important syntactic or semantic features; a group of words in a language that may occur in similar positions or fulfil similar functions in a sentence. The chief parts of speech in English are noun, pronoun, adjective, determiner, adverb, verb, preposition, conjunction, and interjection.

parton ('pɑːˌtɒn) *n Physics.* a hypothetical elementary particle postulated as a constituent of neutrons and protons. [from PART + -ON]

partook (pɑː'tʊk) *vb* the past tense of **partake.**

partridge ('pɑːtrɪdʒ) *n, pl* **partridges** *or* **partridge.** any of various small Old World game birds of the pheasant family, esp. the common or European partridge. [C13: from OF *perdriz,* from L *perdix,* from Gk]

parts Ⓣ (pɑːts) *pl n* **1** personal abilities or talents: *a man of many parts.* **2** short for **private parts.**

part song *n* **1** a song composed in harmonized parts. **2** (*in more technical usage*) a piece of homophonic choral music in which the topmost part carries the melody.

part-time *adj* **1** occupying less than the full time normally associated with an activity: *a part-time job.* ◆ *adv* **part time. 2** on a part-time basis: *he works part time.* ◆ Cf. **full-time.**
▸ˌ**part-'timer** *n*

parturient (pɑː'tjʊərɪənt) *adj* **1** of or relating to childbirth. **2** giving birth. **3** producing a new idea, etc. [C16: via L *parturīre,* from *parere* to bring forth]
▸**par'turiency** *n*

parturition (ˌpɑːtjʊ'rɪʃən) *n* the act or process of giving birth. [C17: from LL *parturītiō,* from *parturīre* to be in labour]

THESAURUS

particular *adj* **1** = **specific,** distinct, exact, express, peculiar, precise, special **2** = **special,** especial, exceptional, marked, notable, noteworthy, remarkable, singular, uncommon, unusual **3** = **detailed,** blow-by-blow, circumstantial, itemized, minute, painstaking, precise, selective, thorough **4** = **fussy,** choosy (*inf.*), critical, dainty, demanding, discriminating, exacting, fastidious, finicky, meticulous, nice (*rare*), overnice, pernickety (*inf.*), picky (*inf.*) ◆ *n* **8** *often plural* = **detail,** circumstance, fact, feature, item, specification **9 in particular** = **especially,** distinctly, exactly, expressly, particularly, specifically
Antonyms *adj* ≠ **specific:** general, imprecise, indefinite, indistinct, inexact, unspecified, vague ≠ **fussy:** casual, easy, easy to please, indiscriminate, negligent, slack, sloppy, uncritical

particularity *n* **1** *often plural* = **circumstance,** detail, fact, instance, item, point **2, 3** = **meticulousness,** accuracy, carefulness, choosiness (*inf.*), detail, fastidiousness, fussiness, precision, thoroughness **4** = **individuality,** characteristic, distinctiveness, feature, idiosyncrasy, peculiarity, property, singularity, trait

particularize *vb* **1, 2** = **specify,** detail, enumerate, give details, itemize, spell out, stipulate

particularly *adv* **1** = **specifically,** distinctly, especially, explicitly, expressly, in particular **2** = **especially,** decidedly, exceptionally, markedly, notably, outstandingly, peculiarly, singularly, surprisingly, uncommonly, unusually

parting *n* **1** = **division,** breaking, detachment, divergence, partition, rift, rupture, separation, split **3** = **going,** adieu, departure, farewell, goodbye, leave-taking, valediction ◆ *adj* **6** *Literary* = **farewell,** departing, final, last, valedictory

partisan *n* **1** = **supporter,** adherent, backer, champion, devotee, disciple, follower, stalwart, upholder, votary **2** = **underground fighter,** guerrilla, irregular, resistance fighter ◆ *adj* **3** = **underground,** guerrilla, irregular, resistance **4** = **prejudiced,** biased, factional, interested, one-sided, partial, sectarian, tendentious
Antonyms *n* ≠ **supporter:** adversary, contender, critic, detractor, foe, knocker (*inf.*), leader, opponent, rival ◆ *adj* ≠ **prejudiced:** bipartisan, broad-minded, disinterested, impartial, non-partisan, unbiased, unprejudiced

partition *n* **1** = **division,** dividing, segregation, separation, severance, splitting **2** = **screen,** barrier, divider, room divider, wall **3** = **allotment,** apportionment, distribution, portion, rationing out, share ◆ *vb* **5** = **separate,** divide, fence off, screen, wall off **5** = **divide,** apportion, cut up, parcel out, portion, section, segment, separate, share, split up, subdivide

partly *adv* = **partially,** halfway, incompletely, in part, in some measure, not fully, relatively, slightly, somewhat, to a certain degree *or* extent, up to a certain point
Antonyms *adv* completely, entirely, fully, in full, totally, wholly

partner *n* **1, 3** = **companion,** accomplice, ally, associate, bedfellow, collaborator, colleague, comrade, confederate, copartner, helper, mate, participant, team-mate **4** = **spouse,** bedfellow, better half (*Brit. inf.*), consort, helpmate, her indoors (*Brit. sl.*), husband *or* wife, mate, significant other (*US inf.*)

partnership *n* **1** = **company,** alliance, association, combine, conglomerate, cooperative, corporation, firm, house, society, union **2** = **cooperation,** companionship, connection, copartnership, fellowship, interest, participation, sharing

parts *pl n* **1** = **talents,** abilities, accomplishments, attributes, calibre, capabilities, endowments, faculties, genius, gifts, intellect, intelligence

part work *n Brit.* a series of magazines issued weekly or monthly, which are designed to be bound together to form a complete book.

party ⓘ ('pɑːtɪ) *n, pl* **parties. 1a** a social gathering for pleasure, often held as a celebration. **1b** (*as modifier*): *party spirit.* **1c** (*in combination*): *partygoer.* **2** a group of people associated in some activity: *a rescue party.* **3a** (*often cap.*) a group of people organized together to further a common political aim, etc. **3b** (*as modifier*): *party politics.* **4** a person, esp. one entering into a contract. **5** the person or persons taking part in legal proceedings: *a party to the action.* **6** *Inf., humorous.* a person. ◆ *vb* **parties, partying, partied.** (*intr*) **7** *Inf.* to celebrate; revel. ◆ *adj* **8** *Heraldry.* (of a shield) divided vertically into two colours, metals, or furs. [C13: from OF *partie* part, from L *partīre* to divide; see PART]

party line *n* **1** a telephone line serving two or more subscribers. **2** the policies or dogma of a political party, etc.

party list *n* (*modifier*) of or relating to a system of voting in which people vote for a party rather than for a candidate. Parties are assigned the number of seats that reflects their share of the vote. See **proportional representation.**

party pooper ('puːpə) *n Inf.* a person whose behaviour or personality spoils other people's enjoyment. [C20: orig. US]

party wall *n Property law.* a wall separating two properties or pieces of land and over which each of the adjoining owners has certain rights.

par value *n* the value imprinted on the face of a share certificate or bond and used to assess dividend, capital ownership, or interest.

parvenu ⓘ *or* (*fem*) **parvenue** ('pɑːvəˌnjuː) *n* **1** a person who, having risen socially or economically, is considered to be an upstart. ◆ *adj* **2** of or characteristic of a parvenu. [C19: from F, from *parvenir* to attain, from L *pervenīre,* from *per* through + *venīre* to come]

parvovirus ('pɑːvəʊˌvaɪrəs) *n* any of a group of viruses characterized by their very small size, each of which is specific to a particular species, as for example canine parvovirus. [C20: NL, from L *parvus* little + VIRUS]

pas (pɑː) *n, pl* **pas.** a dance step or movement, esp. in ballet. [C18: from F, lit.: step]

pascal ('pæskᵊl) *n* the derived SI unit of pressure; the pressure exerted on an area of 1 square metre by a force of 1 newton; equivalent to 10 dynes per square centimetre or 1.45×10^{-4} pound per square inch. Symbol: Pa [C20: after B. *Pascal* (1623–62), F mathematician & scientist]

PASCAL ('pæsˌkæl) *n* a high-level computer-programming language developed as a teaching language.

Pascal's triangle *n* a triangle consisting of rows of numbers; the apex is 1 and each row starts and ends with 1, other numbers being obtained by adding together the two numbers on either side in the row above: used to calculate probabilities. [C17: after B. *Pascal*; see PASCAL]

paschal ('pæskᵊl) *adj* **1** of or relating to **Passover** (sense 1). **2** of or relating to **Easter.** [C15: from OF *pascal,* via Church L from Heb. *pesakh* Passover]

Paschal Lamb *n* **1** (*sometimes not caps.*) *Old Testament.* the lamb killed and eaten on the first day of the Passover. **2** Christ regarded as this sacrifice.

pas de basque (ˌpɑː də 'bɑː) *n, pl* **pas de basque.** a dance step performed usually on the spot and used esp. in reels and jigs. [from F, lit.: Basque step]

pas de deux (*French* pɑddø) *n, pl* **pas de deux.** *Ballet.* a sequence for two dancers. [F: step for two]

pash (pæʃ) *n Sl.* infatuation. [C20: from PASSION]

pasha *or* **pacha** ('pɑːʃə, 'pæʃə) *n* (formerly) a high official of the Ottoman Empire or the modern Egyptian kingdom: placed after a name when used as a title. [C17: from Turkish *paşa*]

pashm ('pæʃəm) *n* the underfur of various Tibetan animals, esp. goats, used for Cashmere shawls. [from Persian, lit.: wool]

Pashto, Pushto ('pʌʃtəʊ), *or* **Pushtu** *n* **1** a language of Afghanistan and NW Pakistan. **2** (*pl* **Pashto** *or* **Pashtos, Pashtu** *or* **Pashtus; Pushto** *or* **Pushtos, Pushtu** *or* **Pushtus**) a speaker of the Pashto language; a Pathan. ◆ *adj* **3** denoting or relating to this language or a speaker of it.

paso doble ('pæsəʊ 'dəʊbleɪ) *n, pl* **paso dobles** *or* **pasos dobles. 1** a modern ballroom dance in fast duple time. **2** a piece of music composed for or in the rhythm of this dance. [Sp.: double step]

pas op ('pɑːs ˌɒp) *interj S. African.* beware. [Afrik.]

pasqueflower ('pɑːskˌflaʊə) *n* **1** a small purple-flowered plant of N and Central Europe and W Asia. **2** any of several related North American plants. [C16: from F *passefleur,* from *passer* to excel + *fleur* flower; changed to *pasqueflower* Easter flower, because it blooms at Easter]

pasquinade (ˌpæskwɪ'neɪd) *n* an abusive lampoon or satire, esp. one posted in a public place. [C17: from It. *Pasquino* name given to an ancient Roman statue disinterred in 1501, which was annually posted with satirical verses]

pass ⓘ (pɑːs) *vb* **1** to go onwards or move by or past (a person, thing, etc.). **2** to run, extend, or lead through, over, or across (a place): *the route passes through the city.* **3** to go through or cause to go through (an obstacle or barrier): *to pass a needle through cloth.* **4** to move or cause to move onwards or over: *he passed his hand over her face.* **5** (*tr*) to go beyond or exceed: *this victory passes all expectation.* **6** to gain or cause to gain an adequate mark or grade in (an examination, course, etc.). **7** (often foll. by *away* or *by*) to elapse or allow to elapse: *we passed the time talking.* **8** (*intr*) to take place or happen: *what passed at the meeting?* **9** to speak or exchange or be spoken or exchanged: *angry words passed between them.* **10** to spread or cause to spread: *we passed the news round the class.* **11** to transfer or exchange or be transferred or exchanged: *the bomb passed from hand to hand.* **12** (*intr*) to undergo change or transition: *to pass from joy to despair.* **13** (when *tr,* often foll. by *down*) to transfer or be transferred by inheritance: *the house passed to the younger son.* **14** to agree to or be agreed to by a legislative body, etc.: *the assembly passed 10 resolutions.* **15** (*tr*) (of a legislative measure) to undergo (a procedural stage) and be agreed: *the bill passed the committee stage.* **16** (when *tr,* often foll. by *on* or *upon*) to pronounce (judgment, findings, etc.): *the court passed sentence.* **17** to go or allow to go without comment or censure: *the insult passed unnoticed.* **18** (*intr*) to opt not to exercise a right, as by not answering a question or not making a bid or a play in card games. **19** to discharge (urine, etc.) from the body. **20** (*intr*) to come to an end or disappear: *his anger soon passed.* **21** (*intr;* usually foll. by *for* or *as*) to be likely to be mistaken for (someone or something else): *you could easily pass for your sister.* **22** (*intr;* foll. by *away, on,* or *over*) *Euphemistic.* to die. **23** *Sport.* to hit, kick, or throw (the ball, etc.) to another player. **24 bring to pass.** *Arch.* to cause to happen. **25 come to pass.** *Arch.* to happen. ◆ *n* **26** the act of passing. **27** a route through a range of mountains where there is a gap between peaks. **28** a permit, licence, or authorization to do something without restriction. **29a** a document allowing entry to and exit from a military installation. **29b** a document authorizing leave of absence. **30** *Brit.* **30a** the passing of a college or university examination to a satisfactory standard but not as high as honours. **30b** (*as modifier*): *a pass degree.* **31** a dive, sweep, or bombing or landing run by an aircraft. **32** a motion of the hand or of a wand as part of a conjuring trick. **33** *Inf.* an attempt to invite sexual intimacy (esp. in **make a pass at**). **34** a state of affairs, esp. a bad one (esp. in **a pretty pass**). **35** *Sport.* the transfer of a ball, etc., from one player to another. **36** *Fencing.* a thrust or lunge. **37** *Bridge, etc.* the act of passing (making no bid). ◆ *sentence substitute.* **38** *Bridge, etc.* a call indicating that a player has no bid to make. ◆ See also **pass off, pass out,** etc. [C13: from OF *passer* to pass, surpass, from L *passūs* step]

pass. *abbrev. for:* **1** passive. **2** passenger. **3** passage.

passable ⓘ ('pɑːsəbᵊl) *adj* **1** adequate, fair, or acceptable. **2** (of an obstacle) capable of being crossed. **3** (of currency) valid for circulation. **4** (of a proposed law) able to be enacted.
▸ **'passableness** *n* ▸ **'passably** *adv*

passacaglia (ˌpæsə'kɑːljə) *n* **1** an old Spanish dance in slow triple time. **2** a slow instrumental piece characterized by a series of variations on a

THESAURUS

party *n* **1** = **get-together** (*inf.*), at-home, bash (*inf.*), beano (*Brit. sl.*), celebration, do (*inf.*), festivity, function, gathering, hooley *or* hoolie (*chiefly Irish & NZ*), knees-up (*Brit. inf.*), rave (*Brit. sl.*), rave-up (*Brit. sl.*), reception, shindig (*inf.*), social, social gathering, soirée **2** = **group**, band, body, bunch (*inf.*), company, crew, detachment (*Military*), gang, gathering, squad, team, unit **3** = **faction**, alliance, association, cabal, camp, clique, coalition, combination, confederacy, coterie, grouping, league, schism, set, side **4** = **person**, individual, somebody, someone **5** = **litigant**, contractor (*Law*), defendant, participant, plaintiff

parvenu *n* **1** = **upstart**, arriviste, *nouveau riche,* social climber ◆ *adj* **2** = **upstart**, *nouveau riche*

pass *vb* **1, 7** = **go by** *or* **past**, depart, elapse, flow, go, lapse, leave, move, move onwards, proceed, roll, run **5** = **exceed**, beat, excel, go beyond, outdistance, outdo, outstrip, overtake, surmount, surpass, transcend **6** = **qualify**, answer, come up to scratch, do, get through, graduate, pass muster, succeed, suffice, suit **7** = **spend**, beguile, devote, employ, experience, fill, occupy, suffer, undergo, while away **8** = **happen**, befall, come up, develop, fall out, occur, take place **11** = **give**, convey, deliver, exchange, hand, kick, let have, reach, send, throw, transfer, transmit **14** = **approve**, accept, adopt, authorize, decree, enact, establish, legislate, ordain, ratify, sanction, validate **16** = **pronounce**, declare, deliver, express, utter **17** = **ignore**, disregard, miss, neglect, not heed, omit, overlook, skip (*inf.*) **19** = **excrete**, crap (*taboo sl.*), defecate, discharge, eliminate, empty, evacuate, expel, shit (*taboo sl.*), void **20** = **end**, blow over, cease, die, disappear, dissolve, dwindle, ebb, evaporate, expire, fade, go, melt away, terminate, vanish, wane **21** *with* **for** *or* **as** = **be mistaken for**, be accepted as, be regarded as, be taken for, impersonate, serve as **22** *foll. by* **away**, **on** *or* **over** *Euphemistic* = **die**, buy it (*US sl.*), croak (*sl.*), decease, depart (this life), expire, kick the bucket (*sl.*), peg out (*inf.*), pop one's clogs (*inf.*), shuffle off this mortal coil, snuff it (*inf.*) ◆ *n* **27** = **gap**, canyon, col, defile, gorge, ravine, route **28, 29** = **licence**, authorization, identification, identity card, passport, permission, permit, safe-conduct, ticket, warrant **33** *Informal As in* **make a pass at** = **advances**, approach, overture, play (*inf.*), proposition, suggestion **34** *As in* **a pretty pass** = **predicament**, condition, juncture, pinch, plight, situation, stage, state, state of affairs, straits
Antonyms *vb* ≠ **go by** *or* past: bring *or* come to a standstill, cease, halt, pause, stop ≠ **qualify:** be inadequate, be inferior to, be unsuccessful, come a cropper (*inf.*), fail, lose, suffer defeat ≠ **approve:** ban, disallow, invalidate, overrule, prohibit, refuse, reject, veto ≠ **ignore:** acknowledge, heed, note, notice, observe, pay attention to

passable *adj* **1** = **adequate**, acceptable, admissible, allowable, all right, average, fair, fair enough, mediocre, middling, moderate, not too bad, ordinary, presentable, so-so (*inf.*), tolerable, unexceptional **2** = **clear**, crossable, navigable, open, traversable, unobstructed
Antonyms *adj* ≠ **adequate:** A1 *or* A-one (*inf.*), exceptional, extraordinary, first-class, inadequate, inadmissible, marvellous, outstanding, superb, tops (*sl.*), unacceptable, unsatisfactory ≠ **clear:** blocked, closed, impassable, obstructed, sealed off, unnavigable

passably *adv* **1** = **well enough**, acceptably, adequately, after a fashion, fairly, moderately,

particular theme played over a repeated bass part. [C17: earlier *passacalle,* from Sp. *pasacalle* street dance, from *paso* step + *calle* street]

passage ➊ ('pæsɪdʒ) *n* **1** a channel, opening, etc., through or by which a person or thing may pass. **2** *Music.* a section or division of a piece, movement, etc. **3** a way, as in a hall or lobby. **4** a section of a written work, speech, etc. **5** a journey, esp. by ship. **6** the act or process of passing from one place, condition, etc., to another: *passage of a gas through a liquid.* **7** the permission, right, or freedom to pass: *to be denied passage through a country.* **8** the enactment of a law by a legislative body. **9** *Rare.* an exchange, as of blows, words, etc. [C13: from OF from *passer* to PASS]

passageway ➊ ('pæsɪdʒ,weɪ) *n* a way, esp. one in or between buildings; passage.

pass band *n* the band of frequencies that is transmitted with maximum efficiency through a circuit, filter, etc.

passbook ('pɑːs,bʊk) *n* **1** a book for keeping a record of withdrawals from and payments into a building society. **2** another name for **bankbook. 3** *S. African.* an official document to identify the bearer, his race, residence, and employment.

passé ➊ ('pɑːseɪ, 'pæseɪ) *adj* **1** out-of-date: *passé ideas.* **2** past the prime; faded: *a passé society beauty.* [C18: from F, p.p. of *passer* to PASS]

passenger ➊ ('pæsɪndʒə) *n* **1a** a person travelling in a car, train, boat, etc., not driven by him. **1b** *(as modifier): a passenger seat.* **2** *Chiefly Brit.* a member of a group or team who is not participating fully in the work. [C14: from OF *passager* passing, from PASSAGE]

passenger pigeon *n* a gregarious North American pigeon, now extinct.

passe-partout (,pæspɑː'tuː) *n* **1** a mounting for a picture in which strips of gummed paper bind together the glass, picture, and backing. **2** the gummed paper used for this. **3** a mat on which a photograph, etc., is mounted. **4** something that secures entry everywhere, esp. a master key. [C17: from F, lit.: pass everywhere]

passepied (pɑːs'pjeɪ) *n, pl* **passepieds** (-'pjeɪ). **1** a lively minuet in triple time, popular in the 17th century. **2** a piece of music composed for or in the rhythm of this dance. [C17: from F: pass foot]

passer-by ➊ *n, pl* **passers-by.** a person who is passing or going by, esp. on foot.

passerine ('pæsə,raɪn, -,riːn) *adj* **1** of, relating to, or belonging to an order of birds characterized by the perching habit: includes the larks, finches, starlings, etc. ◆ *n* **2** any bird belonging to this order. [C18: from L *passer* sparrow]

passim *Latin.* ('pæsɪm) *adv* here and there; throughout: used to indicate that what is referred to occurs frequently in the work cited.

passing ➊ ('pɑːsɪŋ) *adj* **1** transitory or momentary: *a passing fancy.* **2** cursory or casual in action or manner: *a passing reference.* ◆ *adv, adj* **3** *Arch.* to an extreme degree: *the events were passing strange.* ◆ *n* **4** a place where or means by which one may pass, cross, ford, etc. **5** a euphemistic word for **death. 6 in passing.** by the way; incidentally.

passing bell *n* a bell rung to announce a death or a funeral. Also called: **death knell.**

passing note *or US* **passing tone** *n* a nonharmonic note through which a melody passes from one harmonic note to the next.

passion ➊ ('pæʃən) *n* **1** ardent love or affection. **2** intense sexual love. **3** a strong affection or enthusiasm for an object, concept, etc.: *a passion for poetry.* **4** any strongly felt emotion, such as love, hate, envy, etc. **5** an outburst of anger: *he flew into a passion.* **6** the object of an intense desire, ardent affection, or enthusiasm. **7** an outburst expressing intense emotion: *he burst into a passion of sobs.* **8** the sufferings and death of a Christian martyr. [C12: via F from Church L *passiō* suffering, from L *patī* to suffer]
▸'**passional** *adj* ▸'**passionless** *adj*

Passion ('pæʃən) *n* **1** the sufferings of Christ from the Last Supper to his death on the cross. **2** any of the four Gospel accounts of this. **3** a musical setting of this: *the St Matthew Passion.*

passionate ➊ ('pæʃənɪt) *adj* **1** manifesting or exhibiting intense sexual feeling or desire. **2** capable of, revealing, or characterized by intense emotion. **3** easily roused to anger; quick-tempered.
▸'**passionately** *adv*

passionflower ('pæʃən,flaʊə) *n* any plant of a tropical American genus cultivated for their red, yellow, greenish, or purple showy flowers: some species have edible fruit. [C17: from alleged resemblance between parts of the flower and the instruments of the Crucifixion]

passion fruit *n* the edible fruit of any of various passionflowers, esp. granadilla.

Passion play *n* a play depicting the Passion of Christ.

passive ➊ ('pæsɪv) *adj* **1** not active or not participating perceptibly in an activity, organization, etc. **2** unresisting and receptive to external forces; submissive. **3** affected or acted upon by an external object or force. **4** *Grammar.* denoting a voice of verbs in sentences in which the grammatical subject is the recipient of the action described by the verb, as *was broken* in the sentence *The glass was broken by a boy.* **5** *Chem.* (of a substance, esp. a metal) apparently chemically unreactive. **6** *Electronics, telecomm.* **6a** capable only of attenuating a signal: *a passive network.* **6b** not capable of amplifying a signal or controlling a function: *a passive communications satellite.* **7** *Finance.* (of a bond, share, debt, etc.) yielding no interest. ◆ *n* **8** *Grammar.* **8a** the passive voice. **8b** a passive verb. [C14: from L *passīvus* susceptible of suffering, from *patī* to undergo]
▸'**passively** *adv* ▸**pas'sivity** *or* '**passiveness** *n*

passive resistance *n* resistance to a government, law, etc., without violence, as by fasting, demonstrating, or refusing to cooperate.

passive smoking *n* the inhalation of smoke from other people's cigarettes by a nonsmoker.

passkey ('pɑːs,kiː) *n* **1** any of various keys, esp. a latchkey. **2** another term for **master key** or **skeleton key.**

pass law *n* (formerly, in South Africa) a law restricting the movement of Black Africans.

pass off ➊ *vb (adv)* **1** to be or cause to be accepted in a false character: *he passed the fake diamonds off as real.* **2** *(intr)* to come to a gradual end; disappear: *eventually the pain passed off.* **3** *(intr)* to take place: *the meeting passed off without disturbance.* **4** *(tr)* to set aside or disregard: *I managed to pass off his insult.*

pass out ➊ *vb (adv)* **1** *(intr) Inf.* to become unconscious; faint. **2** *(intr) Brit.* (esp. of an officer cadet) to qualify for a military commission, etc. **3** *(tr)* to distribute.

pass over ➊ *vb* **1** *(tr, adv)* to take no notice of; disregard: *they passed me over in the last round of promotions.* **2** *(intr, prep)* to disregard (something bad or embarrassing).

Passover ('pɑːs,əʊvə) *n* **1** an eight-day Jewish festival celebrated in commemoration of the passing over or sparing of the Israelites in Egypt (Exodus 12). **2** another term for the **Paschal Lamb.** [C16: from *pass over,* translation of Heb. *pesah,* from *pāsah* to pass over]

THESAURUS

pretty much, rather, relatively, somewhat, tolerably

passage *n* **1** = **way**, alley, avenue, channel, course, lane, opening, path, road, route, thoroughfare **3** = **corridor**, aisle, doorway, entrance, entrance hall, exit, hall, hallway, lobby, passageway, vestibule **4** = **extract**, clause, excerpt, paragraph, piece, quotation, reading, section, sentence, text, verse **5** = **journey**, crossing, tour, trek, trip, voyage **6** = **movement**, advance, change, conversion, flow, motion, passing, progress, progression, transit, transition **7** = **safe-conduct**, allowance, authorization, freedom, permission, right, visa, warrant **8** = **establishment**, acceptance, enactment, legalization, legislation, passing, ratification

passageway *n* = **corridor**, aisle, alley, cut, entrance, exit, hall, hallway, lane, lobby, passage, wynd (*Scot.*)

passé *adj* **1** = **out-of-date**, antiquated, dated, *démodé*, obsolete, old-fashioned, old hat, outdated, outmoded, outworn, unfashionable

passenger *n* **1** = **traveller**, fare, hitchhiker, pillion rider, rider

passer-by *n* = **bystander**, onlooker, witness

passing *adj* **1** = **momentary**, brief, ephemeral, fleeting, short, short-lived, temporary, transient, transitory **2** = **superficial**, casual, cursory, glancing, hasty, quick, shallow, short, slight ◆ *n* **5** = **end**, death, decease, demise, finish, loss, termination **6 in passing** = **incidentally**, accidentally, by the bye, by the way, en passant, on the way

passion *n* **1, 2** = **love**, adoration, affection, ardour, attachment, concupiscence, desire, fondness, infatuation, itch, keenness, lust, the hots (*sl.*) **3** = **mania**, bug (*inf.*), craving, craze, enthusiasm, fancy, fascination, idol, infatuation, obsession **5, 7** = **rage**, anger, fit, flare-up (*inf.*), frenzy, fury, indignation, ire, outburst, paroxysm, resentment, storm, vehemence, wrath
Antonyms *n* ≠ **emotion**: apathy, calmness, coldness, coolness, frigidity, hate, indifference, unconcern

passionate *adj* **1** = **loving**, amorous, ardent, aroused, desirous, erotic, hot, lustful, sensual, sexy (*inf.*), steamy (*inf.*), wanton **2** = **emotional**, ablaze, animated, ardent, eager, enthusiastic, excited, fervent, fervid, fierce, flaming, frenzied, heartfelt, impassioned, impetuous, impulsive, intense, strong, vehement, warm, wild, zealous **3** = **quick-tempered**, choleric, excitable, fiery, hot-headed, hot-tempered, irascible, irritable, peppery, stormy, tempestuous, violent
Antonyms *adj* ≠ **loving**: cold, frigid, passionless, unloving, unresponsive ≠ **emotional**: apathetic, calm, cold, half-hearted, indifferent, languorous, nonchalant, subdued, unemotional, unenthusiastic ≠ **quick-tempered**: agreeable, calm, easy-going, even-tempered, nonviolent, placid, unexcitable

passionately *adv* **1** = **lovingly**, amorously, ardently, desirously, erotically, hot-bloodedly, libidinously, lustfully, sensually, sexily (*inf.*), steamily (*inf.*), with passion **2** = **emotionally**, animatedly, ardently, eagerly, enthusiastically, excitedly, fervently, fervidly, fiercely, frenziedly, impetuously, impulsively, intensely, strongly, vehemently, warmly, wildly, with all one's heart, zealously **3** = **furiously**, angrily, excitably, fierily, hot-headedly, irascibly, stormily, tempestuously, violently
Antonyms *adv* ≠ **lovingly**: coldly, frigidly, unlovingly, unresponsively ≠ **emotionally**: apathetically, calmly, coldly, half-heartedly, indifferently, nonchalantly, unemotionally, unenthusiastically ≠ **furiously**: calmly, placidly, unexcitably

passive *adj* **1, 2** = **submissive**, acquiescent, compliant, docile, enduring, inactive, inert, lifeless, long-suffering, nonviolent, patient, quiescent, receptive, resigned, unassertive, uninvolved, unresisting
Antonyms *adj* active, alive, assertive, bossy (*inf.*), defiant, domineering, energetic, feisty (*inf., chiefly US & Canad.*), impatient, involved, lively, rebellious, spirited, violent, zippy (*inf.*)

pass off *vb* **1** = **fake**, counterfeit, feign, make a pretence of, palm off **2** = **come to an end**, die away, disappear, fade out, vanish **3** = **take place**, be completed, go off, happen, occur, turn out

pass out *vb* **1** *Informal* = **faint**, become unconscious, black out (*inf.*), drop, flake out (*inf.*), keel over (*inf.*), lose consciousness, swoon (*literary*) **2** = **hand out**, deal out, distribute, dole out

pass over *vb* **1, 2** = **disregard**, discount, forget,

passport ('pɑːspɔːt) *n* **1** an official document issued by a government, identifying an individual, granting him permission to travel abroad, and requesting the protection of other governments for him. **2** a quality, asset, etc., that gains a person admission or acceptance. [C15: from F *passeport,* from *passer* to PASS + PORT[1]]

pass up ❶ *vb (tr, adv) Inf.* to let go by; ignore: *I won't pass up this opportunity.*

password ❶ ('pɑːsˌwɜːd) *n* **1** a secret word, phrase, etc., that ensures admission by proving identity, membership, etc. **2** an action, quality, etc., that gains admission or acceptance. **3** *Computing.* a sequence of characters used to gain access to a computer system.

past ❶ (pɑːst) *adj* **1** completed, finished, and no longer in existence: *past happiness.* **2** denoting or belonging to the time that has elapsed at the present moment: *the past history of the world.* **3** denoting a specific unit of time that immediately precedes the present one: *the past month.* **4** (*prenominal*) denoting a person who has held an office or position; former: *a past president.* **5** *Grammar.* denoting any of various tenses of verbs that are used in describing actions, events, or states that have been begun or completed at the time of utterance. ◆ *n* **6 the past.** the period of time that has elapsed: *forget the past.* **7** the history, experience, or background of a nation, person, etc. **8** an earlier period of someone's life, esp. one regarded as disreputable. **9** *Grammar.* **9a** a past tense. **9b** a verb in a past tense. ◆ *adv* **10** at a time before the present; ago: *three years past.* **11** on or onwards: *I greeted him but he just walked past.* ◆ *prep* **12** beyond in time: *it's past midnight.* **13** beyond in place or position: *the library is past the church.* **14** moving beyond: *he walked past me.* **15** beyond or above the reach, limit, or scope of: *his foolishness is past comprehension.* **16 past it.** *Inf.* unable to perform the tasks one could do when one was younger. **17 not put it past someone.** to consider someone capable of (the action specified). [C14: from *passed,* p.p. of PASS]

> **USAGE NOTE** The past participle of *pass* is sometimes wrongly spelt *past*: *the time for recrimination has passed* (not *past*).

pasta ('pæstə) *n* any of several variously shaped edible preparations made from a flour and water dough, such as spaghetti. [It., from LL: PASTE]

paste ❶ (peɪst) *n* **1** a mixture of a soft or malleable consistency, such as toothpaste. **2** an adhesive made from water and flour or starch, used for joining pieces of paper, etc. **3** a preparation of food, such as meat, that has been pounded to a creamy mass, for spreading on bread, etc. **4** any of various sweet doughy confections: *almond paste.* **5** dough, esp. for making pastry. **6a** a hard shiny glass used for making imitation gems. **6b** an imitation gem made of this glass. **7** the combined ingredients of porcelain. See also **hard paste, soft paste.** ◆ *vb* **pastes, pasting, pasted.** (*tr*) **8** (often foll. by *on* or *onto*) to attach as by using paste: *he pasted posters onto the wall.* **9** (usually foll. by *with*) to cover (a surface) with paper, etc.: *he pasted the wall with posters.* **10** *Sl.* to thrash or beat; defeat. [C14: via OF from LL *pasta* dough, from Gk *pastē* barley porridge, from *passein* to sprinkle]

pasteboard ('peɪstˌbɔːd) *n* **1** a stiff board formed from layers of paper or pulp pasted together. ◆ *adj* **2** flimsy or fake.

pastel ❶ ('pæstᵊl, pæ'stel) *n* **1a** a substance made of ground pigment bound with gum. **1b** a crayon of this. **1c** a drawing done in such crayons. **2** the medium or technique of pastel drawing. **3** a pale delicate colour. ◆ *adj* **4** (of a colour) pale; delicate: *pastel blue.* [C17: via F from It. *pastello,* from LL *pastellus* woad, dim. of *pasta* PASTE]
▸ **'pastelist** *or* **'pastellist** *n*

pastern ('pæstən) *n* the part of a horse's foot between the fetlock and the hoof. [C14: from OF *pasturon,* from *pasture* a hobble, from L *pāstōrius* of a shepherd, from PASTOR]

paste-up *n Printing.* a sheet of paper or board on which are pasted artwork, proofs, etc., for photographing prior to making a plate.

pasteurism ('pæstəˌrɪzəm, -stjə-, 'pɑː-) *n Med.* a method of securing immunity from rabies or of treating patients with other viral infections by the serial injection of progressively more virulent suspensions of the causative virus. Also called: **Pasteur treatment.** [C19: after Louis *Pasteur* (1822–95), F chemist & bacteriologist]

pasteurization *or* **pasteurisation** (ˌpæstəraɪ'zeɪʃən, -stjə-, ˌpɑː-) *n* the process of heating beverages, such as milk, beer, wine, or cider, or solid foods, such as cheese or crab meat, to destroy harmful microorganisms.

pasteurize *or* **pasteurise** ('pæstəˌraɪz, -stjə-, 'pɑː-) *vb* **pasteurizes, pasteurizing, pasteurized** *or* **pasteurises, pasteurising, pasteurised.** (*tr*) to subject (milk, beer, etc.) to pasteurization.
▸ **'pasteurˌizer** *or* **'pasteurˌiser** *n*

pastiche ❶ (pæ'stiːʃ) *or* **pasticcio** (pæ'stɪtʃəʊ) *n, pl* **pastiches** *or* **pasticcios. 1** a work of art that mixes styles, materials, etc. **2** a work of art that imitates the style of another artist or period. [C19: F *pastiche,* It. *pasticcio,* lit.: piecrust (hence, something blended) from LL *pasta* PASTE]

pastille ❶ *or* **pastil** ('pæstɪl) *n* **1** a small flavoured or medicated lozenge. **2** an aromatic substance burnt to fumigate the air. [C17: via F from L *pastillus* small loaf, from *pānis* bread]

pastime ❶ ('pɑːsˌtaɪm) *n* an activity or entertainment which makes time pass pleasantly.

past master ❶ *n* **1** a person with talent for, or experience in, a particular activity. **2** a person who has held the office of master in a guild, etc.

pastor ❶ ('pɑːstə) *n* **1** a clergyman or priest in charge of a congregation. **2** a person who exercises spiritual guidance over a number of people. **3** a S Asian starling having a black head and wings and a pale pink body. [C14: from L: shepherd, from *pascere* to feed]
▸ **'pastorship** *n*

pastoral ❶ ('pɑːstərəl) *adj* **1** of, characterized by, or depicting rural life, scenery, etc. **2** (of a literary work) dealing with an idealized form of rural existence. **3** (of land) used for pasture. **4** of or relating to a clergyman or priest in charge of a congregation or his duties as such. **5** of or relating to shepherds, their work, etc. **6** of or relating to a teacher's responsibility for the personal, as distinct from the educational, development of pupils. ◆ *n* **7** a literary work or picture portraying rural life, esp. in an idealizing way. **8** *Music.* a variant spelling of **pastorale. 9a** a letter from a clergyman to the people under his charge. **9b** the letter of a bishop to the clergy or people of his diocese. **9c** Also called: **pastoral staff.** the crosier carried by a bishop. [C15: from L, from PASTOR]
▸ **'pastoralism** *n* ▸ **'pastorally** *adv*

pastorale (ˌpæstə'rɑːl) *n, pl* **pastorales.** *Music.* **1** a composition evocative of rural life, sometimes with a droning accompaniment. **2** a musical play based on a rustic story. [C18: It., from L: PASTORAL]

pastoralist ('pɑːstərəlɪst) *n Austral.* a grazier raising sheep, cattle, etc., on a large scale.

pastorate ('pɑːstərɪt) *n* **1** the office or term of office of a pastor. **2** a body of pastors.

pastourelle (ˌpɑːstuː'rɛl) *n Music.* **1** a pastoral piece of music. **2** one of the figures in a quadrille. [C19: from F: little shepherdess]

past participle *n* a participial form of verbs used to modify a noun that is logically the object of a verb, also used in certain compound tenses and passive forms of the verb.

past perfect *Grammar.* ◆ *adj* **1** denoting a tense of verbs used in relating past events where the action had already occurred at the time of the action of a main verb that is itself in a past tense. In English this is a compound tense formed with *had* plus the past participle. ◆ *n* **2a** the past perfect tense. **2b** a verb in this tense.

pastrami (pə'strɑːmɪ) *n* highly seasoned smoked beef. [from Yiddish, from Romanian *pastramă,* from *păstra* to preserve]

pastry ('peɪstrɪ) *n, pl* **pastries. 1** a dough of flour, water, and fat. **2** baked foods, such as tarts, made with this dough. **3** an individual cake or pastry pie. [C16: from PASTE]

pasturage ('pɑːstʃərɪdʒ) *n* **1** the business of grazing cattle. **2** another word for **pasture.**

pasture ❶ ('pɑːstʃə) *n* **1** land covered with grass or herbage and grazed by or suitable for grazing by livestock. **2** the grass or herbage growing on it. ◆ *vb* **pastures, pasturing, pastured. 3** (*tr*) to cause (livestock) to graze or (of livestock) to graze (a pasture). [C13: via OF from LL *pāstūra,* from *pascere* to feed]

pasty[1] ❶ ('peɪstɪ) *adj* **pastier, pastiest. 1** of or like the colour, texture, etc., of paste. **2** (esp. of the complexion) pale or unhealthy-looking.
▸ **'pastily** *adv* ▸ **'pastiness** *n*

THESAURUS

ignore, not dwell on, omit, overlook, pass by, take no notice of

pass up *vb Informal* = **miss**, abstain, decline, forgo, give (something) a miss (*inf.*), ignore, let slip, let (something) go by, neglect, refuse, reject

password *n* **1** = **signal**, countersign, key word, open sesame, watchword

past *adj* **1** = **over**, accomplished, completed, done, elapsed, ended, extinct, finished, forgotten, gone, over and done with, spent **2, 4** = **former**, ancient, bygone, early, erstwhile, foregoing, late, long-ago, olden, preceding, previous, prior, quondam, recent ◆ *n* **6 the past** = **former times**, antiquity, days gone by, days of yore, good old days, history, long ago, olden days, old times, times past, yesteryear (*literary*) **7** = **background**, experience, history, life, past life ◆ *prep* **12, 13** = **after**, beyond, farther than, later than, outside, over, subsequent to **14** = **beyond**, across, by, on, over

Antonyms *adj* ≠ **former:** arrived, begun, coming, future, now, present ◆ *n* ≠ **former times:** future, now, present, time to come, today, tomorrow

paste *n* **2** = **adhesive**, cement, glue, gum, mucilage ◆ *vb* **8** = **stick**, cement, fasten, fix, glue, gum

pastel *adj* **3** = **pale**, delicate, light, muted, soft, soft-hued

Antonyms *adj* bright, deep, rich, strong, vibrant, vivid

pastiche *n* **1** = **medley**, blend, farrago, gallimaufry, hotchpotch, *mélange,* miscellany, mixture, motley

pastille *n* **1** = **lozenge**, cough drop, jujube, tablet, troche (*Medical*)

pastime *n* = **activity**, amusement, distraction, diversion, entertainment, game, hobby, leisure, play, recreation, relaxation, sport

past master *n* **1** = **expert**, ace, artist, dab hand (*Brit. inf.*), old hand, virtuoso, wizard

pastor *n* **1** = **clergyman**, churchman, divine, ecclesiastic, minister, parson, priest, rector, vicar

pastoral *adj* **1** = **rustic**, agrestic, Arcadian, bucolic, country, georgic (*literary*), idyllic, rural, simple **4** = **ecclesiastical**, clerical, ministerial, priestly

pasture *n* **1, 2** = **grassland**, grass, grazing, grazing land, lea (*poetic*), meadow, pasturage, shieling (*Scot.*)

pasty[1] *adj* **1** = **sticky**, doughy, glutinous, mucilaginous, starchy **2** = **pale**, anaemic, like death warmed up (*inf.*), pallid, sallow, sickly, unhealthy, wan, wheyfaced

pasty[2] ('pæstɪ) *n, pl* **pasties.** a round of pastry folded over a filling of meat, vegetables, etc. [C13: from OF *pastée,* from LL *pasta* dough]

PA system *n* See **public-address system.**

pat[1] Ⓣ (pæt) *vb* **pats, patting, patted. 1** to hit (something) lightly with the palm of the hand or some other flat surface: *to pat a ball.* **2** to slap (a person or animal) gently, esp. on the back, as an expression of affection, congratulation, etc. **3** (*tr*) to shape, smooth, etc., with a flat instrument or the palm. **4** (*intr*) to walk or run with light footsteps. **5 pat (someone) on the back.** *Inf.* to congratulate. ◆ *n* **6** a light blow with something flat. **7** a gentle slap. **8** a small mass of something: *a pat of butter.* **9** the sound of patting. **10 pat on the back.** *Inf.* a gesture or word indicating approval. [C14: ? imit.]

pat[2] Ⓣ (pæt) *adv* **1** Also: **off pat.** exactly or fluently memorized: *he recited it pat.* **2** opportunely or aptly. **3 stand pat. 3a** *Chiefly US & Canad.* to refuse to abandon a belief, decision, etc. **3b** (in poker, etc.) to play without adding new cards to the hand dealt. ◆ *adj* **4** exactly right; apt: *a pat reply.* **5** too exactly fitting; glib: *a pat answer to a difficult problem.* **6** exactly right: *a pat hand in poker.* [C17: ? adv use ("with a light stroke") of PAT[1]]

pat[3] (pæt) *n* **on one's pat.** *Austral. inf.* alone. [C20: rhyming slang, from *Pat* Malone]

pat. *abbrev. for* patent(ed).

patagium (pə'teɪdʒɪəm) *n, pl* **patagia** (-dʒɪə). **1** a web of skin in bats and gliding mammals that functions as a wing. **2** a membranous fold of skin connecting a bird's wing to the shoulder. [C19: NL, from L, from Gk *patageion* gold border on a tunic]

patch Ⓣ (pætʃ) *n* **1** a piece of material used to mend a garment, etc., or to make patchwork, a sewn-on pocket, etc. **2a** a small plot of land. **2b** its produce: *a patch of cabbages.* **3** *Med.* **3a** a protective covering for an injured eye. **3b** any protective dressing. **4** an imitation beauty spot made of black silk, etc., worn esp. in the 18th century. **5** an identifying piece of fabric worn on the shoulder of a uniform. **6** a small contrasting section: *a patch of cloud in the blue sky.* **7** a scrap; remnant. **8 a bad patch.** a difficult or troubled time. **9 not a patch on.** not nearly as good as. ◆ *vb* (*tr*) **10** to mend or supply (a garment, etc.) with a patch or patches. **11** to put together or produce with patches. **12** (of material) to serve as a patch to. **13** (often foll. by *up*) to mend hurriedly or in a makeshift way. **14** (often foll. by *up*) to make (up) or settle (a quarrel, etc.). **15** to connect (electric circuits) together temporarily by means of a patch board. [C16 *pacche,* ?from F *pieche* PIECE]
▸ **'patcher** *n*

patch board *or* **panel** *n* a device with a large number of sockets into which electrical plugs can be inserted to form many different temporary circuits: used in telephone exchanges, computer systems, etc. Also called: **plugboard.**

patchouli *or* **patchouly** ('pætʃʊlɪ, pə'tʃuːlɪ) *n, pl* **patchoulis** *or* **patchoulies. 1** any of several Asiatic trees, the leaves of which yield a heavy fragrant oil. **2** the perfume made from this oil. [C19: from Tamil *paccilai,* from *paccu* green + *ilai* leaf]

patch pocket *n* a pocket on the outside of a garment.

patch test *n Med.* a test to detect an allergic reaction by applying small amounts of a suspected substance to the skin.

patchwork Ⓣ ('pætʃ,wɜːk) *n* **1** needlework done by sewing pieces of different materials together. **2** something made up of various parts.

patchy Ⓣ ('pætʃɪ) *adj* **patchier, patchiest. 1** irregular in quality, occurrence, intensity, etc.: *a patchy essay.* **2** having or forming patches.
▸ **'patchily** *adv* ▸ **'patchiness** *n*

pate (peɪt) *n* the head, esp. with reference to baldness or (in facetious use) intelligence. [C14: from ?]

pâté ('pæteɪ) *n* **1** a spread of finely minced liver, poultry, etc., served usually as an hors d'oeuvre. **2** a savoury pie. [C18: from F: PASTE]

pâté de foie gras (pɑte də fwa grɑ) *n, pl* **pâtés de foie gras** (pɑte). a smooth rich paste made from the liver of a specially fattened goose. [F: pâté of fat liver]

patella (pə'tɛlə) *n, pl* **patellae** (-liː). *Anat.* a small flat triangular bone in front of and protecting the knee joint. Nontechnical name: **kneecap.** [C17: from L, from *patina* shallow pan]
▸ **pa'tellar** *adj*

paten ('pætᵊn) *n* a plate, usually made of silver or gold, esp. for the bread in the Eucharist. [C13: from OF *patene,* from Med. L, from L *patina* pan]

patency ('peɪtᵊnsɪ) *n* the condition of being obvious.

patent Ⓣ ('peɪtᵊnt, 'pætᵊnt) *n* **1a** a government grant to an inventor assuring him the sole right to make, use, and sell his invention for a limited period. **1b** a document conveying such a grant. **2** an invention, privilege, etc., protected by a patent. **3a** an official document granting a right. **3b** any right granted by such a document. ◆ *adj* **4** open or available for inspection (esp. in **letters patent, patent writ**). **5** ('peɪtᵊnt). obvious: *their scorn was patent to everyone.* **6** concerning protection, appointment, etc., of or by a patent or patents. **7** proprietary. **8** (esp. of a bodily passage or duct) being open or unobstructed. ◆ *vb* (*tr*) **9** to obtain a patent for. **10** to grant by a patent. [C14: via OF from L *patēre* to lie open; n use, short for *letters patent,* from Med. L *litterae patentes* letters lying open (to public inspection)]
▸ **'patentable** *adj* ▸ **,paten'tee** *n* ▸ **,paten'tor** *n*

> **USAGE NOTE** The pronunciation "'pætᵊnt" is heard in *letters patent* and *Patent Office* and is the usual US pronunciation for all senses. In Britain "'pætᵊnt" is sometimes heard for senses 1, 2, and 3, but "peɪtᵊnt" is commoner and is regularly used in collocations like *patent leather.*

patent leather ('peɪtᵊnt) *n* leather processed with lacquer to give a hard glossy surface.

patently ('peɪtᵊntlɪ) *adv* obviously.

patent medicine ('peɪtᵊnt) *n* a medicine with a patent, available without a prescription.

Patent Office ('pætᵊnt) *n* a government department that issues patents.

Patent Rolls ('pætᵊnt) *pl n* (in Britain) the register of patents issued.

pater ('peɪtə) *n Brit. sl.* another word for **father:** now chiefly used facetiously. [from L]

paterfamilias (,peɪtəfə'mɪlɪ,æs) *n, pl* **patresfamilias** (,pɑːtreɪzfə'mɪlɪ,æs). the male head of a household. [L: father of the family]

paternal Ⓣ (pə'tɜːnᵊl) *adj* **1** relating to or characteristic of a father; fatherly. **2** (*prenominal*) related through the father: *his paternal grandfather.* **3** inherited or derived from the male parent. [C17: from LL *paternālis,* from L *pater* father]
▸ **pa'ternally** *adv*

paternalism (pə'tɜːnə,lɪzəm) *n* the attitude or policy of a government or other authority that manages the affairs of a country, company, etc., in the manner of a father, esp. in usurping individual responsibility.
▸ **pa'ternalist** *n, adj* ▸ **pa,ternal'istic** *adj* ▸ **pa,ternal'istically** *adv*

paternity Ⓣ (pə'tɜːnɪtɪ) *n* **1a** the fact or state of being a father. **1b** (*as modifier*): *a paternity suit; paternity leave.* **2** descent or derivation from a father. **3** authorship or origin. [C15: from LL *paternitās,* from L *pater* father]

paternoster (,pætə'nɒstə) *n* **1** *RC Church.* the beads at the ends of each decade of the rosary at which the Paternoster is recited. **2** a type of fishing tackle in which short lines and hooks are attached at intervals to the main line. **3** a type of lift in which platforms are attached to continuous chains: passengers enter while it is moving. [L, lit.: our father (from the opening of the Lord's Prayer)]

Paternoster (,pætə'nɒstə) *n* (*sometimes not cap.*) *RC Church.* **1** the Lord's Prayer, esp. in Latin. **2** the recital of this as an act of devotion.

Paterson's curse ('pætəsᵊnz) *n* an Australian name for **viper's bugloss.**

path Ⓣ (pɑːθ) *n, pl* **paths** (pɑːðz). **1** a road or way, esp. a narrow trodden track. **2** a surfaced walk, as through a garden. **3** the course or direction in which something moves: *the path of a whirlwind.* **4** a course of conduct: *the path of virtue.* [OE *pæth*]
▸ **'pathless** *adj*

path. *abbrev. for:* **1** pathological. **2** pathology.

-path *n combining form.* **1** denoting a person suffering from a specified disease or disorder: *neuropath.* **2** denoting a practitioner of a particular method of treatment: *osteopath.* [back formation from -PATHY]

Pathan (pə'tɑːn) *n* a member of the Pashto-speaking people of Afghanistan, NW Pakistan, and elsewhere. [C17: from Hindi]

pathetic Ⓣ (pə'θɛtɪk) *adj* **1** evoking or expressing pity, sympathy, etc. **2** distressingly inadequate: *the old man sat huddled before a pathetic fire.* **3** *Brit. sl.* ludicrously or contemptibly uninteresting or worthless. **4** *Obs.* of or affecting the feelings. [C16: from F *pathétique,* via LL from Gk *pathetikos* sensitive, from *pathos* suffering]
▸ **pa'thetically** *adv*

pathetic fallacy *n* (in literature) the presentation of inanimate objects in nature as possessing human feelings.

THESAURUS

pat[1] *vb* **1, 2 = stroke,** caress, dab, fondle, pet, slap, tap, touch ◆ *n* **6, 7 = stroke,** clap, dab, light blow, slap, tap **8 = lump,** cake, dab, portion, small piece

pat[2] *adv* **1 = perfectly,** exactly, faultlessly, flawlessly, off pat, precisely ◆ *adj* **5 = glib,** automatic, easy, facile, ready, simplistic, slick, smooth

patch *n* **1 = reinforcement,** piece of material **2 = plot,** area, ground, land, tract **6 = spot,** bit, scrap, shred, small piece, stretch ◆ *vb* **10 = mend,** cover, fix, reinforce, repair, sew up **14** *often foll. by* **up = settle,** bury the hatchet, conciliate, make friends, placate, restore, settle differences, smooth

patchwork *n* **2 = mixture,** confusion, hash, hotchpotch, jumble, medley, mishmash, pastiche

patchy *adj* **1 = uneven,** bitty, erratic, fitful, inconstant, irregular, random, sketchy, spotty, variable, varying
Antonyms *adj* constant, even, regular, unbroken, unvarying

patent *n* **1-3 = copyright,** invention, licence ◆ *adj* **5 = obvious,** apparent, blatant, clear, conspicuous, downright, evident, flagrant, glaring, indisputable, manifest, open, palpable, transparent, unconcealed, unequivocal, unmistakable

paternal *adj* **1 = fatherly,** benevolent, concerned, fatherlike, protective, solicitous, vigilant **3 = patrilineal,** patrimonial

paternity *n* **1 = fatherhood,** fathership **2 = parentage,** descent, extraction, family, lineage **3 = origin,** authorship, derivation, source

path *n* **1 = way,** footpath, footway, pathway, road, towpath, track, trail, walkway (*chiefly US*) **2 = walk,** avenue **3 = course,** avenue, direction, passage, procedure, road, route, track, way

pathetic *adj* **1 = sad,** affecting, distressing, gut-wrenching, harrowing, heartbreaking, heart-rending, melting, moving, pitiable, plaintive, poignant, tender, touching **2 = inadequate,** deplorable, feeble, lamentable, meagre, measly, miserable, paltry, petty, pitiful, poor, puny, sorry, woeful **3** *Brit. slang* **= worthless,** crummy (*sl.*), poxy, rubbishy, trashy, uninteresting, useless

pathfinder ❶ ('pɑːθ,faɪndə) *n* **1** a person who makes or finds a way, esp. through unexplored areas or fields of knowledge. **2** an aircraft or parachutist that indicates a target area by dropping flares, etc. **3** a radar device used for navigation or homing onto a target.

pathfinder prospectus *n* a prospectus regarding the flotation of a new company that contains only sufficient details to test the market reaction.

patho- *or before a vowel* **path-** *combining form.* disease: *pathology.* [from Gk *pathos* suffering]

pathogen ('pæθə,dʒɛn) *n* any agent that can cause disease.
▸,**patho'genic** *adj*

pathogenesis (,pæθə'dʒɛnɪsɪs) *or* **pathogeny** (pə'θɒdʒɪnɪ) *n* the development of a disease.
▸**pathogenetic** (,pæθədʒɪ'nɛtɪk) *adj*

pathological (,pæθə'lɒdʒɪkᵊl) *or (less commonly)* **pathologic** *adj* **1** of or relating to pathology. **2** relating to, involving, or caused by disease. **3** *Inf.* compulsively motivated: *a pathological liar.*
▸,**patho'logically** *adv*

pathology (pə'θɒlədʒɪ) *n, pl* **pathologies. 1** the branch of medicine concerned with the cause, origin, and nature of disease, including the changes occurring as a result of disease. **2** the manifestations of disease, esp. changes occurring in tissues or organs.
▸**pa'thologist** *n*

pathos ❶ ('peɪθɒs) *n* **1** the quality or power, esp. in literature or speech, of arousing feelings of pity, sorrow, etc. **2** a feeling of sympathy or pity. [C17: from Gk: suffering]

pathway ('pɑːθ,weɪ) *n* **1** a path. **2** *Biochem.* a chain of reactions associated with a particular metabolic process.

-pathy *n combining form.* **1** indicating feeling or perception: *telepathy.* **2** indicating disease: *psychopathy.* **3** indicating a method of treating disease: *osteopathy.* [from Gk *patheia* suffering; see PATHOS]
▸**-pathic** *adj combining form.*

patience ❶ ('peɪʃəns) *n* **1** tolerant and even-tempered perseverance. **2** the capacity for calmly enduring pain, trying situations, etc. **3** *Chiefly Brit.* any of various card games for one player only. US word: **solitaire.** [C13: via OF from L *patientia* endurance, from *patī* to suffer]

patient ❶ ('peɪʃənt) *adj* **1** enduring trying circumstances with even temper. **2** tolerant; understanding. **3** capable of accepting delay with equanimity. **4** persevering or diligent: *a patient worker.* ◆ *n* **5** a person who is receiving medical care. [C14: see PATIENCE]
▸'**patiently** *adv*

patina[1] ('pætɪnə) *n, pl* **patinas. 1** a film formed on the surface of a metal, esp. the green oxidation of bronze or copper. **2** any fine layer on a surface: *a patina of frost.* **3** the sheen on a surface caused by much handling. [C18: from It.: coating, from L: PATINA[2]]

patina[2] ('pætɪnə) *n, pl* **patinae** (-,niː). a broad shallow dish used in ancient Rome. [from L, from Gk *patanē* platter]

patio ('pætɪ,əʊ) *n, pl* **patios. 1** an open inner courtyard, esp. one in a Spanish or Spanish-American house. **2** an area adjoining a house, esp. one that is paved. [C19: from Sp.: courtyard]

patisserie (pə'tiːsərɪ) *n* **1** a shop where fancy pastries are sold. **2** such pastries. [C18: F, from *pâtissier* pastry cook, ult. from LL *pasta* PASTE]

Patna rice ('pætnə) *n* a variety of long-grain rice, used for savoury dishes. [after *Patna*, city in NE India]

patois ❶ ('pætwɑː) *n, pl* **patois** ('pætwɑːz). **1** a regional dialect of a language, usually considered substandard. **2** the jargon of a particular group. [C17: from OF: rustic speech, ?from *patoier* to handle awkwardly, from *patte* paw]

pat. pend. *abbrev. for* patent pending.

patri- *combining form.* father: *patricide; patriarch.* [from L *pater*, Gk *patēr* father]

patrial ('peɪtrɪəl) *n* (in Britain, formerly) a person having by statute the right of abode in the United Kingdom. [C20: from L *patria* native land]

patriarch ❶ ('peɪtrɪ,ɑːk) *n* **1** the male head of a tribe or family. **2** a very old or venerable man. **3** *Bible.* **3a** any of a number of persons regarded as the fathers of the human race. **3b** any of the three ancestors of the Hebrew people: Abraham, Isaac, or Jacob. **3c** any of Jacob's twelve sons, regarded as the ancestors of the twelve tribes of Israel. **4** *Early Christian Church.* the bishop of one of several principal sees, esp. those of Rome, Antioch, and Alexandria. **5** *Eastern Orthodox Church.* the bishops of the four ancient principal sees of Constantinople, Antioch, Alexandria, and Jerusalem, and also of Russia, Rumania, and Serbia. **6** *RC Church.* **6a** a title given to the pope. **6b** a title given to a number of bishops, esp. of the Uniat Churches, indicating their rank as immediately below that of the pope. **7** the oldest or most venerable member of a group, community, etc. **8** a person regarded as the founder of a community, tradition, etc. [C12: via OF from Church L *patriarcha*]
▸,**patri'archal** *adj*

patriarchate ('peɪtrɪ,ɑːkɪt) *n* the office, jurisdiction, province, or residence of a patriarch.

patriarchy ('peɪtrɪ,ɑːkɪ) *n, pl* **patriarchies. 1** a form of social organization in which a male is the head of the family and descent, kinship, and title are traced through the male line. **2** any society governed by such a system.

patrician ❶ (pə'trɪʃən) *n* **1** a member of the hereditary aristocracy of ancient Rome. **2** (in medieval Europe) a member of the upper class in numerous Italian republics and German free cities. **3** an aristocrat. **4** a person of refined conduct, tastes, etc. ◆ *adj* **5** (esp. in ancient Rome) of, relating to, or composed of patricians. **6** aristocratic. [C15: from OF *patricien*, from L *patricius* noble, from *pater* father]

patricide ('pætrɪ,saɪd) *n* **1** the act of killing one's father. **2** a person who kills his father.
▸,**patri'cidal** *adj*

patrilineal (,pætrɪ'lɪnɪəl) *adj* tracing descent, kinship, or title through the male line.

patrimony ('pætrɪmənɪ) *n, pl* **patrimonies. 1** an inheritance from one's father or other ancestor. **2** the endowment of a church. [C14 *patrimoyne*, from OF, from L *patrimonium* paternal inheritance]
▸**patrimonial** (,pætrɪ'məʊnɪəl) *adj*

patriot ❶ ('peɪtrɪət, 'pæt-) *n* a person who vigorously supports his country and its way of life. [C16: via F from LL *patriōta*, from Gk *patriōtēs*, from *patris* native land; rel. to Gk *patēr* father; cf. L *pater* father, *patria* fatherland]
▸**patriotic** (,pætrɪ'ɒtɪk) *adj* ▸,**patri'otically** *adv*

Patriot ('peɪtrɪət) *n* a US surface-to-air missile system with multiple launch stations and the capability to track multiple targets by radar.

patriotism ❶ ('pætrɪə,tɪzəm) *n* devotion to one's own country and concern for its defence.

patristic (pə'trɪstɪk) *or* **patristical** *adj* of or relating to the Fathers of the Church, their writings, or the study of these.
▸**pa'tristics** *n (functioning as sing)*

patrol ❶ (pə'trəʊl) *n* **1** the action of going round a town, etc., at regular intervals for purposes of security or observation. **2** a person or group that carries out such an action. **3** a military detachment with the mission of security or combat with enemy forces. **4** a division of a troop of Scouts or Guides. ◆ *vb* **patrols, patrolling, patrolled. 5** to engage in a patrol of (a place). [C17: from F *patrouiller*, from *patouiller* to flounder in mud, from *patte* paw]
▸**pa'troller** *n*

patrol car *n* a police car used for patrolling streets and motorways.

patrology (pə'trɒlədʒɪ) *n* **1** the study of the writings of the Fathers of the Church. **2** a collection of such writings. [C17: from Gk *patr-*, *patēr* father + -LOGY]
▸**pa'trologist** *n*

patrol wagon *n* the usual US, Austral., and NZ term for **Black Maria.**

patron[1] ❶ ('peɪtrən) *n* **1** a person who sponsors or aids artists, charities, etc.; protector or benefactor. **2** a customer of a shop, hotel, etc., esp. a regular one. **3** See **patron saint.** [C14: via OF from L *patrōnus* protector, from *pater* father]
▸'**patroness** *fem n*

patron[2] (patrɔ̃) *n* the owner of a restaurant, hotel. etc., esp. of a French one. [F]

patronage ❶ ('pætrənɪdʒ) *n* **1a** the support given or custom brought by a patron. **1b** the position of a patron. **2** (in politics) **2a** the practice of making appointments to office, granting contracts, etc. **2b** the favours, etc., so distributed. **3a** a condescending manner. **3b** any kindness done in a condescending way.

patronize ❶ *or* **patronise** ('pætrə,naɪz) *vb* **patronizes, patronizing, patron-**

THESAURUS

Antonyms *adj* ≠ **sad:** amusing, comical, droll, entertaining, funny, laughable, ludicrous, ridiculous

pathfinder *n* **1** = **pioneer**, discoverer, explorer, guide, scout, trailblazer

pathos *n* **1** = **sadness**, pitiableness, pitifulness, plaintiveness, poignancy

patience *n* **1** = **forbearance**, calmness, composure, cool (*sl.*), equanimity, even temper, imperturbability, restraint, serenity, sufferance, tolerance, toleration **2** = **endurance**, constancy, fortitude, long-suffering, perseverance, persistence, resignation, stoicism, submission
Antonyms *n* ≠ **forbearance:** agitation, exasperation, excitement, impatience, irritation, nervousness, passion, restlessness

patient *adj* **1** = **long-suffering**, calm, composed, enduring, persevering, persistent, philosophical, quiet, resigned, self-possessed, serene, stoical, submissive, uncomplaining, untiring **2** = **forbearing**, accommodating, even-tempered, forgiving, indulgent, lenient, mild, tolerant, understanding ◆ *n* **5** = **sick person**, case, invalid, sufferer

patois *n* **1** = **dialect 2** = **jargon**, argot, cant, lingo (*inf.*), patter, slang, vernacular

patriarch *n* **1** = **father**, paterfamilias, sire **2** = **elder**, grandfather, greybeard, old man

patrician *n* **3** = **aristocrat**, aristo, childe (*arch.*), noble, nobleman, peer ◆ *adj* **6** = **aristocratic**, blue-blooded, gentle (*arch.*), highborn, high-class, lordly, noble

patriot *n* = **nationalist**, chauvinist, flag-waver (*inf.*), jingo, lover of one's country, loyalist

patriotic *adj* = **nationalistic**, chauvinistic, flag-waving (*inf.*), jingoistic, loyal

patriotism *n* = **nationalism**, flag-waving (*inf.*), jingoism, love of one's country, loyalty

patrol *n* **1** = **policing**, guarding, protecting, rounds, safeguarding, vigilance, watching **2** = **guard**, garrison, patrolman, sentinel, watch, watchman ◆ *vb* **5** = **police**, cruise, guard, inspect, keep guard, keep watch, make the rounds, pound, range, safeguard, walk the beat

patron[1] *n* **1** = **supporter**, advocate, angel (*inf.*), backer, benefactor, champion, defender, friend, guardian, helper, philanthropist, protagonist, protector, sponsor **2** = **customer**, buyer, client, frequenter, habitué, shopper

patronage *n* **1a** = **support**, aid, assistance, backing, benefaction, championship, encouragement, espousal, help, promotion, sponsorship **1a** = **custom**, business, clientele, commerce, trade, trading, traffic **3a** = **condescension**, deigning, disdain, patronizing, stooping

patronize *vb* **1** = **talk down to**, be lofty with, look down on, treat as inferior, treat conde-

DICTIONARY

ized *or* **patronises, patronising, patronised. 1** to behave or treat in a condescending way. **2** *(tr)* to act as a patron by sponsoring or bringing trade to.
▸ **'patron,izer** *or* **'patron,iser** *n* ▸ **'patron,izing** *or* **'patron,ising** *adj* ▸ **'patron,izingly** *or* **'patron,isingly** *adv*

patron saint *n* a saint regarded as the particular guardian of a country, person, etc.

patronymic (,pætrə'nɪmɪk) *adj* **1** (of a name) derived from the name of its bearer's father or ancestor. ◆ *n* **2** a patronymic name. [C17: via LL from Gk *patronumikos*, from *patēr* father + *onoma* NAME]

patroon (pə'truːn) *n US.* a Dutch land holder in New Netherland and New York with manorial rights in the colonial era. [C18: from Du.: PATRON[1]]

patsy ('pætsɪ) *n, pl* **patsies.** *Sl., chiefly US & Canad.* **1** a person who is easily cheated, victimized, etc. **2** a scapegoat. [C20: from ?]

patten ('pætᵊn) *n* a wooden clog or sandal on a raised wooden platform or metal ring. [C14: from OF *patin*, prob. from *patte* paw]

patter[1] Ⓣ ('pætə) *vb* **1** *(intr)* to walk or move with quick soft steps. **2** to strike with or make a quick succession of light tapping sounds. ◆ *n* **3** a quick succession of light tapping sounds, as of feet: *the patter of mice.* [C17: from PAT[1]]

patter[2] Ⓣ ('pætə) *n* **1** the glib rapid speech of comedians, etc. **2** quick idle talk; chatter. **3** the jargon of a particular group, etc.; lingo. ◆ *vb* **4** *(intr)* to speak glibly and rapidly. **5** to repeat (prayers, etc.) in a mechanical or perfunctory manner. [C14: from L *pater* in *Pater Noster* Our Father]

pattern Ⓣ ('pætᵊn) *n* **1** an arrangement of repeated or corresponding parts, decorative motifs, etc. **2** a decorative design: *a paisley pattern.* **3** a style: *various patterns of cutlery.* **4** a plan or diagram used as a guide in making something: *a paper pattern for a dress.* **5** a standard way of moving, acting, etc.: *traffic patterns.* **6** a model worthy of imitation: *a pattern of kindness.* **7** a representative sample. **8** a wooden or metal shape or model used in a foundry to make a mould. ◆ *vb (tr)* **9** (often foll. by *after* or *on*) to model. **10** to arrange as or decorate with a pattern. [C14 *patron*, from Med. L *patrōnus* example, from L: PATRON[1]]

patty ('pætɪ) *n, pl* **patties. 1** a small cake of minced food. **2** a small pie. [C18: from F PÂTÉ]

patu ('pɑːtuː) *n, pl* **patus.** *NZ.* a short Maori club, now ceremonial only. [from Maori]

patulous ('pætjʊləs) *adj Bot.* spreading widely or expanded: *patulous branches.* [C17: from L *patulus* open, from *patēre* to lie open]

paua ('pɑːʊɑ) *n* an edible abalone of New Zealand, having an iridescent shell used for jewellery, etc. [from Maori]

paucity Ⓣ ('pɔːsɪtɪ) *n* **1** insufficiency; dearth. **2** smallness of number; fewness. [C15: from L *paucitās* scarcity, from *paucus* few]

Pauli exclusion principle ('pɔːlɪ) *n Physics.* the principle that two identical fermions cannot occupy the same quantum state in a body, such as an atom; sometimes shortened to **exclusion principle.** [C20: after Wolfgang *Pauli* (1900–58), US physicist]

Pauline ('pɔːlaɪn) *adj* relating to Saint Paul or his doctrines.

Paul Jones (pɔːl dʒəʊnz) *n* an old-time dance in which partners are exchanged. [C19: after John Paul *Jones* (1747–92), US naval commander in the War of Independence]

paulownia (pɔː'ləʊnɪə) *n* a tree of a Japanese genus, esp. one having large heart-shaped leaves and clusters of purplish or white flowers. [C19: NL, after Anna *Paulovna*, daughter of Paul I of Russia]

paunch Ⓣ (pɔːntʃ) *n* **1** the belly or abdomen, esp. when protruding. **2** another name for **rumen.** ◆ *vb (tr)* **3** to stab in the stomach; disembowel. [C14: from Anglo-Norman *paunche*, from OF *pance*, from L *panticēs* (pl) bowels]
▸ **'paunchy** *adj* ▸ **'paunchiness** *n*

pauper Ⓣ ('pɔːpə) *n* **1** a person who is extremely poor. **2** (formerly) a person supported by public charity. [C16: from L: poor]
▸ **'pauper,ism** *n*

pauperize Ⓣ *or* **pauperise** ('pɔːpə,raɪz) *vb* **pauperizes, pauperizing, pauperized** *or* **pauperises, pauperising, pauperised.** *(tr)* to make a pauper of; impoverish.

pause Ⓣ (pɔːz) *vb* **pauses, pausing, paused.** *(intr)* **1** to cease an action temporarily. **2** to hesitate; delay: *she replied without pausing.* ◆ *n* **3** a temporary stop or rest, esp. in speech or action; short break. **4** *Prosody.* another word for **caesura. 5** Also called: **fermata.** *Music.* a continuation of a note or rest beyond its normal length. Usual symbol: 𝄐 **6 give pause to.** to cause to hesitate. [C15: from L *pausa* pause, from Gk *pausis*, from *pauein* to halt]

pav (pæv) *n Austral. & NZ inf.* short for **pavlova.**

pavane *or* **pavan** (pə'vɑːn, 'pævᵊn) *n* **1** a slow and stately dance of the 16th and 17th centuries. **2** a piece of music composed for or in the rhythm of this dance. [C16 *pavan*, via F from Sp. *pavana*, from OIt. *padovana* Paduan (dance), from *Padova* Padua]

pave Ⓣ (peɪv) *vb* **paves, paving, paved.** *(tr)* **1** to cover (a road, etc.) with a firm surface suitable for travel, as with paving stones or concrete. **2** to serve as the material for a pavement or other hard layer: *bricks paved the causeway.* **3** (often foll. by *with*) to cover with a hard layer (of): *shelves paved with marble.* **4** to prepare or make easier (esp. in **pave the way**). [C14: from OF *paver*, from L *pavīre* to ram down]
▸ **'paver** *n*

pavement ('peɪvmənt) *n* **1** a hard-surfaced path for pedestrians alongside and a little higher than a road. US and Canad. word: **sidewalk. 2** the material used in paving. [C13: from L *pavīmentum* hard floor, from *pavīre* to beat hard]

pavilion (pə'vɪljən) *n* **1** *Brit.* a building at a sports ground, esp. a cricket pitch, in which players change, etc. **2** a summerhouse or other decorative shelter. **3** a building or temporary structure, esp. one that is open and ornamental, for housing exhibitions, etc. **4** a large ornate tent, esp. one with a peaked top, as used by medieval armies. **5** one of a set of buildings that together form a hospital or other large institution. ◆ *vb (tr) Literary.* **6** to place as in a pavilion: *pavilioned in splendour.* **7** to provide with a pavilion or pavilions. [C13: from OF *pavillon* canopied structure, from L *pāpiliō* butterfly, tent]

paving ('peɪvɪŋ) *n* **1** a paved surface; pavement. **2** material used for a pavement.

pavlova (pæv'ləʊvə) *n* a meringue cake topped with whipped cream and fruit. [C20: after Anna *Pavlova* (1885–1931), Russian ballerina]

Pavlovian (pæv'ləʊvɪən) *adj* **1** of or relating to the work of Ivan Pavlov (1849–1936), Soviet physiologist, on conditioned reflexes. **2** (of a reaction or response) automatic; involuntary.

paw Ⓣ (pɔː) *n* **1** any of the feet of a four-legged mammal, bearing claws or nails. **2** *Inf.* a hand, esp. one that is large, clumsy, etc. ◆ *vb* **3** to scrape or contaminate with the paws or feet. **4** *(tr) Inf.* to touch or caress in a clumsy, rough, or overfamiliar manner. [C13: via OF from Gmc]

pawky ('pɔːkɪ) *adj* **pawkier, pawkiest.** *Dialect or Scot.* having a dry wit. [C17: from Scot. *pawk* trick, from ?]
▸ **'pawkily** *adv* ▸ **'pawkiness** *n*

pawl (pɔːl) *n* a pivoted lever shaped to engage with a ratchet to prevent motion in a particular direction. [C17: ?from Du. *pal* pawl]

pawn[1] Ⓣ (pɔːn) *vb (tr)* **1** to deposit (an article) as security for the repayment of a loan, esp. from a pawnbroker. **2** to stake: *to pawn one's honour.* ◆ *n* **3** an article deposited as security. **4** the condition of being so deposited (esp. in **in pawn**). **5** a person or thing that is held as a security. **6** the act of pawning. [C15: from OF *pan* security, from L *pannus* cloth, apparently because clothing was often left as a surety]
▸ **'pawnage** *n*

pawn[2] Ⓣ (pɔːn) *n* **1** a chess man of the lowest theoretical value. **2** a person, group, etc., manipulated by another. [C14: from Anglo-Norman *poun*, from OF, from Med. L *pedō* infantryman, from L *pēs* foot]

pawnbroker ('pɔːn,brəʊkə) *n* a dealer licensed to lend money at a spec-

THESAURUS

scendingly, treat like a child **2** = **support**, assist, back, befriend, foster, fund, help, maintain, promote, sponsor, subscribe to **2** = **be a customer** *or* **client of**, buy from, deal with, do business with, frequent, shop at, trade with

patronizing *adj* **1** = **condescending**, contemptuous, disdainful, gracious, haughty, lofty, snobbish, stooping, supercilious, superior, toffee-nosed (*sl., chiefly Brit.*)
Antonyms *adj* deferential, humble, obsequious, respectful, servile

patter[1] *vb* **1** = **walk lightly**, scurry, scuttle, skip, tiptoe, trip **2** = **tap**, beat, pat, pelt, pitapat, pitter-patter, rat-a-tat, spatter ◆ *n* **3** = **tapping**, pattering, pitapat, pitter-patter

patter[2] *n* **1** = **spiel** (*inf.*), line, monologue, pitch **2** = **chatter**, gabble, jabber, nattering, prattle, yak (*sl.*) **3** = **jargon**, argot, cant, lingo (*inf.*), patois, slang, vernacular ◆ *vb* **4** = **chatter**, babble, blab, hold forth, jabber, prate, rattle off, rattle on, spiel (*inf.*), spout (*inf.*), tattle

pattern *n* **1, 2** = **design**, arrangement, decoration, decorative design, device, figure, motif, ornament **3** = **type**, kind, shape, sort, style, variety **4** = **plan**, design, diagram, guide, instructions, original, stencil, template **6** = **model**, archetype, criterion, cynosure, example, exemplar, guide, norm, original, par, paradigm, paragon, prototype, standard **7** = **sample**, example, specimen ◆ *vb* **9** = **model**, copy, emulate, follow, form, imitate, mould, order, shape, style **10** = **decorate**, design, trim

paucity *n* **1, 2** *Formal* = **scarcity**, dearth, deficiency, fewness, insufficiency, lack, meagreness, paltriness, poverty, rarity, scantiness, shortage, slenderness, slightness, smallness, sparseness, sparsity

paunch *n* **1** = **belly**, abdomen, beer-belly (*inf.*), corporation (*inf.*), middle-age spread (*inf.*), pot, potbelly, spare tyre (*Brit. sl.*), spread (*inf.*)

pauper *n* **1** = **down-and-out**, bankrupt, beggar, have-not, indigent, insolvent, mendicant, poor person

pauperism *n* **1** = **poverty**, beggary, destitution, impecuniousness, indigence, mendicancy, need, neediness, pennilessness, penury, privation, want

pauperize *vb* = **impoverish**, bankrupt, beggar, break, bust (*inf.*), cripple financially, reduce to beggary, ruin

pause *vb* **1, 2** = **stop briefly**, break, cease, delay, deliberate, desist, discontinue, halt, have a breather (*inf.*), hesitate, interrupt, rest, take a break, wait, waver ◆ *n* **3** = **stop**, break, breather (*inf.*), breathing space, caesura, cessation, delay, discontinuance, entr'acte, gap, halt, hesitation, interlude, intermission, interruption, interval, let-up (*inf.*), lull, respite, rest, stay, stoppage, wait
Antonyms *vb* ≠ **stop briefly:** advance, continue, proceed, progress ◆ *n* ≠ **stop:** advancement, continuance, progression

pave *vb* **1** = **cover**, asphalt, concrete, flag, floor, macadamize, surface, tar, tile

paw *vb* **4** *Informal* = **manhandle**, grab, handle roughly, maul, molest

pawn[1] *vb* **1, 2** = **hock** (*inf., chiefly US*), deposit, gage (*arch.*), hazard, mortgage, pledge, pop (*inf.*), stake, wager ◆ *n* **3** = **security**, assurance, bond, collateral, gage, guarantee, guaranty, pledge

pawn[2] *n* **2** = **tool**, cat's-paw, creature, dupe, instrument, plaything, puppet, stooge (*sl.*), toy

ified rate of interest on the security of movable personal property, which can be sold if the loan is not repaid within a specified period. ▸ **'pawn,broking** *n*

pawnshop ('pɔːn,ʃɒp) *n* the premises of a pawnbroker.

pawn ticket *n* a receipt for goods pawned.

pawpaw ('pɔː,pɔː) *n* another name for **papaw** or **papaya**.

pax (pæks) *n* **1** *Chiefly RC Church.* **1a** the kiss of peace. **1b** a small metal or ivory plate, formerly used to convey the kiss of peace from the celebrant at Mass to those attending it. ◆ *interj* **2** *Brit. school sl.* a call signalling an end to hostilities or claiming immunity from the rules of a game. [L: peace]

PAX (in Britain) *abbrev. for* private automatic exchange.

pay[1] ❶ (peɪ) *vb* **pays, paying, paid. 1** to discharge (a debt, obligation, etc.) by giving or doing something: *he paid his creditors.* **2** (when *intr*, often foll. by *for*) to give (money, etc.) to (a person) in return for goods or services: *they pay their workers well; they pay by the hour.* **3** to give or afford (a person, etc.) a profit or benefit: *it pays one to be honest.* **4** (*tr*) to give or bestow (a compliment, regards, attention, etc.). **5** (*tr*) to make (a visit or call). **6** (*intr;* often foll. by *for*) to give compensation or make amends. **7** (*tr*) to yield a return of: *the shares pay 15 per cent.* **8** *Austral. inf.* to acknowledge or accept (something) as true, just, etc. **9 pay one's way. 9a** to contribute one's share of expenses. **9b** to remain solvent without outside help. ◆ *n* **10a** money given in return for work or services; a salary or wage. **10b** (*as modifier*): *a pay slip; a pay claim.* **11** paid employment (esp. in **in the pay of**). **12** (*modifier*) requiring the insertion of money before or during use: *a pay phone.* **13** (*modifier*) rich enough in minerals to be profitably worked: *pay gravel.* ◆ See also **pay back, pay for,** etc. [C12: from OF *payer*, from L *pācāre* to appease (a creditor), from *pāx* peace] ▸ **'payer** *n*

pay[2] (peɪ) *vb* **pays, paying, payed.** (*tr*) *Naut.* to caulk (the seams of a wooden vessel) with pitch or tar. [C17: from OF *peier*, from L *picāre*, from *pix* pitch]

payable ❶ ('peɪəbᵊl) *adj* **1** (often foll. by *on*) to be paid: *payable on the third of each month.* **2** that is capable of being paid. **3** capable of being profitable. **4** (of a debt, etc.) imposing an obligation on the debtor to pay, esp. at once.

pay-and-display *adj* denoting a car-parking system in which a motorist buys a permit to park for a specified period, usually from a coin-operated machine, and displays the permit on or near the windscreen of his or her car so that it can be seen by a parking attendant.

pay back ❶ *vb* (*tr, adv*) **1** to retaliate against: *to pay someone back for an insult.* **2** to give or do (something equivalent) in return for a favour, insult, etc. **3** to repay (a loan, etc.).

pay bed *n* an informal name for **private pay bed.**

payday ('peɪ,deɪ) *n* the day on which wages or salaries are paid.

pay dirt *n Chiefly US.* **1** soil, gravel, ore, etc. that contains sufficient minerals to make it worthwhile mining. **2 hit** (*or* **strike**) **pay dirt.** *Inf.* to become wealthy, successful, etc.

PAYE (in Britain and New Zealand) *abbrev. for* pay as you earn; a system by which income tax levied on wage and salary earners is paid by employers directly to the government.

payee (peɪ'iː) *n* the person to whom a cheque, money order, etc., is made out.

pay for ❶ *vb* (*prep*) **1** to make payment for. **2** (*intr*) to suffer or be punished, as for a mistake, wrong decision, etc.

paying guest *n* a euphemism for **lodger.**

payload ('peɪ,ləʊd) *n* **1** that part of a cargo earning revenue. **2a** the passengers, cargo, or bombs carried by an aircraft. **2b** the equipment carried by a rocket, satellite, or spacecraft. **3** the explosive power of a warhead, bomb, etc., carried by a missile or aircraft.

paymaster ('peɪ,mɑːstə) *n* an official of a government, business, etc., responsible for the payment of wages and salaries.

payment ❶ ('peɪmənt) *n* **1** the act of paying. **2** a sum of money paid. **3** something given in return; punishment or reward.

paynim ('peɪnɪm) *n Arch.* **1** a heathen or pagan. **2** a Muslim. [C13: from OF *paienime*, from LL *pāgānismus* paganism, from *pāgānus* PAGAN]

pay off ❶ *vb* **1** (*tr, adv*) to pay all that is due in wages, etc., and discharge from employment. **2** (*tr, adv*) to pay the complete amount of (a debt, bill, etc.). **3** (*intr, adv*) to turn out to be profitable, effective, etc.: *the gamble paid off.* **4** (*tr, adv* or *intr, prep*) to take revenge on (a person) or for (a wrong done): *to pay someone off for an insult.* **5** (*tr, adv*) *Inf.* to give a bribe to. ◆ *n* **payoff. 6** the final settlement, esp. in retribution. **7** *Inf.* the climax, consequence, or outcome of events, a story, etc. **8** the final payment of a debt, salary, etc. **9** the time of such a payment. **10** *Inf.* a bribe.

payola (peɪ'əʊlə) *n Inf.* **1** a bribe given to secure special treatment, esp. to a disc jockey to promote a commercial product. **2** the practice of paying or receiving such bribes. [C20: from PAY[1] + *-ola*, as in PIANOLA]

pay out ❶ *vb* (*adv*) **1** to distribute (money, etc.); disburse. **2** (*tr*) to release (a rope) gradually, hand over hand. ◆ *n* **payout. 3** a sum of money paid out.

pay-per-view *n* **a** a system of television broadcasting by which subscribers pay for each programme they wish to receive. **b** (*as modifier*): *a pay-per-view channel.*

payphone ('peɪ,fəʊn) *n* a public telephone operated by coins or a phonecard.

payroll ('peɪ,rəʊl) *n* **1** a list of employees, specifying the salary or wage of each. **2a** the total of these amounts or the actual money equivalent. **2b** (*as modifier*): *a payroll tax.*

payt *abbrev. for* payment.

pay up *vb* (*adv*) to pay (money) promptly, in full, or on demand.

Pb *the chemical symbol for* lead. [from NL *plumbum*]

PB *Athletics abbrev. for* personal best.

PBS *US abbrev. for* Public Broadcasting Service.

PBX (in Britain) *abbrev. for* private branch exchange; a telephone system that handles the internal and external calls of a building, firm, etc.

pc *abbrev. for:* **1** per cent. **2** postcard. **3** (in prescriptions) post cibum. [L: after meals]

PC *abbrev. for:* **1** personal computer. **2** Parish Council(lor). **3** (in Britain) Police Constable. **4** politically correct. **5** (in Britain) Privy Council(lor). **6** (in Canada) Progressive Conservative.

pc. *abbrev. for:* **1** (*pl* **pcs.**) piece. **2** price.

PCB *abbrev. for* polychlorinated biphenyl; any of a group of compounds in which chlorine atoms replace the hydrogen atoms in biphenyl: used in electrical insulators and in the manufacture of plastics; a toxic pollutant.

PCC (in Britain) *abbrev. for* Press Complaints Commission.

PCP *n Trademark.* phencyclidine; a depressant drug used illegally as a hallucinogen.

PCV (in Britain) *abbrev. for* passenger carrying vehicle.

pd *abbrev. for:* **1** paid. **2** Also: **PD.** per diem. **3** potential difference.

Pd *the chemical symbol for* palladium.

PDR *abbrev. for* price-dividend ratio.

P-D ratio *n* short for **price-dividend ratio.**

PDSA (in Britain) *abbrev. for* People's Dispensary for Sick Animals.

PDT (in the US and Canada) *abbrev. for* Pacific Daylight Time.

PE *abbrev. for:* **1** physical education. **2** potential energy. **3** Presiding Elder. **4** Also: **p.e.** printer's error. **5** *Statistics.* probable error. **6** Protestant Episcopal.

pea (piː) *n* **1** an annual climbing plant with small white flowers and long green pods containing edible green seeds: cultivated in temperate regions. **2** the seed of this plant, eaten as a vegetable. **3** any of several other leguminous plants, such as the sweet pea. [C17: from PEASE (incorrectly assumed to be a pl)]

peace ❶ (piːs) *n* **1a** the state existing during the absence of war. **1b** (*as modifier*): *peace negotiations.* **2** (*often cap.*) a treaty marking the end of a war. **3** a state of harmony between people or groups. **4** law and order within a state: *a breach of the peace.* **5** absence of mental anxiety (often in **peace of mind**). **6** a state of stillness, silence, or serenity. **7 at peace. 7a** in a state of harmony or friendship. **7b** in a state of serenity. **7c** dead: *the old lady is at peace now.* **8 hold** *or* **keep one's peace.** to keep silent. **9 keep the peace.** to maintain law and order. ◆ *vb* **peaces, peacing, peaced. 10** (*intr*) *Obs. except as an imperative.* to be or become silent or still. ◆ *modifier* **11** denoting a person or thing symbolizing support for international peace: *peace women.* [C12: from OF *pais*, from L *pāx*]

peaceable ❶ ('piːsəbᵊl) *adj* **1** inclined towards peace. **2** tranquil; calm. ▸ **'peaceableness** *n* ▸ **'peaceably** *adv*

Peace Corps *n* an agency of the US government that sends volunteers to developing countries to work on educational projects, etc.

peace dividend *n* additional money available to a government from

THESAURUS

pay[1] *vb* **1, 2 = reimburse**, clear, compensate, cough up (*inf.*), discharge, foot, give, honour, liquidate, meet, offer, recompense, remit, remunerate, render, requite, reward, settle, square up **3 = benefit**, be advantageous, be worthwhile, repay, serve **3 = be profitable**, be remunerative, make a return, make money, provide a living **4 = give**, bestow, extend, grant, hand out, present, proffer, render **7 = yield**, bring in, produce, profit, return ◆ *n* **10 = wages**, allowance, compensation, earnings, emoluments, fee, hand-out, hire, income, meed (*arch.*), payment, recompense, reimbursement, remuneration, reward, salary, stipend, takings

payable *adj* **1, 4 = due**, mature, obligatory, outstanding, owed, owing, receivable, to be paid

pay back *vb* **1 = get even with** (*inf.*), get one's own back, hit back, reciprocate, recompense, retaliate, settle a score with **3 = repay**, refund, reimburse, return, settle up, square

pay for *vb* **2 = suffer**, answer for, atone, be punished, compensate, get one's deserts, make amends, suffer the consequences

payment *n* **1 = paying**, defrayal, discharge, outlay, remittance, settlement **2 = remittance**, advance, deposit, instalment, portion, premium **2 = wage**, fee, hire, remuneration, reward

pay off *vb* **1 = settle**, clear, discharge, liquidate, pay in full, square **1 = dismiss**, discharge, fire, lay off, let go, sack (*inf.*) **3 = succeed**, be effective, be profitable, be successful, work **4 = get even with** (*inf.*), pay back, retaliate, settle a score **5** *Informal* **= bribe**, buy off, corrupt, get at, grease the palm of (*sl.*), oil (*inf.*), suborn ◆ *n* **payoff 6 = retribution**, conclusion, day of reckoning, final reckoning, judgment, reward, settlement **7** *Informal* **= outcome**, climax, clincher (*inf.*), consequence, culmination, finale, moment of truth, punch line, result, the crunch (*inf.*), upshot

pay out *vb* **1 = spend**, cough up (*inf.*), disburse, expend, fork out *or* over *or* up (*sl.*), lay out (*inf.*), shell out (*inf.*)

peace *n* **1, 2 = truce**, armistice, cessation of hostilities, conciliation, pacification, treaty **3 = harmony**, accord, agreement, amity, concord **5 = serenity**, calm, composure, contentment, placidity, relaxation, repose **6 = stillness**, calm, calmness, hush, peacefulness, quiet, quietude, repose, rest, silence, tranquillity

peaceable *adj* **1 = peace-loving**, amiable, amicable, conciliatory, dovish, friendly, gentle,

cuts in defence expenditure because of the end of a period of hostilities.

peaceful ➊ ('pi:sfʊl) *adj* **1** not in a state of war or disagreement. **2** calm; tranquil. **3** not involving violence: *peaceful picketing.* **4** of, relating to, or in accord with a time of peace. **5** inclined towards peace.
▸ **'peacefully** *adv* ▸ **'peacefulness** *n*

peacekeeping ('pi:sˌki:pɪŋ) *n* **a** the maintenance of peace, esp. the prevention of further fighting between hostile forces. **b** (*as modifier*): *a UN peacekeeping force.*

peacemaker ➊ ('pi:sˌmeɪkə) *n* a person who establishes peace, esp. between others.
▸ **'peaceˌmaking** *n*

peace offering *n* **1** something given to an adversary in the hope of procuring or maintaining peace. **2** *Judaism.* a sacrificial meal shared between the offerer and Jehovah.

peace pipe *n* a long decorated pipe smoked by North American Indians, esp. as a token of peace. Also called: **calumet.**

peace sign *n* a gesture made with the palm of the hand outwards and the index and middle fingers raised in a V.

peacetime ('pi:sˌtaɪm) *n* **a** a period without war; time of peace. **b** (*as modifier*): *a peacetime agreement.*

peach[1] (pi:tʃ) *n* **1** a small tree with pink flowers and rounded edible fruit: cultivated in temperate regions. **2** the soft juicy fruit of this tree, which has a downy reddish-yellow skin, yellowish-orange sweet flesh, and a single stone. **3a** a pinkish-yellow to orange colour. **3b** (*as adj*): *a peach dress.* **4** *Inf.* a person or thing that is especially pleasing. [C14 *peche*, from OF, from Med. L *persica*, from L *Persicum mālum* Persian apple]

peach[2] (pi:tʃ) *vb* (*intr*) *Sl.* to inform against an accomplice. [C15: var. of earlier *apeche*, from F, from LL *impedicāre* to entangle; see IMPEACH]

peach brandy *n* (esp. in S. Africa) a coarse brandy made from fermented peaches.

peach Melba *n* a dessert made of halved peaches, vanilla ice cream, and raspberries. [C20: after Dame Nellie MELBA]

peachy ('pi:tʃɪ) *adj* **peachier, peachiest. 1** of or like a peach, esp. in colour or texture. **2** *Inf.* excellent; fine.
▸ **'peachiness** *n*

peacock ('pi:ˌkɒk) *n, pl* **peacocks** *or* **peacock. 1** a male peafowl, having a crested head and a very large fanlike tail marked with blue and green eyelike spots. **2** another name for **peafowl. 3** a vain strutting person. ◆ *vb* **4** to display (oneself) proudly. [C14 *pecok*, *pe-* from OE *pāwa* (from L *pāvō* peacock) + COCK[1]]
▸ **'peaˌcockish** *adj* ▸ **'peaˌhen** *fem n*

peacock blue *n* **a** a greenish-blue colour. **b** (*as adj*): *a peacock-blue car.*

peafowl ('pi:ˌfaʊl) *n, pl* **peafowls** *or* **peafowl.** either of two large pheasants of India and Ceylon and of SE Asia. The males (see **peacock** (sense 1)) have a characteristic bright plumage.

pea green *n* **a** a yellowish-green colour. **b** (*as adj*): *a pea-green teapot.*

pea jacket *or* **peacoat** ('pi:ˌkəʊt) *n* a sailor's short heavy woollen overcoat. [C18: from Du. *pijjekker*, from *pij* coat of coarse cloth + *jekker* jacket]

peak[1] ➊ (pi:k) *n* **1** a pointed end, edge, or projection: *the peak of a roof.* **2** the pointed summit of a mountain. **3** a mountain with a pointed summit. **4** the point of greatest development, strength, etc.: *the peak of his career.* **5a** a sharp increase followed by a sharp decrease: *a voltage peak.* **5b** the maximum value of this quantity. **5c** (*as modifier*): *peak voltage.* **6** Also called: **visor.** a projecting piece on the front of some caps. **7** *Naut.* **7a** the extreme forward (**forepeak**) or aft (**afterpeak**) part of the hull. **7b** (of a fore-and-aft quadrilateral sail) the after uppermost corner. **7c** the after end of a gaff. ◆ *vb* **8** to form or reach or cause to form or reach a peak. **9** (*tr*) *Naut.* to set (a gaff) or tilt (oars) vertically. ◆ *adj* **10** of or relating to a period of greatest use or demand: *peak viewing hours.* [C16: ?from PIKE[2], infl. by BEAK[1]]

peak[2] ➊ (pi:k) *vb* (*intr*) to become wan, emaciated, or sickly. [C16: from ?]
▸ **'peaky** *or* **'peakish** *adj*

peaked (pi:kt) *adj* having a peak; pointed.

peak load *n* the maximum load on an electrical power-supply system.

peal ➊ (pi:l) *n* **1** a loud prolonged usually reverberating sound, as of bells, thunder, or laughter. **2** *Bell-ringing.* a series of changes rung in accordance with specific rules. **3** (*not in technical usage*) the set of bells in a belfry. ◆ *vb* **4** (*intr*) to sound with a peal or peals. **5** (*tr*) to give forth loudly and sonorously. **6** (*tr*) to ring (bells) in peals. [C14 *pele*, var. of *apele* APPEAL]

peanut ('pi:ˌnʌt) *n* **a** a leguminous plant widely cultivated for its edible seeds. **b** the edible nutlike seed of this plant, used for food and as a source of oil. Also called: **groundnut, monkey nut.** ◆ See also **peanuts.**

peanut butter *n* a brownish oily paste made from peanuts.

peanuts ('pi:ˌnʌts) *n Sl.* a trifling amount of money.

pear (pɛə) *n* **1** a widely cultivated tree, having white flowers and edible fruits. **2** the sweet gritty-textured juicy fruit of this tree, which has a globular base and tapers towards the apex. **3** the wood of this tree, used for making furniture. **4 go pear-shaped.** *Inf.* to go wrong: *the plan started to go pear-shaped.* [OE *pere*, ult. from L *pirum*]

pearl[1] (pɜ:l) *n* **1** a hard smooth lustrous typically rounded structure occurring on the inner surface of the shell of a clam or oyster around an invading particle such as a sand grain; much valued as a gem. **2** any artificial gem resembling this. **3** See **mother-of-pearl. 4** a person or thing that is like a pearl, esp. in beauty or value. **5** a pale greyish-white colour, often with a bluish tinge. ◆ *adj* **6** of, made of, or set with pearl or mother-of-pearl. **7** having the shape or colour of a pearl. ◆ *vb* **8** (*tr*) to set with or as if with pearls. **9** to shape into or assume a pearl-like form or colour. **10** (*intr*) to dive or search for pearls. [C14: from OF, from Vulgar L *pernula* (unattested), from L *perna* sea mussel]

pearl[2] (pɜ:l) *n, vb* a variant spelling of **purl**[1] (senses 2, 3, 5).

pearl ash *n* the granular crystalline form of potassium carbonate.

pearl barley *n* barley ground into small round grains, used esp. in soups and stews.

pearly ➊ ('pɜ:lɪ) *adj* **pearlier, pearliest. 1** resembling a pearl, esp. in lustre. **2** decorated with pearls or mother-of-pearl. ◆ *n, pl* **pearlies.** *Brit.* **3** a London costermonger or his wife who wear on ceremonial occasions a traditional dress of dark clothes covered with pearl buttons. **4** (*pl*) the clothes or the buttons themselves.
▸ **'pearliness** *n*

Pearly Gates *pl n Inf.* the entrance to heaven.

pearly king *or* (*fem*) **pearly queen** *n* the London costermonger whose ceremonial clothes display the most lavish collection of pearl buttons.

pearly nautilus *n* any of several cephalopod molluscs of warm and tropical seas, having a partitioned pale pearly external shell with brown stripes. Also called: **chambered nautilus.**

pearmain ('pɛəˌmeɪn) *n* any of several varieties of apple having a red skin. [C15: from OF *permain* a type of pear, ?from L *Parmēnsis* of Parma]

peart (pɪət) *adj Dialect.* lively; spirited; brisk. [C15: var. of PERT]
▸ **'peartly** *adv*

peasant ➊ ('pɛz[ə]nt) *n* **1** a member of a class of low social status that depends on either cottage industry or agricultural labour as a means of subsistence. **2** *Inf.* a person who lives in the country; rustic. **3** *Inf.* an uncouth or uncultured person. [C15: from Anglo-F, from OF *païsant*, from *païs* country, from L *pāgus* rural area]

peasantry ('pɛz[ə]ntrɪ) *n* peasants as a class.

pease (pi:z) *n, pl* **pease.** *Arch. or dialect.* another word for **pea.** [OE *peose*, via LL from L *pisa* peas, pl of *pisum*, from Gk *pison*]

peasecod *or* **peascod** ('pi:zˌkɒd) *n Arch.* the pod of a pea plant. [C14: from PEASE + COD[2]]

pease pudding *n* (esp. in Britain) a dish of split peas that have been soaked and boiled.

peashooter ('pi:ˌʃu:tə) *n* a tube through which dried peas are blown, used as a toy weapon.

peasouper (ˌpi:'su:pə) *n* **1** *Inf., chiefly Brit.* dense dirty yellowish fog. **2** *Canad.* a disparaging name for a **French Canadian.**

peat (pi:t) *n* **a** a compact brownish deposit of partially decomposed vegetable matter saturated with water: found in uplands and bogs and used as a fuel (when dried) and as a fertilizer. **b** (*as modifier*): *peat bog.* [C14: from Anglo-L *peta*, ?from Celtic]
▸ **'peaty** *adj*

peat moss *n* any of various mosses, esp. sphagnum, that grow in wet places and decay to form peat. See also **sphagnum.**

pebble ('pɛb[ə]l) *n* **1** a small smooth rounded stone, esp. one worn by the action of water. **2a** a transparent colourless variety of rock crystal, used for making certain lenses. **2b** such a lens. **3** (*modifier*) *Inf.* (of a lens or of spectacles) thick, with a high degree of magnification or distortion. **4a** a grainy irregular surface, esp. on leather. **4b** leather having such a surface. ◆ *vb* **pebbles, pebbling, pebbled.** (*tr*) **5** to cover with pebbles. **6** to impart a grainy surface to (leather). [OE *papolstān*, from *papol-* (? imit.) + *stān* stone]
▸ **'pebbly** *adj*

THESAURUS

inoffensive, mild, nonbelligerent, pacific, peaceful, placid, unwarlike **2** = **calm**, balmy, peaceful, quiet, restful, serene, still, tranquil, undisturbed

peaceful *adj* **1** = **at peace**, amicable, free from strife, friendly, harmonious, nonviolent, on friendly *or* good terms, without hostility **2** = **calm**, gentle, placid, quiet, restful, serene, still, tranquil, undisturbed, unruffled, untroubled **5** = **peace-loving**, conciliatory, irenic, pacific, peaceable, placatory, unwarlike
Antonyms *adj* ≠ **at peace:** antagonistic, bitter, hostile, unfriendly, violent, warring, wartime ≠ **calm:** agitated, disquieted, disturbed, loud, nervous, noisy, raucous, restless, upset ≠ **peace-loving:** belligerent, warlike

peacemaker *n* = **mediator**, appeaser, arbitrator, conciliator, pacifier, peacemonger

peak[1] *n* **1, 2** = **point**, aiguille, apex, brow, crest, pinnacle, summit, tip, top **4** = **high point**, acme, apogee, climax, crown, culmination, maximum point, *ne plus ultra*, zenith ◆ *vb* **8** = **culminate**, be at its height, climax, come to a head, reach its highest point, reach the zenith

peaky *adj* = **off colour**, emaciated, green about the gills, ill, in poor shape, like death warmed up (*inf.*), pale, peelie-wally (*Scot.*), pinched, poorly (*inf.*), sick, sickly, under the weather (*inf.*), unwell, wan

peal *n* **1, 2** = **ring**, blast, carillon, chime, clamour, clang, clap, crash, resounding, reverberation, ringing, roar, rumble, sound, tintinnabulation ◆ *vb* **5, 6** = **ring**, chime, crack, crash, resonate, resound, reverberate, roar, roll, rumble, sound, toll

pearly *adj* **1** = **silvery**, creamy, ivory, milky **1** = **iridescent**, margaric, margaritic, mother-of-pearl, nacreous, opalescent

peasant *n* **1** = **rustic**, churl, countryman, hind (*obs.*), son of the soil, swain (*arch.*) **2** *Informal* = **boor**, churl, country bumpkin, hayseed (*US & Canad. inf.*), hick (*inf., chiefly US & Canad.*), lout, provincial, yokel

pebble dash *n Brit.* a finish for external walls consisting of small stones embedded in plaster.

pec (pɛk) *n (usually pl) Inf.* short for **pectoral muscle.**

pecan (pɪˈkæn, ˈpiːkən) *n* **1** a hickory tree of the southern US having deeply furrowed bark and edible nuts. **2** the smooth oval nut of this tree, which has a sweet oily kernel. [C18: from Algonquian *paccan*]

peccable (ˈpɛkəbᵊl) *adj* liable to sin. [C17: via F from Med. L *peccābilis*, from L *peccāre* to sin]

peccadillo ➊ (ˌpɛkəˈdɪləʊ) *n, pl* **peccadilloes** *or* **peccadillos.** a petty sin or fault. [C16: from Sp., from *pecado* sin, from L *peccātum*, from *peccāre* to transgress]

peccant (ˈpɛkənt) *adj Rare.* **1** guilty of an offence; corrupt. **2** violating or disregarding a rule; faulty. **3** producing disease; morbid. [C17: from L *peccans*, from *peccāre* to sin]
▸ **ˈpeccancy** *n*

peccary (ˈpɛkərɪ) *n, pl* **peccaries** *or* **peccary.** either of two piglike mammals of forests of southern North America, Central and South America. [C17: from Carib]

peck[1] (pɛk) *n* **1** a unit of dry measure equal to 8 quarts or one quarter of a bushel. **2** a container used for measuring this quantity. **3** a large quantity or number. [C13: from Anglo-Norman, from ?]

peck[2] ➊ (pɛk) *vb* **1** (when *intr*, sometimes foll. by *at*) to strike with the beak or with a pointed instrument. **2** (*tr*; sometimes foll. by *out*) to dig (a hole, etc.) by pecking. **3** (*tr*) (of birds) to pick up (corn, worms, etc.) by pecking. **4** (*intr*; often foll. by *at*) to nibble or pick (at one's food). **5** *Inf.* to kiss (a person) quickly and lightly. **6** (*intr*; foll. by *at*) to nag. ◆ *n* **7** a quick light blow, esp. from a bird's beak. **8** a mark made by such a blow. **9** *Inf.* a quick light kiss. [C14: from ?]

pecker (ˈpɛkə) *n Brit. sl.* spirits (esp. in **keep one's pecker up**).

pecking order *n* **1** Also called: **peck order.** a natural hierarchy in a group of gregarious birds, such as domestic fowl. **2** any hierarchical order, as among people in a particular group.

peckish (ˈpɛkɪʃ) *adj Inf., chiefly Brit.* feeling slightly hungry. [C18: from PECK[2]]

pecten (ˈpɛktɪn) *n, pl* **pectens** *or* **pectines** (-tɪˌniːz). **1** a comblike structure in the eye of birds and reptiles, consisting of a network of blood vessels projecting inwards from the retina. **2** any other comblike part or organ. [C18: from L: a comb, from *pectere* to comb]

pectin (ˈpɛktɪn) *n Biochem.* any of the acidic polysaccharides that occur in ripe fruit and vegetables: used in the manufacture of jams because of their ability to solidify to a gel. [C19: from Gk *pēktos* congealed, from *pegnuein* to set]
▸ **ˈpectic** *or* **ˈpectinous** *adj*

pectoral (ˈpɛktərəl) *adj* **1** of or relating to the chest, breast, or thorax: *pectoral fins.* **2** worn on the breast or chest: *a pectoral medallion.* ◆ *n* **3** a pectoral organ or part, esp. a muscle or fin. **4** a medicine for disorders of the chest or lungs. **5** anything worn on the chest or breast for decoration or protection. [C15: from L *pectorālis*, from *pectus* breast]
▸ **ˈpectorally** *adv*

pectoral fin *n* either of a pair of fins, situated just behind the head in fishes, that help to control the direction of movement during locomotion.

pectoral muscle *n* either of two large chest muscles (**pectoralis major** and **pectoralis minor**), that assist in movements of the shoulder and upper arm.

peculate (ˈpɛkjʊˌleɪt) *vb* **peculates, peculating, peculated.** to appropriate or embezzle (public money, etc.). [C18: from L *pecūlārī*, from *pecūlium* private property (orig., cattle); see PECULIAR]
▸ **ˌpecuˈlation** *n* ▸ **ˈpecuˌlator** *n*

peculiar ➊ (pɪˈkjuːlɪə) *adj* **1** strange or unusual; odd: *a peculiar idea.* **2** distinct from others; special. **3** (*postpositive*; foll. by *to*) belonging characteristically or exclusively (to): *peculiar to North America.* [C15: from L *pecūliāris* concerning private property, from *pecūlium*, lit.: property in cattle, from *pecus* cattle]
▸ **peˈculiarly** *adv*

peculiarity ➊ (pɪˌkjuːlɪˈærɪtɪ) *n, pl* **peculiarities. 1** a strange or unusual habit or characteristic. **2** a distinguishing trait, etc., that is characteristic of a particular person; idiosyncrasy. **3** the state or quality of being peculiar.

pecuniary ➊ (pɪˈkjuːnɪərɪ) *adj* **1** of or relating to money. **2** *Law.* (of an offence) involving a monetary penalty. [C16: from L *pecūniāris*, from *pecūnia* money]
▸ **peˈcuniarily** *adv*

pecuniary advantage *n Law.* financial advantage that is dishonestly obtained by deception and that constitutes a criminal offence.

-ped *or* **-pede** *n combining form.* foot or feet: *quadruped; centipede.* [from L *pēs*, *ped-* foot]

pedagogue ➊ *or US* (*sometimes*) **pedagog** (ˈpɛdəˌgɒg) *n* **1** a teacher or educator. **2** a pedantic or dogmatic teacher. [C14: from L *paedagōgus*, from Gk *paidagōgos* slave who looked after his master's son, from *pais* boy + *agōgos* leader]
▸ **ˌpedaˈgogic** *or* **ˌpedaˈgogical** *adj* ▸ **ˌpedaˈgogically** *adv*

pedagogy (ˈpɛdəˌgɒgɪ, -ˌgɒdʒɪ, -ˌgəʊdʒɪ) *n* the principles, practice, or profession of teaching.

pedal[1] (ˈpɛdᵊl) *n* **1a** any foot-operated lever, esp. one of the two levers that drive the chainwheel of a bicycle, the foot brake, clutch control, or accelerator of a car, one of the levers on an organ controlling deep bass notes, or one of the levers on a piano used to mute or sustain tone. **1b** (*as modifier*): *a pedal cycle.* ◆ *vb* **pedals, pedalling, pedalled** *or US* **pedals, pedaling, pedaled. 2** to propel (a bicycle, etc.) by operating the pedals. **3** (*intr*) to operate the pedals of an organ, piano, etc. **4** to work (pedals of any kind). [C17: from L *pedālis*; see PEDAL[2]]

pedal[2] (ˈpiːdᵊl) *adj* of or relating to the foot or feet. [C17: from L *pedālis*, from *pēs* foot]

pedal point (ˈpɛdᵊl) *n Music.* a sustained bass note, over which the other parts move bringing changing harmonies. Often shortened to **pedal.**

pedal steel guitar (ˈpɛdᵊl) *n* a floor-mounted multineck steel guitar with each set of strings tuned to a different open chord and foot pedals to raise or lower the pitch.

pedant ➊ (ˈpɛdᵊnt) *n* **1** a person who relies too much on academic learning or who is concerned chiefly with insignificant detail. **2** *Arch.* a schoolmaster or teacher. [C16: via OF from It. *pedante* teacher]
▸ **pedantic** (pɪˈdæntɪk) *adj* ▸ **peˈdantically** *adv*

pedantry ➊ (ˈpɛdᵊntrɪ) *n, pl* **pedantries.** the habit or an instance of being a pedant, esp. in the display of useless knowledge or minute observance of petty rules or details.

pedate (ˈpɛdeɪt) *adj* **1** (of a plant leaf) deeply divided into several lobes. **2** *Zool.* having or resembling a foot: *a pedate appendage.* [C18: from L *pedātus* equipped with feet, from *pēs* foot]

peddle ➊ (ˈpɛdᵊl) *vb* **peddles, peddling, peddled. 1** to go from place to place selling (goods, esp. small articles). **2** (*tr*) to sell (illegal drugs, esp. narcotics). **3** (*tr*) to advocate (ideas, etc.) persistently: *to peddle a new philosophy.* [C16: back formation from PEDLAR]

peddler (ˈpɛdlə) *n* **1** a person who sells illegal drugs, esp. narcotics. **2** the usual US spelling of **pedlar.**

pederasty *or* **paederasty** (ˈpɛdəˌræstɪ) *n* homosexual relations between men and boys. [C17: from NL *paederastia*, from Gk, from *pais* boy + *erastēs* lover, from *eran* to love]
▸ **ˈpederˌast** *or* **ˈpaederˌast** *n* ▸ **ˌpederˈastic** *or* **ˌpaederˈastic** *adj*

pedestal ➊ (ˈpɛdɪstᵊl) *n* **1** a base that supports a column, statue, etc. **2** a position of eminence or supposed superiority (esp. in **place, put,** *or* **set on a pedestal**). [C16: from F *piédestal*, from OIt. *piedestallo*, from *pie* foot + *di* of + *stallo* a stall]

pedestrian ➊ (pɪˈdɛstrɪən) *n* **1a** a person travelling on foot; walker. **1b** (*as modifier*): *a pedestrian precinct.* ◆ *adj* **2** dull; commonplace: *a pedestrian style of writing.* [C18: from L *pedester*, from *pēs* foot]

pedestrian crossing *n Brit.* a path across a road marked as a crossing for pedestrians.

pedestrianize *or* **pedestrianise** (pɪˈdɛstrɪəˌnaɪz) *vb* **pedestrianizes, pedestrianizing, pedestrianized** *or* **pedestrianises, pedestrianising, pedestrianised.** (*tr*) to convert (a street, etc.) into an area for the use of pedestrians only.
▸ **peˌdestrianiˈzation** *or* **peˌdestrianiˈsation** *n*

pedi- *combining form.* indicating the foot: *pedicure.* [from L *pēs*, *ped-* foot]

pedicab (ˈpɛdɪˌkæb) *n* a pedal-operated tricycle, available for hire in

THESAURUS

peccadillo *n* = **misdeed**, error, indiscretion, infraction, lapse, misdemeanour, petty sin, slip, trifling fault

peck[2] *vb, n* **1-9** = **pick**, bite, dig, hit, jab, kiss, nibble, poke, prick, strike, tap

peculiar *adj* **1** = **odd**, abnormal, bizarre, curious, eccentric, exceptional, extraordinary, far-out, freakish, funny, offbeat, off-the-wall (*sl.*), outlandish, out-of-the-way, outré, quaint, queer, singular, strange, uncommon, unconventional, unusual, weird **2, 3** = **specific**, appropriate, characteristic, distinct, distinctive, distinguishing, endemic, idiosyncratic, individual, local, particular, personal, private, restricted, special, unique
Antonyms *adj* ≠ **odd**: commonplace, conventional, expected, familiar, ordinary, usual ≠ **specific**: common, general, indistinctive, unspecific

peculiarity *n* **1, 3** = **eccentricity**, abnormality, bizarreness, foible, freakishness, idiosyncrasy, mannerism, oddity, odd trait, queerness, quirk **2** = **characteristic**, attribute, distinctiveness, feature, mark, particularity, property, quality, singularity, speciality, trait

pecuniary *adj* **1** = **monetary**, commercial, financial, fiscal

pedagogue *n* **1, 2** = **teacher**, dogmatist, dominie (*Scot.*), educator, instructor, master *or* mistress, pedant, schoolmaster *or* schoolmistress

pedant *n* **1** = **hairsplitter**, casuist, doctrinaire, dogmatist, literalist, nit-picker (*inf.*), pedagogue, pettifogger, precisian, quibbler, scholastic, sophist

pedantic *adj* **1** = **hairsplitting**, abstruse, academic, bookish, didactic, donnish, erudite, formal, fussy, nit-picking (*inf.*), overnice, particular, pedagogic, picky (*inf.*), pompous, precise, priggish, punctilious, scholastic, schoolmasterly, sententious, stilted

pedantry *n* = **hairsplitting**, bookishness, finicality, overnicety, pedagogism, pettifoggery, pomposity, punctiliousness, quibbling, sophistry, stuffiness

peddle *vb* **1, 2** = **sell**, flog (*sl.*), hawk, huckster, market, push (*inf.*), sell door to door, trade, vend

pedestal *n* **1** = **support**, base, dado (*Architecture*), foot, foundation, mounting, pier, plinth, socle, stand

pedestrian *n* **1** = **walker**, footslogger, foot-traveller ◆ *adj* **2** = **dull**, banal, boring, commonplace, flat, ho-hum (*inf.*), humdrum, mediocre, mundane, no great shakes (*inf.*), ordinary, plodding, prosaic, run-of-the-mill, unimaginative, uninspired, uninteresting
Antonyms *n* ≠ **walker**: driver, motorist ◆ *adj* ≠ **dull**: exciting, fascinating, imaginative, important, interesting, noteworthy, outstanding, remarkable, significant

some Asian countries, with an attached seat for one or two passengers.

pedicel (ˈpɛdɪˌsɛl) *n* **1** the stalk bearing a single flower of an inflorescence. **2** Also called: **peduncle.** *Biol.* any short stalk bearing an organ or organism. ◆ Also called: **pedicle.** [C17: from NL *pedicellus*, from L *pedīculus*, from *pēs* foot]
▸**pedicellate** (pɪˈdɪsɪˌleɪt) *adj*

pediculosis (pɪˌdɪkjʊˈləʊsɪs) *n Pathol.* the state of being infested with lice. [C19: via NL from L *pedīculus* louse]
▸**pediculous** (pɪˈdɪkjʊləs) *adj*

pedicure (ˈpɛdɪˌkjʊə) *n* treatment of the feet, either by a medical expert or a cosmetician. [C19: via F from L *pēs* foot + *cūrāre* to care for]

pedigree Ⓣ (ˈpɛdɪˌgriː) *n* **1a** the line of descent of a purebred animal. **1b** (*as modifier*): *a pedigree bull.* **2** a document recording this. **3** a genealogical table, esp. one indicating pure ancestry. [C15: from OF *pie de grue* crane's foot, alluding to the spreading lines used in a genealogical chart]
▸ˈ**pediˌgreed** *adj*

pediment (ˈpɛdɪmənt) *n* a low-pitched gable, esp. one that is triangular as used in classical architecture. [C16: from obs. *periment*, ? workman's corruption of PYRAMID]
▸ˌ**pediˈmental** *adj*

pedipalp (ˈpɛdɪˌpælp) *n* either member of the second pair of head appendages of arachnids: specialized for feeding, locomotion, etc. [C19: from NL *pedipalpi*, from L *pēs* foot + *palpus* palp]

pedlar Ⓣ *or esp. US* **peddler** (ˈpɛdlə) *n* a person who peddles; hawker. [C14: changed from *peder*, from *ped*, *pedde* basket, from ?]

pedo- *or before a vowel* **ped-** a variant (esp. US) of **paedo-**.

pedology (pɪˈdɒlədʒɪ) *n* the study of soils. [C20: from Gk *pedon* ground, earth + -OLOGY]

pedometer (pɪˈdɒmɪtə) *n* a device that records the number of steps taken in walking and hence the distance travelled.

peduncle (pɪˈdʌŋkᵊl) *n* **1** the stalk of a plant bearing an inflorescence or solitary flower. **2** *Anat., pathol.* any stalklike structure. **3** *Biol.* another name for **pedicel** (sense 2). [C18: from NL *pedunculus*, from L *pedīculus* little foot]
▸**peduncular** (pɪˈdʌŋkjʊlə) *or* **pedunculate** (pɪˈdʌŋkjʊlɪt, -ˌleɪt) *adj*

pee (piː) *Inf.* ◆ *vb* **pees, peeing, peed. 1** (*intr*) to urinate. ◆ *n* **2** urine. **3** the act of urinating. [C18: euphemistic for PISS, based on the initial letter]

peek Ⓣ (piːk) *vb* **1** (*intr*) to glance quickly or furtively. ◆ *n* **2** such a glance. [C14 *pike*, rel. to M Du *kiken* to peek]

peekaboo (ˈpiːkəˌbuː) *n* **1** a game for young children, in which one person hides his face and suddenly reveals it and cries "peekaboo". ◆ *adj* **2** (of a garment) made of fabric that is sheer or patterned with small holes. [C16: from PEEK + BOO]

peel[1] Ⓣ (piːl) *vb* **1** (*tr*) to remove (the skin, rind, etc.) of (a fruit, egg, etc.). **2** (*intr*) (of paint, etc.) to be removed from a surface, esp. by weathering. **3** (*intr*) (of a surface) to lose its outer covering of paint, etc., esp. by weathering. **4** (*intr*) (of a person or part of the body) to shed skin in flakes or (of skin) to be shed in flakes, esp. as a result of sunburn. ◆ *n* **5** the skin or rind of a fruit, etc. ◆ See also **peel off.** [OE *pilian* to strip off the outer layer, from L *pilāre* to make bald, from *pilus* a hair]
▸ˈ**peeler** *n*

peel[2] (piːl) *n* a long-handled shovel used by bakers for moving bread in an oven. [C14 *pele*, from OF, from L *pāla* spade, from *pangere* to drive in]

peel[3] (piːl) *n Brit.* a fortified tower of the 16th century on the borders of Scotland. [C14 (fence made of stakes): from OF *piel* stake, from L *pālus*]

peeler (ˈpiːlə) *n Irish & obs. Brit. sl.* another word for **policeman.** [C19: from the founder of the police force, Sir Robert *Peel* (1788–1850), Brit. statesman & prime minister]

peeling (ˈpiːlɪŋ) *n* a strip of skin, rind, bark, etc., that has been peeled off: *a potato peeling.*

peel off *vb* (*adv*) **1** to remove or be removed by peeling. **2** (*intr*) *Sl.* to undress. **3** (*intr*) (of an aircraft) to turn away as by banking, and leave a formation.

peen (piːn) *n* **1** the end of a hammer head opposite the striking face, often rounded or wedge-shaped. ◆ *vb* **2** (*tr*) to strike with the peen of a hammer or a stream of metal shot. [C17: var. of *pane*, ?from F *panne*, ult. from L *pinna* point]

peep[1] Ⓣ (piːp) *vb* (*intr*) **1** to look furtively or secretly, as through a small aperture or from a hidden place. **2** to appear partially or briefly: *the sun peeped through the clouds.* ◆ *n* **3** a quick or furtive look. **4** the first appearance: *the peep of dawn.* [C15: var. of PEEK]

peep[2] Ⓣ (piːp) *vb* (*intr*) **1** (esp. of young birds) to utter shrill small noises. **2** to speak in a weak voice. ◆ *n* **3** a peeping sound. [C15: imit.]

peeper (ˈpiːpə) *n* **1** a person who peeps. **2** (*often pl*) a slang word for **eye**[1] (sense 1).

peephole Ⓣ (ˈpiːpˌhəʊl) *n* a small aperture, as in a door for observing callers before opening.

Peeping Tom *n* a man who furtively observes women undressing; voyeur. [C19: after the tailor who, according to legend, peeped at Lady Godiva when she rode naked through Coventry]

peepshow (ˈpiːpˌʃəʊ) *n* **1** Also called: **raree show.** a box with a peephole through which a series of pictures can be seen. **2** a booth from which a viewer can see a live nude model for a fee.

peepul (ˈpiːpᵊl) *or* **pipal** *n* an Indian tree resembling the banyan: regarded as sacred by Buddhists. Also called: **bo tree.** [C18: from Hindi *pīpal*, from Sansk. *pippala*]

peer[1] Ⓣ (pɪə) *n* **1** a member of a nobility; nobleman. **2** a person who holds any of the five grades of the British nobility: duke, marquess, earl, viscount, and baron. See also **life peer. 3** a person who is an equal in social standing, rank, age, etc.: *to be tried by one's peers.* [C14 (in sense 3): from OF *per*, from L *pār* equal]

peer[2] Ⓣ (pɪə) *vb* (*intr*) **1** to look intently with or as if with difficulty: *to peer into the distance.* **2** to appear partially or dimly: *the sun peered through the fog.* [C16: from Flemish *pieren* to look with narrowed eyes]

peerage Ⓣ (ˈpɪərɪdʒ) *n* **1** the whole body of peers; aristocracy. **2** the position, rank, or title of a peer. **3** (esp. in the British Isles) a book listing the peers and giving their genealogy.

peeress (ˈpɪərɪs) *n* **1** the wife or widow of a peer. **2** a woman holding the rank of a peer in her own right.

peer group *n* a social group composed of individuals of approximately the same age.

peerless Ⓣ (ˈpɪəlɪs) *adj* having no equals; matchless.

peeve Ⓣ (piːv) *Inf.* ◆ *vb* **peeves, peeving, peeved. 1** (*tr*) to irritate; vex; annoy. ◆ *n* **2** something that irritates; vexation. [C20: back formation from PEEVISH]
▸**peeved** *adj*

peevish Ⓣ (ˈpiːvɪʃ) *adj* fretful or irritable. [C14: from ?]
▸ˈ**peevishly** *adv* ▸ˈ**peevishness** *n*

peewee (ˈpiːwiː) *n* a small black-and-white Australian bird with long thin legs. [imit.]

peewit *or* **pewit** (ˈpiːwɪt) *n* another name for **lapwing.** [C16: imit. of its call]

peg Ⓣ (pɛg) *n* **1** a small cylindrical pin or dowel used to join two parts together. **2** a pin pushed or driven into a surface: used to mark scores, define limits, support coats, etc. **3** any of several pins on a violin, etc., which can be turned so as to tune strings wound around them. **4** Also called: **clothes peg.** *Brit., Austral., & NZ.* a split or hinged pin for fastening wet clothes to a line to dry. US and Canad. equivalent: **clothespin. 5** *Brit.* a small drink of wine or spirits. **6** an opportunity or pretext for doing something: *a peg on which to hang a theory.* **7** *Inf.* a level of self-esteem, importance, etc. (esp. in **bring** *or* **take down a peg**). **8** *Inf.* See **peg leg. 9 off the peg.** *Chiefly Brit.* (of clothes) ready-to-wear, as opposed to tailor-made. ◆ *vb* **pegs, pegging, pegged. 10** (*tr*) to knock or insert a peg into. **11** (*tr*) to secure with pegs: *to peg a tent.* **12** (*tr*) to mark (a

THESAURUS

pedigree *n* **1a, 3** = **lineage**, ancestry, blood, breed, derivation, descent, extraction, family, family tree, genealogy, heritage, line, race, stemma, stirps, stock ◆ *modifier* **1b** = **purebred**, full-blooded, thoroughbred

pedlar *n* = **seller**, cheap-jack (*inf.*), colporteur, door-to-door salesman, duffer (*dialect*), hawker, huckster, vendor

peek *vb* **1** = **glance**, eyeball (*sl.*), keek (*Scot.*), look, peep, peer, snatch a glimpse, sneak a look, spy, take a look, take *or* have a gander (*inf.*) ◆ *n* **2** = **glance**, blink, butcher's (*Brit. sl.*), gander (*inf.*), glim (*Scot.*), glimpse, keek (*Scot.*), look, look-see (*sl.*), peep, shufti (*Brit. sl.*)

peel[1] *vb* **1, 2, 4** = **skin**, decorticate, desquamate, flake off, pare, scale, strip off ◆ *n* **5** = **skin**, epicarp, exocarp, peeling, rind

peep[1] *vb* **1** = **peek**, eyeball (*sl.*), keek (*Scot.*), look, look from hiding, look surreptitiously, peer, sneak a look, spy, steal a look **2** = **appear briefly**, emerge, peer out, show partially ◆ *n* **3** = **look**, butcher's, gander (*inf.*), glim (*Scot.*), glimpse, keek (*Scot.*), look-see (*sl.*), peek

peep[2] *vb, n* **1-3** = **tweet**, cheep, chirp, chirrup, pipe, squeak, twitter

peephole *n* = **spyhole**, aperture, chink, crack, crevice, fissure, hole, keyhole, opening, pinhole, slit

peer[1] *n* **1, 2** = **noble**, aristo (*inf.*), aristocrat, baron, count, duke, earl, lord, marquess, marquis, nobleman, viscount **3** = **equal**, coequal, compeer, fellow, like, match

peer[2] *vb* **1** = **squint**, gaze, inspect, peep, scan, scrutinize, snoop, spy **2** = **appear**, become visible, emerge, peep out

peerage *n* **1** = **aristocracy**, lords and ladies, nobility, peers, titled classes

peerless *adj* = **unequalled**, beyond compare, excellent, incomparable, matchless, nonpareil, outstanding, second to none, superlative, unique, unmatched, unparalleled, unrivalled, unsurpassed
Antonyms *adj* commonplace, inferior, mediocre, no great shakes (*inf.*), ordinary, poor, second-rate

peeve *Informal vb* **1** = **irritate**, annoy, bother, bug (*inf.*), exasperate, gall, get (*inf.*), get on one's nerves, irk, nark (*Brit., Austral., & NZ sl.*), nettle, pique, provoke, rile, rub (up) the wrong way, vex ◆ *n* **2** = **irritation**, annoyance, bother, gripe (*inf.*), nuisance, pest, sore point, vexation

peeved *adj* **1** = **irritated**, annoyed, exasperated, galled, hacked (off) (*US sl.*), irked, nettled, piqued, put out, riled, sore, upset, vexed

peevish *adj* = **irritable**, acrimonious, cantankerous, captious, childish, churlish, crabbed, cross, crotchety (*inf.*), crusty, fractious, fretful, grumpy, huffy, ill-natured, ill-tempered, liverish, pettish, petulant, querulous, short-tempered, shrewish, snappy, splenetic, sulky, sullen, surly, testy, tetchy, touchy, waspish, whingeing (*inf.*)
Antonyms *adj* affable, agreeable, cheerful, cheery, easy-going, even-tempered, genial, good-natured, happy, merry, pleasant, sweet

peg *vb* **11** = **fasten**, attach, fix, join, make fast, secure **14** *Chiefly Brit. with* **along** *or* **away** = **work at**, apply oneself to, beaver away, keep at it, keep going, keep on, persist, plod along, plug away at (*inf.*), stick to it, work away **15** = **fix**, control, freeze, limit, set, stabilize

score) with pegs, as in some card games. **13** *(tr) Inf.* to throw (stones, etc.) at a target. **14** *(intr;* foll. by *away, along,* etc.) *Chiefly Brit.* to work steadily: *he pegged away at his job for years.* **15** *(tr)* to stabilize (the price of a commodity, an exchange rate, etc.). [C15: from Low Gmc *pegge*]

pegboard ('pɛɡ,bɔːd) *n* **1** a board having a pattern of holes into which small pegs can be fitted, used for playing certain games or keeping a score. **2** another name for **solitaire** (sense 1). **3** hardboard perforated by a pattern of holes in which articles may be hung, as for display.

peg leg *n Inf.* **1** an artificial leg, esp. one made of wood. **2** a person with an artificial leg.

pegmatite ('pɛɡmə,taɪt) *n* any of a class of coarse-grained intrusive igneous rocks consisting chiefly of quartz and feldspar. [C19: from Gk *pegma* something joined together]

peg out *vb (adv)* **1** *(intr) Inf.* to collapse or die. **2** *(intr) Cribbage.* to score the point that wins the game. **3** *(tr)* to mark or secure with pegs: *to peg out one's claims to a piece of land.*

peg top *n* a child's spinning top, usually made of wood with a metal centre pin.

peg-top *adj* (of skirts, trousers, etc.) wide at the hips then tapering off towards the ankle.

PEI *abbrev. for* Prince Edward Island.

peignoir ('peɪnwɑː) *n* a woman's dressing gown. [C19: from F, from *peigner* to comb, since the garment was worn while the hair was combed]

pejoration (,piːdʒə'reɪʃən) *n* **1** semantic change whereby a word acquires unfavourable connotations. **2** the process of worsening.

pejorative ➊ (pɪ'dʒɒrətɪv, 'piːdʒər-) *adj* **1** (of words, expressions, etc.) having an unpleasant or disparaging connotation. ◆ *n* **2** a pejorative word, etc. [C19: from F *péjoratif,* from LL *pējōrātus,* p.p. of *pējōrāre* to make worse, from L *pēior* worse]
►**pe'joratively** *adv*

pekan ('pɛkən) *n* another name for **fisher** (the animal). [C18: from Canad. F *pékan,* from Amerind]

peke (piːk) *n Inf.* a Pekingese dog.

Pekingese (,piːkɪŋ'iːz) *or* **Pekinese** (,piːkə'niːz) *n* **1** *(pl* **Pekingese** *or* **Pekinese**) a small breed of pet dog with a profuse straight coat, curled plumed tail, and short wrinkled muzzle. **2** the dialect of Mandarin Chinese spoken in Beijing (formerly Peking). **3** *(pl* **Pekingeses**) a native or inhabitant of Beijing (formerly Peking), in NE China. ◆ *adj* **4** of Beijing (formerly Peking) or its inhabitants.

Peking man (piː'kɪŋ) *n* an early type of man, of the Lower Palaeolithic age, remains of which were found in a cave near Beijing (formerly Peking).

pekoe ('piːkəʊ) *n* a high-quality tea made from the downy tips of the young buds of the tea plant. [C18: from Chinese *peh ho,* from *peh* white + *ho* down]

pelage ('pɛlɪdʒ) *n* the coat of a mammal, consisting of hair, wool, fur, etc. [C19: via F from OF *pel* animal's coat, from L *pilus* hair]

Pelagianism (pɛ'leɪdʒɪə,nɪzəm) *n Christianity.* a heretical doctrine, first formulated by Pelagius, a 5th-century British monk, that rejected the concept of original sin.
►**Pe'lagian** *n, adj*

pelagic (pɛ'lædʒɪk) *adj* **1** of or relating to the open sea: *pelagic whaling.* **2** (of marine life) occurring in the upper waters of open sea. [C17: from L *pelagicus,* from *pelagus,* from Gk *pelagos* sea]

pelargonium (,pɛlə'ɡəʊnɪəm) *n* any plant of a chiefly southern African genus having circular or lobed leaves and red, pink, or white aromatic flowers: includes many cultivated geraniums. [C19: via NL from Gk *pelargos* stork, on the model of GERANIUM; from the likeness of the seed vessels to a stork's bill]

pelf (pɛlf) *n Contemptuous.* money or wealth; lucre. [C14: from OF *pelfre* booty]

pelham ('pɛləm) *n* a horse's bit for a double bridle, less severe than a curb but more severe than a snaffle. [prob. from the name *Pelham*]

pelican ('pɛlɪkən) *n* any aquatic bird of a tropical and warm water family. They have a long straight flattened bill, with a distensible pouch for engulfing fish. [OE *pellican,* from LL *pelicānus,* from Gk *pelekān*]

pelican crossing *n* a type of road crossing with a pedestrian-operated traffic-light system. [C20: from *pe(destrian) li(ght) con(trolled) crossing,* with *-con* adapted to *-can* of *pelican*]

pelisse (pɛ'liːs) *n* **1** a fur-trimmed cloak. **2** a loose coat, usually fur-trimmed, worn esp. by women in the early 19th century. [C18: via OF from Med. L *pellicia* cloak, from L *pellis* skin]

pellagra (pə'leɪɡrə, -'læ-) *n Pathol.* a disease caused by a dietary deficiency of nicotinic acid, characterized by scaling of the skin, inflammation of the mouth, diarrhoea, mental impairment, etc. [C19: via It. from *pelle* skin + *-agra,* from Gk *agra* paroxysm]
►**pel'lagrous** *adj*

pellet ('pɛlɪt) *n* **1** a small round ball, esp. of compressed matter. **2a** an imitation bullet used in toy guns. **2b** a piece of small shot. **3** a stone ball formerly used in a catapult. **4** *Ornithol.* a mass of undigested food that is regurgitated by birds of prey. **5** a small pill. ◆ *vb (tr)* **6** to strike with pellets. **7** to make or form into pellets. [C14: from OF *pelote,* from Vulgar L *pilota* (unattested), from L *pila* ball]

pellitory ('pɛlɪtərɪ, -trɪ) *n, pl* **pellitories. 1** any of various plants of a S and W European genus, esp. wall pellitory, that grow in crevices and have long narrow leaves and small pink flowers. **2 pellitory of Spain.** a small Mediterranean plant, the root of which contains an oil formerly used to relieve toothache. [C16 *peletre,* from OF *piretre,* from L, from Gk *purethron,* from *pur* fire, from the hot pungent taste of the root]

pell-mell ➊ ('pɛl'mɛl) *adv* **1** in a confused headlong rush: *the hounds ran pell-mell into the yard.* **2** in a disorderly manner: *the things were piled pell-mell in the room.* ◆ *adj* **3** disordered; tumultuous: *a pell-mell rush for the exit.* ◆ *n* **4** disorder; confusion. [C16: from OF *pesle-mesle,* jingle based on *mesler* to MEDDLE]

pellucid ➊ (pɛ'luːsɪd) *adj* **1** transparent or translucent. **2** extremely clear in style and meaning. [C17: from L *pellūcidus,* var. of *perlūcidus,* from *perlūcēre* to shine through]
►,**pellu'cidity** *or* **pel'lucidness** *n* ►**pel'lucidly** *adv*

pelmet ('pɛlmɪt) *n* an ornamental drapery or board fixed above a window to conceal the curtain rail. [C19: prob. from F *palmette* palm-leaf decoration on cornice moulding]

pelota (pə'lɒtə) *n* any of various games played in Spain, Spanish America, SW France, etc., by two players who use a basket strapped to their wrists or a wooden racket to propel a ball against a specially marked wall. [C19: from Sp.: ball, from OF *pelote;* see PELLET]

peloton ('pɛlə,tɒn) *n* the main field of riders in a cycling race. [C20: F, lit.: pack]

pelt[1] ➊ (pɛlt) *vb* **1** *(tr)* to throw (missiles, etc.) at (a person, etc.). **2** *(tr)* to hurl (insults, etc.) at (a person, etc.). **3** *(intr;* foll. by *along,* etc.) to hurry. **4** *(intr)* to rain heavily. ◆ *n* **5** a blow. **6** speed (esp. in **at full pelt**). [C15: from ?]

pelt[2] ➊ (pɛlt) *n* **1** the skin of a fur-bearing animal, esp. when it has been removed from the carcass. **2** the hide of an animal, stripped of hair. [C15: ? back formation from PELTRY]

peltate ('pɛlteɪt) *adj* (of leaves) having the stalk attached to the centre of the lower surface. [C18: from L *peltātus* equipped with a *pelta* small shield]

peltry ('pɛltrɪ) *n, pl* **peltries.** the pelts of animals collectively. [C15: from OF *peleterie* collection of pelts, from L *pilus* hair]

pelvic fin *n* either of a pair of fins attached to the pelvic girdle of fishes that help to control the direction of movement during locomotion.

pelvic inflammatory disease *n* inflammation of a woman's womb, Fallopian tubes, or ovaries as a result of infection. Abbrev.: **PID.**

pelvimetry (pɛl'vɪmɪtrɪ) *n Obstetrics.* measurement of the dimensions of the female pelvis.

pelvis ('pɛlvɪs) *n, pl* **pelvises** *or* **pelves** (-viːz). **1** the large funnel-shaped structure at the lower end of the trunk of most vertebrates. **2** Also called: **pelvic girdle.** the bones that form this structure. **3** any anatomical cavity or structure shaped like a funnel or cup. [C17: from L: basin]
►**'pelvic** *adj*

pemmican *or* **pemican** ('pɛmɪkən) *n* a small pressed cake of shredded dried meat, pounded into paste, used originally by Native Americans and now chiefly for emergency rations. [C19: from Amerind *pimikân,* from *pimii* grease]

pemphigus ('pɛmfɪɡəs, pɛm'faɪ-) *n Pathol.* any of a group of blistering skin diseases. [C18: via NL from Gk *pemphix* bubble]

pen[1] ➊ (pɛn) *n* **1** an implement for writing or drawing using ink, formerly consisting of a sharpened and split quill, and now of a metal nib attached to a holder. See also **ballpoint, fountain pen. 2** the writing end of such an implement; nib. **3** style of writing. **4 the pen.** writing as an occupation. ◆ *vb* **pens, penning, penned. 5** *(tr)* to write or compose. [OE *pinne,* from LL *penna* (quill) pen, from L: feather]

pen[2] ➊ (pɛn) *n* **1** an enclosure in which domestic animals are kept. **2** any place of confinement. **3** a dock for servicing submarines, esp. having a bombproof roof. ◆ *vb* **pens, penning, penned** *or* **pent. 4** *(tr)* to enclose in a pen. [OE *penn*]

pen[3] (pɛn) *n US & Canad. inf.* short for **penitentiary** (sense 1).

pen[4] (pɛn) *n* a female swan. [C16: from ?]

PEN (pɛn) *n acronym for* International Association of Poets, Playwrights, Editors, Essayists, and Novelists.

Pen. *abbrev. for* Peninsula.

penal ➊ ('piːnᵊl) *adj* **1** of, relating to, constituting, or prescribing punishment. **2** used or designated as a place of punishment: *a penal institution.* [C15: from LL *poenālis* concerning punishment, from L *poena* penalty]
►**'penally** *adv*

THESAURUS

pejorative *adj* **1** = **derogatory,** belittling, debasing, deprecatory, depreciatory, detractive, detractory, disparaging, negative, slighting, uncomplimentary, unpleasant

pell-mell *adv* **1** = **helter-skelter,** full tilt, hastily, heedlessly, hurriedly, impetuously, posthaste, precipitously, rashly, recklessly ◆ *adj* **2** = **disorderly,** chaotic, confused, disorganized, haphazard, tumultuous

pellucid *adj* **1** = **transparent,** bright, clear, crystalline, glassy, limpid, translucent **2** = **clear,** comprehensible, limpid, lucid, perspicuous, plain, straightforward, unambiguous

pelt[1] *vb* **1** = **throw,** assail, batter, beat, belabour, bombard, cast, hurl, pepper, pummel, shower, sling, strike, thrash, wallop *(inf.)* **3** = **rush,** belt *(sl.)*, burn rubber *(inf.)*, career, charge, dash, hurry, run fast, shoot, speed, stampede, tear, whizz *(inf.)* **4** = **pour,** bucket down *(inf.)*, rain cats and dogs *(inf.)*, rain hard, teem

pelt[2] *n* **1, 2** = **coat,** fell, hide, skin

pen[1] *vb* **5** = **write,** commit to paper, compose, draft, draw up, jot down

pen[2] *n* **1** = **enclosure,** cage, coop, corral *(chiefly US & Canad.)*, fold, hutch, pound, sty ◆ *vb* **4** = **enclose,** cage, confine, coop up, fence in, hedge, hem in, hurdle, impound, mew (up), pound, shut up *or* in

penal *adj* **1** = **disciplinary,** corrective, penalizing, punitive, retributive

penal code *n* the codified body of the laws that relate to crime and its punishment.

penalize ⓘ *or* **penalise** ('piːnəˌlaɪz) *vb* **penalizes, penalizing, penalized** *or* **penalises, penalising, penalised.** (*tr*) **1** to impose a penalty on (someone), as for breaking a law or rule. **2** to inflict a disadvantage on. **3** *Sport.* to award a free stroke, point, or penalty against (a player or team). **4** to declare (an act) legally punishable.
▸ˌ**penali'zation** *or* ˌ**penali'sation** *n*

penalty ⓘ ('pɛnᵊltɪ) *n, pl* **penalties. 1** a legal or official punishment, such as a term of imprisonment. **2** some other form of punishment, such as a fine or forfeit for not fulfilling a contract. **3** loss, suffering, or other misfortune occurring as a result of one's own action, error, etc. **4** *Sport, games, etc.* a handicap awarded against a player or team for illegal play, such as a free shot at goal by the opposing team. [C16: from Med. L *poenālitās* penalty; see PENAL]

penalty area *n* another name for **penalty box** (sense 1).

penalty box *n* **1** *Soccer.* a rectangular area in front of the goal, within which a penalty is awarded for a serious foul by the defending team. **2** *Ice hockey.* a bench for players serving time penalties.

penalty corner *n Hockey.* a free hit from the goal line taken by the attacking side. Also called: **short corner.**

penalty rates *pl n Austral. & NZ.* rates of pay for employees working outside normal hours.

penalty shoot-out *n* **1** *Soccer.* a method of deciding the winner of a drawn match, in which players from each team attempt to score with a penalty kick. **2** a similar method of resolving a tie in hockey, ice hockey, polo, etc.

penance ⓘ ('pɛnəns) *n* **1** voluntary self-punishment to atone for a sin, crime, etc. **2** a feeling of regret for one's wrongdoings. **3** *Christianity.* a punishment usually consisting of prayer, fasting, etc., imposed by church authority as a condition of absolution. **4** *RC Church.* a sacrament in which repentant sinners are absolved on condition of confession of their sins to a priest and of performing a penance. ◆ *vb* **penances, penancing, penanced. 5** (*tr*) (of ecclesiastical authorities) to impose a penance upon (a sinner). [C13: via OF from L *paenitentia* repentance]

penates (pə'nɑːtiːz) *pl n* See **lares and penates.**

pence (pɛns) *n* a plural of **penny.**

> **USAGE NOTE** Since the decimalization of British currency and the introduction of the abbreviation **p**, as in *10p, 85p*, etc., the abbreviation has tended to replace *pence* in speech, as in *4p* (ˌfɔː'piː), *12p* (ˌtwɛlv'piː), etc.

penchant ⓘ ('pɒŋʃɒn) *n* strong inclination or liking; bent or taste. [C17: from F, from *pencher* to incline, from L *pendēre* to be suspended]

pencil ('pɛnsᵊl) *n* **1** a thin cylindrical instrument used for writing, drawing, etc., consisting of a rod of graphite or other marking substance usually encased in wood and sharpened. **2** something similar in shape or function: *a styptic pencil.* **3** a narrow set of lines or rays, such as light rays, diverging from or converging to a point. **4** *Rare.* an artist's individual style. **5** a type of artist's brush. ◆ *vb* **pencils, pencilling, pencilled** *or US* **pencils, penciling, penciled.** (*tr*) **6** to draw, colour, or write with a pencil. **7** to mark with a pencil. [C14: from OF *pincel,* from L *pēnicillus* painter's brush, from *pēniculus* a little tail]
▸'**penciller** *or US* '**penciler** *n*

pend (pɛnd) *vb* (*intr*) to await judgment or settlement. [C15: from L *pendēre* to hang]

pendant ('pɛndənt) *n* **1a** an ornament that hangs from a piece of jewellery. **1b** a necklace with such an ornament. **2** a hanging light, esp. a chandelier. **3** a carved ornament that is suspended from a ceiling or roof. ◆ *adj* **4** a variant spelling of **pendent.** [C14: from OF, from *pendre* to hang, from L *pendēre* to hang down]

pendent ('pɛndənt) *adj* **1** dangling. **2** jutting. **3** (of a grammatical construction) incomplete. **4** a less common word for **pending.** ◆ *n* **5** a variant spelling of **pendant.** [C15: from OF *pendant,* from *pendre* to hang; see PENDANT]
▸'**pendency** *n*

pendentive (pɛn'dɛntɪv) *n* any of four triangular sections of vaulting with concave sides, positioned at a corner of a rectangular space to support a dome. [C18: from F *pendentif,* from L *pendens* hanging, from *pendere* to hang]

pending ⓘ ('pɛndɪŋ) *prep* **1** while waiting for. ◆ *adj* (*postpositive*) **2** not yet decided, confirmed, or finished. **3** imminent: *these developments have been pending for some time.*

pendragon (pɛn'drægən) *n* a supreme war chief or leader of the ancient Britons. [Welsh, lit.: head dragon]

pendulous ⓘ ('pɛndjʊləs) *adj* hanging downwards, esp. so as to swing from side to side. [C17: from L *pendulus,* from *pendēre* to hang down]
▸'**pendulously** *adv* ▸'**pendulousness** *n*

pendulum ('pɛndjʊləm) *n* **1** a body mounted so that it can swing freely under the influence of gravity. **2** such a device used to regulate a clock mechanism. **3** something that changes fairly regularly: *the pendulum of public opinion.* [C17: from L *pendulus* PENDULOUS]

peneplain *or* **peneplane** ('piːnɪˌpleɪn) *n* a relatively flat land surface produced by erosion. [C19: from L *paene* almost + PLAIN[1]]

penetrant ('pɛnɪtrənt) *adj* **1** sharp; penetrating. ◆ *n* **2** *Chem.* a substance that lowers the surface tension of a liquid and thus causes it to penetrate or be absorbed more easily. **3** a person or thing that penetrates.

penetrate ⓘ ('pɛnɪˌtreɪt) *vb* **penetrates, penetrating, penetrated. 1** to find or force a way into or through (something); pierce; enter. **2** to diffuse through (a substance, etc.); permeate. **3** (*tr*) to see through: *their eyes could not penetrate the fog.* **4** (*tr*) (of a man) to insert the penis into the vagina of (a woman). **5** (*tr*) to grasp the meaning of (a principle, etc.). **6** (*intr*) to be understood: *his face lit up as the new idea penetrated.* [C16: from L *penetrāre*]
▸'**penetrable** *adj* ▸ˌ**penetra'bility** *n* ▸'**pene**ˌ**trator** *n*

penetrating ⓘ ('pɛnɪˌtreɪtɪŋ) *adj* tending to or able to penetrate: *a penetrating mind; a penetrating voice.*
▸'**pene**ˌ**tratingly** *adv*

penetration ⓘ (ˌpɛnɪ'treɪʃən) *n* **1** the act or an instance of penetrating. **2** the ability or power to penetrate. **3** keen insight or perception. **4** *Mil.* an offensive manoeuvre that breaks through an enemy's defensive position. **5** Also called: **market penetration.** the proportion of the total number of potential purchasers of a product or service who either are aware of its existence or actually buy it.

pen friend *n* a person with whom one exchanges letters, often a person in another country whom one has not met. Also called: **pen pal.**

penguin ('pɛŋgwɪn) *n* a flightless marine bird of cool southern, esp. Antarctic, regions: they have wings modified as flippers, webbed feet, and feathers lacking barbs. [C16: ?from Welsh *pen gwyn,* from *pen* head + *gwyn* white]

penicillin (ˌpɛnɪ'sɪlɪn) *n* any of a group of antibiotics with powerful action against bacteria: originally obtained from the fungus *Penicillium.* [C20: from PENICILLIUM]

penicillium (ˌpɛnɪ'sɪlɪəm) *n, pl* **penicilliums** *or* **penicillia** (-'sɪlɪə). any saprophytic fungus of the genus *Penicillium,* which commonly grow as a green or blue mould on stale food. [C19: NL, from L *pēnicillus* tuft of hairs; from the appearance of the sporangia of this fungus]

penillion *or* **pennillion** (pɪ'nɪlɪən) *pl n, sing* **penill** (pɪ'nɪl). the Welsh art or practice of singing poetry in counterpoint to a traditional melody played on the harp. [from Welsh: verses]

peninsula (pɪ'nɪnsjʊlə) *n* a narrow strip of land projecting into a sea or lake from the mainland. [C16: from L, lit.: almost an island, from *paene* almost + *insula* island]
▸**pen'insular** *adj*

> **USAGE NOTE** The noun *peninsula* is sometimes confused with the adjective *peninsular: the Iberian peninsula* (not *peninsular*).

penis ⓘ ('piːnɪs) *n, pl* **penises** *or* **penes** (-niːz). the male organ of copulation in higher vertebrates, also used for urine excretion in many mammals. [C17: from L: penis]
▸**penile** ('piːnaɪl) *adj*

penitent ⓘ ('pɛnɪtənt) *adj* **1** feeling regret for one's sins; repentant. ◆ *n* **2** a person who is penitent. **3** *Christianity.* **3a** a person who repents

THESAURUS

penalize *vb* **1-3** = **punish**, award a penalty against (*Sport*), correct, discipline, handicap, impose a penalty on, inflict a handicap on, put at a disadvantage

penalty *n* **1, 2** = **punishment**, disadvantage, fine, forfeit, forfeiture, handicap, mulct, price, retribution

penance *n* **1** = **atonement**, mortification, penalty, punishment, reparation, sackcloth and ashes

penchant *n* = **liking**, affinity, bent, bias, disposition, fondness, inclination, leaning, partiality, predilection, predisposition, proclivity, proneness, propensity, taste, tendency, turn

pending *adj* **2, 3** = **undecided**, awaiting, forthcoming, hanging fire, imminent, impending, in the balance, in the offing, undetermined, unsettled, up in the air

pendulous *adj* = **hanging**, dangling, drooping, pendent, sagging, swaying, swinging

penetrable *adj* **1, 2, 5** = **clear**, accessible, comprehensible, fathomable, intelligible, open, passable, permeable, pervious, porous

penetrate *vb* **1** = **pierce**, bore, enter, go through, impale, perforate, prick, probe, stab **2** = **permeate**, diffuse, enter, get in, infiltrate, make inroads (into), pervade, seep, suffuse **5** = **grasp**, comprehend, decipher, discern, fathom, figure out (*inf.*), get to the bottom of, suss (out) (*sl.*), understand, unravel, work out **6** = **be understood**, affect, become clear, come across, get through to, impress, touch

penetrating *adj* **1** = **sharp**, biting, carrying, harsh, intrusive, pervasive, piercing, shrill, stinging, strong **5** = **perceptive**, acute, astute, critical, discerning, discriminating, incisive, intelligent, keen, perspicacious, profound, quick, sagacious, searching, sharp, sharp-witted, shrewd
Antonyms *adj* ≠ **sharp:** blunt, dull, mild, sweet ≠ **perceptive:** apathetic, dull, indifferent, obtuse, shallow, stupid, uncomprehending, unperceptive

penetration *n* **1** = **piercing**, entrance, entry, incision, inroad, invasion, perforation, puncturing **3** = **perception**, acuteness, astuteness, discernment, insight, keenness, perspicacity, sharpness, shrewdness, wit

penis *n* = **phallus**, cock (*taboo sl.*), dick (*taboo sl.*), dong (*sl.*), John Thomas (*taboo sl.*), knob (*Brit. taboo sl.*), member, organ, pizzle (*arch. & dialect*), plonker (*sl.*), prick (*taboo sl.*), tool (*taboo sl.*), willie *or* willy (*Brit. inf.*)

penitence *n* **1** = **repentance**, compunction, contrition, regret, remorse, ruefulness, self-reproach, shame, sorrow

penitent *adj* **1** = **repentant**, abject, apologetic, atoning, conscience-stricken, contrite, regretful, remorseful, rueful, sorrowful, sorry

his sins and seeks forgiveness for them. **3b** *RC Church.* a person who confesses his sins and submits to a penance. [C14: from Church L *paenitēns* regretting, from *paenitēre* to repent, from ?]
▸**'penitence** *n* ▸**'penitently** *adv*

penitential (ˌpɛnɪ'tɛnʃəl) *adj* **1** of, showing, or constituting penance. ◆ *n* **2** *Chiefly RC Church.* a book or compilation of instructions for confessors. **3** a less common word for **penitent** (senses 2, 3).
▸**ˌpeni'tentially** *adv*

penitentiary (ˌpɛnɪ'tɛnʃərɪ) *n, pl* **penitentiaries. 1** (in the US and Canada) a state or federal prison. Also (US and Canad. inf.): **pen. 2** *RC Church.* **2a** a cardinal who presides over a tribunal that decides all matters affecting the sacrament of penance. **2b** this tribunal itself. ◆ *adj* **3** another word for **penitential** (sense 1). **4** *US & Canad.* (of an offence) punishable by imprisonment in a penitentiary. [C15 (meaning also: an officer dealing with penances): from Med. L *poenitentiārius*, from L *paenitēns* PENITENT]

penknife ('pɛnˌnaɪf) *n, pl* **penknives.** a small knife with one or more blades that fold into the handle; pocketknife.

penman ('pɛnmən) *n, pl* **penmen. 1** a person skilled in handwriting. **2** a person who writes by hand in a specified way: *a bad penman.* **3** an author. **4** *Rare.* a scribe.

penmanship ➊ ('pɛnmənʃɪp) *n* style or technique of writing by hand.

penna ('pɛnə) *n, pl* **pennae** (-niː). *Ornithol.* any large feather that has a vane and forms part of the main plumage of a bird. [L: feather]

pen name ➊ *n* an author's pseudonym. Also called: **nom de plume.**

pennant ➊ ('pɛnənt) *n* **1** a type of pennon, esp. one flown from vessels as identification or for signalling. **2** *Chiefly US, Canad., & Austral.* **2a** a flag serving as an emblem of championship in certain sports. **2b** (*as modifier*): *pennant cricket.* [C17: prob. a blend of PENDANT & PENNON]

pennate ('pɛneɪt) *adj Biol.* **1** having feathers, wings, or winglike structures. **2** another word for **pinnate.** [C19: from L *pennātus*, from *penna* wing]

penni ('pɛnɪ) *n, pl* **penniä** (-nɪə) *or* **pennis.** a Finnish monetary unit worth one hundredth of a markka. [Finnish, from Low G *pennig* PENNY]

penniless ➊ ('pɛnɪlɪs) *adj* very poor; almost totally without money.
▸**'pennilessly** *adv* ▸**'pennilessness** *n*

pennon ('pɛnən) *n* **1** a long flag, often tapering and divided at the end, originally a knight's personal flag. **2** a small tapering or triangular flag borne on a ship or boat. **3** a poetic word for **wing.** [C14: via OF ult. from L *penna* feather]

Pennsylvania Dutch (ˌpɛnsɪl'veɪnɪə) *n* **1** a dialect of German spoken in E Pennsylvania. **2** (preceded by *the; functioning as pl*) a group of German-speaking people in E Pennsylvania, descended from 18th-century settlers from SW Germany and Switzerland.

Pennsylvanian (ˌpɛnsɪl'veɪnɪən) *adj* **1** of the state of Pennsylvania, in the US. **2** (in North America) of, denoting, or formed in the upper of two divisions of the Carboniferous period. ◆ *n* **3** an inhabitant or native of the state of Pennsylvania. **4** (preceded by *the*) the Pennsylvanian period or rock system.

penny ('pɛnɪ) *n, pl* **pennies** *or* **pence** (pɛns). **1** Also called: **new penny.** *Brit.* a bronze coin having a value equal to one hundredth of a pound. Abbrev.: **p. 2** *Brit.* (before 1971) a bronze or copper coin having a value equal to one twelfth of a shilling. Abbrev.: **d. 3** a monetary unit of the Republic of Ireland worth one hundredth of a pound. **4** (*pl* **pennies**) *US & Canad.* a cent. **5** a coin of similar value, as used in several other countries. **6** (*used with a negative*) *Inf., chiefly Brit.* the least amount of money: *I don't have a penny.* **7 a pretty penny.** *Inf.* a considerable sum of money. **8 spend a penny.** *Brit. inf.* to urinate. **9 the penny dropped.** *Inf., chiefly Brit.* the explanation of something was finally realized. [OE *penig, pening*]

penny arcade *n Chiefly US.* a public place with various coin-operated machines for entertainment.

Penny Black *n* the first adhesive postage stamp, issued in Britain in 1840.

penny-dreadful *n, pl* **penny-dreadfuls.** *Brit. inf.* a cheap, often lurid book or magazine.

penny-farthing *n Brit.* an early type of bicycle with a large front wheel and a small rear wheel, the pedals being on the front wheel.

penny-pinching ➊ *adj* **1** excessively careful with money; miserly. ◆ *n* **2** miserliness.
▸**'penny-ˌpincher** *n*

pennyroyal (ˌpɛnɪ'rɔɪəl) *n* **1** a Eurasian plant with hairy leaves and small mauve flowers, yielding an aromatic oil used in medicine. **2** a similar and related plant of E North America. [C16: var. of Anglo-Norman *puliol real*, from OF *pouliol* (from L *pūleium* pennyroyal) + *real* ROYAL]

penny shares *pl n Stock Exchange.* securities with a low market price, esp. less than 20p, enabling small investors to purchase a large number for a relatively small outlay.

pennyweight ('pɛnɪˌweɪt) *n* a unit of weight equal to 24 grains or one twentieth of an ounce (Troy).

penny whistle *n* a type of flageolet with six finger holes, esp. a cheap metal one. Also called: **tin whistle.**

penny-wise *adj* **1** greatly concerned with saving small sums of money. **2 penny-wise and pound-foolish.** careful about trifles but wasteful in large ventures.

pennywort ('pɛnɪˌwɜːt) *n* **1** a Eurasian rock plant with whitish-green tubular flowers and rounded leaves. **2** a marsh plant of Europe and North Africa, having circular leaves and greenish-pink flowers. **3** any of various other plants with rounded penny-like leaves.

pennyworth ➊ ('pɛnɪˌwɜːθ) *n* **1** the amount that can be bought for a penny. **2** a small amount: *he hasn't got a pennyworth of sense.*

penology (piː'nɒlədʒɪ) *n* **1** the branch of the social sciences concerned with the punishment of crime. **2** the science of prison management. [C19: from Gk *poinē* punishment]
▸**penological** (ˌpiːnə'lɒdʒɪkᵊl) *adj* ▸**pe'nologist** *n*

pen pal *n* another name for **pen friend.**

penpusher ('pɛnˌpʊʃə) *n* a person who writes a lot, esp. a clerk involved with boring paperwork.
▸**'penˌpushing** *adj, n*

pension[1] ➊ ('pɛnʃən) *n* **1** a regular payment made by the state to people over a certain age to enable them to subsist without having to work. **2** a regular payment made by an employer to former employees after they retire. **3** any regular payment made by way of patronage, or in recognition of merit, service, etc.: *a pension paid to a disabled soldier.* ◆ *vb* **4** (*tr*) to grant a pension to. [C14: via OF from L *pēnsiō* a payment, from *pendere* to pay]
▸**'pensionable** *adj* ▸**'pensionary** *adj* ▸**'pensioner** *n*

pension[2] *French.* (pɑ̃sjɔ̃) *n* (in France and some other countries) a relatively cheap boarding house. [C17: from F; extended meaning of *pension* grant; see PENSION[1]]

pensioneer trustee (ˌpɛnʃə'nɪə) *n* (in Britain) a person authorized by the Inland Revenue to oversee the management of a pension fund.

pension off *vb* (*tr, adv*) **1** to cause to retire from a job and pay a pension to. **2** to discard, because of age: *to pension off submarines.*

pensive ➊ ('pɛnsɪv) *adj* **1** deeply or seriously thoughtful, often with a tinge of sadness. **2** expressing or suggesting pensiveness. [C14: from OF *pensif*, from *penser* to think, from L *pensāre* to consider]
▸**'pensively** *adv* ▸**'pensiveness** *n*

penstemon (pɛn'stiːmən) *n* a variant (esp. US) of **pentstemon.**

penstock ('pɛnˌstɒk) *n* **1** a conduit that supplies water to a hydroelectric power plant. **2** a channel bringing water from the head gates to a water wheel. **3** a sluice for controlling water flow. [C17: from PEN[2] + STOCK]

pent (pɛnt) *vb* a past tense and past participle of **pen**[2] (sense 4).

penta- *or before a vowel* **pent-** *combining form.* five: *pentagon; pentode.* [from Gk *pente*]

pentacle ('pɛntəkᵊl) *n* another name for **pentagram.** [C16: from It. *pentacolo* something having five corners]

pentad ('pɛntæd) *n* **1** a group or series of five. **2** the number or sum of five. **3** a period of five years. **4** *Chem.* a pentavalent element, atom, or radical. **5** *Meteorol.* a period of five days. [C17: from Gk *pentas* group of five]

pentadactyl (ˌpɛntə'dæktɪl) *adj* (of the limbs of amphibians, reptiles, birds, and mammals) having a hand or foot bearing five digits.

pentagon ('pɛntəˌgɒn) *n* a polygon having five sides.
▸**pentagonal** (pɛn'tægənᵊl) *adj*

Pentagon ('pɛntəˌgɒn) *n* **1** the five-sided building in Arlington, Virginia, that houses the headquarters of the US Department of Defense. **2** the military leadership of the US.

pentagram ('pɛntəˌgræm) *n* **1** a star-shaped figure with five points. **2** such a figure used by the Pythagoreans, black magicians, etc. ◆ Also called: **pentacle, pentangle.**

pentahedron (ˌpɛntə'hiːdrən) *n, pl* **pentahedrons** *or* **pentahedra** (-drə). a solid figure having five plane faces.
▸**ˌpenta'hedral** *adj*

pentamerous (pɛn'tæmərəs) *adj* consisting of five parts, esp. (of flowers) having the petals, sepals, and other parts arranged in groups of five.

pentameter (pɛn'tæmɪtə) *n* **1** a verse line consisting of five metrical feet. **2** (in classical prosody) a verse line consisting of two dactyls, one

THESAURUS

Antonyms *adj* callous, impenitent, remorseless, unrepentant

penmanship *n* = **handwriting**, calligraphy, chirography, fist (*inf.*), hand, longhand, script, writing

pen name *n* = **pseudonym**, allonym, nom de plume

pennant *n* **1** = **flag**, banderole, banner, burgee, ensign, jack, pennon, streamer

penniless *adj* = **poor**, bankrupt, broke (*inf.*), cleaned out (*sl.*), destitute, down and out, down at heel, flat broke (*inf.*), impecunious, impoverished, indigent, moneyless, necessitous, needy, on one's uppers, on the breadline, penurious, poverty-stricken, ruined, short, skint (*Brit. sl.*), stony-broke (*Brit. sl.*), strapped (*sl.*), without a penny to one's name
Antonyms *adj* affluent, filthy rich, loaded (*sl.*), rich, rolling (*sl.*), wealthy, well-heeled (*inf.*)

penny-pincher *n* **1** = **miser**, meany (*inf.*), niggard, pinchpenny, screw (*sl.*), Scrooge, skinflint

penny-pinching *adj* **1** = **miserly**, cheeseparing, close, frugal, mean, near (*inf.*), niggardly, scrimping, Scrooge-like, stingy, tightfisted
Antonyms *adj* generous, kind, liberal, munificent, open-handed, prodigal, unstinting

pennyworth *n* **2** = **bit**, crumb, jot, little, mite, modicum, particle, scrap, small amount, tittle

pension[1] *n* **1-3** = **allowance**, annuity, benefit, superannuation

pensioner *n* **1, 2** = **senior citizen**, O.A.P., retired person

pensive *adj* **1** = **thoughtful**, blue (*inf.*), cogitative, contemplative, dreamy, grave, in a brown study (*inf.*), meditative, melancholy, mournful, musing, preoccupied, reflective, ruminative, sad, serious, sober, solemn, sorrowful, wistful
Antonyms *adj* active, carefree, cheerful, frivolous, gay, happy, joyous, light-hearted

stressed syllable, two dactyls, and a final stressed syllable. ◆ *adj* **3** designating a verse line consisting of five metrical feet.

pentamidine (pɛnˈtæmɪˌdiːn, -dɪn) *n* a drug used to treat protozoal infections, esp. pneumonia caused by *Pneumocystis carinii* in AIDS patients.

pentane (ˈpɛnteɪn) *n* an alkane hydrocarbon having three isomers, esp. the isomer with a straight chain of carbon atoms (*n*-pentane) which is a colourless flammable liquid used as a solvent.

pentangle (ˈpɛnˌtæŋgᵊl) *n* another name for **pentagram.**

pentanoic acid (ˌpɛntəˈnəʊɪk) *n* a colourless liquid carboxylic acid used in making perfumes, flavourings, and pharmaceuticals. Formula: $CH_3(CH_2)_3COOH$. Former name: **valeric acid.**

Pentateuch (ˈpɛntəˌtjuːk) *n* the first five books of the Old Testament. [C16: from Church L *pentateuchus,* from Gk PENTA- + *teukhos* tool (in LGk: scroll)]
▸ˌ**Pentaˈteuchal** *adj*

pentathlon (pɛnˈtæθlən) *n* an athletic contest consisting of five different events. [C18: from Gk *pentathlon,* from PENTA- + *athlon* contest]

pentatomic (ˌpɛntəˈtɒmɪk) *adj Chem.* having five atoms in the molecule.

pentatonic scale (ˌpɛntəˈtɒnɪk) *n Music.* any of several scales consisting of five notes.

pentavalent (ˌpɛntəˈveɪlənt) *adj Chem.* having a valency of five. Also: **quinquevalent.**

pentazocine (pɛnˈtæzəʊˌsiːn) *n* a powerful synthetic opiate used in medical practice as an analgesic.

Pentecost (ˈpɛntɪˌkɒst) *n* **1** a Christian festival occurring on Whit Sunday commemorating the descent of the Holy Ghost on the apostles. **2** *Judaism.* the harvest festival, celebrated on the fiftieth day after the second day of Passover. Hebrew name: **Shavuot.** [OE, from Church L, from Gk *pentēkostē* fiftieth]

Pentecostal (ˌpɛntɪˈkɒstᵊl) *adj* **1** (*usually prenominal*) of or relating to any of various Christian groups that emphasize the charismatic aspects of Christianity and adopt a fundamental attitude to the Bible. **2** of or relating to Pentecost or the influence of the Holy Spirit. ◆ *n* **3** a member of a Pentecostal Church.
▸ˌ**Penteˈcostalist** *n, adj*

penthouse (ˈpɛntˌhaʊs) *n* **1** a flat or maisonette built onto the top floor or roof of a block of flats. **2** a construction on the roof of a building, esp. one used to house machinery, etc. **3** a shed built against a building, esp. one that has a sloping roof. [C14 *pentis* (later *penthouse*), from OF *apentis,* from LL *appendicium* appendage, from L *appendere* to hang from; see APPEND]

pentobarbitone sodium (ˌpɛntəˈbɑːbɪˌtəʊn) *n* a barbiturate drug used in medicine as a sedative and hypnotic.

pentode (ˈpɛntəʊd) *n* **1** an electronic valve having five electrodes: a cathode, anode, and three grids. **2** (*modifier*) (of a transistor) having three terminals at the base or gate. [C20: from PENTA- + Gk *hodos* way]

Pentothal sodium (ˈpɛntəˌθæl) *n* a trademark for **thiopentone sodium.**

pentstemon (pɛntˈstiːmən) *or esp. US* **penstemon** *n* any plant of a North American genus having white, pink, red, blue, or purple flowers with five stamens, one of which is sterile. [C18: NL, from PENTA- + Gk *stēmōn* thread (here: stamen)]

pent-up ⓣ *adj* not released; repressed: *pent-up emotions.*

pentyl acetate (ˈpɛntaɪl, -tɪl) *n* a colourless combustible liquid used as a solvent for paints, in the extraction of penicillin, in photographic film, and as a flavouring. Formula: $C_2H_5OOCCH_3$. Also called: **amyl acetate.**

penult (ˈpɛnʌlt, pɪˈnʌlt) *n* the last syllable but one in a word. [C16: L *paenultima syllaba,* from *paene ultima* almost the last]

penultimate (pɪˈnʌltɪmɪt) *adj* **1** next to the last. ◆ *n* **2** anything next to last, esp. a penult.

penumbra (pɪˈnʌmbrə) *n, pl* **penumbrae** (-briː) *or* **penumbras. 1** a fringe region of half shadow resulting from the partial obstruction of light by an opaque object. **2** *Astron.* the lighter and outer region of a sunspot. **3** *Painting.* the area in which light and shade blend. [C17: via NL from L *paene* almost + *umbra* shadow]
▸**peˈnumbral** *adj*

penurious ⓣ (pɪˈnjʊərɪəs) *adj* **1** niggardly with money. **2** lacking money or means. **3** scanty.
▸**peˈnuriously** *adv* ▸**peˈnuriousness** *n*

penury ⓣ (ˈpɛnjʊrɪ) *n* **1** extreme poverty. **2** extreme scarcity. [C15: from L *pēnūria* dearth, from ?]

peon[1] (ˈpiːən, ˈpiːɒn) *n* **1** a Spanish-American farm labourer or unskilled worker. **2** (formerly, in Spanish America) a debtor compelled to work off his debts. **3** any very poor person. [C19: from Sp. *peón* peasant, from Med. L *pedō* man who goes on foot, from L *pēs* foot]
▸ˈ**peonage** *n*

peon[2] (pjuːn, ˈpiːən, ˈpiːɒn) *n* (in India, Sri Lanka, etc., esp. formerly) **1** a messenger or attendant, esp. in an office. **2** a native policeman. **3** a foot soldier. [C17: from Port. *peão* orderly; see PEON[1]]

peony *or* **paeony** (ˈpiːənɪ) *n, pl* **peonies** *or* **paeonies. 1** any of a genus of shrubs and plants of Eurasia and North America, having large pink, red, white, or yellow flowers. **2** the flower of any of these plants. [OE *peonie,* from L *paeōnia,* from Gk *paiōnia;* rel. to *paiōnios* healing, from *paiōn* physician]

people ⓣ (ˈpiːpᵊl) *n* (*usually functioning as pl*) **1** persons collectively or in general. **2** a group of persons considered together: *blind people.* **3** (*pl* **peoples**) the persons living in a country and sharing the same nationality: *the French people.* **4** one's family: *he took her home to meet his people.* **5** persons loyal to someone powerful: *the king's people accompanied him in exile.* **6 the people. 6a** the mass of persons without special distinction, privileges, etc. **6b** the body of persons in a country, etc., esp. those entitled to vote. ◆ *vb* **peoples, peopling, peopled. 7** (*tr*) to provide with or as if with people or inhabitants. [C13: from OF *pople,* from L *populus*]

> **USAGE NOTE** See at **person.**

people carrier *n* another name for **multipurpose vehicle.**

people mover *n* **1** any of various automated forms of transport for large numbers of passengers over short distances, such as a moving pavement, driverless cars, etc. **2** another name for **multipurpose vehicle.**

people's democracy *n* (in Communist ideology) a country or government in transition from bourgeois democracy to socialism.

people's front *n* a less common term for **popular front.**

pep ⓣ (pɛp) *n* **1** high spirits, energy, or vitality. ◆ *vb* **peps, pepping, pepped. 2** (*tr;* usually foll. by *up*) to liven by imbuing with new vigour. [C20: short for PEPPER]

PEP (pɛp) *n acronym for* **1** personal equity plan: a method of saving in the UK with certain tax advantages, in which investments up to a fixed annual value can be purchased. ◆ *abbrev. for* **2** political and economic planning.

peperomia (ˌpɛpəˈrəʊmɪə) *n* any of a genus of tropical plants cultivated for their ornamental foliage. [C19: NL from Gk *peperi* pepper + *omoros* similar]

peplum (ˈpɛpləm) *n, pl* **peplums** *or* **pepla** (-lə). a flared ruffle attached to the waist of a jacket, bodice, etc. [C17: from L: full upper garment, from Gk *peplos* shawl]

pepo (ˈpiːpəʊ) *n, pl* **pepos.** the fruit of any of various plants, such as the melon, cucumber, and pumpkin, having a firm rind, fleshy watery pulp, and numerous seeds. [C19: from L: pumpkin, from Gk *pepōn* edible gourd, from *peptein* to ripen]

pepper ⓣ (ˈpɛpə) *n* **1** a woody climbing plant, *Piper nigrum,* of the East Indies, having small black berry-like fruits. **2** the dried fruit of this plant, which is ground to produce a sharp hot condiment. See also **black pepper, white pepper. 3** any of various other plants of the genus *Piper.* **4** Also called: **capsicum.** any of various tropical plants, the fruits of which are used as a vegetable and a condiment. See also **sweet pepper, red pepper, cayenne pepper. 5** the fruit of any of these capsicums, which has a mild or pungent taste. **6** the condiment made from the fruits of any of these plants. ◆ *vb* (*tr*) **7** to season with pepper. **8** to sprinkle liberally; dot: *his prose was peppered with alliteration.* **9** to pelt with small missiles. [OE *piper,* from L, from Gk *peperi*]

pepper-and-salt *adj* **1** (of cloth, etc.) marked with a fine mixture of black and white. **2** (of hair) streaked with grey.

peppercorn (ˈpɛpəˌkɔːn) *n* **1** the small dried berry of the pepper plant. **2** something trifling.

peppercorn rent *n* a rent that is very low or nominal.

pepper mill *n* a small hand mill used to grind peppercorns.

peppermint (ˈpɛpəˌmɪnt) *n* **1** a temperate mint plant with purple or white flowers and downy leaves, which yield a pungent oil. **2** the oil from this plant, which is used as a flavouring. **3** a sweet flavoured with peppermint.

pepperoni (ˌpɛpəˈrəʊnɪ) *n* a highly seasoned dry sausage of pork and beef spiced with pepper, used esp. on pizza. [C20: from It. *peperoni,* pl of *peperone* cayenne pepper]

pepper pot *n* **1** a small container with perforations in the top for sprinkling pepper. **2** a West Indian stew of meat, etc., highly seasoned with an extract of bitter cassava.

THESAURUS

pent-up *adj* = **suppressed,** bottled up, bridled, checked, constrained, curbed, held back, inhibited, repressed, smothered, stifled

penurious *adj* **1** = **mean,** cheeseparing, close, close-fisted, frugal, grudging, miserly, near (*inf.*), niggardly, parsimonious, skimping, stingy, tightfisted, ungenerous **2** = **poor,** destitute, down and out, down at heel, impecunious, impoverished, indigent, needy, on the breadline, penniless, poverty-stricken **3** = **meagre,** beggarly, deficient, inadequate, miserable, miserly, paltry, pathetic, poor, scanty

penury *n* **1** = **poverty,** beggary, destitution, indigence, need, pauperism, privation, straitened circumstances, want **2** = **scarcity,** dearth, deficiency, lack, paucity, scantiness, shortage, sparseness

people *pl n* **1** = **persons,** human beings, humanity, humans, mankind, men and women, mortals **3** = **nation,** citizens, community, folk, inhabitants, population, public **4** = **family,** clan, race, tribe **6a the people** = **the public,** the commonalty, the crowd, the general public, the grass roots, the herd, (the) hoi polloi, the masses, the mob, the multitude, the plebs, the populace, the proles (*derogatory sl., chiefly Brit.*), the proletariat, the rabble, the rank and file ◆ *vb* **7** = **inhabit,** colonize, occupy, populate, settle

pep *n* **1** = **energy,** animation, brio, get-up-and-go (*inf.*), gusto, high spirits, life, liveliness, spirit, verve, vigour, vim (*sl.*), vitality, vivacity, zip (*inf.*) ◆ *vb* **2** *usually foll. by* **up** = **enliven,** animate, exhilarate, inspire, invigorate, jazz up (*inf.*), quicken, stimulate, vitalize, vivify

pepper *n* **6** = **seasoning,** flavour, spice ◆ *vb* **8** = **sprinkle,** bespatter, dot, fleck, spatter, speck, stipple, stud **9** = **pelt,** bombard, riddle, scatter, shower

pepper tree *n* any of several evergreen trees of a chiefly South American genus having yellowish-white flowers and bright red ornamental fruits.

peppery ❶ ('pɛpərɪ) *adj* **1** flavoured with or tasting of pepper. **2** quick-tempered; irritable. **3** full of bite and sharpness: *a peppery speech.*
▸**'pepperiness** *n*

pep pill *n Inf.* a tablet containing a stimulant drug.

peppy ('pɛpɪ) *adj* **peppier, peppiest.** *Inf.* full of vitality; bouncy or energetic.
▸**'peppily** *adv* ▸**'peppiness** *n*

pepsin ('pɛpsɪn) *n* an enzyme produced in the stomach, which, when activated by acid, splits proteins into peptones. [C19: via G from Gk *pepsis,* from *peptein* to digest]

pep talk *n Inf.* an enthusiastic talk designed to increase confidence, production, cooperation, etc.

peptic ('pɛptɪk) *adj* **1** of, relating to, or promoting digestion. **2** of, relating to, or caused by pepsin or the action of the digestive juices. [C17: from Gk *peptikos* capable of digesting, from *peptein* to digest]

peptic ulcer *n Pathol.* an ulcer of the mucous membrane lining those parts of the alimentary tract exposed to digestive juices. It can occur in the oesophagus, the stomach, the duodenum, the jejunum, or in the ileum.

peptide ('pɛptaɪd) *n* any of a group of compounds consisting of two or more amino acids linked by chemical bonding between their respective carboxyl and amino groups.

peptide bond *n Biochem.* a chemical amide linkage, -NH-CO-, formed by the condensation of the amino group of one amino acid with the carboxyl group of another.

peptone ('pɛptəʊn) *n Biochem.* any of a group of compounds that form an intermediary group in the digestion of proteins to amino acids. [C19: from G *Pepton,* from Gk *pepton* something digested, from *peptein* to digest]
▸**peptonic** (pɛp'tɒnɪk) *adj*

per (pɜː; *unstressed* pə) *determiner* **1** for every: *three pence per pound.* ◆ *prep* **2** (esp. in some Latin phrases) by; through. **3 as per.** according to: *as per specifications.* **4 as per usual.** *Inf.* as usual. [C15: from L: by, for each]

per. *abbrev. for:* **1** period. **2** person.

per- *prefix* **1** through: *pervade.* **2** throughout: *perennial.* **3** away, beyond: *perfidy.* **4** (*intensifier*): *perfervid.* **5** indicating that a chemical compound contains a high proportion of a specified element: *peroxide.* **6** indicating that a chemical element is in a higher than usual state of oxidation: *permanganate.* [from L *per* through]

peracid (pɜːr'æsɪd) *n* an acid, such as perchloric acid ($HClO_4$), in which the element forming the acid radical exhibits its highest valency.

peradventure (pərəd'vɛntʃə, ˌpɜːr-) *Arch.* ◆ *adv* **1** by chance; perhaps. ◆ *n* **2** chance or doubt. [C13: from OF *par aventure* by chance]

perambulate (pə'ræmbjʊˌleɪt) *vb* **perambulates, perambulating, perambulated. 1** to walk about (a place). **2** (*tr*) to walk round in order to inspect. [C16: from L *perambulāre* to traverse, from *per-* through + *ambulāre* to walk]
▸**perˌambu'lation** *n* ▸**perambulatory** (pə'ræmbjʊlətərɪ, -trɪ) *adj*

perambulator (pə'ræmbjʊˌleɪtə) *n* a formal word for **pram**[1].

per annum (pər 'ænəm) *adv* every year or by the year. [L]

P-E ratio *abbrev. for* price-earnings ratio.

percale (pə'keɪl, -'kɑːl) *n* a close-textured woven cotton fabric, used esp. for sheets. [C17: via F from Persian *pargālah* piece of cloth]

per capita (pə 'kæpɪtə) *adj, adv* of or for each person. [L, lit.: according to heads]

perceive ❶ (pə'siːv) *vb* **perceives, perceiving, perceived. 1** to become aware of (something) through the senses; recognize or observe. **2** (*tr; may take a clause as object*) to come to comprehend; grasp. [C13: from OF *perçoivre,* from L *percipere* to seize entirely]
▸**per'ceivable** *adj* ▸**per'ceivably** *adv*

per cent (pə 'sɛnt) *adv* **1** Also: **per centum.** in or for every hundred. Symbol: % ◆ *n also* **percent. 2** a percentage or proportion. **3** (*often pl*) securities yielding a rate of interest as specified: *he bought three percents.* [C16: from Med. L *per centum* out of every hundred]

percentage (pə'sɛntɪdʒ) *n* **1** proportion or rate per hundred parts. **2** *Commerce.* the interest, tax, commission, or allowance on a hundred items. **3** any proportion in relation to the whole. **4** *Inf.* profit or advantage.

percentile (pə'sɛntaɪl) *n* one of 99 actual or notional values of a variable dividing its distribution into 100 groups with equal frequencies. Also called: **centile.**

percept ('pɜːsɛpt) *n* **1** a concept that depends on recognition by the senses, such as sight, of some external object or phenomenon. **2** an object or phenomenon that is perceived. [C19: from L *perceptum,* from *percipere* to PERCEIVE]

perceptible ❶ (pə'sɛptəb°l) *adj* able to be perceived; noticeable or recognizable.
▸**perˌcepti'bility** *n* ▸**per'ceptibly** *adv*

perception ❶ (pə'sɛpʃən) *n* **1** the act or the effect of perceiving. **2** insight or intuition gained by perceiving. **3** the ability or capacity to perceive. **4** way of perceiving; view. **5** the process by which an organism detects and interprets the external world by means of the sensory receptors. [C15: from L *perceptiō* comprehension; see PERCEIVE]
▸**per'ceptional** *adj* ▸**perceptual** (pə'sɛptjʊəl) *adj*

perceptive ❶ (pə'sɛptɪv) *adj* **1** quick at perceiving; observant. **2** perceptual. **3** able to perceive.
▸**per'ceptively** *adv* ▸**per'ceptiveness** *or* **ˌpercep'tivity** *n*

perch[1] ❶ (pɜːtʃ) *n* **1** a pole, branch, or other resting place above ground on which a bird roosts. **2** a similar resting place for a person or thing. **3** another name for **rod** (sense 7). ◆ *vb* **4** (usually foll. by *on*) to alight, rest, or cause to rest on or as if on a perch: *the bird perched on the branch; the cap was perched on his head.* [C13 *perche* stake, from OF, from L *pertica* long staff]

perch[2] (pɜːtʃ) *n, pl* **perch** *or* **perches. 1** any of a family of freshwater spiny-finned teleost fishes of Europe and North America: valued as food and game fishes. **2** any of various similar or related fishes. [C13: from OF *perche,* from L *perca,* from Gk *perkē*]

perchance ❶ (pə'tʃɑːns) *adv Arch. or poetic.* **1** perhaps; possibly. **2** by chance; accidentally. [C14: from Anglo-F *par chance*]

Percheron ('pɜːʃəˌrɒn) *n* a compact heavy breed of carthorse. [C19: from F, from *le Perche,* region of NW France, where the breed originated]

perchloric acid (pə'klɔːrɪk) *n* a colourless syrupy oxyacid of chlorine containing a greater proportion of oxygen than chloric acid. It is a powerful oxidizing agent. Formula: $HClO_4$. Systematic name: **chloric(VII) acid.**

percipient ❶ (pə'sɪpɪənt) *adj* **1** able to perceive. **2** perceptive. ◆ *n* **3** a person who perceives. [C17: from L *percipiens* observing, from *percipere* to grasp]
▸**per'cipience** *n* ▸**per'cipiently** *adv*

percolate ❶ *vb* ('pɜːkəˌleɪt), **percolates, percolating, percolated. 1** to cause (a liquid) to pass through a fine mesh, porous substance, etc., or (of a liquid) to pass through a fine mesh, etc.; trickle: *rain percolated through the roof.* **2** to permeate; penetrate gradually: *water percolated the road.* **3** to make (coffee) or (of coffee) to be made in a percolator. ◆ *n* ('pɜːkəlɪt, -ˌleɪt). **4** a product of percolation. [C17: from L *percolāre,* from PER- + *cōlāre* to strain, from *cōlum* a strainer; see COLANDER]
▸**percolable** ('pɜːkələb°l) *adj* ▸**ˌperco'lation** *n*

percolator ('pɜːkəˌleɪtə) *n* a kind of coffeepot in which boiling water is forced up through a tube and filters down through the coffee grounds into a container.

per contra ('pɜː 'kɒntrə) *adv* on the contrary. [from L]

percuss (pə'kʌs) *vb* (*tr*) **1** to strike sharply or suddenly. **2** *Med.* to tap on (a body surface) with the fingertips or a special hammer to aid diagnosis. [C16: from L *percutere,* from *per-* through + *quatere* to shake]
▸**per'cussor** *n*

percussion ❶ (pə'kʌʃən) *n* **1** the act, an instance, or an effect of percussing. **2** *Music.* the family of instruments in which sound arises from the striking of materials with sticks or hammers. **3** *Music.* instruments of this family constituting a section of an orchestra, etc. **4** *Med.* the act of percussing a body surface. **5** the act of exploding a percussion cap. [C16: from L *percussiō,* from *percutere* to hit; see PERCUSS]
▸**per'cussive** *adj* ▸**per'cussively** *adv* ▸**per'cussiveness** *n*

percussion cap *n* a detonator consisting of a paper or thin metal cap containing material that explodes when struck.

percussion instrument *n* any of various musical instruments that

THESAURUS

peppery *adj* **1 = hot**, fiery, highly seasoned, piquant, pungent, spicy **2 = irritable**, choleric, hot-tempered, irascible, quick-tempered, snappish, testy, touchy, vitriolic, waspish **3 = sharp**, astringent, biting, caustic, incisive, sarcastic, stinging, trenchant, vitriolic
Antonyms *adj* ≠ **hot:** bland, insipid, mild, tasteless, vapid

perceive *vb* **1 = see**, be aware of, behold, descry, discern, distinguish, espy, make out, note, notice, observe, recognize, remark, spot **2 = understand**, appreciate, apprehend, comprehend, conclude, deduce, feel, gather, get (*inf.*), get the message, get the picture, grasp, know, learn, realize, see, sense, suss (out) (*sl.*)

perceptible *adj* **= visible**, apparent, appreciable, blatant, clear, conspicuous, detectable, discernible, distinct, evident, noticeable, observable, obvious, palpable, perceivable, recognizable, tangible
Antonyms *adj* concealed, hidden, imperceptible, inconspicuous, indiscernible, invisible, unapparent, undetectable, unnoticeable

perception *n* **1, 2 = understanding**, apprehension, awareness, conception, consciousness, discernment, feeling, grasp, idea, impression, insight, notion, observation, recognition, sensation, sense, taste

perceptive *adj* **1 = observant**, acute, alert, astute, aware, discerning, insightful, intuitive, penetrating, percipient, perspicacious, quick, responsive, sensitive, sharp
Antonyms *adj* dull, indifferent, insensitive, obtuse, slow-witted, stupid, thick

perch[1] *n* **1, 2 = resting place**, branch, pole, post, roost ◆ *vb* **4 = sit**, alight, balance, land, rest, roost, settle

perchance *adv Archaic or poetic* **1, 2 = perhaps**, by chance, for all one knows, haply (*arch.*), maybe, mayhap (*arch.*), peradventure (*arch.*), possibly, probably

percipient *adj* **1, 2 = perceptive**, alert, alive, astute, aware, bright (*inf.*), discerning, discriminating, intelligent, observant, penetrating, perspicacious, quick-witted, sharp, wide-awake

percolate *vb* **1-3 = filter**, drain, drip, exude, filtrate, leach, ooze, penetrate, perk (*of coffee, inf.*), permeate, pervade, seep, strain, transfuse

percussion *n* **1 = impact**, blow, brunt, bump, clash, collision, concussion, crash, jolt, knock, shock, smash, thump

produce a sound when their resonating surfaces are struck directly, as with a stick or mallet, or by leverage action.

percussionist (pəˈkʌʃənɪst) *n Music.* a person who plays any of several percussion instruments.

percutaneous (ˌpɜːkjuˈteɪnɪəs) *adj Med.* effected through the skin, as in the absorption of an ointment.

per diem (ˈpɜː ˈdaɪɛm, ˈdiːɛm) *adv* **1** every day or by the day. ◆ *n* **2** an allowance for daily expenses. [from L]

perdition ❶ (pəˈdɪʃən) *n* **1** *Christianity.* **1a** final and irrevocable spiritual ruin. **1b** this state as one that the wicked are said to be destined to endure forever. **2** another word for **hell. 3** *Arch.* utter ruin or destruction. [C14: from LL *perditiō* ruin, from L *perdere* to lose, from PER- (away) + *dāre* to give]

perdurable (pəˈdjʊərəbᵊl) *adj Rare.* extremely durable. [C13: from LL *perdūrābilis,* from L *per-* (intensive) + *dūrābilis* long-lasting, from *dūrus* hard]

père *French.* (pɛr; *English* pɛə) *n* an addition to a French surname to specify the father rather than the son of the same name: *Dumas père.*

Père David's deer *n* a large grey deer, surviving only in captivity. [C20: after Father A. *David* (died 1900), F missionary]

peregrinate (ˈpɛrɪgrɪˌneɪt) *vb* **peregrinates, peregrinating, peregrinated. 1** (*intr*) to travel or wander about from place to place; voyage. **2** (*tr*) to travel through (a place). [C16: from L, from *peregrīnārī* to travel; see PEREGRINE]
▸ˌ**peregriˈnation** *n* ▸ˈ**peregriˌnator** *n*

peregrine (ˈpɛrɪgrɪn) *adj Arch.* **1** coming from abroad. **2** travelling. [C14: from L *peregrīnus* foreign, from *pereger* being abroad, from *per* through + *ager* land (that is, beyond one's own land)]

peregrine falcon *n* a falcon occurring in most parts of the world, having a dark plumage on the back and wings and lighter underparts.

peremptory ❶ (pəˈrɛmptərɪ) *adj* **1** urgent or commanding: *a peremptory ring on the bell.* **2** not able to be remitted or debated; decisive. **3** dogmatic. **4** *Law.* **4a** admitting of no denial or contradiction; precluding debate. **4b** obligatory rather than permissive. [C16: from Anglo-Norman *peremptorie,* from L *peremptōrius* decisive, from *perimere* to take away completely]
▸**perˈemptorily** *adv* ▸**perˈemptoriness** *n*

perennial ❶ (pəˈrɛnɪəl) *adj* **1** lasting throughout the year or through many years. **2** everlasting; perpetual. ◆ *n* **3** a woody or herbaceous plant that continues its growth for at least three years. [C17: from L *perennis* continual, from *per* through + *annus* year]
▸**perˈennially** *adv*

perestroika (ˌpɛrəˈstrɔɪkə) *n* the policy of reconstructing the economy, etc., of the former Soviet Union under the leadership of Mikhail Gorbachov. [C20: Russian, lit.: reconstruction]

perfect ❶ *adj* (ˈpɜːfɪkt). **1** having all essential elements. **2** unblemished; faultless: *a perfect gemstone.* **3** correct or precise: *perfect timing.* **4** utter or absolute: *a perfect stranger.* **5** excellent in all respects: *a perfect day.* **6** *Maths.* exactly divisible into equal integral or polynomial roots: *36 is a perfect square.* **7** *Bot.* **7a** (of flowers) having functional stamens and pistils. **7b** (of plants) having all parts present. **8** *Grammar.* denoting a tense of verbs used in describing an action that has been completed. In English this is formed with *have* or *has* plus the past participle. **9** *Music.* **9a** of or relating to the intervals of the unison, fourth, fifth, and octave. **9b** (of a cadence) ending on the tonic chord, giving a feeling of conclusion. Also: **final.** ◆ *n* (ˈpɜːfɪkt). **10** *Grammar.* **10a** the perfect tense. **10b** a verb in this tense. ◆ *vb* (pəˈfɛkt). (*tr*) **11** to make perfect; improve to one's satisfaction: *he is in Paris to perfect his French.* **12** to make fully accomplished. [C13: from L *perfectus,* from *perficere* to perform, from *per-* through + *facere* to do]

> **USAGE NOTE** For most of its meanings, the adjective *perfect* describes an absolute state, i.e. one that cannot be qualified; thus something is either *perfect* or *not perfect,* and cannot be *more perfect.* However when *perfect* means excellent in all respects, a comparative can be used with it without absurdity: *the next day the weather was even more perfect.*

perfect gas *n* another name for **ideal gas.**

perfectible (pəˈfɛktəbᵊl) *adj* capable of becoming or being made perfect.
▸**perˌfectiˈbility** *n*

perfection ❶ (pəˈfɛkʃən) *n* **1** the act of perfecting or the state or quality of being perfect. **2** the highest degree of a quality, etc. **3** an embodiment of perfection. [C13: from L *perfectiō* a completing, from *perficere* to finish]

perfectionism ❶ (pəˈfɛkʃəˌnɪzəm) *n* **1** *Philosophy.* the doctrine that man can attain perfection in this life. **2** the demand for the highest standard of excellence.
▸**perˈfectionist** *n, adj*

perfective (pəˈfɛktɪv) *adj* **1** tending to perfect. **2** *Grammar.* denoting an aspect of verbs used to express that the action or event described by the verb is or was completed: *I lived in London for ten years* is perfective; *I have lived in London for ten years* is imperfective, since the implication is that I still live in London.

perfectly ❶ (ˈpɜːfɪktlɪ) *adv* **1** completely, utterly, or absolutely. **2** in a perfect way.

perfect number *n* an integer, such as 28, that is equal to the sum of all its possible factors, excluding itself.

perfect participle *n* another name for **past participle.**

perfect pitch *n* another name (not in technical usage) for **absolute pitch** (sense 1).

perfervid (pɜːˈfɜːvɪd) *adj Literary.* extremely ardent or zealous. [C19: from NL *perfervidus*]

perfidious ❶ (pəˈfɪdɪəs) *adj* guilty, treacherous, or faithless; deceitful. [C18: from L, from *perfidus* faithless]
▸**perˈfidiously** *adv* ▸**perˈfidiousness** *n* ▸ˈ**perfidy** *n*

perfoliate (pəˈfəʊlɪɪt, -ˌeɪt) *adj* (of a leaf) having a base that completely encloses the stem, so that the stem appears to pass through it. [C17: from NL *perfoliātus,* from L *per-* through + *folium* leaf]
▸**perˌfoliˈation** *n*

perforate ❶ *vb* (ˈpɜːfəˌreɪt), **perforates, perforating, perforated. 1** to make a hole or holes in (something). **2** (*tr*) to punch rows of holes between (stamps, etc.) for ease of separation. ◆ *adj* (ˈpɜːfərɪt). **3** *Biol.* pierced by small holes: *perforate shells.* **4** *Philately.* another word for **perforated.** [C16: from L *perforāre,* from *per-* through + *forāre* to pierce]
▸ˈ**perforable** *adj* ▸ˈ**perfoˌrator** *n*

perforated (ˈpɜːfəˌreɪtɪd) *adj* **1** pierced with holes. **2** (esp. of stamps) having perforations.

perforation (ˌpɜːfəˈreɪʃən) *n* **1** the act of perforating or the state of being perforated. **2** a hole or holes made in something. **3a** a method of making individual stamps, etc. easily separable by punching holes along their margins. **3b** the holes punched in this way. Abbrev.: **perf.**

perforce ❶ (pəˈfɔːs) *adv* by necessity; unavoidably. [C14: from OF *par force*]

perform ❶ (pəˈfɔːm) *vb* **1** to carry out (an action). **2** (*tr*) to fulfil: *to perform someone's request.* **3** to present or enact (a play, concert, etc.): *the group performed Hamlet.* [C14: from Anglo-Norman *perfourmer* (infl. by *forme* FORM), from OF *parfournir,* from *par-* PER- + *fournir* to provide]
▸**perˈformable** *adj* ▸**perˈformer** *n*

performance ❶ (pəˈfɔːməns) *n* **1** the act, process, or art of performing. **2** an artistic or dramatic production: *last night's performance was terri-*

THESAURUS

perdition *n* **1, 2** *Christianity* = **damnation**, condemnation, destruction, doom, downfall, everlasting punishment, hell, hellfire, ruin

peremptory *adj* **1, 2** = **imperative**, absolute, binding, categorical, commanding, compelling, decisive, final, incontrovertible, irrefutable, obligatory, undeniable **3** = **imperious**, arbitrary, assertive, authoritative, autocratic, bossy (*inf.*), dictatorial, dogmatic, domineering, high-handed, intolerant, overbearing

perennial *adj* **1** = **lasting**, abiding, chronic, constant, continual, continuing, enduring, incessant, inveterate, lifelong, persistent, recurrent, unchanging **2** = **eternal**, ceaseless, deathless, everlasting, immortal, imperishable, never-ending, permanent, perpetual, unceasing, undying, unfailing, uninterrupted

perfect *adj* **1, 4** = **complete**, absolute, completed, consummate, entire, finished, full, out-and-out, sheer, unadulterated, unalloyed, unmitigated, utter, whole **2** = **faultless**, blameless, clean, flawless, immaculate, impeccable, pure, spotless, unblemished, unmarred, untarnished **3** = **exact**, accurate, close, correct, faithful, on the money (*US*), precise, right, spot-on (*Brit. inf.*), strict, true, unerring **5** = **excellent**, ideal, splendid, sublime, superb, superlative, supreme ◆ *vb* **11** = **improve**, ameliorate, cultivate, develop, elaborate, hone, polish, refine **12** = **accomplish**, achieve, carry out, complete, consummate, effect, finish, fulfil, perform, realize
Antonyms *adj* ≠ **complete:** incomplete, partial, unfinished ≠ **faultless:** damaged, defective, deficient, faulty, flawed, impaired, imperfect, impure, ruined, spoiled ≠ **excellent:** bad, inferior, poor, unskilled, worthless ◆ *vb* ≠ **improve:** mar

perfection *n* **1** = **accomplishment**, achievement, achieving, completion, consummation, evolution, fulfilment, realization **1** = **completeness**, maturity **1** = **purity**, integrity, perfectness, wholeness **2** = **excellence**, exquisiteness, sublimity, superiority **3** = **ideal**, acme, crown, paragon

perfectionist *n* **2** = **stickler**, formalist, precisian, precisionist, purist

perfectly *adv* **1** = **completely**, absolutely, altogether, consummately, entirely, every inch, fully, quite, thoroughly, totally, utterly, wholly **2** = **flawlessly**, admirably, exquisitely, faultlessly, ideally, impeccably, like a dream, superbly, superlatively, supremely, to perfection, wonderfully
Antonyms *adv* ≠ **completely:** inaccurately, incompletely, mistakenly, partially ≠ **flawlessly:** badly, defectively, faultily, imperfectly, poorly

perfidious *adj* = **treacherous**, corrupt, deceitful, dishonest, disloyal, double-dealing, double-faced, faithless, false, recreant (*arch.*), traitorous, treasonous, two-faced, unfaithful, untrustworthy

perfidy *n* = **treachery**, betrayal, deceit, disloyalty, double-dealing, duplicity, faithlessness, falsity, infidelity, perfidiousness, treason

perforate *vb* **1** = **pierce**, bore, drill, hole, honeycomb, penetrate, punch, puncture

perforce *adv* = **necessarily**, by force of circumstances, by necessity, inevitably, needs must, of necessity, unavoidably, willy-nilly, without choice

perform *vb* **1, 2** = **carry out**, accomplish, achieve, act, bring about, complete, comply with, discharge, do, effect, execute, fulfil, function, observe, pull off, satisfy, transact, work **3** = **present**, act, appear as, depict, enact, play, produce, put on, render, represent, stage

performance *n* **1** = **carrying out**, accomplishment, achievement, act, completion, conduct, consummation, discharge, execution, exploit, feat, fulfilment, work **2** = **presentation**, acting, appearance, exhibition, gig, interpretation,

ble. **3** manner or quality of functioning: *a machine's performance.* **4** *Inf.* mode of conduct or behaviour, esp. when distasteful: *what did you mean by that performance at the restaurant?* **5** *Inf.* any tiresome procedure: *the performance of preparing to go out in the snow.*

performance art *n* a theatrical presentation that incorporates various art forms, such as dance, sculpture, etc.

performative (pəˈfɔːmətɪv) *adj Linguistics, philosophy.* **1a** denoting an utterance that itself constitutes the act described by the verb. For example, the sentence *I confess that I was there* is itself a confession. **1b** (*as n*): *that sentence is a performative.* **2a** denoting a verb that may be used as the main verb in such an utterance. **2b** (*as n*): *"promise" is a performative.*

performing arts the arts, such as a music and drama, that require a public performance.

perfume **T** *n* (ˈpɜːfjuːm). **1** a mixture of alcohol and fragrant essential oils extracted from flowers, etc., or made synthetically. **2** a scent or odour, esp. a fragrant one. ◆ *vb* (pəˈfjuːm), **perfumes, perfuming, perfumed.** **3** (*tr*) to impart a perfume to. **[**C16: from F *parfum,* prob. from OProvençal *perfum,* from *perfumar* to make scented, from *per* through (from L) + *fumar* to smoke, from L *fumāre* to smoke**]**

perfumer (pəˈfjuːmə) *or* **perfumier** (pəˈfjuːmjeɪ) *n* a person who makes or sells perfume.

perfumery (pəˈfjuːmərɪ) *n, pl* **perfumeries.** **1** a place where perfumes are sold. **2** a factory where perfumes are made. **3** the process of making perfumes. **4** perfumes in general.

perfunctory **T** (pəˈfʌŋktərɪ) *adj* **1** done superficially, only as a matter of routine. **2** dull or indifferent. **[**C16: from LL *perfunctōrius* negligent, from *perfunctus* dispatched, from *perfungī* to fulfil**]**
▸**perˈfunctorily** *adv* ▸**perˈfunctoriness** *n*

perfuse (pəˈfjuːz) *vb* **perfuses, perfusing, perfused.** (*tr*) **1** to suffuse or permeate (a liquid, colour, etc.) through or over (something). **2** *Surgery.* to pass (a fluid) through (tissue). **[**C16: from L *perfūsus* wetted, from *perfundere* to pour over**]**
▸**perˈfused** *adj*

perfusionist (pəˈfjuːʒənɪst) *n Surgery.* the person in a surgical team who is responsible for the perfusion of blood through the patient's lung tissue to ensure adequate exchange of oxygen and carbon dioxide.

pergola (ˈpɜːgələ) *n* a horizontal trellis or framework, supported on posts, that carries climbing plants. **[**C17: via It. from L *pergula* projection from a roof, from *pergere* to go forward**]**

perhaps **T** (pəˈhæps; *informal* præps) *adv* **1a** possibly; maybe. **1b** (*as sentence modifier*): *he'll arrive tomorrow, perhaps.* ◆ *sentence substitute.* **2** it may happen, be so, etc.; maybe. **[**C16 *perhappes,* from *per* by + *happes* chance**]**

peri (ˈpɪərɪ) *n, pl* **peris.** **1** (in Persian folklore) one of a race of beautiful supernatural beings. **2** any beautiful fairy-like creature. **[**C18: from Persian: fairy, from Avestan *pairikā* witch**]**

peri- *prefix* **1** enclosing, encircling, or around: *pericardium; pericarp.* **2** near or adjacent: *perihelion.* **[**from Gk *peri* around**]**

perianth (ˈpɛrɪˌænθ) *n* the outer part of a flower, consisting of the calyx and corolla. **[**C18: from F *périanthe,* from NL, from PERI- + Gk *anthos* flower**]**

periapt (ˈpɛrɪˌæpt) *n Rare.* a charm or amulet. **[**C16: via F from Gk *periapton,* from PERI- + *haptos* clasped, from *haptein* to fasten**]**

pericarditis (ˌpɛrɪkɑːˈdaɪtɪs) *n* inflammation of the pericardium.

pericardium (ˌpɛrɪˈkɑːdɪəm) *n, pl* **pericardia** (-dɪə). the membranous sac enclosing the heart. **[**C16: via NL from Gk *perikardion,* from PERI- + *kardia* heart**]**
▸ˌ**periˈcardial** *or* ˌ**periˈcardiˌac** *adj*

pericarp (ˈpɛrɪˌkɑːp) *n* the part of a fruit enclosing the seeds that develops from the wall of the ovary. **[**C18: via F from NL *pericarpium***]**
▸ˌ**periˈcarpial** *adj*

perichondrium (ˌpɛrɪˈkɒndrɪəm) *n, pl* **perichondria** (-drɪə). the fibrous membrane that covers the cartilage. **[**C18: NL, from PERI- + Gk *chondros* cartilage**]**

periclase (ˈpɛrɪˌkleɪs) *n* a mineral consisting of magnesium oxide. **[**C19: from NL *periclasia,* from Gk *peri* very + *klasis* a breaking, referring to its perfect cleavage**]**

pericline (ˈpɛrɪˌklaɪn) *n* **1** a white translucent variety of albite in the form of elongated crystals. **2** Also called: **dome.** a dome-shaped formation of stratified rock with its slopes following the direction of folding. **[**C19: from Gk *periklinēs* sloping on all sides**]**
▸ˌ**periˈclinal** *adj*

pericranium (ˌpɛrɪˈkreɪnɪəm) *n, pl* **pericrania** (-nɪə). the fibrous membrane covering the external surface of the skull. **[**C16: NL, from Gk *perikranion***]**

peridot (ˈpɛrɪˌdɒt) *n* a pale green transparent variety of the olivine chrysolite, used as a gemstone. **[**C14: from OF *peritot,* from ?**]**

perigee (ˈpɛrɪˌdʒiː) *n* the point in its orbit around the earth when the moon or a satellite is nearest the earth. **[**C16: via F from Gk *perigeion,* from PERI- + *gea* earth**]**
▸ˌ**periˈgean** *adj*

periglacial (ˌpɛrɪˈgleɪʃəl) *adj* relating to a region bordering a glacier: *periglacial climate.*

perihelion (ˌpɛrɪˈhiːlɪən) *n, pl* **perihelia** (-lɪə). the point in its orbit when a planet or comet is nearest the sun. **[**C17: from NL *perihēlium,* from PERI- + Gk *hēlios* sun**]**

peril **T** (ˈpɛrɪl) *n* exposure to risk or harm; danger or jeopardy. **[**C13: via OF from L *perīculum***]**

perilous **T** (ˈpɛrɪləs) *adj* very hazardous or dangerous: *a perilous journey.*
▸ˈ**perilously** *adv* ▸ˈ**perilousness** *n*

perilune (ˈpɛrɪˌluːn) *n* the point in a lunar orbit when a spacecraft is nearest the moon. **[**C20: from PERI- + *-lune,* from L *lūna* moon**]**

perimeter **T** (pəˈrɪmɪtə) *n* **1** *Maths.* **1a** the curve or line enclosing a plane area. **1b** the length of this curve or line. **2a** any boundary around something. **2b** (*as modifier*): *a perimeter fence.* **3** a medical instrument for measuring the field of vision. **[**C16: from F *périmètre,* from L *perimetros***]**
▸**perimetric** (ˌpɛrɪˈmɛtrɪk) *adj*

perinatal (ˌpɛrɪˈneɪtᵊl) *adj* of or occurring in the period from about three months before to one month after birth.

perineum (ˌpɛrɪˈniːəm) *n, pl* **perinea** (-ˈniːə). **1** the region of the body between the anus and the genital organs. **2** the surface of the human trunk between the thighs. **[**C17: from NL, from Gk *perinaion,* from PERI- + *inein* to empty**]**
▸ˌ**periˈneal** *adj*

period **T** (ˈpɪərɪəd) *n* **1** a portion of time of indefinable length: *he spent a period away from home.* **2a** a portion of time specified in some way: *Picasso's blue period.* **2b** (*as modifier*): *period costume.* **3** a nontechnical name for an occurence of menstruation. **4** *Geol.* a unit of geological time during which a system of rocks is formed: *the Jurassic period.* **5** a division of time, esp. of the academic day. **6** *Physics, maths.* the time taken to complete one cycle of a regularly recurring phenomenon; the reciprocal of frequency. Symbol: *T* **7** *Astron.* **7a** the time required by a body to make one complete rotation on its axis. **7b** the time interval between two successive maxima or minima of light variation of a variable star. **8** *Chem.* one of the horizontal rows of elements in the periodic table. Each period starts with an alkali metal and ends with a rare gas. **9** another term (esp. US and Canad.) for **full stop.** **10** a complete sentence, esp. one with several clauses. **11** a completion or end. **[**C14 *peryod,* from L *periodus,* from Gk *periodos* circuit, from PERI- + *hodos* way**]**

periodic **T** (ˌpɪərɪˈɒdɪk) *adj* **1** happening or recurring at intervals; intermittent. **2** of, relating to, or resembling a period. **3** having or occurring in a series of repeated periods or cycles.
▸ˌ**periˈodically** *adv* ▸**periodicity** (ˌpɪərɪəˈdɪsɪtɪ) *n*

periodical **T** (ˌpɪərɪˈɒdɪkᵊl) *n* **1** a publication issued at regular intervals, usually monthly or weekly. ◆ *adj* **2** of or relating to such publications. **3** published at regular intervals. **4** periodic or occasional.

periodic function *n Maths.* a function whose value is repeated at constant intervals.

periodic law *n* the principle that the chemical properties of the elements are periodic functions of their atomic weights or, more accurately, of their atomic numbers.

periodic sentence *n Rhetoric.* a sentence in which the completion of the main clause is left to the end, thus creating an effect of suspense.

periodic table *n* a table of the elements, arranged in order of increasing atomic number, based on the periodic law.

periodontal (ˈpɛrɪəˈdɒntᵊl) *adj* of, denoting, or affecting the gums and other tissues surrounding the teeth: *periodontal disease.*

periodontics (ˌpɛrɪəˈdɒntɪks) *n* (*functioning as sing*) the branch of dentistry concerned with diseases affecting the tissues and structures that

THESAURUS

play, portrayal, production, representation, show **3** = **functioning**, action, conduct, efficiency, operation, practice, running, working **4, 5** *Informal* = **carry-on** (*inf., chiefly Brit.*), act, behaviour, bother, business, fuss, pantomime (*inf., chiefly Brit.*), pother, rigmarole, to-do

performer *n* **3** = **artiste**, actor *or* actress, play-actor, player, Thespian, trouper

perfume *n* **1, 2** = **fragrance**, aroma, attar, balminess, bouquet, cologne, essence, incense, niff (*Brit. sl.*), odour, redolence, scent, smell, sweetness

perfunctory *adj* **1, 2** = **offhand**, automatic, careless, cursory, heedless, inattentive, indifferent, mechanical, negligent, routine, sketchy, slipshod, slovenly, stereotyped, superficial, unconcerned, unthinking, wooden

Antonyms *adj* ardent, assiduous, attentive, careful, diligent, keen, spirited, thorough, thoughtful, zealous

perhaps *adv* **1** = **maybe**, as the case may be, conceivably, feasibly, for all one knows, it may be, perchance (*arch.*), possibly

peril *n* = **danger**, exposure, hazard, insecurity, jeopardy, menace, pitfall, risk, uncertainty, vulnerability

Antonyms *n* certainty, impregnability, invulnerability, safety, security, surety

perilous *adj* = **dangerous**, chancy, exposed, fraught with danger, hairy (*sl.*), hazardous, parlous (*arch.*), precarious, risky, threatening, unsafe, unsure, vulnerable

perimeter *n* **1, 2** = **boundary**, ambit, border, borderline, bounds, circumference, confines, edge, limit, margin, periphery

Antonyms *n* central part, centre, core, heart, hub, middle, nucleus

period *n* **1** = **time**, interval, season, space, span, spell, stretch, term, while **2, 4** = **age**, aeon, course, cycle, date, days, epoch, era, generation, season, stage, term, time, years

periodic *adj* **1, 3** = **recurrent**, at fixed intervals, cyclic, cyclical, every once in a while, every so often, infrequent, intermittent, occasional, periodical, regular, repeated, seasonal, spasmodic, sporadic

periodical *n* **1** = **publication**, journal, magazine, monthly, organ, paper, quarterly, review, serial, weekly, zine (*inf.*)

surround teeth. Also called: **periodontology.** [C19: from PERI- + *-odontics,* from Gk *odōn* tooth]
▸ **ˌperioˈdontical** *adj*

periosteum (ˌperɪˈɒstɪəm) *n, pl* **periostea** (-tɪə). a thick fibrous two-layered membrane covering the surface of bones. [C16: NL, from Gk *periosteon,* from PERI- + *osteon* bone]
▸ **ˌperiˈosteal** *adj*

peripatetic (ˌperɪpəˈtetɪk) *adj* **1** itinerant. **2** *Brit.* employed in two or more educational establishments and travelling from one to another: *a peripatetic football coach.* ◆ *n* **3** a peripatetic person. [C16: from L *peripatēticus,* from Gk, from *peripatein* to pace to and fro]
▸ **ˌperipaˈtetically** *adv*

Peripatetic (ˌperɪpəˈtetɪk) *adj* **1** of or relating to the teachings of Aristotle, who used to teach philosophy while walking about the Lyceum in ancient Athens. ◆ *n* **2** a student of Aristotelianism.

peripeteia (ˌperɪpɪˈtaɪə, -ˈtɪə) *n* (esp. in drama) an abrupt turn of events or reversal of circumstances. [C16: from Gk, from PERI- + *piptein* to fall (to change suddenly, lit.: to fall around)]

peripheral Ⓣ (pəˈrɪfərəl) *adj* **1** not relating to the most important part of something; incidental. **2** of or relating to a periphery. **3** *Anat.* of, relating to, or situated near the surface of the body: *a peripheral nerve.*
▸ **peˈripherally** *adv*

peripheral device *or* **unit** *n Computing.* any device, such as a disk, printer, modem, or screen, concerned with input/output, storage, etc. Often shortened to **peripheral.**

periphery Ⓣ (pəˈrɪfərɪ) *n, pl* **peripheries. 1** the outermost boundary of an area. **2** the outside surface of something. [C16: from LL *peripheria,* from Gk, from PERI- + *pherein* to bear]

periphrasis (pəˈrɪfrəsɪs) *n, pl* **periphrases** (-rəˌsiːz). **1** a roundabout way of expressing something; circumlocution. **2** an expression of this kind. [C16: via L from Gk, from PERI- + *phrazein* to declare]

periphrastic (ˌperɪˈfræstɪk) *adj* **1** employing or involving periphrasis. **2** expressed in two or more words rather than by an inflected form of one: used esp. of a tense of a verb where the alternative word is an auxiliary verb, as in *He does go.*
▸ **ˌperiˈphrastically** *adv*

perisarc (ˈperɪˌsɑːk) *n* the outer chitinous layer secreted by colonial hydrozoan coelenterates. [C19: from PERI- + *-sarc,* from Gk *sarx* flesh]

periscope (ˈperɪˌskəʊp) *n* any of a number of optical instruments that enable the user to view objects that are not in the direct line of vision, such as one in a submarine for looking above the surface of the water. They have a system of mirrors or prisms to reflect the light. [C19: from Gk *periskopein* to look around]
▸ **periscopic** (ˌperɪˈskɒpɪk) *adj*

perish Ⓣ (ˈperɪʃ) *vb* **1** (*intr*) to be destroyed or die, esp. in an untimely way. **2** (*tr* sometimes foll. by *with* or *from*) to cause to suffer: *we were perished with cold.* **3** to rot or cause to rot: *leather perishes if exposed to bad weather.* ◆ *n* **4 do a perish.** *Austral. inf.* to die or come near to dying of thirst or starvation. [C13: from OF *périr,* from L *perīre* to pass away entirely]

perishable Ⓣ (ˈperɪʃəbᵊl) *adj* **1** liable to rot. ◆ *n* **2** (*often pl*) a perishable article, esp. food.
▸ **ˌperishaˈbility** *or* **ˈperishableness** *n*

perishing (ˈperɪʃɪŋ) *adj* **1** *Inf.* (of weather, etc.) extremely cold. **2** *Sl.* (intensifier qualifying something undesirable): *it's a perishing nuisance!*
▸ **ˈperishingly** *adv*

perisperm (ˈperɪˌspɜːm) *n* the nutritive tissue surrounding the embryo in certain seeds.

perissodactyl (pəˌrɪsəʊˈdæktɪl) *n* **1** any of an order of placental mammals having hooves with an odd number of toes: includes horses, tapirs, and rhinoceroses. ◆ *adj* **2** of, relating to, or belonging to this order. [C19: from NL *perissodactylus,* from Gk *perissos* uneven + *daktulos* digit]

peristalsis (ˌperɪˈstælsɪs) *n, pl* **peristalses** (-siːz). *Physiol.* the succession of waves of involuntary muscular contraction of various bodily tubes, esp. of the alimentary tract, where it effects transport of food and waste products. [C19: from NL, from PERI- + Gk *stalsis* compression, from *stellein* to press together]
▸ **ˌperiˈstaltic** *adj*

peristome (ˈperɪˌstəʊm) *n* **1** a fringe of pointed teeth surrounding the opening of a moss capsule. **2** any of various parts surrounding the mouth of invertebrates, such as echinoderms and earthworms, and of protozoans. [C18: from NL *peristoma,* from PERI- + Gk *stoma* mouth]

peristyle (ˈperɪˌstaɪl) *n* **1** a colonnade round a court or building. **2** an area surrounded by a colonnade. [C17: via F from L *peristȳlum,* from Gk *peristulon,* from PERI- + *stulos* column]

peritoneum (ˌperɪtəˈniːəm) *n, pl* **peritonea** (-ˈniːə) *or* **peritoneums.** a serous sac that lines the walls of the abdominal cavity and covers the viscera. [C16: via LL from Gk *peritonaion,* from *peritonos* stretched around]
▸ **ˌperitoˈneal** *adj*

peritonitis (ˌperɪtəˈnaɪtɪs) *n* inflammation of the peritoneum.

periwig (ˈperɪˌwɪg) *n* a wig, such as a peruke. [C16 *perwyke,* changed from F *perruque* wig, PERUKE]

periwinkle[1] (ˈperɪˌwɪŋkᵊl) *n* any of various edible marine gastropods having a spirally coiled shell. Often shortened to **winkle.** [C16: from ?]

periwinkle[2] (ˈperɪˌwɪŋkᵊl) *n* any of several Eurasian evergreen plants having trailing stems and blue flowers. [C14 *pervenke,* from OE *perwince,* from LL *pervinca*]

perjure Ⓣ (ˈpɜːdʒə) *vb* **perjures, perjuring, perjured.** (*tr*) *Criminal law.* to render (oneself) guilty of perjury. [C15: from OF *parjurer,* from L *perjūrāre,* from PER- + *jūrāre* to make an oath, from *jūs* law]
▸ **ˈperjurer** *n*

perjured Ⓣ (ˈpɜːdʒəd) *adj Criminal law.* **1a** having sworn falsely. **1b** having committed perjury. **2** involving or characterized by perjury: *perjured evidence.*

perjury Ⓣ (ˈpɜːdʒərɪ) *n, pl* **perjuries.** *Criminal law.* the offence committed by a witness in judicial proceedings who, having been lawfully sworn, wilfully gives false evidence. [C14: from Anglo-F *parjurie,* from L *perjūrium* a false oath; see PERJURE]
▸ **perjurious** (pɜːˈdʒʊərɪəs) *adj*

perk[1] (pɜːk) *adj* **1** pert; brisk; lively. ◆ *vb* **2** See **perk up.** [C16: see PERK UP]

perk[2] (pɜːk) *vb Inf.* short for **percolate** (sense 3).

perk[3] Ⓣ (pɜːk) *n Brit. inf.* short for **perquisite.**

perk up Ⓣ *vb* (*adv*) **1** to make or become more cheerful, hopeful, or lively. **2** to rise or cause to rise briskly: *the dog's ears perked up.* **3** (*tr*) to make smarter in appearance: *she perked up her outfit with a bright scarf.* [C14 *perk,* ?from Norman F *perquer;* see PERCH[1]]

perky Ⓣ (ˈpɜːkɪ) *adj* **perkier, perkiest. 1** jaunty; lively. **2** confident; spirited.
▸ **ˈperkily** *adv* ▸ **ˈperkiness** *n*

Perl (pɜːl) *n* a computer language that is used for text manipulation, esp. on the World Wide Web. [C20: *p(ractical) e(xtraction and) r(eport) l(anguage)*]

perlite (ˈpɜːlaɪt) *n* a variety of obsidian consisting of masses of globules. [C19: from F, from *perle* PEARL[1]]

perm[1] (pɜːm) *n* **1** a hairstyle produced by treatment with heat, chemicals, etc. which gives long-lasting waves or curls. Also called (esp. formerly): **permanent wave.** ◆ *vb* **2** (*tr*) to give a perm to (hair).

perm[2] (pɜːm) *vb, n Inf.* short for **permutate, permutation** (sense 4).

permafrost (ˈpɜːməˌfrɒst) *n* ground that is permanently frozen. [C20: from PERMA(NENT) + FROST]

permalloy (pɜːmˈælɔɪ) *n* any of various alloys containing iron and nickel and sometimes smaller amounts of chromium and molybdenum.

permanence Ⓣ (ˈpɜːmənəns) *n* the state or quality of being permanent.

permanency (ˈpɜːmənənsɪ) *n, pl* **permanencies. 1** a person or thing that is permanent. **2** another word for **permanence.**

permanent Ⓣ (ˈpɜːmənənt) *adj* **1** existing or intended to exist for an indefinite period: *a permanent structure.* **2** not expected to change; not temporary: *a permanent condition.* [C15: from L *permanens* continuing, from *permanēre* to stay to the end]
▸ **ˈpermanently** *adv*

THESAURUS

peripheral *adj* **1 = incidental**, beside the point, borderline, inessential, irrelevant, marginal, minor, secondary, superficial, tangential, unimportant **2 = outermost**, exterior, external, outer, outside, perimetric, surface

periphery *n* **1 = boundary**, ambit, border, brim, brink, circumference, edge, fringe, hem, outer edge, outskirts, perimeter, rim, skirt, verge

perish *vb* **1 = die**, be killed, be lost, decease, expire, lose one's life, pass away **1 = be destroyed**, collapse, decline, disappear, fall, go under, vanish **3 = rot**, break down, decay, decompose, disintegrate, moulder, waste, wither

perishable *adj* **1 = short-lived**, decaying, decomposable, destructible, easily spoilt, liable to rot, unstable
Antonyms *adj* durable, lasting, long-life, long-lived, non-perishable

perjure *vb Criminal law* **= commit perjury**, bear false witness, forswear, give false testimony, lie under oath, swear falsely

perjured *adj* **1** *Criminal law* **= lying**, deceitful, false, forsworn, mendacious, perfidious, traitorous, treacherous, untrue, untruthful

perjury *n Criminal law* **= lying under oath**, bearing false witness, false oath, false statement, false swearing, forswearing, giving false testimony, oath breaking, violation of an oath, wilful falsehood

perk[3] *n Brit. informal* **= bonus**, benefit, dividend, extra, fringe benefit, icing on the cake, perquisite, plus

perk up *vb* **1 = cheer up**, brighten, buck up, liven up, look up, pep up, rally, recover, recuperate, revive, take heart

perky *adj* **1, 2 = lively**, animated, bouncy, bright, bright-eyed and bushy-tailed, bubbly, buoyant, cheerful, cheery, chirpy (*inf.*), full of beans (*inf.*), gay, genial, in fine fettle, jaunty, spirited, sprightly, sunny, upbeat (*inf.*), vivacious

permanence *n* **= continuity**, constancy, continuance, dependability, durability, duration, endurance, finality, fixedness, fixity, immortality, indestructibility, lastingness, perdurability (*rare*), permanency, perpetuity, stability, survival

permanent *adj* **1, 2 = lasting**, abiding, constant, durable, enduring, eternal, everlasting, fixed, immovable, immutable, imperishable, indestructible, invariable, long-lasting, perennial, perpetual, persistent, stable, steadfast, unchanging, unfading
Antonyms *adj* brief, changing, ephemeral, finite, fleeting, impermanent, inconstant, momentary, mortal, passing, short-lived, temporary, transitory, variable

permanently *adv* **1, 2 = for ever**, abidingly, always, constantly, continually, enduringly, eternally, immovably, immutably, indelibly, in perpetuity, invariably, lastingly, perennially, perpetually, persistently, steadfastly, unchangingly, unfadingly, unwaveringly
Antonyms *adv* briefly, ephemerally, fleetingly, im-

permanent health insurance *n* a form of insurance that provides up to 75 per cent of a person's salary, until retirement, in case of prolonged illness or disability.

permanent magnet *n* a magnet, often of steel, that retains its magnetization after the magnetic field producing it has been removed.

permanent press *n* a chemical treatment for clothing that makes the fabric crease-resistant and sometimes provides a garment with a permanent crease or pleats.

permanent wave *n* another name (esp. formerly) for **perm**[1] (sense 1).

permanent way *n Chiefly Brit.* the track of a railway, including the sleepers, rails, etc.

permanganate (pəˈmæŋɡəˌneɪt, -nɪt) *n* a salt of permanganic acid.

permanganic acid (ˌpɜːmænˈɡænɪk) *n* a monobasic acid known only in solution and in the form of permanganate salts. Formula: $HMnO_4$. Systematic name: **manganic(VII) acid.**

permeability (ˌpɜːmɪəˈbɪlɪtɪ) *n* **1** the state or quality of being permeable. **2** a measure of the ability of a medium to modify a magnetic field, expressed as the ratio of the magnetic flux density in the medium to the field strength; measured in henries per metre. Symbol: μ

permeable ❶ (ˈpɜːmɪəbᵊl) *adj* capable of being permeated, esp. by liquids. [C15: from LL *permeābilis,* from L *permeāre* to pervade; see PERMEATE]
▸ **ˈpermeably** *adv*

permeance (ˈpɜːmɪəns) *n* **1** the act of permeating. **2** the reciprocal of the reluctance of a magnetic circuit.
▸ **ˈpermeant** *adj, n*

permeate ❶ (ˈpɜːmɪˌeɪt) *vb* **permeates, permeating, permeated. 1** to penetrate or pervade (a substance, area, etc.): *a lovely smell permeated the room.* **2** to pass through or cause to pass through by osmosis or diffusion: *to permeate a membrane.* [C17: from L *permeāre,* from *per-* through + *meāre* to pass]
▸ **ˌpermeˈation** *n* ▸ **ˈpermeative** *adj*

Permian (ˈpɜːmɪən) *adj* **1** of, denoting, or formed in the last period of the Palaeozoic era, between the Carboniferous and Triassic periods. ◆ *n* **2 the.** the Permian period or rock system. [C19: after *Perm,* Russian port]

permissible ❶ (pəˈmɪsəbᵊl) *adj* permitted; allowable.
▸ **perˌmissiˈbility** *n* ▸ **perˈmissibly** *adv*

permission ❶ (pəˈmɪʃən) *n* authorization to do something.

permissive ❶ (pəˈmɪsɪv) *adj* **1** tolerant; lenient: *permissive parents.* **2** indulgent in matters of sex: *a permissive society.* **3** granting permission.
▸ **perˈmissively** *adv* ▸ **perˈmissiveness** *n*

permit ❶ *vb* (pəˈmɪt), **permits, permitting, permitted. 1** (*tr*) to grant permission to do something: *you are permitted to smoke.* **2** (*tr*) to consent to or tolerate: *she will not permit him to come.* **3** (when *intr,* often foll. by *of;* when *tr,* often foll. by an infinitive) to allow the possibility (of): *the passage permits of two interpretations; his work permits him to relax nowadays.* ◆ *n* (ˈpɜːmɪt). **4** an official document granting authorization; licence. **5** permission. [C15: from L *permittere,* from *per-* through + *mittere* to send]
▸ **perˈmitter** *n*

permittivity (ˌpɜːmɪˈtɪvɪtɪ) *n, pl* **permittivities.** a measure of the ability of a substance to transmit an electric field.

permutate (ˈpɜːmjuˌteɪt) *vb* **permutates, permutating, permutated.** to alter the sequence or arrangement (of): *endlessly permutating three basic designs.*

permutation ❶ (ˌpɜːmjuˈteɪʃən) *n* **1** *Maths.* **1a** an ordered arrangement of the numbers, terms, etc., of a set into specified groups: *the permutations of a, b, and c, taken two at a time, are ab, ba, ac, ca, bc, cb.* **1b** a group formed in this way. **2** a combination of items, etc., made by reordering. **3** an alteration; transformation. **4** a fixed combination for selections of results on football pools. Usually shortened to **perm.** [C14: from L *permūtātiō,* from *permūtāre* to change thoroughly]
▸ **ˌpermuˈtational** *adj*

permute (pəˈmjuːt) *vb* **permutes, permuting, permuted.** (*tr*) **1** to change the sequence of. **2** *Maths.* to subject to permutation. [C14: from L *permūtāre,* from PER- + *mūtāre* to change]

pernicious ❶ (pəˈnɪʃəs) *adj* **1** wicked or malicious: *pernicious lies.* **2** causing grave harm; deadly. [C16: from L *perniciōsus,* from *perniciēs* ruin, from PER- (intensive) + *nex* death]
▸ **perˈniciously** *adv* ▸ **perˈniciousness** *n*

pernicious anaemia *n* a form of anaemia characterized by lesions of the spinal cord, weakness, sore tongue, diarrhoea, etc.: associated with inadequate absorption of vitamin B_{12}.

pernickety ❶ (pəˈnɪkɪtɪ) *adj Inf.* **1** excessively precise; fussy. **2** (of a task) requiring close attention. [C19: orig. Scot. from ?]

peroneal (ˌperəˈniːəl) *adj Anat.* of or relating to the fibula. [C19: from NL *peronē,* from Gk: fibula]

perorate (ˈperəˌreɪt) *vb* **perorates, perorating, perorated.** (*intr*) **1** to speak at length, esp. in a formal manner. **2** to conclude a speech or sum up.

peroration (ˌperəˈreɪʃən) *n* the conclusion of a speech or discourse, in which points made previously are summed up. [C15: from L *perōrātiō,* from PER- (thoroughly) + *ōrāre* to speak]

perovskite (pɛˈrɒvskaɪt) *n* a yellow, brown, or greyish-black mineral. [C19: after *Perovski,* Russian mineralogist]

peroxide (pəˈrɒksaɪd) *n* **1** short for **hydrogen peroxide,** esp. when used for bleaching hair. **2** any of a class of metallic oxides, such as sodium peroxide, Na_2O_2. **3** (*not in technical usage*) any of certain dioxides, such as manganese(VI) oxide, MnO_2, that resemble peroxides in their formula. **4** any of a class of organic compounds whose molecules contain two oxygen atoms bound together. **5** (*modifier*) of, relating to, bleached with, or resembling peroxide: *a peroxide blonde.* ◆ *vb* **peroxides, peroxiding, peroxided. 6** (*tr*) to bleach (the hair) with peroxide.

perpendicular ❶ (ˌpɜːpənˈdɪkjʊlə) *adj* **1** at right angles to a horizontal plane. **2** denoting, relating to, or having the style of Gothic architecture used in England during the 14th and 15th centuries, characterized by tracery having vertical lines. **3** upright; vertical. ◆ *n* **4** *Geom.* a line or plane perpendicular to another. **5** any instrument used for indicating the vertical line through a given point. [C14: from L *perpendiculāris,* from *perpendiculum* a plumb line, from *per-* through + *pendēre* to hang]
▸ **perpendicularity** (ˌpɜːpənˌdɪkjʊˈlærɪtɪ) *n* ▸ **ˌperpenˈdicularly** *adv*

perpetrate ❶ (ˈpɜːpɪˌtreɪt) *vb* **perpetrates, perpetrating, perpetrated.** (*tr*) to perform or be responsible for (a deception, crime, etc.). [C16: from L *perpetrāre,* from *per-* (thoroughly) + *patrāre* to perform]
▸ **ˌperpeˈtration** *n* ▸ **ˈperpeˌtrator** *n*

> **USAGE NOTE** *Perpetrate* and *perpetuate* are sometimes confused: *he must answer for the crimes he has perpetrated* (not *perpetuated*); *the book helped to perpetuate* (not *perpetrate*) *some of the myths surrounding his early life.*

perpetual ❶ (pəˈpɛtjʊəl) *adj* **1** (*usually prenominal*) eternal; permanent. **2** (*usually prenominal*) seemingly ceaseless because often repeated: *your perpetual complaints.* [C14: via OF from L *perpetuālis* universal, from *perpes* continuous, from *per-* (thoroughly) + *petere* to go towards]
▸ **perˈpetually** *adv*

perpetual debenture *n* a bond or debenture that can either never be redeemed or cannot be redeemed on demand.

perpetual motion *n* motion of a hypothetical mechanism that continues indefinitely without any external source of energy. It is impossible in practice because of friction.

perpetuate ❶ (pəˈpɛtjʊˌeɪt) *vb* **perpetuates, perpetuating, perpetuated.** (*tr*) to cause to continue: *to perpetuate misconceptions.* [C16: from L *perpetuāre* to continue without interruption, from *perpetuus* PERPETUAL]
▸ **perˌpetuˈation** *n*

> **USAGE NOTE** See at **perpetrate.**

THESAURUS

permanently, inconstantly, momentarily, temporarily, transitorily

permeable *adj* = **penetrable,** absorbent, absorptive, pervious, porous, spongy

permeate *vb* **1, 2** = **pervade,** charge, diffuse throughout, fill, filter through, imbue, impregnate, infiltrate, pass through, penetrate, percolate, saturate, seep through, soak through, spread through

permissible *adj* = **permitted,** acceptable, admissible, allowable, all right, authorized, kosher (*inf.*), lawful, legal, legit (*sl.*), legitimate, licit, O.K. *or* okay (*inf.*), proper, sanctioned
Antonyms *adj* banned, forbidden, illegal, illicit, prohibited, unauthorized, unlawful

permission *n* = **authorization,** allowance, approval, assent, blank cheque, carte blanche, consent, dispensation, freedom, go-ahead (*inf.*), green light, leave, liberty, licence, permit, sanction, sufferance, tolerance

permissive *adj* **1, 2** = **tolerant,** acquiescent, easy-going, easy-oasy (*sl.*), forbearing, free, indulgent, latitudinarian, lax, lenient, liberal, open-minded
Antonyms *adj* authoritarian, denying, domineering, forbidding, grudging, rigid, strict

permit *vb* **1, 2** = **allow,** admit, agree, authorize, consent, empower, enable, endorse, endure, entitle, give leave *or* permission, give the green light to, grant, let, license, own, sanction, suffer, tolerate, warrant ◆ *n* **4, 5** = **licence,** authorization, liberty, pass, passport, permission, sanction, warrant

permutation *n* **3** = **transformation,** alteration, change, shift, transmutation, transposition

pernicious *adj* **1, 2** = **wicked,** bad, baleful, baneful (*arch.*), damaging, dangerous, deadly, deleterious, destructive, detrimental, evil, fatal, harmful, hurtful, injurious, maleficent, malevolent, malicious, malign, malignant, noisome, noxious, offensive, pestilent, poisonous, ruinous, venomous

pernickety *adj Informal* **1** = **fussy,** careful, carping, difficult to please, exacting, fastidious, finicky, hairsplitting, nice, nit-picking (*inf.*), overprecise, painstaking, particular, picky (*inf.*), punctilious **2** = **tricky,** detailed, exacting, fiddly, fine
Antonyms *adj* ≠ **fussy:** careless, easy to please, haphazard, heedless, inattentive, lax, slack, slapdash, slipshod, sloppy, uncritical ≠ **tricky:** easy, simple

perpendicular *adj* **1, 3** = **upright,** at right angles to, on end, plumb, straight, vertical

perpetrate *vb* = **commit,** be responsible for, bring about, carry out, do, effect, enact, execute, inflict, perform, wreak

perpetual *adj* **1** = **everlasting,** abiding, endless, enduring, eternal, immortal, infinite, lasting, never-ending, perennial, permanent, sempiternal (*literary*), unchanging, undying, unending **2** = **continual,** ceaseless, constant, continuous, endless, incessant, interminable, never-ending, perennial, persistent, recurrent, repeated, unceasing, unfailing, uninterrupted, unremitting
Antonyms *adj* brief, ephemeral, fleeting, impermanent, momentary, passing, short-lived, temporary, transitory

perpetuate *vb* = **maintain,** continue, eternalize, immortalize, keep alive, keep going, keep up, preserve, sustain

perpetuity (ˌpɜːpɪˈtjuːɪtɪ) *n, pl* **perpetuities. 1** eternity. **2** the state of being perpetual. **3** *Property law.* a limitation preventing the absolute disposal of an estate for longer than the period allowed by law. **4** an annuity that is payable indefinitely. **5 in perpetuity.** forever. [C15: from OF *perpetuite,* from L *perpetuitās* continuity; see PERPETUAL]

perplex ❶ (pəˈplɛks) *vb (tr)* **1** to puzzle; bewilder; confuse. **2** to complicate: *to perplex an issue.* [C15: from obs. *perplex* (adj) intricate, from L *perplexus* entangled, from *per-* (thoroughly) + *plectere* to entwine] ▸**perplexedly** (pəˈplɛksɪdlɪ, -ˈplɛkstlɪ) *adv* ▸**perˈplexingly** *adv*

perplexity ❶ (pəˈplɛksɪtɪ) *n, pl* **perplexities. 1** the state of being perplexed. **2** the state of being intricate or complicated. **3** something that perplexes.

per pro (ˈpɜː ˈprəʊ) *prep* by delegation to: through the agency of: used when signing documents on behalf of someone else. [L: abbrev. of *per prōcūrātiōnem*]

USAGE NOTE See at **pp.**

perquisite ❶ (ˈpɜːkwɪzɪt) *n* **1** an incidental benefit gained from a certain type of employment, such as the use of a company car. **2** a customary benefit received in addition to a regular income. **3** a customary tip. **4** something expected or regarded as an exclusive right. ◆ Often shortened (informal) to **perk.** [C15: from Med. L *perquīsītum,* from L *perquīrere* to seek earnestly for something]

Perrier water *or* **Perrier** (ˈpɛrɪeɪ) *n Trademark.* a sparkling mineral water from the south of France. [C20: after a spring, *Source Perrier,* at Vergèze, France]

perron (ˈpɛrən) *n* an external flight of steps, esp. one at the front entrance of a building. [C14: from OF, from *pierre* stone, from L *petra*]

perry (ˈpɛrɪ) *n, pl* **perries.** wine made of pears, similar in taste to cider. [C14 *pereye,* from OF *peré,* ult. from L *pirum* pear]

pers. *abbrev. for:* **1** person. **2** personal.

Pers. *abbrev. for* Persia(n).

perse (pɜːs) *n* **a** a dark greyish-blue colour. **b** *(as adj): perse cloth.* [C14: from OF, from Med. L *persus,* ? changed from L *Persicus* Persian]

per se ❶ (ˈpɜː ˈseɪ) *adv* by or in itself; intrinsically. [L]

persecute ❶ (ˈpɜːsɪˌkjuːt) *vb* **persecutes, persecuting, persecuted.** *(tr)* **1** to oppress, harass, or maltreat, esp. because of race, religion, etc. **2** to bother persistently. [C15: from OF, from *persecuteur,* from LL *persecūtor* pursuer, from L *persequī* to take vengeance upon] ▸ˌ**perseˈcution** *n* ▸ˈ**perseˌcutive** *adj* ▸ˈ**perseˌcutor** *n*

persecution complex *n Psychol.* an acute irrational fear that other people are plotting one's downfall.

perseverance ❶ (ˌpɜːsɪˈvɪərəns) *n* **1** continued steady belief or efforts; persistence. **2** *Christian theol.* continuance in a state of grace.

perseveration (pɜːˌsɛvəˈreɪʃən) *n Psychol.* the tendency for an impression, idea, or feeling to dissipate only slowly and to recur during subsequent experiences.

persevere ❶ (ˌpɜːsɪˈvɪə) *vb* **perseveres, persevering, persevered.** *(intr; often foll. by in)* to show perseverance. [C14: from OF *perseverer,* from L, from *perseverus* very strict; see SEVERE]

Persian (ˈpɜːʃən) *adj* **1** of or relating to ancient Persia or modern Iran, their inhabitants, or their languages. ◆ *n* **2** a native, citizen, or inhabitant of modern Iran; an Iranian. **3** the language of Iran or Persia in any of its ancient or modern forms.

Persian carpet *or* **rug** *n* a carpet or rug made in Persia or the Near East by knotting silk or wool yarn by hand onto a woven backing in rich colours and flowing or geometric designs.

Persian cat *n* a long-haired variety of domestic cat.

Persian lamb *n* **1** a black loosely curled fur from the karakul lamb. **2** a karakul lamb.

persiennes (ˌpɜːsɪˈɛnz) *pl n* outside window shutters having louvres. [C19: from F, from *persien* Persian]

persiflage (ˈpɜːsɪˌflɑːʒ) *n* light frivolous conversation, style, or treatment; friendly teasing. [C18: via F from *persifler* to tease, from *per-* (intensive) + *siffler* to whistle, from L *sībilāre* to whistle]

persimmon (pɜːˈsɪmən) *n* **1** any of several tropical trees, typically having hard wood and large orange-red fruit. **2** Also called: **sharon fruit.** the sweet fruit of any of these trees, which is edible when completely ripe. [C17: from Amerind]

persist ❶ (pəˈsɪst) *vb (intr)* **1** (often foll. by *in*) to continue steadfastly or obstinately despite opposition. **2** to continue without interruption: *the rain persisted throughout the night.* [C16: from L *persistere,* from *per-* (intensive) + *sistere* to stand steadfast] ▸**perˈsister** *n*

persistence ❶ (pəˈsɪstəns) *or* **persistency** *n* **1** the quality of persisting; tenacity. **2** the act of persisting; continued effort or existence.

persistent ❶ (pəˈsɪstənt) *adj* **1** showing persistence. **2** incessantly repeated; unrelenting: *your persistent questioning.* **3** (of plant parts) remaining attached to the plant after the normal time of withering. **4** *Zool.* (of parts normally present only in young stages) present in the adult. **5** (of a chemical, esp. when used as a insecticide) slow to break down. ▸**perˈsistently** *adv*

persistent vegetative state *n Med.* an irreversible condition, resulting from brain damage, characterized by lack of consciousness, thought, and feeling, although reflex activities (such as breathing) continue. Abbrev.: **PVS.**

person ❶ (ˈpɜːsᵊn) *n, pl* **persons. 1** an individual human being. **2** the body of a human being: *guns hidden on his person.* **3** a grammatical category into which pronouns and forms of verbs are subdivided depending on whether they refer to the speaker, the person addressed, or some other individual, thing, etc. **4** a human being or a corporation recognized in law as having certain rights and obligations. **5 in person.** actually present: *the author will be there in person.* [C13: from OF *persone,* from L *persōna* mask, ?from Etruscan *phersu* mask]

USAGE NOTE *People* is the word usually used to refer to more than one individual: *there were a hundred people at the reception. Persons* is rarely used, except in official English: *several persons were interviewed.*

-person *n combining form.* sometimes used instead of *-man* and *-woman* or *-lady: chairperson.*

USAGE NOTE See at **-man.**

persona ❶ (pɜːˈsəʊnə) *n, pl* **personae** (-niː). **1** *(often pl)* a character in a play, novel, etc. **2** (in Jungian psychology) the mechanism that conceals a person's true thoughts and feelings, esp. in adaptation to the outside world. [L: mask]

personable ❶ (ˈpɜːsənəbᵊl) *adj* pleasant in appearance and personality. ▸ˈ**personableness** *n* ▸ˈ**personably** *adv*

personage ❶ (ˈpɜːsənɪdʒ) *n* **1** an important or distinguished person. **2** another word for **person** (sense 1). **3** *Rare.* a figure in literature, history, etc.

THESAURUS

Antonyms *vb* abolish, destroy, end, forget, ignore, put an end to, stamp out, suppress

perplex *vb* **1** = **puzzle**, baffle, befuddle, bemuse, beset, bewilder, confound, confuse, dumbfound, faze, flummox, mix up, muddle, mystify, nonplus, stump **2** = **complicate**, encumber, entangle, involve, jumble, mix up, snarl up, tangle, thicken

perplexing *adj* **1** = **puzzling**, baffling, bewildering, complex, complicated, confusing, difficult, enigmatic, hard, inexplicable, intricate, involved, knotty, labyrinthine, mysterious, mystifying, paradoxical, strange, taxing, thorny, unaccountable, weird

perplexity *n* **1** = **puzzlement**, bafflement, bewilderment, confusion, incomprehension, mystification, stupefaction **2** = **complexity**, difficulty, inextricability, intricacy, involvement, obscurity **3** = **puzzle**, difficulty, dilemma, enigma, fix (*inf.*), how-do-you-do (*inf.*), knotty problem, mystery, paradox, snarl

perquisite *n* **1, 2** = **bonus**, benefit, dividend, extra, fringe benefit, icing on the cake, perk (*Brit. inf.*), plus

per se *adv* = **in itself**, as such, by definition, by itself, by its very nature, essentially, in essence, intrinsically, of itself

persecute *vb* **1** = **victimize**, afflict, be on one's back (*sl.*), distress, dragoon, hound, hunt, ill-treat, injure, maltreat, martyr, molest, oppress, pick on, pursue, torment, torture **2** = **harass**, annoy, badger, bait, bother, hassle (*inf.*), pester, tease, vex, worry

Antonyms *vb* accommodate, back, calm, coddle, comfort, console, cosset, humour, indulge, leave alone, let alone, mollycoddle, pamper, pet, spoil, support

perseverance *n* **1** = **persistence**, constancy, dedication, determination, diligence, doggedness, endurance, indefatigability, pertinacity, purposefulness, resolution, sedulity, stamina, steadfastness, tenacity

persevere *vb* = **keep going**, be determined *or* resolved, carry on, continue, endure, go on, hang on, hold fast, hold on, keep on *or* at, keep one's hand in, maintain, persist, plug away (*inf.*), pursue, remain, stand firm, stay the course, stick at *or* to

Antonyms *vb* be irresolute, dither (*chiefly Brit.*), end, falter, give in, give up, hesitate, quit, shilly-shally (*inf.*), swither (*Scot.*), throw in the towel, vacillate, waver

persist *vb* **1** = **persevere**, be resolute, continue, hold on (*inf.*), insist, stand firm, stay the course **2** = **continue**, abide, carry on, endure, keep up, last, linger, remain

persistence *n* **1, 2** = **determination**, constancy, diligence, doggedness, endurance, grit, indefatigability, perseverance, pertinacity, pluck, resolution, stamina, steadfastness, tenacity, tirelessness

persistent *adj* **1** = **determined**, assiduous, dogged, enduring, fixed, immovable, indefatigable, obdurate, obstinate, persevering, pertinacious, resolute, steadfast, steady, stiff-necked, stubborn, tenacious, tireless, unflagging **2** = **continuous**, constant, continual, endless, incessant, interminable, lasting, never-ending, perpetual, relentless, repeated, unrelenting, unremitting

Antonyms *adj* ≠ **determined:** changeable, flexible, irresolute, tractable, yielding ≠ **continuous:** inconstant, intermittent, irregular, occasional, off-and-on, periodic

person *n* **1, 2** = **individual**, being, body, human, human being, living soul, soul **5 in person** = **personally**, bodily, in the flesh, oneself

persona *n* **1, 2** = **personality**, assumed role, character, façade, face, front, mask, part, public face, role

personable *adj* = **pleasant**, affable, agreeable, amiable, attractive, charming, good-looking, handsome, likable *or* likeable, nice, pleasing, presentable, winning

Antonyms *adj* disagreeable, sullen, surly, ugly, unattractive, unpleasant, unsightly

personage *n* **1** = **personality**, big name, big noise (*inf.*), big shot (*inf.*), celeb (*inf.*), celebrity, dignitary, luminary, megastar (*inf.*), notable,

persona grata *Latin.* (pɜːˈsəʊnə ˈɡrɑːtə) *n, pl* **personae gratae** (pɜːˈsəʊniː ˈɡrɑːtiː). an acceptable person, esp. a diplomat.

personal ❶ (ˈpɜːsənᵊl) *adj* **1** of or relating to the private aspects of a person's life: *personal letters.* **2** (*prenominal*) of or relating to a person's body, its care, or its appearance: *personal hygiene.* **3** belonging to or intended for a particular person and no-one else: *for your personal use.* **4** (*prenominal*) undertaken by an individual: *a personal appearance by a celebrity.* **5** referring to or involving a person's individual personality, intimate affairs, etc., esp. in an offensive way: *personal remarks; don't be so personal.* **6** having the attributes of an individual conscious being: *a personal God.* **7** of, relating to, or denoting grammatical person. **8** *Law.* of or relating to movable property, as money, etc.

personal column *n* a newspaper column containing personal messages and advertisements.

personal computer *n* a small inexpensive computer used in word processing, computer games, etc.

personal equity plan *n* the full name for **PEP.**

personality ❶ (ˌpɜːsəˈnælɪtɪ) *n, pl* **personalities. 1** *Psychol.* the sum total of all the behavioural and mental characteristics by means of which an individual is recognized as being unique. **2** the distinctive character of a person that makes him socially attractive: *a salesman needs a lot of personality.* **3** a well-known person in a certain field, such as entertainment. **4** a remarkable person. **5** (*often pl*) a personal remark.

personalize ❶ *or* **personalise** (ˈpɜːsənəˌlaɪz) *vb* **personalizes, personalizing, personalized** *or* **personalises, personalising, personalised.** (*tr*) **1** to endow with personal or individual qualities. **2** to mark (stationery, clothing, etc.) with a person's initials, name, etc. **3** to take (a remark, etc.) personally. **4** another word for **personify.**

►**ˌpersonaliˈzation** *or* **ˌpersonaliˈsation** *n*

personally ❶ (ˈpɜːsənəlɪ) *adv* **1** without the help or intervention of others: *I'll attend to it personally.* **2** (*sentence modifier*) in one's own opinion or as regards oneself: *personally, I hate onions.* **3** as if referring to oneself: *to take the insults personally.* **4** as a person: *we like him personally, but professionally he's incompetent.*

personal organizer *n* **1** a diary that stores personal records, appointments, notes, etc. **2** a pocket-sized electronic device that performs the same functions.

personal pronoun *n* a pronoun having a definite person or thing as an antecedent and functioning grammatically in the same way as the noun that it replaces. The personal pronouns include *I, you, he, she, it, we,* and *they.*

personal property *n Law.* movable property, such as furniture or money. Also called: **personalty.** Cf. **real property.**

personal stereo *n* a small audio cassette player worn attached to a belt and used with lightweight headphones.

persona non grata *Latin.* (pɜːˈsəʊnə nɒn ˈɡrɑːtə) *n, pl* ***personae non gratae*** (pɜːˈsəʊniː nɒn ˈɡrɑːtiː). **1** an unacceptable or unwelcome person. **2** a diplomat who is not acceptable to the government to whom he or she is accredited.

personate ❶ (ˈpɜːsəˌneɪt) *vb* **personates, personating, personated.** (*tr*) **1** to act the part of (a character in a play); portray. **2** *Criminal law.* to assume the identity of (another person) with intent to deceive.

►**ˌpersonˈation** *n* ►**ˈpersonative** *adj* ►**ˈpersonˌator** *n*

personification ❶ (pɜːˌsɒnɪfɪˈkeɪʃən) *n* **1** the attribution of human characteristics to things, abstract ideas, etc. **2** the representation of an abstract quality or idea in the form of a person, creature, etc., as in art and literature. **3** a person or thing that personifies. **4** a person or thing regarded as an embodiment of a quality: *he is the personification of optimism.*

personify ❶ (pɜːˈsɒnɪˌfaɪ) *vb* **personifies, personifying, personified.** (*tr*) **1** to attribute human characteristics to (a thing or abstraction). **2** to represent (an abstract quality) in human or animal form. **3** (of a person or thing) to represent (an abstract quality), as in art. **4** to be the embodiment of.

►**perˈsoniˌfier** *n*

personnel ❶ (ˌpɜːsəˈnɛl) *n* **1** the people employed in an organization or for a service. **2a** the department that interviews, appoints, or keeps records of employees. **2b** (*as modifier*): *a personnel officer.* [C19: from F, ult. from LL *persōnālis* personal (adj); see PERSON]

perspective ❶ (pəˈspɛktɪv) *n* **1** a way of regarding situations, facts, etc., and judging their relative importance. **2** the proper or accurate point of view or the ability to see it; objectivity: *try to get some perspective on your troubles.* **3** a view over some distance in space or time; prospect. **4** the theory or art of suggesting three dimensions on a two-dimensional surface, in order to recreate the appearance and spatial relationships that objects or a scene in recession present to the eye. **5** the appearance of objects, buildings, etc., relative to each other, as determined by their distance from the viewer, or the effects of this distance on their appearance. [C14: from Med. L *perspectīva ars* the science of optics, from L *perspicere* to inspect carefully]

►**perˈspectively** *adv*

Perspex (ˈpɜːspɛks) *n Trademark.* any of various clear acrylic resins.

perspicacious ❶ (ˌpɜːspɪˈkeɪʃəs) *adj* acutely perceptive or discerning. [C17: from L *perspicax,* from *perspicere* to look at closely]

►**ˌperspiˈcaciously** *adv* ►**perspicacity** (ˌpɜːspɪˈkæsɪtɪ) *or* **ˌperspiˈcaciousness** *n*

perspicuous ❶ (pəˈspɪkjʊəs) *adj* (of speech or writing) easily understood; lucid. [C15: from L *perspicuus* transparent, from *perspicere* to explore thoroughly]

►**perˈspicuously** *adv* ►**perˈspicuousness** *or* **perspicuity** (ˌpɜːspɪˈkjuːɪtɪ) *n*

perspiration ❶ (ˌpɜːspəˈreɪʃən) *n* **1** the salty fluid secreted by the sweat glands of the skin. **2** the act of secreting this fluid.

►**perspiratory** (pəˈspaɪərətərɪ) *adj*

perspire ❶ (pəˈspaɪə) *vb* **perspires, perspiring, perspired.** to secrete or exude (perspiration) through the pores of the skin. [C17: from L *perspīrāre* to blow, from *per-* (through) + *spīrāre* to breathe]

►**perˈspiringly** *adv*

persuade ❶ (pəˈsweɪd) *vb* **persuades, persuading, persuaded.** (*tr; may take a clause as object or an infinitive*) **1** to induce, urge, or prevail upon successfully: *he finally persuaded them to buy it.* **2** to cause to believe; convince: *even with the evidence, the police were not persuaded.* [C16: from L *persuādēre,* from *per-* (intensive) + *suādēre* to urge, advise]

►**perˈsuadable** *or* **perˈsuasible** *adj* ►**perˌsuadaˈbility** *or* **perˌsuasiˈbility** *n*

►**perˈsuader** *n*

persuasion ❶ (pəˈsweɪʒən) *n* **1** the act of persuading or of trying to persuade. **2** the power to persuade. **3** a strong belief. **4** an established creed or belief, esp. a religious one. **5** a sect, party, or faction. [C14: from L *persuāsiō*]

persuasive ❶ (pəˈsweɪsɪv) *adj* having the power or tending to persuade: *a persuasive salesman.*

►**perˈsuasively** *adv* ►**perˈsuasiveness** *n*

pert ❶ (pɜːt) *adj* **1** saucy, impudent, or forward. **2** jaunty: *a pert little hat.*

THESAURUS

public figure, somebody, V.I.P., well-known person, worthy

personal *adj* **1, 3 = private,** exclusive, individual, intimate, own, particular, peculiar, privy, special **2 = physical,** bodily, corporal, corporeal, exterior, material **5 = offensive,** derogatory, disparaging, insulting, nasty, pejorative, slighting

personality *n* **1 = nature,** character, disposition, identity, individuality, make-up, psyche, temper, temperament, traits **2 = character,** attraction, attractiveness, charisma, charm, dynamism, likableness *or* likeableness, magnetism, pleasantness **3 = celebrity,** big name, celeb (*inf.*), famous name, household name, megastar (*inf.*), notable, personage, star, well-known face, well-known person

personalized *adj* **2 = customized,** distinctive, individual, individualized, monogrammed, private, special, tailor-made

personally *adv* **1 = by oneself,** alone, independently, in person, in the flesh, on one's own,.solely **2 = in one's opinion,** for oneself, for one's part, from one's own viewpoint, in one's books, in one's own view **4 = individually,** individualistically, privately, specially, subjectively

personate *vb* **1, 2 = impersonate,** act, depict, do (*inf.*), enact, feign, imitate, play-act, portray, represent

personification *n* **1, 2, 4 = embodiment,** epitome, image, incarnation, likeness, portrayal, recreation, representation, semblance

personify *vb* **1, 2, 4 = embody,** body forth, epitomize, exemplify, express, image (*rare*), incarnate, mirror, represent, symbolize, typify

personnel *n* **1 = employees,** helpers, human resources, liveware, members, men and women, people, staff, workers, workforce

perspective *n* **1 = outlook,** angle, attitude, broad view, context, frame of reference, overview, way of looking **2 = objectivity,** proportion, relation, relative importance, relativity **3 = view,** outlook, panorama, prospect, scene, vista

perspicacious *adj* **= perceptive,** acute, alert, astute, aware, clear-sighted, clever, discerning, keen, observant, penetrating, percipient, sagacious, sharp, sharp-witted, shrewd

perspicacity *n* **= insight,** acumen, acuteness, discernment, discrimination, keenness, penetration, perceptiveness, percipience, perspicaciousness, perspicuity, sagaciousness, sagacity, sharpness, shrewdness, smarts (*sl., chiefly US*), suss (*sl.*), wit

perspicuity *n* **= clarity,** clearness, comprehensibility, distinctness, explicitness, intelligibility, limpidity, limpidness, lucidity, plainness, precision, straightforwardness, transparency

perspicuous *adj* **= clear,** comprehensible, crystal-clear, distinct, easily understood, explicit, intelligible, limpid, lucid, obvious, plain, self-evident, straightforward, transparent, unambiguous, understandable

perspiration *n* **1 = sweat,** exudation, moisture, wetness

perspire *vb* **= sweat,** be damp, be wet, drip, exude, glow, pour with sweat, secrete, swelter

persuade *vb* **1 = talk into,** actuate, advise, allure, bring round (*inf.*), coax, counsel, entice, impel, incite, induce, influence, inveigle, prevail upon, prompt, sway, twist (someone's) arm, urge, win over **2 = convince,** cause to believe, convert, satisfy

Antonyms *vb* ≠ **talk into:** deter, discourage, dissuade, forbid, prohibit

persuasion *n* **1 = urging,** blandishment, cajolery, conversion, enticement, exhortation, inducement, influencing, inveiglement, wheedling **2 = persuasiveness,** cogency, force, potency, power, pull (*inf.*) **3, 4 = creed,** belief, certitude, conviction, credo, faith, firm belief, fixed opinion, opinion, tenet, views **5 = faction,** camp, cult, denomination, party, school, school of thought, sect, side

persuasive *adj* **= convincing,** cogent, compelling, credible, effective, eloquent, forceful, impelling, impressive, inducing, influential, logical, moving, plausible, sound, telling, touching, valid, weighty, winning

Antonyms *adj* feeble, flimsy, illogical, implausible, incredible, ineffective, invalid, unconvincing, unimpressive, weak

pert *adj* **1 = impudent,** bold, brash, cheeky, flip (*inf.*), flippant, forward, fresh (*inf.*), impertinent, insolent, lippy (*US & Canad. sl.*), presump-

3 *Obs.* clever or brisk. [C13: var. of earlier *apert,* from L *apertus* open, from *aperīre* to open]
▸'**pertly** *adv* ▸'**pertness** *n*

pert. *abbrev. for* pertaining.

pertain ⓣ (pəˈteɪn) *vb* (*intr;* often foll. by *to*) **1** to have reference or relevance: *issues pertaining to women.* **2** to be appropriate: *the product pertains to real user needs.* **3** to belong (to) or be a part (of). [C14: from L *pertinēre,* from *per-* (intensive) + *tenēre* to hold]

pertinacious ⓣ (ˌpɜːtɪˈneɪʃəs) *adj* **1** doggedly resolute in purpose or belief; unyielding. **2** stubbornly persistent. [C17: from L *pertinax,* from *per-* (intensive) + *tenāx* clinging, from *tenēre* to hold]
▸ˌ**pertiˈnaciously** *adv* ▸**pertinacity** (ˌpɜːtɪˈnæsɪtɪ) *or* ˌ**pertiˈnaciousness** *n*

pertinent ⓣ (ˈpɜːtɪnənt) *adj* relating to the matter at hand; relevant. [C14: from L *pertinēns,* from *pertinēre* to PERTAIN]
▸ˈ**pertinence** *or* ˈ**pertinency** *n* ▸ˈ**pertinently** *adv*

perturb ⓣ (pəˈtɜːb) *vb* (*tr; often passive*) **1** to disturb the composure of; trouble. **2** to throw into disorder. **3** *Physics, astron.* to cause (a planet, electron, etc.) to undergo a perturbation. [C14: from OF *pertourber,* from L *perturbāre* to confuse, from *per-* (intensive) + *turbāre* to agitate]
▸**perˈturbable** *adj* ▸**perˈturbing** *adj*

perturbation (ˌpɜːtəˈbeɪʃən) *n* **1** the act of perturbing or the state of being perturbed. **2** a cause of disturbance. **3** *Physics.* a secondary influence on a system that modifies simple behaviour, such as the effect of the other electrons on one electron in an atom. **4** *Astron.* a small continuous deviation in the orbit of a planet or comet, due to the attraction of neighbouring planets.

pertussis (pəˈtʌsɪs) *n* the technical name for **whooping cough.** [C18: NL, from L *per-* (intensive) + *tussis* cough]
▸**perˈtussal** *adj*

Peru Current (pəˈruː) *n* a cold ocean current flowing northwards off the Pacific coast of South America. Also called: **Humboldt Current.**

peruke (pəˈruːk) *n* a wig for men in the 17th and 18th centuries. Also called: **periwig.** [C16: from F *perruque,* from It. *perrucca* wig, from ?]

peruse ⓣ (pəˈruːz) *vb* **peruses, perusing, perused.** (*tr*) **1** to read or examine with care; study. **2** to browse or read in a leisurely way. [C15 (meaning: to use up): from PER- (intensive) + USE]
▸**peˈrusal** *n* ▸**peˈruser** *n*

perv (pɜːv) *Sl.* ◆ *n* **1** a pervert. **2** *Austral.* a lascivious look. ◆ *vb also* **perve.** (*intr*) **3** *Austral.* to behave like a voyeur.

pervade ⓣ (pɜːˈveɪd) *vb* **pervades, pervading, pervaded.** (*tr*) to spread through or throughout, esp. subtly or gradually; permeate. [C17: from L *pervādere,* from *per-* through + *vādere* to go]
▸**pervasion** (pɜːˈveɪʒən) *n* ▸**pervasive** (pɜːˈveɪsɪv) *adj* ▸**perˈvasively** *adv* ▸**perˈvasiveness** *n*

perverse ⓣ (pəˈvɜːs) *adj* **1** deliberately deviating from what is regarded as normal, good, or proper. **2** persistently holding to what is wrong. **3** wayward or contrary; obstinate. [C14: from OF *pervers,* from L *perversus* turned the wrong way]
▸**perˈversely** *adv* ▸**perˈverseness** *or* **perˈversity** *n*

perversion ⓣ (pəˈvɜːʃən) *n* **1** any abnormal means of obtaining sexual satisfaction. **2** the act of perverting or the state of being perverted. **3** a perverted form or usage.

pervert ⓣ *vb* (pəˈvɜːt). (*tr*) **1** to use wrongly or badly. **2** to interpret wrongly or badly; distort. **3** to lead into deviant or perverted beliefs or behaviour; corrupt. **4** to debase. ◆ *n* (ˈpɜːvɜːt). **5** a person who practises sexual perversion. [C14: from OF *pervertir,* from L *pervertere* to turn the wrong way]
▸**perˈverted** *adj* ▸**perˈverter** *n* ▸**perˈvertible** *adj* ▸**perˈversive** *adj*

pervious (ˈpɜːvɪəs) *adj* **1** able to be penetrated; permeable. **2** receptive to new ideas, etc.; open-minded. [C17: from L *pervius,* from *per-* (through) + *via* a way]
▸ˈ**perviously** *adv* ▸ˈ**perviousness** *n*

pes (peɪz, piːz) *n, pl* **pedes** (ˈpediːz). the technical name for the human **foot.** [C19: NL: foot]

peseta (pəˈseɪtə; *Spanish* peˈseta) *n* the standard monetary unit of Spain, divided into 100 céntimos. [C19: from Sp., dim. of PESO]

pesky (ˈpeskɪ) *adj* **peskier, peskiest.** *US & Canad. inf.* troublesome. [C19: prob. changed from *pesty;* see PEST]
▸ˈ**peskily** *adv* ▸ˈ**peskiness** *n*

peso (ˈpeɪsəʊ; *Spanish* ˈpeso) *n, pl* **pesos** (-səʊz; *Spanish* -sos). the standard monetary unit of Argentina, Chile, Colombia, Cuba, the Dominican Republic, Guinea-Bissau, Mexico, the Philippines, and Uruguay. [C16: from Sp.: weight, from L *pēnsum* something weighed out, from *pendere* to weigh]

pessary (ˈpesərɪ) *n, pl* **pessaries.** *Med.* **1** a device for inserting into the vagina, either as a support for the uterus or (**diaphragm pessary**) as a contraceptive. **2** a vaginal suppository. [C14: from LL *pessārium,* from L *pessum,* from Gk *pessos* plug]

pessimism ⓣ (ˈpesɪˌmɪzəm) *n* **1** the tendency to expect the worst in all things. **2** the doctrine of the ultimate triumph of evil over good. **3** the doctrine that this world is corrupt and that man's sojourn in it is a preparation for some other existence. [C18: from L *pessimus* worst, sup. of *malus* bad]
▸ˈ**pessimist** *n* ▸ˌ**pessiˈmistic** *adj* ▸ˌ**pessiˈmistically** *adv*

pest ⓣ (pest) *n* **1** a person or thing that annoys, esp. by imposing itself when it is not wanted; nuisance. **2** any organism that damages crops, or injures or irritates livestock or man. **3** *Rare.* an epidemic disease. [C16: from L *pestis* plague, from ?]

pester ⓣ (ˈpestə) *vb* (*tr*) to annoy or nag continually. [C16: from OF *empestrer* to hobble (a horse), from Vulgar L *impāstōriāre* (unattested) to use a hobble, ult. from L *pastor* herdsman]

pesticide (ˈpestɪˌsaɪd) *n* a chemical used for killing pests, esp. insects.
▸ˌ**pestiˈcidal** *adj*

pestiferous (peˈstɪfərəs) *adj* **1** *Inf.* troublesome; irritating. **2** breeding, carrying, or spreading infectious disease. **3** corrupting; pernicious. [C16: from L *pestifer,* from *pestis* contagion + *ferre* to bring]

pestilence ⓣ (ˈpestɪləns) *n* **1a** any epidemic of a deadly infectious disease, such as the plague. **1b** such a disease. **2** an evil influence.

pestilent ⓣ (ˈpestɪlənt) *adj* **1** annoying; irritating. **2** highly destructive morally or physically; pernicious. **3** likely to cause epidemic or infec-

THESAURUS

tuous, pushy (*inf.*), sassy (*US inf.*), saucy, smart **2** = **neat**, brisk, dapper, daring, dashing, gay, jaunty, lively, nimble, perky, smart, spirited, sprightly

pertain *vb* **1-3** = **relate**, appertain, apply, be appropriate, bear on, befit, belong, be part of, be relevant, concern, refer, regard

pertinacious *adj* **1, 2** = **determined**, bull-headed, dogged, headstrong, inflexible, intractable, mulish, obdurate, obstinate, persevering, persistent, perverse, pig-headed, relentless, resolute, self-willed, stiff-necked, strong-willed, stubborn, tenacious, unyielding, wilful

pertinent *adj* = **relevant**, admissible, *ad rem*, applicable, apposite, appropriate, apropos, apt, fit, fitting, germane, material, pat, proper, suitable, to the point, to the purpose
Antonyms *adj* discordant, immaterial, inappropriate, incongruous, irrelevant, unfitting, unrelated, unsuitable

pertness *n* **1** = **impudence**, audacity, brashness, brass (*inf.*), bumptiousness, cheek (*inf.*), cheekiness, chutzpah (*US & Canad. inf.*), cockiness, effrontery, forwardness, front, impertinence, insolence, presumption, rudeness, sauciness

perturb *vb* **1** = **disturb**, agitate, alarm, bother, discompose, disconcert, discountenance, disquiet, faze, fluster, ruffle, trouble, unnerve, unsettle, upset, vex, worry **2** = **disorder**, confuse, disarrange, muddle, unsettle

perturbed *adj* **1** = **disturbed**, agitated, alarmed, anxious, disconcerted, disquieted, fearful, flurried, flustered, ill at ease, nervous, restless, shaken, troubled, uncomfortable, uneasy, upset, worried
Antonyms *adj* assured, at ease, comfortable, composed, cool, impassive, relaxed, unperturbed, unruffled

perusal *n* **1, 2** = **read**, browse, check, examination, inspection, look through, scrutiny, study

peruse *vb* **1, 2** = **read**, browse, check, examine, eyeball (*sl.*), inspect, look through, run one's eye over, scan, scrutinize, study, work over

pervade *vb* = **spread through**, affect, charge, diffuse, extend, fill, imbue, infuse, overspread, penetrate, percolate, permeate, suffuse

pervasive *adj* = **widespread**, common, extensive, general, inescapable, omnipresent, permeating, pervading, prevalent, rife, ubiquitous, universal

perverse *adj* **1** = **abnormal**, depraved, deviant, improper, incorrect, unhealthy **3** = **stubborn**, contradictory, contrary, contumacious, cross-grained, cussed (*inf.*), delinquent, disobedient, dogged, headstrong, intractable, intransigent, miscreant, mulish, obdurate, obstinate, pig-headed, rebellious, refractory, stiff-necked, troublesome, unmanageable, unreasonable, unyielding, wayward, wilful, wrong-headed
Antonyms *adj* ≠ **stubborn:** accommodating, agreeable, complaisant, cooperative, flexible, malleable, obedient, obliging

perversion *n* **1** = **deviation**, aberration, abnormality, debauchery, depravity, immorality, kink (*Brit. inf.*), kinkiness (*sl.*), unnaturalness, vice, vitiation, wickedness **2, 3** = **distortion**, corruption, falsification, misinterpretation, misrepresentation, misuse, twisting

perversity *n* **2** = **contrariness**, contradictiveness, contradictoriness, contumacy, frowardness (*arch.*), intransigence, obduracy, refractoriness, waywardness, wrong-headedness

pervert *vb* **1, 2** = **distort**, abuse, falsify, garble, misconstrue, misinterpret, misrepresent, misuse, twist, warp **3, 4** = **corrupt**, debase, debauch, degrade, deprave, desecrate, initiate, lead astray, subvert ◆ *n* **5** = **deviant**, debauchee, degenerate, weirdo *or* weirdie (*inf.*)

perverted *adj* **2-4** = **unnatural**, aberrant, abnormal, corrupt, debased, debauched, depraved, deviant, distorted, evil, immoral, impaired, kinky (*sl.*), misguided, sick, twisted, unhealthy, vicious, vitiated, warped, wicked

pessimism *n* **1** = **gloominess**, cynicism, dejection, depression, despair, despondency, distrust, gloom, gloomy outlook, glumness, hopelessness, melancholy, the hump (*Brit. inf.*)

pessimist *n* **1** = **wet blanket** (*inf.*), cynic, defeatist, doomster, gloom merchant (*inf.*), killjoy, melancholic, misanthrope, prophet of doom, worrier

pessimistic *adj* **1** = **gloomy**, bleak, cynical, dark, dejected, depressed, despairing, despondent, distrustful, downhearted, fatalistic, foreboding, glum, hopeless, melancholy, misanthropic, morose, resigned, sad
Antonyms *adj* assured, bright, buoyant, cheerful, cheery, encouraged, exhilarated, hopeful, in good heart, optimistic, sanguine

pest *n* **1** = **nuisance**, annoyance, bane, bore, bother, drag (*inf.*), gall, irritation, pain (*inf.*), pain in the neck (*inf.*), thorn in one's flesh, trial, vexation **2** = **infection**, bane, blight, bug, curse, epidemic, pestilence, plague, scourge

pester *vb* = **annoy**, aggravate (*inf.*), badger, bedevil, bother, bug (*inf.*), chivvy, disturb, fret, get at (*inf.*), harass, harry, hassle (*inf.*), irk, nag, pick on, plague, ride (*inf.*), torment, worry

pestilence *n* **1** = **plague**, Black Death, epidemic, pandemic, visitation **2** = **affliction**, bane, blight, cancer, canker, curse, scourge

pestilent *adj* **1** = **annoying**, bothersome, galling, irksome, irritating, plaguy (*inf.*), tiresome, vexing **2** = **harmful**, corrupting, deleterious, destructive, detrimental, evil, injurious, perni-

tious disease. [C15: from L *pestilens* unwholesome, from *pestis* plague]
▸ **'pestilently** *adv* ▸**pestilential** (ˌpɛstɪ'lɛnʃəl) *adj* ▸**ˌpesti'lentially** *adv*

pestle ('pɛsᵊl) *n* **1** a club-shaped instrument for mixing or grinding substances in a mortar. **2** a tool for pounding or stamping. ◆ *vb* **pestles, pestling, pestled. 3** to pound (a substance or object) with or as if with a pestle. [C14: from OF *pestel,* from L *pistillum*]

pesto ('pɛstəʊ) *n* a sauce for pasta, consisting of basil leaves, nuts, garlic, oil, and Parmesan cheese, all crushed together. [It., shortened form of *pestato,* p.p. of *pestare* to pound, crush]

pet[1] **T** (pɛt) *n* **1** a tame animal kept for companionship, amusement, etc. **2** a person who is fondly indulged; favourite: *teacher's pet.* ◆ *adj* **3** kept as a pet: *a pet dog.* **4** of or for pet animals: *pet food.* **5** particularly cherished: *a pet hatred.* **6** familiar or affectionate: *a pet name.* ◆ *vb* **pets, petting, petted. 7** (*tr*) to treat (a person, animal, etc.) as a pet; pamper. **8** (*tr*) to pat or fondle (an animal, child, etc.). **9** (*intr*) *Inf.* (of two people) to caress each other in an erotic manner. [C16: from ?]
▸ **'petter** *n*

pet[2] **T** (pɛt) *n* a fit of sulkiness, esp. at what is felt to be a slight; pique. [C16: from ?]

PET (pɛt) *n acronym for* positron emission tomography.

Pet. *Bible. abbrev. for* Peter.

peta- *prefix* denoting 10^{15}: *petametres.* Symbol: P [C20: so named because it is the SI prefix after TERA-; on the model of PENTA-, the prefix after TETRA-]

petal ('pɛtᵊl) *n* any of the separate parts of the corolla of a flower: often brightly coloured. [C18: from NL *petalum,* from Gk *petalon* leaf]
▸ **'petaline** *adj* ▸ **'petalled** *adj* ▸ **'petal-ˌlike** *adj*

-petal *adj combining form.* seeking: *centripetal.* [from NL *-petus,* from L *petere* to seek]

petard (pɪ'tɑːd) *n* **1** (formerly) a device containing explosives used to breach a wall, doors, etc. **2 hoist with one's own petard.** being the victim of one's own schemes, etc. [C16: from F: firework, from *péter* to break wind, from L *pēdere*]

petaurist (pət'ɒrɪst) *n* another name for **flying phalanger.** [C19: from L, from Gk *petauristēs* performer on the springboard]

petcock ('pɛtˌkɒk) *n* a small valve for checking the water content of a steam boiler or draining waste from the cylinder of a steam engine. [C19: from PET[1] or ? F *pet,* from *péter* to break wind + COCK[1]]

petechia (pɪ'tiːkɪə) *n, pl* **petechiae** (-kɪˌiː). a minute discoloured spot on the surface of the skin. [C18: via NL from It. *petecchia* freckle, from ?]
▸**pe'techial** *adj*

peter[1] **T** ('piːtə) *vb* (*intr;* foll. by *out* or *away*) to fall (off) in volume, intensity, etc., and finally cease. [C19: from ?]

peter[2] ('piːtə) *n Sl.* **1** a safe, till, or cashbox. **2** a prison cell. [C17 (meaning a case): from the name *Peter*]

peterman ('piːtəmən) *n, pl* **petermen.** *Sl.* a burglar skilled in safe-breaking. [C19: from PETER[2]]

Peter Pan *n* a youthful, boyish, or immature man. [C20: after the main character in *Peter Pan* (1904), a play by J. M. Barrie]

Peter Principle *n* **the.** the theory, usually taken facetiously, that all members in a hierarchy rise to their own level of incompetence. [C20: from the book *The Peter Principle* (1969) by Dr Lawrence J. *Peter* and Raymond Hull]

petersham ('piːtəʃəm) *n* **1** a thick corded ribbon used to stiffen belts, etc. **2** a heavy woollen fabric used for coats, etc. **3** a kind of overcoat made of such fabric. [C19: after Viscount *Petersham* (died 1851), E army officer]

Peter's pence *or* **Peter pence** *n* **1** an annual tax, originally of one penny, formerly levied for the maintenance of the Papal See: abolished by Henry VIII in 1534. **2** a voluntary contribution made by Roman Catholics in many countries for the same purpose. [C13: referring to St *Peter,* considered as the first pope]

Peters' projection *n* a form of modified Mercator's map projection that gives prominence to Third World countries. [C20: after Arno *Peters,* G historian]

pethidine ('pɛθɪˌdiːn) *n* a white crystalline water-soluble drug used as an analgesic. [C20: ? a blend of PIPERIDINE + ETHYL]

petiole ('pɛtɪˌəʊl) *n* **1** the stalk by which a leaf is attached to the plant. **2** *Zool.* a slender stalk or stem, as between the thorax and abdomen of ants. [C18: via F from L *petiolus* little foot, from *pēs* foot]
▸**petiolate** ('pɛtɪəˌleɪt) *adj*

petit ('pɛtɪ) *adj* (*prenominal*) *Chiefly law.* of lesser importance; small. [C14: from OF: little, from ?]

petit bourgeois ('bʊəʒwɑː) *n, pl* **petits bourgeois** ('bʊəʒwɑːz). **1** Also called: **petite bourgeoisie, petty bourgeoisie.** the section of the middle class with the lowest social status, as shopkeepers, lower clerical staff, etc. **2** a member of this stratum. ◆ *adj* **3** of, relating to, or characteristic of the petit bourgeois, esp. indicating a sense of self-righteousness and conformity to established standards of behaviour.

petite **T** (pə'tiːt) *adj* (of a woman) small, delicate, and dainty. [C18: from F, fem of *petit* small]

petit four (fɔː) *n, pl* **petits fours** (fɔːz). any of various very small fancy cakes and biscuits. [F, lit.: little oven]

petition **T** (pɪ'tɪʃən) *n* **1** a written document signed by a large number of people demanding some form of action from a government or other authority. **2** any formal request to a higher authority; entreaty. **3** *Law.* a formal application in writing made to a court asking for some specific judicial action: *a petition for divorce.* **4** the action of petitioning. ◆ *vb* **5** (*tr*) to address or present a petition to (a person in authority, government, etc.): *to petition Parliament.* **6** (*intr;* foll. by *for*) to seek by petition: *to petition for a change in the law.* [C14: from L *petītiō,* from *petere* to seek]
▸**pe'titionary** *adj*

petitioner (pɪ'tɪʃənə) *n* **1** a person who presents a petition. **2** *Chiefly Brit.* the plaintiff in a divorce suit.

petitio principii (pɪ'tɪʃɪˌəʊ prɪn'kɪpɪˌaɪ) *n Logic.* a form of fallacious reasoning in which the conclusion has been assumed in the premises; begging the question. [C16: L, translation of Gk *to en arkhei aiteisthai* an assumption at the beginning]

petit jury *n* a jury of 12 persons empanelled to determine the facts of a case and decide the issue pursuant to the direction of the court on points of law. Also called: **petty jury.**
▸**petit juror** *n*

petit larceny *n* (formerly, in England) the stealing of property valued at 12 pence or under. Abolished 1827. Also called: **petty larceny.**

petit mal (mæl) *n* a mild form of epilepsy characterized by periods of impairment or loss of consciousness for up to 30 seconds. Cf. **grand mal.** [C19: F: little illness]

petit point ('pɛtɪ 'pɔɪnt; *French* pəti pwɛ̃) *n* **1** a small diagonal needlepoint stitch used for fine detail. **2** work done with such stitches. [F: small point]

Petrarchan sonnet (pɛ'trɑːkən) *n* a sonnet form associated with the Italian poet Petrarch (1304–74), having an octave rhyming a b b a a b b a and a sestet rhyming either c d e c d e or c d c d c d.

petrel ('pɛtrəl) *n* any of a family of oceanic birds having a hooked bill and tubular nostrils: includes albatrosses, storm petrels, and shearwaters. [C17: var. of earlier *pitteral,* associated by folk etymology with St *Peter,* because the bird appears to walk on water]

Petri dish ('pɛtrɪ) *n* a shallow dish, often with a cover, used in laboratories, esp. for producing cultures of microorganisms. [C19: after J. R. *Petri* (1852–1921), G bacteriologist]

petrifaction (ˌpɛtrɪ'fækʃən) *or* **petrification** (ˌpɛtrɪfɪ'keɪʃən) *n* **1** the act or process of forming petrified organic material. **2** the state of being petrified.

petrify **T** ('pɛtrɪˌfaɪ) *vb* **petrifies, petrifying, petrified. 1** (*tr; often passive*) to convert (organic material) into a fossilized form by impregnation with dissolved minerals so that the original appearance is preserved. **2** to make or become dull, unresponsive, etc.; deaden. **3** (*tr; often passive*) to stun or daze with horror, fear, etc. [C16: from F *pétrifier,* ult. from Gk *petra* stone]
▸ **'petriˌfier** *n*

petro- *or before a vowel* **petr-** *combining form.* **1** indicating stone or rock: *petrology.* **2** indicating petroleum, its products, etc.: *petrochemical.* **3** of or relating to the production, export, or sale of petroleum: *petrostate.* [from Gk *petra* rock or *petros* stone]

petrochemical (ˌpɛtrəʊ'kɛmɪkᵊl) *n* **1** any substance, such as acetone or ethanol, obtained from petroleum. ◆ *adj* **2** of, concerned with, or obtained from petrochemicals or related to petrochemistry.
▸ **ˌpetro'chemistry** *n*

petrodollar ('pɛtrəʊˌdɒlə) *n* money earned by a country by the exporting of petroleum.

petroglyph ('pɛtrəˌglɪf) *n* a drawing or carving on rock, esp. a prehistoric one. [C19: via F from Gk *petra* stone + *gluphē* carving]

petrography (pɛ'trɒgrəfɪ) *n* the branch of petrology concerned with the description and classification of rocks.
▸**pe'trographer** *n* ▸**petrographic** (ˌpɛtrə'græfɪk) *or* **ˌpetro'graphical** *adj*

petrol ('pɛtrəl) *n* any one of various volatile flammable liquid mixtures of hydrocarbons, obtained from petroleum and used as a solvent and

THESAURUS

cious, ruinous, vicious **3** = **contaminated**, catching, contagious, diseased, disease-ridden, infected, infectious, plague-ridden, tainted

pestilential *adj* **2** = **deadly**, dangerous, deleterious, destructive, detrimental, evil, foul, harmful, hazardous, injurious, pernicious, ruinous **3** = **contaminated**, catching, contagious, disease-ridden, infectious, malignant, noxious, pestiferous, poisonous, venomous

pet[1] *n* **2** = **favourite**, apple of one's eye, blue-eyed boy (*inf.*), darling, fave (*inf.*), idol, jewel, treasure ◆ *adj* **3** = **tame**, domesticated, house, house-broken, house-trained (*Brit.*), trained **5** = **favourite**, cherished, dearest, dear to one's heart, fave (*inf.*), favoured, particular, preferred, special ◆ *vb* **7** = **pamper**, baby, coddle, cosset, mollycoddle, spoil **8** = **fondle**, caress, pat, stroke **9** *Informal* = **cuddle**, canoodle (*sl.*), kiss, neck (*inf.*), smooch (*inf.*), snog (*Brit. sl.*)

pet[2] *n* = **sulk**, bad mood, bate (*Brit. sl.*), huff, ill temper, miff (*inf.*), paddy (*Brit. inf.*), paddywhack (*Brit. inf.*), pique, pout, sulks, tantrum, temper

peter[1] *vb, foll. by* **out** *or* **away** = **die out**, come to nothing, dwindle, ebb, evaporate, fade, fail, give out, run dry, run out, stop, taper off, wane

petite *adj* = **small**, dainty, delicate, dinky (*Brit. inf.*), elfin, little, slight

petition *n* **1, 2** = **appeal**, address, application, entreaty, invocation, memorial, plea, prayer, request, round robin, solicitation, suit, supplication ◆ *vb* **5** = **appeal**, adjure, ask, beg, beseech, call upon, crave, entreat, plead, pray, press, solicit, sue, supplicate, urge

petrified *adj* **1** = **fossilized**, ossified, rocklike **3** = **terrified**, aghast, appalled, dazed, dumbfounded, frozen, horrified, numb, scared stiff, shocked, speechless, stunned, stupefied, terror-stricken

petrify *vb* **1** = **fossilize**, calcify, harden, set, solidify, turn to stone **3** = **terrify**, amaze, appal, astonish, astound, confound, dumbfound,

a fuel for internal-combustion engines. US and Canad. name: **gasoline.** [C16: via F from Med. L PETROLEUM]

petrolatum (ˌpetrəˈleɪtəm) *n* a translucent gelatinous substance obtained from petroleum; used as a lubricant and in medicine as an ointment base. Also called: **petroleum jelly.**

petrol bomb *n* **1** a device filled with petrol that bursts into flames on impact. ◆ *vb* **petrol-bomb.** (*tr*) **2** to attack with petrol bombs.

petrol engine *n* an internal-combustion engine that uses petrol as fuel.

petroleum (pəˈtrəʊlɪəm) *n* a dark-coloured thick flammable crude oil occurring in sedimentary rocks, consisting mainly of hydrocarbons. Fractional distillation separates the crude oil into petrol, paraffin, diesel oil, lubricating oil, etc. Fuel oil, paraffin wax, asphalt, and carbon black are extracted from the residue. [C16: from Med. L, from L *petra* stone + *oleum* oil]

petroleum jelly *n* another name for **petrolatum.**

petrology (pɛˈtrɒlədʒɪ) *n, pl* **petrologies.** the study of the composition, origin, structure, and formation of rocks.
▸**petrological** (ˌpetrəˈlɒdʒɪkᵊl) *adj* ▸**peˈtrologist** *n*

petrol station *n Brit.* another term for **filling station.**

petrous (ˈpetrəs, ˈpiː-) *adj Anat.* denoting the dense part of the temporal bone that surrounds the inner ear. [C16: from L *petrōsus* full of rocks]
▸**petrosal** (pɛˈtrəʊsᵊl) *adj*

petticoat (ˈpetɪˌkəʊt) *n* **1** a woman's underskirt. **2** *Inf.* **2a** a humorous or mildly disparaging name for a woman. **2b** (*as modifier*): *petticoat politics.* [C15: see PETTY, COAT]

pettifogger (ˈpetɪˌfɒgə) *n* **1** a lawyer who conducts unimportant cases, esp. one who resorts to trickery. **2** any person who quibbles. [C16: from PETTY + *fogger,* from ?, perhaps from *Fugger,* a family (C15–16) of G financiers]
▸**ˈpettiˌfoggery** *n* ▸**ˈpettiˌfog** *vb* **ˈpettiˌfogs, ˈpettiˌfogging, ˈpettiˌfogged.** (*intr*) ▸**ˈpettiˌfogging** *adj*

pettish **T** (ˈpetɪʃ) *adj* peevish; petulant. [C16: from PET[2]]
▸**ˈpettishly** *adv* ▸**ˈpettishness** *n*

petty **T** (ˈpetɪ) *adj* **pettier, pettiest. 1** trivial; trifling: *petty details.* **2** narrow-minded, mean: *petty spite.* **3** minor or subordinate in rank: *petty officialdom.* **4** *Law.* a variant of **petit.** [C14: from OF PETIT]
▸**ˈpettily** *adv* ▸**ˈpettiness** *n*

petty cash *n* a small cash fund for minor incidental expenses.

petty jury *n* a variant of **petit jury.**

petty larceny *n* a variant of **petit larceny.**

petty officer *n* a noncommissioned officer in a naval service comparable in rank to a sergeant in an army or marine corps.

petty sessions *n* (*functioning as sing or pl*) another term for **magistrates' court.**

petulant **T** (ˈpetjʊlənt) *adj* irritable, impatient, or sullen in a peevish or capricious way. [C16: via OF from L *petulāns* bold, from *petulāre* (unattested) to attack playfully, from *petere* to assail]
▸**ˈpetulance** *or* **ˈpetulancy** *n* ▸**ˈpetulantly** *adv*

petunia (pɪˈtjuːnɪə) *n* any plant of a tropical American genus cultivated for their colourful funnel-shaped flowers. [C19: via NL from obs. F *petun* variety of tobacco, from Tupi *petyn*]

petuntse (pɪˈtʌntsɪ, -ˈtʊn-) *n* a fusible mineral used in hard-paste porcelain. [C18: from Chinese, from *pe* white + *tun* heap + *tzu* offspring]

pew (pjuː) *n* **1** (in a church) **1a** one of several long benchlike seats with backs, used by the congregation. **1b** an enclosed compartment reserved for the use of a family or other small group. **2** *Brit. inf.* a seat (esp. in **take a pew**). [C14 *pywe,* from OF, from L *podium* a balcony, from Gk *podion* supporting structure, from *pous* foot]

pewit *or* **peewit** (ˈpiːwɪt) *n* other names for **lapwing.** [C13: imit. of the bird's cry]

pewter (ˈpjuːtə) *n* **1a** any of various alloys containing tin, lead, and sometimes copper and antimony. **1b** (*as modifier*): *pewter ware; a pewter tankard.* **2** plate or kitchen utensils made from pewter. [C14: from OF *peaultre,* from ?]
▸**ˈpewterer** *n*

peyote (peɪˈəʊtɪ, pɪ-) *n* another name for **mescal** (the plant). [Mexican Sp., from Nahuatl *peyotl*]

pF *abbrev. for* picofarad.

pf. *abbrev for:* **1** perfect. **2** Also: **pfg.** pfennig. **3** preferred.

pfennig (ˈfenɪg; *German* ˈpfenɪç) *n, pl* **pfennigs** *or* **pfennige** (*German* -nɪgə). a German monetary unit worth one hundredth of a Deutschmark. [G: PENNY]

PFI (in Britain) *abbrev. for* Private Finance Initiative.

PG *symbol for* a film certified for viewing by anyone, but which contains scenes that may be unsuitable for children, for whom parental guidance is necessary. [C20: from abbrev. of *parental guidance*]

pg. *abbrev. for* page.

Pg. *abbrev. for:* **1** Portugal. **2** Portuguese.

PGR *abbrev. for* psychogalvanic response.

pH *n* potential of hydrogen; a measure of the acidity or alkalinity of a solution. Pure water has a pH of 7, acid solutions have a pH less than 7, and alkaline solutions a pH greater than 7.

phacelia (fæˈsiːlɪə) *n* any of a genus of N American plants having clusters of blue flowers. [NL from Gk *phakelos* a cluster]

phaeton (ˈfeɪtᵊn) *n* a light four-wheeled horse-drawn carriage with or without a top. [C18: from F, from L, from Gk *Phaethon* son of Helios (the sun god), who borrowed his father's chariot]

-phage *n combining form.* indicating something that eats or consumes something specified: *bacteriophage.* [from Gk *-phagos;* see PHAGO-]
▸**-phagous** *adj combining form.*

phago- *or before a vowel* **phag-** *combining form.* eating, consuming, or destroying: *phagocyte.* [from Gk *phagein* to consume]

phagocyte (ˈfægəˌsaɪt) *n* a cell or protozoan that engulfs particles, such as microorganisms.
▸**phagocytic** (ˌfægəˈsɪtɪk) *adj*

phagocytosis (ˌfægəsaɪˈtəʊsɪs) *n* the process by which a cell, such as a white blood cell, ingests microorganisms, other cells, etc.

-phagy *or* **-phagia** *n combining form.* indicating an eating or devouring: *anthropophagy.* [from Gk *-phagia;* see PHAGO-]

phalange (ˈfælændʒ) *n, pl* **phalanges** (fæˈlændʒiːz). *Anat.* another name for **phalanx** (sense 4). [C16: via F, ult. from Gk PHALANX]

phalangeal (fəˈlændʒɪəl) *adj Anat.* of or relating to a phalanx or phalanges.

phalanger (fəˈlændʒə) *n* any of various Australasian arboreal marsupials having dense fur and a long tail. Also called (Austral. and NZ): **possum.** See also **flying phalanger.** [C18: via NL from Gk *phalaggion* spider's web, referring to its webbed hind toes]

phalanx (ˈfælæŋks) *n, pl* **phalanxes** *or* **phalanges** (fæˈlændʒiːz). **1** an ancient Greek and Macedonian battle formation of hoplites presenting long spears from behind a wall of overlapping shields. **2** any closely ranked unit or mass of people: *the police formed a phalanx to protect the embassy.* **3** a number of people united for a common purpose. **4** *Anat.* any of the bones of the fingers or toes. **5** *Bot.* a bundle of stamens. [C16: via L from Gk: infantry formation in close ranks, bone of finger or toe]

phalarope (ˈfæləˌrəʊp) *n* any of a family of aquatic shore birds of northern oceans and lakes, having a long slender bill and lobed toes. [C18: via F from NL *Phalaropus,* from Gk *phalaris* coot + *pous* foot]

phallic (ˈfælɪk) *adj* **1** of, relating to, or resembling a phallus: *a phallic symbol.* **2** *Psychoanal.* relating to a stage of psychosexual development during which a male child's interest is concentrated on the genital organs. **3** of or relating to phallicism.

phallicism (ˈfælɪˌsɪzəm) *or* **phallism** *n* the worship or veneration of the phallus.

phallus (ˈfæləs) *n, pl* **phalluses** *or* **phalli** (-laɪ). **1** another word for **penis. 2** an image of the male sexual organ, esp. as a symbol of reproductive power. [C17: via LL from Gk *phallos*]

-phane *n combining form.* indicating something resembling a specified substance: *cellophane.* [from Gk *phainein* to shine, appear]

phanerogam (ˈfænərəʊˌgæm) *n* any plant of a former major division which included all seed-bearing plants; a former name for **spermatophyte.** [C19: from NL *phanerogamus,* from Gk *phaneros* visible + *gamos* marriage]
▸ˌ**phaneroˈgamic** *or* **phanerogamous** (ˌfænəˈrɒgəməs) *adj*

phantasm **T** (ˈfæntæzəm) *n* **1** a phantom. **2** an illusory perception of an object, person, etc. [C13: from OF *fantasme,* from L *phantasma,* from Gk]
▸**phanˈtasmal** *or* **phanˈtasmic** *adj*

phantasmagoria **T** (ˌfæntæzməˈgɔːrɪə) *or* **phantasmagory** (fænˈtæzməgərɪ) *n* **1** *Psychol.* a shifting medley of real or imagined figures, as in a dream. **2** *Films.* a sequence of pictures made to vary in size rapidly. **3** a shifting scene composed of different elements. [C19: prob. from F, from PHANTASM + *-agorie,* ?from Gk *ageirein* to gather together]
▸**phantasmagoric** (ˌfæntæzməˈgɒrɪk) *or* ˌ**phantasmaˈgorical** *adj*

phantasy **T** (ˈfæntəsɪ) *n, pl* **phantasies.** an archaic spelling of **fantasy.**

phantom **T** (ˈfæntəm) *n* **1a** an apparition or spectre. **1b** (*as modifier*): *a phantom army marching through the sky.* **2** the visible representation of something abstract, esp. as in a dream or hallucination: *phantoms of*

THESAURUS

horrify, immobilize, paralyse, stun, stupefy, transfix

pettish *adj* = **peevish**, cross, fractious, fretful, grumpy, huffy, ill-humoured, irritable, liverish, petulant, querulous, sulky, tetchy, thin-skinned, touchy, waspish

petty *adj* **1** = **trivial**, contemptible, inconsiderable, inessential, inferior, insignificant, little, measly (*inf.*), negligible, paltry, piddling (*inf.*), slight, small, trifling, unimportant **2** = **small-minded**, cheap, grudging, mean, mean-minded, shabby, spiteful, stingy, ungenerous **3** = **minor**, inferior, junior, lesser, lower, secondary, subordinate

Antonyms *adj* ≠ **trivial:** consequential, considerable, essential, important, major, momentous, significant ≠ **small-minded:** broad-minded, generous, liberal, magnanimous, open-minded, tolerant

petulance *n* = **sulkiness**, bad temper, crabbiness, ill humour, irritability, peevishness, pettishness, pique, pouts, querulousness, spleen, sullenness, waspishness

petulant *adj* = **sulky**, bad-tempered, captious, cavilling, crabbed, cross, crusty, fault-finding, fretful, huffy, ill-humoured, impatient, irritable, moody, peevish, perverse, pouting, querulous, snappish, sour, sullen, ungracious, waspish

Antonyms *adj* affable, cheerful, congenial, easy-going, even-tempered, good-humoured, good-natured, happy, patient, smiling

phantasm *n* **1** = **phantom**, apparition, eidolon, ghost, revenant, shade (*literary*), spectre, spirit, spook (*inf.*), wraith **2** = **illusion**, chimera, figment, figment of the imagination, hallucination, vision

phantasmagoric *adj* **1** = **illusory**, chimerical, dreamlike, hallucinatory, Kafkaesque, kaleidoscopic, nightmarish, phantasmal, psychedelic, surreal, unreal

phantasy *see* **fantasy**

phantom *n* **1** = **spectre**, apparition, eidolon,

evil haunted his sleep. **3** something apparently unpleasant or horrific that has no material form. [C13: from OF *fantosme,* from L *phantasma*]

phantom limb *n* the illusion that a limb still exists following its amputation, sometimes with the sensation of pain (**phantom limb pain**).

phantom pregnancy *n* the occurrence of signs of pregnancy, such as enlarged abdomen and absence of menstruation, when no embryo is present, due to hormonal imbalance. Also called: **false pregnancy.**

-phany *n combining form.* indicating a manifestation: *theophany.* [from Gk *-phania,* from *phainein* to show]
▸**-phanous** *adj combining form.*

phar., Phar., pharm., *or* **Pharm.** *abbrev. for:* **1** pharmaceutical. **2** pharmacist. **3** pharmacopoeia. **4** pharmacy.

Pharaoh ('fɛərəʊ) *n* the title of the ancient Egyptian kings. [OE *Pharaon,* via L, Gk, & Heb., ult. from Egyptian *pr-'o* great house]
▸**Pharaonic** (fɛə'rɒnɪk) *adj*

Pharisaic (ˌfærɪ'seɪɪk) *or* **Pharisaical** *adj* **1** *Judaism.* of, relating to, or characteristic of the Pharisees or Pharisaism. **2** (*often not cap.*) righteously hypocritical.
▸ˌ**Phari'saically** *adv*

Pharisaism ('færɪseɪˌɪzəm) *or* **Phariseeism** ('færɪsiːˌɪzəm) *n* **1** *Judaism.* the tenets and customs of the Pharisees. **2** (*often not cap.*) observance of the external forms of religion without genuine belief; hypocrisy.

Pharisee ⓣ ('færɪˌsiː) *n* **1** a member of an ancient Jewish sect teaching strict observance of Jewish traditions. **2** (*often not cap.*) a self-righteous or hypocritical person. [OE *Farīsēus,* ult. from Aramaic *perīshāiyā,* pl. of *perīsh* separated]

pharmaceutical (ˌfɑːmə'sjuːtɪk°l) *or* (*less commonly*) **pharmaceutic** *adj* of or relating to drugs or pharmacy. [C17: from LL *pharmaceuticus,* from Gk *pharmakeus* purveyor of drugs; see PHARMACY]
▸ˌ**pharma'ceutically** *adv*

pharmaceutics (ˌfɑːmə'sjuːtɪks) *n* **1** (*functioning as sing*) another term for **pharmacy** (sense 1). **2** pharmaceutical remedies.

pharmacist ('fɑːməsɪst) *n* a person qualified to prepare and dispense drugs.

pharmaco- *combining form.* indicating drugs: *pharmacology.* [from Gk *pharmakon* drug]

pharmacognosy (ˌfɑːmə'kɒgnəsɪ) *n* the study of crude drugs of plant and animal origin. [C19: from PHARMACO- + *gnosy,* from Gk *gnosis* knowledge]
▸ˌ**pharma'cognosist** *n*

pharmacology (ˌfɑːmə'kɒlədʒɪ) *n* the science or study of drugs, including their characteristics, action, and uses.
▸**pharmacological** (ˌfɑːməkə'lɒdʒɪk°l) *adj* ▸ˌ**pharmaco'logically** *adv*
▸ˌ**pharma'cologist** *n*

pharmacopoeia *or US* (*sometimes*) **pharmacopeia** (ˌfɑːməkə'piːə) *n* an authoritative book containing a list of medicinal drugs with their uses, preparation, dosages, formulas, etc. [C17: via NL from Gk *pharmakopoiia* art of preparing drugs, from PHARMACO- + *-poiia,* from *poiein* to make]
▸ˌ**pharmaco'poeial** *adj*

pharmacy ('fɑːməsɪ) *n, pl* **pharmacies. 1** Also: **pharmaceutics.** the practice or art of preparing and dispensing drugs. **2** a dispensary. [C14: from Med. L *pharmacia,* from Gk *pharmakeia* making of drugs, from *pharmakon* drug]

pharos ('fɛərɒs) *n* any marine lighthouse or beacon. [C16: after a large Hellenistic lighthouse on an island off Alexandria in Egypt]

pharyngeal (ˌfærɪn'dʒiːəl) *or* **pharyngal** (fə'rɪŋg°l) *adj* **1** of, relating to, or situated in or near the pharynx. **2** *Phonetics.* pronounced with an articulation in or constriction of the pharynx. [C19: from NL *pharyngeus;* see PHARYNX]

pharyngitis (ˌfærɪn'dʒaɪtɪs) *n* inflammation of the pharynx.

pharynx ('færɪŋks) *n, pl* **pharynges** (fæ'rɪndʒiːz) *or* **pharynxes.** the part of the alimentary canal between the mouth and the oesophagus. [C17: via NL from Gk *pharunx* throat]

phase ⓣ (feɪz) *n* **1** any distinct or characteristic period or stage in a sequence of events: *there were two phases to the resolution.* **2** *Astron.* one of the recurring shapes of the portion of the moon or an inferior planet illuminated by the sun. **3** *Physics.* the fraction of a cycle of a periodic quantity that has been completed at a specific reference time, expressed as an angle. **4** *Physics.* a particular stage in a periodic process or phenomenon. **5 in phase.** (of two waveforms) reaching corresponding phases at the same time. **6 out of phase.** (of two waveforms) not in phase. **7** *Chem.* a distinct state of matter characterized by homogeneous composition and properties and the possession of a clearly defined boundary. **8** *Zool.* a variation in the normal form of an animal, esp. a colour variation, brought about by seasonal or geographical change. ◆ *vb* **phases, phasing, phased.** (*tr*) **9** (*often passive*) to execute, arrange, or introduce gradually or in stages: *the withdrawal was phased over several months.* **10** (sometimes foll. by *with*) to cause (a part, process, etc.) to function or coincide with (another part, etc.): *he tried to phase the intake and output of the machine; he phased the intake with the output.* **11** *Chiefly US.* to arrange (processes, goods, etc.) to be supplied or executed when required. [C19: from NL *phases,* pl. of *phasis,* from Gk: aspect]
▸'**phasic** *adj*

phase in *vb* (*tr, adv*) to introduce in a gradual or cautious manner: *the legislation was phased in over two years.*

phase modulation *n* a type of modulation in which the phase of a radio carrier wave is varied by an amount proportional to the instantaneous amplitude of the modulating signal.

phase out ⓣ *vb* (*tr, adv*) **1** to discontinue or withdraw gradually. ◆ *n* **phase-out. 2** *Chiefly US.* the action or an instance of phasing out: *a phase-out of conventional forces.*

phase rule *n* the principle that in any system in equilibrium the number of degrees of freedom is equal to the number of components less the number of phases plus two.

-phasia *n combining form.* indicating speech disorder of a specified kind: *aphasia.* [from Gk, from *phanai* to speak]
▸**-phasic** *adj and n combining form.*

phatic ('fætɪk) *adj* (of speech) used to establish social contact and to express sociability rather than specific meaning. [C20: from Gk *phat(os)* spoken + -IC]

PhD *abbrev. for* Doctor of Philosophy. Also: **DPhil.**

pheasant ('fɛz°nt) *n* **1** any of various long-tailed gallinaceous birds, having a brightly-coloured plumage in the male: native to Asia but introduced elsewhere. **2** any of various other related birds, including the quails and partridges. **3** *US & Canad.* any of several other gallinaceous birds, esp. the ruffed grouse. [C13: from OF *fesan,* from L *phāsiānus,* from Gk *phasianos ornis* Phasian bird, after the River *Phasis,* in Colchis, an ancient country on the Black Sea]

phellem ('fɛləm) *n Bot.* the technical name for **cork** (sense 4). [C20: from Gk *phellos* cork + PHLOEM]

phenacetin (fɪ'næsɪtɪn) *n* a white crystalline solid used in medicine to relieve pain and fever. Also called: **acetophenetidin.** [C19: from PHENO- + ACETYL + -IN]

pheno- *or before a vowel* **phen-** *combining form.* **1** showing or manifesting: *phenotype.* **2** indicating that a molecule contains benzene rings: *phenobarbitone.* [from Gk *phaino-* shining, from *phainein* to show; its use in a chemical sense is exemplified in *phenol,* so called because orig. prepared from illuminating gas]

phenobarbitone (ˌfiːnəʊ'bɑːbɪˌtəʊn) *or* **phenobarbital** (ˌfiːnəʊ'bɑːbɪt°l) *n* a white crystalline derivative of barbituric acid used as a sedative for treating insomnia and epilepsy.

phenocryst ('fiːnəˌkrɪst, 'fɛn-) *n* any of several large crystals in igneous rocks such as porphyry. [C19: from PHENO- (shining) + CRYSTAL]

phenol ('fiːnɒl) *n* **1** Also called: **carbolic acid.** a white crystalline derivative of benzene, used as an antiseptic and disinfectant and in the manufacture of resins, explosives, and pharmaceuticals. Formula: C_6H_5OH. **2** *Chem.* any of a class of organic compounds whose molecules contain one or more hydroxyl groups bound directly to a carbon atom in an aromatic ring.
▸**phe'nolic** *adj*

phenolic resin *n* any one of a class of resins derived from phenol, used in paints, adhesives, and as thermosetting plastics.

phenology (fɪ'nɒlədʒɪ) *n* the study of recurring phenomena, such as animal migration, esp. as influenced by climatic conditions. [C19: from PHENO(MENON) + -LOGY]
▸**phenological** (ˌfiːnə'lɒdʒɪk°l) *adj* ▸**phe'nologist** *n*

phenolphthalein (ˌfiːnɒl'θeɪliːn, -lɪɪn, -'θæl-) *n* a colourless crystalline compound used in medicine as a laxative and in chemistry as an indicator. [from PHENO- + *phthal-,* short form of NAPHTHALENE + -IN]

phenomena (fɪ'nɒmɪnə) *n* a plural of **phenomenon.**

phenomenal ⓣ (fɪ'nɒmɪn°l) *adj* **1** of or relating to a phenomenon. **2** extraordinary; outstanding; remarkable: *a phenomenal achievement.* **3** *Philosophy.* known or perceived by the senses rather than the mind.
▸**phe'nomenally** *adv*

phenomenalism (fɪ'nɒmɪnəˌlɪzəm) *n Philosophy.* the doctrine that statements about physical objects and the external world can be analysed in terms of possible or actual experiences, and that entities, such as physical objects, are only mental constructions out of phenomenal appearances.
▸**phe'nomenalist** *n, adj*

phenomenology (fɪˌnɒmɪ'nɒlədʒɪ) *n Philosophy.* **1** the movement that concentrates on the detailed description of conscious experience. **2** the science of phenomena as opposed to the science of being.
▸**phenomenological** (fɪˌnɒmɪnə'lɒdʒɪk°l) *adj*

phenomenon ⓣ (fɪ'nɒmɪnən) *n, pl* **phenomena** (-ɪnə) *or* **phenomenons. 1**

THESAURUS

ghost, phantasm, revenant, shade (*literary*), spirit, spook (*inf.*), wraith **3** = **illusion,** chimera, figment, figment of the imagination, hallucination, vision

Pharisee *n* **2** *often not cap.* = **hypocrite,** canter, dissembler, dissimulator, fraud, humbug, phoney *or* phony (*inf.*), pietist, whited sepulchre

phase *n* **1** = **stage,** aspect, chapter, condition, development, juncture, period, point, position, state, step, time

phase out *vb* **1** = **wind down,** axe (*inf.*), close, deactivate, dispose of gradually, ease off, eliminate, pull, pull out, remove, replace, run down, taper off, terminate, wind up, withdraw
Antonyms *vb* activate, begin, create, establish, form, initiate, open, set up, start

phenomenal *adj* **1, 2** = **extraordinary,** exceptional, fantastic, marvellous, miraculous, notable, outstanding, prodigious, remarkable, sensational, singular, stellar (*inf.*), uncommon, unique, unparalleled, unusual, wondrous (*arch. or literary*)
Antonyms *adj* average, common, mediocre, no great shakes (*inf.*), ordinary, poor, run-of-the-mill, second-rate, unexceptional, unremarkable, usual

phenomenon *n* **1** = **occurrence,** circumstance, episode, event, fact, happening, incident **2** = **wonder,** exception, marvel, miracle,

anything that can be perceived as an occurrence or fact by the senses. **2** any remarkable occurrence or person. **3** *Philosophy.* **3a** the object of perception, experience, etc. **3b** (in the writings of Kant (1724–1804), German philosopher) a thing as it appears, as distinguished from its real nature as a thing-in-itself. [C16: via LL from Gk *phainomenon,* from *phainesthai* to appear, from *phainein* to show]

USAGE NOTE Although *phenomena* is often treated as if it were singular, correct usage is to employ *phenomenon* with a singular construction and *phenomena* with a plural: *that is an interesting phenomenon* (not *phenomena*); *several new phenomena were recorded in his notes.*

phenotype ('fiːnəʊˌtaɪp) *n* the physical constitution of an organism as determined by the interaction of its genetic constitution and the environment.
▸**phenotypic** (ˌfiːnəʊ'tɪpɪk) *or* ˌ**pheno'typical** *adj* ▸ˌ**pheno'typically** *adv*

phenyl ('fiːnaɪl, 'fɛnɪl) *n* (*modifier*) of, containing, or consisting of the monovalent group C_6H_5, derived from benzene: *a phenyl group.*

phenylalanine (ˌfiːnaɪl'æləˌniːn) *n* an essential amino acid; a component of proteins.

phenylbutazone (ˌfiːnaɪl'bjuːtəˌzəʊn) *n* an anti-inflammatory drug used in the treatment of rheumatic diseases. [C20: from *(dioxodi)phenylbut(ylpyr)azo(lidi)ne*]

phenylketonuria (ˌfiːnaɪlˌkiːtə'njʊərɪə) *n* a congenital metabolic disorder characterized by the abnormal accumulation of phenylalanine in the body fluids, resulting in mental deficiency. [C20: NL; see PHENYL, KETONE, -URIA]

pheromone ('fɛrəˌməʊn) *n* a chemical substance, secreted externally by certain animals, such as insects, affecting the behaviour of other animals of the same species. [C20 *phero-,* from Gk *pherein* to bear + (HOR)MONE]

phew (fjuː) *interj* an exclamation of relief, surprise, disbelief, weariness, etc.

phi (faɪ) *n, pl* **phis.** the 21st letter in the Greek alphabet, Φ, φ.

phial ('faɪəl) *n* a small bottle for liquids, etc.; vial. [C14: from OF *fiole,* from L *phiola* saucer, from Gk *phialē* wide shallow vessel]

Phi Beta Kappa ('faɪ 'beɪtə 'kæpə, 'biːtə) *n* (in the US) **1** a national honorary society, founded in 1776, membership of which is based on high academic ability. **2** a member of this society. [from the initials of the Gk motto *philosophia biou kubernētēs* philosophy the guide of life]

phil. *abbrev. for:* **1** philharmonic. **2** philosophy.

Phil. *abbrev. for:* **1** Philadelphia. **2** *Bible.* Philippians. **3** Philippines. **4** Philharmonic.

philadelphus (ˌfɪlə'dɛlfəs) *n* any of a N temperate genus of shrubs cultivated for their strongly scented showy flowers. See also **mock orange** (sense 1). [C19: NL, from Gk *philadelphon* mock orange, lit.: loving one's brother]

philander ⓘ (fɪ'lændə) *vb* (*intr;* often foll. by *with*) (of a man) to flirt with women. [C17: from Gk *philandros* fond of men, used as a name for a lover in literary works]
▸**phi'landerer** *n*

philanthropic ⓘ (ˌfɪlən'θrɒpɪk) *or* **philanthropical** *adj* showing concern for humanity, esp. by performing charitable actions, donating money, etc.
▸ˌ**philan'thropically** *adv*

philanthropy ⓘ (fɪ'lænθrəpɪ) *n, pl* **philanthropies. 1** the practice of performing charitable or benevolent actions. **2** love of mankind in general. [C17: from LL *philanthrōpia,* from Gk: love of mankind, from *philos* loving + *anthrōpos* man]
▸**phi'lanthropist** *or* **philanthrope** ('fɪlənˌθrəʊp) *n*

philately (fɪ'lætəlɪ) *n* the collection and study of postage stamps. [C19: from F *philatélie,* from PHILO- + Gk *ateleia* exemption from charges (here referring to stamps)]
▸**philatelic** (ˌfɪlə'tɛlɪk) *adj* ▸ˌ**phila'telically** *adv* ▸**phi'latelist** *n*

-phile *or* **-phil** *n combining form.* indicating a person or thing having a fondness for something specified: *bibliophile.* [from Gk *philos* loving]

Philem. *Bible. abbrev. for* Philemon.

philharmonic (ˌfɪlhɑː'mɒnɪk, ˌfɪlə-) *adj* **1** fond of music. **2** (*cap. when part of a name*) denoting an orchestra, choir, society, etc., devoted to music. ◆ *n* **3** (*cap. when part of a name*) a specific philharmonic choir, orchestra, or society. [C18: from F *philharmonique,* from It. *filarmonico* music-loving]

philhellene (fɪl'hɛliːn) *n* **1** a lover of Greece and Greek culture. **2** *European history.* a supporter of the cause of Greek national independence.
▸**philhellenic** (ˌfɪlhɛ'liːnɪk) *adj*

-philia *n combining form.* **1** indicating a tendency towards: *haemophilia.* **2** indicating an abnormal liking for: *necrophilia.* [from Gk *philos* loving]
▸**-philiac** *n combining form.* ▸**-philous** *or* **-philic** *adj combining form.*

philibeg ('fɪlɪˌbɛg) *n* a variant spelling of **filibeg.**

philippic (fɪ'lɪpɪk) *n* a bitter or impassioned speech of denunciation; invective. [C16: after the orations of Demosthenes, 4th-century orator, against Philip of Macedon (382–336 B.C.)]

Philippine ('fɪlɪˌpiːn) *n, adj* another word for **Filipino.**

Philistine ⓘ ('fɪlɪˌstaɪn) *n* **1** a person who is hostile towards culture, the arts, etc.; a smug boorish person. **2** a member of the non-Semitic people who inhabited ancient Philistia, a country on the coast of SW Palestine. ◆ *adj* **3** (*sometimes not cap.*) boorishly uncultured. **4** of or relating to the ancient Philistines.
▸**Philistinism** ('fɪlɪstɪˌnɪzəm) *n*

phillumenist (fɪ'ljuːmənɪst, -'luː-) *n* a person who collects matchbox labels. [C20: from PHILO- + L *lumen* light + -IST]

philo- *or before a vowel* **phil-** *combining form.* indicating a love of: *philology; philanthropic.* [from Gk *philos* loving]

philodendron (ˌfɪlə'dɛndrən) *n, pl* **philodendrons** *or* **philodendra** (-drə). an evergreen climbing plant of a tropical American genus: cultivated as a house plant. [C19: NL from Gk: lover of trees]

philogyny (fɪ'lɒdʒɪnɪ) *n Rare.* fondness for women. [C17: from Gk *philogunia,* from PHILO- + *gunē* woman]
▸**phi'logynist** *n*

philology (fɪ'lɒlədʒɪ) *n* **1** comparative and historical linguistics. **2** the scientific analysis of written records and literary texts. **3** (no longer in scholarly use) the study of literature. [C17: from L *philologia,* from Gk: love of language]
▸**philological** (ˌfɪlə'lɒdʒɪkəl) *adj* ▸ˌ**philo'logically** *adv* ▸**phi'lologist** *or* (*less commonly*) **phi'lologer** *n*

philomel ('fɪləˌmɛl) *or* **philomela** (ˌfɪləʊ'miːlə) *n* poetic names for a **nightingale.** [C14 *philomene,* via Med. L from L *philomēla,* from Gk]

philoprogenitive (ˌfɪləʊprəʊ'dʒɛnɪtɪv) *adj Rare.* **1** fond of children. **2** producing many offspring.

philos. *abbrev. for:* **1** philosopher. **2** philosophical.

philosopher ⓘ (fɪ'lɒsəfə) *n* **1** a student, teacher, or devotee of philosophy. **2** a person of philosophical temperament, esp. one who is patient, wise, and stoical. **3** (formerly) an alchemist or devotee of occult science.

philosopher's stone *n* a stone or substance thought by alchemists to be capable of transmuting base metals into gold.

philosophical ⓘ (ˌfɪlə'sɒfɪkəl) *or* **philosophic** *adj* **1** of or relating to philosophy or philosophers. **2** reasonable, wise, or learned. **3** calm and stoical, esp. in the face of difficulties or disappointments.
▸ˌ**philo'sophically** *adv*

philosophical analysis *n* a philosophical method in which language and experience are analysed in an attempt to provide new insights into various philosophical problems.

philosophize *or* **philosophise** (fɪ'lɒsəˌfaɪz) *vb* **philosophizes, philosophizing, philosophized** *or* **philosophises, philosophising, philosophised. 1** (*intr*) to make philosophical pronouncements and speculations. **2** (*tr*) to explain philosophically.
▸**phi'losoˌphizer** *or* **phi'losoˌphiser** *n*

philosophy ⓘ (fɪ'lɒsəfɪ) *n, pl* **philosophies. 1** the academic discipline concerned with making explicit the nature and significance of ordinary and scientific beliefs and investigating the intelligibility of concepts by means of rational argument concerning their presuppositions, implications, and interrelationships. **2** the particular doctrines relating to these issues of a specific individual or school: *the philosophy of Descartes.* **3** the basic principles of a discipline: *the philosophy of law.* **4** any system of belief, values, or tenets. **5** a personal

THESAURUS

nonpareil, prodigy, rarity, sensation, sight, spectacle

philander *vb* = **womanize** (*inf.*), coquet, court, dally, flirt, fool around (*inf.*), toy, trifle

philanderer *n* = **womanizer** (*inf.*), Casanova, dallier, Don Juan, flirt, gallant, gay dog, ladies' man, lady-killer (*inf.*), Lothario, playboy, stud (*sl.*), trifler, wolf (*inf.*)

philanthropic *adj* **1** = **humanitarian,** almsgiving, altruistic, beneficent, benevolent, benignant, charitable, eleemosynary, generous, gracious, humane, kind, kind-hearted, munificent, public-spirited
Antonyms *adj* egoistic, mean, miserly, niggardly, penurious, selfish, self-seeking, stingy

philanthropist *n* **1** = **humanitarian,** almsgiver, altruist, benefactor, contributor, donor, giver, patron

philanthropy *n* **1, 2** = **humanitarianism,** almsgiving, altruism, beneficence, benevo-le nce, benignity, bounty, brotherly love, charitableness, charity, generosity, generousness, kind-heartedness, largesse *or* largess, liberality, munificence, open-handedness, patronage, public-spiritedness

Philistine *n* **1** = **boor,** barbarian, bourgeois, Goth, ignoramus, lout, lowbrow, vulgarian, yahoo ◆ *adj* **3** *sometimes not cap.* = **uncultured,** anti-intellectual, boorish, bourgeois, crass, ignorant, inartistic, lowbrow, tasteless, uncultivated, uneducated, unrefined

philosopher *n* **1** = **thinker,** dialectician, logician, mahatma, metaphysician, sage, seeker after truth, theorist, wise man

philosophical *adj* **1, 2** = **rational,** abstract, erudite, learned, logical, sagacious, theoretical, thoughtful, wise **3** = **stoical,** calm, collected, composed, cool, impassive, imperturbable, patient, resigned, sedate, serene, tranquil, unruffled
Antonyms *adj* ≠ **rational:** factual, illogical, irrational, practical, pragmatic, scientific ≠ **stoical:** emotional, hot-headed, impulsive, perturbed, rash, restless, upset

philosophy *n* **1** = **thought,** aesthetics, knowledge, logic, metaphysics, rationalism, reason, reasoning, thinking, wisdom **2-5** = **outlook,** attitude to life, basic idea, beliefs, convictions, doctrine, ideology, principles, tenets, thinking, values, viewpoint, *Weltanschauung,* world view **6** = **stoicism,** calmness, composure, coolness, dispassion, equanimity, resignation, restraint, self-possession, serenity

outlook or viewpoint. **6** serenity of temper. [C13: from OF *filosofie,* from L *philosophia,* from Gk, from *philosophos* lover of wisdom]

-philous *or* **-philic** *adj combining form.* indicating love of or fondness for: *heliophilous.* [from L *-philus,* from Gk *-philos*]

philtre *or US* **philter** ('fɪltə) *n* a drink supposed to arouse desire. [C16: from L *philtrum,* from Gk *philtron* love potion, from *philos* loving]

phimosis (faɪ'məʊsɪs) *n* abnormal tightness of the foreskin, preventing its being retracted. [C17: via NL from Gk: a muzzling]

phiz (fɪz) *n Sl., chiefly Brit.* the face or a facial expression. Also called: **phizog** (fɪ'zɒg). [C17: colloquial shortening of PHYSIOGNOMY]

phlebitis (flɪ'baɪtɪs) *n* inflammation of a vein. [C19: via NL from Gk]
▸**phlebitic** (flɪ'bɪtɪk) *adj*

phlebo- *or before a vowel* **phleb-** *combining form.* indicating a vein: *phlebotomy.* [from Gk *phleps, phleb-* vein]

phlebotomy (flɪ'bɒtəmɪ) *n, pl* **phlebotomies.** surgical incision into a vein. [C14: from OF *flebothomie,* from LL *phlebotomia,* from Gk]

phlegm (flɛm) *n* **1** the viscid mucus secreted by the walls of the respiratory tract. **2** *Arch.* one of the four bodily humours. **3** apathy; stolidity. **4** imperturbability; coolness. [C14: from OF *fleume,* from LL *phlegma,* from Gk: inflammation, from *phlegein* to burn]
▸'**phlegmy** *adj*

phlegmatic ❶ (flɛg'mætɪk) *or* **phlegmatical** *adj* **1** having a stolid or unemotional disposition. **2** not easily excited.
▸**phleg'matically** *adv*

phloem ('fləʊɛm) *n* tissue in higher plants that conducts synthesized food substances to all parts of the plant. [C19: via G from Gk *phloos* bark]

phlogiston (flɒ'dʒɪstɒn, -tən) *n Chem.* a hypothetical substance formerly thought to be present in all combustible materials. [C18: via NL from Gk, from *phlogizein* to set alight]

phlox (flɒks) *n, pl* **phlox** *or* **phloxes.** any of a chiefly North American genus of plants cultivated for their clusters of white, red, or purple flowers. [C18: via L from Gk: a plant of glowing colour, lit.: flame]

phlyctena (flɪk'tiːnə) *n, pl* **phlyctenae** (-niː). *Pathol.* a small blister, vesicle, or pustule. [C17: via NL from Gk *phluktaina,* from *phluzein* to swell]

-phobe *n combining form.* indicating one that fears or hates: *xenophobe.* [from Gk *-phobos* fearing]
▸**-phobic** *adj combining form.*

phobia ❶ ('fəʊbɪə) *n Psychiatry.* an abnormal intense and irrational fear of a given situation, organism, or object. [C19: from Gk *phobos* fear]
▸'**phobic** *adj, n*

-phobia *n combining form.* indicating an extreme abnormal fear of or aversion to: *acrophobia; claustrophobia.* [via L from Gk, from *phobos* fear]
▸**-phobic** *adj combining form.*

phocomelia (ˌfəʊkəʊ'miːlɪə) *n* a congenital deformity characterized esp. by short stubby hands or feet attached close to the body. [C19: via NL from Gk *phōkē* a seal + *melos* a limb]

phoebe ('fiːbɪ) *n* any of several greyish-brown North American flycatchers. [C19: imit.]

Phoenician (fə'nɪʃən, -'niːʃɪən) *n* **1** a member of an ancient Semitic people of NW Syria. **2** the extinct language of this people. ◆ *adj* **3** of Phoenicia, an ancient E Mediterranean maritime country, the Phoenicians, or their language.

phoenix *or US* **phenix** ('fiːnɪks) *n* **1** a legendary Arabian bird said to set fire to itself and rise anew from the ashes every 500 years. **2** a person or thing of surpassing beauty or quality. [OE *fenix,* via L from Gk *phoinix*]

phon (fɒn) *n* a unit of loudness that measures the intensity of a sound by the number of decibels it is above a reference tone. [C20: via G from Gk *phōnē* sound]

phonate (fəʊ'neɪt) *vb* **phonates, phonating, phonated.** (*intr*) to articulate speech sounds, esp. voiced speech sounds. [C19: from Gk *phōnē* voice]
▸**pho'nation** *n*

phone[1] ❶ (fəʊn) *n, vb* **phones, phoning, phoned.** short for **telephone.**

phone[2] (fəʊn) *n Phonetics.* a single speech sound. [C19: from Gk *phōnē* sound, voice]

-phone *combining form.* **1** (*forming nouns*) indicating a device giving off sound: *telephone.* **2** (*forming nouns and adjectives*) (a person) speaking a particular language: *Francophone.* [from Gk *phōnē* voice, sound]
▸**-phonic** *adj combining form.*

phonecard ('fəʊnˌkɑːd) *n* a card used instead of coins to operate certain public telephones.

phone-in *n* **a** a radio or television programme in which listeners' or viewers' questions, comments, etc., are telephoned to the studio and broadcast live as part of a discussion. **b** (*as modifier*): *a phone-in programme.*

phoneme ('fəʊniːm) *n Linguistics.* one of the set of speech sounds in any given language that serve to distinguish one word from another. [C20: via F from Gk *phōnēma* sound, speech]
▸**phonemic** (fə'niːmɪk) *adj*

phonemics (fə'niːmɪks) *n* (*functioning as sing*) that aspect of linguistics concerned with the classification and analysis of the phonemes of a language.
▸**pho'nemicist** *n*

phonetic (fə'nɛtɪk) *adj* **1** of or relating to phonetics. **2** denoting any perceptible distinction between one speech sound and another. **3** conforming to pronunciation: *phonetic spelling.* [C19: from NL *phōnēticus,* from Gk, from *phōnein* to make sounds, speak]
▸**pho'netically** *adv*

phonetics (fə'nɛtɪks) *n* (*functioning as sing*) the science concerned with the study of speech processes, including the production, perception, and analysis of speech sounds.
▸**phonetician** (ˌfəʊnɪ'tɪʃən) *or* **phonetist** ('fəʊnɪtɪst) *n*

phoney ❶ *or esp. US* **phony** ('fəʊnɪ) *Inf.* ◆ *adj* **phonier, phoniest. 1** not genuine; fake. **2** (of a person) insincere or pretentious. ◆ *n, pl* **phoneys** *or esp. US* **phonies. 3** an insincere or pretentious person. **4** something that is not genuine; a fake. [C20: from ?]
▸'**phoneyness** *or esp. US* '**phoniness** *n*

phonics ('fɒnɪks) *n* (*functioning as sing*) **1** an obsolete name for **acoustics** (sense 1). **2** a method of teaching people to read by training them to associate letters with their phonetic values.
▸'**phonic** *adj* ▸'**phonically** *adv*

phono- *or before a vowel* **phon-** *combining form.* indicating a sound or voice: *phonograph; phonology.* [from Gk *phōnē* sound, voice]

phonogram ('fəʊnəˌgræm) *n* any written symbol standing for a sound, syllable, morpheme, or word.
▸ˌ**phono'gramic** *or* ˌ**phono'grammic** *adj*

phonograph ('fəʊnəˌgrɑːf) *n* **1** an early form of gramophone capable of recording and reproducing sound on wax cylinders. **2** another US and Canad. word for **gramophone** or **record player.**

phonography (fəʊ'nɒgrəfɪ) *n* **1** a writing system that represents sounds by individual symbols. **2** the employment of such a writing system.
▸**phonographic** (ˌfəʊnə'græfɪk) *adj*

phonology (fə'nɒlədʒɪ) *n, pl* **phonologies. 1** the study of the sound system of a language or of languages in general. **2** such a sound system.
▸**phonological** (ˌfəʊnə'lɒdʒɪkᵊl, ˌfɒn-) *adj* ▸ˌ**phono'logically** *adv* ▸**pho'nologist** *n*

phonon ('fəʊnɒn) *n Physics.* a quantum of vibrational energy in the acoustic vibrations of a crystal lattice. [C20: from PHONO- + -ON]

-phony *n combining form.* indicating a specified type of sound: *cacophony; euphony.* [from Gk *-phōnia,* from *phōnē* sound]
▸**-phonic** *adj combining form.*

phooey ('fuːɪ) *interj Inf.* an exclamation of scorn, contempt, etc. [C20: prob. var. of PHEW]

-phore *n combining form.* indicating one that bears or produces: *semaphore.* [from NL *-phorus,* from Gk *-phoros* bearing, from *pherein* to bear]
▸**-phorous** *adj combining form.*

-phoresis *n combining form.* indicating a transmission: *electrophoresis.* [from Gk *phorēsis* being carried, from *pherein* to bear]

phormium ('fɔːmɪəm) *n* any of a genus of plants of the lily family with tough leathery evergreen leaves. Also called: **New Zealand flax, flax lily.** [C19: NL from Gk *phormos* basket]

phosgene ('fɒzdʒiːn) *n* a colourless poisonous gas: used in chemical warfare and in the manufacture of pesticides, dyes, and polyurethane resins. [C19: from Gk *phōs* light + *-gene,* var. of -GEN]

phosphate ('fɒsfeɪt) *n* **1** any salt or ester of any phosphoric acid. **2** (*often pl*) any of several chemical fertilizers containing phosphorous compounds. [C18: from F *phosphat;* see PHOSPHORUS, -ATE[1]]
▸**phosphatic** (fɒs'fætɪk) *adj*

phosphatide ('fɒsfəˌtaɪd) *n* another name for **phospholipid.**

phosphatidylcholine (ˌfɒsfæˌtaɪdaɪl'kəʊliːn) *n* the systematic name for **lecithin.**

phosphene ('fɒsfiːn) *n* the sensation of light caused by pressure on the eyelid of a closed eye. [C19: from Gk *phōs* light + *phainein* to show]
▸**phos'phenic** *adj*

phosphide ('fɒsfaɪd) *n* any compound of phosphorus with another element, esp. a more electropositive element.

phosphine ('fɒsfiːn) *n* a colourless flammable gas that is slightly soluble in water and has a strong fishy odour: used as a pesticide. Formula: PH_3.

THESAURUS

phlegmatic *adj* **1, 2** = **unemotional,** apathetic, bovine, cold, dull, frigid, heavy, impassive, indifferent, lethargic, listless, lymphatic, matter-of-fact, placid, sluggish, stoical, stolid, undemonstrative, unfeeling
Antonyms *adj* active, alert, animated, emotional, energetic, excited, hyper (*inf.*), lively, passionate

phobia *n Psychiatry* = **terror,** aversion, detestation, dislike, distaste, dread, fear, hatred, horror, irrational fear, loathing, obsession, overwhelming anxiety, repulsion, revulsion, thing (*inf.*)
Antonyms *n* bent, fancy, fondness, inclination, liking, love, partiality, passion, penchant, soft spot

phone[1] *n* = **telephone,** blower (*inf.*), dog and bone (*sl.*), = **call,** bell (*Brit. sl.*), buzz (*inf.*), ring (*inf., chiefly Brit.*), tinkle (*Brit. inf.*) ◆ *vb* = **call,** buzz (*inf.*), get on the blower (*inf.*), give someone a bell (*Brit. sl.*), give someone a buzz (*inf.*), give someone a call, give someone a ring (*inf., chiefly Brit.*), make a call, ring (up) (*inf., chiefly Brit.*), telephone

phoney *Informal adj* **1** = **fake,** affected, assumed, bogus, counterfeit, ersatz, false, feigned, forged, imitation, pseudo (*inf.*), put-on, sham, spurious, trick ◆ *n* **4** = **fake,** counterfeit, faker, forgery, fraud, humbug, impostor, pretender, sham
Antonyms *adj* ≠ **fake:** authentic, bona fide, genuine, original, real, sincere, unaffected, unassumed, unfeigned

phosphite (ˈfɒsfaɪt) *n* any salt or ester of phosphorous acid.

phospho- *or before a vowel* **phosph-** *combining form.* containing phosphorus: *phosphoric.* [from F, from *phosphore* PHOSPHORUS]

phospholipid (ˌfɒsfəˈlɪpɪd) *n* any of a group of fatty compounds: important constituents of all membranes. Also called: **phosphatide.**

phosphonic acid (fɒsˈfɒnɪk) *n* the systematic name for **phosphorous acid.**

phosphor (ˈfɒsfə) *n* a substance capable of emitting light when irradiated with particles of electromagnetic radiation. [C17: from F, ult. from Gk *phōsphoros* PHOSPHORUS]

phosphorate (ˈfɒsfəˌreɪt) *vb* **phosphorates, phosphorating, phosphorated.** to treat or combine with phosphorus.

phosphor bronze *n* any of various hard corrosion-resistant alloys containing phosphorus: used in gears, bearings, cylinder casings, etc.

phosphoresce (ˌfɒsfəˈrɛs) *vb* **phosphoresces, phosphorescing, phosphoresced.** (*intr*) to exhibit phosphorescence.

phosphorescence (ˌfɒsfəˈrɛsəns) *n* **1** *Physics.* a fluorescence that persists after the bombarding radiation producing it has stopped. **2** the light emitted in phosphorescence. **3** the emission of light in which insufficient heat is evolved to cause fluorescence. Cf. **fluorescence.**
▸ˌ**phosphoˈrescent** *adj*

phosphoric (fɒsˈfɒrɪk) *adj* of or containing phosphorus in the pentavalent state.

phosphoric acid *n* **1** a colourless solid tribasic acid used in the manufacture of fertilizers and soap. Formula: H_3PO_4. Systematic name: **phosphoric(V) acid.** Also called: **orthophosphoric acid. 2** any oxyacid of phosphorus produced by reaction between phosphorus pentoxide and water.

phosphorous (ˈfɒsfərəs) *adj* of or containing phosphorus in the trivalent state.

phosphorous acid *n* **1** a white or yellowish hygroscopic crystalline dibasic acid. Formula: H_3PO_3. Systematic name: **phosphonic acid.** Also called: **orthophosphorous acid. 2** any oxyacid of phosphorus containing less oxygen than the corresponding phosphoric acid.

phosphorus (ˈfɒsfərəs) *n* **1** an allotropic nonmetallic element occurring in phosphates and living matter. Ordinary phosphorus is a toxic flammable phosphorescent white solid; the red form is less reactive and nontoxic: used in matches, pesticides, and alloys. The radioisotope **phosphorus-32 (radiophosphorus),** with a half-life of 14.3 days, is used in radiotherapy and as a tracer. Symbol: P; atomic no.: 15; atomic wt.: 30.974. **2** a less common name for a **phosphor.** [C17: via L from Gk *phōsphoros* light-bringing, from *phōs* light + *pherein* to bring]

Phosphorus (ˈfɒsfərəs) *n* a morning star, esp. Venus.

phossy jaw (ˈfɒsɪ) *n* a gangrenous condition of the lower jawbone caused by prolonged exposure to phosphorus fumes. [C19: *phossy,* colloquial shortening of PHOSPHORUS]

phot (fɒt, fəʊt) *n* a unit of illumination equal to one lumen per square centimetre. 1 phot is equal to 10 000 lux. [C20: from Gk *phōs* light]

phot. *abbrev. for:* **1** photograph. **2** photographic. **3** photography.

photic (ˈfəʊtɪk) *adj* **1** of or concerned with light. **2** designating the zone of the sea where photosynthesis takes place.

photo (ˈfəʊtəʊ) *n, pl* **photos.** short for **photograph.**

photo- *combining form.* **1** of, relating to, or produced by light: *photosynthesis.* **2** indicating a photographic process: *photolithography.* [from Gk *phōs, phōt-* light]

photo call *n* a time arranged for photographers, esp. press photographers, to take pictures of a celebrity.

photocell (ˈfəʊtəʊˌsɛl) *n* a device in which the photoelectric or photovoltaic effect or photoconductivity is used to produce a current or voltage when exposed to light or other electromagnetic radiation. They are used in exposure meters, burglar alarms, etc. Also called: **photoelectric cell, electric eye.**

photochemistry (ˌfəʊtəʊˈkɛmɪstrɪ) *n* the branch of chemistry concerned with the chemical effects of light and other electromagnetic radiations.
▸**photochemical** (ˌfəʊtəʊˈkɛmɪkᵊl) *adj*

photochromic (ˌfəʊtəʊˈkrəʊmɪk) *adj* (of glass) changing colour with the intensity of incident light, used, for example, in sunglasses that darken as the sunlight becomes brighter.

photocomposition (ˌfəʊtəʊˌkɒmpəˈzɪʃən) *n* another name (esp. US and Canad.) for **filmsetting.**

photoconductivity (ˌfəʊtəʊˌkɒndʌkˈtɪvɪtɪ) *n* the change in the electrical conductivity of certain substances, such as selenium, as a result of the absorption of electromagnetic radiation.
▸**photoconductive** (ˌfəʊtəʊkənˈdʌktɪv) *adj* ▸ˌ**photoconˈductor** *n*

photocopier (ˈfəʊtəʊˌkɒpɪə) *n* an instrument using light-sensitive photographic materials to reproduce written, printed, or graphic work.

photocopy (ˈfəʊtəʊˌkɒpɪ) *n, pl* **photocopies. 1** a photographic reproduction of written, printed, or graphic work. ◆ *vb* **photocopies, photocopying, photocopied. 2** to reproduce (written, printed, or graphic work) on photographic material.

photodegradable (ˌfəʊtəʊdɪˈgreɪdəbᵊl) *adj* (of plastic) capable of being decomposed by prolonged exposure to light.

photoelectric (ˌfəʊtəʊɪˈlɛktrɪk) *adj* of or concerned with electric or electronic effects caused by light or other electromagnetic radiation.
▸**photoelectricity** (ˌfəʊtəʊɪlɛkˈtrɪsɪtɪ) *n*

photoelectric cell *n* another name for **photocell.**

photoelectric effect *n* **1** the ejection of electrons from a solid by an incident beam of sufficiently energetic electromagnetic radiation. **2** any phenomenon involving electric current and electromagnetic radiation, such as photoemission.

photoelectron (ˌfəʊtəʊɪˈlɛktrɒn) *n* an electron ejected from an atom, molecule, or solid by an incident photon.

photoemission (ˌfəʊtəʊɪˈmɪʃən) *n* the emission of electrons due to the impact of electromagnetic radiation.

photoengraving (ˌfəʊtəʊɪnˈgreɪvɪŋ) *n* **1** a photomechanical process for producing letterpress printing plates. **2** a plate made by this process. **3** a print made from such a plate.
▸ˌ**photoenˈgrave** *vb (tr)*

photo finish *n* **1** a finish of a race in which contestants are so close that a photograph is needed to decide the result. **2** any race or competition in which the winners are separated by a very small margin.

Photofit (ˈfəʊtəʊˌfɪt) *n Trademark.* **a** a method of combining photographs of facial features, hair, etc., into a composite picture of a face: used by the police to trace suspects, criminals, etc. **b** (*as modifier*): *a Photofit picture.*

photoflash (ˈfəʊtəʊˌflæʃ) *n* another name for **flashbulb.**

photoflood (ˈfəʊtəʊˌflʌd) *n* a highly incandescent tungsten lamp used for indoor photography, television, etc.

photog. *abbrev. for:* **1** photograph. **2** photographer. **3** photographic. **4** photography.

photogenic (ˌfəʊtəˈdʒɛnɪk) *adj* **1** (esp. of a person) having a general facial appearance that looks attractive in photographs. **2** *Biol.* producing or emitting light.
▸ˌ**photoˈgenically** *adv*

photogram (ˈfəʊtəˌgræm) *n* **1** a picture, usually abstract, produced on a photographic material without the use of a camera. **2** *Obs.* a photograph.

photogrammetry (ˌfəʊtəʊˈgræmɪtrɪ) *n* the process of making measurements from photographs, used esp. in the construction of maps from aerial photographs.

photograph ❶ (ˈfəʊtəˌgrɑːf) *n* **1** an image of an object, person, scene, etc., in the form of a print or slide recorded by a camera. Often shortened to **photo.** ◆ *vb* **2** to take a photograph of (an object, person, scene, etc.).

photographic ❶ (ˌfəʊtəˈgræfɪk) *adj* **1** of or relating to photography. **2** like a photograph in accuracy or detail. **3** (of a person's memory) able to retain facts, appearances, etc., in precise detail.
▸ˌ**photoˈgraphically** *adv*

photography (fəˈtɒgrəfɪ) *n* **1** the process of recording images on sensitized material by the action of light, X-rays, etc. **2** the art, practice, or occupation of taking photographs.
▸**phoˈtographer** *n*

photogravure (ˌfəʊtəʊgrəˈvjʊə) *n* **1** any of various methods in which an intaglio plate for printing is produced by the use of photography. **2** matter printed from such a plate. [C19: from PHOTO- + F *gravure* engraving]

photojournalism (ˌfəʊtəʊˈdʒɜːnᵊˌlɪzəm) *n* journalism in which photographs are the predominant feature.
▸ˌ**photoˈjournalist** *n*

photokinesis (ˌfəʊtəʊkɪˈniːsɪs, -kaɪ-) *n Biol.* the movement of an organism in response to the stimulus of light.

photolithography (ˌfəʊtəʊlɪˈθɒgrəfɪ) *n* **1** a lithographic printing process using photographically made plates. Often shortened to **photolitho. 2** *Electronics.* a process used in the manufacture of semiconductor devices and printed circuits in which a particular pattern is transferred from a photograph onto a substrate.
▸ˌ**photoliˈthographer** *n*

photoluminescence (ˌfəʊtəʊˌluːmɪˈnɛsəns) *n* luminescence resulting from the absorption of light or infrared or ultraviolet radiation.

photolysis (fəʊˈtɒlɪsɪs) *n* chemical decomposition caused by light or other electromagnetic radiation.
▸**photolytic** (ˌfəʊtəʊˈlɪtɪk) *adj*

photomechanical (ˌfəʊtəʊmɪˈkænɪkᵊl) *adj* of or relating to any of various methods by which printing plates are made using photography.
▸ˌ**photomeˈchanically** *adv*

photometer (fəʊˈtɒmɪtə) *n* an instrument used in photometry, usually one that compares the illumination produced by a particular light source with that produced by a standard source.

photometry (fəʊˈtɒmɪtrɪ) *n* **1** the measurement of the intensity of light. **2** the branch of physics concerned with such measurements.
▸**phoˈtometrist** *n*

photomicrograph (ˌfəʊtəʊˈmaɪkrəˌgrɑːf) *n* a photograph of a microscope image.
▸**photomicrography** (ˌfəʊtəʊmaɪˈkrɒgrəfɪ) *n*

photomontage (ˌfəʊtəʊmɒnˈtɑːʒ) *n* **1** the technique of producing a

THESAURUS

photograph *n* **1** = **picture,** image, likeness, photo (*inf.*), print, shot, slide, snap (*inf.*), snapshot, transparency ◆ *vb* **2** = **take a picture of,** capture on film, film, get a shot of, record, shoot, snap (*inf.*), take, take (someone's) picture

photographic *adj* **2** = **lifelike,** graphic, natural, pictorial, realistic, visual, vivid **3** = **accurate,** detailed, exact, faithful, minute, precise, retentive

composite picture by combining several photographs. **2** the composite picture so produced.

photomultiplier (ˌfəʊtəʊˈmʌltɪˌplaɪə) *n* a device sensitive to electromagnetic radiation which produces a detectable pulse of current.

photon (ˈfəʊtɒn) *n* a quantum of electromagnetic radiation with energy equal to the product of the frequency of the radiation and the Planck constant.

photo-offset *n Printing.* an offset process in which the plates are produced photomechanically.

photo opportunity *n* an opportunity, either preplanned or accidental, for the press to photograph a politician, celebrity, or event.

photoperiodism (ˌfəʊtəʊˈpɪərɪəˌdɪzəm) *n* the response of plants and animals by behaviour, growth, etc., to the period of daylight in every 24 hours (**photoperiod**).
▸ˌ**photoˌperiˈodic** *adj*

photophobia (ˌfəʊtəʊˈfəʊbɪə) *n* **1** *Pathol.* abnormal sensitivity of the eyes to light. **2** *Psychiatry.* abnormal fear of sunlight or well-lit places.
▸ˌ**photoˈphobic** *adj*

photopolymer (ˌfəʊtəʊˈpɒlɪmə) *n* a polymeric material that is sensitive to light: used in printing plates, microfilms, etc.

photoreceptor (ˌfəʊtəʊrɪˈsɛptə) *n Zool., physiol.* a light-sensitive cell or organ that conveys impulses through the sensory neuron connected to it.

photosensitive (ˌfəʊtəʊˈsɛnsɪtɪv) *adj* sensitive to electromagnetic radiation, esp. light.
▸ˌ**photoˌsensiˈtivity** *n* ▸ˌ**photoˈsensiˌtize** *or* ˌ**photoˈsensiˌtise** *vb (tr)*

photoset (ˈfəʊtəʊˌsɛt) *vb* **photosets, photosetting, photoset.** another word for **filmset.**
▸ˈ**photoˌsetter** *n*

photosphere (ˈfəʊtəʊˌsfɪə) *n* the visible surface of the sun.
▸**photospheric** (ˌfəʊtəʊˈsfɛrɪk) *adj*

photostat (ˈfəʊtəʊˌstæt) *n* **1** a machine or process used to make photographic copies of written, printed, or graphic matter. **2** any copy made by such a machine. ◆ *vb* **photostats, photostatting** *or* **photostating, photostatted** *or* **photostated. 3** to make a photostat copy (of).

photosynthesis (ˌfəʊtəʊˈsɪnθɪsɪs) *n* (in plants) the synthesis of organic compounds from carbon dioxide and water using light energy absorbed by chlorophyll.
▸ˌ**photoˈsynthesize** *or* ˌ**photoˈsynthesise** *vb* ▸**photosynthetic** (ˌfəʊtəʊsɪnˈθɛtɪk) *adj* ▸ˌ**photosynˈthetically** *adv*

phototaxis (ˌfəʊtəʊˈtæksɪs) *n* the movement of an entire organism in response to light.

phototropism (ˌfəʊtəʊˈtrəʊpɪzəm) *n* the growth response of plant parts to the stimulus of light, producing a bending towards the light source.
▸ˌ**photoˈtropic** *adj*

photovoltaic effect (ˌfəʊtəʊvɒlˈteɪɪk) *n* the effect when electromagnetic radiation falls on a thin film of one solid deposited on the surface of a dissimilar solid producing a difference in potential between the two materials.

phrasal verb *n* a phrase that consists of a verb plus an adverbial or prepositional particle, esp. one the meaning of which cannot be deduced from the constituents: *"take in" meaning "deceive" is a phrasal verb.*

phrase ❶ (freɪz) *n* **1** a group of words forming a syntactic constituent of a sentence. Cf. **clause** (sense 1). **2** an idiomatic or original expression. **3** manner or style of speech or expression. **4** *Music.* a small group of notes forming a coherent unit of melody. ◆ *vb* **phrases, phrasing, phrased.** *(tr)* **5** *Music.* to divide (a melodic line, part, etc.) into musical phrases, esp. in performance. **6** to express orally or in a phrase. [C16: from L *phrasis*, from Gk: speech, from *phrazein* to tell]
▸ˈ**phrasal** *adj*

phrase book *n* a book containing frequently used expressions and their equivalents in a foreign language.

phrase marker *n Linguistics.* a representation, esp. a tree diagram, of the constituent structure of a sentence.

phraseogram (ˈfreɪzɪəˌɡræm) *n* a symbol representing a phrase, as in shorthand.

phraseology ❶ (ˌfreɪzɪˈɒlədʒɪ) *n, pl* **phraseologies. 1** the manner in which words or phrases are used. **2** a set of phrases used by a particular group of people.
▸**phraseological** (ˌfreɪzɪəˈlɒdʒɪkᵊl) *adj*

phrasing (ˈfreɪzɪŋ) *n* **1** the way in which something is expressed, esp. in writing; wording. **2** *Music.* the division of a melodic line, part, etc., into musical phrases.

phrenetic (frɪˈnɛtɪk) *adj* an obsolete spelling of **frenetic.**
▸**phreˈnetically** *adv*

phrenic (ˈfrɛnɪk) *adj* **1a** of or relating to the diaphragm. **1b** *(as n): the phrenic.* **2** *Obs.* of or relating to the mind. [C18: from NL *phrenicus*, from Gk *phrēn* mind, diaphragm]

phrenology (frɪˈnɒlədʒɪ) *n* (formerly) the branch of science concerned with determination of the strength of the faculties by the shape and size of the skull overlying the parts of the brain thought to be responsible for them.
▸**phrenological** (ˌfrɛnəˈlɒdʒɪkᵊl) *adj* ▸**phreˈnologist** *n*

phrensy (ˈfrɛnzɪ) *n, pl* **phrensies** an obsolete spelling of **frenzy.**

Phrygian (ˈfrɪdʒɪən) *adj* **1** of or relating to ancient Phrygia, a country of W central Asia Minor, its inhabitants, or their extinct language. **2** *Music.* of or relating to an authentic mode represented by the natural diatonic scale from E to E. ◆ *n* **3** a native or inhabitant of ancient Phrygia. **4** an ancient language of Phrygia.

Phrygian cap *n* a conical cap of soft material worn during ancient times, that became a symbol of liberty during the French Revolution.

phthisis (ˈθaɪsɪs, ˈfθaɪ-, ˈtaɪ-) *n* any disease that causes wasting of the body, esp. pulmonary tuberculosis. [C16: via L from Gk, from *phthinein* to waste away]

phut (fʌt) *Inf.* ◆ *n* **1** a representation of a muffled explosive sound. ◆ *adv* **2 go phut.** to break down or collapse. [C19: imit.]

phycomycete (ˌfaɪkəʊˈmaɪsiːt) *n* any of a primitive group of fungi formerly included in the class *Phycomycetes*, but now classified in different phyla: includes certain mildews and moulds. [from Gk *phukos* seaweed + -MYCETE]

phyla (ˈfaɪlə) *n* the plural of **phylum.**

phylactery (fɪˈlæktərɪ) *n, pl* **phylacteries. 1** *Judaism.* either of the pair of blackened square cases containing parchments inscribed with biblical passages, bound by leather thongs to the head and left arm, and worn by Jewish men during weekday morning prayers. **2** a reminder. **3** *Arch.* an amulet or charm. [C14: from LL *phylactērium*, from Gk *phulaktērion* outpost, from *phulax* a guard]

phyletic (faɪˈlɛtɪk) *adj* of or relating to the evolutionary development of organisms. [C19: from Gk *phuletikos* tribal]

-phyll *or* **-phyl** *n combining form.* leaf: *chlorophyll.* [from Gk *phullon*]

phyllo- *or before a vowel* **phyll-** *combining form.* leaf: *phyllopod.* [from Gk *phullon* leaf]

phyllode (ˈfɪləʊd) *n* a flattened leafstalk that resembles and functions as a leaf. [C19: from NL *phyllodium*, from Gk *phullōdēs* leaflike]

phylloquinone (ˌfɪləʊkwɪˈnəʊn) *n* a viscous fat-soluble liquid occurring in plants: essential for the production of prothrombin, required in blood clotting. Also called: **vitamin K_1.**

phyllotaxis (ˌfɪləˈtæksɪs) *or* **phyllotaxy** *n, pl* **phyllotaxes** (-ˈtæksiːz) *or* **phyllotaxies. 1** the arrangement of the leaves on a stem. **2** the study of this arrangement.
▸ˌ**phylloˈtactic** *adj*

-phyllous *adj combining form.* having leaves of a specified number or type: *monophyllous.* [from Gk *-phullos* of a leaf]

phylloxera (ˌfɪlɒkˈsɪərə, fɪˈlɒksərə) *n, pl* **phylloxerae** (-riː) *or* **phylloxeras.** any of a genus of homopterous insects, such as vine phylloxera, typically feeding on plant juices. [C19: NL, from PHYLLO- + *xēros* dry]

phylo- *or before a vowel* **phyl-** *combining form.* tribe; race; phylum: *phylogeny.* [from Gk *phulon* race]

phylogeny (faɪˈlɒdʒɪnɪ) *or* **phylogenesis** (ˌfaɪləʊˈdʒɛnɪsɪs) *n, pl* **phylogenies** *or* **phylogeneses** (-ˈdʒɛnɪˌsiːz). *Biol.* the sequence of events involved in the evolution of a species, genus, etc. Cf. **ontogeny.** [C19: from PHYLO- + -GENY]
▸**phylogenic** (ˌfaɪləʊˈdʒɛnɪk) *or* **phylogenetic** (ˌfaɪləʊdʒɪˈnɛtɪk) *adj*

phylum (ˈfaɪləm) *n, pl* **phyla. 1** a major taxonomic division of living organisms that contain one or more classes. **2** a group of related language families or linguistic stocks. [C19: NL, from Gk *phulon* race]

phys. *abbrev. for:* **1** physical. **2** physician. **3** physics. **4** physiological. **5** physiology.

physalis (faɪˈseɪlɪs) *n* any of a genus of plants producing inflated orange seed vessels. See **Chinese lantern.** [NL from Gk *physallis* bladder]

physic (ˈfɪzɪk) *n* **1** *Rare.* a medicine, esp. a cathartic. **2** *Arch.* the art or skill of healing. ◆ *vb* **physics, physicking, physicked. 3** *(tr) Arch.* to treat (a patient) with medicine. [C13: from OF *fisique*, via L, from Gk *phusikē*, from *phusis* nature]

physical ❶ (ˈfɪzɪkᵊl) *adj* **1** of or relating to the body, as distinguished from the mind or spirit. **2** of, relating to, or resembling material things or nature: *the physical universe.* **3** involving or requiring bodily contact: *rugby is a physical sport.* **4** of or concerned with matter and energy. **5** of or relating to physics. **6** perceptible to the senses; apparent: *a physical manifestation.* ◆ See also **physicals.**
▸ˈ**physically** *adv*

physical anthropology *n* the branch of anthropology dealing with the genetic aspect of human development and its physical variations.

physical chemistry *n* the branch of chemistry concerned with the way in which the physical properties of substances depend on their chemical structure, properties, and reactions.

physical education *n* training and practice in sports, gymnastics, etc. Abbrev.: **PE.**

physical geography *n* the branch of geography that deals with the natural features of the earth's surface.

physical jerks *pl n Brit. inf.* See **jerk**[1] (sense 6).

physicals (ˈfɪzɪkᵊlz) *pl n Commerce.* commodities that can be purchased and used, as opposed to those bought and sold in a futures market. Also called: **actuals.**

physical science *n* any of the sciences concerned with nonliving matter, such as physics, chemistry, astronomy, and geology.

physical therapy *n Chiefly US.* another term for **physiotherapy.**

physician ❶ (fɪˈzɪʃən) *n* **1** a person legally qualified to practise medi-

THESAURUS

phrase *n* **1-3** = **expression**, group of words, idiom, locution, motto, remark, saying, tag, utterance, way of speaking ◆ *vb* **6** = **express**, couch, formulate, frame, present, put, put into words, say, term, utter, voice, word

phraseology *n* **1** = **wording**, choice of words, diction, expression, idiom, language, parlance, phrase, phrasing, speech, style, syntax

physical *adj* **1** = **bodily**, carnal, corporal, corporeal, earthly, fleshly, incarnate, mortal, somatic, unspiritual **2** = **material**, natural, palpable, real, sensible, solid, substantial, tangible, visible

physician *n* **1** = **doctor**, doc, doctor of medicine, general practitioner, G.P., healer, M.D.,

cine, esp. other than surgery; doctor of medicine. **2** *Arch.* any person who treats diseases; healer. [C13: from OF *fisicien,* from *fisique* PHYSIC]

physicist ('fɪzɪsɪst) *n* a person versed in or studying physics.

physics ('fɪzɪks) *n* (*functioning as sing*) **1** the branch of science concerned with the properties of matter and energy and the relationships between them. It is based on mathematics and traditionally includes mechanics, optics, electricity and magnetism, acoustics, and heat. Modern physics, based on quantum theory, includes atomic, nuclear, particle, and solid-state studies. **2** physical properties of behaviour: *the physics of the electron.* **3** *Arch.* natural science. [C16: from L *physica,* translation of Gk *ta phusika* natural things, from *phusis* nature]

physio ('fɪzɪəʊ) *n Inf.* **1** short for **physiotherapy. 2** (*pl* **physios**) short for **physiotherapist.**

physio- *or before a vowel* **phys-** *combining form.* **1** of or relating to nature or natural functions: *physiology.* **2** physical: *physiotherapy.* [from Gk *phusio,* ult. from *phuein* to make grow]

physiocrat ('fɪzɪəʊˌkræt) *n* a believer in the 18th-century French economic theory that the inherent natural order governing society was based on land and its natural products as the only true form of wealth. [C18: from F *physiocrate;* see PHYSIO-, -CRAT]
▸**physiocracy** (ˌfɪzɪ'ɒkrəsɪ) *n*

physiognomy ❶ (ˌfɪzɪ'ɒnəmɪ) *n* **1** a person's features considered as an indication of personality. **2** the art or practice of judging character from facial features. **3** the outward appearance of something. [C14: from OF *phisonomie,* via Med. L, from LGk *phusiognōmia,* from *phusis* nature + *gnōmōn* judge]
▸**physiognomic** (ˌfɪzɪə'nɒmɪk) *or* ˌ**physiog'nomical** *adj* ▸ˌ**physiog'nomically** *adv* ▸ˌ**physi'ognomist** *n*

physiography (ˌfɪzɪ'ɒgrəfɪ) *n* another name for **geomorphology** or **physical geography.**
▸ˌ**physi'ographer** *n* ▸**physiographic** (ˌfɪzɪə'græfɪk) *or* ˌ**physio'graphical** *adj*

physiol. *abbrev. for:* **1** physiological. **2** physiology.

physiology (ˌfɪzɪ'ɒləd͡ʒɪ) *n* **1** the branch of science concerned with the functioning of organisms. **2** the processes and functions of all or part of an organism. [C16: from L *physiologia,* from Gk]
▸ˌ**physi'ologist** *n* ▸**physiological** (ˌfɪzɪə'lɒd͡ʒɪk'l) *adj* ▸ˌ**physio'logically** *adv*

physiotherapy (ˌfɪzɪəʊ'θɛrəpɪ) *n* the treatment of disease, injury, etc., by physical means, such as massage or exercises, rather than by drugs.
▸ˌ**physio'therapist** *n*

physique ❶ (fɪ'ziːk) *n* the general appearance of the body with regard to size, shape, muscular development, etc. [C19: via F from *physique* (adj) natural, from L *physicus* physical]

-phyte *n combining form.* indicating a plant of a specified type or habitat: *lithophyte.* [from Gk *phuton* plant]
▸**-phytic** *adj combining form.*

phyto- *or before a vowel* **phyt-** *combining form.* indicating a plant or vegetation: *phytogenesis.* [from Gk *phuton* plant, from *phuein* to make grow]

phytochrome ('faɪtəʊˌkrəʊm) *n Bot.* a blue-green pigment, present in most plants, that mediates many light-dependent processes, including photoperiodism and the greening of leaves.

phytogenesis (ˌfaɪtəʊ'd͡ʒɛnɪsɪs) *or* **phytogeny** (faɪ'tɒd͡ʒənɪ) *n* the branch of botany concerned with the origin and evolution of plants.

phyton ('faɪtɒn) *n* a unit of plant structure, usually considered as the smallest part of the plant that is capable of growth when detached from the parent plant. [C20: from Gk; see -PHYTE]

phytopathology (ˌfaɪtəʊpə'θɒləd͡ʒɪ) *n* the branch of botany concerned with diseases of plants.

phytoplankton (ˌfaɪtə'plæŋktən) *n* the photosynthesizing constituent of plankton, mainly unicellular algae.

phytotoxin (ˌfaɪtə'tɒksɪn) *n* a toxin, such as strychnine, that is produced by a plant.
▸ˌ**phyto'toxic** *adj*

pi[1] (paɪ) *n, pl* **pis. 1** the 16th letter in the Greek alphabet (Π, π). **2** *Maths.* a transcendental number, fundamental to mathematics, that is the ratio of the circumference of a circle to its diameter. Approximate value: 3.141 592... ; symbol: π [C18 (mathematical use): representing the first letter of Gk *periphereia* PERIPHERY]

pi[2] *or* **pie** (paɪ) *n, pl* **pies. 1** a jumbled pile of printer's type. **2** a jumbled mixture. ◆ *vb* **pies, piing, pied** *or* **pies, pieing, pied.** (*tr*) **3** to spill and mix (set type) indiscriminately. **4** to mix up. [C17: from ?]

pi[3] (paɪ) *adj Brit. sl.* short for **pious** (sense 3).

PI *abbrev. for:* **1** Phillipine Islands. **2** private investigator.

piacevole (piːætʃ'eɪvəʊleɪ) *adv Music.* in an agreeable, pleasant manner. [It.]

piacular (paɪ'ækjʊlə) *adj* **1** making expiation. **2** requiring expiation. [C17: from L *piāculum* propitiatory sacrifice, from *piāre* to appease]

piaffe (pɪ'æf) *n Dressage.* a slow trot done on the spot. [C18: from F, from *piaffer* to strut]

pia mater ('paɪə 'meɪtə) *n* the innermost of the three membranes (see **meninges**) that cover the brain and spinal cord. [C16: from Med. L, lit.: pious mother]

pianism ('piːəˌnɪzəm) *n* technique, skill, or artistry in playing the piano.
▸ˌ**pia'nistic** *adj*

pianissimo (pɪə'nɪsɪˌməʊ) *adj, adv Music.* to be performed very quietly. Symbol: *pp* [C18: from It., sup. of *piano* soft]

pianist ('pɪənɪst) *n* a person who plays the piano.

piano[1] (pɪ'ænəʊ) *n, pl* **pianos.** a musical stringed instrument played by depressing keys that cause hammers to strike the strings and produce audible vibrations. [C19: short for PIANOFORTE]

piano[2] ('pjɑːnəʊ) *adj, adv Music.* to be performed softly. [C17: from It., from L *plānus* flat]

piano accordion (pɪ'ænəʊ) *n* an accordion in which the right hand plays a piano-like keyboard. See **accordion.**
▸**piano accordionist** *n*

pianoforte (pɪˌænəʊ'fɔːtɪ) *n* the full name for **piano**[1]. [C18: from It., orig. (*gravecembalo col*) *piano e forte* (harpsichord with) soft & loud; see PIANO[2], FORTE[2]]

Pianola (pɪə'nəʊlə) *n Trademark.* a type of mechanical piano in which the keys are depressed by air pressure, this air flow being regulated by perforations in a paper roll.

piano roll (pɪ'ænəʊ) *n* a perforated roll of paper for a Pianola.

piastre *or* **piaster** (pɪ'æstə) *n* **1** (formerly) the standard monetary unit of South Vietnam. **2a** a fractional monetary unit of Egypt, Lebanon, and Syria worth one hundredth of a pound: also used in the Sudan but its use is being phased out. **2b** Also called: **kurus.** a Turkish monetary unit worth one hundredth of a lira. **2c** a Libyan monetary unit worth one hundredth of a dinar. [C17: from F *piastre,* from It. *piastra d'argento* silver plate]

piazza (pɪ'ætsə; *Italian* 'pjattsa) *n* **1** a large open square in an Italian town. **2** *Chiefly Brit.* a covered passageway or gallery. [C16: from It.: marketplace, from L *platēa* courtyard, from Gk *plateia;* see PLACE]

pibroch ('piːbrɒk; *Gaelic* 'piːbrɒx) *n* a form of music for Scottish bagpipes, consisting of a theme and variations. [C18: from Gaelic *piobaireachd,* from *piobair* piper]

pic (pɪk) *n, pl* **pics** *or* **pix.** *Inf.* a photograph or illustration. [C20: shortened from PICTURE]

pica[1] ('paɪkə) *n* **1** another word for **em. 2** (formerly) a size of printer's type equal to 12 point. **3** a typewriter type size having 10 characters to the inch. [C15: from Anglo-L *pīca* list of ecclesiastical regulations, apparently from L *pīca* magpie, with reference to its habit of collecting things; the connection between the orig. sense & the typography meanings is obscure]

pica[2] ('paɪkə) *n Pathol.* an abnormal craving to ingest substances such as clay, dirt, or hair. [C16: from Medical L, from L: magpie, an allusion to its omnivorous feeding habits]

picador ('pɪkəˌdɔː) *n Bullfighting.* a horseman who pricks the bull with a lance to weaken it. [C18: from Sp., lit.: pricker, from *picar* to prick]

picaresque (ˌpɪkə'rɛsk) *adj* of or relating to a type of fiction in which the hero, a rogue, goes through a series of episodic adventures. [C19: via F from Sp. *picaresco,* from *pícaro* a rogue]

picaroon (ˌpɪkə'ruːn) *n Arch.* an adventurer or rogue. [C17: from Sp. *picarón,* from *pícaro*]

picayune (ˌpɪkə'juːn) *adj also* **picayunish.** *US & Canad. inf.* **1** of small value or importance. **2** mean; petty. ◆ *n* **3** any coin of little value, esp. a five-cent piece. **4** an unimportant person or thing. [C19: from F *picaillon* coin from Piedmont, from Provençal *picaioun,* from ?]

piccalilli ('pɪkəˌlɪlɪ) *n* a pickle of mixed vegetables in a mustard sauce. [C18 *piccalillo,* ? based on PICKLE]

piccanin ('pɪkəˌnɪn) *n S. African offens.* a Black African child. [var. of PICCANINNY]

piccaninny *or esp. US* **pickaninny** (ˌpɪkə'nɪnɪ) *n, pl* **piccaninnies** *or esp. US* **pickaninnies.** *Offens.* a small Black child. [C17: ?from Port. *pequenino* tiny one, from *pequeno* small]

piccolo ('pɪkəˌləʊ) *n, pl* **piccolos.** a woodwind instrument an octave higher than the flute. [C19: from It.: small]

pick[1] ❶ (pɪk) *vb* **1** to choose (something) deliberately or carefully, as from a number; select. **2** to pluck or gather (fruit, berries, or crops) from (a tree, bush, field, etc.). **3** (*tr*) to remove loose particles from (the teeth, the nose, etc.). **4** (esp. of birds) to nibble or gather (corn, etc.). **5** (*tr*) to pierce, dig, or break up (a hard surface) with a pick. **6** (*tr*) to form (a hole, etc.) in this way. **7** (when *intr,* foll. by *at*) to nibble (at) fussily or without appetite. **8** to separate (strands, fibres, etc.), as in weaving. **9** (*tr*) to provoke (an argument, fight, etc.) deliberately. **10** (*tr*) to steal (money or valuables) from (a person's pocket). **11** (*tr*) to open (a lock) with an instrument other than a key. **12** to pluck the strings of (a guitar, banjo, etc.). **13** (*tr*) to make (one's way) carefully on foot: *they picked their way through the rubble.* **14 pick and choose.** to select fastidiously, fussily, etc. **15 pick someone's brains.** to obtain information or ideas from someone. ◆ *n* **16** freedom or right of selection (esp. in **take one's pick**). **17** a person, thing, etc., that is chosen first or preferred: *the pick of the bunch.* **18** the act of picking. **19** the amount of

THESAURUS

medic (*inf.*), medical practitioner, medico (*inf.*), sawbones (*sl.*), specialist

physiognomy *n* **1** = **face**, clock (*Brit. sl.*), countenance, dial (*Brit. sl.*), features, look, phiz (*sl.*), phizog (*sl.*), visage

physique *n* = **build**, body, constitution, figure, form, frame, make-up, shape, structure

pick[1] *vb* **1** = **select**, cherry-pick, choose, decide upon, elect, fix upon, hand-pick, mark out, opt for, settle upon, sift out, single out, sort out **2** = **gather**, collect, cull, cut, harvest, pluck, pull **7** = **nibble**, have no appetite, peck at, play *or* toy with, push the food round the plate **9** = **provoke**, foment, incite, instigate, start **11** = **open**, break into, break open, crack, force, jemmy, prise open ◆ *n* **16** = **choice**, choosing, decision, option, preference, selection **17** = **the best**, choicest, *crème de la crème,* elect, elite, flower, pride, prize, the cream, the tops (*sl.*)

Antonyms *vb* ≠ **select**: cast aside, decline, discard, dismiss, reject, spurn, turn down

a crop picked at one period or from one area. ◆ See also **pick at, pick off**, etc. [C15: from earlier *piken* to pick, infl. by F *piquer* to pierce]
▸**'picker** *n*

pick[2] (pɪk) *n* **1** a tool with a handle carrying a long steel head curved and tapering to a point at one or both ends, used for loosening soil, breaking rocks, etc. **2** any of various tools used for picking, such as an ice pick or toothpick. **3** a plectrum. [C14: ? a var. of PIKE[2]]

pickaback ('pɪkəˌbæk) *n, adv* another word for **piggyback**.

pick at ❶ *vb* (*intr, prep*) to make criticisms of in a niggling or petty manner.

pickaxe *or US* **pickax** ('pɪkˌæks) *n* **1** a large pick or mattock. ◆ *vb* **pickaxes, pickaxing, pickaxed. 2** to use a pickaxe on (earth, rocks, etc.). [C15: from earlier *pikois* (but infl. also by AXE), from OF, from *pic* PICK[2]]

pickerel ('pɪkərəl, 'pɪkrəl) *n, pl* **pickerel** *or* **pickerels. 1** a small pike. **2** any of several North American freshwater game fishes of the pike family. [C14: dim. of PIKE[1]]

picket ❶ ('pɪkɪt) *n* **1** a pointed stake that is driven into the ground to support a fence, etc. **2** an individual or group standing outside an establishment to make a protest, to dissuade or prevent employees or clients from entering, etc. **3** a small detachment of troops positioned to give early warning of attack. ◆ *vb* **4** to post or serve as pickets at (a factory, embassy, etc.). **5** to guard (a main body or place) by using or acting as a picket. **6** (*tr*) to fasten (a horse or other animal) to a picket. **7** (*tr*) to fence (an area, etc.) with pickets. [C18: from F *piquet*, from OF *piquer* to prick; see PIKE[2]]
▸**'picketer** *n*

picket fence *n* a fence consisting of pickets driven into the ground.

picket line *n* a line of people acting as pickets.

pickings ❶ ('pɪkɪŋz) *pl n* (*sometimes sing*) money, profits, etc., acquired easily; spoils.

pickle ❶ ('pɪk[ə]l) *n* **1** (*often pl*) vegetables, such as onions, etc., preserved in vinegar, brine, etc. **2** any food preserved in this way. **3** a liquid or marinade, such as spiced vinegar, for preserving vegetables, meat, fish, etc. **4** *Chiefly US & Canad.* a cucumber that has been preserved and flavoured in a pickling solution, as brine or vinegar. **5** *Inf.* an awkward or difficult situation: *to be in a pickle.* **6** *Brit. inf.* a mischievous child. ◆ *vb* **pickles, pickling, pickled.** (*tr*) **7** to preserve in a pickling liquid. **8** to immerse (a metallic object) in a liquid, such as an acid, to remove surface scale. [C14: ?from MDu. *pekel*]
▸**'pickler** *n*

pickled ('pɪk[ə]ld) *adj* **1** preserved in a pickling liquid. **2** *Inf.* intoxicated; drunk.

picklock ('pɪkˌlɒk) *n* **1** a person who picks locks. **2** an instrument for picking locks.

pick-me-up ❶ *n Inf.* a tonic or restorative, esp. a special drink taken as a stimulant.

pick off *vb* (*tr, adv*) to aim at and shoot one by one.

pick on ❶ *vb* (*intr, prep*) to select for something unpleasant, esp. in order to bully or blame.

pick out ❶ *vb* (*tr, adv*) **1** to select for use or special consideration, etc., as from a group. **2** to distinguish (an object from its surroundings), as in painting: *she picked out the woodwork in white.* **3** to recognize (a person or thing): *we picked out his face among the crowd.* **4** to distinguish (sense or meaning) as from a mass of detail or complication. **5** to play (a tune) tentatively, as by ear.

pickpocket ('pɪkˌpɒkɪt) *n* a person who steals from the pockets of others in public places.

pick-up ❶ *n* **1** the light balanced arm of a record player that carries the wires from the cartridge to the preamplifier. **2** an electromagnetic transducer that converts vibrations into electric signals. **3** another name for **cartridge** (sense 2). **4** Also called: **pick-up truck.** a small truck with an open body used for light deliveries. **5** *Inf., chiefly US.* an ability to accelerate rapidly: *this car has good pick-up.* **6** *Inf.* a casual acquaintance, usually one made with sexual intentions. **7** *Inf.* **7a** a stop to collect passengers, goods, etc. **7b** the people or things collected. **8** *Inf.* an improvement. **9** *Sl.* a pick-me-up. ◆ *adj* **10** *US & Canad.* organized or assembled hastily and without planning: *a pick-up game.* ◆ *vb* **pick up.** (*adv*) **11** (*tr*) to gather up in the hand or hands. **12** (*reflexive*) to raise (oneself) after a fall or setback. **13** (*tr*) to obtain casually, incidentally, etc. **14** (*intr*) to improve in health, condition, activity, etc.: *the market began to pick up.* **15** (*tr*) to learn gradually or as one goes along. **16** to resume; return to. **17** (*tr*) to accept the responsibility for paying (a bill). **18** (*tr*) to collect or give a lift to (passengers, goods, etc.). **19** (*tr*) *Inf.* to become acquainted with, esp. with a view to having sexual relations. **20** (*tr*) *Inf.* to arrest. **21** to increase (speed). **22** (*tr*) to receive (electrical signals, a radio signal, sounds, etc.).

Pickwickian (pɪk'wɪkɪən) *adj* **1** of, relating to, or resembling Mr Pickwick in Charles Dickens' *The Pickwick Papers*, esp. in being naive or benevolent. **2** (of the use or meaning of a word) odd or unusual.

picky ❶ ('pɪkɪ) *adj* **pickier, pickiest.** *Inf.* fussy; finicky.
▸**'pickily** *adv* ▸**'pickiness** *n*

picnic ❶ ('pɪknɪk) *n* **1** a trip or excursion on which people bring food to be eaten in the open air. **2a** any informal meal eaten outside. **2b** (*as modifier*): *a picnic lunch.* **3** *Inf.* an easy or agreeable task. ◆ *vb* **picnics, picnicking, picnicked. 4** (*intr*) to eat or take part in a picnic. [C18: from F *piquenique*, from ?]
▸**'picnicker** *n*

picnic races *pl n Austral.* horse races for amateur riders held in rural areas.

pico- *prefix* denoting 10^{-12}: *picofarad.* Symbol: p [from Sp. *pico* small quantity, odd number, peak]

picot ('piːkəʊ) *n* any of a pattern of small loops, as on lace. [C19: from F: small point, from *pic* point]

picotee (ˌpɪkə'tiː) *n* a type of carnation having pale petals edged with a darker colour. [C18: from F *picoté* marked with points, from *picot* PICOT]

picric acid ('pɪkrɪk) *n* a toxic sparingly soluble crystalline yellow acid used as a dye, antiseptic, and explosive. Formula: $C_6H_3(NO_2)_3$. Systematic name: **2,4,6-trinitrophenol.** [C19: from Gk *pikros* bitter + -IC]

Pict (pɪkt) *n* a member of any of the peoples who lived in N Britain in the first to the fourth centuries A.D. [OE *Peohtas;* later forms from LL *Pictī* painted men, from *pingere* to paint]
▸**'Pictish** *adj*

pictograph ('pɪktəˌgrɑːf) *n* **1** a picture or symbol standing for a word or group of words, as in written Chinese. **2** a chart on which symbols are used to represent values. ◆ Also called: **pictogram.** [C19: from L *pictus*, from *pingere* to paint]
▸**pictographic** (ˌpɪktə'græfɪk) *adj* ▸**pictography** (pɪk'tɒgrəfɪ) *n*

pictorial ❶ (pɪk'tɔːrɪəl) *adj* **1** relating to, consisting of, or expressed by pictures. **2** (of language, style, etc.) suggesting a picture; vivid; graphic. ◆ *n* **3** a magazine, newspaper, etc., containing many pictures. [C17: from LL *pictōrius*, from L *pictor* painter, from *pingere* to paint]
▸**pic'torially** *adv*

picture ❶ ('pɪktʃə) *n* **1a** a visual representation of something, such as a person or scene, produced on a surface, as in a photograph, painting, etc. **1b** (*as modifier*): *picture gallery; picture postcard.* **2** a mental image: *a clear picture of events.* **3** a verbal description, esp. one that is vivid. **4** a situation considered as an observable scene: *the political picture.* **5** a person or thing resembling another: *he was the picture of his father.* **6** a person, scene, etc., typifying a particular state: *the picture of despair.* **7** the image on a television screen. **8** a motion picture; film. **9 the pictures.** *Chiefly Brit.* a cinema or film show. **10** another name for **tableau vivant. 11 in the picture.** informed about a situation. ◆ *vb* **pictures, picturing, pictured.** (*tr*) **12** to visualize or imagine. **13** to describe or depict, esp. vividly. **14** (*often passive*) to put in a picture or make a picture of: *they were pictured sitting on the rocks.* [C15: from L *pictūra* painting, from *pingere* to paint]

picture card *n* another name for **court card.**

picture hat *n* a hat with a very wide brim.

THESAURUS

pick at *vb* = **criticize**, carp, cavil, find fault, get at, nag, pick holes, pick to pieces, quibble

picket *n* **1** = **stake**, pale, paling, palisade, peg, post, stanchion, upright **2** = **protester**, demonstrator, flying picket, picketer **3** = **lookout**, guard, patrol, scout, sentinel, sentry, spotter, vedette (*Military*), watch ◆ *vb* **4** = **blockade**, boycott, demonstrate **7** = **fence**, corral, enclose, hedge in, palisade, pen in, rail in, shut in, wall in

pickings *pl n* = **profits**, booty, earnings, gravy (*sl.*), ill-gotten gains, loot, plunder, proceeds, returns, rewards, spoils, yield

pickle *n* **5** *Informal* = **predicament**, bind (*inf.*), difficulty, dilemma, fix (*inf.*), hot water (*inf.*), jam, quandary, scrape (*inf.*), spot (*inf.*), tight spot ◆ *vb* **7** = **preserve**, cure, keep, marinade, steep

pick-me-up *n Informal* = **tonic**, bracer (*inf.*), drink, pick-up, refreshment, restorative, shot in the arm (*inf.*), stimulant

pick on *vb* = **torment**, badger, bait, blame, bully, goad, hector, tease

pick out *vb* **1** = **select**, choose, cull, hand-pick, separate the sheep from the goats, single out, sort out **2, 3** = **identify**, discriminate, distinguish, make distinct, make out, notice, perceive, recognize, tell apart

pick-up *n* **5** *Informal, chiefly U.S.* = **acceleration**, response, revving (*inf.*), speed-up **8** *Informal* = **improvement**, change for the better, gain, rally, recovery, revival, rise, strengthening, upswing, upturn ◆ *vb* **pick up 11, 12** = **lift**, gather, grasp, hoist, raise, take up, uplift **13** = **obtain**, buy, come across, find, garner, happen upon, purchase, score (*sl.*) **14** = **recover**, be on the mend, gain, gain ground, get better, improve, make a comeback, mend, perk up, rally, take a turn for the better, turn the corner **15** = **learn**, acquire, get the hang of (*inf.*), master **18** = **collect**, call for, get, give someone a lift, go to get, uplift (*Scot.*) **20** *Informal* = **arrest**, apprehend, bust (*inf.*), collar (*inf.*), do (*sl.*), lift (*sl.*), nab (*inf.*), nail (*inf.*), nick (*sl., chiefly Brit.*), pinch (*inf.*), run in (*sl.*), take into custody

picky *adj Informal* = **fussy**, captious, carping, cavilling, choosy, critical, dainty, fastidious, fault-finding, finicky, nice, particular, pernickety (*inf.*)

picnic *n* **1, 2** = **excursion**, outdoor meal, outing **3** *Informal* = **walkover** (*inf.*), cakewalk, child's play (*inf.*), cinch (*sl.*), piece of cake (*Brit. inf.*), pushover (*sl.*), snap (*inf.*)

pictorial *adj* **1, 2** = **graphic**, expressive, illustrated, picturesque, representational, scenic, striking, vivid

picture *n* **1** = **representation**, delineation, drawing, effigy, engraving, illustration, image, likeness, painting, photograph, portrait, portrayal, print, similitude, sketch **3** = **description**, account, depiction, image, impression, recreation, report **5** = **double**, carbon copy, copy, dead ringer, duplicate, image, likeness, living image, lookalike, replica, ringer (*sl.*), spit (*inf., chiefly Brit.*), spit and image (*inf.*), spitting image (*inf.*), twin **6** = **personification**, archetype, embodiment, epitome, essence, living example, perfect example **8** = **film**, flick (*sl.*), motion picture, movie (*US inf.*) ◆ *vb* **12** = **imagine**, conceive of, envision, see, see in the mind's eye, visualize **13, 14** = **represent**, delineate, de-

picture moulding *n* **1** the edge around a framed picture. **2** Also called: **picture rail.** the moulding or rail near the top of a wall from which pictures are hung.

picture palace *or* **house** *n Brit., old-fashioned.* another name for **cinema.**

picturesque ➊ (ˌpɪktʃəˈrɛsk) *adj* **1** visually pleasing, esp. in being striking or quaint: *a picturesque view.* **2** (of language) graphic; vivid. [C18: from F *pittoresque* (but also infl. by PICTURE), from It., from *pittore* painter, from L *pictor*]
▸ˌ**picturˈesquely** *adv* ▸ˌ**picturˈesqueness** *n*

picture tube *n* another name for **television tube.**

picture window *n* a large window having a single pane of glass, usually facing a view.

picture writing *n* **1** any writing system that uses pictographs. **2** a system of artistic expression and communication using pictures.

PID *abbrev. for* pelvic inflammatory disease.

piddle (ˈpɪdᵊl) *vb* **piddles, piddling, piddled. 1** (*intr*) *Inf.* to urinate. **2** (when *tr*, often foll. by *away*) to spend (one's time) aimlessly; fritter. [C16: from ?]
▸ˈ**piddler** *n*

piddling ➊ (ˈpɪdlɪŋ) *adj Inf.* petty; trifling; trivial.

piddock (ˈpɪdək) *n* a marine bivalve boring into rock, clay, or wood by means of sawlike shell valves. [C19: from ?]

pidgin (ˈpɪdʒɪn) *n* a language made up of elements of two or more other languages and used for contacts, esp. trading contacts, between the speakers of other languages. [C19: ?from Chinese pronunciation of E *business*]

pidgin English *n* a pidgin in which one of the languages involved is English.

pie[1] (paɪ) *n* **1** a baked sweet or savoury filling in a pastry-lined dish, often covered with a pastry crust. **2 pie in the sky.** illusory hope or promise of some future good. [C14: from ?]

pie[2] (paɪ) *n* an archaic or dialect name for **magpie.** [C13: via OF from L *pīca* magpie]

pie[3] (paɪ) *n, vb* **pies, pieing, pied.** *Printing.* a variant spelling of **pi**[2].

piebald ➊ (ˈpaɪˌbɔːld) *adj* **1** marked in two colours, esp. black and white. ◆ *n* **2** a black-and-white horse. [C16: PIE[2] + BALD; see also PIED]

pie cart *n NZ.* a mobile van selling warmed-up food and drinks.

piece ➊ (piːs) *n* **1** an amount or portion forming a separate mass or structure; bit: *a piece of wood.* **2** a small part, item, or amount forming part of a whole, esp. when broken off or separated: *a piece of bread.* **3** a length by which a commodity is sold, esp. cloth, wallpaper, etc. **4** an instance or occurrence: *a piece of luck.* **5** an example or specimen of a style or type: *a beautiful piece of Dresden.* **6** *Inf.* an opinion or point of view: *to state one's piece.* **7** a literary, musical, or artistic composition. **8** a coin: *a fifty-pence piece.* **9** a small object used in playing certain games: *chess pieces.* **10** a firearm or cannon. **11** any chessman other than a pawn. **12** *Brit. dialect.* a packed lunch taken to work. **13** *NZ.* fragments of fleece wool. **14 go to pieces. 14a** (of a person) to lose control of oneself; have a breakdown. **14b** (of a building, organization, etc.) to disintegrate. **15 nasty piece of work.** *Brit. inf.* a cruel or mean person. **16 of a piece.** of the same kind; alike. ◆ *vb* **pieces, piecing, pieced.** (*tr*) **17** (often foll. by *together*) to fit or assemble piece by piece. **18** (often foll. by *up*) to patch or make up (a garment, etc.) by adding pieces. [C13 *pece*, from OF, of Gaulish origin]

pièce de résistance ➊ *French.* (pjɛs də rezistɑ̃s) *n* **1** the principal or most outstanding item in a series. **2** the main dish of a meal. [lit.: piece of resistance]

piece goods *pl n* goods, esp. fabrics, made in standard widths and lengths.

piecemeal ➊ (ˈpiːsˌmiːl) *adv* **1** by degrees; bit by bit; gradually. **2** in or into pieces. ◆ *adj* **3** fragmentary or unsystematic: *a piecemeal approach.* [C13 *pecemele*, from PIECE + *-mele*, from OE *mælum* quantity taken at one time]

piece of eight *n, pl* **pieces of eight.** a former Spanish coin worth eight reals; peso.

piecework (ˈpiːsˌwɜːk) *n* work paid for according to the quantity produced.

pie chart *n* a circular graph divided into sectors proportional to the magnitudes of the quantities represented.

piecrust table (ˈpaɪˌkrʌst) *n* a round table, edged with moulding suggestive of a pie crust.

pied ➊ (paɪd) *adj* having markings of two or more colours. [C14: from PIE[2]; an allusion to the magpie's colouring]

pied-à-terre (ˌpjeɪtɑːˈtɛə) *n, pl* **pieds-à-terre** (ˌpjeɪtɑːˈtɛə). a flat or other lodging for occasional use. [from F, lit.: foot on (the) ground]

piedmont (ˈpiːdmɒnt) *adj* (*prenominal*) (of glaciers, plains, etc.) formed or situated at the foot of a mountain. [via F from It. *piémonte*, from *pié*, var. of *piede* foot + *mont* mountain]

pied wagtail *n* a British songbird with a black throat and back, long black tail, and white underparts and face.

pie-eyed *adj Sl.* drunk.

pier ➊ (pɪə) *n* **1** a structure with a deck that is built out over water, and used as a landing place, promenade, etc. **2** a pillar that bears heavy loads. **3** the part of a wall between two adjacent openings. **4** another name for **buttress** (sense 1). [C12 *per*, from Anglo-L *pera* pier supporting a bridge]

pierce ➊ (pɪəs) *vb* **pierces, piercing, pierced.** (*mainly tr*) **1** to form or cut (a hole) in (something) as with a sharp instrument. **2** to thrust into sharply or violently: *the thorn pierced his heel.* **3** to force (a way, route, etc.) through (something). **4** (of light, etc.) to shine through or penetrate (darkness). **5** (*also intr*) to discover or realize (something) suddenly or (of an idea, etc.) to become suddenly apparent. **6** (of sounds or cries) to sound sharply through (the silence, etc.). **7** to move or affect deeply or sharply: *the cold pierced their bones.* **8** (*intr*) to penetrate: *piercing cold.* [C13 *percen*, from OF *percer*, ult. from L *pertundere*, from *per* through + *tundere* to strike]
▸ˈ**piercing** *adj* ▸ˈ**piercingly** *adv*

pier glass *n* a tall narrow mirror, designed to hang on the wall between windows.

pieris (ˈpaɪrɪs) *n* an evergreen shrub with white flowers like lily of the valley in spring. [C19: from L, from Gk *Pīeria* the haunt of the Muses]

Pierrot (ˈpɪərəʊ; *French* pjero) *n* **1** a male character from French pantomime with a whitened face, white costume, and pointed hat. **2** (*usually not cap.*) a clown so made up.

pier table *n* a side table designed to stand against a wall between windows.

pietà (pɪɛˈtɑː) *n* a sculpture, painting, or drawing of the dead Christ, supported by the Virgin Mary. [It.: pity, from L *pietās* PIETY]

pietism (ˈpaɪɪˌtɪzəm) *n* exaggerated or affected piety.
▸ˈ**pietist** *n* ▸ˌ**pieˈtistic** *or* ˌ**pieˈtistical** *adj*

piet-my-vrou (ˈpɪtˌmeɪˈfrəʊ) *n S. African.* a red-breasted cuckoo. [imit.]

piety ➊ (ˈpaɪɪtɪ) *n, pl* **pieties. 1** dutiful devotion to God and observance of religious principles. **2** the quality of being pious. **3** a pious action, saying, etc. **4** *Now rare.* devotion and obedience to parents or superiors. [C13 *piete*, from OF, from L *pietās* piety, dutifulness, from *pius* pious]

piezoelectric effect (paɪˌiːzəʊɪˈlɛktrɪk) *or* **piezoelectricity** (paɪˌiːzəʊɪlɛkˈtrɪsɪtɪ) *n Physics.* **a** the production of electricity or electric polarity by applying a mechanical stress to certain crystals. **b** the converse effect in which stress is produced in a crystal as a result of an applied potential difference. [C19: from Gk *piezein* to press]
▸**piˌezoeˈlectrically** *adv*

piffle ➊ (ˈpɪfᵊl) *Inf.* ◆ *n* **1** nonsense. ◆ *vb* **piffles, piffling, piffled. 2** (*intr*) to talk or behave feebly. [C19: from ?]

THESAURUS

pict, describe, draw, illustrate, paint, photograph, portray, render, show, sketch

picturesque *adj* **1** = **interesting**, attractive, beautiful, charming, pretty, quaint, scenic, striking **2** = **vivid**, colourful, graphic
Antonyms *adj* ≠ **interesting:** commonplace, everyday, inartistic, unattractive, uninteresting ≠ **vivid:** drab, dull

piddling *adj Informal* = **trivial**, derisory, fiddling, insignificant, little, measly (*inf.*), Mickey Mouse (*sl.*), nickel-and-dime (*US sl.*), paltry, petty, piffling, puny, trifling, unimportant, useless, worthless
Antonyms *adj* considerable, important, major, significant, sizable *or* sizeable, substantial, tidy (*inf.*), useful, valuable

piebald *adj* **1** = **pied**, black and white, brindled, dappled, flecked, mottled, speckled, spotted

piece *n* **1, 2** = **bit**, allotment, chunk, division, fraction, fragment, length, morsel, mouthful, part, portion, quantity, scrap, section, segment, share, shred, slice **4, 5** = **instance**, case, example, occurrence, sample, specimen, stroke **7** = **work**, article, bit (*inf.*), composition, creation, item, production, study, work of art **14 go to pieces** = **break down**, crack up (*inf.*), crumple, disintegrate, fall apart, lose control, lose one's head **16 of a piece** = **alike**, analogous, consistent, identical, of the same kind, similar, the same, uniform ◆ *vb* **17** *often foll. by* **together** = **assemble**, compose, fix, join, mend, patch, repair, restore, unite

pièce de résistance *n* **1** = **masterpiece**, *chef-d'oeuvre*, jewel, masterwork, showpiece

piecemeal *adv* **1** = **bit by bit**, at intervals, by degrees, by fits and starts, fitfully, gradually, intermittently, little by little, partially, slowly ◆ *adj* **3** = **unsystematic**, fragmentary, intermittent, interrupted, partial, patchy, spotty

pied *adj* = **variegated**, dappled, flecked, irregular, motley, mottled, multicoloured, particoloured, piebald, spotted, streaked, varicoloured

pier *n* **1** = **jetty**, landing place, promenade, quay, wharf **2** = **pillar**, buttress, column, pile, piling, post, support, upright

pierce *vb* **1, 2** = **penetrate**, bore, drill, enter, impale, lance, perforate, prick, probe, puncture, run through, spike, stab, stick into, transfix **7** = **hurt**, affect, cut, cut to the quick, excite, move, pain, rouse, sting, stir, strike, thrill, touch, wound

piercing *adj* **2** = **sharp**, acute, agonizing, excruciating, exquisite, fierce, intense, painful, powerful, racking, severe, shooting, stabbing **5** = **perceptive**, alert, aware, bright (*inf.*), keen, penetrating, perspicacious, probing, quick-witted, searching, sharp, shrewd **6** = **penetrating**, ear-splitting, high-pitched, loud, sharp, shattering, shrill **7** = **cold**, arctic, biting, bitter, freezing, frosty, keen, nipping, nippy, numbing, raw, wintry
Antonyms *adj* ≠ **perceptive:** obtuse, slow, slow-witted, thick, unperceptive ≠ **penetrating:** inaudible, low, low-pitched, mellifluous, quiet, soundless

piety *n* **1, 2** = **holiness**, devotion, devoutness, dutifulness, duty, faith, godliness, grace, piousness, religion, reverence, sanctity, veneration

piffle *n* **1** *Informal* = **nonsense**, balderdash, bilge (*inf.*), bunk (*inf.*), bunkum *or* buncombe (*chiefly US*), codswallop, drivel, eyewash (*inf.*), garbage (*inf.*), hogwash, hot air (*inf.*), moonshine, pap, poppycock (*inf.*), rot, rubbish, tommyrot, tosh (*sl., chiefly Brit.*), trash, tripe (*inf.*), twaddle

piffling Ⓣ ('pɪflɪŋ) *adj Inf.* worthless; trivial.

pig Ⓣ (pɪg) *n* **1** any artiodactyl mammal of an African and Eurasian family, esp. the domestic pig, typically having a long head with a movable snout and a thick bristle-covered skin. Related adj: **porcine. 2** *Inf.* a dirty, greedy, or bad-mannered person. **3** the meat of swine; pork. **4** *Derog.* a slang word for **policeman. 5a** a mass of metal cast into a simple shape. **5b** the mould used. **6** *Brit. inf.* something that is difficult or unpleasant. **7 a pig in a poke.** something bought or received without prior sight or knowledge. **8 make a pig of oneself.** *Inf.* to overindulge oneself. ◆ *vb* **pigs, pigging, pigged. 9** *(intr)* (of a sow) to give birth. **10** *(intr)* Also: **pig it.** *Inf.* to live in squalor. **11** *(tr) Inf.* to devour (food) greedily. [C13 *pigge,* from ?]

pigeon[1] Ⓣ ('pɪdʒɪn) *n* **1** any of numerous related birds having a heavy body, small head, short legs, and long pointed wings. **2** *Sl.* a victim or dupe. [C14: from OF *pijon* young dove, from LL *pīpiō* young bird, from *pīpīre* to chirp]

pigeon[2] Ⓣ ('pɪdʒɪn) *n Brit. inf.* concern or responsibility (often in **it's his, her,** etc., **pigeon**). [C19: altered from PIDGIN]

pigeon breast *n* a deformity of the chest characterized by an abnormal protrusion of the breastbone, caused by rickets.

pigeonhole Ⓣ ('pɪdʒɪn,həʊl) *n* **1** a small compartment for papers, letters, etc., as in a bureau. **2** a hole or recess in a dovecote for pigeons to nest in. ◆ *vb* **pigeonholes, pigeonholing, pigeonholed.** *(tr)* **3** to put aside or defer. **4** to classify or categorize.

pigeon-toed *adj* having the toes turned inwards.

pigface ('pɪg,feɪs) *n Austral.* a creeping succulent plant having bright-coloured flowers and red fruits and often grown for ornament.

piggery ('pɪgərɪ) *n, pl* **piggeries. 1** a place where pigs are kept. **2** great greediness.

piggish Ⓣ ('pɪgɪʃ) *adj* **1** like a pig, esp. in appetite or manners. **2** *Inf., chiefly Brit.* obstinate or mean.
▸**'piggishly** *adv* ▸**'piggishness** *n*

piggy ('pɪgɪ) *n, pl* **piggies. 1** a child's word for a **pig. 2** a child's word for a **toe.** ◆ *adj* **piggier, piggiest. 3** another word for **piggish.**

piggyback ('pɪgɪ,bæk) *or* **pickaback** *n* **1** a ride on the back and shoulders of another person. **2** a system whereby a vehicle, aircraft, etc., is transported for part of its journey on another vehicle. ◆ *adv* **3** on the back and shoulders of another person. **4** on or as an addition. ◆ *adj* **5** of or for a piggyback: *a piggyback ride; piggyback lorry trains.* **6** of or relating to a type of heart transplant in which the transplanted heart functions in conjunction with the patient's own heart.

piggy bank *n* a child's coin bank shaped like a pig with a slot for coins.

pig-headed Ⓣ *adj* stupidly stubborn.
▸**,pig-'headedly** *adv* ▸**,pig-'headedness** *n*

pig iron *n* crude iron produced in a blast furnace and poured into moulds.

piglet ('pɪglɪt) *n* a young pig.

pigmeat ('pɪg,mi:t) *n* a less common name for pork, ham, or bacon.

pigment Ⓣ ('pɪgmənt) *n* **1** a substance occurring in plant or animal tissue and producing a characteristic colour. **2** any substance used to impart colour. **3** a powder that is mixed with a liquid to give a paint, ink, etc. [C14: from L *pigmentum,* from *pingere* to paint]
▸**'pigmentary** *adj*

pigmentation (,pɪgmən'teɪʃən) *n* **1** coloration in plants, animals, or man caused by the presence of pigments. **2** the deposition of pigment in animals, plants, or man.

Pigmy ('pɪgmɪ) *n, pl* **Pigmies.** a variant spelling of **Pygmy.**

pignut ('pɪg,nʌt) *n* **1** Also called: **hognut. 1a** the bitter nut of any of several North American hickory trees. **1b** any of the trees bearing such a nut. **2** another name for **earthnut.**

pig-root *vb (intr) Austral. & NZ sl.* (of a horse) to buck slightly.

pigs (pɪgz) *interj Austral. sl.* an expression of derision or disagreement. Also: **pig's arse, pig's bum.**

pigskin ('pɪg,skɪn) *n* **1** the skin of the domestic pig. **2** leather made of this skin. **3** *US & Canad. inf.* a football. ◆ *adj* **4** made of pigskin.

pigsticking ('pɪg,stɪkɪŋ) *n* the sport of hunting wild boar.
▸**'pig,sticker** *n*

pigsty ('pɪg,staɪ) *or US & Canad.* **pigpen** *n, pl* **pigsties** *or US & Canad.* **pigpens. 1** a pen for pigs; sty. **2** *Brit.* an untidy place.

pigswill ('pɪg,swɪl) *n* waste food or other edible matter fed to pigs. Also called: **pig's wash.**

pigtail ('pɪg,teɪl) *n* **1** a plait of hair or one of two plaits on either side of the face. **2** a twisted roll of tobacco.

pika ('paɪkə) *n* a burrowing mammal of mountainous regions of North America and Asia, having short rounded ears, a rounded body, and rudimentary tail. [C19: from E Siberian *piika*]

pikau ('pi:kaʊ) *n NZ.* a pack, knapsack, or rucksack. [Maori]

pike[1] (paɪk) *n, pl* **pike** *or* **pikes. 1** any of several large predatory freshwater teleost fishes having a broad flat snout, strong teeth, and an elongated body covered with small scales. **2** any of various similar fishes. [C14: short for *pikefish,* from OE *pīc* point, with reference to the shape of its jaw]

pike[2] (paɪk) *n* **1** a medieval weapon consisting of a metal spearhead joined to a long pole. **2** a point or spike. ◆ *vb* **pikes, piking, piked. 3** *(tr)* to pierce using a pike. [OE *pīc* point, from ?]
▸**'pikeman** *n*

pike[3] (paɪk) *n* short for **turnpike** (sense 1).

pike[4] (paɪk) *n Northern English dialect.* a pointed or conical hill. [OE *pīc*]

pike[5] (paɪk) *or* **piked** (paɪkt) *adj* (of the body position of a diver) bent at the hips but with the legs straight.

pike[6] (paɪk) *vb* **pikes, piking, piked.** *(intr;* foll. by *out) Austral. sl.* to shirk. [from PIKER]

pikeperch ('paɪk,pɜ:tʃ) *n, pl* **pikeperch** *or* **pikeperches.** any of various pike-like freshwater teleost fishes of the perch family of Europe.

piker ('paɪkə) *n US, Austral., & NZ sl.* **1** a person who will not accept a challenge; shirker. **2** a mean person. [C19: from *Pike* county, Missouri, US]

pikestaff ('paɪk,stɑ:f) *n* the wooden handle of a pike.

pilaster (pɪ'læstə) *n* a shallow rectangular column attached to the face of a wall. [C16: from F *pilastre,* from L *pīla* pillar]
▸**pi'lastered** *adj*

pilau (pɪ'laʊ), **pilaf, pilaff** ('pɪlæf), *or* **pilaw** (pɪ'lɔ:) *n* a dish originating from the East, consisting of rice flavoured with spices and cooked in stock, to which meat, poultry, or fish may be added. [C17: from Turkish *pilāw,* from Persian]

pilchard ('pɪltʃəd) *n* a European food fish of the herring family, with a rounded body covered with large scales. [C16 *pylcher,* from ?]

pile[1] Ⓣ (paɪl) *n* **1** a collection of objects laid on top of one another; heap; mound. **2** *Inf.* a large amount of money (esp. in **make a pile**). **3** *(often pl) Inf.* a large amount: *a pile of work.* **4** a less common word for **pyre. 5** a large building or group of buildings. **6** *Physics.* a structure of uranium and a moderator used for producing atomic energy; nuclear reactor. ◆ *vb* **piles, piling, piled. 7** (often foll. by *up*) to collect or be collected into or as if into a pile: *snow piled up in the drive.* **8** *(intr;* foll. by *in, into, off, out,* etc.) to move in a group, esp. in a hurried or disorganized manner: *to pile off the bus.* **9 pile it on.** *Inf.* to exaggerate. ◆ See also **pile up.** [C15: via OF from L *pīla* stone pier]

pile[2] Ⓣ (paɪl) *n* **1** a long column of timber, concrete, or steel, driven into the ground as a foundation for a structure. ◆ *vb* **piles, piling, piled.** *(tr)* **2** to drive (piles) into the ground. **3** to support (a structure) with piles. [OE *pīl,* from L *pīlum*]

pile[3] Ⓣ (paɪl) *n* **1** the yarns in a fabric that stand up or out from the weave, as in carpeting, velvet, etc. **2** soft fine hair, fur, wool, etc. [C15: from Anglo-Norman *pyle,* from L *pilus* hair]

pileate ('paɪlɪɪt, -,eɪt, 'pɪl-) *or* **pileated** ('paɪlɪ,eɪtɪd, 'pɪl-) *adj* **1** (of birds) having a crest. **2** *Bot.* having a pileus. [C18: from L *pīleātus* wearing a felt cap, from PILEUS]

pile-driver *n* a machine that drives piles into the ground.

pileous ('paɪlɪəs, 'pɪl-) *adj Biol.* **1** hairy. **2** of or relating to hair. [C19: ult. from L *pilus* a hair]

piles Ⓣ (paɪlz) *pl n* a nontechnical name for **haemorrhoids.** [C15: from L *pilae* balls (referring to the external piles)]

pileum ('paɪlɪəm, 'pɪl-) *n, pl* **pilea** (-lɪə). the top of a bird's head from the base of the bill to the occiput. [C19: NL, from L PILEUS]

pile up Ⓣ *vb (adv)* **1** to gather or be gathered in a pile. **2** *Inf.* to crash or cause to crash. ◆ *n* **pile-up. 3** *Inf.* a multiple collision of vehicles.

pileus ('paɪlɪəs) *n, pl* **pilei** (-lɪ,aɪ). the upper cap-shaped part of a mushroom. [C18: (botanical use): NL, from L: felt cap]

THESAURUS

piffling *adj Informal* = **trivial,** derisory, fiddling, insignificant, little, measly (*inf.*), Mickey Mouse (*sl.*), paltry, petty, piddling (*inf.*), puny, trifling, unimportant, useless, worthless

pig *n* **1** = **hog,** boar, grunter, piggy, piglet, porker, shoat, sow, swine **2** *Informal* = **slob** (*sl.*), animal, beast, boor, brute, glutton, greedy guts (*sl.*), guzzler, hog (*inf.*), sloven, swine

pigeon[1] *n* **1** = **dove,** bird, culver (*arch.*), cushat, squab **2** *Slang* = **victim,** dupe, fall guy (*inf.*), gull (*arch.*), mug (*Brit. sl.*), sitting duck, sitting target, sucker (*sl.*)

pigeon[2] *n Brit. informal* = **responsibility,** baby (*sl.*), business, concern, lookout (*inf.*), worry

pigeonhole *n* **1** = **compartment,** cubbyhole, cubicle, locker, niche, place, section **2** = **classification,** category, class, slot (*inf.*) ◆ *vb* **3** = **put off,** defer, file, postpone, shelve **4** = **classify,** catalogue, categorize, characterize, codify, compartmentalize, ghettoize, label, slot (*inf.*), sort

piggish *adj* **1** = **greedy,** boorish, crude, gluttonous, hoggish, piggy, rude, swinish, voracious **2** *Informal* = **stubborn,** mean, obstinate, pig-headed, possessive, selfish

pig-headed *adj* = **stubborn,** bull-headed, contrary, cross-grained, dense, froward (*arch.*), inflexible, mulish, obstinate, perverse, self-willed, stiff-necked, stupid, unyielding, wilful, wrong-headed
Antonyms *adj* agreeable, amiable, complaisant, cooperative, flexible, obliging, open-minded, tractable

pigment *n* **2** = **colour,** colorant, colouring, colouring matter, dye, dyestuff, paint, stain, tincture, tint

pile[1] *n* **1** = **heap,** accumulation, assemblage, assortment, collection, hoard, mass, mound, mountain, rick, stack, stockpile **2** *Informal* = **fortune,** big money, bomb (*Brit. sl.*), mint, money, packet (*sl.*), pot, pretty penny (*inf.*), tidy sum (*inf.*), wealth **3** *often plural Informal* = **a lot,** great deal, ocean, oodles (*inf.*), quantity, stacks **5** = **building,** edifice, erection, structure ◆ *vb* **7** = **collect,** accumulate, amass, assemble, gather, heap, hoard, load up, mass, stack, store **8** = **crowd,** charge, crush, flock, flood, jam, pack, rush, stream

pile[2] *n* **1** = **foundation,** beam, column, pier, piling, pillar, post, support, upright

pile[3] *n* **1, 2** = **nap,** down, fibre, filament, fur, hair, plush, shag, surface

piles *pl n* = **haemorrhoids**

pile up *n* **pile-up 3** *Informal* = **collision,** accident, crash, multiple collision, smash, smash-up (*inf.*)

pilewort ('paɪlˌwɜːt) *n* any of several plants, such as lesser celandine, thought to be effective in treating piles.

pilfer ❶ ('pɪlfə) *vb* to steal (minor items), esp. in small quantities. [C14 *pylfre* (n) from OF *pelfre* booty]
▸**'pilferage** *n* ▸**'pilferer** *n*

pilgrim ❶ ('pɪlgrɪm) *n* **1** a person who undertakes a journey to a sacred place. **2** any wayfarer. [C12: from Provençal *pelegrin*, from L *peregrīnus* foreign, from *per* through + *ager* land]

pilgrimage ❶ ('pɪlgrɪmɪdʒ) *n* **1** a journey to a shrine or other sacred place. **2** a journey or long search made for exalted or sentimental reasons. ◆ *vb* **pilgrimages, pilgrimaging, pilgrimaged. 3** (*intr*) to make a pilgrimage.

Pilgrim Fathers *or* **Pilgrims** *pl n* **the.** the English Puritans who sailed on the Mayflower to New England, where they founded Plymouth Colony in SE Massachusetts (1620).

piliferous (paɪ'lɪfərəs) *adj* (esp. of plants) bearing or ending in a hair or hairs. [C19: from L *pilus* hair + -FEROUS]
▸**'piliˌform** *adj*

piling ('paɪlɪŋ) *n* **1** the act of driving piles. **2** a number of piles. **3** a structure formed of piles.

pill[1] ❶ (pɪl) *n* **1** a small spherical or ovoid mass of a medicinal substance, intended to be swallowed whole. **2 the pill.** (*sometimes cap.*) *Inf.* an oral contraceptive. **3** something unpleasant that must be endured (esp. in **bitter pill to swallow**). **4** *Sl.* a ball or disc. **5** *Sl.* an unpleasant or boring person. ◆ *vb* **6** (*tr*) to give pills to. [C15: from MFlemish *pille*, from L *pilula* a little ball, from *pila* ball]

pill[2] (pɪl) *vb* **1** *Arch. or dialect.* to peel or skin (something). **2** *Arch.* to pillage or plunder (a place, etc.). [OE *pilian*, from L *pilāre* to strip]

pillage ❶ ('pɪlɪdʒ) *vb* **pillages, pillaging, pillaged. 1** to rob (a town, village, etc.) of (booty or spoils). ◆ *n* **2** the act of pillaging. **3** something obtained by pillaging; booty. [C14: via OF from *piller* to despoil, prob. from *peille* rag, from L *pīleus* felt cap]
▸**'pillager** *n*

pillar ❶ ('pɪlə) *n* **1** an upright structure of stone, brick, metal, etc. that supports a superstructure. **2** something resembling this in shape or function: *a pillar of smoke.* **3** a prominent supporter: *a pillar of the Church.* **4 from pillar to post.** from one place to another. [C13: from OF *pilier*, from L *pīla*]

pillar box *n* (in Britain) a red pillar-shaped public letter box situated on a pavement.

pillbox ('pɪlˌbɒks) *n* **1** a box for pills. **2** a small enclosed fortified emplacement, made of reinforced concrete. **3** a small round hat.

pillion ('pɪljən) *n* **1** a seat or place behind the rider of a motorcycle, scooter, horse, etc. ◆ *adv* **2** on a pillion: *to ride pillion.* [C16: from Gaelic; cf. Scot. *pillean*, Irish *pillīn* couch]

pilliwinks ('pɪlɪˌwɪŋks) *pl n* a medieval instrument of torture for the fingers. [C14: from ?]

pillock ('pɪlək) *n Brit. sl.* a stupid or annoying person. [C14: from Scand. dialect *pillicock* penis]

pillory ❶ ('pɪlərɪ) *n, pl* **pillories. 1** a wooden framework into which offenders were formerly locked by the neck and wrists and exposed to public abuse and ridicule. **2** exposure to public scorn or abuse. ◆ *vb* **pillories, pillorying, pilloried.** (*tr*) **3** to expose to public scorn or ridicule. **4** to punish by putting in a pillory. [C13: from Anglo-L *pillorium*, from OF *pilori*, from ?]

pillow ('pɪləʊ) *n* **1** a cloth case stuffed with feathers, foam rubber, etc., used to support the head, esp. during sleep. **2** Also called: **cushion.** a padded cushion or board on which pillow lace is made. **3** anything like a pillow in shape or function. ◆ *vb* (*tr*) **4** to rest (one's head) on or as if on a pillow. **5** to serve as a pillow for. [OE *pylwe*, from L *pulvīnus* cushion]

pillowcase ('pɪləʊˌkeɪs) *or* **pillowslip** ('pɪləʊˌslɪp) *n* a removable washable cover of cotton, linen, nylon, etc., for a pillow.

pillow fight *n* a mock fight in which participants thump each other with pillows.

pillow lace *n* lace made by winding thread around bobbins on a padded cushion or board. Cf. **point lace.**

pillow talk *n* confidential talk between sexual partners in bed.

pilose ('paɪləʊz) *adj Biol.* covered with fine soft hairs: *pilose leaves.* [C18: from L *pilōsus*, from *pilus* hair]
▸**pilosity** (paɪ'lɒsɪtɪ) *n*

pilot ❶ ('paɪlət) *n* **1** a person who is qualified to operate an aircraft or spacecraft in flight. **2a** a person who is qualified to steer or guide a ship into or out of a port, river mouth, etc. **2b** (*as modifier*): *a pilot ship.* **3** a person who steers a ship. **4** a person who acts as a leader or guide. **5** *Machinery.* a guide used to assist in joining two mating parts together. **6** an experimental programme on radio or television. **7** (*modifier*) serving as a test or trial: *a pilot project.* **8** (*modifier*) serving as a guide: *a pilot beacon.* ◆ *vb* (*tr*) **9** to act as pilot of. **10** to control the course of. **11** to guide or lead (a project, people, etc.). [C16: from F *pilote*, from Med. L *pilotus*, ult. from Gk *pēdon* oar]

pilotage ('paɪlətɪdʒ) *n* **1** the act of piloting an aircraft or ship. **2** a pilot's fee.

pilot balloon *n* a meteorological balloon used to observe air currents.

pilot fish *n* a small fish of tropical and subtropical seas, marked with dark vertical bands: often accompanies sharks.

pilot house *n Naut.* an enclosed structure on the bridge of a vessel from which it can be navigated; a wheelhouse.

pilot lamp *n* a small light in an electric circuit or device that lights when the current is on.

pilot light *n* **1** a small auxiliary flame that ignites the main burner of a gas appliance. **2** a small electric light used as an indicator.

pilot officer *n* the most junior commissioned rank in the British Royal Air Force and in certain other air forces.

pilot study *n* a small-scale experiment undertaken to decide whether and how to launch a full-scale project.

Pils (pɪlz, pɪls) *n* a type of lager-like beer. [C20: abbrev. of PILSNER]

Pilsner ('pɪlznə) *or* **Pilsener** *n* a type of pale beer with a strong flavour of hops. [after *Pilsen*, city in the N Czech Republic, where it was orig. brewed]

pilule ('pɪljuːl) *n* a small pill. [C16: via F from L *pilula* little ball, from *pila* ball]
▸**'pilular** *adj*

pimento (pɪ'mɛntəʊ) *n, pl* **pimentos.** another name for **allspice** or **pimiento.** [C17: from Sp. *pimiento* pepper plant, from Med. L *pigmenta* spiced drink, from L *pigmentum* PIGMENT]

pi meson *n* another name for **pion.**

pimiento (pɪ'mjɛntəʊ, -'mɛn-) *n, pl* **pimientos.** a Spanish pepper with a red fruit used as a vegetable. Also called: **pimento.** [var. of PIMENTO]

pimp[1] ❶ (pɪmp) *n* **1** a man who solicits for a prostitute or brothel. **2** a man who procures sexual gratification for another; procurer; pander. ◆ *vb* **3** (*intr*) to act as a pimp. [C17: from ?]

pimp[2] (pɪmp) *Sl., chiefly Austral. & NZ.* ◆ *n* **1** a spy or informer. ◆ *vb* **2** (*intr; often foll. by on*) to inform (on). [from ?]

pimpernel ('pɪmpəˌnɛl, -nᵊl) *n* any of several plants, such as the scarlet pimpernel, typically having small star-shaped flowers. [C15: from OF *pimpernelle*, ult. from L *piper* PEPPER]

pimple ❶ ('pɪmpᵊl) *n* a small round usually inflamed swelling of the skin. [C14: rel. to OE *pipilian* to break out in spots]
▸**'pimpled** *adj* ▸**'pimply** *adj* ▸**'pimpliness** *n*

pin ❶ (pɪn) *n* **1** a short stiff straight piece of wire pointed at one end and either rounded or having a flattened head at the other: used mainly for fastening pieces of cloth, paper, etc. **2** short for **cotter pin, hairpin, panel pin, rolling pin,** or **safety pin. 3** an ornamental brooch, esp. a narrow one. **4** a badge worn fastened to the clothing by a pin. **5** something of little or no importance (esp. in **not care** *or* **give a pin (for)**). **6** a peg or dowel. **7** anything resembling a pin in shape, function, etc. **8** (in various bowling games) a usually club-shaped wooden object set up in groups as a target. **9** Also called: **safety pin.** a clip on a hand grenade that prevents its detonation until removed or released. **10** *Naut.* **10a** See **belaying pin. 10b** the sliding closure for a shackle. **11** *Music.* a metal tuning peg on a piano. **12** *Surgery.* a metal rod, esp. of stainless steel, for holding together adjacent ends of fractured bones during healing. **13** *Chess.* a position in which a piece is pinned against a more valuable piece or the king. **14** *Golf.* the flagpole marking the hole on a green. **15** (*usually pl*) *Inf.* a leg. ◆ *vb* **pins, pinning, pinned.** (*tr*) **16** to attach, hold, or fasten with or as if with a pin or pins. **17** to transfix with a pin, spear, etc. **18** (foll. by *on*) *Inf.* to place (the blame for something): *he pinned the charge on his accomplice.* **19** *Chess.* to cause (an enemy piece) to be effectively immobilized since moving it would reveal a check or expose a more valuable piece to capture. ◆ See also **pin down.** [OE *pinn*]

PIN (pɪn) *n acronym for* personal identification number: a number used by a holder of a cash card or credit card used in EFTPOS.

pinaceous (paɪ'neɪʃəs) *adj* of, relating to, or belonging to a family of conifers with needle-like leaves: includes pine, spruce, fir, larch, and cedar. [C19: via NL from L *pīnus* a pine]

pinafore ('pɪnəˌfɔː) *n* **1** *Chiefly Brit.* an apron, esp. one with a bib. **2** Also called: **pinafore dress.** a dress with a sleeveless bodice or bib top, worn over a jumper or blouse. [C18: from PIN + AFORE]

THESAURUS

pilfer *vb* = **steal**, appropriate, blag, embezzle, filch, lift (*inf.*), pinch (*inf.*), purloin, rifle, rob, snaffle (*Brit. inf.*), snitch (*sl.*), swipe (*sl.*), take, thieve, walk off with

pilgrim *n* **1, 2** = **traveller**, crusader, hajji, palmer, wanderer, wayfarer

pilgrimage *n* **1, 2** = **journey**, crusade, excursion, expedition, hajj, mission, tour, trip

pill[1] *n* **1** = **tablet**, bolus, capsule, pellet, pilule **2 the pill** = **oral contraceptive 5** *Slang* = **trial**, bore, drag (*inf.*), nuisance, pain (*inf.*), pain in the neck (*inf.*), pest

pillage *vb* **1** = **plunder**, depredate (*rare*), despoil, freeboot, loot, maraud, raid, ransack, ravage, reive (*dialect*), rifle, rob, sack, spoil (*arch.*), spoliate, strip ◆ *n* **2** = **plunder**, depredation, devastation, marauding, rapine, robbery, sack, spoliation **3** = **booty**, loot, plunder, spoils

pillar *n* **1** = **support**, column, obelisk, pier, pilaster, piling, post, prop, shaft, stanchion, upright **3** = **supporter**, leader, leading light (*inf.*), mainstay, rock, torchbearer, tower of strength, upholder, worthy

pillory *vb* **3** = **ridicule**, brand, cast a slur on, denounce, expose to ridicule, heap *or* pour scorn on, hold up to shame, lash, show up, stigmatize

pilot *n* **1** = **airman**, aviator, captain, flyer **2-4** = **helmsman**, conductor, coxswain, director, guide, leader, navigator, steersman ◆ *modifier* **7** = **trial**, experimental, model, test ◆ *vb* **9-11** = **fly**, conduct, control, direct, drive, guide, handle, lead, manage, navigate, operate, shepherd, steer

pimp[1] *n* **1, 2** = **procurer**, bawd (*arch.*), go-between, pander, panderer, white-slaver, whoremaster (*arch.*) ◆ *vb* **3** = **procure**, live off immoral earnings, sell, solicit, tout

pimple *n* = **spot**, boil, papule, plook (*Scot.*), pustule, swelling, zit (*sl.*)

pin *vb* **16** = **fasten**, affix, attach, fix, join, secure

pinaster (paɪˈnæstə) *n* a Mediterranean pine tree with paired needles and prickly cones. Also called: **maritime** (*or* **cluster**) **pinaster.** [C16: from L: wild pine, from *pīnus* pine]

pinball (ˈpɪnˌbɔːl) *n* **a** a game in which the player shoots a small ball through several hazards on a table, electrically operated machine, etc. **b** (*as modifier*): *a pinball machine.*

pince-nez (ˈpænsˌneɪ, ˈpɪns-; *French* pɛ̃sne) *n, pl* **pince-nez.** eyeglasses that are held in place only by means of a clip over the bridge of the nose. [C19: F, lit.: pinch-nose]

pincers (ˈpɪnsəz) *pl n* **1** Also called: **pair of pincers.** a gripping tool consisting of two hinged arms with handles at one end and, at the other, curved bevelled jaws that close on the workpiece. **2** the pair or pairs of jointed grasping appendages in lobsters and certain other arthropods. [C14: from OF *pinceour,* from OF *pincier* to pinch]

pinch 🅣 (pɪntʃ) *vb* **1** to press (something, esp. flesh) tightly between two surfaces, esp. between a finger and thumb. **2** to confine, squeeze, or painfully press (toes, fingers, etc.) because of lack of space: *these shoes pinch.* **3** (*tr*) to cause stinging pain to: *the cold pinched his face.* **4** (*tr*) to make thin or drawn-looking, as from grief, lack of food, etc. **5** (usually foll. by *on*) to provide (oneself or another person) with meagre allowances, amounts, etc. **6 pinch pennies.** to live frugally because of meanness or to economize. **7** (usually foll. by *off, out,* or *back*) to remove the tips of (buds, shoots, etc.) to correct or encourage growth. **8** (*tr*) *Inf.* to steal or take without asking. **9** (*tr*) *Inf.* to arrest. ◆ *n* **10** a squeeze or sustained nip. **11** the quantity of a substance, such as salt, that can be taken between a thumb and finger. **12** a very small quantity. **13** (usually preceded by *the*) sharp, painful, or extreme stress, need, etc.: *feeling the pinch of poverty.* **14** *Sl.* a robbery. **15** *Sl.* a police raid or arrest. **16 at a pinch.** if absolutely necessary. [C16: prob. from OF *pinchier* (unattested)]

pinchbeck (ˈpɪntʃˌbɛk) *n* **1** an alloy of copper and zinc, used as imitation gold. **2** a spurious or cheap imitation. ◆ *adj* **3** made of pinchbeck. **4** sham or cheap. [C18 (the alloy), C19 (something spurious): after C. *Pinchbeck* (?1670–1732), E watchmaker who invented it]

pinchpenny (ˈpɪntʃˌpɛnɪ) *adj* **1** niggardly; miserly. ◆ *n, pl* **pinchpennies.** **2** a miserly person.

pincushion (ˈpɪnˌkʊʃən) *n* a small well-padded cushion in which pins are stuck ready for use.

pin down 🅣 *vb* (*tr, adv*) **1** to force (someone) to make a decision or carry out a promise. **2** to define clearly: *he had a vague suspicion that he couldn't quite pin down.* **3** to confine to a place.

pine[1] (paɪn) *n* **1** any of a genus of evergreen resinous coniferous trees of the N hemisphere, with long needle-shaped leaves (**pine needles**) and brown cones. **2** the wood of any of these trees. [OE *pīn,* from L *pīnus* pine]

pine[2] 🅣 (paɪn) *vb* **pines, pining, pined. 1** (*intr;* often foll. by *for* or an infinitive) to feel great longing or desire; yearn. **2** (*intr;* often foll. by *away*) to become ill or thin through worry, longing, etc. [OE *pīnian* to torture, from *pīn* pain, from Med. L *pēna,* from L *poena* PAIN]

pineal eye (ˈpɪnɪəl) *n* an outgrowth of the pineal gland that forms an eyelike structure on the top of the head in certain cold-blooded vertebrates. [C19: from F, from L *pīnea* pine cone]

pineal gland *or* **body** *n* a pea-sized organ situated at the base of the brain that secretes a hormone, melatonin, into the bloodstream. Technical names: **epiphysis, epiphysis cerebri.**

pineapple (ˈpaɪnˌæpᵊl) *n* **1** a tropical American plant cultivated for its large fleshy edible fruit. **2** the fruit of this plant, consisting of an inflorescence clustered around a fleshy axis and surmounted by a tuft of leaves. **3** *Mil. sl.* a hand grenade. [C14 *pinappel* pine cone; C17: applied to the fruit because of its appearance]

pine cone *n* the seed-producing structure of a pine tree. See **cone** (sense 3a).

pine marten *n* a marten of N European and Asian coniferous woods, having dark brown fur with a creamy-yellow patch on the throat.

pinene (ˈpaɪniːn) *n* either of two isomeric terpenes, found in many essential oils and constituting the main part of oil of turpentine. [C20: from PINE[1] + -ENE]

pine nut *or* **kernel** *n* the edible seed of certain pine trees.

pine tar *n* a brown or black semisolid, produced by the destructive distillation of pine wood, used in roofing compositions, paints, medicines, etc.

pinfeather (ˈpɪnˌfɛðə) *n Ornithol.* a feather emerging from the skin and still enclosed in its horny sheath.

pinfold (ˈpɪnˌfəʊld) *n* **1** a pound for stray cattle. ◆ *vb* **2** (*tr*) to gather or confine in or as if in a pinfold. [OE *pundfald*]

ping (pɪŋ) *n* **1** a short high-pitched resonant sound, as of a bullet striking metal or a sonar echo. ◆ *vb* **2** (*intr*) to make such a noise. [C19: imit.]

pinger (ˈpɪŋə) *n* a device that makes a pinging sound, esp. one that can be preset to ring at a particular time.

Ping-Pong (ˈpɪŋˌpɒŋ) *n Trademark.* another name for **table tennis.** Also: **ping pong.**

pinhead (ˈpɪnˌhɛd) *n* **1** the head of a pin. **2** something very small. **3** *Inf.* a stupid person.
▸ **ˈpinˌheaded** *adj* ▸ **ˈpinˌheadedness** *n*

pinhole (ˈpɪnˌhəʊl) *n* a small hole made with or as if with a pin.

pinion[1] 🅣 (ˈpɪnjən) *n* **1** *Chiefly poetic.* a bird's wing. **2** the part of a bird's wing including the flight feathers. ◆ *vb* (*tr*) **3** to hold or bind (the arms) of (a person) so as to restrain or immobilize him. **4** to confine or shackle. **5** to make (a bird) incapable of flight by removing the flight feathers. [C15: from OF *pignon* wing, from L *pinna* wing]

pinion[2] (ˈpɪnjən) *n* a cogwheel that engages with a larger wheel or rack. [C17: from F *pignon* cogwheel, from OF *peigne* comb, from L *pecten*]

pink[1] 🅣 (pɪŋk) *n* **1** a pale reddish colour. **2** pink cloth or clothing: *dressed in pink.* **3** any of various Old World plants, such as the garden pink, cultivated for their fragrant flowers. See also **carnation** (sense 1). **4** the flower of any of these plants. **5** the highest or best degree, condition, etc. (esp. in **in the pink**). **6a** a huntsman's scarlet coat. **6b** a huntsman who wears a scarlet coat. ◆ *adj* **7** of the colour pink. **8** *Brit. inf.* left-wing. **9** *Inf.* of or relating to homosexuals or homosexuality: *the pink vote.* **10** (of a huntsman's coat) scarlet or red. ◆ *vb* **11** (*intr*) another word for **knock** (sense 7). [C16 (the flower), C18 (the colour): ? short for PINKEYE]
▸ **ˈpinkish** *or* **ˈpinky** *adj* ▸ **ˈpinkness** *n*

pink[2] 🅣 (pɪŋk) *vb* (*tr*) **1** to prick lightly with a sword, etc. **2** to decorate (leather, etc.) with a perforated or punched pattern. **3** to cut with pinking shears. [C14: ? of Low G origin]

pink[3] (pɪŋk) *n* a sailing vessel with a narrow overhanging transom. [C15: from MDu. *pinke,* from ?]

pinkeye (ˈpɪŋkˌaɪ) *n* **1** Also called: **acute conjunctivitis.** an acute contagious inflammation of the conjunctiva of the eye, characterized by redness, discharge, etc. **2** Also called: **infectious keratitis.** a similar condition affecting the cornea of horses and cattle. [C16: partial translation of obs. Du. *pinck oogen* small eyes]

pinkie *or* **pinky** (ˈpɪŋkɪ) *n, pl* **pinkies.** *Scot., US, & Canad.* the little finger. [C19: from Du. *pinkje*]

pinking shears *pl n* scissors with a serrated edge on one or both blades, producing a wavy edge to material cut, thus preventing fraying.

pink salmon *n* **1** any salmon having pale pink flesh. **2** the flesh of such a fish.

pin money *n* **1** an allowance by a husband to his wife for personal expenditure. **2** money saved or earned for incidental expenses.

pinna (ˈpɪnə) *n, pl* **pinnae** (-niː) *or* **pinnas. 1** any leaflet of a pinnate compound leaf. **2** *Zool.* a feather, wing, fin, etc. **3** another name for **auricle** (sense 2). [C18: via NL from L: wing]

pinnace (ˈpɪnɪs, -əs) *n* any of various kinds of ship's tender. [C16: from F *pinace,* ?from OSp. *pinaza,* lit.: something made of pine, ult. from L *pīnus* pine]

pinnacle 🅣 (ˈpɪnəkᵊl) *n* **1** the highest point, esp. of fame, success, etc. **2** a towering peak, as of a mountain. **3** a slender upright structure in the form of a spire on the top of a buttress, gable, or tower. ◆ *vb* **pinnacles, pinnacling, pinnacled.** (*tr*) **4** to set as on a pinnacle. **5** to furnish with a pinnacle or pinnacles. **6** to crown with a pinnacle. [C14: via OF from LL *pinnāculum* a peak, from L *pinna* wing]

pinnate (ˈpɪneɪt, ˈpɪnɪt) *adj* **1** like a feather in appearance. **2** (of compound leaves) having the leaflets growing opposite each other in pairs on either side of the stem. [C18: from L *pinnātus,* from *pinna* feather]
▸ **ˈpinnately** *adv* ▸ **pinˈnation** *n*

pinniped (ˈpɪnɪˌpɛd) *adj* **1** of, relating to, or belonging to an order of aquatic placental mammals having a streamlined body and limbs specialized as flippers: includes seals, sea lions, and the walrus. ◆ *n* **2** any pinniped animal. [C19: from NL *pinnipēs,* from L *pinna* fin + *pēs* foot]

pinnule (ˈpɪnjuːl) *n* **1** any of the lobes of a leaflet of a pinnate com-

THESAURUS

pinch *vb* **1** = **squeeze**, compress, grasp, nip, press, tweak **2** = **hurt**, chafe, confine, cramp, crush, pain **5** = **scrimp**, afflict, be stingy, distress, economize, oppress, pinch pennies, press, skimp, spare, stint, tighten one's belt **8** *Informal* = **steal**, filch, knock off (*sl.*), lift (*inf.*), nick (*sl., chiefly Brit.*), pilfer, purloin, rob, snaffle (*Brit. inf.*), snatch, snitch (*sl.*), swipe (*sl.*) **9** *Informal* = **arrest**, apprehend, bust (*inf.*), collar (*inf.*), do (*sl.*), lift (*sl.*), nab (*inf.*), nail (*inf.*), pick up (*sl.*), pull in (*Brit. sl.*), run in (*sl.*), take into custody ◆ *n* **10** = **squeeze**, nip, tweak **12** = **dash**, bit, jot, mite, small quantity, *soupçon,* speck, taste **13** = **hardship**, crisis, difficulty, emergency, exigency, necessity, oppression, pass, plight, predicament, pressure, strait, stress

Antonyms *vb* ≠ **scrimp:** be extravagant, blow (*sl.*), fritter away, spend like water, squander, waste ≠ **arrest:** free, let go, let out, release, set free

pinched *adj* **4** = **thin**, careworn, drawn, gaunt, haggard, peaky, starved, worn
Antonyms *adj* blooming, chubby, fat, glowing, hale and hearty, healthy, plump, radiant, ruddy, well-fed

pin down *vb* **1** = **force**, compel, constrain, make, press, pressurize **2** = **determine**, designate, home in on, identify, locate, name, pinpoint, specify **3** = **fix**, bind, confine, constrain, hold, hold down, immobilize, nail down, tie down

pine[2] *vb* **1** *often foll. by* **for** = **long**, ache, carry a torch for, covet, crave, desire, eat one's heart out over, hanker, hunger for, lust after, sigh, suspire (*arch. or poetic*), thirst for, wish for, yearn for **2** = **waste**, decay, decline, droop, dwindle, fade, flag, languish, peak, sicken, sink, weaken, wilt, wither

pinion[1] *vb* **4** = **immobilize**, bind, chain, confine, fasten, fetter, manacle, pin down, shackle, tie

pink[1] *n* **5** = **best**, acme, height, peak, perfection, summit ◆ *adj* **7** = **rosy**, flesh, flushed, reddish, rose, roseate, salmon

pink[2] *vb* **1, 3** = **cut**, incise, notch, perforate, prick, punch, scallop, score

pinnacle *n* **1, 2** = **peak**, acme, apex, apogee, crest, crown, eminence, height, meridian, summit, top, vertex, zenith **3** = **spire**, belfry, cone, needle, obelisk, pyramid, steeple

pound leaf, which is itself pinnately divided. **2** *Zool.* any feather-like part, such as any of the arms of a sea lily. [C16: from L *pinnula*, dim. of *pinna* feather]
▸'**pinnular** *adj*

pinny ('pɪnɪ) *n, pl* **pinnies.** a child's or informal name for **pinafore** (sense 1).

pinochle *or* **pinocle** ('piːnʌkᵊl) *n* **1** a card game for two to four players similar to bezique. **2** the combination of queen of spades and jack of diamonds in this game. [C19: from ?]

pinpoint ➊ ('pɪn,pɔɪnt) *vb (tr)* **1** to locate or identify exactly: *to pinpoint a problem; to pinpoint a place on a map.* ◆ *n* **2** an insignificant or trifling thing. **3** the point of a pin. **4** (*modifier*) exact: *a pinpoint aim.*

pinprick ('pɪn,prɪk) *n* **1** a slight puncture made by or as if by a pin. **2** a small irritation. ◆ *vb* **3** (*tr*) to puncture with or as if with a pin.

pins and needles *n* (*functioning as sing*) *Inf.* **1** a tingling sensation in the fingers, toes, legs, etc., caused by the return of normal blood circulation after its temporary impairment. **2 on pins and needles.** in a state of anxious suspense.

pinstripe ('pɪn,straɪp) *n* (in textiles) a very narrow stripe in fabric or the fabric itself.

pint ➊ (paɪnt) *n* **1** a unit of liquid measure of capacity equal to one eighth of a gallon. 1 Brit. pint is equal to 0.568 litre, 1 US pint to 0.473 litre. **2** a unit of dry measure of capacity equal to one half of a quart. 1 US dry pint is equal to one sixty-fourth of a US bushel or 0.5506 litre. **3** a measure having such a capacity. **4** *Brit. inf.* **4a** a pint of beer. **4b** a drink of beer: *he's gone out for a pint.* [C14: from OF *pinte*, from ?; ?from Med. L *pincta* marks used in measuring liquids, ult. from L *pingere* to paint]

pinta ('paɪntə) *n Inf.* a pint of milk. [C20: phonetic rendering of *pint of*]

pintail ('pɪn,teɪl) *n, pl* **pintails** *or* **pintail.** a greyish-brown duck with a pointed tail.

pintle ('pɪntᵊl) *n* **1** a pin or bolt forming the pivot of a hinge. **2** the link bolt, hook, or pin on a vehicle's towing bracket. **3** the needle or plunger of the injection valve of an oil engine. [OE *pintel* penis]

pinto ('pɪntəʊ) *US & Canad.* ◆ *adj* **1** marked with patches of white; piebald. ◆ *n, pl* **pintos. 2** a pinto horse. [C19: from American Sp. (orig.: painted, spotted), ult. from L *pingere* to paint]

pint-size ➊ *or* **pint-sized** *adj Inf.* very small.

pin tuck *n* a narrow, ornamental fold, esp. used on shirt fronts and dress bodices.

pin-up *n* **1** *Inf.* **1a** a picture of a sexually attractive person, esp. when partially or totally undressed. **1b** (*as modifier*): *a pin-up magazine.* **2** *Sl.* a person who has appeared in such a picture. **3** a photograph of a famous personality.

pinus radiata ('paɪnəs ,reɪdɪ'ɑːtə) *n* a pine tree grown in New Zealand and Australia to produce building timber.

pinwheel ('pɪn,wiːl) *n* another name for a **Catherine wheel** (sense 1).

pinworm ('pɪn,wɜːm) *n* a parasitic nematode worm, infecting the colon, rectum, and anus of humans. Also called: **threadworm.**

piny ('paɪnɪ) *adj* **pinier, piniest.** of, resembling, or covered with pine trees.

Pinyin ('pɪn'jɪn) *n* a system of spelling used to transliterate Chinese characters into the Roman alphabet.

pion ('paɪɒn) *or* **pi meson** *n Physics.* a meson having a positive or negative charge and a rest mass 273 times that of the electron, or no charge and a rest mass 264 times that of the electron. [C20: from Gk letter PI + -ON]

pioneer ➊ (,paɪə'nɪə) *n* **1a** a colonist, explorer, or settler of a new land, region, etc. **1b** (*as modifier*): *a pioneer wagon.* **2** an innovator or developer of something new. **3** *Mil.* a member of an infantry group that digs entrenchments, makes roads, etc. ◆ *vb* **4** to be a pioneer (in or of). **5** (*tr*) to initiate, prepare, or open up: *to pioneer a medical programme.* [C16: from OF *paonier* infantryman, from *paon* PAWN²]

pious ➊ ('paɪəs) *adj* **1** having or expressing reverence for a god or gods; religious; devout. **2** marked by reverence. **3** marked by false reverence; sanctimonious. **4** sacred; not secular. [C17: from L *pius*]
▸'**piously** *adv* ▸'**piousness** *n*

pip¹ (pɪp) *n* **1** the seed of a fleshy fruit, such as an apple or pear. **2** any of the segments marking the surface of a pineapple. [C18: short for PIPPIN]

pip² (pɪp) *n* **1** a short high-pitched sound, a sequence of which can act as a time signal, esp. on radio. **2** a radar blip. **3a** a device, such as a spade, diamond, heart, or club on a playing card. **3b** any of the spots on dice or dominoes. **4** *Inf.* the emblem worn on the shoulder by junior officers in the British Army, indicating their rank. ◆ *vb* **pips, pipping, pipped. 5** (of a young bird) **5a** (*intr*) to chirp; peep. **5b** to pierce (the shell of its egg) while hatching. **6** (*intr*) to make a short high-pitched sound. [C16 (in the sense: spot); C17 (vb); C20 (in the sense: short high-pitched sound): ? imit.]

pip³ (pɪp) *n* **1** a contagious disease of poultry characterized by the secretion of thick mucus in the mouth and throat. **2** *Facetious sl.* a minor human ailment. **3** *Brit. sl.* a bad temper or depression (esp. in **give (someone) the pip**). ◆ *vb* **pips, pipping, pipped. 4** *Brit. sl.* to cause to be annoyed or depressed. [C15: from MDu. *pippe*, ult. from L *pituita* phlegm]

pip⁴ (pɪp) *vb* **pips, pipping, pipped.** (*tr*) *Brit. sl.* **1** to wound, esp. with a gun. **2** to defeat (a person), esp. when his success seems certain (often in **pip at the post**). **3** to blackball or ostracize. [C19 (orig. in the sense: to blackball): prob. from PIP²]

pipal ('piːpᵊl) *n* a variant of **peepul.**

pipe¹ ➊ (paɪp) *n* **1** a long tube of metal, plastic, etc., used to convey water, oil, gas, etc. **2** a long tube or case. **3** an object made in various shapes and sizes, consisting of a small bowl with an attached tubular stem, in which tobacco or other substances are smoked. **4** Also called: **pipeful.** the amount of tobacco that fills the bowl of a pipe. **5 put that in your pipe and smoke it.** *Inf.* accept that fact if you can. **6** *Zool., bot.* any of various hollow organs, such as the respiratory passage of certain animals. **7a** any musical instrument whose sound production results from the vibration of an air column in a simple tube. **7b** any of the tubular devices on an organ. **8 the pipes.** See **bagpipes. 9** a shrill voice or sound, as of a bird. **10a** a boatswain's pipe. **10b** the sound it makes. **11** (*pl*) *Inf.* the respiratory tract or vocal cords. **12** *Metallurgy.* a conical hole in the head of an ingot. **13** a cylindrical vein of rich ore. **14** Also called: **volcanic pipe.** a vertical cylindrical passage in a volcano through which molten lava is forced during eruption. ◆ *vb* **pipes, piping, piped. 15** to play (music) on a pipe. **16** (*tr*) to summon or lead by a pipe: *to pipe the dancers.* **17** to utter (something) shrilly. **18a** to signal orders to (the crew) by a boatswain's pipe. **18b** (*tr*) to signal the arrival or departure of: *to pipe the admiral aboard.* **19** (*tr*) to convey (water, gas, etc.) by a pipe or pipes. **20** (*tr*) to provide with pipes. **21** (*tr*) to trim (an article, esp. of clothing) with piping. **22** to force cream or icing, etc., through a shaped nozzle to decorate food. ◆ See also **pipe down, pipe up.** [OE *pīpe* (n), *pīpian* (vb), ult. from L *pīpāre* to chirp]

pipe² (paɪp) *n* **1** a large cask for wine, oil, etc. **2** a measure of capacity for wine equal to four barrels or 105 Brit. gallons. **3** a cask holding this quantity with its contents. [C14: via OF (in the sense: tube), ult. from L *pīpāre* to chirp]

pipe bomb *n* a small explosive device hidden in a pipe or drain, detonated by means of a timer.

pipeclay ('paɪp,kleɪ) *n* **1** a fine white pure clay, used in the manufacture of tobacco pipes and pottery and for whitening leather and similar materials. ◆ *vb* **2** (*tr*) to whiten with pipeclay.

pipe cleaner *n* a short length of thin wires twisted so as to hold tiny tufts of yarn: used to clean the stem of a tobacco pipe.

piped music *n* light popular music prerecorded and played through amplifiers in a shop, restaurant, factory, etc., as background music.

pipe down ➊ *vb* (*intr, adv*) *Inf.* to stop talking, making noise, etc.

pipe dream ➊ *n* a fanciful or impossible plan or hope. [alluding to dreams produced by smoking an opium pipe]

pipefish ('paɪp,fɪʃ) *n, pl* **pipefish** *or* **pipefishes.** any of various teleost fishes having a long tubelike snout and an elongated body covered with bony plates. Also called: **needlefish.**

pipefitting ('paɪp,fɪtɪŋ) *n* **a** the act or process of bending and joining pipes. **b** the branch of plumbing involving this.
▸'**pipe,fitter** *n*

pipeline ➊ ('paɪp,laɪn) *n* **1** a long pipe used to transport oil, natural gas, etc. **2** a medium of communication, esp. a private one. **3 in the pipeline.** in the process of being completed, delivered, or produced. ◆ *vb* **pipelines, pipelining, pipelined.** (*tr*) **4** to convey by pipeline. **5** to supply with a pipeline.

pipe major *n* the noncommissioned officer responsible for the training of a pipe band.

pipe organ *n* another name for **organ** (the musical instrument).

piper ('paɪpə) *n* **1** a person who plays a pipe or bagpipes. **2 pay the piper and call the tune.** to bear the cost of an undertaking and control it.

piperidine (pɪ'perɪ,diːn) *n* a liquid compound with a peppery ammoniacal odour: used in making rubbers and curing epoxy resins.

piperine ('pɪpə,raɪn) *n* an alkaloid that is the active ingredient of pepper, used as a flavouring and as an insecticide. [C19: from L *piper* PEPPER]

THESAURUS

pinpoint *vb* **1** = **identify**, define, distinguish, get a fix on, home in on, locate, spot

pint *n* **4** *Brit. informal* = **beer**, ale, jar (*Brit. inf.*), jug (*Brit. inf.*)

pint-size *adj Informal* = **small**, diminutive, little, midget, miniature, pocket, pygmy *or* pigmy, teensy-weensy, teeny-weeny, tiny, wee

pioneer *n* **1** = **settler**, colonist, colonizer, explorer, frontiersman **2** = **founder**, developer, founding father, innovator, leader, trailblazer ◆ *vb* **4, 5** = **develop**, create, discover, establish, initiate, instigate, institute, invent, launch, lay the groundwork, map out, open up, originate, prepare, show the way, start, take the lead

pious *adj* **1, 2** = **religious**, dedicated, devoted, devout, God-fearing, godly, holy, reverent, righteous, saintly, spiritual **3** = **self-righteous**, goody-goody, holier-than-thou, hypocritical, pietistic, religiose, sanctimonious, unctuous
Antonyms *adj* ≠ **religious:** impious, irreligious, irreverent, ungodly, unholy ≠ **self-righteous:** humble, meek, sincere

pipe¹ *n* **1** = **tube**, conduit, conveyor, duct, hose, line, main, passage, pipeline **3** = **clay**, briar, meerschaum **7a** = **whistle**, fife, horn, tooter, wind instrument ◆ *vb* **15, 17** = **whistle**, cheep, peep, play, sing, sound, tootle, trill, tweet, twitter, warble **19** = **convey**, bring in, channel, conduct, siphon, supply, transmit

pipe down *vb Informal* = **be quiet**, belt up (*sl.*), button it (*sl.*), button one's lip (*sl.*), hold one's tongue, hush, put a sock in it (*Brit. sl.*), quieten down, shush, shut one's mouth, shut up (*inf.*)

pipe dream *n* = **daydream**, castle in the air, chimera, delusion, dream, fantasy, notion, reverie, vagary

pipeline *n* **1** = **tube**, conduit, conveyor, duct, line, passage, pipe **3 in the pipeline** = **on the way**,

piperonal ('pɪpərəʊˌnæl) *n* a white fragrant aldehyde used in flavourings, perfumery, and suntan lotions.

pipette (pɪ'pɛt) *n* a calibrated glass tube drawn to a fine bore at one end, filled by sucking liquid into the bulb, and used to transfer or measure known volumes of liquid. [C19: via F: little pipe]

pipe up ❶ *vb (intr, adv)* **1** to commence singing or playing a musical instrument: *the band piped up.* **2** to speak up, esp. in a shrill voice.

pipi ('pɪpi:) *n, pl* **pipi** *or* **pipis. 1** an edible shellfish of New Zealand. **2** an Australian mollusc of sandy beaches, widely used as bait. [from Maori]

piping ('paɪpɪŋ) *n* **1** pipes collectively, as in the plumbing of a house. **2** a cord of icing, whipped cream, etc., often used to decorate desserts and cakes. **3** a thin strip of covered cord or material, used to edge hems, etc. **4** the sound of a pipe or bagpipes. **5** the art or technique of playing a pipe or bagpipes. **6** a shrill voice or sound, esp. a whistling sound. ◆ *adj* **7** making a shrill sound. **8 piping hot.** extremely hot.

pipistrelle (ˌpɪpɪ'strɛl) *n* any of a genus of numerous small brownish insectivorous bats, occurring in most parts of the world. [C18: via F from It. *pipistrello,* from L *vespertīliō* a bat, from *vesper* evening, because of its nocturnal habits]

pipit ('pɪpɪt) *n* any of various songbirds, esp. the **meadow pipit,** having brownish speckled plumage and a long tail. [C18: prob. imit.]

pipkin ('pɪpkɪn) *n* a small earthenware vessel. [C16: ? dim. of PIPE[2]; see -KIN]

pippin ('pɪpɪn) *n* any of several varieties of eating apple. [C13: from OF *pepin,* from ?]

pipsissewa (pɪp'sɪsəwə) *n* any of several ericaceous plants of an Asian and American genus, having jagged evergreen leaves and white or pinkish flowers. Also called: **wintergreen.** [C19: from Algonquian *pipisisikweu,* lit.: it breaks it into pieces, so called because believed to be efficacious in treating bladder stones]

pipsqueak ❶ ('pɪpˌskwi:k) *n Inf.* a person or thing that is insignificant or contemptible.

piquant ❶ ('pi:kənt, -kɑ:nt) *adj* **1** having an agreeably pungent or tart taste. **2** lively or stimulating to the mind. [C16: from F (lit.: prickling), from *piquer* to prick, goad]
▸ **'piquancy** *n* ▸ **'piquantly** *adv*

pique ❶ (pi:k) *n* **1** a feeling of resentment or irritation, as from having one's pride wounded. ◆ *vb* **piques, piquing, piqued.** *(tr)* **2** to cause to feel resentment or irritation. **3** to excite or arouse. **4** (foll. by *on* or *upon*) to pride or congratulate (oneself). [C16: from F, from *piquer* to prick]

piqué ('pi:keɪ) *n* a close-textured fabric of cotton, silk, or spun rayon woven with lengthwise ribs. [C19: from F *piqué* pricked, from *piquer* to prick]

piquet (pɪ'kɛt, -'keɪ) *n* a card game for two people played with a reduced pack. [C17: from F, from ?]

piracy ❶ ('paɪrəsɪ) *n, pl* **piracies. 1** *Brit.* robbery on the seas. **2** a felony, such as robbery or hijacking, committed aboard a ship or aircraft. **3** the unauthorized use or appropriation of patented or copyrighted material, ideas, etc. [C16: from Anglo-L *pirātia,* from LGk *peirāteia;* see PIRATE]

piranha *or* **piraña** (pɪ'rɑ:njə) *n* any of various small freshwater voracious fishes of tropical America, having strong jaws and sharp teeth. [C19: via Port. from Tupi: fish with teeth, from *pirá* fish + *sainha* tooth]

pirate ❶ ('paɪrɪt) *n* **1** a person who commits piracy. **2a** a vessel used by pirates. **2b** *(as modifier): a pirate ship.* **3** a person who illicitly uses or appropriates someone else's literary, artistic, or other work. **4a** a person or group of people who broadcast illegally. **4b** *(as modifier): a pirate radio station.* ◆ *vb* **pirates, pirating, pirated. 5** *(tr)* to use, appropriate, or reproduce (artistic work, ideas, etc.) illicitly. [C15: from L *pīrāta,* from Gk *peirātēs* one who attacks, from *peira* an attack]
▸ **pi'ratical** *or* **piratic** (paɪ'rætɪk) *adj* ▸ **pi'ratically** *adv*

pirogue (pɪ'rəʊg) *or* **piragua** (pɪ'rɑ:gwə, -'ræg-) *n* any of various kinds of dugout canoes. [C17: via F from Sp., of Amerind origin]

pirouette ❶ (ˌpɪrʊ'ɛt) *n* **1** a body spin, esp. in dancing, on the toes or the ball of the foot. ◆ *vb* **pirouettes, pirouetting, pirouetted. 2** *(intr)* to perform a pirouette. [C18: from F, from OF *pirouet* spinning top]

piscatorial (ˌpɪskə'tɔ:rɪəl) *or* **piscatory** ('pɪskətərɪ, -trɪ) *adj* **1** of or relating to fish, fishing, or fishermen. **2** devoted to fishing. [C19: from L *piscātōrius,* from *piscātor* fisherman]
▸ **ˌpisca'torially** *adv*

Pisces ('paɪsi:z, 'pɪ-) *n, Latin genitive* **Piscium** ('paɪsɪəm). **1** *Astron.* a faint extensive zodiacal constellation lying between Aquarius and Aries on the ecliptic. **2** *Astrol.* Also called: the **Fishes.** the twelfth sign of the zodiac. The sun is in this sign between about Feb. 19 and March 20. **3a** a taxonomic group that comprises all fishes. See **fish** (sense 1). **3b** a taxonomic group that comprises the bony fishes only. See **teleost.** [C14: L: the fish (pl)]

pisci- *combining form.* fish: *pisciculture.* [from L *piscis*]

pisciculture ('pɪsɪˌkʌltʃə) *n* the rearing and breeding of fish under controlled conditions.
▸ **ˌpisci'cultural** *adj* ▸ **ˌpisci'culturist** *n, adj*

piscina (pɪ'si:nə) *n, pl* **piscinae** (-ni:) *or* **piscinas.** *RC Church.* a stone basin, with a drain, in a church or sacristy where water used at Mass is poured away. [C16: from L: fish pond, from *piscis* a fish]

piscine ('pɪsaɪn) *adj* of, relating to, or resembling a fish.

piscivorous (pɪ'sɪvərəs) *adj* feeding on fish.

pish (pʃ, pɪʃ) *interj* **1** an exclamation of impatience or contempt. ◆ *vb* **2** to make this exclamation at (someone or something).

pisiform ('pɪsɪˌfɔ:m) *adj* **1** *Zool., bot.* resembling a pea. ◆ *n* **2** a small pealike bone on the ulnar side of the carpus. [C18: via NL from L *pīsum* pea + *forma* shape]

pismire ('pɪsˌmaɪə) *n* an archaic or dialect word for an **ant.** [C14 (lit.: urinating ant, from the odour of formic acid): from PISS + obs. *mire* ant, from ON]

piss (pɪs) *Sl.* ◆ *vb* **1** *(intr) Taboo.* to urinate. **2** *(tr) Taboo.* to discharge as or in one's urine: *to piss blood.* ◆ *n* **3** *Taboo.* an act of urinating. **4** *Taboo.* urine. **5 take the piss.** to tease or make fun of someone or something. [C13: from OF *pisser,* prob. imit.]

piss artist *n Sl.* **1** a boastful or incompetent person. **2** a person who drinks heavily and gets drunk frequently.

pissed (pɪst) *adj Sl.* **1** *Brit. taboo.* drunk. **2** *US.* annoyed, irritated, or disappointed.

piss off *vb (adv) Taboo sl.* **1** *(tr; often passive)* to annoy, irritate, or disappoint. **2** *(intr) Chiefly Brit.* to go away; depart: often used to dismiss a person.

piss-up *n Sl.* a party involving a considerable amount of drinking.

pistachio (pɪ'stɑ:ʃɪˌəʊ) *n, pl* **pistachios. 1** a tree of the Mediterranean region and W Asia, with small hard-shelled nuts. **2** Also called: **pistachio nut.** the nut of this tree, having an edible green kernel. **3** the sweet flavour of the pistachio nut, used in ice creams, etc. ◆ *adj* **4** of a yellowish-green colour. [C16: via It. & L from Gk *pistakion* pistachio nut, from *pistakē* pistachio tree, from Persian *pistah*]

piste (pi:st) *n* a slope or course for skiing. [C18: via OF from OIt. *pista,* from *pistare* to tread down]

pistil ('pɪstɪl) *n* the female reproductive part of a flower, consisting of one or more separate or fused carpels. [C18: from L *pistillum* pestle]

pistillate ('pɪstɪlɪt, -ˌleɪt) *adj* (of plants) **1** having pistils but no anthers. **2** having or producing pistils.

pistol ('pɪstᵊl) *n* **1** a short-barrelled handgun. **2 hold a pistol to a person's head.** to threaten a person in order to force him to do what one wants. ◆ *vb* **pistols, pistolling, pistolled** *or US* **pistols, pistoling, pistoled. 3** *(tr)* to shoot with a pistol. [C16: from F *pistole,* from G, from Czech *pišt'ala* pistol, pipe]

pistole (pɪs'təʊl) *n* any of various gold coins of varying value, formerly used in Europe. [C16: from OF, shortened from *pistolet,* lit.: little PISTOL]

pistol grip *n* **a** a handle shaped like the butt of a pistol. **b** *(as modifier): a pistol-grip camera.*

pistol-whip *vb* **pistol-whips, pistol-whipping, pistol-whipped.** *(tr) US.* to beat or strike with a pistol barrel.

piston ('pɪstən) *n* a disc or cylindrical part that slides to and fro in a hollow cylinder. In an internal-combustion engine it is attached by a pivoted connecting rod to a crankshaft or flywheel, thus converting reciprocating motion into rotation. [C18: via F from OIt. *pistone,* from *pistare* to grind, from L *pinsere* to beat]

piston ring *n* a split ring that fits into a groove on the rim of a piston to provide a spring-loaded seal against the cylinder wall.

piston rod *n* **1** the rod that connects the piston of a reciprocating steam engine to the crosshead. **2** a less common name for a **connecting rod.**

pit[1] ❶ (pɪt) *n* **1** a large, usually deep opening in the ground. **2a** a mine or excavation, esp. for coal. **2b** the shaft in a mine. **2c** *(as modifier): pit*

THESAURUS

brewing, coming, getting ready, in preparation, in process, in production, under way

pipe up *vb* **2** = **speak**, have one's say, make oneself heard, put one's oar in, raise one's voice, speak up, volunteer

pipsqueak *n Informal* = **squirt** (*inf.*), creep (*sl.*), nobody, nonentity, nothing, upstart, whippersnapper

piquancy *n* **1** = **spiciness**, bite (*inf.*), edge, flavour, kick (*inf.*), pungency, relish, sharpness, spice, tang, zest **2** = **interest**, colour, excitement, pep, pizzazz *or* pizazz (*inf.*), raciness, spirit, vigour, vitality, zing (*inf.*), zip (*inf.*)

piquant *adj* **1** = **spicy**, biting, highly-seasoned, peppery, pungent, savoury, sharp, stinging, tangy, tart, with a kick (*inf.*), zesty **2** = **interesting**, lively, provocative, racy, salty, scintillating, sparkling, spirited, stimulating
Antonyms *adj* ≠ **spicy:** bland, insipid, mild ≠ **interesting:** banal, bland, boring, dull, insipid, tame, uninteresting, vapid

pique *n* **1** = **resentment**, annoyance, displeasure, huff, hurt feelings, irritation, miff (*inf.*), offence, umbrage, vexation, wounded pride ◆ *vb* **2** = **displease**, affront, annoy, gall, get (*inf.*), incense, irk, irritate, miff (*inf.*), mortify, nettle, offend, peeve (*inf.*), provoke, put out, rile, sting, vex, wound **3** = **arouse**, excite, galvanize, goad, kindle, provoke, rouse, spur, stimulate, stir, whet

piracy *n* **1, 2** = **robbery**, buccaneering, freebooting, hijacking, infringement, rapine, stealing, theft

pirate *n* **1** = **buccaneer**, corsair, filibuster, freebooter, marauder, raider, rover, sea robber, sea rover, sea wolf **3** = **plagiarist**, cribber, infringer, plagiarizer ◆ *vb* **5** = **copy**, appropriate, borrow, crib (*inf.*), lift (*inf.*), plagiarize, poach, reproduce, steal

piratical *adj* **1** = **buccaneering**, criminal, dishonest, felonious, fraudulent, lawless, pillaging, plundering, rapacious, thieving, unprincipled, wolfish

pirouette *n, vb* **1, 2** = **spin**, pivot, turn, twirl, whirl

pit[1] *n* **1, 2, 7, 8** = **hole**, abyss, cavity, chasm, coal mine, crater, dent, depression, dimple, excavation, gulf, hollow, indentation, mine, pockmark, pothole, trench ◆ *vb* **13** *often with* **against** = **set against**, match, oppose, put in opposition

pony; pit prop. **3** a concealed danger or difficulty. **4 the pit.** hell. **5** Also called: **orchestra pit.** the area that is occupied by the orchestra in a theatre, located in front of the stage. **6** an enclosure for fighting animals or birds. **7** *Anat.* **7a** a small natural depression on the surface of a body, organ, or part. **7b** the floor of any natural bodily cavity: *the pit of the stomach.* **8** *Pathol.* a small indented scar at the site of a former pustule; pockmark. **9** a working area at the side of a motor-racing track for servicing or refuelling vehicles. **10** a section on the floor of a commodity exchange devoted to a special line of trading. **11** the ground floor of the auditorium of a theatre. **12** another word for **pitfall** (sense 2). ◆ *vb* **pits, pitting, pitted. 13** (*tr*; often foll. by *against*) to match in opposition, esp. as antagonists. **14** to mark or become marked with pits. **15** (*tr*) to place or bury in a pit. [OE *pytt,* from L *puteus*]

pit[2] (pɪt) *Chiefly US & Canad.* ◆ *n* **1** the stone of a cherry, etc. ◆ *vb* **pits, pitting, pitted.** (*tr*) **2** to extract the stone from (a fruit). [C19: from Du.: kernel]

pitapat (ˈpɪtəˌpæt) *adv* **1** with quick light taps. ◆ *vb* **pitapats, pitapatting, pitapatted. 2** (*intr*) to make quick light taps. ◆ *n* **3** such taps. [C16: imit.]

pit bull terrier *n* a dog resembling the Staffordshire bull terrier but somewhat larger: originally developed for dogfighting.

pitch[1] Ⓣ (pɪtʃ) *vb* **1** to hurl or throw (something); cast; fling. **2** (*usually tr*) to set up (a camp, tent, etc.). **3** (*tr*) to aim or fix (something) at a particular level, position, style, etc.: *if you advertise privately you may pitch the price too low.* **4** (*tr*) to aim to sell (a product) to a specified market or on a specified basis. **5** (*intr*) to slope downwards. **6** (*intr*) to fall forwards or downwards. **7** (*intr*) (of a vessel) to dip and raise its bow and stern alternately. **8** *Cricket.* to bowl (a ball) so that it bounces on a certain part of the wicket, or (of a ball) to bounce on a certain part of the wicket. **9** (*intr*) (of a missile, aircraft, etc.) to deviate from a stable flight attitude by movement of the longitudinal axis about the lateral axis. **10** (*tr*) (in golf, etc.) to hit (a ball) steeply into the air. **11** (*tr*) *Music.* **11a** to sing or play accurately (a note, interval, etc.). **11b** (*usually passive*) (of a wind instrument) to specify or indicate its basic key or harmonic series by its size, manufacture, etc. **12** *Baseball, softball.* **12a** (*tr*) to throw (a ball) to a batter. **12b** (*intr*) to act as a pitcher in a game. ◆ *n* **13** the degree of elevation or depression. **14a** the angle of descent of a downward slope. **14b** such a slope. **15** the extreme height or depth. **16** *Mountaineering.* a section of a route between two belay points. **17** the degree of slope of a roof. **18** the distance between corresponding points on adjacent members of a body of regular form, esp. the distance between teeth on a gearwheel or between threads on a screw thread. **19** the pitching motion of a ship, missile, etc. **20** *Music.* **20a** the height or depth of a note as determined by its frequency relative to that of other notes: *high pitch; low pitch.* **20b** an absolute frequency assigned to a specific note, fixing the relative frequencies of all other notes. **21** *Cricket.* the rectangular area between the stumps, 22 yards long and 10 feet wide; the wicket. **22** the act or manner of pitching a ball, as in cricket, etc. **23** *Chiefly Brit.* a vendor's station, esp. on a pavement. **24** *Sl.* a persuasive sales talk, esp. one routinely repeated. **25** *Chiefly Brit.* (in many sports) the field of play. **26** *Golf.* Also called: **pitch shot.** an approach shot in which the ball is struck in a high arc. **27 queer someone's pitch.** *Brit. inf.* to upset someone's plans. ◆ See also **pitch in, pitch into.** [C13 *picchen*]

pitch[2] (pɪtʃ) *n* **1** any of various heavy dark viscid substances obtained as a residue from the distillation of tars. **2** any of various similar substances, such as asphalt, occurring as natural deposits. **3** crude turpentine obtained as sap from pine trees. ◆ *vb* **4** (*tr*) to apply pitch to (something). [OE *pic,* from L *pix*]

pitch-black Ⓣ *adj* **1** extremely dark; unlit: *the room was pitch-black.* **2** of a deep black colour.

pitchblende (ˈpɪtʃˌblɛnd) *n* a blackish mineral that occurs in veins, frequently associated with silver: the principal source of uranium and radium. [C18: partial translation of G *Pechblende,* from *Pech* PITCH[2] (from its black colour) + BLENDE]

pitch-dark Ⓣ *adj* extremely or completely dark.

pitched battle *n* **1** a battle ensuing from the deliberate choice of time and place. **2** any fierce encounter, esp. one with large numbers.

pitcher[1] (ˈpɪtʃə) *n* a large jug, usually rounded with a narrow neck and often of earthenware, used mainly for holding water. [C13: from OF *pichier,* from Med. L *picārium,* var. of *bicārium* BEAKER]

pitcher[2] (ˈpɪtʃə) *n Baseball.* the player on the fielding team who throws the ball to the batter.

pitcher plant *n* any of various insectivorous plants, having leaves modified to form pitcher-like organs that attract and trap insects, which are then digested.

pitchfork (ˈpɪtʃˌfɔːk) *n* **1** a long-handled fork with two or three long curved tines for tossing hay. ◆ *vb* (*tr*) **2** to use a pitchfork on (something). **3** to thrust (someone) unwillingly into a position.

pitch in Ⓣ *vb* (*intr, adv*) **1** to cooperate or contribute. **2** to begin energetically.

pitch into Ⓣ *vb* (*intr, prep*) *Inf.* **1** to assail physically or verbally. **2** to get on with doing (something).

pitch pine *n* **1** any of various coniferous trees of North America: valued as a source of turpentine and pitch. **2** the wood of any of these trees.

pitch pipe *n* a small pipe that sounds a note or notes of standard frequency. It is used for establishing the correct starting note for unaccompanied singing.

pitchy Ⓣ (ˈpɪtʃɪ) *adj* **pitchier, pitchiest. 1** full of or covered with pitch. **2** resembling pitch.
▸ˈ**pitchiness** *n*

piteous Ⓣ (ˈpɪtɪəs) *adj* exciting or deserving pity.
▸ˈ**piteously** *adv* ▸ˈ**piteousness** *n*

pitfall Ⓣ (ˈpɪtˌfɔːl) *n* **1** an unsuspected difficulty or danger. **2** a trap in the form of a concealed pit, designed to catch men or wild animals. [OE *pytt* PIT[1] + *fealle* trap]

pith Ⓣ (pɪθ) *n* **1** the soft fibrous tissue lining the inside of the rind in fruits such as the orange. **2** the essential or important part, point, etc. **3** weight; substance. **4** *Bot.* the central core of unspecialized cells surrounded by conducting tissue in stems. **5** the soft central part of a bone, feather, etc. ◆ *vb* (*tr*) **6** to kill (animals) by severing the spinal cord. **7** to remove the pith from (a plant). [OE *pitha*]

pithead (ˈpɪtˌhɛd) *n* the top of a mine shaft and the buildings, hoisting gear, etc., around it.

pithecanthropus (ˌpɪθɪkænˈθrəʊpəs) *n, pl* **pithecanthropi** (-ˌpaɪ). any primitive apelike man of the former genus *Pithecanthropus,* now included in the genus *Homo.* See **Java man.** [C19: NL, from Gk *pithēkos* ape + *anthrōpos* man]

pith helmet *n* a lightweight hat made of the pith of the sola, an E Indian swamp plant, that protects the wearer from the sun. Also called: **topee, topi.**

pithos (ˈpɪθɒs, ˈpaɪ-) *n, pl* **pithoi** (-θɔɪ). a large ceramic container for oil or grain. [from Gk]

pithy Ⓣ (ˈpɪθɪ) *adj* **pithier, pithiest. 1** terse and full of meaning or substance. **2** of, resembling, or full of pith.
▸ˈ**pithily** *adv* ▸ˈ**pithiness** *n*

pitiable Ⓣ (ˈpɪtɪəbᵊl) *adj* exciting or deserving pity or contempt.
▸ˈ**pitiableness** *n* ▸ˈ**pitiably** *adv*

pitiful Ⓣ (ˈpɪtɪfʊl) *adj* **1** arousing or deserving pity. **2** arousing or deserving contempt. **3** *Arch.* full of pity or compassion.
▸ˈ**pitifully** *adv* ▸ˈ**pitifulness** *n*

pitiless Ⓣ (ˈpɪtɪlɪs) *adj* having or showing little or no pity or mercy.
▸ˈ**pitilessly** *adv* ▸ˈ**pitilessness** *n*

pitman (ˈpɪtmən) *n, pl* **pitmen.** *Chiefly Scot. & N English.* a person who works in a pit, esp. a coal miner.

piton (ˈpiːtɒn) *n Mountaineering.* a metal spike that may be driven into a crevice and used to secure a rope, etc. [C20: from F: ringbolt]

pits (pɪts) *pl n* **the.** *Sl.* the worst possible person, place, or thing. [C20: from ? *armpits*]

pit stop *n* **1** *Motor racing.* a brief stop made at a pit by a racing car for re-

THESAURUS

14 = **scar**, dent, dint, gouge, hole, indent, mark, nick, notch, pockmark

pitch[1] *vb* **1** = **throw**, bung (*Brit. sl.*), cast, chuck (*inf.*), fling, heave, hurl, launch, lob, sling, toss **2** = **set up**, erect, fix, locate, place, plant, put up, raise, settle, station **6** = **fall**, dive, drop, stagger, topple, tumble **7** = **toss**, flounder, lurch, make heavy weather, plunge, roll, wallow, welter ◆ *n* **13, 15** = **level**, degree, height, highest point, point, summit **14, 17** = **slope**, angle, cant, dip, gradient, incline, steepness, tilt **20** = **tone**, harmonic, modulation, sound, timbre **24** *Slang* = **sales talk**, line, patter, spiel (*inf.*) **25** *Chiefly Brit.* = **sports field**, field of play, ground, park

pitch-black *adj* **1, 2** = **jet-black**, dark, ebony, inky, jet, pitch-dark, raven, sable, unlit

pitch-dark *adj* = **black**, dark, pitch-black, pitchy, Stygian, unilluminated, unlit

pitch in *vb* **1** = **help**, chip in, contribute, cooperate, do one's bit, join in, lend a hand, lend a helping hand, participate **2** = **begin**, fall to, get busy, get cracking (*inf.*), plunge into, set about, set to, tackle

pitch into *vb* **1** *Informal* = **attack**, assail, assault, get stuck into (*inf.*), lace into, light into (*inf.*), sail into (*inf.*), tear into (*inf.*)

pitchy *adj* **2** = **black**, coal-black, dark, ebony, inky, jet, jetty, moonless, pitch-black, raven, sable, unilluminated, unlighted

piteous *adj* = **pathetic**, affecting, deplorable, dismal, distressing, doleful, grievous, gut-wrenching, harrowing, heartbreaking, heart-rending, lamentable, miserable, mournful, moving, pitiable, pitiful, plaintive, poignant, sad, sorrowful, woeful, wretched

pitfall *n* **1** = **danger**, banana skin (*inf.*), catch, difficulty, drawback, hazard, peril, snag, trap **2** = **trap**, deadfall, downfall, pit, snare

pith *n* **2** = **essence**, core, crux, gist, heart, heart of the matter, kernel, marrow, meat, nub, point, quintessence, salient point, the long and the short of it **3** = **importance**, consequence, depth, force, import, matter, moment, power, significance, strength, substance, value, weight

pithy *adj* **1** = **succinct**, brief, cogent, compact, concise, epigrammatic, expressive, finely honed, forceful, laconic, meaningful, pointed, short, terse, to the point, trenchant

Antonyms *adj* diffuse, garrulous, long, long-winded, loquacious, prolix, verbose, wordy

pitiable *adj* = **pathetic**, deplorable, dismal, distressing, doleful, grievous, gut-wrenching, harrowing, lamentable, miserable, mournful, piteous, poor, sad, sorry, woeful, wretched

pitiful *adj* **1** = **pathetic**, deplorable, distressing, grievous, gut-wrenching, harrowing, heartbreaking, heart-rending, lamentable, miserable, piteous, pitiable, sad, woeful, wretched **2** = **contemptible**, abject, base, beggarly, despicable, dismal, inadequate, insignificant, low, mean, measly, miserable, paltry, scurvy, shabby, sorry, vile, worthless

Antonyms *adj* ≠ **pathetic:** amusing, cheerful, cheering, comical, funny, happy, heartening, laughable, merry ≠ **contemptible:** adequate, admirable, honourable, laudable, praiseworthy, significant, valuable

pitiless *adj* = **merciless**, brutal, callous, cold-blooded, cold-hearted, cruel, hardhearted, harsh, heartless, implacable, inexorable, inhuman, relentless, ruthless, uncaring, unfeeling, unmerciful, unsympathetic

pairs, refuelling, etc. **2** *Inf.* any stop made during a car journey for refreshment, rest, or refuelling.

pitta bread *or* **pitta** ('pɪtə) *n* a flat rounded slightly leavened bread, originally from the Middle East. [from Mod. Gk: a cake]

pittance Ⓣ ('pɪtᵊns) *n* a small amount or portion, esp. a meagre allowance of money. [C16: from OF *pietance* ration, ult. from L *pietās* duty]

pitter-patter ('pɪtəˌpætə) *n* **1** the sound of light rapid taps or pats, as of raindrops. ◆ *vb* **2** (*intr*) to make such a sound. ◆ *adv* **3** with such a sound.

pituitary (pɪ'tju:ɪtərɪ) *n, pl* **pituitaries. 1** See **pituitary gland.** ◆ *adj* **2** of or relating to the pituitary gland. [C17: from LL *pītuītārius* slimy, from *pītuīta* phlegm]

pituitary gland *or* **body** *n* the master endocrine gland, attached by a stalk to the base of the brain. Its two lobes secrete hormones affecting skeletal growth, development of the sex glands, and the functioning of the other endocrine glands.

pit viper *n* any venomous snake of a New World family, having a heat-sensitive organ in a pit on each side of the head: includes the rattlesnakes.

pity Ⓣ ('pɪtɪ) *n, pl* **pities. 1** sympathy or sorrow felt for the sufferings of another. **2 have** (*or* **take**) **pity on.** to have sympathy or show mercy for. **3** something that causes regret. **4** an unfortunate chance: *what a pity you can't come.* ◆ *vb* **pities, pitying, pitied.** (*tr*) **5** to feel pity for. [C13: from OF *pité*, from L *pietās* duty]
▸ **'pitying** *adj* ▸ **'pityingly** *adv*

pityriasis (ˌpɪtə'raɪəsɪs) *n* any of a group of skin diseases characterized by the shedding of dry flakes of skin. [C17: via NL from Gk *pituriasis* scurfiness, from *pituron* bran]

più (pju:) *adv* (*in combination*) *Music.* more (quickly, etc.): *più allegro.* [It., from L *plus* more]

piupiu ('pi:u:ˌpi:u:) *n* a skirt made from leaves of the New Zealand flax, worn by Maoris on ceremonial occasions. [from Maori]

pivot Ⓣ ('pɪvət) *n* **1** a short shaft or pin supporting something that turns; fulcrum. **2** the end of a shaft or arbor that terminates in a bearing. **3** a person or thing upon which progress, success, etc., depends. **4** the person or position from which a military formation takes its reference when altering position, etc. ◆ *vb* **5** (*tr*) to mount on or provide with a pivot or pivots. **6** (*intr*) to turn on or as if on a pivot. [C17: from OF]

pivotal Ⓣ ('pɪvətᵊl) *adj* **1** of, involving, or acting as a pivot. **2** of crucial importance.

pix[1] (pɪks) *n* a plural of **pic.**

pix[2] (pɪks) *n* a less common spelling of **pyx.**

pixel ('pɪksəl) *n* any of a number of very small picture elements that make up a picture, as on a visual display unit. [C20: from *pix* pictures + *el(ement)*]

pixie Ⓣ *or* **pixy** ('pɪksɪ) *n, pl* **pixies.** (in folklore) a fairy or elf. [C17: from ?]

pixilated *or* **pixillated** ('pɪksɪˌleɪtɪd) *adj Chiefly US.* **1** eccentric or whimsical. **2** *Sl.* drunk. [C20: from PIXIE + *-lated*, as in *stimulated, titillated,* etc.]

pizza ('pi:tsə) *n* a dish of Italian origin consisting of a baked disc of dough covered with cheese and tomatoes, plus ham, mushrooms, etc. [C20: from It., ?from Vulgar L *picea* (unattested), ? rel. to Mod. Gk *pitta* cake]

pizzazz *or* **pizazz** (pə'zæz) *n Inf.* an attractive combination of energy and style; sparkle. Also: **bezazz.** [C20: ?]

pizzeria (ˌpi:tsə'ri:ə) *n* a place where pizzas are made, sold, or eaten.

pizzicato (ˌpɪtsɪ'kɑ:təʊ) *Music.* ◆ *adj, adv* **1** (in music for the violin family) to be plucked with the finger. ◆ *n* **2** this style or technique of playing. [C19: from It.: pinched, from *pizzicare* to twist]

pizzle ('pɪzᵊl) *n Arch. or dialect.* the penis of an animal, esp. a bull. [C16: of Gmc origin]

pk *pl* **pks** *abbrev. for:* **1** pack. **2** park. **3** peak.

pkg. *pl* **pkgs.** *abbrev. for* package.

pl *abbrev. for:* **1** place. **2** plate. **3** plural.

Pl. (in street names) *abbrev. for* Place.

PLA *abbrev. for* Port of London Authority.

plaas (plɑ:s) *n S. African.* a farm. [from Afrik., from Du.]

placable ('plækəbᵊl) *adj* easily placated or appeased. [C15: via OF from L *plācābilis*, from *plācāre* to appease]
▸ ˌ**placa'bility** *n*

placard Ⓣ ('plækɑ:d) *n* **1** a notice for public display; poster. **2** a small plaque or card. ◆ *vb* (*tr*) **3** to post placards on or in. **4** to advertise by placards. **5** to display as a placard. [C15: from OF *plaquart*, from *plaquier* to plate, lay flat; see PLAQUE]

placate Ⓣ (plə'keɪt) *vb* **placates, placating, placated.** (*tr*) to pacify or appease. [C17: from L *plācāre*]
▸ **pla'cation** *n* ▸ **pla'catory** *adj*

place Ⓣ (pleɪs) *n* **1** a particular point or part of space or of a surface, esp. that occupied by a person or thing. **2** a geographical point, such as a town, city, etc. **3** a position or rank in a sequence or order. **4** an open square lined with houses in a city or town. **5** space or room. **6** a house or living quarters. **7** a country house with grounds. **8** any building or area set aside for a specific purpose. **9** a passage in a book, play, film, etc.: *to lose one's place.* **10** proper, right, or customary surroundings (esp. in **out of place, in place**). **11** right, prerogative, or duty: *it is your place to give a speech.* **12** appointment, position, or job: *a place at college.* **13** position, condition, or state: *if I were in your place.* **14a** a space or seat, as at a dining table. **14b** (*as modifier*): *place mat.* **15** *Maths.* the relative position of a digit in a number. **16** any of the best times in a race. **17** *Horse racing.* **17a** *Brit., Austral., & NZ.* the first, second, or third position at the finish. **17b** *US & Canad.* the first or usually the second position at the finish. **17c** (*as modifier*): *a place bet.* **18 all over the place.** in disorder or disarray. **19 give place (to).** to make room (for) or be superseded (by). **20 go places.** *Inf.* **20a** to travel. **20b** to become successful. **21 in place of. 21a** instead of; in lieu of: *go in place of my sister.* **21b** in exchange for: *he gave her it in place of her ring.* **22 know one's place.** to be aware of one's inferior position. **23 put someone in his** (*or* **her**) **place.** to humble someone who is arrogant, conceited, forward, etc. **24 take one's place.** to take up one's usual or specified position. **25 take place.** to happen or occur. **26 take the place of.** to be a substitute for. ◆ *vb* **places, placing, placed.** (*mainly tr*) **27** to put or set in a particular or appropriate place. **28** to find or indicate the place of. **29** to identify or classify by linking with an appropriate context: *to place a face.* **30** to regard or view as being: *to place prosperity above sincerity.* **31** to make (an order, bet, etc.). **32** to find a home or job for (someone). **33** to appoint to an office or position. **34** (often foll. by *with*) to put under the care (of). **35** to direct or aim carefully. **36** (*passive*) *Brit.* to cause (a racehorse, greyhound, athlete, etc.) to arrive in first, second, third, or sometimes fourth place. **37** (*intr*) *US & Canad.* (of a racehorse, greyhound, etc.) to finish among the first three in a contest, esp. in second position. **38** to invest (funds). **39** (*tr*) to insert (an advertisement) in a newspaper, journal, etc. [C13: via OF from L *platēa* courtyard, from Gk *plateia*, from *platus* broad]

placebo (plə'si:bəʊ) *n, pl* **placebos** *or* **placeboes. 1** *Med.* an inactive substance administered to a patient usually to compare its effects with those of a real drug but sometimes for the psychological benefit to the patient through his believing he is receiving treatment. **2** something said or done to please or humour another. **3** *RC Church.* a traditional name for the vespers of the office for the dead. [C13 (in the ecclesiastical sense): from L *Placebo Domino* I shall please the Lord; C19 (in the medical sense)]

placebo effect *n Med.* a positive therapeutic effect claimed by a patient after receiving a placebo believed by him to be an active drug.

place card *n* a card placed on a dinner table before a seat, indicating who is to sit there.

place kick *Football, etc.* ◆ *n* **1** a kick in which the ball is placed in position before it is kicked. ◆ *vb* **place-kick. 2** to kick (a ball) in this way.

placement Ⓣ ('pleɪsmənt) *n* **1** the act of placing or the state of being placed. **2** arrangement or position. **3** the process of finding employment.

placenta (plə'sentə) *n, pl* **placentas** *or* **placentae** (-ti:). **1** the vascular

THESAURUS

Antonyms *adj* caring, compassionate, kind, merciful, relenting, responsive, soft-hearted, sparing

pittance *n* = **peanuts** (*sl.*), allowance, chicken feed (*sl.*), drop, mite, modicum, portion, ration, slave wages, trifle

pity *n* **1** = **compassion**, charity, clemency, commiseration, condolence, fellow feeling, forbearance, kindness, mercy, quarter, sympathy, tenderness, understanding **2 take pity on** = **have mercy on**, feel compassion for, forgive, melt, pardon, put out of one's misery, relent, reprieve, show mercy, spare **3, 4** = **shame**, bummer (*sl.*), crime, crying shame, misfortune, regret, sad thing, sin ◆ *vb* **5** = **feel sorry for**, bleed for, commiserate with, condole with, feel for, grieve for, have compassion for, sympathize with, weep for

Antonyms *n* ≠ **compassion:** anger, apathy, brutality, cruelty, disdain, fury, hard-heartedness, indifference, inhumanity, mercilessness, pitilessness, ruthlessness, scorn, severity, unconcern, wrath

pivot *n* **1** = **axis**, axle, fulcrum, spindle, swivel **3** = **hub**, centre, focal point, heart, hinge, kingpin ◆ *vb* **6** = **turn**, revolve, rotate, spin, swivel, twirl **6** = **rely**, be contingent, depend, hang, hinge, revolve round, turn

pivotal *adj* **2** = **crucial**, central, climactic, critical, decisive, determining, focal, vital

pixie *n* = **elf**, brownie, fairy, peri, sprite

placard *n* **1** = **notice**, advertisement, *affiche*, bill, poster, public notice, sticker

placate *vb* = **calm**, appease, assuage, conciliate, humour, mollify, pacify, propitiate, satisfy, soothe, win over

placatory *adj* = **calming**, appeasing, conciliatory, designed to please, pacificatory, peacemaking, propitiative

place *n* **1** = **spot**, area, location, locus, point, position, site, situation, station, venue, whereabouts **2** = **region**, city, district, hamlet, locale, locality, neighbourhood, quarter, town, vicinity, village **3** = **position**, grade, rank, station, status **5** = **space**, accommodation, room, stead **6, 7** = **home**, abode, apartment, domicile, dwelling, flat, house, manor, mansion, pad (*sl.*), property, residence, seat **11** = **duty**, affair, charge, concern, function, prerogative, responsibility, right, role **12** = **job**, appointment, berth (*inf.*), billet, employment, position, post **21 in place of** = **instead of**, as an alternative to, as a substitute for, in exchange for, in lieu of, taking the place of **23 put (someone) in his place** = **humble**, bring down, cut down to size, humiliate, make (someone) eat humble pie, make (someone) swallow his pride, mortify, take down a peg (*inf.*) **25 take place** = **happen**, befall, betide, come about, come to pass (*arch.*), go on, occur, transpire (*inf.*) ◆ *vb* **27** = **put**, bung (*Brit. sl.*), deposit, dispose, establish, fix, install, lay, locate, plant, position, rest, set, settle, situate, stand, station, stick (*inf.*) **28** = **classify**, arrange, class, grade, group, order, rank, sort **29** = **identify**, associate, know, put one's finger on, recognize, remember, set in context **34** = **assign**, allocate, appoint, charge, commission, entrust, give

placement *n* **1, 2** = **positioning**, arrangement, deployment, disposition, distribution, emplacement, installation, locating, location, or-

organ formed in the uterus of most mammals during pregnancy, consisting of both maternal and embryonic tissues and providing oxygen and nutrients for the fetus. **2** *Bot.* the part of the ovary of flowering plants to which the ovules are attached. [C17: via L from Gk *plakoeis* flat cake, from *plax* flat]
▸**pla'cental** *adj*

placer ('plæsə) *n* **a** surface sediment containing particles of gold or some other valuable mineral. **b** (*in combination*): *placer-mining.* [C19: from American Sp.: deposit, from Sp. *plaza* PLACE]

place setting *n* the cutlery, crockery, and glassware laid for one person at a dining table.

placet ('pleɪset) *n* a vote or expression of assent by saying *placet.* [C16: from L, lit.: it pleases]

placid ● ('plæsɪd) *adj* having a calm appearance or nature. [C17: from L *placidus* peaceful]
▸**placidity** (plə'sɪdɪtɪ) *or* '**placidness** *n* ▸'**placidly** *adv*

placing ('pleɪsɪŋ) *n Stock Exchange.* a method of issuing securities to the public using an intermediary, such as a stockbroking firm.

placket ('plækɪt) *n Dressmaking.* **1** a piece of cloth sewn in under a closure with buttons, zips, etc. **2** the closure itself. [C16: ?from MDu. *plackaet* breastplate, from Med. L *placca* metal plate]

placoid ('plækɔɪd) *adj* **1** platelike or flattened. **2** (of the scales of sharks) toothlike; composed of dentine with an enamel tip and basal pulp cavity. [C19: from Gk *plac-*, *plax* flat]

plafond (plə'fɒn; *French* plafɔ̃) *n* a ceiling, esp. one having ornamentation. [C17: from F, from *plat* flat + *fond* bottom, from L *fundus*]

plagal ('pleɪgᵊl) *adj* **1** (of a cadence) progressing from the subdominant to the tonic chord, as in the *Amen* of a hymn. **2** (of a mode) commencing upon the dominant of an authentic mode, but sharing the same final as the authentic mode. ◆ Cf. **authentic** (sense 5). [C16: from Med. L *plagālis,* from *plaga,* ?from Gk *plagos* side]

plage (plɑːʒ) *n Astron.* a bright patch in the sun's chromosphere. [F, lit.: beach]

plagiarism ● ('pleɪdʒə,rɪzəm) *n* **1** the act of plagiarizing. **2** something plagiarized. [C17: from L *plagiārus* plunderer, from *plagium* kidnapping]
▸'**plagiarist** *n* ▸,**plagia'ristic** *adj*

plagiarize ● *or* **plagiarise** ('pleɪdʒə,raɪz) *vb* **plagiarizes, plagiarizing, plagiarized** *or* **plagiarises, plagiarising, plagiarised.** to appropriate (ideas, passages, etc.) from (another work or author).
▸'**plagia,rizer** *or* '**plagia,riser** *n*

plagioclase ('pleɪdʒɪəʊ,kleɪz) *n* a series of feldspar minerals consisting of a mixture of sodium and calcium aluminium silicates in triclinic crystalline form. [C19: from Gk, from *plagos* side + -CLASE]
▸**plagioclastic** (,pleɪdʒɪəʊ'klæstɪk) *adj*

plague ● (pleɪg) *n* **1** any widespread and usually highly contagious disease with a high fatality rate. **2** an infectious disease of rodents, esp. rats, transmitted to man by the bite of the rat flea. **3** See **bubonic plague. 4** something that afflicts or harasses. **5** *Inf.* an annoyance or nuisance. **6** a pestilence, affliction, or calamity on a large scale, esp. when regarded as sent by God. ◆ *vb* **plagues, plaguing, plagued.** (*tr*) **7** to afflict or harass. **8** to bring down a plague upon. **9** *Inf.* to annoy. [C14: from LL *plāga* pestilence, from L: a blow]

plaguy *or* **plaguey** ('pleɪgɪ) *Arch., inf.* ◆ *adj* **1** disagreeable or vexing. ◆ *adv* **2** disagreeably or annoyingly.
▸'**plaguily** *adv*

plaice (pleɪs) *n, pl* **plaice** *or* **plaices. 1** a European flatfish having an oval brown body marked with red or orange spots and valued as a food fish. **2** *US & Canad.* any of various other related fishes. [C13: from OF *plaïz,* from LL *platessa* flatfish, from Gk *platus* flat]

plaid (plæd, pleɪd) *n* **1** a long piece of cloth of a tartan pattern, worn over the shoulder as part of Highland costume. **2a** a crisscross weave or cloth. **2b** (*as modifier*): *a plaid scarf.* [C16: from Scot. Gaelic *plaide,* from ?]

Plaid Cymru (,plaɪd 'kʌmrɪ) *n* the Welsh nationalist party. [Welsh]

plain[1] ● (pleɪn) *adj* **1** flat or smooth; level. **2** not complicated; clear: *the plain truth.* **3** not difficult; simple or easy: *a plain task.* **4** honest or straightforward. **5** lowly, esp. in social rank or education. **6** without adornment or show: *a plain coat.* **7** (of fabric) without pattern or of simple untwilled weave. **8** not attractive. **9** not mixed; simple: *plain vodka.* **10** (of knitting) done in plain stitch. ◆ *n* **11** a level or almost level tract of country. **12** a simple stitch in knitting made by passing the wool round the front of the needle. ◆ *adv* **13** (intensifier): *just plain tired.* [C13: from OF: simple, from L *plānus* level, clear]
▸'**plainly** *adv* ▸'**plainness** *n*

plain[2] (pleɪn) *vb* a dialect or poetic word for **complain.** [C14 *pleignen,* from OF *plaindre* to lament, from L *plangere* to beat]

plainchant ('pleɪn,tʃɑːnt) *n* another name for **plainsong.** [C18: from F, for Med. L *cantus plānus*]

plain chocolate *n* chocolate with a slightly bitter flavour and dark colour.

plain clothes *pl n* **a** ordinary clothes, as distinguished from uniform, as worn by a police detective on duty. **b** (*as modifier*): *a plain-clothes policeman.*

plain flour *n* flour to which no raising agent has been added.

plain sailing *n* **1** *Inf.* smooth or easy progress. **2** *Naut.* sailing in a body of water that is unobstructed; clear sailing.

plainsman ('pleɪnzmən) *n, pl* **plainsmen.** a person who lives in a plains region, esp. in the Great Plains of North America.

plainsong ('pleɪn,sɒŋ) *n* the style of unison unaccompanied vocal music used in the medieval Church, esp. in Gregorian chant. [C16: translation of Med. L *cantus plānus*]

plain-spoken ● *adj* candid; frank; blunt.

plaint (pleɪnt) *n* **1** *Arch.* a complaint or lamentation. **2** *Law.* a statement in writing of grounds of complaint made to a court of law. [C13: from OF *plainte,* from L *planctus* lamentation, from *plangere* to beat]

plaintiff ('pleɪntɪf) *n* a person who brings a civil action in a court of law. [C14: from legal F *plaintif,* from OF *plaintif* (adj) complaining, from *plainte* PLAINT]

plaintive ● ('pleɪntɪv) *adj* expressing melancholy; mournful. [C14: from OF *plaintif* grieving, from PLAINT]
▸'**plaintively** *adv* ▸'**plaintiveness** *n*

plait (plæt) *n* **1** a length of hair, etc., that has been plaited. **2** a rare spelling of **pleat.** ◆ *vb* **3** (*tr*) to intertwine (strands or strips) in a pattern. [C15 *pleyt,* from OF *pleit,* from L *plicāre* to fold]

plan ● (plæn) *n* **1** a detailed scheme, method, etc., for attaining an objective. **2** (*sometimes pl*) a proposed, usually tentative idea for doing something. **3** a drawing to scale of a horizontal section through a building taken at a given level. **4** an outline, sketch, etc. ◆ *vb* **plans, planning, planned. 5** to form a plan (for) or make plans (for). **6** (*tr*) to make a plan of (a building). **7** (*tr; takes a clause as object or an infinitive*) to have in mind as a purpose; intend. [C18: via F from L *plānus* flat]

planar ('pleɪnə) *adj* **1** of or relating to a plane. **2** lying in one plane; flat. [C19: from LL *plānāris* on level ground, from L *plānus* flat]

planarian (plə'nɛərɪən) *n* any of various free-living mostly aquatic flatworms, having a three-branched intestine. [C19: from NL *Plānāria* type genus, from LL *plānārius* flat; see PLANE[1]]

planar process *n* a method of producing diffused junctions in semiconductor devices. A pattern of holes is etched into an oxide layer formed on a silicon substrate, into which impurities are diffused through the holes.

THESAURUS

dering, stationing **3** = **appointment**, assignment, employment, engagement

placid *adj* = **calm**, collected, composed, cool, equable, even, even-tempered, gentle, halcyon, imperturbable, mild, peaceful, quiet, self-possessed, serene, still, tranquil, undisturbed, unexcitable, unfazed (*inf.*), unmoved, unruffled, untroubled
Antonyms *adj* agitated, disturbed, emotional, excitable, impulsive, passionate, rough, temperamental, tempestuous

plagiarism *n* **1** = **copying**, appropriation, borrowing, cribbing (*inf.*), infringement, lifting (*inf.*), piracy, theft

plagiarize *vb* = **copy**, appropriate, borrow, crib (*inf.*), infringe, lift (*inf.*), pirate, steal, thieve

plague *n* **1** = **disease**, contagion, epidemic, infection, lurgy (*inf.*), pandemic, pestilence **4** = **affliction**, bane, blight, calamity, cancer, curse, evil, scourge, torment, trial **5** *Informal* = **nuisance**, aggravation, annoyance, bother, hassle (*inf.*), irritant, pain (*inf.*), pest, problem, thorn in one's flesh, vexation ◆ *vb* **7, 9** = **pester**, afflict, annoy, badger, bedevil, be on one's back (*sl.*), bother, disturb, fret, get in one's hair (*inf.*), get on one's nerves (*inf.*), harass, harry, hassle (*inf.*), haunt, molest, pain, persecute, tease, torment, torture, trouble, vex

plain[1] *adj* **1** = **flat**, even, level, plane, smooth **2** = **clear**, apparent, bold, comprehensible, distinct, evident, legible, lucid, manifest, obvious, overt, patent, transparent, unambiguous, understandable, unmistakable, visible **4** = **straightforward**, artless, blunt, candid, direct, downright, forthright, frank, guileless, honest, ingenuous, open, outspoken, round, sincere, upfront (*inf.*) **5** = **ordinary**, common, commonplace, everyday, frugal, homely, lowly, modest, simple, unaffected, unpretentious, workaday **6** = **unadorned**, austere, bare, basic, discreet, modest, muted, pure, restrained, severe, simple, Spartan, stark, unembellished, unfussy, unornamented, unpatterned, unvarnished **8** = **ugly**, ill-favoured, no oil painting (*inf.*), not beautiful, not striking, ordinary, unalluring, unattractive, unlovely, unprepossessing ◆ *n* **11** = **flatland**, grassland, llano, lowland, mesa, open country, pampas, plateau, prairie, steppe, tableland, veld
Antonyms *adj* ≠ **flat**: bumpy, not level, uneven ≠ **clear**: ambiguous, complex, concealed, deceptive, difficult, disguised, hidden, illegible, incomprehensible, inconspicuous, indiscernible, indistinct, obscure, vague, veiled ≠ **straightforward**: circuitous, indirect, meandering, rambling, roundabout ≠ **ordinary**: affected, distinguished, egotistic, ostentatious, pretentious, sophisticated, worldly ≠ **unadorned**: adorned, decorated, fancy, ornate ≠ **ugly**: attractive, beautiful, comely, good-looking, gorgeous, handsome

plain-spoken *adj* = **blunt**, candid, direct, downright, explicit, forthright, frank, open, outright, outspoken, straightforward, unequivocal, upfront (*inf.*)
Antonyms *adj* diplomatic, discreet, evasive, guarded, indirect, reticent, subtle, tactful, thoughtful

plaintive *adj* = **sorrowful**, disconsolate, doleful, grief-stricken, grievous, heart-rending, melancholy, mournful, pathetic, piteous, pitiful, rueful, sad, wistful, woebegone, woeful

plan *n* **1, 2** = **scheme**, contrivance, design, device, idea, method, plot, procedure, programme, project, proposal, proposition, scenario, strategy, suggestion, system **3, 4** = **diagram**, blueprint, chart, delineation, drawing, illustration, layout, map, representation, scale drawing, sketch ◆ *vb* **5** = **devise**, arrange, concoct, contrive, design, draft, formulate, frame, invent, organize, outline, plot, prepare, represent, scheme, think out **7** = **intend**, aim, contemplate, envisage, foresee, mean, propose, purpose

planchet ('plɑːntʃɪt) *n* a piece of metal ready to be stamped as a coin, medal, etc.; flan. [C17: from F: little board, from *planche* PLANK]

planchette (plɑːn'ʃɛt) *n* a heart-shaped board on wheels, on which messages are written under supposed spirit guidance. [C19: from F: little board, from *planche* PLANK]

Planck constant (plæŋk) *or* **Planck's constant** *n* a fundamental constant equal to the energy of any quantum of radiation divided by its frequency. [C19: after Max *Planck* (1858–1947), G physicist]

plane[1] ➊ (pleɪn) *n* **1** *Maths.* a flat surface in which a straight line joining any two of its points lies entirely on that surface. **2** a level surface. **3** a level of existence, attainment, etc. **4a** short for **aeroplane. 4b** a wing or supporting surface of an aircraft. ◆ *adj* **5** level or flat. **6** *Maths.* lying entirely in one plane. ◆ *vb* **planes, planing, planed.** (*intr*) **7** to glide. **8** (of a boat) to rise partly and skim over the water when moving at a certain speed. [C17: from L *plānum* level surface]

plane[2] (pleɪn) *n* **1** a tool with a steel blade set obliquely in a wooden or iron body, for smoothing timber surfaces, cutting grooves, etc. **2** a flat tool, usually metal, for smoothing the surface of clay or plaster in a mould. ◆ *vb* **planes, planing, planed.** (*tr*) **3** to smooth or cut (timber, etc.) using a plane. **4** (often foll. by *off*) to remove using a plane. [C14: via OF from LL *plāna* plane, from *plānāre* to level]

plane[3] (pleɪn) *n* See **plane tree.**

plane geometry *n* the study of the properties of plane curves, figures, etc.

plane polarization *n* a type of polarization in which waves of light or other radiation are restricted to vibration in a single plane.

planet ('plænɪt) *n* **1** Also called: **major planet.** any of the nine celestial bodies, Mercury, Venus, Earth, Mars, Jupiter, Saturn, Uranus, Neptune, or Pluto, that revolve around the sun in elliptical orbits. **2** any celestial body revolving around a star. **3** *Astrol.* any of the planets of the solar system, excluding the earth but including the sun and moon, each thought to rule one or sometimes two signs of the zodiac. [C12: via OF from LL *planēta*, from Gk *planētēs* wanderer, from *planaein* to wander]

plane table *n* a surveying instrument consisting of a drawing board mounted on adjustable legs.

planetarium (ˌplænɪ'tɛərɪəm) *n, pl* **planetariums** *or* **planetaria** (-ɪə). **1** an instrument for simulating the apparent motions of the sun, moon, and planets by projecting images of these bodies onto a domed ceiling. **2** a building in which such an instrument is housed. **3** a model of the solar system.

planetary ➊ ('plænɪtərɪ, -trɪ) *adj* **1** of a planet. **2** mundane; terrestrial. **3** wandering or erratic. **4** *Astrol.* under the influence of one of the planets. **5** (of a gear) having an axis that rotates around that of another gear.

planetesimal hypothesis (ˌplænɪ'tɛsɪməl) *n* the discredited theory that the close passage of a star to the sun caused many small bodies (**planetesimals**) to be drawn from the sun, eventually coalescing to form the planets. [C20: *planetesimal*, from PLANET + INFINITESIMAL]

planetoid ('plænɪˌtɔɪd) *n* another name for **asteroid** (sense 1).
▸ˌ**plane'toidal** *adj*

plane tree *or* **plane** *n* a tree with ball-shaped heads of fruit and leaves with pointed lobes. [C14 *plane*, from OF, from L *platanus*, from Gk, from *platos* wide, referring to the leaves]

plangent ('plændʒənt) *adj* **1** having a loud deep sound. **2** resonant and mournful. [C19: from L *plangere* to beat (esp. the breast, in grief)]

planimeter (plæ'nɪmɪtə) *n* a mechanical instrument for measuring the area of an irregular plane figure by moving a point attached to an arm.
▸**pla'nimetry** *n*

planish ('plænɪʃ) *vb* (*tr*) to give a final finish to (metal, etc.) by hammering or rolling. [C16: from OF *planir* to smooth out, from L *plānus* flat]

planisphere ('plænɪˌsfɪə) *n* a projection or representation of all or part of a sphere on a plane surface. [C14: from Med. L *plānisphaerium*, from L *plānus* flat + Gk *sphaira* globe]

plank (plæŋk) *n* **1** a stout length of sawn timber. **2** something that supports or sustains. **3** one of the policies in a political party's programme. **4 walk the plank.** to be forced by pirates, etc., to walk to one's death off the end of a plank jutting out from the side of a ship. ◆ *vb* **5** (*tr*) to cover or provide with planks. [C13: from OF *planke*, from LL *planca* board, from *plancus* flat-footed]

planking ('plæŋkɪŋ) *n* a number of planks.

plankton ('plæŋktən) *n* the organisms inhabiting the surface layer of a sea or lake, consisting of small drifting plants and animals. [C19: via G from Gk *planktos* wandering, from *plazesthai* to roam]

planned economy *n* another name for **command economy.**

planned obsolescence *n* the policy of deliberately limiting the life of a product in order to encourage the purchaser to replace it. Also called: **built-in obsolescence.**

planner ('plænə) *n* **1** a person who makes plans, esp. for the development of a town, building, etc. **2** a chart for recording future appointments, tasks, goals, etc.

planning permission *n* (in Britain) formal permission granted by a local authority for the development or changed use of land or buildings.

plano- *or sometimes before a vowel* **plan-** *combining form.* indicating flatness or planeness: *plano-concave.* [from L *plānus* flat]

plano-concave (ˌpleɪnəʊ'kɒnkeɪv) *adj* (of a lens) having one side concave and the other plane.

plano-convex (ˌpleɪnəʊ'kɒnvɛks) *adj* (of a lens) having one side convex and the other plane.

plant[1] ➊ (plɑːnt) *n* **1** any living organism that typically synthesizes its food from inorganic substances, lacks specialized sense organs, and has no powers of locomotion. **2** such an organism that is smaller than a shrub or tree; a herb. **3** a cutting, seedling, or similar structure, esp. when ready for transplantation. **4** *Inf.* a thing positioned secretly for discovery by another, esp. in order to incriminate an innocent person. **5** *Inf.* a person, placed in an audience, whose rehearsed responses, etc., seem spontaneous to the rest of the audience. **6** *Inf.* a person placed secretly in a group or organization to obtain information, etc. ◆ *vb* (*tr*) **7** (often foll. by *out*) to set (seeds, crops, etc.) into (ground) to grow. **8** to place firmly in position. **9** to establish; found. **10** (foll. by *with*) to stock or furnish. **11** to implant in the mind. **12** *Sl.* to deliver (a blow). **13** *Inf.* to position or hide, esp. in order to deceive or observe. **14** *Inf.* to hide or secrete, esp. for some illegal purpose or in order to incriminate someone. [OE, from *planta* a shoot]
▸'**plantable** *adj*

plant[2] ➊ (plɑːnt) *n* **1** the land, buildings, and equipment used in carrying on an industry or business. **2** a factory or workshop. **3** mobile mechanical equipment for construction, road-making, etc. [C20: special use of PLANT[1]]

plantain[1] ('plæntɪn) *n* any of various N temperate plants, esp. the great plantain, which has a rosette of broad leaves and a slender spike of small greenish flowers. See also **ribwort.** [C14 *plauntein*, from OF, from L *plantāgō*, from *planta* sole of the foot]

plantain[2] ('plæntɪn) *n* a large tropical plant with a green-skinned banana-like fruit which is eaten as a staple food in many tropical regions. [C16: Sp. *platano* plantain, PLANE TREE]

plantain lily *n* any of several Asian plants of the genus *Hosta*, having broad ribbed leaves.

plantar ('plæntə) *adj* of or on the sole of the foot. [C18: from L *plantāris*, from *planta* sole of the foot]

plantation (plæn'teɪʃən) *n* **1** an estate, esp. in tropical countries, where cash crops such as rubber, oil palm, etc., are grown on a large scale. **2** a group of cultivated trees or plants. **3** (formerly) a colony or group of settlers.

planter ('plɑːntə) *n* **1** the owner or manager of a plantation. **2** a machine designed for rapid and efficient planting of seeds. **3** a colonizer or settler. **4** a decorative pot for house plants.

plantigrade ('plæntɪˌgreɪd) *adj* **1** walking with the entire sole of the foot touching the ground, as man and bears. ◆ *n* **2** a plantigrade animal. [C19: via F from NL *plantigradus*, from L *planta* sole of the foot + *gradus* a step]

plant louse *n* another name for an **aphid.**

plaque ➊ (plæk, plɑːk) *n* **1** an ornamental or commemorative inscribed tablet. **2** a small flat brooch or badge. **3** *Pathol.* any small abnormal patch on or within the body. **4** short for **dental plaque.** [C19: from F, from *plaquier* to plate, from MDu. *placken* to beat into a thin plate]

plash (plæʃ) *vb, n* a less common word for **splash.** [OE *plæsc*, prob. imit.]
▸'**plashy** *adj*

-plasia *or* **-plasy** *n combining form.* indicating growth, development, or change. [from NL, from Gk *plasis* a moulding, from *plassein* to mould]

plasm ('plæzəm) *n* **1** protoplasm of a specified type: *germ plasm.* **2** a variant of **plasma.**

-plasm *n combining form.* (in biology) indicating the material forming cells: *protoplasm; cytoplasm.* [from Gk *plasma* something moulded; see PLASMA]
▸**-plasmic** *adj combining form.*

plasma ('plæzmə) *or* **plasm** *n* **1** the clear yellowish fluid portion of blood or lymph in which the corpuscles and cells are suspended. **2** Also called: **blood plasma.** a sterilized preparation of such fluid, taken from the blood, for use in transfusions. **3** a former name for **protoplasm** or **cytoplasm. 4** *Physics.* a hot ionized gas containing positive ions and electrons. **5** a green variety of chalcedony. [C18: from LL: something moulded, from Gk, from *plassein* to mould]
▸**plasmatic** (plæz'mætɪk) *or* '**plasmic** *adj*

plasma torch *n* an electrical device for converting a gas into a plasma, used for melting metal, etc.

plasmid ('plæzmɪd) *n* a small circle of bacterial DNA that is independent of the main bacterial chromosome. Plasmids often contain genes for drug resistances and can be transmitted between bacteria of the

THESAURUS

plane[1] *n* **1, 2** = **flat surface**, level surface **3** = **level**, condition, degree, footing, position, stratum **4** = **aeroplane**, aircraft, jet ◆ *adj* **5** = **level**, even, flat, flush, horizontal, plain, regular, smooth, uniform ◆ *vb* **7** = **skim**, glide, sail, skate

planetary *adj* **2** = **terrestrial**, earthly, mundane, sublunary, tellurian, terrene **3** = **moving**, aberrant, erratic, journeying, travelling, vacillating, variable, wandering

plant[1] *n* **1, 2** = **vegetable**, bush, flower, herb, shrub, weed ◆ *vb* **7** = **sow**, implant, put in the ground, scatter, seed, set out, transplant **8, 9** = **place**, establish, fix, found, imbed, insert, institute, lodge, put, root, set, settle, sow the seeds

plant[2] *n* **1, 3** = **machinery**, apparatus, equipment, gear **2** = **factory**, foundry, mill, shop, works, yard

plaque *n* **1, 2** = **plate**, badge, brooch, cartouch(e), medal, medallion, panel, slab, tablet

same and different species: used in genetic engineering. [C20: from PLASM + -ID[1]]

plasmodium (plæz'məʊdɪəm) *n, pl* **plasmodia** (-dɪə). **1** an amoeboid mass of protoplasm, containing many nuclei: a stage in the life cycle of certain organisms. **2** a parasitic protozoan which causes malaria. [C19: NL; see PLASMA, -ODE[1]]
▸**plas'modial** *adj*

plasmolysis (plæz'mɒlɪsɪs) *n* the shrinkage of protoplasm away from cell walls that occurs as a result of excessive water loss, esp. in plant cells.

-plast *n combining form.* indicating a living cell or particle of living matter: *protoplast.* [from Gk *plastos* formed, from *plassein* to form]

plaster ⓣ ('plɑːstə) *n* **1** a mixture of lime, sand, and water that is applied to a wall or ceiling as a soft paste that hardens when dry. **2** *Brit., Austral., & NZ.* an adhesive strip of material for dressing a cut, wound, etc. **3** short for **mustard plaster** or **plaster of Paris.** ◆ *vb* **4** to coat (a wall, ceiling, etc.) with plaster. **5** (*tr*) to apply like plaster: *she plastered make-up on her face.* **6** (*tr*) to cause to lie flat or to adhere. **7** (*tr*) to apply a plaster cast to. **8** (*tr*) *Sl.* to strike or defeat with great force. [OE, from Med. L *plastrum* medicinal salve, building plaster, via L from Gk *emplastron* curative dressing]
▸**'plasterer** *n*

plasterboard ('plɑːstəˌbɔːd) *n* a thin rigid board, in the form of a layer of plaster compressed between two layers of fibreboard, used to form or cover walls, etc.

plastered ('plɑːstəd) *adj Sl.* intoxicated; drunk.

plaster of Paris *n* **1** a white powder that sets to a hard solid when mixed with water, used for making sculptures and casts, as an additive for lime plasters, and for making casts for setting broken limbs. **2** the hard plaster produced when this powder is mixed with water. [C15: from Med. L *plastrum parisiense,* orig. made from the gypsum of *Paris*]

plastic ⓣ ('plæstɪk) *n* **1** any one of a large number of synthetic materials that have a polymeric structure and can be moulded when soft and then set. Plastics are used in the manufacture of many articles and in coatings, artificial fibres, etc. ◆ *adj* **2** made of plastic. **3** easily influenced; impressionable. **4** capable of being moulded or formed. **5a** of moulding or modelling: *the plastic arts.* **5b** produced or apparently produced by moulding: *the plastic draperies of Giotto's figures.* **6** having the power to form or influence: *the plastic forces of the imagination.* **7** *Biol.* able to change, develop, or grow: *plastic tissues.* **8** *Sl.* superficially attractive yet unoriginal or artificial: *plastic food.* [C17: from L *plasticus* relating to moulding, from Gk *plastikos,* from *plassein* to form]
▸**'plastically** *adv* ▸**plasticity** (plæ'stɪsɪtɪ) *n*

-plastic *adj combining form.* growing or forming. [from Gk *plastikos;* see PLASTIC]

plastic bomb *n* a bomb consisting of plastic explosive fitted around a detonator.

plastic bullet *n* a bullet consisting of a cylinder of plastic about four inches long, generally causing less severe injuries than an ordinary bullet, and used esp. for riot control. Also called: **baton round.**

plastic explosive *n* an adhesive jelly-like explosive substance.

Plasticine ('plæstɪˌsiːn) *n Trademark.* a soft coloured material used, esp. by children, for modelling.

plasticize *or* **plasticise** ('plæstɪˌsaɪz) *vb* **plasticizes, plasticizing, plasticized** *or* **plasticises, plasticising, plasticised.** to make or become plastic, as by the addition of a plasticizer.
▸**ˌplastici'zation** *or* **ˌplastici'sation** *n*

plasticizer *or* **plasticiser** ('plæstɪˌsaɪzə) *n* any of a number of substances added to materials. Their uses include softening and improving the flexibility of plastics and preventing dried paint coatings from becoming too brittle.

plastic money *n* credit cards as opposed to cash.

plastic surgery *n* the branch of surgery concerned with therapeutic or cosmetic repair or re-formation of missing, injured, or malformed tissues or parts.
▸**plastic surgeon** *n*

plastid ('plæstɪd) *n* any of various small particles in the cells of plants and some animals which contain starch, oil, protein, etc. [C19: via G from Gk *plastēs* sculptor, from *plassein* to form]

plastron ('plæstrən) *n* the bony plate forming the ventral part of the shell of a tortoise or turtle. [C16: via F from It. *piastrone,* from *piastra* breastplate, from L *emplastrum* PLASTER]
▸**'plastral** *adj*

-plasty *n combining form.* indicating plastic surgery: *rhinoplasty.* [from Gk *-plastia;* see -PLAST]

plat[1] (plæt) *n* a small area of ground; plot. [C16 (also in ME place names): orig. a var. of PLOT[2]]

plat[2] (plæt) *vb* **plats, platting, platted,** *n* a dialect variant spelling of **plait.** [C16]

platan ('plætᵊn) *n* another name for **plane tree.** [C14: see PLANE TREE]

plat du jour ('plɑː də 'ʒʊə; *French* pla dy zur) *n, pl* **plats du jour** ('plɑːz də 'ʒʊə; *French* pla dy zur). the specially prepared or recommended dish of the day on a restaurant's menu. [F, lit.: dish of the day]

plate ⓣ (pleɪt) *n* **1a** a shallow usually circular dish made of porcelain, earthenware, glass, etc., on which food is served. **1b** (*as modifier*): *a plate rack.* **2a** Also called: **plateful.** the contents of a plate. **2b** *Austral. & NZ.* a plate of cakes, sandwiches, etc., brought by a guest to a party: *everyone was asked to bring a plate.* **3** an entire course of a meal: *a cold plate.* **4** any shallow receptacle, esp. for receiving a collection in church. **5** flat metal of uniform thickness obtained by rolling, usually having a thickness greater than about three millimetres. **6** a thin coating of metal usually on another metal, as produced by electrodeposition. **7** metal or metalware that has been coated in this way: *Sheffield plate.* **8** dishes, cutlery, etc., made of gold or silver. **9** a sheet of metal, plastic, rubber, etc., having a printing surface produced by a process such as stereotyping. **10** a print taken from such a sheet or from a woodcut. **11** a thin flat sheet of a substance, such as metal or glass. **12** a small piece of metal, plastic, etc., designed to bear an inscription and to be fixed to another surface. **13** armour made of overlapping or articulated pieces of thin metal. **14** *Photog.* a sheet of glass, or sometimes metal, coated with photographic emulsion on which an image can be formed by exposure to light. **15** a device for straightening teeth. **16** an informal word for **denture** (sense 1). **17** *Anat.* any flat platelike structure. **18a** a cup awarded to the winner of a sporting contest, esp. a horse race. **18b** a race or contest for such a prize. **19** any of the rigid layers of the earth's lithosphere. **20** *Electronics, chiefly US.* the anode in an electronic valve. **21** a horizontal timber joist that supports rafters. **22** a light horseshoe for flat racing. **23** *RC Church.* Also called: **Communion plate.** a flat plate held under the chin of a communicant in order to catch any fragments of the consecrated Host. **24 on a plate.** acquired without trouble: *he was handed the job on a plate.* **25 on one's plate.** waiting to be done or dealt with. ◆ *vb* **plates, plating, plated.** (*tr*) **26** to coat (a surface, usually metal) with a thin layer of other metal by electrolysis, etc. **27** to cover with metal plates, as for protection. **28** *Printing.* to make a stereotype or electrotype from (type or another plate). **29** to form (metal) into plate, esp. by rolling. [C13: from OF: thin metal sheet, something flat, from Vulgar L *plattus* (unattested)]

plateau ⓣ ('plætəʊ) *n, pl* **plateaus** *or* **plateaux** (-əʊz). **1** a wide mainly level area of elevated land. **2** a relatively long period of stability; levelling off: *the rising prices reached a plateau.* ◆ *vb* (*intr*) **3** to remain at a stable level for a relatively long period. [C18: from F, from OF *platel* something flat, from *plat* flat]

plated ('pleɪtɪd) *adj* **a** coated with a layer of metal. **b** (*in combination*): *gold-plated.*

plate glass *n* glass formed into a sheet by rolling, used for windows, etc.

platelayer ('pleɪtˌleɪə) *n Brit.* a workman who lays and maintains railway track. US equivalent: **trackman.**

platelet ('pleɪtlɪt) *n* a minute particle occurring in the blood of vertebrates and involved in the clotting of the blood. [C19: a small PLATE]

platen ('plætᵊn) *n* **1** a flat plate in a printing press that presses the paper against the type. **2** the roller on a typewriter, against which the keys strike. [C15: from OF *platine,* from *plat* flat]

plater ('pleɪtə) *n* **1** a person or thing that plates. **2** *Horse racing.* a mediocre horse entered chiefly for minor races.

plate tectonics *n* (*functioning as sing*) *Geol.* the study of the earth's crust with reference to the theory that the lithosphere is divided into rigid blocks (plates) that float on semimolten rock and are thus able to interact with each other at their boundaries.

platform ⓣ ('plætfɔːm) *n* **1** a raised floor or other horizontal surface. **2** a raised area at a railway station, from which passengers have access to the trains. **3** See **drilling platform. 4** the declared principles, aims, etc., of a political party, etc. **5a** the thick raised sole of some shoes. **5b** (*as modifier*): *platform shoes.* **6** a vehicle or level place on which weapons are mounted and fired. **7** a specific type of computer hardware or computer operating system. [C16: from F *plateforme,* from *plat* flat + *forme* layout]

platform ticket *n* a ticket for admission to railway platforms but not for travel.

plating ('pleɪtɪŋ) *n* **1** a coating or layer of material, esp. metal. **2** a layer or covering of metal plates.

platiniridium (ˌplætɪnɪ'rɪdɪəm) *n* any alloy of platinum and iridium.

platinize *or* **platinise** ('plætɪˌnaɪz) *vb* **platinizes, platinizing, platinized** *or* **platinises, platinising, platinised.** (*tr*) to coat with platinum.
▸**ˌplatini'zation** *or* **ˌplatini'sation** *n*

platinum ('plætɪnəm) *n* a ductile malleable silvery-white metallic ele-

THESAURUS

plaster *n* **1** = **mortar**, gesso, gypsum, plaster of Paris, stucco **2** = **bandage**, adhesive plaster, dressing, Elastoplast (*Trademark*), sticking plaster ◆ *vb* **4, 5** = **cover**, bedaub, besmear, coat, daub, overlay, smear, spread

plastic *adj* **3** = **manageable**, compliant, docile, easily influenced, impressionable, malleable, pliable, receptive, responsive, tractable **4** = **pliant**, ductile, fictile, flexible, mouldable, pliable, soft, supple, tensile **8** *Slang* = **false**, artificial, meretricious, mock, phoney *or* phony (*inf.*), pseudo (*inf.*), sham, specious, spurious, superficial, synthetic
Antonyms *adj* ≠ **manageable:** intractable, rebellious, recalcitrant, refractory, unmanageable, unreceptive ≠ **pliant:** brittle, hard, inflexible, rigid, stiff, unbending, unyielding ≠ **false:** authentic, genuine, natural, real, sincere, true

plasticity *n* **3, 4** = **pliability**, flexibility, malleability, pliableness, suppleness, tractability

plate *n* **1** = **platter**, dish, trencher (*arch.*) **3** = **helping**, course, dish, portion, serving **5, 11** = **layer**, panel, sheet, slab **10** = **illustration**, lithograph, print ◆ *vb* **26** = **coat**, anodize, cover, electroplate, face, gild, laminate, nickel, overlay, platinize, silver

plateau *n* **1** = **upland**, highland, mesa, table, tableland **2** = **levelling off**, level, stability, stage

platform *n* **1** = **stage**, dais, podium, rostrum,

ment, very resistant to heat and chemicals: used in jewellery, laboratory apparatus, electrical contacts, dentistry, electroplating, and as a catalyst. Symbol: Pt; atomic no.: 78; atomic wt.: 195.08. [C19: NL, from Sp. *platina* silvery element, from *plata* silver, from Provençal: silver plate + the suffix *-um*]

platinum black *n Chem.* a black powder consisting of very finely divided platinum metal.

platinum-blond *or (fem)* **platinum-blonde** *adj* **1** (of hair) of a pale silver-blond colour. **2a** having hair of this colour. **2b** *(as n): she was a platinum blonde.*

platinum disc *n* **1** (in Britain) an LP record certified to have sold 300 000 copies or a single certified to have sold 600 000 copies. **2** (in the US) an LP record or single certified to have sold one million copies.

platinum metal *n* any of the group of precious metallic elements consisting of ruthenium, rhodium, palladium, osmium, iridium, and platinum.

platitude ⓣ ('plætɪˌtjuːd) *n* **1** a trite, dull, or obvious remark. **2** staleness or insipidity of thought or language; triteness. [C19: from F, lit.: flatness, from *plat* flat]
▸ˌ**plati'tudinous** *adj*

platitudinize *or* **platitudinise** (ˌplætɪ'tjuːdɪˌnaɪz) *vb* **platitudinizes, platitudinizing, platitudinized** *or* **platitudinises, platitudinising, platitudinised.** *(intr)* to speak or write in platitudes.

Platonic ⓣ (plə'tɒnɪk) *adj* **1** of or relating to Plato or his teachings. **2** *(often not cap.)* free from physical desire: *Platonic love.*
▸**Pla'tonically** *adv*

Platonic solid *n* any of the five possible regular polyhedrons: cube, tetrahedron, octahedron, icosahedron, and dodecahedron.

Platonism ('pleɪtəˌnɪzəm) *n* the teachings of Plato (?427–?347 B.C.), Greek philosopher, and his followers; esp. the philosophical theory that the meanings of general words are real entities (Forms) and that particular objects have properties in common by virtue of their relationship with these Forms.
▸'**Platonist** *n*

platoon ⓣ (plə'tuːn) *n* **1** *Mil.* a subunit of a company, usually comprising three sections of ten to twelve men. **2** a group of people sharing a common activity, etc. [C17: from F *peloton* little ball, group of men, from *pelote* ball; see PELLET]

Plattdeutsch *(German* 'platdɔytʃ) *n* another name for **Low German.** [lit.: flat German]

platteland ('platəˌlant) *n* **the.** (in South Africa) the country districts or rural areas. [C20: from Afrik., from Du. *plat* flat + *land* country]

platter ⓣ ('plætə) *n* **1** a large shallow usually oval dish or plate. **2** a course of a meal, usually consisting of several different foods served on the same plate: *a seafood platter.* [C14: from Anglo-Norman *plater,* from *plat* dish, from OF *plat* flat; see PLATE]

platy- *combining form.* indicating something flat, as **platyhelminth,** the flatworm. [from Gk *platus* flat]

platypus ('plætɪpəs) *n, pl* **platypuses.** See **duck-billed platypus.** [C18: NL, from PLATY- + *-pus,* from Gk *pous* foot]

platyrrhine ('plætɪˌraɪn) *or* **platyrrhinian** (ˌplætɪ'rɪnɪən) *adj* **1** (esp. of New World monkeys) having widely separated nostrils opening to the side of the face. **2** (of a human) having an unusually short wide nose. [C19: from NL *platyrrhinus,* from PLATY- + *-rrhinus,* from Gk *rhis* nose]

plaudit ⓣ ('plɔːdɪt) *n (usually pl)* **1** an expression of enthusiastic approval. **2** a round of applause. [C17: from earlier *plauditē,* from L: applaud!, from *plaudere* to APPLAUD]

plausible ⓣ ('plɔːzɪbᵊl) *adj* **1** apparently reasonable, valid, truthful, etc.: *a plausible excuse.* **2** apparently trustworthy or believable: *a plausible speaker.* [C16: from L *plausibilis* worthy of applause, from *plaudere* to APPLAUD]
▸ˌ**plausi'bility** *or* '**plausibleness** *n* ▸'**plausibly** *adv*

play ⓣ (pleɪ) *vb* **1** to occupy oneself in (a sport or diversion). **2** *(tr)* to contend against (an opponent) in a sport or game: *Ed played Tony at chess and lost.* **3** to fulfil or cause to fulfil (a particular role) in a team game: *he plays in the defence.* **4** *(intr;* often foll. by *about* or *around)* to behave carelessly, esp. in a way that is unconsciously cruel or hurtful: *to play about with a young girl's affections.* **5** (when *intr,* often foll. by *at)* to perform or act the part (of) in or as in a dramatic production. **6** to perform (a dramatic production). **7a** to have the ability to perform on (a musical instrument): *David plays the harp.* **7b** to perform as specified: *he plays out of tune.* **8** *(tr)* **8a** to reproduce (a piece of music, note, etc.) on an instrument. **8b** to perform works by: *to play Brahms.* **9** to discharge or cause to discharge: *he played the water from the hose onto the garden.* **10** to cause (a radio, etc.) to emit sound. **11** to move freely, quickly, or irregularly: *lights played on the scenery.* **12** *(tr) Stock Exchange.* to speculate or operate aggressively for gain in (a market). **13** *(tr) Angling.* to attempt to tire (a hooked fish) by alternately letting out and reeling in line. **14** to put (a card, counter, piece, etc.) into play. **15** to gamble. **16 play fair** *(or* **false).** (often foll. by *with)* to prove oneself fair *(or* unfair) in one's dealings. **17 play for time.** to delay the outcome of some activity so as to gain time to one's own advantage. **18 play into the hands of.** to act directly to the advantage of (an opponent). ◆ *n* **19** a dramatic composition written for performance by actors on a stage, etc.; drama. **20** the performance of a dramatic composition. **21a** games, exercise, or other activity undertaken for pleasure, esp. by children. **21b** *(in combination): playroom.* **22** conduct: *fair play.* **23** the playing of a game or the period during which a game is in progress: *rain stopped play.* **24** *US.* a manoeuvre in a game: *a brilliant play.* **25** the situation of a ball, etc., that is within the defined area and being played according to the rules (in **in play, out of play**). **26** gambling. **27** activity or operation: *the play of the imagination.* **28** freedom of movement: *too much play in the rope.* **29** light, free, or rapidly shifting motion: *the play of light on the water.* **30** fun, jest, or joking: *I only did it in play.* **31 call into play.** to bring into operation. **32 make a play for.** *Inf.* to make an obvious attempt to gain. ◆ See also **play along, playback,** etc. [OE *plega* (n), *plegan* (vb)]
▸'**playable** *adj*

play-act *vb* **1** *(intr)* to pretend or make believe. **2** *(intr)* to behave in an overdramatic or affected manner. **3** to act in or as in (a play).
▸'**play-ˌacting** *n* ▸'**play-ˌactor** *n*

play along *vb (adv)* **1** *(intr;* usually foll. by *with)* to cooperate (with), esp. as a temporary measure. **2** *(tr)* to manipulate as if in a game, esp. for one's own advantage: *he played the widow along until she gave him her money.*

playback ('pleɪˌbæk) *n* **1** the act or process of reproducing a recording, esp. on magnetic tape. **2** the part of a tape recorder serving to reproduce or used for reproducing recorded material. ◆ *vb* **play back.** *(adv)* **3** to reproduce (recorded material) on (a magnetic tape) by means of a tape recorder.

playbill ('pleɪˌbɪl) *n* **1** a poster or bill advertising a play. **2** the programme of a play.

playboy ⓣ ('pleɪˌbɔɪ) *n* a man, esp. one of private means, who devotes himself to the pleasures of nightclubs, female company, etc.

play down ⓣ *vb (tr, adv)* to make little or light of; minimize the importance of.

player ⓣ ('pleɪə) *n* **1** a person who participates in or is skilled at some game or sport. **2** a person who plays a game or sport professionally. **3** a person who plays a musical instrument. **4** an actor. **5** *Inf.* a participant, esp. a powerful one, in a particular field of activity: *a leading city player.*

player piano *n* a mechanical piano; Pianola.

playful ⓣ ('pleɪfʊl) *adj* **1** full of high spirits and fun: *a playful kitten.* **2** good-natured and humorous: *a playful remark.*
▸'**playfully** *adv*

playgoer ('pleɪˌgəʊə) *n* a person who goes to theatre performances, esp. frequently.

playground ('pleɪˌgraʊnd) *n* **1** an outdoor area for children's play, esp. one having swings, slides, etc., or adjoining a school. **2** a place popular as a sports or holiday resort.

THESAURUS

stand **4** = **policy**, manifesto, objective(s), party line, principle, programme, tenet(s)

platitude *n* **1** = **cliché**, banality, bromide, commonplace, hackneyed saying, inanity, stereotype, trite remark, truism **2** = **triteness**, banality, dullness, inanity, insipidity, triviality, vapidity, verbiage

platitudinous *adj* **1, 2** = **clichéd**, banal, commonplace, corny *(sl.)*, hack, hackneyed, overworked, set, stale, stereotyped, stock, tired, trite, truistic, vapid, well-worn

Platonic *adj* **2** *often not cap.* = **nonphysical**, ideal, idealistic, intellectual, spiritual, transcendent

platoon *n* **1, 2** = **squad**, company, group, outfit *(inf.)*, patrol, squadron, team

platter *n* **1** = **plate**, charger, dish, salver, tray, trencher *(arch.)*

plaudit *n* **1, 2** *usually plural* = **approval**, acclaim, acclamation, applause, approbation, clapping, commendation, congratulation, hand, kudos, ovation, praise, round of applause

plausible *adj* **1** = **believable**, colourable, conceivable, credible, likely, persuasive, possible, probable, reasonable, tenable, verisimilar **2** = **glib**, fair-spoken, smooth, smooth-talking, smooth-tongued, specious
Antonyms *adj* ≠ **believable**: genuine, illogical, implausible, impossible, improbable, inconceivable, incredible, real, unbelievable, unlikely

play *vb* **1** = **amuse oneself**, caper, engage in games, entertain oneself, fool, frisk, frolic, gambol, have fun, revel, romp, sport, trifle **2** = **compete**, be in a team, challenge, contend against, participate, rival, take on, take part, vie with **4** *often foll. by* **about** *or* **around** = **philander**, dally, fool around, mess around, take lightly, trifle, womanize **5, 6** = **act**, act the part of, execute, impersonate, perform, personate, portray, represent, take the part of **12** *Stock Exchange* = **gamble**, bet, chance, hazard, punt *(chiefly Brit.)*, risk, speculate, take, wager ◆ *n* **19** = **drama**, comedy, dramatic piece, entertainment, farce, masque, pantomime, performance, piece, radio play, show, soap opera, stage show, television drama, tragedy **21** = **amusement**, caper, diversion, entertainment, frolic, fun, gambol, game, jest, pastime, prank, recreation, romp, sport **26** = **gambling**, gaming **27** = **action**, activity, employment, function, operation, transaction, working **28** = **space**, elbowroom, give *(inf.)*, latitude, leeway, margin, motion, movement, range, room, scope, sweep, swing **30** = **fun**, foolery, humour, jest, joking, lark *(inf.)*, prank, sport, teasing

playboy *n* = **womanizer**, ladies' man, lady-killer, lover boy *(sl.)*, man about town, philanderer, pleasure seeker, rake, roué, socialite

play down *vb* = **minimize**, gloss over, make light of, make little of, set no store by, soft-pedal *(inf.)*, underplay, underrate

player *n* **1, 2** = **sportsman** *or* **sportswoman**, competitor, contestant, participant, team member **3** = **musician**, artist, instrumentalist, music maker, performer, virtuoso **4** = **performer**, actor *or* actress, entertainer, Thespian, trouper

playful *adj* **1** = **lively**, cheerful, coltish, frisky, frolicsome, gay, impish, joyous, kittenish, larkish *(inf.)*, merry, mischievous, puckish, rol-

playgroup ('pleɪˌgruːp) *n* a regular meeting of small children for supervised creative play.

playhouse ('pleɪˌhaʊs) *n* **1** a theatre. **2** *US.* a small house for children to play in.

playing card *n* one of a pack of 52 rectangular pieces of stiff card, used for playing a wide variety of games, each card having one or more symbols of the same kind on the face, but an identical design on the reverse.

playing field *n Chiefly Brit.* a field or open space used for sport.

playlet ('pleɪlɪt) *n* a short play.

playlist ('pleɪˌlɪst) *n* **1** a list of records chosen for playing, as on a radio station. ◆ *vb* **2** (*tr*) to put (a song or record) on a playlist.

playmaker ('pleɪˌmeɪkə) *n Sport.* a player whose role is to create scoring opportunities for his or her team-mates.

playmate ('pleɪˌmeɪt) *or* **playfellow** *n* a friend or partner in play or recreation.

play off *vb* (*adv*) **1** (*tr;* usually foll. by *against*) to manipulate as if in playing a game: *to play one person off against another.* **2** (*intr*) to take part in a play-off. ◆ *n* **play-off. 3** *Sport.* an extra contest to decide the winner when competitors are tied. **4** *Chiefly US & Canad.* a contest or series of games to determine a championship.

play on *vb* (*intr*) **1** (*adv*) to continue to play. **2** (*prep*) Also: **play upon.** to exploit or impose upon (the feelings or weakness of another).

play on words *n* another term for **pun**[1].

playpen ('pleɪˌpɛn) *n* a small enclosure, usually portable, in which a young child can be left to play in safety.

playschool ('pleɪˌskuːl) *n* an informal nursery group for preschool children.

plaything ('pleɪˌθɪŋ) *n* **1** a toy. **2** a person regarded or treated as a toy.

playtime ('pleɪˌtaɪm) *n* a time for play or recreation, esp. the school break.

play up *vb* (*adv*) **1** (*tr*) to highlight: *to play up one's best features.* **2** *Brit. inf.* to behave irritatingly (towards). **3** (*intr*) *Brit. inf.* (of a machine, etc.) to function erratically: *the car is playing up again.* **4** to hurt; give (one) trouble: *my back's playing up again.* **5 play up to. 5a** to support (another actor) in a performance. **5b** to try to gain favour with by flattery.

playwright ('pleɪˌraɪt) *n* a person who writes plays.

plaza ('plɑːzə) *n* **1** an open space or square, esp. in Spain. **2** *Chiefly US & Canad.* a modern complex of shops, buildings, and parking areas. [C17: from Sp., from L *platēa* courtyard; see PLACE]

plc *or* **PLC** *abbrev. for* public limited company.

plea (pliː) *n* **1** an earnest entreaty or request. **2a** *Law.* something alleged by or on behalf of a party to legal proceedings in support of his claim or defence. **2b** *Criminal law.* the answer made by an accused to the charge: *a plea of guilty.* **2c** (in Scotland and formerly in England) a suit or action at law. **3** an excuse, justification, or pretext: *he gave the plea of a previous engagement.* [C13: from Anglo-Norman *plai,* from OF *plaid* lawsuit, from Med. L *placitum* court order (lit.: what is pleasing), from L *placēre* to please]

plea bargaining *n* an agreement between the prosecution and defence, sometimes including the judge, in which the accused agrees to plead guilty to a lesser charge in return for more serious charges being dropped.

plead (pliːd) *vb* **pleads, pleading; pleaded, plead** (plɛd), *or esp. Scot. & US.* **pled. 1** (when *intr,* often foll. by *with*) to appeal earnestly or humbly (to). **2** (*tr; may take a clause as object*) to give as an excuse: *to plead ignorance.* **3** *Law.* to declare oneself to be (guilty or not guilty) in answer to the charge. **4** *Law.* to advocate (a case) in a court of law. **5** (*intr*) *Law.* **5a** to file pleadings. **5b** to address a court as an advocate. [C13: from OF *plaidier,* from Med. L *placitāre* to have a lawsuit, from L *placēre* to please]
▸ **'pleadable** *adj* ▸ **'pleader** *n*

pleadings ('pliːdɪŋz) *pl n Law.* the formal written statements presented alternately by the plaintiff and defendant in a lawsuit.

pleasance ('plɛzəns) *n* **1** a secluded part of a garden laid out with trees, walks, etc. **2** *Arch.* enjoyment or pleasure. [C14 *plesaunce,* from OF *plaisance,* ult. from *plaisir* to PLEASE]

pleasant ('plɛzᵊnt) *adj* **1** giving or affording pleasure; enjoyable. **2** having pleasing or agreeable manners, appearance, habits, etc. **3** *Obs.* merry and lively. [C14: from OF *plaisant,* from *plaisir* to PLEASE]
▸ **'pleasantly** *adv*

pleasantry ('plɛzᵊntrɪ) *n, pl* **pleasantries. 1** (*often pl*) an agreeable or amusing remark, etc., often one made in order to be polite: *they exchanged pleasantries.* **2** an agreeably humorous manner or style. [C17: from F *plaisanterie,* from *plaisant* PLEASANT]

please (pliːz) *vb* **pleases, pleasing, pleased. 1** to give satisfaction, pleasure, or contentment to (a person). **2** to be the will of or have the will (to): *if it pleases you; the court pleases.* **3 if you please.** if you will or wish, sometimes used in ironic exclamation. **4 pleased with.** happy because of. **5 please oneself.** to do as one likes. ◆ *adv* **6** (*sentence modifier*) used in making polite requests, pleading, etc. **7 yes please.** a polite formula for accepting an offer, invitation, etc. [C14 *plese,* from OF *plaisir,* from L *placēre*]
▸ **pleased** *adj* ▸ **pleasedly** ('pliːzɪdlɪ) *adv*

pleasing ('pliːzɪŋ) *adj* giving pleasure; likable or gratifying.
▸ **'pleasingly** *adv*

pleasurable ('plɛʒərəbᵊl) *adj* enjoyable, agreeable, or gratifying.
▸ **'pleasurably** *adv*

pleasure ('plɛʒə) *n* **1** an agreeable or enjoyable sensation or emotion: *the pleasure of hearing good music.* **2** something that gives enjoyment: *his garden was his only pleasure.* **3a** amusement, recreation, or enjoyment. **3b** (*as modifier*): *a pleasure ground.* **4** *Euphemistic.* sexual gratification: *he took his pleasure of her.* **5** a person's preference. ◆ *vb* **pleasures, pleasuring, pleasured. 6** (when *intr,* often foll. by *in*) *Arch.* to give pleasure to or take pleasure (in). [C14 *plesir,* from OF]

pleat (pliːt) *n* **1** any of various types of fold formed by doubling back fabric, etc., and pressing, stitching, or steaming into place. ◆ *vb* **2** (*tr*) to arrange (material, part of a garment, etc.) in pleats. [C16: var. of PLAIT]

pleb (plɛb) *n* **1** short for **plebeian. 2** *Brit. inf., often derog.* a common vulgar person.

plebeian (plə'biːən) *adj* **1** of or characteristic of the common people, esp. those of ancient Rome. **2** lacking refinement; philistine or vulgar: *plebeian tastes.* ◆ *n* **3** one of the common people, esp. one of the Roman plebs. **4** a person who is coarse, vulgar, etc. [C16: from L *plēbēius* of the people, from *plēbs* the common people of ancient Rome]
▸ **ple'beianˌism** *n*

plebiscite ('plɛbɪˌsaɪt, -sɪt) *n* **1** a direct vote by the electorate of a state,

THESAURUS

licking, spirited, sportive, sprightly, vivacious **2** = **joking**, arch, coy, flirtatious, good-natured, humorous, jesting, jokey, roguish, teasing, tongue-in-cheek, waggish
Antonyms *adj* despondent, gloomy, grave, morose, sedate, serious

playmate *n* = **friend**, chum (*inf.*), companion, comrade, neighbour, pal (*inf.*), playfellow

play on *vb* **2** = **take advantage of**, abuse, capitalize on, exploit, impose on, milk, profit by, trade on, turn to account, utilize

plaything *n* **1** = **toy**, amusement, bauble, game, gewgaw, gimcrack, pastime, trifle, trinket

play up *vb* **1** = **emphasize**, accentuate, bring to the fore, call attention to, highlight, magnify, point up, stress, turn the spotlight on, underline **2** *Brit. informal* = **be awkward**, be bolshie (*Brit. inf.*), be cussed (*inf.*), be disobedient, be stroppy (*Brit. sl.*), give trouble, misbehave **3** *Brit. informal* = **malfunction**, be on the blink, be wonky (*Brit. sl.*), not work properly **4** = **hurt**, be painful, be sore, bother, give one gyp (*Brit. & NZ sl.*), give one trouble, pain, trouble **5b play up to** *Informal* = **butter up**, bootlick (*inf.*), brown-nose (*taboo sl.*), crawl to, curry favour, fawn, flatter, get in with, ingratiate oneself, keep (someone) sweet, pander to, suck up to (*inf.*), toady

playwright *n* = **dramatist**, dramaturge, dramaturgist

plea *n* **1** = **appeal**, begging, entreaty, intercession, overture, petition, prayer, request, suit, supplication **2** *Law* = **suit**, action, allegation, cause **3** = **excuse**, apology, claim, defence, explanation, extenuation, justification, pretext, vindication

plead *vb* **1** = **appeal**, ask, beg, beseech, crave, entreat, implore, importune, petition, request, solicit, supplicate **2** = **allege**, adduce, argue, assert, maintain, put forward, use as an excuse

pleasant *adj* **1** = **pleasing**, acceptable, agreeable, amusing, delectable, delightful, enjoyable, fine, gratifying, lovely, nice, pleasurable, refreshing, satisfying, welcome **2** = **friendly**, affable, agreeable, amiable, charming, cheerful, cheery, congenial, engaging, genial, good-humoured, likable *or* likeable, nice
Antonyms *adj* ≠ **pleasing:** awful, disagreeable, distasteful, horrible, horrid, miserable, offensive, repulsive, unpleasant ≠ **friendly:** cold, disagreeable, horrible, horrid, impolite, offensive, rude, unfriendly, unlikable *or* unlikeable

pleasantry *n* **1** = **joke**, badinage, banter, bon mot, good-natured remark, jest, josh (*sl., chiefly US & Canad.*), quip, sally, witticism

please *vb* **1** = **delight**, amuse, charm, cheer, content, entertain, give pleasure to, gladden, gratify, humour, indulge, rejoice, satisfy, suit, tickle, tickle pink (*inf.*) **2** = **want**, be inclined, choose, desire, like, opt, prefer, see fit, will, wish
Antonyms *vb* ≠ **delight:** anger, annoy, depress, disgust, displease, dissatisfy, grieve, incense, offend, provoke, sadden, vex

pleased *adj* **1** = **happy**, chuffed (*Brit. sl.*), contented, delighted, euphoric, glad, gratified, in high spirits, over the moon (*inf.*), pleased as punch (*inf.*), rapt, satisfied, thrilled, tickled, tickled pink (*inf.*)

pleasing *adj* = **enjoyable**, agreeable, amiable, amusing, attractive, charming, delightful, engaging, entertaining, gratifying, likable *or* likeable, pleasurable, polite, satisfying, winning
Antonyms *adj* boring, disagreeable, dull, monotonous, rude, unattractive, unlikable *or* unlikeable, unpleasant

pleasurable *adj* = **enjoyable**, agreeable, congenial, delightful, diverting, entertaining, fun, good, gratifying, lovely, nice, pleasant, welcome

pleasure *n* **1-3** = **happiness**, amusement, beer and skittles (*inf.*), bliss, comfort, contentment, delectation, delight, diversion, ease, enjoyment, gladness, gratification, jollies (*sl.*), joy, recreation, satisfaction, solace **5** = **wish**, choice, command, desire, inclination, mind, option, preference, purpose, will
Antonyms *n* ≠ **happiness:** abstinence, anger, displeasure, duty, labour, misery, necessity, obligation, pain, sadness, sorrow, suffering, unhappiness

plebeian *adj* **1, 2** = **common**, base, coarse, ignoble, low, lowborn, lower-class, mean, non-U (*Brit. inf.*), proletarian, uncultivated, unrefined, vulgar, working-class ◆ *n* **3** = **commoner**, common man, man in the street, peasant, pleb, prole (*derogatory sl., chiefly Brit.*), proletarian
Antonyms *adj* ≠ **common:** aristocratic, cultivated, highborn, high-class, patrician, polished, refined, upper-class, well-bred

region, etc., on some question, usually of national importance. **2** any expression of public opinion on some matter. ◆ See also **referendum.** [C16: from OF *plébiscite,* from L *plēbiscītum* decree of the people, from *plēbs* the populace + *scīscere* to decree, from *scīre* to know]
▸**plebiscitary** (plə'bɪsɪtərɪ, -trɪ) *adj*

plectrum ('plɛktrəm) *n, pl* **-trums** *or* **-tra** (-trə). any implement for plucking a string, such as a small piece of plastic, wood, etc., used to strum a guitar. [C17: from L, from Gk *plektron,* from *plessein* to strike]

pled (plɛd) *vb US or (esp. in legal usage) Scot.* a past tense and past participle of **plead.**

pledge 🅣 (plɛdʒ) *n* **1** a formal or solemn promise or agreement. **2a** collateral for the payment of a debt or the performance of an obligation. **2b** the condition of being collateral (esp. in **in pledge**). **3** a token: *the gift is a pledge of their sincerity.* **4** an assurance of support or goodwill, conveyed by drinking a toast: *we drank a pledge to their success.* **5** a person who binds himself, as by becoming bail or surety for another. **6 take** *or* **sign the pledge.** to make a vow to abstain from alcoholic drink. ◆ *vb* **pledges, pledging, pledged. 7** to promise formally or solemnly. **8** (*tr*) to bind by or as if by a pledge: *they were pledged to secrecy.* **9** to give or offer (one's word, freedom, property, etc.) as a guarantee, as for the repayment of a loan. **10** to drink a toast to (a person, cause, etc.). [C14: from OF *plege,* from LL *plebium* security, from *plebīre* to pledge, of Gmc origin]
▸**'pledgable** *adj* ▸**'pledger** *or* **'pledgor** *n*

pledgee (plɛdʒ'iː) *n* **1** a person to whom a pledge is given. **2** a person to whom property is delivered as a pledge.

pledget ('plɛdʒɪt) *n* a small flattened pad of wool, cotton, etc., esp. for use as a pressure bandage to be applied to wounds. [C16: from ?]

-plegia *n combining form.* indicating a specified type of paralysis: *paraplegia.* [from Gk, from *plēgē* stroke, from *plēssein* to strike]
▸**-plegic** *adj and n combining form.*

pleiad ('plaɪəd) *n* a brilliant or talented group, esp. one with seven members. [C16: orig. F *Pléiade,* name given by P. de Ronsard (1524–85) to himself and six other poets, ult. after the *Pleiades,* the seven daughters of the Gk god Atlas]

Pleiocene ('plaɪəʊˌsiːn) *adj, n* a variant spelling of **Pliocene.**

Pleistocene ('plaɪstəˌsiːn) *adj* **1** of, denoting, or formed in the first epoch of the Quaternary period. It was characterized by extensive glaciations of the N hemisphere and the evolutionary development of man. ◆ *n* **2 the.** the Pleistocene epoch or rock series. [C19: from Gk *pleistos* most + *kainos* recent]

plenary 🅣 ('pliːnərɪ, 'plɛn-) *adj* **1** full, unqualified, or complete: *plenary powers; plenary indulgence.* **2** (of assemblies, councils, etc.) attended by all the members. [C15: from LL *plēnārius,* from L *plēnus* full]
▸**'plenarily** *adv*

plenipotentiary 🅣 (ˌplɛnɪpə'tɛnʃərɪ) *adj* **1** (esp. of a diplomatic envoy) invested with or possessing full authority. **2** conferring full authority. **3** (of power or authority) full; absolute. ◆ *n, pl* **plenipotentiaries. 4** a person invested with full authority to transact business, esp. a diplomat authorized to represent a country. See also **envoy**[1] (sense 1). [C17: from Med. L *plēnipotentiārius,* from L *plēnus* full + *potentia* POWER]

plenitude 🅣 ('plɛnɪˌtjuːd) *n* **1** abundance. **2** the condition of being full or complete. [C15: via OF from L *plēnitūdō,* from *plēnus* full]

plenteous 🅣 ('plɛntɪəs) *adj* **1** ample; abundant: *a plenteous supply of food.* **2** producing or yielding abundantly: *a plenteous grape harvest.* [C13 *plenteus,* from OF, from *plentif,* from *plenté* PLENTY]
▸**'plenteously** *adv* ▸**'plenteousness** *n*

plentiful 🅣 ('plɛntɪfʊl) *adj* **1** ample; abundant. **2** having or yielding an abundance: *a plentiful year.*
▸**'plentifully** *adv* ▸**'plentifulness** *n*

plenty 🅣 ('plɛntɪ) *n, pl* **plenties. 1** (often foll. by *of*) a great number, amount, or quantity; lots: *plenty of time; there are plenty of cars on display here.* **2** ample supplies or resources: *the age of plenty.* **3 in plenty.** existing in abundance: *food in plenty.* ◆ *determiner* **4a** very many; ample: *plenty of people believe in ghosts.* **4b** (*as pron*): *that's plenty, thanks.* ◆ *adv* **5** *Inf.* fully or abundantly: *the coat was plenty big enough.* [C13: from OF *plenté,* from LL *plēnitās* fullness, from L *plēnus* full]

plenum ('pliːnəm) *n, pl* **plenums** *or* **plena** (-nə). **1** an enclosure containing gas at a higher pressure than the surrounding environment. **2** a fully attended meeting. **3** (esp. in the philosophy of the Stoics) space regarded as filled with matter. [C17: from L: space filled with matter, from *plēnus* full]

pleochroism (plɪ'ɒkrəʊˌɪzəm) *n* a property of certain crystals of absorbing light waves selectively and therefore of showing different colours when looked at from different directions. [C19: from Gk *pleiōn* more, from *polus* many + *-chroism* from *khrōs* skin colour]
▸**pleochroic** (ˌpliːə'krəʊɪk) *adj*

pleomorphism (ˌpliːə'mɔːfɪzəm) *or* **pleomorphy** ('pliːəˌmɔːfɪ) *n* **1** the occurrence of more than one different form in the life cycle of a plant or animal. **2** another word for **polymorphism** (sense 2).
▸ˌ**pleo'morphic** *adj*

pleonasm ('pliːəˌnæzəm) *n Rhetoric.* **1** the use of more words than necessary or an instance of this, such as *a tiny little child.* **2** a word or phrase that is superfluous. [C16: from L *pleonasmus,* from Gk *pleonasmos* excess, from *pleonazein* to be redundant]
▸ˌ**pleo'nastic** *adj*

plesiosaur ('pliːsɪəˌsɔː) *n* any of various marine reptiles of Jurassic and Cretaceous times, having a long neck, short tail, and paddle-like limbs. [C19: from NL *plēsiosaurus,* from Gk *plēsios* near + *sauros* a lizard]

plethora 🅣 ('plɛθərə) *n* **1** superfluity or excess; overabundance. **2** *Pathol., obs.* a condition caused by dilation of superficial blood vessels, characterized esp. by a reddish face. [C16: via Med. L from Gk *plēthōrē* fullness, from *plēthein* to grow full]
▸**plethoric** (plɛ'θɒrɪk) *adj*

pleura ('plʊərə) *n, pl* **pleurae** ('plʊəriː). the thin transparent membrane enveloping the lungs and lining the walls of the thoracic cavity. [C17: via Med. L from Gk: side, rib]
▸**'pleural** *adj*

pleurisy ('plʊərɪsɪ) *n* inflammation of the pleura, characterized by pain that is aggravated by deep breathing or coughing. [C14: from OF *pleurisie,* from LL, from Gk *pleuritis,* from *pleura* side]
▸**pleuritic** (plʊ'rɪtɪk) *adj, n*

pleuro- *or before a vowel* **pleur-** *combining form.* **1** of or relating to the side. **2** indicating the pleura. [from Gk *pleura* side]

pleuropneumonia (ˌplʊərəʊnjuː'məʊnɪə) *n* the combined disorder of pleurisy and pneumonia.

Plexiglas ('plɛksɪˌglɑːs) *n US. trademark.* a transparent plastic, polymethylmethacrylate, used for combs, plastic sheeting, etc.

plexor ('plɛksə) *or* **plessor** *n Med.* a small hammer with a rubber head for use in percussion of the chest and testing reflexes. [C19: from Gk *plēxis* a stroke, from *plēssein* to strike]

plexus ('plɛksəs) *n, pl* **plexuses** *or* **plexus. 1** any complex network of nerves, blood vessels, or lymphatic vessels. **2** an intricate network or arrangement. [C17: NL, from L *plectere* to braid]

pliable 🅣 ('plaɪəbᵊl) *adj* easily moulded, bent, influenced, or altered.
▸ˌ**plia'bility** *or* **'pliableness** *n* ▸**'pliably** *adv*

pliant 🅣 ('plaɪənt) *adj* **1** easily bent; supple: *a pliant young tree.* **2** adaptable; yielding readily to influence; compliant. [C14: from OF, from *plier* to fold; see PLY[2]]
▸**'pliancy** *n* ▸**'pliantly** *adv*

plicate ('plaɪkeɪt) *or* **plicated** *adj* having or arranged in parallel folds or ridges; pleated: *a plicate leaf; plicate rock strata.* [C18: from L *plicātus* folded, from *plicāre* to fold]
▸**pli'cation** *n*

plié ('pliːeɪ) *n* a classic ballet practice posture with back erect and knees bent. [F: bent]

plier ('plaɪə) *n* a person who plies a trade.

pliers ('plaɪəz) *pl n* a gripping tool consisting of two hinged arms usually with serrated jaws. [C16: from PLY[1]]

THESAURUS

pledge *n* **1 = promise**, assurance, covenant, oath, undertaking, vow, warrant, word, word of honour **2 = guarantee**, bail, bond, collateral, deposit, earnest, gage, pawn, security, surety **4 = toast**, health ◆ *vb* **7, 8 = promise**, contract, engage, give one's oath, give one's word, give one's word of honour, swear, undertake, vouch, vow **9 = bind**, engage, gage (*arch.*), guarantee, mortgage, plight **10 = drink to**, drink the health of, toast

plenary *adj* **1 = complete**, absolute, full, sweeping, thorough, unconditional, unlimited, unqualified, unrestricted **2 = full**, complete, entire, general, open, whole

plenipotentiary *n* **4 = ambassador**, emissary, envoy, legate, minister

plenitude *n* **1 = abundance**, bounty, copiousness, cornucopia, excess, plenteousness, plenty, plethora, profusion, wealth **2 = completeness**, amplitude, fullness, repletion

plenteous *adj* **1 = plentiful**, abundant, ample, bounteous (*literary*), bountiful, copious, generous, inexhaustible, infinite, lavish, liberal, overflowing, profuse, thick on the ground **2 = productive**, bumper, fertile, fruitful, luxuriant, plentiful, prolific

plentiful *adj* **1 = abundant**, ample, bounteous (*literary*), bountiful, complete, copious, generous, inexhaustible, infinite, lavish, liberal, overflowing, plenteous, profuse, thick on the ground **2 = productive**, bumper, fertile, fruitful, luxuriant, plenteous, prolific
Antonyms *adj* ≠ **abundant**: deficient, inadequate, insufficient, scant, scarce, skimpy, small, sparing, sparse, thin on the ground

plenty *n* **1 = lots** (*inf.*), abundance, enough, fund, good deal, great deal, heap(s), mass, masses, mine, mountain(s), oodles (*inf.*), pile(s) (*inf.*), plethora, quantities, quantity, stack(s), store, sufficiency, volume **2 = abundance**, affluence, copiousness, fertility, fruitfulness, luxury, opulence, plenitude, plenteousness, plentifulness, profusion, prosperity, wealth

plethora *n* **1 = excess**, glut, overabundance, profusion, superabundance, superfluity, surfeit, surplus
Antonyms *n* dearth, deficiency, lack, scarcity, shortage, want

pliability *n* **= flexibility**, bendability, ductility, elasticity, malleability, mobility, plasticity, pliancy **= impressionableness**, adaptability, amenability, compliance, docility, susceptibility, tractableness

pliable *adj* **= flexible**, bendable, bendy, ductile, limber, lithe, malleable, plastic, pliant, supple, tensile **= compliant**, adaptable, docile, easily led, impressionable, influenceable, like putty in one's hands, manageable, persuadable, pliant, receptive, responsive, susceptible, tractable, yielding
Antonyms *adj* ≠ **flexible**: rigid, stiff ≠ **compliant**: headstrong, inflexible, intractable, obdurate, obstinate, stubborn, unadaptable, unbending, unyielding, wilful

pliant *adj* **1 = flexible**, bendable, bendy, ductile, lithe, plastic, pliable, supple, tensile **2 = impressionable**, adaptable, biddable, compliant, easily led, influenceable, manageable, persuadable, pliable, susceptible, tractable, yielding

plight[1] ❶ (plaɪt) *n* a condition of extreme hardship, danger, etc. [C14 *plit,* from OF *pleit* fold; prob. infl. by OE *pliht* PLIGHT[2]]

plight[2] ❶ (plaɪt) *vb (tr)* **1** to promise formally or pledge (allegiance, support, etc.). **2 plight one's troth.** to make a promise, esp. of marriage. ◆ *n* **3** *Arch. or dialect.* a solemn promise, esp. of engagement; pledge. [OE *pliht* peril]
►'**plighter** *n*

plimsoll *or* **plimsole** ('plɪmsəl) *n Brit.* a light rubber-soled canvas shoe worn for various sports. Also called: **gym shoe, sandshoe.** [C20: from the resemblance of the sole to a Plimsoll line]

Plimsoll line ('plɪmsəl) *n* another name for **load line.** [C19: after Samuel *Plimsoll* (1824–98), Brit. politician who advocated its adoption]

plinth (plɪnθ) *n* **1** the rectangular slab or block that forms the lowest part of the base of a column, statue, pedestal, or pier. **2** Also called: **plinth course.** the lowest part of the wall of a building, esp. one that is formed of a course of stone or brick. **3** a flat block on either side of a doorframe, where the architrave meets the skirting. [C17: from L *plinthus,* from Gk *plinthos* brick]

Pliocene *or* **Pleiocene** ('plaɪəʊˌsiːn) *adj* **1** of, denoting, or formed in the last epoch of the Tertiary period, during which many modern mammals appeared. ◆ *n* **2 the.** the Pliocene epoch or rock series. [C19: from Gk *pleiōn* more, from *polus* many + *-cene* from *kainos* recent]

plissé ('pliːseɪ, 'plɪs-) *n* **1** fabric with a wrinkled finish, achieved by treatment involving caustic soda: *cotton plissé.* **2** such a finish on a fabric. [F: pleated]

PLO *abbrev. for* Palestine Liberation Organization.

plod ❶ (plɒd) *vb* **plods, plodding, plodded. 1** to make (one's way) or walk along (a path, etc.) with heavy usually slow steps. **2** *(intr)* to work slowly and perseveringly. ◆ *n* **3** the act of plodding. **4** *Brit.* a slang word for **policeman.** [C16: imit.]
►'**plodder** *n* ►'**plodding** *adj* ►'**ploddingly** *adv*

-ploid *adj and n combining form.* indicating a specific multiple of a single set of chromosomes: *diploid.* [from Gk *-pl(oos)* -fold + -OID]
►**-ploidy** *n combining form.*

plonk[1] (plɒŋk) *vb* **1** (often foll. by *down*) to drop or be dropped heavily: *he plonked the money on the table.* ◆ *n* **2** the act or sound of plonking. [var. of PLUNK]

plonk[2] (plɒŋk) *n Inf.* alcoholic drink, usually wine, esp. of inferior quality. [C20: ?from F *blanc* white, as in *vin blanc* white wine]

plonker ('plɒŋkə) *n Sl.* a stupid person. [C20: from PLONK[1]]

plop (plɒp) *n* **1** the characteristic sound made by an object dropping into water without a splash. ◆ *vb* **plops, plopping, plopped. 2** to fall or cause to fall with the sound of a plop: *the stone plopped into the water.* ◆ *interj* **3** an exclamation imitative of this sound: *to go plop.* [C19: imit.]

plosion ('pləʊʒən) *n Phonetics.* the sound of an abrupt break or closure, esp. the audible release of a stop. Also called: **explosion.**

plosive ('pləʊsɪv) *Phonetics.* ◆ *adj* **1** accompanied by plosion. ◆ *n* **2** a plosive consonant; stop. [C20: from F, from *explosif* EXPLOSIVE]

plot[1] ❶ (plɒt) *n* **1** a secret plan to achieve some purpose, esp. one that is illegal or underhand. **2** the story or plan of a play, novel, etc. **3** *Mil.* a graphic representation of an individual or tactical setting that pinpoints an artillery target. **4** *Chiefly US.* a diagram or plan. **5 lose the plot.** *Inf.* to lose one's ability or judgment in a given situation. ◆ *vb* **plots, plotting, plotted. 6** to plan secretly (something illegal, revolutionary, etc.); conspire. **7** *(tr)* to mark (a course, as of a ship or aircraft) on a map. **8** *(tr)* to make a plan or map of. **9a** to locate and mark (points) on a graph by means of coordinates. **9b** to draw (a curve) through these points. **10** *(tr)* to construct the plot of (a literary work, etc.). [C16: from PLOT[2], infl. by obs. *complot* conspiracy, from OF, from ?]
►'**plotter** *n*

plot[2] ❶ (plɒt) *n* a small piece of land: *a vegetable plot.* [OE]

plough ❶ *or esp. US* **plow** (plaʊ) *n* **1** an agricultural implement with sharp blades for cutting or turning over the earth. **2** any of various similar implements, such as a device for clearing snow. **3** ploughed land. **4 put one's hand to the plough.** to begin or undertake a task. ◆ *vb* **5** to till (the soil, etc.) with a plough. **6** to make (furrows or grooves) in (something) with or as if with a plough. **7** (when *intr,* usually foll. by *through*) to move (through something) in the manner of a plough. **8** *(intr;* foll. by *through)* to work at slowly or perseveringly. **9** *(intr;* foll. by *into* or *through)* (of a vehicle) to run uncontrollably into something in its path. **10** *(intr) Brit. sl.* to fail an examination. [OE *plōg* plough land]
►'**plougher** *or esp. US* '**plower** *n*

Plough (plaʊ) *n* **the.** the group of the seven brightest stars in the constellation Ursa Major. Also called: **Charles's Wain.** Usual US name: the **Big Dipper.**

plough back *vb (tr, adv)* to reinvest (the profits of a business) in the same business.

ploughman *or esp. US* **plowman** ('plaʊmən) *n, pl* **ploughmen** *or esp. US* **plowmen.** a man who ploughs, esp. using horses.

ploughman's lunch *n* a snack lunch, served esp. in a pub, consisting of bread and cheese with pickle.

ploughshare *or esp. US* **plowshare** ('plaʊˌʃɛə) *n* the horizontal pointed cutting blade of a mouldboard plough.

plover ('plʌvə) *n* **1** any of a family of shore birds, typically having a round head, straight bill, and large pointed wings. **2 green plover.** another name for **lapwing.** [C14: from OF *plovier* rainbird, from L *pluvia* rain]

plow (plaʊ) *n, vb* the usual US spelling of **plough.**

ploy ❶ (plɔɪ) *n* **1** a manoeuvre or tactic in a game, conversation, etc. **2** any business, job, hobby, etc., with which one is occupied: *angling is his latest ploy.* **3** *Chiefly Brit.* a frolic, escapade, or practical joke. [C18: orig. Scot. & N English, obs. n sense of EMPLOY meaning an occupation]

PLP (in Britain) *abbrev. for* Parliamentary Labour Party.

PLR *abbrev. for* Public Lending Right.

pluck ❶ (plʌk) *vb* **1** *(tr)* to pull off (feathers, fruit, etc.) from (a fowl, tree, etc.). **2** (when *intr,* foll. by *at*) to pull or tug. **3** *(tr;* foll. by *off, away,* etc.) *Arch.* to pull (something) forcibly or violently (from something or someone). **4** *(tr)* to sound (the strings) of (a musical instrument) with the fingers, a plectrum, etc. **5** *(tr) Sl.* to fleece or swindle. ◆ *n* **6** courage, usually in the face of difficulties or hardship. **7** a sudden pull or tug. **8** the heart, liver, and lungs, esp. of an animal used for food. [OE *pluccian, plyccan*]
►'**plucker** *n*

pluck up *vb (tr, adv)* **1** to pull out; uproot. **2** to muster (courage, one's spirits, etc.).

plucky ❶ ('plʌkɪ) *adj* **pluckier, pluckiest.** having or showing courage in the face of difficulties, danger, etc.
►'**pluckily** *adv* ►'**pluckiness** *n*

plug ❶ (plʌg) *n* **1** a piece of wood, cork, or other material, used to stop up holes or waste pipes or as a wedge for taking a screw or nail. **2** a device having one or more pins to which an electric cable is attached: used to make an electrical connection when inserted into a socket. **3** Also called: **volcanic plug.** a mass of solidified magma filling the neck of an extinct volcano. **4** See **sparking plug. 5a** a cake of pressed or twisted tobacco, esp. for chewing. **5b** a small piece of such a cake. **6** *Inf.* a favourable mention of a product, show, etc., as on television. ◆ *vb* **plugs, plugging, plugged. 7** *(tr)* to stop up or secure (a hole, gap, etc.) with or as if with a plug. **8** *(tr)* to insert or use (something) as a plug: *to plug a finger into one's ear.* **9** *(tr) Inf.* to make favourable and often-repeated mentions of (a song, product, show, etc.), as on television. **10** *(tr) Sl.* to shoot: *he plugged six rabbits.* **11** *(tr) Sl.* to punch. **12** *(intr;* foll. by *along, away,* etc.) *Inf.* to work steadily or persistently. [C17: from MDu. *plugge*]
►'**plugger** *n*

plug-and-play *adj Computing.* capable of detecting the addition of a new input or output device and automatically activating the appropriate control software.

THESAURUS

plight[1] *n* = **difficulty,** case, circumstances, condition, dilemma, extremity, hole (*sl.*), hot water (*inf.*), jam (*inf.*), perplexity, pickle (*inf.*), predicament, scrape (*inf.*), situation, spot (*inf.*), state, straits, tight spot, trouble

plight[2] *vb* **1** = **promise,** contract, covenant, engage, guarantee, pledge, propose, swear, vouch, vow

plod *vb* **1** = **trudge,** clump, drag, lumber, slog, stomp (*inf.*), tramp, tread **2** = **slog,** drudge, grind (*inf.*), grub, labour, peg away, persevere, plough through, plug away, soldier on, toil

plodder *n* **1** = **slowcoach** (*Brit. inf.*), dawdler, laggard, slowpoke (*US & Canad. inf.*), tortoise **2** = **slogger,** drudge, hack, toiler, workhorse

plot[1] *n* **1** = **plan,** cabal, conspiracy, covin, intrigue, machination, scheme, stratagem **2** = **story,** action, narrative, outline, scenario, story line, subject, theme, thread ◆ *vb* **6** = **plan,** cabal, collude, conspire, contrive, hatch, intrigue, machinate, manoeuvre, scheme **7** = **chart,** calculate, compute, draft, draw, locate, map, mark, outline **10** = **devise,** brew, conceive, concoct, contrive, cook up (*inf.*), design, frame, hatch, imagine, lay, project

plot[2] *n* = **patch,** allotment, area, ground, lot, parcel, tract

plotter *n* **6** = **conspirator,** architect, cabalist, conniver, conspirer, intriguer, Machiavellian, planner, schemer, strategist

plough *vb* **5** = **turn over,** break ground, cultivate, dig, furrow, ridge, till **7** *usually foll. by* **through** = **forge,** cut, drive, flounder, plod, plunge, press, push, stagger, surge, wade **9** *foll. by* **into** *or* **through** = **plunge into,** bulldoze into, career into, crash into, hurtle into, shove into, smash into

ploy *n* **1** = **tactic,** contrivance, device, dodge, gambit, game, manoeuvre, move, ruse, scheme, stratagem, subterfuge, trick, wile

pluck *vb* **1** = **pull out** *or* **off,** collect, draw, gather, harvest, pick **2** = **tug,** catch, clutch, jerk, pull at, snatch, tweak, yank **4** = **strum,** finger, pick, plunk, thrum, twang ◆ *n* **6** = **courage,** backbone, boldness, bottle (*Brit. sl.*), bravery, determination, grit, guts (*inf.*), hardihood, heart, intrepidity, mettle, nerve, resolution, spirit, spunk (*inf.*)

plucky *adj* = **courageous,** bold, brave, daring, doughty, feisty (*inf.*), game, gritty, gutsy (*sl.*), hardy, have-a-go (*inf.*), heroic, intrepid, mettlesome, spirited, spunky (*inf.*), undaunted, unflinching, valiant
Antonyms *adj* afraid, chicken (*sl.*), cowardly, dastardly, dispirited, scared, spineless, spiritless, timid, yellow (*inf.*)

plug *n* **1** = **stopper,** bung, cork, spigot, stopple **5** = **wad,** cake, chew, pigtail, quid, twist **6** *Informal* = **mention,** advert (*Brit. inf.*), advertisement, good word, hype, publicity, puff, push ◆ *vb* **7** = **seal,** block, bung, choke, close, cork, cover, fill, pack, stop, stopper, stopple, stop up, stuff **9** *Informal* = **mention,** advertise, build up, hype, promote, publicize, puff, push, write up **10** *Slang* = **shoot,** blow away (*sl., chiefly US*), gun down, pick off, pop, pot, put a bullet in **12** *foll. by* **along, away** *etc. Informal* = **slog,** drudge, grind (*inf.*), labour, peg away, plod, toil

plughole ('plʌg,həʊl) *n* a hole in a sink, etc., through which waste water drains and which can be closed with a plug.

plug in *vb* (*tr, adv*) to connect (an electrical appliance, etc.) with a power source by means of an electrical plug.

plug-ugly *adj* **1** *Inf.* extremely ugly. ◆ *n, pl* **plug-uglies. 2** *US sl.* a city tough; ruffian. [C19: from ?]

plum ❶ (plʌm) *n* **1** a small rosaceous tree with an edible oval fruit that is purple, yellow, or green and contains an oval stone. **2** the fruit of this tree. **3** a raisin, as used in a cake or pudding. **4a** a dark reddish-purple colour. **4b** (*as adj*): *a plum carpet.* **5** *Inf.* **5a** something of a superior or desirable kind, such as a financial bonus. **5b** (*as modifier*): *a plum job.* [OE *plūme*]

plumage ('plu:mɪdʒ) *n* the layer of feathers covering the body of a bird. [C15: from OF, from *plume* feather, from L *plūma* down]

plumate ('plu:meɪt, -mɪt) *or* **plumose** *adj Zool., bot.* **1** of or possessing feathers or plumes. **2** covered with small hairs: *a plumate seed.* [C19: from L *plumātus* covered with feathers; see PLUME]

plumb ❶ (plʌm) *n* **1** a weight, usually of lead, suspended at the end of a line and used to determine water depth or verticality. **2** the perpendicular position of a freely suspended plumb line (esp. in **out of plumb, off plumb**). ◆ *adv also* **plum. 3** vertically or perpendicularly. **4** *Inf., chiefly US.* (intensifier): *plumb stupid.* **5** *Inf.* exactly; precisely. ◆ *vb* **6** (*tr;* often foll. by *up*) to test the alignment of or adjust to the vertical with a plumb line. **7** (*tr*) to experience (the worst extremes of): *to plumb the depths of despair.* **8** (*tr*) to understand or master (something obscure): *to plumb a mystery.* **9** to connect or join (a device such as a tap) to a water pipe or drainage system. [C13: from OF *plomb* (unattested) lead line, from *plon* lead, from L *plumbum*]
▸ **'plumbable** *adj*

plumbago (plʌm'beɪgəʊ) *n, pl* **plumbagos. 1** a plant of warm regions, having clusters of blue, white, or red flowers. **2** another name for **graphite.** [C17: from L: lead ore, translation of Gk *polubdaina,* from *polubdos* lead]

plumber ('plʌmə) *n* a person who installs and repairs pipes, fixtures, etc., for water, drainage, and gas. [C14: from OF *plommier* worker in lead, from LL *plumbārius,* from L *plumbum* lead]

plumbing ('plʌmɪŋ) *n* **1** the trade or work of a plumber. **2** the pipes, fixtures, etc., used in a water, drainage, or gas installation. **3** the act or procedure of using a plumb.

plumbism ('plʌm,bɪzəm) *n* chronic lead poisoning. [C19: from L *plumbum* lead]

plumb line *n* a string with a metal weight, or **plumb bob,** at one end that, when suspended, points directly towards the earth's centre of gravity and so is used to determine verticality, depth, etc.

plumb rule *n* a plumb line attached to a narrow board, used by builders, surveyors, etc.

plume ❶ (plu:m) *n* **1** a feather, esp. one that is large or ornamental. **2** a feather or cluster of feathers worn esp. formerly as a badge or ornament in a headband, hat, etc. **3** *Biol.* any feathery part. **4** something that resembles a plume: *a plume of smoke.* **5** a token or decoration of honour; prize. ◆ *vb* **plumes, pluming, plumed.** (*tr*) **6** to adorn with feathers or plumes. **7** (of a bird) to clean or preen (itself or its feathers). **8** (foll. by *on* or *upon*) to pride or congratulate (oneself). [C14: from OF, from L *plūma* downy feather]

plummet ❶ ('plʌmɪt) *vb* **plummets, plummeting, plummeted. 1** (*intr*) to drop down; plunge. ◆ *n* **2** the weight on a plumb line; plumb bob. **3** a lead plumb used by anglers. [C14: from OF *plommet* ball of lead, from *plomb* lead, from L *plumbum*]

plummy ❶ ('plʌmɪ) *adj* **plummier, plummiest. 1** of, full of, or resembling plums. **2** *Brit. inf.* (of speech) deep, refined, and somewhat drawling. **3** *Brit. inf.* choice; desirable.

plumose ('plu:məʊs, -məʊz) *adj* another word for **plumate.** [C17: from L *plūmōsus* feathery]

plump[1] ❶ (plʌmp) *adj* **1** well filled out or rounded; chubby: *a plump turkey.* **2** bulging; full: *a plump wallet.* ◆ *vb* **3** (often foll. by *up* or *out*) to make or become plump: *to plump up a pillow.* [C15 (meaning: dull, rude), C16 (in current senses): ?from MDu. *plomp* blunt]
▸ **'plumply** *adv* ▸ **'plumpness** *n*

plump[2] ❶ (plʌmp) *vb* **1** (often foll. by *down, into,* etc.) to drop or fall suddenly and heavily. **2** (*intr;* foll. by *for*) to give support (to) or make a choice (of) one out of a group or number. ◆ *n* **3** a heavy abrupt fall or the sound of this. ◆ *adv* **4** suddenly or heavily. **5** straight down; directly: *the helicopter landed plump in the middle of the field.* ◆ *adj, adv* **6** in a blunt, direct, or decisive manner. [C14: prob. imit.]

plum pudding *n Brit.* a boiled or steamed pudding made with flour, suet, sugar, and dried fruit.

plumule ('plu:mju:l) *n* **1** the embryonic shoot of seed-bearing plants. **2** a down feather of young birds. [C18: from LL *plūmula* a little feather]

plumy ('plu:mɪ) *adj* **plumier, plumiest. 1** plumelike; feathery. **2** consisting of, covered with, or adorned with feathers.

plunder ❶ ('plʌndə) *vb* **1** to steal (valuables, goods, sacred items, etc.) from (a town, church, etc.) by force, esp. in time of war; loot. **2** (*tr*) to rob or steal (choice or desirable things) from (a place): *to plunder an orchard.* ◆ *n* **3** anything taken by plundering; booty. **4** the act of plundering; pillage. [C17: prob. from Du. *plunderen* (orig.: to plunder household goods)]
▸ **'plunderer** *n*

plunge ❶ (plʌndʒ) *vb* **plunges, plunging, plunged. 1** (usually foll. by *into*) to thrust or throw (something, oneself, etc.): *they plunged into the sea.* **2** to throw or be thrown into a certain condition: *the room was plunged into darkness.* **3** (usually foll. by *into*) to involve or become involved deeply (in). **4** (*intr*) to move or dash violently or with great speed or impetuosity. **5** (*intr*) to descend very suddenly or steeply: *the ship plunged in heavy seas; a plunging neckline.* **6** (*intr*) *Inf.* to speculate or gamble recklessly, for high stakes, etc. ◆ *n* **7** a leap or dive. **8** *Inf.* a swim; dip. **9** a pitching or tossing motion. **10 take the plunge.** *Inf.* to resolve to do something dangerous or irrevocable. [C14: from OF *plongier,* from Vulgar L *plumbicāre* (unattested) to sound with a plummet, from L *plumbum* lead]

plunger ('plʌndʒə) *n* **1** a rubber suction cup used to clear blocked drains, etc. **2** a device or part of a machine that has a plunging or thrusting motion; piston. **3** *Inf.* a reckless gambler.

plunk (plʌŋk) *vb* **1** to pluck (the strings) of (a banjo, etc.) or (of such an instrument) to give forth a sound when plucked. **2** (often foll. by *down*) to drop or be dropped, esp. heavily or suddenly. ◆ *n* **3** the act or sound of plunking. [C20: imit.]

pluperfect (plu:'pɜ:fɪkt) *adj, n Grammar.* another term for **past perfect.** [C16: from L *plūs quam perfectum* more than perfect]

plural ('plʊərəl) *adj* **1** containing, involving, or composed of more than one. **2** denoting a word indicating that more than one referent is being referred to or described. ◆ *n* **3** *Grammar.* **3a** the plural number. **3b** a plural form. [C14: from OF *plurel,* from LL *plūrālis* concerning many, from L *plūs* more]
▸ **'plurally** *adv*

pluralism ('plʊərə,lɪzəm) *n* **1** the holding by a single person of more than one ecclesiastical benefice or office; plurality. **2** *Sociol.* a theory of society as several autonomous but interdependent groups. **3** the existence in a society of groups having distinctive ethnic origin, cultural forms, religions, etc. **4** *Philosophy.* **4a** the metaphysical doctrine that reality consists of more than two basic types of substance. Cf. **monism** (sense 1), **dualism** (sense 2). **4b** the metaphysical doctrine that reality consists of independent entities rather than one unchanging whole.
▸ **'pluralist** *n, adj* ▸ **,plural'istic** *adj*

plurality ❶ (plʊə'rælɪtɪ) *n, pl* **pluralities. 1** the state of being plural. **2** *Maths.* a number greater than one. **3** the US term for **relative majority. 4** a large number. **5** the greater number; majority. **6** another word for **pluralism** (sense 1).

pluralize *or* **pluralise** ('plʊərə,laɪz) *vb* **pluralizes, pluralizing, pluralized** *or* **pluralises, pluralising, pluralised. 1** (*intr*) to hold more than one ecclesiastical benefice or office at the same time. **2** to make or become plural.

pluri- *combining form.* denoting several. [from L *plur-, plus* more, *plures* several]

plus ❶ (plʌs) *prep* **1** increased by the addition of: *four plus two.* **2** with or with the addition of: *a good job, plus a new car.* ◆ *adj* **3** (*prenominal*) indicating or involving addition: *a plus sign.* **4** another word for **positive** (senses 7, 8). **5** on the positive part of a scale or coordinate axis: *a value of +x.* **6** indicating the positive side of an electrical circuit. **7** involving advantage: *a plus factor.* **8** (*postpositive*) *Inf.* having a value above that which is stated: *she had charm plus.* **9** (*postpositive*) slightly above a specified standard: *he received a B+ grade for his essay.* ◆ *n* **10** short for **plus sign. 11** a positive quantity. **12** *Inf.* something positive or to the good. **13** a gain, surplus, or advantage. ◆ Mathematical symbol: + [C17: from L: more]

> **USAGE NOTE** *Plus, together with,* and *along with* do not create compound subjects in the way that *and* does: the number of the verb depends on that of the subject to which *plus, together with,* or *along with* is added: *this task, plus all the others, was* (not *were*) *undertaken by the government; the doctor, together with the nurses, was* (not *were*) *waiting for the patient.*

THESAURUS

plum *Informal* ◆ *n* **5a** = **prize**, bonus, cream, find, pick, treasure ◆ *modifier* **5b** = **choice**, best, first-class, prize

plumb *n* **1** = **weight**, lead, plumb bob, plummet ◆ *adv* **3** = **vertically**, perpendicularly, up and down **5** *Informal* = **exactly**, bang, precisely, slap, spot-on (*Brit. inf.*)

plume *n* **1, 2** = **feather**, aigrette, crest, pinion, quill ◆ *vb* **8** *foll. by* **on** *or* **upon** = **pride oneself**, congratulate oneself, pat oneself on the back, pique oneself, preen oneself

plummet *vb* **1** = **plunge**, crash, descend, dive, drop down, fall, nose-dive, stoop, swoop, tumble

plummy *adj* **2** *Brit. informal* = **deep**, fruity, posh (*inf., chiefly Brit.*), refined, resonant, upper-class

plump[1] *adj* **1** = **chubby**, beefy, burly, buxom, corpulent, dumpy, fat, fleshy, full, obese, podgy, portly, roly-poly, rotund, round, stout, tubby, well-upholstered (*inf.*)
Antonyms *adj* anorexic, bony, emaciated, lanky, lean, scrawny, skinny, slender, slim, sylphlike, thin

plump[2] *vb* **1** = **flop**, drop, dump, fall, sink, slump **2** *foll. by* **for** = **choose**, back, come down in favour of, favour, opt for, side with, support

plunder *vb* **1, 2** = **loot**, despoil, devastate, pillage, raid, ransack, ravage, rifle, rob, sack, spoil, steal, strip ◆ *n* **3** = **loot**, booty, ill-gotten gains, pillage, prey, prize, rapine, spoils, swag (*sl.*)

plunge *vb* **1** = **throw**, cast, pitch **4** = **hurtle**, career, charge, dash, jump, lurch, rush, swoop, tear **5** = **descend**, dip, dive, douse, drop, fall, go down, immerse, nose-dive, plummet, sink, submerge, tumble ◆ *n* **7, 9** = **dive**, descent, drop, fall, immersion, jump, submersion, swoop

plurality *n* **5** = **majority**, bulk, mass, most, nearly all, overwhelming number, preponderance

plus *prep* **1, 2** = **and**, added to, coupled with, with, with the addition of ◆ *adj* **3, 4** = **additional**, added, add-on, extra, positive, supple-

plus fours *pl n* men's baggy knickerbockers reaching below the knee, now only worn for golf, etc. [C20: because made with four inches of material to hang over at the knee]

plush ❶ (plʌʃ) *n* **1** a fabric with a cut pile that is longer and softer than velvet. ◆ *adj* **2** Also: **plushy.** *Inf.* lavishly appointed; rich; costly. [C16: from F *pluche,* from OF *peluchier* to pluck, ult. from L *pilus* a hair] ▸**'plushly** *adv*

plus sign *n* the symbol +, indicating addition or positive quantity.

Pluto[1] ('plu:təʊ) *n Gk myth.* the god of the underworld; Hades. ▸**Plu'tonian** *adj*

Pluto[2] ('plu:təʊ) *n* the smallest planet and the farthest known from the sun. [L, from Gk *Ploutōn,* lit.: the rich one]

plutocracy (plu:'tɒkrəsɪ) *n, pl* **plutocracies. 1** the rule of society by the wealthy. **2** a state or government characterized by the rule of the wealthy. **3** a class that exercises power by virtue of its wealth. [C17: from Gk *ploutokratia,* from *ploutos* wealth + *-kratia* rule] ▸**plutocratic** (ˌplu:tə'krætɪk) *adj* ▸ˌ**pluto'cratically** *adv*

plutocrat ❶ ('plu:təˌkræt) *n* a member of a plutocracy.

pluton ('plu:tɒn) *n* any mass of igneous rock that has solidified below the surface of the earth. [C20: back formation from PLUTONIC]

plutonic (plu:'tɒnɪk) *adj* (of igneous rocks) derived from magma that has cooled and solidified below the surface of the earth. [C20: after PLUTO[1]]

plutonium (plu:'təʊnɪəm) *n* a highly toxic metallic transuranic element. It occurs in trace amounts in uranium ores and is produced in a nuclear reactor by neutron bombardment of uranium-238. The most stable isotope, **plutonium-239,** readily undergoes fission and is used as a reactor fuel. Symbol: Pu; atomic no.: 94; half-life of ^{239}Pu: 24 360 years. [C20: after PLUTO[2] because Pluto lies beyond Neptune and plutonium was discovered soon after NEPTUNIUM]

pluvial ('plu:vɪəl) *adj* **1** of, characterized by, or due to the action of rain; rainy. ◆ *n* **2** *Geol.* a period of persistent rainfall. [C17: from L *pluviālis* rainy, from *pluvia* rain]

pluviometer (ˌplu:vɪ'ɒmɪtə) *n* another name for **rain gauge.** ▸**pluviometric** (ˌplu:vɪə'mɛtrɪk) *adj* ▸ˌ**pluvio'metrically** *adv*

ply[1] ❶ (plaɪ) *vb* **plies, plying, plied.** (*mainly tr*) **1** to carry on, pursue, or work at (a job, trade, etc.). **2** to manipulate or wield (a tool, etc.). **3** to sell (goods, wares, etc.), esp. at a regular place. **4** (usually foll. by *with*) to provide (with) or subject (to) repeatedly or persistently: *he plied us with drink; he plied the speaker with questions.* **5** (*intr*) to work steadily or diligently. **6** (*also intr*) (esp. of a ship, etc.) to travel regularly along (a route) or in (an area): *to ply the trade routes.* [C14 *plye,* short for *aplye* to APPLY]

ply[2] ❶ (plaɪ) *n, pl* **plies. 1a** a layer, fold, or thickness, as of yarn. **1b** (*in combination*): *four-ply.* **2** a thin sheet of wood glued to other similar sheets to form plywood. **3** one of the strands twisted together to make rope, yarn, etc. [C15: from OF *pli* fold, from *plier* to fold, from L *plicāre*]

Plymouth Brethren ('plɪməθ) *pl n* a religious sect founded about 1827, strongly Puritanical in outlook and having no organized ministry.

plywood ('plaɪˌwʊd) *n* a structural board consisting of thin layers of wood glued together under pressure, with the grain of one layer at right angles to the grain of the adjoining layer.

pm *abbrev. for* premium.

Pm *the chemical symbol for* promethium.

PM *abbrev. for:* **1** Past Master (of a fraternity). **2** Paymaster. **3** Postmaster. **4** Prime Minister. **5** *Mil.* Provost Marshal.

p.m., P.M., pm, *or* **PM** *abbrev. for:* **1** (indicating the time from midday to midnight) post meridiem. [L: after noon] **2** postmortem (examination).

PMG *abbrev. for:* **1** Paymaster General. **2** Postmaster General.

PMS *abbrev. for* premenstrual syndrome.

PMT *abbrev. for* premenstrual tension.

PNdB *abbrev. for* perceived noise decibel.

pneumatic (nju'mætɪk) *adj* **1** of or concerned with air, gases, or wind. **2** (of a machine or device) operated by compressed air or by a vacuum. **3** containing compressed air: *a pneumatic tyre.* **4** (of the bones of birds) containing air spaces which reduce their weight as an adaptation to flying. ◆ *n* **5** a pneumatic tyre. [C17: from LL *pneumaticus* of air or wind, from Gk, from *pneuma* breath, wind] ▸**pneu'matically** *adv*

pneumatics (nju'mætɪks) *n* (*functioning as sing*) the branch of physics concerned with the mechanical properties of gases, esp. air.

pneumatology (ˌnju:mə'tɒlədʒɪ) *n* **1** the branch of theology concerned with the Holy Ghost and other spiritual beings. **2** an obsolete name for **psychology** (the science).

pneumatophore (nju:'mætəʊˌfɔ:) *n* **1** a specialized root of certain swamp plants, such as the mangrove, that branches upwards and undergoes gaseous exchange with the atmosphere. **2** a polyp such as the Portuguese man-of-war, that is specialized as a float.

pneumococcus (ˌnju:məʊ'kɒkəs) *n, pl* **pneumococci** (-'kɒksaɪ). a bacterium that causes pneumonia.

pneumoconiosis (ˌnju:məʊˌkəʊnɪ'əʊsɪs) *or* **pneumonoconiosis** (ˌnju:mənəʊˌkəʊnɪ'əʊsɪs) *n* any disease of the lungs or bronchi caused by the inhalation of metallic or mineral particles. [C19: shortened from *pneumonoconiosis,* from Gk *pneumōn* lung + *-coniosis,* from *konis* dust]

pneumoencephalogram (ˌnju:məʊɛn'sɛfələˌgræm) *n* See **encephalogram.**

pneumogastric (ˌnju:məʊ'gæstrɪk) *adj Anat.* **1** of or relating to the lungs and stomach. **2** a former term for **vagus.**

pneumonectomy (ˌnju:məʊ'nɛktəmɪ) *or* **pneumectomy** *n, pl* **pneumonectomies** *or* **pneumectomies.** the surgical removal of a lung or part of a lung. [C20: from Gk *pneumōn* lung + -ECTOMY]

pneumonia (nju:'məʊnɪə) *n* inflammation of one or both lungs, in which the air sacs (alveoli) become filled with liquid. [C17: NL from Gk from *pneumōn* lung] ▸**pneumonic** (nju:'mɒnɪk) *adj*

pneumothorax (ˌnju:məʊ'θɔ:ræks) *n* the abnormal presence of air between the lung and the wall of the chest (pleural cavity), resulting in collapse of the lung.

p-n junction *n Electronics.* a boundary between a p-type and n-type semiconductor that functions as a rectifier and is used in diodes and junction transistors.

po (pəʊ) *n, pl* **pos.** *Brit.* an informal word for **chamber pot.** [C19: from POT[1]]

Po *the chemical symbol for* polonium.

PO *abbrev. for:* **1** Personnel Officer. **2** petty officer. **3** Pilot Officer. **4** Also: **p.o.** postal order. **5** Post Office.

poach[1] ❶ (pəʊtʃ) *vb* **1** to catch (game, fish, etc.) illegally by trespassing on private property. **2** to encroach on or usurp (another person's rights, duties, etc.) or steal (an idea, employee, etc.). **3** *Tennis, badminton, etc.* to take or play (shots that should belong to one's partner). **4** to break up (land) into wet muddy patches, as by riding over it. [C17: from OF *pocher,* of Gmc origin] ▸**'poacher** *n*

poach[2] (pəʊtʃ) *vb* to simmer (eggs, fish, etc.) very gently in water, milk, stock, etc. [C15: from OF *pochier* to enclose in a bag (as the yolks are enclosed by the whites)] ▸**'poacher** *n*

pochard ('pəʊtʃəd) *n, pl* **pochards** *or* **pochard.** any of various diving ducks, esp. a European variety, the male of which has a grey-and-black body and a reddish head. [C16: from ?]

pock ❶ (pɒk) *n* **1** any pustule resulting from an eruptive disease, esp. from smallpox. **2** another word for **pockmark** (sense 1). [OE *pocc*] ▸**'pocky** *adj*

pocket ❶ ('pɒkɪt) *n* **1** a small bag or pouch in a garment for carrying small articles, money, etc. **2** any bag or pouch or anything resembling this. **3** *S. African.* a bag or sack of vegetables or fruit. **4** a cavity in the earth, etc., such as one containing ore. **5** a small enclosed or isolated area: *a pocket of resistance.* **6** any of the six holes with pouches or nets let into the corners and sides of a billiard table. **7 in one's pocket.** under one's control. **8 in** *or* **out of pocket.** having made a profit or loss. **9 line one's pockets.** to make money, esp. by dishonesty when in a position of trust. **10** (*modifier*) small: *a pocket edition.* ◆ *vb* **pockets, pocketing, pocketed.** (*tr*) **11** to put into one's pocket. **12** to take surreptitiously or unlawfully; steal. **13** (*usually passive*) to confine in or as if in a pocket. **14** to conceal or keep back: *he pocketed his pride and asked for help.* **15** *Billiards, etc.* to drive (a ball) into a pocket. [C15: from Anglo-Norman *poket* a little bag, from *poque* bag, from MDu. *poke* bag] ▸**'pocketless** *adj*

pocket battleship *n* a small heavily armed battle cruiser specially built to conform with treaty limitations on tonnage and armament.

pocket billiards *n* (*functioning as sing*) *Billiards.* **1** another name for **pool**[2] (sense 5). **2** any game played on a table in which the object is to pocket the balls, esp. snooker and pool.

pocketbook ('pɒkɪtˌbʊk) *n* **1** *Chiefly US.* a small bag or case for money, papers, etc. **2** a pocket-sized notebook.

pocket borough *n* (before the Reform Act of 1832) an English borough constituency controlled by one person or family who owned the land.

pocketful ('pɒkɪtfʊl) *n, pl* **pocketfuls.** as much as a pocket will hold.

pocketknife ('pɒkɪtˌnaɪf) *n, pl* **pocketknives.** a small knife with one or more blades that fold into the handle; penknife.

pocket money *n* **1** *Brit.* a small weekly sum of money given to children by parents as an allowance. **2** money for day-to-day spending, incidental expenses, etc.

THESAURUS

mentary ◆ *n* **12, 13** = **advantage**, asset, benefit, bonus, extra, gain, good point, icing on the cake, perk (*Brit. inf.*), surplus

plush *adj* **2** = **luxurious**, costly, de luxe, lavish, luxury, opulent, palatial, rich, ritzy (*sl.*), sumptuous
Antonyms *adj* cheap, cheap and nasty, inexpensive, ordinary, plain, spartan

plutocrat *n* = **rich man**, capitalist, Croesus, Dives, fat cat, magnate, millionaire, moneybags (*sl.*), tycoon

ply[1] *vb* **1** = **work at**, carry on, exercise, follow, practise, pursue **2** = **use**, employ, handle, manipulate, swing, utilize, wield **4** = **bombard**, assail, beset, besiege, harass, importune, press, urge

ply[2] *n* **1** = **thickness**, fold, layer, leaf, sheet

poach[1] *vb* **1** = **steal**, hunt *or* fish illegally, plunder, rob, steal game **2** = **encroach**, appropriate, infringe, intrude, trespass

pock *n* **1, 2** = **scar**, blemish, flaw, mark, pimple, pockmark, pustule, spot

pocket *n* **1, 2** = **pouch**, bag, compartment, hollow, receptacle, sack ◆ *modifier* **10** = **small**, abridged, compact, concise, little, miniature, pint-size(d) (*inf.*), portable, potted (*inf.*) ◆ *vb* **12** = **steal**, appropriate, cabbage (*Brit. sl.*), filch,

pockmark ⓣ ('pɒkˌmɑːk) *n* **1** Also called: **pock.** a pitted scar left on the skin after the healing of a smallpox or similar pustule. **2** any pitting of a surface that resembles such scars. ◆ *vb* **3** (*tr*) to scar or pit with pockmarks.

poco ('pəʊkəʊ; *Italian* 'pɔːko) *or* **un poco** *adj, adv* (*in combination*) *Music.* a little; to a small degree. [from It.: little, from L *paucus* few]

poco a poco *adv* (*in combination*) *Music.* little by little: *poco a poco rall.* [It.]

pod ⓣ (pɒd) *n* **1a** the fruit of any leguminous plant, consisting of a long two-valved case that contains seeds. **1b** the seedcase as distinct from the seeds. **2** any similar fruit. **3** a streamlined structure attached to an aircraft and used to house a jet engine, fuel tank, armament, etc. ◆ *vb* **pods, podding, podded. 4** (*tr*) to remove the pod from. [C17: ? back formation from earlier *podware* bagged vegetables]

-pod *or* **-pode** *n combining form.* indicating a certain type or number of feet: *arthropod; tripod.* [from Gk *-podos* footed, from *pous* foot]

podagra (pə'dægrə) *n* gout of the foot or big toe. [C15: via L from Gk, from *pous* foot + *agra* a trap]

poddy ('pɒdɪ) *n, pl* **poddies.** *Austral.* a handfed calf or lamb. [?from *poddy* (adj) fat]

podgy ⓣ ('pɒdʒɪ) *adj* **podgier, podgiest. 1** short and fat; chubby. **2** (of the face, arms, etc.) unpleasantly chubby and pasty-looking. [C19: from *podge* a short plump person]
▸**'podgily** *adv* ▸**'podginess** *n*

podium ⓣ ('pəʊdɪəm) *n, pl* **podiums** *or* **podia** (-dɪə). **1** a small raised platform used by lecturers, conductors, etc. **2** a plinth that supports a colonnade or wall. **3** a low wall surrounding the arena of an ancient amphitheatre. **4** *Zool.* any footlike organ, such as the tube foot of a starfish. [C18: from L: platform, from Gk *podion* little foot, from *pous* foot]

-podium *n combining form.* a part resembling a foot: *pseudopodium.* [from NL: footlike; see PODIUM]

podophyllin (ˌpɒdəʊ'fɪlɪn) *n* a bitter yellow resin obtained from the dried underground stems of the May apple and mandrake: used as a cathartic. [C19: from NL *Podophyllum,* genus of herbs, from *podo-,* from Gk *pous* foot + *phullon* leaf]

-podous *adj combining form.* having feet of a certain kind or number: *cephalopodous.*

podzol ('pɒdzɒl) *or* **podsol** ('pɒdsɒl) *n* a type of soil characteristic of coniferous forest regions having a greyish-white colour in its upper layers from which certain minerals have leached. [C20: from Russian: ash ground]

poem ⓣ ('pəʊɪm) *n* **1** a composition in verse, usually characterized by words chosen for their sound and suggestive power as well as for their sense, and using such techniques as metre, rhyme, and alliteration. **2** a literary composition that is not in verse but exhibits the intensity of imagination and language common to it: *a prose poem.* **3** anything resembling a poem in beauty, effect, etc. [C16: from L *poēma,* from Gk, var. of *poiēma* something created, from *poiein* to make]

poesy ('pəʊɪzɪ) *n, pl* **poesies. 1** an archaic word for **poetry. 2** *Poetic.* the art of writing poetry. [C14: via OF from L *poēsis,* from Gk, from *poiēsis* poetic art, from *poiein* to make]

poet ⓣ ('pəʊɪt) *or* (*sometimes when fem*) **poetess** *n* **1** a person who writes poetry. **2** a person with great imagination and creativity. [C13: from L *poēta,* from Gk *poiētēs* maker, poet]

poetaster (ˌpəʊɪ'tæstə, -'teɪ-) *n* a writer of inferior verse. [C16: from Med. L; see POET, -ASTER]

poetic ⓣ (pəʊ'ɛtɪk) *or* **poetical** *adj* **1** of poetry. **2** characteristic of poetry, as in being elevated, sublime, etc. **3** characteristic of a poet. **4** recounted in verse.
▸**po'etically** *adv*

poeticize, poeticise (pəʊ'ɛtɪˌsaɪz) *or* **poetize, poetise** ('pəʊɪˌtaɪz) *vb* **poeticizes, poeticizing, poeticized; poeticises, poeticising, poeticised** *or* **poetizes, poetizing, poetized; poetises, poetising, poetised. 1** (*tr*) to put into poetry or make poetic. **2** (*intr*) to speak or write poetically.

poetic justice *n* fitting retribution.

poetic licence *n* justifiable departure from conventional rules of form, fact, etc., as in poetry.

poetics (pəʊ'ɛtɪks) *n* (*usually functioning as sing*) **1** the principles and forms of poetry or the study of these. **2** a treatise on poetry.

poet laureate *n, pl* **poets laureate.** *Brit.* the poet appointed as court poet of Britain who is given a lifetime post in the Royal Household.

poetry ⓣ ('pəʊɪtrɪ) *n* **1** literature in metrical form; verse. **2** the art or craft of writing verse. **3** poetic qualities, spirit, or feeling in anything. **4** anything resembling poetry in rhythm, beauty, etc. [C14: from Med. L *poētria,* from L *poēta* POET]

po-faced ⓣ *adj* **1** wearing a disapproving stern expression. **2** narrow-minded; strait-laced. [C20: from PO + POKER-FACED]

pogo stick ('pəʊgəʊ) *n* a stout pole with a handle at the top, steps for the feet and a spring at the bottom, so that the user can spring up, down, and along on it. [C20: from ?]

pogrom ('pɒgrəm) *n* an organized persecution or extermination of an ethnic group, esp. of Jews. [C20: via Yiddish from Russian: destruction, from *po-* like + *grom* thunder]

pohutukawa (pəˌhuːtuː'kɑːwə) *n* a New Zealand tree which grows on the coast and produces red flowers in the summer. Also called: **Christmas tree.**

poi (pɔɪ) *n NZ.* a ball of woven New Zealand flax swung rhythmically by Maori women while performing poi dances.

poi dance *n NZ.* a women's formation dance that involves singing and manipulating a poi.

-poiesis *n combining form.* indicating the act of making or producing something specified. [from Gk, from *poiēsis* a making; see POESY]
▸**-poietic** *adj combining form.*

poignant ⓣ ('pɔɪnjənt, -nənt) *adj* **1** sharply distressing or painful to the feelings. **2** to the point; cutting or piercing: *poignant wit.* **3** keen or pertinent in mental appeal: *a poignant subject.* **4** pungent in smell. [C14: from OF, from L *pungens* pricking, from *pungere* to sting]
▸**'poignancy** *or* **'poignance** *n* ▸**'poignantly** *adv*

poikilothermic (ˌpɔɪkɪləʊ'θɜːmɪk) *or* **poikilothermal** (ˌpɔɪkɪləʊ'θɜːməl) *adj* (of all animals except birds and mammals) having a body temperature that varies with the temperature of the surroundings. [C19: from Gk *poikilos* various + THERMAL]
▸**ˌpoikilo'thermy** *n*

poinciana (ˌpɔɪnsɪ'ɑːnə) *n* a tree of a tropical genus having large orange or red flowers. [C17: NL, after M. de *Poinci,* 17th-cent. governor of the French Antilles]

poind (pɔɪnd) *vb* (*tr*) *Scots Law.* **1** to take (property of a debtor, etc.) in execution of distress; distrain. **2** to impound (stray cattle, etc.). [C15: from Scot., var. of OE *pyndan* to impound]

poinsettia (pɔɪn'sɛtɪə) *n* a shrub of Mexico and Central America, widely cultivated for its showy scarlet bracts, which resemble petals. [C19: NL, after J. P. *Poinsett* (1799–1851), US Minister to Mexico]

point ⓣ (pɔɪnt) *n* **1** a dot or tiny mark. **2** a location, spot, or position. **3** any dot used in writing or printing, such as a decimal point or a full stop. **4** the sharp tapered end of a pin, knife, etc. **5** *Maths.* **5a** a geometric element having no dimensions whose position is located by means of its coordinates. **5b** a location: *point of inflection.* **6** a small promontory. **7** a specific condition or degree. **8** a moment: *at that point he left the room.* **9** a reason, aim, etc.: *the point of this exercise is to train new teachers.* **10** an essential element in an argument: *I take your point.* **11** a suggestion or tip. **12** a detail or item. **13** a characteristic, physical attribute, etc.: *he has his good points.* **14** a distinctive characteristic or quality of an animal, esp. one used as a standard in judging livestock. **15** (*often pl*) any of the extremities, such as the tail, ears, or feet, of a domestic animal. **16** (*often pl*) *Ballet.* the tip of the toes. **17** a single unit for measuring or counting, as in the scoring of a game. **18** *Printing.* a unit of measurement equal to one twelfth of a pica. There are approximately 72 points to the inch. **19** *Finance.* a unit of value used to quote security and commodity prices and their fluctuations. **20** *Navigation.* **20a** one of the 32 marks on the compass indicating direction. **20b** the angle of 11°15′ between two adjacent marks. **21** *Cricket.* a fielding position at right angles to the batsman on the off side and relatively near the pitch. **22** either of the two electrical contacts that make or break the current flow in the distributor of an internal-combustion engine. **23** *Brit., Austral., & NZ.* (*often pl*) a junction of railway tracks in which a pair of rails can be moved so that a train can be directed onto either of two lines. US and Canad. equivalent: **switch. 24** (*often pl*) a piece of ribbon, cord, etc., with metal tags at the end: used during the 16th and 17th centuries to fasten clothing. **25** *Brit.* short for **power point. 26** the position of the body of a pointer or setter when it discovers game. **27** *Boxing.* a mark awarded for a scoring blow, knockdown, etc. **28** any diacritic used in a writing system, esp. in a phonetic transcription, to indicate modifications of vowels or consonants. **29** *Jewellery.* a unit of weight equal to 0.01 carat. **30** the act of pointing. **31 beside the point.** irrelevant. **32 case in point.** a specific

THESAURUS

help oneself to, lift (*inf.*), pilfer, purloin, snaffle (*Brit. inf.*), take

pockmark *n* **1** = **scar**, blemish, pit, pock

pod *n, vb* **1, 4** = **shell**, hull, husk, shuck

podgy *adj* **1** = **tubby**, chubby, chunky, dumpy, fat, fleshy, plump, roly-poly, rotund, short and fat, squat, stout, stubby, stumpy

podium *n* **1** = **platform**, dais, rostrum, stage

poem *n* **1** = **verse**, lyric, ode, rhyme, song, sonnet

poet *n* **1** = **bard**, lyricist, maker (*arch.*), rhymer, versifier

poetic *adj* **1, 2** = **lyrical**, elegiac, lyric, metrical, rhythmic, rhythmical, songlike

poetry *n* **1, 2** = **verse**, metrical composition, poems, poesy, rhyme, rhyming

po-faced *adj* **2** = **humourless**, disapproving, narrow-minded, prim, prudish, puritanical, solemn, stolid, strait-laced

poignancy *n* **1** = **sadness**, emotion, emotionalism, evocativeness, feeling, pathos, piteousness, plaintiveness, sentiment, tenderness **2** = **sharpness**, bitterness, intensity, keenness **4** = **pungency**, piquancy, sharpness

poignant *adj* **1** = **moving**, affecting, agonizing, bitter, distressing, gut-wrenching, harrowing, heartbreaking, heart-rending, intense, painful, pathetic, sad, touching, upsetting **2** = **cutting**, acute, biting, caustic, keen, penetrating, piercing, pointed, sarcastic, severe, sharp **4** = **pungent**, acrid, piquant, sharp, stinging, tangy

point *n* **1, 3** = **full stop**, dot, mark, period, speck, stop **2** = **place**, location, position, site, spot, stage, station **4** = **end**, apex, nib, prong, sharp end, spike, spur, summit, tine, tip, top **6** = **headland**, bill, cape, foreland, head, ness (*arch.*), promontory **7** = **stage**, circumstance, condition, degree, extent, position **8** = **moment**, instant, juncture, time, very minute **9** = **aim**, design, end, goal, intent, intention, motive, object, objective, purpose, reason, use, usefulness, utility **10** = **essence**, burden, core, crux, drift, gist, heart, import, main idea, marrow, matter, meaning, nub, pith, proposition, question, subject, text, theme, thrust **12** = **item**, aspect, detail, facet, feature, instance, nicety, particular **13** = **characteristic**, aspect, attribute, peculiarity, property, quality, respect, side, trait

or relevant instance. **33 make a point of.** **33a** to make (something) one's regular habit. **33b** to do (something) because one thinks it important. **34 not to put too fine a point on it.** to speak plainly and bluntly. **35 on** (*or* **at**) **the point of.** at the moment immediately before: *on the point of leaving the room.* **36 score points off.** to gain an advantage at someone else's expense. **37 to the point.** relevant. **38 up to a point.** not completely. ◆ *vb* **39** (usually foll. by *at* or *to*) to indicate the location or direction of by or as by extending (a finger or other pointed object) towards it: *he pointed to the front door; don't point that gun at me.* **40** (*intr;* usually foll. by *at* or *to*) to indicate or identify a specific person or thing among several: *all evidence pointed to Donald as the murderer.* **41** (*tr*) to direct or face in a specific direction: *point me in the right direction.* **42** (*tr*) to sharpen or taper. **43** (*intr*) (of gun dogs) to indicate the place where game is lying by standing rigidly with the muzzle turned in its direction. **44** (*tr*) to finish or repair the joints of (brickwork, masonry, etc.) with mortar or cement. **45** (*tr*) *Music.* to mark (a psalm text) with vertical lines to indicate the points at which the music changes during chanting. **46** (*tr*) *Phonetics.* to provide (a letter or letters) with diacritics. **47** (*tr*) to provide (a Hebrew or similar text) with vowel points. ◆ See also **point off, point out, point up.** [C13: from OF: spot, from L *punctum* a point, from *pungere* to pierce]

point after *n American football.* a score given for a successful kick between the goalposts and above the crossbar, following a touchdown.

point-blank ❶ *adj* **1a** aimed or fired at a target so close that it is unnecessary to make allowance for the drop in the course of the projectile. **1b** permitting such aim or fire without loss of accuracy: *at point-blank range.* **2** aimed or fired at nearly zero range. **3** plain or blunt: *a point-blank question.* ◆ *adv* **4** directly or straight. **5** plainly or bluntly. [C16: from POINT + BLANK (in the sense: centre spot of an archery target)]

point duty *n* **1** the stationing of a policeman or traffic warden at a road junction to control and direct traffic. **2** the position at the head of a military control, regarded as being the most dangerous.

pointe (pɔɪnt) *n Ballet.* the tip of the toe (esp. in **on pointes**). [from F: point]

pointed ❶ ('pɔɪntɪd) *adj* **1** having a point. **2** cutting or incisive: *a pointed wit.* **3** obviously directed at a particular person or aspect: *pointed criticism.* **4** emphasized or made conspicuous: *pointed ignorance.* **5** (of an arch or style of architecture) Gothic. **6** *Music.* (of a psalm text) marked to show changes in chanting. **7** (of Hebrew text) with vowel points marked.
▸ **'pointedly** *adv*

pointer ❶ ('pɔɪntə) *n* **1** a person or thing that points. **2** an indicator on a measuring instrument. **3** a long rod or cane used by a lecturer to point to parts of a map, blackboard, etc. **4** one of a breed of large smooth-coated gun dogs, usually white with black, liver, or lemon markings. **5** a helpful piece of information.

pointillism ('pwæntɪˌlɪzəm) *n* the technique of painting elaborated from impressionism, in which dots of unmixed colour are juxtaposed on a white ground so that from a distance they fuse in the viewer's eye into appropriate intermediate tones. [C19: from F, from *pointiller* to mark with tiny dots, from *pointille* little point, from It., from *punto* POINT]
▸ **'pointillist** *n, adj*

pointing ('pɔɪntɪŋ) *n* the act or process of repairing or finishing joints in brickwork, masonry, etc., with mortar.

point lace *n* lace made by a needle with buttonhole stitch on a paper pattern. Also called: **needlepoint.** Cf. **pillow lace.**

pointless ❶ ('pɔɪntlɪs) *adj* **1** without a point. **2** without meaning, relevance, or force. **3** *Sport.* without a point scored.
▸ **'pointlessly** *adv*

point off *vb* (*tr, adv*) to mark off from the right-hand side (a number of decimal places) in a whole number to create a mixed decimal: *point off three decimal places in 12345 and you get 12.345.*

point of honour *n, pl* **points of honour.** a circumstance, event, etc., that involves the defence of one's principles, social honour, etc.

point of no return *n* **1** a point at which an irreversible commitment must be made to an action, progression, etc. **2** a point in a journey at which, if one continues, supplies will be insufficient for a return to the starting place.

point of order *n, pl* **points of order.** a question raised in a meeting as to whether the rules governing procedures are being breached.

point of sale *n* (in retail distribution) **a** the place at which a sale is made. Abbrev.: **POS. b** (*as modifier*): *a point-of-sale display.*

point of view ❶ *n, pl* **points of view. 1** a position from which someone or something is observed. **2** a mental viewpoint or attitude.

point out ❶ *vb* (*tr, adv*) to indicate or specify.

pointsman ('pɔɪntsˌmæn, -mən) *n, pl* **pointsmen. 1** a person who operates railway points. **2** a policeman or traffic warden on point duty.

point source *n Optics.* a source of light or other radiation that can be considered to have negligible dimensions.

points system *n Brit.* a system used to assess applicants' eligibility for local authority housing, based on (points awarded for) such factors as the length of time the applicant has lived in the area, how many children are in the family, etc.

point-to-point *n Brit.* a steeplechase organized by a recognized hunt or other body, usually restricted to amateurs riding horses that have been regularly used in hunting.

point up ❶ *vb* (*tr, adv*) to emphasize, esp. by identifying: *he pointed up the difficulties.*

poise[1] ❶ (pɔɪz) *n* **1** composure or dignity of manner. **2** physical balance. **3** equilibrium; stability. **4** the position of hovering. ◆ *vb* **poises, poising, poised. 5** to be or cause to be balanced or suspended. **6** (*tr*) to hold, as in readiness: *to poise a lance.* [C16: from OF *pois* weight, from L *pēnsum,* from *pendere* to weigh]

poise[2] (pwɑːz, pɔɪz) *n* the cgs unit of viscosity; the viscosity of a fluid in which a tangential force of 1 dyne per square centimetre maintains a difference in velocity of 1 centimetre per second between two parallel planes 1 centimetre apart. Symbol: P [C20: after Jean Louis Marie *Poiseuille* (1799–1869), F physician]

poised ❶ (pɔɪzd) *adj* **1** self-possessed; dignified. **2** balanced and prepared for action.

poison ❶ ('pɔɪzᵊn) *n* **1** any substance that can impair function or otherwise injure the body. **2** something that destroys, corrupts, etc. **3** a substance that retards a chemical reaction or the activity of a catalyst. **4** a substance that absorbs neutrons in a nuclear reactor and thus slows down the reaction. ◆ *vb* (*tr*) **5** to give poison to (a person or animal), esp. with intent to kill. **6** to add poison to. **7** to taint or infect with or as if with poison. **8** (foll. by *against*) to turn (a person's mind) against: *he poisoned her mind against me.* **9** to retard or stop (a chemical or nuclear reaction) by the action of a poison. [C13: from OF *puison* potion, from L *pōtiō* a drink, esp. a poisonous one, from *pōtāre* to drink]
▸ **'poisoner** *n*

poison ivy *n* any of several North American shrubs or climbing plants that cause an itching rash on contact.

poisonous ❶ ('pɔɪzənəs) *adj* **1** having the effects or qualities of a poison. **2** capable of killing or inflicting injury. **3** corruptive or malicious.
▸ **'poisonously** *adv* ▸ **'poisonousness** *n*

poison-pen letter *n* a letter written in malice, usually anonymously, and intended to abuse, frighten, or insult the recipient.

poison pill *n Finance.* a tactic used by a company fearing an unwelcome takeover bid, in which the value of the company is automatically reduced, as by the sale of an issue of shares having an option unfavourable to the bidders, if the bid is successful.

THESAURUS

17 = **unit**, score, tally **31 beside the point** = **irrelevant**, extraneous, immaterial, inapplicable, inapposite, inappropriate, incidental, inconsequential, neither here nor there, not to the purpose, off the subject, out of the way, pointless, unconnected, unimportant, without connection **37 to the point** = **relevant**, applicable, apposite, appropriate, apropos, apt, brief, fitting, germane, pertinent, pithy, pointed, short, suitable, terse ◆ *vb* **39, 40** = **indicate**, bespeak, call attention to, denote, designate, direct, show, signify **41** = **aim**, bring to bear, direct, level, train **42** = **sharpen**, barb, edge, taper, whet

point-blank *adj* **3** = **direct**, abrupt, blunt, categorical, downright, explicit, express, plain, straight-from-the-shoulder, unreserved ◆ *adv* **4, 5** = **directly**, bluntly, brusquely, candidly, explicitly, forthrightly, frankly, openly, overtly, plainly, straight, straightforwardly

pointed *adj* **1** = **sharp**, acicular, acuminate, acute, barbed, cuspidate, edged, mucronate **2** = **cutting**, accurate, acute, biting, incisive, keen, penetrating, pertinent, sharp, telling, trenchant

pointer *n* **2** = **indicator**, guide, hand, needle **5** = **hint**, advice, caution, information, recommendation, suggestion, tip, warning

pointless *adj* **2** = **senseless**, absurd, aimless, dumb-ass, fruitless, futile, inane, ineffectual, irrelevant, meaningless, nonsensical, silly, stupid, unavailing, unproductive, unprofitable, useless, vague, vain, without rhyme or reason, worthless
Antonyms *adj* appropriate, beneficial, desirable, fitting, fruitful, logical, meaningful, productive, profitable, proper, sensible, to the point, useful, worthwhile

point of view *n* **1** = **perspective**, angle, orientation, outlook, position, standpoint **2** = **opinion**, approach, attitude, belief, judgment, slant, view, viewpoint, way of looking at it

point out *vb* = **mention**, allude to, bring up, call attention to, identify, indicate, remind, reveal, show, specify

point up *vb* = **emphasize**, accent, accentuate, make clear, stress, underline

poise[1] *n* **1** = **composure**, aplomb, assurance, calmness, cool (*sl.*), coolness, dignity, elegance, equanimity, equilibrium, grace, presence, presence of mind, sang-froid, savoir-faire, self-possession, serenity ◆ *vb* **5** = **position**, balance, float, hang, hang in midair, hang suspended, hold, hover, support, suspend

poised *adj* **1** = **composed**, calm, collected, debonair, dignified, graceful, nonchalant, self-confident, self-possessed, serene, suave, together (*inf.*), unfazed (*inf.*), unruffled, urbane **2** = **ready**, all set, in the wings, on the brink, prepared, standing by, waiting
Antonyms *adj* ≠ **composed:** agitated, annoyed, discomposed, disturbed, excited, irritated, ruffled, worked up

poison *n* **1** = **toxin**, bane, venom **2** = **contamination**, bane, blight, cancer, canker, contagion, corruption, malignancy, miasma, virus ◆ *vb* **5** = **murder**, give (someone) poison, kill **6, 7** = **contaminate**, adulterate, envenom, infect, pollute **8** = **corrupt**, defile, deprave, pervert, subvert, taint, undermine, vitiate, warp

poisonous *adj* **1, 2** = **toxic**, baneful, deadly, fatal, lethal, mephitic, mortal, noxious, venomous, virulent **3** = **evil**, baleful, baneful (*arch.*), corrupting, malicious, noxious, pernicious, pestiferous, pestilential, vicious

poison sumach *n* a swamp shrub of the southeastern US that causes an itching rash on contact with the skin.

Poisson distribution ('pwɑːsᵊn) *n Statistics.* a distribution that represents the number of events occurring randomly in a fixed time at an average rate λ. [C19: after S. D. *Poisson* (1781–1840), F mathematician]

poke[1] ❶ (pəʊk) *vb* **pokes, poking, poked. 1** (*tr*) to jab or prod, as with the elbow, a stick, etc. **2** (*tr*) to make (a hole) by or as by poking. **3** (when *intr*, often foll. by *at*) to thrust (at). **4** (*tr*) *Inf.* to hit with the fist; punch. **5** (usually foll. by *in, through,* etc.) to protrude or cause to protrude: *don't poke your arm out of the window.* **6** (*tr*) to stir (a fire, etc.) by poking. **7** (*intr*) to meddle or intrude. **8** (*intr;* often foll. by *about* or *around*) to search or pry. **9 poke one's nose into.** to interfere with or meddle in. ◆ *n* **10** a jab or prod. **11** *Inf.* a blow with one's fist; punch. [C14: from Low G & MDu. *poken* to prod]

poke[2] (pəʊk) *n* **1** *Dialect.* a pocket or bag. **2 a pig in a poke.** See **pig.** [C13: from OF *poque,* of Gmc origin]

poke[3] (pəʊk) *n* **1** Also called: **poke bonnet.** a bonnet with a brim that projects at the front, popular in the 18th and 19th centuries. **2** the brim itself. [C18: from POKE[1] (in the sense: to project)]

poker[1] ('pəʊkə) *n* a metal rod, usually with a handle, for stirring a fire.

poker[2] ('pəʊkə) *n* a card game of bluff and skill in which bets are made on the hands dealt, the highest-ranking hand winning the pool. [C19: prob. from F *poque* similar card game]

poker face *n Inf.* a face without expression, as that of a poker player attempting to conceal the value of his cards.
▸ **'poker-ˌfaced** *adj*

poker machine *n Austral. & NZ.* a fruit machine.

pokerwork ('pəʊkəˌwɜːk) *n* the art of producing pictures or designs on wood by charring it with a heated tool.

pokeweed ('pəʊkˌwiːd), **pokeberry,** *or* **pokeroot** *n* a tall North American plant that has a poisonous purple root used medicinally. [C18 *poke,* from Algonquian *puccoon* plant used in dyeing, from *pak* blood]

pokie ('pəʊkɪ) *n Austral. inf.* short for **poker machine.**

poky ❶ *or* **pokey** ('pəʊkɪ) *adj* **pokier, pokiest. 1** (esp. of rooms) small and cramped. **2** *Inf., chiefly US.* without speed or energy; slow. [C19: from POKE[1] (in sl. sense: to confine)]
▸ **'pokily** *adv* ▸ **'pokiness** *n*

pol. *abbrev. for:* **1** political. **2** politics.

Pol. *abbrev. for:* **1** Poland. **2** Polish.

polar ❶ ('pəʊlə) *adj* **1** at, near, or relating to either of the earth's poles or the area inside the Arctic or Antarctic Circles: *polar regions.* **2** having or relating to a pole or poles. **3** pivotal or guiding in the manner of the Pole Star. **4** directly opposite, as in tendency or character. **5** *Chem.* (of a molecule) having an uneven distribution of electrons and thus a permanent dipole moment: *water has polar molecules.*

polar bear *n* a white carnivorous bear of coastal regions of the North Pole.

polar circle *n* a term for either the **Arctic Circle** or **Antarctic Circle.**

polar coordinates *pl n* a pair of coordinates for locating a point in a plane by means of the length of a radius vector, *r,* which pivots about the origin to establish the angle, θ, that the position of the point makes with a fixed line. Usually written (*r,* θ).

polar distance *n* the angular distance of a star, planet, etc., from the celestial pole; the complement of the declination.

polar front *n Meteorol.* a front dividing cold polar air from warmer temperate or tropical air.

Polari (pə'lɑːrɪ) *n* an English slang derived from the Lingua Franca of Mediterranean ports; brought to England by sailors from the 16th century onwards. [C19: from It. *parlare* to speak]

polarimeter (ˌpəʊlə'rɪmɪtə) *n* an instrument for measuring the polarization of light.
▸ **polarimetric** (ˌpəʊlərɪ'mɛtrɪk) *adj*

Polaris (pə'lɑːrɪs) *n* **1** Also called: the **Pole Star,** the **North Star.** the brightest star in the constellation Ursa Minor, situated slightly less than 1° from the north celestial pole. **2** a type of US two-stage intermediate-range ballistic missile, usually fired by a submerged submarine. [from Med. L *stella polāris* polar star]

polariscope (pəʊ'lærɪˌskəʊp) *n* an instrument for detecting polarized light or for observing objects under polarized light, esp. for detecting strain in transparent materials.

polarity ❶ (pəʊ'lærɪtɪ) *n, pl* **polarities. 1** the condition of having poles. **2** the condition of a body or system in which it has opposing physical properties, esp. magnetic poles or electric charge. **3** the particular state of a part that has polarity: *an electrode with positive polarity.* **4** the state of having or expressing two directly opposite tendencies, opinions, etc.

polarization *or* **polarisation** (ˌpəʊləraɪ'zeɪʃən) *n* **1** the condition of having or giving polarity. **2** *Physics.* the phenomenon in which waves of light or other radiation are restricted to certain directions of vibration.

polarize *or* **polarise** ('pəʊləˌraɪz) *vb* **polarizes, polarizing, polarized** *or* **polarises, polarising, polarised. 1** to acquire or cause to acquire polarity or polarization. **2** (*tr*) to cause (people) to adopt extreme opposing positions: *to polarize opinion.*
▸ **'polarˌizer** *or* **'polarˌiser** *n*

polar lights *pl n* the aurora borealis in the N hemisphere or the aurora australis in the S hemisphere.

polarography (ˌpəʊlə'rɒgrəfɪ) *n* a technique for analysing and studying ions in solution by using an electrolytic cell with a very small cathode and obtaining a graph (**polarogram**) of the current against the potential to determine the concentration and nature of the ions.

Polaroid ('pəʊləˌrɔɪd) *n Trademark.* **1** a type of plastic sheet that can polarize a transmitted beam of normal light because it is composed of long parallel molecules. It only transmits plane-polarized light if these molecules are parallel to the plane of polarization. **2 Polaroid Land Camera.** any of several types of camera yielding a finished print by means of a special developing and processing technique that occurs inside the camera and takes only a few seconds. **3** (*pl*) sunglasses with lenses made from Polaroid plastic.

polder ('pəʊldə, 'pɒl-) *n* a stretch of land reclaimed from the sea or a lake, esp. in the Netherlands. [C17: from MDu. *polre*]

pole[1] ❶ (pəʊl) *n* **1** a long slender usually round piece of wood, metal, or other material. **2** the piece of timber on each side of which a pair of carriage horses are hitched. **3** another name for **rod** (sense 7). **4 up the pole.** *Brit., Austral., & NZ inf.* **4a** slightly mad. **4b** mistaken; on the wrong track. ◆ *vb* **poles, poling, poled. 5** (*tr*) to strike or push with a pole. **6** (*tr*) **6a** to set out (an area of land or garden) with poles. **6b** to support (a crop, such as hops) on poles. **7** to punt (a boat). [OE *pāl,* from L *pālus* a stake]

pole[2] ❶ (pəʊl) *n* **1** either of the two antipodal points where the earth's axis of rotation meets the earth's surface. See also **North Pole, South Pole. 2** *Physics.* **2a** either of the two regions at the extremities of a magnet to which the lines of force converge. **2b** either of two points at which there are opposite electric charges, as at the terminals of a battery. **3** *Biol.* either end of the axis of a cell, spore, ovum, or similar body. **4** either of two mutually exclusive or opposite actions, opinions, etc. **5 poles apart** (*or* **asunder**). having widely divergent opinions, tastes, etc. [C14: from L *polus* end of an axis, from Gk *polos* pivot]

Pole (pəʊl) *n* a native, inhabitant, or citizen of Poland or a speaker of Polish.

poleaxe *or US* **poleax** ('pəʊlˌæks) *n* **1** another term for a battle-axe or a butcher's axe. ◆ *vb* **poleaxes, poleaxing, poleaxed. 2** (*tr*) to hit or fell with or as if with a poleaxe. [C14 *pollax* battle-axe, from POLL + AXE]

polecat ('pəʊlˌkæt) *n, pl* **polecats** *or* **polecat. 1** a dark brown musteline mammal of Europe, Asia, and N Africa, that is closely related to but larger than the weasel and gives off an unpleasant smell. **2** *US.* a nontechnical name for **skunk** (sense 1). [C14 *polcat,* ?from OF *pol* cock, from L *pullus,* + CAT; from its preying on poultry]

polemic ❶ (pə'lɛmɪk) *adj also* **polemical. 1** of or involving dispute or controversy. ◆ *n* **2** an argument or controversy, esp. over a doctrine, belief, etc. **3** a person engaged in such controversy. [C17: from Med. L *polemicus,* from Gk *polemikos* relating to war, from *polemos* war]
▸ **po'lemically** *adv* ▸ **polemicist** (pə'lɛmɪsɪst) *n*

polemics ❶ (pə'lɛmɪks) *n* (*functioning as sing*) the art or practice of dispute or argument, as in attacking or defending a doctrine or belief.

pole position *n* **1** (in motor racing) the starting position on the inside of the front row, generally considered the best one. **2** an advantageous starting position.

pole star *n* a guiding principle, rule, etc.

Pole Star *n* **the.** the star closest to the N celestial pole at any particular time. At present this is Polaris, but it will eventually be replaced owing to precession of the earth's axis.

pole vault *n* **1 the.** a field event in which competitors attempt to clear a high bar with the aid of an extremely flexible long pole. ◆ *vb* **pole-vault. 2** (*intr*) to perform a pole vault or compete in the pole vault.
▸ **'pole-ˌvaulter** *n*

poley ('pəʊlɪ) *adj Austral.* (of cattle) hornless or polled.

police ❶ (pə'liːs) *n* **1** (often preceded by *the*) the organized civil force of a state, concerned with maintenance of law and order. **2** (*functioning as pl*) the members of such a force collectively. **3** any organized body with a similar function: *security police.* ◆ *vb* **polices, policing, policed.** (*tr*)

THESAURUS

poke[1] *vb* **1, 3, 4 = jab,** butt, dig, elbow, hit, nudge, prod, punch, push, shove, stab, stick, thrust **7 = interfere,** butt in, intrude, meddle, nose, peek, poke one's nose into (*inf.*), pry, put one's two cents in (*US sl.*), snoop (*inf.*), tamper ◆ *n* **10, 11 = jab,** butt, dig, hit, nudge, prod, punch, thrust

poky *adj* **1 = small,** confined, cramped, incommodious, narrow, tiny
Antonyms *adj* capacious, commodious, large, open, roomy, spacious, wide

polar *adj* **1 = freezing,** Antarctic, Arctic, cold, extreme, frozen, furthest, glacial, icy, terminal **3 = pivotal,** beacon-like, cardinal, guiding, leading **4 = opposite,** antagonistic, antipodal, antithetical, contradictory, contrary, diametric, opposed

polarity *n* **4 = opposition,** ambivalence, contradiction, contrariety, dichotomy, duality, paradox

pole[1] *n* **1 = rod,** bar, mast, post, shaft, spar, staff, standard, stick

pole[2] *n* **1 = extremity,** antipode, limit, terminus **5 poles apart = at opposite extremes,** at opposite ends of the earth, incompatible, irreconcilable, miles apart, widely separated, worlds apart

polemic *adj* **1 = controversial,** argumentative, contentious, disputatious, polemical ◆ *n* **2 = argument,** controversy, debate, dispute

polemics *n* **= dispute,** argument, argumentation, contention, controversy, debate, disputation

police *n* **1, 2 = the law** (*inf.*), boys in blue (*inf.*), constabulary, fuzz (*sl.*), law enforcement agency, police force, the Old Bill (*sl.*) ◆ *vb* **4 = control,** guard, keep in order, keep the peace,

4 to regulate, control, or keep in order by means of a police or similar force. **5** to observe or record the activity or enforcement of: *a committee was set up to police the new agreement on picketing.* [C16: via F from L *polītia* administration; see POLITY]

police dog *n* a dog, often an Alsatian, trained to help the police, as in tracking.

policeman ❶ (pəˈliːsmən) *or* (*fem*) **policewoman** *n, pl* **policemen** *or* **policewomen.** a member of a police force, esp. one holding the rank of constable.

police officer *n* a member of a police force, esp. a constable; policeman.

police procedural *n* a novel, film, or television drama that deals realistically with police work.

police state *n* a state or country in which a repressive government maintains control through the police.

police station *n* the office or headquarters of the police force of a district.

policing (pəˈliːsɪŋ) *n* the policies, techniques, and practice of a police force in keeping order, preventing crime, etc.

policy[1] ❶ (ˈpɒlɪsɪ) *n, pl* **policies. 1** a plan of action adopted or pursued by an individual, government, party, business, etc. **2** wisdom, shrewdness, or sagacity. **3** (*often pl*) *Scot.* the improved grounds surrounding a country house. [C14: from OF *policie*, from L *polītia* administration, POLITY]

policy[2] (ˈpɒlɪsɪ) *n, pl* **policies.** a document containing a contract of insurance. [C16: from OF *police* certificate, from OIt. from L *apodixis* proof, from Gk *apodeixis*]
▸ **ˈpolicyˌholder** *n*

polio (ˈpəʊlɪəʊ) *n* short for **poliomyelitis.**

poliomyelitis (ˌpəʊlɪəʊˌmaɪəˈlaɪtɪs) *n* an acute infectious viral disease, esp. affecting children. In its paralytic form the brain and spinal cord are involved, causing paralysis and wasting of muscle. Also called: **infantile paralysis.** [C19: NL, from Gk *polios* grey + *muelos* marrow]

polish ❶ (ˈpɒlɪʃ) *vb* **1** to make or become smooth and shiny by rubbing, esp. with wax or an abrasive. **2** (*tr*) to make perfect or complete. **3** to make or become elegant or refined. ◆ *n* **4** a finish or gloss. **5** the act of polishing. **6** a substance used to produce a shiny, often protective surface. **7** elegance or refinement, esp. in style, manner, etc. [C13 *polis*, from OF *polir*, from L *polīre* to polish]
▸ **ˈpolisher** *n*

Polish (ˈpəʊlɪʃ) *adj* **1** of, relating to, or characteristic of Poland, its people, or their language. ◆ *n* **2** the official language of Poland.

polished ❶ (ˈpɒlɪʃt) *adj* **1** accomplished: *a polished actor.* **2** impeccably or professionally done: *a polished performance.* **3** (of rice) milled to remove the outer husk.

polish off ❶ *vb* (*tr, adv*) *Inf.* **1** to finish or process completely. **2** to dispose of or kill.

polish up *vb* (*adv*) **1** to make or become smooth and shiny by polishing. **2** (when *intr*, foll. by *on*) to study or practise until adept (at): *he's polishing up on his German.*

Politburo (ˈpɒlɪtˌbjʊərəʊ) *n* **1** the executive and policy-making committee of a Communist Party. **2** the supreme policy-making authority in most Communist countries. [C20: from Russian: contraction of *Politicheskoe Buro* political bureau]

polite ❶ (pəˈlaɪt) *adj* **1** showing a great regard for others, as in manners, etc.; courteous. **2** cultivated or refined: *polite society.* **3** elegant or polished: *polite letters.* [C15: from L *polītus* polished]
▸ **poˈlitely** *adv* ▸ **poˈliteness** *n*

politesse (ˌpɒlɪˈtɛs) *n* formal or genteel politeness. [C18: via F from It. *politezza*, ult. from L *polīre* to polish]

politic ❶ (ˈpɒlɪtɪk) *adj* **1** artful or shrewd; ingenious. **2** crafty or unscrupulous; cunning. **3** wise or prudent, esp. in statesmanship: *a politic choice.* **4** an archaic word for **political.** ◆ See also **body politic.** [C15: from OF *politique*, from L *polīticus* concerning civil administration, from Gk, from *politēs* citizen, from *polis* city]
▸ **ˈpoliticly** *adv*

political ❶ (pəˈlɪtɪkᵊl) *adj* **1** of or relating to the state, government, public administration, etc. **2a** of or relating to government policy-making as distinguished from administration or law. **2b** of or relating to the civil aspects of government as distinguished from the military. **3** of, dealing with, or relating to politics: *a political person.* **4** of or relating to the parties and the partisan aspects of politics. **5** organized with respect to government: *a political unit.*
▸ **poˈlitically** *adv*

political economy *n* the former name for **economics** (sense 1).

politically correct *adj* demonstrating liberal ideals, esp. by using vocabulary that is intended to avoid prejudice of any kind. Often abbreviated to **PC.**

political prisoner *n* a person imprisoned for holding or expressing particular political beliefs.

political science *n* the study of the state, government, and politics: one of the social sciences.
▸ **political scientist** *n*

politician ❶ (ˌpɒlɪˈtɪʃən) *n* **1** a person actively engaged in politics, esp. a full-time professional member of a deliberative assembly. **2** a person who is experienced or skilled in government or administration; statesman. **3** *Disparaging, chiefly US.* a person who engages in politics out of a wish for personal gain.

politicize *or* **politicise** (pəˈlɪtɪˌsaɪz) *vb* **politicizes, politicizing, politicized** *or* **politicises, politicising, politicised. 1** (*tr*) to render political in tone, interest, or awareness. **2** (*intr*) to participate in political discussion or activity.
▸ **poˌliticiˈzation** *or* **poˌliticiˈsation** *n*

politicking (ˈpɒlɪtɪkɪŋ) *n* political activity, esp. seeking votes.

politico (pəˈlɪtɪˌkəʊ) *n, pl* **politicos.** *Chiefly US.* an informal word for a **politician** (senses 1, 3). [C17: from It. or Sp.]

politics ❶ (ˈpɒlɪtɪks) *n* **1** (*functioning as sing*) the art and science of directing and administrating states and other political units; government. **2** (*functioning as sing*) the complex or aggregate of relationships of people in society, esp. those relationships involving authority or power. **3** (*functioning as pl*) political activities or affairs: *party politics.* **4** (*functioning as sing*) the business or profession of politics. **5** (*functioning as sing or pl*) any activity concerned with the acquisition of power, etc.: *company politics are frequently vicious.* **6** manoeuvres or factors leading up to or influencing (something): *the politics of the decision.* **7** (*functioning as pl*) opinions, sympathies, etc., with respect to politics: *his conservative politics.*

polity (ˈpɒlɪtɪ) *n, pl* **polities. 1** a form of government or organization of a society, etc.; constitution. **2** a politically organized society, etc. **3** the management of public affairs. **4** political organization. [C16: from L *polītia*, from Gk *politeia* citizenship, civil administration, from *politēs* citizen, from *polis* city]

polka (ˈpɒlkə) *n* **1** a 19th-century Bohemian dance with three steps and a hop, in fast duple time. **2** a piece of music composed for or in the rhythm of this dance. ◆ *vb* **polkas, polkaing, polkaed. 3** (*intr*) to dance a polka. [C19: via F from Czech *pulka* half-step]

polka dot *n* one of a pattern of small circular regularly spaced spots on a fabric.

poll ❶ (pəʊl) *n* **1** the casting, recording, or counting of votes in an election; a voting. **2** the result of such a voting: *a heavy poll.* **3** Also called: **opinion poll. 3a** a canvassing of a representative sample of people on some question in order to determine the general opinion. **3b** the results of such a canvassing. **4** any counting or enumeration, esp. for taxation or voting purposes. **5** the back part of the head of an animal. ◆ *vb* (*mainly tr*) **6** to receive (a vote or quantity of votes): *he polled 10 000 votes.* **7** to receive, take, or record the votes of: *he polled the whole town.* **8** to canvass (a person, group, area, etc.) as part of a survey of opinion. **9** (*sometimes intr*) to cast (a vote) in an election. **10** to clip or shear. **11** to remove or cut short the horns of (cattle). [C13 (in the sense: a human head) & C17 (in the sense: votes): from MLow G *polle* hair of the head, head, top of a tree]

pollack *or* **pollock** (ˈpɒlək) *n, pl* **pollacks, pollack** *or* **pollocks, pollock.** a gadoid food fish that has a projecting lower jaw and occurs in northern seas. [C17: from earlier Scot. *podlok*, from ?]

THESAURUS

patrol, protect, regulate, watch **5** = **monitor**, check, observe, oversee, supervise

policeman *n* = **cop** (*sl.*), bizzy (*inf.*), bobby (*inf.*), constable, copper (*sl.*), flatfoot (*sl.*), fuzz (*sl.*), gendarme (*sl.*), officer, peeler (*obs. Brit. sl.*), plod (*Brit. sl.*), rozzer (*sl.*)

policy[1] *n* **1** = **procedure**, action, approach, code, course, custom, guideline, line, plan, practice, programme, protocol, rule, scheme, stratagem, theory **2** = **wisdom**, discretion, good sense, prudence, sagacity, shrewdness

polish *vb* **1** = **shine**, brighten, buff, burnish, clean, furbish, rub, smooth, wax **2** = **perfect**, brush up, correct, cultivate, emend, enhance, finish, improve, refine, touch up ◆ *n* **4** = **sheen**, brightness, brilliance, finish, glaze, gloss, lustre, smoothness, sparkle, veneer **6** = **varnish**, wax **7** = **style**, breeding, class (*inf.*), elegance, finesse, finish, grace, politesse, refinement, suavity, urbanity

polished *adj* **1, 2** = **accomplished**, adept, expert, faultless, fine, flawless, impeccable, masterly, outstanding, professional, skilful, superlative
Antonyms *adj* amateurish, inept, inexpert, unaccomplished, unskilled

polish off *vb* **2** *Informal* = **kill**, blow away, bump off (*inf.*), dispose of, do away with, do in (*sl.*), eliminate, get rid of, liquidate, murder, take out (*sl.*)

polite *adj* **1** = **mannerly**, affable, civil, complaisant, courteous, deferential, gracious, obliging, respectful, well-behaved, well-mannered **2, 3** = **refined**, civilized, courtly, cultured, elegant, genteel, polished, sophisticated, urbane, well-bred
Antonyms *adj* ≠ **mannerly:** crude, discourteous, ill-mannered, impertinent, impolite, impudent, insulting, rude ≠ **refined:** uncultured, unrefined

politeness *n* **1** = **courtesy**, civility, common courtesy, complaisance, correctness, courteousness, decency, deference, etiquette, grace, graciousness, mannerliness, obligingness, respectfulness

politic *adj* **1, 2** = **shrewd**, artful, astute, canny, crafty, cunning, designing, ingenious, intriguing, Machiavellian, scheming, sly, subtle, unscrupulous **3** = **wise**, advisable, diplomatic, discreet, expedient, in one's best interests, judicious, prudent, sagacious, sensible, tactful

political *adj* **1, 2** = **governmental**, civic, parliamentary, policy-making **4** = **factional**, partisan, party

politician *n* **1** = **statesman**, legislator, Member of Parliament, M.P., office bearer, politico (*inf.*, *chiefly US*), public servant, stateswoman

politics *n* **1** = **statesmanship**, affairs of state, civics, government, government policy, political science, polity, statecraft **5** = **power struggle**, Machiavellianism, machination, *Realpolitik*

poll *n* **1, 3** = **canvass**, ballot, census, count, Gallup Poll, (public) opinion poll, sampling, survey **2** = **vote**, figures, returns, tally, voting ◆ *vb* **6** = **tally**, register **8** = **question**, ballot, canvass, fly a kite, interview, sample, survey

pollan ('pɒlən) *n* any of several varieties of whitefish that occur in lakes in Northern Ireland. [C18: prob. from Irish *poll* lake]

pollard ('pɒləd) *n* **1** an animal, such as a sheep or deer, that has either shed its horns or antlers or has had them removed. **2** a tree that has had its branches cut back to encourage a more bushy growth. ◆ *vb* **3** (*tr*) to convert into a pollard; poll. [C16: hornless animal; see POLL]

pollen ('pɒlən) *n* a substance produced by the anthers of seed-bearing plants, consisting of numerous fine grains containing the male gametes. [C16: from L: powder]
▸**pollinic** (pə'lɪnɪk) *adj*

pollen analysis *n* another name for **palynology.**

pollen count *n* a measure of the pollen present in the air over a 24-hour period, often published to enable sufferers from hay fever to predict the severity of their attacks.

pollex ('pɒlɛks) *n, pl* **pollices** (-lɪ,si:z). the first digit of the forelimb of amphibians, reptiles, birds, and mammals, such as the thumb of man. [C19: from L: thumb, big toe]
▸**pollical** ('pɒlɪkᵊl) *adj*

pollinate ('pɒlɪ,neɪt) *vb* **pollinates, pollinating, pollinated.** (*tr*) to transfer pollen from the anthers to the stigma of (a flower).
▸**,polli'nation** *n* ▸**'polli,nator** *n*

polling booth *n* a semienclosed space in which a voter stands to mark a ballot paper during an election.

polling station *n* a building, such as a school, designated as the place to which voters go during an election in order to cast their votes.

polliwog *or* **pollywog** ('pɒlɪ,wɒg) *n Dialect, US, & Canad.* a tadpole. [C15 *polwygle*]

pollster ('pəʊlstə) *n* a person who conducts opinion polls.

poll tax *n* **1** a tax levied per head of adult population. **2** an informal name for **community charge.**

pollutant (pə'lu:tᵊnt) *n* a substance that pollutes, esp. a chemical produced as a waste product of an industrial process.

pollute Ⓣ (pə'lu:t) *vb* **pollutes, polluting, polluted.** (*tr*) **1** to contaminate, as with poisonous or harmful substances. **2** to make morally corrupt. **3** to desecrate. [C14 *polute,* from L *polluere* to defile]
▸**pol'luter** *n* ▸**pol'lution** *n*

Pollyanna (,pɒlɪ'ænə) *n* a person who is optimistic. [C20: after the chief character in *Pollyanna* (1913), a novel by Eleanor Porter (1868–1920), US writer]

polo ('pəʊləʊ) *n* **1** a game similar to hockey played on horseback using long-handled mallets (**polo sticks**) and a wooden ball. **2** short for **water polo. 3** Also called: **polo neck. 3a** a collar on a garment, worn rolled over to fit closely round the neck. **3b** a garment, esp. a sweater, with such a collar. [C19: from Balti (dialect of Kashmir): ball, from Tibetan *pulu*]

polonaise (,pɒlə'neɪz) *n* **1** a ceremonial marchlike dance in three-four time from Poland. **2** a piece of music composed for or in the rhythm of this dance. **3** a woman's costume with a tight bodice and an overskirt drawn back to show a decorative underskirt. [C18: from F *danse polonaise* Polish dance]

polonium (pə'ləʊnɪəm) *n* a very rare radioactive element that occurs in trace amounts in uranium ores. Symbol: Po; atomic no.: 84; half-life of most stable isotope, ^{209}Po: 103 years. [C19: NL, from Med. L *Polōnia* Poland; in honour of the nationality of its discoverer, Marie Curie]

polony (pə'ləʊnɪ) *n, pl* **polonies.** *Brit.* another name for **bologna sausage.**

polo shirt *n* a knitted cotton short-sleeved shirt with a collar and three-button opening at the neck.

poltergeist ('pɒltə,gaɪst) *n* a spirit believed to manifest its presence by noises and acts of mischief, such as throwing furniture about. [C19: from G, from *poltern* to be noisy + *Geist* GHOST]

poltroon (pɒl'tru:n) *n* an abject or contemptible coward. [C16: from OF *poultron,* from OIt. *poltrone* lazy good-for-nothing, apparently from *poltrire* to lie indolently in bed]

poly ('pɒlɪ) *n, pl* **polys.** *Inf.* short for **polytechnic.**

poly- *combining form.* **1** more than one; many or much: *polyhedron.* **2** having an excessive or abnormal number or amount: *polyphagia.* [from Gk *polus* much, many]

polyamide (,pɒlɪ'æmaɪd, -mɪd) *n* any of a class of synthetic polymeric materials, including nylon.

polyandry ('pɒlɪ,ændrɪ) *n* **1** the practice or condition of being married to more than one husband at the same time. **2** the practice in animals of a female mating with more than one male during one breeding season. **3** the condition in flowers of having a large indefinite number of stamens. [C18: from Gk *poluandria,* from POLY- + *-andria* from *anēr* man]
▸**,poly'androus** *adj*

polyanthus (,pɒlɪ'ænθəs) *n, pl* **polyanthuses.** any of several hybrid garden primroses with brightly coloured flowers. [C18: NL, from Gk: having many flowers]

polyatomic (,pɒlɪə'tɒmɪk) *adj* (of a molecule) containing more than two atoms.

poly bag ('pɒlɪ) *n Brit. inf.* a polythene bag, esp. one used to store or protect food or household articles.

polybasic (,pɒlɪ'beɪsɪk) *adj* (of an acid) having two or more replaceable hydrogen atoms per molecule.

polycarboxylate (,pɒlɪkɑ:'bɒksɪ,leɪt) *n* a salt or ester of a polycarboxylic acid. Polycarboxylate esters are used in certain detergents.

polycarboxylic acid ('pɒlɪ,kɑ:bɒk'sɪlɪk) *n* a type of carboxylic acid containing two or more carboxyl groups.

polycarpic (,pɒlɪ'kɑ:pɪk) *or* **polycarpous** *adj* (of a plant) able to produce flowers and fruit several times in succession.
▸**'poly,carpy** *n*

polycentrism (,pɒlɪ'sɛntrɪzəm) *n* (formerly) the fact or advocacy of the existence of more than one predominant ideological or political centre in a political system, alliance, etc., in the Communist world.

polychaete ('pɒlɪ,ki:t) *n* **1** a marine annelid worm having a distinct head and paired fleshy appendages (parapodia) that bear bristles and are used in swimming. ◆ *adj also* **polychaetous. 2** of or denoting such a creature. [C19: from NL, from Gk *polukhaitēs* having much hair]

polychromatic (,pɒlɪkrəʊ'mætɪk), **polychromic** (,pɒlɪ'krəʊmɪk), *or* **polychromous** *adj* **1** having various or changing colours. **2** (of light or other radiation) containing radiation with more than one wavelength.
▸**polychromatism** (,pɒlɪ'krəʊmə,tɪzəm) *n*

polyclinic (,pɒlɪ'klɪnɪk) *n* a hospital or clinic able to treat a wide variety of diseases.

polycotton ('pɒlɪkɒtᵊn) *n* a fabric made from a mixture of polyester and cotton.

polycotyledon (,pɒlɪ,kɒtɪ'li:dᵊn) *n* any of various plants, esp. gymnosperms, that have or appear to have more than two cotyledons.
▸**,poly,coty'ledonous** *adj*

polycyclic (,pɒlɪ'saɪklɪk) *adj* **1** (of a molecule or compound) having molecules that contain two or more closed rings of atoms. **2** *Biol.* having two or more rings or whorls: *polycyclic shells.* ◆ *n* **3** a polycyclic compound.

polycystic (,pɒlɪ'sɪstɪk) *adj Med.* containing many cysts: *a polycystic ovary.*

polydactyl (,pɒlɪ'dæktɪl) *adj also* **polydactylous. 1** (of man and other vertebrates) having more than the normal number of digits. ◆ *n* **2** a human or other vertebrate having more than the normal number of digits.

polyester (,pɒlɪ'ɛstə) *n* any of a large class of synthetic materials that are polymers containing recurring -COO- groups: used as plastics, textile fibres, and adhesives.

polyethene (,pɒlɪ'ɛθi:n) *n* the systematic name for **polythene.**

polyethylene (,pɒlɪ'ɛθɪ,li:n) *n* another name for **polythene.**

polygamy (pə'lɪgəmɪ) *n* **1** the practice of having more than one wife or husband at the same time. **2** the condition of having male, female, and hermaphrodite flowers on the same plant or on separate plants of the same species. **3** the practice in male animals of having more than one mate during one breeding season. [C16: via F from Gk *polugamia*]
▸**po'lygamist** *n* ▸**po'lygamous** *adj* ▸**po'lygamously** *adv*

polygene ('pɒlɪ,dʒi:n) *n* any of a group of genes that each produce a small quantitative effect on a particular characteristic, such as height.

polygenesis (,pɒlɪ'dʒɛnɪsɪs) *n* **1** *Biol.* evolution of organisms from different ancestral groups. **2** the hypothetical descent of different races from different ultimate ancestors.
▸**polygenetic** (,pɒlɪdʒɪ'nɛtɪk) *adj*

polyglot ('pɒlɪ,glɒt) *adj* **1** having a command of many languages. **2** written in or containing many languages. ◆ *n* **3** a person with a command of many languages. **4** a book, esp. a Bible, containing several versions of the same text written in various languages. **5** a mixture of languages. [C17: from Gk *poluglōttos,* lit.: many-tongued]

polygon ('pɒlɪ,gɒn) *n* a closed plane figure bounded by three or more straight sides that meet in pairs in the same number of vertices and do not intersect other than at these vertices. Specific polygons are named according to the number of sides, such as triangle, pentagon, etc. [C16: via L from Gk *polugōnon* figure with many angles]
▸**polygonal** (pə'lɪgənᵊl) *adj* ▸**po'lygonally** *adv*

polygonum (pə'lɪgənəm) *n* a plant having stems with knotlike joints and spikes of small white, green, or pink flowers. [C18: NL, from Gk *polugonon* knotgrass, from *polu-* POLY- + *-gonon,* from *gonu* knee]

polygraph ('pɒlɪ,grɑ:f) *n* **1** an instrument for the simultaneous recording of several involuntary physiological activities, including pulse rate and perspiration, used esp. as a lie detector. **2** a device for producing copies of written matter. [C18: from Gk *polugraphos* writing copiously]

polygyny (pə'lɪdʒɪnɪ) *n* **1** the practice or condition of being married to more than one wife at the same time. **2** the practice in animals of a male mating with more than one female during one breeding season. **3** the condition in flowers of having many styles. [C18: from POLY- + *-gyny,* from Gk *gunē* a woman]
▸**po'lygynous** *adj*

polyhedron (,pɒlɪ'hi:drən) *n, pl* **polyhedrons** *or* **polyhedra** (-drə). a solid figure consisting of four or more plane faces (all polygons), pairs of which meet along an edge, three or more edges meeting at a vertex.

THESAURUS

pollute *vb* **1 = contaminate,** adulterate, befoul, dirty, foul, infect, make filthy, mar, poison, smirch, soil, spoil, stain, taint **2, 3 = defile,** besmirch, corrupt, debase, debauch, deprave, desecrate, dishonour, profane, sully, violate

Antonyms *vb* ≠ **contaminate:** clean, cleanse, decontaminate, disinfect, purge, sanitize, sterilize ≠ **defile:** esteem, honour

pollution *n* **1 = contamination,** adulteration, corruption, defilement, dirtying, foulness, impurity, taint, uncleanness, vitiation

Specific polyhedrons are named according to the number of faces, such as tetrahedron, icosahedron, etc. [C16: from Gk *poluedron*, from POLY- + *hedron* side]
▸ˌ**polyˈhedral** *adj*

Polyhymnia (ˌpɒlɪˈhɪmnɪə) *n Greek myth.* the Muse of singing, mime, and sacred dance. [L, from Gk *Polumnia* full of songs]

polymath (ˈpɒlɪˌmæθ) *n* a person of great and varied learning. [C17: from Gk *polumathēs* having much knowledge]
▸**polymathy** (pəˈlɪməθɪ) *n*

polymer (ˈpɒlɪmə) *n* a naturally occurring or synthetic compound, such as starch or Perspex, that has large molecules made up of many relatively simple repeated units.
▸**polymerism** (pəˈlɪməˌrɪzəm, ˈpɒlɪmə-) *n*

polymerase (ˈpɒlɪməˌreɪs, -ˌreɪz) *n* any enzyme that catalyses the synthesis of a polymer, esp. the synthesis of DNA or RNA.

polymeric (ˌpɒlɪˈmɛrɪk) *adj* of, concerned with, or being a polymer: *a polymeric compound.* [C19: from Gk *polumerēs* having many parts]

polymerization *or* **polymerisation** (pəˌlɪməraɪˈzeɪʃən, ˌpɒlɪməraɪ-) *n* the act or process of forming a polymer or copolymer.

polymerize *or* **polymerise** (ˈpɒlɪməˌraɪz, pəˈlɪmə-) *vb* **polymerizes, polymerizing, polymerized** *or* **polymerises, polymerising, polymerised.** to react or cause to react to form a polymer.

polymerous (pəˈlɪmərəs) *adj Biol.* having or being composed of many parts.

polymorph (ˈpɒlɪˌmɔːf) *n* a species of animal or plant, or a crystalline form of a chemical compound, that exhibits polymorphism. [C19: from Gk *polumorphos* having many forms]

polymorphic function *n Computing.* a function in a computer program that can deal with a number of different types of data.

polymorphism (ˌpɒlɪˈmɔːfɪzəm) *n* **1** the occurrence of more than one form of individual in a single species within an interbreeding population. **2** the existence or formation of different types of crystal of the same chemical compound.

polymorphous (ˌpɒlɪˈmɔːfəs) *or* **polymorphic** *adj* **1** having, taking, or passing through many different forms or stages. **2** exhibiting or undergoing polymorphism.

Polynesian (ˌpɒlɪˈniːʒən, -ʒɪən) *adj* **1** of or relating to Polynesia, a group of Pacific islands, or to its people, or any of their languages. ◆ *n* **2** a member of the people that inhabit Polynesia, generally of Caucasoid features with light skin and wavy hair. **3** a branch of the Malayo-Polynesian family of languages, including Maori and Hawaiian.

polyneuritis (ˌpɒlɪnjʊˈraɪtɪs) *n* inflammation of many nerves at the same time.

polynomial (ˌpɒlɪˈnəʊmɪəl) *adj* **1** of, consisting of, or referring to two or more names or terms. ◆ *n* **2a** a mathematical expression consisting of a sum of terms each of which is the product of a constant and one or more variables raised to a positive or zero integral power. **2b** Also called: **multinomial.** any mathematical expression consisting of the sum of a number of terms. **3** *Biol.* a taxonomic name consisting of more than two terms, such as *Parus major minor* in which *minor* designates the subspecies.

polynucleotide (ˌpɒlɪˈnjuːklɪəˌtaɪd) *n Biochem.* a molecular chain of nucleotides chemically bonded by a series of ester linkages between the phosphoryl group of one nucleotide and the hydroxyl group of the sugar in the adjacent nucleotide.

polynya (ˈpɒlənˌjɑː) *n* a stretch of open water surrounded by ice, esp. near the mouths of large rivers, in arctic seas. [C19: from Russian, from *poly* open]

polyp (ˈpɒlɪp) *n* **1** *Zool.* one of the two forms of individual that occur in coelenterates. It usually has a hollow cylindrical body with a ring of tentacles around the mouth. **2** Also called: **polypus.** *Pathol.* a small growth arising from the surface of a mucous membrane. [C16 *polip*, from F *polype* nasal polyp, from L *pōlypus*, from Gk *polupous* having many feet]
▸ˈ**polypous** *or* ˈ**polypoid** *adj*

polypeptide (ˌpɒlɪˈpɛptaɪd) *n* any of a group of natural or synthetic polymers made up of amino acids chemically linked together; includes the proteins.

polypetalous (ˌpɒlɪˈpɛtələs) *adj* (of flowers) having many distinct or separate petals.

polyphagia (ˌpɒlɪˈfeɪdʒə) *n* **1** an abnormal desire to consume excessive amounts of food. **2** the habit of certain animals, esp. certain insects, of feeding on many different types of food. [C17: NL, from Gk, from *poluphagos* eating much]
▸**polyphagous** (pəˈlɪfəgəs) *adj*

polyphase (ˈpɒlɪˌfeɪz) *adj* **1** (of an electrical system, circuit, or device) having or using alternating voltages of the same frequency, the phases of which are cyclically displaced by fractions of a period. **2** having more than one phase.

polyphone (ˈpɒlɪˌfəʊn) *n* a letter or character having more than one phonetic value, such as *c* in English.

polyphonic (ˌpɒlɪˈfɒnɪk) *adj* **1** *Music.* composed of relatively independent parts; contrapuntal. **2** many-voiced. **3** *Phonetics.* denoting a polyphone.
▸ˌ**polyˈphonically** *adv*

polyphony (pəˈlɪfənɪ) *n, pl* **polyphonies. 1** polyphonic style of composition or a piece of music utilizing it. **2** the use of polyphones in a writing system. [C19: from Gk *poluphōnia* diversity of tones]
▸**poˈlyphonous** *adj* ▸**poˈlyphonously** *adv*

polyploid (ˈpɒlɪˌplɔɪd) *adj* (of cells, organisms, etc.) having more than twice the basic (haploid) number of chromosomes.
▸ˌ**polyˈploidal** *adj* ▸ˈ**polyˌploidy** *n*

polypod (ˈpɒlɪˌpɒd) *adj* **1** (esp. of insect larvae) having many legs or similar appendages. ◆ *n* **2** an animal of this type.

polypody (ˈpɒlɪˌpəʊdɪ) *n, pl* **polypodies.** any of various ferns having deeply divided leaves and round naked sporangia. [C15: from L *polypodium*, from Gk, from POLY- + *pous* foot]

polypropylene (ˌpɒlɪˈprəʊpɪˌliːn) *n* any of various tough flexible synthetic thermoplastic materials made by polymerizing propylene. Systematic name: **polypropene** (ˌpɒlɪˈprəʊpiːn).

polypus (ˈpɒlɪpəs) *n, pl* **polypi** (-paɪ). *Pathol.* another word for **polyp** (sense 2). [C16: via L from Gk: POLYP]

polysaccharide (ˌpɒlɪˈsækəˌraɪd, -rɪd) *or* **polysaccharose** (ˌpɒlɪˈsækəˌrəʊz, -ˌrəʊs) *n* any one of a class of carbohydrates whose molecules contain linked monosaccharide units: includes starch, inulin, and cellulose.

polysemy (ˌpɒlɪˈsiːmɪ, pəˈlɪsəmɪ) *n* the existence of several meanings in a single word. [C20: from NL *polysēmia*, from Gk *polusēmos* having many meanings]
▸ˌ**polyˈsemous** *adj*

polysomic (ˌpɒlɪˈsəʊmɪk) *adj* of, relating to, or designating a basically diploid chromosome complement, in which some but not all the chromosomes are represented more than twice.

polystyrene (ˌpɒlɪˈstaɪriːn) *n* a synthetic thermoplastic material obtained by polymerizing styrene; used as a white rigid foam (**expanded polystyrene**) for insulating and packing and as a glasslike material in light fittings.

polysyllable (ˈpɒlɪˌsɪləbᵊl) *n* a word consisting of more than two syllables.
▸**polysyllabic** (ˌpɒlɪsɪˈlæbɪk) *adj* ▸ˌ**polysylˈlabically** *adv*

polysyndeton (ˌpɒlɪˈsɪndɪtən) *n Rhetoric.* the use of several conjunctions in close succession, esp. where some might be omitted, as in *he ran and jumped and laughed for joy.* [C16: POLY- + *-syndeton*, from Gk *sundetos* bound together]

polytechnic (ˌpɒlɪˈtɛknɪk) *n* **1** *Brit.* (formerly) a college offering advanced courses in many fields at and below degree standard. ◆ *adj* **2** of or relating to technical instruction and training. [C19: via F from Gk *polutekhnos* skilled in many arts]

polytetrafluoroethylene (ˌpɒlɪˌtɛtrəˌflʊərəʊˈɛθɪˌliːn) *n* a white thermoplastic material with a waxy texture, made by polymerizing tetrafluoroethylene. It is used for making gaskets, hoses, insulators, bearings, and for coating metal surfaces. Abbrev.: **PTFE.** Also called (trademark): **Teflon.**

polytheism (ˈpɒlɪθiːˌɪzəm, ˌpɒlɪˈθiːɪzəm) *n* the worship of or belief in more than one god.
▸ˌ**polytheˈistic** *adj* ▸ˌ**polytheˈistically** *adv*

polythene (ˈpɒlɪˌθiːn) *n* any one of various light thermoplastic materials made from ethylene with properties depending on the molecular weight of the polymer. Systematic name: **polyethene.** Also called: **polyethylene.**

polytonality (ˌpɒlɪtəʊˈnælɪtɪ) *or* **polytonalism** *n Music.* the simultaneous use of more than two different keys or tonalities.
▸ˌ**polyˈtonal** *adj* ▸ˌ**polyˈtonally** *adv*

polyunsaturated (ˌpɒlɪʌnˈsætʃəˌreɪtɪd) *adj* of or relating to a class of animal and vegetable fats, the molecules of which consist of long carbon chains with many double bonds. Polyunsaturated compounds are less likely to be converted into cholesterol in the body. See also **monounsaturated.**

polyurethane (ˌpɒlɪˈjʊərəˌθeɪn) *n* a class of synthetic materials commonly used as a foam for insulation and packing.

polyvalent (ˌpɒlɪˈveɪlənt, pəˈlɪvələnt) *adj* **1** *Chem.* having more than one valency. **2** (of a vaccine) effective against several strains of the same disease-producing microorganism, antigen, or toxin.
▸ˌ**polyˈvalency** *n*

polyvinyl (ˌpɒlɪˈvaɪnɪl, -ˈvaɪnᵊl) *n* (*modifier*) designating a plastic or resin formed by polymerization of a vinyl derivative.

polyvinyl acetate *n* a colourless odourless tasteless resin used in emulsion paints, adhesives, sealers, a substitute for chicle in chewing gum, and for sealing porous surfaces.

polyvinyl chloride *n* the full name of **PVC.**

polyvinyl resin *n* any of a class of thermoplastic resins made by polymerizing a vinyl compound. The commonest type is PVC.

polyzoan (ˌpɒlɪˈzəʊən) *n, adj* another word for **bryozoan.** [C19: from NL, *Polyzoa* class name, from POLY- + *-zoan*, from Gk *zōion* an animal]

pom (pɒm) *n Austral. & NZ sl.* short for **pommy.**

POM *abbrev. for* prescription only medicine (*or* medication). Cf. **OTC.**

pomace (ˈpʌmɪs) *n* **1** the pulpy residue of apples or similar fruit after crushing and pressing, as in cider-making. **2** any pulpy substance left after crushing, mashing, etc. [C16: from Med. L *pōmācium* cider, from L *pōmum* apple]

pomaceous (pɒˈmeɪʃəs) *adj* of, relating to, or bearing pomes, such as the apple and quince trees. [C18: from NL *pōmāceus*, from L *pōmum* apple]

pomade (pəˈmɑːd) *n* **1** a perfumed oil or ointment put on the hair, as to make it smooth and shiny. ◆ *vb* **pomades, pomading, pomaded. 2** (*tr*) to put pomade on. ◆ Also: **pomatum.** [C16: from F *pommade*, from It. *pomato* (orig. made partly from apples), from L *pōmum* apple]

pomander (pəʊˈmændə) *n* **1** a mixture of aromatic substances in a sachet or an orange, formerly carried as scent or as a protection against disease. **2** a container for such a mixture. [C15: from OF *pome d'ambre*, from Med. L *pōmum ambrae* apple of amber]

pome (pəʊm) *n* the fleshy fruit of the apple and related plants, consisting of an enlarged receptacle enclosing the ovary and seeds. [C15: from OF, from LL *pōma*, pl. of L *pōmum* apple]

pomegranate ('pɒmɪˌɡrænɪt, 'pɒmˌɡrænɪt) *n* **1** an Asian shrub or small tree cultivated in semitropical regions for its edible fruit. **2** the many-chambered globular fruit of this tree, which has tough reddish rind, juicy red pulp, and many seeds. [C14: from OF *pome grenate*, from L *pōmum* apple + *grenate*, from *grānātus* full of seeds]

pomelo ('pɒmɪˌləʊ) *n, pl* **pomelos.** **1** Also called: **shaddock.** the edible yellow fruit, resembling a grapefruit, of a tropical tree widely grown in oriental regions. **2** *US.* another name for **grapefruit.** [C19: from Du. *pompelmoes*]

Pomeranian (ˌpɒmə'reɪnɪən) *adj* **1** of or relating to Pomerania, a region of N central Europe now chiefly in Poland. ♦ *n* **2** a breed of toy dog of the spitz type with a long thick straight coat.

pomfret ('pʌmfrɪt, 'pɒm-) *or* **pomfret-cake** *n* a small black rounded confection of liquorice. Also called: **Pontefract cake.** [C19: from *Pomfret*, earlier form of *Pontefract*, West Yorkshire, where orig. made]

pomiculture ('pɒmɪˌkʌltʃə) *n* the cultivation of fruit. [C19: from L *pōmum* fruit + CULTURE]

pommel ('pʌməl, 'pɒm-) *n* **1** the raised part on the front of a saddle. **2** a knob at the top of a sword or similar weapon. ♦ *vb* **pommels, pommelling, pommelled** *or US* **pommels, pommeling, pommeled.** **3** a less common word for **pummel.** [C14: from OF *pomel* knob, from Vulgar L *pōmellum* (unattested) little apple, from L *pōmum* apple]

pommy ('pɒmɪ) *n, pl* **pommies.** (*sometimes cap.*) *Sl.* a mildly offensive word used by Australians and New Zealanders for a British person. Sometimes shortened to **pom.** [C20: from ?, ? a blend of IMMIGRANT & POMEGRANATE (alluding to the red cheeks of British immigrants)]

pomology (pɒ'mɒlədʒɪ) *n* the branch of horticulture concerned with the study and cultivation of fruit. [C19: from NL *pōmologia*, from L *pōmum* fruit]
▸**pomological** (ˌpɒmə'lɒdʒɪkᵊl) *adj*

pomp ⓣ (pɒmp) *n* **1** stately or magnificent display; ceremonial splendour. **2** vain display, esp. of dignity or importance. **3** *Obs.* a procession or pageant. [C14: from OF *pompe*, from L *pompa* procession, from Gk *pompē*]

pompadour ('pɒmpəˌdʊə) *n* an early 18th-century hairstyle for women, having the front hair arranged over a pad to give it greater height and bulk. [C18: after the Marquise de *Pompadour*, mistress of Louis XV of France, who originated it]

pompano ('pɒmpəˌnəʊ) *n, pl* **pompano** *or* **pompanos.** **1** any of several food fishes of American coastal regions of the Atlantic. **2** a spiny-finned food fish of North American coastal regions of the Pacific. [C19: from Sp. *pámpano*, from ?]

pompom ('pɒmpɒm) *or* **pompon** *n* **1** a ball of tufted silk, wool, feathers, etc., worn on a hat for decoration. **2a** the small globelike flower head of certain varieties of dahlia and chrysanthemum. **2b** (*as modifier*): *pompom dahlia.* [C18: from F, from OF *pompe* knot of ribbons, from ?]

pom-pom ('pɒmpɒm) *n* an automatic rapid-firing small-calibre cannon, esp. a type of anti-aircraft cannon used in World War II. Also called: **pompom.** [C19: imit.]

pomposo (pɒm'pəʊsəʊ) *adv Music.* in a pompous manner. [It.]

pompous ⓣ ('pɒmpəs) *adj* **1** exaggeratedly or ostentatiously dignified or self-important. **2** ostentatiously lofty in style: *a pompous speech.* **3** *Rare.* characterized by ceremonial pomp or splendour.
▸**pomposity** (pɒm'pɒsɪtɪ) *or* '**pompousness** *n* ▸'**pompously** *adv*

'pon (pɒn) *Poetic or arch. contraction of* upon.

ponce ⓣ (pɒns) *Derog. sl., chiefly Brit.* ♦ *n* **1** a man given to ostentatious or effeminate display. **2** another word for **pimp**[1]. ♦ *vb* **ponces, poncing, ponced.** **3** (*intr;* often foll. by *around* or *about*) to act like a ponce. [C19: from Polari, from Sp. *pu(n)to* male prostitute or F *pront* prostitute]
▸'**poncy** *or* '**poncey** *adj*

poncho ('pɒntʃəʊ) *n, pl* **ponchos.** a cloak of a kind originally worn in South America, made of a rectangular or circular piece of cloth with a hole in the middle for the head. [C18: from American Sp., of Amerind origin, from *pantho* woollen material]

pond ⓣ (pɒnd) *n* a pool of still water, often artificially created. [C13 *ponde* enclosure]

ponder ⓣ ('pɒndə) *vb* (when *intr*, sometimes foll. by *on* or *over*) to give thorough or deep consideration (to); meditate (upon). [C14: from OF *ponderer*, from L *ponderāre* to weigh, consider, from *pondus* weight]
▸'**ponderable** *adj*

ponderous ⓣ ('pɒndərəs) *adj* **1** heavy; huge. **2** (esp. of movement) lacking ease or lightness; lumbering or graceless. **3** dull or laborious: *a ponderous oration.* [C14: from L *ponderōsus* of great weight, from *pondus* weight]
▸'**ponderously** *adv* ▸'**ponderousness** *or* **ponderosity** (ˌpɒndə'rɒsɪtɪ) *n*

pond lily *n* another name for **water lily.**

pondok ('pɒndɒk) *or* **pondokkie** *n* (in southern Africa) a crudely made house built of tin sheet, reeds, etc. [C20: from Malay *pondók* leaf house]

pond scum *n* a greenish layer floating on the surface of stagnant waters, consisting of algae.

pondweed ('pɒndˌwiːd) *n* **1** any of various water plants of the genus *Potamogeton*, which grow in ponds and slow streams. **2** Also called: **waterweed.** *Brit.* any of various water plants, such as mare's-tail, that have thin or much-divided leaves.

pone[1] (pəʊn, 'pəʊnɪ) *n Cards.* the player to the right of the dealer, or the nondealer in two-handed games. [C19: from L: put!, that is, play, from *ponere* to put]

pone[2] (pəʊn) *n Southern US.* bread made of maize. Also called: **pone bread, corn pone.** [C17: of Amerind origin]

pong (pɒŋ) *Brit. inf.* ♦ *n* **1** a disagreeable or offensive smell; stink. ♦ *vb* **2** (*intr*) to stink. [C20: ?from Romany *pan* to stink]
▸'**pongy** *adj*

ponga ('pɒŋə) *n* a tall New Zealand tree fern with large leathery leaves.

pongee (pɒn'dʒiː, 'pɒndʒiː) *n* **1** a thin plain-weave silk fabric from China or India, left in its natural colour. **2** a cotton or rayon fabric similar to this. [C18: from Mandarin Chinese (Peking) *pen-chī* woven at home, from *pen* own + *chi* loom]

pongid ('pɒŋɡɪd, 'pɒndʒɪd) *n* **1** any primate of the family Pongidae, which includes the gibbons and the great apes. ♦ *adj* **2** of this family. [from NL *Pongo* type genus, from Congolese *mpongo* ape]

pongo ('pɒŋɡəʊ) *n, pl* **pongos.** an anthropoid ape, esp. an orang-utan or (formerly) a gorilla. [C17: from Congolese *mpongo*]

poniard ('pɒnjəd) *n* **1** a small dagger with a slender blade. ♦ *vb* **2** (*tr*) to stab with a poniard. [C16: from OF *poignard*, from *poing* fist, from L *pugnus*]

pons Varolii (pɒnz və'rəʊlɪˌaɪ) *n, pl* **pontes Varolii** ('pɒntiːz). a broad white band of connecting nerve fibres that bridges the hemispheres of the cerebellum in mammals. Sometimes shortened to **pons.** [C16: NL, lit.: bridge of Varoli, after Costanzo *Varoli* (?1543–75), It. anatomist]

pontifex ('pɒntɪˌfɛks) *n, pl* **pontifices** (pɒn'tɪfɪˌsiːz). (in ancient Rome) any of the senior members of the Pontifical College, presided over by the **Pontifex Maximus.** [C16: from L, ?from Etruscan but infl. by folk etymology as if meaning lit.: bridge-maker]

pontiff ('pɒntɪf) *n* a former title of the pagan high priest at Rome, later used of popes and occasionally of other bishops, and now confined to the pope. [C17: from F *pontife*, from L PONTIFEX]

pontifical ⓣ (pɒn'tɪfɪkᵊl) *adj* **1** of, relating to, or characteristic of a pontiff. **2** having an excessively authoritative manner; pompous. ♦ *n* **3** *RC Church, Church of England.* a book containing the prayers and ritual instructions for ceremonies restricted to a bishop.
▸**pon'tifically** *adv*

pontificals (pɒn'tɪfɪkᵊlz) *pl n Chiefly RC Church.* the insignia and special vestments worn by a bishop, esp. when celebrating High Mass.

pontificate ⓣ *vb* (pɒn'tɪfɪˌkeɪt), **pontificates, pontificating, pontificated.** (*intr*) **1** to speak or behave in a pompous or dogmatic manner. **2** to serve or officiate at a Pontifical Mass. ♦ *n* (pɒn'tɪfɪkɪt). **3** the office or term of office of a pope.

pontoon[1] (pɒn'tuːn) *n* **a** a watertight float or vessel used where buoyancy is required in water, as in supporting a bridge, in salvage work, or where a temporary or mobile structure is required in military operations. **b** (*as modifier*): *a pontoon bridge.* [C17: from F *ponton*, from L *pontō* punt, from *pōns* bridge]

pontoon[2] (pɒn'tuːn) *n* a gambling game in which players try to obtain card combinations worth 21 points. Also called: **twenty-one** (esp. US), **vingt-et-un.** [C20: prob. an alteration of F *vingt-et-un*, lit.: twenty-one]

THESAURUS

pomp *n* **1** = **ceremony**, éclat, flourish, grandeur, magnificence, pageant, pageantry, parade, solemnity, splendour, state **2** = **show**, display, grandiosity, ostentation, pomposity, vainglory

pomposity *n* **1** = **self-importance**, affectation, airs, arrogance, flaunting, grandiosity, haughtiness, pompousness, portentousness, presumption, pretension, pretentiousness, vainglory, vanity **2** = **grandiloquence**, bombast, fustian, hot air (*inf.*), loftiness, magniloquence, rant, turgidity

pompous *adj* **1** = **self-important**, affected, arrogant, bloated, grandiose, imperious, magisterial, ostentatious, overbearing, pontifical, portentous, pretentious, puffed up, showy, supercilious, vainglorious **2** = **grandiloquent**, boastful, bombastic, flatulent, fustian, high-flown, inflated, magniloquent, orotund, overblown, turgid, windy
Antonyms *adj* ≠ **self-important:** humble, modest, natural, self-effacing, simple, unaffected, unpretentious ≠ **grandiloquent:** direct, plain-spoken, simple, succinct

ponce *n Derogatory slang, chiefly Brit.* **1** = **fop**, beau, coxcomb (*arch.*), dandy, popinjay, swell **2** = **pimp**, bawd (*arch.*), pander, procurer

pond *n* = **pool**, dew pond, duck pond, fish pond, lochan, millpond, small lake, tarn

ponder *vb* = **think**, brood, cerebrate, cogitate, consider, contemplate, deliberate, examine, excogitate, give thought to, meditate, mull over, muse, puzzle over, rack one's brains, reflect, ruminate, study, weigh

ponderous *adj* **1** = **unwieldy**, bulky, clunky (*inf.*), cumbersome, cumbrous, heavy, hefty, huge, massive, weighty **2** = **clumsy**, awkward, elephantine, graceless, heavy-footed, laborious, lumbering **3** = **dull**, dreary, heavy, laboured, lifeless, long-winded, pedantic, pedestrian, plodding, prolix, stilted, stodgy, tedious, tiresome, verbose
Antonyms *adj* ≠ **unwieldy:** handy, light, little, small, tiny, weightless ≠ **clumsy:** graceful, light, light-footed

pontifical *adj* **1** = **papal**, apostolic, ecclesiastical, prelatic **2** = **pompous**, bloated, condescending, dogmatic, imperious, magisterial, overbearing, portentous, pretentious, self-important

pontificate *vb* **1** = **expound**, declaim, dogmatize, hold forth, lay down the law, pontify, preach, pronounce, sound off

pony ('pəʊnɪ) *n, pl* **ponies. 1** any of various breeds of small horse, usually under 14.2 hands. **2** a small drinking glass, esp. for liqueurs. **3** anything small of its kind. **4** *Brit. sl.* a sum of £25, esp. in bookmaking. **5** Also called: **trot.** *US sl.* a translation used by students, often illicitly; crib. [C17: from Scot. *powney,* ?from obs. F *poulenet* a little colt, from L *pullus* young animal, foal]

ponytail ('pəʊnɪˌteɪl) *n* a hairstyle in which the hair is gathered together tightly by a band into a bunch at the back of the head.

pony trekking *n* the act of riding ponies cross-country, esp. as a pastime.

pooch (puːtʃ) *n Chiefly US & Canad.* a slang word for **dog.** [from ?]

poodle ('puːdᵊl) *n* **1** a breed of dog with curly hair, which is generally clipped from ribs to tail. **2** a servile person; lackey. [C19: from G *Pudel,* short for *Pudelhund,* from *pudeln* to splash + *Hund* dog; formerly trained as water dogs]

poof (pʊf, puːf), **poove** (puːv), *or* **poofter** ('puːftə) *n Brit. & Austral. derog. sl.* a male homosexual. [C20: from F *pouffe* puff]
► **'poofy** *adj*

pooh (puː) *interj* an exclamation of disdain, contempt, or disgust.

Pooh-Bah ('puː'bɑː) *n* a pompous self-important official holding several offices at once and fulfilling none of them. [C19: after the character, the Lord-High-Everything-Else, in *The Mikado* (1885), by Gilbert & Sullivan]

pooh-pooh 🅣 ('puː'puː) *vb (tr)* to express disdain or scorn for; dismiss or belittle.

pool[1] 🅣 (puːl) *n* **1** a small body of still water, usually fresh; small pond. **2** a small isolated collection of spilt liquid; puddle: *a pool of blood.* **3** a deep part of a stream or river where the water runs very slowly. **4** an underground accumulation of oil or gas. **5** See **swimming pool.** [OE *pōl*]

pool[2] 🅣 (puːl) *n* **1** any communal combination of resources, funds, etc.: *a typing pool.* **2** the combined stakes of the betters in many gambling games; kitty. **3** *Commerce.* a group of producers who agree to establish and maintain output levels and high prices, each member of the group being allocated a maximum quota. **4** *Finance, chiefly US.* a joint fund organized by security-holders for speculative or manipulative purposes on financial markets. **5** any of various billiard games in which the object is to pot all the balls with the cue ball, esp. that played with 15 coloured and numbered balls, popular in the US. Also called: **pocket billiards.** ◆ *vb (tr)* **6** to combine (investments, money, interests, etc.) into a common fund, as for a joint enterprise. **7** *Commerce.* to organize a pool of (enterprises). [C17: from F *poule,* lit.: hen used to signify stakes in a card game, from Med. L *pulla* hen, from L *pullus* young animal]

pools (puːlz) *pl n* **the** *Brit.* an organized nationwide principally postal gambling pool betting on the result of football matches. Also called: **football pools.**

poop[1] (puːp) *Naut.* ◆ *n* **1** a raised structure at the stern of a vessel, esp. a sailing ship. **2** Also called: **poop deck.** a raised deck at the stern of a ship. ◆ *vb* **3** *(tr)* (of a wave or sea) to break over the stern of (a vessel). **4** *(intr)* (of a vessel) to ship a wave or sea over the stern, esp. repeatedly. [C15: from OF *pupe,* from L *puppis*]

poop[2] (puːp) *vb US & Canad. sl.* **1** *(tr; usually passive)* to cause to become exhausted; tire: *he was pooped after the race.* **2** *(intr;* usually foll. by *out)* to give up or fail: *he pooped out of the race.* [C14 *poupen* to blow, ? imit.]

poop[3] (puːp) *Inf.* ◆ *vb (intr)* **1** to defecate. ◆ *n* **2** faeces; excrement. [perhaps related to POOP[2]]

pooper-scooper *n* a device used to remove dogs' excrement from public areas. [C20: POOP[3] + -ER[1] + SCOOP]

poor 🅣 (pʊə, pɔː) *adj* **1** lacking financial or other means of subsistence; needy. **2** characterized by or indicating poverty: *the country had a poor economy.* **3** scanty or inadequate: *a poor salary.* **4** (when *postpositive,* usually foll. by *in)* badly supplied (with resources, etc.): *a region poor in wild flowers.* **5** inferior. **6** contemptible or despicable. **7** disappointing or disagreeable: *a poor play.* **8** *(prenominal)* deserving of pity; unlucky: *poor John is ill again.* [C13: from OF *povre,* from L *pauper*]
► **'poorness** *n*

poor box *n* a box, esp. one in a church, used for the collection of alms or money for the poor.

poorhouse ('pʊəˌhaʊs, 'pɔː-) *n* another name for **workhouse** (sense 1).

poor law *n English history.* a law providing for the relief or support of the poor from parish funds.

poorly 🅣 ('pʊəlɪ, 'pɔː-) *adv* **1** badly. ◆ *adj* **2** *(usually postpositive) Inf.* in poor health; rather ill.

poort (pʊət) *n* (in South Africa) a steep narrow mountain pass, usually following a river or stream. [C19: from Afrik., from Du.: gateway]

poor White *n Often offens.* **a** a poverty-stricken and underprivileged White person, esp. in the southern US and South Africa. **b** *(as modifier): poor White trash.*

pop[1] 🅣 (pɒp) *vb* **pops, popping, popped. 1** to make or cause to make a light sharp explosive sound. **2** to burst open with such a sound. **3** *(intr;* often foll. by *in, out,* etc.) *Inf.* to come (to) or go (from) rapidly or suddenly. **4** *(intr)* (esp. of the eyes) to protrude: *her eyes popped with amazement.* **5** to shoot at (a target) with a firearm. **6** *(tr)* to place with a sudden movement: *she popped some tablets into her mouth.* **7** *(tr) Inf.* to pawn: *he popped his watch yesterday.* **8** *(tr) Sl.* to take (a drug) in pill form or as an injection. **9 pop the question.** *Inf.* to propose marriage. ◆ *n* **10** a light sharp explosive sound; crack. **11** *Inf.* a flavoured nonalcoholic carbonated beverage. ◆ *adv* **12** with a popping sound. ◆ See also **pop off.** [C14: imit.]

pop[2] (pɒp) *n* **1a** music of general appeal, esp. among young people, that originated as a distinctive genre in the 1950s. It is generally characterized by a heavy rhythmic element and the use of electrical amplification. **1b** *(as modifier): a pop group.* **2** *Inf.* a piece of popular or light classical music. ◆ *adj* **3** *Inf.* short for **popular.**

pop[3] (pɒp) *n* **1** an informal word for **father. 2** *Inf.* a name used in addressing an old man.

POP *abbrev. for* Post Office Preferred (size of envelopes, etc.).

pop. *abbrev. for:* **1** popular(ly). **2** population.

pop art *n* a movement in modern art that imitates the methods, styles, and themes of popular culture and mass media, such as comic strips, advertising, and science fiction.

popcorn ('pɒpˌkɔːn) *n* **1** a variety of maize having hard pointed kernels that puff up and burst when heated. **2** the puffed edible kernels of this plant.

pope 🅣 (pəʊp) *n* **1** *(often cap.)* the bishop of Rome as head of the Roman Catholic Church. **2** *Eastern Orthodox Churches.* a title sometimes given to a parish priest or to the Greek Orthodox patriarch of Alexandria. [OE *papa,* from Church L: bishop, esp. of Rome, from LGk *papas* father-in-God, from Gk *pappas* father]
► **'popedom** *n*

popery ('pəʊpərɪ) *n* a derogatory name for **Roman Catholicism.**

popeyed ('pɒpˌaɪd) *adj* **1** having bulging prominent eyes. **2** staring in astonishment.

popgun ('pɒpˌgʌn) *n* a toy gun that fires a pellet or cork by means of compressed air.

popinjay ('pɒpɪnˌdʒeɪ) *n* **1** a conceited, foppish, or excessively talkative person. **2** an archaic word for **parrot. 3** the figure of a parrot used as a target. [C13 *papeniai,* from OF *papegay* a parrot, from Sp., from Ar. *babaghā*]

popish ('pəʊpɪʃ) *adj Derog.* belonging to or characteristic of Roman Catholicism.

poplar ('pɒplə) *n* **1** a tree of N temperate regions, having triangular leaves, flowers borne in catkins, and light soft wood. **2** *US.* the tulip tree. [C14: from OF *poplier,* from L *pōpulus*]

poplin ('pɒplɪn) *n* a strong fabric, usually of cotton, in plain weave with fine ribbing. [C18: from F *papeline,* ?from *Poperinge,* a centre of textile manufacture in Flanders]

popliteal (pɒp'lɪtɪəl, ˌpɒplɪ'tiːəl) *adj* of, relating to, or near the part of the leg behind the knee. [C18: from NL *popliteus* the muscle behind the knee joint, from L *poples* the ham of the knee]

popmobility (ˌpɒpməʊ'bɪlɪtɪ) *n* a form of exercise that combines aerobics in a continuous dance routine, performed to pop music. [C20: POP[2] + MOBILITY]

pop off *vb (intr, adv) Inf.* **1** to depart suddenly or unexpectedly. **2** to die, esp. suddenly.

THESAURUS

pooh-pooh *vb* = **scorn**, belittle, brush aside, deride, disdain, dismiss, disregard, make little of, play down, scoff, slight, sneer, sniff at, spurn, turn up one's nose at *(inf.)*
Antonyms *vb* exalt, extol, glorify, praise

pool[1] *n* **1** = **pond**, lake, mere, puddle, splash, tarn **5** = **swimming pool**, swimming bath

pool[2] *n* **1** = **syndicate**, collective, combine, consortium, group, team, trust **2** = **kitty**, bank, funds, jackpot, pot, stakes ◆ *vb* **6** = **combine**, amalgamate, join forces, league, merge, put together, share

poor *adj* **1** = **impoverished**, badly off, broke, destitute, dirt-poor *(inf.)*, down and out, down at heel, flat broke *(inf.)*, hard up *(inf.)*, impecunious, indigent, in need, in queer street, in want, necessitous, needy, on one's uppers, on the breadline, penniless, penurious, poverty-stricken, short, skint *(Brit. sl.)*, stony-broke *(Brit. sl.)* **3, 4** = **meagre**, deficient, exiguous, inadequate, incomplete, insufficient, lacking, measly, miserable, niggardly, pathetic, pitiable, reduced, scant, scanty, skimpy, slight, sparse, straitened **5** = **inferior**, below par, faulty, feeble, low-grade, low-rent *(inf., chiefly US)*, mediocre, no great shakes *(inf.)*, not much cop *(Brit. sl.)*, rotten *(inf.)*, rubbishy, second-rate, shabby, shoddy, sorry, substandard, unsatisfactory, valueless, weak, worthless **8** = **unfortunate**, hapless, ill-fated, luckless, miserable, pathetic, pitiable, unhappy, unlucky, wretched
Antonyms *adj* ≠ **impoverished:** affluent, comfortable *(inf.)*, prosperous, rich, wealthy, well-heeled *(inf.)*, well-off ≠ **meagre:** abundant, adequate, ample, complete, dense, plentiful, satisfactory, sufficient, thick ≠ **inferior:** excellent, exceptional, first-class, first-rate, satisfactory, superior, valuable ≠ **unfortunate:** fortunate, happy, lucky, successful

poorly *adv* **1** = **badly**, crudely, inadequately, incompetently, inexpertly, inferiorly, insufficiently, meanly, shabbily, unsatisfactorily, unsuccessfully ◆ *adj* **2** *Informal* = **ill**, ailing, below par, indisposed, off colour, out of sorts, rotten *(inf.)*, seedy *(inf.)*, sick, under the weather *(inf.)*, unwell
Antonyms *adv* ≠ **badly:** acceptably, adequately, competently, expertly, satisfactorily, sufficiently, well ◆ *adj* ≠ **ill:** fit, hale and hearty, healthy, in good health, in the pink, well

pop[1] *vb* **1, 2** = **burst**, bang, crack, explode, go off, report, snap **3** *often foll. by* **in, out,** *etc. Informal* = **call**, appear, come *or* go suddenly, drop in *(inf.)*, leave quickly, nip in *or* out *(Brit. inf.)*, visit **4** = **protrude**, bulge, stick out **6** = **put**, insert, push, shove, slip, stick, thrust, tuck ◆ *n* **10** = **bang**, burst, crack, explosion, noise, report **11** *Informal* = **soft drink**, fizzy drink, ginger *(Scot.)*, lemonade, mineral water, soda water

pope *n* **1** = **Holy Father**, Bishop of Rome, pontiff, Vicar of Christ

poppadom *or* **poppadum** ('pɒpədəm) *n* a thin round crisp Indian bread, fried or roasted and served with curry, etc. [from Hindi]

popper ('pɒpə) *n* **1** a person or thing that pops. **2** *Brit.* an informal name for **press stud. 3** *Chiefly US & Canad.* a container for cooking popcorn in. **4** *Sl.* an amyl nitrite capsule, crushed and inhaled by drug users.

poppet ('pɒpɪt) *n* **1** a term of affection for a small child or sweetheart. **2** Also called: **poppet valve.** a mushroom-shaped valve that is lifted from its seating by applying an axial force to its stem. **3** *Naut.* a temporary supporting brace for a vessel hauled on land. [C14: early var. of PUPPET]

popping crease *n Cricket.* a line four feet in front of and parallel with the bowling crease, at or behind which the batsman stands. [C18: from POP[1] (in the obs. sense: to hit) + CREASE]

popple ('pɒpᵊl) *vb* **popples, poppling, poppled.** (*intr*) **1** (of boiling water or a choppy sea) to heave or toss; bubble. **2** (often foll. by *along*) (of a stream or river) to move with an irregular tumbling motion. [C14: imit.]

poppy ('pɒpɪ) *n, pl* **poppies. 1** any of numerous papaveraceous plants having red, orange, or white flowers and a milky sap. **2** any of several similar or related plants, such as the California poppy and Welsh poppy. **3** any of the drugs, such as opium, that are obtained from these plants. **4a** a strong red to reddish-orange colour. **4b** (*as adj*): *a poppy dress.* **5** an artificial red poppy flower worn to mark Remembrance Sunday. [OE *popæg,* ult. from L *papāver*]

poppycock ❶ ('pɒpɪˌkɒk) *n Inf.* nonsense. [C19: from Du. dialect *pappekak,* lit.: soft excrement]

Poppy Day *n* an informal name for **Remembrance Sunday.**

poppyhead ('pɒpɪˌhɛd) *n* **1** the hard dry seed-containing capsule of a poppy. **2** a carved ornament, esp. one used on the top of the end of a pew or bench in Gothic church architecture.

poppy seed *n* the small grey seeds of the opium poppy, used esp. on loaves.

pop socks *pl n* knee-length nylon stockings.

popsy ('pɒpsɪ) *n, pl* **popsies.** *Old-fashioned Brit. sl.* an attractive young woman. [C19: dim. from *pop,* shortened from POPPET; orig. a nursery term]

populace ❶ ('pɒpjʊləs) *n* (*sometimes functioning as pl*) **1** local inhabitants. **2** the common people; masses. [C16: via F from It. *popolaccio* the common herd, from *popolo* people, from L *populus*]

popular ❶ ('pɒpjʊlə) *adj* **1** widely favoured or admired. **2** favoured by an individual or limited group: *I'm not very popular with her.* **3** prevailing among the general public; common: *popular discontent.* **4** appealing to or comprehensible to the layman: *a popular lecture on physics.* ◆ *n* **5** (*usually pl*) a cheap newspaper with a mass circulation. [C15: from L *populāris* of the people, democratic]
▸**popularity** (ˌpɒpjʊ'lærɪtɪ) *n* ▸**'popularly** *adv*

popular front *n* (*often cap.*) any of the left-wing groups or parties that were organized from 1935 onwards to oppose the spread of fascism.

popularize ❶ *or* **popularise** ('pɒpjʊləˌraɪz) *vb* **popularizes, popularizing, popularized** *or* **popularises, popularising, popularised.** (*tr*) **1** to make popular. **2** to make or cause to become easily understandable or acceptable.
▸ˌ**populari'zation** *or* ˌ**populari'sation** *n* ▸**'popularˌizer** *or* **'popularˌiser** *n*

populate ❶ ('pɒpjʊˌleɪt) *vb* **populates, populating, populated.** (*tr*) **1** (*often passive*) to live in; inhabit. **2** to provide a population for; colonize or people. [C16: from Med. L *populāre,* from L *populus* people]

population ❶ (ˌpɒpjʊ'leɪʃən) *n* **1** (*sometimes functioning as pl*) all the persons inhabiting a specified place. **2** the number of such inhabitants. **3** (*sometimes functioning as pl*) all the people of a particular class in a specific area: *the Chinese population of San Francisco.* **4** the act or process of providing a place with inhabitants; colonization. **5** *Ecology.* a group of individuals of the same species inhabiting a given area. **6** *Astron.* either of two main groups of stars classified according to age and location. **7** *Statistics.* the entire aggregate of individuals or items from which samples are drawn.

population explosion *n* a rapid increase in the size of a population caused by such factors as a sudden decline in infant mortality or an increase in life expectancy.

population pyramid *n* a pyramid-shaped diagram illustrating the age distribution of a population: the youngest are represented by a rectangle at the base, the oldest by one at the apex.

populism ('pɒpjʊˌlɪzəm) *or* **popularism** *n* the practice, esp. by a politician of making a calculated appeal to the interests, tastes, or prejudices of ordinary people.

populist ('pɒpjʊˌlɪst) *adj* **1** appealing to the interests or prejudices of ordinary people. ◆ *n* **2** a person, esp. a politician, who appeals to the interests or prejudices of ordinary people.

Populist ('pɒpjʊlɪst) *n* **1** *US history.* a member of the People's Party, formed largely by agrarian interests to contest the 1892 presidential election. ◆ *adj* **2** of or relating to the People's Party or any individual or movement with similar aims. Also: **Populistic.**
▸**'Popuˌlism** *n*

populous ❶ ('pɒpjʊləs) *adj* containing many inhabitants. [C15: from LL *populōsus*]
▸**'populously** *adv* ▸**'populousness** *n*

porangi ('pɔːræŋɪ) *adj NZ inf.* crazy; mad. [from Maori]

porbeagle ('pɔːˌbiːgᵊl) *n* any of several voracious sharks of northern seas. Also called: **mackerel shark.** [C18: from Cornish *porgh-bugel,* from ?]

porcelain ('pɔːslɪn) *n* **1** a more or less translucent ceramic material, the principal ingredients being kaolin and petuntse (hard paste) or other clays, bone ash, etc. **2** an object made of this or such objects collectively. **3** (*modifier*) of, relating to, or made from this material: *a porcelain cup.* [C16: from F *porcelaine,* from It. *porcellana* cowrie shell, lit.: relating to a sow, from *porcella* little sow, from *porca* sow, from L; see PORK]
▸**porcellaneous** (ˌpɔːsə'leɪnɪəs) *adj*

porch (pɔːtʃ) *n* **1** a low structure projecting from the doorway of a house and forming a covered entrance. **2** *US & Canad.* a veranda. [C13: from F *porche,* from L *porticus* portico]

porcine ('pɔːsaɪn) *adj* of or characteristic of pigs. [C17: from L *porcīnus,* from *porcus* a pig]

porcupine ('pɔːkjʊˌpaɪn) *n* any of various large rodents that have a body covering of protective spines or quills. [C14 *porc despyne* pig with spines, from OF *porc espin;* see PORK, SPINE]
▸**'porcuˌpinish** *adj* ▸**'porcuˌpiny** *adj*

porcupine fish *n* any of various fishes of temperate and tropical seas having a body that is covered with sharp spines and can be inflated into a globe. Also called: **globefish.**

porcupine grass *n Austral.* another name for **spinifex.**

porcupine provisions *pl n Finance.* provisions, such as poison pills or staggered directorships, made in the bylaws of a company to deter takeover bids. Also called: **shark repellents.**

pore[1] ❶ (pɔː) *vb* **pores, poring, pored.** (*intr*) **1** (foll. by *over*) to make a close intent examination or study (of): *he pored over the documents for several hours.* **2** (foll. by *over, on,* or *upon*) to think deeply (about). **3** (foll. by *over, on,* or *upon*) *Rare.* to gaze fixedly (upon). [C13 *pouren*]

> **USAGE NOTE** See at **pour.**

pore[2] ❶ (pɔː) *n* **1** any small opening in the skin or outer surface of an animal. **2** *Bot.* any small aperture, esp. that of a stoma, through which water vapour and gases pass. **3** any other small hole, such as a space in a rock, etc. [C14: from LL *porus,* from Gk *poros* passage, pore]

porgy ('pɔːgɪ) *n, pl* **porgy** *or* **porgies.** any of various perchlike fishes, many of which occur in American Atlantic waters. [C18: from Sp. *pargo,* from L *phager,* from Gk *phagros* sea bream]

poriferan (pɔː'rɪfərən) *n* any invertebrate of the phylum *Porifera,* which comprises the sponges. [C19: from NL *porifer* bearing pores]

pork (pɔːk) *n* the flesh of pigs used as food. [C13: from OF *porc,* from L *porcus* pig]

porker ('pɔːkə) *n* a pig, esp. a young one, fattened to provide meat.

pork pie *n* **1** a pie filled with minced seasoned pork. **2** See **porky**[2].

porkpie hat ('pɔːkˌpaɪ) *n* a hat with a round flat crown and a brim that can be turned up or down.

porky[1] ('pɔːkɪ) *adj* **porkier, porkiest. 1** characteristic of pork. **2** *Inf.* fat; obese.

porky[2] ('pɔːkɪ) *n, pl* **porkies.** *Brit. sl.* a lie. Also called: **pork pie.** [from rhyming slang *pork pie* lie]

porn (pɔːn) *or* **porno** ('pɔːnəʊ) *n, adj Inf.* short for **pornography** or **pornographic.**

pornography ❶ (pɔː'nɒgrəfɪ) *n* **1** writings, pictures, films, etc., de-

THESAURUS

poppycock *n Informal* = **nonsense**, babble, balderdash, baloney (*inf.*), bilge (*inf.*), bunk (*inf.*), bunkum *or* buncombe (*chiefly US*), drivel, eyewash (*inf.*), garbage (*inf.*), gibberish, gobbledegook (*inf.*), guff (*sl.*), hogwash, hokum (*sl., chiefly US & Canad.*), hot air (*inf.*), moonshine, pap, piffle (*inf.*), rot, rubbish, tommyrot, trash, tripe (*inf.*), twaddle

populace *n* **1, 2** = **people**, commonalty, crowd, general public, hoi polloi, inhabitants, Joe (and Eileen) Public (*sl.*), Joe Six-Pack (*US sl.*), masses, mob, multitude, rabble, throng

popular *adj* **1** = **well-liked**, accepted, approved, celebrated, famous, fashionable, fave (*inf.*), favoured, favourite, in, in demand, in favour, liked, sought-after **3** = **common**, conventional, current, general, prevailing, prevalent, public, standard, stock, ubiquitous, universal, widespread
Antonyms *adj* ≠ **well-liked:** despised, detested, disliked, hated, loathed, unaccepted, unpopular ≠ **common:** infrequent, rare, uncommon, unusual

popularity *n* **1** = **favour**, acceptance, acclaim, adoration, approval, celebrity, currency, esteem, fame, idolization, lionization, recognition, regard, renown, reputation, repute, vogue

popularize *vb* **1, 2** = **make popular**, disseminate, familiarize, give currency to, give mass appeal, make available to all, simplify, spread, universalize

popularly *adv* **3** = **generally**, commonly, conventionally, customarily, ordinarily, regularly, traditionally, universally, usually, widely

populate *vb* **1, 2** = **inhabit**, colonize, live in, occupy, people, settle

population *n* **1** = **inhabitants**, citizenry, community, denizens, folk, natives, people, populace, residents, society

populous *adj* = **populated**, crowded, heavily populated, overpopulated, packed, swarming, teeming, thronged

pore[1] *vb* **1, 2** *foll. by* **over** = **study**, brood, contemplate, dwell on, examine, go over, peruse, ponder, read, scrutinize, work over

pore[2] *n* **1-3** = **opening**, hole, orifice, outlet, stoma

pornographic *adj* **1** = **obscene**, blue, dirty, filthy, indecent, lewd, offensive, prurient, salacious, smutty, X-rated (*inf.*)

pornography *n* **1** = **obscenity**, dirt, erotica, filth, indecency, porn (*inf.*), porno (*inf.*), smut

signed to stimulate sexual excitement. **2** the production of such material. ◆ Sometimes (informal) shortened to **porn** or **porno.** [C19: from Gk *pornographos* writing of harlots]
▸**por'nographer** *n* ▸**pornographic** (ˌpɔːnəˈɡræfɪk) *adj* ▸ˌ**porno'graphically** *adv*

poromeric (ˌpɔːrəˈmɛrɪk) *adj* **1** (of a plastic) permeable to water vapour. ◆ *n* **2** a substance having this characteristic, esp. one used in place of leather in making shoe uppers. [C20: from PORO(SITY) + (POLY)MER + -IC]

porous ❶ (ˈpɔːrəs) *adj* **1** permeable to water, air, or other fluids. **2** *Biol. & geol.* having pores. [C14: from Med. L *porōsus,* from LL *porus* PORE[2]]
▸ˈ**porously** *adv* ▸**porosity** (pɔːˈrɒsɪtɪ) *or* ˈ**porousness** *n*

porphyria (pɔːˈfɪrɪə) *n* a hereditary disease of body metabolism, producing abdominal pain, mental confusion, etc. [C19: from NL, from *porphyrin* a purple substance excreted by patients suffering from this condition, from Gk *porphura* purple]

porphyry (ˈpɔːfɪrɪ) *n, pl* **porphyries. 1** a reddish-purple rock consisting of large crystals of feldspar in a finer groundmass of feldspar, hornblende, etc. **2** any igneous rock with large crystals embedded in a finer groundmass of minerals. [C14 *porfurie,* from LL, from Gk *porphuritēs (lithos)* purple (stone), from *porphuros* purple]
▸ˌ**porphy'ritic** *adj*

porpoise (ˈpɔːpəs) *n, pl* **porpoises** *or* **porpoise.** any of various small cetacean mammals having a blunt snout and many teeth. [C14: from F *pourpois,* from Med. L *porcopiscus,* from L *porcus* pig + *piscis* fish]

porridge (ˈpɒrɪdʒ) *n* **1** a dish made from oatmeal or another cereal, cooked in water or milk to a thick consistency. **2** *Sl.* a term of imprisonment. [C16: var. (infl. by ME *porray* pottage) of POTTAGE]

porringer (ˈpɒrɪndʒə) *n* a small dish, often with a handle, for soup, porridge, etc. [C16: changed from ME *potinger, poteger,* from OF, from *potage* soup; see POTTAGE]

port[1] ❶ (pɔːt) *n* **1** a town or place alongside navigable water with facilities for the loading and unloading of ships. **2** See **port of entry.** [OE, from L *portus*]

port[2] (pɔːt) *n* **1** Also called (formerly): **larboard.** the left side of an aircraft or vessel when facing the nose or bow. Cf. **starboard** (sense 1). ◆ *vb* **2** to turn or be turned towards the port. [C17: from ?]

port[3] (pɔːt) *n* a sweet fortified dessert wine. [C17: after *Oporto,* Portugal, from where it came orig.]

port[4] (pɔːt) *n* **1** *Naut.* **1a** an opening in the side of a ship, fitted with a watertight door, for access to the holds. **1b** See **porthole** (sense 1). **2** a small opening in a wall, armoured vehicle, etc., for firing through. **3** an aperture by which fluid enters or leaves the cylinder head of an engine, compressor, etc. **4** *Electronics.* a logical circuit for the input and ouput of data. **5** *Chiefly Scot.* a gate in a town or fortress. [OE, from L *porta* gate]

port[5] (pɔːt) *vb (tr) Mil.* to carry (a rifle, etc.) in a position diagonally across the body with the muzzle near the left shoulder. [C14: from OF, from *porter* to carry, from L *portāre*]

port[6] (pɔːt) *n Austral.* (esp. in Queensland) a suitcase or school case. [C20: shortened from PORTMANTEAU]

Port. *abbrev. for:* **1** Portugal. **2** Portuguese.

portable ❶ (ˈpɔːtəbᵊl) *adj* **1** able to be carried or moved easily, esp. by hand. **2** (of computer software, files, etc.) able to be transferred from one type of computer system to another. ◆ *n* **3** an article designed to be readily carried by hand, such as a television, typewriter, etc. [C14: from LL *portābilis,* from L *portāre* to carry]
▸ˌ**porta'bility** *n* ▸ˈ**portably** *adv*

portage (ˈpɔːtɪdʒ) *n* **1** the act of carrying; transport. **2** the cost of carrying or transporting. **3** the transporting of boats, supplies, etc., overland between navigable waterways. **4** the route used for such transport. ◆ *vb* **portages, portaging, portaged. 5** to transport (boats, supplies, etc.) thus. [C15: from F, from OF *porter* to carry]

Portakabin (ˈpɔːtəˌkæbɪn) *n Trademark.* a portable building quickly set up for use as a temporary office, etc.

portal ❶ (ˈpɔːtᵊl) *n* **1** an entrance, gateway, or doorway, esp. one that is large and impressive ◆ *adj* **2** *Anat.* of or relating to a portal vein: *hepatic portal system.* [C14: via OF from Med. L *portāle,* from L *porta* gate]

portal vein *n* any vein connecting two capillary networks, esp. in the liver.

portamento (ˌpɔːtəˈmɛntəʊ) *n, pl* **portamenti** (-tɪ). *Music.* a smooth slide from one note to another in which intervening notes are not separately discernible. [C18: from It.: a carrying, from L *portāre* to carry]

portative (ˈpɔːtətɪv) *adj* **1** a less common word for **portable. 2** concerned with the act of carrying. [C14: from F, from L *portāre* to carry]

portcullis (pɔːtˈkʌlɪs) *n* an iron or wooden grating suspended vertically in grooves in the gateway of a castle or town and able to be lowered so as to bar the entrance. [C14 *port colice,* from OF *porte coleïce* sliding gate, from *porte* door + *coleïce,* from *couler* to slide, from LL *cōlāre* to filter]

Porte (pɔːt) *n* short for Sublime Porte; the court or government of the Ottoman Empire. [C17: shortened from F *Sublime Porte* High Gate, rendering the Turkish title *Babi Ali,* the imperial gate, regarded as the seat of government]

porte-cochere (ˌpɔːtkɒˈʃɛə) *n* **1** a large covered entrance for vehicles leading into a courtyard. **2** a large roof projecting over a drive to shelter travellers entering or leaving vehicles. [C17: from F: carriage entrance]

portend ❶ (pɔːˈtɛnd) *vb (tr)* to give warning of; foreshadow. [C15: from L *portendere* to indicate]

portent ❶ (ˈpɔːtɛnt) *n* **1** a sign of a future event; omen. **2** momentous or ominous significance: *a cry of dire portent.* **3** a marvel. [C16: from L *portentum* sign, from *portendere* to portend]

portentous ❶ (pɔːˈtɛntəs) *adj* **1** of momentous or ominous significance. **2** miraculous, amazing, or awe-inspiring. **3** self-important or pompous.

porter[1] ❶ (ˈpɔːtə) *n* **1** a person employed to carry luggage, parcels, supplies, etc., at a railway station or hotel. **2** (in hospitals) a person employed to move patients from place to place. **3** *US & Canad.* a railway employee who waits on passengers, esp. in a sleeper. [C14: from OF *portour,* from LL *portātōr,* from L *portāre* to carry]
▸ˈ**porterage** *n*

porter[2] ❶ (ˈpɔːtə) *n* **1** *Chiefly Brit.* a person in charge of a gate or door; doorman or gatekeeper. **2** a person employed as a caretaker and doorkeeper who also answers inquiries. **3** a person in charge of the maintenance of a building, esp. a block of flats. [C13: from OF *portier,* from LL *portārius,* from L *porta* door]

porter[3] (ˈpɔːtə) *n Brit.* a dark sweet ale brewed from black malt. [C18: from *porter's ale,* apparently because it was a favourite beverage of porters]

porterhouse (ˈpɔːtəˌhaʊs) *n* **1** Also called: **porterhouse steak.** a thick choice steak of beef cut from the middle ribs or sirloin. **2** (formerly) a place in which porter, beer, etc., and sometimes chops and steaks, were served. [C19 (sense 1): said to be after a porterhouse in New York]

portfire (ˈpɔːtˌfaɪə) *n* a slow-burning fuse used for firing rockets and fireworks and, in mining, for igniting explosives. [C17: from F *porte-feu,* from *porter* to carry + *feu* fire]

portfolio (pɔːtˈfəʊlɪəʊ) *n, pl* **portfolios. 1** a flat case, esp. of leather, used for carrying maps, drawings, etc. **2** the contents of such a case, such as drawings or photographs, that demonstrate recent work. **3** such a case used for carrying ministerial or state papers. **4** the responsibilities or role of the head of a government department: *the portfolio for foreign affairs.* **5 Minister without portfolio.** a cabinet minister who is not responsible for any government department. **6** the complete investments held by an individual investor or a financial organization. [C18: from It. *portafoglio,* from *portāre* to carry + *foglio* leaf, from L *folium*]

portfolio management *n* the service provided by an investment adviser who manages a financial portfolio on behalf of the investor.

porthole (ˈpɔːtˌhəʊl) *n* **1** a small aperture in the side of a vessel to admit light and air, fitted with a watertight cover. Sometimes shortened to **port. 2** an opening in a wall or parapet through which a gun can be fired.

portico (ˈpɔːtɪkəʊ) *n, pl* **porticoes** *or* **porticos. 1** a covered entrance to a building; porch. **2** a covered walkway in the form of a roof supported by columns or pillars, esp. one built on to the exterior of a building. [C17: via It. from L *porticus*]

portière (ˌpɔːtɪˈɛə; *French* pɔrtjɛr) *n* a curtain hung in a doorway. [C19: via F from Med. L *portāria,* from L *porta* door]
▸ˌ**porti'èred** *adj*

portion ❶ (ˈpɔːʃən) *n* **1** a part of a whole. **2** a part allotted or belonging to a person or group. **3** an amount of food served to one person; helping. **4** *Law.* **4a** a share of property, esp. one coming to a child from the estate of his parents. **4b** a dowry. **5** a person's lot or destiny. ◆ *vb (tr)* **6** to divide up; share out. **7** to give a share to (a person). [C13: via OF from L *portiō*]
▸ˈ**portionless** *adj*

Portland cement (ˈpɔːtlənd) *n* a cement that hardens under water and is made by heating clay and crushed chalk or limestone. [C19: after

THESAURUS

porous *adj* **1 = permeable**, absorbent, absorptive, penetrable, pervious, spongy
Antonyms *adj* impenetrable, impermeable, impervious, nonporous

port[1] *n* **1 = harbour**, anchorage, haven, roads, roadstead, seaport

portable *adj* **1 = light**, compact, convenient, easily carried, handy, lightweight, manageable, movable, portative

portal *n* **1 = doorway**, door, entrance, entrance way, entry, gateway, way in

portend *vb* **= foretell**, adumbrate, augur, bespeak, betoken, bode, foreshadow, foretoken, forewarn, harbinger, herald, indicate, omen, point to, predict, presage, prognosticate, promise, threaten, warn of

portent *n* **1 = omen**, augury, foreboding, foreshadowing, forewarning, harbinger, indication, premonition, presage, presentiment, prognostic, prognostication, sign, threat, warning

portentous *adj* **1 = significant**, alarming, crucial, fateful, forbidding, important, menacing, minatory, momentous, ominous, sinister, threatening **2 = remarkable**, amazing, astounding, awe-inspiring, extraordinary, miraculous, phenomenal, prodigious, wondrous (*arch. or literary*) **3 = pompous**, bloated, elephantine, heavy, ponderous, pontifical, self-important, solemn

porter[1] *n* **1 = baggage attendant**, bearer, carrier

porter[2] *n* **1-3 = doorman**, caretaker, concierge, gatekeeper, janitor

portion *n* **1 = part**, bit, fraction, fragment, morsel, piece, scrap, section, segment **2 = share**, allocation, allotment, allowance, division, lot, measure, parcel, quantity, quota, ration **3 = helping**, piece, serving **5 = destiny**, cup, fate, fortune, lot, luck ◆ *vb* **6 = divide**, allocate, allot, apportion, assign, deal, distribute, divvy up (*inf.*), dole out, parcel out, partition, share out

the *Isle of Portland*, a peninsula in Dorset, because its colour resembles that of the stone quarried there]

portly ❶ ('pɔːtlɪ) *adj* **portlier, portliest.** **1** stout or corpulent. **2** *Arch.* stately; impressive. [C16: from PORT[5] (in the sense: deportment)]
▸ **'portliness** *n*

portmanteau (pɔːt'mæntəʊ) *n, pl* **portmanteaus** *or* **portmanteaux** (-təʊz). **1** (formerly) a large travelling case made of stiff leather, esp. one hinged at the back so as to open out into two compartments. **2** (*modifier*) embodying several uses or qualities: *the heroine is a portmanteau figure of all the virtues.* [C16: from F: cloak carrier]

portmanteau word *n* another name for **blend** (sense 7). [C19: from the idea that two meanings are packed into one word]

port of call *n* **1** a port where a ship stops. **2** any place visited on a traveller's itinerary.

port of entry *n Law.* an airport, harbour, etc., where customs officials are stationed to supervise the entry into and exit from a country of persons and merchandise.

portrait ❶ ('pɔːtrɪt, -treɪt) *n* **1** a painting or other likeness of an individual, esp. of the face. **2** a verbal description, esp. of a person's character. ◆ *adj* **3** *Printing.* (of an illustration in a book, magazine, etc.) of greater height than width. Cf. **landscape** (sense 5a). [C16: from F, from *portraire* to PORTRAY]
▸ **'portraitist** *n*

portraiture ('pɔːtrɪtʃə) *n* **1** the practice or art of making portraits. **2a** a portrait. **2b** portraits collectively. **3** a verbal description.

portray ❶ (pɔː'treɪ) *vb (tr)* **1** to make a portrait of. **2** to depict in words. **3** to play the part of (a character) in a play or film. [C14: from OF *portraire* to depict, from L *prōtrahere* to drag forth]
▸ **por'trayal** *n* ▸ **por'trayer** *n*

Port-Salut ('pɔː sə'luː; *French* pɔrsaly) *n* a mild semihard whole-milk cheese of a round flat shape. Also called: **Port du Salut.** [C19: named after the Trappist monastery at *Port du Salut* in NW France where it was first made]

Portuguese (ˌpɔːtjʊ'giːz) *n* **1** the official language of Portugal and Brazil; it belongs to the Romance group of the Indo-European family. **2** (*pl* **Portuguese**) a native, citizen, or inhabitant of Portugal. ◆ *adj* **3** of Portugal, its inhabitants, or their language.

Portuguese man-of-war *n* any of several large hydrozoans having an aerial float and long stinging tentacles. Sometimes shortened to **man-of-war.**

portulaca (ˌpɔːtjʊ'lækə, -'leɪkə) *n* any of a genus of plants of tropical and subtropical America, having yellow, pink, or purple showy flowers. [C16: from L: PURSLANE]

POS *abbrev. for* point of sale.

pose[1] ❶ (pəʊz) *vb* **poses, posing, posed.** **1** to assume or cause to assume a physical attitude, as for a photograph or painting. **2** (*intr;* often foll. by *as*) to present oneself (as something one is not). **3** (*intr*) to affect an attitude in order to impress others. **4** (*tr*) to put forward or ask: *to pose a question.* **5** (*intr*) *Sl.* to adopt a particular style of appearance and stand or strut around, esp. in bars, discotheques, etc., in order to attract attention. ◆ *n* **6** a physical attitude, esp. one deliberately adopted for an artist or photographer. **7** a mode of behaviour that is adopted for effect. [C14: from OF *poser* to set in place, from LL *pausāre* to cease, put down (infl. by L *pōnere* to place)]

pose[2] (pəʊz) *vb* **poses, posing, posed.** (*tr*) *Rare.* to puzzle or baffle. [C16: from obs. *appose,* from L *appōnere* to put to]

poser[1] ('pəʊzə) *n* **1** a person who poses. **2** *Inf.* a person who likes to be seen in trendsetting clothes in fashionable bars, discos, etc.

poser[2] ❶ ('pəʊzə) *n* a baffling or insoluble question.

poseur ❶ (pəʊ'zɜː) *n* a person who strikes an attitude or assumes a pose in order to impress others. [C19: from F, from *poser* to POSE[1]]

posh ❶ (pɒʃ) *adj Inf., chiefly Brit.* **1** smart, elegant, or fashionable. **2** upper-class or genteel. [C19: often said to be an acronym of *port out, starboard home,* the most desirable location for a cabin in British ships sailing to & from the East, being the shaded side; but more likely from obs. sl. *posh* (n) a dandy]

posit ❶ ('pɒzɪt) *vb (tr)* **1** to assume or put forward as fact or the factual basis for an argument; postulate. **2** to put in position. [C17: from L *pōnere* to place]

position ❶ (pə'zɪʃən) *n* **1** place, situation, or location: *he took up a position to the rear.* **2** the appropriate or customary location: *the telescope is in position for use.* **3** the manner in which a person or thing is placed; arrangement. **4** *Mil.* an area or point occupied for tactical reasons. **5** point of view; stand: *what's your position on this issue?* **6** social status, esp. high social standing. **7** a post of employment; job. **8** the act of positing a fact or viewpoint. **9** something posited, such as an idea. **10** *Sport.* the part of a field or playing area where a player is placed or where he generally operates. **11** *Music.* the vertical spacing or layout of the written notes in a chord. **12** (in classical prosody) the situation in which a short vowel may be regarded as long, that is, when it occurs before two or more consonants. **13** *Finance.* the market commitment of a dealer in securities, currencies, or commodities: *a short position.* **14** **in a position.** (foll. by an infinitive) able (to). ◆ *vb (tr)* **15** to put in the proper or appropriate place; locate. **16** *Sport.* to place (oneself or another player) in a particular part of the field or playing area. [C15: from LL *positiō* a positioning, affirmation, from *pōnere* to place]
▸ **po'sitional** *adj*

positional notation *n* the method of denoting numbers by the use of a finite number of digits, each digit having its value multiplied by its place value, as in $936 = (9 \times 100) + (3 \times 10) + 6$.

position audit *n Commerce.* a systematic assessment of the current strengths and weaknesses of an organization as a prerequisite for future strategic planning.

positive ❶ ('pɒzɪtɪv) *adj* **1** expressing certainty or affirmation: *a positive answer.* **2** possessing actual or specific qualities; real: *a positive benefit.* **3** tending to emphasize what is good or laudable; constructive: *he takes a very positive attitude when correcting pupils' mistakes.* **4** tending towards progress or improvement. **5** *Philosophy.* constructive rather than sceptical. **6** (*prenominal*) *Inf.* (intensifier): *a positive delight.* **7** *Maths.* having a value greater than zero: *a positive number.* **8** *Maths.* **8a** measured in a direction opposite to that regarded as negative. **8b** having the same magnitude as but opposite sense to an equivalent negative quantity. **9** *Grammar.* denoting the usual form of an adjective as opposed to its comparative or superlative form. **10** *Physics.* **10a** (of an electric charge) having an opposite polarity to the charge of an electron and the same polarity as the charge of a proton. **10b** (of a body, system, ion, etc.) having a positive electric charge. **11** short for **electropositive.** **12** *Med.* (of the results of an examination or test) indicating the presence of a suspected disorder or organism. **13** *Economics.* of or denoting an analysis that is free of ethical, political, or value judgments. ◆ *n* **14** something that is positive. **15** *Maths.* a quantity greater than zero. **16** *Photog.* a print or slide showing a photographic image whose colours or tones correspond to those of the original subject. **17** *Grammar.* the positive degree of an adjective or adverb. **18** a positive object, such as a terminal or plate in a voltaic cell. [C13: from LL *positīvus,* from *pōnere* to place]
▸ **'positiveness** *or* ˌ**posi'tivity** *n*

positive discrimination *n* the provision of special opportunities for a disadvantaged group.

positive feedback *n* See **feedback** (sense 2).

positively ❶ ('pɒzɪtɪvlɪ) *adv* **1** in a positive manner. **2** (intensifier): *he disliked her; in fact, he positively hated her.*

THESAURUS

portly *adj* **1** = **stout,** ample, beefy (*inf.*), bulky, burly, corpulent, fat, fleshy, heavy, large, obese, overweight, plump, rotund, tubby (*inf.*)

portrait *n* **1** = **picture,** image, likeness, painting, photograph, portraiture, representation, sketch **2** = **description,** account, characterization, depiction, portrayal, profile, thumbnail sketch, vignette

portray *vb* **1** = **represent,** delineate, depict, draw, figure, illustrate, limn, paint, picture, render, sketch **2** = **describe,** characterize, depict, paint a mental picture of, put in words **3** = **play,** act the part of, represent

portrayal *n* **1-3** = **representation,** characterization, delineation, depiction, description, impersonation, interpretation, performance, picture, rendering, take (*inf., chiefly US*)

pose[1] *vb* **1** = **position,** arrange, model, sit, sit for **2** *often foll. by* **as** = **impersonate,** feign, masquerade as, pass oneself off as, pretend to be, profess to be, sham **3** = **put on airs,** affect, attitudinize, posture, show off (*inf.*), strike an attitude **4** = **present,** advance, ask, posit, propound, put, put forward, set, state, submit ◆ *n* **6** = **posture,** attitude, bearing, mien (*literary*), position, stance **7** = **act,** affectation, air, attitudinizing, façade, front, mannerism, masquerade, posturing, pretence, role

poser[2] *n* = **puzzle,** brain-teaser, conundrum, enigma, knotty point, problem, question, riddle, teaser, tough one, vexed question

poseur *n* = **show-off** (*inf.*), attitudinizer, exhibitionist, hot dog (*chiefly US*), impostor, mannerist, masquerader, poser, posturer, self-publicist

posh *adj* **1, 2** *Informal, chiefly Brit.* = **upper-class,** classy (*sl.*), elegant, exclusive, fashionable, grand, high-class, high-toned, la-di-da (*inf.*), luxurious, luxury, ritzy (*sl.*), smart, stylish, swanky (*inf.*), swish (*inf., chiefly Brit.*), top-drawer, up-market

posit *vb* **1** = **put forward,** advance, assert, assume, postulate, predicate, presume, propound, state, submit

position *n* **1** = **place,** area, bearings, locale, locality, location, point, post, reference, site, situation, spot, station, whereabouts **3** = **posture,** arrangement, attitude, disposition, pose, stance **5** = **attitude,** angle, belief, opinion, outlook, point of view, slant, stance, stand, standpoint, view, viewpoint **6** = **status,** caste, class, consequence, eminence, importance, place, prestige, rank, reputation, standing, station, stature **7** = **job,** berth (*inf.*), billet (*inf.*), capacity, duty, employment, function, occupation, office, place, post, role, situation ◆ *vb* **15** = **place,** arrange, array, dispose, fix, lay out, locate, put, sequence, set, settle, stand, stick (*inf.*)

positive *adj* **1** = **certain,** assured, confident, convinced, sure **2** = **definite,** absolute, actual, affirmative, categorical, certain, clear, clear-cut, conclusive, concrete, decisive, direct, explicit, express, firm, incontrovertible, indisputable, real, unequivocal, unmistakable **3** = **helpful,** beneficial, constructive, effective, efficacious, forward-looking, practical, productive, progressive, useful **6** *Informal* = **absolute,** complete, consummate, downright, out-and-out, perfect, rank, thorough, thoroughgoing, unmitigated, utter

Antonyms *adj* ≠ **certain:** not confident, unassured, uncertain, unconvinced, unsure ≠ **definite:** contestable, disputable, doubtful, inconclusive, indecisive, indefinite, uncertain ≠ **helpful:** conservative, detrimental, harmful, impractical, reactionary, unhelpful, useless

positively *adv* **1, 2** = **definitely,** absolutely, assuredly, categorically, certainly, emphatically, firmly, surely, undeniably, unequivocally, unmistakably, unquestionably, with certainty, without qualification

positive vetting *n* the checking of a person's background, to assess his suitability for a position that may involve national security.

positivism (ˈpɒzɪtɪˌvɪzəm) *n* **1** a form of empiricism, esp. as established by Auguste Comte, that rejects metaphysics and theology and holds that experimental investigation and observation are the only sources of substantial knowledge. See also **logical positivism. 2** the quality of being definite, certain, etc.
▸ˈ**positivist** *n, adj*

positron (ˈpɒzɪˌtrɒn) *n Physics.* the antiparticle of the electron, having the same mass but an equal and opposite charge. [C20: from *posi(tive + elec)tron*]

positron emission tomography *n* a technique for assessing brain activity and function by recording the emission of positrons when radioactively labelled glucose, introduced into the brain, is metabolized.

positronium (ˌpɒzɪˈtrəʊnɪəm) *n Physics.* a short-lived entity consisting of a positron and an electron bound together.

posology (pəˈsɒlədʒɪ) *n* the branch of medicine concerned with the determination of appropriate doses of drugs or agents. [C19: from F *posologie,* from Gk *posos* how much]

poss. *abbrev. for:* **1** possession. **2** possessive. **3** possible. **4** possibly.

posse (ˈpɒsɪ) *n* **1** *US.* short for **posse comitatus,** the able-bodied men of a district forming a group upon whom the sheriff may call for assistance in maintaining law and order. **2** *Sl.* a Jamaican street gang in the US. **3** *Inf.* a group of friends or associates. **4** (in W Canada) a troop of trained horses and riders who perform at stampedes. **5** *Law.* possibility (esp. in **in posse**). [C16: from Med. L (n): power, from L (vb): to be able]

posse comitatus (ˌkɒmɪˈtɑːtəs) *n* the formal legal term for **posse** (sense 1). [Med. L: strength (manpower) of the county]

possess Ⓣ (pəˈzɛs) *vb (tr)* **1** to have as one's property; own. **2** to have as a quality, characteristic, etc.: *to possess good eyesight.* **3** to have knowledge of: *to possess a little French.* **4** to gain control over or dominate: *whatever possessed you to act so foolishly?* **5** (foll. by *of*) to cause to be the owner or possessor: *I am possessed of the necessary information.* **6** to have sexual intercourse with. **7** *Now rare.* to maintain (oneself or one's feelings) in a certain state or condition: *possess yourself in patience until I tell you the news.* [C15: from OF *possesser,* from L *possidēre*]
▸**posˈsessor** *n* ▸**posˈsessory** *adj*

possessed Ⓣ (pəˈzɛst) *adj* **1** (foll. by *of*) owning or having. **2** (*usually postpositive*) under the influence of a powerful force, such as a spirit or strong emotion. **3** a less common term for **self-possessed.**

possession Ⓣ (pəˈzɛʃən) *n* **1** the act of possessing or state of being possessed: *in possession of the crown.* **2** anything that is owned or possessed. **3** (*pl*) wealth or property. **4** the state of being controlled by or as if by evil spirits. **5** the occupancy of land, property, etc., whether or not accompanied by ownership: *to take possession of a house.* **6** a territory subject to a foreign state: *colonial possessions.* **7** *Sport.* control of the ball, puck, etc., as exercised by a player or team: *he got possession in his own half.*

possessive Ⓣ (pəˈzɛsɪv) *adj* **1** of or relating to possession. **2** having or showing an excessive desire to possess or dominate: *a possessive husband.* **3** *Grammar.* **3a** another word for **genitive. 3b** denoting an inflected form of a noun or pronoun used to convey the idea of possession, association, etc., as *my* or *Harry's.* ◆ *n* **4** *Grammar.* **4a** the possessive case. **4b** a word or speech element in the possessive case.
▸**posˈsessively** *adv* ▸**posˈsessiveness** *n*

posset (ˈpɒsɪt) *n* a drink of hot milk curdled with ale, beer, etc., flavoured with spices, formerly used as a remedy for colds. [C15 *poshoote,* from ?]

possibility Ⓣ (ˌpɒsɪˈbɪlɪtɪ) *n, pl* **possibilities. 1** the state or condition of being possible. **2** anything that is possible. **3** a competitor, candidate, etc., who has a moderately good chance of winning, being chosen, etc. **4** (*often pl*) a future prospect or potential: *my new house has great possibilities.*

possible Ⓣ (ˈpɒsɪbᵊl) *adj* **1** capable of existing, taking place, or proving true without contravention of any natural law. **2** capable of being achieved: *it is not possible to finish in three weeks.* **3** having potential: *the idea is a possible money-spinner.* **4** feasible but less than probable: *it is possible that man will live on Mars.* **5** *Logic.* (of a statement, formula, etc.) capable of being true under some interpretation or in some circumstances. ◆ *n* **6** another word for **possibility** (sense 3). [C14: from L *possibilis* that may be, from *posse* to be able]

> **USAGE NOTE** Although it is very common to talk about something being *very possible* or *more possible,* these uses are generally thought to be incorrect, since *possible* describes an absolute state, and therefore something can only be *possible* or *not possible: it is very likely* (not *very possible*) *that he will resign; it has now become easier* (not *more possible*) *to obtain an entry visa.*

possibly Ⓣ (ˈpɒsɪblɪ) *sentence substitute, adv* **1a** perhaps or maybe. **1b** (*as sentence modifier*): *possibly he'll come.* ◆ *adv* **2** by any chance; at all: *he can't possibly come.*

possum (ˈpɒsəm) *n* **1** an informal name for **opossum. 2** an Australian and New Zealand name for **phalanger. 3 play possum.** to pretend to be dead, ignorant, asleep, etc., in order to deceive an opponent. **4 stir the possum** *Austral. sl.* to cause trouble.

post[1] Ⓣ (pəʊst) *n* **1** a length of wood, metal, etc., fixed upright to serve as a support, marker, point of attachment, etc. **2** *Horse racing.* **2a** either of two upright poles marking the beginning (**starting post**) and end (**winning post**) of a racecourse. **2b** the finish of a horse race. ◆ *vb (tr)* **3** (sometimes foll. by *up*) to fasten or put up (a notice) in a public place. **4** to announce by or as if by means of a poster: *to post banns.* **5** to publish (a name) on a list. **6** to denounce publicly; brand. [OE, from L *postis*]

post[2] Ⓣ (pəʊst) *n* **1** a position to which a person is appointed or elected; appointment; job. **2** a position to which a person, such as a sentry, is assigned for duty. **3** a permanent military establishment. **4** *Brit.* either of two military bugle calls (**first post** and **last post**) giving notice of the time to retire for the night. **5** See **trading post.** ◆ *vb* **6** *(tr)* to assign to or station at a particular place or position. **7** *Chiefly Brit.* to transfer to a different unit or ship on taking up a new appointment, etc. [C16: from F *poste,* from It. *posto,* ult. from L *pōnere* to place]

post[3] Ⓣ (pəʊst) *n* **1** *Chiefly Brit.* letters, packages, etc., that are transported and delivered by the Post Office; mail. **2** *Chiefly Brit.* a single collection or delivery of mail. **3** *Brit.* an official system of mail delivery. **4** (formerly) any of a series of stations furnishing relays of men and horses to deliver mail over a fixed route. **5** a rider who carried mail between such stations. **6** *Brit.* a postbox or post office: *take this to the post.* **7** any of various book sizes, esp. 5¼ by 8¼ inches (**post octavo**). **8 by return of post.** *Brit.* by the next mail in the opposite direction. ◆ *vb* **9** *(tr) Chiefly Brit.* to send by post. US and Canad. word: **mail. 10** *(tr) Book-keeping.* **10a** to enter (an item) in a ledger. **10b** (often foll. by *up*) to compile or enter all paper items in (a ledger). **11** *(tr)* to inform of the latest news. **12** *(intr)* (formerly) to travel with relays of post horses. **13** *Arch.* to travel or dispatch with speed; hasten. ◆ *adv* **14** with speed; rapidly. **15** (formerly) by means of post horses. [C16: via F from It. *poste,* from L *posita* something placed, from *pōnere* to put]

post- *prefix* **1** after in time or sequence; following; subsequent: *postgraduate.* **2** behind; posterior to: *postorbital.* [from L, from *post* after, behind]

postage (ˈpəʊstɪdʒ) *n* **a** the charge for delivering a piece of mail. **b** (*as modifier*): *postage charges.*

postage meter *n Chiefly US & Canad.* a postal franking machine. Also called: **postal meter.**

postage stamp *n* **1** a printed paper label with a gummed back for attaching to mail as an official indication that the required postage has been paid. **2** a mark printed on an envelope, etc., serving the same function.

postal (ˈpəʊstᵊl) *adj* of or relating to a Post Office or to the mail-delivery service.
▸ˈ**postally** *adv*

postal note *n Austral. & NZ.* the usual name for **postal order.**

postal order *n* a written order for the payment of a sum of money, to a named payee, obtainable and payable at a post office.

postbag (ˈpəʊstˌbæg) *n* **1** *Chiefly Brit.* another name for **mailbag. 2** the mail received by a magazine, radio programme, public figure, etc.

postbox (ˈpəʊstˌbɒks) *n* another name for **letter box** (sense 2).

postcard (ˈpəʊstˌkɑːd) *n* a card, often bearing a photograph, picture, etc., on one side (**picture postcard**), for sending a message by post without an envelope. Also called (US): **postal card.**

THESAURUS

possess *vb* **1, 2** = **have**, be blessed with, be born with, be endowed with, enjoy, have to one's name, hold, own **4** = **seize**, acquire, control, dominate, hold, occupy, take over, take possession of

possessed *adj* **2** = **crazed**, bedevilled, berserk, bewitched, consumed, cursed, demented, enchanted, frenetic, frenzied, hag-ridden, haunted, maddened, obsessed, raving, under a spell

possession *n* **1** = **ownership**, control, custody, hold, occupancy, occupation, proprietorship, tenure, title **3** *plural* = **property**, assets, belongings, chattels, effects, estate, goods and chattels, things, wealth **6** = **province**, colony, dominion, protectorate, territory

possessive *adj* **2** = **jealous**, acquisitive, controlling, covetous, dominating, domineering, grasping, overprotective, selfish

possibility *n* **1** = **feasibility**, likelihood, plausibility, potentiality, practicability, workableness **2** = **likelihood**, chance, hazard, hope, liability, odds, probability, prospect, risk **4** *often plural* = **potential**, capabilities, potentiality, promise, prospects, talent

possible *adj* **1** = **conceivable**, credible, hypothetical, imaginable, likely, potential **2** = **feasible**, attainable, doable, on (*inf.*), practicable, realizable, viable, within reach, workable **3** = **likely**, hopeful, potential, probable, promising
Antonyms *adj* ≠ **conceivable:** impossible, inconceivable, incredible, unimaginable, unlikely, unthinkable ≠ **feasible:** impossible, impracticable, unfeasible, unobtainable, unreasonable ≠ **likely:** impossible, improbable

possibly *adv* **1** = **perhaps**, God willing, haply, maybe, mayhap (*arch.*), peradventure (*arch.*), perchance (*arch.*) **2** = **at all**, by any chance, by any means, in any way

post[1] *n* **1** = **support**, column, newel, pale, palisade, picket, pillar, pole, shaft, stake, standard, stock, upright ◆ *vb* **3-5** = **put up**, advertise, affix, announce, display, make known, pin up, proclaim, promulgate, publicize, publish, stick up

post[2] *n* **1** = **job**, appointment, assignment, berth (*inf.*), billet (*inf.*), employment, office, place, position, situation **2** = **station**, beat, place, position ◆ *vb* **6** = **station**, assign, establish, locate, place, position, put, situate

post[3] *n* **2, 3** = **mail**, collection, delivery, postal service ◆ *vb* **9** = **send**, dispatch, mail, transmit

post chaise *n* a closed four-wheeled horse-drawn coach used as a rapid means for transporting mail and passengers in the 18th and 19th centuries. [C18: from POST[3] + CHAISE]

postclassical (pəʊst'klæsɪkᵊl) *adj* (esp. of Greek or Roman literature) later than the classical period.

postcode ('pəʊst,kəʊd) *n* a code of letters and digits used as part of a postal address to aid the sorting of mail. Also called: **postal code.** US name: **zip code.**

postconsonantal (pəʊst,kɒnsə'næntᵊl) *adj* (of a speech sound) immediately following a consonant.

postdate (pəʊst'deɪt) *vb* **postdates, postdating, postdated.** (*tr*) **1** to write a future date on (a document, etc.), as on a cheque to prevent it being paid until then. **2** to assign a date to (an event, period, etc.) that is later than its previously assigned date of occurrence. **3** to be or occur at a later date than.

postdoctoral (pəʊst'dɒktərəl) *adj* of, relating to, or designating studies, research, or professional work above the level of a doctorate.

poster ❶ ('pəʊstə) *n* **1** a large printed picture, used for decoration. **2** a placard or bill posted in a public place as an advertisement. **3** a person who posts bills.

poste restante ('pəʊst rɪ'stænt) *n* **1** an address on mail indicating that it should be kept at a specified post office until collected by the addressee. **2** the mail-delivery service or post-office department that handles mail having this address. ◆ US and Canad. equivalent: **general delivery.** [F, lit.: mail remaining]

posterior ❶ (pɒ'stɪərɪə) *adj* **1** situated at the back of or behind something. **2** coming after or following another in a series. **3** coming after in time. ◆ *n* **4** the buttocks; rump. [C16: from L: latter, from *posterus* coming next, from *post* after]
▸**pos'teriorly** *adv*

posterity ❶ (pɒ'stɛrɪtɪ) *n* **1** future or succeeding generations. **2** all of one's descendants. [C14: from F *postérité,* from L *posteritās,* from *posterus* coming after, from *post* after]

postern ('pɒstən) *n* a back door or gate, esp. one that is for private use. [C13: from OF *posterne,* from LL *posterula* (*jānua*) a back (entrance), from *posterus* coming behind]

poster paint *or* **colour** *n* a gum-based opaque watercolour paint used for writing posters, etc.

postfeminist (pəʊst'fɛmɪnɪst) *adj* **1** resulting from or including the beliefs and ideas of feminism. **2** differing from or showing moderation of these beliefs and ideas. ◆ *n* **3** a person who believes in or advocates any of the ideas that have developed from the feminist movement.

post-Fordism (,pəʊst'fɔːdɪzəm) *n* the idea that modern industrial production has moved away from mass production in huge factories, as pioneered by Henry Ford (1863–1947), US car manufacturer, towards specialized markets based on small flexible manufacturing units.
▸**,post-'Fordist** *adj*

post-free *adv, adj* **1** *Brit.* with the postage prepaid; postpaid. **2** free of postal charge.

postglacial (pəʊst'gleɪsɪəl, -ʃəl) *adj* formed or occurring after a glacial period.

postgraduate (pəʊst'grædjʊɪt) *n* **1** a student who has obtained a degree from a university, etc., and is pursuing studies for a more advanced qualification. **2** (*modifier*) of or relating to such a student or his studies. ◆ Also (US and Canad.): **graduate.**

posthaste ❶ ('pəʊst'heɪst) *adv* **1** with great haste. ◆ *n* **2** *Arch.* great haste.

post horn *n* a simple valveless natural horn consisting of a long tube of brass or copper.

post horse *n* (formerly) a horse kept at an inn or post house for use by postriders or for hire to travellers.

post house *n* (formerly) a house or inn where horses were kept for postriders or for hire to travellers.

posthumous ('pɒstjʊməs) *adj* **1** happening or continuing after one's death. **2** (of a book, etc.) published after the author's death. **3** (of a child) born after the father's death. [C17: from L *postumus* the last, but modified as though from L *post* after + *humus* earth, that is, after the burial]
▸**'posthumously** *adv*

posthypnotic suggestion (,pəʊsthɪp'nɒtɪk) *n* a suggestion made to the subject while he is in a hypnotic trance, to be acted upon at some time after emerging from the trance.

postiche (pɒ'stiːʃ) *adj* **1** (of architectural ornament) inappropriately applied; sham. **2** false or artificial; spurious. ◆ *n* **3** another term for **hairpiece** (sense 2). **4** anything that is false; sham or pretence. [C19: from F, from It. *apposticcio* (n), from LL *appositīcius* (adj); see APPOSITE]

postilion *or* **postillion** (pɒ'stɪljən) *n* a person who rides the near horse of the leaders in order to guide a team of horses drawing a coach. [C16: from F *postillon,* from It. *postiglione,* from *posta* POST[3]]

postimpressionism (,pəʊstɪm'prɛʃə,nɪzəm) *n* a movement in painting in France at the end of the 19th century which rejected the naturalism and momentary effects of impressionism but adapted its use of pure colour to paint subjects with greater subjective emotion.
▸**,postim'pressionist** *n, adj*

post-industrial (,pəʊstɪn'dʌstrɪəl) *adj* denoting work or a society that is no longer based on heavy industry.

posting ('pəʊstɪŋ) *n* **1** an appointment to a position or post, usually in another town or country. **2** *Computing.* an electronic message sent to a bulletin board, website, etc., and intended for access by every user.

postliminy (pəʊst'lɪmɪnɪ) *or* **postliminium** (,pəʊstlɪ'mɪnɪəm) *n, pl* **postliminies** *or* **postliminia** (-ɪə). *International law.* the right by which persons and property seized in war are restored to their former status on recovery. [C17: from L *post* behind + *limen, liminis* threshold]

postlude ('pəʊstluːd) *n Music.* a final or concluding piece or movement. [C19: from POST- + *-lude,* from L *lūdus* game; cf. PRELUDE]

postman ('pəʊstmən) *or* (*fem*) **postwoman** *n, pl* **postmen** *or* **postwomen.** a person who carries and delivers mail as a profession.

postman's knock *n* a children's party game in which a kiss is exchanged for a pretend letter.

postmark ('pəʊst,mɑːk) *n* **1** any mark stamped on mail by postal officials, usually showing the date and place of posting. ◆ *vb* **2** (*tr*) to put such a mark on (mail).

postmaster ('pəʊst,mɑːstə) *n* **1** Also (*fem*) **postmistress.** an official in charge of a local post office. **2** the person responsible for managing the electronic mail at a site.

postmaster general *n, pl* **postmasters general.** the executive head of the postal service in certain countries.

postmeridian (,pəʊstmə'rɪdɪən) *adj* after noon; in the afternoon or evening. [C17: from L *postmerīdiānus* in the afternoon]

post meridiem ('pəʊst mə'rɪdɪəm) the full form of **p.m.** [C17: L: after noon]

post mill *n* a windmill built around a central post on which the whole mill can be turned so that the sails catch the wind.

postmillennialism (,pəʊstmɪ'lɛnɪə,lɪzəm) *n Christian theol.* the doctrine or belief that the Second Coming of Christ will be preceded by the millennium.
▸**,postmil'lennialist** *n*

postmodernism (pəʊst'mɒdə,nɪzəm) *n* (in the arts, architecture, etc.) a style and school of thought that rejects the dogma and practices of any form of modernism; in architecture it contrasts with international modernism and features elements from several periods, esp. the Classical, often with ironic use of decoration.
▸**post'modernist** *n, adj*

postmortem ❶ (pəʊst'mɔːtəm) *adj* **1** (*prenominal*) occurring after death. ◆ *n* **2** analysis or study of a recent event: *a postmortem on a game of chess.* **3** See **postmortem examination.** [C18: from L, lit.: after death]

postmortem examination *n* dissection and examination of a dead body to determine the cause of death. Also called: **autopsy, necropsy.**

postnatal (pəʊst'neɪtᵊl) *adj* of or relating to the period after childbirth.

post-obit (pəʊst'əʊbɪt, -'ɒbɪt) *Chiefly law.* ◆ *n* **1** a bond given by a borrower, payable after the death of a specified person, esp. one given to a moneylender by an expectant heir promising to repay when his interest falls into possession. ◆ *adj* **2** taking effect after death. [C18: from L *post obitum* after death]

post office *n* a building or room where postage stamps are sold and other postal business is conducted.

Post Office *n* a government department or authority in many countries responsible for postal services and often telecommunications.

post office box *n* a private numbered place in a post office, in which letters received are kept until called for.

postoperative (pəʊst'ɒpərətɪv) *adj* of or occurring in the period following a surgical operation.

post-paid *adv, adj* with the postage prepaid.

postpone ❶ (pəʊst'pəʊn, pə'spəʊn) *vb* **postpones, postponing, postponed.** (*tr*) **1** to put off or delay until a future time. **2** to put behind in order of importance; defer. [C16: from L *postpōnere* to put after]
▸**post'ponement** *n*

postpositive (pəʊst'pɒzɪtɪv) *adj* **1** (of an adjective or other modifier) placed after the word modified, either immediately after, as in *two men abreast,* or as part of a complement, as in *those men are bad.* ◆ *n* **2** a postpositive modifier.

postprandial (pəʊst'prændɪəl) *adj usually humorous.* after a meal.

postrider ('pəʊst,raɪdə) *n* (formerly) a person who delivered post on horseback.

postscript ❶ ('pəʊs,skrɪpt, 'pəʊst-) *n* **1** a message added at the end of a letter, after the signature. **2** any supplement, as to a document or book. [C16: from LL *postscribere* to write after]

THESAURUS

poster *n* **2** = **notice**, advertisement, *affiche*, announcement, bill, placard, public notice, sticker

posterior *adj* **1** = **behind**, after, back, hind, hinder, rear **2, 3** = **later**, ensuing, following, latter, subsequent

posterity *n* **1** = **future**, future generations, succeeding generations **2** = **descendants**, children, family, heirs, issue, offspring, progeny, scions, seed (*chiefly Biblical*)

posthaste *adv* **1** = **speedily**, at once, directly, double-quick, full tilt, hastily, hotfoot, promptly, pronto (*inf.*), quickly, straightaway, swiftly

postmortem *n* **3** = **examination**, analysis, autopsy, dissection, necropsy

postpone *vb* **1, 2** = **put off**, adjourn, defer, delay, hold over, put back, put on ice (*inf.*), put on the back burner (*inf.*), shelve, suspend, table, take a rain check on (*US & Canad. inf.*)
Antonyms *vb* advance, bring forward, call to order, carry out, go ahead with

postponement *n* **1, 2** = **delay**, adjournment, deferment, deferral, moratorium, respite, stay, suspension

postscript *n* **1, 2** = **P.S.**, addition, afterthought, afterword, appendix, supplement

poststructuralism (pəʊst'strʌktʃərəˌlɪzəm) *n* an approach to literature that, proceeding from the tenets of structuralism, maintains that, as words have no absolute meaning, any text is open to an unlimited range of interpretations.
▸**post'structuralist** *n, adj*

post-traumatic stress disorder *n* a psychological condition, characterized by anxiety, withdrawal, and a proneness to physical illness, that may follow a traumatic experience.

postulant ('pɒstjʊlənt) *n* a person who makes a request or application, esp. a candidate for admission to a religious order. [C18: from L *postulāns* asking, from *postulāre* to ask]

postulate Ⓣ *vb* ('pɒstjʊˌleɪt), **postulates, postulating, postulated.** (*tr; may take a clause as object*) **1** to assume to be true or existent; take for granted. **2** to ask, demand, or claim. **3** to nominate (a person) to a post or office subject to approval by a higher authority. ◆ *n* ('pɒstjʊlɪt). **4** something taken as self-evident or assumed as the basis of an argument. **5** a prerequisite. **6** a fundamental principle. **7** *Logic, maths.* an unproved statement that should be taken for granted: used as an initial premise in a process of reasoning. [C16: from L *postulāre* to ask for]
▸ˌ**postu'lation** *n*

postulator ('pɒstjʊˌleɪtə) *n RC Church.* a person who presents a plea for the beatification or canonization of some deceased person.

posture Ⓣ ('pɒstʃə) *n* **1** a position or attitude of the limbs or body. **2** a characteristic manner of bearing the body: *good posture.* **3** the disposition of the parts of a visible object. **4** a mental attitude. **5** a state or condition. **6** a false or affected attitude; pose. ◆ *vb* **postures, posturing, postured. 7** to assume or cause to assume a bodily attitude. **8** (*intr*) to assume an affected posture; pose. [C17: via F from It. *postura,* from L *positūra,* from *pōnere* to place]
▸**'postural** *adj* ▸**'posturer** *n*

postwar (pəʊst'wɔː) *adj* happening or existing after a war.

posy Ⓣ ('pəʊzɪ) *n, pl* **posies. 1** a small bunch of flowers. **2** *Arch.* a brief motto or inscription, esp. one on a trinket or a ring. [C16: var. of POESY]

pot[1] Ⓣ (pɒt) *n* **1** a container, usually round and deep and often having a handle and lid, used for cooking and other domestic purposes. **2** the amount that a pot will hold; potful. **3** a large mug or tankard. **4** *Austral.* any of various measures used for serving beer. **5** the money or stakes in the pool in gambling games. **6** a wicker trap for catching fish, esp. crustaceans: *a lobster pot.* **7** *Billiards, etc.* a shot by which a ball is pocketed. **8** a chamber pot, esp. a small one designed for a baby or toddler. **9** (*often pl*) *Inf.* a large amount (esp. of money). **10** *Inf.* a prize or trophy. **11** *Chiefly Brit.* short for **chimneypot. 12** short for **flowerpot, teapot. 13** See **potbelly. 14 go to pot.** to go to ruin. ◆ *vb* **pots, potting, potted.** (*mainly tr*) **15** to put or preserve (meat, etc.) in a pot. **16** to plant (a cutting, seedling, etc.) in soil in a flowerpot. **17** to cause (a baby or toddler) to use or sit on a pot. **18** to shoot (game) for food rather than for sport. **19** (*also intr*) to shoot casually or without careful aim. **20** (*also intr*) to shape clay as a potter. **21** *Billiards, etc.* to pocket (a ball). **22** *Inf.* to capture or win. [LOE *pott,* from Med. L *pottus* (unattested), ?from L *pōtus* a drink]

pot[2] (pɒt) *n Sl.* cannabis used as a drug in any form. [C20: ? shortened from Mexican Indian *potiguaya*]

potable ('pəʊtəbᵊl) *adj* drinkable. [C16: from LL *pōtābilis* drinkable, from L *pōtāre* to drink]
▸ˌ**pota'bility** *n*

potae ('pɒtaɪ) *n NZ.* a hat. [Maori]

potage *French.* (pɔtaʒ; *English* pəʊ'tɑːʒ) *n* any thick soup. [C16: from OF; see POTTAGE]

potamic (pə'tæmɪk) *adj* of or relating to rivers. [C19: from Gk *potamos* river]

potash ('pɒtˌæʃ) *n* **1** another name for **potassium carbonate** or **potassium hydroxide. 2** potassium chemically combined in certain compounds: *chloride of potash.* [C17 *pot ashes,* translation of obs. Du. *potaschen;* because orig. obtained by evaporating the lye of wood ashes in pots]

potassium (pə'tæsɪəm) *n* a light silvery element of the alkali metal group that is highly reactive and rapidly oxidizes in air. Symbol: K; atomic no.: 19; atomic wt.: 39.098. [C19: NL *potassa* potash]
▸**po'tassic** *adj*

potassium-argon dating *n* a technique for determining the age of minerals based on the occurrence in natural potassium of a small fixed amount of radioisotope ^{40}K that decays to the stable argon isotope ^{40}Ar with a half-life of 1.28×10^9 years. Measurement of the ratio of these isotopes thus gives the age of the mineral.

potassium bromide *n* a white crystalline soluble substance with a bitter saline taste used in making photographic papers and plates and in medicine as a sedative. Formula: KBr.

potassium carbonate *n* a white odourless substance used in making glass and soft soap and as an alkaline cleansing agent. Formula: K_2CO_3.

potassium chlorate *n* a white crystalline soluble substance used in explosives and as a disinfectant and bleaching agent. Formula: $KClO_3$.

potassium cyanide *n* a white poisonous granular soluble solid substance used in photography. Formula: KCN.

potassium hydrogen tartrate *n* a white soluble crystalline salt used in baking powders, soldering fluxes, and laxatives. Formula: $KHC_4H_4O_6$. Also called: **cream of tartar.**

potassium hydroxide *n* a white deliquescent alkaline solid used in the manufacture of soap, liquid shampoos, and detergents. Formula: KOH.

potassium nitrate *n* a colourless or white crystalline compound used in gunpowders, pyrotechnics, fertilizers, and as a preservative for foods (**E 252**). Formula: KNO_3. Also called: **saltpetre, nitre.**

potassium permanganate *n* a dark purple poisonous odourless soluble crystalline solid, used as a bleach, disinfectant, and antiseptic. Formula: $KMnO_4$. Systematic name: **potassium manganate(VII).**

potation (pəʊ'teɪʃən) *n* **1** the act of drinking. **2** a drink or draught, esp. of alcoholic drink. [C15: from L *pōtātiō,* from *pōtāre* to drink]

potato (pə'teɪtəʊ) *n, pl* **potatoes. 1a** a plant of South America widely cultivated for its edible tubers. **1b** the starchy oval tuber of this plant, which has a brown or red skin and is cooked and eaten as a vegetable. **2** any of various similar plants, esp. the sweet potato. [C16: from Sp. *patata* white potato, from Taino *batata* sweet potato]

potato beetle *n* another name for the **Colorado beetle.**

potato chip *n* (*usually pl*) **1** another name for **chip** (sense 4). **2** the US, Canad., Austral., and NZ term for **crisp** (sense 10).

potato crisp *n* (*usually pl*) another name for **crisp** (sense 10).

potbelly Ⓣ ('pɒtˌbelɪ) *n, pl* **potbellies. 1** a protruding or distended belly. **2** a person having such a belly.
▸**'potˌbellied** *adj*

potboiler ('pɒtˌbɔɪlə) *n Inf.* an artistic work of little merit produced quickly to make money.

pot-bound *adj* (of a pot plant) having grown to fill all the available root space and therefore lacking room for continued growth.

potboy ('pɒtˌbɔɪ) *or* **potman** ('pɒtmən) *n, pl* **potboys** *or* **potmen.** *Chiefly Brit.* (esp. formerly) a man employed at a public house to serve beer, etc.

potch (pɒtʃ) *n Chiefly Austral., sl.* inferior quality opal. [C20: from ?]

poteen ('pɒtiːn) *or* **poitín** (pɒ'tʃiːn) *n* (in Ireland) illicit spirit, often distilled from potatoes. [C19: from Irish *poitín* little pot, from *pota* pot]

potent[1] Ⓣ ('pəʊtᵊnt) *adj* **1** possessing great strength; powerful. **2** (of arguments, etc.) persuasive or forceful. **3** influential or authoritative. **4** tending to produce violent physical or chemical effects: *a potent poison.* **5** (of a male) capable of having sexual intercourse. [C15: from L *potēns* able, from *posse* to be able]
▸**'potency** *or* **'potence** *n* ▸**'potently** *adv*

potent[2] ('pəʊtᵊnt) *adj Heraldry.* (of a cross) having flat bars across the ends of the arms. [C17: from obs. *potent* a crutch, from L *potentia* power]

potentate Ⓣ ('pəʊtᵊnˌteɪt) *n* a ruler or monarch. [C14: from LL *potentātus,* from L: rule, from *potens* powerful, from *posse* to be able]

potential Ⓣ (pə'tenʃəl) *adj* **1a** possible but not yet actual. **1b** (*prenominal*) capable of being or becoming; latent. **2** *Grammar.* (of a verb) expressing possibility, as English *may* and *might.* ◆ *n* **3** latent but unrealized ability: *Jones has great potential as a sales manager.* **4** *Grammar.* a potential verb or verb form. **5** short for **electric potential.** [C14: from OF *potencial,* from LL *potentiālis,* from L *potentia* power]
▸**po'tentially** *adv*

potential difference *n* the difference in electric potential between two points in an electric field; the work that has to be done in trans-

THESAURUS

postulate *vb* **1, 3** = **presuppose**, advance, assume, hypothesize, posit, predicate, propose, put forward, suppose, take for granted, theorize

posture *n* **1, 2** = **bearing**, attitude, carriage, disposition, mien (*literary*), pose, position, set, stance **4** = **attitude**, disposition, feeling, frame of mind, inclination, mood, outlook, point of view, stance, standpoint **5** = **state**, circumstance, condition, mode, phase, position, situation ◆ *vb* **8** = **show off** (*inf.*), affect, attitudinize, do for effect, hot-dog (*chiefly US*), make a show, pose, put on airs, try to attract attention

posy *n* **1** = **bouquet**, boutonniere, buttonhole, corsage, nosegay, spray

pot[1] *n* **1** = **container**, bowl, crock, jug, pan, urn, utensil, vase, vessel **5** = **pool**, bank, jackpot, kitty, stakes **10** *Informal* = **trophy**, cup **13** = **paunch**, beer belly *or* gut (*inf.*), bulge, corporation (*inf.*), gut, potbelly, spare tyre (*Brit. sl.*), spread (*inf.*) **14 go to pot** = **decline**, deteriorate, go downhill (*inf.*), go to rack and ruin, go to the dogs (*inf.*), run to seed, slump, worsen ◆ *vb* **19** = **shoot**, hit, plug (*inf.*), strike

potbellied *adj* **1** = **fat**, bloated, corpulent, distended, obese, overweight, paunchy

potbelly *n* **1** = **paunch**, beer belly (*inf.*), corporation (*inf.*), gut, middle-age spread (*inf.*), pot, spare tyre (*Brit. sl.*), spread (*inf.*)

potency *n* **1, 3** = **power**, authority, capacity, control, effectiveness, efficacy, energy, force, influence, might, muscle, potential, puissance, strength, sway, vigour

potent[1] *adj* **1** = **strong**, efficacious, forceful, mighty, powerful, puissant, vigorous **2** = **persuasive**, cogent, compelling, convincing, effective, forceful, impressive, telling **3** = **powerful**, authoritative, commanding, dominant, dynamic, influential
Antonyms *adj* ≠ **strong:** impotent, weak ≠ **persuasive:** ineffective, unconvincing

potentate *n* = **ruler**, emperor, king, mogul, monarch, overlord, prince, sovereign

potential *adj* **1** = **possible**, budding, dormant, embryonic, future, hidden, inherent, latent, likely, promising, undeveloped, unrealized ◆ *n* **3** = **ability**, aptitude, capability, capacity, possibility, potentiality, power, the makings, what it takes (*inf.*), wherewithal

ferring unit positive charge from one point to the other, measured in volts. Abbrev.: **pd.**

potential energy *n* the energy of a body or system as a result of its position in an electric, magnetic, or gravitational field. Abbrev.: **PE.**

potentiality ❶ (pəˌtɛnʃɪˈælɪtɪ) *n, pl* **potentialities. 1** latent or inherent capacity for growth, fulfilment, etc. **2** a person or thing that possesses this.

potentiate (pəˈtɛnʃɪˌeɪt) *vb* **potentiates, potentiating, potentiated.** (*tr*) **1** to cause to be potent. **2** *Med.* to increase (the individual action or effectiveness) of two drugs by administering them in combination.

potentilla (ˌpəʊtᵊnˈtɪlə) *n* any rosaceous plant or shrub of the N temperate genus *Potentilla*, having five-petalled flowers. [C16: NL, from Med. L: garden valerian, from L *potēns* powerful]

potentiometer (pəˌtɛnʃɪˈɒmɪtə) *n* **1** an instrument for determining a potential difference of electromotive force. **2** a device used in electronic circuits, esp. as a volume control. Sometimes shortened to **pot.**
▸**poˌtentiˈometry** *n*

potful (ˈpɒtfʊl) *n* the amount held by a pot.

pother (ˈpɒðə) *n* **1** a commotion, fuss, or disturbance. **2** a choking cloud of smoke, dust, etc. ◆ *vb* **3** to make or be troubled or upset. [C16: from ?]

potherb (ˈpɒtˌhɜːb) *n* any plant having leaves, flowers, stems, etc., that are used in cooking.

pothole (ˈpɒtˌhəʊl) *n* **1** *Geog.* **1a** a deep hole in limestone areas resulting from action by running water. **1b** a circular hole in the bed of a river produced by abrasion. **2** a deep hole produced in a road surface by wear or weathering.

potholing (ˈpɒtˌhəʊlɪŋ) *n Brit.* a sport in which participants explore underground caves.
▸ˈ**potˌholer** *n*

pothook (ˈpɒtˌhʊk) *n* **1** a curved or S-shaped hook used for suspending a pot over a fire. **2** a long hook used for lifting hot pots, lids, etc. **3** an S-shaped mark, often made by children when learning to write.

pothouse (ˈpɒtˌhaʊs) *n Brit.* (formerly) a small tavern or pub.

pothunter (ˈpɒtˌhʌntə) *n* **1** a person who hunts for profit without regard to the rules of sport. **2** *Inf.* a person who enters competitions for the sole purpose of winning prizes.

potion ❶ (ˈpəʊʃən) *n* a drink, esp. of medicine, poison, or some supposedly magic beverage. [C13: via OF from L *pōtiō* a drink, esp. a poisonous one, from *pōtāre* to drink]

potlatch (ˈpɒtˌlætʃ) *n Anthropol.* a competitive ceremonial activity among certain North American Indians, involving a lavish distribution of gifts to emphasize the wealth and status of the chief or clan. [C19: of Amerind origin, from *patshatl* a present]

pot luck *n Inf.* **1** whatever food happens to be available without special preparation. **2** whatever is available (esp. in **take pot luck**).

pot marigold *n* a Central European and Mediterranean plant grown for its rayed orange-and-yellow showy flowers.

potometer (pəˈtɒmɪtə) *n* an apparatus that measures the rate of water uptake by a plant or plant part. [from L *pōtāre* to drink + -METER]

potoroo (ˌpɒtəˈruː) *n* another name for **kangaroo rat.** [from Abor.]

potpourri ❶ (ˌpəʊˈpʊərɪ) *n, pl* **potpourris. 1** a collection of mixed flower petals dried and preserved in a pot to scent the air. **2** a collection of unrelated items; miscellany. **3** a medley of popular tunes. [C18: from F, lit.: rotten pot, translation of Sp. *olla podrida* miscellany]

pot roast *n* meat cooked slowly in a covered pot with very little water.

potsherd (ˈpɒtˌʃɜːd) *or* **potshard** (ˈpɒtˌʃɑːd) *n* a broken fragment of pottery. [C14: from POT[1] + *schoord* piece of broken crockery; see SHARD]

pot shot *n* **1** a chance shot taken casually, hastily, or without careful aim. **2** a shot fired to kill game in disregard of the rules of sport. **3** a shot fired at quarry within easy range.

pot still *n* a type of still in which heat is applied directly to the pot in which the wash is contained: used in distilling whisky.

pottage (ˈpɒtɪdʒ) *n* a thick soup. [C13: from OF *potage* contents of a pot, from *pot* POT[1]]

potted (ˈpɒtɪd) *adj* **1** placed or grown in a pot. **2** cooked or preserved in a pot: *potted shrimps.* **3** *Inf.* abridged: *a potted version of a novel.*

potter[1] (ˈpɒtə) *n* a person who makes pottery.

potter[2] ❶ (ˈpɒtə) *or esp. US & Canad.* **putter** *vb* **1** (*intr;* often foll. by *about* or *around*) to busy oneself in a desultory though agreeable manner. **2** (*intr;* often foll. by *along* or *about*) to move with little energy or direction: *to potter about town.* **3** (*tr;* usually foll. by *away*) to waste (time): *to potter the day away.* [C16 (in the sense: to poke repeatedly): from OE *potian* to thrust]
▸ˈ**potterer** *or esp. US* ˈ**putterer** *n*

Potteries (ˈpɒtərɪz) *pl n* **the.** (*sometimes functioning as sing*) a region of W central England, in Staffordshire, in which the china industries are concentrated.

potter's field *n* **1** *New Testament.* the land bought by the Sanhedrin with the money paid for the betrayal of Jesus, to be used as a burial place for strangers (Acts 1:19; Matthew 27:7). **2** *US.* a cemetery where the poor or unidentified are buried at the public's expense.

potter's wheel *n* a device with a horizontal rotating disc, on which clay is shaped by hand.

pottery ❶ (ˈpɒtərɪ) *n, pl* **potteries. 1** articles made from earthenware and baked in a kiln. **2** a place where such articles are made. **3** the craft or business of making such articles. [C15: from OF *poterie,* from *potier* potter, from *pot* POT[1]]

potting shed *n* a building in which plants are set in flowerpots and in which empty pots, potting compost, etc., are stored.

pottle (ˈpɒtᵊl) *n Arch.* a liquid measure equal to half a gallon. [C14 *potel,* from OF: a small POT[1]]

potto (ˈpɒtəʊ) *n, pl* **pottos.** a short-tailed prosimian primate having vertebral spines protruding through the skin in the neck region. Also called: **kinkajou.** [C18: of W African origin]

Pott's disease (pɒts) *n* a disease of the spine, characterized by weakening and gradual disintegration of the vertebrae. [C18: after Percivall *Pott* (1714–88), Brit. surgeon]

Pott's fracture *n* a fracture of the lower part of the fibula, usually with the dislocation of the ankle. [C18: see POTT'S DISEASE]

potty[1] ❶ (ˈpɒtɪ) *adj* **pottier, pottiest.** *Brit. inf.* **1** foolish or slightly crazy. **2** trivial or insignificant. **3** (foll. by *about*) very keen (on). [C19: ?from POT[1]]
▸ˈ**pottiness** *n*

potty[2] (ˈpɒtɪ) *n, pl* **potties.** a child's word for **chamber pot.**

pouch ❶ (paʊtʃ) *n* **1** a small flexible baglike container: *a tobacco pouch.* **2** a saclike structure in any of various animals, such as the cheek fold in rodents. **3** *Anat.* any sac, pocket, or pouchlike cavity. **4** a Scot. word for **pocket.** ◆ *vb* **5** (*tr*) to place in or as if in a pouch. **6** to arrange or become arranged in a pouchlike form. **7** (*tr*) (of certain birds and fishes) to swallow. [C14: from OF *pouche,* from OF *poche* bag]
▸ˈ**pouchy** *adj*

pouf *or* **pouffe** (puːf) *n* **1** a large solid cushion used as a seat. **2a** a woman's hairstyle, fashionable esp. in the 18th century, in which the hair is piled up in rolled puffs. **2b** a pad set in the hair to make such puffs. **3** (*also* pʊf). *Brit. derog. sl.* less common spellings of **poof.** [C19: from F]

poulard *or* **poularde** (ˈpuːlɑːd) *n* a hen that has been spayed for fattening. Cf. **capon.** [C18: from OF *pollarde,* from *polle* hen]

poult (pəʊlt) *n* the young of a gallinaceous bird, esp. of domestic fowl. [C15: var. of *poulet* PULLET]

poulterer (ˈpəʊltərə) *n Brit.* another word for a **poultryman.** [C17: from obs. *poulter,* from OF *pouletier,* from *poulet* PULLET]

poultice (ˈpəʊltɪs) *n Med.* a local moist and often heated application for the skin used to improve the circulation, treat inflamed areas, etc. [C16: from earlier *pultes,* from L *puls* a thick porridge]

poultry (ˈpəʊltrɪ) *n* domestic fowls collectively. [C14: from OF *pouletrie,* from *pouletier* poultry dealer]

poultryman (ˈpəʊltrɪmən) *or* **poulterer** *n, pl* **poultrymen** *or* **poulterers. 1** Also called: **chicken farmer.** a person who rears domestic fowls for their eggs or meat. **2** a dealer in poultry.

pounce[1] ❶ (paʊns) *vb* **pounces, pouncing, pounced. 1** (*intr;* often foll. by *on* or *upon*) to spring or swoop, as in capturing prey. ◆ *n* **2** the act of pouncing; a spring or swoop. **3** the claw of a bird of prey. [C17: apparently from ME *punson* pointed tool]
▸ˈ**pouncer** *n*

pounce[2] (paʊns) *n* **1** a very fine resinous powder, esp. of cuttlefish bone, formerly used to dry ink. **2** a fine powder, esp. of charcoal, that is tapped through perforations in paper in order to transfer the design to another surface. ◆ *vb* **pounces, pouncing, pounced.** (*tr*) **3** to dust (paper) with pounce. **4** to transfer (a design) by means of pounce. [C18: from OF *ponce,* from L *pūmex* pumice]

pouncet box (ˈpaʊnsɪt) *n* a box with a perforated top used for perfume. [C16 *pouncet,* ? alteration of *pounced* perforated]

pound[1] ❶ (paʊnd) *vb* **1** (when *intr,* often foll. by *on* or *at*) to strike heavily and often. **2** (*tr*) to beat to a pulp; pulverize. **3** (*tr;* foll. by *out*) to produce, as by typing heavily. **4** to walk or move with heavy steps or thuds. **5** (*intr*) to throb heavily. ◆ *n* **6** the act of pounding. [OE *pūnian*]
▸ˈ**pounder** *n*

pound[2] (paʊnd) *n* **1** an avoirdupois unit of weight that is divided into 16 ounces and is equal to 0.453 592 kilograms. Abbrev.: **lb. 2** a troy unit of weight divided into 12 ounces equal to 0.373 242 kilograms.

THESAURUS

potentiality *n* **1** = **capacity**, ability, aptitude, capability, likelihood, potential, promise, prospect, the makings

potion *n* = **concoction**, brew, cup, dose, draught, elixir, mixture, philtre, tonic

potpourri *n* **2** = **mixture**, collection, combination, gallimaufry, hotchpotch, medley, *mélange,* miscellany, mixed bag (*inf.*), motley, pastiche, patchwork, salmagundi

potter[2] *vb* **1** = **mess about**, dabble, fiddle (*inf.*), footle (*inf.*), fribble, fritter, poke along, tinker

pottery *n* **1** = **ceramics**, earthenware, stoneware, terracotta

potty[1] *adj Brit. informal* **1** = **crazy**, barmy, crackpot (*inf.*), daft (*inf.*), dippy (*sl.*), dotty (*sl., chiefly Brit.*), eccentric, foolish, loopy (*inf.*), oddball (*inf.*), silly, soft (*inf.*), touched, up the pole (*inf.*) **2** = **trivial**, footling (*inf.*), insignificant, petty, piddling, trifling

pouch *n* **1** = **bag**, container, pocket, poke (*dialect*), purse, sack

pounce[1] *vb* **1** = **spring**, ambush, attack, bound onto, dash at, drop, fall upon, jump, leap at, snatch, strike, swoop, take by surprise, take unawares ◆ *n* **2** = **spring**, assault, attack, bound, jump, leap, swoop

pound[1] *vb* **1** = **beat**, batter, beat the living daylights out of, belabour, clobber (*sl.*), hammer, pelt, pummel, strike, thrash, thump **2** = **crush**, bray (*dialect*), bruise, comminute, powder, pulverize, triturate **3** *with* **out** = **thump**, bang, beat, hammer **4** = **stomp** (*inf.*), clomp, march, thunder, tramp **5** = **pulsate**, beat, palpitate, pitapat, pulse, throb

3a the standard monetary unit of the United Kingdom, divided into 100 pence. Official name: **pound sterling. 3b** *(as modifier): a pound coin.* **4** the standard monetary unit of various other countries, including Cyprus, Egypt, Israel, and Syria. **5** Also called: **pound Scots.** a former Scottish monetary unit originally worth an English pound but later declining in value to 1 shilling 8 pence. [OE *pund,* from L *pondō*]

pound[3] ❶ (paʊnd) *n* **1** an enclosure for keeping officially removed vehicles or distrained goods or animals, esp. stray dogs. **2** a place where people are confined. **3** a trap for animals. ◆ *vb* **4** *(tr)* to confine in or as if in a pound; impound, imprison, or restrain. [C14: from LOE *pund-,* as in *pundfeald* PINFOLD]

poundage ('paʊndɪdʒ) *n* **1** a charge of so much per pound of weight. **2** a charge of so much per pound sterling. **3** a weight expressed in pounds.

poundal ('paʊndᵊl) *n* the fps unit of force; the force that imparts an acceleration of 1 foot per second per second to a mass of 1 pound. Abbrev.: **pdl.** [C19: from POUND[2] + QUINTAL]

pound cost averaging *n Stock Exchange.* a method of accumulating capital by investing a fixed sum in a particular security at regular intervals, in order to achieve an average purchase price below the arithmetic average of the market prices on the purchase dates.

-pounder ('paʊndə) *n (in combination)* **1** something weighing a specified number of pounds: *a 200-pounder.* **2** something worth a specified number of pounds: *a ten-pounder.* **3** a gun that discharges a shell weighing a specified number of pounds: *a two-pounder.*

pound sterling *n* See **pound**[2] (sense 3).

pour ❶ (pɔː) *vb* **1** to flow or cause to flow in a stream. **2** *(tr)* to emit in a profuse way. **3** *(intr; often foll. by down)* Also: **pour with rain.** to rain heavily. **4** *(intr)* to move together in large numbers; swarm. **5** *(intr)* to serve tea, coffee, etc.: *shall I pour?* **6 it never rains but it pours.** events, esp. unfortunate ones, come in rapid succession. **7 pour oil on troubled waters.** to calm a quarrel, etc. ◆ *n* **8** a pouring, downpour, etc. [C13: from ?]
▸ **'pourer** *n*

> **USAGE NOTE** The verbs *pour* and *pore* are sometimes confused: *she poured cream over her strudel; she pored* (not *poured*) *over the manuscript.*

pourboire *French.* (purbwar) *n* a tip; gratuity. [lit.: for drinking]

poussin *(French* pusɛ̃) *n* a young chicken reared for eating. [from F]

pout[1] ❶ (paʊt) *vb* **1** to thrust out (the lips), as when sullen or (of the lips) to be thrust out. **2** *(intr)* to swell out; protrude. **3** *(tr)* to utter with a pout. ◆ *n* **4** Also: **the pouts.** a fit of sullenness. **5** the act or state of pouting. [C14: from ?]
▸ **'poutingly** *adv*

pout[2] (paʊt) *n, pl* **pout** *or* **pouts. 1** short for **eelpout. 2** Also called: **horned pout.** a N American catfish with barbels round the mouth. **3** any of various gadoid food fishes. [OE *-pūte,* as in *ǣlepūte* eelpout]

pouter ('paʊtə) *n* **1** a person or thing that pouts. **2** a breed of domestic pigeon with a large crop capable of being greatly puffed out.

poverty ❶ ('pɒvətɪ) *n* **1** the condition of being without adequate food, money, etc. **2** scarcity: *a poverty of wit.* **3** a lack of elements conducive to fertility in soil. [C12: from OF *poverté,* from L *paupertās* restricted means, from *pauper* poor]

poverty-stricken ❶ *adj* suffering from extreme poverty.

poverty trap *n* the situation of being unable to raise one's living standard because one is dependent on state benefits which are reduced or withdrawn if one gains any extra income.

pow (paʊ) *interj* an exclamation imitative of a collision, explosion, etc.

POW *abbrev. for* prisoner of war.

powan ('paʊən) *n* a freshwater whitefish occurring in some Scottish lakes. [C17: Scot. var. of POLLAN]

powder ❶ ('paʊdə) *n* **1** a substance in the form of tiny loose particles. **2** any of various preparations in this form, such as gunpowder, face powder, or soap powder. ◆ *vb* **3** to turn into powder; pulverize. **4** *(tr)* to cover or sprinkle with or as if with powder. [C13: from OF *poldre,* from L *pulvis* dust]
▸ **'powderer** *n* ▸ **'powdery** *adj*

powder blue *n* a dusty pale blue colour.

powder burn *n* a superficial burn of the skin caused by a momentary intense explosion.

powder flask *n* a small flask or case formerly used to carry gunpowder.

powder horn *n* a powder flask consisting of the hollow horn of an animal.

powder keg *n* **1** a small barrel to hold gunpowder. **2** a potential source of violence, disaster, etc.

powder metallurgy *n* the science and technology of producing solid metal components from metal powder by compaction and sintering.

powder monkey *n* (formerly) a boy who carried powder from the magazine to the guns on warships.

powder puff *n* a soft pad of fluffy material used for applying cosmetic powder to the skin.

powder room *n* a ladies' cloakroom.

powdery mildew *n* a plant disease characterized by a white powdery growth on stems and leaves, caused by parasitic fungi.

power ❶ ('paʊə) *n* **1** ability to do something. **2** *(often pl)* a specific ability, capacity, or faculty. **3** political, financial, social, etc., force or influence. **4** control or dominion or a position of control, dominion, or authority. **5** a state or other political entity with political, industrial, or military strength. **6** a person or group that exercises control, influence, or authority: *he's a power in the state.* **7** a prerogative, privilege, or liberty. **8** legal authority to act for another. **9a** a military force. **9b** military potential. **10** *Maths.* **10a** the value of a number or quantity raised to some exponent. **10b** another name for **exponent** (sense 4). **11** *Physics, engineering.* a measure of the rate of doing work expressed as the work done per unit time. It is measured in watts, horsepower, etc. **12a** the rate at which electrical energy is fed into or taken from a device or system. It is measured in watts. **12b** *(as modifier): a power amplifier.* **13** the ability to perform work. **14a** mechanical energy as opposed to manual labour. **14b** *(as modifier): a power tool.* **15** a particular form of energy: *nuclear power.* **16a** a measure of the ability of a lens or optical system to magnify an object. **16b** another word for **magnification. 17** *Inf.* a large amount: *a power of good.* **18 in one's power.** *(often foll. by an infinitive)* able or allowed (to). **19 in (someone's) power.** under the control of (someone). **20 the powers that be.** established authority. ◆ *vb* **21** *(tr)* to give or provide power to. **22** *(tr)* to fit (a machine) with a motor or engine. **23** *Inf.* to move or cause to move by the exercise of physical power. [C13: from Anglo-Norman *poer,* from Vulgar L *potēre* (unattested), from L *posse* to be able]

power amplifier *n Electronics.* an amplifier that is usually the final amplification stage in a device and is designed to give the required power output.

powerboat ('paʊəˌbəʊt) *n* a boat, esp. a fast one, propelled by an inboard or outboard motor.

powerboating ('paʊəˌbəʊtɪŋ) *n* the sport of driving powerboats in racing competitions.

power cut *n* a temporary interruption or reduction in the supply of electrical power.

power dive *n* **1** a steep dive by an aircraft with its engines at high power. ◆ *vb* **power-dive, power-dives, power-diving, power-dived. 2** to cause (an aircraft) to perform a power dive or (of an aircraft) to perform a power dive.

power dressing *n* a style of dressing in severely tailored suits, adopted by some women executives to project an image of efficiency.

powerful ❶ ('paʊəfʊl) *adj* **1** having great power. **2** extremely effective or efficient: *a powerful drug.* ◆ *adv* **3** *Dialect.* very: *he ran powerful fast.*
▸ **'powerfully** *adv* ▸ **'powerfulness** *n*

powerhouse ('paʊəˌhaʊs) *n* **1** an electrical generating station or plant. **2** *Inf.* a forceful or powerful person or thing.

powerless ❶ ('paʊəlɪs) *adj* without power or authority.
▸ **'powerlessly** *adv* ▸ **'powerlessness** *n*

power lunch *n* a high-powered business meeting conducted over lunch.

power of attorney *n* **1** legal authority to act for another person in certain specified matters. **2** the document conferring such authority.

power pack *n* a device for converting the current from a supply into

THESAURUS

pound[3] *n* **1** = **enclosure**, compound, corral *(chiefly US & Canad.)*, pen, yard

pour *vb* **1, 2** = **flow**, course, emit, gush, run, rush, spew, spout, stream **3** = **rain**, bucket down *(inf.)*, come down in torrents, pelt (down), rain cats and dogs *(inf.)*, rain hard *or* heavily, sheet, teem **4** = **stream**, crowd, swarm, teem, throng **5** = **let flow**, decant, spill, splash

pout[1] *vb* **1** = **sulk**, glower, look petulant, look sullen, lour *or* lower, make a *moue*, mope, pull a long face, purse one's lips, turn down the corners of one's mouth ◆ *n* **5** = **sullen look**, glower, long face, *moue*

poverty *n* **1** = **pennilessness**, beggary, destitution, distress, hand-to-mouth existence, hardship, indigence, insolvency, necessitousness, necessity, need, pauperism, penury, privation, want **2** = **scarcity**, dearth, deficiency, insufficiency, lack, paucity, shortage **3** = **barrenness**, aridity, bareness, deficiency, infertility, meagreness, poorness, sterility, unfruitfulness
Antonyms *n* ≠ **pennilessness:** affluence, comfort, luxury, opulence, richness, wealth ≠ **scarcity:** abundance, plethora, sufficiency ≠ **barrenness:** fecundity, fertility, fruitfulness, productiveness

poverty-stricken *adj* = **penniless**, bankrupt, beggared, broke, destitute, dirt-poor *(inf.)*, distressed, down and out, down at heel, flat broke *(inf.)*, impecunious, impoverished, indigent, needy, on one's uppers, on the breadline, penurious, poor, short, skint *(Brit. sl.)*

powder *n* **1** = **dust**, fine grains, loose particles, pounce, talc ◆ *vb* **3** = **grind**, crush, granulate, pestle, pound, pulverize **4** = **dust**, cover, dredge, scatter, sprinkle, strew

powdery *adj* **1** = **fine**, chalky, crumbling, crumbly, dry, dusty, friable, grainy, granular, loose, pulverized, sandy

power *n* **1** = **ability**, capability, capacity, competence, competency, faculty, potential **3, 4** = **control**, ascendancy, authority, bottom, command, dominance, domination, dominion, influence, mastery, rule, sovereignty, supremacy, sway **7, 8** = **authority**, authorization, licence, prerogative, privilege, right, warrant
Antonyms *n* ≠ **ability:** inability, incapability, incapacity, incompetence

powerful *adj* **1** = **controlling**, authoritative, commanding, dominant, influential, prevailing, puissant, sovereign, supreme

powerless *adj* = **defenceless**, dependent, disenfranchised, disfranchised, ineffective, over a barrel *(inf.)*, subject, tied, unarmed, vulnerable = **weak**, debilitated, disabled, etiolated, feeble, frail, helpless, impotent, incapable, incapacitated, ineffectual, infirm, paralysed, prostrate
Antonyms *adj* ≠ **weak:** able-bodied, fit, healthy, lusty, powerful, robust, strong, sturdy

direct or alternating current at the voltage required by a particular electrical or electronic device.

power plant *n* **1** the complex, including machinery, associated equipment, and the structure housing it, that is used in the generation of power, esp. electrical power. **2** the equipment supplying power to a particular machine.

power point *n* an electrical socket mounted on or recessed into a wall.

power-sharing *n* a political arrangement in which opposing groups in a society participate in government.

power station *n* an electrical generating station.

power steering *n* a form of steering used on vehicles, where the torque applied to the steering wheel is augmented by engine power. Also called: **power-assisted steering.**

power structure *n* the structure or distribution of power and authority in a community.

powwow ❶ ('paʊˌwaʊ) *n* **1** a talk, conference, or meeting. **2** a magical ceremony of certain North American Indians. **3** (among certain North American Indians) a medicine man. **4** a meeting of North American Indians. ◆ *vb* **5** (*intr*) to hold a powwow. [C17: of Amerind origin]

pox (pɒks) *n* **1** any disease characterized by the formation of pustules on the skin that often leave pockmarks when healed. **2** (usually preceded by *the*) an informal name for **syphilis. 3 a pox on (someone** *or* **something).** (*interj*) *Arch.* an expression of intense disgust or aversion. [C15: changed from *pocks,* pl. of POCK]

pozzuolana (ˌpɒtswəˈlɑːnə) *or* **pozzolana** (ˌpɒtsəˈlɑːnə) *n* **1** a type of porous volcanic ash used in making hydraulic cements. **2** any of various artificial substitutes for this ash used in cements. [C18: from It.: of *Pozzuoli,* port in SW Italy]

pp *abbrev. for:* **1** past participle. **2** (in formal correspondence) per pro. [L: *per procurationem*: by delegation to] ◆ **3** *Music. symbol for* pianissimo.

> **USAGE NOTE** In formal correspondence, when Brenda Smith is signing on behalf of Peter Jones, she should write *Peter Jones pp* (or *per pro*) *Brenda Smith,* not the other way about.

pp *or* **PP** *abbrev. for:* **1** parcel post. **2** post-paid. **3** (in prescriptions) post prandium. [L: after a meal] **4** prepaid.

PP *abbrev. for:* **1** Parish Priest. **2** past President.

pp. *abbrev. for* pages.

ppd *abbrev. for:* **1** post-paid. **2** prepaid.

PPE *abbrev. for* philosophy, politics, and economics: a university course.

ppm *Chem. abbrev. for* parts per million.

PPP *abbrev. for* purchasing power parity: a rate of exchange between two currencies that gives them equal purchasing powers in their own economies.

ppr *or* **p.pr.** *abbrev. for* present participle.

PPS *abbrev. for:* **1** parliamentary private secretary. **2** Also: **pps** post postscriptum. [L: after postscript; additional postscript]

PQ *abbrev. for:* **1** (in Canada) Parti Québecois. **2** Province of Quebec.

pr *abbrev. for:* **1** (*pl* **prs**) pair. **2** paper. **3** power.

Pr *the chemical symbol for* praseodymium.

PR *abbrev. for:* **1** proportional representation. **2** public relations. **3** Puerto Rico.

pr. *abbrev. for:* **1** price. **2** pronoun.

practicable ❶ ('præktɪkəbᵊl) *adj* **1** capable of being done; feasible. **2** usable. [C17: from F *praticable,* from *pratiquer* to practise; see PRACTICAL]
▸ˌ**practica'bility** *or* **'practicableness** *n* ▸**'practicably** *adv*

> **USAGE NOTE** See at **practical.**

practical ❶ ('præktɪkᵊl) *adj* **1** of or concerned with experience or actual use; not theoretical. **2** of or concerned with ordinary affairs, work, etc. **3** adapted or adaptable for use. **4** of, involving, or trained by practice. **5** being such for all general purposes; virtual. ◆ *n* **6** an examination or lesson in a practical subject. [C17: from earlier *practic,* from F *pratique,* via LL from Gk *praktikos,* from *prassein* to experience]
▸ˌ**practi'cality** *or* **'practicalness** *n*

> **USAGE NOTE** A distinction is usually made between *practical* and *practicable. Practical* refers to a person, idea, project, etc., as being more concerned with or relevant to practice than theory: *he is a very practical person; the idea had no practical application. Practicable* refers to a project or idea as being capable of being done or put into effect: *the plan was expensive, yet practicable.*

practical joke *n* a prank or trick usually intended to make the victim appear foolish.
▸**practical joker** *n*

practically ❶ ('præktɪkəlɪ, -klɪ) *adv* **1** virtually; almost: *it rained practically every day.* **2** in actuality rather than in theory: *what can we do practically to help?*

practice ❶ ('præktɪs) *n* **1** a usual or customary action: *it was his practice to rise at six.* **2** repetition of an activity in order to achieve mastery and fluency: *they had one last practice the day before the show.* **3** the condition of having mastery of a skill or activity through repetition (esp. in **in practice, out of practice**). **4** the exercise of a profession: *he set up practice as a lawyer.* **5** the act of doing something: *he put his plans into practice.* **6** the established method of conducting proceedings in a court of law. ◆ *vb* **practices, practicing, practiced. 7** the US spelling of **practise.** [C16: from Med. L *practicāre* to practise, from Gk *praktikē* practical work, from *prattein* to do]

practise ❶ *or US* **practice** ('præktɪs) *vb* **practises, practising, practised** *or US* **practices, practicing, practiced. 1** to do or cause to do repeatedly in order to gain skill. **2** (*tr*) to do (something) habitually or frequently: *they practise ritual murder.* **3** to observe or pursue (something): *to practise Christianity.* **4** to work at (a profession, etc.): *he practises medicine.* [C15: see PRACTICE]

practised ❶ *or US* **practiced** ('præktɪst) *adj* **1** expert; skilled; proficient. **2** acquired or perfected by practice.

practitioner (præk'tɪʃənə) *n* **1** a person who practises a profession or art. **2** *Christian Science.* a person authorized to practise spiritual healing. [C16: from *practician,* from OF, from *pratiquer* to PRACTISE]

prae- *prefix* an archaic variant of **pre-.**

praedial *or* **predial** ('priːdɪəl) *adj* **1** of or relating to land, farming, etc. **2** attached to or occupying land. [C16: from Med. L *praediālis,* from L *praedium* farm, estate]

praesidium (prɪ'sɪdɪəm) *n* a variant of **presidium.**

praetor *or esp. US* **pretor** ('priːtə, -tɔː) *n* (in ancient Rome) any of several senior magistrates ranking just below the consuls. [C15: from L: one who leads the way, prob. from *praeīre,* from *prae-* before + *īre* to go]
▸**prae'torian** *or* **pre'torian** *adj, n* ▸**'praetorship** *or* **'pretorship** *n*

pragmatic ❶ (præg'mætɪk) *adj* **1** advocating behaviour dictated more by practical consequences than by theory. **2** *Philosophy.* of pragmatism. **3** involving everyday or practical business. **4** of or concerned with the affairs of a state or community. **5** *Rare.* meddlesome; officious. Also (for senses 3, 5): **pragmatical.** [C17: from LL *prāgmaticus,* from Gk *prāgmatikos* from *pragma* act, from *prattein* to do]
▸**prag**ˌ**mati'cality** *n* ▸**prag'matically** *adv*

pragmatic sanction *n* an edict, decree, or ordinance issued with the force of fundamental law by a sovereign.

pragmatism ('prægməˌtɪzəm) *n* **1** action or policy dictated by consideration of the practical consequences rather than by theory. **2** *Philosophy.* the doctrine that the content of a concept consists only in its practical applicability.
▸**'pragmatist** *n, adj*

prairie ('prɛərɪ) *n* (*often pl*) a treeless grassy plain of the central US and S Canada. [C18: from F, from OF *praierie,* from L *prātum* meadow]

prairie chicken, fowl, grouse, *or* **hen** *n* either of two mottled brown-and-white grouse of North America.

THESAURUS

powwow *n* **1** = **meeting**, chinwag (*Brit. inf.*), confab (*inf.*), confabulation, conference, congress, consultation, council, discussion, get-together (*inf.*), huddle (*inf.*), palaver, parley, seminar, talk ◆ *vb* **5** = **meet**, confab (*inf.*), confer, discuss, get together, go into a huddle (*inf.*), palaver, parley, talk

practicability *n* **1** = **feasibility**, advantage, operability, possibility, practicality, use, usefulness, value, viability, workability

practicable *adj* **1** = **feasible**, achievable, attainable, doable, performable, possible, viable, within the realm of possibility, workable
Antonyms *adj* beyond the bounds of possibility, impossible, out of the question, unachievable, unattainable, unfeasible, unworkable

practical *adj* **1** = **functional**, applied, efficient, empirical, experimental, factual, pragmatic, realistic, utilitarian **2** = **sensible**, businesslike, down-to-earth, everyday, hard-headed, matter-of-fact, mundane, ordinary, realistic, workaday **3** = **feasible**, doable, practicable, serviceable, sound, useful, workable **4** = **skilled**, accomplished, efficient, experienced, proficient, qualified, seasoned, trained, veteran, working
Antonyms *adj* ≠ **functional:** impracticable, impractical, inefficient, speculative, theoretical, unpractical, unrealistic ≠ **sensible:** impractical, unrealistic ≠ **feasible:** impossible, impractical, unpractical, unsound, unworkable, useless ≠ **skilled:** inefficient, inexperienced, unaccomplished, unqualified, unskilled, untrained

practically *adv* **1** = **almost**, all but, basically, close to, essentially, fundamentally, in effect, just about, nearly, to all intents and purposes, very nearly, virtually, well-nigh

practice *n* **1** = **custom**, habit, method, mode, praxis, routine, rule, system, tradition, usage, use, usual procedure, way, wont **2** = **rehearsal**, discipline, drill, exercise, preparation, repetition, study, training, work-out **4** = **profession**, business, career, vocation, work **5** = **use**, action, application, effect, exercise, experience, operation

practise *vb* **1** = **rehearse**, discipline, drill, exercise, go over, go through, keep one's hand in, polish, prepare, repeat, study, train, warm up, work out **3** = **do**, apply, carry out, follow, live up to, observe, perform, put into practice **4** = **work at**, carry on, engage in, ply, pursue, specialize in, undertake

practised *adj* **1** = **skilled**, able, accomplished, experienced, expert, proficient, qualified, seasoned, trained, versed
Antonyms *adj* amateurish, bungling, incompetent, inexperienced, inexpert, unqualified, unskilled, untrained

pragmatic *adj* **1, 3** = **practical**, businesslike, down-to-earth, efficient, hard-headed, matter-of-fact, realistic, sensible, utilitarian
Antonyms *adj* airy-fairy, idealistic, impractical, inefficient, starry-eyed, stupid, theoretical, unprofessional, unrealistic

prairie dog *n* any of several rodents that live in large complex burrows in the prairies of North America. Also called: **prairie marmot.**

prairie oyster *n* a drink consisting of raw unbeaten egg, vinegar or Worcester sauce, salt, and pepper: a supposed cure for a hangover.

prairie schooner *n Chiefly US.* a horse-drawn covered wagon used in the 19th century to cross the prairies of North America.

prairie wolf *n* another name for **coyote.**

praise ❶ (preɪz) *n* **1** the act of expressing commendation, admiration, etc. **2** the rendering of homage and gratitude to a deity. **3 sing someone's praises.** to commend someone highly. ◆ *vb* **praises, praising, praised.** (*tr*) **4** to express commendation, admiration, etc., for. **5** to proclaim the glorious attributes of (a deity) with homage and thanksgiving. [C13: from OF *preisier,* from LL *pretiāre* to esteem highly, from L *pretium* prize]

praiseworthy ❶ ('preɪzˌwɜːðɪ) *adj* deserving of praise; commendable.
▸**'praise,worthily** *adv* ▸**'praise,worthiness** *n*

Prakrit ('prɑːkrɪt) *n* any of the vernacular Indic languages as distinguished from Sanskrit: spoken from about 300 B.C. to the Middle Ages. [C18: from Sansk. *prākrta* original]
▸**Pra'kritic** *adj*

praline ('prɑːliːn) *n* **1** a confection of nuts with caramelized sugar. **2** Also called: **sugared almond.** a sweet consisting of an almond encased in sugar. [C18: from F, after César de Choiseul, comte de Plessis-*Praslin* (1598–1675), F field marshal whose chef first concocted it]

pralltriller ('prɑːlˌtrɪlə) *n* an ornament used in 18th-century music consisting of an inverted mordent with an added initial upper note. [G: bouncing trill]

pram[1] (præm) *n Brit.* a cotlike four-wheeled carriage for a baby. US term: **baby carriage.** [C19: shortened & altered from PERAMBULATOR]

pram[2] (prɑːm) *n Naut.* a light tender with a flat bottom and a bow formed from the ends of the side and bottom planks meeting in a small raised transom. [C16: from MDu. *prame*]

prance ❶ (prɑːns) *vb* **prances, prancing, pranced. 1** (*intr*) to swagger or strut. **2** (*intr*) to caper, gambol, or dance about. **3** (*intr*) (of a horse) to move with high lively springing steps. **4** (*tr*) to cause to prance. ◆ *n* **5** the act or an instance of prancing. [C14 *prauncen,* from ?]
▸**'prancer** *n* ▸**'prancing** *adj*

prandial ('prændɪəl) *adj Facetious.* of or relating to a meal. [C19: from L *prandium* meal, luncheon]

prang (præŋ) *Chiefly Brit. sl.* ◆ *n* **1** an accident or crash in an aircraft, car, etc. **2** an aircraft bombing raid. ◆ *vb* **3** to crash or damage (an aircraft, car, etc.). **4** to damage (a town, etc.) by bombing. [C20: ? imit.]

prank[1] ❶ (præŋk) *n* a mischievous trick or joke. [C16: from ?]
▸**'prankish** *adj* ▸**'prankster** *n*

prank[2] (præŋk) *vb* **1** (*tr*) to dress or decorate showily or gaudily. **2** (*intr*) to make an ostentatious display. [C16: from MDu. *pronken*]

prase (preɪz) *n* a light green translucent variety of chalcedony. [C14: from F, from L *prasius* a leek-green stone, from Gk *prasios,* from *prason* a leek]

praseodymium (ˌpreɪzɪəʊ'dɪmɪəm) *n* a malleable ductile silvery-white element of the lanthanide series of metals. Symbol: Pr; atomic no.: 59; atomic wt.: 140.91. [C20: NL, from Gk *prasios* of a leek-green colour + DIDYMIUM]

prate ❶ (preɪt) *vb* **prates, prating, prated. 1** (*intr*) to talk idly and at length; chatter. **2** (*tr*) to utter in an idle or empty way. ◆ *n* **3** idle or trivial talk; chatter. [C15: of Gmc origin]
▸**'prater** *n* ▸**'prating** *adj*

pratfall ('prætˌfɔːl) *n US & Canad. sl.* a fall upon one's buttocks. [C20: from C16 *prat* buttocks (from ?) + FALL]

pratincole ('prætɪŋˌkəʊl, 'preɪ-) *n* any of various swallow-like shore birds of the Old World, having long pointed wings, short legs, and a short bill. [C18: from NL *pratincola* field-dwelling, from L *prātum* meadow + *incola* inhabitant]

prattle ❶ ('prætᵊl) *vb* **prattles, prattling, prattled. 1** (*intr*) to talk in a foolish or childish way; babble. **2** (*tr*) to utter in a foolish or childish way. ◆ *n* **3** foolish or childish talk. [C16: from MLow G *pratelen* to chatter]
▸**'prattler** *n* ▸**'prattling** *adj*

prau (praʊ) *n* a variant of **proa.**

prawn (prɔːn) *n* **1** any of various small edible marine decapod crustaceans having a slender flattened body with a long tail and two pairs of pincers. **2 come the raw prawn with.** *Austral. inf.* to attempt to deceive. [C15: from ?]

praxis ('præksɪs) *n, pl* **praxes** ('præksiːz) *or* **praxises. 1** the practice of a field of study, as opposed to the theory. **2** a practical exercise. **3** accepted practice or custom. [C16: via Med. L from Gk: deed, action, from *prassein* to do]

pray ❶ (preɪ) *vb* **1** (when *intr*, often foll. by *for;* when *tr, usually takes a clause as object*) to utter prayers (to God or other object of worship). **2** (when *tr, usually takes a clause as object or an infinitive*) to beg or implore: *she prayed to be allowed to go.* ◆ *sentence substitute.* **3** *Arch.* I beg you; please: *pray, leave us alone.* [C13: from OF *preier,* from L *precārī* to implore, from *prex* an entreaty]

prayer[1] ❶ (prɛə) *n* **1** a personal communication or petition addressed to a deity, esp. in the form of supplication, adoration, praise, contrition, or thanksgiving. **2** a similar personal communication that does not involve adoration, addressed to beings closely associated with a deity, such as saints. **3** the practice of praying: *prayer is our solution to human problems.* **4** (*often pl*) a form of devotion spent mainly or wholly praying: *morning prayers.* **5** (*cap. when part of a recognized name*) a form of words used in praying: *the Lord's Prayer.* **6** an object or benefit prayed for. **7** an earnest request or entreaty. [C13 *preiere,* from OF, from Med. L, from L *precārius* obtained by begging, from *prex* prayer]
▸**'prayerful** *adj*

prayer[2] ('preɪə) *n* a person who prays.

prayer book (prɛə) *n* a book containing the prayers used at church services or recommended for private devotions.

prayer rug (prɛə) *n* the small carpet on which a Muslim kneels and prostrates himself while saying his prayers. Also called: **prayer mat.**

prayer wheel (prɛə) *n Buddhism.* (esp. in Tibet) a wheel or cylinder inscribed with or containing prayers, each revolution of which is counted as an uttered prayer, so that such prayers can be repeated by turning it.

praying mantis *or* **mantid** *n* another name for **mantis.**

PRB *abbrev. for* Pre-Raphaelite Brotherhood.

pre- *prefix* before in time, position, etc.: *predate; pre-eminent.* [from L *prae* before]

preach ❶ (priːtʃ) *vb* **1** to make known (religious truth) or give religious or moral instruction or exhortation in (sermons). **2** to advocate (a virtue, action, etc.), esp. in a moralizing way. [C13: from OF *prechier,* from Church L *praedicāre,* from L: to proclaim in public; see PREDICATE]

preacher ❶ ('priːtʃə) *n* a person who preaches, esp. a Protestant clergyman.

preachify ('priːtʃɪˌfaɪ) *vb* **preachifies, preachifying, preachified.** (*intr*) *Inf.* to preach or moralize in a tedious manner.
▸**ˌpreachifi'cation** *n*

preachment ('priːtʃmənt) *n* **1** the act of preaching. **2** a tedious or pompous sermon.

preachy ❶ ('priːtʃɪ) *adj* **preachier, preachiest.** *Inf.* inclined to or marked by preaching.

preacquisition profit (ˌpriːækwɪ'zɪʃən) *n* the retained profit of a company earned before a takeover and therefore not eligible for distribution as a dividend to the shareholders of the acquiring company.

preamble ❶ (priː'æmbᵊl) *n* **1** a preliminary or introductory statement, esp. attached to a statute setting forth its purpose. **2** a preliminary event, fact, etc. [C14: from OF *préambule,* from LL *praeambulum,* from L *prae-* before + *ambulāre* to walk]

preamplifier (priː'æmplɪˌfaɪə) *n* an electronic amplifier used to improve the signal-to-noise ratio of an electronic device. It boosts a low-level signal to an intermediate level before it is transmitted to the main amplifier.

prebend ('prɛbənd) *n* **1** the stipend assigned by a cathedral or collegiate church to a canon or member of the chapter. **2** the land, tithe, or other source of such a stipend. **3** a less common word for **prebendary. 4** *Church of England.* the office of a prebendary. [C15: from OF *prébende,* from Med. L *praebenda* stipend, from L *praebēre* to offer, from *prae* forth + *habēre* to have]
▸**prebendal** (prɪ'bɛndᵊl) *adj*

prebendary ('prɛbəndərɪ, -drɪ) *n, pl* **prebendaries. 1** a canon or member of the chapter of a cathedral or collegiate church who holds a preb-

THESAURUS

praise *n* **1** = **approval**, acclaim, acclamation, accolade, applause, approbation, cheering, commendation, compliment, congratulation, encomium, eulogy, good word, kudos, laudation, ovation, panegyric, plaudit, tribute **2** = **thanks**, adoration, devotion, glory, homage, worship ◆ *vb* **4** = **approve**, acclaim, admire, applaud, cheer, compliment, congratulate, crack up (*inf.*), cry up, eulogize, extol, honour, laud, pat on the back, pay tribute to, sing the praises of, take one's hat off to **5** = **give thanks to**, adore, bless, exalt, glorify, magnify (*arch.*), pay homage to, worship

praiseworthy *adj* = **creditable**, admirable, commendable, estimable, excellent, exemplary, fine, honourable, laudable, meritorious, worthy
Antonyms *adj* condemnable, deplorable, despicable, discreditable, disgraceful, dishonourable, ignoble, reprehensible

prance *vb* **1** = **strut**, parade, show off (*inf.*), stalk, swagger, swank (*inf.*) **2** = **dance**, bound, caper, cavort, cut a rug (*inf.*), frisk, gambol, jump, leap, romp, skip, spring, trip

prank[1] *n* = **trick**, antic, caper, escapade, frolic, jape, lark, practical joke, skylarking (*inf.*)

prate *vb* **1, 2** = **chatter**, babble, blather, blether, boast, brag, drivel, gab (*inf.*), gas (*inf.*), go on, jaw (*sl.*), rabbit (on) (*Brit. inf.*), waffle (*inf., chiefly Brit.*), witter (*inf.*), yak (*sl.*)

prattle *vb* **1** = **chatter**, babble, blather, blether, clack, drivel, gabble, jabber, patter, rabbit (on) (*Brit. inf.*), rattle on, run on, twitter, waffle (*inf., chiefly Brit.*), witter (*inf.*)

pray *vb* **1** = **say one's prayers**, offer a prayer, recite the rosary **2** = **beg**, adjure, ask, beseech, call upon, crave, cry for, entreat, implore, importune, invoke, petition, plead, request, solicit, sue, supplicate, urge

prayer[1] *n* **1, 2** = **orison**, communion, devotion, invocation, litany, supplication **7** = **plea**, appeal, entreaty, petition, request, suit, supplication

preach *vb* **1** = **deliver a sermon**, address, evangelize, exhort, orate **2** = **lecture**, admonish, advocate, exhort, harangue, moralize, sermonize, urge

preacher *n* = **clergyman**, evangelist, minister, missionary, parson, revivalist

preachy *adj Informal* = **moralizing**, canting, didactic, edifying, holier-than-thou, homiletic, pharisaic, pietistic, pontifical, religiose, sanctimonious, self-righteous

preamble *n* **1** = **introduction**, exordium, foreword, opening move, opening statement *or* re-

end. **2** *Church of England.* an honorary canon with the title of prebendary.

Precambrian *or* **Pre-Cambrian** (priːˈkæmbrɪən) *adj* **1** of, denoting, or formed in the earliest geological era, which lasted for about 4 000 000 000 years before the Cambrian period. ◆ *n* **2 the.** the Precambrian era.

precancel (priːˈkænsᵊl) *vb* **precancels, precancelling, precancelled** *or US* **precancels, precanceling, precanceled.** (*tr*) to cancel (postage stamps) before placing them on mail.

precancerous *adj* (esp. of cells) displaying characteristics that may develop into cancer.

precarious **T** (prɪˈkɛərɪəs) *adj* **1** liable to failure or catastrophe; insecure; perilous. **2** *Arch.* dependent on another's will. [C17: from L *precārius* obtained by begging, from *prex* PRAYER[1]]
▸**preˈcariously** *adv* ▸**preˈcariousness** *n*

precast (ˈpriːˌkɑːst) *adj* (esp. of concrete when employed as a structural element in building) cast in a particular form before being used.

precaution **T** (prɪˈkɔːʃən) *n* **1** an action taken to avoid a dangerous or undesirable event. **2** caution practised beforehand; circumspection. [C17: from F, from LL *praecautiō*, from L, from *prae* before + *cavēre* to beware]
▸**preˈcautionary** *adj*

precede **T** (prɪˈsiːd) *vb* **precedes, preceding, preceded. 1** to go or be before (someone or something) in time, place, rank, etc. **2** (*tr*) to preface or introduce. [C14: via OF from L *praecēdere* to go before]

precedence **T** (ˈprɛsɪdəns) *or* **precedency** *n* **1** the act of preceding or the condition of being precedent. **2** the ceremonial order or priority to be observed on formal occasions: *the officers are seated according to precedence.* **3** a right to preferential treatment: *I take precedence over you.*

precedent **T** *n* (ˈprɛsɪdənt). **1** *Law.* a judicial decision that serves as an authority for deciding a later case. **2** an example or instance used to justify later similar occurrences. ◆ *adj* (prɪˈsiːdᵊnt, ˈprɛsɪdənt). **3** preceding.

precedented (ˈprɛsɪˌdɛntɪd) *adj* (of a decision, etc.) supported by having a precedent.

precedential (ˌprɛsɪˈdɛnʃəl) *adj* **1** of or serving as a precedent. **2** having precedence.

preceding **T** (prɪˈsiːdɪŋ) *adj* (*prenominal*) going or coming before; former.

precentor (prɪˈsɛntə) *n* **1** a cleric who directs the choral services in a cathedral. **2** a person who leads a congregation or choir in the sung parts of church services. [C17: from LL *praecentor*, from *prae* before + *canere* to sing]
▸**precentorial** (ˌpriːsɛnˈtɔːrɪəl) *adj* ▸**preˈcentorˌship** *n*

precept **T** (ˈpriːsɛpt) *n* **1** a rule or principle for action. **2** a guide or rule for morals; maxim. **3** a direction, esp. for a technical operation. **4** *Law.* **4a** a writ or warrant. **4b** (in England) an order to collect money under a rate. [C14: from L *praeceptum* injunction, from *praecipere* to admonish, from *prae* before + *capere* to take]
▸**preˈceptive** *adj*

preceptor (prɪˈsɛptə) *n Rare.* a tutor or instructor.
▸**preceptorial** (ˌpriːsɛpˈtɔːrɪəl) *or* **preˈceptoral** *adj* ▸**preˈceptress** *fem n*

precession (prɪˈsɛʃən) *n* **1** the act of preceding. **2** See **precession of the equinoxes. 3** the motion of a spinning body, such as a top, gyroscope, or planet, in which it wobbles so that the axis of rotation sweeps out a cone. [C16: from LL *praecessiō*, from L *praecādere* to precede]
▸**preˈcessional** *adj* ▸**preˈcessionally** *adv*

precession of the equinoxes *n* the slightly earlier occurrence of the equinoxes each year due to the slow continuous westward shift of the equinoctial points along the ecliptic.

precinct **T** (ˈpriːsɪŋkt) *n* **1a** an enclosed area or building marked by a fixed boundary such as a wall. **1b** such a boundary. **2** an area in a town, often closed to traffic, that is designed or reserved for a particular activity: *a shopping precinct.* **3** *US.* **3a** a district of a city for administrative or police purposes. **3b** a polling district. [C15: from Med. L *praecinctum* (something) surrounded, from L *praecingere* to gird around]

precincts **T** (ˈpriːsɪŋkts) *pl n* the surrounding region or area.

preciosity (ˌprɛʃɪˈɒsɪtɪ) *n, pl* **preciosities.** fastidiousness or affectation.

precious **T** (ˈprɛʃəs) *adj* **1** beloved; dear; cherished. **2** very costly or valuable. **3** very fastidious or affected, as in speech, manners, etc. **4** *Inf.* worthless: *you and your precious ideas!* ◆ *adv* **5** *Inf.* (intensifier): *there's precious little left.* [C13: from OF *precios*, from L *pretiōsus* valuable, from *pretium* price]
▸**ˈpreciously** *adv* ▸**ˈpreciousness** *n*

precious metal *n* gold, silver, or platinum.

precious stone *n* any of certain rare minerals, such as diamond, ruby, or opal, that are highly valued as gemstones.

precipice **T** (ˈprɛsɪpɪs) *n* **1** the steep sheer face of a cliff or crag. **2** the cliff or crag itself. [C16: from L *praecipitium* steep place, from *praeceps* headlong]
▸**ˈprecipiced** *adj*

precipitant (prɪˈsɪpɪtənt) *adj* **1** hasty or impulsive; rash. **2** rushing or falling rapidly or without heed. **3** abrupt or sudden. ◆ *n* **4** *Chem.* a substance that causes a precipitate to form.
▸**preˈcipitance** *or* **preˈcipitancy** *n*

precipitate **T** *vb* (prɪˈsɪpɪˌteɪt), **precipitates, precipitating, precipitated. 1** (*tr*) to cause to happen too soon; bring on. **2** to throw or fall from or as from a height. **3** to cause (moisture) to condense and fall as snow, rain, etc., or (of moisture, rain, etc.) to condense and fall thus. **4** *Chem.* to undergo or cause to undergo a process in which a dissolved substance separates from solution as a fine suspension of solid particles. ◆ *adj* (prɪˈsɪpɪtɪt). **5** rushing ahead. **6** done rashly or with undue haste. **7** sudden and brief. ◆ *n* (prɪˈsɪpɪtɪt). **8** *Chem.* a precipitated solid. [C16: from L *praecipitāre* to throw down headlong, from *praeceps* steep, from *prae* before + *caput* head]
▸**preˈcipitable** *adj* ▸**preˌcipitaˈbility** *n* ▸**preˈcipitately** *adv* ▸**preˈcipiˌtator** *n*

precipitation (prɪˌsɪpɪˈteɪʃən) *n* **1** *Meteorol.* **1a** rain, snow, sleet, dew, etc., formed by condensation of water vapour in the atmosphere. **1b** the deposition of these on the earth's surface. **2** the formation of a chemical precipitate. **3** the act of precipitating or the state of being precipitated. **4** rash or undue haste.

precipitous **T** (prɪˈsɪpɪtəs) *adj* **1** resembling a precipice. **2** very steep. **3** hasty or precipitate.
▸**preˈcipitously** *adv* ▸**preˈcipitousness** *n*

> **USAGE NOTE** The use of *precipitous* to mean *hasty* is thought by some people to be incorrect.

precis *or* **précis** **T** (ˈpreɪsiː) *n, pl* **precis** *or* **précis** (ˈpreɪsiːz). **1** a summary of a text; abstract. ◆ *vb* **2** (*tr*) to make a precis of. [C18: from F: PRECISE]

precise **T** (prɪˈsaɪs) *adj* **1** strictly correct in amount or value: *a precise sum.* **2** particular: *this precise location.* **3** using or operating with total accuracy: *precise instruments.* **4** strict in observance of rules, standards, etc.: *a precise mind.* [C16: from F *précis*, from L *praecīdere* to curtail, from *prae* before + *caedere* to cut]
▸**preˈcisely** *adv* ▸**preˈciseness** *n*

THESAURUS

marks, overture, preface, prelude, proem, prolegomenon

precarious *adj* **1** = **dangerous**, built on sand, chancy (*inf.*), dicey (*inf., chiefly Brit.*), dodgy (*Brit., Austral., & NZ inf.*), doubtful, dubious, hazardous, insecure, perilous, risky, shaky, slippery, touch and go, tricky, uncertain, unreliable, unsafe, unsettled, unstable, unsteady, unsure
Antonyms *adj* certain, dependable, reliable, safe, secure, stable, steady

precaution *n* **1** = **safeguard**, belt and braces (*inf.*), insurance, preventative measure, protection, provision, safety measure **2** = **forethought**, anticipation, care, caution, circumspection, foresight, providence, prudence, wariness

precede *vb* **1, 2** = **go before**, antecede, antedate, come first, forerun, go ahead of, head, herald, introduce, lead, pave the way, preface, take precedence, usher

precedence *n* **1, 3** = **priority**, antecedence, lead, pre-eminence, preference, primacy, rank, seniority, superiority, supremacy

precedent *n* **2** = **instance**, antecedent, authority, criterion, example, exemplar, model, paradigm, pattern, previous example, prototype, standard

preceding *adj* = **previous**, above, aforementioned, aforesaid, anterior, earlier, foregoing, former, past, prior

precept *n* **1** = **rule**, behest, canon, command, commandment, decree, dictum, direction, instruction, law, mandate, order, ordinance, principle, regulation, statute **2** = **maxim**, axiom, byword, dictum, guideline, motto, principle, rule, saying

precinct *n* **1** = **enclosure**, bound, boundary, confine, limit **2** = **area**, district, quarter, section, sector, zone

precincts *pl n* = **district**, borders, bounds, confines, environs, limits, milieu, neighbourhood, purlieus, region, surrounding area

precious *adj* **1** = **loved**, adored, beloved, cherished, darling, dear, dearest, fave (*inf.*), favourite, idolized, prized, treasured, valued **2** = **valuable**, choice, costly, dear, expensive, exquisite, fine, high-priced, inestimable, invaluable, priceless, prized, rare, recherché **3** = **affected**, alembicated, artificial, chichi, fastidious, overnice, overrefined, twee (*Brit. inf.*)

precipice *n* **1, 2** = **cliff**, bluff, brink, cliff face, crag, height, rock face, sheer drop, steep

precipitate *vb* **1** = **quicken**, accelerate, advance, bring on, dispatch, expedite, further, hasten, hurry, press, push forward, speed up, trigger **2** = **throw**, cast, discharge, fling, hurl, launch, let fly, send forth ◆ *adj* **5** = **swift**, breakneck, headlong, plunging, rapid, rushing, violent **6** = **hasty**, frantic, harum-scarum, heedless, hurried, ill-advised, impetuous, impulsive, indiscreet, madcap, precipitous, rash, reckless **7** = **sudden**, abrupt, brief, quick, unexpected, without warning

precipitous *adj* **2** = **sheer**, abrupt, dizzy, falling sharply, high, perpendicular, steep **3** = **hasty**, abrupt, careless, harum-scarum, heedless, hurried, ill-advised, precipitate, rash, reckless, sudden

precis *n* **1** = **summary**, abridgment, abstract, *aperçu*, compendium, condensation, digest, outline, résumé, rundown, sketch, synopsis ◆ *vb* **2** = **summarize**, abridge, abstract, compress, condense, outline, shorten, sum up

precise *adj* **1, 2** = **exact**, absolute, accurate, actual, clear-cut, correct, definite, explicit, express, fixed, literal, particular, specific, strict, unequivocal **4** = **strict**, careful, ceremonious, exact, fastidious, finicky, formal, inflexible, meticulous, nice, particular, prim, punctilious, puritanical, rigid, scrupulous, stiff
Antonyms *adj* ≠ **exact:** ambiguous, equivocal, incorrect, indefinite, indistinct, inexact, loose, vague ≠ **strict:** careless, flexible, haphazard, inexact, informal, relaxed, unceremonious

precisely *adv* **1, 2** = **exactly**, absolutely, accurately, bang, correctly, just, just so, literally, neither more nor less, on the button (*inf.*), plumb (*inf.*), slap (*inf.*), smack (*inf.*), square, squarely, strictly, to the letter

precision ⓘ (prɪˈsɪʒən) *n* **1** the quality of being precise; accuracy. **2** (*modifier*) characterized by a high degree of exactness: *precision grinding*. [C17: from L *praecīsiō* a cutting off; see PRECISE]
▸**preˈcisionism** *n* ▸**preˈcisionist** *n*

preclassical (priːˈklæsɪkᵊl) *adj* (of music, literature, etc.) before a period regarded as classical.

preclude ⓘ (prɪˈkluːd) *vb* **precludes, precluding, precluded.** (*tr*) **1** to exclude or debar. **2** to make impossible, esp. beforehand. [C17: from L *praeclūdere* to shut up, from *prae* before + *claudere* to close]
▸**preclusion** (prɪˈkluːʒən) *n* ▸**preclusive** (prɪˈkluːsɪv) *adj*

precocial (prɪˈkəʊʃəl) *adj* **1** denoting birds whose young, after hatching, are covered with down and capable of leaving the nest within a few days. ◆ *n* **2** a precocial bird. ◆ Cf. **altricial.**

precocious ⓘ (prɪˈkəʊʃəs) *adj* **1** ahead in development, such as the mental development of a child. **2** *Bot.* flowering or ripening early. [C17: from L *praecox*, from *prae* early + *coquere* to ripen]
▸**preˈcociously** *adv* ▸**preˈcociousness** *or* **precocity** (prɪˈkɒsɪtɪ) *n*

precognition (ˌpriːkɒgˈnɪʃən) *n Psychol.* the alleged ability to foresee future events. [C17: from LL *praecognitiō* foreknowledge, from *praecognoscere* to foresee]
▸**precognitive** (priːˈkɒgnɪtɪv) *adj*

preconceive ⓘ (ˌpriːkənˈsiːv) *vb* **preconceives, preconceiving, preconceived.** (*tr*) to form an idea of beforehand.
▸**preconception** (ˌpriːkənˈsɛpʃən) *n*

precondition ⓘ (ˌpriːkənˈdɪʃən) *n* **1** a necessary or required condition; prerequisite. ◆ *vb* **2** (*tr*) *Psychol.* to present successively two stimuli to (an organism) without reinforcement so that they become associated; if a response is then conditioned to the second stimulus on its own, the same response will be evoked by the first stimulus.

preconize *or* **preconise** (ˈpriːkəˌnaɪz) *vb* **preconizes, preconizing, preconized** *or* **preconises, preconising, preconised.** (*tr*) **1** to announce or commend publicly. **2** to summon publicly. **3** (of the pope) to approve the appointment of (a nominee) to one of the higher dignities in the Roman Catholic Church. [C15: from Med. L *praecōnīzāre* to make an announcement, from L *praecō* herald]
▸**ˌpreconiˈzation** *or* **ˌpreconiˈsation** *n*

precursor ⓘ (prɪˈkɜːsə) *n* **1** a person or thing that precedes and announces someone or something to come. **2** a predecessor. **3** a chemical substance that gives rise to another more important substance. [C16: from L *praecursor* one who runs in front, from *praecurrere*, from *prae* in front + *currere* to run]

precursory ⓘ (prɪˈkɜːsərɪ) *or* **precursive** *adj* **1** serving as a precursor. **2** preliminary.

pred. *abbrev. for* predicate.

predacious *or* **predaceous** (prɪˈdeɪʃəs) *adj* (of animals) habitually hunting and killing other animals for food. [C18: from L *praeda* plunder]
▸**preˈdaciousness, preˈdaceousness,** *or* **predacity** (prɪˈdæsɪtɪ) *n*

predate (priːˈdeɪt) *vb* **predates, predating, predated.** (*tr*) **1** to affix a date to (a document, paper, etc.) that is earlier than the actual date. **2** to assign a date to (an event, period, etc.) that is earlier than the actual or previously assigned date of occurrence. **3** to be or occur at an earlier date than; precede in time.

predation (prɪˈdeɪʃən) *n* a relationship between two species of animal in a community, in which one hunts, kills, and eats the other.

predator (ˈprɛdətə) *n* **1** any carnivorous animal. **2** a predatory person or thing.

predatory ⓘ (ˈprɛdətərɪ) *adj* **1** *Zool.* another word for **predacious. 2** of or characterized by plundering, robbing, etc. [C16: from L *praedātōrius* rapacious, from *praedārī* to pillage, from *praeda* booty]
▸**ˈpredatorily** *adv* ▸**ˈpredatoriness** *n*

predecease (ˌpriːdɪˈsiːs) *vb* **predeceases, predeceasing, predeceased.** to die before (some other person).

predecessor ⓘ (ˈpriːdɪˌsɛsə) *n* **1** a person who precedes another, as in an office. **2** something that precedes something else. **3** an ancestor. [C14: via OF from LL *praedēcessor*, from *prae* before + *dēcēdere* to go away]

predella (prɪˈdɛlə) *n, pl* **predelle** (-liː). **1** a painting or a series of small paintings in a long strip forming the lower edge of an altarpiece or the face of an altar step. **2** a platform in a church upon which the altar stands. [C19: from It.: step, prob. from OHG *bret* board]

predestinarian (ˌpriːdɛstɪˈnɛərɪən) *n* **1** a person who believes in divine predestination. ◆ *adj* **2** of or relating to predestination or those who believe in it.

predestinate *vb* (priːˈdɛstɪˌneɪt), **predestinates, predestinating, predestinated. 1** another word for **predestine.** ◆ *adj* (priːˈdɛstɪnɪt, -ˌneɪt). **2** predestined.

predestination ⓘ (priːˌdɛstɪˈneɪʃən) *n* **1** *Christian theol.* **1a** the act of God foreordaining every event from eternity. **1b** the doctrine or belief, esp. associated with Calvin, that the final salvation of some of mankind is foreordained from eternity by God. **2** the act of predestining or the state of being predestined.

predestine ⓘ (priːˈdɛstɪn) *or* **predestinate** *vb* **predestines, predestining, predestined** *or* **predestinates, predestinating, predestinated.** (*tr*) **1** to determine beforehand. **2** *Christian theol.* (of God) to decree from eternity (any event, esp. the final salvation of individuals). [C14: from L *praedestināre* to resolve beforehand]

predetermine ⓘ (ˌpriːdɪˈtɜːmɪn) *vb* **predetermines, predetermining, predetermined.** (*tr*) **1** to determine beforehand. **2** to influence or bias.
▸**ˌpredeˈterminable** *adj* ▸**ˌpredeˈterminate** *adj* ▸**ˌpredeˌtermiˈnation** *n*

predicable (ˈprɛdɪkəbᵊl) *adj* **1** capable of being predicated or asserted. ◆ *n* **2** a quality that can be predicated. **3** *Logic, obs.* any of the five Aristotelian classes of predicates, namely genus, species, difference, property, and relation. [C16: from L *praedicābilis*, from *praedicāre* to assert publicly; see PREDICATE]
▸**ˌpredicaˈbility** *n*

predicament ⓘ *n* **1** (prɪˈdɪkəmənt) a perplexing, embarrassing, or difficult situation. **2** (ˈprɛdɪkəmənt). *Logic.* a logical category. [C14: from LL *praedicāmentum* what is predicated, from *praedicāre* to announce; see PREDICATE]

predicant (ˈprɛdɪkənt) *adj* **1** of or relating to preaching. ◆ *n* **2** a member of a religious order founded for preaching, esp. a Dominican. [C17: from L *praedicāns* preaching, from *praedicāre* to say publicly; see PREDICATE]

predicate ⓘ *vb* (ˈprɛdɪˌkeɪt), **predicates, predicating, predicated.** (*mainly tr*) **1** (*also intr; when tr, may take a clause as object*) to declare or affirm. **2** to imply or connote. **3** (foll. by *on* or *upon*) *Chiefly US.* to base (a proposition, argument, etc.). **4** *Logic.* to assert (a property or condition) of the subject of a proposition. ◆ *n* (ˈprɛdɪkɪt). **5** *Grammar.* the part of a sentence in which something is asserted or denied of the subject of a sentence. **6** *Logic.* a term, property, or condition that is affirmed or denied concerning the subject of a proposition. ◆ *adj* (ˈprɛdɪkɪt). **7** of or relating to something that has been predicated. [C16: from L *praedicāre* to assert publicly, from *prae* in front + *dīcere* to say]
▸**ˌprediˈcation** *n*

predicate calculus *n* the system of symbolic logic concerned not only with relations between propositions as wholes but also with the representation by symbols of individuals and predicates in propositions. See also **propositional calculus.**

predicative (prɪˈdɪkətɪv) *adj Grammar.* relating to or occurring within the predicate of a sentence: *a predicative adjective.* Cf. **attributive.**
▸**preˈdicatively** *adv*

predict ⓘ (prɪˈdɪkt) *vb* (*tr; may take a clause as object*) to state or make a declaration about in advance; foretell. [C17: from L *praedīcere* to mention beforehand]
▸**preˈdictable** *adj* ▸**preˌdictaˈbility** *n* ▸**preˈdictably** *adv* ▸**preˈdictive** *adj* ▸**preˈdictor** *n*

prediction ⓘ (prɪˈdɪkʃən) *n* **1** the act of predicting. **2** something predicted; a forecast.

predigest (ˌpriːdaɪˈdʒɛst, -dɪ-) *vb* (*tr*) to treat (food) artificially to aid subsequent digestion in the body.
▸**ˌpreˈdiˈgestion** *n*

predikant (ˌprɛdɪˈkænt) *n* a minister in the Dutch Reformed Church,

THESAURUS

precision *n* **1** = **exactness**, accuracy, care, correctness, definiteness, dotting the i's and crossing the t's, exactitude, fidelity, meticulousness, nicety, particularity, preciseness, rigour

preclude *vb* **1, 2** = **prevent**, check, debar, exclude, forestall, hinder, inhibit, make impossible, make impracticable, obviate, prohibit, put a stop to, restrain, rule out, stop

precocious *adj* **1** = **advanced**, ahead, bright, developed, forward, quick, smart
Antonyms *adj* backward, dense, dull, retarded, slow, underdeveloped, unresponsive

preconceived *adj* = **presumed**, forejudged, predetermined, prejudged, premature, presupposed

preconception *n* = **preconceived idea** *or* **notion**, bias, notion, predisposition, prejudice, prepossession, presumption, presupposition

precondition *n* **1** = **necessity**, essential, must, prerequisite, requirement, *sine qua non*

precursor *n* **1** = **herald**, forerunner, harbinger, messenger, usher, vanguard **2** = **forerunner**, antecedent, forebear, originator, pioneer, predecessor

precursory *adj* **1, 2** = **preceding**, antecedent, introductory, prefatory, preliminary, preparatory, previous, prior

predatory *adj* **1** = **hunting**, carnivorous, predacious, rapacious, raptorial, ravening **2** = **rapacious**, despoiling, greedy, marauding, pillaging, plundering, ravaging, thieving, voracious, vulturine, vulturous

predecessor *n* **1** = **previous job holder**, antecedent, forerunner, former job holder, precursor, prior job holder **3** = **ancestor**, antecedent, forebear, forefather

predestination *n* **1, 2** = **fate**, destiny, doom, election (*Theology*), foreordainment, foreordination, lot, necessity, predetermination

predestined *adj* **1** = **fated**, doomed, foreordained, meant, predestinated, predetermined, pre-elected, preordained

predetermined *adj* **1** = **prearranged**, agreed, arranged in advance, cut and dried (*inf.*), decided beforehand, fixed, preplanned, set, settled, set up

predicament *n* **1** = **fix** (*inf.*), corner, dilemma, emergency, hole (*sl.*), hot water (*inf.*), how-do-you-do (*inf.*), jam (*inf.*), mess, pickle (*inf.*), pinch, plight, quandary, scrape (*inf.*), situation, spot (*inf.*), state, tight spot

predicate *vb* **1** = **declare**, affirm, assert, aver, avouch, avow, contend, maintain, proclaim, state **2** = **imply**, connote, indicate, intimate, signify, suggest **3** *Chiefly U.S. foll. by* **on** *or* **upon** = **base**, build, establish, found, ground, postulate, rest

predict *vb* = **foretell**, augur, call, divine, forebode, forecast, foresee, portend, presage, prognosticate, prophesy, soothsay, vaticinate (*rare*)

predictable *adj* = **likely**, anticipated, calculable, certain, expected, foreseeable, foreseen, on the cards, reliable, sure, sure-fire (*inf.*)
Antonyms *adj* out of the blue, surprising, unexpected, unforeseen, unlikely, unpredictable

prediction *n* **1, 2** = **prophecy**, augury, divina-

esp. in South Africa. [from Du., from OF *predicant,* from LL, from *praedicāre* to PREACH]

predilection ➊ (ˌpriːdɪˈlɛkʃən) *n* a predisposition, preference, or bias. [C18: from F *prédilection,* from Med. L *praedīligere* to prefer, from L *prae* before + *dīligere* to love]

predispose ➊ (ˌpriːdɪˈspəuz) *vb* **predisposes, predisposing, predisposed.** (*tr*) (often foll. by *to* or *towards*) to incline or make (someone) susceptible to something beforehand.
▸ˌ**predisˈposal** *n* ▸ˌ**predispoˈsition** *n*

prednisolone (prɛdˈnɪsəˌləun) *n* a steroid drug derived from prednisone and having the same uses as cortisone. [C20: altered from PREDNISONE]

prednisone (ˈprɛdnɪˌsəun) *n* a steroid drug derived from cortisone and having the same uses. [C20: perhaps from PRE(GNANT) + -D(IE)N(E) + (CORT)ISONE]

predominant ➊ (prɪˈdɒmɪnənt) *adj* **1** superior in power, influence, etc., over others. **2** prevailing.
▸**preˈdominance** *n* ▸**preˈdominantly** *adv*

predominate ➊ *vb* (prɪˈdɒmɪˌneɪt), **predominates, predominating, predominated.** (*intr*) **1** (often foll. by *over*) to have power, influence, or control. **2** to prevail or preponderate. ◆ *adj* (prɪˈdɒmɪnɪt). **3** another word for **predominant.** [C16: from Med. L *praedominārī,* from L *prae* before + *dominārī* to bear rule]
▸**preˈdominately** *adv* ▸**preˌdomiˈnation** *n*

pre-eclampsia (ˌpriːɪˈklæmpsɪə) *n* a serious condition that can occur late in pregnancy. If not treated it can lead to eclampsia.

pre-embryo (priːˈɛmbrɪˌəu) *n, pl* **pre-embryos.** the structure formed after fertilization of an ovum but before differentiation of embryonic tissue.

pre-eminent ➊ (prɪˈɛmɪnənt) *adj* extremely eminent or distinguished; outstanding.
▸**pre-ˈeminence** *n* ▸**pre-ˈeminently** *adv*

pre-empt ➊ (prɪˈɛmpt) *vb* **1** (*tr*) to acquire in advance of or to the exclusion of others; appropriate. **2** (*tr*) *Chiefly US.* to occupy (public land) in order to acquire a prior right to purchase. **3** (*intr*) *Bridge.* to make a high opening bid, often on a weak hand, to shut out opposition bidding.
▸**pre-ˈemptor** *n*

pre-emption (prɪˈɛmpʃən) *n* **1** *Law.* the purchase of or right to purchase property in preference to others. **2** *International law.* the right of a government to intercept and seize property of the subjects of another state while in transit, esp. in time of war. [C16: from Med. L *praeemptiō,* from *praeemere* to buy beforehand]

pre-emptive (prɪˈɛmptɪv) *adj* **1** of, involving, or capable of pre-emption. **2** *Bridge.* (of a high bid) made to shut out opposition bidding. **3** *Mil.* designed to reduce or destroy an enemy's attacking strength before it can use it: *a pre-emptive strike.*

preen ➊ (priːn) *vb* **1** (of birds) to maintain (feathers) in a healthy condition by arrangement, cleaning, and other contact with the bill. **2** to dress or array (oneself) carefully; primp. **3** (usually foll. by *on*) to pride or congratulate (oneself). [C14 *preinen,* prob. from *prunen,* infl. by *prenen* to prick; suggestive of the pricking movement of the bird's beak]
▸ˈ**preener** *n*

pre-exist (prɪɪgˈzɪst) *vb* (*intr*) to exist at an earlier time.
▸**pre-exˈistent** *adj* ▸**pre-exˈistence** *n*

pref. *abbrev. for:* **1** preface. **2** prefatory. **3** preference. **4** preferred. **5** prefix.

prefab (ˈpriːˌfæb) *n* a building that is prefabricated, esp. a small house.

prefabricate (priːˈfæbrɪˌkeɪt) *vb* **prefabricates, prefabricating, prefabricated.** (*tr*) to manufacture sections of (a building) so that they can be easily transported to and rapidly assembled on a building site.
▸**preˌfabriˈcation** *n*

preface ➊ (ˈprɛfɪs) *n* **1** a statement written as an introduction to a literary or other work, typically explaining its scope, intention, method, etc.; foreword. **2** anything introductory. ◆ *vb* **prefaces, prefacing, prefaced.** (*tr*) **3** to furnish with a preface. **4** to serve as a preface to. [C14: from Med. L *praefātia,* from L *praefātiō* a saying beforehand, from *praefārī* to utter in advance]
▸ˈ**prefacer** *n*

prefatory ➊ (ˈprɛfətərɪ, -trɪ) *or* **prefatorial** (ˌprɛfəˈtɔːrɪəl) *adj* of or serving as a preface; introductory. [C17: from L *praefārī* to say in advance]

prefect (ˈpriːfɛkt) *n* **1** (in France, Italy, etc.) the chief administrative officer in a department. **2** (in France, etc.) the head of a police force. **3** *Brit., Austral., & NZ.* a schoolchild appointed to a position of limited power over his fellows. **4** (in ancient Rome) any of several magistrates or military commanders. **5** *RC Church.* one of two senior masters in a Jesuit school or college. [C14: from L *praefectus* one put in charge, from *praeficere* to place in authority over, from *prae* before + *facere* to do]
▸**prefectorial** (ˌpriːfɛkˈtɔːrɪəl) *adj*

prefecture (ˈpriːfɛkˌtjuə) *n* **1** the office, position, or area of authority of a prefect. **2** the official residence of a prefect in France, etc.

prefer ➊ (prɪˈfɜː) *vb* **prefers, preferring, preferred. 1** (when *tr, may take a clause as object or an infinitive*) to like better or value more highly: *I prefer to stand.* **2** *Law.* (esp. of the police) to put (charges) before a court, magistrate, etc., for consideration and judgment. **3** (*tr; often passive*) to advance in rank over another or others; promote. [C14: from L *praeferre* to carry in front, prefer]

> **USAGE NOTE** Normally, *to* is used after *prefer* and *preferable,* not *than: I prefer Brahms to Tchaikovsky; a small income is preferable to no income at all.* However, *than* or *rather* should be used to link infinitives: *I prefer to walk than/rather than to catch the train.*

preferable ➊ (ˈprɛfərəbᵊl) *adj* preferred or more desirable.
▸ˈ**preferably** *adv*

> **USAGE NOTE** Since *preferable* already means *more desirable,* one should not say something is *more preferable.* See also at **prefer.**

preference ➊ (ˈprɛfərəns, ˈprɛfrəns) *n* **1** the act of preferring. **2** something or someone preferred. **3** *International trade.* the granting of favour or precedence to particular foreign countries, as by levying differential tariffs.

preference shares *pl n Brit. & Austral.* fixed-interest shares issued by a company and giving their holders a prior right over ordinary shareholders to payment of dividend and to repayment of capital if the company is liquidated. US and Canad. name: **preferred stock.** Cf. **ordinary shares, preferred ordinary shares.**

preferential ➊ (ˌprɛfəˈrɛnʃəl) *adj* **1** showing or resulting from prefer-

THESAURUS

tion, forecast, prognosis, prognostication, soothsaying, sortilege

predilection *n* = **liking,** bag (*sl.*), bias, cup of tea (*inf.*), fancy, fondness, inclination, leaning, love, partiality, penchant, predisposition, preference, proclivity, proneness, propensity, taste, tendency, weakness

predispose *vb* = **incline,** affect, bias, dispose, induce, influence, lead, make (one) of a mind to, prejudice, prepare, prime, prompt, sway

predisposed *adj* = **inclined,** agreeable, amenable, given, liable, minded, prone, ready, subject, susceptible, willing

predisposition *n* = **inclination,** bent, bias, disposition, likelihood, penchant, potentiality, predilection, proclivity, proneness, propensity, susceptibility, tendency, willingness

predominance *n* **1, 2** = **prevalence,** ascendancy, control, dominance, dominion, edge, greater number, hold, leadership, mastery, paramountcy, preponderance, supremacy, sway, upper hand, weight

predominant *adj* **1, 2** = **main,** ascendant, capital, chief, controlling, dominant, important, leading, notable, paramount, preponderant, prevailing, prevalent, primary, prime, principal, prominent, ruling, sovereign, superior, supreme, top-priority
Antonyms *adj* inferior, minor, secondary, subordinate, unimportant, uninfluential

predominantly *adv* **2** = **mainly,** chiefly, for the most part, generally, in the main, largely, mostly, on the whole, preponderantly, primarily, principally, to a great extent

predominate *vb* **1, 2** = **prevail,** be most noticeable, carry weight, get the upper hand, hold sway, outweigh, overrule, overshadow, preponderate, reign, rule, tell

pre-eminence *n* = **superiority,** distinction, excellence, paramountcy, predominance, prestige, prominence, renown, supremacy, transcendence

pre-eminent *adj* = **outstanding,** chief, consummate, distinguished, excellent, foremost, incomparable, matchless, paramount, peerless, predominant, renowned, superior, supreme, transcendent, unequalled, unrivalled, unsurpassed

pre-eminently *adv* = **particularly,** above all, by far, conspicuously, eminently, emphatically, exceptionally, far and away, incomparably, inimitably, matchlessly, notably, *par excellence,* second to none, signally, singularly, strikingly, superlatively, supremely

pre-empt *vb* **1** = **anticipate,** acquire, appropriate, arrogate, assume, seize, take over, usurp

preen *vb* **1** = **clean,** plume **2** = **smarten,** array, deck out, doll up (*sl.*), dress up, prettify, primp, prink, spruce up, titivate, trig (*arch. or dialect*), trim **3** *usually foll. by* **on** = **pride oneself,** congratulate oneself, pique oneself, plume oneself

preface *n* **1** = **introduction,** exordium, foreword, preamble, preliminary, prelude, proem, prolegomenon, prologue ◆ *vb* **4** = **introduce,** begin, launch, lead up to, open, precede, prefix

prefatory *adj* = **introductory,** antecedent, opening, precursory, prefatorial, preliminary, prelusive, prelusory, preparatory, proemial, prolegomenal

prefer *vb* **1** = **like better,** adopt, be partial to, choose, desire, elect, fancy, favour, go for, incline towards, opt for, pick, plump for, select, single out, wish, would rather, would sooner **2** *Law* = **put forward,** file, lodge, place, present, press **3** = **promote,** advance, aggrandize, elevate, move up, raise, upgrade

preferable *adj* = **better,** best, choice, chosen, favoured, more desirable, more eligible, superior, worthier
Antonyms *adj* average, fair, ineligible, inferior, mediocre, poor, second-rate, undesirable

preferably *adv* = **rather,** as a matter of choice, by choice, first, in *or* for preference, much rather, much sooner, sooner, willingly

preference *n* **1** = **priority,** advantage, favoured treatment, favouritism, first place, precedence, pride of place **2** = **first choice,** bag (*sl.*), choice, cup of tea (*inf.*), desire, election, fave (*inf.*), favourite, option, partiality, pick, predilection, selection, top of the list

preferential *adj* **1** = **privileged,** advantageous, better, favoured, partial, partisan, special, superior

ence. **2** giving, receiving, or originating from preference in international trade.
▸ **ˌprefer'entially** *adv*

preferment ⓣ (prɪ'fɜːmənt) *n* **1** the act of promoting to a higher position, office, etc. **2** the state of being preferred for promotion or social advancement. **3** the act of preferring.

preferred ordinary shares *pl n Brit.* shares issued by a company that rank between preference shares and ordinary shares in the payment of dividends. Cf. **preference shares, ordinary shares.**

prefigure ⓣ (priː'fɪgə) *vb* **prefigures, prefiguring, prefigured.** (*tr*) **1** to represent or suggest in advance. **2** to imagine beforehand.
▸ **ˌprefigu'ration** *n* ▸ **pre'figurement** *n*

prefix *n* ('priːfɪks). **1** *Grammar.* an affix that precedes the stem to which it is attached, as for example *un-* in *unhappy*. Cf. **suffix** (sense 1). **2** something coming or placed before. ◆ *vb* (priː'fɪks, 'priːfɪks). (*tr*) **3** to put or place before. **4** *Grammar.* to add (a morpheme) as a prefix to the beginning of a word.
▸ **prefixion** (priː'fɪkʃən) *n*

prefrontal (priː'frʌntᵊl) *adj* in or relating to the foremost part of the frontal lobe of the brain.

preglacial (priː'gleɪsɪəl, -ʃəl) *adj* formed or occurring before a glacial period, esp. before the Pleistocene epoch.

pregnable ('prɛgnəbᵊl) *adj* capable of being assailed or captured. [C15 *prenable*, from OF *prendre* to take, from L *prehendere* to catch]

pregnant ⓣ ('prɛgnənt) *adj* **1** carrying a fetus or fetuses within the womb. **2** full of meaning or significance. **3** inventive or imaginative. **4** prolific or fruitful. [C16: from L *praegnāns* with child, from *prae* before + (*g*)*nascī* to be born]
▸ **'pregnancy** *n* ▸ **'pregnantly** *adv*

prehensile (prɪ'hɛnsaɪl) *adj* adapted for grasping, esp. by wrapping around a support: *a prehensile tail*. [C18: from F *préhensile*, from L *prehendere* to grasp]
▸ **prehensility** (ˌpriːhɛn'sɪlɪtɪ) *n*

prehension (prɪ'hɛnʃən) *n* **1** the act of grasping. **2** apprehension by the mind.

prehistoric ⓣ (ˌpriːhɪ'stɒrɪk) *or* **prehistorical** *adj* of or relating to man's development before the appearance of the written word.
▸ **ˌprehis'torically** *adv* ▸ **pre'history** *n*

pre-ignition (ˌpriːɪg'nɪʃən) *n* ignition of all or part of the explosive charge in an internal-combustion engine before the exact instant necessary for correct operation.

prejudge ⓣ (priː'dʒʌdʒ) *vb* **prejudges, prejudging, prejudged.** (*tr*) to judge beforehand, esp. without sufficient evidence.

prejudice ⓣ ('prɛdʒʊdɪs) *n* **1** an opinion formed beforehand, esp. an unfavourable one based on inadequate facts. **2** the act or condition of holding such opinions. **3** intolerance of or dislike for people of a specific race, religion, etc. **4** disadvantage or injury resulting from prejudice. **5 in** (*or* **to**) **the prejudice of.** to the detriment of. **6 without prejudice.** *Law.* without dismissing or detracting from an existing right or claim. ◆ *vb* **prejudices, prejudicing, prejudiced.** (*tr*) **7** to cause to be prejudiced. **8** to disadvantage or injure by prejudice. [C13: from OF *préjudice*, from L *praejūdicium*, from *prae* before + *jūdicium* sentence, from *jūdex* a judge]

prejudicial ⓣ (ˌprɛdʒʊ'dɪʃəl) *adj* causing prejudice; damaging.
▸ **ˌpreju'dicially** *adv*

prelacy ('prɛləsɪ) *n, pl* **prelacies. 1** Also called: **prelature. 1a** the office or status of a prelate. **1b** prelates collectively. **2** *Often derog.* government of the Church by prelates.

prelapsarian (ˌpriːlæp'sɛərɪən) *adj* of or relating to the human state before the Fall: *prelapsarian innocence*.

prelate ('prɛlɪt) *n* a Church dignitary of high rank, such as a cardinal, bishop, or abbot. [C13: from OF *prélat*, from Church L *praelātus*, from L *praeferre* to hold in special esteem]
▸ **prelatic** (prɪ'lætɪk) *or* **pre'latical** *adj*

preliminaries (prɪ'lɪmɪnərɪz) *pl n* the full word for **prelims.**

preliminary ⓣ (prɪ'lɪmɪnərɪ) *adj* **1** (*usually prenominal*) occurring before or in preparation; introductory. ◆ *n, pl* **preliminaries. 2** a preliminary event or occurrence. **3** an eliminating contest held before the main competition. [C17: from NL *praelīminăris*, from L *prae* before + *līmen* threshold]
▸ **pre'liminarily** *adv*

prelims ('priːlɪmz, prə'lɪmz) *pl n* **1** Also called: **front matter.** the pages of a book, such as the title page and contents, before the main text. **2** the first public examinations taken for the bachelor's degree in some universities. **3** (in Scotland) the school examinations taken before public examinations. [C19: a contraction of PRELIMINARIES]

prelude ⓣ ('prɛljuːd) *n* **1a** a piece of music that precedes a fugue, or forms the first movement of a suite, or an introduction to an act in an opera, etc. **1b** (esp. for piano) a self-contained piece of music. **2** an introduction or preceding event, occurrence, etc. ◆ *vb* **preludes, preluding, preluded. 3** to serve as a prelude to (something). **4** (*tr*) to introduce by a prelude. [C16: from Med. L *praelūdium*, from *prae* before + L *lūdere* to play]
▸ **preludial** (prɪ'ljuːdɪəl) *adj*

premarital (priː'mærɪtᵊl) *adj* (esp. of sexual relations) occurring before marriage.

premature ⓣ (ˌprɛmə'tjʊə, 'prɛməˌtjʊə) *adj* **1** occurring or existing before the normal or expected time. **2** impulsive or hasty: *a premature judgment*. **3** (of an infant) born before the end of the full period of gestation. [C16: from L *praemātūrus* very early, from *prae* in advance + *mātūrus* ripe]
▸ **ˌprema'turely** *adv*

premedical (priː'mɛdɪkᵊl) *adj* **1** of or relating to a course of study prerequisite for entering medical school. **2** of or relating to a person engaged in such a course of study.

premedication (ˌpriːmɛdɪ'keɪʃən) *n Surgery.* any drugs administered to sedate and otherwise prepare a patient for general anaesthesia.

premeditate ⓣ (prɪ'mɛdɪˌteɪt) *vb* **premeditates, premeditating, premeditated.** to plan or consider (something, such as a violent crime) beforehand.
▸ **pre'mediˌtator** *n*

premeditation ⓣ (prɪˌmɛdɪ'teɪʃən) *n* **1** *Law.* prior resolve to do some act or to commit a crime. **2** the act of premeditating.

premenstrual syndrome *or* **tension** *n* symptoms, esp. nervous tension, that may be experienced because of hormonal changes in the days before a menstrual period starts. Abbrevs.: **PMS, PMT.**

premier ⓣ ('prɛmjə) *n* **1** another name for **prime minister. 2** any of the heads of government of the Canadian provinces and the Australian states. **3** *Austral.* a team that wins a premiership. ◆ *adj* (*prenominal*) **4** first in importance, rank, etc. **5** first in occurrence; earliest. [C15: from OF: first, from L *prīmārius* principal, from *prīmus* first]

premiere ⓣ ('prɛmɪˌɛə, 'prɛmɪə) *n* **1** the first public performance of a film, play, opera, etc. **2** the leading lady in a theatre company. ◆ *vb* **premieres, premiering, premiered. 3** (*tr*) to give a premiere of: *the show will be premiered on Broadway*. [C19: from F, fem of *premier* first]

premiership ('prɛmjəʃɪp) *n* **1** the office of premier. **2a** a championship competition held among a number of sporting clubs. **2b** a victory in such a championship.

premillennialism (ˌpriːmɪ'lɛnɪəˌlɪzəm) *n* the doctrine or belief that the millennium will be preceded by the Second Coming of Christ.
▸ **ˌpremil'lennialist** *n* ▸ **ˌpremille'narian** *n, adj*

THESAURUS

preferment *n* **1 = promotion**, advancement, dignity, elevation, exaltation, rise, upgrading

prefigure *vb* **1 = foreshadow**, adumbrate, foretoken, indicate, intimate, portend, presage, shadow forth, suggest **2 = imagine**, consider, fancy, picture, presuppose

pregnancy *n* **1 = gestation**, gravidity

pregnant *adj* **1 = expectant**, big *or* heavy with child, enceinte, expecting (*inf.*), gravid, in the club (*Brit. sl.*), in the family way (*inf.*), in the pudding club (*sl.*), preggers (*Brit. inf.*), with child **2 = meaningful**, charged, eloquent, expressive, loaded, pointed, significant, suggestive, telling, weighty **3 = imaginative**, creative, inventive, original, seminal **4 = prolific**, abounding in, abundant, fecund, fertile, fraught, fruitful, full, productive, replete, rich in, teeming

prehistoric *adj* **= earliest**, early, primeval, primitive, primordial

prejudge *vb* **= jump to conclusions**, anticipate, forejudge, make a hasty assessment, presume, presuppose

prejudice *n* **1 = bias**, jaundiced eye, partiality, preconceived notion, preconception, prejudgment, warp **3 = discrimination**, bigotry, chauvinism, injustice, intolerance, narrow-mindedness, racism, sexism, unfairness **4 = harm**, damage, detriment, disadvantage, hurt, impairment, loss, mischief ◆ *vb* **7 = bias**, colour, distort, influence, jaundice, poison, predispose, prepossess, slant, sway, warp **8 = harm**, damage, hinder, hurt, impair, injure, mar, spoil, undermine

prejudiced *adj* **1, 3 = biased**, bigoted, conditioned, discriminatory, influenced, intolerant, jaundiced, narrow-minded, one-sided, opinionated, partial, partisan, prepossessed, unfair
Antonyms *adj* fair, impartial, just, neutral, not bigoted, not prejudiced, open-minded, unbiased

prejudicial *adj* **= harmful**, counterproductive, damaging, deleterious, detrimental, disadvantageous, hurtful, inimical, injurious, undermining, unfavourable

preliminary *adj* **1 = first**, exploratory, initial, initiatory, introductory, opening, pilot, precursory, prefatory, preparatory, prior, qualifying, test, trial ◆ *n* **2 = introduction**, beginning, foundation, groundwork, initiation, opening, overture, preamble, preface, prelims, prelude, preparation, start

prelude *n* **2 = introduction**, beginning, commencement, curtain-raiser, exordium, foreword, intro (*inf.*), overture, preamble, preface, preliminary, preparation, proem, prolegomenon, prologue, start

premature *adj* **1 = early**, forward, unseasonable, untimely **2 = hasty**, ill-considered, ill-timed, impulsive, inopportune, jumping the gun, overhasty, precipitate, previous (*inf.*), rash, too soon, untimely **3 = immature**, abortive, embryonic, incomplete, predeveloped, undeveloped, unfledged

prematurely *adv* **1 = too early**, before one's time, too soon, untimely **2 = overhastily**, at half-cock, half-cocked, precipitately, rashly, too hastily, too soon

premeditated *adj* **= planned**, aforethought, calculated, conscious, considered, contrived, deliberate, intended, intentional, prepense, studied, wilful
Antonyms *adj* accidental, inadvertent, unintentional, unplanned, unpremeditated, unwitting

premeditation *n* **1, 2 = planning**, deliberation, design, determination, forethought, intention, malice aforethought, plotting, prearrangement, predetermination, purpose

premier *n* **1, 2 = head of government**, chancellor, chief minister, P.M., prime minister ◆ *adj* **4 = chief**, arch, first, foremost, head, highest, leading, main, primary, prime, principal, top **5 = first**, earliest, inaugural, initial, original

premiere *n* **1 = first night**, debut, first performance, first showing, opening

premise ➊ *n* (ˈprɛmɪs), also **premiss. 1** *Logic.* a statement that is assumed to be true for the purpose of an argument from which a conclusion is drawn. ◆ *vb* (prɪˈmaɪz, ˈprɛmɪs), **premises, premising, premised. 2** (when *tr, may take a clause as object*) to state or assume (a proposition) as a premise in an argument, etc. [C14: from OF *prémisse,* from Med. L *praemissa* sent on before, from L *praemittere* to dispatch in advance]

premises ➊ (ˈprɛmɪsɪz) *pl n* **1** a piece of land together with its buildings, esp. considered as a place of business. **2** *Law.* (in a deed, etc.) the matters referred to previously; the aforesaid.

premium ➊ (ˈpriːmɪəm) *n* **1** an amount paid in addition to a standard rate, price, wage, etc.; bonus. **2** the amount paid or payable, usually in regular instalments, for an insurance policy. **3** the amount above nominal or par value at which something sells. **4** an offer of something free or at a reduced price as an inducement to buy a commodity or service. **5** a prize given to the winner of a competition. **6** *US.* an amount sometimes charged for a loan of money in addition to the interest. **7** great value or regard: *to put a premium on someone's services.* **8 at a premium. 8a** in great demand, usually because of scarcity. **8b** above par. [C17: from L *praemium* prize]

Premium Savings Bonds *pl n* (in Britain) bonds issued by the Treasury since 1956 for purchase by the public. No interest is paid but there is a monthly draw for cash prizes of various sums. Also called: **premium bonds.**

premolar (priːˈməʊlə) *adj* **1** situated before a molar tooth. ◆ *n* **2** any one of eight bicuspid teeth in the human adult, two on each side of both jaws between the first molar and the canine.

premonition ➊ (ˌprɛməˈnɪʃən) *n* **1** an intuition of a future, usually unwelcome, occurrence; foreboding. **2** an early warning of a future event. [C16: from LL *praemonitiō,* from L *praemonēre* to admonish beforehand, from *prae* before + *monēre* to warn]
▸**premonitory** (prɪˈmɒnɪtərɪ, -trɪ) *adj*

Premonstratensian (ˌpriːmɒnstrəˈtɛnsɪən) *adj* **1** of or denoting an order of regular canons founded in 1119 at Prémontré, in France. ◆ *n* **2** a member of this order.

prenatal (priːˈneɪtᵊl) *adj* **1** occurring or present before birth; during pregnancy. ◆ *n* **2** *Inf.* a prenatal examination. ◆ Also: **antenatal.**

prenominal (priːˈnɒmɪnᵊl) *adj* placed before a noun, esp. (of an adjective or sense of an adjective) used only before a noun.

prentice (ˈprɛntɪs) *n* an archaic word for **apprentice.**

prenuptial agreement *n* a contract made between a man and woman before they marry, agreeing on the distribution of their assets in the event of divorce.

preoccupation ➊ (priːˌɒkjʊˈpeɪʃən) *n* **1** the state of being preoccupied, esp. mentally. **2** something that preoccupies the mind.

preoccupied ➊ (priːˈɒkjʊˌpaɪd) *adj* **1** engrossed or absorbed in something, esp. one's own thoughts. **2** already occupied or used.

preoccupy (priːˈɒkjʊˌpaɪ) *vb* **preoccupies, preoccupying, preoccupied.** (*tr*) **1** to engross the thoughts or mind of. **2** to occupy before or in advance of another. [C16: from L *praeoccupāre* to capture in advance]

preordain ➊ (ˌpriːɔːˈdeɪn) *vb* (*tr*) to ordain, decree, or appoint beforehand.

prep (prɛp) *n Inf.* **1** short for **preparation** (sense 5) or (chiefly US) **preparatory school.** ◆ *vb* **preps, prepping, prepped. 2** (*tr*) to prepare (a patient) for a medical operation or procedure.

prep. *abbrev. for:* **1** preparation. **2** preparatory. **3** preposition.

preparation ➊ (ˌprɛpəˈreɪʃən) *n* **1** the act or process of preparing. **2** the state of being prepared; readiness. **3** (*often pl*) a measure done in order to prepare for something; provision: *to make preparations for something.* **4** something that is prepared, esp. a medicine. **5** (esp. in a boarding school) **5a** homework. **5b** the period reserved for this. Usually shortened to **prep. 6** *Music.* **6a** the anticipation of a dissonance so that the note producing it in one chord is first heard in the preceding chord as a consonance. **6b** a note so employed.

preparative (prɪˈpærətɪv) *adj* **1** preparatory. ◆ *n* **2** something that prepares.
▸**preˈparatively** *adv*

preparatory ➊ (prɪˈpærətərɪ, -trɪ) *adj* **1** serving to prepare. **2** introductory. **3** occupied in preparation. **4 preparatory to.** before: *a drink preparatory to eating.*
▸**preˈparatorily** *adv*

preparatory school *n* **1** (in Britain) a private school, usually single-sex and for children between the ages of 6 and 13, generally preparing pupils for public school. **2** (in the US) a private secondary school preparing pupils for college. ◆ Often shortened to **prep school.**

prepare ➊ (prɪˈpɛə) *vb* **prepares, preparing, prepared. 1** to make ready or suitable in advance for some use, event, etc.: *to prepare a meal; to prepare to go.* **2** to put together using parts or ingredients; construct. **3** (*tr*) to equip or outfit, as for an expedition. **4** (*tr*) *Music.* to soften the impact of (a dissonant note) by the use of preparation. **5 be prepared.** (*foll. by an infinitive*) to be willing and able: *I'm not prepared to reveal these figures.* [C15: from L *praeparāre,* from *prae* before + *parāre* to make ready]
▸**preˈparer** *n*

preparedness ➊ (prɪˈpɛərɪdnɪs) *n* the state of being prepared, esp. militarily ready for war.

prepay (priːˈpeɪ) *vb* **prepays, prepaying, prepaid.** (*tr*) to pay for in advance.
▸**preˈpayable** *adj*

prepense (prɪˈpɛns) *adj* (*postpositive*) (usually in legal contexts) premeditated (esp. in **malice prepense**). [C18: from Anglo-Norman *purpensé,* from OF *purpenser* to consider in advance, from L *pēnsāre* to consider]

preponderant ➊ (prɪˈpɒndərənt) *adj* greater in weight, force, influence, etc.
▸**preˈponderance** *n* ▸**preˈponderantly** *adv*

preponderate ➊ (prɪˈpɒndəˌreɪt) *vb* **preponderates, preponderating, preponderated.** (*intr*) **1** (often foll. by *over*) to be more powerful, important, numerous, etc. (than). **2** to be of greater weight than something else. [C17: from LL *praeponderāre* to be of greater weight, from *pondus* weight]
▸**preˌponderˈation** *n*

preposition (ˌprɛpəˈzɪʃən) *n* a word or group of words used before a noun or pronoun to relate it grammatically or semantically to some other constituent of a sentence. [C14: from L *praepositiō* a putting before, from *pōnere* to place]
▸**ˌprepoˈsitional** *adj* ▸**ˌprepoˈsitionally** *adv*

> **USAGE NOTE** The practice of ending a sentence with a preposition (*Venice is a place I should like to go to*) was formerly regarded as incorrect, but is now acceptable and is the preferred form in many contexts.

prepossess ➊ (ˌpriːpəˈzɛs) *vb* (*tr*) **1** to preoccupy or engross mentally. **2** to influence in advance, esp. to make a favourable impression on beforehand.
▸**ˌpreposˈsession** *n*

prepossessing ➊ (ˌpriːpəˈzɛsɪŋ) *adj* creating a favourable impression; attractive.

preposterous ➊ (prɪˈpɒstərəs) *adj* contrary to nature, reason, or sense;

THESAURUS

premise *n* **1** = **assumption**, argument, assertion, ground, hypothesis, postulate, postulation, presupposition, proposition, supposition, thesis ◆ *vb* **2** = **assume**, hypothesize, posit, postulate, predicate, presuppose, state

premises *pl n* **1** = **building**, establishment, place, property, site

premium *n* **1** = **bonus**, boon, bounty, fee, percentage (*inf.*), perk (*Brit. inf.*), perquisite, prize, recompense, remuneration, reward **7** = **regard**, appreciation, stock, store, value **8 at a premium** = **in great demand**, beyond one's means, costly, expensive, hard to come by, in short supply, like gold dust, not to be had for love or money, rare, scarce, valuable

premonition *n* **1, 2** = **feeling**, apprehension, feeling in one's bones, foreboding, forewarning, funny feeling (*inf.*), hunch, idea, intuition, misgiving, omen, portent, presage, presentiment, sign, suspicion, warning

preoccupation *n* **1** = **absorption**, absence of mind, absent-mindedness, abstraction, brown study, daydreaming, engrossment, immersion, inattentiveness, musing, oblivion, pensiveness, prepossession, reverie, woolgathering **2** = **obsession**, bee in one's bonnet, concern, fixation, hang-up (*inf.*), hobbyhorse, *idée fixe*, pet subject

preoccupied *adj* **1** = **absorbed**, absent-minded, abstracted, caught up in, distracted, distrait, engrossed, faraway, heedless, immersed, in a brown study, intent, lost in, lost in thought, oblivious, rapt, taken up, unaware, wrapped up

preordained *adj* = **predetermined**, destined, doomed, fated, mapped out in advance, predestined

preparation *n* **1** = **groundwork**, development, getting ready, preparing, putting in order **2** = **readiness**, alertness, anticipation, expectation, foresight, precaution, preparedness, provision, safeguard **3** *often plural* = **arrangement**, measure, plan, provision **4** = **mixture**, composition, compound, concoction, medicine, tincture **5a** = **homework**, prep (*inf.*), revision, schoolwork, study, swotting (*Brit. inf.*)

preparatory *adj* **1, 2** = **introductory**, basic, elementary, opening, prefatory, preliminary, preparative, primary **4 preparatory to** = **before**, in advance of, in anticipation of, in preparation for, prior to

prepare *vb* **1** = **make** *or* **get ready**, adapt, adjust, anticipate, arrange, coach, dispose, form, groom, make provision, plan, practise, prime, put in order, train, warm up **2** = **put together**, assemble, concoct, construct, contrive, draw up, fashion, fix up, get up (*inf.*), make, produce, turn out **3** = **equip**, accoutre, fit, fit out, furnish, outfit, provide, supply

prepared *adj* **1** = **ready**, all set, all systems go, arranged, fit, in order, in readiness, planned, primed, set **5** = **willing**, able, disposed, inclined, minded, of a mind, predisposed

preparedness *n* = **readiness**, alertness, fitness, order, preparation

preponderance *n* = **predominance**, ascendancy, bulk, dominance, domination, dominion, extensiveness, greater numbers, greater part, lion's share, mass, power, prevalence, superiority, supremacy, sway, weight

preponderant *adj* = **prevalent**, ascendant, dominant, extensive, foremost, greater, important, larger, paramount, predominant, prevailing, significant

preponderate *vb* **1** = **predominate**, dominate, hold sway, outnumber, prevail, reign supreme, rule

prepossessing *adj* = **attractive**, alluring, amiable, appealing, beautiful, bewitching, captivating, charming, engaging, fair, fascinating, fetching, glamorous, good-looking, handsome, inviting, likable *or* likeable, lovable, magnetic, pleasing, striking, taking, winning
Antonyms *adj* disagreeable, displeasing, objectionable, offensive, repulsive, ugly, unattractive, uninviting, unlikable *or* unlikeable

prepossession *n* **1** = **preoccupation**, absorption, engrossment **2** = **partiality**, bias, inclination, liking, predilection, predisposition, prejudice

preposterous *adj* = **ridiculous**, absurd, asi-

absurd; ridiculous. [C16: from L *praeposterus* reversed, from *prae* in front + *posterus* following]
▸**pre'posterously** *adv* ▸**pre'posterousness** *n*

prepotency (prɪ'pəʊtᵊnsɪ) *n* **1** the quality of possessing greater power or influence. **2** *Genetics.* the ability of one parent to transmit more characteristics to its offspring than the other parent. **3** *Bot.* the ability of pollen from one source to bring about fertilization more readily than that from other sources.
▸**pre'potent** *adj*

preppy ('prɛpɪ) *Inf.* ◆ *adj* **1** of or denoting a style of neat, understated, and often expensive clothes; young but classic. ◆ *n, pl* **preppies. 2** a person exhibiting such style. [C20: orig. US, from *preppy* a person who attends a PREPARATORY SCHOOL]

prep school *n Inf.* See **preparatory school.**

prepuce ('priːpjuːs) *n* **1** the retractable fold of skin covering the tip of the penis. Nontechnical name: **foreskin. 2** a similar fold of skin covering the tip of the clitoris. [C14: from L *praepūtium*]

prequel ('priːkwəl) *n* a film that is made about an earlier stage of a story or character's life because the later part of it has already made a successful film. [C20: from PRE- + *(se)quel*]

Pre-Raphaelite (ˌpriː'ræfəlaɪt) *n* **1** a member of the **Pre-Raphaelite Brotherhood**, an association of painters and writers founded in 1848 to revive the fidelity to nature and the vivid realistic colour considered typical of Italian painting before Raphael. ◆ *adj* **2** of, in the manner of, or relating to Pre-Raphaelite painting and painters.
▸ˌ**Pre-'Raphaelitˌism** *n*

prerequisite ⓣ (priː'rɛkwɪzɪt) *adj* **1** required as a prior condition. ◆ *n* **2** something required as a prior condition.

prerogative ⓣ (prɪ'rɒgətɪv) *n* **1** an exclusive privilege or right exercised by a person or group of people holding a particular office or hereditary rank. **2** any privilege or right. **3** a power, privilege, or immunity restricted to a sovereign or sovereign government. ◆ *adj* **4** having or able to exercise a prerogative. [C14: from L *praerogātīva* privilege, earlier: group with the right to vote first, from *prae* before + *rogāre* to ask]

pres. *abbrev. for:* **1** present (time). **2** presidential.

Pres. *abbrev. for* President.

presage ⓣ *n* ('prɛsɪdʒ). **1** an intimation or warning of something about to happen; portent; omen. **2** a sense of what is about to happen; foreboding. ◆ *vb* ('prɛsɪdʒ, prɪ'seɪdʒ). **presages, presaging, presaged.** *(tr)* **3** to have a presentiment of. **4** to give a forewarning of; portend. [C14: from L *praesāgium,* from *praesāgīre* to perceive beforehand]
▸**pre'sageful** *adj* ▸**pre'sager** *n*

presale ('priːˌseɪl) *n* the practice of arranging the sale of a product before it is available.
▸**pre'sell** *vb (tr)*

presbyopia (ˌprɛzbɪ'əʊpɪə) *n* a progressively diminishing ability of the eye to focus, noticeable from middle to old age, caused by loss of elasticity of the crystalline lens. [C18: NL, from Gk *presbus* old man + *ōps* eye]
▸**presbyopic** (ˌprɛzbɪ'ɒpɪk) *adj*

presbyter ('prɛzbɪtə) *n* **1a** an elder of a congregation in the early Christian Church. **1b** (in some Churches having episcopal politics) an official who is subordinate to a bishop and has administrative and sacerdotal functions. **2** (in some hierarchical Churches) another name for **priest. 3** (in the Presbyterian Church) an elder. [C16: from LL, from Gk *presbuteros* an older man, from *presbus* old man]
▸ˌ**presby'terial** *adj*

presbyterian (ˌprɛzbɪ'tɪərɪən) *adj* **1** of or designating Church government by presbyters or lay elders. ◆ *n* **2** an upholder of this type of Church government.
▸ˌ**presby'terianism** *n*

Presbyterian (ˌprɛzbɪ'tɪərɪən) *adj* **1** of or relating to any of various Protestant Churches governed by presbyters or lay elders and adhering to various modified forms of Calvinism. ◆ *n* **2** a member of a Presbyterian Church.
▸ˌ**Presby'terianism** *n*

presbytery ('prɛzbɪtərɪ) *n, pl* **presbyteries. 1** *Presbyterian Church.* **1a** a local Church court. **1b** the congregations within the jurisdiction of any such court. **2** the part of a church east of the choir, in which the main altar is situated; a sanctuary. **3** presbyters or elders collectively. **4** *RC Church.* the residence of a parish priest. [C15: from OF *presbiterie,* from Church L, from Gk *presbyterion;* see PRESBYTER]

prescience ⓣ ('prɛsɪəns) *n* knowledge of events before they take place; foreknowledge. [C14: from L *praescīre* to foreknow]
▸'**prescient** *adj*

prescribe ⓣ (prɪ'skraɪb) *vb* **prescribes, prescribing, prescribed. 1** *(tr)* to lay down as a rule or directive. **2** *Med.* to recommend or order the use of (a drug or other remedy). [C16: from L *praescrībere* to write previously]
▸**pre'scriber** *n*

prescript ('priːskrɪpt) *n* something laid down or prescribed. [C16: from L *praescriptum* something written down beforehand, from *praescrībere* to PRESCRIBE]

prescription ⓣ (prɪ'skrɪpʃən) *n* **1a** written instructions from a physician to a pharmacist stating the form, dosage, strength, etc., of a drug to be issued to a specific patient. **1b** the drug or remedy prescribed. **2a** written instructions for an optician specifying the lenses needed to correct defects of vision. **2b** *(as modifier)*: *prescription glasses.* **3** the act of prescribing. **4** something that is prescribed. **5** a long-established custom or a claim based on one. **6** *Law.* **6a** the uninterrupted possession of property over a stated time, after which a right or title is acquired (**positive prescription**). **6b** the barring of adverse claims to property, etc., after a specified time has elapsed, allowing the possessor to acquire title (**negative prescription**). [C14: from legal L *praescriptiō* an order; see PRESCRIBE]

prescriptive ⓣ (prɪ'skrɪptɪv) *adj* **1** making or giving directions, rules, or injunctions. **2** sanctioned by long-standing custom. **3** based upon legal prescription: *a prescriptive title.*
▸**pre'scriptively** *adv* ▸**pre'scriptiveness** *n*

presence ⓣ ('prɛzəns) *n* **1** the state or fact of being present. **2** immediate proximity. **3** personal appearance or bearing, esp. of a dignified nature. **4** an imposing or dignified personality. **5** an invisible spirit felt to be nearby. **6** *Electronics.* a recording control that boosts mid-range frequencies. **7** *Obs.* assembly or company. [C14: via OF from L *praesentia* a being before, from *praeesse* to be before]

presence chamber *n* the room in which a great person, such as a monarch, receives guests, assemblies, etc.

presence of mind ⓣ *n* the ability to remain calm and act constructively during times of crisis.

presenile dementia (priː'siːnaɪl) *n* a form of dementia, of unknown cause, starting before a person is old.

present[1] ⓣ ('prɛzᵊnt) *adj* **1** *(prenominal)* in existence at the time at which something is spoken or written. **2** *(postpositive)* being in a specified place, thing, etc.: *the murderer is present in this room.* **3** *(prenominal)* now being dealt with or under discussion: *the present author.* **4** *Grammar.* denoting a tense of verbs used when the action or event described is occurring at the time of utterance or when the speaker does not wish to make any explicit temporal reference. **5** *Arch.* instant: *present help is at hand.* ◆ *n* **6** *Grammar.* **6a** the present tense. **6b** a verb in this tense. **7 at present.** now. **8 for the present.** for the time being; temporarily. **9 the present.** the time being; now. ◆ See also **presents.** [C13: from L *praesens,* from *praeesse* to be in front of]

present[2] ⓣ *vb* (prɪ'zɛnt). *(mainly tr)* **1** to introduce (a person) to another, esp. to someone of higher rank. **2** to introduce to the public: *to present a play.* **3** to introduce and compere (a radio or television show). **4** to show; exhibit: *he presented a brave face to the world.* **5** to bring or suggest to the mind: *to present a problem.* **6** to put forward; submit: *she*

THESAURUS

nine, bizarre, crazy, excessive, exorbitant, extravagant, extreme, foolish, impossible, incredible, insane, irrational, laughable, ludicrous, monstrous, nonsensical, out of the question, outrageous, risible, senseless, shocking, unreasonable, unthinkable

prerequisite *adj* **1** = **required**, called for, essential, imperative, indispensable, mandatory, necessary, needful, obligatory, of the essence, requisite, vital ◆ *n* **2** = **requirement**, condition, essential, imperative, must, necessity, precondition, qualification, requisite, *sine qua non*

prerogative *n* **1-3** = **right**, advantage, authority, birthright, choice, claim, droit, due, exemption, immunity, liberty, perquisite, privilege, sanction, title

presage *n* **1** = **omen**, augury, auspice, forecast, forewarning, harbinger, intimation, portent, prediction, prognostic, prognostication, prophecy, sign, warning **2** = **misgiving**, apprehension, boding, feeling, foreboding, forewarning, intuition, premonition, presentiment ◆ *vb* **3** = **sense**, divine, feel, foresee, have a feeling, intuit **3** = **predict**, forecast, foretell, forewarn, prognosticate, prophesy, soothsay, vaticinate *(rare)* **4** = **portend**, adumbrate, augur, betoken, bode, forebode, foreshadow, foretoken, omen, point to, signify, warn

prescience *n Formal* = **foresight**, clairvoyance, foreknowledge, precognition, prevision *(rare)*, second sight

prescient *adj* = **foresighted**, clairvoyant, discerning, divinatory, divining, far-sighted, mantic, perceptive, prophetic, psychic

prescribe *vb* **1** = **order**, appoint, assign, command, decree, define, dictate, direct, enjoin, establish, fix, impose, lay down, ordain, recommend, require, rule, set, specify, stipulate

prescription *n* **1a** = **instruction**, direction, formula, recipe **1b** = **medicine**, drug, mixture, preparation, remedy

prescriptive *adj* **1** = **dictatorial**, authoritarian, didactic, dogmatic, legislating, preceptive, rigid

presence *n* **1** = **being**, attendance, companionship, company, existence, habitation, inhabitance, occupancy, residence **2** = **proximity**, closeness, immediate circle, nearness, neighbourhood, propinquity, vicinity **3** = **personality**, air, appearance, aspect, aura, bearing, carriage, comportment, demeanour, ease, mien *(literary)*, poise, self-assurance **5** = **spirit**, apparition, eidolon, ghost, manifestation, revenant, shade *(literary)*, spectre, supernatural being, wraith

presence of mind *n* = **level-headedness**, alertness, aplomb, calmness, composure, cool *(sl.)*, coolness, imperturbability, phlegm, quickness, sang-froid, self-assurance, self-command, self-possession, wits

present[1] *adj* **1** = **current**, contemporary, existent, existing, extant, immediate, instant, present-day **2** = **here**, accounted for, at hand, available, in attendance, near, nearby, ready, there, to hand ◆ *n* **7 at present** = **just now**, at the moment, now, nowadays, right now **8 for the present** = **for now**, for a while, for the moment, for the nonce, for the time being, in the meantime, not for long, provisionally, temporarily **9 the present** = **now**, here and now, the present moment, the time being, this day and age, today

present[2] *vb* **1** = **introduce**, acquaint with, make known **4** = **put on**, demonstrate, display, exhibit, give, mount, put before the public, show,

presented a proposal for a new book. **7** to award: *to present a prize; to present a university with a foundation scholarship.* **8** to offer formally: *to present one's compliments.* **9** to hand over for action or settlement: *to present a bill.* **10** to depict in a particular manner: *the actor presented Hamlet as a very young man.* **11** to salute someone with (one's weapon) (usually in **present arms**). **12** to aim (a weapon). **13** to nominate (a clergyman) to a bishop for institution to a benefice in his diocese. **14** to lay (a charge, etc.) before a court, magistrate, etc., for consideration or trial. **15** to bring a formal charge or accusation against (a person); indict. **16** (*intr*) *Med.* to seek treatment for a particular problem: *she presented with postnatal depression.* **17** (*intr*) *Inf.* to produce a specified impression: *she presents well in public.* **18 present oneself.** to appear, esp. at a specific time and place. ◆ *n* ('prɛzᵊnt). **19** a gift. [C13: from OF *presenter,* from L *praesentāre* to exhibit, from *praesens* PRESENT[1]]

presentable ❶ (prɪ'zɛntəbᵊl) *adj* **1** fit to be presented or introduced to other people. **2** fit to be displayed or offered.
▸**pre'sentableness** *or* **pre,senta'bility** *n* ▸**pre'sentably** *adv*

presentation ❶ (,prɛzən'teɪʃən) *n* **1** the act of presenting or state of being presented. **2** the manner of presenting; delivery or overall impression. **3** a verbal report, often with illustrative material: *a presentation on the company results.* **4a** an offering, as of a gift. **4b** (*as modifier*): *a presentation copy of a book.* **5** a performance or representation, as of a play. **6** the formal introduction of a person, as at court; debut. **7** the act or right of nominating a clergyman to a benefice.
▸**,presen'tational** *adj*

presentationism (,prɛzən'teɪʃə,nɪzəm) *n Philosophy.* the theory that objects are identical with our perceptions of them. Cf. **representationalism.**
▸**,presen'tationist** *n, adj*

presentative (prɪ'zɛntətɪv) *adj* **1** *Philosophy.* able to be known or perceived immediately. **2** conferring the right of ecclesiastical presentation.

present-day ❶ *n* (*modifier*) of the modern day; current: *I don't like present-day fashions.*

presenter (prɪ'zɛntə) *n* **1** a person who presents something or someone. **2** *Radio, television.* a person who introduces a show, links items, etc.

presentient (prɪ'senʃənt) *adj* characterized by or experiencing a presentiment. [C19: from L *praesentiens,* from *praesentire,* from *prae-* PRE- + *sentire* to feel]

presentiment ❶ (prɪ'zɛntɪmənt) *n* a sense of something about to happen; premonition. [C18: from obs. F, from *pressentir* to sense beforehand]

presently ❶ ('prɛzəntlɪ) *adv* **1** in a short while; soon. **2** at the moment. **3** an archaic word for **immediately.**

presentment (prɪ'zɛntmənt) *n* **1** the act of presenting or state of being presented; presentation. **2** something presented, such as a picture, play, etc. **3** *Law.* a statement on oath by a jury of something within their own knowledge or observation. **4** *Commerce.* the presenting of a bill of exchange, promissory note, etc.

present participle ('prɛzᵊnt) *n* a participial form of verbs used adjectivally when the action it describes is contemporaneous with that of the main verb of a sentence and also used in the formation of certain compound tenses. In English this form ends in *-ing.*

present perfect ('prɛzᵊnt) *adj, n Grammar.* another term for **perfect** (senses 8, 10).

presents ('prɛzənts) *pl n Law.* used in a deed or document to refer to itself: *know all men by these presents.*

preservative (prɪ'zɜːvətɪv) *n* **1** something that preserves, esp. a chemical added to foods. ◆ *adj* **2** tending or intended to preserve.

preserve ❶ (prɪ'zɜːv) *vb* **preserves, preserving, preserved.** (*mainly tr*) **1** to keep safe from danger or harm; protect. **2** to protect from decay or dissolution; maintain: *to preserve old buildings.* **3** to maintain possession of; keep up: *to preserve a façade of indifference.* **4** to prevent from decomposition or chemical change. **5** to prepare (food), as by salting, so that it will resist decomposition. **6** to make preserves of (fruit, etc.). **7** to rear and protect (game) in restricted places for hunting or fishing. **8** (*intr*) to maintain protection for game in preserves. ◆ *n* **9** something that preserves or is preserved. **10** a special domain: *archaeology is the preserve of specialists.* **11** (*usually pl*) fruit, etc., prepared by cooking with sugar. **12** areas where game is reared for private hunting or fishing. [C14: via OF, from LL *praeservāre,* lit.: to keep safe in advance, from L *prae* before + *servāre* to keep safe]
▸**pre'servable** *adj* ▸**preservation** (,prɛzə'veɪʃən) *n* ▸**pre'server** *n*

preset *vb* (priː'sɛt), **presets, presetting, preset.** (*tr*) **1** to set (a timing device) so that something begins to operate at the time specified. ◆ *n* ('priːsɛt). **2** *Electronics.* a control, such as a variable resistor, that is not as accessible as the main controls and is used to set initial conditions.

preshrunk (priː'ʃrʌŋk) *adj* (of fabrics) having undergone shrinking during manufacture so that further shrinkage will not occur.

preside ❶ (prɪ'zaɪd) *vb* **presides, presiding, presided.** (*intr*) **1** to sit in or hold a position of authority, as over a meeting. **2** to exercise authority; control. [C17: via F from L *praesidēre* to superintend, from *prae* before + *sedēre* to sit]

presidency ('prɛzɪdənsɪ) *n, pl* **presidencies. 1** the office, dignity, or term of a president. **2** (*often cap.*) the office of president of a republic, esp. of the President of the US.

president ('prɛzɪdənt) *n* **1** (*often cap.*) the head of state of a republic, esp. of the US **2** (in the US) the chief executive officer of a company, corporation, etc. **3** a person who presides over an assembly, meeting, etc. **4** the chief executive officer of certain establishments of higher education. [C14: via OF from LL *praesidens* ruler; see PRESIDE]
▸**presidential** (,prɛzɪ'dɛnʃəl) *adj* ▸**,presi'dentially** *adv* ▸**'presidentship** *n*

presidium *or* **praesidium** (prɪ'sɪdɪəm) *n* **1** (*often cap.*) (in Communist countries) a permanent committee of a larger body, such as a legislature, that acts for it when it is in recess. **2** a collective presidency. [C20: from Russian *prezidium,* from L *praesidium,* from *praesidēre* to superintend; see PRESIDE]

press[1] ❶ (pres) *vb* **1** to apply or exert weight, force, or steady pressure (on): *he pressed the button on the camera.* **2** (*tr*) to squeeze or compress so as to alter in shape. **3** to apply heat or pressure to (clothing) so as to smooth out creases. **4** to make (objects) from soft material by pressing with a mould, etc., esp. to make gramophone records from plastic. **5** (*tr*) to clasp; embrace. **6** (*tr*) to extract or force out (juice) by pressure (from). **7** (*tr*) to force or compel. **8** to importune (a person) insistently: *they pressed for an answer.* **9** to harass or cause harassment. **10** (*tr*) to plead or put forward strongly: *to press a claim.* **11** (*intr*) to be urgent. **12** (*tr;* usually passive) to have little of: *we're hard pressed for time.* **13** (when *intr,* often foll. by *on* or *forward*) to hasten or advance or cause to hasten or advance in a forceful manner. **14** (*intr*) to crowd; push. **15** (*tr*) *Arch.* to trouble or oppress. ◆ *n* **16** any machine that exerts pressure to form, shape, or cut materials or to extract liquids, compress solids, or hold components together while an adhesive joint is formed. **17** See **printing press. 18** the art or process of printing. **19 to (the) press.** to be printed: *when is this book going to press?* **20 the press. 20a** news media collectively, esp. newspapers. **20b** (*as modifier*): *press relations.* **21** the opinions and reviews in the newspapers, etc.: *the play received a poor press.* **22** the act of pressing or state of being pressed. **23** the act of crowding or pushing together. **24** a closely packed throng; crowd. **25** a cupboard, esp. a large one used for storing clothes or linen. **26** a wood or metal clamp to prevent tennis rackets, etc., from warping when not in use. [C14 *pressen,* from OF *presser,* from L, from *premere* to press]

press[2] (pres) *vb* (*tr*) **1** to recruit (men) by forcible measures for military service. **2** to use for a purpose other than intended (esp. in **press into**

THESAURUS

stage **6, 8** = **put forward,** adduce, advance, declare, expound, extend, hold out, introduce, offer, pose, produce, proffer, raise, recount, relate, state, submit, suggest, tender **7** = **give,** award, bestow, confer, donate, entrust, furnish, grant, hand out, hand over, offer, proffer, put at (someone's) disposal ◆ *n* **19** = **gift,** benefaction, boon, bounty, donation, endowment, favour, grant, gratuity, hand-out, largesse *or* largess, offering, prezzie (*inf.*)

presentable *adj* **1, 2** = **decent,** acceptable, becoming, fit to be seen, good enough, not bad (*inf.*), O.K. *or* okay (*inf.*), passable, proper, respectable, satisfactory, suitable, tolerable
Antonyms *adj* below par, not good enough, not up to scratch, poor, rubbishy, unacceptable, unpresentable, unsatisfactory

presentation *n* **1** = **giving,** award, bestowal, conferral, donation, investiture, offering **3** = **performance,** demonstration, display, exhibition, production, representation, show **5** = **portrayal,** appearance, arrangement, delivery, exposition, production, rendition, staging, submission **6** = **debut,** coming out, introduction, launch, launching, reception

present-day *modifier* = **current,** contemporary, latter-day, modern, newfangled, present, recent, up-to-date

presentiment *n* = **premonition,** anticipation, apprehension, expectation, fear, feeling, foreboding, forecast, forethought, hunch, intuition, misgiving, presage

presently *adv* **1** = **soon,** anon (*arch.*), before long, by and by, erelong (*arch. or poetic*), in a minute, in a moment, in a short while, pretty soon (*inf.*), shortly

preservation *n* **1, 2** = **protection,** conservation, defence, keeping, maintenance, perpetuation, safeguarding, safekeeping, safety, salvation, security, storage, support, upholding

preserve *vb* **1** = **protect,** care for, conserve, defend, guard, keep, safeguard, save, secure, shelter, shield **2** = **maintain,** continue, keep, keep up, perpetuate, retain, sustain, uphold **3** = **keep,** conserve, put up, save, store ◆ *n* **10** = **area,** domain, field, realm, specialism, sphere **11** *usually plural* = **jam,** confection, confiture, conserve, jelly, marmalade, sweetmeat **12** = **reserve,** game reserve, reservation, sanctuary
Antonyms *vb* ≠ **protect:** assail, assault, attack, leave unprotected, turn out ≠ **maintain:** abandon, discontinue, drop, end, give up ≠ **keep:** blow (*sl.*), consume, fritter away, spend, squander, waste

preside *vb* **1, 2** = **run,** administer, be at the head of, be in authority, chair, conduct, control, direct, govern, head, lead, manage, officiate, supervise

press[1] *vb* **1, 2** = **compress,** bear down on, condense, crush, depress, force down, jam, mash, push, reduce, squeeze, stuff **3** = **smooth,** calender, finish, flatten, iron, mangle, put the creases in, steam **5** = **hug,** clasp, crush, embrace, encircle, enfold, fold in one's arms, hold close, squeeze **7** = **force,** compel, constrain, demand, enforce, enjoin, insist on **8** = **urge,** beg, entreat, exhort, implore, importune, petition, plead, pressurize, sue, supplicate **12** *usually passive* = **be hard put,** be hurried, be pushed, be rushed (*inf.*), be short of **14** = **crowd,** cluster, flock, gather, hasten, herd, hurry, mill, push, rush, seethe, surge, swarm, throng **15** *Archaic* = **trouble,** afflict, assail, beset, besiege, disquiet, harass, plague, torment, vex, worry ◆ *n* **20 the press: a** = **newspapers,** columnists, correspondents, Fleet Street, fourth estate, gentlemen of the press, journalism, journalists, journos (*sl.*), news media, newsmen, photographers, pressmen, reporters, the papers **24** = **crowd,** bunch, crush, flock, herd, horde, host, mob, multitude, pack, push (*inf.*), swarm, throng

service). ◆ *n* **3** recruitment into military service by forcible measures, as by a press gang. [C16: back formation from *prest* to recruit soldiers; also infl. by PRESS[1]]

press agent *n* a person employed to obtain favourable publicity, such as notices in newspapers, for an organization, actor, etc.

press box *n* an area reserved for reporters, as in a sports stadium.

press conference *n* an interview for press reporters given by a politician, film star, etc.

press fit *n Engineering.* a type of fit for mating parts, usually tighter than a sliding fit, used when the parts do not have to move relative to each other.

press gallery *n* an area for newspaper reporters, esp. in a legislative assembly.

press gang *n* **1** (formerly) a detachment of men used to press civilians for service in the navy or army. ◆ *vb* **press-gang.** *(tr)* **2** to force (a person) to join the navy or army by a press gang. **3** to induce (a person) to perform a duty by forceful persuasion.

pressing Ⓣ ('prɛsɪŋ) *adj* **1** demanding immediate attention. **2** persistent or importunate. ◆ *n* **3** a large specified number of gramophone records produced at one time from a master record. **4** *Football.* the tactic of trying to stay very close to the opposition when they are in possession of the ball.
▸**'pressingly** *adv*

pressman ('prɛsmən, -ˌmæn) *n, pl* **pressmen. 1** a journalist. **2** a person who operates a printing press.

press of sail *n Naut.* the most sail a vessel can carry under given conditions. Also called: **press of canvas.**

press release *n* an official announcement or account of a news item circulated to the press.

pressroom ('prɛsˌruːm, -ˌrʊm) *n* the room in a printing establishment that houses the printing presses.

press stud *n* a fastening device consisting of one part with a projecting knob that snaps into a hole on another like part, used esp. on clothing. Canad. equivalent: **dome fastener.**

press-up *n* an exercise in which the body is alternately raised from and lowered to the floor by the arms only, the trunk being kept straight. Also called (US and Canad.): **push-up.**

pressure Ⓣ ('prɛʃə) *n* **1** the state of pressing or being pressed. **2** the exertion of force by one body on the surface of another. **3** a moral force that compels: *to bring pressure to bear.* **4** urgent claims or demands: *to work under pressure.* **5** a burdensome condition that is hard to bear: *the pressure of grief.* **6** the force applied to a unit area of a surface, usually measured in pascals, millibars, torrs, or atmospheres. **7** short for **atmospheric pressure** or **blood pressure.** ◆ *vb* **pressures, pressuring, pressured.** *(tr)* **8** to constrain or compel, as by moral force. **9** another word for **pressurize.** [C14: from LL *pressūra* a pressing, from L *premere* to press]

pressure cooker *n* a strong hermetically sealed pot in which food may be cooked quickly under pressure at a temperature above the normal boiling point of water.
▸**'pressure-ˌcook** *vb*

pressure group *n* a group of people who seek to exert pressure on legislators, public opinion, etc., in order to promote their own ideas or welfare.

pressure point *n* any of several points on the body above an artery that, when firmly pressed, will control bleeding from the artery at a point farther away from the heart.

pressure suit *n* an inflatable suit worn by a person flying at high altitudes or in space, to provide protection from low pressure.

pressurize Ⓣ *or* **pressurise** ('prɛʃəˌraɪz) *vb* **pressurizes, pressurizing, pressurized** *or* **pressurises, pressurising, pressurised.** *(tr)* **1** to increase the pressure in (an enclosure, such as an aircraft cabin) in order to maintain approximately atmospheric pressure when the external pressure is low. **2** to increase pressure on (a fluid). **3** to make insistent demands of (someone); coerce.
▸**ˌpressuri'zation** *or* **ˌpressuri'sation** *n*

pressurized-water reactor *n* a type of nuclear reactor that uses water under pressure as both coolant and moderator.

presswork ('prɛsˌwɜːk) *n* the operation of, or matter printed by, a printing press.

Prestel ('prɛstɛl) *n Trademark.* (in Britain) the viewdata service operated by British Telecom.

Prester John ('prɛstə) *n* a legendary Christian priest and king, believed in the Middle Ages to have ruled in the Far East, but identified in the 14th century with the king of Ethiopia. [C14 *Prestre Johan,* from Med. L *presbyter Iohannes* Priest John]

prestidigitation (ˌprɛstɪˌdɪdʒɪ'teɪʃən) *n* another name for **sleight of hand.** [C19: from F: quick-fingeredness, from L *praestigiae* tricks, prob. infl. by F *preste* nimble, & L *digitus* finger]
▸**ˌpresti'digiˌtator** *n*

prestige Ⓣ (prɛ'stiːʒ) *n* **1** high status or reputation achieved through success, influence, wealth, etc.; renown. **2a** the power to impress; glamour. **2b** *(modifier): a prestige car.* [C17: via F from L *praestigiae* tricks]
▸**prestigious** (prɛ'stɪdʒəs) *adj*

prestissimo (prɛ'stɪsɪˌməʊ) *Music.* ◆ *adj, adv* **1** to be played as fast as possible. ◆ *n, pl* **prestissimos. 2** a piece to be played in this way. [C18: from It.: very quickly, from *presto* fast]

presto ('prɛstəʊ) *adj, adv* **1** *Music.* to be played very fast. ◆ *adv* **2** immediately (esp. in **hey presto**). ◆ *n, pl* **prestos. 3** *Music.* a passage directed to be played very quickly. [C16: from It.: fast, from LL *praestus* (adj) ready to hand, L *praestō* (adv) present]

prestressed concrete (ˌpriː'strɛst) *n* concrete that contains steel wires that are stretched to counteract the stresses that will occur under load.

presumably Ⓣ (prɪ'zjuːməblɪ) *adv (sentence modifier)* one supposes that: *presumably he won't see you, if you're leaving tomorrow.*

presume Ⓣ (prɪ'zjuːm) *vb* **presumes, presuming, presumed. 1** (when *tr, often takes a clause as object*) to take (something) for granted; assume. **2** (when *tr, often foll. by an infinitive*) to dare (to do something): *do you presume to copy my work?* **3** *(intr;* foll. by *on* or *upon)* to rely or depend: *don't presume on his agreement.* **4** *(intr;* foll. by *on* or *upon)* to take advantage (of): *don't presume upon his good nature too far.* **5** *(tr) Law.* to take as proved until contrary evidence is produced. [C14: via OF from L *praesūmere* to take in advance, from *prae* before + *sūmere* to ASSUME]
▸**presumedly** (prɪ'zjuːmɪdlɪ) *adv* ▸**pre'suming** *adj*

presumption Ⓣ (prɪ'zʌmpʃən) *n* **1** the act of presuming. **2** bold or insolent behaviour. **3** a belief or assumption based on reasonable evidence. **4** a basis on which to presume. **5** *Law.* an inference of the truth of a fact from other facts proved. [C13: via OF from L *praesumptiō* anticipation, from *praesūmere* to take beforehand; see PRESUME]

presumptive Ⓣ (prɪ'zʌmptɪv) *adj* **1** based on presumption or probability. **2** affording reasonable ground for belief.
▸**pre'sumptively** *adv*

presumptuous Ⓣ (prɪ'zʌmptjʊəs) *adj* characterized by presumption or tending to presume; bold; forward.
▸**pre'sumptuously** *adv* ▸**pre'sumptuousness** *n*

presuppose Ⓣ (ˌpriːsə'pəʊz) *vb* **presupposes, presupposing, presupposed.** *(tr)* **1** to take for granted. **2** to require as a necessary prior condition.
▸**presupposition** (ˌpriːsʌpə'zɪʃən) *n*

preteen (priː'tiːn) *n* a boy or girl approaching his or her teens.

pretence Ⓣ *or US* **pretense** (prɪ'tɛns) *n* **1** the act of pretending. **2** a false display; affectation. **3** a claim, esp. a false one, to a right, title, or distinction. **4** make-believe. **5** a pretext.

pretend Ⓣ (prɪ'tɛnd) *vb* **1** (when *tr, usually takes a clause as object or an in-*

THESAURUS

pressing *adj* **1, 2 = urgent**, burning, constraining, crucial, exigent, high-priority, imperative, important, importunate, now or never, serious, vital
Antonyms *adj* dispensable, regular, routine, unimportant, unnecessary

pressure *n* **1, 2 = force**, compressing, compression, crushing, heaviness, squeezing, weight **3 = power**, coercion, compulsion, constraint, force, influence, obligation, sway **5 = stress**, adversity, affliction, burden, demands, difficulty, distress, exigency, hassle (*inf.*), heat, hurry, load, press, strain, urgency

pressurize *vb* **2 = compress**, condense, constrict, press, squash, squeeze **3 = force**, breathe down someone's neck, browbeat, coerce, compel, dragoon, drive, intimidate, press-gang, put the screws on (*sl.*), turn on the heat (*inf.*), twist one's arm (*inf.*)

prestige *n* **1 = status**, authority, bottom, Brownie points, cachet, celebrity, credit, distinction, eminence, esteem, fame, honour, importance, influence, kudos, regard, renown, reputation, standing, stature, weight

prestigious *adj* **1 = celebrated**, eminent, esteemed, exalted, great, illustrious, important, imposing, impressive, influential, notable, prominent, renowned, reputable, respected
Antonyms *adj* humble, lowly, minor, obscure, unimportant, unimpressive, unknown

presumably *adv* **= it would seem**, apparently, doubtless, doubtlessly, in all likelihood, in all probability, likely, most likely, on the face of it, probably, seemingly

presume *vb* **1 = believe**, assume, conjecture, guess (*inf., chiefly US & Canad.*), infer, posit, postulate, presuppose, suppose, surmise, take for granted, take it, think **2 = dare**, go so far, have the audacity, make bold, make so bold, take the liberty, undertake, venture **3 = depend**, bank on, count on, rely, trust

presumption *n* **2 = cheek** (*inf.*), assurance, audacity, boldness, brass (*inf.*), brass neck (*Brit. inf.*), chutzpah (*US & Canad. inf.*), effrontery, forwardness, front, gall (*inf.*), impudence, insolence, neck (*inf.*), nerve (*inf.*), presumptuousness, temerity **3 = assumption**, anticipation, belief, conjecture, guess, hypothesis, opinion, premise *or* premiss, presupposition, supposition, surmise **4 = probability**, basis, chance, grounds, likelihood, plausibility, reason

presumptive *adj* **1 = assumed**, believed, expected, hypothetical, inferred, supposed, understood **2 = possible**, believable, conceivable, credible, likely, plausible, probable, reasonable, verisimilar

presumptuous *adj* **= pushy** (*inf.*), arrogant, audacious, bigheaded (*inf.*), bold, conceited, foolhardy, forward, insolent, overconfident, overfamiliar, overweening, presuming, rash
Antonyms *adj* bashful, humble, modest, retiring, shy, timid, unassuming

presuppose *vb* **1 = presume**, accept, assume, consider, imply, posit, postulate, suppose, take as read, take for granted, take it

presupposition *n* **1 = assumption**, belief, hypothesis, preconceived idea, preconception, premise, presumption, supposition, theory

pretence *n* **1, 4 = deception**, acting, charade, deceit, fabrication, fakery, faking, falsehood, feigning, invention, make-believe, sham, simulation, subterfuge, trickery **2 = show**, affectation, appearance, artifice, display, façade, hokum (*sl., chiefly US & Canad.*), posing, posturing, pretentiousness, veneer **3, 5 = pretext**, claim, cloak, colour, cover, excuse, façade, garb, guise, mask, masquerade, ruse, semblance, show, veil, wile
Antonyms *n* ≠ **deception:** candour, frankness, honesty, ingenuousness, openness ≠ **show:** actuality, fact, reality

pretend *vb* **1 = feign**, affect, allege, assume, counterfeit, dissemble, dissimulate, fake, falsify, impersonate, make out, pass oneself off as, pro-

finitive) to claim or allege (something untrue). **2** (*tr; may take a clause as object or an infinitive*) to make believe, as in a play: *you pretend to be Ophelia.* **3** (*intr;* foll. by *to*) to present a claim, esp. a dubious one: *to pretend to the throne.* **4** (*intr;* foll. by *to*) *Obs.* to aspire as a candidate or suitor (for). ◆ *adj* **5** make-believe; imaginary. [C14: from L *praetendere* to stretch forth, feign]

pretender ⓣ (prɪˈtɛndə) *n* **1** a person who pretends or makes false allegations. **2** a person who mounts a claim, as to a throne or title.

pretension ⓣ (prɪˈtɛnʃən) *n* **1** (*often pl*) a false claim, esp. to merit, worth, or importance. **2** a specious or unfounded allegation; pretext. **3** the quality of being pretentious.

pretentious ⓣ (prɪˈtɛnʃəs) *adj* **1** making claim to distinction or importance, esp. undeservedly. **2** ostentatious.
▸**preˈtentiously** *adv* ▸**preˈtentiousness** *n*

preterite *or esp. US* **preterit** (ˈprɛtərɪt) *Grammar.* ◆ *n* **1** a tense of verbs used to relate past action, formed in English by inflection of the verb, as *jumped, swam.* **2** a verb in this tense. ◆ *adj* **3** denoting this tense. [C14: from LL *praeteritum* (*tempus*) past (time), from L *praeterīre* to go by, from *preter-* beyond + *īre* to go]

preterm (priːˈtɜːm) *adj* **1** (of a baby) born prematurely. ◆ *adv* **2** prematurely.

pretermit (ˌpriːtəˈmɪt) *vb* **pretermits, pretermitting, pretermitted.** (*tr*) *Rare.* **1** to disregard. **2** to fail to do; neglect; omit. [C16: from L *praetermittere* to let pass, from *preter-* beyond + *mittere* to send]

preternatural ⓣ (ˌpriːtəˈnætʃrəl) *adj* **1** beyond what is ordinarily found in nature; abnormal. **2** another word for **supernatural.** [C16: from Med. L *praeternātūrālis,* from L *praeter natūram* beyond the scope of nature]
▸ˌ**preterˈnaturally** *adv*

pretext ⓣ (ˈpriːtɛkst) *n* **1** a fictitious reason given in order to conceal the real one. **2** a pretence. [C16: from L *praetextum* disguise, from *praetexere* to weave in front, disguise]

pretor (ˈpriːtə, -tɔː) *n* a variant (esp. US) spelling of **praetor.**

prettify ⓣ (ˈprɪtɪˌfaɪ) *vb* **prettifies, prettifying, prettified.** (*tr*) to make pretty, esp. in a trivial fashion; embellish.
▸ˌ**prettifiˈcation** *n* ▸ˈ**prettiˌfier** *n*

pretty ⓣ (ˈprɪtɪ) *adj* **prettier, prettiest. 1** pleasing or appealing in a delicate or graceful way. **2** dainty, neat, or charming. **3** *Inf., often ironical.* excellent, grand, or fine: *here's a pretty mess!* **4** commendable; good of its kind: *he replied with a pretty wit.* **5** *Inf.* effeminate; foppish. **6** *Arch. or Scot.* vigorous or brave. **7 sitting pretty.** *Inf.* well placed or established financially, socially, etc. ◆ *n, pl* **pretties. 8** a pretty person or thing. ◆ *adv Inf.* **9** fairly; somewhat. **10** very. ◆ *vb* **pretties, prettying, prettied. 11** (*tr;* often foll. by *up*) to make pretty; adorn. [OE *prættig* clever]
▸ˈ**prettily** *adv* ▸ˈ**prettiness** *n*

pretty-pretty *adj Inf.* excessively or ostentatiously pretty.

pretzel (ˈprɛtsəl) *n* a brittle savoury biscuit, in the form of a knot or stick, eaten esp. in Germany and the US. [C19: from G, from OHG *brezitella*]

prevail ⓣ (prɪˈveɪl) *vb* (*intr*) **1** (often foll. by *over* or *against*) to prove superior; gain mastery: *skill will prevail.* **2** to be the most important feature; be prevalent. **3** to exist widely; be in force. **4** (often foll. by *on* or *upon*) to succeed in persuading or inducing. [C14: from L *praevalēre* to be superior in strength]
▸**preˈvailer** *n*

prevailing ⓣ (prɪˈveɪlɪŋ) *adj* **1** generally accepted; widespread: *the prevailing opinion.* **2** most frequent; predominant: *the prevailing wind is from the north.*
▸**preˈvailingly** *adv*

prevalent ⓣ (ˈprɛvələnt) *adj* **1** widespread or current. **2** superior in force or power; predominant.
▸ˈ**prevalence** *n* ▸ˈ**prevalently** *adv*

prevaricate ⓣ (prɪˈværɪˌkeɪt) *vb* **prevaricates, prevaricating, prevaricated.** (*intr*) to speak or act falsely or evasively with intent to deceive. [C16: from L *praevāricārī* to walk crookedly, from *prae* beyond + *vāricare* to straddle the legs]
▸**preˌvariˈcation** *n* ▸**preˈvariˌcator** *n*

prevent ⓣ (prɪˈvɛnt) *vb* **1** (*tr*) to keep from happening, esp. by taking precautionary action. **2** (*tr;* often foll. by *from*) to keep (someone from doing something). **3** (*intr*) to interpose or act as a hindrance. **4** (*tr*) *Arch.* to anticipate or precede. [C15: from L *praevenīre,* from *prae* before + *venīre* to come]
▸**preˈventable** *or* **preˈventible** *adj* ▸**preˈventably** *or* **preˈventibly** *adv*

prevention ⓣ (prɪˈvɛnʃən) *n* **1** the act of preventing. **2** a hindrance or impediment.

preventive ⓣ (prɪˈvɛntɪv) *adj* **1** tending or intended to prevent or hinder. **2** *Med.* tending to prevent disease; prophylactic. **3** (in Britain) of, relating to, or belonging to the customs and excise service or the coastguard. ◆ *n* **4** something that serves to prevent or hinder. **5** *Med.* any drug or agent that tends to prevent disease. Also (for senses 1, 2, 4, 5): **preventative.**
▸**preˈventively** *or* **preˈventatively** *adv*

preview ⓣ (ˈpriːvjuː) *n* **1** an advance view or sight. **2** an advance showing before public presentation of a film, art exhibition, etc., usually before an invited audience. ◆ *vb* **3** (*tr*) to view in advance.

previous ⓣ (ˈpriːvɪəs) *adj* **1** (*prenominal*) existing or coming before something else. **2** (*postpositive*) *Inf.* taking place or done too soon; premature. **3 previous to.** before. [C17: from L *praevius* leading the way, from *prae* before + *via* way]
▸ˈ**previously** *adv* ▸ˈ**previousness** *n*

previous question *n* **1** (in the House of Commons) a motion to drop

THESAURUS

fess, put on, sham, simulate **2** = **make believe,** act, imagine, make up, play, play the part of, suppose **3** = **lay claim,** allege, aspire, claim, profess, purport

pretended *adj* **1, 2** = **feigned,** alleged, avowed, bogus, counterfeit, fake, false, fictitious, imaginary, ostensible, phoney *or* phony (*inf.*), pretend (*inf.*), professed, pseudo (*inf.*), purported, sham, so-called, spurious

pretender *n* **2** = **claimant,** aspirant, claimer

pretension *n* **1** = **claim,** aspiration, assertion, assumption, demand, pretence, profession **3** = **affectation,** airs, conceit, hypocrisy, ostentation, pomposity, pretentiousness, self-importance, show, showiness, snobbery, snobbishness, vainglory, vanity

pretentious *adj* **1, 2** = **affected,** arty-farty (*inf.*), assuming, bombastic, conceited, exaggerated, extravagant, flaunting, grandiloquent, grandiose, highfalutin (*inf.*), high-flown, high-sounding, hollow, inflated, magniloquent, mannered, ostentatious, overambitious, pompous, puffed up, showy, snobbish, specious, vainglorious
Antonyms *adj* modest, natural, plain, simple, unaffected, unassuming, unpretentious

preternatural *adj* **1, 2** = **supernatural,** abnormal, anomalous, extraordinary, inexplicable, irregular, marvellous, miraculous, mysterious, odd, peculiar, strange, unaccountable, unearthly, unnatural, unusual

pretext *n* **1, 2** = **guise,** affectation, alleged reason, appearance, cloak, cover, device, excuse, mask, ploy, pretence, red herring, ruse, semblance, show, simulation, veil

prettify *vb* = **adorn,** deck out, decorate, doll up (*sl.*), do up, embellish, garnish, gild, ornament, pretty up, tart up (*Brit. sl.*), titivate, trick out, trim

pretty *adj* **1** = **attractive,** appealing, beautiful, bonny, charming, comely, cute, fair, good-looking, graceful, lovely, personable **2** = **pleasant,** bijou, dainty, delicate, elegant, fine, neat, nice, pleasing, tasteful, trim ◆ *adv* **9** *Informal* = **fairly,** kind of (*inf.*), moderately, quite, rather, reasonably, somewhat
Antonyms *adj* ≠ **attractive:** plain, ugly, unattractive, unshapely, unsightly

prevail *vb* **1** = **win,** be victorious, carry the day, gain mastery, overcome, overrule, prove superior, succeed, triumph **2, 3** = **be widespread,** abound, be current, be prevalent, exist generally, obtain, predominate, preponderate **4** *often foll. by* **on** *or* **upon** = **persuade,** bring round, convince, dispose, incline, induce, influence, prompt, sway, talk into, win over

prevailing *adj* **1** = **widespread,** common, current, customary, established, fashionable, general, in style, in vogue, ordinary, popular, prevalent, set, usual **2** = **predominating,** dominant, influential, main, operative, preponderating, principal, ruling

prevalence *n* **1** = **commonness,** acceptance, common occurrence, currency, frequency, pervasiveness, popularity, profusion, regularity, ubiquity, universality **2** = **predominance,** ascendancy, hold, mastery, preponderance, primacy, rule, sway

prevalent *adj* **1** = **common,** accepted, commonplace, current, customary, established, everyday, extensive, frequent, general, habitual, popular, rampant, rife, ubiquitous, universal, usual, widespread **2** = **predominant,** ascendant, compelling, dominant, governing, powerful, prevailing, successful, superior
Antonyms *adj* ≠ **common:** confined, infrequent, limited, localized, rare, restricted, uncommon, unusual

prevaricate *vb* = **evade,** beat about the bush, beg the question, cavil, deceive, dodge, equivocate, flannel (*Brit. inf.*), give a false colour to, hedge, lie, palter, quibble, shift, shuffle, stretch the truth, tergiversate
Antonyms *vb* be blunt, be direct, be frank, be straightforward, come straight to the point, not beat about the bush

prevarication *n* = **evasion,** cavilling, deceit, deception, equivocation, falsehood, falsification, lie, misrepresentation, pretence, quibbling, tergiversation, untruth

prevaricator *n* = **dissembler,** deceiver, dodger, equivocator, evader, fibber, hypocrite, liar, pettifogger, quibbler, sophist

prevent *vb* **1-3** = **stop,** anticipate, avert, avoid, balk, bar, block, check, counteract, defend against, foil, forestall, frustrate, hamper, head off, hinder, impede, inhibit, intercept, nip in the bud, obstruct, obviate, preclude, restrain, stave off, thwart, ward off
Antonyms *vb* allow, encourage, help, incite, permit, support, urge

prevention *n* **1** = **elimination,** anticipation, avoidance, deterrence, forestalling, obviation, precaution, preclusion, prophylaxis, safeguard, thwarting

preventive *adj* **1** = **hindering,** hampering, impeding, obstructive **2** *Medical* = **protective,** counteractive, deterrent, inhibitory, precautionary, prophylactic, shielding ◆ *n* **4** = **hindrance,** block, impediment, obstacle, obstruction **5** *Medical* = **protection,** deterrent, neutralizer, prevention, prophylactic, protective, remedy, safeguard, shield

preview *n* **1, 2** = **sample,** advance showing, foretaste, sampler, sneak preview, taster, trailer ◆ *vb* **3** = **sample,** foretaste, taste

previous *adj* **1** = **earlier,** antecedent, anterior, erstwhile, ex-, foregoing, former, one-time, past, preceding, prior, quondam, sometime **2** *Informal* = **premature,** ahead of oneself, precipitate, too early, too soon, untimely
Antonyms *adj* ≠ **earlier:** consequent, following, later, subsequent, succeeding

previously *adv* **1** = **before,** at one time, a while ago, beforehand, earlier, formerly, heretofore, hitherto, in advance, in anticipation, in days *or* years gone by, in the past, once, then, until now

the present topic under debate, put in order to prevent a vote. **2** (in the House of Lords and US legislative bodies) a motion to vote on a bill without delay.

previse (prɪˈvaɪz) *vb* **previses, prevising, prevised.** (*tr*) *Rare.* **1** to predict or foresee. **2** to notify in advance. [C16: from L *praevidēre* to foresee]
▸**prevision** (prɪˈvɪʒən) *n*

prey ⓣ (preɪ) *n* **1** an animal hunted or captured by another for food. **2** a person or thing that becomes the victim of a hostile person, influence, etc. **3 bird** *or* **beast of prey.** a bird or animal that preys on others for food. **4** an archaic word for **booty.** ◆ *vb* (*intr;* often foll. by *on* or *upon*) **5** to hunt food by killing other animals. **6** to make a victim (of others), as by profiting at their expense. **7** to exert a depressing or obsessive effect (on the mind, spirits, etc.). [C13: from OF *preie,* from L *praeda* booty]
▸ˈ**preyer** *n*

priapic (praɪˈæpɪk, -ˈeɪ-) *or* **priapean** (ˌpraɪəˈpiːən) *adj* **1** (*sometimes cap.*) of or relating to Priapus, in classical antiquity the god of male procreative power and of gardens and vineyards. **2** a less common word for **phallic.**

priapism (ˈpraɪəˌpɪzəm) *n Pathol.* prolonged painful erection of the penis, caused by neurological disorders, etc. [C17: from LL *priāpismus,* ult. from Gk *Priapus;* see PRIAPIC]

price ⓣ (praɪs) *n* **1** the sum in money or goods for which anything is or may be bought or sold. **2** the cost at which anything is obtained. **3** the cost of bribing a person. **4** a sum of money offered as a reward for a capture or killing. **5** value or worth, esp. high worth. **6** *Gambling.* another word for **odds. 7 at any price.** whatever the price or cost. **8 at a price.** at a high price. **9 what price (something)?** what are the chances of (something) happening now? ◆ *vb* **prices, pricing, priced.** (*tr*) **10** to fix the price of. **11** to discover the price of. **12 price out of the market.** to charge so highly for as to prevent the sale, hire, etc., of. [C13 *pris,* from OF, from L *pretium*]
▸ˈ**pricer** *n*

price control *n* the establishment and maintenance of maximum price levels for basic goods and services by a government.

price-dividend ratio *n* the ratio of the price of a share on a stock exchange to the dividends per share paid in the previous year, used as a measure of a company's potential as an investment. Abbrevs.: **P-D ratio, PDR.**

price-earnings ratio *n* the ratio of the price of a share on the stock exchange to the earnings per share, used as a measure of a company's future profitability. Abbrev.: **P-E ratio.**

price-fixing *n* **1** the setting of prices by agreement among producers and distributors. **2** another name for **price control** or **resale price maintenance.**

price leadership *n Marketing.* the setting of the price of a product or service by a dominant firm at a level that competitors can match, in order to avoid a price war.

priceless ⓣ (ˈpraɪslɪs) *adj* **1** of inestimable worth; invaluable. **2** *Inf.* extremely amusing or ridiculous.
▸ˈ**pricelessly** *adv* ▸ˈ**pricelessness** *n*

price ring *n* a group of traders formed to maintain the prices of their goods.

price-sensitive *adj* likely to affect the price of property, esp. shares and securities: *price-sensitive information.*

pricey ⓣ *or* **pricy** (ˈpraɪsɪ) *adj* **pricier, priciest.** an informal word for **expensive.**

prick ⓣ (prɪk) *vb* (*mainly tr*) **1a** to make (a small hole) in (something) by piercing lightly with a sharp point. **1b** to wound in this manner. **2** (*intr*) to cause or have a piercing or stinging sensation. **3** to cause to feel a sharp emotional pain: *knowledge of such poverty pricked his conscience.* **4** to puncture. **5** to outline by dots or punctures. **6** (*also intr;* usually foll. by *up*) to rise or raise erect: *the dog pricked his ears up.* **7** (usually foll. by *out* or *off*) to transplant (seedlings) into a larger container. **8** *Arch.* to urge on, esp. to spur a horse on. **9 prick up one's ears.** to start to listen attentively; become interested. ◆ *n* **10** the act of pricking or the sensation of being pricked. **11** a mark made by a sharp point; puncture. **12** a sharp emotional pain: *a prick of conscience.* **13** a taboo slang word for **penis. 14** *Sl., derog.* an obnoxious or despicable person. **15** an instrument or weapon with a sharp point. **16** the track of an animal, esp. a hare. **17 kick against the pricks.** to hurt oneself by struggling against something in vain. [OE *prica* point, puncture]
▸ˈ**pricker** *n*

pricket (ˈprɪkɪt) *n* **1** a male deer in the second year of life having unbranched antlers. **2** a sharp metal spike on which to stick a candle. [C14 *priket,* from *prik* PRICK]

prickle ⓣ (ˈprɪkᵊl) *n* **1** *Bot.* a pointed process arising from the outer layer of a stem, leaf, etc., and containing no woody tissue. Cf. **thorn. 2** a pricking or stinging sensation. ◆ *vb* **prickles, prickling, prickled. 3** to feel or cause to feel a stinging sensation. **4** (*tr*) to prick, as with a thorn. [OE *pricel*]

prickly ⓣ (ˈprɪklɪ) *adj* **pricklier, prickliest. 1** having or covered with prickles. **2** stinging. **3** irritable. **4** full of difficulties: *a prickly problem.*
▸ˈ**prickliness** *n*

prickly heat *n* a nontechnical name for **miliaria.**

prickly pear *n* **1** any of various tropical cactuses having flattened or cylindrical spiny joints and oval fruit that is edible in some species. **2** the fruit of any of these plants.

pride ⓣ (praɪd) *n* **1** a feeling of honour and self-respect; a sense of personal worth. **2** excessive self-esteem; conceit. **3** a source of pride. **4** satisfaction or pleasure in one's own or another's success, achievements, etc. (esp. in **take (a) pride in**). **5** the better or superior part of something. **6** the most flourishing time. **7** a group (of lions). **8** courage; spirit. **9** *Arch.* pomp or splendour. **10 pride of place.** the most important position. ◆ *vb* **prides, priding, prided. 11** (*tr;* foll. by *on* or *upon*) to take pride in (oneself) for. [OE *prȳda*]
▸ˈ**prideful** *adj* ▸ˈ**pridefully** *adv*

prie-dieu (priːˈdjɜː) *n* a piece of furniture consisting of a low surface for kneeling upon and a narrow front surmounted by a rest, for use when praying. [C18: from F, from *prier* to pray + *Dieu* God]

prier *or* **pryer** (ˈpraɪə) *n* a person who pries.

priest ⓣ (priːst) *n* **1** a person ordained to act as a mediator between God and man in administering the sacraments, preaching, etc. **2** (in episcopal Churches) a minister in the second grade of the hierarchy of holy orders, ranking below a bishop but above a deacon. **3** a minister of any religion. **4** an official who offers sacrifice on behalf of the people and performs other religious ceremonies. ◆ *vb* **5** (*tr*) to make a priest; ordain. [OE *prēost,* apparently from PRESBYTER]
▸ˈ**priestess** *fem n* ▸ˈ**priestˌhood** *n* ▸ˈ**priestˌlike** *adj* ▸ˈ**priestly** *adj*

priestcraft (ˈpriːstˌkrɑːft) *n* **1** the art and skills involved in the work of a priest. **2** *Derog.* the influence of priests upon politics.

priest-hole *or* **priest's hole** *n* a secret chamber in certain houses in England, built as a hiding place for Roman Catholic priests when they were proscribed in the 16th and 17th centuries.

prig[1] ⓣ (prɪg) *n* a person who is smugly self-righteous and narrow-minded. [C18: from ?]
▸ˈ**priggery** *or* ˈ**priggishness** *n* ▸ˈ**priggish** *adj* ▸ˈ**priggishly** *adv*

prig[2] (prɪg) *Brit. arch. sl.* ◆ *vb* **prigs, prigging, prigged. 1** another word for **steal.** ◆ *n* **2** another word for **thief.** [C16: from ?]

prim ⓣ (prɪm) *adj* **primmer, primmest. 1** affectedly proper, precise, or for-

THESAURUS

prey *n* **1** = **quarry**, game, kill **2** = **victim**, dupe, fall guy (*inf.*), mark, mug (*Brit. sl.*), target ◆ *vb* **5** = **hunt**, devour, eat, feed upon, live off, seize **6** = **victimize**, blackmail, bleed (*inf.*), bully, exploit, intimidate, take advantage of, terrorize **7** = **worry**, burden, distress, hang over, haunt, oppress, trouble, weigh down, weigh heavily

price *n* **1** = **cost**, amount, asking price, assessment, bill, charge, damage (*inf.*), estimate, expenditure, expense, face value, fee, figure, outlay, payment, rate, valuation, value, worth **2** = **consequences**, cost, penalty, sacrifice, toll **4** = **reward**, bounty, compensation, premium, recompense **7 at any price** = **whatever the cost**, anyhow, cost what it may, expense no object, no matter what the cost, regardless ◆ *vb* **10** = **evaluate**, assess, cost, estimate, put a price on, rate, value

priceless *adj* **1** = **valuable**, beyond price, cherished, costly, dear, expensive, incalculable, incomparable, inestimable, invaluable, irreplaceable, precious, prized, rare, rich, treasured, worth a king's ransom **2** *Informal* = **hilarious**, absurd, amusing, comic, droll, funny, killing (*inf.*), rib-tickling, ridiculous, riotous, side-splitting
Antonyms *adj* ≠ **valuable:** cheap, cheapo (*inf.*), common, inexpensive, worthless

pricey *adj* = **expensive**, costly, dear, exorbitant, extortionate, high-priced, over the odds (*Brit. inf.*), steep (*inf.*)

prick *vb* **1, 4** = **pierce**, bore, impale, jab, lance, perforate, pink, punch, puncture, stab **2** = **sting**, bite, itch, prickle, smart, tingle **3** = **distress**, cut, grieve, move, pain, stab, touch, trouble, wound **6** *usually foll. by* **up** = **raise**, point, rise, stand erect ◆ *n* **11** = **puncture**, cut, gash, hole, perforation, pinhole, wound **12** = **pang**, gnawing, prickle, smart, spasm, sting, twinge

prickle *n* **1** = **spike**, barb, needle, point, spine, spur, thorn **2** = **tingling**, chill, formication, goose bumps, goose flesh, paraesthesia (*Medical*), pins and needles (*inf.*), smart, tickle, tingle ◆ *vb* **3** = **tingle**, itch, smart, sting, twitch **4** = **prick**, jab, nick, stick

prickly *adj* **1** = **spiny**, barbed, brambly, briery, bristly, thorny **2** = **itchy**, crawling, pricking, prickling, scratchy, sharp, smarting, stinging, tingling **3** = **irritable**, bad-tempered, cantankerous, edgy, fractious, grumpy, liverish, peevish, pettish, petulant, ratty (*Brit. & NZ inf.*), shirty (*sl., chiefly Brit.*), snappish, stroppy (*Brit. sl.*), tetchy, touchy, waspish **4** = **difficult**, complicated, intricate, involved, knotty, thorny, ticklish, tricky, troublesome, trying

pride *n* **1** = **self-respect**, *amour-propre,* dignity, honour, self-esteem, self-worth **2** = **conceit**, arrogance, bigheadedness (*inf.*), egotism, haughtiness, hauteur, hubris, loftiness, *morgue,* presumption, pretension, pretentiousness, self-importance, self-love, smugness, snobbery, superciliousness, vainglory, vanity **3** = **gem**, boast, jewel, pride and joy, prize, treasure **4** = **satisfaction**, delight, gratification, joy, pleasure **5** = **elite**, best, choice, cream, flower, glory, pick ◆ *vb* **11** *foll. by* **on** *or* **upon** = **be proud of**, boast of, brag about, congratulate oneself on, crow about, exult in, flatter oneself, glory in, pique oneself, plume oneself, revel in, take pride in, vaunt
Antonyms *n* ≠ **conceit:** humility, meekness, modesty

priest *n* **1-3** = **clergyman**, churchman, cleric, curate, divine, ecclesiastic, father, father confessor, holy man, man of God, man of the cloth, minister, padre (*inf.*), pastor, vicar

priestly *adj* **1-3** = **ecclesiastic**, canonical, clerical, hieratic, pastoral, priestlike, sacerdotal

prig[1] *n* = **goody-goody** (*inf.*), Holy Joe (*inf.*), Holy Willie (*inf.*), Mrs Grundy, old maid (*inf.*), pedant, prude, puritan, stuffed shirt (*inf.*)

priggish *adj* = **self-righteous**, goody-goody, holier-than-thou, narrow-minded, pedantic, prim, prudish, puritanical, self-satisfied, smug, starchy (*inf.*), stiff, stuffy

prim *adj* **1** = **prudish**, demure, fastidious, formal, fussy, niminy-piminy, old-maidish (*inf.*), partic-

mal. ◆ *vb* **prims, primming, primmed. 2** (*tr*) to make prim. **3** to purse (the mouth) primly or (of the mouth) to be so pursed. [C18: from ?]
▸**'primly** *adv* ▸**'primness** *n*

prima ballerina ('priːmə) *n* a leading female ballet dancer. [from It., lit.: first ballerina]

primacy ❶ ('praɪməsɪ) *n, pl* **primacies. 1** the state of being first in rank, grade, etc. **2** *Christianity.* the office, rank, or jurisdiction of a primate, senior bishop, or pope.

prima donna ❶ ('priːmə 'dɒnə) *n, pl* **prima donnas. 1** a leading female operatic star. **2** *Inf.* a temperamental person. [C19: from It.: first lady]

prima facie ('praɪmə 'feɪʃɪ) *adv* at first sight; as it seems at first. [C15: from L, from *prīmus* first + *faciēs* FACE]

prima-facie evidence *n Law.* evidence that is sufficient to establish a fact or to raise a presumption of the truth unless controverted.

primal ❶ ('praɪməl) *adj* **1** first or original. **2** chief or most important. [C17: from Med. L *prīmālis,* from L *prīmus* first]

primaquine ('praɪmə,kwiːn) *n* a synthetic drug used in the treatment of malaria. [C20: from *prima-,* from L *prīmus* first + QUIN(OLIN)E]

primarily ❶ ('praɪmərɪlɪ, praɪ'mærɪlɪ, -'meərɪlɪ) *adv* **1** principally; chiefly; mainly. **2** at first; originally.

primary ❶ ('praɪmərɪ) *adj* **1** first in importance, degree, rank, etc. **2** first in position or time, as in a series. **3** fundamental; basic. **4** being the first stage; elementary. **5** (*prenominal*) of or relating to the education of children up to the age of 11. **6** (of the flight feathers of a bird's wing) growing from the manus. **7a** being the part of an electric circuit, such as a transformer, in which a changing current induces a current in a neighbouring circuit: *a primary coil.* **7b** (of a current) flowing in such a circuit. **8a** (of a product) consisting of a natural raw material; unmanufactured. **8b** (of production or industry) involving the extraction or winning of such products. **9** (of Latin, Greek, or Sanskrit tenses) referring to present or future time. **10** *Geol., obs.* relating to the Palaeozoic or earlier eras. ◆ *n, pl* **primaries. 11** a person or thing that is first in rank, occurrence, etc. **12** (in the US) a preliminary election in which the voters of a state or region choose a party's convention delegates, nominees for office, etc. Full name: **primary election. 13** short for **primary colour** or **primary school. 14** any of the flight feathers growing from the manus of a bird's wing. **15** a primary coil, winding, inductance, or current in an electric circuit. **16** *Astron.* a celestial body around which one or more specified secondary bodies orbit: *the sun is the primary of the earth.* [C15: from L *prīmārius* principal, from *prīmus* first]

primary accent *or* **stress** *n Linguistics.* the strongest accent in a word or breath group, as that on the first syllable of *agriculture.*

primary cell *n* an electric cell that generates an electromotive force by the direct and usually irreversible conversion of chemical energy into electrical energy. Also called: **voltaic cell.**

primary colour *n* **1** any of three colours (usually red, green, and blue) that can be mixed to match any other colour, including white light but excluding black. **2** any one of the colours cyan, magenta, or yellow. An equal mixture of the three produces a black pigment. **3** any one of the colours red, yellow, green, or blue. All other colours look like a mixture of two or more of these colours.

primary school *n* **1** (in England and Wales) a school for children below the age of 11. It is usually divided into an infant and a junior section. **2** (in Scotland) a school for children below the age of 12. **3** (in the US and Canad.) a school equivalent to the first three or four grades of elementary school.

primate[1] ('praɪmeɪt) *n* **1** any placental mammal of the order *Primates,* typically having flexible hands, good eyesight, and, in the higher apes, a highly developed brain: includes lemurs, apes, and man. ◆ *adj* **2** of, relating to, or belonging to the order *Primates.* [C18: from NL *primates,* pl. of *prīmās* principal, from *prīmus* first]
▸**primatial** (praɪ'meɪʃəl) *adj*

primate[2] ('praɪmeɪt) *n* **1** another name for an **archbishop. 2 Primate of all England.** the Archbishop of Canterbury. **3 Primate of England.** the Archbishop of York. [C13: from OF, from L *prīmās* principal, from *prīmus* first]

prime ❶ (praɪm) *adj* **1** (*prenominal*) first in quality or value; first-rate. **2** (*prenominal*) fundamental; original. **3** (*prenominal*) first in importance; chief. **4** *Maths.* **4a** having no factors except itself or one: $x^2 + x + 3$ *is a prime polynomial.* **4b** (foll. by *to*) having no common factors (with): *20 is prime to 21.* **5** *Finance.* having the best credit rating: *prime investments.* ◆ *n* **6** the time when a thing is at its best. **7** a period of power, vigour, etc. (esp. in **the prime of life**). **8** *Maths.* short for **prime number. 9** *Chiefly RC Church.* the second of the seven canonical hours of the divine office, originally fixed for the first hour of the day, at sunrise. **10** the first of eight basic positions from which a parry or attack can be made in fencing. ◆ *vb* **primes, priming, primed. 11** to prepare (something). **12** (*tr*) to apply a primer, such as paint or size, to (a surface). **13** (*tr*) to fill (a pump) with its working fluid before starting, in order to expel air from it before starting. **14 prime the pump. 14a** See **pump priming. 14b** to make an initial input in order to set a process going. **15** (*tr*) to increase the quantity of fuel in the float chamber of (a carburettor) in order to facilitate the starting of an engine. **16** (*tr*) to insert a primer into (a gun, mine, etc.) preparatory to detonation or firing. **17** (*tr*) to provide with facts beforehand; brief. [(adj) C14: from L *prīmus* first; (n) C13: from L *prīma* (*hora*) the first (hour); (vb) C16: from ?]
▸**'primeness** *n*

prime cost *n* the portion of the cost of a commodity that varies directly with the amount of it produced, principally comprising materials and labour. Also called: **variable cost.**

prime meridian *n* the 0° meridian from which the other meridians are calculated, usually taken to pass through Greenwich.

prime minister *n* **1** the head of a parliamentary government. **2** the chief minister of a sovereign or a state.

prime mover *n* **1** the original force behind an idea, enterprise, etc. **2a** the source of power, such as fuel, wind, electricity, etc., for a machine. **2b** the means of extracting power from such a source, such as a steam engine.

prime number *n* an integer that cannot be factorized into other integers but is only divisible by itself or 1, such as 2, 3, 7, and 11.

primer[1] ('praɪmə) *n* an introductory text, such as a school textbook. [C14: via Anglo-Norman, from Med. L *prīmārius* (*liber*) a first (book), from L *prīmārius* PRIMARY]

primer[2] ('praɪmə) *n* **1** a person or thing that primes. **2** a device, such as a tube containing explosive, for detonating the main charge in a gun, mine, etc. **3** a substance, such as paint, applied to a surface as a base, sealer, etc. [C15: see PRIME (vb)]

prime rate *n* the lowest commercial interest rate charged by a bank at a particular time.

primers ('prɪməz) *n* (*functioning as sing*) *NZ inf.* the youngest classes in a primary school: *in the primers.*

prime time *n* the peak viewing time on television, for which advertising rates are the highest.

primeval ❶ *or* **primaeval** (praɪ'miːvᵊl) *adj* of or belonging to the first ages of the world. [C17: from L *prīmaevus* youthful, from *prīmus* first + *aevum* age]
▸**pri'mevally** *or* **pri'maevally** *adv*

priming ('praɪmɪŋ) *n* **1** something used to prime. **2** a substance used to ignite an explosive charge.

primitive ❶ ('prɪmɪtɪv) *adj* **1** of or belonging to the beginning; original. **2** characteristic of an early state, esp. in being crude or uncivilized: *a primitive dwelling.* **3** *Anthropol.* denoting a preliterate and nonindustrial social system. **4** *Biol.* of, relating to, or resembling an early stage in development: *primitive amphibians.* **5** showing the characteristics of primitive painters; untrained, childlike, or naive. **6** *Geol.* of or denoting rocks formed in or before the Palaeozoic era. **7** denoting a word from which another word is derived, as for example *hope,* from which *hopeless* is derived. **8** *Protestant theol.* of or associated with a group that breaks away from a sect, denomination, or Church in order to return to what is regarded as the original simplicity of the Gospels. ◆ *n* **9** a primitive person or thing. **10a** an artist whose work does not conform to traditional standards of Western painting, such as a painter from an African civilization. **10b** a painter of the pre-Renaissance era in European painting. **10c** a painter of any era whose work appears childlike or untrained. ◆ Also called (for a, c): **naive. 11** a work by such an artist. **12** a word from which another word is derived. **13** *Maths.* a curve or other form from which another is derived. [C14: from L *prīmitīvus* earliest of its kind from *prīmus* first]
▸**'primitively** *adv* ▸**'primitiveness** *n*

THESAURUS

ular, precise, priggish, prissy (*inf.*), proper, puritanical, schoolmarmish (*Brit. inf.*), starchy (*inf.*), stiff, strait-laced
Antonyms *adj* carefree, casual, easy-going, informal, laid-back, relaxed

primacy *n* **1** = **supremacy**, ascendancy, command, dominance, dominion, leadership, preeminence, superiority

prima donna *n* **1** = **diva**, leading lady, star

primal *adj* **1** = **first**, earliest, initial, original, primary, prime, primitive, primordial, pristine **2** = **chief**, central, first, greatest, highest, main, major, most important, paramount, prime, principal

primarily *adv* **1** = **chiefly**, above all, basically, especially, essentially, for the most part, fundamentally, generally, largely, mainly, mostly, on the whole, principally **2** = **at first**, at *or* from the start, first and foremost, initially, in the beginning, in the first place, originally

primary *adj* **1** = **chief**, best, capital, cardinal, dominant, first, greatest, highest, leading, main, paramount, prime, principal, top **2** = **earliest**, aboriginal, initial, original, primal, primeval, primitive, primordial, pristine **3** = **basic**, beginning, bog-standard (*inf.*), elemental, essential, fundamental, radical, ultimate, underlying **4** = **elementary**, introductory, rudimentary, simple
Antonyms *adj* ≠ **chief**: inferior, lesser, lowest, subordinate, supplementary, unimportant ≠ **elementary**: ensuing, following, later, secondary, subsequent, succeeding

prime *adj* **1** = **best**, capital, choice, excellent, first-class, first-rate, grade A, highest, quality, select, selected, superior, top **2** = **fundamental**, basic, bog-standard (*inf.*), earliest, original, primary, underlying **3** = **main**, chief, leading, predominant, pre-eminent, primary, principal, ruling, senior ◆ *n* **6** = **peak**, best days, bloom, flower, full flowering, height, heyday, maturity, perfection, zenith ◆ *vb* **11** = **prepare**, break in, coach, fit, get ready, groom, make ready, train **17** = **inform**, brief, clue in (*inf.*), clue up (*inf.*), fill in (*inf.*), gen up (*Brit. inf.*), give someone the lowdown (*inf.*), notify, tell

primeval *adj* = **earliest**, ancient, early, first, old, original, prehistoric, primal, primitive, primordial, pristine

primitive *adj* **1** = **early**, earliest, elementary, first, original, primary, primeval, primordial, pristine **2** = **crude**, rough, rude, rudimentary, simple, unrefined **2** = **uncivilized**, barbarian, barbaric, savage, uncultivated, undeveloped **5** = **simple**, childlike, naive, undeveloped, unsophisticated, untrained, untutored

primitivism ('prɪmɪtɪˌvɪzəm) *n* **1** the condition of being primitive. **2** the belief that the value of primitive cultures is superior to that of the modern world.
▸**'primitivist** *n, adj*

primo ('pri:məʊ) *n, pl* **primos** *or* **primi** (-mi:). *Music.* **1** the upper or right-hand part of a piano duet. **2 tempo primo.** at the same speed as at the beginning of the piece. [It.: first, from L *prīmus*]

primogenitor (ˌpraɪməʊ'dʒɛnɪtə) *n* **1** a forefather; ancestor. **2** an earliest parent or ancestor, as of a race. [C17: alteration of PROGENITOR after PRIMOGENITURE]

primogeniture (ˌpraɪməʊ'dʒɛnɪtʃə) *n* **1** the state of being a first-born. **2** *Law.* the right of an eldest son to succeed to the estate of his ancestor to the exclusion of all others. [C17: from Med. L *prīmōgenitūra* birth of a first child, from L *prīmō* at first + LL *genitūra* a birth]
▸**primogenitary** (ˌpraɪməʊ'dʒɛnɪtərɪ, -trɪ) *adj*

primordial Ⓣ (praɪ'mɔ:dɪəl) *adj* **1** existing at or from the beginning; primeval. **2** constituting an origin; fundamental. **3** *Biol.* relating to an early stage of development. [C14: from LL *prīmōrdiālis* original, from L *prīmus* first + *ōrdīrī* to begin]
▸**priˌmordi'ality** *n* ▸**pri'mordially** *adv*

primp Ⓣ (prɪmp) *vb* to dress (oneself), esp. in fine clothes; prink. [C19: prob. from PRIM]

primrose ('prɪmˌrəʊz) *n* **1** any of various temperate plants of the genus *Primula,* esp. a European variety which has pale yellow flowers. **2** short for **evening primrose. 3** Also called: **primrose yellow.** a light yellow, sometimes with a greenish tinge. ◆ *adj* **4** of or abounding in primroses. **5** of the colour primrose. [C15: from OF *primerose,* from Med. L *prīma rosa* first rose]

primrose path *n* (often preceded by *the*) a pleasurable way of life.

primula ('prɪmjʊlə) *n* any plant of the N temperate genus *Primula,* having white, yellow, pink, or purple funnel-shaped flowers with five spreading petals: includes the primrose, oxlip, cowslip, and polyanthus. [C18: NL, from Med. L *prīmula* (*vēris*) little first one (of the spring)]

primum mobile *Latin.* ('praɪmʊm 'məʊbɪlɪ) *n* **1** a prime mover. **2** *Astron.* the outermost empty sphere in the Ptolemaic system that was thought to revolve around the earth from east to west in 24 hours carrying with it the inner spheres of the planets, sun, moon, and fixed stars. [C15: from Med. L: first moving (thing)]

Primus ('praɪməs) *n Trademark.* a portable paraffin cooking stove, used esp. by campers. Also called: **Primus stove.**

prince Ⓣ (prɪns) *n* **1** (in Britain) a son of the sovereign or of one of the sovereign's sons. **2** a nonreigning male member of a sovereign family. **3** the monarch of a small territory that was at some time subordinate to an emperor or king. **4** any monarch. **5** a nobleman in various countries, such as Italy and Germany. **6** an outstanding member of a specified group: *a merchant prince.* [C13: via OF from L *princeps* first man, ruler]
▸**'princedom** *n* ▸**'princeˌlike** *adj*

prince consort *n* the husband of a female sovereign, who is himself a prince.

princeling ('prɪnslɪŋ) *n* **1** a young prince. **2** Also called: **princelet.** the ruler of an insignificant territory.

princely Ⓣ ('prɪnslɪ) *adj* **princelier, princeliest. 1** generous or lavish. **2** of or characteristic of a prince. ◆ *adv* **3** in a princely manner.
▸**'princeliness** *n*

Prince of Darkness *n* another name for **Satan.**

Prince of Peace *n Bible.* the future Messiah (Isaiah 9:6): held by Christians to be Christ.

Prince of Wales *n* the eldest son and heir apparent of the British sovereign.

prince regent *n* a prince who acts as regent during the minority, disability, or absence of the legal sovereign.

prince's-feather *n* **1** a garden plant with spikes of bristly brownish-red flowers. **2** a tall tropical plant with hanging spikes of pink flowers.

princess (prɪn'sɛs) *n* **1** (in Britain) a daughter of the sovereign or of one of the sovereign's sons. **2** a nonreigning female member of a sovereign family. **3** the wife and consort of a prince. **4** *Arch.* a female sovereign. **5** Also: **princess dress.** a style of dress having a fitted bodice and A-line skirt without a seam at the waistline.

princess royal *n* the eldest daughter of a British or (formerly) a Prussian sovereign.

principal Ⓣ ('prɪnsɪpᵊl) *adj* (*prenominal*) **1** first in importance, rank, value, etc. **2** denoting capital or property as opposed to interest, etc. ◆ *n* **3** a person who is first in importance or directs some event, organization, etc. **4** *Law.* **4a** a person who engages another to act as his agent. **4b** an active participant in a crime. **4c** the person primarily liable to fulfil an obligation. **5** the head of a school or other educational institution. **6** (in Britain) a civil servant of an executive grade who is in charge of a section. **7** the leading performer in a play. **8** *Finance.* **8a** capital or property, as contrasted with income. **8b** the original amount of a debt on which interest is calculated. **9** a main roof truss or rafter. **10** *Music.* either of two types of open diapason organ stops. [C13: via OF from L *principālis* chief, from *princeps* chief man]
▸**'principally** *adv* ▸**'principalship** *n*

> **USAGE NOTE** See at **principle.**

principal boy *n* the leading male role in a pantomime, traditionally played by a woman.

principality (ˌprɪnsɪ'pælɪtɪ) *n, pl* **principalities. 1** a territory ruled by a prince or from which a prince draws his title. **2** the authority of a prince.

principal nursing officer *n* a grade of nurse concerned with administration in the British National Health Service.

principal parts *pl n Grammar.* the main inflected forms of a verb, from which all other inflections may be deduced.

principate ('prɪnsɪˌpeɪt) *n* **1** a state ruled by a prince. **2** a form of rule in the early Roman Empire in which some republican forms survived.

principle Ⓣ ('prɪnsɪpᵊl) *n* **1** a standard or rule of personal conduct: *he would stoop to anything – he has no principles.* **2** a set of such moral rules: *he was a man of principle.* **3** a fundamental or general truth. **4** the essence of something. **5** a source; origin. **6** a law concerning a natural phenomenon or the behaviour of a system: *the principle of the conservation of mass.* **7** *Chem.* a constituent of a substance that gives the substance its characteristics. **8 in principle.** in theory. **9 on principle.** because of or in demonstration of a principle. [C14: from L *principium* beginning, basic tenet]

> **USAGE NOTE** *Principle* and *principal* are often confused: *the principal* (not *principle*) *reason for his departure; the plan was approved in principle* (not *principal*).

principled Ⓣ ('prɪnsɪpᵊld) *adj* **a** having high moral principles. **b** (*in combination*): *high-principled.*

prink Ⓣ (prɪŋk) *vb* **1** to dress (oneself, etc.) finely; deck out. **2** (*intr*) to preen oneself. [C16: prob. changed from PRANK[2] (to adorn)]

print Ⓣ (prɪnt) *vb* **1** to reproduce (text, pictures, etc.), esp. in large numbers, by applying ink to paper or other material. **2** to produce or reproduce (a manuscript, data, etc.) in print, as for publication. **3** to write (letters, etc.) in the style of printed matter. **4** to mark or indent (a surface) by pressing (something) onto it. **5** to produce a photographic print from (a negative). **6** (*tr*) to fix in the mind or memory. **7** (*tr*) to make (a mark) by applying pressure. ◆ *n* **8** printed matter such as newsprint. **9** a printed publication such as a book. **10 in print. 10a** in printed or published form. **10b** (of a book, etc.) offered for sale by the publisher. **11 out of print.** no longer available from a publisher. **12** a design or picture printed from an engraved plate, wood block, or other medium. **13** printed text, esp. with regard to the typeface: *small print.* **14** a positive photographic image produced from a negative image on film. **15a** a fabric with a printed design. **15b** (*as modifier*): *a print dress.* **16a** a mark made by pressing something onto a surface. **16b** a stamp, die, etc., that makes such an impression. **17** See **fingerprint.** ◆ See also

THESAURUS

Antonyms *adj* ≠ **early:** advanced, later, modern ≠ **crude:** comfortable, elaborate, refined ≠ **uncivilized:** civilized, developed ≠ **simple:** adult, developed, mature, sophisticated, trained, tutored

primordial *adj* **1** = **primeval,** earliest, first, prehistoric, primal, primitive, pristine **2** = **fundamental,** basic, elemental, original, radical

primp *vb* = **preen,** deck out, doll up (*sl.*), dress up (*sl.*), prank, prink, put on one's best bib and tucker (*inf.*), put on one's glad rags (*sl.*)

prince *n* **3, 4** = **ruler,** lord, monarch, potentate, sovereign

princely *adj* **1** = **generous,** bounteous, bountiful, gracious, lavish, liberal, magnanimous, munificent, open-handed, rich **2** = **regal,** august, dignified, grand, high-born, imperial, imposing, lofty, magnificent, majestic, noble, royal, sovereign, stately

principal *adj* **1** = **main,** arch, capital, cardinal, chief, controlling, dominant, essential, first, foremost, highest, key, leading, most important, paramount, pre-eminent, primary, prime, strongest ◆ *n* **3** = **head,** boss (*inf.*), chief, director, leader, master, ruler, superintendent **5** = **headmaster** *or* **headmistress,** dean, director, head (*inf.*), head teacher, master *or* mistress, rector **7** = **star,** lead, leader **8a** = **capital,** assets, capital funds, money
Antonyms *adj* ≠ **main:** auxiliary, inferior, minor, subordinate, subsidiary, supplementary, weakest

principally *adv* **1** = **mainly,** above all, chiefly, especially, first and foremost, for the most part, in the main, largely, mostly, particularly, predominantly, primarily

principle *n* **1, 3** = **rule,** assumption, axiom, canon, criterion, dictum, doctrine, dogma, ethic, formula, fundamental, golden rule, law, maxim, moral law, precept, proposition, standard, truth, verity **2** = **morals,** conscience, integrity, probity, rectitude, scruples, sense of duty, sense of honour, uprightness **8 in principle** = **in theory,** ideally, in essence, theoretically

principled *adj* = **moral,** conscientious, correct, decent, ethical, high-minded, honourable, just, righteous, right-minded, scrupulous, upright, virtuous

prink *vb* **1** = **dress up,** deck, dress to kill (*inf.*), dress (up) to the nines (*inf.*), fig up (*sl.*), trick out **2** = **preen,** adorn, doll up (*sl.*), groom, prank, primp, titivate

print *vb* **1, 2** = **publish,** engrave, go to press, impress, imprint, issue, mark, put to bed (*inf.*), run off, stamp ◆ *n* **8, 9** = **publication,** book, magazine, newspaper, newsprint, periodical, printed matter, typescript, zine (*inf.*) **10 in print: a** = **available,** in black and white, on paper, on the streets, out, printed **b** current, in the shops, obtainable, on the market, on the shelves **11 out of print** = **unavailable,** no longer published, o.p., unobtainable **12, 14** = **reproduction,** copy, engraving, photo, photograph, picture **13** = **typeface,** characters, face, font (*chiefly US*), fount, lettering, letters, type

print out. [C13 *priente,* from OF: something printed, from *preindre* to make an impression, from L *premere* to press]
▸**'printable** *adj*

printed circuit *n* an electronic circuit in which certain components and the connections between them are formed by etching a metallic coating or by electrodeposition on one or both sides of a thin insulating board.

printer ('prɪntə) *n* **1** a person or business engaged in printing. **2** a machine or device that prints. **3** *Computing.* an output device for printing results on paper.

printer's devil *n* an apprentice or errand boy in a printing establishment.

printing ('prɪntɪŋ) *n* **1** the business or art of producing printed matter. **2** printed text. **3** Also called: **impression.** all the copies of a book, etc., printed at one time. **4** a form of writing in which letters resemble printed letters.

printing press *n* any of various machines used for printing.

printmaker ('prɪntˌmeɪkə) *n* a person who makes print or prints, esp. a craftsman or artist.

print out *vb* (*tr, adv*) **1** (of a computer output device) to produce (printed information). ◆ *n* **print-out, printout. 2** such printed information.

print shop *n* a place in which printing is carried out.

prion ('priːɒn) *n* a protein in the brain, an abnormal transmissible form of which is thought to be the agent responsible for certain spongiform encephalopathies, such as BSE, scrapie, Creutzfeldt-Jakob disease, and kuru. [C20: from *pro(teinaceous) in(fectious particle)*]

prior[1] Ⓣ ('praɪə) *adj* **1** (*prenominal*) previous. **2 prior to.** before; until. [C18: from L: previous]

prior[2] ('praɪə) *n* **1** the superior of a community in certain religious orders. **2** the deputy head of a monastery or abbey, immediately below the abbot. [C11: from LL: head, from L (adj): previous, from OL *pri* before]
▸**'priorate** *n* ▸**'prioress** *fem n*

priority Ⓣ (praɪ'ɒrɪtɪ) *n, pl* **priorities. 1** the condition of being prior; antecedence; precedence. **2** the right of precedence over others. **3** something given specified attention: *my first priority.*

priory Ⓣ ('praɪərɪ) *n, pl* **priories.** a religious house governed by a prior, sometimes being subordinate to an abbey. [C13: from Med. L *priōria*]

prise *or* **prize** (praɪz) *vb* **prises, prising, prised** *or* **prizes, prizing, prized.** (*tr*) **1** to force open by levering. **2** to extract or obtain with difficulty: *they had to prise the news out of him.* [C17: from OF *prise* a taking, from *prendre* to take, from L *prehendere;* see PRIZE[1]]

prism ('prɪzəm) *n* **1** a transparent polygonal solid, often having triangular ends and rectangular sides, for dispersing light into a spectrum or for reflecting light: used in binoculars, periscopes, etc. **2** *Maths.* a polyhedron having parallel bases and sides that are parallelograms. [C16: from Med. L *prisma,* from Gk: something shaped by sawing, from *prizein* to saw]

prismatic (prɪz'mætɪk) *adj* **1** of or produced by a prism. **2** exhibiting bright spectral colours: *prismatic light.* **3** *Crystallog.* another word for **orthorhombic.**
▸**pris'matically** *adv*

prison Ⓣ ('prɪzən) *n* **1** a public building used to house convicted criminals and accused persons awaiting trial. **2** any place of confinement. [C12: from OF *prisun,* from L *prēnsiō* a capturing, from *prehendere* to lay hold of]

prisoner Ⓣ ('prɪzənə) *n* **1** a person kept in custody as a punishment for a crime, while awaiting trial, or for some other reason. **2** a person confined by any of various restraints: *we are all prisoners of time.* **3 take (someone) prisoner.** to capture and hold (someone) as a prisoner.

prisoner of war *n* a person, esp. a serviceman, captured by an enemy in time of war. Abbrev.: **POW.**

prisoner's base *n* a children's game involving two teams, members of which chase and capture each other.

prissy Ⓣ ('prɪsɪ) *adj* **prissier, prissiest.** fussy and prim, esp. in a prudish way. [C20: prob. from PRIM + SISSY]
▸**'prissily** *adv* ▸**'prissiness** *n*

pristine Ⓣ ('prɪstaɪn, -tiːn) *adj* **1** of or involving the earliest period, state, etc.; original. **2** pure; uncorrupted. **3** fresh, clean, and unspoiled: *his pristine new car.* [C15: from L *pristinus* primitive]

> **USAGE NOTE** The use of *pristine* to mean *fresh, clean, and unspoiled* is considered by some people to be incorrect.

prithee ('prɪðɪ) *interj Arch.* pray thee; please. [C16: shortened from *I pray thee*]

privacy Ⓣ ('praɪvəsɪ, 'prɪvəsɪ) *n* **1** the condition of being private. **2** secrecy.

private Ⓣ ('praɪvɪt) *adj* **1** not widely or publicly known: *they had private reasons for the decision.* **2** confidential; secret: *a private conversation.* **3** not for general or public use: *a private bathroom.* **4** of or provided by a private individual or organization rather than by the state. **5** (*prenominal*) individual; special: *my own private recipe.* **6** (*prenominal*) having no public office, rank, etc.: *a private man.* **7** (*prenominal*) denoting a soldier of the lowest military rank. **8** (of a place) retired; not overlooked. ◆ *n* **9** a soldier of the lowest rank in many armies and marine corps. **10 in private.** in secret. [C14: from L *prīvātus* belonging to one individual, withdrawn from public life, from *prīvāre* to deprive]
▸**'privately** *adv*

private bill *n* a bill presented to Parliament or Congress on behalf of a private individual, corporation, etc.

private company *n* a limited company that does not issue shares for public subscription and whose owners do not enjoy an unrestricted right to transfer their shareholdings. Cf. **public company.**

private detective *n* an individual privately employed to investigate a crime or make other inquiries. Also called: **private investigator.**

private enterprise *n* economic activity undertaken by private individuals or organizations under private ownership.

privateer (ˌpraɪvə'tɪə) *n* **1** an armed privately owned vessel commissioned for war service by a government. **2** Also called: **privateersman.** a member of the crew of a privateer. ◆ *vb* **3** (*intr*) to serve as a privateer.

private eye *n Inf.* a private detective.

Private Finance Initiative *n* (in Britain) a government scheme to encourage private investment in public projects. Abbrev.: **PFI.**

private health insurance *n* insurance against the need for medical treatment as a private patient.

private hotel *n* **1** a hotel in which the proprietor has the right to refuse to accept a person as a guest. **2** *Austral. & NZ.* a hotel not having a licence to sell alcoholic liquor.

private income *n* an income from sources other than employment, such as investment. Also called: **private means.**

private life *n* the social life or personal relationships of an individual, esp. of a celebrity.

private member *n* a member of a legislative assembly not having an appointment in the government.

private member's bill *n* a parliamentary bill sponsored by a Member of Parliament who is not a government minister.

private parts *or* **privates** *pl n* euphemistic terms for **genitals.**

private patient *n Brit.* a patient receiving medical treatment not paid for by the National Health Service.

private pay bed *n* (in Britain) a hospital bed reserved for private patients who are charged by the health service for use of hospital facilities.

private practice *n Brit.* medical practice that is not part of the National Health Service.

private school *n* a school under the financial and managerial control of a private body, accepting mostly fee-paying pupils.

private secretary *n* **1** a secretary entrusted with the personal and confidential matters of a business executive. **2** a civil servant who acts as aide to a minister or senior government official.

private sector *n* the part of a country's economy that consists of privately owned enterprises.

privation Ⓣ (praɪ'veɪʃən) *n* **1** loss or lack of the necessities of life, such as food and shelter. **2** hardship resulting from this. **3** the state of being deprived. [C14: from L *prīvātiō* deprivation]

privative ('prɪvətɪv) *adj* **1** causing privation. **2** expressing lack or negation, as for example the English suffix *-less* and prefix *un-*. [C16: from L *prīvātīvus* indicating loss]
▸**'privatively** *adv*

privatize *or* **privatise** ('praɪvɪˌtaɪz) *vb* **privatizes, privatizing, privatized** *or*

THESAURUS

prior[1] *adj* **1** = **earlier**, aforementioned, antecedent, anterior, foregoing, former, preceding, pre-existent, pre-existing, previous **2 prior to** = **before**, earlier than, preceding, previous to

priority *n* **1-3** = **precedence**, first concern, greater importance, pre-eminence, preference, prerogative, rank, right of way, seniority, superiority, supremacy, the lead

priory *n* = **monastery**, abbey, cloister, convent, nunnery, religious house

prison *n* **1** = **jail**, can (*sl.*), choky (*sl.*), clink (*sl.*), confinement, cooler (*sl.*), dungeon, lockup, nick (*Brit. sl.*), penal institution, penitentiary (*US*), poky *or* pokey (*US & Canad. sl.*), pound, quod (*sl.*), slammer (*sl.*), stir (*sl.*)

prisoner *n* **1** = **convict**, con (*sl.*), jailbird, lag (*sl.*) **1** = **captive**, detainee, hostage, internee

prissy *adj* = **prim**, fastidious, finicky, fussy, niminy-piminy, old-maidish (*inf.*), overnice, precious, prim and proper, prudish, schoolmarmish (*Brit. inf.*), squeamish, strait-laced

pristine *adj* **1** = **original**, earliest, first, former, initial, primal, primary, primeval, primitive, primordial **2, 3** = **new**, immaculate, pure, uncorrupted, undefiled, unspoiled, unsullied, untouched, virgin, virginal

privacy *n* **1** = **seclusion**, isolation, privateness, retirement, retreat, separateness, sequestration, solitude **2** = **secrecy**, clandestineness, concealment, confidentiality

private *adj* **2** = **secret**, clandestine, closet, confidential, covert, hush-hush (*inf.*), in camera, inside, off the record, privy (*arch.*), unofficial **3, 5** = **exclusive**, individual, intimate, own, particular, personal, reserved, special **4** = **nonpublic**, independent **8** = **secluded**, concealed, isolated, not overlooked, retired, secret, separate, sequestered ◆ *n* **9** = **enlisted man** (*US*), private soldier, squaddie *or* squaddy (*Brit. sl.*), tommy (*Brit. inf.*), Tommy Atkins (*Brit. inf.*) ◆ *adj* **10 in private** = **in secret**, behind closed doors, confidentially, in camera, personally, privately
Antonyms *adj* ≠ **secret:** disclosed, known, official, open, public, revealed ≠ **exclusive:** common, general, open, public, unlimited, unrestricted ≠ **secluded:** bustling, busy, frequented, unsecluded

privation *n* **1, 2** = **want**, destitution, distress, hardship, indigence, lack, loss, misery, necessity, need, neediness, penury, poverty, suffering

privatises, privatising, privatised. (*tr*) to take into, or return to, private ownership, a company or concern that has previously been owned by the state.
▸ ˌ**privati'zation** *or* ˌ**privati'sation** *n*

privet ('prɪvɪt) *n* **a** any of a genus of shrubs, esp. one having oval dark green leaves, white flowers, and purplish-black berries. **b** (*as modifier*): *a privet hedge*. [C16: from ?]

privilege Ⓣ ('prɪvɪlɪdʒ) *n* **1** a benefit, immunity, etc., granted under certain conditions. **2** the advantages and immunities enjoyed by a small usually powerful group or class, esp. to the disadvantage of others: *one of the obstacles to social harmony is privilege*. **3** *US Stock Exchange*. a speculative contract permitting its purchaser to make optional purchases or sales of securities at a specified time over a limited period. ◆ *vb* **privileges, privileging, privileged.** (*tr*) **4** to bestow a privilege or privileges upon. **5** (foll. by *from*) to free or exempt. [C12: from OF *privilège*, from L *prīvilēgium* law relevant to rights of an individual, from *prīvus* an individual + *lēx* law]

privileged Ⓣ ('prɪvɪlɪdʒd) *adj* **1** enjoying or granted as a privilege or privileges. **2** *Law*. **2a** not actionable as a libel or slander. **2b** (of a communication, document, etc.) that a witness cannot be compelled to divulge.

privity ('prɪvɪtɪ) *n, pl* **privities. 1** a legally recognized relationship existing between two parties, such as that between the parties to a contract: *privity of contract*. **2** secret knowledge that is shared. [C13: from OF *privete*]

privy Ⓣ ('prɪvɪ) *adj* **privier, priviest. 1** (*postpositive*; foll. by *to*) participating in the knowledge of something secret. **2** *Arch*. secret, hidden, etc. ◆ *n, pl* **privies. 3** a lavatory, esp. an outside one. **4** *Law*. a person in privity with another. See **privity**. [C13: from OF *privé* something private, from L *prīvātus* PRIVATE]
▸ '**privily** *adv*

privy council *n* **1** the council of state of a monarch, esp. formerly. **2** *Arch*. a secret council.

Privy Council *n* **1** the private council of the British sovereign, consisting of all current and former ministers of the Crown and other distinguished subjects, all of whom are appointed for life. **2** (in Canada) a ceremonial body of advisers of the governor general, the chief of them being the Federal cabinet ministers.
▸ **Privy Counsellor** *n*

privy purse *n* (*often cap*.) **1** an allowance voted by Parliament for the private expenses of the monarch. **2** an official of the royal household responsible for dealing with the monarch's private expenses. Full name: **Keeper of the Privy Purse.**

privy seal *n* (*often cap*.) (in Britain) a seal affixed to certain documents issued by royal authority: of less importance than the great seal.

Prix Goncourt (*French* pri) *n* an annual prize for a work of French fiction. [C20: after the Académie Goncourt, which awards it]

prize[1] Ⓣ (praɪz) *n* **1a** a reward or honour for having won a contest, competition, etc. **1b** (*as modifier*): *prize jockey; prize essay*. **2** something given to the winner of any game of chance, lottery, etc. **3** something striven for. **4** any valuable property captured in time of war, esp. a vessel. [C14: from OF *prise* a capture, from L *prehendere* to seize; infl. by ME *prise* reward]

prize[2] Ⓣ (praɪz) *vb* **prizes, prizing, prized.** (*tr*) to esteem greatly; value highly. [C15 *prise*, from OF *preisier* to PRAISE]

prize court *n Law*. a court having jurisdiction to determine how property captured at sea in wartime is to be distributed.

prizefight Ⓣ ('praɪzˌfaɪt) *n* a boxing match for a prize or purse.
▸ '**prizeˌfighter** *n* ▸ '**prizeˌfighting** *n*

prize ring *n* **1** the enclosed area or ring used by prizefighters. **2 the prize ring.** the sport of prizefighting.

pro[1] (prəʊ) *adv* **1** in favour of a motion, issue, course of action, etc. ◆ *prep* **2** in favour of. ◆ *n, pl* **pros. 3** (*usually pl*) an argument or vote in favour of a proposal or motion. See also **pros and cons.** [from L *prō* (prep) in favour of]

pro[2] (prəʊ) *n, pl* **pros**, *adj Inf*. **1** short for **professional. 2** a prostitute. [C19]

PRO *abbrev. for*: **1** Public Records Office. **2** public relations officer.

pro-[1] *prefix* **1** in favour of; supporting: *pro-Chinese*. **2** acting as a substitute for: *proconsul; pronoun*. [from L *prō* (adv & prep). In compound words borrowed from L, *prō-* indicates: forward, out (*project*); away from (*prodigal*); onward (*proceed*); in front of (*provide, protect*); on behalf of (*procure*); substitute for (*pronominal*); and sometimes intensive force (*promiscuous*)]

pro-[2] *prefix* before in time or position; anterior; forward: *prognathous*. [from Gk *pro* (prep) before (in time, position, etc.)]

proa ('prəʊə) *or* **prau** *n* any of several kinds of canoe-like boats used in the South Pacific, esp. one equipped with an outrigger and sails. [C16: from Malay *parāhū* a boat]

proactive (prəʊ'æktɪv) *adj* **1** tending to initiate change rather than reacting to events. **2** *Psychol*. of or denoting a mental process that affects a subsequent process. [C20: from PRO-[2] + (RE)ACTIVE]

pro-am ('prəʊ'æm) *adj* (of a golf tournament, etc.) involving both professional and amateur players.

probability Ⓣ (ˌprɒbə'bɪlɪtɪ) *n, pl* **probabilities. 1** the condition of being probable. **2** an event or other thing that is probable. **3** *Statistics*. a measure of the degree of confidence one may have in the occurrence of an event, measured on a scale from zero (impossibility) to one (certainty).

probable Ⓣ ('prɒbəbəl) *adj* **1** likely to be or to happen but not necessarily so. **2** most likely: *the probable cause of the accident*. ◆ *n* **3** a person who is probably to be chosen for a team, event, etc. [C14: via OF from L *probābilis* that may be proved, from *probāre* to prove]

probably Ⓣ ('prɒbəblɪ) *adv* **1** (*sentence modifier*) in all likelihood or probability: *I'll probably see you tomorrow*. ◆ *sentence substitute*. **2** I believe such a thing may be the case.

proband ('prəʊbænd) *n* another name (esp. US) for **propositus.** [C20: from L *probandus*, *probāre* to test]

probang ('prəʊbæŋ) *n Surgery*. a long flexible rod, often with a small sponge at one end, for inserting into the oesophagus, as to apply medication. [C17: var., apparently by association with PROBE, of *provang*, coined by W. Rumsey (1584–1660), Welsh judge, its inventor; from ?]

probate ('prəʊbɪt, -beɪt) *n* **1** the process of officially proving the validity of a will. **2** the official certificate stating a will to be genuine and conferring on the executors power to administer the estate. **3** (*modifier*) relating to probate: *a probate court*. ◆ *vb* **probates, probating, probated. 4** (*tr*) *Chiefly US*. to establish officially the validity of (a will). [C15: from L *probāre* to inspect]

probation Ⓣ (prə'beɪʃən) *n* **1** a system of dealing with offenders by placing them under the supervision of a probation officer. **2 on probation. 2a** under the supervision of a probation officer. **2b** undergoing a test period. **3** a trial period, as for a teacher.
▸ **pro'bational** *or* **pro'bationary** *adj*

probationer (prə'beɪʃənə) *n* a person on probation.

probation officer *n* an officer of a court who supervises offenders placed on probation and assists and befriends them.

probe Ⓣ (prəʊb) *vb* **probes, probing, probed. 1** (*tr*) to search into closely. **2** to examine (something) with or as if with a probe. ◆ *n* **3** something that probes or tests. **4** *Surgery*. a slender instrument for exploring a wound, sinus, etc. **5** a thorough inquiry, such as one by a newspaper into corrupt practices. **6** *Electronics*. a lead connecting to or containing a monitoring circuit used for testing. **7** anything which provides or acts as a coupling, esp. a flexible tube extended from an aircraft to link it with another so that it can refuel. **8** See **space probe.** [C16: from Med. L *proba* investigation, from L *probāre* to test]
▸ '**probeable** *adj* ▸ '**prober** *n*

probity Ⓣ ('prəʊbɪtɪ) *n* confirmed integrity. [C16: from L *probitās* honesty, from *probus* virtuous]

problem Ⓣ ('prɒbləm) *n* **1a** any thing, matter, person, etc., that is difficult to deal with. **1b** (*as modifier*): *a problem child*. **2** a puzzle, question, etc., set for solution. **3** *Maths*. a statement requiring a solution usually by means of several operations or constructions. **4** (*modifier*) designating a literary work that deals with difficult moral questions: *a problem play*. [C14: from LL *problēma*, from Gk: something put forward]

problematic Ⓣ (ˌprɒblə'mætɪk) *or* **problematical** *adj* **1** having the na-

THESAURUS

privilege *n* **1** = **right**, advantage, benefit, birthright, claim, concession, due, entitlement, franchise, freedom, immunity, liberty, prerogative, sanction

privileged *adj* **1** = **special**, advantaged, elite, entitled, favoured, honoured, indulged, powerful, ruling **1** = **allowed**, empowered, exempt, free, granted, licensed, sanctioned, vested **2b** = **confidential**, exceptional, inside, not for publication, off the record, privy, special

privy *adj* **1** *foll. by* **to** = **informed of**, apprised of, aware of, cognizant of, hip to (*sl*.), in on, in the know about (*inf*.), in the loop, wise to (*sl*.) **2** *Archaic* = **secret**, confidential, hidden, hush-hush (*inf*.), off the record, personal, private ◆ *n* **3** = **lavatory**, bog (*sl*.), closet, earth closet, latrine, outside toilet

prize[1] *n* **1a** = **reward**, accolade, award, honour, premium, trophy ◆ *modifier* **1b** = **champion**, award-winning, best, first-rate, outstanding, top, top-notch (*inf*.), winning ◆ *n* **2** = **winnings**, haul, jackpot, purse, stakes, windfall **3** = **goal**, aim, ambition, conquest, desire, gain, Holy Grail (*inf*.), hope **4** = **booty**, capture, loot, pickings, pillage, plunder, spoil(s), trophy

prize[2] *vb* = **value**, appreciate, cherish, esteem, hold dear, regard highly, set store by, treasure

prizefighter *n* = **boxer**, bruiser (*inf*.), fighter, pug (*sl*.), pugilist

prizefighting *n* = **boxing**, fighting, pugilism, the noble art *or* science, the prize ring, the ring

probability *n* **1, 3** = **likelihood**, chance(s), expectation, liability, likeliness, odds, presumption, prospect

probable *adj* **1, 2** = **likely**, apparent, credible, feasible, most likely, odds-on, on the cards, ostensible, plausible, possible, presumable, presumed, reasonable, seeming, verisimilar
Antonyms *adj* doubtful, improbable, not likely, unlikely

probably *adv* **1** = **likely**, as likely as not, doubtless, in all likelihood, in all probability, maybe, most likely, perchance (*arch*.), perhaps, possibly, presumably

probation *n* **3** = **trial period**, apprenticeship, examination, initiation, novitiate, test, trial

probe *vb* **1** = **examine**, explore, go into, investigate, look into, query, research, scrutinize, search, sift, sound, test, verify, work over **2** = **explore**, feel around, poke, prod ◆ *n* **5** = **examination**, detection, exploration, inquest, inquiry, investigation, research, scrutiny, study

probity *n* = **integrity**, equity, fairness, fidelity, goodness, honesty, honour, justice, morality, rectitude, righteousness, sincerity, trustworthiness, truthfulness, uprightness, virtue, worth

problem *n* **1a** = **difficulty**, can of worms (*inf*.), complication, dilemma, disagreement, dispute, disputed point, doubt, Gordian knot, hard nut to crack (*inf*.), how-do-you-do (*inf*.), point at issue, predicament, quandary, trouble ◆ *modifier* **1b** = **difficult**, delinquent, intractable, uncontrollable, unmanageable, unruly ◆ *n* **2** = **puzzle**, brain-teaser (*inf*.), conundrum, enigma, poser, question, riddle, teaser

problematic *adj* **1** = **tricky**, chancy (*inf*.), de-

ture of a problem; uncertain; questionable. **2** *Logic, obs.* (of a proposition) asserting that a property may or may not hold.
▸ **ˌproblemˈatically** *adv*

pro bono publico *Latin.* (ˈprəʊ ˈbəʊnəʊ ˈpʊblɪkəʊ) for the public good.

proboscidean *or* **proboscidian** (ˌprəʊbɒˈsɪdɪən) *adj* **1** of or belonging to an order of massive herbivorous placental mammals having tusks and a long trunk: contains the elephants. ◆ *n* **2** any proboscidean animal.

proboscis (prəʊˈbɒsɪs) *n, pl* **proboscises** *or* **proboscides** (-sɪˌdiːz). **1** a long flexible prehensile trunk or snout, as of an elephant. **2** the elongated mouthpart of certain insects. **3** any similar organ. **4** *Inf., facetious.* a person's nose. [C17: via L from Gk *proboskis* trunk of an elephant, from *boskein* to feed]

procaine (ˈprəʊkeɪn, prəʊˈkeɪn) *n* a colourless or white crystalline water-soluble substance used, as **procaine hydrochloride**, as a local anaesthetic. [C20: from PRO-[1] + (CO)CAINE]

procathedral (ˌprəʊkəˈθiːdrəl) *n* a church serving as a cathedral.

procedure ➊ (prəˈsiːdʒə) *n* **1** a way of acting or progressing, esp. an established method. **2** the established form of conducting the business of a legislature, the enforcement of a legal right, etc. **3** *Computing.* another name for **subroutine.**
▸ **proˈcedural** *adj* ▸ **proˈcedurally** *adv*

proceed ➊ (prəˈsiːd) *vb* (*intr*) **1** (often foll. by *to*) to advance or carry on, esp. after stopping. **2** (often foll. by *with*) to continue: *he proceeded with his reading.* **3** (often foll. by *against*) to institute or carry on a legal action. **4** to originate; arise: *evil proceeds from the heart.* [C14: from L *prōcēdere* to advance]
▸ **proˈceeder** *n*

proceeding ➊ (prəˈsiːdɪŋ) *n* **1** an act or course of action. **2a** a legal action. **2b** any step taken in a legal action. **3** (*pl*) the minutes of the meetings of a society, etc. **4** (*pl*) legal action; litigation. **5** (*pl*) the events of an occasion.

proceeds ➊ (ˈprəʊsiːdz) *pl n* **1** the profit or return derived from a commercial transaction, investment, etc. **2** the result, esp. the total sum, accruing from some undertaking.

process[1] ➊ (ˈprəʊses) *n* **1** a series of actions which produce a change or development: *the process of digestion.* **2** a method of doing or producing something. **3** progress or course of time. **4 in the process of.** during or in the course of. **5a** a summons commanding a person to appear in court. **5b** the whole proceedings in an action at law. **6** a natural outgrowth or projection of a part or organism. **7** (*modifier*) relating to the general preparation of a printing forme or plate by the use, at some stage, of photography. ◆ *vb* (*tr*) **8** to subject to a routine procedure; handle. **9** to treat or prepare by a special method, esp. to treat (food) in order to preserve it: *to process cheese.* **10a** to institute legal proceedings against. **10b** to serve a process on. **11** *Photog.* **11a** to develop, rinse, fix, wash, and dry (exposed film, etc.). **11b** to produce final prints or slides from (undeveloped film). **12** *Computing.* to perform operations on (data) according to programmed instructions in order to obtain the required information. [C14: from OF *procès*, from L *prōcessus* an advancing, from *prōcēdere* to proceed]

process[2] (prəˈses) *vb* (*intr*) to proceed in a procession. [C19: back formation from PROCESSION]

process industry *n* a manufacturing industry, such as oil refining, which converts bulk raw materials into a workable form.

procession ➊ (prəˈseʃən) *n* **1** the act of proceeding in a regular formation. **2** a group of people or things moving forwards in an orderly, regular, or ceremonial manner. **3** *Christianity.* the emanation of the Holy Spirit. ◆ *vb* **4** (*intr*) *Rare.* to go in procession. [C12: via OF from L *prōcessiō* a marching forwards]

processional (prəˈseʃənəl) *adj* **1** of or suitable for a procession. ◆ *n* **2** *Christianity.* **2a** a book containing the prayers, hymns, etc., prescribed for processions. **2b** a hymn, etc., used in a procession.

processor (ˈprəʊsesə) *n* **1** *Computing.* another name for **central processing unit. 2** a person or thing that carries out a process.

process-server *n* a sheriff's officer who serves legal documents such as writs for appearance in court.

procès-verbal *French.* (prɔsɛvɛrbal) *n, pl* ***-baux*** (-bo). a written record of an official proceeding; minutes. [C17: from F: see PROCESS, VERBAL]

pro-choice *adj* (of an organization, pressure group, etc.) supporting the right of a woman to have an abortion. Cf. **pro-life.**

prochronism (ˈprəʊkrəˌnɪzəm) *n* an error in dating that places an event earlier than it actually occurred. [C17: from PRO-[2] + Gk *khronos* time + -ISM, by analogy with ANACHRONISM]

proclaim ➊ (prəˈkleɪm) *vb* (*tr*) **1** (*may take a clause as object*) to announce publicly. **2** (*may take a clause as object*) to indicate plainly. **3** to praise or extol. [C14: from L *prōclāmāre* to shout aloud]
▸ **proclamation** (ˌprɒkləˈmeɪʃən) *n* ▸ **proˈclaimer** *n* ▸ **proclamatory** (prəˈklæmətərɪ, -trɪ) *adj*

proclitic (prəʊˈklɪtɪk) *adj* **1a** denoting a monosyllabic word or form having no stress and pronounced as a prefix of the following word, as in English *'t* for *it* in *'twas.* **1b** (in classical Greek) denoting a word that throws its accent onto the following word. ◆ *n* **2** a proclitic word or form. [C19: from NL *proclīticus*, from Gk *proklinein* to lean forwards; on the model of ENCLITIC]

proclivity ➊ (prəˈklɪvɪtɪ) *n, pl* **proclivities.** a tendency or inclination. [C16: from L *prōclīvitās*, from *prōclīvis* steep, from *clīvus* a slope]

proconsul (prəʊˈkɒnsəl) *n* **1** a governor of a colony or other dependency. **2** (in ancient Rome) the governor of a senatorial province.
▸ **proconsular** (prəʊˈkɒnsjʊlə) *adj*

procrastinate ➊ (prəʊˈkræstɪˌneɪt, prə-) *vb* **procrastinates, procrastinating, procrastinated.** (*usually intr*) to put off (an action) until later; delay. [C16: from L *prōcrāstināre* to postpone until tomorrow, from PRO-[1] + *crās* tomorrow]
▸ **proˌcrastiˈnation** *n* ▸ **proˈcrastiˌnator** *n*

procreate ➊ (ˈprəʊkrɪˌeɪt) *vb* **procreates, procreating, procreated. 1** to beget or engender (offspring). **2** (*tr*) to bring into being. [C16: from L *prōcreāre*, from PRO-[1] + *creāre* to create]
▸ **ˈprocreant** *or* **ˈprocreˌative** *adj* ▸ **ˌprocreˈation** *n* ▸ **ˈprocreˌator** *n*

Procrustean (prəʊˈkrʌstɪən) *adj* tending or designed to produce conformity by violent or ruthless methods. [C19: from *Procrustes*, Gk robber who fitted travellers into his bed by stretching or lopping off their limbs]

proctology (prɒkˈtɒlədʒɪ) *n* the branch of medical science concerned with the rectum. [from Gk *prōktos* rectum + -OLOGY]

proctor (ˈprɒktə) *n* **1** a member of the staff of certain universities having duties including the enforcement of discipline. **2** (formerly) an agent, esp. one engaged to conduct another's case in a court. **3** *Church of England.* one of the elected representatives of the clergy in Convocation. [C14: syncopated var. of PROCURATOR]
▸ **proctorial** (prɒkˈtɔːrɪəl) *adj*

procumbent (prəʊˈkʌmbənt) *adj* **1** (of stems) trailing loosely along the ground. **2** leaning forwards or lying on the face. [C17: from L *prōcumbere* to fall forwards]

procurator (ˈprɒkjʊˌreɪtə) *n* **1** (in ancient Rome) a civil official of the emperor's administration, often employed as the governor of a minor province. **2** *Rare.* a person engaged by another to manage his affairs. [C13: from L: a manager, from *prōcūrāre* to attend to]
▸ **procuracy** (ˈprɒkjʊrəsɪ) *or* **ˈprocuˌratorship** *n* ▸ **procuratorial** (ˌprɒkjʊrəˈtɔːrɪəl) *adj*

procurator fiscal *n* (in Scotland) a legal officer who performs the functions of public prosecutor and coroner.

procure ➊ (prəˈkjʊə) *vb* **procures, procuring, procured. 1** (*tr*) to obtain or acquire; secure. **2** to obtain (women or girls) to act as prostitutes. [C13: from L *prōcūrāre* to look after]
▸ **proˈcurable** *adj* ▸ **proˈcurement, proˈcural,** *or* **procuration** (ˌprɒkjʊˈreɪʃən) *n*

procurer ➊ (prəˈkjʊərə) *n* a person who procures, esp. one who procures women as prostitutes.

THESAURUS

batable, doubtful, dubious, enigmatic, moot, open to doubt, problematical, puzzling, questionable, uncertain, unsettled
Antonyms *adj* beyond question, certain, clear, definite, indisputable, settled, undebatable, unquestionable

procedure *n* **1 = method**, action, conduct, course, custom, form, formula, modus operandi, operation, performance, plan of action, policy, practice, process, routine, scheme, step, strategy, system, transaction

proceed *vb* **1, 2 = go on**, advance, carry on, continue, get going, get on with, get under way with, go ahead, make a start, move on, press on, progress, set in motion **4 = arise**, come, derive, emanate, ensue, flow, follow, issue, originate, result, spring, stem
Antonyms *vb* ≠ **go on**: break off, cease, discontinue, end, get behind, halt, leave off, pack in (*Brit. inf.*), retreat, stop

proceeding *n* **1 = action**, act, course of action, deed, measure, move, occurrence, procedure, process, step, undertaking, venture **3** *plural* = **business**, account, affairs, annals, archives, dealings, doings, matters, minutes, records, report, transactions

proceeds *pl n* **1 = income**, earnings, gain, produce, products, profit, receipts, returns, revenue, takings, yield

process[1] *n* **1, 2 = procedure**, action, course, course of action, manner, means, measure, method, mode, operation, performance, practice, proceeding, system, transaction **3 = development**, advance, course, evolution, formation, growth, movement, progress, progression, stage, step, unfolding **5b = action**, case, suit, trial ◆ *vb* **8 = handle**, deal with, dispose of, fulfil, take care of **9 = prepare**, alter, convert, refine, transform, treat

procession *n* **2 = parade**, cavalcade, column, cortege, file, march, motorcade, train

proclaim *vb* **1, 2 = declare**, advertise, affirm, announce, blaze (abroad), blazon (abroad), circulate, enunciate, give out, herald, indicate, make known, profess, promulgate, publish, shout from the housetops (*inf.*), show, trumpet
Antonyms *vb* conceal, hush up, keep back, keep secret, suppress, withhold

proclamation *n* **1, 2 = declaration**, announcement, decree, edict, manifesto, notice, notification, promulgation, pronouncement, pronunciamento, publication

proclivity *n* **= tendency**, bent, bias, disposition, facility, inclination, leaning, liableness, penchant, predilection, predisposition, proneness, propensity, weakness

procrastinate *vb* **= delay**, adjourn, be dilatory, dally, defer, drag one's feet (*inf.*), gain time, play a waiting game, play for time, postpone, prolong, protract, put off, retard, stall, temporize
Antonyms *vb* advance, expedite, get on with, hasten, hurry (up), proceed, speed up

procrastination *n* **= delay**, dilatoriness, hesitation, slackness, slowness, temporization *or* temporisation

procreate *vb* **1, 2 = reproduce**, beget, breed, bring into being, engender, father, generate, mother, produce, propagate, sire

procure *vb* **1 = obtain**, acquire, appropriate, buy, come by, earn, effect, find, gain, get, get hold of, land, lay hands on, manage to get, pick up, purchase, score (*sl.*), secure, win

procurer *n* **= pimp**, bawd (*arch.*), madam, pan-

prod ⓣ (prɒd) *vb* **prods, prodding, prodded. 1** to poke or jab with or as if with a pointed object. **2** (*tr*) to rouse to action. ◆ *n* **3** the act or an instance of prodding. **4** a sharp object. **5** a stimulus or reminder. [C16: from ?]
▸**'prodder** *n*

prod. *abbrev. for:* **1** produce. **2** produced. **3** product.

prodigal ⓣ ('prɒdɪgᵊl) *adj* **1** recklessly wasteful or extravagant, as in disposing of goods or money. **2** lavish: *prodigal of compliments.* ◆ *n* **3** a person who spends lavishly or squanders money. [C16: from Med. L *prōdigālis* wasteful, from L, from *prōdigere* to squander, from *agere* to drive]
▸**,prodi'gality** *n* ▸**'prodigally** *adv*

prodigious ⓣ (prə'dɪdʒəs) *adj* **1** vast in size, extent, power, etc. **2** wonderful or amazing. [C16: from L *prōdigiōsus* marvellous, from *prōdigium;* see PRODIGY]
▸**pro'digiously** *adv* ▸**pro'digiousness** *n*

prodigy ⓣ ('prɒdɪdʒɪ) *n, pl* **prodigies. 1** a person, esp. a child, of unusual or marvellous talents. **2** anything that is a cause of wonder. **3** something monstrous or abnormal. [C16: from L *prōdigium* an unnatural happening]

produce ⓣ *vb* (prə'djuːs), **produces, producing, produced. 1** to bring (something) into existence; yield. **2** (*tr*) to make: *she produced a delicious dinner.* **3** (*tr*) to give birth to. **4** (*tr*) to present to view: *to produce evidence.* **5** (*tr*) to bring before the public: *he produced a film last year.* **6** (*tr*) to act as producer of. **7** (*tr*) *Geom.* to extend (a line). ◆ *n* ('prɒdjuːs). **8** anything produced; a product. **9** agricultural products collectively: *farm produce.* [C15: from L *prōdūcere* to bring forward]
▸**pro'ducible** *adj* ▸**pro,duci'bility** *n*

producer ⓣ (prə'djuːsə) *n* **1** a person or thing that produces. **2** *Brit.* a person responsible for the artistic direction of a play. **3** *US & Canad.* a person who organizes the stage production of a play, including the finance, management, etc. **4** the person who takes overall administrative responsibility for a film or television programme. Cf. **director** (sense 4). **5** the person who supervises the arrangement, recording, and mixing of a record. **6** *Econ.* a person or business enterprise that generates goods or services for sale. Cf. **consumer** (sense 1). **7** *Chem.* an apparatus or plant for making producer gas.

producer gas *n* a mixture of carbon monoxide and nitrogen produced by passing air over hot coke, used mainly as a fuel.

product ⓣ ('prɒdʌkt) *n* **1** something produced by effort, or some mechanical or industrial process. **2** the result of some natural process. **3** a result or consequence. **4** *Maths.* the result of the multiplication of two or more numbers, quantities, etc. [C15: from L *prōductum* (something) produced, from *prōdūcere* to bring forth]

product differentiation *n Commerce.* the real or illusory distinction between competing products in a market.

production ⓣ (prə'dʌkʃən) *n* **1** the act of producing. **2** anything that is produced; a product. **3** the amount produced or the rate at which it is produced. **4** *Econ.* the creation or manufacture of goods and services with exchange value. **5** any work created as a result of literary or artistic effort. **6** the presentation of a play, opera, etc. **7** *Brit.* the artistic direction of a play. **8** (*modifier*) manufactured by mass production: *a production model of a car.*
▸**pro'ductional** *adj*

production line *n* a factory system in which parts or components of the end product are transported by a conveyor through a number of different sites at each of which a manual or machine operation is performed on them.

productive ⓣ (prə'dʌktɪv) *adj* **1** producing or having the power to produce; fertile. **2** yielding favourable results. **3** *Econ.* **3a** producing goods and services that have exchange value: *productive assets.* **3b** relating to such production: *the productive processes of an industry.* **4** (*postpositive;* foll. by *of*) resulting in: *productive of good results.*
▸**pro'ductively** *adv* ▸**pro'ductiveness** *n*

productivity ⓣ (,prɒdʌk'tɪvɪtɪ) *n* **1** the output of an industrial concern in relation to the materials, labour, etc., it employs. **2** the state of being productive.

product liability *n* the liability to the public of a manufacturer or trader for selling a faulty product.

product life cycle *n Marketing.* the four stages (introduction, growth, maturity, and decline) into one of which the sales of a product fall during its market life.

product line *n Marketing.* a group of related products marketed by the same company.

product placement *n* the practice of a company paying for its product to be placed in a prominent position in a film or television programme as a form of advertising.

proem ('prəʊɛm) *n* an introduction or preface, such as to a work of literature. [C14: from L *prooemium* introduction, from Gk *prooimion,* from PRO-² + *hoimē* song]
▸**proemial** (prəʊ'iːmɪəl) *adj*

proenzyme (prəʊ'ɛnzaɪm) *n* the inactive form of an enzyme; zymogen.

Prof. *abbrev. for* Professor.

profane ⓣ (prə'feɪn) *adj* **1** having or indicating contempt, irreverence, or disrespect for a divinity or something sacred. **2** not designed for religious purposes; secular. **3** not initiated into the inner mysteries or sacred rites. **4** coarse or blasphemous: *profane language.* ◆ *vb* **profanes, profaning, profaned.** (*tr*) **5** to treat (something sacred) with irreverence. **6** to put to an unworthy use. [C15: from L *profānus* outside the temple]
▸**profanation** (,prɒfə'neɪʃən) *n* ▸**pro'fanely** *adv* ▸**pro'faneness** *n* ▸**pro'faner** *n*

profanity ⓣ (prə'fænɪtɪ) *n, pl* **profanities. 1** the state or quality of being profane. **2** vulgar or irreverent action, speech, etc.

profess ⓣ (prə'fɛs) *vb* **1** (*tr*) to affirm or acknowledge: *to profess ignorance; to profess a belief in God.* **2** (*tr*) to claim (something), often insincerely or falsely: *to profess to be a skilled driver.* **3** to receive or be received into a religious order, as by taking vows. [C14: from L *prōfitērī* to confess openly]

professed ⓣ (prə'fɛst) *adj* (*prenominal*) **1** avowed or acknowledged. **2**

THESAURUS

der, panderer, white-slaver, whoremaster (*arch.*)

prod *vb* **1** = **poke**, dig, drive, elbow, jab, nudge, prick, propel, push, shove **2** = **prompt**, egg on, goad, impel, incite, motivate, move, put a bomb under (*inf.*), rouse, spur, stimulate, stir up, urge ◆ *n* **3** = **poke**, boost, dig, elbow, jab, nudge, push, shove **4** = **goad**, poker, spur, stick **5** = **prompt**, boost, cue, reminder, signal, stimulus

prodigal *adj* **1** = **extravagant**, excessive, immoderate, improvident, intemperate, profligate, reckless, spendthrift, squandering, wanton, wasteful **2** = **lavish**, bounteous, bountiful, profuse ◆ *n* **3** = **spendthrift**, big spender, profligate, squanderer, wastrel
Antonyms *adj* ≠ **extravagant:** economical, frugal, miserly, parsimonious, sparing, stingy, thrifty, tight ≠ **lavish:** deficient, lacking, meagre, scanty, scarce, short, sparse

prodigality *n* **1** = **wastefulness**, abandon, dissipation, excess, extravagance, immoderation, intemperance, profligacy, recklessness, squandering, wantonness, waste **2** = **lavishness**, bounteousness, profusion

prodigious *adj* **1** = **huge**, colossal, enormous, giant, gigantic, immeasurable, immense, inordinate, mammoth, massive, monstrous, monumental, stellar (*inf.*), stupendous, tremendous, vast **2** = **wonderful**, abnormal, amazing, astounding, dramatic, exceptional, extraordinary, fabulous, fantastic (*inf.*), impressive, marvellous, miraculous, phenomenal, remarkable, staggering, startling, striking, stupendous, unusual
Antonyms *adj* ≠ **huge:** negligible, small, tiny ≠ **wonderful:** normal, ordinary, unexceptional, unimpressive, unremarkable, usual

prodigy *n* **1** = **genius**, brainbox, child genius, mastermind, talent, whizz (*inf.*), whizz kid (*inf.*), wizard, wonder child, wunderkind **2** = **wonder**, marvel, miracle, one in a million, phenomenon, rare bird (*inf.*), sensation **3** = **monster**, abnormality, curiosity, freak, grotesque, monstrosity, mutation, spectacle

produce *vb* **1** = **cause**, bring about, effect, generate, give rise to, make for, occasion, provoke, set off **1** = **yield**, afford, engender, furnish, give, render, supply **2** = **make**, compose, construct, create, develop, fabricate, invent, manufacture, originate, put together, turn out **3** = **bring forth**, bear, beget, breed, deliver **4** = **show**, advance, bring forward, bring to light, demonstrate, exhibit, offer, present, put forward, set forth **5** = **present**, direct, do, exhibit, mount, put before the public, put on, show, stage **7** *Geometry* = **extend**, lengthen, prolong, protract ◆ *n* **9** = **fruit and vegetables**, crop, greengrocery, harvest, product, yield

producer *n* **1** = **maker**, farmer, grower, manufacturer **2-5** = **director**, impresario, *régisseur*

product *n* **1** = **goods**, artefact, commodity, concoction, creation, invention, merchandise, produce, production, work **3** = **result**, consequence, effect, end result, fruit, issue, legacy, offshoot, outcome, returns, spin-off, upshot, yield

production *n* **1** = **producing**, assembly, construction, creation, fabrication, formation, making, manufacture, manufacturing, origination, preparation **6, 7** = **presentation**, direction, management, staging

productive *adj* **1** = **fertile**, creative, dynamic, energetic, fecund, fruitful, generative, inventive, plentiful, producing, prolific, rich, teeming, vigorous **2** = **useful**, advantageous, beneficial, constructive, effective, fruitful, gainful, gratifying, profitable, rewarding, valuable, worthwhile
Antonyms *adj* ≠ **fertile:** barren, poor, sterile, unfertile, unfruitful, unproductive ≠ **useful:** unproductive, unprofitable, useless

productivity *n* **1, 2** = **output**, abundance, mass production, production, productive capacity, productiveness, work rate, yield

profane *adj* **1** = **sacrilegious**, disrespectful, godless, heathen, idolatrous, impious, impure, irreligious, irreverent, pagan, sinful, ungodly, wicked **2** = **secular**, lay, temporal, unconsecrated, unhallowed, unholy, unsanctified, worldly **4** = **crude**, abusive, blasphemous, coarse, filthy, foul, obscene, vulgar ◆ *vb* **5, 6** = **desecrate**, abuse, commit sacrilege, contaminate, debase, defile, misuse, pervert, pollute, prostitute, violate, vitiate
Antonyms *adj* ≠ **sacrilegious:** clean, decorous, holy, proper, religious, respectful, reverent, sacred, spiritual

profanity *n* **1** = **sacrilege**, blasphemy, impiety, profaneness **2** = **swearing**, abuse, curse, cursing, execration, foul language, four-letter word, imprecation, irreverence, malediction, obscenity, swearword

profess *vb* **1** = **state**, acknowledge, admit, affirm, announce, assert, asseverate, aver, avow, certify, confess, confirm, declare, maintain, own, proclaim, vouch **2** = **claim**, act as if, allege, call oneself, dissemble, fake, feign, let on, make out, pretend, purport, sham

professed *adj* **1** = **declared**, avowed, certified, confessed, confirmed, proclaimed, self-acknowledged, self-confessed **2** = **supposed**, alleged, apparent, ostensible, pretended, pur-

alleged or pretended. **3** professing to be qualified as: *a professed philosopher.* **4** having taken vows of a religious order.
▸**professedly** (prəˈfɛsɪdlɪ) *adv*

profession ⓘ (prəˈfɛʃən) *n* **1** an occupation requiring special training in the liberal arts or sciences, esp. one of the three learned professions, law, theology, or medicine. **2** the body of people in such an occupation. **3** an avowal; declaration. **4** Also called: **profession of faith.** a declaration of faith in a religion, esp. as made on entering the Church or an order belonging to it. [C13: from Med. L *professiō* the taking of vows upon entering a religious order, from L: public acknowledgment; see PROFESS]

professional ⓘ (prəˈfɛʃənᵊl) *adj* **1** of, suitable for, or engaged in as a profession. **2** engaging in an activity as a means of livelihood. **3a** extremely competent in a job, etc. **3b** (of a piece of work or anything performed) produced with competence or skill. **4** undertaken or performed by people who are paid. ◆ *n* **5** a person who belongs to one of the professions. **6** a person who engages for his livelihood in some activity also pursued by amateurs. **7** a person who engages in an activity with great competence. **8** an expert player of a game who gives instruction, esp. to members of a club by whom he is hired.
▸**proˈfessionaˌlism** *n* ▸**proˈfessionally** *adv*

professional foul *n Football.* a deliberate foul committed as a last-ditch tactic to prevent an opponent from scoring.

professor ⓘ (prəˈfɛsə) *n* **1** the principal teacher in a field of learning at a university or college; a holder of a university chair. **2** *Chiefly US & Canad.* any teacher in a university or college. **3** a person who professes his opinions, beliefs, etc. [C14: from Med. L: one who has made his profession in a religious order, from L: a public teacher; see PROFESS]
▸**professorial** (ˌprɒfɪˈsɔːrɪəl) *adj* ▸**ˌprofesˈsorially** *adv* ▸**ˌprofesˈsoriate** *or* **proˈfessorship** *n*

proffer ⓘ (ˈprɒfə) *vb* **1** (*tr*) to offer for acceptance. ◆ *n* **2** the act of proffering. [C13: from OF *proffrir,* from PRO-[1] + *offrir* to offer]

proficient ⓘ (prəˈfɪʃənt) *adj* **1** having great facility (in an art, occupation, etc.); skilled. ◆ *n* **2** an expert. [C16: from L *prōficere* to make progress]
▸**proˈficiency** *n* ▸**proˈficiently** *adv*

profile ⓘ (ˈprəʊfaɪl) *n* **1** a side view or outline of an object, esp. of a human head. **2** a short biographical sketch. **3** a graph, table, etc., representing the extent to which a person, field, or object exhibits various tested characteristics: *a population profile.* **4** a vertical section of soil or rock showing the different layers. **5** the outline of the shape of a river valley either from source to mouth (**long profile**) or at right angles to the flow of the river (**cross profile**). ◆ *vb* **profiles, profiling, profiled. 6** (*tr*) to draw, write, or make a profile of. [C17: from It. *profilo,* from *profilare* to sketch lightly, from L *filum* thread]
▸**ˈprofiler** *or* **profilist** (ˈprəʊfɪlɪst) *n*

profile component *n Brit. education.* attainment targets in different subjects brought together for the general assessment of a pupil.

profit ⓘ (ˈprɒfɪt) *n* **1** (*often pl*) excess of revenues over outlays and expenses in a business enterprise. **2** the monetary gain derived from a transaction. **3** income derived from property or an investment, as contrasted with capital gains. **4a** *Econ.* the income accruing to a successful entrepreneur and held to be the motivating factor of a capitalist economy. **4b** (*as modifier*): *the profit motive.* **5** a gain, benefit, or advantage. ◆ *vb* **6** to gain or cause to gain profit. [C14: from L *prōfectus* advance, from *prōficere* to make progress]
▸**ˈprofitless** *adj*

profitable ⓘ (ˈprɒfɪtəbᵊl) *adj* affording gain or profit.
▸**ˌprofitaˈbility** *n* ▸**ˈprofitably** *adv*

profit and loss *n Book-keeping.* an account compiled at the end of a financial year showing that year's revenue and expense items and indicating gross and net profit or loss.

profit centre *n* a section of a commercial organization which is allocated financial targets in its own right.

profiteer ⓘ (ˌprɒfɪˈtɪə) *n* **1** a person who makes excessive profits, esp. by charging exorbitant prices for goods in short supply. ◆ *vb* **2** (*intr*) to make excessive profits.

profiterole (ˈprɒfɪtəˌrəʊl, prəˈfɪtəˌrəʊl) *n* a small case of choux pastry with a sweet or savoury filling. [C16: from F, lit.: a small profit]

profit-sharing *n* a system in which a portion of the net profit of a business is distributed to its employees, usually in proportion to their wages or their length of service.

profit taking *n* selling commodities, securities, etc., at a profit after a rise in market values or before an expected fall in values.

profligate ⓘ (ˈprɒflɪgɪt) *adj* **1** shamelessly immoral or debauched. **2** wildly extravagant or wasteful. ◆ *n* **3** a profligate person. [C16: from L *prōflīgātus* corrupt, from *prōflīgāre* to overthrow, from PRO-[1] + *flīgere* to beat]
▸**profligacy** (ˈprɒflɪgəsɪ) *n* ▸**ˈprofligately** *adv*

pro forma (ˈprəʊ ˈfɔːmə) *adj* **1** prescribing a set form or procedure. ◆ *adv* **2** performed in a set manner. [L: for form's sake]

profound ⓘ (prəˈfaʊnd) *adj* **1** penetrating deeply into subjects or ideas: *a profound mind.* **2** showing or requiring great knowledge or understanding: *a profound treatise.* **3** situated at or extending to a great depth. **4** stemming from the depths of one's nature: *profound regret.* **5** intense or absolute: *profound silence.* **6** thoroughgoing; extensive: *profound changes.* ◆ *n* **7** *Arch. or literary.* a great depth; abyss. [C14: from OF *profund,* from L *profundus* deep, from *fundus* bottom]
▸**proˈfoundly** *adv* ▸**profundity** (prəˈfʌndɪtɪ) *n*

profuse ⓘ (prəˈfjuːs) *adj* **1** plentiful or abundant: *profuse compliments.* **2**

THESAURUS

ported, self-styled, so-called, *soi-disant,* would-be

professedly *adv* **1** = **admittedly**, avowedly, by open declaration, confessedly **2** = **supposedly**, allegedly, apparently, by one's own account, falsely, ostensibly, purportedly, under the pretext of

profession *n* **1** = **occupation**, business, calling, career, employment, line, line of work, métier, office, position, sphere, vocation, walk of life **3** = **declaration**, acknowledgment, affirmation, assertion, attestation, avowal, claim, confession, statement, testimony, vow

professional *adj* **3** = **expert**, ace (*inf.*), adept, competent, crack (*sl.*), efficient, experienced, finished, masterly, polished, practised, proficient, qualified, skilled, slick, trained ◆ *n* **7** = **expert**, adept, authority, buff (*inf.*), dab hand (*Brit. inf.*), guru, hotshot (*inf.*), maestro, master, maven (*US*), past master, pro (*inf.*), specialist, virtuoso, whizz (*inf.*), wizard
Antonyms *adj* ≠ **expert**: amateurish, incapable, incompetent, inefficient, inept, inexperienced, unpolished, unqualified, unskilled, untrained

professor *n* **1** = **don** (*Brit.*), fellow (*Brit.*), head of faculty, prof (*inf.*)

proffer *vb* **1** = **offer**, extend, hand, hold out, present, propose, propound, submit, suggest, tender, volunteer

proficiency *n* **1** = **skill**, ability, accomplishment, aptitude, competence, craft, dexterity, expertise, expertness, facility, knack, know-how (*inf.*), mastery, skilfulness, talent

proficient *adj* **1** = **skilled**, able, accomplished, adept, apt, capable, clever, competent, conversant, efficient, experienced, expert, gifted, masterly, qualified, skilful, talented, trained, versed
Antonyms *adj* bad, incapable, incompetent, inept, unaccomplished, unskilled

profile *n* **1** = **outline**, contour, drawing, figure, form, portrait, shape, side view, silhouette, sketch **2** = **biography**, characterization, character sketch, sketch, thumbnail sketch, vignette **3** = **analysis**, chart, diagram, examination, graph, review, study, survey, table

profit *n* **1** *often plural* = **earnings**, boot, bottom line, emoluments, gain, percentage (*inf.*), proceeds, receipts, return, revenue, surplus, takings, winnings, yield **5** = **benefit**, advancement, advantage, avail, gain, good, interest, mileage (*inf.*), use, value ◆ *vb* **6** = **benefit**, aid, avail, be of advantage to, better, contribute, gain, help, improve, promote, serve, stand in good stead **6** = **capitalize on**, cash in on (*inf.*), exploit, learn from, make capital of, make good use of, make the most of, put to good use, reap the benefit of, take advantage of, turn to advantage *or* account, use, utilize

profitable *adj* = **money-making**, commercial, cost-effective, fruitful, gainful, lucrative, paying, remunerative, rewarding, worthwhile = **beneficial**, advantageous, economic, expedient, fruitful, productive, rewarding, serviceable, useful, valuable, worthwhile
Antonyms *adj* disadvantageous, fruitless, unremunerative, unrewarding, useless, vain, worthless

profiteer *n* **1** = **racketeer**, exploiter ◆ *vb* **2** = **exploit**, fleece, make a quick buck (*sl.*), make someone pay through the nose, overcharge, racketeer, skin (*sl.*), sting (*inf.*)

profitless *adj* **1, 5** = **unprofitable**, bootless, fruitless, futile, idle, ineffective, ineffectual, pointless, thankless, to no purpose, unavailing, unproductive, unremunerative, useless, vain, worthless

profligacy *n* **1** = **immorality**, abandon, corruption, debauchery, degeneracy, depravity, dissipation, dissoluteness, dolce vita, laxity, libertinism, licentiousness, promiscuity, unrestraint, wantonness **2** = **extravagance**, excess, improvidence, lavishness, prodigality, recklessness, squandering, waste, wastefulness

profligate *adj* **1** = **depraved**, abandoned, corrupt, debauched, degenerate, dissipated, dissolute, immoral, iniquitous, libertine, licentious, loose, promiscuous, shameless, sink, unprincipled, vicious, vitiated, wanton, wicked, wild **2** = **extravagant**, immoderate, improvident, prodigal, reckless, spendthrift, squandering, wasteful ◆ *n* **3** = **spendthrift**, prodigal, squanderer, waster, wastrel **3** = **degenerate**, debauchee, dissipater, libertine, rake, reprobate, roué, swinger (*sl.*)
Antonyms *adj* ≠ **depraved**: chaste, decent, moral, principled, pure, upright, virginal, virtuous

profound *adj* **1, 2** = **wise**, abstruse, deep, discerning, erudite, learned, penetrating, philosophical, recondite, sagacious, sage, serious, skilled, subtle, thoughtful, weighty **3** = **deep**, abysmal, bottomless, cavernous, fathomless, yawning **4** = **sincere**, abject, acute, deeply felt, extreme, great, heartfelt, heartrending, hearty, intense, keen **5** = **complete**, absolute, consummate, exhaustive, extensive, extreme, far-reaching, intense, out-and-out, pronounced, serious (*inf.*), thoroughgoing, total, unqualified, utter
Antonyms *adj* ≠ **wise**: imprudent, stupid, thoughtless, uneducated, uninformed, unknowledgeable, unwise ≠ **sincere**: insincere, shallow ≠ **complete**: slight, superficial

profoundly *adv* **4** = **greatly**, abjectly, acutely, deeply, extremely, from the bottom of one's heart, heartily, intensely, keenly, seriously, sincerely, thoroughly, to the core, to the nth degree, very

profundity *n* **1, 2** = **insight**, acuity, acumen, depth, erudition, intelligence, learning, penetration, perceptiveness, perspicacity, perspicuity, sagacity, wisdom **4** = **intensity**, depth, extremity, seriousness, severity, strength

profuse *adj* **1** = **plentiful**, abundant, ample, bountiful, copious, luxuriant, overflowing, prolific, teeming **2** = **extravagant**, excessive, exuberant, fulsome, generous, immoderate, lavish, liberal, open-handed, prodigal, unstinting
Antonyms *adj* ≠ **plentiful**: deficient, inadequate, meagre, scanty, scarce, skimpy, sparse ≠ **extravagant**: frugal, illiberal, moderate, provident, thrifty

(often foll. by *in*) free or generous in the giving (of): *profuse in thanks.* [C15: from L *profundere* to pour lavishly]
▸pro'fusely *adv* ▸pro'fuseness *or* pro'fusion *n*

progenitive (prəʊ'dʒɛnɪtɪv) *adj* capable of bearing offspring.
▸pro'genitiveness *n*

progenitor (prəʊ'dʒɛnɪtə) *n* **1** a direct ancestor. **2** an originator or founder. [C14: from L: ancestor, from *gignere* to beget]

progeny ('prɒdʒɪnɪ) *n, pl* **progenies. 1** the immediate descendant or descendants of a person, animal, etc. **2** a result or outcome. [C13: from L *prōgeniēs* lineage; see PROGENITOR]

progesterone (prəʊ'dʒɛstəˌrəʊn) *n* a steroid hormone, secreted mainly by the corpus luteum in the ovary, that prepares and maintains the uterus for pregnancy. [C20: from PRO-[1] + GE(STATION) + STER(OL) + -ONE]

progestogen (prəʊ'dʒɛstədʒən) *or* **progestin** (prə'dʒɛstɪn) *n* any of a group of steroid hormones with progesterone-like activity, used in oral contraceptives and in treating gynaecological disorders.

prognathous (prɒg'neɪθəs) *or* **prognathic** (prɒg'næθɪk) *adj* having a projecting lower jaw. [C19: from PRO-[2] + Gk *gnathos* jaw]

prognosis (prɒg'nəʊsɪs) *n, pl* **prognoses** (-'nəʊsiːz). **1** *Med.* a prediction of the course or outcome of a disease. **2** any prediction. [C17: via L from Gk: knowledge beforehand]

prognostic (prɒg'nɒstɪk) *adj* **1** of or serving as a prognosis. **2** predicting. ♦ *n* **3** *Med.* any symptom or sign used in making a prognosis. **4** a sign of some future occurrence. [C15: from OF *pronostique,* from L *prognōsticum,* from Gk, from *progignōskein* to know in advance]

prognosticate (prɒg'nɒstɪˌkeɪt) *vb* **prognosticates, prognosticating, prognosticated. 1** to foretell (future events); prophesy. **2** (*tr*) to foreshadow or portend. [C16: from Med. L *prognōsticāre* to predict]
▸progˌnosti'cation *n* ▸prog'nosticative *adj* ▸prog'nostiˌcator *n*

program *or* (*sometimes*) **programme** ('prəʊgræm) *n* **1** a sequence of coded instructions fed into a computer, enabling it to perform specified logical and arithmetical operations on data. ♦ *vb* **programs** *or* **programmes, programming, programmed. 2** (*tr*) to feed a program into (a computer). **3** (*tr*) to arrange (data) in a suitable form so that it can be processed by a computer. **4** (*intr*) to write a program.
▸'programmer *n*

programmable *or* **programable** (prəʊ'græməbəl) *adj* capable of being programmed for automatic operation or computer processing.

programme *or US* **program** ('prəʊgræm) *n* **1** a written or printed list of the events, performers, etc., in a public performance. **2** a performance presented at a scheduled time, esp. on radio or television. **3** a specially arranged selection of things to be done: *what's the programme for this afternoon?* **4** a plan, schedule, or procedure. **5** a syllabus or curriculum. ♦ *vb* **programmes, programming, programmed** *or US* **programs, programing, programed. 6** to design or schedule (something) as a programme. ♦ *n, vb* **7** *Computing.* a variant spelling of **program.** [C17: from LL *programma,* from Gk: written public notice, from PRO-[2] + *graphein* to write]
▸ˌprogram'matic *adj*

programmed learning *n* a teaching method in which the material to be learned is broken down into easily understandable parts on which the pupil is able to test himself.

programme music *n* music that is intended to depict or evoke a scene or idea.

programme of study *n Brit. education.* the prescribed syllabus that pupils must be taught at each key stage in the National Curriculum.

programming language *n* a simple language system designed to facilitate the writing of computer programs.

program statement *n* a single instruction in a computer program.

program trading *n* trading on international stock exchanges using a computer program to exploit differences between stock index futures and actual share prices on world equity markets.

progress *n* ('prəʊgrɛs). **1** movement forwards, esp. towards a place or objective. **2** satisfactory development or advance. **3** advance towards completion or perfection. **4** (*modifier*) of or relating to progress: *a progress report.* **5** (formerly) a stately royal journey. **6 in progress.** taking place. ♦ *vb* (prə'grɛs). **7** (*intr*) to move forwards or onwards. **8** (*intr*) to move towards completion or perfection. **9** (*tr*) to be responsible for the satisfactory progress of (a project, etc.) to completion. [C15: from L *prōgressus,* from *prōgredī* to advance, from *gradī* to step]

progression (prə'grɛʃən) *n* **1** the act of progressing; advancement. **2** the act or an instance of moving from one thing in a sequence to the next. **3** *Maths.* a sequence of numbers in which each term differs from the succeeding term by a constant relation. See also **arithmetic progression, geometric progression, harmonic progression. 4** *Music.* movement from one note or chord to the next.
▸pro'gressional *adj*

progressive (prə'grɛsɪv) *adj* **1** of or relating to progress. **2** progressing by steps or degrees. **3** (*often cap.*) favouring or promoting political or social reform: *a progressive policy.* **4** denoting an educational system that allows flexibility in learning procedures, based on activities determined by the needs and capacities of the individual child. **5** (esp. of a disease) advancing in severity, complexity, or extent. **6** (of a dance, card game, etc.) involving a regular change of partners. **7** denoting an aspect of verbs in some languages, including English, used to express continuous activity: *a progressive aspect of the verb "to walk" is "is walking".* ♦ *n* **8** a person who advocates progress, as in education, politics, etc. **9a** the progressive aspect of a verb. **9b** a verb in this aspect.
▸pro'gressively *adv* ▸pro'gressiveness *n* ▸pro'gressivism *n* ▸pro'gressivist *n*

progress payment *n* an instalment of a larger payment made to a contractor for work carried out up to a specified stage of the job.

prohibit (prə'hɪbɪt) *vb* (*tr*) **1** to forbid by law or other authority. **2** to hinder or prevent. [C15: from L *prohibēre* to prevent, from PRO-[1] + *habēre* to hold]
▸pro'hibiter *or* pro'hibitor *n*

prohibition (ˌprəʊɪ'bɪʃən) *n* **1** the act of prohibiting or state of being prohibited. **2** an order or decree that prohibits. **3** (*sometimes cap.*) (esp. in the US) a policy of legally forbidding the manufacture, sale, or consumption of alcoholic beverages. **4** *Law.* an order of a superior court forbidding an inferior court to determine a matter outside its jurisdiction.
▸ˌprohi'bitionary *adj* ▸ˌprohi'bitionist *n*

Prohibition (ˌprəʊɪ'bɪʃən) *n* the period (1920–33) when the manufacture, sale, and transportation of intoxicating liquors was banned in the US.
▸ˌProhi'bitionist *n*

prohibitive (prə'hɪbɪtɪv) *or* (*less commonly*) **prohibitory** (prə'hɪbɪtərɪ, -trɪ) *adj* **1** prohibiting or tending to prohibit. **2** (esp. of prices) tending or designed to discourage sale or purchase.
▸pro'hibitively *adv* ▸pro'hibitiveness *n*

project *n* ('prɒdʒɛkt). **1** a proposal, scheme, or design. **2a** a task requiring considerable or concerted effort, such as one by students. **2b** the subject of such a task. ♦ *vb* (prə'dʒɛkt). **3** (*tr*) to propose or plan. **4** (*tr*) to throw forwards. **5** to jut or cause to jut out. **6** (*tr*) to make a prediction based on known data and observations. **7** (*tr*) to transport in the imagination: *to project oneself into the future.* **8** (*tr*) to cause (an

THESAURUS

profusion *n* **1, 2** = **abundance**, bounty, copiousness, cornucopia, excess, extravagance, exuberance, glut, lavishness, luxuriance, multitude, oversupply, plenitude, plethora, prodigality, quantity, riot, superabundance, superfluity, surplus, wealth

progenitor *n* **1** = **ancestor**, begetter, forebear, forefather, parent, primogenitor, procreator **2** = **originator**, antecedent, forerunner, instigator, precursor, predecessor, source

progeny *n* **1** = **children**, breed, descendants, family, issue, lineage, offspring, posterity, race, scions, seed (*chiefly Biblical*), stock, young

prognosis *n* **1, 2** = **forecast**, diagnosis, expectation, prediction, prognostication, projection, speculation, surmise

prognosticate *vb* **1** = **foretell**, divine, forecast, predict, presage, prophesy, soothsay, vaticinate (*rare*) **2** = **indicate**, augur, betoken, forebode, foreshadow, harbinger, herald, point to, portend, presage

prognostication *n* **1** = **prediction**, expectation, forecast, prognosis, projection, prophecy, speculation, surmise

programme *n* **1, 3, 5** = **schedule**, agenda, curriculum, line-up, list, listing, list of players, order of events, order of the day, plan, syllabus, timetable **2** = **show**, broadcast, performance, presentation, production **4** = **plan**, design, order of the day, plan of action, procedure, project, scheme ♦ *vb* **6** = **schedule**, arrange, bill, book, design, engage, formulate, itemize, lay on, line up, list, map out, plan, prearrange, work out

progress *n* **1** = **movement**, advance, course, onward course, passage, progression, way **2, 3** = **development**, advance, advancement, amelioration, betterment, breakthrough, gain, gaining ground, growth, headway, improvement, increase, progression, promotion, step forward **6 in progress** = **going on**, being done, happening, occurring, proceeding, taking place, under way ♦ *vb* **7** = **move on**, advance, come on, continue, cover ground, forge ahead, gain ground, gather way, get on, go forward, make headway, make inroads (into), make one's way, make strides, proceed, travel **8** = **develop**, advance, ameliorate, better, blossom, gain, grow, improve, increase, mature
Antonyms *n* ≠ **movement:** regression, retrogression ≠ **development:** decline, failure, recession, regression, relapse, retrogression ♦ *vb* ≠ **move on:** get behind, recede, regress, retrogress ≠ **develop:** decrease, get behind, lose, lose ground, regress, retrogress

progression *n* **1** = **progress**, advance, advancement, furtherance, gain, headway, movement forward **2** = **sequence**, chain, course, cycle, order, series, string, succession

progressive *adj* **3, 4** = **enlightened**, advanced, avant-garde, dynamic, enterprising, forward-looking, go-ahead, liberal, modern, radical, reformist, revolutionary, up-and-coming **5** = **growing**, accelerating, advancing, continuing, continuous, developing, escalating, increasing, intensifying, ongoing

prohibit *vb* **1** = **forbid**, ban, debar, disallow, interdict, outlaw, proscribe, veto **2** = **prevent**, constrain, hamper, hinder, impede, make impossible, obstruct, preclude, restrict, rule out, stop
Antonyms *vb* ≠ **forbid:** allow, authorize, command, consent to, endure, further, give leave, let, license, order, permit, suffer, tolerate ≠ **prevent:** allow, let, permit

prohibited *adj* **1** = **forbidden**, banned, barred, not allowed, off limits, proscribed, taboo, *verboten*, vetoed

prohibition *n* **1** = **prevention**, constraint, disqualification, exclusion, forbiddance, interdiction, negation, obstruction, restriction **2** = **ban**, bar, boycott, disallowance, embargo, injunction, interdict, proscription, veto

prohibitive *adj* **1** = **prohibiting**, forbidding, proscriptive, repressive, restraining, restrictive, suppressive **2** = **exorbitant**, beyond one's means, excessive, extortionate, high-priced, preposterous, sky-high, steep (*inf.*)

project *n* **1, 2** = **scheme**, activity, assignment, design, enterprise, job, occupation, plan,

image) to appear on a surface. **9** to cause (one's voice) to be heard clearly at a distance. **10** *Psychol.* **10a** (*intr*) (esp. of a child) to believe that others share one's subjective mental life. **10b** to impute to others (one's hidden desires). **11** (*tr*) *Geom.* to draw a projection of. **12** (*intr*) to communicate effectively, esp. to a large gathering. [C14: from L *prōicere* to throw down]

projectile ❶ (prəˈdʒɛktaɪl) *n* **1** an object thrown forwards. **2** any self-propelling missile, esp. a rocket. **3** any object that can be fired from a gun, such as a shell. ◆ *adj* **4** designed to be hurled forwards. **5** projecting forwards. **6** *Zool.* another word for **protrusile**. [C17: from NL *prōjectilis* jutting forwards]

projection ❶ (prəˈdʒɛkʃən) *n* **1** the act of projecting or the state of being projected. **2** a part that juts out. **3** See **map projection**. **4** the representation of a line, figure, or solid on a given plane as it would be seen from a particular direction or in accordance with an accepted set of rules. **5** a scheme or plan. **6** a prediction based on known evidence and observations. **7a** the process of showing film on a screen. **7b** the images shown. **8** *Psychol.* **8a** the belief that others share one's subjective mental life. **8b** the process of projecting one's own hidden desires and impulses.
▸**proˈjectional** *adj* ▸**proˈjective** *adj*

projectionist (prəˈdʒɛkʃənɪst) *n* a person responsible for the operation of film projection machines.

projective geometry *n* the branch of geometry concerned with the properties of solids that are invariant under projection and section.

projector (prəˈdʒɛktə) *n* **1** an optical instrument that projects an enlarged image of individual slides. Full name: **slide projector**. **2** an optical instrument in which a film is wound past a lens so that the frames can be viewed as a continuously moving sequence. Full name: **film** *or* **cine projector**. **3** a device for projecting a light beam. **4** a person who devises projects.

prokaryote *or* **procaryote** (prəʊˈkærɪɒt) *n* any organism of the kingdom *Prokaryotae* having cells in which the genetic material is in a single filament of DNA, not enclosed in a nucleus. Cf. **eukaryote**. [from PRO-[2] + KARYO- + *-ote* as in *zygote*]
▸**prokaryotic** *or* **procaryotic** (prəʊˌkærɪˈɒtɪk) *adj*

prolactin (prəʊˈlæktɪn) *n* a gonadotrophic hormone secreted by the anterior lobe of the pituitary gland. In mammals it stimulates the secretion of progesterone by the corpus luteum and initiates and maintains lactation.

prolapse (ˈprəʊlæps, prəʊˈlæps) *Pathol.* ◆ *n* **1** Also: **prolapsus** (prəʊˈlæpsəs). the sinking or falling down of an organ or part, esp. the womb. ◆ *vb* **prolapses, prolapsing, prolapsed.** (*intr*) **2** (of an organ, etc.) to sink from its normal position. [C17: from L *prōlābi* to slide along]

prolate (ˈprəʊleɪt) *adj* having a polar diameter of greater length than the equatorial diameter. Cf. **oblate**[1]. [C17: from L *prōferre* to enlarge]
▸ˈ**prolately** *adv*

prole (prəʊl) *n, adj Derog. sl., chiefly Brit.* short for **proletarian**.

prolegomenon (ˌprəʊleˈgɒmɪnən) *n, pl* **prolegomenona** (-nə). (*often pl*) a preliminary discussion, esp. a formal critical introduction to a lengthy text. [C17: from Gk, from *prolegein*, from PRO-[2] + *legein* to say]
▸ˌ**proleˈgomenal** *adj*

prolepsis (prəʊˈlɛpsɪs) *n, pl* **prolepses** (-siːz). **1** a rhetorical device by which objections are anticipated and answered in advance. **2** use of a word after a verb in anticipation of its becoming applicable through the action of the verb, as *flat* in *hammer it flat*. [C16: via LL from Gk: anticipation, from *prolambanein* to anticipate, from PRO-[2] + *lambanein* to take]
▸**proˈleptic** *adj*

proletarian ❶ (ˌprəʊlɪˈtɛərɪən) *adj* **1** of or belonging to the proletariat. ◆ *n* **2** a member of the proletariat. [C17: from L *prōlētārius* one whose only contribution to the state was his offspring, from *prōlēs* offspring]
▸ˌ**proleˈtarianism** *n*

proletariat ❶ (ˌprəʊlɪˈtɛərɪət) *n* **1** all wage-earners collectively. **2** the lower or working class. **3** (in Marxist theory) the class of wage-earners, esp. industrial workers, in a capitalist society, whose only possession of significant material value is their labour. **4** (in ancient Rome) the lowest class of citizens, who had no property. [C19: via F from L *prōlētārius* PROLETARIAN]

pro-life *adj* (of an organization, pressure group, etc.) supporting the right to life of the unborn; against abortion, experiments on embryos, etc.
▸ˌ**pro-ˈlifer** *n*

proliferate ❶ (prəˈlɪfəˌreɪt) *vb* **proliferates, proliferating, proliferated.** **1** to grow or reproduce (new parts, cells, etc.) rapidly. **2** to grow or increase rapidly. [C19: from Med. L *prōlifer* having offspring, from L *prōlēs* offspring + *ferre* to bear]
▸**proˌliferˈation** *n* ▸**proˈliferative** *adj*

prolific ❶ (prəˈlɪfɪk) *adj* **1** producing fruit, offspring, etc., in abundance. **2** producing constant or successful results. **3** (often foll. by *in* or *of*) rich or fruitful. [C17: from Med. L *prōlificus*, from L *prōlēs* offspring]
▸**proˈlifically** *adv* ▸**proˈlificness** *or* **proˈlificacy** *n*

prolix (ˈprəʊlɪks, prəʊˈlɪks) *adj* **1** (of a speech, book, etc.) so long as to be boring. **2** long-winded. [C15: from L *prōlixus* stretched out widely, from *līquī* to flow]
▸**proˈlixity** *n* ▸**proˈlixly** *adv*

prolocutor (prəʊˈlɒkjʊtə) *n* a chairman, esp. of the lower house of clergy in a convocation of the Anglican Church. [C15: from L: advocate, from *loqui* to speak]
▸**proˈlocutorship** *n*

PROLOG *or* **Prolog** (ˈprəʊlɒg) *n* a computer programming language based on mathematical logic. [C20: from *pro(gramming in) log(ic)*]

prologue ❶ *or US* (*often*) **prolog** (ˈprəʊlɒg) *n* **1** the prefatory lines introducing a play or speech. **2** a preliminary act or event. **3** (in early opera) **3a** an introductory scene in which a narrator summarizes the main action of the work. **3b** a brief independent play preceding the opera, esp. one in honour of a patron. ◆ *vb* **prologues, prologuing, prologued** *or US* **prologs, prologing, prologed.** **4** (*tr*) to introduce with a prologue. [C13: from L *prologus*, from Gk, from PRO-[2] + *logos* discourse]

prolong ❶ (prəˈlɒŋ) *vb* (*tr*) to lengthen; extend. [C15: from LL *prōlongāre* to extend, from L PRO-[1] + *longus* long]
▸**prolongation** (ˌprəʊlɒŋˈgeɪʃən) *n*

prolusion (prəˈluːʒən) *n* **1** a preliminary written exercise. **2** an introductory essay. [C17: from L *prōlūsiō*, from *prōlūdere* to practise beforehand, from PRO-[1] + *lūdere* to play]
▸**prolusory** (prəˈluːzərɪ) *adj*

prom (prɒm) *n* **1** *Brit.* short for **promenade** (sense 1) or **promenade concert**. **2** *US & Canad. inf.* a formal dance held at a high school or college.

PROM (prɒm) *n Computing. acronym for* programmable read only memory.

promenade ❶ (ˌprɒməˈnɑːd) *n* **1** *Chiefly Brit.* a public walk, esp. at a seaside resort. **2** a leisurely walk, esp. one in a public place for pleasure or display. **3** a marchlike step in dancing. **4** a marching sequence in a square or country dance. ◆ *vb* **promenades, promenading, promenaded.** **5** to take a promenade in or through (a place). **6** (*intr*) *Dancing.* to perform a promenade. **7** (*tr*) to display or exhibit (someone or oneself) on or as if on a promenade. [C16: from F, from *promener* to lead out for a walk, from LL *prōmināre* to drive (cattle) along, from *mināre* to drive, prob. from *minārī* to threaten]
▸ˌ**promeˈnader** *n*

promenade concert *n* a concert at which some of the audience stand rather than sit.

promenade deck *n* an upper covered deck of a passenger ship for the use of the passengers.

promethazine (prəʊˈmɛθəˌziːn) *n* an antihistamine drug used to treat allergies and to prevent vomiting. [C20: from PRO(PYL) + *(di)meth(ylamine)* + *(phenothi)azine*]

Promethean (prəˈmiːθɪən) *adj* **1** of or relating to Prometheus, in Greek myth the Titan who stole fire from Olympus to give to mankind. He was punished by being chained to a rock and having an eagle tear out his liver. **2** creative, original, or life-enhancing.

promethium (prəˈmiːθɪəm) *n* a radioactive element of the lanthanide series artificially produced by the fission of uranium. Symbol: Pm; atomic no.: 61; half-life of most stable isotope, ^{145}Pm: 17.7 years. [C20: NL from *Prometheus*; see PROMETHEAN]

prominence ❶ (ˈprɒmɪnəns) *n* **1** the state of being prominent. **2** something that is prominent, such as a protuberance. **3** relative impor-

THESAURUS

programme, proposal, task, undertaking, venture, work ◆ *vb* **3** = **plan**, contemplate, contrive, design, devise, draft, frame, map out, outline, propose, purpose, scheme **4** = **throw**, cast, discharge, fling, hurl, launch, make carry, propel, shoot, transmit **5** = **stick out**, beetle, bulge, extend, jut, overhang, protrude, stand out **6** = **forecast**, calculate, call, estimate, extrapolate, gauge, predetermine, predict, reckon

projectile *n* **2, 3** = **missile**, bullet, rocket, shell

projection *n* **1** = **forecast**, calculation, computation, estimate, estimation, extrapolation, prediction, reckoning **2** = **protrusion**, bulge, eaves, jut, ledge, overhang, protuberance, ridge, shelf, sill **4** = **plan**, blueprint, diagram, map, outline, representation

proletarian *adj* **1** = **working-class**, cloth-cap (*inf.*), common, plebeian ◆ *n* **2** = **worker**, commoner, Joe Bloggs (*Brit. inf.*), man of the people, pleb, plebeian, prole (*derogatory sl., chiefly Brit.*)

proletariat *n* **1, 2** = **working class**, commonalty, commoners, hoi polloi, labouring classes, lower classes, lower orders, plebs, proles (*derogatory sl., chiefly Brit.*), the common people, the great unwashed (*inf. & derogatory*), the herd, the masses, the rabble, wage-earners
Antonyms *n* aristo (*inf.*), aristocracy, gentry, nobility, peerage, ruling class, upper class, upper crust (*inf.*)

proliferate *vb* **1, 2** = **increase**, breed, burgeon, escalate, expand, grow rapidly, multiply, mushroom, run riot, snowball

proliferation *n* **2** = **multiplication**, build-up, concentration, escalation, expansion, extension, increase, intensification, spread, step-up (*inf.*)

prolific *adj* **1, 3** = **productive**, abundant, bountiful, copious, fecund, fertile, fruitful, generative, luxuriant, profuse, rank, rich, teeming
Antonyms *adj* barren, fruitless, infertile, sterile, unfruitful, unproductive, unprolific

prologue *n* **1** = **introduction**, exordium, foreword, preamble, preface, preliminary, prelude, proem

prolong *vb* = **lengthen**, carry on, continue, delay, drag out, draw out, extend, make longer, perpetuate, protract, spin out, stretch
Antonyms *vb* abbreviate, abridge, curtail, cut, cut down, shorten, summarize

promenade *n* **1** = **walkway**, boulevard, esplanade, parade, prom, public walk **2** = **stroll**, airing, constitutional, saunter, turn, walk ◆ *vb* **5** = **stroll**, perambulate, saunter, stretch one's legs, take a walk, walk **7** = **parade**, flaunt, strut, swagger

prominence *n* **1** = **conspicuousness**, markedness, outstandingness, precedence, salience, specialness, top billing, weight **2** = **protrusion**, bulge, jutting, projection, protuberance, swelling **2** = **rising ground**, cliff, crag, crest, elevation, headland, height, high point, hummock,

tance. 4 *Astron.* an eruption of incandescent gas from the sun's surface, visible during a total eclipse.

prominent ❶ ('prɒmɪnənt) *adj* **1** jutting or projecting outwards. **2** standing out from its surroundings; noticeable. **3** widely known; eminent. [C16: from L *prōminēre* to jut out, from PRO-[1] + *ēminēre* to project]
▸**'prominently** *adv*

promiscuous ❶ (prə'mɪskjuəs) *adj* **1** indulging in casual and indiscriminate sexual relationships. **2** consisting of a number of dissimilar parts or elements mingled indiscriminately. **3** indiscriminate in selection. **4** casual or heedless. [C17: from L *prōmiscuus* indiscriminate, from PRO-[1] + *miscēre* to mix]
▸**pro'miscuously** *adv* ▸**promiscuity** (ˌprɒmɪ'skjuːɪtɪ) *or* **pro'miscuousness** *n*

promise ❶ ('prɒmɪs) *vb* **promises, promising, promised. 1** (often foll. by *to;* when *tr, may take a clause as object or an infinitive*) to give an assurance of (something to someone): *I promise that I will come.* **2** (*tr*) to undertake to give (something to someone): *he promised me a car for my birthday.* **3** (when *tr, takes an infinitive*) to cause people to expect that one is likely (to be or do something): *she promises to be a fine soprano.* **4** (*tr; usually passive*) *Obs.* to betroth: *I'm promised to Bill.* **5** (*tr*) to assure (someone) of the authenticity or inevitability of something: *there'll be trouble, I promise you.* ◆ *n* **6** an assurance given by one person to another agreeing or guaranteeing to do or not to do something. **7** indication of forthcoming excellence: *a writer showing considerable promise.* **8** the thing of which an assurance is given. [C14: from L *prōmissum* a promise, from *prōmittere* to send forth]
▸**ˌpromi'see** *n* ▸**'promiser** *or* (*Law*) **'promisor** *n*

Promised Land *n* **1** *Old Testament.* the land of Canaan, promised by God to Abraham and his descendants as their heritage (Genesis 12:7). **2** *Christianity.* heaven. **3** any longed-for place where one expects to find greater happiness.

promising ❶ ('prɒmɪsɪŋ) *adj* showing promise of future success.
▸**'promisingly** *adv*

promissory ('prɒmɪsərɪ) *adj* **1** containing, relating to, or having the nature of a promise. **2** *Insurance.* stipulating how the provisions of an insurance contract will be fulfilled.

promissory note *n Commerce, chiefly US.* a document containing a signed promise to pay a stated sum of money to a specified person at a designated date or on demand. Also called: **note, note of hand.**

promo ('prəʊməʊ) *n, pl* **promos.** *Inf.* something used to promote a product, esp. a videotape film used to promote a pop record. [C20: shortened from *promotion*]

promontory ❶ ('prɒməntərɪ, -trɪ) *n, pl* **promontories. 1** a high point of land, esp. of rocky coast, that juts out into the sea. **2** *Anat.* any of various projecting structures. [C16: from L *prōmunturium* headland]

promote ❶ (prə'məʊt) *vb* **promotes, promoting, promoted.** (*tr*) **1** to encourage the progress or existence of. **2** to raise to a higher rank, status, etc. **3** to advance (a pupil or student) to a higher course, class, etc. **4** to work for: *to promote reform.* **5** to encourage the sale of (a product) by advertising or securing financial support. [C14: from L *prōmovēre* to push onwards]
▸**pro'motion** *n* ▸**pro'motional** *adj*

promoter ❶ (prə'məʊtə) *n* **1** a person or thing that promotes. **2** a person who helps to organize, develop, or finance an undertaking. **3** a person who organizes and finances a sporting event, esp. a boxing match.

prompt ❶ (prɒmpt) *adj* **1** performed or executed without delay. **2** quick or ready to act or respond. ◆ *adv* **3** *Inf.* punctually. ◆ *vb* **4** (*tr*) to urge (someone to do something). **5** to remind (an actor, singer, etc.) of lines forgotten during a performance. **6** (*tr*) to refresh the memory of. **7** (*tr*) to give rise to by suggestion: *his affairs will prompt discussion.* ◆ *n* **8** *Commerce.* **8a** the time limit allowed for payment of the debt incurred by purchasing on credit. **8b** Also called: **prompt note.** a memorandum sent to a purchaser to remind him of the time limit and the sum due. **9** anything that serves to remind. [C15: from L *promptus* evident, from *prōmere* to produce, from *emere* to buy]
▸**'promptly** *adv* ▸**'promptness** *n*

prompter ❶ ('prɒmptə) *n* **1** a person offstage who reminds the actors of forgotten lines or cues. **2** a person, thing, etc., that prompts.

promptitude ('prɒmptɪˌtjuːd) *n* the quality of being prompt; punctuality.

prompt side *n Theatre.* the side of the stage where the prompter is, usually to the actor's left in Britain and to his right in the United States.

promulgate ❶ ('prɒməlˌgeɪt) *vb* **promulgates, promulgating, promulgated.** (*tr*) **1** to put into effect (a law, decree, etc.), esp. by formal proclamation. **2** to announce officially. **3** to make widespread. [C16: from L *prōmulgāre* to bring to public knowledge]
▸**ˌpromul'gation** *n* ▸**'promulˌgator** *n*

pron. *abbrev. for:* **1** pronominal. **2** pronoun. **3** pronounced. **4** pronunciation.

pronate (prəʊ'neɪt) *vb* **pronates, pronating, pronated.** (*tr*) to turn (the forearm or hand) so that the palmar surface is directed downwards. [C19: from LL *prōnāre* to bow]
▸**pro'nation** *n* ▸**pro'nator** *n*

prone ❶ (prəʊn) *adj* **1** lying flat or face downwards; prostrate. **2** sloping or tending downwards. **3** having an inclination to do something. [C14: from L *prōnus* bent forward, from PRO-[1]]
▸**'pronely** *adv* ▸**'proneness** *n*

-prone *adj combining form.* liable or disposed to suffer: *accident-prone.*

THESAURUS

mound, pinnacle, projection, promontory, rise, spur **3** = **fame**, celebrity, distinction, eminence, greatness, importance, name, notability, pre-eminence, prestige, rank, reputation, standing

prominent *adj* **1** = **jutting**, bulging, hanging over, projecting, protruding, protrusive, protuberant, standing out **2** = **noticeable**, blatant, conspicuous, easily seen, eye-catching, in the foreground, obtrusive, obvious, outstanding, pronounced, remarkable, salient, striking, to the fore, unmistakable **3** = **famous**, big-time (*inf.*), celebrated, chief, distinguished, eminent, foremost, important, leading, main, major league (*inf.*), notable, noted, outstanding, popular, pre-eminent, renowned, respected, top, well-known, well-thought-of
Antonyms *adj* ≠ **jutting:** concave, indented, receding ≠ **noticeable:** inconspicuous, indistinct, insignificant, unnoticeable ≠ **famous:** insignificant, minor, secondary, undistinguished, unimportant, unknown, unnotable

promiscuity *n* **1** = **licentiousness**, abandon, amorality, debauchery, depravity, dissipation, immorality, incontinence, laxity, laxness, lechery, libertinism, looseness, permissiveness, profligacy, promiscuousness, sleeping around (*inf.*), wantonness

promiscuous *adj* **1** = **licentious**, abandoned, debauched, dissipated, dissolute, fast, immoral, lax, libertine, loose, of easy virtue, profligate, unbridled, unchaste, wanton, wild **2** = **mixed**, chaotic, confused, disordered, diverse, heterogeneous, ill-assorted, indiscriminate, intermingled, intermixed, jumbled, mingled, miscellaneous, motley **3, 4** = **indiscriminate**, careless, casual, haphazard, heedless, indifferent, irregular, irresponsible, random, slovenly, uncontrolled, uncritical, undiscriminating, unfastidious, unselective
Antonyms *adj* ≠ **licentious:** chaste, decent, innocent, modest, moral, pure, undefiled, unsullied, vestal, virginal, virtuous ≠ **mixed:** homogeneous, identical, neat, ordered, orderly, organized, shipshape, uniform, unmixed ≠ **indiscriminate:** careful, critical, discriminating, fastidious, responsible, selective

promise *vb* **1, 2** = **guarantee**, assure, contract, cross one's heart, engage, give an undertaking, give one's word, pledge, plight, stipulate, swear, take an oath, undertake, vouch, vow, warrant **3** = **seem likely**, augur, bespeak, betoken, bid fair, denote, give hope of, hint at, hold a probability, hold out hopes of, indicate, lead one to expect, look like, show signs of, suggest ◆ *n* **6** = **guarantee**, assurance, bond, commitment, compact, covenant, engagement, oath, pledge, undertaking, vow, word, word of honour **7** = **potential**, ability, aptitude, capability, capacity, flair, talent

promising *adj* = **encouraging**, auspicious, bright, favourable, full of promise, hopeful, likely, propitious, reassuring, rosy = **talented**, able, gifted, likely, rising, up-and-coming
Antonyms *adj* ≠ **encouraging:** discouraging, unauspicious, unfavourable, unpromising

promontory *n* **1** = **point**, cape, foreland, head, headland, ness, spur

promote *vb* **1** = **help**, advance, aid, assist, back, boost, contribute to, develop, encourage, forward, foster, further, gee up, nurture, stimulate, support **2** = **raise**, aggrandize, dignify, elevate, exalt, honour, kick upstairs (*inf.*), prefer, upgrade **4** = **work for**, advocate, call attention to, champion, endorse, espouse, popularize, prescribe, push for, recommend, speak for, sponsor, support, urge **5** = **advertise**, beat the drum for (*inf.*), hype, plug (*inf.*), publicize, puff, push, sell
Antonyms *vb* ≠ **help:** discourage, hinder, hold back, impede, obstruct, oppose, prevent ≠ **raise:** demote, downgrade, lower *or* reduce in rank

promoter *n* **1** = **supporter**, advocate, campaigner, champion, helper, mainstay, proponent, stalwart, upholder **2, 3** = **organizer**, arranger, entrepreneur, impresario, matchmaker

promotion *n* **1** = **encouragement**, advancement, advocacy, backing, boosting, cultivation, development, espousal, furtherance, progress, support **2** = **rise**, advancement, aggrandizement, elevation, ennoblement, exaltation, honour, move up, preferment, upgrading **5** = **publicity**, advertising, advertising campaign, ballyhoo (*inf.*), hard sell, hype, media hype, plugging (*inf.*), propaganda, puffery (*inf.*), pushing

prompt *adj* **1** = **immediate**, early, instant, instantaneous, on time, punctual, quick, rapid, speedy, swift, timely, unhesitating **2** = **quick**, alert, brisk, eager, efficient, expeditious, ready, responsive, smart, willing ◆ *adv* **3** *Informal* = **exactly**, on the dot, promptly, punctually, sharp ◆ *vb* **4** = **motivate**, cause, impel, incite, induce, inspire, instigate, move, provoke, spur, stimulate, urge **5, 6** = **remind**, assist, cue, help out, jog the memory, prod, refresh the memory **7** = **cause**, call forth, elicit, evoke, give rise to, occasion, provoke ◆ *n* **9** = **reminder**, cue, help, hint, jog, jolt, prod, spur, stimulus
Antonyms *adj* ≠ **immediate:** hesitating, late, slow ≠ **quick:** inactive, inattentive, inefficient, remiss, slack, tardy, unresponsive ◆ *vb* ≠ **motivate:** deter, discourage, prevent, restrain, talk out of

prompter *n* **2** = **autocue**, idiot board (*sl.*), Teleprompter (*Trademark*) **2** = **instigator**, agitator, catalyst, gadfly, inspirer, moving spirit, prime mover

promptly *adv* **1** = **immediately**, at once, by return, directly, hotfoot, instantly, on the dot, on time, posthaste, pronto (*inf.*), punctually, quickly, speedily, swiftly, unhesitatingly

promptness *n* **1, 2** = **swiftness**, alacrity, alertness, briskness, dispatch, eagerness, haste, promptitude, punctuality, quickness, readiness, speed, willingness

promulgate *vb* **2, 3** = **make known**, advertise, announce, broadcast, circulate, communicate, declare, decree, disseminate, issue, make public, notify, proclaim, promote, publish, spread

prone *adj* **1** = **face down**, flat, horizontal, lying down, procumbent, prostrate, recumbent **3** = **liable**, apt, bent, disposed, given, inclined,

prong ⓘ (prɒŋ) *n* **1** a sharply pointed end of an instrument, such as on a fork. **2** any pointed projecting part. ◆ *vb* **3** (*tr*) to prick or spear with or as if with a prong. [C15]
▸**pronged** *adj*

pronghorn (ˈprɒŋˌhɔːn) *n* a ruminant mammal inhabiting rocky deserts of North America and having small branched horns. Also called: **American antelope.**

pronominal (prəʊˈnɒmɪnᵊl) *adj* relating to or playing the part of a pronoun. [C17: from LL *prōnōminālis,* from *prōnōmen* a PRONOUN]
▸**proˈnominally** *adv*

pronoun (ˈprəʊˌnaʊn) *n* one of a class of words that serves to replace a noun or noun phrase that has already been or is about to be mentioned in the sentence or context. Abbrev.: **pron.** [C16: from L *prōnōmen,* from PRO-[1] + *nōmen* noun]

pronounce ⓘ (prəˈnaʊns) *vb* **pronounces, pronouncing, pronounced. 1** to utter or articulate (a sound or sounds). **2** (*tr*) to utter (words) in the correct way. **3** (*tr; may take a clause as object*) to proclaim officially: *I now pronounce you man and wife.* **4** (when *tr, may take a clause as object*) to declare as one's judgment: *to pronounce the death sentence upon someone.* [C14: from L *prōnuntiāre* to announce]
▸**proˈnounceable** *adj* ▸**proˈnouncer** *n*

pronounced ⓘ (prəˈnaʊnst) *adj* **1** strongly marked or indicated. **2** (of a sound) articulated with vibration of the vocal cords; voiced.
▸**pronouncedly** (prəˈnaʊnsɪdlɪ) *adv*

pronouncement ⓘ (prəˈnaʊnsmənt) *n* **1** an official or authoritative announcement. **2** the act of declaring or uttering formally.

pronto (ˈprɒntəʊ) *adv Inf.* at once. [C20: from Sp.: quick, from L *promptus* PROMPT]

pronunciation ⓘ (prəˌnʌnsɪˈeɪʃən) *n* **1** the act, instance, or manner of pronouncing sounds. **2** the supposedly correct manner of pronouncing sounds in a given language. **3** a phonetic transcription of a word.

proof ⓘ (pruːf) *n* **1** any evidence that establishes or helps to establish the truth, validity, quality, etc., of something. **2** *Law.* the whole body of evidence upon which the verdict of a court is based. **3** *Maths, logic.* a sequence of steps or statements that establishes the truth of a proposition. **4** the act of testing the truth of something (esp. in **put to the proof**). **5** *Scots Law.* trial before a judge without a jury. **6** *Printing.* a trial impression made from composed type for the correction of errors. **7** (in engraving, etc.) a print made by an artist or under his supervision for his own satisfaction before he hands the plate over to a professional printer. **8** *Photog.* a trial print from a negative. **9a** the alcoholic strength of proof spirit. **9b** the strength of a liquor as measured on a scale in which the strength of proof spirit is 100 degrees. ◆ *adj* **10** (*usually postpositive;* foll. by *against*) impervious (to): *the roof is proof against rain.* **11** having the alcoholic strength of proof spirit. **12** of proved impenetrability: *proof armour.* ◆ *vb* **13** (*tr*) to take a proof from (type matter, a plate, etc.). **14** to proofread (text) or inspect (a print, etc.), as for approval. **15** to render (something) proof, esp. to waterproof. [C13: from OF *preuve* a test, from LL *proba,* from L *probāre* to test]

-proof *adj, vb combining form.* (to make) impervious to; secure against (damage by): *waterproof.* [from PROOF (adj)]

proofread (ˈpruːfˌriːd) *vb* **proofreads, proofreading, proofread** (-ˌrɛd). to read (copy or printer's proofs) and mark errors to be corrected.
▸ˈ**proofˌreader** *n*

proof spirit *n* (in Britain) a mixture of alcohol and water or an alcoholic beverage that contains 49.28 per cent of alcohol by weight, 57.1 per cent by volume at 51°F: used until 1980 as a standard of alcoholic liquids.

prop[1] ⓘ (prɒp) *vb* **props, propping, propped.** (*tr;* often foll. by *up*) **1** to support with a rigid object, such as a stick. **2** (usually also foll. by *against*) to place or lean. **3** to sustain or support. ◆ *n* **4** something that gives rigid support, such as a stick. **5** short for **clothes prop. 6** a person or thing giving support, as of a moral nature. **7** *Rugby.* either of the forwards at either end of the front row of a scrum. [C15: rel. to M Du. *proppe* vine prop]

prop[2] (prɒp) *n* short for **property** (sense 8).

prop[3] (prɒp) *n* an informal word for **propeller.**

prop. *abbrev. for:* **1** proper(ly). **2** property. **3** proposition. **4** proprietor.

propaedeutic (ˌprəʊpɪˈdjuːtɪk) *n* **1** (*often pl*) preparatory instruction basic to further study of an art or science. ◆ *adj also* **propaedeutical. 2** of, relating to, or providing such instruction. [C19: from Gk *propaideuein* to teach in advance, from PRO-[2] + *paideuein* to rear]

propaganda ⓘ (ˌprɒpəˈgændə) *n* **1** the organized dissemination of information, allegations, etc., to assist or damage the cause of a government, movement, etc. **2** such information, allegations, etc. [C18: from It., use of *propāgandā* in the NL title *Sacra Congregatio de Propaganda Fide* Sacred Congregation for Propagating the Faith]
▸ˌ**propaˈgandism** *n* ▸ˌ**propaˈgandist** *n, adj*

Propaganda (ˌprɒpəˈgændə) *n RC Church.* a congregation responsible for directing the work of the foreign missions.

propagandize ⓘ *or* **propagandise** (ˌprɒpəˈgænˌdaɪz) *vb* **propagandizes, propagandizing, propagandized** *or* **propagandises, propagandising, propagandised. 1** (*tr*) to spread by, or subject to, propaganda. **2** (*intr*) to spread or organize propaganda.

propagate ⓘ (ˈprɒpəˌgeɪt) *vb* **propagates, propagating, propagated. 1** *Biol.* to reproduce or cause to reproduce; breed. **2** (*tr*) *Horticulture.* to produce (plants) by layering, grafting, cuttings, etc. **3** (*tr*) to promulgate. **4** *Physics.* to transmit, esp. in the form of a wave: *to propagate sound.* **5** (*tr*) to transmit (characteristics) from one generation to the next. [C16: from L *propāgāre* to increase (plants) by cuttings, from *propāgēs* a cutting, from *pangere* to fasten]
▸ˌ**propaˈgation** *n* ▸ˌ**propaˈgational** *adj* ▸ˈ**propagative** *adj* ▸ˈ**propaˌgator** *n*

propane (ˈprəʊpeɪn) *n* a flammable gaseous alkane found in petroleum and used as a fuel. Formula: $CH_3CH_2CH_3$. [C19: from PROPIONIC (ACID) + -ANE]

propanoic acid (ˌprəʊpəˈnəʊɪk) *n* a colourless liquid carboxylic acid used in inhibiting the growth of moulds in bread. Formula: CH_3CH_2COOH. Former name: **propionic acid.** [C20: from PROPANE + -OIC]

pro patria *Latin.* (ˈprəʊ ˈpætrɪˌɑː) for one's country.

propel ⓘ (prəˈpɛl) *vb* **propels, propelling, propelled.** (*tr*) to impel, drive, or cause to move forwards. [C15: from L *prōpellere*]
▸**proˈpellant** *or* **proˈpellent** *n*

propeller (prəˈpɛlə) *n* **1** a device having blades radiating from a central hub that is rotated to produce thrust to propel a ship, aircraft, etc. **2** a person or thing that propels.

propelling pencil *n* a pencil consisting of a metal or plastic case containing a replaceable lead. As the point is worn away the lead can be extended, usually by turning part of the case.

propene (ˈprəʊpiːn) *n* a colourless gaseous alkene obtained by cracking petroleum. Formula: $CH_3CH{:}CH_2$. Also called: **propylene.**

propensity ⓘ (prəˈpɛnsɪtɪ) *n, pl* **propensities. 1** a natural tendency. **2** *Obs.* partiality. [C16: from L *prōpensus* inclined to, from *prōpendēre* to hang forwards]

proper ⓘ (ˈprɒpə) *adj* **1** (*usually prenominal*) appropriate or usual: *in its proper place.* **2** suited to a particular purpose: *use the proper knife to cut the bread.* **3** correct in behaviour. **4** vigorously or excessively moral. **5** up to a required or regular standard. **6** (*immediately postpositive*) (of an object, quality, etc.) referred to so as to exclude anything not directly connected with it: *his claim is connected with the deed proper.* **7**

THESAURUS

likely, predisposed, subject, susceptible, tending
Antonyms *adj* ≠ **face down:** erect, face up, perpendicular, supine, upright, vertical ≠ **liable:** averse, disinclined, indisposed, not likely, unlikely

proneness *n* **3** = **tendency,** bent, bias, disposition, inclination, leaning, liability, partiality, proclivity, propensity, susceptibility, weakness

prong *n* **1, 2** = **point,** projection, spike, tine, tip

pronounce *vb* **1** = **say,** accent, articulate, enunciate, sound, speak, stress, utter, vocalize, voice **3, 4** = **declare,** affirm, announce, assert, decree, deliver, judge, proclaim

pronounced *adj* **1** = **noticeable,** broad, clear, conspicuous, decided, definite, distinct, evident, marked, obvious, salient, striking, strong, unmistakable
Antonyms *adj* concealed, hidden, imperceptible, inconspicuous, unapparent, unnoticeable, vague

pronouncement *n* **1** = **announcement,** declaration, decree, dictum, edict, judgment, manifesto, notification, proclamation, promulgation, pronunciamento, statement

pronunciation *n* **1** = **intonation,** accent, accentuation, articulation, diction, elocution, enunciation, inflection, speech, stress

proof *n* **1** = **evidence,** attestation, authentication, certification, confirmation, corroboration, demonstration, substantiation, testimony, verification **4** *As in* **put to the proof** = **test,** assay, examination, experiment, ordeal, scrutiny, trial **6** *Printing* = **trial print,** galley, galley proof, page proof, pull, slip, trial impression ◆ *adj* **10** = **impervious,** impenetrable, repellent, resistant, strong, tight, treated

prop[1] *vb* **1, 3** = **support,** bolster, brace, buttress, hold up, maintain, shore, stay, sustain, truss, uphold **2** = **rest,** lean, place, set, stand ◆ *n* **4** = **support,** brace, buttress, mainstay, stanchion, stay, truss

propaganda *n* **1, 2** = **information,** advertising, agitprop, ballyhoo (*inf.*), boosterism, brainwashing, disinformation, hype, newspeak, promotion, publicity

propagandist *n* **1** = **publicist,** advocate, evangelist, indoctrinator, pamphleteer, promoter, proponent, proselytizer

propagandize *vb* **1, 2** = **persuade,** brainwash, convince, indoctrinate, instil, proselytize

propagate *vb* **1** = **reproduce,** beget, breed, engender, generate, increase, multiply, procreate, produce, proliferate **3** = **spread,** broadcast, circulate, diffuse, disseminate, make known, proclaim, promote, promulgate, publicize, publish, transmit
Antonyms *vb* ≠ **spread:** cover up, hide, hush up, keep under wraps, stifle, suppress, withhold

propagation *n* **1** = **reproduction,** breeding, generation, increase, multiplication, procreation, proliferation **3** = **spreading,** circulation, communication, diffusion, dissemination, distribution, promotion, promulgation, spread, transmission

propel *vb* = **drive,** force, impel, launch, push, send, set in motion, shoot, shove, start, thrust
Antonyms *vb* check, delay, hold back, pull, slow, stop

propensity *n* **1** = **tendency,** aptness, bent, bias, disposition, inclination, leaning, liability, penchant, predisposition, proclivity, proneness, susceptibility, weakness

proper *adj* **1** = **suitable,** appropriate, apt, becoming, befitting, fit, fitting, legitimate, meet (*arch.*), right, suited **3** = **polite,** *comme il faut,* decent, decorous, *de rigueur,* genteel, gentlemanly, ladylike, mannerly, punctilious, refined, respectable, seemly **7** = **characteristic,** individual, own, particular, peculiar, personal, respective, special, specific
Antonyms *adj* ≠ **suitable:** improper, inappropriate, unbecoming, unsuitable ≠ **polite:** coarse, common, crude, discourteous, impolite, indecent,

(*postpositive;* foll. by *to*) belonging to or characteristic of a person or thing. **8** (*prenominal*) *Brit. inf.* (intensifier): *I felt a proper fool.* **9** (*usually postpositive*) (of heraldic colours) considered correct for the natural colour of the object depicted: *three martlets proper.* **10** *Arch.* pleasant or good. **11 good and proper.** *Inf.* thoroughly. ◆ *n* **12** the parts of the Mass that vary according to the particular day or feast on which the Mass is celebrated. [C13: via OF from L *prōprius* special]
▸ **'properly** *adv* ▸ **'properness** *n*

proper fraction *n* a fraction in which the numerator has a lower absolute value than the denominator, as ½ or $x/(3 + x^2)$.

proper motion *n* the very small continuous change in the direction of motion of a star relative to the sun.

proper noun *or* **name** *n* the name of a person, place, or object, as for example *Iceland, Patrick,* or *Uranus.* Cf. **common noun.**

propertied ('prɒpətɪd) *adj* owning land or property.

property ❶ ('prɒpətɪ) *n, pl* **properties. 1** something of value, either tangible, such as land, or intangible, such as copyrights. **2** *Law.* the right to possess, use, and dispose of anything. **3** possessions collectively. **4a** land or real estate. **4b** (*as modifier*): *property rights.* **5** *Chiefly Austral.* a ranch or station. **6** a quality or characteristic attribute, such as the density or strength of a material. **7** *Logic, obs.* Also called: **proprium** ('prəʊprɪəm). an attribute that is not essential to a species but is common and peculiar to it. **8** any movable object used on the set of a stage play or film. Usually shortened to **prop.** [C13: from OF *propriété,* from L *proprietās* something personal, from *proprius* one's own]

property bond *n* a bond issued by a life-assurance company, the premiums for which are invested in a property-owning fund.

property centre *n* a service for buying and selling property, including conveyancing, provided by a group of local solicitors. In full: **solicitors' property centre.**

property man *n* a member of the stage crew in charge of the stage properties. Usually shortened to **propman.**

prophecy ❶ ('prɒfɪsɪ) *n, pl* **prophecies. 1a** a message of divine truth revealing God's will. **1b** the act of uttering such a message. **2** a prediction or guess. **3** the charismatic endowment of a prophet. [C13: ult. from Gk *prophētēs* PROPHET]

prophesy ❶ ('prɒfɪˌsaɪ) *vb* **prophesies, prophesying, prophesied. 1** to foretell (something) by or as if by divine inspiration. **2** (*intr*) *Arch.* to give instructions in religious subjects. [C14 *prophecien,* from PROPHECY]
▸ **'propheˌsiable** *adj* ▸ **'propheˌsier** *n*

prophet ❶ ('prɒfɪt) *n* **1** a person who supposedly speaks by divine inspiration, esp. one through whom a divinity expresses his will. **2** a person who predicts the future: *a prophet of doom.* **3** a spokesman for a movement, doctrine, etc. [C13: from OF *prophète,* from L, from Gk *prophētēs* one who declares the divine will, from PRO-² + *phanai* to speak]
▸ **'prophetess** *fem n*

Prophet ('prɒfɪt) *n* **the. 1** the principal designation of Mohammed as the founder of Islam. **2** a name for Joseph Smith as the founder of the Mormon Church.

prophetic ❶ (prə'fɛtɪk) *adj* **1** of or relating to a prophet or prophecy. **2** of the nature of a prophecy; predictive.
▸ **pro'phetically** *adv*

prophylactic (ˌprɒfɪ'læktɪk) *adj* **1** protecting from or preventing disease. **2** protective or preventive. ◆ *n* **3** a prophylactic drug or device. **4** *Chiefly US.* another name for **condom.** [C16: via F from Gk *prophulaktikos,* from *prophulassein* to guard by taking advance measures, from PRO-² + *phulax* a guard]

prophylaxis (ˌprɒfɪ'læksɪs) *n* the prevention of disease or control of its possible spread.

propinquity (prə'pɪŋkwɪtɪ) *n* **1** nearness in place or time. **2** nearness in relationship. [C14: from L *propinquitās,* from *propinquus* near, from *prope* nearby]

propionic acid (ˌprəʊpɪ'ɒnɪk) *n* the former name for **propanoic acid.** [C19: from Gk *pro-* first + *pionic,* from *piōn* fat, because it is first in order of the fatty acids]

propitiate ❶ (prə'pɪʃɪˌeɪt) *vb* **propitiates, propitiating, propitiated.** (*tr*) to appease or make well disposed; conciliate. [C17: from L *propitiāre,* from *propitius* gracious]
▸ **pro'pitiable** *adj* ▸ **proˌpiti'ation** *n* ▸ **pro'pitiative** *adj* ▸ **pro'pitiˌator** *n* ▸ **pro'pitiatory** *adj*

propitious ❶ (prə'pɪʃəs) *adj* **1** favourable; auguring well. **2** gracious or favourably inclined. [C15: from L *propitius* well disposed, from *prope* close to]
▸ **pro'pitiously** *adv* ▸ **pro'pitiousness** *n*

propjet ('prɒpˌdʒɛt) *n* another name for **turboprop.**

propolis ('prɒpəlɪs) *n* a greenish-brown resinous aromatic substance collected by bees from the buds of trees for use in the construction of hives. Also called: **bee glue, hive dross.** [C17: via L from Gk: suburb, bee glue, from *pro-* before + *polis* city]

proponent ❶ (prə'pəʊnənt) *n* a person who argues in favour of something or puts forward a proposal, etc. [C16: from L *prōpōnere* to PROPOSE]

proportion ❶ (prə'pɔːʃən) *n* **1** relative magnitude or extent; ratio. **2** correct or desirable relationship between parts; symmetry. **3** a part considered with respect to the whole. **4** (*pl*) dimensions or size: *a building of vast proportions.* **5** a share or quota. **6** a relationship that maintains a constant ratio between two variable quantities: *prices increase in proportion to manufacturing costs.* **7** *Maths.* a relationship between four numbers or quantities in which the ratio of the first pair equals the ratio of the second pair. ◆ *vb* (*tr*) **8** to adjust in relative amount, size, etc. **9** to cause to be harmonious in relationship of parts. [C14: from L *prōportiō,* from *prō portione,* lit.: for (its, one's) PORTION]
▸ **pro'portionable** *adj* ▸ **pro'portionably** *adv* ▸ **pro'portionment** *n*

proportional ❶ (prə'pɔːʃənᵊl) *adj* **1** of, involving, or being in proportion. ◆ *n* **2** *Maths.* an unknown term in a proportion: *in $a/b = c/x$, x is the fourth proportional.*
▸ **proˌportion'ality** *n* ▸ **pro'portionally** *adv*

proportional representation *n* representation of parties in an elective body in proportion to the votes they win. Abbrev.: **PR.** Cf. **first-past-the-post.** See also **Additional Member System, Alternative Vote, party list, Single Transferable Vote.**

proportionate *adj* (prə'pɔːʃənɪt). **1** being in proper proportion. ◆ *vb* (prə'pɔːʃəˌneɪt), **proportionates, proportionating, proportionated. 2** (*tr*) to make proportionate.
▸ **pro'portionately** *adv*

proposal ❶ (prə'pəʊzᵊl) *n* **1** the act of proposing. **2** something proposed, as a plan. **3** an offer, esp. of marriage.

propose ❶ (prə'pəʊz) *vb* **proposes, proposing, proposed. 1** (when *tr, may take a clause as object*) to put forward (a plan, etc.) for consideration. **2** (*tr*) to nominate, as for a position. **3** (*tr*) to intend (to do something): *I propose to leave town now.* **4** (*tr*) to announce the drinking of (a toast). **5** (*intr;* often foll. by *to*) to make an offer of marriage. [C14: from OF *proposer,* from L *prōpōnere* to display, from PRO-¹ + *pōnere* to place]
▸ **pro'posable** *adj* ▸ **pro'poser** *n*

proposition ❶ (ˌprɒpə'zɪʃən) *n* **1** a proposal for consideration. **2** *Philosophy.* the content of a sentence that affirms or denies something and is capable of being true or false. **3** *Maths.* a statement or theorem, usually containing its proof. **4** *Inf.* a person or matter to be dealt with: *he's a difficult proposition.* **5** *Inf.* an invitation to engage in sexual intercourse. ◆ *vb* **6** (*tr*) to propose a plan, deal, etc., to, esp. to engage in

THESAURUS

rude, ungentlemanly, unladylike, unrefined, unseemly

properly *adv* **1 = suitably,** appropriately, aptly, deservedly, fittingly, legitimately, rightly **3 = politely,** decently, decorously, ethically, punctiliously, respectably, respectfully
Antonyms *adv* ≠ **suitably:** improperly, inappropriately, inaptly, unfittingly, unsuitably, wrongly ≠ **politely:** badly, disrespectfully, impolitely, improperly, indecently, indecorously, unethically

property *n* **1, 3 = possessions,** assets, belongings, building(s), capital, chattels, effects, estate, goods, holdings, house(s), means, resources, riches, wealth **4 = land,** acres, estate, freehold, holding, real estate, real property, realty, title **6 = quality,** ability, attribute, characteristic, feature, hallmark, idiosyncrasy, mark, peculiarity, trait, virtue

prophecy *n* **1, 2 = prediction,** augury, divination, forecast, foretelling, prognosis, prognostication, revelation, second sight, soothsaying, sortilege, vaticination (*rare*)

prophesy *vb* **1 = predict,** augur, call, divine, forecast, foresee, foretell, forewarn, presage, prognosticate, soothsay, vaticinate (*rare*)

prophet *n* **1, 2 = soothsayer,** augur, Cassandra, clairvoyant, diviner, forecaster, oracle, prognosticator, prophesier, seer, sibyl

prophetic *adj* **1, 2 = predictive,** augural, divinatory, fatidic (*rare*), foreshadowing, mantic, oracular, presaging, prescient, prognostic, sibylline, vatic (*rare*)

propitiate *vb* **= appease,** conciliate, make peace, mollify, pacify, placate, reconcile, satisfy

propitiation *n* **= appeasement,** conciliation, mollification, peacemaking, placation, reconciliation

propitiatory *adj* **= appeasing,** assuaging, conciliatory, pacificatory, pacifying, peacemaking, placative, placatory, propitiative, reconciliatory

propitious *adj* **1 = favourable,** advantageous, auspicious, bright, encouraging, fortunate, full of promise, happy, lucky, opportune, promising, prosperous, rosy, timely **2 = well-disposed,** benevolent, benign, favourably inclined, friendly, gracious, kind

proponent *n* **= supporter,** advocate, apologist, backer, champion, defender, enthusiast, exponent, friend, partisan, patron, spokesman *or* spokeswoman, subscriber, upholder, vindicator

proportion *n* **1 = relative amount,** distribution, ratio, relationship **2 = balance,** agreement, congruity, correspondence, harmony, symmetry **3, 5 = part,** amount, cut, division, fraction, measure, percentage, quota, segment, share **4** *plural* **= dimensions,** amplitude, breadth, bulk, capacity, expanse, extent, magnitude, measurements, range, scope, size, volume

proportional *adj* **1 = balanced,** commensurate, comparable, compatible, consistent, correspondent, corresponding, equitable, equivalent, even, in proportion, just
Antonyms *adj* different, discordant, disproportionate, dissimilar, incommensurable, incompatible, inconsistent, unequal

proposal *n* **2, 3 = suggestion,** bid, design, motion, offer, overture, plan, presentation, proffer, programme, project, proposition, recommendation, scheme, tender, terms

propose *vb* **1 = put forward,** advance, come up with, present, proffer, propound, submit, suggest, tender **2 = nominate,** introduce, invite, name, present, put up, recommend **3 = intend,** aim, design, have every intention, have in mind, mean, plan, purpose, scheme **5 = offer marriage,** ask for someone's hand (in marriage), pay suit, pop the question (*inf.*)

proposition *n* **1 = proposal,** motion, plan, programme, project, recommendation, scheme, suggestion ◆ *vb* **6 = make a pass at,** accost, make an improper suggestion, make an indecent proposal, solicit

sexual intercourse. [C14 *proposicioun,* from L *prōpositiō* a setting forth; see PROPOSE]
▸ˌpropoˈsitional *adj*

propositional calculus *n* the system of symbolic logic concerned only with the relations between propositions as wholes, taking no account of their internal structure. Cf. **predicate calculus.**

propositus (prəˈpɒzɪtəs) *or (fem)* **proposita** (prəˈpɒzɪtə) *n, pl* **propositi** (-ˌtaɪ) *or (fem)* **propositae** (-tiː). *Med.* the first patient to be investigated in a family study, to whom all relationships are referred. Also called (esp. US): **proband.**

propound ❶ (prəˈpaʊnd) *vb (tr)* **1** to put forward for consideration. **2** *English law.* to produce (a will or similar instrument) to the proper court or authority for its validity to be established. [C16 *propone,* from L *prōpōnere* to set forth, from PRO-[1] + *pōnere* to place]
▸**proˈpounder** *n*

propranolol (prəʊˈprænəˌlɒl) *n* a drug used in the treatment of heart disease.

proprietary (prəˈpraɪətərɪ, -trɪ) *adj* **1** of or belonging to property or proprietors. **2** privately owned and controlled. **3** *Med.* denoting a drug manufactured and distributed under a trade name. ◆ *n, pl* **proprietaries. 4** *Med.* a proprietary drug. **5** a proprietor or proprietors collectively. **6a** right to property. **6b** property owned. **7** (in Colonial America) an owner of a **proprietary colony,** a colony which was granted by the Crown to a particular person or group. [C15: from LL *proprietārius* an owner, from *proprius* one's own]
▸**proˈprietarily** *adv*

proprietary name *n* a name which is restricted in use by virtue of being a trade name.

proprietor ❶ (prəˈpraɪətə) *n* **1** an owner of a business. **2** a person enjoying exclusive right of ownership to some property.
▸**proprietorial** (prəˌpraɪəˈtɔːrɪəl) *adj* ▸**proˈprietress** *or* **proˈprietrix** *fem n*

propriety ❶ (prəˈpraɪətɪ) *n, pl* **proprieties. 1** the quality or state of being appropriate or fitting. **2** conformity to the prevailing standard of behaviour, speech, etc. **3 the proprieties.** the standards of behaviour considered correct by polite society. [C15: from OF *propriété,* from L *proprietās* a peculiarity, from *proprius* one's own]

proprioceptor (ˌprəʊprɪəˈsɛptə) *n Physiol.* any receptor, as in the gut, blood vessels, muscles, etc., that supplies information about the state of the body. [C20: from *proprio-,* from L *proprius* one's own + RECEPTOR]
▸ˌproprioˈceptive *adj*

proptosis (prɒpˈtəʊsɪs) *n, pl* **proptoses** (-siːz). *Pathol.* the forward displacement of an organ or part, such as the eyeball. [C17: via LL from Gk, from *propiptein* to fall forwards]

propulsion ❶ (prəˈpʌlʃən) *n* **1** the act of propelling or the state of being propelled. **2** a propelling force. [C15: from L *prōpellere* to propel]
▸**propulsive** (prəˈpʌlsɪv) *or* **proˈpulsory** *adj*

propyl (ˈprəʊpɪl) *n (modifier)* of or containing the monovalent group of atoms C_3H_7 -. [C19: from PROP(IONIC ACID) + -YL]

propylaeum (ˌprɒpɪˈliːəm) *or* **propylon** (ˈprɒpɪˌlɒn) *n, pl* **propylaea** (-ˈliːə) *or* **propylons, propyla** (-lə). a portico, esp. one that forms the entrance to a temple. [C18: via L from Gk *propulaion* before the gate, from PRO-[2] + *pulē* gate]

propylene (ˈprəʊpɪˌliːn) *n* another name for **propene.** [C19]

propylene glycol *n* a colourless viscous compound used as an antifreeze and brake fluid. Formula: $CH_3CH(OH)CH_2OH$. Systematic name: **1,2-dihydroxypropane.**

pro rata (ˈprəʊ ˈrɑːtə) in proportion. [Med. L]

prorate (prəʊˈreɪt, ˈprəʊreɪt) *vb* **prorates, prorating, prorated.** *Chiefly US & Canad.* to divide, assess, or distribute proportionately. [C19: from PRO RATA]
▸**proˈratable** *adj* ▸**proˈration** *n*

prorogue (prəˈrəʊg) *vb* **prorogues, proroguing, prorogued.** to discontinue the meetings of (a legislative body) without dissolving it. [C15: from L *prorogāre,* lit.: to ask publicly]
▸**prorogation** (ˌprəʊrəˈgeɪʃən) *n*

prosaic ❶ (prəʊˈzeɪɪk) *adj* **1** lacking imagination. **2** having the characteristics of prose. [C16: from LL *prōsaicus,* from L *prōsa* PROSE]
▸**proˈsaically** *adv*

pros and cons *pl n* the various arguments in favour of and against a motion, course of action, etc. [C16: from L *prō* for + *con,* from *contrā* against]

proscenium (prəˈsiːnɪəm) *n, pl* **proscenia** (-nɪə) *or* **prosceniums. 1** the arch or opening separating the stage from the auditorium together with the area immediately in front of the arch. **2** (in ancient theatres) the stage itself. [C17: via L from Gk *proskēnion,* from *pro-* before + *skēnē* scene]

prosciutto (prəʊˈʃuːtəʊ; *Italian* proˈʃutto) *n* cured ham from Italy: usually served as an hors d'oeuvre. [It., lit.: dried beforehand]

proscribe ❶ (prəʊˈskraɪb) *vb* **proscribes, proscribing, proscribed.** *(tr)* **1** to condemn or prohibit. **2** to outlaw; banish; exile. [C16: from L *prōscrībere* to put up a public notice, from *prō-* in public + *scrībere* to write]
▸**proˈscriber** *n* ▸**proscription** (prəʊˈskrɪpʃən) *n*

prose (prəʊz) *n* **1** spoken or written language distinguished from poetry by its lack of a marked metrical structure. **2** a passage set for translation into a foreign language. **3** commonplace or dull discourse, expression, etc. **4** *(modifier)* written in prose. **5** *(modifier)* matter-of-fact. ◆ *vb* **proses, prosing, prosed. 6** to write (something) in prose. **7** *(intr)* to speak or write in a tedious style. [C14: via OF from L *prōsa ōrātiō* straightforward speech, from *prorsus* prosaic, from *prōvertere* to turn forwards]
▸ˈ**proseˌlike** *adj*

prosecute ❶ (ˈprɒsɪˌkjuːt) *vb* **prosecutes, prosecuting, prosecuted. 1** *(tr)* to bring a criminal action against (a person). **2** *(intr)* **2a** to seek redress by legal proceedings. **2b** to institute or conduct a prosecution. **3** *(tr)* to practise (a profession or trade). **4** *(tr)* to continue to do (a task, etc.). [C15: from L *prōsequī* to follow]
▸ˈ**proseˌcutable** *adj* ▸ˈ**proseˌcutor** *n*

prosecution (ˌprɒsɪˈkjuːʃən) *n* **1** the act of prosecuting or the state of being prosecuted. **2a** the institution and conduct of legal proceedings against a person. **2b** the proceedings brought in the name of the Crown to put an accused on trial. **3** the lawyers acting for the Crown to put the case against a person. **4** the following up or carrying on of something begun.

proselyte ❶ (ˈprɒsɪˌlaɪt) *n* **1** a person newly converted to a religious faith, esp. a Gentile converted to Judaism. ◆ *vb* **proselytes, proselyting, proselyted. 2** a less common word for **proselytize.** [C14: from Church L *prosēlytus,* from Gk *prosēlutos* recent arrival, convert, from *proserchesthai* to draw near]
▸**proselytism** (ˈprɒsɪlɪˌtɪzəm) *n* ▸**proselytic** (ˌprɒsɪˈlɪtɪk) *adj*

proselytize ❶ *or* **proselytise** (ˈprɒsɪlɪˌtaɪz) *vb* **proselytizes, proselytizing, proselytized** *or* **proselytises, proselytising, proselytised.** to convert (someone) from one religious faith to another.
▸ˈ**proselytˌizer** *or* ˈ**proselytˌiser** *n*

prosencephalon (ˌprɒsɛnˈsɛfəlɒn) *n, pl* **prosencephala** (-lə). the part of the brain that develops from the anterior portion of the neural tube. Nontechnical name: **forebrain.** [C19: from NL, from Gk *prosō* forward + *enkephalos* brain]

prosenchyma (prɒsˈɛŋkɪmə) *n* a plant tissue consisting of long narrow cells with pointed ends: occurs in conducting tissue. [C19: from NL, from Gk *pros-* towards + *enkhuma* infusion]

prosimian (prəʊˈsɪmɪən) *n* **1** any of a primitive suborder of primates, including lemurs, lorises, and tarsiers. ◆ *adj* **2** of or belonging to this suborder. [C19: via NL from L *sīmia* ape]

prosit *German.* (ˈproːzɪt) *sentence substitute.* good health! cheers! [G, from L, lit.: may it prove beneficial]

prosody (ˈprɒsədɪ) *n* **1** the study of poetic metre and of the art of versification. **2** a system of versification. **3** the patterns of stress and intonation in a language. [C15: from L *prosōdia* accent of a syllable, from Gk *prosōidia* song set to music, from *pros* towards + *ōidē,* from *aoidē* song; see ODE]
▸**prosodic** (prəˈsɒdɪk) *adj* ▸ˈ**prosodist** *n*

prosopopoeia *or* **prosopopeia** (ˌprɒsəpəˈpiːə) *n* **1** *Rhetoric.* another word for **personification. 2** a figure of speech that represents an imaginary, absent, or dead person speaking or acting. [C16: via L from Gk *prosōpopoiia* dramatization, from *prosōpon* face + *poiein* to make]

THESAURUS

propound *vb* **1 = put forward,** advance, advocate, contend, lay down, postulate, present, propose, set forth, submit, suggest

proprietor *n* **1, 2 = owner,** deed holder, freeholder, landlord *or* landlady, landowner, possessor, titleholder

propriety *n* **1 = correctness,** appropriateness, aptness, becomingness, fitness, rightness, seemliness, suitableness **2 = decorum,** breeding, courtesy, decency, delicacy, etiquette, good form, good manners, modesty, politeness, protocol, punctilio, rectitude, refinement, respectability, seemliness **3 the proprieties = etiquette,** accepted conduct, amenities, civilities, niceties, rules of conduct, social code, social conventions, social graces, the done thing
Antonyms *n* ≠ **decorum:** bad form, bad manners, immodesty, impoliteness, indecency, indecorum, indelicacy, vulgarity

propulsion *n* **2 = drive,** impetus, impulse, impulsion, momentum, motive power, power, pressure, propelling force, push, thrust

prosaic *adj* **1 = dull,** banal, boring, commonplace, dry, everyday, flat, hackneyed, humdrum, matter-of-fact, mundane, ordinary, pedestrian, routine, stale, tame, trite, unimaginative, uninspiring, vapid, workaday
Antonyms *adj* entertaining, exciting, extraordinary, fascinating, imaginative, interesting, poetical, unusual

proscribe *vb* **1 = prohibit,** ban, boycott, censure, condemn, damn, denounce, doom, embargo, forbid, interdict, reject **2 = outlaw,** attaint *(arch.),* banish, blackball, deport, exclude, excommunicate, exile, expatriate, expel, ostracize
Antonyms *vb* ≠ **prohibit:** allow, authorize, endorse, give leave, give permission, license, permit, sanction, warrant

proscription *n* **1 = prohibition,** ban, boycott, censure, condemnation, damning, denunciation, dooming, embargo, interdict, rejection **2 = banishment,** attainder *(arch.),* deportation, ejection, eviction, exclusion, excommunication, exile, expatriation, expulsion, ostracism, outlawry

prosecute *vb* **1** *Law* **= put on trial,** arraign, bring action against, bring suit against, bring to trial, do *(sl.),* indict, litigate, prefer charges, put in the dock, seek redress, sue, summon, take to court, try **3 = conduct,** carry on, direct, discharge, engage in, manage, perform, practise, work at **4 = continue,** carry through, follow through, persevere, persist, pursue, see through

proselyte *n* **1 = convert,** catechumen, initiate, neophyte, new believer, novice, tyro

proselytize *vb* **= convert,** bring into the fold, bring to God, evangelize, make converts, propagandize, spread the gospel, win over

prospect ❶ *n* ('prɒspɛkt). **1** (*sometimes pl*) a probability of future success. **2** a view or scene. **3** a mental outlook. **4** expectation, or what one expects. **5** a prospective buyer, project, etc. **6** a survey or observation. **7** *Mining.* **7a** a known or likely deposit of ore. **7b** the location of a deposit of ore. **7c** the yield of mineral obtained from a sample of ore. ◆ *vb* (prə'spɛkt). **8** (when *intr*, often foll. by *for*) to explore (a region) for gold or other valuable minerals. **9** (*tr*) to work (a mine) to discover its profitability. **10** (*intr;* often foll. by *for*) to search (for). [C15: from L *prōspectus* distant view, from *prōspicere* to look into the distance]

prospective ❶ (prə'spɛktɪv) *adj* **1** looking towards the future. **2** (*prenominal*) expected or likely.
▸**pro'spectively** *adv*

prospector (prə'spɛktə) *n* a person who searches for gold, petroleum, etc.

prospectus ❶ (prə'spɛktəs) *n, pl* **prospectuses. 1** a formal statement giving details of a forthcoming event, such as the issue of shares. **2** a brochure giving details of courses, as at a school.

prosper ❶ ('prɒspə) *vb* (*usually intr*) to thrive, succeed, etc., or cause to thrive, etc., in a healthy way. [C15: from L *prosperāre* to succeed, from *prosperus* fortunate, from PRO-[1] + *spēs* hope]

prosperity ❶ (prɒ'spɛrɪtɪ) *n* the condition of prospering; success or wealth.

prosperous ❶ ('prɒspərəs) *adj* **1** flourishing; prospering. **2** wealthy.
▸**'prosperously** *adv*

prostaglandin (ˌprɒstə'glændɪn) *n* any of a group of hormone-like compounds found in all mammalian tissues, which stimulate the muscles of the uterus and affect the blood vessels; used to induce abortion or birth. [C20: from *prosta(te) gland* + -IN; orig. believed to be secreted by the prostate gland]

prostate ('prɒsteɪt) *n* **1** Also called: **prostate gland.** a gland in male mammals that surrounds the neck of the bladder and secretes a liquid constituent of the semen. ◆ *adj* **2** Also: **prostatic** (prɒ'stætɪk). of the prostate gland. ◆ See also **PSA.** [C17: via Med. L from Gk *prostatēs* something standing in front (of the bladder), from *pro-* in front + *histanai* to cause to stand]

prosthesis ('prɒsθɪsɪs) *n, pl* **prostheses** (-ˌsiːz). **1** *Surgery.* **1a** the replacement of a missing bodily part with an artificial substitute. **1b** an artificial part such as a limb, eye, or tooth. **2** *Linguistics.* another word for **prothesis.** [C16: via LL from Gk: an addition, from *prostithenai* to add, from *pros-* towards + *tithenai* to place]
▸**prosthetic** (prɒs'θɛtɪk) *adj* ▸**pros'thetically** *adv*

prosthetics (prɒs'θɛtɪks) *n* (*functioning as sing*) the branch of surgery concerned with prosthesis.

prostitute ❶ ('prɒstɪˌtjuːt) *n* **1** a woman who engages in sexual intercourse for money. **2** a man who engages in such activity, esp. in homosexual practices. **3** a person who offers his talent for unworthy purposes. ◆ *vb* **prostitutes, prostituting, prostituted.** (*tr*) **4** to offer (oneself or another) in sexual intercourse for money. **5** to offer for unworthy purposes. [C16: from L *prōstituere* to expose to prostitution, from *prō-* in public + *statuere* to cause to stand]
▸ˌ**prosti'tution** *n* ▸**'prostiˌtutor** *n*

prostrate ❶ *adj* ('prɒstreɪt). **1** lying face downwards, as in submission. **2** exhausted physically or emotionally. **3** helpless or defenceless. **4** (of a plant) growing closely along the ground. ◆ *vb* (prɒ'streɪt), **prostrates, prostrating, prostrated.** (*tr*) **5** to cast (oneself) down, as in submission. **6** to lay or throw down flat. **7** to make helpless. **8** to make exhausted. [C14: from L *prōsternere* to throw to the ground, from *prō-* before + *sternere* to lay low]
▸**pros'tration** *n*

prostyle ('prəʊstaɪl) *adj* **1** (of a building) having a row of columns in front, esp. as in the portico of a Greek temple. ◆ *n* **2** a prostyle building, portico, etc. [C17: from L *prostȳlos,* from Gk: with pillars in front, from PRO-[2] + *stulos* pillar]

prosy ❶ ('prəʊzɪ) *adj* **prosier, prosiest. 1** of the nature of or similar to prose. **2** dull, tedious, or long-winded.
▸**'prosily** *adv* ▸**'prosiness** *n*

Prot. *abbrev. for:* **1** Protectorate. **2** Protestant.

protactinium (ˌprəʊtæk'tɪnɪəm) *n* a toxic radioactive element that occurs in uranium ores and is produced by neutron irradiation of thorium. Symbol: Pa; atomic no.: 91; half-life of most stable isotope, ^{231}Pa: 32 500 years.

protagonist ❶ (prəʊ'tægənɪst) *n* **1** the principal character in a play, story, etc. **2** a supporter, esp. when important or respected, of a cause, party, etc. [C17: from Gk *prōtagōnistēs,* from *prōtos* first + *agōnistēs* actor]
▸**pro'tagonism** *n*

protasis ('prɒtəsɪs) *n, pl* **protases** (-siːz). **1** *Logic, grammar.* the antecedent of a conditional statement, such as *it rains* in *if it rains the game will be cancelled.* **2** (in classical drama) the introductory part of a play. [C17: via L from Gk: a proposal, from *pro-* before + *teinein* to extend]

protea ('prəʊtɪə) *n* a shrub of tropical and southern Africa, having flowers with coloured bracts arranged in showy heads. [C20: from NL, from *Proteus,* a sea god who could change shape, referring to the many forms of the plant]

protean ❶ (prəʊ'tiːən, 'prəʊtɪən) *adj* readily taking on various shapes or forms; variable. [C20: from *Proteus;* see PROTEA]

protease ('prəʊtɪˌeɪs) *n* any enzyme involved in proteolysis. [C20: from PROTEIN + -ASE]

protease inhibitor *n* any one of a class of antiviral drugs that impair the growth and replication of HIV by inhibiting the action of protease produced by the virus: used in the treatment of AIDS.

protect ❶ (prə'tɛkt) *vb* (*tr*) **1** to defend from trouble, harm, etc. **2** *Econ.* to assist (domestic industries) by the imposition of protective tariffs on imports. **3** *Commerce.* to provide funds in advance to guarantee payment of (a note, etc.). [C16: from L *prōtegere* to cover before]

protectant (prə'tɛktənt) *n* a chemical substance that affords protection, as against frost, rust, insects, etc.

protection ❶ (prə'tɛkʃən) *n* **1** the act of protecting or the condition of being protected. **2** something that protects. **3a** the imposition of duties on imports, for the protection of domestic industries against overseas competition, etc. **3b** Also called: **protectionism.** the system or theory of such restrictions. **4** *Inf.* **4a** Also called: **protection money.** money demanded by gangsters for freedom from molestation. **4b** freedom from molestation purchased in this way.
▸**pro'tectionˌism** *n* ▸**pro'tectionist** *n, adj*

protective ❶ (prə'tɛktɪv) *adj* **1** giving or capable of giving protection. **2**

THESAURUS

prospect *n* **1** *sometimes plural* = **likelihood,** chance, possibility **2** = **view,** landscape, outlook, panorama, perspective, scene, sight, spectacle, vision, vista **4** = **expectation,** anticipation, calculation, contemplation, future, hope, odds, opening, outlook, plan, presumption, probability, promise, proposal, thought ◆ *vb* **10** = **look for,** explore, go after, search for, seek, survey

prospective *adj* **1, 2** = **future,** about to be, anticipated, approaching, awaited, coming, destined, eventual, expected, forthcoming, hoped-for, imminent, intended, likely, looked-for, on the cards, possible, potential, soon-to-be, -to-be, to come, upcoming

prospectus *n* **1, 2** = **catalogue,** announcement, conspectus, list, outline, plan, programme, scheme, syllabus, synopsis

prosper *vb* = **succeed,** advance, be fortunate, bloom, do well, fare well, flourish, flower, get on, grow rich, make good, make it (*inf.*), progress, thrive

prosperity *n* = **success,** affluence, boom, ease, fortune, good fortune, good times, life of luxury, life of Riley (*inf.*), luxury, plenty, prosperousness, riches, the good life, wealth, well-being
Antonyms *n* adversity, depression, destitution, failure, indigence, misfortune, poverty, shortage, want

prosperous *adj* **1** = **successful,** blooming, booming, doing well, flourishing, fortunate, lucky, on a roll, on the up and up (*Brit.*), palmy, prospering, thriving **2** = **wealthy,** affluent, in clover (*inf.*), in the money (*inf.*), moneyed, opulent, rich, well-heeled (*inf.*), well-off, well-to-do
Antonyms *adj* ≠ **successful:** defeated, failing, inauspicious, unfavourable, unfortunate, unlucky, unpromising, unsuccessful, untimely ≠ **wealthy:** impoverished, poor

prostitute *n* **1** = **whore,** bawd (*arch.*), brass (*sl.*), call girl, camp follower, cocotte, courtesan, fallen woman, *fille de joie,* harlot, hooker (*US sl.*), hustler (*US & Canad. sl.*), loose woman, moll (*sl.*), pro (*sl.*), scrubber (*Brit. & Austral. sl.*), streetwalker, strumpet, tart (*inf.*), trollop, white slave, working girl (*facetious sl.*) ◆ *vb* **5** = **cheapen,** debase, degrade, demean, devalue, misapply, pervert, profane

prostitution *n* **1** = **harlotry,** harlot's trade, Mrs. Warren's profession, streetwalking, the game (*sl.*), the oldest profession, vice, whoredom

prostrate *adj* **1** = **prone,** abject, bowed low, flat, horizontal, kowtowing, procumbent **2** = **exhausted,** at a low ebb, dejected, depressed, desolate, drained, fagged out (*inf.*), fallen, inconsolable, overcome, spent, worn out **3** = **helpless,** brought to one's knees, defenceless, disarmed, impotent, overwhelmed, paralysed, powerless, reduced ◆ *vb* **5** = **bow down to,** abase oneself, bend the knee to, bow before, cast oneself before, cringe, fall at (someone's) feet, fall on one's knees before, grovel, kneel, kowtow, submit **7** = **lay low,** bring low, crush, depress, disarm, overcome, overthrow, overturn, overwhelm, paralyse, reduce, ruin **8** = **exhaust,** drain, fag out (*inf.*), fatigue, sap, tire, wear out, weary

prostration *n* **5** = **bow,** abasement, genuflection, kneeling, kowtow, obeisance, submission **7, 8** = **exhaustion,** collapse, dejection, depression, depth of misery, desolation, despair, despondency, grief, helplessness, paralysis, weakness, weariness

prosy *adj* **2** = **dull,** boring, commonplace, flat, humdrum, long, long-drawn-out, long-winded, monotonous, overlong, pedestrian, prosaic, prosing, stale, tedious, tiresome, unimaginative, uninteresting, wordy

protagonist *n* **1** = **leading character,** central character, hero *or* heroine, lead, principal **2** = **supporter,** advocate, champion, exponent, leader, mainstay, moving spirit, prime mover, standard-bearer, torchbearer

protean *adj* = **changeable,** ever-changing, many-sided, mercurial, multiform, mutable, polymorphous, temperamental, variable, versatile, volatile

protect *vb* **1** = **keep safe,** care for, chaperon, cover, cover up for, defend, foster, give sanctuary, guard, harbour, keep, look after, mount *or* stand guard over, preserve, safeguard, save, screen, secure, shelter, shield, stick up for (*inf.*), support, take under one's wing, watch over
Antonyms *vb* assail, assault, attack, betray, endanger, expose, expose to danger, threaten

protection *n* **1** = **safety,** aegis, care, charge, custody, defence, guardianship, guarding, preservation, protecting, safeguard, safekeeping, security **2** = **safeguard,** armour, barrier, buffer, bulwark, cover, guard, refuge, screen, shelter, shield

protective *adj* **1** = **protecting,** careful, cover-

Econ. of or intended for protection of domestic industries. ◆ *n* **3** something that protects. **4** a condom.
▸**pro'tectively** *adv* ▸**pro'tectiveness** *n*

protective coloration *n* the coloration of an animal that enables it to blend with its surroundings and therefore escape the attention of predators.

protector Ⓣ (prəˈtɛktə) *n* **1** a person or thing that protects. **2** *History.* a person who exercised royal authority during the minority, absence, or incapacity of the monarch.
▸**pro'tectress** *fem n*

Protector (prəˈtɛktə) *n* short for **Lord Protector**, the title borne by Oliver Cromwell (1653–58) and by Richard Cromwell (1658–59) as heads of state during the period known as the Protectorate.

protectorate (prəˈtɛktərɪt) *n* **1a** a territory largely controlled by but not annexed to a stronger state. **1b** the relation of a protecting state to its protected territory. **2** the office or period of office of a protector.

protégé Ⓣ *or (fem)* **protégée** (ˈprəʊtɪˌʒeɪ) *n* a person who is protected and aided by the patronage of another. [C18: from F *protéger* to PROTECT]

protein (ˈprəʊtiːn) *n* any of a large group of nitrogenous compounds of high molecular weight that are essential constituents of all living organisms. [C19: via G from Gk *prōteios* primary, from *protos* first + -IN]
▸ˌ**protein'aceous, pro'teinic,** *or* **pro'teinous** *adj*

pro tempore *Latin.* (ˈprəʊ ˈtɛmpərɪ) *adv, adj* for the time being. Often shortened to **pro tem** (ˈprəʊ ˈtɛm).

proteolysis (ˌprəʊtɪˈɒlɪsɪs) *n* the hydrolysis of proteins into simpler compounds by the action of enzymes. [C19: from NL, from *proteo-* (from PROTEIN) + -LYSIS]
▸**proteolytic** (ˌprəʊtɪəˈlɪtɪk) *adj*

protest Ⓣ *n* (ˈprəʊtɛst). **1a** public, often organized, manifestation of dissent. **1b** (*as modifier*): *a protest march.* **2** a formal or solemn objection. **3** a formal notarial statement drawn up on behalf of a creditor and declaring that the debtor has dishonoured a bill of exchange, etc. **4** the act of protesting. ◆ *vb* (prəˈtɛst). **5** (when *intr*, foll. by *against, at, about*, etc.; when *tr, may take a clause as object*) to make a strong objection (to something, esp. a supposed injustice or offence). **6** (when *tr, may take a clause as object*) to disagree; object: *"I'm O.K." she protested.* **7** (when *tr, may take a clause as object*) to assert in a formal or solemn manner. **8** (*tr*) *Chiefly US.* to object forcefully to: *leaflets protesting Dr King's murder.* **9** (*tr*) to declare formally that (a bill of exchange or promissory note) has been dishonoured. [C14: from L *prōtestārī* to make a formal declaration, from *prō-* before + *testārī* to assert]
▸**pro'testant** *adj, n* ▸**pro'tester** *or* **pro'testor** *n* ▸**pro'testingly** *adv*

Protestant (ˈprɒtɪstənt) *n* **a** an adherent of Protestantism. **b** (*as modifier*): *the Protestant Church.*

Protestantism (ˈprɒtɪstənˌtɪzəm) *n* the religion of any of the Churches of Western Christendom that are separated from the Roman Catholic Church and adhere substantially to principles established during the Reformation.

protestation Ⓣ (ˌprəʊtɛsˈteɪʃən) *n* **1** the act of protesting. **2** a strong declaration.

prothalamion (ˌprəʊθəˈleɪmɪən) *or* **prothalamium** *n, pl* **prothalamia** (-mɪə). a song or poem in celebration of a marriage. [C16: from Gk *pro-* before + *thalamos* marriage]

prothallus (prəʊˈθæləs) *or* **prothallium** (prəʊˈθælɪəm) *n, pl* **prothalli** (-laɪ) *or* **prothallia** (-lɪə). *Bot.* the small flat green disc of tissue that bears the reproductive organs of ferns, horsetails, and club mosses. [C19: from NL, from *pro-* before + Gk *thallus* a young shoot]

prothesis (ˈprɒθɪsɪs) *n, pl* **protheses** (-siːz). **1** a development of a language by which a syllable is prefixed to a word to facilitate pronunciation: *Latin "scala" gives Spanish "escala" by prothesis.* **2** *Eastern Orthodox Church.* the solemn preparation of the Eucharistic elements before consecration. [C16: via LL from Gk: a setting out in public, from *pro-* forth + *thesis* a placing]
▸**prothetic** (prəˈθɛtɪk) *adj* ▸**pro'thetically** *adv*

prothrombin (prəʊˈθrɒmbɪn) *n Biochemistry.* a zymogen found in blood that gives rise to thrombin on activation.

protist (ˈprəʊtɪst) *n* (in some classification systems) any organism belonging to a large group, including bacteria, protozoans, and fungi, regarded as distinct from plants and animals. The group is usually now restricted to protozoans, unicellular algae, and simple fungi. Cf. **protoctist.** [C19: from NL *Protista* most primitive organisms, from Gk *prōtistos* the very first, from *prōtos* first]

protium (ˈprəʊtɪəm) *n* the most common isotope of hydrogen, having a mass number of 1. [C20: NL, from PROTO- + -IUM]

proto- *or sometimes before a vowel* **prot-** *combining form.* **1** first: *protomartyr.* **2** primitive or original: *prototype.* **3** first in a series of chemical compounds: *protoxide.* [from Gk *prōtos* first, from *pro* before]

protocol Ⓣ (ˈprəʊtəˌkɒl) *n* **1** the formal etiquette and procedure for state and diplomatic ceremonies. **2** a record of an agreement, esp. in international negotiations, etc. **3a** an amendment to a treaty or convention. **3b** an annexe appended to a treaty to deal with subsidiary matters. **4** *Chiefly US.* a record of data or observations on a particular experiment or proceeding. **5** *Computing.* the set form in which data must be presented for handling by a particular computer configuration, esp. in the transmission of information between different computer systems. [C16: from Med. L *prōtocollum*, from LGk *prōtokollon* sheet glued to the front of a manuscript, from PROTO- + *kolla* glue]

protoctist (prəʊˈtɒktɪst) *n* (in modern biological classifications) any unicellular or simple multicellular organism belonging to the kingdom that includes protozoans, algae, and slime moulds. [C19: from NL *protoctista*, ?from Gk *prototokos* first born]

protohuman (ˌprəʊtəʊˈhjuːmən) *n* **1** any of various prehistoric primates that resembled modern man. ◆ *adj* **2** of these primates.

Proto-Indo-European *n* the prehistoric unrecorded language that was the ancestor of all Indo-European languages.

protomartyr (ˌprəʊtəʊˈmɑːtə) *n* **1** St Stephen as the first Christian martyr. **2** the first martyr to lay down his life in any cause.

proton (ˈprəʊtɒn) *n* a stable, positively charged elementary particle, found in atomic nuclei in numbers equal to the atomic number of the element. [C20: from Gk *prōtos* first]

protoplasm (ˈprəʊtəˌplæzəm) *n Biol.* the living contents of a cell: a complex translucent colourless colloidal substance. [C19: from NL, from PROTO- + Gk *plasma* form]
▸ˌ**proto'plasmic,** ˌ**proto'plasmal,** *or* ˌ**protoplas'matic** *adj*

prototype Ⓣ (ˈprəʊtəˌtaɪp) *n* **1** one of the first units manufactured of a product, which is tested so that the design can be changed if necessary before the product is manufactured commercially. **2** a person or thing that serves as an example of a type. **3** *Biol.* the ancestral or primitive form of a species.
▸ˌ**proto'typal, prototypic** (ˌprəʊtəˈtɪpɪk), *or* ˌ**proto'typical** *adj*

protozoan (ˌprəʊtəˈzəʊən) *n, pl* **protozoa** (-ˈzəʊə). **1** Also **protozoon.** any of various minute unicellular organisms formerly regarded as invertebrates of the phylum *Protozoa*, but now usually classified in certain phyla of protoctists. Protozoans include amoebas and foraminifers. ◆ *adj also* **protozoic. 2** of or belonging to protozoans. [C19: via NL from Gk PROTO- + *zoion* animal]

protract Ⓣ (prəˈtrækt) *vb* (*tr*) **1** to lengthen or extend (a speech, etc.). **2** (of a muscle) to draw, thrust, or extend (a part, etc.) forwards. **3** to plot using a protractor and scale. [C16: from L *prōtrahere* to prolong, from PRO-[1] + *trahere* to drag]
▸**pro'tracted** *adj* ▸**protractedly** *adv* ▸**pro'traction** *n*

protractile (prəˈtræktaɪl) *adj* able to be extended: *protractile muscle.*

protractor (prəˈtræktə) *n* **1** an instrument for measuring or drawing angles, usually a flat semicircular transparent plastic sheet graduated in degrees. **2** *Anat.* a former term for **extensor.**

protrude Ⓣ (prəˈtruːd) *vb* **protrudes, protruding, protruded. 1** to thrust forwards or outwards. **2** to project or cause to project. [C17: from L, from PRO-[2] + *trudere* to thrust]
▸**pro'trusion** *n* ▸**pro'trusive** *adj*

protrusile (prəˈtruːsaɪl) *adj Zool.* capable of being thrust forwards: *protrusile jaws.*

protuberant Ⓣ (prəˈtjuːbərənt) *adj* swelling out; bulging. [C17: from LL *prōtūberāre* to swell, from PRO-[1] + *tūber* swelling]
▸**pro'tuberance** *or* **pro'tuberancy** *n* ▸**pro'tuberantly** *adv*

proud Ⓣ (praʊd) *adj* **1** (foll. by *of*, an infinitive, or a clause) pleased or

THESAURUS

ing, defensive, fatherly, insulating, jealous, maternal, motherly, paternal, possessive, safeguarding, sheltering, shielding, vigilant, warm, watchful

protector *n* **1** = **defender**, advocate, benefactor, bodyguard, champion, counsel, guard, guardian, guardian angel, knight in shining armour, patron, safeguard, tower of strength

protégé *n* = **charge**, dependant, discovery, pupil, student, ward

protest *n* **1, 2** = **objection**, complaint, declaration, demur, demurral, disapproval, dissent, formal complaint, outcry, protestation, remonstrance ◆ *vb* **5, 6** = **object**, complain, cry out, demonstrate, demur, disagree, disapprove, expostulate, express disapproval, kick (against) (*inf.*), oppose, remonstrate, say no to, take exception, take up the cudgels **7** = **assert**, affirm, argue, asseverate, attest, avow, contend, declare, insist, maintain, profess, testify, vow

protestation *n* **1** = **objection**, complaint, disagreement, dissent, expostulation, outcry, protest, remonstrance, remonstration **2** = **declaration**, affirmation, asseveration, avowal, oath, pledge, profession, vow

protester *n* **5, 6** = **demonstrator**, agitator, dissenter, dissident, protest marcher, rebel

protocol *n* **1** = **code of behaviour**, conventions, courtesies, customs, decorum, etiquette, formalities, good form, manners, politesse, propriety, p's and q's, rules of conduct **2** = **agreement**, compact, concordat, contract, convention, covenant, pact, treaty

prototype *n* **1, 2** = **original**, archetype, example, first, mock-up, model, norm, paradigm, pattern, precedent, standard, type

protract *vb* **1** = **extend**, continue, drag on *or* out, draw out, keep going, lengthen, prolong, spin out, stretch out
Antonyms *vb* abbreviate, abridge, compress, curtail, reduce, shorten, summarize

protracted *adj* **1** = **extended**, dragged out, drawn-out, interminable, lengthy, long, long-drawn-out, never-ending, overlong, prolonged, spun out, time-consuming

protrude *vb* **1, 2** = **stick out**, bulge, come through, extend, jut, obtrude, point, pop (*of eyes*), project, shoot out, stand out, start (from), stick out like a sore thumb

protrusion *n* **1, 2** = **projection**, bulge, bump, hump, jut, lump, outgrowth, protuberance, swelling

protuberance *n* = **bulge**, bump, excrescence, hump, knob, lump, outgrowth, process, projection, prominence, protrusion, swelling, tumour

protuberant *adj* = **bulging**, beetling, bulbous, gibbous, hanging over, jutting, popping (*of eyes*), prominent, protruding, protrusive, proud (*dialect*), swelling, swollen
Antonyms *adj* concave, flat, indented, receding, sunken

proud *adj* **1, 2** = **satisfied**, appreciative, con-

satisfied, as with oneself, one's possessions, achievements, etc. **2** feeling honoured or gratified by some distinction. **3** having an inordinately high opinion of oneself; haughty. **4** characterized by or proceeding from a sense of pride: *a proud moment.* **5** having a proper sense of self-respect. **6** stately or distinguished. **7** bold or fearless. **8** (of a surface, edge, etc.) projecting or protruding. **9** (of animals) restive or excited, often sexually. ◆ *adv* **10 do (someone) proud. 10a** to entertain (someone) on a grand scale: *they did us proud at the hotel.* **10b** to honour (someone): *his honesty did him proud.* [LOE *prūd,* from OF *prud, prod* brave, from LL *prōde* useful, from L *prōdesse* to be of value]
▸**'proudly** *adv* ▸**'proudness** *n*

proud flesh *n* a mass of tissue formed around a healing wound.

Prov. *abbrev. for:* **1** Provençal. **2** *Bible.* Proverbs. **3** Province. **4** Provost.

prove Ⓣ (pruːv) *vb* **proves, proving, proved; proved** *or* **proven.** (*mainly tr*) **1** (*may take a clause as object or an infinitive*) to demonstrate the truth or validity of, esp. by using an established sequence of procedures. **2** to establish the quality of, esp. by experiment. **3** *Law.* to establish the genuineness of (a will). **4** to show (oneself) able or courageous. **5** (*copula*) to be found (to be): *this has proved useless.* **6** (*intr*) (of dough) to rise in a warm place before baking. [C12: from OF *prover,* from L *probāre* to test, from *probus* honest]
▸**'provable** *adj* ▸**'provably** *adv* ▸**ˌprova'bility** *n*

proven Ⓣ ('pruːvᵊn, 'prəʊ-) *vb* **1** a past participle of **prove. 2** See **not proven.** ◆ *adj* **3** tried; tested: *a proven method.*

provenance Ⓣ ('prɒvɪnəns) *n* a place of origin, as of a work of art. [C19: from F, from *provenir,* from L *prōvenīre* to originate, from *venīre* to come]

Provençal (ˌprɒvɒn'sɑːl; *French* prɔvɑ̃sal) *adj* **1** denoting or characteristic of Provence, a former province of SE France, its inhabitants, their dialect of French, or their Romance language. ◆ *n* **2** a language of Provence, closely related to French and Italian, belonging to the Romance group of the Indo-European family. **3** a native or inhabitant of Provence.

provender Ⓣ ('prɒvɪndə) *n* **1** fodder for livestock. **2** food in general. [C14: from OF *provendre,* from LL *praebenda* grant, from L *praebēre* to proffer]

proverb Ⓣ ('prɒvɜːb) *n* **1** a short memorable saying embodying some commonplace fact. **2** a person or thing exemplary of a characteristic: *Antarctica is a proverb for extreme cold.* **3** *Bible.* a wise saying providing guidance. [C14: via OF from L *prōverbium,* from *verbum* word]

proverbial Ⓣ (prə'vɜːbɪəl) *adj* **1** (*prenominal*) commonly or traditionally referred to as an example of some peculiarity, characteristic, etc. **2** of, embodied in, or resembling a proverb.
▸**pro'verbially** *adv*

provide Ⓣ (prə'vaɪd) *vb* **provides, providing, provided.** (*mainly tr*) **1** to furnish or supply. **2** to afford; yield: *this meeting provides an opportunity to talk.* **3** (*intr;* often foll. by *for* or *against*) to take careful precautions: *he provided against financial ruin by wise investment.* **4** (*intr;* foll. by *for*) to supply means of support (to): *he provides for his family.* **5** (of a person, law, etc.) to state as a condition; stipulate. **6** to confer and induct into ecclesiastical offices. [C15: from L *prōvidēre* to provide for, from *prō-* beforehand + *vidēre* to see]
▸**pro'vider** *n*

providence Ⓣ ('prɒvɪdəns) *n* **1a** *Christianity.* God's foreseeing protection and care of his creatures. **1b** such protection and care as manifest by some other force. **2** a supposed manifestation of such care and guidance. **3** the foresight or care exercised by a person in the management of his affairs.

Providence ('prɒvɪdəns) *n Christianity.* God, esp. as showing foreseeing care of his creatures.

provident Ⓣ ('prɒvɪdənt) *adj* **1** providing for future needs. **2** exercising foresight in the management of one's affairs. **3** characterized by foresight. [C15: from L *prōvidens* foreseeing, from *prōvidēre* to PROVIDE]
▸**'providently** *adv*

providential Ⓣ (ˌprɒvɪ'dɛnʃəl) *adj* characteristic of or presumed to proceed from or as if from divine providence.
▸**ˌprovi'dentially** *adv*

provident society *n* a mutual insurance society catering esp. for those on a low income, providing sickness, death, and pension benefits.

providing Ⓣ (prə'vaɪdɪŋ) *or* **provided** *conj* (*subordinating;* sometimes foll. by *that*) on the condition or understanding (that): *I'll play, providing you pay me.*

province Ⓣ ('prɒvɪns) *n* **1** a territory governed as a unit of a country or empire. **2** (*pl;* usually preceded by *the*) those parts of a country lying outside the capital and other large cities and regarded as outside the mainstream of sophisticated culture. **3** an area of learning, activity, etc. **4** the extent of a person's activities or office. **5** an ecclesiastical territory, having an archbishop or metropolitan at its head. **6** an administrative and territorial subdivision of a religious order. **7** *History.* a region of the Roman Empire outside Italy ruled by a governor from Rome. [C14: from OF, from L *prōvincia* conquered territory]

provincewide ('prɒvɪnsˌwaɪd) *Canad.* ◆ *adj* **1** covering or available to the whole of a province: *a provincewide referendum.* ◆ *adv* **2** throughout a province: *an advertising campaign to go provincewide.*

provincial Ⓣ (prə'vɪnʃəl) *adj* **1** of or connected with a province. **2** characteristic of or connected with the provinces. **3** having attitudes and opinions supposedly common to people living in the provinces; unsophisticated; limited. **4** *NZ.* denoting a football team representing a province, one of the historical administrative areas of New Zealand. ◆ *n* **5** a person lacking the sophistications of city life; rustic or narrow-minded individual. **6** a person coming from or resident in a province or the provinces. **7** the head of an ecclesiastical province. **8** the head of a territorial subdivision of a religious order.
▸**provinciality** (prəˌvɪnʃɪ'ælɪtɪ) *n* ▸**pro'vincially** *adv*

provincialism Ⓣ (prə'vɪnʃəˌlɪzəm) *n* **1** narrowness of mind; lack of sophistication. **2** a word or attitude characteristic of a provincial. **3** attention to the affairs of one's local area rather than the whole nation. **4** the state or quality of being provincial.

provirus ('prəʊˌvaɪrəs) *n* the inactive form of a virus in a host cell.

provision Ⓣ (prə'vɪʒən) *n* **1** the act of supplying food, etc. **2** something that is supplied. **3** preparations (esp. in **make provision for**). **4** (*pl*) food and other necessities, as for an expedition. **5** a condition or stipula-

THESAURUS

tent, contented, glad, gratified, honoured, pleased, self-respecting, well-pleased **3** = **conceited**, arrogant, boastful, disdainful, egotistical, haughty, high and mighty (*inf.*), imperious, lordly, narcissistic, orgulous (*arch.*), overbearing, presumptuous, self-important, self-satisfied, snobbish, snooty (*inf.*), stuck-up (*inf.*), supercilious, toffee-nosed (*sl., chiefly Brit.*), vain **4** = **glorious**, exalted, gratifying, illustrious, memorable, pleasing, red-letter, rewarding, satisfying **6** = **distinguished**, august, eminent, grand, great, illustrious, imposing, magnificent, majestic, noble, splendid, stately
Antonyms *adj* ≠ **satisfied:** discontented, displeased, dissatisfied ≠ **conceited:** abject, ashamed, deferential, humble, meek, modest, submissive, unobtrusive ≠ **distinguished:** base, humble, ignoble, ignominious, lowly, unassuming, undignified

provable *adj* **1, 2** = **verifiable**, attestable, demonstrable, evincible, testable

prove *vb* **1** = **verify**, ascertain, attest, authenticate, bear out, confirm, corroborate, demonstrate, determine, establish, evidence, evince, justify, show, show clearly, substantiate **2** = **test**, analyse, assay, check, examine, experiment, put to the test, put to trial, try **5** = **turn out**, be found to be, come out, end up, result
Antonyms *vb* ≠ **verify:** discredit, disprove, give the lie to, refute, rule out

proven *adj* **3** = **established**, accepted, attested, authentic, certified, checked, confirmed, definite, dependable, proved, reliable, tested, tried, trustworthy, undoubted, valid, verified

provenance *n* = **origin**, birthplace, derivation, source

provender *n* **1** = **fodder**, feed, forage **2** = **food**, comestibles, eatables, eats (*sl.*), edibles, fare, feed, foodstuffs, groceries, grub (*sl.*), nosebag (*sl.*), nosh (*sl.*), provisions, rations, supplies, sustenance, tack (*inf.*), victuals, vittles (*obs. or dialect*)

proverb *n* **1** = **saying**, adage, aphorism, apophthegm, byword, dictum, gnome, maxim, saw

proverbial *adj* **1** = **conventional**, accepted, acknowledged, archetypal, axiomatic, current, customary, famed, famous, legendary, notorious, self-evident, time-honoured, traditional, typical, unquestioned, well-known

provide *vb* **1** = **supply**, accommodate, cater, contribute, equip, furnish, outfit, provision, purvey, stock up **2** = **give**, add, afford, bring, impart, lend, present, produce, render, serve, yield **3** *often foll. by* **for** *or* **against** = **take precautions**, anticipate, arrange for, forearm, get ready, make arrangements, make plans, plan ahead, plan for, prepare for, take measures **4** *foll. by* **for** = **support**, care for, keep, look after, maintain, sustain, take care of **5** = **stipulate**, determine, lay down, require, specify, state
Antonyms *vb* ≠ **supply:** deprive, keep back, refuse, withhold ≠ **take precautions:** disregard, fail to notice, miss, neglect, overlook ≠ **support:** neglect

providence *n* **1** = **fate**, destiny, divine intervention, fortune, God's will, predestination **3** = **foresight**, care, caution, discretion, farsightedness, forethought, perspicacity, presence of mind, prudence

provident *adj* **1** = **thrifty**, economical, frugal, prudent **2, 3** = **foresighted**, canny, careful, cautious, discreet, equipped, far-seeing, farsighted, forearmed, sagacious, shrewd, vigilant, well-prepared, wise
Antonyms *adj* ≠ **thrifty:** improvident, imprudent, prodigal, profligate, spendthrift, thriftless, uneconomical, unthrifty, wasteful ≠ **foresighted:** careless, heedless, improvident, negligent, reckless, short-sighted, thoughtless

providential *adj* = **lucky**, fortuitous, fortunate, happy, heaven-sent, opportune, timely, welcome

provider *n* **1** = **supplier**, benefactor, donor, giver, source **4** = **breadwinner**, earner, mainstay, supporter, wage earner

providing *conj* = **on condition that**, as long as, contingent upon, given, if and only if, in case, in the event, on the assumption, subject to, upon these terms, with the proviso, with the understanding

province *n* **1** = **region**, colony, county, department, dependency, district, division, domain, patch, section, territory, tract, turf (*US sl.*), zone **4** = **area**, business, capacity, charge, concern, duty, employment, field, function, line, orbit, part, pigeon (*Brit. inf.*), post, responsibility, role, sphere, turf (*US sl.*)

provincial *adj* **2** = **rural**, country, hick (*inf., chiefly US & Canad.*), home-grown, homespun, local, rustic **3** = **parochial**, insular, inward-looking, limited, narrow, narrow-minded, parish-pump, small-minded, small-town (*chiefly US*), uninformed, unsophisticated, upcountry ◆ *n* **5** = **yokel**, country cousin, hayseed (*US & Canad. inf.*), hick (*inf., chiefly US & Canad.*), rustic
Antonyms *adj* ≠ **rural:** urban ≠ **parochial:** cosmopolitan, fashionable, polished, refined, sophisticated, urbane

provincialism *n* **1** = **narrow-mindedness**, insularity, lack of sophistication, parochialism, sectionalism **2** = **regionalism**, dialect, idiom, localism, patois, vernacularism

provision *n* **1** = **supplying**, accoutrement, ca-

tion incorporated in a document; proviso. **6** the conferring of and induction into ecclesiastical offices. ◆ *vb* **7** (*tr*) to supply with provisions. [C14: from L *prōvīsiō* a providing; see PROVIDE]
▸**pro'visioner** *n*

provisional ❶ (prə'vɪʒən°l) *adj* subject to later alteration; temporary or conditional: *a provisional decision.*
▸**pro'visionally** *adv*

Provisional (prə'vɪʒən°l) *adj* **1** designating one of the two factions of the IRA and Sinn Féin that have existed since a split in late 1969. The Provisional movement advocates terrorism to achieve Irish unity. ◆ *n* **2** Also called: **Provo.** a member of the Provisional IRA or Sinn Féin.

proviso ❶ (prə'vaɪzəʊ) *n, pl* **provisos** *or* **provisoes. 1** a clause in a document or contract that embodies a condition or stipulation. **2** a condition or stipulation. [C15: from Med. L *prōvīsō quod* it being provided that, from L *prōvīsus* provided]

provisory (prə'vaɪzərɪ) *adj* **1** containing a proviso; conditional. **2** provisional. **3** making provision.
▸**pro'visorily** *adv*

Provo ('prəʊvəʊ) *n, pl* **Provos.** another name for a **Provisional** (sense 2).

provocation ❶ (ˌprɒvə'keɪʃən) *n* **1** the act of provoking or inciting. **2** something that causes indignation, anger, etc.

provocative ❶ (prə'vɒkətɪv) *adj* serving or intended to provoke or incite, esp. to anger or sexual desire: *a provocative look; a provocative remark.*
▸**pro'vocatively** *adv*

provoke ❶ (prə'vəʊk) *vb* **provokes, provoking, provoked.** (*tr*) **1** to anger or infuriate. **2** to incite or stimulate. **3** to promote (anger, etc.) in a person. **4** to cause; bring about: *the accident provoked an inquiry.* [C15: from L *prōvocāre* to call forth]
▸**pro'voking** *adj* ▸**pro'vokingly** *adv*

provost ('prɒvəst) *n* **1** the head of certain university colleges or schools. **2** (in Scotland) the chairman and civic head of certain district councils or (formerly) of a burgh council. Cf. **convener** (sense 2). **3** *Church of England.* the senior dignitary of one of the more recent cathedral foundations. **4** *RC Church.* **4a** the head of a cathedral chapter. **4b** (formerly) the member of a monastic community second in authority under the abbot. **5** (in medieval times) an overseer, steward, or bailiff. [OE *profost,* from Med. L *prōpositus* placed at the head (of), from L *praepōnere* to place first]

provost marshal (prə'vəʊ) *n* the officer in charge of military police in a camp or city.

prow ❶ (praʊ) *n* the bow of a vessel. [C16: from OF *proue,* from L *prora,* from Gk *prōra*]

prowess ❶ ('praʊɪs) *n* **1** outstanding or superior skill or ability. **2** bravery or fearlessness, esp. in battle. [C13: from OF *proesce,* from *prou* good]

prowl ❶ (praʊl) *vb* **1** (when *intr,* often foll. by *around* or *about*) to move stealthily around (a place) as if in search of prey or plunder. ◆ *n* **2** the act of prowling. **3 on the prowl. 3a** moving around stealthily. **3b** pursuing members of the opposite sex. [C14 *prollen,* from ?]
▸**'prowler** *n*

prox. *abbrev. for* proximo (next month).

proximal ('prɒksɪməl) *adj Anat.* situated close to the centre, median line, or point of attachment or origin.
▸**'proximally** *adv*

proximate ('prɒksɪmɪt) *adj* **1** next or nearest in space or time. **2** very near; close. **3** immediately preceding or following in a series. **4** a less common word for **approximate.** [C16: from LL *proximāre* to draw near, from L *proximus* next, from *prope* near]
▸**'proximately** *adv*

proximity ❶ (prɒk'sɪmɪtɪ) *n* **1** nearness in space or time. **2** nearness or closeness in a series. [C15: from L *proximitās* closeness; see PROXIMATE]

proximo ('prɒksɪməʊ) *adv Now rare except when abbreviated in formal correspondence.* in or during the next or coming month: *a letter of the seventh proximo.* Abbrev.: **prox.** Cf. **instant, ultimo.** [C19: from L: in or on the next]

proxy ❶ ('prɒksɪ) *n, pl* **proxies. 1** a person authorized to act on behalf of someone else; agent: *vote by proxy.* **2** authority, esp. in the form of a document, given to a person to act on behalf of someone else. [C15 *prokesye,* from *procuracy,* from L *prōcūrātiō* procuration; see PROCURE]

PRP *abbrev. for:* **1** performance-related pay. **2** profit-related pay.

PRT *abbrev. for* petroleum revenue tax.

prude ❶ (pru:d) *n* a person who affects or shows an excessively modest, prim, or proper attitude, esp. regarding sex. [C18: from F, from *prudefemme,* from OF *prode femme* respectable woman; see PROUD]
▸**'prudery** *n* ▸**'prudish** *adj* ▸**'prudishly** *adv*

prudence ❶ ('pru:dəns) *n* **1** caution in practical affairs; discretion. **2** care taken in the management of one's resources. **3** consideration for one's own interests. **4** the quality of being prudent.

prudent ❶ ('pru:d°nt) *adj* **1** discreet or cautious in managing one's activities; circumspect. **2** practical and careful in providing for the future. **3** exercising good judgment. [C14: from L *prūdēns* far-sighted, from *prōvidens* acting with foresight; see PROVIDENT]
▸**'prudently** *adv*

prudential (pru:'dɛnʃəl) *adj* **1** characterized by or resulting from prudence. **2** exercising sound judgment.
▸**pru'dentially** *adv*

pruinose ('pru:ɪˌnəʊs, -ˌnəʊz) *adj Bot.* coated with a powdery or waxy bloom. [C19: from L *pruīnōsus* frost-covered, from *pruīna* hoarfrost]

prune[1] (pru:n) *n* **1** a purplish-black partially dried fruit of any of several varieties of plum tree. **2** *Sl., chiefly Brit.* a dull or foolish person. **3 prunes and prisms.** denoting an affected and mincing way of speaking. [C14: from OF *prune,* from L *prūnum* plum, from Gk *prounon*]

prune[2] ❶ (pru:n) *vb* **prunes, pruning, pruned. 1** to remove (dead or superfluous twigs, branches, etc.) from (a tree, shrub, etc.), esp. by cutting off. **2** to remove (anything undesirable or superfluous) from (a book, etc.). [C15: from OF *proignier* to clip, prob. from *provigner* to prune vines, ult. from L *propāgo* a cutting]
▸**'prunable** *adj* ▸**'pruner** *n*

prunella (pru:'nɛlə) *n* a strong fabric, esp. a twill-weave worsted, formerly used for academic gowns and the uppers of some shoes. [C17: ?from *prunelle,* a green French liqueur, with reference to the colour of the cloth]

pruning hook *n* a tool with a curved steel blade terminating in a hook, used for pruning.

THESAURUS

tering, equipping, fitting out, furnishing, providing, victualling **3** *As in* **make provision for** = **arrangement**, plan, prearrangement, precaution, preparation **4** *plural* = **food**, comestibles, eatables, eats (*sl.*), edibles, fare, feed, foodstuff, groceries, grub (*sl.*), nosebag (*sl.*), provender, rations, stores, supplies, sustenance, tack (*inf.*), viands, victuals, vittles (*obs. or dialect*) **5** = **condition**, agreement, clause, demand, proviso, requirement, rider, specification, stipulation, term

provisional *adj* = **temporary**, interim, pro tem, stopgap, transitional = **conditional**, contingent, limited, provisory, qualified, tentative
Antonyms *adj* ≠ **temporary:** permanent ≠ **conditional:** definite, fixed

proviso *n* **1, 2** = **condition**, clause, limitation, provision, qualification, requirement, reservation, restriction, rider, stipulation, strings

provocation *n* **2** = **cause**, *casus belli*, grounds, incitement, inducement, instigation, justification, motivation, reason, stimulus **2** = **offence**, affront, annoyance, challenge, dare, grievance, indignity, injury, insult, red rag, taunt, vexation

provocative *adj* = **offensive**, aggravating (*inf.*), annoying, challenging, disturbing, galling, goading, incensing, insulting, outrageous, provoking, stimulating = **suggestive**, alluring, arousing, erotic, exciting, inviting, seductive, sexy (*inf.*), stimulating, tantalizing, tempting

provoke *vb* **1** = **anger**, affront, aggravate (*inf.*), annoy, chafe, enrage, exasperate, gall, hassle (*inf.*), incense, infuriate, insult, irk, irritate, madden, make one's blood boil, offend, pique, put one's back up, put out, rile, try one's patience, vex **2, 4** = **rouse**, bring about, bring on *or* down, call forth, cause, draw forth, elicit, evoke, excite, fire, foment, generate, give rise to, incite, induce, inflame, inspire, instigate, kindle, lead to, motivate, move, occasion, precipitate, produce, promote, prompt, stimulate, stir
Antonyms *vb* ≠ **anger:** appease, calm, conciliate, mollify, pacify, placate, propitiate, quiet, soothe, sweeten ≠ **rouse:** abate, allay, assuage, blunt, curb, ease, lessen, lull, mitigate, moderate, modify, relieve, temper

provoking *adj* **1** = **annoying**, aggravating (*inf.*), exasperating, galling, irking, irksome, irritating, maddening, obstructive, offensive, tiresome, vexatious, vexing

prow *n* = **bow(s)**, fore, forepart, front, head, nose, sharp end (*jocular*), stem

prowess *n* **1** = **skill**, ability, accomplishment, adeptness, adroitness, aptitude, attainment, command, dexterity, excellence, expertise, expertness, facility, genius, mastery, talent **2** = **bravery**, boldness, courage, daring, dauntlessness, doughtiness, fearlessness, gallantry, hardihood, heroism, intrepidity, mettle, valiance, valour
Antonyms *n* ≠ **skill:** clumsiness, inability, incapability, incompetence, ineptitude, ineptness, inexpertise ≠ **bravery:** cowardice, faintheartedness, fear, gutlessness, timidity

prowl *vb* **1** = **move stealthily**, cruise, hunt, lurk, nose around, patrol, range, roam, rove, scavenge, skulk, slink, sneak, stalk, steal

proximity *n* **1** = **nearness**, adjacency, closeness, contiguity, juxtaposition, neighbourhood, propinquity, vicinity

proxy *n* **1** = **representative**, agent, attorney, delegate, deputy, factor, substitute, surrogate

prude *n* = **prig**, old maid (*inf.*), puritan, schoolmarm (*Brit. inf.*)

prudence *n* **1** = **common sense**, canniness, care, caution, circumspection, discretion, good sense, heedfulness, judgment, judiciousness, sagacity, vigilance, wariness, wisdom **2** = **thrift**, careful budgeting, economizing, economy, far-sightedness, foresight, forethought, frugality, good management, husbandry, planning, precaution, preparedness, providence, saving

prudent *adj* **1, 3** = **sensible**, canny, careful, cautious, circumspect, discerning, discreet, judicious, politic, sagacious, sage, shrewd, vigilant, wary, wise **2** = **thrifty**, canny, careful, economical, far-sighted, frugal, provident, sparing
Antonyms *adj* ≠ **sensible:** careless, heedless, impolitic, imprudent, inconsiderate, indiscreet, injudicious, irrational, rash, thoughtless, unwise ≠ **thrifty:** careless, extravagant, improvident, imprudent, wasteful

prudery *n* = **primness**, old-maidishness (*inf.*), overmodesty, priggishness, prudishness, puritanicalness, squeamishness, starchiness (*inf.*), strictness, stuffiness

prudish *adj* = **prim**, demure, formal, narrow-minded, niminy-piminy, old-maidish, overmodest, overnice, priggish, prissy (*inf.*), proper, puritanical, schoolmarmish (*Brit. inf.*), squeamish, starchy (*inf.*), strait-laced, stuffy, Victorian
Antonyms *adj* broad-minded, liberal, open-minded, permissive

prune[2] *vb* **1** = **cut**, clip, cut back, dock, lop, pare down, reduce, shape, shorten, snip, trim

prurient ❶ ('prʊərɪənt) *adj* **1** unusually or morbidly interested in sexual thoughts or practices. **2** exciting lustfulness. [C17: from L *prūrīre* to lust after, itch]
▸ **'prurience** *n* ▸ **'pruriently** *adv*

prurigo (prʊə'raɪgəʊ) *n* a chronic inflammatory disease of the skin characterized by intense itching. [C19: from L: an itch]
▸ **pruriginous** (prʊə'rɪdʒɪnəs) *adj*

pruritus (prʊə'raɪtəs) *n Pathol.* any intense sensation of itching. [C17: from L: an itching; see PRURIENT]
▸ **pruritic** (prʊə'rɪtɪk) *adj*

Prussian ('prʌʃən) *adj* **1** of Prussia, a former state in N Germany, or its people, esp. of the Junkers and their military tradition. ◆ *n* **2** a native or inhabitant of Prussia. **3 Old Prussian.** the extinct Baltic language of the non-German inhabitants of Prussia.

Prussian blue *n* **1** any of a number of blue pigments containing ferrocyanide or ferricyanide ions. **2a** the blue or deep greenish-blue colour of this. **2b** (*as adj*): *a Prussian-blue carpet.*

prussic acid ('prʌsɪk) *n* the extremely poisonous aqueous solution of hydrogen cyanide. [C18: from F *acide prussique* Prussian acid, because obtained from Prussian blue]

pry[1] ❶ (praɪ) *vb* **pries, prying, pried. 1** (*intr; often foll. by into*) to make an impertinent or uninvited inquiry (about a private matter, topic, etc.). ◆ *n, pl* **pries. 2** the act of prying. **3** a person who pries. [C14: from ?]

pry[2] (praɪ) *vb* **pries, prying, pried.** the US and Canad. word for **prise.** [C14: from ?]

pryer ('praɪə) *n* a variant spelling of **prier.**

Przewalski's horse (ˌpɜːʒə'vælskɪz) *n* a wild horse of W Mongolia, having an erect mane and no forelock: extinct in the wild, a few survive in captivity. [C19: after the Russian explorer Nikolai *Przewalski* (1839–88), who discovered it]

PS *abbrev. for:* **1** Passenger Steamer. **2** Police-Sergeant. **3** Also: **ps.** postscript. **4** private secretary. **5** prompt side.

Ps. *or* **Psa.** *Bible. abbrev. for* Psalm(s).

PSA *abbrev. for* prostatic specific antigen: an enzyme secreted by the prostate gland, increased levels of which are found in the blood of patients with cancer of the prostate.

psalm ❶ (sɑːm) *n* **1** (*often cap.*) any of the sacred songs that constitute a book (Psalms) of the Old Testament. **2** a musical setting of one of these. **3** any sacred song. [OE, from LL *psalmus,* from Gk *psalmos* song accompanied on the harp, from *psallein* to play (the harp)]
▸ **psalmic** ('sɑːmɪk, 'sæl-) *adj*

psalmist ('sɑːmɪst) *n* the composer of a psalm or psalms, esp. (when *cap.* and preceded by *the*) David, traditionally regarded as the author of The Book of Psalms.

psalmody ('sɑːmədɪ, 'sæl-) *n, pl* **psalmodies. 1** the act of singing psalms or hymns. **2** the art of setting psalms to music. [C14: via LL from Gk *psalmōdia* singing accompanied by a harp, from *psalmos* (see PSALM) + *ōidē* ODE]
▸ **'psalmodist** *n* ▸ **psalmodic** (sæl'mɒdɪk) *adj*

Psalter ('sɔːltə) *n* **1** another name for the Book of Psalms, esp. in the version in the Book of Common Prayer. **2** a translation, musical, or metrical version of the Psalms. **3** a book containing a version of Psalms. [OE *psaltere,* from LL *psaltērium,* from Gk *psaltērion* stringed instrument, from *psallein* to play a stringed instrument]

psalterium (sɔːl'tɪərɪəm) *n, pl* **psalteria** (-'tɪərɪə). the third compartment of the stomach of ruminants. Also called: **omasum.** [C19: from L *psaltērium* PSALTER; from the similarity of its folds to the pages of a book]

psaltery ('sɔːltərɪ) *n, pl* **psalteries.** *Music.* an ancient stringed instrument similar to the lyre, but having a trapezoidal sounding board over which the strings are stretched.

p's and q's *pl n* behaviour; manners (esp. in **mind one's p's and q's**). [altered from *p(lea)se and (than)k yous*]

PSBR (in Britain) *abbrev. for* public sector borrowing requirement; the money required by the public sector of the economy for expenditure on items that are not financed from income.

psephology (sɛ'fɒlədʒɪ) *n* the statistical and sociological study of elections. [C20: from Gk *psephos* pebble, vote + -LOGY, from the ancient Greeks' custom of voting with pebbles]
▸ **psephological** (ˌsɛfə'lɒdʒɪkˀl) *adj* ▸ **ˌpsepho'logically** *adv* ▸ **pse'phologist** *n*

pseud ❶ (sjuːd) *n* **1** *Inf.* a false or pretentious person. ◆ *adj* **2** another word for **pseudo.**

Pseudepigrapha (ˌsjuːdɪ'pɪgrəfə) *pl n* various Jewish writings from the first century B.C. to the first century A.D. that claim to have been divinely revealed but which have been excluded from the Greek canon of the Old Testament. [C17: from Gk *pseudepigraphos* falsely entitled, from PSEUDO- + *epigraphein* to inscribe]
▸ **Pseudepigraphic** (ˌsjuːdɛpɪ'græfɪk) *or* **ˌPseudepi'graphical** *adj*

pseudo ('sjuːdəʊ) *adj Inf.* not genuine.

pseudo- ❶ *or sometimes before a vowel* **pseud-** *combining form.* **1** false, pretending, or unauthentic: *pseudo-intellectual.* **2** having a close resemblance to: *pseudopodium.* [from Gk *pseudēs* false, from *pseudein* to lie]

pseudocarp ('sjuːdəʊˌkɑːp) *n* a fruit, such as the apple, that includes parts other than the ripened ovary.
▸ **ˌpseudo'carpous** *adj*

pseudomorph ('sjuːdəʊˌmɔːf) *n* a mineral that has an uncharacteristic crystalline form as a result of assuming the shape of another mineral that it has replaced.
▸ **ˌpseudo'morphic** *or* **ˌpseudo'morphous** *adj* ▸ **ˌpseudo'morphism** *n*

pseudonym ❶ ('sjuːdəˌnɪm) *n* a fictitious name adopted esp. by an author. [C19: via F from Gk *pseudōnumon*]
▸ **ˌpseudo'nymity** *n* ▸ **pseudonymous** (sjuː'dɒnɪməs) *adj*

pseudopodium (ˌsjuːdəʊ'pəʊdɪəm) *n, pl* **pseudopodia** (-dɪə). a temporary projection from the cell of a protozoan, etc., used for feeding and locomotion.

pseudovector (ˌsjuːdəʊ'vɛktə) *n Maths.* a variable quantity, such as angular momentum, that has magnitude and orientation with respect to an axis.

psf *abbrev. for* pounds per square foot.

pshaw (pʃɔː) *interj Becoming rare.* an exclamation of disgust, impatience, disbelief, etc.

psi[1] (psaɪ) *n* **1** the 23rd letter of the Greek alphabet (Ψ, ψ), a composite consonant, transliterated as *ps.* **2** paranormal or psychic phenomena collectively.

psi[2] *abbrev. for* pounds per square inch.

psilocybin (ˌsɪlə'saɪbɪn, ˌsaɪlə-) *n* a crystalline phosphate ester that is the active principle of the hallucinogenic fungus *Psilocybe mexicana.* Formula: $C_{12}H_{17}N_2O_4P$. [C20: from NL *Psilocybe* (from Gk *psilos* bare + *kubē* head) + -IN]

psi particle *n* See **J/psi particle.**

psittacine ('sɪtəˌsaɪn, -sɪn) *adj* of, relating to, or resembling a parrot. [C19: from LL *psittacīnus,* from L *psittacus* a parrot]

psittacosis (ˌsɪtə'kəʊsɪs) *n* a disease of parrots that can be transmitted to man, in whom it produces pneumonia. Also called: **parrot fever.** [C19: from NL, from L *psittacus* a parrot, from Gk *psittakos;* see -OSIS]

psoas ('səʊəs) *n* either of two muscles of the loins that aid in flexing and rotating the thigh. [C17: from NL, from Gk *psoai* (pl)]

psoriasis (sə'raɪəsɪs) *n* a skin disease characterized by the formation of reddish spots and patches covered with silvery scales. [C17: via NL from Gk: itching disease, from *psōra* itch]
▸ **psoriatic** (ˌsɔːrɪ'ætɪk) *adj*

psst (pst) *interj* an exclamation made to attract someone's attention, esp. one made surreptitiously.

PST (in the US and Canada) *abbrev. for* Pacific Standard Time.

PSV (in Britain) *abbrev. for* public service vehicle (now called passenger carrying vehicle).

psych *or* **psyche** (saɪk) *vb* **psychs** *or* **psyches, psyching, psyched.** (*tr*) *Inf.* to psychoanalyse. See also **psych out, psych up.** [C20: shortened from PSYCHOANALYSE]

psyche ❶ ('saɪkɪ) *n* the human mind or soul. [C17: from L, from Gk *psukhē* breath, soul]

psychedelic ❶ (ˌsaɪkɪ'dɛlɪk) *adj* **1** relating to or denoting new or altered perceptions or sensory experiences, as through the use of hallucinogenic drugs. **2** denoting any of the drugs, esp. LSD, that produce these effects. **3** *Inf.* (of painting, etc.) having the vivid colours and complex patterns popularly associated with the visual effects of psychedelic states. [C20: from PSYCHE + Gk *delos* visible]
▸ **ˌpsyche'delically** *adv*

psychiatry ❶ (saɪ'kaɪətrɪ) *n* the branch of medicine concerned with the diagnosis and treatment of mental disorders.
▸ **psychiatric** (ˌsaɪkɪ'ætrɪk) *or* **ˌpsychi'atrical** *adj* ▸ **ˌpsychi'atrically** *adv* ▸ **psy'chiatrist** *n*

psychic ❶ ('saɪkɪk) *adj* **1a** outside the possibilities defined by natural laws, as mental telepathy. **1b** (of a person) sensitive to forces not rec-

THESAURUS

prurient *adj* **1** = **lecherous,** concupiscent, desirous, hankering, itching, lascivious, libidinous, longing, lustful, salacious **2** = **indecent,** dirty, erotic, lewd, obscene, pornographic, salacious, smutty, steamy (*Inf.*), voyeuristic, X-rated (*inf.*)

pry[1] *vb* **1** = **be inquisitive,** be a busybody, be nosy (*inf.*), ferret about, interfere, intrude, meddle, nose into, peep, peer, poke, poke one's nose in *or* into (*inf.*), snoop (*inf.*)

prying *adj* **1** = **inquisitive,** curious, eavesdropping, impertinent, interfering, intrusive, meddlesome, meddling, nosy (*inf.*), snooping (*inf.*), snoopy (*inf.*), spying

psalm *n* **1, 3** = **hymn,** carol, chant, paean, song of praise

pseud *n* **1** *Informal* = **poser** (*inf.*), fraud, humbug, phoney *or* phony, trendy (*Brit. inf.*)

pseudo- *combining form* **1** = **false,** artificial, bogus, counterfeit, ersatz, fake, imitation, mock, not genuine, phoney *or* phony (*inf.*), pretended, quasi-, sham, spurious
Antonyms *adj* actual, authentic, bona fide, genuine, heartfelt, honest, real, sincere, true, unfeigned

pseudonym *n* = **false name,** alias, assumed name, incognito, nom de guerre, nom de plume, pen name, professional name, stage name

psyche *n* = **soul,** anima, essential nature, individuality, inner man, innermost self, mind, personality, pneuma (*Philosophy*), self, spirit, subconscious, true being

psychedelic *adj* **1, 2** = **hallucinogenic,** consciousness-expanding, hallucinatory, mind-bending (*inf.*), mind-blowing (*inf.*), mind-expanding, psychoactive, psychotomimetic, psychotropic **3** *Informal* = **multicoloured,** crazy, freaky (*sl.*), kaleidoscopic, wild

psychiatrist *n* = **psychotherapist,** analyst, headshrinker (*sl.*), psychoanalyser, psychoanalyst, psychologist, shrink (*sl.*), therapist

psychic *adj* **1** = **supernatural,** clairvoyant, extrasensory, mystic, occult, preternatural, tele-

ognized by natural laws. **2** mental as opposed to physical. ◆ *n* **3** a person who is sensitive to parapsychological forces or influences. ▸**'psychical** *adj* ▸**'psychically** *adv*

psycho ('saɪkəʊ) *n, pl* **psychos,** *adj* an informal word for **psychopath** or **psychopathic.**

psycho- *or sometimes before a vowel* **psych-** *combining form.* indicating the mind or psychological or mental processes: *psychology.* [from Gk *psukhē* spirit, breath]

psychoactive (ˌsaɪkəʊ'æktɪv) *adj* (of drugs such as LSD and barbiturates) capable of affecting mental activity. Also: **psychotropic.**

psychoanalyse *or esp. US* **psychoanalyze** (ˌsaɪkəʊ'ænəˌlaɪz) *vb* **psychoanalyses, psychoanalysing, psychoanalysed** *or US* **psychoanalyzes, psychoanalyzing, psychoanalyzed.** (*tr*) to examine or treat (a person) by psychoanalysis.

psychoanalysis (ˌsaɪkəʊə'nælɪsɪs) *n* a method of studying the mind and treating mental and emotional disorders based on revealing and investigating the role of the unconscious mind. ▸**psychoanalyst** (ˌsaɪkəʊ'ænəlɪst) *n* ▸**psychoanalytic** (ˌsaɪkəʊˌænə'lɪtɪk) *or* **ˌpsychoˌana'lytical** *adj* ▸**ˌpsychoˌana'lytically** *adv*

psychobiology (ˌsaɪkəʊbaɪ'ɒlədʒɪ) *n Psychol.* the attempt to understand the psychology of organisms in terms of their biological functions and structures. ▸**psychobiological** (ˌsaɪkəʊˌbaɪə'lɒdʒɪkᵊl) *adj* ▸**ˌpsychobi'ologist** *n*

psychochemical (ˌsaɪkəʊ'kemɪkᵊl) *n* **1** any of various chemicals whose primary effect is the alteration of the normal state of consciousness. ◆ *adj* **2** of such compounds.

psychodrama ('saɪkəʊˌdrɑːmə) *n* **1** *Psychiatry.* a form of group therapy in which individuals act out situations from their past. **2** a film, television drama, etc., in which the psychological development of the characters is emphasized.

psychodynamics (ˌsaɪkəʊdaɪ'næmɪks) *n* (*functioning as sing*) *Psychol.* the study of interacting motives and emotions. ▸**ˌpsychody'namic** *adj*

psychogenic (ˌsaɪkəʊ'dʒenɪk) *adj Psychol.* (esp. of disorders or symptoms) of mental, rather than organic, origin. ▸**ˌpsycho'genically** *adv*

psychokinesis (ˌsaɪkəʊkɪ'niːsɪs, -kaɪ-) *n* (in parapsychology) alteration of the state of an object supposedly by mental influence alone. [C20: from PSYCHO- + Gk *kinēsis* motion]

psycholinguistics (ˌsaɪkəʊlɪŋ'gwɪstɪks) *n* (*functioning as sing*) the psychology of language, including language acquisition by children, language disorders, etc. ▸**ˌpsycho'linguist** *n*

psychological ❶ (ˌsaɪkə'lɒdʒɪkᵊl) *adj* **1** of or relating to psychology. **2** of or relating to the mind or mental activity. **3** having no real or objective basis; arising in the mind: *his backaches are all psychological.* **4** affecting the mind. ▸**ˌpsycho'logically** *adv*

psychological moment *n* the most appropriate time for producing a desired effect.

psychological warfare *n* the application of psychology, esp. to attempts to influence morale in time of war.

psychologize *or US* **psychologise** (saɪ'kɒləˌdʒaɪz) *vb* **psychologizes, psychologizing, psychologized** *or US* **psychologises, psychologising, psychologised.** (*intr*) **1** to make interpretations of mental processes. **2** to carry out investigation in psychology.

psychology ❶ (saɪ'kɒlədʒɪ) *n, pl* **psychologies. 1** the scientific study of all forms of human and animal behaviour. **2** *Inf.* the mental make-up of an individual that causes him to think or act in the way he does. ▸**psy'chologist** *n*

psychometrics (ˌsaɪkəʊ'metrɪks) *n* (*functioning as sing*) **1** the branch of psychology concerned with the design and use of psychological tests. **2** the application of statistical techniques to psychological testing.

psychometry (saɪ'kɒmɪtrɪ) *n Psychol.* **1** measurement and testing of mental states and processes. **2** (in parapsychology) the supposed ability to deduce facts about events by touching objects related to them. ▸**psychometric** (ˌsaɪkəʊ'metrɪk) *or* **ˌpsycho'metrical** *adj* ▸**ˌpsycho'metrically** *adv*

psychomotor (ˌsaɪkəʊ'məʊtə) *adj* of, relating to, or characterizing movements of the body associated with mental activity.

psychoneurosis (ˌsaɪkəʊnjʊ'rəʊsɪs) *n, pl* **psychoneuroses** (-'rəʊsiːz). another word for **neurosis.**

psychopath ❶ ('saɪkəʊˌpæθ) *n* a person with a personality disorder characterized by a tendency to commit antisocial and sometimes violent acts without feeling guilt. ▸**ˌpsycho'pathic** *adj* ▸**ˌpsycho'pathically** *adv*

psychopathology (ˌsaɪkəʊpə'θɒlədʒɪ) *n* the scientific study of mental disorders. ▸**psychopathological** (ˌsaɪkəʊˌpæθə'lɒdʒɪkᵊl) *adj*

psychopathy (saɪ'kɒpəθɪ) *n* any mental disorder or disease.

psychopharmacology (ˌsaɪkəʊˌfɑːmə'kɒlədʒɪ) *n* the study of drugs that affect the mind.

psychophysics (ˌsaɪkəʊ'fɪzɪks) *n* (*functioning as sing*) the branch of psychology concerned with the relationship between physical stimuli and their effects in the mind. ▸**ˌpsycho'physical** *adj*

psychophysiology (ˌsaɪkəʊˌfɪzɪ'ɒlədʒɪ) *n* the branch of psychology concerned with the physiological basis of mental processes. ▸**psychophysiological** (ˌsaɪkəʊˌfɪzɪə'lɒdʒɪkᵊl) *adj*

psychosexual (ˌsaɪkəʊ'seksjʊəl) *adj* of or relating to the mental aspects of sex, such as sexual fantasies. ▸**ˌpsycho'sexually** *adv*

psychosis (saɪ'kəʊsɪs) *n, pl* **psychoses** (-'kəʊsiːz). any form of severe mental disorder in which the individual's contact with reality becomes highly distorted. [C19: NL, from PSYCHO- + -OSIS]

psychosocial (ˌsaɪkəʊ'səʊʃəl) *adj* of or relating to processes or factors that are both social and psychological in origin.

psychosomatic (ˌsaɪkəʊsə'mætɪk) *adj* of disorders, such as stomach ulcers, thought to be caused or aggravated by psychological factors such as stress.

psychosurgery (ˌsaɪkəʊ'sɜːdʒərɪ) *n* any surgical procedure on the brain, such as a frontal lobotomy, to relieve serious mental disorders. ▸**psychosurgical** (ˌsaɪkəʊ'sɜːdʒɪkᵊl) *adj*

psychotherapy (ˌsaɪkəʊ'θerəpɪ) *n* the treatment of nervous disorders by psychological methods. ▸**ˌpsychoˌthera'peutic** *adj* ▸**ˌpsychoˌthera'peutically** *adv* ▸**ˌpsycho'therapist** *n*

psychotic ❶ (saɪ'kɒtɪk) *Psychiatry.* ◆ *adj* **1** of or characterized by psychosis. ◆ *n* **2** a person suffering from psychosis. ▸**psy'chotically** *adv*

psychotomimetic (saɪˌkɒtəʊmɪ'metɪk) *adj* (of drugs such as LSD and mescaline) capable of inducing psychotic symptoms.

psych out *vb* (*mainly tr, adv*) *Inf.* **1** to guess correctly the intentions of (another). **2** to analyse (a problem, etc.) psychologically. **3** to intimidate or frighten.

psychrometer (saɪ'krɒmɪtə) *n* a type of hygrometer consisting of two thermometers, one of which has a dry bulb and the other a bulb that is kept moist and ventilated.

psych up *vb* (*tr, adv*) *Inf.* to get (oneself or another) into a state of psychological readiness for an action, performance, etc.

pt *abbrev. for:* **1** part. **2** patient. **3** payment. **4** point. **5** port. **6** pro tempore.

Pt *abbrev. for* (in place names): **1** Point. **2** Port. ◆ **3.** *the chemical symbol for* platinum.

PT *abbrev. for:* **1** physical therapy. **2** physical training. **3** postal telegraph.

pt. *abbrev. for:* **1** pint. **2** preterite.

PTA *abbrev. for:* **1** Parent-Teacher Association. **2** (in Britain) Passenger Transport Authority.

ptarmigan ('tɑːmɪgən) *n, pl* **ptarmigans** *or* **ptarmigan.** any of several arctic and subarctic grouse, esp. one which has a white winter plumage. [C16: changed (? infl. by Gk *pteron* wing) from Scot. Gaelic *tarmachan,* from ?]

Pte *Mil. abbrev. for* private.

pteridology (ˌterɪ'dɒlədʒɪ) *n* the branch of botany concerned with the study of ferns. [C19: from *pterido-,* from Gk *pteris* fern + -LOGY] ▸**pteridological** (ˌterɪdəʊ'lɒdʒɪkᵊl) *adj*

pteridophyte ('terɪdəʊˌfaɪt) *n* (in traditional classification) a plant, such as a fern, horsetail, or club moss, reproducing by spores and having vascular tissue, roots, stems, and leaves. In modern classifications these plants are placed in separate phyla. [C19: from *pterido-,* from Gk *pteris* fern + -PHYTE]

ptero- *combining form.* a wing, or a part resembling a wing: *pterodactyl.* [from Gk *pteron*]

pterodactyl (ˌterə'dæktɪl) *n* an extinct flying reptile having membranous wings supported on an elongated fourth digit.

pteropod ('terəˌpɒd) *n* a small marine gastropod mollusc in which the foot is expanded into two winglike lobes for swimming. Also called: **sea butterfly.**

pterosaur ('terəˌsɔː) *n* any of an order of extinct flying reptiles of Jurassic and Cretaceous times: included the pterodactyls.

-pterous *or* **-pteran** *adj combining form.* indicating a specified number or type of wings: *dipterous.* [from Gk *-pteros,* from *pteron* wing]

pterygoid process ('terɪˌgɔɪd) *n Anat.* either of two long bony plates extending downwards from each side of the sphenoid bone within the skull. [C18 *pterygoid,* from Gk *pterugoeidēs,* from *pterux* wing; see -OID]

PTN *abbrev. for* public telephone network: the telephone network provided in Britain by British Telecom.

PTO *or* **pto** *abbrev. for* please turn over.

Ptolemaic (ˌtɒlɪ'meɪɪk) *adj* **1** of or relating to the ancient astronomer Ptolemy, 2nd-century A.D. Greek astronomer, or to his conception of the universe. **2** of or relating to the Macedonian dynasty that ruled

THESAURUS

kinetic, telepathic **2** = **mental,** psychogenic, psychological, spiritual

psychological *adj* **2** = **mental,** cerebral, cognitive, intellectual **3** = **imaginary,** all in the mind, emotional, irrational, psychosomatic, subconscious, subjective, unconscious, unreal

psychology *n* **1** = **behaviourism,** science of mind, study of personality **2** *Informal* = **way of thinking,** attitude, mental make-up, mental processes, thought processes, what makes one tick

psychopath *n* = **madman,** headbanger (*inf.*), headcase (*inf.*), insane person, lunatic, maniac, mental case (*sl.*), nutcase (*sl.*), nutter (*Brit. sl.*), psychotic, sociopath

psychotic *adj* **1** = **mad,** certifiable, demented, deranged, insane, lunatic, mental (*sl.*), *non compos mentis,* not right in the head, off one's head (*sl.*), psychopathic, round the bend (*Brit. sl.*), unbalanced

Egypt from the death of Alexander the Great (323 B.C.) to the death of Cleopatra (30 B.C.).

Ptolemaic system *n* the theory of planetary motion developed by Ptolemy from the hypotheses of earlier philosophers, stating that the earth lay at the centre of the universe with the sun, the moon, and the known planets revolving around it in complicated orbits. Beyond the largest of these orbits lay a sphere of fixed stars.

ptomaine *or* **ptomain** ('təʊmeɪn) *n* any of a group of amines formed by decaying organic matter. [C19: from It. *ptomaina,* from Gk *ptoma* corpse, from *piptein* to fall]

ptomaine poisoning *n* a popular term for **food poisoning.** Ptomaines were once erroneously thought to be a cause of food poisoning.

ptosis ('təʊsɪs) *n, pl* **ptoses** ('təʊsiːz). prolapse or drooping of a part, esp. the eyelid. [C18: from Gk: a falling]
▸**ptotic** ('tɒtɪk) *adj*

PTSD *abbrev. for* post-traumatic stress disorder.

pty *Austral., NZ, & S. African. abbrev. for* proprietary.

ptyalin ('taɪəlɪn) *n Biochemistry.* an amylase secreted in the saliva of man and other animals. [C19: from Gk *ptualon* saliva, from *ptuein* to spit]

p-type *adj* **1** (of a semiconductor) having a density of mobile holes in excess of that of conduction electrons. **2** associated with or resulting from the movement of holes in a semiconductor: *p-type conductivity.*

Pu *the chemical symbol for* plutonium.

pub ➊ (pʌb) *n* **1** *Chiefly Brit.* a building with a bar and one or more public rooms licensed for the sale and consumption of alcoholic drink, often also providing light meals. Formal name: **public house. 2** *Austral. & NZ.* a hotel. ◆ *vb* **pubs, pubbing, pubbed. 3** *(intr) Inf.* to visit a pub or pubs (esp. in **go pubbing**).

pub. *abbrev. for:* **1** public. **2** publication. **3** published. **4** publisher. **5** publishing.

pub-crawl *Inf., chiefly Brit.* ◆ *n* **1** a drinking tour of a number of pubs or bars. ◆ *vb* **2** *(intr)* to make such a tour.

puberty ➊ ('pjuːbətɪ) *n* the period at the beginning of adolescence when the sex glands become functional. Also called: **pubescence.** [C14: from L *pūbertās* maturity, from *pūber* adult]
▸'**pubertal** *adj*

pubes ('pjuːbiːz) *n, pl* **pubes. 1** the region above the external genital organs, covered with hair from the time of puberty. **2** pubic hair. **3** the pubic bones. **4** the plural of **pubis.** [from L]

pubescent (pjuː'bes°nt) *adj* **1** arriving or arrived at puberty. **2** (of certain plants and animals or their parts) covered with a layer of fine short hairs or down. [C17: from L *pūbēscere* to reach manhood, from *pūber* adult]
▸**pu'bescence** *n*

pubic ('pjuːbɪk) *adj* of or relating to the pubes or pubis: *pubic hair.*

pubis ('pjuːbɪs) *n, pl* **pubes.** one of the three sections of the hipbone that forms part of the pelvis. [C16: shortened from NL *os pūbis* bone of the PUBES]

public ➊ ('pʌblɪk) *adj* **1** of or concerning the people as a whole. **2** open to all: *public gardens.* **3** performed or made openly: *public proclamation.* **4** *(prenominal)* well-known: *a public figure.* **5** *(usually prenominal)* maintained at the expense of, serving, or for the use of a community: *a public library.* **6** open, acknowledged, or notorious: *a public scandal.* **7** **go public.** (of a private company) to issue shares for subscription by the public. ◆ *n* **8** the community or people in general. **9** a section of the community grouped because of a common interest, activity, etc.: *the racing public.* [C15: from L *pūblicus,* changed from *pōplicus* of the people, from *populus* people]
▸'**publicly** *adv*

public-address system *n* a system of microphones, amplifiers, and loudspeakers for increasing the sound level, used in auditoriums, public gatherings, etc. Sometimes shortened to **PA system.**

publican ('pʌblɪkən) *n* **1** (in Britain) a person who keeps a public house. **2** (in ancient Rome) a public contractor, esp. one who farmed the taxes of a province. [C12: from OF *publicain,* from L *pūblicānus* tax gatherer, from *pūblicum* state revenues]

publication ➊ (ˌpʌblɪ'keɪʃən) *n* **1** the act or process of publishing a printed work. **2** any printed work offered for sale or distribution. **3** the act or an instance of making information public. [C14: via OF from L *pūblicātiō* confiscation of property, from *pūblicāre* to seize for public use]

public bar *n Brit.* a bar in a public house usually serving drinks at a cheaper price than in the lounge bar.

public company *n* a limited company whose shares may be purchased by the public and traded freely on the open market and whose share capital is not less than a statutory minimum; public limited company. Cf. **private company.**

public convenience *n* a public lavatory.

public corporation *n* (in Britain) an organization established to run a nationalized industry or state-owned enterprise. The chairman and board members are appointed by a government minister, and the government has overall control.

public domain *n* **1** the status of a published work upon which the copyright has expired or which has not been subject to copyright. **2** **in the public domain.** generally known or accessible.

public enemy *n* a notorious person, such as a criminal, who is regarded as a menace to the public.

public house *n* **1** *Brit.* the formal name for a **pub. 2** *US & Canad.* an inn, tavern, or small hotel.

publicist ('pʌblɪsɪst) *n* **1** a person who publicizes something, esp. a press or publicity agent. **2** a journalist. **3** *Rare.* a person learned in public or international law.

publicity ➊ (pʌ'blɪsɪtɪ) *n* **1a** the technique or process of attracting public attention to people, products, etc., as by the use of the mass media. **1b** *(as modifier): a publicity agent.* **2** public interest aroused by such a technique or process. **3** information used to draw public attention to people, products, etc. **4** the state of being public. [C18: via F from Med. L *pūblicitās;* see PUBLIC]

publicize ➊ *or* **publicise** ('pʌblɪˌsaɪz) *vb* **publicizes, publicizing, publicized** *or* **publicises, publicising, publicised.** *(tr)* to bring to public notice; advertise.

Public Lending Right *n* the right of authors to receive payment when their books are borrowed from public libraries.

public-liability insurance *n* (in Britain) a form of insurance, compulsory for any business in contact with the public, which pays compensation to a member of the public suffering injury or damage as a result of the policyholder or his employees failing to take reasonable care.

public limited company *n* another name for **public company.** Abbrev.: **plc** *or* **PLC.**

public nuisance *n* **1** *Law.* an illegal act causing harm to members of a community rather than to any individual. **2** *Inf.* a person generally considered objectionable.

public opinion *n* the attitude of the public, esp. as a factor in determining action, policy, etc.

public prosecutor *n Law.* an official in charge of prosecuting important cases.

Public Record Office *n* an institution in which official records are stored and kept available for inspection by the public.

public relations *n (functioning as sing or pl)* **1a** the practice of creating, promoting, or maintaining goodwill and a favourable image among the public towards an institution, public body, etc. **1b** the professional staff employed for this purpose. Abbrev.: **PR. 1c** the techniques employed. **1d** *(as modifier): the public-relations industry.* **2** the relationship between an organization and the public.

public school *n* **1** (in England and Wales) a private independent fee-paying secondary school. **2** in certain Canadian provinces, a public elementary school as distinguished from a separate school. **3** (in the US) any school that is part of a free local educational system.

public sector *n* the part of an economy which consists of state-owned institutions, including nationalized industries and services provided by local authorities.

public servant *n* **1** an elected or appointed holder of a public office. **2** the Austral. and NZ equivalent of **civil servant.**

public service *n* the Austral. and NZ equivalent of the **civil service.**

public-spirited ➊ *adj* having or showing active interest in the good of the community.

public utility *n* an enterprise concerned with the provision to the public of essentials, such as electricity or water. Also called (in the US): **public-service corporation.**

public works *pl n* engineering projects and other constructions, financed and undertaken by a government for the community.

publish ➊ ('pʌblɪʃ) *vb* **1** to produce and issue (printed matter) for distribution and sale. **2** *(intr)* to have one's written work issued for publica-

THESAURUS

pub 1 *n* = **tavern**, alehouse *(arch.)*, bar, boozer *(Brit., Austral., & NZ inf.)*, hostelry, inn, local *(Brit. inf.)*, roadhouse, taproom, watering hole *(facetious sl.)*

puberty *n* = **adolescence**, awkward age, juvenescence, pubescence, teenage, teens, young adulthood

public *adj* 1 = **general**, civic, civil, common, national, popular, social, state, universal, widespread 2 = **open**, accessible, communal, community, free to all, not private, open to the public, unrestricted 4 = **well-known**, important, prominent, respected 5 = **known**, acknowledged, exposed, in circulation, notorious, obvious, open, overt, patent, plain, published, recognized ◆ *n* 8 = **people**, citizens, commonalty, community, country, electorate, everyone, hoi polloi, Joe (and Eileen) Public *(sl.)*, Joe Six-Pack *(US sl.)*, masses, multitude, nation, populace, population, society, voters 9 = **clientele**, audience, buyers, followers, following, patrons, supporters, those interested, trade
Antonyms *adj* ≠ **open:** barred, closed, exclusive, inaccessible, personal, private, restricted, unavailable ≠ **known:** hidden, secluded, secret, unknown, unrevealed

publication *n* 1, 3 = **announcement**, advertisement, airing, appearance, broadcasting, declaration, disclosure, dissemination, notification, proclamation, promulgation, publishing, reporting 2 = **pamphlet**, book, booklet, brochure, handbill, hardback, issue, leaflet, magazine, newspaper, paperback, periodical, title, zine *(inf.)*

publicity *n* 1, 2 = **advertising**, attention, ballyhoo *(inf.)*, boost, boosterism, build-up, hype, plug *(inf.)*, press, promotion, public notice, puff, puffery *(inf.)*

publicize *vb* = **advertise**, beat the drum for *(inf.)*, bring to public notice, broadcast, give publicity to, hype, make known, play up, plug *(inf.)*, promote, puff, push, spotlight, spread about, write up
Antonyms *vb* conceal, contain, cover up, keep dark, keep secret, smother, stifle, suppress, withhold

public-spirited *adj* = **altruistic**, charitable, community-minded, generous, humanitarian, philanthropic, unselfish

publish *vb* 1 = **put out**, bring out, issue, print, produce 3 = **announce**, advertise, blow wide

tion. **3** (*tr*) to announce formally or in public. **4** (*tr*) to communicate (defamatory matter) to someone other than the person defamed: *to publish a libel.* [C14: from OF *puplier*, from L *pūblicāre* to make PUBLIC]
▸ **'publishable** *adj*

publisher ('pʌblɪʃə) *n* **1** a company or person engaged in publishing periodicals, books, music, etc. **2** *US & Canad.* the proprietor of a newspaper.

puce (pju:s) *n, adj* (of) a colour varying from deep red to dark purplish brown. [C18: shortened from F *couleur puce* flea colour, from L *pūlex* flea]

puck[1] (pʌk) *n* **1** a small disc of hard rubber used in ice hockey. **2** a stroke at the ball in hurling. **3** *Irish sl.* a sharp blow. ◆ *vb* (*tr*) **4** to strike (the ball) in hurling. **5** *Irish sl.* to strike hard; punch. [C19: from ?]

puck[2] ❶ (pʌk) *n* a mischievous or evil spirit. [OE *pūca*, from ?]
▸ **'puckish** *adj*

pucka ('pʌkə) *adj* a less common spelling of **pukka.**

pucker ❶ ('pʌkə) *vb* **1** to gather (a soft surface such as the skin) into wrinkles, or (of such a surface) to be so gathered. ◆ *n* **2** a wrinkle, crease, or irregular fold. [C16: ? rel. to POKE[2], from the baglike wrinkles]

pudding ❶ ('pʊdɪŋ) *n* **1** a sweetened usually cooked dessert made in many forms and of various ingredients. **2** a savoury dish, usually consisting partially of pastry or batter: *steak-and-kidney pudding.* **3** the dessert course in a meal. **4** a sausage-like mass of meat, oatmeal, etc., stuffed into a prepared skin or bag and boiled. [C13 *poding*]
▸ **'puddingy** *adj*

pudding stone *n* a conglomerate rock in which there is a difference in colour and composition between the pebbles and the matrix.

puddle ('pʌdəl) *n* **1** a small pool of water, esp. of rain. **2** a small pool of any liquid. **3** a worked mixture of wet clay and sand that is impervious to water and is used to line a pond or canal. ◆ *vb* **puddles, puddling, puddled.** (*tr*) **4** to make (clay, etc.) into puddle. **5** to subject (iron) to puddling. [C14 *podel*, dim. of OE *pudd* ditch, from ?]
▸ **'puddler** *n* ▸ **'puddly** *adj*

puddling ('pʌdlɪŋ) *n* a process for converting pig iron into wrought iron by heating it with ferric oxide in a furnace and stirring it to oxidize the carbon.

pudency ('pju:dənsɪ) *n* modesty or prudishness. [C17: from LL *pudentia*, from L *pudēre* to feel shame]

pudendum (pju:'dɛndəm) *n, pl* **pudenda** (-də). (*often pl*) the human external genital organs collectively, esp. of a female. [C17: from LL, from L *pudenda* the shameful (parts), from *pudēre* to be ashamed]
▸ **pu'dendal** *or* **pudic** ('pju:dɪk) *adj*

pudgy ('pʌdʒɪ) *adj* **pudgier, pudgiest.** a variant spelling (esp. US) of **podgy.** [C19: from ?]
▸ **'pudgily** *adv* ▸ **'pudginess** *n*

pueblo ('pwɛbləʊ; *Spanish* 'pweβlo) *n, pl* **pueblos** (-ləʊz; *Spanish* -los). **1** a communal village, built by certain Indians of the southwestern US and parts of Latin America, consisting of one or more flat-roofed houses. **2** (in Spanish America) a village or town. [C19: from Sp.: people, from L *populus*]

puerile ❶ ('pjʊəraɪl) *adj* **1** exhibiting silliness; immature; trivial. **2** of or characteristic of a child. [C17: from L *puerīlis* childish, from *puer* a boy]
▸ **'puerilely** *adv* ▸ **puerility** (pjʊə'rɪlɪtɪ) *n*

puerperal (pju:'ɜ:pərəl) *adj* of or occurring during the period following childbirth. [C18: from NL *puerperālis*, from L *puerperium* childbirth, ult. from *puer* boy + *parere* to bear]

puerperal fever *n* a serious, formerly widespread, form of blood poisoning caused by infection contracted during childbirth.

puerperal psychosis *n* a mental disorder sometimes occurring in women after childbirth, characterized by deep depression.

puff ❶ (pʌf) *n* **1** a short quick gust or emission, as of wind, smoke, etc. **2** the amount of wind, smoke, etc., released in a puff. **3** the sound made by a puff. **4** an instance of inhaling and expelling the breath as in smoking. **5** a light aerated pastry usually filled with cream, jam, etc. **6** a powder puff. **7** exaggerated praise, as of a book, product, etc., esp. through an advertisement. **8** a piece of clothing fabric gathered up so as to bulge in the centre while being held together at the edges. **9** a cylindrical roll of hair pinned in place in a coiffure. **10** *US.* a quilted bed cover. **11** one's breath (esp. in **out of puff**). **12** *Derog. sl.* a male homosexual. ◆ *vb* **13** to blow or breathe or cause to blow or breathe in short quick draughts. **14** (*tr; often foll. by out; usually passive*) to cause to be out of breath. **15** to take draws at (a cigarette, etc.). **16** (*intr*) to move with or by the emission of puffs: *the steam train puffed up the incline.* **17** (often foll. by *up, out*, etc.) to swell, as with air, pride, etc. **18** (*tr*) to praise with exaggerated empty words, often in advertising. **19** (*tr*) to apply (powder, dust, etc.) to (something). [OE *pyffan*]
▸ **'puffy** *adj*

puff adder *n* **1** a large venomous African viper that inflates its body when alarmed. **2** another name for **hognose snake.**

puffball ('pʌf,bɔ:l) *n* **1** any of various fungi having a round fruiting body that discharges a cloud of brown spores when mature. **2** short for **puffball skirt.**

puffball skirt *n* a skirt or a dress with a skirt that puffs out wide and is nipped into a narrow hem.

puffer ('pʌfə) *n* **1** a person or thing that puffs. **2** Also called: **blowfish, globefish.** a marine fish with an elongated spiny body that can be inflated to form a globe.

puffin ('pʌfɪn) *n* any of various northern diving birds, having a black-and-white plumage and a brightly coloured vertically flattened bill. [C14: ? of Cornish origin]

puff pastry *or US* **puff paste** *n* a dough used for making a rich flaky pastry.

puff-puff *n Brit.* a children's name for a steam locomotive or railway train.

pug[1] (pʌg) *n* a small compact breed of dog with a smooth coat, lightly curled tail, and a short wrinkled nose. [C16: from ?]
▸ **'puggish** *adj*

pug[2] (pʌg) *vb* **pugs, pugging, pugged.** (*tr*) **1** to mix (clay) with water to form a malleable mass or paste, often in a **pug mill. 2** to fill or stop with clay or a similar substance. [C19: from ?]

pug[3] (pʌg) *n* a slang name for **boxer** (sense 1). [C20: shortened from PUGILIST]

pugging ('pʌgɪŋ) *n* material such as clay, sawdust, etc., inserted between wooden flooring and ceiling to deaden sound. Also called: **pug.**

puggree, pugree ('pʌgrɪ) *or* **puggaree, pugaree** ('pʌgərɪ) *n* **1** the usual Indian word for **turban. 2** a scarf, usually pleated, around the crown of some hats, esp. sun helmets. [C17: from Hindi *pagrī*, from Sansk. *parikara*]

pugilism ❶ ('pju:dʒɪ,lɪzəm) *n* the art, practice, or profession of fighting with the fists; boxing. [C18: from L *pugil* a boxer]
▸ **'pugilist** *n* ▸ **,pugi'listic** *adj* ▸ **,pugi'listically** *adv*

pugnacious ❶ (pʌg'neɪʃəs) *adj* readily disposed to fight; belligerent. [C17: from L *pugnāx*]
▸ **pug'naciously** *adv* ▸ **pugnacity** (pʌg'næsɪtɪ) *n*

pug nose *n* a short stubby upturned nose. [C18: from PUG[1]]
▸ **'pug-,nosed** *adj*

puisne ('pju:nɪ) *adj* (esp. of a subordinate judge) of lower rank. [C16: from Anglo-F, from OF *puisné* born later, from L *posteā* afterwards + *nascī* to be born]

puissance ('pju:ɪsəns, 'pwi:sɑ:ns) *n* **1** a competition in showjumping that tests a horse's ability to jump large obstacles. **2** *Arch. or poetic.* power. [C15: from OF; see PUISSANT]

puissant ('pju:ɪsənt) *adj Arch. or poetic.* powerful. [C15: from OF, ult. from L *potēns* mighty, from *posse* to have power]
▸ **'puissantly** *adv*

puke ❶ (pju:k) *Sl.* ◆ *vb* **pukes, puking, puked. 1** to vomit. ◆ *n* **2** the act of vomiting. **3** the matter vomited. [C16: prob. imit.]

pukeko ('pʊkəkəʊ) *n, pl* **pukekos.** a New Zealand wading bird with bright plumage. [from Maori]

pukka ❶ *or* **pucka** ('pʌkə) *adj Anglo-Indian.* properly or perfectly done, constructed, etc.; good; genuine. [C17: from Hindi *pakkā* firm, from Sansk. *pakva*]

pulchritude ('pʌlkrɪ,tju:d) *n Formal or literary.* physical beauty. [C15: from L *pulchritūdō*, from *pulcher* beautiful]
▸ **,pulchri'tudinous** *adj*

pule (pju:l) *vb* **pules, puling, puled.** (*intr*) to cry plaintively; whimper. [C16: ? imit.]
▸ **'puler** *n*

Pulitzer prize ('pʊlɪtzə) *n* one of a group of prizes awarded yearly since 1917 for excellence in American journalism, literature, and music. [after Joseph *Pulitzer* (1847–1911), Hungarian-born US newspaper publisher]

THESAURUS

open (*sl.*), broadcast, circulate, communicate, declare, disclose, distribute, divulge, impart, leak, proclaim, promulgate, publicize, reveal, shout from the rooftops (*inf.*), spread

pucker *vb* **1** = **wrinkle**, compress, contract, crease, crinkle, crumple, draw together, furrow, gather, knit, pout, purse, ruckle, ruck up, ruffle, screw up, tighten ◆ *n* **2** = **wrinkle**, crease, crinkle, crumple, fold, ruck, ruckle

puckish *adj* = **mischievous**, frolicsome, impish, naughty, playful, roguish, sly, sportive, teasing, waggish, whimsical

pudding *n* **1, 3** = **dessert**, afters (*Brit. inf.*), last course, pud (*inf.*), second course, sweet

puerile *adj* **1** = **childish**, babyish, foolish, immature, inane, infantile, irresponsible, jejune, juvenile, naive, petty, ridiculous, silly, trivial, weak

Antonyms *adj* adult, grown-up, mature, responsible, sensible

puff *n* **1** = **blast**, breath, draught, emanation, flurry, gust, whiff **4** = **smoke**, drag, pull **7** = **advertisement**, commendation, favourable mention, good word, plug (*inf.*), sales talk **8** = **bulge**, bunching, swelling ◆ *vb* **13** = **blow**, breathe, exhale, gasp, gulp, pant, wheeze **15** = **smoke**, drag, draw, inhale, pull at *or* on, suck **17** *often foll. by with* **up, out** *etc.* = **swell**, bloat, dilate, distend, expand, inflate **18** = **promote**, crack up (*inf.*), hype, overpraise, plug (*inf.*), praise, publicize, push

puffy *adj* **17** = **swollen**, bloated, distended, enlarged, inflamed, inflated, puffed up

pugilism *n* = **boxing**, fighting, prizefighting, the noble art *or* science, the prize ring, the ring

pugilist *n* = **boxer**, bruiser (*inf.*), fighter, prizefighter, pug (*sl.*)

pugnacious *adj* = **aggressive**, antagonistic, argumentative, bellicose, belligerent, choleric, combative, contentious, disputatious, hot-tempered, irascible, irritable, petulant, quarrelsome

Antonyms *adj* calm, conciliatory, gentle, irenic, pacific, peaceable, peaceful, peace-loving, placatory, placid, quiet

puke *vb* **1** *Slang* = **vomit**, barf, be nauseated, be sick, chuck (up) (*sl., chiefly US*), chunder (*sl., chiefly Austral.*), disgorge, heave, regurgitate, retch, spew, throw up (*inf.*)

pukka *adj Anglo-Indian* = **genuine**, authentic, bona fide, official, on the level (*inf.*), proper, real, the real McCoy

pull ❶ (pʊl) *vb* (*mainly tr*) **1** (*also intr*) to exert force on (an object) so as to draw it towards the source of the force. **2** to remove; extract: *to pull a tooth.* **3** to strip of feathers, hair, etc.; pluck. **4** to draw the entrails from (a fowl). **5** to rend or tear. **6** to strain (a muscle or tendon). **7** (usually foll. by *off*) *Inf.* to bring about: *to pull off a million-pound deal.* **8** (often foll. by *on*) *Inf.* to draw out (a weapon) for use: *he pulled a knife on his attacker.* **9** *Inf.* to attract: *the pop group pulled a crowd.* **10** (*also intr*) *Sl.* to attract (a sexual partner). **11** (*intr;* usually foll. by *on* or *at*) to drink or inhale deeply: *to pull at one's pipe.* **12** to make (a grimace): *to pull a face.* **13** (*also intr;* foll. by *away, out, over,* etc.) to move (a vehicle) or (of a vehicle) to be moved in a specified manner. **14** (*intr*) to possess or exercise the power to move: *this car doesn't pull well on hills.* **15** to withdraw or remove: *the board decided to pull their support.* **16** *Printing.* to take (a proof) from type. **17** *Golf, baseball, etc.* to hit (a ball) so that it veers away from the direction in which the player intended to hit it. **18** *Cricket.* to hit (a ball pitched straight or on the off side) to the leg side. **19** *Hurling.* to strike (a fast-moving ball) in the same direction as it is already moving. **20** (*also intr*) to row (a boat) or take a stroke of (an oar) in rowing. **21** (of a rider) to restrain (a horse), esp. to prevent it from winning a race. **22 pull a fast one.** *Sl.* to play a sly trick. **23 pull apart** *or* **to pieces.** to criticize harshly. **24 pull (one's) punches. 24a** *Inf.* to restrain the force of one's criticisms or actions. **24b** *Boxing.* to restrain the force of one's blows. ◆ *n* **25** an act or an instance of pulling or being pulled. **26** the force or effort used in pulling: *the pull of the moon affects the tides.* **27** the act or an instance of taking in drink or smoke. **28** *Printing.* a proof taken from type: *the first pull was smudged.* **29** something used for pulling, such as a handle. **30** *Inf.* special advantage or influence: *his uncle is chairman of the company, so he has quite a lot of pull.* **31** *Inf.* the power to attract attention or support. **32** a period of rowing. **33** a single stroke of an oar in rowing. **34** the act of pulling the ball in golf, cricket, etc. **35** the act of reining in a horse. ◆ See also **pull down, pull in,** etc. [OE *pullian*]
▸**'puller** *n*

pull down ❶ *vb* (*tr, adv*) to destroy or demolish: *the old houses were pulled down.*

pullet ('pʊlɪt) *n* a young hen of the domestic fowl, less than one year old. [C14: from OF *poulet* chicken, from L *pullus* a young animal or bird]

pulley ('pʊlɪ) *n* **1** a wheel with a grooved rim in which a rope can run in order to change the direction of a force applied to the rope, etc. **2** a number of such wheels pivoted in parallel in a block, used to raise heavy loads. **3** a wheel with a flat, convex, or grooved rim mounted on a shaft and driven by or driving a belt passing around it. [C14 *poley*, from OF *polie*, from Vulgar L *polidium* (unattested), apparently from LGk *polidion* (unattested) a little pole, from Gk *polos* axis]

pull in ❶ *vb* (*adv*) **1** (*intr;* often foll. by *to*) to reach a destination: *the train pulled in at the station.* **2** (*intr*) Also: **pull over.** (of a motor vehicle) **2a** to draw in to the side of the road. **2b** to stop (at a café, lay-by, etc.). **3** (*tr*) to attract: *his appearance will pull in the crowds.* **4** (*tr*) *Sl.* to arrest. **5** (*tr*) to earn or gain (money). ◆ *n* **pull-in. 6** *Brit.* a roadside café, esp. for lorry drivers.

Pullman ('pʊlmən) *n, pl* **Pullmans.** a luxurious railway coach. Also called: **Pullman car.** [C19: after G. M. *Pullman* (1831–97), its US inventor]

pull off ❶ *vb* (*tr*) **1** to remove (clothing) forcefully. **2** (*adv*) to succeed in performing (a difficult feat).

pull out ❶ *vb* (*adv*) **1** (*tr*) to extract. **2** (*intr*) to depart: *the train pulled out of the station.* **3** *Mil.* to withdraw or be withdrawn: *the troops were pulled out of the ruined city.* **4** (*intr*) (of a motor vehicle) **4a** to draw away from the side of the road. **4b** to draw out from behind another vehicle to overtake. **5** (*intr*) to abandon a position or situation. **6** (foll. by *of*) to level out (from a dive). ◆ *n* **pull-out. 7** an extra leaf of a book that folds out. **8** a removable section of a magazine, etc.

pullover ('pʊlˌəʊvə) *n* a garment, esp. a sweater, that is pulled on over the head.

pull through ❶ *vb* to survive or recover or cause to survive or recover, esp. after a serious illness or crisis. Also: **pull round.**

pull together *vb* **1** (*intr, adv*) to cooperate, or work harmoniously. **2 pull oneself together.** *Inf.* to regain one's self-control or composure.

pullulate ('pʌljʊˌleɪt) *vb* **pullulates, pullulating, pullulated.** (*intr*) **1** (of animals, etc.) to breed abundantly. **2** (of plants) to sprout, bud, or germinate. [C17: from L *pullulāre* to sprout, from *pullulus* a baby animal, from *pullus* young animal]
▸ˌ**pullu'lation** *n*

pull up ❶ *vb* (*adv*) **1** (*tr*) to remove by the roots. **2** (often foll. by *with* or *on*) to move level (with) or ahead (of), esp. in a race. **3** to stop: *the car pulled up suddenly.* **4** (*tr*) to rebuke. ◆ *n* **pull-up. 5** *Brit.* a roadside café; pull-in.

pulmonary ('pʌlmənərɪ, 'pʊl-) *adj* **1** of or affecting the lungs. **2** having lungs or lunglike organs. [C18: from L *pulmōnārius*, from *pulmō* a lung]

pulmonary artery *n* either of the two arteries that convey oxygen-depleted blood from the heart to the lungs.

pulmonary vein *n* any one of the four veins that convey oxygen-rich blood from the lungs to the heart.

pulp ❶ (pʌlp) *n* **1** soft or fleshy plant tissue, such as the succulent part of a fleshy fruit. **2** a moist mixture of cellulose fibres, as obtained from wood, from which paper is made. **3a** a magazine or book containing trite or sensational material, and usually printed on cheap rough paper. **3b** (*as modifier*): *a pulp novel.* **4** *Dentistry.* the soft innermost part of a tooth, containing nerves and blood vessels. **5** any soft soggy mass. **6** *Mining.* pulverized ore. ◆ *vb* **7** to reduce (a material) to pulp or (of a material) to be reduced to pulp. **8** (*tr*) to remove the pulp from (fruit, etc.). [C16: from L *pulpa*]
▸**'pulpy** *adj*

pulpit ('pʊlpɪt) *n* **1** a raised platform, usually surrounded by a barrier, set up in churches as the appointed place for preaching, etc. **2** a medium for expressing an opinion, such as a newspaper column. **3** (usually preceded by *the*) **3a** the preaching of the Christian message. **3b** the clergy or their influence. [C14: from L *pulpitum* a platform]

pulpwood ('pʌlpˌwʊd) *n* pine, spruce, or any other soft wood used to make paper.

pulque ('pʊlkɪ) *n* a light alcoholic drink from Mexico made from the juice of various agave plants. [C17: from Mexican Sp., apparently from Nahuatl, from *puliuhqui* decomposed, since it will only keep for a day]

pulsar ('pʌlˌsɑː) *n* any of a number of very small stars first discovered in 1967, which rotate fast, emitting regular pulses of polarized radiation. [C20: from PULS(ATING ST)AR, on the model of QUASAR]

pulsate ❶ (pʌl'seɪt) *vb* **pulsates, pulsating, pulsated.** (*intr*) **1** to expand and contract with a rhythmic beat; throb. **2** *Physics.* to vary in intensity, magnitude, etc. **3** to quiver or vibrate. [C18: from L *pulsāre* to push]
▸**pulsative** ('pʌlsətɪv) *adj* ▸**pul'sation** *n* ▸**pul'sator** *n* ▸**pulsatory** ('pʌlsətərɪ, -trɪ) *adj*

pulsatilla (ˌpʌlsə'tɪlə) *n* any of a genus of plants related to the anemone, with feathery or hairy foliage. [C16: from Med. L, from *pulsāta* beaten (by the wind)]

pulsating star *n* a type of variable star, the variation in brightness resulting from expansion and subsequent contraction of the star.

pulse[1] ❶ (pʌls) *n* **1** *Physiol.* **1a** the rhythmic contraction and expansion of an artery at each beat of the heart. **1b** a single such pulsation. **2** *Physics, electronics.* **2a** a transient sharp change in some quantity normally constant in a system. **2b** one of a series of such transient disturbances, usually recurring at regular intervals. **3a** a recurrent rhythmic series of beats, vibrations, etc. **3b** any single beat, wave, etc., in such a series. **4** an inaudible electronic "ping" to operate a slide projector. **5** bustle, vitality, or excitement: *the pulse of a city.* **6 keep one's finger on the pulse.** to be well informed about current events, opinions, etc. ◆ *vb* **pulses, pulsing, pulsed. 7** (*intr*) to beat, throb, or vibrate. **8** (*tr*) to provide an electronic pulse to operate (a slide projector). [C14 *pous*, from L *pulsus* a beating, from *pellere* to beat]
▸**'pulseless** *adj*

pulse[2] (pʌls) *n* **1** the edible seeds of any of several leguminous plants, such as peas, beans, and lentils. **2** the plant producing any of these. [C13 *pols*, from OF, from L *puls* pottage of pulse]

pulsejet ('pʌlsˌdʒet) *n* a type of ramjet engine in which air is admitted through movable vanes that are closed by the pressure resulting from

THESAURUS

pull *vb* **1 = draw**, drag, haul, jerk, tow, trail, tug, yank **2, 3 = extract**, cull, draw out, gather, pick, pluck, remove, take out, uproot, weed **5, 6 = strain**, dislocate, rend, rip, sprain, stretch, tear, wrench **9** *Informal* **= attract**, draw, entice, lure, magnetize **23 pull apart** *or* to pieces **= criticize**, attack, blast, find fault, flay, lambast(e), lay into (*inf.*), pan (*inf.*), pick holes in, put down, run down, slam (*sl.*), slate (*inf.*), tear into (*inf.*) ◆ *n* **25 = tug**, jerk, twitch, yank **27 = puff**, drag (*sl.*), inhalation **30** *Informal* **= influence**, advantage, bottom, clout (*inf.*), leverage, muscle, power, weight **31** *Informal* **= attraction**, drawing power, effort, exertion, force, forcefulness, influence, lure, magnetism
Antonyms *vb* ≠ **draw:** drive, nudge, push, ram, shove, thrust ≠ **extract:** implant, insert, plant ≠ **attract:** deter, discourage, put one off, repel ◆ *n* ≠ **tug:** nudge, push, shove, thrust

pull down *vb* **= demolish**, bulldoze, destroy, raze, remove
Antonyms *vb* build, construct, erect, put up, raise, set up

pull in *vb* **1, 2 = draw in**, arrive, come in, draw up, reach, stop **3 = attract**, bring in, draw **4** *Slang* **= arrest**, bust (*inf.*), collar (*inf.*), feel one's collar (*sl.*), lift (*sl.*), nab (*inf.*), nail (*inf.*), pinch (*inf.*), run in (*sl.*), take into custody **5 = earn**, clear, gain, gross, make, net, pocket, take home

pull off *vb* **1 = remove**, detach, doff, rip off, tear off, wrench off **2 = succeed**, accomplish, bring off, carry out, crack it (*inf.*), cut it (*inf.*), do the trick, manage, score a success, secure one's object

pull out *vb* **2, 3 = withdraw**, abandon, back off, depart, evacuate, leave, quit, retreat, stop participating

pull through *vb* **= survive**, come through, get better, get over, pull round, rally, recover, turn the corner, weather

pull up *vb* **1 = uproot**, dig out, lift, raise **3 = stop**, brake, come to a halt, halt, reach a standstill **4 = reprimand**, admonish, bawl out (*inf.*), carpet (*inf.*), castigate, dress down (*inf.*), read the riot act, rebuke, reprove, slap on the wrist, take to task, tell off (*inf.*), tick off (*inf.*)

pulp *n* **1 = flesh**, marrow, soft part ◆ *modifier* **3b = cheap**, lurid, mushy (*inf.*), rubbishy, sensational, trashy ◆ *n* **5 = paste**, mash, mush, pap, pomace, semiliquid, semisolid, triturate ◆ *vb* **7 = crush**, mash, pulverize, squash, triturate

pulpy *adj* **1, 5 = soft**, fleshy, mushy, pappy, squashy, succulent

pulsate *vb* **1, 3 = throb**, beat, hammer, oscillate, palpitate, pound, pulse, quiver, thud, thump, tick, vibrate

pulse[1] *n* **1, 3 = beat**, beating, oscillation, pulsa-

each intermittent explosion of the fuel in the combustion chamber, thus causing a pulsating thrust. Also called: **pulsejet engine, pulsojet.**

pulse modulation *n Electronics.* a type of modulation in which a train of pulses is used as the carrier wave, one or more of its parameters, such as amplitude, being modulated or modified in order to carry information.

pulsimeter (pʌl'sɪmɪtə) *n Med.* an instrument for measuring the rate of the pulse.

pulverize ❶ *or* **pulverise** ('pʌlvəˌraɪz) *vb* **pulverizes, pulverizing, pulverized** *or* **pulverises, pulverising, pulverised. 1** to reduce (a substance) to fine particles, as by grinding, or (of a substance) to be so reduced. **2** (*tr*) to destroy completely. [C16: from LL *pulverizare,* from L *pulvis* dust] ▸ **'pulverˌizable** *or* **'pulverˌisable** *adj* ▸ **ˌpulveri'zation** *or* **ˌpulveri'sation** *n* ▸ **'pulverˌizer** *or* **'pulverˌiser** *n*

pulverulent (pʌl'vɛrʊlənt) *adj* consisting of, covered with, or crumbling to dust or fine particles. [C17: from L *pulverulentus,* from *pulvis* dust]

puma ('pjuːmə) *n* a large American feline mammal that resembles a lion, having a plain greyish-brown coat and long tail. Also called: **cougar, mountain lion.** [C18: via Sp. from Quechua]

pumice ('pʌmɪs) *n* **1** Also called: **pumice stone.** a light porous volcanic rock used for scouring and, in powdered form, as an abrasive and for polishing. ◆ *vb* **pumices, pumicing, pumiced. 2** (*tr*) to rub or polish with pumice. [C15 *pomys,* from OF *pomis,* from L *pūmex*] ▸ **pumiceous** (pjuː'mɪʃəs) *adj*

pummel ❶ ('pʌməl) *vb* **pummels, pummelling, pummelled** *or US* **pummels, pummeling, pummeled.** (*tr*) to strike repeatedly with or as if with the fists. Also (less commonly): **pommel.** [C16: see POMMEL]

pump[1] ❶ (pʌmp) *n* **1** any device for compressing, driving, raising, or reducing the pressure of a fluid, esp. by means of a piston or set of rotating impellers. **2** *Biol.* a mechanism for the active transport of ions, such as protons, calcium ions, and sodium ions, across cell membranes: *a sodium pump.* ◆ *vb* **3** (when *tr,* usually foll. by *from, out,* etc.) to raise or drive (air, liquid, etc., esp. into or from something) with a pump. **4** (*tr;* usually foll. by *in* or *into*) to supply in large amounts: *to pump capital into a project.* **5** (*tr*) to deliver (bullets, etc.) repeatedly. **6** to operate (something, esp. a handle) in the manner of a pump or (of something) to work in this way: *to pump the pedals of a bicycle.* **7** (*tr*) to obtain (information) from (a person) by persistent questioning. **8** (*intr;* usually foll. by *from* or *out of*) (of liquids) to flow freely in large spurts: *oil pumped from the fissure.* **9** **pump iron.** *Sl.* to exercise with weights; do body-building exercises. [C15: from MDu. *pumpe* pipe, prob. from Sp. *bomba,* imit.]

pump[2] (pʌmp) *n* **1** a low-cut low-heeled shoe without fastenings, worn esp. for dancing. **2** a type of shoe with a rubber sole, used in games such as tennis; plimsoll. [C16: from ?]

pumpernickel ('pʌmpəˌnɪkəl) *n* a slightly sour black bread, originating in Germany, made of coarse rye flour. [C18: from G, from ?]

pumpkin ('pʌmpkɪn) *n* **1** any of several creeping plants of the genus *Cucurbita.* **2** the large round fruit of any of these plants, which has a thick orange rind, pulpy flesh, and numerous seeds. [C17: from earlier *pumpion,* from OF, from L *pepo,* from Gk, from *peptein* to ripen]

pump priming *n* **1** the process of introducing fluid into a pump to improve starting and to expel air from it. **2** government expenditure designed to stimulate economic activity in stagnant or depressed areas. **3** another term for **deficit financing.**

pun[1] ❶ (pʌn) *n* **1** the use of words to exploit ambiguities and innuendoes for humorous effect; a play on words. An example is: *"Ben Battle was a soldier bold, And used to war's alarms: But a cannonball took off his legs, So he laid down his arms."* (Thomas Hood). ◆ *vb* **puns, punning, punned. 2** (*intr*) to make puns. [C17: ?from It. *puntiglio* wordplay; see PUNCTILIO]

pun[2] (pʌn) *vb* **puns, punning, punned.** (*tr*) *Brit.* to pack (earth, rubble, etc.) by pounding. [C16: var. of POUND[1]]

puna *Spanish.* ('puna) *n* **1** a high cold dry plateau. **2** another name for **mountain sickness.** [C17: from American Sp., of Amerind origin]

punch[1] ❶ (pʌntʃ) *vb* **1** to strike at, esp. with a clenched fist. **2** (*tr*) *Western US.* to herd or drive (cattle), esp. for a living. **3** (*tr*) to poke with a stick, etc. ◆ *n* **4** a blow with the fist. **5** *Inf.* point or vigour: *his arguments lacked punch.* [C15: ? var. of *pounce,* from OF *poinçonner* to stamp] ▸ **'puncher** *n*

punch[2] ❶ (pʌntʃ) *n* **1** a tool or machine for piercing holes in a material. **2** a tool or machine used for stamping a design on something or shaping it by impact. **3** the solid die of a punching machine. **4** *Computing.* a device for making holes in a card or paper tape. ◆ *vb* **5** (*tr*) to pierce, cut, stamp, shape, or drive with a punch. [C14: shortened from *puncheon,* from OF *ponçon;* see PUNCHEON[2]]

punch[3] (pʌntʃ) *n* any mixed drink containing fruit juice and, usually, alcoholic liquor, generally hot and spiced. [C17: ?from Hindi *pānch,* from Sansk. *pañca* five; it orig. had five ingredients]

Punch (pʌntʃ) *n* the main character in the traditional children's puppet show **Punch and Judy.**

punchbag ('pʌntʃˌbæg) *n* a suspended stuffed bag that is punched for exercise, esp. boxing training. Also called (US and Canad.): **punching bag.**

punchball ('pʌntʃˌbɔːl) *n* **1** a stuffed or inflated ball, supported by a flexible rod, that is punched for exercise, esp. boxing training. **2** *US.* a game resembling baseball.

punchbowl ('pʌntʃˌbəʊl) *n* **1** a large bowl for serving punch, often having small drinking glasses hooked around the rim. **2** *Brit.* a bowl-shaped depression in the land.

punch-drunk ❶ *adj* **1** demonstrating or characteristic of the behaviour of a person who has suffered repeated blows to the head, esp. a professional boxer. **2** dazed; stupefied.

punched card *or esp. US* **punch card** *n* a card on which data can be coded in the form of punched holes, formerly used in computing.

punched tape *or US* (*sometimes*) **perforated tape** *n* other terms for **paper tape.**

puncheon[1] ('pʌntʃən) *n* a large cask of variable capacity, usually between 70 and 120 gallons. [C15 *poncion,* from OF *ponchon,* from ?]

puncheon[2] ('pʌntʃən) *n* **1** a short wooden post used as a vertical strut. **2** a less common name for **punch**[2] (sense 1). [C14 *ponson,* from OF *ponçon,* from L *punctiō* a puncture, from *pungere* to prick]

Punchinello (ˌpʌntʃɪ'nɛləʊ) *n, pl* **Punchinellos** *or* **Punchinelloes. 1** a clown from Italian puppet shows, the prototype of Punch. **2** (*sometimes not cap.*) any grotesque or absurd character. [C17: from earlier *Polichinello,* from It. *Polecenella,* from *pulcino* chicken, ult. from L *pullus* young animal]

punch line *n* the culminating part of a joke, funny story, etc., that gives it its point.

punch-up ❶ *n Brit. inf.* a fight or brawl.

punchy ❶ ('pʌntʃɪ) *adj* **punchier, punchiest. 1** an informal word for **punch-drunk. 2** *Inf.* incisive or forceful. ▸ **'punchily** *adv* ▸ **'punchiness** *n*

punctate ('pʌŋkteɪt) *adj* having or marked with minute spots or depressions. [C18: from NL *punctātus,* from L *punctum* a point] ▸ **punc'tation** *n*

punctilio (pʌŋk'tɪlɪˌəʊ) *n, pl* **punctilios. 1** strict attention to minute points of etiquette. **2** a petty formality or fine point of etiquette. [C16: from It. *puntiglio* small point, from L *punctum* point]

punctilious ❶ (pʌŋk'tɪlɪəs) *adj* **1** paying scrupulous attention to correctness in etiquette. **2** attentive to detail. ▸ **punc'tiliously** *adv* ▸ **punc'tiliousness** *n*

punctual ❶ ('pʌŋktjʊəl) *adj* **1** arriving or taking place at an arranged time. **2** (of a person) having the characteristic of always keeping to arranged times. **3** *Obs.* precise; exact. **4** *Maths.* consisting of or confined to a point. [C14: from Med. L *punctuālis* concerning detail, from L *punctum* point] ▸ **ˌpunctu'ality** *n* ▸ **'punctually** *adv*

punctuate ❶ ('pʌŋktjʊˌeɪt) *vb* **punctuates, punctuating, punctuated.** (*mainly tr*) **1** (*also intr*) to insert punctuation marks into (a written text). **2** to interrupt or insert at frequent intervals: *a meeting punctuated by heckling.* **3** to give emphasis to. [C17: from Med. L *punctuāre* to prick, from L, from *pungere* to puncture]

punctuation (ˌpʌŋktjʊ'eɪʃən) *n* **1** the use of symbols not belonging to the alphabet of a writing system to indicate aspects of the intonation and meaning not otherwise conveyed in the written language. **2** the symbols used for this purpose.

THESAURUS

tion, rhythm, stroke, throb, throbbing, vibration ◆ *vb* **7** = **beat**, pulsate, throb, tick, vibrate

pulverize *vb* **1** = **crush**, bray, comminute, granulate, grind, levigate (*Chemistry*), mill, pestle, pound, triturate **2** = **defeat**, annihilate, crush, demolish, destroy, flatten, lick (*inf.*), smash, stuff (*sl.*), tank (*sl.*), vanquish, wreck

pummel *vb* = **beat**, bang, batter, belt (*inf.*), clobber (*sl.*), hammer, knock, lambast(e), pound, punch, rain blows upon, strike, thump

pump[1] *vb* **3** *usually foll. by* **from, out** *etc.* = **drive out**, bail out, drain, draw off, empty, force out, siphon **3** *foll. by* **up** = **inflate**, blow up, dilate **4** *often with* **into** = **drive**, force, inject, pour, push, send, supply **7** = **interrogate**, cross-examine, give (someone) the third degree, grill (*inf.*), probe, question closely, quiz, worm out of

pun[1] *n* **1** = **play on words**, double entendre, equivoque, paronomasia (*Rhetoric*), quip, witticism

punch[1] *vb* **1** = **hit**, bash (*inf.*), belt (*inf.*), biff, bop (*inf.*), box, clout (*inf.*), plug (*sl.*), pummel, slam, slug, smash, sock (*sl.*), strike, swipe (*inf.*), wallop (*inf.*) ◆ *n* **4** = **blow**, bash (*inf.*), biff (*sl.*), bop (*inf.*), clout (*inf.*), hit, jab, knock, plug (*sl.*), sock (*sl.*), swipe (*inf.*), thump, wallop (*inf.*) **5** *Informal* = **effectiveness**, bite, drive, force, forcefulness, impact, point, verve, vigour

punch[2] *vb* **5** = **pierce**, bore, cut, drill, perforate, pink, prick, puncture, stamp

punch-drunk *adj* **1, 2** = **dazed**, befuddled, confused, groggy (*inf.*), in a daze, knocked silly, punchy (*inf.*), reeling, slaphappy (*inf.*), staggering, stupefied, unsteady, woozy (*inf.*)

punch-up *n Brit. informal* = **fight**, argument, battle royal, brawl, dust-up (*inf.*), free-for-all (*inf.*), row, scrap (*inf.*), set-to (*inf.*), shindig (*inf.*), shindy (*inf.*), stand-up fight (*inf.*)

punchy *adj* **2** *Informal* = **effective**, aggressive, dynamic, forceful, incisive, in-your-face (*sl.*), lively, spirited, storming (*inf.*), vigorous

punctilious *adj* **1, 2** = **particular**, careful, ceremonious, conscientious, exact, finicky, formal, fussy, meticulous, nice, precise, proper, scrupulous, strict

punctual *adj* **1** = **on time**, early, exact, in good time, on the dot, precise, prompt, seasonable, strict, timely

Antonyms *adj* behind, behindhand, belated, delayed, late, overdue, tardy, unpunctual

punctuality *n* **1** = **promptness**, promptitude, readiness, regularity

punctuate *vb* **2** = **interrupt**, break, interject, intersperse, pepper, sprinkle **3** = **emphasize**, ac-

punctuation mark *n* any of the signs used in punctuation, such as a comma.

puncture ➊ ('pʌŋktʃə) *n* **1** a small hole made by a sharp object. **2** a perforation and loss of pressure in a pneumatic tyre. **3** the act of puncturing or perforating. ◆ *vb* **punctures, puncturing, punctured. 4** (*tr*) to pierce a hole in (something) with a sharp object. **5** to cause (something pressurized, esp. a tyre) to lose pressure by piercing, or (of a tyre, etc.) to collapse in this way. **6** (*tr*) to depreciate (a person's self-esteem, pomposity, etc.). [C14: from L *punctūra,* from *pungere* to prick]

pundit ➊ ('pʌndɪt) *n* **1** an expert. **2** (formerly) a learned person. **3** Also: **pandit.** a Brahman learned in Sanskrit, Hindu religion, philosophy or law. [C17: from Hindi *pandit,* from Sansk. *pandita* learned man]

punga ('pʌŋə) *n* a variant spelling of **ponga.**

pungent ➊ ('pʌndʒənt) *adj* **1** having an acrid smell or sharp bitter flavour. **2** (of wit, satire, etc.) biting; caustic. **3** *Biol.* ending in a sharp point. [C16: from L *pungens* piercing, from *pungere* to prick]
▸'**pungency** *n* ▸'**pungently** *adv*

Punic ('pju:nɪk) *adj* **1** of or relating to ancient Carthage or the Carthaginians. **2** treacherous; faithless. ◆ *n* **3** the language of the Carthaginians; a late form of Phoenician. [C15: from L *Pūnicus,* var. of *Poenicus* Carthaginian, from Gk *Phoinix*]

punish ➊ ('pʌnɪʃ) *vb* **1** to force (someone) to undergo a penalty for some crime or misdemeanour. **2** (*tr*) to inflict punishment for (some crime, etc.). **3** (*tr*) to treat harshly, esp. as by overexertion: *to punish a horse.* **4** (*tr*) *Inf.* to consume in large quantities: *to punish the bottle.* [C14 *punisse,* from OF *punir,* from L *pūnīre* to punish, from *poena* penalty]
▸'**punishable** *adj* ▸'**punisher** *n* ▸'**punishing** *adj*

punishment ➊ ('pʌnɪʃmənt) *n* **1** a penalty for a crime or offence. **2** the act of punishing or state of being punished. **3** *Inf.* rough treatment.

punitive ➊ ('pju:nɪtɪv) *adj* relating to, involving, or with the intention of inflicting punishment: *a punitive expedition.* [C17: from Med. L *pūnītīvus* concerning punishment, from L *pūnīre* to punish]
▸'**punitively** *adv*

Punjabi (pʌn'dʒɑ:bɪ) *n* **1** (*pl* **Punjabis**) a member of the chief people of the Punjab, in NW India. **2** the language of the Punjab, belonging to the Indic branch of the Indo-European family. ◆ *adj* **3** of the Punjab, its people, or their language.

punk[1] (pʌŋk) *n* **1** a youth movement of the late 1970s, characterized by anti-Establishment slogans and outrageous clothes and hairstyles. **2** an inferior, rotten, or worthless person or thing. **3** worthless articles collectively. **4** short for **punk rock. 5** *Obs.* a young male homosexual; catamite. **6** *Obs.* a prostitute. ◆ *adj* **7** rotten or worthless. [C16: from ?]

punk[2] (pʌŋk) *n* dried decayed wood or other substance that smoulders when ignited: used as tinder. [C18: from ?]

punka *or* **punkah** ('pʌŋkə) *n* **1** a fan made of a palm leaf or leaves. **2** a large fan made of palm leaves, etc., worked mechanically to cool a room. [C17: from Hindi *pankhā,* from Sansk. *paksaka* fan, from *paksa* wing]

punk rock *n* a fast abrasive style of rock music of the late 1970s, characterized by aggressive lyrics and performance, usually expressing rage and frustration.
▸**punk rocker** *n*

punnet ('pʌnɪt) *n Chiefly Brit.* a small basket for fruit. [C19: ? dim. of dialect *pun* POUND[2]]

punster ('pʌnstə) *n* a person who is fond of making puns, esp. one who makes a tedious habit of this.

punt[1] (pʌnt) *n* **1** an open flat-bottomed boat with square ends, propelled by a pole. ◆ *vb* **2** to propel (a boat, esp. a punt) by pushing with a pole on the bottom of a river, etc. [OE *punt* shallow boat, from L *pontō* punt]

punt[2] (pʌnt) *n* **1** a kick in certain sports, such as rugby, in which the ball is released and kicked before it hits the ground. **2** any long high kick. ◆ *vb* **3** to kick (a ball, etc.) using a punt. [C19: ? var. of dialect *bunt* to push]

punt[3] ➊ (pʌnt) *Chiefly Brit.* ◆ *vb* **1** (*intr*) to gamble; bet. ◆ *n* **2** a gamble or bet, esp. against the bank, as in roulette, or on horses. **3** Also called: **punter.** a person who bets. **4 take a punt at.** *Austral. & NZ inf.* to make an attempt at. [C18: from F *ponter* to punt, from *ponte* bet laid against the banker, from Sp. *punto* point, from L *punctum*]

punt[4] (pʊnt) *n* the Irish pound. [Irish Gaelic: pound]

punter[1] ('pʌntə) *n* a person who punts a boat.

punter[2] ('pʌntə) *n* a person who kicks a ball.

punter[3] ➊ ('pʌntə) *n* **1** a person who gambles or bets. **2** *Sl.* any client or customer, esp. a prostitute's client. **3** *Sl.* a victim of a con man.

puny ➊ ('pju:nɪ) *adj* **punier, puniest. 1** small and weakly. **2** paltry; insignificant. [C16: from OF *puisne* PUISNE]
▸'**puniness** *n*

pup ➊ (pʌp) *n* **1a** a young dog; puppy. **1b** the young of various other animals, such as the seal. **2 in pup.** (of a bitch) pregnant. **3** *Inf., chiefly Brit.* a conceited young man (esp. in **young pup**). **4 sell (someone) a pup.** to swindle (someone) by selling him something worthless. ◆ *vb* **pups, pupping, pupped. 5** (of dogs, seals, etc.) to give birth to (young). [C18: back formation from PUPPY]

pupa ('pju:pə) *n, pl* **pupae** (-pi:) *or* **pupas.** an insect at the immobile nonfeeding stage of development between larva and adult, when many internal changes occur. [C19: via NL, from L: a doll]
▸'**pupal** *adj*

pupate (pju:'peɪt) *vb* **pupates, pupating, pupated.** (*intr*) (of an insect larva) to develop into a pupa.
▸**pu'pation** *n*

pupil[1] ➊ ('pju:pᵊl) *n* **1** a student who is taught by a teacher. **2** *Civil & Scots Law.* a boy under 14 or a girl under 12 who is in the care of a guardian. [C14: from L *pupillus* an orphan, from *pūpus* a child]
▸'**pupillage** *or US* '**pupilage** *n* ▸'**pupillary** *or* '**pupilary** *adj*

pupil[2] ('pju:pᵊl) *n* the dark circular aperture at the centre of the iris of the eye, through which light enters. [C16: from L *pūpilla,* dim. of *pūpa* doll; from the tiny reflections in the eye]
▸'**pupillary** *or* '**pupilary** *adj*

pupiparous (pju:'pɪpərəs) *adj* (of certain dipterous flies) producing young that have already reached the pupa stage at the time of hatching. [C19: from NL *pupiparus,* from PUPA + *parere* to bring forth]

puppet ➊ ('pʌpɪt) *n* **1a** a small doll or figure moved by strings attached to its limbs or by the hand inserted in its cloth body. **1b** (*as modifier*): *a puppet theatre.* **2a** a person, state, etc., that appears independent but is controlled by another. **2b** (*as modifier*): *a puppet government.* [C16 *popet,* ?from OF *poupette* little doll, ult. from L *pūpa* doll]

puppeteer (ˌpʌpɪ'tɪə) *n* a person who manipulates puppets.

puppetry ('pʌpɪtrɪ) *n* **1** the art of making and manipulating puppets and presenting puppet shows. **2** unconvincing or specious presentation.

puppy ('pʌpɪ) *n, pl* **puppies. 1** a young dog; pup. **2** *Inf., contemptuous.* a brash or conceited young man; pup. [C15 *popi,* from OF *popée* doll]
▸'**puppyhood** *n* ▸'**puppyish** *adj*

puppy fat *n* fatty tissue that develops in childhood or adolesence and usually disappears with maturity.

puppy love *n* another term for **calf love.**

Purana (pʊ'rɑ:nə) *n* any of a class of Sanskrit writings not included in the Vedas, characteristically recounting the birth and deeds of Hindu gods and the creation of the universe. [C17: from Sansk.: ancient, from *purā* formerly]

Purbeck marble *or* **stone** ('pɜ:bɛk) *n* a fossil-rich limestone that takes a high polish. [C15: after *Purbeck,* Dorset, where quarried]

purblind ('pɜ:ˌblaɪnd) *adj* **1** partly or nearly blind. **2** lacking in insight or understanding; obtuse. [C13: see PURE, BLIND]

purchase ➊ ('pɜ:tʃɪs) *vb* **purchases, purchasing, purchased.** (*tr*) **1** to obtain

THESAURUS

centuate, lay stress on, mark, point up, stress, underline

puncture *n* **1** = **hole**, break, cut, damage, leak, nick, opening, perforation, rupture, slit **2** = **flat tyre**, flat ◆ *vb* **4** = **pierce**, bore, cut, impale, nick, penetrate, perforate, prick, rupture **5** = **deflate**, go down, go flat **6** = **humble**, deflate, discourage, disillusion, flatten, take down a peg (*inf.*)

pundit *n* **1** = **expert**, buff (*inf.*), guru, maestro, one of the cognoscenti, (self-appointed) expert *or* authority

pungent *adj* **1** = **strong**, acid, acrid, aromatic, bitter, highly flavoured, hot, peppery, piquant, seasoned, sharp, sour, spicy, stinging, tangy, tart **2** = **cutting**, acrimonious, acute, barbed, biting, caustic, incisive, keen, mordacious, mordant, penetrating, piercing, poignant, pointed, sarcastic, scathing, sharp, stinging, stringent, telling, trenchant, vitriolic
Antonyms *adj* ≠ **strong**: bland, dull, mild, moderate, tasteless, unsavoury, unstimulating, weak ≠ **cutting**: dull, inane

punish *vb* **1, 2** = **discipline**, beat, bring to book, cane, castigate, chasten, chastise, correct, flog, give a lesson to, give (someone) the works (*sl.*), lash, penalize, rap someone's knuckles, scourge, sentence, slap someone's wrist, throw the book at, whip **3** = **mistreat**, abuse, batter, give (someone) a going-over (*inf.*), harm, hurt, injure, knock about, manhandle, misuse, oppress, rough up

punishable *adj* **1** = **culpable**, blameworthy, chargeable, convictable, criminal, indictable

punishing *adj* **3** = **hard**, arduous, backbreaking, burdensome, demanding, exhausting, grinding, gruelling, strenuous, taxing, tiring, uphill, wearing
Antonyms *adj* cushy (*inf.*), easy, effortless, light, simple, undemanding, unexacting, untaxing

punishment *n* **1, 2** = **penalty**, chastening, chastisement, comeuppance (*sl.*), correction, discipline, just deserts, penance, punitive measures, retribution, sanction, what for (*inf.*) **3** *Informal* = **rough treatment**, abuse, beating, hard work, maltreatment, manhandling, pain, slave labour, torture, victimization

punitive *adj* = **retaliatory**, in reprisal, in retaliation, punitory, retaliative, revengeful, vindictive

punt[3] *vb* **1** = **bet**, back, gamble, lay, stake, wager ◆ *n* **2** = **bet**, gamble, stake, wager

punter[3] *n* **1** = **gambler**, backer, better, punt (*chiefly Brit.*) **2** *Slang* = **customer**, client

puny *adj* **1** = **feeble**, diminutive, dwarfish, frail, little, pint-sized (*inf.*), pygmy *or* pigmy, sickly, stunted, tiny, underfed, undersized, undeveloped, weak, weakly **2** = **insignificant**, inconsequential, inferior, minor, paltry, petty, piddling (*inf.*), trifling, trivial, worthless
Antonyms *adj* ≠ **feeble**: brawny, burly, healthy, hefty (*inf.*), husky (*inf.*), powerful, robust, strong, sturdy, well-built, well-developed

pup *n* **3** *Informal, chiefly Brit.* = **whippersnapper**, braggart, jackanapes, popinjay, whelp

pupil[1] *n* **1** = **learner**, beginner, catechumen, disciple, neophyte, novice, scholar, schoolboy *or* schoolgirl, student, trainee, tyro
Antonyms *n* coach, guru, instructor, master *or* mistress, schoolmaster *or* schoolmistress, schoolteacher, teacher, trainer, tutor

puppet *n* **1** = **marionette**, doll **2** = **pawn**, cat's-paw, creature, dupe, figurehead, gull (*arch.*), instrument, mouthpiece, stooge, tool

purchasable *adj* **1** = **for sale**, available, in stock, obtainable, on sale, on the market, to be had

purchase *vb* **1** = **buy**, acquire, come by, gain,

(goods, etc.) by payment. **2** to obtain by effort, sacrifice, etc.: *to purchase one's freedom.* **3** to draw or lift (a load) with mechanical apparatus. ◆ *n* **4** something that is purchased. **5** the act of buying. **6** acquisition of an estate by any lawful means other than inheritance. **7** the mechanical advantage achieved by a lever. **8** a firm foothold, grasp, etc., as for climbing something. [C13: from OF *porchacier* to strive to obtain; see CHASE[1]]
▸ **'purchasable** *adj* ▸ **'purchaser** *n*

purchase tax *n* (in Britain, formerly) a tax levied on nonessential consumer goods and added to selling prices by retailers.

purdah ('pɜːdə) *n* **1** the custom in some Muslim and Hindu communities of keeping women in seclusion, with clothing that conceals them completely when they go out. **2** a screen in a Hindu house used to keep the women out of view. [C19: from Hindi *parda* veil, from Persian *pardah*]

pure ❶ (pjʊə) *adj* **1** not mixed with any extraneous or dissimilar materials, elements, etc. **2** free from tainting or polluting matter: *pure water.* **3** free from moral taint or defilement: *pure love.* **4** (*prenominal*) (intensifier): *a pure coincidence.* **5** (of a subject, etc.) studied in its theoretical aspects rather than for its practical applications: *pure mathematics.* **6** (of a vowel) pronounced with more or less unvarying quality without any glide. **7** (of a consonant) not accompanied by another consonant. **8** of unmixed descent. **9** *Genetics, biol.* breeding true; homozygous. [C13: from OF *pur,* from L *pūrus* unstained]
▸ **'purely** *adv* ▸ **'pureness** *n*

purebred ❶ *adj* ('pjʊə'brɛd). **1** denoting a pure strain obtained through many generations of controlled breeding. ◆ *n* ('pjʊə,brɛd). **2** a purebred animal.

purée ('pjʊəreɪ) *n* **1** a smooth thick pulp of sieved fruit, vegetables, meat, or fish. ◆ *vb* **purées, puréeing, puréed. 2** (*tr*) to make (cooked foods) into a purée. [C19: from F *purer* to PURIFY]

purfle ('pɜːfᵊl) *n also* **purfling. 1** a ruffled or curved ornamental band, as on clothing, furniture, etc. ◆ *vb* **purfles, purfling, purfled. 2** (*tr*) to decorate with such a band. [C14: from OF *purfiler* to decorate with a border, from *fil* thread, from L *fīlum*]

purgation (pɜː'geɪʃən) *n* the act of purging or state of being purged; purification.

purgative ❶ ('pɜːgətɪv) *Med.* ◆ *n* **1** a drug or agent for purging the bowels. ◆ *adj* **2** causing evacuation of the bowels.
▸ **'purgatively** *adv*

purgatory ❶ ('pɜːgətərɪ, -trɪ) *n* **1** *Chiefly RC Church.* a state or place in which the souls of those who have died in a state of grace are believed to undergo a limited amount of suffering to expiate their venial sins. **2** a place or condition of suffering or torment, esp. one that is temporary. [C13: from OF *purgatoire,* from Med. L *pūrgātōrium,* lit.: place of cleansing, from L *pūrgāre* to purge]
▸ **,purga'torial** *adj*

purge ❶ (pɜːdʒ) *vb* **purges, purging, purged. 1** (*tr*) to rid (something) of (impure elements). **2** (*tr*) to rid (a state, political party, etc.) of (dissident people). **3** (*tr*) **3a** to empty (the bowels) by evacuation of faeces. **3b** to cause (a person) to evacuate his bowels. **4a** to clear (a person) of a charge. **4b** to free (oneself) of guilt, as by atonement. **5** (*intr*) to be purified. ◆ *n* **6** the act or process of purging. **7** the elimination of opponents or dissidents from a state, political party, etc. **8** a purgative drug or agent. [C14: from OF *purger,* from L *pūrgāre* to purify]

purificator ('pjʊərɪfɪ,keɪtə) *n Christianity.* a small white linen cloth used to wipe the chalice and paten at the Eucharist.

purify ❶ ('pjʊərɪ,faɪ) *vb* **purifies, purifying, purified. 1** to free (something) of contaminating or debasing matter. **2** (*tr*) to free (a person, etc.) from sin or guilt. **3** (*tr*) to make clean, as in a ritual. [C14: from OF *purifier,* from LL *pūrificāre* to cleanse, from *pūrus* pure + *facere* to make]
▸ **,purifi'cation** *n* ▸ **purificatory** ('pjʊərɪfɪ,keɪtərɪ, -trɪ) *adj* ▸ **'puri,fier** *n*

Purim ('pʊərɪm; *Hebrew* puː'riːm) *n* a Jewish holiday in February or March to commemorate the deliverance of the Jews from the massacre planned by Haman (Esther 9). [Heb. *pūrīm,* pl. of *pūr* lot; from the casting of lots by Haman]

purine ('pjʊəriːn) *or* **purin** ('pjʊərɪn) *n* **1** a colourless crystalline solid that can be prepared from uric acid. Formula: $C_5H_5N_4$. **2** Also called: **purine base.** any of a number of nitrogenous bases that are derivatives of purine. [C19: from G *Purin*]

puriri (puː'riːriː) *n* a New Zealand tree with hard timber and red berries. [from Maori]

purism ❶ ('pjʊə,rɪzəm) *n* insistence on traditional canons of correctness of form or purity of style or content.
▸ **'purist** *adj, n* ▸ **pu'ristic** *adj*

puritan ❶ ('pjʊərɪtᵊn) *n* **1** a person who adheres to strict moral or religious principles, esp. one opposed to luxury and sensual enjoyment. ◆ *adj* **2** characteristic of a puritan. [C16: from LL *pūritās* purity]
▸ **'puritan,ism** *n*

Puritan ('pjʊərɪtᵊn) (in the late 16th and 17th centuries) ◆ *n* **1** any of the extreme English Protestants who wished to purify the Church of England of most of its ceremony and other aspects that they deemed to be Catholic. ◆ *adj* **2** of or relating to the Puritans.
▸ **'Puritan,ism** *n*

puritanical ❶ (,pjʊərɪ'tænɪkᵊl) *adj* **1** *Usually disparaging.* strict in moral or religious outlook, esp. in shunning sensual pleasures. **2** (*sometimes cap.*) of or relating to a puritan or the Puritans.
▸ **,puri'tanically** *adv*

purity ❶ ('pjʊərɪtɪ) *n* the state or quality of being pure.

purl[1] (pɜːl) *n* **1** a knitting stitch made by doing a plain stitch backwards. **2** a decorative border, as of lace. **3** gold or silver wire thread. ◆ *vb* **4** to knit in purl stitch. **5** to edge (something) with a purl. ◆ Also (for senses 2, 3, 5): **pearl.** [C16: from dialect *pirl* to twist into a cord]

purl[2] (pɜːl) *vb* **1** (*intr*) (of a stream, etc.) to flow with a gentle swirling or rippling movement and a murmuring sound. ◆ *n* **2** a swirling movement of water; eddy. **3** a murmuring sound, as of a shallow stream. [C16: rel. to Norwegian *purla* to bubble]

purler[1] ('pɜːlə) *n Inf.* a headlong or spectacular fall (esp. in **come a purler**).

purler[2] ('pɜːlə) *n Austral. sl.* something outstanding in its class. [from ?]

purlieu ❶ ('pɜːljuː) *n* **1** *English history.* land on the edge of a forest once included within the bounds of the royal forest but later separated although still subject to some of the forest laws. **2** (*usually pl*) a neighbouring area; outskirts. **3** (*often pl*) a place one frequents; haunt. [C15 *purlewe,* from Anglo-F *puralé* a going through (infl. also by OF *lieu* place), from OF *puraler,* from *pur* through + *aler* to go]

purlin *or* **purline** ('pɜːlɪn) *n* a horizontal beam that supports the common rafters of a roof and is carried by the principal rafters or trusses. [C15: from ?]

purloin ❶ (pɜː'lɔɪn) *vb* to steal. [C15: from OF *porloigner* to put at a distance, from *por-* for + *loin* distant, from L *longus* long]
▸ **pur'loiner** *n*

THESAURUS

get, get hold of, invest in, make a purchase, obtain, pay for, pick up, procure, score (*sl.*), secure, shop for **2 = achieve**, attain, earn, gain, realize, win ◆ *n* **4 = buy**, acquisition, asset, gain, investment, possession, property **7, 8 = grip**, advantage, edge, foothold, footing, grasp, hold, influence, lever, leverage, support, toehold
Antonyms *vb* ≠ **buy:** hawk, market, merchandise, peddle, retail, sell, trade in, vend

purchaser *n* **1 = buyer**, consumer, customer, vendee (*Law*)
Antonyms *n* dealer, merchant, retailer, salesman *or* saleswoman, salesperson, seller, shopkeeper, tradesman, vendor

pure *adj* **1 = unmixed**, authentic, clear, flawless, genuine, natural, neat, perfect, real, simple, straight, true, unalloyed **2 = clean**, disinfected, germ-free, immaculate, pasteurized, sanitary, spotless, squeaky-clean, sterile, sterilized, unadulterated, unblemished, uncontaminated, unpolluted, untainted, wholesome **3 = innocent**, blameless, chaste, guileless, honest, immaculate, impeccable, maidenly, modest, squeaky-clean, true, uncorrupted, undefiled, unspotted, unstained, unsullied, upright, virgin, virginal, virtuous **4 = complete**, absolute, mere, outright, sheer, thorough, unmitigated, unqualified, utter **5 = theoretical**, abstract, academic, philosophical, speculative
Antonyms *adj* ≠ **unmixed:** adulterated, alloyed, flawed, imperfect, mixed ≠ **clean:** contaminated, dirty, filthy, impure, infected, polluted, tainted ≠ **innocent:** contaminated, corrupt, defiled, guilty, immodest, immoral, impure, indecent, obscene, sinful, spoiled, unchaste, unclean, untrue ≠ **complete:** qualified ≠ **theoretical:** applied, practical

purebred *adj* **1 = thoroughbred**, blood, full-blooded, pedigree

purely *adv* **4 = absolutely**, completely, entirely, exclusively, just, merely, only, plainly, simply, solely, totally, wholly

purgative *n* **1 = purge**, aperient, cathartic, depurative, emetic, enema, evacuant, laxative, physic (*rare*) ◆ *adj* **2 = purging**, aperient (*Medical*), cleansing, depurative, evacuant, laxative

purgatory *n* **2 = torment**, agony, hell (*inf.*), hell on earth, misery, murder (*inf.*), the rack, torture

purge *vb* **1 = cleanse**, clean out, clear, expiate, purify, wash **2 = get rid of**, dismiss, do away with, eject, eradicate, expel, exterminate, kill, liquidate, oust, remove, rid of, rout out, sweep out, wipe out **4 = absolve**, exonerate, forgive, pardon ◆ *n* **7 = removal**, cleanup, crushing, ejection, elimination, eradication, expulsion, liquidation, reign of terror, suppression, witch hunt **8 = purgative** (*Medical*), aperient (*Medical*), cathartic, dose of salts, emetic, enema, laxative, physic (*rare*)

purify *vb* **1 = clean**, clarify, cleanse, decontaminate, disinfect, filter, fumigate, refine, sanitize, wash **2 = absolve**, cleanse, exculpate, exonerate, lustrate, redeem, sanctify, shrive
Antonyms *vb* ≠ **clean:** adulterate, befoul, contaminate, corrupt, defile, foul, infect, pollute, soil, taint ≠ **absolve:** stain, sully, taint, vitiate

purist *n* **= stickler**, classicist, formalist, pedant, precisian

puritan *n* **1 = moralist**, fanatic, pietist, prude, rigorist, zealot ◆ *adj* **2 = strict**, ascetic, austere, hidebound, intolerant, moralistic, narrow, narrow-minded, prudish, puritanical, severe, strait-laced

puritanical *adj* **1 = strict**, ascetic, austere, bigoted, disapproving, fanatical, forbidding, narrow, narrow-minded, prim, proper, prudish, puritan, rigid, severe, stiff, strait-laced, stuffy
Antonyms *adj* broad-minded, hedonistic, indulgent, latitudinarian, liberal, permissive, tolerant

puritanism *n* **2 = strictness**, asceticism, austerity, fanaticism, moralism, narrowness, piety, piousness, prudishness, rigidity, rigorism, severity, zeal

purity *n* **= cleanness**, brilliance, clarity, cleanliness, clearness, faultlessness, fineness, genuineness, immaculateness, pureness, untaintedness, wholesomeness **= innocence**, blamelessness, chasteness, chastity, decency, guilelessness, honesty, integrity, piety, rectitude, sincerity, virginity, virtue, virtuousness
Antonyms *n* ≠ **cleanness:** cloudiness, contamination, impurity ≠ **innocence:** immodesty, immorality, impurity, unchasteness, vice, wickedness

purlieu *n* **2** *usually plural* **= outskirts**, borders, confines, environs, fringes, limits, neighbourhood, periphery, precincts, suburbs, vicinity **3** *often plural* **= stamping ground**, hang-out (*inf.*), haunt, patch, resort, territory

purloin *vb* **= steal**, appropriate, blag (*sl.*), filch,

purple ('pɜːpᵊl) *n* **1** a colour between red and blue. **2** a dye or pigment producing such a colour. **3** cloth of this colour, often used to symbolize royalty or nobility. **4** (usually preceded by *the*) high rank; nobility. **5a** the official robe of a cardinal. **5b** the rank of a cardinal as signified by this. ◆ *adj* **6** of the colour purple. **7** (of writing) excessively elaborate or full of imagery: *purple prose.* [OE, from L *purpura* purple dye, from Gk *porphura* the purple fish (murex)]
▸**'purpleness** *n* ▸**'purplish** *or* **'purply** *adj*

purple heart *n* **1** any of several tropical American trees. **2** *Inf., chiefly Brit.* a heart-shaped purple tablet consisting mainly of amphetamine.

Purple Heart *n* a decoration awarded to members of the US Armed Forces for a wound received in action.

purple patch *n* **1** Also called: **purple passage.** a section in a piece of writing characterized by fanciful or ornate language. **2** *Sl.* a period of good fortune.

purport ❶ *vb* (pɜː'pɔːt). (*tr*) **1** to claim to be (true, official, etc.) by manner or appearance, esp. falsely. **2** (esp. of speech or writing) to signify or imply. ◆ *n* ('pɜːpɔːt). **3** meaning; significance. **4** object; intention. [C15: from Anglo-F: contents, from OF *porporter* to convey, from L *portāre*]

purpose ❶ ('pɜːpəs) *n* **1** the reason for which anything is done, created, or exists. **2** a fixed design or idea that is the object of an action or other effort. **3** determination: *a man of purpose.* **4** practical advantage or use: *to work to good purpose.* **5** that which is relevant (esp. in **to** *or* **from the purpose**). **6** *Arch.* purport. **7 on purpose.** intentionally. ◆ *vb* **purposes, purposing, purposed. 8** (*tr*) to intend or determine to do (something). [C13: from OF *porpos,* from *porposer* to plan, from L *prōpōnere* to PROPOSE]
▸**'purposeless** *adj*

purpose-built *adj* made to serve a specific purpose.

purposeful ❶ ('pɜːpəsfʊl) *adj* **1** having a definite purpose in view. **2** determined.
▸**'purposefully** *adv* ▸**'purposefulness** *n*

> **USAGE NOTE** *Purposefully* is sometimes wrongly used where *purposely* is meant: *he had purposely* (not *purposefully*) *left the door unlocked.*

purposely ❶ ('pɜːpəslɪ) *adv* on purpose.

> **USAGE NOTE** See at **purposeful.**

purposive ('pɜːpəsɪv) *adj* **1** having or indicating conscious intention. **2** serving a purpose; useful.
▸**'purposively** *adv* ▸**'purposiveness** *n*

purpura ('pɜːpjʊrə) *n Pathol.* any of several blood diseases causing purplish spots on the skin due to subcutaneous bleeding. [C18: via L from Gk *porphura* a shellfish yielding purple dye]

purr (pɜː) *vb* **1** (*intr*) (esp. of cats) to make a low vibrant sound, usually considered as expressing pleasure, etc. **2** (*tr*) to express (pleasure, etc.) by this sound or by a sound suggestive of purring. ◆ *n* **3** a purring sound. [C17: imit.]

purse ❶ (pɜːs) *n* **1** a small bag or pouch for carrying money, esp. coins. **2** *US & Canad.* a woman's handbag. **3** anything resembling a small bag or pouch in form or function. **4** wealth; funds; resources. **5** a sum of money that is offered, esp. as a prize. ◆ *vb* **purses, pursing, pursed. 6** (*tr*) to contract (the mouth, lips, etc.) into a small rounded shape. [OE *purs,* prob. from LL *bursa* bag, ult. from Gk: leather]

purser ('pɜːsə) *n* an officer aboard a ship or aircraft who keeps the accounts and attends to the welfare of the passengers.

purse seine *n* a large net that encloses fish and is then closed at the bottom by means of a line resembling the string formerly used to draw shut the neck of a money pouch.

purse strings *pl n* control of expenditure (esp. in **hold** *or* **control the purse strings**).

purslane ('pɜːslɪn) *n* a plant with fleshy leaves used (esp. formerly) in salads and as a potherb. [C14 *purcelane,* from OF *porcelaine,* from LL, from L *porcillāca,* var. of *portulāca*]

pursuance ❶ (pə'sjuːəns) *n* the carrying out or pursuing of an action, plan, etc.

pursuant (pə'sjuːənt) *adj* **1** (*usually postpositive;* often foll. by *to*) *Chiefly law.* in agreement or conformity. **2** *Arch.* pursuing. [C17: rel. to ME *poursuivant* following after, from OF; see PURSUE]
▸**pur'suantly** *adv*

pursue ❶ (pə'sjuː) *vb* **pursues, pursuing, pursued.** (*mainly tr*) **1** (*also intr*) to follow (a fugitive, etc.) in order to capture or overtake. **2** to follow closely or accompany: *ill health pursued her.* **3** to seek or strive to attain (some desire, etc.). **4** to follow the precepts of (a plan, policy, etc.). **5** to apply oneself to (studies, interests, etc.). **6** to follow persistently or seek to become acquainted with. **7** to continue to discuss or argue (a point, subject, etc.). [C13: from Anglo-Norman *pursiwer,* from OF *poursivre,* from L *prōsequī* to follow after]
▸**pur'suer** *n*

pursuit ❶ (pə'sjuːt) *n* **1a** the act of pursuing. **1b** (*as modifier*): *a pursuit plane.* **2** an occupation or pastime. **3** (in cycling) a race in which the riders set off at intervals along the track and attempt to overtake each other. [C14: from OF *poursieute,* from *poursivre* to PURSUE]

pursuivant ('pɜːsɪvənt) *n* **1** the lowest rank of heraldic officer. **2** *History.* a state or royal messenger. **3** *History.* a follower or attendant. [C14: from OF, from *poursivre* to PURSUE]

purulent ('pjʊərʊlənt) *adj* of, relating to, or containing pus. [C16: from L *pūrulentus,* from *pūs*]
▸**'purulence** *n* ▸**'purulently** *adv*

purvey ❶ (pə'veɪ) *vb* (*tr*) **1** to sell or provide (commodities, esp. foodstuffs) on a large scale. **2** to publish (lies, scandal, etc.). [C13: from OF *porveeir,* from L *prōvidēre* to PROVIDE]
▸**pur'veyor** *n*

purveyance (pə'veɪəns) *n* **1** *History.* the collection or requisition of provisions for a sovereign. **2** *Rare.* the act of purveying.

purview ❶ ('pɜːvjuː) *n* **1** scope of operation. **2** breadth or range of outlook. **3** *Law.* the body of a statute, containing the enacting clauses. [C15: from Anglo-Norman *purveu,* from *porveeir* to furnish; see PURVEY]

pus (pʌs) *n* the yellow or greenish fluid product of inflammation. [C16: from L *pūs*]

push ❶ (pʊʃ) *vb* **1** (when *tr,* often foll. by *off, away,* etc.) to apply steady force to in order to move. **2** to thrust (one's way) through something, such as a crowd. **3** (*tr*) to encourage or urge (a person) to some action, decision, etc. **4** (when *intr,* often foll. by *for*) to be an advocate or promoter (of): *to push for acceptance of one's theories.* **5** (*tr*) to use one's influence to help (a person): *to push one's own candidate.* **6** to bear upon (oneself or another person) in order to achieve better results, etc. **7** *Cricket, etc.* to hit (a ball) with a stiff pushing stroke. **8** (*tr*) *Inf.* to sell (narcotic drugs) illegally. **9** (*intr;* foll. by *out, into,* etc.) to extend: *the*

THESAURUS

knock off (*sl.*), lift (*inf.*), nick (*sl., chiefly Brit.*), pilfer, pinch (*inf.*), rob, snaffle (*Brit. inf.*), snitch (*sl.*), swipe (*sl.*), thieve, walk off with

purport *vb* **1** = **claim**, allege, assert, declare, maintain, pose as, pretend, proclaim, profess **2** = **signify**, betoken, convey, denote, express, imply, import, indicate, intend, mean, point to, suggest ◆ *n* **3** = **significance**, bearing, drift, gist, idea, implication, import, meaning, sense, spirit, tendency, tenor **4** = **intention**, aim, design, intent, object, objective, plan, purpose

purpose *n* **1** = **reason**, aim, design, function, idea, intention, object, point, principle, the why and wherefore **2** = **aim**, ambition, aspiration, design, desire, end, goal, Holy Grail (*inf.*), hope, intention, object, objective, plan, project, scheme, target, view, wish **3** = **determination**, constancy, firmness, persistence, resolution, resolve, single-mindedness, steadfastness, tenacity, will **4** = **use**, advantage, avail, benefit, effect, gain, good, mileage (*inf.*), outcome, profit, result, return, utility **7 on purpose** = **deliberately**, by design, designedly, intentionally, knowingly, purposely, wilfully, wittingly ◆ *vb* **8** = **intend**, aim, aspire, commit oneself, contemplate, decide, design, determine, have a mind to, make up one's mind, mean, meditate, plan, propose, resolve, set one's sights on, think to, work towards

purposeful *adj* **2** = **determined**, decided, deliberate, firm, fixed, immovable, positive, resolute, resolved, settled, single-minded, steadfast, strong-willed, tenacious, unfaltering
Antonyms *adj* aimless, faltering, irresolute, otiose, purposeless, undecided, undetermined, vacillating, wavering

purposeless *adj* **1** = **pointless**, aimless, empty, goalless, motiveless, needless, otiose, senseless, uncalled-for, unnecessary, useless, vacuous, wanton, without rhyme or reason

purposely *adv* = **deliberately**, by design, calculatedly, consciously, designedly, expressly, intentionally, knowingly, on purpose, wilfully, with intent
Antonyms *adv* accidentally, by accident, by chance, by mistake, inadvertently, unconsciously, unintentionally, unknowingly, unwittingly

purse *n* **1** = **pouch**, money-bag, wallet **4** = **money**, coffers, exchequer, funds, means, resources, treasury, wealth, wherewithal **5** = **prize**, award, gift, reward ◆ *vb* **6** = **pucker**, close, contract, knit, pout, press together, tighten, wrinkle

pursuance *n* = **carrying out**, bringing about, discharge, doing, effecting, execution, following, performance, prosecution, pursuing

pursue *vb* **1, 2** = **follow**, accompany, attend, chase, dog, give chase to, go after, harass, harry, haunt, hound, hunt, hunt down, plague, run after, shadow, stalk, tail (*inf.*), track **3** = **try for**, aim for, aspire to, desire, have as one's goal, purpose, seek, strive for, work towards **4** = **continue**, adhere to, carry on, cultivate, hold to, keep on, maintain, persevere in, persist in, proceed, see through **5** = **engage in**, apply oneself, carry on, conduct, perform, ply, practise, prosecute, tackle, wage, work at **6** = **court**, chase after, make up to (*inf.*), pay attention to, pay court to, set one's cap at, woo
Antonyms *vb* ≠ **follow:** avoid, flee, give (someone *or* something) a wide berth, keep away from, run away from, shun, steer clear of ≠ **try for:** eschew, fight shy of

pursuit *n* **1** = **pursuing**, chase, hunt, hunting, inquiry, quest, search, seeking, tracking, trail, trailing **2** = **occupation**, activity, hobby, interest, line, pastime, pleasure, vocation

purvey *vb* **1** = **supply**, cater, deal in, furnish, provide, provision, retail, sell, trade in, victual **2** = **communicate**, make available, pass on, publish, retail, spread, transmit

purview *n* **1** = **scope**, ambit, compass, confine(s), extent, field, limit, orbit, province, range, reach, sphere **2** = **understanding**, comprehension, ken, overview, perspective, range of view

push *vb* **1** = **shove**, depress, drive, poke, press, propel, ram, thrust **2** = **make** *or* **force one's way**, elbow, jostle, move, shoulder, shove, squeeze, thrust **3** = **urge**, egg on, encourage, expedite, gee up, hurry, impel, incite, persuade, press, prod, speed (up), spur **4** = **promote**, advertise, boost, cry up, hype, make known, plug (*inf.*), propagandize, publicize, puff ◆ *n* **11** = **shove**,

DICTIONARY

cliffs pushed out to the sea. **10 push one's luck** *or* **push it. 10a** to take undue risks, esp. through overconfidence. **10b** (*intr*) to act overconfidently. ◆ *n* **11** the act of pushing; thrust. **12** a part or device that is pressed to operate some mechanism. **13** *Inf.* drive, energy, etc. **14** *Inf.* a special effort or attempt to advance, as of an army: *to make a push.* **15** *Austral. sl.* a group, gang, or clique. **16** *Cricket, etc.* a stiff pushing stroke. **17 at a push.** *Inf.* with difficulty; only just. **18 the push.** *Inf., chiefly Brit.* dismissal, esp. from employment. ◆ See also **push off, push in,** etc. [C13: from OF *pousser,* from L *pulsāre,* from *pellere* to drive]

push-bike *n Brit.* an informal name for **bicycle.**

push button *n* **1** an electrical switch operated by pressing a button, which closes or opens a circuit. ◆ *modifier.* **push-button. 2a** operated by a push button: *a push-button radio.* **2b** initiated as simply as by pressing a button: *push-button warfare.*

pushcart (ˈpʊʃˌkɑːt) *n* another name (esp. US and Canad.) for **barrow**[1] (sense 3).

pushchair (ˈpʊʃˌtʃɛə) *n* a usually collapsible chair-shaped carriage for a small child. Also called: **baby buggy, buggy.** US and Canad. word: **stroller.** Austral. words: **pusher, stroller.**

pushed ❶ (pʊʃt) *adj* (often foll. by *for*) *Inf.* short (of) or in need (of time, money, etc.).

pusher (ˈpʊʃə) *n* **1** *Inf.* a person who sells illegal drugs, esp. narcotics such as heroin. **2** *Inf.* an aggressively ambitious person. **3** a person or thing that pushes. **4** *Austral.* the usual name for **pushchair.**

push in *vb* (*intr, adv*) to force one's way into a group of people, queue, etc.

pushing ❶ (ˈpʊʃɪŋ) *adj* **1** enterprising or aggressively ambitious. **2** impertinently self-assertive. ◆ *adv* **3** almost or nearly (a certain age, speed, etc.): *pushing fifty.*
▸ˈ**pushingly** *adv*

push money *n* a cash inducement provided by a manufacturer or distributor for a retailer or his staff, to reward successful selling.

push off ❶ *vb* (*adv*) **1** Also: **push out.** to move into open water, as by being cast off from a mooring. **2** (*intr*) *Inf.* to go away; leave.

pushover ❶ (ˈpʊʃˌəʊvə) *n Inf.* **1** something that is easily achieved. **2** a person, team, etc., that is easily taken advantage of or defeated.

push-pull *n* (*modifier*) using two similar electronic devices made to operate out of phase with each other to produce a signal that replicates the input waveform: *a push-pull amplifier.*

push-start *vb* (*tr*) **1** to start (a motor vehicle) by pushing it while it is in gear, thus turning the engine. ◆ *n* **2** this process.

push through *vb* (*tr*) to compel to accept: *the bill was pushed through Parliament.*

Pushto (ˈpʌʃtəʊ) *or* **Pushtu** (ˈpʌʃtuː) *n, adj* variant spellings of **Pashto.**

push-up *n* the US and Canad. term for **press-up.**

pushy ❶ (ˈpʊʃɪ) *adj* **pushier, pushiest.** *Inf.* **1** offensively assertive. **2** aggressively or ruthlessly ambitious.
▸ˈ**pushily** *adv* ▸ˈ**pushiness** *n*

pusillanimous ❶ (ˌpjuːsɪˈlænɪməs) *adj* characterized by a lack of courage or determination. [C16: from LL *pusillanimis* from L *pusillus* weak + *animus* courage]
▸**pusillanimity** (ˌpjuːsɪləˈnɪmɪtɪ) *n* ▸ˌ**pusilˈlanimously** *adv*

puss (pʊs) *n* **1** an informal name for a **cat. 2** *Sl.* a girl or woman. **3** an informal name for a **hare.** [C16: rel. to MLow G *pūs*]

pussy[1] (ˈpʊsɪ) *n, pl* **pussies. 1** Also called: **puss, pussycat.** an informal name for a **cat. 2** a furry catkin. **3** *Taboo sl.* the female pudenda. [C18: from PUSS]

pussy[2] (ˈpʌsɪ) *adj* **pussier, pussiest.** containing or full of pus.

pussycat (ˈpʊsɪˌkæt) *n* **1** an informal or child's name for **cat**[1]. **2** *Brit. inf.* an endearing or gentle person.

pussyfoot ❶ (ˈpʊsɪˌfʊt) *vb* (*intr*) *Inf.* **1** to move about stealthily or warily like a cat. **2** to avoid committing oneself.

pussy willow (ˈpʊsɪ) *n* a willow tree with silvery silky catkins.

pustulant (ˈpʌstjʊlənt) *adj* **1** causing the formation of pustules. ◆ *n* **2** an agent causing such formation.

pustulate *vb* (ˈpʌstjʊˌleɪt), **pustulates, pustulating, pustulated. 1** to form or cause to form into pustules. ◆ *adj* (ˈpʌstjʊlɪt). **2** covered with pustules.
▸ˌ**pustuˈlation** *n*

pustule ❶ (ˈpʌstjuːl) *n* **1** a small inflamed elevated area of skin containing pus. **2** any spot resembling a pimple. [C14: from L *pustula* a blister, var. of *pūsula*]
▸**pustular** (ˈpʌstjʊlə) *adj*

put ❶ (pʊt) *vb* **puts, putting, put.** (*mainly tr*) **1** to cause to be (in a position or place): *to put a book on the table.* **2** to cause to be (in a state, relation, etc.): *to put one's things in order.* **3** (foll. by *to*) to cause (a person) to experience or suffer: *to put to death.* **4** to set or commit (to an action, task, or duty), esp. by force: *he put him to work.* **5** to render or translate: *to put into English.* **6** to set (words) in a musical form (esp. in **put to music**). **7** (foll. by *at*) to estimate: *he put the distance at fifty miles.* **8** (foll. by *to*) to utilize: *he put his knowledge to use.* **9** (foll. by *to*) to couple (a female animal) with a male for breeding: *the farmer put his heifer to the bull.* **10** to express: *to put it bluntly.* **11** to make (an end or limit): *he put an end to the proceedings.* **12** to present for consideration; propose: *he put the question to the committee.* **13** to invest (money) in or expend (time, energy, etc.) on: *he put five thousand pounds into the project.* **14** to impart: *to put zest into a party.* **15** to throw or cast. **16 not know where to put oneself.** to feel embarrassed. **17 stay put.** to remain in one place; keep one's position. ◆ *n* **18** a throw, esp. in putting the shot. **19** Also called: **put option.** *Stock Exchange.* an option to sell a stated number of securities at a specified price during a limited period. ◆ See also **put about, put across,** etc. [C12 *puten* to push]

put about *vb* (*adv*) **1** *Naut.* to change course. **2** (*tr*) to make widely known: *he put about the news of the air disaster.* **3** (*tr; usually passive*) to disconcert or disturb.

put across ❶ *vb* (*tr*) **1** (*adv*) to communicate in a comprehensible way: *he couldn't put things across very well.* **2 put one across.** *Inf.* to get (someone) to believe a claim, excuse, etc., by deception: *they put one across their teacher.*

put aside ❶ *vb* (*tr, adv*) **1** to move (an object, etc.) to one side, esp. in rejection. **2** to save: *to put money aside for a rainy day.* **3** to disregard: *let us put aside our differences.*

putative ❶ (ˈpjuːtətɪv) *adj* (*prenominal*) **1** commonly regarded as being: *the putative father.* **2** considered to exist or have existed; inferred. [C15: from LL *putātīvus* supposed, from L *putāre* to consider]
▸ˈ**putatively** *adv*

put away ❶ *vb* (*tr, adv*) **1** to return (something) to the proper place. **2** to save: *to put away money for the future.* **3** to lock up in a prison, mental institution, etc.: *they put him away for twenty years.* **4** to eat or drink, esp. in large amounts.

put back *vb* (*tr, adv*) **1** to return to its former place. **2** to move to a later time: *the wedding was put back a fortnight.* **3** to impede the progress of: *the strike put back production.*

put by *vb* (*tr, adv*) to set aside for the future; save.

put down ❶ *vb* (*tr, adv*) **1** to make a written record of. **2** to repress: *to put down a rebellion.* **3** to consider: *they put him down for an ignoramus.* **4** to attribute: *I put the mistake down to inexperience.* **5** to put (an animal) to

THESAURUS

butt, jolt, nudge, poke, prod, thrust **13** *Informal* = **drive,** ambition, determination, dynamism, energy, enterprise, get-up-and-go (*inf.*), go (*inf.*), gumption (*inf.*), initiative, pep, vigour, vitality **14** *Informal* = **effort,** advance, assault, attack, campaign, charge, offensive, onset, thrust **18 the push** *Informal, chiefly Brit.* = **dismissal,** discharge, marching orders (*inf.*), one's books (*inf.*), one's cards (*inf.*), the boot (*sl.*), the (old) heave-ho (*inf.*), the sack (*inf.*)
Antonyms *vb* ≠ **shove:** drag, draw, haul, jerk, pull, tow, trail, tug, yank ≠ **urge:** deter, discourage, dissuade, put off ◆ *n* ≠ **shove:** jerk, pull, tug, yank

pushed *adj Informal often foll. by* **for** = **short of,** hurried, in difficulty, pressed, rushed, tight, under pressure, up against it (*inf.*)

pushing *adj* **1** = **ambitious,** determined, driving, dynamic, enterprising, go-ahead, on the go, purposeful, resourceful **2** = **self-assertive,** assertive, bold, brash, bumptious, forward, impertinent, intrusive, presumptuous, pushy (*inf.*)

push off *vb* **2** *Informal* = **go away,** beat it (*sl.*), depart, get lost (*inf.*), launch, leave, light out (*inf.*), make oneself scarce (*inf.*), make tracks, pack one's bags (*inf.*), shove off (*inf.*), slope off, take off (*inf.*)

pushover *Informal n* **1** = **piece of cake** (*Brit. inf.*), breeze (*US & Canad. inf.*), cakewalk (*inf.*), child's play (*inf.*), cinch (*sl.*), doddle (*Brit. sl.*), duck soup (*US sl.*), picnic (*inf.*), plain sailing, walkover (*inf.*) **2** = **sucker** (*sl.*), chump (*inf.*), easy game (*inf.*), easy *or* soft mark (*inf.*), mug (*Brit. sl.*), soft touch (*sl.*), stooge (*sl.*), walkover (*inf.*)
Antonyms *n* ≠ **piece of cake:** challenge, hassle (*inf.*), ordeal, test, trial, undertaking

pushy *adj* **1, 2** = **forceful,** aggressive, ambitious, assertive, bold, brash, bumptious, loud, obnoxious, obtrusive, offensive, officious, presumptuous, pushing, self-assertive
Antonyms *adj* diffident, inoffensive, meek, mousy, quiet, reserved, retiring, self-effacing, shy, timid, unassertive, unassuming, unobtrusive

pusillanimous *adj* = **cowardly,** abject, chicken-hearted, craven, faint-hearted, fearful, feeble, gutless (*inf.*), lily-livered, recreant (*arch.*), spineless, timid, timorous, weak, yellow (*inf.*)
Antonyms *adj* bold, brave, courageous, daring, dauntless, fearless, gallant, heroic, intrepid, plucky, valiant, valorous

pussyfoot *vb* **1** = **creep,** prowl, slink, steal, tiptoe, tread warily **2** = **hedge,** beat about the bush, be noncommittal, equivocate, flannel (*Brit. inf.*), hum and haw, prevaricate, sit on the fence, tergiversate

pustule *n* **1** = **boil,** abscess, blister, fester, gathering, pimple, ulcer, zit (*sl.*)

put *vb* **1** = **place,** bring, deposit, establish, fix, lay, position, rest, set, settle, situate **3** = **impose,** commit, condemn, consign, doom, enjoin, inflict, levy, subject **4** = **make,** assign, constrain, employ, force, induce, oblige, require, set, subject to **10** = **express,** phrase, pose, set, state, utter, word **12** = **present,** advance, bring forward, forward, offer, posit, propose, set before, submit, tender **15** = **throw,** cast, fling, heave, hurl, lob, pitch, toss

put across *vb* **1** = **communicate,** convey, explain, get across, get through, make clear, make oneself understood, spell out

put aside *vb* **2** = **save,** cache, deposit, keep in reserve, lay by, salt away, squirrel away, stockpile, store, stow away **3** = **disregard,** bury, discount, forget, ignore

putative *adj* **1** = **supposed,** alleged, assumed, commonly believed, imputed, presumed, presumptive, reported, reputed

put away *vb* **1** = **put back,** replace, return to (its) place, tidy away **2** = **save,** deposit, keep, lay in, put by, set aside, store away **3** = **commit,** certify, confine, institutionalize, lock up **4** = **consume,** devour, eat up, gobble, gulp down, wolf down

put down *vb* **1** = **record,** enter, inscribe, log, set down, take down, transcribe, write down **2** = **repress,** crush, quash, quell, silence, stamp out, suppress **4** = **attribute,** ascribe, impute, set down **5** = **put to sleep,** destroy, do away with, put away, put out of its misery **7** *Slang* = **humiliate,** condemn, crush, deflate, dismiss, dispar-

death, because of old age or illness. **6** to table on the agenda: *the MPs put down a motion on the increase in crime.* **7** *Sl.* to reject or humiliate. ◆ *n* **put-down. 8** a cruelly crushing remark.

put forth *vb (tr, adv) Formal.* **1** to propose. **2** (of a plant) to produce or bear (leaves, etc.).

put forward Ⓣ *vb (tr, adv)* **1** to propose; suggest. **2** to offer the name of; nominate.

put in *vb (adv)* **1** *(intr) Naut.* to bring a vessel into port. **2** (often foll. by *for*) to apply (for a job, etc.). **3** *(tr)* to submit: *he put in his claims form.* **4** to intervene with (a remark) during a conversation. **5** *(tr)* to devote (time, effort, etc.): *he put in three hours overtime last night.* **6** *(tr)* to establish or appoint: *he put in a manager.* **7** *(tr) Cricket.* to cause to bat: *England won the toss and put the visitors in to bat.*

put off Ⓣ *vb (tr)* **1** *(adv)* to postpone: *they have put off the dance until tomorrow.* **2** *(adv)* to evade (a person) by postponement or delay: *they tried to put him off, but he came anyway.* **3** *(adv)* to cause aversion: *he was put off by her appearance.* **4** *(prep)* to cause to lose interest in: *the accident put him off driving.*

put on Ⓣ *vb (tr, mainly adv)* **1** to clothe oneself in. **2** *(usually passive)* to adopt (an attitude or feeling) insincerely: *his misery was just put on.* **3** to present (a play, show, etc.). **4** to add: *she put on weight.* **5** to cause (an electrical device) to function. **6** *(also prep)* to wager (money) on a horse race, game, etc. **7** *(also prep)* to impose: *to put a tax on cars.* **8** *Cricket.* to cause (a bowler) to bowl.

put out Ⓣ *vb (tr, adv)* **1** *(often passive)* **1a** to annoy; anger. **1b** to disturb; confuse. **2** to extinguish (a fire, light, etc.). **3** to poke forward: *to put out one's tongue.* **4** to be a source of inconvenience to: *I hope I'm not putting you out.* **5** to publish; broadcast: *the authorities put out a leaflet.* **6** to render unconscious. **7** to dislocate: *he put out his shoulder in the accident.* **8** to give out (work to be done) at different premises. **9** to lend (money) at interest. **10** *Cricket, etc.* to dismiss (a player or team).

put over *vb (tr, adv)* **1** *Inf.* to communicate (facts, information, etc.). **2** *Chiefly US.* to postpone. **3 put (a fast) one over on.** *Inf.* to get (someone) to believe a claim, excuse, etc., by deception: *he put one over on his boss.*

put-put ('pʌtˌpʌt) *Inf.* ◆ *n* **1** a light chugging or popping sound, as made by a petrol engine. ◆ *vb* **put-puts, put-putting, put-putted. 2** *(intr)* to make such a sound.

putrefy Ⓣ ('pju:trɪˌfaɪ) *vb* **putrefies, putrefying, putrefied.** (of organic matter) to decompose or rot with an offensive smell. [C15: from OF *putrefier* + L *putrefacere,* from *puter* rotten + *facere* to make]
▸**putrefaction** (ˌpju:trɪ'fækʃən) *n* ▸ˌ**putre'factive** *or* **putrefacient** (ˌpju:trɪ'feɪʃənt) *adj*

putrescent Ⓣ (pju:'tresᵊnt) *adj* **1** becoming putrid; rotting. **2** characterized by or undergoing putrefaction. [C18: from L *putrescere* to become rotten]
▸**pu'trescence** *n*

putrid Ⓣ ('pju:trɪd) *adj* **1** (of organic matter) in a state of decomposition: *putrid meat.* **2** morally corrupt. **3** sickening; foul: *a putrid smell.* **4** *Inf.* deficient in quality or value: *a putrid film.* [C16: from L *putridus,* from *putrēre* to be rotten]
▸**pu'tridity** *or* **'putridness** *n* ▸**'putridly** *adv*

putsch (putʃ) *n* a violent and sudden uprising; political revolt. [C20: from G, from Swiss G: a push, imit.]

putt (pʌt) *Golf.* ◆ *n* **1** a stroke on the green with a putter to roll the ball into or near the hole. ◆ *vb* **2** to strike (the ball) in this way. [C16: of Scot. origin]

puttee *or* **putty** ('pʌtɪ) *n, pl* **puttees** *or* **putties.** *(usually pl)* a strip of cloth worn wound around the leg from the ankle to the knee, esp. as part of a military uniform in World War I. [C19: from Hindi *paṭṭī,* from Sansk. *paṭṭikā,* from *paṭṭa* cloth]

putter[1] ('pʌtə) *n Golf.* **1** a club for putting, usually having a solid metal head. **2** a golfer who putts: *he is a good putter.*

putter[2] ('pʌtə) *vb* the usual US and Canad. word for **potter**[2].
▸**'putterer** *n*

putter[3] ('putə) *n* **1** a person who puts: *the putter of a question.* **2** a person who puts the shot.

put through Ⓣ *vb (tr, mainly adv)* **1** to carry out to a conclusion: *he put through his plan.* **2** *(also prep)* to organize the processing of: *she put through his application to join the organization.* **3** to connect by telephone. **4** to make (a telephone call).

putting green ('pʌtɪŋ) *n* **1** (on a golf course) the area of closely mown grass at the end of a fairway where the hole is. **2** an area of smooth grass with several holes for putting games.

putto ('putəu) *n, pl* **putti** (-ti:). a representation of a small boy, a cherub or cupid, esp. in baroque painting or sculpture. [from It., from L *putus* boy]

putty ('pʌtɪ) *n, pl* **putties. 1** a stiff paste made of whiting and linseed oil that is used to fix glass into frames and to fill cracks in woodwork, etc. **2** any substance with a similar function or appearance. **3** a mixture of lime and water with sand or plaster of Paris used on plaster as a finishing coat. **4** *(as modifier): a putty knife.* **5** a person who is easily influenced: *he's putty in her hands.* **6a** a colour varying from greyish yellow to greyish brown. **6b** *(as adj): putty wool.* ◆ *vb* **putties, puttying, puttied. 7** *(tr)* to fix, fill, or coat with putty. [C17: from F *potée* a potful]

put up Ⓣ *vb (adv, mainly tr)* **1** to build; erect: *to put up a statue.* **2** to accommodate or be accommodated at: *can you put me up for tonight?* **3** to increase (prices). **4** to submit (a plan, case, etc.). **5** to offer: *to put a house up for sale.* **6** to give: *to put up a good fight.* **7** to provide (money) for: *they put up five thousand for the new project.* **8** to preserve or can (jam, etc.). **9** to pile up (long hair) on the head in any of several styles. **10** *(also intr)* to nominate or be nominated as a candidate: *he put up for president.* **11** *Arch.* to return (a weapon) to its holder: *put up your sword!* **12 put up to. 12a** to inform or instruct (a person) about (tasks, duties, etc.). **12b** to incite to. **13 put up with.** *Inf.* to endure; tolerate. ◆ *adj* **put-up. 14** dishonestly or craftily prearranged (esp. in **put-up job**).

put upon Ⓣ *vb (intr, prep; usually passive)* **1** to presume on (a person's generosity, good nature, etc.): *he's always being put upon.* **2** to impose hardship on: *he was sorely put upon.*

putz (pʌts) *n US sl.* a despicable or stupid person. [from Yiddish *puts* ornament]

puzzle Ⓣ ('pʌzᵊl) *vb* **puzzles, puzzling, puzzled. 1** to perplex or be perplexed. **2** *(intr;* foll. by *over)* to ponder about the cause of: *he puzzled over her absence.* **3** *(tr;* usually foll. by *out)* to solve by mental effort: *he puzzled out the meaning.* ◆ *n* **4** a person or thing that puzzles. **5** a problem that cannot be easily solved. **6** the state of being puzzled. **7** a toy, game, or question presenting a problem that requires skill or ingenuity for its solution. [C16: from ?]
▸**'puzzlement** *n* ▸**'puzzler** *n* ▸**'puzzling** *adj* ▸**'puzzlingly** *adv*

PVC *abbrev. for* polyvinyl chloride; a synthetic thermoplastic material

THESAURUS

age, mortify, reject, shame, slight, snub ◆ *n* **put-down 8 = humiliation**, barb, dig, disparagement, gibe, rebuff, sarcasm, slight, sneer, snub

put forward *vb* **1, 2 = recommend**, advance, introduce, move, nominate, prescribe, present, press, proffer, propose, submit, suggest, tender

put off *vb* **1 = postpone**, defer, delay, hold over, put back, put on ice, put on the back burner *(inf.)*, reschedule **3 = disconcert**, abash, confuse, discomfit, dismay, distress, faze, nonplus, perturb, rattle *(inf.)*, throw *(inf.)*, unsettle **4 = discourage**, dishearten, dissuade
Antonyms *vb* ≠ **discourage:** egg on, encourage, gee up, incite, persuade, prompt, push, spur, urge

put on *vb* **1 = don**, change into, dress, get dressed in, slip into **2 = fake**, affect, assume, feign, make believe, play-act, pretend, sham, simulate **3 = present**, do, mount, produce, show, stage **4 = add**, gain, increase by **6 = bet**, back, lay, place, wager
Antonyms *vb* ≠ **don:** cast off, doff, remove, shed, slip off, slip out of, take off, throw off, undress

put out *vb* **1a = annoy**, anger, confound, disturb, exasperate, harass, irk, irritate, nettle, perturb, provoke, vex **1b = disconcert**, discompose, discountenance, disturb, embarrass, put on the spot, take the wind out of someone's sails **2 = extinguish**, blow out, douse, quench, smother, snuff out, stamp out **4 = inconvenience**, bother, discomfit, discommode, disturb, impose upon, incommode, trouble, upset **5 = issue**, bring out, broadcast, circulate, make known, make public, publish, release

putrefy *vb* **= rot**, break down, corrupt, decay, decompose, deteriorate, go bad, spoil, stink, taint

putrescent *adj* **1, 2 = rotting**, decaying, decomposing, going bad, stinking

putrid *adj* **1, 3 = rotten**, bad, contaminated, corrupt, decayed, decomposed, fetid, foul, off, olid, putrefied, rancid, rank, reeking, rotting, spoiled, stinking, tainted
Antonyms *adj* clean, fresh, pure, sweet, uncontaminated, untainted, wholesome

put through *vb* **1 = carry out**, accomplish, achieve, bring off, conclude, do, effect, execute, manage, pull off, realize

put up *vb* **1 = build**, construct, erect, fabricate, raise **2 = accommodate**, board, entertain, give one lodging, house, lodge, take in **4 = submit**, float, nominate, offer, present, propose, put forward, recommend **7 = provide**, advance, give, invest, pay, pledge, supply **12b put up to = encourage**, egg on, goad, incite, instigate, prompt, put the idea into one's head, urge **13 put up with** *Informal* **= stand**, abide, bear, brook, endure, hack *(sl.)*, lump *(inf.)*, stand for, stomach, suffer, swallow, take, tolerate
Antonyms *vb* ≠ **build:** demolish, destroy, flatten, knock down, level, pull down, raze, tear down ≠ **stand:** not stand for, object to, oppose, protest against, reject, take exception to

put upon *vb* **1, 2 = take advantage of**, abuse, beset, exploit, harry, impose upon, inconvenience, overwork, put out, saddle, take for a fool, take for granted, trouble

puzzle *vb* **1 = perplex**, baffle, beat *(sl.)*, bewilder, confound, confuse, flummox, mystify, nonplus, stump **2** *usually foll. by* **over = think about**, ask oneself, brood, cudgel *or* rack one's brains, mull over, muse, ponder, study, think hard, wonder **3** *usually foll. by* **out = solve**, clear up, crack, crack the code, decipher, figure out, find the key, get it, get the answer, resolve, see, sort out, suss (out) *(sl.)*, think through, unravel, work out ◆ *n* **4, 5, 7 = problem**, brain-teaser *(inf.)*, conundrum, enigma, labyrinth, maze, mystery, paradox, poser, question, question mark, riddle, teaser **6 = perplexity**, bafflement, bewilderment, confusion, difficulty, dilemma, quandary, uncertainty

puzzled *adj* **1 = perplexed**, at a loss, at sea, baffled, beaten, bewildered, clueless, confused, doubtful, flummoxed, in a fog, lost, mixed up, mystified, nonplussed, stuck, stumped, without a clue

puzzlement *n* **1 = perplexity**, bafflement, bewilderment, confusion, disorientation, doubt, doubtfulness, mystification, questioning, surprise, uncertainty, wonder

puzzling *adj* **1 = perplexing**, abstruse, ambiguous, baffling, bewildering, beyond one, enigmatic, full of surprises, hard, incomprehensible, inexplicable, involved, knotty, labyrinthine, misleading, mystifying, oracular, unaccountable, unclear, unfathomable
Antonyms *adj* clear, comprehensible, easy, evident, intelligible, lucid, manifest, obvious, patent, plain, simple, unambiguous, unequivocal, unmistakable

made by polymerizing vinyl chloride. The flexible forms are used in insulation, shoes, etc. Rigid PVC is used for moulded articles.

PVS *abbrev. for:* **1** persistent vegetative state. **2** postviral syndrome.

Pvt. *Mil. abbrev. for* private.

PW *abbrev. for* policewoman.

PWA *abbrev. for* person with AIDS.

PWR *abbrev. for* pressurized-water reactor.

pyaemia *or* **pyemia** (paɪ'iːmɪə) *n* blood poisoning characterized by pus-forming microorganisms in the blood. [C19: from NL, from Gk *puon* pus + *haima* blood]
▸**py'aemic** *or* **py'emic** *adj*

pye-dog, pie-dog, *or* **pi-dog** ('paɪˌdɒg) *n* an ownerless half-wild Asian dog. [C19: Anglo-Indian, from Hindi *pāhī* outsider]

pyelitis (ˌpaɪə'laɪtɪs) *n* inflammation of the pelvis of the kidney. [C19: NL, from Gk *puelos* trough]
▸**pyelitic** (ˌpaɪə'lɪtɪk) *adj*

pygmy ⓘ *or* **pigmy** ('pɪgmɪ) *n, pl* **pygmies** *or* **pigmies. 1** an abnormally undersized person. **2** something that is a very small example of its type. **3** a person of little importance or significance. **4** (*modifier*) very small. [C14 *pigmeis* the Pygmies, from L *Pygmaeus* a Pygmy, from Gk *pugmaios* undersized, from *pugmē* fist]
▸**pygmaean** *or* **pygmean** (pɪg'miːən) *adj*

Pygmy *or* **Pigmy** ('pɪgmɪ) *n, pl* **Pygmies** *or* **Pigmies.** a member of one of the dwarf peoples of Equatorial Africa, noted for their hunting and forest culture.

pyinkado (pjɪŋ'kɑːdəʊ) *n, pl* **pyinkados. 1** a leguminous tree, native to India and Myanmar. **2** the heavy durable timber of this tree, used for construction. [C19: from Burmese]

pyjamas *or US* **pajamas** (pə'dʒɑːməz) *pl n* **1** loose-fitting nightclothes comprising a jacket or top and trousers. **2** full loose-fitting ankle-length trousers worn by either sex in various Eastern countries. [C19: from Hindi, from Persian *pai* leg + *jāma* garment]

pyknic ('pɪknɪk) *adj* characterized by a broad squat fleshy physique with a large chest and abdomen. [C20: from Gk *puknos* thick]

pylon ('paɪlən) *n* **1** a large vertical steel tower-like structure supporting high-tension electrical cables. **2** a post or tower for guiding pilots or marking a turning point in a race. **3** a streamlined aircraft structure for attaching an engine pod, etc., to the main body of the aircraft. **4** a monumental gateway, such as one at the entrance to an ancient Egyptian temple. [C19: from Gk *pulōn* a gateway]

pylorus (paɪ'lɔːrəs) *n, pl* **pylori** (-raɪ). the small circular opening at the base of the stomach through which partially digested food passes to the duodenum. [C17: via LL from Gk *pulōrus* gatekeeper, from *pulē* gate + *ouros* guardian]

pyo- *or before a vowel* **py-** *combining form.* denoting pus: *pyosis.* [from Gk *puon*]

pyorrhoea *or esp. US* **pyorrhea** (ˌpaɪə'rɪə) *n* inflammation of the gums characterized by the discharge of pus and loosening of the teeth; periodontal disease.
▸ˌ**pyor'rhoeal,** ˌ**pyor'rhoeic** *or esp. US* ˌ**pyor'rheal,** ˌ**pyor'rheic** *adj*

pyracantha (ˌpaɪrə'kænθə) *n* any of a genus of shrubs with yellow, orange, or scarlet berries, widely cultivated for ornament. [C17: from Gk *purakantha,* from PYRO- + *akantha* thorn]

pyramid ('pɪrəmɪd) *n* **1** a huge masonry construction that has a square base and, as in the case of the ancient Egyptian royal tombs, four sloping triangular sides. **2** an object or structure resembling such a construction. **3** *Maths.* a solid having a polygonal base and triangular sides that meet in a common vertex. **4** *Crystallography.* a crystal form in which three planes intersect all three axes of the crystal. **5** *Finance.* a group of enterprises containing a series of holding companies structured so that the top holding company controls the entire group with a relatively small proportion of the total capital invested. **6** (*pl*) a game similar to billiards. ◆ *vb* **pyramids, pyramiding, pyramided. 7** to build up or be arranged in the form of a pyramid. **8** *Finance.* to form (companies) into a pyramid. [C16 (earlier *pyramis*): from L *pyramis,* from Gk *puramis,* prob. from Egyptian]
▸**pyramidal** (pɪ'ræmɪdᵊl), ˌ**pyra'midical,** *or* ˌ**pyra'midic** *adj* ▸**py'ramidally** *or* ˌ**pyra'midically** *adv*

pyramid selling *n* a practice adopted by some manufacturers of advertising for distributors and selling them batches of goods. The first distributors then advertise for more distributors who are sold subdivisions of the original batches at an increased price. This process continues until the final distributors are left with a stock that is unsaleable except at a loss.

pyre ('paɪə) *n* a pile of wood or other combustible material, esp. one for cremating a corpse. [C17: from L *pyra,* from Gk *pura* hearth, from *pur* fire]

pyrethrin (paɪ'riːθrɪn) *n* either of two oily compounds found in pyrethrum and used as insecticides. [C19: from PYRETHRUM + -IN]

pyrethrum (paɪ'riːθrəm) *n* **1** any of several cultivated Eurasian chrysanthemums with white, pink, red, or purple flowers. **2** any insecticide prepared from the dried flowers of any of these plants. [C16: via L from Gk *purethron* feverfew, prob. from *puretos* fever; see PYRETIC]

pyretic (paɪ'rɛtɪk) *adj Pathology.* of, relating to, or characterized by fever. [C18: from NL *pyreticus,* from Gk *puretos* fever, from *pur* fire]

Pyrex ('paɪrɛks) *n Trademark.* **a** any of a variety of glasses that have low coefficients of expansion, making them suitable for heat-resistant glassware used in cookery and chemical apparatus. **b** (*as modifier*): *a Pyrex dish.*

pyrexia (paɪ'rɛksɪə) *n* a technical name for **fever.** [C18: from NL, from Gk *purexis,* from *puressein* to be feverish, from *pur* fire]
▸**py'rexial** *or* **py'rexic** *adj*

pyridine ('pɪrɪˌdiːn) *n* a colourless hygroscopic liquid heterocyclic compound with a characteristic odour: used as a solvent and in preparing other organic chemicals. Formula: C_5H_5N. [C19: from PYRO- + -ID[2] + -INE[2]]

pyridoxine (ˌpɪrɪ'dɒksiːn) *n Biochemistry.* a derivative of pyridine that is a precursor of the compounds pyridoxal and pyridoxamine. Also called: **vitamin** B_6.

pyrimidine (paɪ'rɪmɪˌdiːn) *n* **1** a liquid or crystalline organic compound with a penetrating odour. Formula: $C_4H_4N_2$. **2** Also called: **pyrimidine base.** any of a number of similar compounds having a basic structure that is derived from pyrimidine, and which are constituents of nucleic acids. [C20: var. of PYRIDINE]

pyrite ('paɪraɪt) *n* a yellow mineral consisting of iron sulphide in cubic crystalline form. It occurs in igneous and metamorphic rocks and in veins, associated with various metals, and is used mainly in the manufacture of sulphuric acid and paper. Formula: FeS_2. Also called: **iron pyrites, pyrites.** [C16: from L *pyrites* flint, from Gk *purītēs* (*lithos*) fire(stone), from *pur* fire]
▸**pyritic** (paɪ'rɪtɪk) *or* **py'ritous** *adj*

pyrites (paɪ'raɪtiːz; *in combination* 'paɪraɪts) *n, pl* **pyrites. 1** another name for **pyrite. 2** any of a number of other disulphides of metals, esp. of copper and tin.

pyro- *or before a vowel* **pyr-** *combining form.* **1** denoting fire or heat: *pyromania; pyrometer.* **2** *Chem.* denoting a new substance obtained by heating another: *pyroboric acid is obtained by heating boric acid.* **3** *Mineralogy.* **3a** having a property that changes upon the application of heat. **3b** having a flame-coloured appearance: *pyroxylin.* [from Gk *pur* fire]

pyroelectricity (ˌpaɪrəʊɪlɛk'trɪsɪtɪ) *n* the development of opposite charges at the ends of the axis of certain crystals as a result of a change in temperature.

pyrogallol (ˌpaɪrəʊ'gælɒl) *n* a crystalline soluble phenol with weakly acidic properties: used as a photographic developer and for absorbing oxygen in gas analysis. Formula: $C_6H_3(OH)_3$. [C20: from PYRO- + GALL(IC ACID) + -OL[1]]

pyrogenic (ˌpaɪrəʊ'dʒɛnɪk) *or* **pyrogenous** (paɪ'rɒdʒɪnəs) *adj* **1** produced by or producing heat. **2** *Pathology.* causing or resulting from fever. **3** *Geol.* less common words for **igneous.**

pyrography (paɪ'rɒgrəfɪ) *n* another name for **pokerwork.**

pyroligneous (ˌpaɪrəʊ'lɪgnɪəs) *or* **pyrolignic** *adj* (of a substance) produced by the action of heat on wood, esp. by destructive distillation.

pyrolysis (paɪ'rɒlɪsɪs) *n* **1** the application of heat to chemical compounds in order to cause decomposition. **2** such chemical decomposition.
▸**pyrolytic** (ˌpaɪrəʊ'lɪtɪk) *adj*

pyromania (ˌpaɪrəʊ'meɪnɪə) *n Psychiatry.* the uncontrollable impulse and practice of setting things on fire.
▸ˌ**pyro'maniˌac** *n*

pyrometer (paɪ'rɒmɪtə) *n* an instrument for measuring high temperatures, esp. by measuring the brightness or total quantity of the radiation produced.
▸**pyrometric** (ˌpaɪrəʊ'mɛtrɪk) *or* ˌ**pyro'metrical** *adj* ▸ˌ**pyro'metrically** *adv* ▸**py'rometry** *n*

pyrope ('paɪrəʊp) *n* a deep yellowish-red garnet that consists of magnesium aluminium silicate and is used as a gemstone. [C14 (used loosely of a red gem; modern sense C19): from OF *pirope,* from L *pyrōpus* bronze, from Gk *purōpus* fiery-eyed]

pyrophoric (ˌpaɪrəʊ'fɒrɪk) *adj* **1** (of a chemical) igniting spontaneously on contact with air. **2** (of an alloy) producing sparks when struck or scraped: *lighter flints are made of pyrophoric alloy.* [C19: from NL *pyrophorus,* from Gk *purophoros* fire-bearing, from *pur* fire + *pherein* to bear]

pyrosis (paɪ'rəʊsɪs) *n Pathology.* a technical name for **heartburn.** [C18: from NL, from Gk: a burning, from *puroun* to burn, from *pur* fire]

pyrostat ('paɪrəʊˌstæt) *n* **1** a device that activates an alarm or extinguisher in the event of a fire. **2** a thermostat for use at high temperatures.
▸ˌ**pyro'static** *adj*

pyrotechnics (ˌpaɪrəʊ'tɛknɪks) *n* **1** (*functioning as sing*) the art of making fireworks. **2** (*functioning as sing or pl*) a firework display. **3** (*functioning as sing or pl*) brilliance of display, as in the performance of music.
▸ˌ**pyro'technic** *or* ˌ**pyro'technical** *adj*

pyroxene (paɪ'rɒksiːn) *n* any of a large group of minerals consisting of the silicates of magnesium, iron, and calcium. They occur in basic igneous rocks. [C19: PYRO- + *-xene* from Gk *xenos* foreign, because mistakenly thought to have originated elsewhere when found in igneous rocks]

THESAURUS

pygmy *n* **1** = **midget,** dwarf, homunculus, Lilliputian, manikin, shrimp (*inf.*), Tom Thumb **3** = **nonentity,** cipher, lightweight (*inf.*), mediocrity, nobody, pipsqueak (*inf.*), small fry ◆ *modifier* **4** = **small,** baby, diminutive, dwarf, dwarfish, elfin, Lilliputian, midget, miniature, minuscule, pocket, pygmean, stunted, teensy-weensy, teeny-weeny, tiny, undersized, wee

pyromaniac *n* = **arsonist,** firebug (*inf.*), fire raiser, incendiary

pyroxylin (paɪˈrɒksɪlɪn) *n* a yellow substance obtained by nitrating cellulose with a mixture of nitric and sulphuric acids; guncotton: used to make collodion, plastics, lacquers, and adhesives.

pyrrhic (ˈpɪrɪk) *Prosody*. ◆ *n* **1** a metrical foot of two short or unstressed syllables. ◆ *adj* **2** of or composed in pyrrhics. [C16: via L, from Gk *purrhikhē*, said to be after its inventor *Purrhikhos*]

Pyrrhic victory *n* a victory in which the victor's losses are as great as those of the defeated. Also called: **Cadmean victory.** [after *Pyrrhus* (319–272 B.C.), who defeated the Romans at Asculum in 279 B.C. but suffered heavy losses]

Pyrrhonism (ˈpɪrəˌnɪzəm) *n* the doctrine of Pyrrho (?365–?275 B.C.), Greek sceptic philosopher, that certain knowledge is impossible to obtain.

pyruvic acid (paɪˈruːvɪk) *n* a liquid formed during the metabolism of proteins and carbohydrates, helping to release energy to the body. [C19: from PYRO- + L *ūva* grape]

Pythagoras' theorem *n* (paɪˈθægərəs) the theorem that in a right-angled triangle the square of the length of the hypotenuse equals the sum of the squares of the other two sides. [after *Pythagoras* (?580–?500 B.C.) Gk philosopher and mathematician]

Pythagorean (paɪˌθægəˈriːən) *adj* **1** of or relating to Pythagoras. ◆ *n* **2** a follower of Pythagoras.

Pythian (ˈpɪθɪən) *adj also* **Pythic. 1** of or relating to Delphi or its oracle. ◆ *n* **2** the priestess of Apollo at the oracle of Delphi. [C16: via L *Pȳthius* from Gk *Puthios* of Delphi]

python (ˈpaɪθən) *n* any of a family of large nonvenomous snakes of Africa, S Asia, and Australia. They can reach a length of more than 20 feet and kill their prey by constriction. [C16: NL, after *Python*, a dragon killed by Apollo]
▸**pythonic** (paɪˈθɒnɪk) *adj*

pythoness (ˈpaɪθənɛs) *n* a woman, such as Apollo's priestess at Delphi, believed to be possessed by an oracular spirit. [C14: *phitonesse*, ult. from Gk *Puthōn* Python; see PYTHON]

pyuria (paɪˈjʊərɪə) *n Pathol.* any condition characterized by the presence of pus in the urine. [C19: from NL, from Gk *puon* pus + *ouron* urine]

pyx (pɪks) *n* **1** Also called: **pyx chest.** the chest in which coins from the British mint are placed to be tested for weight, etc. **2** *Christianity.* any receptacle in which the Eucharistic Host is kept. [C14: from L *pyxis* small box, from Gk, from *puxos* box tree]

pyxidium (pɪkˈsɪdɪəm) *or* **pyxis** (ˈpɪksɪs) *n, pl* **pyxidia** (-ɪə) *or* **pyxides** (ˈpɪksɪˌdiːz). the dry fruit of such plants as the plantain: a capsule whose upper part falls off when mature so that the seeds are released. [C19: via NL from Gk *puxidion* a little box, from *puxis* box]

pyxis (ˈpɪksɪs) *n, pl* **pyxides** (ˈpɪksɪˌdiːz). **1** a small box used by the ancient Greeks and Romans to hold medicines, etc. **2** another name for **pyxidium.** [C14: via L from Gk: box]

q *or* **Q** (kjuː) *n, pl* **q's, Q's,** *or* **Qs. 1** the 17th letter of the English alphabet. **2** a speech sound represented by this letter.
q *symbol for* quintal.
Q *symbol for:* **1** *Physics.* heat. **2** *Chess.* queen. **3** question.
q. *abbrev. for:* **1** quart. **2** quarter. **3** quarterly. **4** query. **5** question. **6** quire.
Q. *abbrev. for:* **1** quartermaster. **2** (*pl* **Qq., qq.**) Also: **q.** quarto. **3** Quebec. **4** Queen. **5** question. **6** *Electronics.* Q factor.
qadi (ˈkɑːdɪ, ˈkeɪdɪ) *n, pl* **qadis.** a variant spelling of **cadi.**
QANTAS (ˈkwɒntəs) *n* the national airline of Australia. [C20: from *Q(ueensland) a(nd) N(orthern) T(erritory) A(erial) S(ervices Ltd.)*]
QARANC *abbrev. for* Queen Alexandra's Royal Army Nursing Corps.
qawwali (kəˈvɑːlɪ) *n* an Islamic religious song, esp. in Asia.
QB *abbrev. for* Queen's Bench.
QC *abbrev. for* Queen's Counsel.
QED *abbrev. for:* **1** quantum electrodynamics. **2** quod erat demonstrandum. [L: which was to be shown or proved]
Q factor *n* **1** a measure of the relationship between stored energy and rate of energy dissipation in certain electrical components, devices, etc. **2** Also called: **Q value.** the heat released in a nuclear reaction. ◆ Symbol: Q [C20: short for *quality factor*]
Q fever *n* an acute disease characterized by fever and pneumonia, transmitted to man by a rickettsia. [C20: from *q(uery) fever* (the cause being orig. unknown)]
qi (tʃiː) *n* a variant spelling of **chi**[2].
Qld *or* **QLD** *abbrev. for* Queensland.
QM *abbrev. for* Quartermaster.
QMG *abbrev. for* Quartermaster General.
QMV *abbrev. for* Qualified Majority Voting.
qr. *pl* **qrs.** *abbrev. for:* **1** quarter. **2** quarterly. **3** quire.
Q-ship *n* a merchant ship with concealed guns, used to decoy enemy ships. [C20: from Q short for QUERY]
QSM (in New Zealand) *abbrev. for* Queen's Service Medal.
QSO *abbrev. for:* **1** quasi-stellar object. **2** (in New Zealand) Queen's Service Order.
qt *pl* **qt** *or* **qts** *abbrev. for* quart.
q.t. *Inf.* **1** *abbrev. for* quiet. **2 on the q.t.** secretly.
qua (kweɪ, kwɑː) *prep* in the capacity of; by virtue of being. [C17: from L, ablative sing (fem) of *qui* who]
quack[1] (kwæk) *vb* (*intr*) **1** (of a duck) to utter a harsh guttural sound. **2** to make a noise like a duck. ◆ *n* **3** the sound made by a duck. [C17: imit.]
quack[2] ❶ (kwæk) *n* **1a** an unqualified person who claims medical knowledge or other skills. **1b** (*as modifier*): *a quack doctor.* **2** *Brit., Austral., & NZ inf.* a doctor; physician or surgeon. ◆ *vb* **3** (*intr*) to act in the manner of a quack. [C17: short for QUACKSALVER]
▸ˈ**quackish** *adj*
quackery (ˈkwækərɪ) *n, pl* **quackeries.** the activities or methods of a quack.
quack grass *n* another name for **couch grass.**
quacksalver (ˈkwækˌsælvə) *n* an archaic word for **quack**[2]. [C16: from Du., from *quack,* apparently: to hawk + *salf* SALVE]
quad[1] (kwɒd) *n* short for **quadrangle.**
quad[2] (kwɒd) *n Printing.* a block of type metal used for spacing. [C19: shortened from QUADRAT]
quad[3] (kwɒd) *n* short for **quadruplet.**
quad[4] (kwɒd) *n, adj Inf.* short for **quadraphonics** *or* **quadraphonic.**
quad bike *or* **quad** *n* a vehicle like a motorcycle, with four large wheels, designed for agricultural, sporting, and other off-road uses.
Quadragesima (ˌkwɒdrəˈdʒɛsɪmə) *n* the first Sunday in Lent. Also called: **Quadragesima Sunday.** [C16: from Med. L *quadrāgēsima dies* the fortieth day]
Quadragesimal (ˌkwɒdrəˈdʒɛsɪməl) *adj* of, relating to, or characteristic of Lent.
quadrangle (ˈkwɒdˌræŋgᵊl) *n* **1** *Geom.* a plane figure consisting of four points connected by four lines. **2** a rectangular courtyard, esp. one having buildings on all four sides. **3** the building surrounding such a courtyard. [C15: from LL *quadrangulum* figure having four corners]
▸**quadrangular** (kwɒˈdræŋgjʊlə) *adj*
quadrant (ˈkwɒdrənt) *n* **1** *Geom.* **1a** a quarter of the circumference of a circle. **1b** the area enclosed by two perpendicular radii of a circle. **1c** any of the four sections into which a plane is divided by two coordinate axes. **2** a piece of a mechanism in the form of a quarter circle. **3** an instrument formerly used in astronomy and navigation for measuring the altitudes of stars. [C14: from L *quadrāns* a quarter]
▸**quadrantal** (kwɒˈdræntᵊl) *adj*
quadraphonics *or* **quadrophonics** (ˌkwɒdrəˈfɒnɪks) *n* (*functioning as sing*) a system of sound recording and reproduction that uses four independent loudspeakers to give directional sources of sound.
▸ˌ**quadraˈphonic** *or* ˌ**quadroˈphonic** *adj*
quadrat (ˈkwɒdrət) *n* **1** *Ecology.* an area of vegetation selected at random for study. **2** *Printing.* an archaic name for **quad**[2]. [C14 (meaning "a square"): var. of QUADRATE]
quadrate *n* (ˈkwɒdrɪt, -ˌdreɪt). **1** a cube, square, or a square or cubelike object. **2** one of a pair of bones of the upper jaw of fishes, amphibians, reptiles, and birds. ◆ *adj* (ˈkwɒdrɪt, -ˌdreɪt). **3** of or relating to this bone. **4** square or rectangular. ◆ *vb* (kwɒˈdreɪt), **quadrates, quadrating, quadrated. 5** (*tr*) to make square or rectangular. **6** (often foll. by *with*) to conform or cause to conform. [C14: from L *quadrāre* to make square]
quadratic (kwɒˈdrætɪk) *Maths.* ◆ *n* **1** Also called: **quadratic equation.** an equation containing one or more terms in which the variable is raised to the power of two, but to no higher power. ◆ *adj* **2** of or relating to the second power.
quadrature (ˈkwɒdrətʃə) *n* **1** *Maths.* the process of determining a square having an area equal to that of a given figure or surface. **2** the process of making square or dividing into squares. **3** *Astron.* a configuration in which two celestial bodies form an angle of 90° with a third body. **4** *Electronics.* the relationship between two waves that are 90° out of phase.
quadrella (kwɒˈdrɛlə) *n Austral.* a form of betting in which the punter must select the winner of four specified races.
quadrennial (kwɒˈdrɛnɪəl) *adj* **1** occurring every four years. **2** lasting four years. ◆ *n* **3** a period of four years.
▸**quadˈrennially** *adv*
quadrennium (kwɒˈdrɛnɪəm) *n, pl* **quadrenniums** *or* **quadrennia** (-nɪə). a period of four years. [C17: from L *quadriennium,* from QUADRI- + *annus* year]
quadri- *or before a vowel* **quadr-** *combining form.* four: *quadrilateral.* [from L; cf. *quattuor* four]
quadric (ˈkwɒdrɪk) *Maths.* ◆ *adj* **1** having or characterized by an equation of the second degree. **2** of the second degree. ◆ *n* **3** a quadric curve, surface, or function.
quadriceps (ˈkwɒdrɪˌsɛps) *n, pl* **quadricepses** (-ˌsɛpsɪz) *or* **quadriceps.** *Anat.* a large four-part muscle of the front of the thigh, which extends the leg. [C19: NL, from QUADRI- + *-ceps* as in BICEPS]
quadrifid (ˈkwɒdrɪfɪd) *adj Bot.* divided into four lobes or other parts: *quadrifid leaves.*
quadrilateral (ˌkwɒdrɪˈlætərəl) *adj* **1** having or formed by four sides. ◆ *n* **2** Also called: **tetragon.** a polygon having four sides.
quadrille[1] (kwɒˈdrɪl) *n* **1** a square dance for four couples. **2** a piece of music for such a dance. [C18: via F from Sp. *cuadrilla,* dim. of *cuadro* square, from L *quadra*]
quadrille[2] (kwɒˈdrɪl, kwə-) *n* an old card game for four players. [C18: from F, from Sp. *cuartillo,* from *cuarto* fourth, from L *quartus,* infl. by QUADRILLE[1]]
quadrillion (kwɒˈdrɪljən) *n, pl* **quadrillions** *or* **quadrillion. 1** (in Britain, France, and Germany) the number represented as one followed by 24 zeros (10^{24}). US and Canad. word: **septillion. 2** (in the US and Canada) the number represented as one followed by 15 zeros (10^{15}). ◆ *determiner* **3** amounting to this number: *a quadrillion atoms.* [C17: from F *quadrillon,* from QUADRI- + *-illion,* on the model of *million*]
▸**quadˈrillionth** *adj*
quadrinomial (ˌkwɒdrɪˈnəʊmɪəl) *n* an algebraic expression containing four terms.
quadriplegia (ˌkwɒdrɪˈpliːdʒɪə) *n* paralysis of all four limbs. Also called: **tetraplegia.** [C20: from QUADRI- + Gk *plēssein* to strike]
▸**quadriplegic** (ˌkwɒdrɪˈpliːdʒɪk) *adj*
quadrivalent (ˌkwɒdrɪˈveɪlənt) *adj Chem.* another word for **tetravalent.**
▸ˌ**quadriˈvalency** *or* ˌ**quadriˈvalence** *n*
quadrivium (kwɒˈdrɪvɪəm) *n, pl* **quadrivia** (ɪə). (in medieval learning) a course consisting of arithmetic, geometry, astronomy, and music. [from Med. L, from L: crossroads, from QUADRI- + *via* way]
quadroon (kwɒˈdruːn) *n* a person who is one-quarter Black. [C18: from Sp. *cuarterón,* from *cuarto* quarter, from L *quartus*]
quadrumanous (kwɒˈdruːmənəs) *adj* (of monkeys and apes) having all four feet specialized for use as hands. [C18: from NL *quadrumanus,* from QUADRI- + L *manus* hand]
quadruped (ˈkwɒdrʊˌpɛd) *n* **1** an animal, esp. a mammal, that has all four limbs specialized for walking. ◆ *adj* **2** having four feet. [C17: from L *quadrupēs,* from *quadru-* (see QUADRI-) + *pēs* foot]
▸**quadrupedal** (kwɒˈdruːpɪdᵊl) *adj*
quadruple (ˈkwɒdrʊpᵊl, kwɒˈdruːpᵊl) *vb* **quadruples, quadrupling, quadrupled. 1** to multiply by four or increase fourfold. ◆ *adj* **2** four times as much or as many; fourfold. **3** consisting of four parts. **4** *Music.* having four beats in each bar. ◆ *n* **5** a quantity or number four times as great as another. [C16: via OF from L *quadruplus,* from *quadru-* (see QUADRI-) + *-plus* -fold]
▸ˈ**quadruply** *adv*

THESAURUS

quack[2] *n* **1a** = **charlatan,** fake, fraud, humbug, impostor, mountebank, phoney *or* phony (*inf.*), pretender, quacksalver (*arch.*) ◆ *modifier* **1b** = **fake,** counterfeit, fraudulent, phoney *or* phony (*inf.*), pretended, sham

quadruplet ('kwɒdrʊplɪt, kwɒ'dru:plɪt) *n* **1** one of four offspring born at one birth. **2** a group of four similar things. **3** *Music.* a group of four notes to be played in a time value of three.

quadruplicate *adj* (kwɒ'dru:plɪkɪt). **1** fourfold or quadruple. ◆ *vb* (kwɒ'dru:plɪˌkeɪt), **quadruplicates, quadruplicating, quadruplicated. 2** to multiply or be multiplied by four. ◆ *n* (kwɒ'dru:plɪkɪt). **3** a group or set of four things. [C17: from L *quadruplicāre* to increase fourfold]

quaestor ('kwi:stə) *or US (sometimes)* **questor** ('kwɛstə) *n* any of several magistrates of ancient Rome, usually a financial administrator. [C14: from L, from *quaerere* to inquire]
▸**quaestorial** (kwɛ'stɔ:rɪəl) *adj*

quaff ⓣ (kwɒf) *vb* to drink heartily or in one draught. [C16: ? imit.; cf. MLow G *quassen* to eat or drink excessively]
▸'**quaffer** *n*

quag (kwæg) *n* a quagmire. [C16: ? rel. to QUAKE]

quagga ('kwægə) *n, pl* **quaggas** *or* **quagga.** a recently extinct member of the horse family of southern Africa: it had zebra-like stripes on the head and shoulders. [C18: from obs. Afrik., from Khoikhoi *qŭagga*]

quaggy ⓣ ('kwægɪ) *adj* **quaggier, quaggiest. 1** resembling a quagmire; boggy. **2** soft or flabby.

quagmire ⓣ ('kwægˌmaɪə) *n* **1** a soft wet area of land that gives way under the feet; bog. **2** an awkward, complex, or embarrassing situation. [C16: from QUAG + MIRE]

quahog ('kwɑ:ˌhɒg) *n* an edible clam native to the Atlantic coast of North America, having a large heavy rounded shell. [C18: from Amerind, short for *poquauhock,* from *pohkeni* dark + *hogki* shell]

quaich *or* **quaigh** (kweɪx) *n Scot.* a small shallow drinking cup, usually with two handles. [from Gaelic *cuach* cup]

Quai d'Orsay (*French* ke dɔrse) *n* the quay along the S bank of the Seine, Paris, where the French foreign office is situated.

quail[1] (kweɪl) *n, pl* **quails** *or* **quail.** any of various small Old World game birds having rounded bodies and small tails. [C14: from OF *quaille,* from Med. L *quaccula,* prob. imit.]

quail[2] ⓣ (kweɪl) *vb* (*intr*) to shrink back with fear; cower. [C15: ?from OF *quailler,* from L *coāgulāre* to curdle]

quaint ⓣ (kweɪnt) *adj* **1** attractively unusual, esp. in an old-fashioned style. **2** odd or inappropriate. [C13 (in the sense: clever): from OF *cointe,* from L *cognitus* known, from *cognoscere* to ascertain]
▸'**quaintly** *adv* ▸'**quaintness** *n*

quair (kwɛə) *n Scot.* a book. [var. of QUIRE[1]]

quake ⓣ (kweɪk) *vb* **quakes, quaking, quaked.** (*intr*) **1** to shake or tremble with or as with fear. **2** to convulse or quiver, as from instability. ◆ *n* **3** a quaking. **4** *Inf.* an earthquake. [OE *cwacian*]

Quaker ('kweɪkə) *n* **1** a member of the Religious Society of Friends, a Christian sect founded by George Fox about 1650. Quakers reject sacraments, ritual, and formal ministry, and have promoted many causes for social reform. ◆ *adj* **2** of the Religious Society of Friends or its beliefs or practices. [C17: orig. a derog. nickname]
▸'**Quakeress** *fem n* ▸'**Quakerish** *adj* ▸'**Quakerism** *n*

quaking ('kweɪkɪŋ) *adj* unstable or unsafe to walk on, as a bog or quicksand.

quaking grass *n* any of various grasses having delicate branches that shake in the wind.

quaky ('kweɪkɪ) *adj* **quakier, quakiest.** inclined to quake; shaky.
▸'**quakiness** *n*

qualification ⓣ (ˌkwɒlɪfɪ'keɪʃən) *n* **1** an official record of achievement awarded on the successful completion of a course of training or passing of an examination. **2** an ability, quality, or attribute, esp. one that fits a person to perform a particular job or task. **3** a condition that modifies or limits; restriction. **4** a qualifying or being qualified.

qualified ⓣ ('kwɒlɪˌfaɪd) *adj* **1** having the abilities, qualities, attributes, etc., necessary to perform a particular job or task. **2** limited, modified, or restricted; not absolute.

Qualified Majority Voting *n* a voting system, used by the EU Council of Ministers, by which resolutions concerning certain areas of policy may be passed without unanimity. Abbrev.: **QMV.**

qualify ⓣ ('kwɒlɪˌfaɪ) *vb* **qualifies, qualifying, qualified. 1** to provide or be provided with the abilities or attributes necessary for a task, office, duty, etc.: *his degree qualifies him for the job.* **2** (*tr*) to make less strong, harsh, or violent; moderate or restrict. **3** (*tr*) to modify or change the strength or flavour of. **4** (*tr*) *Grammar.* another word for **modify. 5** (*tr*) to attribute a quality to; characterize. **6** (*intr*) to progress to the final stages of a competition, as by winning preliminary contests. [C16: from OF *qualifier,* from Med. L *quālificāre* to characterize, from L *quālis* of what kind + *facere* to make]
▸'**qualiˌfiable** *adj* ▸'**qualiˌfier** *n*

qualitative ('kwɒlɪtətɪv) *adj* involving or relating to distinctions based on quality or qualities.
▸'**qualitatively** *adv*

qualitative analysis *n* See **analysis** (sense 4).

quality ⓣ ('kwɒlɪtɪ) *n, pl* **qualities. 1** a distinguishing characteristic or attribute. **2** the basic character or nature of something. **3** a feature of personality. **4** degree or standard of excellence, esp. a high standard. **5** (formerly) high social status or the distinction associated with it. **6** musical tone colour; timbre. **7** *Logic.* the characteristic of a proposition that makes it affirmative or negative. **8** *Phonetics.* the distinctive character of a vowel, determined by the configuration of the mouth, tongue, etc. **9** (*modifier*) having or showing excellence or superiority: *a quality product.* [C13: from OF *qualité,* from L *quālitās* state, from *quālis* of what sort]

quality control *n* control of the quality of a manufactured product, usually by statistical sampling techniques.

quality time *n* a short period during the day in which a person gives the whole of his or her attention to some matter other than work, esp. family relationships.

qualm ⓣ (kwɑ:m) *n* **1** a sudden feeling of sickness or nausea. **2** a pang of doubt, esp. concerning moral conduct; scruple. **3** a sudden sensation of misgiving. [OE *cwealm* death or plague]
▸'**qualmish** *adj*

quandary ⓣ ('kwɒndrɪ) *n, pl* **quandaries.** a difficult situation; predicament. [C16: from ?; ? rel. to L *quandō* when]

quandong, quandang ('kwɒnˌdɒŋ), *or* **quantong** ('kwɒnˌtɒŋ) *n* **1** Also called: **native peach. 1a** a small Australian tree. **1b** the edible fruit or nut of this tree. **2** *Austral. sl.* a sponger or parasite. **3 silver quandong. 3a** an Australian tree. **3b** its timber. [from Abor.]

quango ('kwæŋgəʊ) *n, pl* **quangos.** a semipublic government-financed administrative body whose members are appointed by the government. [C20: *qu(asi-)a(utonomous) n(on) g(overnmental) o(rganization)*]

quant[1] (kwɒnt) *n* **1** a long pole for propelling a boat, esp. a punt. ◆ *vb* **2** to propel (a boat) with a quant. [C15: prob. from L *contus* pole, from Gk *kontos*]

quant[2] (kwɒnt) *n Inf.* a highly paid analyst with a degree in a quantitative science, employed by a financial house to predict price movements of securities, commodities, etc. [C20: from QUANTITATIVE]

quanta ('kwɒntə) *n* the plural of **quantum.**

quantic ('kwɒntɪk) *n* a homogeneous function of two or more variables in a rational and integral form. [C19: from L *quantus* how great]

quantifier ('kwɒntɪˌfaɪə) *n* **1** *Logic.* a symbol indicating the quantity of a term: *the existential quantifier corresponds to the words "there is something, such that".* **2** *Grammar.* a word or phrase, such as *some, all,* or *no,* expressing quantity.

quantify ('kwɒntɪˌfaɪ) *vb* **quantifies, quantifying, quantified.** (*tr*) **1** to discover or express the quantity of. **2** *Logic.* to specify the quantity of (a term) by using a quantifier, such as *all, some,* or *no.* [C19: from Med. L *quantificāre,* from L *quantus* how much + *facere* to make]
▸'**quantifiable** *adj* ▸ˌ**quantifi'cation** *n*

THESAURUS

quaff *vb* = **drink,** bend the elbow (*inf.*), bevvy (*dialect*), carouse, down, gulp, guzzle, imbibe, swallow, swig (*inf.*), tope

quaggy *adj* **1** = **boggy,** fenny, marshy, miry, muddy, mushy, paludal, soft, soggy, squelchy, swampy, yielding

quagmire *n* **1** = **bog,** fen, marsh, mire, morass, quicksand, slough, swamp **2** = **entanglement,** difficulty, dilemma, fix (*inf.*), imbroglio, impasse, jam (*inf.*), muddle, pass, pickle (*inf.*), pinch, plight, predicament, quandary, scrape (*inf.*)

quail[2] *vb* = **shrink,** blanch, blench, cower, cringe, faint, falter, flinch, recoil, shudder, tremble

quaint *adj* **1** = **old-fashioned,** antiquated, antique, artful, charming, gothic, ingenious, old-world, picturesque **2** = **unusual,** bizarre, curious, droll, eccentric, fanciful, fantastic, odd, original, peculiar, queer, rum (*Brit. sl.*), singular, strange, whimsical
Antonyms ≠ **old-fashioned:** fashionable, modern, new, up-to-date *adj* ≠ **unusual:** normal, ordinary

quake *vb* **1, 2** = **shake,** convulse, quiver, rock, shiver, shudder, totter, tremble, vibrate, wobble

qualification *n* **2** = **attribute,** ability, accomplishment, aptitude, capability, capacity, eligibility, endowment(s), fitness, quality, skill, suitability, suitableness **3** = **condition,** allowance, caveat, criterion, exception, exemption, limitation, modification, objection, prerequisite, proviso, requirement, reservation, restriction, rider, stipulation

qualified *adj* **1** = **capable,** able, accomplished, adept, certificated, competent, efficient, eligible, equipped, experienced, expert, fit, knowledgeable, licensed, practised, proficient, skilful, talented, trained **2** = **restricted,** bounded, circumscribed, conditional, confined, contingent, equivocal, guarded, limited, modified, provisional, reserved
Antonyms *adj* ≠ **capable:** amateur, apprentice, self-styled, self-taught, trainee, uncertificated, unqualified, untrained ≠ **restricted:** categorical, outright, unconditional, unequivocal, wholehearted

qualify *vb* **1** = **certify,** capacitate, commission, condition, empower, endow, equip, fit, ground, permit, prepare, ready, sanction, train **2, 3** = **moderate,** abate, adapt, assuage, circumscribe, diminish, ease, lessen, limit, mitigate, modify, modulate, reduce, regulate, restrain, restrict, soften, temper, vary **5** = **be described,** be characterized, be designated, be distinguished, be named
Antonyms *vb* ≠ **certify:** ban, debar, disqualify, forbid, preclude, prevent

quality *n* **1** = **characteristic,** aspect, attribute, condition, feature, mark, peculiarity, property, trait **2** = **nature,** character, constitution, description, essence, kind, make, sort, worth **4** = **excellence,** calibre, distinction, grade, merit, position, pre-eminence, rank, standing, status, superiority, value **5** = **nobility,** aristocracy, gentry, ruling class, upper class

qualm *n* **1** = **nausea,** agony, attack, pang, queasiness, sickness, spasm, throe (*rare*), twinge **2** = **misgiving,** anxiety, apprehension, compunction, disquiet, doubt, hesitation, regret, reluctance, remorse, scruple, twinge *or* pang of conscience, uncertainty, uneasiness

quandary *n* = **difficulty,** bewilderment, cleft stick, delicate situation, dilemma, doubt, embarrassment, impasse, perplexity, plight, predicament, puzzle, strait, uncertainty

quantity *n* **1** = **amount,** aggregate, allotment, lot, number, part, portion, quota, sum, total

quantitative (ˈkwɒntɪtətɪv) *or* **quantitive** *adj* **1** involving or relating to considerations of amount or size. **2** capable of being measured. **3** *Prosody.* of a metrical system that is based on the length of syllables. ▸ **ˈquantitatively** *or* **ˈquantitively** *adv*

quantitative analysis *n* See **analysis** (sense 4).

quantity Ⓣ (ˈkwɒntɪtɪ) *n, pl* **quantities. 1a** a specified or definite amount, number, etc. **1b** (*as modifier*): *a quantity estimate.* **2** the aspect of anything that can be measured, weighed, counted, etc. **3 unknown quantity.** a person or thing whose action, effort, etc., is unknown or unpredictable. **4** a large amount. **5** *Maths.* an entity having a magnitude that may be denoted by a numerical expression. **6** *Physics.* a specified magnitude or amount. **7** *Logic.* the characteristic of a proposition that makes it universal or particular. **8** *Prosody.* the relative duration of a syllable or the vowel in it. [C14: from OF *quantité,* from L *quantitās* amount, from *quantus* how much]

> **USAGE NOTE** The use of a plural noun after *quantity of* as in *a large quantity of bananas* was formerly considered incorrect, but is now acceptable.

quantity surveyor *n* a person who estimates the cost of the materials and labour necessary for a construction job.

quantize *or* **quantise** (ˈkwɒntaɪz) *vb* **quantizes, quantizing, quantized** *or* **quantises, quantising, quantised.** (*tr*) **1** *Physics.* to restrict (a physical quantity) to one of a set of fixed values. **2** *Maths.* to limit to values that are multiples of a basic unit. ▸ **ˌquantiˈzation** *or* **ˌquantiˈsation** *n*

quantum (ˈkwɒntəm) *n, pl* **quanta. 1** *Physics.* **1a** the smallest quantity of some physical property that a system can possess according to the quantum theory. **1b** a particle with such a unit of energy. **2** amount or quantity, esp. a specific amount. ◆ *adj* **3** of or designating a major breakthrough or sudden advance: *a quantum leap forward.* [C17: from L *quantus* (adj) how much]

quantum electrodynamics *n Physics.* the study of electromagnetic radiation and its interaction with charged particles in terms of quantum theory. Abbrev.: **QED.**

quantum mechanics *n* (*functioning as sing*) the branch of mechanics, based on the quantum theory, used for interpreting the behaviour of elementary particles and atoms, which do not obey Newtonian mechanics.

quantum meruit *Latin.* (ˈmɛruːɪt) as much as he has earned.

quantum number *n Physics.* one of a set of integers or half-integers characterizing the energy states of a particle or system of particles.

quantum theory *n* a theory concerning the behaviour of physical systems based on the idea that they can only possess certain properties, such as energy and angular momentum, in discrete amounts (quanta).

quaquaversal (ˌkwɑːkwəˈvɜːsəl) *adj Geol.* directed outwards in all directions from a common centre. [C18: from L *quāquā* in every direction + *versus* towards]

quarantine (ˈkwɒrənˌtiːn) *n* **1** a period of isolation or detention, esp. of persons or animals arriving from abroad, to prevent the spread of disease. **2** the place where such detention is enforced. **3** any period or state of enforced isolation. ◆ *vb* **quarantines, quarantining, quarantined. 4** (*tr*) to isolate in or as if in quarantine. [C17: from It. *quarantina* period of forty days, from *quaranta* forty, from L *quadrāgintā*]

quarantine flag *n Naut.* the yellow signal flag for the letter Q, flown alone from a vessel to indicate that there is no disease aboard or, with a second signal flag, to indicate that there is disease aboard. Also called: **yellow jack.**

quark[1] (kwɑːk) *n Physics.* any of a set of six elementary particles that, together with their antiparticles, are thought to be fundamental units of all baryons and mesons but unable to exist in isolation. [C20: coined by James Joyce in the novel *Finnegans Wake* (1939) & given special application in physics]

quark[2] (kwɑːk) *n* a type of low-fat soft cheese. [from G]

quarrel[1] Ⓣ (ˈkwɒrəl) *n* **1** an angry disagreement; argument. **2** a cause of dispute; grievance. ◆ *vb* **quarrels, quarrelling, quarrelled** *or US* **quarrels, quarreling, quarreled.** (*intr;* often foll. by *with*) **3** to engage in a disagreement or dispute; argue. **4** to find fault; complain. [C14: from OF *querele,* from L *querēlla* complaint, from *querī* to complain] ▸ **ˈquarreller** *or US* **ˈquarreler** *n*

quarrel[2] (ˈkwɒrəl) *n* **1** an arrow having a four-edged head, fired from a crossbow. **2** a small square or diamond-shaped pane of glass. [C13: from OF *quarrel* pane, from Med. L *quadrellus,* dim. of L *quadrus* square]

quarrelsome Ⓣ (ˈkwɒrəlsəm) *adj* inclined to quarrel or disagree; belligerent.

quarrian *or* **quarrion** (ˈkwɒrɪən) *n* a cockatiel of inland Australia that feeds on seeds and grasses. [C20: prob. from Abor.]

quarry[1] (ˈkwɒrɪ) *n, pl* **quarries. 1** an open surface excavation for the extraction of building stone, slate, marble, etc. **2** a copious source, esp. of information. ◆ *vb* **quarries, quarrying, quarried. 3** to extract (stone, slate, etc.) from or as if from a quarry. **4** (*tr*) to excavate a quarry in. **5** to obtain (something) diligently and laboriously. [C15: from OF *quarriere,* from *quarre* (unattested) square-shaped stone, from L *quadrāre* to make square]

quarry[2] Ⓣ (ˈkwɒrɪ) *n, pl* **quarries. 1** an animal, etc., that is hunted, esp. by other animals; prey. **2** anything pursued. [C14 *quirre* entrails offered to the hounds, from OF *cuirée* what is placed on the hide, from *cuir* hide, from L *corium* leather; prob. also infl. by OF *coree* entrails, from L *cor* heart]

quarryman (ˈkwɒrɪmən) *n, pl* **quarrymen.** a man who works in or manages a quarry.

quarry tile *n* an unglazed floor tile.

quart (kwɔːt) *n* **1** a unit of liquid measure equal to a quarter of a gallon or two pints. 1 US quart (0.946 litre) is equal to 0.8326 UK quart. 1 UK quart (1.136 litres) is equal to 1.2009 US quarts. **2** a unit of dry measure equal to 2 pints or one eighth of a peck. [C14: from OF *quarte,* from L *quartus* fourth]

quartan (ˈkwɔːtᵊn) *adj* (of a fever) occurring every third day. [C13: from L *febris quartāna* fever occurring every fourth day, reckoned inclusively]

quarte (kɑːt) *n* the fourth of eight basic positions from which a parry or attack can be made in fencing. [C18: F from OF *quarte,* from L *quartus* fourth]

quarter Ⓣ (ˈkwɔːtə) *n* **1** one of four equal parts of an object, quantity, etc. **2** the fraction equal to one divided by four (¼). **3** *US, Canad., etc.* a 25-cent piece. **4** a unit of weight equal to a quarter of a hundredweight. 1 US quarter is equal to 25 pounds; 1 Brit. quarter is equal to 28 pounds. **5** short for **quarter-hour. 6** a fourth part of a year; three months. **7** *Astron.* **7a** one fourth of the moon's period of revolution around the earth. **7b** either of two phases of the moon when half of the lighted surface is visible. **8** *Inf.* a unit of weight equal to a quarter of a pound or 4 ounces. **9** *Brit.* a unit of capacity for grain, etc., usually equal to 8 UK bushels. **10** *Sport.* one of the four periods into which certain games are divided. **11** *Naut.* the part of a vessel's side towards the stern. **12** a region or district of a town or city: *the Spanish quarter.* **13** a region, direction, or point of the compass. **14** (*sometimes pl*) an unspecified person or group of people: *to get word from the highest quarter.* **15** mercy or pity, as shown to a defeated opponent (esp. in **ask for** *or* **give quarter**). **16** any of the four limbs, including the adjacent parts, of a quadruped or bird. **17** *Heraldry.* one of four quadrants into which a shield may be divided. ◆ *vb* **18** (*tr*) to divide into four equal parts. **19** (*tr*) to divide into any number of parts. **20** (*tr*) (esp. formerly) to dismember (a human body). **21** to billet or be billeted in lodgings, esp. (of military personnel) in civilian lodgings. **22** (*intr*) (of hounds) to range over an area of ground in search of game or the scent of quarry. **23** (*intr*) *Naut.* (of the wind) to blow onto a vessel's quarter. **24** (*tr*) *Heraldry.* **24a** to divide (a shield) into four separate bearings. **24b** to place (one set of arms) in diagonally opposite quarters to another. ◆ *adj* **25** being or consisting of one of four equal parts. ◆ See also **quarters.** [C13: from OF *quartier,* from L *quartārius* a fourth part, from *quartus* fourth]

quarterback (ˈkwɔːtəˌbæk) *n* a player in American football who directs attacking play.

quarter-bound *adj* (of a book) having a binding consisting of two types of material, the better type being used on the spine.

quarter day *n* any of four days in the year when certain payments become due. In England, Wales, and Northern Ireland these are Lady Day, Midsummer's Day, Michaelmas, and Christmas. In Scotland they are Candlemas, Whit Sunday, Lammas, and Martinmas.

quarterdeck (ˈkwɔːtəˌdɛk) *n Naut.* the after part of the upper deck of a ship, traditionally the deck for official or ceremonial use.

quartered (ˈkwɔːtəd) *adj* **1** *Heraldry.* (of a shield) divided into four sections, each having contrasting arms or having two sets of arms, each repeated in diagonally opposite corners. **2** (of a log) sawn into four equal parts along two diameters at right angles to each other.

quarterfinal (ˌkwɔːtəˈfaɪnᵊl) *n* the round before the semifinal in a competition.

quarter-hour *n* **1** a period of 15 minutes. **2** either of the points on a timepiece that mark 15 minutes before or after the hour.

quartering (ˈkwɔːtərɪŋ) *n* **1** *Mil.* the allocation of accommodation to

THESAURUS

4 = size, bulk, capacity, expanse, extent, greatness, length, magnitude, mass, measure, volume

quarrel[1] *n* **1 = disagreement,** affray, altercation, argument, brawl, breach, commotion, contention, controversy, difference (of opinion), discord, disputation, dispute, dissension, dissidence, disturbance, feud, fight, fracas, fray, row, scrap (*inf.*), shindig (*inf.*), shindy (*inf.*), skirmish, spat, squabble, strife, tiff, vendetta, wrangle ◆ *vb* **3 = disagree,** altercate, argue, bicker, brawl, clash, differ, dispute, fall out (*inf.*), fight, fight like cat and dog, go at it hammer and tongs, row, spar, squabble, wrangle **4 = object to,** carp, cavil, complain, decry, disapprove, find fault, take exception to

Antonyms *n* ≠ **disagreement:** accord, agreement, concord ◆ *vb* ≠ **disagree:** agree, get on *or* along (with)

quarrelsome *adj* **= argumentative,** belligerent, cantankerous, cat-and-dog (*inf.*), choleric, combative, contentious, cross, disputatious, fractious, ill-tempered, irascible, irritable, litigious, peevish, petulant, pugnacious, querulous

Antonyms *adj* easy-going, equable, even-tempered, placid

quarry[2] *n* **1 = prey,** game, victim **2 = goal,** aim, objective, prize

quarter *n* **12 = district,** area, direction, locality, location, neighbourhood, part, place, point, position, province, region, side, spot, station, territory, zone **15 = mercy,** clemency, compassion, favour, forgiveness, leniency, pity ◆ *vb* **21 = accommodate,** billet, board, house, install, lodge, place, post, put up, station

service personnel. **2** *Heraldry.* **2a** the marshalling of several coats of arms on one shield, usually representing intermarriages. **2b** any coat of arms marshalled in this way.

quarterlight (ˈkwɔːtəˌlaɪt) *n Brit.* a small pivoted window in the door of a car for ventilation.

quarterly (ˈkwɔːtəlɪ) *adj* **1** occurring, done, paid, etc., at intervals of three months. **2** of, relating to, or consisting of a quarter. ◆ *n, pl* **quarterlies. 3** a periodical issued every three months. ◆ *adv* **4** once every three months.

quartermaster (ˈkwɔːtəˌmɑːstə) *n* **1** an officer responsible for accommodation, food, and equipment in a military unit. **2** a rating in the navy, usually a petty officer, with particular responsibility for navigational duties.

quarter-miler *n* an athlete who specializes in running the quarter mile.

quartern (ˈkwɔːtən) *n* **1** a fourth part of certain weights or measures. **2** Also called: **quartern loaf.** *Brit.* **2a** a type of loaf 4 inches square. **2b** any loaf weighing 1600 g. [C13: from OF *quarteron,* from *quart* a quarter]

quarter note *n* the usual US and Canad. name for **crotchet** (sense 1).

quarter plate *n* a photographic plate measuring 3¼ × 4¼ inches (8.3 × 10.8 cm).

quarters Ⓣ (ˈkwɔːtəz) *pl n* **1** accommodation, esp. as provided for military personnel. **2** the stations assigned to crew members of a warship: *general quarters.*

quarter sessions *n* (*functioning as sing or pl*) (formerly) any of various courts held four times a year before justices of the peace or a recorder.

quarterstaff (ˈkwɔːtəˌstɑːf) *n, pl* **quarterstaves** (-ˌsteɪvz). a stout iron-tipped wooden staff about 6ft long, formerly used as a weapon. [C16: from ?]

quarter tone *n Music.* a quarter of a whole tone.

quartet *or* **quartette** (kwɔːˈtɛt) *n* **1** a group of four singers or instrumentalists or a piece of music composed for such a group. **2** any group of four. [C18: from It. *quartetto,* dim. of *quarto* fourth]

quartic (ˈkwɔːtɪk) *adj, n* another word for **biquadratic.** [C19: from L *quartus* fourth]

quartile (ˈkwɔːtaɪl) *n* **1** *Statistics.* one of three values of a variable dividing its distribution into four groups with equal frequencies. ◆ *adj* **2** *Statistics.* of a quartile. **3** *Astrol.* denoting an aspect of two heavenly bodies when their longitudes differ by 90°. [C16: from Med. L *quartīlis,* from L *quartus* fourth]

quarto (ˈkwɔːtəʊ) *n, pl* **quartos.** a book size resulting from folding a sheet of paper into four leaves or eight pages. [C16: from NL *in quartō* in quarter]

quartz (kwɔːts) *n* a hard glossy mineral consisting of silicon dioxide in crystalline form. It occurs as colourless rock crystal and as several impure coloured varieties including agate, chalcedony, flint, and amethyst. Formula: SiO_2. [C18: from G *Quarz,* of Slavic origin]

quartz clock *or* **watch** *n* a clock or watch that is operated by a vibrating quartz crystal.

quartz crystal *n* a thin plate or rod cut from a piece of piezoelectric quartz and ground so that it vibrates at a particular frequency.

quartz glass *n* a colourless glass composed of almost pure silica, resistant to very high temperatures.

quartz-iodine lamp *or* **quartz lamp** *n* a type of tungsten-halogen lamp containing small amounts of iodine and having a quartz envelope, operating at high temperature and producing an intense light for use in car headlamps, etc.

quartzite (ˈkwɔːtsaɪt) *n* **1** a sandstone composed of quartz. **2** a very hard rock consisting of intergrown quartz crystals.

quasar (ˈkweɪzɑː, -sɑː) *n* any of a class of quasi-stellar objects that emit an immense amount of energy in the form of light, infrared radiation, etc., from a compact source. They are extremely distant and hence the youngest objects observed in the universe, and their energy generation is thought to involve a black hole located in a galaxy. [C20: *quasi(i-stell)ar (object)*]

quash Ⓣ (kwɒʃ) *vb* (*tr*) **1** to subdue forcefully and completely. **2** to annul or make void (a law, etc.). **3** to reject (an indictment, etc.) as invalid. [C14: from OF *quasser,* from L *quassāre* to shake]

quasi- Ⓣ *combining form.* **1** almost but not really; seemingly: *a quasi-religious cult.* **2** resembling but not actually being; so-called: *a quasi-scholar.* [from L, lit.: as if]

quasi-stellar object (ˈkwɑːzɪ, ˈkweɪsaɪ) *n* a member of any of several classes of astronomical bodies, including **quasars** and **quasi-stellar galaxies,** both of which have exceptionally large red shifts. Abbrev.: **QSO.**

quassia (ˈkwɒʃə) *n* **1** any of a genus of tropical American trees having bitter bark and wood. **2** the wood of this tree or a bitter compound extracted from it, formerly used as a tonic and vermifuge, now used in insecticides. [C18: from NL, after Graman *Quassi,* a slave who discovered (1730) the medicinal value of the root]

quatercentenary (ˌkwætəsɛnˈtiːnərɪ) *n, pl* **quatercentenaries.** a 400th anniversary. [C19: from L *quater* four times + CENTENARY]
▸ˌ**quatercenˈtennial** (ˌkwætəsɛnˈtɛnɪəl) *adj, n*

quaternary (kwəˈtɜːnərɪ) *adj* **1** consisting of fours or by fours. **2** fourth in a series. **3** *Chem.* containing or being an atom bound to four other atoms or groups. ◆ *n, pl* **quaternaries. 4** the number four or a set of four. [C15: from L *quaternārius* each containing four, from *quaternī* by fours, from *quattuor* four]

Quaternary (kwəˈtɜːnərɪ) *adj* **1** of or denoting the most recent period of geological time, which succeeded the Tertiary period one million years ago. ◆ *n* **2 the.** the Quaternary period or rock system.

quaternion (kwəˈtɜːnɪən) *n* **1** *Maths.* a generalized complex number consisting of four components, $x = x_0 + x_1\mathrm{i} + x_2\mathrm{j} + x_3\mathrm{k}$, where $x, x_0 \ldots x_3$ are real numbers and $\mathrm{i}^2 = \mathrm{j}^2 = \mathrm{k}^2 = -1$, $\mathrm{ij} = -\mathrm{ji} = \mathrm{k}$, etc. **2** a set of four. [C14: from LL, from L *quaternī* four at a time]

quatrain (ˈkwɒtreɪn) *n* a stanza or poem of four lines. [C16: from F, from *quatre* four, from L *quattuor*]

quatrefoil (ˈkætrəˌfɔɪl) *n* **1** a leaf composed of four leaflets. **2** *Archit.* a carved ornament having four foils arranged about a common centre. [C15: from OF, from *quatre* four + *-foil* leaflet]

quattrocento (ˌkwætrəʊˈtʃɛntəʊ) *n* the 15th century, esp. in reference to Renaissance Italian art and literature. [It., lit.: four hundred (short for fourteen hundred)]

quaver Ⓣ (ˈkweɪvə) *vb* **1** to say or sing (something) with a trembling voice. **2** (*intr*) (esp. of the voice) to quiver or tremble. **3** (*intr*) *Rare.* to sing or play trills. ◆ *n* **4** *Music.* a note having the time value of an eighth of a semibreve. Usual US and Canad. name: **eighth note. 5** a tremulous sound or note. [C15 (in the sense: to vibrate): from *quaven* to tremble, of Gmc origin]
▸ˈ**quavering** *adj* ▸ˈ**quaveringly** *adv*

quay (kiː) *n* a wharf, typically one built parallel to the shoreline. [C14 *keye,* from OF *kai,* of Celtic origin]

quayage (ˈkiːɪdʒ) *n* **1** a system of quays. **2** a charge for the use of a quay.

quayside (ˈkiːˌsaɪd) *n* the edge of a quay along the water.

Que. *abbrev. for* Quebec.

quean (kwiːn) *n* **1** *Arch.* **1a** a boisterous impudent woman. **1b** a prostitute. **2** *Scot.* an unmarried girl. [OE *cwene*]

queasy Ⓣ (ˈkwiːzɪ) *adj* **queasier, queasiest. 1** having the feeling that one is about to vomit; nauseous. **2** feeling or causing uneasiness. [C15: from ?]
▸ˈ**queasily** *adv* ▸ˈ**queasiness** *n*

Quebecker *or* **Quebecer** (kwɪˈbɛkə, kəˈbɛkə) *n* a native or inhabitant of Quebec.

Québecois (*French* kebɛkwa) *n, pl* **Québecois** (-kwa). a native or inhabitant of the province of Quebec, esp. a French-speaking one.

quebracho (keɪˈbrɑːtʃəʊ) *n, pl* **quebrachos** (-tʃəʊz). **1** either of two South American trees having a tannin-rich hard wood used in tanning and dyeing. **2** a South American tree, whose bark yields alkaloids used in medicine and tanning. **3** the wood or bark of any of these trees. [C19: from American Sp., from *quiebracha,* from *quebrar* to break (from L *crepāre* to rattle) + *hacha* axe (from F)]

Quechua (ˈkɛtʃwə) *n* **1** (*pl* **Quechuas** *or* **Quechua**) a member of any of a group of South American Indian peoples of the Andes, including the Incas. **2** the language or family of languages spoken by these peoples.
▸ˈ**Quechuan** *adj, n*

queen Ⓣ (kwiːn) *n* **1** a female sovereign who is the official ruler or head of state. **2** the wife of a king. **3** a woman or a thing personified as a woman considered the best or most important of her kind: *the queen of ocean liners.* **4** *Sl.* an effeminate male homosexual. **5** the only fertile female in a colony of bees, ants, etc. **6** an adult female cat. **7** a playing card bearing the picture of a queen. **8** the most powerful chess piece, able to move in a straight line in any direction or diagonally. ◆ *vb* **9** *Chess.* to promote (a pawn) to a queen when it reaches the eighth rank. **10** (*tr*) to crown as queen. **11** (*intr*) to reign as queen. **12 queen it.** (often foll. by *over*) *Inf.* to behave in an overbearing manner. [OE *cwēn*]

Queen-Anne *n* **1** a style of furniture popular in England about 1700–20 and in America about 1720–70, characterized by walnut veneer and cabriole legs. ◆ *adj* **2** in or of this style. **3** of a style of architecture popular in early 18th-century England, characterized by red-brick construction with classical ornamentation.

Queen Anne's lace *n* another name for the **wild carrot.**

queen bee *n* **1** the fertile female bee in a hive. **2** *Inf.* a woman in a position of dominance over her associates.

queen consort *n* the wife of a reigning king.

queen dowager *n* the widow of a king.

queenly Ⓣ (ˈkwiːnlɪ) *adj* **queenlier, queenliest. 1** resembling or appropriate to a queen. ◆ *adv* **2** in a manner appropriate to a queen.

THESAURUS

quarters *pl n* **1** = **lodgings**, abode, accommodation, barracks, billet, cantonment (*Military*), digs (*Brit. inf.*), domicile, dwelling, habitation, lodging, post, residence, rooms, shelter, station

quash *vb* **1** = **suppress**, beat, crush, destroy, extinguish, extirpate, overthrow, put down, quell, quench, repress, squash, subdue **2, 3** = **annul**, cancel, declare null and void, invalidate, nullify, overrule, overthrow, rescind, reverse, revoke, set aside, void

quasi- *combining form* **1** = **almost**, apparently, partly, seemingly, supposedly **2** = **pseudo-**, apparent, fake, mock, near, nominal, pretended, seeming, semi-, sham, so-called, synthetic, virtual, would-be

quaver *vb* **2** = **tremble**, quake, quiver, shake, shudder, thrill, trill, twitter, vibrate, waver ◆ *n* **5** = **trembling**, break, quiver, shake, sob, throb, tremble, tremor, trill, vibration, warble

queasy *adj* **1** = **sick**, bilious, giddy, green around the gills (*inf.*), groggy (*inf.*), ill, indisposed, nauseated, off colour, queer, sickish, squeamish, uncomfortable, unwell, upset **2** = **uneasy**, anxious, concerned, fidgety, ill at ease, restless, troubled, uncertain, worried

queen *n* **1, 2** = **sovereign**, consort, monarch, ruler **3** = **ideal**, diva, doyenne, idol, mistress, model, perfection, prima donna, star

queenly *adj* **1** = **majestic**, grand, imperial, noble, regal, royal, stately

queen mother *n* the widow of a former king who is also the mother of the reigning sovereign.

queen olive *n* a variety of olive having large fleshy fruit suitable for pickling.

queen post *n* one of a pair of vertical posts that connect the tie beam of a truss to the principal rafters. Cf. **king post.**

Queen's Award *n* either of two awards instituted by royal warrant (1976) for increased export earnings by a British firm (**Queen's Award for Export Achievement**) or for an advance in technology (**Queen's Award for Technological Achievement**).

Queen's Bench *n* (in England when the sovereign is female) one of the divisions of the High Court of Justice.

Queensberry rules ('kwi:nzbərɪ) *pl n* **1** the code of rules followed in modern boxing. **2** *Inf.* gentlemanly conduct, esp. in a dispute. [C19: after the ninth Marquess of *Queensberry,* who originated the rules in 1869]

Queen's Counsel *n* (when the sovereign is female) **1** a barrister (in England and Wales) or an advocate (in Scotland) appointed Counsel to the Crown by the sovereign on the recommendation of the Lord Chancellor (in England and Wales) or the Lord President (in Scotland). **2** (in Australia) a similar appointment, usually made on the recommendation of the Chief Justice of each state, through the state governor. **3** (in Canada) an honorary title which may be bestowed by the government on lawyers with long experience.

Queen's English *n* (when the British sovereign is female) standard Southern British English.

queen's evidence *n English law.* (when the sovereign is female) evidence given for the Crown against his former associates in crime by an accomplice (esp. in **turn queen's evidence**). US equivalent: **state's evidence.**

Queen's Guide *n* (in Britain and the Commonwealth when the sovereign is female) a Guide who has passed the highest tests of proficiency.

queen's highway *n* **1** (in Britain when the sovereign is female) any public road or right of way. **2** (in Canada) a main road maintained by the provincial government.

queen-size *or* **queen-sized** *adj* (of a bed, etc.) larger or longer than normal size but smaller or shorter than king-size.

Queensland nut ('kwi:nz,lænd) *n* another name for **macadamia.**

Queen's Scout *n* (in Britain and the Commonwealth when the sovereign is female) a Scout who has passed the highest tests of proficiency. US equivalent: **Eagle Scout.**

queer **T** (kwɪə) *adj* **1** differing from the normal or usual; odd or strange. **2** dubious; shady. **3** faint, giddy, or queasy. **4** *Inf., derog.* homosexual. **5** *Inf.* eccentric or slightly mad. **6** *Sl.* worthless or counterfeit. ◆ *n* **7** *Inf., derog.* a homosexual. ◆ *vb (tr) Inf.* **8** to spoil or thwart (esp. in **queer someone's pitch**). **9** to put in a difficult position. [C16: ? from G *quer* oblique, ult. from OHG *twërh*]
▸'**queerly** *adv* ▸'**queerness** *n*

> **USAGE NOTE** Although the term *queer* meaning homosexual is still considered derogatory when used by nonhomosexuals, it is now used by homosexuals of themselves as a positive term, as in *queer politics, queer cinema.*

queer fish *n Brit. inf.* an odd person.

queer street *n (sometimes cap.) Inf.* a difficult situation, such as debt or bankruptcy (in **in queer street**).

quell **T** (kwɛl) *vb (tr)* **1** to suppress (rebellion, etc.); subdue. **2** to overcome or allay. [OE *cwellan* to kill]
▸'**queller** *n*

quench **T** (kwɛntʃ) *vb (tr)* **1** to satisfy (one's thirst, desires, etc.); slake. **2** to put out (a fire, etc.); extinguish. **3** to put down; suppress; subdue. **4** to cool (hot metal) by plunging it into cold water. [OE *ācwencan* to extinguish]
▸'**quenchable** *adj* ▸'**quencher** *n*

quenelle (kə'nɛl) *n* a ball of sieved meat or fish. [C19: from F, from G *Knödel* dumpling, from OHG *knodo* knot]

querist ('kwɪərɪst) *n* a person who makes inquiries or queries; questioner.

quern (kwɜ:n) *n* a stone hand mill for grinding corn. [OE *cweorn*]

quernstone ('kwɜ:n,stəʊn) *n* **1** another name for **millstone** (sense 1). **2** one of the two stones used in a quern.

querulous **T** ('kwɛrʊləs, 'kwɛrjʊ-) *adj* **1** inclined to make whining or peevish complaints. **2** characterized by or proceeding from a complaining fretful attitude or disposition. [C15: from L *querulus,* from *querī* to complain]
▸'**querulously** *adv* ▸'**querulousness** *n*

query **T** ('kwɪərɪ) *n, pl* **queries. 1** a question, esp. one expressing doubt. **2** a question mark. ◆ *vb* **queries, querying, queried.** *(tr)* **3** to express uncertainty, doubt, or an objection concerning (something). **4** to express as a query. **5** *US.* to put a question to (a person); ask. [C17: from earlier *quere,* from L *quaerē* ask!, from *quaerere* to seek]

query language *n Computing.* the instructions and procedures used to retrieve information from a database.

quest **T** (kwɛst) *n* **1** a looking for or seeking; search. **2** (in medieval romance) an expedition by a knight or knights to accomplish a task, such as finding the Holy Grail. **3** the object of a search; a goal or target. ◆ *vb (mainly intr)* **4** (foll. by *for* or *after*) to go in search (of). **5** (of dogs, etc.) to search for game. **6** *(also tr) Arch.* to seek. [C14: from OF *queste,* from L *quaesita* sought, from *quaerere* to seek]
▸'**quester** *n* ▸'**questing** *adj* ▸'**questingly** *adv*

question **T** ('kwɛstʃən) *n* **1** a form of words addressed to a person in order to elicit information or evoke a response; interrogative sentence. **2** a point at issue: *it's only a question of time until she dies.* **3** a difficulty or uncertainty. **4a** an act of asking. **4b** an investigation into some problem. **5** a motion presented for debate. **6 put the question.** to require members of a deliberative assembly to vote on a motion presented. **7** *Law.* a matter submitted to a court or other tribunal. **8 beyond (all) question.** beyond (any) dispute or doubt. **9 call in** *or* **into question. 9a** to make (something) the subject of disagreement. **9b** to cast doubt upon the truth, etc., of (something). **10 in question.** under discussion: *this is the man in question.* **11 out of the question.** beyond consideration; unthinkable or impossible. **12 put to the question.** (formerly) to interrogate by torture. ◆ *vb (mainly tr)* **13** to put a question or questions to (a person); interrogate. **14** to make (something) the subject of dispute. **15** to express uncertainty about the truth of (something); doubt. [C13: via OF from L *quaestiō,* from *quaerere* to seek]
▸'**questioner** *n*

> **USAGE NOTE** *The question whether* should be used rather than *the question of whether* or *the question as to whether: this leaves open the question whether he acted correctly.*

questionable **T** ('kwɛstʃənəbᵊl) *adj* **1** (esp. of a person's morality or honesty) admitting of some doubt; dubious. **2** of disputable value or authority.
▸'**questionableness** *n* ▸'**questionably** *adv*

questioning ('kwɛstʃənɪŋ) *adj* **1** proceeding from or characterized by a feeling of doubt or uncertainty. **2** intellectually inquisitive: *a questioning mind.*
▸'**questioningly** *adv*

questionless ('kwɛstʃənlɪs) *adj* **1** blindly adhering; unquestioning. **2** a less common word for **unquestionable.**
▸'**questionlessly** *adv*

question mark *n* **1** the punctuation mark **?**, used at the end of ques-

THESAURUS

queer *adj* **1** = **strange**, abnormal, anomalous, atypical, curious, disquieting, droll, eerie, erratic, extraordinary, funny, left-field (*inf.*), odd, outlandish, outré, peculiar, remarkable, rum (*Brit. sl.*), singular, uncanny, uncommon, unconventional, unnatural, unorthodox, unusual, weird **2** = **dubious**, doubtful, fishy (*inf.*), irregular, mysterious, puzzling, questionable, shady (*inf.*), suspicious **3** = **faint**, dizzy, giddy, light-headed, queasy, reeling, uneasy **5** *Informal* = **eccentric**, crazy, demented, idiosyncratic, irrational, mad, odd, touched, unbalanced, unhinged ◆ *vb Informal* **8** = **spoil**, bodge (*inf.*), botch, endanger, harm, impair, imperil, injure, jeopardize, mar, ruin, thwart, wreck
Antonyms *adj* ≠ **strange:** believable, common, conventional, customary, natural, normal, ordinary, orthodox, rational, regular, straight, unexceptional, unoriginal ◆ *vb* ≠ **spoil:** aid, boost, enhance, help

quell *vb* **1** = **suppress**, conquer, crush, defeat, extinguish, overcome, overpower, put down, quash, squelch, stamp out, stifle, subdue, vanquish **2** = **assuage**, allay, alleviate, appease, calm, compose, deaden, dull, mitigate, moderate, mollify, pacify, quiet, silence, soothe

quench *vb* **1** = **satisfy**, allay, appease, cool, sate, satiate, slake **2** = **put out**, douse, extinguish, smother, snuff out **3** = **suppress**, check, crush, destroy, end, squelch, stifle

querulous *adj* **1, 2** = **complaining**, cantankerous, captious, carping, censorious, critical, cross, discontented, dissatisfied, fault-finding, fretful, grouchy (*inf.*), grumbling, hard to please, irascible, irritable, peevish, petulant, plaintive, ratty (*Brit. & NZ inf.*), sour, testy, tetchy, touchy, whining
Antonyms *adj* contented, easy to please, equable, placid, uncomplaining, uncritical, undemanding

query *n* **1** = **question**, demand, doubt, hesitation, inquiry, objection, problem, reservation, scepticism, suspicion ◆ *vb* **3** = **doubt**, challenge, disbelieve, dispute, distrust, mistrust, suspect **4, 5** = **ask**, inquire *or* enquire, question

quest *n* **1** = **search**, hunt, pursuit **2** = **expedition**, adventure, crusade, enterprise, exploration, journey, mission, pilgrimage, voyage

question *n* **3** = **difficulty**, argument, can of worms (*inf.*), confusion, contention, controversy, debate, dispute, doubt, dubiety, misgiving, problem, query, uncertainty **4b** = **inquiry**, examination, interrogation, investigation **5** = **motion**, issue, point, proposal, proposition, subject, theme, topic **9 call into question** = **dispute**, cast doubt upon, challenge, controvert, disbelieve, distrust, doubt, impugn, mistrust, oppose, query, suspect **10 in question** = **under discussion**, at issue, in doubt, open to debate **11 out of the question** = **impossible**, inconceivable, not to be thought of, unthinkable ◆ *vb* **13** = **ask**, catechize, cross-examine, examine, grill (*inf.*), inquire, interrogate, interview, investigate, probe, pump (*inf.*), quiz, sound out
Antonyms *n* ≠ **inquiry:** answer, reply ◆ *vb* ≠ **ask:** answer, reply

questionable *adj* **1** = **dubious**, dodgy, doubtful, fishy (*inf.*), iffy (*inf.*), shady (*inf.*), suspect, suspicious **2** = **disputable**, arguable, controversial, controvertible, debatable, dubitable, equivocal, moot, paradoxical, problematical, uncertain, unproven, unreliable
Antonyms *adj* ≠ **disputable:** authoritative, certain, incontrovertible, indisputable, straightforward, unequivocal

tions and in other contexts where doubt or ignorance is implied. **2** this mark used for any other purpose, as to draw attention to a possible mistake.

question master *n Brit.* the chairman of a quiz or panel game.

questionnaire (ˌkwɛstʃəˈnɛə, ˌkɛs-) *n* a set of questions on a form, submitted to a number of people in order to collect statistical information.

question time *n* (in parliamentary bodies of the British type) the time set aside each day for questions to government ministers.

quetzal (ˈkɛtsəl) *n, pl* **quetzals** *or* **quetzales** (-ˈsɑːlɛs). **1** a crested bird of Central and N South America, which has a brilliant green, red, and white plumage and, in the male, long tail feathers. **2** the standard monetary unit of Guatemala. [via American Sp. from Nahuatl *quetzalli* brightly coloured tail feather]

queue ❶ (kjuː) *Chiefly Brit.* ◆ *n* **1** a line of people, vehicles, etc., waiting for something. **2** *Computing.* a list in which entries are deleted from one end and inserted at the other. **3** a pigtail. ◆ *vb* **queues, queuing** *or* **queueing, queued. 4** (*intr*, often foll. by *up*) to form or remain in a line while waiting. **5** *Computing.* to arrange (a number of programs) in a predetermined order for accessing by a computer. ◆ Usual US word (senses 1, 4): **line.** [C16 (in the sense: tail); C18 (in the sense: pigtail): via F from L *cauda* tail]

queue-jump *vb* (*intr*) **1** to take a place in a queue ahead of those already queuing; push in. **2** to obtain some advantage out of turn or unfairly.
▸**ˈqueue-ˌjumper** *n*

quibble ❶ (ˈkwɪbᵊl) *vb* **quibbles, quibbling, quibbled.** (*intr*) **1** to make trivial objections. **2** *Arch.* to play on words; pun. ◆ *n* **3** a trivial objection or equivocation, esp. one used to avoid an issue. **4** *Arch.* a pun. [C17: prob. from obs. *quib*, ?from L *quibus* (from *quī* who, which), as used in legal documents, with reference to their obscure phraseology]
▸**ˈquibbler** *n* ▸**ˈquibbling** *adj*

quiche (kiːʃ) *n* an open savoury tart with an egg custard filling to which bacon, onion, cheese, etc., are added. [F, from G *Kuchen* cake]

quick ❶ (kwɪk) *adj* **1** performed or occurring during a comparatively short time: *a quick move.* **2** lasting a short time; brief. **3** accomplishing something in a time that is shorter than normal: *a quick worker.* **4** characterized by rapidity of movement; fast. **5** immediate or prompt. **6** (*postpositive*) eager or ready to perform (an action): *quick to criticize.* **7** responsive to stimulation; alert; lively. **8** eager or enthusiastic for learning. **9** easily excited or aroused. **10** nimble in one's movements or actions; deft: *quick fingers.* **11** *Arch.* **11a** alive; living. **11b** (*as n*) living people (esp. in **the quick and the dead**). **12 quick with child.** *Arch.* pregnant. ◆ *n* **13** any area of sensitive flesh, esp. that under a toenail or fingernail. **14** the most important part (of a thing). **15 cut (someone) to the quick.** to hurt (someone's) feelings deeply. ◆ *adv Inf.* **16** in a rapid manner; swiftly. **17** soon: *I hope he comes quick.* ◆ *sentence substitute.* **18** a command to perform an action immediately. [OE *cwicu* living]
▸**ˈquickly** *adv* ▸**ˈquickness** *n*

quick-change artist *n* an actor or entertainer who undertakes several rapid changes of costume during his performance.

quicken ❶ (ˈkwɪkən) *vb* **1** to make or become faster; accelerate. **2** to impart to or receive vigour, enthusiasm, etc.: *science quickens man's imagination.* **3** to make or become alive; revive. **4a** (of an unborn fetus) to begin to show signs of life. **4b** (of a pregnant woman) to reach the stage of pregnancy at which movements of the fetus can be felt.

quick-freeze *vb* **quick-freezes, quick-freezing, quick-froze, quick-frozen.** (*tr*) to preserve (food) by subjecting it to rapid refrigeration at temperatures of 0°C or lower.

quickie (ˈkwɪkɪ) *n Inf.* **1** Also called (esp. Brit.): **quick one.** a speedily consumed alcoholic drink. **2a** anything made or done rapidly. **2b** (*as modifier*): *a quickie divorce.*

quicklime (ˈkwɪkˌlaɪm) *n* another name for **calcium oxide.**

quick march *n* **1** a march at quick time or the order to proceed at such a pace. ◆ *interj* **2** a command to commence such a march.

quicksand (ˈkwɪkˌsænd) *n* a deep mass of loose wet sand that sucks anything on top of it inextricably into it.

quickset (ˈkwɪkˌsɛt) *Chiefly Brit.* ◆ *n* **1a** a plant or cutting, esp. of hawthorn, set so as to form a hedge. **1b** such plants or cuttings collectively. **2** a hedge composed of such plants. ◆ *adj* **3** composed of such plants.

quicksilver (ˈkwɪkˌsɪlvə) *n* **1** another name for **mercury** (sense 1). ◆ *adj* **2** rapid or unpredictable in movement or change.

quickstep (ˈkwɪkˌstɛp) *n* **1** a modern ballroom dance in rapid quadruple time. **2** a piece of music composed for or in the rhythm of this dance. ◆ *vb* **quicksteps, quickstepping, quickstepped. 3** (*intr*) to perform this dance.

quick-tempered ❶ *adj* readily roused to anger; irascible.

quickthorn (ˈkwɪkˌθɔːn) *n* hawthorn, esp. when planted as a hedge. [C17: prob. from *quick* in the sense "fast-growing": cf. QUICKSET]

quick time *n Mil.* the normal marching rate of 120 paces to the minute.

quick-witted ❶ *adj* having a keenly alert mind, esp. as used to avert danger, make effective reply, etc.
▸**ˌquick-ˈwittedly** *adv* ▸**ˌquick-ˈwittedness** *n*

quid[1] (kwɪd) *n* a piece of tobacco, suitable for chewing. [OE *cwidu* chewing resin]

quid[2] (kwɪd) *n, pl* **quid.** *Brit. sl.* **1** a pound (sterling). **2** (**be**) **quids in.** (to be) in a very favourable or advantageous position. [C17: from ?]

quiddity (ˈkwɪdɪtɪ) *n, pl* **quiddities. 1** the essential nature of something. **2** a petty or trifling distinction; quibble. [C16: from Med. L *quidditās*, from L *quid* what]

quidnunc (ˈkwɪdˌnʌŋk) *n* a person eager to learn news and scandal; gossipmonger. [C18: from L, lit.: what now]

quid pro quo ❶ (ˈkwɪd prəʊ ˈkwəʊ) *n, pl* **quid pro quos. 1** a reciprocal exchange. **2** something given in compensation, esp. an advantage or object given in exchange for another. [C16: from L: something for something]

quiescent ❶ (kwɪˈɛsᵊnt) *adj* quiet, inactive, or dormant. [C17: from L *quiescere* to rest]
▸**quiˈescence** *or* **quiˈescency** *n* ▸**quiˈescently** *adv*

quiet ❶ (ˈkwaɪət) *adj* **1** characterized by an absence of noise. **2** calm or tranquil: *the sea is quiet tonight.* **3** free from activities, distractions, etc.; untroubled: *a quiet life.* **4** short of work, orders, etc.; not busy: *business is quiet today.* **5** private; not public; secret: *a quiet word with someone.* **6** free from anger, impatience, or other extreme emotion. **7** free from pretentiousness; modest or reserved: *quiet humour.* **8** *Astron.* (of the sun) exhibiting a very low number of sunspots, solar flares, etc.; inactive. ◆ *n* **9** the state of being silent, peaceful, or untroubled. **10 on the quiet.** without other people knowing. ◆ *vb* **11** a less common word for **quieten.** [C14: from L *quiētus*, p.p. of *quiēscere* to rest, from *quiēs* repose]
▸**ˈquietness** *n*

quieten ❶ (ˈkwaɪətᵊn) *vb Chiefly Brit.* **1** (often foll. by *down*) to make or become calm, silent, etc. **2** (*tr*) to allay (fear, doubts, etc.).

quietism (ˈkwaɪəˌtɪzəm) *n* **1** a form of religious mysticism originating

THESAURUS

queue *n* **1** = **line**, chain, concatenation, file, order, progression, sequence, series, string, succession, train

quibble *vb* **1** = **split hairs**, carp, cavil, equivocate, evade, pretend, prevaricate, shift ◆ *n* **3** = **objection**, cavil, complaint, criticism, nicety, niggle, prevarication, protest, sophism, subtlety

quibbling *adj* **1** = **hair-splitting**, carping, caviling, critical, jesuitical, niggling, nit-picking (*inf.*), overnice, sophistical

quick *adj* **1, 4** = **fast**, active, brisk, express, fleet, hasty, rapid, speedy, swift **2** = **brief**, cursory, hasty, hurried, perfunctory **5** = **prompt**, expeditious, sudden **7, 8** = **intelligent**, acute, alert, all there (*inf.*), astute, bright (*inf.*), clever, discerning, nimble-witted, perceptive, quick on the uptake (*inf.*), quick-witted, receptive, sharp, shrewd, smart **9** = **excitable**, passionate **10** = **nimble**, able, adept, adroit, agile, deft, dexterous, skilful **11a** *Archaic* = **alive**, animate, existing, live, living, viable
Antonyms *adj* ≠ **fast**: dull, heavy, inactive, lazy, lethargic ≠ **fast**: slow, sluggish, unresponsive ≠ **brief**: gradual, long ≠ **intelligent**: stupid, unintelligent ≠ **excitable**: calm, deliberate, patient, restrained ≠ **deft**: inexpert, maladroit, unskilful

quicken *vb* **1** = **speed**, accelerate, dispatch, expedite, hasten, hurry, impel, precipitate **2, 3** = **invigorate**, activate, animate, arouse, energize, excite, galvanize, incite, inspire, kindle, refresh, reinvigorate, resuscitate, revitalize, revive, rouse, stimulate, strengthen, vitalize, vivify

quickly *adv* **1, 4** = **swiftly**, abruptly, apace, at a rate of knots (*inf.*), at *or* on the double, at speed, briskly, expeditiously, fast, hastily, hell for leather (*inf.*), hotfoot, hurriedly, immediately, instantly, like greased lightning (*inf.*), like lightning, like the clappers (*Brit. inf.*), posthaste, promptly, pronto (*inf.*), quick, rapidly, soon, speedily, with all speed
Antonyms *adv* carefully, eventually, slowly, sluggishly, unhurriedly

quick-tempered *adj* = **hot-tempered**, cantankerous, choleric, excitable, fiery, impatient, impulsive, irascible, irritable, petulant, quarrelsome, ratty (*Brit. & NZ inf.*), shrewish, splenetic, testy, tetchy, waspish
Antonyms *adj* cool, dispassionate, phlegmatic, placid, slow to anger, tolerant

quick-witted *adj* = **clever**, alert, astute, bright (*inf.*), keen, perceptive, sharp, shrewd, smart
Antonyms *adj* dull, obtuse, slow, slow-witted, stupid, thick (*inf.*), unperceptive

quid pro quo *n* **1, 2** = **exchange**, compensation, equivalent, interchange, reprisal, retaliation, substitution, tit for tat

quiescent *adj* = **quiet**, calm, dormant, in abeyance, inactive, latent, motionless, peaceful, placid, resting, serene, silent, smooth, still, tranquil, unagitated, undisturbed, unmoving, unruffled

quiet *adj* **1** = **silent**, dumb, hushed, inaudible, low, low-pitched, noiseless, peaceful, soft, soundless **2** = **calm**, contented, gentle, mild, motionless, pacific, peaceful, placid, restful, serene, smooth, still, tranquil, untroubled **5** = **undisturbed**, isolated, private, retired, secluded, secret, sequestered, unfrequented **6** = **reserved**, collected, docile, even-tempered, gentle, imperturbable, meek, mild, phlegmatic, retiring, sedate, shy, unexcitable **7** = **unobtrusive**, conservative, modest, plain, reserved, restrained, simple, sober, subdued, unassuming, unpretentious ◆ *n* **9** = **peace**, calmness, ease, quietness, repose, rest, serenity, silence, stillness, tranquillity
Antonyms *adj* ≠ **silent**: deafening, ear-splitting, high-decibel, high-volume, loud, noisy, stentorian ≠ **calm**: agitated, alert, excitable, exciting, frenetic, troubled, turbulent, violent ≠ **undisturbed**: bustling, busy, crowded, exciting, fashionable, lively, popular, vibrant ≠ **reserved**: excitable, excited, high-spirited, impatient, loquacious, passionate, restless, talkative, verbose, violent ◆ *n* ≠ **peace**: activity, bustle, commotion, din, disturbance, noise, racket

quieten *vb* **1** = **silence**, compose, hush, muffle, mute, quell, quiet, shush (*inf.*), stifle, still, stop, subdue **2** = **soothe**, allay, alleviate, appease, as-

in Spain in the late 17th century, requiring complete passivity to God's will. **2** passivity and calmness of mind towards external events.
▸**'quietist** *n, adj*

quietly ('kwaɪətlɪ) *adv* **1** in a quiet manner. **2** **just quietly.** *Austral.* confidentially.

quietude ('kwaɪə,tju:d) *n* the state or condition of being quiet, peaceful, calm, or tranquil.

quietus Ⓣ (kwaɪ'i:təs, -'eɪtəs) *n, pl* **quietuses.** **1** anything that serves to quash, eliminate, or kill. **2** a release from life; death. **3** the discharge or settlement of debts, duties, etc. [C16: from L *quiētus est*, lit.: he is at rest]

quiff (kwɪf) *n Brit.* a tuft of hair brushed up above the forehead. [C19: from ?]

quill (kwɪl) *n* **1a** any of the large stiff feathers of the wing or tail of a bird. **1b** the long hollow part of a feather; calamus. **2** Also called: **quill pen.** a feather made into a pen for writing. **3** any of the stiff hollow spines of a porcupine or hedgehog. **4** a device, formerly made from a crow quill, for plucking a harpsichord string. **5** a small roll of bark, esp. one of dried cinnamon. **6** a bobbin or spindle. **7** a fluted fold, as in a ruff. ◆ *vb (tr)* **8** to wind (thread, etc.) onto a spool or bobbin. **9** to make or press fluted folds in (a ruff, etc.). [C15 (in the sense: hollow reed or pipe): from ?; cf. MLow G *quiele* quill]

quilt Ⓣ (kwɪlt) *n* **1** a cover for a bed, consisting of a soft filling sewn between two layers of material, usually with crisscross seams. **2** short for **continental quilt.** **3** a bedspread. **4** anything resembling a quilt. ◆ *vb (tr)* **5** to stitch together (two pieces of fabric) with (a thick padding or lining) between them. **6** to create (a garment, etc.) in this way. **7** to pad with material. [C13: from OF *coilte* mattress, from L *culcita* stuffed item of bedding]
▸**'quilted** *adj* ▸**'quilter** *n*

quilting ('kwɪltɪŋ) *n* **1** material for quilts. **2** the act of making a quilt. **3** quilted work.

quin (kwɪn) *n Brit.* short for **quintuplet** (sense 1). US and Canad. word: **quint.**

quinary ('kwaɪnərɪ) *adj* **1** of or by fives. **2** fifth in a series. **3** (of a number system) having a base of five. [C17: from L *quīnārius* containing five, from *quīnī* five each]

quince (kwɪns) *n* **1** a small widely cultivated Asian tree with edible pear-shaped fruits. **2** the fruit of this tree, much used in preserves. [C14 *qwince* pl. of *quyn*, from OF *coin*, from L *cotōneum*, from Gk *kudōnion* quince]

quincentenary (,kwɪnsɛn'ti:nərɪ) *n, pl* **quincentenaries.** a 500th anniversary. [C19: irregularly from L *quinque* five + CENTENARY]
▸**quincentennial** (,kwɪnsɛn'tɛnɪəl) *adj, n*

quincunx ('kwɪnkʌŋks) *n* a group of five objects arranged in the shape of a rectangle with one at each of the four corners and the fifth in the centre. [C17: from L: five twelfths, from *quinque* five + *uncia* twelfth; in ancient Rome, this was a coin worth five twelfths of an AS² and marked with five spots]
▸**quincuncial** (kwɪn'kʌnʃəl) *adj*

quinella (kwɪ'nɛlə) *n Austral.* a form of betting in which the punter must select the first and second place winners, in any order. [from American Sp. *quiniela*]

quinidine ('kwɪnɪ,di:n) *n* a crystalline alkaloid drug used to treat heart arrhythmias.

quinine (kwɪ'ni:n; *US* 'kwaɪnaɪn) *n* a bitter crystalline alkaloid extracted from cinchona bark, the salts of which are used as a tonic, analgesic, etc., and in malaria therapy. [C19: from Sp. *quina* cinchona bark, from Quechua *kina* bark]

quinol ('kwɪnɒl) *n* another name for **hydroquinone.**

quinoline ('kwɪnə,li:n, -lɪn) *n* an oily colourless insoluble compound synthesized by heating aniline, nitrobenzene, glycerol, and sulphuric acid: used as a food preservative and in the manufacture of dyes and antiseptics. Formula: C_9H_7N.

quinquagenarian (,kwɪŋkwədʒɪ'nɛərɪən) *n* **1** a person between 50 and 59 years old. ◆ *adj* **2** being between 50 and 59 years old. **3** of a quinquagenarian. [C16: from L *quinquāgēnārius* containing fifty, from *quinquāgēnī* fifty each]

Quinquagesima (,kwɪŋkwə'dʒɛsɪmə) *n* the Sunday preceding Lent. Also called: **Quinquagesima Sunday.** [C14: via Med. L from L *quinquāgēsima diēs* fiftieth day]

quinquecentenary (,kwɪŋkwɪsɛn'ti:nərɪ) *n, pl* **quinquecentenaries.** another name for **quincentenary.**

quinquennial (kwɪn'kwɛnɪəl) *adj* **1** occurring once every five years or over a period of five years. ◆ *n* **2** a fifth anniversary.
▸**quin'quennially** *adv*

quinquennium (kwɪn'kwɛnɪəm) *n, pl* **quinquennia** (-nɪə). a period or cycle of five years. [C17: from L *quinque* five + *annus* year]

quinquereme (,kwɪŋkwɪ'ri:m) *n* an ancient Roman galley with five banks of oars. [C16: from L *quinquerēmis*, from *quinque-* five + *rēmus* oar]

quinquevalent (,kwɪŋkwɪ'veɪlənt) *adj Chem.* another word for **pentavalent.**
▸**,quinque'valency** *or* **,quinque'valence** *n*

quinsy ('kwɪnzɪ) *n* inflammation of the tonsils and surrounding tissues with the formation of abscesses. [C14: via OF & Med. L from Gk *kunankhē*, from *kuōn* dog + *ankhein* to strangle]

quint[1] *n* **1** (kwɪnt). an organ stop sounding a note a fifth higher. **2** (kɪnt). *Piquet.* a sequence of five cards in the same suit. [C17: from F *quinte*, from L *quintus* fifth]

quint[2] (kwɪnt) *n* the US and Canad. word for **quin.**

quintain ('kwɪntɪn) *n* (esp. in medieval Europe) a post or target set up for tilting exercises for mounted knights or foot soldiers. [C14: from OF *quintaine*, from L: street in a Roman camp between the fifth & sixth maniples (the maniple was a unit of 120–200 soldiers in ancient Rome), from *quintus* fifth]

quintal ('kwɪntᵊl) *n* **1** a unit of weight equal to (esp. in Britain) 112 pounds or (esp. in US) 100 pounds. **2** a unit of weight equal to 100 kilograms. [C15: via OF from Ar. *qintār*, possibly from L *centēnārius* consisting of a hundred]

quintan ('kwɪntən) *adj* (of a fever) occurring every fourth day. [C17: from L *febris quintāna* fever occurring every fifth day, reckoned inclusively]

quinte (kænt) *n* the fifth of eight basic positions from which a parry or attack can be made in fencing. [C18: F from L *quintus* fifth]

quintessence Ⓣ (kwɪn'tɛsəns) *n* **1** the most typical representation of a quality, state, etc. **2** an extract of a substance containing its principle in its most concentrated form. **3** (in ancient philosophy) ether, the fifth essence or element, which was thought to be the constituent matter of the heavenly bodies and latent in all things. [C15: via F from Med. L *quinta essentia* the fifth essence, translation of Gk]
▸**quintessential** (,kwɪntɪ'sɛnʃəl) *adj* ▸**,quintes'sentially** *adv*

quintet *or* **quintette** (kwɪn'tɛt) *n* **1** a group of five singers or instrumentalists or a piece of music composed for such a group. **2** any group of five. [C19: from It. *quintetto*, from *quinto* fifth]

quintillion (kwɪn'tɪljən) *n, pl* **quintillions** *or* **quintillion.** **1** (in Britain, France, and Germany) the number represented as one followed by 30 zeros (10^{30}). US and Canad. word: **nonillion.** **2** (in the US and Canada) the number represented as one followed by 18 zeros (10^{18}). Brit. word: **trillion.** [C17: from L *quintus* fifth + *-illion*, as in MILLION]
▸**quin'tillionth** *adj*

quintuple ('kwɪntjʊpᵊl, kwɪn'tju:pᵊl) *vb* **quintuples, quintupling, quintupled.** **1** to multiply by five. ◆ *adj* **2** five times as much or as many; fivefold. **3** consisting of five parts. ◆ *n* **4** a quantity or number five times as great as another. [C16: from F, from L *quintus*, on the model of QUADRUPLE]

quintuplet ('kwɪntjʊplɪt, kwɪn'tju:plɪt) *n* **1** one of five offspring born at one birth. **2** a group of five similar things. **3** *Music.* a group of five notes to be played in a time value of three or four.

quintuplicate *adj* (kwɪn'tju:plɪkɪt). **1** fivefold or quintuple. ◆ *vb* (kwɪn'tju:plɪ,keɪt), **quintuplicates, quintuplicating, quintuplicated.** **2** to multiply or be multiplied by five. ◆ *n* (kwɪn'tju:plɪkɪt). **3** a group or set of five things.

quip Ⓣ (kwɪp) *n* **1** a sarcastic remark. **2** a witty saying. **3** *Arch.* another word for **quibble.** ◆ *vb* **quips, quipping, quipped.** **4** *(intr)* to make a quip. [C16: from earlier *quippy*, prob. from L *quippe* indeed, to be sure]
▸**'quipster** *n*

quire[1] ('kwaɪə) *n* **1** a set of 24 or 25 sheets of paper. **2** four sheets of paper folded to form 16 pages. **3** a set of all the sheets in a book. [C15 *quayer*, from OF *quaier*, from L *quaternī* four at a time, from *quater* four times]

quire[2] ('kwaɪə) *n* an obsolete spelling of **choir.**

quirk Ⓣ (kwɜ:k) *n* **1** a peculiarity of character; mannerism or foible. **2** an unexpected twist or turn: *a quirk of fate.* **3** a continuous groove in an architectural moulding. **4** a flourish, as in handwriting. [C16: from ?]
▸**'quirky** *adj* ▸**'quirkiness** *n*

quirt (kwɜ:t) *US & S. African.* ◆ *n* **1** a whip with a leather thong at one end. ◆ *vb (tr)* **2** to strike with a quirt. [C19: from Sp. *cuerda* CORD]

quisling Ⓣ ('kwɪzlɪŋ) *n* a traitor who aids an occupying enemy force; collaborator. [C20: after Major Vidkun *Quisling* (1887–1945), Norwegian collaborator with the Nazis]

quit Ⓣ (kwɪt) *vb* **quits, quitting, quitted** *or* **quit.** **1** *(tr)* to depart from; leave. **2**

THESAURUS

suage, blunt, calm, deaden, dull, lull, mitigate, mollify, palliate, tranquillize
Antonyms *vb* ≠ **soothe:** aggravate, exacerbate, intensify, provoke, upset, worsen

quietness *n* **1** = **peace,** hush, quiet, silence **2** = **calmness,** calm, placidity, quiescence, quietude, repose, rest, serenity, still, stillness, tranquillity

quietus *n* **1** = **death,** clincher (*inf.*), *coup de grâce*, deathblow, demise, end, final blow, finish

quilt *n* **1-3** = **bedspread,** comforter (*US*), continental quilt, counterpane, coverlet, doona (*Austral.*), duvet, eiderdown

quintessence *n* **1** = **essence,** gist, heart, kernel, lifeblood, marrow, pith, soul, spirit **2** = **extract,** core, distillation, essence

quintessential *adj* **1** = **ultimate,** archetypal, definitive, essential, fundamental, prototypical, typical

quip *n* **2** = **joke,** badinage, bon mot, jest, pleasantry, repartee, retort, riposte, sally, wisecrack (*inf.*), witticism

quirk *n* **1** = **peculiarity,** aberration, bee in one's bonnet, caprice, characteristic, eccentricity, fancy, fetish, foible, habit, *idée fixe*, idiosyncrasy, kink, mannerism, oddity, singularity, trait, vagary, whim

quirky *adj* **1** = **odd,** capricious, curious, eccentric, fanciful, idiosyncratic, offbeat, peculiar, rum (*Brit. sl.*), singular, unpredictable, unusual, whimsical

quisling *n* = **traitor,** betrayer, collaborator, fifth columnist, Judas, renegade, turncoat

quit *vb* **1** = **depart,** abandon, decamp, desert, exit, forsake, go, leave, pack one's bags (*inf.*), pull out, take off (*inf.*), withdraw **2** = **resign,** abdicate, go, leave, pull out, relinquish,

to resign; give up (a job). **3** (*intr*) (of a tenant) to give up occupancy of premises and leave them. **4** to desist or cease from (something or doing something). **5** (*tr*) to pay off (a debt). **6** (*tr*) *Arch.* to conduct or acquit (oneself); comport (oneself). ◆ *adj* **7** (*usually predicative;* foll. by *of*) free (from); released (from). [C13: from OF *quitter,* from L *quiētus* QUIET]

quitch grass (kwɪtʃ) *n* another name for **couch grass.** Sometimes shortened to **quitch.** [OE *cwice;* ? rel. to *cwicu* living, QUICK (with the implication that the grass cannot be killed)]

quitclaim ('kwɪtˌkleɪm) *Law.* ◆ *n* **1** a renunciation of a claim or right. ◆ *vb* **2** (*tr*) to renounce (a claim). [C14: from Anglo-F *quiteclame,* from *quite* QUIT + *clamer* to declare (from L *clamāre* to shout)]

quite ● (kwaɪt) *adv* **1** completely or absolutely: *you're quite right.* **2** (*not used with a negative*) somewhat: *she's quite pretty.* **3** in actuality; truly. **4** **quite a** *or* **an.** (*not used with a negative*) of an exceptional, considerable, or noticeable kind: *quite a girl.* **5** **quite something.** a remarkable or noteworthy thing or person. ◆ *sentence substitute.* **6** Also: **quite so.** an expression used to indicate agreement. [C14: adverbial use of *quite* (adj) QUIT]

USAGE NOTE See at **very.**

quitrent ('kwɪtˌrɛnt) *n* (formerly) a rent payable by a freeholder or copyholder to his lord in lieu of services.

quits (kwɪts) *adj* (*postpositive*) *Inf.* **1** on an equal footing; even. **2** **call it quits.** to agree to end a dispute, contest, etc., agreeing that honours are even.

quittance ('kwɪtᵊns) *n* **1** release from debt or other obligation. **2** a receipt or other document certifying this. [C13: from OF, from *quitter* to release from obligation; see QUIT]

quitter ('kwɪtə) *n* a person who gives up easily.

quiver[1] ● ('kwɪvə) *vb* **1** (*intr*) to shake with a tremulous movement; tremble. ◆ *n* **2** the state, process, or noise of shaking or trembling. [C15: from obs. *cwiver* quick, nimble]
▸'**quivering** *adj* ▸'**quivery** *adj*

quiver[2] ('kwɪvə) *n* a case for arrows. [C13: from OF *cuivre*]

qui vive (ˌkiː 'viːv) *n* **on the qui vive.** on the alert; attentive. [C18: from F, lit.: long live who?, sentry's challenge (equivalent to "Whose side are you on?")]

Quixote ('kwɪksət; *Spanish* ki'xote) *n* See **Don Quixote.**

quixotic ● (kwɪk'sɒtɪk) *adj* preoccupied with an unrealistically optimistic or chivalrous approach to life; impractically idealistic. [C18: after DON QUIXOTE]
▸**quix'otically** *adv*

quiz ● (kwɪz) *n, pl* **quizzes. 1a** an entertainment in which the knowledge of the players is tested by a series of questions. **1b** (*as modifier*): *a quiz programme.* **2** any set of quick questions designed to test knowledge. **3** an investigation by close questioning. **4** *Obs.* a practical joke. **5** *Obs.* a puzzling individual. **6** *Obs.* a person who habitually looks quizzically at others. ◆ *vb* **quizzes, quizzing, quizzed.** (*tr*) **7** to investigate by close questioning; interrogate. **8** *US & Canad. inf.* to test the knowledge of (a student or class). **9** (*tr*) *Obs.* to look quizzically at, esp. through a small monocle. [C18: from ?]
▸'**quizzer** *n*

quizzical ● ('kwɪzɪkᵊl) *adj* questioning and mocking or supercilious.
▸'**quizzically** *adv*

quod (kwɒd) *n Chiefly Brit.* a slang word for **jail.** [C18: from ?]

quod erat demonstrandum *Latin.* ('kwɒd 'ɛræt ˌdɛmən'strændʊm) (at the conclusion of a proof, esp. of a theorem in Euclidean geometry) which was to be proved. Abbrev.: **QED.**

quodlibet ('kwɒdlɪˌbɛt) *n* **1** a light piece of music. **2** a subtle argument, esp. one prepared as an exercise on a theological topic. [C14: from L, from *quod* what + *libet* pleases, that is, whatever you like]

quoin (kwɔɪn, kɔɪn) *n* **1** an external corner of a wall. **2** a stone forming the external corner of a wall. **3** another name for **keystone** (sense 1). **4** *Printing.* a wedge or an expanding device used to lock type up in a chase. **5** a wedge used for any of various other purposes. [C16: var. of *coin* (in former sense of corner)]

quoit (kɔɪt) *n* a ring of iron, plastic, etc., used in the game of quoits. [C15: from ?]

quoits (kɔɪts) *pl n* (*usually functioning as sing*) a game in which quoits are tossed at a stake in the ground in attempts to encircle it.

quokka ('kwɒkə) *n* a small wallaby of Western Australia, now rare. [of Abor. origin]

quondam ● ('kwɒndæm) *adj* (*prenominal*) of an earlier time; former. [C16: from L]

quorate ('kwɔːˌreɪt) *adj Brit.* consisting of or being a quorum: *the meeting was quorate.*

Quorn (kwɔːn) *n Trademark.* a vegetable protein developed from a type of fungus and used as a meat substitute.

quorum ('kwɔːrəm) *n* a minimum number of members in an assembly, etc., required to be present before any business can be transacted. [C15: from L, lit.: of whom, occurring in L commissions in the formula *quorum vos...duos* (etc.) *volumus* of whom we wish that you be...two (etc.)]

quota ● ('kwəʊtə) *n* **1** the proportional share or part that is due from, due to, or allocated to a person or group. **2** a prescribed number or quantity, as of items to be imported or students admitted to a college, etc. [C17: from L *quota pars* how big a share?, from *quotus* of what number]

quotable ('kwəʊtəbᵊl) *adj* apt or suitable for quotation.
▸ˌ**quota'bility** *n*

quotation ● (kwəʊ'teɪʃən) *n* **1** a phrase or passage from a book, speech, etc., remembered and repeated, usually with an acknowledgment of its source. **2** the act or habit of quoting. **3a** a cost estimate for goods or services given to a prospective client. **3b** the current market price of a commodity, security, etc. **4** *Printing.* a quad used to fill up spaces.

quotation mark *n* either of the punctuation marks used to begin or end a quotation, respectively " and " or ' and '. Also called: **inverted comma.**

quote ● (kwəʊt) *vb* **quotes, quoting, quoted. 1** to recite a quotation. **2** (*tr*) to put quotation marks round (a phrase, etc.). **3a** to give (a cost estimate for specified goods or services) to a prospective client. **3b** to state (the current market price) of (a security or commodity). ◆ *n* **4** an informal word for **quotation. 5** (*often pl*) an informal word for **quotation mark.** ◆ *interj* **6** an expression used to indicate that the words that follow it form a quotation. [C14: from Med. L *quotāre* to assign reference numbers to passages, from L *quot* how many]

quoted company *n* a company whose shares are quoted on a stock exchange.

quote-driven *adj* denoting an electronic market system, esp. for stock exchanges, in which prices are determined by quotations made by market makers or dealers. Cf. **order-driven.**

quote-unquote *interj* an expression used before or part before and part after a quotation to identify it as such, and sometimes to dissociate the writer or speaker from it.

quoth (kwəʊθ) *vb Arch.* (used with all pronouns except *thou* and *you,* and with nouns) said. [OE *cwæth,* third person sing of *cwethan* to say]

quotha ('kwəʊθə) *interj Arch.* an expression of mild sarcasm, used in picking up a word or phrase used by someone else. [C16: from *quoth a* quoth he]

quotidian (kwəʊ'tɪdɪən) *adj* **1** (esp. of fever) recurring daily. **2** commonplace. ◆ *n* **3** a fever characterized by attacks that recur daily. [C14: from L *quotīdiānus,* var. of *cottīdiānus* daily]

quotient ('kwəʊʃənt) *n* **1a** the result of the division of one number or quantity by another. **1b** the integral part of the result of division. **2** a ratio of two numbers or quantities to be divided. [C15: from L *quotiens* how often]

quo vadis ('kwəʊ 'vɑːdɪs) whither goest thou? [L from the Vulgate version of John 16:5]

quo warranto ('kwəʊ wɒ'ræntəʊ) *n Law.* a proceeding initiated to determine or (formerly) a writ demanding by what authority a person claims an office, franchise, or privilege. [from Med. L: by what warrant]

Qur'an (kʊ'rɑːn, -'ræn) *n* a variant spelling of **Koran.**

q.v. (denoting a cross-reference) *abbrev. for* quod vide. [NL: which (word, item, etc.) see]

qwerty *or* **QWERTY keyboard** ('kwɜːtɪ) *n* the standard English language typewriter keyboard layout with the characters q, w, e, r, t, and y at the top left of the keyboard.

THESAURUS

renounce, retire, step down (*inf.*), surrender **4** = **stop**, abandon, belay (*Nautical*), cease, conclude, discontinue, drop, end, give up, halt, suspend, throw in the towel
Antonyms *vb* ≠ **stop:** complete, continue, finish, go on with, see through

quite *adv* **1** = **absolutely**, completely, considerably, entirely, fully, in all respects, largely, perfectly, precisely, totally, wholly, without reservation **2** = **somewhat**, fairly, moderately, rather, reasonably, relatively, to a certain extent, to some degree **3** = **truly**, in fact, in reality, in truth, really

quiver[1] *vb* **1** = **shake**, agitate, convulse, oscillate, palpitate, pulsate, quake, quaver, shiver, shudder, tremble, vibrate ◆ *n* **2** = **shake**, convulsion, oscillation, palpitation, pulsation, shiver, shudder, spasm, throb, tic, tremble, tremor, vibration

quixotic *adj* = **unrealistic**, absurd, dreamy, fanciful, fantastical, idealistic, imaginary, impracticable, impractical, romantic, unworldly, Utopian, visionary

quiz *n* **3** = **examination**, investigation, questioning, test ◆ *vb* **7** = **question**, ask, catechize, examine, grill (*inf.*), interrogate, investigate, pump (*inf.*)

quizzical *adj* = **mocking**, arch, curious, derisive, inquiring, questioning, sardonic, supercilious, teasing

quondam *adj* = **former**, bygone, earlier, ex-, foregoing, late, one-time, past, previous, retired, sometime

quota *n* **1** = **share**, allocation, allowance, assignment, cut (*inf.*), part, portion, proportion, ration, slice, whack (*inf.*)

quotation *n* **1** = **passage**, citation, cutting, excerpt, extract, quote (*inf.*), reference, selection **3** = **estimate**, bid price, charge, cost, figure, price, quote (*inf.*), rate, tender

quote *vb* **1** = **repeat**, cite, detail, extract, instance, name, paraphrase, recite, refer to, retell

Rr

r *or* **R** (ɑː) *n, pl* **r's, R's,** *or* **Rs. 1** the 18th letter of the English alphabet. **2** a speech sound represented by this letter. **3** See **three Rs.**

R *symbol for:* **1** *Chem.* gas constant. **2** *Chem.* radical. **3** *Currency.* **3a** rand. **3b** rupee. **4** Réaumur (scale). **5** *Physics, electronics.* resistance. **6** roentgen *or* röntgen. **7** *Chess.* rook. **8** Royal. **9** (in the US and Australia) **9a** restricted exhibition (used to describe a category of film certified as unsuitable for viewing by anyone under the age of 18). **9b** (*as modifier*): *an R film.*

r. *abbrev. for:* **1** rare. **2** recto. **3** Also: **r** rod (unit of length). **4** ruled. **5** *Cricket.* run(s).

R. *abbrev. for:* **1** rabbi. **2** rector. **3** Regiment. **4** Regina. [L: Queen] **5** Republican. **6** Rex. [L: King] **7** River. **8** Royal.

R. *or* **r.** *abbrev. for:* **1** radius. **2** railway. **3** registered (trademark). **4** right. **5** river. **6** road. **7** rouble.

Ra *the chemical symbol for* radium.

RA *abbrev. for:* **1** rear admiral. **2** *Astron.* right ascension. **3** (in Britain) Royal Academician *or* Academy. **4** (in Britain) Royal Artillery.

RAAF *abbrev. for* Royal Australian Air Force.

rabbet ('ræbɪt) *or* **rebate** *n* **1** a recess, groove, or step, usually of rectangular section, cut into a piece of timber to receive a mating piece. ◆ *vb* **rabbets, rabbeting, rabbeted** *or* **rebates, rebating, rebated.** (*tr*) **2** to cut a rabbet in (timber). **3** to join (pieces of timber) using a rabbet. [C15: from OF *rabattre* to beat down]

rabbi ('ræbaɪ) *n, pl* **rabbis. 1** the spiritual leader of a Jewish congregation; the chief religious minister of a synagogue. **2** a scholar learned in Jewish Law, esp. one authorized to teach it. [Heb., from *rabh* master + -ī my]

rabbinate ('ræbɪnɪt) *n* **1** the position, function, or tenure of office of a rabbi. **2** rabbis collectively.

rabbinic (rə'bɪnɪk) *or* **rabbinical** (rə'bɪnɪk^{ə}l) *adj* of or relating to the rabbis, their teachings, writings, views, language, etc.
▸**rab'binically** *adv*

Rabbinic (rə'bɪnɪk) *n* the form of the Hebrew language used by the rabbis of the Middle Ages.

rabbit ('ræbɪt) *n, pl* **rabbits** *or* **rabbit. 1** any of various common gregarious burrowing mammals of Europe and North Africa. They are closely related and similar to hares but are smaller and have shorter ears. **2** the fur of such an animal. **3** *Brit. inf.* a poor performer at a game or sport. ◆ *vb* **4** (*intr*) to hunt or shoot rabbits. **5** (*intr*) (often foll. by *on* or *away*) *Brit. inf.* to talk inconsequentially; chatter. [C14: ?from Walloon *robett,* dim. of Flemish *robbe* rabbit, from ?]

rabbit fever *n Pathol.* another name for **tularaemia.**

rabbit punch *n* a short sharp blow to the back of the neck that can cause loss of consciousness or even death. Austral. name: **rabbit killer.**

rabble Ⓣ ('ræb^{ə}l) *n* **1** a disorderly crowd; mob. **2 the rabble.** *Contemptuous.* the common people. [C14 (in the sense: a pack of animals): from ?]

rabble-rouser Ⓣ *n* a person who manipulates the passions of the mob; demagogue.
▸**'rabble-ˌrousing** *adj, n*

Rabelaisian Ⓣ (ˌræbə'leɪzɪən, -ʒən) *adj* **1** of, relating to, or resembling the work of François Rabelais (?1494–1553), French writer, esp. by broad, often bawdy, humour and sharp satire. ◆ *n* **2** a student or admirer of Rabelais.
▸**ˌRabe'laisianism** *n*

rabid Ⓣ ('ræbɪd, 'reɪ-) *adj* **1** relating to or having rabies. **2** zealous; fanatical; violent; raging. [C17: from L *rabidus* frenzied, from *rabere* to be mad]
▸**rabidity** (rə'bɪdɪtɪ) *or* **'rabidness** *n* ▸**'rabidly** *adv*

rabies ('reɪbiːz) *n Pathol.* an acute infectious viral disease of the nervous system transmitted by the saliva of infected animals, esp. dogs. [C17: from L: madness, from *rabere* to rave]
▸**rabic** ('ræbɪk) *or* **rabietic** (ˌreɪbɪ'ɛtɪk) *adj*

RAC *abbrev. for:* **1** Royal Armoured Corps. **2** Royal Automobile Club.

raccoon *or* **racoon** (rə'kuːn) *n, pl* **raccoons, raccoon** *or* **racoons, racoon. 1** an omnivorous mammal, esp. the **North American raccoon,** inhabiting forests of North and Central America. Raccoons have a pointed muzzle, long tail, and greyish-black fur with black bands around the tail and across the face. **2** the fur of the raccoon. [C17: from Algonquian *ärähkun,* from *ärähkuněm* he scratches with his hands]

race[1] Ⓣ (reɪs) *n* **1** a contest of speed, as in running, etc. **2** any competition or rivalry. **3** rapid or constant onward movement: *the race of time.* **4** a rapid current of water, esp. one through a narrow channel that has a tidal range greater at one end than the other. **5** a channel of a stream, esp. one for conducting water to or from a water wheel for energy: *a mill race.* **6a** a channel or groove that contains ball bearings or roller bearings. **6b** the inner or outer cylindrical ring in a ball bearing or roller bearing. **7** *Austral. & NZ.* a narrow passage or enclosure in a sheep yard through which sheep pass individually, as to a sheep dip. **8** *Austral.* a wire tunnel through which footballers pass from the changing room onto a football field. **9** *Arch.* the span or course of life. ◆ *vb* **races, racing, raced. 10** to engage in a contest of speed with (another). **11** to cause (animals, etc.) to engage in a race: *to race pigeons.* **12** to move or go as fast as possible. **13** to run (an engine, propeller, etc.) or (of an engine, propeller, etc.) to run at high speed, esp. after reduction of the load. ◆ See also **races.** [C13: from ON *rās* running]

race[2] Ⓣ (reɪs) *n* **1** a group of people of common ancestry, distinguished from others by physical characteristics, such as hair type, colour of skin, stature, etc. **2 the human race.** human beings collectively. **3** a group of animals or plants having common characteristics that distinguish them from other members of the same species, usually forming a geographically isolated group; subspecies. **4** a group of people sharing the same interests, characteristics, etc.: *race of authors.* [C16: from F, from It. *razza,* from ?]

racecard ('reɪsˌkɑːd) *n* a card at a race meeting with the races and runners, etc., printed on it.

racecourse ('reɪsˌkɔːs) *n* a long broad track, over which horses are raced. Also called (esp. US and Canad.): **racetrack.**

racehorse ('reɪsˌhɔːs) *n* a horse specially bred for racing.

raceme (rə'siːm) *n* an inflorescence in which the flowers are borne along the main stem. [C18: from L *racēmus* bunch of grapes]
▸**racemose** ('ræsɪˌməʊs, -məʊz) *adj*

race meeting *n* a prearranged fixture for racing horses (or greyhounds) over a set course.

racemic (rə'siːmɪk, -'sɛm-) *adj Chem.* of, or being a mixture of dextrorotatory and laevorotatory isomers in such proportions that the mixture has no optical activity. [C19: from RACEME + -IC]
▸**racemism** ('ræsɪˌmɪzəm) *n*

racer ('reɪsə) *n* **1** a person, animal, or machine that races. **2** a turntable used to traverse a heavy gun. **3** any of several slender nonvenomous North American snakes, such as the **striped racer.**

race relations *n* **1** (*functioning as pl*) the relations between members of two or more human races, esp. within a single community. **2** (*functioning as sing*) the branch of sociology concerned with such relations.

race riot *n* a riot among members of different races in the same community.

races ('reɪsɪz) *pl n* **the races.** a series of contests of speed between horses (or greyhounds) over a set course.

racetrack ('reɪsˌtræk) *n* **1** a circuit or course, esp. an oval one, used for motor racing, etc. **2** the usual US and Canad. word for **racecourse.**

raceway ('reɪsˌweɪ) *n* **1** another word for **race**[1] (senses 5, 6). **2** *Chiefly US.* a racetrack.

rachis *or* **rhachis** ('reɪkɪs) *n, pl* **rachises, rhachises** *or* **rachides, rhachides** ('rækɪˌdiːz, 'reɪ-). **1** *Bot.* the main axis or stem of an inflorescence or compound leaf. **2** *Ornithol.* the shaft of a feather, esp. the part that carries the barbs. **3** another name for **spinal column.** [C17: via NL from Gk *rhakhis* ridge]
▸**rachial, rhachial** ('reɪkɪəl) *or* **rachidial, rhachidial** (rə'kɪdɪəl) *adj*

rachitis (rə'kaɪtɪs) *n Pathol.* another name for **rickets.**
▸**rachitic** (rə'kɪtɪk) *adj*

Rachmanism ('rækməˌnɪzəm) *n* extortion or exploitation by a landlord of tenants of slum property. [C20: after Perec *Rachman* (1920–62), Brit. property-owner]

racial Ⓣ ('reɪʃəl) *adj* **1** denoting or relating to the division of the human species into races on grounds of physical characteristics. **2** characteristic of any such group.
▸**'racially** *adv*

racism ('reɪsɪzəm) *or* **racialism** ('reɪʃəˌlɪzəm) *n* **1** the belief that races have distinctive cultural characteristics determined by hereditary factors and that this endows some races with an intrinsic superiority. **2**

THESAURUS

rabble *n* **1 = mob,** crowd, herd, horde, swarm, throng **2 the rabble** *Contemptuous* **= commoners,** canaille, commonalty, common people, crowd, dregs, hoi polloi, lower classes, lumpenproletariat, masses, peasantry, populace, proletariat, riffraff, scum, the great unwashed (*inf. & derogatory*), trash (*chiefly US & Canad.*)
Antonyms *n* ≠ **commoners:** aristocracy, bourgeoisie, elite, gentry, high society, nobility, upper classes

rabble-rouser *n* **= agitator,** demagogue, firebrand, incendiary, stirrer (*inf.*), troublemaker

Rabelaisian *adj* **1 = bawdy,** broad, coarse, earthy, extravagant, exuberant, gross, lusty, raunchy (*sl.*), robust, satirical, uninhibited, unrestrained

rabid *adj* **1 = mad,** hydrophobic **2 = fanatical,** bigoted, extreme, fervent, intemperate, intolerant, irrational, narrow-minded, zealous
Antonyms *adj* ≠ **fanatical:** half-hearted, moderate, wishy-washy (*inf.*)

race[1] *n* **1, 2 = contest,** chase, competition, contention, dash, pursuit, rivalry ◆ *vb* **10 = compete,** contest, run **13 = run,** barrel (along), burn rubber (*inf.*), career, dart, dash, fly, gallop, go like a bomb (*Brit. & NZ inf.*), hare (*Brit. inf.*), hasten, hurry, run like mad (*inf.*), speed, tear, zoom

race[2] *n* **1 = people,** blood, breed, clan, ethnic group, family, folk, house, issue, kin, kindred, line, lineage, nation, offspring, progeny, seed (*chiefly Biblical*), stock, tribe, type

racial *adj* **1, 2 = ethnic,** ethnological, folk, genealogical, genetic, national, tribal

abusive or aggressive behaviour towards members of another race on the basis of such a belief.
▸ **'racist** *or* **'racialist** *n, adj*

rack[1] ❶ (ræk) *n* **1** a framework for holding, carrying, or displaying a specific load or object. **2** a toothed bar designed to engage a pinion to form a mechanism that will adjust the position of something. **3** (preceded by *the*) an instrument of torture that stretched the body of the victim. **4** a cause or state of mental or bodily stress, suffering, etc. (esp. in **on the rack**). **5** *US & Canad.* (in pool, snooker, etc.) **5a** the triangular frame used to arrange the balls for the opening shot. **5b** the balls so grouped. Brit. equivalent: **frame.** ◆ *vb (tr)* **6** to torture on the rack. **7** to cause great suffering to: *guilt racked his conscience.* **8** to strain or shake (something) violently: *the storm racked the town.* **9** to place or arrange in or on a rack. **10** to move (parts of machinery or a mechanism) using a toothed rack. **11** to raise (rents) exorbitantly. **12 rack one's brains.** to strain in mental effort. [C14 *rekke,* prob. from MDu. *rec* framework]
▸ **'racker** *n*

USAGE NOTE See at **wrack**[1].

rack[2] (ræk) *n* destruction; wreck (obs. except in **go to rack and ruin**). [C16: var. of WRACK[1]]

rack[3] (ræk) *n* another word for **single-foot.** [C16: ? based on ROCK[2]]

rack[4] (ræk) *n* **1** a group of broken clouds moving in the wind. ◆ *vb* **2** *(intr)* (of clouds) to be blown along by the wind. [OE *wrǣc* what is driven]

rack[5] (ræk) *vb (tr)* to clear (wine, beer, etc.) as by siphoning it off from the dregs. [C15: from OProvençal *arraca,* from *raca* dregs of grapes after pressing]

rack-and-pinion *n* **1** a device for converting rotary into linear motion and vice versa, in which a gearwheel (the pinion) engages with a flat toothed bar (the rack). ◆ *adj* **2** (of a type of steering gear in motor vehicles) having a track rod with a rack along part of its length that engages with a pinion attached to the steering column.

racket[1] ❶ ('rækɪt) *n* **1** a noisy disturbance or loud commotion; clamour; din. **2** an illegal enterprise carried on for profit, such as extortion, fraud, etc. **3** *Sl.* a business or occupation: *what's your racket?* **4** *Music.* a medieval woodwind instrument of deep bass pitch. ◆ *vb* **5** *(intr; often foll. by about) Now rare.* to go about gaily or noisily, in search of pleasure, etc. [C16: prob. imit.]
▸ **'rackety** *adj*

racket[2] *or* **racquet** ('rækɪt) *n* **1** a bat consisting of an open network of strings stretched in an oval frame with a handle, used to strike a tennis ball, etc. **2** a snowshoe shaped like a tennis racket. ◆ *vb* **3** *(tr)* to strike (a ball, etc.) with a racket. ◆ See also **rackets.** [C16: from F *raquette,* from Ar. *rāhat* palm of the hand]

racketeer (ˌrækɪ'tɪə) *n* **1** a person engaged in illegal enterprises for profit. ◆ *vb* **2** *(intr)* to operate an illegal enterprise.
▸ **ˌracket'eering** *n*

racket press *n* a device consisting of a frame closed by a spring mechanism, for keeping taut the strings of a tennis racket, squash racket, etc.

rackets ('rækɪts) *n (functioning as sing)* **a** a game similar to squash played in a four-walled court by two or four players using rackets and a small hard ball. **b** *(as modifier): a rackets court.*

rack railway *n* a steep mountain railway having a middle rail fitted with a rack that engages a pinion on the locomotive to provide traction. Also called: **cog railway.**

rack-rent *n* **1** a high rent that annually equals the value of the property upon which it is charged. **2** any extortionate rent. ◆ *vb* **3** to charge an extortionate rent for.
▸ **'rack-ˌrenter** *n*

rack saw *n Building trades.* a wide-toothed saw.

racon ('reɪkɒn) *n* another name for **radar beacon.** [C20: from RA(DAR) + (BEA)CON]

raconteur (ˌrækɒn'tɜː) *n* a person skilled in telling stories. [C19: F, from *raconter* to tell]

racoon (rə'kuːn) *n, pl* **racoons** *or* **racoon.** a variant spelling of **raccoon.**

racquet ('rækɪt) *n* a variant spelling of **racket**[2].

racy ❶ ('reɪsɪ) *adj* **racier, raciest. 1** (of a person's manner, literary style, etc.) having a distinctively lively and spirited quality. **2** having a characteristic or distinctive flavour: *a racy wine.* **3** suggestive; slightly indecent; risqué.
▸ **'racily** *adv* ▸ **'raciness** *n*

rad[1] (ræd) *n* a former unit of absorbed ionizing radiation dose equivalent to an energy absorption per unit mass of 0.01 joule per kilogram of irradiated material. [C20: from RADIATION]

rad[2] *symbol for* radian.

rad. *abbrev. for:* **1** radical. **2** radius.

RADA ('rɑːdə) *n* (in Britain) *acronym for* Royal Academy of Dramatic Art.

radar ('reɪdɑː) *n* **1** a method for detecting the position and velocity of a distant object. A narrow beam of extremely high-frequency radio pulses is transmitted and reflected by the object back to the transmitter. The direction of the reflected beam and the time between transmission and reception of a pulse determine the position of the object. **2** the equipment used in such detection. [C20: *ra(dio) d(etecting) a(nd) r(anging)*]

radar astronomy *n* the use of radar to map the surfaces of the planets, their satellites, and other bodies.

radar beacon *n* a device for transmitting a coded radar signal in response to a signal from an aircraft or ship. The coded signal is then used by the navigator to determine his position. Also called: **racon.**

radarscope ('reɪdɑːˌskəʊp) *n* a cathode-ray oscilloscope on which radar signals can be viewed.

radar trap *n* a device using radar to detect motorists who exceed the speed limit.

raddle ('ræd°l) *vb* **raddles, raddling, raddled. 1** *(tr) Chiefly Brit.* to paint (the face) with rouge. ◆ *n, vb* **2** another word for **ruddle.** [C16: var. of RUDDLE]

raddled ❶ ('ræd°ld) *adj* (esp. of a person) unkempt or run-down in appearance.

radial ('reɪdɪəl) *adj* **1** (of lines, etc.) emanating from a common central point; arranged like the radii of a circle. **2** of, like, or relating to a radius or ray. **3** short for **radial-ply. 4** *Anat.* of or relating to the radius or forearm. **5** *Astron.* (of velocity) in a direction along the line of sight of a celestial object and measured by means of the red shift (or blue shift) of the spectral lines of the object. ◆ *n* **6** a radial part or section. [C16: from Med. L *radiālis,* from RADIUS]
▸ **'radially** *adv*

radial engine *n* an internal-combustion engine having a number of cylinders arranged about a central crankcase.

radial-ply *adj* (of a motor tyre) having the fabric cords in the outer casing running radially to enable the sidewalls to be flexible.

radial symmetry *n* a type of structure of an organism in which a vertical cut through the axis in any of two or more planes produces two halves that are mirror images of each other. Cf. **bilateral symmetry.**

radian ('reɪdɪən) *n* an SI unit of plane angle; the angle between two radii of a circle that cut off on the circumference an arc equal in length to the radius. 1 radian is equivalent to 57.296 degrees. Symbol: rad. [C19: from RADIUS]

radiance ❶ ('reɪdɪəns) *or* **radiancy** *n, pl* **radiances** *or* **radiancies. 1** the quality or state of being radiant. **2** a measure of the amount of electromagnetic radiation leaving or arriving at a point on a surface.

radiant ❶ ('reɪdɪənt) *adj* **1** sending out rays of light; bright; shining. **2** characterized by health, happiness, etc.: *a radiant smile.* **3** emitted or propagated by or as radiation; radiated: *radiant heat.* **4** sending out heat by radiation: *a radiant heater.* **5** *Physics.* (of a physical quantity in photometry) evaluated by absolute energy measurements: *radiant flux.* ◆ *n* **6** a point or object that emits radiation, esp. the part of a heater that gives out heat. **7** *Astron.* the point in the sky from which a meteor shower appears to emanate. [C15: from L *radiāre* to shine, from *radius* ray of light]
▸ **'radiancy** *n* ▸ **'radiantly** *adv*

radiant energy *n* energy that is emitted or propagated in the form of particles or electromagnetic radiation.

radiant heat *n* heat transferred in the form of electromagnetic radiation rather than by conduction or convection; infrared radiation.

radiata pine (ˌreɪdɪ'ɑːtə) *n* a pine tree grown in Australia and New Zealand to produce building timber. Often shortened to **radiata.** [from NL]

radiate ❶ *vb* ('reɪdɪˌeɪt), **radiates, radiating, radiated. 1** Also: **eradiate.** to emit (heat, light, or other forms of radiation) or (of heat, light, etc.) to be emitted as radiation. **2** *(intr)* (of lines, beams, etc.) to spread out from a centre or be arranged in a radial pattern. **3** *(tr)* (of a person) to show (happiness, etc.) to a great degree. ◆ *adj* ('reɪdɪɪt, -ˌeɪt). **4** having rays; radiating. **5** (of a capitulum) consisting of ray flowers. **6** (of animals) showing radial symmetry. [C17: from L *radiāre* to emit rays]
▸ **'radiative** *adj*

THESAURUS

rack[1] *n* **1** = **frame,** framework, stand, structure **4** = **torture,** affliction, agony, anguish, misery, pain, pang, persecution, suffering, torment ◆ *vb* **7** = **torture,** afflict, agonize, crucify, distress, excruciate, harass, harrow, oppress, pain, torment **8** = **strain,** force, pull, shake, stress, stretch, tear, wrench

racket[1] *n* **1** = **noise,** babel, ballyhoo *(inf.),* clamour, commotion, din, disturbance, fuss, hubbub, hullabaloo, outcry, pandemonium, row, rumpus, shouting, tumult, uproar **2** = **fraud,** criminal activity, illegal enterprise, scheme **3** *Slang* = **business,** game *(inf.),* line, occupation

rackety *adj* **1** = **noisy,** blaring, boisterous, clamorous, disorderly, rowdy, uproarious

racy *adj* **1** = **lively,** animated, buoyant, dramatic, energetic, entertaining, exciting, exhilarating, heady, sexy *(inf.),* sparkling, spirited, stimulating, vigorous, zestful **3** = **risqué,** bawdy, blue, broad, immodest, indecent, indelicate, naughty, near the knuckle *(inf.),* off colour, smutty, spicy *(inf.),* suggestive

raddled *adj* = **run-down,** broken-down, coarsened, dilapidated, dishevelled, haggard, tattered, the worse for wear, unkempt

radiance *n* **1** = **brightness,** brilliance, effulgence, glare, gleam, glitter, glow, incandescence, light, luminosity, lustre, resplendence, shine **1** = **happiness,** delight, gaiety, joy, pleasure, rapture, warmth

radiant *adj* **1** = **bright,** beaming, brilliant, effulgent, gleaming, glittering, glorious, glowing, incandescent, luminous, lustrous, resplendent, shining, sparkling, sunny **2** = **happy,** beaming, beatific, blissful, delighted, ecstatic, floating on air, gay, glowing, joyful, joyous, on cloud nine *(inf.),* rapt, rapturous, sent
Antonyms *adj* ≠ **bright:** black, dark, dull, gloomy, sombre ≠ **happy:** disconsolate, down in the dumps *(inf.),* gloomy, joyless, low, miserable, sad, sombre, sorrowful

radiate *vb* **1** = **emit,** diffuse, disseminate, emanate, give off *or* out, gleam, glitter, pour, scatter, send out, shed, shine, spread **2** = **spread out,** branch out, diverge, issue

radiation ⓘ (ˌreɪdɪˈeɪʃən) *n* **1** *Physics.* **1a** the emission or transfer of radiant energy as particles, electromagnetic waves, sound, etc. **1b** the particles, etc., emitted, esp. the particles and gamma rays emitted in nuclear decay. **2** Also called: **radiation therapy.** *Med.* treatment using a radioactive substance. **3** the act, state, or process of radiating or being radiated.
▸ˌ**radiˈational** *adj*

radiation sickness *n Pathol.* illness caused by overexposure of the body to ionizing radiations from radioactive material or X-rays.

radiator (ˈreɪdɪˌeɪtə) *n* **1** a device for heating a room, building, etc., consisting of a series of pipes through which hot water or steam passes. **2** a device for cooling an internal-combustion engine, consisting of thin-walled tubes through which water passes. **3** *Electronics.* the part of an aerial or transmission line that radiates electromagnetic waves.

radical ⓘ (ˈrædɪkᵊl) *adj* **1** of, relating to, or characteristic of the basic or inherent constitution of a person or thing; fundamental: *a radical fault.* **2** concerned with or tending to concentrate on fundamental aspects of a matter; searching or thoroughgoing: *radical thought.* **3** favouring or tending to produce extreme or fundamental changes in political, economic, or social conditions, institutions, etc.: *a radical party.* **4** *Med.* (of treatment) aimed at removing the source of a disease: *radical surgery.* **5** *Sl., chiefly US.* very good; excellent. **6** of or arising from the root or the base of the stem of a plant: *radical leaves.* **7** *Maths.* of, relating to, or containing roots of numbers or quantities. **8** *Linguistics.* of or relating to the root of a word. ◆ *n* **9** a person who favours extreme or fundamental change in existing institutions or in political, social, or economic conditions. **10** *Maths.* a root of a number or quantity, such as $\sqrt[3]{5}$, $\sqrt{x}$. **11** *Chem.* **11a** short for **free radical. 11b** another name for **group** (sense 9). **12** *Linguistics.* another word for **root**[1] (sense 8). [C14: from LL *rādīcālis* having roots, from L *rādix* a root]
▸ˈ**radicalness** *n*

radicalism (ˈrædɪkəˌlɪzəm) *n* **1** the principles, desires, or practices of political radicals. **2** a radical movement, esp. in politics.
▸ˌ**radicalˈistic** *adj* ▸ˌ**radicalˈistically** *adv*

radically (ˈrædɪkəlɪ) *adv* thoroughly; completely; fundamentally: *to alter radically.*

radical sign *n* the symbol √ placed before a number or quantity to indicate the extraction of a root, esp. a square root. The value of a higher root is indicated by a raised digit in front of the symbol, as in $\sqrt[3]{}$.

radicand (ˈrædɪˌkænd, ˌrædɪˈkænd) *n* a number or quantity from which a root is to be extracted, usually preceded by a radical sign: 3 *is the radicand of* $\sqrt{3}$. [C20: from L *rādīcandum,* lit.: that which is to be rooted, from *rādīcāre,* from *rādīx* root]

radicchio (ræˈdiːkɪəʊ) *n, pl* **radicchios.** an Italian variety of chicory, having purple leaves streaked with white that are eaten raw in salads.

radices (ˈreɪdɪˌsiːz) *n* a plural of **radix.**

radicle (ˈrædɪkᵊl) *n* **1** *Bot.* **1a** the part of the embryo of seed-bearing plants that develops into the main root. **1b** a very small root or rootlike part. **2** *Anat.* any bodily structure resembling a rootlet, esp. one of the smallest branches of a vein or nerve. **3** *Chem.* a variant spelling of **radical** (sense 11). [C18: from L *rādīcula,* from *rādīx* root]

radii (ˈreɪdɪˌaɪ) *n* a plural of **radius.**

radio (ˈreɪdɪəʊ) *n, pl* **radios. 1** the use of electromagnetic waves, lying in the radio-frequency range, for broadcasting, two-way communications, etc. **2** an electronic device designed to receive, demodulate, and amplify radio signals from sound broadcasting stations, etc. **3** the broadcasting, content, etc., of radio programmes: *he thinks radio is poor these days.* **4** the occupation or profession concerned with any aspect of the broadcasting of radio programmes. **5** short for **radiotelegraph, radiotelegraphy,** or **radiotelephone. 6** (*modifier*) **6a** of, relating to, or sent by radio signals: *a radio station.* **6b** of, concerned with, using, or operated by radio frequencies: *radio spectrum.* **6c** relating to or produced for radio: *radio drama.* ◆ *vb* **radios, radioing, radioed. 7** to transmit (a message, etc.) to (a person, etc.) by means of radio waves. ◆ Also called (esp. Brit.): **wireless.** [C20: short for *radiotelegraphy*]

radio- *combining form.* **1** denoting radio, broadcasting, or radio frequency: *radiogram.* **2** indicating radioactivity or radiation: *radiocarbon; radiochemistry.* [from F, from L *radius* ray]

radioactive (ˌreɪdɪəʊˈæktɪv) *adj* exhibiting, using, or concerned with radioactivity.
▸ˌ**radioˈactively** *adv*

radioactive dating *n* another term for **radiometric dating.**

radioactive decay *n* disintegration of a nucleus that occurs spontaneously or as a result of electron capture. Also called: **disintegration.**

radioactive series *n Physics.* a series of nuclides each of which undergoes radioactive decay into the next member of the series, ending with a stable element, usually lead.

radioactive tracer *n Med.* See **tracer** (sense 3).

radioactive waste *n* any waste material containing radionuclides. Also called: **nuclear waste.**

radioactivity (ˌreɪdɪəʊækˈtɪvɪtɪ) *n* the spontaneous emission of radiation from atomic nuclei. The radiation can consist of alpha, beta, or gamma radiation.

radio astronomy *n* a branch of astronomy in which a radio telescope is used to detect and analyse radio signals received on earth from radio sources in space.

radio beacon *n* a fixed radio transmitting station that broadcasts a characteristic signal by means of which a vessel or aircraft can determine its bearing or position.

radiobiology (ˌreɪdɪəʊbaɪˈɒlədʒɪ) *n* the branch of biology concerned with the effects of radiation on living organisms and the study of biological processes using radioactive substances as tracers.
▸**radiobiological** (ˌreɪdɪəʊˌbaɪəˈlɒdʒɪkᵊl) *adj* ▸ˌ**radioˌbioˈlogically** *adv* ▸ˌ**radiobiˈologist** *n*

radiocarbon (ˌreɪdɪəʊˈkɑːbᵊn) *n* a radioactive isotope of carbon, esp. carbon-14. See **carbon** (sense 1).

radiocarbon dating *n* See **carbon dating.**

radiochemistry (ˌreɪdɪəʊˈkɛmɪstrɪ) *n* the chemistry of radioactive elements and their compounds.
▸ˌ**radioˈchemical** *adj* ▸ˌ**radioˈchemist** *n*

radio compass *n* any navigational device that gives a bearing by determining the direction of incoming radio waves transmitted from a particular radio station or beacon. See also **goniometer** (sense 2).

radio control *n* remote control by means of radio signals from a transmitter.
▸ˈ**radio-conˈtrolled** *adj*

radioelement (ˌreɪdɪəʊˈɛlɪmənt) *n* an element that is naturally radioactive.

radio frequency *n* **1a** any frequency that lies in the range 10 kilohertz to 300 000 megahertz and can be used for broadcasting. Abbrevs.: **rf, RF. 1b** (*as modifier*): *a radio-frequency amplifier.* **2** the frequency transmitted by a particular radio station.

radio galaxy *n* a galaxy that is a strong emitter of radio waves.

radiogram (ˈreɪdɪəʊˌgræm) *n* **1** *Brit.* a unit comprising a radio and record player. **2** a message transmitted by radiotelegraphy. **3** another name for **radiograph.**

radiograph (ˈreɪdɪəʊˌgrɑːf) *n* an image produced on a specially sensitized photographic film or plate by radiation, usually by X-rays or gamma rays.

radiography (ˌreɪdɪˈɒgrəfɪ) *n* the production of radiographs of opaque objects for use in medicine, surgery, industry, etc.
▸ˌ**radiˈographer** *n* ▸**radiographic** (ˌreɪdɪəʊˈgræfɪk) *adj* ▸ˌ**radioˈgraphically** *adv*

radio-immuno-assay (ˈreɪdɪəʊˌɪmjʊnəʊˈæseɪ) *n* a sensitive immunological assay, making use of radioactive labelling, of such things as hormone levels in the blood.

radioisotope (ˌreɪdɪəʊˈaɪsətəʊp) *n* a radioactive isotope.
▸**radioisotopic** (ˌreɪdɪəʊˌaɪsəˈtɒpɪk) *adj*

radiolarian (ˌreɪdɪəʊˈlɛərɪən) *n* any of various marine protozoans typically having a siliceous shell and stiff radiating cytoplasmic projections. [C19: from NL *Radiolaria,* from LL *radiolus* little sunbeam, from L *radius* ray]

radiology (ˌreɪdɪˈɒlədʒɪ) *n* the use of X-rays and radioactive substances in the diagnosis and treatment of disease.
▸ˌ**radiˈologist** *n*

radiometer (ˌreɪdɪˈɒmɪtə) *n* any instrument for the detection or measurement of radiant energy.
▸**radiometric** (ˌreɪdɪəʊˈmɛtrɪk) *adj* ▸ˌ**radiˈometry** *n*

radiometric dating *n* any method of dating material based on the decay of its constituent radioactive atoms, such as potassium-argon dating or rubidium-strontium dating. Also called: **radioactive dating.**

radiopager (ˈreɪdɪəʊˌpeɪdʒə) *n* a small radio receiver fitted with a buzzer to alert a person to telephone their home, office, etc., to receive a message.
▸ˈ**radioˌpaging** *n*

radiopaque (ˌreɪdɪəʊˈpeɪk) *or* **radio-opaque** *adj* not permitting X-rays or other radiation to pass through.
▸**radiopacity** (ˌreɪdɪəʊˈpæsɪtɪ) *or* ˌ**radio-oˈpacity** *n*

radio receiver *n* an apparatus that receives incoming modulated radio waves and converts them into sound.

radioscopy (ˌreɪdɪˈɒskəpɪ) *n* another word for **fluoroscopy.**
▸**radioscopic** (ˌreɪdɪəʊˈskɒpɪk) *adj* ▸ˌ**radioˈscopically** *adv*

radiosonde (ˈreɪdɪəʊˌsɒnd) *n* an airborne instrument to send meteorological information back to earth by radio. [C20: RADIO- + F *sonde* sounding line]

radio source *n* a celestial object, such as a supernova remnant or quasar, that is a source of radio waves.

radio spectrum *n* the range of electromagnetic frequencies used in radio transmission, between 10 kilohertz and 300 000 megahertz.

radio star *n* a former name for **radio source.**

radiotelegraphy (ˌreɪdɪəʊtɪˈlɛgrəfɪ) *n* a type of telegraphy in which messages (formerly in Morse code) are transmitted by radio waves.
▸ˌ**radioˈteleˌgraph** *vb, n* ▸**radiotelegraphic** (ˌreɪdɪəʊˌtɛlɪˈgræfɪk) *adj*

radiotelephone (ˌreɪdɪəʊˈtɛlɪˌfəʊn) *n* **1** a device for communications by means of radio waves rather than by transmitting along wires or cables. ◆ *vb* **radiotelephones, radiotelephoning, radiotelephoned. 2** to telephone (a person) by radiotelephone.

THESAURUS

radiation *n* **1** = **emission,** emanation, rays

radical *adj* **1** = **fundamental,** basic, constitutional, deep-seated, essential, innate, natural, organic **2** = **thoroughgoing,** profound **3** = **extreme,** drastic, excessive, extremist, fanatical, revolutionary, sweeping ◆ *n* **9** = **extremist,** fanatic, militant, revolutionary

Antonyms *adj* ≠ **fundamental:** insignificant, minor, superficial, token, trivial ◆ *n* ≠ **extremist:** conservative, moderate, reactionary

▸**radiotelephonic** (ˌreɪdɪəʊˌtelɪˈfɒnɪk) *adj* ▸**radiotelephony** (ˌreɪdɪəʊtɪˈlefənɪ) *n*
radio telescope *n* an instrument consisting of an antenna or system of antennas connected to one or more radio receivers, used in radio astronomy to detect and analyse radio waves from space.
radioteletype (ˌreɪdɪəʊˈtelɪˌtaɪp) *n* **1** a teleprinter that transmits or receives information by means of radio waves. **2** a network of such devices widely used for communicating news, messages, etc. Abbrevs.: **RTT, RTTY.**
radiotherapy (ˌreɪdɪəʊˈθerəpɪ) *n* the treatment of disease by means of alpha or beta particles emitted from an implanted or ingested radioisotope, or by means of a beam of high-energy radiation. Cf. **chemotherapy.**
▸**radiotherapeutic** (ˌreɪdɪəʊˌθerəˈpjuːtɪk) *adj* ▸ˌ**radioˈtherapist** *n*
radio wave *n* an electromagnetic wave of radio frequency.
radish (ˈrædɪʃ) *n* **1** any of a genus of plants of Europe and Asia, with petals arranged like a cross, cultivated for their edible roots. **2** the root of this plant, which has a pungent taste and is eaten raw in salads. [OE *rǣdīc*, from L *rādīx* root]
radium (ˈreɪdɪəm) *n* **a** a highly radioactive luminescent white element of the alkaline earth group of metals. It occurs in pitchblende and other uranium ores. Symbol: Ra; atomic no.: 88; half-life of most stable isotope, ^{226}Ra: 1620 years. **b** (*as modifier*): *radium needle.* [C20: from L *radius* ray]
radium therapy *n* treatment of disease, esp. cancer, by exposing affected tissues to radiation from radium.
radius (ˈreɪdɪəs) *n, pl* **radii** *or* **radiuses. 1** a straight line joining the centre of a circle or sphere to any point on the circumference or surface. **2** the length of this line, usually denoted by the symbol *r.* **3** *Anat.* the outer, slightly shorter of the two bones of the human forearm, extending from the elbow to the wrist. **4** a corresponding bone in other vertebrates. **5** any of the veins of an insect's wing. **6** a group of ray flowers, occurring in such plants as the daisy. **7a** any radial or radiating part, such as a spoke. **7b** (*as modifier*): *a radius arm.* **8** a circular area of a size indicated by the length of its radius: *the police stopped every lorry within a radius of four miles.* **9** the operational limit of a ship, aircraft, etc. [C16: from L: rod, ray, spoke]
radix (ˈreɪdɪks) *n, pl* **radices** *or* **radixes. 1** *Maths.* any number that is the base of a number system or of a system of logarithms: *10 is the radix of the decimal system.* **2** *Biol.* the root or point of origin of a part or organ. **3** *Linguistics.* a less common word for **root**[1] (sense 8). [C16: from L *rādīx* root]
radix point *n* a point, such as the decimal point in the decimal system, separating the integral part of a number from the fractional part.
radome (ˈreɪdəʊm) *n* a protective housing for a radar antenna made from a material that is transparent to radio waves. [C20: RA(DAR) + DOME]
radon (ˈreɪdɒn) *n* a colourless radioactive element of the rare gas group, the most stable isotope of which, radon-222, is a decay product of radium. Symbol: Rn; atomic no.: 86; half-life of ^{222}Rn: 3.82 days. [C20: from RADIUM + -ON]
radula (ˈrædjʊlə) *n, pl* **radulae** (-ˌliː). a horny tooth-bearing strip on the tongue of molluscs that is used for rasping food. [C19: from LL: a scraping iron, from L *rādere* to scrape]
▸ˈ**radular** *adj*
RAF (*Not standard* ræf) *abbrev. for* Royal Air Force.
Rafferty (ˈræfətɪ) *or* **Rafferty's rules** *pl n Austral. & NZ sl.* no rules at all. [C20: from ?]
raffia *or* **raphia** (ˈræfɪə) *n* **1** a palm tree, native to Madagascar, that has large plumelike leaves, the stalks of which yield a useful fibre. **2** the fibre obtained from this plant, used for weaving, etc. **3** any of several related palms or the fibre obtained from them. [C19: from Malagasy]
raffish 🅣 (ˈræfɪʃ) *adj* **1** careless or unconventional in dress, manners, etc.; rakish. **2** tawdry; flashy; vulgar. [C19: from *raff* rubbish, rabble]
▸ˈ**raffishly** *adv* ▸ˈ**raffishness** *n*
raffle 🅣 (ˈræfᵊl) *n* **1a** a lottery in which the prizes are goods rather than money. **1b** (*as modifier*): *a raffle ticket.* ◆ *vb* **raffles, raffling, raffled. 2** (*tr;* often foll. by *off*) to dispose of (goods) in a raffle. [C14 (a dice game): from OF, from ?]
▸ˈ**raffler** *n*
rafflesia (ræˈfliːzɪə) *n* any of various tropical Asian parasitic leafless plants, the flowers of which grow up to 45 cm (18 inches) across, smell of putrid meat, and are pollinated by carrion flies. [C19: NL, after Sir Stamford *Raffles* (1781–1826), Brit. colonial administrator, who discovered it]
raft[1] (rɑːft) *n* **1** a buoyant platform of logs, planks, etc., used as a vessel or moored platform. **2** a thick slab of reinforced concrete laid over soft ground to provide a foundation for a building. ◆ *vb* **3** to convey on or travel by raft, or make a raft from. [C15: from ON *raptr* RAFTER]
raft[2] (rɑːft) *n Inf.* a large collection or amount: *a raft of old notebooks discovered in a cupboard.*
rafter (ˈrɑːftə) *n* any one of a set of parallel sloping beams that form the framework of a roof. [OE *ræfter*]
RAFVR *abbrev. for* Royal Air Force Volunteer Reserve.
rag[1] (ræg) *n* **1a** a small piece of cloth, such as one torn from a discarded garment, or such pieces of cloth collectively. **1b** (*as modifier*): *a rag doll.* **2** a fragmentary piece of any material; scrap; shred. **3** *Inf.* a newspaper, esp. one considered as worthless, sensational, etc. **4** *Inf.* an item of clothing. **5** *Inf.* a handkerchief. **6** *Brit. sl., esp. naval.* a flag or ensign. **7 from rags to riches.** *Inf.* **7a** from poverty to great wealth. **7b** (*as modifier*): *a rags-to-riches tale.* [C14: prob. back formation from RAGGED from OE *raggig*]
rag[2] (ræg) *vb* **rags, ragging, ragged.** (*tr*) **1** to draw attention facetiously and persistently to the shortcomings of (a person). **2** *Brit.* to play rough practical jokes on. ◆ *n* **3** *Brit.* a boisterous practical joke. **4** (in British universities, etc.) **4a** a period in which various events are organized to raise money for charity. **4b** (*as modifier*): *rag day.* [C18: from ?]
rag[3] (ræg) *Jazz.* ◆ *n* **1** a piece of ragtime music. ◆ *vb* **rags, ragging, ragged. 2** (*tr*) to compose or perform in ragtime. [C20: from RAGTIME]
raga (ˈrɑːgə) *n* (in Indian music) **1** any of several conventional patterns of melody and rhythm that form the basis for freely interpreted compositions. **2** a composition based on one of these patterns. [C18: from Sansk. *rāga* tone, colour]
ragamuffin 🅣 (ˈrægəˌmʌfɪn) *n* **1** a ragged unkempt person, esp. a child. **2** another name for **ragga.** [C14 *Ragamoffyn*, a demon in the poem *Piers Plowman* (1393); prob. based on RAG[1]]
rag-and-bone man *n Brit.* a man who buys and sells discarded clothing, etc. US equivalent: **junkman.**
ragbag 🅣 (ˈrægˌbæg) *n* **1** a bag for storing odd rags. **2** a confused assortment; jumble.
ragbolt (ˈrægˌbəʊlt) *n* a bolt that has angled projections on it to prevent it working loose.
rage 🅣 (reɪdʒ) *n* **1** intense anger; fury. **2** violent movement or action, esp. of the sea, wind, etc. **3** great intensity of hunger or other feelings. **4** a fashion or craze (esp. in **all the rage**). **5** *Austral. & NZ inf.* a dance or party. ◆ *vb* **rages, raging, raged.** (*intr*) **6** to feel or exhibit intense anger. **7** (esp. of storms, fires, etc.) to move or surge with great violence. **8** (esp. of a disease) to spread rapidly and uncontrollably. **9** *Austral. & NZ inf.* to have a good time. [C13: via OF from L *rabiēs* madness]
ragga (ˈrægə) *n* a dance-oriented style of reggae. Also called: **ragamuffin.** [C20: shortened from RAGAMUFFIN]
ragged 🅣 (ˈrægɪd) *adj* **1** (of clothes) worn to rags; tattered. **2** (of a person) dressed in tattered clothes. **3** having a neglected or unkempt appearance: *ragged weeds.* **4** having a rough or uneven surface or edge; jagged. **5** uneven or irregular: *a ragged beat; a ragged shout.* [C13: prob. from *ragge* RAG[1]]
▸ˈ**raggedly** *adv* ▸ˈ**raggedness** *n*
ragged robin *n* a plant related to the carnation family and native to Europe and Asia, that has pink or white flowers with ragged petals. See also **catchfly.**
raggedy (ˈrægɪdɪ) *adj Inf., chiefly US & Canad.* somewhat ragged; tattered: *a raggedy doll.*
ragi, raggee, *or* **raggy** (ˈrægɪ) *n* a cereal grass, cultivated in Africa and Asia for its edible grain. [C18: from Hindi]
raglan (ˈræglən) *n* **1** a coat, jumper, etc., with sleeves that continue to the collar instead of having armhole seams. ◆ *adj* **2** cut in this design: *a raglan sleeve.* [C19: after Lord *Raglan* (1788–1855), Brit. field marshal]
ragout (ræˈguː) *n* **1** a richly seasoned stew of meat and vegetables. ◆ *vb* **ragouts** (-ˈguːz), **ragouting** (-ˈguːɪŋ), **ragouted** (-ˈguːd). **2** (*tr*) to make into a ragout. [C17: from F, from *ragoûter* to stimulate the appetite again, from *ra-* RE- + *goûter* from L *gustāre* to taste]
rag-rolling *n* a decorating technique in which paint is applied with a roughly folded cloth in order to create a marbled effect.
ragtag (ˈrægˌtæg) *n Derog.* the common people; rabble (esp. in **ragtag and bobtail**). [C19: from RAG[1] + TAG[1]]
ragtime (ˈrægˌtaɪm) *n* a style of jazz piano music, developed by Scott Joplin around 1900, having a two-four rhythm base and a syncopated melody. [C20: prob. from RAGGED + TIME]
rag trade *n Inf.* the clothing business.

THESAURUS

raffish *adj* **1 = dashing,** bohemian, careless, casual, devil-may-care, disreputable, jaunty, rakish, sporty, unconventional **2 = vulgar,** coarse, flashy, garish, gaudy, gross, loud, meretricious, showy, tasteless, tawdry, trashy, uncouth
raffle *n* **1 = draw,** lottery, sweep, sweepstake
ragamuffin *n* **1 = urchin,** gamin, guttersnipe, scarecrow (*inf.*), street arab (*offens.*), tatterdemalion (*rare*)
ragbag *n* **2 = mixture,** confusion, hotchpotch, jumble, medley, miscellany, mixed bag (*inf.*), omnium-gatherum, potpourri
rage *n* **1 = fury,** agitation, anger, high dudgeon, ire, madness, passion, rampage, raving, wrath **3 = frenzy,** fury, mania, obsession, passion, vehemence, violence **4 = craze,** enthusiasm, fad (*inf.*), fashion, latest thing, vogue ◆ *vb* **6 = be furious,** be beside oneself, be incandescent, blow a fuse (*sl., chiefly US*), blow one's top, blow up (*inf.*), crack up (*inf.*), fly off the handle (*inf.*), foam at the mouth, fret, fume, go ballistic (*sl., chiefly US*), go off the deep end (*inf.*), go up the wall (*sl.*), lose it (*inf.*), lose one's rag (*sl.*), lose one's temper, lose the plot (*inf.*), see red (*inf.*), seethe, storm, throw a fit (*inf.*) **7 = be at its height,** be uncontrollable, rampage, storm, surge
Antonyms *n* ≠ **fury:** acceptance, calmness, equanimity, gladness, good humour, joy, pleasure, resignation ◆ *vb* ≠ **be furious:** accept, keep one's cool, remain unruffled, resign oneself to, stay calm
ragged *adj* **1 = shabby,** down at heel, frayed, in holes, in rags, in tatters, mean, poor, tattered, tatty, threadbare, torn, worn-out **4 = rough,** crude, jagged, notched, rugged, serrated, uneven, unfinished **5 = irregular,** broken, desultory, disorganized, fragmented, uneven
Antonyms *adj* ≠ **shabby:** fashionable, smart
raging *adj* **6 = furious,** beside oneself, boiling mad (*inf.*), doing one's nut (*Brit. sl.*), enraged, fit to be tied (*sl.*), fizzing (*Scot.*), foaming at the

ragweed ('ræg,wi:d) *n* a North American plant of the composite family such as the **common ragweed.** Its green tassel-like flowers produce large amounts of pollen, which causes hay fever. Also called: **ambrosia.**

ragworm ('ræg,wɜ:m) *n* any polychaete worm living chiefly in burrows in sand and having a flattened body with a row of fleshy lateral appendages along each side. US name: **clamworm.**

ragwort ('ræg,wɜ:t) *n* any of several European plants of the composite family that have yellow daisy-like flowers. See also **groundsel.**

rah (rɑ:) *interj Inf., chiefly US.* short for **hurrah.**

rai (raɪ) *n* a type of Algerian popular music based on traditional Algerian music influenced by modern Western pop. [C20: Ar., lit.: opinion]

raid ❶ (reɪd) *n* **1** a sudden surprise attack. **2** a surprise visit by police searching for criminals or illicit goods: *a fraud-squad raid.* See also **bear raid, dawn raid, ram raid.** ◆ *vb* **3** to make a raid against (a person, thing, etc.). **4** to sneak into (a place) in order to take something, steal, etc.: *raiding the larder.* [C15: Scot. dialect, from OE *rād* military expedition]
▸ **'raider** *n*

rail[1] (reɪl) *n* **1** a horizontal bar of wood, etc., supported by vertical posts, functioning as a fence, barrier, etc. **2** a horizontal bar fixed to a wall on which to hang things: *a picture rail.* **3** a horizontal framing member in a door. Cf. **stile**[2]. **4** short for **railing. 5** one of a pair of parallel bars laid on a track, roadway, etc., that serve as a guide and running surface for the wheels of a train, tramcar, etc. **6a** short for **railway. 6b** (*as modifier*): *rail transport.* **7** *Naut.* a trim for finishing the top of a bulwark. **8 off the rails. 8a** into or in a state of disorder. **8b** eccentric or mad. ◆ *vb (tr)* **9** to provide with a rail or railings. **10** (usually foll. by *in* or *off*) to fence (an area) with rails. [C13: from OF *raille* rod, from L *rēgula* ruler]

rail[2] ❶ (reɪl) *vb (intr;* foll. by *at* or *against*) to complain bitterly or vehemently. [C15: from OF *railler* to mock, from OProvençal *ralhar* to chatter, from LL *ragere* to yell]
▸ **'railer** *n*

rail[3] (reɪl) *n* any of various small cranelike wading marsh birds with short wings and neck, long legs, and dark plumage. [C15: from OF *raale,* ?from L *rādere* to scrape]

railcar ('reɪl,kɑ:) *n* a passenger-carrying railway vehicle consisting of a single coach with its own power unit.

railcard ('reɪl,kɑ:d) *n Brit.* a card issued to students or senior citizens to entitle them to cheap rail fares.

railhead ('reɪl,hɛd) *n* **1** a terminal of a railway. **2** the farthest point reached by completed track on an unfinished railway.

railing ❶ ('reɪlɪŋ) *n* **1** (*often pl*) a fence, balustrade, or barrier that consists of rails supported by posts. **2** rails collectively or material for making rails.

raillery ❶ ('reɪlərɪ) *n, pl* **railleries. 1** light-hearted satire or ridicule; banter. **2** a bantering remark. [C17: from F, from *railler* to tease; see RAIL[2]]

railroad ('reɪl,rəʊd) *n* **1** the usual US word for **railway.** ◆ *vb* **2** *(tr) Inf.* to force (a person) into (an action) with haste or by unfair means.

railway ('reɪl,weɪ) *or US* **railroad** *n* **1** a permanent track composed of a line of parallel metal rails fixed to sleepers, for transport of passengers and goods in trains. **2** any track for the wheels of a vehicle to run on: *a cable railway.* **3** the entire equipment, rolling stock, buildings, property, and system of tracks used in such a transport system. **4** the organization responsible for operating a railway network. **5** (*modifier*) of, relating to, or used on a railway: *a railway engine.*

raiment ('reɪmənt) *n Arch. or poetic.* attire; clothing. [C15: from *arrayment,* from OF *areement;* see ARRAY]

rain ❶ (reɪn) *n* **1a** precipitation from clouds in the form of drops of water, formed by the condensation of water vapour in the atmosphere. **1b** a fall of rain; shower. **1c** (*in combination*): *a raindrop.* **2** a large quantity of anything falling rapidly or in quick succession: *a rain of abuse.* **3 (come) rain or (come) shine.** regardless of the weather or circumstances. **4 right as rain.** *Brit. inf.* perfectly all right. ◆ *vb* **5** *(intr;* with *it* as subject) to be the case that rain is falling. **6** (often with *it* as subject) to fall or cause to fall like rain. **7** *(tr)* to bestow in large measure: *to rain abuse on someone.* **8 rained off.** cancelled or postponed on account of rain. US and Canad. term: **rained out.** ◆ See also **rains.** [OE *regn*]
▸ **'rainless** *adj*

rainbow ('reɪn,bəʊ) *n* **1a** a bow-shaped display in the sky of the colours of the spectrum, caused by the refraction and reflection of the sun's rays through rain. **1b** (*as modifier*): *a rainbow pattern.* **2** an illusory hope: *to chase rainbows.* **3** (*modifier*) of or relating to a political grouping together by several minorities, esp. of different races: *the rainbow coalition.*

rainbow nation *n S. African.* an epithet, alluding to its multiracial population, of South Africa. [C20: coined by Nelson Mandela (born 1918), South African statesman, following the end of apartheid]

rainbow trout *n* a freshwater trout of North American origin, marked with many black spots and two longitudinal red stripes.

rain check *n US & Canad.* **1** a ticket stub for a baseball game that allows readmission on a future date if the event is cancelled because of rain. **2** the deferral of acceptance of an offer. **3 take a rain check.** *Inf.* to accept or request the postponement of an offer.

raincoat ('reɪn,kəʊt) *n* a coat made of a waterproof material.

rainfall ('reɪn,fɔ:l) *n* **1** precipitation in the form of raindrops. **2** *Meteorol.* the amount of precipitation in a specified place and time.

rainforest ('reɪn,fɒrɪst) *n* dense forest found in tropical areas of heavy rainfall.

rain gauge *n* an instrument for measuring rainfall or snowfall, consisting of a cylinder covered by a funnel-like lid.

rainproof ('reɪn,pru:f) *adj* **1** Also: **'rain,tight.** (of garments, materials, etc.) impermeable to rainwater. ◆ *vb* **2** *(tr)* to make rainproof.

rains (reɪnz) *pl n* **the rains.** the season of heavy rainfall, esp. in the tropics.

rain shadow *n* the relatively dry area on the leeward side of high ground in the path of rain-bearing winds.

rainstorm ('reɪn,stɔ:m) *n* a storm with heavy rain.

rainwater ('reɪn,wɔ:tə) *n* pure water from rain (as distinguished from spring water, tap water, etc., which may contain minerals and impurities).

rainy ❶ ('reɪnɪ) *adj* **rainier, rainiest. 1** characterized by a large rainfall: *a rainy climate.* **2** wet or showery; bearing rain.
▸ **'rainily** *adv* ▸ **'raininess** *n*

rainy day *n* a future time of need, esp. financial.

raise ❶ (reɪz) *vb* **raises, raising, raised.** (*mainly tr*) **1** to move or elevate to a higher position or level; lift. **2** to set or place in an upright position. **3** to construct, build, or erect: *to raise a barn.* **4** to increase in amount, size, value, etc.: *to raise prices.* **5** to increase in degree, strength, intensity, etc.: *to raise one's voice.* **6** to advance in rank or status; promote. **7** to arouse or awaken from sleep or death. **8** to stir up or incite; activate: *to raise a mutiny.* **9 raise Cain** (*or* **the devil, hell, the roof,** etc.). **9a** to create a disturbance, esp. by making a great noise. **9b** to protest vehemently. **10** to give rise to; cause or provoke: *to raise a smile.* **11** to put forward for consideration: *to raise a question.* **12** to cause to assemble or gather together: *to raise an army.* **13** to grow or cause to grow: *to raise a crop.* **14** to bring up; rear: *to raise a family.* **15** to cause to be heard or known; utter or express: *to raise a shout.* **16** to bring to an end; remove: *to raise a siege.* **17** to cause (bread, etc.) to rise, as by the addition of yeast. **18** *Poker.* to bet more than (the previous player). **19** *Bridge.* to bid (one's partner's suit) at a higher level. **20** *Naut.* to cause (something) to seem to rise above the horizon by approaching: *we raised land after 20 days.* **21** to establish radio communications with: *we raised Moscow last night.* **22** to obtain (money, funds, etc.). **23** to bring (a surface, a design, etc.) into relief; cause to project. **24** to cause (a blister, etc.) to form on the skin. **25** *Maths.* to multiply (a number) by itself a specified number of times: *8 is 2 raised to the power 3.* **26 raise one's glass (to).** to drink a toast (to). **27 raise one's hat.** *Old-fashioned.* to take one's hat briefly off one's head as a greeting or mark of respect. ◆ *n* **28** the act or an instance of raising. **29** *Chiefly US & Canad.* an increase, esp. in salary, wages, etc.; rise. [C12: from ON *reisa*]
▸ **'raisable** *or* **'raiseable** *adj*

raised beach *n* a wave-cut platform raised above the shoreline by a relative fall in the water level.

raisin ('reɪzᵊn) *n* a dried grape. [C13: from OF: grape, ult. from L *racēmus* cluster of grapes]
▸ **'raisiny** *adj*

THESAURUS

mouth, frenzied, fuming, incandescent, incensed, infuriated, mad, raving, seething

raid *n* **1 = attack,** break-in, descent, foray, hit-and-run attack, incursion, inroad, invasion, irruption, onset, sally, seizure, sortie, surprise attack ◆ *vb* **3 = attack,** assault, break into, descend on, fall upon, forage (*Military*), foray, invade, pillage, plunder, reive (*dialect*), rifle, sack, sally forth, swoop down upon

raider *n* **1 = attacker,** forager (*Military*), invader, marauder, plunderer, reiver (*dialect*), robber, thief

rail[2] *vb* **= complain,** abuse, attack, blast, censure, criticize, fulminate, inveigh, lambast(e), put down, revile, scold, tear into (*inf.*), upbraid, vituperate, vociferate

railing *n* **1 = fence,** balustrade, barrier, paling, rails

raillery *n* **1 = teasing,** badinage, banter, chaff, irony, jesting, joke, joking, josh (*sl., chiefly US & Canad.*), kidding (*inf.*), mockery, persiflage, pleasantry, repartee, ridicule, satire, sport

rain *n* **1 = rainfall,** cloudburst, deluge, downpour, drizzle, fall, precipitation, raindrops, showers **2 = shower,** deluge, flood, hail, spate, stream, torrent, volley ◆ *vb* **5 = pour,** bucket down (*inf.*), come down in buckets (*inf.*), drizzle, fall, pelt (down), rain cats and dogs (*inf.*), shower, teem **6 = fall,** deposit, drop, shower, sprinkle **7 = bestow,** lavish, pour, shower

rainy *adj* **1, 2 = wet,** damp, drizzly, showery
Antonyms *adj* arid, dry, fine, sunny

raise *vb* **1 = lift,** elevate, exalt, heave, hoist, move up, rear, uplift **3 = build,** construct, erect, put up **4, 5 = increase,** advance, aggravate, amplify, augment, boost, enhance, enlarge, escalate, exaggerate, heighten, hike (up) (*inf.*), inflate, intensify, jack up, magnify, put up, reinforce, strengthen **6 = promote,** advance, aggrandize, elevate, exalt, prefer, upgrade **8 = stir up,** activate, arouse, awaken, cause, evoke, excite, foment, foster, incite, instigate, kindle, motivate, provoke, rouse, set on foot, summon up, whip up **10 = cause,** bring about, create, engender, give rise to, occasion, originate, produce, provoke, start **11 = put forward,** advance, bring up, broach, introduce, moot, suggest **12 = collect,** assemble, form, gather, get, levy, mass, mobilize, muster, obtain, rally, recruit **13 = grow,** breed, cultivate, produce, propagate, rear **14 = bring up,** develop, nurture, rear **16 = end,** abandon, give up, lift, relieve, relinquish, remove, terminate
Antonyms *vb* ≠ **build:** demolish, destroy, level, ruin, wreck ≠ **increase:** cut, decrease, diminish, drop, lessen, lower, reduce, sink ≠ **promote:** demote, downgrade, reduce ≠ **stir up:** calm, depress, lessen, lower, quash, quell, reduce, sink, soothe, suppress ≠ **end:** begin, establish, start

raison d'être *French.* (rɛzɔ̃ dɛtrə) *n, pl* **raisons d'être** (rɛzɔ̃ dɛtrə). reason or justification for existence.

raita ('raɪtə) *n* an Indian dish of finely chopped cucumber, peppers, mint, etc., in yogurt, served with curries. [C20: from Hindi]

raj (rɑːdʒ) *n* **1** (in India) government; rule. **2** (cap. and preceded by *the*) the British government in India before 1947. [C19: from Hindi, from Sansk., from *rājati* he rules]

rajah *or* **raja** ('rɑːdʒə) *n* **1** (in India, formerly) a ruler: sometimes used as a title preceding a name. **2** a Malayan or Javanese prince or chieftain. [C16: from Hindi, from Sansk. *rājan* king]

Rajput *or* **Rajpoot** ('rɑːdʒpʊt) *n Hinduism.* one of a Hindu military caste claiming descent from the Kshatriya, the original warrior caste. [C16: from Hindi, from Sansk. *rājan* king]

rake[1] **T** (reɪk) *n* **1** a hand implement consisting of a row of teeth set in a headpiece attached to a long shaft and used for gathering hay, straw, etc., or for smoothing loose earth. **2** any of several mechanical farm implements equipped with rows of teeth or rotating wheels mounted with tines and used to gather hay, straw, etc. **3** any of various implements similar in shape or function. **4** the act of raking. ◆ *vb* **rakes, raking, raked. 5** to scrape, gather, or remove (leaves, refuse, etc.) with a rake. **6** to level or prepare (a surface) with a rake. **7** (*tr;* sometimes foll. by *out*) to clear (ashes, etc.) from (a fire). **8** (*tr;* foll. by *up* or *together*) to gather (items or people) with difficulty, as from a scattered area or limited supply. **9** (*tr;* often foll. by *through, over,* etc.) to search or examine carefully. **10** (when *intr,* foll. by *against, along,* etc.) to scrape or graze: *the ship raked the side of the quay.* **11** (*tr*) to direct (gunfire) along the length of (a target): *machine-guns raked the column.* **12** (*tr*) to sweep (one's eyes) along the length of (something); scan. ◆ See also **rake in, rake-off,** etc. [OE *raca*]
▸ **'raker** *n*

rake[2] **T** (reɪk) *n* a dissolute man, esp. one in fashionable society; roué. [C17: short for *rakehell* a dissolute man]

rake[3] (reɪk) *vb* **rakes, raking, raked.** (*mainly intr*) **1** to incline from the vertical by a perceptible degree, esp. (of a ship's mast) towards the stern. **2** (*tr*) to construct with a backward slope. ◆ *n* **3** the degree to which an object, such as a ship's mast, inclines from the perpendicular, esp. towards the stern. **4** *Theatre.* the slope of a stage from the back towards the footlights. **5** the angle between the working face of a cutting tool and a plane perpendicular to the surface of the workpiece. [C17: from ?; ? rel. to G *ragen* to project, Swedish *raka*]

rake in *vb* (*tr, adv*) *Inf.* to acquire (money) in large amounts.

rake-off *Sl.* ◆ *n* **1** a share of profits, esp. one that is illegal or given as a bribe. ◆ *vb* **rake off. 2** (*tr, adv*) to take or receive (such a share of profits).

rake up *vb* (*tr, adv*) to revive, discover, or bring to light (something forgotten): *to rake up an old quarrel.*

raki *or* **rakee** (rɑː'kiː, 'rækɪ) *n* a strong spirit distilled in Turkey from grain, usually flavoured with aniseed or other aromatics. [C17: from Turkish *rāqī*]

rakish[1] **T** ('reɪkɪʃ) *adj* dissolute; profligate. [C18: from RAKE[2]]
▸ **'rakishly** *adv* ▸ **'rakishness** *n*

rakish[2] **T** ('reɪkɪʃ) *adj* **1** dashing; jaunty: *a hat set at a rakish angle.* **2** *Naut.* (of a ship or boat) having lines suggestive of speed. [C19: prob. from RAKE[3]]

rale *or* **râle** (rɑːl) *n Med.* an abnormal crackling sound heard on auscultation of the chest, usually caused by the accumulation of fluid in the lungs. [C19: from F, from *râler* to breathe with a rattling sound]

rallentando (ˌrælən'tændəʊ) *adj, adv Music.* becoming slower. Also: **ritardando.** [C19: It., from *rallentare* to slow down]

rally[1] **T** ('rælɪ) *vb* **rallies, rallying, rallied. 1** to bring (a group, unit, etc.) into order, as after dispersal, or (of such a group) to reform and come to order. **2** (when *intr,* foll. by *to*) to organize (supporters, etc.) for a common cause or (of such people) to come together for a purpose. **3** to summon up (one's strength, spirits, etc.) or (of a person's health, strength, or spirits) to revive or recover. **4** (*intr*) *Stock Exchange.* to increase sharply after a decline. **5** (*intr*) *Tennis, squash, etc.* to engage in a rally. ◆ *n, pl* **rallies. 6** a large gathering of people for a common purpose. **7** a marked recovery of strength or spirits, as during illness. **8** a return to order after dispersal or rout, as of troops, etc. **9** *Stock Exchange.* a sharp increase in price or trading activity after a decline. **10** *Tennis, squash, etc.* an exchange of several shots before one player wins the point. **11** a type of motoring competition over public roads. [C16: from OF *rallier,* from RE- + *alier* to unite]
▸ **'rallier** *n*

rally[2] **T** ('rælɪ) *vb* **rallies, rallying, rallied.** to mock or ridicule (someone) in a good-natured way; chaff; tease. [C17: from OF *railler* to tease; see RAIL[2]]

rallycross ('rælɪˌkrɒs) *n* a form of motor sport in which cars race over a one-mile circuit of rough grass with some hard-surfaced sections.

rally round *vb* (*intr*) to come to the aid of (someone); offer moral or practical support.

ram **T** (ræm) *n* **1** an uncastrated adult male sheep. **2** a piston or moving plate, esp. one driven hydraulically or pneumatically. **3** the falling weight of a pile driver. **4** short for **battering ram. 5** a pointed projection in the stem of an ancient warship for puncturing the hull of enemy ships. **6** a warship equipped with a ram. ◆ *vb* **rams, ramming, rammed. 7** (*tr;* usually foll. by *into*) to force or drive, as by heavy blows: *to ram a post into the ground.* **8** (of a moving object) to crash with force (against another object) or (of two moving objects) to collide in this way. **9** (*tr;* often foll. by *in* or *down*) to stuff or cram (something into a hole, etc.). **10** (*tr;* foll. by *onto, against,* etc.) to thrust violently: *he rammed the books onto the desk.* **11** (*tr*) to present (an idea, argument, etc.) forcefully or aggressively (esp. in **ram** (**something**) **down someone's throat**). **12** (*tr*) to drive (a charge) into a firearm. [OE *ramm*]
▸ **'rammer** *n*

Ram (ræm) *n* **the.** the constellation Aries, the first sign of the zodiac.

RAM[1] (ræm) *n Computing. acronym for* random access memory: semiconductor memory in which all storage locations can be rapidly accessed in the same amount of time. It forms the main memory of a computer, used by applications to perform tasks while the device is operating.

RAM[2] *abbrev. for* Royal Academy of Music.

Ramadan *or* **Rhamadhan** (ˌræmə'dɑːn) *n* **1** the ninth month of the Muslim year, lasting 30 days, during which strict fasting is observed from sunrise to sunset. **2** the fast itself. [C16: from Ar., lit.: the hot month, from *ramad* dryness]

Raman effect ('rɑːmən) *n* the change in wavelength of light that is scattered by electrons within a material: used in **Raman spectroscopy** for studying molecules. [C20: after Sir Chandasekhara *Raman* (1888–1970), Indian physicist]

ramble **T** ('ræmbᵊl) *vb* **rambles, rambling, rambled.** (*intr*) **1** to stroll about freely, as for relaxation, with no particular direction. **2** (of paths, streams, etc.) to follow a winding course; meander. **3** to grow or develop in a random fashion. **4** (of speech, writing, etc.) to lack organization. ◆ *n* **5** a leisurely stroll, esp. in the countryside. [C17: prob. rel. to MDu. *rammelen* to ROAM (of animals)]

rambler **T** ('ræmblə) *n* **1** a weak-stemmed plant that straggles over other vegetation. **2** a person who rambles, esp. one who takes country walks. **3** a person who lacks organization in his speech or writing.

rambling **T** ('ræmblɪŋ) *adj* **1** straggling or sprawling haphazardly: *a rambling old house.* **2** (of speech or writing) diffuse and disconnected. **3** (of a plant, esp. a rose) climbing and straggling. **4** nomadic; wandering.

Ramboesque (ˌræmbəʊ'esk) *adj* looking or behaving like or characteristic of Rambo, a mindlessly brutal fictional film character.
▸ **'Rambo,ism** *n*

rambunctious (ræm'bʌŋkʃəs) *adj Inf.* boisterous; unruly. [C19: prob. from Icelandic *ram* (intensifying prefix) + *-bunctious,* from BUMPTIOUS]
▸ **ram'bunctiousness** *n*

rambutan (ræm'buːtᵊn) *n* **1** a tree related to the soapberry, native to SE Asia, that has bright red edible fruit covered with hairs. **2** the fruit of this tree. [C18: from Malay, from *rambut* hair]

RAMC *abbrev. for* Royal Army Medical Corps.

ramekin *or* **ramequin** ('ræmɪkɪn) *n* **1** a savoury dish made from a

THESAURUS

rake[1] *vb* **5 = gather**, collect, remove, scrape up **6 = scrape**, break up, harrow, hoe, scour, scratch **8** *with* **together** *or* **up = collect**, assemble, dig up, dredge up, gather, scrape together **9 = search**, comb, examine, forage, hunt, ransack, scan, scour, scrutinize **10 = graze**, scrape, scratch **11 = sweep**, enfilade, pepper

rake[2] *n* **= libertine**, debauchee, dissolute man, lech *or* letch, lecher, playboy, profligate, roué, sensualist, swinger (*sl.*), voluptuary
Antonyms *n* ascetic, celibate, monk, puritan

rakish[1] *adj* **= immoral**, abandoned, debauched, depraved, dissipated, dissolute, lecherous, licentious, loose, prodigal, profligate, sinful, wanton

rakish[2] *adj* **1 = dashing**, breezy, dapper, debonair, devil-may-care, flashy, jaunty, natty (*inf.*), raffish, smart, snazzy (*inf.*), sporty

rally[1] *vb* **1 = reassemble**, bring *or* come to order, re-form, regroup, reorganize, unite **2 = gather**, assemble, bond together, bring *or* come together, collect, convene, get together, marshal, mobilize, muster, organize, round up, summon, unite **3 = recover**, be on the mend, come round, get better, get one's second wind, improve, perk up, pick up, pull through, recuperate, regain one's strength, revive, take a turn for the better, turn the corner ◆ *n* **6 = gathering**, assembly, conference, congregation, congress, convention, convocation, mass meeting, meeting, muster **7 = recovery**, comeback (*inf.*), improvement, recuperation, renewal, resurgence, revival, turn for the better **8 = regrouping**, reorganization, reunion, stand
Antonyms *vb* ≠ **gather:** disband, disperse, separate, split up ≠ **recover:** deteriorate, fail, get worse, relapse, take a turn for the worse, worsen ◆ *n* ≠ **recovery:** collapse, deterioration, relapse, turn for the worse

rally[2] *vb* **= tease**, chaff, make fun of, mock, poke fun at, ridicule, send up (*Brit. inf.*), take the mickey out of (*inf.*), taunt, twit

ram *vb* **7, 9 = cram**, beat, crowd, drum, force, hammer, jam, pack, pound, stuff, tamp, thrust **8 = hit**, butt, collide with, crash, dash, drive, force, impact, run into, slam, smash, strike

ramble *vb* **1 = walk**, amble, drift, perambulate, peregrinate, range, roam, rove, saunter, straggle, stravaig (*Scot. & N English dialect*), stray, stroll, traipse (*inf.*), wander **2 = meander**, snake, twist and turn, wind, zigzag **4 = babble**, chatter, digress, expatiate, maunder, rabbit (on) (*Brit. inf.*), rattle on, run off at the mouth (*sl.*), waffle (*inf., chiefly Brit.*), wander, witter on (*inf.*) ◆ *n* **5 = walk**, excursion, hike, perambulation, peregrination, roaming, roving, saunter, stroll, tour, traipse (*inf.*), trip

rambler *n* **2 = walker**, drifter, hiker, roamer, rover, stroller, wanderer, wayfarer

rambling *adj* **1 = sprawling**, irregular, spreading, straggling, trailing **2 = long-winded**, circuitous, desultory, diffuse, digressive, disconnected, discursive, disjointed, incoherent, irregular, periphrastic, prolix, wordy

cheese mixture baked in a fireproof container. **2** the container itself. [C18: F *ramequin,* of Gmc origin]

ramification ➊ (ˌræmɪfɪˈkeɪʃən) *n* **1** the act or process of ramifying or branching out. **2** an offshoot or subdivision. **3** a structure of branching parts.

ramify ➊ (ˈræmɪˌfaɪ) *vb* **ramifies, ramifying, ramified. 1** to divide into branches or branchlike parts. **2** (*intr*) to develop complicating consequences. [C16: from F *ramifier,* from L *rāmus* branch + *facere* to make]

ramjet *or* **ramjet engine** (ˈræmˌdʒɛt) *n* **a** a type of jet engine in which fuel is burned in a duct using air compressed by the forward speed of the aircraft. **b** an aircraft powered by such an engine.

ramose (ˈreɪməʊs, ræˈməʊs) *or* **ramous** (ˈreɪməs) *adj* having branches. [C17: from L *rāmōsus,* from *rāmus* branch]
▸ˈ**ramosely** *or* ˈ**ramously** *adv* ▸**ramosity** (ræˈmɒsɪtɪ) *n*

ramp ➊ (ræmp) *n* **1** a sloping floor, path, etc., that joins two surfaces at different levels. **2** a place where the level of a road surface changes because of roadworks. **3** a movable stairway by which passengers enter and leave an aircraft. **4** the act of ramping. **5** *Brit. sl.* a swindle, esp. one involving exorbitant prices. ◆ *vb* **6** (*intr*) (often foll. by *about* or *around*) (esp. of animals) to rush around in a wild excited manner. **7** (*intr*) to act in a violent or threatening manner (esp. in **ramp and rage**). **8** (*tr*) *Finance.* to buy (a security) in the market with the object of raising its price and enhancing the image of the company behind it for financial gain. [C18 (n): from C13 *rampe,* from OF *ramper* to crawl or rear, prob. of Gmc origin]

rampage ➊ *vb* (ræmˈpeɪdʒ), **rampages, rampaging, rampaged. 1** (*intr*) to rush about in a violent or agitated fashion. ◆ *n* (ˈræmpeɪdʒ, ræmˈpeɪdʒ). **2** angry or destructive behaviour. **3 on the rampage.** behaving violently or destructively. [C18: from Scot., from ?; ? based on RAMP]
▸**ramˈpageous** *adj* ▸**ramˈpageously** *adv* ▸ˈ**rampager** *n*

rampant ➊ (ˈræmpənt) *adj* **1** unrestrained or violent in behaviour, etc. **2** growing or developing unchecked. **3** (*postpositive*) *Heraldry.* (of a beast) standing on the hind legs, the right foreleg raised above the left. **4** (of an arch) having one abutment higher than the other. [C14: from OF *ramper* to crawl, rear; see RAMP]
▸ˈ**rampancy** *n* ▸ˈ**rampantly** *adv*

rampart ➊ (ˈræmpɑːt) *n* **1** the surrounding embankment of a fort, often including any walls, parapets, etc., that are built on the bank. **2** any defence or bulwark. ◆ *vb* **3** (*tr*) to provide with a rampart; fortify. [C16: from OF, from RE- + *emparer* to take possession of, from OProvençal *antparar,* from L *ante* before + *parāre* to prepare]

rampike (ˈræmˌpaɪk) *n Canad.* a tall tree that has been burned or is bare of branches.

rampion (ˈræmpɪən) *n* a plant, native to Europe and Asia, that has clusters of bell-shaped bluish flowers and an edible white tuberous root used in salads. [C16: prob. from OF *raiponce,* from OIt. *raponzo,* from *rapa* turnip, from L *rāpum*]

ram raid *n Inf.* a raid in which a stolen car is driven through a shop window in order to steal goods from the shop.
▸**ram raiding** *n* ▸**ram raider** *n*

ramrod (ˈræmˌrɒd) *n* **1** a rod for cleaning the barrel of a rifle, etc. **2** a rod for ramming in the charge of a muzzle-loading firearm.

ramshackle ➊ (ˈræmˌʃækᵊl) *adj* (esp. of buildings) rickety, shaky, or derelict. [C17 *ramshackled,* from obs. *ransackle* to RANSACK]

ramsons (ˈræmzənz, -sənz) *pl n* (*usually functioning as sing*) **1** a broad-leaved garlic native to Europe and Asia. **2** the bulbous root of this plant, eaten as a relish. [OE *hramesa*]

ran (ræn) *vb* the past tense of **run.**

RAN *abbrev. for* Royal Australian Navy.

ranch (rɑːntʃ) *n* **1** a large tract of land, esp. one in North America, together with the necessary personnel, buildings, and equipment, for rearing livestock, esp. cattle. **2a** any large farm for the rearing of a particular kind of livestock or crop: *a mink ranch.* **2b** the buildings, land, etc., connected with it. ◆ *vb* **3** (*intr*) to run a ranch. **4** (*tr*) to raise (animals) on or as if on a ranch. [C19: from Mexican Sp. *rancho* small farm]
▸ˈ**rancher** *n*

rancherie (ˈrɑːntʃərɪ) *n* (in British Columbia, Canada) a settlement of North American Indians, esp. on a reserve. [from Sp. *rancheria*]

rancid ➊ (ˈrænsɪd) *adj* **1** (of food) having an unpleasant stale taste or smell as the result of decomposition. **2** (of a taste or smell) rank or sour; stale. [C17: from L *rancidus,* from *rancēre* to stink]
▸**rancidity** (rænˈsɪdɪtɪ) *or* ˈ**rancidness** *n*

rancour ➊ *or US* **rancor** (ˈræŋkə) *n* malicious resentfulness or hostility; spite. [C14: from OF, from LL *rancor* rankness]
▸ˈ**rancorous** *adj* ▸ˈ**rancorously** *adv*

rand[1] (rænd, rɒnt) *n* the standard monetary unit of South Africa, divided into 100 cents. [C20: from Afrik., from *Witwatersrand,* S Transvaal, referring to the gold-mining there; rel. to RAND[2]]

rand[2] (rænd) *n* **1** *Shoemaking.* a leather strip put in the heel of a shoe before the lifts are put on. **2** *Dialect.* **2a** a strip or margin; border. **2b** a strip of cloth; selvage. [OE; rel. to OHG *rant* border, rim of a shield, ON *rönd* shield, rim]

Rand (rænd) *n* **the.** short for Witwatersrand, an area in South Africa rich in mineral deposits, esp. gold.

R & B *abbrev. for* rhythm and blues.

R & D *abbrev. for* research and development.

random ➊ (ˈrændəm) *adj* **1** lacking any definite plan or prearranged order; haphazard: *a random selection.* **2** *Statistics.* **2a** having a value which cannot be determined but only described in terms of probability: *a random variable.* **2b** chosen without regard to any characteristics of the individual members of the population so that each has an equal chance of being selected: *random sampling.* ◆ *n* **3 at random.** not following any prearranged order. [C14: from OF *randon,* from *randir* to gallop, of Gmc origin]
▸ˈ**randomly** *adv* ▸ˈ**randomness** *n*

random access *n* another name for **direct access.**

randomize *or* **randomise** (ˈrændəˌmaɪz) *vb* **randomizes, randomizing, randomized** *or* **randomises, randomising, randomised.** (*tr*) to set up (a selection process, sample, etc.) in a deliberately random way in order to enhance the statistical validity of any results obtained.
▸ˌ**randomiˈzation** *or* ˌ**randomiˈsation** *n* ▸ˈ**randomˌizer** *or* ˈ**randomˌiser** *n*

random walk theory *n Stock Exchange.* the theory that the future movement of share prices does not reflect past movements and therefore will not follow a discernible pattern.

R and R *US mil. abbrev. for* rest and recreation.

randy ➊ (ˈrændɪ) *adj* **randier, randiest. 1** *Inf., chiefly Brit.* sexually eager or lustful. **2** *Chiefly Scot.* lacking any sense of propriety; reckless. ◆ *n, pl* **randies. 3** *Chiefly Scot.* a rude or reckless person. [C17: prob. from obs. *rand* to RANT]
▸ˈ**randily** *adv* ▸ˈ**randiness** *n*

ranee (ˈrɑːnɪ) *n* a variant spelling of **rani.**

rang (ræŋ) *vb* the past tense of **ring**[2].

USAGE NOTE See at **ring**[2].

rangatira (ˌrʌŋgəˈtɪərə) *n NZ.* a Maori chief of either sex. [from Maori]

range ➊ (reɪndʒ) *n* **1** the limits within which a person or thing can function effectively: *the violin has a range of five octaves.* **2** the limits within which any fluctuation takes place: *a range of values.* **3** the total products of a manufacturer, designer, or stockist: *the new spring range.* **4a** the maximum effective distance of a projectile fired from a weapon. **4b** the distance between a target and a weapon. **5** an area set aside for shooting practice or rocket testing. **6** the total distance which a ship, aircraft, or land vehicle is capable of covering without taking on fresh fuel: *the range of this car is about 160 miles.* **7** *Maths.* (of a function or variable) the set of values that a function or variable can

THESAURUS

Antonyms *adj* ≠ **long-winded:** coherent, concise, direct, to the point

ramification *n* **1** = **consequences,** complications, developments, results, sequel, upshot **2** = **outgrowth,** branch, development, divarication, division, excrescence, extension, forking, offshoot, subdivision

ramify *vb* **1** = **divide,** branch, divaricate, fork, separate, split up **2** = **become complicated,** multiply, thicken

ramp *n* **1** = **slope,** grade, gradient, incline, inclined plane, rise

rampage *vb* **1** = **go berserk,** go ape (*sl.*), go ballistic (*sl., chiefly US*), rage, run amok, run riot, run wild, storm, tear ◆ *n* **2** = **frenzy,** destruction, fury, rage, storm, tempest, tumult, uproar, violence **3 on the rampage** = **berserk,** amok, destructive, out of control, raging, rampant, riotous, violent, wild

rampant *adj* **1** = **unrestrained,** aggressive, dominant, excessive, flagrant, on the rampage, out of control, out of hand, outrageous, raging, rampaging, riotous, unbridled, uncontrollable, ungovernable, vehement, violent, wanton, wild **2** = **widespread,** epidemic, exuberant, luxuriant, prevalent, profuse, rank, rife, spreading like wildfire, unchecked, uncontrolled, unrestrained **3** *Heraldry* = **upright,** erect, rearing, standing

rampart *n* **1, 2** = **defence,** barricade, bastion, breastwork, bulwark, earthwork, embankment, fence, fort, fortification, guard, parapet, security, stronghold, wall

ramshackle *adj* = **rickety,** broken-down, crumbling, decrepit, derelict, dilapidated, flimsy, jerry-built, shaky, tottering, tumbledown, unsafe, unsteady
Antonyms *adj* solid, stable, steady, well-built

rancid *adj* **1, 2** = **rotten,** bad, fetid, foul, frowsty, fusty, musty, off, putrid, rank, sour, stale, strong-smelling, tainted
Antonyms *adj* fresh, pure, undecayed

rancorous *adj* = **bitter,** acrimonious, hostile, implacable, malevolent, malicious, malign, malignant, resentful, spiteful, splenetic, venomous, vindictive, virulent

rancour *n* = **hatred,** animosity, animus, antipathy, bad blood, bitterness, chip on one's shoulder (*inf.*), enmity, grudge, hate, hostility, ill feeling, ill will, malevolence, malice, malignity, resentfulness, resentment, spite, spleen, venom

random *adj* **1** = **chance,** accidental, adventitious, aimless, arbitrary, casual, desultory, fortuitous, haphazard, hit or miss, incidental, indiscriminate, purposeless, spot, stray, unplanned, unpremeditated ◆ *n* **3 at random** = **haphazardly,** accidentally, adventitiously, aimlessly, arbitrarily, by chance, casually, indiscriminately, irregularly, purposelessly, randomly, unsystematically, willy-nilly
Antonyms *adj* ≠ **chance:** definite, deliberate, intended, planned, premeditated, specific

randy *adj* **1** *Informal* = **lustful,** amorous, aroused, concupiscent, horny (*sl.*), hot, lascivious, lecherous, raunchy (*sl.*), satyric, sexually excited, sexy (*inf.*), turned-on (*sl.*)

range *n* **1, 2** = **limits,** ambit, amplitude, area, bounds, compass, confines, distance, domain, extent, field, latitude, orbit, pale, parameters (*inf.*), province, purview, radius, reach, scope, span, sphere, sweep **3** = **series,** assortment, class, collection, gamut, kind, lot, order, selection, sort, variety **10** = **sequence,** chain, file, line, rank, row, series, string, tier ◆ *vb* **14** = **ar-**

take. **8** *US & Canad.* **8a** an extensive tract of open land on which livestock can graze. **8b** (*as modifier*): *range cattle.* **9** the geographical region in which a species of plant or animal normally grows or lives. **10** a rank, row, or series of items. **11** a series or chain of mountains. **12** a large stove with burners and one or more ovens, usually heated by solid fuel. **13** the act or process of ranging. ◆ *vb* **ranges, ranging, ranged. 14** to establish or be situated in a line, row, or series. **15** (*tr; often reflexive,* foll. by *with*) to put into a specific category; classify: *she ranges herself with the angels.* **16** (foll. by *on*) to aim or point (a telescope, gun, etc.) or (of a gun, telescope, etc.) to be pointed or aimed. **17** to establish the distance of (a target) from (a weapon). **18** (*intr*) (of a gun or missile) to have a specified range. **19** (when *intr,* foll. by *over*) to wander about (in) an area; roam (over). **20** (*intr;* foll. by *over*) (of an animal or plant) to live or grow in its normal habitat. **21** (*tr*) to put (cattle) to graze on a range. **22** (*intr*) to fluctuate within specific limits. **23** (*intr*) to extend or run in a specific direction. **24** (*intr*) *Naut.* (of a vessel) to swing back and forth while at anchor. **25** (*tr*) to make (lines of printers' type) level or even at the margin. [C13: from OF: row, from *ranger* to position, from *renc* line]

rangefinder ('reɪndʒ,faɪndə) *n* an instrument for determining the distance of an object from the observer, esp. in order to sight a gun or focus a camera.

ranger ('reɪndʒə) *n* **1** (*sometimes cap.*) an official in charge of a forest, park, nature reserve, etc. **2** *Orig. US.* a person employed to patrol a State or national park. Brit. equivalent: **warden. 3** *US.* one of a body of armed troops employed to police a State or district: *a Texas ranger.* **4** (in the US) a commando specially trained in making raids. **5** a person who wanders about; a rover.

Ranger *or* **Ranger Guide** ('reɪndʒə) *n Brit.* a member of the senior branch of the Guides.

rangiora (,ræŋgɪ'ɔ:rə) *n* a broad-leaved shrub of New Zealand. [from Maori]

rangy ❶ ('reɪndʒɪ) *adj* **rangier, rangiest. 1** having long slender limbs. **2** adapted to wandering or roaming. **3** allowing considerable freedom of movement; spacious.
▸**'rangily** *adv* ▸**'ranginess** *n*

rani *or* **ranee** ('rɑ:nɪ) *n* an Indian queen or princess; the wife of a rajah. [C17: from Hindi: queen, from Sansk. *rājñī*]

rank[1] ❶ (ræŋk) *n* **1** a position, esp. an official one, within a social organization: *the rank of captain.* **2** high social or other standing; status. **3** a line or row of people or things. **4** the position of an item in any ordering or sequence. **5** *Brit.* a place where taxis wait to be hired. **6** a line of soldiers drawn up abreast of each other. **7** any of the eight horizontal rows of squares on a chessboard. **8 close ranks.** to maintain discipline or solidarity. **9 pull rank.** to get one's own way by virtue of one's superior position or rank. **10 rank and file. 10a** the ordinary soldiers, excluding the officers. **10b** the great mass or majority of any group, as opposed to the leadership. **10c** (*modifier*): *rank-and-file support.* ◆ *vb* **11** (*tr*) to arrange (people or things) in rows or lines; range. **12** to accord or be accorded a specific position in an organization or group. **13** (*tr*) to array a set of objects as a sequence: *to rank students by their test scores.* **14** (*intr*) to be important; rate: *money ranks low in her order of priorities.* **15** *Chiefly US.* to take precedence or surpass in rank. [C16: from OF *ranc* row, rank, of Gmc origin]

rank[2] ❶ (ræŋk) *adj* **1** showing vigorous and profuse growth: *rank weeds.* **2** highly offensive or disagreeable, esp. in smell or taste. **3** (*prenominal*) complete or absolute; utter: *a rank outsider.* **4** coarse or vulgar; gross: *his language was rank.* [OE *ranc* straight, noble]
▸**'rankly** *adv* ▸**'rankness** *n*

ranker ('ræŋkə) *n* **1** a soldier in the ranks. **2** a commissioned officer who entered service as a noncommissioned recruit.

ranking ('ræŋkɪŋ) *adj* **1** *Chiefly US & Canad.* prominent; high ranking. **2** *Caribbean sl.* possessed of style; exciting. ◆ *n* **3** a position on a scale; rating: *a ranking in a tennis tournament.*

rankle ❶ ('ræŋk^{ə}l) *vb* **rankles, rankling, rankled.** (*intr*) to cause severe and continuous irritation, anger, or bitterness; fester. [C14 *ranclen,* from OF *draoncle* ulcer, from L *dracunculus* dim. of *dracō* serpent]

ransack ❶ ('rænsæk) *vb* (*tr*) **1** to search through every part of (a house, box, etc.); examine thoroughly. **2** to plunder; pillage. [C13: from ON *rann* house + *saka* to search]
▸**'ransacker** *n*

ransom ❶ ('rænsəm) *n* **1** the release of captured prisoners, property, etc., on payment of a stipulated price. **2** the price demanded or stipulated for such a release. **3 hold to ransom. 3a** to keep (prisoners, etc.) in confinement until payment for their release is received. **3b** to attempt to force (a person) to comply with one's demands. **4 a king's ransom.** a very large amount of money or valuables. ◆ *vb* (*tr*) **5** to pay a stipulated price and so obtain the release of (prisoners, property, etc.). **6** to set free (prisoners, property, etc.) upon receiving the payment demanded. **7** to redeem; rescue: *Christ ransomed men from sin.* [C14: from OF *ransoun,* from L *redemptiō* a buying back]
▸**'ransomer** *n*

rant ❶ (rænt) *vb* **1** to utter (something) in loud, violent, or bombastic tones. ◆ *n* **2** loud, declamatory, or extravagant speech; bombast. [C16: from Du. *ranten* to rave]
▸**'ranter** *n* ▸**'ranting** *adj, n* ▸**'rantingly** *adv*

ranunculaceous (rə,nʌŋkju'leɪʃəs) *adj* of, relating to, or belonging to a N temperate family of flowering plants typically having flowers with five petals and numerous anthers and styles. The family includes the buttercup, clematis, and columbine.

ranunculus (rə'nʌŋkjuləs) *n, pl* **ranunculuses** *or* **ranunculi** (-,laɪ). any of a genus of ranunculaceous plants having finely divided leaves and typically yellow five-petalled flowers. The genus includes buttercup, crowfoot, and spearwort. [C16: from L: tadpole, from *rāna* frog]

RAOC *abbrev. for* Royal Army Ordnance Corps.

rap[1] ❶ (ræp) *vb* **raps, rapping, rapped. 1** to strike (a fist, stick, etc.) against (something) with a sharp quick blow; knock. **2** (*intr*) to make a sharp loud sound, esp. by knocking. **3** (*tr*) to rebuke or criticize sharply. **4** (*tr;* foll. by *out*) to put (forth) in sharp rapid speech; utter in an abrupt fashion: *to rap out orders.* **5** (*intr*) *Sl.* to talk, esp. volubly. **6** (*intr*) to perform a rhythmic monologue with musical backing. **7 rap over the knuckles.** to reprimand. ◆ *n* **8** a sharp quick blow or the sound produced by such a blow. **9** a sharp rebuke or criticism. **10** *Sl.* voluble talk; chatter. **11a** a fast, rhythmic monologue over a musical backing. **11b** (*as modifier*): *rap music.* **12 beat the rap.** *US & Canad. sl.* to escape punishment or be acquitted of a crime. **13 take the rap.** *Sl.* to suffer the punishment for a crime, whether guilty or not. [C14: prob. from ON; cf. Swedish *rappa* to beat]

rap[2] (ræp) *n* (*used with a negative*) the least amount (esp. in **not care a rap**). [C18: prob. from *ropaire* counterfeit coin formerly current in Ireland]

rap[3] (ræp) *vb* **raps, rapping, rapped,** *n Austral. inf.* a variant spelling of **wrap** (senses 8, 14).

rapacious ❶ (rə'peɪʃəs) *adj* **1** practising pillage or rapine. **2** greedy or grasping. **3** (of animals, esp. birds) subsisting by catching living prey. [C17: from L *rapāx,* from *rapere* to seize]
▸**ra'paciously** *adv* ▸**rapacity** (rə'pæsɪtɪ) *or* **ra'paciousness** *n*

rape[1] ❶ (reɪp) *n* **1** the offence of forcing a person, esp. a woman, to submit to sexual intercourse against that person's will. **2** the act of despoiling a country in warfare. **3** any violation or abuse: *the rape of justice.* **4** *Arch.* abduction: *the rape of the Sabine women.* ◆ *vb* **rapes, raping, raped.** (*mainly tr*) **5** to commit rape upon (a person). **6** *Arch.* to carry off by force; abduct. [C14: from L *rapere* to seize]
▸**'rapist** *n*

THESAURUS

range, align, array, dispose, draw up, line up, order, sequence **15** = **group**, arrange, bracket, catalogue, categorize, class, classify, file, grade, pigeonhole, rank **16** = **point**, aim, align, direct, level, train **19** = **roam**, cruise, explore, ramble, rove, straggle, stray, stroll, sweep, traverse, wander **22** = **vary**, extend, fluctuate, go, reach, run, stretch

rangy *adj* **1** = **long-limbed**, gangling, lanky, leggy, long-legged

rank[1] *n* **1, 2** = **status**, caste, class, classification, degree, dignity, division, echelon, grade, level, nobility, order, position, quality, sort, standing, station, stratum, type **3** = **row**, column, file, formation, group, line, range, series, tier **10 rank and file: a** = **lower ranks**, men, other ranks, private soldiers, soldiers, troops **b** = **general public**, body, Joe (and Eileen) Public (*sl.*), Joe Six-Pack (*US sl.*), majority, mass, masses ◆ *vb* **11, 13** = **arrange**, align, array, class, classify, dispose, grade, line up, locate, marshal, order, position, range, sequence, sort

rank[2] *adj* **1** = **abundant**, dense, exuberant, flourishing, lush, luxuriant, productive, profuse, strong-growing, vigorous **2** = **foul**, bad, disagreeable, disgusting, fetid, fusty, gamey, mephitic, musty, noisome, noxious, off, offensive, olid, pungent, putrid, rancid, revolting, stale, stinking, strong-smelling, yucky *or* yukky (*sl.*) **3** = **absolute**, arrant, blatant, complete, downright, egregious, excessive, extravagant, flagrant, glaring, gross, rampant, sheer, thorough, total, undisguised, unmitigated, utter **4** = **vulgar**, abusive, atrocious, coarse, crass, filthy, foul, gross, indecent, nasty, obscene, outrageous, scurrilous, shocking

rankle *vb* = **annoy**, anger, chafe, embitter, fester, gall, get one's goat (*sl.*), get on one's nerves (*inf.*), irk, irritate, rile

ransack *vb* **1** = **search**, comb, explore, forage, go through, rake, rummage, scour, turn inside out **2** = **plunder**, despoil, gut, loot, pillage, raid, ravage, rifle, sack, strip

ransom *n* **1** = **release**, deliverance, liberation, redemption, rescue **2** = **payment**, money, payoff, price ◆ *vb* **5** = **buy the freedom of**, buy (someone) out (*inf.*), deliver, liberate, obtain *or* pay for the release of, redeem, release, rescue, set free

rant *vb* **1** = **shout**, bellow, bluster, cry, declaim, rave, roar, spout (*inf.*), vociferate, yell ◆ *n* **2** = **tirade**, bluster, bombast, diatribe, fanfaronade (*rare*), harangue, philippic, rhetoric, vociferation

rap[1] *vb* **1, 2** = **hit**, crack, knock, strike, tap **3** = **reprimand**, blast, carpet, castigate, censure, chew out (*US & Canad. inf.*), criticize, give a rocket (*Brit. & NZ inf.*), knock (*inf.*), lambast(e), pan (*inf.*), read the riot act, scold, tick off (*inf.*) **4** = **bark**, speak abruptly, spit **5** *Slang* = **talk**, chat, confabulate, converse, discourse, shoot the breeze (*sl., chiefly US*) ◆ *n* **8** = **blow**, clout (*inf.*), crack, knock, tap **9** *Slang* = **rebuke**, blame, censure, chiding, punishment, responsibility, sentence **10** *Slang, chiefly U.S.* = **talk**, chat, colloquy, confabulation, conversation, dialogue, discourse, discussion

rapacious *adj* **1** = **marauding**, plundering **2** = **greedy**, avaricious, extortionate, grasping, insatiable, ravenous, voracious, wolfish **3** = **predatory**, preying

rapacity *n* **2** = **greed**, avarice, avidity, cupidity, graspingness, greediness, insatiableness, rapaciousness, ravenousness, voraciousness, voracity, wolfishness **3** = **predatoriness**

rape[1] *n* **1** = **sexual assault**, outrage, ravishment, violation **2** = **desecration**, abuse, defilement, maltreatment, perversion, violation **3** = **plundering**, depredation, despoilment, despoliation, pillage, rapine, sack, spoliation ◆ *vb* **5** = **sexually assault**, abuse, force, outrage, ravish, violate

rape[2] (reɪp) *n* a Eurasian plant that is cultivated for its seeds, **rapeseed**, which yield a useful oil, **rape oil**, and as a fodder plant. Also called: **colza, cole.** [C14: from L *rāpum* turnip]

rape[3] (reɪp) *n* (*often pl*) the skins and stalks of grapes left after wine-making: used in making vinegar. [C17: from F *râpe*, of Gmc origin]

raphia ('ræfɪə) *n* a variant spelling of **raffia.**

raphide ('reɪfaɪd) *or* **raphis** ('reɪfɪs) *n, pl* **raphides** ('ræfɪˌdiːz). needle-shaped crystals, usually of calcium oxalate, that occur in many plant cells. [C18: from F, from Gk *rhaphis* needle]

rapid ➊ ('ræpɪd) *adj* **1** (of an action) performed or occurring during a short interval of time; quick. **2** acting or moving quickly; fast: *a rapid worker.* ◆ See also **rapids.** [C17: from L *rapidus* tearing away, from *rapere* to seize]
▸ **'rapidly** *adv* ▸ **rapidity** (rəˈpɪdɪtɪ) *or* **'rapidness** *n*

rapid eye movement *n* movement of the eyeballs during paradoxical sleep, while the sleeper is dreaming. Abbrev.: **REM.**

rapid fire *n* **1** a fast rate of gunfire. ◆ *adj* **rapid-fire. 2** firing shots rapidly. **3** done, delivered, or occurring in rapid succession.

rapids ('ræpɪdz) *pl n* part of a river where the water is very fast and turbulent.

rapier ('reɪpɪə) *n* **1** a long narrow two-edged sword with a guarded hilt, used as a thrusting weapon, popular in the 16th and 17th centuries. **2** a smaller single-edged 18th-century sword, used principally in France. [C16: from OF *espee rapiere*, lit.: rasping sword]

rapine ➊ ('ræpaɪn) *n* the seizure of property by force; pillage. [C15: from L *rapīna* plundering, from *rapere* to snatch]

rappee (ræˈpiː) *n* a moist English snuff. [C18: from F *tabac râpé*, lit.: scraped tobacco]

rappel (ræˈpɛl) *vb* **rappels, rappelling, rappelled,** *n* **1** another word for **abseil.** ◆ *n* **2** (formerly) a drumbeat to call soldiers to arms. [C19: from F, from *rappeler* to call back, from L *appellāre* to summon]

rapport ➊ (ræˈpɔː) *n* (often foll. by *with*) a sympathetic relationship or understanding. See also **en rapport.** [C15: from F, from *rapporter* to bring back, from RE- + *aporter*, from L *apportāre*, from *ad*- to + *portāre* to carry]

rapprochement ➊ *French.* (raprɔʃmɑ̃) *n* a resumption of friendly relations, esp. between two countries. [C19: lit.: bringing closer]

rapscallion (ræpˈskæljən) *n* a disreputable person; rascal or rogue. [C17: from earlier *rascallion*; see RASCAL]

rapt[1] ➊ (ræpt) *adj* **1** totally absorbed; engrossed; spellbound, esp. through or as if through emotion: *rapt with wonder.* **2** characterized by or proceeding from rapture: *a rapt smile.* [C14: from L *raptus* carried away, from *rapere* to seize]
▸ **'raptly** *adv*

rapt[2] (ræpt) *adj Austral. inf.* Also: **wrapped.** very pleased; delighted.

raptor ('ræptə) *n* another name for **bird of prey.** [C17: from L: plunderer, from *rapere* to take by force]

raptorial (ræpˈtɔːrɪəl) *adj Zool.* **1** (of the feet of birds) adapted for seizing prey. **2** of or relating to birds of prey. [C19: from L *raptor* robber, from *rapere* to snatch]

rapture ➊ ('ræptʃə) *n* **1** the state of mind resulting from feelings of high emotion; joyous ecstasy. **2** (*often pl*) an expression of ecstatic joy. **3** the act of transporting a person from one sphere of existence to another. ◆ *vb* **raptures, rapturing, raptured. 4** (*tr*) *Arch. or literary.* to enrapture. [C17: from Med. L *raptūra*, from L *raptus* RAPT[1]]
▸ **'rapturous** *adj*

RAR *abbrev. for* Royal Australian Regiment.

rara avis ('rɛərə 'eɪvɪs) *n, pl* **rarae aves** ('rɛəriː 'eɪviːz). an unusual, uncommon, or exceptional person or thing. [L: rare bird]

rare[1] ➊ (rɛə) *adj* **1** not widely known; not frequently used or experienced; uncommon or unusual: *a rare word.* **2** not widely distributed; not generally occurring: *a rare herb.* **3** (of a gas, esp. the atmosphere at high altitudes) having a low density; thin; rarefied. **4** uncommonly great; extreme: *kind to a rare degree.* **5** exhibiting uncommon excellence: *rare skill.* [C14: from L *rārus* sparse]
▸ **'rareness** *n*

rare[2] ➊ (rɛə) *adj* (of meat, esp. beef) very lightly cooked. [OE *hrēr*; rel. to *hreaw* RAW]

rarebit ('rɛəbɪt) *n* another term for **Welsh rabbit.** [C18: by folk etymology from (WELSH) RABBIT; see RARE[2], BIT[1]]

rare earth *n* **1** any oxide of a lanthanide. **2** Also called: **rare-earth element.** any element of the lanthanide series.

raree show ('rɛəriː) *n* **1** a street show or carnival. **2** another name for **peepshow.** [C17: *raree* from RARE[1]]

rarefaction (ˌrɛərɪˈfækʃən) *or* **rarefication** (ˌrɛərɪfɪˈkeɪʃən) *n* the act or process of making less dense or the state of being less dense.
▸ ˌ**rare'factive** *adj*

rarefied ➊ ('rɛərɪˌfaɪd) *adj* **1** exalted in nature or character; lofty: *a rarefied spiritual existence.* **2** current within only a small group. **3** thin: *air rarefied at altitude.*

rarefy ➊ ('rɛərɪˌfaɪ) *vb* **rarefies, rarefying, rarefied.** to make or become rarer or less dense; thin out. [C14: from OF *raréfier*, from L *rārēfacere*, from *rārus* RARE[1] + *facere* to make]
▸ **'rareˌfiable** *adj* ▸ **'rareˌfier** *n*

rare gas *n* another name for **inert gas.**

rarely ➊ ('rɛəlɪ) *adv* **1** hardly ever; seldom. **2** to an unusual degree; exceptionally. **3** *Dialect.* uncommonly well; excellently: *he did rarely at market yesterday.*

> **USAGE NOTE** Since *rarely* means *hardly ever*, one should not say something *rarely ever* happens.

raring ➊ ('rɛərɪŋ) *adj* ready; willing; enthusiastic (esp. in **raring to go**). [C20: from *rare*, var. of REAR[2]]

rarity ➊ ('rɛərɪtɪ) *n, pl* **rarities. 1** a rare person or thing, esp. something valued because it is uncommon. **2** the state of being rare.

rasbora (ræzˈbɔːrə) *n* any of the small cyprinid fishes of tropical Asia and East Africa. Many species are brightly coloured and are popular aquarium fishes. [from NL, from an East Indian language]

rascal ➊ ('rɑːskᵊl) *n* **1** a disreputable person; villain. **2** a mischievous or impish rogue. **3** an affectionate or mildly reproving term, esp. for a child: *you little rascal.* **4** *Obs.* a person of lowly birth. ◆ *adj* **5** (*prenominal*) *Obs.* **5a** belonging to the rabble. **5b** dishonest; knavish. [C14: from OF *rascaille* rabble, ?from OF *rasque* mud]

rascality (rɑːˈskælɪtɪ) *n, pl* **rascalities.** mischievous or disreputable character or action.

rascally ➊ ('rɑːskəlɪ) *adj* **1** dishonest or mean; base. ◆ *adv* **2** in a dishonest or mean fashion.

rase (reɪz) *vb* **rases, rasing, rased.** a variant spelling of **raze.**

rash[1] ➊ (ræʃ) *adj* **1** acting without due thought; impetuous. **2** resulting from excessive haste or impetuosity: *a rash word.* [C14: from OHG *rasc* hurried, clever]
▸ **'rashly** *adv* ▸ **'rashness** *n*

THESAURUS

rapid *adj* **1 = quick**, brisk, expeditious, express, fast, fleet, flying, hasty, hurried, precipitate, prompt, quickie (*inf.*), speedy, swift
Antonyms *adj* deliberate, gradual, leisurely, slow, tardy, unhurried

rapidity *n* **1 = speed**, alacrity, briskness, celerity, dispatch, expedition, fleetness, haste, hurry, precipitateness, promptitude, promptness, quickness, rush, speediness, swiftness, velocity

rapidly *adv* **1 = quickly**, apace, at speed, briskly, expeditiously, fast, hastily, hell for leather, hotfoot, hurriedly, in a hurry, in a rush, in haste, like a shot, like greased lightning, like lightning, like the clappers (*Brit. inf.*), posthaste, precipitately, promptly, pronto (*inf.*), speedily, swiftly, with dispatch

rapine *n* **= pillage**, depredation, despoilment, despoliation, looting, marauding, plundering, ransacking, rape, robbery, sack, seizure, spoliation, theft

rapport *n* **= bond**, affinity, empathy, harmony, interrelationship, link, relationship, sympathy, tie, understanding

rapprochement *French n* **= reconciliation**, détente, reconcilement, restoration of harmony, reunion, softening
Antonyms *n* antagonism, dissension, exacerbation, falling-out, quarrel, resumption of hostilities, schism

rapt[1] *adj* **1 = spellbound**, absorbed, carried away, engrossed, enthralled, entranced, fascinated, gripped, held, intent, preoccupied **2 = blissful**, bewitched, blissed out, captivated, charmed, delighted, ecstatic, enchanted, enraptured, rapturous, ravished, sent, transported
Antonyms *adj* ≠ **spellbound:** bored, detached, left cold, unaffected, uninterested, uninvolved, unmoved

rapture *n* **1 = ecstasy**, beatitude, bliss, cloud nine, delectation, delight, enthusiasm, euphoria, exaltation, felicity, happiness, joy, ravishment, rhapsody, seventh heaven, spell, transport

rapturous *adj* **1 = ecstatic**, blissed out, blissful, delighted, enthusiastic, euphoric, exalted, floating on air, happy, in seventh heaven, joyful, joyous, on cloud nine (*inf.*), overjoyed, over the moon (*inf.*), rapt, ravished, rhapsodic, sent, transported

rare[1] *adj* **1 = uncommon**, exceptional, few, infrequent, out of the ordinary, recherché, scarce, singular, sparse, sporadic, strange, thin on the ground, unusual **5 = superb**, admirable, choice, excellent, exquisite, extreme, fine, great, incomparable, peerless, superlative
Antonyms *adj* ≠ **uncommon:** abundant, bountiful, common, frequent, habitual, manifold, many, plentiful, profuse, regular

rare[2] *adj* **= underdone**, bloody, half-cooked, half-raw, undercooked

rarefied *adj* **1 = exalted**, elevated, high, lofty, noble, spiritual, sublime **2 = exclusive**, clannish, cliquish, esoteric, occult, private, select

rarefy *vb* **= thin out**, attenuate, clarify, purify, refine, sublimate

rarely *adv* **1 = seldom**, almost never, hardly, hardly ever, infrequently, little, once in a blue moon, once in a while, only now and then, on rare occasions, scarcely ever **2 = exceptionally**, extraordinarily, finely, notably, remarkably, singularly, uncommonly, unusually
Antonyms *adv* ≠ **seldom:** commonly, frequently, often, regularly, usually

raring *adj* **= eager**, athirst, avid, champing at the bit (*inf.*), desperate, enthusiastic, impatient, keen, keen as mustard, longing, ready, willing, yearning

rarity *n* **1 = curio**, collector's item, curiosity, find, gem, one-off, pearl, treasure **2 = uncommonness**, infrequency, scarcity, shortage, singularity, sparseness, strangeness, unusualness

rascal *n* **1 = rogue**, bad egg (*old-fashioned inf.*), blackguard, caitiff (*arch.*), devil, disgrace, good-for-nothing, knave (*arch.*), miscreant, ne'er-do-well, rake, rapscallion, reprobate, scally (*Northwest English dialect*), scoundrel, varmint (*inf.*), villain, wastrel, wretch **2, 3 = scamp**, imp, pickle (*Brit. inf.*), scallywag (*inf.*)

rascally *adj* **1 = villainous**, bad, base, crooked, dishonest, disreputable, evil, good-for-nothing, low, mean, reprobate, scoundrelly, unscrupulous, vicious, wicked

rash[1] *adj* **1 = reckless**, audacious, brash, care-

rash[2] ➊ (ræʃ) *n* **1** *Pathol.* any skin eruption. **2** a series of unpleasant and unexpected occurrences: *a rash of forest fires.* [C18: from OF *rasche,* from *raschier* to scratch, from L *rādere* to scrape]
rasher ('ræʃə) *n* a thin slice of bacon or ham. [C16: from ?]
rasp ➊ (rɑːsp) *n* **1** a harsh grating noise. **2** a coarse file with rows of raised teeth. ◆ *vb* **3** (*tr*) to scrape or rub (something) roughly, esp. with a rasp; abrade. **4** to utter with or make a harsh grating noise. **5** to irritate (one's nerves); grate (upon). [C16: from OF *raspe,* of Gmc origin; cf. OHG *raspōn* to scrape]
▸ **'rasper** *n* ▸ **'rasping** *adj* ▸ **'raspish** *adj*
raspberry ('rɑːzbərɪ, -brɪ) *n, pl* **raspberries. 1** a prickly rosaceous shrub of North America and Europe that has pinkish-white flowers and typically red berry-like fruits (drupelets). See also **bramble. 2a** the fruit of any such plant. **2b** (*as modifier*): *raspberry jelly.* **3a** a dark purplish-red colour. **3b** (*as adj*): *a raspberry dress.* **4** a spluttering noise made with the tongue and lips to express contempt (esp. in **blow a raspberry**). [C17: from earlier *raspis* raspberry, from ? + BERRY]
Rastafarian (ˌræstə'fɛərɪən) *n* **1** a member of an originally Jamaican religion that regards Ras Tafari, the former emperor of Ethiopia, Haile Selassie, as God. ◆ *adj* **2** of, characteristic of, or relating to the Rastafarians. ◆ Often shortened to **Rasta.**
raster ('ræstə) *n* a pattern of horizontal scanning lines, esp. those traced by an electron beam on a television screen or those in a digitized bitmap image. [C20: via G from L: rake, from *rādere* to scrape]
rat ➊ (ræt) *n* **1** any of numerous long-tailed Old World rodents, that are similar to but larger than mice and are now distributed all over the world. **2** *Inf.* a person who deserts his friends or associates, esp. in time of trouble. **3** *Inf.* a worker who works during a strike; blackleg; scab. **4** *Inf.* a despicable person. **5 have** *or* **be rats.** *Austral. sl.* to be mad or eccentric. **6 smell a rat.** to detect something suspicious. ◆ *vb* **rats, ratting, ratted. 7** (*intr;* usually foll. by *on*) **7a** to divulge secret information (about); betray the trust (of). **7b** to default (on); abandon. **8** to hunt and kill rats. [OE *rætt*]
rata ('rɑːtə) *n* a New Zealand tree with red flowers. [from Maori]
ratable *or* **rateable** ('reɪtəbᵊl) *adj* **1** able to be rated or evaluated. **2** *Brit.* (of property) liable to payment of rates.
▸ ˌ**rata'bility** *or* ˌ**ratea'bility** *n* ▸ **'ratably** *or* **'rateably** *adv*
ratable value *n Brit.* (formerly) a fixed value assigned to a property by a local authority, on the basis of which variable annual rates are charged.
ratafia (ˌrætə'fɪə) *or* **ratafee** (ˌrætə'fiː) *n* **1** any liqueur made from fruit or from brandy with added fruit. **2** a flavouring essence made from almonds. **3** *Chiefly Brit.* Also called: **ratafia biscuit.** a small macaroon flavoured with almonds. [C17: from West Indian Creole F]
ratan (ræ'tæn) *n* a variant spelling of **rattan.**
rat-arsed *adj Brit. sl.* drunk.
rat-a-tat-tat ('rætəˌtæt'tæt) *or* **rat-a-tat** ('rætə'tæt) *n* the sound of knocking on a door.
ratatouille (ˌrætə'twiː) *n* a vegetable casserole made of tomatoes, aubergines, peppers, etc., fried in oil and stewed slowly. [C19: from F, from *touiller* to stir, from L, from *tudes* hammer]
ratbag ('rætˌbæg) *n Sl.* an eccentric, stupid, or unreliable person.
rat-catcher *n* a person whose job is to destroy or drive away vermin, esp. rats.
ratchet ('rætʃɪt) *n* **1** a device in which a toothed rack or wheel is engaged by a pawl to permit motion in one direction only. **2** the toothed rack or wheel forming part of such a device. [C17: from F *rochet,* from OF *rocquet* blunt head of a lance, of Gmc origin]
ratchet effect *n Econ.* an effect that occurs when a price or wage increases as a result of temporary pressure but fails to fall back when the pressure is removed.
rate[1] ➊ (reɪt) *n* **1** a quantity or amount considered in relation to or measured against another quantity or amount: *a rate of 70 miles an hour.* **2a** a price or charge with reference to a standard or scale: *rate of interest.* **2b** (*as modifier*): *a rate card.* **3** a charge made per unit for a commodity, service, etc. **4** See **rates. 5** the relative speed of progress or change of something variable; pace: *the rate of production has doubled.* **6a** relative quality; class or grade. **6b** (*in combination*): *first-rate ideas.* **7 at any rate.** in any case; at all events; anyway. ◆ *vb* **rates, rating, rated.** (*mainly tr*) **8** (*also intr*) to assign or receive a position on a scale of relative values; rank: *he is rated fifth in the world.* **9** to estimate the value of; evaluate: *we rate your services highly.* **10** to be worthy of; deserve: *this hotel does not rate four stars.* **11** to consider; regard: *I rate him among my friends.* **12** *Brit.* to assess the value of (property) for the purpose of local taxation. [C15: from OF, from Med. L *rata,* from L *prō ratā parte* according to a fixed proportion, from *ratus* fixed, from *rērī* to think, decide]
rate[2] ➊ (reɪt) *vb* **rates, rating, rated.** (*tr*) to scold or criticize severely; rebuke harshly. [C14: ? rel. to Swedish *rata* to chide]
rateable ('reɪtəbᵊl) *adj* a variant spelling of **ratable.**
rate-cap ('reɪtˌkæp) *vb* **rate-caps, rate-capping, rate-capped.** (*tr*) (formerly in Britain) to impose on (a local authority) an upper limit on the rate it may levy.
▸ **'rate-ˌcapping** *n*
ratel ('reɪtᵊl) *n* **1** a carnivorous mammal related to the badger family, inhabiting wooded regions of Africa and S Asia. It has a massive body, strong claws, and a thick coat that is paler on the back. It feeds on honey and small animals. **2** *S. African.* a six-wheeled armoured vehicle. [C18: from Afrik.]
rate of exchange *n* See **exchange rate.**
rate of return *n Finance.* the ratio of the annual income from an investment to the original investment, often expressed as a percentage.
ratepayer ('reɪtˌpeɪə) *n Brit.* (formerly) a person who paid local rates, esp. a householder.
rates (reɪts) *pl n Brit.* a tax formerly levied on property by a local authority.
rather ➊ ('rɑːðə) *adv* (*in senses 1-4, not used with a negative*) **1** relatively or fairly; somewhat: *it's rather dull.* **2** to a significant or noticeable extent; quite: *she's rather pretty.* **3** to a limited extent or degree: *I rather thought that was the case.* **4** with better or more just cause: *this text is rather to be deleted than rewritten.* **5** more readily or willingly; sooner: *I would rather not see you tomorrow.* ◆ *sentence connector.* **6** on the contrary: *it's not cold. Rather, it's very hot.* ◆ *sentence substitute.* ('rɑː'ðɜː). **7** an expression of strong affirmation: *Is it worth seeing? Rather!* [OE *hrathor* comp. of *hræth* READY, quick]

> **USAGE NOTE** Both *would* and *had* are used with *rather* in sentences such as *I would rather* (or *had rather*) *go to the film than to the play. Had rather* is less common and now widely regarded as slightly old-fashioned.

ratify ➊ ('rætɪˌfaɪ) *vb* **ratifies, ratifying, ratified.** (*tr*) to give formal approval or consent to. [C14: via OF from L *ratus* fixed (see RATE[1]) + *facere* to make]
▸ **'ratiˌfiable** *adj* ▸ ˌ**ratifi'cation** *n* ▸ **'ratiˌfier** *n*
rating[1] ➊ ('reɪtɪŋ) *n* **1** a classification according to order or grade; ranking. **2** an ordinary seaman. **3** *Sailing.* a handicap assigned to a racing boat based on its dimensions, draught, etc. **4** the estimated financial or credit standing of a business enterprise or individual. **5** *Radio, television, etc.* a figure based on statistical sampling indicating what proportion of the total audience tune in to a specific programme.
rating[2] ➊ ('reɪtɪŋ) *n* a sharp scolding or rebuke.
ratio ➊ ('reɪʃɪəʊ) *n, pl* **ratios. 1** a measure of the relative size of two classes expressible as a proportion: *the ratio of boys to girls is 2 to 1.* **2** *Maths.* a quotient of two numbers or quantities. See also **proportion** (sense 6). [C17: from L: a reckoning, from *rērī* to think]

THESAURUS

less, foolhardy, harebrained, harum-scarum, hasty, headlong, headstrong, heedless, helter-skelter, hot-headed, ill-advised, impetuous, imprudent, impulsive, incautious, indiscreet, injudicious, madcap, precipitate, premature, thoughtless, unguarded, unthinking, unwary
Antonyms *adj* canny, careful, cautious, considered, premeditated, prudent
rash[2] *n* **1** = **outbreak**, eruption **2** = **spate**, epidemic, flood, outbreak, plague, series, succession, wave
rashness *n* **1** = **recklessness**, adventurousness, audacity, brashness, carelessness, foolhardiness, hastiness, heedlessness, indiscretion, precipitation, temerity, thoughtlessness
rasp *n* **1** = **grating**, grinding, scrape, scratch ◆ *vb* **3** = **scrape**, abrade, excoriate, file, grind, rub, sand, scour **5** = **irritate**, grate (upon), irk, jar (upon), rub (someone) up the wrong way, set one's teeth on edge, wear upon
rasping *adj* **4** = **harsh**, creaking, croaking, croaky, grating, gravelly, gruff, hoarse, husky, jarring, rough
rat *n* **2** *Informal* = **traitor**, betrayer, deceiver, defector, deserter, double-crosser, grass (*Brit. inf.*), informer, nark (*sl.*), quisling, snake in the grass, stool pigeon, two-timer (*inf.*) **4** *Informal* = **rogue**, bad lot, bastard (*offens.*), bounder (*old-fashioned Brit. sl.*), cad (*old-fashioned Brit. inf.*), heel (*sl.*), ratfink (*sl., chiefly US and Canad.*), rotter (*sl., chiefly Brit.*), scoundrel, shyster (*inf., chiefly US*) ◆ *vb* **7** *usually foll. by* **on** = **betray**, abandon, defect, desert, do the dirty on (*Brit. inf.*), leave high and dry, leave (someone) in the lurch, run out on (*inf.*), sell down the river (*inf.*)
rate[1] *n* **1** = **degree**, percentage, proportion, ratio, relation, scale, standard **3** = **charge**, cost, dues, duty, fee, figure, hire, price, tariff, tax, toll **5** = **speed**, gait, measure, pace, tempo, time, velocity **6a** = **grade**, class, classification, degree, position, quality, rank, rating, status, value, worth **7 at any rate** = **in any case**, anyhow, anyway, at all events, nevertheless ◆ *vb* **8** = **rank**, class, classify, grade **9** = **evaluate**, adjudge, appraise, assess, estimate, measure, value, weigh **10** = **deserve**, be entitled to, be worthy of, merit **11** = **consider**, count, reckon, regard
rate[2] *vb* = **rebuke**, bawl out, berate, blame, carpet (*inf.*), castigate, censure, chew out (*US & Canad. inf.*), chide, criticize severely, give a rocket (*Brit. & NZ inf.*), haul over the coals (*inf.*), read the riot act, reprimand, reprove, scold, take to task, tear into (*inf.*), tear (someone) off a strip (*inf.*), tell off (*inf.*), tongue-lash, upbraid
rather *adv* **1** = **to some extent**, a bit, a little, fairly, kind of (*inf.*), moderately, pretty (*inf.*), quite, relatively, slightly, somewhat, sort of (*inf.*), to some degree **2** = **significantly**, a good bit, noticeably, very **5** = **preferably**, instead, more readily, more willingly, sooner
ratify *vb* = **approve**, affirm, authenticate, authorize, bear out, certify, confirm, consent to, corroborate, endorse, establish, sanction, sign, uphold, validate
Antonyms *vb* abrogate, annul, cancel, reject, repeal, repudiate, revoke
rating[1] *n* **1** = **position**, class, classification, degree, designation, estimate, evaluation, grade, order, placing, rank, rate, standing, status
rating[2] *n* = **rebuke**, chiding, dressing down (*inf.*), lecture, piece of one's mind, reprimand, reproof, roasting (*inf.*), row (*inf.*), scolding, telling-off (*inf.*), ticking-off (*inf.*), tongue-lashing
ratio *n* **1** = **proportion**, arrangement, correlation, correspondence, equation, fraction, percentage, rate, relation, relationship

ratiocinate (ˌrætɪˈɒsɪˌneɪt) *vb* **ratiocinates, ratiocinating, ratiocinated.** (*intr*) to think or argue logically and methodically; reason. [C17: from L *ratiōcinārī* to calculate, from *ratiō* REASON]
▸ˌ**ratiˌociˈnation** *n* ▸ˌ**ratiˈociˌnative** *adj* ▸ˌ**ratiˈociˌnator** *n*

ration ◑ (ˈræʃən) *n* **1a** a fixed allowance of food, provisions, etc., esp. a statutory one for civilians in time of scarcity or soldiers in time of war. **1b** (*as modifier*): *a ration book*. **2** a sufficient or adequate amount: *you've had your ration of television for today*. ◆ *vb* (*tr*) **3** (often foll. by *out*) to distribute (provisions), esp. to an army. **4** to restrict the distribution or consumption of (a commodity) by (people): *the government has rationed sugar*. ◆ See also **rations.** [C18: via F from L *ratiō* REASON]

rational ◑ (ˈræʃənᵊl) *adj* **1** using reason or logic in thinking out a problem. **2** in accordance with the principles of logic or reason; reasonable. **3** of sound mind; sane: *the patient seemed rational*. **4** endowed with the capacity to reason: *rational beings*. **5** *Maths*. **5a** expressible as a ratio of two integers. **5b** (of an expression, equation, etc.) containing no variable either in irreducible radical form or raised to a fractional power. ◆ *n* **6** a rational number. [C14: from L *ratiōnālis*, from *ratiō* REASON]
▸ˌ**ratioˈnality** *n* ▸ˈ**rationally** *adv* ▸ˈ**rationalness** *n*

rationale ◑ (ˌræʃəˈnɑːl) *n* a reasoned exposition, esp. one defining the fundamental reasons for an action, etc. [C17: from NL, from L *ratiōnālis*]

rationalism (ˈræʃənəˌlɪzəm) *n* **1** reliance on reason rather than intuition to justify one's beliefs or actions. **2** *Philosophy*. the doctrine that knowledge is acquired by reason without regard to experience. **3** the belief that knowledge and truth are ascertained by rational thought and not by divine or supernatural revelation.
▸ˈ**rationalist** *n* ▸ˌ**rationalˈistic** *adj* ▸ˌ**rationalˈistically** *adv*

rationalize ◑ *or* **rationalise** (ˈræʃənəˌlaɪz) *vb* **rationalizes, rationalizing, rationalized** *or* **rationalises, rationalising, rationalised. 1** to justify (one's actions) with plausible reasons, esp. after the event. **2** to apply logic or reason to (something). **3** (*tr*) to eliminate unnecessary equipment, etc., from (a group of businesses, factory, etc.), in order to make it more efficient. **4** (*tr*) *Maths*. to eliminate radicals without changing the value of (an expression) or the roots of (an equation).
▸ˌ**rationaliˈzation** *or* ˌ**rationaliˈsation** *n* ▸ˈ**rationalˌizer** *or* ˈ**rationalˌiser** *n*

rational number *n* any real number of the form *a*/*b*, where *a* and *b* are integers and *b* is not zero, as 7 or 7/3.

rations (ˈræʃənz) *pl n* (*sometimes sing*) a fixed daily allowance of food, esp. to military personnel or when supplies are limited.

ratite (ˈrætaɪt) *adj* **1** (of flightless birds) having a breastbone that lacks a keel for the attachment of flight muscles. **2** of or denoting the flightless birds, that have a flat breastbone, feathers lacking vanes, and reduced wings. ◆ *n* **3** a bird, such as an ostrich that belongs to this group; a flightless bird. [C19: from L *ratis* raft]

rat kangaroo *n* any of several ratlike kangaroos that occur in Australia and Tasmania.

ratline *or* **ratlin** (ˈrætlɪn) *n Naut*. any of a series of light lines tied across the shrouds of a sailing vessel for climbing aloft. [C15: from ?]

ratoon *or* **rattoon** (ræˈtuːn) *n* **1** a new shoot that grows from near the root of crop plants, esp. the sugar cane, after the old growth has been cut back. ◆ *vb* **2** to propagate by such a growth. [C18: from Sp. *retoño*, from RE- + *otoñar* to sprout in autumn, from *otoño* AUTUMN]

ratpack (ˈrætˌpæk) *n Derog. sl*. those members of the press who pursue celebrities and give wide, often intrusive, coverage of their private lives: *the royal ratpack*.

rat race *n* a continual routine of hectic competitive activity: *working in the City is a real rat race*.

rat-running *n* the practice of driving through residential side streets to avoid congested main roads.
▸**rat-run** *n* ▸**rat-runner** *n*

ratsbane (ˈrætsˌbeɪn) *n* rat poison, esp. arsenic oxide.

rat-tail *n* **1a** a horse's tail that has no hairs. **1b** a horse having such a tail. **2** a style of spoon in which the line of the handle is prolonged in a tapering moulding along the back of the bowl.

rattan *or* **ratan** (ræˈtæn) *n* **1** a climbing palm having tough stems used for wickerwork and canes. **2** the stems of such a plant collectively. **3** a stick made from one of these stems. [C17: from Malay *rōtan*]

ratter (ˈrætə) *n* **1** a dog or cat that catches and kills rats. **2** another word for **rat** (sense 3).

rattle ◑ (ˈrætᵊl) *vb* **rattles, rattling, rattled. 1** to make a rapid succession of short sharp sounds, as of loose pellets colliding when shaken in a container. **2** to shake with such a sound. **3** to send, move, drive, etc., with such a sound: *the car rattled along the country road*. **4** (*intr*; foll. by *on*) to chatter idly: *he rattled on about his work*. **5** (*tr*; foll. by *off*, *out*, etc.) to recite perfunctorily or rapidly. **6** (*tr*) *Inf*. to disconcert; make frightened or anxious. ◆ *n* **7** a rapid succession of short sharp sounds. **8** a baby's toy filled with small pellets that rattle when shaken. **9** a series of loosely connected horny segments on the tail of a rattlesnake, vibrated to produce a rattling sound. **10** any of various European scrophulariaceous plants having a capsule in which the seeds rattle, such as the **red rattle** and the **yellow rattle. 11** idle chatter. **12** *Med*. another name for **rale.** [C14: from MDu. *ratelen*, imit.]
▸ˈ**rattly** *adj*

rattler (ˈrætlə) *n* **1** a person or thing that rattles. **2** *Inf*. a rattlesnake.

rattlesnake (ˈrætᵊlˌsneɪk) *n* any of the venomous New World snakes such as the **black** or **timber rattlesnake** belonging to the family of pit vipers. They have a series of loose horny segments on the tail that are vibrated to produce a buzzing or whirring sound.

rattletrap (ˈrætᵊlˌtræp) *n Inf*. a broken-down old vehicle, esp. an old car.

rattling (ˈrætlɪŋ) *adv Inf*. (intensifier qualifying something good, fine, etc.): *a rattling good lunch*.

ratty ◑ (ˈrætɪ) *adj* **rattier, rattiest. 1** *Brit. & NZ inf*. irritable; annoyed. **2** *Inf*. (of the hair) straggly, unkempt, or greasy. **3** *US & Canad. sl*. shabby; dilapidated. **4** *Austral. sl*. mad, eccentric, or odd. **5** of, like, or full of rats.
▸ˈ**rattily** *adv* ▸ˈ**rattiness** *n*

raucous ◑ (ˈrɔːkəs) *adj* (of voices, cries, etc.) harshly or hoarsely loud. [C18: from L *raucus* hoarse]
▸ˈ**raucously** *adv* ▸ˈ**raucousness** *n*

raunchy ◑ (ˈrɔːntʃɪ) *adj* **raunchier, raunchiest.** *Sl*. **1** openly sexual; lusty; earthy. **2** *Chiefly US*. slovenly; dirty. [C20: from ?]
▸ˈ**raunchily** *adv* ▸ˈ**raunchiness** *n*

raupo (ˈraupəʊ) *n, pl* **raupos.** a marsh reed common in New Zealand. [from Maori]

rauwolfia (rɔːˈwʊlfɪə, raʊ-) *n* **1** a tropical flowering tree or shrub of SE Asia with latex in its stem. **2** the powdered root of this plant: a source of various drugs, esp. reserpine. [C19: NL, after Leonhard *Rauwolf* (died 1596), G botanist]

ravage ◑ (ˈrævɪdʒ) *vb* **ravages, ravaging, ravaged. 1** to cause extensive damage to. ◆ *n* **2** (*often pl*) destructive action: *the ravages of time*. [C17: from F, from OF *ravir* to snatch away, RAVISH]
▸ˈ**ravager** *n*

rave ◑ (reɪv) *vb* **raves, raving, raved. 1** to utter (something) in a wild or incoherent manner, as when delirious. **2** (*intr*) to speak in an angry uncontrolled manner. **3** (*intr*) (of the sea, wind, etc.) to rage or roar. **4** (*intr*; foll. by *over* or *about*) *Inf*. to write or speak (about) with great enthusiasm. **5** (*intr*) *Brit. sl*. to enjoy oneself wildly or uninhibitedly. ◆ *n* **6** *Inf*. **6a** enthusiastic or extravagant praise. **6b** (*as modifier*): *a rave review*. **7** *Brit. sl*. **7a** Also called: **rave-up.** a party. **7b** a professionally organized party for young people, with electronic dance music, sometimes held in a field or disused building. **8** a name given to various types of dance music, such as techno, that feature fast electronic rhythm. [C14 *raven*, apparently from OF *resver* to wander]

ravel (ˈrævᵊl) *vb* **ravels, ravelling, ravelled** *or US* **ravels, raveling, raveled. 1** to tangle (threads, fibres, etc.) or (of threads, etc.) to become entangled. **2** (often foll. by *out*) to tease or draw out (the fibres of a fabric) or (of a fabric) to fray out in loose ends; unravel. **3** (*tr*; usually foll. by *out*) to disentangle or resolve: *to ravel out a complicated story*. ◆ *n* **4** a tangle or complication. [C16: from MDu. *ravelen*]
▸ˈ**raveller** *n* ▸ˈ**ravelly** *adj*

raven[1] (ˈreɪvᵊn) *n* **1** a large passerine bird of the crow family, having a

THESAURUS

ration *n* **1a** = **allowance**, allotment, dole, helping, measure, part, portion, provision, quota, share ◆ *vb* **3** = **distribute**, allocate, allot, apportion, deal, dole, give out, issue, measure out, mete, parcel out **4** = **limit**, budget, conserve, control, restrict, save

rational *adj* **1, 4** = **reasoning**, cerebral, cognitive, ratiocinative, thinking **2** = **sensible**, enlightened, intelligent, judicious, logical, lucid, realistic, reasonable, sagacious, sane, sound, wise **3** = **sane**, all there (*inf.*), balanced, *compos mentis*, in one's right mind, lucid, normal, of sound mind
Antonyms *adj* insane, irrational, unreasonable, unsound

rationale *n* = **reason**, exposition, grounds, logic, motivation, philosophy, principle, *raison d'être*, theory

rationalize *vb* **1** = **justify**, account for, excuse, explain away, extenuate, make allowance for, make excuses for, vindicate **2** = **reason out**, apply logic to, elucidate, resolve, think through **3** = **streamline**, make cuts, make more efficient, trim

rattle *vb* **1** = **clatter**, bang, jangle **2, 3** = **shake**, bounce, jar, jiggle, jolt, jounce, vibrate **4** *with* **on** *or* **away** = **prattle**, blether, cackle, chatter, gabble, gibber, jabber, prate, rabbit (on) (*Brit. inf.*), run on, witter (*inf.*), yak (away) (*sl.*) **5** *with* **off** *or* **out** = **recite**, list, reel off, rehearse, run through, spiel off (*inf.*) **6** *Informal* = **fluster**, discomfit, discompose, disconcert, discountenance, disturb, faze, frighten, perturb, put (someone) off his stride, put (someone) out of countenance, scare, shake, upset

ratty *adj* **1** *Brit. & N.Z. informal* = **irritable**, angry, annoyed, crabbed, cross, impatient, short-tempered, snappy, testy, tetchy, touchy

raucous *adj* = **harsh**, grating, hoarse, husky, loud, noisy, rasping, rough, strident
Antonyms *adj* dulcet, mellifluous, quiet, smooth, sweet

raunchy *adj* **1** *Slang* = **sexy**, bawdy, coarse, earthy, lecherous, lewd, lustful, lusty, ribald, salacious, sexual, smutty, steamy (*inf.*), suggestive

ravage *vb* **1** = **destroy**, demolish, desolate, despoil, devastate, gut, lay waste, leave in ruins, loot, pillage, plunder, ransack, raze, ruin, sack, shatter, spoil, wreak havoc on, wreck ◆ *n* **2** *often plural* = **damage**, demolition, depredation, desolation, destruction, devastation, havoc, pillage, plunder, rapine, ruin, ruination, spoliation, waste

rave *vb* **1, 2** = **rant**, babble, be delirious, fume, go mad (*inf.*), rage, roar, splutter, storm, talk wildly, thunder **4** *Informal* = **enthuse**, be delighted by, be mad about (*inf.*), be wild about (*inf.*), cry up, gush, praise, rhapsodize ◆ *n* **6a** *Informal* = **praise**, acclaim, applause, encomium ◆ *modifier* **6b** *Informal* = **enthusiastic**, ecstatic, excellent, favourable, laudatory ◆ *n* **7a** = **party**, affair, bash, beano (*Brit. sl.*), blow-out (*sl.*), celebration, do (*inf.*), hooley *or* hoolie (*chiefly Irish & NZ*)

large straight bill, long wedge-shaped tail, and black plumage. **2a** a shiny black colour. **2b** *(as adj): raven hair.* [OE *hræfn*]

raven[2] ('ræv°n) *vb* **1** to seize or seek (plunder, prey, etc.). **2** to eat (something) voraciously or greedily. [C15: from OF *raviner* to attack impetuously; see RAVENOUS]

ravening ('rævənɪŋ) *adj* (of animals) voracious; predatory.
▸**'raveningly** *adv*

ravenous ❶ ('rævənəs) *adj* **1** famished; starving. **2** rapacious; voracious. [C16: from OF *ravineux,* from L *rapīna* plunder, from *rapere* to seize]
▸**'ravenously** *adv* ▸**'ravenousness** *n*

raver ('reɪvə) *n* **1** *Brit. sl.* a person who leads a wild or uninhibited social life. **2** *Sl.* a person who enjoys rave music, esp. one who frequents raves.

ravine ❶ (rə'vi:n) *n* a deep narrow steep-sided valley. [C15: from OF: torrent, from L *rapīna* robbery, infl. by L *rapidus* RAPID, both from *rapere* to snatch]

raving ❶ ('reɪvɪŋ) *adj* **1a** delirious; frenzied. **1b** *(as adv): raving mad.* **2** *Inf.* (intensifier): *a raving beauty.* ◆ *n* **3** *(usually pl)* frenzied or wildly extravagant talk or utterances.
▸**'ravingly** *adv*

ravioli (ˌrævɪ'əʊlɪ) *n* small squares of pasta containing a savoury mixture of meat, cheese, etc. [C19: It. dialect, lit.: little turnips, from It. *rava* turnip, from L *rāpa*]

ravish ❶ ('rævɪʃ) *vb (tr)* **1** *(often passive)* to enrapture. **2** to rape. **3** *Arch.* to carry off by force. [C13: from OF *ravir,* from L *rapere* to seize]
▸**'ravisher** *n* ▸**'ravishment** *n*

ravishing ❶ ('rævɪʃɪŋ) *adj* delightful; lovely; entrancing.
▸**'ravishingly** *adv*

raw ❶ (rɔ:) *adj* **1** (of food) not cooked. **2** *(prenominal)* in an unfinished, natural, or unrefined state; not treated by manufacturing or other processes: *raw materials.* **3** (of the skin, a wound, etc.) having the surface exposed or abraded, esp. painfully. **4** (of an edge of material) unhemmed; liable to fray. **5** ignorant, inexperienced, or immature: *a raw recruit.* **6** *(prenominal)* not selected or modified: *raw statistics.* **7** frank or realistic: *a raw picture of a marriage.* **8** (of spirits) undiluted. **9** *Chiefly US.* coarse, vulgar, or obscene. **10** (of the weather) harshly cold and damp. **11** *Inf.* unfair; unjust (esp. in **a raw deal**). ◆ *n* **12 in the raw. 12a** *Inf.* without clothes; naked. **12b** in a natural or unmodified state. **13 the raw.** *Brit. inf.* a sensitive point: *his criticism touched me on the raw.* [OE *hreaw*]
▸**'rawish** *adj* ▸**'rawly** *adv* ▸**'rawness** *n*

rawboned ('rɔ:'bəʊnd) *adj* having a lean bony physique.

rawhide ('rɔ:ˌhaɪd) *n* **1** untanned hide. **2** a whip or rope made of strips cut from such a hide.

rawhide hammer *n* a hammer, used to avoid damaging a surface, having a head consisting of a metal tube from each end of which a tight roll of hide protrudes.

rawinsonde ('reɪwɪnˌsɒnd) *n* a hydrogen balloon carrying meteorological instruments and a radar target, enabling the velocity of winds in the atmosphere to be measured. [C20: blend of *radar* + *wind* + *radiosonde*]

Rawlplug ('rɔ:lplʌg) *n Trademark.* a short fibre or plastic tube used to provide a fixing in a wall for a screw.

raw material *n* **1** material on which a particular manufacturing process is carried out. **2** a person or thing regarded as suitable for some particular purpose: *raw material for the army.*

raw silk *n* **1** untreated silk fibres reeled from the cocoon. **2** fabric woven from such fibres.

ray[1] ❶ (reɪ) *n* **1** a narrow beam of light; gleam. **2** a slight indication: *a ray of solace.* **3** *Maths.* a straight line extending from a point. **4** a thin beam of electromagnetic radiation or particles. **5** any of the bony or cartilaginous spines of the fin of a fish that form the support for the soft part of the fin. **6** any of the arms or branches of a starfish. **7** *Bot.* any strand of tissue that runs radially through the vascular tissue of some higher plants. ◆ *vb* **8** (of an object) to emit (light) in rays or (of light) to issue in the form of rays. **9** *(intr)* (of lines, etc.) to extend in rays or on radiating paths. **10** *(tr)* to adorn (an ornament, etc.) with rays or radiating lines. [C14: from OF *rai,* from L *radius* spoke]

ray[2] (reɪ) *n* any of various marine selachian fishes typically having a flattened body, greatly enlarged winglike pectoral fins, gills on the undersurface of the fins, and a long whiplike tail. [C14: from OF *raie,* from L *raia*]

ray[3] (reɪ) *n Music.* (in tonic sol-fa) the second degree of any major scale; supertonic. [C18: later variant of *re;* see GAMUT]

Raybans ('reɪˌbænz) *pl n Trademark.* a brand of sunglasses.

ray flower *or* **floret** *n* any of the small strap-shaped flowers in the flower head of certain composite plants, such as the daisy.

ray gun *n* (in science fiction) a gun that emits rays to paralyse, stun, or destroy.

rayless ('reɪlɪs) *adj* **1** dark; gloomy. **2** lacking rays: *a rayless flower.*

raylet ('reɪlɪt) *n* a small ray.

rayon ('reɪɒn) *n* **1** any of a number of textile fibres made from wood pulp or other forms of cellulose. **2** any fabric made from such a fibre. **3** *(as modifier): a rayon shirt.* [C20: from F, from OF *rai* RAY[1]]

raze ❶ *or* **rase** (reɪz) *vb* **razes, razing, razed** *or* **rases, rasing, rased.** *(tr)* **1** to demolish (buildings, etc.) completely (esp. in **raze to the ground**). **2** to delete; erase. **3** *Arch.* to graze. [C16: from OF *raser,* from L *rādere* to scrape]
▸**'razer** *or* **'raser** *n*

razoo (rɑ:'zu:) *n, pl* **razoos.** *Austral. & NZ inf.* an imaginary coin: *not a brass razoo; they took every last razoo.* [C20: from ?]

razor ('reɪzə) *n* **1** a sharp implement used esp. for shaving the face. **2 on a razor's edge** *or* **razor-edge.** in an acute dilemma. ◆ *vb* **3** *(tr)* to cut or shave with a razor. [C13: from OF *raseor,* from *raser* to shave; see RAZE]

razorback ('reɪzəˌbæk) *n* **1** Also called: **finback.** another name for the **common rorqual** (see **rorqual**). **2** a wild pig of the US, having a narrow body, long legs, and a ridged back.

razorbill ('reɪzəˌbɪl) *or* **razor-billed auk** *n* a common auk of the North Atlantic, having a thick laterally compressed bill with white markings.

razor blade *n* a small rectangular piece of metal sharpened on one or both long edges for use in a razor for shaving.

razor-shell *n* any of various sand-burrowing bivalve molluscs which have a long tubular shell. US name: **razor clam.**

razor wire *n* strong wire with pieces of sharp metal set across it at close intervals.

razz (ræz) *US & Canad. sl.* ◆ *vb* **1** *(tr)* to make fun of; deride. ◆ *n* **2** short for **raspberry** (sense 4).

razzle-dazzle ❶ ('ræz°l'dæz°l) *or* **razzmatazz** ('ræzmə'tæz) *n Sl.* **1** noisy or showy fuss or activity. **2** a spree or frolic. [C19: rhyming compound from DAZZLE]

Rb *the chemical symbol for* rubidium.

RBT *abbrev. for* random breath testing.

RC *abbrev. for:* **1** Red Cross. **2** Roman Catholic.

RCA *abbrev. for:* **1** (formerly) Radio Corporation of America. **2** Royal College of Art.

RCAF *abbrev. for* Royal Canadian Air Force.

RC CH *abbrev. for* Roman Catholic Church.

RCM *abbrev. for* Royal College of Music.

RCMP *abbrev. for* Royal Canadian Mounted Police.

RCN *abbrev. for:* **1** Royal Canadian Navy. **2** Royal College of Nursing.

RCP *abbrev. for* Royal College of Physicians.

RCS *abbrev. for:* **1** Royal College of Science. **2** Royal College of Surgeons. **3** Royal Corps of Signals.

rd *abbrev. for:* **1** road. **2** rod (unit of length). **3** round. **4** *Physics.* rutherford.

Rd *abbrev. for* Road.

RDC (in Britain, formerly) *abbrev. for* Rural District Council.

re[1] (reɪ, ri:) *n Music.* the syllable used in the fixed system of solmization for the note D. [C14: see GAMUT]

re[2] ❶ (ri:) *prep* with reference to. [C18: from L *rē,* ablative case of *rēs* thing]

> **USAGE NOTE** *Re,* in contexts such as *re your letter, your remarks have been noted* or *he spoke to me re your complaint,* is common in business or official correspondence. In general English *with reference to* is preferable in the former case and *about* or *concerning* in the latter. Even in business correspondence, the use of *re* is often restricted to the letter heading.

THESAURUS

ravenous *adj* **1** = **starving,** esurient, famished, starved, very hungry **2** = **voracious,** devouring, edacious, gluttonous, insatiable, predatory, rapacious, ravening
Antonyms *adj* ≠ **starving:** full, glutted, sated, satiated

ravine *n* = **canyon,** clough (*dialect*), defile, flume, gap (*US*), gorge, gulch (*US*), gully, linn (*Scot.*), pass

raving *adj* **1a** = **mad,** berserk, crazed, crazy, delirious, frantic, frenzied, furious, hysterical, insane, irrational, out of one's mind, rabid, raging, wild

ravish *vb* **1** = **enchant,** captivate, charm, delight, enrapture, entrance, fascinate, overjoy, spellbind, transport **2** = **rape,** abuse, force, outrage, sexually assault, violate

ravishing *adj* = **enchanting,** beautiful, bewitching, charming, dazzling, delightful, drop-dead (*sl.*), entrancing, gorgeous, lovely, radiant, stunning (*inf.*)

raw *adj* **1** = **uncooked,** bloody (*of meat*), fresh, natural, undressed, unprepared **2** = **unrefined,** basic, coarse, crude, green, natural, organic, rough, unfinished, unprocessed, unripe, untreated **3** = **sore,** abraded, chafed, grazed, open, scratched, sensitive, skinned, tender **5** = **inexperienced,** callow, green, ignorant, immature, new, undisciplined, unpractised, unseasoned, unskilled, untrained, untried **7** = **frank,** bare, blunt, brutal, candid, naked, plain, realistic, unembellished, unvarnished **10** = **chilly,** biting, bitter, bleak, chill, cold, damp, freezing, harsh, parky (*Brit. inf.*), piercing, unpleasant, wet
Antonyms *adj* ≠ **uncooked:** baked, cooked, done ≠ **unrefined:** finished, prepared, refined ≠ **inexperienced:** experienced, practised, professional, skilled, trained ≠ **frank:** embellished, gilded

ray[1] *n* **1** = **beam,** bar, flash, gleam, shaft **2** = **trace,** flicker, glimmer, hint, indication, scintilla, spark

raze *vb* **1** = **destroy,** bulldoze, demolish, flatten, knock down, level, pull down, remove, ruin, tear down, throw down **2** = **erase,** delete, efface, excise, expunge, extinguish, extirpate, obliterate, rub out, scratch out, strike out, wipe from the face of the earth, wipe out

razzle-dazzle *n* **1** *Slang* = **fuss,** carry-on (*inf., chiefly Brit.*), commotion, hullabaloo, performance (*inf.*), rigmarole, song and dance (*inf.*), to-do

re[2] *prep* = **concerning,** about, anent (*Scot.*), apropos, in respect of, on the subject of, regarding, respecting, with reference to, with regard to

Re *the chemical symbol for* rhenium.
RE *abbrev. for:* **1** Religious Education. **2** Royal Engineers.
re- *prefix* **1** indicating return to a previous condition, withdrawal, etc.: *rebuild; renew.* **2** indicating repetition of an action: *remarry.* [L]

> **USAGE NOTE** Verbs beginning with *re-* indicate repetition or restoration. It is unnecessary to add an adverb such as *back* or *again: This must not occur again* (not *recur again*); *we recounted the votes* (not *recounted the votes again*, which implies that the votes were counted three times, not twice).

reach ❶ (riːtʃ) *vb* **1** (*tr*) to arrive at or get to (a place, person, etc.) in the course of movement or action: *to reach the office.* **2** to extend as far as (a point or place): *to reach the ceiling; can you reach?* **3** (*tr*) to come to (a certain condition or situation): *to reach the point of starvation.* **4** (*intr*) to extend in influence or operation: *the Roman conquest reached throughout England.* **5** (*tr*) *Inf.* to pass or give (something to a person) with the outstretched hand. **6** (*intr;* foll. by *out, for,* or *after*) to make a movement (towards), as if to grasp or touch. **7** (*tr*) to make contact or communication with (someone): *we tried to reach him all day.* **8** (*tr*) to strike, esp. in fencing or boxing. **9** (*tr*) to amount to (a certain sum): *to reach five million.* **10** (*intr*) *Naut.* to sail on a tack with the wind on or near abeam. ◆ *n* **11** the act of reaching. **12** the extent or distance of reaching: *within reach.* **13** the range of influence, power, etc. **14** an open stretch of water, esp. on a river. **15** *Naut.* the direction or distance sailed by a vessel on one tack. **16** *Advertising.* the proportion of a market that an advertiser hopes to reach at least once in a campaign. [OE *rǣcan*]
▸ **'reachable** *adj* ▸ **'reacher** *n*

reach-me-down *n* **1a** (*often pl*) a cheaply ready-made or second-hand garment. **1b** (*as modifier*): *reach-me-down finery.* **2** (*modifier*) not original; derivative: *reach-me-down ideas.*

react ❶ (rɪ'ækt) *vb* **1** (*intr;* foll. by *to, upon,* etc.) (of a person or thing) to act in response to another person, a stimulus, etc. **2** (*intr;* foll. by *against*) to act in an opposing or contrary manner. **3** (*intr*) *Physics.* to exert an equal force in the opposite direction to an acting force. **4** *Chem.* to undergo or cause to undergo a chemical reaction. [C17: from LL *reagere,* from RE- + L *agere* to do]

re-act (riː'ækt) *vb* (*tr*) to act or perform again.

reactance (rɪ'æktəns) *n* the opposition to the flow of alternating current by the capacitance or inductance of an electrical circuit.

reactant (rɪ'æktənt) *n* a substance that participates in a chemical reaction.

reaction ❶ (rɪ'ækʃən) *n* **1** a response to some foregoing action or stimulus. **2** the reciprocal action of two things acting together. **3** opposition to change, esp. political change, or a desire to return to a former system. **4** a response indicating a person's feelings or emotional attitude. **5** *Med.* **5a** any effect produced by the action of a drug. **5b** any effect produced by a substance (allergen) to which a person is allergic. **6** *Chem.* a process that involves changes in the structure and energy content of atoms, molecules, or ions. **7** the equal and opposite force that acts on a body whenever it exerts a force on another body.
▸ **re'actional** *adj*

> **USAGE NOTE** *Reaction* is used to refer both to an instant response (*her reaction was one of amazement*) and to a considered response in the form of a statement (*the Minister gave his reaction to the court's decision*). Some people think this second use is incorrect.

reactionary ❶ (rɪ'ækʃənərɪ, -ʃənrɪ) *or* **reactionist** *adj* **1** of, relating to, or characterized by reaction, esp. against radical political or social change. ◆ *n, pl* **reactionaries** *or* **reactionists. 2** a person opposed to radical change.
▸ **re'actionism** *n*

reaction engine *or* **motor** *n* an engine, such as a jet engine, that ejects gas at high velocity and develops its thrust from the ensuing reaction.

reaction turbine *n* a turbine in which the working fluid is accelerated by expansion in both the static nozzles and the rotor blades.

reactivate (rɪ'æktɪˌveɪt) *vb* **reactivates, reactivating, reactivated.** (*tr*) to make (something) active again.
▸ **reˌacti'vation** *n*

reactive (rɪ'æktɪv) *adj* **1** readily partaking in chemical reactions: *sodium is a reactive metal.* **2** of, concerned with, or having a reactance. **3** responsive to stimulus. **4** (of mental illnesses) precipitated by an external cause.
▸ **reactivity** (ˌriːæk'tɪvɪtɪ) *or* **re'activeness** *n*

reactor (rɪ'æktə) *n* **1** short for **nuclear reactor. 2** a vessel in which a chemical reaction takes occurs. **3** a coil of low resistance and high inductance that introduces reactance into a circuit. **4** *Med.* a person sensitive to a particular drug or agent. **5** *Chem.* a substance that takes part in a reaction.

read[1] ❶ (riːd) *vb* **reads, reading, read** (rɛd). **1** to comprehend the meaning of (something written or printed) by looking at and interpreting the written or printed characters. **2** (when *tr,* often foll. by *out*) to look at, interpret, and speak aloud (something written or printed). **3** (*tr*) to interpret the significance or meaning of through scrutiny and recognition: *to read a map.* **4** (*tr*) to interpret or understand the meaning of (signs, characters, etc.) other than by visual means: *to read Braille.* **5** (*tr*) to have sufficient knowledge of (a language) to understand the written or printed word. **6** (*tr*) to discover or make out the true nature or mood of: *to read someone's mind.* **7** to interpret or understand (something read) in a specified way: *I read this speech as satire.* **8** (*tr*) to adopt as a reading in a particular passage: *for "boon" read "bone".* **9** (*intr*) to have or contain a certain form or wording: *the sentence reads as follows.* **10** to undertake a course of study in (a subject): *to read history.* **11** to gain knowledge by reading: *he read about the war.* **12** (*tr*) to register, indicate, or show: *the meter reads 100.* **13** (*tr*) to put into a specified condition by reading: *to read a child to sleep.* **14** (*tr*) to hear and understand, esp. when using a two-way radio: *we are reading you loud and clear.* **15** *Computing.* to obtain (data) from a storage device, such as magnetic tape. **16 read a lesson** (*or* **lecture**). *Inf.* to censure or reprimand. ◆ *n* **17** matter suitable for reading: *this book is a very good read.* **18** the act or a spell of reading. ◆ See also **read into, read out,** etc. [OE *rǣdan* to advise, explain]

read[2] (rɛd) *vb* **1** the past tense and past participle of **read**[1]. ◆ *adj* **2** having knowledge gained from books (esp. in **widely read** and **well-read**). **3 take (something) as read.** to take (something) for granted as a fact; understand or presume.

readable ❶ ('riːdəbᵊl) *adj* **1** (of handwriting, etc.) able to be read or deciphered; legible. **2** (of style of writing) interesting, easy, or pleasant to read.
▸ **ˌreada'bility** *or* **'readableness** *n* ▸ **'readably** *adv*

reader ('riːdə) *n* **1** a person who reads. **2** *Chiefly Brit.* a member of staff below a professor but above a senior lecturer at a university. **3a** a book that is part of a planned series for those learning to read. **3b** a standard textbook, esp. for foreign-language learning. **4** a person who reads aloud in public. **5** a person who reads and assesses the merit of manuscripts submitted to a publisher. **6** a proofreader. **7** short for **lay reader.**

readership ('riːdəʃɪp) *n* all the readers collectively of a publication or author: *a readership of five million.*

reading ❶ ('riːdɪŋ) *n* **1a** the act of a person who reads. **1b** (*as modifier*): *a reading room.* **2a** ability to read. **2b** (*as modifier*): *a child of reading age.* **3** any matter that can be read; written or printed text. **4** a public recital or rendering of a literary work. **5** the form of a particular word or passage in a given text, esp. where more than one version exists. **6** an interpretation, as of a piece of music, a situation, or something said or written. **7** knowledge gained from books: *a person of little reading.* **8** a measurement indicated by a gauge, dial, scientific instrument, etc. **9** *Parliamentary procedure.* **9a** the formal recital of the body or title of a bill in a legislative assembly in order to begin one of the stages of its

THESAURUS

reach *vb* **1** = **arrive at,** attain, get as far as, get to, land at, make **2** = **touch,** contact, extend to, get (a) hold of, go as far as, grasp, stretch to **5** *Informal* = **pass,** hand, hold out, stretch **7** = **contact,** communicate with, establish contact with, find, get, get hold of, get in touch with, get through to, make contact with **9** = **come to,** amount to, arrive at, attain, climb to, drop to, fall to, move to, rise to, sink to ◆ *n* **12** = **range,** distance, extension, extent, grasp, stretch, sweep **13** = **power,** ambit, capacity, command, compass, influence, jurisdiction, mastery, scope, spread

react *vb* **1** = **respond,** behave, conduct oneself, function, operate, proceed, work

reaction *n* **1, 2** = **counteraction,** backlash, compensation, counterbalance, counterpoise, recoil **3** = **conservatism,** counter-revolution, obscurantism, the right **4** = **response,** acknowledgment, answer, feedback, reply

reactionary *adj* **1** = **conservative,** blimpish, counter-revolutionary, obscurantist, right-wing ◆ *n* **2** = **conservative,** Colonel Blimp, counter-revolutionary, die-hard, obscurantist, rightist, right-winger
Antonyms *adj, n* ≠ **conservative:** leftist, progressive, radical, reformist, revolutionary, socialist

read[1] *vb* **1** = **look at,** glance at, peruse, pore over, refer to, run one's eye over, scan, study **2** = **recite,** announce, declaim, deliver, speak, utter **3** = **understand,** comprehend, construe, decipher, discover, interpret, perceive the meaning of, see **12** = **register,** display, indicate, record, show

readable *adj* **1** = **legible,** clear, comprehensible, decipherable, intelligible, plain, understandable **2** = **enjoyable,** easy to read, entertaining, enthralling, gripping, interesting, pleasant, worth reading
Antonyms *adj* ≠ **legible:** illegible, incomprehensible, indecipherable, unintelligible, unreadable ≠ **enjoyable:** as dry as dust, badly-written, boring, dull, heavy, heavy going, pretentious, turgid, unreadable

readily *adv* **2** = **willingly,** cheerfully, eagerly, freely, gladly, lief (*rare*), quickly, voluntarily, with good grace, with pleasure **3** = **promptly,** at once, easily, effortlessly, hotfoot, in no time, quickly, right away, smoothly, speedily, straight away, unhesitatingly, without delay, without demur, without difficulty, without hesitation
Antonyms *adv* ≠ **willingly:** reluctantly, unwillingly ≠ **promptly:** hesitatingly, slowly, with difficulty

readiness *n* **1** = **preparedness,** fitness, maturity, preparation, ripeness **2** = **willingness,** aptness, eagerness, gameness (*inf.*), inclination, keenness **3** = **promptness,** promptitude, quickness, rapidity

reading *n* **1a** = **perusal,** examination, inspection, review, scrutiny, study **4** = **recital,** homily, lecture, lesson, performance, rendering, rendition, sermon **6** = **interpretation,** conception, construction, grasp, impression, take (*inf., chiefly US*), treatment, understanding, version **7** = **learning,** book-learning, edification, education, erudition, knowledge, scholarship

passage. **9b** one of the three stages in the passage of a bill through a legislative assembly. See **first reading, second reading, third reading. 10** the formal recital of something written, esp. a will.

read into (riːd) *vb* (*tr, prep*) to discern in or infer from a statement (meanings not intended by the speaker or writer).

read out (riːd) *vb* (*adv*) **1** (*tr*) to read (something) aloud. **2** to retrieve (information) from a computer memory or storage device. **3** (*tr*) *US & Canad.* to expel (someone) from a political party or other society. ◆ *n* **read-out. 4a** the act of retrieving information from a computer memory or storage device. **4b** the information retrieved.

read up (riːd) *vb* (*adv; when intr,* often foll. by *on*) to acquire information about (a subject) by reading intensively.

read-write head (ˈriːdˈraɪt) *n Computing.* an electromagnet that can both read and write information on a magnetic tape or disk.

ready 🅣 (ˈrɛdɪ) *adj* **readier, readiest. 1** in a state of completion or preparedness, as for use or action. **2** willing or eager: *ready helpers.* **3** prompt or rapid: *a ready response.* **4** (*prenominal*) quick in perceiving; intelligent: *a ready mind.* **5** (*postpositive*) (foll. by *to*) on the point (of) or liable (to): *ready to collapse.* **6** (*postpositive*) conveniently near (esp. in **ready to hand**). **7 make** *or* **get ready.** to prepare (oneself or something) for use or action. ◆ *n* **8** *Inf.* (*often preceded by* the) short for **ready money. 9 at** *or* **to the ready. 9a** (of a rifle) in the position adopted prior to aiming and firing. **9b** poised for use or action: *with pen at the ready.* ◆ *vb* **readies, readying, readied. 10** (*tr*) to put in a state of readiness; prepare. [OE (*ge*)*rǣde*]
▸ˈ**readily** *adv* ▸ˈ**readiness** *n*

ready-made *adj* **1** made for purchase and immediate use by any customer. **2** extremely convenient or ideally suited: *a ready-made solution.* **3** unoriginal or conventional: *ready-made phrases.* ◆ *n* **4** a ready-made article, esp. a garment.

ready-mix *n* **1** (*modifier*) consisting of ingredients blended in advance, esp. of food that is ready to cook or eat after addition of milk or water: *a ready-mix cake.* **2** concrete that is mixed before or during delivery to a building site.

ready money *or* **cash** *n* funds for immediate use; cash. Also: **the ready, the readies.**

ready reckoner *n* a table of numbers for facilitating simple calculations, esp. for working out interest, etc.

ready-to-wear *adj* (**ready to wear** *when postpositive*). **1** (of clothes) not tailored for the wearer; of a standard size. ◆ *n* **2** an article or suit of such clothes.

reafforest (ˌriːəˈfɒrɪst) *or* **reforest** *vb* (*tr*) to replant (an area that was formerly forested).
▸ˌ**reafˌforestˈation** *or* ˌ**reforestˈation** *n*

reagent (riːˈeɪdʒənt) *n* a substance for use in a chemical reaction, esp. for use in chemical synthesis and analysis.

real[1] 🅣 (rɪəl) *adj* **1** existing or occurring in the physical world; not imaginary, fictitious, or theoretical; actual. **2** (*prenominal*) true; actual; not false: *the real reason.* **3** (*prenominal*) deserving the name; rightly so called: *a real friend.* **4** not artificial or simulated; genuine: *real fur.* **5** (of food, etc.) traditionally made and having a distinct flavour: *real ale; real cheese.* **6** *Philosophy.* existent or relating to actual existence (as opposed to nonexistent, potential, contingent, or apparent). **7** (*prenominal*) *Econ.* (of prices, incomes, etc.) considered in terms of purchasing power rather than nominal currency value. **8** (*prenominal*) denoting or relating to immovable property such as land and tenements: *real estate.* **9** *Maths.* involving or containing real numbers alone; having no imaginary part. **10** *Inf.* (intensifier): *a real genius.* **11 the real thing.** the genuine article, not a substitute. ◆ *n* **12 for real.** *Sl.* not as a test or trial; in earnest. **13 the real.** that which exists in fact; reality. [C15: from OF *réel,* from LL *reālis,* from L *rēs* thing]
▸ˈ**realness** *n*

real[2] (reɪˈɑːl) *n, pl* **reals** *or* **reales** (*Spanish* reˈales). a former small Spanish or Spanish-American silver coin. [C17: from Sp., lit.: royal, from L *rēgālis;* see REGAL]

real ale *n* any beer which is allowed to ferment in the barrel and which is pumped up from the keg without using carbon dioxide.

real estate *n* another term, chiefly US and Canad., for **real property.**

realgar (rɪˈælgə) *n* a rare orange-red soft mineral consisting of arsenic sulphide in monoclinic crystalline form. [C14: via Med. L from Ar. *rahj al-ghar* powder of the mine]

realism (ˈrɪəˌlɪzəm) *n* **1** awareness or acceptance of the physical universe, events, etc., as they are, as opposed to the abstract or ideal. **2** a style of painting and sculpture that seeks to represent the familiar or typical in real life. **3** any similar style in other arts, esp. literature. **4** *Philosophy.* the thesis that general terms refer to entities that have a real existence separate from the individuals which fall under them. **5** *Philosophy.* the theory that physical objects continue to exist whether they are perceived or not.
▸ˈ**realist** *n*

realistic 🅣 (ˌrɪəˈlɪstɪk) *adj* **1** showing awareness and acceptance of reality. **2** practical or pragmatic rather than ideal or moral. **3** (of a book, etc.) depicting what is real and actual. **4** of or relating to philosophical realism.
▸ˌ**realˈistically** *adv*

reality 🅣 (rɪˈælɪtɪ) *n, pl* **realities. 1** the state of things as they are or appear to be, rather than as one might wish them to be. **2** something that is real. **3** the state of being real. **4** *Philosophy.* **4a** that which exists, independent of human awareness. **4b** the totality of facts. **5 in reality.** actually; in fact.

reality principle *n Psychoanal.* control of behaviour by the ego to meet the conditions imposed by the external world.

realize 🅣 *or* **realise** (ˈrɪəˌlaɪz) *vb* **realizes, realizing, realized** *or* **realises, realising, realised. 1** (when *tr, may take a clause as object*) to become conscious or aware of (something). **2** (*tr, often passive*) to bring (a plan, ambition, etc.) to fruition. **3** (*tr*) to give (a drama or film) the appearance of reality. **4** (*tr*) (of goods, property, etc.) to sell for or make (a certain sum): *this table realized £800.* **5** (*tr*) to convert (property or goods) into cash. **6** (*tr*) (of a musicologist or performer) to reconstruct (a composition) from an incomplete set of parts.
▸ˈ**realˌizable** *or* ˈ**realˌisable** *adj* ▸ˈ**realˌizably** *or* ˈ**realˌisably** *adv* ▸ˌ**realiˈzation** *or* ˌ**realiˈsation** *n* ▸ˈ**realˌizer** *or* ˈ**realˌiser** *n*

real life *n* actual human life, as lived by real people, esp. contrasted with the lives of fictional characters: *miracles don't happen in real life.*

really 🅣 (ˈrɪəlɪ) *adv* **1** in reality; in actuality; assuredly: *it's really quite harmless.* **2** truly; genuinely: *really beautiful.* ◆ *interj* **3** an exclamation of dismay, disapproval, doubt, surprise, etc. **4 not really?** an exclamation of surprise or polite doubt.

USAGE NOTE See at **very.**

realm 🅣 (rɛlm) *n* **1** a royal domain; kingdom: *peer of the realm.* **2** a field of interest, study, etc.: *the realm of the occult.* [C13: from OF *reialme,* from L *regimen* rule, infl. by OF *reial,* from L *rēgālis* REGAL]

real number *n* any rational or irrational number. See **number.**

real presence *n* the doctrine that the body of Christ is actually present in the Eucharist.

real property *n Property law.* immovable property, esp. freehold land. Cf. **personal property.**

real tennis *n* an ancient form of tennis played in a four-walled indoor court.

real-time *adj* denoting or relating to a data-processing system in which a computer is on-line to a source of data and processes the data as it is generated.

realtor (ˈrɪəltə, -ˌtɔː) *n* a US word for an **estate agent,** esp. an accredited one. [C20: from REALTY + -OR[1]]

realty (ˈrɪəltɪ) *n* another term for **real property.**

ream[1] (riːm) *n* **1** a number of sheets of paper, formerly 480 sheets (**short ream**), now 500 sheets (**long ream**) or 516 sheets (**printer's ream** or **perfect**

THESAURUS

ready *adj* **1** = **prepared**, all set, arranged, completed, fit, in readiness, organized, primed, ripe, set **2** = **willing**, agreeable, apt, disposed, eager, game (*inf.*), glad, happy, have-a-go (*inf.*), inclined, keen, minded, predisposed, prone **3** = **prompt**, quick, rapid, smart **4** = **intelligent**, acute, alert, astute, bright, clever, keen, perceptive, quick-witted, sharp, smart **5** *foll. by* **to** = **on the point of**, about to, close to, in danger of, liable to, likely to, on the brink of, on the verge of **6** = **available**, accessible, at *or* on hand, at one's fingertips, at the ready, close to hand, convenient, handy, near, on call, on tap (*inf.*), present ◆ *n* **9b at** *or* **to the ready** = **poised**, all systems go, in readiness, prepared, ready for action, waiting ◆ *vb* **10** = **prepare**, arrange, equip, fit out, get ready, make ready, order, organize, set
Antonyms *adj* ≠ **prepared:** immature, unequipped, unfit, unprepared ≠ **willing:** disinclined, hesitant, loath, reluctant, unprepared, unwilling ≠ **prompt:** slow ≠ **available:** distant, inaccessible, late, unavailable

real[1] *adj* **1** = **actual**, existent, factual, veritable **2** = **true**, genuine **4** = **genuine**, authentic, bona fide, heartfelt, honest, sincere, unaffected, unfeigned
Antonyms *adj* ≠ **genuine:** affected, counterfeit, fake, faked, false, feigned, imitation, insincere

realistic *adj* **1, 2** = **practical**, businesslike, common-sense, down-to-earth, hard-headed, level-headed, matter-of-fact, pragmatic, rational, real, sensible, sober, unromantic, unsentimental **3** = **lifelike**, authentic, faithful, genuine, graphic, natural, naturalistic, representational, true, true to life, truthful, vérité
Antonyms *adj* ≠ **practical:** fanciful, idealistic, impractical, unrealistic

reality *n* **1** = **realism**, truth **2** = **truth**, certainty, fact, verity **3** = **genuineness**, actuality, authenticity, corporeality, materiality, validity, verisimilitude **5 in reality** = **in fact**, actually, as a matter of fact, in actuality, in point of fact, in truth, really

realization *n* **1** = **awareness**, appreciation, apprehension, cognizance, comprehension, conception, consciousness, grasp, imagination, perception, recognition, understanding **2** = **achievement**, accomplishment, carrying-out, completion, consummation, effectuation, fulfilment

realize *vb* **1** = **become aware of**, appreciate, apprehend, be cognizant of, become conscious of, catch on (*inf.*), comprehend, conceive, get the message, grasp, imagine, recognize, take in, twig (*Brit. inf.*), understand **2** = **achieve**, accomplish, actualize, bring about, bring off, bring to fruition, carry out *or* through, complete, consummate, do, effect, effectuate, fulfil, incarnate, make concrete, make happen, perform, reify **4** = **sell for**, acquire, bring *or* take in, clear, earn, gain, get, go for, make, net, obtain, produce

really *adv* **1, 2** = **truly**, absolutely, actually, assuredly, categorically, certainly, genuinely, in actuality, indeed, in fact, in reality, positively, surely, undoubtedly, verily, without a doubt

realm *n* **1** = **kingdom**, country, domain, dominion, empire, land, monarchy, principality, province, state **2** = **field**, area, branch, department, orbit, patch, province, region, sphere, territory, turf (*US sl.*), world, zone

ream). One ream is equal to 20 quires. **2** (*often pl*) *Inf.* a large quantity, esp. of written matter: *he wrote reams.* [C14: from OF, from Sp., from Ar. *rizmah* bale]
ream² (riːm) *vb* (*tr*) **1** to enlarge (a hole) by use of a reamer. **2** *US.* to extract (juice) from (a citrus fruit) using a reamer. [C19: ?from C14 *remen* to open up, from OE *rȳman* to widen]
reamer (ˈriːmə) *n* **1** a steel tool with a cylindrical or tapered shank around which longitudinal teeth are ground, used for smoothing the bores of holes accurately to size. **2** *US.* a utensil with a conical projection used for extracting juice from citrus fruits.
reap ➊ (riːp) *vb* **1** to cut or harvest (a crop) from (a field). **2** (*tr*) to gain or get (something) as a reward for or result of some action or enterprise. [OE *riopan*]
▸ˈ**reapable** *adj*
reaper (ˈriːpə) *n* **1** a person who reaps or a machine for reaping. **2 the grim reaper.** death.
rear¹ ➊ (rɪə) *n* **1** the back or hind part. **2** the area or position that lies at the back: *a garden at the rear of the house.* **3** the section of a military force farthest from the front. **4** an informal word for **buttocks** (see **buttock**). **5 bring up the rear.** to be at the back in a procession, race, etc. **6 in the rear.** at the back. **7** (*modifier*) of or in the rear: *the rear side.* [C17: prob. from REARWARD or REARGUARD]
rear² ➊ (rɪə) *vb* **1** (*tr*) to care for and educate (children) until maturity; raise. **2** (*tr*) to breed (animals) or grow (plants). **3** (*tr*) to place or lift (a ladder, etc.) upright. **4** (*tr*) to erect (a monument, building, etc.). **5** (*intr; often foll. by up*) (esp. of horses) to lift the front legs in the air and stand nearly upright. **6** (*intr; often foll. by up or over*) (esp. of tall buildings) to rise high; tower. **7** (*intr*) to start with anger, resentment, etc. [OE *rǣran*]
▸ˈ**rearer** *n*
rear admiral *n* an officer holding flag rank in any of certain navies, junior to a vice admiral.
rearguard (ˈrɪəˌgɑːd) *n* **1** a detachment detailed to protect the rear of a military formation, esp. in retreat. **2** an entrenched or conservative element, as in a political party. **3** (*modifier*) of, relating to, or characteristic of a rearguard: *a rearguard action.* [C15: from OF *rereguarde,* from *rer,* from L *retro* back + *guarde* GUARD]
rear light *or* **lamp** *n* a red light, usually one of a pair, attached to the rear of a motor vehicle. Also called: **tail-light, tail lamp.**
rearm (riːˈɑːm) *vb* **1** to arm again. **2** (*tr*) to equip (an army, etc.) with better weapons.
▸**reˈarmament** *n*
rearmost (ˈrɪəˌməʊst) *adj* nearest the rear; coming last.
rear-view mirror *n* a mirror on a motor vehicle enabling the driver to see traffic behind him.
rearward (ˈrɪəwəd) *adj, adv* **1** Also (for adv only): **rearwards.** towards or in the rear. ◆ *n* **2** a position in the rear, esp. the rear division of a military formation. [C14 (*as n:* the part of an army behind the main body of troops): from Anglo-F *rerewarde,* var. of *reregarde;* see REARGUARD]
reason ➊ (ˈriːzᵊn) *n* **1** the faculty of rational argument, deduction, judgment, etc. **2** sound mind; sanity. **3** a cause or motive, as for a belief, action, etc. **4** an argument in favour or a justification for something. **5** *Philosophy.* the intellect regarded as a source of knowledge, as contrasted with experience. **6** *Logic.* a premise of an argument in favour of the given conclusion. **7 by reason of.** because of. **8 in** *or* **within reason.** within moderate or justifiable bounds. **9 it stands to reason.** it is logical or obvious. **10 listen to reason.** to be persuaded peaceably. **11 reasons of State.** political justifications for an immoral act. ◆ *vb* **12** (*when tr, takes a clause as object*) to think logically or draw (logical conclusions) from facts or premises. **13** (*intr; usually foll. by with*) to seek to persuade by reasoning. **14** (*tr; often foll. by out*) to work out or resolve (a problem) by reasoning. [C13: from OF *reisun,* from L *ratiō* reckoning, from *rērī* to think]
▸ˈ**reasoner** *n*

> **USAGE NOTE** The expression *the reason is because...* should be avoided. Instead one should say either *this is because...* or *the reason is that...*

reasonable ➊ (ˈriːzənəbᵊl) *adj* **1** showing reason or sound judgment. **2** having the ability to reason. **3** having modest or moderate expectations. **4** moderate in price. **5** fair; average: *reasonable weather.*
▸ˈ**reasonably** *adv* ▸ˈ**reasonableness** *n*
reasoned ➊ (ˈriːzᵊnd) *adj* well thought-out or well presented: *a reasoned explanation.*
reasoning ➊ (ˈriːzənɪŋ) *n* **1** the act or process of drawing conclusions from facts, evidence, etc. **2** the arguments, proofs, etc., so adduced.
reassure ➊ (ˌriːəˈʃʊə) *vb* **reassures, reassuring, reassured.** (*tr*) **1** to relieve (someone) of anxieties; restore confidence to. **2** to insure again.
▸ˌ**reasˈsurance** *n* ▸ˌ**reasˈsurer** *n* ▸ˌ**reasˈsuringly** *adv*
Réaumur (ˈreɪəˌmjʊə) *adj* indicating measurement on the Réaumur scale.
Réaumur scale *n* a scale of temperature in which the freezing point of water is taken as 0° and the boiling point as 80°. [C18: after René de *Réaumur* (1683–1757), F physicist, who introduced it]
reave (riːv) *vb* **reaves, reaving, reaved** *or* **reft.** *Arch.* **1** to carry off (property, prisoners, etc.) by force. **2** (*tr;* foll. by *of*) to deprive; strip. See **reive.** [OE *reāfian*]
rebarbative (rɪˈbɑːbətɪv) *adj* fearsome; forbidding. [C19: from F *rébarbatif,* from OF *rebarber* to repel (an enemy)]
rebate¹ ➊ *n* (ˈriːbeɪt). **1** a refund of a fraction of the amount payable; discount. ◆ *vb* (rɪˈbeɪt), **rebates, rebating, rebated.** (*tr*) **2** to deduct (a part) of a payment from (the total). **3** *Arch.* to reduce. [C15: from OF *rabattre* to beat down, hence reduce, from RE- + *abatre* to put down]
▸**reˈbatable** *or* **reˈbateable** *adj* ▸ˈ**rebater** *n*
rebate² (ˈriːbeɪt, ˈræbɪt) *n, vb* **rebates, rebating, rebated.** another word for **rabbet.**
rebec *or* **rebeck** (ˈriːbɛk) *n* a medieval stringed instrument resembling the violin but having a lute-shaped body. [C16: from OF *rebebe,* from Ar. *rebāb;* ? infl. by OF *bec* beak]
rebel ➊ *vb* (rɪˈbɛl), **rebels, rebelling, rebelled.** (*intr; often foll. by against*) **1** to resist or rise up against a government or authority, esp. by force of arms. **2** to dissent from an accepted moral code or convention of behaviour, etc. **3** to show repugnance (towards). ◆ *n* (ˈrɛbᵊl). **4a** a person who rebels. **4b** (*as modifier*): *a rebel soldier.* **5** a person who dissents from some accepted moral code or convention of behaviour, etc. [C13: from OF *rebelle,* from L *rebellis* insurgent, from RE- + *bellum* war]
rebellion ➊ (rɪˈbɛljən) *n* **1** organized opposition to a government or other authority. **2** dissent from an accepted moral code or convention of behaviour, etc. [C14: via OF from L *rebelliō* revolt (of those conquered); see REBEL]
rebellious ➊ (rɪˈbɛljəs) *adj* **1** showing a tendency towards rebellion. **2** (of a problem, etc.) difficult to overcome; refractory.
▸**reˈbelliously** *adv* ▸**reˈbelliousness** *n*
rebirth ➊ (riːˈbɜːθ) *n* **1** a revival or renaissance: *the rebirth of learning.* **2** a second or new birth.

THESAURUS

reap *vb* **1 = collect**, bring in, cut, garner, gather, harvest **2 = get**, acquire, derive, gain, obtain, win
rear¹ *n* **1 = back**, back end, end, rearguard, stern, tail, tail end ◆ *modifier* **7 = back**, aft, after (*Nautical*), following, hind, hindmost, last, trailing
Antonyms *n* ≠ **back**: bow, forward end, front, nose, stem, vanguard ◆ *modifier* ≠ **back**: foremost, forward, front, leading
rear² *vb* **1 = bring up**, care for, educate, foster, nurse, nurture, raise, train **2 = breed**, cultivate, grow **3 = raise**, elevate, hoist, hold up, lift, set upright **4 = build**, construct, erect, fabricate, put up **6 = rise**, loom, soar, tower
reason *n* **1 = logic**, apprehension, brains, comprehension, intellect, judgment, ratiocination, reasoning, sense, understanding **2 = sanity**, mentality, mind, rationality, sense, sound mind, soundness **3 = cause**, aim, basis, design, end, goal, grounds, impetus, incentive, inducement, intention, motive, object, occasion, purpose, target, warrant, why and wherefore (*inf.*) **4 = justification**, apologia, apology, argument, case, defence, excuse, explanation, exposition, ground, rationale, vindication **8 in** *or* **within reason = in moderation**, proper, reasonable, sensible, warrantable, within bounds, within limits ◆ *vb* **12 = deduce**, conclude, draw conclusions, infer, make out, ratiocinate, resolve, solve, syllogize, think, work out **13** *usually foll. by* **with = persuade**, argue with, bring round, debate with, dispute with, dissuade, expostulate with, move, prevail upon, remonstrate with, show (someone) the error of his ways, talk into *or* out of, urge, win over
Antonyms *n* ≠ **logic**: emotion, feeling, instinct, sentiment
reasonable *adj* **1 = sensible**, advisable, arguable, believable, credible, intelligent, judicious, justifiable, logical, plausible, practical, reasoned, tenable, well-advised, well-thought-out, wise **2 = sane**, rational, sober, sound **3, 4 = fair**, acceptable, equitable, fit, just, moderate, proper, right, within reason **5 = average**, fair, moderate, modest, O.K. *or* okay (*inf.*), tolerable
Antonyms *adj* ≠ **sensible**: impossible, irrational, unintelligent, unreasonable, unsound ≠ **fair**: unfair, unreasonable
reasoned *adj* **= sensible**, clear, judicious, logical, systematic, well-expressed, well-presented, well-thought-out
reasoning *n* **1 = thinking**, analysis, cogitation, deduction, logic, ratiocination, reason, thought **2 = case**, argument, exposition, hypothesis, interpretation, proof, train of thought
reassure *vb* **1 = encourage**, bolster, buoy up, cheer up, comfort, gee up, hearten, inspirit, put *or* set one's mind at rest, relieve (someone) of anxiety, restore confidence to
rebate¹ *n* **1 = refund**, allowance, bonus, deduction, discount, reduction
rebel *vb* **1 = revolt**, man the barricades, mutiny, resist, rise up, take to the streets, take up arms **2 = defy**, come out against, dig one's heels in (*inf.*), disobey, dissent, refuse to obey **3 = recoil**, flinch, show repugnance, shrink, shy away ◆ *n* **4a = revolutionary**, insurgent, insurrectionary, mutineer, resistance fighter, revolutionist, secessionist ◆ *modifier* **4b = rebellious**, insubordinate, insurgent, insurrectionary, mutinous, revolutionary ◆ *n* **5 = nonconformist**, apostate, dissenter, heretic, schismatic
rebellion *n* **1 = resistance**, insurgence, insurgency, insurrection, mutiny, revolt, revolution, rising, uprising **2 = nonconformity**, apostasy, defiance, disobedience, dissent, heresy, insubordination, schism
rebellious *adj* **1 = revolutionary**, disaffected, disloyal, disobedient, disorderly, insubordinate, insurgent, insurrectionary, mutinous, rebel, recalcitrant, seditious, turbulent, ungovernable, unruly **2 = defiant**, contumacious, difficult, incorrigible, intractable, obstinate, recalcitrant, refractory, resistant, unmanageable
Antonyms *adj* ≠ **revolutionary:** dutiful, loyal, obedient, patriotic, subordinate ≠ **defiant:** dutiful, obedient, subservient
rebirth *n* **1 = revival**, new beginning, regeneration, reincarnation, renaissance, renascence, renewal, restoration, resurgence, resurrection, revitalization

reboot (riːˈbuːt) *vb* to shut down and then restart (a computer system) or (of a computer system) to shut down and restart.

rebore *n* (ˈriːˌbɔː). **1** the process of boring out the cylinders of a worn reciprocating engine and fitting oversize pistons. ◆ *vb* (riːˈbɔː), **rebores, reboring, rebored. 2** (*tr*) to carry out this process.

rebound ⓣ *vb* (rɪˈbaʊnd). (*intr*) **1** to spring back, as from a sudden impact. **2** to misfire, esp. so as to hurt the perpetrator. ◆ *n* (ˈriːbaʊnd). **3** the act or an instance of rebounding. **4 on the rebound. 4a** in the act of springing back. **4b** *Inf.* in a state of recovering from rejection, etc.: *he married her on the rebound from an unhappy love affair.* [C14: from OF *rebondir,* from RE- + *bondir* to BOUND[2]]

rebounder (rɪˈbaʊndə) *n* a type of small trampoline used for aerobic exercising.

rebozo (rɪˈbəʊzəʊ) *n, pl* **rebozos.** a long wool or linen scarf covering the shoulders and head, worn by Latin American women. [C19: from Sp., from *rebozar* to muffle]

rebrand (ˌriːˈbrænd) *vb* (*tr*) to change or update the image of (an organization or product).

rebuff ⓣ (rɪˈbʌf) *vb* (*tr*) **1** to snub, reject, or refuse (help, sympathy, etc.). **2** to beat back (an attack); repel. ◆ *n* **3** a blunt refusal or rejection; snub. [C16: from OF *rebuffer,* from It., from *ribuffo* a reprimand, from *ri-* RE- + *buffo* puff, gust, apparently imit.]

rebuke ⓣ (rɪˈbjuːk) *vb* **rebukes, rebuking, rebuked. 1** (*tr*) to scold or reprimand (someone). ◆ *n* **2** a reprimand or scolding. [C14: from OF *rebuker,* from RE- + *buchier* to hack down, from *busche* log, of Gmc origin]
▸**reˈbukable** *adj* ▸**reˈbuker** *n* ▸**reˈbukingly** *adv*

rebus (ˈriːbəs) *n, pl* **rebuses. 1** a puzzle consisting of pictures, symbols, etc., representing syllables and words; the word *hear* might be represented by H and a picture of an ear. **2** a heraldic device that is a pictorial representation of the name of the bearer. [C17: from F *rébus,* from L *rēbus* by things, from RES]

rebut ⓣ (rɪˈbʌt) *vb* **rebuts, rebutting, rebutted.** (*tr*) to refute or disprove, esp. by offering a contrary contention or argument. [C13: from OF *reboter,* from RE- + *boter* to thrust, BUTT[3]]
▸**reˈbuttable** *adj* ▸**reˈbuttal** *n*

rebutter (rɪˈbʌtə) *n* **1** *Law.* a defendant's pleading in reply to a plaintiff's surrejoinder. **2** a person who rebuts.

rec. *abbrev. for:* **1** receipt. **2** recipe. **3** record.

recalcitrant ⓣ (rɪˈkælsɪtrənt) *adj* **1** not susceptible to control; refractory. ◆ *n* **2** a recalcitrant person. [C19: via F from L, from RE- + *calcitrāre* to kick, from *calx* heel]
▸**reˈcalcitrance** *n*

recalescence (ˌriːkəˈlɛsəns) *n* a sudden spontaneous increase in the temperature of cooling iron. [C19: from L *recalēscere* to grow warm again, from RE- + *calēscere,* from *calēre* to be hot]
▸ˌ**recalˈesce** *vb* (*intr*) ▸ˌ**recaˈlescent** *adj*

recall ⓣ (rɪˈkɔːl) *vb* (*tr*) **1** (*may take a clause as object*) to bring back to mind; recollect; remember. **2** to order to return. **3** to revoke or take back. **4** to cause (one's thoughts, attention, etc.) to return from a reverie or digression. ◆ *n* **5** the act of recalling or state of being recalled. **6** revocation or cancellation. **7** the ability to remember things; recollection. **8** *Mil.* (formerly) a signal to call back troops, etc. **9** *US.* the process by which elected officials may be deprived of office by popular vote.
▸**reˈcallable** *adj*

recant ⓣ (rɪˈkænt) *vb* to repudiate or withdraw (a former belief or statement), esp. formally in public. [C16: from L *recantāre,* from RE- + *cantāre* to sing]
▸**recantation** (ˌriːkænˈteɪʃən) *n* ▸**reˈcanter** *n*

recap *vb* (ˈriːˌkæp, riːˈkæp), **recaps, recapping, recapped,** *n* (ˈriːˌkæp). *Inf.* short for **recapitulate** *or* **recapitulation.**
▸**reˈcappable** *adj*

recapitulate ⓣ (ˌriːkəˈpɪtjʊˌleɪt) *vb* **recapitulates, recapitulating, recapitulated. 1** to restate the main points of (an argument, speech, etc.). **2** (*tr*) (of an animal) to repeat (stages of its evolutionary development) during the embryonic stages of its life. [C16: from LL *recapitulāre,* lit.: to put back under headings; see CAPITULATE]
▸ˌ**recaˈpitulative** *or* ˌ**recaˈpitulatory** *adj*

recapitulation (ˌriːkəˌpɪtjʊˈleɪʃən) *n* **1** the act of recapitulating, esp. summing up, as at the end of a speech. **2** Also called: **palingenesis.** *Biol.* the apparent repetition in the embryonic development of an animal of the changes that occurred during its evolutionary history. **3** *Music.* the repeating of earlier themes, esp. in the final section of a movement in sonata form.

recapture (riːˈkæptʃə) *vb* **recaptures, recapturing, recaptured.** (*tr*) **1** to capture or take again. **2** to recover, renew, or repeat (a lost or former ability, sensation, etc.). ◆ *n* **3** the act of recapturing or fact of being recaptured.

recce (ˈrɛkɪ) *n, vb* **recces, recceing, recced** *or* **recceed.** a slang word for **reconnaissance** or **reconnoitre.**

recd *or* **rec'd** *abbrev. for* received.

recede ⓣ (rɪˈsiːd) *vb* **recedes, receding, receded.** (*intr*) **1** to withdraw from a point or limit; go back: *the tide receded.* **2** to become more distant: *hopes of rescue receded.* **3** to slope backwards: *apes have receding foreheads.* **4a** (of a man's hair) to cease to grow at the temples and above the forehead. **4b** (of a man) to start to go bald in this way. **5** to decline in value. **6** (usually foll. by *from*) to draw back or retreat, as from a promise. [C15: from L *recēdere* to go back, from RE- + *cēdere* to yield]

re-cede (riːˈsiːd) *vb* **re-cedes, re-ceding, re-ceded.** (*tr*) to restore to a former owner.

receipt ⓣ (rɪˈsiːt) *n* **1** a written acknowledgment by a receiver of money, goods, etc., that payment or delivery has been made. **2** the act of receiving or fact of being received. **3** (*usually pl*) an amount or article received. **4** *Obs.* another word for **recipe.** ◆ *vb* **5** (*tr*) to acknowledge payment of (a bill), as by marking it. [C14: from OF *receite,* from Med. L *recepta,* from L *recipere* to RECEIVE]

receivable (rɪˈsiːvəbᵊl) *adj* **1** suitable for or capable of being received, esp. as payment or legal tender. **2** (of a bill, etc.) awaiting payment: *accounts receivable.* ◆ *n* **3** (*usually pl*) the part of the assets of a business represented by accounts due for payment.

receive ⓣ (rɪˈsiːv) *vb* **receives, receiving, received.** (*mainly tr*) **1** to take (something offered) into one's hand or possession. **2** to have (an honour, blessing, etc.) bestowed. **3** to accept delivery or transmission of (a letter, etc.). **4** to be informed of (news). **5** to hear and consent to or acknowledge (a confession, etc.). **6** (of a container) to take or hold (a substance, commodity, or certain amount). **7** to support or sustain (the weight of something); bear. **8** to apprehend or perceive (ideas, etc.). **9** to experience, undergo, or meet with: *to receive a crack on the skull.* **10** (*also intr*) to be at home to (visitors). **11** to greet or welcome (guests), esp. in formal style. **12** to admit (a person) to a place, society, condition, etc.: *he was received into the priesthood.* **13** to accept or acknowledge (a precept or principle) as true or valid. **14** to convert (incoming radio signals) into sounds, pictures, etc., by means of a receiver. **15** (*also intr*) *Tennis, etc.* to play at the other end from the server. **16** (*also intr*) to partake of (the Christian Eucharist). **17** (*intr*) *Chiefly Brit.* to buy and sell stolen goods. [C13: from OF *receivre,* from L *recipere,* from RE- + *capere* to take]

received (rɪˈsiːvd) *adj* generally accepted or believed: *received wisdom.*

Received Pronunciation *n* the accent of standard Southern British English. Abbrev.: **RP.**

receiver (rɪˈsiːvə) *n* **1** a person who receives something; recipient. **2** a person appointed by a court to manage property pending the outcome of litigation, during the infancy of the owner, or after the owner has been declared bankrupt or insane. **3** *Chiefly Brit.* a person

THESAURUS

rebound *vb* **1** = **bounce,** recoil, resound, return, ricochet, spring back **2** = **misfire,** backfire, boomerang, recoil ◆ *n* **3** = **bounce,** comeback, kickback, repercussion, return, ricochet

rebuff *vb* **1** = **reject,** brush off, check, cold-shoulder, cut, decline, deny, discourage, knock back (*sl.*), put off, refuse, repulse, resist, slight, snub, spurn, turn down ◆ *n* **3** = **rejection,** brush-off (*sl.*), check, cold shoulder, defeat, denial, discouragement, kick in the teeth (*sl.*), knock-back (*sl.*), opposition, refusal, repulse, slap in the face (*inf.*), slight, snub, thumbs down
Antonyms *vb* ≠ **reject:** encourage, lead on (*inf.*), submit to, welcome ◆ *n* ≠ **rejection:** come-on (*inf.*), encouragement, thumbs up, welcome

rebuke *vb* **1** = **scold,** admonish, bawl out (*inf.*), berate, blame, carpet (*inf.*), castigate, censure, chew out (*US & Canad. inf.*), chide, dress down (*inf.*), give a rocket (*Brit. & NZ inf.*), haul (someone) over the coals (*inf.*), lecture, read the riot act, reprehend, reprimand, reproach, reprove, take to task, tear into (*inf.*), tear (someone) off a strip (*inf.*), tell off (*inf.*), tick off (*inf.*), upbraid ◆ *n* **2** = **scolding,** admonition, blame, castigation, censure, dressing down (*inf.*), lecture, reprimand, reproach, reproof, reproval, row, telling-off (*inf.*), ticking-off (*inf.*), tongue-lashing
Antonyms *vb* ≠ **scold:** applaud, approve, commend, compliment, congratulate, laud, praise ◆ *n* ≠ **scolding:** commendation, compliment, laudation, praise

rebut *vb* = **disprove,** confute, defeat, invalidate, negate, overturn, prove wrong, quash, refute

rebuttal *n* = **disproof,** confutation, defeat, invalidation, negation, refutation

recalcitrant *adj* **1** = **disobedient,** contrary, contumacious, defiant, insubordinate, intractable, obstinate, refractory, stubborn, uncontrollable, ungovernable, unmanageable, unruly, unwilling, wayward, wilful
Antonyms *adj* amenable, compliant, docile, obedient, submissive

recall *vb* **1** = **recollect,** bring *or* call to mind, call *or* summon up, evoke, look *or* think back to, mind (*dialect*), remember, reminisce about **3** = **annul,** abjure, call back, call in, cancel, countermand, nullify, repeal, rescind, retract, revoke, take back, withdraw ◆ *n* **6** = **annulment,** cancellation, nullification, recision, repeal, rescindment, rescission, retraction, revocation, withdrawal **7** = **recollection,** memory, remembrance

recant *vb* = **withdraw,** abjure, apostatize, deny, disavow, disclaim, disown, forswear, recall, renege, renounce, repudiate, retract, revoke, take back, unsay
Antonyms *vb* insist, maintain, profess, reaffirm, reiterate, repeat, restate, uphold

recapitulate *vb* **1** = **restate,** epitomize, go over again, outline, recap (*inf.*), recount, reiterate, repeat, review, run over, run through again, summarize, sum up

recede *vb* **1** = **fall back,** abate, back off, draw back, ebb, go back, regress, retire, retreat, retrocede, retrogress, return, subside, withdraw **5** = **lessen,** decline, diminish, dwindle, fade, shrink, sink, wane

receipt *n* **1** = **sales slip,** acknowledgment, counterfoil, proof of purchase, stub, voucher **2** = **receiving,** acceptance, delivery, reception, recipience **3** *usually plural* = **takings,** gains, gate, income, proceeds, profits, return

receive *vb* **1** = **get,** accept, accept delivery of, acquire, be given, be in receipt of, collect, derive, obtain, pick up, take **4** = **be informed of,** be told, gather, hear **8** = **perceive,** apprehend **9** = **experience,** bear, be subjected to, encounter,

who receives stolen goods knowing that they have been stolen. **4** the equipment in a telephone, radio, or television that receives incoming electrical signals or modulated radio waves and converts them into the original audio or video signals. **5** the detachable part of a telephone that is held to the ear. **6** *Chem.* a vessel in which the distillate is collected during distillation. **7** *US sport.* a player whose function is to receive the ball.

receivership (rɪˈsiːvəʃɪp) *n Law.* **1** the office or function of a receiver. **2** the condition of being administered by a receiver.

receiving order *n Brit.* a court order appointing a receiver to manage the property of a debtor or bankrupt.

recension (rɪˈsɛnʃən) *n* **1** a critical revision of a literary work. **2** a text revised in this way. [C17: from L *recēnsiō,* from *recēnsēre,* from RE- + *cēnsēre* to assess]

recent Ⓣ (ˈriːsᵊnt) *adj* having appeared, happened, or been made not long ago; modern, fresh, or new. [C16: from L *recens* fresh; rel. to Gk *kainos* new]
▸**ˈrecently** *adv* ▸**ˈrecentness** *or* **ˈrecency** *n*

Recent (ˈriːsᵊnt) *adj, n Geol.* another word for **Holocene.**

receptacle Ⓣ (rɪˈsɛptəkᵊl) *n* **1** an object that holds something; container. **2** *Bot.* **2a** the enlarged or modified tip of the flower stalk that bears the parts of the flower. **2b** the part of lower plants that bears the reproductive organs or spores. [C15: from L *receptāculum* store-place, from *receptāre,* from *recipere* to RECEIVE]

reception Ⓣ (rɪˈsɛpʃən) *n* **1** the act of receiving or state of being received. **2** the manner in which something, such as a guest or a new idea, is received: *a cold reception.* **3** a formal party for guests, such as after a wedding. **4** an area in an office, hotel, etc., where visitors or guests are received and appointments or reservations dealt with. **5** short for **reception room. 6** the quality or fidelity of a received radio or television broadcast: *the reception was poor.* [C14: from L *receptiō,* from *recipere* to RECEIVE]

reception centre *n* a place to which distressed people, such as vagrants, addicts, victims of a disaster, refugees, etc., go pending more permanent arrangements.

receptionist (rɪˈsɛpʃənɪst) *n* a person employed in an office, surgery, etc., to receive clients or guests, arrange appointments, etc.

reception room *n* **1** a room in a private house suitable for entertaining guests. **2** a room in a hotel suitable for receptions, etc.

receptive Ⓣ (rɪˈsɛptɪv) *adj* **1** able to apprehend quickly. **2** tending to receive new ideas or suggestions favourably. **3** able to hold or receive.
▸**reˈceptively** *adv* ▸**receptivity** (ˌriːsɛpˈtɪvɪtɪ) *or* **reˈceptiveness** *n*

receptor (rɪˈsɛptə) *n* **1** *Physiol.* a sensory nerve ending that changes specific stimuli into nerve impulses. **2** any of various devices that receive information, signals, etc.

recess Ⓣ *n* (rɪˈsɛs, ˈriːsɛs). **1** a space, such as a niche or alcove, set back or indented. **2** (*often pl*) a secluded or secret place: *recesses of the mind.* **3** a cessation of business, such as the closure of Parliament during a vacation. **4** *Anat.* a small cavity or depression in a bodily organ. **5** *US & Canad.* a break between classes at a school. ◆ *vb* (rɪˈsɛs). **6** (*tr*) to place or set (something) in a recess. **7** (*tr*) to build a recess in (a wall, etc.). [C16: from L *recessus* a retreat, from *recēdere* to RECEDE]

recession[1] Ⓣ (rɪˈsɛʃən) *n* **1** a temporary depression in economic activity or prosperity. **2** the withdrawal of the clergy and choir in procession after a church service. **3** the act of receding. **4** a part of a building, wall, etc., that recedes. [C17: from L *recessio;* see RECESS]

recession[2] (riːˈsɛʃən) *n* the act of restoring possession to a former owner. [C19: from RE- + CESSION]

recessional (rɪˈsɛʃənᵊl) *adj* **1** of or relating to recession. ◆ *n* **2** a hymn sung as the clergy and choir withdraw after a church service.

recessive (rɪˈsɛsɪv) *adj* **1** tending to recede or go back. **2** *Genetics.* **2a** (of a gene) capable of producing its characteristic phenotype in the organism only when its allele is identical. **2b** (of a character) controlled by such a gene. Cf. **dominant** (sense 4). **3** *Linguistics.* (of stress) tending to be placed on or near the initial syllable of a polysyllabic word. ◆ *n* **4** *Genetics.* a recessive gene or character.
▸**reˈcessively** *adv* ▸**reˈcessiveness** *n*

recharge (ˌriːˈtʃɑːdʒ) *vb* **recharges, recharging, recharged.** (*tr*) **1** to cause (an accumulator, capacitor, etc.) to take up and store electricity again. **2** to revive or renew (one's energies) (esp. in **recharge one's batteries**).
▸**reˈchargeable** *adj*

recherché Ⓣ (rəˈʃɛəʃeɪ) *adj* **1** known only to connoisseurs; choice or rare. **2** studiedly refined or elegant. [C18: from F: p.p. of *rechercher* to make a thorough search for]

recidivism (rɪˈsɪdɪˌvɪzəm) *n* habitual relapse into crime. [C19: from L *recidīvus* falling back, from RE- + *cadere* to fall]
▸**reˈcidivist** *n, adj* ▸**reˌcidiˈvistic** *or* **reˈcidivous** *adj*

recipe Ⓣ (ˈrɛsɪpɪ) *n* **1** a list of ingredients and directions for making something, esp. when preparing food. **2** *Med.* (formerly) a medical prescription. **3** a method for achieving some desired objective: *a recipe for success.* [C14: from L, lit.: take (it)! from *recipere* to take]

recipient (rɪˈsɪpɪənt) *n* **1** a person who or thing that receives. ◆ *adj* **2** receptive. [C16: via F from L, from *recipere* to RECEIVE]
▸**reˈcipience** *or* **reˈcipiency** *n*

reciprocal Ⓣ (rɪˈsɪprəkᵊl) *adj* **1** of, relating to, or designating something given by each of two people, countries, etc., to the other; mutual: *reciprocal trade.* **2** given or done in return: *a reciprocal favour.* **3** (of a pronoun) indicating that action is given and received by each subject; for example, *each other* in *they started to shout at each other.* **4** *Maths.* of or relating to a number or quantity divided into one. ◆ *n* **5** something that is reciprocal. **6** Also called: **inverse.** *Maths.* a number or quantity that when multiplied by a given number or quantity gives a product of one: *the reciprocal of 2 is 0.5.* [C16: from L *reciprocus* alternating]
▸**reˌciproˈcality** *n* ▸**reˈciprocally** *adv*

reciprocate Ⓣ (rɪˈsɪprəˌkeɪt) *vb* **reciprocates, reciprocating, reciprocated. 1** to give or feel in return. **2** to move or cause to move backwards and forwards. **3** (*intr*) to be correspondent or equivalent. [C17: from L *reciprocāre,* from *reciprocus* RECIPROCAL]
▸**reˌcipro'cation** *n* ▸**reˈciprocative** *or* **reˈcipro,catory** *adj* ▸**reˈcipro,cator** *n*

reciprocating engine *n* an engine in which one or more pistons move backwards and forwards inside a cylinder or cylinders.

reciprocity (ˌrɛsɪˈprɒsɪtɪ) *n* **1** reciprocal action or relation. **2** a mutual exchange of commercial or other privileges. [C18: via F from L *reciprocus* RECIPROCAL]

recision (rɪˈsɪʒən) *n* the act of cancelling or rescinding; annulment: *the recision of a treaty.* [C17: from L *recīsiō,* from *recīdere* to cut back]

recital Ⓣ (rɪˈsaɪtᵊl) *n* **1** a musical performance by a soloist or soloists. **2** the act of reciting or repeating something learned or prepared. **3** an account, narration, or description. **4** (*often pl*) *Law.* the preliminary statement in a deed showing the reason for its existence and explaining the operative part.
▸**reˈcitalist** *n*

recitation Ⓣ (ˌrɛsɪˈteɪʃən) *n* **1a** the act of reciting from memory. **1b** a formal reading of verse before an audience. **2** something recited.

recitative[1] (ˌrɛsɪtəˈtiːv) *n* a passage in a musical composition, esp. the narrative parts in an oratorio, reflecting the natural rhythms of speech. [C17: from It. *recitativo;* see RECITE]

recitative[2] (rɪˈsaɪtətɪv) *adj* of or relating to recital.

recite Ⓣ (rɪˈsaɪt) *vb* **recites, reciting, recited. 1** to repeat (a poem, etc.) aloud from memory before an audience. **2** (*tr*) to give a detailed account of. **3** (*tr*) to enumerate (examples, etc.). [C15: from L *recitāre* to cite again, from RE- + *citāre* to summon]
▸**reˈcitable** *adj* ▸**reˈciter** *n*

reck (rɛk) *vb Arch.* (*used mainly with a negative*) **1** to mind or care about (something): *to reck nought.* **2** (*usually impersonal*) to concern or interest (someone). [OE *reccan*]

reckless Ⓣ (ˈrɛklɪs) *adj* having or showing no regard for danger or consequences; heedless; rash: *a reckless driver.* [OE *recceleās;* see RECK, -LESS]
▸**ˈrecklessly** *adv* ▸**ˈrecklessness** *n*

THESAURUS

go through, meet with, suffer, sustain, undergo **10, 11** = **greet**, accommodate, admit, be at home to, entertain, meet, take in, welcome

recent *adj* = **new**, contemporary, current, fresh, happening (*inf.*), late, latter, latter-day, modern, novel, present-day, up-to-date, young
Antonyms *adj* ancient, antique, earlier, early, former, historical, old

recently *adv* = **newly**, currently, freshly, lately, latterly, not long ago, of late

receptacle *n* **1** = **container**, holder, repository

reception *n* **1** = **receiving**, acceptance, admission, receipt, recipience **2** = **response**, acknowledgment, greeting, reaction, recognition, treatment, welcome **3** = **party**, do (*inf.*), entertainment, function, levee, soirée

receptive *adj* **1** = **perceptive**, alert, bright, quick on the uptake (*inf.*), responsive, sensitive **2** = **open**, accessible, amenable, approachable, favourable, friendly, hospitable, interested, open-minded, open to suggestions, susceptible, sympathetic, welcoming
Antonyms *adj* ≠ **perceptive:** unreceptive, unresponsive ≠ **open:** biased, narrow-minded, prejudiced, unreceptive, unresponsive

recess *n* **1** = **alcove**, bay, cavity, corner, depression, hollow, indentation, niche, nook, oriel **2** *often plural* = **depths**, bowels, heart, innards (*inf.*), innermost parts, reaches, retreats, secret places **3** = **break**, cessation of business, closure, holiday, intermission, interval, respite, rest, vacation

recession[1] *n* **1** = **depression**, decline, downturn, drop, slump
Antonyms *n* boom, upturn

recherché *adj* **1** = **rare**, arcane, choice, esoteric, exotic

recipe *n* **1** = **directions**, ingredients, instructions, receipt (*obs.*) **3** = **method**, formula, modus operandi, prescription, procedure, process, programme, technique

reciprocal *adj* **1, 2** = **mutual**, alternate, complementary, correlative, corresponding, equivalent, exchanged, give-and-take, interchangeable, interdependent, reciprocative, reciprocatory
Antonyms *adj* one-way, unilateral, unreciprocated

reciprocate *vb* **1** = **return**, barter, exchange, feel in return, interchange, reply, requite, respond, return the compliment, swap, trade **3** = **be equivalent**, correspond, equal, match

recital *n* **1** = **performance**, rehearsal, rendering **2** = **recitation**, repetition **3** = **account**, description, detailing, narration, narrative, recapitulation, relation, statement, story, tale, telling

recitation *n* **1** = **recital**, lecture, narration, performance, reading, rendering, telling **2** = **piece**, passage

recite *vb* **1** = **repeat**, declaim, deliver, do one's party piece (*inf.*), narrate, perform, rehearse, speak **2** = **recount**, describe, detail, recapitulate, relate, tell **3** = **enumerate**, itemize

reckless *adj* = **careless**, daredevil, devil-may-care, foolhardy, harebrained, harum-scarum, hasty, headlong, heedless, ill-advised, imprudent, inattentive, incautious, indiscreet, irresponsible, madcap, mindless, negligent, precipitate, rash, regardless, thoughtless, wild

reckon Ⓣ ('rɛkən) *vb* **1** to calculate or ascertain by calculating; compute. **2** (*tr*) to include; count as part of a set or class. **3** (*usually passive*) to consider or regard: *he is reckoned clever.* **4** (when *tr, takes a clause as object*) to think or suppose; be of the opinion: *I reckon you don't know.* **5** (*intr;* foll. by *with*) to settle accounts (with). **6** (*intr;* foll. by *with* or *without*) to take into account or fail to take into account: *they reckoned without John.* **7** (*intr;* foll. by *on* or *upon*) to rely or depend: *I reckon on your support.* **8** (*tr*) *Inf.* to have a high opinion of. **9 to be reckoned with.** of considerable importance or influence. [OE *(ge)recenian* recount]

reckoner ('rɛkənə) *n* any of various devices or tables used to facilitate reckoning, esp. a ready reckoner.

reckoning Ⓣ ('rɛkənɪŋ) *n* **1** the act of counting or calculating. **2** settlement of an account or bill. **3** a bill or account. **4** retribution for one's actions (esp. in **day of reckoning**). **5** *Navigation.* short for **dead reckoning.**

reclaim Ⓣ (rɪ'kleɪm) *vb* (*tr*) **1** to claim back: *reclaim baggage.* **2** to convert (desert, marsh, etc.) into land suitable for growing crops. **3** to recover (useful substances) from waste products. **4** to convert (someone) from sin, folly, vice, etc. ◆ *n* **5** the act of reclaiming or state of being reclaimed. [C13: from OF *réclamer,* from L *reclāmāre* to cry out, from RE- + *clāmāre* to shout]
▸**re'claimable** *adj* ▸**re'claimant** *or* **re'claimer** *n*

reclamation (ˌrɛklə'meɪʃən) *n* **1** the conversion of desert, marsh, etc., into land suitable for cultivation. **2** the recovery of useful substances from waste products. **3** the act of reclaiming or state of being reclaimed.

réclame *French.* (reklam) *n* **1** public acclaim or attention; publicity. **2** the capacity for attracting publicity.

reclinate ('rɛklɪˌneɪt) *adj Bot.* naturally curved or bent backwards so that the upper part rests on the ground. [C18: from L *reclīnātus* bent back]

recline Ⓣ (rɪ'klaɪn) *vb* **reclines, reclining, reclined.** to rest in a leaning position. [C15: from OF *recliner,* from L *reclīnāre,* from RE- + *clīnāre* to LEAN[1]]
▸**re'clinable** *adj* ▸**reclination** (ˌrɛklɪ'neɪʃən) *n*

recliner (rɪ'klaɪnə) *n* a person or thing that reclines, esp. a type of armchair having a back that can be adjusted to slope at various angles.

recluse Ⓣ (rɪ'kluːs) *n* **1** a person who lives in seclusion, esp. to devote himself to prayer and religious meditation; a hermit. ◆ *adj* **2** solitary; retiring. [C13: from OF *reclus,* from LL *reclūdere* to shut away, from L RE- + *claudere* to close]
▸**reclusion** (rɪ'kluːʒən) *n* ▸**re'clusive** *adj*

recognition Ⓣ (ˌrɛkəg'nɪʃən) *n* **1** the act of recognizing or fact of being recognized. **2** acceptance or acknowledgment of a claim, duty, etc. **3** a token of thanks. **4** formal acknowledgment of a government or of the independence of a country. [C15: from L *recognitiō,* from *recognoscere,* from RE- + *cognoscere* to know]
▸**recognitive** (rɪ'kɒgnɪtɪv) *or* **re'cognitory** *adj*

recognizance *or* **recognisance** (rɪ'kɒgnɪzəns) *n Law.* **a** a bond entered into before a court or magistrate by which a person binds himself to do a specified act, as to appear in court on a stated day, keep the peace, or pay a debt. **b** a monetary sum pledged to the performance of such an act. [C14: from OF *reconoissance,* from *reconoistre* to RECOGNIZE]
▸**re'cognizant** *or* **re'cognisant** *adj*

recognize Ⓣ *or* **recognise** ('rɛkəgˌnaɪz) *vb* **recognizes, recognizing, recognized** *or* **recognises, recognising, recognised.** (*tr*) **1** to perceive (a person or thing) to be the same as or belong to the same class as something previously seen or known; know again. **2** to accept or be aware of (a fact, problem, etc.): *to recognize necessity.* **3** to give formal acknowledgment of the status or legality of (a government, a representative, etc.). **4** *Chiefly US & Canad.* to grant (a person) the right to speak in a deliberative body. **5** to give a token of thanks for (a service rendered, etc.). **6** to make formal acknowledgment of (a claim, etc.). **7** to show approval or appreciation of (something good). **8** to acknowledge or greet (a person). [C15: from L *recognoscere,* from RE- + *cognoscere* to know]
▸**'recogˌnizable** *or* **'recogˌnisable** *adj* ▸**ˌrecogˌniza'bility** *or* **ˌrecogˌnisa'bility** *n* ▸**'recogˌnizably** *or* **'recogˌnisably** *adv* ▸**'recogˌnizer** *or* **'recogˌniser** *n*

recoil Ⓣ *vb* (rɪ'kɔɪl). (*intr*) **1** to jerk back, as from an impact or violent thrust. **2** (often foll. by *from*) to draw back in fear, horror, or disgust. **3** (foll. by *on* or *upon*) to go wrong, esp. so as to hurt the perpetrator. **4** (of an atom, etc.) to change momentum as a result of the emission of a particle. ◆ *n* (rɪ'kɔɪl, 'riːkɔɪl). **5a** the backward movement of a gun when fired. **5b** the distance moved. **6** the motion acquired by an atom, etc., as a result of its emission of a particle. **7** the act of recoiling. [C13: from OF *reculer,* from RE- + *cul* rump, from L *cūlus*]
▸**re'coiler** *n*

recollect Ⓣ (ˌrɛkə'lɛkt) *vb* (when *tr, often takes a clause as object*) to recall from memory; remember. [C16: from L *recolligere,* from RE- + *colligere* to COLLECT]
▸**ˌrecol'lection** *n* ▸**ˌrecol'lective** *adj* ▸**ˌrecol'lectively** *adv*

recombinant (riː'kɒmbɪnənt) *Genetics.* ◆ *adj* **1** produced by the combining of genetic material from more than one origin. ◆ *n* **2** a chromosome, cell, organism, etc., the genetic makeup of which results from recombination.

recombinant DNA *n* DNA molecules that are extracted from different sources and chemically joined together.

recombination (ˌriːkɒmbɪ'neɪʃən) *n Genetics.* any of several processes by which genetic material of different origins becomes combined.

recommend Ⓣ (ˌrɛkə'mɛnd) *vb* (*tr*) **1** (*may take a clause as object or an infinitive*) to advise as the best course or choice; counsel. **2** to praise or commend: *to recommend a new book.* **3** to make attractive or advisable: *the trip has little to recommend it.* **4** *Arch.* to entrust (a person or thing) to someone else's care; commend. [C14: via Med. L from L RE- + *commendāre* to COMMEND]
▸**ˌrecom'mendable** *adj* ▸**ˌrecom'mendatory** *adj* ▸**ˌrecom'mender** *n*

recommendation Ⓣ (ˌrɛkəmɛn'deɪʃən) *n* **1** the act of recommending. **2** something that recommends, esp. a letter. **3** something that is recommended, such as a course of action.

recommit (ˌriːkə'mɪt) *vb* **recommits, recommitting, recommitted.** (*tr*) **1** to send (a bill) back to a committee for further consideration. **2** to commit again.
▸**ˌrecom'mitment** *or* **ˌrecom'mittal** *n*

recompense Ⓣ ('rɛkəmˌpɛns) *vb* **recompenses, recompensing, recompensed.** (*tr*) **1** to pay or reward for service, work, etc. **2** to compensate for loss, injury, etc. ◆ *n* **3** compensation for loss, injury, etc. **4** reward, remuneration, or repayment. [C15: from OF *recompenser,* from L RE- + *compensāre* to balance in weighing]
▸**'recomˌpensable** *adj* ▸**'recomˌpenser** *n*

reconcile Ⓣ ('rɛkənˌsaɪl) *vb* **reconciles, reconciling, reconciled.** (*tr*) **1** (*often passive;* usually foll. by *to*) to make (oneself or another) no longer opposed; cause to acquiesce in something unpleasant: *she reconciled herself to poverty.* **2** to become friendly with (someone) after estrangement or to re-establish friendly relations between (two or

THESAURUS

Antonyms *adj* careful, cautious, heedful, mindful, observant, responsible, thoughtful, wary

reckon *vb* **1** = **count**, add up, calculate, compute, enumerate, figure, number, tally, total **3** = **consider**, account, appraise, count, deem, esteem, estimate, evaluate, gauge, hold, judge, look upon, rate, regard, think of **4** = **think**, assume, believe, be of the opinion, conjecture, expect, fancy, guess (*inf., chiefly US & Canad.*), imagine, suppose, surmise **5** *foll. by* **with** = **deal**, cope, face, handle, settle accounts, treat **6** = **take into account**, anticipate, bargain for, bear in mind, be prepared for, expect, foresee, plan for, take cognizance of **7** *with* **on** *or* **upon** = **rely on**, bank on, calculate, count on, depend on, hope for, take for granted, trust in **9 to be reckoned with** = **powerful**, consequential, considerable, important, influential, significant, strong, weighty

reckoning *n* **1** = **count**, adding, addition, calculation, computation, counting, estimate, summation, working **3** = **bill**, account, charge, due, score **4** = **retribution**, doom, judgment, last judgment

reclaim *vb* **1** = **regain**, get *or* take back, recover, retrieve **3** = **salvage**

recline *vb* = **lean**, be recumbent, lay (something) down, lie (down), loll, lounge, repose, rest, sprawl, stretch out
Antonyms *vb* get up, rise, sit up, stand, stand up, stand upright

recluse *n* **1** = **hermit**, anchoress, anchorite, ascetic, eremite, monk, solitary

reclusive *adj* **1, 2** = **solitary**, ascetic, cloistered, eremitic, hermitic, hermit-like, isolated, monastic, recluse, retiring, secluded, sequestered, withdrawn
Antonyms *adj* gregarious, sociable

recognition *n* **1** = **identification**, detection, discovery, recall, recollection, remembrance **2** = **acceptance**, admission, allowance, avowal, awareness, concession, confession, perception, realization, understanding **3** = **approval**, acknowledgment, appreciation, gratitude, greeting, honour, respect, salute

recognize *vb* **1** = **identify**, know, know again, make out, notice, place, put one's finger on, recall, recollect, remember, spot **2** = **acknowledge**, accept, admit, allow, avow, be aware of, concede, confess, grant, own, perceive, realize, see, take on board, understand **7** = **approve**, acknowledge, appreciate, honour, respect **8** = **greet**, acknowledge, salute
Antonyms *vb* ≠ **acknowledge:** be unaware of, forget, ignore, overlook

recoil *vb* **1** = **jerk back**, kick, react, rebound, resile, spring back **2** = **draw back**, balk at, falter, flinch, quail, shrink, shy away **3** = **backfire**, boomerang, go pear-shaped (*inf.*), go wrong, misfire, rebound ◆ *n* **5a** = **reaction**, backlash, kick

recollect *vb* = **remember**, call to mind, mind (*dialect*), place, recall, reminisce, summon up

recollection *n* = **memory**, impression, mental image, recall, remembrance, reminiscence

recommend *vb* **1** = **advise**, advance, advocate, counsel, enjoin, exhort, prescribe, propose, put forward, suggest, urge **2** = **commend**, approve, endorse, praise, put in a good word for, speak well of, vouch for **3** = **make attractive**, make acceptable, make appealing, make interesting
Antonyms *vb* ≠ **advise, commend:** argue against, disapprove of, reject, veto

recommendation *n* **1, 3** = **advice**, counsel, proposal, suggestion, urging **2** = **commendation**, advocacy, approbation, approval, blessing, endorsement, favourable mention, good word, plug (*inf.*), praise, reference, sanction, testimonial

recompense *vb* **1** = **reward**, pay, remunerate **2** = **compensate**, indemnify, make amends for, make good, make restitution for, make up for, pay for, redress, reimburse, repay, requite, satisfy ◆ *n* **3** = **compensation**, amends, damages, emolument, indemnification, indemnity, payment, reparation, repayment, requital, restitution, satisfaction **4** = **reward**, meed (*arch.*), pay, payment, remuneration, repayment, return, wages

reconcile *vb* **1** = **accept**, accommodate, get used, make the best of, put up with (*inf.*), resign oneself, submit, yield **2** = **make peace between**, appease, bring to terms, conciliate, pacify, placate, propitiate, re-establish friendly relations

more people). **3** to settle (a quarrel). **4** to make (two apparently conflicting things) compatible or consistent with each other. **5** to reconsecrate (a desecrated church, etc.). [C14: from L *reconciliāre*, from RE- + *conciliāre* to make friendly, CONCILIATE]
▸**'recon,cilement** *n* ▸**'recon,ciler** *n* ▸**reconciliation** (,rɛkən,sɪlɪ'eɪʃən) *n* ▸**reconciliatory** (,rɛkən'sɪlɪətərɪ, -trɪ) *adj*

recondite ❶ (rɪ'kɒndaɪt, 'rɛkən,daɪt) *adj* **1** requiring special knowledge; abstruse. **2** dealing with abstruse or profound subjects. [C17: from L *reconditus* hidden away, from RE- + *condere* to conceal]
▸**re'conditely** *adv* ▸**re'conditeness** *n*

recondition ❶ (,riːkən'dɪʃən) *vb* (*tr*) to restore to good condition or working order: *to recondition an engine.*
▸**,recon'ditioned** *adj*

reconnaissance ❶ (rɪ'kɒnɪsəns) *n* **1** the act of reconnoitring. **2** the process of obtaining information about the position, etc., of an enemy. **3** a preliminary inspection of an area of land. [C18: from F, from OF *reconoistre* to explore, RECOGNIZE]

reconnoitre ❶ *or US* **reconnoiter** (,rɛkə'nɔɪtə) *vb* **reconnoitres, reconnoitring, reconnoitred** *or US* **reconnoiters, reconnoitering, reconnoitered. 1** to survey or inspect (an enemy's position, region of land, etc.). ◆ *n* **2** the act or process of reconnoitring; a reconnaissance. [C18: from obs. F *reconnoître* to inspect, explore; see RECOGNIZE]
▸**,recon'noitrer** *or US* **,recon'noiterer** *n*

reconsider ❶ (,riːkən'sɪdə) *vb* to consider (something) again, with a view to changing one's policy or course of action.
▸**,recon,sider'ation** *n*

reconstitute (riː'kɒnstɪ,tjuːt) *vb* **reconstitutes, reconstituting, reconstituted.** (*tr*) **1** to restore (food, etc.) to its former or natural state, as by the addition of water to a concentrate. **2** to reconstruct; form again.
▸**reconstituent** (,riːkən'stɪtjuənt) *adj, n* ▸**,reconsti'tution** *n*

reconstruct ❶ (,riːkən'strʌkt) *vb* (*tr*) **1** to construct or form again; rebuild. **2** to form a picture of (a crime, past event, etc.) by piecing together evidence.
▸**,recon'structible** *adj* ▸**,recon'struction** *n* ▸**,recon'structive** *or* **,recon'structional** *adj* ▸**,recon'structor** *n*

reconvert (,riːkən'vɜːt) *vb* (*tr*) **1** to change (something) back to a previous state or form. **2** to bring (someone) back to his former religion.
▸**reconversion** (,riːkən'vɜːʃən) *n*

record ❶ *n* ('rɛkɔːd). **1** an account in permanent form, esp. in writing, preserving knowledge or information. **2** a written account of some transaction that serves as legal evidence of the transaction. **3** a written official report of the proceedings of a court of justice or legislative body. **4** anything serving as evidence or as a memorial: *the First World War is a record of human folly.* **5** (*often pl*) information or data on a specific subject collected methodically over a long period: *weather records.* **6a** the best or most outstanding amount, rate, height, etc., ever attained, as in some field of sport: *a world record.* **6b** (*as modifier*): *a record time.* **7** the sum of one's recognized achievements, career, or performance. **8** a list of crimes of which an accused person has previously been convicted. **9 have a record.** to be a known criminal. **10** Also called: **gramophone record, disc.** a thin disc of a plastic material upon which sound has been recorded. Each side has a spiral groove, which undulates in accordance with the frequency and amplitude of the sound. **11** the markings made by a recording instrument such as a seismograph. **12** *Computing.* a group of data or piece of information preserved as a unit in machine-readable form. **13 for the record.** for the sake of strict factual accuracy. **14 go on record.** to state one's views publicly. **15 off the record.** confidential or confidentially. **16 on record. 16a** stated in a public document. **16b** publicly known. **17 set** *or* **put the record straight.** to correct an error. ◆ *vb* (rɪ'kɔːd). (*mainly tr*) **18** to set down in some permanent form so as to preserve the true facts of: *to record the minutes of a meeting.* **19** to contain or serve to relate (facts, information, etc.). **20** to indicate, show, or register: *his face recorded his disappointment.* **21** to remain as or afford evidence of: *these ruins record the life of the Romans in Britain.* **22** (*also intr*) to make a recording of (music, speech, etc.) for reproduction, esp. on a record player or tape recorder, or for later broadcasting. **23** (*also intr*) (of an instrument) to register or indicate (information) on a scale: *the barometer recorded a low pressure.* [C13: from OF *recorder*, from L *recordārī* to remember, from RE- + *cor* heart]
▸**re'cordable** *adj*

recorded delivery *n* a Post Office service by which an official record of posting and delivery is obtained for a letter or package.

recorder ❶ (rɪ'kɔːdə) *n* **1** a person who records, such as an official or historian. **2** something that records, esp. an apparatus that provides a permanent record of experiments, etc. **3** short for **tape recorder. 4** *Music.* a wind instrument of the flute family, blown through a fipple in the mouth end, having a reedlike quality of tone. **5** (in England) a barrister or solicitor of at least ten years' standing appointed to sit as a part-time judge in the crown court.
▸**re'cordership** *n*

recording ❶ (rɪ'kɔːdɪŋ) *n* **1a** the act or process of making a record, esp. of sound on a gramophone record or magnetic tape. **1b** (*as modifier*): *recording studio.* **2** the record or tape so produced. **3** something that has been recorded, esp. a radio or television programme.

Recording Angel *n* an angel who supposedly keeps a record of every person's good and bad acts.

record of achievement *n Brit.* a statement of the personal and educational development of each pupil.

record player *n* a device for reproducing the sounds stored on a record. A stylus vibrates in accordance with the undulations of the walls of the groove in the record as it rotates.

recount ❶ (rɪ'kaʊnt) *vb* (*tr*) to tell the story or details of; narrate. [C15: from OF *reconter*, from RE- + *conter* to tell; see COUNT[1]]
▸**re'countal** *n*

re-count *vb* (riː'kaʊnt). **1** to count (votes, etc.) again. ◆ *n* ('riː,kaʊnt). **2** a second or further count, esp. of votes in an election.

recoup ❶ (rɪ'kuːp) *vb* **1** to regain or make good (a financial or other loss). **2** (*tr*) to reimburse or compensate (someone), as for a loss. **3** *Law.* to keep back (something due), having rightful claim to do so. ◆ *n* **4** *Rare.* the act of recouping; recoupment. [C15: from OF *recouper* to cut back, from RE- + *couper*, from *coper* to behead]
▸**re'coupable** *adj* ▸**re'coupment** *n*

recourse ❶ (rɪ'kɔːs) *n* **1** the act of resorting to a person, course of action, etc., in difficulty (esp. in **have recourse to**). **2** a person, organization, or course of action that is turned to for help, etc. **3** the right to demand payment, esp. from the drawer or endorser of a bill of exchange or other negotiable instrument when the person accepting it fails to pay. **4 without recourse.** a qualified endorsement on such a negotiable instrument, by which the endorser protects himself from liability to subsequent holders. [C14: from OF *recours*, from LL *recursus* a running back, from RE- + L *currere* to run]

recover ❶ (rɪ'kʌvə) *vb* **1** (*tr*) to find again or obtain the return of (something lost). **2** to regain (loss of money, time, etc.). **3** (of a person) to regain (health, spirits, composure, etc.). **4** to regain (a former and better condition): *industry recovered after the war.* **5** *Law.* **5a** (*tr*) to gain (something) by the judgment of a court of law: *to recover damages.* **5b** (*intr*) to succeed in a lawsuit. **6** (*tr*) to obtain (useful substances) from waste. **7** (*intr*) (in fencing, rowing, etc.) to make a recovery. [C14: from OF *recoverer*, from L *recuperāre* RECUPERATE]
▸**re'coverable** *adj* ▸**re,covera'bility** *n* ▸**re'coverer** *n*

THESAURUS

between, restore harmony between, reunite **3** = **resolve**, adjust, compose, harmonize, patch up, put to rights, rectify, settle, square

reconciliation *n* **1** = **accommodation**, adjustment, compromise, settlement **2** = **pacification**, appeasement, conciliation, détente, propitiation, *rapprochement*, reconcilement, reunion, understanding
Antonyms *n* ≠ **pacification:** alienation, antagonism, break-up, estrangement, falling-out, separation

recondite *adj* **1, 2** = **obscure**, abstruse, arcane, cabbalistic, concealed, dark, deep, difficult, esoteric, hidden, involved, mysterious, mystical, occult, profound, secret
Antonyms *adj* exoteric, simple, straightforward

recondition *vb* = **restore**, do up (*inf.*), fix up (*inf., chiefly US & Canad.*), overhaul, remodel, renew, renovate, repair, revamp

reconnaissance *n* **1-3** = **inspection**, exploration, investigation, observation, patrol, recce (*sl.*), reconnoitring, scan, scouting, scrutiny, survey

reconnoitre *vb* **1** = **inspect**, case (*sl.*), explore, get the lie of the land, investigate, make a reconnaissance (of), observe, patrol, recce (*sl.*), scan, scout, scrutinize, see how the land lies, spy out, survey

reconsider *vb* = **rethink**, change one's mind, have second thoughts, reassess, re-evaluate, re-examine, review, revise, take another look at, think again, think better of, think over, think twice

reconstruct *vb* **1** = **rebuild**, reassemble, recreate, re-establish, reform, regenerate, remake, remodel, renovate, reorganize, restore **2** = **deduce**, build up, build up a picture of, piece together

record *n* **1** = **document**, account, annals, archives, chronicle, diary, entry, file, journal, log, memoir, memorandum, memorial, minute, register, report **2, 3** = **documentation**, evidence **4** = **evidence**, memorial, remembrance, testimony, witness **7** = **background**, career, curriculum vitae, history, performance, track record (*inf.*) **10** = **disc**, album, black disc, EP, forty-five, gramophone record, LP, platter (*US sl.*), recording, release, seventy-eight, single, vinyl, waxing (*inf.*) **15 off the record** = **not for publication**, confidential, confidentially, in confidence, in private, private, sub rosa, under the rose, unofficial, unofficially ◆ *vb* **18** = **set down**, chalk up (*inf.*), chronicle, document, enrol, enter, inscribe, log, minute, note, preserve, put down, put on file, put on record, register, report, take down, transcribe, write down **22** = **make a recording of**, cut, lay down (*sl.*), put on wax (*inf.*), tape, tape-record, video, video-tape, wax (*inf.*) **23** = **register**, contain, give evidence of, indicate, read, say, show

recorder *n* **1** = **chronicler**, annalist, archivist, clerk, diarist, historian, registrar, scorekeeper, scorer, scribe

recording *n* **2** = **record**, cut (*inf.*), disc, gramophone record, tape, video

recount *vb* = **tell**, delineate, depict, describe, detail, enumerate, give an account of, narrate, portray, recite, rehearse, relate, repeat, report, tell the story of

recoup *vb* **1** = **regain**, make good, recover, redeem, retrieve, win back **2** = **compensate**, make redress for, make up for, refund, reimburse, remunerate, repay, requite, satisfy

recourse *n* **2** = **option**, alternative, appeal, choice, expedient, refuge, remedy, resort, resource, way out

recover *vb* **1, 2** = **regain**, find again, get back, make good, recapture, reclaim, recoup, redeem, repair, repossess, restore, retake, retrieve, take back, win back **3** = **get better**, be on the mend, bounce back, come round, convalesce, feel oneself again, get back on one's feet, get well, heal, improve, mend, pick up, pull through, rally, recuperate, regain one's health *or* strength, revive, take a turn for the better, turn the corner
Antonyms *vb* ≠ **regain:** abandon, forfeit, lose ≠ **get**

re-cover (riːˈkʌvə) *vb (tr)* **1** to cover again. **2** to provide (furniture, etc.) with a new cover.

recovery ⓘ (rɪˈkʌvərɪ) *n, pl* **recoveries. 1** the act or process of recovering, esp. from sickness, a shock, or a setback. **2** restoration to a former or better condition. **3** the regaining of something lost. **4** the extraction of useful substances from waste. **5** the retrieval of a space capsule after a spaceflight. **6** *Law.* the obtaining of a right, etc., by the judgment of a court. **7** *Fencing.* a return to the position of guard after making an attack. **8** *Swimming, rowing, etc.* the action of bringing the arm, an oar, etc., forward for another stroke. **9** *Golf.* a stroke played from the rough or a bunker to the fairway or green.

recovery stock *n Stock Exchange.* a security that has fallen in price but is believed to have the ability to recover.

recreant (ˈrɛkrɪənt) *Arch.* ◆ *adj* **1** cowardly; faint-hearted. **2** disloyal. ◆ *n* **3** a disloyal or cowardly person. [C14: from OF, from *recroire* to surrender, from RE- + L *crēdere* to believe]
▸ˈ**recreance** *or* ˈ**recreancy** *n* ▸ˈ**recreantly** *adv*

recreate (ˈrɛkrɪˌeɪt) *vb* **recreates, recreating, recreated.** *Rare.* to amuse (oneself or someone else). [C15: from L *recreāre* to invigorate, renew, from RE- + *creāre* to CREATE]
▸ˈ**recreative** *adj* ▸ˈ**recreatively** *adv* ▸ˈ**recreˌator** *n*

re-create (ˌriːkrɪˈeɪt) *vb* **re-creates, re-creating, re-created.** to create anew; reproduce.
▸ˌ**re-creˈation** *n* ▸ˌ**re-creˈator** *n*

recreation ⓘ (ˌrɛkrɪˈeɪʃən) *n* **1** refreshment of health or spirits by relaxation and enjoyment. **2** an activity that promotes this. **3a** an interval of free time between school lessons. **3b** *(as modifier): recreation period.*

recreational (ˌrɛkrɪˈeɪʃənᵊl) *adj* **1** of, relating to, or used for recreation: *recreational facilities.* **2** (of a drug) taken for pleasure rather than for medical reasons or because of an addiction.

recreational vehicle *n Chiefly US.* a large vanlike vehicle equipped to be lived in. Abbrev.: **RV.**

recriminate ⓘ (rɪˈkrɪmɪˌneɪt) *vb* **recriminates, recriminating, recriminated.** *(intr)* to return an accusation against someone or engage in mutual accusations. [C17: via Med. L, from L *crīmināri* to accuse, from *crīmen* accusation]
▸**reˌcrimiˈnation** *n* ▸**reˈcriminative** *or* **reˈcriminatory** *adj* ▸**reˈcrimiˌnator** *n*

recrudesce (ˌriːkruːˈdɛs) *vb* **recrudesces, recrudescing, recrudesced.** *(intr)* (of a disease, trouble, etc.) to break out or appear again after a period of dormancy. [C19: from L *recrūdēscere,* from RE- + *crūdēscere* to grow worse, from *crūdus* bloody, raw]
▸ˌ**recruˈdescence** *n*

recruit ⓘ (rɪˈkruːt) *vb* **1a** to enlist (men) for military service. **1b** to raise or strengthen (an army, etc.) by enlistment. **2** *(tr)* to enrol or obtain (members, support, etc.). **3** to furnish or be furnished with a fresh supply; renew. **4** *Arch.* to recover (health, spirits, etc.). ◆ *n* **5** a newly joined member of a military service. **6** any new member or supporter. [C17: from F *recrute* lit.: new growth, from *recroître,* from L, from RE- + *crēscere* to grow]
▸**reˈcruitable** *adj* ▸**reˈcruiter** *n* ▸**reˈcruitment** *n*

recta (ˈrɛktə) *n* a plural of **rectum.**

rectal (ˈrɛktəl) *adj* of or relating to the rectum.
▸ˈ**rectally** *adv*

rectangle (ˈrɛkˌtæŋgᵊl) *n* a parallelogram having four right angles. [C16: from Med. L *rectangulum,* from L *rectus* straight + *angulus* angle]

rectangular (rɛkˈtæŋgjʊlə) *adj* **1** shaped like a rectangle. **2** having or relating to right angles. **3** mutually perpendicular: *rectangular coordinates.* **4** having a base or section shaped like a rectangle.
▸**recˌtanguˈlarity** *n* ▸**recˈtangularly** *adv*

rectangular coordinates *pl n* the Cartesian coordinates in a system of mutually perpendicular axes.

rectangular hyperbola *n* a hyperbola with perpendicular asymptotes.

recti (ˈrɛktaɪ) *n* the plural of **rectus.**

recti- *or before a vowel* **rect-** *combining form.* straight or right: *rectangle.* [from L *rectus*]

rectifier (ˈrɛktɪˌfaɪə) *n* **1** an electronic device that converts an alternating current to a direct current. **2** *Chem.* an apparatus for condensing a hot vapour to a liquid in distillation; condenser. **3** a thing or person that rectifies.

rectify ⓘ (ˈrɛktɪˌfaɪ) *vb* **rectifies, rectifying, rectified.** *(tr)* **1** to put right; correct; remedy. **2** to separate (a substance) from a mixture or refine (a substance) by fractional distillation. **3** to convert (alternating current) into direct current. **4** *Maths.* to determine the length of (a curve). [C14: via OF from Med. L *rectificāre,* from L *rectus* straight + *facere* to make]
▸ˈ**rectiˌfiable** *adj* ▸ˌ**rectifiˈcation** *n*

rectilinear (ˌrɛktɪˈlɪnɪə) *or* **rectilineal** *adj* **1** in, moving in, or characterized by a straight line. **2** consisting of, bounded by, or formed by a straight line.
▸ˌ**rectiˈlinearly** *or* ˌ**rectiˈlineally** *adv*

rectitude ⓘ (ˈrɛktɪˌtjuːd) *n* **1** moral or religious correctness. **2** correctness of judgment. [C15: from LL *rectitūdō,* from L *rectus* right, from *regere* to rule]

recto (ˈrɛktəʊ) *n, pl* **rectos. 1** the front of a sheet of printed paper. **2** the right-hand pages of a book. Cf. **verso** (sense 1b). [C19: from L *rectō foliō* on the right-hand page]

rectocele (ˈrɛktəʊˌsiːl) *n Pathol.* a protrusion or herniation of the rectum into the vagina.

rector (ˈrɛktə) *n* **1** *Church of England.* a clergyman in charge of a parish in which, as its incumbent, he would formerly have been entitled to the whole of the tithes. **2** *RC Church.* a cleric in charge of a college, religious house, or congregation. **3** *Protestant Episcopal Church.* a clergyman in charge of a parish. **4** *Chiefly Brit.* the head of certain schools, colleges, or universities. **5** (in Scotland) a high-ranking official in a university. **6** (in South Africa) a principal of an Afrikaans university. [C14: from L: director, ruler, from *regere* to rule]
▸ˈ**rectorate** *n* ▸**rectorial** (rɛkˈtɔːrɪəl) *adj* ▸ˈ**rectorship** *n*

rectory (ˈrɛktərɪ) *n, pl* **rectories. 1** the official house of a rector. **2** *Church of England.* the office and benefice of a rector.

rectrix (ˈrɛktrɪks) *n, pl* **rectrices** (ˈrɛktrɪˌsiːz, rɛkˈtraɪsiːz). any of the large stiff feathers of a bird's tail, used in controlling the direction of flight. [C17: from LL, fem of L *rector* RECTOR]
▸**rectricial** (rɛkˈtrɪʃəl) *adj*

rectum (ˈrɛktəm) *n, pl* **rectums** *or* **recta.** the lower part of the alimentary canal, between the sigmoid flexure of the colon and the anus. [C16: from NL *rectum intestinum* the straight intestine]

rectus (ˈrɛktəs) *n, pl* **recti.** *Anat.* a straight muscle. [C18: from NL *rectus musculus*]

recumbent ⓘ (rɪˈkʌmbənt) *adj* **1** lying down; reclining. **2** (of an organ) leaning or resting against another organ. [C17: from L *recumbere* to lie back, from RE- + *cumbere* to lie]
▸**reˈcumbence** *or* **reˈcumbency** *n* ▸**reˈcumbently** *adv*

recuperate ⓘ (rɪˈkuːpəˌreɪt, -ˈkjuː-) *vb* **recuperates, recuperating, recuperated. 1** *(intr)* to recover from illness or exhaustion. **2** to recover (financial losses, etc.). [C16: from L *recuperāre* to recover, from RE- + *capere* to gain]
▸**reˌcuperˈation** *n* ▸**reˈcuperative** *adj*

recur ⓘ (rɪˈkɜː) *vb* **recurs, recurring, recurred.** *(intr)* **1** to happen again. **2** (of a thought, etc.) to come back to the mind. **3** (of a problem, etc.) to come up again. **4** *Maths.* (of a digit or group of digits) to be repeated an infinite number of times at the end of a decimal fraction. [C15: from L *recurrere,* from RE- + *currere* to run]
▸**reˈcurring** *adj*

recurrent ⓘ (rɪˈkʌrənt) *adj* **1** tending to happen again or repeatedly. **2** *Anat.* (of certain nerves, etc.) turning back, so as to run in the opposite direction.
▸**reˈcurrence** *n* ▸**reˈcurrently** *adv*

recurrent fever *n* another name for **relapsing fever.**

recurring decimal *n* a rational number that contains a pattern of digits repeated indefinitely after the decimal point.

recursion (rɪˈkɜːʃən) *n* **1** the act or process of returning or running back. **2** *Maths, logic.* the application of a function to its own values to generate an infinite sequence of values. [C17: from L *recursio,* from *recurrere* RECUR]
▸**reˈcursive** *adj*

recurve (rɪˈkɜːv) *vb* **recurves, recurving, recurved.** to curve or bend (some-

THESAURUS

better: deteriorate, go downhill, relapse, take a turn for the worse, weaken, worsen

recovery *n* **1 = improvement,** convalescence, healing, mending, rally, recuperation, return to health, revival, turn for the better **2 = revival,** amelioration, betterment, improvement, rally, rehabilitation, restoration, upturn **3 = retrieval,** recapture, reclamation, redemption, repair, repossession, restoration

recreation *n* **1, 2 = pastime,** amusement, beer and skittles *(inf.)*, distraction, diversion, enjoyment, entertainment, exercise, fun, hobby, leisure activity, play, pleasure, refreshment, relaxation, relief, sport

recrimination *n* **= bickering,** counterattack, countercharge, mutual accusation, name-calling, quarrel, retaliation, retort, squabbling

recruit *vb* **1 = enlist,** draft, enrol, impress, levy, mobilize, muster, raise **2 = win (over),** engage, enrol, gather, obtain, procure, proselytize, round up, take on ◆ *n* **5 = beginner,** apprentice, convert, greenhorn *(inf.)*, helper, initiate, learner, neophyte, novice, proselyte, rookie *(inf.)*, trainee, tyro
Antonyms *vb* ≠ **enlist:** dismiss, fire, lay off, make redundant, sack *(inf.)*

rectify *vb* **1 = correct,** adjust, amend, emend, fix, improve, make good, mend, put right, redress, reform, remedy, repair, right, set the record straight, square **2 = separate,** distil, purify, refine

rectitude *n* **1 = morality,** correctness, decency, equity, goodness, honesty, honour, incorruptibility, integrity, justice, principle, probity, righteousness, scrupulousness, uprightness, virtue **2 = correctness,** accuracy, exactness, justice, precision, rightness, soundness, verity
Antonyms *n* ≠ **morality:** baseness, corruption, dishonesty, dishonour, immorality, scandalousness

recumbent *adj* **1 = lying down,** flat, flat on one's back, horizontal, leaning, lying, prone, prostrate, reclining, resting, stretched out, supine

recuperate *vb* **1 = recover,** be on the mend, convalesce, get back on one's feet, get better, improve, mend, pick up, regain one's health, turn the corner

recur *vb* **1, 3 = happen again,** come again, come and go, come back, persist, reappear, repeat, return, revert **2 = return to mind,** be remembered, come back, haunt one's thoughts, run through one's mind

recurrent *adj* **1 = periodic,** continued, cyclical, frequent, habitual, recurring, regular, repeated, repetitive
Antonyms *adj* isolated, one-off

thing) back or down or (of something) to be so curved or bent. [C16: from L *recurvāre,* from RE- + *curvāre* to CURVE]

recusant (ˈrɛkjuzənt) *n* **1** (in 16th to 18th century England) a Roman Catholic who did not attend the services of the Church of England. **2** any person who refuses to submit to authority. ◆ *adj* **3** (formerly, of Catholics) refusing to attend services of the Church of England. **4** refusing to submit to authority. [C16: from L *recūsāns* refusing, from *recūsāre,* from RE- + *causārī* to dispute, from *causa* a CAUSE]
▸ **ˈrecusance** *or* **ˈrecusancy** *n*

recycle Ⓣ (riːˈsaɪkəl) *vb* **recycles, recycling, recycled.** (*tr*) **1** to pass (a substance) through a system again for further treatment or use. **2** to reclaim (packaging or products with a limited useful life) for further use: *to recycle water.* ◆ *n* **3** the repetition of a fixed sequence of events.
▸ **reˈcyclable** *or* **reˈcycleable** *adj*

red[1] Ⓣ (rɛd) *n* **1** any of a group of colours, such as that of a ripe tomato or fresh blood. **2** a pigment or dye of or producing these colours. **3** red cloth or clothing: *dressed in red.* **4** a red ball in snooker, etc. **5** (in roulette) one of two colours on which players may place even bets. **6** *Inf.* red wine: *a bottle of red.* **7 in the red.** *Inf.* in debt. **8 see red.** *Inf.* to become very angry. ◆ *adj* **redder, reddest. 9** of the colour red. **10** reddish in colour or having parts or marks that are reddish: *red deer.* **11** having the face temporarily suffused with blood, being a sign of anger, shame, etc. **12** (of the complexion) rosy; florid. **13** (of the eyes) bloodshot. **14** (of the hands) stained with blood. **15** bloody or violent: *red revolution.* **16** denoting the highest degree of urgency in an emergency; used by the police and the army and informally (esp. in the phrase **red alert**). **17** (of wine) made from black grapes and coloured by their skins. ◆ *vb* **reds, redding, redded. 18** another word for **redden.** [OE *rēad*]
▸ **ˈreddish** *adj* ▸ **ˈredness** *n*

red[2] (rɛd) *vb* **reds, redding, red** *or* **redded.** (*tr*) a variant spelling of **redd.**

Red (rɛd) *Inf.* ◆ *adj* **1** Communist, Socialist, or Soviet. **2** radical, leftist, or revolutionary. ◆ *n* **3** a member or supporter of a Communist or Socialist Party or a national of the Soviet Union. **4** a radical, leftist, or revolutionary. [C19: from the colour chosen to symbolize revolutionary socialism]

redact (rɪˈdækt) *vb* (*tr*) **1** to compose or draft (an edict, proclamation, etc.). **2** to put (a literary work, etc.) into appropriate form for publication; edit. [C15: from L *redigere* to bring back, from *red-* RE- + *agere* to drive]
▸ **reˈdaction** *n* ▸ **reˈdactional** *adj* ▸ **reˈdactor** *n*

red admiral *n* a butterfly of temperate Europe and Asia, having black wings with red and white markings. See also **white admiral.**

red algae *pl n* the numerous algae which contain a red pigment in addition to chlorophyll. The group includes carrageen and dulse.

redback (ˈrɛdˌbæk) *n Austral.* a small, venomous spider, the female of which has a red stripe on its back. Also called: **redback spider.**

red bark *n* a kind of cinchona containing a high proportion of alkaloids.

red biddy *n Inf.* cheap red wine fortified with methylated spirits.

red blood cell *n* another name for **erythrocyte.**

red-blooded Ⓣ *adj Inf.* vigorous; virile.
▸ **ˌred-ˈbloodedness** *n*

red book *n Brit.* (sometimes caps.) a government publication bound in red, esp. the Treasury's annual forecast of revenue, expenditure, growth, and inflation.

redbreast (ˈrɛdˌbrɛst) *n* any of various birds having a red breast, esp. the Old World robin.

redbrick (ˈrɛdˌbrɪk) *n* (*modifier*) denoting, relating to, or characteristic of a provincial British university of relatively recent foundation.

redcap (ˈrɛdˌkæp) *n* **1** *Brit. inf.* a military policeman. **2** *US & Canad.* a porter at an airport or station.

red card *Soccer, etc.* ◆ *n* **1** a card of a red colour displayed by a referee to indicate that a player has been sent off. ◆ *vb* **red-card. 2** (*tr*) to send off (a player).

red carpet *n* **1** a strip of red carpeting laid for important dignitaries to walk on. **2a** deferential treatment accorded to a person of importance. **2b** (*as modifier*): *a red-carpet reception.*

red cedar *n* **1** any of several North American coniferous trees, esp. a juniper that has fragrant reddish wood. **2** the wood of any of these trees. **3** any of several Australian timber trees.

red cent *n* (*used with a negative*) *Inf., chiefly US.* a cent considered as a trivial amount of money (esp. in **not have a red cent,** etc.).

redcoat (ˈrɛdˌkəut) *n* **1** (formerly) a British soldier. **2** *Canad. inf.* another name for **Mountie.**

red coral *n* any of several corals, the skeletons of which are pinkish red in colour and used to make ornaments, etc.

red corpuscle *n* another name for **erythrocyte.**

Red Crescent *n* the emblem of the Red Cross Society in a Muslim country.

Red Cross *n* **1** an international humanitarian organization (**Red Cross Society**) formally established by the Geneva Convention of 1864. **2** the emblem of this organization, consisting of a red cross on a white background.

redcurrant (ˌrɛdˈkʌrənt) *n* **1** a N temperate shrub having greenish flowers and small edible rounded red berries. **2a** the fruit of this shrub. **2b** (*as modifier*): *redcurrant jelly.*

redd *or* **red** (rɛd) *Scot. & N English dialect.* ◆ *vb* **redds, redding, redd** *or* **redded. 1** (*tr;* often foll. by *up*) to bring order to; tidy (up). ◆ *n* **2** the act or an instance of redding. [C15: *redden* to clear, ? a variant of RID]
▸ **ˈredder** *n*

red deer *n* a large deer formerly widely distributed in the woodlands of Europe and Asia. The coat is reddish brown in summer and the short tail is surrounded by a patch of light-coloured hair.

redden Ⓣ (ˈrɛdən) *vb* **1** to make or become red. **2** (*intr*) to flush with embarrassment, anger, etc.

reddle (ˈrɛdəl) *n, vb* **reddles, reddling, reddled.** a variant spelling of **ruddle.**

red duster *n Brit.* an informal name for the **Red Ensign.**

red dwarf *n* one of a class of stars of relatively small mass and low luminosity.

rede (riːd) *Arch.* ◆ *n* **1** advice or counsel. **2** an explanation. ◆ *vb* **redes, reding, reded.** (*tr*) **3** to advise; counsel. **4** to explain. [OE *rǣdan* to rule]

red earth *n* a clayey zonal soil of tropical savanna lands, formed by extensive chemical weathering and coloured by iron compounds.

redeem Ⓣ (rɪˈdiːm) *vb* (*tr*) **1** to recover possession or ownership of by payment of a price or service; regain. **2** to convert (bonds, shares, etc.) into cash. **3** to pay off (a loan, etc.). **4** to recover (something pledged, mortgaged, or pawned). **5** to convert (paper money) into bullion or specie. **6** to fulfil (a promise, pledge, etc.). **7** to exchange (coupons, etc.) for goods. **8** to reinstate in someone's estimation or good opinion: *he redeemed himself by his altruistic action.* **9** to make amends for. **10** to recover from captivity, esp. by a money payment. **11** *Christianity.* (of Christ as Saviour) to free (humanity) from sin by death on the Cross. [C15: from OF *redimer,* from L *redimere,* from *red-* RE- + *emere* to buy]
▸ **reˈdeemable** *or* **reˈdemptible** *adj* ▸ **reˈdeemer** *n*

Redeemer (rɪˈdiːmə) *n* **the.** Jesus Christ as having brought redemption to mankind.

redeeming (rɪˈdiːmɪŋ) *adj* serving to compensate for faults or deficiencies.

redemption Ⓣ (rɪˈdɛmpʃən) *n* **1** the act or process of redeeming. **2** the state of being redeemed. **3** *Christianity.* **3a** deliverance from sin through the incarnation, sufferings, and death of Christ. **3b** atonement for guilt. [C14: via OF from L *redemptiō* a buying back; see REDEEM]
▸ **reˈdemptional, reˈdemptive,** *or* **reˈdemptory** *adj* ▸ **reˈdemptively** *adv*

redemption yield *n Stock Exchange.* the yield produced by a redeemable gilt-edged security taking into account the annual interest it pays and an annualized amount to account for any profit or loss when it is redeemed.

Red Ensign *n* the ensign of the British Merchant Navy, having the Union Jack on a red background at the upper corner of the vertical edge alongside the hoist. It was also the national flag of Canada until 1965.

redeploy (ˌriːdɪˈplɔɪ) *vb* to assign new positions or tasks to (labour, troops, etc.).
▸ **ˌredeˈployment** *n*

redevelopment area (ˌriːdɪˈvɛləpmənt) *n* an urban area in which all or most of the buildings are demolished and rebuilt.

redeye (ˈrɛdˌaɪ) *n* **1** *US sl.* inferior whisky. **2** *Sl., chiefly US.* a flight that departs late at night and arrives early next morning. **3** another name for **rudd.**

red-faced *adj* **1** flushed with embarrassment or anger. **2** having a florid complexion.
▸ **red-facedly** (ˌrɛdˈfeɪsɪdlɪ, -ˈfeɪstlɪ) *adv*

redfin (ˈrɛdˌfɪn) *n* any of various small cyprinid fishes with reddish fins.

THESAURUS

recycle *vb* **1** = **reprocess,** reuse **2** = **reclaim,** reuse, salvage, save

red[1] *n, adj* **1, 9** = **crimson,** cardinal, carmine, cherry, claret, coral, gules (*Heraldry*), maroon, pink, rose, ruby, scarlet, vermeil, vermilion, wine ◆ *n* **7 in the red** *Informal* = **in debt,** bankrupt, in arrears, in debit, in deficit, insolvent, on the rocks, overdrawn, owing money, showing a loss **8 see red** *Informal* = **lose one's temper,** be beside oneself with rage (*inf.*), become enraged, blow a fuse, blow one's top, boil, crack up (*inf.*), fly off the handle (*inf.*), go ballistic (*sl., chiefly US*), go mad (*inf.*), go off one's head (*sl.*), go off the deep end (*inf.*), go up the wall (*sl.*), lose it (*inf.*), lose one's rag (*sl.*), lose the plot (*inf.*), seethe ◆ *adj* **10** = **chestnut,** bay, carroty, flame-coloured, flaming, foxy, reddish, sandy, titian **11** = **flushed,** blushing, embarrassed, florid, rubicund, shamefaced, suffused **12** = **rosy,** blooming, glowing, healthy, roseate, ruddy **13** = **bloodshot,** inflamed, red-rimmed **14** = **bloody,** bloodstained, ensanguined (*literary*), gory, sanguine

red-blooded *adj Informal* = **vigorous,** hearty, lusty, manly, robust, strong, virile, vital

redden *vb* **2** = **flush,** blush, colour (up), crimson, go red, suffuse

redeem *vb* **1** = **buy back,** reclaim, recover, recover possession of, regain, repossess, repurchase, retrieve, win back **2, 7** = **trade in,** cash (in), change, exchange **6** = **fulfil,** abide by, acquit, adhere to, be faithful to, carry out, discharge, hold to, keep, keep faith with, make good, meet, perform, satisfy **8** = **reinstate,** absolve, rehabilitate, restore to favour **9** = **make up for,** atone for, compensate for, defray, make amends for, make good, offset, outweigh, redress, save **10** = **save,** buy the freedom of, deliver, emancipate, extricate, free, liberate, pay the ransom of, ransom, rescue, set free

redemption *n* **1** = **recovery,** reclamation, repossession, repurchase, retrieval **2** = **salvation,** deliverance, emancipation, liberation, ransom, release, rescue **3b** = **compensation,** amends, atonement, expiation, reparation

redfish ('rɛd,fɪʃ) *n, pl* **redfish** *or* **redfishes. 1** a male salmon that has recently spawned. Cf. **blackfish** (sense 2). **2** *Canad.* another name for **kokanee.**
red flag *n* **1** a symbol of socialism, communism, or revolution. **2** a warning of danger or a signal to stop.
red fox *n* the common European fox which has a reddish-brown coat.
red giant *n* a giant star that emits red light.
red grouse *n* a reddish-brown grouse of upland moors of Great Britain.
Red Guard *n* a member of a Communist Chinese youth movement that attempted to effect the Cultural Revolution (1966–69).
red-handed ⓘ *adj* (*postpositive*) in the act of committing a crime or doing something wrong or shameful (esp. in **catch red-handed**). [C19 (earlier, C15 *red hand*)]
▸,**red-'handedly** *adv* ▸,**red-'handedness** *n*
red hat *n* the broad-brimmed crimson hat given to cardinals as the symbol of their rank.
redhead ('rɛd,hɛd) *n* a person with red hair.
▸**'red,headed** *adj*
red heat *n* **1** the temperature at which a substance is red-hot. **2** the state or condition of being red-hot.
red herring *n* **1** anything that diverts attention from a topic or line of inquiry. **2** a herring cured by salting and smoking.
red-hot *adj* **1** (esp. of metal) heated to the temperature at which it glows red. **2** extremely hot. **3** keen, excited, or eager. **4** furious; violent: *red-hot anger.* **5** very recent or topical: *red-hot information.* **6** *Austral. sl.* extreme, unreasonable, or unfair.
red-hot poker *n* a liliaceous plant: widely cultivated for its showy spikes of red or yellow flowers.
Red Indian *n, adj* another name, now considered offensive, for **American Indian.** [see REDSKIN]
redingote ('rɛdɪŋ,gəʊt) *n* **1** a man's full-skirted outer coat of the 18th and 19th centuries. **2** a woman's coat of the 18th century, with an open-fronted skirt, revealing a decorative underskirt. **3** a woman's coat with a close-fitting top and a full skirt. [C19: from F, from E *riding coat*]
redintegrate (re'dɪntɪ,greɪt) *vb* **redintegrates, redintegrating, redintegrated.** (*tr*) to make whole or complete again; restore to a perfect state; renew. [C15: from L *redintegrāre* to renew, from *red-* RE- + *integer* complete]
▸**re,dinte'gration** *n* ▸**red'integrative** *adj*
redistribution (,ri:dɪstrɪ'bju:ʃən) *n* **1** the act or an instance of distributing again. **2** a revision of the number of seats in the Canadian House of Commons allocated to each province, made every ten years on the basis of a new census.
redivivus (,rɛdɪ'vaɪvəs) *adj Rare.* returned to life; revived. [C17: from LL, from L *red-* RE- + *vīvus* alive]
red lead (lɛd) *n* a bright-red poisonous insoluble oxide of lead.
red-letter day *n* a memorably important or happy occasion. [C18: from the red letters used in ecclesiastical calendars to indicate saints' days and feasts]
red light *n* **1** a signal to stop, esp. a red traffic signal. **2** a danger signal. **3a** a red lamp indicating that a house is a brothel. **3b** (*as modifier*): *a red-light district.*
redline ('rɛd,laɪn) *vb* **redlines, redlining, redlined.** (*tr*) (esp. of a bank or group of banks) to refuse to consider giving a loan to (a person or country) because of the presumed risks involved.
red meat *n* any meat that is dark in colour, esp. beef and lamb. Cf. **white meat.**
red mullet *n* a food fish of European waters with a pair of long barbels beneath the chin and a reddish coloration. US name: **goatfish.**
redneck ('rɛd,nɛk) *n Disparaging.* **1** (in the southwestern US) a poor uneducated White farm worker. **2** a person or institution that is extremely reactionary. ◆ *adj* **3** reactionary and bigoted: *redneck laws.*
redo (ri:'du:) *vb* **redoes, redoing, redid, redone.** (*tr*) **1** to do over again. **2** *Inf.* to redecorate, esp. thoroughly: *we redid the house last summer.*
red ochre *n* any of various natural red earths containing ferric oxide: used as pigments.
redolent ⓘ ('rɛdəʊlənt) *adj* **1** having a pleasant smell; fragrant. **2** (*postpositive;* foll. by *of* or *with*) having the odour or smell (of): *a room redolent of flowers.* **3** (*postpositive;* foll. by *of* or *with*) reminiscent or suggestive (of): *a picture redolent of the 18th century.* [C14: from L *redolens* smelling (of), from *redolēre* to give off an odour, from *red-* RE- + *olēre* to smell]
▸**'redolence** *or* **'redolency** *n* ▸**'redolently** *adv*
redouble (rɪ'dʌbᵊl) *vb* **redoubles, redoubling, redoubled. 1** to make or become much greater in intensity, number, etc.: *to redouble one's efforts.* **2** to send back (sounds) or (of sounds) to be sent back. **3** *Bridge.* to double (an opponent's double). ◆ *n* **4** the act of redoubling.
redoubt (rɪ'daʊt) *n* **1** an outwork or fieldwork defending a hilltop, pass, etc. **2** a temporary defence work built inside a fortification as a last defensive position. [C17: via F from obs. It. *ridotta,* from Med. L *reductus* shelter, from L *redūcere,* from RE- + *dūcere* to lead]
redoubtable ⓘ (rɪ'daʊtəbᵊl) *adj* **1** to be feared; formidable. **2** worthy of respect. [C14: from OF, from *redouter* to dread, from RE- + *douter* to be afraid, DOUBT]
▸**re'doubtableness** *n* ▸**re'doubtably** *adv*
redound ⓘ (rɪ'daʊnd) *vb* **1** (*intr;* foll. by *to*) to have an advantageous or disadvantageous effect (on): *brave deeds redound to your credit.* **2** (*intr;* foll. by *on* or *upon*) to recoil or rebound. **3** (*tr*) *Arch.* to reflect; bring: *his actions redound dishonour upon him.* [C14: from OF *redonder,* from L *redundāre* to stream over, from *red-* RE- + *undāre* to rise in waves]
redox ('ri:dɒks) *n* (*modifier*) another term for **oxidation-reduction.** [C20: from RED(UCTION) + OX(IDATION)]
red pepper *n* **1** any of several varieties of the pepper plant cultivated for their hot pungent red podlike fruits. **2** the fruit of any of these plants. **3** the ripe red fruit of the sweet pepper. **4** another name for **cayenne pepper.**
Red Planet *n* **the.** an informal name for **Mars**[2].
redpoll ('rɛd,pɒl) *n* either of two widely distributed types of finches, having a greyish-brown plumage with a red crown and pink breast.
red rag *n* a provocation; something that infuriates. [so called because red objects supposedly infuriate bulls]
redress ⓘ (rɪ'drɛs) *vb* (*tr*) **1** to put right (a wrong), esp. by compensation; make reparation for. **2** to correct or adjust (esp. in **redress the balance**). **3** to make compensation to (a person) for a wrong. ◆ *n* **4** the act or an instance of setting right a wrong; remedy or cure. **5** compensation, amends, or reparation for a wrong, injury, etc. [C14: from OF *redrecier* to set up again, from RE- + *drecier* to straighten; see DRESS]
▸**re'dressable** *or* **re'dressible** *adj* ▸**re'dresser** *or* **re'dressor** *n*
re-dress (ri:'drɛs) *vb* (*tr*) to dress (something) again.
Red River cart *n Canad. history.* a strongly-built, two-wheeled, ox- or horse-drawn cart used in W Canada.
red rose *n English history.* the emblem of the House of Lancaster.
red salmon *n* any salmon having reddish flesh, esp. the sockeye salmon.
redshank ('rɛd,ʃæŋk) *n* any of various large common European sandpipers, esp. the **spotted redshank,** having red legs.
red shift *n* a shift in the lines of the spectrum of an astronomical object towards a longer wavelength (the red end of an optical spectrum), relative to the wavelength of these lines in the terrestrial spectrum, usually as a result of the Doppler effect caused by the recession of the object.
redskin ('rɛd,skɪn) *n* an informal name, now considered offensive, for an **American Indian.** [so called because one now extinct tribe painted themselves with red ochre]
red snapper *n* any of various marine percoid food fishes of the snapper family, having a reddish coloration, common in American coastal regions of the Atlantic.
red spider *n* short for **red spider mite** (see **spider mite**).
red squirrel *n* a reddish-brown squirrel, inhabiting woodlands of Europe and parts of Asia.
redstart ('rɛd,stɑ:t) *n* **1** a European songbird of the thrush family: the male has a black throat, orange-brown tail and breast, and grey back. **2** a North American warbler. [OE *rēad* red + *steort* tail]
red tape *n* obstructive official routine or procedure; time-consuming bureaucracy. [C18: from the red tape used to bind official government documents]
reduce ⓘ (rɪ'dju:s) *vb* **reduces, reducing, reduced.** (*mainly tr*) **1** (*also intr*) to make or become smaller in size, number, etc. **2** to bring into a certain state, condition, etc.: *to reduce a forest to ashes; he was reduced to tears.* **3** (*also intr*) to make or become slimmer; lose or cause to lose excess weight. **4** to impoverish (esp. in **in reduced circumstances**). **5** to bring into a state of submission to one's authority; subjugate: *the whole country was reduced after three months.* **6** to bring down the price of (a commodity). **7** to lower the rank or status of; demote: *reduced to the ranks.* **8** to set out systematically as an aid to understanding; simplify: *his theories have been reduced in a treatise.* **9** *Maths.* to modify or simplify the form of (an expression or equation), esp. by substitution of one term by another. **10** *Cookery.* to make (a sauce, stock, etc.) more con-

THESAURUS

red-handed *adj* = **in the act,** bang to rights (*sl.*), (in) flagrante delicto, with one's fingers *or* hand in the till (*inf.*), with one's pants down (*US sl.*)
redolent *adj* **1** = **scented,** aromatic, fragrant, odorous, perfumed, sweet-smelling **2** = **reminiscent,** evocative, remindful, suggestive
redoubtable *adj* **1** = **formidable,** awful, doughty, dreadful, fearful, fearsome, mighty, powerful, resolute, strong, terrible, valiant
redound *vb* **1** *foll. by* **to** = **contribute to,** conduce, effect, lead to, militate for, tend towards **2** *foll. by* **on** *or* **upon** = **rebound,** accrue, come back, ensue, recoil, reflect, result
redress *vb* **1** = **make amends for,** compensate for, make reparation for, make restitution for, make up for, pay for, put right, recompense for **2** = **put right,** adjust, amend, balance, correct, ease, even up, mend, rectify, reform, regulate, relieve, remedy, repair, restore the balance, square ◆ *n* **4** = **rectification,** aid, assistance, correction, cure, ease, help, justice, relief, remedy, satisfaction **5** = **amends,** atonement, compensation, payment, quittance, recompense, reparation, requital, restitution
reduce *vb* **1** = **lessen,** abate, abridge, contract, curtail, cut, cut down, debase, decrease, depress, dilute, diminish, downsize, impair, lower, moderate, shorten, slow down, tone down, truncate, turn down, weaken, wind down **3** = **slim,** be *or* go on a diet, diet, lose weight, shed weight, slenderize (*chiefly US*), trim **4** = **impoverish,** bankrupt, break, pauperize, ruin **5** = **drive,** bring, bring to the point of, conquer, force, master, overpower, subdue, vanquish **6** = **cheapen,** bring down the price of, cut, discount, lower, mark down, slash **7** = **degrade,** break, bring low, demote, downgrade,

centrated by boiling away some of the water in it. **11** to thin out (paint) by adding oil, turpentine, etc. **12** (*also intr*) *Chem.* **12a** to undergo or cause to undergo a chemical reaction with hydrogen. **12b** to lose or cause to lose oxygen atoms. **12c** to undergo or cause to undergo an increase in the number of electrons. **13** *Photog.* to lessen the density of (a negative or print). **14** *Surgery.* to manipulate or reposition (a broken or displaced bone, organ, or part) back to its normal site. [C14: from L *redūcere* to bring back, from RE- + *dūcere* to lead]
▸**re'ducible** *adj* ▸**re,duci'bility** *n* ▸**re'ducibly** *adv*

reducer (rɪ'dju:sə) *n* **1** *Photog.* a chemical solution used to lessen the density of a negative or print by oxidizing some of the blackened silver to soluble silver compounds. **2** a pipe fitting connecting two pipes of different diameters. **3** a person or thing that reduces.

reducing agent *n Chem.* a substance that reduces another substance in a chemical reaction, being itself oxidized in the process.

reducing glass *n* a lens or curved mirror that produces an image smaller than the object observed.

reductase (rɪ'dʌkteɪz) *n* any enzyme that catalyses a biochemical reduction reaction. [C20: from REDUCTION + -ASE]

reductio ad absurdum (rɪ'dʌktɪəʊ æd æb'sɜ:dəm) *n* **1** a method of disproving a proposition by showing that its inevitable consequences would be absurd. **2** a method of indirectly proving a proposition by assuming its negation to be true and showing that this leads to an absurdity. **3** application of a principle or proposed principle to an instance in which it is absurd. [L, lit.: reduction to the absurd]

reduction (rɪ'dʌkʃən) *n* **1** the act or process or an instance of reducing. **2** the state or condition of being reduced. **3** the amount by which something is reduced. **4** a form of an original resulting from a reducing process, such as a copy on a smaller scale. **5** *Maths.* **5a** the process of converting a fraction into its decimal form. **5b** the process of dividing out the common factors in the numerator and denominator of a fraction.
▸**re'ductive** *adj*

reduction formula *n Maths.* a formula expressing the values of a trigonometric function of any angle greater than 90° in terms of a function of an acute angle.

reductionism (rɪ'dʌkʃə,nɪzəm) *n* **1** the analysis of complex things, data, etc., into less complex constituents. **2** *Often disparaging.* any theory or method that holds that a complex idea, system, etc., can be completely understood in terms of its simpler parts or components.
▸**re'ductionist** *n, adj* ▸**re,duction'istic** *adj*

redundancy ❶ (rɪ'dʌndənsɪ) *n, pl* **redundancies. 1a** the state or condition of being redundant or superfluous, esp. superfluous in one's job. **1b** (*as modifier*): *a redundancy payment.* **2** excessive proliferation or profusion, esp. of superfluity.

redundant ❶ (rɪ'dʌndənt) *adj* **1** surplus to requirements; unnecessary or superfluous. **2** verbose or tautological. **3** deprived of one's job because it is no longer necessary. [C17: from L *redundans* overflowing, from *redundāre* to stream over; see REDOUND]
▸**re'dundantly** *adv*

red underwing *n* a large noctuid moth having hind wings coloured red and black.

reduplicate *vb* (rɪ'dju:plɪ,keɪt), **reduplicates, reduplicating, reduplicated. 1** to make or become double; repeat. **2** to repeat (a sound or syllable) in a word or (of a sound or syllable) to be repeated. ◆ *adj* (rɪ'dju:plɪkɪt). **3** doubled or repeated. **4** (of petals or sepals) having the margins curving outwards.
▸**re,dupli'cation** *n* ▸**re'duplicative** *adj*

red-water *n* a disease of cattle which destroys the red blood cells, characterized by the passage of red or blackish urine.

redwing ('rɛd,wɪŋ) *n* a small European thrush having a speckled breast, reddish flanks, and brown back.

redwood ('rɛd,wʊd) *n* a giant coniferous tree of coastal regions of California, having reddish fibrous bark and durable timber.

reebok ('ri:bʌk, -bɒk) *n, pl* **reeboks** *or* **reebok.** a variant spelling of **rhebuck** *or* **rhebok.**

re-echo (ri:'ɛkəʊ) *vb* **re-echoes, re-echoing, re-echoed. 1** to echo (a sound that is already an echo); resound. **2** (*tr*) to repeat like an echo.

reed (ri:d) *n* **1** any of various widely distributed tall grasses that grow in swamps and shallow water and have jointed hollow stalks. **2** the stalk, or stalks collectively, of any of these plants, esp. as used for thatching. **3** *Music.* **3a** a thin piece of cane or metal inserted into the tubes of certain wind instruments, which sets in vibration the air column inside the tube. **3b** a wind instrument or organ pipe that sounds by means of a reed. **4** one of the several vertical parallel wires on a loom that may be moved upwards to separate the warp threads. **5** a small semicircular architectural moulding. **6** an archaic word for **arrow. 7 broken reed.** a weak, unreliable, or ineffectual person. ◆ *vb* (*tr*) **8** to fashion into or supply with reeds or reeding. **9** to thatch using reeds. [OE *hreod*]

reedbuck ('ri:d,bʌk) *n, pl* **reedbucks** *or* **reedbuck.** an antelope of Africa south of the Sahara, having a buff-coloured coat and inward-curving horns.

reed bunting *n* a common European bunting that has a brown streaked plumage with, in the male, a black head.

reed grass *n* a tall perennial grass of rivers and ponds of Europe, Asia, and Canada.

reeding ('ri:dɪŋ) *n* **1** a set of small semicircular architectural mouldings. **2** the milling on the edges of a coin.

reedling ('ri:dlɪŋ) *n* a titlike Eurasian songbird, common in reed beds, which belongs to the family of Old World flycatchers and has a tawny back and tail and, in the male, a grey-and-black head. Also called: **bearded tit.**

reed mace *n* a tall reedlike marsh plant, with straplike leaves and flowers in long brown spikes. Also called: (popularly) **bulrush, cat's-tail.**

reed organ *n* **1** a wind instrument, such as the harmonium, accordion, or harmonica, in which the sound is produced by reeds, each reed producing one note only. **2** a type of pipe organ in which all the pipes are fitted with reeds.

reed pipe *n* an organ pipe sounded by a vibrating reed.

reed stop *n* an organ stop controlling a rank of reed pipes.

reed warbler *n* any of various common Old World warblers that inhabit marshy regions and have a brown plumage.

reedy ('ri:dɪ) *adj* **reedier, reediest. 1** (of a place) abounding in reeds. **2** of or like a reed. **3** having a tone like a reed instrument; shrill or piping.
▸**'reedily** *adv* ▸**'reediness** *n*

reef[1] (ri:f) *n* **1** a ridge of rock, sand, coral, etc., the top of which lies close to the surface of the sea. **2** a vein of ore, esp. one of gold-bearing quartz. **3** (*cap.*) **the. 3a** the Great Barrier Reef in Australia. **3b** the Witwatersrand in South Africa, a gold-bearing ridge. [C16: from MDu. *ref*, from ON *rif* RIB[1], REEF[2]]

reef[2] (ri:f) *Naut.* ◆ *n* **1** the part gathered in when sail area is reduced, as in a high wind. ◆ *vb* **2** to reduce the area of (sail) by taking in a reef. **3** (*tr*) to shorten or bring inboard (a spar). [C14: from MDu. *rif*; rel. to ON *rif* reef, RIB[1]]

reefer ('ri:fə) *n* **1** *Naut.* a person who reefs, such as a midshipman. **2** another name for **reefing jacket. 3** *Sl.* a hand-rolled cigarette containing cannabis. [C19: from REEF[2]; applied to the cigarette from its resemblance to the rolled reef of a sail]

reefing jacket *n* a man's short double-breasted jacket of sturdy wool.

reef knot *n* a knot consisting of two overhand knots turned opposite ways. Also called: **square knot.**

reef point *n Naut.* one of several short lengths of line stitched through a sail for tying a reef.

reek ❶ (ri:k) *vb* **1** (*intr*) to give off or emit a strong unpleasant odour; smell or stink. **2** (*intr*; often foll. by *of*) to be permeated (by): *the letter reeks of subservience.* **3** (*tr*) to treat with smoke; fumigate. **4** (*tr*) *Chiefly dialect.* to give off or emit (smoke, fumes, etc.). ◆ *n* **5** a strong offensive smell; stink. **6** *Chiefly dialect.* smoke or steam; vapour. [OE *rēocan*]
▸**'reeky** *adj*

reel[1] (ri:l, rɪəl) *n* **1** any of various cylindrical objects or frames that turn on an axis and onto which film, tape, wire, etc., may be wound. US equivalent: **spool. 2** *Angling.* a device for winding, casting, etc., consisting of a revolving spool with a handle, attached to a fishing rod. ◆ *vb* (*tr*) **3** to wind (cotton, thread, etc.) onto a reel. **4** (foll. by *in, out,* etc.) to wind or draw with a reel: *to reel in a fish.* [OE *hrēol*]
▸**'reelable** *adj* ▸**'reeler** *n*

reel[2] ❶ (ri:l, rɪəl) *vb* (*mainly intr*) **1** to sway, esp. under the shock of a blow or through dizziness or drunkenness. **2** to whirl about or have the feeling of whirling about: *his brain reeled.* ◆ *n* **3** a staggering or swaying motion or sensation. [C14 *relen*, prob. from REEL[1]]

reel[3] (ri:l, rɪəl) *n* **1** any of various lively Scottish dances for a fixed number of couples who combine in square and circular formations. **2** a piece of music composed for or in the rhythm of this dance. [C18: from REEL[2]]

reel-fed *adj Printing.* involving or printing on a web of paper: *a reel-fed press.*

reelman ('ri:lmən, 'rɪəl-) *n, pl* **reelmen.** *Austral. & NZ.* (formerly) the member of a beach life-saving team who controlled the reel on which the line was wound.

reel off *vb* (*tr, adv*) to recite or write fluently and without apparent effort.

reel-to-reel *adj* **1** (of magnetic tape) wound from one reel to another in use. **2** (of a tape recorder) using magnetic tape wound from one reel to another, as opposed to cassettes.

re-entrant (ri:'ɛntrənt) *adj* **1** (of an angle) pointing inwards. ◆ *n* **2** an angle or part that points inwards.

re-entry (ri:'ɛntrɪ) *n, pl* **re-entries. 1** the act of retaking possession of land, etc. **2** the return of a spacecraft into the earth's atmosphere.

re-entry vehicle *n* the portion of a ballistic missile that carries a nuclear warhead and re-enters the earth's atmosphere.

THESAURUS

humble, humiliate, lower in rank, lower the status of, take down a peg (*inf.*)
Antonyms *vb* ≠ **lessen:** augment, enhance, enlarge, extend, heighten, increase ≠ **degrade:** elevate, enhance, exalt, promote

redundancy *n* **1a** = **unemployment**, joblessness, layoff, the axe, the sack (*inf.*) **2** = **superfluity**, superabundance, surfeit, surplus

redundant *adj* **1** = **superfluous**, *de trop*, excessive, extra, inessential, inordinate, supererogatory, supernumerary, surplus, unnecessary, unwanted **2** = **tautological**, diffuse, iterative, padded, periphrastic, pleonastic, prolix, repetitious, verbose, wordy
Antonyms *adj* ≠ **superfluous:** essential, necessary, needed, vital

reek *vb* **1** = **stink**, hum (*sl.*), pong (*Brit. inf.*), smell, smell to high heaven **2** *often foll. by* **of** = **be redolent of**, be characterized by, be permeated by **4** *Chiefly dialect* = **be redolent of**, fume, give off smoke *or* fumes, smoke, steam ◆ *n* **5** = **stink**, effluvium, fetor, malodour, mephitis, niff (*Brit. sl.*), odour, pong (*Brit. inf.*), smell, stench **6** *Chiefly dialect* = **smoke**, exhalation, fumes, steam, vapour

reel[2] *vb* **1** = **stagger**, falter, lurch, pitch, rock, roll, stumble, sway, totter, waver, wobble **2** = **whirl**,

DICTIONARY

reeve[1] (riːv) *n* **1** *English history.* the local representative of the king in a shire until the early 11th century. **2** (in medieval England) a manorial steward who supervised the daily affairs of the manor. **3** *Canad. government.* (in some provinces) a president of a local council, esp. in a rural area. **4** (formerly) a minor local official in England and the US. [OE *gerēva*]

reeve[2] (riːv) *vb* **reeves, reeving, reeved** *or* **rove.** (*tr*) *Naut.* **1** to pass (a rope or cable) through an eye or other narrow opening. **2** to fasten by passing through or around something. [C17: ?from Du. *rēven* REEF[2]]

reeve[3] (riːv) *n* the female of the ruff (the bird). [C17: from ?]

re-export *vb* (ˌriːɪkˈspɔːt, ˌriːˈɛkspɔːt). **1** to export (imported goods, esp. after processing). ◆ *n* (riːˈɛkspɔːt). **2** the act of re-exporting. **3** a re-exported commodity.
▸**ˌre-exporˈtation** *n* ▸**ˌre-exˈporter** *n*

ref (rɛf) *n Inf.* short for **referee.**

ref. *abbrev. for:* **1** referee. **2** reference. **3** reformed.

refection (rɪˈfɛkʃən) *n* refreshment with food and drink. [C14: from L *refectiō* a restoring, from *reficere,* from RE- + *facere* to make]

refectory (rɪˈfɛktərɪ, -trɪ) *n, pl* **refectories.** a dining hall in a religious or academic institution. [C15: from LL *refectōrium,* from L *refectus* refreshed]

refectory table *n* a long narrow dining table.

refer ⓘ (rɪˈfɜː) *vb* **refers, referring, referred.** (often foll. by *to*). **1** (*intr*) to make mention (of). **2** (*tr*) to direct the attention of (someone) for information, facts, etc.: *the reader is referred to Chomsky, 1965.* **3** (*intr*) to seek information (from): *he referred to his notes.* **4** (*intr*) to be relevant (to); pertain or relate (to). **5** (*tr*) to assign or attribute: *Cromwell referred his victories to God.* **6** (*tr*) to hand over for consideration, reconsideration, or decision: *to refer a complaint to another department.* **7** (*tr*) to hand back to the originator as unacceptable or unusable. **8** (*tr*) *Brit.* to fail (a student) in an examination. **9 refer to drawer.** a request by a bank that the payee consult the drawer concerning a cheque payable by that bank. **10** (*tr*) to direct (a patient, client, etc.) to another doctor, agency, etc. [C14: from L *referre,* from RE- + *ferre* to BEAR[1]]
▸**referable** (ˈrɛfərəbᵊl) *or* **referrable** (rɪˈfɜːrəbᵊl) *adj* ▸**reˈferral** *n* ▸**reˈferrer** *n*

> **USAGE NOTE** The common practice of adding *back* to *refer* is tautologous, since this meaning is already contained in the *re-* of *refer: this refers to* (not *back to*) *what has already been said.* However, when *refer* is used in the sense of passing a document or question for further consideration to the person from whom it was received, it may be appropriate to say *he referred the matter back.*

referee ⓘ (ˌrɛfəˈriː) *n* **1** a person to whom reference is made, esp. for an opinion, information, or a decision. **2** the umpire or judge in any of various sports, esp. football and boxing. **3** a person who is willing to testify to the character or capabilities of someone. **4** *Law.* a person appointed by a court to report on a matter. ◆ *vb* **referees, refereeing, refereed. 5** to act as a referee (in); preside (over).

reference ⓘ (ˈrɛfərəns, ˈrɛfrəns) *n* **1** the act or an instance of referring. **2** something referred, esp. proceedings submitted to a referee in law. **3** a direction of the attention to a passage elsewhere or to another book, etc. **4** a book or passage referred to. **5** a mention or allusion: *this book contains several references to the Civil War.* **6** the relation between a word or phrase and the object or idea to which it refers. **7a** a source of information or facts. **7b** (*as modifier*): *a reference book; a reference library.* **8** a written testimonial regarding one's character or capabilities. **9** a person referred to for such a testimonial. **10a** (foll. by *to*) relation or delimitation, esp. to or by membership of a specific group: *without reference to sex or age.* **10b** (*as modifier*): *a reference group.* **11 terms of reference.** the specific limits of responsibility that determine the activities of an investigating body, etc. ◆ *vb* **references, referencing, referenced.** (*tr*) **12** to furnish or compile a list of references for (a publication, etc.). **13** to make a reference to; refer to. ◆ *prep* **14** *Business jargon.* with reference to: *reference your letter of the 9th inst.* Abbrev.: **re.**
▸**referential** (ˌrɛfəˈrɛnʃəl) *adj*

referendum ⓘ (ˌrɛfəˈrɛndəm) *n, pl* **referendums** *or* **referenda** (-də). **1** submission of an issue of public importance to the direct vote of the electorate. **2** a vote on such a measure. ◆ See also **plebiscite.** [C19: from L: something to be carried back, from *referre* to REFER]

referent (ˈrɛfərənt) *n* the object or idea to which a word or phrase refers. [C19: from L *referens* from *referre* to REFER]

referred pain *n Psychol.* pain felt at some place other than its actual place of origin.

refill *vb* (riːˈfɪl). **1** to fill (something) again. ◆ *n* (ˈriːfɪl). **2** a replacement for a consumable substance in a permanent container. **3** a second or subsequent filling.
▸**reˈfillable** *adj*

refine ⓘ (rɪˈfaɪn) *vb* **refines, refining, refined. 1** to make or become free from impurities or foreign matter; purify. **2** (*tr*) to separate (a mixture) into pure constituents, as in an oil refinery. **3** to make or become elegant or polished. **4** (*intr;* often foll. by *on* or *upon*) to enlarge or improve (upon) by making subtle or fine distinctions. **5** (*tr*) to make (language) more subtle or polished. [C16: from RE- + FINE[1]]
▸**reˈfinable** *adj* ▸**reˈfiner** *n*

refined ⓘ (rɪˈfaɪnd) *adj* **1** not coarse or vulgar; genteel, elegant, or polite. **2** subtle; discriminating. **3** freed from impurities; purified.

refinement ⓘ (rɪˈfaɪnmənt) *n* **1** the act of refining or the state of being refined. **2** a fine or delicate point or distinction; a subtlety. **3** fineness or precision of thought, expression, manners, etc. **4** an improvement to a piece of equipment, etc.

refinery (rɪˈfaɪnərɪ) *n, pl* **refineries.** a factory for the purification of some crude material, such as sugar, oil, etc.

refit *vb* (riːˈfɪt), **refits, refitting, refitted. 1** to make or be made ready for use again by repairing, re-equipping, or resupplying. ◆ *n* (ˈriːˌfɪt). **2** a repair or re-equipping, as of a ship, for further use.
▸**reˈfitment** *n*

refl. *abbrev. for:* **1** reflection. **2** reflective. **3** reflex(ive).

reflate (riːˈfleɪt) *vb* **reflates, reflating, reflated.** to inflate or be inflated again. [C20: back formation from REFLATION]

reflation (riːˈfleɪʃən) *n* **1** an increase in economic activity. **2** an increase in the supply of money and credit designed to cause such economic activity. ◆ Cf. **inflation** (sense 2). [C20: from RE- + *-flation,* as in INFLATION]

reflect ⓘ (rɪˈflɛkt) *vb* **1** to undergo or cause to undergo a process in which light, other electromagnetic radiation, sound, particles, etc., are thrown back after impinging on a surface. **2** (of a mirror, etc.) to form an image of (something) by reflection. **3** (*tr*) to show or express: *his tactics reflect his desire for power.* **4** (*tr*) to bring as a consequence: *their success reflected great credit on them.* **5** (*intr;* foll. by *on* or *upon*) to cause to be regarded in a specified way: *her behaviour reflects well on her.* **6** (*intr;* often foll. by *on* or *upon*) to cast dishonour or honour, credit or discredit, etc. (on). **7** (*intr;* usually foll. by *on*) to think, meditate, or ponder. [C15: from L *reflectere,* from RE- + *flectere* to bend]
▸**reˈflectingly** *adv*

reflectance (rɪˈflɛktəns) *or* **reflection factor** *n* a measure of the ability of a surface to reflect light or other electromagnetic radiation, equal to the ratio of the reflected flux to the incident flux.

reflecting telescope *n* a type of telescope in which the initial image is formed by a concave mirror. Also called: **reflector.** Cf. **refracting telescope.**

reflection ⓘ *or* **reflexion** (rɪˈflɛkʃən) *n* **1** the act of reflecting or the state of being reflected. **2** something reflected or the image so produced, as by a mirror. **3** careful or long consideration or thought. **4** attribution of discredit or blame. **5** *Maths.* a transformation in which the direction of one axis is reversed or changes the polarity of one of the variables. **6** *Anat.* the bending back of a structure or part upon itself.
▸**reˈflectional** *or* **reˈflexional** *adj*

reflection density *n Physics.* a measure of the extent to which a surface reflects light or other electromagnetic radiation. Symbol: *D*

reflective ⓘ (rɪˈflɛktɪv) *adj* **1** characterized by quiet thought or con-

THESAURUS

go round and round, revolve, spin, swim, swirl, twirl

refer *vb* **1** = **allude**, advert, bring up, cite, hint, invoke, make mention of, make reference, mention, speak of, touch on **2** = **direct**, guide, point, recommend, send **3** = **consult**, apply, go, have recourse to, look up, seek information from, turn to **4** = **relate**, apply, be directed to, belong, be relevant to, concern, pertain **5** = **attribute**, accredit, ascribe, assign, credit, impute, put down to **6** = **pass on**, commit, consign, deliver, hand over, submit, transfer, turn over

referee *n* **2** = **umpire**, adjudicator, arbiter, arbitrator, judge, ref ◆ *vb* **5** = **umpire**, adjudicate, arbitrate, judge, mediate

reference *n* **5** = **citation**, allusion, mention, note, quotation, remark **8** = **testimonial**, certification, character, credentials, endorsement, good word, recommendation **10a** *foll. by* **to** = **relevance**, applicability, bearing, concern, connection, consideration, regard, relation, respect

referendum *n* **1, 2** = **public vote**, plebiscite, popular vote

refine *vb* **1, 2** = **purify**, clarify, cleanse, distil, filter, process, rarefy **5** = **improve**, hone, perfect, polish

refined *adj* **1** = **cultured**, civil, civilized, courtly, cultivated, elegant, genteel, gentlemanly, gracious, ladylike, polished, polite, sophisticated, urbane, well-bred, well-mannered **2** = **discerning**, delicate, discriminating, exact, fastidious, fine, nice, precise, punctilious, sensitive, sublime, subtle **2** = **purified**, clarified, clean, distilled, filtered, processed, pure
Antonyms *adj* ≠ **cultured:** boorish, coarse, common, ill-bred, inelegant, uncultured, ungentlemanly, unladylike, unmannerly, unrefined ≠ **purified:** coarse, impure, unrefined

refinement *n* **1** = **purification**, clarification, cleansing, distillation, filtering, processing, rarefaction, rectification **2** = **subtlety**, fine point, fine tuning, nicety, nuance **3** = **sophistication**, breeding, civility, civilization, courtesy, courtliness, cultivation, culture, delicacy, discrimination, elegance, fastidiousness, fineness, finesse, finish, gentility, good breeding, good manners, grace, graciousness, polish, politeness, politesse, precision, style, taste, urbanity

reflect *vb* **1, 2** = **throw back**, echo, give back, imitate, mirror, reproduce, return **3** = **show**, bear out, bespeak, communicate, demonstrate, display, evince, exhibit, express, indicate, manifest, reveal **7** = **consider**, cogitate, contemplate, deliberate, meditate, mull over, muse, ponder, ruminate, think, wonder

reflection *n* **2** = **image**, counterpart, echo, mirror image **3** = **consideration**, cerebration, cogitation, contemplation, deliberation, idea, impression, meditation, musing, observation, opinion, perusal, pondering, rumination, study, thinking, thought, view **4** = **criticism**, aspersion, censure, derogation, imputation, reproach, slur

reflective *adj* **1** = **thoughtful**, cogitating, con-

templation. **2** capable of reflecting: *a reflective surface.* **3** produced by reflection.
▸**re'flectively** *adv*

reflectivity (ˌriːflɛk'tɪvɪtɪ) *n* **1** *Physics.* a measure of the ability of a surface to reflect radiation, equal to the reflectance of a layer of material sufficiently thick for the reflectance not to depend on the thickness. **2** Also: **reflectiveness.** the quality or capability of being reflective.

reflector (rɪ'flɛktə) *n* **1** a person or thing that reflects. **2** a surface or object that reflects light, sound, heat, etc. **3** another name for **reflecting telescope.**

reflet (rə'fleɪ) *n* an iridescent glow or lustre, as on ceramic ware. [C19: from F: a reflection, from It. *riflesso,* from L *reflexus,* from *reflectere* to reflect]

reflex *n* ('riːflɛks). **1a** an immediate involuntary response, such as coughing, evoked by a given stimulus. **1b** (*as modifier*): *a reflex action.* See also **reflex arc. 2a** a mechanical response to a particular situation, involving no conscious decision. **2b** (*as modifier*): *a reflex response.* **3** a reflection; an image produced by or as if by reflection. ◆ *adj* ('riːflɛks). **4** *Maths.* (of an angle) between 180° and 360°. **5** (*prenominal*) turned, reflected, or bent backwards. ◆ *vb* (rɪ'flɛks). **6** (*tr*) to bend, turn, or reflect backwards. [C16: from L *reflexus* bent back, from *reflectere* to reflect]
▸**re'flexible** *adj* ▸**reˌflexi'bility** *n*

reflex arc *n Physiol.* the neural pathway over which impulses travel to produce a reflex action.

reflex camera *n* a camera in which the image is composed and focused on a ground-glass viewfinder screen.

reflexion (rɪ'flɛkʃən) *n Brit.* a less common spelling of **reflection.**
▸**re'flexional** *adj*

reflexive (rɪ'flɛksɪv) *adj* **1** denoting a class of pronouns that refer back to the subject of a sentence or clause. Thus, in *that man thinks a great deal of himself,* the pronoun *himself* is reflexive. **2** denoting a verb used transitively with the reflexive pronoun as its direct object, as in *to dress oneself.* **3** *Physiol.* of or relating to a reflex. ◆ *n* **4** a reflexive pronoun or verb.
▸**re'flexively** *adv* ▸**re'flexiveness** *or* **reflexivity** (ˌriːflɛk'sɪvɪtɪ) *n*

reflexology (ˌriːflɛk'sɒlədʒɪ) *n* a form of therapy in alternative medicine in which the soles of the feet are massaged: designed to stimulate the blood supply and nerves and thus relieve tension.
▸ˌ**reflex'ologist** *n*

reflux ('riːflʌks) *vb* **1** *Chem.* to boil or be boiled in a vessel attached to a condenser, so that the vapour condenses and flows back into the vessel. ◆ *n* **2** *Chem.* **2a** an act of refluxing. **2b** (*as modifier*): *a reflux condenser.* **3** the act or an instance of flowing back; ebb. [C15: from Med. L *refluxus,* from L *refluere* to flow back]

reflux oesophagitis (iːˌsɒfə'dʒaɪtɪs) *n* inflammation of the gullet caused by regurgitation of stomach acids, producing heartburn: may be associated with a hiatus hernia.

reform ❶ (rɪ'fɔːm) *vb* **1** (*tr*) to improve (an existing institution, law, etc.) by alteration or correction of abuses. **2** to give up or cause to give up a reprehensible habit or immoral way of life. ◆ *n* **3** an improvement or change for the better, esp. as a result of correction of legal or political abuses or malpractices. **4** a principle, campaign, or measure aimed at achieving such change. **5** improvement of morals or behaviour. [C14: via OF from L *reformāre* to form again]
▸**re'formable** *adj* ▸**re'formative** *adj* ▸**re'former** *n*

re-form (riː'fɔːm) *vb* to form anew.
▸ˌ**re-for'mation** *n*

reformation (ˌrɛfə'meɪʃən) *n* **1** the act or an instance of reforming or the state of being reformed. **2** (*usually cap.*) a religious and political movement of 16th-century Europe that began as an attempt to reform the Roman Catholic Church and resulted in the establishment of the Protestant Churches.
▸ˌ**refor'mational** *adj*

reformatory (rɪ'fɔːmətərɪ, -trɪ) *n, pl* **reformatories. 1** Also called: **reform school.** (formerly) a place of instruction where young offenders were sent for corrective training. ◆ *adj* **2** having the purpose or function of reforming.

Reformed (rɪ'fɔːmd) *adj* **1** of or designating a Protestant Church, esp. the Calvinist. **2** of or designating Reform Judaism.

reformism (rɪ'fɔːmɪzəm) *n* a doctrine advocating reform, esp. political or religious reform rather than abolition.
▸**re'formist** *n, adj*

Reform Judaism *n* a movement in Judaism that does not require strict observance of the law, but adapts to the contemporary world.

refract (rɪ'frækt) *vb* **1** to cause to undergo refraction. **2** (*tr*) to measure the amount of refraction of (the eye, a lens, etc.). [C17: from L *refractus* broken up, from *refringere,* from RE- + *frangere* to break]
▸**re'fractable** *adj* ▸**re'fractive** *adj*

refracting telescope *n* a type of telescope in which the image is formed by a set of lenses. Also called: **refractor.** Cf. **reflecting telescope.**

refraction (rɪ'frækʃən) *n* **1** *Physics.* the change in direction of a propagating wave, such as light or sound, in passing from one medium to another in which it has a different velocity. **2** the amount by which a wave is refracted. **3** the ability of the eye to refract light.
▸**re'fractional** *adj*

refractive index *n Physics.* a measure of the extent to which a medium refracts light; the ratio of the speed of light in free space to that in the medium.

refractometer (ˌriːfræk'tɒmɪtə) *n* any instrument for measuring the refractive index.
▸**refractometric** (rɪˌfræktə'mɛtrɪk) *adj* ▸ˌ**refrac'tometry** *n*

refractor (rɪ'fræktə) *n* **1** an object or material that refracts. **2** another name for **refracting telescope.**

refractory ❶ (rɪ'fræktərɪ) *adj* **1** unmanageable or obstinate. **2** *Med.* not responding to treatment. **3** *Physiol.* (of a nerve or muscle) incapable of responding to stimulation. **4** (of a material) able to withstand high temperatures without fusion or decomposition. ◆ *n, pl* **refractories. 5** a material, such as fire clay, that is able to withstand high temperatures.
▸**re'fractorily** *adv* ▸**re'fractoriness** *n*

refrain[1] ❶ (rɪ'freɪn) *vb* (*intr*; usually foll. by *from*) to abstain (from action); forbear. [C14: from L *refrēnāre* to check with a bridle, from RE- + *frēnum* a bridle]
▸**re'frainer** *n* ▸**re'frainment** *n*

refrain[2] ❶ (rɪ'freɪn) *n* **1** a regularly recurring melody, such as the chorus of a song. **2** a much repeated saying or idea. [C14: via OF, ult. from L *refringere* to break into pieces]

refrangible (rɪ'frændʒɪbᵊl) *adj* capable of being refracted. [C17: from L *refringere* to break up, from RE- + *frangere* to break]
▸**reˌfrangi'bility** *or* **re'frangibleness** *n*

refresh ❶ (rɪ'frɛʃ) *vb* **1** (*usually tr or reflexive*) to make or become fresh or vigorous, as through rest, drink, or food; revive or reinvigorate. **2** (*tr*) to enliven (something worn or faded), as by adding new decorations. **3** to pour cold water over previously blanched and drained food. **4** (*tr*) to stimulate (the memory, etc.). **5** (*tr*) to replenish, as with new equipment or stores. [C14: from OF *refreschir;* see RE-, FRESH]
▸**re'fresher** *n* ▸**re'freshing** *adj*

refresher course *n* a short educational course for people to review their subject and developments in it.

refreshment ❶ (rɪ'frɛʃmənt) *n* **1** the act of refreshing or the state of being refreshed. **2** (*pl*) snacks and drinks served as a light meal.

refrigerant (rɪ'frɪdʒərənt) *n* **1** a fluid capable of changes of phase at low temperatures: used as the working fluid of a refrigerator. **2** a cooling substance, such as ice or solid carbon dioxide. **3** *Med.* an agent that provides a sensation of coolness or reduces fever. ◆ *adj* **4** causing cooling or freezing.

refrigerate ❶ (rɪ'frɪdʒəˌreɪt) *vb* **refrigerates, refrigerating, refrigerated.** to make or become frozen or cold, esp. for preservative purposes; chill or freeze. [C16: from L *refrīgerāre* to make cold, from RE- + *frīgus* cold]
▸**reˌfriger'ation** *n* ▸**re'frigerative** *adj* ▸**re'frigeratory** *adj, n*

refrigerator (rɪ'frɪdʒəˌreɪtə) *n* a chamber in which food, drink, etc., are kept cool. Informal name: **fridge.**

refringent (rɪ'frɪndʒənt) *adj Physics.* of, concerned with, or causing refraction; refractive. [C18: from L *refringere;* see REFRACT]
▸**re'fringency** *or* **re'fringence** *n*

reft (rɛft) *vb* a past tense and past participle of **reave.**

refuel (riː'fjuːəl) *vb* **refuels, refuelling, refuelled** *or US* **refuels, refueling, refueled.** to supply or be supplied with fresh fuel.

refuge ❶ ('rɛfjuːdʒ) *n* **1** shelter or protection, as from the weather or danger. **2** any place, person, action, or thing that offers protection, help, or relief. [C14: via OF from L *refugium,* from *refugere,* from RE- + *fugere* to escape]

refugee ❶ (ˌrɛfjʊ'dʒiː) *n* **a** a person who has fled from some danger or problem, esp. political persecution. **b** (*as modifier*): *a refugee camp.*
▸ˌ**refu'geeism** *n*

THESAURUS

templative, deliberative, meditative, pensive, pondering, reasoning, ruminative

reform *vb* **1** = **improve**, ameliorate, amend, better, correct, emend, mend, rebuild, reclaim, reconstitute, reconstruct, rectify, regenerate, rehabilitate, remodel, renovate, reorganize, repair, restore, revolutionize **2** = **mend one's ways**, clean up one's act (*inf.*), get back on the straight and narrow (*inf.*), get it together (*inf.*), get one's act together (*inf.*), go straight (*inf.*), pull one's socks up (*Brit. inf.*), shape up (*inf.*), turn over a new leaf ◆ *n* **3** = **improvement**, amelioration, amendment, betterment, correction, rectification, rehabilitation, renovation

refractory *adj* **1** = **unmanageable**, cantankerous, contentious, contumacious, difficult, disobedient, disputatious, headstrong, intractable, mulish, obstinate, perverse, recalcitrant, stiff-necked, stubborn, uncontrollable, uncooperative, unruly, wilful

refrain[1] *vb* = **stop**, abstain, avoid, cease, desist, do without, eschew, forbear, give up, kick (*inf.*), leave off, renounce

refrain[2] *n* **1** = **chorus**, burden, melody, song, tune

refresh *vb* **1** = **revive**, brace, breathe new life into, cheer, cool, enliven, freshen, inspirit, invigorate, kick-start (*inf.*), reanimate, rejuvenate, revitalize, revivify, stimulate **2** = **renovate**, renew, repair, restore **4** = **stimulate**, brush up (*inf.*), jog, prod, prompt, renew **5** = **replenish**, top up

refreshing *adj* **1** = **stimulating**, bracing, cooling, fresh, inspiriting, invigorating, revivifying, thirst-quenching **2** = **new**, different, novel, original
Antonyms *adj* ≠ **stimulating:** enervating, exhausting, soporific, tiring, wearisome

refreshment *n* **1** = **revival**, enlivenment, freshening, reanimation, renewal, renovation, repair, restoration, stimulation **2** *plural* = **food and drink**, drinks, snacks, titbits

refrigerate *vb* = **cool**, chill, freeze, keep cold

refuge *n* **1, 2** = **shelter**, asylum, bolt hole, harbour, haven, hide-out, protection, resort, retreat, sanctuary, security

refugee *n* **a** = **exile**, displaced person, émigré, escapee, fugitive, runaway

refugee capital *n Finance.* money from abroad invested, esp. for a short term, in the country offering the highest interest rate.
refugium (rɪˈfjuːdʒɪəm) *n, pl* **refugia** (-dʒɪə). a geographical region that has remained unaltered by a climatic change affecting surrounding regions and that therefore forms a haven for relict fauna and flora. [C20: L: REFUGE]
refulgent (rɪˈfʌldʒənt) *adj Literary.* shining, brilliant, or radiant. [C16: from L *refulgēre*, from RE- + *fulgēre* to shine]
▸**reˈfulgence** *or* **reˈfulgency** *n* ▸**reˈfulgently** *adv*
refund ➊ *vb* (rɪˈfʌnd). *(tr)* **1** to give back (money, etc.), as when an article purchased is unsatisfactory. **2** to reimburse (a person). ◆ *n* (ˈriːˌfʌnd). **3** return of money to a purchaser or the amount so returned. [C14: from L *refundere*, from RE- + *fundere* to pour]
▸**reˈfundable** *adj* ▸**reˈfunder** *n*
re-fund (riːˈfʌnd) *vb (tr) Finance.* to discharge (an old or matured debt) by new borrowing, as by a new bond issue. [C20: from RE- + FUND]
refurbish ➊ (riːˈfɜːbɪʃ) *vb (tr)* to renovate, re-equip, or restore.
▸**reˈfurbishment** *n*
refusal ➊ (rɪˈfjuːzᵊl) *n* **1** the act or an instance of refusing. **2** the opportunity to reject or accept; option.
refuse[1] ➊ (rɪˈfjuːz) *vb* **refuses, refusing, refused. 1** *(tr)* to decline to accept (something offered): *to refuse promotion.* **2** to decline to give or grant (something) to (a person, etc.). **3** (when *tr, takes an infinitive*) to express determination not (to do something); decline: *he refuses to talk about it.* **4** (of a horse) to be unwilling to take (a jump). [C14: from OF *refuser*, from L *refundere* to pour back]
▸**reˈfusable** *adj* ▸**reˈfuser** *n*
refuse[2] ➊ (ˈrɛfjuːs) *n* **a** anything thrown away; waste; rubbish. **b** *(as modifier): a refuse collection.* [C15: from OF *refuser* to REFUSE[1]]
refusenik *or* **refusnik** (rɪˈfjuːznɪk) *n* **1** (formerly) a Jew in the Soviet Union who had been refused permission to emigrate. **2** a person who refuses to cooperate with a system or comply with a law because of a moral conviction. [C20: from REFUSE[1] + -NIK]
refute ➊ (rɪˈfjuːt) *vb* **refutes, refuting, refuted.** *(tr)* to prove (a statement, theory, charge, etc.) of (a person) to be false or incorrect; disprove. [C16: from L *refūtāre* to rebut]
▸**refutable** (ˈrɛfjʊtəbᵊl, rɪˈfjuː-) *adj* ▸**ˈrefutably** *adv* ▸**ˌrefuˈtation** *n* ▸**reˈfuter** *n*

> **USAGE NOTE** The use of *refute* to mean *deny* is thought by many people to be incorrect.

reg. *abbrev. for:* **1** regiment. **2** register(ed). **3** registrar. **4** regular(ly). **5** regulation.
regain ➊ (rɪˈgeɪn) *vb (tr)* **1** to take or get back; recover. **2** to reach again.
▸**reˈgainer** *n*
regal ➊ (ˈriːgᵊl) *adj* of, relating to, or befitting a king or queen; royal. [C14: from L *rēgālis*, from *rēx* king]
▸**reˈgality** *n* ▸**ˈregally** *adv*
regale ➊ (rɪˈgeɪl) *vb* **regales, regaling, regaled.** *(tr;* usually foll. by *with)* **1** to give delight or amusement to: *he regaled them with stories.* **2** to provide with choice or abundant food or drink. ◆ *n* **3** *Arch.* **3a** a feast. **3b** a delicacy of food or drink. [C17: from F *régaler*, from *gale* pleasure]
▸**reˈgalement** *n*
regalia ➊ (rɪˈgeɪlɪə) *n (pl, sometimes functioning as sing)* **1** the ceremonial emblems or robes of royalty, high office, an order, etc. **2** any splendid or special clothes; finery. [C16: from Med. L: royal privileges, from L *rēgālis* REGAL]
regard ➊ (rɪˈgɑːd) *vb* **1** to look closely or attentively at (something or someone); observe steadily. **2** *(tr)* to hold (a person or thing) in respect, admiration, or affection: *we regard your work very highly.* **3** *(tr)* to look upon or consider in a specified way: *she regarded her brother as her responsibility.* **4** *(tr)* to relate to; concern; have a bearing on. **5** to take notice of or pay attention to (something); heed: *he has never regarded the conventions.* **6 as regards.** *(prep)* in respect of; concerning. ◆ *n* **7** a gaze; look. **8** attention; heed: *he spends without regard to his bank balance.* **9** esteem, affection, or respect. **10** reference, relation, or connection (esp. in **with regard to** *or* **in regard to**). **11** *(pl)* good wishes or greetings (esp. in **with kind regards,** used at the close of a letter). **12 in this regard.** on this point. [C14: from OF *regarder* to look at, care about, from RE- + *garder* to GUARD]
regardant (rɪˈgɑːdᵊnt) *adj (usually postpositive) Heraldry.* (of a beast) shown looking backwards over its shoulder. [C15: from OF; see REGARD]
regardful ➊ (rɪˈgɑːdfʊl) *adj* **1** (often foll. by *of*) showing regard (for); heedful (of). **2** showing regard, respect, or consideration.
▸**reˈgardfully** *adv*
regarding ➊ (rɪˈgɑːdɪŋ) *prep* in respect of; on the subject of.
regardless ➊ (rɪˈgɑːdlɪs) *adj* **1** (usually foll. by *of*) taking no regard or heed; heedless. ◆ *adv* **2** in spite of everything; disregarding drawbacks.
▸**reˈgardlessly** *adv* ▸**reˈgardlessness** *n*
regatta (rɪˈgætə) *n* an organized series of races of yachts, rowing boats, etc. [C17: from obs. It. *rigatta* contest, from ?]
regd *abbrev. for* registered.
regelation (ˌriːdʒɪˈleɪʃən) *n* the rejoining together of two pieces of ice as a result of melting under pressure at the interface between them and subsequent refreezing.
▸**ˈregeˌlate** *vb*
regency (ˈriːdʒənsɪ) *n, pl* **regencies. 1** government by a regent. **2** the office of a regent. **3** a territory under the jurisdiction of a regent. [C15: from Med. L *regentia*, from L *regere* to rule]
Regency (ˈriːdʒənsɪ) *n* (preceded by *the*) **1** (in Britain) the period (1811–20) of the regency of the Prince of Wales (later George IV). **2** (in France) the period (1715-23) of the regency of Philip, Duke of Orleans. ◆ *adj* **3** characteristic of or relating to the Regency periods or to the styles of architecture, art, etc., produced in them.
regenerate ➊ *vb* (rɪˈdʒɛnəˌreɪt), **regenerates, regenerating, regenerated. 1** to undergo or cause to undergo moral, spiritual, or physical renewal or invigoration. **2** to form or be formed again; come or bring into existence once again. **3** to replace (lost or damaged tissues or organs) by new growth, or to cause (such tissues) to be replaced. **4** *(tr) Electronics.* to use positive feedback to improve the demodulation and amplification of a signal. ◆ *adj* (rɪˈdʒɛnərɪt). **5** morally, spiritually, or physically renewed or reborn.
▸**reˈgeneracy** *n* ▸**reˌgenerˈation** *n* ▸**reˈgenerative** *adj* ▸**reˈgeneratively** *adv* ▸**reˈgenerˌator** *n*
regent (ˈriːdʒənt) *n* **1** the ruler or administrator of a country during the minority, absence, or incapacity of its monarch. **2** *US & Canad.* a member of the governing board of certain schools and colleges. ◆ *adj* **3** *(usually postpositive)* acting or functioning as a regent: *a queen regent.* [C14: from L *regēns*, from *regere* to rule]
▸**ˈregental** *adj* ▸**ˈregentship** *n*
regent-bird *n Austral.* a bowerbird, the male of which has showy yellow and velvety-black plumage. [after the Prince *Regent*]
reggae (ˈrɛgeɪ) *n* a type of West Indian popular music having four beats to the bar, the upbeat being strongly accented. [C20: of West Indian origin]
regicide (ˈrɛdʒɪˌsaɪd) *n* **1** the killing of a king. **2** a person who kills a king. [C16: from L *rēx* king + -CIDE]
▸**ˌregiˈcidal** *adj*
regime ➊ *or* **régime** (reɪˈʒiːm) *n* **1** a system of government or a particu-

THESAURUS

refund *vb* **1 = give back,** make good, pay back, reimburse, repay, restore, return **2 = reimburse,** pay back, repay ◆ *n* **3 = repayment,** reimbursement, return
refurbish *vb* **= renovate,** clean up, do up, fix up (*inf., chiefly US & Canad.*), mend, overhaul, re-equip, refit, remodel, repair, restore, revamp, set to rights, spruce up
refusal *n* **1 = rejection,** defiance, denial, kick in the teeth (*sl.*), knock-back (*sl.*), negation, no, rebuff, repudiation, thumbs down **2 = option,** choice, consideration, opportunity
refuse[1] *vb* **1 = turn down,** decline, reject, repudiate, say no, spurn **2 = withhold,** deny **3 = abstain,** decline
Antonyms *vb* ≠ **turn down:** accept, agree, consent ≠ **withhold:** allow, approve, give, permit
refuse[2] *n* **= rubbish,** dregs, dross, garbage, junk (*inf.*), leavings, lees, litter, offscourings, scum, sediment, sweepings, trash, waste
refute *vb* **= disprove,** blow out of the water (*sl.*), confute, counter, discredit, give the lie to, negate, overthrow, prove false, rebut, silence
Antonyms *vb* confirm, prove, substantiate
regain *vb* **1 = recover,** get back, recapture, recoup, redeem, repossess, retake, retrieve, take back, win back **2 = get back to,** reach again, reattain, return to
regal *adj* **= royal,** fit for a king *or* queen, kingly *or* queenly, magnificent, majestic, noble, princely, proud, sovereign
regale *vb* **1 = entertain,** amuse, delight, divert, gratify **2 = serve,** feast, ply, refresh
regalia *pl n* **1, 2 = trappings,** accoutrements, finery, garb, gear, paraphernalia, rigout (*inf.*)
regard *vb* **1 = look at,** behold, check, check out (*inf.*), clock (*Brit. sl.*), eye, eyeball, gaze at, get a load of (*inf.*), mark, notice, observe, remark, scrutinize, take a dekko at (*Brit. sl.*), view, watch **3 = consider,** account, adjudge, believe, deem, esteem, estimate, hold, imagine, judge, look upon, rate, see, suppose, think, treat, value, view **5 = heed,** attend, listen to, mind, note, pay attention to, respect, take into consideration, take notice of **6 as regards = concerning,** pertaining to, regarding, relating to ◆ *n* **7 = look,** gaze, glance, scrutiny, stare **8 = heed,** attention, interest, mind, notice **9 = respect,** account, affection, attachment, care, concern, consideration, deference, esteem, honour, love, note, reputation, repute, store, sympathy, thought **10 = relation,** bearing, concern, connection, reference, relevance **11** *plural* **= good wishes,** best wishes, compliments, devoirs, greetings, respects, salutations **12** *As in* **in this regard = point,** aspect, detail, feature, item, matter, particular, respect
regardful *adj* **1, 2 = mindful,** attentive, aware, careful, considerate, dutiful, heedful, observant, respectful, thoughtful, watchful
regarding *prep* **= concerning,** about, apropos, as regards, as to, in *or* with regard to, in re, in respect of, in the matter of, on the subject of, re, respecting, with reference to
regardless *adj* **1 = heedless,** disregarding, inattentive, inconsiderate, indifferent, neglectful, negligent, rash, reckless, remiss, unconcerned, unmindful ◆ *adv* **2 = in spite of everything,** anyway, come what may, despite everything, for all that, in any case, nevertheless, no matter what, nonetheless, rain or shine
Antonyms *adj* ≠ **heedless:** heedful, mindful, regardful
regenerate *vb* **1 = renew,** breathe new life into, change, give a shot in the arm, inspirit, invigorate, kick-start, reawaken, reconstruct, re-establish, reinvigorate, rejuvenate, renovate, reproduce, restore, revive, revivify, uplift
Antonyms *vb* become moribund, decline, degenerate, stagnate, stultify
regime *n* **1, 2 = government,** administration, establishment, leadership, management, reign, rule, system

lar administration: *a fascist regime.* **2** a social system or order. **3** another word for **regimen** (sense 1). [C18: from F, from L *regimen* guidance, from *regere* to rule]

regimen ('rɛdʒɪˌmɛn) *n* **1** Also called: **regime.** a systematic course of therapy, often including a recommended diet. **2** administration or rule. [C14: from L: guidance]

regiment *n* ('rɛdʒɪmənt). **1** a military formation varying in size from a battalion to a number of battalions. **2** a large number in regular or organized groups. ◆ *vb* ('rɛdʒɪˌmɛnt). (*tr*) **3** to force discipline or order on, esp. in a domineering manner. **4** to organize into a regiment. **5** to form into organized groups. [C14: via OF from LL *regimentum* government, from L *regere* to rule]
▸**ˌregi'mental** *adj* ▸**ˌregi'mentally** *adv* ▸**ˌregimen'tation** *n*

regimentals (ˌrɛdʒɪ'mɛntᵊlz) *pl n* **1** the uniform and insignia of a regiment. **2** military dress.

Regina (rɪ'dʒaɪnə) *n* queen: now used chiefly in documents, inscriptions, etc. Cf. **Rex.** [L]

region 🅣 ('riːdʒən) *n* **1** any large, indefinite, and continuous part of a surface or space. **2** an area considered as a unit for geographical, functional, social, or cultural reasons. **3** an administrative division of a country, or a Canadian province. **4** a realm or sphere of activity or interest. **5** range, area, or scope: *in what region is the price likely to be?* **6** a division or part of the body: *the lumbar region.* [C14: from L *regiō*, from *regere* to govern]

regional 🅣 ('riːdʒənᵊl) *adj* of, characteristic of, or limited to a region.
▸**'regionally** *adv*

regionalism ('riːdʒənəˌlɪzəm) *n* **1** division of a country into administrative regions having partial autonomy. **2** loyalty to one's home region; regional patriotism.
▸**'regionalist** *n, adj*

régisseur *French.* (reʒisœr) *n* an official in a dance company with varying duties, usually including directing productions. [F, from *régir* to manage]

register 🅣 ('rɛdʒɪstə) *n* **1** an official or formal list recording names, events, or transactions. **2** the book in which such a list is written. **3** an entry in such a list. **4** a recording device that accumulates data, totals sums of money, etc.: *a cash register.* **5** a movable plate that controls the flow of air into a furnace, chimney, room, etc. **6** *Music.* **6a** the timbre characteristic of a certain manner of voice production. **6b** any of the stops on an organ as classified in respect of its tonal quality: *the flute register.* **7** *Printing.* the exact correspondence of lines of type, etc., on the two sides of a printed sheet of paper. **8** a form of a language associated with a particular social situation or subject matter. **9** the act or an instance of registering. ◆ *vb* **10** (*tr*) to enter or cause someone to enter (an event, person's name, ownership, etc.) on a register. **11** to show or be shown on a scale or other measuring instrument: *the current didn't register on the meter.* **12** to show or be shown in a person's face, bearing, etc.: *his face registered surprise.* **13** (*intr*) *Inf.* to have an effect; make an impression: *the news of her uncle's death just did not register.* **14** to send (a letter, package, etc.) by registered post. **15** (*tr*) *Printing.* to adjust (a printing press, forme, etc.) to ensure that the printed matter is in register. [C14: from Med. L *registrum*, from L *regerere* to transcribe, from RE- + *gerere* to bear]
▸**'registrable** *adj*

Registered General Nurse *n* (in Britain) a nurse who has completed a three-year training course and has been registered with the United Kingdom Central Council for Nursing, Midwifery, and Health Visiting. Abbrev.: **RGN.**

registered post *n* **1** a Post Office service by which compensation is paid for loss or damage to mail for which a registration fee has been paid. **2** mail sent by this service.

Registered Trademark *n* See **trademark** (sense 1).

register office *n Brit.* a government office where civil marriages are performed and births, marriages, and deaths are recorded. Often called: **registry office.**

register ton *n* the full name for **ton**[1] (sense 6).

registrar (ˌrɛdʒɪ'strɑː, 'rɛdʒɪˌstrɑː) *n* **1** a person who keeps official records. **2** an administrative official responsible for student records, enrolment procedure, etc., in a school, college, or university. **3** *Brit. & NZ.* a hospital doctor senior to a houseman but junior to a consultant. **4** *Austral.* the chief medical administrator of a large hospital. **5** *Chiefly US.* a person employed by a company to maintain a register of its security issues.
▸**'regisˌtrarship** *n*

registration (ˌrɛdʒɪ'streɪʃən) *n* **1a** the act of registering or state of being registered. **1b** (*as modifier*): *a registration number.* **2** an entry in a register. **3** a group of people, such as students, who register at a particular time. **4** *Austral.* **4a** a tax payable by the owner of a motor vehicle. **4b** the period paid for.

registration document *n Brit.* a document giving identification details of a motor vehicle, including its manufacturer, date of registration, and owner's name.

registration number *n* a sequence of letters and numbers assigned to a motor vehicle when it is registered, usually indicating the year and place of registration, displayed on numberplates at the front and rear of the vehicle.

registration plate *n Austral. & NZ.* the numberplate of a vehicle.

registry ('rɛdʒɪstrɪ) *n, pl* **registries. 1** a place where registers are kept. **2** the registration of a ship's country of origin: *a ship of Liberian registry.* **3** another word for **registration.**

registry office *n Brit.* another term for **register office.**

Regius professor ('riːdʒɪəs) *n Brit.* a person appointed by the Crown to a university chair founded by a royal patron. [C17: *regius*, from L: royal, from *rex* king]

reglet ('rɛglɪt) *n* **1** a flat narrow architectural moulding. **2** *Printing.* a strip of oiled wood used for spacing between lines. [C16: from OF, lit.: a little rule, from *régle* rule, from L *rēgula*]

regmaker ('rɛxˌmɑːkə) *n S. African.* a drink to relieve the symptoms of a hangover. [from Afrik., right maker]

regnal ('rɛgnəl) *adj* **1** of a sovereign or reign. **2** designating a year of a sovereign's reign calculated from the date of accession. [C17: from Med. L *rēgnālis*, from L *rēgnum* sovereignty; see REIGN]

regnant ('rɛgnənt) *adj* **1** (*postpositive*) reigning. **2** prevalent; current. [C17: from L *regnāre* to REIGN]
▸**'regnancy** *n*

regorge (rɪ'gɔːdʒ) *vb* **regorges, regorging, regorged. 1** (*tr*) to vomit up; disgorge. **2** (*intr*) (esp. of water) to flow or run back. [C17: from F *regorger*; see GORGE]

regress 🅣 *vb* (rɪ'grɛs). **1** (*intr*) to return or revert, as to a former place, condition, or mode of behaviour. **2** (*tr*) *Statistics.* to measure the extent to which (a dependent variable) is associated with one or more independent variables. ◆ *n* ('riːgrɛs). **3** movement in a backward direction; retrogression. [C14: from L *regressus*, from *regredī* to go back, from RE- + *gradī* to go]
▸**re'gressive** *adj* ▸**re'gressor** *n*

regression (rɪ'grɛʃən) *n* **1** *Psychol.* the adoption by an adult of behaviour more appropriate to a child. **2** *Statistics.* **2a** the measure of the association between one variable (the dependent variable) and other variables (the independent variables). **2b** (*as modifier*): *regression curve.* **3** *Geol.* the retreat of the sea from the land. **4** the act of regressing.

regret 🅣 (rɪ'grɛt) *vb* **regrets, regretting, regretted.** (*tr*) **1** (*may take a clause as object or an infinitive*) to feel sorry, repentant, or upset about. **2** to bemoan or grieve the death or loss of. ◆ *n* **3** a sense of repentance, guilt, or sorrow. **4** a sense of loss or grief. **5** (*pl*) a polite expression of sadness, esp. in a formal refusal of an invitation. [C14: from OF *regreter*, from ON]
▸**re'gretful** *adj* ▸**re'gretfully** *adv* ▸**re'gretfulness** *n* ▸**re'grettable** *adj* ▸**re'grettably** *adv*

> **USAGE NOTE** *Regretful* and *regretfully* are sometimes wrongly used where *regrettable* and *regrettably* are meant: *he gave a regretful smile; he smiled regretfully; this is a regrettable* (not *a regretful*) *mistake; regrettably* (not *regretfully*), *I shall be unable to attend.*

regroup (riː'gruːp) *vb* **1** to reorganize (military forces), esp. after an attack or a defeat. **2** (*tr*) to rearrange into a new grouping.

Regt *abbrev. for:* **1** Regent. **2** Regiment.

regulable ('rɛgjʊləbᵊl) *adj* able to be regulated.

regular 🅣 ('rɛgjʊlə) *adj* **1** normal, customary, or usual. **2** according to a uniform principle, arrangement, or order. **3** occurring at fixed or prearranged intervals: *a regular call on a customer.* **4** following a set rule or nor-

THESAURUS

region *n* **1, 2** = **area**, country, district, division, expanse, land, locality, part, patch, place, province, quarter, section, sector, territory, tract, turf (*US sl.*), zone **4** = **sphere**, domain, field, province, realm, world **5** = **vicinity**, area, neighbourhood, range, scope, sphere

regional *adj* = **local**, district, parochial, provincial, sectional, zonal

register *n* **1, 2** = **list**, annals, archives, catalogue, chronicle, diary, file, ledger, log, memorandum, record, roll, roster, schedule ◆ *vb* **10** = **record**, catalogue, check in, chronicle, enlist, enrol, enter, inscribe, list, note, set down, sign on *or* up, take down **12** = **show**, be shown, bespeak, betray, display, exhibit, express, indicate, manifest, record, reflect, reveal, say **13** *Informal* = **have an effect**, come home, dawn on, get through, impress, make an impression, sink in, tell

regress *vb* **1** = **revert**, backslide, degenerate, deteriorate, ebb, fall away *or* off, fall back, go back, lapse, lose ground, recede, relapse, retreat, retrocede, retrogress, return, turn the clock back, wane
Antonyms *vb* advance, improve, progress, wax

regret *vb* **1** = **feel sorry about**, be upset, bewail, cry over spilt milk, deplore, feel remorse about, lament, repent, rue, weep over **2** = **grieve**, bemoan, miss, mourn ◆ *n* **3** = **sorrow**, bitterness, compunction, contrition, lamentation, pang of conscience, penitence, remorse, repentance, ruefulness, self-reproach **4** = **grief**
Antonyms *vb* ≠ **feel sorry about:** be happy, be satisfied, feel satisfaction, have not looked back, rejoice ◆ *n* ≠ **sorrow:** callousness, contentment, impenitence, lack of compassion, pleasure, satisfaction

regretful *adj* **1** = **sorry**, apologetic, ashamed, contrite, disappointed, mournful, penitent, remorseful, repentant, rueful, sad, sorrowful

regrettable *adj* **1** = **unfortunate**, deplorable, disappointing, distressing, ill-advised, lamentable, pitiable, sad, shameful, unhappy, woeful, wrong

regular *adj* **1** = **normal**, common, commonplace, customary, daily, everyday, habitual, ordinary, routine, typical, unvarying, usual **2** = **systematic**, consistent, constant, established, even, ordered, set, stated, steady, uniform **3** = **periodic**, fixed, rhythmic, set, systematic **4** = **methodical**, dependable, efficient, formal, orderly, standardized, steady, systematic **5** = **even**, balanced, flat, level, smooth, straight,

mal practice; methodical or orderly. **5** symmetrical in appearance or form; even: *regular features.* **6** (*prenominal*) organized, elected, conducted, etc., in a proper or officially prescribed manner. **7** (*prenominal*) officially qualified or recognized: *he's not a regular doctor.* **8** (*prenominal*) (intensifier): *a regular fool.* **9** *US & Canad. inf.* likable, dependable, or nice: *a regular guy.* **10** denoting or relating to the personnel or units of the permanent military services: *a regular soldier.* **11** (of flowers) having any of their parts, esp. petals, alike in size, etc.; symmetrical. **12** *Grammar.* following the usual pattern of formation in a language. **13** *Maths.* **13a** (of a polygon) equilateral and equiangular. **13b** (of a polyhedron) having identical regular polygons as faces. **13c** (of a prism) having regular polygons as bases. **13d** (of a pyramid) having a regular polygon as a base and the altitude passing through the centre of the base. **14** *Bot.* (of a flower) having radial symmetry. **15** (*postpositive*) subject to the rule of an established religious order or community: *canons regular.* ◆ *n* **16** a professional long-term serviceman in a military unit. **17** *Inf.* a person who does something regularly, such as attending a theatre. **18** a member of a religious order or congregation, as contrasted with a secular. [C14: from OF *reguler,* from L *rēgulāris* of a bar of wood or metal, from *rēgula* ruler, model]
▸ˌ**reguˈlarity** *n* ▸ˈ**regularˌize** *or* ˈ**regularˌise** *vb* ▸ˈ**regularly** *adv*

regulate Ⓣ (ˈrɛgjʊˌleɪt) *vb* **regulates, regulating, regulated.** (*tr*) **1** to adjust (the amount of heat, sound, etc.) as required; control. **2** to adjust (an instrument or appliance) so that it operates correctly. **3** to bring into conformity with a rule, principle, or usage. [C17: from LL *rēgulāre* to control, from L *rēgula* ruler]
▸ˈ**regulative** *or* ˈ**regulatory** *adj* ▸ˈ**regulatively** *adv*

regulation Ⓣ (ˌrɛgjʊˈleɪʃən) *n* **1** the act or process of regulating. **2** a rule, principle, or condition that governs procedure or behaviour. **3** (*modifier*) as required by official rules: *regulation uniform.* **4** (*modifier*) normal; usual; conforming to accepted standards: *a regulation haircut.*

regulator (ˈrɛgjʊˌleɪtə) *n* **1** a person or thing that regulates. **2** the mechanism by which the speed of a timepiece is regulated. **3** any of various mechanisms or devices, such as a governor valve, for controlling fluid flow, pressure, temperature, etc.

regulo (ˈrɛgjʊləʊ) *n* any of a number of temperatures to which a gas oven may be set: *cook at regulo 4.* [C20: from *Regulo,* trademark for a type of thermostatic control on gas ovens]

regulus (ˈrɛgjʊləs) *n, pl* **reguluses** *or* **reguli** (-ˌlaɪ). impure metal forming beneath the slag during the smelting of ores. [C16: from L: a petty king, from *rēx* king; formerly used for *antimony,* because it combines readily with gold, the king of metals]
▸ˈ**reguline** *adj*

regurgitate Ⓣ (rɪˈgɜːdʒɪˌteɪt) *vb* **regurgitates, regurgitating, regurgitated. 1** to vomit forth (partially digested food). **2** (of some birds and animals) to bring back to the mouth (undigested or partly digested food to feed the young). **3** (*intr*) to be cast up or out, esp. from the mouth. **4** (*intr*) *Med.* (of blood) to flow in a direction opposite to the normal one, esp. through a defective heart valve. [C17: from Med. L *regurgitāre,* from RE- + *gurgitāre* to flood, from L *gurges* whirlpool]
▸**reˈgurgitant** *n, adj* ▸**reˌgurgiˈtation** *n*

rehabilitate Ⓣ (ˌriːəˈbɪlɪˌteɪt) *vb* **rehabilitates, rehabilitating, rehabilitated.** (*tr*) **1** to help (a physically or mentally disabled person or an ex-prisoner) to readapt to society or a new job, as by vocational guidance, retraining, or therapy. **2** to restore to a former position or rank. **3** to restore the good reputation of. [C16: from Med. L *rehabilitāre* to restore, from RE- + L *habilitās* skill]
▸ˌ**rehaˌbiliˈtation** *n* ▸ˌ**rehaˈbilitative** *adj*

Rehabilitation Department *n NZ.* a government department set up after World War II to assist ex-servicemen. Often shortened to **rehab.**

rehash Ⓣ *vb* (riːˈhæʃ). **1** (*tr*) to rework, reuse, or make over (old or already used material). ◆ *n* (ˈriːˌhæʃ). **2** something consisting of old, reworked, or reused material. [C19: from RE- + HASH[1] (to chop into pieces)]

rehearsal Ⓣ (rɪˈhɜːsᵊl) *n* **1** a session of practising a play, concert, etc., in preparation for public performance. **2 in rehearsal.** being prepared for public performance.

rehearse Ⓣ (rɪˈhɜːs) *vb* **rehearses, rehearsing, rehearsed. 1** to practise (a play, concert, etc.), in preparation for public performance. **2** (*tr*) to run through; recount; recite: *he rehearsed the grievances of the committee.* **3** (*tr*) to train or drill (a person) for public performance. [C16: from Anglo-Norman *rehearser,* from OF *rehercier* to harrow a second time, from RE- + *herce* harrow]
▸**reˈhearser** *n*

reheat *vb* (riːˈhiːt). **1** to heat or be heated again: *to reheat yesterday's soup.* **2** (*tr*) to add fuel to (the exhaust gases of an aircraft jet engine) to produce additional heat and thrust. ◆ *n* (ˈriːˌhiːt), *also* **reheating. 3** a process in which additional fuel is ignited in the exhaust gases of a jet engine to produce additional thrust.
▸**reˈheater** *n*

rehoboam (ˌriːəˈbəʊəm) *n* a wine bottle holding the equivalent of six normal bottles. [after *Rehoboam,* a son of King Solomon, from Heb., lit.: the nation is enlarged]

Reich (raɪk) *n* **1** the Holy Roman Empire (962–1806) (**First Reich**). **2** the Hohenzollern empire in Germany from 1871 to 1918 (**Second Reich**). **3** the Nazi dictatorship (1933–45) in Germany (**Third Reich**). [G: kingdom]

Reichsmark (ˈraɪksˌmɑːk) *n, pl* **Reichsmarks** *or* **Reichsmark.** the standard monetary unit of Germany between 1924 and 1948.

Reichstag (ˈraɪksˌtɑːg) *n* **1** the legislative assembly of Germany (1867–1933). **2** the building in Berlin in which this assembly met.

reify (ˈriːɪˌfaɪ) *vb* **reifies, reifying, reified.** (*tr*) to consider or make (an abstract idea or concept) real or concrete. [C19: from L *rēs* thing]
▸ˌ**reifiˈcation** *n* ▸ˌ**reifiˈcatory** *adj* ▸ˈ**reiˌfier** *n*

reign Ⓣ (reɪn) *n* **1** the period during which a monarch is the official ruler of a country. **2** a period during which a person or thing is dominant or powerful: *the reign of violence.* ◆ *vb* (*intr*) **3** to exercise the power and authority of a sovereign. **4** to be accorded the rank and title of a sovereign without having ruling authority. **5** to predominate; prevail: *darkness reigns.* **6** (*usually present participle*) to be the most recent winner of a contest, etc.: *the reigning champion.* [C13: from OF *reigne,* from L *rēgnum* kingdom, from *rēx* king]

> **USAGE NOTE** *Reign* is sometimes wrongly written for *rein* in certain phrases: *he gave full rein* (not *reign*) *to his feelings; it will be necessary to rein in* (not *reign in*) *public spending.*

reiki (ˈreɪkɪ) *n* a form of therapy in which the practitioner is believed to channel energy into the patient in order to encourage healing or restore well-being. [Japanese, from *rei* universal + *ki* life force]

reimburse Ⓣ (ˌriːɪmˈbɜːs) *vb* **reimburses, reimbursing, reimbursed.** (*tr*) to repay or compensate (someone) for (money already spent, losses, damages, etc.). [C17: from RE- + *imburse,* from Med. L *imbursāre* to put in a moneybag, from *bursa* PURSE]
▸ˌ**reimˈbursable** *adj* ▸ˌ**reimˈbursement** *n* ▸ˌ**reimˈburser** *n*

reimport *vb* (ˌriːɪmˈpɔːt, riːˈɪmpɔːt). **1** (*tr*) to import (goods manufactured from exported raw materials). ◆ *n* (riːˈɪmpɔːt). **2** the act of reimporting. **3** a reimported commodity.
▸ˌ**reimporˈtation** *n*

rein Ⓣ (reɪn) *n* **1** (*often pl*) one of a pair of long straps, usually connected together and made of leather, used to control a horse. **2** a similar device used to control a very young child. **3** any form or means of control: *to take up the reins of government.* **4** the direction in which a rider turns (in **on a left rein**). **5** something that restrains, controls, or guides. **6 give (a) free rein.** to allow considerable freedom; remove restraints. **7 keep a tight rein on.** to control carefully; limit: *we have to keep a tight rein on expenditure.* ◆ *vb* **8** (*tr*) to check, restrain, hold back, or halt with or as if with reins. **9** to control or guide (a horse) with a rein or reins: *they reined left.* ◆ See also **rein in.** [C13: from OF *resne,* from L *retinēre* to hold back, from RE- + *tenēre* to hold]

> **USAGE NOTE** See at **reign.**

THESAURUS

symmetrical, uniform **7** = **official**, approved, bona fide, classic, correct, established, formal, orthodox, prevailing, proper, sanctioned, standard, time-honoured, traditional
Antonyms *adj* ≠ **normal:** abnormal, exceptional, infrequent, irregular, occasional, rare, uncommon, unconventional, unusual ≠ **systematic:** erratic, inconsistent, inconstant, irregular, varied ≠ **methodical:** disorderly, unmethodical ≠ **even:** erratic, irregular, uneven

regulate *vb* **1, 2** = **adjust**, balance, fit, moderate, modulate, tune **3** = **control**, administer, arrange, conduct, direct, govern, guide, handle, manage, monitor, order, organize, oversee, rule, run, settle, superintend, supervise, systematize

regulation *n* **1** = **adjustment**, modulation, tuning **1** = **control**, administration, arrangement, direction, governance, government, management, supervision **2** = **rule**, canon, commandment, decree, dictate, direction, edict, law, order, ordinance, precept, procedure, requirement, standing order, statute ◆ *adj* **3** = **official**, mandatory, prescribed, required **4** = **usual**, conventional, customary, normal, standard

regurgitate *vb* **1** = **vomit**, barf (*US sl.*), chuck (up) (*sl., chiefly US*), chunder, disgorge, puke (*sl.*), sick up (*inf.*), spew (out *or* up), throw up (*inf.*)

rehabilitate *vb* **1** = **reintegrate**, adjust **2** = **restore**, re-establish, reinstate **3** = **redeem**, clear, reform, restore, save

rehash *vb* **1** = **rework**, alter, change, make over, rearrange, refashion, rejig (*inf.*), reshuffle, reuse, rewrite ◆ *n* **2** = **reworking**, new version, rearrangement, rewrite

rehearsal *n* **1** = **practice**, drill, going-over (*inf.*), practice session, preparation, reading, rehearsing, run-through

rehearse *vb* **1** = **practise**, act, drill, go over, prepare, ready, recite, repeat, run through, study, train, try out **2** = **recite**, delineate, depict, describe, detail, enumerate, go over, list, narrate, recount, relate, review, run through, spell out, tell, trot out (*inf.*)

reign *n* **1, 2** = **rule**, ascendancy, command, control, dominion, empire, hegemony, influence, monarchy, power, sovereignty, supremacy, sway ◆ *vb* **3** = **rule**, administer, be in power, command, govern, hold sway, influence, occupy *or* sit on the throne, wear the crown, wield the sceptre **5** = **be supreme**, be rampant, be rife, hold sway, obtain, predominate, prevail

reimburse *vb* = **pay back**, compensate, indemnify, recompense, refund, remunerate, repay, restore, return, square up

rein *n* **1, 3** = **control**, brake, bridle, check, curb, harness, hold, restraint, restriction **6 give (a) free rein** = **give a free hand**, free, give a blank cheque, give carte blanche, give (someone) his *or* her head, give way to, indulge, let go, remove restraints ◆ *vb* **8** = **control**, bridle, check, curb, halt, hold, hold back, limit, restrain, restrict, slow down

DICTIONARY

reincarnate *vb* (ˌriːɪnˈkɑːˌneɪt), **reincarnates, reincarnating, reincarnated.** (*tr; often passive*) **1** to cause to undergo reincarnation; be born again. ◆ *adj* (ˌriːɪnˈkɑːnɪt). **2** born again in a new body.

reincarnation Ⓣ (ˌriːɪnkɑːˈneɪʃən) *n* **1** the belief that on the death of the body the soul transmigrates to or is born again in another body. **2** the incarnation or embodiment of a soul in a new body after it has left the old one at physical death. **3** embodiment again in a new form, as of a principle or idea.
▸ˌ**reincarˈnationist** *n, adj*

reindeer (ˈreɪnˌdɪə) *n, pl* **reindeer** *or* **reindeers.** a large deer, having large branched antlers in the male and female and inhabiting the arctic regions. It also occurs in North America, where it is known as a caribou. [C14: from ON *hreindýri*, from *hreinn* reindeer + *dyr* animal]

reindeer moss *n* any of various lichens which occur in arctic and subarctic regions, providing food for reindeer.

reinforce Ⓣ (ˌriːɪnˈfɔːs) *vb* **reinforces, reinforcing, reinforced.** (*tr*) **1** to give added strength or support to. **2** to give added emphasis to; stress or increase: *his rudeness reinforced my determination.* **3** to give added support to (a military force) by providing more men, supplies, etc. [C17: from F *renforcer*]
▸ˌ**reinˈforcement** *n*

reinforced concrete *n* concrete with steel bars, mesh, etc., embedded in it to enable it to withstand tensile and shear stresses.

reinforced plastic *n* plastic with fibrous matter, such as carbon fibre, embedded in it to strengthen it.

rein in *vb* (*adv*) to stop (a horse) by pulling on the reins.

reins (reɪnz) *pl n Arch.* the kidneys or loins. [C14: from OF, from L *rēnēs* the kidneys]

reinstate Ⓣ (ˌriːɪnˈsteɪt) *vb* **reinstates, reinstating, reinstated.** (*tr*) to restore to a former rank or condition.
▸ˌ**reinˈstatement** *n* ▸ˌ**reinˈstator** *n*

reinsurer (ˌriːɪnˈʃʊərə) *n* an insurance company which will accept business from other insurance companies, thus enabling the risks to be spread.
▸ˌ**reinˈsurance** *n*

reinvent (ˌriːɪnˈvɛnt) *vb* (*tr*) **1** to replace (a product, etc.) with an entirely new version. **2** to duplicate (something that already exists) in what is therefore a wasted effort (esp. in **reinvent the wheel**).

reissue (ˌriːˈɪʃjuː) *n* **1** a book, record, etc., that is published or released again after being unavailable for a time. ◆ *vb* **2** (*tr*) to publish or release (a book, record, etc.) again after a period of unavailability.

reiterate Ⓣ (riːˈɪtəˌreɪt) *vb* **reiterates, reiterating, reiterated.** (*tr; may take a clause as object*) to say or do again or repeatedly. [C16: from L *reiterāre*, from RE- + *iterāre* to do again, from *iterum* again]
▸**reˌiterˈation** *n* ▸**reˈiterative** *adj* ▸**reˈiteratively** *adv*

reive (riːv) *vb* **reives, reiving, reived.** (*intr*) *Scot. & N English dialect.* to go on a plundering raid. [var. of REAVE]
▸ˈ**reiver** *n*

reject Ⓣ *vb* (rɪˈdʒɛkt). (*tr*) **1** to refuse to accept, use, believe, etc. **2** to throw out as useless or worthless; discard. **3** to rebuff (a person). **4** (of an organism) to fail to accept (a foreign tissue graft or organ transplant). ◆ *n* (ˈriːdʒɛkt). **5** something rejected as imperfect, unsatisfactory, or useless. [C15: from L *rēicere* to throw back, from RE- + *jacere* to hurl]
▸**reˈjecter** *or* **reˈjector** *n* ▸**reˈjection** *n* ▸**reˈjective** *adj*

rejig Ⓣ (riːˈdʒɪɡ) *vb* **rejigs, rejigging, rejigged.** (*tr*) **1** to re-equip (a factory or plant). **2** *Inf.* to rearrange, manipulate, etc., sometimes in an unscrupulous way. ◆ *n* **3** the act or process of rejigging.
▸**reˈjigger** *n*

rejoice Ⓣ (rɪˈdʒɔɪs) *vb* **rejoices, rejoicing, rejoiced.** (when *tr, takes a clause as object or an infinitive;* when *intr,* often foll. by *in*) to feel or express great joy or happiness. [C14: from OF *resjoir*, from RE- + *joir* to be glad, from L *gaudēre* to rejoice]
▸**reˈjoicer** *n*

rejoin[1] (riːˈdʒɔɪn) *vb* **1** to come again into company with (someone or something). **2** (*tr*) to put or join together again; reunite.

rejoin[2] Ⓣ (rɪˈdʒɔɪn) *vb* (*tr*) **1** to answer or reply. **2** *Law.* to answer (a plaintiff's reply). [C15: from OF *rejoign-*, stem of *rejoindre;* see RE-, JOIN]

rejoinder Ⓣ (rɪˈdʒɔɪndə) *n* **1** a reply or response to a question or remark. **2** *Law.* (in pleading) the answer made by a defendant to the plaintiff's reply. [C15: from OF *rejoindre* to REJOIN[2]]

rejuvenate Ⓣ (rɪˈdʒuːvɪˌneɪt) *vb* **rejuvenates, rejuvenating, rejuvenated.** (*tr*) **1** to give new youth, restored vitality, or youthful appearance to. **2** (*usually passive*) *Geog.* to cause (a river) to begin eroding more vigorously to a new lower base level. [C19: from RE- + L *juvenis* young]
▸**reˌjuveˈnation** *n* ▸**reˈjuveˌnator** *n*

rejuvenesce (rɪˌdʒuːvəˈnɛs) *vb* **rejuvenesces, rejuvenescing, rejuvenesced.** **1** to make or become youthful or restored to vitality. **2** *Biol.* to convert (cells) or (of cells) to be converted into a more active form.
▸**reˌjuveˈnescence** *n* ▸**reˌjuveˈnescent** *adj*

rel. *abbrev. for:* **1** relating. **2** relative(ly). **3** released. **4** religion. **5** religious.

relapse Ⓣ (rɪˈlæps) *vb* **relapses, relapsing, relapsed.** (*intr*) **1** to lapse back into a former state or condition, esp. one involving bad habits. **2** to become ill again after apparent recovery. ◆ *n* **3** the act or an instance of relapsing. **4** the return of ill health after an apparent or partial recovery. [C16: from L *relabī*, from RE- + *labī* to slip, slide]
▸**reˈlapser** *n*

relapsing fever *n* any of various infectious diseases characterized by recurring fever, caused by the bite of body lice or ticks. Also called: **recurrent fever.**

relate Ⓣ (rɪˈleɪt) *vb* **relates, relating, related.** **1** (*tr*) to tell or narrate (a story, etc.). **2** (often foll. by *to*) to establish association (between two or more things) or (of something) to have relation or reference (to something else). **3** (*intr;* often foll. by *to*) to form a sympathetic or significant relationship (with other people, things, etc.). [C16: from L *relātus* brought back, from *referre*, from RE- + *ferre* to bear]
▸**reˈlatable** *adj* ▸**reˈlater** *n*

related Ⓣ (rɪˈleɪtɪd) *adj* **1** connected; associated. **2** connected by kinship or marriage. **3** (in diatonic music) denoting or relating to a key that has notes in common with another key or keys.
▸**reˈlatedness** *n*

relation Ⓣ (rɪˈleɪʃən) *n* **1** the state or condition of being related or the manner in which things are related. **2** connection by blood or marriage; kinship. **3** a person who is connected by blood or marriage; relative. **4** reference or regard (esp. in **in** *or* **with relation to**). **5** the position, association, connection, or status of one person or thing with regard to another. **6** the act of relating or narrating. **7** an account or narrative. **8** *Law.* the statement of grounds of complaint made by a relator. **9** *Logic, maths.* **9a** an association between ordered pairs of objects, numbers, etc., such as ... is greater than .... **9b** the set of ordered pairs whose members have such an association. ◆ See also **relations.** [C14: from L *relātiō* a narration, a relation (between philosophical concepts)]

relational (rɪˈleɪʃənᵊl) *adj* **1** *Grammar.* indicating or expressing syntactic relation, as for example the case endings in Latin. **2** having relation or

THESAURUS

reincarnation *n* **1** = **rebirth**, metempsychosis, transmigration of souls

reinforce *vb* **1** = **strengthen**, augment, bolster, buttress, fortify, harden, prop, shore up, stiffen, supplement, support, toughen **2** = **stress**, emphasize, increase, underline
Antonyms *vb* undermine, weaken

reinforcement *n* **1** = **support**, brace, buttress, prop, shore, stay **2** = **strengthening**, addition, amplification, augmentation, enlargement, fortification, increase, supplement **3** *plural* = **reserves**, additional *or* fresh troops, auxiliaries, support

reinstate *vb* = **restore**, bring back, recall, re-establish, rehabilitate, replace, return

reiterate *vb Formal* = **repeat**, do again, iterate, recapitulate, restate, retell, say again

reject *vb* **1** = **deny**, decline, disallow, exclude, renounce, repudiate, veto **2** = **discard**, bin, cast aside, eliminate, jettison, scrap, throw away *or* out **3** = **rebuff**, jilt, refuse, repulse, say no to, spurn, turn down ◆ *n* **5** = **castoff**, discard, failure, flotsam, second
Antonyms *vb* ≠ **deny**: accept, agree, allow, approve, permit ≠ **rebuff**: accept ≠ **discard**: accept, receive, select ◆ *n* ≠ **castoff**: prize, treasure

rejection *n* **1** = **denial**, dismissal, exclusion, renunciation, repudiation, thumbs down, veto **3** = **rebuff**, brushoff, bum's rush (*sl.*), kick in the teeth (*sl.*), knock-back (*sl.*), refusal, the (old) heave-ho (*inf.*)
Antonyms *n* ≠ **denial**: acceptance, affirmation, approval ≠ **rebuff**: acceptance, selection

rejig *vb* **2** *Informal* = **rearrange**, alter, juggle, manipulate, massage, reorganize, reshuffle, tweak

rejoice *vb* = **be glad**, be happy, be overjoyed, celebrate, delight, exult, glory, joy, jump for joy, make merry, revel, triumph
Antonyms *vb* be sad, be unhappy, be upset, grieve, lament, mourn

rejoicing *n* = **happiness**, celebration, cheer, delight, elation, exultation, festivity, gaiety, gladness, joy, jubilation, merrymaking, revelry, triumph

rejoin[2] *vb* **1** = **reply**, answer, come back with, respond, retort, return, riposte

rejoinder *n* **1** = **reply**, answer, comeback (*inf.*), counter, counterattack, response, retort, riposte

rejuvenate *vb* **1** = **revitalize**, breathe new life into, give new life to, make young again, reanimate, refresh, regenerate, reinvigorate, renew, restore, restore vitality to, revivify

relapse *vb* **1** = **lapse**, backslide, degenerate, fail, fall back, regress, retrogress, revert, slip back, weaken **2** = **worsen**, deteriorate, fade, fail, sicken, sink, weaken ◆ *n* **3** = **lapse**, backsliding, fall from grace, recidivism, regression, retrogression, reversion **4** = **worsening**, deterioration, recurrence, setback, turn for the worse, weakening
Antonyms *vb* ≠ **worsen**: get better, improve, rally, recover ◆ *n* ≠ **worsening**: improvement, rally, recovery, turn for the better

relate *vb* **1** = **tell**, chronicle, describe, detail, give an account of, impart, narrate, present, recite, recount, rehearse, report, set forth **2** = **connect**, ally, associate, coordinate, correlate, couple, join, link **2** = **concern**, appertain, apply, bear upon, be relevant to, have reference to, have to do with, pertain, refer
Antonyms *vb* ≠ **connect**: detach, disconnect, dissociate, divorce ≠ **concern**: be irrelevant to, be unconnected, have nothing to do with

related *adj* **1** = **associated**, accompanying, affiliated, agnate, akin, allied, cognate, concomitant, connected, correlated, interconnected, joint, linked **2** = **akin**, agnate, cognate, consanguineous, kin, kindred
Antonyms *adj* ≠ **associated**: separate, unconnected, unrelated ≠ **akin**: unrelated

relation *n* **1** = **connection**, application, bearing, bond, comparison, correlation, interdependence, link, pertinence, similarity, tie-in **2** = **kinship**, affiliation, affinity, consanguinity, kindred, propinquity, relationship **3** = **relative**, kin, kinsman *or* kinswoman **4** = **regard**, reference **6** = **narration**, description, recital, recountal **7** = **account**, description, narrative, report, story, tale

being related. **3** *Computing.* based on data that is interconnected, often in tabular form.

relations ⓣ (rɪˈleɪʃənz) *pl n* **1** social, political, or personal connections or dealings between or among individuals, groups, nations, etc. **2** family or relatives. **3** *Euphemistic.* sexual intercourse.

relationship ⓣ (rɪˈleɪʃənʃɪp) *n* **1** the state of being connected or related. **2** association by blood or marriage; kinship. **3** the mutual dealings, connections, or feelings that exist between two countries, people, etc. **4** an emotional or sexual affair or liaison.

relative ⓣ (ˈrɛlətɪv) *adj* **1** having meaning or significance only in relation to something else; not absolute. **2** (*prenominal*) (of a scientific quantity) being measured or stated relative to some other substance or measurement: *relative density.* **3** (*prenominal*) comparative or respective: *the relative qualities of speed and accuracy.* **4** (*postpositive;* foll. by *to*) in proportion (to); corresponding (to): *earnings relative to production.* **5** having reference (to); pertinent (to). **6** *Grammar.* denoting or belonging to a class of words that function as subordinating conjunctions in introducing relative clauses such as *who, which,* and *that.* Cf. **demonstrative. 7** *Grammar.* denoting or relating to a clause (**relative clause**) that modifies a noun or pronoun occurring earlier in the sentence. **8** (of a musical key or scale) having the same key signature as another key or scale. ◆ *n* **9** a person who is related by blood or marriage; relation. **10** a relative pronoun, clause, or grammatical construction. [C16: from LL *relātīvus* referring]
▸ˈ**relatively** *adv* ▸ˈ**relativeness** *n*

relative aperture *n Photog.* the ratio of the equivalent focal length of a lens to the effective aperture of the lens.

relative atomic mass *n* the ratio of the average mass per atom of the naturally occurring form of an element to one-twelfth of the mass of an atom of carbon-12. Symbol: A_r Abbrev.: **r.a.m.** Former name: **atomic weight.**

relative density *n* the ratio of the density of a substance to the density of a standard substance under specified conditions. For liquids and solids the standard is usually water at 4°C. For gases the standard is air or hydrogen at the same temperature and pressure as the substance. See also **specific gravity, vapour density.**

relative frequency *n Statistics.* the ratio of the actual number of favourable events to the total possible number of events.

relative humidity *n* the mass of water vapour present in the air expressed as a percentage of the mass present in an equal volume of saturated air at the same temperature.

relative majority *n Brit.* the excess of votes or seats won by the winner of an election over the runner-up when no candidate or party has more than 50 per cent. Cf. **absolute majority.**

relative molecular mass *n* the sum of all the relative atomic masses of the atoms in a molecule; the ratio of the average mass per molecule of a specified isotopic composition of a substance to one-twelfth the mass of an atom of carbon-12. Symbol: M_r Abbrev.: **r.m.m.** Former name: **molecular weight.**

relative permeability *n* the ratio of the permeability of a medium to that of free space.

relative permittivity *n* the ratio of the permittivity of a substance to that of free space.

relativism (ˈrɛlətɪˌvɪzəm) *n* any theory holding that truth or moral or aesthetic value, etc., is not universal or absolute but may differ between individuals or cultures.
▸ˈ**relativist** *n, adj* ▸ˌ**relativˈistic** *adj*

relativity (ˌrɛləˈtɪvɪtɪ) *n* **1** either of two theories developed by Albert Einstein, the **special theory of relativity**, which requires that the laws of physics shall be the same as seen by any two different observers in uniform relative motion, and the **general theory of relativity**, which considers observers with relative acceleration and leads to a theory of gravitation. **2** the state or quality of being relative.

relator (rɪˈleɪtə) *n* **1** a person who relates a story; narrator. **2** *English law.* a person who gives information upon which the attorney general brings an action.

relatum (rɪˈleɪtəm) *n, pl* **relata** (-tə). *Logic.* one of the objects between which a relation is said to hold.

relax ⓣ (rɪˈlæks) *vb* **1** to make (muscles, a grip, etc.) less tense or rigid or (of muscles, a grip, etc.) to become looser or less rigid. **2** (*intr*) to take rest, as from work or effort. **3** to lessen the force of (effort, concentration) or (of effort) to become diminished. **4** to make (rules or discipline) less rigid or strict or (of rules, etc.) to diminish in severity. **5** (*intr*) (of a person) to become less formal; unbend. [C15: from L *relaxāre* to loosen, from RE- + *laxāre,* from *laxus* loose]
▸**reˈlaxed** *adj* ▸**relaxedly** (rɪˈlæksɪdlɪ) *adv* ▸**reˈlaxer** *n*

relaxant (rɪˈlæksᵊnt) *n* **1** *Med.* a drug or agent that relaxes, esp. one that relaxes tense muscles. ◆ *adj* **2** of or tending to produce relaxation.

relaxation ⓣ (ˌriːlækˈseɪʃən) *n* **1** rest or refreshment, as after work or effort; recreation. **2** a form of rest or recreation: *his relaxation is cricket.* **3** a partial lessening of a punishment, duty, etc. **4** the act of relaxing or state of being relaxed. **5** *Physics.* the return of a system to equilibrium after a displacement from this state.

relaxin (rɪˈlæksɪn) *n* **1** a mammalian polypeptide hormone secreted during pregnancy, which relaxes the pelvic ligaments. **2** a preparation of this hormone, used to facilitate childbirth. [C20: from RELAX + -IN]

relay ⓣ *n* (ˈriːleɪ). **1** a person or team of people relieving others, as on a shift. **2** a fresh team of horses, etc., posted along a route to relieve others. **3** the act of relaying or process of being relayed. **4** short for **relay race. 5** an automatic device that controls a valve, switch, etc., by means of an electric motor, solenoid, or pneumatic mechanism. **6** *Electronics.* an electrical device in which a small change in current or voltage controls the switching on or off of circuits. **7** *Radio.* **7a** a combination of a receiver and transmitter designed to receive radio signals and retransmit them. **7b** (*as modifier*): *a relay station.* ◆ *vb* (rɪˈleɪ). (*tr*) **8** to carry or spread (news or information) by relays. **9** to supply or replace with relays. **10** to retransmit (a signal) by means of a relay. **11** *Brit.* to broadcast (a performance) by sending out signals through a transmitting station. [C15 *relaien,* from OF *relaier* to leave behind, from RE- + *laier* to leave, ult. from L *laxāre* to loosen]

relay race *n* a race between two or more teams of contestants in which each contestant covers a specified portion of the distance.

release ⓣ (rɪˈliːs) *vb* **releases, releasing, released.** (*tr*) **1** to free (a person or animal) from captivity or imprisonment. **2** to free (someone) from obligation or duty. **3** to free (something) from (one's grip); let fall. **4** to issue (a record, film, or book) for sale or circulation. **5** to make (news or information) known or allow (news, etc.) to be made known. **6** *Law.* to relinquish (a right, claim, or title) in favour of someone else. ◆ *n* **7** the act of freeing or state of being freed. **8** the act of issuing for sale or publication. **9** something issued for sale or public showing, esp. a film or a record: *a new release from Bob Dylan.* **10** a news item, etc., made available for publication, broadcasting, etc. **11** *Law.* the surrender of a claim, right, title, etc., in favour of someone else. **12** a control mechanism for starting or stopping an engine. **13** the control mechanism for the shutter in a camera. [C13: from OF *relesser,* from L *relaxāre* to slacken]
▸**reˈleaser** *n*

relegate ⓣ (ˈrɛlɪˌgeɪt) *vb* **relegates, relegating, relegated.** (*tr*) **1** to move to a position of less authority, importance, etc.; demote. **2** (*usually passive*) *Chiefly Brit.* to demote (a football team, etc.) to a lower division. **3** to assign or refer (a matter) to another. **4** (foll. by *to*) to banish or exile. **5** to assign (something) to a particular group or category. [C16: from L *relēgāre,* from RE- + *lēgāre* to send]
▸ˈ**releˌgatable** *adj* ▸ˌ**releˈgation** *n*

relent ⓣ (rɪˈlɛnt) *vb* (*intr*) **1** to change one's mind about some decision, esp. a harsh one; become more mild or amenable. **2** (of the pace or in-

THESAURUS

relations *pl n* **1** = **dealings**, affairs, associations, communications, connections, contact, interaction, intercourse, liaison, meetings, rapport, relationship, terms **2** = **family**, clan, kin, kindred, kinsfolk, kinsmen, relatives, tribe

relationship *n* **1** = **connection**, correlation, link, parallel, proportion, ratio, similarity, tie-up **3** = **association**, affinity, bond, communications, conjunction, connection, exchange, kinship, rapport **4** = **affair**, liaison

relative *adj* **1, 3** = **dependent**, allied, associated, comparative, connected, contingent, corresponding, proportionate, reciprocal, related, respective **4** *foll. by* **to** = **in proportion to**, corresponding to, proportional to **5** = **relevant**, applicable, apposite, appropriate, appurtenant, apropos, germane, pertinent ◆ *n* **9** = **relation**, connection, kinsman *or* kinswoman, member of one's *or* the family

relatively *adv* **3** = **comparatively**, in *or* by comparison, rather, somewhat, to some extent

relax *vb* **2** = **rest**, laze, put one's feet up, take it easy, take one's ease **3** = **lessen**, abate, diminish, ease, ebb, let up, loosen, lower, mitigate, moderate, reduce, relieve, slacken, weaken **5** = **be** *or* **feel at ease**, chill out (*sl., chiefly US*), hang loose (*sl.*), let oneself go (*inf.*), let one's hair down (*inf.*), lighten up (*sl.*), loosen up, make oneself at home, mellow out (*inf.*), take it easy, unbend, unwind
Antonyms *vb* ≠ **lessen:** heighten, increase, intensify, tense, tighten, work ≠ **be** *or* feel at ease: be alarmed, be alert

relaxation *n* **1, 2** = **leisure**, amusement, beer and skittles (*inf.*), enjoyment, entertainment, fun, pleasure, recreation, refreshment, rest **3** = **lessening**, abatement, diminution, easing, letup (*inf.*), moderation, reduction, slackening, weakening

relaxed *adj* **5** = **easy-going**, casual, comfortable, downbeat (*inf.*), easy, free and easy, informal, insouciant, laid-back (*inf.*), leisurely, mellow, mild, nonchalant, unhurried, untaxing

relay *n* **1** = **shift**, relief, turn ◆ *vb* **8** = **pass on**, broadcast, carry, communicate, hand on, send, spread, transmit

release *vb* **1** = **set free**, deliver, discharge, disengage, drop, emancipate, extricate, free, let go, let out, liberate, loose, manumit, turn loose, unbridle, unchain, undo, unfasten, unfetter, unloose, unshackle, untie **2** = **acquit**, absolve, dispense, excuse, exempt, exonerate, let go, let off **4** = **issue**, circulate, disseminate, distribute, launch, present, publish, put out **5** = **make known**, break, make public, unveil ◆ *n* **7** = **liberation**, deliverance, delivery, discharge, emancipation, freedom, liberty, manumission, relief **8, 9** = **publication**, issue **10** = **announcement**, proclamation
Antonyms *vb* ≠ **set free:** detain, engage, fasten, hold, imprison, incarcerate, keep ≠ **issue:** suppress, withhold ◆ *n* ≠ **liberation:** detention, imprisonment, incarceration, internment

relegate *vb* **1** = **demote**, downgrade **3** = **pass on**, assign, consign, delegate, entrust, refer, transfer **4** = **banish**, deport, eject, exile, expatriate, expel, oust, throw out

relent *vb* **1** = **be merciful**, acquiesce, capitulate, change one's mind, come round, forbear, give in, give quarter, give way, have pity, melt, show mercy, soften, unbend, yield **2** = **ease**, die down, drop, fall, let up, relax, slacken, slow, weaken
Antonyms *vb* ≠ **be merciful:** be unyielding, give no

tensity of something) to slacken. **3** (of the weather) to become more mild. [C14: from RE- + L *lentāre* to bend, from *lentus* flexible]

relentless Ⓣ (rɪˈlɛntlɪs) *adj* **1** (of an enemy, etc.) implacable; inflexible; inexorable. **2** (of pace or intensity) sustained; unremitting.
▸**reˈlentlessly** *adv* ▸**reˈlentlessness** *n*

relevant Ⓣ (ˈrɛlɪvənt) *adj* having direct bearing on the matter in hand; pertinent. [C16: from Med. L *relevans*, from L *relevāre*, from RE- + *levāre* to raise, RELIEVE]
▸**ˈrelevance** *or* **ˈrelevancy** *n* ▸**ˈrelevantly** *adv*

reliable Ⓣ (rɪˈlaɪəbᵊl) *adj* able to be trusted; dependable.
▸**reˌliaˈbility** *or* **reˈliableness** *n* ▸**reˈliably** *adv*

reliance Ⓣ (rɪˈlaɪəns) *n* **1** dependence, confidence, or trust. **2** something or someone upon which one relies.
▸**reˈliant** *adj* ▸**reˈliantly** *adv*

relic Ⓣ (ˈrɛlɪk) *n* **1** something that has survived from the past, such as an object or custom. **2** something treasured for its past associations; keepsake. **3** (*usually pl*) a remaining part or fragment. **4** *RC Church, Eastern Church.* part of the body of a saint or his belongings, venerated as holy. **5** *Inf.* an old or old-fashioned person or thing. **6** (*pl*) *Arch.* the remains of a dead person; corpse. [C13: from OF *relique*, from L *reliquiae* remains, from *relinquere* to leave behind]

relict (ˈrɛlɪkt) *n* **1** *Ecology.* **1a** a group of animals or plants that exists as a remnant of a formerly widely distributed group. **1b** (*as modifier*): *a relict fauna.* **2** *Geol.* a mountain, lake, glacier, etc., that is a remnant of a pre-existing formation after a destructive process has occurred. **3** an archaic word for **widow. 4** an archaic word for **relic.** [C16: from L *relictus* left behind, from *relinquere* to RELINQUISH]

relief Ⓣ (rɪˈliːf) *n* **1** a feeling of cheerfulness or optimism that follows the removal of anxiety, pain, or distress. **2** deliverance from or alleviation of anxiety, pain, etc. **3a** help or assistance, as to the poor or needy. **3b** (*as modifier*): *relief work.* **4** a diversion from monotony. **5** a person who replaces another at some task or duty. **6** a bus, plane, etc., that carries additional passengers when a scheduled service is full. **7** a road (**relief road**) carrying traffic round an urban area; bypass. **8a** the act of freeing a beleaguered town, fortress, etc.: *the relief of Mafeking.* **8b** (*as modifier*): *a relief column.* **9** Also called: **relievo, rilievo.** *Sculpture, archit.* **9a** the projection of forms or figures from a flat ground, so that they are partly or wholly free of it. **9b** a piece of work of this kind. **10** a printing process that employs raised surfaces from which ink is transferred to the paper. **11** any vivid effect resulting from contrast: *comic relief.* **12** variation in altitude in an area; difference between highest and lowest level. **13** *Law.* redress of a grievance or hardship: *to seek relief through the courts.* **14 on relief.** *US & Canad.* (of people) in receipt of government aid because of personal need. [C14: from OF, from *relever*; see RELIEVE]

relief map *n* a map that shows the configuration and height of the land surface, usually by means of contours.

relieve Ⓣ (rɪˈliːv) *vb* **relieves, relieving, relieved.** (*tr*) **1** to bring alleviation of (pain, distress, etc.) to (someone). **2** to bring aid or assistance to (someone in need, etc.). **3** to take over the duties or watch of (someone). **4** to bring aid or a relieving force to (a besieged town, etc.). **5** to free (someone) from an obligation. **6** to make (something) less unpleasant, arduous, or monotonous. **7** to bring into relief or prominence, as by contrast. **8** (foll. by *of*) *Inf.* to take from: *the thief relieved him of his watch.* **9 relieve oneself.** to urinate or defecate. [C14: from OF *relever*, from L *relevāre* to lift up, relieve, from RE- + *levāre* to lighten]
▸**reˈlievable** *adj* ▸**reˈliever** *n*

relieved (rɪˈliːvd) *adj* (*postpositive; often foll. by at, about, etc.*) experiencing relief, esp. from worry or anxiety.

religieuse *French.* (rəliʒjøz) *n* a nun. [C18: fem of RELIGIEUX]

religieux *French.* (rəliʒjø) *n, pl* ***religieux*** (-ʒjø). a member of a monastic order or clerical body. [C17: from L *religiōsus* religious]

religion (rɪˈlɪdʒən) *n* **1** belief in, worship of, or obedience to a supernatural power or powers considered to be divine or to have control of human destiny. **2** any formal or institutionalized expression of such belief: *the Christian religion.* **3** the attitude and feeling of one who believes in a transcendent controlling power or powers. **4** *Chiefly RC Church.* the way of life entered upon by monks and nuns: *to enter religion.* **5** something of overwhelming importance to a person: *football is his religion.* [C12: via OF from L *religiō* fear of the supernatural, piety, prob. from *religāre*, from RE- + *ligāre* to bind]

religionism (rɪˈlɪdʒəˌnɪzəm) *n* extreme religious fervour.
▸**reˈligionist** *n, adj*

religiose (rɪˈlɪdʒɪˌəʊs) *adj* affectedly or extremely pious; sanctimoniously religious.
▸**reˈligiˌosely** *adv* ▸**religiosity** (rɪˌlɪdʒɪˈɒsɪtɪ) *n*

religious Ⓣ (rɪˈlɪdʒəs) *adj* **1** of, relating to, or concerned with religion. **2a** pious; devout; godly. **2b** (*as collective n; preceded by the*): *the religious.* **3** appropriate to or in accordance with the principles of a religion. **4** scrupulous, exact, or conscientious. **5** *Christianity.* of or relating to a way of life dedicated to religion and defined by a monastic rule. ◆ *n* **6** *Christianity.* a monk or nun.
▸**reˈligiously** *adv* ▸**reˈligiousness** *n*

Religious Society of Friends *n* the official name for the **Quakers.**

relinquish Ⓣ (rɪˈlɪŋkwɪʃ) *vb* (*tr*) **1** to give up (a task, struggle, etc.); abandon. **2** to surrender or renounce (a claim, right, etc.). **3** to release; let go. [C15: from F *relinquir*, from L *relinquere*, from RE- + *linquere* to leave]
▸**reˈlinquisher** *n* ▸**reˈlinquishment** *n*

reliquary (ˈrɛlɪkwərɪ) *n, pl* **reliquaries.** a receptacle or repository for relics, esp. relics of saints. [C17: from OF *reliquaire*, from *relique* RELIC]

relique (rəˈliːk, ˈrɛlɪk) *n* an archaic spelling of **relic.**

reliquiae (rɪˈlɪkwɪˌiː) *pl n* fossil remains of animals or plants. [C19: from L: remains]

relish Ⓣ (ˈrɛlɪʃ) *vb* (*tr*) **1** to savour or enjoy (an experience) to the full. **2** to anticipate eagerly; look forward to. **3** to enjoy the taste or flavour of (food, etc.); savour. ◆ *n* **4** liking or enjoyment, as of something eaten or experienced (esp. in **with relish**). **5** pleasurable anticipation: *he didn't have much relish for the idea.* **6** an appetizing or spicy food added to a main dish to enhance its flavour. **7** an appetizing taste or flavour. **8** a zestful trace or touch: *there was a certain relish in all his writing.* [C16: from earlier *reles* aftertaste, from OF, from *relaisser* to leave behind; see RELEASE]
▸**ˈrelishable** *adj*

relive (riːˈlɪv) *vb* **relives, reliving, relived.** (*tr*) to experience (a sensation, event, etc.) again, esp. in the imagination.
▸**reˈlivable** *adj*

relocate (ˌriːləʊˈkeɪt) *vb* **relocates, relocating, relocated.** to move or be moved to a new place, esp. (of an employee, a business, etc.) to a new area or place of employment.
▸**ˌreloˈcation** *n*

reluctance Ⓣ (rɪˈlʌktəns) *or* **reluctancy** *n* **1** lack of eagerness or willingness; disinclination. **2** *Physics.* a measure of the resistance of a closed magnetic circuit to a magnetic flux. [C16: from L *reluctārī* to resist, from RE- + *luctārī* to struggle]

reluctant Ⓣ (rɪˈlʌktənt) *adj* not eager; unwilling; disinclined. [C17: from L *reluctārī* to resist]
▸**reˈluctantly** *adv*

reluctivity (ˌrɛlʌkˈtɪvɪtɪ) *n, pl* **reluctivities.** *Physics.* a specific or relative

THESAURUS

quarter, remain firm, show no mercy ≠ **ease:** increase, intensify, strengthen

relentless *adj* **1** = **merciless**, cruel, fierce, grim, hard, harsh, implacable, inexorable, inflexible, pitiless, remorseless, ruthless, uncompromising, undeviating, unforgiving, unrelenting, unstoppable, unyielding **2** = **unremitting**, incessant, nonstop, persistent, punishing, sustained, unabated, unbroken, unfaltering, unflagging, unrelenting, unrelieved, unstoppable
Antonyms *adj* ≠ **merciless:** compassionate, forgiving, merciful, submissive, yielding

relevant *adj* = **significant**, admissible, *ad rem*, applicable, apposite, appropriate, appurtenant, apt, fitting, germane, material, pertinent, proper, related, relative, suited, to the point, to the purpose
Antonyms *adj* beside the point, extraneous, extrinsic, immaterial, inapplicable, inappropriate, irrelevant, unconnected, unrelated

reliable *adj* = **dependable**, certain, faithful, honest, predictable, regular, reputable, responsible, safe, sound, stable, staunch, sure, tried and true, true, trustworthy, trusty, unfailing, upright
Antonyms *adj* irresponsible, undependable, unreliable, untrustworthy

reliance *n* **1** = **trust**, assurance, belief, confidence, credence, credit, dependence, faith

relic *n* **1** = **remnant**, fragment, scrap, survival, token, trace, vestige **2** = **keepsake**, memento, remembrance, souvenir

relief *n* **2** = **ease**, abatement, alleviation, assuagement, balm, comfort, cure, deliverance, easement, mitigation, palliation, release, remedy, solace **3a** = **aid**, assistance, help, succour, support, sustenance **4** = **rest**, break, breather (*inf.*), diversion, let-up (*inf.*), refreshment, relaxation, remission, respite

relieve *vb* **1** = **ease**, abate, allay, alleviate, appease, assuage, calm, comfort, console, cure, diminish, dull, mitigate, mollify, palliate, relax, salve, soften, solace, soothe **2** = **help**, aid, assist, bring aid to, succour, support, sustain **3** = **take over from**, give (someone) a break *or* rest, stand in for, substitute for, take the place of **5** = **free**, deliver, discharge, disembarrass, disencumber, exempt, release, unburden **6** = **interrupt**, break, brighten, let up on (*inf.*), lighten, slacken, vary
Antonyms *vb* ≠ **ease:** aggravate, exacerbate, heighten, intensify, worsen

religious *adj* **1-3** = **devout**, churchgoing, devotional, divine, doctrinal, faithful, god-fearing, godly, holy, pious, pure, reverent, righteous, sacred, scriptural, sectarian, spiritual, theological **4** = **conscientious**, exact, faithful, fastidious, meticulous, punctilious, rigid, rigorous, scrupulous, unerring, unswerving

Antonyms *adj* ≠ **devout:** godless, infidel, irreligious, rational, secular, unbelieving

relinquish *vb* **1** = **give up**, abandon, drop **2** = **renounce**, abandon, abdicate, cede, drop, forgo, forsake, give up, hand over, lay aside, quit, repudiate, resign, retire from, surrender, vacate, waive, yield **3** = **release**, let go

relish *vb* **1** = **enjoy**, appreciate, delight in, fancy, lick one's lips, like, look forward to, luxuriate in, prefer, revel in, savour, taste ◆ *n* **5** = **enjoyment**, appetite, appreciation, fancy, fondness, gusto, liking, love, partiality, penchant, predilection, stomach, taste, zest, zing (*inf.*) **6** = **condiment**, appetizer, sauce, seasoning **7** = **flavour**, piquancy, savour, smack, spice, tang, taste, trace
Antonyms *vb* ≠ **enjoy:** be unenthusiastic about, dislike, loathe ◆ *n* ≠ **enjoyment:** dislike, distaste, loathing

reluctance *n* **1** = **unwillingness**, aversion, backwardness, disinclination, dislike, disrelish, distaste, hesitancy, indisposition, loathing, repugnance

reluctant *adj* = **unwilling**, averse, backward, disinclined, grudging, hesitant, indisposed, loath, recalcitrant, slow, unenthusiastic
Antonyms *adj* eager, enthusiastic, inclined, keen, willing

reluctance of a magnetic material. [C19: from obs. *reluct* to struggle + -*ivity*]

rely ⓣ (rɪ'laɪ) *vb* **relies, relying, relied.** (*intr;* foll. by *on* or *upon*) **1** to be dependent (on): *he relies on his charm.* **2** to have trust or confidence (in): *you can rely on us.* [C14: from OF *relier* to fasten together, from L *religāre,* from RE- + *ligāre* to tie]

REM *abbrev. for* rapid eye movement.

remain ⓣ (rɪ'meɪn) *vb* (*mainly intr*) **1** to stay behind or in the same place: *to remain at home.* **2** (*copula*) to continue to be: *to remain cheerful.* **3** to be left, as after use, the passage of time, etc. **4** to be left to be done, said, etc.: *it remains to be pointed out.* [C14: from OF *remanoir,* from L *remanēre,* from RE- + *manēre* to stay]

remainder ⓣ (rɪ'meɪndə) *n* **1** a part or portion that is left, as after use, subtraction, expenditure, the passage of time, etc.: *the remainder of the milk.* **2** *Maths.* **2a** the amount left over when one quantity cannot be exactly divided by another: *for 10 ÷ 3, the remainder is 1.* **2b** another name for **difference** (sense 7). **3** *Property law.* a future interest in property; an interest in a particular estate that will pass to one at some future date, as on the death of the current possessor. **4** a number of copies of a book left unsold when demand ceases, which are sold at a reduced price. ◆ *vb* **5** (*tr*) to sell (copies of a book) as a remainder.

remains ⓣ (rɪ'meɪnz) *pl n* **1** any pieces, fragments, etc., that are left unused or still extant, as after use, consumption, the passage of time: *archaeological remains.* **2** the body of a dead person; corpse. **3** Also called: **literary remains.** the unpublished writings of an author at the time of his death.

remake *n* ('riːˌmeɪk). **1** something that is made again, esp. a new version of an old film. **2** the act of making again. ◆ *vb* (riː'meɪk), **remakes, remaking, remade. 3** (*tr*) to make again or anew.

remand (rɪ'mɑːnd) *vb* (*tr*) **1** *Law.* (of a court or magistrate) to send (a prisoner or accused person) back into custody. **2** to send back. ◆ *n* **3** the sending of a prisoner or accused person back into custody to await trial. **4** the act of remanding or state of being remanded. **5 on remand.** in custody or on bail awaiting trial. [C15: from Med. L *remandāre* to send back word, from L RE- + *mandāre* to command]

remand centre *n* (in Britain) an institution to which accused persons are sent for detention while awaiting appearance before a court.

remanence ('rɛmənəns) *n Physics.* the ability of a material to retain magnetization after the removal of the magnetizing field. [C17: from L *remanēre* to stay behind]

remark ⓣ (rɪ'mɑːk) *vb* **1** (when *intr*, often foll. by *on* or *upon;* when *tr*, *may take a clause as object*) to pass a casual comment (about); reflect in informal speech or writing. **2** (*tr; may take a clause as object*) to perceive; observe; notice. ◆ *n* **3** a brief casually expressed thought or opinion. **4** notice, comment, or observation: *the event passed without remark.* **5** a variant of **remarque.** [C17: from OF *remarquer* to observe, from RE- + *marquer* to note, MARK[1]]

▸**re'marker** *n*

remarkable ⓣ (rɪ'mɑːkəbᵊl) *adj* **1** worthy of note or attention: *a remarkable achievement.* **2** unusual, striking, or extraordinary: *a remarkable sight.*

▸**re'markableness** *n* ▸**re'markably** *adv*

remarque (rɪ'mɑːk) *n* a mark in the margin of an engraved plate to indicate the stage of production. [C19: from F; see REMARK]

remaster (riː'mɑːstə) *vb* (*tr*) to make a new master audio recording, now usually digital, from (an earlier original recording), in order to produce compact discs or stereo records with improved sound reproduction.

REME ('riːmɪ) *n acronym for* Royal Electrical and Mechanical Engineers.

remedial (rɪ'miːdɪəl) *adj* **1** affording a remedy; curative. **2** denoting or relating to special teaching for backward and slow learners: *remedial education.*

▸**re'medially** *adv*

remedy ⓣ ('rɛmɪdɪ) *n, pl* **remedies. 1** (usually foll. by *for* or *against*) any drug or agent that cures a disease or controls its symptoms. **2** (usually foll. by *for* or *against*) anything that serves to cure defects, improve conditions, etc.: *a remedy for industrial disputes.* **3** the legally permitted variation from the standard weight or quality of coins. ◆ *vb* (*tr*) **4** to relieve or cure (a disease, etc.) by a remedy. **5** to put to rights (a fault, error, etc.); correct. [C13: from Anglo-Norman *remedie,* from L *remedium* a cure, from *remedērī,* from RE- + *medērī* to heal]

▸**remediable** (rɪ'miːdɪəbᵊl) *adj* ▸**re'mediably** *adv* ▸**'remediless** *adj*

remember ⓣ (rɪ'mɛmbə) *vb* **1** to become aware of (something forgotten) again; bring back to one's consciousness. **2** to retain (an idea, intention, etc.) in one's conscious mind: *remember to do one's shopping.* **3** (*tr*) to give money, etc., to (someone), as in a will or in tipping. **4** (*tr;* foll. by *to*) to mention (a person's name) to another person, as by way of greeting: *remember me to your mother.* **5** (*tr*) to mention (a person) favourably, as in prayer. **6** (*tr*) to commemorate (a person, event, etc.): *to remember the dead of the wars.* **7 remember oneself.** to recover one's good manners after a lapse. [C14: from OF *remembrer,* from LL *rememorārī* to recall to mind, from L RE- + *memor* mindful]

▸**re'memberer** *n*

remembrance ⓣ (rɪ'mɛmbrəns) *n* **1** the act of remembering or state of being remembered. **2** something that is remembered; reminiscence. **3** a memento or keepsake. **4** the extent in time of one's power of recollection. **5** the act of honouring some past event, person, etc.

Remembrance Day *n* **1** (in Britain) another name for **Remembrance Sunday. 2** (in Canada) a statutory holiday observed on November 11 in memory of the dead of both World Wars.

remembrancer (rɪ'mɛmbrənsə) *n* **1** *Arch.* a reminder, memento, or keepsake. **2** (*usually cap.*) (in Britain) any of several officials of the Exchequer, esp. one (**Queen's** *or* **King's Remembrancer**) whose duties include collecting debts due to the Crown. **3** (*usually cap.*) an official (**City Remembrancer**) appointed by the Corporation of the City of London to represent its interests to Parliament.

Remembrance Sunday *n* (in Britain) the Sunday closest to November 11, on which the dead of both World Wars are commemorated. Also called: **Remembrance Day.**

remex ('riːmɛks) *n, pl* **remiges** ('rɛmɪˌdʒiːz). any of the large flight feathers of a bird's wing. [C18: from L: rower, from *rēmus* oar]

▸**remigial** (rɪ'mɪdʒɪəl) *adj*

remind ⓣ (rɪ'maɪnd) *vb* (*tr;* usually foll. by *of; may take a clause as object or an infinitive*) to cause (a person) to remember (something or to do something); put (a person) in mind (of something): *remind me to phone home; flowers remind me of holidays.*

▸**re'minder** *n*

remindful (rɪ'maɪndfʊl) *adj* **1** serving to remind. **2** (*postpositive*) mindful.

reminisce ⓣ (ˌrɛmɪ'nɪs) *vb* **reminisces, reminiscing, reminisced.** (*intr*) to talk or write about old times, past experiences, etc.

reminiscence ⓣ (ˌrɛmɪ'nɪsəns) *n* **1** the act of recalling or narrating past experiences. **2** (*often pl*) some past experience, event, etc., that is recalled. **3** an event, phenomenon, or experience that reminds one of something else. **4** *Philosophy.* the doctrine that the mind has seen the universal forms of all things in a previous disembodied existence.

reminiscent ⓣ (ˌrɛmɪ'nɪsᵊnt) *adj* **1** (*postpositive;* foll. by *of*) stimulating memories (of) or comparisons (with). **2** characterized by reminiscence. **3** (of a person) given to reminiscing. [C18: from L *reminiscī* to call to mind, from RE- + *mēns* mind]

▸ˌ**remi'niscently** *adv*

remise (rɪ'maɪz) *vb* **remises, remising, remised. 1** (*tr*) *Law.* to give up or relinquish (a right, claim, etc.). **2** (*intr*) *Fencing.* to make a remise. ◆ *n* **3** *Fencing.* a second thrust made on the same lunge after the first has missed. **4** *Obs.* a coach house. [C17: from F *remettre* to put back, from L *remittere,* from RE- + *mittere* to send]

THESAURUS

rely *vb* **2** = **depend**, bank, be confident of, be sure of, bet, count, have confidence in, lean, reckon, repose trust in, swear by, trust

remain *vb* **1** = **continue**, abide, bide, dwell, endure, go on, last, persist, prevail, stand, stay, survive **3** = **stay behind**, be left, delay, hang in the air, linger, stay put (*inf.*), tarry, wait
Antonyms *vb* ≠ **stay behind:** depart, go, leave

remainder *n* **1** = **rest**, balance, butt, dregs, excess, leavings, oddment, relic, remains, remnant, residue, residuum, stub, surplus, tail end, trace, vestige(s)

remaining *adj* **3** = **left-over**, abiding, lasting, lingering, outstanding, residual, surviving, unfinished

remains *pl n* **1** = **remnants**, balance, crumbs, debris, detritus, dregs, fragments, leavings, leftovers, oddments, odds and ends, pieces, relics, remainder, residue, rest, scraps, traces, vestiges **2** = **corpse**, body, cadaver, carcass

remark *vb* **1** = **comment**, animadvert, declare, mention, observe, pass comment, reflect, say, state **2** = **notice**, espy, heed, make out, mark, note, observe, perceive, regard, see, take note or notice of ◆ *n* **3** = **comment**, assertion, declaration, observation, opinion, reflection, statement, thought, utterance, word **4** = **notice**, acknowledgment, attention, comment, consideration, heed, mention, observation, recognition, regard, thought

remarkable *adj* **1** = **noteworthy**, distinguished, famous, impressive, notable, outstanding, pre-eminent, prominent **2** = **extraordinary**, conspicuous, miraculous, odd, phenomenal, rare, signal, singular, strange, striking, surprising, uncommon, unusual, wonderful
Antonyms *adj* banal, common, commonplace, everyday, insignificant, mundane, ordinary, unexceptional, unimpressive, unsurprising, usual

remediable *adj* **4** = **curable**, medicable, repairable, soluble, solvable, treatable

remedy *n* **1** = **cure**, antidote, counteractive, medicament, medicine, nostrum, panacea, physic (*rare*), relief, restorative, specific, therapy, treatment **2** = **solution**, antidote, corrective, countermeasure, panacea, redress, relief ◆ *vb* **3** = **cure**, alleviate, assuage, control, ease, heal, help, mitigate, palliate, relieve, restore, soothe, treat **4** = **put right**, ameliorate, correct, fix, rectify, redress, reform, relieve, repair, set to rights, solve

remember *vb* **1** = **recall**, call to mind, call up, commemorate, look back (on), put one's finger on, recognize, recollect, reminisce, retain, summon up, think back **2** = **bear in mind**, keep in mind
Antonyms *vb* disregard, forget, ignore, neglect, overlook

remembrance *n* **1, 2** = **memory**, mind, recall, recognition, recollection, regard, reminiscence, retrospect, thought **3** = **souvenir**, commemoration, keepsake, memento, memorial, monument, relic, remembrancer (*arch.*), reminder, testimonial, token

remind *vb* = **call to mind**, awaken memories of, bring back to, bring to mind, call up, jog one's memory, make (someone) remember, prompt, put in mind, refresh one's memory

reminisce *vb* = **recall**, go over in the memory, hark back, live in the past, look back, recollect, remember, review, think back

reminiscence *n* **1, 2** = **recollection**, anecdote, memoir, memory, recall, reflection, remembrance, retrospection, review

reminiscent *adj* **1** = **suggestive**, evocative, redolent, remindful, similar

remiss ⓣ (rɪ'mɪs) *adj* (*postpositive*) **1** lacking in care or attention to duty; negligent. **2** lacking in energy. [C15: from L *remissus,* from *remittere,* from RE- + *mittere* to send]
▸**re'missly** *adv* ▸**re'missness** *n*

remissible (rɪ'mɪsɪbᵊl) *adj* able to be remitted. [C16: from L *remissibilis;* see REMIT]
▸**re,missi'bility** *n*

remission ⓣ (rɪ'mɪʃən) *or* (*less commonly*) **remittal** (rɪ'mɪtᵊl) *n* **1** the act of remitting or state of being remitted. **2** a reduction of the term of a sentence of imprisonment, as for good conduct. **3** forgiveness for sin. **4** discharge or release from penalty, obligation, etc. **5** lessening of intensity; abatement, as in the symptoms of a disease. **6** *Rare.* the act of sending a remittance.
▸**re'missive** *adj* ▸**re'missively** *adv*

remit ⓣ *vb* (rɪ'mɪt), **remits, remitting, remitted.** (*mainly tr*) **1** (*also intr*) to send (payment, etc.), as for goods or service, esp. by post. **2** *Law.* (esp. of an appeal court) to send back (a case) to an inferior court for further consideration. **3** to cancel or refrain from exacting (a penalty or punishment). **4** (*also intr*) to relax (pace, intensity, etc.) or (of pace) to slacken or abate. **5** to postpone; defer. **6** *Arch.* to pardon or forgive (crime, sins, etc.). ◆ *n* ('riːmɪt, rɪ'mɪt). **7** area of authority (of a committee, etc.). **8** *Law.* the transfer of a case from one court or jurisdiction to another. **9** the act of remitting. [C14: from L *remittere,* from RE- + *mittere* to send]
▸**re'mittable** *adj* ▸**re'mitter** *n*

remittance ⓣ (rɪ'mɪtəns) *n* **1** payment for goods or services received or as an allowance, esp. when sent by post. **2** the act of remitting.

remittance man *n* a man living abroad on money sent from home, esp. in the days of the British Empire.

remittent (rɪ'mɪtᵊnt) *adj* (of the symptoms of a disease) characterized by periods of diminished severity.
▸**re'mittence** *n* ▸**re'mittently** *adv*

remix *vb* (riː'mɪks). **1** to change the balance and separation of (a recording). ◆ *n* ('riː,mɪks). **2** a remixed version of a recording.

remnant ⓣ ('rɛmnənt) *n* **1** (*often pl*) a part left over after use, processing, etc. **2** a surviving trace or vestige: *a remnant of imperialism.* **3** a piece of material from the end of a roll. ◆ *adj* **4** remaining; left over. [C14: from OF *remenant* remaining, from *remanoir* to REMAIN]

remonetize *or* **remonetise** (riː'mʌnɪ,taɪz) *vb* **remonetizes, remonetizing, remonetized** *or* **remonetises, remonetising, remonetised.** (*tr*) to reinstate as legal tender: *to remonetize silver.*
▸**re,moneti'zation** *or* **re,moneti'sation** *n*

remonstrance ⓣ (rɪ'mɒnstrəns) *n* **1** the act of remonstrating. **2** a protest or reproof, esp. a petition protesting against something.

remonstrant (rɪ'mɒnstrənt) *n* **1** a person who remonstrates, esp. one who signs a remonstrance. ◆ *adj* **2** *Rare.* remonstrating.

remonstrate ⓣ ('rɛmən,streɪt) *vb* **remonstrates, remonstrating, remonstrated.** (*intr*) (usually foll. by *with, against,* etc.) to argue in protest or objection: *to remonstrate with the government.* [C16: from Med. L *remonstrāre* to point out (errors, etc.), from L RE- + *monstrāre* to show]
▸**,remon'stration** *n* ▸**remonstrative** (rɪ'mɒnstrətɪv) *adj* ▸**'remon,strator** *n*

remontant (rɪ'mɒntənt) *adj* **1** (esp. of roses) flowering more than once in a single season. ◆ *n* **2** a rose having such a growth. [C19: from F: coming up again, from *remonter*]

remora ('rɛmərə) *n* a marine spiny-finned fish which has a flattened elongated body and attaches itself to larger fish, rocks, etc., by a sucking disc on the top of the head. [C16: from L, from RE- + *mora* delay; from its alleged habit of delaying ships]

remorse ⓣ (rɪ'mɔːs) *n* **1** a sense of deep regret and guilt for some misdeed. **2** compunction; pity; compassion. [C14: from Med. L *remorsus* a gnawing, from L *remordēre,* from RE- + *mordēre* to bite]
▸**re'morseful** *adj* ▸**re'morsefully** *adv* ▸**re'morsefulness** *n* ▸**re'morseless** *adj*

remote ⓣ (rɪ'məʊt) *adj* **1** located far away; distant. **2** far from society or civilization; out-of-the-way. **3** distant in time. **4** distantly related or connected: *a remote cousin.* **5** slight or faint (esp. in **not the remotest idea**). **6** (of a person's manner) aloof or abstracted. **7** operated from a distance; remote-controlled: *a remote monitor.* [C15: from L *remōtus* far removed, from *removēre,* from RE- + *movēre* to move]
▸**re'motely** *adv* ▸**re'moteness** *n*

remote access *n Computing.* access to a computer from a physically separate terminal.

remote control *n* control of a system or activity from a distance, usually by radio, ultrasonic, or electrical signals.
▸**re,mote-con'trolled** *adj*

remote sensor *n* any instrument, such as a radar device or camera, that scans the earth or another planet from space in order to collect data about some aspect of it.
▸**remote sensing** *adj, n*

rémoulade (,rɛmə'leɪd) *n* a mayonnaise sauce flavoured with herbs, mustard, and capers, served with salads, cold meat, etc. [C19: from F, from dialect *ramolas* horseradish, from L *armoracea*]

remould *vb* (,riː'məʊld). (*tr*) **1** to mould again. **2** to bond a new tread onto the casing of (a worn pneumatic tyre). ◆ *n* ('riː,məʊld). **3** a tyre made by this process.

remount *vb* (riː'maʊnt). **1** to get on (a horse, bicycle, etc.) again. **2** (*tr*) to mount (a picture, jewel, exhibit, etc.) again. ◆ *n* ('riː,maʊnt). **3** a fresh horse.

removal ⓣ (rɪ'muːvᵊl) *n* **1** the act of removing or state of being removed. **2a** a change of residence. **2b** (*as modifier*): *a removal company.* **3** dismissal from office.

removalist (rɪ'muːvəlɪst) *n Austral.* a person or company that transports household effects to a new home.

remove ⓣ (rɪ'muːv) *vb* **removes, removing, removed.** (*mainly tr*) **1** to take away and place elsewhere. **2** to dismiss (someone) from office. **3** to do away with; abolish; get rid of. **4** *Euphemistic.* to assassinate; kill. **5** (*intr*) *Formal.* to change the location of one's home or place of business. ◆ *n* **6** the act of removing, esp. (formal) a removal of one's residence or place of work. **7** the degree of difference: *only one remove from madness.* **8** *Brit.* (in certain schools) a class or form. [C14: from OF *removoir,* from L *removēre;* see MOVE]
▸**re'movable** *adj* ▸**re,mova'bility** *n* ▸**re'mover** *n*

removed (rɪ'muːvd) *adj* **1** separated by distance or abstract distinction. **2** (*postpositive*) separated by a degree of descent or kinship: *the child of a person's first cousin is his first cousin once removed.*

remunerate ⓣ (rɪ'mjuːnə,reɪt) *vb* **remunerates, remunerating, remunerated.** (*tr*) to reward or pay for work, service, etc. [C16: from L *remūnerārī* to reward, from RE- + *mūnerāre* to give, from *mūnus* a gift]

THESAURUS

remiss *adj* **1** = **negligent**, careless, culpable, delinquent, derelict, dilatory, forgetful, heedless, inattentive, indifferent, lax, neglectful, regardless, slack, slapdash, slipshod, sloppy (*inf.*), tardy, thoughtless, unmindful **2** = **lackadaisical**, slothful, slow
Antonyms *adj* ≠ **negligent**: attentive, careful, diligent, painstaking, scrupulous

remission *n* **2** = **reduction**, decrease, diminution, lessening, suspension **3, 4** = **pardon**, absolution, acquittal, amnesty, discharge, excuse, exemption, exoneration, forgiveness, indulgence, release, reprieve **5** = **lessening**, abatement, abeyance, alleviation, amelioration, ebb, let-up (*inf.*), lull, moderation, relaxation, respite

remit *vb* **1** = **send**, dispatch, forward, mail, post, transmit **3** = **cancel**, desist, forbear, halt, repeal, rescind, stop **4** = **lessen**, abate, alleviate, decrease, diminish, dwindle, ease up, fall away, mitigate, moderate, reduce, relax, sink, slacken, soften, wane, weaken **5** = **postpone**, defer, delay, put off, put on the back burner (*inf.*), shelve, suspend, take a rain check on (*US & Canad. inf.*) ◆ *n* **7** = **instructions**, authorization, brief, guidelines, orders, terms of reference

remittance *n* **1** = **payment**, allowance, consideration, fee

remnant *n* **1** = **remainder**, balance, bit, butt, end, fragment, leftovers, oddment, piece, remains, residue, residuum, rest, rump, scrap, shred, stub, tail end **2** = **vestige**, hangover, survival, trace

remonstrance *n* **2** = **protest**, complaint, expostulation, grievance, objection, petition, protestation, reprimand, reproof

remonstrate *vb* = **protest**, argue, challenge, complain, dispute, dissent, expostulate, object, take exception, take issue

remorse *n* **1** = **regret**, anguish, bad *or* guilty conscience, contrition, grief, guilt, pangs of conscience, penitence, repentance, ruefulness, self-reproach, shame, sorrow **2** = **pity**, compassion, compunction

remorseful *adj* **1** = **regretful**, apologetic, ashamed, chastened, conscience-stricken, contrite, guilt-ridden, guilty, penitent, repentant, rueful, sad, self-reproachful, sorrowful, sorry

remorseless *adj* **1** = **pitiless**, callous, cruel, hard, hardhearted, harsh, implacable, inhumane, merciless, ruthless, savage, uncompassionate, unforgiving, unmerciful

remote *adj* **2** = **out-of-the-way**, backwoods, distant, far, faraway, far-off, godforsaken, inaccessible, in the middle of nowhere, isolated, lonely, off the beaten track, outlying, secluded **5** = **slight**, doubtful, dubious, faint, implausible, inconsiderable, meagre, negligible, outside, poor, slender, slim, small, unlikely **6** = **aloof**, abstracted, cold, detached, distant, faraway, indifferent, introspective, introverted, removed, reserved, standoffish, unapproachable, uncommunicative, uninterested, uninvolved, withdrawn
Antonyms *adj* ≠ **out-of-the-way**: adjacent, central, close, just round the corner, near, nearby, neighbouring ≠ **slight**: considerable, good, likely, strong ≠ **aloof**: alert, attentive, aware, gregarious, interested, involved, outgoing, sociable

removal *n* **1** = **taking away** *or* **off** *or* **out**, abstraction, dislodgment, displacement, dispossession, ejection, elimination, eradication, erasure, expunction, extraction, purging, stripping, subtraction, uprooting, withdrawal **2** = **move**, departure, flitting (*Scot. & N English dialect*), relocation, transfer **33** = **dismissal**, expulsion

remove *vb* **1** = **take away** *or* **off** *or* **out**, abstract, amputate, carry off *or* away, cart off (*sl.*), delete, detach, dislodge, displace, doff, extract, move, pull, purge, shed, transfer, withdraw **2** = **dismiss**, depose, dethrone, discharge, expel, give the bum's rush (*sl.*), oust, relegate, show one the door, throw out, throw out on one's ear (*inf.*), transport, unseat **3** = **do away with**, abolish, eject, eliminate, erase, excise, expunge, get rid of, see the back of, strike out, wipe from the face of the earth, wipe out **4** *Euphemistic* = **kill**, assassinate, bump off, dispose of, do away with, do in (*sl.*), eliminate, execute, get rid of, liquidate, murder, take out (*sl.*), wipe from the face of the earth **5** *Formal* = **move**, depart, flit (*Scot. & N English dialect*), move away, quit, relocate, shift, transfer, transport, vacate
Antonyms *vb* ≠ **take away** *or* **off** *or* **out**: don, insert, join, link, place, put, put back, put in, put on, replace, set ≠ **dismiss**: appoint, install

remunerate *vb* = **pay**, compensate, indemnify, recompense, redress, reimburse, repay, requite, reward

remuneration *n* = **payment**, compensation, earnings, emolument, fee, income, indemnity, meed (*arch.*), pay, profit, recompense, reim-

▸re‚muner'ation *n* ▸re'munerable *adj* ▸re'munerative *adj* ▸re'muneratively *adv* ▸re'muner‚ator *n*

renaissance ❶ (rə'neɪsəns, 'rɛnə‚sɑːns) *or* **renascence** *n* a revival or rebirth, esp. of culture and learning. [C19: from F, from L RE- + *nascī* to be born]

Renaissance (rə'neɪsəns, 'rɛnə‚sɑːns) *n* **1 the.** the great revival of art, literature, and learning in Europe in the 14th, 15th, and 16th centuries. **2** the spirit, culture, art, science, and thought of this period. ◆ *adj* **3** of, characteristic of, or relating to the Renaissance, its culture, etc.

renal ('riːnᵊl) *adj* of, relating to, resembling, or situated near the kidney. [C17: from F, from LL *rēnālis,* from L *rēnēs* kidneys, from ?]

renal pelvis *n* a small funnel-shaped cavity of the kidney into which urine is discharged before passing into the ureter.

renascent (rɪ'næsᵊnt, -'neɪ-) *adj* becoming active or vigorous again; reviving: *renascent nationalism.* [C18: from L *renascī* to be born again]

rencounter (rɛn'kaʊntə) *Arch.* ◆ *n also* **rencontre** (rɛn'kɒntə). **1** an unexpected meeting. **2** a hostile clash, as of two armies, adversaries, etc.; skirmish. ◆ *vb* **3** to meet (someone) unexpectedly. [C16: from F *rencontre,* from *rencontrer;* as ENCOUNTER]

rend ❶ (rɛnd) *vb* **rends, rending, rent. 1** to tear with violent force or to be torn in this way; rip. **2** (*tr*) to tear or pull (one's clothes, etc.), esp. as a manifestation of rage or grief. **3** (*tr*) (of a noise or cry) to disturb (the silence) with a shrill or piercing tone. [OE *rendan*]
▸'rendible *adj*

render ❶ ('rɛndə) *vb* (*tr*) **1** to present or submit (accounts, etc.) for payment, etc. **2** to give or provide (aid, charity, a service, etc.). **3** to show (obedience), as expected. **4** to give or exchange, as by way of return or requital: *to render blow for blow.* **5** to cause to become: *grief had rendered him simple-minded.* **6** to deliver (a verdict or opinion) formally. **7** to portray or depict (something), as in painting, music, or acting. **8** to translate (something). **9** (sometimes foll. by *up*) to yield or give: *the tomb rendered up its secret.* **10** (often foll. by *back*) to return (something); give back. **11** to cover the surface of (brickwork, etc.) with a coat of plaster. **12** (often foll. by *down*) to extract (fat) from (meat) by melting. ◆ *n* **13** a first thin coat of plaster applied to a surface. **14** one who or that which rends. [C14: from OF *rendre,* from L *reddere* to give back (infl. by L *prendere* to grasp), from RE- + *dare* to give]
▸'renderable *adj* ▸'renderer *n* ▸'rendering *n*

rendezvous ❶ ('rɒndɪ‚vuː) *n, pl* **rendezvous** (-‚vuːz). **1** a meeting or appointment to meet at a specified time and place. **2** a place where people meet. ◆ *vb* (*intr*) **3** to meet at a specified time or place. [C16: from F, from *rendez-vous!* present yourselves! from *se rendre* to present oneself; see RENDER]

rendition ❶ (rɛn'dɪʃən) *n* **1** a performance of a musical composition, dramatic role, etc. **2** a translation. **3** the act of rendering. [C17: from obs. F, from LL *redditiō;* see RENDER]

renegade ❶ ('rɛnɪ‚geɪd) *n* **1a** a person who deserts his cause or faith for another; traitor. **1b** (*as modifier*): *a renegade priest.* **2** any outlaw or rebel. [C16: from Sp. *renegado,* ult. from L RE- + *negāre* to deny]

renege ❶ *or* **renegue** (rɪ'niːg, -'neɪg) *vb* **reneges, reneging, reneged** *or* **renegues, reneguing, renegued. 1** (*intr;* often foll. by *on*) to go back (on one's promise, etc.). ◆ *vb, n* **2** *Cards.* other words for **revoke.** [C16 (in the sense: to deny, renounce): from Med. L *renegāre* to renounce]
▸re'neger *or* re'neguer *n*

renew ❶ (rɪ'njuː) *vb* (*mainly tr*) **1** to take up again. **2** (*also intr*) to begin (an activity) again; recommence. **3** to restate or reaffirm (a promise, etc.). **4** (*also intr*) to make (a lease, etc.) valid for a further period. **5** to regain or recover (vigour, strength, activity, etc.). **6** to restore to a new or fresh condition. **7** to replace (an old or worn-out part or piece). **8** to replenish (a supply, etc.).
▸re'newable *adj* ▸re'newal *n* ▸re'newer *n*

renewable energy *n* another name for **alternative energy.**

renewables *pl n* sources of alternative energy, such as wind and wave power.

reni- *combining form.* kidney or kidneys: *reniform.* [from L *rēnēs*]

reniform ('rɛnɪ‚fɔːm) *adj* having the shape or profile of a kidney: *a reniform leaf.*

renin ('riːnɪn) *n* a proteolytic enzyme secreted by the kidneys, which plays an important part in the maintenance of blood pressure. [C20: from RENI- + -IN]

rennet ('rɛnɪt) *n* **1** the membrane lining the fourth stomach of a young calf. **2** a substance prepared esp. from the stomachs of calves and used for curdling milk in making cheese. [C15: rel. to OE *gerinnan* to curdle, RUN]

rennin ('rɛnɪn) *n* an enzyme that occurs in gastric juice and is an active constituent of rennet. It coagulates milk. [C20: from RENNET + -IN]

renounce ❶ (rɪ'naʊns) *vb* **renounces, renouncing, renounced. 1** (*tr*) to give up formally (a claim or right): *to renounce a title.* **2** (*tr*) to repudiate: *to renounce Christianity.* **3** (*tr*) to give up (some habit, etc.) voluntarily: *to renounce one's old ways.* **4** (*intr*) *Cards.* to fail to follow suit because one has no more cards of the suit led. ◆ *n* **5** *Cards.* a failure to follow suit. [C14: from OF *renoncer,* from L *renuntiāre,* from RE- + *nuntiāre* to announce, from *nuntius* messenger]
▸re'nouncement *n* ▸re'nouncer *n*

renovate ❶ ('rɛnə‚veɪt) *vb* **renovates, renovating, renovated.** (*tr*) **1** to restore (something) to good condition. **2** to revive or refresh (one's spirits, health, etc.). [C16: from L *renovāre,* from RE- + *novāre* to make new]
▸‚reno'vation *n* ▸'reno‚vative *adj* ▸'reno‚vator *n*

renown ❶ (rɪ'naʊn) *n* widespread reputation, esp. of a good kind; fame. [C14: from Anglo-Norman *renoun,* from OF *renom,* from *renomer* to celebrate, from RE- + *nomer* to name, from L *nōmināre*]
▸re'nowned *adj*

rent[1] ❶ (rɛnt) *n* **1** a payment made periodically by a tenant to a landlord or owner for the occupation or use of land, buildings, etc. **2** *Econ.* the return derived from the cultivation of land in excess of production costs. **3 for rent.** *Chiefly US & Canad.* available for use and occupation subject to the payment of rent. ◆ *vb* **4** (*tr*) to grant (a person) the right to use one's property in return for periodic payments. **5** (*tr*) to occupy or use (property) in return for periodic payments. **6** (*intr;* often foll. by *at*) to be let or rented (for a specified rental). [C12: from OF *rente* revenue, from Vulgar L *rendere* (unattested) to yield; see RENDER]
▸'rentable *adj* ▸'renter *n*

rent[2] ❶ (rɛnt) *n* **1** a slit or opening made by tearing or rending. **2** a breach or division. ◆ *vb* **3** the past tense and past participle of **rend.**

rent-a- *prefix* **1** denoting a rental service. **2** *Derog. or facetious.* denoting a person or group that performs a function as if hired from a rental service: *rent-a-mob.*

rental ('rɛntᵊl) *n* **1a** the amount paid by a tenant as rent. **1b** an income derived from rents received. **2** property available for renting. ◆ *adj* **3** of or relating to rent.

rent boy *n* a young male prostitute.

rent control *n* regulation by law of the rent a landlord can charge for domestic accommodation and of his right to evict tenants.

rent-free *adj, adv* without payment of rent.

rentier *French.* (rɑ̃tje) *n* a person whose income consists primarily of fixed unearned amounts, such as rent or interest. [from *rente;* see RENT[1]]

rent-roll *n* **1** a register of lands and buildings owned by a person, company, etc., showing the rent due from each tenant. **2** the total income arising from rented property.

renunciation ❶ (rɪ‚nʌnsɪ'eɪʃən) *n* **1** the act or an instance of renouncing. **2** a formal declaration renouncing something. **3** *Stock Exchange.*

THESAURUS

bursement, reparation, repayment, retainer, return, reward, salary, stipend, wages

remunerative *adj* = **profitable**, economic, gainful, lucrative, moneymaking, paying, recompensing, rewarding, rich, worthwhile

renaissance *n* = **rebirth**, awakening, new birth, new dawn, reappearance, reawakening, re-emergence, regeneration, renewal, restoration, resurgence, resurrection, revival

rend *vb* **1** = **tear**, break, burst, cleave, crack, divide, fracture, lacerate, pierce, pull, rip, rupture, separate, sever, shatter, smash, splinter, split, sunder (*literary*), tear to pieces, wrench

render *vb* **2** = **provide**, contribute, deliver, furnish, give, hand out, make available, pay, present, show, submit, supply, tender, turn over, yield **5** = **make**, cause to become, leave **7** = **represent**, act, depict, do, give, interpret, perform, play, portray, present **8** = **translate**, construe, explain, interpret, put, reproduce, restate, transcribe **9** = **give up**, cede, deliver, give, hand over, relinquish, surrender, turn over, yield

rendezvous *n* **1** = **appointment**, assignation, date, engagement, meeting, tryst (*arch.*) **2** = **meeting place**, gathering point, place of assignation, trysting-place (*arch.*), venue ◆ *vb* **3** = **meet**, assemble, be reunited, collect, come together, converge, gather, get together, join up, muster, rally

rendition *n* **1** = **performance**, arrangement, delivery, depiction, execution, interpretation, portrayal, presentation, reading, rendering, take (*inf., chiefly US*), version **2** = **translation**, construction, explanation, interpretation, reading, transcription, version

renegade *n* **1a** = **deserter**, apostate, backslider, betrayer, defector, dissident, recreant (*arch.*), runaway, traitor, turncoat ◆ *modifier* **1b** = **traitorous**, apostate, backsliding, disloyal, dissident, recreant, runaway, unfaithful

renege *vb* **1** = **break one's word**, back out, break a promise, default, go back, repudiate, welsh (*sl.*)

renew *vb* **1, 2** = **recommence**, begin again, breathe new life into, bring up to date, continue, extend, prolong, recreate, re-establish, regenerate, rejuvenate, reopen, resume, revitalize **3** = **reaffirm**, repeat, restate **6** = **restore**, fix up, mend, modernize, overhaul, refit, refurbish, renovate, repair, transform **8** = **replace**, refresh, replenish, restock

renounce *vb* **1** = **give up**, abandon, abdicate, abjure, abnegate, abstain from, cast off, decline, discard, disown, eschew, forgo, forsake, forswear, leave off, quit, relinquish, renege, resign, retract, swear off, throw off, waive, wash one's hands of **2** = **deny**, disclaim, recant, reject, repudiate, spurn
Antonyms *vb* assert, avow, claim, maintain, reassert

renovate *vb* **1** = **restore**, do up, fix up (*inf., chiefly US & Canad.*), modernize, overhaul, recondition, reconstitute, recreate, refit, reform, refurbish, rehabilitate, remodel, renew, repair, revamp

renown *n* = **fame**, acclaim, celebrity, distinction, eminence, glory, honour, illustriousness, lustre, mark, note, reputation, repute, stardom

renowned *adj* = **famous**, acclaimed, celebrated, distinguished, eminent, esteemed, famed, illustrious, notable, noted, well-known
Antonyms *adj* forgotten, little-known, neglected, obscure, unknown

rent[1] *n* **1** = **hire**, fee, lease, payment, rental, tariff ◆ *vb* **4** = **let**, charter, hire, lease **5** = **hire**, charter, lease

rent[2] *n* **1** = **tear**, breach, break, chink, crack, flaw, gash, hole, opening, perforation, rip, slash, slit, split **2** = **division**, breach, break, cleavage, discord, dissension, disunity, faction, rift, rupture, schism, split

renunciation *n* **1, 2** = **giving up**, abandonment, abdication, abjuration, abnegation,

the surrender to another of the rights to buy new shares in a rights issue. [C14: from L *renunciātiō* a declaration, from *renuntiāre* to report]
▸**re'nunciative** *or* **re'nunciatory** *adj*

rep[1] *or* **repp** (rɛp) *n* a silk, wool, rayon, or cotton fabric with a transversely corded surface. [C19: from F *reps*, ?from E *ribs*]
▸**repped** *adj*

rep[2] (rɛp) *n Theatre.* short for **repertory company.**

rep[3] (rɛp) *n* **1** short for **representative** (sense 2). **2** *NZ inf.* a rugby player selected to represent his district.

rep[4] (rɛp) *n US inf.* short for **reputation.**

rep. *abbrev. for:* **1** report. **2** reporter. **3** reprint.

Rep. *abbrev. for:* **1** *US.* Representative. **2** Republic. **3** *US.* Republican.

repair[1] Ⓣ (rɪ'pɛə) *vb* (*tr*) **1** to restore (something damaged or broken) to good condition or working order. **2** to heal (a breach or division) in (something): *to repair a broken marriage.* **3** to make amends for (a mistake, injury, etc.). ◆ *n* **4** the act, task, or process of repairing. **5** a part that has been repaired. **6** state or condition: *in good repair.* [C14: from OF *reparer*, from L *reparāre*, from RE- + *parāre* to make ready]
▸**re'pairable** *adj* ▸**re'pairer** *n*

repair[2] Ⓣ (rɪ'pɛə) *vb* (*intr*) **1** (usually foll. by *to*) to go (to a place). **2** (usually foll. by *to*) to have recourse (to) for help, etc.: *to repair to one's lawyer.* ◆ *n* **3** a haunt or resort. [C14: from OF *repairier*, from LL *repatriāre* to return to one's native land, from L RE- + *patria* fatherland]

repairman (rɪ'pɛə,mæn) *n, pl* **repairmen.** a man whose job it is to repair machines, etc.

repand (rɪ'pænd) *adj Bot.* having a wavy margin: *a repand leaf.* [C18: from L *repandus* bent backwards, from RE- + *pandus* curved]
▸**re'pandly** *adv*

reparable Ⓣ ('rɛpərəbᵊl, 'rɛprə-) *adj* able to be repaired, recovered, or remedied. [C16: from L *reparābilis*, from *reparāre* to REPAIR[1]]
▸**'reparably** *adv*

reparation Ⓣ (,rɛpə'reɪʃən) *n* **1** the act or process of making amends. **2** (*usually pl*) compensation exacted as an indemnity from a defeated nation by the victors. **3** the act or process of repairing or state of having been repaired. [C14 *reparacioun*, ult. from L *reparāre* to REPAIR[1]]
▸**reparative** (rɪ'pærətɪv) *or* **re'paratory** *adj*

repartee Ⓣ (,rɛpɑː'tiː) *n* **1** a sharp, witty, or aphoristic remark made as a reply. **2** skill in making sharp witty replies. [C17: from F *repartie*, from *repartir* to retort, from RE- + *partir* to go away]

repast Ⓣ (rɪ'pɑːst) *n* a meal or the food provided at a meal: *a light repast.* [C14: from OF, from *repaistre* to feed, from LL *repāscere*, from L RE- + *pāscere* to feed, pasture (of animals)]

repatriate *vb* (riː'pætrɪ,eɪt), **repatriates, repatriating, repatriated.** (*tr*) **1** to send back (a refugee, prisoner of war, etc.) to the country of his birth or citizenship. **2** to send back (a sum of money previously invested abroad) to its country of origin. ◆ *n* (riː'pætrɪɪt). **3** a person who has been repatriated. [C17: from LL *repatriāre*, from L RE- + *patria* fatherland]
▸**re,patri'ation** *n*

repay Ⓣ (rɪ'peɪ) *vb* **repays, repaying, repaid. 1** to pay back (money, etc.) to (a person); refund or reimburse. **2** to make a return for (something): *to repay kindness.*
▸**re'payable** *adj* ▸**re'payment** *n*

repeal Ⓣ (rɪ'piːl) *vb* (*tr*) **1** to annul or rescind officially; revoke: *these laws were repealed.* ◆ *n* **2** an instance or the process of repealing; annulment. [C14: from OF *repeler*, from RE- + *apeler* to call, APPEAL]
▸**re'pealable** *adj* ▸**re'pealer** *n*

repeat Ⓣ (rɪ'piːt) *vb* **1** (when *tr, may take a clause as object*) to do or experience (something) again once or several times, esp. to say or write (something) again. **2** (*intr*) to occur more than once: *the last figure repeats.* **3** (*tr; may take a clause as object*) to reproduce (the words, sounds, etc.) uttered by someone else; echo. **4** (*tr*) to utter (a poem, etc.) from memory; recite. **5** (*intr*) (of food) to be tasted again after ingestion as the result of belching. **6** (*tr; may take a clause as object*) to tell to another person (the secrets imparted to one by someone else). **7** (*intr*) (of a clock) to strike the hour or quarter-hour just past. **8** (*intr*) *US.* to vote (illegally) more than once in a single election. **9 repeat oneself.** to say or do the same thing more than once, esp. so as to be tedious. ◆ *n* **10a** the act or an instance of repeating. **10b** (*as modifier*): *a repeat performance.* **11** a word, action, etc., that is repeated. **12** an order made out for goods, etc., that duplicates a previous order. **13** *Radio, television.* a broadcast of a programme which has been broadcast before. **14** *Music.* a passage that is an exact restatement of the passage preceding it. [C14: from OF *repeter*, from L *repetere*, from RE- + *petere* to seek]
▸**re'peatable** *adj*

> **USAGE NOTE** Since *again* is part of the meaning of *repeat*, one should not say something is *repeated again.*

repeated (rɪ'piːtɪd) *adj* done, made, or said again and again; continual.
▸**re'peatedly** *adv*

repeater (rɪ'piːtə) *n* **1** a person or thing that repeats. **2** Also called: **repeating firearm.** a firearm capable of discharging several shots without reloading. **3** a timepiece that strikes the hour or quarter-hour just past, when a spring is pressed. **4** a device that amplifies incoming electrical signals and retransmits them.

repeating decimal *n* another name for **recurring decimal.**

repechage (,rɛpɪ'ʃɑːʒ) *n* a heat of a competition, esp. in rowing or fencing, in which eliminated contestants have another chance to qualify for the next round or the final. [C19: from F *repêchage*, lit.: fishing out again, from RE- + *pêcher* to fish + -AGE]

repel Ⓣ (rɪ'pɛl) *vb* **repels, repelling, repelled.** (*mainly tr*) **1** to force or drive back (something or somebody). **2** (*also intr*) to produce a feeling of aversion or distaste in (someone or something); be disgusting (to). **3** to be effective in keeping away, controlling, or resisting: *a spray that repels flies.* **4** to have no affinity for; fail to mix with or absorb: *water and oil repel each other.* **5** to disdain to accept (something); turn away from or spurn: *she repelled his advances.* [C15: from L *repellere*, from RE- + *pellere* to push]
▸**re'peller** *n* ▸**re'pellingly** *adv*

> **USAGE NOTE** See at **repulse.**

repellent Ⓣ (rɪ'pɛlənt) *adj* **1** distasteful or repulsive. **2** driving or forcing away or back; repelling. ◆ *n also* **repellant. 3** something, esp. a chemical substance, that repels: *insect repellent.* **4** a substance with which fabrics are treated to increase their resistance to water.
▸**re'pellence** *or* **re'pellency** *n* ▸**re'pellently** *adv*

repent[1] Ⓣ (rɪ'pɛnt) *vb* to feel remorse (for); be contrite (about); show penitence (for). [C13: from OF *repentir*, from RE- + *pentir*, from L *paenitēre* to repent]
▸**re'penter** *n*

repent[2] ('riːpᵊnt) *adj Bot.* lying or creeping along the ground: *repent stems.* [C17: from L *rēpere* to creep]

repentance Ⓣ (rɪ'pɛntəns) *n* **1** remorse or contrition for one's past actions. **2** an act or the process of being repentant; penitence.
▸**re'pentant** *adj*

repercussion Ⓣ (,riːpə'kʌʃən) *n* **1** (*often pl*) a result or consequence of

THESAURUS

abstention, denial, disavowal, disclaimer, eschewal, forswearing, rejection, relinquishment, repudiation, resignation, spurning, surrender, waiver

repair[1] *vb* **1** = **mend**, fix, heal, make good, patch, patch up, put back together, recover, renew, renovate, restore, restore to working order **3** = **put right**, compensate for, make up for, rectify, redress, retrieve, square ◆ *n* **5** = **mend**, adjustment, darn, overhaul, patch, restoration **6** = **condition**, fettle, form, nick (*inf.*), shape (*inf.*), state
Antonyms *vb* ≠ **mend:** damage, destroy, harm, ruin, wreck

repair[2] *vb* **1** = **go**, betake oneself, head for, leave for, move, remove, retire, set off for, withdraw **2** = **have recourse**, resort, turn

reparable *adj* = **curable**, recoverable, rectifiable, remediable, restorable, retrievable, salvageable

reparation *n* **1** = **compensation**, amends, atonement, damages, indemnity, propitiation, recompense, redress, renewal, repair, requital, restitution, satisfaction

repartee *n* **1** = **witticism**, badinage, banter, bon mot, persiflage, pleasantry, raillery, riposte, sally, wit, wittiness, wordplay

repast *n* = **meal**, collation, food, nourishment, refection, spread (*inf.*), victuals

repay *vb* **1** = **pay back**, compensate, make restitution, recompense, refund, reimburse, remunerate, requite, restore, return, reward, settle up with, square **2** = **reciprocate**, avenge, even *or* settle the score with, get back at, get even with (*inf.*), get one's own back on (*inf.*), hit back, make reprisal, pay (someone) back in his *or* her own coin, retaliate, return the compliment, revenge

repeal *vb* **1** = **abolish**, abrogate, annul, cancel, countermand, declare null and void, invalidate, nullify, obviate, recall, rescind, reverse, revoke, set aside, withdraw ◆ *n* **2** = **abolition**, abrogation, annulment, cancellation, invalidation, nullification, rescinding, rescindment, rescission, revocation, withdrawal
Antonyms *vb* ≠ **abolish:** confirm, enact, introduce, pass, ratify, reaffirm, validate ◆ *n* ≠ **abolition:** confirmation, enactment, introduction, passing, ratification, reaffirmation, validation

repeat *vb* **1** = **redo**, duplicate, recapitulate, renew, replay, reproduce, rerun, reshow **3** = **reiterate**, echo, iterate, quote, relate, restate, retell **4** = **recite** ◆ *n* **10a** = **repetition**, duplicate, echo, recapitulation, reiteration, replay, reproduction, rerun, reshowing

repeatedly *adv* **1** = **over and over**, again and again, frequently, many a time and oft (*arch.* or *poetic*), many times, often, time after time, time and (time) again

repel *vb* **1** = **drive off**, beat off, check, confront, decline, fight, hold off, keep at arm's length, oppose, parry, put to flight, rebuff, refuse, reject, repulse, resist, ward off **2** = **disgust**, give one the creeps (*inf.*), gross out (*US sl.*), make one shudder, make one sick, nauseate, offend, put one off, revolt, sicken, turn one off (*inf.*), turn one's stomach
Antonyms *vb* ≠ **disgust:** attract, delight, draw, entrance, fascinate, invite, please

repellent *adj* **1** = **disgusting**, abhorrent, abominable, cringe-making (*Brit. inf.*), discouraging, distasteful, hateful, horrid, loathsome, nauseating, noxious, obnoxious, obscene, odious, offensive, off-putting (*Brit. inf.*), repugnant, repulsive, revolting, sickening, yucky *or* yukky (*sl.*)

repent[1] *vb* = **regret**, atone, be ashamed, be contrite, be sorry, deplore, feel remorse, lament, relent, reproach oneself, rue, see the error of one's ways, show penitence, sorrow

repentance *n* **1, 2** = **regret**, compunction, contrition, grief, guilt, penitence, remorse, sackcloth and ashes, self-reproach, sorriness, sorrow

repentant *adj* **1, 2** = **regretful**, apologetic, ashamed, chastened, contrite, penitent, remorseful, rueful, self-reproachful, sorry

an action or event: *the repercussions of the war are still felt.* **2** a recoil after impact; a rebound. **3** a reflection, esp. of sound; echo or reverberation. [C16: from L *repercussiō*, from *repercutere* to strike back]
▸ **ˌreperˈcussive** *adj*

repertoire Ⓣ (ˈrɛpəˌtwɑː) *n* **1** all the works collectively that a company, actor, etc., is competent to perform. **2** the entire stock of things available in a field or of a kind. **3 in repertoire.** denoting the performance of two or more plays, etc., by the same company in the same venue on different evenings over a period of time: *"Tosca" returns to Leeds next month in repertoire with "Wozzeck".* [C19: from F, from LL *repertōrium* inventory; see REPERTORY]

repertory Ⓣ (ˈrɛpətərɪ, -trɪ) *n, pl* **repertories. 1** the entire stock of things available in a field or of a kind; repertoire. **2** a place where a stock of things is kept; repository. **3** short for **repertory company.** [C16: from LL *repertōrium* storehouse, from L *reperīre* to obtain, from RE- + *parere* to bring forth]
▸ **repertorial** (ˌrɛpəˈtɔːrɪəl) *adj*

repertory company *n* a theatrical company that performs plays from a repertoire. US name: **stock company.**

repetend (ˈrɛpɪˌtɛnd) *n* **1** *Maths.* the digit in a recurring decimal that repeats itself. **2** anything repeated. [C18: from L *repetendum* what is to be repeated, from *repetere* to REPEAT]

répétiteur *French.* (repetitœr) *n* a member of an opera company who coaches the singers.

repetition Ⓣ (ˌrɛpɪˈtɪʃən) *n* **1** the act or an instance of repeating; reiteration. **2** a thing, word, action, etc., that is repeated. **3** a replica or copy.
▸ **repetitive** (rɪˈpɛtɪtɪv) *adj*

repetitious Ⓣ (ˌrɛpɪˈtɪʃəs) *adj* characterized by unnecessary repetition.
▸ **ˌrepeˈtitiously** *adv* ▸ **ˌrepeˈtitiousness** *n*

repetitive strain *or* **stress injury** *n* a condition, characterized by arm or wrist pains, that can affect musicians, computer operators, etc., who habitually perform awkward hand movements. Abbrev.: **RSI.**

repine Ⓣ (rɪˈpaɪn) *vb* **repines, repining, repined.** (*intr*) to be fretful or low-spirited through discontent. [C16: from RE- + PINE[2]]

replace Ⓣ (rɪˈpleɪs) *vb* **replaces, replacing, replaced.** (*tr*) **1** to take the place of; supersede. **2** to substitute a person or thing for (another); put in place of: *to replace an old pair of shoes.* **3** to restore to its rightful place.
▸ **reˈplaceable** *adj* ▸ **reˈplacer** *n*

replacement Ⓣ (rɪˈpleɪsmənt) *n* **1** the act or process of replacing. **2** a person or thing that replaces another.

replay *n* (ˈriːˌpleɪ). **1** Also called: **action replay.** a showing again of a sequence of action in slow motion immediately after it happens. **2** a second match between a pair or group of contestants. ◆ *vb* (riːˈpleɪ). **3** to play again (a record, sporting contest, etc.).

replenish Ⓣ (rɪˈplɛnɪʃ) *vb* (*tr*) **1** to make full or complete again by supplying what has been used up. **2** to put fresh fuel on (a fire). [C14: from OF *replenir*, from RE- + *plenir*, from L *plēnus* full]
▸ **reˈplenisher** *n* ▸ **reˈplenishment** *n*

replete Ⓣ (rɪˈpliːt) *adj* (*usually postpositive*) **1** (often foll. by *with*) copiously supplied (with); abounding (in). **2** having one's appetite completely or excessively satisfied; gorged; satiated. [C14: from L *replētus*, from *replēre*, from RE- + *plēre* to fill]
▸ **reˈpletely** *adv* ▸ **reˈpleteness** *n* ▸ **reˈpletion** *n*

replevin (rɪˈplɛvɪn) *Law.* ◆ *n* **1** the recovery of goods unlawfully taken, made subject to establishing the validity of the recovery in a legal action and returning the goods if the decision is adverse. **2** (formerly) a writ of replevin. ◆ *vb* **3** another word for **replevy.** [C15: from Anglo-F, from OF *replevir* to give security for, from RE- + *plevir* to PLEDGE]

replevy (rɪˈplɛvɪ) *Law.* ◆ *vb* **replevies, replevying, replevied.** (*tr*) **1** to recover possession of (goods) by replevin. ◆ *n, pl* **replevies. 2** another word for **replevin.** [C15: from OF *replevir*; see REPLEVIN]
▸ **reˈpleviable** *or* **reˈplevisable** *adj*

replica Ⓣ (ˈrɛplɪkə) *n* an exact copy or reproduction, esp. on a smaller scale. [C19: from It., lit.: a reply, from *replicare*, from L: to bend back, repeat]

replicate Ⓣ *vb* (ˈrɛplɪˌkeɪt), **replicates, replicating, replicated.** (*mainly tr*) **1** (*also intr*) to make or be a copy (of); reproduce. **2** to fold (something) over on itself; bend back. ◆ *adj* (ˈrɛplɪkɪt). **3** folded back on itself: *a replicate leaf.* [C19: from L *replicātus* bent back; see REPLICA]
▸ **ˌrepliˈcation** *n* ▸ **ˈreplicative** *adj*

reply Ⓣ (rɪˈplaɪ) *vb* **replies, replying, replied.** (*mainly intr*) **1** to make answer (to) in words or writing or by an action; respond. **2** (*tr; takes a clause as object*) to say (something) in answer: *he replied that he didn't want to come.* **3** *Law.* to answer a defendant's plea. **4** to return (a sound); echo. ◆ *n, pl* **replies. 5** an answer; response. **6** the answer made by a plaintiff or petitioner to a defendant's case. [C14: from OF *replier* to fold again, reply, from L *replicāre*, from RE- + *plicāre* to fold]
▸ **reˈplier** *n*

repo (ˈriːpəʊ) *n Inf.* short for: **1** repurchase agreement. **2a** repossession of property. **2b** (*as modifier*): *a repo car.*

repoint (ˌriːˈpɔɪnt) *vb* (*tr*) to repair the joints of (brickwork, masonry, etc.) with mortar or cement.

report Ⓣ (rɪˈpɔːt) *n* **1** an account prepared after investigation and published or broadcast. **2** a statement made widely known; rumour: *according to report, he is not dead.* **3** an account of the deliberations of a committee, body, etc.: *a report of parliamentary proceedings.* **4** *Brit.* a statement on the progress of each schoolchild. **5** a written account of a case decided at law. **6** comment on a person's character or actions; reputation: *he is of good report here.* **7** a sharp loud noise, esp. one made by a gun. ◆ *vb* (when *tr, may take a clause as object;* when *intr,* often foll. by *on*) **8** to give an account (of); describe. **9** to give an account of the results of an investigation (into): *to report on housing conditions.* **10** (of a committee, legislative body, etc.) to make a formal report on (a bill). **11** (*tr*) to complain about (a person), esp. to a superior. **12** to present (oneself) or be present at an appointed place or for a specific purpose: *report to the manager's office.* **13** (*intr*) to say or show that one is (in a certain state): *to report fit.* **14** (*intr;* foll. by *to*) to be responsible (to) and under the authority (of). **15** (*intr*) to act as a reporter. **16** *Law.* to take down in writing details of (the proceedings of a court of law, etc.) as a record or for publication. [C14: from OF, from *reporter*, from L *reportāre*, from RE- + *portāre* to carry]
▸ **reˈportable** *adj* ▸ **reˈportedly** *adv*

reportage (rɪˈpɔːtɪdʒ, ˌrɛpɔːˈtɑːʒ) *n* **1** the act or process of reporting news or other events of general interest. **2** a journalist's style of reporting.

reported speech *n* another term for **indirect speech.**

reporter Ⓣ (rɪˈpɔːtə) *n* **1** a person who reports, esp. one employed to gather news for a newspaper or broadcasting organization. **2** a person authorized to report the proceedings of a legislature.

report stage *n* the stage preceding the third reading in the passage of a bill through Parliament.

repose[1] Ⓣ (rɪˈpəʊz) *n* **1** a state of quiet restfulness; peace or tranquillity. **2** dignified calmness of manner; composure. ◆ *vb* **reposes, reposing, reposed. 3** to lie or lay down at rest. **4** (*intr*) to lie when dead, as in the grave. **5** (*intr;* foll. by *on, in,* etc.) *Formal.* to be based (on): *your plan re-*

THESAURUS

repercussion *n* **1** *often plural* = **consequences**, backlash, result, sequel, side effects **3** = **reverberation**, echo, rebound, recoil

repertoire *n* **2** = **range**, collection, list, repertory, repository, stock, store, supply

repertory *n* **1** = **repertoire**, collection, list, range, stock, store, supply **2** = **repository**

repetition *n* **1** = **repeating**, duplication, echo, iteration, reappearance, recapitulation, recital, recurrence, redundancy, rehearsal, reiteration, relation, renewal, repetitiousness, replication, restatement, return, tautology

repetitious *adj* = **long-winded**, iterative, pleonastic, prolix, redundant, tautological, tedious, verbose, windy, wordy

repetitive *adj* **1** = **monotonous**, boring, dull, mechanical, recurrent, samey (*inf.*), tedious, unchanging, unvaried

repine *vb* = **complain**, brood, eat one's heart out, fret, grieve, grumble, lament, languish, moan, mope, murmur, sulk

replace *vb* **1** = **take the place of**, fill (someone's) shoes *or* boots, follow, oust, stand in lieu of, step into (someone's) shoes *or* boots, substitute, succeed, supersede, supplant, supply, take over from **3** = **put back**, re-establish, reinstate, restore

replacement *n* **2** = **successor**, double, fill-in, proxy, stand-in, substitute, surrogate, understudy

replenish *vb* **1** = **refill**, fill, furnish, make up, provide, reload, renew, replace, restock, restore, stock, supply, top up
Antonyms *vb* consume, drain, empty, exhaust, use up

replete *adj* **1** = **filled**, abounding, brimful, brimming, charged, chock-full, crammed, full to bursting, glutted, jammed, jam-packed, stuffed, teeming, well-provided, well-stocked **2** = **sated**, full, full up, gorged, satiated
Antonyms *adj* ≠ **filled:** bare, barren, empty, lacking, wanting ≠ **sated:** empty, esurient, famished, hungry, starving

repletion *n* **1** = **surfeit**, completeness, glut, plethora, superfluity **2** = **fullness**, overfullness, satiation, satiety

replica *n* = **duplicate**, carbon copy, copy, facsimile, imitation, model, reproduction
Antonyms *n* master, original, prototype

replicate *vb* **1** = **copy**, ape, duplicate, follow, mimic, recreate, reduplicate, repeat, reproduce

reply *vb* **1, 2** = **answer**, acknowledge, come back, counter, make answer, react, reciprocate, rejoin, respond, retaliate, retort, return, riposte, write back ◆ *n* **5** = **answer**, acknowledgment, comeback (*inf.*), counter, counterattack, echo, reaction, reciprocation, rejoinder, response, retaliation, retort, return, riposte

report *n* **1** = **account**, announcement, communication, declaration, description, detail, information, narrative, news, note, recital, record, relation, statement, summary, tale, tidings, version, word **2** = **rumour**, buzz, gossip, hearsay, scuttlebutt (*US sl.*), talk **3** = **article**, communiqué, dispatch, message, paper, piece, story, write-up **6** = **repute**, character, eminence, esteem, fame, regard, reputation **7** = **bang**, blast, boom, crack, crash, detonation, discharge, explosion, noise, reverberation, sound ◆ *vb* **8** = **communicate**, air, announce, bring word, broadcast, circulate, cover, declare, describe, detail, document, give an account of, inform of, mention, narrate, note, notify, pass on, proclaim, publish, recite, record, recount, relate, relay, state, tell, write up **12** = **present oneself**, appear, arrive, be present, clock in *or* on, come, show up (*inf.*), turn up

reporter *n* **1** = **journalist**, announcer, correspondent, hack (*derogatory*), journo (*sl.*), newscaster, newshound (*inf.*), newspaperman *or* newspaperwoman, pressman, writer

repose[1] *n* **1** = **peace**, ease, inactivity, quiet, quietness, quietude, relaxation, respite, rest, restfulness, stillness, tranquillity **2** = **composure**, aplomb, calmness, dignity, equanimity, peace

poses on a fallacy. [C15: from OF *reposer,* from LL *repausāre,* from RE- + *pausāre* to stop]
▸re'posal *n* ▸re'poser *n* ▸re'poseful *adj* ▸re'posefully *adv*

repose[2] ➊ (rɪ'pəʊz) *vb* **reposes, reposing, reposed.** (*tr*) **1** to put (trust) in a person or thing. **2** to place or put (an object) somewhere. [C15: from L *repōnere* to store up, from RE- + *pōnere* to put]
▸re'posal *n*

reposition (ˌriːpə'zɪʃən) *n* **1** the act or process of depositing or storing. ◆ *vb* (*tr*) **2** to place in a new position. **3** to target (a product or brand) at a new market by changing its image.

repository ➊ (rɪ'pɒzɪtərɪ, -trɪ) *n, pl* **repositories. 1** a place or container in which things can be stored for safety. **2** a place where things are kept for exhibition; museum. **3** a place of burial; sepulchre. **4** a person to whom a secret is entrusted; confidant. [C15: from L *repositōrium,* from *repōnere* to place]

repossess (ˌriːpə'zɛs) *vb* (*tr*) to take back possession of (property), esp. for nonpayment of money due under a hire-purchase agreement.
▸repossession (ˌriːpə'zɛʃən) *n* ▸ˌrepos'sessor *n*

repoussé (rə'puːseɪ) *adj* **1** raised in relief, as a design on a thin piece of metal hammered through from the underside. ◆ *n* **2** a design or surface made in this way. [C19: from F, from *repousser,* from RE- + *pousser* to PUSH]

repp (rɛp) *n* a variant spelling of **rep**[1].

reprehend (ˌrɛprɪ'hɛnd) *vb* (*tr*) to find fault with; criticize. [C14: from L *reprehendere* to hold fast, rebuke, from RE- + *prendere* to grasp]
▸ˌrepre'hender *n* ▸ˌrepre'hension *n*

reprehensible ➊ (ˌrɛprɪ'hɛnsɪbᵊl) *adj* open to criticism or rebuke; blameworthy. [C14: from LL *reprehensibilis,* from L *reprehendere;* see REPREHEND]
▸ˌrepreˌhensi'bility *n* ▸ˌrepre'hensibly *adv*

represent ➊ (ˌrɛprɪ'zɛnt) *vb* (*tr*) **1** to stand as an equivalent of; correspond to. **2** to act as a substitute or proxy (for). **3** to act as or be the authorized delegate or agent for (a person, country, etc.): *an MP represents his constituency.* **4** to serve or use as a means of expressing: *letters represent the sounds of speech.* **5** to exhibit the characteristics of; exemplify; typify: *romanticism in music is represented by Beethoven.* **6** to present an image of through the medium of a picture or sculpture; portray. **7** to bring clearly before the mind. **8** to set forth in words; state or explain. **9** to describe as having a specified character or quality: *he represented her as a saint.* **10** to act out the part of on stage; portray. [C14: from L *repraesentāre* to exhibit, from RE- + *praesentāre* to PRESENT[2]]
▸ˌrepre'sentable *adj* ▸ˌrepreˌsenta'bility *n*

re-present (ˌriːprɪ'zɛnt) *vb* (*tr*) to present again.
▸re-presentation (ˌriːˌprɛzən'teɪʃən) *n*

representation ➊ (ˌrɛprɪzɛn'teɪʃən) *n* **1** the act or an instance of representing or the state of being represented. **2** anything that represents, such as a verbal or pictorial portrait. **3** anything that is represented, such as an image brought clearly to mind. **4** the principle by which delegates act for a constituency. **5** a body of representatives. **6** an instance of acting for another in a particular capacity, such as executor. **7** a dramatic production or performance. **8** (*often pl*) a statement of facts, true or alleged, esp. one set forth by way of remonstrance or expostulation.

representational (ˌrɛprɪzɛn'teɪʃənᵊl) *adj* **1** *Art.* depicting objects, scenes, etc., directly as seen; naturalistic. **2** of or relating to representation.

representationalism (ˌrɛprɪzɛn'teɪʃənəˌlɪzəm) *or* **representationism** *n* **1** *Philosophy.* the doctrine that in perceptions of objects what is before the mind is not the object but a representation of it. Cf. **presentationism. 2** *Art.* the practice of depicting objects, scenes, etc., directly as seen.
▸ˌrepresenˌtational'istic *adj* ▸ˌrepresen'tationist *n, adj*

representative ➊ (ˌrɛprɪ'zɛntətɪv) *n* **1** a person or thing that represents another. **2** a person who represents and tries to sell the products or services of a firm. **3** a typical example. **4** a person representing a constituency in a deliberative, legislative, or executive body, esp. (*cap.*) a member of the **House of Representatives** (the lower house of Congress). ◆ *adj* **5** serving to represent; symbolic. **6a** exemplifying a class or kind; typical. **6b** containing or including examples of all the interests, types, etc., in a group. **7** acting as deputy or proxy for another. **8** representing a constituency or the whole people in the process of government: *a representative council.* **9** of or relating to the political representation of the people: *representative government.* **10** of or relating to a mental picture or representation.
▸ˌrepre'sentatively *adv* ▸ˌrepre'sentativeness *n*

repress ➊ (rɪ'prɛs) *vb* (*tr*) **1** to keep (feelings, etc.) under control; suppress or restrain. **2** to put into a state of subjugation: *to repress a people.* **3** *Psychol.* to banish (unpleasant thoughts) from one's conscious mind. [C14: from L *reprimere* to press back, from RE- + *premere* to PRESS[1]]
▸re'pressed *adj* ▸re'presser *or* re'pressor *n* ▸re'pressible *adj* ▸re'pression *n* ▸re'pressive *adj*

reprieve ➊ (rɪ'priːv) *vb* **reprieves, reprieving, reprieved.** (*tr*) **1** to postpone or remit the punishment of (a person, esp. one condemned to death). **2** to give temporary relief to (a person or thing), esp. from otherwise irrevocable harm. ◆ *n* **3** a postponement or remission of punishment. **4** a warrant granting a postponement. **5** a temporary relief from pain or harm; respite. [C16: from OF *repris* (something) taken back, from *reprendre,* from L *reprehendere;* ? also infl. by obs. E *repreve* to reprove]
▸re'prievable *adj* ▸re'priever *n*

reprimand ➊ ('rɛprɪˌmɑːnd) *n* **1** a reproof or formal admonition; rebuke. ◆ *vb* **2** (*tr*) to admonish or rebuke, esp. formally. [C17: from F *réprimande,* from L *reprimenda* (things) to be repressed; see REPRESS]
▸ˌrepri'manding *adj*

reprint *n* ('riːˌprɪnt). **1** a reproduction in print of any matter already published. **2** a reissue of a printed work using the same type, plates, etc., as the original. ◆ *vb* (riː'prɪnt). **3** (*tr*) to print again.
▸re'printer *n*

reprisal ➊ (rɪ'praɪzᵊl) *n* **1** the act or an instance of retaliation in any form. **2** (*often pl*) retaliatory action against an enemy in wartime. **3** (formerly) the forcible seizure of the property or subjects of one nation by another. [C15: from OF *reprisaille,* from OIt., from *riprendere* to recapture, from L *reprehendere;* see REPREHEND]

reprise (rɪ'priːz) *Music.* ◆ *n* **1** the repeating of an earlier theme. ◆ *vb* **reprises, reprising, reprised. 2** to repeat (an earlier theme). [C14: from OF, from *reprendre* to take back, from L *reprehendere;* see REPREHEND]

repro ('riːprəʊ) *n, pl* **repros. 1** short for **reproduction** (sense 2): *repro furniture.* **2** short for **reproduction proof.**

reproach ➊ (rɪ'prəʊtʃ) *vb* (*tr*) **1** to impute blame to (a person) for an ac-

THESAURUS

of mind, poise, self-possession, serenity, tranquillity ◆ *vb* **3** = **rest,** drowse, lay down, lie, lie down, lie upon, recline, relax, rest upon, sleep, slumber, take it easy, take one's ease

repose[2] *vb* **1** = **entrust,** confide **2** = **place,** deposit, lodge, put, store

repository *n* **1** = **store,** archive, depository, depot, emporium, magazine, receptacle, storehouse, treasury, vault, warehouse

reprehensible *adj* = **blameworthy,** bad, censurable, condemnable, culpable, delinquent, discreditable, disgraceful, errant, erring, ignoble, objectionable, opprobrious, remiss, shameful, unworthy
Antonyms *adj* acceptable, admirable, forgivable, laudable, pardonable, praiseworthy, unobjectionable

represent *vb* **1, 2** = **stand for,** act for, be, betoken, correspond to, equal, equate with, express, mean, serve as, speak for, substitute for, symbolize **5** = **exemplify,** embody, epitomize, personify, symbolize, typify **6** = **depict,** delineate, denote, describe, designate, evoke, express, illustrate, outline, picture, portray, render, reproduce, show, sketch **9** = **make out to be,** describe as, pass off as, pose as, pretend to be **10** = **portray,** act, appear as, assume the role of, enact, exhibit, perform, play the part of, produce, put on, show, stage

representation *n* **1** = **portrayal,** account, delineation, depiction, description, narration, narrative, relation, resemblance **2** = **picture,** illustration, image, likeness, model, portrait, sketch **5** = **body of representatives,** committee, delegates, delegation, embassy **7** = **performance,** exhibition, play, production, show, sight, spectacle **8** *often plural* = **statement,** account, argument, explanation, exposition, expostulation, remonstrance

representative *n* **1** = **delegate,** agent, commissioner, councillor, depute (*Scot.*), deputy, member, member of parliament, M.P., proxy, spokesman *or* spokeswoman **2** = **salesman,** agent, commercial traveller, rep, traveller **3** = **typical example,** archetype, embodiment, epitome, exemplar, personification, type ◆ *adj* **5** = **typical,** archetypal, characteristic, emblematic, evocative, exemplary, illustrative, symbolic **8** = **chosen,** delegated, elected, elective
Antonyms *adj* ≠ **typical:** atypical, extraordinary, uncharacteristic

repress *vb* **1** = **control,** bottle up, check, curb, hold back, hold in, inhibit, keep in check, master, muffle, overcome, overpower, restrain, silence, smother, stifle, suppress, swallow **2** = **subdue,** crush, quash, quell, subjugate
Antonyms *vb* ≠ **control:** encourage, express, give free rein to, let out, release ≠ **subdue:** free, liberate

repression *n* **2** = **subjugation,** authoritarianism, censorship, coercion, constraint, control, despotism, domination, restraint, suppression, tyranny

repressive *adj* **2** = **oppressive,** absolute, authoritarian, coercive, despotic, dictatorial, harsh, severe, tough, tyrannical
Antonyms *adj* democratic, liberal, libertarian

reprieve *vb* **1** = **grant a stay of execution to,** let off the hook (*sl.*), pardon, postpone *or* remit the punishment of **2** = **relieve,** abate, allay, alleviate, mitigate, palliate, respite ◆ *n* **3, 4** = **stay of execution,** abeyance, amnesty, deferment, pardon, postponement, remission, suspension **5** = **relief,** abatement, alleviation, let-up (*inf.*), mitigation, palliation, respite

reprimand *n* **1** = **blame,** admonition, castigation, censure, dressing-down (*inf.*), flea in one's ear (*inf.*), lecture, rebuke, reprehension, reproach, reproof, row, talking-to (*inf.*), telling-off (*inf.*), ticking-off (*inf.*), tongue-lashing ◆ *vb* **2** = **blame,** admonish, bawl out, carpet (*inf.*), castigate, censure, check, chew out (*US & Canad. inf.*), chide, dress down (*inf.*), give a rocket (*Brit. & NZ inf.*), give (someone) a row (*inf.*), haul over the coals (*inf.*), lecture, rap over the knuckles, read the riot act, rebuke, reprehend, reproach, reprove, scold, slap on the wrist (*inf.*), take to task, tear into (*inf.*), tear (someone) off a strip (*Brit. inf.*), tell off (*inf.*), tick off (*inf.*), upbraid
Antonyms *n* ≠ **blame:** commendation, compliment, congratulations, praise ◆ *vb* ≠ **blame:** applaud, commend, compliment, congratulate, praise

reprisal *n* **1** = **retaliation,** an eye for an eye, counterstroke, requital, retribution, revenge, vengeance

reproach *vb* **1** = **blame,** abuse, bawl out (*inf.*), blast, carpet (*inf.*), censure, chew out (*US & Canad. inf.*), chide, condemn, criticize, defame, discredit, disparage, find fault with, give a rocket (*Brit. & NZ inf.*), have a go at (*inf.*), lambast(e), read the riot act, rebuke, reprehend, reprimand, reprove, scold, take to task, tear

tion or fault; rebuke. ◆ *n* **2** the act of reproaching. **3** rebuke or censure; reproof. **4** disgrace or shame: *to bring reproach upon one's family.* **5** **above** *or* **beyond reproach.** perfect; beyond criticism. [C15: from OF *reprochier,* from L RE- + *prope* near]
▸**re'proachable** *adj* ▸**re'proacher** *n* ▸**re'proachingly** *adv*

reproachful ➊ (rɪ'prəʊtʃfʊl) *adj* full of or expressing reproach.
▸**re'proachfully** *adv* ▸**re'proachfulness** *n*

reprobate ➊ ('reprəʊˌbeɪt) *adj* **1** morally unprincipled; depraved. **2** *Christianity.* condemned to eternal punishment in hell. ◆ *n* **3** an unprincipled, depraved, or damned person. **4** a disreputable or roguish person. ◆ *vb* **reprobates, reprobating, reprobated.** (*tr*) **5** to disapprove of; condemn. **6** (of God) to condemn to eternal punishment in hell. [C16: from LL *reprobātus* held in disfavour, from L RE- + *probāre* to test, APPROVE]
▸**reprobacy** ('reprəbəsɪ) *n* ▸**'reproˌbater** *n* ▸**ˌrepro'bation** *n*

reprocess (riː'prəʊses) *vb* (*tr*) to treat again (something already made and used) in order to make it reusable in some form.
▸**re'processing** *n, adj*

reproduce ➊ (ˌriːprə'djuːs) *vb* **reproduces, reproducing, reproduced.** (*mainly tr*) **1** to make a copy, representation, or imitation of; duplicate. **2** (*also intr*) *Biol.* to undergo or cause to undergo a process of reproduction. **3** to produce again; bring back into existence again; re-create. **4** (*intr*) to come out (well, badly, etc.) when copied.
▸**ˌrepro'ducer** *n* ▸**ˌrepro'ducible** *adj* ▸**ˌrepro'ducibly** *adv* ▸**ˌreproˌduci'bility** *n*

reproduction ➊ (ˌriːprə'dʌkʃən) *n* **1** *Biol.* any of various processes, either sexual or asexual, by which an animal or plant produces one or more individuals similar to itself. **2a** an imitation or facsimile of a work of art. **2b** (*as modifier*): *a reproduction portrait.* **3** the quality of sound from an audio system. **4** the act or process of reproducing.

reproduction proof *n Printing.* a proof of very good quality used for photographic reproduction to make a printing plate.

reproductive (ˌriːprə'dʌktɪv) *adj* of, relating to, characteristic of, or taking part in reproduction.
▸**ˌrepro'ductively** *adv* ▸**ˌrepro'ductiveness** *n*

reprography (rɪ'prɒgrəfɪ) *n* the art or process of copying, reprinting, or reproducing printed material.
▸**reprographic** (ˌreprə'græfɪk) *adj* ▸**ˌrepro'graphically** *adv*

reproof ➊ (rɪ'pruːf) *n* an act or expression of rebuke or censure. Also: **reproval** (rɪ'pruːvᵊl). [C14 *reproffe,* from OF *reprove,* from LL *reprobāre* to disapprove of; see REPROBATE]

re-proof (riː'pruːf) *vb* (*tr*) **1** to treat (a coat, jacket, etc.) so as to renew its texture, waterproof qualities, etc. **2** to provide a new proof of (a book, galley, etc.).

reprove ➊ (rɪ'pruːv) *vb* **reproves, reproving, reproved.** (*tr*) to rebuke or scold. [C14: from OF *reprover,* from LL *reprobāre,* from L RE- + *probāre* to examine]
▸**re'provable** *adj* ▸**re'prover** *n* ▸**re'provingly** *adv*

reptant ('reptənt) *adj Biol.* creeping, crawling, or lying along the ground. [C17: from L *reptāre* to creep]

reptile ('reptaɪl) *n* **1** any of the cold-blooded vertebrates characterized by lungs, an outer covering of horny scales or plates, and young produced in eggs, such as the tortoises, turtles, snakes, lizards, and crocodiles. **2** a grovelling insignificant person: *you miserable little reptile!* ◆ *adj* **3** creeping, crawling, or squirming. [C14: from LL *reptilis* creeping, from L *rēpere* to crawl]
▸**reptilian** (rep'tɪlɪən) *n, adj*

republic (rɪ'pʌblɪk) *n* **1** a form of government in which the people or their elected representatives possess the supreme power. **2** a political or national unit possessing such a form of government. **3** a constitutional form in which the head of state is an elected or nominated president. [C17: from F *république,* from L *rēspublica,* lit.: the public thing, from *rēs* thing + *publica* PUBLIC]

republican (rɪ'pʌblɪkən) *adj* **1** of, resembling, or relating to a republic. **2** supporting or advocating a republic. ◆ *n* **3** a supporter or advocate of a republic.

Republican (rɪ'pʌblɪkən) *adj* **1** of, belonging to, or relating to a Republican Party. **2** of, belonging to, or relating to the Irish Republican Army. ◆ *n* **3** a member or supporter of a Republican Party. **4** a member or supporter of the Irish Republican Army.

republicanism (rɪ'pʌblɪkəˌnɪzəm) *n* **1** the principles or theory of republican government. **2** support for a republic. **3** (*often cap.*) support for a Republican Party.

Republican Party *n* **1** one of the two major political parties in the US: established around 1854. **2** any of a number of political parties in other countries, usually so named to indicate their opposition to monarchy.

repudiate ➊ (rɪ'pjuːdɪˌeɪt) *vb* **repudiates, repudiating, repudiated.** (*tr*) **1** to reject the authority or validity of; refuse to accept or ratify. **2** to refuse to acknowledge or pay (a debt). **3** to cast off or disown (a son, lover, etc.). [C16: from L *repudiāre* to put away, from *repudium* separation, divorce, from RE- + *pudēre* to be ashamed]
▸**re'pudiable** *adj* ▸**reˌpudi'ation** *n* ▸**re'pudiative** *adj* ▸**re'pudiˌator** *n*

repugnant ➊ (rɪ'pʌgnənt) *adj* **1** repellent to the senses; causing aversion. **2** distasteful; offensive; disgusting. **3** contradictory; inconsistent or incompatible. [C14: from L *repugnāns* resisting, from *repugnāre,* from RE- + *pugnāre* to fight]
▸**re'pugnance** *n* ▸**re'pugnantly** *adv*

repulse ➊ (rɪ'pʌls) *vb* **repulses, repulsing, repulsed.** (*tr*) **1** to drive back or ward off (an attacking force); repel; rebuff. **2** to reject with coldness or discourtesy: *she repulsed his advances.* ◆ *n* **3** the act or an instance of driving back or warding off; rebuff. **4** a cold discourteous rejection or refusal. [C16: from L *repellere* to drive back]
▸**re'pulser** *n*

> **USAGE NOTE** Some people think that the use of *repulse* in sentences such as *he was repulsed by what he saw* is incorrect and that the correct word is *repel.*

repulsion ➊ (rɪ'pʌlʃən) *n* **1** a feeling of disgust or aversion. **2** *Physics.* a force separating two objects, such as the force between two like electric charges.

repulsive ➊ (rɪ'pʌlsɪv) *adj* **1** causing or occasioning repugnance; loathsome; disgusting or distasteful. **2** tending to repel, esp. by coldness and discourtesy. **3** *Physics.* concerned with, producing, or being a repulsion.
▸**re'pulsively** *adv* ▸**re'pulsiveness** *n*

repurchase (riː'pɜːtʃɪs) *vb* **1** (*tr*) to buy back or buy again (goods, securities, assets, etc.). ◆ *n* **2** an act or instance of repurchasing.

reputable ➊ ('repjʊtəbᵊl) *adj* **1** having a good reputation; honoured, trustworthy, or respectable. **2** (of words) acceptable as good usage; standard.
▸**'reputably** *adv*

reputation ➊ (ˌrepjʊ'teɪʃən) *n* **1** the estimation in which a person or

THESAURUS

into (*inf.*), tear (someone) off a strip (*Brit. inf.*), upbraid ◆ *n* **3** = **blame**, abuse, blemish, censure, condemnation, contempt, disapproval, discredit, disgrace, dishonour, disrepute, ignominy, indignity, obloquy, odium, opprobrium, rebuke, scorn, shame, slight, slur, stain, stigma

reproachful *adj* = **critical**, abusive, admonitory, castigatory, censorious, condemnatory, contemptuous, disappointed, disapproving, fault-finding, reproving, scolding, upbraiding

reprobate *adj* **1** = **unprincipled**, abandoned, bad, base, corrupt, degenerate, depraved, dissolute, hardened, immoral, incorrigible, profligate, shameless, sinful, vile, wicked ◆ *n* **3, 4** = **scoundrel**, bastard (*offens.*), blackguard, degenerate, evildoer, miscreant, ne'er-do-well, outcast, rake, rascal, roué, scumbag (*sl.*), shit (*taboo sl.*), sinner, son-of-a-bitch (*sl., chiefly US & Canad.*), villain, wretch, wrongdoer ◆ *vb* **5** = **condemn**, damn, denounce, disapprove of, frown upon, reprehend, vilify

reproduce *vb* **1** = **copy**, duplicate, echo, emulate, imitate, match, mirror, parallel, print, recreate, repeat, replicate, represent, transcribe **2** *Biology* = **breed**, generate, multiply, procreate, produce young, proliferate, propagate, spawn

reproduction *n* **1** *Biology* = **breeding**, generation, increase, multiplication, procreation, proliferation, propagation **2** = **copy**, duplicate, facsimile, imitation, picture, print, replica
Antonyms *n* ≠ **copy**: master, original, prototype

reproof *n* = **rebuke**, admonition, blame, castigation, censure, chiding, condemnation, criticism, dressing-down (*inf.*), reprehension, reprimand, reproach, reproval, scolding, ticking-off (*inf.*), tongue-lashing, upbraiding
Antonyms *n* commendation, compliment, encouragement, praise

reprove *vb* = **rebuke**, abuse, admonish, bawl out (*inf.*), berate, blame, carpet (*inf.*), censure, check, chew out (*US & Canad. inf.*), chide, condemn, give a rocket (*Brit. & NZ inf.*), read the riot act, reprehend, reprimand, scold, take to task, tear into (*inf.*), tear (someone) off a strip (*Brit. inf.*), tell off (*inf.*), tick off (*inf.*), upbraid
Antonyms *vb* applaud, commend, compliment, encourage, praise

repudiate *vb* **1** = **deny**, abjure, disavow, disclaim, reject, renounce, rescind, retract, reverse, revoke **3** = **disown**, abandon, cast off, desert, discard, forsake, reject, turn one's back on, wash one's hands of
Antonyms *vb* ≠ **deny**: accept, acknowledge, admit, assert, avow, defend, proclaim, ratify

repugnance *n* **1, 2** = **distaste**, abhorrence, antipathy, aversion, disgust, dislike, disrelish, hatred, loathing, odium, reluctance, repulsion, revulsion

repugnant *adj* **1, 2** = **distasteful**, abhorrent, abominable, disgusting, foul, hateful, horrid, loathsome, nauseating, objectionable, obnoxious, odious, offensive, repellent, revolting, sickening, vile, yucky *or* yukky (*sl.*) **3** = **incompatible**, adverse, antagonistic, antipathetic, averse, contradictory, hostile, inconsistent, inimical, opposed
Antonyms *adj* ≠ **distasteful**: agreeable, attractive, pleasant, unobjectionable ≠ **incompatible**: compatible

repulse *vb* **1** = **drive back**, beat off, check, defeat, fight off, rebuff, repel, throw back, ward off **2** = **reject**, disdain, disregard, give the cold shoulder to, rebuff, refuse, snub, spurn, turn down ◆ *n* **3** = **defeat**, check, disappointment, failure, reverse **4** = **rejection**, cold shoulder, kick in the teeth, knock-back (*sl.*), rebuff, refusal, snub, spurning, the (old) heave-ho (*inf.*)

repulsion *n* **1** = **disgust**, abhorrence, aversion, detestation, disrelish, distaste, hatred, loathing, odium, repugnance, revulsion

repulsive *adj* **1** = **disgusting**, abhorrent, abominable, disagreeable, distasteful, forbidding, foul, hateful, hideous, horrid, loathsome, nauseating, objectionable, obnoxious, obscene, odious, offensive, repellent, revolting, sickening, ugly, unpleasant, vile
Antonyms *adj* appealing, attractive, delightful, enticing, lovely, pleasant

reputable *adj* **1** = **respectable**, creditable, estimable, excellent, good, honourable, honoured, legitimate, of good repute, reliable, trustworthy, upright, well-thought-of, worthy
Antonyms *adj* cowboy (*inf.*), disreputable, fly-by-night, shady (*inf.*), unreliable, untrustworthy

reputation *n* **1** = **name**, character, estimation, opinion, renown, repute, standing, stature **2** =

thing is generally held; opinion. **2** a high opinion generally held about a person or thing; esteem. **3** notoriety or fame, esp. for some specified characteristic. [C14: from L *reputātiō*, from *reputāre* to calculate; see REPUTE]

repute ❶ (rɪ'pjuːt) *vb* **reputes, reputing, reputed. 1** (*tr; usually passive*) to consider (a person or thing) to be as specified: *he is reputed to be rich.* ◆ *n* **2** public estimation; reputation: *a writer of little repute.* [C15: from OF *reputer*, from L *reputāre*, from RE- + *putāre* to think]

reputed ❶ (rɪ'pjuːtɪd) *adj* (*prenominal*) generally reckoned or considered; supposed: *the reputed writer of two epic poems.*
▸**re'putedly** *adv*

request ❶ (rɪ'kwɛst) *vb* (*tr*) **1** to express a desire for, esp. politely; ask for or demand: *to request a bottle of wine.* ◆ *n* **2** the act or an instance of requesting, esp. in the form of a written statement, etc.; petition or solicitation. **3 by request.** in accordance with someone's desire. **4 in request.** in demand; popular: *he is in request all over the world.* **5 on request.** on the occasion of a demand or request: *application forms are available on request.* [C14: from OF *requeste*, from Vulgar L *requaerere*; see REQUIRE, QUEST]
▸**re'quester** *n*

request stop *n* a point on a route at which a bus, etc., will stop only if signalled to do so. US equivalent: **flag stop.**

Requiem ('rɛkwɪəm) *n* **1** *RC Church.* a Mass celebrated for the dead. **2** a musical setting of this Mass. **3** any piece of music composed or performed as a memorial to a dead person. [C14: from L *requiēs* rest, from the introit, *Requiem aeternam dona eis* Rest eternal grant unto them]

requiem shark *n* any of a family of sharks occurring mostly in tropical seas and characterized by a nictitating membrane.

requiescat (ˌrɛkwɪ'ɛskæt) *n* a prayer for the repose of the souls of the dead. [L, from *requiescat in pace* may he rest in peace]

require ❶ (rɪ'kwaɪə) *vb* **requires, requiring, required.** (*mainly tr; may take a clause as object or an infinitive*) **1** to have need of; depend upon; want. **2** to impose as a necessity; make necessary: *this work requires precision.* **3** (*also intr*) to make formal request (for); insist upon. **4** to call upon or oblige (a person) authoritatively; order or command: *to require someone to account for his actions.* [C14: from OF *requerre*, via Vulgar L from L *requīrere* to seek to know; also infl. by *quaerere* to seek]
▸**re'quirer** *n*

> **USAGE NOTE** The use of *require to* as in *I require to see the manager* or *you require to complete a special form* is thought by many people to be incorrect: *I need to see the manager; you are required to complete a special form.*

requirement ❶ (rɪ'kwaɪəmənt) *n* **1** something demanded or imposed as an obligation. **2** a thing desired or needed. **3** the act or an instance of requiring.

requisite ❶ ('rɛkwɪzɪt) *adj* **1** absolutely essential; indispensable. ◆ *n* **2** something indispensable; necessity. [C15: from L *requisītus* sought after, from *requīrere* to seek for]
▸**'requisitely** *adv*

requisition ❶ (ˌrɛkwɪ'zɪʃən) *n* **1** a request or demand, esp. an authoritative or formal one. **2** an official form on which such a demand is made. **3** the act of taking something over, esp. temporarily for military or public use. ◆ *vb* (*tr*) **4** to demand and take for use, esp. by military or public authority. **5** (*may take an infinitive*) to require (someone) formally to do (something): *to requisition a soldier to drive an officer's car.*
▸ˌ**requi'sitionary** *adj* ▸ˌ**requi'sitionist** *n*

requite ❶ (rɪ'kwaɪt) *vb* **requites, requiting, requited.** (*tr*) to make return to (a person for a kindness or injury); repay with a similar action. [C16: RE- + obs. *quite* to discharge, repay; see QUIT]
▸**re'quitable** *adj* ▸**re'quital** *n* ▸**re'quitement** *n* ▸**re'quiter** *n*

reredos ('rɪədɒs) *n* **1** a screen or wall decoration at the back of an altar. **2** another word for **fireback.** [C14: from OF *areredos*, from *arere* behind + *dos* back, from L *dorsum*]

rerun *vb* (riː'rʌn), **reruns, rerunning, reran, rerun.** (*tr*) **1** to broadcast or put on (a film, etc.) again. **2** to run (a race, etc.) again. ◆ *n* ('riːˌrʌn). **3** a film, etc., that is broadcast again; repeat. **4** a race that is run again. **5** *Computing.* the repeat of a part of a computer program.

res (reɪs) *n, pl* **res.** *Latin.* a thing, matter, or object.

res. *abbrev. for:* **1** research. **2** reserve. **3** residence. **4** resides. **5** resigned. **6** resolution.

resale price maintenance ('riːseɪl) *n* the practice by which a manufacturer establishes a fixed or minimum price for the resale of a brand product by retailers or other distributors. US equivalent: **fair trade.** Abbrev.: **rpm.**

reschedule (riː'ʃɛdjuːl; *also, esp. US* -'skɛdʒʊəl) *vb* (*tr*) **1** to change the time, date, or schedule of. **2** to arrange a revised schedule for repayment of (a debt).

rescind ❶ (rɪ'sɪnd) *vb* (*tr*) to annul or repeal. [C17: from L *rēscindere* to cut off, from *re-* (intensive) + *scindere* to cut]
▸**re'scindable** *adj* ▸**re'scinder** *n* ▸**re'scindment** *n*

rescission (rɪ'sɪʒən) *n* **1** the act of rescinding. **2** *Law.* the right to have a contract set aside if it has been entered into mistakenly, as a result of misrepresentation, undue influence, etc.

rescript ('riːˌskrɪpt) *n* **1** (in ancient Rome) a reply by the emperor to a question on a point of law. **2** any official announcement or edict; a decree. **3** something rewritten. [C16: from L *rēscriptum* reply, from *rēscribere* to write back]

rescue ❶ ('rɛskjuː) *vb* **rescues, rescuing, rescued.** (*tr*) **1** to bring (someone or something) out of danger, etc.; deliver or save. **2** to free (a person) from legal custody by force. **3** *Law.* to seize (goods) by force. ◆ *n* **4a** the act or an instance of rescuing. **4b** (*as modifier*): *a rescue party.* **5** the forcible removal of a person from legal custody. **6** *Law.* the forcible seizure of goods or property. [C14: *rescowen*, from OF *rescourre*, from RE- + *escourre* to pull away, from L *excutere* to shake off, from *quatere* to shake]
▸**'rescuer** *n*

research ❶ (rɪ'sɜːtʃ) *n* **1** systematic investigation to establish facts or collect information on a subject. ◆ *vb* **2** to carry out investigations into (a subject, etc.). [C16: from OF *recercher* to seek, search again, from RE- + *cercher* to SEARCH]
▸**re'searchable** *adj* ▸**re'searcher** *n*

research and development *n* a commercial company's application of scientific research to develop new products. Abbrev.: **R & D.**

reseat (riː'siːt) *vb* (*tr*) **1** to show (a person) to a new seat. **2** to put a new seat on (a chair, etc.). **3** to provide new seats for (a theatre, etc.). **4** to re-form the seating of (a valve).

resect (rɪ'sɛkt) *vb* (*tr*) *Surgery.* to cut out part of (a bone, organ, or other structure or part). [C17: from L *resecāre*, from RE- + *secāre* to cut]

resection (rɪ'sɛkʃən) *n* **1** *Surgery.* excision of part of a bone, organ, or other part. **2** *Surveying.* a method of fixing the position of a point by making angular observations to three fixed points.
▸**re'sectional** *adj*

resemblance ❶ (rɪ'zɛmbləns) *n* **1** the state or quality of resembling; likeness or similarity. **2** the degree or extent to which a likeness exists. **3** semblance; likeness.
▸**re'semblant** *adj*

THESAURUS

esteem, credit, honour **3** = **fame**, distinction, eminence

repute *n* **2** = **reputation**, celebrity, distinction, eminence, esteem, estimation, fame, name, renown, standing, stature

reputed *adj* = **supposed**, accounted, alleged, believed, considered, deemed, estimated, held, ostensible, putative, reckoned, regarded, rumoured, said, seeming, thought

reputedly *adv* = **supposedly**, allegedly, apparently, ostensibly, seemingly

request *vb* **1** = **ask (for)**, appeal for, apply for, beg, beseech, call for, demand, desire, entreat, invite, petition, pray, put in for, requisition, seek, solicit, sue for, supplicate ◆ *n* **2** = **asking**, appeal, application, begging, call, demand, desire, entreaty, petition, prayer, requisition, solicitation, suit, supplication
Antonyms *vb* ≠ **ask (for)**: command, order ◆ *n* ≠ **asking**: command, order

require *vb* **1** = **need**, crave, depend upon, desire, have need of, lack, miss, stand in need of, want, wish **2** = **demand**, call for, entail, involve, necessitate, take **3, 4** = **order**, ask, bid, call upon, command, compel, constrain, demand, direct, enjoin, exact, insist upon, instruct, oblige

required *adj* **2** = **necessary**, called for, compulsory, demanded, *de rigueur*, essential, mandatory, needed, obligatory, prescribed, recommended, requisite, set, unavoidable, vital
Antonyms *adj* elective, noncompulsory, not necessary, not vital, optional, unimportant, voluntary

requirement *n* **1** = **necessity**, demand, desideratum, essential, must, precondition, prerequisite, qualification, requisite, *sine qua non*, specification, stipulation **2** = **need**, lack, want

requisite *adj* **1** = **necessary**, called for, essential, indispensable, mandatory, needed, needful, obligatory, prerequisite, required, vital ◆ *n* **2** = **necessity**, condition, desideratum, essential, must, need, precondition, prerequisite, requirement, *sine qua non*

requisition *n* **1** = **demand**, application, call, request, summons **3** = **takeover**, appropriation, commandeering, occupation, seizure ◆ *vb* **4** = **take over**, appropriate, commandeer, occupy, seize, take possession of **5** = **demand**, apply for, call for, put in for, request

requital *n* = **return**, amends, compensation, payment, recompense, redress, reimbursement, remuneration, repayment, restitution, reward

requite *vb* = **return**, compensate, get even, give in return, give tit for tat, make amends, make good, make restitution, pay, pay (someone) back in his *or* her own coin, reciprocate, recompense, redress, reimburse, remunerate, repay, respond, retaliate, return like for like, reward, satisfy

rescind *vb* = **annul**, abrogate, cancel, countermand, declare null and void, invalidate, obviate, overturn, quash, recall, repeal, retract, reverse, revoke, set aside, void
Antonyms *vb* confirm, enact, implement, reaffirm, support, uphold, validate

rescue *vb* **1** = **save**, deliver, extricate, free, get out, liberate, recover, redeem, release, salvage, save (someone's) bacon (*Brit. inf.*), save the life of, set free ◆ *n* **4a** = **liberation**, deliverance, extrication, recovery, redemption, release, relief, salvage, salvation, saving
Antonyms *vb* ≠ **save**: abandon, desert, leave, leave behind, lose, strand

research *n* **1** = **investigation**, analysis, delving, examination, experimentation, exploration, fact-finding, groundwork, inquiry, probe, scrutiny, study ◆ *vb* **2** = **investigate**, analyse, consult the archives, do tests, examine, experiment, explore, look into, make inquiries, probe, scrutinize, study, work over

resemblance *n* **1, 2** = **similarity**, affinity, analogy, closeness, comparability, comparison, conformity, correspondence, counterpart, kin-

resemble ➊ (rɪ'zɛmb°l) *vb* **resembles, resembling, resembled.** (*tr*) to possess some similarity to; be like. [C14: from OF *resembler*, from RE- + *sembler* to look like, from L *similis* like]
▸**re'sembler** *n*

resent ➊ (rɪ'zɛnt) *vb* (*tr*) to feel bitter, indignant, or aggrieved at. [C17: from F *ressentir*, from RE- + *sentir* to feel, from L *sentīre* to perceive; see SENSE]
▸**re'sentful** *adj* ▸**re'sentment** *n*

reserpine ('rɛsəpɪn) *n* an insoluble alkaloid, extracted from the roots of a rauwolfia, used medicinally to lower blood pressure and as a sedative and tranquillizer. [C20: from G *Reserpin*, prob. from the NL name of the plant]

reservation ➊ (ˌrɛzə'veɪʃən) *n* **1** the act or an instance of reserving. **2** something reserved, esp. accommodation or a seat. **3** (*often pl*) a stated or unstated qualification of opinion that prevents one's wholehearted acceptance of a proposal, etc. **4** an area of land set aside, esp. (in the US) for American Indian peoples. **5** *Brit.* the strip of land between the two carriageways of a dual carriageway. **6** the act or process of keeping back, esp. for oneself; withholding. **7** *Law.* a right or interest retained by the grantor in property dealings.

reserve ➊ (rɪ'zɜːv) *vb* **reserves, reserving, reserved.** (*tr*) **1** to keep back or set aside, esp. for future use or contingency; withhold. **2** to keep for oneself; retain: *I reserve the right to question these men later.* **3** to obtain or secure by advance arrangement: *I have reserved two tickets for tonight's show.* **4** to delay delivery of (a judgment). ◆ *n* **5a** something kept back or set aside, esp. for future use or contingency. **5b** (*as modifier*): *a reserve stock.* **6** the state or condition of being reserved: *I have plenty in reserve.* **7** a tract of land set aside for a special purpose: *a nature reserve.* **8** *Austral. & NZ.* a public park. **9** the usual Canadian name for **reservation** (sense 4). **10** *Sport.* a substitute. **11** (*often pl*) **11a** a part of an army not committed to immediate action in a military engagement. **11b** that part of a nation's armed services not in active service. **12** coolness or formality of manner; restraint, silence, or reticence. **13** (*often pl*) *Finance.* liquid assets or a portion of capital not invested or a portion of profits not distributed by a bank or business enterprise and held to meet future liabilities or contingencies. **14 without reserve.** without reservations; fully. [C14: from OF *reserver*, from L *reservāre*, from RE- + *servāre* to keep]
▸**re'servable** *adj* ▸**re'server** *n*

re-serve (riː'sɜːv) *vb* **re-serves, re-serving, re-served.** (*tr*) to serve again.

reserve bank *n* one of the twelve banks forming part of the US Federal Reserve System.

reserve currency *n* foreign currency that is acceptable as a medium of international payments and is held in reserve by many countries.

reserved ➊ (rɪ'zɜːvd) *adj* **1** set aside for use by a particular person. **2** cool or formal in manner; restrained or reticent. **3** destined; fated: *a man reserved for greatness.*
▸**reservedly** (rɪ'zɜːvɪdlɪ) *adv* ▸**re'servedness** *n*

reserved list *n Brit.* a list of retired naval, army, or air-force officers available for recall to active service in an emergency.

reserved occupation *n Brit.* an occupation from which one will not be called up for military service in time of war.

reserve-grade *adj Austral.* denoting a sporting team of the second rank in a club.

reserve price *n Brit.* the minimum price acceptable to the owner of property being auctioned or sold. Also called (esp. Scot. and US): **upset price.**

reserve tranche *n* the quota of 25 per cent to which a member of the IMF has unconditional access. Prior to 1978 it was paid in gold and known as the **gold tranche.**

reservist (rɪ'zɜːvɪst) *n* one who serves in the reserve formations of a nation's armed forces.

reservoir ➊ ('rɛzəˌvwɑː) *n* **1** a natural or artificial lake or large tank used for collecting and storing water for community use. **2** *Biol.* a cavity in an organism containing fluid. **3** a place where a great stock of anything is accumulated. **4** a large supply of something: *a reservoir of talent.* [C17: from F *réservoir*, from *réserver* to RESERVE]

reservoir rock *n* porous and permeable rock containing producible oil or gas in its pore spaces.

reset[1] *vb* (riː'sɛt), **resets, resetting, reset.** (*tr*) **1** to set again (a broken bone, matter in type, a gemstone, etc.). **2** to restore (a gauge, etc.) to zero. ◆ *n* ('riːˌsɛt). **3** the act or an instance of setting again. **4** a thing that is set again.
▸**re'setter** *n*

reset[2] *Scot.* ◆ *vb* (riː'sɛt), **resets, resetting, reset. 1** to receive or handle goods knowing they have been stolen. ◆ *n* ('riːsɛt). **2** the receiving of stolen goods. [C14: from OF *receter*, from L *receptāre*, from *recipere* to receive]
▸**re'setter** *n*

res gestae ('dʒɛstiː) *pl n* **1** things done or accomplished; achievements. **2** *Law.* incidental facts and circumstances that are admissible in evidence because they explain the matter at issue. [L]

reside ➊ (rɪ'zaɪd) *vb* **resides, residing, resided.** (*intr*) *Formal.* **1** to live permanently (in a place); have one's home (in): *he resides in London.* **2** (of things, qualities, etc.) to be inherently present (in); be vested (in): *political power resides in military strength.* [C15: from L *residēre* to sit back, from RE- + *sedēre* to sit]
▸**re'sider** *n*

residence ➊ ('rɛzɪdəns) *n* **1** the place in which one resides; abode or home. **2** a large imposing house; mansion. **3** the fact of residing in a place or a period of residing. **4 in residence. 4a** actually resident: *the Queen is in residence.* **4b** designating a creative artist resident and active for a set period at a college, gallery, etc.: *writer in residence.*

residency ('rɛzɪdənsɪ) *n, pl* **residencies. 1** a variant of **residence. 2** a regular series of concerts by a band or singer at one venue. **3** *US & Canad.* the period, following internship, during which a physician undergoes specialized training. **4** (in India, formerly) the official house of the governor general at the court of a native prince.

resident ➊ ('rɛzɪdənt) *n* **1** a person who resides in a place. **2** (esp. formerly) a representative of the British government in a British protectorate. **3** (in India, formerly) a representative of the British governor general at the court of a native prince. **4** a bird or animal that does not migrate. **5** *Brit. & NZ.* a junior doctor who lives in the hospital where he works. **6** *US & Canad.* a physician who lives in the hospital while undergoing specialist training after completing his internship. ◆ *adj* **7** living in a place; residing. **8** living or staying at a place in order to discharge a duty, etc. **9** (of qualities, etc.) existing or inherent (in). **10** (of birds and animals) not in the habit of migrating.
▸**'residentship** *n*

residential (ˌrɛzɪ'dɛnʃəl) *adj* **1** suitable for or allocated for residence: *a residential area.* **2** relating to residence.
▸ˌ**resi'dentially** *adv*

residentiary (ˌrɛzɪ'dɛnʃərɪ) *adj* **1** residing in a place, esp. officially. **2** obliged to reside in an official residence: *a residentiary benefice.* ◆ *n, pl* **residentiaries. 3** a clergyman obliged to reside in the place of his official appointment.

residual ➊ (rɪ'zɪdjuəl) *adj* **1** of, relating to, or designating a residue or remainder; remaining; leftover. **2** *US.* of or relating to the payment of residuals. ◆ *n* **3** something left over as a residue; remainder. **4** *Statistics.* **4a** the difference between the mean of a set of observations and one particular observation. **4b** the difference between the numerical

THESAURUS

ship, likeness, parallel, parity, sameness, similitude **3** = **semblance**, facsimile, image, likeness
Antonyms *n* ≠ **similarity:** difference, disparity, dissimilarity, heterogeneity, unlikeness, variation

resemble *vb* = **be like**, bear a resemblance to, be similar to, duplicate, echo, favour (*inf.*), look like, mirror, parallel, put one in mind of, remind one of, take after

resent *vb* = **be bitter about**, be angry about, bear a grudge about, begrudge, be in a huff about, be offended by, dislike, grudge, harbour a grudge against, have hard feelings about, object to, take amiss, take as an insult, take exception to, take offence at, take umbrage at
Antonyms *vb* accept, approve, be content with, be pleased by, feel flattered by, like, welcome

resentful *adj* = **bitter**, aggrieved, angry, choked, embittered, exasperated, grudging, huffish, huffy, hurt, in a huff, incensed, indignant, in high dudgeon, irate, jealous, miffed (*inf.*), offended, peeved (*inf.*), piqued, put out, revengeful, unforgiving, wounded
Antonyms *adj* content, flattered, gratified, pleased, satisfied

resentment *n* = **bitterness**, anger, animosity, bad blood, chip on one's shoulder (*inf.*), displeasure, fury, grudge, huff, hurt, ill feeling, ill will, indignation, ire, irritation, malice, pique, rage, rancour, umbrage, vexation, wrath

reservation *n* **3** = **doubt**, demur, hesitancy, scepticism, scruple **3** = **condition**, proviso, qualification, rider, stipulation **4** = **reserve**, enclave, homeland, preserve, sanctuary, territory, tract

reserve *vb* **1, 2** = **keep**, conserve, hang on to, hoard, hold, husband, keep back, lay up, preserve, put by, retain, save, set aside, stockpile, store, withhold **3** = **book**, bespeak, engage, prearrange, pre-engage, retain, secure **4** = **delay**, defer, keep back, postpone, put off, withhold ◆ *n* **5a** = **store**, backlog, cache, capital, fall-back, fund, hoard, reservoir, savings, stock, stockpile, supply ◆ *modifier* **5b** = **substitute**, alternate, auxiliary, extra, fall-back, secondary, spare ◆ *n* **7** = **reservation**, park, preserve, sanctuary, tract **12** = **shyness**, aloofness, constraint, coolness, formality, modesty, reluctance, reservation, restraint, reticence, secretiveness, silence, taciturnity

reserved *adj* **1** = **set aside**, booked, engaged, held, kept, restricted, retained, spoken for, taken **2** = **uncommunicative**, aloof, cautious, close-mouthed, cold, cool, demure, formal, modest, prim, restrained, reticent, retiring, secretive, shy, silent, standoffish, taciturn, unapproachable, undemonstrative, unforthcoming, unresponsive, unsociable
Antonyms *adj* ≠ **uncommunicative:** ardent, demonstrative, forward, open, sociable, uninhibited, unreserved, warm

reservoir *n* **1** = **lake**, basin, pond, tank **3** = **repository**, container, holder, receptacle, store, tank **4** = **store**, accumulation, fund, pool, reserves, source, stock, stockpile, supply

reside *vb Formal* **1** = **live**, abide, dwell, hang out (*inf.*), have one's home, inhabit, lodge, remain, settle, sojourn, stay **2** = **be present**, abide, be intrinsic to, be vested, consist, dwell, exist, inhere, lie, rest with
Antonyms *vb* ≠ **live:** holiday in, visit

residence *n* **1** = **home**, abode, domicile, dwelling, flat, habitation, house, household, lodging, pad (*sl.*), place, quarters **2** = **mansion**, hall, manor, palace, seat, villa **3** = **stay**, occupancy, occupation, sojourn, tenancy

resident *n* **1** = **inhabitant**, citizen, denizen, indweller, local, lodger, occupant, tenant ◆ *adj* **7** = **inhabiting**, dwelling, living, local, neighbourhood, settled
Antonyms *n* ≠ **inhabitant:** nonresident, visitor ◆ *adj* ≠ **inhabiting:** nonresident, visiting

residual *adj* **1** = **remaining**, leftover, net, nett, unconsumed, unused, vestigial

value of one particular observation and the theoretical result. **5** (*often pl*) payment made to an actor, musician, etc., for subsequent use of film in which the person appears.
▸**re'sidually** *adv*

residual unemployment *n* the unemployment that remains in periods of full employment, as a result of those mentally, physically, or emotionally unfit to work.

residuary (rɪ'zɪdjʊərɪ) *adj* **1** of, relating to, or constituting a residue; residual. **2** *Law.* entitled to the residue of an estate after payment of debts and distribution of specific gifts.

residue Ⓣ ('rɛzɪˌdjuː) *n* **1** matter remaining after something has been removed. **2** *Law.* what is left of an estate after the discharge of debts and distribution of specific gifts. [C14: from OF *residu*, from L *residuus* remaining over, from *residēre* to stay behind]

residuum (rɪ'zɪdjʊəm) *n, pl* **residua** (-jʊə). a more formal word for **residue.**

resign Ⓣ (rɪ'zaɪn) *vb* **1** (when *intr*, often foll. by *from*) to give up tenure of (a job, office, etc.). **2** (*tr*) to reconcile (oneself) to; yield: *to resign oneself to death.* **3** (*tr*) to give up (a right, claim, etc.); relinquish. [C14: from OF *resigner*, from L *resignāre* to unseal, destroy, from RE- + *signāre* to seal]
▸**re'signer** *n*

re-sign (riː'saɪn) *vb* to sign again.

resignation Ⓣ (ˌrɛzɪg'neɪʃən) *n* **1** the act of resigning. **2** a formal document stating one's intention to resign. **3** a submissive unresisting attitude; passive acquiescence.

resigned Ⓣ (rɪ'zaɪnd) *adj* characteristic of or proceeding from an attitude of resignation; acquiescent or submissive.
▸**resignedly** (rɪ'zaɪnɪdlɪ) *adv* ▸**re'signedness** *n*

resile (rɪ'zaɪl) *vb* **resiles, resiling, resiled.** (*intr*) to spring or shrink back; recoil or resume original shape. [C16: from OF *resilir*, from L *resilīre* to jump back, from RE- + *salīre* to jump]
▸**re'silement** *n*

resilient Ⓣ (rɪ'zɪlɪənt) *adj* **1** (of an object) capable of regaining its original shape or position after bending, stretching, or other deformation; elastic. **2** (of a person) recovering easily and quickly from illness, hardship, etc.
▸**re'silience** *or* **re'siliency** *n* ▸**re'siliently** *adv*

resin ('rɛzɪn) *n* **1** any of a group of solid or semisolid amorphous compounds that are obtained directly from certain plants as exudations. **2** any of a large number of synthetic, usually organic, materials that have a polymeric structure, esp. such a substance in a raw state before it is moulded or treated with plasticizer, etc. ◆ *vb* **3** (*tr*) to treat or coat with resin. [C14: from OF *resine*, from L *rēsīna*, from Gk *rhētinē* resin from a pine]
▸**'resinous** *adj* ▸**'resinously** *adv* ▸**'resinousness** *n*

resinate ('rɛzɪˌneɪt) *vb* **resinates, resinating, resinated.** (*tr*) to impregnate with resin.

resipiscence (ˌrɛsɪ'pɪsəns) *n Literary.* acknowledgment that one has been mistaken. [C16: from LL *resipiscentia*, from *resipiscere* to recover one's senses, from L *sapere* to know]
▸**ˌresi'piscent** *adj*

resist Ⓣ (rɪ'zɪst) *vb* **1** to stand firm (against); not yield (to); fight (against). **2** (*tr*) to withstand the deleterious action of; be proof against: *to resist corrosion.* **3** (*tr*) to oppose; refuse to accept or comply with: *to resist arrest.* **4** (*tr*) to refrain from, esp. in spite of temptation (esp. in **cannot resist (something)**). ◆ *n* **5** a substance used to protect something, esp. a coating that prevents corrosion. [C14: from L *resistere*, from RE- + *sistere* to stand firm]
▸**re'sister** *n* ▸**re'sistible** *adj* ▸**reˌsisti'bility** *n* ▸**re'sistibly** *adv* ▸**re'sistless** *adj*

resistance Ⓣ (rɪ'zɪstəns) *n* **1** the act or an instance of resisting. **2** the capacity to withstand something, esp. the body's natural capacity to withstand disease. **3a** the opposition to a flow of electric current through a circuit component, medium, or substance. It is measured in ohms. Symbol: R **3b** (*as modifier*): *a resistance thermometer.* **4** any force that tends to retard or oppose motion: *air resistance; wind resistance.* **5 line of least resistance.** the easiest, but not necessarily the best or most honourable, course of action. **6** See **passive resistance.**
▸**re'sistant** *adj, n*

Resistance Ⓣ (rɪ'zɪstəns) *n* **the.** an illegal organization fighting for national liberty in a country under enemy occupation.

resistance thermometer *n* an accurate type of thermometer in which temperature is calculated from the resistance of a coil of wire or of a semiconductor placed at the point at which the temperature is to be measured.

resistivity (ˌriːzɪs'tɪvɪtɪ) *n* **1** the electrical property of a material that determines the resistance of a piece of given dimensions. It is measured in ohms. Former name: **specific resistance. 2** the power or capacity to resist; resistance.

resistor (rɪ'zɪstə) *n* an electrical component designed to introduce a known value of resistance into a circuit.

resit *vb* (riː'sɪt), **resits, resitting, resat.** (*tr*) **1** to sit (an examination) again. ◆ *n* ('riːsɪt). **2** an examination which one must sit again.

res judicata (ˌdʒuːdɪ'kɑːtə) *or* **res adjudicata** *n Law.* a matter already adjudicated upon that cannot be raised again. [L]

resoluble (rɪ'zɒljʊb^{ə}l, 'rɛzəl-) *adj* another word for **resolvable.**

re-soluble (riː'sɒljʊb^{ə}l) *adj* capable of being dissolved again.
▸**re-'solubleness** *or* **re-ˌsolu'bility** *n* ▸**re-'solubly** *adv*

resolute Ⓣ ('rɛzəˌluːt) *adj* **1** firm in purpose or belief; steadfast. **2** characterized by resolution; determined: *a resolute answer.* [C16: from L *resolutus*, from *resolvere* to RESOLVE]
▸**'resoˌlutely** *adv* ▸**'resoˌluteness** *n*

resolution Ⓣ (ˌrɛzə'luːʃən) *n* **1** the act or an instance of resolving. **2** firmness or determination. **3** something resolved or determined; decision. **4** a formal expression of opinion by a meeting. **5** a judicial decision on some matter; verdict; judgment. **6** the act of separating something into its constituent parts or elements. **7** *Med.* subsidence of the symptoms of a disease, esp. the disappearance of inflammation without pus. **8** *Music.* the process in harmony whereby a dissonant note or chord is followed by a consonant one. **9** the ability of a television or film image to reproduce fine detail. **10** *Physics.* another word for **resolving power.**
▸**ˌreso'lutioner** *or* **ˌreso'lutionist** *n*

resolvable (rɪ'zɒlvəb^{ə}l) *or* **resoluble** *adj* able to be resolved or analysed.
▸**reˌsolva'bility, reˌsolu'bility** *or* **re'solvableness, re'solubleness** *n*

resolve Ⓣ (rɪ'zɒlv) *vb* **resolves, resolving, resolved.** (*mainly tr*) **1** (*takes a clause as object or an infinitive*) to decide or determine firmly. **2** to express (an opinion) formally, esp. by a vote. **3** (*also intr;* usually foll. by *into*) to separate or cause to separate (into) (constituent parts). **4** (*usually reflexive*) to change; alter: *the ghost resolved itself into a tree.* **5** to make up the mind of; cause to decide: *the tempest resolved him to stay at home.* **6** to find the answer or solution to. **7** to explain away or dispel: *to resolve a doubt.* **8** to bring to an end; conclude: *to resolve an argument.* **9** *Med.* to cause (an inflammation) to subside, esp. without the formation of pus. **10** *Music.* (*also intr*) to follow (a dissonant note or chord) by one producing a consonance. **11** *Physics.* to distinguish between (separate parts) of (an image) as in a microscope, telescope, or other optical instrument. ◆ *n* **12** something determined or decided; resolution: *he had made a resolve to work all day.* **13** firmness of purpose; determination: *nothing can break his resolve.* [C14: from L *resolvere* to unfasten, reveal, from RE- + *solvere* to loosen]
▸**re'solvable** *adj* ▸**reˌsolva'bility** *n* ▸**re'solver** *n*

resolved (rɪ'zɒlvd) *adj* fixed in purpose or intention; determined.
▸**resolvedly** (rɪ'zɒlvɪdlɪ) *adv* ▸**re'solvedness** *n*

THESAURUS

residue *n* **1** = **remainder**, balance, dregs, excess, extra, leftovers, remains, remnant, residuum, rest, surplus

resign *vb* **1** = **quit**, abdicate, call it a day *or* night, give in one's notice, leave, step down (*inf.*), vacate **2** = **accept**, acquiesce, bow, give in, give up, reconcile, submit, succumb, yield **3** = **give up**, abandon, cede, forgo, forsake, hand over, relinquish, renounce, surrender, turn over, yield

resignation *n* **1** = **leaving**, abandonment, abdication, departure, notice, relinquishment, renunciation, retirement, surrender **3** = **acceptance**, acquiescence, compliance, endurance, forbearing, fortitude, nonresistance, passivity, patience, submission, sufferance
Antonyms *n* ≠ **acceptance:** defiance, dissent, kicking up a fuss, protest, resistance

resigned *adj* = **stoical**, acquiescent, compliant, long-suffering, patient, subdued, submissive, unprotesting, unresisting

resilient *adj* **1** = **flexible**, bouncy, elastic, plastic, pliable, rubbery, springy, supple **2** = **tough**, bouncy, buoyant, feisty, hardy, irrepressible, quick to recover, strong
Antonyms *adj* ≠ **flexible:** flaccid, inflexible, limp, rigid, stiff ≠ **tough:** delicate, effete, sensitive, sickly, weak

resist *vb* **1, 3** = **oppose**, battle, check, combat, confront, contend with, counteract, countervail, curb, defy, dispute, fight, hinder, hold out against, put up a fight (against), refuse, stand up to, struggle against, thwart, weather **2** = **withstand**, be proof against, repel **4** = **refrain from**, abstain from, avoid, forbear, forgo, keep from, leave alone, prevent oneself from, refuse, turn down
Antonyms *vb* ≠ **oppose:** accept, acquiesce, cave in (*inf.*), give in, submit, succumb, surrender, welcome, yield ≠ **refrain from:** enjoy, give in to, indulge in, surrender to

resistance *n* **1** = **fighting**, battle, combat, contention, counteraction, defiance, fight, hindrance, impediment, intransigence, obstruction, opposition, refusal, struggle

Resistance *n* = **freedom fighters**, guerrillas, irregulars, maquis, partisans, underground

resistant *adj* **1** = **opposed**, antagonistic, combative, defiant, dissident, hostile, intractable, intransigent, recalcitrant, unwilling **2** = **impervious**, hard, insusceptible, proof against, strong, tough, unaffected by, unyielding

resolute *adj* **1, 2** = **determined**, bold, constant, dogged, firm, fixed, immovable, inflexible, obstinate, persevering, purposeful, relentless, set, stalwart, staunch, steadfast, strong-willed, stubborn, tenacious, unbending, undaunted, unflinching, unshakable, unshaken, unwavering
Antonyms *adj* doubtful, irresolute, undecided, undetermined, unresolved, unsteady, weak

resolution *n* **1** = **solution**, answer, end, finding, outcome, settlement, solving, sorting out, unravelling, upshot, working out **2** = **determination**, boldness, constancy, courage, dedication, doggedness, earnestness, energy, firmness, fortitude, obstinacy, perseverance, purpose, relentlessness, resoluteness, resolve, sincerity, staunchness, staying power, steadfastness, stubbornness, tenacity, willpower **3, 5** = **decision**, declaration, determination, intent, intention, judgment, motion, purpose, resolve, verdict

resolve *vb* **1** = **decide**, agree, conclude, design, determine, fix, intend, make up one's mind, purpose, settle, undertake **3** = **break down**, analyse, anatomize, clear, disentangle, disintegrate, dissect, dissolve, liquefy, melt, reduce,

resolvent (rɪˈzɒlvənt) *adj* **1** serving to dissolve or separate something into its elements; resolving. ◆ *n* **2** a drug or agent able to reduce swelling or inflammation.

resolving power *n* **1** Also called: **resolution.** *Physics.* the ability of a microscope or telescope to produce separate images of closely placed objects. **2** *Photog.* the ability of an emulsion to show up fine detail in an image.

resonance (ˈrɛzənəns) *n* **1** the condition or quality of being resonant. **2** sound produced by a body vibrating in sympathy with a neighbouring source of sound. **3** the condition of a body or system when it is subjected to a periodic disturbance of the same frequency as the natural frequency of the body or system. **4** amplification of speech sounds by sympathetic vibration in the bone structure of the head and chest, resounding in the cavities of the nose, mouth, and pharynx. **5** *Electronics.* the condition of an electrical circuit when the frequency is such that the capacitive and inductive reactances are equal in magnitude. **6** *Med.* the sound heard when tapping a hollow bodily structure, esp. the chest or abdomen. **7** *Chem.* the phenomenon in which the electronic structure of a molecule can be represented by two or more hypothetical structures involving single, double, and triple chemical bonds. **8** *Physics.* the condition of a system in which there is a sharp maximum probability for the absorption of electromagnetic radiation or capture of particles. [C16: from L *resonāre* to RESOUND]

resonant 🅣 (ˈrɛzənənt) *adj* **1** resounding or re-echoing. **2** producing resonance: *resonant walls.* **3** full of, or intensified by, resonance: *a resonant voice.*
▸**ˈresonantly** *adv*

resonate (ˈrɛzəˌneɪt) *vb* **resonates, resonating, resonated. 1** to resound or cause to resound; reverberate. **2** *Chem., electronics.* to exhibit or cause to exhibit resonance. [C19: from L *resonāre*]
▸**ˌresoˈnation** *n*

resonator (ˈrɛzəˌneɪtə) *n* any body or system that displays resonance, esp. a tuned electrical circuit or a conducting cavity in which microwaves are generated by a resonant current.

resorb (rɪˈsɔːb) *vb (tr)* to absorb again. [C17: from L *resorbēre,* from RE- + *sorbēre* to suck in]
▸**reˈsorbent** *adj* ▸**reˈsorptive** *adj*

resorcinol (rɪˈzɔːsɪˌnɒl) *n* a colourless crystalline phenol, used in making dyes, drugs, resins, and adhesives. Formula: $C_6H_4(OH)_2$. [C19: NL, from RESIN + *orcinol,* a crystalline solid]
▸**reˈsorcinal** *adj*

resorption (rɪˈsɔːpʃən) *n* **1** the process of resorbing or the state of being resorbed. **2** *Geol.* the remelting of a mineral by magma, resulting in a new crystal form being produced.

resort 🅣 (rɪˈzɔːt) *vb (intr)* **1** (usually foll. by *to*) to have recourse (to) for help, use, etc.: *to resort to violence.* **2** to go, esp. often or habitually: *to resort to the beach.* ◆ *n* **3** a place to which many people go for recreation, etc.: *a holiday resort.* **4** the use of something as a means, help, or recourse. **5 last resort.** the last possible course of action open to one. [C14: from OF *resortir,* from RE- + *sortir* to emerge]
▸**reˈsorter** *n*

re-sort (riːˈsɔːt) *vb (tr)* to sort again.

resound 🅣 (rɪˈzaʊnd) *vb (intr)* **1** to ring or echo with sound; reverberate. **2** to make a prolonged echoing noise: *the trumpet resounded.* **3** (of sounds) to echo or ring. **4** to be widely famous: *his fame resounded throughout India.* [C14: from OF *resoner,* from L *resonāre* to sound again]

re-sound (riːˈsaʊnd) *vb* to sound or cause to sound again.

resounding 🅣 (rɪˈzaʊndɪŋ) *adj* **1** clear and emphatic: *a resounding vote of confidence.* **2** resonant; reverberating: *a resounding slap.*
▸**reˈsoundingly** *adv*

resource 🅣 (rɪˈzɔːs, -ˈsɔːs) *n* **1** capability, ingenuity, and initiative; quick-wittedness: *a man of resource.* **2** (*often pl*) a source of economic wealth, esp. of a country or business enterprise. **3** a supply or source of aid or support; something resorted to in time of need. **4** a means of doing something; expedient. [C17: from OF *ressourse* relief, from *resourdre,* from L *resurgere,* from RE- + *surgere* to rise]
▸**reˈsourceless** *adj*

resourceful 🅣 (rɪˈzɔːsfʊl, -ˈsɔːs-) *adj* ingenious, capable, and full of initiative.
▸**reˈsourcefully** *adv* ▸**reˈsourcefulness** *n*

respect 🅣 (rɪˈspɛkt) *n* **1** an attitude of deference, admiration, or esteem; regard. **2** the state of being honoured or esteemed. **3** a detail, point, or characteristic: *they differ in some respects.* **4** reference or relation (esp. in **in respect of, with respect to**). **5** polite or kind regard; consideration: *respect for people's feelings.* **6** (*often pl*) an expression of esteem or regard (esp. in **pay one's respects**). ◆ *vb (tr)* **7** to have an attitude of esteem towards: *to respect one's elders.* **8** to pay proper attention to; not violate: *to respect Swiss neutrality.* **9** *Arch.* to concern or refer to. [C14: from L *rēspicere* to look back, pay attention to, from RE- + *specere* to look]
▸**reˈspecter** *n*

respectable 🅣 (rɪˈspɛktəbᵊl) *adj* **1** having or deserving the respect of other people; estimable; worthy. **2** having good social standing or reputation. **3** having socially or conventionally acceptable morals, etc.: *a respectable woman.* **4** relatively or fairly good; considerable: *a respectable salary.* **5** fit to be seen by other people; presentable.
▸**reˌspectaˈbility** *n* ▸**reˈspectably** *adv*

respectful 🅣 (rɪˈspɛktfʊl) *adj* full of, showing, or giving respect.
▸**reˈspectfully** *adv* ▸**reˈspectfulness** *n*

respecting (rɪˈspɛktɪŋ) *prep* concerning; regarding.

respective 🅣 (rɪˈspɛktɪv) *adj* belonging or relating separately to each of several people or things; several: *we took our respective ways home.*
▸**reˈspectiveness** *n*

respectively (rɪˈspɛktɪvlɪ) *adv* (in listing a number of items or attributes that refer to another list) separately in the order given: *he gave Janet and John a cake and a chocolate respectively.*

respirable (ˈrɛspɪrəbᵊl) *adj* **1** able to be breathed. **2** suitable or fit for breathing.
▸**ˌrespiraˈbility** *n*

respiration (ˌrɛspɪˈreɪʃən) *n* **1** the process in living organisms of taking in oxygen from the surroundings and giving out carbon dioxide. **2** the chemical breakdown of complex organic substances that takes place in the cells and tissues of animals and plants, during which energy is released and carbon dioxide produced.
▸**respiratory** (ˈrɛspɪrətərɪ, -trɪ) *or* **ˌrespiˈrational** *adj*

respirator (ˈrɛspɪˌreɪtə) *n* **1** an apparatus for providing long-term artificial respiration. **2** a device worn over the mouth and nose to prevent inhalation of noxious fumes or to warm cold air before it is breathed.

respiratory failure *n* a condition in which the respiratory system is unable to provide an adequate supply of oxygen or to remove carbon dioxide efficiently.

respiratory quotient *n Biol.* the ratio of the volume of carbon dioxide expired to the volume of oxygen consumed by an organism, tissue, or cell in a given time.

respiratory system *n* the specialized organs, collectively, concerned with external respiration: in humans and other mammals it includes the trachea, bronchi, bronchioles, lungs, and diaphragm.

respire (rɪˈspaɪə) *vb* **respires, respiring, respired. 1** to inhale and exhale (air); breathe. **2** (*intr*) to undergo the process of respiration. [C14: from L *rēspīrāre* to exhale, from RE- + *spīrāre* to breathe]

respite 🅣 (ˈrɛspɪt, -paɪt) *n* **1** a pause from exertion; interval of rest. **2** a temporary delay. **3** a temporary stay of execution; reprieve. ◆ *vb* **re-**

THESAURUS

separate, solve, split up, unravel **4** = **change**, alter, convert, metamorphose, transform, transmute **6** = **work out**, answer, clear up, crack, elucidate, fathom, find the solution to, suss (out) (*sl.*) **7** = **dispel**, banish, clear up, explain, remove ◆ *n* **12** = **decision**, conclusion, design, intention, objective, project, purpose, resolution, undertaking **13** = **determination**, boldness, courage, earnestness, firmness, resoluteness, resolution, steadfastness, willpower
Antonyms *n* ≠ **determination:** cowardice, half-heartedness, indecision, vacillation, wavering

resonant *adj* **1, 3** = **echoing**, booming, full, resounding, reverberant, reverberating, rich, ringing, sonorous, vibrant

resort *vb* **1** *usually foll. by* **to** = **have recourse to**, avail oneself of, bring into play, employ, exercise, fall back on, look to, make use of, turn to, use, utilize **2** = **go**, frequent, haunt, head for, repair, visit ◆ *n* **3** = **holiday centre**, haunt, refuge, retreat, spot, tourist centre, watering place (*Brit.*) **4** = **recourse**, reference

resound *vb* = **echo**, fill the air, re-echo, resonate, reverberate, ring

resounding *adj* **2** = **echoing**, booming, full, powerful, resonant, reverberating, rich, ringing, sonorous, sounding, vibrant

resource *n* **1** = **ingenuity**, ability, capability, cleverness, initiative, inventiveness, quick-wittedness, resourcefulness, talent **2** *often plural* = **funds**, assets, capital, holdings, materials, means, money, property, reserves, riches, supplies, wealth, wherewithal **3** = **supply**, hoard, reserve, source, stockpile **4** = **means**, appliance, contrivance, course, device, expedient, resort

resourceful *adj* = **ingenious**, able, bright, capable, clever, creative, imaginative, inventive, quick-witted, sharp, talented
Antonyms *adj* gormless (*Brit. inf.*), unimaginative, uninventive

respect *n* **1, 2** = **regard**, admiration, appreciation, approbation, consideration, deference, esteem, estimation, honour, recognition, reverence, veneration **3** = **particular**, aspect, characteristic, detail, facet, feature, matter, point, sense, way **4** *As in* **in respect of** *or* **with respect to** = **relation**, bearing, connection, reference, regard **6** *often plural* = **greetings**, compliments, devoirs, good wishes, regards, salutations ◆ *vb* **7** = **think highly of**, admire, adore, appreciate, defer to, esteem, have a good *or* high opinion of, honour, look up to, recognize, regard, revere, reverence, set store by, value, venerate **8** = **abide by**, adhere to, attend, comply with, follow, heed, honour, notice, obey, observe, pay attention to, regard, show consideration for
Antonyms *n* ≠ **regard:** contempt, disdain, disregard, disrespect, irreverence, scorn ◆ *vb* ≠ **abide by:** abuse, disregard, disrespect, ignore, neglect, scorn

respectable *adj* **1-3** = **honourable**, admirable, decent, decorous, dignified, estimable, good, honest, proper, reputable, respected, upright, venerable, worthy **4** = **reasonable**, ample, appreciable, considerable, decent, fair, fairly good, goodly, presentable, sizable *or* sizeable, substantial, tidy (*inf.*), tolerable
Antonyms *adj* ≠ **honourable:** dishonourable, disreputable, ignoble, impolite, improper, indecent, unrefined, unworthy ≠ **reasonable:** paltry, poor, small

respectful *adj* = **polite**, civil, courteous, courtly, deferential, dutiful, gracious, humble, mannerly, obedient, regardful, reverent, reverential, self-effacing, solicitous, submissive, well-mannered

respective *adj* = **specific**, corresponding, individual, own, particular, personal, relevant, separate, several, various

respite *n* **1** = **pause**, break, breather (*inf.*), breathing space, cessation, halt, hiatus, inter-

spites, respiting, respited. 4 (*tr*) to grant a respite to; reprieve. [C13: from OF *respit*, from L *respectus* a looking back; see RESPECT]

resplendent ❶ (rɪˈsplɛndənt) *adj* having a brilliant or splendid appearance. [C15: from L *resplendēre*, from RE- + *splendēre* to shine]
▸reˈsplendence *or* reˈsplendency *n* ▸reˈsplendently *adv*

respond ❶ (rɪˈspɒnd) *vb* 1 to state or utter (something) in reply. 2 (*intr*) to act in reply; react: *to respond by issuing an invitation.* 3 (*intr*; foll. by *to*) to react favourably: *this patient will respond to treatment.* 4 an archaic word for **correspond**. ◆ *n* 5 *Archit.* a pilaster or an engaged column that supports an arch or a lintel. 6 *Christianity.* a choral anthem chanted in response to a lesson read. [C14: from OF *respondre*, from L *rēspondēre* to return like for like, from RE- + *spondēre* to pledge]
▸reˈspondence *or* reˈspondency *n* ▸reˈsponder *n*

respondent (rɪˈspɒndənt) *n* 1 *Law.* a person against whom a petition is brought. ◆ *adj* 2 a less common word for **responsive**.

response ❶ (rɪˈspɒns) *n* 1 the act of responding; reply or reaction. 2 *Bridge.* a bid replying to a partner's bid or double. 3 (*usually pl*) *Christianity.* a short sentence or phrase recited or sung in reply to the officiant at a church service. 4 *Electronics.* the ratio of the output to the input level of an electrical device. 5 a glandular, muscular, or electrical reaction that arises from stimulation of the nervous system. [C14: from L *rēsponsum* answer, from *rēspondēre* to RESPOND]
▸reˈsponseless *adj*

responser *or* **responsor** (rɪˈspɒnsə) *n* a radio or radar receiver used to receive and display signals from a transponder.

responsibility ❶ (rɪˌspɒnsɪˈbɪlɪtɪ) *n, pl* **responsibilities.** 1 the state or position of being responsible. 2 a person or thing for which one is responsible.

responsible ❶ (rɪˈspɒnsɪbᵊl) *adj* 1 (*postpositive;* usually foll. by *for*) having control or authority (over). 2 (*postpositive;* foll. by *to*) being accountable for one's actions and decisions (to): *responsible to one's commanding officer.* 3 (of a position, duty, etc.) involving decision and accountability. 4 (often foll. by *for*) being the agent or cause (of some action): *responsible for a mistake.* 5 able to take rational decisions without supervision; accountable for one's own actions. 6 able to meet financial obligations; of sound credit. [C16: from L *rēsponsus*, from *rēspondēre* to RESPOND]
▸reˈsponsibleness *n* ▸reˈsponsibly *adv*

responsive ❶ (rɪˈspɒnsɪv) *adj* 1 reacting or replying quickly or favourably, as to a suggestion, initiative, etc. 2 (of an organism) reacting to a stimulus.
▸reˈsponsively *adv* ▸reˈsponsiveness *n*

responsory (rɪˈspɒnsərɪ) *n, pl* **responsories.** an anthem or chant recited or sung after a lesson in a church service. [C15: from LL *rēsponsōrium*, from L *rēspondēre* to answer]

rest[1] ❶ (rɛst) *n* 1a relaxation from exertion or labour. 1b (*as modifier*): *a rest period.* 2 repose; sleep. 3 any relief or refreshment, as from worry. 4 calm; tranquillity. 5 death regarded as repose: *eternal rest.* 6 cessation from motion. 7 **at rest.** 7a not moving. 7b calm. 7c dead. 7d asleep. 8 a pause or interval. 9 a mark in a musical score indicating a pause of specific duration. 10 *Prosody.* a pause at the end of a line; caesura. 11 a shelter or lodging: *a seaman's rest.* 12 a thing or place on which to put something for support or to steady it. 13 *Billiards, snooker.* any of various special poles sometimes used as supports for the cue. 14 **come to rest.** to slow down and stop. 15 **lay to rest.** to bury (a dead person). 16 **set (someone's mind) at rest.** to reassure (someone) or settle (someone's mind). ◆ *vb* 17 to take or give rest, as by sleeping, lying down, etc. 18 to place or position (oneself, etc.) for rest or relaxation. 19 (*tr*) to place or position for support or steadying: *to rest one's elbows on the table.* 20 (*intr*) to be at ease; be calm. 21 to cease or cause to cease from motion or exertion. 22 (*intr*) to remain without further attention or action: *let the matter rest.* 23 to direct (one's eyes) or (of one's eyes) to be directed: *her eyes rested on the child.* 24 to depend or cause to depend; base; rely: *the whole argument rests on one crucial fact.* 25 (*intr;* foll. by *with, on, upon,* etc.) to be a responsibility (of): *it rests with us to apportion blame.* 26 *Law.* to finish the introduction of evidence in (a case). 27 to put pastry in a cool place to allow the gluten to contract. 28 **rest on one's oars.** to stop doing anything for a time. [OE *ræst, reste,* of Gmc origin]
▸ˈrester *n*

rest[2] ❶ (rɛst) *n* (usually preceded by *the*) 1 something left or remaining; remainder. 2 the others: *the rest of the world.* ◆ *vb* 3 (*copula*) to continue to be (as specified); remain: *rest assured.* [C15: from OF *rester* to remain, from L *rēstāre*, from RE- + *stāre* to stand]

rest area *n Austral. & NZ.* a motorists' stopping place, usually off a highway, equipped with tables, seats, etc.

restaurant ❶ (ˈrɛstəˌrɒŋ, ˈrɛstrɒŋ) *n* a commercial establishment where meals are prepared and served to customers. [C19: from F, from *restaurer* to RESTORE]

restaurant car *n Brit.* a railway coach in which meals are served. Also called: **dining car.**

restaurateur (ˌrɛstərəˈtɜː) *n* a person who owns or runs a restaurant. [C18: via F from LL *restaurātor*, from L *restaurāre* to RESTORE]

rest-cure *n* 1 a rest taken as part of a course of medical treatment, so as to relieve stress, anxiety, etc. 2 an easy time or assignment: usually used with a negative: *it's no rest-cure, I assure you.*

restful ❶ (ˈrɛstful) *adj* 1 giving or conducive to rest. 2 being at rest; tranquil; calm.
▸ˈrestfully *adv* ▸ˈrestfulness *n*

restharrow (ˈrɛstˌhærəʊ) *n* any of a genus of Eurasian papilionaceous plants with tough woody stems and roots. [C16: from *rest*, var. of ARREST (to hinder, stop) + HARROW]

resting (ˈrɛstɪŋ) *adj* 1 not moving or working; at rest. 2 *Euphemistic.* (of an actor) out of work. 3 (esp. of plant spores) undergoing a period of dormancy before germination.

restitution ❶ (ˌrɛstɪˈtjuːʃən) *n* 1 the act of giving back something that has been lost or stolen. 2 *Law.* compensating for loss or injury by reverting as far as possible to the original position. 3 the return of an object or system to its original state, esp. after elastic deformation. [C13: from L *rēstitūtiō*, from *rēstituere* to rebuild, from RE- + *statuere* to set up]
▸ˈrestiˌtutive *or* ˌrestiˈtutory *adj*

restive ❶ (ˈrɛstɪv) *adj* 1 restless, nervous, or uneasy. 2 impatient of control or authority. [C16: from OF *restif* balky, from *rester* to remain]
▸ˈrestively *adv* ▸ˈrestiveness *n*

restless ❶ (ˈrɛstlɪs) *adj* 1 unable to stay still or quiet. 2 ceaselessly active or moving: *the restless wind.* 3 worried; anxious; uneasy. 4 not restful; without repose: *a restless night.*
▸ˈrestlessly *adv* ▸ˈrestlessness *n*

THESAURUS

mission, interruption, interval, let-up (*inf.*), lull, recess, relaxation, relief, rest 2 = **delay**, adjournment, moratorium, postponement, suspension 3 = **reprieve**, stay

resplendent *adj* = **brilliant**, beaming, bright, dazzling, effulgent, gleaming, glittering, glorious, irradiant, luminous, lustrous, radiant, refulgent (*literary*), shining, splendid

respond *vb* 1, 2 = **answer**, acknowledge, act in response, come back, counter, react, reciprocate, rejoin, reply, retort, return, rise to the bait, take the bait
Antonyms *vb* ignore, remain silent, turn a blind eye

response *n* 1 = **answer**, acknowledgment, comeback (*inf.*), counterattack, counterblast, feedback, reaction, rejoinder, reply, retort, return, riposte

responsibility *n* 1 = **authority**, importance, power 1 = **accountability**, amenability, answerability, liability 1 = **fault**, blame, burden, culpability, guilt, liability 1 = **level-headedness**, conscientiousness, dependability, maturity, rationality, reliability, sensibleness, soberness, stability, trustworthiness 2 = **duty**, care, charge, liability, obligation, onus, pigeon (*inf.*), trust

responsible *adj* 1 = **in charge**, at the helm, carrying the can (*inf.*), in authority, in control 2 = **accountable**, amenable, answerable, bound, chargeable, duty-bound, liable, subject, under obligation 3 = **authoritative**, decision-making, executive, high, important 4 = **to blame**, at fault, culpable, guilty 5 = **sensible**, adult, conscientious, dependable, level-headed, mature, rational, reliable, sober, sound, stable, trustworthy
Antonyms *adj* ≠ **accountable**: unaccountable ≠ **sensible**: irresponsible, unconscientious, undependable, unreliable, untrustworthy

responsive *adj* 1 = **sensitive**, alive, awake, aware, forthcoming, impressionable, open, perceptive, quick to react, reactive, receptive, sharp, susceptible, sympathetic
Antonyms *adj* apathetic, impassive, insensitive, silent, unresponsive, unsympathetic

rest[1] *n* 1 = **relaxation**, idleness, leisure 2 = **repose**, doze, forty winks (*inf.*), kip (*Brit. sl.*), lie-down, nap, siesta, sleep, slumber, snooze (*inf.*) 3 = **refreshment**, relief 4 = **calm**, somnolence, stillness, tranquillity 6 = **inactivity**, motionlessness, standstill 7 **at rest: a** = **asleep**, at a standstill, still, stopped, unmoving **b** = **peaceful**, tranquil **c** = **at peace d** = **resting**, sleeping 8 = **pause**, break, breather (*inf.*), breathing space, cessation, halt, holiday, interlude, intermission, interval, lull, respite, stop, time off, vacation 12 = **support**, base, holder, prop, shelf, stand, trestle ◆ *vb* 17 = **relax**, doze, drowse, have a snooze (*inf.*), have forty winks (*inf.*), idle, kip (*Brit. sl.*), laze, lie down, lie still, nap, put one's feet up, refresh oneself, sit down, sleep, slumber, snooze (*inf.*), take a nap, take it easy, take one's ease 19 = **place**, be supported, lay, lean, lie, prop, recline, repose, sit, stand, stretch out 20 = **be calm**, be at ease, take it easy 21 = **stop**, break off, cease, come to a standstill, desist, discontinue, halt, have a break, knock off (*inf.*), stay, take a breather (*inf.*) 24 = **depend**, base, be based, be founded, found, hang, hinge, lie, rely, reside, turn
Antonyms *n* ≠ **relaxation, pause**: activity, bustle, work ◆ *vb* ≠ **relax, stop**: keep going, slog away (*inf.*), work

rest[2] *n* 1 = **remainder**, balance, excess, leftovers, remains, remnants, residue, residuum, rump, surplus 2 = **others** ◆ *vb* 3 = **continue being**, be left, go on being, keep, remain, stay

restaurant *n* = **café**, bistro, cafeteria, diner (*chiefly US & Canad.*), eatery *or* eaterie, tearoom, trattoria

restful *adj* 1, 2 = **relaxing**, calm, calming, comfortable, pacific, peaceful, placid, quiet, relaxed, serene, sleepy, soothing, tranquil, tranquillizing, undisturbed, unhurried
Antonyms *adj* agitated, busy, disturbing, restless, uncomfortable, unrelaxed

restitution *n* 1 = **return**, restoration 2 *Law* = **compensation**, amends, indemnification, indemnity, recompense, redress, refund, reimbursement, remuneration, reparation, repayment, requital, satisfaction

restive *adj* 1 = **restless**, agitated, edgy, fidgety, ill at ease, impatient, jittery (*inf.*), jumpy, nervous, on edge, uneasy, unquiet 2 = **unruly**, fractious, recalcitrant, refractory
Antonyms *adj* ≠ **restless**: at ease, calm, content, peaceful, relaxed, satisfied, serene, tranquil

restless *adj* 1, 2 = **moving**, active, bustling, changeable, footloose, having itchy feet, hurried, inconstant, irresolute, nomadic, roving, transient, turbulent, unsettled, unstable, unsteady, wandering 3 = **uneasy**, agitated, anxious, disturbed, edgy, fidgeting, fidgety, fitful,

rest mass *n* the mass of an object that is at rest relative to an observer. It is the mass used in Newtonian mechanics.

restoration ❶ (ˌrestəˈreɪʃən) *n* **1** the act of restoring to a former or original condition, place, etc. **2** the giving back of something lost, stolen, etc. **3** something restored, replaced, or reconstructed. **4** a model or representation of an extinct animal, etc. **5** (*usually cap.*) *Brit. history.* the re-establishment of the monarchy in 1660 or the reign of Charles II (1660–85).

restorative (rɪˈstɒrətɪv) *adj* **1** tending to revive or renew health, spirits, etc. ◆ *n* **2** anything that restores or revives, esp. a drug.

restore ❶ (rɪˈstɔː) *vb* **restores, restoring, restored.** (*tr*) **1** to return (something) to its original or former condition. **2** to bring back to health, good spirits, etc. **3** to return (something lost, stolen, etc.) to its owner. **4** to reintroduce or re-enforce: *to restore discipline.* **5** to reconstruct (an extinct animal, etc.). [C13: from OF, from L *restaurāre* to rebuild, from RE- + *-staurāre,* as in *instaurāre* to renew]
▸**reˈstorable** *adj* ▸**reˈstorer** *n*

restrain ❶ (rɪˈstreɪn) *vb* (*tr*) **1** to hold (someone) back from some action, esp. by force. **2** to deprive (someone) of liberty, as by imprisonment. **3** to limit or restrict. [C14 *restreyne,* from OF *restreindre,* from L *restringere,* from RE- + *stringere* to draw, bind]
▸**reˈstrainable** *adj* ▸**restrainedly** (rɪˈstreɪnɪdlɪ) *adv* ▸**reˈstrainer** *n*

restraint ❶ (rɪˈstreɪnt) *n* **1** the ability to control or moderate one's impulses, passions, etc. **2** the act of restraining or the state of being restrained. **3** something that restrains; restriction. [C15: from OF *restreinte,* from *restreindre* to RESTRAIN]

restraint of trade *n* action interfering with the freedom to compete in business.

restrict ❶ (rɪˈstrɪkt) *vb* (often foll. by *to*) to confine or keep within certain, often specified, limits or selected bounds. [C16: from L *restrictus* bound up, from *restringere;* see RESTRAIN]

restricted (rɪˈstrɪktɪd) *adj* **1** limited or confined. **2** not accessible to the general public or (*esp. US*) out of bounds to military personnel. **3** *Brit.* denoting a zone in which a speed limit or waiting restrictions for vehicles apply.
▸**reˈstrictedly** *adv* ▸**reˈstrictedness** *n*

restriction ❶ (rɪˈstrɪkʃən) *n* **1** something that restricts; a restrictive measure, law, etc. **2** the act of restricting or the state of being restricted.
▸**reˈstrictionist** *n, adj*

restrictive (rɪˈstrɪktɪv) *adj* **1** restricting or tending to restrict. **2** *Grammar.* denoting a relative clause or phrase that restricts the number of possible referents of its antecedent. The relative clause in *Americans who live in New York* is restrictive; the relative clause in *Americans, who are generally extrovert,* is nonrestrictive.
▸**reˈstrictively** *adv* ▸**reˈstrictiveness** *n*

restrictive practice *n Brit.* **1** a trading agreement against the public interest. **2** a practice of a union or other group tending to limit the freedom of other workers or employers.

rest room *n* a room in a public building with toilets, washbasins, and, sometimes, couches.

restructure (riːˈstrʌktʃə) *vb* (*tr*) to organize (a system, business, society, etc.) in a different way: *radical attempts to restructure the economy.*
▸**reˈstructuring** *n*

result ❶ (rɪˈzʌlt) *n* **1** something that ensues from an action, policy, etc.; outcome; consequence. **2** a number, quantity, or value obtained by solving a mathematical problem. **3** *US.* a decision of a legislative body. **4** (*often pl*) the final score or outcome of a sporting contest. **5** a favourable result, esp. a victory or success. ◆ *vb* (*intr*) **6** (often foll. by *from*) to be the outcome or consequence (of). **7** (foll. by *in*) to issue or terminate (in a specified way, etc.); end: *to result in tragedy.* [C15: from L *resultāre* to rebound, spring from, from RE- + *saltāre* to leap]

resultant (rɪˈzʌltənt) *adj* **1** that results; resulting. ◆ *n* **2** *Maths, physics.* a single vector that is the vector sum of two or more other vectors.

resume ❶ (rɪˈzjuːm) *vb* **resumes, resuming, resumed. 1** to begin again or go on with (something interrupted). **2** (*tr*) to occupy again, take back, or recover: *to resume one's seat; resume the presidency.* **3** *Arch.* to summarize; make a résumé of. [C15: from L *resūmere,* from RE- + *sūmere* to take up]
▸**reˈsumable** *adj* ▸**reˈsumer** *n*

résumé ❶ (ˈrezjuˌmeɪ) *n* **1** a short descriptive summary, as of events, etc. **2** *US & Canad.* another name for **curriculum vitae.** [C19: from F, from *résumer* to RESUME]

resumption ❶ (rɪˈzʌmpʃən) *n* the act of resuming or beginning again. [C15: via OF from LL *resumptiō,* from L *resūmere* to RESUME]
▸**reˈsumptive** *adj* ▸**reˈsumptively** *adv*

resupinate (rɪˈsjuːpɪnɪt) *adj Bot.* (of plant parts) reversed or inverted in position, so as to appear to be upside down. [C18: from L *resupīnātus* bent back, from *resupīnāre,* from RE- + *supīnāre* to place on the back]
▸**reˌsupiˈnation** *n*

resurge (rɪˈsɜːdʒ) *vb* **resurges, resurging, resurged.** (*intr*) *Rare.* to rise again as if from the dead. [C16: from L *resurgere* to rise again, reappear, from RE- + *surgere* to lift, arise]

resurgent ❶ (rɪˈsɜːdʒənt) *adj* rising again, as to new life, vigour, etc.: *resurgent nationalism.*
▸**reˈsurgence** *n*

resurrect ❶ (ˌrezəˈrekt) *vb* **1** to rise or raise from the dead; bring or be brought back to life. **2** (*tr*) to bring back into use or activity; revive. **3** (*tr*) *Facetious.* (formerly) to exhume and steal (a body) from its grave.

resurrection ❶ (ˌrezəˈrekʃən) *n* **1** a supposed act or instance of a dead person coming back to life. **2** belief in the possibility of this as part of a religious or mystical system. **3** the condition of those who have risen from the dead: *we shall all live in the resurrection.* **4** (*usually cap.*) *Christian theol.* the rising again of Christ from the tomb three days after his death. **5** (*usually cap.*) the rising again from the dead of all men at the Last Judgment. [C13: via OF from LL *resurrectiō,* from L *resurgere* to rise again]
▸ˌ**resurˈrectional** *or* ˌ**resurˈrectionary** *adj*

resurrectionism (ˌrezəˈrekʃəˌnɪzəm) *n* belief that men will rise again from the dead, esp. according to Christian doctrine.

resurrectionist (ˌrezəˈrekʃənɪst) *n* **1** *Facetious.* (formerly) a body snatcher. **2** a person who believes in the Resurrection.

resurrection plant *n* any of several unrelated desert plants that form a tight ball when dry and unfold and bloom when moistened.

resuscitate ❶ (rɪˈsʌsɪˌteɪt) *vb* **resuscitates, resuscitating, resuscitated.** (*tr*) to restore to consciousness; revive. [C16: from L *resuscitāre,* from RE- +

THESAURUS

fretful, ill at ease, jumpy, nervous, on edge, restive, troubled, unquiet, unruly, unsettled, worried **4 = sleepless**, tossing and turning, unsettled
Antonyms *adj* ≠ **moving**: settled, stable, steady ≠ **uneasy**: comfortable, composed, easy, quiet, relaxed ≠ **sleepless**: restful, undisturbed

restlessness *n* **1, 2 = movement**, activity, bustle, hurry, hurry-scurry, inconstancy, instability, transience, turbulence, turmoil, unrest, unsettledness **3 = restiveness**, agitation, ants in one's pants (*sl.*), anxiety, disquiet, disturbance, edginess, fitfulness, fretfulness, heebie-jeebies (*sl.*), inquietude, insomnia, jitters (*inf.*), jumpiness, nervousness, uneasiness, worriedness

restoration *n* **1 = repair**, reconstruction, recovery, refreshment, refurbishing, rehabilitation, rejuvenation, renewal, renovation, revitalization, revival **2 = reinstatement**, re-establishment, reinstallation, replacement, restitution, return
Antonyms *n* ≠ **repair**: demolition, scrapping, wrecking ≠ **reinstatement**: abolition, overthrow

restore *vb* **1 = repair**, fix, mend, rebuild, recondition, reconstruct, recover, refurbish, rehabilitate, renew, renovate, retouch, set to rights, touch up **2 = revive**, bring back to health, build up, reanimate, refresh, rejuvenate, revitalize, revivify, strengthen **3 = return**, bring back, give back, hand back, recover, re-establish, reinstate, replace, retrocede, send back **4 = reinstate**, reconstitute, re-enforce, re-establish, reimpose, reintroduce
Antonyms *vb* ≠ **repair**: demolish, scrap, wreck ≠ **revive**: make worse, sicken, weaken ≠ **reinstate**: abolish, abrogate, repeal, rescind

restrain *vb* **2 = imprison**, arrest, bind, chain, confine, detain, fetter, hold, jail, lock up, manacle, pinion, tie up **3 = hold back**, bridle, check, confine, constrain, contain, control, curb, curtail, debar, govern, hamper, handicap, harness, have on a tight leash, hinder, hold, inhibit, keep, keep under control, limit, muzzle, prevent, rein, repress, restrict, straiten, subdue, suppress
Antonyms *vb* ≠ **imprison**: free, liberate, release ≠ **hold back**: assist, encourage, gee up, help, incite, urge on

restraint *n* **1 = self-control**, coercion, command, compulsion, constraint, control, curtailment, hindrance, hold, inhibition, limitation, moderation, prevention, pulling one's punches, restriction, self-discipline, self-possession, self-restraint, suppression **2 = confinement**, arrest, bondage, captivity, detention, fetters, imprisonment **3 = limitation**, ban, boycott, bridle, check, curb, disqualification, embargo, interdict, limit, rein, restriction, taboo **3 = bonds**, chains, manacles, pinions, straitjacket
Antonyms *n* ≠ **self-control**: excess, immoderation, intemperance, licence, self-indulgence ≠ **limitation**: freedom, liberty

restrict *vb* **= limit**, bound, circumscribe, clip someone's wings, confine, contain, cramp, demarcate, hamper, handicap, hem in, impede, inhibit, keep within bounds *or* limits, regulate, restrain, straiten
Antonyms *vb* allow, broaden, encourage, foster, free, permit, promote, widen

restriction *n* **1 = limitation**, check, condition, confinement, constraint, containment, control, curb, demarcation, handicap, inhibition, regulation, restraint, rule, stipulation

result *n* **1 = consequence**, conclusion, development, effect, end, end result, event, fruit, issue, outcome, product, reaction, sequel, termination, upshot ◆ *vb* **6 = arise**, appear, derive, develop, emanate, ensue, eventuate, flow, follow, happen, issue, spring, stem, turn out **7 result in = end in**, culminate in, finish with, pan out (*inf.*), terminate in, wind up
Antonyms *n* ≠ **consequence**: beginning, cause, germ, origin, outset, root, source

resume *vb* **1 = begin again**, carry on, continue, go on, proceed, recommence, reinstitute, reopen, restart, take up *or* pick up where one left off **2 = occupy again**, assume again, reoccupy, take back, take up again
Antonyms *vb* ≠ **begin again**: cease, discontinue, stop

résumé *n* **1 = summary**, abstract, digest, epitome, précis, recapitulation, review, rundown, synopsis

resumption *n* **= continuation**, carrying on, fresh outbreak, new beginning, re-establishment, renewal, reopening, restart, resurgence

resurgence *n* **= revival**, rebirth, recrudescence, re-emergence, renaissance, renascence, resumption, resurrection, return

resurrect *vb* **1 = restore to life**, raise from the dead **2 = revive**, breathe new life into, bring back, kick-start (*inf.*), reintroduce, renew

resurrection *n* **1 = raising** *or* **rising from the dead**, return from the dead
Antonyms *n* ≠ **raising** *or* **rising from the dead**: burial, demise

resuscitate *vb* **= revive**, breathe new life into,

suscitāre to raise, from *sub-* up from below + *citāre* to rouse, from *citus* quick]
▸**re,susci'tation** *n* ▸**re'suscitative** *adj* ▸**re'susci,tator** *n*

ret (rɛt) *vb* **rets, retting, retted.** (*tr*) to moisten or soak (flax, hemp, etc.) in order to separate the fibres from the woody tissue by beating. [C15: of Gmc origin]

ret. *abbrev. for:* **1** retain. **2** retired. **3** return(ed).

retable (rɪ'teɪbᵊl) *n* an ornamental screenlike structure above and behind an altar. [C19: from F, from Sp. *retablo,* from L *retrō* behind + *tabula* board]

retail ('riːteɪl) *n* **1** the sale of goods individually or in small quantities to consumers. Cf. **wholesale.** ◆ *adj* **2** of, relating to, or engaged in such selling: *retail prices.* ◆ *adv* **3** in small amounts or at a retail price. ◆ *vb* **4** to sell or be sold in small quantities to consumers. **5** (rɪ'teɪl). (*tr*) to relate (gossip, scandal, etc.) in detail. [C14: from OF *retaillier,* from RE- + *taillier* to cut; see TAILOR]
▸**'retailer** *n*

retail price index *n* a measure of the changes in the average level of retail prices of selected goods, usually on a monthly basis. Abbrev.: **RPI.**

retain ❶ (rɪ'teɪn) *vb* (*tr*) **1** to keep in one's possession. **2** to be able to hold or contain: *soil that retains water.* **3** (of a person) to be able to remember (information, etc.) without difficulty. **4** to hold in position. **5** to keep for one's future use, as by paying a retainer or nominal charge. **6** *Law.* to engage the services of (a barrister) by payment of a preliminary fee. [C14: from OF *retenir,* from L *retinēre* to hold back, from RE- + *tenēre* to hold]
▸**re'tainable** *adj* ▸**re'tainment** *n*

retained object *n Grammar.* a direct or indirect object of a passive verb. The phrase *the drawings* in *she was given the drawings* is a retained object.

retainer ❶ (rɪ'teɪnə) *n* **1** *History.* a supporter or dependant of a person of rank. **2** a servant, esp. one who has been with a family for a long time. **3** a clip, frame, or similar device that prevents a part of a machine, etc., from moving. **4** a fee paid in advance to secure first option on the services of a barrister, jockey, etc. **5** a reduced rent paid for a flat, etc., to reserve it for future use.

retaining wall *n* a wall constructed to hold back earth, loose rock, etc. Also called: **revetment.**

retake *vb* (riː'teɪk), **retakes, retaking, retook, retaken.** (*tr*) **1** to take back or capture again: *to retake a fortress.* **2** *Films.* to shoot (a scene) again. **3** to tape (a recording) again. ◆ *n* ('riː,teɪk). **4** *Films.* a rephotographed scene. **5** a retaped recording.
▸**re'taker** *n*

retaliate ❶ (rɪ'tælɪ,eɪt) *vb* **retaliates, retaliating, retaliated.** (*intr*) **1** to take retributory action, esp. by returning some injury or wrong in kind. **2** to cast (accusations) back upon a person. [C17: from LL *retāliāre,* from L RE- + *tālis* of such kind]
▸**re,tali'ation** *n* ▸**re'taliative** *or* **re'taliatory** *adj*

retard ❶ (rɪ'tɑːd) *vb* (*tr*) to delay or slow down (the progress or speed) of (something). [C15: from OF *retarder,* from L *retardāre,* from RE- + *tardāre* to make slow, from *tardus* sluggish]

retardant (rɪ'tɑːdᵊnt) *n* **1** a substance that reduces the rate of a chemical reaction. ◆ *adj* **2** having a slowing effect.

retardation (,riːtɑː'deɪʃən) *or* **retardment** (rɪ'tɑːdmənt) *n* **1** the act of retarding or the state of being retarded. **2** something that retards.
▸**re'tardative** *or* **re'tardatory** *adj*

retarded (rɪ'tɑːdɪd) *adj* underdeveloped, usually mentally and esp. having an IQ of 70 to 85.

retarder (rɪ'tɑːdə) *n* **1** a person or thing that retards. **2** a substance added to slow down the rate of a chemical change, such as one added to cement to delay its setting.

retch ❶ (rɛtʃ, riːtʃ) *vb* **1** (*intr*) to undergo an involuntary spasm of ineffectual vomiting. ◆ *n* **2** an involuntary spasm of ineffectual vomiting. [OE *hrǣcan;* rel. to ON *hrǣkja* to spit]

retd *abbrev. for:* **1** retired. **2** retained. **3** returned.

rete ('riːtɪ) *n, pl* **retia** ('riːʃɪə, -tɪə). *Anat.* any network of nerves or blood vessels; plexus. [C14 (referring to a metal network used with an astrolabe): from L *rēte* net]
▸**retial** ('riːʃɪəl) *adj*

retention (rɪ'tɛnʃən) *n* **1** the act of retaining or state of being retained. **2** the capacity to hold or retain liquid, etc. **3** the capacity to remember. **4** *Pathol.* the abnormal holding within the body of urine, faeces, etc. **5** *Commerce.* a sum of money owed to a contractor but not paid for an agreed period as a safeguard against the appearance of any faults. **6** (*pl*) *Account.* profits earned by a company but not distributed as dividends; retained earnings. [C14: from L *retentiō,* from *retinēre* to RETAIN]

retentive (rɪ'tɛntɪv) *adj* having the capacity to retain or remember.
▸**re'tentively** *adv* ▸**re'tentiveness** *n*

retiarius (,riːtɪ'ɛərɪəs, ,riːʃɪ-) *n, pl* **retiarii** (-'ɛərɪ,aɪ). (in ancient Rome) a gladiator armed with a net and trident. [L, from *rēte* net]

reticent ❶ ('rɛtɪsənt) *adj* not communicative; not saying all that one knows; taciturn; reserved. [C19: from L *reticēre* to keep silent, from RE- + *tacēre* to be silent]
▸**'reticence** *n* ▸**'reticently** *adv*

reticle ('rɛtɪkᵊl) *or* (*less commonly*) **reticule** *n* a network of fine lines, wires, etc., placed in the focal plane of an optical instrument. [C17: from L *rēticulum* a little net, from *rēte* net]

reticulate *adj* (rɪ'tɪkjʊlɪt) *also* **reticular. 1** in the form of a network or having a network of parts: *a reticulate leaf.* ◆ *vb* (rɪ'tɪkjʊ,leɪt), **reticulates, reticulating, reticulated. 2** to form or be formed into a net. [C17: from LL *rēticulātus* made like a net]
▸**re'ticulately** *adv* ▸**re,ticu'lation** *n*

reticule ('rɛtɪ,kjuːl) *n* **1** (formerly) a woman's small bag or purse, usually with a drawstring and made of net, beading, brocade, etc. **2** a less common variant of **reticle.** [C18: from F *réticule,* from L *rēticulum* RETICLE]

reticulum (rɪ'tɪkjʊləm) *n, pl* **reticula** (-lə). **1** any fine network, esp. one in the body composed of cells, fibres, etc. **2** the second compartment of the stomach of ruminants. [C17: from L: little net, from *rēte* net]

retiform ('riːtɪ,fɔːm, 'rɛt-) *adj Rare.* netlike; reticulate. [C17: from L *rēte* net + *forma* shape]

retina ('rɛtɪnə) *n, pl* **retinas** *or* **retinae** (-,niː). the light-sensitive membrane forming the inner lining of the posterior wall of the eyeball. [C14: from Med. L, ?from L *rēte* net]
▸**'retinal** *adj*

retinene ('rɛtɪ,niːn) *n* a yellow pigment, the aldehyde of vitamin A, that is involved in the formation of rhodopsin. [C20: from RETINA + -ENE]

retinitis (,rɛtɪ'naɪtɪs) *n* inflammation of the retina. [C20: from NL, from RETINA + -ITIS]

retinoscopy (,rɛtɪ'nɒskəpɪ) *n Ophthalmol.* a procedure for detecting errors of refraction in the eye by means of an instrument (**retinoscope**) that reflects a beam of light from a mirror into the eye.
▸**retinoscopic** (,rɛtɪnə'skɒpɪk) *adj* ▸**,retino'scopically** *adv* ▸**,reti'noscopist** *n*

retinue ❶ ('rɛtɪ,njuː) *n* a body of aides and retainers attending an important person. [C14: from OF *retenue,* from *retenir* to RETAIN]

retiral (rɪ'taɪərᵊl) *n esp. Scot.* the act of retiring; retirement.

retire ❶ (rɪ'taɪə) *vb* **retires, retiring, retired.** (*mainly intr*) **1** (*also tr*) to give up or to cause (a person) to give up his work, esp. on reaching pensionable age. **2** to go away, as into seclusion, for recuperation, etc. **3** to go to bed. **4** to recede or disappear: *the sun retired behind the clouds.* **5** to withdraw from a sporting contest, esp. because of injury. **6** (*also tr*) to pull back (troops, etc.) from battle or (of troops, etc.) to fall back. **7** (*tr*) to remove (money, bonds, shares, etc.) from circulation. [C16: from F *retirer,* from OF RE- + *tirer* to pull, draw]
▸**re'tired** *adj* ▸**re'tirement** *n* ▸**re'tirer** *n*

retirement pension *n Brit.* a weekly payment made by the government to a retired man over 65 or a woman over 60.

retirement relief *n* (in Britain) relief from capital-gains tax given to persons over 60 when disposing of business assets.

retiring ❶ (rɪ'taɪərɪŋ) *adj* shunning contact with others; shy; reserved.
▸**re'tiringly** *adv*

THESAURUS

bring round, bring to life, give artificial respiration to, give the kiss of life, quicken, reanimate, renew, rescue, restore, resurrect, revitalize, revivify, save

retain *vb* **1** = **keep**, contain, detain, grasp, grip, hang *or* hold onto, hold, hold back, hold fast, keep possession of, maintain, preserve, reserve, restrain, save **3** = **remember**, bear in mind, impress on the memory, keep in mind, memorize, recall, recollect **5** = **hire**, commission, employ, engage, pay, reserve
Antonyms *vb* ≠ **keep:** let go, lose, release, use up ≠ **remember:** forget

retainer *n* **2** = **servant**, attendant, dependant, domestic, flunky, footman, henchman, lackey, supporter, valet **4** = **fee**, advance, deposit

retaliate *vb* **1** = **pay (someone) back**, even the score, exact retribution, get back at, get even with (*inf.*), get one's own back (*inf.*), give as good as one gets (*inf.*), give (someone) a taste of his *or* her own medicine, give tit for tat, hit back, make reprisal, reciprocate, return like for like, strike back, take an eye for an eye, take revenge, wreak vengeance
Antonyms *vb* accept, submit, turn the other cheek

retaliation *n* **1** = **revenge**, an eye for an eye, a taste of one's own medicine, counterblow, counterstroke, reciprocation, repayment, reprisal, requital, retribution, tit for tat, vengeance

retard *vb* = **slow down**, arrest, brake, check, clog, decelerate, defer, delay, detain, encumber, handicap, hinder, hold back *or* up, impede, obstruct, set back, stall
Antonyms *vb* accelerate, advance, expedite, hasten, speed, speed up, stimulate

retch *vb* **1** = **gag**, barf (*US sl.*), be sick, chuck (up) (*sl., chiefly US*), chunder (*sl., chiefly Austral.*), disgorge, heave, puke (*sl.*), regurgitate, spew, throw up (*inf.*), toss one's cookies (*US sl.*), vomit

reticence *n* = **silence**, quietness, reserve, restraint, secretiveness, taciturnity, uncommunicativeness, unforthcomingness

reticent *adj* = **uncommunicative**, close-lipped, mum, quiet, reserved, restrained, secretive, silent, taciturn, tight-lipped, unforthcoming, unspeaking
Antonyms *adj* candid, communicative, expansive, frank, open, talkative, voluble

retinue *n* = **attendants**, aides, cortege, entourage, escort, followers, following, servants, suite, train

retire *vb* **1** = **stop working**, be pensioned off, (be) put out to grass, give up work **2** = **withdraw**, absent oneself, betake oneself, depart, exit, go away, leave, remove **3** = **go to bed**, go to one's room, go to sleep, hit the hay (*sl.*), hit the sack (*sl.*), kip down (*Brit. sl.*), turn in (*inf.*) **6** = **fall back**, back off, decamp, give ground, give way, pull back, pull out, recede, retreat, withdraw

retirement *n* **2** = **withdrawal**, loneliness, obscurity, privacy, retreat, seclusion, solitude

retiring *adj* = **shy**, bashful, coy, demure, diffident, humble, meek, modest, quiet, reclusive, reserved, reticent, self-effacing, shrinking, timid, timorous, unassertive, unassuming

retool (riːˈtuːl) *vb* **1** to replace, re-equip, or rearrange the tools in (a factory, etc.). **2** (*tr*) *Chiefly US & Canad.* to revise or reorganize.

retort[1] **T** (rɪˈtɔːt) *vb* **1** (when *tr*, *takes a clause as object*) to utter (something) quickly, wittily, or angrily, in response. **2** to use (an argument) against its originator. ◆ *n* **3** a sharp, angry, or witty reply. **4** an argument used against its originator. [C16: from L *retorquēre*, from RE- + *torquēre* to twist, wrench]
▸**reˈtorter** *n*

retort[2] (rɪˈtɔːt) *n* **1** a glass vessel with a long tapering neck that is bent down, used for distillation. **2** a vessel used for heating ores in the production of metals or heating coal to produce gas. ◆ *vb* **3** (*tr*) to heat in a retort. [C17: from F *retorte*, from Med. L *retorta*, from L *retorquēre* to twist back; see RETORT[1]]

retouch **T** (riːˈtʌtʃ) *vb* (*tr*) **1** to restore, correct, or improve (a painting, make-up, etc.) with new touches. **2** *Photog.* to alter (a negative or print) by painting over blemishes or adding details. ◆ *n* **3** the art or practice of retouching. **4** a detail that is the result of retouching. **5** a photograph, painting, etc., that has been retouched.
▸**reˈtoucher** *n*

retrace (rɪˈtreɪs) *vb* **retraces, retracing, retraced.** (*tr*) **1** to go back over (one's steps, a route, etc.) again. **2** to go over (a past event) in the mind; recall. **3** to go over (a story, account, etc.) from the beginning.

re-trace (riːˈtreɪs) *vb* **re-traces, re-tracing, re-traced.** (*tr*) to trace (a map, etc.) again.

retract **T** (rɪˈtrækt) *vb* **1** (*tr*) to draw in (a part or appendage): *a snail can retract its horns; to retract the landing gear of an aircraft.* **2** to withdraw (a statement, opinion, charge, etc.) as invalid or unjustified. **3** to go back on (a promise or agreement). [C16: from L *retractāre* to withdraw, from *tractāre*, from *trahere* to drag]
▸**reˈtractable** *or* **reˈtractible** *adj* ▸**reˈtraction** *n* ▸**reˈtractive** *adj*

retractile (rɪˈtræktaɪl) *adj* capable of being drawn in: *the retractile claws of a cat.*
▸**retractility** (ˌriːtrækˈtɪlɪtɪ) *n*

retractor (rɪˈtræktə) *n* **1** *Anat.* any of various muscles that retract an organ or part. **2** *Surgery.* an instrument for holding back an organ or part. **3** a person or thing that retracts.

retral (ˈriːtrəl, ˈrɛtrəl) *adj Rare.* at, near, or towards the back. [C19: from L *retrō* backwards]
▸**ˈretrally** *adv*

retread *vb* (riːˈtrɛd), **retreads, retreading, retreaded. 1** (*tr*) another word for **remould** (sense 2). ◆ *n* (ˈriːˌtrɛd). **2** another word for **remould** (sense 3). **3** *NZ sl.* a pensioner who has resumed employment, esp. in the same profession as formerly.

re-tread (riːˈtrɛd) *vb* **re-treads, re-treading, re-trod, re-trodden** *or* **re-trod.** (*tr*) to tread (one's steps, etc.) again.

retreat **T** (rɪˈtriːt) *vb* (*mainly intr*) **1** *Mil.* to withdraw or retire in the face of or from action with an enemy. **2** to retire or withdraw, as to seclusion or shelter. **3** (of a person's features) to slope back; recede. **4** (*tr*) *Chess.* to move (a piece) back. ◆ *n* **5** the act of retreating or withdrawing. **6** *Mil.* **6a** a withdrawal or retirement in the face of the enemy. **6b** a bugle call signifying withdrawal or retirement. **7** retirement or seclusion. **8** a place to which one may retire for religious contemplation. **9** a period of seclusion, esp. for religious contemplation. **10** an institution for the care and treatment of the mentally ill, infirm, elderly, etc. [C14: from OF *retret*, from *retraire* to withdraw, from L *retrahere* to pull back]

retrench **T** (rɪˈtrɛntʃ) *vb* **1** to reduce (costs); economize. **2** (*tr*) to shorten, delete, or abridge. [C17: from OF *retrenchier*, from RE- + *trenchier* to cut, from L *truncāre* to lop]
▸**reˈtrenchment** *n*

retribution **T** (ˌrɛtrɪˈbjuːʃən) *n* **1** the act of punishing or taking vengeance for wrongdoing, sin, or injury. **2** punishment or vengeance. [C14: via OF from Church L *retribūtiō*, from L *retribuere*, from RE- + *tribuere* to pay]
▸**retributive** (rɪˈtrɪbjʊtɪv) *adj* ▸**reˈtributively** *adv*

retrieval (rɪˈtriːvᵊl) *n* **1** the act or process of retrieving. **2** the possibility of recovery, restoration, or rectification. **3** a computer operation that recalls data from a file.

retrieve **T** (rɪˈtriːv) *vb* **retrieves, retrieving, retrieved.** (*mainly tr*) **1** to get or fetch back again; recover. **2** to bring back to a more satisfactory state; revive. **3** to rescue or save. **4** to recover or make newly available (stored information) from a computer system. **5** (*also intr*) (of dogs) to find and fetch (shot game, etc.). **6** *Tennis, etc.* to return successfully (a shot difficult to reach). **7** to recall; remember. ◆ *n* **8** the act of retrieving. **9** the chance of being retrieved. [C15: from OF *retrover*, from RE- + *trouver* to find, ?from Vulgar L *tropāre* (unattested) to compose]
▸**reˈtrievable** *adj*

retriever (rɪˈtriːvə) *n* **1** one of a breed of large dogs that can be trained to retrieve game. **2** any dog used to retrieve shot game. **3** a person or thing that retrieves.

retro **T** (ˈrɛtrəʊ) *n, pl* **retros. 1** short for **retrorocket.** ◆ *adj* **2** denoting something associated with or revived from the past: *retro fashion.*

retro- *prefix* **1** back or backwards: *retroactive.* **2** located behind: *retrochoir.* [from L *retrō* behind, backwards]

retroact (ˈrɛtrəʊˌækt) *vb* (*intr*) **1** to act in opposition. **2** to influence or have reference to past events.
▸ˌ**retroˈaction** *n*

retroactive (ˌrɛtrəʊˈæktɪv) *adj* **1** applying or referring to the past: *retroactive legislation.* **2** effective from a date or for a period in the past.
▸ˌ**retroˈactively** *adv* ▸ˌ**retroacˈtivity** *n*

retrocede (ˌrɛtrəʊˈsiːd) *vb* **retrocedes, retroceding, retroceded. 1** (*tr*) to give back; return. **2** (*intr*) to go back; recede.
▸**retrocession** (ˌrɛtrəʊˈsɛʃən) *or* ˌ**retroˈcedence** *n* ▸ˌ**retroˈcessive** *or* ˌ**retroˈcedent** *adj*

retrochoir (ˈrɛtrəʊˌkwaɪə) *n* the space in a large church or cathedral behind the high altar.

retrofire (ˈrɛtrəʊˌfaɪə) *n* **1** the act of firing a retrorocket. **2** the moment at which it is fired.

retrofit (ˈrɛtrəʊˌfɪt) *vb* **retrofits, retrofitting, retrofitted.** (*tr*) to equip (a vehicle, piece of equipment, etc.) with new parts, safety devices, etc., after manufacture.

retroflex (ˈrɛtrəʊˌflɛks) *or* **retroflexed** *adj* **1** bent or curved backwards. **2** *Phonetics.* of or involving retroflexion. [C18: from L *retrōflexus*, from *retrōflectere*, from RETRO- + *flectere* to bend]

retroflexion *or* **retroflection** (ˌrɛtrəʊˈflɛkʃən) *n* **1** the act or condition of bending or being bent backwards. **2** the act of turning the tip of the tongue upwards and backwards in the articulation of a vowel or a consonant.

retrograde **T** (ˈrɛtrəʊˌgreɪd) *adj* **1** moving or bending backwards. **2** (esp. of order) reverse or inverse. **3** tending towards an earlier worse condition; declining or deteriorating. **4** *Astron.* **4a** occurring or orbiting in a direction opposite to that of the earth's motion around the sun. Cf. **direct** (sense 18). **4b** occurring or orbiting in a direction around a planet opposite to the planet's rotational direction. **4c** appearing to move in a clockwise direction due to the rotational period exceeding the period of revolution around the sun: *Venus has retrograde rotation.* ◆ *vb* **retrogrades, retrograding, retrograded.** (*intr*) **5** to move in a retrograde direction; retrogress. [C14: from L *retrōgradī*, from *gradi* to walk, go]
▸ˌ**retrograˈdation** *n* ▸ˈ**retroˌgradely** *adv*

retrogress **T** (ˌrɛtrəʊˈgrɛs) *vb* (*intr*) **1** to go back to an earlier, esp. worse, condition; degenerate or deteriorate. **2** to move backwards; recede. [C19: from L *retrōgressus* having moved backwards; see RETROGRADE]
▸ˌ**retroˈgression** *n* ▸ˌ**retroˈgressive** *adj* ▸ˌ**retroˈgressively** *adv*

retrorocket (ˈrɛtrəʊˌrɒkɪt) *n* a small auxiliary rocket engine on a larger rocket, missile, or spacecraft, that produces thrust in the opposite direction to the direction of flight in order to decelerate. Often shortened to **retro.**

retrorse (rɪˈtrɔːs) *adj* (esp. of plant parts) pointing backwards. [C19: from L *retrōrsus*, from *retrōversus* turned back, from RETRO- + *vertere* to turn]
▸**reˈtrorsely** *adv*

retrospect **T** (ˈrɛtrəʊˌspɛkt) *n* the act of surveying things past (often in **in retrospect**). [C17: from L *retrōspicere* to look back, from RETRO- + *specere* to look]
▸ˌ**retroˈspection** *n*

THESAURUS

Antonyms *adj* audacious, bold, brassy, forward, gregarious, outgoing, sociable

retort[1] *vb* **1 = reply,** answer, answer back, come back with, counter, rejoin, respond, retaliate, return, riposte ◆ *n* **3 = reply,** answer, comeback (*inf.*), rejoinder, response, riposte

retouch *vb* **1 = touch up,** brush up, correct, finish, improve, recondition, renovate, restore

retract *vb* **1 = draw in,** pull back, pull in, reel in, sheathe **2 = withdraw,** abjure, cancel, deny, disavow, disclaim, disown, eat one's words, recall, recant, renege, renounce, repeal, repudiate, rescind, reverse, revoke, take back, unsay **3 = go back on,** back out of, renege on

retreat *vb* **1, 2 = withdraw,** back away, back off, depart, draw back, fall back, give ground, go back, leave, pull back, recede, recoil, retire, shrink, turn tail ◆ *n* **5, 6a = withdrawal,** departure, evacuation, flight, retirement **7, 9 = seclusion,** privacy, retirement **8 = refuge,** asylum, den, haunt, haven, hideaway, resort, sanctuary, shelter
Antonyms *vb* ≠ **withdraw:** advance, engage, move forward ◆ *n* ≠ **withdrawal:** advance, charge, entrance

retrench *vb* **1 = economize,** cut back, husband, make economies, save, tighten one's belt **2 = reduce,** curtail, cut, cut back, decrease, diminish, lessen, limit, pare, prune, trim

retrenchment *n* **1 = cutback,** cost-cutting, economy, tightening one's belt **2 = reduction,** contraction, curtailment, cut, cutback, pruning, rundown
Antonyms *n* ≠ **cutback:** expansion, investment

retribution *n* **1, 2 = punishment,** an eye for an eye, compensation, justice, Nemesis, reckoning, recompense, redress, repayment, reprisal, requital, retaliation, revenge, reward, satisfaction, vengeance

retrieve *vb* **1, 3 = get back,** fetch back, recall, recapture, recoup, recover, redeem, regain, repair, repossess, rescue, restore, salvage, save, win back

retro *adj* **2 = old-time,** antique, bygone, former, nostalgia, of yesteryear, old, old-fashioned, old-world, past, period

retrograde *adj* **3 = deteriorating,** backward, declining, degenerative, downward, inverse, negative, regressive, relapsing, retreating, retrogressive, reverse, waning, worsening ◆ *vb* **5 = deteriorate,** backslide, decline, degenerate, go downhill (*inf.*), regress, relapse, retreat, retrogress, revert, wane, worsen

retrogress *vb* **1 = deteriorate,** backslide, decline, go back, go downhill (*inf.*), regress, relapse, retrocede, retrograde, return, revert, worsen **2 = recede,** drop, ebb, fall, go back, lose ground, retire, retreat, sink, wane, withdraw

retrospect *n* **= hindsight,** afterthought, recollection, re-examination, remembrance, reminiscence, review, survey
Antonyms *n* anticipation, foresight

retrospective (ˌretrəʊˈspektɪv) *adj* **1** looking or directed backwards, esp. in time; characterized by retrospection. **2** applying to the past; retroactive. ◆ *n* **3** an exhibition of an artist's life's work.
▸ˌ**retroˈspectively** *adv*

retroussé (rəˈtruːseɪ) *adj* (of a nose) turned up. [C19: from F *retrousser* to tuck up]

retroversion (ˌretrəʊˈvɜːʃən) *n* **1** the act of turning or condition of being turned backwards. **2** the condition of a part or organ, esp. the uterus, that is turned backwards.
▸ˈ**retroˌverted** *adj*

Retrovir (ˈretrəʊˌvɪə) *n Trademark.* the brand name for AZT.

retrovirus (ˈretrəʊˌvaɪrəs) *n* any of several viruses that are able to reverse the normal flow of genetic information from DNA to RNA by transcribing RNA into DNA: many retroviruses are known to cause cancer in animals.
▸ˈ**retroˌviral** *adj*

retsina (retˈsiːnə) *n* a Greek wine flavoured with resin. [Mod. Gk, from It. *resina* RESIN]

retune (riːˈtjuːn) *vb* **retunes, retuning, retuned.** (*tr*) **1** to tune (a musical instrument) differently or again. **2** to tune (a radio, television, etc.) to another frequency.

return 🅣 (rɪˈtɜːn) *vb* **1** (*intr*) to come back to a former place or state. **2** (*tr*) to give, take, or carry back; replace or restore. **3** (*tr*) to repay or recompense, esp. with something of equivalent value: *return the compliment.* **4** (*tr*) to earn or yield (profit or interest) as an income from an investment or venture. **5** (*intr*) to come back or revert in thought or speech: *I'll return to that later.* **6** (*intr*) to recur or reappear: *the symptoms have returned.* **7** to answer or reply. **8** (*tr*) to vote into office; elect. **9** (*tr*) *Law.* (of a jury) to deliver or render (a verdict). **10** (*tr*) to submit (a report, etc.) about (someone or something) to someone in authority. **11** (*tr*) *Cards.* to lead back (the suit led by one's partner). **12** (*tr*) *Ball games.* to hit, throw, or play (a ball) back. **13 return thanks.** (of Christians) to say grace before a meal. ◆ *n* **14** the act or an instance of coming back. **15** something that is given or sent back, esp. unsatisfactory merchandise or a theatre ticket for resale. **16** the act or an instance of putting, sending, or carrying back; replacement or restoration. **17** (*often pl*) the yield or profit from an investment or venture. **18** the act or an instance of reciprocation or repayment (esp. in **in return for**). **19** a recurrence or reappearance. **20** an official report, esp. of the financial condition of a company. **21a** a form (a **tax return**) on which a statement of one's taxable income is made. **21b** the statement itself. **22** (*often pl*) a statement of the votes counted at an election. **23** an answer or reply. **24** *Brit.* short for **return ticket. 25** *Archit.* a part of a building that forms an angle with the façade. **26** *Law.* a report by a bailiff or other officer on the outcome of a formal document such as a writ, summons, etc. **27** *Cards.* a lead of a card in the suit that one's partner has previously led. **28** *Ball games.* the act of playing or throwing a ball, etc., back. **29 by return (of post).** *Brit.* by the next post back to the sender. **30 many happy returns (of the day).** a conventional birthday greeting. ◆ *adj* **31** of, relating to, or characterized by a return: *a return visit.* **32** denoting a second, reciprocal occasion: *a return match.* [C14: from OF *retorner;* see RE-, TURN]
▸**reˈturnable** *adj*

return crease *n Cricket.* one of two lines marked at right-angles to each bowling crease, from inside which a bowler must deliver the ball.

returned soldier *n Austral. & NZ.* a soldier who has served abroad. Also (Austral. and Canad.): **returned man.**

returner (rɪˈtɜːnə) *n* **1** a person or thing that returns. **2** a person who goes back to work after a break, esp. a woman who has had children.

returning officer *n* (in Britain, Canada, Australia, etc.) an official in charge of conducting an election in a constituency, etc.

return ticket *n Brit., Austral., & NZ.* a ticket entitling a passenger to travel to his destination and back.

retuse (rɪˈtjuːs) *adj Bot.* having a rounded apex and a central depression. [C18: from L *retundere* to make blunt, from RE- + *tundere* to pound]

reunify (riːˈjuːnɪˌfaɪ) *vb* **reunifies, reunifying, reunified.** (*tr*) to bring together again (something, esp. a country previously divided).
▸ˌ**reunifiˈcation** *n*

reunion (riːˈjuːnjən) *n* **1** the act of coming together again. **2** the state or condition of having been brought together again. **3** a gathering of relatives, friends, or former associates.

reunite (ˌriːjuːˈnaɪt) *vb* **reunites, reuniting, reunited.** to bring or come together again.
▸ˌ**reuˈnitable** *adj*

Reuters (ˈrɔɪtəz) *n* a private news agency in London that distributes news to member newspapers. It was founded by Baron Paul Julius von Reuter (1816–99), German telegrapher.

rev (rev) *Inf.* ◆ *n* **1** revolution per minute. ◆ *vb* **revs, revving, revved. 2** (often foll. by *up*) to increase the speed of revolution of (an engine).

rev. *abbrev. for:* **1** revenue. **2** reverse(d). **3** review. **4** revise(d). **5** revision. **6** revolution. **7** revolving.

Rev. *abbrev. for:* **1** *Bible.* Revelation (of Saint John the Divine). **2** Reverend.

revalue (riːˈvæljuː) *or US* **revaluate** *vb* **revalues, revaluing, revalued** *or US* **revaluates, revaluating, revaluated. 1** to adjust the exchange value of (a currency), esp. upwards. Cf. **devalue. 2** (*tr*) to make a fresh valuation of.
▸**reˌvaluˈation** *n*

revamp 🅣 (riːˈvæmp) *vb* (*tr*) **1** to patch up or renovate; repair or restore. ◆ *n* **2** something that has been renovated or revamped. **3** the act or process of revamping. [C19: from RE- + VAMP[2]]

revanchism (rɪˈvæntʃɪzəm) *n* **1** a foreign policy aimed at revenge or the regaining of lost territories. **2** support for such a policy. [C20: from F *revanche* REVENGE]
▸**reˈvanchist** *n, adj*

rev counter *n Brit.* an informal name for **tachometer.**

Revd *abbrev. for* Reverend.

reveal 🅣 (rɪˈviːl) *vb* (*tr*) **1** (*may take a clause as object or an infinitive*) to disclose (a secret); divulge. **2** to expose to view or show (something concealed). **3** (of God) to disclose (divine truths). ◆ *n* **4** *Archit.* the vertical side of an opening in a wall, esp. the side of a window or door between the frame and the front of the wall. [C14: from OF *reveler,* from L *revēlāre* to unveil, from RE- + *vēlum* a VEIL]
▸**reˈvealable** *adj* ▸**reˈvealer** *n* ▸**reˈvealment** *n*

revealed religion *n* **1** religion based on the revelation by God to man of ideas that he would not have arrived at by reason alone. **2** religion in which the existence of God depends on revelation.

revealing (rɪˈviːlɪŋ) *adj* **1** of significance or import: *a very revealing experience.* **2** showing more of the body than is usual: *a revealing costume.*
▸**reˈvealingly** *adv*

reveille (rɪˈvælɪ) *n* **1** a signal, given by a bugle, drum, etc., to awaken soldiers or sailors in the morning. **2** the hour at which this takes place. [C17: from F *réveillez!* awake! from RE- + OF *esveillier* to be wakeful, ult. from L *vigilāre* to keep watch]

revel 🅣 (ˈrevᵊl) *vb* **revels, revelling, revelled** *or US* **revels, reveling, reveled.** (*intr*) **1** (foll. by *in*) to take pleasure or wallow: *to revel in success.* **2** to take part in noisy festivities; make merry. ◆ *n* **3** (*often pl*) an occasion of noisy merrymaking. [C14: from OF *reveler* to be merry, noisy, from L *rebellāre* to revolt]
▸ˈ**reveller** *n*

revelation 🅣 (ˌrevəˈleɪʃən) *n* **1** the act or process of disclosing something previously secret or obscure, esp. something true. **2** a fact disclosed or revealed, esp. in a dramatic or surprising way. **3** *Christianity.* God's disclosure of his own nature and his purpose for mankind. [C14: from Church L *revēlātiō,* from L *revēlāre* to REVEAL]
▸ˌ**reveˈlational** *or* ˌ**reveˈlatory** *adj*

Revelation (ˌrevəˈleɪʃən) *n* (*popularly, often pl*) the last book of the New Testament, containing visionary descriptions of heaven, and of the end of the world. Also called: the **Apocalypse,** the **Revelation of Saint John the Divine.**

revelationist (ˌrevəˈleɪʃənɪst) *n* a person who believes that God has revealed certain truths to man.

revelry 🅣 (ˈrevᵊlrɪ) *n, pl* **revelries.** noisy or unrestrained merrymaking.

THESAURUS

return *vb* **1** = **come back,** come round again, go back, reappear, rebound, recoil, recur, repair, retreat, revert, turn back **2** = **put back,** carry back, convey, give back, re- establish, reinstate, remit, render, replace, restore, retrocede, send, send back, take back, transmit **3** = **give back,** pay back, reciprocate, recompense, refund, reimburse, repay, requite **4** = **earn,** bring in, make, net, repay, yield **7** = **reply,** answer, come back (with), communicate, rejoin, respond, retort **8** = **elect,** choose, pick, vote in **9** *Law* = **announce,** arrive at, bring in, come to, deliver, render, report, submit ◆ *n* **16** = **restoration,** re-establishment, reinstatement, replacement **17** = **profit,** advantage, benefit, boot (*dialect*), gain, income, interest, proceeds, revenue, takings, yield **18** = **repayment,** compensation, meed (*arch.*), reciprocation, recompense, reimbursement, reparation, requital, retaliation, reward **19** = **reappearance,** recurrence **20, 21** = **statement,** account, form, list, report, summary **23** = **reply,** answer, comeback (*inf.*), rejoinder, response, retort, riposte

Antonyms *vb* ≠ **come back:** depart, disappear, go away, leave ≠ **put back, give back:** hold, keep, leave, remove, retain ≠ **earn:** lose ◆ *n* ≠ **restoration:** removal

revamp *vb* **1** = **renovate,** do up (*inf.*), fix up (*inf., chiefly US & Canad.*), give a face-lift to, overhaul, patch up, recondition, refit, refurbish, rehabilitate, repair, restore

reveal *vb* **1** = **make known,** announce, betray, blow wide open (*sl.*), broadcast, communicate, disclose, divulge, get off one's chest (*inf.*), give away, give out, impart, leak, let on, let out, let slip, make public, proclaim, publish, take the wraps off (*inf.*), tell **2** = **show,** bare, bring to light, display, exhibit, expose to view, lay bare, manifest, open, uncover, unearth, unmask, unveil

Antonyms *vb* ≠ **make known:** conceal, cover up, hide, keep quiet about, sweep under the carpet (*inf.*) ≠ **show:** conceal, cover up, hide

revel *vb* **1** *foll. by* **in** = **enjoy,** bask in, crow about, delight in, drool over, gloat about, indulge in, lap up, luxuriate in, rejoice over, relish, rub one's hands, savour, take pleasure in, thrive on, wallow in **2** = **celebrate,** carouse, go on a spree, live it up (*inf.*), make merry, paint the town red (*inf.*), push the boat out (*Brit. inf.*), rave (*Brit. sl.*), roister, whoop it up (*inf.*) ◆ *n* **3** *often plural* = **merrymaking,** bacchanal, beano, carousal, carouse, celebration, debauch, festivity, gala, hooley *or* hoolie (*chiefly Irish & NZ*), jollification, party, rave (*Brit. sl.*), rave-up (*Brit. sl.*), saturnalia, spree

Antonyms *vb* ≠ **enjoy:** abhor, be uninterested in, dislike, hate, have no taste for

revelation *n* **1** = **disclosure,** announcement, betrayal, broadcasting, communication, discovery, display, exhibition, exposé, exposition, exposure, giveaway, leak, manifestation, news, proclamation, publication, telling, uncovering, unearthing, unveiling

reveller *n* **2** = **merrymaker,** carouser, celebrator, partygoer, pleasure-seeker, roisterer

revelry *n* = **merrymaking,** beano (*Brit. sl.*), carousal, carouse, celebration, debauch, debauchery, festivity, fun, hooley *or* hoolie (*chiefly

revenant ('rɛvɪnənt) *n* something, esp. a ghost, that returns. [C19: from F: ghost, from *revenir,* from L *revenīre,* from RE- + *venīre* to come]

revenge ❶ (rɪ'vɛndʒ) *n* **1** the act of retaliating for wrongs or injury received; vengeance. **2** something done as a means of vengeance. **3** the desire to take vengeance. **4** a return match, regarded as a loser's opportunity to even the score. ◆ *vb* **revenges, revenging, revenged.** (*tr*) **5** to inflict equivalent injury or damage for (injury received). **6** to take vengeance for (oneself or another); avenge. [C14: from OF *revenger,* from LL *revindicāre,* from RE- + *vindicāre* to VINDICATE]
▸**re'venger** *n* ▸**re'venging** *adj* ▸**re'vengingly** *adv*

revengeful ❶ (rɪ'vɛndʒfʊl) *adj* full of or characterized by desire for vengeance; vindictive.
▸**re'vengefully** *adv* ▸**re'vengefulness** *n*

revenue ❶ ('rɛvɪˌnjuː) *n* **1** the income accruing from taxation to a government. **2a** a government department responsible for the collection of government revenue. **2b** (*as modifier*): *revenue men.* **3** the gross income from a business enterprise, investment, etc. **4** a particular item of income. **5** a source of income. [C16: from OF, from *revenir* to return, from L *revenīre;* see REVENANT]

revenue cutter *n* a small lightly armed boat used to enforce customs regulations and catch smugglers.

reverb (rɪ'vɜːb) *n* an electronic device that creates artificial acoustics.

reverberate ❶ (rɪ'vɜːbəˌreɪt) *vb* **reverberates, reverberating, reverberated. 1** (*intr*) to resound or re-echo. **2** to reflect or be reflected many times. **3** (*intr*) to rebound or recoil. **4** (*intr*) (of the flame or heat in a reverberatory furnace) to be deflected onto the metal or ore on the hearth. **5** (*tr*) to heat, melt, or refine (a metal or ore) in a reverberatory furnace. [C16: from L *reverberāre,* from RE- + *verberāre* to beat, from *verber* a lash]
▸**re'verberantly** *adv* ▸**reˌverber'ation** *n* ▸**re'verberative** *adj* ▸**re'verbeˌrator** *n* ▸**re'verberatory** *adj*

reverberation time *n* a measure of the acoustic properties of a room, equal to the time taken for a sound to fall in intensity by 60 decibels. It is usually measured in seconds.

reverberatory furnace *n* a metallurgical furnace having a curved roof that deflects heat onto the charge so that the fuel is not in direct contact with the ore.

revere ❶ (rɪ'vɪə) *vb* **reveres, revering, revered.** (*tr*) to be in awe of and respect deeply; venerate. [C17: from L *reverērī,* from RE- + *verērī* to fear, be in awe of]

reverence ❶ ('rɛvərəns) *n* **1** a feeling or attitude of profound respect, usually reserved for the sacred or divine. **2** an outward manifestation of this feeling, esp. a bow or act of obeisance. **3** the state of being revered or commanding profound respect. ◆ *vb* **reverences, reverencing, reverenced. 4** (*tr*) to revere or venerate.

Reverence ('rɛvərəns) *n* (preceded by *Your* or *His*) a title sometimes used to address or refer to a Roman Catholic priest.

reverend ('rɛvərənd) *adj* **1** worthy of reverence. **2** relating to or designating a clergyman. ◆ *n* **3** *Inf.* a clergyman. [C15: from L *reverendus* fit to be revered]

Reverend ('rɛvərənd) *adj* a title of respect for a clergyman. Abbrev.: **Rev., Revd.**

> **USAGE NOTE** *Reverend* with a surname alone (*Reverend Smith*), as a term of address (*"Yes, Reverend"*), or in the salutation of a letter (*Dear Rev. Mr Smith*) are all generally considered to be wrong usage. Preferred are (*the*) *Reverend John Smith* or *Reverend Mr Smith* and *Dear Mr Smith.*

reverent ❶ ('rɛvərənt, 'rɛvrənt) *adj* feeling, expressing, or characterized by reverence. [C14: from L *reverēns* respectful]
▸**'reverently** *adv*

reverential (ˌrɛvə'rɛnʃəl) *adj* resulting from or showing reverence.
▸ˌ**rever'entially** *adv*

reverie ❶ ('rɛvərɪ) *n* **1** an act or state of absent-minded daydreaming: *to fall into a reverie.* **2** a piece of instrumental music suggestive of a daydream. **3** *Arch.* a fanciful or visionary notion; daydream. [C14: from OF *resverie* wildness, from *resver* to behave wildly, from ?]

revers (rɪ'vɪə) *n, pl* **revers** (-'vɪəz). (*usually pl*) the turned-back lining of part of a garment, esp. of a lapel or cuff. [C19: from F, lit.: REVERSE]

reversal (rɪ'vɜːsᵊl) *n* **1** the act or an instance of reversing. **2** a change for the worse; reverse. **3** the state of being reversed. **4** the annulment of a judicial decision, esp. by an appeal court.

reverse ❶ (rɪ'vɜːs) *vb* **reverses, reversing, reversed.** (*mainly tr*) **1** to turn or set in an opposite direction, order, or position. **2** to change into something different or contrary; alter completely: *reverse one's policy.* **3** (*also intr*) to move or cause to move backwards or in an opposite direction: *to reverse a car.* **4** to run (machinery, etc.) in the opposite direction to normal. **5** to turn inside out. **6** *Law.* to revoke or set aside (a judgment, decree, etc.); annul. **7 reverse the charge(s).** to make a telephone call at the recipient's expense. ◆ *n* **8** the opposite or contrary of something. **9** the back or rear side of something. **10** a change to an opposite position, state, or direction. **11** a change for the worse; setback or defeat. **12a** the mechanism or gears by which machinery, a vehicle, etc., can be made to reverse its direction. **12b** (*as modifier*): *reverse gear.* **13** the side of a coin bearing a secondary design. **14a** printed matter in which normally black or coloured areas, esp. lettering, appear white, and vice versa. **14b** (*as modifier*): *reverse plates.* **15 in reverse.** in an opposite or backward direction. **16 the reverse of.** emphatically not; not at all: *he was the reverse of polite when I called.* ◆ *adj* **17** opposite or contrary in direction, position, order, nature, etc.; turned backwards. **18** back to front; inverted. **19** operating or moving in a manner contrary to that which is usual. **20** denoting or relating to a mirror image. [C14: from OF, from L *reversus,* from *revertere* to turn back]
▸**re'versely** *adv* ▸**re'verser** *n*

reverse-charge *adj* (*prenominal*) (of a telephone call) made at the recipient's expense.

reverse takeover *n Finance.* the purchase of a larger company by a smaller company, esp. of a public company by a private company.

reverse transcriptase (træn'skrɪpteɪz) *n* an enzyme present in retroviruses that copies RNA into DNA, thus reversing the usual flow of genetic information in which DNA is copied into RNA.

reverse video *n Computing.* highlighting by reversing the colours of normal characters and background on a visual display unit.

reversible (rɪ'vɜːsɪbᵊl) *adj* **1** capable of being reversed: *a reversible decision.* **2** capable of returning to an original condition. **3** *Chem., physics.* capable of assuming or producing either of two possible states and changing from one to the other: *a reversible reaction.* **4** (of a fabric or garment) woven, printed, or finished so that either side may be used as the outer side. ◆ *n* **5** a reversible garment, esp. a coat.
▸**reˌversi'bility** *n* ▸**re'versibly** *adv*

reversing lights *pl n* lights on the rear of a motor vehicle that go on when the vehicle is being reversed.

reversion (rɪ'vɜːʃən) *n* **1** a return to an earlier condition, practice, or belief; act of reverting. **2** *Biol.* the return of individuals, organs, etc., to a more primitive condition or type. **3** *Property law.* **3a** an interest in an estate that reverts to the grantor or his heirs at the end of a period, esp. at the end of the life of a grantee. **3b** an estate so reverting. **3c** the right to succeed to such an estate. **4** the benefit payable on the death of a life-insurance policyholder.
▸**re'versionary** *or* **re'versional** *adj*

reversionary bonus *n Insurance.* a bonus added to the sum payable on death or at the maturity of a with-profits assurance policy.

revert ❶ (rɪ'vɜːt) *vb* (*intr;* foll. by *to*). **1** to go back to a former practice, condition, belief, etc.: *he reverted to his old wicked ways.* **2** to take up again or come back to a former topic. **3** *Biol.* (of individuals, organs, etc.) to return to a more primitive, earlier, or simpler condition or type. **4** *Property law.* (of an estate or interest in land) to return to its former owner or his heirs. **5 revert to type.** to resume characteristics that were

THESAURUS

Irish & NZ), jollification, jollity, party, rave (*Brit. sl.*), rave-up (*Brit. sl.*), roistering, saturnalia, spree

revenge *n* **1, 2** = **retaliation**, an eye for an eye, reprisal, requital, retribution, satisfaction, vengeance ◆ *vb* **5, 6** = **avenge**, even the score for, get even, get one's own back for (*inf.*), hit back, make reprisal for, pay (someone) back, repay, requite, retaliate, take an eye for an eye for, take revenge for, vindicate

revengeful *adj* = **vengeful**, bitter, malevolent, malicious, malignant, merciless, pitiless, resentful, spiteful, unforgiving, unmerciful, vindictive

revenue *n* **1, 3** = **income**, gain, interest, proceeds, profits, receipts, returns, rewards, takings, yield
Antonyms *n* expenditure, expenses, outgoings

reverberate *vb* **1** = **echo**, rebound, recoil, re-echo, resound, ring, vibrate

reverberation *n* **1** = **echo**, rebound, recoil, re-echoing, resonance, resounding, ringing, vibration

revere *vb* = **be in awe of**, adore, defer to, exalt, have a high opinion of, honour, look up to, put on a pedestal, respect, reverence, think highly of, venerate, worship
Antonyms *vb* deride, despise, hold in contempt, scorn, sneer at

reverence *n* **1** = **respect**, admiration, adoration, awe, deference, devotion, high esteem, homage, honour, veneration, worship ◆ *vb* **4** = **revere**, admire, adore, be in awe of, hold in awe, honour, pay homage to, respect, venerate, worship
Antonyms *n* ≠ **respect**: contempt, contumely, derision, disdain, scorn

reverent *adj* = **respectful**, adoring, awed, deferential, devout, humble, loving, meek, pious, reverential, solemn, submissive
Antonyms *adj* cheeky, disrespectful, flippant, impious, irreverent, mocking, sacrilegious

reverie *n* **1** = **daydream**, absent-mindedness, abstraction, brown study, castles in the air *or* Spain, daydreaming, inattention, musing, preoccupation, trance, woolgathering

reverse *vb* **1** = **turn round**, invert, transpose, turn back, turn over, turn upside down, upend **3** = **go backwards**, back, backtrack, back up, move backwards, retreat **6** *Law* = **change**, alter, annul, cancel, countermand, declare null and void, invalidate, negate, obviate, overrule, overset, overthrow, overturn, quash, repeal, rescind, retract, revoke, set aside, undo, upset ◆ *n* **8** = **opposite**, antithesis, contradiction, contrary, converse, inverse **9** = **back**, flip side, other side, rear, underside, verso, wrong side **11** = **misfortune**, adversity, affliction, blow, check, defeat, disappointment, failure, hardship, misadventure, mishap, repulse, reversal, setback, trial, vicissitude ◆ *adj* **18** = **opposite**, back to front, backward, contrary, converse, inverse, inverted
Antonyms *vb* ≠ **go backwards**: advance, go forward, move forward ≠ **change**: carry out, enforce, implement, validate ◆ *n* ≠ **back**: forward side, front, obverse, recto, right side

revert *vb* **1** = **return**, backslide, come back, go back, lapse, recur, regress, relapse, resume

thought to have disappeared. [C13: from L *revertere,* from RE- + *vertere* to turn]
▸**re'verter** *n* ▸**re'vertible** *adj*

USAGE NOTE Since *back* is part of the meaning of *revert,* one should not say that someone *reverts back* to a certain type of behaviour.

revet (rɪ'vɛt) *vb* **revets, revetting, revetted.** to face (a wall or embankment) with stones. [C19: from F *revêt,* from OF *revestir* to reclothe; see REVETMENT]

revetment (rɪ'vɛtmənt) *n* **1** a facing of stones, sandbags, etc., to protect a wall, embankment, or earthworks. **2** another name for **retaining wall.** [C18: from F *revêtement,* lit.: a reclothing, from *revêtir;* ult. from L RE- + *vestīre* to clothe]

review ❶ (rɪ'vjuː) *vb* (*mainly tr*) **1** to look at or examine again: *to review a situation.* **2** to look back upon (a period of time, sequence of events, etc.); remember: *he reviewed his achievements with pride.* **3** to inspect, esp. formally or officially: *the general reviewed his troops.* **4** *Law.* to re-examine (a decision) judicially. **5** to write a critical assessment of (a book, film, play, concert, etc.), esp. as a profession. ◆ *n* **6** Also called: **reviewal.** the act or an instance of reviewing. **7** a general survey or report: *a review of the political situation.* **8** a critical assessment of a book, film, play, concert, etc., esp. one printed in a newspaper or periodical. **9** a publication containing such articles. **10** a second consideration; re-examination. **11** a retrospective survey. **12** a formal or official inspection. **13** a US and Canad. word for **revision** (sense 2). **14** *Law.* judicial re-examination of a case, esp. by a superior court. **15** a less common spelling of **revue.** [C16: from F, from *revoir* to see again, from L RE- + *vidēre* to see]
▸**re'viewer** *n*

revile ❶ (rɪ'vaɪl) *vb* **reviles, reviling, reviled.** to use abusive or scornful language against (someone or something). [C14: from OF *reviler,* from RE- + *vil* VILE]
▸**re'vilement** *n* ▸**re'viler** *n*

revise ❶ (rɪ'vaɪz) *vb* **revises, revising, revised. 1** (*tr*) to change or amend: *to revise one's opinion.* **2** *Brit.* to reread (a subject or notes on it) so as to memorize it, esp. for an examination. **3** (*tr*) to prepare a new version or edition of (a previously printed work). ◆ *n* **4** the act, process, or result of revising; revision. [C16: from L *revīsere,* from RE- + *vīsere* to inspect, from *vidēre* to see]
▸**re'visal** *n* ▸**re'viser** *n*

Revised Standard Version *n* a revision by American scholars of the American Standard Version of the Bible. The New Testament was published in 1946 and the entire Bible in 1953.

Revised Version *n* a revision of the Authorized Version of the Bible by two committees of British scholars, the New Testament being published in 1881 and the Old in 1885.

revision ❶ (rɪ'vɪʒən) *n* **1** the act or process of revising. **2** *Brit.* the process of rereading a subject or notes on it, esp. for an examination. **3** a corrected or new version of a book, article, etc.
▸**re'visionary** *adj*

revisionism (rɪ'vɪʒəˌnɪzəm) *n* **1** (*sometimes cap.*) **1a** a moderate, nonrevolutionary version of Marxism developed in Germany around 1900. **1b** (in Marxist-Leninist ideology) any dangerous departure from the true interpretation of Marx's teachings. **2** the advocacy of revision of some political theory, etc.
▸**re'visionist** *n, adj*

revisory (rɪ'vaɪzərɪ) *adj* of, relating to, or having the power of revision.

revitalize ❶ *or* **revitalise** (riː'vaɪtᵊˌlaɪz) *vb* **revitalizes, revitalizing, revitalized** *or* **revitalises, revitalising, revitalised.** (*tr*) to restore vitality or animation to.

revival ❶ (rɪ'vaɪvᵊl) *n* **1** the act or an instance of reviving or the state of being revived. **2** an instance of returning to life or consciousness; restoration of vigour or vitality. **3** a renewed use, acceptance of, or interest in (past customs, styles, etc.): *the Gothic revival.* **4** a new production of a play that has not been recently performed. **5** a reawakening of faith. **6** an evangelistic meeting or meetings intended to effect such a reawakening in those present.

revivalism (rɪ'vaɪvəˌlɪzəm) *n* **1** a movement that seeks to reawaken faith. **2** the tendency or desire to revive former customs, styles, etc.
▸**re'vivalist** *n* ▸**reˌvival'istic** *adj*

revive ❶ (rɪ'vaɪv) *vb* **revives, reviving, revived. 1** to bring or be brought back to life, consciousness, or strength: *revived by a drop of whisky.* **2** to give or assume new vitality; flourish again or cause to flourish again. **3** to make or become operative or active again: *the youth movement was revived.* **4** to bring or come back to mind. **5** (*tr*) *Theatre.* to mount a new production of (an old play). [C15: from OF *revivre* to live again, from L *revīvere,* from RE- + *vīvere* to live]
▸**re'vivable** *adj* ▸**reˌviva'bility** *n* ▸**re'viver** *n* ▸**re'viving** *adj*

revivify ❶ (rɪ'vɪvɪˌfaɪ) *vb* **revivifies, revivifying, revivified.** (*tr*) to give new life or spirit to.
▸**reˌvivifi'cation** *n*

revocable ('rɛvəkəbᵊl) *or* **revokable** (rɪ'vəʊkəbᵊl) *adj* capable of being revoked.
▸**ˌrevoca'bility** *or* **reˌvoka'bility** *n* ▸**'revocably** *or* **re'vokably** *adv*

revocation (ˌrɛvə'keɪʃən) *n* **1** the act of revoking or state of being revoked. **2a** the cancellation or annulment of a legal instrument. **2b** the withdrawal of an offer, power of attorney, etc.
▸**revocatory** ('rɛvəkətərɪ, -trɪ) *adj*

revoice (riː'vɔɪs) *vb* **revoices, revoicing, revoiced.** (*tr*) **1** to utter again; echo. **2** to adjust the design of (an organ pipe or wind instrument) as after disuse or to conform with modern pitch.

revoke ❶ (rɪ'vəʊk) *vb* **revokes, revoking, revoked. 1** (*tr*) to take back or withdraw; cancel; rescind. **2** (*intr*) *Cards.* to break a rule by failing to follow suit when able to do so. ◆ *n* **3** *Cards.* the act of revoking. [C14: from L *revocāre* to call back, withdraw, from RE- + *vocāre* to call]
▸**re'voker** *n*

revolt ❶ (rɪ'vəʊlt) *n* **1** a rebellion or uprising against authority. **2 in revolt.** in the process or state of rebelling. ◆ *vb* **3** (*intr*) to rise up in rebellion against authority. **4** (*usually passive*) to feel or cause to feel revulsion, disgust, or abhorrence. [C16: from F *révolter,* from OIt. *rivoltare* to overturn, ult. from L *revolvere* to roll back]

revolting ❶ (rɪ'vəʊltɪŋ) *adj* **1** causing revulsion; nauseating, disgusting, or repulsive. **2** *Inf.* unpleasant or nasty.
▸**re'voltingly** *adv*

revolute ('rɛvəˌluːt) *adj* (esp. of the margins of a leaf) rolled backwards and downwards. [C18: from L *revolūtus* rolled back; see REVOLVE]

revolution ❶ (ˌrɛvə'luːʃən) *n* **1** the overthrow or repudiation of a regime or political system by the governed. **2** (in Marxist theory) the inevitable, violent transition from one system of production in a society to the next. **3** a far-reaching and drastic change, esp. in ideas, methods, etc. **4a** movement in or as if in a circle. **4b** one complete turn in such a circle: *33 revolutions per minute.* **5a** the orbital motion of one body, such as a planet, around another. **5b** one complete turn in such motion. **6** a cycle of successive events or changes. [C14: via OF from LL *revolūtiō,* from L *revolvere* to REVOLVE]

THESAURUS

review *vb* **1 = reconsider,** go over again, look at again, reassess, recapitulate, re-evaluate, re-examine, rethink, revise, run over, take another look at, think over **2 = look back on,** call to mind, recall, recollect, reflect on, remember, summon up **3 = inspect,** examine, scrutinize **5 = assess,** criticize, discuss, evaluate, give one's opinion of, judge, read through, study, weigh, write a critique of ◆ *n* **7 = report,** analysis, examination, perusal, scrutiny, study, survey **8 = critique,** commentary, critical assessment, criticism, evaluation, judgment, notice, study **9 = magazine,** journal, periodical, zine (*inf.*) **10 = re-examination,** another look, fresh look, reassessment, recapitulation, reconsideration, re-evaluation, rethink, retrospect, revision, second look **12 = inspection,** display, march past, parade, procession

reviewer *n* **5 = critic,** arbiter, commentator, connoisseur, essayist, judge

revile *vb* **= malign,** abuse, asperse, bad-mouth (*sl., chiefly US & Canad.*), calumniate, defame, denigrate, knock (*inf.*), libel, reproach, rubbish (*inf.*), run down, scorn, slag (off) (*sl.*), slander, smear, traduce, vilify, vituperate

revise *vb* **1 = change,** alter, amend, correct, edit, emend, modify, reconsider, redo, re-examine, revamp, review, rework, rewrite, update **2 = study,** cram (*inf.*), go over, memorize, reread, run through, swot up (*Brit. inf.*)

revision *n* **1 = change,** alteration, amendment, correction, editing, emendation, modification, re-examination, review, rewriting, updating **2 = studying,** cramming (*inf.*), homework, memorizing, rereading, swotting (*Brit. inf.*)

revitalize *vb* **= reanimate,** breathe new life into, bring back to life, refresh, rejuvenate, renew, restore, resurrect, revivify

revival *n* **1, 2 = renewal,** awakening, quickening, reanimation, reawakening, rebirth, recrudescence, refreshment, renaissance, renascence, restoration, resurgence, resurrection, resuscitation, revitalization, revivification
Antonyms *n* disappearance, extinction, falling off, suppression

revive *vb* **1-3 = revitalize,** animate, awaken, breathe new life into, bring back to life, bring round, cheer, come round, comfort, invigorate, kick-start, quicken, rally, reanimate, recover, refresh, rekindle, renew, renovate, restore, resuscitate, rouse, spring up again
Antonyms *vb* die out, disappear, enervate, exhaust, tire out, weary

revivify *vb* **= revive,** breathe new life into, give new life to, inspirit, invigorate, kick-start (*inf.*), reanimate, refresh, renew, restore, resuscitate

revoke *vb* **1 = cancel,** abolish, abrogate, annul, call back, countermand, declare null and void, disclaim, invalidate, negate, nullify, obviate, quash, recall, recant, renege, renounce, repeal, repudiate, rescind, retract, reverse, set aside, take back, withdraw
Antonyms *vb* confirm, endorse, implement, maintain, put into effect, uphold

revolt *n* **1 = uprising,** defection, insurgency, insurrection, mutiny, putsch, rebellion, revolution, rising, sedition ◆ *vb* **3 = rebel,** defect, mutiny, resist, rise, take to the streets, take up arms (against) **4 = disgust,** give one the creeps (*inf.*), gross out (*US sl.*), make one's flesh creep, nauseate, offend, repel, repulse, shock, sicken, turn off (*inf.*), turn one's stomach

revolting *adj* **1, 2 = disgusting,** abhorrent, abominable, appalling, cringe-making (*Brit. inf.*), distasteful, foul, horrible, horrid, loathsome, nasty, nauseating, nauseous, noisome, obnoxious, obscene, offensive, repellent, repugnant, repulsive, shocking, sickening, yucky or yukky (*sl.*)
Antonyms *adj* agreeable, attractive, delightful, fragrant, palatable, pleasant

revolution *n* **1 = revolt,** coup, coup d'état, insurgency, mutiny, putsch, rebellion, rising, uprising **3 = transformation,** drastic *or* radical change, innovation, metamorphosis, reformation, sea change, shift, upheaval **4 = rotation,** circle, circuit, cycle, gyration, lap, round, spin, turn, wheel, whirl **5 = orbit,** circuit

revolutionary ➊ (ˌrɛvəˈluːʃənərɪ) *n, pl* **revolutionaries. 1** a person who advocates or engages in revolution. ◆ *adj* **2** relating to or characteristic of a revolution. **3** advocating or engaged in revolution. **4** radically new or different: *a revolutionary method of making plastics.*

Revolutionary (ˌrɛvəˈluːʃənərɪ) *adj* **1** *Chiefly US.* of or relating to the War of American Independence (1775–83). **2** of or relating to any of various other Revolutions, esp. the **Russian Revolution** (1917) or the **French Revolution** (1789).

revolutionist (ˌrɛvəˈluːʃənɪst) *n* **1** a less common word for a **revolutionary.** ◆ *adj* **2** of or relating to revolution or revolutionaries.

revolutionize ➊ *or* **revolutionise** (ˌrɛvəˈluːʃəˌnaɪz) *vb* **revolutionizes, revolutionizing, revolutionized** *or* **revolutionises, revolutionising, revolutionised.** (*tr*) **1** to bring about a radical change in: *science has revolutionized civilization.* **2** to inspire or infect with revolutionary ideas: *they revolutionized the common soldiers.* **3** to cause a revolution in (a country, etc.).
▸ˌ**revoˈlutionˌizer** *or* ˌ**revoˈlutionˌiser** *n*

revolve ➊ (rɪˈvɒlv) *vb* **revolves, revolving, revolved. 1** to move or cause to move around a centre or axis; rotate. **2** (*intr*) to occur periodically or in cycles. **3** to consider or be considered. **4** (*intr*; foll. by *around* or *about*) to be centred or focused (upon): *Juliet's thoughts revolved around Romeo.* ◆ *n* **5** *Theatre.* a circular section of a stage that can be rotated by electric power to provide a scene change. [C14: from L *revolvere,* from RE- + *volvere* to roll, wind]
▸**reˈvolvable** *adj*

revolver (rɪˈvɒlvə) *n* a pistol having a revolving multichambered cylinder that allows several shots to be discharged without reloading.

revolving (rɪˈvɒlvɪŋ) *adj* **1** moving round a central axis: *revolving door.* **2** (of a fund) constantly added to from income from its investments to offset outgoing payments. **3** (of a letter of credit, loan, etc.) available to be repeatedly drawn on by the beneficiary provided that a specified amount is never exceeded.

revue (rɪˈvjuː) *n* a light entertainment consisting of topical sketches, songs, dancing, etc. [C20: from F; see REVIEW]

revulsion ➊ (rɪˈvʌlʃən) *n* **1** a sudden violent reaction in feeling, esp. one of extreme loathing. **2** the act or an instance of drawing back or recoiling from something. **3** the diversion of disease from one part of the body to another by cupping, counterirritants, etc. [C16: from L *revulsiō* a pulling away, from *revellere,* from RE- + *vellere* to pull, tear]

revulsive (rɪˈvʌlsɪv) *adj* **1** of or causing revulsion. ◆ *n* **2** *Med.* a counterirritant.
▸**reˈvulsively** *adv*

reward ➊ (rɪˈwɔːd) *n* **1** something given in return for a deed or service rendered. **2** a sum of money offered, esp. for help in finding a criminal or for the return of lost or stolen property. **3** profit or return. **4** something received in return for good or evil; deserts. ◆ *vb* **5** (*tr*) to give something to (someone), esp. in gratitude for (a service rendered); recompense. [C14: from OF *rewarder,* from RE- + *warder* to care for, guard, of Gmc origin]
▸**reˈwardless** *adj*

reward claim *n Austral. history.* a claim granted to a miner who discovered gold in a new area.

rewarding ➊ (rɪˈwɔːdɪŋ) *adj* giving personal satisfaction; gratifying.

rewa-rewa (ˈreɪwəˈreɪwə) *n* a tall tree of New Zealand, yielding reddish timber. [C19: from Maori]

rewind *vb* (riːˈwaɪnd), **rewinds, rewinding, rewound. 1** (*tr*) to wind back, esp. a film or tape onto the original reel. ◆ *n* (ˈriːˌwaɪnd, riːˈwaɪnd). **2** something rewound. **3** the act of rewinding.
▸**reˈwinder** *n*

rewire (riːˈwaɪə) *vb* **rewires, rewiring, rewired.** (*tr*) to provide (a house, engine, etc.) with new wiring.
▸**reˈwirable** *adj*

reword ➊ (riːˈwɜːd) *vb* (*tr*) to alter the wording of; express differently.

rework (riːˈwɜːk) *vb* (*tr*) **1** to use again in altered form. **2** to rewrite or revise. **3** to reprocess for use again.

rewrite ➊ *vb* (riːˈraɪt), **rewrites, rewriting, rewrote, rewritten.** (*tr*) **1** to write (material) again, esp. changing the words or form. ◆ *n* (ˈriːˌraɪt). **2** *Computing.* to return (data) to a store when it has been erased during reading. **3** something rewritten.

Rex (rɛks) *n* king: part of the official title of a king, now used chiefly in documents, legal proceedings, on coins, etc. Cf. **Regina.** [L]

Rexine (ˈrɛksiːn) *n Trademark.* a form of artificial leather.

Reye's syndrome (raɪz, reɪz) *n* a rare metabolic disease in children that can be fatal, involving damage to the brain, liver, and kidneys. [C20: after R.D.K. *Reye* (1912–78), Austral. paediatrician]

Reynard *or* **Renard** (ˈrɛnəd, ˈrɛnɑːd) *n* a name for a fox, used in fables, etc.

RF *abbrev. for* radio frequency.

RFC *abbrev. for:* **1** Royal Flying Corps. **2** Rugby Football Club.

RGN (in Britain) *abbrev. for* Registered General Nurse.

RGS *abbrev. for* Royal Geographical Society.

rh *or* **RH** *abbrev. for* right hand.

Rh 1 *the chemical symbol for* rhodium. ◆ **2** *abbrev. for* rhesus (esp. in **Rh factor**).

RHA *abbrev. for:* **1** Regional Health Authority. **2** Royal Horse Artillery.

rhabdomancy (ˈræbdəˌmænsɪ) *n* divination for water or mineral ore by means of a rod or wand. [C17: via LL from LGk *rhabdomanteia,* from Gk *rhabdos* rod + *manteia* divination]
▸ˈ**rhabdoˌmantist** *or* ˈ**rhabdoˌmancer** *n*

rhachis (ˈreɪkɪs) *n, pl* **rhachises** *or* **rhachides** (ˈrækɪˌdiːz, ˈreɪ-). a variant spelling of **rachis.**

Rhadamanthine (ˌrædəˈmænθaɪn) *adj* impartial; judicially strict. [C19: after *Rhadamanthus,* in Gk myth one of the judges of the dead in the underworld]

rhapsodic (ræpˈsɒdɪk) *adj* **1** of or like a rhapsody. **2** lyrical or romantic.

rhapsodize ➊ *or* **rhapsodise** (ˈræpsəˌdaɪz) *vb* **rhapsodizes, rhapsodizing, rhapsodized** *or* **rhapsodises, rhapsodising, rhapsodised. 1** to speak or write (something) with extravagant enthusiasm. **2** (*intr*) to recite or write rhapsodies.
▸ˈ**rhapsodist** *n*

rhapsody (ˈræpsədɪ) *n, pl* **rhapsodies. 1** *Music.* a composition free in structure and highly emotional in character. **2** an expression of ecstatic enthusiasm. **3** (in ancient Greece) an epic poem or part of an epic recited by a rhapsodist. **4** a literary work composed in an intense or exalted style. **5** rapturous delight or ecstasy. [C16: via L from Gk *rhapsōidia,* from *rhaptein* to sew together + *ōidē* song]

rhatany (ˈrætənɪ) *n, pl* **rhatanies. 1** either of two South American leguminous shrubs that have thick fleshy roots. **2** the dried roots used as an astringent. ◆ Also called: **krameria.** [C19: from NL *rhatānia,* ult. from Quechua *ratánya*]

rhea (rɪə) *n* either of two large fast-running flightless birds inhabiting the open plains of S South America. They are similar to but smaller than the ostrich. [C19: NL; arbitrarily after *Rhea,* in Gk myth., mother of Zeus]

rhebuck *or* **rhebok** (ˈriːbʌk) *n, pl* **rhebucks, rhebuck** *or* **reboks, rhebok.** an antelope of southern Africa, having woolly brownish-grey hair. [C18: Afrik., from Du. *reebok* ROEBUCK]

Rhenish (ˈrɛnɪʃ, ˈriː-) *adj* **1** of or relating to the River Rhine or the lands adjacent to it. ◆ *n* **2** another word for **hock**[2].

rhenium (ˈriːnɪəm) *n* a dense silvery-white metallic element that has a high melting point. Symbol: Re; atomic no.: 75; atomic wt.: 186.2. [C19: NL, from *Rhēnus* the Rhine]

rheo- *combining form.* indicating stream, flow, or current: *rheostat.* [from Gk *rheos* stream, anything flowing, from *rhein* to flow]

rheology (rɪˈɒlədʒɪ) *n* the branch of physics concerned with the flow and change of shape of matter, esp. the viscosity of liquids.
▸**rheological** (ˌriːəˈlɒdʒɪkᵊl) *adj* ▸**rheˈologist** *n*

rheostat (ˈrɪəˌstæt) *n* a variable resistance, usually a coil of wire with a terminal at one end and a sliding contact that moves along the coil to tap off the current.
▸ˌ**rheoˈstatic** *adj*

rhesus baby (ˈriːsəs) *n* a baby suffering from haemolytic disease at birth as its red blood cells (which are Rh positive) have been attacked in the womb by antibodies from its Rh negative mother. [C20: see RH FACTOR]

rhesus factor *n* See **Rh factor.**

rhesus monkey *n* a macaque monkey of S Asia. [C19: NL, arbitrarily from Gk *Rhesos,* mythical Thracian king]

rhetoric ➊ (ˈrɛtərɪk) *n* **1** the study of the technique of using language effectively. **2** the art of using speech to persuade, influence, or please; oratory. **3** excessive ornamentation and contrivance in spoken or written discourse; bombast. **4** speech or discourse that pretends to

THESAURUS

revolutionary *n* **1** = **rebel**, insurgent, insurrectionary, insurrectionist, mutineer, revolutionist ◆ *adj* **3** = **rebel**, extremist, insurgent, insurrectionary, mutinous, radical, seditious, subversive **4** = **innovative**, avant-garde, different, drastic, experimental, fundamental, ground-breaking, new, novel, progressive, radical, thoroughgoing
Antonyms *adj, n* ≠ **rebel:** counter-revolutionary, loyalist, reactionary ◆ *adj* ≠ **innovative:** conservative, conventional, mainstream, minor, traditional, trivial

revolutionize *vb* **1** = **transform**, break with the past, metamorphose, modernize, reform, revamp

revolve *vb* **1** = **go round**, circle, gyrate, orbit, rotate, spin, turn, twist, wheel, whirl **3** = **consider**, deliberate, meditate, mull over, ponder, reflect, ruminate, study, think about, think over, turn over (in one's mind)

revulsion *n* **1** = **disgust**, abhorrence, abomination, aversion, detestation, distaste, loathing, odium, recoil, repugnance, repulsion
Antonyms *n* attraction, desire, fascination, liking, pleasure

reward *n* **1, 2** = **payment**, benefit, bounty, compensation, honour, meed, merit, prize, recompense, remuneration, repayment, requital **3** = **profit**, bonus, gain, premium, return, wages **4** = **punishment**, comeuppance (*sl.*), desert, just deserts, requital, retribution ◆ *vb* **5** = **compensate**, honour, make it worth one's while, pay, recompense, remunerate, repay, requite
Antonyms *n* ≠ **payment:** fine, penalty, punishment ◆ *vb* ≠ **compensate:** fine, penalize, punish

rewarding *adj* = **satisfying**, advantageous, beneficial, economic, edifying, enriching, fruitful, fulfilling, gainful, gratifying, pleasing, productive, profitable, remunerative, valuable, worthwhile
Antonyms *adj* barren, boring, fruitless, unproductive, unprofitable, unrewarding, vain

reword *vb* = **put in other words**, express differently, paraphrase, put another way, recast, rephrase

rewrite *vb* **1** = **revise**, correct, edit, emend, recast, redraft, touch up

rhapsodize *vb* **1** = **enthuse**, drool, go into ecstasies, gush, rave (*inf.*), wax lyrical

rhetoric *n* **2** = **oratory**, eloquence **3, 4** = **hyperbole**, bombast, fustian, grandiloquence, hot air (*inf.*), magniloquence, pomposity, rant, verbosity, wordiness

significance but lacks true meaning: *mere rhetoric.* [C14: via L from Gk *rhētorikē (tekhnē)* (the art of) rhetoric, from *rhētōr* teacher of rhetoric, orator]

rhetorical ❶ (rɪ'tɒrɪkᵊl) *adj* **1** concerned with effect or style rather than content or meaning; bombastic. **2** of or relating to rhetoric or oratory.
▸**rhe'torically** *adv*

rhetorical question *n* a question to which no answer is required: used esp. for dramatic effect. An example is *Who knows?* (with the implication *Nobody knows*).

rhetorician (ˌrɛtə'rɪʃən) *n* **1** a teacher of rhetoric. **2** a stylish or eloquent writer or speaker. **3** a pompous or extravagant speaker.

rheum (ruːm) *n* a watery discharge from the eyes or nose. [C14: from OF *reume,* ult. from Gk *rheuma* bodily humour, stream, from *rhein* to flow]
▸**'rheumy** *adj*

rheumatic (ruː'mætɪk) *adj* **1** of, relating to, or afflicted with rheumatism. ◆ *n* **2** a person afflicted with rheumatism. [C14: ult. from Gk *rheumatikos,* from *rheuma* a flow; see RHEUM]
▸**rheu'matically** *adv*

rheumatic fever *n* a disease characterized by inflammation and pain in the joints.

rheumatics (ruː'mætɪks) *n* (*functioning as sing*) *Inf.* rheumatism.

rheumatism ('ruːməˌtɪzəm) *n* any painful disorder of joints, muscles, or connective tissue. [C17: from L *rheumatismus* catarrh, from Gk *rheumatismos;* see RHEUM]

rheumatoid ('ruːməˌtɔɪd) *adj* (of symptoms) resembling rheumatism.

rheumatoid arthritis *n* a chronic disease characterized by inflammation and swelling of joints (esp. in the hands, wrists, knees, and feet), muscle weakness, and fatigue.

rheumatology (ˌruːmə'tɒlədʒɪ) *n* the study of rheumatic diseases.
▸**rheumatological** (ˌruːmətə'lɒdʒɪkᵊl) *adj*

Rh factor *n* an antigen commonly found in human blood: the terms **Rh positive** and **Rh negative** are used to indicate its presence or absence. It may cause a haemolytic reaction, esp. during pregnancy or following transfusion of blood that does not contain this antigen. Full name: **rhesus factor.** [after the rhesus monkey, in which it was first discovered]

rhinal ('raɪnᵊl) *adj* of or relating to the nose.

rhinestone ('raɪnˌstəʊn) *n* an imitation gem made of paste. [C19: translation of F *caillou du Rhin,* referring to Strasbourg, where such gems were made]

Rhine wine (raɪn) *n* any wine produced along the Rhine, characteristically a white table wine.

rhinitis (raɪ'naɪtɪs) *n* inflammation of the mucous membrane that lines the nose.
▸**rhinitic** (raɪ'nɪtɪk) *adj*

rhino[1] ('raɪnəʊ) *n, pl* **rhinos** *or* **rhino.** short for **rhinoceros.**

rhino[2] ('raɪnəʊ) *n Brit.* a slang word for **money.** [C17: from ?]

rhino- *or before a vowel* **rhin-** *combining form.* the nose: *rhinology.* [from Gk *rhis, rhin*]

rhinoceros (raɪ'nɒsərəs, -'nɒsrəs) *n, pl* **rhinoceroses** *or* **rhinoceros.** any of several mammals constituting a family of SE Asia and Africa and having either one horn on the nose, like the **Indian rhinoceros,** or two horns, like the African **white rhinoceros.** They have a very thick skin and a massive body. [C13: via L from Gk *rhinokerōs,* from *rhis* nose + *keras* horn]
▸**rhinocerotic** (ˌraɪnəʊsɪ'rɒtɪk) *adj*

rhinology (raɪ'nɒlədʒɪ) *n* the branch of medical science concerned with the nose.
▸**rhinological** (ˌraɪnᵊ'lɒdʒɪkᵊl) *adj* ▸**rhi'nologist** *n*

rhinoplasty ('raɪnəʊˌplæstɪ) *n* plastic surgery of the nose.
▸**ˌrhino'plastic** *adj*

rhinoscopy (raɪ'nɒskəpɪ) *n Med.* examination of the nasal passages, esp. with a special instrument called a **rhinoscope** ('raɪnəʊˌskəʊp).

rhizo- *or before a vowel* **rhiz-** *combining form.* root: *rhizocarpous.* [from Gk *rhiza*]

rhizocarpous (ˌraɪzəʊ'kɑːpəs) *adj* **1** (of plants) producing subterranean flowers and fruit. **2** (of plants) having perennial roots but stems and leaves that wither.

rhizoid ('raɪzɔɪd) *n* any of various hairlike structures that function as roots in mosses, ferns, and fungi.
▸**rhi'zoidal** *adj*

rhizome ('raɪzəʊm) *n* a thick horizontal underground stem whose buds develop into new plants. Also called: **rootstock, rootstalk.** [C19: from NL *rhizoma,* from Gk, from *rhiza* a root]
▸**rhizomatous** (raɪ'zɒmətəs, -'zəʊ-) *adj*

rhizopod ('raɪzəʊˌpɒd) *n* **1** any of various protozoans characterized by naked protoplasmic processes (pseudopodia). ◆ *adj* **2** of, relating to, or belonging to rhizopods.

rho (rəʊ) *n, pl* **rhos.** the 17th letter in the Greek alphabet (Ρ, ρ).

rhodamine ('rəʊdəˌmiːn, -mɪn) *n* any one of a group of synthetic red or pink basic dyestuffs used for wool and silk. [C20: from RHODO- + AMINE]

Rhode Island Red *n* a breed of domestic fowl, originating in America, characterized by a dark reddish-brown plumage and the production of brown eggs.

Rhodesian man *n* a type of early man, occurring in Africa in late Pleistocene times and resembling Neanderthal man.

Rhodes scholarship (rəʊdz) *n* one of 72 scholarships founded by Cecil Rhodes (1853–1902), South African statesman and financier, awarded annually to Commonwealth and US students to study at Oxford University.
▸**Rhodes scholar** *n*

rhodium ('rəʊdɪəm) *n* a hard silvery-white element of the platinum metal group. Used as an alloying agent to harden platinum and palladium. Symbol: Rh; atomic no.: 45; atomic wt.: 102.90. [C19: NL, from Gk *rhodon* rose, from the pink colour of its compounds]

rhodo- *or before a vowel* **rhod-** *combining form.* rose or rose-coloured: *rhododendron; rhodolite.* [from Gk *rhodon* rose]

rhodochrosite (ˌrəʊdəʊ'krəʊsaɪt) *n* a pink, grey, or brown mineral that consists of manganese carbonate in hexagonal crystalline form. Formula: $MnCO_3$. [C19: from Gk *rhodokhrōs,* from *rhodon* rose + *khrōs* colour]

rhododendron (ˌrəʊdə'dɛndrən) *n* any of various shrubs native to S Asia but widely cultivated in N temperate regions. They are mostly evergreen and have clusters of showy red, purple, pink, or white flowers. [C17: from L: oleander, from Gk, from *rhodon* rose + *dendron* tree]

rhodolite ('rɒdəˌlaɪt) *n* a pale violet or red variety of garnet, used as a gemstone.

rhodonite ('rɒdəˌnaɪt) *n* a brownish translucent mineral consisting of manganese silicate in crystalline form with calcium, iron, or magnesium sometimes replacing the manganese. It is used as an ornamental stone, glaze, and pigment. [C19: from G *Rhodonit,* from Gk *rhodon* rose + -ITE[1]]

rhodopsin (rəʊ'dɒpsɪn) *n* a red pigment in the rods of the retina in vertebrates. Also called: **visual purple.** See also **iodopsin.** [C20: from RHODO- + Gk *opsis* sight + -IN]

rhomb (rɒm) *n* another name for **rhombus.**

rhombencephalon (ˌrɒmbɛn'sɛfəˌlɒn) *n* the part of the brain that develops from the posterior portion of the embryonic neural tube. Nontechnical name: **hindbrain.** [C20: from RHOMBUS + ENCEPHALON]

rhombic aerial *n* a directional travelling-wave aerial, usually horizontal, consisting of two conductors forming a rhombus.

rhombohedral (ˌrɒmbəʊ'hiːdrəl) *adj* **1** of or relating to a rhombohedron. **2** *Crystallog.* another term for **trigonal** (sense 2).

rhombohedron (ˌrɒmbəʊ'hiːdrən) *n, pl* **rhombohedrons** *or* **rhombohedra** (-drə). a six-sided prism whose sides are parallelograms. [C19: from RHOMBUS + -HEDRON]

rhomboid ('rɒmbɔɪd) *n* **1** a parallelogram having adjacent sides of unequal length. ◆ *adj also* **rhom'boidal.** **2** having such a shape. [C16: from LL, from Gk *rhomboeidēs* shaped like a RHOMBUS]

rhombus ('rɒmbəs) *n, pl* **rhombuses** *or* **rhombi** (-baɪ). an oblique-angled parallelogram having four equal sides. Also called: **rhomb.** [C16: from Gk *rhombos* something that spins; rel. to *rhembein* to whirl]
▸**'rhombic** *adj*

rhonchus ('rɒŋkəs) *n, pl* **rhonchi** (-kaɪ). a rattling or whistling respiratory sound resembling snoring, caused by secretions in the trachea or bronchi. [C19: from L, from Gk *rhenkhos* snoring]

RHS *abbrev. for:* **1** Royal Historical Society. **2** Royal Horticultural Society. **3** Royal Humane Society.

rhubarb ('ruːbɑːb) *n* **1** any of several temperate and subtropical plants, esp. **common garden rhubarb,** which has long green and red acid-tasting edible leafstalks, usually eaten sweetened and cooked. **2** the leafstalks of this plant. **3** a related plant of central Asia, having a bitter-tasting underground stem that can be dried and used as a laxative or astringent. **4** *US & Canad. sl.* a heated discussion or quarrel. ◆ *interj, n, vb* **5** the noise made by actors to simulate conversation, esp. by repeating the word *rhubarb.* [C14: from OF *reubarbe,* from Med. L *reubarbum,* prob. var. of *rha barbarum,* from *rha* rhubarb (from Gk, ?from *Rha,* ancient name of the Volga) + L *barbarus* barbarian]

rhumb (rʌm) *n* short for **rhumb line.**

rhumba ('rʌmbə, 'rʊm-) *n, pl* **rhumbas.** a variant spelling of **rumba.**

rhumb line *n* **1** an imaginary line on the surface of a sphere that intersects all meridians at the same angle. **2** the course navigated by a vessel or aircraft that maintains a uniform compass heading. [C16: from OSp. *rumbo,* apparently from MDu. *ruum* space, ship's hold, infl. by RHOMBUS]

rhyme ❶ *or* (*arch.*) **rime** (raɪm) *n* **1** identity of the terminal sounds in lines of verse or in words. **2** a word that is identical to another in its terminal sound: *"while" is a rhyme for "mile".* **3** a piece of poetry, esp. having corresponding sounds at the ends of the lines. **4 rhyme or reason.** sense, logic, or meaning. ◆ *vb* **rhymes, rhyming, rhymed** *or* **rimes, riming, rimed.** **5** to use (a word) or (of a word) to be used so as to form a rhyme. **6** to render (a subject) into rhyme. **7** to compose (verse) in a metrical structure. ◆ See also **eye rhyme.** [C12: from OF *rime,* ult. from OHG *rīm* a number; spelling infl. by RHYTHM]

rhymester, rimester ('raɪmstə), **rhymer,** *or* **rimer** *n* a poet, esp. one considered to be mediocre; poetaster or versifier.

THESAURUS

rhetorical *adj* **1** = **high-flown,** arty-farty (*inf.*), bombastic, declamatory, flamboyant, flashy, florid, flowery, grandiloquent, high-sounding, hyperbolic, magniloquent, oratorical, pompous, pretentious, showy, silver-tongued, verbose, windy **2** = **oratorical,** linguistic, stylistic, verbal

rhyme *n* **3** = **poetry,** ode, poem, song, verse **4 rhyme or reason** = **sense,** logic, meaning, method, plan ◆ *vb* **5** = **sound like,** chime, harmonize

rhyming slang *n* slang in which a word is replaced by another word or phrase that rhymes with it; e.g. *apples and pears* meaning *stairs.*

rhyolite ('raɪəˌlaɪt) *n* a fine-grained igneous rock consisting of quartz, feldspars, and mica or amphibole. [C19: *rhyo-* from Gk *rhuax* a stream of lava + -LITE]
▸**rhyolitic** (ˌraɪə'lɪtɪk) *adj*

rhythm ❶ ('rɪðəm) *n* **1a** the arrangement of the durations of and accents on the notes of a melody, usually laid out into regular groups (**bars**) of beats. **1b** any specific arrangement of such groupings; time: *quadruple rhythm.* **2** (in poetry) **2a** the arrangement of words into a sequence of stressed and unstressed or long and short syllables. **2b** any specific such arrangement; metre. **3** (in painting, sculpture, etc.) a harmonious sequence or pattern of masses alternating with voids, of light alternating with shade, of alternating colours, etc. **4** any sequence of regularly recurring functions or events, such as certain physiological functions of the body. [C16: from L *rhythmus,* from Gk *rhuthmos;* rel. to *rhein* to flow]

rhythm and blues *n* (*functioning as sing*) any of various kinds of popular music derived from or influenced by the blues. Abbrev.: **R & B.**

rhythmic ❶ ('rɪðmɪk) *or* **rhythmical** ('rɪðmɪkᵊl) *adj* of, relating to, or characterized by rhythm, as in movement or sound; metrical, periodic, or regularly recurring.
▸'**rhythmically** *adv* ▸**rhythmicity** (rɪð'mɪsɪtɪ) *n*

rhythm method *n* a method of contraception by restricting sexual intercourse to those days in a woman's menstrual cycle on which conception is considered least likely to occur.

rhythm section *n* those instruments in a band or group (usually piano, double bass, and drums) whose prime function is to supply the rhythm.

RI *abbrev. for:* **1** Regina et Imperatrix. [L: Queen and Empress] **2** Rex et Imperator. [L: King and Emperor] **3** Royal Institution. **4** religious instruction.

ria (rɪə) *n* a long narrow inlet of the seacoast, being a former valley that was submerged by the sea. [C19: from Sp., from *ría* river]

riata *or* **reata** (rɪ'ɑːtə) *n South & West US.* a lariat or lasso. [C19: from American Sp., from Sp. *reatar* to tie together again, from RE- + *atar* to tie, from L *aptāre* to fit]

rib[1] (rɪb) *n* **1** any of the 24 elastic arches of bone that together form the chest wall in man. All are attached behind to the thoracic part of the spinal column. **2** the corresponding bone in other vertebrates. **3** a cut of meat including one or more ribs. **4** a part or element similar in function or appearance to a rib, esp. a structural member or a ridge. **5** a structural member in a wing that extends from the leading edge to the trailing edge. **6** a projecting moulding or band on the underside of a vault or ceiling. **7** one of a series of raised rows in knitted fabric. **8** a raised ornamental line on the spine of a book where the stitching runs across it. **9** any of the transverse stiffening timbers or joists forming the frame of a ship's hull. **10** any of the larger veins of a leaf. **11** a vein of ore in rock. **12** a projecting ridge of a mountain; spur. ◆ *vb* **ribs, ribbing, ribbed.** (*tr*) **13** to furnish or support with a rib or ribs. **14** to mark with or form into ribs or ridges. **15** to knit plain and purl stitches alternately in order to make raised rows in (knitting). [OE *ribb;* rel. to OHG *rippi,* ON *rif* REEF[1]]
▸'**ribless** *adj*

rib[2] (rɪb) *vb* **ribs, ribbing, ribbed.** (*tr*) *Inf.* to tease or ridicule. [C20: short for *rib-tickle* (vb)]

RIBA *abbrev. for* Royal Institute of British Architects.

ribald ❶ ('rɪbᵊld) *adj* **1** coarse, obscene, or licentious, usually in a humorous or mocking way. ◆ *n* **2** a ribald person. [C13: from OF *ribauld,* from *riber* to live licentiously, of Gmc origin]

ribaldry ❶ ('rɪbᵊldrɪ) *n* ribald language or behaviour.

riband *or* **ribband** ('rɪbənd) *n* a ribbon, esp. one awarded for some achievement. [C14: var. of RIBBON]

ribbing ('rɪbɪŋ) *n* **1** a framework or structure of ribs. **2** a pattern of ribs in woven or knitted material. **3** *Inf.* teasing.

ribbon ('rɪbᵊn) *n* **1** a narrow strip of fine material, esp. silk, used for trimming, tying, etc. **2** something resembling a ribbon; a long strip. **3** a long thin flexible band of metal used as a graduated measure, spring, etc. **4** a long narrow strip of ink-impregnated cloth for making the impression of type characters on paper in a typewriter, etc. **5** (*pl*) ragged strips or shreds (esp. in **torn to ribbons**). **6** a small strip of coloured cloth signifying membership of an order or award of military decoration, prize, etc. **7** a small, usually looped, strip of coloured cloth worn to signify support for a charity or cause: *a red AIDS ribbon.* ◆ *vb* (*tr*) **8** to adorn with a ribbon or ribbons. **9** to mark with narrow ribbon-like marks. [C14 *ryban,* from OF *riban,* apparently of Gmc origin]

ribbon development *n Brit.* the building of houses in a continuous row along a main road.

ribbonfish ('rɪbᵊnˌfɪʃ) *n, pl* **ribbonfish** *or* **ribbonfishes.** any of various soft-finned deep-sea fishes that have an elongated compressed body.

ribbonwood ('rɪbᵊnˌwʊd) *n* a small evergreen malvaceous tree of New Zealand. Its wood is used in furniture making. Also: **lacebark.**

ribcage ('rɪbˌkeɪdʒ) *n* the bony structure of the ribs and their connective tissue that encloses the lungs, heart, etc.

riboflavin *or* **riboflavine** (ˌraɪbəʊ'fleɪvɪn) *n* a vitamin of the B complex that occurs in green vegetables, milk, fish, egg yolk, liver, and kidney: used as a yellow or orange food colouring (**E 101**). Also called: **vitamin B_2.** [C20: from RIBOSE + FLAVIN]

ribonuclease (ˌraɪbəʊ'njuːklɪˌeɪz) *n* any of a group of enzymes that catalyse the hydrolysis of RNA. [C20: from RIBONUCLE(IC ACID) + -ASE]

ribonucleic acid (ˌraɪbəʊnjuː'kliːɪk, -'kleɪ-) *n* the full name of **RNA.** [C20: from RIBO(SE) + NUCLEIC ACID]

ribose ('raɪbəʊz, -bəʊs) *n* a sugar that occurs in RNA and riboflavin. [C20: changed from *arabinose,* from (GUM) ARAB(IC) + -IN+ -OSE[2]]

ribosomal RNA (ˌraɪbə'səʊməl) *n* a type of RNA thought to form the component of ribosomes on which the translation of messenger RNA into protein chains is accomplished.

ribosome ('raɪbəˌsəʊm) *n* any of numerous minute particles in the cytoplasm of cells that contain RNA and protein and are the site of protein synthesis. [C20: from RIBO(NUCLEIC ACID) + -SOME[3]]
▸ˌ**ribo'somal** *adj*

rib-tickler *n* a very amusing joke or story.
▸'**rib-**ˌ**tickling** *adj*

ribwort ('rɪbˌwɜːt) *n* a Eurasian plant that has lancelike ribbed leaves. Also called: **ribgrass.** See also **plantain**[1].

rice (raɪs) *n* **1** an erect grass that grows in warm climates on wet ground and has yellow oblong edible grains that become white when polished. **2** the grain of this plant. ◆ *vb* **rices, ricing, riced.** **3** (*tr*) *US & Canad.* to sieve (potatoes or other vegetables) to a coarse mashed consistency. [C13 *rys,* via F, It., & L from Gk *orūza,* of Oriental origin]

rice bowl *n* **1** a small bowl used for eating rice. **2** a fertile rice-producing region.

rice paper *n* **1** a thin edible paper made from the straw of rice, on which macaroons and similar cakes are baked. **2** a thin delicate Chinese paper made from the **rice-paper plant**, the pith of which is pared and flattened into sheets.

ricercare (ˌriːtʃə'kɑːreɪ) *or* **ricercar** ('riːtʃəˌkɑː) *n, pl* **ricercari** (-'kɑːriː) *or* **ricercars.** (in music of the 16th and 17th centuries) **1** an elaborate polyphonic composition making extensive use of contrapuntal imitation and usually very slow in tempo. **2** an instructive composition to illustrate instrumental technique; étude. [It., lit.: to seek again]

rich ❶ (rɪtʃ) *adj* **1a** well supplied with wealth, property, etc.; owning much. **1b** (*as collective n; preceded by the*): *the rich.* **2** (when *postpositive,* usually foll. by *in*) having an abundance of natural resources, minerals, etc.: *a land rich in metals.* **3** producing abundantly; fertile: *rich soil.* **4** (when *postpositive,* foll. by *in* or *with*) well supplied (with desirable qualities); abundant (in): *a country rich with cultural interest.* **5** of great worth or quality: *a rich collection of antiques.* **6** luxuriant or prolific: *a rich growth of weeds.* **7** expensively elegant, elaborate, or fine; costly: *a rich display.* **8** (of food) having a large proportion of flavoursome or fatty ingredients. **9** having a full-bodied flavour: *a rich ruby port.* **10** (of a smell) pungent or fragrant. **11** (of colour) intense or vivid; deep: *a rich red.* **12** (of sound or a voice) full, mellow, or resonant. **13** (of a fuel-air mixture) containing a relatively high proportion of fuel. **14** very amusing or ridiculous: *a rich joke.* ◆ *n* **15** See **riches.** [OE *rīce* (orig. of persons: great, mighty), of Gmc origin, ult. from Celtic]

riches ❶ ('rɪtʃɪz) *pl n* wealth; an abundance of money, valuable possessions, or property.

richly ❶ ('rɪtʃlɪ) *adv* **1** in a rich or elaborate manner: *a richly decorated carving.* **2** fully and appropriately: *he was richly rewarded.*

THESAURUS

rhythm *n* **1, 2** = **beat**, accent, cadence, flow, lilt, measure (*Prosody*), metre, movement, pattern, periodicity, pulse, swing, tempo, time

rhythmic *adj* = **cadenced**, flowing, harmonious, lilting, melodious, metrical, musical, periodic, pulsating, throbbing

ribald *adj* **1** = **coarse**, bawdy, blue, broad, earthy, filthy, gross, indecent, licentious, naughty, near the knuckle (*inf.*), obscene, off colour, Rabelaisian, racy, raunchy (*sl.*), risqué, rude, scurrilous, smutty, vulgar, X-rated (*inf.*)
Antonyms *adj* chaste, decent, decorous, genteel, inoffensive, polite, proper, refined, tasteful

ribaldry *n* = **coarseness**, bawdiness, billingsgate, earthiness, filth, grossness, indecency, licentiousness, naughtiness, obscenity, raciness, rudeness, scurrility, smut, smuttiness, vulgarity

rich *adj* **1** = **wealthy**, affluent, filthy rich, flush, loaded (*sl.*), made of money (*inf.*), moneyed, opulent, propertied, prosperous, rolling (*sl.*), stinking rich (*inf.*), well-heeled (*inf.*), well-off, well-to-do **2** = **well-stocked**, abounding, full, productive, well-endowed, well-provided, well-supplied **3, 6** = **fruitful**, abounding, abundant, ample, copious, exuberant, fecund, fertile, full, lush, luxurious, plenteous, plentiful, productive, prolific **5, 7** = **costly**, beyond price, elaborate, elegant, expensive, exquisite, fine, gorgeous, lavish, palatial, precious, priceless, splendid, sumptuous, superb, valuable **8, 9** = **full-bodied**, creamy, delicious, fatty, flavoursome, heavy, highly-flavoured, juicy, luscious, savoury, spicy, succulent, sweet, tasty **11** = **vivid**, bright, deep, gay, intense, strong, vibrant, warm **12** = **resonant**, deep, dulcet, full, mellifluous, mellow **14** = **funny**, amusing, comical, hilarious, humorous, laughable, ludicrous, ridiculous, risible, side-splitting
Antonyms *adj* ≠ **wealthy:** destitute, impoverished, needy, penniless, poor ≠ **well-stocked:** lacking, poor, scarce, wanting ≠ **fruitful:** barren, poor, unfertile, unfruitful, unproductive ≠ **costly:** cheap, cheapo (*inf.*), inexpensive, valueless, worthless ≠ **full-bodied:** bland, dull ≠ **vivid:** dull, insipid, weak ≠ **resonant:** high-pitched

riches *pl n* = **wealth**, abundance, affluence, assets, fortune, gold, money, opulence, plenty, property, resources, richness, substance, treasure
Antonyms *pl n* dearth, indigence, lack, need, paucity, poverty, scantiness, scarcity, want

richly *adv* **1** = **elaborately**, elegantly, expensively, exquisitely, gorgeously, lavishly, luxuriously, opulently, palatially, splendidly,

richness ('rɪtʃnɪs) *n* **1** the state or quality of being rich. **2** *Ecology.* the number of individuals of a species in a given area.

Richter scale ('rɪxtə) *n* a scale for expressing the magnitude of an earthquake, ranging from 0 to over 8. [C20: after Charles *Richter* (1900–85), US seismologist]

rick[1] (rɪk) *n* **1** a large stack of hay, corn, etc., built in a regular-shaped pile, esp. with a thatched top. ◆ *vb* **2** (*tr*) to stack into ricks. [OE *hrēac*]

rick[2] (rɪk) *n* **1** a wrench or sprain, as of the back. ◆ *vb* **2** (*tr*) to wrench or sprain (a joint, a limb, the back, etc.). [C18: var. of *wrick*]

rickets ('rɪkɪts) *n* (*functioning as sing or pl*) a disease mainly of children, characterized by softening of developing bone, and hence bow legs, caused by a deficiency of vitamin D. [C17: from ?]

rickettsia (rɪ'kɛtsɪə) *n, pl* **rickettsiae** (-sɪ,iː) *or* **rickettsias.** any of a group of parasitic microorganisms, that live in the tissues of ticks, mites, etc., and cause disease when transmitted to man. [C20: after Howard T. *Ricketts* (1871–1910), US pathologist]
▸**rick'ettsial** *adj*

rickettsial disease *n* any of several acute infectious diseases, such as typhus, caused by ticks, mites, or body lice infected with rickettsiae.

rickety ❶ ('rɪkɪtɪ) *adj* **1** (of a structure, piece of furniture, etc.) likely to collapse or break. **2** feeble. **3** resembling or afflicted with rickets. [C17: from RICKETS]
▸**'ricketiness** *n*

rickrack *or* **ricrac** ('rɪk,ræk) *n* a zigzag braid used for trimming. [C20: reduplication of RACK[1]]

rickshaw ('rɪkʃɔː) *or* **ricksha** ('rɪkʃə) *n* **1** Also called: **jinrikisha.** a small two-wheeled passenger vehicle drawn by one or two men, used in parts of Asia. **2** Also called: **trishaw.** a similar vehicle with three wheels, propelled by a man pedalling as on a tricycle. [C19: shortened from JINRIKISHA]

ricochet ('rɪkə,ʃeɪ, 'rɪkə,ʃɛt) *vb* **ricochets** (-,ʃeɪz), **ricocheting** (-,ʃeɪɪŋ), **ricocheted** (-,ʃeɪd) *or* **ricochets** (-,ʃɛtz), **ricochetting** (-,ʃɛtɪŋ), **ricochetted** (-,ʃɛtɪd). **1** (*intr*) (esp. of a bullet) to rebound from a surface, usually with a whining or zipping sound. ◆ *n* **2** the motion or sound of a rebounding object, esp. a bullet. **3** an object that ricochets. [C18: from F]

ricotta (rɪ'kɒtə) *n* a soft white unsalted cheese made from sheep's milk. [It., from L *recocta* recooked, from *recoquere*, from RE- + *coquere* to COOK]

RICS *abbrev. for* Royal Institution of Chartered Surveyors.

rictus ('rɪktəs) *n, pl* **rictus** *or* **rictuses. 1.** the gap or cleft of an open mouth or beak. **2** a fixed or unnatural grin or grimace as in horror or death. [C18: from L, from *ringī* to gape]
▸**'rictal** *adj*

rid ❶ (rɪd) *vb* **rids, ridding, rid** *or* **ridded.** (*tr*) **1** (foll. by *of*) to relieve from something disagreeable or undesirable; make free (of). **2 get rid of.** to relieve or free oneself of (something unpleasant or undesirable). [C13 (meaning: to clear land): from ON *rythja*]

riddance ('rɪdᵊns) *n* the act of getting rid of something; removal (esp. in **good riddance**).

ridden ('rɪdᵊn) *vb* **1** the past participle of **ride.** ◆ *adj* **2** (*in combination*) afflicted or dominated by something specified: *disease-ridden.*

riddle[1] ❶ ('rɪdᵊl) *n* **1** a question, puzzle, or verse so phrased that ingenuity is required for elucidation of the answer or meaning. **2** a person or thing that puzzles, perplexes, or confuses. ◆ *vb* **riddles, riddling, riddled. 3** to solve, explain, or interpret (a riddle). **4** (*intr*) to speak in riddles. [OE *rǣdelle, rǣdelse,* from *rǣd* counsel]
▸**'riddler** *n*

riddle[2] ❶ ('rɪdᵊl) *vb* **riddles, riddling, riddled.** (*tr*) **1** (usually foll. by *with*) to pierce or perforate with numerous holes: *riddled with bullets.* **2** to put through a sieve; sift. ◆ *n* **3** a sieve, esp. a coarse one used for sand, grain, etc. [OE *hriddel* a sieve]
▸**'riddler** *n*

ride ❶ (raɪd) *vb* **rides, riding, rode, ridden. 1** to sit on and control the movements of (a horse or other animal). **2** (*tr*) to sit on and propel (a bicycle or similar vehicle). **3** (*intr;* often foll. by *on* or *in*) to be carried along or travel on or in a vehicle: *she rides to work on the bus.* **4** (*tr*) to travel over or traverse: *they rode the countryside in search of shelter.* **5** (*tr*) to take part in by riding: *to ride a race.* **6** to travel through or be carried across (sea, sky, etc.): *the small boat rode the waves; the moon was riding high.* **7** (*tr*) *US & Canad.* to cause to be carried: *to ride someone out of town.* **8** (*intr*) to be supported as if floating: *the candidate rode to victory on his new policies.* **9** (*intr*) (of a vessel) to lie at anchor. **10** (*tr*) (of a vessel) to be attached to (an anchor). **11** (*tr*) **11a** *Sl.* to have sexual intercourse with (someone). **11b** (of a male animal) to copulate with; mount. **12** (*tr; usually passive*) to tyrannize over or dominate: *ridden by fear.* **13** (*tr*) *Inf.* to persecute, esp. by constant or petty criticism: *don't ride me so hard.* **14** (*intr*) *Inf.* to continue undisturbed: *let it ride.* **15** (*tr*) to endure successfully; ride out. **16** (*tr*) to yield slightly to (a punch, etc.) to lessen its impact. **17** (*intr;* often foll. by *on*) (of a bet) to remain placed: *let your winnings ride on the same number.* **18 ride again.** *Inf.* to return to a former activity or scene. **19 ride for a fall.** to act in such a way as to invite disaster. **20 riding high.** confident, popular, and successful. ◆ *n* **21** a journey or outing on horseback or in a vehicle. **22** a path specially made for riding on horseback. **23** transport in a vehicle; lift: *can you give me a ride to the station?* **24** a device or structure, such as a roller coaster at a fairground, in which people ride for pleasure or entertainment. **25** *Sl.* an act of sexual intercourse. **26** *Sl.* a partner in sexual intercourse. **27 take for a ride.** *Inf.* **27a** to cheat, swindle, or deceive. **27b** to take (someone) away in a car and murder him. [OE *rīdan*]
▸**'ridable** *or* **'rideable** *adj*

ride out *vb* (*tr, adv*) to endure successfully; survive (esp. in **ride out the storm**).

rider ('raɪdə) *n* **1** a person or thing that rides. **2** an additional clause, amendment, or stipulation added to a document, esp. (in Britain) a legislative bill at its third reading. **3** *Brit.* a statement made by a jury in addition to its verdict, such as a recommendation for mercy. **4** any of various objects or devices resting on or strengthening something else.
▸**'riderless** *adj*

ride up *vb* (*intr, adv*) to work away from the proper position: *her new skirt rode up.*

ridge (rɪdʒ) *n* **1** a long narrow raised land formation with sloping sides. **2** any long narrow raised strip or elevation, as on a fabric or in ploughed land. **3** *Anat.* any elongated raised margin or border on a bone, tissue, etc. **4a** the top of a roof at the junction of two sloping sides. **4b** (*as modifier*): *a ridge tile.* **5** *Meteorol.* an elongated area of high pressure, esp. an extension of an anticyclone. Cf. **trough** (sense 4). ◆ *vb* **ridges, ridging, ridged. 6** to form into a ridge or ridges. [OE *hrycg*]
▸**'ridge,like** *adj* ▸**'ridgy** *adj*

ridgepole ('rɪdʒ,pəʊl) *n* **1** a timber along the ridge of a roof, to which the rafters are attached. **2** the horizontal pole at the apex of a tent.

ridgeway ('rɪdʒ,weɪ) *n Brit.* a road or track along a ridge, esp. one of great antiquity.

ridicule ❶ ('rɪdɪ,kjuːl) *n* **1** language or behaviour intended to humiliate or mock. ◆ *vb* **ridicules, ridiculing, ridiculed. 2** (*tr*) to make fun of or mock. [C17: from F, from L *rīdiculus,* from *rīdēre* to laugh]

ridiculous ❶ (rɪ'dɪkjʊləs) *adj* worthy of or exciting ridicule; absurd, preposterous, laughable, or contemptible. [C16: from L *rīdiculōsus,* from *rīdēre* to laugh]
▸**ri'diculousness** *n*

riding[1] ('raɪdɪŋ) *n* **1a** the art or practice of horsemanship. **1b** (*as modifier*): *a riding school.* **2** a track for riding.

riding[2] ('raɪdɪŋ) *n* (*cap. when part of a name*) any of the three former administrative divisions of Yorkshire: **North Riding, East Riding,** and **West Riding.** [from OE *thriding,* from ON *thrithjungr* a third]

riding crop *n* a short whip with a handle at one end for opening gates.

riding lamp *or* **light** *n* a light on a boat or ship showing that it is at anchor.

riempie ('rɪmpɪ) *n S. African.* a leather thong or lace used mainly to make chair seats. [C19: Afrik., dim. of *riem,* from Du.: RIM]

riesling ('riːzlɪŋ, 'raɪz-) *n* **1** a white wine from the Rhine valley in Germany and from certain districts in other countries. **2** the grape used to make this wine. [C19: from G, from earlier *Rüssling,* from ?]

rife ❶ (raɪf) *adj* (*postpositive*) **1** of widespread occurrence; current. **2** very plentiful; abundant. **3** (foll. by *with*) abounding (in): *a garden rife with weeds.* [OE *rīfe*]
▸**'rifely** *adv* ▸**'rifeness** *n*

riff (rɪf) *Jazz, rock.* ◆ *n* **1** an ostinato played over changing harmonies. ◆ *vb* **2** (*intr*) to play riffs. [C20: prob. altered from REFRAIN[2]]

riffle ('rɪfᵊl) *vb* **riffles, riffling, riffled. 1** (when *intr,* often foll. by *through*) to flick rapidly through (pages of a book, etc.). **2** to shuffle (cards) by

THESAURUS

sumptuously **2** = **fully**, amply, appropriately, in full measure, properly, suitably, thoroughly, well

rickety *adj* **1** = **shaky**, broken, broken-down, decrepit, derelict, dilapidated, imperfect, infirm, insecure, jerry-built, precarious, ramshackle, tottering, unsound, unsteady, wobbly **2** = **feeble**, flimsy, frail, weak

rid *vb* **1** = **free**, clear, deliver, disabuse, disburden, disembarrass, disencumber, lighten, make free, purge, relieve, unburden **2 get rid of** = **dispose of**, dispense with, do away with, dump, eject, eliminate, expel, give the bum's rush (*sl.*), jettison, remove, see the back of, shake off, throw away *or* out, unload, weed out, wipe from the face of the earth

riddle[1] *n* **1** = **puzzle**, brain-teaser (*inf.*), Chinese puzzle, conundrum, enigma, mystery, poser, problem, rebus, teaser

riddle[2] *vb* **1** = **pierce**, honeycomb, pepper, perforate, puncture **2** = **sieve**, bolt, filter, screen, sift, strain, winnow ◆ *n* **3** = **sieve**, filter, screen, strainer

riddled *adj* **1** = **filled**, corrupted, damaged, impaired, infested, marred, permeated, pervaded, spoilt

ride *vb* **1, 2** = **control**, handle, manage, sit on **3** = **travel**, be borne, be carried, be supported, float, go, journey, move, progress, sit **12** = **dominate**, enslave, grip, haunt, oppress, tyrannize over ◆ *n* **21** = **journey**, drive, jaunt, lift, outing, spin (*inf.*), trip, whirl (*inf.*)

ridicule *n* **1** = **mockery**, banter, chaff, derision, gibe, irony, jeer, laughter, raillery, rib, sarcasm, satire, scorn, sneer, taunting ◆ *vb* **2** = **laugh at**, banter, caricature, chaff, deride, humiliate, jeer, lampoon, laugh out of court, laugh to scorn, make a fool of, make a monkey out of, make fun of, make one a laughing stock, mock, parody, poke fun at, pooh-pooh, satirize, scoff, send up (*Brit. inf.*), sneer, take the mickey out of (*inf.*), taunt

ridiculous *adj* = **laughable**, absurd, comical, contemptible, derisory, farcical, foolish, funny, hilarious, inane, incredible, ludicrous, nonsensical, outrageous, preposterous, risible, silly, stupid, unbelievable, zany
Antonyms *adj* bright, clever, intelligent, logical, prudent, rational, reasonable, sagacious, sane, sensible, serious, smart, solemn, well-thought-out, wise

rife *adj* **1** = **widespread**, common, current, epidemic, frequent, general, prevailing, prevalent, raging, ubiquitous, universal **2** = **abundant**, plentiful, rampant, teeming

halving the pack and flicking the corners together. **3** to cause or form a ripple on water. ◆ *n* **4** *US & Canad.* **4a** a rapid in a stream. **4b** a rocky shoal causing a rapid. **4c** a ripple on water. **5** *Mining.* a contrivance on the bottom of a sluice, containing grooves for trapping particles of gold. **6** the act or an instance of riffling. [C18: prob. from RUFFLE[1], infl. by RIPPLE[1]]

riffraff ❶ ('rɪf,ræf) *n* (*sometimes functioning as pl*) worthless people, esp. collectively; rabble. [C15 *rif and raf,* from OF *rif et raf;* rel. to *rifler* to plunder, and *rafle* a sweeping up]

rifle[1] ('raɪf°l) *n* **1a** a firearm having a long barrel with a spirally grooved interior, which imparts to the bullet spinning motion and thus greater accuracy over a longer range. **1b** (*as modifier*): *rifle fire.* **2** (formerly) a large cannon with a rifled bore. **3** one of the grooves in a rifled bore. **4** (*pl*) **4a** a unit of soldiers equipped with rifles. **4b** (*cap. when part of a name*): *the King's Own Rifles.* ◆ *vb* **rifles, rifling, rifled.** (*tr*) **5** to make spiral grooves inside the barrel of (a gun). [C18: from OF *rifler* to scratch; rel. to Low G *rifeln* from *riefe* groove]

rifle[2] ❶ ('raɪf°l) *vb* **rifles, rifling, rifled.** (*tr*) **1** to search (a house, safe, etc.) and steal from it; ransack. **2** to steal and carry off: *to rifle goods.* [C14: from OF *rifler* to plunder, scratch, of Gmc origin]
▸ **'rifler** *n*

riflebird ('raɪf°l,bɜːd) *n* any of various Australian birds of paradise whose plumage has a metallic sheen.

rifleman ('raɪf°lmən) *n, pl* **riflemen. 1** a person skilled in the use of a rifle, esp. a soldier. **2** a wren of New Zealand.

rifle range *n* an area used for target practice with rifles.

rifling ('raɪflɪŋ) *n* **1** the cutting of spiral grooves on the inside of a firearm's barrel. **2** the series of grooves so cut.

rift ❶ (rɪft) *n* **1** a gap or space made by cleaving or splitting. **2** *Geol.* a fault produced by tension on either side of the fault plane. **3** a gap between two cloud masses; break or chink. **4** a break in friendly relations between people, nations, etc. ◆ *vb* **5** to burst or cause to burst open; split. [C13: from ON]

rift valley *n* a long narrow valley resulting from the subsidence of land between two faults.

rig ❶ (rɪg) *vb* **rigs, rigging, rigged.** (*tr*) **1** *Naut.* to equip (a vessel, mast, etc.) with (sails, rigging, etc.). **2** *Naut.* to set up or prepare ready for use. **3** to put the components of (an aircraft, etc.) into their correct positions. **4** to manipulate in a fraudulent manner, esp. for profit: *to rig prices.* ◆ *n* **5** *Naut.* the distinctive arrangement of the sails, masts, etc., of a vessel. **6** the installation used in drilling for and exploiting natural gas and oil deposits: *an oil rig.* **7** apparatus or equipment. **8** *US & Canad.* an articulated lorry. ◆ See also **rig out, rig up.** [C15: of Scand. origin; rel. to Norwegian *rigga* to wrap]

rigadoon (,rɪgə'duːn) *n* **1** an old Provençal couple dance, light and graceful, in lively duple time. **2** a piece of music composed for or in the rhythm of this dance. [C17: from F, allegedly after *Rigaud,* a dancing master at Marseilles]

rigamarole ('rɪgəmə,rəʊl) *n* a variant of **rigmarole.**

-rigged *adj* (*in combination*) (of a sailing vessel) having a rig of a certain kind: *ketch-rigged; schooner-rigged.*

rigger ('rɪgə) *n* **1** a workman who rigs vessels, etc. **2** *Rowing.* a bracket on a boat to support a projecting rowlock. **3** a person skilled in the use of pulleys, cranes, etc.

rigging ('rɪgɪŋ) *n* **1** the shrouds, stays, etc., of a vessel. **2** the bracing wires, struts, and lines of a biplane, etc. **3** any form of lifting gear.

right ❶ (raɪt) *adj* **1** in accordance with accepted standards of moral or legal behaviour, justice, etc.: *right conduct.* **2** correct or true: *the right answer.* **3** appropriate, suitable, or proper: *the right man for the job.* **4** most favourable or convenient: *the right time to act.* **5** in a satisfactory condition: *things are right again now.* **6** indicating or designating the correct time: *the clock is right.* **7** correct in opinion or judgment. **8** sound in mind or body. **9** (*usually prenominal*) of, designating, or located near the side of something or someone that faces east when the front is turned towards the north. **10** (*usually prenominal*) worn on a right hand, foot, etc. **11** (*sometimes cap.*) of, designating, belonging to, or relating to the political or intellectual right (see sense 36). **12** (*sometimes cap.*) conservative: *the right wing of the party.* **13** *Geom.* **13a** formed by or containing a line or plane perpendicular to another line or plane. **13b** having the axis perpendicular to the base: *a right circular cone.* **13c** straight: *a right line.* **14** relating to or designating the side of cloth worn or facing outwards. **15 in one's right mind.** sane. **16 she'll be right.** *Austral. & NZ inf.* that's all right; not to worry. **17 the right side of. 17a** in favour with: *you'd better stay on the right side of him.* **17b** younger than: *she's still on the right side of fifty.* **18 too right.** *Austral. & NZ inf.* an exclamation of agreement. ◆ *adv* **19** in accordance with correctness or truth: *to guess right.* **20** in the appropriate manner: *do it right next time!* **21** in a straight line: *right to the top.* **22** in the direction of the east from the point of view of a person or thing facing north. **23** absolutely or completely: *he went right through the floor.* **24** all the way: *the bus goes right into town.* **25** without delay: *I'll be right over.* **26** exactly or precisely: *right here.* **27** in a manner consistent with a legal or moral code: *do right by me.* **28** in accordance with propriety; fittingly: *it serves you right.* **29** to good or favourable advantage: *it all came out right in the end.* **30** (esp. in religious titles) most or very: *right reverend.* **31 right, left, and centre.** on all sides. ◆ *n* **32** any claim, title, etc., that is morally just or legally granted as allowable or due to a person: *I know my rights.* **33** anything that accords with the principles of legal or moral justice. **34** the fact or state of being in accordance with reason, truth, or accepted standards (esp. in **in the right**) **35** the right side, direction, position, area, or part: *the right of the army.* **36** (*often cap.* and preceded by *the*) the supporters or advocates of social, political, or economic conservatism or reaction. **37** *Boxing.* **37a** a punch with the right hand. **37b** the right hand. **38** (*often pl*) *Finance.* the privilege of a company's shareholders to subscribe for new issues of the company's shares on advantageous terms. **39 by right** (*or* **rights**). properly: *by rights you should be in bed.* **40 in one's own right.** having a claim or title oneself rather than through marriage or other connection. **41 to rights.** consistent with justice or orderly arrangement: *he put the matter to rights.* ◆ *vb* (*mainly tr*) **42** (*also intr*) to restore to or attain a normal, esp. an upright, position: *the raft righted in a few seconds.* **43** to make (something) accord with truth or facts. **44** to restore to an orderly state or condition. **45** to compensate for or redress (esp. in **right a wrong**). ◆ *interj* **46** an expression of agreement or compliance. [OE *riht, reoht*]
▸ **'rightable** *adj* ▸ **'righter** *n* ▸ **'rightness** *n*

right about *n* **1** a turn executed through 180°. ◆ *adj, adv* **2** in the opposite direction.

right angle *n* **1** the angle between radii of a circle that cut off on the circumference an arc equal in length to one quarter of the circumference; an angle of 90° or $\pi/2$ radians. **2 at right angles.** perpendicular or perpendicularly.
▸ **'right-,angled** *adj*

right-angled triangle *n* a triangle one angle of which is a right angle. US and Canad. name: **right triangle.**

right ascension *n Astron.* the angular distance measured eastwards along the celestial equator from the vernal equinox to the point at which the celestial equator intersects a great circle passing through the celestial pole and the heavenly object in question.

right away ❶ *adv* without delay.

righteous ❶ ('raɪtʃəs) *adj* **1a** characterized by, proceeding from, or in accordance with accepted standards of morality or uprightness: *a righteous man.* **1b** (*as collective n;* preceded by *the*): *the righteous.* **2** mor-

THESAURUS

riffraff *n* = **rabble**, *canaille,* dregs of society, hoi polloi, ragtag and bobtail, scum, undesirables

rifle[2] *vb* **1** = **ransack**, burgle, despoil, go through, gut, loot, pillage, plunder, rob, rummage, sack, strip

rift *n* **1** = **split**, breach, break, chink, cleavage, cleft, crack, cranny, crevice, fault, fissure, flaw, fracture, gap, opening, space **4** = **breach**, alienation, difference, disagreement, division, estrangement, falling out (*inf.*), quarrel, schism, separation, split

rig *vb* **1** *Nautical* = **equip**, accoutre, fit out, furnish, kit out, outfit, provision, supply, turn out **4** = **fix** (*inf.*), arrange, doctor, engineer, fake, falsify, fiddle with (*inf.*), gerrymander, juggle, manipulate, tamper with, trump up ◆ *n* **7** = **apparatus**, accoutrements, equipage, equipment, fitments, fittings, fixtures, gear, machinery, outfit, tackle

right *adj* **1** = **just**, equitable, ethical, fair, good, honest, honourable, lawful, moral, proper, righteous, true, upright, virtuous **2** = **correct**, accurate, admissible, authentic, exact, factual, genuine, on the money (*US*), precise, satisfactory, sound, spot-on (*Brit. inf.*), true, unerring, valid, veracious **3** = **proper**, appropriate, becoming, *comme il faut,* desirable, done, fit, fitting, seemly, suitable **4** = **favourable**, advantageous, convenient, deserved, due, ideal, opportune, propitious, rightful **8** = **healthy**, all there (*inf.*), balanced, *compos mentis,* fine, fit, in good health, in the pink, lucid, normal, rational, reasonable, sane, sound, unimpaired, up to par, well **11, 12** = **conservative**, reactionary, Tory ◆ *adv* **19** = **correctly**, accurately, aright, exactly, factually, genuinely, precisely, truly **20** = **suitably**, appropriately, aptly, befittingly, fittingly, properly, satisfactorily **23** = **completely**, absolutely, altogether, entirely, perfectly, quite, thoroughly, totally, utterly, wholly **25** = **straight**, directly, immediately, instantly, promptly, quickly, straightaway, without delay **26** = **exactly**, bang, precisely, slap-bang (*inf.*), squarely **27** = **fairly**, ethically, honestly, honourably, justly, morally, righteously, virtuously **28** = **properly**, fittingly **29** = **favourably**, advantageously, beneficially, for the better, fortunately, to advantage, well ◆ *n* **32** = **prerogative**, authority, business, claim, due, freedom, interest, liberty, licence, permission, power, privilege, title **33, 34** = **justice**, equity, fairness, good, goodness, honour, integrity, lawfulness, legality, morality, propriety, reason, rectitude, righteousness, truth, uprightness, virtue **39 by right** *or* **rights** = **in fairness**, equitably, justly, properly **41 to rights** = **in order**, arranged, straight, tidy ◆ *vb* **45** = **rectify**, compensate for, correct, fix, put right, redress, repair, settle, sort out, straighten, vindicate

Antonyms *adj* ≠ **just:** bad, dishonest, immoral, improper, indecent, unethical, unfair, unjust, wrong ≠ **correct:** counterfeit, erroneous, fake, false, fraudulent, illegal, illicit, inaccurate, incorrect, inexact, invalid, mistaken, questionable, uncertain, unlawful, untruthful, wrong ≠ **proper:** inappropriate, undesirable, unfitting, unseemly, unsuitable, wrong ≠ **favourable:** disadvantageous, inconvenient, unfavourable ≠ **healthy:** abnormal, unsound ≠ **conservative:** left, leftist, left-wing, liberal, radical, right-on (*inf.*), socialist ◆ *adv* ≠ **correctly:** inaccurately, incorrectly ≠ **completely:** improperly, incompletely ≠ **straight:** indirectly, slowly ≠ **favourably:** badly, poorly, unfavourably ◆ *n* ≠ **justice:** badness, dishonour, evil, immorality, impropriety

right away *adv* = **immediately**, at once, directly, forthwith, instantly, now, posthaste, promptly, pronto (*inf.*), right off, straightaway, straight off (*inf.*), this instant, without delay, without hesitation

righteous *adj* **1** = **virtuous**, blameless, equitable, ethical, fair, good, honest, honourable,

ally justifiable or right: *righteous indignation.* [OE *rihtwīs,* from RIGHT + WISE[2]]
▸'**righteously** *adv* ▸'**righteousness** *n*

rightful ➊ ('raɪtful) *adj* **1** in accordance with what is right. **2** (*prenominal*) having a legally or morally just claim: *the rightful owner.* **3** (*prenominal*) held by virtue of a legal or just claim: *my rightful property.*
▸'**rightfully** *adv*

right-hand *adj* (*prenominal*) **1** of, located on, or moving towards the right: *a right-hand bend.* **2** for use by the right hand. **3 right-hand man.** one's most valuable assistant.

right-handed *adj* **1** using the right hand with greater skill or ease than the left. **2** performed with the right hand. **3** made for use by the right hand. **4** turning from left to right.
▸,**right-'handedness** *n*

rightist ('raɪtɪst) *adj* **1** of, tending towards, or relating to the political right or its principles. ◆ *n* **2** a person who supports or belongs to the political right.
▸'**rightism** *n*

rightly ('raɪtlɪ) *adv* **1** in accordance with the true facts. **2** in accordance with principles of justice or morality. **3** with good reason: *he was rightly annoyed with her.* **4** properly or suitably. **5** (*used with a negative*) *Inf.* with certainty (usually in **I don't rightly know**).

right-minded *adj* holding opinions or principles that accord with what is right or with the opinions of the speaker.

righto *or* **right oh** (ˈraɪtˈəʊ) *sentence substitute. Brit. inf.* an expression of agreement or compliance.

right off *adv* immediately; right away.

right of way *n, pl* **rights of way. 1** the right of one vehicle or vessel to take precedence over another, as laid down by law or custom. **2a** the legal right of someone to pass over another's land, acquired by grant or by long usage. **2b** the path used by this right. **3** *US.* the strip of land over which a power line, road, etc., extends.

right-on *adj Inf.* modern, trendy, and socially aware or relevant: *right-on green politics.*

Right Reverend *adj* (in Britain) a title of respect for an Anglican or Roman Catholic bishop.

rights issue *n Stock Exchange.* an issue of new shares offered by a company to its existing shareholders on favourable terms.

rightsize ('raɪt,saɪz) *vb* to restructure (an organization) to cut costs and improve effectiveness without ruthlessly downsizing.

right-thinking ('raɪt,θɪŋkɪŋ) *adj* possessing reasonable and generally acceptable opinions.

rightward ('raɪtwəd) *adj* **1** situated on or directed towards the right. ◆ *adv* **2** a variant of **rightwards.**

rightwards ('raɪtwədz) *or* **rightward** *adv* towards or on the right.

right whale *n* a large whalebone whale which is grey or black, has a large head and no dorsal fin, and is hunted as a source of whalebone and oil. See also **bowhead.** [C19: ? because it was *right* for hunting]

right wing *n* **1** (*often cap.*) the conservative faction of an assembly, party, etc. **2** the part of an army or field of battle on the right from the point of view of one facing the enemy. **3a** the right-hand side of the field of play from the point of view of a team facing its opponent's goal. **3b** a player positioned in this area in any of various games. ◆ *adj* **right-wing. 4** of, belonging to, or relating to the right wing.
▸,**right-'winger** *n*

rigid ➊ ('rɪdʒɪd) *adj* **1** physically inflexible or stiff: *a rigid piece of plastic.* **2** rigorously strict: *rigid rules.* [C16: from L *rigidus,* from *rigēre* to be stiff]
▸**ri'gidity** *n* ▸'**rigidly** *adv*

rigidify (rɪ'dʒɪdɪ,faɪ) *vb* **rigidifies, rigidifying, rigidified.** to make or become rigid.

rigmarole ➊ ('rɪgmə,rəʊl) *or* **rigamarole** *n* **1** any long complicated procedure. **2** a set of incoherent or pointless statements. [C18: from earlier *ragman roll* a list, prob. a roll used in a medieval game, wherein characters were described in verse, beginning with *Ragemon le bon* Ragman the good]

rigor ('raɪgɔː, 'rɪgə) *n* **1** *Med.* a sudden feeling of chilliness, often accompanied by shivering: it sometimes precedes a fever. **2** ('rɪgə). *Pathol.* rigidity of a muscle. **3** a state of rigidity assumed in reaction to shock. [see RIGOUR]

rigor mortis ('rɪgə 'mɔːtɪs) *n Pathol.* the stiffness of joints and muscular rigidity of a dead body. [C19: L, lit.: rigidity of death]

rigorous ➊ ('rɪgərəs) *adj* **1** harsh, strict, or severe: *rigorous discipline.* **2** severely accurate: *rigorous book-keeping.* **3** (esp. of weather) extreme or harsh. **4** *Maths, logic.* (of a proof) making the validity of each step explicit.
▸'**rigorously** *adv*

rigour ➊ *or US* **rigor** ('rɪgə) *n* **1** harsh but just treatment or action. **2** a severe or cruel circumstance: *the rigours of famine.* **3** strictness, harshness, or severity of character. **4** strictness in judgment or conduct. [C14: from L *rigor*]

rig out ➊ *vb* **1** (*tr, adv;* often foll. by *with*) to equip or fit out (with): *his car is rigged out with gadgets.* **2** to dress or be dressed: *rigged out smartly.* ◆ *n* **rigout. 3** *Inf.* a person's clothing or costume, esp. a bizarre outfit.

rig up ➊ *vb* (*tr, adv*) to erect or construct, esp. as a temporary measure: *cameras were rigged up.*

Rig-Veda (rɪg'veɪdə) *n* a compilation of Hindu poems dating from 2000 B.C. or earlier. [C18: from Sansk. *rigveda,* from *ric* song of praise + VEDA]

rile ➊ (raɪl) *vb* **riles, riling, riled.** (*tr*) **1** to annoy or anger. **2** *US & Canad.* to agitate (water, etc.). [C19: var. of ROIL]

rill (rɪl) *n* **1** a brook or stream. **2** a channel or gulley, such as one formed during soil erosion. **3** Also: **rille.** one of many winding cracks on the moon. [C15: from Low G *rille*]

rim ➊ (rɪm) *n* **1** the raised edge of an object, esp. of something more or less circular such as a cup or crater. **2** the peripheral part of a wheel, to which the tyre is attached. **3** *Basketball.* the hoop from which the net is suspended. ◆ *vb* **rims, rimming, rimmed.** (*tr*) **4** to put a rim on (a pot, cup, wheel, etc.). **5** *Sl.* to lick, kiss, or suck the anus of (one's sexual partner). [OE *rima*]

rime[1] (raɪm) *n* **1** frost formed by the freezing of water droplets in fog onto solid objects. ◆ *vb* **rimes, riming, rimed. 2** (*tr*) to cover with rime or something resembling rime. [OE *hrīm*]

rime[2] (raɪm) *n, vb* **rimes, riming, rimed.** an archaic spelling of **rhyme.**

rim-fire *adj* **1** (of a cartridge) having the primer in the rim of the base. **2** (of a firearm) adapted for such cartridges.

rimose (raɪ'məʊs, -'məʊz) *adj* (esp. of plant parts) having the surface marked by a network of cracks. [C18: from L *rīmōsus,* from *rīma* a split]

rimu ('riːmuː) *n* a New Zealand tree. Also called: **red pine.** [from Maori]

rimy ('raɪmɪ) *adj* **rimier, rimiest.** coated with rime.

rind ➊ (raɪnd) *n* **1** a hard outer layer or skin on bacon, cheese, etc. **2** the outer layer of a fruit or of the spore-producing body of certain fungi. **3** the outer layer of the bark of a tree. [OE *rinde*]

rinderpest ('rɪndə,pest) *n* an acute contagious viral disease of cattle, characterized by severe inflammation of the intestinal tract and diarrhoea. [C19: from G *Rinderpest* cattle pest]

ring[1] ➊ (rɪŋ) *n* **1** a circular band of a precious metal often set with gems and worn upon the finger as an adornment or as a token of engage-

THESAURUS

just, law-abiding, moral, pure, squeaky-clean, upright
Antonyms *adj* bad, corrupt, dishonest, dishonourable, evil, false, guilty, immoral, improper, indecent, insincere, sinful, unethical, unfair, unjust, unprincipled, unrighteous, unscrupulous, unseemly, wicked

righteousness *n* **1 = virtue**, blamelessness, equity, ethicalness, faithfulness, goodness, honesty, honour, integrity, justice, morality, probity, purity, rectitude, uprightness

rightful *adj* **1 = just**, due, proper, suitable **2, 3 = lawful**, authorized, bona fide, de jure, legal, legitimate, real, true, valid

rigid *adj* **1 = stiff**, inelastic, inflexible, unyielding **2 = strict**, adamant, austere, exact, fixed, harsh, inflexible, intransigent, invariable, rigorous, set, severe, stern, stringent, unalterable, unbending, uncompromising, undeviating, unrelenting, unyielding
Antonyms *adj* ≠ **stiff**: bending, elastic, flexible, limber, lissom(e), mobile, pliable, pliant, soft, supple, yielding ≠ **strict**: flexible, indulgent, lax, lenient, merciful, soft, tolerant

rigmarole *n* **1 = procedure**, bother, carry-on (*inf., chiefly Brit.*), fuss, hassle (*inf.*), nonsense, palaver, pantomime (*inf.*), performance (*inf.*), red tape, to-do **2 = twaddle**, balderdash, gibberish, jargon, trash

rigorous *adj* **1 = strict**, austere, challenging, demanding, exacting, firm, hard, harsh, inflexible, rigid, severe, stern, stringent, tough **2 = thorough**, accurate, conscientious, exact, meticulous, nice, painstaking, precise, punctilious, scrupulous
Antonyms *adj* ≠ **strict**: easy, flexible, friendly, genial, gentle, humane, indulgent, kind, lax, lenient, loose, mild, permissive, relaxed, soft, sympathetic, tolerant, weak ≠ **thorough**: careless, half-hearted, haphazard, imperfect, inaccurate, incorrect, inexact, loose, negligent, slapdash, sloppy, slovenly, unscrupulous

rigour *n* **2 = hardship**, ordeal, privation, suffering, trial **3 = strictness**, asperity, austerity, firmness, hardness, harshness, inflexibility, rigidity, sternness, stringency **4 = thoroughness**, accuracy, conscientiousness, exactitude, exactness, meticulousness, preciseness, precision, punctiliousness

rig out *vb* **1 = dress**, array, attire, clothe, costume, kit out **2 = equip**, accoutre, fit, furnish, kit out, outfit, set up ◆ *n* **rigout 3** *Informal* **= outfit**, apparel, clobber, clothing, costume, dress, garb, gear (*inf.*), get-up (*inf.*), habit, raiment (*arch. or poetic*), togs

rig up *vb* **= set up**, arrange, assemble, build, cobble together, construct, erect, fix up, improvise, put together, put up, throw together

rile *vb* **1 = anger**, aggravate (*inf.*), annoy, bug (*inf.*), gall, get *or* put one's back up, get one's goat (*sl.*), get on one's nerves (*inf.*), get under one's skin (*inf.*), irk, irritate, nark (*Brit., Austral., & NZ sl.*), nettle, peeve (*inf.*), pique, provoke, rub one up the wrong way, try one's patience, upset, vex

rim *n* **1 = edge**, border, brim, brink, circumference, flange, lip, margin, verge

rind *n* **1 = skin**, crust, outer layer, peel **2 = skin**, epicarp, husk, integument

ring[1] *n* **1, 2 = circle**, band, circuit, halo, hoop, loop, round **5 = arena**, circus, enclosure, rink **9 = gang**, association, band, cabal, cartel, cell, circle, clique, combine, coterie, crew (*inf.*), group, junta, knot, mob, organization, syndicate ◆ *vb* **20 = encircle**, circumscribe, enclose, encompass, gird, girdle, hem in, seal off, surround

ment or marriage. **2** any object or mark that is circular in shape. **3** a circular path or course: *to run around in a ring.* **4** a group of people or things standing or arranged so as to form a circle: *a ring of spectators.* **5** an enclosed space, usually circular in shape, where circus acts are performed. **6** a square raised platform, marked off by ropes, in which contestants box or wrestle. **7 the ring.** the sport of boxing. **8 throw one's hat in the ring.** to announce one's intention to be a candidate or contestant. **9** a group of people usually operating illegally and covertly: *a drug ring; a paedophile ring.* **10** (esp. at country fairs) an enclosure where horses, cattle, and other livestock are paraded and auctioned. **11** an area reserved for betting at a racecourse. **12** a circular strip of bark cut from a tree or branch. **13** a single turn in a spiral. **14** *Geom.* the area of space lying between two concentric circles. **15** *Maths.* a set that is subject to two binary operations, addition and multiplication, such that the set is a commutative group under addition and is closed under multiplication, this latter operation being associative. **16** *Bot.* short for **annual ring. 17** *Chem.* a closed loop of atoms in a molecule. **18** *Astron.* any of the thin circular bands of small bodies orbiting a giant planet, esp. Saturn. **19 run rings round.** *Inf.* to outclass completely. ◆ *vb* **rings, ringing, ringed.** (*tr*) **20** to surround with, or as if with, or form a ring. **21** to mark a bird with a ring or clip for subsequent identification. **22** to fit a ring in the nose of (a bull, etc.) so that it can be led easily. **23** to ringbark. [OE *hring*]
▸**ringed** *adj*

ring[2] 🅣 (rɪŋ) *vb* **rings, ringing, rang, rung. 1** to emit or cause to emit a resonant sound, characteristic of certain metals when struck. **2** to cause (a bell, etc.) to emit a ringing sound by striking it once or repeatedly or (of a bell) to emit such a sound. **3a** (*tr*) to cause (a large bell) to emit a ringing sound by pulling on a rope attached to a wheel on which the bell swings back and forth, being sounded by a clapper inside it. **3b** (*intr*) (of a bell) to sound by being swung in this way. **4** (*intr*) (of a building, place, etc.) to be filled with sound: *the church rang with singing.* **5** (*intr;* foll. by *for*) to call by means of a bell, etc.: *to ring for the butler.* **6** Also: **ring up.** *Chiefly Brit.* to call (a person) by telephone. **7** (*tr*) to strike or tap (a coin) in order to assess its genuineness by the sound produced. **8** *Sl.* to change the identity of (a stolen vehicle) by using the licence plate, serial number, etc., of another, usually disused, vehicle. **9** (*intr*) (of the ears) to have or give the sensation of humming or ringing. **10 ring a bell.** to bring something to the mind or memory: *that rings a bell.* **11 ring down the curtain. 11a** to lower the curtain at the end of a theatrical performance. **11b** (foll. by *on*) to put an end (to). **12 ring false.** to give the impression of being false. **13 ring true.** to give the impression of being true. ◆ *n* **14** the act of or a sound made by ringing. **15** a sound produced by or suggestive of a bell. **16** any resonant or metallic sound: *the ring of trumpets.* **17** *Inf., chiefly Brit.* a telephone call. **18** the complete set of bells in a tower or belfry: *a ring of eight bells.* **19** an inherent quality or characteristic: his words had the ring of sincerity. ◆ See also **ring in, ring off,** etc. [OE *hringan*]

> **USAGE NOTE** *Rang* and *sang* are the correct forms of the past tenses of *ring* and *sing,* although *rung* and *sung* are still heard informally and dialectally: *he rung (rang) the bell.*

ringbark (ˈrɪŋˌbɑːk) *vb* (*tr*) to kill (a tree) by cutting away a strip of bark from around the trunk.

ring binder *n* a loose-leaf binder with metal rings that can be opened to insert perforated paper.

ringbolt (ˈrɪŋˌbəʊlt) *n* a bolt with a ring fitted through an eye attached to the bolt head.

ringdove (ˈrɪŋˌdʌv) *n* **1** another name for **wood pigeon. 2** an Old World turtledove, having a black neck band.

ringed plover *n* a European shorebird with a greyish-brown back, white underparts, a black throat band, and orange legs.

ringer (ˈrɪŋə) *n* **1** a person or thing that rings a bell, etc. **2** Also called: **dead ringer.** *Sl.* a person or thing that is almost identical to another. **3** *Sl.* a stolen vehicle the identity of which has been changed by the use of the licence plate, serial number, etc., of another, usually disused, vehicle. **4** *Chiefly US.* a contestant, esp. a horse, entered in a competition under false representations of identity, record, or ability. **5** *Austral.* a stockman; station hand. **6** *Austral.* the fastest shearer in a shed. **7** *Austral. inf.* the fastest or best at anything. **8** a quoit thrown so as to encircle a peg. **9** such a throw.

ring-fence *vb* **1** to assign (money, a grant, fund, etc.) to one particular purpose, so as to restrict its use: *to ring-fence a financial allowance.* **2** to oblige (a person or organization) to use money for a particular purpose: *to ring-fence a local authority.* ◆ *n* **ring fence. 3** an agreement, contract, etc., in which the use of money is restricted to a particular purpose.

ring finger *n* the third finger, esp. of the left hand, on which a wedding ring is worn.

ring in *vb* (*adv*) **1** (*intr*) *Chiefly Brit.* to report to someone by telephone. **2** (*tr*) to accompany the arrival of with bells (esp. in **ring in the new year**). ◆ *n* **ring-in. 3** *Austral. & NZ inf.* a person or thing that is not normally a member of a particular group; outsider.

ringing tone *n Brit.* a sequence of pairs of tones heard by the dialler on a telephone when the number dialled is ringing. Cf. **engaged tone, dialling tone.**

ringleader (ˈrɪŋˌliːdə) *n* a person who leads others in unlawful or mischievous activity.

ringlet (ˈrɪŋlɪt) *n* **1** a lock of hair hanging down in a spiral curl. **2** a butterfly that occurs in S Europe and has dark brown wings marked with small black-and-white eyespots.
▸ˈ**ringleted** *adj*

ring main *n* a domestic electrical supply in which outlet sockets are connected to the mains supply through a continuous closed circuit (**ring circuit**).

ringmaster (ˈrɪŋˌmɑːstə) *n* the master of ceremonies in a circus.

ring-necked *adj* (of animals, esp. birds and snakes) having a band of distinctive colour around the neck.

ring-necked pheasant *n* a common pheasant originating in Asia. The male has a bright plumage with a band of white around the neck and the female is mottled brown.

ring off *vb* (*intr, adv*) *Chiefly Brit.* to terminate a telephone conversation by replacing the receiver; hang up.

ring out *vb* (*adv*) **1** (*tr*) to accompany the departure of with bells (esp. in **ring out the old year**). **2** (*intr*) to send forth a loud resounding noise.

ring ouzel *n* a European thrush common in rocky areas. The male has a blackish plumage and the female is brown.

ring road *n* a main road that bypasses a town or town centre. US names: **belt, beltway.**

ringside (ˈrɪŋˌsaɪd) *n* **1** the row of seats nearest a boxing or wrestling ring. **2a** any place affording a close uninterrupted view. **2b** (*as modifier*): *a ringside seat.*

ringtail (ˈrɪŋˌteɪl) *n Austral.* any of several tree-living phalangers having curling prehensile tails used to grasp branches while climbing.

ring up *vb* (*adv*) **1** *Chiefly Brit.* to make a telephone call (to). **2** (*tr*) to record on a cash register. **3 ring up the curtain. 3a** to begin a theatrical performance. **3b** (often foll. by *on*) to make a start (on).

ringworm (ˈrɪŋˌwɜːm) *n* any of various fungal infections of the skin or nails, often appearing as itching circular patches. Also called: **tinea.**

rink (rɪŋk) *n* **1** an expanse of ice for skating on, esp. one that is artificially prepared and under cover. **2** an area for roller-skating on. **3** a building or enclosure for ice-skating or roller-skating. **4** *Bowls.* a strip of the green on which a game is played. **5** *Curling.* the strip of ice on which the game is played. **6** (in bowls and curling) the players on one side in a game. [C14 (Scots): from OF *renc* row]

rinkhals (ˈrɪŋkˌhæls) *or* **ringhals** (ˈrɪŋgˌhæls) *n, pl* **rinkhals, rinkhalses, ringhals** *or* **ringhalses.** a venomous snake of southern Africa, which can spit venom over 2 m (7 ft). [Afrik., lit.: ring neck]

rink rat *n Canad. sl.* a youth who helps with odd chores around an ice-hockey rink in return for free admission to games, etc.

rinse 🅣 (rɪns) *vb* **rinses, rinsing, rinsed.** (*tr*) **1** to remove soap from (clothes, etc.) by applying clean water in the final stage in washing. **2** to wash lightly, esp. without using soap. **3** to give a light tint to (hair). ◆ *n* **4** the act or an instance of rinsing. **5** *Hairdressing.* a liquid preparation put on the hair when wet to give a tint to it: *a blue rinse.* [C14: from OF *rincer,* from L *recens* fresh]
▸ˈ**rinser** *n*

rioja (rɪˈəʊxə) *n* a red or white wine, with a distinctive vanilla bouquet and flavour, produced around the Ebro river in central N Spain. [C20: from *La Rioja,* the area where it is produced]

riot 🅣 (ˈraɪət) *n* **1a** a disturbance made by an unruly mob or (in law) three or more persons. **1b** (*as modifier*): *a riot shield.* **2** unrestrained revelry. **3** an occasion of boisterous merriment. **4** *Sl.* a person who occasions boisterous merriment. **5** a dazzling display: *a riot of colour.* **6** *Hunting.* the indiscriminate following of any scent by hounds. **7** *Arch.* wanton lasciviousness. **8 run riot. 8a** to behave without restraint. **8b** (of plants) to grow profusely. ◆ *vb* **9** (*intr*) to take part in a riot. **10** (*intr*) to indulge in unrestrained revelry. **11** (*tr;* foll. by *away*) to spend (time or money) in wanton or loose living. [C13: from OF *riote* dispute, from *ruihoter* to quarrel, prob. from *ruir* to make a commotion, from L *rugīre* to roar]
▸ˈ**rioter** *n*

Riot Act *n* **1** *Criminal law.* (formerly, in England) a statute of 1715 by which persons committing a riot had to disperse within an hour of the reading of the act by a magistrate. **2 read the riot act to.** to warn or reprimand severely.

riotous 🅣 (ˈraɪətəs) *adj* **1** proceeding from or of the nature of riots or ri-

THESAURUS

ring[2] *vb* **1-3 = chime,** clang, peal, resonate, resound, reverberate, sound, toll **6 = phone,** buzz, call, telephone ◆ *n* **14, 15 = chime,** knell, peal **17 = call,** buzz, phone call

rinse *vb* **2 = wash,** bathe, clean, cleanse, dip, splash, wash out, wet ◆ *n* **4 = wash,** bath, dip, splash, wetting

riot *n* **1a = disturbance,** anarchy, commotion, confusion, disorder, donnybrook, fray, lawlessness, mob violence, quarrel, row, street fighting, strife, tumult, turbulence, turmoil, upheaval, uproar **2, 3 = merrymaking,** blast (*US sl.*), boisterousness, carousal, excess, festivity, frolic, high jinks, jollification, revelry, romp **5 = display,** extravaganza, flourish, profusion, show, splash **8 run riot: a = grow profusely,** be out of control, break *or* cut loose, go wild, let oneself go, raise hell, throw off all restraint **b** grow like weeds, luxuriate, spread like wildfire ◆ *vb* **9 = rampage,** fight in the streets, go on the rampage, raise an uproar, run riot, take to the streets **10 = make merry,** carouse, cut loose, frolic, go on a binge, go on a spree, paint the town red (*inf.*), revel, roister, romp

riotous *adj* **1 = unruly,** anarchic, disorderly, insubordinate, lawless, mutinous, rampageous, rebellious, refractory, rowdy, tumultuous, ungovernable, violent **2 = unrestrained,** boister-

oting. **2** characterized by wanton revelry: *riotous living.* **3** characterized by unrestrained merriment: *riotous laughter.*
▸ **'riotously** *adv* ▸ **'riotousness** *n*

riot shield *n* (in Britain) a shield used by police controlling crowds.

rip[1] ⓣ (rɪp) *vb* **rips, ripping, ripped. 1** to tear or be torn violently or roughly. **2** (*tr; foll. by off or out*) to remove hastily or roughly. **3** (*intr*) *Inf.* to move violently or precipitously. **4** (*intr; foll. by into*) *Inf.* to pour violent abuse (on). **5** (*tr*) to saw or split (wood) in the direction of the grain. **6 let rip.** to act or speak without restraint. ◆ *n* **7** a tear or split. **8** short for **ripsaw.** ◆ See also **rip off.** [C15: ?from Flemish *rippen*]

rip[2] (rɪp) *n* short for **riptide.** [C18: ?from RIP[1]]

rip[3] (rɪp) *n Inf., arch.* **1** a debauched person. **2** an old worn-out horse. [C18: ?from *rep,* shortened from REPROBATE]

RIP *abbrev. for* requiescat *or* requiescant in pace. [L: may he, she, *or* they rest in peace]

riparian (raɪ'pɛərɪən) *adj* **1** of, inhabiting, or situated on the bank of a river. **2** denoting or relating to the legal rights of the owner of land on a river bank, such as fishing. ◆ *n* **3** *Property law.* a person who owns land on a river bank. [C19: from L, from *rīpa* river bank]

ripcord ('rɪp,kɔːd) *n* **1** a cord that when pulled opens a parachute from its pack. **2** a cord on the gas bag of a balloon that when pulled enables gas to escape and the balloon to descend.

ripe ⓣ (raɪp) *adj* **1** (of fruit, grain, etc.) mature and ready to be eaten or used. **2** mature enough to be eaten or used: *ripe cheese.* **3** fully developed in mind or body. **4** resembling ripe fruit, esp. in redness or fullness: *a ripe complexion.* **5** (*postpositive;* foll. by *for*) ready or eager (to undertake or undergo an action). **6** (*postpositive;* foll. by *for*) suitable: *the time is not yet ripe.* **7** mature in judgment or knowledge. **8** advanced but healthy (esp. in **a ripe old age**). **9** *Sl.* **9a** complete; thorough. **9b** excessive; exorbitant. **10** *Sl.* slightly indecent; risqué. [OE *rīpe*]
▸ **'ripely** *adv* ▸ **'ripeness** *n*

ripen ⓣ ('raɪpᵊn) *vb* to make or become ripe.

ripieno (,rɪpɪ'eɪnəʊ) *n, pl* **ripieni** (-niː) *or* **ripienos.** *Music.* a supplementary instrument or player. [It.]

rip off ⓣ *vb* (*tr*) **1** to tear roughly (from). **2** (*adv*) *Sl.* to steal from or cheat (someone). ◆ *n* **rip-off. 3** *Sl.* a grossly overpriced article. **4** *Sl.* the act of stealing or cheating.

riposte ⓣ (rɪ'pɒst, rɪ'pəʊst) *n* **1** a swift sharp reply in speech or action. **2** *Fencing.* a counterattack made immediately after a successful parry. ◆ *vb* **ripostes, riposting, riposted. 3** (*intr*) to make a riposte. [C18: from F, from It., from *rispondere* to reply]

ripper ('rɪpə) *n* **1** a person or thing that rips. **2** a murderer who dissects or mutilates his victim's body. **3** *Inf., chiefly Austral. & NZ.* a fine or excellent person or thing.

ripping ('rɪpɪŋ) *adj Arch. Brit. sl.* excellent; splendid.
▸ **'rippingly** *adv*

ripple[1] ⓣ ('rɪpᵊl) *n* **1** a slight wave or undulation on the surface of water. **2** a small wave or undulation in fabric, hair, etc. **3** a sound reminiscent of water flowing quietly in ripples: *a ripple of laughter.* **4** *Electronics.* an oscillation of small amplitude superimposed on a steady value. **5** *US & Canad.* another word for **riffle** (sense 4). ◆ *vb* **ripples, rippling, rippled. 6** (*intr*) to form ripples or flow with an undulating motion. **7** (*tr*) to stir up (water) so as to form ripples. **8** (*tr*) to make ripple marks. **9** (*intr*) (of sounds) to rise and fall gently. [C17: ?from RIP[1]]
▸ **'rippler** *n* ▸ **'rippling** *or* **'ripply** *adj*

ripple[2] ('rɪpᵊl) *n* **1** a special kind of comb designed to separate the seed from the stalks in flax or hemp. ◆ *vb* **ripples, rippling, rippled. 2** (*tr*) to comb with this tool. [C14: of Gmc origin]
▸ **'rippler** *n*

ripple effect *n* the repercussions of an event or situation experienced far beyond its immediate location.

ripple mark *n* one of a series of small wavy ridges of sand formed by waves on a beach, by a current in a sandy riverbed, or by wind on land: sometimes found fossilized on bedding planes of sedimentary rock.

rip-roaring *adj Inf.* characterized by excitement, intensity, or boisterous behaviour.

ripsaw ('rɪp,sɔː) *n* a handsaw for cutting along the grain of timber.

ripsnorter ('rɪp,snɔːtə) *n Sl.* a person or thing noted for intensity or excellence.
▸ **'rip,snorting** *adj*

riptide ('rɪp,taɪd) *n* **1** Also called: **rip.** a stretch of turbulent water in the sea, caused by the meeting of currents. **2** Also called: **rip current.** a strong current, esp. one flowing outwards from the shore.

rise ⓣ (raɪz) *vb* **rises, rising, rose, risen** ('rɪzᵊn). (*mainly intr*) **1** to get up from a lying, sitting, kneeling, or prone position. **2** to get out of bed, esp. to begin one's day: *he always rises early.* **3** to move from a lower to a higher position or place. **4** to ascend or appear above the horizon: *the sun is rising.* **5** to increase in height or level: *the water rose above the normal level.* **6** to attain higher rank, status, or reputation: *he will rise in the world.* **7** to be built or erected: *those blocks of flats are rising fast.* **8** to appear: *new troubles rose to afflict her.* **9** to increase in strength, degree, etc.: *the wind is rising.* **10** to increase in amount or value: *house prices are always rising.* **11** to swell up: *dough rises.* **12** to become erect, stiff, or rigid: *the hairs on his neck rose in fear.* **13** (of one's stomach or gorge) to manifest nausea. **14** to revolt: *the people rose against their oppressors.* **15** to slope upwards: *the ground rises beyond the lake.* **16** to be resurrected. **17** to originate: *that river rises in the mountains.* **18** (of a session of a court, legislative assembly, etc.) to come to an end. **19** *Angling.* (of fish) to come to the surface of the water. **20** (often foll. by *to*) *Inf.* to respond (to teasing, etc.). ◆ *n* **21** the act or an instance of rising. **22** an increase in height. **23** an increase in rank, status, or position. **24** an increase in amount, cost, or value. **25** an increase in degree or intensity. **26** *Brit.* an increase in salary or wages. US and Canad. word: **raise. 27** the vertical height of a step or of a flight of stairs. **28** the vertical height of a roof above the walls or columns. **29** *Angling.* the act or instance of fish coming to the surface of the water to take flies, etc. **30** the beginning, origin, or source. **31** a piece of rising ground; incline. **32 get** *or* **take a rise out of.** *Sl.* to provoke an angry or petulant reaction from. **33 give rise to.** to cause the development of. [OE *rīsan*]

riser ('raɪzə) *n* **1** a person who rises, esp. from bed: *an early riser.* **2** the vertical part of a stair. **3** a vertical pipe, esp. one within a building.

rise to *vb* (*intr, prep*) to respond adequately to (the demands of something, esp. a testing challenge).

risibility (,rɪzɪ'bɪlɪtɪ) *n, pl* **risibilities. 1** a tendency to laugh. **2** hilarity; laughter.

risible ⓣ ('rɪzɪbᵊl) *adj* **1** having a tendency to laugh. **2** causing laughter; ridiculous. [C16: from LL *rīsibilis,* from L *rīdēre* to laugh]
▸ **'risibly** *adv*

rising ('raɪzɪŋ) *n* **1** a rebellion; revolt. **2** the leaven used to make dough rise in baking. ◆ *adj* (*prenominal*) **3** increasing in rank, status, or reputation: *a rising young politician.* **4** growing up to adulthood: *the rising generation.* ◆ *adv* **5** *Inf.* approaching: *he's rising 50.*

rising damp *n* capillary movement of moisture from the ground into the walls of buildings, resulting in damage up to a level of 3 feet.

rising trot *n* a horse's trot in which the rider rises from the saddle every second beat.

risk ⓣ (rɪsk) *n* **1** the possibility of incurring misfortune or loss. **2** *Insurance.* **2a** chance of a loss or other event on which a claim may be filed. **2b** the type of such an event, such as fire or theft. **2c** the amount of the claim should such an event occur. **2d** a person or thing considered with respect to the characteristics that may cause an insured event to occur. **3 at risk.** vulnerable. **4 take** *or* **run a risk.** to proceed in an action without regard to the possibility of danger involved. ◆ *vb* (*tr*) **5** to expose to danger or loss. **6** to act in spite of the possibility of (in-

THESAURUS

ous, loud, luxurious, noisy, orgiastic, rambunctious (*inf.*), roisterous, rollicking, saturnalian, uproarious, wanton, wild **3** = **uproarious,** side-splitting
Antonyms *adj* ≠ **unruly, unrestrained:** calm, civilized, disciplined, gentle, lawful, mild, obedient, orderly, peaceful, quiet, restrained, well-behaved

rip[1] *vb* **1** = **tear,** be rent, burst, claw, cut, gash, hack, lacerate, rend, score, slash, slit, split ◆ *n* **7** = **tear,** cleavage, cut, gash, hole, laceration, rent, slash, slit, split

ripe *adj* **1, 2** = **mature,** fully developed, fully grown, mellow, ready, ripened, seasoned **5** *foll. by* **for** = **ready for,** eager for, in readiness for, prepared for **6** = **suitable,** auspicious, favourable, ideal, opportune, right, timely
Antonyms *adj* ≠ **mature:** green, immature, undeveloped, unripe ≠ **suitable:** disadvantageous, inappropriate, inconvenient, inopportune, unfavourable, unfitting, unseemly, unsuitable, untimely

ripen *vb* = **mature,** burgeon, come of age, come to fruition, develop, get ready, grow ripe, make ripe, prepare, season

rip off *vb Slang* **2** = **steal,** cabbage (*Brit. sl.*), filch, knock off (*sl.*), lift (*inf.*), pilfer, pinch (*inf.*), swipe (*sl.*), thieve *Slang* **2** = **cheat,** con (*inf.*), cozen, defraud, diddle (*inf.*), do the dirty on (*Brit. inf.*), dupe, fleece, gyp (*sl.*), rob, skin (*sl.*), steal from, stiff (*sl.*), swindle, trick ◆ *n* **rip-off 4** *Slang* = **cheat,** con (*inf.*), con trick (*inf.*), exploitation, fraud, robbery, scam (*sl.*), sting (*inf.*), swindle, theft

riposte *n* **1** = **retort,** answer, comeback (*inf.*), counterattack, rejoinder, repartee, reply, response, return, sally ◆ *vb* **3** = **retort,** answer, come back, reciprocate, rejoin, reply, respond, return

ripple[1] *n* **1, 2** = **wave,** undulation

rise *vb* **2** = **get up,** arise, get out of bed, get to one's feet, rise and shine, stand up, surface **3** = **go up,** ascend, climb, levitate, move up **6** = **advance,** be promoted, climb the ladder, get on, get somewhere, go places (*inf.*), progress, prosper, work one's way up **8** = **originate,** appear, become apparent, crop up, emanate, emerge, eventuate, flow, happen, issue, occur, spring, turn up **9** = **increase,** enlarge, go up, grow, intensify, lift, mount, soar, swell, wax **14** = **rebel,** mount the barricades, mutiny, resist, revolt, take up arms **15** = **get steeper,** ascend, climb, go uphill, mount, slope upwards ◆ *n* **22** = **upward slope,** acclivity, ascent, elevation, hillock, incline, rising ground **23** = **promotion,** advance, aggrandizement, climb, progress **25** = **increase,** advance, ascent, climb, improvement, upsurge, upswing, upturn, upward turn **26** = **pay increase,** increment, raise (*US*) **33 give rise to** = **cause,** bring about, bring on, effect, produce, provoke, result in
Antonyms *vb* ≠ **go up, get steeper:** descend, drop, fall, plunge, sink ≠ **increase:** abate, abbreviate, abridge, condense, curtail, decline, decrease, descend, diminish, drop, dwindle, fall, lessen, plunge, reduce, shrink, sink, wane ◆ *n* ≠ **increase:** blip, decline, decrease, downswing, downturn, drop, fall

risible *adj* **2** = **ridiculous,** absurd, amusing, comical, droll, farcical, funny, hilarious, humorous, laughable, ludicrous, rib-tickling (*inf.*), side-splitting

risk *n* **1** = **danger,** chance, gamble, hazard, jeopardy, peril, pitfall, possibility, speculation, uncertainty, venture ◆ *vb* **5, 6** = **dare,** chance, endanger, expose to danger, gamble, hazard, imperil, jeopardize, put in jeopardy, skate on

jury or loss): *to risk a fall in climbing.* [C17: from F, from It., from *rischiare* to be in peril, from Gk *rhiza* cliff (from the hazards of sailing along rocky coasts)]

risk capital *n Chiefly Brit.* capital invested in an issue of ordinary shares, esp. of a speculative enterprise. Also called: **venture capital.**

risk factor *n Med.* a factor, such as a habit or an environmental condition, that predisposes an individual to develop a particular disease.

risky ❶ ('rɪskɪ) *adj* **riskier, riskiest.** involving danger.
►'**riskily** *adv* ►'**riskiness** *n*

risotto (rɪ'zɒtəʊ) *n, pl* **risottos.** a dish of rice cooked in stock and served variously with tomatoes, cheese, chicken, etc. [C19: from It., from *riso* RICE]

risqué ❶ ('rɪskeɪ) *adj* bordering on impropriety or indecency: *a risqué joke.* [C19: from F *risquer* to hazard, RISK]

rissole ('rɪsəʊl) *n* a mixture of minced cooked meat coated in egg and breadcrumbs and fried. [C18: from F, prob. ult. from L *russus* red]

risus sardonicus ('ri:səs sɑ:'dɒnɪkəs) *n Pathol.* fixed contraction of the facial muscles resulting in a peculiar distorted grin, caused esp. by tetanus. Also called: **trismus cynicus** ('trɪzməs 'sɪnɪkəs). [C17: NL, lit.: sardonic laugh]

rit. *Music. abbrev. for:* **1** ritardando. **2** ritenuto.

ritardando (ˌrɪtɑ:'dændəʊ) *adj, adv* another term for **rallentando.** Abbrev.: **rit.** [C19: from It., from *ritardare* to slow down]

rite ❶ (raɪt) *n* **1** a formal act prescribed or customary in religious ceremonies: *the rite of baptism.* **2** a particular body of such acts, esp. of a particular Christian Church: *the Latin rite.* **3** a Christian Church: *the Greek rite.* [C14: from L *rītus* religious ceremony]

ritenuto (ˌrɪtə'nu:təʊ) *adj, adv Music.* **1** held back momentarily. **2** Abbrev.: **rit.** another term for **rallentando.** [C19: from It., from L *retinēre* to hold back]

rite of passage *n* a ceremony performed in some cultures at times when an individual changes his status, as at puberty and marriage.

ritornello (ˌrɪtə'nɛləʊ) *n, pl* **ritornellos** *or* **ritornelli** (-li:). *Music.* a short piece of instrumental music interpolated in a song. [It., lit.: a little return]

ritual ❶ ('rɪtjʊəl) *n* **1** the prescribed or established form of a religious or other ceremony. **2** such prescribed forms in general or collectively. **3** stereotyped activity or behaviour. **4** any formal act, institution, or procedure that is followed consistently: *the ritual of the law.* ◆ *adj* **5** of or characteristic of religious, social, or other rituals. [C16: from L *rītuālis,* from *rītus* RITE]
►'**ritually** *adv*

ritualism ('rɪtjʊəˌlɪzəm) *n* **1** exaggerated emphasis on the importance of rites and ceremonies. **2** the study of rites and ceremonies, esp. magical or religious ones.
►'**ritualist** *n* ►ˌ**ritual'istic** *adj* ►ˌ**ritual'istically** *adv*

ritualize *or* **ritualise** ('rɪtjʊəˌlaɪz) *vb* **ritualizes, ritualizing, ritualized** *or* **ritualises, ritualising, ritualised. 1** *(intr)* to engage in ritualism or devise rituals. **2** *(tr)* to make (something) into a ritual.

ritzy ❶ ('rɪtsɪ) *adj* **ritzier, ritziest.** *Sl.* luxurious or elegant. [C20: after the hotels established by César *Ritz* (1850–1918), Swiss hotelier]
►'**ritzily** *adv* ►'**ritziness** *n*

rival ❶ ('raɪvᵊl) *n* **1a** a person, organization, team, etc., that competes with another for the same object or in the same field. **1b** *(as modifier): rival suitors.* **2** a person or thing that is considered the equal of another: *she is without rival in the field of physics.* ◆ *vb* **rivals, rivalling, rivalled** *or US* **rivals, rivaling, rivaled.** *(tr)* **3** to be the equal or near equal of: *an empire that rivalled Rome.* **4** to try to equal or surpass. [C16: from L *rīvalis,* lit.: one who shares the same brook, from *rīvus* a brook]

rivalry ❶ ('raɪvəlrɪ) *n, pl* **rivalries. 1** the act of rivalling. **2** the state of being a rival or rivals.

rive (raɪv) *vb* **rives, riving, rived; rived** *or* **riven** ('rɪvᵊn). *(usually passive)* **1** to split asunder: *a tree riven by lightning.* **2** to tear apart: *riven to shreds.* [C13: from ON *rīfa*]

river ❶ ('rɪvə) *n* **1a** a large natural stream of fresh water flowing along a definite course, usually into the sea, being fed by tributary streams. **1b** *(as modifier): river traffic.* **1c** *(in combination): riverside; riverbed.* Related adjs.: **fluvial, potamic. 2** any abundant stream or flow: *a river of blood.* [C13: from OF, from L *rīpārius* of a river bank, from *rīpa* bank]
►'**riverless** *adj*

riverine ('rɪvəˌraɪn) *adj* **1** of, like, relating to, or produced by a river. **2** located or dwelling near a river; riparian.

rivet ❶ ('rɪvɪt) *n* **1** a short metal pin for fastening two or more pieces together, having a head at one end, the other end being hammered flat after being passed through holes in the pieces. ◆ *vb* **rivets, riveting, riveted.** *(tr)* **2** to join by riveting. **3** to hammer in order to form into a head. **4** *(often passive)* to cause to be fixed, as in fascinated attention, horror, etc.: *to be riveted to the spot.* [C14: from OF, from *river* to fasten, from ?]
►'**riveter** *n* ►'**riveting** *adj*

riviera (ˌrɪvɪ'ɛərə) *n* a coastal region reminiscent of the mediterranean coast of France and N Italy. [C20: from *Riviera,* from It., lit.: shore, ult. from L *ripa* shore]

rivière (ˌrɪvɪ'ɛə) *n* a necklace the diamonds or other precious stones of which gradually increase in size up to a large centre stone. [C19: from F: brook, RIVER]

rivulet ('rɪvjʊlɪt) *n* a small stream. [C16: from It. *rivoletto,* from L *rīvulus,* from *rīvus* stream]

riyal (rɪ'jɑ:l) *n* the standard monetary and currency unit of Saudi Arabia or Yemen. [from Ar. *riyāl,* from Sp. *real*]

RL *abbrev. for* Rugby League.

rly *abbrev. for* railway.

rm *abbrev. for:* **1** ream. **2** room.

RM *abbrev. for:* **1** Royal Mail. **2** Royal Marines. **3** (in Canada) Rural Municipality.

RMA *abbrev. for* Royal Military Academy (Sandhurst).

rms *abbrev. for* root mean square.

Rn *the chemical symbol for* radon.

RN *abbrev. for:* **1** (in Canada) Registered Nurse. **2** Royal Navy.

RNA *n Biochem.* ribonucleic acid; any of a group of nucleic acids, present in all living cells, that play an essential role in the synthesis of proteins.

RNAS *abbrev. for:* **1** Royal Naval Air Service(s). **2** Royal Naval Air Station.

RNIB (in Britain) *abbrev. for* Royal National Institute for the Blind.

RNID (in Britain) *abbrev. for* Royal National Institute for Deaf People.

RNLI *abbrev. for* Royal National Lifeboat Institution.

RNZAF *abbrev. for* Royal New Zealand Air Force.

RNZN *abbrev. for* Royal New Zealand Navy.

roach[1] (rəʊtʃ) *n, pl* **roaches** *or* **roach.** a European freshwater food fish having a deep compressed body and reddish ventral and tail fins. [C14: from OF *roche,* from ?]

roach[2] (rəʊtʃ) *n* **1** short for **cockroach. 2** *Sl.* the butt of a cannabis cigarette.

roach[3] (rəʊtʃ) *n Naut.* the curve at the foot of a square sail. [C18: from ?]

roach clip *n Sl.* a small clip resembling tweezers, used to hold the butt of a cannabis cigarette, in order to avoid burning one's fingers.

road ❶ (rəʊd) *n* **1a** an open way, usually surfaced with tarmac or concrete, providing passage from one place to another. **1b** *(as modifier): road traffic; a road sign.* **1c** *(in combination): the roadside.* **2a** a street. **2b** *(cap. when part of a name): London Road.* **3** *Brit.* one of the tracks of a railway. **4** a way, path, or course: *the road to fame.* **5** *(often pl) Naut.* Also called: **roadstead.** a partly sheltered anchorage. **6** a drift or tunnel in a mine, esp. a level one. **7 hit the road.** *Sl.* to start or resume travelling. **8 one for the road.** *Inf.* a last alcoholic drink before leaving. **9 on the road. 9a** travelling about; on tour. **9b** leading a wandering life. **10 take (to) the road.** to begin a journey or tour. [OE *rād;* rel. to *rīdan* to RIDE]
►'**roadless** *adj*

road allowance *n Canad.* land reserved by the government to be used for public roads.

roadblock ('rəʊdˌblɒk) *n* a barrier set up across a road by the police or military, in order to stop a fugitive, inspect traffic, etc.

road-fund licence *n Brit.* a paper disc showing that the tax in respect of a motor vehicle has been paid. [C20: from the former *road fund* for the maintenance of public highways]

road hog *n Inf.* a selfish or aggressive driver.

roadholding ('rəʊdˌhəʊldɪŋ) *n* the extent to which a motor vehicle is stable and does not skid, esp. on sharp bends or wet roads.

THESAURUS

thin ice, take a chance on, take the plunge, venture

risky *adj* = **dangerous,** chancy *(inf.),* dicey *(inf., chiefly Brit.),* dodgy *(Brit., Austral., & NZ inf.),* fraught with danger, hazardous, perilous, precarious, touch-and-go, tricky, uncertain, unsafe
Antonyms *adj* certain, reliable, safe, secure, stable, sure

risqué *adj* = **suggestive,** bawdy, blue, daring, immodest, improper, indelicate, naughty, near the knuckle *(inf.),* off colour, Rabelaisian, racy, ribald

rite *n* **1** = **ceremony,** act, ceremonial, communion, custom, form, formality, liturgy, mystery, observance, ordinance, practice, procedure, ritual, sacrament, service, solemnity, usage

ritual *n* **1** = **ceremony,** ceremonial, communion, liturgy, mystery, observance, rite, sacrament, service, solemnity **4** = **custom,** convention, form, formality, habit, ordinance, practice, prescription, procedure, protocol, red tape, routine, tradition, usage ◆ *adj* **5** = **ceremonial,** ceremonious, conventional, customary, formal, habitual, prescribed, procedural, routine, stereotyped

ritzy *adj Slang* = **luxurious,** de luxe, elegant, glamorous, glittering, grand, high-class, luxury, opulent, plush *(inf.),* posh *(inf., chiefly Brit.),* stylish, sumptuous, swanky *(inf.)*

rival *n* **1a** = **opponent,** adversary, antagonist, challenger, competitor, contender, contestant, emulator ◆ *modifier* **1b** = **competing,** competitive, conflicting, emulating, opposed, opposing ◆ *n* **2** = **equal,** compeer, equivalent, fellow, match, peer ◆ *vb* **3** = **equal,** be a match for, bear comparison with, come up to, compare with, match, measure up to **4** = **compete,** contend, emulate, oppose, seek to displace, vie with
Antonyms *n* ≠ **opponent:** ally, friend, helper, supporter ◆ *vb* ≠ **compete:** aid, back, help, support

rivalry *n* **1, 2** = **competition,** antagonism, competitiveness, conflict, contention, contest, duel, emulation, opposition, struggle, vying

river *n* **1a** = **stream,** beck, brook, burn *(Scot.),* creek, rivulet, tributary, watercourse, waterway **2** = **flow,** flood, rush, spate, torrent

riveting *adj* **4** = **enthralling,** absorbing, arresting, captivating, engrossing, fascinating, gripping, hypnotic, spellbinding

road *n* **1** = **way,** avenue, course, direction, highway, lane, motorway, path, pathway, roadway, route, thoroughfare, track **2** = **street 5** *Nautical* = **roadstead,** anchorage

roadhouse ('rəʊdˌhaʊs) *n* a pub, restaurant, etc., that is situated at the side of a road.
road hump *n* the official name for **sleeping policeman.**
roadie ('rəʊdɪ) *n Inf.* a person who transports and sets up equipment for a band or group. [C20: shortened from *road manager*]
road metal *n* crushed rock, broken stone, etc., used to construct a road.
road movie *n* a genre of film in which the chief character takes to the road, esp. to escape the law, his own past, etc.
road pricing *n* the practice of charging motorists for using certain stretches of road, in order to reduce congestion.
road rage *n* aggressive behaviour by a motorist in response to the actions of another road user.
roadroller ('rəʊdˌrəʊlə) *n* a motor vehicle with heavy rollers for compressing road surfaces during road-making.
road show *n* **1** *Radio.* **1a** a live programme, usually with some audience participation, transmitted from a radio van taking a particular show on the road. **1b** the personnel and equipment needed for such a show. **2** a group of entertainers on tour. **3** any occasion when an organization attracts publicity while touring or visiting: *the royal road show.*
roadstead ('rəʊdˌstɛd) *n Naut.* another word for **road** (sense 5).
roadster ('rəʊdstə) *n* **1** an open car, esp. one seating only two. **2** a kind of bicycle.
road tax *n* a tax paid, usually annually, on motor vehicles in use on the roads.
road test *n* **1** a test to ensure that a vehicle is roadworthy, esp. after repair or servicing, by driving it on roads. **2** a test of something in actual use. ◆ *vb* **road-test.** (*tr*) **3** to test (a vehicle, etc.) in this way.
road train *n Austral.* a truck pulling one or more large trailers, esp. on western roads.
roadway ('rəʊdˌweɪ) *n* **1** the surface of a road. **2** the part of a road that is used by vehicles.
roadwork ('rəʊdˌwɜːk) *n* sports training by running along roads.
roadworks ('rəʊdˌwɜːks) *pl n* repairs to a road or cable under a road, esp. when forming a hazard or obstruction to traffic.
roadworthy ('rəʊdˌwɜːðɪ) *adj* (of a motor vehicle) mechanically sound; fit for use on the roads.
▸**'roadˌworthiness** *n*
roam ⓣ (rəʊm) *vb* **1** to travel or walk about with no fixed purpose or direction. ◆ *n* **2** the act of roaming. [C13: from ?]
▸**'roamer** *n*
roan (rəʊn) *adj* **1** (of a horse) having a bay (**red roan**), chestnut (**strawberry roan**), or black (**blue roan**) coat sprinkled with white hairs. ◆ *n* **2** a horse having such a coat. **3** a soft sheepskin leather used in bookbinding, etc. [C16: from OF, from Sp. *roano,* prob. from Gothic *rauths* red]
roar ⓣ (rɔː) *vb* (*mainly intr*) **1** (of lions and other animals) to utter characteristic loud growling cries. **2** (*also tr*) (of people) to utter (something) with a loud deep cry, as in anger or triumph. **3** to laugh in a loud hearty unrestrained manner. **4** (of horses) to breathe with laboured rasping sounds. **5** (of the wind, waves, etc.) to blow or break loudly and violently, as during a storm. **6** (of a fire) to burn fiercely with a roaring sound. **7** (*tr*) to bring (oneself) into a certain condition by roaring: *to roar oneself hoarse.* ◆ *n* **8** a loud deep cry, uttered by a person or crowd, esp. in anger or triumph. **9** a prolonged loud cry of certain animals, esp. lions. **10** any similar noise made by a fire, the wind, waves, an engine, etc. [OE *rārian*]
▸**'roarer** *n*
roaring ('rɔːrɪŋ) *adj* **1** *Inf.* very brisk and profitable (esp. in **a roaring trade**). ◆ *adv* **2** noisily or boisterously (esp. in **roaring drunk**). ◆ *n* **3** a loud prolonged cry.
▸**'roaringly** *adv*
roast (rəʊst) *vb* (*mainly tr*) **1** to cook (meat or other food) by dry heat, usually with added fat and esp. in an oven. **2** to brown or dry (coffee, etc.) by exposure to heat. **3** *Metallurgy.* to heat (an ore) in order to produce a concentrate that is easier to smelt. **4** to heat (oneself or something) to an extreme degree, as when sunbathing, etc. **5** (*intr*) to be excessively and uncomfortably hot. **6** (*tr*) *Inf.* to criticize severely. ◆ *n* **7** something that has been roasted, esp. meat. [C13: from OF *rostir,* of Gmc origin]
▸**'roaster** *n*
roasting ('rəʊstɪŋ) *Inf.* ◆ *adj* **1** extremely hot. ◆ *n* **2** severe criticism.
rob ⓣ (rɒb) *vb* **robs, robbing, robbed. 1** to take something from (someone) illegally, as by force. **2** (*tr*) to plunder (a house, etc.). **3** (*tr*) to deprive unjustly: *to be robbed of an opportunity.* [C13: from OF *rober,* of Gmc origin]
▸**'robber** *n*
robbery ⓣ ('rɒbərɪ) *n, pl* **robberies. 1** *Criminal law.* the stealing of property from a person by using or threatening to use force. **2** the act or an instance of robbing.
robe ⓣ (rəʊb) *n* **1** any loose flowing garment, esp. the official vestment of a peer, judge, or academic. **2** a dressing gown or bathrobe. ◆ *vb* **robes, robing, robed. 3** to put a robe, etc., on (oneself or someone else). [C13: from OF; of Gmc origin]
robin ('rɒbɪn) *n* **1** Also called: **robin redbreast.** a small Old World songbird related to the thrushes. The adult has a brown back, orange-red breast and face, and grey underparts. **2** a North American thrush similar to but larger than the Old World robin. [C16: arbitrary use of name *Robin*]
Robin Hood *n* a legendary English outlaw, who lived in Sherwood Forest (in the reign of Richard I) and robbed the rich to give to the poor.
robinia (rəˈbɪnɪə) *n* any tree of the leguminous genus *Robinia,* esp. the locust tree.
roborant ('rəʊbərənt, 'rɒb-) *adj* **1** tending to fortify or increase strength. ◆ *n* **2** a drug or agent that increases strength. [C17: from L *roborāre* to strengthen, from *rōbur* an oak]
robot ⓣ ('rəʊbɒt) *n* **1** any automated machine programmed to perform specific mechanical functions in the manner of a human. **2** (*modifier*) automatic: *a robot pilot.* **3** a person who works or behaves like a machine. **4** *S. African.* a set of traffic lights. [C20: (used in *R.U.R.,* a play by Karel Čapek (1890–1938), Czech writer) from Czech *robota* work]
▸**ro'botic** *adj* ▸**'robot-ˌlike** *adj*
robot bomb *n* another name for the **V-1.**
robot dancing *or* **robotic dancing** (rəʊˈbɒtɪk) *n* a dance of the 1980s, characterized by jerky, mechanical movements. Also called: **robotics.**
robotics (rəʊˈbɒtɪks) *n* (*functioning as sing*) **1** the science or technology of designing, building, and using robots. **2** another name for **robot dancing.**
robust ⓣ (rəʊˈbʌst, 'rəʊbʌst) *adj* **1** strong in constitution. **2** sturdily built: *a robust shelter.* **3** requiring or suited to physical strength: *a robust sport.* **4** (esp. of wines) having a full-bodied flavour. **5** rough or boisterous. **6** (of thought, intellect, etc.) straightforward. [C16: from L *rōbustus,* from *rōbur* an oak, strength]
▸**ro'bustly** *adv*
robusta (rəʊˈbʌstə) *n* **1** a species of coffee tree, *Coffea canephora.* **2** coffee or coffee beans obtained from this plant. [from L *rōbustus* robust]
robustious (rəʊˈbʌstʃəs) *adj Arch.* **1** rough; boisterous. **2** strong, robust, or stout.
▸**ro'bustiously** *adv* ▸**ro'bustiousness** *n*
robustness (rəʊˈbʌstnɪs) *n* **1** the quality of being robust. **2** *Computing.* the ability of a computer system to cope with errors during execution.
roc (rɒk) *n* (in Arabian legend) a bird of enormous size and power. [C16: from Ar., from Persian *rukh*]
ROC *abbrev. for* Royal Observer Corps.
rocaille (rɒˈkaɪ) *n* decorative rock or shell work, esp. as ornamentation in a rococo fountain, grotto, or interior. [from F, from *roc* ROCK[1]]
rocambole ('rɒkəmˌbəʊl) *n* a variety of alliaceous plant whose garlic-like bulb is used for seasoning. [C17: from F, from G *Rockenbolle,* lit.: distaff bulb (with reference to its shape)]
Rochelle salt (rɒˈʃɛl) *n* a white crystalline double salt used in Seidlitz powder. Formula: $KNaC_4H_4O_6.4H_2O$. [C18: after *La Rochelle,* port in W France]
roche moutonnée (rəʊʃ ˌmuːtəˈneɪ) *n, pl* **roches moutonnées** (rəʊʃ ˌmuːtəˈneɪz). a rounded mass of rock smoothed and striated by ice that has flowed over it. [C19: F, lit.: fleecy rock, from *mouton* sheep]
rochet ('rɒtʃɪt) *n* a white surplice with tight sleeves, worn by bishops, abbots, and certain other Church dignitaries. [C14: from OF, from *roc* coat, of Gmc origin]
rock[1] ⓣ (rɒk) *n* **1** *Geol.* any aggregate of minerals that makes up part of the earth's crust. It may be unconsolidated, such as a sand, clay, or mud, or consolidated, such as granite, limestone, or coal. **2** any hard mass of consolidated mineral matter, such as a boulder. **3** *US, Canad., & Austral.* a stone. **4** a person or thing suggesting a rock, esp. in being dependable, unchanging, or providing firm foundation. **5** *Brit.* a hard sweet, typically a long brightly coloured peppermint-flavoured stick,

THESAURUS

roam *vb* **1 = wander,** drift, meander, peregrinate, prowl, ramble, range, rove, stravaig (*Scot. & N English dialect*), stray, stroll, travel, walk
roar *vb* **1, 2 = cry,** bawl, bay, bell, bellow, clamour, howl, rumble, shout, thunder, vociferate, yell **3 = guffaw,** bust a gut (*inf.*), crack up (*inf.*), hoot, laugh heartily, split one's sides (*inf.*) ◆ *n* **8, 9 = cry,** bellow, clamour, howl, outcry, rumble, shout, thunder, yell
rob *vb* **1 = steal from,** bereave, cheat, con, defraud, deprive, despoil, dispossess, do out of (*inf.*), gyp (*sl.*), hold up, mug (*inf.*), rip off (*sl.*), skin (*sl.*), stiff (*sl.*), swindle **2 = plunder,** burgle, loot, pillage, raid, ransack, rifle, sack, strip
robber *n* **1 = thief,** bandit, brigand, cheat, con man, footpad (*arch.*), fraud, fraudster, highwayman, mugger (*inf.*), pirate, stealer, swindler **2 = plunderer,** burglar, looter, raider
robbery *n* **1, 2 = theft,** burglary, depredation, embezzlement, filching, fraud, hold-up, larceny, mugging (*inf.*), pillage, plunder, raid, rip-off (*sl.*), spoliation, stealing, steaming (*inf.*), stick-up (*sl., chiefly US*), swindle, thievery
robe *n* **1 = gown,** costume, habit, vestment **2 = dressing gown,** bathrobe, housecoat, negligee, peignoir, wrapper ◆ *vb* **3 = clothe,** apparel (*arch.*), attire, drape, dress, garb
robot *n* **1 = machine,** android, automaton, mechanical man
robust *adj* **1 = strong,** able-bodied, alive and kicking, athletic, brawny, fighting fit, fit, fit as a fiddle (*inf.*), hale, hardy, healthy, hearty, husky (*inf.*), in fine fettle, in good health, lusty, muscular, powerful, rude, rugged, sinewy, sound, staunch, stout, strapping, sturdy, thickset, tough, vigorous, well **5 = rough,** boisterous, coarse, earthy, indecorous, raunchy (*sl.*), raw, roisterous, rollicking, rude, unsubtle **6 = straightforward,** common-sensical, down-to-earth, hard-headed, practical, pragmatic, realistic, sensible
Antonyms *adj* ≠ **strong:** delicate, feeble, frail, hothouse (*inf., often disparaging*), infirm, sickly, slender, unfit, unhealthy, unsound, weak, weedy (*inf.*), wimpish *or* wimpy (*inf.*) ≠ **rough:** refined
rock[1] *n* **2 = stone,** boulder **4 = tower of strength,** anchor, bulwark, cornerstone, foundation, mainstay, protection, support

sold esp. in holiday resorts. **6** *Sl.* a jewel, esp. a diamond. **7** *Sl.* another name for **crack** (sense 28). **8 on the rocks. 8a** in a state of ruin or destitution. **8b** (of drinks, esp. whisky) served with ice. [C14: from OF *roche,* from ?]

rock[2] ➊ (rɒk) *vb* **1** to move or cause to move from side to side or backwards and forwards. **2** to reel or sway or cause (someone) to reel or sway, as with a violent shock or emotion. **3** (*tr*) to shake or move (something) violently. **4** (*intr*) to dance in the rock-and-roll style. ◆ *n* **5** a rocking motion. **6** short for **rock and roll. 7** Also called: **rock music.** any of various styles of pop music having a heavy beat, derived from rock and roll. [OE *roccian*]

rockabilly (ˈrɒkəˌbɪlɪ) *n* a fast, spare style of White rock music which originated in the mid-1950s in the US South. [C20: from ROCK (AND ROLL) + (HILL)BILLY]

rock and roll *or* **rock'n'roll** *n* **1a** a type of pop music originating in the 1950s as a blend of rhythm and blues and country and western. **1b** (*as modifier*): *the rock-and-roll era.* **2** dancing performed to such music, with exaggerated body movements stressing the beat. ◆ *vb* **3** (*intr*) to perform this dance.
▸**rock and roller** *or* **rock'n'roller** *n*

rock bass (bæs) *n* an eastern North American freshwater food fish, related to the sunfish family.

rock bottom *n* **a** the lowest possible level. **b** (*as modifier*): *rock-bottom prices.*

rock-bound *adj* hemmed in or encircled by rocks. Also (poetic): **rock-girt.**

rock cake *n* a small cake containing dried fruit and spice, with a rough surface supposed to resemble a rock.

rock crystal *n* a pure transparent colourless quartz, used in electronic and optical equipment.

rock dove *or* **pigeon** *n* a common dove from which domestic and feral pigeons are descended.

rocker (ˈrɒkə) *n* **1** any of various devices that transmit or operate with a rocking motion. See also **rocker arm. 2** another word for **rocking chair. 3** either of two curved supports on the legs of a chair on which it may rock. **4a** an ice skate with a curved blade. **4b** the curve itself. **5** a rock-music performer, fan, or song. **6** *Brit.* an adherent of a youth movement rooted in the 1950s, characterized by motorcycle trappings. **7 off one's rocker.** *Sl.* crazy.

rocker arm *n* a lever that rocks about a pivot, esp. a lever in an internal-combustion engine that transmits the motion of a pushrod or cam to a valve.

rockery (ˈrɒkərɪ) *n, pl* **rockeries.** a garden constructed with rocks, esp. one where alpine plants are grown.

rocket[1] (ˈrɒkɪt) *n* **1** a self-propelling device, esp. a cylinder containing a mixture of solid explosives, used as a firework, distress signal, etc. **2a** any vehicle that carries its own fuel and oxidant to burn in a rocket engine, esp. one used to carry a spacecraft, etc. **2b** (*as modifier*): *rocket launcher.* **3** *Brit. & NZ inf.* a severe reprimand (esp. in **get a rocket**). ◆ *vb* **rockets, rocketing, rocketed. 4** (*tr*) to propel (a missile, spacecraft, etc.) by means of a rocket. **5** (*intr;* foll. by *off, away,* etc.) to move off at high speed. **6** (*intr*) to rise rapidly: *he rocketed to the top.* [C17: from OF, from It. *rochetto,* dim. of *rocca* distaff, of Gmc origin]

rocket[2] (ˈrɒkɪt) *n* any of several plants of the mustard family, typically having yellowish flowers, such as **London rocket** and **yellow rocket.** See also **arugula, wall rocket.** [C16: from F *roquette,* from It. *rochetta,* from L *ērūca* hairy plant]

rocket engine *n* a reaction engine in which a fuel and oxidizer are burnt in a combustion chamber, the products of combustion expanding through a nozzle and producing thrust.

rocketry (ˈrɒkɪtrɪ) *n* the science and technology of the design, operation, maintenance, and launching of rockets.

rockfish (ˈrɒkˌfɪʃ) *n, pl* **rockfish** *or* **rockfishes. 1** any of various fishes that live among rocks, such as the goby, bass, etc. **2** *Brit.* any of several coarse fishes when used as food, esp. the dogfish or wolffish.

rock garden *n* a garden featuring rocks or rockeries.

rocking chair *n* a chair set on curving supports so that the sitter may rock backwards and forwards.

rocking horse *n* a toy horse mounted on a pair of rockers on which a child can rock to and fro in a seesaw movement.

rocking stone *n* a boulder so delicately poised that it can be rocked.

rockling (ˈrɒklɪŋ) *n, pl* **rocklings** *or* **rockling.** a small gadoid fish which has an elongated body with barbels around the mouth and occurs mainly in the North Atlantic Ocean. [C17: from ROCK[1] + -LING[1]]

rock lobster *n* another name for the **spiny lobster.**

rock melon *n US, Austral., & NZ.* another name for **cantaloupe.**

rock pigeon *n* another name for **rock dove.**

rock plant *n* any plant that grows on rocks or in rocky ground.

rock rabbit *n S. African.* another name for **dassie.** See **hyrax.**

rockrose (ˈrɒkˌrəuz) *n* any of various shrubs or herbaceous plants cultivated for their yellow-white or reddish roselike flowers.

rock salmon *n Brit.* a former term for **rockfish** (sense 2).

rock salt *n* another name for **halite.**

rock snake *or* **python** *n* any large Australasian python of the genus *Liasis.*

rock tripe *n Canad.* any of various edible lichens that grow on rocks and are used in the North as a survival food.

rock wool *n* another name for **mineral wool.**

rocky[1] ➊ (ˈrɒkɪ) *adj* **rockier, rockiest. 1** consisting of or abounding in rocks: *a rocky shore.* **2** unyielding: *rocky determination.* **3** hard like rock: *rocky muscles.*
▸ˈ**rockiness** *n*

rocky[2] ➊ (ˈrɒkɪ) *adj* **rockier, rockiest. 1** weak or unstable. **2** *Inf.* (of a person) dizzy; nauseated.
▸ˈ**rockily** *adv* ▸ˈ**rockiness** *n*

Rocky Mountain spotted fever *n* an acute rickettsial disease characterized by high fever, chills, pain in muscles and joints, etc. It is caused by the bite of an infected tick.

rococo (rəˈkəukəu) *n* (*often cap.*) **1** a style of architecture and decoration that originated in France in the early 18th century, characterized by elaborate but graceful ornamentation. **2** an 18th-century style of music characterized by prettiness and extreme use of ornamentation. **3** any florid or excessively ornamental style. ◆ *adj* **4** denoting, being in, or relating to the rococo. **5** florid or excessively elaborate. [C19: from F, from ROCAILLE, from *roc* ROCK[1]]

rod ➊ (rɒd) *n* **1** a slim cylinder of metal, wood, etc. **2** a switch or bundle of switches used to administer corporal punishment. **3** any of various staffs of insignia or office. **4** power, esp. of a tyrannical kind: *a dictator's iron rod.* **5** a straight slender shoot, stem, or cane of a woody plant. **6** See **fishing rod. 7** Also called: **pole, perch. 7a** a unit of length equal to 5½ yards. **7b** a unit of square measure equal to 30¼ square yards. **8** *Surveying.* another name (esp. US) for **staff**[1] (sense 8). **9** Also called: **retinal rod.** any of the elongated cylindrical cells in the retina of the eye, which are sensitive to dim light but not to colour. **10** any rod-shaped bacterium. **11** *US.* a slang name for **pistol. 12** short for **hot rod.** [OE *rodd*]
▸ˈ**rodˌlike** *adj*

rode (rəud) *vb* the past tense of **ride.**

rodent (ˈrəudᵊnt) *n* **a** any of the relatively small placental mammals having constantly growing incisor teeth specialized for gnawing. The group includes rats, mice, squirrels, etc. **b** (*as modifier*): *rodent characteristics.* [C19: from L *rōdere* to gnaw]
▸ˈ**rodent-ˌlike** *adj*

rodent ulcer *n* a slow-growing malignant tumour on the face, usually occurring at the edge of the eyelids, lips, or nostrils.

rodeo (ˈrəudɪˌəu) *n, pl* **rodeos.** *Chiefly US & Canad.* **1** a display of the skills of cowboys, including bareback riding. **2** the rounding up of cattle for branding, etc. **3** an enclosure for cattle that have been rounded up. [C19: from Sp., from *rodear* to go around, from *rueda* a wheel, from L *rota*]

rodomontade (ˌrɒdəmɒnˈteɪd, -ˈtɑːd) *Literary.* ◆ *n* **1a** boastful words or behaviour. **1b** (*as modifier*): *rodomontade behaviour.* ◆ *vb* **rodomontades, rodomontading, rodomontaded. 2** (*intr*) to boast or rant. [C17: from F, from It. *rodomonte* a boaster, from *Rodomonte,* the name of a braggart king of Algiers in epic poems]

roe[1] (rəu) *n* **1** Also called: **hard roe.** the ovary of a female fish filled with mature eggs. **2** Also called: **soft roe.** the testis of a male fish filled with mature sperm. [C15: from MDu. *roge,* from OHG *roga*]

roe[2] (rəu) *n, pl* **roes** *or* **roe.** short for **roe deer.** [OE *rā(ha)*]

Roe (rəu) *n* **Richard.** *Law.* (formerly) the defendant in a fictitious action, Doe versus Roe, to test a point of law. See also **Doe.**

roebuck (ˈrəuˌbʌk) *n, pl* **roebucks** *or* **roebuck.** the male of the roe deer.

roe deer *n* a small graceful deer of woodlands of Europe and Asia. The antlers are small and the summer coat is reddish-brown.

roentgen *or* **röntgen** (ˈrɒntgən, -tjən, ˈrɛnt-) *n* a unit of dose of electromagnetic radiation equal to the dose that will produce in air a charge of 0.258×10^{-3} coulomb on all ions of one sign. [C19: after Wilhelm Konrad *Roentgen* (1845–1923), G physicist who discovered x-rays]

roentgen ray *n* a former name for **X-ray.**

rogation (rəuˈgeɪʃən) *n* (*usually pl*) *Christianity.* a solemn supplication, esp. in a form of ceremony prescribed by the Church. [C14: from L *rogātiō,* from *rogāre* to ask, make supplication]

Rogation Days *pl n* April 25 (the **Major Rogation**) and the Monday, Tuesday, and Wednesday before Ascension Day, observed by Christians as days of solemn supplication and marked by processions and special prayers.

roger (ˈrɒdʒə) *interj* **1** (used in signalling, telecommunications, etc.) message received and understood. **2** an expression of agreement. ◆ *vb* **3** *Taboo sl.* (of a man) to copulate (with). [C20: from the name *Roger,* representing *R* for *received*]

rogue ➊ (rəug) *n* **1** a dishonest or unprincipled person, esp. a man. **2** *Often jocular.* a mischievous or wayward person, often a child. **3** a crop plant which is inferior, diseased, or of a different, unwanted variety. **4a** any inferior or defective specimen. **4b** (*as modifier*): *rogue heroin.* **5** *Arch.* a vagrant. **6a** an animal of vicious character that leads a solitary

THESAURUS

rock[2] *vb* **1** = **sway,** lurch, pitch, reel, roll, swing, toss, wobble **2** = **shock,** astonish, astound, daze, dumbfound, jar, set one back on one's heels (*inf.*), shake, stagger, stun, surprise

rocky[1] *adj* **1** = **rough,** boulder-strewn, craggy, pebbly, rugged, stony

rocky[2] *adj* **1** = **unstable,** doubtful, rickety, shaky, uncertain, undependable, unreliable, unsteady, weak, wobbly

rod *n* **2** = **cane,** birch, switch **3** = **stick,** bar, baton, crook, dowel, mace, pole, sceptre, shaft, staff, wand

rogue *n* **1** = **scoundrel,** blackguard, charlatan, cheat, con man (*inf.*), crook (*inf.*), deceiver, devil, fraud, fraudster, knave (*arch.*), mountebank, ne'er-do-well, rapscallion, rascal, reprobate, scally (*Northwest English dialect*), scumbag (*sl.*), sharper, swindler, villain **2** = **scamp,** rascal

life. **6b** (*as modifier*): *a rogue elephant.* ◆ *vb* **rogues, roguing, rogued. 7** (*tr*) to rid (a field or crop) of plants that are inferior, diseased, etc. [C16: from ?]

roguery ('rəʊgərɪ) *n, pl* **rogueries. 1** behaviour characteristic of a rogue. **2** a roguish or mischievous act.

rogues' gallery *n* **1** a collection of photographs of known criminals kept by the police for identification purposes. **2** a group of undesirable people.

roguish ('rəʊgɪʃ) *adj* **1** dishonest or unprincipled. **2** mischievous.
▸ **'roguishly** *adv*

roil (rɔɪl) *vb* **1** (*tr*) to make (a liquid) cloudy or turbid by stirring up dregs or sediment. **2** (*intr*) (esp. of a liquid) to be agitated. **3** (*intr*) *Dialect.* to be noisy. **4** (*tr*) *Now rare.* another word for **rile** (sense 1). [C16: from ?]

roister ('rɔɪstə) *vb* (*intr*) **1** to engage in noisy or unrestrained merrymaking. **2** to brag, bluster, or swagger. [C16: from OF *rustre* lout, from *ruste* uncouth, from L *rusticus* rural]
▸ **'roisterer** *n* ▸ **'roisterous** *adj* ▸ **'roisterously** *adv*

Roland ('rəʊlənd) *n* **1** the greatest of the legendary 12 peers or paladins (of whom Oliver was another) in attendance on Charlemagne. **2 a Roland for an Oliver.** an effective retort or retaliation.

role *or* **rôle** (rəʊl) *n* **1** a part or character in a play, film, etc., to be played by an actor or actress. **2** *Psychol.* the part played by a person in a particular social setting, influenced by his expectation of what is appropriate. **3** usual function: *what is his role in the organization?* [C17: from F *rôle* ROLL, an actor's script]

role model *n* a person regarded by others, esp. younger people, as a good example to follow.

role-playing *n Psychol.* activity in which a person imitates, consciously or unconsciously, a role uncharacteristic of himself. See also **psychodrama.**

roll (rəʊl) *vb* **1** to move or cause to move along by turning over and over. **2** to move or cause to move along on wheels or rollers. **3** to flow or cause to flow onwards in an undulating movement. **4** (*intr*) (of animals, etc.) to turn onto the back and kick. **5** (*intr*) to extend in undulations: *the hills roll down to the sea.* **6** (*intr;* usually foll. by *around*) to move or occur in cycles. **7** (*intr*) (of a planet, the moon, etc.) to revolve in an orbit. **8** (*intr;* foll. by *on, by,* etc.) to pass or elapse: *the years roll by.* **9** to rotate or cause to rotate wholly or partially: *to roll one's eyes.* **10** to curl, cause to curl, or admit of being curled, so as to form a ball, tube, or cylinder. **11** to make or form by shaping into a ball, tube, or cylinder: *to roll a cigarette.* **12** (often foll. by *out*) to spread or cause to spread out flat or smooth under or as if under a roller: *to roll pastry.* **13** to emit or utter with a deep prolonged reverberating sound: *the thunder rolled continuously.* **14** to trill or cause to be trilled: *to roll one's r's.* **15** (*intr*) (of a vessel, aircraft, rocket, etc.) to turn from side to side around the longitudinal axis. **16** to cause (an aircraft) to execute a roll or (of an aircraft) to execute a roll (sense 34). **17** (*intr*) to walk with a swaying gait, as when drunk. **18** *Chiefly US.* to throw (dice). **19** (*intr*) to operate or begin to operate: *the presses rolled.* **20** (*intr*) *Inf.* to make progress: *let the good times roll.* **21** (*tr*) *Inf., chiefly US & NZ.* to rob (a helpless person). ◆ *n* **22** the act or an instance of rolling. **23** anything rolled up in a cylindrical form: *a roll of newspaper.* **24** an official list or register, esp. of names: *an electoral roll.* **25** a rounded mass: *rolls of flesh.* **26** a cylinder used to flatten something; roller. **27** a small cake of bread for one person. **28** a flat pastry or cake rolled up with a meat (**sausage roll**), jam (**jam roll**), or other filling. **29** a swell or undulation on a surface: *the roll of the hills.* **30** a swaying, rolling, or unsteady movement or gait. **31** a deep prolonged reverberating sound: *the roll of thunder.* **32** a trilling sound; trill. **33** a very rapid beating of the sticks on a drum. **34** a flight manoeuvre in which an aircraft makes one complete rotation about its longitudinal axis without loss of height or change in direction. **35** *Sl.* an act of sexual intercourse or petting (esp. in **a roll in the hay**). **36** *US sl.* an amount of money, esp. a wad of paper money. **37 on a roll.** *Sl.* experiencing continued good luck or success. **38 strike off the roll(s). 38a** to expel from membership. **38b** to debar (a solicitor) from practising, usually because of dishonesty. ◆ See also **roll in, roll on,** etc. [C14 *rollen,* from OF *roler,* from L *rotulus,* dim. of *rota* a wheel]

rollbar ('rəʊl,bɑː) *n* a bar that reinforces the frame of a car used for racing, rallying, etc., to protect the driver if the car should turn over.

roll call *n* the reading aloud of an official list of names, those present responding when their names are read out.

rolled gold *n* a metal, such as brass, coated with a thin layer of gold. Also (US): **filled gold.**

rolled-steel joist *n* a steel beam, esp. one with a cross section in the form of a letter *H* or *I.* Abbrev.: **RSJ.**

roller ('rəʊlə) *n* **1** a cylinder having an absorbent surface and a handle, used for spreading paint. **2** Also called: **garden roller.** a heavy cast-iron cylinder on an axle to which a handle is attached; used for flattening lawns. **3** a long heavy wave of the sea, advancing towards the shore. **4** a hardened cylinder of precision-ground steel that forms one of the rolling components of a roller bearing or of a linked driving chain. **5** a cylinder fitted on pivots, used to enable heavy objects to be easily moved. **6** *Printing.* a cylinder, usually of hard rubber, used to ink a plate before impression. **7** any of various other cylindrical devices that rotate about a cylinder, used for any of various purposes. **8** a small cylinder onto which a woman's hair may be rolled to make it curl. **9** *Med.* a bandage consisting of a long strip of muslin rolled tightly into a cylindrical form before application. **10** any of various Old World birds, such as the **European roller**, that have a blue, green, and brown plumage, a slightly hooked bill, and an erratic flight. **11** (*often cap.*) a variety of tumbler pigeon. **12** a person or thing that rolls. **13** short for **steamroller.**

rollerball ('rəʊlə,bɔːl) *n* a pen having a small moving nylon, plastic, or metal ball as a writing point.

roller bearing *n* a bearing in which a shaft runs on a number of hardened-steel rollers held within a cage.

roller chain *n Engineering.* a chain for transmitting power in which each link consists of two free-moving rollers held in position by pins connected to sideplates.

roller coaster *n* another term for **big dipper.**

roller derby *n* a race on roller skates, esp. one involving aggressive tactics.

roller skate *n* **1** a device having straps for fastening to a shoe and four small wheels that enable the wearer to glide swiftly over a floor. ◆ *vb* **roller-skate, roller-skates, roller-skating, roller-skated. 2** (*intr*) to move on roller skates.
▸ **roller skater** *n*

roller towel *n* **1** a towel with the two ends sewn together, hung on a roller. **2** a towel wound inside a roller enabling a clean section to be pulled out when needed.

rollick ('rɒlɪk) *vb* **1** (*intr*) to behave in a carefree or boisterous manner. ◆ *n* **2** a boisterous or carefree escapade. [C19: Scot. dialect, prob. from ROMP + FROLIC]

rollicking[1] ('rɒlɪkɪŋ) *adj* boisterously carefree. [C19: from ROLLICK]

rollicking[2] ('rɒlɪkɪŋ) *n Brit. inf.* a very severe telling-off. [C20: from ROLLICK (vb) (in former sense: to be angry, make a fuss); ? infl. by BOLLOCKING]

roll in *vb* (*mainly intr*) **1** (*adv*) to arrive in abundance or in large numbers. **2** (*adv*) *Inf.* to arrive at one's destination. **3 be rolling in.** (*prep*) *Sl.* to abound or luxuriate in (wealth, money, etc.).

rolling ('rəʊlɪŋ) *adj* **1** having gentle rising and falling slopes: *rolling country.* **2** progressing by stages or by occurrences in different places in succession: *a rolling strike.* **3** subject to regular review and updating: *a rolling plan for overseas development.* **4** reverberating: *rolling thunder.* **5** *Sl.* extremely rich. **6** that may be turned up or down: *a rolling hat brim.* ◆ *adv* **7** *Sl.* swaying or staggering (in **rolling drunk**).

rolling launch *n Marketing.* the process of introducing a product onto a market gradually. Cf. **roll out** (sense 3).

rolling mill *n* **1** a mill or factory where ingots of heated metal are passed between rollers to produce sheets or bars of a required cross section and form. **2** a machine having rollers that may be used for this purpose.

rolling pin *n* a cylinder with handles at both ends used for rolling dough, pastry, etc., out flat.

rolling stock *n* the wheeled vehicles collectively used on a railway, including the locomotives, coaches, etc.

rolling stone *n* a restless or wandering person.

rollmop ('rəʊl,mɒp) *n* a herring fillet rolled, usually around onion slices, and pickled in spiced vinegar. [C20: from G *Rollmops,* from *rollen* to ROLL + *Mops* pug dog]

rollneck ('rəʊl,nɛk) *adj* **1** (of a garment) having a high neck that may be rolled over. ◆ *n* **2** a rollneck sweater or other garment.

roll of honour *n* a list of those who have died in war for their country.

roll on *vb* **1** *Brit.* used to express the wish that an eagerly anticipated event or date will come quickly: *roll on Saturday.* ◆ *adj* **roll-on. 2** (of a deodorant, etc.) dispensed by means of a revolving ball fitted into the

THESAURUS

roguish *adj* **1** = **unprincipled**, criminal, crooked, deceitful, deceiving, dishonest, fraudulent, knavish, raffish, rascally, shady (*inf.*), swindling, unscrupulous, villainous **2** = **mischievous**, arch, cheeky, coquettish, frolicsome, impish, playful, puckish, sportive, waggish

roister *vb* **1** = **make merry**, carouse, celebrate, frolic, go on a spree, live it up (*inf.*), paint the town red (*inf.*), push the boat out (*Brit. inf.*), revel, rollick, romp, whoop it up (*inf.*) **2** = **swagger**, bluster, boast, brag, show off (*inf.*), strut

role *n* **1** = **part**, character, impersonation, portrayal, representation **3** = **job**, capacity, duty, function, part, position, post, task

roll *vb* **1, 2** = **turn**, go round, gyrate, pivot, reel, revolve, rotate, spin, swivel, trundle, twirl, wheel, whirl **3** = **flow**, run, undulate **10** = **wind**, bind, coil, curl, enfold, entwine, envelop, furl, swathe, twist, wrap **12** = **level**, even, flatten, press, smooth, spread **13** = **rumble**, boom, drum, echo, grumble, resound, reverberate, roar, thunder **15** = **toss**, billow, lurch, reel, rock, sway, swing, tumble, wallow, welter **17** = **sway**, lumber, lurch, reel, stagger, swagger, waddle ◆ *n* **22** = **turn**, cycle, gyration, reel, revolution, rotation, run, spin, twirl, undulation, wheel, whirl **23** = **spool**, ball, bobbin, cylinder, reel, scroll **24** = **register**, annals, catalogue, census, chronicle, directory, index, inventory, list, record, roster, schedule, scroll, table **29** = **undulation**, billowing, swell, waves **30** = **tossing**, lurching, pitching, rocking, rolling, wallowing **31** = **rumble**, boom, drumming, growl, grumble, resonance, reverberation, roar, thunder

rollick *vb* **1** = **romp**, caper, cavort, frisk, galumph (*inf.*), gambol, make merry, revel

rollicking[1] *adj* = **boisterous**, carefree, cavorting, devil-may-care, exuberant, frisky, frolicsome, full of beans (*inf.*), hearty, jaunty, jovial, joyous, lively, merry, playful, rip-roaring (*inf.*), romping, spirited, sportive, sprightly, swashbuckling

Antonyms *adj* cheerless, despondent, dull, gloomy, lifeless, melancholy, morose, sad, sedate, serious, unhappy

rollicking[2] *n Brit. informal* = **scolding**, dressing-down, lecture, reprimand, roasting (*inf.*),

neck of the container. ◆ *n* **roll-on. 3** a woman's foundation garment, made of elasticized material and having no fastenings.

roll-on/roll-off *adj* denoting a cargo ship or ferry designed so that vehicles can be driven on and off.

roll out *vb (tr, adv)* **1** to cause (pastry) to become flatter and thinner by pressure with a rolling pin. **2** to show (a new type of aircraft) to the public for the first time. **3** to launch (a new film, product, etc.) in a series of successive waves, as over the whole country. ◆ *n* **roll-out. 4** a presentation to the public of a new aircraft, product, etc.; a launch.

roll over *vb (adv)* **1** *(intr)* to overturn. **2** *(intr)* (of an animal, esp. a dog) to lie on its back while kicking its legs in the air. **3** *(intr)* to capitulate. **4** *(tr)* to allow (a loan, prize, etc.) to continue in force for a further period. ◆ *n* **rollover. 5** an instance of such continuance of a loan, prize, etc.

roll-top desk *n* a desk having a slatted wooden panel that can be pulled down over the writing surface when not in use.

roll up *vb (adv)* **1** to form or cause to form a cylindrical shape. **2** *(tr)* to wrap (an object) round on itself or on an axis: *to roll up a map.* **3** *(intr) Inf.* to arrive, esp. in a vehicle. **4** *(intr) Austral.* to assemble; congregate. ◆ *n* **roll-up. 5** *Brit. inf.* a cigarette made by hand from loose tobacco and cigarette papers. **6** *Austral.* the number attending a meeting, etc.

Rolodex ('rəulə,deks) *n Trademark, chiefly US.* a small file for holding names, addresses, and telephone numbers, consisting of cards attached horizontally to a rotatable central cylinder.

roly-poly ❶ ('rəulɪ'pəulɪ) *adj* **1** plump, buxom, or rotund. ◆ *n, pl* **roly-polies. 2** *Brit.* a strip of suet pastry spread with jam, fruit, or a savoury mixture, rolled up, and baked or steamed. [C17: apparently by reduplication from *roly,* from ROLL]

ROM (rɒm) *n Computing. acronym for* read only memory: a storage device that holds data permanently and cannot be altered by the programmer.

rom. *Printing. abbrev. for* roman (type).

Rom. *abbrev. for:* **1** Roman. **2** Romance (languages). **3** Romania(n). **4** *Bible.* Romans.

Romaic (rəu'meɪɪk) *Obs.* ◆ *n* **1** the modern Greek vernacular. ◆ *adj* **2** of or relating to Greek. [C19: from Gk *Rhōmaikos* Roman, with reference to the Eastern Roman Empire]

roman ('rəumən) *adj* **1** of, relating to, or denoting a vertical style of printing type: the usual form of type for most printed matter. Cf. **italic.** ◆ *n* **2** roman type. [C16: so called because the style of letters is that used in ancient Roman inscriptions]

Roman ('rəumən) *adj* **1** of or relating to Rome or its inhabitants in ancient or modern times. **2** of or relating to Roman Catholicism or the Roman Catholic Church. ◆ *n* **3** a citizen or inhabitant of ancient or modern Rome.

roman à clef *French.* (rɔmɑ̃ a kle) *n, pl* ***romans à clef*** (rɔmɑ̃ a kle). a novel in which real people are depicted under fictitious names. [lit.: novel with a key]

Roman alphabet *n* the alphabet evolved by the ancient Romans for the writing of Latin, derived ultimately from the Phoenicians. The alphabet serves for writing most of the languages of W Europe.

Roman blind *n* a window blind consisting of a length of material which, when drawn up, gathers into horizontal folds from the bottom.

Roman candle *n* a firework that produces a continuous shower of sparks punctuated by coloured balls of fire. [C19: it originated in Italy]

Roman Catholic *adj* **1** of or relating to the Roman Catholic Church. ◆ *n* **2** a member of this Church. ◆ Often shortened to **Catholic.**
▸**Roman Catholicism** *n*

Roman Catholic Church *n* the Christian Church over which the pope presides, with administrative headquarters in the Vatican. Also called: **Catholic Church, Church of Rome.**

romance ❶ *n* (rə'mæns, 'rəumæns). **1** a love affair. **2** love, esp. romantic love idealized for its purity or beauty. **3** a spirit of or inclination for adventure or mystery. **4** a mysterious, exciting, sentimental, or nostalgic quality, esp. one associated with a place. **5** a narrative in verse or prose, written in a vernacular language in the Middle Ages, dealing with adventures of chivalrous heroes. **6** any similar narrative work dealing with events and characters remote from ordinary life. **7** a story, novel, film, etc., dealing with love, usually in an idealized or sentimental way. **8** an extravagant, absurd, or fantastic account. **9** a lyrical song or short instrumental composition having a simple melody. ◆ *vb* (rə'mæns), **romances, romancing, romanced. 10** *(intr)* to tell, invent, or write extravagant or romantic fictions. **11** *(intr)* to tell extravagant or improbable lies. **12** *(intr)* to have romantic thoughts. **13** *(intr)* (of a couple) to indulge in romantic behaviour. **14** *(tr)* to be romantically involved with. [C13: *romauns,* from OF *romans,* ult. from L *Rōmānicus* Roman]
▸**ro'mancer** *n*

Romance (rə'mæns, 'rəumæns) *adj* **1** denoting, relating to, or belonging to the languages derived from Latin, including Italian, Spanish, Portuguese, French, and Romanian. **2** denoting a word borrowed from a Romance language. ◆ *n* **3** this group of languages.

Roman Empire *n* **1** the territories ruled by ancient Rome. At its height the Roman Empire included W and S Europe, N Africa, and SW Asia. In 395 A.D. it was divided into the **Eastern Roman Empire,** whose capital was Byzantium, and the **Western Roman Empire,** whose capital was Rome. **2** the government of Rome and its dominions by the emperors from 27 B.C. **3** the Byzantine Empire. **4** the Holy Roman Empire.

Romanesque (,rəumə'nɛsk) *adj* **1** denoting or having the style of architecture used in W and S Europe from the 9th to the 12th century, characterized by the rounded arch and massive-masonry wall construction. **2** denoting a corresponding style in painting, sculpture, etc. [C18: see ROMAN, -ESQUE]

Roman holiday *n* entertainment or pleasure that depends on the suffering of others. [C19: from Byron's poem *Childe Harold* (IV, 141)]

Romanian (rəu'meɪnɪən), **Rumanian,** *or* **Roumanian** *n* **1** the official language of Romania in SE Europe. **2** a native, citizen, or inhabitant of Romania. ◆ *adj* **3** relating to, denoting, or characteristic of Romania, its people, or their language.

Romanic (rəu'mænɪk) *adj* another word for **Roman** or **Romance.**

Romanism ('rəumə,nɪzəm) *n* Roman Catholicism, esp. when regarded as excessively or superstitiously ritualistic.
▸**'Romanist** *n*

Romanize *or* **Romanise** ('rəumə,naɪz) *vb* **Romanizes, Romanizing, Romanized** *or* **Romanises, Romanising, Romanised. 1** *(tr)* to impart a Roman Catholic character to (a ceremony, etc.). **2** *(intr)* to be converted to Roman Catholicism. **3** *(tr)* to transcribe (a language) into the Roman alphabet.
▸**,Romani'zation** *or* **,Romani'sation** *n*

Roman law *n* the system of jurisprudence of ancient Rome, codified under Justinian and forming the basis of many modern legal systems.

Roman nose *n* a nose having a high prominent bridge.

Roman numerals *pl n* the letters used by the Romans for the representation of cardinal numbers, still used occasionally today. The integers are represented by the following letters: I (= 1), V (= 5), X (= 10), L (= 50), C (= 100), D (= 500), and M (= 1000). VI = 6 (V + I) but IV = 4 (V – I).

Romansch *or* **Romansh** (rəu'mænʃ) *n* a group of Romance dialects spoken in the Swiss canton of Grisons; an official language of Switzerland since 1938. [C17: from Romansch, lit.: Romance language]

romantic ❶ (rəu'mæntɪk) *adj* **1** of, relating to, imbued with, or characterized by romance. **2** evoking or given to thoughts and feelings of love, esp. idealized or sentimental love: *a romantic setting.* **3** impractical, visionary, or idealistic: *a romantic scheme.* **4** *Often euphemistic.* imaginary or fictitious: *a romantic account of one's war service.* **5** *(often cap.)* of or relating to a movement in European art, music, and literature in the late 18th and early 19th centuries, characterized by an emphasis on feeling and content rather than order and form. ◆ *n* **6** a person who is romantic, as in being idealistic, amorous, or soulful. **7** a person whose tastes in art, literature, etc., lie mainly in romanticism. **8** *(often cap.)* a poet, composer, etc., of the romantic period or whose main inspiration is romanticism. [C17: from F, from obs. *romant* story, romance, from OF *romans* ROMANCE]
▸**ro'mantically** *adv*

romanticism (rəu'mæntɪ,sɪzəm) *n* **1** *(often cap.)* the theory, practice, and style of the romantic art, music, and literature of the late 18th and early 19th centuries, usually opposed to classicism. **2** romantic attitudes, ideals, or qualities.
▸**ro'manticist** *n*

romanticize *or* **romanticise** (rəu'mæntɪ,saɪz) *vb* **romanticizes, romanticizing, romanticized** *or* **romanticises, romanticising, romanticised. 1** *(intr)* to think or act in a romantic way. **2** *(tr)* to interpret according to romantic precepts. **3** to make or become romantic, as in style.
▸**ro,mantici'zation** *or* **ro,mantici'sation** *n*

Romany *or* **Romani** ('rɒmənɪ, 'rəu-) *n* **1a** *(pl* **Romanies** *or* **Romanis)** another name for a **Gypsy. 1b** *(as modifier): Romany customs.* **2** the language of the Gypsies, belonging to the Indic branch of the Indo-European family. [C19: from Romany *romani* (adj) Gypsy, ult. from Sansk. *domba* man of a low caste of musicians, of Dravidian origin]

THESAURUS

telling-off *(inf.)*, ticking off *(inf.)*, tongue-lashing

roly-poly *adj* **1** = **plump**, buxom, chubby, fat, overweight, podgy, pudgy, rotund, rounded, tubby

romance *n* **1** = **love affair**, affair, *affaire (du coeur)*, affair of the heart, amour, attachment, intrigue, liaison, passion, relationship **3** = **excitement**, adventure, charm, colour, exoticness, fascination, glamour, mystery, nostalgia, sentiment **7** = **story**, fairy tale, fantasy, fiction, idyll, legend, love story, melodrama, novel, tale, tear-jerker *(inf.)* **8** = **tall story** *(inf.)*, absurdity, exaggeration, fabrication, fairy tale, falsehood, fiction, flight of fancy, invention, lie, trumped-up story, urban legend, urban myth ◆ *vb* **10** = **exaggerate**, be economical with the truth, fantasize, let one's imagination run away with one, lie, make up stories, stretch the truth, tell stories

romantic *adj* **1** = **exciting**, charming, colourful, exotic, fascinating, glamorous, mysterious, nostalgic, picturesque **2** = **loving**, amorous, fond, lovey-dovey, mushy *(inf.)*, passionate, sentimental, sloppy *(inf.)*, soppy *(Brit. inf.)*, tender **3** = **idealistic**, dreamy, high-flown, impractical, quixotic, starry-eyed, unrealistic, utopian, visionary, whimsical **4** = **fictitious**, chimerical, exaggerated, extravagant, fabulous, fairy-tale, fanciful, fantastic, idyllic, imaginary, imaginative, improbable, legendary, made-up, unrealistic, wild ◆ *n* **6** = **idealist**, Don Quixote, dreamer, romancer, sentimentalist, utopian, visionary

Antonyms *adj* ≠ **exciting:** uninspiring ≠ **loving:** cold-hearted, insensitive, unaffectionate, unimpassioned, unloving, unromantic, unsentimental ≠ **idealistic:** practical, realistic ≠ **fictitious:** realistic

romanza (rəʊ'mænzə) *n* a short instrumental piece of songlike character. [It.]
romaunt (rə'mɔ:nt) *n Arch.* a verse romance. [C16: from OF; see ROMANTIC]
Romeo ('rəʊmɪəʊ) *n, pl* **Romeos.** an ardent male lover. [after the hero of Shakespeare's *Romeo and Juliet* (1594)]
Romish ('rəʊmɪʃ) *adj Usually derog.* of or resembling Roman Catholic beliefs or practices.
romp ⓣ (rɒmp) *vb* (*intr*) **1** to play or run about wildly, boisterously, or joyfully. **2 romp home** (*or* **in**). to win a race, etc., easily. ◆ *n* **3** a noisy or boisterous game or prank. **4** an instance of sexual activity between two or more people that is entered into light-heartedly and without emotional commitment: *naked sex romps.* **5** *Arch.* a playful or boisterous child, esp. a girl. **6** an easy victory. [C18: prob. var. of RAMP, from OF *ramper* to crawl, climb]
rompers ('rɒmpəz) *pl n* **1** a one-piece baby garment consisting of trousers and a bib with straps. **2** *NZ.* a type of costume worn by schoolgirls for games and gymnastics.
rondavel (ˌrɒn'dɑ:vəl) *n S. African.* a circular, often thatched, building with a conical roof. [from ?]
rondeau ('rɒndəʊ) *n, pl* **rondeaux** (-dəʊ, -dəʊz). a poem consisting of 13 or 10 lines with two rhymes and having the opening words of the first line used as an unrhymed refrain. [C16: from OF, from *rondel* a little round, from *rond* ROUND]
rondel ('rɒndᵊl) *n* a rondeau consisting of three stanzas of 13 or 14 lines with a two-line refrain appearing twice or three times. [C14: from OF, lit.: a little circle, from *rond* ROUND]
rondo ('rɒndəʊ) *n, pl* **rondos.** a piece of music in which a refrain is repeated between episodes: often constitutes the form of the last movement of a sonata or concerto. [C18: from It., from F RONDEAU]
rone (rəʊn) *or* **ronepipe** *n Scot.* a drainpipe for carrying rainwater from a roof. [C19: from ?]
röntgen ('rɒntgən, -tjən, 'rɛnt-) *n* a variant spelling of **roentgen.**
roo (ru:) *n Austral. inf.* a kangaroo.
rood (ru:d) *n* **1a** a crucifix, esp. one set on a beam or screen at the entrance to the chancel of a church. **1b** (*as modifier*): *rood screen.* **2** the Cross on which Christ was crucified. **3** a unit of area equal to one quarter of an acre or 0.10117 hectare. **4** a unit of area equal to 40 square rods. [OE *rōd*]
roof (ru:f) *n, pl* **roofs** (ru:fs, ru:vz). **1a** a structure that covers or forms the top of a building. **1b** (*in combination*): *the rooftop.* **1c** (*as modifier*): *a roof garden.* **2** the top covering of a vehicle, oven, or other structure: *the roof of a car.* **3** *Anat.* any structure that covers an organ or part: *the roof of the mouth.* **4** a highest or topmost point or part: *Mount Everest is the roof of the world.* **5** a house or other shelter: *a poor man's roof.* **6 hit** (*or* **raise** *or* **go through**) **the roof.** *Inf.* to get extremely angry. ◆ *vb* **7** (*tr*) to provide or cover with a roof or rooflike part. [OE *hrōf*]
▸**'roofer** *n* ▸**'roofless** *adj*
roof garden *n* a garden on a flat roof of a building.
roofing ('ru:fɪŋ) *n* **1** material used to construct a roof. **2** the act of constructing a roof.
roof rack *n* a rack attached to the roof of a motor vehicle for carrying luggage, skis, etc.
rooftree ('ru:fˌtri:) *n* another name for **ridgepole.**
rooibos ('rɔɪˌbɒs, 'rʊɪˌbɒs) *n* any of various South African trees with red leaves. [from Afrik. *rooi* red + *bos* bush]
rooibos tea *n S. African.* a tealike drink made from the leaves of the rooibos.
rooikat ('rɔɪˌkæt, 'rʊɪˌkæt) *n* a South African lynx. [from Afrik. *rooi* red + *kat* cat]
rooinek ('rɔɪˌnɛk, 'rʊɪˌnɛk) *n S. African.* a contemptuous name for an **Englishman.** [C19: Afrik., lit.: red neck]
rook[1] ⓣ (rʊk) *n* **1** a large Eurasian passerine bird, with a black plumage and a whitish base to its bill. **2** *Sl.* a swindler or cheat, esp. one who cheats at cards. ◆ *vb* **3** (*tr*) *Sl.* to overcharge, swindle, or cheat. [OE *hrōc*]
rook[2] (rʊk) *n* a chesspiece that may move any number of unoccupied squares in a straight line, horizontally or vertically. Also called: **castle.** [C14: from OF *rok*, ult. from Ar. *rukhkh*]
rookery ('rʊkərɪ) *n, pl* **rookeries. 1** a group of nesting rooks. **2** a clump of trees containing rooks' nests. **3a** a breeding ground or communal living area of certain other birds or mammals, esp. penguins or seals. **3b** a colony of any such creatures. **4** *Arch.* an overcrowded slum.
rookie ('rʊkɪ) *n Inf.* a newcomer, esp. a raw recruit in the army. [C20: changed from RECRUIT]
room ⓣ (ru:m, rʊm) *n* **1** space or extent, esp. unoccupied or unobstructed space for a particular purpose: *is there room to pass?* **2** an area within a building enclosed by a floor, a ceiling, and walls or partitions. **3** (*functioning as sing or pl*) the people present in a room: *the whole room was laughing.* **4** (foll. by *for*) opportunity or scope: *room for manoeuvre.* **5** (*pl*) a part of a house, hotel, etc., that is rented out as separate accommodation: *living in dingy rooms in Dalry.* ◆ *vb* **6** (*intr*) to occupy or share a room or lodging: *where does he room?* [OE *rūm*]
▸**'roomer** *n*
roomful ('ru:mˌfʊl, 'rʊm-) *n, pl* **roomfuls.** a number or quantity sufficient to fill a room: *a roomful of furniture.*
rooming house *n US & Canad.* a house having self-contained furnished rooms or flats for renting.
roommate ('ru:mˌmeɪt, 'rʊm-) *n* a person with whom one shares a room or lodging.
room service *n* service in a hotel providing meals, drinks, etc., in guests' rooms.
roomy ⓣ ('ru:mɪ, 'rʊmɪ) *adj* **roomier, roomiest.** spacious.
▸**'roomily** *adv* ▸**'roominess** *n*
roost (ru:st) *n* **1** a place, perch, branch, etc., where birds, esp. domestic fowl, rest or sleep. **2** a temporary place to rest or stay. ◆ *vb* **3** (*intr*) to rest or sleep on a roost. **4** (*intr*) to settle down or stay. **5 come home to roost.** to have unfavourable repercussions. [OE *hrōst*]
Roost (ru:st) *n* **the.** a powerful current caused by conflicting tides around the Shetland and Orkney Islands. [C16: from ON *röst*]
rooster ('ru:stə) *n Chiefly US & Canad.* the male of the domestic fowl; a cock.
root[1] ⓣ (ru:t) *n* **1a** the organ of a higher plant that anchors the rest of the plant in the ground and absorbs water and mineral salts from the soil. **1b** (loosely) any of the branches of such an organ. **2** any plant part, such as a tuber, that is similar to a root in function or appearance. **3a** the essential part or nature of something: *your analysis strikes at the root of the problem.* **3b** (*as modifier*): *the root cause of the problem.* **4** *Anat.* the embedded portion of a tooth, nail, hair, etc. **5** origin or derivation. **6** (*pl*) a person's sense of belonging in a community, place, etc., esp. the one in which he was born or brought up. **7** *Bible.* a descendant. **8** *Linguistics.* the form of a word that remains after removal of all affixes. **9** *Maths.* a quantity that when multiplied by itself a certain number of times equals a given quantity: *3 is a cube root of 27.* **10** Also called: **solution.** *Maths.* a number that when substituted for the variable satisfies a given equation. **11** *Music.* (in harmony) the note forming the foundation of a chord. **12** *Austral. & NZ sl.* sexual intercourse. **13 root and branch.** (*adv*) entirely; utterly. ◆ Related adj: **radical.** ◆ *vb* **14** (*intr*) Also: **take root.** to establish a root and begin to grow. **15** (*intr*) Also: **take root.** to become established, embedded, or effective. **16** (*tr*) to embed with or as if with a root or roots. **17** *Austral. & NZ sl.* to have sexual intercourse (with). ◆ See also **root out, roots.** [OE *rōt*, from ON]
▸**'rooter** *n* ▸**'rootˌlike** *adj* ▸**'rooty** *adj* ▸**'rootiness** *n*
root[2] ⓣ (ru:t) *vb* (*intr*) **1** (of a pig) to burrow in or dig up the earth in search of food, using the snout. **2** (foll. by *about, around, in,* etc.) *Inf.* to search vigorously but unsystematically. [C16: changed (through infl. of ROOT[1]) from earlier *wroot*, from OE *wrōtan*; rel. to OE *wrōt* snout]
▸**'rooter** *n*
root[3] (ru:t) *vb* (*intr;* usually foll. by *for*) *Inf.* to give support to (a contestant, team, etc.), as by cheering. [C19: ? var. of Scot. *rout* to make a loud noise, from ON *rauta* to roar]
root beer *n US & Canad.* an effervescent drink made from extracts of various roots and herbs.
root canal *n* the passage in the root of a tooth through which its nerves and blood vessels enter the pulp cavity.
root-canal therapy *n* another name for **root treatment.**
root climber *n* any of various climbing plants, such as the ivy, that adhere to a supporting structure by means of small roots growing from the side of the stem.
root crop *n* a crop, as of turnips or beets, cultivated for the food value of its roots.
rooted ⓣ ('ru:tɪd) *adj* **1** having roots. **2** deeply felt: *rooted objections.*
root ginger *n* the raw underground stem of the ginger plant used finely chopped or grated, esp. in Chinese dishes.
root hair *n* any of the hollow hairlike outgrowths of the outer cells of a root, just behind the tip, that absorb water and salts from the soil.
rooting compound *n Horticulture.* a substance, usually a powder, containing auxins in which plant cuttings are dipped in order to promote root growth.
rootle ('ru:tᵊl) *vb* **rootles, rootling, rootled.** (*intr*) *Brit.* another word for **root**[2].

THESAURUS

romp *vb* **1** = **frolic**, caper, cavort, cut capers, frisk, gambol, have fun, make merry, revel, roister, rollick, skip, sport **2 romp home** *or* **in** = **win easily**, run away with it, walk it (*inf.*), win by a mile (*inf.*), win hands down ◆ *n* **3** = **frolic**, caper, lark (*inf.*)
rook[1] *vb* **3** *Slang* = **cheat**, bilk, clip (*sl.*), cozen, defraud, diddle (*inf.*), do (*sl.*), fleece, gyp (*sl.*), overcharge, rip off (*sl.*), skin (*sl.*), stiff (*sl.*), sting (*inf.*), swindle
room *n* **1** = **space**, allowance, area, capacity, compass, elbowroom, expanse, extent, latitude, leeway, margin, play, range, scope, territory, volume **2** = **chamber**, apartment, office **4** = **opportunity**, chance, occasion, scope
roomy *adj* = **spacious**, ample, broad, capacious, commodious, extensive, generous, large, sizable *or* sizeable, wide
Antonyms *adj* bounded, confined, cramped, narrow, small, tiny
root[1] *n* **1, 2** = **stem**, radicle, radix, rhizome, tuber **3** = **heart**, core, crux, essence, fundamental, nub, nucleus **5** = **source**, base, beginnings, bottom, cause, derivation, foundation, fountainhead, germ, mainspring, origin, seat, seed, starting point **6** *plural* = **sense of belonging**, birthplace, cradle, family, heritage, home, origins **13 root and branch** = **completely**, entirely, finally, radically, thoroughly, totally, to the last man, utterly, wholly, without exception ◆ *vb* **15** = **become established**, anchor, become settled, embed, entrench, establish, fasten, fix, ground, implant, moor, set, stick, take root
root[2] *vb* **1, 2** = **dig**, burrow, delve, ferret, forage, hunt, nose, poke, pry, rootle, rummage
rooted *adj* **2** = **deep-seated**, confirmed, deep, deeply felt, entrenched, established, firm, fixed, ingrained, radical, rigid

rootless Ⓣ ('ruːtlɪs) *adj* having no roots, esp. (of a person) having no ties with a particular place.

rootlet ('ruːtlɪt) *n* a small root.

root mean square *n* the square root of the average of the squares of a set of numbers or quantities: *the root mean square of* 1, 2, *and* 4 *is* $\sqrt{[(1^2 + 2^2 + 4^2)/3]} = \sqrt{7}$. Abbrev.: **rms.**

root nodule *n* a swelling on the root of a leguminous plant, such as clover, that contains bacteria capable of nitrogen fixation.

root out Ⓣ *vb (tr, adv)* to remove or eliminate completely: *we must root out inefficiency.*

roots (ruːts) *adj* (of popular music) going back to the origins of a style, esp. in being genuine and unpretentious: *roots rock.*

roots music *n* **1** another name for **world music. 2** reggae, esp. when regarded as authentic and uncommercialized.

rootstock ('ruːtˌstɒk) *n* **1** another name for **rhizome. 2** another name for **stock** (sense 7). **3** *Biol.* a basic structure from which offshoots have developed.

root treatment *n Dentistry.* a procedure, used for treating an abscess at the tip of the root of a tooth, in which the pulp is removed and a filling (**root filling**) inserted in the root canal. Also called: **root-canal therapy.**

ropable *or* **ropeable** ('rəʊpəbᵊl) *adj* **1** capable of being roped. **2** *Austral. & NZ inf.* **2a** angry. **2b** wild or intractable: *a ropable beast.*

rope Ⓣ (rəʊp) *n* **1a** a fairly thick cord made of intertwined hemp or other fibres or of wire or other strong material. **1b** *(as modifier): a rope ladder.* **2** a row of objects fastened to form a line: *a rope of pearls.* **3** a quantity of material wound in the form of a cord. **4** a filament or strand, esp. of something viscous or glutinous: *a rope of slime.* **5 give (someone) enough** (*or* **plenty of**) **rope to hang himself.** to allow (someone) to accomplish his own downfall by his own foolish acts. **6 know the ropes.** to have a thorough understanding of a particular sphere of activity. **7 on the ropes. 7a** *Boxing.* driven against the ropes enclosing the ring by an opponent's attack. **7b** in a hopeless position. **8 the rope. 8a** a rope halter used for hanging. **8b** death by hanging. ◆ *vb* **ropes, roping, roped. 9** *(tr)* to bind or fasten with or as if with a rope. **10** *(tr;* usually foll. by *off)* to enclose or divide by means of a rope. **11** (when *intr,* foll. by *up*) *Mountaineering.* to tie (climbers) together with a rope. [OE *rāp*]

rope in Ⓣ *vb (tr, adv)* **1** *Brit.* to persuade to take part in some activity. **2** *US & Canad.* to trick or entice into some activity.

rope's end *n* a short piece of rope, esp. as formerly used for flogging sailors.

ropewalk ('rəʊpˌwɔːk) *n* a long narrow usually covered path or shed where ropes are made.

ropey Ⓣ *or* **ropy** ('rəʊpɪ) *adj* **ropier, ropiest. 1** *Brit. inf.* **1a** inferior. **1b** slightly unwell. **2** (of a viscous or sticky substance) forming strands. **3** resembling a rope.

▸ **'ropily** *adv* ▸ **'ropiness** *n*

Roquefort ('rɒkfɔː) *n* a blue-veined cheese with a strong flavour, made from ewe's and goat's milk. [C19: after *Roquefort,* village in S France]

roquet ('rəʊkɪ) *Croquet.* ◆ *vb* **roquets** (-kɪz), **roqueting** (-kɪɪŋ), **roqueted** (-kɪd). **1** to drive one's ball against (another person's ball) in order to be allowed to croquet. ◆ *n* **2** the act of roqueting. [C19: var. of CROQUET]

ro-ro ('rəʊrəʊ) *adj acronym for* roll-on/roll-off.

rorqual ('rɔːkwəl) *n* any of several whalebone whales that have a dorsal fin and a series of grooves along the throat and chest. Also called: **finback.** [C19: from F, from Norwegian *rörhval,* from ON *reytharhvalr,* from *reythr* (from *rauthr* red) + *hvalr* whale]

Rorschach test ('rɔːʃɑːk) *n Psychol.* a personality test consisting of a number of unstructured inkblots presented for interpretation. [C20: after Hermann *Rorschach* (1884–1922), Swiss psychiatrist]

rort (rɔːt) *Austral. inf.* ◆ *n* **1** a rowdy party or celebration. **2** a fraud; deception. ◆ *vb (tr)* **3** to take unfair advantage of (something): *our voting system can be rorted.* [C20: back formation from E dialect *rorty* (in the sense: good, splendid)]

▸ **'rorty** *adj*

rosace ('rəʊzeɪs) *n* **1** another name for **rose window. 2** another name for **rosette.** [C19: from F, from L *rosāceus* ROSACEOUS]

rosaceous (rəʊ'zeɪʃəs) *adj* **1** of or belonging to the Rosaceae, a family of plants typically having white, yellow, pink, or red five-petalled flowers. The family includes the rose, strawberry, blackberry, and many fruit trees. **2** like a rose, esp., rose-coloured. [C18: from L *rosāceus* composed of roses, from *rosa* ROSE[1]]

rosarian (rəʊ'zɛərɪən) *n* a person who cultivates roses, esp. professionally.

rosarium (rəʊ'zɛərɪəm) *n, pl* **rosariums** *or* **rosaria** (-'zɛərɪə). a rose garden. [C19: NL]

rosary ('rəʊzərɪ) *n, pl* **rosaries. 1** *RC Church.* **1a** a series of prayers counted on a string of beads, usually five or 15 decades of Aves, each decade beginning with a Paternoster and ending with a Gloria. **1b** a string of 55 or 165 beads used to count these prayers as they are recited. **2** (in other religions) a similar string of beads used in praying. **3** an archaic word for a **garland** (of flowers, etc.). [C14: from L *rosārium* rose garden, from *rosārius* of roses, from *rosa* ROSE[1]]

rose[1] (rəʊz) *n* **1a** a shrub or climbing plant having prickly stems, compound leaves, and fragrant flowers. **1b** *(in combination): rosebush.* **2** the flower of any of these plants. **3** any of various similar plants, such as the Christmas rose. **4a** a purplish-pink colour. **4b** *(as adj): rose paint.* **5** a rose, or a representation of one, as the national emblem of England. **6a** a cut for a gemstone, having a hemispherical faceted crown and a flat base. **6b** a gem so cut. **7** a perforated cap fitted to a watering can or hose, causing the water to issue in a spray. **8** a design or decoration shaped like a rose; rosette. **9** Also called: **ceiling rose.** *Electrical engineering.* a circular boss attached to a ceiling through which the flexible lead of an electric-light fitting passes. **10** *History.* See **red rose, white rose. 11 bed of roses.** a situation of comfort or ease. **12 under the rose.** in secret; privately; sub rosa. ◆ *vb* **roses, rosing, rosed. 13** *(tr)* to make rose-coloured; cause to blush or redden. [OE, from L *rosa,* prob. from Gk *rhodon* rose]

▸ **'roseˌlike** *adj*

rose[2] (rəʊz) *vb* the past tense of **rise.**

rosé ('rəʊzeɪ) *n* any pink wine, made either by removing the skins of red grapes after only a little colour has been extracted or by mixing red and white wines. [C19: from F, lit.: pink, from L *rosa* ROSE[1]]

roseate Ⓣ ('rəʊzɪˌeɪt) *adj* **1** of the colour rose or pink. **2** excessively or idealistically optimistic.

rosebay ('rəʊzˌbeɪ) *n* **1** any of several rhododendrons. **2 rosebay willowherb.** a perennial plant that has spikes of deep pink flowers and is widespread in N temperate regions. **3** another name for **oleander.**

rosebud ('rəʊzˌbʌd) *n* **1** the bud of a rose. **2** *Literary.* a pretty young woman.

rose campion *n* a European plant widely cultivated for its pink flowers. Its stems and leaves are covered with white woolly down. Also called: **dusty miller.**

rose chafer *or* **beetle** *n* a British beetle that has a greenish-golden body with a metallic lustre and feeds on plants.

rose-coloured *adj* **1** of the colour rose; rosy. **2** Also: **rose-tinted.** excessively optimistic. **3 see through rose-coloured** *or* **rose-tinted glasses** (*or* **spectacles**). to view in an excessively optimistic light.

rose-cut *adj* (of a gemstone) cut with a hemispherical faceted crown and a flat base.

rosehip ('rəʊzˌhɪp) *n* the berry-like fruit of a rose plant.

rosella (rəʊ'zɛlə) *n* any of various Australian parrots. [C19: prob. alteration of *Rose-hiller,* after *Rose Hill,* Parramatta, near Sydney]

rosemary ('rəʊzmərɪ) *n, pl* **rosemaries.** an aromatic European shrub widely cultivated for its grey-green evergreen leaves, which are used in cookery and in the manufacture of perfumes. It is the traditional flower of remembrance. [C15: earlier *rosmarine,* from L *rōs* dew + *marīnus* marine; modern form infl. by folk etymology, as if ROSE[1] + *Mary*]

rose of Sharon ('ʃærən) *n* a creeping shrub native to SE Europe but widely cultivated, having large yellow flowers. Also called: **Aaron's beard.**

roseola (rəʊ'ziːələ) *n Pathol.* **1** any red skin rash. **2** another name for **rubeola.** [C19: from NL, dim. of L *roseus* rosy]

▸ **ro'seolar** *adj*

rosery ('rəʊzərɪ) *n, pl* **roseries.** a bed or garden of roses.

Rosetta stone *n* a basalt slab discovered in 1799 at Rosetta, N Egypt, dating to the reign of Ptolemy V (196 B.C.) and carved with parallel inscriptions in hieroglyphics, Egyptian demotic, and Greek, which provided the key to the decipherment of ancient Egyptian texts.

rosette (rəʊ'zɛt) *n* **1** a decoration resembling a rose, esp. an arrangement of ribbons in a rose-shaped design worn as a badge or presented as a prize. **2** another name for **rose window. 3** *Bot.* a circular cluster of leaves growing from the base of a stem. [C18: from OF: a little ROSE[1]]

rose-water *n* **1** scented water made by the distillation of rose petals or by impregnation with oil of roses. **2** *(modifier)* elegant or delicate, esp. excessively so.

rose window *n* a circular window, esp. one that has ornamental tracery radiating from the centre to form a symmetrical roselike pattern. Also called: **wheel window, rosette.**

rosewood ('rəʊzˌwʊd) *n* the hard dark wood of any of various tropical trees. It has a roselike scent and is used in cabinetwork.

Rosh Hashanah *or* **Rosh Hashana** ('rɒʃ hə'ʃɑːnə; *Hebrew* 'rɔʃ haʃa'na) *n* the Jewish New Year festival, celebrated on the first and second of Tishri. [from Heb., lit.: beginning of the year, from *rōsh* head + *hash-shānāh* year]

Rosicrucian (ˌrəʊzɪ'kruːʃən) *n* **1** a member of a society professing esoteric religious doctrines, venerating the rose and Cross as symbols of Christ's Resurrection and Redemption, and claiming various occult powers. ◆ *adj* **2** of or designating the Rosicrucians or Rosicrucianism.

THESAURUS

rootless *adj* = **footloose,** homeless, itinerant, roving, transient, vagabond

root out *vb* = **get rid of,** abolish, cut out, destroy, dig up by the roots, do away with, efface, eliminate, eradicate, erase, exterminate, extirpate, remove, tear out by the roots, uproot, weed out, wipe from the face of the earth

rope *n* **1** = **cord,** cable, hawser, line, strand **6 know the ropes** = **be experienced,** be an old hand, be knowledgeable, know all the ins and outs, know one's way around, know the score (*inf.*), know what's what, know where it's at (*sl.*) **8 the rope** = **hanging,** capital punishment, halter, lynching, noose ◆ *vb* **9** = **tie,** bind, fasten, hitch, lash, lasso, moor, pinion, tether

rope in *vb* **1** *Brit.* = **persuade,** drag in, engage, enlist, inveigle, involve, talk into

ropey *adj Brit. informal* **1a** = **inferior,** deficient, inadequate, indifferent, mediocre, no great shakes (*inf.*), of poor quality, poor, sketchy, substandard **1b** = **unwell,** below par, off colour, poorly (*inf.*), rough (*inf.*), sickish, under the weather (*inf.*)

roseate *adj* **1** = **pink,** blooming, blushing, pinkish, red, rose-coloured, rosy, rubicund, ruddy **2**

[C17: from L *Rosae Crucis* Rose of the Cross, translation of the G name Christian *Rosenkreuz,* supposed founder of the society]

rosin ('rɒzɪn) *n* **1** Also called: **colophony.** a translucent brittle amber substance produced in the distillation of crude turpentine oleoresin and used esp. in making varnishes, printing inks, and sealing waxes and for treating the bows of stringed instruments. **2** (not in technical usage) another name for **resin** (sense 1). ◆ *vb* **3** (*tr*) to treat or coat with rosin. [C14: var. of RESIN]
▸'**rosiny** *adj*

ROSPA ('rɒspə) *n* (in Britain) *acronym for* Royal Society for the Prevention of Accidents.

roster ➊ ('rɒstə) *n* **1** a list or register, esp. one showing the order of people enrolled for duty. ◆ *vb* **2** (*tr*) to place on a roster. [C18: from Du. *rooster* grating or list (the lined paper looking like a grid)]

rostrum ➊ ('rɒstrəm) *n, pl* **rostrums** *or* **rostra** (-trə). **1** any platform on which public speakers stand to address an audience. **2** a platform in front of an orchestra on which the conductor stands. **3** another word for **ram** (sense 5). **4** the prow of an ancient Roman ship. **5** *Biol., zool.* a beak or beaklike part. [C16: from L *rōstrum* beak, ship's prow, from *rōdere* to nibble, gnaw; in pl, *rōstra* orator's platform, because this platform in the Roman forum was adorned with the prows of captured ships]
▸'**rostral** *adj*

rosy ➊ ('rəuzɪ) *adj* **rosier, rosiest. 1** of the colour rose or pink. **2** having a healthy pink complexion: *rosy cheeks.* **3** optimistic, esp. excessively so: *a rosy view of social improvements.* **4** resembling or abounding in roses.
▸'**rosily** *adv* ▸'**rosiness** *n*

rot ➊ (rɒt) *vb* **rots, rotting, rotted. 1** to decay or cause to decay as a result of bacterial or fungal action. **2** (*intr;* usually foll. by *off* or *away*) to crumble (off) or break (away), as from decay or long use. **3** (*intr*) to become weak or depressed through inertia, confinement, etc.; languish: *rotting in prison.* **4** to become or cause to become morally degenerate. ◆ *n* **5** the process of rotting or the state of being rotten. **6** something decomposed. Related adj: **putrid. 7** short for **dry rot. 8** *Pathol.* any putrefactive decomposition of tissues. **9** a condition in plants characterized by decay of tissues, caused by bacteria, fungi, etc. **10** *Vet. science.* a contagious fungal disease of sheep. **11** (*also interj*) nonsense; rubbish. [OE *rotian* (vb); rel. to ON, *rotna;* C13 (n), from ON]

rota ('rəutə) *n Chiefly Brit.* a register of names showing the order in which people take their turn to perform certain duties. [C17: from L: a wheel]

Rota ('rəutə) *n RC Church.* the supreme ecclesiastical tribunal.

rotachute ('rəutə,ʃuːt) *n* a device serving the same purpose as a parachute, in which the canopy is replaced by freely revolving rotor blades, used for the delivery of stores or recovery of missiles.

rotaplane ('rəutə,pleɪn) *n* an aircraft that derives its lift from freely revolving rotor blades.

rotary ➊ ('rəutərɪ) *adj* **1** operating by rotation. **2** turning; revolving. ◆ *n, pl* **rotaries. 3** a part of a machine that rotates about an axis. **4** *US & Canad.* another term for **roundabout** (sense 2). [C18: from Med. L *rotārius,* from L *rota* wheel]

Rotary Club *n* any of the local clubs that form **Rotary International,** an international association of professional and businessmen founded in the US in 1905 to promote community service.
▸**Rotarian** (rəu'tɛərɪən) *n, adj*

rotary engine *n* **1** an internal-combustion engine having radial cylinders that rotate about a fixed crankshaft. **2** an engine, such as a turbine or wankel engine, in which power is transmitted directly to rotating components.

rotary plough *or* **tiller** *n* an implement with a series of blades mounted on a power-driven shaft which rotates so as to break up soil.

rotary press *n* a machine for printing from a revolving cylindrical forme, usually onto a continuous strip of paper.

rotary table *n* a chain or gear-driven unit, mounted in the derrick floor which rotates the drill pipe and bit.

rotate ➊ *vb* (rəu'teɪt), **rotates, rotating, rotated. 1** to turn or cause to turn around an axis; revolve or spin. **2** to follow or cause to follow a set sequence. **3** to replace (one set of personnel) with another. ◆ *adj* ('rəuteɪt). **4** *Bot.* designating a corolla the petals of which radiate like the spokes of a wheel.
▸**ro'tatable** *adj*

rotation ➊ (rəu'teɪʃən) *n* **1** the act of rotating; rotary motion. **2** a regular cycle of events in a set order or sequence. **3** a planned sequence of cropping according to which the crops grown in successive seasons on the same land are varied so as to make a balanced demand on its resources of fertility. **4** the spinning motion of a body, such as a planet, about an internal axis. **5** *Maths.* **5a** a circular motion of a configuration about a given point, without a change in shape. **5b** a transformation in which the coordinate axes are rotated by a fixed angle about the origin.
▸**ro'tational** *adj*

rotator (rəu'teɪtə) *n* **1** a person, device, or part that rotates or causes rotation. **2** *Anat.* any of various muscles that revolve a part on its axis.

rotatory ('rəutətərɪ, -trɪ) *or* (*less commonly*) **rotative** *adj* of, possessing, or causing rotation.
▸'**rotatorily** *adv*

Rotavator ('rəutə,veɪtə) *n Trademark.* a mechanical cultivator with rotary blades. [C20: from ROTA(RY) + (CULTI)VATOR]
▸'**Rota,vate** *vb* (*tr*)

rote (rəut) *n* **1** a habitual or mechanical routine or procedure. **2 by rote.** by repetition; by heart (often in **learn by rote**). [C14: from ?]

rotenone ('rəutɪ,nəun) *n* a white odourless crystalline substance extracted from the roots of derris: a powerful insecticide. [C20: from Japanese *rōten* derris + -ONE]

rotgut ('rɒt,gʌt) *n Facetious sl.* alcoholic drink, esp. spirits, of inferior quality.

rotifer ('rəutɪfə) *n* a minute aquatic multicellular invertebrate having a ciliated wheel-like organ used in feeding and locomotion: common constituents of freshwater plankton. Also called: **wheel animalcule.** [C18: from NL *Rotifera,* from L *rota* wheel + *ferre* to bear]
▸**rotiferal** (rəu'tɪfərəl) *or* **ro'tiferous** *adj*

rotisserie (rəu'tɪsərɪ) *n* **1** a rotating spit on which meat, poultry, etc., can be cooked. **2** a shop or restaurant where meat is roasted to order. [C19: from F, from OF *rostir* to ROAST]

rotogravure (,rəutəugrə'vjuə) *n* **1** a printing process using cylinders with many small holes, from which ink is transferred to a moving web of paper, etc., in a rotary press. **2** printed material produced in this way, esp. magazines. [C20: from L *rota* wheel + GRAVURE]

rotor ('rəutə) *n* **1** the rotating member of a machine or device, such as the revolving arm of the distributor of an internal-combustion engine. **2** a rotating device having radiating blades projecting from a hub which produces thrust to lift and propel a helicopter. [C20: shortened form of ROTATOR]

rotten ➊ ('rɒtᵊn) *adj* **1** decomposing, decaying, or putrid. **2** breaking up, esp. through age or hard use: *rotten ironwork.* **3** morally corrupt. **4** disloyal or treacherous. **5** *Inf.* unpleasant: *rotten weather.* **6** *Inf.* unsatisfactory or poor: *rotten workmanship.* **7** *Inf.* miserably unwell. **8** *Inf.* distressed and embarrassed: *I felt rotten breaking the bad news to him.* ◆ *adv Inf.* **9** extremely; very much: *men fancy her rotten.* [C13: from ON *rottin;* rel. to OE *rotian* to ROT]
▸'**rottenly** *adv* ▸'**rottenness** *n*

rotten borough *n* (before the Reform Act of 1832) any of certain English parliamentary constituencies with few or no electors.

rottenstone ('rɒtᵊn,stəun) *n* a much-weathered limestone, rich in silica: used in powdered form for polishing metal.

rotter ➊ ('rɒtə) *n Sl., chiefly Brit.* a worthless, unpleasant, or despicable person.

Rottweiler ('rɒt,waɪlə, -,vaɪlə) *n* **1** a breed of large dog with a smooth black and tan coat, noted for strength and aggression. **2** (*often not cap.*) **2a** an aggressive and unscrupulous person. **2b** (*as modifier*): *rottweiler*

THESAURUS

= **overoptimistic,** idealistic, rose-coloured, unrealistic, utopian

roster *n* **1** = **rota,** agenda, catalogue, inventory, list, listing, register, roll, schedule, scroll, table

rostrum *n* **1, 2** = **stage,** dais, platform, podium, stand

rosy *adj* **1** = **pink,** red, roseate, rose-coloured **2** = **glowing,** blooming, blushing, flushed, fresh, healthy-looking, radiant, reddish, roseate, rubicund, ruddy **3** = **promising,** auspicious, bright, cheerful, encouraging, favourable, hopeful, optimistic, reassuring, roseate, rose-coloured, sunny
Antonyms *adj* ≠ **glowing:** ashen, colourless, grey, pale, pallid, sickly, wan, white ≠ **promising:** cheerless, depressing, discouraging, dismal, down in the dumps (*inf.*), dull, gloomy, hopeless, miserable, pessimistic, unhappy, unpromising

rot *vb* **1** = **decay,** break down, corrode, corrupt, decompose, degenerate, deteriorate, disintegrate, fester, go bad, moulder, perish, putrefy, spoil, taint **3** = **deteriorate,** decline, degenerate, languish, waste away, wither away ◆ *n* **5** = **decay,** blight, canker, corrosion, corruption, decomposition, deterioration, disintegration, mould, putrefaction, putrescence **11** *Informal* = **nonsense,** balderdash, bilge (*inf.*), bosh (*inf.*), bunk (*inf.*), bunkum *or* buncombe (*chiefly US*), claptrap (*inf.*), cobblers (*Brit. taboo sl.*), codswallop (*Brit. sl.*), crap (*sl.*), drivel, garbage (*chiefly US*), hogwash, hokum (*sl., chiefly US & Canad.*), hot air (*inf.*), moonshine, piffle (*inf.*), poppycock (*inf.*), rubbish, shit (*taboo sl.*), stuff and nonsense, tommyrot, tosh (*sl., chiefly Brit.*), trash, tripe (*inf.*), twaddle

rotary *adj* **2** = **revolving,** gyratory, rotating, rotational, rotatory, spinning, turning

rotate *vb* **1** = **revolve,** go round, gyrate, pirouette, pivot, reel, spin, swivel, turn, wheel **2** = **follow in sequence,** alternate, interchange, switch, take turns

rotation *n* **1** = **revolution,** gyration, orbit, pirouette, reel, spin, spinning, turn, turning, wheel **2** = **sequence,** alternation, cycle, interchanging, succession, switching

rotten *adj* **1** = **decaying,** bad, corroded, corrupt, decayed, decomposed, decomposing, festering, fetid, foul, mouldering, mouldy, perished, putrescent, putrid, rank, sour, stinking, tainted, unsound **2** = **disintegrating,** crumbling **3** *Informal* = **corrupt,** base, bent, contemptible, crooked (*inf.*), degenerate, despicable, dirty, disagreeable, dishonest, dishonourable, filthy, immoral, mean, nasty, scurrilous, unpleasant, venal, vicious, vile, wicked **4** = **treacherous,** deceitful, disloyal, faithless, mercenary, perfidious, untrustworthy **5** *Informal* = **bad,** deplorable, disappointing, regrettable, unfortunate, unlucky **6** *Informal* = **inferior,** crummy, duff (*Brit. inf.*), ill-considered, ill-thought-out, inadequate, lousy (*sl.*), low-grade, of a sort *or* of sorts, poor, poxy (*sl.*), ropey *or* ropy (*Brit. inf.*), sorry, substandard, unacceptable, unsatisfactory **7** *Informal* = **unwell,** bad, below par, ill, off colour, poorly (*inf.*), ropey *or* ropy (*Brit. inf.*), rough (*inf.*), sick, under the weather (*inf.*)
Antonyms *adj* ≠ **decaying:** fresh, good, pure, sweet, wholesome ≠ **corrupt:** decent, honest, honourable, moral, scrupulous, trustworthy

rotter *n Slang, chiefly Brit.* = **scoundrel,** bad lot, blackguard, blighter (*Brit. inf.*), bounder (*old-fashioned Brit. sl.*), cad (*Brit. inf.*), cur, louse (*sl.*), rat (*inf.*), scumbag (*sl.*), stinker (*sl.*), swine

politics. [G, from *Rottweil*, town in Swabia, Germany, where the breed originated]

rotund Ⓣ (rəʊˈtʌnd) *adj* **1** rounded or spherical in shape. **2** plump. **3** sonorous or grandiloquent. [C18: from L *rotundus* round, from *rota* wheel]
▸**roˈtundity** *n* ▸**roˈtundly** *adv*

rotunda (rəʊˈtʌndə) *n* a circular building or room, esp. one that has a dome. [C17: from It. *rotonda*, from L *rotundus* round, from *rota* a wheel]

rouble *or* **ruble** (ˈruːbᵊl) *n* the standard monetary unit of Belarus, Russia, and Tajikistan. [C16: from Russian *rubl* silver bar, from ORussian *rublĭ* bar, block of wood, from *rubiti* to cut up]

roué Ⓣ (ˈruːeɪ) *n* a debauched or lecherous man; rake. [C19: from F, lit.: one broken on the wheel; with reference to the fate deserved by a debauchee]

rouge (ruːʒ) *n* **1** a red powder or cream, used as a cosmetic for adding redness to the cheeks. **2** short for **jeweller's rouge.** ◆ *vb* **rouges, rouging, rouged. 3** (*tr*) to apply rouge to. [C18: F: red, from L *rubeus*]

rouge et noir (ˈruːʒ eɪ ˈnwɑː) *n* a card game in which the players put their stakes on any of two red and two black diamond-shaped spots marked on the table. [F, lit.: red and black]

rough Ⓣ (rʌf) *adj* **1** (of a surface) not smooth; uneven or irregular. **2** (of ground) covered with scrub, boulders, etc. **3** denoting or taking place on uncultivated ground: *rough grazing.* **4** shaggy or hairy. **5** turbulent: *a rough sea.* **6** (of performance or motion) uneven; irregular: *a rough engine.* **7** (of behaviour or character) rude, coarse, or violent. **8** harsh or sharp: *rough words.* **9** *Inf.* severe or unpleasant: *a rough lesson.* **10** (of work, etc.) requiring physical rather than mental effort. **11** *Inf.* ill: *he felt rough after an evening of heavy drinking.* **12** unfair: *rough luck.* **13** harsh or grating to the ear. **14** without refinement, luxury, etc. **15** not perfected in any detail; rudimentary: *rough workmanship; rough justice.* **16** not prepared or dressed: *rough gemstones.* **17** (of a guess, etc.) approximate. **18** having the sound of *h*; aspirated. **19 rough on.** *Inf., chiefly Brit.* **19a** severe towards. **19b** unfortunate for (a person). **20 the rough side of one's tongue.** harsh words; a rebuke. ◆ *n* **21** rough ground. **22** a sketch or preliminary piece of artwork. **23** unfinished or crude state (esp. in **in the rough**). **24 the rough.** *Golf.* the part of the course bordering the fairways where the grass is untrimmed. **25** *Inf.* a violent person; thug. **26** the unpleasant side of something (esp. in **take the rough with the smooth**). ◆ *adv* **27** roughly. **28 sleep rough.** to spend the night in the open; be without shelter. ◆ *vb* (*tr*) **29** to make rough; roughen. **30** (foll. by *out, in*, etc.) to prepare (a sketch, report, etc.) in preliminary form. **31 rough it.** *Inf.* to live without the usual comforts of life. ◆ See also **rough up.** [OE *rūh*]
▸**ˈroughly** *adv* ▸**ˈroughness** *n*

roughage (ˈrʌfɪdʒ) *n* **1** the coarse indigestible constituents of food, which provide bulk to the diet and aid digestion. **2** any rough material.

rough-and-ready Ⓣ *adj* **1** crude, unpolished, or hastily prepared, but sufficient for the purpose. **2** (of a person) without formality or refinement.

rough-and-tumble Ⓣ *n* **1** a fight or scuffle without rules. ◆ *adj* **2** characterized by disorderliness and disregard for rules.

rough breathing *n* (in Greek) the sign (ʽ) placed over an initial letter, indicating that (in ancient Greek) it was pronounced with an *h*.

roughcast (ˈrʌfˌkɑːst) *n* **1** a mixture of plaster and small stones used to cover the surface of an external wall. **2** any rough or preliminary form, model, etc. ◆ *adj* **3** covered with roughcast. ◆ *vb* **roughcasts, roughcasting, roughcast. 4** to apply roughcast to (a wall, etc.). **5** to prepare in rough.
▸**ˈroughˌcaster** *n*

rough-cut *n* a first basic edited version of a film with the scenes in sequence and the soundtrack synchronized.

rough diamond *n* **1** an unpolished diamond. **2** an intrinsically trustworthy or good person with uncouth manners or dress.

rough-dry *adj* **1** (of clothes or linen) dried ready for pressing. ◆ *vb* **rough-dries, rough-drying, rough-dried. 2** (*tr*) to dry (clothes, etc.) without ironing them.

roughen (ˈrʌfᵊn) *vb* to make or become rough.

rough-hew *vb* **rough-hews, rough-hewing, rough-hewed; rough-hewed** *or* **rough-hewn.** (*tr*) to cut or shape roughly without finishing the surface.

roughhouse Ⓣ (ˈrʌfˌhaʊs) *n Sl.* rough, disorderly, or noisy behaviour.

roughish (ˈrʌfɪʃ) *adj* somewhat rough.

rough music *n* (formerly) a loud cacophony created with tin pans, drums, etc., esp. as a protest or demonstration of indignation outside someone's house.

roughneck Ⓣ (ˈrʌfˌnɛk) *n Sl.* **1** a rough or violent person; thug. **2** a worker in an oil-drilling operation.

rough puff pastry *n* a rich flaky pastry.

roughrider (ˈrʌfˌraɪdə) *n* a rider of wild or unbroken horses.

roughshod (ˈrʌfˌʃɒd) *adj* **1** (of a horse) shod with rough-bottomed shoes to prevent sliding. ◆ *adv* **2 ride roughshod over.** to domineer over or act with complete disregard for.

rough stuff *n Inf.* violence.

rough trade *n Sl.* (in homosexual use) a tough or violent sexual partner, esp. one casually picked up.

rough up Ⓣ *vb* (*tr, adv*) **1** *Inf.* to treat violently; beat up. **2** to cause (feathers, hair, etc.) to stand up by rubbing against the grain.

roulade (ruːˈlɑːd) *n* **1** something cooked in the shape of a roll, esp. a slice of meat. **2** an elaborate run in vocal music. [C18: from F, lit.: a rolling, from *rouler* to ROLL]

roulette (ruːˈlɛt) *n* **1** a gambling game in which a ball is dropped onto a spinning horizontal wheel divided into numbered slots, with players betting on the slot into which the ball will fall. **2** a toothed wheel for making a line of perforations. **3** a curve generated by a point on one curve rolling on another. ◆ *vb* **roulettes, rouletting, rouletted.** (*tr*) **4** to use a roulette on (something), as in engraving, making stationery, etc. [C18: from F, from *rouelle*, dim. of *roue* a wheel, from L *rota*]

round Ⓣ (raʊnd) *adj* **1** having a flat circular shape, as a hoop. **2** having the shape of a ball. **3** curved; not angular. **4** involving or using circular motion. **5** (*prenominal*) complete: *a round dozen.* **6** *Maths.* **6a** forming or expressed by a whole number, with no fraction. **6b** expressed to the nearest ten, hundred, or thousand: *in round figures.* **7** (of a sum of money) considerable. **8** fully depicted or developed, as a character in a book. **9** full and plump: *round cheeks.* **10** (of sound) full and sonorous. **11** (of pace) brisk; lively. **12** (*prenominal*) (of speech) candid; unmodified: *a round assertion.* **13** (of a vowel) pronounced with rounded lips. ◆ *n* **14** a round shape or object. **15 in the round. 15a** in full detail. **15b** *Theatre.* with the audience all round the stage. **16** a session, as of a negotiation: *a round of talks.* **17** a series: *a giddy round of parties.* **18 the daily round.** the usual activities of one's day. **19** a stage of a competi-

THESAURUS

rotund *adj* **1** = **round**, bulbous, globular, orbicular, rounded, spherical **2** = **plump**, chubby, corpulent, fat, fleshy, heavy, obese, podgy, portly, roly-poly, rounded, stout, tubby **3** = **sonorous**, full, grandiloquent, magniloquent, orotund, pompous, resonant, rich, round
Antonyms *adj* ≠ **plump**: angular, gaunt, lank, lanky, lean, scrawny, skinny, slender, slight, slim, thin

roué *n* = **libertine**, debauchee, dirty old man (*sl.*), lech *or* letch (*inf.*), lecher, profligate, rake, sensualist, wanton

rough *adj* **1, 2** = **uneven**, broken, bumpy, craggy, irregular, jagged, rocky, rugged, stony **4** = **coarse**, bristly, bushy, dishevelled, disordered, fuzzy, hairy, shaggy, tangled, tousled, uncut, unshaven, unshorn **5** = **stormy**, agitated, boisterous, choppy, inclement, squally, tempestuous, turbulent, wild **7** = **rude**, bearish, bluff, blunt, brusque, churlish, coarse, curt, discourteous, ill-bred, ill-mannered, impolite, inconsiderate, indelicate, loutish, unceremonious, uncivil, uncouth, uncultured, ungracious, unmannerly, unpolished, unrefined, untutored **10** = **arduous**, tough **11** *Informal* = **unwell**, below par, ill, not a hundred per cent (*inf.*), off colour, poorly (*inf.*), ropey *or* ropy (*Brit. inf.*), rotten (*inf.*), sick, under the weather (*inf.*), upset **13** = **grating**, cacophonous, discordant, gruff, harsh, husky, inharmonious, jarring, rasping, raucous, unmusical **14** = **uncomfortable**, austere, hard, rugged, spartan, unpleasant **15** = **basic**, crude, cursory, formless, hasty, imperfect, incomplete, quick, raw, rough-and-ready, rough-hewn, rudimentary, shapeless, sketchy, unfinished, unpolished, unrefined **16** = **unprocessed**, crude, raw, rough-hewn, uncut, undressed, unhewn, unpolished, unwrought **17** = **approximate**, estimated, foggy, general, hazy, imprecise, inexact, sketchy, vague **19a** = **harsh**, cruel, curt, drastic, extreme, hard, nasty, severe, sharp, tough, unfeeling, unjust, unpleasant, violent ◆ *n* **22** = **outline**, draft, mock-up, preliminary sketch, suggestion **25** *Informal* = **thug**, bruiser, bully boy, casual, lager lout, roughneck (*sl.*), rowdy, ruffian, tough ◆ *vb* **30** *foll. by* **out** = **outline**, adumbrate, block out, delineate, draft, plan, sketch, suggest
Antonyms *adj* ≠ **uneven**: even, level, regular, smooth, unbroken ≠ **coarse**: smooth, soft ≠ **stormy**: calm, gentle, quiet, smooth, tranquil ≠ **rude**: civil, considerate, courteous, courtly, delicate, elegant, graceful, gracious, pleasant, polite, refined, smooth, sophisticated, urbane, well-bred, well-mannered ≠ **arduous**: comfortable, cushy (*inf.*), easy, pleasant, soft ≠ **grating**: harmonious, smooth ≠ **basic**: complete, detailed, finished, perfected, polished, refined, specific ≠ **approximate**: exact, perfected, specific ≠ **harsh**: gentle, just, kind, mild, pleasant, quiet, soft

rough-and-ready *adj* **1** = **makeshift**, adequate, cobbled together, crude, improvised, provisional, sketchy, stopgap, thrown together, unpolished, unrefined

rough-and-tumble *n* **1** = **fight**, affray (*Law*), brawl, donnybrook, dust-up, fracas, melee *or* mêlée, punch-up (*Brit. inf.*), roughhouse (*sl.*), scrap (*inf.*), scrimmage, scuffle, shindig (*inf.*), shindy (*inf.*), struggle ◆ *adj* **2** = **disorderly**, boisterous, haphazard, indisciplined, irregular, rough, rowdy, scrambled, scrambling

roughhouse *n Slang* = **rough behaviour**, boisterousness, brawl, brawling, disorderliness, disturbance, horseplay, row, rowdiness, rowdyism, skylarking (*inf.*)

roughneck *n Slang* **1** = **thug**, bruiser (*inf.*), bully boy, heavy (*sl.*), rough (*inf.*), rowdy, ruffian, tough

rough up *vb* **1** *Informal* = **beat up**, bash up (*inf.*), batter, beat the living daylights out of (*inf.*), do over (*Brit., Austral., & NZ sl.*), knock about *or* around, maltreat, manhandle, mistreat, thrash, work over (*sl.*)

round *adj* **1-3** = **spherical**, ball-shaped, bowed, bulbous, circular, curved, curvilinear, cylindrical, discoid, disc-shaped, globular, orbicular, ring-shaped, rotund, rounded **5** = **complete**, entire, full, solid, unbroken, undivided, whole **7** = **considerable**, ample, bounteous, bountiful, generous, great, large, liberal, substantial **9** = **plump**, ample, fleshy, full, full-fleshed, roly-poly, rotund, rounded **10** = **sonorous**, full, mellifluous, orotund, resonant, rich, rotund **12** = **candid**, blunt, direct, downright, frank, outspoken, plain, straightforward, unmodified ◆ *n* **14** = **sphere**, ball, band, circle, disc, globe, orb, ring **17** = **series**, bout, cycle, sequence, session, succession **19** = **stage**, division, lap, level, period, session, turn **20** = **course**, ambit, beat, circuit, compass, routine, schedule, series, tour, turn **24, 25** = **bullet**, cartridge, discharge, shell, shot ◆ *vb* **48** = **encircle**, circle, flank, surround

tion: *he was eliminated in the first round.* **20** (*often pl*) a series of calls: *a milkman's round.* **21** a playing of all the holes on a golf course. **22** a single turn of play by each player, as in a card game. **23** one of a number of periods in a boxing, wrestling, or other match. **24** a single discharge by a gun. **25** a bullet or other charge of ammunition. **26** a number of drinks bought at one time for a group of people. **27a** a single slice of bread. **27b** a sandwich made from two slices of bread. **28** a general outburst of applause, etc. **29** movement in a circle. **30** *Music.* a part song in which the voices follow each other at equal intervals at the same pitch. **31** a sequence of bells rung in order of treble to tenor. **32** a cut of beef from the thigh. **33 go** *or* **make the rounds. 33a** to go from place to place, as in making social calls. **33b** (of information, rumour, etc.) to be passed around, so as to be generally known. ◆ *prep* **34** surrounding, encircling, or enclosing: *a band round her head.* **35** on all or most sides of: *to look round one.* **36** on or outside the circumference or perimeter of. **37** from place to place in: *driving round Ireland.* **38** reached by making a partial circuit about: *the shop round the corner.* **39** revolving round (a centre or axis): *the earth's motion round its axis.* ◆ *adv* **40** on all or most sides. **41** on or outside the circumference or perimeter: *the racing track is two miles round.* **42** to all members of a group: *pass the food round.* **43** in rotation or revolution: *the wheels turn round.* **44** by a circuitous route: *the road to the farm goes round by the pond.* **45** to a specific place: *she came round to see me.* **46 all year round.** throughout the year. ◆ *vb* **47** to make or become round. **48** (*tr*) to encircle; surround. **49** to move or cause to move with turning motion: *to round a bend.* **50** (*tr*) **50a** to pronounce (a speech sound) with rounded lips. **50b** to purse (the lips). ◆ See also **round down, round off,** etc. [C13: from OF *ront,* from L *rotundus* round, from *rota* a wheel]
▸ **'roundish** *adj* ▸ **'roundness** *n*

> **USAGE NOTE** See at **around.**

roundabout ➊ ('raʊndəˌbaʊt) *n* **1** *Brit.* a revolving circular platform provided with wooden animals, seats, etc., on which people ride for amusement; merry-go-round. **2** a road junction in which traffic streams circulate around a central island. US and Canad. name: **traffic circle.** ◆ *adj* **3** indirect; devious. ◆ *adv, prep* **round about. 4** on all sides: *spectators standing round about.* **5** approximately: *at round about 5 o'clock.*

round dance *n* **1** a dance in which the dancers form a circle. **2** a ballroom dance, such as the waltz, in which couples revolve.

round down *vb* (*tr, adv*) to lower (a number) to the nearest whole number or ten, hundred, or thousand below it.

rounded ('raʊndɪd) *adj* **1** round or curved. **2** mature or complete. **3** (of the lips) pursed. **4** (of a speech sound) articulated with rounded lips.

roundel ('raʊndᵊl) *n* **1** a form of rondeau consisting of three stanzas each of three lines with a refrain after the first and the third. **2** a circular identifying mark in national colours on military aircraft. **3** a small circular window, medallion, etc. **4** a round plate of armour used to protect the armpit. **5** another word for **roundelay.** [C13: from OF *rondel;* see RONDEL]

roundelay ('raʊndɪˌleɪ) *n* **1** Also called: **roundel.** a slow medieval dance performed in a circle. **2** a song in which a line or phrase is repeated as a refrain. [C16: from OF *rondelet* a little rondel, from *rondel;* also infl. by LAY[4]]

rounders ('raʊndəz) *n* (*functioning as sing*) *Brit.* a ball game in which players run between posts after hitting the ball, scoring a **rounder** if they run round all four before the ball is retrieved.

Roundhead ('raʊndˌhɛd) *n English history.* a supporter of Parliament against Charles I during the Civil War. [referring to their short-cut hair]

roundhouse ('raʊndˌhaʊs) *n* **1** *US & Canad.* a building in which railway locomotives are serviced, radial tracks being fed by a central turntable. **2** *US boxing sl.* a swinging punch or style of punching. **3** an obsolete word for **jail. 4** *Obs.* a cabin on the quarterdeck of a sailing ship.

rounding ('raʊndɪŋ) *n Computing.* a process in which a number is approximated as the closest number that can be expressed using the number of bits or digits available.

roundly ➊ ('raʊndlɪ) *adv* **1** frankly, bluntly, or thoroughly: *to be roundly criticized.* **2** in a round manner or so as to be round.

round off ➊ *vb* (*tr, adv*) **1** (often foll. by *with*) to complete, esp. agreeably: *we rounded off the evening with a brandy.* **2** to make less jagged.

round on ➊ *vb* (*intr, prep*) to attack or reply to (someone) with sudden irritation or anger.

round robin *n* **1** a petition or protest having the signatures in a circle to disguise the order of signing. **2** a tournament in which each player plays against every other player.

round-shouldered *adj* denoting a faulty posture characterized by drooping shoulders and a slight forward bending of the back.

roundsman ('raʊndzmən) *n, pl* **roundsmen. 1** *Brit.* a person who makes rounds, as for inspection or to deliver goods. **2** *Austral. & NZ.* a reporter covering a particular district or topic.

round table *n* **a** a meeting of parties or people on equal terms for discussion. **b** (*as modifier*): *a round-table conference.*

Round Table *n* **the. 1** (in Arthurian legend) the circular table of King Arthur, enabling his knights to sit around it without any having precedence. **2** Arthur and his knights collectively. **3** one of an organization of clubs of young business and professional men who meet in order to further charitable work.

round-the-clock *adj* (*or as adv* **round the clock**) throughout the day and night.

round tower *n* a freestanding circular stone belfry built in Ireland from the 10th century beside a monastery and used as a place of refuge.

round trip *n* a trip to a place and back again, esp. returning by a different route.

roundtripping ('raʊndˌtrɪpɪŋ) *n Finance.* a form of trading in which a company borrows a sum of money from one source and takes advantage of a short-term rise in interest rates to make a profit by lending it to another.

round up ➊ *vb* (*tr, adv*) **1** to gather together: *to round ponies up.* **2** to raise (a number) to the nearest whole number or ten, hundred, or thousand above it. ◆ *n* **roundup. 3** the act of gathering together livestock, esp. cattle, so that they may be branded, counted, or sold. **4** any similar act of bringing together: *a roundup of today's news.*

roundworm ('raʊndˌwɜːm) *n* a nematode worm that is a common intestinal parasite of man and pigs.

roup (raʊp) *Scot. & N English dialect.* ◆ *vb* (*tr*) **1** to sell by auction. ◆ *n* **2** an auction. [C16 (orig.: to shout): of Scand. origin]

rouse ➊ (raʊz) *vb* **rouses, rousing, roused. 1** to bring (oneself or another person) out of sleep, etc., or (of a person) to come to consciousness in this way. **2** (*tr*) to provoke: *to rouse someone's anger.* **3 rouse oneself.** to become energetic. **4** to start or cause to start from cover: *to rouse game birds.* **5** (*intr;* foll. by *on*) *Austral.* to scold or rebuke. [C15 (in sense of hawks ruffling their feathers): from ?]
▸ **'rouser** *n*

rouseabout ('raʊzəˌbaʊt) *n* **1** *Austral. & NZ.* an unskilled labourer in a shearing shed. **2** a variant of **roustabout** (sense 1).

rousing ➊ ('raʊzɪŋ) *adj* tending to excite; lively or vigorous: *a rousing chorus.*
▸ **'rousingly** *adv*

roust (raʊst) *vb* (*tr;* often foll. by *out*) to rout or stir, as out of bed. [C17: ?from ROUSE]

roustabout ('raʊstəˌbaʊt) *n* **1** an unskilled labourer, esp. on an oil rig. **2** *Austral. & NZ.* a variant of **rouseabout** (sense 1).

rout[1] ➊ (raʊt) *n* **1** an overwhelming defeat. **2** a disorderly retreat. **3** a noisy rabble. **4** *Law.* a group of three or more people proceeding to commit an illegal act. **5** *Arch.* a large party or social gathering. ◆ *vb* **6** (*tr*) to defeat and cause to flee in confusion. [C13: from Anglo-Norman *rute,* from OF: disorderly band, from L *ruptus,* from *rumpere* to burst]

rout[2] (raʊt) *vb* **1** to dig over or turn up (something), esp. (of an animal) with the snout; root. **2** (*tr;* usually foll. by *out* or *up*) to find by searching. **3** (*tr;* usually foll. by *out*) to drive out: *they routed him out of bed at midnight.* **4** (*tr;* often foll. by *out*) to hollow or gouge out. **5** (*intr*) to search, poke, or rummage. [C16: var. of ROOT[2]]

route ➊ (ruːt) *n* **1** the choice of roads taken to get to a place. **2** a regular journey travelled. **3** (*cap.*) *US.* a main road between cities: *Route 66.* ◆ *vb* **routes, routeing, routed.** (*tr*) **4** to plan the route of; send by a particular route. [C13: from OF *rute,* from Vulgar L *rupta via* (unattested), lit.: a broken (established) way, from L *ruptus,* from *rumpere* to break]

> **USAGE NOTE** When forming the present participle or verbal noun from the verb *to route* it is preferable to retain the *e* in order to distinguish the word from *routing,* the present participle or verbal noun from *rout*[1], to defeat or *rout*[2], to dig, rummage: *the routeing of buses from the city centre to the suburbs.* The spelling *routing* in this sense is, however, sometimes encountered, esp. in American English.

THESAURUS

49 = **go round**, bypass, circumnavigate, skirt, turn

roundabout *adj* **3** = **indirect**, circuitous, circumlocutory, devious, discursive, evasive, meandering, oblique, periphrastic, tortuous
Antonyms *adj* direct, straight, straightforward

roundly *adv* **1** = **thoroughly**, bitterly, bluntly, fiercely, frankly, intensely, outspokenly, rigorously, severely, sharply, vehemently, violently

round off *vb* **1** = **complete**, bring to a close, cap, close, conclude, crown, finish off, put the finishing touch to, settle
Antonyms *vb* begin, commence, initiate, open, start

round on *vb* = **attack**, abuse, bite (someone's) head off (*inf.*), have a go at (*Brit. sl.*), lose one's temper with, retaliate, snap at, turn on, wade into

round up *vb* **1** = **gather**, assemble, bring together, collect, drive, group, herd, marshal, muster, rally ◆ *n* **roundup 3** = **gathering**, assembly, collection, herding, marshalling, muster, rally **4** = **summary**, collation, survey

rouse *vb* **1** = **wake up**, arouse, awaken, call, get up, rise, wake **2** = **provoke**, agitate, anger, arouse, galvanize, get going, incite, inflame, instigate, move, prod, stimulate, stir, whip up

rousing *adj* = **lively**, brisk, electrifying, exciting, exhilarating, inflammatory, inspiring, moving, spirited, stimulating, stirring, vigorous
Antonyms *adj* boring, dreary, dull, lifeless, sluggish, spiritless, unenergetic, wearisome, wishy-washy (*inf.*)

rout[1] *n* **1** = **defeat**, beating, debacle, disorderly retreat, drubbing, headlong flight, hiding (*inf.*), licking (*inf.*), overthrow, overwhelming defeat, pasting (*sl.*), ruin, shambles, thrashing ◆ *vb* **6** = **defeat**, beat, chase, clobber, conquer, crush, cut to pieces, destroy, dispel, drive off, drub, lick (*inf.*), overpower, overthrow, put to flight, put to rout, scatter, stuff (*sl.*), tank (*sl.*), thrash, throw back in confusion, wipe the floor with (*inf.*), worst

route *n* **1** = **way**, beat, circuit, course, direction, itinerary, journey, passage, path, road, round,

routemarch (ˈruːtˌmɑːtʃ) *n* **1** *Mil.* a long training march. **2** *Inf.* any long exhausting walk.

router (ˈraʊtə) *n* any of various tools or machines for hollowing out, cutting grooves, etc.

routine ⓣ (ruːˈtiːn) *n* **1** a usual or regular method of procedure, esp. one that is unvarying. **2** *Computing.* a program or part of a program performing a specific function: *an input routine.* **3** a set sequence of dance steps. **4** *Inf.* a hackneyed or insincere speech. ◆ *adj* **5** relating to or characteristic of routine. [C17: from OF, from *route* a customary way, ROUTE]
▸**rouˈtinely** *adv*

roux (ruː) *n* a mixture of equal amounts of fat and flour, heated, blended, and used as a basis for sauces. [F: brownish, from L *russus* RUSSET]

rove[1] ⓣ (rəʊv) *vb* **roves, roving, roved. 1** to wander about (a place) with no fixed direction; roam. **2** (*intr*) (of the eyes) to look around; wander. ◆ *n* **3** the act of roving. [C15 *roven* (in archery) to shoot at a target chosen at random (C16: to wander, stray), from ON]

rove[2] (rəʊv) *vb* **roves, roving, roved. 1** (*tr*) to pull out and twist (fibres of wool, cotton, etc.) lightly, as before spinning. ◆ *n* **2** wool, cotton, etc., thus prepared. [C18: from ?]

rove[3] (rəʊv) *vb* a past tense and past participle of **reeve**[2].

rover[1] ⓣ (ˈrəʊvə) *n* **1** a person who roves. **2** *Archery.* a mark selected at random for use as a target. **3** *Australian Rules football.* a player without a fixed position who, with the ruckmen, forms the ruck. [C15: from ROVE[1]]

rover[2] (ˈrəʊvə) *n* a pirate or pirate ship. [C14: prob. from MDu. or MLow G, from *roven* to rob]

Rover *or* **Rover Scout** (ˈrəʊvə) *n Brit.* the former name for **Venture Scout.**

roving commission *n* authority or power given in a general area, without precisely defined terms of reference.

row[1] ⓣ (rəʊ) *n* **1** an arrangement of persons or things in a line: *a row of chairs.* **2** *Chiefly Brit.* a street, esp. a narrow one lined with identical houses. **3** a line of seats, as in a cinema, theatre, etc. **4** *Maths.* a horizontal linear arrangement of numbers, quantities, or terms. **5** a horizontal rank of squares on a chessboard or draughtboard. **6 a hard row to hoe.** a difficult task or assignment. **7 in a row.** in succession; one after the other: *he won two gold medals in a row.* [OE *rāw, rǣw*]

row[2] (rəʊ) *vb* **1** to propel (a boat) by using oars. **2** (*tr*) to carry (people, goods, etc.) in a rowing boat. **3** to be propelled by means of (oars or oarsmen). **4** (*intr*) to take part in the racing of rowing boats as a sport. **5** (*tr*) to race against in a boat propelled by oars: *Oxford row Cambridge every year.* ◆ *n* **6** an act, instance, period, or distance of rowing. **7** an excursion in a rowing boat. [OE *rōwan*]
▸**ˈrower** *n*

row[3] ⓣ (raʊ) *n* **1** a noisy quarrel. **2** a noisy disturbance: *we couldn't hear the music for the row next door.* **3** a reprimand. ◆ *vb* **4** (*intr;* often foll. by *with*) to quarrel noisily. **5** (*tr*) *Arch.* to reprimand. [C18: from ?]

rowan (ˈrəʊən, ˈraʊ-) *n* another name for the (European) **mountain ash.** [C16: of Scand. origin]

rowdy ⓣ (ˈraʊdɪ) *adj* **rowdier, rowdiest. 1** tending to create noisy disturbances; rough, loud, or disorderly: *a rowdy gang of football supporters.* ◆ *n, pl* **rowdies. 2** a person who behaves in such a fashion. [C19: orig. US sl., ? rel. to ROW[3]]
▸**ˈrowdily** *adv* ▸**ˈrowdiness** *or* **ˈrowdyism** *n*

rowel (ˈraʊəl) *n* **1** a small spiked wheel attached to a spur. **2** *Vet. science.* a piece of leather inserted under the skin of a horse to cause a discharge. ◆ *vb* **rowels, rowelling, rowelled** *or US* **rowels, roweling, roweled.** (*tr*) **3** to goad (a horse) using a rowel. **4** *Vet. science.* to insert a rowel in (the skin of a horse) to cause a discharge. [C14: from OF *roel* a little wheel, from *roe* a wheel, from L *rota*]

rowing boat (ˈrəʊɪŋ) *n Chiefly Brit.* a small pleasure boat propelled by one or more pairs of oars. Usual US and Canad. word: **rowboat.**

rowing machine (ˈrəʊɪŋ) *n* a device with oars and a sliding seat, resembling a sculling boat, used to provide exercise.

rowlock (ˈrɒlək) *n* a swivelling device attached to the gunwale of a boat that holds an oar in place. Usual US and Canad. word: **oarlock.**

royal ⓣ (ˈrɔɪəl) *adj* **1** of, relating to, or befitting a king, queen, or other monarch; regal. **2** (*prenominal; often cap.*) established by, chartered by, under the patronage of, or in the service of royalty: *the Royal Society of St George.* **3** being a member of a royal family. **4** above the usual or normal in standing, size, quality, etc. **5** *Inf.* unusually good or impressive; first-rate. **6** *Naut.* just above the topgallant (in **royal mast**). ◆ *n* **7** (*sometimes cap.*) a member of a royal family. **8** Also: **royal stag.** a stag with antlers having 12 or more branches. **9** *Naut.* a sail set next above the topgallant, on a royal mast. **10** a size of printing paper, 20 by 25 inches. [C14: from OF *roial,* from L *rēgālis* fit for a king, from *rēx* king; cf. REGAL]
▸**ˈroyally** *adv*

Royal Academy *n* a society founded by George III in 1768 to foster a national school of painting, sculpture, and design in England. Full name: **Royal Academy of Arts.**

Royal Air Force *n* the air force of Great Britain. Abbrev.: **RAF.**

Royal and Ancient Club *n* **the.** a golf club, headquarters of the sport's ruling body, based in St Andrews, Scotland. Abbrev.: **R&A.**

royal assent *n Brit.* the formal signing of an act of Parliament by the sovereign, by which it becomes law.

royal blue *n* **a** a deep blue colour. **b** (*as adj*): *a royal-blue carpet.*

Royal Commission *n* (in Britain) a body set up by the monarch on the recommendation of the prime minister to gather information about the operation of existing laws or to investigate any social, educational, or other matter.

royal fern *n* a fern of damp regions, having large fronds up to 2 metres (7 feet) in height.

royal flush *n Poker.* a hand made up of the five top honours of a suit.

royalist (ˈrɔɪəlɪst) *n* **1** a supporter of a monarch or monarchy, esp. during the English Civil War. **2** *Inf.* an extreme reactionary: *an economic royalist.* ◆ *adj* **3** of or relating to royalists.
▸**ˈroyalism** *n*

royal jelly *n* a substance secreted by the pharyngeal glands of worker bees and fed to all larvae when very young and to larvae destined to become queens throughout their development.

Royal Marines *pl n Brit.* a corps of soldiers specially trained in amphibious warfare. Abbrev.: **RM.**

Royal Mint *n* a British organization having the sole right to manufacture coins since the 16th century. In 1968 it moved from London to Llantrisant in Wales.

Royal Navy *n* the navy of Great Britain. Abbrev.: **RN.**

royal palm *n* any of several palm trees of tropical America, having a tall trunk with a tuft of feathery pinnate leaves.

royal standard *n* a flag bearing the arms of the British sovereign, flown only when she or he is present.

royal tennis *n* another name for **real tennis.**

royalty (ˈrɔɪəltɪ) *n, pl* **royalties. 1** the rank, power, or position of a king or queen. **2a** royal persons collectively. **2b** a person who belongs to a royal family. **3** any quality characteristic of a monarch. **4** a percentage of the revenue from the sale of a book, performance of a theatrical work, use of a patented invention or of land, etc., paid to the author, inventor, or proprietor.

royal warrant *n* an authorization to a tradesman to supply goods to a royal household.

rozzer (ˈrɒzə) *n Sl.* a policeman. [C19: from ?]

RPG *abbrev. for* report program generator: a business-oriented computer programming language.

RPI (in Britain) *abbrev. for* retail price index.

rpm *abbrev. for:* **1** resale price maintenance. **2** revolutions per minute.

RPV *abbrev. for* remotely piloted vehicle.

RR *abbrev. for:* **1** Right Reverend. **2** *Canad. & US.* rural route.

-rrhagia *n combining form.* (in pathology) an abnormal discharge: *menorrhagia.* [from Gk *-rrhagia* a bursting forth, from *rhēgnunai* to burst]

-rrhoea *or esp. US* **-rrhea** *n combining form.* (in pathology) a flow: *diarrhoea.* [from NL, from Gk *-rrhoia,* from *rhein* to flow]

r-RNA *abbrev. for* ribosomal RNA.

RRP *abbrev. for* recommended retail price.

Rs *symbol for* rupees.

RS (in Britain) *abbrev. for* Royal Society.

RSA *abbrev. for:* **1** Republic of South Africa. **2** (in New Zealand) Returned Services Association. **3** Royal Scottish Academician. **4** Royal Scottish Academy. **5** Royal Society of Arts.

RSFSR (formerly) *abbrev. for* Russian Soviet Federative Socialist Republic.

RSI *abbrev. for* repetitive strain injury.

RSL (in Australia) *abbrev. for* Returned Services League.

THESAURUS

run ◆ *vb* **4** = **send,** convey, direct, dispatch, forward, steer

routine *n* **1** = **procedure,** custom, formula, grind (*inf.*), groove, method, order, pattern, practice, programme, usage, way, wont **4** *Informal* = **performance,** act, bit (*inf.*), line, piece, spiel (*inf.*) ◆ *adj* **5** = **usual,** conventional, customary, everyday, familiar, habitual, normal, ordinary, standard, typical, wonted, workaday
Antonyms *adj* ≠ **usual:** abnormal, different, exceptional, irregular, special, unusual

rove[1] *vb* **1** = **wander,** cruise, drift, gad about, gallivant, meander, ramble, range, roam, stravaig (*Scot. & N English dialect*), stray, stroll, traipse (*inf.*)

rover[1] *n* **1** = **wanderer,** bird of passage, drifter, gadabout (*inf.*), gypsy, itinerant, nomad, rambler, ranger, rolling stone, stroller, transient, traveller, vagrant

row[1] *n* **1** = **line,** bank, column, file, queue, range, rank, sequence, series, string, tier **7 in a row** = **consecutively,** one after the other, successively

row[3] *n* **1** = **quarrel,** altercation, brawl, controversy, dispute, falling-out (*inf.*), fracas, fray, fuss, ruckus (*inf.*), ruction (*inf.*), scrap (*inf.*), shindig (*inf.*), shindy (*inf.*), shouting match (*inf.*), slanging match (*Brit.*), squabble, tiff, trouble **2** = **disturbance,** commotion, noise, racket, rumpus, tumult, uproar **3** = **telling-off** (*inf.*), castigation, dressing-down, flea in one's ear (*inf.*), lecture, reprimand, reproof, rollicking (*Brit. inf.*), talking-to (*inf.*), ticking-off (*inf.*), tongue-lashing ◆ *vb* **4** = **quarrel,** argue, brawl, dispute, fight, go at it hammer and tongs, scrap (*inf.*), spar, squabble, wrangle

rowdy *adj* **1** = **disorderly,** boisterous, loud, loutish, noisy, obstreperous, rough, unruly, uproarious, wild ◆ *n* **2** = **hooligan,** brawler, casual, lager lout, lout, rough (*inf.*), ruffian, tearaway (*Brit.*), tough, troublemaker, yahoo, yob *or* yobbo (*Brit. sl.*)
Antonyms *adj* ≠ **disorderly:** decorous, gentle, law-abiding, mannerly, orderly, peaceful, refined

royal *adj* **1** = **regal,** imperial, kinglike, kingly, monarchical, princely, queenly, sovereign **5** *Informal* = **splendid,** august, grand, impressive, magnificent, majestic, stately, superb, superior

RSM *abbrev. for:* **1** regimental sergeant major. **2** Royal School of Music. **3** Royal Society of Medicine.
RSNZ *abbrev. for* Royal Society of New Zealand.
RSPB (in Britain) *abbrev. for* Royal Society for the Protection of Birds.
RSPCA (in Britain and Australia) *abbrev. for* Royal Society for the Prevention of Cruelty to Animals.
RSV *abbrev. for* Revised Standard Version (of the Bible).
RSVP *abbrev. for* répondez s'il vous plaît. [F: please reply]
rt *abbrev. for* right.
RTE *abbrev. for* Radio Telefis Éireann. [Irish Gaelic: Irish Radio and Television]
Rt Hon. *abbrev. for* Right Honourable.
Ru *the chemical symbol for* ruthenium.
RU *abbrev. for* Rugby Union.
RU486 *n Trademark.* a brand name for the **abortion pill.**
rub ❶ (rʌb) *vb* **rubs, rubbing, rubbed. 1** to apply pressure and friction to (something) with a backward and forward motion. **2** to move (something) with pressure along, over, or against (a surface). **3** to chafe or fray. **4** (*tr*) to bring into a certain condition by rubbing: *rub it clean.* **5** (*tr*) to spread with pressure, esp. in order to cause to be absorbed: *she rubbed ointment into his back.* **6** (*tr*) to mix (fat) into flour with the fingertips, as in making pastry. **7** (foll. by *off, out, away,* etc.) to remove or be removed by rubbing: *the mark would not rub off the chair.* **8** (*intr*) *Bowls.* (of a bowl) to be slowed or deflected by an uneven patch on the green. **9** (*tr;* often foll. by *together*) to move against each other with pressure and friction (esp. in **rub one's hands,** often a sign of glee, keen anticipation, or satisfaction, and **rub noses,** a greeting among Eskimos). **10 rub (up) the wrong way.** to arouse anger in; annoy. ◆ *n* **11** the act of rubbing. **12** (preceded by *the*) an obstacle or difficulty (esp. in **there's the rub**). **13** something that hurts the feelings or annoys; cut; rebuke. **14** *Bowls.* an uneven patch in the green. ◆ See also **rub along, rub down,** etc. [C15: ?from Low G *rubben,* from ?]
rub along *vb* (*intr, adv*) *Brit.* **1** to continue in spite of difficulties. **2** to maintain an amicable relationship; not quarrel.
rubato (ruːˈbɑːtəʊ) *Music.* ◆ *n, pl* **rubatos. 1** flexibility of tempo in performance. ◆ *adj, adv* **2** to be played with a flexible tempo. [C19: from It. *tempo rubato,* lit.: stolen time, from *rubare* to ROB]
rubber[1] (ˈrʌbə) *n* **1** Also called: **India rubber, gum elastic, caoutchouc.** a cream to dark brown elastic material obtained by coagulating and drying the latex from certain plants, esp. the rubber tree. **2** any of a large variety of elastomers produced from natural rubber or by synthetic means. **3** *Chiefly Brit.* a piece of rubber used for erasing something written; eraser. **4** a cloth, pad, etc., used for polishing. **5** a person who rubs something in order to smooth, polish, or massage. **6** (*often pl*) *Chiefly US & Canad.* a rubberized waterproof overshoe. **7** *Sl.* a condom. **8** (*modifier*) made of or producing rubber: *a rubber ball; a rubber factory.* [C17: from RUB + -ER[1]; the tree was so named because its product was used for rubbing out writing]
▸ˈ**rubbery** *adj*
rubber[2] (ˈrʌbə) *n* **1** *Bridge, whist, etc.* **1a** a match of three games. **1b** the deal that wins such a match. **2** a series of matches or games in any of various sports. [C16: from ?]
rubber band *n* a continuous loop of thin rubber, used to hold papers, etc., together. Also called: **elastic band.**
rubber cement *n* any of a number of adhesives made by dissolving rubber in a solvent such as benzene.
rubberize *or* **rubberise** (ˈrʌbəˌraɪz) *vb* **rubberizes, rubberizing, rubberized** *or* **rubberises, rubberising, rubberised.** (*tr*) to coat or impregnate with rubber.
rubberneck (ˈrʌbəˌnɛk) *Sl.* ◆ *n* **1** a person who stares or gapes inquisitively. **2** a sightseer or tourist. ◆ *vb* **3** (*intr*) to stare in a naive or foolish manner.
rubber plant *n* **1** a plant with glossy leathery leaves that grows as a tall tree in India and Malaya but is cultivated as a house plant in Europe and North America. **2** any of several tropical trees, the sap of which yields crude rubber.
rubber stamp *n* **1** a device used for imprinting dates, etc., on forms, invoices, etc. **2** automatic authorization of a payment, proposal, etc. **3** a person who makes such automatic authorizations; a cipher or person of little account. ◆ *vb* **rubber-stamp.** (*tr*) **4** to imprint (forms, invoices, etc.) with a rubber stamp. **5** *Inf.* to approve automatically.
rubber tree *n* a tropical American tree cultivated throughout the tropics, esp. in Malaya, for the latex of its stem, which is the major source of commercial rubber.
rubbing (ˈrʌbɪŋ) *n* an impression taken of an incised or raised surface by laying paper over it and rubbing with wax, graphite, etc.
rubbish ❶ (ˈrʌbɪʃ) *n* **1** worthless, useless, or unwanted matter. **2** discarded or waste matter; refuse. **3** foolish words or speech; nonsense. ◆ *vb* **4** (*tr*) *Inf.* to criticize; attack verbally. [C14 *robys,* from ?]
▸ˈ**rubbishy** *adj*
rubble (ˈrʌbᵊl) *n* **1** fragments of broken stones, bricks, etc. **2** debris from ruined buildings. **3** Also called: **rubblework.** masonry constructed of broken pieces of rock, stone, etc. [C14 *robyl;* ? rel. to RUBBISH, or to ME *rubben* to rub]
▸ˈ**rubbly** *adj*
rub down *vb* (*adv*) **1** to dry or clean (a horse, athlete, oneself, etc.) vigorously, esp. after exercise. **2** to make or become smooth by rubbing. **3** (*tr*) to prepare (a surface) for painting by rubbing it with sandpaper. ◆ *n* **rubdown. 4** the act of rubbing down.
rube (ruːb) *n US sl.* an unsophisticated countryman. [C20: prob. from the name *Reuben*]
rubella (ruːˈbɛlə) *n* a mild contagious viral disease, somewhat similar to measles, characterized by cough, sore throat, and skin rash. Also called: **German measles.** [C19: from NL, from L *rubellus* reddish, from *rubeus* red]
rubellite (ˈruːbɪˌlaɪt, ruːˈbɛl-) *n* a red transparent variety of tourmaline, used as a gemstone. [C18: from L *rubellus* reddish]
rubeola (ruːˈbiːələ) *n* the technical name for **measles.** [C17: from NL, from L *rubeus* reddish]
Rubicon (ˈruːbɪkən) *n* **1** a stream in N Italy: in ancient times the boundary between Italy and Cisalpine Gaul. By leading his army across it and marching on Rome in 49 B.C., Julius Caesar committed himself to civil war with the senatorial party. **2** (*sometimes not cap.*) a point of no return. **3** a penalty in piquet by which the score of a player who fails to reach 100 points in six hands is added to his opponent's. **4 cross** (*or* **pass**) **the Rubicon.** to commit oneself irrevocably to some course of action.
rubicund ❶ (ˈruːbɪkənd) *adj* of a reddish colour; ruddy; rosy. [C16: from L *rubicundus,* from *rubēre* to be ruddy, from *ruber* red]
▸**rubicundity** (ˌruːbɪˈkʌndɪtɪ) *n*
rubidium (ruːˈbɪdɪəm) *n* a soft highly reactive radioactive element of the alkali metal group. It is used in electronic valves, photocells, and special glass. Symbol: Rb; atomic no.: 37; atomic wt.: 85.47; half-life of ^{87}Rb: 5×10^{11} years. [C19: from NL, from L *rubidus* dark red, with reference to the two red lines in its spectrum]
▸**ruˈbidic** *adj*
rubidium-strontium dating *n* a technique for determining the age of minerals based on the occurrence in natural rubidium of a fixed amount of the radioisotope ^{87}Rb which decays to the stable strontium isotope ^{87}Sr with a half-life of 5×10^{11} years.
rubiginous (ruːˈbɪdʒɪnəs) *adj* rust-coloured. [C17: from L *rūbīginōsus,* from *rūbīgō* rust, from *ruber* red]
rub in *vb* (*tr, adv*) **1** to spread with pressure, esp. in order to cause to be absorbed. **2 rub it in.** *Inf.* to harp on something distasteful to a person.
ruble (ˈruːbᵊl) *n* a variant spelling of **rouble.**
rub off *vb* **1** to remove or be removed by rubbing. **2** (*intr;* often foll. by *on* or *onto*) to have an effect through close association or contact: *her crude manners have rubbed off on you.*
rub out ❶ *vb* (*tr, adv*) **1** to remove or be removed with a rubber. **2** *US sl.* to murder.
rubric (ˈruːbrɪk) *n* **1** a title, heading, or initial letter in a book, manuscript, or section of a legal code, esp. one printed or painted in red ink or in some similarly distinguishing manner. **2** a set of rules of conduct or procedure. **3** a set of directions for the conduct of Christian church services, often printed in red in a prayer book or missal. [C15 *rubrike* red ochre, red lettering, from L *rubrīca* (*terra*) red (earth), ruddle, from *ruber* red]
▸ˈ**rubrical** *adj* ▸ˈ**rubrically** *adv*
ruby (ˈruːbɪ) *n, pl* **rubies. 1** a deep red transparent precious variety of corundum: used as a gemstone, in lasers, and for bearings and rollers in watchmaking. **2a** the deep-red colour of a ruby. **2b** (*as adj*): *ruby lips.* **3a** something resembling, made of, or containing a ruby. **3b** (*as modifier*): *a ruby necklace.* **4** (*modifier*) denoting a fortieth anniversary: *our ruby wedding.* [C14: from OF *rubi,* from L *rubeus,* from *ruber* red]
RUC *abbrev. for* Royal Ulster Constabulary.
ruche (ruːʃ) *n* a strip of pleated or frilled lawn, lace, etc., used to decorate blouses, dresses, etc. [C19: from F, lit.: beehive, from Med. L *rūsca* bark of a tree, of Celtic origin]
ruching (ˈruːʃɪŋ) *n* **1** material used for a ruche. **2** a ruche or ruches collectively.
ruck[1] (rʌk) *n* **1** a large number or quantity; mass, esp. of undistinguished people or things. **2** (in a race) a group of competitors who are well behind the leaders. **3** *Rugby.* a loose scrum that forms around the ball when it is on the ground. **4** *Australian Rules football.* the three players who do not have fixed positions but follow the ball closely.

THESAURUS

rub *vb* **1** = **stroke,** caress, knead, massage, smooth **3** = **chafe,** abrade, fray, grate, scrape **5** = **spread,** apply, put, smear **10 rub up the wrong way** = **annoy,** aggravate (*inf.*), anger, bug (*inf.*), get in one's hair (*inf.*), get one's goat (*sl.*), get on one's nerves (*inf.*), get under one's skin (*inf.*), irk, irritate, nark (*Brit., Austral., & NZ sl.*), peeve (*inf.*), vex ◆ *n* **11** = **massage,** caress, kneading **12** *As in* **the rub** = **difficulty,** catch, drawback, hazard, hindrance, hitch, impediment, obstacle, problem, snag, trouble
rubbish *n* **1, 2** = **waste,** crap (*sl.*), debris, dreck (*sl., chiefly US*), dregs, dross, flotsam and jetsam, garbage (*chiefly US*), grot (*sl.*), junk (*inf.*), litter, lumber, offal, offscourings, refuse, scrap, trash **3** = **nonsense,** balderdash, bilge (*inf.*), bosh (*inf.*), bunkum *or* buncombe (*chiefly US*), claptrap (*inf.*), codswallop (*Brit. sl.*), crap (*sl.*), drivel, garbage (*chiefly US*), gibberish, hogwash, hokum (*sl., chiefly US & Canad.*), hot air (*inf.*), moonshine, piffle (*inf.*), poppycock (*inf.*), rot, stuff and nonsense, tommyrot, tosh (*sl., chiefly Brit.*), trash, tripe (*inf.*), twaddle
rubbishy *adj* **1** = **trashy,** cheap, paltry, shoddy, tatty, tawdry, throwaway, twopenny, twopenny-halfpenny, valueless, worthless
rubicund *adj Old-fashioned* = **reddish,** blushing, florid, flushed, pink, roseate, rosy, ruddy
rub out *vb* **1** = **erase,** cancel, delete, efface, excise, expunge, obliterate, remove, wipe out **2** *U.S. slang* = **murder,** assassinate, blow away (*sl., chiefly US*), bump off, butcher, dispatch, do in

◆ *vb* **5** (*intr*) *Rugby.* to try to win the ball by mauling and scrummaging. [C13 (meaning "heap of firewood"): ?from ON]

ruck[2] (rʌk) *n* **1** a wrinkle, crease, or fold. ◆ *vb* **2** (usually foll. by *up*) to become or make wrinkled, creased, or puckered. [C18: of Scand. origin; rel. to ON *hrukka*]

ruckman ('rʌkmən) *n, pl* **ruckmen.** *Australian Rules football.* either of two players who, with the rover, form the ruck.

ruck-rover *n Australian Rules football.* a player playing a role midway between that of the rover and the ruckmen.

rucksack ('rʌk,sæk) *n* a large bag, usually having two straps, carried on the back and often used by climbers, campers, etc. Also called: **backpack.** [C19: from G, lit.: back sack]

ruction ❶ ('rʌkʃən) *n Inf.* **1** an uproar; noisy or quarrelsome disturbance. **2** (*pl*) an unpleasant row; trouble. [C19: ? changed from INSURRECTION]

rudaceous (ru:'deɪʃəs) *adj* (of conglomerate, breccia, and similar rocks) composed of coarse-grained material. [C20: from L *rudis* coarse, rough + -ACEOUS]

rudbeckia (rʌd'bɛkɪə) *n* any of a genus of North American plants of the composite family, cultivated for their showy flowers, which have golden-yellow rays and green or black conical centres. See also **black-eyed Susan.** [C18: NL, after Olaus *Rudbeck* (1630–1702), Swedish botanist]

rudd (rʌd) *n* a European freshwater fish, having a compressed dark greenish body and reddish ventral and tail fins. [C17: prob. from dialect *rud* red colour, from OE *rudu* redness]

rudder ('rʌdə) *n* **1** *Naut.* a pivoted vertical vane that projects into the water at the stern and can be used to steer a vessel. **2** a vertical control surface attached to the rear of the fin used to steer an aircraft. **3** anything that guides or directs. [OE *rōther*]
▸ **'rudderless** *adj*

rudderpost ('rʌdə,pəust) *n Naut.* **1** a postlike member at the forward edge of a rudder. **2** the part of the stern frame of a vessel to which a rudder is fitted.

ruddle ('rʌdᵊl), **raddle,** *or* **reddle** *n* **1** a red ochre, used esp. to mark sheep. ◆ *vb* **ruddles, ruddling, ruddled. 2** (*tr*) to mark (sheep) with ruddle. [C16: dim. formed from OE *rudu* redness; see RUDD]

ruddy ❶ ('rʌdɪ) *adj* **ruddier, ruddiest. 1** (of the complexion) having a healthy reddish colour. **2** coloured red or pink: *a ruddy sky.* ◆ *adv, adj Inf., chiefly Brit.* **3** (intensifier) bloody; damned: *a ruddy fool.* [OE *rudig*, from *rudu* redness]
▸ **'ruddily** *adv* ▸ **'ruddiness** *n*

rude ❶ (ru:d) *adj* **1** insulting or uncivil; discourteous; impolite. **2** lacking refinement; coarse or uncouth. **3** vulgar or obscene: *a rude joke.* **4** unexpected and unpleasant: *a rude awakening.* **5** roughly or crudely made: *we made a rude shelter on the island.* **6** rough or harsh in sound, appearance, or behaviour. **7** humble or lowly. **8** (*prenominal*) robust or sturdy: *in rude health.* **9** (*prenominal*) approximate or imprecise: *a rude estimate.* [C14: via OF from L *rudis* coarse, unformed]
▸ **'rudely** *adv* ▸ **'rudeness** *or* (*inf.*) **'rudery** *n*

ruderal ('ru:dərəl) *n* **1** a plant that grows on waste ground. ◆ *adj* **2** growing in waste places. [C19: from NL *rūderālis*, from L *rūdus* rubble]

rudiment ❶ ('ru:dɪmənt) *n* **1** (*often pl*) the first principles or elementary stages of a subject. **2** (*often pl*) a partially developed version of something. **3** *Biol.* an organ or part in an embryonic or vestigial state. [C16: from L *rudīmentum* a beginning, from *rudis* unformed]

rudimentary ❶ (,ru:dɪ'mɛntərɪ, -trɪ) *or* **rudimental** *adj* **1** basic; fundamental. **2** incompletely developed; vestigial: *rudimentary leaves.*
▸ **,rudi'mentarily** *or* (*less commonly*) **,rudi'mentally** *adv*

rudish ('ru:dɪʃ) *adj* somewhat rude.

rue[1] ❶ (ru:) *vb* **rues, ruing, rued. 1** to feel sorrow, remorse, or regret for (one's own wrongdoing, past events, etc.). ◆ *n* **2** *Arch.* sorrow, pity, or regret. [OE *hrēowan*]
▸ **'ruer** *n*

rue[2] (ru:) *n* an aromatic Eurasian shrub with small yellow flowers and evergreen leaves which yield an acrid volatile oil, formerly used medicinally as a narcotic and stimulant. Archaic name: **herb of grace.** [C14: from OF, from L *rūta*, from Gk *rhutē*]

rueful ❶ ('ru:fʊl) *adj* **1** feeling or expressing sorrow or regret: *a rueful face.* **2** inspiring sorrow or pity.
▸ **'ruefully** *adv* ▸ **'ruefulness** *n*

ruff[1] (rʌf) *n* **1** a circular pleated or fluted collar of lawn, muslin, etc., worn by both men and women in the 16th and 17th centuries. **2** a natural growth of long or coloured hair or feathers around the necks of certain animals or birds. **3** an Old World shore bird of the sandpiper family, the male of which has a large erectile ruff of feathers in the breeding season. [C16: back formation from RUFFLE[1]]
▸ **'ruff,like** *adj*

ruff[2] (rʌf) *Cards.* ◆ *n, vb* **1** another word for **trump**[1] (senses 1, 4). ◆ *n* **2** an old card game similar to whist. [C16: from OF *roffle;* ? changed from It. *trionfa* TRUMP[1]]

ruffe *or* **ruff** (rʌf) *n* a European freshwater teleost fish of the perch family, having a single spiny dorsal fin. [C15: ? alteration of ROUGH (referring to its scales)]

ruffian ❶ ('rʌfɪən) *n* a violent or lawless person; hoodlum. [C16: from OF *rufien*, from It. *ruffiano* pander]
▸ **'ruffianism** *n* ▸ **'ruffianly** *adj*

ruffle[1] ❶ ('rʌfᵊl) *vb* **ruffles, ruffling, ruffled. 1** to make, be, or become irregular or rumpled: *a breeze ruffling the water.* **2** to annoy, irritate, or be annoyed or irritated. **3** (*tr*) to make into a ruffle; pleat. **4** (of a bird) to erect (its feathers) in anger, display, etc. **5** (*tr*) to flick (cards, pages, etc.) rapidly. ◆ *n* **6** an irregular or disturbed surface. **7** a strip of pleated material used as a trim. **8** *Zool.* another name for **ruff**[1] (sense 2). **9** annoyance or irritation. [C13: of Gmc origin; cf. MLow G *ruffelen* to crumple, ON *hrufla* to scratch]

ruffle[2] ('rʌfᵊl) *n* **1** a low continuous drumbeat. ◆ *vb* **ruffles, ruffling, ruffled. 2** (*tr*) to beat (a drum) with a low repetitive beat. [C18: from earlier *ruff*, imit.]

rufous ('ru:fəs) *adj* reddish-brown. [C18: from L *rūfus*]

rufty-tufty (,rʌftɪ 'tʌftɪ) *adj Sl.* rugged in appearance or manner.

rug (rʌg) *n* **1** a floor covering, smaller than a carpet and made of thick wool or of other material, such as an animal skin. **2** *Chiefly Brit.* a blanket, esp. one used for travellers. **3** *Sl.* a wig. **4 pull the rug out from under.** to betray, expose, or leave defenceless. [C16: of Scand. origin]

ruga ('ru:gə) *n, pl* **rugae** (-dʒi:). (*usually pl*) *Anat.* a fold, wrinkle, or crease. [C18: L]

rugby *or* **rugby football** ('rʌgbɪ) *n* **1** a form of football played with an oval ball in which the handling and carrying of the ball is permitted. Also called: **rugger. 2** *Canad.* another name for **Canadian football.** See also **rugby league, rugby union.** [after the public school at *Rugby*, where it was first played]

rugby league *n* a form of rugby football played between teams of 13 players.

rugby union *n* a form of rugby football played between teams of 15 players.

rugged ❶ ('rʌgɪd) *adj* **1** having an uneven or jagged surface. **2** rocky or steep: *rugged scenery.* **3** (of the face) strong-featured or furrowed. **4** rough, severe, or stern in character. **5** without refinement or culture; rude: *rugged manners.* **6** involving hardship; harsh: *he leads a rugged life in the mountains.* **7** difficult or hard: *a rugged test.* **8** (of equipment, machines, etc.) designed to withstand rough treatment or use in rough conditions. **9** *Chiefly US & Canad.* sturdy or strong; robust. [C14: from ON]
▸ **'ruggedly** *adv* ▸ **'ruggedness** *n*

rugger ('rʌgə) *n Chiefly Brit.* an informal name for **rugby.**

rugose ('ru:gəus, -gəuz) *adj* wrinkled: *rugose leaves.* [C18: from L *rūgōsus*, from *rūga* wrinkle]
▸ **'rugosely** *adv* ▸ **rugosity** (ru:'gɒsɪtɪ) *n*

THESAURUS

(*inf.*), eliminate (*sl.*), hit (*sl.*), kill, knock off (*sl.*), slaughter, slay, take out (*sl.*), waste (*inf.*)

ruction *n* **2** *Informal, plural* = **row**, altercation, brawl, commotion, dispute, disturbance, fracas, fuss, hue and cry, quarrel, racket, rumpus, scrap (*inf.*), scrimmage, shindig (*inf.*), shindy (*inf.*), storm, to-do, trouble, uproar

ruddy *adj* **1** = **rosy**, blooming, blushing, florid, flushed, fresh, glowing, healthy, radiant, red, reddish, rosy-cheeked, rubicund, sanguine, sunburnt **2** = **red**, crimson, pink, reddish, roseate, ruby, scarlet
Antonyms *adj* ≠ **rosy:** anaemic, ashen, colourless, grey, pale, pallid, sickly, wan, white

rude *adj* **1** = **impolite**, abrupt, abusive, blunt, brusque, cheeky, churlish, curt, discourteous, disrespectful, ill-mannered, impertinent, impudent, inconsiderate, insolent, insulting, offhand, peremptory, short, uncivil, unmannerly **2** = **coarse**, barbarous, boorish, brutish, crude, graceless, gross, ignorant, illiterate, loutish, low, oafish, rough, savage, scurrilous, uncivilized, uncouth, uncultured, uneducated, ungracious, unpolished, unrefined, untutored, vulgar **4** = **unpleasant**, abrupt, harsh, sharp, startling, sudden, violent **5** = **roughly-made**, artless, crude, inartistic, inelegant, makeshift, primitive, raw, rough, rough-hewn, simple
Antonyms *adj* ≠ **impolite:** civil, considerate, cordial, courteous, courtly, decent, gentlemanly, gracious, ladylike, mannerly, polite, respectful, sociable, urbane, well-bred ≠ **coarse:** civilized, cultured, educated, elegant, learned, polished, refined, sophisticated, urbane ≠ **roughly-made:** artful, even, finished, shapely, smooth, well-made

rudiment *n* **1** *often plural* = **basics**, beginnings, elements, essentials, first principles, foundation, fundamentals, nuts and bolts

rudimentary *adj* **1** = **basic**, early, elementary, fundamental, initial, introductory, primary, primitive **2** = **undeveloped**, embryonic, immature, vestigial
Antonyms *adj* ≠ **basic:** advanced, complete, higher, later, mature, refined, secondary, sophisticated, supplementary

rue[1] *vb* **1** = **regret**, bemoan, be sorry for, bewail, deplore, grieve, kick oneself for, lament, mourn, repent, reproach oneself for, sorrow for, weep over

rueful *adj* **1** = **regretful**, conscience-stricken, contrite, dismal, doleful, grievous, lugubrious, melancholy, mournful, penitent, plaintive, remorseful, repentant, sad, self-reproachful, sorrowful, sorry, woebegone, woeful
Antonyms *adj* cheerful, delighted, glad, happy, joyful, pleased, unrepentant

ruffian *n* = **thug**, bruiser (*inf.*), brute, bully, bully boy, heavy (*sl.*), hoodlum, hooligan, lager lout, miscreant, ned (*Scot. sl.*), rascal, rogue, rough (*inf.*), roughneck (*sl.*), rowdy, scoundrel, tough, villain, wretch, yardie

ruffle[1] *vb* **1** = **disarrange**, derange, discompose, dishevel, disorder, mess up, rumple, tousle, wrinkle **2** = **annoy**, agitate, confuse, disconcert, disquiet, disturb, faze, fluster, harass, hassle (*inf.*), irritate, nettle, peeve (*inf.*), perturb, put out, rattle (*inf.*), shake up (*inf.*), stir, trouble, unnerve, unsettle, upset, vex, worry
Antonyms *vb* ≠ **annoy:** appease, calm, comfort, compose, console, ease, mollify, solace, soothe

rugged *adj* **1, 2** = **rocky**, broken, bumpy, craggy, difficult, irregular, jagged, ragged, rough, stark, uneven **3** = **strong-featured**, furrowed, leathery, lined, rough-hewn, weather-

rug rat *n US & Canad. inf.* a young child not yet walking.

ruin ➊ ('ru:ɪn) *n* **1** a destroyed or decayed building or town. **2** the state of being destroyed or decayed. **3** loss of wealth, position, etc., or something that causes such loss; downfall. **4** something that is severely damaged: *his life was a ruin.* **5** a person who has suffered a downfall, bankruptcy, etc. **6** *Arch.* loss of her virginity by a woman outside marriage. ◆ *vb* **7** (*tr*) to bring to ruin; destroy. **8** (*tr*) to injure or spoil: *the town has been ruined with tower blocks.* **9** (*intr*) *Arch. or poetic.* to fall into ruins; collapse. **10** (*tr*) *Arch.* to seduce and abandon (a woman). [C14: from OF *ruine,* from L *rūīna* a falling down, from *ruere* to fall violently]

ruination (ˌru:ɪ'neɪʃən) *n* **1** the act of ruining or the state of being ruined. **2** something that causes ruin.

ruinous ➊ ('ru:ɪnəs) *adj* causing, tending to cause, or characterized by ruin or destruction.
▸ **'ruinously** *adv* ▸ **'ruinousness** *n*

rule ➊ (ru:l) *n* **1** an authoritative regulation or direction concerning method or procedure, as for a court of law, legislative body, game, or other activity: *judges' rules; play according to the rules.* **2** the exercise of governmental authority or control: *the rule of Caesar.* **3** the period of time in which a monarch or government has power: *his rule lasted 100 days.* **4** a customary form or procedure: *he made a morning swim his rule.* **5** (usually preceded by *the*) the common order of things: *violence was the rule rather than the exception.* **6** a prescribed method or procedure for solving a mathematical problem. **7** any of various devices with a straight edge for guiding or measuring; ruler: *a carpenter's rule.* **8** *Printing.* **8a** a printed or drawn character in the form of a long thin line. **8b** another name for **dash**[1] (sense 12): *en rule; em rule.* **8c** a strip of metal used to print such a line. **9** *Christianity.* a systematic body of prescriptions followed by members of a religious order. **10** *Law.* an order by a court or judge. **11 as a rule.** normally or ordinarily. ◆ *vb* **rules, ruling, ruled. 12** to exercise governing or controlling authority over (a people, political unit, individual, etc.). **13** (when *tr, often takes a clause as object*) to decide authoritatively; decree: *the chairman ruled against the proposal.* **14** (*tr*) to mark with straight parallel lines or one straight line. **15** (*tr*) to restrain or control. **16** (*intr*) to be customary or prevalent: *chaos rules in this school.* **17** (*intr*) to be pre-eminent or superior: *football rules in the field of sport.* **18 rule the roost** (*or* **roast**). to be pre-eminent; be in charge. [C13: from OF *riule,* from L *rēgula* a straight edge]
▸ **'rulable** *adj*

rule of three *n* a mathematical rule asserting that the value of one unknown quantity in a proportion is found by multiplying the denominator of each ratio by the numerator of the other.

rule of thumb *n* **a** a rough and practical approach, based on experience, rather than theory. **b** (*as modifier*): *a rule-of-thumb decision.*

rule out ➊ *vb* (*tr, adv*) **1** to dismiss from consideration. **2** to make impossible; preclude.

ruler ➊ ('ru:lə) *n* **1** a person who rules or commands. **2** Also called: **rule.** a strip of wood, metal, or other material, having straight edges, used for measuring and drawing straight lines.

Rules (ru:lz) *pl n* **1** short for **Australian Rules** (football). **2 the Rules.** *English history.* the neighbourhood around certain prisons in which trusted prisoners were allowed to live under specified restrictions.

ruling ➊ ('ru:lɪŋ) *n* **1** a decision of someone in authority, such as a judge. **2** one or more parallel ruled lines. ◆ *adj* **3** controlling or exercising authority. **4** predominant.

rum[1] (rʌm) *n* spirit made from sugar cane. [C17: ? shortened from C16 *rumbullion,* from ?]

rum[2] ➊ (rʌm) *adj* **rummer, rummest.** *Brit. sl.* strange; peculiar; odd. [C19: ?from Romany *rom* man]
▸ **'rumly** *adv* ▸ **'rumness** *n*

Rumanian (ru:'meɪnɪən) *n, adj* a variant of **Romanian.**

rumba *or* **rhumba** ('rʌmbə, 'rʊm-) *n* **1** a rhythmic and syncopated Cuban dance in duple time. **2** a ballroom dance derived from this. **3** a piece of music composed for or in the rhythm of this dance. [C20: from Sp.: lavish display, from ?]

rumble ('rʌmb°l) *vb* **rumbles, rumbling, rumbled. 1** to make or cause to make a deep resonant sound: *thunder rumbled in the sky.* **2** (*intr*) to move with such a sound: *the train rumbled along.* **3** (*tr*) to utter with a rumbling sound: *he rumbled an order.* **4** (*tr*) *Brit. sl.* to find out about (someone or something): *the police rumbled their plans.* **5** (*intr*) *US sl.* to be involved in a gang fight. ◆ *n* **6** a deep resonant sound. **7** a widespread murmur of discontent. **8** *US, Canad., & NZ sl.* a gang fight. [C14: ?from MDu. *rummelen*]
▸ **'rumbler** *n* ▸ **'rumbling** *adj*

rumble seat *n* a folding outside seat at the rear of some early cars; dicky.

rumbustious ➊ (rʌm'bʌstʃəs) *adj* boisterous or unruly. [C18: prob. var. of ROBUSTIOUS]
▸ **rum'bustiously** *adv* ▸ **rum'bustiousness** *n*

rumen ('ru:mɛn) *n, pl* **rumens** *or* **rumina** (-mɪnə). the first compartment of the stomach of ruminants, in which food is partly digested before being regurgitated as cud. [C18: from L: gullet]

ruminant ('ru:mɪnənt) *n* **1** any of a suborder of artiodactyl mammals which chew the cud and have a stomach of four compartments. The suborder includes deer, antelopes, cattle, sheep, and goats. **2** any other animal that chews the cud, such as a camel. ◆ *adj* **3** of, relating to, or belonging to this suborder. **4** (of members of this suborder and related animals, such as camels) chewing the cud; ruminating. **5** meditating or contemplating in a slow quiet way.

ruminate ➊ ('ru:mɪˌneɪt) *vb* **ruminates, ruminating, ruminated. 1** (of ruminants) to chew (the cud). **2** (when *intr,* often foll. by *upon, on,* etc.) to meditate or ponder (upon). [C16: from L *rūmināre* to chew the cud, from RUMEN]
▸ **ˌrumi'nation** *n* ▸ **'ruminative** *adj* ▸ **'ruminatively** *adv* ▸ **'rumiˌnator** *n*

rummage ➊ ('rʌmɪdʒ) *vb* **rummages, rummaging, rummaged. 1** (when *intr,* often foll. by *through*) to search (through) while looking for something, often causing disorder. ◆ *n* **2** an act of rummaging. **3** a jumble of articles. [C14 (in the sense: to pack a cargo): from OF *arrumage,* from *arrumer* to stow in a ship's hold, prob. of Gmc origin]
▸ **'rummager** *n*

rummage sale *n* **1** the US and Canad. term for **jumble sale. 2** *US.* a sale of unclaimed property.

rummer ('rʌmə) *n* a drinking glass having an ovoid bowl on a short stem. [C17: from Du. *roemer* a glass for drinking toasts, from *roemen* to praise]

rummy ('rʌmɪ) *or* **rum** *n* a card game based on collecting sets and sequences. [C20: ?from RUM[2]]

rumour ➊ *or US* **rumor** ('ru:mə) *n* **1a** information, often a mixture of

THESAURUS

beaten, weathered, worn, wrinkled **4** = **stern**, austere, crabbed, dour, gruff, hard, harsh, rough, rude, severe, sour, surly **5** = **rude**, barbarous, blunt, churlish, crude, graceless, uncouth, uncultured, unpolished, unrefined **7** = **difficult**, arduous, demanding, exacting, hard, harsh, laborious, rigorous, stern, strenuous, taxing, tough, trying, uncompromising **8, 9** = **sturdy**, robust, strong, tough, well-built
Antonyms *adj* ≠ **rocky:** even, gentle, level, regular, smooth, unbroken ≠ **strong-featured:** delicate, pretty, refined, smooth, unmarked, youthful ≠ **rude:** civil, courteous, cultivated, cultured, elegant, polished, polite, refined, sophisticated, subtle, urbane, well-bred ≠ **difficult:** agreeable, easy, gentle, mild, pleasant, simple, soft, tender, uncomplicated, unexacting ≠ **sturdy:** delicate, fragile

ruin *n* **2** = **destruction**, breakdown, collapse, crackup, crash, damage, decay, defeat, devastation, disintegration, disrepair, dissolution, downfall, failure, fall, havoc, overthrow, ruination, subversion, the end, undoing, wreck **3** = **bankruptcy**, destitution, insolvency ◆ *vb* **7** = **destroy**, break, bring down, bring to nothing, bring to ruin, crush, defeat, demolish, devastate, lay in ruins, lay waste, overthrow, overturn, overwhelm, raze, shatter, smash, total (*sl.*), trash (*sl.*), wreak havoc upon, wreck **8** = **spoil**, blow (*sl.*), bodge (*inf.*), botch, damage, disfigure, injure, make a mess of, mangle, mar, mess up, screw up (*inf.*), undo
Antonyms *n* ≠ **destruction:** creation, preservation, success, triumph, victory ◆ *vb* ≠ **destroy:** build, construct, create, keep, preserve, save ≠ **spoil:** enhance, enrich, improve, mend, repair, restore, strengthen, support

ruinous *adj* = **destructive**, baleful, baneful (*arch.*), calamitous, catastrophic, deadly, deleterious, devastating, dire, disastrous, fatal, injurious, murderous, noxious, pernicious, shattering, withering

rule *n* **1** = **regulation**, axiom, canon, criterion, decree, dictum, direction, guide, guideline, law, maxim, order, ordinance, precept, principle, ruling, standard, tenet **2, 3** = **government**, administration, ascendancy, authority, command, control, direction, domination, dominion, empire, influence, jurisdiction, leadership, mastery, power, regime, reign, supremacy, sway **4** = **procedure**, course, formula, method, policy, way **5** = **custom**, condition, convention, form, habit, order *or* way of things, practice, procedure, routine, tradition, wont **11 as a rule** = **usually**, customarily, for the most part, generally, mainly, normally, on the whole, ordinarily ◆ *vb* **12** = **govern**, administer, be in authority, be in power, be number one (*inf.*), command, control, direct, guide, hold sway, lead, manage, preside over, regulate, reign, wear the crown **13** = **decree**, adjudge, adjudicate, decide, determine, establish, find, judge, lay down, pronounce, resolve, settle **16** = **be prevalent**, be customary, hold sway, obtain, predominate, preponderate, prevail **17** = **be pre-eminent**, be superior, dominate

rule out *vb* **1** = **dismiss**, leave out, reject **2** = **exclude**, ban, debar, disqualify, eliminate, forbid, obviate, preclude, prevent, prohibit, proscribe
Antonyms *vb* ≠ **exclude:** allow, approve, authorize, let, license, order, permit, sanction

ruler *n* **1** = **governor**, commander, controller, crowned head, emperor *or* empress, head of state, king *or* queen, leader, lord, monarch, potentate, prince *or* princess, sovereign **2** = **measure**, rule, straight edge, yardstick

ruling *n* **1** = **decision**, adjudication, decree, finding, judgment, pronouncement, resolution, verdict ◆ *adj* **3** = **governing**, commanding, controlling, dominant, leading, regnant, reigning, upper **4** = **predominant**, chief, current, dominant, main, pre-eminent, preponderant, prevailing, prevalent, principal, supreme
Antonyms *adj* ≠ **predominant:** auxiliary, inferior, least, minor, secondary, subordinate, subsidiary, unimportant

rum[2] *adj Brit. slang* = **strange**, curious, dodgy (*Brit., Austral., & NZ inf.*), funny, odd, peculiar, queer, singular, suspect, suspicious, unusual, weird

rumbustious *adj* = **unruly**, boisterous, clamorous, disorderly, exuberant, loud, noisy, obstreperous, refractory, robust, rough, rowdy, unmanageable, uproarious, wayward, wild, wilful

ruminate *vb* **2** = **ponder**, brood, chew over, cogitate, consider, contemplate, deliberate, meditate, mull over, muse, rack one's brains, reflect, revolve, think, turn over in one's mind, weigh

rummage *vb* **1** = **search**, delve, examine, explore, forage, hunt, ransack, root, rootle

rumour *n* **1, 2** = **story**, bruit (*arch.*), bush tele-

truth and untruth, passed around verbally. **1b** (*in combination*): *a rumourmonger*. **2** gossip or hearsay. ◆ *vb* **3** (*tr; usually passive*) to pass around or circulate in the form of a rumour: *it is rumoured that the Queen is coming*. [C14: via OF from L *rūmor* common talk]

rump Ⓣ (rʌmp) *n* **1** the hindquarters of a mammal, not including the legs. **2** the rear part of a bird's back, nearest to the tail. **3** a person's buttocks. **4** Also called: **rump steak**. a cut of beef from behind the loin. **5** an inferior remnant. [C15: from ON]
▸ **'rumpless** *adj*

rumple Ⓣ ('rʌmpᵊl) *vb* **rumples, rumpling, rumpled. 1** to make or become crumpled or dishevelled. ◆ *n* **2** a wrinkle, fold, or crease. [C17: from MDu. *rompelen;* rel. to OE *gerumpen* wrinkled]
▸ **'rumply** *adj*

Rump Parliament *or* **the Rump** *n English history*. the remainder of the Long Parliament after Pride's Purge (the expulsion by Thomas Pride in 1648 of those members hostile to the army). It sat from 1648–53.

rumpus Ⓣ ('rʌmpəs) *n, pl* **rumpuses**. a noisy, confused, or disruptive commotion. [C18: from ?]

rumpus room *n* a room used for noisy activities, such as parties or children's games.

rumpy-pumpy ('rʌmpɪ'pʌmpɪ) *n Inf.* sexual intercourse.

run Ⓣ (rʌn) *vb* **runs, running, ran, run. 1** (*intr*) **1a** (of a two-legged creature) to move on foot at a rapid pace so that both feet are off the ground for part of each stride. **1b** (of a four-legged creature) to move at a rapid gait. **2** (*tr*) to pass over (a distance, route, etc.) in running: *to run a mile*. **3** (*intr*) to run in or finish a race as specified, esp. in a particular position: *John is running third*. **4** (*tr*) to perform as by running: *to run an errand*. **5** (*intr*) to flee; run away. **6** (*tr*) to bring into a specified state by running: *to run oneself to a standstill*. **7** (*tr*) to track down or hunt (an animal): *to run a fox to earth*. **8** (*tr*) to set (animals) loose on (a field or tract of land) so as to graze freely: *he ran stock on that pasture last year*. **9** (*intr;* often foll. by *over, round,* or *up*) to make a short trip or brief visit: *I'll run over this afternoon*. **10** (*intr*) to move quickly and easily on wheels by rolling, or in any of certain other ways: *a sledge running over snow*. **11** to move or cause to move with a specified result: *to run a ship aground; run into a tree*. **12** (often foll. by *over*) to move or pass or cause to move or pass quickly: *to run one's eyes over a page*. **13** (*tr;* foll. by *into, out of, through,* etc.) to force, thrust, or drive: *she ran a needle into her finger*. **14** (*tr*) to drive or maintain and operate (a vehicle). **15** (*tr*) to give a lift to (someone) in a vehicle: *he ran her to the station*. **16** to ply or cause to ply between places on a route: *the bus runs from Piccadilly to Golders Green*. **17** to function or cause to function: *the engine is running smoothly*. **18** (*tr*) to manage: *to run a company*. **19** to extend or continue or cause to extend or continue in a particular direction, for a particular duration or distance, etc.: *the road runs north; the play ran for two years*. **20** (*intr*) *Law.* to have legal force or effect: *the house lease runs for two more years*. **21** (*tr*) to be subjected to, be affected by, or incur: *to run a risk; run a temperature*. **22** (*intr;* often foll. by *to*) to be characterized (by); tend or incline: *to run to fat*. **23** (*intr*) to recur persistently or be inherent: *red hair runs in my family*. **24** to cause or allow (liquids) to flow or (of liquids) to flow: *the well has run dry*. **25** (*intr*) to melt and flow: *the wax grew hot and began to run*. **26** *Metallurgy*. **26a** to melt or fuse. **26b** (*tr*) to cast (molten metal): *to run lead into ingots*. **27** (*intr*) (of waves, tides, rivers, etc.) to rise high, surge, or be at a specified height: *a high sea was running that night*. **28** (*intr*) to be diffused: *the colours in my dress ran when I washed it*. **29** (*intr*) (of stitches) to unravel or come undone or (of a garment) to have stitches unravel or come undone. **30** (*intr*) (of growing creepers, etc.) to trail, spread, or climb: *ivy running over a cottage wall*. **31** (*intr*) to spread or circulate quickly: *a rumour ran through the town*. **32** (*intr*) to be stated or reported: *his story runs as follows*. **33** to publish or print or be published or printed in a newspaper, magazine, etc.: *they ran his story in the next issue*. **34** (often foll. by *for*) *Chiefly US & Canad.* to be a candidate or present as a candidate for political or other office: *Jones is running for president*. **35** (*tr*) to get past or through: *to run a blockade*. **36** (*tr*) to deal in (arms, etc.), esp. by importing illegally: *he runs guns for the rebels*. **37** *Naut.* to sail (a vessel, esp. a sailing vessel) or (of such a vessel) to be sailed with the wind coming from astern. **38** (*intr*) (of fish) to migrate upstream from the sea, esp. in order to spawn. **39** (*tr*) *Cricket*. to score (a run or number of runs) by hitting the ball and running between the wickets. **40** (*tr*) *Billiards, etc.* to make (a number of successful shots) in sequence. **41** (*tr*) *Golf.* to hit (the ball) so that it rolls along the ground. **42** (*tr*) *Bridge*. to cash (all one's winning cards in a long suit) successively. ◆ *n* **43** an act, instance, or period of running. **44** a gait, pace, or motion faster than a walk: *she went off at a run*. **45** a distance covered by running or a period of running: *a run of ten miles*. **46** an instance or period of travelling in a vehicle, esp. for pleasure: *to go for a run in the car*. **47** free and unrestricted access: *we had the run of the house*. **48a** a period of time during which a machine, computer, etc., operates. **48b** the amount of work performed in such a period. **49** a continuous or sustained period: *a run of good luck*. **50** a continuous sequence of performances: *the play had a good run*. **51** *Cards*. a sequence of winning cards in one suit: *a run of spades*. **52** tendency or trend: *the run of the market*. **53** type, class, or category: *the usual run of graduates*. **54** (usually foll. by *on*) a continuous and urgent demand: *a run on the dollar*. **55** a series of unravelled stitches, esp. in tights; ladder. **56** the characteristic pattern or direction of something: *the run of the grain on wood*. **57a** a period during which water or other liquid flows. **57b** the amount of such a flow. **58** a pipe, channel, etc., through which water or other liquid flows. **59** *US.* a small stream. **60** a steeply inclined course, esp. a snow-covered one used for skiing. **61** an enclosure for domestic fowls or other animals: *a chicken run*. **62** (esp. in Australia and New Zealand) a tract of land for grazing livestock. **63** the migration of fish upstream in order to spawn. **64** *Mil.* **64a** a mission in a warplane. **64b** Also called: **bombing run**. an approach by a bomber to a target. **65** the movement of an aircraft along the ground during takeoff or landing. **66** *Music*. a rapid scalelike passage of notes. **67** *Cricket*. a score of one, normally achieved by both batsmen running from one end of the wicket to the other after one of them has hit the ball. **68** *Baseball*. an instance of a batter touching all four bases safely, thereby scoring. **69** *Golf*. the distance that a ball rolls after hitting the ground. **70 a run for (one's) money.** *Inf.* **70a** a close competition. **70b** pleasure derived from an activity. **71 in the long run**. as the eventual outcome of a series of events, etc. **72 in the short run**. as the immediate outcome of a series of events, etc. **73 on the run. 73a** escaping from arrest; fugitive. **73b** in rapid flight; retreating: *the enemy is on the run*. **73c** hurrying from place to place. **74 the runs**. *Sl.* diarrhoea. ◆ See also **runabout, run across,** etc. [OE *runnen*, p.p. of (*ge*)*rinnan*]

runabout ('rʌnəˌbaʊt) *n* **1** a small light vehicle or aeroplane. ◆ *vb* **run about**. **2** (*intr, adv*) to move busily from place to place.

run across Ⓣ *vb* (*intr, prep*) to meet unexpectedly; encounter by chance.

run along *vb* (*intr, adv*) (often said patronizingly) to go away; leave.

run around *Inf.* ◆ *vb* (*intr, adv*) **1** (often foll. by *with*) to associate habitually (with). **2** to behave in a fickle or promiscuous manner. ◆ *n* **run-around**. **3** deceitful or evasive treatment of a person (esp. in **give** *or* **get the run-around**).

run away Ⓣ *vb* (*intr, adv*) **1** to take flight; escape. **2** to go away; depart. **3** (of a horse) to gallop away uncontrollably. **4 run away with. 4a** to abscond or elope with: *he ran away with his boss's daughter*. **4b** to make off with; steal. **4c** to escape from the control of: *his enthusiasm ran away with him*. **4d** to win easily or be assured of victory in (a competition): *he ran away with the race*. ◆ *n* **runaway. 5a** a person or animal that runs away. **5b** (*as modifier*): *a runaway horse*. **6** the act or an instance of running away. **7** (*modifier*) rising rapidly, as prices: *runaway inflation*. **8** (*modifier*) (of a race, victory, etc.) easily won.

THESAURUS

graph, buzz, canard, dirt (*US sl.*), gossip, hearsay, news, report, scuttlebutt (*US sl.*), talk, tidings, whisper, word ◆ *vb* **3** *usually passive* = **be said**, be circulated, be noised abroad, be passed around, be published, be put about, be reported, be told, be whispered

rump *n* **1** = **hindquarters**, haunch, rear, tail **3** = **buttocks**, arse (*taboo sl.*), ass (*US & Canad. taboo sl.*), backside (*inf.*), bottom, bum (*Brit. sl.*), buns (*US sl.*), butt (*US & Canad. inf.*), derrière (*euphemistic*), jacksy (*Brit. sl.*), posterior, rear, rear end, seat, tail (*inf.*)

rumple *vb* **1** = **ruffle**, crease, crinkle, crumple, crush, derange, dishevel, disorder, mess up, pucker, screw up, scrunch, tousle, wrinkle

rumpus *n* = **commotion**, brouhaha, confusion, disruption, disturbance, furore, fuss, hue and cry, kerfuffle (*inf.*), noise, row, shindig (*inf.*), shindy (*inf.*), tumult, uproar

run *vb* **1** = **race**, barrel (along) (*inf., chiefly US & Canad.*), bolt, career, dart, dash, gallop, hare (*Brit. inf.*), hasten, hie, hotfoot, hurry, jog, leg it (*inf.*), lope, rush, scamper, scramble, scud, scurry, speed, sprint, stampede **5** = **flee**, abscond, beat a retreat, beat it (*sl.*), bolt, clear out, cut and run (*inf.*), decamp, depart, do a runner (*sl.*), escape, fly the coop (*US & Canad. inf.*), leg it (*inf.*), make a run for it, make off, scarper (*Brit. sl.*), show a clean pair of heels, skedaddle (*inf.*), slope off, take flight, take off (*inf.*), take to one's heels **10** = **move**, course, glide, go, pass, roll, skim, slide **14** = **operate 15** = **give a lift to**, bear, carry, convey, drive, manoeuvre, operate, propel, transport **17** = **work**, function, go, operate, perform, tick **18** = **manage**, administer, be in charge of, boss (*inf.*), carry on, conduct, control, coordinate, direct, handle, head, lead, look after, mastermind, operate, oversee, own, regulate, superintend, supervise, take care of **19** = **continue**, extend, go, last, lie, proceed, range, reach, stretch **24** = **flow**, cascade, discharge, go, gush, issue, leak, move, pour, proceed, spill, spout, stream **25** = **melt**, dissolve, fuse, go soft, liquefy, turn to liquid **28** = **spread**, be diffused, bleed, lose colour, mix **29** = **unravel**, come apart, come undone, ladder, tear **31** = **circulate**, be current, climb, creep, go round, spread, trail **33** = **publish**, display, feature, print **34** *chiefly U.S. & Canad.* = **compete**, be a candidate, challenge, contend, put oneself up for, stand, take part **36** = **smuggle**, bootleg, deal in, ship, sneak, traffic in ◆ *n* **43, 44** = **race**, dash, gallop, jog, rush, sprint, spurt **46** = **ride**, drive, excursion, jaunt, journey, joy ride (*inf.*), lift, outing, round, spin (*inf.*), trip **49** = **sequence**, chain, course, cycle, passage, period, round, season, series, spell, streak, stretch, string **52** = **tendency**, course, current, direction, drift, flow, motion, movement, passage, path, progress, stream, tenor, tide, trend, way **53** = **type**, category, class, kind, order, sort, variety **54** = **demand**, pressure, rush **55** = **tear**, ladder, rip, snag **61** = **enclosure**, coop, pen **71 in the long run** = **in the end**, at the end of the day, eventually, in the final analysis, in the fullness of time, in time, ultimately, when all is said and done **73 on the run: a** = **escaping**, at liberty, fugitive, in flight, on the lam (*US sl.*), on the loose **b** = **in retreat**, defeated, falling back, fleeing, in flight, retreating, running away **c** = **hurrying**, at speed, hastily, hurriedly, in a hurry, in a rush, in haste
Antonyms *vb* ≠ **race**: crawl, creep, dawdle, walk ≠ **flee**: remain, stay ≠ **continue**: cease, stop

run across *vb* = **meet**, bump into, chance upon, come across, come upon, encounter, meet with, run into

run away *vb* **1** = **flee**, abscond, beat it (*sl.*), bolt, clear out, cut and run, decamp, do a bunk

runcible spoon ('rʌnsɪbᵊl) *n* a forklike utensil with two broad prongs and one sharp curved prong. [*runcible* coined by Edward Lear, E humorist, in a nonsense poem (1871)]

run down ⓣ *vb* (*mainly adv*) **1** to allow (an engine, etc.) to lose power gradually and cease to function or (of an engine, etc.) to do this. **2** to decline or reduce in number or size: *the firm ran down its sales force.* **3** (*tr; usually passive*) to tire, sap the strength of, or exhaust: *he was thoroughly run down.* **4** (*tr*) to criticize adversely; decry. **5** (*tr*) to hit and knock to the ground with a moving vehicle. **6** (*tr*) *Naut.* to collide with and cause to sink. **7** (*tr*) to pursue and find or capture: *to run down a fugitive.* **8** (*tr*) to read swiftly or perfunctorily: *he ran down their list of complaints.* ◆ *adj* **run-down. 9** tired; exhausted. **10** worn-out, shabby, or dilapidated. ◆ *n* **rundown. 11** a brief review, résumé, or summary. **12** the process of a mechanism coming gradually to a standstill after the power is removed. **13** a reduction in number or size.

rune (ru:n) *n* **1** any of the characters of an ancient Germanic alphabet, in use, esp. in Scandinavia, from the 3rd century A.D. to the end of the Middle Ages. **2** any obscure piece of writing using mysterious symbols. **3** a kind of Finnish poem or a stanza in such a poem. [OE *rūn*, from ON *rūn* secret]
▸ **'runic** *adj*

rung[1] (rʌŋ) *n* **1** one of the bars or rods that form the steps of a ladder. **2** a crosspiece between the legs of a chair, etc. **3** *Naut.* a spoke on a ship's wheel or a handle projecting from the periphery. [OE *hrung*]
▸ **'rungless** *adj*

rung[2] (rʌŋ) *vb* the past participle of **ring**[2].

> **USAGE NOTE** See at **ring**[2].

run in ⓣ *vb* (*adv*) **1** to run (an engine) gently, usually when it is new. **2** (*tr*) to insert or include. **3** (*intr*) (of an aircraft) to approach a point or target. **4** (*tr*) *Inf.* to take into custody; arrest. ◆ *n* **run-in. 5** *Inf.* an argument or quarrel. **6** an approach to the end of an event, etc.: *the run-in for the championship.* **7** *Printing.* matter inserted in an existing paragraph.

run into ⓣ *vb* (*prep, mainly intr*) **1** (*also tr*) to collide with or cause to collide with: *her car ran into a tree.* **2** to encounter unexpectedly. **3** (*also tr*) to be beset by: *the project ran into financial difficulties.* **4** to extend to; be of the order of: *debts running into thousands.*

runnel ('rʌnᵊl) *n Literary.* a small stream. [C16: from OE *rynele;* rel. to RUN]

runner ⓣ ('rʌnə) *n* **1** a person who runs, esp. an athlete. **2** a messenger for a bank, etc. **3** a person engaged in the solicitation of business. **4** a person on the run; fugitive. **5a** a person or vessel engaged in smuggling. **5b** (*in combination*): *a gunrunner.* **6** a person who operates, manages, or controls something. **7a** either of the strips of metal or wood on which a sledge runs. **7b** the blade of an ice skate. **8** a roller or guide for a sliding component. **9** *Bot.* **9a** Also called: **stolon.** a slender horizontal stem, as of the strawberry, that grows along the surface of the soil and propagates by producing roots and shoots at the nodes or tip. **9b** a plant that propagates in this way. **10** a strip of lace, linen, etc., placed across a table or dressing table for protection and decoration. **11** another word for **rocker** (on a rocking chair). **12 do a runner.** *Sl.* to run away in order to escape trouble or to avoid paying for something.

runner bean *n* another name for **scarlet runner.**

runner-up *n, pl* **runners-up.** a contestant finishing a race or competition in second place.

running ⓣ ('rʌnɪŋ) *adj* **1** maintained continuously; incessant: *running commentary.* **2** (*postpositive*) without interruption; consecutive: *he lectured for two hours running.* **3** denoting or relating to the scheduled operation of a public vehicle: *the running time of a train.* **4** accomplished at a run: *a running jump.* **5** moving or slipping easily, as a rope or a knot. **6** (of a wound, etc.) discharging pus. **7** prevalent; current: *running prices.* **8** repeated or continuous: *a running design.* **9** (of plants, plant stems, etc.) creeping along the ground. **10** flowing: *running water.* **11** (of handwriting) having the letters run together. ◆ *n* **12** management or organization: *the running of a company.* **13** operation or maintenance: *the running of a machine.* **14** competition or competitive situation (in **in the running, out of the running**). **15 make the running.** to set the pace in a competition or race.

running board *n* a footboard along the side of a vehicle, esp. an early motorcar.

running head *or* **title** *n Printing.* a heading printed at the top of every page of a book.

running light *n Naut.* one of several lights displayed by vessels operating at night.

running mate *n* **1** *US.* a candidate for the subordinate of two linked positions, esp. a candidate for the vice-presidency. **2** a horse that pairs another in a team.

running repairs *pl n* repairs that do not, or do not greatly, interrupt operations.

runny ⓣ ('rʌnɪ) *adj* **runnier, runniest. 1** tending to flow; liquid. **2** (of the nose) exuding mucus.

run off ⓣ *vb* (*adv*) **1** (*intr*) to depart in haste. **2** (*tr*) to produce quickly, as copies on a duplicating machine. **3** to drain (liquid) or (of liquid) to be drained. **4** (*tr*) to decide (a race) by a run-off. **5 run off with. 5a** to steal; purloin. **5b** to elope with. ◆ *n* **run-off. 6** an extra race, contest, election, etc., to decide the winner after a tie. **7** *NZ.* grazing land for store cattle. **8** that portion of rainfall that runs into streams as surface water rather than being absorbed by the soil. **9** the overflow of a liquid from a container.

run-of-the-mill ⓣ *adj* ordinary, average, or undistinguished in quality, character, or nature.

run on *vb* (*adv*) **1** (*intr*) to continue without interruption. **2** to write with linked-up characters. **3** *Printing.* to compose text matter without indentation or paragraphing. ◆ *n* **run-on. 4** *Printing.* **4a** text matter composed without indenting. **4b** an additional quantity required in excess of the originally stated amount, whilst the job is being produced. **5a** a word added at the end of a dictionary entry whose meaning can be easily inferred from the definition of the headword. **5b** (*as modifier*): *a run-on entry.*

run out ⓣ *vb* (*adv*) **1** (*intr;* often foll. by *of*) to exhaust (a supply of something) or (of a supply) to become exhausted. **2 run out on.** *Inf.* to desert or abandon. **3** (*tr*) *Cricket.* to dismiss (a running batsman) by breaking the wicket with the ball, or with the ball in the hand, while he is out of his ground. ◆ *n* **run-out. 4** *Cricket.* dismissal of a batsman by running him out.

run over ⓣ *vb* **1** (*tr, adv*) to knock down (a person) with a moving vehicle. **2** (*intr*) to overflow the capacity of (a container). **3** (*intr, prep*) to examine hastily or make a rapid survey of. **4** (*intr, prep*) to exceed (a limit): *we've run over our time.*

runt (rʌnt) *n* **1** the smallest and weakest young animal in a litter, esp. the smallest piglet in a litter. **2** *Derog.* an undersized or inferior person. **3** a large pigeon, originally bred for eating. [C16: from ?]
▸ **'runtish** *or* **'runty** *adj* ▸ **'runtiness** *n*

THESAURUS

(*Brit. sl.*), do a runner (*sl.*), escape, fly the coop (*US & Canad. inf.*), make a run for it, run off, scarper (*Brit. sl.*), scram (*inf.*), show a clean pair of heels, skedaddle (*inf.*), take flight, take off, take to one's heels, turn tail **4 run away with: a** = **abscond**, abduct, elope **b** = **steal**, abscond, make off, pinch (*inf.*), run off, snatch **d** = **win easily**, romp home, walk it (*inf.*), win by a mile (*inf.*), win hands down ◆ *n* **runaway 5a** = **fugitive**, absconder, deserter, escapee, escaper, refugee, truant ◆ *modifier* **5b** = **escaped**, fleeing, fugitive, loose, out of control, uncontrolled, wild **8** = **easily won**, easy, effortless

run down *vb* **2** = **reduce**, curtail, cut, cut back, decrease, downsize, drop, pare down, trim **3** = **weaken**, debilitate, exhaust, sap the strength of, tire, undermine the health of **4** = **criticize**, asperse, bad-mouth (*sl., chiefly US & Canad.*), belittle, decry, defame, denigrate, disparage, knock (*inf.*), put down, revile, rubbish (*inf.*), slag (off) (*sl.*), speak ill of, vilify **5** = **knock down**, hit, knock over, run into, run over, strike ◆ *adj* **run-down 9** = **exhausted**, below par, debilitated, drained, enervated, fatigued, out of condition, peaky, tired, under the weather (*inf.*), unhealthy, weak, weary, worn-out **10** = **dilapidated**, broken-down, decrepit, dingy, ramshackle, seedy, shabby, tumbledown, worn-out ◆ *n* **rundown 11** = **summary**, briefing, outline, précis, recap (*inf.*), résumé, review, run-through, sketch, synopsis

Antonyms *adj* ≠ **exhausted**: fighting fit, fine, fit, fit as a fiddle, full of beans (*inf.*), healthy, well

run in *vb* **1** = **break in gently**, run gently **4** *Informal* = **arrest**, apprehend, bust (*inf.*), collar (*inf.*), feel one's collar (*sl.*), jail, lift (*sl.*), nab (*inf.*), nail (*inf.*), pick up, pinch (*inf.*), pull in (*Brit. sl.*), take into custody, take to jail, throw in jail ◆ *n* **run-in 5** *Informal* = **fight**, altercation, argument, brush, confrontation, contretemps, dispute, dust-up (*inf.*), encounter, face-off (*sl.*), quarrel, row, set-to (*inf.*), skirmish, tussle

run into *vb* **1** = **collide with**, bump into, crash into, dash against, hit, ram, strike **2** = **meet**, bump into, chance upon, come across *or* upon, encounter, meet with, run across **3** = **be beset by**, be confronted by

runner *n* **1** = **athlete**, harrier, jogger, miler, sprinter **2** = **messenger**, courier, dispatch bearer, errand boy **9a** *Botany* = **stem**, offshoot, shoot, sprig, sprout, stolon (*Botany*), tendril

running *adj* **1, 2** = **continuous**, constant, incessant, in succession, on the trot (*inf.*), perpetual, together, unbroken, unceasing, uninterrupted **10** = **flowing**, moving, streaming ◆ *n* **12** = **management**, administration, charge, conduct, control, coordination, direction, leadership, organization, regulation, superintendency, supervision **13** = **working**, functioning, maintenance, operation, performance

runny *adj* **1** = **flowing**, diluted, fluid, liquefied, liquid, melted, streaming, watery

run off *vb* **1** = **flee**, bolt, clear out, cut and run (*inf.*), decamp, do a runner (*sl.*), escape, fly the coop (*US & Canad. inf.*), hook it (*sl.*), make off, run away, scarper (*Brit. sl.*), show a clean pair of heels, skedaddle (*inf.*), take flight, take to one's heels, turn tail **2** = **produce**, churn out (*inf.*), duplicate, print **3** = **drain**, bleed, flow away, siphon, tap **5 run off with: a** = **steal**, lift (*inf.*), make off with, pinch (*inf.*), purloin, run away with, swipe (*sl.*) **b** = **run away with**, abscond with, elope with

run-of-the-mill *adj* = **ordinary**, average, banal, bog-standard (*Brit. & Irish sl.*), common, commonplace, dime-a-dozen (*inf.*), fair, mediocre, middling, modest, no great shakes (*inf.*), passable, tolerable, undistinguished, unexceptional, unexciting, unimpressive, vanilla (*inf.*)
Antonyms *adj* excellent, exceptional, extraordinary, marvellous, out of the ordinary, splendid, unusual

run out *vb* **1** *often foll. by* **of** = **finish**, be cleaned out, be exhausted, be out of, be used up, cease, dry up, exhaust one's supply of, fail, give out, have no more of, have none left, have no remaining, peter out, use up **2 run out on** *Informal* = **desert**, abandon, forsake, leave high and dry, leave holding the baby, leave in the lurch, rat on (*inf.*), run away from, strand

run over *vb* **1** = **knock down**, hit, knock over, run down, strike **2** = **overflow**, brim over, spill, spill over **3** = **review**, check, examine, go over,

run through ◐ *vb* **1** (*tr, adv*) to transfix with a sword or other weapon. **2** (*intr, prep*) to exhaust (money) by wasteful spending. **3** (*intr, prep*) to practise or rehearse: *let's run through the plan.* **4** (*intr, prep*) to examine hastily. ◆ *n* **run-through. 5** a practice or rehearsal. **6** a brief survey.

run time *n Computing.* the time during which a computer program is executed.

run to *vb* (*intr, prep*) to be sufficient for: *my income doesn't run to luxuries.*

run up ◐ *vb* (*tr, adv*) **1** to amass; incur: *to run up debts.* **2** to make by sewing together quickly. **3** to hoist: *to run up a flag.* ◆ *n* **run-up. 4** an approach run by an athlete for the long jump, pole vault, etc. **5** a preliminary or preparatory period: *the run-up to the election.*

runway ('rʌnˌweɪ) *n* **1** a hard level roadway from which aircraft take off and on which they land. **2** *Forestry, North American.* a chute for sliding logs down. **3** *Chiefly US.* a narrow ramp extending from the stage into the audience in a theatre, etc. esp. as used by models in a fashion show.

rupee (ruː'piː) *n* the standard monetary unit of India, Mauritius, Nepal, Pakistan, the Seychelles, and Sri Lanka. [C17: from Hindi *rupaīyā*, from Sansk. *rūpya* coined silver, from *rūpa* shape, beauty]

rupiah (ruː'piːə) *n, pl* **rupiah** *or* **rupiahs.** the standard monetary unit of Indonesia. [from Hindi: RUPEE]

rupture ◐ ('rʌptʃə) *n* **1** the act of breaking or bursting or the state of being broken or burst. **2** a breach of peaceful or friendly relations. **3** *Pathol.* **3a** the breaking or tearing of a bodily structure or part. **3b** another word for **hernia.** ◆ *vb* **ruptures, rupturing, ruptured. 4** to break or burst. **5** to affect or be affected with a rupture or hernia. **6** to undergo or cause to undergo a breach in relations or friendship. [C15: from L *ruptūra*, from *rumpere* to burst forth]
▸'**rupturable** *adj*

rural ◐ ('rʊərəl) *adj* **1** of, relating to, or characteristic of the country or country life. **2** living in the country. **3** of, relating to, or associated with farming. ◆ Cf. **urban.** [C15: via OF from L *rūrālis*, from *rūs* the country]
▸'**ruralism** *n* ▸'**ruralist** *n* ▸**ru'rality** *n* ▸'**rurally** *adv*

rural dean *n Chiefly Brit.* a clergyman having authority over a group of parishes.

rural district *n* (formerly) a rural division of a county.

ruralize *or* **ruralise** ('rʊərəˌlaɪz) *vb* **ruralizes, ruralizing, ruralized** *or* **ruralises, ruralising, ruralised. 1** (*tr*) to make rural in character, appearance, etc. **2** (*intr*) to go into the country to live.
▸ˌ**rurali'zation** *or* ˌ**rurali'sation** *n*

rural route *n US & Canad.* a mail service or route in a rural area, the mail being delivered by car or van.

Ruritanian (ˌrʊərɪ'teɪnɪən) *adj* of or characteristic of a romantic and idealistic setting in which adventure and intrigue occur. [C19: after the imaginary kingdom created by Anthony Hope (1863–1933), in *The Prisoner of Zenda*]

ruse ◐ (ruːz) *n* an action intended to mislead, deceive, or trick; stratagem. [C15: from OF: trick, esp. to evade capture, from *ruser* to retreat, from L *recūsāre* to refuse]

rush[1] ◐ (rʌʃ) *vb* **1** to hurry or cause to hurry; hasten. **2** (*tr*) to make a sudden attack upon (a fortress, position, person, etc.). **3** (when *intr*, often foll. by *at, in,* or *into*) to proceed or approach in a reckless manner. **4 rush one's fences.** to proceed with precipitate haste. **5** (*intr*) to come, flow, swell, etc., quickly or suddenly: *tears rushed to her eyes.* **6** (*tr*) *Sl.* to cheat, esp. by grossly overcharging. **7** (*tr*) *US & Canad.* to make a concerted effort to secure the agreement, participation, etc., of (a person). **8** (*intr*) *American football.* to gain ground by running forwards with the ball. ◆ *n* **9** the act or condition of rushing. **10** a sudden surge towards someone or something: *a gold rush.* **11** a sudden surge of sensation, esp. from a drug. **12** a sudden demand. ◆ *adj* (*prenominal*) **13** requiring speed or urgency: *a rush job.* **14** characterized by much movement, business, etc.: *a rush period.* [C14 *ruschen*, from OF *ruser* to put to flight, from L *recūsāre* to refuse]
▸'**rusher** *n*

rush[2] (rʌʃ) *n* **1** an annual or perennial plant growing in wet places and typically having grasslike cylindrical leaves and small green or brown flowers. **2** something valueless; a trifle; straw: *not worth a rush.* **3** short for **rush light.** [OE *risce, rysce*]
▸'**rushˌlike** *adj* ▸'**rushy** *adj*

rushes ('rʌʃɪz) *pl n* (*sometimes sing*) (in film-making) the initial prints of a scene or scenes before editing, usually prepared daily.

rush hour *n* a period at the beginning and end of the working day when large numbers of people are travelling to or from work.

rush light *or* **candle** *n* a narrow candle, formerly in use, made of the pith of various types of rush dipped in tallow.

rusk (rʌsk) *n* a light bread dough, sweet or plain, baked twice until it is brown, hard, and crisp: often given to babies. [C16: from Sp. or Port. *rosca* screw, bread shaped in a twist, from ?]

Russ. *abbrev. for* Russia(n).

russet ('rʌsɪt) *n* **1** brown with a yellowish or reddish tinge. **2** a rough homespun fabric, reddish-brown in colour, formerly in use for clothing. **3** any of various apples with rough brownish-red skins. ◆ *adj* **4** *Arch.* simple; homely; rustic: *a russet life.* **5** of the colour russet: *russet hair.* [C13: from Anglo-Norman, from OF *rosset*, from *rous*, from L *russus*; rel. to L *ruber* red]
▸'**russety** *adj*

Russia leather *n* a smooth dyed leather made from calfskin and scented with birch tar oil, originally produced in Russia.

Russian ('rʌʃən) *n* **1** the official language of Russia, and of the former Soviet Union: an Indo-European language belonging to the East Slavonic branch. **2** a native or inhabitant of Russia. ◆ *adj* **3** of, relating to, or characteristic of Russia, its people, or their language.

Russian doll *n* a hollow wooden figure, usually representing a Russian peasant woman, that comes apart to reveal a similar smaller figure, which itself contains another, and so on.

Russianize *or* **Russianise** ('rʌʃəˌnaɪz) *vb* **Russianizes, Russianizing, Russianized** *or* **Russianises, Russianising, Russianised.** to make or become Russian in style, etc.
▸ˌ**Russiani'zation** *or* ˌ**Russiani'sation** *n*

Russian roulette *n* **1** an act of bravado in which each person in turn spins the cylinder of a revolver loaded with only one cartridge and presses the trigger with the barrel against his own head. **2** any foolish or potentially suicidal undertaking.

Russian salad *n* a salad of cold diced cooked vegetables mixed with mayonnaise and pickles.

Russo- ('rʌsəʊ) *combining form.* Russia or Russian: *Russo-Japanese.*

rust ◐ (rʌst) *n* **1** a reddish-brown oxide coating formed on iron or steel by the action of oxygen and moisture. **2** Also called: **rust fungus.** *Plant pathol.* **2a** any of a group of fungi which are parasitic on cereal plants, conifers, etc. **2b** any of various plant diseases characterized by reddish-brown discoloration of the leaves and stem, esp. that caused by the rust fungi. **3a** a strong brown colour, sometimes with a reddish or yellowish tinge. **3b** (*as adj*): *a rust carpet.* **4** any corrosive or debilitating influence, esp. lack of use. ◆ *vb* **5** to become or cause to become coated with a layer of rust. **6** to deteriorate or cause to deteriorate through some debilitating influence or lack of use: *he allowed his talent to rust over the years.* [OE *rūst*]
▸'**rustless** *adj*

rust belt *n* an area where heavy industry is in decline, esp. in the Midwest of the US.

rustic ◐ ('rʌstɪk) *adj* **1** of, characteristic of, or living in the country; rural. **2** having qualities ascribed to country life or people; simple; unsophisticated: *rustic pleasures.* **3** crude, awkward, or uncouth. **4** made of untrimmed branches: *a rustic seat.* **5** (of masonry, etc.) having a rusticated finish. ◆ *n* **6** a person who comes from or lives in the country. **7** an unsophisticated, simple, or clownish person from the country. **8** Also called: **rusticwork.** brick or stone having a rough finish. [C16: from OF *rustique*, from L *rūsticus*, from *rūs* the country]
▸'**rustically** *adv* ▸**rusticity** (rʌ'stɪsɪtɪ) *n*

rusticate ('rʌstɪˌkeɪt) *vb* **rusticates, rusticating, rusticated. 1** to banish or retire to the country. **2** to make or become rustic in style, etc. **3** (*tr*) *Architect.* to finish (an exterior wall) with large blocks of masonry sepa-

THESAURUS

go through, rehearse, reiterate, run through, survey

run through *vb* **1** = **pierce**, impale, spit, stab, stick, transfix **2** = **squander**, blow (*sl.*), dissipate, exhaust, fritter away, spend like water, throw away, waste **3** = **rehearse**, go over, practise, read, run over **4** = **review**, check, examine, go through, look over, run over, survey

run up *n* **run-up 5** = **build-up**, approach, preliminaries

rupture *n* **1** = **break**, breach, burst, cleavage, cleft, crack, fissure, fracture, rent, split, tear **2** = **breach**, altercation, break, bust-up (*inf.*), contention, disagreement, disruption, dissolution, estrangement, falling-out (*inf.*), feud, hostility, quarrel, rift, schism, split **3b** *Medical* = **hernia** ◆ *vb* **4** = **break**, burst, cleave, crack, fracture, puncture, rend, separate, sever, split, tear **6** = **cause a breach**, break off, come between, disrupt, dissever, divide, split

rural *adj* **1, 2** = **rustic**, Arcadian, bucolic, countrified, country, hick (*inf., chiefly US & Canad.*), pastoral, sylvan, upcountry **3** = **agricultural**, agrarian, agrestic
Antonyms *adj* ≠ **rustic:** city, cosmopolitan, town, urban

ruse *n* = **trick**, artifice, blind, deception, device, dodge, hoax, imposture, manoeuvre, ploy, sham, stratagem, subterfuge, wile

rush[1] *vb* **1** = **push**, accelerate, dispatch, expedite, hurry, hustle, press, quicken, speed up **2** = **attack**, capture, charge, overcome, storm, take by storm **3** = **hurry**, barrel (along), bolt, burn rubber (*inf.*), career, dart, dash, fly, hasten, hotfoot, lose no time, make haste, race, run, scramble, scurry, shoot, speed, sprint, stampede, tear ◆ *n* **9** = **attack**, assault, charge, onslaught, push, storm, surge **10** = **hurry**, charge, dash, dispatch, expedition, haste, race, scramble, speed, stampede, surge, swiftness, urgency ◆ *adj* **13** = **hasty**, brisk, cursory, emergency, expeditious, fast, hurried, prompt, quick, rapid, swift, urgent
Antonyms *vb* ≠ **hurry:** dally, dawdle, delay, procrastinate, slow down, tarry, wait ◆ *adj* ≠ **hasty:** careful, detailed, leisurely, not urgent, slow, thorough, unhurried

rust *n* **1** = **corrosion**, oxidation **2** = **mildew**, blight, mould, must, rot ◆ *vb* **5** = **corrode**, oxidize **6** = **deteriorate**, atrophy, decay, decline, go stale, stagnate, tarnish

rustic *adj* **1** = **rural**, agrestic, Arcadian, bucolic, countrified, country, pastoral, sylvan, upcountry **2** = **simple**, artless, homely, homespun, plain, unaffected, unpolished, unrefined, unsophisticated **3** = **uncouth**, awkward, boorish, churlish, cloddish, clodhopping, clownish, coarse, crude, graceless, hick (*inf., chiefly US & Canad.*), loutish, lumpish, maladroit, rough, uncultured, unmannerly ◆ *n* **7** = **yokel**, boor, bumpkin, clod, clodhopper (*inf.*), clown, country boy, country cousin, countryman *or* countrywoman, hayseed (*US & Canad. inf.*), hick (*inf., chiefly US & Canad.*), hillbilly, Hodge, peasant, son of the soil, swain (*arch.*)
Antonyms *adj* ≠ **rural:** cosmopolitan, urban ≠ **simple:** elegant, grand, polished, refined, sophisticated ≠ **uncouth:** courtly, polished, refined,

rated by deep joints. **4** (*tr*) *Brit.* to send down from university for a specified time as a punishment. **[**C17: from L *rūsticārī,* from *rūs* the country**]**
▸ **ˌrustiˈcation** *n* ▸ **ˈrustiˌcator** *n*

rusticated (ˈrʌstɪˌkeɪtɪd) *or* **rusticating** (ˈrʌstɪˌkeɪtɪŋ) *n* (in New Zealand) a wide type of weatherboarding used in older houses.

rustle[1] ➊ (ˈrʌsᵊl) *vb* **rustles, rustling, rustled. 1** to make or cause to make a low crisp whispering or rubbing sound, as of dry leaves or paper. **2** to move with such a sound. ◆ *n* **3** such a sound or sounds. **[**OE *hrūxlian***]**

rustle[2] (ˈrʌsᵊl) *vb* **rustles, rustling, rustled. 1** *Chiefly US & Canad.* to steal (cattle, horses, etc.). **2** *Inf., US & Canad.* to move swiftly and energetically. **[**C19: prob. special use of RUSTLE[1] (in the sense: to move with a quiet sound)**]**
▸ **ˈrustler** *n*

rustle up *vb* (*tr, adv*) *Inf.* **1** to prepare (a meal, etc.) rapidly, esp. at short notice. **2** to forage for and obtain.

rustproof (ˈrʌstˌpruːf) *adj* treated against rusting.

rusty ➊ (ˈrʌstɪ) *adj* **rustier, rustiest. 1** covered with, affected by, or consisting of rust: *a rusty machine.* **2** of the colour rust. **3** discoloured by age: *a rusty coat.* **4** (of the voice) tending to croak. **5** old-fashioned in appearance: *a rusty old gentleman.* **6** impaired in skill or knowledge by inaction or neglect. **7** (of plants) affected by the rust fungus.
▸ **ˈrustily** *adv* ▸ **ˈrustiness** *n*

rut[1] ➊ (rʌt) *n* **1** a groove or furrow in a soft road, caused by wheels. **2** a narrow or predictable way of life; dreary or undeviating routine (esp. in **in a rut**). ◆ *vb* **ruts, rutting, rutted. 3** (*tr*) to make a rut in. **[**C16: prob. from F *route* road**]**

rut[2] (rʌt) *n* **1** a recurrent period of sexual excitement and reproductive activity in certain male ruminants. ◆ *vb* **ruts, rutting, rutted. 2** (*intr*) (of male ruminants) to be in a period of sexual excitement and activity. **[**C15: from OF *rut* noise, roar, from L *rugītus,* from *rugīre* to roar**]**

rutabaga (ˌruːtəˈbeɪgə) *n* the US and Canad. name for **swede. [**C18: from Swedish dialect *rotabagge,* lit.: root bag**]**

rutaceous (ruːˈteɪʃəs) *adj* of, relating to, or belonging to a family of tropical and temperate flowering plants many of which have aromatic leaves. The family includes rue, citrus trees, and dittany. **[**C19: from NL *Rutaceae,* from L *rūta* RUE[2]**]**

ruth (ruːθ) *n Arch.* **1** pity; compassion. **2** repentance; remorse. **[**C12: from *rewen* to RUE[1]**]**

ruthenium (ruːˈθiːnɪəm) *n* a hard brittle white element of the platinum metal group. It is used to harden platinum and palladium. Symbol: Ru; atomic no.: 44; atomic wt.: 101.07. **[**C19: from Med. L *Ruthenia* Russia, where it was discovered**]**

rutherford (ˈrʌðəfəd) *n* a former unit of activity equal to the quantity of a radioactive nuclide required to produce one million disintegrations per second. Abbrev.: **rd. [**C20: after Ernest *Rutherford* (1871–1937), Brit. physicist who discovered the atomic nucleus**]**

rutherfordium (ˌrʌðəˈfɔːdɪəm) *n* the US name for the element with the atomic no. 104.Symbol: Rf **[**C20: after E. *Rutherford;* see RUTHERFORD**]**

ruthful (ˈruːθfʊl) *adj Arch.* full of or causing sorrow or pity.
▸ **ˈruthfully** *adv* ▸ **ˈruthfulness** *n*

ruthless ➊ (ˈruːθlɪs) *adj* feeling or showing no mercy; hardhearted.
▸ **ˈruthlessly** *adv* ▸ **ˈruthlessness** *n*

rutile (ˈruːtaɪl) *n* a mineral consisting of titanium(IV) oxide (TiO_2) in tetragonal crystalline form. It is an important source of titanium. **[**C19: via F from G *Rutil,* from L *rutilus* red, glowing**]**

ruttish (ˈrʌtɪʃ) *adj* **1** (of an animal) in a condition of rut. **2** lascivious or salacious.
▸ **ˈruttishly** *adv* ▸ **ˈruttishness** *n*

rutty (ˈrʌtɪ) *adj* **ruttier, ruttiest.** full of ruts or holes: *a rutty track.*
▸ **ˈruttily** *adv* ▸ **ˈruttiness** *n*

RV *abbrev. for:* **1** *Chiefly US.* recreational vehicle. **2** Revised Version (of the Bible).

-ry *suffix forming nouns.* a variant of **-ery:** *dentistry.*

Ryder Cup *n* **the.** the trophy awarded in a professional golfing competition between teams representing Europe and the US. **[**C20: after Samuel *Ryder* (1859–1936), Brit. businessman and golf patron**]**

rye (raɪ) *n* **1** a tall hardy widely cultivated annual grass having bristly flower spikes and light brown grain. **2** the grain of this grass, used in making flour and whisky, and as a livestock food. **3** Also called: (esp. US): **rye whiskey.** whisky distilled from rye. **4** *US.* short for **rye bread.** **[**OE *ryge***]**

rye bread *n* any of various breads made entirely or partly from rye flour, often with caraway seeds.

rye-grass *n* any of various grasses native to Europe, N Africa, and Asia, and widely cultivated as forage crops. They have flattened flower spikes and hairless leaves.

THESAURUS

sophisticated, urbane ◆ *n* ≠ **yokel:** city slicker, cosmopolitan, courtier, sophisticate, townie, townsman

rustle[1] *vb* **1** = **crackle**, crepitate, crinkle, susurrate (*literary*), swish, whish, whisper, whoosh ◆ *n* **3** = **crackle**, crepitation, crinkling, rustling, susurration *or* susurrus (*literary*), whisper

rusty *adj* **1** = **corroded**, oxidized, rust-covered, rusted **2** = **reddish-brown**, chestnut, coppery, reddish, russet, rust-coloured **4** = **croaking**, cracked, creaking, croaky, hoarse **5** = **old-fashioned**, ancient, antiquated, antique, dated, outmoded, out of date, passé **6** = **out of practice**, deficient, impaired, not what it was, sluggish, stale, unpractised, weak

rut[1] *n* **1** = **groove**, furrow, gouge, indentation, pothole, score, track, trough, wheel mark **2** = **habit**, dead end, groove, humdrum existence, pattern, routine, system

ruthless *adj* = **merciless**, adamant, barbarous, brutal, callous, cruel, ferocious, fierce, hard, hard-hearted, harsh, heartless, inexorable, inhuman, pitiless, relentless, remorseless, savage, severe, stern, unfeeling, unmerciful, unpitying, unrelenting, without pity
Antonyms *adj* compassionate, forgiving, gentle, humane, kind, lenient, merciful, pitying, sparing

rutted *adj* **1** = **grooved**, cut, furrowed, gouged, holed, indented, marked, scored

Ss

s *or* **S** (ɛs) *n, pl* **s's, S's,** *or* **Ss. 1** the 19th letter of the English alphabet. **2** a speech sound represented by this letter, either voiceless, as in *sit,* or voiced, as in *dogs.* **3a** something shaped like an S. **3b** (*in combination*): *an S-bend in a road.*

s *symbol for* second (of time).

S *symbol for:* **1** small. **2** Society. **3** South. **4** *Chem.* sulphur. **5** *Physics.* **5a** entropy. **5b** siemens. **5c** strangeness. **6** *Currency.* Schilling.

s. *abbrev. for:* **1** shilling. **2** singular. **3** son. **4** succeeded.

s. *or* **S.** *Music. abbrev. for* soprano.

S. *abbrev. for:* **1** sabbath. **2** (*pl* **SS**) Saint. **3** Saturday. **4** Saxon. **5** school. **6** September. **7** Signor. **8** Sunday.

-s[1] *or* **-es** *suffix.* forming the plural of most nouns: *boys; boxes.* [from OE *-as,* pl. nominative and accusative ending of some masc nouns]

-s[2] *or* **-es** *suffix.* forming the third person singular present indicative tense of verbs: *he runs.* [from OE (northern dialect) *-es, -s,* orig. the ending of the second person singular]

-'s *suffix.* **1** forming the possessive singular of nouns and some pronouns: *man's; one's.* **2** forming the possessive plural of nouns whose plurals do not end in *-s: children's.* (The possessive plural of nouns ending in *s* and of some singular nouns is formed by the addition of an apostrophe after the final *s: girls'; for goodness' sake.*) **3** forming the plural of numbers, letters, or symbols: *20's.* **4** *Inf.* contraction of *is* or *has: it's gone.* **5** *Inf.* contraction of *us* with *let: let's.* **6** *Inf.* contraction of *does* in some questions: *what's he do?* [senses 1, 2: assimilated contraction from ME *-es,* from OE, masc and neuter genitive sing; sense 3, equivalent to *-s*[1]]

SA *abbrev. for:* **1** Salvation Army. **2** South Africa. **3** South America. **4** South Australia. **5** *Sturmabteilung:* the Nazi terrorist militia.

sabadilla (ˌsæbəˈdɪlə) *n* **1** a tropical American liliaceous plant. **2** the bitter brown seeds of this plant, which contain the alkaloid veratrine used in insecticides. [C19: from Sp. *cebadilla,* dim. of *cebada* barley, from L *cibāre* to feed, from *cibus* food]

Sabaean *or* **Sabean** (səˈbiːən) *n* **1** an inhabitant or native of ancient Saba. **2** the ancient Semitic language of Saba. ◆ *adj* **3** of or relating to ancient Saba, its inhabitants, or their language. [C16: from L *Sabaeus,* from Gk *Sabaios* belonging to Saba (Sheba)]

sabbat (ˈsæbæt, -ət) *n* another word for **Sabbath** (sense 4).

Sabbatarian (ˌsæbəˈtɛərɪən) *n* **1** a person advocating the strict religious observance of Sunday. **2** a person who observes Saturday as the Sabbath. ◆ *adj* **3** of the Sabbath or its observance. [C17: from LL *sabbatārius* a Sabbath-keeper]
▸**ˌSabbaˈtarianism** *n*

Sabbath (ˈsæbəθ) *n* **1** the seventh day of the week, Saturday, devoted to worship and rest from work in Judaism and in certain Christian Churches. **2** Sunday, observed by Christians as the day of worship and rest. **3** (*not cap.*) a period of rest. **4** Also called: **sabbat, witches' Sabbath.** a midnight meeting for practitioners of witchcraft or devil worship. [OE *sabbat,* from L, from Gk *sabbaton,* from Heb., from *shābath* to rest]

sabbatical (səˈbætɪkᵊl) *adj* **1** denoting a period of leave granted to university staff, teachers, etc., esp. originally every seventh year: *a sabbatical year.* ◆ *n* **2** any sabbatical period. [C16: from Gk *sabbatikos;* see SABBATH]

Sabbatical (səˈbætɪkᵊl) *adj* of, relating to, or appropriate to the Sabbath as a day of rest and religious observance.

SABC *abbrev. for* South African Broadcasting Corporation.

saber (ˈseɪbə) *n, vb* the US spelling of **sabre.**

sabin (ˈsæbɪn, ˈseɪ-) *n Physics.* a unit of acoustic absorption. [C20: introduced by Wallace C. *Sabine* (1868–1919), US physicist]

Sabine (ˈsæbaɪn) *n* **1** a member of an ancient people who lived in central Italy. ◆ *adj* **2** of or relating to this people or their language.

sabkha (ˈsæbxə, -kə) *n* a flat coastal plain with a salt crust, common in Arabia. [C19: from Ar.]

sable ❶ (ˈseɪbᵊl) *n, pl* **sables** *or* **sable. 1** a marten of N Asian forests, with dark brown luxuriant fur. **2a** the highly valued fur of this animal. **2b** (*as modifier*): *a sable coat.* **3 American sable.** the brown, slightly less valuable fur of the American marten. **4** a dark brown to yellowish-brown colour. ◆ *adj* **5** of the colour of sable fur. **6** black; dark. **7** (*usually postpositive*) *Heraldry.* of the colour black. [C15: from OF, from OHG *zobel,* of Slavic origin]

sable antelope *n* a large black E African antelope with long backward-curving horns.

sabot (ˈsæbəʊ) *n* **1** a shoe made from a single block of wood. **2** a shoe with a wooden sole and a leather or cloth upper. **3** *Austral.* a small sailing boat with a shortened bow. [C17: from F, prob. from OF *savate* an old shoe, also infl. by *bot* BOOT[1]]

sabotage ❶ (ˈsæbəˌtɑːʒ) *n* **1** the deliberate destruction, disruption, or damage of equipment, a public service, etc., as by enemy agents, dissatisfied employees, etc. **2** any similar action. ◆ *vb* **sabotages, sabotaging, sabotaged. 3** (*tr*) to destroy or disrupt, esp. by secret means. [C20: from F, from *saboter* to spoil through clumsiness (lit.: to clatter in sabots)]

saboteur (ˌsæbəˈtɜː) *n* a person who commits sabotage. [C20: from F]

sabra (ˈsɑːbrə) *n* a native-born Israeli Jew. [from Heb. *Sābēr* prickly pear, common plant in the coastal areas of the country]

sabre *or US* **saber** (ˈseɪbə) *n* **1** a stout single-edged cavalry sword, having a curved blade. **2** a sword used in fencing, having a narrow V-shaped blade. ◆ *vb* **sabres, sabring, sabred** *or US* **sabers, sabering, sabered. 3** (*tr*) to injure or kill with a sabre. [C17: via F from G (dialect) *Sabel,* from MHG *sebel,* ?from Magyar *szablya*]

sabre-rattling *n, adj Inf.* seeking to intimidate by an aggressive display of military power.

sabre-toothed tiger *or* **cat** *n* any of various extinct felines with long curved upper canine teeth.

sac ❶ (sæk) *n* a pouch, bag, or pouchlike part in an animal or plant. [C18: from F, from L *saccus;* see SACK[1]]
▸**saccate** (ˈsækɪt, -eɪt) *adj* ▸**ˈsacˌlike** *adj*

saccharide (ˈsækəˌraɪd) *n* any sugar or other carbohydrate, esp. a simple sugar.

saccharimeter (ˌsækəˈrɪmɪtə) *n* any instrument for measuring the strength of sugar solutions.
▸**ˌsacchaˈrimetry** *n*

saccharin (ˈsækərɪn) *n* a very sweet white crystalline slightly soluble powder used as a nonfattening sweetener. [C19: from SACCHARO- + -IN]

saccharine ❶ (ˈsækəˌriːn) *adj* **1** excessively sweet; sugary: *a saccharine smile.* **2** of the nature of or containing sugar or saccharin.

saccharo- *or before a vowel* **sacchar-** *combining form.* sugar. [via L from Gk *sakkharon,* ult. from Sansk. *śarkarā* sugar]

saccharose (ˈsækəˌrəʊz, -ˌrəʊs) *n* a technical name for **sugar** (sense 1).

saccule (ˈsækjuːl) *or* **sacculus** (ˈsækjʊləs) *n* **1** a small sac. **2** the smaller of the two parts of the membranous labyrinth of the internal ear. Cf. **utricle.** [C19: from L *sacculus* dim. of *saccus* SACK[1]]

sacerdotal (ˌsæsəˈdəʊtᵊl) *adj* of, relating to, or characteristic of priests. [C14: from L *sacerdōtālis,* from *sacerdōs* priest, from *sacer* sacred]
▸**ˌsacerˈdotaˌlism** *n* ▸**ˌsacerˈdotally** *adv*

sachem (ˈseɪtʃəm) *n* **1** *US.* a leader of a political party or organization. **2** another name for **sagamore.** [C17: from Amerind *săchim* chief]

sachet (ˈsæʃeɪ) *n* **1** a small sealed envelope, usually made of plastic, for containing shampoo, etc. **2a** a small soft bag containing perfumed powder, placed in drawers to scent clothing. **2b** the powder contained in such a bag. [C19: from OF: a little bag, from *sac* bag; see SACK[1]]

sack[1] ❶ (sæk) *n* **1** a large bag made of coarse cloth, thick paper, etc., used as a container. **2** Also called: **sackful.** the amount contained in a sack. **3a** a woman's loose tube-shaped dress. **3b** Also called: **sacque** (sæk). a woman's full loose hip-length jacket. **4 the sack.** *Inf.* dismissal from employment. **5** a slang word for **bed. 6 hit the sack.** *Sl.* to go to bed. ◆ *vb* (*tr*) **7** *Inf.* to dismiss from employment. **8** to put into a sack or sacks. [OE *sacc,* from L *saccus* bag, from Gk *sakkos*]
▸**ˈsackˌlike** *adj*

sack[2] ❶ (sæk) *n* **1** the plundering of a place by an army or mob. **2** *American football.* a tackle on a quarterback that brings him down before he has passed the ball. ◆ *vb* (*tr*) **3** to plunder and partially destroy (a place). **4** *American football.* to tackle and bring down (a quarterback) before he has passed the ball. [C16: from F *mettre à sac,* lit.: to put (loot) in a sack, from L *saccus* SACK[1]]
▸**ˈsacker** *n*

sack[3] (sæk) *n Arch. except in trademarks.* any dry white wine from SW Europe. [C16 *wyne seck,* from F *vin sec* dry wine, from L *siccus* dry]

THESAURUS

sable *adj* **6** = **black**, dark, dusty, ebon (*poetic*), ebony, jet, jetty, raven, sombre

sabotage *n* **1** = **damage**, destruction, disruption, subversion, treachery, treason, wrecking ◆ *vb* **3** = **damage**, cripple, destroy, disable, disrupt, incapacitate, sap the foundations of, subvert, throw a spanner in the works (*Brit. inf.*), undermine, vandalize, wreck

sac *n* = **pouch**, bag, bladder, bursa, cyst, pocket, pod, vesicle

saccharine *adj* **1** = **oversweet**, cloying, honeyed, maudlin, mawkish, nauseating, sentimental, sickly, soppy (*Brit. inf.*), sugary, syrupy (*inf.*), treacly

sack[1] *n* **4 the sack** = **dismissal**, discharge, termination of employment, the axe (*inf.*), the boot (*sl.*), the chop (*Brit. sl.*), the (old) heave-ho (*inf.*), the push (*sl.*) **6 hit the sack** *Slang* = **go to bed**, bed down, hit the hay (*sl.*), retire, turn in (*inf.*) ◆ *vb* **7** *Informal* = **dismiss**, axe (*inf.*), discharge, fire (*inf.*), give (someone) his cards, give (someone) his marching orders, give (someone) the boot (*sl.*), kick out (*inf.*)

sack[2] *n* **1** = **plundering**, depredation, despoliation, destruction, devastation, looting, pillage, plunder, rape, rapine, ravage, ruin, waste ◆ *vb* **3** = **plunder**, demolish, despoil, destroy, devastate, lay waste, loot, maraud, pillage, raid, ravage, rifle, rob, ruin, spoil, strip

sackbut ('sæk,bʌt) *n* a medieval form of trombone. [C16: from F *saqueboute,* from OF *saquer* to pull + *bouter* to push]

sackcloth ➊ ('sæk,klɒθ) *n* **1** coarse cloth such as sacking. **2** garments made of such cloth, worn formerly to indicate mourning. **3 sackcloth and ashes.** a public display of extreme grief.

sacking ('sækɪŋ) *n* coarse cloth used for making sacks, woven from flax, hemp, jute, etc.

sack race *n* a race in which the competitors' legs and often bodies are enclosed in sacks.

sacral[1] ('seɪkrəl) *adj* of or associated with sacred rites. [C19: from L *sacrum* sacred object]

sacral[2] ('seɪkrəl) *adj* of or relating to the sacrum. [C18: from NL *sacrālis* of the SACRUM]

sacrament ('sækrəmənt) *n* **1** an outward sign combined with a prescribed form of words and regarded as conferring grace upon those who receive it. The Protestant sacraments are baptism and the Lord's Supper. In the Roman Catholic and Eastern Churches they are baptism, penance, confirmation, the Eucharist, holy orders, matrimony, and the anointing of the sick (formerly extreme unction). **2** (*often cap.*) the Eucharist. **3** the consecrated elements of the Eucharist, esp. the bread. **4** something regarded as possessing a sacred significance. **5** a pledge. [C12: from Church L *sacrāmentum* vow, from L *sacrāre* to consecrate]

sacramental (,sækrə'mentᵊl) *adj* **1** of or having the nature of a sacrament. ◆ *n* **2** *RC Church.* a sacrament-like ritual action, such as the sign of the cross or the use of holy water.
▸**,sacra'menta,lism** *n* ▸**sacramentality** (,sækrəmen'tælɪtɪ) *n*

sacrarium (sæ'krεərɪəm) *n, pl* **sacraria** (-'krεərɪə). **1** the sanctuary of a church. **2** *RC Church.* a place near the altar of a church where materials used in the sacred rites are deposited or poured away. [C18: from L, from *sacer* sacred]

sacred ➊ ('seɪkrɪd) *adj* **1** exclusively devoted to a deity or to some religious ceremony or use. **2** worthy of or regarded with reverence and awe. **3** connected with or intended for religious use: *sacred music.* **4 sacred to.** dedicated to. [C14: from L *sacrāre* to set apart as holy, from *sacer* holy]
▸**'sacredly** *adv* ▸**'sacredness** *n*

sacred cow *n Inf.* a person, custom, etc., held to be beyond criticism. [alluding to the Hindu belief that cattle are sacred]

sacred mushroom *n* **1** any of various hallucinogenic mushrooms that have been eaten in rituals in various parts of the world. **2** a mescal button, used in a similar way.

sacrifice ➊ ('sækrɪ,faɪs) *n* **1** a surrender of something of value as a means of gaining something more desirable or of preventing some evil. **2** a ritual killing of a person or animal with the intention of propitiating or pleasing a deity. **3** a symbolic offering of something to a deity. **4** the person, animal, or object killed or offered. **5** loss entailed by giving up or selling something at less than its value. **6** *Chess.* the act or an instance of sacrificing a piece. ◆ *vb* **sacrifices, sacrificing, sacrificed. 7** to make a sacrifice (of). **8** *Chess.* to permit or force one's opponent to capture a piece freely, as in playing a gambit: *he sacrificed his queen and checkmated his opponent on the next move.* [C13: via OF from L *sacrificium,* from *sacer* holy + *facere* to make]
▸**'sacri,ficer** *n*

sacrifice paddock *n NZ.* a grassed field which is allowed to be grazed completely, so that it can be cultivated and resown later.

sacrificial ➊ (,sækrɪ'fɪʃəl) *adj* used in or connected with a sacrifice.
▸**,sacri'ficially** *adv*

sacrilege ➊ ('sækrɪlɪdʒ) *n* **1** the misuse or desecration of anything regarded as sacred or as worthy of extreme respect. **2** the act or an instance of taking anything sacred for secular use. [C13: from OF, from L, from *sacrilegus* temple-robber, from *sacra* sacred things + *legere* to take]
▸**sacrilegist** (,sækrɪ'li:dʒɪst) *n*

sacrilegious ➊ (,sækrɪ'lɪdʒəs) *adj* **1** of, relating to, or involving sacrilege. **2** guilty of sacrilege.
▸**,sacri'legiously** *adv*

sacring bell ('seɪkrɪŋ) *n Chiefly RC Church.* a small bell rung at the elevation of the Host and chalice during Mass.

sacristan ('sækrɪstən) *or* **sacrist** ('sækrɪst, 'seɪ-) *n* **1** a person who has charge of the contents of a church. **2** a less common word for **sexton.** [C14: from Med. L *sacristānus,* ult. from L *sacer* holy]

sacristy ('sækrɪstɪ) *n, pl* **sacristies.** a room attached to a church or chapel where the sacred vessels, vestments, etc., are kept. [C17: from Med. L *sacristia;* see SACRISTAN]

sacroiliac (,seɪkrəʊ'ɪlɪ,æk) *Anat.* ◆ *adj* **1** of or relating to the sacrum and ilium or their articulation. ◆ *n* **2** the joint where these bones meet.

sacrosanct ➊ ('sækrəʊ,sæŋkt) *adj* very sacred or holy. [C17: from L *sacrōsanctus* made holy by sacred rite, from *sacer* holy + *sanctus,* from *sancīre* to hallow]
▸**,sacro'sanctity** *n*

sacrum ('seɪkrəm) *n, pl* **sacra** (-krə). the large wedge-shaped bone, consisting of five fused vertebrae, in the lower part of the back. [C18: from L *os sacrum* holy bone, because it was used in sacrifices, from *sacer* holy]

sad ➊ (sæd) *adj* **sadder, saddest. 1** feeling sorrow; unhappy. **2** causing, suggestive, or expressive of such feelings: *a sad story.* **3** unfortunate; shabby: *her clothes were in a sad state.* **4** *Brit. inf.* ludicrously contemptible; pathetic: *a sad, boring little wimp.* [OE *sæd* weary]
▸**'sadly** *adv* ▸**'sadness** *n*

SAD *abbrev. for* seasonal affective disorder.

sadden ➊ ('sædᵊn) *vb* to make or become sad.

saddle ➊ ('sædᵊl) *n* **1** a seat for a rider, usually made of leather, placed on a horse's back and secured with a girth under the belly. **2** a similar seat on a bicycle, tractor, etc. **3** a back pad forming part of the harness of a packhorse. **4** anything that resembles a saddle in shape, position, or function. **5** a cut of meat, esp. mutton, consisting of both loins. **6** the part of a horse or similar animal on which a saddle is placed. **7** the part of the back of a domestic chicken that is nearest to the tail. **8** another word for **col** (sense 1). **9 in the saddle.** in a position of control. ◆ *vb* **saddles, saddling, saddled. 10** (sometimes foll. by *up*) to put a saddle on (a horse). **11** (*intr*) to mount into the saddle. **12** (*tr*) to burden: *I didn't ask to be saddled with this job.* [OE *sadol, sædel*]
▸**'saddle-,like** *adj*

saddleback ('sædᵊl,bæk) *n* a marking resembling a saddle on the backs of various animals.
▸**'saddle-,backed** *adj*

saddlebag ('sædᵊl,bæg) *n* a pouch or small bag attached to the saddle of a horse, bicycle, etc.

saddlebill ('sædᵊl,bɪl) *n* a large black-and-white stork of tropical Africa, having a heavy red bill with a black band around the middle. Also called: **jabiru.**

saddlebow ('sædᵊl,bəʊ) *n* the pommel of a saddle.

saddlecloth ('sædᵊl,klɒθ) *n* a light cloth put under a horse's saddle, so as to prevent rubbing.

saddle horse *n* a lightweight horse kept for riding only.

saddler ('sædlə) *n* a person who makes, deals in, or repairs saddles and other leather equipment for horses.

saddle roof *n* a roof that has a ridge and two gables.

saddlery ('sædlərɪ) *n, pl* **saddleries. 1** saddles, harness, and other leather equipment for horses collectively. **2** the business, work, or place of work of a saddler.

saddle soap *n* a soft soap containing neat's-foot oil used to preserve and clean leather.

saddletree ('sædᵊl,tri:) *n* the frame of a saddle.

Sadducee ('sædjʊ,si:) *n Judaism.* a member of an ancient Jewish sect that was opposed to the Pharisees, denying the resurrection of the dead and the validity of oral tradition. [OE *saddūcēas,* via L & Gk from LHeb. *ṣāddūqī,* prob. from *Ṣadoq* Zadok, high priest and supposed founder of the sect]
▸**,Saddu'cean** *adj*

sadhu *or* **saddhu** ('sɑ:du:) *n* a Hindu wandering holy man. [Sansk., from *sādhu* good]

sadiron ('sæd,aɪən) *n* a heavy iron, pointed at both ends for pressing clothes. [C19: from SAD (in the obs. sense: heavy) + IRON]

sadism ➊ ('seɪdɪzəm) *n* the gaining of pleasure or sexual gratification from the infliction of pain and mental suffering on another person. Cf. **masochism.** [C19: from F, after the Marquis de *Sade* (1740–1814), F soldier & writer]
▸**'sadist** *n* ▸**sadistic** (sə'dɪstɪk) *adj* ▸**sa'distically** *adv*

THESAURUS

sackcloth *n* **3 sackcloth and ashes = penitence,** compunction, contrition, grief, hair shirt, mortification, mourning, penance, remorse, repentance

sacred *adj* **1, 2 = holy,** blessed, consecrated, divine, hallowed, revered, sanctified, venerable **3 = religious,** ecclesiastical, holy, solemn
Antonyms *adj* ≠ **holy, religious:** lay, nonspiritual, profane, secular, temporal, unconsecrated, worldly

sacrifice *n* **1 = surrender,** destruction, holocaust (*rare*), loss, renunciation **2 = offering,** hecatomb, immolation, oblation ◆ *vb* **7 = give up,** forego, forfeit, immolate, let go, lose, offer, offer up, say goodbye to, surrender

sacrificial *adj* **= propitiatory,** atoning, expiatory, oblatory, reparative

sacrilege *n* **1 = desecration,** blasphemy, heresy, impiety, irreverence, mockery, profanation, profaneness, profanity, violation
Antonyms *n* piety, respect, reverence

sacrilegious *adj* **1 = profane,** blasphemous, desecrating, godless, impious, irreligious, irreverent, ungodly, unholy

sacrosanct *adj* **= inviolable,** hallowed, inviolate, sacred, sanctified, set apart, untouchable

sad *adj* **1 = unhappy,** blue, cheerless, dejected, depressed, disconsolate, dismal, doleful, down, downcast, down in the dumps (*inf.*), down in the mouth (*inf.*), gloomy, glum, grief-stricken, grieved, heavy-hearted, low, low-spirited, lugubrious, melancholy, mournful, pensive, sick at heart, sombre, wistful, woebegone **2 = tragic,** calamitous, dark, depressing, disastrous, dismal, grievous, harrowing, heart-rending, lachrymose, moving, pathetic, pitiable, pitiful, poignant, sorry, tearful, upsetting **3 = deplorable,** bad, dismal, lamentable, miserable, shabby, sorry, to be deplored, wretched
Antonyms *adj* ≠ **unhappy:** blithe, cheerful, cheery, chirpy (*inf.*), glad, happy, in good spirits, jolly, joyful, joyous, light-hearted, merry, pleased ≠ **deplorable:** good

sadden *vb* **= upset,** aggrieve, bring tears to one's eyes, cast a gloom upon, cast down, dash, deject, depress, desolate, dispirit, distress, grieve, make one's heart bleed, make sad

saddle *vb* **12 = burden,** charge, encumber, load, lumber (*Brit. inf.*), task, tax

sadistic *adj* **= cruel,** barbarous, beastly, brutal, fiendish, inhuman, perverse, perverted, ruthless, savage, vicious

sadness *n* **1 = unhappiness,** bleakness, cheerlessness, dejection, depression, despondency,

sadomasochism (ˌseɪdəʊˈmæsəˌkɪzəm) *n* **1** the combination of sadistic and masochistic elements in one person. **2** sexual practice in which one partner adopts a sadistic role and the other a masochistic one.
▸ **ˌsadomasoˈchistic** *adj*

s.a.e. *abbrev. for* stamped addressed envelope.

safari (səˈfɑːrɪ) *n, pl* **safaris. 1** an overland journey or hunting expedition, esp. in Africa. **2** the people, animals, etc., that go on the expedition. [C19: from Swahili: journey, from Ar., from *safara* to travel]

safari park *n* an enclosed park in which lions and other wild animals are kept uncaged in the open and can be viewed by the public from cars, etc.

safari suit *n* an outfit made of tough cotton, denim, etc., consisting of a bush jacket with matching trousers, shorts, or skirt.

safe ❶ (seɪf) *adj* **1** affording security or protection from harm: *a safe place.* **2** (*postpositive*) free from danger: *you'll be safe here.* **3** secure from risk: *a safe investment.* **4** worthy of trust: *a safe companion.* **5** tending to avoid controversy or risk: *a safe player.* **6** not dangerous: *water safe to drink.* **7 on the safe side.** as a precaution. ◆ *adv* **8** in a safe condition: *the children are safe in bed now.* **9 play safe.** to act in a way least likely to cause danger, controversy, or defeat. ◆ *n* **10** a strong container, usually of metal and provided with a secure lock, for storing money or valuables. **11** a small cupboard-like container for storing food. [C13: from OF *salf,* from L *salvus*]
▸ **ˈsafely** *adv* ▸ **ˈsafeness** *n*

safe-breaker *n* a person who breaks open and robs safes. Also called: **safe-cracker.**

safe-conduct ❶ *n* **1** a document giving official permission to travel through a region, esp. in time of war. **2** the protection afforded by such a document.

safe-deposit *or* **safety-deposit** *n* **a** a place with facilities for the safe storage of money. **b** (*as modifier*): *a safe-deposit box.*

safeguard ❶ (ˈseɪfˌgɑːd) *n* **1** a person or thing that ensures protection against danger, injury, etc. **2** a safe-conduct. ◆ *vb* **3** (*tr*) to protect.

safe house *n* a place used secretly by undercover agents, terrorists, etc., as a refuge.

safekeeping ❶ (ˈseɪfˈkiːpɪŋ) *n* the act of keeping or state of being kept in safety.

safe period *n Inf.* the period during the menstrual cycle when conception is considered least likely to occur.

safe seat *n* a Parliamentary seat that at an election is sure to be held by the same party as held it before.

safe sex *n* sexual intercourse using physical protection, such as a condom, or nonpenetrative methods to prevent the spread of such diseases as AIDS.

safety ❶ (ˈseɪftɪ) *n, pl* **safeties. 1** the quality of being safe. **2** freedom from danger or risk of injury. **3** a contrivance designed to prevent injury. **4** *American football.* Also called: **safetyman.** either of two players who defend the area furthest back in the field.

safety belt *n* **1** another name for **seat belt** (sense 1). **2** a belt or strap worn by a person working at a great height to prevent him from falling.

safety curtain *n* a curtain made of fireproof material that can be lowered to separate the auditorium and stage in a theatre to prevent the spread of a fire.

safety factor *n* the ratio of the breaking stress of a material to the calculated maximum stress in use. Also called: **factor of safety.**

safety glass *n* glass that if broken will not shatter.

safety lamp *n* an oil-burning miner's lamp in which the flame is surrounded by a metal gauze to prevent it from igniting combustible gas.

safety match *n* a match that will light only when struck against a specially prepared surface.

safety net *n* **1** a net used in a circus to catch high-wire and trapeze artistes if they fall. **2** any means of protection from hardship or loss.

safety pin *n* a spring wire clasp with a covering catch, made so as to shield the point when closed.

safety razor *n* a razor with a guard over the blade or blades to prevent deep cuts.

safety valve *n* **1** a valve in a pressure vessel that allows fluid to escape at excess pressure. **2** a harmless outlet for emotion, etc.

saffian (ˈsæfɪən) *n* leather tanned with sumach and usually dyed a bright colour. [C16: via Russian & Turkish from Persian *sakhtiyān* goatskin, from *sakht* hard]

safflower (ˈsæflaʊə) *n* **1** a thistle-like Eurasian annual plant having large heads of orange-yellow flowers and yielding a dye and an oil used in paints, medicines, etc. **2** a red dye used for cotton and for colouring foods and cosmetics. [C16: via Du. *saffloer* or G *safflor* from OF *saffleur*]

saffron (ˈsæfrən) *n* **1** an Old World crocus having purple or white flowers with orange stigmas. **2** the dried stigmas of this plant, used to flavour or colour food. **3 meadow saffron.** another name for **autumn crocus. 4a** an orange to orange-yellow colour. **4b** (*as adj*): *a saffron dress.* [C13: from OF *safran,* from Med. L *safranum,* from Ar. *za'farān*]

S.Afr. *abbrev. for* South Africa(n).

safranine *or* **safranin** (ˈsæfrənɪn) *n* any of a class of azine dyes used for textiles. [C19: from F *safran* SAFFRON + -INE[2]]

sag ❶ (sæg) *vb* **sags, sagging, sagged.** (*mainly intr*) **1** (*also tr*) to sink or cause to sink in parts, as under weight or pressure: *the bed sags in the middle.* **2** to fall in value: *prices sagged to a new low.* **3** to hang unevenly. **4** (of courage, etc.) to weaken. ◆ *n* **5** the act or an instance of sagging: *a sag in profits.* **6** *Naut.* the extent to which a vessel's keel sags at the centre. [C15: from ON]
▸ **ˈsaggy** *adj*

saga ❶ (ˈsɑːgə) *n* **1** any of several medieval prose narratives written in Iceland and recounting the exploits of a hero or a family. **2** any similar heroic narrative. **3** a series of novels about several generations or members of a family. **4** *Inf.* a series of events or a story stretching over a long period. [C18: from ON: a narrative]

sagacious ❶ (səˈgeɪʃəs) *adj* having or showing sagacity; wise. [C17: from L *sagāx,* from *sāgīre* to be astute]
▸ **saˈgaciously** *adv*

sagacity ❶ (səˈgæsɪtɪ) *n* foresight, discernment, or keen perception; ability to make good judgments.

sagamore (ˈsægəˌmɔː) *n* (among some North American Indians) a chief or eminent man. [C17: from Amerind *sāgimau,* lit.: he overcomes]

sage[1] ❶ (seɪdʒ) *n* **1** a man revered for his profound wisdom. ◆ *adj* **2** profoundly wise or prudent. [C13: from OF, from L *sapere* to be sensible]
▸ **ˈsagely** *adv* ▸ **ˈsageness** *n*

sage[2] (seɪdʒ) *n* **1** a perennial Mediterranean plant having grey-green leaves and purple, blue, or white flowers. **2** the leaves of this plant, used in cooking for flavouring. **3** short for **sagebrush.** [C14: from OF *saulge,* from L *salvia,* from *salvus* in good health (from its curative properties)]

sagebrush (ˈseɪdʒˌbrʌʃ) *n* any of a genus of aromatic plants of W North America, having silver-green leaves and large clusters of small white flowers.

saggar *or* **sagger** (ˈsægə) *n* a clay box in which ceramic wares are placed during firing. [C17: ? alteration of SAFEGUARD]

sagittal suture (ˈsædʒɪtᵊl) *n* a serrated line on the top of the skull that marks the junction of the two parietal bones.

Sagittarius (ˌsædʒɪˈtɛərɪəs) *n, Latin genitive* **Sagittarii** (ˌsædʒɪˈtɛərɪˌaɪ). **1** *Astron.* a S constellation. **2** Also called: the **Archer.** *Astrol.* the ninth sign of the zodiac. The sun is in this sign between Nov. 22 and Dec. 21. [C14: from L: an archer, from *sagitta* an arrow]
▸ **Sagittarian** (ˌsædʒɪˈtɛərɪən) *adj*

sagittate (ˈsædʒɪˌteɪt) *adj* (esp. of leaves) shaped like the head of an arrow. [C18: from NL *sagittātus,* from L *sagitta* arrow]

sago (ˈseɪgəʊ) *n* a starchy cereal obtained from the powdered pith of a palm (**sago palm**), used for puddings and as a thickening agent. [C16: from Malay *sāgū*]

saguaro (səˈgwɑːrəʊ) *n, pl* **saguaros.** a giant cactus of desert regions of Arizona, S California, and Mexico. [Mexican Sp., var. of *sahuaro,* an Indian name]

sahib (ˈsɑːhɪb) *n* (in India) a form of address placed after a man's name,

THESAURUS

dolefulness, dolour (*poetic*), gloominess, grief, heavy heart, melancholy, misery, mournfulness, poignancy, sorrow, sorrowfulness, the blues, the dumps (*inf.*), tragedy, wretchedness

safe *adj* **1 = secure,** free from harm, impregnable, in safe hands, in safety, out of danger, out of harm's way, out of the woods, protected, safe and sound **2 = unharmed,** all right, intact, O.K. *or* okay (*inf.*), undamaged, unhurt, unscathed **3 = risk-free,** certain, impregnable, riskless, secure, sound **5 = cautious,** circumspect, conservative, dependable, discreet, on the safe side, prudent, realistic, reliable, sure, tried and true, trustworthy, unadventurous **6 = harmless,** innocuous, nonpoisonous, nontoxic, pure, tame, unpolluted, wholesome ◆ *n* **10 = strongbox,** coffer, deposit box, repository, safe-deposit box, vault
Antonyms *adj* ≠ **secure:** at risk, damaged, endangered, imperilled, insecure, jeopardized, put at risk, put in danger, threatened ≠ **cautious:** imprudent, incautious, reckless, risky, unsafe ≠ **harmless:** baneful, dangerous, harmful, hazardous, hurtful, injurious, noxious, pernicious, unsafe

safe-conduct *n* **1 = permit,** authorization, licence, pass, passport, safeguard, warrant

safeguard *n* **1 = protection,** aegis, armour, bulwark, convoy, defence, escort, guard, security, shield, surety ◆ *vb* **3 = protect,** defend, guard, look after, preserve, screen, shield, watch over

safekeeping *n* **= protection,** care, charge, custody, guardianship, keeping, supervision, surveillance, trust, tutelage, ward

safely *adv* **1-3 = in safety,** in one piece, safe and sound, securely, with impunity, without risk, with safety

safety *n* **1 = security,** assurance, immunity, impregnability, protection

sag *vb* **1 = sink,** bag, bulge, cave in, dip, droop, drop, fall, fall unevenly, give way, hang loosely, seat (*of skirts, etc.*), settle, slump, swag **4 = tire,** decline, droop, fall, flag, slide, slip, slump, wane, weaken, wilt ◆ *n* **5 = drop,** decline, depression, dip, downturn, fall, lapse, slip, slump

saga *n* **2 = tale,** adventure, chronicle, epic, narrative, *roman-fleuve,* soap opera, story, yarn

sagacious *adj* **= wise,** able, acute, apt, astute, canny, clear-sighted, discerning, far-sighted, fly (*sl.*), insightful, intelligent, judicious, knowing, long-headed, perceptive, perspicacious, sage, sharp, sharp-witted, shrewd, smart

sagacity *n* **= wisdom,** acuteness, astuteness, canniness, discernment, foresight, insight, judiciousness, knowingness, penetration, perspicacity, prudence, sapience, sense, sharpness, shrewdness, understanding

sage[1] *n* **1 = wise man,** authority, elder, expert, guru, mahatma, man of learning, master, Nestor, philosopher, pundit, savant, Solomon, Solon ◆ *adj* **2 = wise,** acute, canny, discerning, intelligent, judicious, learned, perspicacious, politic, prudent, sagacious, sapient, sensible

used as a mark of respect. [C17: from Urdu, from Ar. *çāhib*, lit.: friend]

said[1] (sɛd) *adj* **1** (*prenominal*) (in contracts, etc.) aforesaid. ◆ *vb* **2** the past tense and past participle of **say**.

said[2] ('sɑːɪd) *n* a variant of **sayyid**.

saiga ('saɪɡə) *n* either of two antelopes of the plains of central Asia, having a slightly elongated nose. [C19: from Russian]

sail ❶ (seɪl) *n* **1** an area of fabric, usually Terylene or nylon (formerly canvas), with fittings for holding it in any suitable position to catch the wind, used for propelling certain kinds of vessels, esp. over water. **2** a voyage on such a vessel: *a sail down the river.* **3** a vessel with sails or such vessels collectively: *to travel by sail.* **4** a ship's sails collectively. **5** something resembling a sail in shape, position, or function, such as the part of a windmill that is turned by the wind. **6 in sail.** having the sail set. **7 make sail. 7a** to run up the sail or to run up more sail. **7b** to begin a voyage. **8 set sail. 8a** to embark on a voyage by ship. **8b** to hoist sail. **9 under sail. 9a** with sail hoisted. **9b** under way. ◆ *vb* (*mainly intr*) **10** to travel in a boat or ship: *we sailed to Le Havre.* **11** to begin a voyage: *we sail at 5 o'clock.* **12** (of a vessel) to move over the water. **13** (*tr*) to manoeuvre or navigate a vessel: *he sailed the schooner up the channel.* **14** (*tr*) to sail over: *she sailed the Atlantic single-handed.* **15** (often foll. by *over, through,* etc.) to move fast or effortlessly: *we sailed through customs.* **16** to move along smoothly; glide. **17** (often foll. by *in* or *into*) *Inf.* **17a** to begin (something) with vigour. **17b** to make an attack (on) violently. [OE *segl*]
▸**'sailable** *adj* ▸**'sailless** *adj*

sailboard ('seɪlˌbɔːd) *n* the craft used for windsurfing, consisting of a moulded board to which a mast bearing a single sail is attached.

sailboarding ('seɪlˌbɔːdɪŋ) *n* another name for **windsurfing**.

sailcloth ('seɪlˌklɒθ) *n* **1** any of various fabrics from which sails are made. **2** a canvas-like cloth used for clothing, etc.

sailer ('seɪlə) *n* a vessel, with specified sailing characteristics: *a good sailer.*

sailfish ('seɪlˌfɪʃ) *n, pl* **sailfish** *or* **sailfishes. 1** any of several large game fishes of warm and tropical seas. They have an elongated upper jaw and a long sail-like dorsal fin. **2** another name for **basking shark**.

sailing ship *n* a large sailing vessel.

sailor ❶ ('seɪlə) *n* **1** any member of a ship's crew, esp. one below the rank of officer. **2** a person who sails, esp. with reference to the likelihood of his becoming seasick: *a good sailor.*

sailplane ('seɪlˌpleɪn) *n* a high-performance glider.

sainfoin ('sænfɔɪn) *n* a Eurasian perennial plant, widely grown as a forage crop, having pale pink flowers and curved pods. [C17: from F, from Med. L *sānum faenum* wholesome hay, referring to its former use as a medicine]

saint (seɪnt; *unstressed* sənt) *n* **1** a person who after death is formally recognized by a Christian Church as having attained a specially exalted place in heaven and the right to veneration. **2** a person of exceptional holiness. **3** (*pl*) *Bible.* the collective body of those who are righteous in God's sight. ◆ *vb* **4** (*tr*) to recognize formally as a saint. [C12: from OF, from L *sanctus* holy, from *sancīre* to hallow]
▸**'sainthood** *n* ▸**'saintlike** *adj*

Saint Agnes' Eve ('æɡnəs) *n, usually abbreviated to* **St Agnes' Eve.** the night of Jan. 20, when according to tradition a woman can discover the identity of her future husband by performing certain rites.

Saint Andrew's Cross ('ændruːz) *n, usually abbreviated to* **St Andrew's Cross. 1** a diagonal cross with equal arms. **2** a white diagonal cross on a blue ground.

Saint Anthony's fire ('æntənɪz) *n, usually abbreviated to* **St Anthony's fire.** *Pathol.* another name for **ergotism** or **erysipelas**.

Saint Bernard ('bɜːnəd) *n, usually abbreviated to* **St Bernard.** a large breed of dog with a dense red-and-white coat, formerly used as a rescue dog in mountainous areas.

sainted ('seɪntɪd) *adj* **1** canonized. **2** like a saint in character or nature. **3** hallowed or holy.

Saint Elmo's fire ('ɛlməʊz) *n, usually abbreviated to* **St Elmo's fire.** (not in technical usage) a luminous region that sometimes appears around church spires, the masts of ships, etc.

Saint John's wort ('dʒɒnz) *n, usually abbreviated to* **St John's wort.** any of a genus of shrubs or herbaceous plants, having yellow flowers.

Saint Leger ('lɛdʒə) *n, usually abbreviated to* **St Leger. the.** an annual horse race run at Doncaster, England, since 1776.

saintly ❶ ('seɪntlɪ) *adj* like, relating to, or suitable for a saint.
▸**'saintlily** *adv* ▸**'saintliness** *n*

saintpaulia (sənt'pɔːlɪə) *n* another name for **African violet**. [C20: NL, after Baron W. von *Saint Paul,* G soldier (died 1910), who discovered it]

saint's day *n Christianity.* a day in the church calendar commemorating a saint.

Saint Vitus's dance ('vaɪtəsɪz) *n, usually abbreviated to* **St Vitus's dance.** *Pathol.* a nontechnical name for **Sydenham's chorea**.

saith (sɛθ) *vb* (used with *he, she,* or *it*) *Arch.* a form of the present tense of **say**.

saithe (seɪθ) *n Brit.* another name for **coalfish**. [C19: from ON]

sake[1] ❶ (seɪk) *n* **1** benefit or interest (esp. in **for (someone's** *or* **one's own) sake**). **2** the purpose of obtaining or achieving (esp. in **for the sake of (something)**). **3** used in various exclamations of impatience, urgency, etc.: *for heaven's sake.* [C13 (in the phrase *for the sake of,* prob. from legal usage): from OE *sacu* lawsuit (hence, a cause)]

sake[2], **saké,** *or* **saki** ('sækɪ) *n* a Japanese alcoholic drink made from fermented rice. [C17: from Japanese]

saker ('seɪkə) *n* a large falcon of E Europe and Asia. [C14 *sagre,* from OF *sacre,* from Ar. *saqr*]

saki ('sɑːkɪ) *n* **1** any of several small mostly arboreal New World monkeys having a long bushy tail. **2** another name for **sake**[2]. [sense 1: C20: F, from Tupi *saqi*]

sal (sæl) *n* a pharmacological term for **salt** (sense 3). [L]

salaam (sə'lɑːm) *n* **1** a Muslim salutation consisting of a deep bow with the right palm on the forehead. **2** a salutation signifying peace. ◆ *vb* **3** to make a salaam (to). [C17: from Ar. *salām* peace, from *assalām 'alaikum* peace be to you]

salable ('seɪləbᵊl) *adj* the US spelling of **saleable**.

salacious ❶ (sə'leɪʃəs) *adj* **1** having an excessive interest in sex. **2** (of books, etc.) erotic, bawdy, or lewd. [C17: from L *salax* fond of leaping, from *salīre* to leap]
▸**sa'laciously** *adv* ▸**sa'laciousness** *or* **salacity** (sə'læsɪtɪ) *n*

salad ('sæləd) *n* **1** a dish of raw vegetables, such as lettuce, tomatoes, etc., served as a separate course with cold meat, eggs, etc., or as part of a main course. **2** any dish of cold vegetables or fruit served with a dressing: *potato salad.* **3** any green vegetable or herb used in such a dish. [C15: from OF *salade,* from OProvençal *salada,* from *salar* to season with salt, from L *sal* salt]

salad days *pl n* a period of youth and inexperience.

salad dressing *n* a sauce for salad, such as oil and vinegar or mayonnaise.

salade niçoise (sæ'lɑːd niː'swɑːz) *n* a cold dish consisting of a variety of ingredients, usually including hard-boiled eggs, anchovy fillets, olives, tomatoes, and sometimes tuna fish. [C20: from F, lit.: salad of or from *Nice,* S France]

salamander ('sæləˌmændə) *n* **1** any of various amphibians of central and S Europe. They have an elongated body, and only return to water to breed. **2** *Chiefly US & Canad.* any amphibian with a tail, as the newt. **3** a mythical reptilian creature supposed to live in fire. **4** an elemental fire-inhabiting being. [C14: from OF *salamandre,* from L *salamandra,* from Gk]

salami (sə'lɑːmɪ) *n* a highly seasoned type of sausage, usually flavoured with garlic. [C19: from It., pl of *salame,* from Vulgar L *salāre* (unattested) to salt, from L *sal* salt]

sal ammoniac *n* another name for **ammonium chloride**.

salaried ('sælərɪd) *adj* earning or yielding a salary: *a salaried worker; salaried employment.*

salary ❶ ('sælərɪ) *n, pl* **salaries. 1** a fixed payment made by an employer, often monthly, for professional or office work. Cf. **wage**. ◆ *vb* **salaries, salarying, salaried. 2** (*tr*) to pay a salary to. [C14: from Anglo-Norman *salarie,* from L *salārium* the sum given to Roman soldiers to buy salt, from *sal* salt]

salchow ('sælkəʊ) *n Figure skating.* a jump from the inner backward edge of one foot with one, two, or three full turns in the air, returning to the outer backward edge of the opposite foot. [C20: after Ulrich *Salchow* (1877–1949), Swedish figure skater, who originated it]

sale ❶ (seɪl) *n* **1** the exchange of goods, property, or services for an agreed sum of money or credit. **2** the amount sold. **3** the opportunity to sell: *there was no sale for luxuries.* **4a** an event at which goods are sold at reduced prices, usually to clear old stocks. **4b** (*as modifier*): *sale bargains.* **5** an auction. [OE *sala,* from ON *sala*]

saleable *or US* **salable** ('seɪləbᵊl) *adj* fit for selling or capable of being sold.
▸**ˌsalea'bility** *or US* **ˌsala'bility** *n*

sale of work *n* a sale of articles, often handmade, the proceeds of which benefit a charity or charities.

sale or return *n* an arrangement by which a retailer pays only for goods sold, returning those that are unsold.

saleroom ('seɪlˌruːm, -ˌrʊm) *n Chiefly Brit.* a room where objects are displayed for sale, esp. by auction.

THESAURUS

sail *vb* **10** = **go by water**, cruise, ride the waves, voyage **11** = **embark**, cast *or* weigh anchor, get under way, hoist the blue peter, put to sea, set sail **13** = **pilot**, captain, navigate, skipper, steer **16** = **glide**, drift, float, fly, scud, shoot, skim, skirr, soar, sweep, wing **17** *with* **into** *Informal* = **attack**, assault, begin, belabour, fall upon, get going, get to work on, lambast(e), set about, tear into (*inf.*)

sailor *n* **1** = **mariner**, hearty (*inf.*), Jack Tar, lascar, leatherneck (*sl.*), marine, matelot (*sl., chiefly Brit.*), navigator, salt, sea dog, seafarer, seafaring man, seaman, tar (*inf.*)

saintly *adj* = **virtuous**, angelic, beatific, blameless, blessed, devout, full of good works, god-fearing, godly, holy, pious, religious, righteous, sainted, saintlike, sinless, worthy

sake[1] *n* **1** *As in* **for someone's** *or* **one's own sake** = **benefit**, account, advantage, behalf, consideration, gain, good, interest, profit, regard, respect, welfare, wellbeing **2** *As in* **for the sake of** = **purpose**, aim, cause, end, motive, objective, principle, reason

salacious *adj* **2** = **lascivious**, bawdy, blue, carnal, concupiscent, erotic, indecent, lecherous, lewd, libidinous, lustful, obscene, pornographic, prurient, ribald, ruttish, smutty, steamy (*inf.*), wanton, X-rated (*inf.*)

salary *n* **1** = **pay**, earnings, emolument, income, remuneration, stipend, wage, wages

sale *n* **1** = **selling**, auction, deal, disposal, marketing, transaction, vending

salesclerk ('seɪlz,klɜːk) *n US & Canad.* a shop assistant.
salesman ('seɪlzmən) *n, pl* **salesmen. 1** Also called: **saleswoman** *(fem)*, **salesgirl** *(fem)*, *or* **salesperson.** a person who sells merchandise or services in a shop. **2** short for **travelling salesman.**
salesmanship ('seɪlzmənʃɪp) *n* **1** the technique of, skill, or ability in selling. **2** the work of a salesman.
sales pitch *or* **talk** *n* an argument or other persuasion used in selling.
sales resistance *n* opposition of potential customers to selling, esp. aggressive selling.
sales tax *n* a tax levied on retail sales receipts and added to selling prices by retailers.
sales trader *n Stock Exchange.* a person employed by a market maker, or his firm, to find clients.
Salian ('seɪlɪən) *adj* **1** denoting or relating to a group of Franks (the **Salii**) who settled in the Netherlands in the 4th century A.D. ◆ *n* **2** a member of this group.
salicin ('sælɪsɪn) *n* a crystalline water-soluble glucoside obtained from the bark of poplar trees and used as a medical analgesic. [C19: from F, from L *salix* willow]
Salic law ('sælɪk) *n History.* **1** the code of laws of the Salian Franks and other Germanic tribes. **2** a law excluding women from succession to the throne in certain countries, such as France.
salicylate (sə'lɪsɪ,leɪt) *n* any salt or ester of salicylic acid.
salicylic acid (,sælɪ'sɪlɪk) *n* a white crystalline substance with a sweet taste and bitter aftertaste, used in the manufacture of aspirin, and as a fungicide. [C19: *salicyl* (from F, from L *salix* a willow + -YL) + -IC]
salient ⓘ ('seɪlɪənt) *adj* **1** conspicuous or striking: *a salient feature.* **2** projecting outwards at an angle of less than 180°. **3** (esp. of animals) leaping. ◆ *n* **4** *Mil.* a projection of the forward line into enemy-held territory. **5** a salient angle. [C16: from L *salīre* to leap]
▸**'salience** *or* **'saliency** *n* ▸**'saliently** *adv*
salientian (,seɪlɪ'ɛnʃɪən) *n* **1** any of an order of vertebrates with no tail and long hind legs adapted for hopping, as the frog or the toad. ◆ *adj* **2** of or belonging to this order. [C19: from NL *Salientia,* lit.: leapers, from L *salīre* to leap]
salina (sə'laɪnə) *n* a salt marsh or lake. [C17: from Sp., from Med. L: salt pit, from LL *salīnus* SALINE]
saline ('seɪlaɪn) *adj* **1** of, consisting of, or containing common salt: *a saline taste.* **2** *Med.* of or relating to a saline. **3** of, consisting of, or containing any chemical salt, esp. sodium chloride. ◆ *n* **4** *Med.* a solution of sodium chloride and water. [C15: from LL *salīnus,* from L *sal* salt]
▸**salinity** (sə'lɪnɪtɪ) *n*
salinometer (,sælɪ'nɒmɪtə) *n* a hydrometer for determining the amount of salt in a solution.
▸**,sali'nometry** *n*
saliva (sə'laɪvə) *n* the secretion of salivary glands, consisting of a clear usually slightly acid aqueous fluid of variable composition. [C17: from L, from ?]
▸**salivary** (sə'laɪvərɪ) *adj*
salivary gland *n* any of the glands in mammals that secrete saliva.
salivate ('sælɪ,veɪt) *vb* **salivates, salivating, salivated. 1** *(intr)* to secrete saliva, esp. an excessive amount. **2** *(tr)* to cause (an animal, etc.) to produce saliva, as by the administration of mercury.
▸**,sali'vation** *n*
Salk vaccine (sɔːlk) *n* a vaccine against poliomyelitis. [C20: after Jonas *Salk* (1914–95), US virologist, who developed it]
sallee *or* **sally** ('sælɪ) *n Austral.* **1** a SE Australian eucalyptus tree with pale grey bark. **2** any of various acacia trees. [prob. from Abor.]
sallow[1] **ⓘ** ('sæləʊ) *adj* **1** (esp. of human skin) of an unhealthy pale or yellowish colour. ◆ *vb* **2** *(tr)* to make sallow. [OE *salu*]
▸**'sallowish** *adj* ▸**'sallowness** *n*
sallow[2] ('sæləʊ) *n* **1** any of several small willow trees, esp. the common sallow, which has large catkins that appear before the leaves. **2** a twig or the wood of any of these trees. [OE *sealh*]
▸**'sallowy** *adj*
sally ⓘ ('sælɪ) *n, pl* **sallies. 1** a sudden sortie, esp. by troops. **2** a sudden outburst or emergence into action or expression. **3** an excursion. **4** a jocular retort. ◆ *vb* **sallies, sallying, sallied.** *(intr)* **5** to make a sudden violent sortie. **6** (often foll. by *forth*) to go out on an expedition, etc. **7** to come or set out in an energetic manner. **8** to rush out suddenly. [C16: from OF *saillie,* from *saillir* to dash forwards, from L *salīre* to leap]
Sally Lunn (lʌn) *n* a flat round cake made from a sweet yeast dough. [C19: said to be after an 18th-century E baker who invented it]
salmagundi (,sælmə'gʌndɪ) *n* **1** a mixed salad dish of cooked meats, eggs, beetroot, etc., popular in 18th-century England. **2** a miscellany. [C17: from F *salmigondis,* ?from It. *salami conditi* pickled salami]
salmon ('sæmən) *n, pl* **salmons** *or* **salmon. 1** a soft-finned fish of the Atlantic and the Pacific, which is an important food fish. Salmon occur in cold and temperate waters and many species migrate to fresh water to spawn. **2** *Austral.* any of several unrelated fish. [C13: from OF *saumon,* from L *salmō*]
▸**'salmo,noid** *adj*
salmonella (,sælmə'nɛlə) *n, pl* **salmonellae** (-,liː). any of a genus of rod-shaped aerobic bacteria including many species which cause food poisoning. [C19: NL, after Daniel E. *Salmon* (1850–1914), US veterinary surgeon]
salmon ladder *n* a series of steps designed to enable salmon to move upstream to their breeding grounds.
salon ('sælɒn) *n* **1** a room in a large house in which guests are received. **2** an assembly of guests in a fashionable household, esp. a gathering of major literary, artistic, and political figures. **3** a commercial establishment in which hairdressers, etc., carry on their businesses. **4a** a hall for exhibiting works of art. **4b** such an exhibition, esp. one showing the work of living artists. [C18: from F, from It. *salone,* augmented form of *sala* hall, of Gmc origin]
saloon (sə'luːn) *n* **1** Also called: **saloon bar.** *Brit.* another word for **lounge** (sense 5). **2** a large public room on a passenger ship. **3** any large public room used for a purpose: *a dancing saloon.* **4** *Chiefly US & Canad.* a place where alcoholic drink is sold and consumed. **5** a closed two-door or four-door car with four to six seats. US, Canad., and NZ name: **sedan.** [C18: from F SALON]
salopettes (,sælə'pɛts) *pl n* a garment worn for skiing, consisting of quilted trousers held up by shoulder straps. [C20: from F]
salpiglossis (,sælpɪ'glɒsɪs) *n* any of a genus of plants, some species of which are cultivated for their bright funnel-shaped flowers. [C19: NL, from Gk *salpinx* trumpet + *glōssa* tongue]
salpinx ('sælpɪŋks) *n, pl* **salpinges** (sæl'pɪndʒiːz). *Anat.* another name for **Fallopian tube** or **Eustachian tube.** [C19: from Gk: trumpet]
▸**salpingectomy** (,sælpɪn'dʒɛktəmɪ) *n* ▸**salpingitis** (,sælpɪn'dʒaɪtɪs) *n*
salsa ('sælsə) *n* **1** a type of Latin American big-band dance music. **2** a dance performed to this. **3** *Cookery.* a spicy Mexican tomato-based sauce. [C20: from Sp.: sauce]
salsify ('sælsɪfɪ) *n, pl* **salsifies. 1** Also called: **oyster plant, vegetable oyster.** a Mediterranean plant having grasslike leaves, purple flower heads, and a long white edible taproot. **2** the root of this plant, which tastes of oysters and is eaten as a vegetable. [C17: from F, from It. *sassefrica,* from LL, from L *saxum* rock + *fricāre* to rub]
sal soda *n* the crystalline decahydrate of sodium carbonate, $Na_2CO_3.10H_2O$.
salt ⓘ (sɔːlt) *n* **1** a white powder or colourless crystalline solid, consisting mainly of sodium chloride and used for seasoning and preserving food. **2** *(modifier)* preserved in, flooded with, containing, or growing in salt or salty water: *salt pork.* **3** *Chem.* any of a class of crystalline solid compounds that are formed from, or can be regarded as formed from, an acid and a base. **4** liveliness or pungency: *his wit added salt to the discussion.* **5** dry or laconic wit. **6** an experienced sailor. **7** short for **saltcellar. 8 rub salt into someone's wounds.** to make someone's pain, shame, etc., even worse. **9 salt of the earth.** a person or group of people regarded as the finest of their kind. **10 with a grain** (*or* **pinch**) **of salt.** with reservations. **11 worth one's salt.** worthy of one's pay. ◆ *vb (tr)* **12** to season or preserve with salt. **13** to scatter salt over (an iced road, etc.) to melt the ice. **14** to add zest to. **15** (often foll. by *down* or *away*) to preserve or cure with salt. **16** *Chem.* to treat with salt. **17** to give a false appearance of value to, esp. to introduce valuable ore fraudulently into (a mine, sample, etc.). ◆ *adj* **18** not sour, sweet, or bitter; salty. ◆ See also **salt away, salts.** [OE *sealt*]
▸**'salt,like** *adj* ▸**'saltness** *n*
SALT (sɔːlt) *n acronym for* Strategic Arms Limitation Talks *or* Treaty.
saltation (sæl'teɪʃən) *n* **1** *Biol.* an abrupt variation in the appearance of an organism, species, etc. **2** *Geol.* the leaping movement of sand or soil particles carried in water or by the wind. **3** a sudden abrupt movement. [C17: from L *saltātiō* a dance, from *saltāre* to leap about]
▸**saltatorial** (,sæltə'tɔːrɪəl) *or* **'saltatory** *adj*
salt away ⓘ *or (less commonly)* **down** *vb (tr, adv)* to hoard or save (money, valuables, etc.).
saltbush ('sɔːlt,bʊʃ) *n* any of certain shrubs that grow in alkaline desert regions.
salt cake *n* an impure form of sodium sulphate used in the manufacture of detergents, glass, and ceramic glazes.
saltcellar ('sɔːlt,sɛlə) *n* **1** a small container for salt used at the table. **2** *Brit. inf.* either of the two hollows formed above the collarbones. [changed (through infl. of cellar) from C15 *salt saler; saler* from OF *saliere* container for salt, from L *salārius* belonging to salt, from *sal* salt]
salt dome *or* **plug** *n* a domelike structure of stratified rocks containing a central core of salt.
salted ('sɔːltɪd) *adj* seasoned, preserved, or treated with salt.

THESAURUS

salient *adj* **1** = **prominent**, arresting, conspicuous, important, marked, noticeable, outstanding, pronounced, remarkable, signal, striking **2** = **projecting**, jutting, protruding
sallow[1] *adj* **1** = **wan**, anaemic, bilious, jaundiced-looking, pale, pallid, pasty, peely-wally (*Scot.*), sickly, unhealthy, yellowish
Antonyms *adj* glowing, healthy-looking, radiant, rosy, ruddy
sally *n* **1** = **attack**, campaign, foray, incursion, offensive, raid, sortie, thrust **3** = **excursion**, escapade, frolic, jaunt, trip **4** = **witticism**, bon mot, crack, jest, joke, quip, retort, riposte, smart remark, wisecrack (*inf.*) ◆ *vb* **5-8** = **go forth**, erupt, issue, rush, set out, surge
salt *n* **2** *modifier* = **salty**, brackish, briny, saline, salted **4** = **seasoning**, flavour, relish, savour, taste **5** = **wit**, Attic wit, bite, dry humour, liveliness, piquancy, punch, pungency, sarcasm, sharpness, zest, zip (*inf.*) **6** = **sailor**, mariner, sea dog, seaman, tar (*inf.*) **10 with a grain** *or* **pinch of salt** = **sceptically**, cynically, disbelievingly, doubtfully, suspiciously, with reservations
salt away *vb* = **save**, accumulate, amass, bank, cache, hide, hoard up, lay by, lay in, lay up, put by, save for a rainy day, stash away (*inf.*), stockpile

salt flat *n* a flat expanse of salt left by the total evaporation of a body of water.

saltigrade ('sæltɪˌgreɪd) *adj* (of animals) adapted for moving in a series of jumps. [C19: from NL *Saltigradae,* name formerly applied to jumping spiders, from L *saltus* a leap + *gradī* to move]

saltings ('sɔːltɪŋz) *pl n* meadow land or marsh that is periodically flooded by sea water.

saltire *or* **saltier** ('sɔːlˌtaɪə) *n Heraldry.* an ordinary consisting of a diagonal cross on a shield. [C14 *sawturoure,* from OF *sauteour* cross-shaped barricade, from *saulter* to jump, from L *saltāre*]

salt lick *n* **1** a place where wild animals go to lick salt deposits. **2** a block of salt given to domestic animals to lick. **3** *Austral. & NZ.* a soluble cake of minerals used to supplement the diet of farm animals.

saltpan ('sɔːltˌpæn) *n* a shallow basin, usually in a desert region, containing salt, gypsum, etc., that was deposited from an evaporated salt lake.

saltpetre *or US* **saltpeter** (ˌsɔːlt'piːtə) *n* **1** another name for **potassium nitrate. 2** short for **Chile saltpetre.** [C16: from OF *salpetre,* from L *sal petrae* salt of rock]

salt pork *n* pork, esp. taken from the back and belly, that has been cured with salt.

salts (sɔːlts) *pl n* **1** *Med.* any of various mineral salts, such as magnesium sulphate, for use as a cathartic. **2** short for **smelling salts. 3 like a dose of salts.** *Inf.* very quickly.

saltus ('sæltəs) *n, pl* **saltuses.** a break in the continuity of a sequence. [L: a leap]

saltwater ('sɔːltˌwɔːtə) *adj* of or inhabiting salt water, esp. the sea: *saltwater fishes.*

saltworks ('sɔːltˌwɜːks) *n* (*functioning as sing*) a building or factory where salt is produced.

saltwort ('sɔːltˌwɜːt) *n* any of various plants, of beaches and salt marshes, having prickly leaves, striped stems, and small green flowers. Also called: **glasswort, kali.**

salty ⓣ ('sɔːltɪ) *adj* **saltier, saltiest. 1** of, tasting of, or containing salt. **2** (esp. of humour) sharp. **3** relating to life at sea.
▸ **'saltiness** *n*

salubrious ⓣ (sə'luːbrɪəs) *adj* conducive or favourable to health. [C16: from L, from *salūs* health]
▸ **sa'lubriously** *adv* ▸ **sa'lubrity** *n*

Saluki (sə'luːkɪ) *n* a tall breed of hound with a smooth coat and long fringes on the ears and tail. [C19: from Ar. *salūqīy* of Saluq, an ancient Arabian city]

salutary ⓣ ('sæljʊtərɪ) *adj* **1** promoting or intended to promote an improvement: *a salutary warning.* **2** promoting or intended to promote health. [C15: from L *salūtāris* wholesome, from *salūs* safety]
▸ **'salutarily** *adv*

salutation ⓣ (ˌsælјʊ'teɪʃən) *n* **1** an act, phrase, gesture, etc., that serves as a greeting. **2** a form of words used as an opening to a speech or letter, such as *Dear Sir.* [C14: from L *salūtātiō,* from *salūtāre* to greet; see SALUTE]

salutatory (sə'luːtətərɪ) *adj* of, relating to, or resembling a salutation.
▸ **sa'lutatorily** *adv*

salute ⓣ (sə'luːt) *vb* **salutes, saluting, saluted. 1** (*tr*) to address or welcome with friendly words or gestures of respect, such as bowing. **2** (*tr*) to acknowledge with praise: *we salute your gallantry.* **3** *Mil.* to pay formal respect, as by raising the right arm. ◆ *n* **4** the act of saluting. **5** a formal military gesture of respect. [C14: from L *salūtāre* to greet, from *salūs* wellbeing]
▸ **sa'luter** *n*

salvable ('sælvəbᵊl) *adj* capable of or suitable for being saved or salvaged. [C17: from LL *salvāre* to save, from *salvus* safe]

salvage ⓣ ('sælvɪdʒ) *n* **1** the act, process, or business of rescuing vessels or their cargoes from loss at sea. **2a** the act of saving any goods or property in danger of damage or destruction. **2b** (*as modifier*): *a salvage operation.* **3** the goods or property so saved. **4** compensation paid for the salvage of a vessel or its cargo. **5** the proceeds from the sale of salvaged goods. ◆ *vb* **salvages, salvaging, salvaged.** (*tr*) **6** to save or rescue (goods or property) from fire, shipwreck, etc. **7** to gain (something beneficial) from a failure. [C17: from OF, from Med. L *salvāgium,* from *salvāre* to SAVE[1]]
▸ **'salvageable** *adj* ▸ **'salvager** *n*

salvation ⓣ (sæl'veɪʃən) *n* **1** the act of preserving or the state of being preserved from harm. **2** a person or thing that is the means of preserving from harm. **3** *Christianity.* deliverance by redemption from the power of sin. [C13: from OF, from LL *salvātiō,* from L *salvātus* saved, from *salvāre* to SAVE[1]]

Salvation Army *n* a Christian body founded in 1865 by William Booth and organized on quasi-military lines for evangelism and social work among the poor.

salvationist (sæl'veɪʃənɪst) *n* **1** a member of an evangelical sect emphasizing the doctrine of salvation. **2** (*often cap.*) a member of the Salvation Army.

salve ⓣ (sælv, sɑːv) *n* **1** an ointment for wounds, etc. **2** anything that heals or soothes. ◆ *vb* **salves, salving, salved.** (*tr*) **3** to apply salve to (a wound, etc.). **4** to soothe, comfort, or appease. [OE *sealf*]

salver ('sælvə) *n* a tray, esp. one of silver, on which food, letters, visiting cards, etc., are presented. [C17: from F *salve,* from Sp. *salva* tray from which the king's taster sampled food, from L *salvāre* to SAVE[1]]

salvia ('sælvɪə) *n* any of a genus of herbaceous plants or small shrubs, such as the sage, grown for their medicinal or culinary properties or for ornament. [C19: from L: SAGE[2]]

salvo ('sælvəʊ) *n, pl* **salvos** *or* **salvoes. 1** a discharge of fire from weapons in unison, esp. on a ceremonial occasion. **2** concentrated fire from many weapons, as in a naval battle. **3** an outburst, as of applause. [C17: from It. *salva,* from OF *salve,* from L *salvē!* greetings!, ult. from *salvus* safe]

Salvo ('sælvəʊ) *n, pl* **Salvos.** *Austral. sl.* a member of the Salvation Army.

sal volatile (vɒ'lætɪlɪ) *n* a solution of ammonium carbonate in alcohol and aqueous ammonia, used as smelling salts. Also called: **spirits of ammonia.** [C17: from NL: volatile salt]

SAM (sæm) *n acronym for* surface-to-air missile.

Sam. *Bible. abbrev. for* Samuel.

samara (sə'mɑːrə, 'sæmərə) *n* a dry winged one-seeded fruit: occurs in the ash, maple, etc. Also called: **key fruit.** [C16: from NL, from L: seed of an elm]

Samaritan (sə'mærɪtᵊn) *n* **1** a native or inhabitant of Samaria, a kingdom in ancient Palestine. **2** short for **Good Samaritan. 3** (in the UK) a member of a voluntary organization (**the Samaritans**) that offers counselling to people in despair, esp. by telephone.

samarium (sə'mɛərɪəm) *n* a silvery metallic element of the lanthanide series used in carbon-arc lighting, as a doping agent in laser crystals, and as a neutron-absorber. Symbol: Sm; atomic no.: 62; atomic wt.: 150.35. [C19: from NL, from mineral, *samarskite,* after Col. von *Samarski,* 19th-century Russian inspector of mines + -IUM]

samba ('sæmbə) *n, pl* **sambas. 1** a modern ballroom dance from Brazil in bouncy duple time. **2** a piece of music composed for or in the rhythm of this dance. ◆ *vb* **sambas, sambaing, sambaed. 3** (*intr*) to perform such a dance. [Port., of African origin]

sambar *or* **sambur** ('sæmbə) *n, pl* **sambars, sambar** *or* **samburs, sambur.** a S Asian deer with three-tined antlers. [C17: from Hindi, from Sansk. *śambarra,* from ?]

Sam Browne belt (ˌsæm 'braʊn) *n* a military officer's wide belt supported by a strap passing from the left side of the belt over the right shoulder. [C20: after Sir *Samuel J. Browne* (1824–1901), British general, who devised it]

same ⓣ (seɪm) *adj* (usually preceded by *the*) **1** being the very one: *she is wearing the same hat.* **2a** being the one previously referred to. **2b** (*as n*): *a note received about same.* **3a** identical in kind, quantity, etc.: *two girls of the same age.* **3b** (*as n*): *we'd like the same.* **4** unchanged in character or nature: *his attitude is the same as ever.* **5 all the same. 5a** Also: **just the same.** nevertheless; yet. **5b** immaterial: *it's all the same to me.* ◆ *adv* **6** in an identical manner. [C12: from ON *samr*]
▸ **'sameness** *n*

> **USAGE NOTE** The use of *same* exemplified in *if you send us your order for the materials, we will deliver same tomorrow* is common in business and official English. In general English, however, this use of the word is avoided: *may I borrow your book? I will return it* (not *same*) *tomorrow.*

samfoo ('sæmfuː) *n* a style of dress worn by Chinese women, consisting of a waisted blouse and trousers. [from Chinese *sam* dress + *foo* trousers]

Samian ('seɪmɪən) *adj* **1** of or relating to Samos, an island in the Aegean, or its inhabitants. ◆ *n* **2** a native or inhabitant of Samos.

THESAURUS

salty *adj* **1** = **salt**, brackish, briny, over-salted, saline, salted **2** = **witty**, colourful, humorous, lively, piquant, pungent, racy, sharp, snappy (*inf.*), spicy, tangy, tart, zestful

salubrious *adj* = **health-giving**, beneficial, good for one, healthful, healthy, invigorating, salutary, wholesome

salutary *adj* **1** = **beneficial**, advantageous, good, good for one, helpful, practical, profitable, timely, useful, valuable **2** = **healthy**, healthful, salubrious

salutation *n* **1** = **greeting**, address, obeisance, salute, welcome

salute *vb* **1** = **greet**, accost, acknowledge, address, doff one's cap to, hail, kiss, pay one's respects to, salaam, welcome **2** = **honour**, acknowledge, pay tribute *or* homage to, present arms, recognize, take one's hat off to (*inf.*) ◆ *n* **4** = **greeting**, address, kiss, obeisance, recognition, salaam, salutation, tribute

salvage *vb* **6, 7** = **save**, glean, recover, redeem, rescue, restore, retrieve

salvation *n* **1** = **saving**, deliverance, escape, lifeline, preservation, redemption, rescue, restoration
Antonyms *n* condemnation, damnation, doom, downfall, hell, loss, perdition, ruin

salve *n* **1, 2** = **ointment**, balm, cream, dressing, emollient, liniment, lotion, lubricant, medication, unguent

same *adj* **1, 2** = **aforementioned**, aforesaid, selfsame, very **3** = **identical**, alike, corresponding, duplicate, equal, equivalent, indistinguishable, interchangeable, synonymous, twin **4** = **unchanged**, changeless, consistent, constant, invariable, unaltered, unfailing, uniform, unvarying **5 all the same: a** = **unimportant**, after all, anyhow, be that as it may, in any event, just the same, nonetheless, still **b** = **immaterial**, not worth mentioning, of no consequence
Antonyms *adj* ≠ **identical:** different, dissimilar, diverse, miscellaneous, other ≠ **unchanged:** altered, inconsistent, variable

sameness *n* **3** = **similarity**, identicalness, identity, indistinguishability, likeness, oneness, resemblance, standardization, uniformity **4** = **lack of variety**, consistency, monotony, predictability, repetition, tedium

Samian ware *n* a fine earthenware pottery, reddish-brown or black in colour, found in large quantities on Roman sites. [C19: after the island of *Samos*, source of a reddish earth similar to that from which the pottery was made]

samisen ('sæmɪˌsɛn) *n* a Japanese plucked stringed instrument with a long neck and a rectangular soundbox. [Japanese, from Chinese *san-hsien*, from *san* three + *hsien* string]

samite ('sæmaɪt) *n* a heavy fabric of silk, often woven with gold or silver threads, used in the Middle Ages. [C13: from OF *samit*, from Med. L *examitum*, from Gk, from *hexamitos* having six threads]

samizdat (*Russian* səmiz'dat) *n* (formerly, in the Soviet Union) **a** a system of clandestine printing and distribution of banned literature. **b** (*as modifier*): *a samizdat publication*. [from Russian]

samosa (sə'məʊsə) *n, pl* **samosas** *or* **samosa.** (in Indian cookery) a small, fried, triangular spiced meat or vegetable pasty. [C20: from Hindi]

samovar ('sæməˌvɑː) *n* (esp. in Russia) a metal urn for making tea, in which the water is usually heated by an inner container. [C19: from Russian, from *samo-* self + *varit'* to boil]

Samoyed (ˌsæmə'jɛd) *n* **1** (*pl* **Samoyed** *or* **Samoyeds**) a member of a group of peoples who live chiefly in the area of the N Urals: related to the Finns. **2** the languages of these peoples. **3** (sə'mɔɪɛd) a white or cream breed of dog having a dense coat and a tightly curled tail. [C17: from Russian *Samoed*]

samp (sæmp) *n S. African.* crushed maize used for porridge. [from Amerind *nasaump* softened by water]

sampan ('sæmpæn) *n* a small skiff, widely used in the Orient, that is propelled by oars. [C17: from Chinese, from *san* three + *pan* board]

samphire ('sæmˌfaɪə) *n* **1** an umbelliferous plant of Eurasian coasts, having fleshy divided leaves and clusters of small white flowers. **2** **golden samphire.** a Eurasian coastal plant with fleshy leaves and yellow flower heads. **3** **marsh samphire.** another name for **glasswort** (sense 1). **4** any of several other plants of coastal areas. [C16 *sampiere*, from F *herbe de Saint Pierre* Saint Peter's herb]

sample ❶ ('sɑːmpᵊl) *n* **1a** a small part of anything, intended as representative of the whole. **1b** (*as modifier*): *a sample bottle*. **2** Also called: **sampling.** *Statistics.* a set of individuals or items selected from a population and analysed to test hypotheses about or yield estimates of the population. ◆ *vb* **samples, sampling, sampled. 3** (*tr*) to take a sample or samples of. **4** *Music.* **4a** to take a short extract from (one record) and mix it into a different backing track. **4b** to record (a sound) and feed it into a computerized synthesizer so that it can be reproduced at any pitch. [C13: from OF *essample*, from L *exemplum* EXAMPLE]

sampler ('sɑːmplə) *n* **1** a person who takes samples. **2** a piece of embroidery done to show the embroiderer's skill in using many different stitches. **3** *Music.* a piece of electronic equipment used for sampling. **4** a recording comprising a collection of tracks from other albums, to stimulate interest in the featured products.

sampling ('sɑːmplɪŋ) *n* **1** the process of selecting a random sample. **2** a variant of **sample** (sense 2). **3** *Music.* the process of taking a short extract from a record and mixing it into a different backing track.

sampling distribution *n Statistics.* the distribution of a random, experimentally obtained sample.

Samson ('sæmsən) *n* **1** a judge of Israel, who performed feats of strength until he was betrayed by his mistress Delilah (Judges 13–16). **2** any man of outstanding physical strength.

samurai ('sæmʊˌraɪ) *n, pl* **samurai. 1** the Japanese warrior caste from the 11th to the 19th centuries. **2** a member of this aristocratic caste. [C19: from Japanese]

samurai bond *n Finance.* a bond issued in Japan and denominated in yen, available for purchase by nonresidents of Japan. Cf. **shogun bond.**

sanative ('sænətɪv) *adj, n* a less common word for **curative.** [C15: from Med. L *sānātīvus*, from L *sānāre* to heal, from *sānus* healthy]

sanatorium (ˌsænə'tɔːrɪəm) *or US* **sanitarium** *n, pl* **sanatoriums** *or* **sanatoria** (-rɪə). **1** an institution for the medical care and recuperation of persons who are chronically ill. **2** *Brit.* a room as in a boarding school where sick pupils may receive treatment. [C19: from NL, from L *sānāre* to heal]

sanctified ('sæŋktɪˌfaɪd) *adj* **1** consecrated or made holy. **2** sanctimonious.

sanctify ❶ ('sæŋktɪˌfaɪ) *vb* **sanctifies, sanctifying, sanctified.** (*tr*) **1** to make holy. **2** to free from sin. **3** to sanction (an action or practice) as religiously binding: *to sanctify a marriage*. **4** to declare or render (something) productive of or conducive to holiness or grace. [C14: from LL *sanctificāre*, from L *sanctus* holy + *facere* to make]
▸ˌ**sanctifi'cation** *n* ▸'**sanctiˌfier** *n*

sanctimonious ❶ (ˌsæŋktɪ'məʊnɪəs) *adj* affecting piety or making a display of holiness. [C17: from L *sanctimonia* sanctity, from *sanctus* holy]
▸ˌ**sancti'moniously** *adv* ▸ˌ**sancti'moniousness** *or* '**sanctimony** *n*

sanction ❶ ('sæŋkʃən) *n* **1** authorization. **2** aid or encouragement. **3** something, such as an ethical principle, that imparts binding force to a rule, oath, etc. **4** the penalty laid down in a law for contravention of its provisions. **5** (*often pl*) a coercive measure, esp. one taken by one or more states against another guilty of violating international law. ◆ *vb* (*tr*) **6** to give authority to. **7** to confirm. [C16: from L *sanctiō* the establishment of an inviolable decree, from *sancīre* to decree]

sanctitude ('sæŋktɪˌtjuːd) *n* saintliness; holiness.

sanctity ❶ ('sæŋktɪtɪ) *n, pl* **sanctities. 1** the condition of being sanctified; holiness. **2** anything regarded as sanctified or holy. **3** the condition of being inviolable: *the sanctity of marriage*. [C14: from OF *saincteté*, from L *sanctitās*, from *sanctus* holy]

sanctuary ❶ ('sæŋktjʊərɪ) *n, pl* **sanctuaries. 1** a holy place. **2** a consecrated building or shrine. **3** *Old Testament.* **3a** the Israelite temple at Jerusalem. **3b** the tabernacle in which the Ark was enshrined. **4** the chancel, or that part of a sacred building surrounding the main altar. **5a** a sacred building where fugitives were formerly entitled to immunity from arrest or execution. **5b** the immunity so afforded. **6** a place of refuge. **7** a place, protected by law, where animals can live and breed without interference. [C14: from OF *saintuarie*, from LL *sanctuārium* repository for holy things, from L *sanctus* holy]

sanctuary lamp *n Christianity.* a lamp, usually red, placed in a prominent position in the sanctuary of a church, which, when lit, indicates the presence of the Blessed Sacrament.

sanctum ❶ ('sæŋktəm) *n, pl* **sanctums** *or* **sancta** (-tə). **1** a sacred or holy place. **2** a room or place of total privacy. [C16: from L, from *sanctus* holy]

sanctum sanctorum (sæŋk'tɔːrəm) *n* **1** *Bible.* another term for the **holy of holies. 2** *Often facetious.* an especially private place. [C14: from L, lit.: holy of holies, rendering Heb. *qōdesh haqqodāshīm*]

Sanctus ('sæŋktəs) *n* **1** *Liturgy.* the hymn that occurs immediately after the preface in the celebration of the Eucharist. **2** a musical setting of this. [C14: from the hymn, *Sanctus sanctus sanctus* Holy, holy, holy, from L *sancīre* to consecrate]

Sanctus bell *n Chiefly RC Church.* a bell rung as the opening words of the Sanctus are pronounced.

sand (sænd) *n* **1** loose material consisting of rock or mineral grains, esp. rounded grains of quartz. **2** (*often pl*) a sandy area, esp. on the seashore or in a desert. **3a** a greyish-yellow colour. **3b** (*as adj*): *sand upholstery*. **4** the grains of sandlike material in an hourglass. **5** *US inf.* courage. **6** **the sands are running out.** there is not much time left before the end. ◆ *vb* **7** (*tr*) to smooth or polish the surface of with sandpaper or sand. **8** (*tr*) to sprinkle or cover with or as if with sand. **9** to fill or cause to fill with sand: *the channel sanded up*. [OE]
▸'**sandˌlike** *adj*

sandal ('sændᵊl) *n* **1** a light shoe consisting of a sole held on the foot by thongs, straps, etc. **2** a strap passing over the instep or around the ankle to keep a low shoe on the foot. **3** another name for **sandalwood.** [C14: from L *sandalium*, from Gk, from *sandalon* sandal]
▸'**sandalled** *adj*

sandalwood ('sændᵊlˌwʊd) *or* **sandal** *n* **1** any of a genus of evergreen trees, esp. the **white sandalwood,** of S Asia and Australia, having hard light-coloured heartwood. **2** the wood of any of these trees, which is used for carving, is burned as incense, and yields an aromatic oil used in perfumery. **3** any of various similar trees or their wood, esp. a leguminous tree of SE Asia having dark red wood used as a dye. [C14 *sandal*, from Med. L, from LGk *sandanon*, from Sansk. *candana* sandalwood]

sandarac *or* **sandarach** ('sændəˌræk) *n* **1** a pinaceous tree of NW Africa, having hard fragrant dark wood. **2** a brittle pale yellow transparent resin obtained from the bark of this tree and used in making varnish and incense. [C16 *sandaracha*, from L *sandaraca* red pigment, from Gk *sandarakē*]

sandbag ('sændˌbæg) *n* **1** a sack filled with sand used for protection against gunfire, floodwater, etc., or as ballast in a balloon, etc. **2** a bag filled with sand and used as a weapon. ◆ *vb* **sandbags, sandbagging, sandbagged.** (*tr*) **3** to protect or strengthen with sandbags. **4** to hit with or as if with a sandbag. **5** *Finance.* to obstruct (an unwelcome takeover bid) by having prolonged talks in the hope that a more acceptable bidder will come forward.
▸'**sandˌbagger** *n*

THESAURUS

sample *n* **1a** = **specimen**, cross section, example, exemplification, illustration, indication, instance, model, pattern, representative, sign ◆ *modifier* **1b** = **test**, illustrative, pilot, representative, specimen, trial ◆ *vb* **3** = **test**, experience, inspect, partake of, taste, try

sanctify *vb* **1, 2** = **consecrate**, absolve, anoint, bless, cleanse, hallow, purify, set apart

sanctimonious *adj* = **holier-than-thou**, canting, false, goody-goody (*inf.*), hypocritical, pharisaical, pi (*Brit. sl.*), pietistic, pious, priggish, self-righteous, self-satisfied, smug, Tartuffian *or* Tartufian, too good to be true, unctuous

sanction *n* **1** = **permission**, allowance, approbation, approval, authority, authorization, backing, confirmation, countenance, endorsement, O.K. *or* okay (*inf.*), ratification, stamp or seal of approval, support **5** *often plural* = **ban**, boycott, coercive measures, embargo, penalty ◆ *vb* **6** = **permit**, allow, approve, authorize, back, countenance, endorse, entitle, lend one's name to, support, vouch for **7** = **confirm**, ratify, warrant

Antonyms *n* ≠ **permission**: ban, disapproval, embargo, prohibition, proscription, refusal, veto ≠ **ban**: approbation, approval, authority, authorization, dispensation, licence, permission ◆ *vb* ≠ **permit**: ban, boycott, disallow, forbid, refuse, reject, veto

sanctity *n* **1** = **holiness**, devotion, godliness, goodness, grace, piety, purity, religiousness, righteousness, sanctitude, spirituality **3** = **sacredness**, inviolability, solemnity

sanctuary *n* **1** = **shrine**, altar, church, Holy of Holies, sanctum, temple **6** = **protection**, asylum, haven, refuge, retreat, shelter **7** = **reserve**, conservation area, national park, nature reserve

sanctum *n* **1** = **sanctuary**, Holy of Holies, shrine **2** = **refuge**, den, private room, retreat, study

sandbank ('sænd,bæŋk) *n* a bank of sand in a sea or river, that may be exposed at low tide.
sand bar *n* a ridge of sand in a river or sea, built up by the action of tides, currents, etc., and often exposed at low tide.
sandblast ('sænd,blɑːst) *n* **1** a jet of sand blown from a nozzle under air or steam pressure. ◆ *vb* **2** (*tr*) to clean or decorate (a surface) with a sandblast.
▸'**sand,blaster** *n*
sand-blind *adj* not completely blind. Cf. **stone-blind.** [C15: changed (through infl. of SAND) from OE *samblind* (unattested), from *sam-* half, + BLIND]
▸'**sand-,blindness** *n*
sandbox ('sænd,bɒks) *n* **1** a container on a railway locomotive from which sand is released onto the rails to assist the traction. **2** a container of sand for small children to play in.
sandboy ('sænd,bɔɪ) *n* **happy** (*or* **jolly**) **as a sandboy.** very happy; high-spirited.
sand castle *n* a mass of sand moulded into a castle-like shape, esp. by a child on the beach.
sand eel *or* **lance** *n* a silvery eel-like marine spiny-finned fish found burrowing in sand or shingle. Popular name: **launce.**
sander ('sændə) *n* **1** a power-driven tool for smoothing surfaces by rubbing with an abrasive disc. **2** a person who uses such a device.
sanderling ('sændəlɪŋ) *n* a small sandpiper that frequents sandy shores. [C17: ?from SAND + OE *erthling, eorthling* inhabitant of earth]
sand flea *n* another name for the **chigoe** or **sand hopper.**
sandfly ('sænd,flaɪ) *n, pl* **sandflies. 1** any of various small mothlike dipterous flies: the bloodsucking females transmit diseases including leishmaniasis. **2** any of various similar flies.
sandgrouse ('sænd,graʊs) *n* a bird of dry regions of the Old World, having very short feet, a short bill, and long pointed wings and tail.
sand hopper *n* any of various small hopping crustaceans, common in intertidal regions of seashores. Also called: **beach flea, sand flea.**
sandman ('sænd,mæn) *n, pl* **sandmen.** (in folklore) a magical person supposed to put children to sleep by sprinkling sand in their eyes.
sand martin *n* a small brown European songbird with white underparts: it nests in tunnels bored in sand, river banks, etc.
sandpaper ('sænd,peɪpə) *n* **1** a strong paper coated with sand or other abrasive material for smoothing and polishing. ◆ *vb* **2** (*tr*) to polish or grind (a surface) with or as if with sandpaper.
sandpiper ('sænd,paɪpə) *n* **1** any of numerous N hemisphere shore birds having a long slender bill and legs and cryptic plumage. **2** any other bird of the family which includes snipes and woodcocks.
sandpit ('sænd,pɪt) *n* **1** a shallow pit or container holding sand for children to play in. **2** a pit from which sand is extracted.
sandshoe ('sænd,ʃuː) *n* a light canvas shoe with a rubber sole.
sandstone ('sænd,stəʊn) *n* any of a group of common sedimentary rocks consisting of sand grains consolidated with such materials as quartz, haematite, and clay minerals.
sandstorm ('sænd,stɔːm) *n* a strong wind that whips up clouds of sand, esp. in a desert.
sand trap *n* another name (esp. US) for **bunker** (sense 2).
sand viper *n* a S European viper having a yellowish-brown coloration with a zigzag pattern along the back.
sandwich ('sænwɪdʒ, -wɪtʃ) *n* **1** two or more slices of bread, usually buttered, with a filling of meat, cheese, etc. **2** anything that resembles a sandwich in arrangement. ◆ *vb* (*tr*) **3** to insert tightly between two other things. **4** to put into a sandwich. **5** to place between two dissimilar things. [C18: after 4th Earl of *Sandwich* (1718–92), who ate sandwiches rather than leave the gambling table for meals]
sandwich board *n* one of two connected boards that are hung over the shoulders in front of and behind a person to display advertisements.
sandwich course *n* any of several courses consisting of alternate periods of study and industrial work.
sandwich man *n* a man who carries sandwich boards.
sandwort ('sænd,wɜːt) *n* **1** any of various plants which grow in dense tufts on sandy soil and have white or pink solitary flowers. **2** any of various related plants.
sandy ('sændɪ) *adj* **sandier, sandiest. 1** consisting of, containing, or covered with sand. **2** (esp. of hair) reddish-yellow. **3** resembling sand in texture.
▸'**sandiness** *n*
sand yacht *n* a wheeled boat with sails, built to be propelled over sand by the wind.
sandy blight *n Austral. inf.* any inflammation and irritation of the eye.
sane **T** (seɪn) *adj* **1** free from mental disturbance. **2** having or showing reason or sound sense. [C17: from L *sānus* healthy]
▸'**sanely** *adv* ▸'**saneness** *n*
Sanforized *or* **Sanforised** ('sænfə,raɪzd) *adj Trademark.* (of a fabric) preshrunk using a patented process.
sang (sæŋ) *vb* the past tense of **sing.**

> **USAGE NOTE** See at **ring**[2].

sang-froid **T** (*French* sɑ̃frwa) *n* composure; self-possession. [C18: from F, lit.: cold blood]
sangoma (sæŋ'gəʊmə) *n, pl* **sangomas.** *S. African.* a witch doctor. [from Bantu]
Sangraal (sæŋ'greɪl), **Sangrail,** *or* **Sangreal** ('sæŋgrɪəl) *n* another name for the **Holy Grail.**
sangria (sæŋ'griːə) *n* a Spanish drink of red wine, sugar, and orange or lemon juice, sometimes laced with brandy. [Sp.: a bleeding]
sanguinary **T** ('sæŋgwɪnərɪ) *adj* **1** accompanied by much bloodshed. **2** bloodthirsty. **3** consisting of or stained with blood. [C17: from L *sanguinārius*]
▸'**sanguinarily** *adv* ▸'**sanguinariness** *n*
sanguine **T** ('sæŋgwɪn) *adj* **1** cheerful and confident; optimistic. **2** (esp. of the complexion) ruddy in appearance. **3** blood-red. ◆ *n* **4** a red pencil containing ferric oxide, used in drawing. [C14: from L *sanguineus* bloody, from *sanguis* blood]
▸'**sanguinely** *adv* ▸'**sanguineness** *n*
sanguineous (sæŋ'gwɪnɪəs) *adj* **1** of, containing, or associated with blood. **2** a less common word for **sanguine.**
▸**san'guineousness** *n*
Sanhedrin ('sænɪdrɪn) *n Judaism.* the supreme judicial, ecclesiastical, and administrative council of the Jews in New Testament times. [C16: from LHeb., from Gk *sunedrion* council, from *sun-* SYN- + *hedra* seat]
sanies ('seɪnɪ,iːz) *n Pathol.* a thin greenish foul-smelling discharge from a wound, ulcer, etc., containing pus and blood. [C16: from L, from ?]
sanitarium (,sænɪ'tɛərɪəm) *n, pl* **sanitariums** *or* **sanitaria** (-rɪə). the US word for **sanatorium.** [C19: from L *sānitās* health]
sanitary **T** ('sænɪtərɪ) *adj* **1** of or relating to health and measures for the protection of health. **2** free from dirt, germs, etc.; hygienic. [C19: from F *sanitaire*, from L *sānitās* health]
▸**sanitarian** (,sænɪ'tɛərɪən) *n* ▸'**sanitariness** *n*
sanitary engineering *n* the branch of civil engineering associated with the supply of water, disposal of sewage, and other public health services.
▸**sanitary engineer** *n*
sanitary towel *or esp. US* **napkin** *n* an absorbent pad worn externally by women during menstruation to absorb the menstrual flow.
sanitation (,sænɪ'teɪʃən) *n* the study and use of practical measures for the preservation of public health.
sanitize **T** *or* **sanitise** ('sænɪ,taɪz) *vb* **sanitizes, sanitizing, sanitized** *or* **sanitises, sanitising, sanitised.** (*tr*) **1** *Chiefly US & Canad.* to make hygienic, as by sterilizing. **2** to omit unpleasant details from (a news report, document, etc.) to make it more palatable to the recipients.
▸,**saniti'zation** *or* ,**saniti'sation** *n*
sanity **T** ('sænɪtɪ) *n* **1** the state of being sane. **2** good sense or soundness of judgment. [C15: from L *sānitās* health, from *sānus* healthy]
sank (sæŋk) *vb* the past tense of **sink.**
sans (sænz) *prep* an archaic word for **without.** [C13: from OF *sanz*, from L *sine* without, but prob. also infl. by L *absentiā* in the absence of]
Sans. *or* **Sansk.** *abbrev. for* Sanskrit.
sans-culotte (,sænzkju'lɒt) *n* **1** (during the French Revolution) **1a** (originally) a revolutionary of the poorer class. **1b** (later) any revolutionary. **2** any revolutionary extremist. [C18: from F, lit.: without knee breeches, because the revolutionaries wore pantaloons or trousers rather than knee breeches]
sansevieria (,sænsɪ'vɪərɪə) *n* any of a genus of herbaceous perennial plants of Old World tropical regions: some are cultivated as house plants for their bayonet-like leaves; others yield a useful fibre. [NL, after Raimondo di Sangro (1710–71), It. scholar and prince of *San Severo*]
Sanskrit ('sænskrɪt) *n* an ancient language of India. It is the oldest recorded member of the Indic branch of the Indo-European family of languages. Although it is used only for religious purposes, it is one of

THESAURUS

sane *adj* **1** = **rational**, all there (*inf.*), *compos mentis*, in one's right mind, in possession of all one's faculties, lucid, mentally sound, normal, of sound mind **2** = **sensible**, balanced, judicious, level-headed, moderate, reasonable, sober, sound
Antonyms *adj* ≠ **rational:** crazy, daft (*inf.*), doolally (*sl.*), insane, loony (*sl.*), mad, mentally ill, *non compos mentis*, nuts (*sl.*), off one's head (*sl.*), round the bend *or* twist (*sl.*) ≠ **sensible:** foolish, stupid, unreasonable, unsound, up the pole (*inf.*)
sang-froid *n* = **composure**, aplomb, calmness, cool (*sl.*), cool-headedness, coolness, equanimity, imperturbability, indifference, nonchalance, phlegm, poise, self-possession, unflappability (*inf.*)
sanguinary *adj* **2** = **savage**, bloodthirsty, cruel, fell, grim, merciless, murderous, pitiless, ruthless **3** = **bloody**, bloodied, flowing with blood, gory
sanguine *adj* **1** = **cheerful**, animated, assured, buoyant, confident, hopeful, in good heart, lively, optimistic, spirited **2** = **ruddy**, florid, red, rubicund
Antonyms *adj* ≠ **cheerful:** despondent, dispirited, down, gloomy, heavy-hearted, melancholy, pessimistic ≠ **ruddy:** anaemic, ashen, pale, pallid, peely-wally (*Scot.*)
sanitary *adj* **2** = **hygienic**, clean, germ-free, healthy, salubrious, unpolluted, wholesome
sanitize *vb* **1** = **sterilize**, cleanse, decontaminate, disinfect, fumigate, pasteurize, purge, purify
sanity *n* **1** = **mental health**, normality, rationality, reason, right mind (*inf.*), saneness, stability **2** = **good sense**, common sense, judiciousness, level-headedness, rationality, sense, soundness of judgment
Antonyms *n* ≠ **mental health:** craziness, dementia, insanity, lunacy, madness, mental derangement, mental illness ≠ **good sense:** folly, senselessness, stupidity

the official languages of India. [C17: from Sansk. *samskrta* perfected, lit.: put together]
▸**San'skritic** *adj*

sans serif *or* **sanserif** (sæn'serɪf) *n* a style of printer's typeface in which the characters have no serifs.

Santa ('sæntə) *n Inf.* short for **Santa Claus.**

Santa Claus ('sæntə ˌklɔ:z) *n* the legendary patron saint of children, commonly identified with Saint Nicholas. Often shortened to **Santa.** Also called: **Father Christmas.**

Santa Gertrudis ('sæntə gə'tru:dɪs) *n* one of a breed of red beef cattle developed in Texas.

santonica (sæn'tɒnɪkə) *n* **1** an oriental wormwood plant. **2** the dried flower heads of this plant, formerly used as a vermifuge. ◆ Also called: **wormseed.** [C17: NL, from LL *herba santonica* herb of the *Santones* (prob. wormwood), from L *Santonī* a people of Aquitania]

santonin ('sæntənɪn) *n* a white crystalline soluble substance extracted from the dried flower heads of santonica and used in medicine as an anthelmintic. [C19: from SANTONICA + -IN]

sap[1] Ⓣ (sæp) *n* **1** a solution of mineral salts, sugars, etc., that circulates in a plant. **2** any vital body fluid. **3** energy; vigour. **4** *Sl.* a gullible person. **5** another name for **sapwood.** ◆ *vb* **saps, sapping, sapped.** (*tr*) **6** to drain of sap. [OE *sæp*]

sap[2] Ⓣ (sæp) *n* **1** a deep and narrow trench used to approach or undermine an enemy position. ◆ *vb* **saps, sapping, sapped. 2** to undermine (a fortification, etc.) by digging saps. **3** (*tr*) to weaken. [C16 *zappe*, from It. *zappa* spade, from ?]

sapele (sə'pi:lɪ) *n* **1** any of various W African trees yielding a hard timber resembling mahogany. **2** the timber of such a tree, used to make furniture. [C20: West African name]

sapid ('sæpɪd) *adj* **1** having a pleasant taste. **2** agreeable or engaging. [C17: from L *sapidus*, from *sapere* to taste]
▸**sapidity** (sə'pɪdɪtɪ) *n*

sapient Ⓣ ('seɪpɪənt) *adj Often used ironically.* wise or sagacious. [C15: from L *sapere* to taste]
▸**'sapience** *n* ▸**'sapiently** *adv*

sapiential (ˌseɪpɪ'enʃəl) *adj* showing, having, or providing wisdom.

sapling ('sæplɪŋ) *n* **1** a young tree. **2** *Literary.* a youth.

sapodilla (ˌsæpə'dɪlə) *n* **1** a large tropical American evergreen tree, the latex of which yields chicle. **2** Also called: **sapodilla plum.** the edible brown rough-skinned fruit of this tree. [C17: from Sp. *zapotillo*, dim. of *zapote* sapodilla fruit, from Nahuatl *tsapotl*]

saponaceous (ˌsæpəʊ'neɪʃəs) *adj* resembling soap. [C18: from NL, from L *sāpō* soap]

saponify (sə'pɒnɪˌfaɪ) *vb* **saponifies, saponifying, saponified.** *Chem.* **1** to undergo or cause to undergo a process in which a fat is converted into a soap by treatment with alkali. **2** to undergo or cause to undergo a reaction in which an ester is hydrolysed to an acid and an alcohol as a result of treatment with an alkali. [C19: from F *saponifier*, from L *sāpō* soap]
▸**saˌponifi'cation** *n*

saponin ('sæpənɪn) *n* any of a group of plant glycosides with a steroid structure that foam when shaken and are used in detergents. [C19: from F *saponine*, from L *sāpō* soap]

sappanwood *or* **sapanwood** ('sæpənˌwʊd) *n* **1** a small tree of S Asia producing wood that yields a red dye. **2** the wood of this tree. [C16: *sapan*, via Du. from Malay *sapang*]

sapper ('sæpə) *n* **1** a soldier who digs trenches, etc. **2** (in the British Army) a private of the Royal Engineers.

Sapphic ('sæfɪk) *adj* **1** *Prosody.* denoting a metre associated with Sappho, 6th-century B.C. Greek poetess of Lesbos. **2** of or relating to Sappho or her poetry. **3** lesbian. ◆ *n* **4** *Prosody.* a verse, line, or stanza written in the Sapphic form of classical lyric poetry.

sapphire ('sæfaɪə) *n* **1a** any precious corundum gemstone that is not red, esp. the highly valued transparent blue variety. **1b** (*as modifier*): *a sapphire ring.* **2a** the blue colour of sapphire. **2b** (*as adj*): *sapphire eyes.* **3** (*modifier*) denoting a forty-fifth anniversary: *our sapphire wedding.* [C13 *safir*, from OF, from L *sapphīrus*, from Gk *sappheiros*, ?from Sansk. *śanipriya*, lit.: beloved of the planet Saturn]

sappy ('sæpɪ) *adj* **sappier, sappiest. 1** (of plants) full of sap. **2** full of energy or vitality.

sapro- *or before a vowel* **sapr-** *combining form.* indicating dead or decaying matter: *saprogenic.* [from Gk *sapros* rotten]

saprogenic (ˌsæprəʊ'dʒenɪk) *or* **saprogenous** (sæ'prɒdʒɪnəs) *adj* **1** producing or resulting from decay. **2** growing on decaying matter.

saprophyte ('sæprəʊˌfaɪt) *n* any plant that lives and feeds on dead organic matter.
▸**saprophytic** (ˌsæprəʊ'fɪtɪk) *adj*

saprotroph ('sæprəʊtrəʊf) *n* any organism, esp. a fungus or bacterium, that lives and feeds on dead organic matter. Also called: **saprobe, saprobiont.**
▸**saprotrophic** (ˌsæprəʊ'trəʊfɪk) *adj* ▸**ˌsapro'trophically** *adv*

saprozoic (ˌsæprəʊ'zəʊɪk) *adj* (of animals or plants) feeding on dead organic matter.

sapsucker ('sæpˌsʌkə) *n* either of two North American woodpeckers that have white wing patches and feed on the sap from trees.

sapwood ('sæpˌwʊd) *n* the soft wood, just beneath the bark in tree trunks, that consists of living tissue.

sarabande *or* **saraband** ('særəˌbænd) *n* **1** a decorous 17th-century courtly dance. **2** a piece of music composed for or in the rhythm of this dance, in slow triple time. [C17: from F *sarabande*, from Sp. *zarabanda*, from ?]

Saracen ('særəsᵊn) *n* **1** *History.* a member of one of the nomadic Arabic tribes, esp. of the Syrian desert. **2a** a Muslim, esp. one who opposed the crusades. **2b** (in later use) any Arab. ◆ *adj* **3** of or relating to Arabs of either of these periods, regions, or types. [C13: from OF *Sarrazin*, from LL *Saracēnus*, from LGk *Sarakēnos*, ?from Ar. *sharq* sunrise]
▸**Saracenic** (ˌsærə'senɪk) *adj*

sarcasm Ⓣ ('sɑ:kæzəm) *n* **1** mocking or ironic language intended to convey scorn or insult. **2** the use or tone of such language. [C16: from LL *sarcasmus*, from Gk, from *sarkazein* to rend the flesh, from *sarx* flesh]

sarcastic Ⓣ (sɑ:'kæstɪk) *adj* **1** characterized by sarcasm. **2** given to the use of sarcasm.
▸**sar'castically** *adv*

sarcenet *or* **sarsenet** ('sɑ:snɪt) *n* a fine soft silk fabric used for clothing, ribbons, etc. [C15: from OF *sarzinet*, from *Sarrazin* SARACEN]

sarco- *or before a vowel* **sarc-** *combining form.* indicating flesh: *sarcoma.* [from Gk *sark-*, *sarx* flesh]

sarcocarp ('sɑ:kəʊˌkɑ:p) *n Bot.* the fleshy mesocarp of such fruits as the peach or plum.

sarcoma (sɑ:'kəʊmə) *n, pl* **sarcomata** (-mətə) *or* **sarcomas.** *Pathol.* a usually malignant tumour arising from connective tissue. [C17: via NL from Gk *sarkōma* fleshy growth]
▸**sar'comatous** *adj*

sarcomatosis (sɑ:ˌkəʊmə'təʊsɪs) *n Pathol.* a condition characterized by the development of several sarcomas at various bodily sites. [C19: see SARCOMA, -OSIS]

sarcophagus (sɑ:'kɒfəgəs) *n, pl* **sarcophagi** (-ˌgaɪ) *or* **sarcophaguses.** a stone or marble coffin or tomb, esp. one bearing sculpture or inscriptions. [C17: via L from Gk *sarkophagos* flesh-devouring; from the type of stone used, which was believed to destroy the flesh of corpses]

sarcoplasm ('sɑ:kəʊˌplæzəm) *n* the cytoplasm of a muscle fibre.
▸**ˌsarco'plasmic** *adj*

sarcous ('sɑ:kəs) *adj* (of tissue) muscular or fleshy. [C19: from Gk *sarx* flesh]

sard (sɑ:d) *or* **sardius** ('sɑ:dɪəs) *n* an orange, red, or brown variety of chalcedony, used as a gemstone. Also called: **sardine.** [C14: from L *sarda*, from Gk *sardios* stone from Sardis]

sardar *or* **sirdar** (sə'dɑ:) *n* (in India) **1** a title used before the name of Sikh men. **2** a leader. [Hindi, from Persian]

sardine[1] (sɑ:'di:n) *n, pl* **sardines** *or* **sardine. 1** any of various small food fishes of the herring family, esp. a young pilchard. **2 like sardines.** very closely crowded together. [C15: via OF from L *sardīna*, dim. of *sarda* a fish suitable for pickling]

sardine[2] ('sɑ:di:n) *n* another name for **sard.** [C14: from LL *sardinus*, from Gk *sardinos lithos* Sardian stone, from *Sardeis* Sardis]

Sardinian (sɑ:'dɪnɪən) *adj* **1.** of or relating to Sardinia, Italian island in the Mediterranean, its inhabitants, or their language. ◆ *n* **2** a native or inhabitant of Sardinia. **3** the spoken language of Sardinia, sometimes regarded as a dialect of Italian but containing many loan words from Spanish.

sardonic Ⓣ (sɑ:'dɒnɪk) *adj* characterized by irony, mockery, or derision. [C17: from F, from L, from Gk *sardonios* derisive, lit.: of Sardinia, alteration of Homeric *sardanios* scornful (laughter or smile)]
▸**sar'donically** *adv* ▸**sar'donicism** *n*

sardonyx ('sɑ:dənɪks) *n* a variety of chalcedony with alternating reddish-brown and white parallel bands. [C14: via L from Gk *sardonux*, ?from *sardion* SARD + *onux* nail]

sargassum (sɑ:'gæsəm) *n* a floating brown seaweed having ribbon-like fronds containing air sacs, esp. abundant in the **Sargasso Sea** in the N Atlantic. [C16: from Port. *sargaço* from ?]

sarge (sɑ:dʒ) *n Inf.* sergeant.

sari *or* **saree** ('sɑ:rɪ) *n, pl* **saris** *or* **sarees.** the traditional dress of women of India, Pakistan, etc., consisting of a very long piece of cloth swathed around the body. [C18: from Hindi *sārī*, from Sansk. *śāṭī*]

THESAURUS

sap[1] *n* **2** = **vital fluid**, animating force, essence, lifeblood **4** *Slang* = **fool**, chump (*inf.*), drip (*inf.*), idiot, jerk (*sl., chiefly US & Canad.*), muggins (*Brit. sl.*), nincompoop, numskull *or* numbskull, oaf, prat (*sl.*), simpleton, twit (*inf.*), wally (*sl.*), weakling

sap[2] *vb* **3** = **weaken**, bleed, deplete, devitalize, drain, enervate, erode, exhaust, rob, undermine, wear down

sapience *n Often used ironically* = **wisdom**, acuity, acuteness, discernment, insight, mother wit, nous (*Brit. sl.*), perspicacity, sagacity, sense, shrewdness, suss (*sl.*), understanding

sapient *adj Often used ironically* = **wise**, acute, canny, discerning, discriminating, intelligent, judicious, knowing, long-headed, perspicacious, sagacious, sage, shrewd, would-be-wise

sarcasm *n* **1** = **irony**, bitterness, causticness, contempt, cynicism, derision, mockery, mordancy, ridicule, satire, scorn, sneering, venom, vitriol

sarcastic *adj* **1, 2** = **ironical**, acerbic, acid, acrimonious, backhanded, bitchy (*inf.*), biting, caustic, contemptuous, cutting, cynical, derisive, disparaging, mocking, mordacious, mordant, sardonic, sarky (*Brit. inf.*), satirical, sharp, sneering, taunting, vitriolic

sardonic *adj* = **mocking**, bitter, cynical, derisive, dry, ironical, jeering, malevolent, malicious, malignant, mordacious, mordant, sarcastic, sneering, wry

sarking ('sɑːkɪŋ) *n Scot., northern English, & NZ.* flat planking supporting the roof cladding of a building. [C15 in England: from Scot. *sark* shirt]
sarky ('sɑːkɪ) *adj* **sarkier, sarkiest.** *Brit. inf.* sarcastic.
sarmentose (sɑː'mɛntəʊs) *or* **sarmentous** (sɑː'mɛntəs) *adj* (of plants such as the strawberry) having stems in the form of runners. [C18: from L *sarmentōsus* full of twigs, from *sarmentum* brushwood, from *sarpere* to prune]
sarnie ('sɑːnɪ) *n Brit. inf.* a sandwich. [C20: prob. from N or dialect pronunciation of first syllable of *sandwich*]
sarod (sæ'rəʊd) *n* an Indian stringed musical instrument that may be played with a bow or plucked. [C19: from Hindi]
sarong (sə'rɒŋ) *n* **1** a garment worn by men and women in the Malay Archipelago, Sri Lanka, etc., consisting of a long piece of cloth tucked around the waist or under the armpits. **2** a western adaptation of this garment, worn by women as beachwear. [C19: from Malay, lit.: sheath]
saros ('seɪrɒs) *n* a cycle of about 18 years 11 days (6585.32 days) in which eclipses of the sun and moon occur in the same sequence. [C19: from Gk, from Babylonian *šāru* 3600 (years); modern use apparently based on mistaken interpretation of *šāru* as a period of 18½ years]
sarrusophone (sə'ruːzəˌfəʊn) *n* a wind instrument resembling the oboe but made of brass. [C19: after *Sarrus,* F bandmaster, who invented it (1856)]
sarsaparilla (ˌsɑːsəpə'rɪlə) *n* **1** any of a genus of tropical American prickly climbing plants having large aromatic roots and heart-shaped leaves. **2** the dried roots of any of these plants, formerly used as a medicine. **3** a nonalcoholic drink prepared from these roots. [C16: from Sp. *sarzaparrilla,* from *zarza* a bramble + *-parrilla,* from *parra* a climbing plant]
sarsen ('sɑːsᵊn) *n* **1** *Geol.* a boulder of silicified sandstone, probably of Tertiary age. **2** such a stone used in a megalithic monument. ◆ Also called: **greywether.** [C17: prob. a var. of SARACEN]
sarsenet ('sɑːsnɪt) *n* a variant spelling of **sarcenet.**
sartorial (sɑː'tɔːrɪəl) *adj* **1** of or relating to a tailor or to tailoring. **2** *Anat.* of the sartorius. [C19: from LL *sartōrius* from L *sartor* a patcher, from *sarcīre* to patch]
▸**sar'torially** *adv*
sartorius (sɑː'tɔːrɪəs) *n, pl* **sartorii** (-'tɔːrɪˌaɪ). *Anat.* a long ribbon-shaped muscle that aids in flexing the knee. [C18: NL, from *sartorius musculus,* lit.: tailor's muscle, because it is used when one sits in the cross-legged position in which tailors traditionally sat while sewing]
Sarum use *n* the distinctive local rite or system of rites used at Salisbury cathedral in late medieval times. [from *Sarum,* ancient name of Salisbury]
SAS *abbrev. for* Special Air Service.
sash[1] (sæʃ) *n* a long piece of ribbon, etc., worn around the waist or over one shoulder, as a symbol of rank. [C16: from Ar. *shāsh* muslin]
sash[2] (sæʃ) *n* **1** a frame that contains the panes of a window or door. **2** a complete frame together with panes of glass. ◆ *vb* **3** (*tr*) to furnish with a sash, sashes, or sash windows. [C17: orig. pl *sashes,* var. of *shashes,* from CHASSIS]
sashay (sæ'ʃeɪ) *vb* (*intr*) *Inf., chiefly US & Canad.* **1** to move, walk, or glide along casually. **2** to move or walk in a showy way; parade. [C19: from an alteration of *chassé,* a gliding dance step]
sash cord *n* a strong cord connecting a sash weight to a sliding sash.
sashimi ('sæʃɪmɪ) *n* a Japanese dish of thin fillets of raw fish. [C19: from Japanese *sashi* pierce + *mi* flesh]
sash saw *n* a small tenon saw used for cutting sashes.
sash weight *n* a weight used to counterbalance the weight of a sliding sash in a sash window and thus hold it in position at any height.
sash window *n* a window consisting of two sashes placed one above the other so that they can be slid past each other.
sasquatch ('sæsˌkwætʃ) *n* (in Canadian folklore) in British Columbia, a hairy beast or manlike monster said to leave huge footprints. [from Amerind]
sass (sæs) *US & Canad. inf.* ◆ *n* **1** impudent talk or behaviour. ◆ *vb* (*intr*) **2** to talk or answer back in such a way. [C20: back formation from SASSY]
sassaby ('sæsəbɪ) *n, pl* **sassabies.** an African antelope of grasslands and semideserts, having angular curved horns. [C19: from Bantu *tshêsêbê*]
sassafras ('sæsəˌfræs) *n* **1** an aromatic deciduous tree of North America, having three-lobed leaves and dark blue fruits. **2** the aromatic dried root bark of this tree, used as a flavouring, and yielding **sassafras oil. 3** *Austral.* any of several unrelated trees having a similar fragrant bark. [C16: from Sp. *sasafras,* from ?]
Sassenach ('sæsəˌnæx) *n Scot. & occasionally Irish.* an English person or a Lowland Scot. [C18: from Gaelic *Sassunach,* from LL *saxonēs* Saxons]
sassy ('sæsɪ) *adj* **sassier, sassiest.** *US & Canad. inf.* insolent; impertinent. [C19: var. of SAUCY]
▸**'sassily** *adv* ▸**'sassiness** *n*
sat (sæt) *vb* the past tense and past participle of **sit.**
Sat. *abbrev. for:* **1** Saturday. **2** Saturn.
Satan ❶ ('seɪtᵊn) *n* the devil, adversary of God, and tempter of mankind: sometimes identified with Lucifer (Luke 4:5–8). [OE, from LL, from Gk, from Heb.: plotter, from *sātan* to plot against]
satanic ❶ (sə'tænɪk) *adj* **1** of or relating to Satan. **2** supremely evil or wicked.
▸**sa'tanically** *adv*
Satanism ('seɪtᵊˌnɪzəm) *n* **1** the worship of Satan. **2** a form of such worship which includes blasphemous parodies of Christian prayers, etc. **3** a satanic disposition.
▸**'Satanist** *n, adj*
SATB *abbrev. for* soprano, alto, tenor, bass: a combination of voices in choral music.
satchel ('sætʃəl) *n* a rectangular bag, usually made of leather or cloth and provided with a shoulder strap, used for carrying school books. [C14: from OF *sachel,* from LL *saccellus,* from L *saccus* SACK[1]]
▸**'satchelled** *adj*
sate[1] ❶ (seɪt) *vb* **sates, sating, sated.** (*tr*) **1** to satisfy (a desire or appetite) fully. **2** to supply beyond capacity or desire. [OE *sadian*]
sate[2] (sæt, seɪt) *vb Arch.* a past tense and past participle of **sit.**
sateen (sæ'tiːn) *n* a glossy linen or cotton fabric that resembles satin. [C19: changed from SATIN, on the model of VELVETEEN]
satellite ❶ ('sætᵊˌlaɪt) *n* **1** a celestial body orbiting around a planet or star: *the earth is a satellite of the sun.* **2** a man-made device orbiting around the earth, moon, or another planet transmitting to earth scientific information or used for communication. **3** a country or political unit under the domination of a foreign power. **4** a subordinate area that is dependent upon a larger adjacent town. **5** (*modifier*) subordinate to or dependent upon another: *a satellite nation.* **6** (*modifier*) of, used in, or relating to the transmission of television signals from a satellite to the house: *a satellite dish aerial.* [C16: from L *satelles* an attendant, prob. of Etruscan origin]
satiable ('seɪʃɪəbᵊl) *adj* capable of being satiated.
▸ˌ**satia'bility** *n* ▸**'satiably** *adv*
satiate ❶ ('seɪʃɪˌeɪt) *vb* **satiates, satiating, satiated.** (*tr*) **1** to fill or supply beyond capacity or desire. **2** to supply to capacity. [C16: from L *satiāre* to satisfy, from *satis* enough]
▸ˌ**sati'ation** *n*
satiety ❶ (sə'taɪɪtɪ) *n* the state of being satiated. [C16: from L *satietās,* from *satis* enough]
satin ('sætɪn) *n* **1** a fabric of silk, rayon, etc., closely woven to show much of the warp, giving a smooth glossy appearance. **2** (*modifier*) like satin in texture: *a satin finish.* [C14: via OF from Ar. *zaitūnī,* Ar. rendering of Chinese *Tseutung* (now *Tsinkiang*), port from which the cloth was prob. first exported]
▸**'satiny** *adj*
satinet *or* **satinette** (ˌsætɪ'nɛt) *n* a thin satin or satin-like fabric. [C18: from F: small satin]
satinflower ('sætɪnˌflaʊə) *n* another name for **greater stitchwort** (see **stitchwort**).
satinwood ('sætɪnˌwʊd) *n* **1** a tree that occurs in the East Indies and has hard wood with a satiny texture. **2** the wood of this tree, used in veneering, marquetry, etc.
satire ❶ ('sætaɪə) *n* **1** a novel, play, etc., in which topical issues, folly, or evil are held up to scorn by means of ridicule. **2** the genre constituted by such works. **3** the use of ridicule, irony, etc., to create such an effect. [C16: from L *satira* a mixture, from *satur* sated, from *satis* enough]
satirical ❶ (sə'tɪrɪkᵊl) *or* **satiric** *adj* **1** of, relating to, or containing satire. **2** given to the use of satire.
▸**sa'tirically** *adv*
satirist ('sætərɪst) *n* **1** a person who writes satire. **2** a person given to the use of satire.
satirize ❶ *or* **satirise** ('sætəˌraɪz) *vb* **satirizes, satirizing, satirized** *or* **satirises, satirising, satirised.** to deride (a person or thing) by means of satire.
▸ˌ**satiri'zation** *or* ˌ**satiri'sation** *n*
satisfaction ❶ (ˌsætɪs'fækʃən) *n* **1** the act of satisfying or state of being

THESAURUS

Satan *n* = **The Devil,** Apollyon, Beelzebub, Lord of the Flies, Lucifer, Mephistopheles, Old Nick (*inf.*), Old Scratch (*inf.*), Prince of Darkness, The Evil One
satanic *adj* **2** = **evil,** accursed, black, demoniac, demoniacal, demonic, devilish, diabolic, fiendish, hellish, infernal, inhuman, iniquitous, malevolent, malignant, wicked
Antonyms *adj* benevolent, benign, divine, godly, holy
sate[1] *vb* **1** = **satisfy,** indulge to the full, satiate, slake **2** = **overfill,** cloy, glut, gorge, saturate, sicken, surfeit, weary
satellite *n* **1** = **moon 2** = **sputnik,** communications satellite ◆ *adj* **5** = **dependent,** client, puppet, subordinate, tributary, vassal
satiate *vb* **1** = **glut,** cloy, gorge, jade, nauseate, overfill, stuff, surfeit **2** = **satisfy,** sate, slake
satiety *n* = **fullness,** gratification, repletion, satiation, satisfaction, saturation, surfeit
satire *n* **1** = **mockery,** burlesque, caricature, irony, lampoon, parody, pasquinade, raillery, ridicule, sarcasm, send-up (*Brit. inf.*), skit, spoof (*inf.*), takeoff (*inf.*), travesty, wit
satirical *adj* **1** = **mocking,** biting, bitter, burlesque, caustic, censorious, cutting, cynical, incisive, ironical, mordacious, mordant, pungent, Rabelaisian, sarcastic, sardonic, taunting, vitriolic
satirize *vb* = **ridicule,** abuse, burlesque, censure, criticize, deride, hold up to ridicule, lampoon, lash, parody, pillory, send up (*Brit. inf.*), take off (*inf.*), travesty
satisfaction *n* **1** = **contentment,** comfort,

satisfied. **2** the fulfilment of a desire. **3** the pleasure obtained from such fulfilment. **4** a source of fulfilment. **5** compensation for a wrong done or received. **6** *RC Church, Church of England.* the performance of a penance. **7** *Christianity.* the atonement for sin by the death of Christ.

satisfactory ❶ (ˌsætɪs'fæktərɪ) *adj* **1** adequate or suitable; acceptable. **2** giving satisfaction. **3** constituting or involving atonement or expiation for sin.
▸ˌ**satis'factorily** *adv*

satisfice ('sætɪsˌfaɪs) *vb* **satisfices, satisficing, satisficed. 1** (*intr*) to act in such a way as to satisfy the minimum requirements for achieving a particular result. **2** (*tr*) *Obs.* to satisfy. [C16: altered from SATISFY]
▸'**satisˌficer** *n*

satisficing behaviour *n Econ.* the form of behaviour demonstrated by firms who seek satisfactory profits and satisfactory growth rather than maximum profits.

satisfy ❶ ('sætɪsˌfaɪ) *vb* **satisfies, satisfying, satisfied.** (*mainly tr*) **1** (*also intr*) to fulfil the desires or needs of (a person). **2** to provide amply for (a need or desire). **3** to convince. **4** to dispel (a doubt). **5** to make reparation to or for. **6** to discharge or pay off (a debt) to (a creditor). **7** to fulfil the requirements of; comply with: *you must satisfy the terms of your lease.* **8** *Maths, logic.* to fulfil the conditions of (a theorem, assumption, etc.); to yield a truth by substitution of the given value. [C15: from OF *satisfier*, from L *satisfacere*, from *satis* enough + *facere* to make]
▸'**satisˌfiable** *adj* ▸'**satisˌfying** *adj* ▸'**satisˌfyingly** *adv*

satori (sə'tɔːrɪ) *n Zen Buddhism.* a state of sudden intuitive enlightenment. [from Japanese]

satrap ('sætrəp) *n* **1** (in ancient Persia) a provincial governor. **2** a subordinate ruler. [C14: from L *satrapa*, from Gk *satrapēs*, from OPersian *khshathrapāvan*, lit.: protector of the land]

satrapy ('sætrəpɪ) *n, pl* **satrapies.** the province, office, or period of rule of a satrap.

SATs (sæts) *pl n Brit. education. acronym for* standard assessment tasks: see **assessment tests.**

satsuma (sæt'suːmə) *n* **1** a small citrus tree cultivated, esp. in Japan, for its edible fruit. **2** the fruit of this tree, which has easily separable segments. [from name of former province of Japan]

saturable ('sætʃərəbᵊl) *adj Chem.* capable of being saturated.
▸ˌ**satura'bility** *n*

saturate ❶ *vb* ('sætʃəˌreɪt), **saturates, saturating, saturated. 1** to fill, soak, or imbue totally. **2** to make (a chemical compound, solution, etc.) saturated or (of a compound, etc.) to become saturated. **3** (*tr*) *Mil.* to bomb or shell heavily. ◆ *adj* ('sætʃərɪt, -ˌreɪt). **4** saturated. [C16: from L *saturāre*, from *satur* sated, from *satis* enough]

saturated ('sætʃəˌreɪtɪd) *adj* **1** (of a solution or solvent) containing the maximum amount of solute that can normally be dissolved at a given temperature and pressure. **2** (of a chemical compound) containing no multiple bonds: *a saturated hydrocarbon.* **3** (of a fat) containing a high proportion of fatty acids having single bonds. **4** (of a vapour) containing the maximum amount of gaseous material at a given temperature and pressure.

saturation (ˌsætʃə'reɪʃən) *n* **1** the act of saturating or the state of being saturated. **2** *Chem.* the state of a chemical compound, solution, or vapour when it is saturated. **3** *Meteorol.* the state of the atmosphere when it can hold no more water vapour at its particular temperature and pressure. **4** the attribute of a colour that enables an observer to judge its proportion of pure chromatic colour. **5** the level beyond which demand for a product or service is not expected to rise. ◆ *modifier.* **6** denoting the maximum possible intensity of coverage of an area: *saturation bombing.*

saturation point *n* the point at which no more can be absorbed, accommodated, used, etc.

Saturday ('sætədɪ) *n* the seventh and last day of the week: the Jewish Sabbath. [OE *sæternes dæg*, translation of L *Sāturnī diēs* day of Saturn]

Saturn[1] ('sætɜːn) *n* the Roman god of agriculture and vegetation. Greek counterpart: **Cronus.**

Saturn[2] ('sætɜːn) *n* **1** the sixth planet from the sun, around which revolve planar concentric rings (**Saturn's rings**) consisting of small frozen particles. **2** the alchemical name for **lead**[2].
▸**Saturnian** (sæ'tɜːnɪən) *adj*

Saturnalia (ˌsætə'neɪlɪə) *n, pl* **Saturnalia** *or* **Saturnalias. 1** an ancient Roman festival celebrated in December: renowned for its general merrymaking. **2** (*sometimes not cap.*) a period or occasion of wild revelry. [C16: from L *Sāturnālis* relating to SATURN[1]]
▸ˌ**Satur'nalian** *adj*

saturnine ❶ ('sætəˌnaɪn) *adj* **1** having a gloomy temperament. **2** *Arch.* **2a** of or relating to lead. **2b** having lead poisoning. [C15: from F *saturnin*, from Med. L *sāturnīnus* (unattested), from L *Sāturnus* Saturn, from the gloomy influence attributed to the planet Saturn]
▸'**saturˌninely** *adv*

satyagraha ('sɔːtjɑːgrɔːhɑː) *n* the policy of nonviolent resistance adopted by Mahatma Gandhi to oppose British rule in India. [via Hindi from Sansk., lit.: insistence on truth, from *satya* truth + *agraha* fervour]

satyr ('sætə) *n* **1** *Greek myth.* one of a class of sylvan deities, represented as goatlike men who drank and danced in the train of Dionysus and chased the nymphs. **2** a man who has strong sexual desires. **3** any of various butterflies, having dark wings often marked with eyespots. [C14: from L *satyrus*, from Gk *saturos*]
▸**satyric** (sə'tɪrɪk) *adj*

satyriasis (ˌsætɪ'raɪəsɪs) *n* a neurotic compulsion in men to have sexual intercourse with many women without being able to have lasting relationships with them. [C17: via NL from Gk *saturiasis*]

sauce ❶ (sɔːs) *n* **1** any liquid or semiliquid preparation eaten with food to enhance its flavour. **2** anything that adds piquancy. **3** *US & Canad.* stewed fruit. **4** *Inf.* impudent language or behaviour. ◆ *vb* **sauces, saucing, sauced.** (*tr*) **5** to prepare (food) with sauce. **6** to add zest to. **7** *Inf.* to be saucy to. [C14: via OF from L *salsus* salted, from *sal* salt]

saucepan ('sɔːspən) *n* a metal or enamel pan with a long handle and often a lid, used for cooking food.

saucer ('sɔːsə) *n* **1** a small round dish on which a cup is set. **2** any similar dish. [C14: from OF *saussier* container for SAUCE]
▸'**saucerful** *n*

saucy ❶ ('sɔːsɪ) *adj* **saucier, sauciest. 1** impertinent. **2** pert; jaunty: *a saucy hat.*
▸'**saucily** *adv* ▸'**sauciness** *n*

sauerkraut ('saʊəˌkraʊt) *n* finely shredded cabbage which has been fermented in brine. [G, from *sauer* sour + *Kraut* cabbage]

sauger ('sɔːgə) *n* a small North American pikeperch with a spotted dorsal fin: valued as a food and game fish. [C19: from ?]

sault (suː) *n Canad.* a waterfall or rapids. [C17: from Canad. F, from F *saut* a leap]

sauna ('sɔːnə) *n* **1** an invigorating bath originating in Finland in which the bather is subjected to hot steam, usually followed by a cold plunge. **2** the place in which such a bath is taken. [C20: from Finnish]

saunter ❶ ('sɔːntə) *vb* **1** (*intr*) to walk in a casual manner; stroll. ◆ *n* **2** a leisurely pace or stroll. [C17 (meaning: to wander aimlessly), C15 (to muse): from ?]
▸'**saunterer** *n*

-saur *or* **-saurus** *n combining form.* lizard: *dinosaur.* [from NL *saurus*]

saurian ('sɔːrɪən) *adj* **1** of or resembling a lizard. ◆ *n* **2** a former name for **lizard.** [C15: from NL *Sauria*, from Gk *sauros*]

saury ('sɔːrɪ) *n, pl* **sauries.** a fish of tropical and temperate seas, having an elongated body and long toothed jaws. Also called: **skipper.** [C18: ? from LL *saurus*, from ?]

sausage ('sɒsɪdʒ) *n* **1** finely minced meat, esp. pork or beef, mixed with fat, cereal, and seasonings (**sausage meat**), and packed into a tube-

THESAURUS

complacency, content, contentedness, ease, enjoyment, gratification, happiness, peace of mind, pleasure, pride, repletion, satiety, well-being **2 = fulfilment**, achievement, appeasing, assuaging, gratification, resolution, settlement **5 = compensation**, amends, atonement, damages, indemnification, justice, recompense, redress, reimbursement, remuneration, reparation, requital, restitution, settlement, vindication
Antonyms *n* ≠ **contentment:** annoyance, discontent, displeasure, dissatisfaction, frustration, grief, misgivings, pain, shame, unhappiness ≠ **compensation:** injury

satisfactory *adj* **1 = adequate**, acceptable, all right, average, competent, fair, good enough, passable, sufficient, suitable, up to scratch, up to standard, up to the mark
Antonyms *adj* bad, below par, inadequate, insufficient, leaving a lot to be desired, mediocre, no great shakes (*inf.*), not up to scratch (*inf.*), poor, sub-standard, unacceptable, unsatisfactory, unsuitable

satisfied *adj* **1 = contented**, at ease, complacent, content, convinced, easy in one's mind, happy, like the cat that swallowed the canary (*inf.*), pacified, positive, smug, sure

satisfy *vb* **1 = be sufficient**, answer, be adequate, be enough, come up to expectations, cut the mustard, do, fill the bill (*inf.*), fulfil, meet, qualify, serve, serve the purpose, suffice **2 = content**, appease, assuage, feed, fill, gratify, indulge, mollify, pacify, pander to, please, quench, sate, satiate, slake, surfeit **3, 4 = convince**, assure, dispel (someone's) doubts, persuade, put (someone's) mind at rest, quiet, reassure **5 = compensate**, atone, indemnify, make good, make reparation for, recompense, remunerate, requite, reward **6 = pay (off)**, settle, square up **7 = fulfil**, answer, comply with, discharge, meet
Antonyms *vb* ≠ **be sufficient:** fail to meet ≠ **content:** annoy, displease, dissatisfy, exasperate, frustrate, give cause for complaint ≠ **convince:** dissuade, fail to persuade

satisfying *adj* **1 = satisfactory**, cheering, convincing, filling, gratifying, pleasing, pleasurable

saturate *vb* **1 = soak**, douse, drench, imbue, impregnate, seep, souse, steep, suffuse, waterlog, wet through

saturnine *adj* **1 = gloomy**, dour, dull, glum, grave, heavy, morose, phlegmatic, sedate, sluggish, sombre, taciturn, uncommunicative

sauce *n* **4** *Informal* **= impudence**, audacity, backchat (*inf.*), brass (*inf.*), brass neck (*Brit. inf.*), cheek (*inf.*), cheekiness, disrespectfulness, face (*inf.*), front, impertinence, insolence, lip (*sl.*), neck (*inf.*), nerve (*inf.*), rudeness

sauciness *n* **1 = impudence**, backchat (*inf.*), brass (*inf.*), brazenness, cheek (*inf.*), flippancy, impertinence, insolence, lip (*sl.*), pertness, rudeness, sauce (*inf.*)

saucy *adj* **1 = impudent**, cheeky (*inf.*), disrespectful, flip (*inf.*), flippant, forward, fresh (*inf.*), impertinent, insolent, lippy (*US & Canad. sl.*), pert, presumptuous, rude, sassy (*US inf.*), smart-alecky (*inf.*) **2 = jaunty**, dashing, gay, natty (*inf.*), perky, rakish, sporty

saunter *vb* **1 = stroll**, amble, dally, linger, loiter, meander, mosey (*inf.*), ramble, roam, rove, stravaig (*Scot. & N English dialect*), take a stroll, tarry, wander ◆ *n* **2 = stroll**, airing, amble, breather, constitutional, perambulation, promenade, ramble, turn, walk

shaped edible casing. **2** *Scot.* sausage meat. **3** an object shaped like a sausage. **4 not a sausage.** nothing at all. [C15: from OF *saussiche,* from LL *salsīcia,* from L *salsus* salted; see SAUCE]

sausage dog *n* an informal name for **dachshund.**

sausage roll *n Brit.* a roll of sausage meat in pastry.

sauté ('səuteɪ) *vb* **sautés, sautéing** *or* **sautéeing, sautéed. 1** to fry (food) quickly in a little fat. ◆ *n* **2** a dish of sautéed food, esp. meat that is browned and then cooked in a sauce. ◆ *adj* **3** sautéed until lightly brown: *sauté potatoes.* [C19: from F: tossed, from *sauter* to jump, from L, from *salīre* to spring]

savage ➊ ('sævɪdʒ) *adj* **1** wild; untamed: *savage beasts.* **2** ferocious in temper: *a savage dog.* **3** uncivilized; crude: *savage behaviour.* **4** (of peoples) nonliterate or primitive: *a savage tribe.* **5** (of terrain) rugged and uncultivated. ◆ *n* **6** a member of a nonliterate society, esp. one regarded as primitive. **7** a fierce or vicious person or animal. ◆ *vb* **savages, savaging, savaged.** (*tr*) **8** to criticize violently. **9** to attack ferociously and wound. [C13: from OF *sauvage,* from L *silvāticus* belonging to a wood, from *silva* a wood]
▸'**savagely** *adv* ▸'**savageness** *n*

savagery ➊ ('sævɪdʒrɪ) *n, pl* **savageries. 1** an uncivilized condition. **2** a savage act or nature. **3** savages collectively.

savanna *or* **savannah** (sə'vænə) *n* open grasslands, usually with scattered bushes or trees, characteristic of much of tropical Africa. [C16: from Sp. *zavana,* from Amerind *zabana*]

savant ➊ ('sævənt) *n* a man of great learning; sage. [C18: from F, from *savoir* to know, from L *sapere* to be wise]
▸'**savante** *fem n*

savate (sə'væt) *n* a form of boxing in which blows may be delivered with the feet as well as the hands. [C19: from F, lit.: old worn-out shoe]

save[1] ➊ (seɪv) *vb* **saves, saving, saved. 1** (*tr*) to rescue, preserve, or guard (a person or thing) from danger or harm. **2** to avoid the spending, waste, or loss of (money, possessions, etc.). **3** (*tr*) to deliver from sin; redeem. **4** (often foll. by *up*) to set aside or reserve (money, goods, etc.) for future use. **5** (*tr*) to treat with care so as to avoid or lessen wear or degeneration. **6** (*tr*) to prevent the necessity for; obviate the trouble of. **7** (*tr*) *Soccer, hockey, etc.* to prevent (a goal) by stopping (a struck ball or puck). ◆ *n* **8** *Soccer, hockey, etc.* the act of saving a goal. **9** *Computing.* an instruction to write information from the memory onto a tape or disk. [C13: from OF *salver,* via LL from L *salvus* safe]
▸'**savable** *or* '**saveable** *adj* ▸'**saver** *n*

save[2] (seɪv) *Arch.* ◆ *prep* **1** (often foll. by *for*) Also: **saving.** with the exception of. ◆ *conj* **2** but. [C13 *sauf,* from OF, from L *salvō,* from *salvus* safe]

save as you earn *n* (in Britain) a savings scheme operated by the government, in which monthly contributions earn tax-free interest. Abbrev.: **SAYE.**

saveloy ('sævɪˌlɔɪ) *n* a smoked sausage made from salted pork, coloured red with saltpetre. [C19: prob. via F from It. *cervellato,* from *cervello* brain, from L, from *cerebrum* brain]

savin *or* **savine** ('sævɪn) *n* **1** a small spreading juniper bush of Europe, N Asia, and North America. **2** the oil derived from the shoots and leaves of this plant, formerly used in medicine to treat rheumatism, etc. [C14: from OF *savine,* from L *herba Sabīna* the Sabine plant]

saving ➊ ('seɪvɪŋ) *adj* **1** tending to save or preserve. **2** redeeming or compensating (esp. in **saving grace**). **3** thrifty or economical. **4** *Law.* denoting or relating to an exception or reservation: *a saving clause in an agreement.* ◆ *n* **5** preservation or redemption. **6** economy or avoidance of waste. **7** reduction in cost or expenditure. **8** anything saved. **9** (*pl*) money saved for future use. ◆ *prep* **10** with the exception of. ◆ *conj* **11** except.
▸'**savingly** *adv*

savings bank *n* a bank that accepts the savings of depositors and pays interest on them.

savings ratio *n Econ.* the ratio of personal savings to disposable income, esp. using the difference between national figures for disposable income and consumer spending as a measure of savings.

saviour ➊ *or US* **savior** ('seɪvjə) *n* a person who rescues another person or a thing from danger or harm. [C13 *saveour,* from OF, from Church L *Salvātor* the Saviour]

Saviour ➊ *or US* **Savior** ('seɪvjə) *n Christianity.* Jesus Christ regarded as the saviour of men from sin.

savoir-faire ➊ ('sævwɑː'fɛə) *n* the ability to do the right thing in any situation. [F, lit.: a knowing how to do]

savory ('seɪvərɪ) *n, pl* **savories. 1** any of numerous aromatic plants, including the **winter savory** and **summer savory,** of the Mediterranean region, having narrow leaves and white, pink, or purple flowers. **2** the leaves of any of these plants, used as a potherb. [C14: prob. from OE *sætherie,* from L *saturēia,* from ?]

savour ➊ *or US* **savor** ('seɪvə) *n* **1** the quality in a substance that is perceived by the sense of taste or smell. **2** a specific taste or smell: *the savour of lime.* **3** a slight but distinctive quality or trace. **4** the power to excite interest: *the savour of wit has been lost.* ◆ *vb* **5** (*intr;* often foll. by *of*) to possess the taste or smell (of). **6** (*intr;* often foll. by *of*) to have a suggestion (of). **7** (*tr*) to season. **8** (*tr*) to taste or smell, esp. appreciatively. **9** (*tr*) to relish or enjoy. [C13: from OF *savour,* from L *sapor* taste, from *sapere* to taste]
▸'**savourless** *or US* '**savorless** *adj*

savoury ➊ *or US* **savory** ('seɪvərɪ) *adj* **1** attractive to the sense of taste or smell. **2** salty or spicy: *a savoury dish.* **3** pleasant. **4** respectable. ◆ *n, pl* **savouries** *or US* **savories. 5** *Chiefly Brit.* a savoury dish served as an hors d'oeuvre or dessert. [C13 *savure,* from OF, from *savourer* to SAVOUR]
▸'**savouriness** *or US* '**savoriness** *n*

savoy (sə'vɔɪ) *n* a cultivated variety of cabbage having a compact head and wrinkled leaves. [C16: after the *Savoy* region in France]

Savoyard (sə'vɔɪɑːd; *French* savwajar) *n* **1.** a native of Savoy, region in SE France. **2** the dialect of French spoken in Savoy. ◆ *adj* **3** of or relating to Savoy, its inhabitants, or their dialect.

savvy ➊ ('sævɪ) *Sl.* ◆ *vb* **savvies, savvying, savvied. 1** to understand or get the sense of (an idea, etc.). ◆ *n* **2** comprehension. ◆ *adj* **savvier, savviest. 3** *Chiefly US.* shrewd. [C18: corruption of Sp. *sabe* (*usted*) (you) know, from *saber* to know, from L *sapere* to be wise]

saw[1] (sɔː) *n* **1** any of various hand tools for cutting wood, metal, etc., having a blade with teeth along one edge. **2** any of various machines or devices for cutting by use of a toothed blade, such as a power-driven toothed band of metal. ◆ *vb* **saws, sawing, sawed; sawed** *or* **sawn. 3** to cut with a saw. **4** to form by sawing. **5** to cut as if wielding a saw: *to saw the air.* **6** to move (an object) from side to side as if moving a saw. [OE *sagu:* rel. to L *secare* to cut]
▸'**sawer** *n* ▸'**saw,like** *adj*

saw[2] (sɔː) *vb* the past tense of **see**[1].

saw[3] ➊ (sɔː) *n* a wise saying, maxim, or proverb. [OE *sagu* a saying]

sawbones ('sɔːˌbəunz) *n, pl* **sawbones** *or* **sawboneses.** *Sl.* a surgeon or doctor.

sawdust ('sɔːˌdʌst) *n* particles of wood formed by sawing.

sawfish ('sɔːˌfɪʃ) *n, pl* **sawfish** *or* **sawfishes.** a sharklike ray of subtropical coastal waters, having a serrated bladelike mouth.

sawfly ('sɔːˌflaɪ) *n, pl* **sawflies.** any of various hymenopterous insects, the females of which have a sawlike ovipositor.

sawhorse ('sɔːˌhɔːs) *n* a stand for timber during sawing.

sawmill ('sɔːˌmɪl) *n* an industrial establishment where timber is sawn into planks, etc.

sawn (sɔːn) *vb* a past participle of **saw**[1].

THESAURUS

savage *adj* **1** = **wild,** feral, undomesticated, untamed **2** = **cruel,** barbarous, beastly, bestial, bloodthirsty, bloody, brutal, brutish, devilish, diabolical, ferocious, fierce, harsh, inhuman, merciless, murderous, pitiless, ravening, ruthless, sadistic, vicious **3** = **uncultivated,** rough, rugged, uncivilized **4** = **primitive,** in a state of nature, nonliterate, rude, unspoilt ◆ *n* **6** = **primitive,** autochthon, barbarian, heathen, indigene, native **7** = **brute,** beast, fiend, monster ◆ *vb* **8** = **criticise,** attack, tear into (*inf.*) **9** = **attack,** lacerate, mangle, maul
Antonyms *adj* ≠ **wild:** domesticated, tame ≠ **cruel:** gentle, humane, kind, merciful, mild, restrained ≠ **uncultivated:** civilized, cultivated, refined ◆ *vb* ≠ **criticise:** acclaim, celebrate, praise, rave about (*inf.*)

savagery *n* **1, 2** = **cruelty,** barbarity, bestiality, bloodthirstiness, brutality, ferocity, fierceness, inhumanity, ruthlessness, sadism, viciousness

savant *n* = **sage,** authority, intellectual, mahatma, master, mastermind, philosopher, scholar

save[1] *vb* **1** = **rescue,** bail (someone) out, come to (someone's) rescue, deliver, free, liberate, recover, redeem, salvage, save (someone's) bacon (*Brit. inf.*), set free **2** = **protect,** conserve, guard, keep safe, look after, preserve, safeguard, screen, shield, take care of **4** = **keep,** be frugal, be thrifty, collect, economize, gather, hide away, hoard, hold, husband, keep up one's sleeve (*inf.*), lay by, put aside for a rainy day, put by, reserve, retrench, salt away, set aside, store, tighten one's belt (*inf.*), treasure up **6** = **prevent,** obviate, rule out, spare
Antonyms *vb* ≠ **rescue, protect:** abandon, endanger, expose, imperil, risk, threaten ≠ **keep:** be extravagant (with), blow (*sl.*), consume, discard, fritter away, spend, splurge, squander, use, use up, waste

saving *adj* **2** *As in* **saving grace** = **redeeming,** compensatory, extenuating, qualifying ◆ *n* **7** = **economy,** bargain, discount, reduction **9** *plural* = **nest egg,** fall-back, fund, provision for a rainy day, reserves, resources, store

saviour *n* = **rescuer,** defender, deliverer, friend in need, Good Samaritan, guardian, knight in shining armour, liberator, preserver, protector, redeemer, salvation

Saviour *n* = **Christ,** Jesus, Messiah, Redeemer

savoir-faire *n* = **social know-how** (*inf.*), accomplishment, address, diplomacy, discretion, finesse, poise, social graces, tact, urbanity

savour *n* **1** = **flavour,** piquancy, relish, smack, smell, tang, taste, zest, zing (*inf.*) **3** = **trace,** distinctive quality **4** = **zest,** excitement, flavour, interest, salt, spice ◆ *vb* **6** *with* **of** = **suggest,** bear the hallmarks of, be indicative of, be suggestive of, partake of, show signs of, smack of, verge on **9** = **enjoy,** appreciate, delight in, drool, enjoy to the full, gloat over, like, luxuriate in, partake, relish, revel in, smack one's lips over

savoury *adj* **1** = **tasty,** agreeable, appetizing, dainty, delectable, delicious, full-flavoured, good, luscious, mouthwatering, palatable, piquant, rich, scrumptious (*inf.*), spicy, tangy, toothsome **4** = **wholesome,** apple-pie (*inf.*), decent, edifying, honest, reputable, respectable
Antonyms *adj* ≠ **tasty:** insipid, tasteless, unappetizing, unpalatable, unpleasant, wersh (*Scot.*) ≠ **wholesome:** disreputable, distasteful, nasty, unpleasant, unsavoury

savvy *Slang vb* **1** = **understand,** apprehend, catch on, catch the drift, comprehend, get the gist, grasp, perceive, take in ◆ *n* **2** = **understanding,** apprehension, comprehension, grasp, ken, perception

saw[3] *n* = **saying,** adage, aphorism, apophthegm, axiom, byword, dictum, gnome, maxim, proverb

sawn-off *or esp. US* **sawed-off** *adj (prenominal)* (of a shotgun) having the barrel cut short, mainly to facilitate concealment of the weapon.

saw set *n* a tool used for setting the teeth of a saw, consisting of a clamp used to bend each tooth at a slight angle to the plane of the saw, alternate teeth being bent in the same direction.

sawyer (ˈsɔːjə) *n* a person who saws timber for a living. [C14 *sawier,* from SAW[1] + *-ier,* var. of -ER[1]]

sax (sæks) *n Inf.* short for **saxophone.**

saxe blue (sæks) *n* **a** a light greyish-blue colour. **b** *(as adj): a saxe-blue dress.* [C19: from F *Saxe* Saxony, source of a dye of this colour]

saxhorn (ˈsæksˌhɔːn) *n* a valved brass instrument used chiefly in brass and military bands, having a tube of conical bore. It resembles the tuba. [C19: after Adolphe *Sax* (see SAXOPHONE), who invented it (1845)]

saxicolous (sækˈsɪkələs) *adj* living on or among rocks: *saxicolous plants.* Also: **saxicole** (ˈsæksɪˌkəʊl), **saxatile** (ˈsæksəˌtaɪl). [C19: from NL *saxicolus,* from L *saxum* rock + *colere* to dwell]

saxifrage (ˈsæksɪˌfreɪdʒ) *n* a plant having small white, yellow, purple, or pink flowers. [C15: from LL *saxifraga,* lit.: rock-breaker, from L *saxum* rock + *frangere* to break]

Saxon (ˈsæksən) *n* **1** a member of a West Germanic people who raided and settled parts of S Britain in the fifth and sixth centuries A.D. **2** a native or inhabitant of Saxony, in SE Germany. **3a** the Low German dialect of Saxony. **3b** any of the West Germanic dialects spoken by the ancient Saxons. ◆ *adj* **4** of or characteristic of the ancient Saxons, the Anglo-Saxons, or their descendants. **5** of or characteristic of Saxony, its inhabitants, or their Low German dialect. [C13 (replacing OE *Seaxe*): via OF from LL *Saxon-, Saxo,* from Gk; of Gmc origin]

saxophone (ˈsæksəˌfəʊn) *n* a keyed single-reed wind instrument of mellow tone colour, used mainly in jazz and dance music. Often shortened to **sax.** [C19: after Adolphe *Sax* (1814–94), Belgian musical-instrument maker, who invented it (1846)]
►**saxophonic** (ˌsæksəˈfɒnɪk) *adj* ►**saxophonist** (sækˈsɒfənɪst) *n*

say Ⓣ (seɪ) *vb* **says, saying, said.** *(mainly tr)* **1** to speak, pronounce, or utter. **2** *(also intr)* to express (an idea, etc.) in words; tell. **3** *(also intr; may take a clause as object)* to state (an opinion, fact, etc.) positively. **4** to recite: *to say grace.* **5** *(may take a clause as object)* to report or allege: *they say we shall have rain today.* **6** *(may take a clause as object)* to suppose: *let us say that he is lying.* **7** *(may take a clause as object)* to convey by means of artistic expression. **8** to make a case for: *there is much to be said for it.* **9 go without saying.** to be so obvious as to need no explanation. **10 I say!** *Inf., chiefly Brit.* an exclamation of surprise. **11 not to say.** even. **12 that is to say.** in other words. **13 to say the least.** at the very least. ◆ *adv* **14** approximately: *there were, say, 20 people present.* **15** for example: *choose a number, say, four.* ◆ *n* **16** the right or chance to speak: *let him have his say.* **17** authority, esp. to influence a decision: *he has a lot of say.* **18** a statement of opinion: *you've had your say.* ◆ *interj* **19** *US & Canad. inf.* an exclamation to attract attention or express surprise. [OE *secgan*]
►ˈ**sayer** *n*

SAYE (in Britain) *abbrev. for* save as you earn.

saying Ⓣ (ˈseɪɪŋ) *n* a maxim, adage, or proverb.

say-so Ⓣ *n Inf.* **1** an arbitrary assertion. **2** an authoritative decision. **3** the authority to make a final decision.

sayyid (ˈsaɪɪd) *or* **said** *n* **1** a Muslim claiming descent from Mohammed's grandson Husain. **2** a Muslim honorary title. [C17: from Ar.: lord]

Sb *the chemical symbol for* antimony. [from NL *stibium*]

SBU *abbrev. for* strategic business unit: a division within an organization responsible for marketing its own range of products.

sc *Printing. abbrev. for* small capitals.

Sc *the chemical symbol for* scandium.

SC *abbrev. for:* **1** *NZ.* School Certificate. **2** Signal Corps. **3** *Canad.* Social Credit.

sc. *abbrev. for:* **1** scale. **2** scene. **3** science. **4** scilicet. **5** screw. **6** scruple (unit of weight).

scab (skæb) *n* **1** the dried crusty surface of a healing skin wound or sore. **2** a contagious disease of sheep resembling mange, caused by a mite. **3** a fungal disease of plants characterized by crusty spots on the fruits, leaves, etc. **4** *Derog.* **4a** Also called: **blackleg.** a person who refuses to support a trade union's actions, esp. strikes. **4b** *(as modifier): scab labour.* **5** a despicable person. ◆ *vb* **scabs, scabbing, scabbed.** *(intr)* **6** to become covered with a scab. **7** to replace a striking worker. [OE *sceabb*]

scabbard (ˈskæbəd) *n* a holder for a bladed weapon such as a sword or bayonet. [C13 *scauberc,* from Norman F *escaubers,* (pl) of Gmc origin]

scabby (ˈskæbɪ) *adj* **scabbier, scabbiest. 1** *Pathol.* having an area of the skin covered with scabs. **2** *Pathol.* having scabies. **3** *Inf.* despicable.
►ˈ**scabbily** *adv* ►ˈ**scabbiness** *n*

scabies (ˈskeɪbiːz) *n* a contagious skin infection caused by a mite, characterized by intense itching and inflammation. [C15: from L: scurf, from *scabere* to scratch]

scabious[1] (ˈskeɪbɪəs) *adj* **1** having or covered with scabs. **2** of, relating to, or resembling scabies. [C17: from L *scabiōsus,* from SCABIES]

scabious[2] (ˈskeɪbɪəs) *n* any of a genus of plants of the Mediterranean region, having blue, red, or whitish dome-shaped flower heads. [C14: from Med. L *scabiōsa herba* the scabies plant, referring to its use in treating scabies]

scabrous (ˈskeɪbrəs) *adj* **1** roughened because of small projections. **2** indecent or salacious: *scabrous humour.* **3** difficult to deal with. [C17: from L *scaber* rough]
►ˈ**scabrously** *adv*

scad (skæd) *n, pl* **scad** *or* **scads.** any of various marine fishes having a deeply forked tail, such as the large mackerel. [C17: from ?]

scads (skædz) *pl n Inf.* a large amount or number. [C19: from ?]

scaffold (ˈskæfəld) *n* **1** a temporary framework that is used to support workmen and materials during the erection, repair, etc., of a building. **2** a raised wooden platform on which plays are performed, tobacco, etc., is dried, or (esp. formerly) criminals are executed. ◆ *vb (tr)* **3** to provide with a scaffold. **4** to support by means of a scaffold. [C14: from OF *eschaffaut,* from Vulgar L *catafalicum* (unattested)]
►ˈ**scaffolder** *n*

scaffolding (ˈskæfəldɪŋ) *n* **1** a scaffold or system of scaffolds. **2** the building materials used to make scaffolds.

scalable (ˈskeɪləbᵊl) *adj* capable of being climbed.
►ˈ**scalableness** *n* ►ˈ**scalably** *adv*

scalar (ˈskeɪlə) *n* **1** a quantity, such as time or temperature, that has magnitude but not direction. **2** *Maths.* an element of a field associated with a vector space. ◆ *adj* **3** having magnitude but not direction. [C17 (meaning: resembling a ladder): from L *scālāris,* from *scāla* ladder]

scalar product *n* the product of two vectors to form a scalar, whose value is the product of the magnitudes of the vectors and the cosine of the angle between them. Also called: **dot product.**

scalawag (ˈskæləˌwæg) *n* a variant of **scallywag.**

scald[1] (skɔːld) *vb* **1** to burn or be burnt with or as if with hot liquid or steam. **2** *(tr)* to subject to the action of boiling water, esp. so as to sterilize. **3** *(tr)* to heat (a liquid) almost to boiling point. **4** to plunge (tomatoes, etc.) into boiling water in order to skin them more easily. ◆ *n* **5** the act or result of scalding. **6** an abnormal condition in plants, caused by exposure to excessive sunlight, gases, etc. [C13: via OF from LL *excaldāre* to wash in warm water, from *calida (aqua)* warm (water), from *calēre* to be warm]
►ˈ**scalder** *n*

scald[2] (skɔːld) *n* a variant spelling of **skald.**

scaldfish (ˈskɔːldˌfɪʃ, ˈskɑːld-) *n, pl* **scaldfish** *or* **scaldfishes.** a small European flatfish, covered with large fragile scales.

scale[1] Ⓣ (skeɪl) *n* **1** any of the numerous plates, made of various substances, covering the bodies of fishes. **2a** any of the horny or chitinous plates covering a part or the entire body of certain reptiles and mammals. **2b** any of the numerous minute structures covering the wings of lepidoptera. **3** a thin flat piece or flake. **4** a thin flake of dead epidermis shed from the skin. **5** a specialized leaf or bract, esp. the protective covering of a bud or the dry membranous bract of a catkin. **6** See **scale insect. 7** any oxide formed on a metal when heated. **8** tartar formed on the teeth. ◆ *vb* **scales, scaling, scaled. 9** *(tr)* to remove the scales or coating from. **10** to peel off or cause to peel off in flakes or scales. **11** *(intr)* to shed scales. **12** to cover or become covered with scales, incrustation, etc. [C14: from OF *escale,* of Gmc origin]

scale[2] (skeɪl) *n* **1** *(often pl)* a machine or device for weighing. **2** one of the pans of a balance. **3 tip the scales. 3a** to exercise a decisive influence. **3b** (foll. by *at*) to amount in weight (to). ◆ *vb* **scales, scaling, scaled.** *(tr)* **4** to weigh with or as if with scales. [C13: from ON *skāl* bowl]

scale[3] Ⓣ (skeɪl) *n* **1** a sequence of marks either at regular intervals, or representing equal steps, used as a reference in making measurements. **2** a measuring instrument having such a scale. **3a** the ratio between the size of something real and that of a representation of it. **3b** *(as modifier): a scale model.* **4** a line, numerical ratio, etc., for showing

THESAURUS

say *vb* **1 = speak**, add, affirm, announce, assert, asseverate, come out with (*inf.*), declare, express, give voice *or* utterance to, maintain, mention, pronounce, put into words, remark, state, utter, voice **3 = tell**, answer, disclose, divulge, give as one's opinion, make known, reply, respond, reveal **4 = recite**, deliver, do, orate, perform, read, rehearse, render, repeat **5 = report**, allege, bruit, claim, noise abroad, put about, rumour, suggest **6 = suppose**, assume, conjecture, dare say, estimate, guess, hazard a guess, imagine, judge, presume, surmise **7 = express**, communicate, convey, give the impression that, imply **9 go without saying = be obvious**, be accepted, be a matter of course, be self-evident, be taken as read, be taken for granted, be understood **13 to say the least = at the very least**, to put it mildly, without any exaggeration ◆ *n* **16 = chance to speak**, crack (*inf.*), opportunity to speak, turn to speak, voice, vote **17 = influence**, authority, clout (*inf.*), power, sway, weight

saying *n* **= proverb**, adage, aphorism, apophthegm, axiom, byword, dictum, gnome, maxim, saw, slogan

say-so *n Informal* **1 = assertion**, asseveration, assurance, dictum, guarantee, word **2 = authorization**, agreement, assent, authority, consent, O.K. *or* okay (*inf.*), permission, sanction

scale[1] *n* **3 = flake**, lamina, layer, plate, squama (*Biology*)

scale[3] *n* **1 = graduation**, calibration, degrees, gamut, gradation, graduated system, hierarchy, ladder, pecking order (*inf.*), progression, ranking, register, seniority system, sequence, series, spectrum, spread, steps **3 = ratio**, proportion **7 = degree**, extent, range, reach, scope, way ◆ *vb* **10 = climb**, ascend, clamber, escalade, mount, surmount **12 = adjust**, proportion, prorate (*chiefly US*), regulate

this ratio. **5** a progressive or graduated table of things, wages, etc.: *a wage scale for carpenters.* **6** an established standard. **7** a relative degree or extent: *he entertained on a grand scale.* **8** *Music.* a group of notes taken in ascending or descending order, esp. within the compass of one octave. **9** *Maths.* the notation of a given number system: *the decimal scale.* ◆ *vb* **scales, scaling, scaled. 10** to climb to the top of (a height) by or as if by a ladder. **11** (*tr*) to make or draw (a model, etc.) according to a particular ratio of proportionate reduction. **12** (*tr*; usually foll. by *up* or *down*) to increase or reduce proportionately in size, etc. **13** (*intr*) *Austral. inf.* to ride on public transport without paying a fare. [C15: via It. from L *scāla* ladder]

scaleboard (ˈskeɪlˌbɔːd) *n* a very thin piece of board, used for backing a picture, etc.

scale insect *n* a small insect which typically lives and feeds on plants and secretes a protective scale around itself. Many species are pests.

scalene (ˈskeɪliːn) *adj* **1** *Maths.* (of a triangle) having all sides of unequal length. **2** *Anat.* of or relating to any of the scalenus muscles. [C17: from LL *scalēnus* with unequal sides, from Gk *skalēnos*]

scalenus (skəˈliːnəs) *n, pl* **scaleni** (-naɪ). *Anat.* any one of the three muscles situated on each side of the neck extending from the cervical vertebrae to the first or second pair of ribs. [C18: from NL; see SCALENE]

scaling ladder *n* a ladder used to climb high walls, esp. one used formerly to enter a besieged town, fortress, etc.

scallion (ˈskæljən) *n* any of various onions, such as the spring onion, that have a small bulb and long leaves and are eaten in salads. [C14: from Anglo-F *scalun,* from L *Ascalōnia* (*caepa*) Ascalonian (onion), from *Ascalo* Ascalon, a Palestinian port]

scallop (ˈskɒləp, ˈskæl-) *n* **1** any of various marine bivalves having a fluted fan-shaped shell. **2** the edible adductor muscle of certain of these molluscs. **3** either of the shell valves of any of these molluscs. **4** a scallop shell in which fish, esp. shellfish, is cooked and served. **5** one of a series of curves along an edge. **6** the shape of a scallop shell used as the badge of a pilgrim, esp. in the Middle Ages. **7** *Chiefly Austral.* a potato cake fried in batter. ◆ *vb* **8** (*tr*) to decorate (an edge) with scallops. **9** to bake (food) in a scallop shell or similar dish. [C14: from OF *escalope* shell, of Gmc origin]
▸ **ˈscalloper** *n* ▸ **ˈscalloping** *n*

scally (ˈskælɪ) *n, pl* **scallies.** *Northwest English dialect.* a rascal; rogue. [C20: from SCALLYWAG]

scallywag (ˈskælɪˌwæg) *n Inf.* a scamp; rascal. ◆ Also: **scalawag, scallawag.** [C19: (orig. undersized animal): from ?]

scalp (skælp) *n* **1** *Anat.* the skin and subcutaneous tissue covering the top of the head. **2** (among North American Indians) a part of this removed as a trophy from a slain enemy. **3** a trophy or token signifying conquest. **4** *Scot. dialect.* a projection of bare rock from vegetation. ◆ *vb* (*tr*) **5** to cut the scalp from. **6** *Inf., chiefly US.* to purchase and resell (securities) quickly so as to make several small profits. **7** *Inf.* to buy (tickets) cheaply and resell at an inflated price. [C13: prob. from ON]
▸ **ˈscalper** *n*

scalpel (ˈskælpəl) *n* a surgical knife with a short thin blade. [C18: from L *scalpellum,* from *scalper* a knife, from *scalpere* to scrape]

scaly Ⓣ (ˈskeɪlɪ) *adj* **scalier, scaliest. 1** resembling or covered in scales. **2** peeling off in scales.
▸ **ˈscaliness** *n*

scaly anteater *n* another name for **pangolin.**

scamp[1] Ⓣ (skæmp) *n* **1** an idle mischievous person. **2** a mischievous child. [C18: from *scamp* (vb) to be a highway robber, prob. from MDu. *schampen* to decamp, from OF *escamper,* from L *campus* field]
▸ **ˈscampish** *adj*

scamp[2] (skæmp) *vb* a less common word for **skimp.**
▸ **ˈscamper** *n*

scamper Ⓣ (ˈskæmpə) *vb* **1** (*intr*) to run about playfully. **2** (often foll. by *through*) to hurry through (a place, task, etc.) ◆ *n* **3** the act of scampering. [C17: prob. from *scamp* (vb); see SCAMP[1]]

scampi (ˈskæmpɪ) *n* (*usually functioning as sing*) large prawns, usually eaten fried in breadcrumbs. [It.: pl of *scampo* shrimp, from ?]

scan Ⓣ (skæn) *vb* **scans, scanning, scanned. 1** (*tr*) to scrutinize minutely. **2** (*tr*) to glance at quickly. **3** (*tr*) *Prosody.* to read or analyse (verse) according to the rules of metre and versification. **4** (*intr*) *Prosody.* to conform to the rules of metre and versification. **5** (*tr*) *Electronics.* to move a beam of light, electrons, etc., in a predetermined pattern over (a surface or region) to obtain information, esp. to reproduce a television image. **6** (*tr*) to examine data stored on (magnetic tape, etc.), usually in order to retrieve information. **7** to examine or search (a prescribed region) by systematically varying the direction of a radar or sonar beam. **8** *Med.* to obtain an image of (a part of the body) by means of a scanner. ◆ *n* **9** the act or an instance of scanning. **10** *Med.* **10a** the examination of a part of the body by means of a scanner: *a brain scan, an ultrasound scan.* **10b** the image produced by a scanner. [C14: from LL *scandere* to scan (verse), from L: to climb]
▸ **ˈscannable** *adj*

Scand. *or* **Scan.** *abbrev. for* Scandinavia(n).

scandal Ⓣ (ˈskændəl) *n* **1** a disgraceful action or event: *his negligence was a scandal.* **2** censure or outrage arising from an action or event. **3** a person whose conduct causes reproach or disgrace. **4** malicious talk, esp. gossip. **5** *Law.* a libellous action or statement. [C16: from LL *scandalum* stumbling block, from Gk *skandalon* a trap]
▸ **ˈscandalous** *adj* ▸ **ˈscandalously** *adv*

scandalize Ⓣ *or* **scandalise** (ˈskændəˌlaɪz) *vb* **scandalizes, scandalizing, scandalized** *or* **scandalises, scandalising, scandalised.** (*tr*) to shock, as by improper behaviour.
▸ **ˌscandaliˈzation** *or* **ˌscandaliˈsation** *n*

scandalmonger Ⓣ (ˈskændəlˌmʌŋgə) *n* a person who spreads or enjoys scandal, gossip, etc.

Scandinavian (ˌskændɪˈneɪvɪən) *adj* **1** of or characteristic of Scandinavia (Norway, Sweden, Denmark, and Iceland), its inhabitants, or their languages. ◆ *n* **2** a native or inhabitant of Scandinavia. **3** the group of Germanic languages, consisting of Swedish, Danish, Norwegian, Icelandic, and Faeroese.

scandium (ˈskændɪəm) *n* a rare silvery-white metallic element occurring in minute quantities in numerous minerals. Symbol: Sc; atomic no.: 21; atomic wt.: 44.96. [C19: from NL, from L *Scandia* Scandinavia, where discovered]

scanner (ˈskænə) *n* **1** a person or thing that scans. **2** a device, usually electronic, used to measure or sample the distribution of some quantity or condition in a particular system, region, or area. **3** an aerial or similar device designed to transmit or receive signals, esp. radar signals, inside a given solid angle of space. **4** any device used in medical diagnosis to obtain an image of an internal organ or part. **5** short for **optical scanner.**

scanning electron microscope *n* a type of electron microscope that produces a three-dimensional image.

scansion (ˈskænʃən) *n* the analysis of the metrical structure of verse. [C17: from L: climbing up, from *scandere* to climb]

scant Ⓣ (skænt) *adj* **1** scarcely sufficient: *he paid her scant attention.* **2** (*prenominal*) bare: *a scant ten inches.* **3** (*postpositive;* foll. by *of*) having a short supply (of). ◆ *vb* (*tr*) **4** to limit in size or quantity. **5** to provide with a limited supply of. **6** to treat in an inadequate manner. ◆ *adv* **7** scarcely; barely. [C14: from ON *skamt,* from *skammr* short]
▸ **ˈscantly** *adv*

scantling (ˈskæntlɪŋ) *n* **1** a piece of sawn timber, such as a rafter, that has a small cross section. **2** the dimensions of a piece of building material or the structural parts of a ship or aircraft. **3** a building stone. **4** a small quantity or amount. [C16: changed (through infl. of SCANT & -LING[1]) from earlier *scantillon* a carpenter's gauge, from OF *escantillon,* ult. from L *scandere* to climb]

scanty Ⓣ (ˈskæntɪ) *adj* **scantier, scantiest. 1** limited; barely enough. **2** inadequate. **3** lacking fullness.
▸ **ˈscantily** *adv* ▸ **ˈscantiness** *n*

scape *or* **ˈscape** (skeɪp) *vb* **scapes, scaping, scaped,** *n* an archaic word for **escape.**

-scape *suffix forming nouns.* indicating a scene or view of something: *seascape.* [from LANDSCAPE]

scapegoat Ⓣ (ˈskeɪpˌgəʊt) *n* **1** a person made to bear the blame for others. **2** *Bible.* a goat symbolically laden with the sins of the Israelites and sent into the wilderness. ◆ *vb* **3** (*tr*) to make a scapegoat of. [C16: from ESCAPE + GOAT, coined by William Tyndale to translate Biblical Heb. *azāzēl* (prob.) goat for Azazel, mistakenly thought to mean "goat that escapes"]

scapegrace Ⓣ (ˈskeɪpˌgreɪs) *n* a mischievous person. [C19: from SCAPE + GRACE, alluding to a person who lacks God's grace]

scaphoid (ˈskæfɔɪd) *adj Anat.* an obsolete word for **navicular.** [C18: via NL from Gk *skaphoeidēs,* from *skaphē* boat]

scapula (ˈskæpjʊlə) *n, pl* **scapulae** (-liː) *or* **scapulas.** either of two large flat

THESAURUS

scaly *adj* **1** = **flaky,** furfuraceous (*Medical*), scabrous, scurfy, squamous *or* squamose (*Biology*), squamulose

scamp[1] *n* **1** = **rascal,** devil, imp, knave (*arch.*), mischief-maker, monkey, pickle (*Brit. inf.*), prankster, rogue, scallywag (*inf.*), scapegrace, toerag (*sl.*), tyke (*inf.*), whippersnapper, wretch

scamper *vb* **2** = **run,** beetle, dart, dash, fly, hasten, hie (*arch.*), hurry, romp, scoot, scurry, scuttle, sprint

scan *vb* **1** = **scrutinize,** con (*arch.*), investigate, recce (*sl.*), scour, search, survey, sweep, take stock of **2** = **glance over,** check, check out (*inf.*), clock (*Brit. sl.*), examine, eye, eyeball (*sl.*), get a load of (*inf.*), look one up and down, look through, run one's eye over, run over, size up (*inf.*), skim, take a dekko at (*Brit. sl.*)

scandal *n* **1** = **crime,** crying shame (*inf.*), disgrace, embarrassment, offence, sin, skeleton in the cupboard, wrongdoing **2** = **shame,** calumny, defamation, detraction, discredit, disgrace, dishonour, ignominy, infamy, obloquy, offence, opprobrium, reproach, stigma **4** = **gossip,** abuse, aspersion, backbiting, dirt, dirty linen (*inf.*), rumours, slander, talk, tattle

scandalize *vb* = **shock,** affront, appal, cause a few raised eyebrows (*inf.*), disgust, horrify, offend, outrage, raise eyebrows

scandalmonger *n* = **gossip,** calumniator, defamer, destroyer of reputations, muckraker, tattle, tattler, traducer

scandalous *adj* **1** = **shocking,** atrocious, disgraceful, disreputable, highly improper, infamous, monstrous, odious, opprobrious, outrageous, shameful, unseemly **4** = **slanderous,** defamatory, gossiping, libellous, scurrilous, untrue
Antonyms *adj* ≠ **shocking:** decent, proper, reputable, respectable, seemly, upright ≠ **slanderous:** laudatory, unimpeachable

scant *adj* **1** = **meagre,** bare, barely sufficient, deficient, inadequate, insufficient, limited, little, minimal, sparse
Antonyms *adj* abundant, adequate, ample, full, generous, plentiful, satisfactory, sufficient

scanty *adj* **1-3** = **meagre,** bare, deficient, exiguous, inadequate, insufficient, narrow, pathetic, poor, restricted, scant, short, skimpy, slender, sparing, sparse, thin

scapegoat *n* **1** = **whipping boy,** fall guy (*inf.*)

scapegrace *n* = **scamp,** bad lot (*inf.*), good-for-nothing, limb of Satan, ne'er-do-well, rascal, rogue, scallywag (*inf.*)

triangular bones, one on each side of the back part of the shoulder in man. Nontechnical name: **shoulder blade.** [C16: from LL: shoulder]

scapular ('skæpjulə) *adj* **1** *Anat.* of or relating to the scapula. ◆ *n* **2** part of the monastic habit worn by members of many Christian religious orders, consisting of a piece of woollen cloth worn over the shoulders, and hanging down to the ankles. **3** two small rectangular pieces of cloth joined by tapes passing over the shoulders and worn in token of affiliation to a religious order. **4** any of the small feathers of a bird that lie along the shoulder. ◆ Also called (for senses 2 and 3): **scapulary.**

scar[1] ❶ (skɑː) *n* **1** any mark left on the skin or other tissue following the healing of a wound, etc. **2** a permanent change in a person's character resulting from emotional distress. **3** the mark on a plant indicating the former point of attachment of a part. **4** a mark of damage. ◆ *vb* **scars, scarring, scarred. 5** to mark or become marked with a scar. **6** (*intr*) to heal leaving a scar. [C14: via LL from Gk *eskhara* scab]

scar[2] (skɑː) *n* a bare craggy rock formation. [C14: from ON *sker* low reef]

scarab ('skærəb) *n* **1** any scarabaeid beetle, esp. the **sacred scarab,** regarded by the ancient Egyptians as divine. **2** the scarab as represented on amulets, etc. [C16: from L *scarabaeus*]

scarabaeid (ˌskærə'biːɪd) *n* **1** any of a family of beetles including the sacred scarab and other dung beetles, the chafers, and rhinoceros beetles. ◆ *adj* **2** of or belonging to this family. [C19: from NL]

Scaramouch ('skærəˌmuːʃ) *n* a stock character who appears as a boastful coward in commedia dell'arte. [C17: via F from It. *Scaramuccia,* from *scaramuccia* a SKIRMISH]

scarce ❶ (skɛəs) *adj* **1** rarely encountered. **2** insufficient to meet the demand. **3 make oneself scarce.** *Inf.* to go away. ◆ *adv* **4** *Arch. or literary.* scarcely. [C13: from OF *scars,* from Vulgar L *excarpsus* (unattested) plucked out, from L *excerpere* to select]
▸ **'scarceness** *n*

scarcely ❶ ('skɛəslɪ) *adv* **1** hardly at all. **2** *Often used ironically.* probably or definitely not: *that is scarcely justification for your actions.*

> **USAGE NOTE** See at **hardly.**

scarcity ❶ ('skɛəsɪtɪ) *n, pl* **scarcities. 1** inadequate supply. **2** rarity or infrequent occurrence.

scare ❶ (skɛə) *vb* **scares, scaring, scared. 1** to fill or be filled with fear or alarm. **2** (*tr;* often foll. by *away* or *off*) to drive (away) by frightening. ◆ *n* **3** a sudden attack of fear or alarm. **4** a period of general fear or alarm. ◆ *adj* **5** causing (needless) fear or alarm: *a scare story.* [C12: from ON *skirra*]
▸ **'scarer** *n*

scarecrow ('skɛəˌkrəʊ) *n* **1** an object, usually in the shape of a man, made out of sticks and old clothes to scare birds away from crops. **2** a person or thing that appears frightening. **3** *Inf.* an untidy-looking person.

scaremonger ❶ ('skɛəˌmʌŋgə) *n* a person who delights in spreading rumours of disaster.
▸ **'scareˌmongering** *n*

scarf[1] (skɑːf) *n, pl* **scarves** *or* **scarfs.** a rectangular, triangular, or long narrow piece of cloth worn around the head, neck, or shoulders for warmth or decoration. [C16: from ?]

scarf[2] (skɑːf) *n, pl* **scarfs. 1** Also called: **scarf joint, scarfed joint.** a lapped joint between two pieces of timber made by notching the ends and strapping or gluing the two pieces together. **2** the end of a piece of timber shaped to form such a joint. **3** *Whaling.* an incision made along a whale before stripping off the blubber. ◆ *vb* (*tr*) **4** to join (two pieces of timber) by means of a scarf. **5** to make a scarf on (a piece of timber). **6** to cut a scarf in (a whale). [C14: prob. from ON]

scarfskin ('skɑːfˌskɪn) *n* the outermost layer of the skin; epidermis or cuticle. [C17: from SCARF[1] (in the sense: an outer covering)]

scarify ('skɛərɪˌfaɪ, 'skærɪ-) *vb* **scarifies, scarifying, scarified.** (*tr*) **1** *Surgery.* to make tiny punctures or superficial incisions in (the skin or other tissue), as for inoculating. **2** *Agriculture.* to break up and loosen (soil) to a shallow depth. **3** to wound with harsh criticism. [C15: via OF from L *scarīfāre* to scratch open, from Gk *skariphasthai* to draw, from *skariphos* a pencil]
▸ **ˌscarifi'cation** *n* ▸ **'scariˌfier** *n*

> **USAGE NOTE** *Scarify* is sometimes wrongly thought to mean the same as *scare: a frightening* (not *scarifying*) *film.*

scarlatina (ˌskɑːlə'tiːnə) *n* the technical name for **scarlet fever.** [C19: from NL, from It. *scarlattina,* dim. of *scarlatto* scarlet]

scarlet ('skɑːlɪt) *n* **1** a vivid orange-red colour. **2** cloth or clothing of this colour. ◆ *adj* **3** of the colour scarlet. **4** sinful or immoral. [C13: from OF *escarlate* fine cloth, from ?]

scarlet fever *n* an acute communicable disease characterized by fever, strawberry-coloured tongue, and a rash starting on the neck and chest and spreading to the abdomen and limbs. Technical name: **scarlatina.**

scarlet letter *n* (esp. among US Puritans) a scarlet letter *A* formerly worn by a person convicted of adultery.

scarlet pimpernel *n* a plant, related to the primrose, having small red, purple, or white star-shaped flowers that close in bad weather. Also called: **shepherd's** (or **poor man's**) **weatherglass.**

scarlet runner *n* a climbing perennial bean plant of South America, having scarlet flowers: widely cultivated for its long green edible pods containing edible seeds. Also: **runner bean.**

scarlet woman *n* **1** a sinful woman described in the Bible (Rev. 17), interpreted as a symbol of pagan Rome or of the Roman Catholic Church. **2** any sexually promiscuous woman.

scarp (skɑːp) *n* **1** a steep slope, esp. one formed by erosion or faulting. **2** *Fortifications.* the side of a ditch cut nearest to a rampart. ◆ *vb* **3** (*tr; often passive*) to wear or cut so as to form a steep slope. [C16: from It. *scarpa*]

scarper ❶ ('skɑːpə) *Brit. sl.* ◆ *vb* **1** (*intr*) to depart in haste. ◆ *n* **2** a hasty departure. [from ?]

Scart *or* **SCART** (skɑːt) *n Electronics.* **a** a 21-pin plug-and-socket system which carries picture, sound, and other signals, used especially in home entertainment systems. **b** (*as modifier*): *a Scart cable.* [C20: after Syndicat des Constructeurs des Appareils Radiorécepteurs et Téléviseurs, the company that designed it]

scarves (skɑːvz) *n* a plural of **scarf**[1].

scary ❶ ('skɛərɪ) *adj* **scarier, scariest.** *Inf.* **1** causing fear or alarm. **2** timid.

scat[1] (skæt) *vb* **scats, scatting, scatted.** (*intr; usually imperative*) *Inf.* to go away in haste. [C19: ?from a hiss + *cat,* used to frighten away cats]

scat[2] (skæt) *n* **1** a type of jazz singing characterized by improvised vocal sounds instead of words. ◆ *vb* **scats, scatting, scatted. 2** (*intr*) to sing jazz in this way. [C20: ? imit.]

scathe (skeɪð) *vb* **scathes, scathing, scathed.** (*tr*) **1** *Rare.* to attack with severe criticism. **2** *Arch. or dialect.* to injure. ◆ *n* **3** *Arch. or dialect.* harm. [OE *sceatha*]

scathing ❶ ('skeɪðɪŋ) *adj* **1** harshly critical; scornful. **2** damaging.
▸ **'scathingly** *adv*

scatology (skæ'tɒlədʒɪ) *n* **1** the scientific study of excrement, esp. in medicine and in palaeontology. **2** obscenity or preoccupation with obscenity, esp. in the form of references to excrement. [C19: from Gk *skat-* excrement + -LOGY]
▸ **scatological** (ˌskætə'lɒdʒɪkᵊl) *adj*

scatter ❶ ('skætə) *vb* **1** (*tr*) to throw about in various directions. **2** to separate and move or cause to separate and move in various directions. **3** to deviate or cause to deviate in many directions, as in the refraction of light. ◆ *n* **4** the act of scattering. **5** a substance or a number of objects scattered about. [C13: prob. a var. of SHATTER]
▸ **'scatterer** *n*

scatterbrain ❶ ('skætəˌbreɪn) *n* a person who is incapable of serious thought or concentration.
▸ **'scatterˌbrained** *adj*

scatter diagram *n Statistics.* a representation by a Cartesian graph of the correlation between two quantities, such as height and weight.

THESAURUS

scar[1] *n* **1 = mark,** blemish, cicatrix, injury, trauma (*Pathology*), wound ◆ *vb* **5 = mark,** brand, damage, disfigure, traumatize

scarce *adj* **1 = rare,** at a premium, deficient, few, few and far between, infrequent, in short supply, insufficient, seldom met with, thin on the ground, uncommon, unusual, wanting
Antonyms *adj* abundant, ample, common, commonplace, frequent, numerous, plenteous, plentiful, sufficient

scarcely *adv* **1 = hardly,** barely, only just, scarce (*arch.*) **2** *Often used ironically* **= definitely not,** by no means, hardly, not at all, on no account, under no circumstances

scarcity *n* **1 = shortage,** dearth, deficiency, infrequency, insufficiency, lack, paucity, poverty, rareness, undersupply, want
Antonyms *n* abundance, excess, glut, superfluity, surfeit, surplus

scare *vb* **1 = frighten,** affright (*arch.*), alarm, daunt, dismay, give (someone) a fright, give (someone) a turn (*inf.*), intimidate, panic, put the wind up (someone) (*inf.*), shock, startle, terrify, terrorize ◆ *n* **3 = fright,** alarm, alert, panic, shock, start, terror

scared *adj* **1 = frightened,** fearful, panicky, panic-stricken, petrified, shaken, startled, terrified

scaremonger *n* **= alarmist,** Calamity Jane, doom merchant (*inf.*), prophet of doom, spreader of despair and despondency

scarper *vb* **1 = run away,** abscond, beat a hasty retreat, beat it (*sl.*), clear off (*inf.*), cut and run (*inf.*), decamp, depart, disappear, do a bunk (*Brit. sl.*), flee, go, make off, make oneself scarce (*inf.*), run for it, scram (*inf.*), skedaddle (*inf.*), slope off, take flight, take oneself off, take to one's heels, vamoose (*sl., chiefly US*)

scary *adj* **1** *Informal* **= frightening,** alarming, bloodcurdling, chilling, creepy (*inf.*), hair-raising, hairy (*sl.*), horrendous, horrifying, intimidating, shocking, spine-chilling, spooky (*inf.*), terrifying, unnerving

scathing *adj* **1 = critical,** belittling, biting, brutal, caustic, cutting, harsh, mordacious, mordant, sarcastic, savage, scornful, searing, trenchant, vitriolic, withering

scatter *vb* **1 = throw about,** broadcast, diffuse, disseminate, fling, litter, shower, sow, spread, sprinkle, strew **2 = disperse,** disband, dispel, dissipate, disunite, put to flight, separate
Antonyms *vb* ≠ **throw about:** cluster, collect ≠ **disperse:** assemble, congregate, converge, rally, unite

scatterbrain *n* **= featherbrain,** bird-brain (*inf.*), butterfly, flibbertigibbet, grasshopper mind, madcap

scatterbrained *adj* **= empty-headed,** bird-brained (*inf.*), careless, featherbrained, forgetful, frivolous, giddy, goofy (*inf.*), inattentive, irresponsible, madcap, scatty (*Brit. inf.*), silly, slaphappy (*inf.*), thoughtless

scattering ❶ (ˈskætərɪŋ) *n* **1** a small amount. **2** *Physics.* the process in which particles, atoms, etc., are deflected as a result of collision.

scatty (ˈskætɪ) *adj* **scattier, scattiest.** *Brit. inf.* **1** empty-headed or thoughtless. **2** distracted (esp. in **drive someone scatty**). [C20: from SCATTERBRAINED]
▸ˈ**scattily** *adv* ▸ˈ**scattiness** *n*

scaup *or* **scaup duck** (skɔːp) *n* either of two diving ducks, the **greater scaup** or the **lesser scaup**, of Europe and America, having a black-and-white plumage in the male. [C16: Scot. var. of SCALP]

scavenge (ˈskævɪndʒ) *vb* **scavenges, scavenging, scavenged. 1** to search for (anything usable) among discarded material. **2** (*tr*) to purify (a molten metal) by bubbling a suitable gas through it. **3** to clean up filth from (streets, etc.).

scavenger (ˈskævɪndʒə) *n* **1** a person who collects things discarded by others. **2** any animal that feeds on decaying organic matter. **3** a person employed to clean the streets. [C16: from Anglo-Norman *scawager*, from OF *escauwage* examination, from *escauwer* to scrutinize, of Gmc origin]
▸ˈ**scavengery** *n*

ScD *abbrev. for* Doctor of Science.

SCE (in Scotland) *abbrev. for* Scottish Certificate of Education: either of two public examinations in specific subjects taken as school-leaving qualifications or as qualifying examinations for entry into a university, college, etc.

scena (ˈʃeɪnə) *n, pl* **scene** (-ˌneɪ). a solo vocal piece of dramatic style and large scope, esp. in opera. [C19: It., from L *scēna* scene]

scenario ❶ (sɪˈnɑːrɪˌəʊ) *n, pl* **scenarios. 1** a summary of the plot of a play, etc., including information about its characters, scenes, etc. **2** a predicted sequence of events. [C19: via It. from L *scēnārium*, from *scēna*; see SCENE]

scene ❶ (siːn) *n* **1** the place where an action or event, real or imaginary, occurs. **2** the setting for the action of a play, novel, etc. **3** an incident or situation, real or imaginary, esp. as described or represented. **4a** a subdivision of an act of a play, in which the setting is fixed. **4b** a single event, esp. a significant one, in a play. **5** *Films.* a shot or series of shots that constitutes a unit of the action. **6** the backcloths, etc., for a play or film set. **7** the prospect of a place, landscape, etc. **8** a display of emotion. **9** *Inf.* the environment for a specific activity: *the fashion scene.* **10** *Inf.* interest or chosen occupation: *classical music is not my scene.* **11** *Rare.* the stage. **12 behind the scenes.** out of public view. [C16: from L *scēna* theatrical stage, from Gk *skēnē* tent, stage]

scene dock *or* **bay** *n* a place in a theatre where scenery is stored, usually near the stage.

scenery ❶ (ˈsiːnərɪ) *n, pl* **sceneries. 1** the natural features of a landscape. **2** *Theatre.* the painted backcloths, etc., used to represent a location in a theatre or studio. [C18: from It. SCENARIO]

scenic ❶ (ˈsiːnɪk) *adj* **1** of or relating to natural scenery. **2** having beautiful natural scenery: *a scenic drive.* **3** of or relating to the stage or stage scenery. **4** (in painting, etc.) representing a scene.
▸ˈ**scenically** *adv*

scenic railway *n* a miniature railway used for amusement in a park, zoo, etc.

scenic reserve *n NZ.* an area of natural beauty, set aside for public recreation.

scent ❶ (sɛnt) *n* **1** a distinctive smell, esp. a pleasant one. **2** a smell left in passing, by which a person or animal may be traced. **3** a trail, clue, or guide. **4** an instinctive ability for detecting. **5** another word (esp. Brit.) for **perfume.** ◆ *vb* **6** (*tr*) to recognize by or as if by the smell. **7** (*tr*) to have a suspicion of: *I scent foul play.* **8** (*tr*) to fill with odour or fragrance. **9** (*intr*) (of hounds, etc.) to hunt by the sense of smell. **10** to smell (at): *the dog scented the air.* [C14: from OF *sentir* to sense, from L *sentīre* to feel]
▸ˈ**scented** *adj*

sceptic ❶ *or arch. & US* **skeptic** (ˈskɛptɪk) *n* **1** a person who habitually doubts the authenticity of accepted beliefs. **2** a person who mistrusts people, ideas, etc., in general. **3** a person who doubts the truth of religion. [C16: from L *scepticus*, from Gk *skeptikos* one who reflects upon, from *skeptesthai* to consider]
▸ˈ**sceptical** *or arch. & US* ˈ**skeptical** *adj* ▸ˈ**sceptically** *or arch. & US* ˈ**skeptically** *adv* ▸ˈ**scepticism** *or arch. & US* ˈ**skepticism** *n*

Sceptic *or arch. & US* **Skeptic** (ˈskɛptɪk) *n* **1** a member of one of the ancient Greek schools of philosophy, esp. that of Pyrrho ?365–?275 B.C., who believed that real knowledge of things is impossible. ◆ *adj* **2** of or relating to the Sceptics.
▸ˈ**Scepticism** *or arch. & US* ˈ**Skepticism** *n*

sceptre *or US* **scepter** (ˈsɛptə) *n* **1** a ceremonial staff held by a monarch as the symbol of authority. **2** imperial authority; sovereignty. [C13: from OF *sceptre*, from L, from Gk *skēptron* staff]
▸ˈ**sceptred** *or US* ˈ**sceptered** *adj*

schedule ❶ (ˈʃɛdjuːl; *also, esp. US* ˈskɛdʒʊəl) *n* **1** a plan of procedure for a project. **2** a list of items: *a schedule of fixed prices.* **3** a list of times; timetable. **4** a list of tasks to be performed, esp. within a set period. **5** *Law.* a list or inventory. ◆ *vb* **schedules, scheduling, scheduled.** (*tr*) **6** to make a schedule of or place in a schedule. **7** to plan to occur at a certain time. [C14: earlier *cedule, sedule* via OF from LL *schedula* small piece of paper, from L *scheda* sheet of paper]

scheduled castes *pl n* certain classes in Indian society officially granted special concessions. See **Harijan.**

scheduled territories *pl n* **the.** another name for **sterling area.**

scheelite (ˈʃiːlaɪt) *n* a white, brownish, or greenish mineral, usually fluorescent, consisting of calcium tungstate with some tungsten often replaced by molybdenum. It is an important source of tungsten. [C19: from G *Scheelit*, after K. W. *Scheele* (1742–86), Swedish chemist]

schema (ˈskiːmə) *n, pl* **schemata** (-mətə). **1** a plan, diagram, or scheme. **2** (in the philosophy of Kant) a rule or principle that enables the understanding to unify experience. **3** *Logic.* **3a** a syllogistic figure. **3b** a representation of the form of an inference. [C19: from Gk: form]

schematic ❶ (skɪˈmætɪk) *adj* **1** of or relating to the nature of a diagram, plan, or schema. ◆ *n* **2** a schematic diagram, esp. of an electrical circuit, etc.
▸**scheˈmatically** *adv*

schematize ❶ *or* **schematise** (ˈskiːməˌtaɪz) *vb* **schematizes, schematizing, schematized** *or* **schematises, schematising, schematised.** (*tr*) to form into or arrange in a scheme.
▸ˈ**schemaˌtism** *n* ▸ˌ**schematiˈzation** *or* ˌ**schematiˈsation** *n*

scheme ❶ (skiːm) *n* **1** a systematic plan for a course of action. **2** a systematic arrangement of parts. **3** a secret plot. **4** a chart, diagram, or outline. **5** an astrological diagram giving the aspects of celestial bodies. **6** *Chiefly Brit.* a plan formally adopted by a commercial enterprise or governmental body, as for pensions, etc. **7** Short for **housing scheme.** ◆ *vb* **schemes, scheming, schemed. 8** (*tr*) to devise a system for. **9** to form intrigues (for) in an underhand manner. [C16: from L *schema*, from Gk *skhēma* form]
▸ˈ**schemer** *n*

scheming ❶ (ˈskiːmɪŋ) *adj* **1** given to making plots; cunning. ◆ *n* **2** intrigues.

Schengen Convention *or* **Agreement** (ˈʃɛŋən) *n* an agreement, signed in 1985, but not implemented until 1995, to abolish border controls within Europe: thirteen countries had acceded by 1995; the UK is not a signatory.

scherzando (skɛəˈtsændəʊ) *Music.* ◆ *adj, adv* **1** to be performed in a light-hearted manner. ◆ *n, pl* **scherzandi** (-diː) *or* **scherzandos. 2** a movement, passage, etc., directed to be performed in this way. [It., lit.: joking; see SCHERZO]

scherzo (ˈskɛətsəʊ) *n, pl* **scherzos** *or* **scherzi** (-tsiː). a brisk lively move-

THESAURUS

scattering *n* **1** = **sprinkling**, few, handful, scatter, smatter, smattering

scenario *n* **1** = **story line**, outline, résumé, rundown, sketch, summary, synopsis **2** = **sequence of events**, master plan, scheme

scene *n* **1** = **site**, area, locality, place, position, setting, situation, spot, stage, whereabouts **2** = **setting**, backdrop, background, location, *mise en scène*, set **4** = **act**, division, episode, part **7** = **view**, landscape, panorama, prospect, vista **8** = **fuss**, carry-on (*inf., chiefly Brit.*), commotion, confrontation, display of emotion, drama, exhibition, hue and cry, performance, row, tantrum, to-do, upset **9** *Informal* = **world**, arena, business, environment, field of interest, milieu

scenery *n* **1** = **landscape**, surroundings, terrain, view, vista **2** *Theatre* = **set**, backdrop, décor, flats, *mise en scène*, setting, stage set

scenic *adj* **2** = **picturesque**, beautiful, breathtaking, grand, impressive, panoramic, spectacular, striking

scent *n* **1** = **fragrance**, aroma, bouquet, niff (*Brit. sl.*), odour, perfume, redolence, smell **2** = **trail**, spoor, track ◆ *vb* **6** = **detect**, be on the track *or* trail of, discern, get wind of (*inf.*), nose out, recognize, sense, smell, sniff, sniff out

scented *adj* **5** = **fragrant**, ambrosial, aromatic, odoriferous, perfumed, redolent, sweet-smelling

sceptic *n* **1-3** = **doubter**, agnostic, cynic, disbeliever, doubting Thomas, Pyrrhonist, scoffer, unbeliever

sceptical *adj* **1-3** = **doubtful**, cynical, disbelieving, doubting, dubious, hesitating, incredulous, mistrustful, questioning, quizzical, scoffing, unbelieving, unconvinced
Antonyms *adj* believing, certain, convinced, credulous, dogmatic, free from doubt, of fixed mind, sure, trusting, undoubting, unquestioning

scepticism *n* **1-3** = **doubt**, agnosticism, cynicism, disbelief, incredulity, Pyrrhonism, suspicion, unbelief

schedule *n* **1-4** = **plan**, agenda, calendar, catalogue, inventory, itinerary, list, list of appointments, programme, timetable ◆ *vb* **6** = **plan**, appoint, arrange, book, organize, programme, slot (*inf.*), time

schematic *adj* **1** = **diagrammatic**, diagrammatical, graphic, illustrative, representational

schematize *vb* = **systematize**, arrange, catalogue, categorize, classify, file, grade, methodize, order, pigeonhole, put into order, regulate, sort, standardize, systemize, tabulate

scheme *n* **1** = **plan**, contrivance, course of action, design, device, programme, project, proposal, strategy, system, tactics, theory **2** = **system**, arrangement, codification, disposition, layout, pattern, schedule, schema **3** = **plot**, conspiracy, dodge, game (*inf.*), intrigue, machinations, manoeuvre, ploy, ruse, shift, stratagem, subterfuge **4** = **diagram**, blueprint, chart, draft, outline ◆ *vb* **8** = **plan**, contrive, design, devise, frame, imagine, lay plans, project, work out **9** = **plot**, collude, conspire, intrigue, machinate, manoeuvre, wheel and deal (*inf.*)

schemer *n* **9** = **plotter**, conniver, deceiver, intriguer, Machiavelli, slyboots (*inf.*), wangler (*inf.*), wheeler-dealer (*inf.*)

scheming *adj* **1** = **calculating**, artful, conniving, cunning, deceitful, designing, duplicitous, foxy, Machiavellian, slippery, sly, tricky, underhand, wily
Antonyms *adj* above-board, artless, guileless, honest, ingenuous, naive, straightforward, trustworthy, undesigning

ment, developed from the minuet, with a contrastive middle section (a trio). [It.: joke, of Gmc origin]

Schick test (ʃɪk) *n Med.* a skin test to determine immunity to diphtheria. [C20: after Bela *Schick* (1877–1967), US paediatrician]

schilling (ˈʃɪlɪŋ) *n* the standard monetary unit of Austria. [C18: from G: SHILLING]

schism ❶ (ˈsɪzəm, ˈskɪz-) *n* **1** the division of a group into opposing factions. **2** the factions so formed. **3** division within or separation from an established Church, not necessarily involving differences in doctrine. [C14: from Church L *schisma*, from Gk *skhisma* a cleft, from *skhizein* to split]

schismatic ❶ (sɪzˈmætɪk, skɪz-) *or* **schismatical** *adj* **1** of or promoting schism. ◆ *n* **2** a person who causes schism or belongs to a schismatic faction.
▸**schisˈmatically** *adv*

schist (ʃɪst) *n* any metamorphic rock that can be split into thin layers. [C18: from F *schiste*, from L *lapis schistos* stone that may be split, from Gk *skhizein* to split]
▸**ˈschistose** *adj*

schistosome (ˈʃɪstəˌsəʊm) *n* any of a genus of blood flukes which cause disease in man and domestic animals. Also called: **bilharzia**. [C19: from NL *Schistosoma*; see SCHIST, -SOME[3]]

schistosomiasis (ˌʃɪstəsəʊˈmaɪəsɪs) *n* a disease caused by infestation of the body with schistosomes. Also called: **bilharziasis**.

schizanthus (skɪzˈænθəs) *n* a flowering annual plant, native to Chile, that has finely divided leaves. [C19: NL from Gk *skhizein* to cut + *anthos* flower]

schizo (ˈskɪtsəʊ) *Offens.* ◆ *adj* **1** schizophrenic. ◆ *n, pl* **schizos**. **2** a schizophrenic person.

schizo- *or before a vowel* **schiz-** *combining form.* indicating a cleavage, split, or division: *schizophrenia*. [from Gk *skhizein* to split]

schizocarp (ˈskɪzəˌkɑːp) *n Bot.* a dry fruit that splits into two or more one-seeded portions at maturity.
▸**ˌschizoˈcarpous** *adj*

schizoid (ˈskɪtsɔɪd) *adj* **1** *Psychol.* denoting a personality disorder characterized by extreme shyness and oversensitivity. **2** *Inf.* characterized by conflicting or contradictory ideas, attitudes, etc. ◆ *n* **3** a person who has a schizoid personality.

schizomycete (ˌskɪtsəʊmaɪˈsiːt) *n* any microscopic organism of the class *Schizomycetes*, which includes the bacteria.

schizophrenia (ˌskɪtsəʊˈfriːnɪə) *n* **1** any of a group of psychotic disorders characterized by progressive deterioration of the personality, withdrawal from reality, hallucinations, emotional instability, etc. **2** *Inf.* behaviour that seems to be motivated by contradictory or conflicting principles. [C20: from SCHIZO- + Gk *phrēn* mind]
▸**ˌschizoˈphrenic** *adj, n*

schizothymia (ˌskɪtsəʊˈθaɪmɪə) *n Psychiatry.* the condition of being schizoid or introverted. It encompasses elements of schizophrenia. [C20: NL, from SCHIZO- + *-thymia*, from Gk *thumos* spirit]
▸**ˌschizoˈthymic** *adj*

schlieren (ˈʃlɪərən) *n* **1** *Physics.* visible streaks produced in a transparent fluid as a result of variations in the fluid's density. **2** streaks or platelike masses of mineral in a rock mass. [G, pl of *Schliere* streak]

schmaltz ❶ *or* **schmalz** (ʃmælts, ʃmɔːlts) *n* excessive sentimentality. [C20: from G (*Schmalz*) & Yiddish: melted fat, from OHG *smalz*]
▸**ˈschmaltzy** *or* **ˈschmalzy** *adj*

Schmidt telescope *or* **camera** (ʃmɪt) *n* a catadioptric telescope designed to produce a very sharp image of a large area of sky in one photographic exposure. [C20: after B. V. *Schmidt* (1879–1935), Estonian-born G inventor]

schnapper (ˈʃnæpə) *n* a variant spelling of **snapper** (senses 1, 2).

schnapps *or* **schnaps** (ʃnæps) *n* **1** a Dutch spirit distilled from potatoes. **2** (in Germany) any strong spirit. [C19: from G *Schnaps*, from *schnappen* to SNAP]

schnauzer (ˈʃnaʊtsə) *n* a wire-haired breed of dog of the terrier type, originally from Germany, with a greyish coat. [C19: from G *Schnauze* snout]

schnitzel (ˈʃnɪtsəl) *n* a thin slice of meat, esp. veal. [G: cutlet, from *schnitzen* to carve, *schnitzeln* to whittle]

schnorkel (ˈʃnɔːkᵊl) *n, vb* **schnorkels, schnorkelling, schnorkelled.** a less common variant of **snorkel**.

schnozzle (ˈʃnɒzᵊl) *n Chiefly US.* a slang word for **nose**. [alteration of Yiddish *shnoitsl*, from G *Schnauze* snout]

scholar ❶ (ˈskɒlə) *n* **1** a learned person, esp. in the humanities. **2** a person, esp. a child, who studies; pupil. **3** a student receiving a scholarship. **4** *S. African.* a school pupil. [C14: from OF *escoler*, via LL from L *schola* SCHOOL[1]]
▸**ˈscholarly** *adj* ▸**ˈscholarliness** *n*

scholarship ❶ (ˈskɒləʃɪp) *n* **1** academic achievement; learning. **2a** financial aid provided for a scholar because of academic merit. **2b** the position of a student who gains this financial aid. **2c** (*as modifier*): *a scholarship student*. **3** the qualities of a scholar.

scholastic ❶ (skəˈlæstɪk) *adj* **1** of or befitting schools, scholars, or education. **2** pedantic or precise. **3** (*often cap.*) characteristic of or relating to the medieval Schoolmen. ◆ *n* **4** a student or pupil. **5** a person who is given to logical subtleties. **6** (*often cap.*) a disciple or adherent of scholasticism; Schoolman. **7** a Jesuit student who is undergoing a period of probation prior to commencing his theological studies. [C16: via L from Gk *skholastikos* devoted to learning, ult. from *skholē* SCHOOL[1]]
▸**schoˈlastically** *adv*

scholasticism (skəˈlæstɪˌsɪzəm) *n* (*sometimes cap.*) the system of philosophy, theology, and teaching that dominated medieval western Europe and was based on the writings of the Church Fathers and Aristotle.

scholiast (ˈskəʊlɪˌæst) *n* a medieval annotator, esp. of classical texts. [C16: from LGk, ult. from Gk *skholē* school]
▸**ˌscholiˈastic** *adj*

school[1] ❶ (skuːl) *n* **1a** an institution or building at which children and young people receive education. **1b** (*as modifier*): *school day*. **1c** (*in combination*): *schoolwork*. **2** any educational institution or building. **3** a faculty or department specializing in a particular subject: *a law school*. **4** the staff and pupils of a school. **5** the period of instruction in a school or one session of this: *he stayed after school to do extra work*. **6** a place or sphere of activity that instructs: *the school of hard knocks*. **7** a body of people or pupils adhering to a certain set of principles, doctrines, or methods. **8** a group of artists, writers, etc., linked by the same style, teachers, or aims. **9** a style of life: *a gentleman of the old school*. **10** *Inf.* a group assembled for a common purpose, esp. gambling or drinking. ◆ *vb (tr)* **11** to train or educate in or as in a school. **12** to discipline or control. [OE *scōl*, from L *schola* school, from Gk *skholē* leisure spent in the pursuit of knowledge]

school[2] (skuːl) *n* **1** a group of fish or other aquatic animals that swim together. ◆ *vb* **2** (*intr*) to form such a group. [OE *scolu* SHOAL[2]]

school board *n* **1** *English History.* an elected board of ratepayers who provided elementary schools (**board schools**). **2** (in the US and Canada) a local board of education.

schoolboy (ˈskuːlˌbɔɪ) *or* (*fem*) **schoolgirl** *n* a child attending school.

schoolhouse (ˈskuːlˌhaʊs) *n* **1** a building used as a school. **2** a house attached to a school.

schoolie (ˈskuːlɪ) *n Austral. sl.* **1** a schoolteacher. **2** a high school student.

schooling ❶ (ˈskuːlɪŋ) *n* **1** education, esp. when received at school. **2** the process of teaching or being taught in a school. **3** the training of an animal, esp. of a horse for dressage.

schoolman (ˈskuːlmən) *n, pl* **schoolmen**. (*sometimes cap.*) a scholar versed in the learning of the **Schoolmen**, the masters in the universities of the Middle Ages who were versed in scholasticism.

schoolmarm (ˈskuːlˌmɑːm) *n Inf.* **1** a woman schoolteacher. **2** any woman considered to be prim or old-fashioned.
▸**ˈschoolˌmarmish** *adj*

schoolmaster (ˈskuːlˌmɑːstə) *or* (*fem*) **schoolmistress** *n* **1** a person who teaches in or runs a school. **2** a person or thing that acts as an instructor.

schoolmate (ˈskuːlˌmeɪt) *or* **schoolfellow** *n* a companion at school; fellow pupil.

school of arts *n Austral.* a public building in a small town: orig. one used for adult education.

Schools (skuːlz) *pl n* **1 the Schools.** the medieval Schoolmen collectively. **2** (at Oxford University) **2a** the University building in which examinations are held. **2b** *Inf.* the Second Public Examination for the degree of Bachelor of Arts.

schoolteacher ❶ (ˈskuːlˌtiːtʃə) *n* a person who teaches in a school.
▸**ˈschoolˌteaching** *n*

school year *n* **1** a twelve-month period, usually of three terms, during which pupils remain in the same class. **2** the time during this period when the school is open.

schooner (ˈskuːnə) *n* **1** a sailing vessel with at least two masts, with all lower sails rigged fore-and-aft, and with the main mast stepped aft. **2**

THESAURUS

schism *n* **1** = **division**, breach, break, discord, disunion, rift, rupture, separation, splintering, split

schismatic *adj* **1** = **separatist**, discordant, dissentient, dissenting, dissident, heretical, heterodox, seceding, splinter

schmaltzy *adj* = **sentimental**, bathetic, cloying, corny (*sl.*), maudlin, mawkish, mushy (*inf.*), overemotional, sloppy (*inf.*), slushy (*inf.*), soppy (*inf.*), tear-jerking

scholar *n* **1** = **intellectual**, academic, bluestocking (*usually disparaging*), bookworm, egghead (*inf.*), man of letters, savant **2** = **student**, disciple, learner, pupil, schoolboy *or* schoolgirl

scholarly *adj* **1** = **learned**, academic, bookish, erudite, intellectual, lettered, scholastic, studious, well-read
Antonyms *adj* lowbrow, middlebrow, philistine, unacademic, uneducated, unintellectual, unlettered

scholarship *n* **1** = **learning**, accomplishments, attainments, book-learning, education, erudition, knowledge, lore **2** = **bursary**, exhibition, fellowship

scholastic *adj* **1** = **learned**, academic, bookish, lettered, literary, scholarly **2** = **pedantic**, pedagogic, precise

school[1] *n* **1-3** = **academy**, alma mater, college, department, discipline, faculty, institute, institution, seminary **7** = **group**, adherents, circle, class, clique, denomination, devotees, disciples, faction, followers, following, schism, sect, set **9** = **way of life**, creed, faith, outlook, persuasion, school of thought, stamp ◆ *vb* **11** = **train**, coach, discipline, drill, educate, indoctrinate, instruct, prepare, prime, tutor, verse

schooling *n* **1** = **teaching**, book-learning, education, formal education, grounding, guidance, instruction, training, tuition

schoolteacher *n* = **schoolmaster** *or* **schoolmistress**, dominie (*Scot.*), instructor, pedagogue, schoolmarm (*inf.*)

Brit. a large glass for sherry. **3** *US, Canad., Austral., & NZ.* a large glass for beer. [C18: from ?]

schottische (ʃɒ'tiːʃ) *n* **1** a 19th-century German dance resembling a slow polka. **2** a piece of music composed for or in the manner of this dance. [C19: from G *der schottische Tanz* the Scottish dance]

Schottky effect ('ʃɒtkɪ) *n Physics.* a reduction in the energy required to remove an electron from a solid surface in a vacuum when an electric field is applied to the surface. [C20: after W. *Schottky* (1886–1976), G physicist]

schuss (ʃʊs) *Skiing.* ◆ *n* **1** a straight high-speed downhill run. ◆ *vb* **2** (*intr*) to perform a schuss. [G: SHOT[1]]

schwa *or* **shwa** (ʃwɑː) *n* **1** a central vowel represented in the International Phonetic Alphabet by (ə). The sound occurs in unstressed syllables in English, as in *around* and *sofa*. **2** the symbol (ə) used to represent this sound. [C19: via G from Heb. *shewā*, a diacritic indicating lack of a vowel sound]

sci. *abbrev. for:* **1** science. **2** scientific.

sciatic (saɪ'ætɪk) *adj* **1** *Anat.* of or relating to the hip or the hipbone. **2** of or afflicted with sciatica. [C16: from F, from LL, from L *ischiadicus* relating to pain in the hip, from Gk, from *iskhia* hip-joint]

sciatica (saɪ'ætɪkə) *n* a form of neuralgia characterized by intense pain along the body's longest nerve (**sciatic nerve**), extending from the back of the thigh down to the calf of the leg. [C15: from LL *sciatica*; see SCIATIC]

science ⓘ ('saɪəns) *n* **1** the systematic study of the nature and behaviour of the material and physical universe, based on observation, experiment, and measurement. **2** the knowledge so obtained or the practice of obtaining it. **3** any particular branch of this knowledge: *the applied sciences*. **4** any body of knowledge organized in a systematic manner. **5** skill or technique. **6** *Arch.* knowledge. [C14: via OF from L *scientia* knowledge, from *scīre* to know]

science fiction *n* **a** a literary genre that makes imaginative use of scientific knowledge. **b** (*as modifier*): *a science-fiction writer.*

Science Museum *n* a museum in London, originating from 1852 and given its present name and site in 1899: contains collections relating to the history of science, technology, and industry.

science park *n* an area where scientific research and commercial development are carried on in cooperation.

scienter (saɪ'ɛntə) *adv Law.* knowingly; wilfully. [from L]

sciential (saɪ'ɛnʃəl) *adj* **1** of or relating to science. **2** skilful or knowledgeable.

scientific ⓘ (ˌsaɪən'tɪfɪk) *adj* **1** (*prenominal*) of, derived from, or used in science: *scientific equipment*. **2** (*prenominal*) occupied in science: *scientific manpower*. **3** conforming with the methods used in science.
▸ˌ**scien'tifically** *adv*

scientism ('saɪənˌtɪzəm) *n* **1** the application of the scientific method. **2** the uncritical application of scientific methods to inappropriate fields of study.
▸ˌ**scien'tistic** *adj*

scientist ⓘ ('saɪəntɪst) *n* a person who studies or practises any of the sciences or who uses scientific methods.

Scientology (ˌsaɪən'tɒlədʒɪ) *n Trademark.* the philosophy of the Church of Scientology, a nondenominational movement founded in the US in the 1950s, which emphasizes self-knowledge as a means of realizing full spiritual potential. [C20: from L *scient(ia)* SCIENCE + -LOGY]
▸ˌ**Scien'tologist** *n*

sci-fi ('saɪ'faɪ) *n* short for **science fiction**.

scilicet ('sɪlɪˌsɛt) *adv* namely: used esp. in explaining an obscure text or supplying a missing word. [L: from *scīre licet* it is permitted to know]

scilla ('sɪlə) *n* any of a genus of liliaceous plants having small bell-shaped flowers. See also **squill** (sense 3). [C19: via L from Gk *skilla*]

scimitar ('sɪmɪtə) *n* an oriental sword with a curved blade broadening towards the point. [C16: from OIt., prob. from Persian *shimshīr*, from ?]

scintigraphy (ˌsɪn'tɪgrəfɪ) *n Med.* a diagnostic technique using a radioactive tracer and scintillation counter for producing pictures (**scintigrams**) of internal parts of the body. [C20: from SCINTI(LLATION) + -GRAPHY]

scintilla (sɪn'tɪlə) *n* a minute amount; hint, trace, or particle. [C17: from L: a spark]

scintillate ⓘ ('sɪntɪˌleɪt) *vb* **scintillates, scintillating, scintillated.** (*mainly intr*) **1** (*also tr*) to give off (sparks); sparkle. **2** to be animated or brilliant. **3** *Physics.* to give off flashes of light as a result of the impact of photons. [C17: from L *scintillāre*, from *scintilla* a spark]
▸'**scintillant** *adj* ▸'**scintilˌlating** *adj*

scintillation (ˌsɪntɪ'leɪʃən) *n* **1** the act of scintillating. **2** a spark or flash. **3** the twinkling of stars. **4** *Physics.* a flash of light produced when a material scintillates.

scintillation counter *n* an instrument for detecting and measuring the intensity of high-energy radiation. It consists of a phosphor with which particles collide producing flashes of light that are converted into pulses of electric current that are counted by electronic equipment.

sciolism ('saɪəˌlɪzəm) *n Rare.* the practice of opinionating on subjects of which one has only superficial knowledge. [C19: from LL *sciolus* someone with a smattering of knowledge, from L *scīre* to know]
▸'**sciolist** *n* ▸ˌ**scio'listic** *adj*

scion ⓘ ('saɪən) *n* **1** a descendant or young member of a family. **2** a shoot of a plant used to form a graft. [C14: from OF *cion*, of Gmc origin]

scirrhus ('sɪrəs) *n, pl* **scirrhi** (-raɪ) *or* **scirrhuses.** *Pathol.* a firm cancerous growth composed of fibrous tissues. [C17: from NL, from L *scirros*, from Gk, from *skiros* hard]
▸**scirrhoid** ('sɪrɔɪd) *adj*

scission ('sɪʃən) *n* the act or an instance of cutting, splitting, or dividing. [C15: from LL *scissiō*, from *scindere* to split]

scissor ('sɪzə) *vb* to cut (an object) with scissors.

scissors ('sɪzəz) *pl n* **1** Also called: **pair of scissors.** a cutting instrument used for cloth, hair, etc., having two crossed pivoted blades that cut by a shearing action. **2** a wrestling hold in which a wrestler wraps his legs round his opponent's body or head and squeezes. **3** any gymnastic feat in which the legs cross and uncross in a scissor-like movement. [C14 *sisoures*, from OF *cisoires*, from Vulgar L *cīsōria* (unattested), ult. from L *caedere* to cut]

scissors kick *n* a type of swimming kick in which one leg is moved forward and the other bent back and they are then brought together again in a scissor-like action.

sciurine ('saɪjʊrɪn, -ˌraɪn) *adj* of or belonging to a family of rodents inhabiting most parts of the world except Australia and southern South America: includes squirrels, marmots, and chipmunks. [C19: from L *sciūrus*, from Gk *skiouros* squirrel, from *skia* a shadow + *oura* a tail]

sclera ('sklɪərə) *n* the firm white fibrous membrane that forms the outer covering of the eyeball. Also called: **sclerotic.** [C19: from NL, from Gk *sklēros* hard]
▸**scle'ritis** *n*

sclerenchyma (sklɪə'rɛŋkɪmə) *n* a supporting tissue in plants consisting of dead cells with very thick lignified walls. [C19: from SCLERO- + PARENCHYMA]

sclero- *or before a vowel* **scler-** *combining form.* **1** indicating hardness: *sclerosis*. **2** of the sclera: *sclerotomy*. [from Gk *sklēros* hard]

scleroderma (ˌsklɪərəʊ'dɜːmə) *or* **sclerodermia** (ˌsklɪərəʊ'dɜːmɪə) *n* a chronic disease common among women, characterized by thickening and hardening of the skin.

scleroma (sklɪə'rəʊmə) *n, pl* **scleromata** (-mətə). *Pathol.* any small area of abnormally hard tissue, esp. in a mucous membrane. [C17: from NL, from Gk, from *sklēroun* to harden, from *sklēros* hard]

scleroprotein (ˌsklɪərəʊ'prəʊtiːn) *n* any of a group of insoluble stable proteins such as keratin that occur in skeletal and connective tissues. Also called: **albuminoid.**

sclerosis (sklɪə'rəʊsɪs) *n, pl* **scleroses** (-siːz). **1** *Pathol.* a hardening or thickening of organs, tissues, or vessels from inflammation, degeneration, or (esp. on the inner walls of arteries) deposition of fatty plaques. **2** the hardening of a plant cell wall or tissue. [C14: via Med. L from Gk *sklērōsis* a hardening]

sclerotic (sklɪə'rɒtɪk) *adj* **1** of or relating to the sclera. **2** of, relating to, or having sclerosis. ◆ *n* **3** another name for **sclera.** [C16: from Med. L *sclērōticus*, from Gk; see SCLEROMA]

sclerous ('sklɪərəs) *adj Anat., pathol.* hard; bony; indurated. [C19: from Gk *sklēros* hard]

SCM (in Britain) *abbrev. for:* **1** State Certified Midwife. **2** Student Christian Movement.

scoff[1] ⓘ (skɒf) *vb* **1** (*intr;* often foll. by *at*) to speak contemptuously (about); mock. **2** (*tr*) *Obs.* to regard with derision. ◆ *n* **3** an expression of derision. **4** an object of derision. [C14: prob. from ON]
▸'**scoffer** *n* ▸'**scoffing** *adj, n*

scoff[2] ⓘ (skɒf) *Inf., chiefly Brit.* ◆ *vb* **1** to eat (food) fast and greedily. ◆ *n* **2** food or rations. [C19: var of *scaff* food]

scold ⓘ (skəʊld) *vb* **1** to find fault with or reprimand (a person) harshly. **2** (*intr*) to use harsh or abusive language. ◆ *n* **3** a person, esp. a woman, who constantly finds fault. [C13: from ON SKALD]
▸'**scolder** *n* ▸'**scolding** *n*

THESAURUS

science *n* **3, 4** = **discipline**, body of knowledge, branch of knowledge **5** = **skill**, art, technique

scientific *adj* **3** = **systematic**, accurate, controlled, exact, mathematical, precise

scientist *n* = **inventor**, boffin (*inf.*), technophile

scintillate *vb* **1** = **sparkle**, blaze, coruscate, flash, give off sparks, gleam, glint, glisten, glitter, twinkle

scintillating *adj* **2** = **brilliant**, animated, bright, dazzling, ebullient, exciting, glittering, lively, sparkling, stimulating, witty

scion *n* **1** = **descendant**, child, heir, offspring, successor **2** = **offshoot**, branch, graft, shoot, slip, sprout, twig

scoff[1] *vb* **1** = **scorn**, belittle, deride, despise, flout, gibe, jeer, knock (*inf.*), laugh at, make light of, make sport of, mock, poke fun at, pooh-pooh, revile, ridicule, sneer, taunt, twit

scoff[2] *vb* **1** = **gobble (up)**, bolt, cram, cram oneself on, devour, gollop, gorge oneself on, gulp down, guzzle, make a pig of oneself on (*inf.*), put away, stuff oneself with, wolf ◆ *n* **2** = **food**, chow (*inf.*), eats (*sl.*), fare, feed, grub (*sl.*), meal, nosh (*sl.*), nosh-up (*Brit. sl.*), rations

scold *vb* **1** = **reprimand**, bawl out (*inf.*), berate, blame, bring (someone) to book, carpet (*inf.*), castigate, censure, chide, find fault with, give a rocket (*Brit. & NZ inf.*), haul (someone) over the coals (*inf.*), have (someone) on the carpet (*inf.*), lecture, nag, rate, read the riot act, rebuke, remonstrate with, reproach, reprove, slate (*inf., chiefly Brit.*), take (someone) to task, tear into (*inf.*), tear (someone) off a strip (*Brit. inf.*), tell off (*inf.*), tick off (*inf.*), upbraid, vituperate ◆ *n* **3** = **nag**, shrew, termagant (*rare*), Xanthippe
Antonyms *vb* ≠ **reprimand:** acclaim, applaud, approve, commend, compliment, extol, laud, praise

scoliosis (ˌskɒlɪˈəʊsɪs) *n Pathol.* an abnormal lateral curvature of the spine. [C18: from NL, from Gk: a curving, from *skolios* bent]
▸**scoliotic** (ˌskɒlɪˈɒtɪk) *adj*

scollop (ˈskɒləp) *n, vb* a variant spelling of **scallop.**

scombroid (ˈskɒmbrɔɪd) *adj* **1** of, relating to, or belonging to the *Scombroidea,* a suborder of marine spiny-finned fishes having a forked powerful tail: includes the mackerels, tunnies, and sailfish. ◆ *n* **2** any fish belonging to the suborder *Scombroidea.* [C19: from Gk *skombros* a mackerel; see -OID]

sconce[1] (skɒns) *n* **1** a bracket fixed to a wall for holding candles or lights. **2** a flat candlestick with a handle. [C14: from OF *esconse* hiding place, lantern, or from LL *sconsa,* from *absconsa* dark lantern]

sconce[2] (skɒns) *n* a small protective fortification, such as an earthwork. [C16: from Du. *schans,* from MHG *schanze* bundle of brushwood]

scone (skɒn, skəʊn) *n* a light plain doughy cake made from flour with very little fat, cooked in an oven or (esp. originally) on a griddle. [C16: Scot., ?from MDu. *schoonbrot* fine bread]

scoop ➊ (sku:p) *n* **1** a utensil used as a shovel or ladle, esp. a small shovel with deep sides and a short handle, used for taking up flour, etc. **2** a utensil with a long handle and round bowl used for dispensing liquids, etc. **3** anything that resembles a scoop in action, such as the bucket on a dredge. **4** a utensil used for serving mashed potatoes, ice cream, etc. **5** a spoonlike surgical instrument for extracting foreign matter, etc., from the body. **6** the quantity taken up by a scoop. **7** the act of scooping, dredging, etc. **8** a hollow cavity. **9** *Sl.* a large quick gain, as of money. **10** a news story reported in one newspaper before all the others. ◆ *vb (mainly tr)* **11** (often foll. by *up*) to take up and remove (an object or substance) with or as if with a scoop. **12** (often foll. by *out*) to hollow out with or as if with a scoop. **13** to make (a large sudden profit). **14** to beat (rival newspapers) in uncovering a news item. [C14: via MDu. *schōpe* from Gmc]
▸**ˈscooper** *n* ▸**ˈscoopˌful** *n*

scoot ➊ (sku:t) *vb* **1** to go or cause to go quickly or hastily; dart or cause to dart off or away. ◆ *n* **2** the act of scooting. [C19 (US): from ?]

scooter (ˈsku:tə) *n* **1** a child's vehicle consisting of a low footboard on wheels, steered by handlebars. **2** See **motor scooter.**

scope ➊ (skəʊp) *n* **1** opportunity for exercising the faculties or abilities. **2** range of view or grasp. **3** the area covered by an activity, topic, etc.: *the scope of his thesis was vast.* **4** *Naut.* slack left in an anchor cable. **5** *Logic.* the part of a formula that follows a quantifier or an operator. **6** *Inf.* short for **telescope, microscope, oscilloscope,** etc. **7** *Arch.* purpose. [C16: from It. *scopo* goal, from L *scopus,* from Gk *skopos* target]

-scope *n combining form.* indicating an instrument for observing or detecting: *microscope.* [from NL *-scopium,* from Gk *-skopion,* from *skopein* to look at]
▸**-scopic** *adj combining form.*

scopolamine (skəˈpɒləˌmi:n) *n* a colourless viscous liquid alkaloid extracted from certain plants, such as henbane: used in preventing travel sickness and as a sedative and truth serum. Also called: **hyoscine.** [C20: *scopol-* from NL *scopolia Japonica* Japanese belladonna (from which the alkaloid is extracted), after G. A. *Scopoli* (1723–88), It. naturalist, + AMINE]

-scopy *n combining form.* indicating a viewing or observation: *microscopy.* [from Gk *-skopia,* from *skopein* to look at]

scorbutic (skɔ:ˈbju:tɪk) *adj* of or having scurvy. [C17: from NL *scorbūticus,* from Med. L *scorbūtus,* prob. of Gmc origin]
▸**scorˈbutically** *adv*

scorch ➊ (skɔ:tʃ) *vb* **1** to burn or become burnt, esp. so as to affect the colour, taste, etc. **2** to wither or parch or cause to wither from exposure to heat. **3** *(intr) Inf.* to be very hot: *it is scorching outside.* **4** *(tr) Inf.* to criticize harshly. ◆ *n* **5** a slight burn. **6** a mark caused by the application of too great heat. **7** *Horticulture.* a mark on fruit, etc., caused by pests or insecticides. [C15: prob. from ON *skorpna* to shrivel up]
▸**ˈscorching** *adj*

scorched earth policy *n* **1** the policy in warfare of removing or destroying everything that might be useful to an invading enemy. **2** *Business.* a manoeuvre by a company expecting an unwelcome takeover bid in which apparent profitability is greatly reduced by a reversible operation, such as borrowing at an exorbitant interest rate.

scorcher (ˈskɔ:tʃə) *n* **1** a person or thing that scorches. **2** something caustic. **3** *Inf.* a very hot day. **4** *Brit. inf.* something remarkable.

score ➊ (skɔ:) *n* **1** a numerical record of a competitive game or match. **2** the total number of points made by a side or individual in a game. **3** the act of scoring, esp. a point or points. **4 the score.** *Inf.* the actual situation. **5** a group or set of twenty: *three score years and ten.* **6** *(usually pl; foll. by of)* lots: *I have scores of things to do.* **7** *Music.* **7a** the printed form of a composition in which the instrumental or vocal parts appear on separate staves vertically arranged on large pages (**full score**) or in a condensed version, usually for piano (**short score**) or voices and piano (**vocal score**). **7b** the incidental music for a film or play. **7c** the songs, music, etc., for a stage or film musical. **8** a mark or notch, esp. one made in keeping a tally. **9** an account of amounts due. **10** an amount recorded as due. **11** a reason: *the book was rejected on the score of length.* **12** a grievance. **13a** a line marking a division or boundary. **13b** *(as modifier): score line.* **14 over the score.** *Inf.* excessive; unfair. **15 settle** *or* **pay off a score. 15a** to avenge a wrong. **15b** to repay a debt. ◆ *vb* **scores, scoring, scored. 16** to gain (a point or points) in a game or contest. **17** *(tr)* to make a total score of. **18** to keep a record of the score (of). **19** *(tr)* to be worth (a certain amount) in a game. **20** *(tr)* to record by making notches in. **21** to make (cuts, lines, etc.) in or on. **22** *(intr) Sl.* to obtain something desired, esp. to purchase an illegal drug. **23** *(intr) Sl.* (of men) to be successful in seducing a person. **24** *(tr)* **24a** to arrange (a piece of music) for specific instruments or voices. **24b** to write the music for (a film, play, etc.). **25** to achieve (success or an advantage): *your idea scored with the boss.* [OE *scora*]
▸**ˈscorer** *n*

scoreboard (ˈskɔ:ˌbɔ:d) *n Sport, etc.* a board for displaying the score of a game or match.

scorecard (ˈskɔ:ˌkɑ:d) *n* **1** a card on which scores are recorded, as in golf. **2** a card identifying the players in a sports match, esp. cricket.

score off ➊ *vb (intr, prep)* to gain an advantage at someone else's expense.

scoria (ˈskɔ:rɪə) *n, pl* **scoriae** (-rɪˌi:). **1** a mass of solidified lava containing many cavities. **2** refuse obtained from smelted ore. [C17: from L: dross, from Gk *skōria,* from *skōr* excrement]

scorify (ˈskɔ:rɪˌfaɪ) *vb* **scorifies, scorifying, scorified.** to remove (impurities) from metals by forming scoria.
▸ˌ**scorifiˈcation** *n* ▸**ˈscoriˌfier** *n*

scoring (ˈskɔ:rɪŋ) *n* another name for **orchestration** (see **orchestrate**).

scorn ➊ (skɔ:n) *n* **1** open contempt for a person or thing. **2** an object of contempt or derision. ◆ *vb* **3** to treat with contempt or derision. **4** *(tr)* to reject with contempt. [C12 *schornen,* from OF *escharnir,* of Gmc origin]
▸**ˈscorner** *n* ▸**ˈscornful** *adj* ▸**ˈscornfully** *adv*

Scorpio (ˈskɔ:pɪˌəʊ) *n* **1** Also called: **Scorpius.** *Astron.* a large S constellation. **2** Also called: the **Scorpion.** *Astrol.* the eighth sign of the zodiac. The sun is in this sign between about Oct. 23 and Nov. 21. [L: SCORPION]

scorpion (ˈskɔ:pɪən) *n* **1** an arachnid of warm dry regions, having a segmented body with a long tail terminating in a venomous sting. **2 false scorpion.** a small nonvenomous arachnid that superficially resembles the scorpion but lacks the long tail. **3** *Bible.* a barbed scourge (I Kings 12:11). [C13: via OF from L *scorpiō,* from Gk *skorpios,* from ?]

THESAURUS

scolding *n* = **rebuke,** dressing-down, (good) talking-to *(inf.),* lecture, piece of one's mind, telling-off *(inf.),* ticking-off *(inf.),* tongue-lashing, wigging *(Brit. sl.)*

scoop *n* **1-4** = **ladle,** dipper, spoon **10** = **exclusive,** coup, exposé, inside story, revelation, sensation ◆ *vb* **11** *often with* **up** = **lift,** clear away, gather up, pick up, remove, sweep up *or* away, take up **12** *with* **out** = **hollow,** bail, dig, dip, empty, excavate, gouge, ladle, scrape, shovel

scoot *vb* **1** = **dash,** bolt, dart, run, scamper, scurry, scuttle, skedaddle *(inf.),* skitter, sprint, zip

scope *n* **1** = **opportunity,** elbowroom, freedom, latitude, liberty, room, space **2** = **range,** ambit, area, capacity, field of reference, orbit, outlook, purview, reach, span, sphere **3** = **extent,** compass, confines, range

scorch *vb* **1, 2** = **burn,** blacken, blister, char, parch, roast, sear, shrivel, singe, wither

scorching *adj* **3** = **burning,** baking, boiling, broiling, fiery, flaming, red-hot, roasting, searing, sizzling, sweltering, torrid, tropical, unbearably hot

score *n* **1** = **points,** grade, mark, outcome, record, result, total **4 the score** *Informal* = **the situation,** the equation, the facts, the lie of the land, the reality, the setup *(inf.),* the truth **6** *plural* = **lots,** a flock, a great number, an army, a throng, crowds, droves, hosts, hundreds, legions, masses, millions, multitudes, myriads, swarms, very many **9** = **amount due,** account, bill, charge, debt, obligation, reckoning, tab *(US inf.),* tally, total **11** = **grounds,** account, basis, cause, ground, reason **12** = **grievance,** a bone to pick, grudge, injury, injustice, wrong **15a settle** *or* **pay off a score** = **get one's own back** *(inf.),* avenge, get even with, give an eye for an eye, give like for like *or* tit for tat, give (someone) a taste of his own medicine, hit back, pay (someone) back (in his own coin), repay, requite, retaliate ◆ *vb* **16** = **gain,** achieve, amass, chalk up *(inf.),* make, notch up *(inf.),* win **18** = **keep count,** count, keep a tally of, record, register, tally **21** = **cut,** crosshatch, deface, gouge, graze, indent, mar, mark, nick, notch, scrape, scratch, slash **24** *Music* = **arrange,** adapt, orchestrate, set **25** = **go down well with (someone),** gain an advantage, impress, make a hit *(inf.),* make an impact *or* impression, make a point, put oneself across, triumph

score off *vb* = **get the better of,** be one up on *(inf.),* have the laugh on, humiliate, make a fool of, make (someone) look silly, worst

scorn *n* **1** = **contempt,** contemptuousness, contumely, derision, despite, disdain, disparagement, mockery, sarcasm, scornfulness, slight, sneer ◆ *vb* **3, 4** = **despise,** be above, consider beneath one, contemn, curl one's lip at, deride, disdain, flout, hold in contempt, look down on, make fun of, reject, scoff at, scout *(arch.),* slight, sneer at, spurn, turn up one's nose at *(inf.)*
Antonyms *n* ≠ **contempt:** acceptance, admiration, affection, esteem, high regard, respect, tolerance, toleration, veneration, worship ◆ *vb* ≠ **despise:** accept, admire, esteem, look favourably on, respect, revere, tolerate, venerate, worship

scornful *adj* **1** = **contemptuous,** contumelious, defiant, derisive, disdainful, haughty, insolent, insulting, jeering, mocking, sarcastic, sardonic, scathing, scoffing, slighting, sneering, supercilious, withering

scornfully *adv* **1** = **contemptuously,** disdainfully, dismissively, scathingly, slightingly, with a sneer, with contempt, with disdain, witheringly, with lip curled

Scorpion ('skɔːpɪən) *n* **the.** the constellation Scorpio, the eighth sign of the zodiac.
scorpion fish *n* any of a genus of fish of temperate and tropical seas, having venomous spines on the dorsal and anal fins.
Scot (skɒt) *n* **1** a native or inhabitant of Scotland. **2** a member of a tribe of Celtic raiders from the north of Ireland who eventually settled in N Britain during the 5th and 6th centuries.
Scot. *abbrev. for:* **1** Scotch (whisky). **2** Scotland. **3** Scottish.
scot and lot *n Brit. history.* a municipal tax paid by burgesses that came to be regarded as a qualification for the borough franchise in parliamentary elections. [C13 *scot* tax, from Gmc]
scotch[1] (skɒtʃ) *vb (tr)* **1** to put an end to; crush: *bad weather scotched our plans.* **2** *Obs.* to cut or score. ◆ *n* **3** *Arch.* a gash. **4** a line marked down, as for hopscotch. [C15: from ?]
scotch[2] (skɒtʃ) *vb* **1** *(tr)* to block, prop, or prevent from moving with or as if with a wedge. ◆ *n* **2** a block or wedge to prevent motion. [C17: from ?]
Scotch[1] (skɒtʃ) *adj* **1** another word for **Scottish.** ◆ *n* **2** the Scots or their language.

> **USAGE NOTE** In the north of England and in Scotland, *Scotch* is not used outside fixed expressions such as *Scotch whisky.* The use of *Scotch* for *Scots* or *Scottish* is otherwise felt to be incorrect, esp. when applied to people.

Scotch[2] (skɒtʃ) *n* whisky distilled from fermented malted barley and made in Scotland. Also called: **Scotch whisky.**
Scotch broth *n Brit.* a thick soup made from mutton or beef stock, vegetables, and pearl barley.
Scotch egg *n Brit.* a hard-boiled egg enclosed in a layer of sausage meat, covered in egg and crumbs, and fried.
Scotchman ('skɒtʃmən) *or (fem)* **Scotchwoman** *n, pl* **Scotchmen** *or* **Scotchwomen.** *(regarded as bad usage by the Scots)* another word for **Scotsman** or **Scotswoman.**
Scotch mist *n* **1** a heavy wet mist. **2** drizzle.
Scotch snap *n Music.* a rhythmic pattern consisting of a short note followed by a long one. Also called: **Scotch catch.**
Scotch terrier *n* another name for **Scottish terrier.**
scoter ('skəʊtə) *n, pl* **scoters** *or* **scoter.** a sea duck of northern regions. The male plumage is black with white patches around the head and eyes. [C17: from ?]
scot-free Ⓣ *adv, adj (predicative)* without harm, loss, or penalty. [C16: see SCOT AND LOT]
Scotland Yard *n* the headquarters of the police force of metropolitan London. Official name: **New Scotland Yard.**
scotoma (skɒ'təʊmə) *n, pl* **scotomas** *or* **scotomata** (-mətə). **1** *Pathol.* a blind spot. **2** *Psychol.* a mental blind spot. [C16: via Med. L from Gk *skotōma* giddiness, from *skotoun* to make dark, from *skotos* darkness]
Scots Ⓣ (skɒts) *adj* **1** of or characteristic of Scotland, its people, their English dialects, or their Gaelic language. ◆ *n* **2** any of the English dialects spoken or written in Scotland.
Scotsman ('skɒtsmən) *or (fem)* **Scotswoman** *n, pl* **Scotsmen** *or* **Scotswomen.** a native or inhabitant of Scotland.
Scots pine *or* **Scotch pine** *n* **1** a coniferous tree of Europe and W and N Asia, having blue-green needle-like leaves and brown cones with a small prickle on each scale. **2** the wood of this tree.
Scotticism ('skɒtɪˌsɪzəm) *n* a Scottish idiom, word, etc.
Scottie *or* **Scotty** ('skɒtɪ) *n, pl* **Scotties. 1** See **Scottish terrier. 2** *Inf.* a Scotsman.
Scottish ('skɒtɪʃ) *adj* of, relating to, or characteristic of Scotland, its people, their Gaelic language, or their English dialects.
Scottish Certificate of Education *n* See **SCE.**
Scottish Gaelic *n* the Goidelic language of the Celts of Scotland, used esp. in the Highlands and Western Isles.
Scottish National Party *n* a political party advocating the independence of Scotland. Abbrev.: **SNP.**
Scottish terrier *n* a small but sturdy long-haired breed of terrier, usually with a black coat.
scoundrel Ⓣ ('skaʊndrəl) *n* a worthless or villainous person. [C16: from ?]
scour[1] Ⓣ ('skaʊə) *vb* **1** to clean or polish (a surface) by washing and rubbing. **2** to remove dirt from or have the dirt removed from. **3** *(tr)* to clear (a channel) by the force of water. **4** *(tr)* to remove by or as if by rubbing. **5** *(tr)* to cause (livestock) to purge their bowels. ◆ *n* **6** the act of scouring. **7** the place scoured, esp. by running water. **8** something that scours, such as a cleansing agent. **9** *(often pl)* prolonged diarrhoea in livestock, esp. cattle. [C13: via MLow G *schüren,* from OF *escurer,* from LL *excūrāre* to cleanse, from *cūrāre;* see CURE]
▸ **'scourer** *n*
scour[2] Ⓣ ('skaʊə) *vb* **1** to range over (territory), as in making a search. **2** to move swiftly or energetically over (territory). [C14: from ON *skūr*]
scourge Ⓣ (skɜːdʒ) *n* **1** a person who harasses or causes destruction. **2** a means of inflicting punishment or suffering. **3** a whip used for inflicting punishment or torture. ◆ *vb* **scourges, scourging, scourged.** *(tr)* **4** to whip. **5** to punish severely. [C13: from Anglo-F, from OF *escorgier* (unattested) to lash, from *es-* EX-[1] + L *corrigia* whip]
▸ **'scourger** *n*
scourings ('skaʊərɪŋz) *pl n* **1** the residue left after cleaning grain. **2** residue that remains after scouring.
scouse (skaʊs) *n Liverpool dialect.* a stew made from left-over meat. [C19: shortened from LOBSCOUSE]
Scouse (skaʊs) *Brit. inf.* ◆ *n* **1** Also: **Scouser.** a person who comes from Liverpool. **2** the dialect spoken by such a person. ◆ *adj* **3** of or from Liverpool. [C20: from SCOUSE]
scout[1] Ⓣ (skaʊt) *n* **1** a person, ship, or aircraft sent out to gain information. **2** *Mil.* a person or unit despatched to reconnoitre the position of the enemy, etc. **3** the act or an instance of scouting. **4** (esp. at Oxford University) a college servant. **5** *Inf.* a fellow. ◆ *vb* **6** to examine or observe (anything) in order to obtain information. **7** *(tr; sometimes foll. by out or up)* to seek. **8** *(intr; foll. by about or around)* to go in search (for). [C14: from OF *ascouter* to listen to, from L *auscultāre* to AUSCULTATE]
▸ **'scouter** *n*
scout[2] (skaʊt) *vb* to reject (a person, etc.) with contempt. [C17: from ON *skūta* derision]
Scout (skaʊt) *n (sometimes not cap.)* a boy or (in some countries) a girl who is a member of a worldwide movement (the **Scout Association**) founded as the Boy Scouts in England in 1908 by Lord Baden-Powell.
▸ **'Scouting** *n*
Scouter ('skaʊtə) *n* the leader of a troop of Scouts. Also called (esp. formerly): **Scoutmaster.**
scow (skaʊ) *n* an unpowered barge used for freight, etc.; lighter. [C18: via Du. *schouw* from Low G *schalde*]
scowl Ⓣ (skaʊl) *vb* **1** *(intr)* to contract the brows in a threatening or angry manner. ◆ *n* **2** a gloomy or threatening expression. [C14: prob. from ON]
▸ **'scowler** *n*
SCPS (in Britain) *abbrev. for* Society of Civil and Public Servants.
scrabble Ⓣ ('skræbᵊl) *vb* **scrabbles, scrabbling, scrabbled. 1** *(intr; often foll. by about or at)* to scrape (at) or grope (for), as with hands or claws. **2** to struggle (with). **3** *(intr; often foll. by for)* to struggle to gain possession. **4** to scribble. ◆ *n* **5** the act or an instance of scrabbling. **6** a scribble. **7** a disorderly struggle. [C16: from MDu. *shrabbelen,* frequentative of *shrabben* to scrape]
▸ **'scrabbler** *n*
Scrabble ('skræbᵊl) *n Trademark.* a game in which words are formed by placing lettered tiles in a pattern similar to a crossword puzzle.
scrag (skræg) *n* **1** a thin or scrawny person or animal. **2** the lean end of a neck of veal or mutton. **3** *Inf.* the neck of a human being. ◆ *vb* **scrags, scragging, scragged. 4** *(tr) Inf.* to wring the neck of. [C16: ? var. of CRAG]
scraggly ('skræglɪ) *adj* **scragglier, scraggliest.** *Chiefly US.* untidy or irregular.
scraggy Ⓣ ('skrægɪ) *adj* **scraggier, scraggiest. 1** lean or scrawny. **2** rough; unkempt.
▸ **'scraggily** *adv* ▸ **'scragginess** *n*
scram[1] Ⓣ (skræm) *vb* **scrams, scramming, scrammed.** *(intr; often imperative) Inf.* to go away hastily. [C20: from SCRAMBLE]
scram[2] (skræm) *n* **1** an emergency shutdown of a nuclear reactor. ◆ *vb* **scrams, scramming, scrammed. 2** (of a nuclear reactor) to shut down or be shut down in an emergency. [C20: ?from SCRAM[1]]

THESAURUS

scot-free *adj* = **unharmed**, clear, safe, scatheless (*arch.*), undamaged, unhurt, uninjured, unpunished, unscathed, without a scratch
Scots *adj* **1** = **Scottish**, Caledonian
scoundrel *n* = **rogue**, bad egg (*old-fashioned inf.*), bastard (*offens.*), blackguard, caitiff (*arch.*), cheat, good-for-nothing, heel (*sl.*), knave (*arch.*), miscreant, ne'er-do-well, rascal, reprobate, rotter (*sl., chiefly Brit.*), scally (*Northwest English dialect*), scamp, scapegrace, swine, vagabond, villain, wretch
scour[1] *vb* **1** = **rub**, abrade, buff, burnish, clean, cleanse, furbish, polish, scrub, whiten **2** = **wash**, cleanse, flush, purge
scour[2] *vb* **1** = **search**, beat, comb, forage, go over with a fine-tooth comb, hunt, look high and low, rake, ransack
scourge *n* **2** = **affliction**, bane, curse, infliction, misfortune, penalty, pest, plague, punishment, terror, torment, visitation **3** = **whip**, cat, cat-o'-nine-tails, lash, strap, switch, thong ◆ *vb* **4** = **whip**, beat, belt (*inf.*), cane, castigate, chastise, discipline, flog, horsewhip, lash, lather (*inf.*), leather, punish, take a strap to, tan (someone's) hide (*sl.*), thrash, trounce, wallop (*inf.*), whale **5** = **afflict**, curse, excoriate, harass, plague, terrorize, torment
Antonyms *n* ≠ **affliction:** benefit, blessing, boon, favour, gift, godsend
scout[1] *n* **2** = **vanguard**, advance guard, escort, lookout, outrider, precursor, reconnoitrer ◆ *vb* **6** = **reconnoitre**, case (*sl.*), check out, investigate, make a reconnaissance, observe, probe, recce (*sl.*), see how the land lies, spy, spy out, survey, watch **8** *with* **about** *or* **around** = **search for**, cast around for, ferret out, hunt for, look for, rustle up, search out, seek, track down
scowl *vb* **1** = **glower**, frown, grimace, look daggers at, lour *or* lower ◆ *n* **2** = **glower**, black look, dirty look, frown, grimace
scrabble *vb* **1** = **scrape**, clamber, claw, dig, grope, paw, scramble, scratch
scraggy *adj* **1** = **scrawny**, angular, bony, emaciated, gangling, gaunt, lanky, lean, rawboned, skinny, undernourished **2** = **unkempt**, draggle-tailed (*arch.*), grotty (*sl.*), lank, meagre, rough, scanty, scruffy, tousled
scram[1] *vb Informal* = **go away**, abscond, beat it (*sl.*), clear off (*inf.*), depart, disappear, get lost (*inf.*), get on one's bike (*Brit. sl.*), go to hell (*inf.*), leave, make oneself scarce (*inf.*), make tracks, quit, scarper (*Brit. sl.*), scoot, skedaddle (*inf.*),

scramble Ⓣ ('skræmbᵊl) *vb* **scrambles, scrambling, scrambled.** **1** (*intr*) to climb or crawl, esp. by using the hands to aid movement. **2** to proceed hurriedly or in a disorderly fashion. **3** (*intr; often foll. by for*) to compete with others, esp. in a disordered manner. **4** (*intr; foll. by through*) to deal with hurriedly. **5** (*tr*) to throw together in a haphazard manner. **6** (*tr*) to collect in a hurried or disorganized manner. **7** (*tr*) to cook (eggs that have been whisked up with milk) in a pan containing a little melted butter. **8** *Mil.* to order (a crew or aircraft) to take off immediately or (of a crew or aircraft) to take off immediately. **9** (*tr*) to render (speech) unintelligible during transmission by means of an electronic scrambler. ◆ *n* **10** the act of scrambling. **11** a climb or trek over difficult ground. **12** a disorderly struggle, esp. to gain possession. **13** *Mil.* an immediate preparation for action, as of crew, aircraft, etc. **14** *Brit.* a motorcycle rally in which competitors race across rough open ground. [C16: blend of SCRABBLE & RAMP]

scrambler ('skræmblə) *n* an electronic device that renders speech unintelligible during transmission, by altering frequencies.

scrap[1] Ⓣ (skræp) *n* **1** a small piece of something larger; fragment. **2** an extract from something written. **3a** waste material or used articles, esp. metal, often collected and reprocessed. **3b** (*as modifier*): *scrap iron.* **4** (*pl*) pieces of discarded food. ◆ *vb* **scraps, scrapping, scrapped.** (*tr*) **5** to discard as useless. [C14: from ON *skrap*]

scrap[2] Ⓣ (skræp) *Inf.* ◆ *n* **1** a fight or argument. ◆ *vb* **scraps, scrapping, scrapped. 2** (*intr*) to quarrel or fight. [C17: ?from SCRAPE]

scrapbook ('skræpˌbʊk) *n* a book or album of blank pages in which to mount newspaper cuttings, pictures, etc.

scrape Ⓣ (skreɪp) *vb* **scrapes, scraping, scraped. 1** to move (a rough or sharp object) across (a surface), esp. to smooth or clean. **2** (*tr; often foll. by away or off*) to remove (a layer) by rubbing. **3** to produce a harsh or grating sound by rubbing against (a surface, etc.). **4** (*tr*) to injure or damage by rough contact: *to scrape one's knee.* **5** (*intr*) to be very economical (esp. in **scrimp and scrape**). **6** (*intr*) to draw the foot backwards in making a bow. **7 scrape acquaintance with.** to contrive an acquaintance with. ◆ *n* **8** the act of scraping. **9** a scraped place. **10** a harsh or grating sound. **11** *Inf.* an awkward or embarrassing predicament. **12** *Inf.* a conflict or struggle. [OE *scrapian*]
▸'**scraper** *n*

scraperboard ('skreɪpəˌbɔːd) *n* thin card covered with a layer of china clay and a top layer of Indian ink, which can be scraped away with a special tool to leave a white line.

scrape through Ⓣ *vb* (*adv*) **1** (*intr*) to manage or survive with difficulty. **2** to succeed in with difficulty or by a narrow margin.

scrape together Ⓣ *or* **up** *vb* (*tr, adv*) to collect with difficulty: *to scrape together money for a new car.*

scrapheap Ⓣ ('skræpˌhiːp) *n* **1** a pile of discarded material. **2 on the scrapheap.** (of people or things) having outlived their usefulness.

scrappy Ⓣ ('skræpɪ) *adj* **scrappier, scrappiest.** fragmentary; disjointed.
▸'**scrappily** *adv*

scratch Ⓣ (skrætʃ) *vb* **1** to mark or cut (the surface of something) with a rough or sharp instrument. **2** (often foll. by *at, out, off,* etc.) to scrape (the surface of something), as with claws, nails, etc. **3** to scrape (the surface of the skin) with the nails, as to relieve itching. **4** to chafe or irritate (a surface, esp. the skin). **5** to make or cause to make a grating sound. **6** (*tr; sometimes foll. by out*) to erase by or as if by scraping. **7** (*tr*) to write or draw awkwardly. **8** (*intr; sometimes foll. by along*) to earn a living, manage, etc., with difficulty. **9** to withdraw (an entry) from a race, (US) election, etc. ◆ *n* **10** the act of scratching. **11** a slight injury. **12** a mark made by scratching. **13** a slight grating sound. **14** (in a handicap sport) a competitor or the status of a competitor who has no allowance. **15a** the line from which competitors start in a race. **15b** (formerly) a line drawn on the floor of a prize ring at which the contestants stood to begin fighting. **16** *Billiards, etc.* a lucky shot. **17 from scratch.** *Inf.* from the very beginning. **18 up to scratch.** (*usually used with a negative*) *Inf.* up to standard. ◆ *adj* **19** *Sport.* (of a team) assembled hastily. **20** (in a handicap sport) with no allowance or penalty. **21** *Inf.* rough or haphazard. [C15: via OF *escrater* from Gmc]
▸'**scratcher** *n* ▸'**scratchy** *adj*

scratchcard ('skrætʒˌkɑːd) *n* a ticket that reveals whether or not the holder is eligible for a prize when the surface is removed by scratching.

scratch file *n Computing.* a temporary store for use during the execution of a program.

scratching ('skrætʃɪŋ) *n* a percussive effect obtained by rotating a gramophone record manually: a disc-jockey and dub technique.

scratch pad *n* **1** *Chiefly US & Canad.* a notebook, esp. one with detachable leaves. **2** *Computing.* a small semiconductor memory for temporary storage.

scratch video *n* the recycling of images from films or television to make collages.

scrawl Ⓣ (skrɔːl) *vb* **1** to write or draw (words, etc.) carelessly or hastily. ◆ *n* **2** careless or scribbled writing or drawing. [C17: ? a blend of SPRAWL & CRAWL[1]]
▸'**scrawly** *adj*

scrawny Ⓣ ('skrɔːnɪ) *adj* **scrawnier, scrawniest. 1** very thin and bony. **2** meagre or stunted. [C19: var. of dialect *scranny*]
▸'**scrawnily** *adv* ▸'**scrawniness** *n*

scream Ⓣ (skriːm) *vb* **1** to utter or emit (a sharp piercing cry or similar sound), esp. as of fear, pain, etc. **2** (*intr*) to laugh wildly. **3** (*intr*) to speak, shout, or behave in a wild manner. **4** (*tr*) to bring (oneself) into a specified state by screaming: *she screamed herself hoarse.* **5** (*intr*) to be extremely conspicuous: *these orange curtains scream; you need something more restful.* ◆ *n* **6** a sharp piercing cry or sound, esp. one denoting fear or pain. **7** *Inf.* a person or thing that causes great amusement. [C13: from Gmc]

screamer ('skriːmə) *n* **1** a person or thing that screams. **2** a goose-like aquatic bird, such as the **crested screamer** of tropical and subtropical South America. **3** *Inf.* (in printing) an exclamation mark. **4** someone or something that raises screams of laughter or astonishment. **5** *US & Canad. sl.* a sensational headline. **6** *Austral. sl.* a person or thing that is excellent of its kind.

scree (skriː) *n* an accumulation of rock fragments at the foot of a cliff or hillside, often forming a sloping heap. [OE *scrīthan* to slip; rel. to ON *skrītha* to slide]

screech[1] Ⓣ (skriːtʃ) *n* **1** a shrill or high-pitched sound or cry. ◆ *vb* **2** to utter with or produce a screech. [C16: var. of earlier *scritch*, imit.]
▸'**screecher** *n* ▸'**screechy** *adj*

screech[2] (skriːtʃ) *n Canad. sl.* (esp. in Newfoundland) a dark rum. [?from SCREECH[1]]

screech owl *n* **1** *Brit.* another name for **barn owl. 2** a small North American owl having a reddish-brown or grey plumage.

screed Ⓣ (skriːd) *n* **1** a long or prolonged speech or piece of writing. **2** a strip of wood, plaster, or metal placed on a surface to act as a guide to the thickness of the cement or plaster coat to be applied. **3** a mixture of cement, sand, and water applied to a concrete slab, etc., to give a smooth surface finish. [C14: prob. var. of OE *scrēade* shred]

screen Ⓣ (skriːn) *n* **1** a light movable frame, panel, or partition serving to shelter, divide, hide, etc. **2** anything that serves to shelter, protect, or conceal. **3** a frame containing a mesh that is placed over a window to keep out insects. **4** a decorated partition, esp. in a church around the choir. **5** a sieve. **6** the wide end of a cathode-ray tube, esp. in a television set, on which a visible image is formed. **7** a white or silvered surface, placed in front of a projector to receive the enlarged image of

THESAURUS

sling one's hook (*Brit. sl.*), slope off, take oneself off, vamoose (*sl., chiefly US*)

scramble *vb* **1** = **struggle**, clamber, climb, crawl, move with difficulty, push, scrabble, swarm **3** = **strive**, contend, hasten, jockey for position, jostle, make haste, push, run, rush, vie ◆ *n* **11** = **climb**, trek **12** = **struggle**, commotion, competition, confusion, free-for-all (*inf.*), hassle (*inf.*), hustle, melee *or* mêlée, muddle, race, rat race, rush, tussle

scrap[1] *n* **1** = **piece**, atom, bit, bite, crumb, fragment, grain, iota, mite, modicum, morsel, mouthful, part, particle, portion, remnant, sliver, snatch, snippet, trace **3** = **waste**, junk, off cuts **4** *plural* = **leftovers**, bits, leavings, remains, scrapings ◆ *vb* **5** = **get rid of**, abandon, break up, chuck, demolish, discard, dispense with, ditch (*sl.*), drop, jettison, junk (*inf.*), shed, throw away *or* out, throw on the scrapheap, toss out, trash (*sl.*), write off
Antonyms *vb* ≠ **get rid of:** bring back, recall, re-establish, reinstall, reinstate, restore, return

scrap[2] *Informal n* **1** = **fight**, argument, battle, brawl, disagreement, dispute, dust-up (*inf.*), quarrel, row, scrimmage, scuffle, set-to (*inf.*), shindig (*inf.*), squabble, tiff, wrangle ◆ *vb* **2** = **fight**, argue, barney (*inf.*), bicker, come to blows, fall out (*inf.*), have a shouting match (*inf.*), have words, row, spar, squabble, wrangle

scrape *vb* **1** = **rub**, abrade, bark, graze, scratch, scuff, skin **2** = **scour**, clean, erase, file, remove, rub **3** = **grate**, grind, rasp, scratch, screech, set one's teeth on edge, squeak **5** = **scrimp**, live from hand to mouth, pinch, save, skimp, stint, tighten one's belt ◆ *n* **11** *Informal* = **predicament**, awkward situation, difficulty, dilemma, distress, fix (*inf.*), mess, plight, pretty pickle (*inf.*), spot (*inf.*), tight spot, trouble

scrape through *vb* **2** = **get by** (*inf.*), cut it fine (*inf.*), have a close shave (*inf.*), just make it, struggle

scrape together *vb* = **collect**, amass, dredge up, get hold of, glean, hoard, muster, rake up *or* together, save

scrapheap *n* **2 on the scrapheap** = **discarded**, ditched (*sl.*), jettisoned, put out to grass (*inf.*), redundant, written off

scrappy *adj* = **incomplete**, bitty, disjointed, fragmentary, perfunctory, piecemeal, sketchy, thrown together

scratch *vb* **1, 2** = **mark**, claw, cut, damage, etch, grate, graze, incise, lacerate, make a mark on, rub, score, scrape **6** = **erase**, annul, cancel, cross out, delete, eliminate, strike off **9** = **withdraw**, pull out, stand down ◆ *n* **12** = **mark**, blemish, claw mark, gash, graze, laceration, scrape **18 up to scratch** *Informal* = **adequate**, acceptable, capable, competent, satisfactory, sufficient, up to snuff (*inf.*), up to standard ◆ *adj* **19** = **improvised**, haphazard, hastily prepared, impromptu, rough, rough-and-ready

scrawl *vb* **1** = **scribble**, doodle, scratch, squiggle ◆ *n* **2** = **scribble**, doodle, squiggle

scrawny *adj* **1** = **thin**, angular, bony, gaunt, lanky, lean, rawboned, scraggy, skeletal, skin-and-bones (*inf.*), skinny, undernourished

scream *vb* **1** = **cry**, bawl, holler (*inf.*), screech, shriek, shrill, sing out, squeal, yell **5** = **be conspicuous**, clash, jar, shriek ◆ *n* **6** = **cry**, howl, outcry, screech, shriek, wail, yell, yelp **7** *Informal* = **laugh**, card, caution (*inf.*), character (*inf.*), comedian, comic, entertainer, hoot (*inf.*), joker, riot (*sl.*), sensation, wag, wit

screech[1] *n* **1** = **cry**, scream, shriek, squawk, squeal, yelp ◆ *vb* **2** = **cry**, scream, shriek, squawk, squeal, yelp

screed *n* **1** = **passage**, speech

screen *n* **1, 2** = **cover**, awning, canopy, cloak, concealment, guard, hedge, mantle, partition, room divider, shade, shelter, shield, shroud **3** = **mesh**, net ◆ *vb* **12** = **cover**, cloak, conceal, defend, guard, hide, mask, protect, safeguard, shade, shelter, shield, shroud, shut out, veil **14**

a film or of slides. **8 the screen.** the film industry or films collectively. **9** *Photog.* a plate of ground glass in some types of camera on which the image of a subject is focused. **10** men or ships deployed around and ahead of a larger military formation to warn of attack. **11** *Electronics.* See **screen grid.** ◆ *vb* (*tr*) **12** (sometimes foll. by *off*) to shelter, protect, or conceal. **13** to sieve or sort. **14** to test or check (an individual or group) so as to determine suitability for a task, etc. **15** to examine for the presence of a disease, weapons, etc. **16** to provide with a screen or screens. **17** to project (a film) onto a screen, esp. for public viewing. [C15: from OF *escren* (F *écran*)]
► **'screenable** *adj* ► **'screener** *n* ► **'screenful** *n*

screen grid *n Electronics.* an electrode placed between the control grid and anode of a valve which acts as an electrostatic shield, thus increasing the stability of the device. Sometimes shortened to **screen.**

screenings ('skri:nɪŋz) *pl n* refuse separated by sifting.

screening test *n* a simple test performed on a large number of people to identify those who have or are likely to develop a specified disease.

screenplay ('skri:n,pleɪ) *n* the script for a film, including instructions for sets and camera work.

screen process *n* a method of printing using a fine mesh of silk, nylon, etc., treated with an impermeable coating except in the areas through which ink is subsequently forced onto the paper behind. Also called: **silk-screen printing.**

screensaver ('skri:nseɪvə) *n Computing.* a computer program that reduces screen damage resulting from an unchanging display, when the computer is switched on but not in use, by blanking the screen or generating moving patterns, pictures, etc.

screenwriter ('skri:n,raɪtə) *n* a person who writes screenplays.

screw **T** (skru:) *n* **1** a device used for fastening materials together, consisting of a threaded shank that has a slotted head by which it may be rotated so as to cut its own thread. **2** Also called: **screw-bolt.** a threaded cylindrical rod that engages with a similarly threaded cylindrical hole. **3** a thread in a cylindrical hole corresponding with that on the screw with which it is designed to engage. **4** anything resembling a screw in shape or spiral form. **5** a twisting movement of or resembling that of a screw. **6** Also called: **screw-back.** *Billiards, etc.* a stroke in which the cue ball moves backward after striking the object ball. **7** another name for **propeller** (sense 1). **8** *Sl.* a prison guard. **9** *Brit. sl.* salary, wages, or earnings. **10** *Brit.* a small amount of salt, tobacco, etc., in a twist of paper. **11** *Sl.* a person who is mean with money. **12** *Sl.* an old or worthless horse. **13** (*often pl*) *Sl.* force or compulsion (esp. in **put the screws on**). **14** *Taboo sl.* sexual intercourse. **15 have a screw loose.** *Inf.* to be insane. ◆ *vb* **16** (*tr*) to rotate (a screw or bolt) so as to drive it into or draw it out of a material. **17** (*tr*) to cut a screw thread in (a rod or hole) with a tap or die or on a lathe. **18** to turn or cause to turn in the manner of a screw. **19** (*tr*) to attach or fasten with a screw or screws. **20** (*tr*) *Inf.* to take advantage of; cheat. **21** (*tr;* often foll. by *up*) *Inf.* to distort or contort: *he screwed his face into a scowl.* **22** (*tr;* often foll. by *from* or *out of*) *Inf.* to coerce or force out of; extort. **23** *Taboo sl.* to have sexual intercourse (with). **24** (*tr*) *Sl.* to burgle. **25 have one's head screwed on the right way.** *Inf.* to be sensible. ◆ See also **screw up.** [C15: from F *escroe,* from Med. L *scrōfa* screw, from L: sow, presumably because the thread of the screw is like the spiral of the sow's tail]
► **'screwer** *n*

screwball ('skru:,bɔ:l) *Sl., chiefly US & Canad.* ◆ *n* **1** an odd or eccentric person. ◆ *adj* **2** odd; eccentric.

screwdriver ('skru:,draɪvə) *n* **1** a tool used for turning screws, usually having a steel shank with a flattened square-cut tip that fits into a slot in the head of the screw. **2** an alcoholic beverage consisting of orange juice and vodka.

screwed (skru:d) *adj* **1** fastened by a screw or screws. **2** having spiral grooves like a screw. **3** twisted or distorted. **4** *Brit. sl.* drunk.

screw eye *n* a wood screw with its shank bent into a ring.

screw pine *n* any of various tropical Old World plants having a spiral mass of pineapple-like leaves and conelike fruits.

screw propeller *n* an early form of ship's propeller in which an Archimedes' screw is used to produce thrust by accelerating a flow of water.

screw top *n* **1** a bottle top that screws onto the bottle, allowing the bottle to be resealed after use. **2** a bottle with such a top.
► **'screw-,top** *adj*

screw up **T** *vb* (*tr, adv*) **1** to twist out of shape or distort. **2** to summon up: *to screw up one's courage.* **3** (*also intr*) *Inf.* to mishandle or bungle.

screwy **T** ('skru:ɪ) *adj* **screwier, screwiest.** *Inf.* odd, crazy, or eccentric.

scribble **T** ('skrɪbᵊl) *vb* **scribbles, scribbling, scribbled.** **1** to write or draw in a hasty or illegible manner. **2** to make meaningless or illegible marks (on). **3** *Derog. or facetious.* to write poetry, novels, etc. ◆ *n* **4** hasty careless writing or drawing. **5** meaningless or illegible marks. [C15: from Med. L *scrībillāre* to write hastily, from L *scrībere* to write]
► **'scribbler** *n* ► **'scribbly** *adj*

scribbly gum *n Austral.* a eucalypt with smooth white bark, marked with random patterns made by wood-boring insects.

scribe **T** (skraɪb) *n* **1** a person who copies documents, esp. a person who made handwritten copies before the invention of printing. **2** a clerk or public copyist. **3** *Bible.* a recognized scholar and teacher of the Jewish Law. ◆ *vb* **scribes, scribing, scribed.** **4** to score a line on (a surface) with a pointed instrument, as in metalworking. [(in the senses: writer, etc.) C14: from L *scrība* clerk, from *scrībere* to write; C17 (vb): ?from INSCRIBE]
► **'scribal** *adj*

scriber ('skraɪbə) *n* a pointed steel tool used to score materials as a guide to cutting, etc. Also called: **scribe.**

scrim (skrɪm) *n* a fine open-weave fabric, used in upholstery, lining, building, and in the theatre to create the illusion of a solid wall. [C18: from ?]

scrimmage **T** ('skrɪmɪdʒ) *n* **1** a rough or disorderly struggle. **2** *American football.* the clash of opposing linemen at every down. ◆ *vb* **scrimmages, scrimmaging, scrimmaged.** **3** (*intr*) to engage in a scrimmage. **4** (*tr*) to put (the ball) into a scrimmage. [C15: from earlier *scrimish,* var. of SKIRMISH]
► **'scrimmager** *n*

scrimp **T** (skrɪmp) *vb* **1** (when *intr,* sometimes foll. by *on*) to be very sparing in the use (of) (esp. in **scrimp and save**). **2** (*tr*) to treat meanly: *he is scrimping his children.* [C18: Scot., from ?]
► **'scrimpy** *adj* ► **'scrimpiness** *n*

scrimshank ('skrɪm,ʃæŋk) *vb* (*intr*) *Brit. mil. sl.* to shirk work. [C19: from ?]

scrimshaw ('skrɪm,ʃɔ:) *n* **1** the art of decorating or carving shells, bone, ivory, etc., done by sailors as a leisure activity. **2** an article or articles made in this manner. [C19: from ?]

scrip[1] (skrɪp) *n* **1** a written certificate, list, etc. **2** a small scrap, esp. of paper with writing on it. **3** *Finance.* **3a** a certificate representing a claim to part of a share of stock. **3b** the shares issued by a company (**scrip** or **bonus issue**) without charge and distributed among existing shareholders. [C18: in some senses, prob. from SCRIPT; otherwise, short for *subscription receipt*]

scrip[2] (skrɪp) *or* **script** *n Inf.* a medical prescription. [C20: from PRESCRIPTION]

script **T** (skrɪpt) *n* **1** handwriting as distinguished from print. **2** the letters, characters, or figures used in writing by hand. **3** any system or style of writing. **4** written copy for the use of performers in films and plays. **5** *Law.* an original or principal document. **6** an answer paper in an examination. **7** another word for **scrip**[2]. ◆ *vb* **8** (*tr*) to write a script for. [C14: from L *scriptum* something written, from *scrībere* to write]

Script. *abbrev. for* Scripture(s).

scriptorium (skrɪp'tɔ:rɪəm) *n, pl* **scriptoriums** *or* **scriptoria** (-rɪə). a room, esp. in a monastery, set apart for the copying of manuscripts. [from Med. L]

scripture ('skrɪptʃə) *n* a sacred, solemn, or authoritative book or piece of writing. [C13: from L *scriptūra* written material, from *scrībere* to write]
► **'scriptural** *adj*

Scripture **T** ('skrɪptʃə) *n* **1** Also called: **Holy Scripture, Holy Writ, the Scriptures.** *Christianity.* the Old and New Testaments. **2** any book or body of writings, esp. when regarded as sacred by a particular religious group.

scriptwriter ('skrɪpt,raɪtə) *n* a person who prepares scripts, esp. for a film.
► **'script,writing** *n*

scrivener ('skrɪvnə) *n Arch.* **1** a person who writes out deeds, etc. **2** a notary. [C14: from *scrivein* clerk, from OF *escrivain,* ult. from L *scrība* SCRIBE]

scrod (skrɒd) *n US.* a young cod or haddock. [C19: ? from obs. Du. *schrood,* from MDu. *schrode* SHRED (n); the name perhaps refers to the method of preparing the fish for cooking]

scrofula ('skrɒfjʊlə) *n Pathol.* (*no longer in technical use*) tuberculosis of the lymphatic glands. Also called (formerly): (the) **king's evil.** [C14: from Med. L, from LL *scrōfulae* swollen glands in the neck, lit.: little sows (sows were thought to be particularly prone to the disease), from L *scrōfa* sow]
► **'scrofulous** *adj*

THESAURUS

= **vet**, cull, evaluate, examine, filter, gauge, grade, process, riddle, scan, sieve, sift, sort **17** = **broadcast**, present, put on, show

screw *vb* **16, 18** = **turn**, tighten, twist, work in **21** *Informal* = **contort**, contract, crumple, distort, pucker, wrinkle **22** *Informal often with* **from** *or* **out of** = **extort**, bleed, coerce, extract, force, pressurize, squeeze, wrest, wring

screw up *vb* **1** = **contort**, contract, crumple, distort, knit, knot, pucker, wrinkle **3** *Informal* = **bungle**, bitch (up), bodge (*inf.*), botch, cock up (*Brit. sl.*), louse up (*sl.*), make a hash of (*inf.*), make a mess of (*sl.*), make a nonsense of, mess up, mishandle, mismanage, queer (*inf.*), spoil

screwy *adj Informal* = **crazy**, batty (*sl.*), crackers (*Brit. sl.*), crackpot (*inf.*), dotty (*sl., chiefly Brit.*), eccentric, nutty (*sl.*), odd, off-the-wall (*sl.*), outré, out to lunch (*inf.*), queer (*inf.*), round the bend (*Brit. sl.*), rum (*Brit. sl.*), weird

scribble *vb* **1, 2** = **scrawl**, dash off, doodle, jot, pen, scratch, write

scribe *n* **1, 2** = **copyist**, amanuensis, clerk, notary (*arch.*), penman (*rare*), scrivener (*arch.*), secretary, writer

scrimmage *n* **1** = **fight**, affray (*Law*), brawl, disturbance, dust-up (*inf.*), fray, free-for-all (*inf.*), melee *or* mêlée, riot, row, scrap (*inf.*), scuffle, set-to (*inf.*), shindig (*inf.*), skirmish, squabble, struggle

scrimp *vb* **1** = **economize**, be frugal, curtail, limit, pinch, pinch pennies, reduce, save, scrape, shorten, skimp, stint, straiten, tighten one's belt

script *n* **1** = **handwriting**, calligraphy, hand, letters, longhand, penmanship, writing **4** = **text**, book, copy, dialogue, libretto, lines, manuscript, words

Scripture *n* **1** = **The Bible**, Holy Bible, Holy Scripture, Holy Writ, The Book of Books, The Good Book, The Gospels, The Scriptures, The Word, The Word of God

scroll ⓣ (skrəʊl) *n* **1** a roll of parchment, etc., usually inscribed with writing. **2** an ancient book in the form of a roll of parchment, papyrus, etc. **3** a decorative carving or moulding resembling a scroll. ◆ *vb* **4** (*tr*) to saw into scrolls. **5** to roll up like a scroll. **6** *Computing.* to move (text) on a screen in order to view a section that cannot be fitted into a single display. [C15 *scrowle,* from *scrowe,* from OF *escroe* scrap of parchment, but also infl. by ROLL]

scroll saw *n* a saw with a narrow blade for cutting intricate ornamental curves in wood.

scrollwork (ˈskrəʊlˌwɜːk) *n* ornamental work in scroll-like patterns.

Scrooge ⓣ (skruːdʒ) *n* a mean or miserly person. [C19: after a character in Dickens' story *A Christmas Carol* (1843)]

scrophulariaceous (ˌskrɒfjʊˌlɛərɪˈeɪʃəs) *adj* of or belonging to the *Scrophulariaceae,* a family of plants including figwort, snapdragon, foxglove, and mullein. [C19: from NL (*herba*) *scrophularia* scrofula (plant), from the use of such plants in treating scrofula]

scrotum (ˈskrəʊtəm) *n, pl* **scrota** (-tə) *or* **scrotums.** the pouch of skin containing the testes in most mammals. [C16: from L]
▸ˈ**scrotal** *adj*

scrounge ⓣ (skraʊndʒ) *vb* **scrounges, scrounging, scrounged.** *Inf.* **1** (when *intr,* sometimes foll. by *around*) to search in order to acquire (something) without cost. **2** to obtain or seek to obtain (something) by begging. [C20: var. of dialect *scrunge* to steal, from ?]
▸ˈ**scrounger** *n*

scrub[1] ⓣ (skrʌb) *vb* **scrubs, scrubbing, scrubbed. 1** to rub (a surface, etc.) hard, with or as if with a brush, soap, and water, in order to clean it. **2** to remove (dirt) by rubbing, esp. with a brush and water. **3** (*intr;* foll. by *up*) (of a surgeon) to wash the hands and arms thoroughly before operating. **4** (*tr*) to purify (a gas) by removing impurities. **5** (*tr*) *Inf.* to delete or cancel. ◆ *n* **6** the act of or an instance of scrubbing. [C14: from MLow G *schrubben,* or MDu. *schrobben*]

scrub[2] (skrʌb) *n* **1a** vegetation consisting of stunted trees, bushes, and other plants growing in an arid area. **1b** (*as modifier*): *scrub vegetation.* **2** an area of arid land covered with such vegetation. **3a** an animal of inferior breeding or condition. **3b** (*as modifier*): *a scrub bull.* **4** a small person. **5** anything stunted or inferior. **6** *Sport, US & Canad.* a player not in the first team. **7 the scrub.** *Austral. inf.* a remote or uncivilized place. ◆ *adj* (*prenominal*) **8** small or inferior. **9** *Sport, US.* **9a** (of a player) not in the first team. **9b** (of a team) composed of such players. [C16: var. of SHRUB[1]]

scrubber (ˈskrʌbə) *n* **1** a person or thing that scrubs. **2** an apparatus for purifying a gas. **3** *Derog. sl.* a promiscuous woman.

scrubby ⓣ (ˈskrʌbɪ) *adj* **scrubbier, scrubbiest. 1** covered with or consisting of scrub. **2** (of trees, etc.) stunted in growth. **3** *Brit. inf.* messy.

scrubland (ˈskrʌbˌlænd) *n* an area of scrub vegetation.

scrub turkey *n* another term for **megapode.**

scrub typhus *n* a disease characterized by severe headache, skin rash, chills, and swelling of the lymph nodes, caused by the bite of mites infected with a microorganism: occurs mainly in Asia and Australia.

scruff[1] ⓣ (skrʌf) *n* the nape of the neck (esp. in **by the scruff of the neck**). [C18: var. of *scuft,* ?from ON *skoft* hair]

scruff[2] ⓣ (skrʌf) *n Inf.* **1** an untidy scruffy person. **2** a disreputable person; ruffian.

scruffy ⓣ (ˈskrʌfɪ) *adj* **scruffier, scruffiest.** unkempt or shabby.

scrum (skrʌm) *n* **1** *Rugby.* the act or method of restarting play when the two opposing packs of forwards group together with heads down and arms interlocked and push to gain ground while the scrum half throws the ball in and the hookers attempt to scoop it out to their own team. **2** *Inf.* a disorderly struggle. ◆ *vb* **scrums, scrumming, scrummed. 3** (*intr;* usually foll. by *down*) *Rugby.* to form a scrum. [C19: from SCRUMMAGE]

scrum half *n Rugby.* **1** a player who puts in the ball at scrums and tries to get it away to his three-quarter backs. **2** this position in a team.

scrummage (ˈskrʌmɪdʒ) *n, vb* **scrummages, scrummaging, scrummaged. 1** *Rugby.* another word for **scrum. 2** a variant of **scrimmage.** [C19: var. of SCRIMMAGE]

scrump (skrʌmp) *vb Dialect.* to steal (apples) from an orchard or garden. [var. of SCRIMP]

scrumptious ⓣ (ˈskrʌmpʃəs) *adj Inf.* very pleasing; delicious. [C19: prob. changed from SUMPTUOUS]
▸ˈ**scrumptiously** *adv*

scrumpy (ˈskrʌmpɪ) *n* a rough dry cider, brewed esp. in the West Country of England. [from *scrump,* var. of SCRIMP (in obs. sense: withered), referring to the apples used]

scrunch ⓣ (skrʌntʃ) *vb* **1** to crumple or crunch or to be crumpled or crunched. ◆ *n* **2** the act or sound of scrunching. [C19: var. of CRUNCH]

scrunchie (ˈskrʌntʃɪ) *n* a loop of elastic covered loosely with fabric, used to hold the hair in a ponytail.

scruple ⓣ (ˈskruːpᵊl) *n* **1** (*often pl*) a doubt or hesitation as to what is morally right in a certain situation. **2** *Arch.* a very small amount. **3** a unit of weight equal to 20 grains (1.296 grams). ◆ *vb* **scruples, scrupling, scrupled. 4** (*obs. when tr*) to have doubts (about), esp. from a moral compunction. [C16: from L *scrūpulus* a small weight, from *scrūpus* rough stone]

scrupulous ⓣ (ˈskruːpjʊləs) *adj* **1** characterized by careful observation of what is morally right. **2** very careful or precise. [C15: from L *scrūpulōsus* punctilious]
▸ˈ**scrupulously** *adv* ▸ˈ**scrupulousness** *n*

scrutineer (ˌskruːtɪˈnɪə) *n* a person who examines, esp. one who scrutinizes the conduct of an election poll.

scrutinize ⓣ *or* **scrutinise** (ˈskruːtɪˌnaɪz) *vb* **scrutinizes, scrutinizing, scrutinized** *or* **scrutinises, scrutinising, scrutinised.** (*tr*) to examine carefully or in minute detail.
▸ˈ**scrutiˌnizer** *or* ˈ**scrutiˌniser** *n*

scrutiny ⓣ (ˈskruːtɪnɪ) *n, pl* **scrutinies. 1** close or minute examination. **2** a searching look. **3** (in the early Christian Church) a formal testing that catechumens had to undergo before being baptized. [C15: from LL *scrūtinium* an investigation, from *scrūtārī* to search (orig. referring to rag-and-bone men), from *scrūta* rubbish]

scry (skraɪ) *vb* **scries, scrying, scried.** (*intr*) to divine, esp. by crystal gazing. [C16: from DESCRY]

scuba (ˈskjuːbə) *n* an apparatus used in skin diving, consisting of a cylinder or cylinders containing compressed air attached to a breathing apparatus. [C20: from the initials of *self-contained underwater breathing apparatus*]

scud ⓣ (skʌd) *vb* **scuds, scudding, scudded.** (*intr*) **1** (esp. of clouds) to move along swiftly and smoothly. **2** *Naut.* to run before a gale. ◆ *n* **3** the act of scudding. **4a** a formation of low ragged clouds driven by a strong wind beneath rain-bearing clouds. **4b** a sudden shower or gust of wind. [C16: prob. of Scand. origin]

scuff (skʌf) *vb* **1** to drag (the feet) while walking. **2** to scratch (a surface) or (of a surface) to become scratched. **3** (*tr*) *US.* to poke at (something) with the foot. ◆ *n* **4** the act or sound of scuffing. **5** a rubbed place caused by scuffing. **6** a backless slipper. [C19: prob. imit.]

scuffle ⓣ (ˈskʌfᵊl) *vb* **scuffles, scuffling, scuffled.** (*intr*) **1** to fight in a disorderly manner. **2** to move by shuffling. ◆ *n* **3** a disorderly struggle. **4** the sound made by scuffling. [C16: of Scand. origin; cf. Swedish *skuff, skuffa* to push]

scull (skʌl) *n* **1** a single oar moved from side to side over the stern of a boat to propel it. **2** one of a pair of short-handled oars, both of which are pulled by one oarsman. **3** a racing shell propelled by an oarsman or oarsmen pulling two oars. **4** an act, instance, period, or distance of sculling. ◆ *vb* **5** to propel (a boat) with a scull. [C14: from ?]
▸ˈ**sculler** *n*

scullery (ˈskʌlərɪ) *n, pl* **sculleries.** *Chiefly Brit.* a small room or part of a kitchen where washing-up, vegetable preparation, etc., is done. [C15: from Anglo-Norman *squillerie,* from OF, from *escuele* a bowl, from L *scutella,* from *scutra* a flat tray]

THESAURUS

scroll *n* **1, 2** = **roll**, parchment

Scrooge *n* = **miser**, cheapskate (*inf.*), meanie *or* meany (*inf., chiefly Brit.*), money-grubber (*inf.*), niggard, penny-pincher (*inf.*), skinflint, tightwad (*US & Canad. sl.*)

scrounge *vb* **1** *Informal* = **cadge**, beg, blag (*sl.*), bum (*inf.*), forage for, freeload (*sl.*), hunt around (for), mooch (*sl.*), sponge (*inf.*), touch (someone) for (*sl.*), wheedle

scrounger *adj* **1** = **cadger**, bum (*inf.*), freeloader (*sl.*), parasite, sponger (*inf.*)

scrub[1] *vb* **1, 2** = **scour**, clean, cleanse, rub **5** *Informal* = **cancel**, abandon, abolish, call off, delete, discontinue, do away with, drop, forget about, give up

scrubby *adj* **2** = **stunted**, meagre, scrawny, spindly, underdeveloped, undersized

scruff[1] *n* = **nape**, scrag (*inf.*)

scruff[2] *n* **1** *Informal* = **ragamuffin**, ragbag (*inf.*), scarecrow, sloven, tramp

scruffy *adj* = **tatty**, disreputable, draggletailed (*arch.*), frowzy, grungy, ill-groomed, mangy, messy, ragged, run-down, scrubby (*Brit. inf.*), seedy, shabby, slatternly, sloppy (*inf.*), slovenly, sluttish, squalid, tattered, ungroomed, unkempt, untidy
Antonyms *adj* chic, dapper, natty, neat, soigné *or* soignée, spruce, tidy, well-dressed, well-groomed, well-turned-out

scrumptious *adj Informal* = **delicious**, appetizing, delectable, exquisite, inviting, luscious, magnificent, moreish (*inf.*), mouthwatering, succulent, yummy (*sl.*)

scrunch *vb* **1** = **crumple**, champ, chew, crunch, crush, mash, ruck up, squash

scruple *n* **1** = **misgiving**, caution, compunction, difficulty, doubt, hesitation, perplexity, qualm, reluctance, second thoughts, squeamishness, twinge of conscience, uneasiness ◆ *vb* **4** = **have misgivings about**, balk at, be loath, be reluctant, demur, doubt, falter, have qualms about, hesitate, stick at, think twice about, vacillate, waver

scrupulous *adj* **1** = **moral**, conscientious, honourable, principled, upright **2** = **careful**, exact, fastidious, meticulous, minute, nice, painstaking, precise, punctilious, rigorous, strict
Antonyms *adj* ≠ **moral:** amoral, dishonest, uncaring, unconscientious, unprincipled, unscrupulous, without scruples ≠ **careful:** careless, inexact, reckless, slapdash, superficial

scrutinize *vb* = **examine**, analyse, dissect, explore, go over with a fine-tooth comb, inquire into, inspect, investigate, peruse, pore over, probe, research, scan, search, sift, study, work over

scrutiny *n* **1** = **examination**, analysis, close study, exploration, inquiry, inspection, investigation, once-over (*inf.*), perusal, search, sifting, study

scud *vb* **1** = **fly**, blow, haste, hasten, race, sail, shoot, skim, speed

scuffle *vb* **1** = **fight**, clash, come to blows, contend, exchange blows, grapple, jostle, struggle, tussle ◆ *n* **3** = **fight**, affray (*Law*), barney (*inf.*), brawl, commotion, disturbance, fray, ruckus (*inf.*), ruction (*inf.*), rumpus, scrap (*inf.*), scrimmage, set-to (*inf.*), shindig (*inf.*), skirmish, tussle

scullion (ˈskʌljən) *n* **1** a mean or despicable person. **2** *Arch.* a servant employed to work in a kitchen. [C15: from OF *escouillon* cleaning cloth, from *escouve* a broom, from L *scōpa* a broom, twig]

sculpt (skʌlpt) *vb* **1** a variant of **sculpture. 2** (*intr*) to practise sculpture. ◆ Also: **sculp.** [C19: from F *sculpter,* from L *sculpere* to carve]

sculptor (ˈskʌlptə) *or* (*fem*) **sculptress** *n* a person who practises sculpture.

sculpture 🅣 (ˈskʌlptʃə) *n* **1** the art of making figures or designs in relief or the round by carving wood, moulding plaster, etc., or casting metals, etc. **2** works or a work made in this way. **3** ridges or indentations as on a shell, formed by natural processes. ◆ *vb* **sculptures, sculpturing, sculptured.** (*mainly tr*) **4** (*also intr*) to carve, cast, or fashion (stone, bronze, etc.) three-dimensionally. **5** to portray (a person, etc.) by means of sculpture. **6** to form in the manner of sculpture. **7** to decorate with sculpture. [C14: from L *sculptūra* a carving]
▸ **ˈsculptural** *adj*

sculpturesque (ˌskʌlptʃəˈrɛsk) *adj* resembling sculpture.
▸ **ˌsculpturˈesquely** *adv*

scum 🅣 (skʌm) *n* **1** a layer of impure matter that forms on the surface of a liquid, often as the result of boiling or fermentation. **2** the greenish film of algae and similar vegetation surface of a stagnant pond. **3** the skin of oxides or impurities on the surface of a molten metal. **4** waste matter. **5** a worthless person or group of people. ◆ *vb* **scums, scumming, scummed. 6** (*tr*) to remove scum from. **7** (*intr*) *Rare.* to form a layer of or become covered with scum. [C13: of Gmc origin]
▸ **ˈscummy** *adj*

scumbag (ˈskʌmˌbæg) *n Sl* an offensive or despicable person. [C20: ?from earlier US sense: condom, from US slang *scum* semen + bag]

scumble (ˈskʌmbᵊl) *vb* **scumbles, scumbling, scumbled. 1** (in painting and drawing) to soften or blend (an outline or colour) with an upper coat of opaque colour, applied very thinly. **2** to produce an effect of broken colour on doors, panelling, etc., by exposing coats of paint below the top coat. ◆ *n* **3** the upper layer of colour applied in this way. [C18: prob. from SCUM]

scuncheon (ˈskʌntʃən) *n* the inner part of a door jamb or window frame. [C15: from OF *escoinson,* from *coin* angle]

scungy (ˈskʌndʒɪ) *adj* **scungier, scungiest.** *Austral.* & *NZ sl.* miserable; sordid; dirty. [C20: from ?]

scunner (ˈskʌnə) *Dialect, chiefly Scot.* ◆ *vb* **1** (*intr*) to feel aversion. **2** (*tr*) to produce a feeling of aversion in. ◆ *n* **3** a strong aversion (often in **take a scunner**). **4** an object of dislike; nuisance. [C14: from Scot. *skunner,* from ?]

scup (skʌp) *n* a common fish of American coastal regions of the Atlantic. [C19: from Amerind *mishcup,* from *mishe* big + *kuppe* close together; from the form of the scales]

scupper[1] (ˈskʌpə) *n Naut.* a drain or spout allowing water on the deck of a vessel to flow overboard. [C15 *skopper,* from ?]

scupper[2] 🅣 (ˈskʌpə) *vb* (*tr*) *Brit. sl.* **1** to overwhelm, ruin, or disable. **2** to sink (one's ship) deliberately. [C19: from ?]

scurf (skɜːf) *n* **1** another name for **dandruff. 2** flaky or scaly matter adhering to or peeling off a surface. [OE *scurf*]
▸ **ˈscurfy** *adj*

scurrilous 🅣 (ˈskʌrɪləs) *adj* **1** grossly or obscenely abusive or defamatory. **2** characterized by gross or obscene humour. [C16: from L *scurrīlis* derisive, from *scurra* buffoon]
▸ **scurrility** (skəˈrɪlɪtɪ) *n* ▸ **ˈscurrilously** *adv*

scurry 🅣 (ˈskʌrɪ) *vb* **scurries, scurrying, scurried. 1** to move about hurriedly. **2** (*intr*) to whirl about. ◆ *n, pl* **scurries. 3** the act or sound of scurrying. **4** a brisk light whirling movement, as of snow. [C19: prob. from *hurry-scurry,* from HURRY]

scurvy 🅣 (ˈskɜːvɪ) *n* **1** a disease caused by a lack of vitamin C, characterized by anaemia, spongy gums, and bleeding beneath the skin. ◆ *adj* **scurvier, scurviest. 2** mean or despicable. [C16: see SCURF]
▸ **ˈscurvily** *adv* ▸ **ˈscurviness** *n*

scurvy grass *n* any of various plants of Europe and North America, formerly used to treat scurvy.

scut (skʌt) *n* the short tail of animals such as the deer and rabbit. [C15: prob. from ON]

scutage (ˈskjuːtɪdʒ) *n* (in feudal society) a payment sometimes exacted by a lord from his vassal in lieu of military service. [C15: from Med. L *scūtāgium,* lit.: shield dues, from L *scūtum* a shield]

scutate (ˈskjuːteɪt) *adj* **1** (of animals) covered with large bony or horny plates. **2** *Bot.* shaped like a round shield. [C19: from L *scūtātus* armed with a shield, from *scūtum* a shield]

scutcheon (ˈskʌtʃən) *n* **1** a variant of **escutcheon. 2** any rounded or shield-shaped structure.

scutch grass (skʌtʃ) *n* another name for **couch grass.** [var. of COUCH GRASS]

scute (skjuːt) *n Zool.* a horny plate that makes up part of the exoskeleton in armadillos, turtles, etc. [C14 (the name of a F coin; C19 in zoological sense): from L *scūtum* shield]

scutellum (skjuːˈtɛləm) *n, pl* **scutella** (-lə). *Biol.* **1** the last of three plates into which an insect's thorax is divided. **2** one of the scales on the tarsus of a bird's leg. **3** the cotyledon of a developing grass seed. [C18: from NL: a little shield, from L *scūtum* a shield]
▸ **scutellate** (ˈskjuːtɪˌleɪt, -lɪt) *adj*

scutter (ˈskʌtə) *vb, n Brit. inf.* scurry. [C18: prob. from SCUTTLE[2], with -ER[1] as in SCATTER]

scuttle[1] 🅣 (ˈskʌtᵊl) *n* **1** See **coal scuttle. 2** *Dialect, chiefly Brit.* a shallow basket, esp. for carrying vegetables. **3** the part of a motorcar body lying immediately behind the bonnet. [OE *scutel* trencher, from L *scutella* bowl, dim. of *scutra* platter]

scuttle[2] (ˈskʌtᵊl) *vb* **scuttles, scuttling, scuttled. 1** (*intr*) to run or move about with short hasty steps. ◆ *n* **2** a hurried pace or run. [C15: ?from SCUD, infl. by SHUTTLE]

scuttle[3] (ˈskʌtᵊl) *vb* **scuttles, scuttling, scuttled.** (*tr*) **1** *Naut.* to cause (a vessel) to sink by opening the seacocks or making holes in the bottom. **2** to give up (hopes, plans, etc.). ◆ *n* **3** *Naut.* a small hatch or its cover. [C15 (n): via OF from Sp. *escotilla* a small opening, from *escote* opening in a piece of cloth, from *escotar* to cut out]

scuttlebutt (ˈskʌtᵊlˌbʌt) *n Naut.* **1** a drinking fountain. **2** (formerly) a cask of drinking water aboard a ship. **3** *Chiefly US sl.* gossip.

scutum (ˈskjuːtəm) *n, pl* **scuta** (-tə). **1** the middle of three plates into which an insect's thorax is divided. **2** another word for **scute.** [L: shield]

scuzzy (ˈskʌzɪ) *adj* **scuzzier, scuzziest.** *Sl., chiefly US.* unkempt, dirty, or squalid. [C20: ?from *disgusting* or ?from blend of *scum* & *fuzz*]

Scylla (ˈsɪlə) *n* **1** *Greek myth.* a sea nymph transformed into a sea monster believed to drown sailors navigating the Strait of Messina. Cf. **Charybdis. 2 between Scylla and Charybdis.** in a predicament in which avoidance of either of two dangers means exposure to the other.

scythe (saɪð) *n* **1** a long-handled implement for cutting grass, etc., having a curved sharpened blade that moves in a plane parallel to the ground. ◆ *vb* **scythes, scything, scythed. 2** (*tr*) to cut (grass, etc.) with a scythe. [OE *sigthe*]

Scythian (ˈsɪðɪən) *adj* **1** of or relating to ancient Scythia, in SE Europe, its inhabitants, or their language. ◆ *n* **2** a member of an ancient nomadic people of Scythia.

SDI *abbrev. for* Strategic Defense Initiative. See **Star Wars.**

SDLP *abbrev. for* Social Democratic and Labour Party (in Northern Ireland).

SDP *abbrev. for* Social Democratic Party.

SDRs *Finance. abbrev. for* special drawing rights.

Se *the chemical symbol for* selenium.

SE *symbol for* southeast(ern).

sea 🅣 (siː) *n* **1a** (usually preceded by *the*) the mass of salt water on the earth's surface as differentiated from the land. Related adjs.: **marine, maritime. 1b** (*as modifier*): *sea air.* **2** (*cap. when part of place name*) **2a** one of the smaller areas of ocean: *the Irish Sea.* **2b** a large inland area of water: *the Caspian Sea.* **3** turbulence or swell: *heavy seas.* **4** (*cap. when part of a name*) *Astron.* any of many huge dry plains on the surface of the moon: *Sea of Serenity.* See also **mare**[2]. **5** anything resembling the sea in size or apparent limitlessness. **6 at sea. 6a** on the ocean. **6b** in a state of confusion. **7 go to sea.** to become a sailor. **8 put (out) to sea.** to embark on a sea voyage. [OE *sǣ*]

sea anchor *n Naut.* any device, such as a bucket, dragged in the water to keep a vessel heading into the wind or reduce drifting.

sea anemone *n* any of various coelenterates having a polypoid body with oral rings of tentacles.

sea bag *n* a canvas bag used by a seaman for his belongings.

sea bass (bæs) *n* any of various American coastal fishes having an elongated body with a long spiny dorsal fin almost divided into two.

sea bird *n* a bird such as a gull, that lives on the sea.

seaboard (ˈsiːˌbɔːd) *n* land bordering on the sea.

seaborgium (ˈsiːbɔːgɪəm) *n* a synthetic transuranic element, synthesized and identified in 1974. Symbol: Sg; atomic no.: 106. [C20: after Glenn *Seaborg* (1912–99), US scientist]

THESAURUS

sculpture *vb* **4** = **sculpt**, carve, chisel, cut, fashion, form, hew, model, mould, sculp, shape

scum *n* **1-4** = **impurities**, algae, crust, dross, film, froth, offscourings, scruff **5** = **rabble**, *canaille,* dregs of society, dross, lowest of the low, ragtag and bobtail, riffraff, rubbish, trash (*chiefly US & Canad.*)

scupper[2] *vb* **1** *Brit. slang* = **destroy**, defeat, demolish, disable, discomfit, overthrow, overwhelm, put paid to, ruin, torpedo, undo, wreck

scurrility *n* **1, 2** = **slanderousness**, abusiveness, billingsgate, coarseness, grossness, indecency, infamousness, invective, obloquy, obscenity, offensiveness, scurrilousness, vituperation

scurrilous *adj* **1, 2** = **slanderous**, abusive, coarse, defamatory, foul, foul-mouthed, gross, indecent, infamous, insulting, low, obscene, offensive, Rabelaisian, ribald, salacious, scabrous, scandalous, vituperative, vulgar
Antonyms *adj* civilized, decent, polite, proper, refined, respectful

scurry *vb* **1** = **hurry**, beetle, dart, dash, fly, race, scamper, scoot, scud, scuttle, skim, sprint, whisk ◆ *n* **3** = **flurry**, bustle, scampering, whirl
Antonyms *vb* ≠ **hurry**: amble, mooch (*sl.*), mosey (*inf.*), saunter, stroll, toddle, wander

scurvy *adj* **2** = **contemptible**, abject, bad, base, despicable, dishonourable, ignoble, low, low-down (*inf.*), mean, pitiful, rotten, scabby (*inf.*), shabby, sorry, vile, worthless

scuttle[1] *vb* **1** = **run**, beetle, bustle, hare (*Brit. inf.*), hasten, hurry, rush, scamper, scoot, scramble, scud, scurry, scutter (*Brit. inf.*)

sea *n* **1a** = **ocean**, main, the briny (*inf.*), the deep, the drink (*inf.*), the waves **1b** *as modifier* = **marine**, aquatic, briny, maritime, ocean, ocean-going, oceanic, pelagic, salt, saltwater, sea-going **5** = **expanse**, abundance, mass, multitude, plethora, profusion, sheet, vast number **6b at sea** = **bewildered**, adrift, astray, at a loss, at sixes and sevens, baffled, confused, disoriented, lost, mystified, puzzled, upset

seaborne ('siːˌbɔːn) *adj* **1** carried on or by the sea. **2** transported by ship.
sea bream *n* a fish of European seas, valued as a food fish.
sea breeze *n* a wind blowing from the sea to the land, esp. during the day when the land surface is warmer.
SEAC ('siːæk) *n* (in Britain) *acronym for* School Examination and Assessment Council.
sea change *n* a seemingly magical change. [from Ariel's song "Full Fathom Five" in *The Tempest* (1611)]
seacoast ('siːˌkəʊst) *n* land bordering on the sea; a coast.
seacock ('siːˌkɒk) *n Naut.* a valve in the hull of a vessel below the water line for admitting sea water or for pumping out bilge water.
sea cow *n* **1** a dugong or manatee. **2** an archaic name for the **walrus.**
sea cucumber *n* an echinoderm having an elongated body covered with a leathery skin and a cluster of tentacles at the oral end.
sea dog *n* an experienced or old sailor.
sea eagle *n* any of various fish-eating eagles of coastal areas, esp. the **European sea eagle,** having a brown plumage and white tail.
seafarer ('siːˌfɛərə) *n* **1** a traveller who goes by sea. **2** a sailor.
seafaring ❶ ('siːˌfɛərɪŋ) *adj* (*prenominal*) **1** travelling by sea. **2** working as a sailor. ◆ *n* **3** the act of travelling by sea. **4** the work of a sailor.
seafood ('siːˌfuːd) *n* edible saltwater fish or shellfish.
seafront ('siːˌfrʌnt) *n* a built-up area facing the sea.
sea-girt *adj Literary.* surrounded by the sea.
seagoing ('siːˌgəʊɪŋ) *adj* intended for or used at sea.
sea green *n* **a** a moderate green colour, sometimes with a bluish or yellowish tinge. **b** (*as adj*): *a sea-green carpet.*
sea gull *n* **1** a popular name for the **gull** (the bird). **2** *NZ inf.* a casual dock worker.
sea holly *n* a European plant of sandy shores, having bluish-green stems and blue flowers.
sea horse *n* **1** a marine teleost fish of temperate and tropical waters, having a bony-plated body, a prehensile tail, and a horselike head and swimming in an upright position. **2** an archaic name for the **walrus. 3** a fabled sea creature with the tail of a fish and the front parts of a horse.
sea-island cotton *n* **1** a cotton plant of the Sea Islands, off the Florida coast, widely cultivated for its fine long fibres. **2** the fibre of this plant or the material woven from it.
sea kale *n* a European coastal plant with broad fleshy leaves and white flowers: cultivated for its edible asparagus-like shoots. Cf. **kale.**
seal[1] ❶ (siːl) *n* **1** a device impressed on a piece of wax, etc., fixed to a letter, etc., as a mark of authentication. **2** a stamp, ring, etc., engraved with a device to form such an impression. **3** a substance, esp. wax, so placed over an envelope, etc., that it must be broken before the object can be opened or used. **4** any substance or device used to close or fasten tightly. **5** a small amount of water contained in the trap of a drain to prevent the passage of foul smells. **6** anything that gives a pledge or confirmation. **7** a token; sign: *seal of death.* **8** a decorative stamp sold in aid of charity. **9** *RC Church.* Also called: **seal of confession.** the obligation never to reveal anything said in confession. **10 set one's seal on** (*or* **to**). **10a** to mark with one's sign or seal. **10b** to endorse. ◆ *vb* (*tr*) **11** to affix a seal to, as proof of authenticity, etc. **12** to stamp with or as if with a seal. **13** to approve or authorize. **14** (sometimes foll. by *up*) to close or secure with or as if with a seal: *to seal one's lips.* **15** (foll. by *off*) to enclose (a place) with a fence, etc. **16** to decide irrevocably. **17** to close tightly so as to render airtight or watertight. **18** to subject (the outside of meat, etc.) to fierce heat so as to retain the juices during cooking. **19** to paint (a porous material) with a nonporous coating. **20** *Austral.* to cover (a road) with bitumen, asphalt, tarmac, etc. [C13 *seel,* from OF, from L *sigillum* little figure, from *signum* a sign]
▸'**sealable** *adj*
seal[2] (siːl) *n* **1** a fish-eating mammal with four flippers which is aquatic but comes on shore to breed. **2** sealskin. ◆ *vb* **3** (*intr*) to hunt for seals. [OE *seolh*]
▸'**sealer** *n* ▸'**seal-ˌlike** *adj*
sea lane *n* an established route for ships.
sealant ('siːlənt) *n* **1** any substance, such as wax, used for sealing documents, bottles, etc. **2** any of a number of substances used for stopping leaks, waterproofing wood, etc.
sea lavender *n* any of various plants found on temperate salt marshes, having spikes of white, pink, or mauve flowers.
sealed-beam *adj* (esp. of a car headlight) having a lens and prefocused reflector sealed in the lamp vacuum.
sealed road *n Austral. & NZ.* a road surfaced with bitumen or some other hard material.
sea legs *pl n Inf.* **1** the ability to maintain one's balance on board ship. **2** the ability to resist seasickness.
sea level *n* the level of the surface of the sea with respect to the land, taken to be the mean level between high and low tide.
sea lily *n* any of various echinoderms in which the body consists of a long stalk bearing a central disc with delicate radiating arms.
sealing wax *n* a hard material made of shellac, turpentine, and pigment that softens when heated.
sea lion *n* any of various large eared seals, such as the **Californian sea lion,** of the N Pacific, often used as a performing animal.
Sea Lord *n* (in Britain) either of the two serving naval officers (**First** and **Second Sea Lords**) who sit on the admiralty board of the Ministry of Defence.
seal ring *n* another term for **signet ring.**
sealskin ('siːlˌskɪn) *n* **a** the skin or pelt of a fur seal, esp. when dressed with the outer hair removed and the underfur dyed dark brown. **b** (*as modifier*): *a sealskin coat.*
Sealyham terrier ('siːlɪəm) *n* a short-legged wire-haired breed of terrier with a medium-length white coat. [C19: after *Sealyham,* village in S Wales]
seam ❶ (siːm) *n* **1** the line along which pieces of fabric, etc., are joined, esp. by stitching. **2** a ridge or line made by joining two edges. **3** a stratum of coal, ore, etc. **4** a linear indentation, such as a wrinkle or scar. **5** (*modifier*) *Cricket.* of or relating to a style of bowling in which the bowler utilizes the stitched seam round the ball in order to make it swing in flight and after touching the ground: *a seam bowler.* **6 bursting at the seams.** full to overflowing. ◆ *vb* **7** (*tr*) to join or sew together by or as if by a seam. **8** to mark or become marked with or as if with a seam or wrinkle. [OE]
seaman ('siːmən) *n, pl* **seamen. 1** a naval rating trained in seamanship. **2** a man who serves as a sailor. **3** a person skilled in seamanship.
▸'**seamanly** *adj, adv* ▸'**seaman-ˌlike** *adj*
seamanship ('siːmənʃɪp) *n* skill in and knowledge of the work of navigating, maintaining, and operating a vessel.
sea mile *n* a unit of distance used in navigation, defined as the length of one minute of arc, measured along the meridian, in the latitude of the position. Its actual length varies slightly with latitude, but is about 1853 metres (6080 feet). See also **nautical mile.**
seamless ('siːmlɪs) *adj* **1** (of a garment) having no seams. **2** continuous or flowing: *seamless output; a seamless performance.*
sea mouse *n* any of various large worms having a broad flattened body covered dorsally with a dense mat of iridescent hairlike setae.
seamstress ('sɛmstrɪs) *or* (*rarely*) **sempstress** ('sɛmpstrɪs) *n* a woman who sews and makes clothes, esp. professionally.
seamy ❶ ('siːmɪ) *adj* **seamier, seamiest.** showing the least pleasant aspect; sordid.
▸'**seaminess** *n*
Seanad Éireann ('ʃænəð 'eːrən) *n* (in the Republic of Ireland) the upper chamber of parliament. [from Irish, lit.: senate of Ireland]
seance *or* **séance** ('seɪɑ̃ns) *n* a meeting at which spiritualists attempt to receive messages from the spirits of the dead. [C19: from F, lit.: a sitting, from OF *seoir* to sit, from L *sedēre*]
sea otter *n* a large marine otter of N Pacific coasts, formerly hunted for its thick brown fur.
sea pink *n* another name for **thrift** (the plant).
seaplane ('siːˌpleɪn) *n* any aircraft that lands on and takes off from water.
seaport ('siːˌpɔːt) *n* **1** a port or harbour accessible to seagoing vessels. **2** a town or city located at such a place.
SEAQ ('siːˌæk) *n acronym for* Stock Exchange Automated Quotations: an electronic system that collects and displays information needed to trade in equities.
sear ❶ (sɪə) *vb* (*tr*) **1** to scorch or burn the surface of. **2** to brand with a hot iron. **3** to cause to wither. **4** *Rare.* to make unfeeling. ◆ *adj* **5** *Poetic.* dried up. [OE *sēarian* to become withered, from *sēar* withered]
search ❶ (sɜːtʃ) *vb* **1** to look through (a place, etc.) thoroughly in order to find someone or something. **2** (*tr*) to examine (a person) for concealed objects. **3** to look at or examine (something) closely: *to search one's conscience.* **4** (*tr;* foll. by *out*) to discover by investigation. **5** *Surgery.* to probe (a wound, etc.). **6** *Computing.* to review (a file) to locate specific information. **7** *Arch.* to penetrate. **8 search me.** *Inf.* I don't know. ◆ *n* **9** the act or an instance of searching. **10** the examination of a vessel by the right of search. **11 right of search.** *International law.* the right possessed by the warships of a belligerent state to search merchant vessels to ascertain whether ship or cargo is liable to seizure. [C14: from OF *cerchier,* from LL *circāre* to go around, from L *circus* circle]
▸'**searchable** *adj* ▸'**searcher** *n*

THESAURUS

seafaring *adj* **1** = **nautical**, marine, maritime, naval, oceanic

seal[1] *n* **6** = **authentication**, assurance, attestation, confirmation, imprimatur, insignia, notification, ratification, stamp ◆ *vb* **13** = **authenticate**, assure, attest, confirm, establish, ratify, stamp, validate **15** *with* **off** = **isolate**, board up, fence off, put out of bounds, quarantine, segregate **16** = **settle**, clinch, conclude, consummate, finalize, shake hands on (*inf.*) **17** = **close**, bung, cork, enclose, fasten, make airtight, plug, secure, shut, stop, stopper, stop up, waterproof

seam *n* **1** = **joint**, closure, suture (*Surgery*) **3** = **layer**, lode, stratum, vein **4** = **ridge**, furrow, line, scar, wrinkle

seamy *adj* = **sordid**, corrupt, dark, degraded, disagreeable, disreputable, low, nasty, rough, squalid, unpleasant, unwholesome

sear *vb* **1, 2** = **scorch**, brand, burn, cauterize, desiccate, dry up *or* out, sizzle **3** = **wither**, blight, shrivel, wilt

search *vb* **1-3** = **look**, cast around, check, comb, examine, explore, ferret, forage, frisk (*inf.*), go over with a fine-tooth comb, hunt, inquire, inspect, investigate, leave no stone unturned, look high and low, probe, pry, ransack, rifle through, rummage through, scour, scrutinize, seek, sift, turn inside out, turn upside down ◆ *n* **9** = **look**, examination, exploration, going-over (*inf.*), hunt, inquiry, inspection, investigation, pursuit, quest, researches, rummage, scrutiny

search engine *n Computing.* a service provided on the Internet that carries out searches and locates information on the Internet.
searching ➊ ('sɜːtʃɪŋ) *adj* keenly penetrating: *a searching look.*
▸**'searchingly** *adv*
searchlight ('sɜːtʃˌlaɪt) *n* **1** a device that projects a powerful beam of light in a particular direction. **2** the beam of light produced by such a device.
search party *n* a group of people taking part in an organized search, as for a lost, missing, or wanted person.
search warrant *n* a written order issued by a justice of the peace authorizing a constable to enter and search premises for stolen goods, etc.
seascape ('siːˌskeɪp) *n* a sketch, etc., of the sea.
sea scorpion *n* any of various northern marine fishes having a tapering body and a large head covered with bony plates and spines.
Sea Scout *n* a Scout belonging to any of a number of Scout troops whose main activities are canoeing, sailing, etc.
sea serpent *n* a huge legendary creature of the sea resembling a snake or dragon.
sea shanty *n* another name for **shanty**[2].
seashell ('siːˌʃɛl) *n* the empty shell of a marine mollusc.
seashore ('siːˌʃɔː) *n* **1** land bordering on the sea. **2** *Law.* the land between the marks of high and low water.
seasick ➊ ('siːˌsɪk) *adj* suffering from nausea and dizziness caused by the motion of a ship at sea.
▸**'sea,sickness** *n*
seaside ('siːˌsaɪd) *n* **a** any area bordering on the sea, esp. one regarded as a resort. **b** (*as modifier*): *a seaside hotel.*
sea snail *n* a small spiny-finned fish of cold seas, having a soft scaleless tadpole-shaped body with the pelvic fins fused into a sucker.
sea snake *n* a venomous snake of tropical seas that swims by means of a laterally compressed oarlike tail.
season ➊ ('siːzᵊn) *n* **1** one of the four equal periods into which the year is divided by the equinoxes and solstices. These periods (spring, summer, autumn, and winter) have characteristic weather conditions, and occur at opposite times of the year in the N and S hemispheres. **2** a period of the year characterized by particular conditions or activities: *the rainy season.* **3** the period during which any particular species of animal, bird, or fish is legally permitted to be caught or killed: *open season on red deer.* **4** a period during which a particular entertainment, sport, etc., takes place: *the football season.* **5** any definite or indefinite period. **6** any of the major periods into which the ecclesiastical calendar is divided, such as Lent or Easter. **7** fitting or proper time. **8 in good season.** early enough. **9 in season. 9a** (of game) permitted to be killed. **9b** (of fresh food) readily available. **9c** Also: **in** *or* **on heat.** (of some female mammals) sexually receptive. **9d** appropriate. ◆ *vb* **10** (*tr*) to add herbs, salt, pepper, or spice to (food). **11** (*tr*) to add zest to. **12** (in the preparation of timber) to undergo or cause to undergo drying. **13** (*tr; usually passive*) to make or become experienced: *seasoned troops.* **14** (*tr*) to mitigate or temper. [C13: from OF *seson,* from L *satiō* a sowing, from *serere* to sow]
▸**'seasoned** *adj* ▸**'seasoner** *n*
seasonable ➊ ('siːzənəbᵊl) *adj* **1** suitable for the season: *a seasonable Christmas snow scene.* **2** taking place at the appropriate time.
▸**'seasonableness** *n* ▸**'seasonably** *adv*
seasonal ('siːzənᵊl) *adj* of, relating to, or occurring at a certain season or seasons of the year: *seasonal labour.*
▸**'seasonally** *adv*
seasonal affective disorder *n* a state of depression sometimes experienced by people in winter, thought to be related to lack of sunlight. Abbrev.: **SAD.**
seasoning ➊ ('siːzənɪŋ) *n* **1** something that enhances the flavour of food, such as salt or herbs. **2** another term (not now in technical usage) for **drying.**
season ticket *n* a ticket for a series of events, number of journeys, etc., within a limited time, usually obtained at a reduced rate.
sea squirt *n* a minute primitive marine animal, most of which are sedentary, having a saclike body with openings through which water enters and leaves.
sea swallow *n* a popular name for **tern.**
seat ➊ (siːt) *n* **1** a piece of furniture designed for sitting on, such as a chair or sofa. **2** the part of a chair, bench, etc., on which one sits. **3** a place to sit, esp. one that requires a ticket: *I have two seats for the film tonight.* **4** the buttocks. **5** the part of a garment covering the buttocks. **6** the part or area serving as the base of an object. **7** the part or surface on which the base of an object rests. **8** the place or centre in which something is located: *a seat of government.* **9** a place of abode, esp. a country mansion. **10** a membership or the right to membership in a legislative or similar body. **11** *Chiefly Brit.* a parliamentary constituency. **12** the manner in which a rider sits on a horse. ◆ *vb* **13** (*tr*) to bring to or place on a seat. **14** (*tr*) to provide with seats. **15** (*tr; often passive*) to place or centre: *the ministry is seated in the capital.* **16** (*tr*) to set firmly in place. **17** (*tr*) to fix or install in a position of power. **18** (*intr*) (of garments) to sag in the area covering the buttocks: *your skirt has seated badly.* [OE *gesete*]
seat belt *n* **1** Also called: **safety belt.** a belt or strap worn in a vehicle to restrain forward motion in the event of a collision. **2** a similar belt or strap worn in an aircraft at takeoff and landing.
seating ➊ ('siːtɪŋ) *n* **1** the act of providing with a seat or seats. **2a** the provision of seats, as in a theatre, etc. **2b** (*as modifier*): *seating arrangements.* **3** material used for covering seats. **4** a surface on which a part, such as a valve, is supported.
sea trout *n* a silvery marine variety of the brown trout that migrates to fresh water to spawn.
sea urchin *n* any echinoderm such as the **edible sea urchin,** having a globular body enclosed in a rigid spiny test and occurring in shallow marine waters.
sea vegetables *pl n* edible seaweed.
sea wall *n* a wall or embankment built to prevent encroachment or erosion by the sea.
seaward ('siːwəd) *adv* **1** Also called: **seawards.** towards the sea. ◆ *adj* **2** directed or moving towards the sea. **3** (esp. of a wind) coming from the sea.
seaway ('siːˌweɪ) *n* **1** a waterway giving access to an inland port. **2** a vessel's progress. **3** a route across the sea.
seaweed ('siːˌwiːd) *n* any of numerous multicellular marine algae that grow on the seashore, in salt marshes, in brackish water, or submerged in the ocean.
seaworthy ('siːˌwɜːðɪ) *adj* in a fit condition or ready for a sea voyage.
▸**'sea,worthiness** *n*
sebaceous (sɪ'beɪʃəs) *adj* **1** of or resembling sebum, fat, or tallow. **2** secreting fat. [C18: from LL *sēbāceus,* from SEBUM]
sebaceous glands *pl n* the small glands in the skin that secrete sebum into hair follicles and onto most of the body surface except the soles of the feet and the palms of the hands.
seborrhoea *or esp. US* **seborrhea** (ˌsɛbə'rɪə) *n* a disease of the sebaceous glands characterized by excessive secretion of sebum.
sebum ('siːbəm) *n* the oily secretion of the sebaceous glands that acts as a lubricant for the hair and skin and provides some protection against bacteria. [C19: from NL, from L: tallow]
sec[1] (sɛk) *adj* **1** (of wines) dry. **2** (of champagne) of medium sweetness. [C19: from F, from L *siccus*]
sec[2] (sɛk) *n Inf.* short for **second**[2]: *wait a sec.*
sec[3] (sɛk) *abbrev. for* secant.
SEC *abbrev. for* Securities and Exchange Commission.
sec. *abbrev. for:* **1** second (of time). **2** secondary. **3** secretary. **4** section. **5** sector.
secant ('siːkənt) *n* **1** (of an angle) a trigonometric function that in a right-angled triangle is the ratio of the length of the hypotenuse to that of the adjacent side; the reciprocal of cosine. Abbrev.: **sec. 2** a line that intersects a curve. [C16: from L *secāre* to cut]
secateurs ('sɛkətəz) *pl n Chiefly Brit.* a small pair of shears for pruning, having a pair of pivoted handles and usually a single cutting blade that closes against a flat surface. [C19: pl of F *sécateur,* from L *secāre* to cut]
secede ➊ (sɪ'siːd) *vb* **secedes, seceding, seceded.** (*intr;* often foll. by *from*) (of a person, section, etc.) to make a formal withdrawal of membership, as from a political alliance, etc. [C18: from L *sēcēdere* to withdraw, from *sē-* apart + *cēdere* to go]
▸**se'ceder** *n*
secession ➊ (sɪ'sɛʃən) *n* **1** the act of seceding. **2** (*often cap.*) *Chiefly US.* the withdrawal in 1860–61 of 11 Southern states from the Union to form the Confederacy, precipitating the American Civil War. [C17: from L *sēcessiō* a withdrawing, from *sēcēdere* to SECEDE]
▸**se'cession,ism** *n* ▸**se'cessionist** *n, adj*
sech (ʃɛk, sɛtʃ, 'sɛk'eɪtʃ) *n* hyperbolic secant.
seclude (sɪ'kluːd) *vb* **secludes, secluding, secluded.** (*tr*) **1** to remove from contact with others. **2** to shut off or screen from view. [C15: from L *sēclūdere* to shut off, from *sē-* + *claudere* to imprison]

THESAURUS

searching *adj* = **keen**, close, intent, minute, penetrating, piercing, probing, quizzical, severe, sharp, thorough
Antonyms *adj* cursory, perfunctory, peripheral, sketchy, superficial
seasickness *n* = **mal de mer**
season *n* **1-7** = **period**, division, interval, juncture, occasion, opportunity, spell, term, time, time of year ◆ *vb* **10, 11** = **flavour**, colour, enliven, lace, leaven, pep up, salt, salt and pepper, spice **13** = **make experienced**, acclimatize, accustom, anneal, discipline, habituate, harden, inure, mature, prepare, toughen, train **14** = **mitigate**, moderate, qualify, temper
seasonable *adj* **1, 2** = **appropriate**, convenient, fit, opportune, providential, suitable, timely, welcome, well-timed
seasoned *adj* **13** = **experienced**, battle-scarred, hardened, long-serving, mature, old, practised, time-served, veteran, weathered, well-versed
Antonyms *adj* callow, green, inexperienced, new, novice, unpractised, unseasoned, unskilled
seasoning *n* **1** = **flavouring**, condiment, dressing, relish, salt and pepper, sauce, spice
seat *n* **1** = **chair**, bench, pew, settle, stall, stool, throne **6** = **base**, bed, bottom, cause, footing, foundation, ground, groundwork **8** = **centre**, axis, capital, cradle, headquarters, heart, hub, location, place, site, situation, source, station **9** = **mansion**, abode, ancestral hall, house, residence **10** = **membership**, chair, constituency, incumbency, place ◆ *vb* **13** = **sit**, deposit, fix, install, locate, place, set, settle
seating *n* **2** = **accommodation**, chairs, places, room, seats
secede *vb* = **withdraw**, apostatize, break with, disaffiliate, leave, pull out, quit, resign, retire, separate, split from
secession *n* **1** = **withdrawal**, apostasy, break, defection, disaffiliation, seceding, split

secluded Ⓣ (sɪˈkluːdɪd) *adj* **1** kept apart from the company of others: *a secluded life.* **2** private.
▸**seˈcludedly** *adv* ▸**seˈcludedness** *n*

seclusion Ⓣ (sɪˈkluːʒən) *n* **1** the act of secluding or the state of being secluded. **2** a secluded place. [C17: from Med. L *sēclūsiō*; see SECLUDE]

second[1] Ⓣ (ˈsɛkənd) *adj* (*usually prenominal*) **1a** coming directly after the first in numbering or counting order, position, time, etc.; being the ordinal number of *two:* often written 2nd. **1b** (*as n*): *the second in line.* **2** graded or ranked between the first and third levels. **3** alternate: *every second Thursday.* **4** extra: *a second opportunity.* **5** resembling a person or event from an earlier period of history: *a second Wagner.* **6** of lower quality; inferior. **7** denoting the lowest but one forward ratio of a gearbox in a motor vehicle. **8** *Music.* denoting a musical part, voice, or instrument subordinate to or lower in pitch than another (the first): *the second tenors.* **9 at second hand.** by hearsay. ◆ *n* **10** *Brit. education.* an honours degree of the second class, usually further divided into an upper and lower designation. Full term: **second-class honours degree. 11** the lowest but one forward ratio of a gearbox in a motor vehicle. **12** (in boxing, duelling, etc.) an attendant who looks after a competitor. **13** a speech seconding a motion or the person making it. **14** *Music.* the interval between one note and another lying next above or below it in the diatonic scale. **15** (*pl*) goods of inferior quality. **16** (*pl*) *Inf.* a second helping of food. **17** (*pl*) the second course of a meal. ◆ *vb* (*tr*) **18** to give aid or backing to. **19** (in boxing, etc.) to act as second to (a competitor). **20** to express formal support for (a motion already proposed). ◆ *adv* **21** Also: **secondly.** in the second place. ◆ *sentence connector.* **22** Also: **secondly.** as the second point. [C13: via OF from L *secundus* coming next in order, from *sequī* to follow]
▸**ˈseconder** *n*

second[2] Ⓣ (ˈsɛkənd) *n* **1a** 1/60 of a minute of time. **1b** the basic SI unit of time: the duration of 9 192 631 770 periods of radiation corresponding to the transition between two hyperfine levels of the ground state of caesium-133. Symbol: s **2** 1/60 of a minute of angle. Symbol: ″ **3** a very short period of time. [C14: from OF, from Med. L *pars minūta secunda* the second small part (a minute being the first small part of an hour); see SECOND[1]]

second[3] (sɪˈkɒnd) *vb* (*tr*) *Brit.* **1** to transfer (an employee) temporarily to another branch, etc. **2** *Mil.* to transfer (an officer) to another post. [C19: from F *en second* in second rank (or position)]
▸**seˈcondment** *n*

secondary Ⓣ (ˈsɛkəndərɪ) *adj* **1** one grade or step after the first. **2** derived from or depending on what is primary or first: *a secondary source.* **3** below the first in rank, importance, etc. **4** (*prenominal*) of or relating to the education of young people between the ages of 11 and 18: *secondary education.* **5** (of the flight feathers of a bird's wing) growing from the ulna. **6a** being the part of an electric circuit, such as a transformer or induction coil, in which a current is induced by a changing current in a neighbouring coil: *a secondary coil.* **6b** (of a current) flowing in such a circuit. **7** *Chem.* **7a** (of an amine) containing the group NH. **7b** (of a salt) derived from a tribasic acid by replacement of two acidic hydrogen atoms with metal atoms. ◆ *n, pl* **secondaries. 8** a person or thing that is secondary. **9** a subordinate, deputy, or inferior. **10** a secondary coil, winding, inductance, or current in an electric circuit. **11** *Ornithol.* any of the flight feathers that grow from the ulna of a bird's wing. **12** *Astron.* a celestial body that orbits around a specified primary body: *the moon is the secondary of the earth.* **13** *American football.* **13a** (usually preceded by *the*) cornerbacks and safeties collectively. **13b** their area in the field. **14** short for **secondary colour.**
▸**ˈsecondarily** *adv* ▸**ˈsecondariness** *n*

secondary cell *n* an electric cell that can be recharged and can therefore be used to store electrical energy in the form of chemical energy.

secondary colour *n* a colour formed by mixing two primary colours.

secondary emission *n Physics.* the emission of electrons (**secondary electrons**) from a solid as a result of bombardment with a beam of electrons, ions, or metastable atoms.

secondary picketing *n* the picketing by striking workers of a factory, distribution outlet, etc., that supplies goods to or distributes goods from their employer.

secondary sexual characteristic *n* any of various features distinguishing individuals of different sex but not directly concerned in reproduction. Examples are the antlers of a stag and the beard of a man.

second ballot *n* an electoral procedure in which, after a first ballot, candidates at the bottom of the poll are eliminated and another ballot is held among the remaining candidates.

second-best *adj* **1** next to the best. **2 come off second best.** *Inf.* to be worsted by someone. ◆ *n* **3 second best.** an inferior alternative.

second chamber *n* the upper house of a bicameral legislative assembly.

second childhood Ⓣ *n* dotage; senility (esp. in **in his, her,** etc., **second childhood**).

second class Ⓣ *n* **1** the class or grade next in value, quality, etc., to the first. ◆ *adj* (**second-class** *when prenominal*). **2** of the class or grade next to the best in quality, etc. **3** shoddy or inferior. **4** of or denoting the class of accommodation in a hotel or on a train, etc., lower in quality and price than first class. **5** (in Britain) of mail that is processed more slowly than first-class mail. **6** *Education.* See **second**[1] (sense 10). ◆ *adv* **7** by second-class mail, transport, etc.

second-class citizen *n* a person whose rights and opportunities are treated as less important than those of other people in the same society.

Second Coming *n* the prophesied return of Christ to earth at the Last Judgment.

second cousin *n* the child of a first cousin of either of one's parents.

second-degree burn *n Pathol.* a burn in which blisters appear on the skin.

seconde (sɪˈkɒnd) *n* the second of eight positions from which a parry or attack can be made in fencing. [C18: from F *seconde parade* the second parry]

Second Empire *n* the style of furniture and decoration of the Second Empire in France (1852–70), reviving the Empire style, but with fussier ornamentation.

second fiddle *n Inf.* **1a** the second violin in a string quartet or an orchestra. **1b** the musical part assigned to such an instrument. **2** a person who has a secondary status.

second floor *n Brit.* the storey of a building immediately above the first and two floors up from the ground. US and Canad. term: **third floor.**

second generation *n* **1** offspring of parents born in a given country. **2** (*modifier*) of a refined stage of development in manufacture: *a second-generation robot.*

second growth *n* natural regrowth of a forest after fire, cutting, etc.

second hand *n* a pointer on the face of a timepiece that indicates the seconds.

second-hand Ⓣ *adj* **1** previously owned or used. **2** not from an original source or experience. **3** dealing in or selling goods that are not new: *a second-hand car dealer.* ◆ *adv* **4** from a source of previously owned or used goods: *he prefers to buy second-hand.* **5** not directly: *he got the news second-hand.*

second language *n* **1** a language other than the mother tongue used for business transactions, teaching, debate, etc. **2** a language that is officially recognized in a country, other than the main national language.

second lieutenant *n* an officer holding the lowest commissioned rank in the armed forces of certain nations.

secondly Ⓣ (ˈsɛkəndlɪ) *adv* another word for **second**[1], usually used to precede the second item in a list of topics.

second nature *n* a habit, characteristic, etc., long practised or acquired so as to seem innate.

second person *n* a grammatical category of pronouns and verbs used when referring to or describing the individual or individuals being addressed.

second-rate Ⓣ *adj* **1** not of the highest quality; mediocre. **2** second in importance, etc.

second reading *n* the second presentation of a bill in a legislative assembly, as to approve its general principles (in Britain), or to discuss a committee's report on it (in the US).

second sight *n* the alleged ability to foresee the future, see actions taking place elsewhere, etc.
▸**ˈsecond-ˈsighted** *adj*

THESAURUS

secluded *adj* **1, 2** = **private**, cloistered, cut off, isolated, lonely, off the beaten track, out-of-the-way, reclusive, remote, retired, sequestered, sheltered, solitary, tucked away, unfrequented
Antonyms *adj* accessible, busy, frequented, open, public

seclusion *n* **1** = **privacy**, concealment, hiding, isolation, ivory tower, purdah, remoteness, retirement, retreat, shelter, solitude

second[1] *adj* **1** = **next**, following, subsequent, succeeding **4** = **additional**, alternative, extra, further, other, repeated **5** = **duplicate**, double, reproduction, twin **6** = **inferior**, lesser, lower, secondary, subordinate, supporting ◆ *n* **12** = **supporter**, assistant, backer, helper ◆ *vb* **18** = **support**, advance, aid, approve, assist, back, commend, encourage, endorse, forward, further, give moral support to, go along with, help, promote

second[2] *n* **1** = **moment**, bat of an eye (*inf.*), flash, instant, jiffy (*inf.*), minute, sec (*inf.*), split second, tick (*Brit. inf.*), trice, twinkling, twinkling of an eye, two shakes of a lamb's tail (*inf.*)

secondary *adj* **1** = **backup**, alternate, auxiliary, extra, fall-back, relief, reserve, second, subsidiary, supporting **2** = **resultant**, consequential, contingent, derivative, derived, indirect, resulting, second-hand **3** = **subordinate**, inferior, lesser, lower, minor, second-rate, unimportant
Antonyms *adj* ≠ **backup:** only, primary ≠ **resultant:** original, preceding ≠ **subordinate:** cardinal, chief, head, larger, main, major, more important, prime, principal, superior

second childhood *n* = **senility**, caducity, dotage

second class *adj* **second-class 3** = **inferior**, déclassé, indifferent, mediocre, no great shakes (*inf.*), outclassed, second-best, second-rate, undistinguished, uninspiring

second-hand *adj* **1** = **used**, handed down, hand-me-down (*inf.*), nearly new, reach-me-down (*inf.*) ◆ *adv* **5** = **indirectly**, at second-hand, on the grapevine (*inf.*)

secondly *adv* = **next**, in the second place, second

second-rate *adj* **1** = **inferior**, bush-league (*Austral. & NZ inf.*), cheap, cheap and nasty (*inf.*), commonplace, dime-a-dozen (*inf.*), end-of-the-pier (*Brit. inf.*), for the birds (*inf.*), low-grade, low quality, mediocre, no great shakes (*inf.*), not much cop (*Brit. sl.*), poor, rubbishy, shoddy, strictly for the birds (*inf.*), substandard, tacky (*inf.*), tawdry, tinhorn (*US sl.*), two-bit (*US & Canad. sl.*)
Antonyms *adj* a cut above (*inf.*), choice, de luxe,

second string *n* **1** *Chiefly Brit.* an alternative course of action, etc., intended to come into use should the first fail (esp. in **a second string to one's bow**). **2** *Chiefly US & Canad.* a substitute or reserve player or team.

second thought *n* (*usually pl*) a revised opinion or idea on a matter already considered.

second wind (wɪnd) *n* **1** the return of the ability to breathe at a comfortable rate, esp. following a period of exertion. **2** renewed ability to continue in an effort.

secrecy Ⓣ ('si:krɪsɪ) *n, pl* **secrecies. 1** the state or quality of being secret. **2** the state of keeping something secret. **3** the ability or tendency to keep things secret.

secret Ⓣ ('si:krɪt) *adj* **1** kept hidden or separate from the knowledge of others. Related adj: **cryptic. 2** known only to initiates: *a secret password.* **3** hidden from general view or use: *a secret garden.* **4** able or tending to keep things private or to oneself. **5** operating without the knowledge of outsiders: *a secret society.* ◆ *n* **6** something kept or to be kept hidden. **7** something unrevealed; a mystery. **8** an underlying explanation, reason, etc.: *the secret of success.* **9** a method, plan, etc., known only to initiates. **10** *Liturgy.* a prayer said by the celebrant of the Mass after the offertory and before the preface. [C14: via OF from L *sēcrētus* concealed, from *sēcernere* to sift]
▸ **'secretly** *adv*

secret agent Ⓣ *n* a person employed in espionage.

secretaire (ˌsɛkrɪ'tɛə) *n* an enclosed writing desk, usually having an upper cabinet section. [C19: from F; see SECRETARY]

secretariat (ˌsɛkrɪ'tɛərɪət) *n* **1a** an office responsible for the secretarial, clerical, and administrative affairs of a legislative body or international organization. **1b** the staff of such an office. **2** a body of secretaries. **3** a secretary's place of work; office. **4** the position of a secretary. [C19: via F from Med. L *sēcrētāriātus,* from *sēcrētārius* SECRETARY]

secretary ('sɛkrətrɪ) *n, pl* **secretaries. 1** a person who handles correspondence, keeps records, and does general clerical work for an individual, organization, etc. **2** the official manager of the day-to-day business of a society or board. **3** (in Britain) a senior civil servant who assists a government minister. **4** (in the US) the head of a government administrative department. **5** (in Britain) See **secretary of state. 6** Another name for **secretaire.** [C14: from Med. L *sēcrētārius,* from L *sēcrētum* something hidden; see SECRET]
▸ **secretarial** (ˌsɛkrɪ'tɛərɪəl) *adj* ▸ **'secretaryship** *n*

secretary bird *n* a large African long-legged bird of prey having a crest and tail of long feathers and feeding chiefly on snakes.

secretary-general *n, pl* **secretaries-general.** a chief administrative official, as of the United Nations.

secretary of state *n* **1** (in Britain) the head of any of several government departments. **2** (in the US) the head of the government department in charge of foreign affairs (**State Department**).

secrete[1] Ⓣ (sɪ'kri:t) *vb* **secretes, secreting, secreted.** (of a cell, organ, etc.) to synthesize and release (a secretion). [C18: back formation from SECRETION]
▸ **se'cretor** *n* ▸ **se'cretory** *adj*

secrete[2] Ⓣ (sɪ'kri:t) *vb* **secretes, secreting, secreted.** (*tr*) to put in a hiding place. [C18: var. of obs. *secret* to hide away]

secretion Ⓣ (sɪ'kri:ʃən) *n* **1** a substance that is released from a cell, esp. a glandular cell. **2** the process involved in producing and releasing such a substance from the cell. [C17: from Med. L *sēcrētiō,* from L: a separation]

secretive Ⓣ ('si:krɪtɪv) *adj* inclined to secrecy.
▸ **'secretively** *adv* ▸ **'secretiveness** *n*

secretory (sɪ'kri:tərɪ) *adj* of, relating to, or producing a secretion: *secretory function.*

secret police *n* a police force that operates relatively secretly to check subversion or political dissent.

secret service *n* a government agency or department that conducts intelligence or counterintelligence operations.

sect Ⓣ (sɛkt) *n* **1** a subdivision of a larger religious group (esp. the Christian Church as a whole) the members of which have to some extent diverged from the rest by developing deviating beliefs, practices, etc. **2** *Often disparaging.* **2a** a schismatic religious body. **2b** a religious group regarded as extreme or heretical. **3** a group of people with a common interest, doctrine, etc. [C14: from L *secta* faction, from *sequī* to follow]

-sect *vb combining form.* to cut or divide, esp. into a specified number of parts: *trisect.* [from L *sectus* cut, from *secāre* to cut]

sectarian Ⓣ (sɛk'tɛərɪən) *adj* **1** of, relating to, or characteristic of sects or sectaries. **2** adhering to a particular sect, faction, or doctrine. **3** narrow-minded, esp. as a result of adherence to a particular sect. ◆ *n* **4** a member of a sect or faction, esp. one who is intolerant towards other sects, etc.
▸ **sec'tarianˌism** *n*

sectary ('sɛktərɪ) *n, pl* **sectaries. 1** a member of a sect, esp. a religous sect. **2** a member of a Nonconformist denomination, esp. one that is small. [C16: from Med. L *sectārius,* from L *secta* SECT]

section Ⓣ ('sɛkʃən) *n* **1** a part cut off or separated from the main body of something. **2** a part or subdivision of a piece of writing, book, etc.: *the sports section of the newspaper.* **3** one of several component parts. **4** a distinct part of a country, community, etc. **5** *US & Canad.* an area one mile square. **6** *NZ.* a plot of land for building, esp. in a suburban area. **7** the section of a railway track that is controlled by a particular signal box. **8** the act or process of cutting or separating by cutting. **9** a representation of an object cut by an imaginary vertical plane so as to show its construction and interior. **10** *Geom.* a plane surface formed by cutting through a solid. **11** a thin slice of biological tissue, etc., prepared for examination by microscope. **12** a segment of an orange or other citrus fruit. **13** a small military formation. **14** *Austral. & NZ.* a fare stage on a bus, tram, etc. **15** *Music.* **15a** an extended division of a composition or movement: *the development section.* **15b** a division in an orchestra, band, etc., containing instruments belonging to the same class: *the brass section.* **16** Also called: **signature, gathering.** a folded printing sheet or sheets ready for gathering and binding. ◆ *vb* (*tr*) **17** to cut or divide into sections. **18** to cut through so as to reveal a section. **19** (in drawing, esp. mechanical drawing) to shade so as to indicate sections. [C16: from L *sectiō,* from *secāre* to cut]

sectional Ⓣ ('sɛkʃənᵊl) *adj* **1** composed of several sections. **2** of or relating to a section. **3** of or concerned with a particular group within a community, esp. to the exclusion of others.
▸ **'sectionaˌlize** *or* **'sectionaˌlise** *vb* (*tr*) ▸ **'sectionally** *adv*

sectionalism ('sɛkʃənəˌlɪzəm) *n* excessive or narrow-minded concern for local or regional interests.
▸ **'sectionalist** *n, adj*

sector Ⓣ ('sɛktə) *n* **1** a part or subdivision, esp. of a society or an economy: *the private sector.* **2** *Geom.* either portion of a circle included between two radii and an arc. **3** a measuring instrument consisting of two graduated arms hinged at one end. **4** a part or subdivision of an area of military operations. **5** *Computing.* the smallest addressable portion of the track on a magnetic tape, disk, or drum store. [C16: from LL: sector, from L: a cutter, from *secāre* to cut]
▸ **'sectoral** *adj*

sectorial (sɛk'tɔ:rɪəl) *adj* **1** of or relating to a sector. **2** *Zool.* adapted for cutting: *the sectorial teeth of carnivores.*

secular Ⓣ ('sɛkjʊlə) *adj* **1** of or relating to worldly as opposed to sacred things. **2** not concerned with or related to religion. **3** not within the control of the Church. **4** (of an education, etc.) having no particular religious affinities. **5** (of clerics) not bound by religious vows to a monastic or other order. **6** occurring or appearing once in an age or cen-

THESAURUS

excellent, fine, first-class, first-rate, good quality, high-class, quality, superior

secrecy *n* **1** = **mystery,** cloak and dagger, concealment, confidentiality, huggermugger (*rare*), privacy, retirement, seclusion, silence, solitude, surreptitiousness **2** = **secretiveness,** clandestineness, covertness, furtiveness, stealth

secret *adj* **1** = **concealed,** backstairs, behind someone's back, camouflaged, cloak-and-dagger, close, closet (*inf.*), confidential, conspiratorial, covered, covert, disguised, furtive, hidden, hole-and-corner (*inf.*), hush-hush (*inf.*), reticent, shrouded, undercover, underground, under wraps, undisclosed, unknown, unpublished, unrevealed, unseen **2** = **mysterious,** abstruse, arcane, cabbalistic, clandestine, classified, cryptic, esoteric, occult, recondite **4** = **stealthy,** close, deep, discreet, reticent, secretive, sly, underhand ◆ *n* **6-9** = **mystery,** code, confidence, enigma, formula, key, recipe, skeleton in the cupboard
Antonyms *adj* ≠ **concealed, stealthy:** apparent, candid, disclosed, frank, manifest, obvious, open, overt, public, unconcealed, visible ≠ **mysterious:** exoteric, straightforward, well-known

secret agent *n* = **spy,** cloak-and-dagger man, nark (*Brit., Austral., & NZ sl.*), spook (*US & Canad. inf.*), undercover agent

secrete[1] *vb* = **give off,** emanate, emit, extravasate (*Medical*), extrude, exude

secrete[2] *vb* = **hide,** bury, cache, conceal, cover, disguise, harbour, screen, secure, shroud, stash (*inf.*), stash away (*inf.*), stow, veil
Antonyms *vb* bare, display, exhibit, expose to view, leave in the open, reveal, show, uncover, unmask, unveil

secretion *n* **2** = **discharge,** emission, excretion, extravasation (*Medical*), exudation

secretive *adj* = **reticent,** cagey, clamlike, close, cryptic, deep, enigmatic, playing one's cards close to one's chest, reserved, tight-lipped, uncommunicative, unforthcoming, withdrawn
Antonyms *adj* candid, communicative, expansive, forthcoming, frank, open, unreserved

secretly *adv* **1-5** = **in secret,** behind closed doors, behind (someone's) back, clandestinely, confidentially, covertly, furtively, in camera, in confidence, in one's heart, in one's heart of hearts, in one's innermost thoughts, on the fly (*sl., chiefly Brit.*), on the q.t. (*inf.*), on the sly, privately, quietly, stealthily, surreptitiously, under the counter, unobserved

sect *n* **1-3** = **group,** camp, denomination, division, faction, party, schism, school, school of thought, splinter group, wing

sectarian *adj* **3** = **narrow-minded,** bigoted, clannish, cliquish, doctrinaire, dogmatic, exclusive, factional, fanatic, fanatical, hidebound, insular, limited, parochial, partisan, rigid ◆ *n* **4** = **bigot,** adherent, disciple, dogmatist, extremist, fanatic, partisan, true believer, zealot
Antonyms *adj* ≠ **narrow-minded:** broad-minded, catholic, free-thinking, liberal, non-sectarian, open-minded, tolerant, unbigoted, unprejudiced

section *n* **1** = **part,** component, cross section, division, fraction, fragment, instalment, passage, piece, portion, sample, segment, slice, subdivision **4** = **district,** area, department, region, sector, zone

sectional *adj* **3** = **regional,** divided, exclusive, factional, local, localized, partial, separate, separatist

sector *n* **1** = **part,** area, category, district, division, quarter, region, stratum, subdivision, zone

secular *adj* **1-3** = **worldly,** civil, earthly, laic, laical, lay, nonspiritual, profane, state, temporal

tury. **7** lasting for a long time. **8** *Astron.* occurring slowly over a long period of time. ◆ *n* **9** a member of the secular clergy. [C13: from OF *seculer,* from LL *saeculāris* temporal, from L: concerning an age, from *saeculum* an age]
▸**secularity** (ˌsɛkjuˈlærɪtɪ) *n* ▸ˈ**secularly** *adv*

secularism (ˈsɛkjuləˌrɪzəm) *n* **1** *Philosophy.* a doctrine that rejects religion, esp. in ethics. **2** the attitude that religion should have no place in civil affairs.
▸ˈ**secularist** *n, adj*

secularize *or* **secularise** (ˈsɛkjuləˌraɪz) *vb* **secularizes, secularizing, secularized** *or* **secularises, secularising, secularised.** (*tr*) **1** to change from religious or sacred to secular functions, etc. **2** to dispense from allegiance to a religious order. **3** *Law.* to transfer (property) from ecclesiastical to civil possession or use.
▸ˌ**seculariˈzation** *or* ˌ**seculariˈsation** *n*

secund (sɪˈkʌnd) *adj Bot.* having parts arranged on or turned to one side of the axis. [C18: from L *secundus* following, from *sequī* to follow]

secure ➊ (sɪˈkjʊə) *adj* **1** free from danger, damage, etc. **2** free from fear, care, etc. **3** in safe custody. **4** not likely to fail, become loose, etc. **5** able to be relied on: *a secure investment.* **6** *Arch.* overconfident. ◆ *vb* **secures, securing, secured.** **7** (*tr*) to obtain: *I will secure some good seats.* **8** (when *intr,* often foll. by *against*) to make or become free from danger, fear, etc. **9** (*tr*) to make fast or firm. **10** (when *intr,* often foll. by *against*) to make or become certain: *this plan will secure your happiness.* **11** (*tr*) to assure (a creditor) of payment, as by giving security. **12** (*tr*) to make (a military position) safe from attack. **13** *Naut.* to make (a vessel or its contents) safe or ready by battening down hatches, etc. [C16: from L *sēcūrus* free from care]
▸**seˈcurable** *adj* ▸**seˈcurely** *adv* ▸**seˈcurement** *n* ▸**seˈcurer** *n*

Securities and Investment Board *n* a British regulatory body set up in 1986 to oversee London's financial markets, each of which has its own self-regulatory organization. Abbrev.: **SIB.**

securitization *or* **securitisation** (sɪˌkjʊərɪtaɪˈzeɪʃən) *n Finance.* the use of such securities as eurobonds to enable investors to lend directly to borrowers with a minimum of risk but without using banks as intermediaries.

security ➊ (sɪˈkjʊərɪtɪ) *n, pl* **securities.** **1** the state of being secure. **2** assured freedom from poverty or want: *he needs the security of a permanent job.* **3** a person or thing that secures, guarantees, etc. **4** precautions taken to ensure against theft, espionage, etc. **5** (*often pl*) **5a** a certificate of creditorship or property carrying the right to receive interest or dividend, such as shares or bonds. **5b** the financial asset represented by such a certificate. **6** the specific asset that a creditor can claim in the event of default on an obligation. **7** something given or pledged to secure the fulfilment of a promise or obligation. **8** the protection of data to ensure that only authorised personnel have access to computer files.

security blanket *n* **1** a policy of temporary secrecy by police or those in charge of security, in order to protect a person, place, etc., threatened with danger, from further risk. **2** a baby's blanket, soft toy, etc., to which a baby or young child becomes very attached, using it as a comforter. **3** *Inf.* anything used or thought of as providing reassurance.

Security Council *n* an organ of the United Nations established to maintain world peace.

security guard *n* someone employed to protect buildings, people, etc., and to collect and deliver large sums of money.

security risk *n* a person deemed to be a threat to state security in that he could be open to pressure, have subversive political beliefs, etc.

secy. *or* **sec'y.** *abbrev. for* secretary.

sedan (sɪˈdæn) *n* **1** *US, Canad., & NZ.* a saloon car. **2** short for **sedan chair.** [C17: from ?]

sedan chair *n* a closed chair for one passenger, carried on poles by two bearers, commonly used in the 17th and 18th centuries.

sedate[1] ➊ (sɪˈdeɪt) *adj* **1** habitually calm and composed in manner. **2** sober or decorous. [C17: from L *sēdāre* to soothe]
▸**seˈdately** *adv* ▸**seˈdateness** *n*

sedate[2] (sɪˈdeɪt) *vb* **sedates, sedating, sedated.** (*tr*) to administer a sedative to. [C20: back formation from SEDATIVE]

sedation (sɪˈdeɪʃən) *n* **1** a state of calm or reduced nervous activity. **2** the administration of a sedative.

sedative ➊ (ˈsɛdətɪv) *adj* **1** having a soothing or calming effect. **2** of or relating to sedation. ◆ *n* **3** *Med.* a sedative drug or agent. [C15: from Med. L *sēdātīvus,* from L *sēdātus* assuaged; see SEDATE[1]]

sedentary ➊ (ˈsɛdᵊntərɪ) *adj* **1** characterized by or requiring a sitting position: *sedentary work.* **2** tending to sit about without taking much exercise. **3** (of animals) moving about very little. **4** (of birds) not migratory. [C16: from L *sedentārius,* from *sedēre* to sit]
▸ˈ**sedentarily** *adv* ▸ˈ**sedentariness** *n*

Seder (ˈseɪdə) *n Judaism.* a ceremonial meal on the first night or first two nights of Passover. [from Heb. *sēdher* order]

sedge (sɛdʒ) *n* a grasslike plant growing on wet ground and having rhizomes, triangular stems, and minute flowers in spikelets. [OE *secg*]
▸ˈ**sedgy** *adj*

sedge warbler *n* a European songbird of reed beds and swampy areas, having a streaked brownish plumage with white eye stripes.

sedilia (sɛˈdaɪlɪə) *n* (*functioning as sing*) the group of three seats, each called a **sedile** (sɛˈdaɪlɪ) on the south side of a sanctuary where the celebrant and ministers sit during High Mass. [C18: from L, from *sedīle* a chair, from *sedēre* to sit]

sediment ➊ (ˈsɛdɪmənt) *n* **1** matter that settles to the bottom of a liquid. **2** material that has been deposited from water, ice, or wind. [C16: from L *sedimentum* a settling, from *sedēre* to sit]
▸ˌ**sedimenˈtation** *n*

sedimentary (ˌsɛdɪˈmɛntərɪ) *adj* **1** characteristic of, resembling, or containing sediment. **2** (of rocks) formed by the accumulation of mineral and organic fragments that have been deposited by water, ice, or wind.
▸ˌ**sediˈmentarily** *adv*

sedimentation tank *n* a tank into which sewage is passed to allow suspended solid matter to separate out.

sedition ➊ (sɪˈdɪʃən) *n* **1** speech or behaviour directed against the peace of a state. **2** an offence that tends to undermine the authority of a state. **3** an incitement to public disorder. [C14: from L *sēditiō* discord, from *sēd-* apart + *itiō* a going, from *īre* to go]
▸**seˈditionary** *n, adj*

seditious ➊ (sɪˈdɪʃəs) *adj* **1** of, like, or causing sedition. **2** inclined to or taking part in sedition.

seduce ➊ (sɪˈdjuːs) *vb* **seduces, seducing, seduced.** (*tr*) **1** to persuade to engage in sexual intercourse. **2** to lead astray, as from the right action. **3** to win over, attract, or lure. [C15: from L *sēdūcere* to lead apart]
▸**seˈducible** *adj*

seducer ➊ (sɪˈdjuːsə) *or* (*fem*) **seductress** (sɪˈdʌktrɪs) *n* a person who entices, allures, or seduces, esp. one who entices another to engage in sexual intercourse.

seduction ➊ (sɪˈdʌkʃən) *n* **1** the act of seducing or the state of being seduced. **2** a means of seduction.

seductive ➊ (sɪˈdʌktɪv) *adj* tending to seduce or capable of seducing; enticing; alluring.
▸**seˈductively** *adv* ▸**seˈductiveness** *n*

sedulous ➊ (ˈsɛdjuləs) *adj* assiduous; diligent. [C16: from L *sēdulus,* from ?]
▸**sedulity** (sɪˈdjuːlɪtɪ) *or* ˈ**sedulousness** *n* ▸ˈ**sedulously** *adv*

THESAURUS

Antonyms *adj* divine, holy, religious, sacred, spiritual, theological

secure *adj* **1** = **safe**, immune, impregnable, in safe hands, out of harm's way, protected, sheltered, shielded, unassailable, undamaged, unharmed **2** = **sure**, assured, certain, confident, easy, reassured **4** = **fixed**, dependable, fast, fastened, firm, fortified, immovable, stable, steady, tight **5** = **reliable**, absolute, conclusive, definite, in the bag (*inf.*), solid, steadfast, tried and true, well-founded ◆ *vb* **7** = **obtain**, acquire, come by, gain, get, get hold of, land, make sure of, pick up, procure, score (*sl.*), win possession of **9** = **fasten**, attach, batten down, bolt, chain, fix, lash, lock, lock up, make fast, moor, padlock, rivet, tie up **10** = **guarantee**, assure, ensure, insure
Antonyms *adj* ≠ **safe:** endangered, unprotected, unsafe ≠ **sure:** ill-at-ease, insecure, unassured, uncertain, uneasy, unsure ≠ **fixed:** insecure, loose, not fastened, precarious, unfixed, unsafe, unsound ◆ *vb* ≠ **obtain:** give up, let (something) slip through (one's) fingers, lose ≠ **fasten:** loose, unloose, untie ≠ **guarantee:** endanger, imperil, leave unguaranteed

security *n* **1** = **safety**, asylum, care, cover, custody, immunity, preservation, protection, refuge, retreat, safekeeping, sanctuary **3** = **assurance**, certainty, confidence, conviction, ease of mind, freedom from doubt, positiveness, reliance, sureness **4** = **precautions**, defence, guards, protection, safeguards, safety measures, surveillance **6** = **pledge**, collateral, gage, guarantee, hostage, insurance, pawn, surety
Antonyms *n* ≠ **safety:** exposure, jeopardy, vulnerability ≠ **assurance:** insecurity, uncertainty

sedate[1] *adj* **1-2** = **calm**, collected, composed, cool, decorous, demure, dignified, earnest, grave, imperturbable, placid, proper, quiet, seemly, serene, serious, sober, solemn, staid, tranquil, unflappable (*inf.*), unhurried, unruffled
Antonyms *adj* ≠ **calm:** agitated, excitable, excited, flighty, impassioned, jumpy, nervous, undignified, unsteady, wild

sedative *adj* **1** = **calming**, allaying, anodyne, calmative, lenitive, relaxing, sleep-inducing, soothing, soporific, tranquillizing ◆ *n* **3** = **tranquillizer**, anodyne, calmative, downer *or* down (*sl.*), narcotic, opiate, sleeping pill

sedentary *adj* **1, 2** = **inactive**, desk, deskbound, motionless, seated, sitting, torpid
Antonyms *adj* active, mobile, motile, moving, on the go (*inf.*)

sediment *n* **1** = **dregs**, deposit, grounds, lees, precipitate, residue, settlings

sedition *n* **1-3** = **rabble-rousing**, agitation, disloyalty, incitement to riot, subversion, treason

seditious *adj* **1, 2** = **revolutionary**, disloyal, dissident, insubordinate, mutinous, rebellious, refractory, subversive, treasonable

seduce *vb* **1** = **corrupt**, betray, debauch, deflower, deprave, dishonour, ruin (*arch.*) **2, 3** = **tempt**, allure, attract, beguile, deceive, decoy, ensnare, entice, inveigle, lead astray, lure, mislead

seduction *n* **1** = **corruption**, defloration, ruin (*arch.*) **2** = **temptation**, allure, enticement, lure, snare

seductive *adj* = **alluring**, attractive, beguiling, bewitching, captivating, come-hither (*inf.*), come-to-bed (*inf.*), enticing, flirtatious, inviting, irresistible, provocative, ravishing, sexy (*inf.*), siren, specious, tempting

seductress *n* = **temptress**, Circe, enchantress, *femme fatale*, Lorelei, siren, vamp (*inf.*)

sedulous *adj* = **diligent**, assiduous, busy, conscientious, constant, industrious, laborious, painstaking, persevering, persistent, tireless, unflagging, unremitting

sedum ('siːdəm) *n* a rock plant having thick fleshy leaves and clusters of white, yellow, or pink flowers. [C15: from L: houseleek]

see[1] Ⓣ (siː) *vb* **sees, seeing, saw, seen. 1** to perceive with the eyes. **2** (when *tr, may take a clause as object*) to understand: *I explained the problem but he could not see it.* **3** (*tr*) to perceive with any or all of the senses: *I hate to see you so unhappy.* **4** (*tr; may take a clause as object*) to foresee: *I can see what will happen if you don't help.* **5** (when *tr, may take a clause as object*) to ascertain or find out (a fact): *see who is at the door.* **6** (when *tr, takes a clause as object;* when *intr,* foll. by *to*) to make sure (of something) or take care (of something): *see that he gets to bed early.* **7** (when *tr, may take a clause as object*) to consider, deliberate, or decide: *see if you can come next week.* **8** (*tr*) to have experience of: *he had seen much unhappiness in his life.* **9** (*tr*) to allow to be in a specified condition: *I cannot stand by and see a child in pain.* **10** (*tr*) to be characterized by: *this period of history has seen much unrest.* **11** (*tr*) to meet or pay a visit to: *to see one's solicitor.* **12** (*tr*) to receive: *the Prime Minister will see the deputation now.* **13** (*tr*) to frequent the company of: *she is seeing a married man.* **14** (*tr*) to accompany: *I saw her to the door.* **15** (*tr*) to refer to or look up: *for further information see the appendix.* **16** (in gambling, esp. in poker) to match (another player's bet) or match the bet of (another player) by staking an equal sum. **17 as far as I can see.** to the best of my judgment. **18 see fit.** (*takes an infinitive*) to consider proper, etc.: *I don't see fit to allow her to come here.* **19 see (someone) hanged** *or* **damned first.** *Inf.* to refuse absolutely to do what one has been asked. **20 see you, see you later,** *or* **be seeing you.** an expression of farewell. ◆ See also **see about, see into,** etc. [OE *sēon*]

see[2] Ⓣ (siː) *n* the diocese of a bishop, or the place within it where his cathedral is situated. [C13: from OF *sed,* from L *sēdēs* a seat]

see about Ⓣ *vb* (*intr, prep*) **1** to take care of: *he couldn't see about the matter because he was ill.* **2** to investigate: *to see about a new car.*

Seebeck effect ('siːbɛk) *n* the phenomenon in which a current is produced in a circuit containing two or more different metals when the junctions between the metals are maintained at different temperatures. Also called: **thermoelectric effect.** [C19: after Thomas *Seebeck* (1770–1831), G physicist]

seed Ⓣ (siːd) *n* **1** *Bot.* a mature fertilized plant ovule, consisting of an embryo and its food store surrounded by a protective seed coat (testa). Related adj: **seminal. 2** the small hard seedlike fruit of plants such as wheat. **3** any propagative part of a plant, such as a tuber, spore, or bulb. **4** the source, beginning, or germ of anything: *the seeds of revolt.* **5** *Chiefly Bible.* descendants: *the seed of Abraham.* **6** an archaic term for **sperm** or **semen. 7** *Sport.* a seeded player. **8** *Chem.* a small crystal added to a supersaturated solution to induce crystallization. **9 go** *or* **run to seed. 9a** (of plants) to produce and shed seeds. **9b** to lose vigour, usefulness, etc. ◆ *vb* **10** to plant (seeds, grain, etc.) in (soil): *we seeded this field with oats.* **11** (*intr*) (of plants) to form or shed seeds. **12** (*tr*) to remove the seeds from (fruit, etc.). **13** (*tr*) *Chem.* to add a small crystal to (a supersaturated solution) in order to cause crystallization. **14** (*tr*) to scatter certain substances, such as silver iodide, in (clouds) in order to cause rain. **15** (*tr*) to arrange (the draw of a tournament) so that outstanding teams or players will not meet in the early rounds. [OE *sǣd*]
▸'**seeder** *n* ▸'**seedless** *adj*

seedbed ('siːdˌbɛd) *n* **1** a plot of land in which seedlings are grown before being transplanted. **2** the place where something develops.

seedcake ('siːdˌkeɪk) *n* a sweet cake flavoured with caraway seeds and lemon rind or essence.

seed capital *n Finance.* a small amount of capital required to finance the research necessary to produce a business plan for a new company.

seed coral *n* small pieces of coral used in jewellery, etc.

seed corn *n* **1** the good quality ears or kernels of corn that are used as seed. **2** assets that are expected to provide future benefits.

seed leaf *n* the nontechnical name for **cotyledon.**

seedling ('siːdlɪŋ) *n* a plant produced from a seed, esp. a very young plant.

seed money *n* money used for the establishment of an enterprise.

seed oyster *n* a young oyster, esp. a cultivated oyster, ready for transplantation.

seed pearl *n* a tiny pearl weighing less than a quarter of a grain.

seed pod *n* a carpel or pistil enclosing the seeds of a plant, esp. a flowering plant.

seed potato *n* a potato tuber used for planting.

seed vessel *n Bot.* a dry fruit, such as a capsule.

seedy Ⓣ ('siːdɪ) *adj* **seedier, seediest. 1** shabby in appearance: *seedy clothes.* **2** (of a plant) at the stage of producing seeds. **3** *Inf.* not physically fit.
▸'**seedily** *adv* ▸'**seediness** *n*

seeing Ⓣ ('siːɪŋ) *n* **1** the sense or faculty of sight. **2** *Astron.* the condition of the atmosphere with respect to observation of stars, planets, etc. ◆ *conj* **3** (*subordinating;* often foll. by *that*) in light of the fact (that).

> **USAGE NOTE** The use of *seeing as how* as in *seeing as (how) the bus is always late, I don't need to hurry* is generally thought to be incorrect or nonstandard.

see into *vb* (*intr, prep*) to discover the true nature of: *I can't see into your thoughts.*

seek Ⓣ (siːk) *vb* **seeks, seeking, sought.** (*mainly tr*) **1** (when *intr,* often foll. by *for* or *after*) to try to find by searching: *to seek a solution.* **2** (*also intr*) to try to obtain or acquire: *to seek happiness.* **3** to attempt (to do something): *I'm only seeking to help.* **4** (*also intr*) to inquire about or request (something). **5** to resort to: *to seek the garden for peace.* [OE *sēcan*]
▸'**seeker** *n*

seek out *vb* (*tr, adv*) to search hard for and find a specific person or thing: *she sought out her friend from amongst the crowd.*

seem Ⓣ (siːm) *vb* (*may take an infinitive*) **1** (*copula*) to appear to the mind or eye; look: *the car seems to be running well.* **2** to appear to be: *there seems no need for all this nonsense.* **3** used to diminish the force of a following infinitive to be polite, more noncommittal, etc.: *I can't seem to get through to you.* [C12: ?from ON *soma* to beseem, from *sœmr* befitting]

> **USAGE NOTE** See at **like.**

seeming Ⓣ ('siːmɪŋ) *adj* **1** (*prenominal*) apparent but not actual or genuine. ◆ *n* **2** outward or false appearance.
▸'**seemingly** *adv*

seemly Ⓣ ('siːmlɪ) *adj* **seemlier, seemliest. 1** proper or fitting. **2** *Obs.* pleasing in appearance. ◆ *adv* **3** *Arch.* decorously. [C13: from ON *sœmiligr,* from *sœmr* befitting]

seen (siːn) *vb* the past participle of **see**[1].

see off *vb* (*tr, adv*) **1** to be present at the departure of (a person making a journey). **2** *Inf.* to cause to leave or depart, esp. by force.

seep Ⓣ (siːp) *vb* **1** (*intr*) to pass gradually or leak as if through small openings. ◆ *n* **2** a small spring or place where water, oil, etc., has oozed through the ground. [OE *sīpian*]
▸'**seepage** *n*

seer[1] Ⓣ (sɪə) *n* **1** a person who can supposedly see into the future. **2** a person who professes supernatural powers. **3** a person who sees.

seer[2] (sɪə) *n* a varying unit of weight used in India, usually about two pounds or one kilogram. [from Hindi]

seersucker ('sɪəˌsʌkə) *n* a light cotton, linen, or other fabric with a

THESAURUS

see[1] *vb* **1 = perceive**, behold, catch a glimpse of, catch sight of, check, check out, clock (*Brit. sl.*), descry, discern, distinguish, espy, eye, eyeball (*sl.*), get a load of (*sl.*), glimpse, heed, identify, lay *or* clap eyes on (*inf.*), look, make out, mark, note, notice, observe, recognize, regard, sight, spot, take a dekko at (*Brit. sl.*), view, witness **2 = understand**, appreciate, catch on (*inf.*), comprehend, fathom, feel, follow, get, get the drift of, get the hang of (*inf.*), grasp, know, make out, realize, take in **4 = foresee**, anticipate, divine, envisage, foretell, imagine, picture, visualize **5 = find out**, ascertain, determine, discover, investigate, learn, make inquiries, refer to **6 = make sure**, ensure, guarantee, make certain, mind, see to it, take care **7 = consider**, decide, deliberate, give some thought to, judge, make up one's mind, mull over, reflect, think over **11 = visit**, confer with, consult, encounter, interview, meet, receive, run into, speak to **13 = go out with**, consort *or* associate with, court, date (*inf., chiefly US*), go steady with (*inf.*), keep company with, walk out with (*obs.*) **14 = accompany**, attend, escort, lead, show, usher, walk

see[2] *n* **= diocese**, bishopric

see about *vb* **1 = take care of**, attend to, consider, deal with, give some thought to, look after, see to **2 = investigate**, look into, make inquiries, research

seed *n* **1 = grain**, egg, egg cell, embryo, germ, kernel, ovule, ovum, pip, spore **4 = origin**, beginning, germ, inkling, nucleus, source, start, suspicion **5** *Chiefly Bible* **= offspring**, children, descendants, heirs, issue, progeny, race, scions, spawn, successors **9 go** *or* run to seed **= decline**, decay, degenerate, deteriorate, go downhill (*inf.*), go to pieces, go to pot, go to rack and ruin, go to waste, let oneself go, retrogress

seedy *adj* **1 = shabby**, crummy (*sl.*), decaying, dilapidated, down at heel, faded, grotty (*sl.*), grubby, mangy, manky (*Scot. dialect*), old, rundown, scruffy, sleazy, slovenly, squalid, tatty, unkempt, worn **3** *Informal* **= unwell**, ailing, ill, off colour, out of sorts, peely-wally (*Scot.*), poorly (*inf.*), sickly, under the weather (*inf.*)
Antonyms *adj* ≠ **shabby:** classy, elegant, fashionable, high-toned, posh (*inf., chiefly Brit.*), ritzy (*sl.*), smart, swanky (*inf.*), swish (*inf., chiefly Brit.*), top-drawer, up-market

seeing *conj* **3 = since**, as, inasmuch as, in view of the fact that

seek *vb* **1, 2 = look for**, be after, follow, go gunning for, go in pursuit of, go in quest of, go in search of, hunt, inquire, pursue, search for **3 = try**, aim, aspire to, attempt, endeavour, essay, have a go (*inf.*), strive **4 = request**, ask, beg, entreat, inquire, invite, petition, solicit

seem *vb* **1 = appear**, assume, give the impression, have the *or* every appearance of, look, look as if, look like, look to be, pretend, sound like, strike one as being

seeming *adj* **1 = apparent**, appearing, illusory, ostensible, outward, quasi-, specious, surface

seemingly *adv* **1 = apparently**, as far as anyone could tell, on the face of it, on the surface, ostensibly, outwardly, to all appearances, to all intents and purposes

seemly *adj* **1 = fitting**, appropriate, becoming, befitting, *comme il faut,* decent, decorous, fit, in good taste, meet (*arch.*), nice, proper, suitable, suited, the done thing
Antonyms *adj* improper, inappropriate, indecorous, in poor taste, out of keeping, out of place, unbecoming, unbefitting, unseemly, unsuitable

seep *vb* **1 = ooze**, bleed, exude, leach, leak, percolate, permeate, soak, trickle, weep, well

seepage *n* **1 = leakage**, exudation, leak, oozing, percolation

seer[1] *n* **1 = prophet**, augur, predictor, sibyl, soothsayer

crinkled surface and often striped. [C18: from Hindi *śīrśakar,* from Persian *shīr o shakkar,* lit.: milk and sugar]

seesaw ❶ ('si:ˌsɔ:) *n* **1** a plank balanced in the middle so that two people seated on the ends can ride up and down by pushing on the ground with their feet. **2** the pastime of riding up and down on a seesaw. **3** an up-and-down or back-and-forth movement. ◆ *vb* **4** (*intr*) to move up and down or back and forth in such a manner. [C17: reduplication of SAW[1], alluding to the movement from side to side, as in sawing]

seethe ❶ (si:ð) *vb* **seethes, seething, seethed. 1** (*intr*) to boil or to foam as if boiling. **2** (*intr*) to be in a state of extreme agitation, esp. through anger. **3** (*tr*) to soak in liquid. **4** (*tr*) *Arch.* to cook by boiling. [OE *sēothan*]
▸**'seething** *adj* ▸**'seethingly** *adv*

see through ❶ *vb* **1** (*tr*) to help out in time of need or trouble. **2** (*tr, adv*) to remain with until the end or completion: *let's see the job through.* **3** (*intr, prep*) to perceive the true nature of: *I can see through your evasion.* ◆ *adj* **see-through. 4** partly or wholly transparent or translucent, esp. (of clothes) in a titillating way.

segment ❶ *n* ('sɛgmənt). **1** *Maths.* **1a** a part of a line or curve between two points. **1b** a part of a plane or solid figure cut off by an intersecting line, plane, or planes. **2** one of several parts or sections into which an object is divided. **3** *Zool.* any of the parts into which the body or appendages of an annelid or arthropod are divided. **4** *Linguistics.* a speech sound considered in isolation. ◆ *vb* (sɛg'mɛnt). **5** to cut or divide (a whole object) into segments. [C16: from L *segmentum,* from *secāre* to cut]
▸**seg'mental** *adj* ▸**'segmentary** *adj*

segmentation (ˌsɛgmɛn'teɪʃən) *n* **1** the act or an instance of dividing into segments. **2** *Embryol.* another name for **cleavage** (sense 4).

segregate ❶ ('sɛgrɪˌgeɪt) *vb* **segregates, segregating, segregated. 1** to set or be set apart from others or from the main group. **2** (*tr*) to impose segregation on (a racial or minority group). **3** *Genetics.* to undergo or cause to undergo segregation. [C16: from L *sēgregāre,* from *sē-* apart + *grex* a flock]
▸**'segreˌgative** *adj* ▸**'segreˌgator** *n*

segregation ❶ (ˌsɛgrɪ'geɪʃən) *n* **1** the act of segregating or state of being segregated. **2** *Sociol.* the practice or policy of creating separate facilities within the same society for the use of a particular group. **3** *Genetics.* the separation at meiosis of the two members of any pair of alleles into separate gametes.
▸**ˌsegre'gational** *adj* ▸**ˌsegre'gationist** *n*

segue ('seɪgwɪ) *vb* **segues, segueing, segued.** (*intr*) **1** (often foll. by *into*) to proceed from one piece of music to another without a break. ◆ *n* **2** the practice or an instance of segueing. [from It: follows, from *seguire* to follow, from L *sequī*]

seguidilla (ˌsɛgɪ'di:ljə) *n* **1** a Spanish dance in a fast triple rhythm. **2** a piece of music composed for or in the rhythm of this dance. [Sp.: a little dance, from *seguida* a dance, from *seguir* to follow, from L *sequī*]

seiche (seɪʃ) *n* a tide-like movement of a body of water caused by barometric pressure, earth tremors, etc. [C19: from Swiss F, from ?]

Seidlitz powder *or* **powders** ('sɛdlɪts) *n* a laxative consisting of two powders, tartaric acid and a mixture of sodium bicarbonate and Rochelle salt. [C19: after *Seidlitz,* a village in Bohemia with mineral springs having similar laxative effects]

seif dune (seɪf) *n* (in deserts, esp. the Sahara) a long ridge of blown sand, often several miles long. [*seif,* from Ar.: sword, from the shape of the dune]

seigneur (se'njɜ:; *French* sɛɲœr) *n* a feudal lord, esp. in France. [C16: from OF, from Vulgar L *senior,* from L: an elderly man; see SENIOR]
▸**sei'gneurial** *adj*

seigneury ('seɪnjərɪ) *n, pl* **seigneuries.** the estate of a seigneur.

seignior ('seɪnjə) *n* **1** a less common name for a **seigneur. 2** (in England) the lord of a seigniory. [C14: from Anglo-F *segnour*]
▸**seigniorial** (seɪ'njɔ:rɪəl) *adj*

seigniory ('seɪnjərɪ) *or* **signory** ('si:njərɪ) *n, pl* **seigniories** *or* **seignories. 1** less common names for a **seigneury. 2** (in England) the fee or manor of a seignior; a feudal domain. **3** the authority of a seignior.

seine (seɪn) *n* **1** a large fishing net that hangs vertically in the water by means of floats at the top and weights at the bottom. ◆ *vb* **seines, seining, seined. 2** to catch (fish) using this net. [OE *segne,* from L *sagēna,* from Gk *sagēnē*]

seise *or US* **seize** (si:z) *vb* **seises, seising, seised** *or US* **seizes, seizing, seized.** to put into legal possession of (property, etc.).
▸**'seiser** *n*

seisin *or US* **seizin** ('si:zɪn) *n Property law.* feudal possession of an estate in land. [C13: from OF *seisine,* from *seisir* to SEIZE]

seismic ('saɪzmɪk) *adj* relating to or caused by earthquakes or artificially produced earth tremors.

seismo- *or before a vowel* **seism-** *combining form.* earthquake: *seismology.* [from Gk *seismos*]

seismograph ('saɪzməˌgrɑ:f) *n* an instrument that registers and records earthquakes. A **seismogram** is the record from such an instrument.
▸**seismographic** (ˌsaɪzmə'græfɪk) *adj* ▸**seismographer** (saɪz'mɒgrəfə) *n* ▸**seis'mography** *n*

seismology (saɪz'mɒlədʒɪ) *n* the branch of geology concerned with the study of earthquakes.
▸**seismologic** (ˌsaɪzmə'lɒdʒɪk) *or* **ˌseismo'logical** *adj* ▸**ˌseismo'logically** *adv* ▸**seis'mologist** *n*

seize[1] ❶ (si:z) *vb* **seizes, seizing, seized.** (*mainly tr*) **1** (also *intr,* foll. by *on*) to take hold of quickly; grab. **2** (sometimes foll. by *on* or *upon*) to grasp mentally, esp. rapidly: *she immediately seized his idea.* **3** to take mental possession of: *alarm seized the crowd.* **4** to take possession of rapidly and forcibly: *the thief seized the woman's purse.* **5** to take legal possession of. **6** to take by force or capture: *the army seized the undefended town.* **7** to take immediate advantage of: *to seize an opportunity.* **8** *Naut.* to bind (two ropes together). **9** (*intr;* often foll. by *up*) (of mechanical parts) to become jammed, esp. because of excessive heat. [C13 *saisen,* from OF *saisir,* from Med. L *sacīre* to position, of Gmc origin]
▸**'seizable** *adj*

seize[2] (si:z) *vb* **seizes, seizing, seized.** the US spelling of **seise.**

seizure ❶ ('si:ʒə) *n* **1** the act or an instance of seizing or the state of being seized. **2** *Pathol.* a sudden manifestation or recurrence of a disease, such as an epileptic convulsion.

selachian (sɪ'leɪkɪən) *adj* of or belonging to a large subclass of cartilaginous fishes including the sharks, rays, dogfish, and skates. [C19: from NL *Selachiī,* from Gk *selakhē* a shark]

seldom ❶ ('sɛldəm) *adv* rarely. [OE *seldon*]

select ❶ (sɪ'lɛkt) *vb* **1** to choose (someone or something) in preference to another or others. ◆ *adj also* **selected. 2** chosen in preference to others. **3** of particular quality. **4** limited as to membership or entry: *a select gathering.* ◆ *n Austral. history.* **5** a piece of land acquired by a free-selector. **6** the process of free-selection. [C16: from L *sēligere* to sort, from *sē-* apart + *legere* to choose]
▸**se'lectness** *n* ▸**se'lector** *n*

select committee *n* (in Britain) a small committee of members of parliament, set up to investigate and report on a specified matter.

selection ❶ (sɪ'lɛkʃən) *n* **1** the act or an instance of selecting or the state of being selected. **2** a thing or number of things that have been selected. **3** a range from which something may be selected: *a good selection of clothes.* **4** *Biol.* the process by which certain organisms or characters are reproduced and perpetuated in the species in preference to others.

selective ❶ (sɪ'lɛktɪv) *adj* **1** of or characterized by selection. **2** tending to choose carefully or characterized by careful choice. **3** *Electronics.* occurring at or operating at a particular frequency or band of frequencies.
▸**se'lectively** *adv*

selectivity (sɪˌlɛk'tɪvɪtɪ) *n* **1** the state or quality of being selective. **2** the degree to which a radio receiver, etc., can respond to the frequency of a desired signal.

selenite ('sɛlɪˌnaɪt) *n* a colourless glassy variety of gypsum.

THESAURUS

seesaw *vb* **4 = alternate,** fluctuate, go from one extreme to the other, oscillate, pitch, swing, teeter

seethe *vb* **1 = boil,** bubble, churn, ferment, fizz, foam, froth **2 = be furious,** be in a state (*inf.*), be incandescent, be incensed, be livid, foam at the mouth, fume, get hot under the collar (*inf.*), go ballistic (*sl., chiefly US*), rage, see red (*inf.*), simmer, storm

see through *vb* **1 = help out,** stick by, support **2 = persevere (with),** keep at, persist, see out, stay to the bitter end, stick out (*inf.*) **3 = be undeceived by,** be wise to (*inf.*), fathom, get to the bottom of, have (someone's) number (*inf.*), not fall for, penetrate, read (someone) like a book ◆ *adj* **see-through 4 = transparent,** diaphanous, filmy, fine, flimsy, gauzy, gossamer, sheer, thin, translucent

segment *n* **2 = section,** bit, compartment, division, part, piece, portion, slice, wedge

segregate *vb* **1, 2 = set apart,** discriminate against, dissociate, isolate, separate, single out
Antonyms *vb* amalgamate, desegregate, join together, mix, unify, unite

segregation *n* **1, 2 = separation,** apartheid, discrimination, isolation

seize[1] *vb* **1 = grab,** catch up, clutch, fasten, grasp, grip, lay hands on, snatch, take **5 = confiscate,** appropriate, commandeer, impound, take possession of **6 = capture,** abduct, annex, apprehend, arrest, catch, collar (*inf.*), get, grasp, nab (*inf.*), nail (*inf.*), take by storm, take captive
Antonyms *vb* ≠ **grab:** let go, loose ≠ **confiscate:** hand back, relinquish ≠ **capture:** free, release, set free, turn loose

seizure *n* **1 = capture,** abduction, annexation, apprehension, arrest, commandeering, confiscation, grabbing, taking **2 = attack,** convulsion, fit, paroxysm, spasm

seldom *adv* **= rarely,** hardly ever, infrequently, not often, occasionally, once in a blue moon (*inf.*), scarcely ever
Antonyms *adv* again and again, frequently, many a time, much, often, over and over again, time after time, time and again

select *vb* **1 = choose,** cherry-pick, opt for, pick, prefer, single out, sort out ◆ *adj* **2, 3 = choice,** excellent, first-class, first-rate, hand-picked, picked, posh (*inf., chiefly Brit.*), preferable, prime, rare, recherché, selected, special, superior, top-notch (*inf.*) **4 = exclusive,** cliquish, elite, limited, privileged
Antonyms *vb* ≠ **choose:** eliminate, reject, turn down ◆ *adj* ≠ **choice:** cheap, indifferent, inferior, ordinary, random, run-of-the-mill, second-rate, shoddy, substandard, unremarkable ≠ **exclusive:** indiscriminate

selection *n* **1 = choice,** choosing, option, pick, preference **2, 3 = range,** anthology, assortment, choice, collection, line-up, medley, miscellany, mixed bag (*inf.*), pick 'n' mix, potpourri, variety

selective *adj* **2 = particular,** careful, discerning, discriminating, discriminatory, eclectic
Antonyms *adj* all-embracing, careless, desultory, indiscriminate, unselective

selenium (sɪˈliːnɪəm) *n* a nonmetallic element that exists in several allotropic forms. The common form is a grey crystalline solid that is photoconductive, photovoltaic, and semiconducting: used in photocells, solar cells, and in xerography. Symbol: Se; atomic no.: 34; atomic wt.: 78.96. [C19: from NL, from Gk *selēnē* moon; by analogy to TELLURIUM (from L *tellus* earth)]

seleno- *or before a vowel* **selen-** *combining form.* denoting the moon: *selenography.* [from Gk *selēnē* moon]

selenography (ˌsiːlɪˈnɒgrəfɪ) *n* the branch of astronomy concerned with the description and mapping of the surface features of the moon.
▸ **ˌseleˈnographer** *n* ▸ **selenographic** (sɪˌliːnəʊˈgræfɪk) *adj*

self (sɛlf) *n, pl* **selves. 1** the distinct individuality or identity of a person or thing. **2** a person's typical bodily make-up or personal characteristics: *she's looking her old self again.* **3** one's own welfare or interests: *he only thinks of self.* **4** an individual's consciousness of his own identity or being. **5** a bird, animal, etc., that is a single colour throughout. ◆ *pron* **6** *Not standard.* myself, yourself, etc.: *seats for self and wife.* ◆ *adj* **7** of the same colour or material. **8** *Obs.* the same. [OE *seolf*]

self- *combining form.* **1** of oneself or itself: *self-defence.* **2** by, to, in, due to, for, or from the self: *self-employed; self-respect.* **3** automatic or automatically: *self-propelled.*

self-abnegation *n* the denial of one's own interests in favour of the interests of others.

self-absorption *n* **1** preoccupation with oneself to the exclusion of others. **2** *Physics.* the process in which some of the radiation emitted by a material is absorbed by the material itself.

self-abuse *n* **1** disparagement or misuse of one's own abilities, etc. **2** a censorious term for **masturbation.**

self-acting *adj* not requiring an external influence or control to function; automatic.

self-addressed *adj* **1** addressed for return to the sender. **2** directed to oneself: *a self-addressed remark.*

self-aggrandizement *n* the act of increasing one's own power, importance, etc.
▸ **ˌself-agˈgranˌdizing** *adj*

self-appointed *adj* having assumed authority without the agreement of others: *a self-appointed critic.*

self-assertion *n* the act or an instance of putting forward one's own opinions, etc., esp. in an aggressive or conceited manner.
▸ **ˌself-asˈserting** *adj* ▸ **ˌself-asˈsertive** *adj*

self-assurance ❶ *n* confidence in the validity, value, etc., of one's own ideas, opinions, etc.
▸ **ˌself-asˈsured** *adj* ▸ **ˌself-asˈsuredly** *adv*

self-centred ❶ *adj* totally preoccupied with one's own concerns.
▸ **ˌself-ˈcentredness** *n*

self-certification *n* (in Britain) a formal assertion by a worker to his employer that absence from work for up to seven days was due to sickness.

self-coloured *adj* **1** having only a single and uniform colour: *a self-coloured dress.* **2** (of cloth, etc.) having the natural or original colour.

self-command *n* another term for **self-control.**

self-confessed *adj* according to one's own testimony or admission: *a self-confessed liar.*

self-confidence ❶ *n* confidence in one's own powers, judgment, etc.
▸ **ˌself-ˈconfident** *adj* ▸ **ˌself-ˈconfidently** *adv*

self-conscious ❶ *adj* **1** unduly aware of oneself as the object of the attention of others. **2** conscious of one's existence.
▸ **ˌself-ˈconsciously** *adv* ▸ **ˌself-ˈconsciousness** *n*

self-contained *adj* **1** containing within itself all parts necessary for completeness. **2** (of a flat) having its own kitchen, bathroom, and lavatory not shared by others. **3** able or tending to keep one's feelings, thoughts, etc., to oneself.
▸ **ˌself-conˈtainedness** *n*

self-contradictory *adj Logic.* (of a proposition) both asserting and denying a given proposition.

self-control ❶ *n* the ability to exercise restraint or control over one's feelings, emotions, reactions, etc.
▸ **ˌself-conˈtrolled** *adj*

self-deception *or* **self-deceit** *n* the act or an instance of deceiving oneself.
▸ **ˌself-deˈceptive** *adj*

self-defence *n* **1** the act of defending oneself, one's actions, ideas, etc. **2** boxing as a means of defending the person (esp. in **noble art of self-defence**). **3** *Law.* the right to defend one's person, family, or property against attack or threat of attack.
▸ **ˌself-deˈfensive** *adj*

self-denial ❶ *n* the denial or sacrifice of one's own desires.
▸ **ˌself-deˈnying** *adj*

self-deprecating *or* **self-depreciating** *adj* having a tendency to disparage oneself.

self-determination *n* **1** the ability to make a decision for oneself without influence from outside. **2** the right of a nation or people to determine its own form of government.
▸ **ˌself-deˈtermined** *adj* ▸ **ˌself-deˈtermining** *adj*

self-discipline *n* the act of disciplining or power to discipline one's own feelings, desires, etc.
▸ **ˌself-ˈdisciplined** *adj*

self-drive *adj* denoting or relating to a hired car that is driven by the hirer.

self-educated *adj* **1** educated through one's own efforts without formal instruction. **2** educated at one's own expense.

self-effacement *n* the act of making oneself, one's actions, etc., inconspicuous, esp. because of timidity.
▸ **ˌself-efˈfacing** *adj*

self-employed *adj* earning one's living in one's own business or through freelance work, rather than as the employee of another.
▸ **ˌself-emˈployment** *n*

self-esteem ❶ *n* **1** respect for or a favourable opinion of oneself. **2** an unduly high opinion of oneself.

self-evident ❶ *adj* containing its own evidence or proof without need of further demonstration.
▸ **ˌself-ˈevidence** *n* ▸ **ˌself-ˈevidently** *adv*

self-existent *adj Philosophy.* existing independently of any other being or cause.

self-explanatory *adj* understandable without explanation; self-evident.

self-expression *n* the expression of one's own personality, feelings, etc., as in painting or poetry.
▸ **ˌself-exˈpressive** *adj*

self-government ❶ *n* **1** the government of a country, nation, etc., by its own people. **2** the state of being self-controlled.
▸ **ˌself-ˈgoverned** *adj* ▸ **ˌself-ˈgoverning** *adj*

selfheal (ˈsɛlfˌhiːl) *n* **1** a low-growing European herbaceous plant with tightly clustered violet-blue flowers and reputedly having healing powers. **2** any of several other plants thought to have healing powers.

self-help *n* **1** the act or state of providing the means to help oneself without relying on the assistance of others. **2a** the practice of solving one's problems by joining or forming a group designed to help those suffering from a particular problem. **2b** (*as modifier*): *a self-help group.*

self-image *n* one's own idea of oneself or sense of one's worth.

self-important ❶ *adj* having or showing an unduly high opinion of one's own abilities, importance, etc.
▸ **ˌself-imˈportantly** *adv* ▸ **ˌself-imˈportance** *n*

self-improvement *n* the improvement of one's status, position, education, etc., by one's own efforts.

self-induced *adj* **1** induced or brought on by oneself or itself. **2** *Electronics.* produced by self-induction.

self-induction *n* the production of an electromotive force in a circuit when the magnetic flux linked with the circuit changes as a result of a change in current in the same circuit.

self-indulgent *adj* tending to indulge one's own desires, etc.
▸ **ˌself-inˈdulgence** *n*

self-interest *n* **1** one's personal interest or advantage. **2** the act or an instance of pursuing one's own interest.
▸ **ˌself-ˈinterested** *adj*

selfish ❶ (ˈsɛlfɪʃ) *adj* **1** chiefly concerned with one's own interest, advantage, etc., esp. to the exclusion of the interests of others. **2** relating to or characterized by self-interest.
▸ **ˈselfishly** *adv* ▸ **ˈselfishness** *n*

self-justification *n* the act or an instance of justifying or providing excuses for one's own behaviour, etc.

selfless ❶ (ˈsɛlflɪs) *adj* having little concern for one's own interests.
▸ **ˈselflessly** *adv* ▸ **ˈselflessness** *n*

THESAURUS

self-assurance *n* = **confidence**, assertiveness, nerve, poise, positiveness, self-confidence, self-possession

self-centred *adj* = **selfish**, egotistic, inward looking, narcissistic, self-absorbed, self-seeking, wrapped up in oneself

self-confidence *n* = **self-assurance**, aplomb, confidence, high morale, nerve, poise, self-reliance, self-respect

self-confident *adj* = **self-assured**, assured, confident, fearless, poised, secure, self-reliant, sure of oneself

self-conscious *adj* **1** = **embarrassed**, affected, awkward, bashful, diffident, ill at ease, insecure, like a fish out of water, nervous, out of countenance, shamefaced, sheepish, uncomfortable

self-control *n* = **willpower**, calmness, cool, coolness, restraint, self-discipline, self-mastery, self-restraint, strength of mind *or* will

self-denial *n* = **abstemiousness**, asceticism, renunciation, self-abnegation, selflessness, self-sacrifice, unselfishness

self-esteem *n* **1, 2** = **self-respect**, *amour-propre,* confidence, faith in oneself, pride, self-assurance, self-regard, vanity

self-evident *adj* = **obvious**, axiomatic, clear, cut-and-dried (*inf.*), incontrovertible, inescapable, manifestly *or* patently true, undeniable, written all over (something)

self-government *n* **1** = **autonomy**, democracy, devolution, home rule, independence, self-determination, self-rule, sovereignty

self-important *adj* = **conceited**, arrogant, bigheaded, bumptious, cocky, full of oneself, overbearing, pompous, presumptuous, pushy (*inf.*), strutting, swaggering, swollen-headed

self-indulgence *n* = **intemperance**, dissipation, excess, extravagance, incontinence, self-gratification, sensualism

selfish *adj* **1** = **self-centred**, egoistic, egoistical, egotistic, egotistical, greedy, looking out for number one (*inf.*), mean, mercenary, narrow, self-interested, self-seeking, ungenerous
Antonyms *adj* altruistic, benevolent, considerate, generous, magnanimous, philanthropic, self-denying, selfless, self-sacrificing, ungrudging, unselfish

selfless *adj* = **unselfish**, altruistic, generous, magnanimous, self-denying, self-sacrificing, ungrudging

self-loading *adj* (of a firearm) utilizing some of the force of the explosion to eject the empty shell and replace it with a new one.
▸ ˌ**self-ˈloader** *n*

self-love *n* the instinct to seek one's own well-being or to further one's own interest.

self-made *adj* **1** having achieved wealth, status, etc., by one's own efforts. **2** made by oneself.

self-opinionated *adj* **1** having an unduly high regard for oneself or one's own opinions. **2** clinging stubbornly to one's own opinions.

self-pity *n* the act or state of pitying oneself, esp. in an exaggerated or self-indulgent manner.
▸ ˌ**self-ˈpitying** *adj* ▸ ˌ**self-ˈpityingly** *adv*

self-pollination *n* the transfer of pollen from the anthers to the stigma of the same flower.
▸ ˌ**self-ˈpolliˌnated** *adj*

self-possessed ❶ *adj* having control of one's emotions, etc.
▸ ˌ**self-posˈsession** *n*

self-preservation *n* the preservation of oneself from danger or injury.

self-pronouncing *adj* (in a phonetic transcription) of or denoting a word that, except for marks of stress, keeps the letters of its ordinary orthography to represent its pronunciation.

self-propelled *adj* (of a vehicle) provided with its own source of tractive power rather than requiring an external means of propulsion.
▸ ˌ**self-proˈpelling** *adj*

self-raising *adj* (of flour) having a raising agent, such as baking powder, already added.

self-realization *n* the realization or fulfilment of one's own potential or abilities.

self-regard *n* **1** concern for one's own interest. **2** proper esteem for oneself.

self-regulating organization *n* one of several British organizations set up in 1986 under the auspices of the Securities and Investment Board to regulate the activities of London investment markets. Abbrev.: **SRO**.

self-reliance ❶ *n* reliance on one's own abilities, decisions, etc.
▸ ˌ**self-reˈliant** *adj*

self-reproach *n* the act of finding fault with or blaming oneself.
▸ ˌ**self-reˈproachful** *adj*

self-respect ❶ *n* a proper sense of one's own dignity and integrity.
▸ ˌ**self-reˈspecting** *adj*

self-restraint ❶ *n* restraint imposed by oneself on one's own feelings, desires, etc.

self-righteous ❶ *adj* having an exaggerated awareness of one's own virtuousness.
▸ ˌ**self-ˈrighteously** *adv* ▸ ˌ**self-ˈrighteousness** *n*

self-rule *n* another term for **self-government** (sense 1).

self-sacrifice ❶ *n* the sacrifice of one's own desires, etc., for the sake of duty or for the well-being of others.
▸ ˌ**self-ˈsacriˌficing** *adj*

selfsame (ˈsɛlfˌseɪm) *adj* (*prenominal*) the very same.

self-satisfied ❶ *adj* having or showing a complacent satisfaction with oneself, one's own actions, behaviour, etc.
▸ ˌ**self-ˌsatisˈfaction** *n*

self-sealing *adj* (esp. of an envelope) designed to become sealed with the application of pressure only.

self-seeking ❶ *n* **1** the act or an instance of seeking one's own profit or interest. ◆ *adj* **2** having or showing an exclusive preoccupation with one's own profit or interest: *a self-seeking attitude.*
▸ ˌ**self-ˈseeker** *n*

self-service *adj* **1** of or denoting a shop, restaurant, petrol station, etc., where the customer serves himself. ◆ *n* **2** the practice of serving oneself, as in a shop, etc.

self-serving *adj* habitually seeking one's own advantage, esp. at the expense of others.

self-sown *adj* (of plants) growing from seed dispersed by any means other than by the agency of man or animals. Also: **self-seeded.**

self-starter *n* **1** an electric motor used to start an internal-combustion engine. **2** the switch that operates this motor. **3** a person who is strongly motivated and shows initiative, esp. at work.

self-styled ❶ *adj* (*prenominal*) claiming to be of a specified nature, quality, profession, etc.: *a self-styled expert.*

self-sufficient *or* **self-sufficing** *adj* **1** able to provide for or support oneself without the help of others. **2** *Rare.* having undue confidence in oneself.
▸ ˌ**self-sufˈficiency** *n* ▸ ˌ**self-sufˈficiently** *adv*

self-supporting *adj* **1** able to support or maintain oneself without the help of others. **2** able to stand up or hold firm without support, props, attachments, etc.

self-tender *n* an offer by a company to buy back some or all of its shares from its shareholders, esp. as a protection against an unwelcome takeover bid.

self-will ❶ *n* stubborn adherence to one's own will, desires, etc., esp. at the expense of others.
▸ ˌ**self-ˈwilled** *adj*

self-winding *adj* (of a wrist watch) having a mechanism in which a rotating or oscillating weight rewinds the mainspring.

Seljuk (sɛlˈdʒuːk) *n* **1** a member of any of the pre-Ottoman Turkish dynasties ruling over large parts of Asia in the 11th, 12th, and 13th centuries A.D. ◆ *adj* **2** of or relating to these dynasties. [C19: from Turkish]

sell ❶ (sɛl) *vb* **sells, selling, sold. 1** to dispose of or transfer or be disposed of or transferred to a purchaser in exchange for money or other consideration. **2** to deal in (objects, property, etc.): *he sells used cars.* **3** (*tr*) to give up or surrender for a price or reward: *to sell one's honour.* **4** to promote or facilitate the sale of (objects, property, etc.): *publicity sells many products.* **5** to gain acceptance of: *to sell an idea.* **6** (*intr*) to be in demand on the market: *these dresses sell well.* **7** (*tr*) *Inf.* to deceive. **8 sell down the river.** *Inf.* to betray. **9 sell oneself. 9a** to convince someone else of one's potential or worth. **9b** to give up one's moral standards, etc. **10 sell short. 10a** *Inf.* to belittle. **10b** *Finance.* to sell securities or goods without owning them in anticipation of buying them before delivery at a lower price. ◆ *n* **11** the act or an instance of selling: *a soft sell.* **12** *Inf.* a hoax or deception. ◆ See also **sell off, sell out,** etc. [OE *sellan* to lend, deliver]
▸ ˈ**sellable** *adj* ▸ ˈ**seller** *n*

sell-by date *n* **1** a date printed on the packaging of perishable goods, indicating the date after which the goods should not be offered for sale. **2 past one's sell-by date.** *Inf.* beyond one's prime.

selling race *or* **plate** *n* a horse race in which the winner must be offered for sale at auction.

sell off *vb* (*tr, adv*) to sell (remaining or unprofitable items), esp. at low prices.

Sellotape (ˈsɛləˌteɪp) *n* **1** *Trademark.* a type of transparent adhesive tape. ◆ *vb* **Sellotapes, Sellotaping, Sellotaped.** (*tr*) **2** to seal or stick using adhesive tape.

sell out ❶ *vb* (*adv*) **1** Also (*chiefly Brit.*): **sell up.** to dispose of (something) completely by selling. **2** (*tr*) *Inf.* to betray. **3** (*intr*) *Inf.* to abandon one's principles, standards, etc. ◆ *n* **sellout. 4** *Inf.* a performance for which all tickets are sold. **5** a commercial success. **6** *Inf.* a betrayal.

sell-through *adj* **1** (of prerecorded video cassettes) sold without first being available for hire only. ◆ *n* **2** the sale of prerecorded video cassettes in this way.

sell up *vb* (*adv*) *Chiefly Brit.* **1** (*tr*) to sell all (the possessions) of (a bankrupt debtor) in order to discharge his debts. **2** (*intr*) to sell a business.

selsyn (ˈsɛlsɪn) *n* another name for **synchro.** [from SEL(F-) + SYN(CHRONOUS)]

Seltzer (ˈsɛltsə) *n* **1** a natural effervescent water with a high content of minerals. **2** a similar synthetic water, used as a beverage. [C18: changed from G *Selterser Wasser* water from (*Nieder*) *Selters,* district where mineral springs are located, near Wiesbaden, Germany]

selva (ˈsɛlvə) *n* **1** dense equatorial forest, esp. in the Amazon basin,

THESAURUS

self-possessed *adj* = **self-assured,** collected, confident, cool, cool as a cucumber (*inf.*), poised, sure of oneself, together (*sl.*), unruffled

self-possession *n* = **self-assurance,** aplomb, composure, confidence, cool (*sl.*), poise, sang-froid, self-command, unflappability (*inf.*)

self-reliant *adj* = **independent,** able to stand on one's own two feet (*inf.*), capable, self-sufficient, self-supporting
Antonyms *adj* dependent, helpless, reliant, relying on

self-respect *n* = **pride,** *amour-propre,* dignity, faith in oneself, morale, one's own image, self-esteem

self-restraint *n* = **self-control,** abstemiousness, forbearance, patience, self-command, self-discipline, willpower

self-righteous *adj* = **sanctimonious,** complacent, goody-goody (*inf.*), holier-than-thou, hypocritical, pharisaic, pi (*Brit. sl.*), pietistic, pious, priggish, self-satisfied, smug, superior, too good to be true

self-sacrifice *n* = **selflessness,** altruism, generosity, self-abnegation, self-denial

self-satisfaction *n* = **smugness,** complacency, contentment, ease of mind, flush of success, glow of achievement, pride, self-approbation, self-approval

self-satisfied *adj* = **smug,** complacent, flushed with success, like a cat that has swallowed the canary, pleased with oneself, proud of oneself, puffed up, self-congratulatory, too big for one's boots *or* breeches, well-pleased

self-seeking *adj* **1** = **selfish,** acquisitive, calculating, careerist, fortune-hunting, gold-digging, looking out for number one (*inf.*), mercenary, on the make (*sl.*), opportunistic, out for what one can get, self-interested, self-serving

self-styled *adj* = **so-called,** professed, quasi-, self-appointed, *soi-disant,* would-be

self-willed *adj* = **stubborn,** cussed (*inf.*), headstrong, intractable, obstinate, opinionated, pig-headed, refractory, stiff-necked, stubborn as a mule, ungovernable, wilful

sell *vb* **1** = **trade,** barter, dispose of, exchange, put up for sale **2** = **deal in,** be in the business of, handle, hawk, market, merchandise, peddle, retail, stock, trade in, traffic in, vend **3** = **give up,** betray, deliver up, sell down the river (*inf.*), sell out (*inf.*), surrender **4, 5** = **promote,** gain acceptance for, put across
Antonyms *vb* ≠ **trade, deal in:** acquire, buy, get, invest in, obtain, pay for, procure, purchase, shop for

seller *n* **2** = **dealer,** agent, merchant, purveyor, rep, representative, retailer, salesman *or* saleswoman, shopkeeper, supplier, tradesman, traveller, vendor

sell out *vb* **1** = **dispose of,** be out of stock of, get rid of, run out of, sell up **2** *Informal* = **betray,** break faith with, double-cross (*inf.*), fail, give away, play false, rat on (*inf.*), sell down the river (*inf.*), stab in the back

characterized by tall broad-leaved evergreen trees. **2** a tract of such forest. [C19: from Sp. & Port., from L *silva* forest]

selvage *or* **selvedge** ('sɛlvɪdʒ) *n* **1** the finished nonfraying edge of a length of woven fabric. **2** a similar strip of material allowed in fabricating a metal or plastic article. [C15: from SELF + EDGE]
▸**'selvaged** *adj*

selves (sɛlvz) *n* **a** the plural of **self. b** (*in combination*): *ourselves, yourselves, themselves.*

Sem. *abbrev. for:* **1** Seminary. **2** Semitic.

semantic (sɪ'mæntɪk) *adj* **1** of or relating to the meanings of different words or symbols. **2** of or relating to semantics. [C19: from Gk *sēmantikos* having significance, from *sēmainein* to signify, from *sēma* a sign]
▸**se'mantically** *adv*

semantics (sɪ'mæntɪks) *n* (*functioning as sing*) **1** the branch of linguistics that deals with the study of meaning. **2** the study of the relationships between signs and symbols and what they represent. **3** *Logic.* the principles that determine the truth-values of the formulas in a logical system.
▸**se'manticist** *n*

semaphore ('sɛmə,fɔː) *n* **1** an apparatus for conveying information by means of visual signals, as with flags, etc. **2** a system of signalling by holding a flag in each hand and moving the arms to designated positions for each letter of the alphabet. ◆ *vb* **semaphores, semaphoring, semaphored. 3** to signal (information) by means of semaphore. [C19: via F, from Gk *sēma* a signal + -PHORE]
▸**semaphoric** (,sɛmə'fɒrɪk) *adj*

semasiology (sɪ,meɪsɪ'ɒlədʒɪ) *n* another name for **semantics.** [C19: from Gk *sēmasia* meaning, from *sēmainein* to signify + -LOGY]

sematic (sɪ'mætɪk) *adj* (of the conspicuous coloration of certain animals) acting as a warning. [C19: from Gk *sēma* a sign]

semblance ⓣ ('sɛmbləns) *n* **1** outward appearance, esp. without any inner substance. **2** a resemblance. [C13: from OF, from *sembler* to seem, from L *simulāre* to imitate, from *similis* like]

sememe ('siːmiːm) *n Linguistics.* the meaning of a morpheme. [C20 (coined in 1933 by L. Bloomfield, US linguist): from Gk *sēma* a sign + -EME]

semen ⓣ ('siːmɛn) *n* **1** the thick whitish fluid containing spermatozoa that is ejaculated from the male genital tract. **2** another name for **sperm**[1]. [C14: from L: seed]

semester (sɪ'mɛstə) *n* **1** *Chiefly US & Canad.* either of two divisions of the academic year. **2** (in German universities) a session of six months. [C19: via G from L *sēmestris* half-yearly, from *sex* six + *mensis* a month]

semi ('sɛmɪ) *n, pl* **semis.** *Inf.* **1** *Brit.* short for **semidetached (house). 2** short for **semifinal.**

semi- *prefix* **1** half: *semicircle.* **2** partially, partly, or almost: *semiprofessional.* **3** occurring twice in a specified period of time: *semiweekly.* [from L]

semiannual (,sɛmɪ'ænjʊəl) *adj* **1** occurring every half-year. **2** lasting for half a year.
▸**,semi'annually** *adv*

semiarid (,sɛmɪ'ærɪd) *adj* characterized by scanty rainfall and scrubby vegetation, often occurring in continental interiors.

semiautomatic (,sɛmɪ,ɔːtə'mætɪk) *adj* **1** partly automatic. **2** (of a firearm) self-loading but firing only one shot at each pull of the trigger. ◆ *n* **3** a semiautomatic firearm.
▸**,semi,auto'matically** *adv*

semibreve ('sɛmɪ,briːv) *n Music.* a note, now the longest in common use, having a time value that may be divided by any power of 2 to give all other notes. Usual US and Canad. name: **whole note.**

semicircle ('sɛmɪ,sɜːkᵊl) *n* **1a** one half of a circle. **1b** half the circumference of a circle. **2** anything having the shape or form of half a circle.
▸**semicircular** (,sɛmɪ'sɜːkjʊlə) *adj*

semicircular canal *n Anat.* any of the three looped fluid-filled membranous tubes, at right angles to one another, that comprise the labyrinth of the ear.

semicolon (,sɛmɪ'kəʊlən) *n* the punctuation mark ; used to indicate a pause intermediate in value or length between that of a comma and that of a full stop.

semiconductor (,sɛmɪkən'dʌktə) *n* **1** a substance, such as germanium or silicon, that has an electrical conductivity that increases with temperature. **2a** a device, such as a transistor or integrated circuit, that depends on the properties of such a substance. **2b** (*as modifier*): *a semiconductor diode.*

semiconscious (,sɛmɪ'kɒnʃəs) *adj* not fully conscious.
▸**,semi'consciously** *adv* ▸**,semi'consciousness** *n*

semidetached (,sɛmɪdɪ'tætʃt) *adj* **a** (of a building) joined to another building on one side by a common wall. **b** (*as n*): *they live in a semidetached.*

semifinal (,sɛmɪ'faɪnᵊl) *n* **a** the round before the final in a competition. **b** (*as modifier*): *the semifinal draw.*
▸**,semi'finalist** *n*

semifluid (,sɛmɪ'fluːɪd) *adj* **1** having properties between those of a liquid and those of a solid. ◆ *n* **2** a substance that has such properties because of high viscosity: *tar is a semifluid.* ◆ Also: **semiliquid.**

semiliterate (,sɛmɪ'lɪtərɪt) *adj* **1** hardly able to read or write. **2** able to read but not to write.

semilunar (,sɛmɪ'luːnə) *adj* shaped like a crescent or half-moon.

semilunar valve *n Anat.* either of two crescent-shaped valves, one in the aorta and one in the pulmonary artery, that prevent regurgitation of blood into the heart.

seminal ⓣ ('sɛmɪnəl) *adj* **1** potentially capable of development. **2** highly original and important. **3** rudimentary or unformed. **4** of or relating to semen: *seminal fluid.* **5** *Biol.* of or relating to seed. [C14: from LL *sēminālis* belonging to seed, from L *sēmen* seed]
▸**'seminally** *adv*

seminar ('sɛmɪ,nɑː) *n* **1** a small group of students meeting regularly under the guidance of a tutor, professor, etc. **2** one such meeting or the place in which it is held. **3** a higher course for postgraduates. **4** any group or meeting for holding discussions or exchanging information. [C19: via G from L *sēminārium* SEMINARY]

seminary ⓣ ('sɛmɪnərɪ) *n, pl* **seminaries. 1** an academy for the training of priests, etc. **2** *Arch.* a private secondary school, esp. for girls. [C15: from L *sēminārium* a nursery garden, from *sēmen* seed]
▸**,semi'narial** *adj* ▸**seminarian** (,sɛmɪ'nɛərɪən) *n*

seminiferous (,sɛmɪ'nɪfərəs) *adj* **1** containing, conveying, or producing semen. **2** (of plants) bearing or producing seeds.

semiotics (,sɛmɪ'ɒtɪks) *n* (*functioning as sing*) **1** the study of signs and symbols, esp. the relations between written or spoken signs and their referents in the physical world or the world of ideas. **2** the scientific study of the symptoms of disease. ◆ Also called: **semiology.** [from Gk *sēmeiōtikos,* from *sēmeion* a sign]
▸**,semi'otic** *adj*

semipermeable (,sɛmɪ'pɜːmɪəbᵊl) *adj* (esp. of a cell membrane) selectively permeable.
▸**,semi,permea'bility** *n*

semiprecious (,sɛmɪ'prɛʃəs) *adj* (of certain stones) having less value than a precious stone.

semiprofessional (,sɛmɪprə'fɛʃənᵊl) *adj* **1** (of a person) engaged in an activity or sport part-time but for pay. **2** (of an activity or sport) engaged in by semiprofessional people. **3** of or relating to a person whose activities are professional in some respects. ◆ *n* **4** a semiprofessional person.
▸**,semipro'fessionally** *adv*

semiquaver ('sɛmɪ,kweɪvə) *n Music.* a note having the time value of one-sixteenth of a semibreve. Usual US and Canad. name: **sixteenth note.**

semirigid (,sɛmɪ'rɪdʒɪd) *adj* **1** partly but not wholly rigid. **2** (of an airship) maintaining shape by means of a main supporting keel and internal gas pressure.

semiskilled (,sɛmɪ'skɪld) *adj* partly skilled or trained but not sufficiently so to perform specialized work.

semisolid (,sɛmɪ'sɒlɪd) *adj* having a viscosity and rigidity intermediate between that of a solid and a liquid.

semisolus (,sɛmɪ'səʊləs) *n* an advertisement that appears on the same page as another advertisement but not adjacent to it.

semisweet ('sɛmɪ,swiːt) *adj* (of biscuits, etc.) slightly sweetened.

Semite ('siːmaɪt) *n* a member of the group of peoples who speak a Semitic language, including the Jews and Arabs as well as the ancient Babylonians, Assyrians, and Phoenicians. [C19: from NL *sēmīta* descendant of Shem, eldest of Noah's sons (Genesis 10:21)]

Semitic (sɪ'mɪtɪk) *n* **1** a branch or subfamily of the Afro-Asiatic family of languages that includes Arabic, Hebrew, Aramaic, and such ancient languages as Phoenician. ◆ *adj* **2** denoting or belonging to this group of languages. **3** denoting or characteristic of any of the peoples speaking a Semitic language, esp. the Jews or the Arabs. **4** another word for **Jewish.**

semitone ('sɛmɪ,təʊn) *n* an interval denoting the pitch difference between certain adjacent degrees of the diatonic scale (**diatonic semitone**) or between one note and its sharpened or flattened equivalent (**chromatic semitone**); minor second. Also called (US and Canad.): **half step.** Cf. **whole tone.**
▸**semitonic** (,sɛmɪ'tɒnɪk) *adj*

semitrailer (,sɛmɪ'treɪlə) *n* a type of trailer or articulated lorry that has wheels only at the rear, the front end being supported by the towing vehicle.

semitropical (,sɛmɪ'trɒpɪkᵊl) *adj* partly tropical.
▸**,semi'tropics** *pl n*

semivowel ('sɛmɪ,vaʊəl) *n Phonetics.* a vowel-like sound that acts like a consonant. In English and many other languages the chief semivowels are (w) in *well* and (j), represented as *y,* in *yell.* Also called: **glide.**

semiyearly (,sɛmɪ'jɪəlɪ) *adj* another word for **semiannual.**

semolina (,sɛmə'liːnə) *n* the large hard grains of wheat left after flour has been bolted, used for puddings, soups, etc. [C18: from It. *semolino,* dim. of *semola* bran, from L *simila* very fine wheat flour]

THESAURUS

semblance *n* **1 = appearance**, air, aspect, bearing, façade, figure, form, front, guise, image, likeness, mask, mien, pretence, resemblance, show, similarity, veneer

semen *n* **1 = sperm**, seed (*arch. or dialect*), seminal fluid, spermatic fluid, spunk (*taboo*)

seminal *adj* **2 = influential**, creative, formative, ground-breaking, imaginative, important, innovative, original, productive

seminary *n* **1, 2 = college**, academy, high school, institute, institution, school

sempervivum (ˌsɛmpəˈvaɪvəm) *n* any of a genus of hardy perennials including the houseleek. [C16 (used of the houseleek, adopted C18 by Linnaeus (1707-78), Swedish botanist, for the genus): L, from *sempervivus* ever-living]

sempiternal (ˌsɛmpɪˈtɜːnᵊl) *adj Literary.* everlasting; eternal. [C15: from OF, from LL *sempiternālis,* from L, from *semper* always + *aeternus* ETERNAL]
▸**ˌsempiˈternally** *adv*

semplice (ˈsɛmplɪtʃɪ) *adj, adv Music.* to be performed in a simple manner. [It.: simple, from L *simplex*]

sempre (ˈsɛmprɪ) *adv Music.* (preceding a tempo or dynamic marking) always; consistently. It is used to indicate that a specified volume, tempo, etc., is to be sustained throughout a piece or passage. [It.: always, from L *semper*]

sempstress (ˈsɛmpstrɪs) *n* a rare word for **seamstress.**

Semtex (ˈsɛmtɛks) *n* a pliable plastic explosive. [orig. a trade name]

SEN (in Britain) *abbrev. for:* **1** (formerly) State Enrolled Nurse. **2** special educational needs: needs arising from any of a wide range of problems that affect a pupil's normal educational development and for which special provisions are made.

Sen. *or* **sen.** *abbrev. for:* **1** senate. **2** senator. **3** senior.

senate (ˈsɛnɪt) *n* **1** any legislative body considered to resemble a Senate. **2** the main governing body at some universities. [C13: from L *senātus* council of the elders, from *senex* an old man]

Senate (ˈsɛnɪt) *n (sometimes not cap.)* **1** the upper chamber of the legislatures of the US, Canada, Australia, and many other countries. **2** the legislative council of ancient Rome.

senator (ˈsɛnətə) *n* **1** *(often cap.)* a member of a Senate or senate. **2** any legislator.
▸**senatorial** (ˌsɛnəˈtɔːrɪəl) *adj*

send ➊ (sɛnd) *vb* **sends, sending, sent. 1** *(tr)* to cause or order (a person or thing) to be taken, directed, or transmitted to another place: *to send a letter.* **2** (when *intr,* foll. by *for;* when *tr, takes an infinitive*) to dispatch a request or command (for something or to do something): *he sent for a bottle of wine.* **3** *(tr)* to direct or cause to go to a place or point: *his blow sent the champion to the floor.* **4** *(tr)* to bring to a state or condition: *this noise will send me mad.* **5** *(tr;* often foll. by *forth, out,* etc.) to cause to issue: *his cooking sent forth a lovely smell.* **6** *(tr)* to cause to happen or come: *misery sent by fate.* **7** to transmit (a message) by radio. **8** *(tr) Sl.* to move to excitement or rapture: *this music really sends me.* ◆ *n* **9** another word for **swash** (sense 4). [OE *sendan*]
▸**ˈsendable** *adj* ▸**ˈsender** *n*

send down *vb (tr, adv)* **1** *Brit.* to expel from a university. **2** *Inf.* to send to prison.

sendoff ➊ (ˈsɛndˌɒf) *n Inf.* **1** a demonstration of good wishes to a person about to set off on a journey, etc. ◆ *vb* **send off.** *(tr, adv)* **2** to cause to depart. **3** *Soccer, rugby, etc.* (of the referee) to dismiss (a player) from the field of play for some offence. **4** *Inf.* to give a sendoff to.

send up ➊ *vb (tr, adv)* **1** *Sl.* to send to prison. **2** *Brit. inf.* to make fun of, esp. by doing an imitation or parody of. ◆ *n* **send-up. 3** *Brit. inf.* a parody or imitation.

senescent (sɪˈnesᵊnt) *adj* **1** growing old. **2** characteristic of old age. [C17: from L *senēscere* to grow old, from *senex* old]
▸**seˈnescence** *n*

seneschal (ˈsɛnɪʃəl) *n* **1** a steward of the household of a medieval prince or nobleman. **2** *Brit.* a cathedral official. [C14: from OF, from Med. L *siniscalcus,* of Gmc origin]

senile ➊ (ˈsiːnaɪl) *adj* **1** of or characteristic of old age. **2** mentally or physically weak or infirm on account of old age. [C17: from L *senīlis,* from *senex* an old man]
▸**senility** (sɪˈnɪlɪtɪ) *n*

senile dementia *n* dementia starting in old age with no clear physical cause.

senior ➊ (ˈsiːnjə) *adj* **1** higher in rank or length of service. **2** older in years: *senior citizens.* **3** of or relating to maturity or old age: *senior privileges.* **4** *Education.* **4a** of or designating more advanced or older pupils. **4b** of or relating to a secondary school. **4c** *US.* denoting a student in the last year of school or university. ◆ *n* **5** a senior person. **6** a senior pupil, student, etc. [C14: from L: older, from *senex* old]

Senior (ˈsiːnjə) *adj Chiefly US.* being the older: used to distinguish the father from the son: *Charles Parker, Senior.* Abbrevs.: **Sr., Sen.**

senior aircraftman *n* a rank in the Royal Air Force comparable to that of a private in the army, though not the lowest rank in the Royal Air Force.

senior citizen ➊ *n* an old age pensioner.

senior common room *n* (in British universities, colleges, etc.) a common room for the use of academic staff.

seniority ➊ (ˌsiːnɪˈɒrɪtɪ) *n, pl* **seniorities. 1** the state of being senior. **2** precedence in rank, etc., due to senior status.

senior service *n Brit.* the Royal Navy.

senna (ˈsɛnə) *n* **1** any of a genus of tropical plants having typically yellow flowers and long pods. **2 senna leaf.** the dried leaflets of any of these plants, used as a cathartic and laxative. **3 senna pods.** the dried fruits of any of these plants, used as a cathartic and laxative. [C16: via NL from Ar. *sanā*]

sennight *or* **se'nnight** (ˈsɛnaɪt) *n* an archaic word for **week.** [OE *seofan nihte;* see SEVEN, NIGHT]

señor (sɛˈnjɔː; *Spanish* seˈɲor) *n, pl* **señors** *or* **señores** (*Spanish* -ˈɲores). a Spaniard: a title of address equivalent to *Mr* when placed before a name or *sir* when used alone. [Sp., from L *senior* an older man, SENIOR]

señora (sɛˈnjɔːrə; *Spanish* seˈɲora) *n, pl* **señoras** (-rəz; *Spanish* -ras). a married Spanish woman: a title of address equivalent to *Mrs* when placed before a name or *madam* when used alone.

señorita (ˌsɛnjɔːˈriːtə; *Spanish* ˌseɲoˈrita) *n, pl* **señoritas** (-təz; *Spanish* -tas). an unmarried Spanish woman: title of address equivalent to *Miss* when placed before a name or *madam* or *miss* when used alone.

sensation ➊ (sɛnˈseɪʃən) *n* **1** the power of perceiving through the senses. **2** a physical experience resulting from the stimulation of one of the sense organs. **3** a general feeling or awareness: *a sensation of fear.* **4** a state of widespread public excitement: *his announcement caused a sensation.* **5** anything that causes such a state: *your speech was a sensation.* [C17: from Med. L, from LL *sensātus* endowed with SENSE]

sensational ➊ (sɛnˈseɪʃənᵊl) *adj* **1** causing or intended to cause intense feelings, esp. of curiosity, horror, etc.: *sensational disclosures in the press.* **2** *Inf.* extremely good: *a sensational skater.* **3** of or relating to the faculty of sensation.
▸**senˈsationally** *adv*

sensationalism (sɛnˈseɪʃənᵊˌlɪzəm) *n* **1** the use of sensational language, etc., to arouse an intense emotional response. **2** such sensational matter itself. **3** *Philosophy.* the doctrine that knowledge cannot go beyond the analysis of experience.
▸**senˈsationalist** *n* ▸**senˌsationalˈistic** *adj*

sensationalize *or* **sensationalise** (sɛnˈseɪʃənᵊˌlaɪz) *vb* **sensationalizes, sensationalizing, sensationalized** *or* **sensationalises, sensationalising, sensationalised.** *(tr)* to cause (events, esp. in newspaper reports) to seem more vivid, shocking, etc., than they really are.

sense ➊ (sɛns) *n* **1** any of the faculties by which the mind receives information about the external world or the state of the body. The five traditional senses are sight, hearing, touch, taste, and smell. **2** the ability to perceive. **3** a feeling perceived through one of the senses: *a sense of warmth.* **4** a mental perception or awareness: *a sense of happiness.* **5** moral discernment: *a sense of right and wrong.* **6** *(sometimes pl)*

THESAURUS

send *vb* **1** = **dispatch**, communicate, consign, convey, direct, forward, remit, transmit **2** *with* **for** = **summon**, call for, demand, order, request **5** *with* **forth, out,** *etc.* = **emit**, broadcast, discharge, exude, give off, radiate **8** *Slang* = **enrapture**, charm, delight, electrify, enthrall, excite, intoxicate, move, please, ravish, stir, thrill, titillate, turn (someone) on (*sl.*)

sendoff *n* **1** = **farewell**, departure, going-away party, leave-taking, start, valediction

send up *vb* **2** = **imitate**, burlesque, lampoon, make fun of, mimic, mock, parody, satirize, spoof (*inf.*), take off (*inf.*), take the mickey out of (*inf.*) ◆ *n* **send-up 3** = **imitation**, mickey-take (*inf.*), mockery, parody, satire, skit, spoof (*inf.*), take-off (*inf.*)

senile *adj* **2** = **doddering**, decrepit, doting, failing, gaga (*inf.*), imbecile, in one's dotage, in one's second childhood

senility *n* **2** = **dotage**, caducity, decrepitude, infirmity, loss of one's faculties, second childhood, senescence, senile dementia

senior *adj* **1** = **higher ranking**, superior **2** = **older**, elder, major (*Brit.*)
Antonyms *adj* ≠ **higher ranking:** inferior, junior, lesser, lower, minor, subordinate ≠ **older:** junior, younger

senior citizen *n* = **pensioner**, elder, O.A.P., old age pensioner, old *or* elderly person, retired person

seniority *n* **1, 2** = **superiority**, eldership, longer service, precedence, priority, rank

sensation *n* **1-3** = **feeling**, awareness, consciousness, impression, perception, sense, tingle **4** = **excitement**, agitation, commotion, furore, scandal, stir, surprise, thrill, vibes (*sl.*) **5** = **hit** (*inf.*), crowd puller (*inf.*), wow (*sl., chiefly US*)

sensational *adj* **1** = **exciting**, amazing, astounding, breathtaking, dramatic, electrifying, hair-raising, horrifying, lurid, melodramatic, revealing, scandalous, sensationalistic, shock- horror (*facetious*), shocking, spectacular, staggering, startling, thrilling, yellow (*of the press*) **2** *Informal* = **excellent**, awesome (*sl.*), brilliant, cracking (*Brit. inf.*), crucial, exceptional, fabulous (*inf.*), first class, impressive, jim-dandy (*sl.*), marvellous, mean (*sl.*), mind-blowing (*inf.*), out of this world (*inf.*), smashing (*inf.*), sovereign, superb
Antonyms *adj* ≠ **exciting:** boring, dull, humdrum, understated, undramatic, unexaggerated, unexciting ≠ **excellent:** commonplace, mediocre, no great shakes (*inf.*), ordinary, prosaic, run-of-the-mill, vanilla (*inf.*)

sense *n* **1** = **faculty**, feeling, sensation, sensibility **3, 4** = **feeling**, appreciation, atmosphere, aura, awareness, consciousness, impression, intuition, perception, premonition, presentiment, sentiment **6** *sometimes plural* = **intelligence**, brains (*inf.*), clear-headedness, cleverness, common sense, discernment, discrimination, gumption (*Brit. inf.*), judgment, mother wit, nous (*Brit. sl.*), quickness, reason, sagacity, sanity, sharpness, smarts (*sl., chiefly US*), tact, understanding, wisdom, wit(s) **7** = **point**, advantage, good, logic, purpose, reason, use, value, worth **8** = **meaning**, definition, denotation, drift, gist, implication, import, interpretation, message, nuance, purport, significance, signification, substance ◆ *vb* **15, 16** = **perceive**, appreciate, apprehend, be aware of, discern, divine, feel, get the impression, grasp, have a (funny) feeling (*inf.*), have a hunch, just know, notice, observe, pick up, realize, suspect, understand
Antonyms *n* ≠ **intelligence:** folly, foolishness, idiocy, nonsense, silliness, stupidity ◆ *vb* ≠ **perceive:** be unaware of, fail to grasp *or* notice, miss, misunderstand, overlook

sound practical judgment or intelligence. **7** reason or purpose: *what is the sense of going out?* **8** meaning: *what is the sense of this proverb?* **9** specific meaning; definition: *in what sense are you using the word?* **10** an opinion or consensus. **11** *Maths.* one of two opposite directions in which a vector can operate. **12 make sense.** to be understandable. **13 take leave of one's senses.** *Inf.* to go mad. ◆ *vb* **senses, sensing, sensed.** (*tr*) **14** to perceive through one or more of the senses. **15** to apprehend or detect without or in advance of the evidence of the senses. **16** to understand. **17** *Computing.* **17a** to test or locate the position of (a part of computer hardware). **17b** to read (data). [C14: from L *sēnsus,* from *sentīre* to feel]

sense datum *n* a unit of sensation, such as a sharp pain, detached both from any information it may convey and from its putative source in the external world.

senseless Ⓣ ('sɛnslɪs) *adj* **1** foolish: *a senseless plan.* **2** lacking in feeling; unconscious. **3** lacking in perception.
▸**'senselessly** *adv* ▸**'senselessness** *n*

sense organ *n* a structure in animals that is specialized for receiving external or internal stimuli and transmitting them in the form of nervous impulses to the brain.

sensibility Ⓣ (ˌsɛnsɪ'bɪlɪtɪ) *n, pl* **sensibilities. 1** the ability to perceive or feel. **2** (*often pl*) the capacity for responding to emotion, etc. **3** (*often pl*) the capacity for responding to aesthetic stimuli. **4** discernment; awareness. **5** (*usually pl*) emotional or moral feelings: *cruelty offends most people's sensibilities.*

sensible Ⓣ ('sɛnsɪbᵊl) *adj* **1** having or showing good sense or judgment. **2** (of clothing) serviceable; practical. **3** having the capacity for sensation; sensitive. **4** capable of being apprehended by the senses. **5** perceptible to the mind. **6** (sometimes foll. by *of*) having perception; aware: *sensible of your kindness.* **7** readily perceived: *a sensible difference.* [C14: from OF, from LL *sēnsibilis,* from L *sentīre* to sense]
▸**'sensibleness** *n* ▸**'sensibly** *adv*

sensitive Ⓣ ('sɛnsɪtɪv) *adj* **1** having the power of sensation. **2** responsive to or aware of feelings, moods, etc. **3** easily irritated; delicate. **4** affected by external conditions or stimuli. **5** easily offended. **6** of or relating to the senses or the power of sensation. **7** capable of registering small differences or changes in amounts, etc.: *a sensitive instrument.* **8** *Photog.* responding readily to light: *a sensitive emulsion.* **9** *Chiefly US.* connected with matters affecting national security. **10** (of a stock market or prices) quickly responsive to external influences. [C14: from Med. L *sēnsitīvus,* from L *sentīre* to feel]
▸**'sensitively** *adv* ▸**ˌsensi'tivity** *n*

sensitive plant *n* a tropical American mimosa plant, the leaflets and stems of which fold if touched.

sensitize *or* **sensitise** ('sɛnsɪˌtaɪz) *vb* **sensitizes, sensitizing, sensitized** *or* **sensitises, sensitising, sensitised. 1** to make or become sensitive. **2** (*tr*) to render (an individual) sensitive to a drug, etc. **3** (*tr*) *Photog.* to make (a material) sensitive to light by coating it with a photographic emulsion often containing special chemicals, such as dyes.
▸**ˌsensiti'zation** *or* **ˌsensiti'sation** *n* ▸**'sensiˌtizer** *or* **'sensiˌtiser** *n*

sensitometer (ˌsɛnsɪ'tɒmɪtə) *n* an instrument for measuring the sensitivity to light of a photographic material over a range of exposures.

sensor ('sɛnsə) *n* anything, such as a photoelectric cell, that receives a signal or stimulus and responds to it. [C19: from L *sēnsus* perceived, from *sentīre* to observe]

sensorimotor (ˌsɛnsərɪ'məʊtə) *or* **sensomotor** (ˌsɛnsə'məʊtə) *adj* of or relating to both the sensory and motor functions of an organism or to the nerves controlling them.

sensorium (sɛn'sɔːrɪəm) *n, pl* **sensoriums** *or* **sensoria** (-rɪə). **1** the area of the brain considered responsible for receiving and integrating sensations from the outside world. **2** *Physiol.* the entire sensory and intellectual apparatus of the body. [C17: from LL, from L *sēnsus* felt, from *sentīre* to perceive]

sensory ('sɛnsərɪ) *adj* of or relating to the senses or the power of sensation. [C18: from L *sensōrius,* from *sentīre* to feel]

sensual Ⓣ ('sɛnsjʊəl) *adj* **1** of or relating to any of the senses or sense organs; bodily. **2** strongly or unduly inclined to gratification of the senses. **3** tending to arouse the bodily appetites, esp. the sexual appetite. [C15: from LL *sensuālis,* from L *sēnsus* SENSE]
▸**'sensually** *adv*

sensualism ('sɛnsjʊəˌlɪzəm) *n* **1** the quality or state of being sensual. **2** the doctrine that the ability to gratify the senses is the only criterion of goodness.

sensuality Ⓣ (ˌsɛnsjʊ'ælɪtɪ) *n, pl* **sensualities. 1** the quality or state of being sensual. **2** excessive indulgence in sensual pleasures.
▸**sensualist** ('sɛnsjʊəlɪst) *n*

sensuous Ⓣ ('sɛnsjʊəs) *adj* **1** aesthetically pleasing to the senses. **2** appreciative of qualities perceived by the senses. **3** of or derived from the senses. [C17, but not common until C19: apparently coined by Milton to avoid the sexual overtones of SENSUAL]
▸**'sensuously** *adv* ▸**'sensuousness** *n*

sent (sɛnt) *vb* the past tense and past participle of **send.**

sentence Ⓣ ('sɛntəns) *n* **1** a sequence of words capable of standing alone to make an assertion, ask a question, or give a command, usually consisting of a subject and a predicate. **2** the judgment formally pronounced upon a person convicted in criminal proceedings, esp. the decision as to what punishment is to be imposed. **3** *Music.* a passage or division of a piece of music, usually consisting of two or more contrasting musical phrases and ending in a cadence. **4** *Arch.* a proverb, maxim, or aphorism. ◆ *vb* **sentences, sentencing, sentenced. 5** (*tr*) to pronounce sentence on (a convicted person) in a court of law. [C13: via OF from L *sententia* a way of thinking, from *sentīre* to feel]
▸**sentential** (sɛn'tɛnʃəl) *adj*

sentence connector *n* a word or phrase that introduces a clause or sentence and serves as a transition between it and a previous clause or sentence, as for example *also* in *I'm buying eggs and also I'm looking for a dessert for tonight.*

sentence substitute *n* a word or phrase, esp. one traditionally classified as an adverb, that is used in place of a finite sentence, such as *yes, no, certainly,* and *never.*

sententious Ⓣ (sɛn'tɛnʃəs) *adj* **1** characterized by or full of aphorisms or axioms. **2** constantly using aphorisms, etc. **3** tending to indulge in pompous moralizing. [C15: from L *sententiōsus* full of meaning, from *sententia;* see SENTENCE]
▸**sen'tentiously** *adv* ▸**sen'tentiousness** *n*

sentient Ⓣ ('sɛnʃənt, 'sɛntɪənt) *adj* **1** having the power of sense perception or sensation; conscious. ◆ *n* **2** *Rare.* a sentient person or thing. [C17: from L *sentiēns* feeling, from *sentīre* to perceive]
▸**sentience** ('sɛnʃəns) *n*

sentiment Ⓣ ('sɛntɪmənt) *n* **1** susceptibility to tender or romantic emotion: *she has too much sentiment to be successful.* **2** (*often pl*) a thought, opinion, or attitude. **3** exaggerated or mawkish feeling or emotion. **4** an expression of response to deep feeling, esp. in art. **5** a feeling or awareness: *a sentiment of pity.* **6** a mental attitude determined by feeling: *there is a strong revolutionary sentiment in his country.* **7**

THESAURUS

senseless *adj* **1** = **stupid**, absurd, asinine, crazy, daft (*inf.*), fatuous, foolish, halfwitted, idiotic, illogical, imbecilic, inane, incongruous, inconsistent, irrational, ludicrous, mad, meaningless, mindless, moronic, nonsensical, pointless, ridiculous, silly, simple, unintelligent, unreasonable, unwise, without rhyme or reason **2** = **unconscious**, anaesthetized, cold, deadened, insensate, insensible, numb, numbed, out, out cold, stunned, unfeeling
Antonyms *adj* ≠ **stupid:** intelligent, meaningful, rational, reasonable, sensible, useful, valid, wise, worthwhile ≠ **unconscious:** conscious, feeling, sensible

sensibility *n* **1** = **sensitivity**, responsiveness, sensitiveness, susceptibility **2** *often plural* = **feelings**, emotions, moral sense, sentiments, susceptibilities **4** = **awareness**, appreciation, delicacy, discernment, insight, intuition, perceptiveness, taste
Antonyms *n* ≠ **sensitivity:** deadness, insensibility, insensitivity, numbness, unresponsiveness ≠ **awareness:** insensibility, lack of awareness, unconsciousness, unperceptiveness

sensible *adj* **1** = **wise**, canny, discreet, discriminating, down-to-earth, far-sighted, intelligent, judicious, matter-of-fact, practical, prudent, rational, realistic, reasonable, sagacious, sage, sane, shrewd, sober, sound, well-reasoned, well-thought-out **5** = **perceptible**, appreciable, considerable, discernable, noticeable, palpable, significant, tangible, visible **6** *usually with* **of** = **aware**, acquainted with, alive to, conscious, convinced, mindful, observant, sensitive to, understanding
Antonyms *adj* ≠ **wise:** daft (*inf.*), dumb-ass (*sl.*), foolish, idiotic, ignorant, injudicious, irrational, senseless, silly, stupid, unreasonable, unwise ≠ **aware:** blind, ignorant, insensible, insensitive, unaware, unmindful

sensitive *adj* **2** = **susceptible**, delicate, easily affected, impressionable, reactive, responsive, sentient, touchy-feely (*inf.*) **3** = **easily hurt**, delicate, tender **5** = **touchy**, easily offended, easily upset, irritable, temperamental, thin-skinned **7** = **precise**, acute, fine, keen, perceptive, responsive
Antonyms *adj* ≠ **susceptible, touchy:** callous, hard, hardened, insensitive, thick-skinned, tough, uncaring, unfeeling ≠ **easily hurt:** insensitive, tough ≠ **precise:** approximate, imprecise, inexact, unperceptive

sensitivity *n* **2** = **sensitiveness**, delicacy, reactiveness, reactivity, receptiveness, responsiveness, susceptibility

sensual *adj* **1, 2** = **physical**, animal, bodily, carnal, epicurean, fleshly, luxurious, unspiritual, voluptuous **3** = **erotic**, lascivious, lecherous, lewd, libidinous, licentious, lustful, randy (*inf., chiefly Brit.*), raunchy (*sl.*), sexual, sexy (*inf.*), steamy (*inf.*), unchaste

sensualist *n* **2** = **pleasure-lover**, *bon vivant,* bon viveur, epicure, epicurean, hedonist, sybarite, voluptuary

sensuality *n* **1** = **eroticism**, animalism, carnality, lasciviousness, lecherousness, lewdness, libidinousness, licentiousness, prurience, salaciousness, sexiness (*inf.*), voluptuousness

sensuous *adj* **1, 2** = **pleasurable**, bacchanalian, epicurean, gratifying, hedonistic, lush, rich, sensory, sumptuous, sybaritic
Antonyms *adj* abstemious, ascetic, celibate, plain, self-denying, Spartan

sentence *n* **2** = **punishment**, condemnation, decision, decree, doom, judgment, order, pronouncement, ruling, verdict ◆ *vb* **5** = **condemn**, doom, mete out justice to, pass judgment on, penalize

sententious *adj* **1** = **gnomic**, aphoristic, axiomatic, brief, compact, concise, epigrammatic, laconic, pithy, pointed, short, succinct, terse **3** = **pompous**, canting, judgmental, moralistic, ponderous, preachifying (*inf.*), sanctimonious

sentient *adj* **1** = **feeling**, conscious, live, living, reactive, sensitive

sentiment *n* **1** = **emotion**, sensibility, soft-heartedness, tender feeling, tenderness **2** *often plural* = **feeling**, attitude, belief, idea, judgment, opinion, persuasion, saying, thought, view, way of thinking **3** = **sentimentality**, emotionalism, mawkishness, overemotionalism, romanticism, slush (*inf.*)

a feeling conveyed, or intended to be conveyed, in words. [C17: from Med. L *sentīmentum,* from L *sentīre* to feel]

sentimental ❶ (ˌsɛntɪˈmɛntᵊl) *adj* **1** tending to indulge the emotions excessively. **2** making a direct appeal to the emotions, esp. to romantic feelings. **3** relating to or characterized by sentiment.
▸ **ˌsentiˈmentaˌlism** *n* ▸ **ˌsentiˈmentalist** *n* ▸ **ˌsentiˈmentally** *adv*

sentimentality ❶ (ˌsɛntɪmɛnˈtælɪtɪ) *n, pl* **sentimentalities. 1** the state, quality, or an instance of being sentimental. **2** an act, statement, etc., that is sentimental.

sentimentalize *or* **sentimentalise** (ˌsɛntɪˈmɛntᵊˌlaɪz) *vb* **sentimentalizes, sentimentalizing, sentimentalized** *or* **sentimentalises, sentimentalising, sentimentalised.** to make sentimental or behave sentimentally.
▸ **ˌsentiˌmentaliˈzation** *or* **ˌsentiˌmentaliˈsation** *n*

sentimental value *n* the value of an article in terms of its sentimental associations for a particular person.

sentinel ❶ (ˈsɛntɪnᵊl) *n* **1** a person, such as a sentry, assigned to keep guard. ◆ *vb* **sentinels, sentinelling, sentinelled** *or US* **sentinels, sentineling, sentineled.** (*tr*) **2** to guard as a sentinel. **3** to post as a sentinel. [C16: from OF *sentinelle,* from OIt., from *sentina* watchfulness, from *sentire* to notice, from L]

sentry (ˈsɛntrɪ) *n, pl* **sentries.** a soldier who guards or prevents unauthorized access to a place, etc. [C17: ? shortened from obs. *centrinel,* C16 var. of SENTINEL]

sentry box *n* a small shelter with an open front in which a sentry may stand to be sheltered from the weather.

senza (ˈsɛntsɑː) *prep Music.* omitting. [It.]

Sep. *abbrev. for:* **1** September. **2** Septuagint.

sepal (ˈsɛpᵊl) *n* any of the separate parts of the calyx of a flower. [C19: from NL *sepalum: sep-* from Gk *skepē* a covering + *-alum,* from NL *petalum* PETAL]

-sepalous *adj combining form.* having sepals of a specified type or number: *polysepalous.*
▸ **-sepaly** *n combining form.*

separable ❶ (ˈsɛpərəbᵊl) *adj* able to be separated, divided, or parted.
▸ **ˌseparaˈbility** *or* **ˈseparableness** *n* ▸ **ˈseparably** *adv*

separate ❶ *vb* (ˈsɛpəˌreɪt), **separates, separating, separated. 1** (*tr*) to act as a barrier between: *a range of mountains separates the two countries.* **2** to part or be parted from a mass or group. **3** (*tr*) to discriminate between: *to separate the men from the boys.* **4** to divide or be divided into component parts. **5** to sever or be severed. **6** (*intr*) (of a married couple) to cease living together. ◆ *adj* (ˈsɛprɪt, ˈsɛpərɪt). **7** existing or considered independently: *a separate problem.* **8** disunited or apart. **9** set apart from the main body or mass. **10** distinct, individual, or particular. **11** solitary or withdrawn. [C15: from L *sēparāre,* from *sē-* apart + *parāre* to obtain]
▸ **ˈseparately** *adv* ▸ **ˈseparateness** *n* ▸ **ˈseparative** *adj* ▸ **ˈsepaˌrator** *n*

separates (ˈsɛprɪts, ˈsɛpərɪts) *pl n* women's outer garments that only cover part of the body; skirts, blouses, jackets, trousers, etc.

separate school *n* **1** (in certain Canadian provinces) a school for a large religious minority financed by provincial grants in addition to the education tax. **2** a Roman Catholic school.

separation ❶ (ˌsɛpəˈreɪʃən) *n* **1** the act of separating or state of being separated. **2** the place or line where a separation is made. **3** a gap that separates. **4** *Family law.* the cessation of cohabitation between a man and wife, either by mutual agreement or under a decree of a court.

separatist (ˈsɛpərətɪst) *n* **a** a person who advocates secession from an organization, federation, union, etc. **b** (*as modifier*): *a separatist movement.*
▸ **ˈsepara,tism** *n*

Sephardi (sɪˈfɑːdiː) *n, pl* **Sephardim** (-dɪm). *Judaism.* **1** a Jew of Spanish, Portuguese, or North African descent. **2** the pronunciation of Hebrew used by these Jews, and of Modern Hebrew as spoken in Israel. ◆ Cf. **Ashkenazi.** [C19: from LHeb., from Heb. *sepharad* a region mentioned in Obadiah 20, thought to have been Spain]
▸ **Seˈphardic** *adj*

sepia (ˈsiːpɪə) *n* **1** a dark reddish-brown pigment obtained from the inky secretion of the cuttlefish. **2** a brownish tone imparted to a photograph, esp. an early one. **3** a brownish-grey to dark yellowish-brown colour. **4** a drawing or photograph in sepia. ◆ *adj* **5** of the colour sepia or done in sepia: *a sepia print.* [C16: from L: a cuttlefish, from Gk]

sepoy (ˈsiːpɔɪ) *n* (formerly) an Indian soldier in the service of the British. [C18: from Port. *sipaio,* from Urdu *sipāhī,* from Persian: horseman, from *sipāh* army]

seppuku (sɛˈpuːkuː) *n* another word for **hara-kiri.** [from Japanese, from Chinese *ch'ieh* to cut + *fu* bowels]

sepsis (ˈsɛpsɪs) *n* the presence of pus-forming bacteria in the body. [C19: via NL from Gk *sēpsis* a rotting]

sept (sɛpt) *n* **1** *Anthropol.* a clan that believes itself to be descended from a common ancestor. **2** a branch of a tribe, esp. in Ireland or Scotland. [C16: ? a var. of SECT]

Sept. *abbrev. for:* **1** September. **2** Septuagint.

septa (ˈsɛptə) *n* the plural of **septum.**

septal (ˈsɛptəl) *adj* of or relating to a septum.

September (sɛpˈtɛmbə) *n* the ninth month of the year, consisting of 30 days. [OE, from L: the seventh (month) according to the original calendar of ancient Rome, from *septem* seven]

septenary (ˈsɛptɪnərɪ) *adj* **1** of or relating to the number seven. **2** forming a group of seven. ◆ *n, pl* **septenaries. 3** the number seven. **4** a group of seven things. **5** a period of seven years. [C16: from L *septēnārius,* from *septēnī* seven each, from *septem* seven]

septennial (sɛpˈtɛnɪəl) *adj* **1** occurring every seven years. **2** relating to or lasting seven years. [C17: from L, from *septem* seven + *annus* a year]

septet (sɛpˈtɛt) *n* **1** *Music.* a group of seven singers or instrumentalists or a piece of music composed for such a group. **2** a group of seven people or things. [C19: from G, from L *septem* seven]

septic ❶ (ˈsɛptɪk) *adj* **1** of or caused by sepsis. **2** of or caused by putrefaction. ◆ *n* **3** *Austral. & NZ inf.* short for **septic tank.** [C17: from L *sēpticus,* from Gk, from *sēptos* decayed, from *sēpein* to make rotten]
▸ **ˈseptically** *adv* ▸ **septicity** (sɛpˈtɪsɪtɪ) *n*

septicaemia *or US* **septicemia** (ˌsɛptɪˈsiːmɪə) *n* any of various diseases caused by microorganisms in the blood. Nontechnical name: **blood poisoning.** [C19: from NL, from Gk *sēptik(os)* SEPTIC + -AEMIA]
▸ **ˌseptiˈcaemic** *or US* **ˌseptiˈcemic** *adj*

septic tank *n* a tank, usually below ground, for containing sewage to be decomposed by anaerobic bacteria. Also called (Austral.): **septic system.**

septillion (sɛpˈtɪljən) *n, pl* **septillions** *or* **septillion. 1** (in Britain, France, and Germany) the number represented as one followed by 42 zeros (10^{42}). **2** (in the US and Canada) the number represented as one followed by 24 zeros (10^{24}). Brit. word: **quadrillion.** [C17: from F, from *sept* seven + *-illion,* on the model of *million*]
▸ **sepˈtillionth** *adj, n*

septime (ˈsɛptiːm) *n* the seventh of eight basic positions from which a parry or attack can be made in fencing. [C19: from L *septimus* seventh, from *septem* seven]

septuagenarian (ˌsɛptjuədʒɪˈnɛərɪən) *n* **1** a person who is from 70 to 79 years old. ◆ *adj* **2** being between 70 and 79 years old. **3** of or relating to a septuagenarian. [C18: from L, from *septuāgintā* seventy]

Septuagesima (ˌsɛptjuəˈdʒɛsɪmə) *n* the third Sunday before Lent. [C14: from Church L *septuāgēsima* (*dīes*) the seventieth (day)]

Septuagint (ˈsɛptjuəˌdʒɪnt) *n* the principal Greek version of the Old Testament, including the Apocrypha, believed to have been translated by 70 or 72 scholars. [C16: from L *septuāgintā* seventy]

septum (ˈsɛptəm) *n, pl* **septa.** *Biol., anat.* a dividing partition between two tissues or cavities. [C18: from L *saeptum* wall, from *saepīre* to enclose]

septuple (ˈsɛptjupᵊl) *adj* **1** seven times as much or as many. **2** consisting of seven parts or members. ◆ *vb* **septuples, septupling, septupled. 3** (*tr*) to multiply by seven. [C17: from LL *septuplus,* from *septem* seven]
▸ **septuplicate** (sɛpˈtjuːplɪkɪt) *n, adj*

sepulchral ❶ (sɪˈpʌlkrəl) *adj* **1** suggestive of a tomb; gloomy. **2** of or relating to a sepulchre.
▸ **seˈpulchrally** *adv*

sepulchre ❶ *or US* **sepulcher** (ˈsɛpəlkə) *n* **1** a burial vault, tomb, or grave. **2** Also called: **Easter sepulchre.** an alcove in some churches in

THESAURUS

sentimental *adj* **1** = **romantic**, corny (*sl.*), dewy-eyed, emotional, gushy, impressionable, maudlin, mawkish, mushy (*inf.*), nostalgic, overemotional, pathetic, schmaltzy (*sl.*), simpering, sloppy (*inf.*), slushy (*inf.*), soft-hearted, tearful, tear-jerking (*inf.*), tender, touching, weepy (*inf.*)
Antonyms *adj* commonsensical, dispassionate, down-to-earth, earthy, hard-headed, practical, realistic, undemonstrative, unemotional, unfeeling, unromantic, unsentimental

sentimentality *n* **1** = **romanticism**, bathos, corniness (*sl.*), emotionalism, gush (*inf.*), mawkishness, mush (*inf.*), nostalgia, pathos, play on the emotions, schmaltz (*sl.*), sloppiness (*inf.*), slush (*inf.*), tenderness

sentinel *n* **1** = **guard**, lookout, picket, sentry, watch, watchman

separable *adj* = **distinguishable**, detachable, divisible, scissile, severable

separate *vb* **1** = **divide**, come between, keep apart, split **2** = **divide**, break off, cleave, come apart, come away, disentangle, disjoin **3** = **isolate**, discriminate between, put on one side, segregate, single out, sort out **4, 5** = **disunite**, bifurcate, detach, disconnect, diverge, divide, remove, sever, sunder, uncouple **6** = **part**, break up, divorce, estrange, go different ways, part company, split up ◆ *adj* **7** = **unconnected**, detached, disconnected, discrete, disjointed, divided, divorced, isolated, unattached **10** = **individual**, alone, apart, autonomous, distinct, independent, particular, single, solitary
Antonyms *vb* ≠ **divide, part, isolate:** amalgamate, combine, connect, join, link, merge, mix, unite ◆ *adj* ≠ **unconnected, individual:** affiliated, alike, connected, interdependent, joined, similar, unified, united

separated *adj* **2, 4-6** = **disconnected**, apart, broken up, disassociated, disunited, divided, living apart, parted, put asunder, separate, split up, sundered

separately *adv* **7** = **individually**, alone, apart, independently, one at a time, one by one, personally, severally, singly
Antonyms *adv* as a group, as one, collectively, in a body, in concert, in unison, jointly, together

separation *n* **1** = **division**, break, detachment, disconnection, disengagement, disjunction, dissociation, disunion, gap, segregation, severance **4** = **split-up**, break-up, divorce, estrangement, farewell, leave-taking, parting, rift, split

septic *adj* **1, 2** = **infected**, festering, poisoned, pussy, putrefactive, putrefying, putrid, suppurating, toxic

sepulchral *adj* **1** = **gloomy**, cheerless, dismal, funereal, grave, lugubrious, melancholy, morbid, mournful, sad, sombre, Stygian, woeful

sepulchre *n* **1** = **tomb**, burial place, grave, mausoleum, sarcophagus, vault

which the Eucharistic elements were kept from Good Friday until Easter. ◆ *vb* **sepulchres, sepulchring, sepulchred** *or US* **sepulchers, sepulchering, sepulchered.** **3** (*tr*) to bury in a sepulchre. [C12: from OF *sépulcre,* from L *sepulcrum,* from *sepelīre* to bury]

sepulture (ˈsɛpəltʃə) *n* the act of placing in a sepulchre. [C13: via OF from L *sepultūra,* from *sepultus* buried, from *sepelīre* to bury]

seq. *abbrev. for:* **1** sequel. **2** sequens. [L: the following (one)]

sequel ❶ (ˈsiːkwəl) *n* **1** anything that follows from something else. **2** a consequence. **3** a novel, play, etc., that continues a previously related story. [C15: from LL *sequēla,* from L *sequī* to follow]

sequela (sɪˈkwiːlə) *n, pl* **sequelae** (-liː). (*often pl*) *Med.* **1** any abnormal bodily condition or disease arising from a pre-existing disease. **2** any complication of a disease. [C18: from L: SEQUEL]

sequence ❶ (ˈsiːkwəns) *n* **1** an arrangement of two or more things in a successive order. **2** the successive order of two or more things: *chronological sequence.* **3** an action or event that follows another or others. **4a** *Cards.* a set of three or more consecutive cards, usually of the same suit. **4b** *Bridge.* a set of two or more consecutive cards. **5** *Music.* an arrangement of notes or chords repeated several times at different pitches. **6** *Maths.* an ordered set of numbers or other mathematical entities in one-to-one correspondence with the integers 1 to *n* **7** a section of a film constituting a single continuous uninterrupted episode. **8** *Biochem.* the unique order of amino acids in a protein or of nucleotides in DNA or RNA. ◆ *vb* (*tr*) **9** to arrange in a sequence. [C14: from Med. L *sequentia* that which follows, from L *sequī* to follow]

sequence of tenses *n Grammar.* the sequence according to which the tense of a subordinate verb in a sentence is determined by the tense of the principal verb, as in *I believe he is lying, I believed he was lying,* etc.

sequencing (ˈsiːkwənsɪŋ) *n Biochem.* the procedure of determining the order of amino acids in the polypeptide chain of a protein (**protein sequencing**) or of nucleotides in a DNA section comprising a gene (**gene sequencing**).

sequent (ˈsiːkwənt) *adj* **1** following in order or succession. **2** following as a result. ◆ *n* **3** something that follows. [C16: from L *sequēns,* from *sequī* to follow]
▸ˈ**sequently** *adv*

sequential (sɪˈkwɛnʃəl) *adj* **1** characterized by or having a regular sequence. **2** another word for **sequent.**
▸**sequentiality** (sɪˌkwɛnʃɪˈælɪtɪ) *n* ▸**seˈquentially** *adv*

sequential access *n* a method of reading data from a computer file by reading through the file from the beginning.

sequester (sɪˈkwɛstə) *vb* (*tr*) **1** to remove or separate. **2** (*usually passive*) to retire into seclusion. **3** *Law.* to take (property) temporarily out of the possession of its owner, esp. until creditors are satisfied or a court order is complied with. **4** *International law.* to appropriate (enemy property). [C14: from LL *sequestrāre* to surrender for safekeeping, from L *sequester* a trustee]

sequestrate (sɪˈkwɛstreɪt) *vb* **sequestrates, sequestrating, sequestrated.** (*tr*) *Law.* a variant of **sequester** (sense 3). [C16: from LL *sequestrāre* to SEQUESTER]
▸**sequestrator** (ˈsiːkwɛsˌtreɪtə) *n*

sequestration (ˌsiːkwɛˈstreɪʃən) *n* **1** the act of sequestering or state of being sequestered. **2** *Law.* the sequestering of property. **3** *Chem.* the effective removal of ions from a solution by coordination with another type of ion or molecule to form complexes.

sequestrum (sɪˈkwɛstrəm) *n, pl* **sequestra** (-trə). *Pathol.* a detached piece of dead bone that often migrates to a wound, etc. [C19: from NL, from L: something deposited]
▸**seˈquestral** *adj*

sequin (ˈsiːkwɪn) *n* **1** a small piece of shiny often coloured metal foil, usually round, used to decorate garments, etc. **2** a gold coin formerly minted in Italy. [C17: via F from It. *zecchino,* from *zecca* mint, from Ar. *sikkah* die for striking coins]
▸ˈ**sequined** *adj*

sequoia (sɪˈkwɔɪə) *n* either of two giant Californian coniferous trees, the **redwood,** or the **big tree** or **giant sequoia.** [C19: NL, after *Sequoya,* known also as George Guess, (?1770–1843), American Indian scholar and leader]

sérac (ˈsɛræk) *n* a pinnacle of ice among crevasses on a glacier, usually on a steep slope. [C19: from Swiss F: a variety of white cheese (hence the ice that resembles it), from Med. L *serācium,* from L *serum* whey]

seraglio (sɛˈrɑːlɪˌəʊ) *or* **serail** (səˈraɪ) *n, pl* **seraglios** *or* **serails. 1** the harem of a Muslim house or palace. **2** a sultan's palace, esp. in the former Turkish empire. [C16: from It. *serraglio* animal cage, from Med. L *serrāculum* bolt, from L *sera* a door bar; associated also with Turkish *seray* palace]

serape (səˈrɑːpɪ) *n* **1** a blanket-like shawl, often of brightly coloured wool, worn by men in Latin America. **2** a large shawl worn around the shoulders by women as a fashion garment. [C19: Mexican Sp.]

seraph ❶ (ˈsɛrəf) *n, pl* **seraphs** *or* **seraphim** (-əfɪm). *Theol.* a member of the highest order of angels in the celestial hierarchies, often depicted as the winged head of a child. [C17: back formation from pl *seraphim,* via LL from Heb.]
▸**seraphic** (sɪˈræfɪk) *adj*

Serb (sɜːb) *n, adj* another word for **Serbian.** [C19: from Serbian *Srb*]

Serbian (ˈsɜːbɪən) *adj* **1** of, relating to, or characteristic of Serbia, in Yugoslavia, its people, or their dialect of Serbo-Croatian. ◆ *n* **2** the dialect of Serbo-Croat spoken in Serbia. **3** a native or inhabitant of Serbia.

Serbo-Croat *or* **Serbo-Croatian** (ˈsɜːbəʊ-) *n* **1** the language of the Serbs and the Croats. The Serbian dialect is usually written in the Cyrillic alphabet, the Croatian in Roman. ◆ *adj* **2** of or relating to this language.

SERC (in Britain) *abbrev. for* Science and Engineering Research Council.

sere[1] (sɪə) *adj* **1** *Arch.* dried up. ◆ *vb* **seres, sering, sered,** *n* **2** a rare spelling of **sear.** [OE *sēar*]

sere[2] (sɪə) *n* the series of changes occurring in the ecological succession of a community. [C20: from SERIES]

serenade (ˌsɛrɪˈneɪd) *n* **1** a piece of music characteristically played outside the house of a woman. **2** a piece of music suggestive of this. **3** an extended composition in several movements similar to the modern suite. ◆ *vb* **serenades, serenading, serenaded. 4** (*tr*) to play a serenade for (someone). **5** (*intr*) to play a serenade. [C17: from F *sérénade,* from It. *serenata,* from *sereno* peaceful, from L *serēnus;* also infl. in meaning by It. *sera* evening, from L *sērus* late]
▸ˌ**sereˈnader** *n*

serendipity (ˌsɛrənˈdɪpɪtɪ) *n* the faculty of making fortunate discoveries by accident. [C18: coined by Horace Walpole, from the Persian fairytale *The Three Princes of Serendip,* in which the heroes possess this gift]
▸ˌ**serenˈdipitous** *adj*

serene ❶ (sɪˈriːn) *adj* **1** peaceful or tranquil; calm. **2** clear or bright: *a serene sky.* **3** (*often cap.*) honoured: *His Serene Highness.* [C16: from L *serēnus*]
▸**seˈrenely** *adv* ▸**serenity** (sɪˈrɛnɪtɪ) *n*

serf ❶ (sɜːf) *n* (esp. in medieval Europe) an unfree person, esp. one bound to the land. [C15: from OF, from L *servus* a slave]
▸ˈ**serfdom** *or* ˈ**serfhood** *n*

serge (sɜːdʒ) *n* **1** a twill-weave woollen or worsted fabric used for clothing. **2** a similar twilled cotton, silk, or rayon fabric. [C14: from OF *sarge,* from Vulgar L *sārica* (unattested), from L *sēricum,* from Gk *sērikon* silk, ult. from *sēr* silkworm]

sergeant (ˈsɑːdʒənt) *n* **1** a noncommissioned officer in certain armies, air forces, and marine corps, usually ranking immediately above a corporal. **2a** (in Britain) a police officer ranking between constable and inspector. **2b** (in the US) a police officer ranking below a captain. **3** a court or municipal officer who has ceremonial duties. ◆ Also: **serjeant.** [C12: from OF *sergent,* from L *serviēns,* lit.: serving, from *servīre* to SERVE]

sergeant at arms *n* an officer of a legislative or fraternal body responsible for maintaining internal order. Also: **sergeant, serjeant at arms.**

Sergeant Baker (ˈbeɪkə) *n* a large brightly coloured Australian sea fish.

sergeant major *n* the chief administrative noncommissioned officer of a military headquarters. See also **warrant officer.**

Sergt *abbrev. for* Sergeant.

serial (ˈsɪərɪəl) *n* **1** a novel, film, etc., presented in instalments at regular intervals. **2** a publication, regularly issued and consecutively numbered. ◆ *adj* **3** of or resembling a series. **4** published or presented as a serial. **5** of or relating to such publication or presentation. **6** *Computing.* of or operating on items of information, etc., in the order in which they occur. **7** of or using the techniques of serialism. [C19: from NL *seriālis,* from L *seriēs* SERIES]
▸ˈ**serially** *adv*

serialism (ˈsɪərɪəˌlɪzəm) *n* (in 20th-century music) the use of a sequence of notes in a definite order as a thematic basis for a composition. See also **twelve-tone.**

serialize *or* **serialise** (ˈsɪərɪəˌlaɪz) *vb* **serializes, serializing, serialized** *or* **serialises, serialising, serialised.** (*tr*) to publish or present in the form of a serial.
▸ˌ**serialiˈzation** *or* ˌ**serialiˈsation** *n*

serial killer *n* a person who carries out a series of murders, selecting victims at random or according to a perverse pattern.

serial monogamy *n* the practice of having a number of long-term monogamous romantic or sexual relationships or marriages in succession.

serial number *n* any of the consecutive numbers assigned to machines, tools, books, etc.

seriate (ˈsɪərɪɪt) *adj* forming a series.

seriatim (ˌsɪərɪˈætɪm) *adv* one after another in order. [C17: from Med. L, from L *seriēs* SERIES]

THESAURUS

sequel *n* **1** = **follow-up,** continuation, development **2** = **consequence,** conclusion, end, issue, outcome, payoff (*inf.*), result, upshot

sequence *n* **1, 2** = **succession,** arrangement, chain, course, cycle, order, procession, progression, series

seraphic *adj* = **angelic,** beatific, blissful, celestial, divine, heavenly, holy, pure, sublime

serene *adj* **1** = **calm,** composed, imperturbable, peaceful, placid, sedate, tranquil, undisturbed, unruffled, untroubled **2** = **clear,** bright, cloudless, fair, halcyon, unclouded
Antonyms *adj* ≠ **calm:** agitated, anxious, disturbed, excitable, flustered, perturbed, troubled, uptight (*inf.*)

serenity *n* **1** = **calmness,** calm, composure, peace, peacefulness, peace of mind, placidity, quietness, quietude, stillness, tranquillity **2** = **clearness,** brightness, fairness

serf *n* = **vassal,** bondsman, helot, liegeman, servant, slave, thrall, varlet (*arch.*), villein

sericeous (sɪ'rɪʃəs) *adj Bot.* **1** covered with a layer of small silky hairs: *a sericeous leaf.* **2** silky. [C18: from LL *sēriceus* silken, from L *sēricus;* see SERGE]

sericulture ('serɪ,kʌltʃə) *n* the rearing of silkworms for the production of raw silk. [C19: via F; *seri-* from L *sēricum* silk, ult. from Gk *sēr* a silkworm]
▸**,seri'cultural** *adj* ▸**,seri'culturist** *n*

series ❶ ('sɪəri:z) *n, pl* **series. 1** a group or succession of related things, usually arranged in order. **2** a set of radio or television programmes having the same characters but different stories. **3** a set of books having the same format, related content, etc., published by one firm. **4** a set of stamps, coins, etc., issued at a particular time. **5** *Maths.* the sum of a finite or infinite sequence of numbers or quantities. **6** *Electronics.* an arrangement of two or more components connected in a circuit so that the same current flows in turn through each of them (esp. in **in series**). Cf. **parallel** (sense 10). **7** *Geol.* a stratigraphical unit that represents the rocks formed during an epoch. [C17: from L: a row, from *serere* to link]

series-wound ('sɪəri:z,waʊnd) *adj* (of a motor or generator) having the field and armature circuits connected in series.

serif ('serɪf) *n Printing.* a small line at the extremities of a main stroke in a type character. [C19: ?from Du. *schreef* dash, prob. of Gmc origin]

serigraph ('serɪ,grɑ:f) *n* a colour print made by an adaptation of the silk-screen process. [C19: from *seri-,* from L *sēricum* silk + -GRAPH]
▸**serigraphy** (sə'rɪgrəfɪ) *n*

serin ('serɪn) *n* any of various small yellow-and-brown finches of parts of Europe. [C16: from F, ?from OProvençal *sirena* a bee-eater, from L *sīrēn,* a kind of bird, from SIREN]

seringa (sə'rɪŋgə) *n* **1** any of a Brazilian genus of trees that yield rubber. **2** a deciduous tree of southern Africa with a graceful shape. [C18: from Port., var. of SYRINGA]

seriocomic (,sɪərɪəʊ'kɒmɪk) *adj* mixing serious and comic elements.
▸**,serio'comically** *adv*

serious ❶ ('sɪərɪəs) *adj* **1** grave in nature or disposition: *a serious person.* **2** marked by deep feeling; sincere: *is he serious or joking?* **3** concerned with important matters: *a serious conversation.* **4** requiring effort or concentration: *a serious book.* **5** giving rise to fear or anxiety: *a serious illness.* **6** *Inf.* worthy of regard because of substantial quantity or quality: *serious money; serious wine.* **7** *Inf.* extreme or remarkable: *a serious haircut.* [C15: from LL *sēriōsus,* from L *sērius*]
▸**'seriousness** *n*

serjeant ('sɑ:dʒənt) *n* a variant spelling of **sergeant.**

serjeant at law *n* (formerly, in England) a barrister of a special rank. Also: **serjeant, sergeant at law, sergeant.**

sermon ❶ ('sɜ:mən) *n* **1a** an address of religious instruction or exhortation, often based on a passage from the Bible, esp. one delivered during a church service. **1b** a written version of such an address. **2** a serious speech, esp. one administering reproof. [C12: via OF from L *sermō* discourse, prob. from *serere* to join together]

sermonize *or* **sermonise** ('sɜ:mə,naɪz) *vb* **sermonizes, sermonizing, sermonized** *or* **sermonises, sermonising, sermonised.** to address (a person or audience) as if delivering a sermon.
▸**'sermon,izer** *or* **'sermon,iser** *n*

Sermon on the Mount *n Bible.* a major discourse delivered by Christ, including the Beatitudes and the Lord's Prayer (Matthew 5–7).

sero- *combining form.* indicating a serum: *serology.*

seroconvert (,sɪərəʊkən'vɜ:t) *vb* (*intr*) (of an individual) to produce antibodies specific to, and in response to the presence in the blood of, a particular antigen, such as a virus or vaccine.
▸**,serocon'version** *n*

serology (sɪ'rɒlədʒɪ) *n* the branch of science concerned with serums.
▸**serologic** (,sɪərə'lɒdʒɪk) *or* **,sero'logical** *adj*

seropositive (,sɪərəʊ'pɒzɪtɪv) *adj* (of a person whose blood has been tested for a specific disease, such as AIDS) showing a serological reaction indicating the presence of the disease.

serotine ('serə,taɪn) *adj* **1** *Biol.* produced, flowering, or developing late in the season. ◆ *n* **2** a reddish-coloured European insectivorous bat. [C16: from L *sērōtinus* late, from *sērus* late; applied to the bat because it flies late in the evening]

serotonin (,serə'təʊnɪn) *n* a compound that occurs in the brain, intestines, and blood platelets and induces vasoconstriction.

serous ('sɪərəs) *adj* of, producing, or containing serum. [C16: from L *serōsus*]
▸**serosity** (sɪ'rɒsɪtɪ) *n*

serous fluid *n* a thin watery fluid found in many body cavities.

serous membrane *n* any of the smooth moist delicate membranes, such as the pleura, that line the closed cavities of the body.

serow ('serəʊ) *n* either of two antelopes of mountainous regions of S and SE Asia, having a dark coat and conical backward-pointing horns. [C19: from native name *să-ro* Tibetan goat]

serpent ('sɜ:pənt) *n* **1** a literary word for **snake. 2** *Bible.* a manifestation of Satan as a guileful tempter (Genesis 3:1–5). **3** a sly or unscrupulous person. **4** an obsolete wind instrument resembling a snake in shape. [C14: via OF from L *serpēns* a creeping thing, from *serpere* to creep]

serpentine[1] ❶ ('sɜ:pən,taɪn) *adj* **1** of, relating to, or resembling a serpent. **2** twisting; winding. [C14: from LL *serpentīnus,* from *serpēns* SERPENT]

serpentine[2] ('sɜ:pən,taɪn) *n* any of several secondary minerals, consisting of hydrated magnesium silicate, that are green to brown in colour and greasy to the touch. [C15 *serpentyn,* from Med. L *serpentīnum* SERPENTINE[1]; referring to the snakelike patterns of these minerals]

serpigo (sɜ:'paɪgəʊ) *n Pathol.* any progressive skin eruption, such as ringworm or herpes. [C14: from Med. L, from L *serpere* to creep]

SERPS *or* **Serps** (sɜ:ps) *n* (in Britain) *acronym for* state earnings-related pension scheme.

serrate ❶ *adj* ('serɪt, -eɪt). **1** (of leaves) having a margin of forward pointing teeth. **2** having a notched or sawlike edge. ◆ *vb* (se'reɪt), **serrates, serrating, serrated. 3** (*tr*) to make serrate. [C17: from L *serrātus* saw-shaped, from *serra* a saw]
▸**ser'rated** *adj*

serration (se'reɪʃən) *n* **1** the state or condition of being serrated. **2** a row of toothlike projections on an edge. **3** a single notch.

serried ❶ ('serɪd) *adj* in close or compact formation: *serried ranks of troops.* [C17: from OF *serré* close-packed, from *serrer* to shut up]

serriform ('serɪ,fɔ:m) *adj Biol.* resembling a notched or sawlike edge. [*serri-,* from L *serra* saw]

serrulate ('serʊ,leɪt, -lɪt) *adj* (esp. of leaves) minutely serrate. [C18: from NL *serrulātus,* from L *serrula* dim. of *serra* a saw]
▸**,serru'lation** *n*

serum ('sɪərəm) *n, pl* **serums** *or* **sera** (-rə). **1** Also called: **blood serum.** blood plasma from which the clotting factors have been removed. **2** antitoxin obtained from the blood serum of immunized animals. **3** *Physiol., zool.* clear watery fluid, esp. that exuded by serous membranes. **4** a less common word for **whey.** [C17: from L: whey]

serum albumin *n* a form of albumin that is the most abundant protein constituent of blood plasma.

serum hepatitis *n* a former name for **hepatitis B.**

serum sickness *n* an allergic reaction, such as vomiting, skin rash, etc., that sometimes follows injection of a foreign serum.

serval ('sɜ:vᵊl) *n, pl* **servals** *or* **serval.** a slender feline mammal of the African bush, having an orange-brown coat with black spots. [C18: via F from LL *cervālis* staglike, from L *cervus* a stag]

servant ❶ ('sɜ:vᵊnt) *n* **1** a person employed to work for another, esp. one who performs household duties. **2** See **public servant.** [C13: via OF from *servant* serving, from *servir* to SERVE]

serve ❶ (sɜ:v) *vb* **serves, serving, served. 1** to be in the service of (a person). **2** to render or be of service to (a person, cause, etc.); help. **3** to attend to (customers) in a shop, etc. **4** (*tr*) to provide (guests, etc.) with food, drink, etc.: *she served her guests with cocktails.* **5** to distribute or provide (food, etc.) for guests, etc.: *do you serve coffee?* **6** (*tr;* sometimes foll. by *up*) to present (food, etc.) in a specified manner: *peaches served with cream.* **7** (*tr*) to provide with a regular supply of. **8** (*tr*) to work actively for: *to serve the government.* **9** (*tr*) to pay homage to: *to serve God.* **10** to suit: *this will serve my purpose.* **11** (*intr; may take an infinitive*) to function: *this wood will serve to build a fire.* **12** to go through (a period of service, enlistment, etc.). **13** (*intr*) (of weather, conditions, etc.) to be suitable. **14** (*tr*) Also: **service.** (of a male animal) to copulate with (a female animal). **15** *Tennis, squash, etc.* to put (the ball) into play. **16** (*tr*) to deliver (a legal document) to (a person). **17** (*tr*) *Naut.* to bind (a rope, etc.) with fine cord to protect it from chafing, etc. **18 serve (a person) right.** *Inf.* to pay (a person) back, esp. for wrongful or foolish treatment or behaviour. ◆ *n* **19** *Tennis, squash, etc.* short for **service. 20**

THESAURUS

series *n* **1 = sequence**, arrangement, chain, course, line, order, progression, run, set, string, succession, train

serious *adj* **1 = solemn**, grave, humourless, long-faced, pensive, sedate, sober, stern, thoughtful, unsmiling **2 = sincere**, deliberate, determined, earnest, genuine, honest, in earnest, resolute, resolved **3 = important**, crucial, deep, difficult, far-reaching, fateful, grim, momentous, no laughing matter, of moment *or* consequence, pressing, significant, urgent, weighty, worrying **5 = grave**, acute, alarming, critical, dangerous, severe
Antonyms *adj* ≠ **solemn:** carefree, flippant, frivolous, jolly, joyful, light-hearted, smiling ≠ **sincere:** capricious, flighty, flippant, frivolous, insincere, uncommitted, undecided ≠ **important:** insignificant, minor, slight, trivial, unimportant

seriously *adv* **1 = sincerely**, acutely, badly, critically, dangerously, distressingly, earnestly, grievously, in earnest, severely, solemnly, sorely, thoughtfully, with a straight face

seriousness *n* **1 = solemnity**, earnestness, gravitas, gravity, humourlessness, sedateness, sobriety, staidness, sternness **3 = importance**, danger, gravity, moment, significance, urgency, weight

sermon *n* **1 = homily**, address, exhortation **2 = lecture**, dressing-down (*inf.*), harangue, talking-to (*inf.*)

serpentine[1] *adj* **2 = twisting**, coiling, crooked, meandering, sinuous, snaking, snaky, tortuous, twisty, winding

serrated *adj* **3 = notched**, sawlike, sawtoothed, serrate, serriform (*Biology*), serrulate, toothed

serried *adj Literary* **= massed**, assembled, close, compact, dense, phalanxed

servant *n* **1 = attendant**, domestic, drudge, help, helper, lackey, liegeman, maid, menial, retainer, servitor (*arch.*), skivvy (*chiefly Brit.*), slave, vassal

serve *vb* **1-3 = work for**, aid, assist, attend to, be in the service of, be of assistance, be of use, help, minister to, oblige, succour, wait on **5 = provide**, arrange, deal, deliver, dish up, distribute, handle, present, purvey, set out, supply **10, 11 = be adequate**, answer, answer the purpose, be acceptable, be good enough, content, do, do duty as, do the work of, fill the bill (*inf.*), function as, satisfy, suffice, suit **12 = perform**, act, attend, complete, discharge, do, fulfil, go through, observe, officiate, pass

Austral. inf. hostile or critical remarks. [C13: from OF *servir*, from L *servīre*, from *servus* a slave]
▸'**servable** *or* '**serveable** *adj*

server ('sɜːvə) *n* **1** a person who serves. **2** *RC Church.* a person who assists the priest at Mass. **3** something that is used in serving food and drink. **4** the player who serves in racket games. **5** *Computing.* a computer or program that supplies data or resources to other machines on a network.

service ➊ ('sɜːvɪs) *n* **1** an act of help or assistance. **2** an organized system of labour and material aids used to supply the needs of the public: *telephone service.* **3** the supply, installation, or maintenance of goods carried out by a dealer. **4** the state of availability for use by the public (esp. in **into** *or* **out of service**). **5** a periodic overhaul made on a car, etc. **6** the act or manner of serving guests, customers, etc., in a shop, hotel, etc. **7** a department of public employment and its employees: *civil service.* **8** employment in or performance of work for another: *in the service of his firm.* **9a** one of the branches of the armed forces. **9b** (*as modifier*): *service life.* **10** the state or duties of a domestic servant (esp. in **in service**). **11** the act or manner of serving food. **12** a set of dishes, cups, etc., for use at table. **13** public worship carried out according to certain prescribed forms: *divine service.* **14** the prescribed form according to which a specific kind of religious ceremony is to be carried out: *the burial service.* **15** *Tennis, squash, etc.* **15a** the act, manner, or right of serving a ball. **15b** the game in which a particular player serves: *he has lost his service.* **16** the serving of a writ, summons, etc., upon a person. **17** (of male animals) the act of mating. **18** (*modifier*) of or for the use of servants or employees. **19** (*modifier*) serving the public rather than producing goods: *service industry.* ◆ *vb* **services, servicing, serviced.** (*tr*) **20** to provide service or services to. **21** to make fit for use. **22** to supply with assistance. **23** to overhaul (a car, machine, etc.). **24** (of a male animal) to mate with (a female). **25** *Brit.* to meet interest on (debt). ◆ See also **services.** [C12 *servise*, from OF, from L *servitium* condition of a slave, from *servus* a slave]

serviceable ➊ ('sɜːvɪsəb^{ə}l) *adj* **1** capable of or ready for service. **2** capable of giving good service.
▸,**servicea'bility** *n* ▸'**serviceably** *adv*

service area *n* a place on a motorway providing garage services, restaurants, toilet facilities, etc.

service car *n NZ.* a bus operating on a long-distance route.

service charge *n* a percentage of a bill, as at a hotel, added to the total to pay for service.

service contract *n* a contract between an employer and a senior employee, esp. a director, executive, etc.

service flat *n Brit.* a flat in which domestic services are provided by the management. Also called (esp. Austral.): **serviced flat.**

serviceman ('sɜːvɪsmən) *n, pl* **servicemen. 1** a person who serves in the armed services of a country. **2** a man employed to service and maintain equipment.
▸'**service,woman** *fem n*

service road *n Brit.* a narrow road running parallel to a main road and providing access to houses, shops, etc., situated along its length.

services ('sɜːvɪsɪz) *pl n* **1** work performed for remuneration. **2** (usually preceded by *the*) the armed forces. **3** (*sometimes sing*) *Econ.* commodities, such as banking, that are mainly intangible and usually consumed concurrently with their production. **4** a system of providing the public with gas, water, etc.

service station *n* a place that supplies fuel, oil, etc., for motor vehicles and often carries out repairs, servicing, etc.

service tree *n* **1** Also called: **sorb.** a Eurasian rosaceous tree, cultivated for its white flowers and brown edible apple-like fruits. **2 wild service tree.** a similar and related Eurasian tree. [*service* from OE *syrfe*, from Vulgar L *sorbea* (unattested), from L *sorbus* sorb]

serviette (,sɜːvɪ'ɛt) *n Chiefly Brit.* a small square of cloth or paper used while eating to protect the clothes, etc. [C15: from OF, from *servir* to SERVE; on the model of OUBLIETTE]

servile ➊ ('sɜːvaɪl) *adj* **1** obsequious or fawning in attitude or behaviour. **2** of or suitable for a slave. **3** existing in or relating to a state of slavery. **4** (when *postpositive*, foll. by *to*) submitting or obedient. [C14: from L *servīlis*, from *servus* slave]
▸**servility** (sɜː'vɪlɪtɪ) *n*

serving ➊ ('sɜːvɪŋ) *n* a portion or helping of food or drink.

servitor ('sɜːvɪtə) *n Arch.* a person who serves another. [C14: from OF, from LL, from L *servīre* to SERVE]

servitude ➊ ('sɜːvɪ,tjuːd) *n* **1** the state or condition of a slave. **2** the state or condition of being subjected to or dominated by a person or thing. **3** *Law.* a burden attaching to an estate for the benefit of an adjoining estate or of some definite person. See also **easement.** [C15: via OF from L *servitūdō*, from *servus* a slave]

servo ('sɜːvəʊ) *adj* **1** (*prenominal*) of or activated by a servomechanism: *servo brakes.* ◆ *n, pl* **servos. 2** *Inf.* short for **servomechanism.** [from *servomotor* from F, from L *servus* slave + F *moteur* motor]

servomechanism ('sɜːvəʊ,mɛkə,nɪzəm) *n* a mechanical or electromechanical system for control of the position or speed of an output transducer.

servomotor ('sɜːvəʊ,məʊtə) *n* any motor that supplies power to a servomechanism.

servqual ('sɜːv,kwɒl) *n Marketing.* the provision of high-quality products by an organization backed by a high level of service for consumers. [C20: from SERV(ICE) + QUAL(ITY)]

sesame ('sɛsəmɪ) *n* **1** a tropical herbaceous plant of the East Indies, cultivated, esp. in India, for its small oval seeds. **2** the seeds of this plant, used in flavouring bread and yielding an edible oil (**benne oil** or **gingili**). [C15: from L *sēsamum*, from Gk *sēsamon*, *sēsamē*, of Semitic origin]

sesamoid ('sɛsə,mɔɪd) *adj Anat.* **1** of or relating to various small bones formed in tendons, such as the patella. **2** of or relating to any of various small cartilages, esp. those of the nose. [C17: from L *sēsamoīdēs* like sesame (seed), from Gk]

sesqui- *prefix* **1** indicating one and a half: *sesquicentennial.* **2** (in a chemical compound) indicating a ratio of two to three. [from L, contraction of SEMI- + *as* AS[2] + *-que* and]

sesquicentennial (,sɛskwɪsɛn'tɛnɪəl) *adj* **1** of a period of 150 years. ◆ *n* **2** a period of 150 years. **3** a 150th anniversary or its celebration.
▸,**sesquicen'tennially** *adv*

sessile ('sɛsaɪl) *adj* **1** (of flowers or leaves) having no stalk. **2** (of animals such as the barnacle) permanently attached. [C18: from L *sēssilis* concerning sitting, from *sedēre* to sit]
▸**sessility** (sɛ'sɪlɪtɪ) *n*

sessile oak *n* another name for the **durmast.**

session ➊ ('sɛʃən) *n* **1** the meeting of a court, legislature, judicial body, etc., for the execution of its function or the transaction of business. **2** a single continuous meeting of such a body. **3** a series or period of such meetings. **4** *Education.* **4a** the time during which classes are held. **4b** a school or university year. **5** *Presbyterian Church.* the body presiding over a local congregation and consisting of the minister and elders. **6** a meeting of a group of musicians to record in a studio. **7** any period devoted to an activity. [C14: from L *sessiō* a sitting, from *sedēre* to sit]
▸'**sessional** *adj*

sesterce ('sɛstəs) *or* **sestertius** (sɛ'stɜːtɪəs) *n* a silver or, later, bronze coin of ancient Rome worth a quarter of a denarius. [C16: from L *sēstertius* a coin worth two and a half asses, from *sēmis* half + *tertius* a third]

sestet (sɛ'stɛt) *n* **1** *Prosody.* the last six lines of a sonnet. **2** another word for **sextet** (sense 1). [C19: from It., from *sesto* sixth, from L, from *sex* six]

sestina (sɛ'stiːnə) *n* an elaborate verse form of Italian origin in which the six final words of the lines in the first stanza are repeated in a different order in each of the remaining five stanzas. [C19: from It., from *sesto* sixth, from L *sextus*]

set[1] ➊ (sɛt) *vb* **sets, setting, set.** (*mainly tr*) **1** to put or place in position or into a specified state or condition: *to set someone free.* **2** (*also intr*; foll. by *to* or *on*) to put or be put (to); apply or be applied: *he set fire to the house.* **3** to put into order or readiness for use: *to set the table for dinner.* **4** (*also intr*) to put, form, or be formed into a jelled, firm, or rigid state: *the jelly set in three hours.* **5** (*also intr*) to put or be put into a position that will restore a normal state: *to set a broken bone.* **6** to adjust (a clock

THESAURUS

service *n* **1, 4** = **help**, advantage, assistance, avail, benefit, ministrations, supply, use, usefulness, utility **5** = **overhaul**, check, maintenance, servicing **8** = **work**, business, duty, employ, employment, labour, office **13** = **ceremony**, function, observance, rite, worship ◆ *vb* **23** = **overhaul**, check, fine tune, go over, maintain, recondition, repair, tune (up)

serviceable *adj* **1** = **useful**, advantageous, beneficial, convenient, dependable, durable, efficient, functional, hard-wearing, helpful, operative, practical, profitable, usable, utilitarian
Antonyms *adj* impractical, inefficient, unserviceable, unusable, useless, worn-out

servile *adj* **1** = **subservient**, abject, base, bootlicking (*inf.*), craven, cringing, fawning, grovelling, humble, low, mean, menial, obsequious, slavish, submissive, sycophantic, toadying, toadyish, unctuous

servility *n* **1** = **subservience**, abjection, baseness, bootlicking (*inf.*), fawning, grovelling, meanness, obsequiousness, self-abasement, slavishness, submissiveness, sycophancy, toadyism, unctuousness

serving *n* = **portion**, helping, plateful

servitude *n* **1** = **slavery**, bondage, bonds, chains, enslavement, obedience, serfdom, subjugation, thraldom, thrall, vassalage

session *n* **1** = **meeting**, assembly, conference, congress, discussion, get-together (*inf.*), hearing, period, seminar, sitting, term

set[1] *vb* **1** = **put**, aim, apply, deposit, direct, embed, fasten, fix, install, lay, locate, lodge, mount, park (*inf.*), place, plant, plonk, plump, position, rest, seat, situate, station, stick, turn **3** = **prepare**, arrange, lay, make ready, spread **4** = **harden**, cake, condense, congeal, crystallize, gelatinize, jell, solidify, stiffen, thicken **6** = **adjust**, coordinate, rectify, regulate, synchronize **7** = **arrange**, agree upon, allocate, appoint, conclude, decide (upon), designate, determine, establish, fix, fix up, name, ordain, regulate, resolve, schedule, settle, specify **8** = **assign**, allot, decree, impose, lay down, ordain, prescribe, specify **18** = **go down**, decline, dip, disappear, sink, subside, vanish ◆ *n* **30** = **position**, attitude, bearing, carriage, fit, hang, posture, turn **31** = **scenery**, *mise-en-scène*, scene, setting, stage set, stage setting ◆ *adj* **36** = **fixed**, agreed, appointed, arranged, customary, decided, definite, established, firm, prearranged, predetermined, prescribed, regular, scheduled, settled, usual **37** = **inflexible**, entrenched, firm, hard and fast, hardened, hidebound, immovable, rigid, strict, stubborn **39** = **conventional**, artificial, formal, hackneyed, rehearsed, routine, standard, stereotyped, stock, traditional, unspontaneous **40** *with* **on** *or* **upon** = **determined**, bent, intent, resolute

or other instrument) to a position. **7** to establish: *we have set the date for our wedding.* **8** to prescribe (an undertaking, course of study, etc.): *the examiners have set "Paradise Lost".* **9** to arrange in a particular fashion, esp. an attractive one: *she set her hair.* **10** Also: **set to music.** to provide music for (a poem or other text to be sung). **11** Also: **set up.** *Printing.* to arrange or produce (type, film, etc.) from (text or copy). **12** to arrange (a stage, television studio, etc.) with scenery and props. **13** to describe (a scene or the background to a literary work, etc.) in words: *his novel is set in Russia.* **14** to present as a model of good or bad behaviour (esp. in **set an example**). **15** (foll. by *on* or *by*) to value (something) at a specified price or estimation of worth: *he set a high price on his services.* **16** (*also intr*) to give or be given a particular direction: *his course was set to the East.* **17** (*also intr*) to rig (a sail) or (of a sail) to be rigged so as to catch the wind. **18** (*intr*) (of the sun, moon, etc.) to disappear beneath the horizon. **19** to leave (dough, etc.) in one place so that it may prove. **20** to sink (the head of a nail) below the surface surrounding it by using a nail set. **21** *Computing.* to give (a binary circuit) the value 1. **22** (of plants) to produce (fruits, seeds, etc.) after pollination or (of fruits or seeds) to develop after pollination. **23** to plant (seeds, seedlings, etc.). **24** to place (a hen) on (eggs) for the purpose of incubation. **25** (*intr*) (of a gun dog) to turn in the direction of game. **26** *Bridge.* to defeat (one's opponents) in their attempt to make a contract. **27** a dialect word for **sit.** ◆ *n* **28** the act of setting or the state of being set. **29** a condition of firmness or hardness. **30** bearing, carriage, or posture: *the set of a gun dog when pointing.* **31** the scenery and other props used in a dramatic production, film, etc. **32** Also called: **set width.** *Printing.* **32a** the width of the body of a piece of type. **32b** the width of the lines of type in a page or column. **33** *Psychol.* a temporary bias disposing an organism to react to a stimulus in one way rather than in others. **34** a seedling, cutting, or similar part that is ready for planting: *onion sets.* **35** a variant spelling of **sett.** ◆ *adj* **36** fixed or established by authority or agreement: *set hours of work.* **37** (*usually postpositive*) rigid or inflexible: *she is set in her ways.* **38** unmoving; fixed: *a set expression on his face.* **39** conventional, artificial, or stereotyped: *she made her apology in set phrases.* **40** (*postpositive;* foll. by *on* or *upon*) resolute in intention: *he is set upon marrying.* **41** (of a book, etc.) prescribed for students' preparation for an examination. ◆ See also **set about, set against,** etc. [OE *settan,* causative of *sittan* to SIT]

set[2] ⓘ (sɛt) *n* **1** a number of objects or people grouped or belonging together, often having certain features or characteristics in common: *a set of coins.* **2** a group of people who associate together, etc.: *he's part of the jet set.* **3** *Maths.* a collection of numbers, objects, etc., that are treated as an entity: {3, the moon} is the set the two members of which are the number 3 and the moon. **4** any apparatus that receives or transmits television or radio signals. **5** *Tennis, squash, etc.* one of the units of a match, in tennis, one in which one player or pair of players must win at least six games: *Hingis lost the first set.* **6a** the number of couples required for a formation dance. **6b** a series of figures that make up a formation dance. **7a** a band's or performer's concert repertoire on a given occasion: *the set included no new songs.* **7b** a continuous performance: *the Who played two sets.* **8 make a dead set at. 8a** to attack by arguing or ridiculing. **8b** (of a woman) to try to gain the affections of (a man). ◆ *vb* **sets, setting, set. 9** (*intr*) (in square and country dancing) to perform a sequence of steps while facing towards another dancer. **10** (*usually tr*) to divide into sets: *in this school we set our older pupils for English.* [C14 (in the obs. sense: a religious sect): from OF *sette,* from L *secta* SECT; later sense infl. by the verb SET[1]]

seta ('siːtə) *n, pl* **setae** (-tiː). (in invertebrates and plants) any bristle or bristle-like appendage. [C18: from L]
▸**setaceous** (sɪ'teɪʃəs) *adj*

set about ⓘ *vb* (*intr, prep*) **1** to start or begin. **2** to attack physically or verbally.

set against ⓘ *vb* (*tr, prep*) **1** to balance or compare. **2** to cause to be unfriendly to.

set aside ⓘ *vb* (*tr, adv*) **1** to reserve for a special purpose. **2** to discard or quash. ◆ *n* **set-aside. 3a** (in the European Union) a scheme in which a proportion of farmland is taken out of production in order to reduce surpluses or maintain or increase prices of a specific crop. **3b** (*as modifier*): *set-aside land.*

set back ⓘ *vb* (*tr, adv*) **1** to hinder; impede. **2** *Inf.* to cost (a person) a specified amount. ◆ *n* **setback. 3** anything that serves to hinder or impede. **4** a recession in the upper part of a high building. **5** a steplike shelf where a wall is reduced in thickness.

set down *vb* (*tr, adv*) **1** to record. **2** to judge or regard: *he set him down as an idiot.* **3** (foll. by *to*) to attribute: *his attitude was set down to his illness.* **4** to rebuke. **5** to snub. **6** *Brit.* to allow (passengers) to alight from a bus, etc.

set forth *vb* (*adv*) *Formal or arch.* **1** (*tr*) to state, express, or utter. **2** (*intr*) to start out on a journey.

SETI ('sɛtɪ) *n acronym for* Search for Extraterrestrial Intelligence; a scientific programme attempting, by radio transmissions, to make contact with beings from other planets.

setiferous (sɪ'tɪfərəs) *or* **setigerous** (sɪ'tɪdʒərəs) *adj Biol.* bearing bristles. [C19: see SETA, -FEROUS, -GEROUS]

set in *vb* (*intr, adv*) **1** to become established: *the winter has set in.* **2** (of wind) to blow or (of current) to move towards shore. ◆ *adj* **set-in. 3** (of a part) made separately and then added to a larger whole: *a set-in sleeve.*

setline ('sɛt,laɪn) *n* any of various types of fishing line that consist of a long suspended line having shorter hooked and baited lines attached.

set off ⓘ *vb* (*adv*) **1** (*intr*) to embark on a journey. **2** (*tr*) to cause (a person) to act or do something, such as laugh. **3** (*tr*) to cause to explode. **4** (*tr*) to act as a foil or contrast to: *that brooch sets your dress off well.* **5** (*tr*) *Accounting.* to cancel a credit on (one account) against a debit on another. ◆ *n* **setoff. 6** anything that serves as a counterbalance. **7** anything that serves to contrast with or enhance something else; foil. **8** a cross claim brought by a debtor that partly offsets the creditor's claim.

set-off *n Printing.* a fault in which ink is transferred from a heavily inked or undried printed sheet to the sheet next to it in a pile.

set on ⓘ *vb* **1** (*prep*) Also: **set upon.** to attack or cause to attack: *they set the dogs on him.* **2** (*tr, adv*) to instigate or incite; urge.

setose ('siːtəʊs) *adj Biol.* covered with setae; bristly. [C17: from L *saetōsus,* from *saeta* a bristle]

set out ⓘ *vb* (*adv, mainly tr*) **1** to present, arrange, or display. **2** to give a full account of: *he set out the matter in full.* **3** to plan or lay out (a garden, etc.). **4** (*intr*) to begin or embark on an undertaking, esp. a journey.

set piece *n* **1** a work of literature, music, etc., often having a conventional or prescribed theme, intended to create an impressive effect. **2** a display of fireworks. **3** *Sport.* a rehearsed team manoeuvre usually attempted at a restart of play.

setscrew ('sɛt,skruː) *n* a screw that fits into the boss or hub of a wheel, coupling, cam, etc., and prevents motion of the part relative to the shaft on which it is mounted.

set square *n* a thin flat piece of plastic, metal, etc., in the shape of a right-angled triangle, used in technical drawing.

sett *or* **set** (sɛt) *n* **1** a small rectangular paving block made of stone. **2** the burrow of a badger. **3a** a square in a pattern of tartan. **3b** the pattern itself. [C19: var. of SET[1] (n)]

settee (sɛ'tiː) *n* a seat, for two or more people, with a back and usually with arms. [C18: changed from SETTLE[2]]

setter ('sɛtə) *n* any of various breeds of large long-haired gun dog trained to point out game by standing rigid.

set theory *n Maths.* the branch of mathematics concerned with the properties and interrelationships of sets.

setting ⓘ ('sɛtɪŋ) *n* **1** the surroundings in which something is set. **2** the scenery, properties, or background used to create the location for a stage play, film, etc. **3** *Music.* a composition consisting of a certain text and music arranged for it. **4** the metal mounting and surround of a gem. **5** the tableware, cutlery, etc., for a single place at table. **6** any of a set of points on a scale or dial that can be selected to control the speed, temperature, etc., at which a machine operates.

settle[1] ⓘ ('sɛtᵊl) *vb* **settles, settling, settled. 1** (*tr*) to put in order: *he settled his affairs before he died.* **2** to arrange or be arranged in a fixed or comfortable position: *he settled himself by the fire.* **3** (*intr*) to come to rest or a halt: *a bird settled on the hedge.* **4** to take up or cause to take up resi-

THESAURUS

Antonyms *adj* ≠ **inflexible:** flexible, free, open, open-minded, undecided

set[2] *n* **1** = **series**, assemblage, assortment, batch, collection, compendium, coordinated group, kit, outfit **2** = **group**, band, circle, class, clique, company, coterie, crew (*inf.*), crowd, faction, gang, outfit, posse (*inf.*), schism, sect

set about *vb* **1** = **begin**, address oneself to, attack, get cracking (*inf.*), get down to, get to work, make a start on, put one's shoulder to the wheel (*inf.*), roll up one's sleeves, sail into (*inf.*), set to, start, tackle, take the first step, wade into **2** = **assault**, assail, attack, belabour, lambast(e), mug (*inf.*), sail into (*inf.*)

set against *vb* **1** = **balance**, compare, contrast, juxtapose, weigh **2** = **alienate**, disunite, divide, drive a wedge between, estrange, make bad blood, make mischief, oppose, set at cross purposes, set at odds, sow dissension

set aside *vb* **1** = **reserve**, earmark, keep, keep back, put on one side, save, select, separate, set apart, single out **2** = **reject**, abrogate, annul, cancel, discard, dismiss, nullify, overrule, overturn, quash, render null and void, repudiate, reverse

set back *vb* **1** = **hold up**, delay, hinder, impede, retard, slow ◆ *n* **setback 3** = **hold-up**, bit of trouble, blow, bummer, check, defeat, disappointment, hitch, misfortune, rebuff, reverse, upset, whammy (*inf., chiefly US*)

set off *vb* **1** = **leave**, depart, embark, sally forth, set out, start out **3** = **detonate**, explode, ignite, kick-start, light, set in motion, touch off, trigger (off) **4** = **enhance**, bring out the highlights in, show off, throw into relief

set on *vb* **1** = **attack**, ambush, assail, assault, beat up, fall upon, fly at, go for, lay into (*inf.*), let fly at, mug (*inf.*), pitch into (*inf.*), pounce on, put the boot in (*sl.*), sail into (*inf.*), set about, sic, turn on, work over (*sl.*)

set out *vb* **1** = **arrange**, array, display, dispose, exhibit, expose to view, lay out, present, set forth **2** = **explain**, describe, detail, elaborate, elucidate **4** = **embark**, begin, get under way, hit the road (*sl.*), sally forth, set off, start out, take to the road

setting *n* **1, 2** = **surroundings**, backdrop, background, context, frame, locale, location, *mise en scène,* perspective, scene, scenery, set, site, surround

settle[1] *vb* **1** = **put in order**, adjust, dispose, order, regulate, set to rights, straighten out, work out **2** = **make oneself comfortable**, bed down **3** = **land**, alight, come to rest, descend, light **4** = **move to**, dwell, inhabit, live, make one's home, put down roots, reside, set up home, take up residence **6** = **colonize**, found, people, pioneer, plant, populate **7** = **calm**, allay, compose, lull, pacify, quell, quiet, quieten, reassure, relax, relieve, sedate, soothe, tranquillize **9** = **subside**, decline, fall, sink **10** = **pay**, acquit oneself of,

dence: *the family settled in the country.* **5** to establish or become established in a way of life, job, etc. **6** (*tr*) to migrate to and form a community; colonize. **7** to make or become quiet, calm, or stable. **8** to cause (sediment) to sink to the bottom, as in a liquid, or (of sediment) to sink thus. **9** to subside or cause to subside: *the dust settled.* **10** (sometimes foll. by *up*) to pay off or account for (a bill, debt, etc.). **11** (*tr*) to decide or dispose of: *to settle an argument.* **12** (*intr;* often foll. by *on* or *upon*) to agree or fix: *to settle upon a plan.* **13** (*tr;* usually foll. by *on* or *upon*) to secure (title, property, etc.) to a person: *he settled his property on his wife.* **14** to determine (a legal dispute, etc.) by agreement of the parties without resort to court action (esp. in **settle out of court**). [OE *setlan*]
▸ **'settleable** *adj*

settle[2] ('sɛtᵊl) *n* a seat, for two or more people, usually made of wood with a high back and arms, and sometimes having a storage space in the boxlike seat. [OE *setl*]

settle down *vb* (*adv, mainly intr*) **1** (*also tr*) to make or become quiet and orderly. **2** (often foll. by *to*) to apply oneself diligently: *please settle down to work.* **3** to adopt an orderly and routine way of life, esp. after marriage.

settle for *vb* (*intr, prep*) to accept or agree to in spite of dispute or dissatisfaction.

settlement ➊ ('sɛtᵊlmənt) *n* **1** the act or state of settling or being settled. **2** the establishment of a new region; colonization. **3** a place newly settled; colony. **4** a community formed by members of a group, esp. of a religious sect. **5** a public building used to provide educational and general welfare facilities for persons living in deprived areas. **6** a subsidence of all or part of a structure. **7a** the payment of an outstanding account, invoice, charge, etc. **7b** (*as modifier*): *settlement day.* **8** an agreement reached in matters of finance, business, etc. **9** *Law.* **9a** a conveyance, usually to trustees, of property to be enjoyed by several persons in succession. **9b** the deed conveying such property.

settler ➊ ('sɛtlə) *n* a person who settles in a new country or a colony.

settlings ('sɛtlɪŋz) *pl n* any matter that has settled at the bottom of a liquid.

set to *vb* (*intr, adv*) **1** to begin working. **2** to start fighting. ◆ *n* **set-to. 3** *Inf.* a brief disagreement or fight.

set-top box *n* a device which converts the signals from a digital television broadcast into a form which can be viewed on a standard analogue television set.

set up ➊ *vb* (*adv, mainly tr*) **1** (*also intr*) to put into a position of power, etc. **2** (*also intr*) to begin or enable (someone) to begin (a new venture), as by acquiring or providing means, etc. **3** to build or construct: *to set up a shed.* **4** to raise or produce: *to set up a wail.* **5** to advance or propose: *to set up a theory.* **6** to restore the health of: *the sea air will set you up again.* **7** to establish (a record). **8** *Inf.* to cause (a person) to be blamed, accused, etc. ◆ *n* **setup. 9** *Inf.* the way in which anything is organized or arranged. **10** *Sl.* an event the result of which is prearranged: *it's a setup.* **11** a prepared arrangement of materials, machines, etc., for a job or undertaking. ◆ *adj* **set-up. 12** physically well-built.

seven ('sɛvᵊn) *n* **1** the cardinal number that is the sum of six and one and is a prime number. **2** a numeral, 7, VII, etc., representing this number. **3** the amount or quantity that is one greater than six. **4** anything representing, represented by, or consisting of seven units, such as a playing card with seven symbols on it. **5** Also called: **seven o'clock.** seven hours after noon or midnight. ◆ *determiner* **6a** amounting to seven: *seven swans a-swimming.* **6b** (*as pron*): *you've eaten seven already.* ◆ See also **sevens.** [OE *seofon*]

seven deadly sins *pl n* a fuller name for the **deadly sins.**

sevenfold ('sɛvᵊn,fəʊld) *adj* **1** equal to or having seven times as many or as much. **2** composed of seven parts. ◆ *adv* **3** by or up to seven times as many or as much.

sevens ('sɛvᵊnz) *n* (*functioning as sing*) a rugby union match or competition played with seven players on each side.

seven seas *pl n* the oceans of the world considered as the N and S Pacific, the N and S Atlantic, and the Arctic, Antarctic, and Indian Oceans.

seven-segment display *n* an arrangement of seven bars forming a square figure of eight, used in electronic displays of alphanumeric characters: any letter or figure can be represented by illuminating selected bars.

seventeen ('sɛvᵊn'ti:n) *n* **1** the cardinal number that is the sum of ten and seven and is a prime number. **2** a numeral, 17, XVII, etc., representing this number. **3** the amount or quantity that is seven more than ten. **4** something represented by, representing, or consisting of 17 units. ◆ *determiner* **5a** amounting to seventeen: *seventeen attempts.* **5b** (*as pron*): *seventeen were sold.* [OE *seofontīene*]
▸ **'seven'teenth** *adj, n*

seventh ('sɛvᵊnθ) *adj* **1** (*usually prenominal*) **1a** coming after the sixth and before the eighth in numbering, position, etc.; being the ordinal number of *seven:* often written 7th. **1b** (*as n*): *she left on the seventh.* ◆ *n* **2a** one of seven equal parts of an object, quantity, measurement, etc. **2b** (*as modifier*): *a seventh part.* **3** the fraction equal to one divided by seven (1/7). **4** *Music.* **4a** the interval between one note and another seven notes away from it in a diatonic scale. **4b** one of two notes constituting such an interval in relation to the other. ◆ *adv* **5** Also: **seventhly.** after the sixth person, event, etc.

Seventh-Day Adventist *n* a member of that branch of the Adventists which constituted itself as a separate body after the expected Second Coming of Christ failed to be realized in 1844. They believe that Christ's coming is imminent and observe Saturday instead of Sunday as their Sabbath.

seventh heaven *n* **1** the final state of eternal bliss. **2** a state of supreme happiness.

seventy ('sɛvᵊntɪ) *n, pl* **seventies. 1** the cardinal number that is the product of ten and seven. **2** a numeral, 70, LXX, etc., representing this number. **3** (*pl*) the numbers 70–79, esp. the 70th to the 79th year of a person's life or of a particular century. **4** the amount or quantity that is seven times as big as ten. **5** something represented by, representing, or consisting of 70 units. ◆ *determiner* **6a** amounting to seventy: *the seventy varieties of fabric.* **6b** (*as pron*): *to invite seventy to the wedding.* [OE *seofontig*]
▸ **'seventieth** *adj, n*

Seven Wonders of the World *pl n* the seven structures considered by ancient and medieval scholars to be the most wondrous of the ancient world. The list varies, but generally consists of the Pyramids of Egypt, the Hanging Gardens of Babylon, Phidias' statue of Zeus at Olympia, the temple of Artemis at Ephesus, the mausoleum of Halicarnassus, the Colossus of Rhodes, and the Pharos (or lighthouse) of Alexandria.

Seven Years' War *n* the war (1756–63) of Britain and Prussia, who emerged in the ascendant, against France and Austria, resulting from commercial and colonial rivalry between Britain and France and from the conflict in Germany between Prussia and Austria.

sever ➊ ('sɛvə) *vb* **1** to put or be put apart. **2** to divide or be divided into parts. **3** (*tr*) to break off or dissolve (a tie, relationship, etc.). [C14 *severen,* from OF, from L *sēparāre* to SEPARATE]
▸ **'severable** *adj*

several ➊ ('sɛvrəl) *determiner* **1a** more than a few: *several people objected.* **1b** (*as pronoun; functioning as pl*): *several of them know.* ◆ *adj* **2** (*prenominal*) various; separate: *the members with their several occupations.* **3** (*prenominal*) distinct; different: *three several times.* **4** *Law.* capable of being dealt with separately. [C15: via Anglo-F from Med. L *sēparālis,* from L *sēpār,* from *sēparāre* to SEPARATE]

severally ('sɛvrəlɪ) *adv* **1** separately or distinctly. **2** each in turn.

severalty ('sɛvrəltɪ) *n, pl* **severalties. 1** the state of being several or separate. **2** (usually preceded by *in*) *Property law.* the tenure of property, esp. land, in a person's own right.

severance ('sɛvərəns) *n* **1** the act of severing or state of being severed. **2** a separation. **3** *Law.* the division into separate parts of a joint estate, contract, etc.

severance pay *n* compensation paid by a firm to employees for loss of employment.

severe ➊ (sɪ'vɪə) *adj* **1** rigorous or harsh in the treatment of others: *a severe parent.* **2** serious in appearance or manner. **3** critical or dangerous: *a severe illness.* **4** causing discomfort by its harshness: *severe weather.* **5**

THESAURUS

clear, discharge, liquidate, quit, square (up) **11** = **resolve**, clear up, complete, conclude, decide, dispose of, put an end to, reconcile **12** *often with* **on** *or* **upon** = **decide**, agree, appoint, arrange, choose, come to an agreement, confirm, determine, establish, fix
Antonyms *vb* ≠ **calm:** agitate, bother, discompose, disquieten, disturb, rattle, trouble, unsettle, upset

settlement *n* **1** = **agreement**, adjustment, arrangement, completion, conclusion, confirmation, disposition, establishment, resolution, termination, working out **2** = **agreement**, colonization, peopling **3** = **colony**, community, encampment, hamlet, outpost **7** = **payment**, clearance, clearing, defrayal, discharge, liquidation, satisfaction

settler *n* = **colonist**, colonizer, frontiersman, immigrant, pioneer, planter

set up *vb* **2** = **establish**, arrange, begin, compose, found, initiate, install, institute, make provision for, organize, prearrange, prepare **3** = **build**, assemble, construct, elevate, erect, put together, put up, raise ◆ *n* **setup 9** = **arrangement**, circumstances, conditions, organization, regime, structure, system

sever *vb* **1, 2** = **cut**, bisect, cleave, cut in two, detach, disconnect, disjoin, disunite, divide, part, rend, separate, split, sunder **3** = **discontinue**, abandon, break off, dissociate, dissolve, put an end to, terminate
Antonyms *vb* ≠ **cut:** attach, connect, fix together, join, link, unite ≠ **discontinue:** continue, maintain, uphold

several *adj* **2** = **various**, assorted, different, disparate, divers (*arch.*), diverse, indefinite, manifold, many, sundry **3** = **different**, distinct, individual, particular, respective, single

severe *adj* **1** = **strict**, austere, cruel, Draconian, drastic, hard, harsh, inexorable, iron-handed, oppressive, pitiless, relentless, rigid, unbending, unrelenting **2** = **grim**, cold, disapproving, dour, flinty, forbidding, grave, serious, sober, stern, strait-laced, tight-lipped, unsmiling **3** = **critical**, acute, dangerous, distressing **4** = **intense**, bitter, extreme, fierce, grinding, inclement, violent **5** = **plain**, ascetic, austere, chaste, classic, functional, restrained, simple, Spartan, unadorned, unembellished, unfussy **6** = **tough**, arduous, demanding, difficult, exacting, fierce, hard, punishing, rigorous, stringent, taxing, unrelenting
Antonyms *adj* ≠ **strict:** easy, lax, lenient, relaxed, tractable ≠ **grim:** affable, genial ≠ **intense:** gentle, mild, minor, moderate, temperate ≠ **plain:** embellished, fancy, ornamental, ornate ≠ **tough:** easy, manageable

strictly restrained in appearance: *a severe way of dressing.* **6** hard to perform or accomplish: *a severe test.* [C16: from L *sevērus*]
▸**se'verely** *adv* ▸**severity** (sɪ'verɪtɪ) *n*

Seville orange *n* **1** an orange tree of tropical and semitropical regions: grown for its bitter fruit, which is used to make marmalade. **2** the fruit of this tree. [C16: after *Seville* in Spain]

Sèvres (*French* sɛvrə) *n* porcelain ware manufactured at Sèvres, near Paris, from 1756, characterized by the use of clear colours and elaborate decorative detail.

sew (səʊ) *vb* **sews, sewing, sewed; sewn** *or* **sewed. 1** to join or decorate (pieces of fabric, etc.) by means of a thread repeatedly passed through with a needle. **2** (*tr;* often foll. by *on* or *up*) to attach, fasten, or close by sewing. **3** (*tr*) to make (a garment, etc.) by sewing. ◆ See also **sew up.** [OE *sēowan*]

sewage ('suːɪdʒ) *n* waste matter from domestic or industrial establishments that is carried away in sewers or drains. [C19: back formation from SEWER[1]]

sewage farm *n* a place where sewage is treated, esp. for use as manure.

sewer[1] (sʊə) *n* **1** a drain or pipe, esp. one that is underground, used to carry away surface water or sewage. ◆ *vb* **2** (*tr*) to provide with sewers. [C15: from OF, from *essever* to drain, from Vulgar L *exaquāre* (unattested), from L EX-[1] + *aqua* water]

sewer[2] ('səʊə) *n* a person or thing that sews.

sewerage ('sʊərɪdʒ) *n* **1** an arrangement of sewers. **2** the removal of surface water or sewage by means of sewers. **3** another word for **sewage.**

sewing ('səʊɪŋ) *n* **a** a piece of cloth, etc., that is sewn or to be sewn. **b** (*as modifier*): *sewing basket.*

sewing machine *n* any machine designed to sew material. It is now usually driven by electric motor but is sometimes operated by a foot treadle or by hand.

sewn (səʊn) *vb* a past participle of **sew.**

sew up *vb* (*tr, adv*) **1** to fasten or mend completely by sewing. **2** *US.* to acquire sole use or control of. **3** *Inf.* to complete or negotiate successfully: *to sew up a deal.*

sex ❶ (sɛks) *n* **1** the sum of the characteristics that distinguish organisms on the basis of their reproductive function. **2** either of the two categories, male or female, into which organisms are placed on this basis. **3** short for **sexual intercourse. 4** feelings or behaviour resulting from the urge to gratify the sexual instinct. **5** sexual matters in general. ◆ *modifier.* **6** of or concerning sexual matters: *sex education.* **7** based on or arising from the difference between the sexes: *sex discrimination.* ◆ *vb* **8** (*tr*) to ascertain the sex of. [C14: from L *sexus*]

sex- *combining form.* six: *sexcentenary.* [from L]

sexagenarian (ˌsɛksədʒɪ'nɛərɪən) *n* **1** a person from 60 to 69 years old. ◆ *adj* **2** being from 60 to 69 years old. **3** of or relating to a sexagenarian. [C18: from L, from *sexāgēnī* sixty each, from *sexāgintā* sixty]

Sexagesima (ˌsɛksə'dʒɛsɪmə) *n* the second Sunday before Lent. [C16: from L: sixtieth, from *sexāgintā* sixty]

sexagesimal (ˌsɛksə'dʒɛsɪməl) *adj* **1** relating to or based on the number 60: *sexagesimal measurement of angles.* ◆ *n* **2** a fraction in which the denominator is some power of 60.

sex-and-shopping *adj* (*prenomial*) (of a novel) belonging to a genre of novel in which the central character, a woman, has a number of sexual encounters, and the author mentions the name of many upmarket products.

sex appeal ❶ *n* the quality or power of attracting the opposite sex.

sexcentenary (ˌsɛksɛn'tiːnərɪ) *adj* **1** of or relating to 600 or a period of 600 years. **2** of or celebrating a 600th anniversary. ◆ *n, pl* **sexcentenaries. 3** a 600th anniversary or its celebration. [C18: from L *sexcentēnī* six hundred each]

sex chromosome *n* either of the chromosomes determining the sex of animals.

sexed (sɛkst) *adj* **1** (*in combination*) having a specified degree of sexuality: *undersexed.* **2** of, relating to, or having sexual differentiation.

sex hormone *n* an animal hormone affecting development and growth of reproductive organs and related parts.

sexism ('sɛksɪzəm) *n* discrimination on the basis of sex, esp. the oppression of women by men.
▸**'sexist** *n, adj*

sexless ❶ ('sɛkslɪs) *adj* **1** having or showing no sexual differentiation. **2** having no sexual desires. **3** sexually unattractive.

sex linkage *n Genetics.* the condition in which a gene is located on a sex chromosome so that the character controlled by the gene is associated with either of the sexes.
▸**'sex-ˌlinked** *adj*

sex object *n* someone, esp. a woman, regarded only from the point of view of someone else's sexual desires.

sexology (sɛk'sɒlədʒɪ) *n* the study of sexual behaviour in human beings.
▸**sex'ologist** *n* ▸**sexological** (ˌsɛksə'lɒdʒɪk°l) *adj*

sexpartite (sɛks'pɑːtaɪt) *adj* **1** (esp. of vaults, arches, etc.) divided into or composed of six parts. **2** involving six participants.

sex shop *n* a shop selling aids to sexual activity, pornographic material, etc.

sext (sɛkst) *n Chiefly RC Church.* the fourth of the seven canonical hours of the divine office or the prayers prescribed for it. [C15: from Church L *sexta hōra* the sixth hour]

sextan ('sɛkstən) *adj* (of a fever) marked by paroxysms that recur every fifth day. [C17: from Med. L *sextana (febris)* (fever) of the sixth (day)]

sextant ('sɛkstənt) *n* **1** an instrument used in navigation and consisting of a telescope through which a sighting of a heavenly body is taken, with protractors for determining its angular distance above the horizon. **2** a sixth part of a circle. [C17: from L *sextāns* one sixth of a unit]

sextet *or* **sextette** (sɛks'tɛt) *n* **1** *Music.* a group of six singers or instrumentalists or a piece of music composed for such a group. **2** a group of six people or things. [C19: var. of SESTET]

sextillion (sɛks'tɪljən) *n, pl* **sextillions** *or* **sextillion. 1** (in Britain, France, and Germany) the number represented as one followed by 36 zeros (10^{36}). **2** (in the US and Canada) the number represented as one followed by 21 zeros (10^{21}). [C17: from F, from SEX- + *-illion,* on the model of SEPTILLION]

sexton ('sɛkstən) *n* a person employed to act as caretaker of a church and often also as a bell-ringer, grave-digger, etc. [C14: from OF, from Med. L *sacristānus* SACRISTAN]

sextuple ('sɛkstjʊp°l) *n* **1** a quantity or number six times as great as another. ◆ *adj* **2** six times as much or as many. **3** consisting of six parts or members. [C17: L *sextus* sixth + *-uple,* as in QUADRUPLE]

sextuplet ('sɛkstjʊplɪt) *n* **1** one of six offspring at one birth. **2** a group of six. **3** *Music.* a group of six notes played in a time value of four.

sexual ❶ ('sɛksjʊəl) *adj* **1** of or characterized by sex. **2** (of reproduction) characterized by the union of male and female gametes. Cf. **asexual** (sense 2). [C17: from LL *sexuālis*]
▸**sexuality** (ˌsɛksjʊ'ælɪtɪ) *n* ▸**'sexually** *adv*

sexual harassment *n* the persistent unwelcome directing of sexual remarks and looks, and unnecessary physical contact, at a person, usually a woman, esp. in the work place.

sexual intercourse ❶ *n* the sexual act in which the male's erect penis is inserted into the female's vagina; copulation; coitus.

sexually transmitted disease *n* any of various diseases, such as syphilis or gonorrhoea, transmitted by sexual intercourse. Also called: **venereal disease.**

sexual selection *n* an evolutionary process in animals, in which selection by females of males with certain characters results in the preservation of these characters in the species.

sexy ❶ ('sɛksɪ) *adj* **sexier, sexiest.** *Inf.* **1** provoking or intended to provoke sexual interest: *a sexy dress.* **2** feeling sexual interest; aroused. **3** interesting, exciting, or trendy: *a sexy project; a sexy new car.*
▸**'sexily** *adv* ▸**'sexiness** *n*

sf *or* **sfz** *Music. abbrev. for* sforzando.

SF *or* **sf** *abbrev. for* science fiction.

SFA *abbrev. for:* **1** Scottish Football Association. **2** sweet Fanny Adams. See **fanny adams.**

SFO *abbrev. for* Serious Fraud Office: the department of the British government which investigates cases of serious financial fraud.

sforzando (sfɔː'tsɑːndəʊ) *or* **sforzato** (sfɔː'tsɑːtəʊ) *Music.* ◆ *adj, adv* **1** to be played with strong initial attack. Abbrevs.: **sf, sfz.** ◆ *n* **2** a symbol, mark, etc., indicating this. [C19: from It., from *sforzare* to force, from Vulgar L *fortiāre* (unattested) to FORCE]

SG *abbrev. for* solicitor general.

sgd *abbrev. for* signed.

S. Glam *abbrev. for* South Glamorgan.

SGML *abbrev. for* standard generalized mark-up language: an international standard used in publishing for defining the structure and formatting of documents.

sgraffito (sgræ'fiːtəʊ) *n, pl* **sgraffiti** (-tɪ). **1** a technique in mural or ceramic decoration in which the top layer of glaze, plaster, etc., is incised with a design to reveal parts of the ground. **2** such a decoration. [C18: from It., from *sgraffire* to scratch]

Sgt *abbrev. for* Sergeant.

sh (*spelling pron* ʃʃʃ) *interj* an exclamation to request silence or quiet.

THESAURUS

severely *adv* **1 = strictly,** harshly, like a ton of bricks (*inf.*), rigorously, sharply, sternly, with an iron hand, with a rod of iron **3 = seriously,** acutely, badly, critically, dangerously, extremely, gravely, hard, sorely

severity *n* **1, 2 = strictness,** austerity, hardness, harshness, rigour, seriousness, severeness, sternness, stringency, toughness

sex *n* **2 = gender 3 = (sexual) intercourse,** coition, coitus, copulation, fornication, going to bed (with someone), intimacy, lovemaking, nookie (*sl.*), rumpy-pumpy (*sl.*), sexual relations, the other (*inf.*) **4, 5 = facts of life,** desire, libido, reproduction, sexuality, the birds and the bees (*inf.*)

sex appeal *n* **= desirability,** allure, attractiveness, glamour, it (*inf.*), magnetism, oomph (*inf.*), seductiveness, sensuality, sexiness (*inf.*), voluptuousness

sexless *adj* **1 = asexual,** androgynous, epicene, hermaphrodite, neuter, nonsexual, parthenogenetic

sexual *adj* **1 = carnal,** coital, erotic, intimate, of the flesh, sensual, sexy **2 = reproductive,** genital, procreative, sex, venereal

sexual intercourse *n* **= copulation,** bonking (*inf.*), carnal knowledge, coition, coitus, commerce (*arch.*), congress, consummation, coupling, intimacy, mating, nookie (*sl.*), penetration, rumpy-pumpy (*sl.*), sex (*inf.*), the other (*inf.*), union

sexuality *n* **1 = desire,** bodily appetites, carnality, eroticism, lust, sensuality, sexiness (*inf.*), virility, voluptuousness

sexy *adj* **1 = erotic,** arousing, beddable, bedroom, come-hither (*inf.*), cuddly, flirtatious, inviting, kissable, naughty, provocative, provoking, seductive, sensual, sensuous, slinky, suggestive, titillating, voluptuous

DICTIONARY

sh. *abbrev. for:* **1** *Stock Exchange.* share. **2** sheep. **3** *Bookbinding.* sheet.

shabby Ⓣ (ˈʃæbɪ) *adj* **shabbier, shabbiest. 1** threadbare or dilapidated in appearance. **2** wearing worn and dirty clothes. **3** mean or unworthy: *shabby treatment.* **4** dirty or squalid. [C17: from OE *sceabb* scab]
▸**ˈshabbily** *adv* ▸**ˈshabbiness** *n*

shack Ⓣ (ʃæk) *n* **1** a roughly built hut. ◆ *vb* **2** See **shack up.** [C19: ?from dialect *shackly* ramshackle, from dialect *shack* to shake]

shackle Ⓣ (ˈʃækᵊl) *n* **1** (*often pl*) a metal ring or fastening, usually part of a pair used to secure a person's wrists or ankles. **2** (*often pl*) anything that confines or restricts freedom. **3** a U-shaped bracket, the open end of which is closed by a bolt (**shackle pin**), used for securing ropes, chains, etc. ◆ *vb* **shackles, shackling, shackled.** (*tr*) **4** to confine with or as if with shackles. **5** to fasten or connect with a shackle. [OE *sceacel*]
▸**ˈshackler** *n*

shack up *vb* (*intr, adv;* usually foll. by *with*) *Sl.* to live, esp. with a lover.

shad (ʃæd) *n, pl* **shad** *or* **shads.** any of various herring-like food fishes that migrate from the sea to fresh water to spawn. [OE *sceadd*]

shaddock (ˈʃædək) *n* another name for **pomelo** (sense 1). [C17: after Captain *Shaddock,* who brought its seed from the East Indies to Jamaica in 1696]

shade Ⓣ (ʃeɪd) *n* **1** relative darkness produced by the blocking out of light. **2** a place made relatively darker or cooler than other areas by the blocking of light, esp. sunlight. **3** a position of relative obscurity. **4** something used to provide a shield or protection from a direct source of light, such as a lampshade. **5** a darker area indicated in a painting, drawing, etc., by shading. **6** a colour that varies slightly from a standard colour: *a darker shade of green.* **7** a slight amount: *a shade of difference.* **8** *Literary.* a ghost. ◆ *vb* **shades, shading, shaded.** (*mainly tr*) **9** to screen or protect from heat, light, view, etc. **10** to make darker or dimmer. **11** to represent (a darker area) in (a painting, etc.), by means of hatching, etc. **12** (*also intr*) to change or cause to change slightly. **13** to lower (a price) slightly. [OE *sceadu*]
▸**ˈshadeless** *adj*

shades (ʃeɪdz) *pl n* **1** gathering darkness at nightfall. **2** *Sl.* sunglasses. **3** (*often cap.;* preceded by *the*) a literary term for **Hades. 4** (foll. by *of*) undertones: *shades of my father!*

shading (ˈʃeɪdɪŋ) *n* the graded areas of tone, lines, dots, etc., indicating light and dark in a painting or drawing.

shadoof (ʃəˈduːf) *n* a mechanism for raising water, consisting of a pivoted pole with a bucket at one end and a counterweight at the other, esp. as used in Egypt. [C19: from Egyptian Ar.]

shadow Ⓣ (ˈʃædəʊ) *n* **1** a dark image or shape cast on a surface by the interception of light rays by an opaque body. **2** an area of relative darkness. **3** the dark portions of a picture. **4** a hint or faint semblance: *beyond a shadow of a doubt.* **5** a remnant or vestige: *a shadow of one's past self.* **6** a reflection. **7** a threatening influence: *a shadow over one's happiness.* **8** a spectre. **9** an inseparable companion. **10** a person who trails another in secret, such as a detective. **11** *Med.* a dark area on an X-ray film representing an opaque structure or part. **12** (in Jungian psychology) the archetype that represents man's animal ancestors. **13** *Arch.* shelter. **14** (*modifier*) *Brit.* designating a member or members of the main opposition party in Parliament who would hold ministerial office if their party were in power: *shadow cabinet.* ◆ *vb* (*tr*) **15** to cast a shadow over. **16** to make dark or gloomy. **17** to shade from light. **18** to follow or trail secretly. **19** (often foll. by *forth*) to represent vaguely. [OE *sceadwe,* oblique case of *sceadu* shade]
▸**ˈshadower** *n*

shadow-box *vb* (*intr*) *Boxing.* to practise blows and footwork against an imaginary opponent.
▸**ˈshadow-ˌboxing** *n*

shadowgraph (ˈʃædəʊˌgrɑːf) *n* **1** a silhouette made by casting a shadow on a lighted surface. **2** another name for **radiograph.**

shadow play *n* a theatrical entertainment using shadows thrown by puppets or actors onto a lighted screen.

shadow price *n Econ.* the calculated price of a good or service for which no market price exists.

shadowy Ⓣ (ˈʃædəʊɪ) *adj* **1** dark; shady. **2** resembling a shadow in faintness. **3** illusory or imaginary. **4** mysterious or secretive: *a shadowy underworld figure.*
▸**ˈshadowiness** *n*

shady Ⓣ (ˈʃeɪdɪ) *adj* **shadier, shadiest. 1** shaded. **2** affording or casting a shade. **3** quiet or concealed. **4** *Inf.* questionable as to honesty or legality.
▸**ˈshadily** *adv* ▸**ˈshadiness** *n*

SHAEF (ʃeɪf) (in WWII) *n acronym for* Supreme Headquarters Allied Expeditionary Forces.

shaft Ⓣ (ʃɑːft) *n* **1** the long narrow pole that forms the body of a spear, arrow, etc. **2** something directed at a person in the manner of a missile. **3** a ray or streak, esp. of light. **4** a rod or pole forming the handle of a hammer, golf club, etc. **5** a revolving rod that transmits motion or power. **6** one of the two wooden poles by which an animal is harnessed to a vehicle. **7** *Anat.* the middle part of a long bone. **8** the middle part of a column or pier, between the base and the capital. **9** *Archit.* a column that supports a vaulting rib, sometimes one of a set. **10** a vertical passageway through a building, as for a lift. **11** a vertical passageway into a mine. **12** *Ornithol.* the central rib of a feather. **13** an archaic or literary word for **arrow.** ◆ *vb* **14** *US & Canad. sl.* to trick or cheat. [OE *sceaft*]

shag[1] (ʃæg) *n* **1** a matted tangle, esp. of hair, etc. **2** a napped fabric, usually a rough wool. **3** shredded coarse tobacco. [OE *sceacga*]

shag[2] (ʃæg) *n* another name for **green cormorant** (*Phalacrocorax aristotelis*). [C16: special use of SHAG[1], with reference to its crest]

shag[3] (ʃæg) *Brit. sl.* ◆ *vb* **shags, shagging, shagged. 1** *Taboo.* to have sexual intercourse with (a person). **2** (*tr;* often foll. by *out; usually passive*) to exhaust. ◆ *n* **3** *Taboo.* an act of sexual intercourse. [C20: from ?]

shaggy Ⓣ (ˈʃægɪ) *adj* **shaggier, shaggiest. 1** having or covered with rough unkempt fur, hair, wool, etc.: *a shaggy dog.* **2** rough or unkempt.
▸**ˈshaggily** *adv* ▸**ˈshagginess** *n*

shaggy dog story *n Inf.* a long rambling joke ending in a deliberate anticlimax, such as a pointless punch line.

shagreen (ʃæˈgriːn) *n* **1** the rough skin of certain sharks and rays, used as an abrasive. **2** a rough grainy leather made from certain animal hides. [C17: from F *chagrin,* from Turkish *çagri* rump]

shah (ʃɑː) *n* a ruler of certain Middle Eastern countries, esp. (formerly) Iran. [C16: from Persian: king]
▸**ˈshahdom** *n*

shake Ⓣ (ʃeɪk) *vb* **shakes, shaking, shook, shaken. 1** to move or cause to move up and down or back and forth with short quick movements. **2** to sway or totter or cause to sway or totter. **3** to clasp or grasp (the hand) of (a person) in greeting, agreement, etc.: *he shook John's hand.* **4** **shake hands.** to clasp hands in greeting, agreement, etc. **5** **shake on it.** *Inf.* to shake hands in agreement, reconciliation, etc. **6** to bring or come to a specified condition by or as if by shaking: *he shook free and ran.* **7** (*tr*) to wave or brandish: *he shook his sword.* **8** (*tr;* often foll. by *up*) to rouse or agitate. **9** (*tr*) to shock, disturb, or upset: *he was shaken by the news.* **10** (*tr*) to undermine or weaken: *the crisis shook his faith.* **11** to mix (dice) by rattling in a cup or the hand before throwing. **12** *Austral. old-fashioned sl.* to steal. **13** (*tr*) *US & Canad. inf.* to get rid of. **14** *Music.* to perform a trill on (a note). **15** **shake in one's shoes.** to tremble with fear or apprehension. **16** **shake one's head.** to indicate disagreement or disapproval by moving the head from side to side. ◆ *n* **17** the act or

THESAURUS

shabby *adj* **1** = **tatty**, dilapidated, down at heel, faded, frayed, having seen better days, mean, neglected, poor, ragged, run-down, scruffy, seedy, tattered, the worse for wear, threadbare, worn, worn-out **3** = **mean**, cheap, contemptible, despicable, dirty, dishonourable, ignoble, low, low-down (*inf.*), rotten (*inf.*), scurvy, shameful, shoddy, ungentlemanly, unworthy
Antonyms *adj* ≠ **tatty:** handsome, in mint condition, neat, new, smart, well-dressed, well-kempt, well-kept, well-to-do ≠ **mean:** fair, generous, honourable, praiseworthy, worthy

shack *n* **1** = **hut**, cabin, dump (*inf.*), hovel, lean-to, shanty, shiel (*Scot.*), shieling (*Scot.*)

shackle *n* **1** *often plural* = **fetter**, bond, chain, handcuff, hobble, iron, leg-iron, manacle, rope, tether ◆ *vb* **4** = **fetter**, bind, chain, constrain, handcuff, hobble, manacle, pinion, put in irons, restrain, restrict, secure, tether, tie, trammel

shade *n* **1** = **dimness**, coolness, dusk, gloom, gloominess, obscurity, screen, semidarkness, shadiness, shadow, shadows **3** **put into the shade** = **outshine**, eclipse, make pale by comparison, outclass, overshadow **4** = **screen**, blind, canopy, cover, covering, curtain, shield, veil **6** = **hue**, colour, stain, tinge, tint, tone **7** = **dash**, amount, degree, difference, gradation, graduation, hint, nuance, semblance, suggestion, suspicion, trace **8** *Literary* = **ghost**, apparition, eidolon, manes, phantom, shadow, spectre, spirit ◆ *vb* **9** = **cover**, conceal, hide, mute, obscure, protect, screen, shield, veil **10** = **darken**, cast a shadow over, cloud, dim, shadow, shut out the light

shadow *n* **1, 2** = **dimness**, cover, darkness, dusk, gathering darkness, gloaming (*Scot. or poetic*), gloom, obscurity, protection, shade, shelter **4** = **trace**, hint, suggestion, suspicion **7** = **cloud**, blight, gloom, sadness **8** = **ghost**, eidolon, image, phantom, remnant, representation, spectre, vestige ◆ *vb* **15-17** = **shade**, cast a shadow over, darken, overhang, screen, shield **18** = **follow**, dog, spy on, stalk, tail (*inf.*), trail

shadowy *adj* **1** = **dark**, crepuscular, dim, dusky, funereal, gloomy, indistinct, murky, obscure, shaded, shady, tenebrious, tenebrous **3, 4** = **vague**, dim, dreamlike, faint, ghostly, illusory, imaginary, impalpable, intangible, nebulous, obscure, phantom, spectral, undefined, unreal, unsubstantial, wraithlike

shady *adj* **1** = **shaded**, bosky (*literary*), bowery, cool, dim, leafy, shadowy, umbrageous **4** *Informal* = **crooked**, disreputable, dodgy (*Brit., Austral., & NZ inf.*), dubious, fishy (*inf.*), questionable, shifty, slippery, suspect, suspicious, unethical, unscrupulous, untrustworthy
Antonyms *adj* ≠ **shaded:** bright, exposed, open, out in the open, sunlit, sunny, unshaded ≠ **crooked:** above-board, ethical, honest, honourable, reputable, respectable, straight, trustworthy, upright

shaft *n* **1** = **handle**, pole, rod, shank, stem, upright **2** *As in* **shaft of wit** *or* **humour** = **gibe**, barb, cut, dart, sting, thrust **3** = **ray**, beam, gleam, streak

shaggy *adj* **1, 2** = **unkempt**, hairy, hirsute, long-haired, rough, tousled, unshorn
Antonyms *adj* close-cropped, crew-cut, cropped, flat-woven, neatly-trimmed, shorn, short-haired, short-piled, smooth

shake *vb* **1, 2** = **vibrate**, bump, fluctuate, jar, joggle, jolt, jounce, oscillate, quake, quiver, rock, shiver, shudder, sway, totter, tremble, waver, wobble **7** = **wave**, brandish, flourish **8** *often with* **up** = **agitate**, churn, convulse, rouse, stir **9** = **upset**, discompose, distress, disturb, frighten, intimidate, move, rattle (*inf.*), shock, unnerve **10** = **undermine**, impair, pull the rug out from under (*inf.*), weaken ◆ *n* **17, 18** = **vibration**, agitation, convulsion, disturbance, jar, jerk, jolt, jounce, pulsation, quaking, shiver, shock, shudder, trembling, tremor **20** *Informal* = **moment**, instant, jiffy (*inf.*), second, tick (*Brit. inf.*), trice

an instance of shaking. **18** a tremor or vibration. **19 the shakes.** *Inf.* a state of uncontrollable trembling or a condition that causes it, such as a fever. **20** *Inf.* a very short period of time: *in half a shake.* **21** a fissure or crack in timber or rock. **22** an instance of shaking dice before casting. **23** *Music.* another word for **trill** (sense 1). **24** an informal name for **earthquake. 25** short for **milk shake. 26 no great shakes.** *Inf.* of no great merit or value. ◆ See also **shake down, shake off, shake up.** [OE *sceacan*]
▸ **'shakable** *or* **'shakeable** *adj*

shake down *vb* (*adv*) **1** to fall or settle or cause to fall or settle by shaking. **2** (*tr*) *US sl.* to extort money from, esp. by blackmail. **3** (*tr*) *Inf., chiefly US.* to submit (a vessel, etc.) to a shakedown test. **4** (*intr*) to go to bed, esp. to a makeshift bed. ◆ *n* **shakedown. 5** *US sl.* a swindle or act of extortion. **6** a makeshift bed, esp. of straw, blankets, etc. **7** *Inf., chiefly US.* **7a** a voyage to test the performance of a ship or aircraft or to familiarize the crew with their duties. **7b** (*as modifier*): *a shakedown run.*

shake off ❶ *vb* (*adv*) **1** to remove or be removed with or as if with a quick movement: *she shook off her depression.* **2** (*tr*) to escape from; elude: *they shook off the police.*

shaker ('ʃeɪkə) *n* **1** a person or thing that shakes. **2** a container from which a condiment is shaken. **3** a container in which the ingredients of alcoholic drinks are shaken together.

Shakers ('ʃeɪkəz) *pl n* **the.** an American millenarian sect, founded in 1747 as an offshoot of the Quakers, given to ecstatic shaking and practising common ownership of property.

Shakespearean *or* **Shakespearian** (ʃeɪk'spɪərɪən) *adj* **1** of, relating to, or characteristic of William Shakespeare (1564–1616), English dramatist and poet, or his works. ◆ *n* **2** a student of or specialist in Shakespeare's works.

Shakespearean sonnet *n* a sonnet form developed in 16th-century England and employed by Shakespeare, having the rhyme scheme a b a b c d c d e f e f g g.

shake up ❶ *vb* (*tr, adv*) **1** to shake in order to mix. **2** to reorganize drastically. **3** to stir. **4** to restore the shape of (a pillow, etc.). **5** *Inf.* to shock mentally or physically. ◆ *n* **shake-up. 6** *Inf.* a radical reorganization.

shako ('ʃækəʊ) *n, pl* **shakos** *or* **shakoes.** a tall usually cylindrical military headdress, having a plume and often a peak. [C19: via F from Hungarian *csákó,* from MHG *zacke* a sharp point]

shaky ❶ ('ʃeɪkɪ) *adj* **shakier, shakiest. 1** tending to shake or tremble. **2** liable to prove defective. **3** uncertain or questionable: *your arguments are very shaky.*
▸ **'shakily** *adv* ▸ **'shakiness** *n*

shale (ʃeɪl) *n* a dark fine-grained sedimentary rock formed by compression of successive layers of clay. [OE *scealu* shell]
▸ **'shaly** *adj*

shale oil *n* an oil distilled from shales and used as fuel.

shall (ʃæl; *unstressed* ʃəl) *vb past* **should.** (takes an infinitive without *to* or an implied infinitive) used as an auxiliary: **1** (esp. with *I* or *we* as subject) to make the future tense: *we shall see you tomorrow.* Cf. **will**[1] (sense 1). **2** (with *you, he, she, it, they,* or a noun as subject) **2a** to indicate determination on the part of the speaker, as in issuing a threat: *you shall pay for this!* **2b** to indicate compulsion, now esp. in official documents. **2c** to indicate certainty or inevitability: *our day shall come.* **3** (*with any noun or pronoun as subject, esp. in conditional clauses or clauses expressing doubt*) to indicate nonspecific futurity: *I don't think I shall ever see her again.* [OE *sceal*]

> **USAGE NOTE** The usual rule given for the use of *shall* and *will* is that where the meaning is one of simple futurity, *shall* is used for the first person of the verb and *will* for the second and third: *I shall go tomorrow; they will be there now.* Where the meaning involves command, obligation, or determination, the positions are reversed: *it shall be done; I will definitely go.* However, *shall* has come to be largely neglected in favour of *will,* which has become the commonest form of the future in all three persons.

shallop ('ʃæləp) *n* a light boat used for rowing in shallow water. [C16: from F *chaloupe,* from Du. *sloep* sloop]

shallot (ʃə'lɒt) *n* **1** an alliaceous plant cultivated for its edible bulb. **2** the bulb of this plant, which divides into small sections and is used in cooking for flavouring. [C17: from OF, from *eschaloigne,* from L *Ascalōnia caepa* Ascalonian onion, from *Ascalon,* a Palestinian town]

shallow ❶ ('ʃæləʊ) *adj* **1** having little depth. **2** lacking intellectual or mental depth or subtlety. ◆ *n* **3** (*often pl*) a shallow place in a body of water. ◆ *vb* **4** to make or become shallow. [C15: rel. to OE *sceald* shallow]
▸ **'shallowly** *adv* ▸ **'shallowness** *n*

shalom aleichem *Hebrew.* (ʃa'lɔm a'lexɛm) *sentence substitute.* peace be to you: used by Jews as a greeting or farewell. Often shortened to **shalom.**

shalt (ʃælt) *vb Arch. or dialect.* (used with the pronoun *thou*) a singular form of the present tense (indicative mood) of **shall.**

sham ❶ (ʃæm) *n* **1** anything that is not what it appears to be. **2** something false or fictitious that purports to be genuine. **3** a person who pretends to be something other than he is. ◆ *adj* **4** counterfeit or false. ◆ *vb* **shams, shamming, shammed. 5** to assume the appearance of (something); counterfeit: *to sham illness.* [C17: ? a N English dialect var. of SHAME]

shaman ('ʃæmən) *n* **1** a priest of shamanism. **2** a medicine man of a similar religion, esp. among certain tribes of North American Indians. [C17: from Russian *shaman,* ult. from Sansk. *śrama* religious exercise]

shamanism ('ʃæmə,nɪzəm) *n* **1** the religion of certain peoples of northern Asia, based on the belief that the world is pervaded by good and evil spirits who can be influenced or controlled only by the shamans. **2** any similar religion involving forms of spiritualism.
▸ **'shamanist** *n, adj*

shamateur ('ʃæmətə) *n* a sportsperson who is officially an amateur but accepts payment. [C20: from SHAM + AMATEUR]

shamble ❶ ('ʃæmb[ə]l) *vb* **shambles, shambling, shambled. 1** (*intr*) to walk or move along in an awkward or unsteady way. ◆ *n* **2** an awkward or unsteady walk. [C17: from *shamble* (adj) ungainly, ?from *shamble legs* legs resembling those of a meat vendor's table; see SHAMBLES]
▸ **'shambling** *adj, n*

shambles ❶ ('ʃæmb[ə]lz) *n* (*functioning as sing or pl*) **1** a place of great disorder: *the room was a shambles after the party.* **2** a place where animals are brought to be slaughtered. **3** any place of slaughter or carnage. [C14 *shamble* table used by meat vendors, from OE *sceamel* stool, from LL *scamellum* a small bench, from L *scamnum* stool]

shambolic ❶ (ʃæm'bɒlɪk) *adj Inf.* completely disorganized; chaotic. [C20: from SHAMBLES]

shame ❶ (ʃeɪm) *n* **1** a painful emotion resulting from an awareness of having done something dishonourable, unworthy, etc. **2** capacity to feel such an emotion. **3** ignominy or disgrace. **4** a person or thing that causes this. **5** an occasion for regret, disappointment, etc.: *it's a shame you can't come with us.* **6 put to shame. 6a** to disgrace. **6b** to surpass totally. ◆ *vb* **shames, shaming, shamed.** (*tr*) **7** to cause to feel shame. **8** to bring shame on. **9** (often foll. by *into*) to compel through a sense of shame. ◆ *interj* **10** *S. African inf.* **10a** an expression of sympathy. **10b** an expression of pleasure or endearment. [OE *scamu*]
▸ **'shamable** *or* **'shameable** *adj*

shamefaced ❶ ('ʃeɪm,feɪst) *adj* **1** bashful or modest. **2** showing a sense of shame. [C16: alteration of earlier *shamefast,* from OE *sceamfaest*]
▸ **shamefacedly** (,ʃeɪm'feɪsɪdlɪ) *adv*

shameful ❶ ('ʃeɪmfʊl) *adj* causing or deserving shame.
▸ **'shamefully** *adv* ▸ **'shamefulness** *n*

THESAURUS

shake off *vb* **1, 2** = **get rid of,** dislodge, elude, get away from, get shot of (*sl.*), give the slip, leave behind, lose, rid oneself of, throw off

shake up *vb* **1** = **stir (up),** agitate, churn (up), mix **2** = **reorganize,** overturn, turn upside down **5** *Informal* = **upset,** disturb, shock, unsettle

shaky *adj* **1** = **unsteady,** all of a quiver (*inf.*), faltering, insecure, precarious, quivery, rickety, tottering, trembling, tremulous, unstable, weak, wobbly **2, 3** = **uncertain,** dubious, iffy (*inf.*), questionable, suspect, undependable, unreliable, unsound, unsupported
Antonyms *adj* ≠ **unsteady:** firm, secure, stable, steady, strong ≠ **uncertain:** dependable

shallow *adj* **2** = **superficial,** empty, flimsy, foolish, frivolous, idle, meaningless, simple, skin-deep, slight, surface, trivial ◆ *n* **3** *often plural* = **bank,** flat, sandbank, sand bar, shelf, shoal
Antonyms *adj* ≠ **superficial:** analytical, comprehensive, deep, in-depth, meaningful, penetrating, perceptive, profound, searching, serious, weighty

sham *n* **1-3** = **phoney** *or* **phony** (*inf.*), counterfeit, feint, forgery, fraud, hoax, humbug, imitation, impostor, imposture, pretence, pretender, pseud (*inf.*), wolf in sheep's clothing ◆ *adj* **4** = **false,** artificial, bogus, counterfeit, ersatz, feigned, imitation, mock, phoney *or* phony (*inf.*), pretended, pseudo (*inf.*), simulated, spurious, synthetic ◆ *vb* **5** = **fake,** affect, assume, counterfeit, feign, imitate, play possum, pretend, put on, simulate
Antonyms *n* ≠ **phoney** *or* **phony:** master, original, the genuine article, the real McCoy (*or* McKay), the real thing ◆ *adj* ≠ **false:** authentic, bona fide, genuine, legitimate, natural, real, sound, true, unfeigned, veritable

shambles *n* **1** = **chaos,** anarchy, confusion, disarray, disorder, disorganization, havoc, madhouse, mess, muddle

shambling *adj* **1** = **clumsy,** awkward, lumbering, lurching, shuffling, ungainly, unsteady

shambolic *adj Informal* = **disorganized,** anarchic, at sixes and sevens, chaotic, confused, disordered, inefficient, in total disarray, muddled, topsy-turvy, unsystematic

shame *n* **1** = **embarrassment,** abashment, chagrin, compunction, humiliation, ignominy, loss of face, mortification, shamefacedness **3** = **disgrace,** blot, contempt, degradation, derision, discredit, dishonour, disrepute, ill repute, infamy, obloquy, odium, opprobrium, reproach, scandal, skeleton in the cupboard, smear **6 put to shame** = **outdo,** disgrace, eclipse, outclass, outstrip, show up, surpass ◆ *vb* **7** = **embarrass,** abash, confound, disconcert, disgrace, humble, humiliate, mortify, reproach, ridicule, take (someone) down a peg (*inf.*) **8** = **dishonour,** blot, debase, defile, degrade, discredit, smear, stain
Antonyms *n* ≠ **embarrassment:** brass neck (*Brit. inf.*), brazenness, cheek, shamelessness, unabashedness ≠ **disgrace:** credit, distinction, esteem, glory, honour, pride, renown, self-respect ◆ *vb* ≠ **embarrass:** do credit to, make proud ≠ **dishonour:** acclaim, credit, enhance the reputation of, honour

shamefaced *adj* **1** = **shy,** bashful, blushing, diffident, hesitant, modest, shrinking, timid **2** = **embarrassed,** abashed, ashamed, chagrined, conscience-stricken, contrite, discomfited, humiliated, mortified, red-faced, remorseful, sheepish

shameful *adj* = **disgraceful,** atrocious, base, dastardly, degrading, dishonourable, ig-

shameless ❶ (ˈʃeɪmlɪs) *adj* **1** having no sense of shame. **2** without decency or modesty.
▸ˈ**shamelessly** *adv* ▸ˈ**shamelessness** *n*

shammy (ˈʃæmɪ) *n, pl* **shammies.** *Inf.* another word for **chamois** (sense 3). Also called: **shammy leather.** [C18: variant of CHAMOIS]

shampoo (ʃæmˈpuː) *n* **1** a preparation of soap or detergent to wash the hair. **2** a similar preparation for washing carpets, etc. **3** the process of shampooing. ◆ *vb* **shampoos, shampooing, shampooed.** (*tr*) **4** to wash (the hair, etc.) with such a preparation. [C18: from Hindi, from *chāmpnā* to knead]

shamrock (ˈʃæmˌrɒk) *n* a plant having leaves divided into three leaflets: the national emblem of Ireland. [C16: from Irish Gaelic *seamrōg*, dim. of *seamar* clover]

shamus (ˈʃɑːməs, ˈʃeɪ-) *n, pl* **shamuses.** *US sl.* a police or private detective. [prob. from *shammes* caretaker of a synagogue, infl. by Irish *Séamas* James]

shandy (ˈʃændɪ) *n, pl* **shandies.** an alcoholic drink made of beer and ginger beer or lemonade. [C19: from ?]

shanghai (ˈʃæŋhaɪ, ʃæŋˈhaɪ) *Sl.* ◆ *vb* **shanghais, shanghaiing, shanghaied.** (*tr*) **1** to kidnap (a man or seaman) for enforced service at sea. **2** to force or trick (someone) into doing something, etc. **3** *Austral. & NZ.* to shoot with a catapult. ◆ *n* **4** *Austral. & NZ.* a catapult. [C19: from the port of *Shanghai*, in E China, from the forceful methods formerly used to collect crews for voyages to the Orient]

Shangri-la (ˌʃæŋgrɪˈlɑː) *n* a remote or imaginary utopia. [C20: from the name of an imaginary valley in the Himalayas, from *Lost Horizon* (1933), a novel by James Hilton]

shank (ʃæŋk) *n* **1** *Anat.* the shin. **2** the corresponding part of the leg in vertebrates other than man. **3** a cut of meat from the top part of an animal's shank. **4** the main part of a tool, between the working part and the handle. **5** the part of a bolt between the thread and the head. **6** the ring or stem on the back of some buttons. **7** the stem or long narrow part of a key, hook, spoon handle, nail, etc. **8** the band of a ring as distinguished from the setting. **9** the part of a shoe connecting the wide part of the sole with the heel. **10** *Printing.* the body of a piece of type. ◆ *vb* **11** (*intr*) (of fruits, roots, etc.) to show disease symptoms, esp. discoloration. **12** (*tr*) *Golf.* to mishit (the ball) with the foot of the shaft. [OE *scanca*]

shanks's pony *or US* **shanks's mare** (ˈʃæŋksɪz) *n Inf.* one's own legs as a means of transportation.

shanny (ˈʃænɪ) *n, pl* **shannies.** a European blenny of rocky coastal waters. [C19: from ?]

shan't (ʃɑːnt) *contraction of* shall not.

shantung (ˌʃænˈtʌŋ) *n* **1** a heavy silk fabric with a knobbly surface. **2** a cotton or rayon imitation of this. [C19: after province of NE China]

shanty[1] ❶ (ˈʃæntɪ) *n, pl* **shanties.** **1** a ramshackle hut; crude dwelling. **2** *Austral. & NZ.* a public house, esp. an unlicensed one. [C19: from Canad. F *chantier* cabin built in a lumber camp, from OF *gantier* GANTRY]

shanty[2] (ˈʃæntɪ) *or* **chanty** *n, pl* **shanties** *or* **chanties.** a song originally sung by sailors, esp. a rhythmic one forming an accompaniment to work. [C19: from F *chanter* to sing; see CHANT]

shantytown (ˈʃæntɪˌtaʊn) *n* a town or section of a town or city inhabited by very poor people living in shanties.

shape ❶ (ʃeɪp) *n* **1** the outward form of an object defined by outline. **2** the figure or outline of the body of a person. **3** a phantom. **4** organized or definite form: *my plans are taking shape.* **5** the form that anything assumes. **6** pattern; mould. **7** condition or state of efficiency: *to be in good shape.* **8** **out of shape. 8a** in bad physical condition. **8b** bent, twisted, or deformed. **9** **take shape.** to assume a definite form. ◆ *vb* **shapes, shaping, shaped. 10** (when *intr*, often foll. by *into* or *up*) to receive or cause to receive shape or form. **11** (*tr*) to mould into a particular pattern or form. **12** (*tr*) to plan, devise, or prepare: *to shape a plan of action.* ◆ See also **shape up.** [OE *gesceap*, lit.: that which is created, from *sceppan* to create]
▸ˈ**shapable** *or* ˈ**shapeable** *adj* ▸ˈ**shaper** *n*

SHAPE (ʃeɪp) *n acronym for* Supreme Headquarters Allied Powers Europe.

-shaped (ʃeɪpt) *adj combining form.* having the shape of: *an L-shaped room; a pear-shaped figure.*

shapeless ❶ (ˈʃeɪplɪs) *adj* **1** having no definite shape or form: *a shapeless mass.* **2** lacking a symmetrical or aesthetically pleasing shape: *a shapeless figure.*
▸ˈ**shapelessness** *n*

shapely ❶ (ˈʃeɪplɪ) *adj* **shapelier, shapeliest.** (esp. of a woman's body or legs) pleasing or attractive in shape.
▸ˈ**shapeliness** *n*

shape up ❶ *vb* (*intr, adv*) *Inf.* **1** to proceed or develop satisfactorily. **2** to develop a definite or proper form.

shard (ʃɑːd) *or* **sherd** *n* **1** a broken piece or fragment of a brittle substance, esp. of pottery. **2** *Zool.* a tough sheath, scale, or shell, esp. the elytra of a beetle. [OE *sceard*]

share[1] ❶ (ʃɛə) *n* **1** a part or portion of something owned or contributed by a person or group. **2** (*often pl*) any of the equal parts, usually of low par value, into which the capital stock of a company is divided. **3** **go shares.** *Inf.* to share (something) with another or others. ◆ *vb* **shares, sharing, shared. 4** (*tr*; often foll. by *out*) to divide or apportion, esp. equally. **5** (when *intr*, often foll. by *in*) to receive or contribute a portion of: *we can share the cost of the petrol.* **6** to join with another or others in the use of (something): *can I share your umbrella?* [OE *scearu*]
▸ˈ**sharable** *or* ˈ**shareable** *adj* ▸ˈ**sharer** *n*

share[2] (ʃɛə) *n* short for **ploughshare.** [OE *scear*]

sharecrop (ˈʃɛəˌkrɒp) *vb* **sharecrops, sharecropping, sharecropped.** *Chiefly US.* to cultivate (farmland) as a sharecropper.

sharecropper (ˈʃɛəˌkrɒpə) *n Chiefly US.* a farmer, esp. a tenant farmer, who pays over a proportion of a crop or crops as rent.

shared ownership *n* (in Britain) a form of house purchase whereby the purchaser buys a proportion of the dwelling, usually from a local authority or housing association, and rents the rest.

share-farmer *n Chiefly Austral.* a farmer who pays a fee to another in return for use of land to raise crops, etc.

shareholder (ˈʃɛəˌhəʊldə) *n* the owner of one or more shares in a company.

share index *n* an index showing the movement of share prices. See **FT Index.**

share-milker *n* (in New Zealand) a person who lives on a dairy farm and milks the farmer's herd in return for an agreed share of the profits.

share option *n* a scheme giving employees an option to buy shares in the company for which they work at a favourable price or discount.

share premium *n Brit.* the excess of the amount actually subscribed for an issue of corporate capital over its par value.

share shop *n* a stockbroker, bank, or other financial intermediary that handles the buying and selling of shares for members of the public, esp. during a privatization issue.

shareware (ˈʃɛəˌwɛə) *n Computing.* software available to all users without the need for a licence and for which a token fee is requested.

sharia *or* **sheria** (ʃəˈriːə) *n* the body of doctrines that regulate the lives of those who profess Islam. [Ar.]

sharif (ʃæˈriːf) *n* a variant transliteration of **sherif.**

shark[1] (ʃɑːk) *n* any of various usually ferocious fishes, with a long body, two dorsal fins, and rows of sharp teeth. [C16: from ?]
▸ˈ**sharkˌlike** *adj*

shark[2] (ʃɑːk) *n* a person who preys on or victimizes others, esp. by swindling or extortion. [C18: prob. from G *Schurke* rogue]

shark repellent *pl n* **1** any of various substances used by divers to deter shark attack. **2** (*pl*) *Finance.* another name for **porcupine provisions.**

sharkskin (ˈʃɑːkˌskɪn) *n* a smooth glossy fabric of acetate rayon, used for sportswear, etc.

shark watcher *n Inf.* a business consultant who assists companies in identifying and preventing unwelcome takeover bids.

sharon fruit (ˈʃærən) *n* another name for **persimmon** (sense 2).

sharp ❶ (ʃɑːp) *adj* **1** having a keen edge suitable for cutting. **2** having an edge or point. **3** involving a sudden change, esp. in direction: *a sharp bend.* **4** moving, acting, or reacting quickly, etc.: *sharp reflexes.* **5** clearly defined. **6** mentally acute; keen-witted; attentive. **7** sly or artful: *sharp practice.* **8** bitter or harsh: *sharp words.* **9** shrill or penetrating:

THESAURUS

nominious, indecent, infamous, low, mean, outrageous, reprehensible, scandalous, unbecoming, unworthy, vile, wicked
Antonyms *adj* admirable, creditable, estimable, exemplary, honourable, laudable, right, worthy

shameless *adj* **2** = **brazen**, abandoned, audacious, barefaced, brash, corrupt, depraved, dissolute, flagrant, hardened, immodest, improper, impudent, incorrigible, indecent, insolent, profligate, reprobate, unabashed, unashamed, unblushing, unprincipled, wanton

shanty[1] *n* **1** = **shack**, bothy (*Scot.*), cabin, hovel, hut, lean-to, shed, shiel (*Scot.*), shieling (*Scot.*)

shape *n* **1** = **form**, build, configuration, contours, cut, figure, lines, make, outline, profile, silhouette **2** = **appearance**, aspect, form, guise, likeness, semblance **6** = **pattern**, frame, model, mould **7** = **condition**, fettle, health, kilter, state, trim ◆ *vb* **11** = **form**, create, fashion, make, model, mould, produce **12** = **develop**, accommodate, adapt, convert, define, devise, frame, guide, modify, plan, prepare, regulate, remodel

shapeless *adj* **1, 2** = **formless**, amorphous, asymmetrical, irregular, misshapen, unstructured
Antonyms *adj* well-formed, well-proportioned, well-turned

shapely *adj* = **well-formed**, comely, curvaceous, elegant, graceful, neat, sightly, trim, well-proportioned, well-turned

shape up *vb* **1** *Informal* = **progress**, be promising, come on, develop, look good, proceed, turn out

share[1] *n* **1** = **part**, allotment, allowance, contribution, cut (*inf.*), division, due, lot, portion, proportion, quota, ration, whack (*inf.*) ◆ *vb* **4** = **divide**, apportion, assign, distribute, divvy up (*inf.*), parcel out, split **5** = **go halves**, go Dutch (*inf.*), go fifty-fifty (*inf.*) **6** = **partake**, participate, receive, use in common

sharp *adj* **1** = **keen**, acute, cutting, honed, jagged, knife-edged, knifelike, pointed, razor-sharp, serrated, sharpened, spiky **3** = **sudden**, abrupt, distinct, extreme, marked **5** = **clear**, clear-cut, crisp, distinct, well-defined **6** = **quick-witted**, alert, apt, astute, bright, clever, discerning, knowing, long-headed, observant, on the ball (*inf.*), penetrating, perceptive, quick, ready, subtle **7** = **cunning**, artful, crafty, dishonest, fly (*sl.*), shrewd, sly, smart, unscrupulous, wily **8** = **cutting**, acerb, acrimonious, barbed, biting, bitter, caustic, harsh, hurtful, mordacious, mordant, sarcastic, sardonic, scathing, severe, trenchant, vitriolic **10** = **sour**, acerb, acerbic, acetic, acid, acrid, burning, hot, piquant, pungent, tart, vinegary **13** *Informal* = **stylish**, chic, classy (*sl.*), dressy, fashionable, natty (*inf.*), smart, snappy, trendy (*inf.*) ◆ *adv*

a sharp cry. **10** having an acrid taste. **11** keen; biting: *a sharp wind.* **12** *Music.* **12a** *(immediately postpositive)* denoting a note that has been raised in pitch by one chromatic semitone: *F sharp.* **12b** (of an instrument, voice, etc.) out of tune by being too high in pitch. Cf. **flat**[1] (sense 20). **13** *Inf.* **13a** stylish. **13b** too smart. **14 at the sharp end.** involved in the most competitive or difficult aspect of any activity. ◆ *adv* **15** in a sharp manner. **16** exactly: *six o'clock sharp.* **17** *Music.* **17a** higher than a standard pitch. **17b** out of tune by being too high in pitch: *she sings sharp.* Cf. **flat**[1] (sense 25). ◆ *n* **18** *Music.* **18a** an accidental that raises the pitch of a note by one chromatic semitone. Usual symbol: ♯ **18b** a note affected by this accidental. Cf. **flat**[1] (sense 31). **19** a thin needle with a sharp point. **20** *Inf.* a sharper. ◆ *vb* **21** *(tr) Music.* the usual US and Canad. word for **sharpen.** [OE *scearp*]
▸**'sharply** *adv* ▸**'sharpness** *n*

sharpbender ('ʃɑːpˌbɛndə) *n Inf.* an organization that has been underperforming its competitors but suddenly becomes more successful, often as a result of new management or changes in its business strategy. [C20: from the sharp upward bend in its sales or profits]

sharpen ❶ ('ʃɑːpᵊn) *vb* **1** to make or become sharp or sharper. **2** *Music.* to raise the pitch of (a note), esp. by one semitone.
▸**'sharpener** *n*

sharper ('ʃɑːpə) *n* a person who cheats or swindles; fraud.

sharpish ('ʃɑːpɪʃ) *adj* **1** rather sharp. ◆ *adv* **2** *Inf.* quickly; fairly sharply: *quick sharpish.*

sharp-set *adj* **1** set to give an acute cutting angle. **2** keenly hungry. **3** keen or eager.

sharpshooter ('ʃɑːpˌʃuːtə) *n* an expert marksman.
▸**'sharpˌshooting** *n*

sharp-tongued *adj* bitter or critical in speech; sarcastic.

sharp-witted *adj* having or showing a keen intelligence; perceptive.
▸ˌ**sharp-'wittedly** *adv* ▸ˌ**sharp-'wittedness** *n*

Shasta daisy ('ʃæstə) *n* a plant widely cultivated for its large white daisy-like flowers.

shastra ('ʃɑːstrə), **shaster** ('ʃɑːstə), *or* **sastra** ('sɑːstrə) *n* any of the sacred writings of Hinduism. [C17: from Sansk. *śāstra,* from *śās* to teach]

shat (ʃæt) *vb Taboo.* a past tense and past participle of **shit.**

shatter ❶ ('ʃætə) *vb* **1** to break or be broken into many small pieces. **2** *(tr)* to impair or destroy: *his nerves were shattered by the torture.* **3** *(tr)* to dumbfound or thoroughly upset: *she was shattered by the news.* **4** *(tr) Inf.* to cause to be tired out or exhausted. [C12: ? obscurely rel. to SCATTER]
▸**'shattered** *adj* ▸**'shattering** *adj* ▸**'shatteringly** *adv*

shatterproof ('ʃætəˌpruːf) *adj* designed to resist shattering.

shave ❶ (ʃeɪv) *vb* **shaves, shaving, shaved; shaved** *or* **shaven.** *(mainly tr)* **1** *(also intr)* to remove (the beard, hair, etc.) from (the face, head, or body) by scraping the skin with a razor. **2** to cut or trim very closely. **3** to reduce to shavings. **4** to remove thin slices from (wood, etc.) with a sharp cutting tool. **5** to touch or graze in passing. **6** *Inf.* to reduce (a price) by a slight amount. ◆ *n* **7** the act or an instance of shaving. **8** any tool for scraping. **9** a thin slice or shaving. [OE *sceafan*]
▸**'shavable** *or* **'shaveable** *adj*

shaveling ('ʃeɪvlɪŋ) *n Arch.* **1** *Derog.* a priest or clergyman with a shaven head. **2** a young fellow; youth.

shaven ('ʃeɪvᵊn) *adj* **a** closely shaved or tonsured. **b** *(in combination): clean-shaven.*

shaver ('ʃeɪvə) *n* **1** a person or thing that shaves. **2** Also called: **electric razor, electric shaver.** an electrically powered implement for shaving, having rotating blades behind a fine metal comb. **3** *Inf.* a youngster, esp. a young boy.

Shavian ('ʃeɪvɪən) *adj* **1** of or like George Bernard Shaw (1856–1950), Irish dramatist, his works, ideas, etc. ◆ *n* **2** an admirer of Shaw or his works.

shaving ('ʃeɪvɪŋ) *n* **1** a thin paring or slice, esp. of wood, that has been shaved from something. ◆ *modifier.* **2** used when shaving the face, etc.: *shaving cream.*

Shavuot *or* **Shabuoth** (ʃə'vuːəs, -əʊs; *Hebrew* ʃavuː'ɔt) *n* the Hebrew name for **Pentecost** (sense 2). [from Heb. *shābhū'ōth,* pl of *shābhūā'* week]

shawl (ʃɔːl) *n* a piece of fabric or knitted or crocheted material worn around the shoulders by women or wrapped around a baby. [C17: from Persian *shāl*]

shawm (ʃɔːm) *n Music.* a medieval form of the oboe with a conical bore and flaring bell. [C14 *shalmye,* from OF *chalemie,* ult. from L *calamus* a reed, from Gk *kalamos*]

shay (ʃeɪ) *n* a dialect word for **chaise.** [C18: back formation from CHAISE, mistaken for pl]

she (ʃiː) *pron (subjective)* **1** refers to a female person or animal: *she is a doctor.* **2** refers to things personified as feminine, such as cars, ships, and nations. **3** *Austral. & NZ.* a pronoun often used instead of *it,* as in **she'll be right** (it will be all right). ◆ *n* **4a** a female person or animal. **4b** *(in combination): she-cat.* [OE *sīe,* accusative of *sēo,* fem. demonstrative pron]

shea (ʃɪə) *n* **1** a tropical African tree with oily seeds. **2 shea butter.** the white butter-like fat obtained from the seeds of this plant and used as food, etc. [C18: from W African *si*]

sheading ('ʃiːdɪŋ) *n* any of the six subdivisions of the Isle of Man. [var. of *shedding*]

sheaf (ʃiːf) *n, pl* **sheaves. 1** a bundle of reaped but unthreshed corn tied with one or two bonds. **2** a bundle of objects tied together. **3** the arrows contained in a quiver. ◆ *vb* **4** *(tr)* to bind or tie into a sheaf. [OE *sceaf*]

shear (ʃɪə) *vb* **shears, shearing, sheared** *or (arch., Austral., & NZ) sometimes* **shore; sheared** *or* **shorn. 1** *(tr)* to remove (the fleece or hair) of (sheep, etc.) by cutting or clipping. **2** to cut or cut through (something) with shears or a sharp instrument. **3** *Engineering.* to cause (a part, member, etc.) to deform or fracture or (of a part, etc.) to deform or fracture as a result of excess torsion. **4** *(tr;* often foll. by *of)* to strip or divest: *to shear someone of his power.* **5** (when *intr,* foll. by *through)* to move through (something) by or as if by cutting. ◆ *n* **6** the act, process, or an instance of shearing. **7** a shearing of a sheep or flock of sheep: *a sheep of two shears.* **8** a form of deformation or fracture in which parallel planes in a body slide over one another. **9** *Physics.* the deformation of a body, part, etc., expressed as the lateral displacement between two points in parallel planes divided by the distance between the planes. **10** either one of the blades of a pair of shears, scissors, etc. ◆ See also **shears.** [OE *sceran*]
▸**'shearer** *n*

shearling ('ʃɪəlɪŋ) *n* **1** a young sheep after its first shearing. **2** the skin of such an animal.

shear pin *n* an easily replaceable pin in a machine designed to break and stop the machine if the stress becomes too great.

shears (ʃɪəz) *pl n* **1a** large scissors, as for cutting cloth, jointing poultry, etc. **1b** a large scissor-like and usually hand-held cutting tool with flat blades, as for cutting hedges. **2** any of various analogous cutting implements.

shearwater ('ʃɪəˌwɔːtə) *n* any of several oceanic birds specialized for an aerial or aquatic existence.

sheatfish ('ʃiːtˌfɪʃ) *n, pl* **sheatfish** *or* **sheatfishes.** another name for **European catfish** (see **silurid** (sense 1)). [C16: var. of *sheathfish;* ? infl. by G *Schaid* sheatfish]

sheath (ʃiːθ) *n, pl* **sheaths** (ʃiːðz). **1** a case or covering for the blade of a knife, sword, etc. **2** any similar close-fitting case. **3** *Biol.* an enclosing or protective structure. **4** the protective covering on an electric cable. **5** a figure-hugging dress with a narrow tapering skirt. **6** another name for **condom.** [OE *scēath*]

sheathe (ʃiːð) *vb* **sheathes, sheathing, sheathed.** *(tr)* **1** to insert (a knife, sword, etc.) into a sheath. **2** (esp. of cats) to retract (the claws). **3** to surface with or encase in a sheath or sheathing.

sheathing ('ʃiːðɪŋ) *n* **1** any material used as an outer layer, as on a ship's hull. **2** boarding, etc., used to cover a timber frame.

sheath knife *n* a knife carried in or protected by a sheath.

sheave[1] (ʃiːv) *vb* **sheaves, sheaving, sheaved.** *(tr)* to gather or bind into sheaves.

sheave[2] (ʃiːv) *n* a wheel with a grooved rim, esp. one used as a pulley. [C14: of Gmc origin]

sheaves (ʃiːvz) *n* the plural of **sheaf.**

shebang (ʃɪ'bæŋ) *n Sl., chiefly US & Canad.* a situation or affair (esp. in **the whole shebang**). [C19: from ?]

shebeen *or* **shebean** (ʃə'biːn) *n* **1** *Irish, Scot., & S. African.* a place where alcoholic drink is sold illegally. **2** (in Ireland) alcohol, esp. home-distilled whiskey, sold without a licence. **3** (in South Africa) a place where Black African men engage in social drinking. [C18: from Irish Gaelic *sībīn* beer of poor quality]

shebeen king *or (fem)* **shebeen queen** *n* (in South Africa) the proprietor of a shebeen.

shed[1] ❶ (ʃɛd) *n* **1** a small building or lean-to of light construction, used for storage, shelter, etc. **2** a large roofed structure, esp. one with open sides, used for storage, repairing locomotives, etc. **3** *Austral. & NZ.* the building in which sheep are shorn. [OE *sced;* prob. var. of *scead* shelter]

shed[2] ❶ (ʃɛd) *vb* **sheds, shedding, shed.** *(mainly tr)* **1** to pour forth or cause to pour forth: *to shed tears.* **2 shed light on** *or* **upon.** to clarify (a problem,

THESAURUS

16 = **promptly**, exactly, on the dot, on time, precisely, punctually

Antonyms *adj* ≠ **keen:** blunt, dull, edgeless, rounded, unsharpened ≠ **sudden:** even, gentle, gradual, moderate, progressive ≠ **clear:** blurred, fuzzy, ill-defined, indistinct, unclear ≠ **quick-witted:** dim, dull-witted, dumb (*inf.*), slow, slow on the uptake, stupid ≠ **cunning:** artless, guileless, ingenuous, innocent, naïve, simple, undesigning ≠ **cutting:** amicable, courteous, friendly, gentle, kindly, mild ≠ **sour:** bland, mild, tasteless ◆ *adv* ≠ **promptly:** approximately, more or less, roughly, round about, vaguely

sharpen *vb* **1** = **whet**, edge, grind, hone, put an edge on, strop

shatter *vb* **1** = **smash**, break, burst, crack, crush, crush to smithereens, demolish, explode, implode, pulverize, shiver, split **2** = **destroy**, blast, blight, bring to nought, demolish, disable, exhaust, impair, overturn, ruin, torpedo, wreck **3** = **upset**, break (someone's) heart, crush, devastate, dumbfound, knock the stuffing out of (someone)

shattered *adj* **3** = **devastated**, crushed, gutted (*sl.*) **4** *Informal* = **exhausted**, all in (*sl.*), clapped out (*Austral. & NZ inf.*), dead beat (*inf.*), dead tired (*inf.*), dog-tired (*inf.*), done in (*inf.*), drained, jiggered (*inf.*), knackered (*sl.*), ready to drop, spent, tired out, weary, wiped out (*inf.*), worn out

shattering *adj* **3** = **devastating**, crushing, overwhelming, paralysing, severe, stunning

shave *vb* **2** = **trim**, crop, pare, plane, shear **5** = **brush**, graze, touch

shed[1] *n* **1** = **hut**, bothy, lean-to, lockup, outhouse, shack

shed[2] *vb* **1** = **give out**, afford, cast, diffuse, drop, emit, give, pour forth, radiate, scatter, shower, spill, throw **2** **shed light on** *or* **upon** = **explain**,

etc.). **3** to cast off or lose: *the snake shed its skin.* **4** (of a lorry) to drop (its load) on the road by accident. **5** to repel: *this coat sheds water.* **6** to separate or divide a group of sheep: *a good dog can shed his sheep in minutes.* **7** *Dialect.* to make a parting in (the hair). ◆ *n* **8** short for **watershed. 9** the action of separating or dividing a group of sheep: *the old dog was better at the shed than the young one.* [OE *sceadan*]
▸ **'shedable** *or* **'sheddable** *adj*

she'd (ʃiːd) *contraction of* she had *or* she would.

shedder[1] ('ʃɛdə) *n* **1** a person or thing that sheds. **2** an animal, such as a llama, snake, or lobster, that moults.

shedder[2] ('ʃɛdə) *n NZ.* a person who milks cows in a cow shed.

shed hand *n Chiefly Austral.* an unskilled worker in a sheepshearing shed.

shed out *vb* (*tr, adv*) *NZ.* to separate off (sheep that have lambed) and move them to better pasture.

sheen ➊ (ʃiːn) *n* **1** a gleaming or glistening brightness; lustre. **2** *Poetic.* splendid clothing. ◆ *adj* **3** *Rare.* beautiful. [OE *sciene*]
▸ **'sheeny** *adj*

sheep (ʃiːp) *n, pl* **sheep. 1** any of a genus of ruminant mammals having transversely ribbed horns and a narrow face. **2 Barbary sheep.** another name for **aoudad. 3** a meek or timid person. **4 separate the sheep from the goats.** to pick out the members of a group who are superior in some respects. [OE *sceap*]
▸ **'sheep,like** *adj*

sheepcote ('ʃiːp,kəʊt) *n Chiefly Brit.* another word for **sheepfold.**

sheep-dip *n* **1** any of several liquid disinfectants and insecticides in which sheep are immersed. **2** a deep trough containing such a liquid.

sheepdog ('ʃiːp,dɒg) *n* **1** a dog used for herding sheep. **2** any of various breeds of dog reared originally for herding sheep. See **Old English sheepdog, Shetland sheepdog.**

sheepdog trial *n* (*often pl*) a competition in which sheepdogs are tested in their tasks.

sheepfold ('ʃiːp,fəʊld) *n* a pen or enclosure for sheep.

sheepish ➊ ('ʃiːpɪʃ) *adj* **1** abashed or embarrassed, esp. through looking foolish. **2** resembling a sheep in timidity.
▸ **'sheepishly** *adv* ▸ **'sheepishness** *n*

sheepo ('ʃiːpəʊ) *n, pl* **sheepos.** *NZ.* a person employed to bring sheep to the catching pen in a shearing shed.

sheep's eyes *pl n Old-fashioned.* amorous or inviting glances.

sheepshank ('ʃiːp,ʃæŋk) *n* a knot made in a rope to shorten it temporarily.

sheepskin ('ʃiːp,skɪn) *n* **a** the skin of a sheep, esp. when used for clothing, etc. **b** (*as modifier*): *a sheepskin coat.*

sheepwalk ('ʃiːp,wɔːk) *n Chiefly Brit.* a tract of land for grazing sheep.

sheer[1] ➊ (ʃɪə) *adj* **1** perpendicular; very steep: *a sheer cliff.* **2** (of textiles) so fine as to be transparent. **3** (*prenominal*) absolute: *sheer folly.* **4** *Obs.* bright. ◆ *adv* **5** steeply. **6** completely or absolutely. [OE *scīr*]
▸ **'sheerly** *adv* ▸ **'sheerness** *n*

sheer[2] (ʃɪə) *vb* (foll. by *off* or *away* (*from*)). **1** to deviate or cause to deviate from a course. **2** (*intr*) to avoid an unpleasant person, thing, topic, etc. ◆ *n* **3** *Naut.* the position of a vessel relative to its mooring. [C17: ? var. of SHEAR]

sheerlegs *or* **shearlegs** ('ʃɪə,lɛgz) *n* (*functioning as sing*) a device for lifting weights consisting of two spars lashed together at the upper ends from which a lifting tackle is suspended. Also called: **shears.** [C19: var. of *shear legs*]

sheet[1] ➊ (ʃiːt) *n* **1** a large rectangular piece of cloth, generally one of a pair used as inner bedclothes. **2a** a thin piece of a substance such as paper or glass, usually rectangular in form. **2b** (*as modifier*): *sheet iron.* **3** a broad continuous surface: *a sheet of water.* **4** a newspaper, esp. a tabloid. **5** a piece of printed paper to be folded into a section for a book. ◆ *vb* **6** (*tr*) to provide with, cover, or wrap in a sheet. [OE *sciete*]

sheet[2] (ʃiːt) *n Naut.* a line or rope for controlling the position of a sail relative to the wind. [OE *scēata* corner of a sail]

sheet anchor *n* **1** *Naut.* a large strong anchor for use in emergency. **2** a person or thing to be relied on in an emergency. [C17: from earlier *shute anker,* from *shoot* (obs.) the sheet of a sail]

sheet bend *n* a knot used esp. for joining ropes of different sizes.

sheeting ('ʃiːtɪŋ) *n* fabric from which sheets are made.

sheet lightning *n* lightning that appears as a broad sheet, caused by the reflection of more distant lightning.

sheet metal *n* metal in the form of a sheet, the thickness being intermediate between that of plate and that of foil.

sheet music *n* **1** the printed or written copy of a short composition or piece. **2** music in its written or printed form.

sheikh *or* **sheik** (ʃeɪk) *n* (in Muslim countries) **a** the head of an Arab tribe, village, etc. **b** a religious leader. [C16: from Ar. *shaykh* old man]
▸ **'sheikhdom** *or* **'sheikdom** *n*

sheila ('ʃiːlə) *n Austral. & NZ old-fashioned.* an informal word for **girl** or **woman.** [C19: from the girl's name *Sheila*]

shekel ('ʃɛkᵊl) *n* **1** the standard monetary unit of modern Israel, divided into 100 agorot. **2** any of several former coins and units of weight of the Near East. **3** (*often pl*) *Inf.* any coin or money. [C16: from Heb. *sheqel*]

shelduck ('ʃɛl,dʌk) *or* (*masc*) **sheldrake** ('ʃɛl,dreɪk) *n, pl* **shelducks, shelduck** *or* **sheldrakes, sheldrake.** any of various large usually brightly coloured gooselike ducks of the Old World. [C14: *shel,* prob. from dialect *sheld* pied]

shelf (ʃɛlf) *n, pl* **shelves. 1** a thin flat plank of wood, metal, etc., fixed horizontally against a wall, etc., for the purpose of supporting objects. **2** something resembling this in shape or function. **3** the objects placed on a shelf: *a shelf of books.* **4** a projecting layer of ice, rock, etc., on land or in the sea. **5** See **off the shelf. 6 on the shelf.** put aside or abandoned; used esp. of unmarried women considered to be past the age of marriage. [OE *scylfe* ship's deck]
▸ **'shelf,like** *adj*

shelf life *n* the length of time a packaged food, etc., will last without deteriorating.

shell ➊ (ʃɛl) *n* **1** the protective outer layer of an egg, esp. a bird's egg. **2** the hard outer covering of many molluscs. **3** any other hard outer layer, such as the exoskeleton of many arthropods. **4** the hard outer layer of some fruits, esp. of nuts. **5** any hard outer case. **6** a hollow artillery projectile filled with explosive primed to explode either during flight or on impact. **7** a small-arms cartridge. **8** a pyrotechnic cartridge designed to explode in the air. **9** *Rowing.* a very light narrow racing boat. **10** the external structure of a building, esp. one that is unfinished. **11** *Physics.* **11a** a class of electron orbits in an atom in which the electrons have the same principal quantum number and little difference in their energy levels. **11b** an analogous energy state of nucleons in certain theories (**shell models**) of the structure of the atomic nucleus. **12 come** (*or* **bring**) **out of one's shell.** to become (or help to become) less shy and reserved. ◆ *vb* **13** to divest or be divested of a shell, husk, etc. **14** to separate or be separated from an ear, husk, etc. **15** (*tr*) to bombard with artillery shells. ◆ See also **shell out.** [OE *sciell*]
▸ **'shell-less** *adj* ▸ **'shell-,like** *adj* ▸ **'shelly** *adj*

she'll (ʃiːl; *unstressed* ʃɪl) *contraction of* she will *or* she shall.

shellac (ʃə'læk, 'ʃɛlæk) *n* **1** a yellowish resin secreted by the lac insect, esp. a commercial preparation of this used in varnishes, polishes, etc. **2** Also called: **shellac varnish.** a varnish made by dissolving shellac in ethanol or a similar solvent. ◆ *vb* **shellacs, shellacking, shellacked.** (*tr*) **3** to coat (an article) with a shellac varnish. [C18: SHELL + LAC[1], translation of F *laque en écailles,* lit.: lac in scales, that is, in thin plates]

shellback ('ʃɛl,bæk) *n* an experienced or old sailor.

shell company *n Business.* **1** a near-defunct company, esp. one with a stock-exchange listing, used as a vehicle for a thriving company. **2** a company that has ceased to trade but retains its registration and is sold for a small sum to enable its new owners to avoid the cost and trouble of registering a new company.

shellfire ('ʃɛl,faɪə) *n* the firing of artillery shells.

shellfish ('ʃɛl,fɪʃ) *n, pl* **shellfish** *or* **shellfishes.** any aquatic invertebrate having a shell or shell-like carapace, esp. such an animal used as human food. Examples are crustaceans such as crabs and lobsters and molluscs such as oysters.

shell out ➊ *vb* (*adv*) *Inf.* to pay out or hand over (money).

shell program *n Computing.* a basic low-cost computer program that provides a framework within which the user can develop the program to suit his personal requirements.

shellproof ('ʃɛl,pruːf) *adj* designed, intended, or able to resist shellfire.

shell shock *n* loss of sight, etc., resulting from psychological strain during prolonged engagement in warfare.
▸ **'shell-,shocked** *adj*

shell suit *n* a lightweight tracksuit consisting of an inner cotton layer covered by a waterproof nylon layer.

Shelta ('ʃɛltə) *n* a secret language used by some itinerant tinkers in Ireland and parts of Britain, based on Gaelic. [C19: from earlier *sheldrū,* ? an arbitrary alteration of OIrish *bēlre* speech]

shelter ➊ ('ʃɛltə) *n* **1** something that provides cover or protection, as from weather or danger. **2** the protection afforded by such a cover. **3** the state of being sheltered. ◆ *vb* **4** (*tr*) to provide with or protect by a

THESAURUS

clarify, clear up, elucidate, simplify **3** = **cast off**, discard, exuviate, moult, slough

sheen *n* **1** = **shine**, brightness, burnish, gleam, gloss, lustre, patina, polish, shininess

sheepish *adj* **1** = **embarrassed**, abashed, ashamed, chagrined, foolish, mortified, self-conscious, shamefaced, silly, uncomfortable
Antonyms *adj* assertive, audacious, bold, brash, brass-necked (*Brit. inf.*), brazen, confident, unabashed, unapologetic, unblushing, unembarrassed

sheer[1] *adj* **1** = **steep**, abrupt, headlong (*arch.*), perpendicular, precipitous **2** = **fine**, diaphanous, gauzy, gossamer, see-through, thin, transparent **3** = **total**, absolute, arrant, complete, downright, out-and-out, pure, rank, thoroughgoing, unadulterated, unalloyed, unmitigated, unqualified, utter
Antonyms *adj* ≠ **steep:** gentle, gradual, horizontal, slanting, sloping ≠ **fine:** coarse, heavy, impenetrable, opaque, thick ≠ **total:** moderate

sheet[1] *n* **2** = **piece**, folio, pane, panel, plate, slab **3** = **expanse**, area, blanket, covering, stretch, sweep

shell *n* **5** = **case**, carapace, husk, pod, shuck **10** = **frame**, chassis, framework, hull, skeleton, structure ◆ *vb* **13, 14** = **husk**, shuck **15** = **bomb**, attack, barrage, blitz, bombard, strafe, strike

shell out *vb* = **pay out**, ante up (*inf., chiefly US*), disburse, expend, fork out (*sl.*), give, hand over, lay out (*inf.*)

shelter *n* **1** = **protection**, awning, cover, covert, defence, guard, roof over one's head, screen, shiel (*Scot.*), umbrella **2, 3** = **safety**, asylum, haven, refuge, retreat, sanctuary, security ◆ *vb* **4** = **protect**, cover, defend, guard, harbour, hide, safeguard, shield, take in **5** = **take shelter**, hide, seek refuge

shelter. **5** (*intr*) to take cover, as from rain. **6** (*tr*) to act as a shelter for. [C16: from ?]
▸ **'shelterer** *n*

sheltered Ⓣ ('ʃɛltəd) *adj* **1** protected from wind or weather. **2** protected from outside influences: *a sheltered upbringing.* **3** specially designed to provide a safe environment for the elderly, handicapped, or disabled: *sheltered housing.*

sheltie *or* **shelty** ('ʃɛltɪ) *n, pl* **shelties.** another name for **Shetland pony** or **Shetland sheepdog.** [C17: prob. from Orkney dialect *sjalti,* from ON *Hjalti* Shetlander, from *Hjaltland* Shetland]

shelve[1] Ⓣ (ʃɛlv) *vb* **shelves, shelving, shelved.** (*tr*) **1** to place on a shelf. **2** to provide with shelves. **3** to put aside or postpone from consideration. **4** to dismiss or cause to retire. [C16: from *shelves,* pl of SHELF]
▸ **'shelver** *n*

shelve[2] (ʃɛlv) *vb* **shelves, shelving, shelved.** (*intr*) to slope away gradually. [C16: from ?]

shelves (ʃɛlvz) *n* the plural of **shelf.**

shelving ('ʃɛlvɪŋ) *n* **1** material for making shelves. **2** a set of shelves; shelves collectively.

shemozzle (ʃɪ'mɒzᵊl) *n Inf.* a noisy confusion or dispute; uproar. [C19: ?from Yiddish *shlimazl* misfortune]

shenanigan (ʃɪ'nænɪgən) *n Inf.* **1** (*usually pl*) roguishness; mischief. **2** an act of treachery; deception. [C19: from ?]

she-oak *n* any of various Australian trees of the genus *Casuarina.* See **casuarina.** [C18: *she* (in the sense: inferior) + OAK]

Sheol ('ʃiːəʊl, -ɒl) *n Bible.* **1** the abode of the dead. **2** (*often not cap.*) hell. [C16: from Heb. *shĕ'ōl*]

shepherd Ⓣ ('ʃɛpəd) *n* **1** a person employed to tend sheep. Fem. equivalent: **shepherdess. 2** a person, such as a clergyman, who watches over a group of people. ◆ *vb* (*tr*) **3** to guide or watch over in the manner of a shepherd. **4** *Australian Rules, rugby, etc.* to prevent opponents from tackling (a member of one's own team) by blocking their path: illegal in rugby.

shepherd dog *n* another term for **sheepdog** (sense 1).

shepherd's pie *n Chiefly Brit.* a baked dish of minced meat covered with mashed potato.

shepherd's-purse *n* a plant having small white flowers and flattened triangular seed pods.

shepherd's weatherglass *n Brit.* another name for the **scarlet pimpernel.**

Sheraton ('ʃɛrətən) *adj* denoting furniture made by or in the style of Thomas Sheraton (1751–1806), British furniture maker, characterized by lightness and elegance.

sherbet ('ʃɜːbət) *n* **1** a fruit-flavoured slightly effervescent powder, eaten as a sweet or used to make a drink. **2** another word (esp. US and Canad.) for **sorbet** (sense 1). **3** *Austral. sl.* beer. **4** a cooling Oriental drink of sweetened fruit juice. [C17: from Turkish, from Persian, from Ar. *sharbah* drink, from *shariba* to drink]

sherd (ʃɜːd) *n* a variant of **shard.**

sherif *or* **shereef** (ʃɛ'riːf) *or* **sharif** *n Islam.* **1** a descendant of Mohammed through his daughter Fatima. **2** an honorific title accorded to any Muslim ruler. [C16: from Ar. *sharīf* noble]

sheriff ('ʃɛrɪf) *n* **1** (in the US) the chief elected law-enforcement officer in a county. **2** (in Canada) a municipal official who enforces court orders, escorts convicted criminals to prison, etc. **3** (in England and Wales) the chief executive officer of the Crown in a county, having chiefly ceremonial duties. **4** (in Scotland) a judge in any of the sheriff courts. **5** (in New Zealand) an officer of the High Court. [OE *scīrgerēfa,* from *scīr* SHIRE + *gerēfa* REEVE[1]]
▸ **'sheriffdom** *n*

sheriff court *n* (in Scotland) a court having jurisdiction to try all but the most serious crimes and to deal with most civil actions.

Sherpa ('ʃɜːpə) *n, pl* **Sherpas** *or* **Sherpa.** a member of a people of Mongolian origin living on the southern slopes of the Himalayas in Nepal, noted as mountaineers.

sherry ('ʃɛrɪ) *n, pl* **sherries.** a fortified wine, originally only from the Jerez region of southern Spain. [C16: from earlier *sherris* (assumed to be pl), from Sp. *Xeres,* now *Jerez*]

sherwani (ʃɛə'wɑːnɪ) *n* a long coat closed up to the neck, worn by men in India. [Hindi]

she's (ʃiːz) *contraction of* she is *or* she has.

Shetland pony ('ʃɛtlənd) *n* a very small sturdy breed of pony with a long shaggy mane and tail. Also called: **sheltie.**

Shetland sheepdog *n* a small dog similar in appearance to a collie. Also called: **sheltie.**

shew (ʃəʊ) *vb* **shews, shewing, shewed; shewn** *or* **shewed.** an archaic spelling of **show.**

shewbread *or* **showbread** ('ʃəʊˌbrɛd) *n Bible.* the loaves of bread placed every Sabbath on the table beside the altar of incense in the tabernacle or temple of ancient Israel.

SHF *or* **shf** *Radio. abbrev. for* superhigh frequency.

Shiah *or* **Shia** ('ʃiːə) *n* **1** one of the two main branches of Islam (the other being the Sunni), now mainly in Iran, which regards Mohammed's cousin Ali and his successors as the true imams. ◆ *adj* **2** designating or characteristic of this sect or its beliefs and practices. [C17: from Ar. *shī'ah* sect, from *shā'a* to follow]

shiatsu (ʃiː'ætsuː) *n* a type of massage in which pressure is applied to the same points of the body as in acupuncture. Also called: **acupressure.** [Japanese from Chinese *chǐ* finger + *yā* pressure]

shibboleth ('ʃɪbəˌlɛθ) *n* **1** a slogan or catch phrase, usually considered outworn, characteristic of a particular party or sect. **2** a custom, phrase, or use of language that acts as a test of belonging to, or as a stumbling block to joining a particular social class, profession, etc. [C14: from Heb., lit.: ear of grain; the word is used in the Old Testament by the Gileadites as a test word for the Ephraimites, who could not pronounce the sound *sh*]

shickered ('ʃɪkəd) *adj Austral. & NZ sl.* drunk; intoxicated. [via Yiddish from Heb.]

shied (ʃaɪd) *vb* the past tense and past participle of **shy**[1] and **shy**[2].

shield Ⓣ (ʃiːld) *n* **1** any protection used to intercept blows, missiles, etc., such as a tough piece of armour carried on the arm. **2** any similar protective device. **3** *Heraldry.* a pointed stylized shield used for displaying armorial bearings. **4** anything that resembles a shield in shape, such as a prize in a sports competition. **5** *Physics.* a structure of concrete, lead, etc., placed around a nuclear reactor. **6** a broad stable plateau of ancient Precambrian rocks forming the rigid nucleus of a particular continent. **7 the shield.** *NZ.* the Bledisloe Shield, a trophy competed for by provincial rugby teams. ◆ *vb* **8** (*tr*) to protect, hide, or conceal (something) from danger or harm. [OE *scield*]
▸ **'shieldˌlike** *adj*

Shield (ʃiːld) *n* **the.** *Canad.* another term for the **Canadian Shield.**

shield match *n* **1** *Austral.* a cricket match for the Sheffield Shield. **2** *NZ.* a rugby match for the Ranfurly Shield.

shield volcano *n* a broad volcano built up from the repeated nonexplosive eruption of basalt to form a low dome or shield, usually having a large caldera at the summit.

shieling ('ʃiːlɪŋ) *or* **shiel** (ʃiːl) *n Chiefly Scot.* **1** a temporary shelter used by people tending cattle on high or remote ground. **2** pasture land for the grazing of cattle in summer. [C16: from earlier *shiel,* from ME *shale* hut, from ?]

shier ('ʃaɪə) *adj* a comparative of **shy**[1].

shiest ('ʃaɪɪst) *adj* a superlative of **shy**[1].

shift Ⓣ (ʃɪft) *vb* **1** to move or cause to move from one place or position to another. **2** (*tr*) to change for another or others. **3** to change (gear) in a motor vehicle. **4** (*intr*) (of a sound or set of sounds) to alter in a systematic way. **5** (*intr*) to provide for one's needs (esp. in **shift for oneself**). **6** to remove or be removed, esp. with difficulty: *no detergent can shift these stains.* **7** (*intr*) *Sl.* to move quickly. **8** (*tr*) *Computing.* to move (bits held in a store location) to the left or right. ◆ *n* **9** the act or an instance of shifting. **10** a group of workers who work for a specific period. **11** the period of time worked by such a group. **12** an expedient, contrivance, or artifice. **13** an underskirt or dress with little shaping. [OE *sciftan*]
▸ **'shifter** *n*

shiftless Ⓣ ('ʃɪftlɪs) *adj* lacking in ambition or initiative.
▸ **'shiftlessness** *n*

shifty Ⓣ ('ʃɪftɪ) *adj* **shiftier, shiftiest. 1** given to evasions. **2** furtive in character or appearance.
▸ **'shiftily** *adv* ▸ **'shiftiness** *n*

shigella (ʃɪ'gɛlə) *n* any of a genus of rod-shaped bacteria, some species of which cause dysentery. [C20: after K. *Shiga* (1870–1957), Japanese bacteriologist, who discovered them]

THESAURUS

Antonyms *vb* ≠ **protect:** endanger, expose, hazard, imperil, lay open, leave open, make vulnerable, risk, subject

sheltered *adj* **2** = **protected,** cloistered, conventual, ensconced, hermitic, isolated, quiet, reclusive, retired, screened, secluded, shaded, shielded, withdrawn
Antonyms *adj* exposed, laid bare, made public, open, public, unconcealed, unprotected, unsheltered

shelve[1] *vb* **3** = **postpone,** defer, dismiss, freeze, hold in abeyance, hold over, lay aside, mothball, pigeonhole, put aside, put off, put on ice, put on the back burner (*inf.*), suspend, table (*US*), take a rain check on (*US & Canad. inf.*)

shepherd *n* **1** = **herdsman,** drover, grazier, stockman ◆ *vb* **3** = **guide,** conduct, convoy, herd, marshal, steer, usher

shield *n* **1** = **buckler,** escutcheon (*Heraldry*), targe (*arch.*) **2** = **protection,** aegis, bulwark, cover, defence, guard, rampart, safeguard, screen, shelter, ward (*arch.*) ◆ *vb* **8** = **protect,** cover, defend, guard, safeguard, screen, shelter, ward off

shift *vb* **1** = **move,** alter, budge, change, displace, fluctuate, move around, rearrange, relocate, remove, reposition, swerve, switch, transfer, transpose, vary, veer **5** *As in* **shift for oneself** = **manage,** assume responsibility, contrive, devise, fend, get along, look after, make do, plan, scheme, take care of ◆ *n* **9** = **move,** about-turn, alteration, change, displacement, fluctuation, modification, permutation, rearrangement, removal, shifting, switch, transfer, veering **12** = **scheme,** artifice, contrivance, craft, device, dodge, equivocation, evasion, expedient, move, resource, ruse, stratagem, subterfuge, trick, wile

shiftless *adj* = **lazy,** aimless, good-for-nothing, idle, incompetent, indolent, inefficient, inept, irresponsible, lackadaisical, slothful, unambitious, unenterprising

shifty *adj* **1, 2** = **untrustworthy,** contriving, crafty, deceitful, devious, duplicitous, evasive, fly-by-night (*inf.*), furtive, scheming, slippery, sly, tricky, underhand, unprincipled, wily
Antonyms *adj* dependable, guileless, honest, honourable, open, reliable, trustworthy, upright

Shiite (ˈʃiːaɪt) *or* **Shiah** *Islam.* ◆ *n* **1** an adherent of Shiah. ◆ *adj* **2** of or relating to Shiah.
▸**Shiism** (ˈʃiːɪzəm) *n* ▸**Shiitic** (ʃiːˈɪtɪk) *adj*

shillelagh *or* **shillala** (ʃəˈleɪlə, -lɪ) *n* (in Ireland) a stout club or cudgel. [C18: from Irish Gaelic *sail* cudgel + *éille* leash, thong]

shilling (ˈʃɪlɪŋ) *n* **1** a former British or Australian silver or cupronickel coin worth one twentieth of a pound, not minted in Britain since 1970. Abbrevs.: **s., sh. 2** the standard monetary unit of Kenya, Somalia, Tanzania, and Uganda. [OE *scilling*]

shillyshally ❶ (ˈʃɪlɪˌʃælɪ) *Inf.* ◆ *vb* **shillyshallies, shillyshallying, shillyshallied. 1** (*intr*) to be indecisive, esp. over unimportant matters. ◆ *adv* **2** in an indecisive manner. ◆ *adj* **3** indecisive or hesitant. ◆ *n, pl* **shillyshallies. 4** vacillation. [C18: from *shill I shall I*, by reduplication of *shall I*]
▸ˈ**shilly,shallier** *n*

shily (ˈʃaɪlɪ) *adv* a less common spelling of **shyly**. See **shy**[1].

shim (ʃɪm) *n* **1** a thin washer or strip often used with a number of similar washers or strips to adjust a clearance for gears, etc. ◆ *vb* **shims, shimming, shimmed. 2** (*tr*) to modify clearance on (a gear, etc.) by use of shims. [C18: from ?]

shimmer ❶ (ˈʃɪmə) *vb* **1** (*intr*) to shine with a glistening or tremulous light. ◆ *n* **2** a faint, glistening, or tremulous light. [OE *scimerian*]
▸ˈ**shimmering** *or* ˈ**shimmery** *adj*

shimmy (ˈʃɪmɪ) *n, pl* **shimmies. 1** an American ragtime dance with much shaking of the hips and shoulders. **2** abnormal wobbling motion in a motor vehicle, esp. in the front wheels or steering. ◆ *vb* **shimmies, shimmying, shimmied.** (*intr*) **3** to dance the shimmy. **4** to vibrate or wobble. [C19: changed from CHEMISE, mistaken for pl]

shin ❶ (ʃɪn) *n* **1** the front part of the lower leg. **2** the front edge of the tibia. **3** *Chiefly Brit.* a cut of beef, the lower foreleg. ◆ *vb* **shins, shinning, shinned. 4** (when *intr*, often foll. by *up*) to climb (a pole, tree, etc.) by gripping with the hands or arms and the legs and hauling oneself up. **5** (*tr*) to kick (a person) in the shins. [OE *scinu*]

shinbone (ˈʃɪnˌbəʊn) *n* the nontechnical name for **tibia** (sense 1).

shindig (ˈʃɪnˌdɪg) *or* **shindy** (ˈʃɪndɪ) *n, pl* **shindigs** *or* **shindies.** *Sl.* **1** a noisy party, dance, etc. **2** a quarrel or commotion. [C19: var. of SHINTY]

shine ❶ (ʃaɪn) *vb* **shines, shining, shone. 1** (*intr*) to emit light. **2** (*intr*) to glow or be bright with reflected light. **3** (*tr*) to direct the light of (a lamp, etc.): *he shone the torch in my eyes.* **4** (*tr; p.t. & p.p.* **shined**) to cause to gleam by polishing: *to shine shoes.* **5** (*intr*) to excel: *she shines at tennis.* **6** (*intr*) to appear clearly. ◆ *n* **7** the state or quality of shining; sheen; lustre. **8** *Inf.* a liking or fancy (esp. in **take a shine to**). [OE *scīnan*]

shiner (ˈʃaɪnə) *n* **1** something that shines, such as a polishing device. **2** any of numerous small North American freshwater cyprinid fishes. **3** *Inf.* a black eye. **4** *NZ. old-fashioned inf.* a tramp.

shingle[1] (ˈʃɪŋgᵊl) *n* **1** a thin rectangular tile, esp. one made of wood, that is laid with others in overlapping rows to cover a roof or a wall. **2** a woman's short-cropped hairstyle. **3** *US & Canad.* a small signboard fixed outside the office of a doctor, lawyer, etc. ◆ *vb* **shingles, shingling, shingled.** (*tr*) **4** to cover (a roof or a wall) with shingles. **5** to cut (the hair) in a short-cropped style. [C12 *scingle*, from LL *scindula* a split piece of wood, from L *scindere* to split]
▸ˈ**shingler** *n*

shingle[2] (ˈʃɪŋgᵊl) *n* **1** coarse gravel, esp. the pebbles found on beaches. **2** a place or area strewn with shingle. [C16: of Scand. origin]
▸ˈ**shingly** *adj*

shingles (ˈʃɪŋgᵊlz) *n* (*functioning as sing*) an acute viral disease characterized by inflammation, pain, and skin eruptions along the course of affected nerves. Technical names: **herpes zoster, zoster.** [C14: from Med. L *cingulum* girdle, rendering Gk *zōnē* zone]

Shinto (ˈʃɪntəʊ) *n* the indigenous religion of Japan, incorporating the worship of a number of ethnic divinities. [C18: from Japanese: the way of the gods, from Chinese *shên* gods + *tao* way]
▸ˈ**Shintoism** *n* ▸ˈ**Shintoist** *n, adj*

shinty (ˈʃɪntɪ) *n* **1** a game resembling hockey played with a ball and sticks curved at the lower end. **2** (*pl* **shinties**) the stick used in this game. [C17: ? from Scot. Gaelic *sinteag* a pace, bound]

shiny ❶ (ˈʃaɪnɪ) *adj* **shinier, shiniest. 1** glossy or polished; bright. **2** (of clothes or material) worn to a smooth and glossy state, as by continual rubbing.
▸ˈ**shininess** *n*

ship ❶ (ʃɪp) *n* **1** a vessel propelled by engines or sails for navigating on the water, esp. a large vessel. **2** *Naut.* a large sailing vessel with three or more square-rigged masts. **3** the crew of a ship. **4** short for **airship** or **spaceship. 5 when one's ship comes in** (*or* **home**). when one has become successful. ◆ *vb* **ships, shipping, shipped. 6** to place, transport, or travel on any conveyance, esp. aboard a ship. **7** (*tr*) *Naut.* to take (water) over the side. **8** to bring or go aboard a vessel: *to ship oars.* **9** (*tr; often foll. by off*) *Inf.* to send away: *they shipped the children off to boarding school.* **10** (*intr*) to engage to serve aboard a ship: *I shipped aboard a Liverpool liner.* [OE *scip*]
▸ˈ**shippable** *adj*

-ship *suffix forming nouns.* **1** indicating state or condition: *fellowship.* **2** indicating rank, office, or position: *lordship.* **3** indicating craft or skill: *scholarship.* [OE *-scipe*]

shipboard (ˈʃɪpˌbɔːd) *n* (*modifier*) taking place, used, or intended for use aboard a ship: *a shipboard encounter.*

shipbuilder (ˈʃɪpˌbɪldə) *n* a person or business engaged in building ships.
▸ˈ**ship,building** *n*

ship chandler *n* a person or business dealing in supplies for ships.
▸**ship chandlery** *n*

shipload (ˈʃɪpˌləʊd) *n* the quantity carried by a ship.

shipmaster (ˈʃɪpˌmɑːstə) *n* the master or captain of a ship.

shipmate (ˈʃɪpˌmeɪt) *n* a sailor who serves on the same ship as another.

shipment (ˈʃɪpmənt) *n* **1a** goods shipped together as part of the same lot: *a shipment of grain.* **1b** (*as modifier*): *a shipment schedule.* **2** the act of shipping cargo.

ship money *n English history.* a tax levied to finance the fitting out of warships: abolished 1640.

ship of the line *n Naut.* (formerly) a warship large enough to fight in the first line of battle.

shipowner (ˈʃɪpˌəʊnə) *n* a person who owns or has shares in a ship or ships.

shipper (ˈʃɪpə) *n* a person or company in the business of shipping freight.

shipping (ˈʃɪpɪŋ) *n* **1a** the business of transporting freight, esp. by ship. **1b** (*as modifier*): *a shipping magnate; shipping line.* **2** ships collectively: *there is a lot of shipping in the Channel.*

ship's biscuit *n* another name for **hardtack.**

shipshape ❶ (ˈʃɪpˌʃeɪp) *adj* **1** neat; orderly. ◆ *adv* **2** in a neat and orderly manner.

shipworm (ˈʃɪpˌwɜːm) *n* any of a genus of wormlike marine bivalve molluscs that bore into wooden piers, ships, etc., by means of drill-like shell valves.

shipwreck (ˈʃɪpˌrɛk) *n* **1** the partial or total destruction of a ship at sea. **2** a wrecked ship or part of such a ship. **3** ruin or destruction: *the shipwreck of all my hopes.* ◆ *vb* (*tr*) **4** to wreck or destroy (a ship). **5** to bring to ruin or destruction. [OE *scipwræc*, from SHIP + *wræc* something driven by the sea]

shipwright (ˈʃɪpˌraɪt) *n* an artisan skilled in one or more of the tasks required to build vessels.

shipyard (ˈʃɪpˌjɑːd) *n* a place or facility for the building, maintenance, and repair of ships.

shiralee (ˌʃɪrəˈliː) *n Austral. sl.* a swagman's bundle. [from ?]

shire (ˈʃaɪə) *n* **1a** one of the British counties. **1b** (*in combination*): *Yorkshire.* **2** (in Australia) a rural district having its own local council. **3** See **shire horse. 4 the Shires.** the Midland counties of England, famous for hunting, etc. [OE *scīr* office]

shire horse *n* a large heavy breed of carthorse with long hair on the fetlocks.

shirk ❶ (ʃɜːk) *vb* **1** to avoid discharging (work, a duty, etc.); evade. ◆ *n also* **shirker. 2** a person who shirks. [C17: prob. from G *Schurke* rogue]

shirr (ʃɜː) *vb* **1** to gather (fabric) into two or more parallel rows to decorate a dress, blouse, etc., often using elastic thread. **2** (*tr*) to bake (eggs) out of their shells. ◆ *n also* **shirring. 3** a series of gathered rows decorating a dress, blouse, etc. [C19: from ?]

shirt (ʃɜːt) *n* **1** a garment worn on the upper part of the body, esp. by men, usually having a collar and sleeves and buttoning up the front. **2** short for **nightshirt. 3 keep your shirt on.** *Inf.* refrain from losing your temper. **4 put** *or* **lose one's shirt on.** *Inf.* to bet or lose all one has on (a horse, etc.). [OE *scyrte*]

shirting (ˈʃɜːtɪŋ) *n* fabric used in making men's shirts.

shirt-lifter *n Derog. sl.* a male homosexual.

shirtsleeve (ˈʃɜːtˌsliːv) *n* **1** the sleeve of a shirt. **2 in one's shirtsleeves.** not wearing a jacket.

shirt-tail *n* the part of a shirt that extends below the waist.

THESAURUS

shillyshally *vb* **1** *Informal* = **be irresolute** *or* **indecisive**, dilly-dally (*inf.*), dither (*chiefly Brit.*), falter, fluctuate, haver (*Brit.*), hem and haw *or* hum and haw, hesitate, seesaw, swither (*Scot.*), vacillate, waver, yo-yo (*inf.*)

shimmer *vb* **1** = **gleam**, dance, glimmer, glisten, phosphoresce, scintillate, twinkle ◆ *n* **2** = **gleam**, diffused light, glimmer, glow, incandescence, iridescence, lustre, phosphorescence, unsteady light

shin *vb* **4** *with* **up** = **climb**, ascend, clamber, scale, scramble, swarm

shine *vb* **1, 2** = **gleam**, beam, emit light, flash, give off light, glare, glimmer, glisten, glitter, glow, radiate, scintillate, shimmer, sparkle, twinkle **4** = **polish**, brush, buff, burnish, rub up **5** = **be outstanding**, be conspicuous, be distinguished, be pre-eminent, excel, stand out, stand out in a crowd, star, steal the show ◆ *n* **7** = **brightness**, glaze, gloss, light, luminosity, lustre, patina, radiance, sheen, shimmer, sparkle

shining *adj* **2** = **bright**, aglow, beaming, brilliant, effulgent, gleaming, glistening, glittering, luminous, radiant, resplendent, shimmering, sparkling **5** = **outstanding**, brilliant, celebrated, conspicuous, distinguished, eminent, glorious, illustrious, leading, splendid

shiny *adj* **1** = **bright**, agleam, burnished, gleaming, glistening, glossy, lustrous, nitid (*poetic*), polished, satiny, sheeny

ship *n* **1** = **vessel**, boat, craft

shipshape *adj* **1** = **tidy**, Bristol fashion, businesslike, neat, orderly, spick-and-span, trig (*arch. or dialect*), trim, uncluttered, well-ordered, well-organized, well-regulated

shirk *vb* **1** = **dodge**, avoid, body-swerve (*Scot.*), duck (out of) (*inf.*), evade, get out of, scrimshank (*Brit. military sl.*), shun, sidestep, skive (*Brit. sl.*), slack

shirker *n* **2** = **slacker**, clock-watcher, dodger, gold brick (*US sl.*), idler, malingerer, quitter, scrimshanker (*Brit. military sl.*), shirk, skiver (*Brit. sl.*)

shirtwaister ('ʃɜːtˌweɪstə) *or US* **shirtwaist** *n* a woman's dress with a tailored bodice resembling a shirt.

shirty ('ʃɜːtɪ) *adj* **shirtier, shirtiest.** *Sl., chiefly Brit.* bad-tempered or annoyed. [C19: ? based on such phrases as *to get someone's shirt out* to annoy someone]
▸ '**shirtily** *adv*

shish kebab ('ʃiːʃ kə'bæb) *n* a dish consisting of small pieces of meat and vegetables threaded onto skewers and grilled. [from Turkish *şiş kebab*, from *şiş* skewer; see KEBAB]

shit (ʃɪt) *Taboo.* ◆ *vb* **shits, shitting; shitted, shit,** *or* **shat. 1** to defecate. **2** (usually foll. by *on*) *Sl.* to give the worst possible treatment (to). ◆ *n* **3** faeces; excrement. **4** an act of defecation. **5** *Sl.* rubbish; nonsense. **6** *Sl.* an obnoxious or worthless person. ◆ *interj* **7** *Sl.* an exclamation expressing anger, disgust, etc. [OE *scite* (unattested) dung, *scītan* to defecate, of Gmc origin]
▸ '**shitty** *adj*

shiv (ʃɪv) *n* a variant of **chiv.**

Shiva ('ʃiːvə, 'ʃɪvə) *n* a variant spelling of **Siva.**

shivaree (ˌʃɪvə'riː) *n* a variant spelling (esp. US and Canad.) of **charivari.**

shiver[1] ❶ ('ʃɪvə) *vb* (*intr*) **1** to shake or tremble, as from cold or fear. ◆ *n* **2** the act of shivering; a tremulous motion. **3 the shivers.** an attack of shivering, esp. through fear or illness. [C13 *chiveren*, ? var. of *chevelen* to chatter (used of teeth), from OE *ceafl* jowl]
▸ '**shiverer** *n* ▸ '**shivering** *n, adj* ▸ '**shivery** *adj*

shiver[2] ❶ ('ʃɪvə) *vb* **1** to break or cause to break into fragments. ◆ *n* **2** a splintered piece. [C13: of Gmc origin]

shoal[1] ❶ (ʃəʊl) *n* **1** a stretch of shallow water. **2** a sandbank or rocky area, esp. one that is visible at low water. ◆ *vb* **3** to make or become shallow. **4** (*intr*) *Naut.* to sail into shallower water. ◆ *adj also* **shoaly. 5** a less common word for **shallow.** [OE *sceald* shallow]

shoal[2] (ʃəʊl) *n* **1** a large group of fish. **2** a large group of people or things. ◆ *vb* **3** (*intr*) to collect together in such a group. [OE *scolu*]

shock[1] ❶ (ʃɒk) *vb* **1** to experience or cause to experience extreme horror, disgust, surprise, etc.: *the atrocities shocked us.* **2** to cause a state of shock in (a person). **3** to come or cause to come into violent contact. ◆ *n* **4** a sudden and violent jarring blow or impact. **5** something that causes a sudden and violent disturbance in the emotions. **6** *Pathol.* a state of bodily collapse, as from severe bleeding, burns, fright, etc. **7** Also: **electric shock.** pain and muscular spasm as the physical reaction to an electric current passing through the body. [C16: from OF *choc*, from *choquier* to make violent contact with, of Gmc origin]
▸ '**shockable** *adj* ▸ ˌ**shocka'bility** *n*

shock[2] (ʃɒk) *n* **1** a number of sheaves set on end in a field to dry. **2** a pile or stack of unthreshed corn. ◆ *vb* **3** (*tr*) to set up (sheaves) in shocks. [C14: prob. of Gmc origin]

shock[3] (ʃɒk) *n* a thick bushy mass, esp. of hair. [C19: ?from SHOCK[2]]

shock absorber *n* any device designed to absorb mechanical shock, esp. one fitted to a motor vehicle to damp the recoil of the road springs.

shocker ('ʃɒkə) *n Inf.* **1** a person or thing that shocks. **2** a sensational novel, film, or play.

shockheaded ('ʃɒkˌhedɪd) *adj* having a head of bushy or tousled hair.

shock-horror *adj Facetious.* (esp. of newspaper headlines) sensationalistic: *shock-horror stories about the British diet.*

shocking ❶ ('ʃɒkɪŋ) *adj* **1** causing shock, horror, or disgust. **2 shocking pink. 2a** of a garish shade of pink. **2b** (*as n*): *dressed in shocking pink.* **3** *Inf.* very bad or terrible: *shocking weather.*
▸ '**shockingly** *adv*

shockproof ('ʃɒkˌpruːf) *adj* capable of absorbing shock without damage.

shock therapy *or* **treatment** *n* the treatment of certain psychotic conditions by injecting drugs or by passing an electric current through the brain (**electroconvulsive therapy**) to produce convulsions or coma.

shock troops *pl n* soldiers specially trained and equipped to carry out an assault.

shock wave *n* a region across which there is a rapid pressure, temperature, and density rise caused by a body moving supersonically in a gas or by a detonation. See also **sonic boom.**

shod (ʃɒd) *vb* the past participle of **shoe.**

shoddy ❶ ('ʃɒdɪ) *adj* **shoddier, shoddiest. 1** imitating something of better quality. **2** of poor quality. ◆ *n, pl* **shoddies. 3** a yarn or fabric made from wool waste or clippings. **4** anything of inferior quality that is designed to simulate superior quality. [C19: from ?]
▸ '**shoddily** *adv* ▸ '**shoddiness** *n*

shoe (ʃuː) *n* **1a** one of a matching pair of coverings shaped to fit the foot, esp. one ending below the ankle, having an upper of leather, plastic, etc., on a sole and heel of heavier material. **1b** (*as modifier*): *shoe cleaner.* **2** anything resembling a shoe in shape, function, position, etc., such as a horseshoe. **3** a band of metal or wood on the bottom of the runner of a sledge. **4** *Engineering.* a lining to protect from wear: see **brake shoe. 5 be in (a person's) shoes.** *Inf.* to be in (another person's) situation. ◆ *vb* **shoes, shoeing, shod.** (*tr*) **6** to furnish with shoes. **7** to fit (a horse) with horseshoes. **8** to furnish with a hard cover, such as a metal plate, for protection against friction or bruising. [OE *scōh*]

shoeblack ('ʃuːˌblæk) *n* (esp. formerly) a person who shines boots and shoes.

shoehorn ('ʃuːˌhɔːn) *n* **1** a smooth curved implement of horn, metal, plastic, etc., inserted at the heel of a shoe to ease the foot into it. ◆ *vb* (*tr*) **2** to cram (people or things) into a small space.

shoelace ('ʃuːˌleɪs) *n* a cord for fastening shoes.

shoe leather *n* **1** leather used to make shoes. **2 save shoe leather.** to avoid wearing out shoes, as by taking a bus rather than walking.

shoemaker ❶ ('ʃuːˌmeɪkə) *n* a person who makes or repairs shoes or boots.
▸ '**shoeˌmaking** *n*

shoer ('ʃuːə) *n Rare.* a person who shoes horses; farrier.

shoeshine ('ʃuːˌʃaɪn) *n* the act or an instance of polishing a pair of shoes.

shoestring ('ʃuːˌstrɪŋ) *n* **1** another word for **shoelace. 2** *Inf.* a very small or petty amount of money (esp. in **on a shoestring**).

shoetree ('ʃuːˌtriː) *n* a wooden or metal form inserted into a shoe or boot to stretch it or preserve its shape.

shofar *or* **shophar** (*Hebrew* ʃɔ'far) *n, pl* **shofars, shophars** *or* **shofroth, shophroth** (*Hebrew* -'frɔt). *Judaism.* a ram's horn sounded on certain religious occasions. [from Heb. *shōphār* ram's horn]

shogun ('ʃəʊˌguːn) *n Japanese history.* (from about 1192 to 1867) any of a line of hereditary military dictators who relegated the emperors to a position of purely theoretical supremacy. [C17: from Japanese, from Chinese *chiang chün* general, from *chiang* to lead + *chün* army]
▸ '**shogunate** *n*

shogun bond *n* a bond sold on the Japanese market by a foreign institution and denominated in a foreign currency. Cf. **samurai bond.**

shone (ʃɒn; *US* ʃəʊn) *vb* a past tense and past participle of **shine.**

shoo (ʃuː) *sentence substitute.* **1** go away!: used to drive away unwanted or annoying people, animals, etc. ◆ *vb* **shoos, shooing, shooed. 2** (*tr*) to drive away by or as if by crying "shoo". **3** (*intr*) to cry "shoo". [C15: imit.]

shoo-in *n US & Canad.* **1** a person or thing that is certain to win or succeed. **2** a match or contest that is easy to win.

shook[1] (ʃʊk) *n* **1** a set of parts ready for assembly, esp. of a barrel. **2** a group of sheaves piled together on end; shock. [C18: from ?]

shook[2] (ʃʊk) *vb* the past tense of **shake.**

shoon (ʃuːn) *n Dialect, chiefly Scot.* a plural of **shoe.**

shoot ❶ (ʃuːt) *vb* **shoots, shooting, shot. 1** (*tr*) to hit, wound, damage, or kill with a missile discharged from a weapon. **2** to discharge (a missile or missiles) from a weapon. **3** to fire (a weapon) or (of a weapon) to be fired. **4** to send out or be sent out as if from a weapon: *he shot questions at her.* **5** (*intr*) to move very rapidly. **6** (*tr*) to slide or push into or out of a fastening: *to shoot a bolt.* **7** to emit (a ray of light) or (of a ray of light) to be emitted. **8** (*tr*) to go or pass quickly over or through: *to shoot rapids.* **9** (*intr*) to hunt game with a gun for sport. **10** (*tr*) to pass over (an area) in hunting game. **11** (*intr*) (of a plant) to produce (buds, branches, etc.). **12** to photograph or record (a sequence, etc.). **13** (*tr; usually passive*) to variegate or streak, as with colour. **14** *Soccer, hockey, etc.* to hit or propel (the ball, etc.) towards the goal. **15** (*tr*) *Sport, chiefly US & Canad.* to score (strokes, etc.): *he shot 72 on the first round.* **16** (*tr*) to measure the altitude of (a celestial body). **17** (often foll. by *up*) *Sl.* to inject (someone, esp. oneself) with (a drug, esp. heroin). **18 shoot a line.** *Sl.* **18a** to boast. **18b** to tell a lie. **19 shoot oneself in the foot.** *Inf.* to

THESAURUS

shiver[1] *vb* **1** = **tremble**, palpitate, quake, quiver, shake, shudder ◆ *n* **2** = **trembling**, flutter, *frisson*, quiver, shudder, thrill, tremble, tremor **3 the shivers** = **the shakes** (*inf.*), chattering teeth, chill, goose flesh, goose pimples

shiver[2] *vb* **1** = **splinter**, break, crack, fragment, shatter, smash, smash to smithereens

shivery *adj* **2** = **shaking**, chilled, chilly, cold, quaking, quivery, shuddery, trembly

shoal[1] *n* **1** = **shallow 2** = **sandbank**, sand bar, shelf

shock[1] *vb* **1** = **horrify**, agitate, appal, disgust, disquiet, give (someone) a turn (*inf.*), gross out (*US sl.*), nauseate, offend, outrage, raise eyebrows, revolt, scandalize, sicken, traumatize, unsettle **2** = **astound**, jar, jolt, numb, paralyse, shake, shake out of one's complacency, shake up (*inf.*), stagger, stun, stupefy ◆ *n* **4** = **impact**, blow, clash, collision, encounter, jarring, jolt **5** = **upset**, blow, bolt from the blue, bombshell, breakdown, collapse, consternation, distress, disturbance, prostration, rude awakening, state of shock, stupefaction, stupor, trauma, turn (*inf.*), whammy (*inf., chiefly US*)

shocking *adj* **1** = **dreadful**, abominable, appalling, atrocious, detestable, disgraceful, disgusting, disquieting, distressing, foul, frightful, from hell (*inf.*), ghastly, hideous, horrible, horrifying, loathsome, monstrous, nauseating, obscene, odious, offensive, outrageous, repulsive, revolting, scandalous, sickening, stupefying, unspeakable, X-rated (*inf.*)
Antonyms *adj* admirable, decent, delightful, excellent, fine, first-rate, gratifying, honourable, laudable, marvellous, pleasant, praiseworthy, satisfying, wonderful

shoddy *adj* **1, 2** = **inferior**, cheap, cheap-jack (*inf.*), cheapo (*inf.*), junky (*inf.*), low-rent (*inf., chiefly US*), poor, rubbishy, second-rate, slipshod, tacky (*inf.*), tatty, tawdry, trashy
Antonyms *adj* accurate, careful, considerate, craftsman-like, excellent, fine, first-rate, meticulous, quality, superlative, well-made

shoemaker *n* = **cobbler**, bootmaker, souter (*Scot.*)

shoot *vb* **1** = **hit**, bag, blast, blow away (*sl., chiefly US*), bring down, kill, open fire, pick off, plug (*sl.*), pump full of lead (*sl.*), zap (*sl.*) **2, 3** = **fire**, discharge, emit, fling, hurl, launch, let fly, project, propel **5** = **speed**, barrel (along) (*inf., chiefly US & Canad.*), bolt, burn rubber (*inf.*), charge, dart, dash, flash, fly, hurtle, race, rush, scoot, spring, streak, tear, whisk, whizz (*inf.*) **11** = **sprout**, bud, burgeon, germinate, put forth new growth ◆ *n* **22, 23** = **sprout**, branch, bud, offshoot, scion, slip, sprig, twig

damage one's own cause inadvertently. ◆ *n* **20** the act of shooting. **21** the action or motion of something that is shot. **22** the first aerial part of a plant to develop from a germinating seed. **23** any new growth of a plant, such as a bud, etc. **24** *Chiefly Brit.* a meeting or party organized for hunting game with guns. **25** an area where game can be hunted with guns. **26** a steep descent in a stream; rapid. **27** *Inf.* a photographic assignment **28 the whole shoot.** *Sl.* everything. ◆ *interj* **29** *US & Canad.* an exclamation expressing disbelief, scepticism, disappointment, etc. ◆ See also **shoot down, shoot through.** [OE *sceōtan*]

shoot down *vb* (*tr, adv*) **1** to shoot callously. **2** to defeat or disprove: *he shot down her argument.*

shoot-'em-up *or* **shoot-em-up** *n Inf.* **1** a type of computer game, the object of which is to shoot as many enemies, targets, etc. as possible. **2** a fast-moving film involving many gunfights, battles, etc.

shooter ('ʃuːtə) *n* **1** a person or thing that shoots. **2** *Sl.* a gun.

shooting box *n* a small country house providing accommodation for a shooting party. Also called: **shooting lodge.**

shooting brake *n Brit.* another name for **estate car.**

shooting star *n Inf.* a meteor.

shooting stick *n* a device that resembles a walking stick, having a spike at one end and a folding seat at the other.

shoot through *vb* (*intr, adv*) *Austral. inf.* to leave; go away.

shop ❶ (ʃɒp) *n* **1** a place, esp. a small building, for the retail sale of goods and services. **2** an act or instance of shopping. **3** a place for the performance of a specified type of work; workshop. **4 all over the shop.** *Inf.* **4a** in disarray: *his papers were all over the shop.* **4b** in every direction: *I've searched for it all over the shop.* **5 shut up shop.** to close business at the end of the day or permanently. **6 talk shop.** *Inf.* to discuss one's business, profession, etc., esp. on a social occasion. ◆ *vb* **shops, shopping, shopped.** **7** (*intr;* often foll. by *for*) to visit a shop or shops in search of (goods) with the intention of buying them. **8** (*tr*) *Sl., chiefly Brit.* to inform on (someone), esp. to the police. [OE *sceoppa* stall]
▸**'shopping** *n*

shop around *vb* (*intr, adv*) *Inf.* **1** to visit a number of shops or stores to compare goods and prices. **2** to consider a number of possibilities before making a choice.

shop assistant *n* a person who serves in a shop.

shop floor *n* **1** the part of a factory housing the machines and men directly involved in production. **2** workers, esp. factory workers organized in a union.

shopkeeper ('ʃɒpˌkiːpə) *n* a person who owns or manages a shop or small store.
▸**'shopˌkeeping** *n*

shoplifter ('ʃɒpˌlɪftə) *n* a customer who steals goods from a shop.
▸**'shopˌlifting** *n*

shopper ('ʃɒpə) *n* **1** a person who buys goods in a shop. **2** a bag for shopping.

shopping centre *n* **1** a purpose-built complex of stores, restaurants, etc. **2** the area of a town where most of the shops are situated.

shopping mall *n* a large enclosed shopping centre.

shopping plaza *n Chiefly US & Canad.* a shopping centre, esp. a small group of stores built as a strip.

shopsoiled ('ʃɒpˌsɔɪld) *adj* worn, faded, etc., from being displayed in a shop or store.

shop steward *n* an elected representative of the union workers in a shop, factory, etc.

shoptalk ('ʃɒpˌtɔːk) *n* conversation concerning one's work, esp. when carried on outside business hours.

shopwalker ('ʃɒpˌwɔːkə) *n Brit.* a person employed by a departmental store to supervise sales personnel, assist customers, etc.

shoran ('ʃɔːræn) *n* a short-range radar system by which an aircraft, ship, etc., can accurately determine its position. [C20: *sho(rt-)ra(nge) n(avigation)*]

shore[1] ❶ (ʃɔː) *n* **1** the land along the edge of a sea, lake, or wide river. Related adj: **littoral. 2a** land, as opposed to water. **2b** (*as modifier*)*: shore duty.* **3** *Law.* the tract of coastland lying between the ordinary marks of high and low water. **4** (*often pl*) a country: *his native shores.* [C14: prob. from MLow G, MDu. *schōre*]

shore[2] ❶ (ʃɔː) *n* **1** a prop or beam used to support a wall, building, etc. ◆ *vb* **shores, shoring, shored. 2** (*tr;* often foll. by *up*) to make safe with or as if with a shore. [C15: from MDu. *schōre*]
▸**'shoring** *n*

shore[3] (ʃɔː) *vb Arch., Austral., & NZ.* a past tense of **shear.**

shore bird *n* any of various birds that live close to water, esp. plovers, sandpipers, etc. Also called (Brit.): **wader.**

shore leave *n Naval.* **1** permission to go ashore. **2** time spent ashore during leave.

shoreless ('ʃɔːlɪs) *adj* **1** without a shore suitable for landing. **2** *Poetic.* boundless; vast.

shoreline ('ʃɔːˌlaɪn) *n* the edge of a body of water.

shoreward ('ʃɔːwəd) *adj* **1** near or facing the shore. ◆ *adv also* **shorewards. 2** towards the shore.

shorn (ʃɔːn) *vb* a past participle of **shear.**

short ❶ (ʃɔːt) *adj* **1** of little length; not long. **2** of little height; not tall. **3** of limited duration. **4** deficient: *the number of places laid at the table was short by four.* **5** (*postpositive;* often foll. by *of* or *on*) lacking (in) or needful (of): *I'm always short of money.* **6** concise; succinct. **7** (of drinks) consisting chiefly of a spirit, such as whisky. **8** *Cricket.* (of a fielding position) near the batsman: *short leg.* **9** lacking in the power of retentiveness: *a short memory.* **10** abrupt to the point of rudeness: *the salesgirl was very short with him.* **11** (of betting odds) almost even. **12** *Finance.* **12a** not possessing the securities or commodities that have been sold under contract and therefore obliged to make a purchase before the delivery date. **12b** of or relating to such sales, which depend on falling prices for profit. **13** *Phonetics.* **13a** denoting a vowel of relatively brief temporal duration. **13b** (in popular usage) denoting the qualities of the five English vowels represented orthographically in the words *pat, pet, pit, pot, put,* and *putt.* **14** *Prosody.* **14a** denoting a vowel that is phonetically short or a syllable containing such a vowel. **14b** (of a vowel or syllable in verse) not carrying emphasis or accent. **15** (of pastry) crumbly in texture. **16 in short supply.** scarce. **17 short and sweet.** unexpectedly brief. **18 short for.** an abbreviation for. ◆ *adv* **19** abruptly: *to stop short.* **20** briefly or concisely. **21** rudely or curtly. **22** *Finance.* without possessing the securities or commodities at the time of their contractual sale: *to sell short.* **23 caught** *or* **taken short.** having a sudden need to urinate or defecate. **24 go short.** not to have a sufficient amount, etc. **25 short of.** except: *nothing short of a miracle can save him now.* ◆ *n* **26** anything that is short. **27** a drink of spirits. **28** *Phonetics, prosody.* a short vowel or syllable. **29** *Finance.* **29a** a short contract or sale. **29b** a short seller. **30** a short film, usually of a factual nature. **31** See **short circuit. 32 for short.** *Inf.* as a shortened form: *he is called J.R. for short.* **33 in short. 33a** as a summary. **33b** in a few words. ◆ *vb* **34** See **short circuit** (sense 2). ◆ See also **shorts.** [OE *scort*]
▸**'shortness** *n*

short-acting *adj* (of a drug) quickly effective, but requiring regularly repeated doses for long-term treatment. Cf. **intermediate-acting, long-acting.**

shortage ❶ ('ʃɔːtɪdʒ) *n* a deficiency or lack in the amount needed, expected, or due; deficit.

shortbread ('ʃɔːtˌbrɛd) *n* a rich crumbly biscuit made with a large proportion of butter.

shortcake ('ʃɔːtˌkeɪk) *n* **1** shortbread. **2** a dessert made of layers of biscuit or cake filled with fruit and cream.

short-change *vb* **short-changes, short-changing, short-changed.** (*tr*) **1** to give less than correct change to. **2** *Sl.* to treat unfairly or dishonestly, esp. by giving less than is expected or deserved.

short circuit *n* **1** a faulty or accidental connection between two points of different potential in an electric circuit, establishing a path of low resistance through which an excessive current can flow. ◆ *vb* **short-circuit. 2** to develop or cause to develop a short circuit. **3** (*tr*) to bypass (a procedure, etc.). **4** (*tr*) to hinder or frustrate (plans, etc.). ◆ Sometimes (for senses 1, 2) shortened to **short.**

shortcoming ❶ ('ʃɔːtˌkʌmɪŋ) *n* a failing, defect, or deficiency.

short corner *n Hockey.* another name for **penalty corner.**

short covering *n* the purchase of securities or commodities by a short seller to meet delivery requirements.

shortcrust pastry ('ʃɔːtˌkrʌst) *n* a basic type of pastry that has a crisp but crumbly texture. Also: **short pastry.**

short cut *n* **1** a route that is shorter than the usual one. **2** a means of saving time or effort. ◆ *vb* **short-cut, short-cuts, short-cutting, short-cut. 3** (*intr*) to use a short cut.

short-dated *adj* (of a gilt-edged security) having less than five years to run before redemption. Cf. **medium-dated, long-dated.**

short-day *adj* (of plants) able to flower only if exposed to short periods of daylight, each followed by a long dark period. Cf. **long-day.**

THESAURUS

shop *n* **1** = **store**, boutique, emporium, hypermarket, market, mart, supermarket

shore[1] *n* **1** = **beach**, coast, foreshore, lakeside, sands, seaboard (*chiefly US*), seashore, strand (*poetic*), waterside

shore[2] *vb* **2** *with* **up** = **support**, augment, brace, buttress, hold, prop, reinforce, strengthen, underpin

short *adj* **1** = **concise**, abridged, brief, clipped, compendious, compressed, curtailed, laconic, pithy, sententious, succinct, summary, terse **2** = **small**, diminutive, dumpy, fubsy (*arch. or dialect*), knee high to a gnat, knee high to a grasshopper, little, low, petite, squat, wee **3** = **brief**, fleeting, momentary, short-lived, short-term **5** *often with* **of** *or* **on** = **lacking**, deficient, inadequate, in need of, insufficient, limited, low (on), meagre, missing, poor, scant, scanty, scarce, short-handed, slender, slim, sparse, strapped (for) (*sl.*), tight, wanting **10** = **abrupt**, blunt, brusque, crusty, curt, discourteous, gruff, impolite, offhand, sharp, terse, testy, uncivil **15** = **crumbly**, brittle, crisp, friable ◆ *adv* **19** = **abruptly**, by surprise, suddenly, unaware, without warning **25 short of** = **except**, apart from, other than, unless ◆ *n* **33 in short** = **briefly**, in a nutshell, in a word, in essence, to come to the point, to cut a long story short, to put it briefly
Antonyms *adj* ≠ **concise:** diffuse, lengthy, long, long-drawn-out, long-winded, prolonged, rambling, unabridged, verbose, wordy ≠ **small:** big, high, lanky, lofty, tall ≠ **brief:** extended, long, long-term ≠ **lacking:** abundant, adequate, ample, bountiful, copious, inexhaustible, plentiful, sufficient, well-stocked ≠ **abrupt:** civil, courteous, polite ◆ *adv* ≠ **abruptly:** bit by bit, gently, gradually, little by little, slowly

shortage *n* = **deficiency**, dearth, deficit, failure, inadequacy, insufficiency, lack, leanness, paucity, poverty, scarcity, shortfall, want
Antonyms *n* abundance, adequate amount, excess, overabundance, plethora, profusion, sufficiency, surfeit, surplus

shortcoming *n* = **failing**, defect, drawback, fault, flaw, foible, frailty, imperfection, weakness, weak point

shorten ➊ (ˈʃɔːtᵊn) *vb* **1** to make or become short or shorter. **2** (*tr*) *Naut.* to reduce the area of (sail). **3** (*tr*) to make (pastry, etc.) short, by adding fat. **4** *Gambling.* to cause (the odds) to lessen or (of odds) to become less.

shortening (ˈʃɔːtᵊnɪŋ) *n* butter or other fat, used in a dough, etc., to make the mixture short.

Shorter Catechism *n Chiefly Presbyterian Church.* the more widely used of two catechisms of religious instruction drawn up in 1647.

shortfall (ˈʃɔːtˌfɔːl) *n* **1** failure to meet a goal or a requirement. **2** the amount of such a failure.

shorthand (ˈʃɔːtˌhænd) *n* **a** a system of rapid handwriting employing simple strokes and other symbols to represent words or phrases. **b** (*as modifier*): *a shorthand typist.*

short-handed *adj* **1** lacking the usual or necessary number of assistants, workers, etc. **2** *Sport, US & Canad.* with less than the full complement of players.

shorthand typist *n Brit.* a person skilled in the use of shorthand and in typing. US and Canad. name: **stenographer.**

short head *n Horse racing.* a distance shorter than the length of a horse's head.

shorthorn (ˈʃɔːtˌhɔːn) *n* a short-horned breed of cattle with several regional varieties.

shortie *or* **shorty** (ˈʃɔːtɪ) *n, pl* **shorties.** *Inf.* **a** a person or thing that is extremely short. **b** (*as modifier*): *a shortie nightdress.*

short list *Chiefly Brit.* ◆ *n* **1** Also called (Scot.): **short leet.** a list of suitable applicants for a job, post, etc., from which the successful candidate will be selected. ◆ *vb* **short-list.** (*tr*) **2** to put (someone) on a short list.

short-lived ➊ *adj* living or lasting only for a short time.

shortly ➊ (ˈʃɔːtlɪ) *adv* **1** in a short time; soon. **2** briefly. **3** in a curt or rude manner.

short-order *adj Chiefly US.* of or connected with food that is easily and quickly prepared.

short-range *adj* of small or limited extent in time or distance: *a short-range forecast.*

shorts (ʃɔːts) *pl n* **1** trousers reaching the top of the thigh or partway to the knee, worn by both sexes for sport, etc. **2** *Chiefly US & Canad.* men's underpants that usually reach mid-thigh. **3** short-dated gilt-edged securities. **4** short-term bonds. **5** securities or commodities that have been sold short. **6** a livestock feed containing a large proportion of bran and wheat germ.

short shrift *n* **1** brief and unsympathetic treatment. **2** (formerly) a brief period allowed to a condemned prisoner to make confession. **3 make short shrift of.** to dispose of quickly.

short-sighted ➊ *adj* **1** relating to or suffering from myopia. **2** lacking foresight: *a short-sighted plan.*
▸ **ˌshort-ˈsightedly** *adv* ▸ **ˌshort-ˈsightedness** *n*

short-spoken *adj* tending to be abrupt in speech.

short story *n* a prose narrative of shorter length than the novel.

short-tempered ➊ *adj* easily moved to anger.

short-term *adj* **1** of, for, or extending over a limited period. **2** *Finance.* extending over, maturing within, or required within a short period of time, usually twelve months: *short-term credit; short-term capital.*

short-termism (-ˈtɜːmɪzəm) *n* the tendency to focus attention on short-term gains, often at the expense of long-term success or stability.

short time *n* the state or condition of working less than the normal working week, esp. because of a business recession.

short ton *n* the full name for **ton**[1] (sense 2).

short-waisted *adj* unusually short from the shoulders to the waist.

short wave *n* **a** a radio wave with a wavelength in the range 10–100 metres. **b** (*as modifier*): *a short-wave broadcast.*

short-winded *adj* **1** tending to run out of breath, esp. after exertion. **2** (of speech or writing) terse or abrupt.

shot[1] ➊ (ʃɒt) *n* **1** the act or an instance of discharging a projectile. **2** (*pl* **shot**) a solid missile, such as an iron ball or a lead pellet, discharged from a firearm. **3a** small round pellets of lead collectively, as used in cartridges. **3b** metal in the form of coarse powder or small pellets. **4** the distance that a discharged projectile travels or is capable of travelling. **5** a person who shoots, esp. with regard to his ability: *he is a good shot.* **6** *Inf.* an attempt. **7** *Inf.* a guess. **8** any act of throwing or hitting something, as in certain sports. **9** the launching of a rocket, etc., esp. to a specified destination: *a moon shot.* **10a** a single photograph. **10b** a length of film taken by a single camera without breaks. **11** *Inf.* an injection, as of a vaccine or narcotic drug. **12** *Inf.* a glass of alcoholic drink, esp. spirits. **13** *Sport.* a heavy metal ball used in the shot put. **14 call the shots.** *Sl.* to have control over an organization, etc. **15 have a shot at.** *Inf.* to attempt. **16 like a shot.** very quickly, esp. willingly. **17 shot in the arm.** *Inf.* anything that regenerates, increases confidence or efficiency, etc. **18 shot in the dark.** a wild guess. [OE *scot*]

shot[2] ➊ (ʃɒt) *vb* **1** the past tense and past participle of **shoot.** ◆ *adj* **2** (of textiles) woven to give a changing colour effect: *shot silk.* **3** streaked with colour.

shotgun (ˈʃɒtˌgʌn) *n* **1** a shoulder firearm with unrifled bore used mainly for hunting small game. **2** *American football.* an offensive formation in which the quarterback lines up for a snap unusually far behind the line of scrimmage. ◆ *adj* **3** *Chiefly US.* involving coercion or duress: *a shotgun merger.*

shotgun wedding *n Inf.* a wedding into which one or both partners are coerced, usually because the woman is pregnant.

shot put *n* an athletic event in which contestants hurl or put a heavy metal ball or shot as far as possible.
▸ **ˈshot-ˌputter** *n*

shotten (ˈʃɒtᵊn) *adj* **1** (of fish, esp. herring) having recently spawned. **2** *Arch.* worthless. [C15: from obs. p.p. of SHOOT]

shot tower *n* a building formerly used in the production of shot, in which molten lead was graded and dropped from a great height into water, thus cooling it and forming the shot.

should (ʃʊd) *vb* the past tense of **shall:** used as an auxiliary verb to indicate that an action is considered by the speaker to be obligatory (*you should go*) or to form the subjunctive mood with *I* or *we* (*I should like to see you*). [OE *sceold*]

> **USAGE NOTE** *Should* has, as its most common meaning in modern English, the sense *ought* as in *I should go to the graduation, but I don't see how I can.* However, the older sense of the subjunctive of *shall* is often used with *I* or *we* to indicate a more polite form than *would: I should like to go, but I can't.* In much speech and writing, *should* has been replaced by *would* in contexts of this kind, but it remains in formal English when a conditional subjunctive is used: *should he choose to remain, he would be granted asylum.*

shoulder ➊ (ˈʃəʊldə) *n* **1** the part of the vertebrate body where the arm or a corresponding forelimb joins the trunk. **2** the joint at the junction of the forelimb with the pectoral girdle. **3** a cut of meat including the upper part of the foreleg. **4** *Printing.* the flat surface of a piece of type from which the face rises. **5** the part of a garment that covers the shoulder. **6** anything that resembles a shoulder in shape or position. **7** the strip of unpaved land that borders a road. **8 a shoulder to cry on.** a person one turns to for sympathy with one's troubles. **9 give (someone) the cold shoulder.** *Inf.* **9a** to treat in a cold manner; snub. **9b** to ignore or shun. **10 put one's shoulder to the wheel.** *Inf.* to work very hard. **11 rub shoulders with.** *Inf.* to mix with socially or associate with. **12 shoulder to shoulder. 12a** side by side. **12b** in a corporate effort. ◆ *vb* **13** (*tr*) to bear or carry (a burden, etc.) as if on one's shoulders. **14** to push (something) with or as if with the shoulder. **15** (*tr*) to lift or carry on the shoulders. **16 shoulder arms.** *Mil.* to bring the rifle vertically close to the right side with the muzzle uppermost. [OE *sculdor*]

shoulder blade ➊ *n* the nontechnical name for **scapula.**

shoulder strap *n* a strap over the shoulders, as to hold up a garment or to support a bag, etc.

shouldn't (ˈʃʊdᵊnt) *contraction of* should not.

shouldst (ʃʊdst) *or* **shouldest** (ˈʃʊdɪst) *vb Arch. or dialect.* (used with the pronoun *thou*) a form of the past tense of **shall.**

shout ➊ (ʃaʊt) *n* **1** a loud cry, esp. to convey emotion or a command. **2** *Inf.* **2a** a round, esp. of drinks. **2b** one's turn to buy a round of drinks. ◆ *vb* **3** to utter (something) in a loud cry. **4** (*intr*) to make a loud noise.

THESAURUS

shorten *vb* **1** = **cut**, abbreviate, abridge, curtail, cut back, cut down, decrease, diminish, dock, downsize, lessen, prune, reduce, trim, truncate, turn up
Antonyms *vb* draw out, elongate, expand, extend, increase, lengthen, make longer, prolong, protract, spin out, stretch

short-lived *adj* = **brief**, ephemeral, fleeting, impermanent, passing, short, temporary, transient, transitory

shortly *adv* **1** = **soon**, anon, any minute now, before long, erelong (*arch. or poetic*), in a little while, presently **2** = **briefly**, concisely, in a few words, succinctly **3** = **curtly**, abruptly, sharply, tartly, tersely

short-sighted *adj* **1** = **near-sighted**, blind as a bat, myopic **2** = **unthinking**, careless, ill-advised, ill-considered, impolitic, impractical, improvident, imprudent, injudicious, seeing no further than (the end of) one's nose

short-tempered *adj* = **quick-tempered**, choleric, fiery, hot-tempered, impatient, irascible, peppery, ratty (*Brit. & NZ inf.*), testy, touchy

shot[1] *n* **1** = **throw**, discharge, lob, pot shot **2** = **pellet**, ball, bullet, lead, projectile, slug **5** = **marksman**, shooter **6** *Informal* = **attempt**, chance, crack (*inf.*), effort, endeavour, essay, go (*inf.*), opportunity, stab (*inf.*), try, turn **7** *Informal* = **guess**, conjecture, surmise **15 have a shot at** *Informal* = **attempt**, have a bash (*inf.*), have a crack (*inf.*), have a go, have a stab (*inf.*), tackle, try, try one's luck **16 like a shot** = **at once**, eagerly, immediately, like a bat out of hell (*sl.*), like a flash, quickly, unhesitatingly **17 shot in the arm** *Informal* = **boost**, encouragement, fillip, geeing-up, impetus, lift, stimulus

shot[2] *adj* **2, 3** = **iridescent**, moiré, opalescent, watered

shoulder *n* **9 give (someone) the cold shoulder** *Informal* = **snub**, blank, cut (*inf.*), ignore, kick in the teeth (*sl.*), ostracize, put down, rebuff, send (someone) to Coventry, shun **10 put one's shoulder to the wheel** *Informal* = **work hard**, apply oneself, buckle down to (*inf.*), exert oneself, get down to, make every effort, set to work, strive **11 rub shoulders with** *Informal* = **mix with**, associate with, consort with, fraternize with, hobnob with, socialize with **12 shoulder to shoulder: a** = **side by side b** = **together** as one, in cooperation, in partnership, in unity, jointly, united ◆ *vb* **13** = **bear**, accept, assume, be responsible for, carry, take on, take upon oneself **14** = **push**, elbow, jostle, press, shove, thrust

shoulder blade *n* = **scapula**

shout *n* **1** = **cry**, bellow, call, roar, scream, yell ◆ *vb* **3, 4** = **cry (out)**, bawl, bay, bellow, call (out), holler (*inf.*), hollo, raise one's voice, roar, scream, yell

5 (*tr*) *Austral. & NZ inf.* to treat (someone) to (something, esp. a round of drinks). [C14: prob. from ON *skūta* taunt]
▸'**shouter** *n*

shout down vb (*tr, adv*) to drown, overwhelm, or silence by talking loudly.

shove (ʃʌv) *vb* **shoves, shoving, shoved. 1** to give a thrust or push to (a person or thing). **2** (*tr*) to give a violent push to. **3** (*intr*) to push one's way roughly. **4** (*tr*) *Inf.* to put (something) somewhere: *shove it in the bin.* ◆ *n* **5** the act or an instance of shoving. ◆ See also **shove off.** [OE *scūfan*]
▸'**shover** *n*

shove-halfpenny *n Brit.* a game in which players try to propel coins, originally old halfpennies, with the hand into lined sections of a wooden board.

shovel ('ʃʌvᵊl) *n* **1** an instrument for lifting or scooping loose material, such as earth, coal, etc., consisting of a curved blade or a scoop attached to a handle. **2** any machine or part resembling a shovel in action. **3** Also called: **shovelful.** the amount that can be contained in a shovel. ◆ *vb* **shovels, shovelling, shovelled** *or US* **shovels, shoveling, shoveled. 4** to lift (earth, etc.) with a shovel. **5** (*tr*) to clear or dig (a path) with or as if with a shovel. **6** (*tr*) to gather, load, or unload in a hurried or careless way. [OE *scofl*]
▸'**shoveller** *or US* '**shoveler** *n*

shoveler ('ʃʌvələ) *n* a duck of ponds and marshes, having a spoon-shaped bill, a blue patch on each wing, and in the male a green head, white breast, and reddish-brown body.

shovelhead ('ʃʌvᵊl,hɛd) *n* a common shark of the Atlantic and Pacific Oceans, having a shovel-shaped head.

shove off *vb* (*intr, adv; often imperative*) **1** to move from the shore in a boat. **2** *Inf.* to go away; depart.

show (ʃəʊ) *vb* **shows, showing, showed; shown** *or* **showed. 1** to make, be, or become visible or noticeable: *to show one's dislike.* **2** (*tr*) to exhibit: *he showed me a picture.* **3** (*tr*) to indicate or explain; prove: *to show that the earth moves round the sun.* **4** (*tr*) to present (oneself or itself) in a specific character: *to show oneself to be trustworthy.* **5** (*tr*; foll. by *how* and an infinitive) to instruct by demonstration: *show me how to swim.* **6** (*tr*) to indicate: *a barometer shows changes in the weather.* **7** (*tr*) to grant or bestow: *to show favour to someone.* **8** (*intr*) to appear: *to show to advantage.* **9** to exhibit, display, or offer (goods, etc.) for sale: *three artists were showing at the gallery.* **10** (*tr*) to allege, as in a legal document: *to show cause.* **11** to present (a film, etc.) or (of a play, etc.) to be presented, as at a theatre or cinema. **12** (*tr*) to guide or escort: *please show me to my room.* **13 show in** *or* **out.** to conduct a person into or out of a room or building by opening the door for him. **14** (*intr*) *Inf.* to arrive. ◆ *n* **15** a display or exhibition. **16** a public spectacle. **17** an ostentatious display. **18** a theatrical or other entertainment. **19** a trace or indication. **20** *Obstetrics.* a discharge of blood at the onset of labour. **21** *US, Austral., & NZ inf.* a chance (esp. in **give someone a show**). **22** *Sl., chiefly Brit.* a thing or affair (esp. in **good show, bad show,** etc.). **23 for show.** in order to attract attention. **24 run the show.** *Inf.* to take charge of or manage an affair, business, etc. **25 steal the show.** *Inf.* to be looked upon as the most interesting, popular, etc., esp. unexpectedly. ◆ See also **show off, show up.** [OE *scēawian*]

showboat ('ʃəʊ,bəʊt) *n* **1** a paddle-wheel river steamer with a theatre and a repertory company. ◆ *vb* **2** (*intr*) to perform or behave in a showy flamboyant way.

showbread ('ʃəʊ,brɛd) *n* a variant spelling of **shewbread.**

show business *n* the entertainment industry, including theatre, films, television, and radio. Informal term: **show biz.**

show card *n Commerce.* a card containing a tradesman's advertisement; poster.

showcase ('ʃəʊ,keɪs) *n* **1** a glass case used to display objects in a museum or shop. **2** a setting in which anything may be displayed to best advantage. ◆ *vb* **showcases, showcasing, showcased. 3** (*tr*) to display or exhibit.

show day *n* (in Australia) a public holiday in a state on the date of its annual agricultural and industrial show.

showdown ('ʃəʊ,daʊn) *n* **1** *Inf.* an action that brings matters to a head or acts as a conclusion. **2** *Poker.* the exposing of the cards in the players' hands at the end of the game.

shower[1] ('ʃaʊə) *n* **1** a brief period of rain, hail, sleet, or snow. **2** a sudden abundant fall or downpour, as of tears, sparks, or light. **3** a rush: *a shower of praise.* **4a** a kind of bath in which a person stands upright and is sprayed with water from a nozzle. **4b** the room, booth, etc., containing such a bath. Full name: **shower bath. 5** *Brit. sl.* a derogatory term applied to a person or group. **6** *US, Canad., Austral., & NZ.* a party held to honour and present gifts to a person, as to a prospective bride. **7** a large number of particles formed by the collision of a cosmic-ray particle with a particle in the atmosphere. **8** *NZ.* a light fabric put over a tea table to protect the food from flies, etc. ◆ *vb* **9** (*tr*) to sprinkle or spray with or as if with a shower. **10** (often with *it* as subject) to fall or cause to fall in the form of a shower. **11** (*tr*) to give (gifts, etc.) in abundance or present (a person) with (gifts, etc.): *they showered gifts on him.* **12** (*intr*) to take a shower. [OE *scūr*]
▸'**showery** *adj*

shower[2] ('ʃəʊə) *n* a person or thing that shows.

showgirl ('ʃəʊ,gɜːl) *n* a girl who appears in variety shows, nightclub acts, etc.

show house *n* a house on a newly built estate that is decorated and furnished for prospective buyers to view.

showing ('ʃəʊɪŋ) *n* **1** a presentation, exhibition, or display. **2** manner of presentation.

showjumping ('ʃəʊ,dʒʌmpɪŋ) *n* the riding of horses in competitions to demonstrate skill in jumping over or between various obstacles.
▸'**show-,jumper** *n*

showman ('ʃəʊmən) *n, pl* **showmen. 1** a person who presents or produces a theatrical show, etc. **2** a person skilled at presenting anything in an effective manner.
▸'**showmanship** *n*

shown (ʃəʊn) *vb* a past participle of **show.**

show off *vb* (*adv*) **1** (*tr*) to exhibit or display so as to invite admiration. **2** (*intr*) *Inf.* to behave in such a manner as to make an impression. ◆ *n* **show-off. 3** *Inf.* a person who makes a vain display of himself.

showpiece ('ʃəʊ,piːs) *n* **1** anything displayed or exhibited. **2** anything prized as a very fine example of its type.

showplace ('ʃəʊ,pleɪs) *n* a place exhibited or visited for its beauty, historic interest, etc.

showroom ('ʃəʊ,ruːm, -,rʊm) *n* a room in which goods for sale, such as cars, are on display.

show up *vb* (*adv*) **1** to reveal or be revealed clearly. **2** (*tr*) to expose or reveal the faults or defects of by comparison. **3** (*tr*) *Inf.* to put to shame; embarrass. **4** (*intr*) *Inf.* to appear or arrive.

showy ('ʃəʊɪ) *adj* **showier, showiest. 1** gaudy or ostentatious. **2** making an imposing display.
▸'**showily** *adv* ▸'**showiness** *n*

shrank (ʃræŋk) *vb* a past tense of **shrink.**

shrapnel ('ʃræpnᵊl) *n* **1** a projectile containing a number of small pellets or bullets exploded before impact. **2** fragments from this type of shell. [C19: after H. *Shrapnel* (1761–1842), E army officer, who invented it]

shred (ʃrɛd) *n* **1** a long narrow strip or fragment torn or cut off. **2** a very small piece or amount. ◆ *vb* **shreds, shredding, shredded** *or* **shred. 3** (*tr*) to tear or cut into shreds. [OE *scread*]
▸'**shredder** *n*

shrew (ʃruː) *n* **1** Also called: **shrewmouse.** a small mouselike long-

THESAURUS

shout down *vb* = **silence**, drown, drown out, overwhelm

shove *vb* **1-3** = **push**, crowd, drive, elbow, impel, jostle, press, propel, shoulder, thrust

shovel *vb* **4** = **move**, convey, dredge, heap, ladle, load, scoop, shift, spoon, toss

shove off *vb* **2** *Informal* = **go away**, bugger off (*taboo sl.*), clear off (*inf.*), depart, get on one's bike, go to hell (*inf.*), leave, pack one's bags (*inf.*), push off (*inf.*), scram (*inf.*), sling one's hook (*Brit. sl.*), slope off, take oneself off, vamoose (*sl., chiefly US*)

show *vb* **1, 2** = **present**, display, exhibit **3** = **prove**, assert, clarify, demonstrate, elucidate, evince, point out **5** = **instruct**, demonstrate, explain, teach **6** = **indicate**, demonstrate, disclose, display, divulge, evidence, evince, make known, manifest, register, reveal, testify to **7** = **act with**, accord, bestow, confer, grant **8** = **be visible**, appear **12** = **guide**, accompany, attend, conduct, escort, lead ◆ *n* **15** = **exhibition**, array, demonstration, display, expo (*inf.*), exposition, fair, manifestation, pageant, pageantry, parade, representation, sight, spectacle, view **17** = **pretence**, affectation, air, appearance, display, illusion, likeness, ostentation, parade, pose, pretext, profession, semblance **18** = **entertainment**, presentation, production
Antonyms *vb* ≠ **present, indicate:** conceal, hide, keep secret, mask, obscure, suppress, veil, withhold ≠ **prove:** deny, disprove, gainsay (*arch. or literary*), refute ≠ **be visible:** be invisible

showdown *n* **1** *Informal* = **confrontation**, breaking point, clash, climax, crisis, culmination, denouement, exposé, face-off (*sl.*), moment of truth

shower[1] *n* **2** = **deluge**, barrage, downpour, fusillade, plethora, rain, stream, torrent, volley **5** *Brit. slang* = **rabble**, bunch of layabouts, crew ◆ *vb* **9** = **spray**, pour, rain, sprinkle **11** = **inundate**, deluge, heap, lavish, load

showing *n* **1** = **display**, demonstration, exhibition, presentation, staging

showman *n* **1** = **impresario**, publicist, stage manager **2** = **performer**, entertainer

show off *vb* **1** = **exhibit**, advertise, demonstrate, display, flaunt, parade, spread out **2** *Informal* = **boast**, blow one's own trumpet, brag, hot-dog (*chiefly US*), make a spectacle of oneself, shoot a line (*inf.*), strut one's stuff (*chiefly US*), swagger ◆ *n* **show-off 3** *Informal* = **exhibitionist**, boaster, braggadocio, braggart, egotist, hot dog (*chiefly US*), peacock, poseur, swaggerer

show up *vb* **1** = **stand out**, appear, be conspicuous, be visible, catch the eye, leap to the eye **2** = **reveal**, expose, highlight, lay bare, pinpoint, put the spotlight on, unmask **3** *Informal* = **embarrass**, let down, mortify, put to shame, shame, show in a bad light **4** *Informal* = **arrive**, appear, come, make an appearance, put in an appearance, show one's face, turn up

showy *adj* **1** = **ostentatious**, brash, flamboyant, flash (*inf.*), flashy, garish, gaudy, over the top (*inf.*), pompous, pretentious, splashy (*inf.*), tawdry, tinselly
Antonyms *adj* discreet, low-key, muted, quiet, restrained, subdued, tasteful, unobtrusive

shred *n* **1** = **strip**, bit, fragment, piece, rag, ribbon, scrap, sliver, snippet, tatter **2** = **particle**, atom, grain, iota, jot, scrap, trace, whit

shrew *n* **2** = **nag**, ballbreaker (*sl.*), dragon (*inf.*), fury, harpy, harridan, scold, spitfire, termagant (*rare*), virago, vixen, Xanthippe

DICTIONARY

snouted insectivorous mammal. **2** a bad-tempered or mean-spirited woman. [OE *scrēawa*]

shrewd Ⓣ (ʃruːd) *adj* **1** astute and penetrating, often with regard to business. **2** artful: *a shrewd politician.* **3** *Obs.* piercing: *a shrewd wind.* [C14: from *shrew* (obs. vb) to curse, from SHREW]
▸ **ˈshrewdly** *adv* ▸ **ˈshrewdness** *n*

shrewish Ⓣ (ˈʃruːɪʃ) *adj* (esp. of a woman) bad-tempered and nagging.

shriek Ⓣ (ʃriːk) *n* **1** a shrill and piercing cry. ◆ *vb* **2** to produce or utter (words, sounds, etc.) in a shrill piercing tone. [C16: prob. from ON *skrækja* to screech]
▸ **ˈshrieker** *n*

shrieval (ˈʃriːvəl) *adj* of or relating to a sheriff.

shrievalty (ˈʃriːvəltɪ) *n, pl* **shrievalties. 1** the office or term of office of a sheriff. **2** the jurisdiction of a sheriff. [C16: from arch. *shrieve* sheriff, on the model of *mayoralty*]

shrift (ʃrɪft) *n Arch.* the act or an instance of shriving or being shriven. See also **short shrift.** [OE *scrift*, from L *scriptum* SCRIPT]

shrike (ʃraɪk) *n* an Old World songbird having a heavy hooked bill and feeding on smaller animals which it sometimes impales on thorns, etc. Also called: **butcherbird.** [OE *scrīc* thrush]

shrill Ⓣ (ʃrɪl) *adj* **1** sharp and high-pitched in quality. **2** emitting a sharp high-pitched sound. ◆ *vb* **3** to utter (words, sounds, etc.) in a shrill tone. [C14: prob. from OE *scralletan*]
▸ **ˈshrillness** *n* ▸ **ˈshrilly** *adv*

shrimp (ʃrɪmp) *n* **1** any of a genus of chiefly marine decapod crustaceans having a slender flattened body with a long tail and a single pair of pincers. **2** *Inf.* a diminutive person, esp. a child. ◆ *vb* **3** (*intr*) to fish for shrimps. [C14: prob. of Gmc origin]
▸ **ˈshrimper** *n*

shrine (ʃraɪn) *n* **1** a place of worship hallowed by association with a sacred person or object. **2** a container for sacred relics. **3** the tomb of a saint or other holy person. **4** a place or site venerated for its association with a famous person or event. **5** *RC Church.* a building, alcove, or shelf arranged as a setting for a statue, picture, etc., of Christ, the Virgin Mary, or a saint. ◆ *vb* **shrines, shrining, shrined. 6** short for **enshrine.** [OE *scrīn*, from L *scrīnium* bookcase]
▸ **ˈshrine,like** *adj*

shrink Ⓣ (ʃrɪŋk) *vb* **shrinks, shrinking; shrank** *or* **shrunk; shrunk** *or* **shrunken. 1** to contract or cause to contract as from wetness, heat, cold, etc. **2** to become or cause to become smaller in size. **3** (*intr*; often foll. by *from*) **3a** to recoil or withdraw: *to shrink from the sight of blood.* **3b** to feel great reluctance (at). ◆ *n* **4** the act or an instance of shrinking. **5** a slang word for **psychiatrist.** [OE *scrincan*]
▸ **ˈshrinkable** *adj* ▸ **ˈshrinker** *n* ▸ **ˈshrinking** *adj*

shrinkage (ˈʃrɪŋkɪdʒ) *n* **1** the act or fact of shrinking. **2** the amount by which anything decreases in size, value, weight, etc. **3** *Commerce.* the loss of merchandise through shoplifting or damage.

shrinking violet *n Inf.* a shy person.

shrink-wrap *vb* **shrink-wraps, shrink-wrapping, shrink-wrapped.** (*tr*) to package a product in a flexible plastic wrapping designed to shrink about its contours to protect and seal it.

shrive (ʃraɪv) *vb* **shrives, shriving; shrove** *or* **shrived; shriven** (ˈʃrɪvən) *or* **shrived.** *Chiefly RC Church.* **1** to hear the confession of (a penitent). **2** (*tr*) to impose a penance upon (a penitent) and grant him absolution. **3** (*intr*) to confess one's sins to a priest in order to obtain forgiveness. [OE *scrīfan*, from L *scrībere* to write]
▸ **ˈshriver** *n*

shrivel Ⓣ (ˈʃrɪvəl) *vb* **shrivels, shrivelling, shrivelled** *or US* **shrivels, shriveling, shriveled. 1** to make or become shrunken and withered. **2** to lose or cause to lose vitality. [C16: prob. of Scand. origin]

shroud Ⓣ (ʃraud) *n* **1** a garment or piece of cloth used to wrap a dead body. **2** anything that envelops like a garment: *a shroud of mist.* **3** a protective covering for a piece of equipment. **4** *Astronautics.* a streamlined protective covering used to protect the payload during a rocket-powered launch. **5** *Naut.* one of a pattern of ropes or cables used to stay a mast. ◆ *vb* (*tr*) **6** to wrap in a shroud. **7** to cover, envelop, or hide. [OE *scrūd* garment]
▸ **ˈshroudless** *adj*

shrove (ʃrəuv) *vb* a past tense of **shrive.**

Shrovetide (ˈʃrəuv,taɪd) *n* the Sunday, Monday, and Tuesday before Ash Wednesday, formerly a time when confessions were made for Lent.

shrub[1] (ʃrʌb) *n* a woody perennial plant, smaller than a tree, with several major branches arising from near the base of the main stem. [OE *scrybb*]
▸ **ˈshrub,like** *adj*

shrub[2] (ʃrʌb) *n* a mixed drink of rum, fruit juice, sugar, and spice. [C18: from Ar. *sharāb*, var. of *shurb* drink; see SHERBET]

shrubbery (ˈʃrʌbərɪ) *n, pl* **shrubberies. 1** a place where a number of shrubs are planted. **2** shrubs collectively.

shrubby (ˈʃrʌbɪ) *adj* **shrubbier, shrubbiest. 1** consisting of, planted with, or abounding in shrubs. **2** resembling a shrub.
▸ **ˈshrubbiness** *n*

shrug (ʃrʌg) *vb* **shrugs, shrugging, shrugged. 1** to draw up and drop (the shoulders) abruptly in a gesture expressing indifference, ignorance, etc. ◆ *n* **2** the gesture so made. [C14: from ?]

shrug off *vb* (*tr, adv*) **1** to minimize the importance of; dismiss. **2** to get rid of.

shrunk (ʃrʌŋk) *vb* a past participle and past tense of **shrink.**

shrunken (ˈʃrʌŋkən) *vb* **1** a past participle of **shrink.** ◆ *adj* **2** (*usually prenominal*) reduced in size.

shtoom (ʃtum) *adj Sl.* silent, dumb (esp. in **keep shtoom**). [from Yiddish, from G *stumm* silent]

shuck (ʃʌk) *n* **1** the outer covering of something, such as the husk of a grain of maize, a pea pod, or an oyster shell. ◆ *vb* (*tr*) **2** to remove the shucks from. [C17: US dialect, from ?]
▸ **ˈshucker** *n*

shucks (ʃʌks) *interj US & Canad. inf.* an exclamation of disappointment, annoyance, etc.

shudder Ⓣ (ˈʃʌdə) *vb* **1** (*intr*) to shake or tremble suddenly and violently, as from horror, fear, aversion, etc. ◆ *n* **2** a convulsive shiver. [C18: from MLow G *schōderen*]
▸ **ˈshuddering** *adj* ▸ **ˈshudderingly** *adv* ▸ **ˈshuddery** *adj*

shuffle Ⓣ (ˈʃʌfəl) *vb* **shuffles, shuffling, shuffled. 1** to walk or move (the feet) with a slow dragging motion. **2** to change the position of (something), esp. in order to deceive others. **3** (*tr*) to mix together in a careless manner: *he shuffled the papers nervously.* **4** to mix up (cards in a pack) to change their order. **5** (*intr*) to behave in an evasive or underhand manner. **6** (when *intr*, often foll. by *into* or *out of*) to move or cause to move clumsily: *he shuffled out of the door.* ◆ *n* **7** the act or an instance of shuffling. **8** a rearrangement: *a Cabinet shuffle.* **9** a dance or dance step with short dragging movements of the feet. [C16: prob. from Low G *schüffeln*]
▸ **ˈshuffler** *n*

shuffleboard (ˈʃʌfəl,bɔːd) *n* a game in which players push wooden or plastic discs with a long cue towards numbered scoring sections marked on a floor, esp. a ship's deck.

shuffle off *vb* (*tr, adv*) to thrust off or put aside: *shuffle off responsibility.*

shuffle play *n* a facility on a compact disc player that selects tracks at random from a number of compact discs.

shufty *or* **shufti** (ˈʃuftɪ, ˈʃʌftɪ) *n, pl* **shufties.** *Brit. sl.* a look; peep. [C20: from Ar.]

shun Ⓣ (ʃʌn) *vb* **shuns, shunning, shunned.** (*tr*) to avoid deliberately. [OE *scunian*, from ?]

shunt (ʃʌnt) *vb* **1** to turn or cause to turn to one side. **2** *Railways.* to transfer (rolling stock) from track to track. **3** *Electronics.* to divert or be diverted through a shunt. **4** (*tr*) to evade by putting off onto someone else. ◆ *n* **5** the act or an instance of shunting. **6** a railway point. **7** *Electronics.* a low-resistance conductor connected in parallel across a part of a circuit to provide an alternative path for a known fraction of the

THESAURUS

shrewd *adj* **1, 2** = **clever**, acute, artful, astute, calculated, calculating, canny, crafty, cunning, discerning, discriminating, far-seeing, far-sighted, fly (*sl.*), intelligent, keen, knowing, long-headed, perceptive, perspicacious, sagacious, sharp, sly, smart, wily
Antonyms *adj* artless, dull, gullible, imprudent, ingenuous, innocent, naive, obtuse, slow-witted, stupid, trusting, undiscerning, unsophisticated, unworldly

shrewdly *adv* **1, 2** = **cleverly**, artfully, astutely, cannily, far-sightedly, knowingly, perceptively, perspicaciously, sagaciously, with all one's wits about one, with consummate skill

shrewdness *n* **1, 2** = **cleverness**, acumen, acuteness, astuteness, canniness, discernment, grasp, judgment, penetration, perspicacity, quick wits, sagacity, sharpness, smartness, suss (*sl.*)

shrewish *adj* = **bad-tempered**, cantankerous, complaining, discontented, fault-finding, ill-humoured, ill-natured, ill-tempered, litigious, nagging, peevish, petulant, quarrelsome, scolding, sharp-tongued, vixenish

shriek *n* **1** = **cry**, holler, howl, scream, screech, squeal, wail, whoop, yell ◆ *vb* **2** = **cry**, holler, howl, scream, screech, squeal, wail, whoop, yell

shrill *adj* **1** = **piercing**, acute, ear-piercing, ear-splitting, high, high-pitched, penetrating, piping, screeching, sharp
Antonyms *adj* deep, dulcet, mellifluous, silver-toned, soft, soothing, sweet-sounding, velvety, well-modulated

shrink *vb* **1, 2** = **decrease**, contract, deflate, diminish, downsize, drop off, dwindle, fall off, grow smaller, lessen, narrow, shorten, shrivel, wither, wrinkle **3** = **recoil**, cower, cringe, draw back, flinch, hang back, quail, retire, shy away, wince, withdraw
Antonyms *vb* ≠ **decrease:** balloon, dilate, distend, enlarge, expand, increase, inflate, mushroom, stretch, swell ≠ **recoil:** attack, challenge, confront, embrace, face, receive, welcome

shrivel *vb* **1** = **wither**, dehydrate, desiccate, dry up, dwindle, shrink, wilt, wizen, wrinkle

shrivelled *adj* **1** = **withered**, desiccated, dried up, dry, sere (*arch.*), shrunken, wizened, wrinkled

shroud *n* **1** = **winding sheet**, cerecloth, cerement, covering, grave clothes **2** = **covering**, cloud, mantle, pall, screen, veil ◆ *vb* **7** = **conceal**, blanket, cloak, cover, envelop, hide, screen, swathe, veil

shudder *vb* **1** = **shiver**, convulse, quake, quiver, shake, tremble ◆ *n* **2** = **shiver**, convulsion, quiver, spasm, trembling, tremor

shuffle *vb* **1** = **scuffle**, drag, scrape, scuff, shamble **2, 3** = **rearrange**, confuse, disarrange, disorder, intermix, jumble, mix, shift **5** = **be evasive**, beat about the bush, beg the question, cavil, dodge, equivocate, evade, flannel (*Brit. inf.*), gloss over, hedge, prevaricate, pussyfoot (*inf.*), quibble

shun *vb* = **avoid**, body-swerve (*Scot.*), cold-shoulder, elude, eschew, evade, fight shy of, give (someone *or* something) a wide berth, have no part in, keep away from, shy away from, steer clear of

current. **8** *Med.* a channel that bypasses the normal circulation of the blood. **9** *Brit. inf.* a collision that occurs when a vehicle runs into the back of the vehicle in front. [C13: ?from *shunen* to SHUN]

shunt-wound ('ʃʌnt,waʊnd) *adj Electrical engineering.* (of a motor or generator) having the field and armature circuits connected in parallel.

shush (ʃʊʃ) *interj* **1** be quiet! hush! ◆ *vb* **2** to silence or calm (someone) by or as if by saying "shush". [C20: reduplication of SH, infl. by HUSH]

shut ⓣ (ʃʌt) *vb* **shuts, shutting, shut. 1** to move (something) so as to cover an aperture: *to shut a door.* **2** to close (something) by bringing together the parts: *to shut a book.* **3** (*tr;* often foll. by *up*) to close or lock the doors of: *to shut up a house.* **4** (*tr;* foll. by *in, out,* etc.) to confine, enclose, or exclude. **5** (*tr*) to prevent (a business, etc.) from operating. **6** **shut the door on. 6a** to refuse to think about. **6b** to render impossible. ◆ *adj* **7** closed or fastened. ◆ *n* **8** the act or time of shutting. ◆ See also **shutdown, shut-off,** etc. [OE *scyttan*]

shutdown ⓣ ('ʃʌt,daʊn) *n* **1a** the closing of a factory, shop, etc. **1b** (*as modifier*): *shutdown costs.* ◆ *vb* **shut down.** (*adv*) **2** to cease or cause to cease operation. **3** (*tr*) to close by lowering.

shuteye ('ʃʌt,aɪ) *n* a slang term for **sleep.**

shut-in *n Chiefly US.* **a** a person confined indoors by illness. **b** (*as modifier*): *a shut-in patient.*

shut-off *n* **1** a device that shuts something off, esp. a machine control. **2** a stoppage or cessation. ◆ *vb* **shut off.** (*tr, adv*) **3** to stem the flow of. **4** to block off the passage through. **5** to isolate or separate.

shutout ⓣ ('ʃʌt,aʊt) *n* **1** a less common word for a **lockout. 2** *Sport.* a match in which the opposition does not score. ◆ *vb* **shut out.** (*tr, adv*) **3** to keep out or exclude. **4** to conceal from sight: *we planted trees to shut out the view of the road.*

shutter ('ʃʌtə) *n* **1** a hinged doorlike cover, often louvred and usually one of a pair, for closing off a window. **2** **put up the shutters.** to close business at the end of the day or permanently. **3** *Photog.* an opaque shield in a camera that, when tripped, admits light to expose the film or plate for a predetermined period, usually a fraction of a second. **4** *Music.* one of the louvred covers over the mouths of organ pipes, operated by the swell pedal. **5** a person or thing that shuts. ◆ *vb* (*tr*) **6** to close with a shutter or shutters. **7** to equip with a shutter or shutters.

shuttering ('ʃʌtərɪŋ) *n* another word (esp. Brit.) for **formwork.**

shuttle ⓣ ('ʃʌtᵊl) *n* **1** a bobbin-like device used in weaving for passing the weft thread between the warp threads. **2** a small bobbin-like device used to hold the thread in a sewing machine, etc. **3a** a bus, train, aircraft, etc., that plies between two points. **3b** short for **space shuttle. 4a** the movement between various countries of a diplomat in order to negotiate with rulers who refuse to meet each other. **4b** (*as modifier*): *shuttle diplomacy.* **5** *Badminton, etc.* short for **shuttlecock.** ◆ *vb* **shuttles, shuttling, shuttled. 6** to move or cause to move by or as if by a shuttle. [OE *scytel* bolt]

shuttlecock ('ʃʌtᵊl,kɒk) *n* **1** a light cone consisting of a cork stub with feathered flights, struck to and fro in badminton and battledore. **2** anything moved to and fro, as in an argument.

shut up ⓣ *vb* (*adv*) **1** (*tr*) to prevent all access to. **2** (*tr*) to confine or imprison. **3** *Inf.* to cease to talk or make a noise or cause to cease to talk or make a noise: often used in commands.

shwa (ʃwɑː) *n* a variant spelling of **schwa.**

shy[1] ⓣ (ʃaɪ) *adj* **shyer, shyest** *or* **shier, shiest. 1** not at ease in the company of others. **2** easily frightened; timid. **3** (often foll. by *of*) watchful or wary. **4** (foll. by *of*) *Inf., chiefly US & Canad.* short (of). **5** (*in combination*) showing reluctance or disinclination: *workshy.* ◆ *vb* **shies, shying, shied.** (*intr*) **6** to move suddenly, as from fear: *the horse shied at the snake in the road.* **7** (usually foll. by *off* or *away*) to draw back. ◆ *n, pl* **shies. 8** a sudden movement, as from fear. [OE *sceoh*]
▸**'shyer** *n* ▸**'shyly** *adv* ▸**'shyness** *n*

shy[2] ⓣ (ʃaɪ) *vb* **shies, shying, shied. 1** to throw (something) with a sideways motion. ◆ *n, pl* **shies. 2** a quick throw. **3** *Inf.* a gibe. **4** *Inf.* an attempt. [C18: of Gmc origin]
▸**'shyer** *n*

Shylock ('ʃaɪ,lɒk) *n* a heartless or demanding creditor. [C19: after *Shylock,* the heartless usurer in Shakespeare's *The Merchant of Venice* (1596)]

shyster ('ʃaɪstə) *n Sl., chiefly US.* a person, esp. a lawyer or politician, who uses discreditable methods. [C19: prob. based on *Scheuster,* a disreputable 19th-cent. New York lawyer]

si (siː) *n Music.* the syllable used in the fixed system of solmization for the note B. [C14: see GAMUT]

Si *the chemical symbol for* silicon.

SI 1 *symbol for* Système International (d'Unités). See **SI unit. 2** *NZ abbrev. for* South Island.

sial ('saɪəl) *n* the silicon-rich and aluminium-rich rocks of the earth's continental upper crust. [C20: *si(licon)* + *al(uminium)*]
▸**sialic** (saɪ'ælɪk) *adj*

siamang ('saɪə,mæŋ) *n* a large black gibbon of Sumatra and the Malay Peninsula, having the second and third toes united. [C19: from Malay]

Siamese (,saɪə'miːz) *n, pl* **Siamese. 1** See **Siamese cat.** ◆ *adj* **2** characteristic of, relating to, or being a Siamese twin. ◆ *adj, n, pl* **Siamese. 3** another word for **Thai.**

Siamese cat *n* a short-haired breed of cat with a tapering tail, blue eyes, and dark ears, mask, tail, and paws.

Siamese fighting fish *n* a brightly coloured labyrinth fish of Thailand and Malaysia: the males are very pugnacious.

Siamese twins *pl n* twin babies born joined together at some point, such as at the hips.

sib (sɪb) *n* **1** a blood relative. **2** kinsmen collectively; kindred. [OE *sibb*]

SIB (in Britain) *abbrev. for* Securities and Investments Board: a body that regulates financial dealings in the City of London.

Siberian (saɪ'bɪərɪən) *adj* **1** of or relating to Siberia or to its peoples. ◆ *n* **2** a native or inhabitant of Siberia.

sibilant ('sɪbɪlənt) *adj* **1** *Phonetics.* relating to or denoting the consonants (s, z, ʃ, ʒ), all pronounced with a characteristic hissing sound. **2** having a hissing sound. ◆ *n* **3** a sibilant consonant. [C17: from L *sībilāre* to hiss, imit.]
▸**'sibilance** *or* **'sibilancy** *n* ▸**'sibilantly** *adv*

sibilate ('sɪbɪ,leɪt) *vb* **sibilates, sibilating, sibilated.** to pronounce or utter (words or speech) with a hissing sound.
▸**,sibi'lation** *n*

sibling ('sɪblɪŋ) *n* **a** a person's brother or sister. **b** (*as modifier*): *sibling rivalry.* [C19: specialized modern use of OE *sibling* relative, from SIB]

sibyl ⓣ ('sɪbɪl) *n* **1** (in ancient Greece and Rome) any of a number of women believed to be oracles or prophetesses. **2** a witch, fortune-teller, or sorceress. [C13: ult. from Gk *Sibulla,* from ?]
▸**sibylline** ('sɪbɪ,laɪn) *adj*

sic[1] (sɪk) *adv* so or thus: inserted in brackets in a text to indicate that an odd or questionable reading is what was actually written or printed. [L]

sic[2] (sɪk) *vb* **sics, sicking, sicked.** (*tr*) **1** to attack: used only in commands, as to a dog. **2** to urge (a dog) to attack. [C19: dialect var. of SEEK]

siccative ('sɪkətɪv) *n* a substance added to a liquid to promote drying: used in paints and some medicines. [C16: from LL *siccātīvus,* from L *siccāre* to dry up, from *siccus* dry]

Sicilian (sɪ'sɪlɪən) *adj* **1** of or relating to the island of Sicily, in the Mediterranean. ◆ *n* **2** a native or inhabitant of Sicily.

siciliano (,siːtʃiː'ljɑːnəʊ) *n, pl* **sicilianos. 1** an old dance in six-beat or twelve-beat time. **2** a piece of music composed for or in the rhythm of this dance. [It.]

sick[1] ⓣ (sɪk) *adj* **1** inclined or likely to vomit. **2a** suffering from ill health. **2b** (*as collective n;* preceded by *the*): *the sick.* **3a** of or used by people who are unwell: *sick benefits.* **3b** (*in combination*): *a sickroom.* **4** deeply affected with a mental or spiritual feeling akin to physical sickness: *sick at heart.* **5** mentally or spiritually disturbed. **6** *Inf.* delighting in or catering for the macabre: *sick humour.* **7** Also: **sick and tired.** (often foll. by *of*) *Inf.* disgusted or weary: *I am sick of his everlasting laughter.* **8** (often foll. by *for*) weary with longing: *I am sick for my own country.* **9** pallid or sickly. **10** not in working order. ◆ *n, vb* **11** an informal word for **vomit.** [OE *sēoc*]
▸**'sickish** *adj*

sick[2] (sɪk) *vb* a variant spelling of **sic**[2].

sickbay ('sɪk,beɪ) *n* a room for the treatment of the sick or injured, as on board a ship or at a boarding school.

sick building syndrome *n* a group of symptoms, such as headaches, eye irritation, and lethargy, that may be experienced by workers in offices that are totally air-conditioned.

THESAURUS

shut *vb* **1** = **close,** bar, draw to, fasten, push to, seal, secure, slam **4** = **confine,** cage, enclose, exclude, impound, imprison, keep, pound, wall off *or* up
Antonyms *vb* ≠ **close:** open, throw wide, unbar, unclose, undo, unfasten, unlock

shutdown *vb* **shut down 2** = **stop,** cease, cease operating, discontinue, halt, switch off **3** = **close,** shut up

shutout *vb* **shut out 3** = **exclude,** bar, black, blackball, debar, keep out, lock out, ostracize **4** = **conceal,** block out, cover, hide, mask, screen, veil

shuttle *vb* **6** = **go back and forth,** alternate, commute, go to and fro, ply, seesaw, shunt

shut up *vb* **2** = **confine,** bottle up, box in, cage, coop up, immure, imprison, incarcerate, intern, keep in **3** *Informal* = **be quiet,** button one's lip (*sl.*), fall silent, gag, hold one's tongue, hush, keep one's trap shut (*sl.*), muzzle, pipe down (*sl.*), put a sock in it (*Brit. sl.*), silence

shy[1] *adj* **1, 2** = **timid,** backward, bashful, coy, diffident, modest, mousy, nervous, reserved, reticent, retiring, self-conscious, self-effacing, shrinking **3** **shy of** = **cautious of,** chary of, distrustful of, hesitant about, suspicious of, wary of ◆ *vb* **7** *usually with* **off** *or* **away** = **recoil,** balk, buck, draw back, flinch, quail, rear, start, swerve, take fright, wince
Antonyms *adj* ≠ **timid:** assured, bold, brash, cheeky, confident, fearless, forward, pushy (*inf.*), self-assured, self-confident ≠ **cautious of:** rash, reckless, unsuspecting, unwary

shy[2] *vb* **1** = **throw,** cast, chuck (*inf.*), fling, hurl, lob (*inf.*), pitch, propel, send, sling, toss

shyness *n* **1, 2** = **timidness,** bashfulness, diffidence, lack of confidence, modesty, mousiness, nervousness, reticence, self-consciousness, timidity, timorousness

sibyl *n* **1, 2** = **prophetess,** Cassandra, oracle, Pythia, pythoness, seer

sick[1] *adj* **1** = **nauseous,** green about the gills (*inf.*), ill, nauseated, puking (*sl.*), qualmish, queasy **2** = **unwell,** ailing, diseased, feeble, indisposed, laid up, on the sick list (*inf.*), poorly (*inf.*), under par (*inf.*), under the weather, weak **6** *Informal* = **morbid,** black, ghoulish, macabre, sadistic **7** *with* **of** = **tired,** blasé, bored, disgusted, displeased, fed up, jaded, revolted, satiated, weary
Antonyms *adj* ≠ **unwell:** able-bodied, fine, fit, fit and well, fit as a fiddle, hale and hearty, healthy, robust, up to par, well

sicken ● ('sɪkən) *vb* **1** to make or become nauseated or disgusted. **2** (*intr*; often foll. by *for*) to show symptoms (of an illness).
▸'**sickener** *n*

sickening ● ('sɪkənɪŋ) *adj* **1** causing sickness or revulsion. **2** *Inf.* extremely annoying.
▸'**sickeningly** *adv*

sick headache *n* **1** a headache accompanied by nausea. **2** a nontechnical name for **migraine.**

sickie ('sɪkɪ) *n Inf.* a day of sick leave from work. [C20: from SICK[1] + -IE]

sickle ('sɪkəl) *n* an implement for cutting grass, corn, etc., having a curved blade and a short handle. [OE *sicol*, from L *sēcula*]

sick leave *n* leave of absence from work through illness.

sicklebill ('sɪkəl,bɪl) *n* any of various birds having a markedly curved bill, such as certain hummingbirds and birds of paradise.

sickle-cell anaemia *n* a hereditary form of anaemia occurring mainly in Black populations, in which a large number of red blood cells become sickle-shaped.

sick list *n* **1** a list of the sick, esp. in the army or navy. **2 on the sick list.** ill.

sickly ● ('sɪklɪ) *adj* **sicklier, sickliest. 1** disposed to frequent ailments; not healthy; weak. **2** of or caused by sickness. **3** (of a smell, taste, etc.) causing revulsion or nausea. **4** (of light or colour) faint or feeble. **5** mawkish; insipid. ◆ *adv* **6** in a sick or sickly manner.
▸'**sickliness** *n*

sick-making *adj Inf.* galling; sickening.

sickness ● ('sɪknɪs) *n* **1** an illness or disease. **2** nausea or queasiness. **3** the state or an instance of being sick.

sick pay *n* wages paid to an employee while he is on sick leave.

sic transit gloria mundi *Latin.* ('sɪk 'trænsɪt 'glɔːrɪ,ɑː 'mʊndiː) thus passes the glory of the world.

sidalcea (sɪ'dælsɪə) *n* any of a genus of hardy perennial plants with pink flowers. Also called **Greek mallow.** [from NL]

side ● (saɪd) *n* **1** a line or surface that borders anything. **2** *Geom.* **2a** any line segment forming part of the perimeter of a plane geometric figure. **2b** another name for **face** (sense 13). **3** either of two parts into which an object, surface, area, etc., can be divided: *the right side and the left side.* **4** either of the two surfaces of a flat object: *the right and wrong side of the cloth.* **5** a surface or part of an object that extends vertically: *the side of a cliff.* **6** either half of a human or animal body, esp. the area around the waist: *I have a pain in my side.* **7** the area immediately next to a person or thing: *he stood at her side.* **8** a district, point, or direction within an area identified by reference to a central point: *the south side of the city.* **9** the area at the edge of a room, road, etc. **10** aspect or part: *look on the bright side.* **11** one of two or more contesting factions, teams, etc. **12** a page in an essay, etc. **13** a position, opinion, etc., held in opposition to another in a dispute. **14** line of descent: *he gets his brains from his mother's side.* **15** *Inf.* a television channel. **16** *Billiards, etc.* spin imparted to a ball by striking it off-centre with the cue. **17** *Brit. sl.* insolence or pretentiousness: *to put on side.* **18 on one side.** set apart from the rest, as provision for emergencies, etc. **19 on the side. 19a** apart from or in addition to the main object. **19b** as a sideline. **19c** *US.* as a side dish. **20 take sides.** to support one group, opinion, etc., as against another. ◆ *adj* **21** being on one side; lateral. **22** from or viewed as if from one side. **23** directed towards one side. **24** subordinate or incidental: *side road.* ◆ *vb* **sides, siding, sided. 25** (*intr*; usually foll. by *with*) to support or associate oneself (with a faction, interest, etc.). [OE *sīde*]

side arms *pl n* weapons carried on the person, by belt or holster, such as a sword, pistol, etc.

sideband ('saɪd,bænd) *n* the frequency band either above (**upper sideband**) or below (**lower sideband**) the carrier frequency, within which fall the components produced by modulation of a carrier wave.

sideboard ('saɪd,bɔːd) *n* a piece of furniture intended to stand at the side of a dining room, with drawers, cupboards, and shelves to hold silver, china, linen, etc.

sideboards ('saɪd,bɔːdz) *pl n* another term for **sideburns.**

sideburns ('saɪd,bɜːnz) *pl n* a man's whiskers grown down either side of the face in front of the ears. Also called: **sideboards, side whiskers,** (*Austral.*) **sidelevers.**

sidecar ('saɪd,kɑː) *n* a small car attached on one side to a motorcycle, the other side being supported by a single wheel.

side chain *n Chem.* a group of atoms bound to an atom, usually a carbon atom, that forms part of a larger chain or ring in a molecule.

-sided *adj* (*in combination*) having a side or sides as specified: *three-sided; many-sided.*

side deal *n* a transaction between two people for their private benefit, which is subsidiary to a contract negotiated by them on behalf of the organizations they represent.

side dish *n* a portion of food served in addition to the main dish.

side drum *n* a small double-headed drum carried at the side with snares that produce a rattling effect.

side effect *n* **1** any unwanted nontherapeutic effect caused by a drug. **2** any secondary effect, esp. an undesirable one.

side-foot *Soccer.* ◆ *n* **1** a shot or pass played with the side of the foot. ◆ *vb* **2** (*tr*) to strike (a ball) with the side of the foot.

sidekick ('saɪd,kɪk) *n Inf.* a close friend or follower who accompanies another on adventures, etc.

sidelight ('saɪd,laɪt) *n* **1** light coming from the side. **2** a side window. **3** either of the two navigational running lights used by vessels at night, a red light on the port and a green on the starboard. **4** *Brit.* either of two small lights on the front of a motor vehicle. **5** additional or incidental information.

sideline ● ('saɪd,laɪn) *n* **1** *Sport.* a line that marks the side boundary of a playing area. **2** a subsidiary interest or source of income. **3** an auxiliary business activity or line of merchandise. ◆ *vb* **sidelines, sidelining, sidelined. 4** (*tr*) *Chiefly US & Canad.* to prevent (a player) from taking part in a game.

sidelines ● ('saɪd,laɪnz) *pl n* **1** *Sport.* the area immediately outside the playing area, where substitute players sit. **2** the peripheral areas of any region, organization, etc.

sidelong ● ('saɪd,lɒŋ) *adj* (*prenominal*) **1** directed or inclining to one side. **2** indirect or oblique. ◆ *adv* **3** from the side; obliquely.

sidereal (saɪ'dɪərɪəl) *adj* **1** of or involving the stars. **2** determined with reference to one or more stars: *the sidereal day.* [C17: from L *sīdereus*, from *sīdus* a star]
▸**si'dereally** *adv*

sidereal day *n* See **day** (sense 5).

sidereal period *n Astron.* the period of revolution of a body about another with respect to one or more stars.

sidereal time *n* time based upon the rotation of the earth with respect to a particular star, the **sidereal day** being the unit of measurement.

sidereal year *n* See **year** (sense 5).

siderite ('saɪdə,raɪt) *n* **1** a pale yellow to brownish-black mineral consisting chiefly of iron(II) carbonate. It occurs mainly in ore veins and sedimentary rocks and is an important source of iron. Formula: $FeCO_3$. **2** a meteorite consisting principally of metallic iron.

sidero- *or before a vowel* **sider-** *combining form.* indicating iron: *siderolite.* [from Gk *sidēros*]

siderolite ('saɪdərə,laɪt) *n* a meteorite consisting of a mixture of iron, nickel, and such ferromagnesian minerals as olivine.

siderosis (,saɪdə'rəʊsɪs) *n* a lung disease caused by breathing in fine particles of iron or other metallic dust.

siderostat ('saɪdərəʊ,stæt) *n* an astronomical instrument consisting of a plane mirror rotated by a clock mechanism about two axes so that light from a celestial body, esp. the sun, is reflected along a constant direction for a long period of time. [C19: from *sidero-*, from L *sidus* a star + -STAT]

side-saddle *n* **1** a riding saddle originally designed for women riders in skirts who sit with both legs on the near side of the horse. ◆ *adv* **2** on or as if on a side-saddle.

sideshow ('saɪd,ʃəʊ) *n* **1** a small show or entertainment offered in conjunction with a larger attraction, as at a circus or fair. **2** a subordinate event or incident.

sideslip ('saɪd,slɪp) *n* **1** a sideways skid, as of a motor vehicle. ◆ *vb* **sideslips, sideslipping, sideslipped. 2** another name for **slip**[1] (sense 11).

sidesman ('saɪdzmən) *n, pl* **sidesmen.** *Church of England.* a man elected to help the parish church-warden.

side-splitting ● *adj* **1** producing great mirth. **2** (of laughter) uproarious or very hearty.

sidestep ● ('saɪd,stɛp) *vb* **sidesteps, sidestepping, sidestepped. 1** to step aside from or out of the way of (something). **2** (*tr*) to dodge or circum-

THESAURUS

sicken *vb* **1** = **disgust**, gross out (*US sl.*), make one's gorge rise, nauseate, repel, revolt, turn one's stomach **2** = **fall ill**, ail, be stricken by, contract, go down with, show symptoms of, take sick

sickening *adj* **1** = **disgusting**, cringe-making (*Brit. inf.*), distasteful, foul, gut-wrenching, loathsome, nauseating, nauseous, noisome, offensive, putrid, repulsive, revolting, stomach-turning (*inf.*), vile, yucky *or* yukky (*sl.*)
Antonyms *adj* beneficial, curative, delightful, health-giving, heartening, inviting, marvellous, mouth-watering, pleasant, salutary, tempting, therapeutic, wholesome, wonderful

sickly *adj* **1** = **unhealthy**, ailing, bilious, bloodless, delicate, faint, feeble, indisposed, infirm, in poor health, lacklustre, languid, pallid, peaky, pining, wan, weak **3** = **nauseating**, bilious (*inf.*), cloying, mawkish, revolting (*inf.*), syrupy (*inf.*)

sickness *n* **1** = **illness**, affliction, ailment, bug (*inf.*), complaint, disease, disorder, indisposition, infirmity, lurgy (*inf.*), malady **2** = **nausea**, barfing (*US sl.*), (the) collywobbles (*sl.*), puking (*sl.*), queasiness, vomiting

side *n* **1** = **border**, boundary, division, edge, limit, margin, part, perimeter, periphery, rim, sector, verge **3, 4** = **part**, aspect, face, facet, flank, hand, surface, view **11** = **party**, camp, cause, faction, sect, team **13** = **point of view**, angle, light, opinion, position, slant, stand, standpoint, viewpoint **17** *Brit. slang* = **conceit**, airs, arrogance, insolence, pretentiousness ◆ *adj* **21** = **lateral**, flanking **24** = **subordinate**, ancillary, incidental, indirect, lesser, marginal, minor, oblique, roundabout, secondary, subsidiary ◆ *vb* **25** *usually with* **with** = **support**, ally with, associate oneself with, befriend, favour, go along with, join with, second, take the part of, team up with (*inf.*)
Antonyms *n* ≠ **border:** centre, core, heart, middle ◆ *adj* ≠ **subordinate:** central, essential, focal, fundamental, key, main, middle, primary, principal ◆ *vb* ≠ **support:** counter, oppose, stand against, withstand

sideline *n* **2** = **supplement**, subsidiary

sidelines *pl n* **2** = **periphery**, border, boundary, edge, fringe, margin

sidelong *adj* **2** = **sideways**, covert, indirect, oblique

side-splitting *adj* **1** = **hilarious**, farcical, hysterical, rollicking, uproarious

sidestep *vb* **1, 2** = **avoid**, body-swerve (*Scot.*), bypass, circumvent, dodge, duck (*inf.*), elude, evade, find a way round, skip, skirt

vent. ◆ *n* **side step. 3** a movement to one side, as in dancing, boxing, etc.
▸ **'side,stepper** *n*

sidestroke ('saɪd,strəʊk) *n* a type of swimming stroke in which the swimmer lies sideways in the water making a scissors kick with his legs.

sideswipe ('saɪd,swaɪp) *n* **1** a glancing blow or hit along or from the side. **2** an unexpected criticism of someone or something while discussing another subject. ◆ *vb* **sideswipes, sideswiping, sideswiped. 3** to strike (someone) with a glancing blow from the side.
▸ **'side,swiper** *n*

sidetrack ❶ ('saɪd,træk) *vb* **1** to distract or be distracted from a main subject or topic. ◆ *n* **2** *US & Canad.* a railway siding. **3** a digression.

side-valve engine *n* a type of internal-combustion engine in which the inlet and exhaust valves are in the cylinder block at the side of the pistons.

sidewalk ('saɪd,wɔːk) *n* the US and Canad. word for **pavement.**

sidewall ('saɪd,wɔːl) *n* either of the sides of a pneumatic tyre between the tread and the rim.

sideward ('saɪdwəd) *adj* **1** directed or moving towards one side. ◆ *adv also* **sidewards. 2** towards one side.

sideways ❶ ('saɪd,weɪz) *adv* **1** moving, facing, or inclining towards one side. **2** from one side; obliquely. **3** with one side forward. ◆ *adj (prenominal)* **4** moving or directed to or from one side. **5** towards or from one side.

side whiskers *pl n* another name for **sideburns.**

sidewinder ('saɪd,waɪndə) *n* **1** a North American rattlesnake that moves forwards by a sideways looping motion. **2** *Boxing, US.* a heavy swinging blow from the side.

siding ('saɪdɪŋ) *n* **1** a short stretch of railway track connected to a main line, used for storing rolling stock. **2** a short railway line giving access to the main line for freight from a factory, etc. **3** *US & Canad.* material attached to the outside of a building to make it weatherproof.

sidle ❶ ('saɪdᵊl) *vb* **sidles, sidling, sidled.** *(intr)* **1** to move in a furtive or stealthy manner. **2** to move along sideways. [C17: back formation from obs. *sideling* sideways]

SIDS *abbrev. for* sudden infant death syndrome. See **cot death.**

siege (siːdʒ) *n* **1a** the offensive operations carried out to capture a fortified place by surrounding it and deploying weapons against it. **1b** *(as modifier): siege warfare.* **2** a persistent attempt to gain something. **3** *Obs.* a seat or throne. **4 lay siege to. 4a** to besiege. **4b** to importune. [C13: from OF *sege* a seat, from Vulgar L *sēdicāre* (unattested) to sit down, from L *sedēre*]

siege mentality *n* a state of mind in which a person believes that he or she is being constantly oppressed or attacked.

siemens ('siːmənz) *n, pl* **siemens.** the derived SI unit of electrical conductance equal to 1 reciprocal ohm. Symbol: S Formerly called: **mho.** [C20: after Ernst Werner von *Siemens* (1816–92) G engineer]

sienna (sɪ'ɛnə) *n* **1** a natural earth containing ferric oxide used as a yellowish-brown pigment when untreated (**raw sienna**) or a reddish-brown pigment when roasted (**burnt sienna**). **2** the colour of this pigment. [C18: from It. *terra di Siena* earth of Siena]

sierra (sɪ'ɛərə) *n* a range of mountains with jagged peaks, esp. in Spain or America. [C17: from Sp., lit.: saw, from L *serra*]
▸ **si'erran** *adj*

siesta ❶ (sɪ'ɛstə) *n* a rest or nap, usually taken in the early afternoon, as in hot countries. [C17: from Sp., from L *sexta hōra* the sixth hour, i.e. noon]

sieve ❶ (sɪv) *n* **1** a device for separating lumps from powdered material, straining liquids, etc., consisting of a container with a mesh or perforated bottom through which the material is shaken or poured. ◆ *vb* **sieves, sieving, sieved. 2** to pass or cause to pass through a sieve. **3** *(tr; often foll. by out)* to separate or remove (lumps, materials, etc.) by use of a sieve. [OE *sife*]
▸ **'sieve,like** *adj*

sift ❶ (sɪft) *vb* **1** *(tr)* to sieve (sand, flour, etc.) in order to remove the coarser particles. **2** to scatter (something) over a surface through a sieve. **3** *(tr)* to separate with or as if with a sieve. **4** *(tr)* to examine minutely: *to sift evidence.* **5** *(intr)* to move as if through a sieve. [OE *siftan*]
▸ **'sifter** *n*

siftings ('sɪftɪŋz) *pl n* material or particles separated out by or as if by a sieve.

sigh ❶ (saɪ) *vb* **1** *(intr)* to draw in and exhale audibly a deep breath as an expression of weariness, relief, etc. **2** *(intr)* to make a sound resembling this. **3** *(intr; often foll. by for)* to yearn, long, or pine. **4** *(tr)* to utter or express with sighing. ◆ *n* **5** the act or sound of sighing. [OE *sīcan,* from ?]
▸ **'sigher** *n*

sight ❶ (saɪt) *n* **1** the power or faculty of seeing; vision. Related adj: **visual. 2** the act or an instance of seeing. **3** the range of vision: *within sight of land.* **4** point of view; judgment: *in his sight she could do no wrong.* **5** a glimpse or view (esp. in **catch** *or* **lose sight of**). **6** anything that is seen. **7** *(often pl)* anything worth seeing: *the sights of London.* **8** *Inf.* anything unpleasant or undesirable to see: *his room was a sight!* **9** any of various devices or instruments used to assist the eye in making alignments or directional observations, esp. such a device used in aiming a gun. **10** an observation or alignment made with such a device. **11 a sight.** *Inf.* a great deal: *she's a sight too good for him.* **12 a sight for sore eyes.** a person or thing that one is pleased or relieved to see. **13 at** *or* **on sight. 13a** as soon as seen. **13b** on presentation: *a bill payable at sight.* **14 know by sight.** to be familiar with the appearance of without having personal acquaintance. **15 not by a long sight.** *Inf.* on no account. **16 set one's sights on.** to have (a specified goal) in mind. **17 sight unseen.** without having seen the object at issue: *to buy a car sight unseen.* ◆ *vb* **18** *(tr)* to see, view, or glimpse. **19** *(tr)* **19a** to furnish with a sight or sights. **19b** to adjust the sight of. **20** to aim (a firearm) using the sight. [OE *sihth*]
▸ **'sightable** *adj*

sighted ('saɪtɪd) *adj* **1** not blind. **2** *(in combination)* having sight of a specified kind: *short-sighted.*

sighting ('saɪtɪŋ) *n* **1** an occasion on which something is seen, esp. something rare or unusual. **2** another name for **sight** (sense 10).

sighting shot *n* an experimental shot made to assist gunmen in setting their sights.

sightless ('saɪtlɪs) *adj* **1** blind. **2** invisible.
▸ **'sightlessly** *adv* ▸ **'sightlessness** *n*

sightly ('saɪtlɪ) *adj* **sightlier, sightliest.** pleasing or attractive to see.
▸ **'sightliness** *n*

sight-read ('saɪt,riːd) *vb* **sight-reads, sight-reading, sight-read** (-,rɛd). to sing or play (music in a printed or written form) without previous preparation.
▸ **'sight-,reader** *n* ▸ **'sight-,reading** *n*

sightscreen ('saɪt,skriːn) *n Cricket.* a large white screen placed near the boundary behind the bowler to help the batsman see the ball.

sightsee ('saɪt,siː) *vb* **sightsees, sightseeing, sightsaw, sightseen.** to visit the famous or interesting sights of (a place).
▸ **'sight,seeing** *n* ▸ **'sight,seer** *n*

sigla ('sɪglə) *n* the list of symbols used in a book, usually collected together as part of the preliminaries. [L: pl of *siglum,* dim. of *signum* sign]

sigma ('sɪgmə) *n* **1** the 18th letter in the Greek alphabet (Σ, σ, or, when final, ς), a consonant, transliterated as *S.* **2** *Maths.* the symbol Σ, indicating summation of the numbers of quantities indicated. [C17: from Gk]

sigma notation *n* an algebraic notation in which a capital Greek sigma (Σ) is used to indicate that all values of the expression following the sigma are to be added together (usually for values of a variable between specified limits).

sigmoid ('sɪgmɔɪd) *or* **sigmoidal** *adj* **1** shaped like the letter S. **2** of or relating to the sigmoid flexure of the large intestine. [C17: from Gk *sigmoeidēs* sigma-shaped]

sigmoid flexure *n* the S-shaped bend in the final portion of the large intestine.

sign ❶ (saɪn) *n* **1** something that indicates a fact, condition, etc., that is not immediately or outwardly observable. **2** an action or gesture intended to convey information, a command, etc. **3a** a board, placard, etc., displayed in public and intended to inform, warn, etc. **3b** *(as modifier): a sign painter.* **4** an arbitrary mark or device that stands for a word, phrase, etc. **5** *Maths, logic.* **5a** any symbol used to indicate an operation: *a plus sign.* **5b** the positivity or negativity of a number, expression, etc. **6** an indication or vestige: *the house showed no signs of being occupied.* **7** a portentous or significant event. **8** the scent or spoor of an animal. **9** *Med.* any objective evidence of the presence of a disease or disorder. **10** *Astrol.* See **sign of the zodiac.** ◆ *vb* **11** to write (one's name) as a signature to (a document, etc.) in attestation, confirmation, etc. **12** *(intr; often foll. by to)* to make a sign. **13** to engage or be engaged by written agreement, as a player for a team, etc. **14** *(tr)* to outline in gestures a sign over, esp. the sign of the cross. **15** *(tr)* to indicate by or as if

THESAURUS

sidetrack *vb* **1** = **distract**, deflect, divert, lead off the subject

sideways *adv* **1, 2** = **obliquely**, crabwise, edgeways, laterally, sidelong, sidewards, to the side ◆ *adj* **4, 5** = **oblique**, side, sidelong, slanted

sidle *vb* **1** = **edge**, creep, inch, slink, sneak, steal

siesta *n* = **nap**, catnap, doze, forty winks (*inf.*), kip (*Brit. sl.*), rest, sleep, snooze (*inf.*)

sieve *n* **1** = **strainer**, colander, riddle, screen, sifter, tammy cloth ◆ *vb* **2, 3** = **sift**, bolt, remove, riddle, separate, strain

sift *vb* **1** = **sieve**, bolt, filter, pan, part, riddle, separate **4** = **examine**, analyse, fathom, go through, investigate, pore over, probe, research, screen, scrutinize, work over

sigh *vb* **1** = **breathe**, complain, grieve, lament, moan, sorrow, sough, suspire (*arch.*) **3 sigh for** = **long for**, eat one's heart out over, languish over, mourn for, pine for, yearn for

sight *n* **1** = **vision**, eye, eyes, eyesight, seeing **3** = **view**, appearance, apprehension, eyeshot, field of vision, ken, perception, range of vision, viewing, visibility **7** = **spectacle**, display, exhibition, pageant, scene, show, vista **8** *Informal* = **eyesore**, blot on the landscape (*inf.*), fright (*inf.*), mess, monstrosity, spectacle ◆ *vb* **18** = **spot**, behold, discern, distinguish, make out, observe, perceive, see

sign *n* **1** = **indication**, clue, evidence, giveaway, hint, manifestation, mark, note, proof, signal, suggestion, symptom, token, trace, vestige **3** = **notice**, board, placard, warning **4** = **symbol**, badge, character, cipher, device, emblem, ensign, figure, logo, mark, representation **7** = **omen**, augury, auspice, foreboding, forewarning, portent, presage, warning, writing on the wall ◆ *vb* **11** = **autograph**, endorse, initial, inscribe, set one's hand to, subscribe **12** = **gesture**, beckon, gesticulate, indicate, signal, use sign language, wave

by a sign; betoken. ◆ See also **sign away, sign in,** etc. [C13: from OF, from L *signum* a sign]
▸'**signable** *adj* ▸'**signer** *n*

signal ⓘ ('sɪgnᵊl) *n* **1** any sign, gesture, etc., that serves to communicate information. **2** anything that acts as an incitement to action: *the rise in prices was a signal for rebellion.* **3a** a variable parameter, such as a current or electromagnetic wave, by which information is conveyed through an electronic circuit, etc. **3b** the information so conveyed. **3c** *(as modifier): a signal generator.* ◆ *adj* **4** distinguished or conspicuous. **5** used to give or act as a signal. ◆ *vb* **signals, signalling, signalled** *or US* **signals, signaling, signaled. 6** to communicate (a message, etc.) to (a person). [C16: from OF *seignal,* from Med. L *signāle,* from L *signum* sign]
▸'**signaller** *or US* '**signaler** *n*

signal box *n* **1** a building containing signal levers for all the railway lines in its section. **2** a control point for a large area of a railway system.

signalize *or* **signalise** ('sɪgnə,laɪz) *vb* **signalizes, signalizing, signalized** *or* **signalises, signalising, signalised.** *(tr)* **1** to make noteworthy. **2** to point out carefully.

signally ('sɪgnəlɪ) *adv* conspicuously or especially.

signalman ('sɪgnᵊlmən) *n, pl* **signalmen.** a railway employee in charge of the signals and points within a section.

signal-to-noise ratio *n* the ratio of one parameter, such as power of a wanted signal, to the same parameter of the noise at a specified point in an electronic circuit, etc.

signatory ('sɪgnətərɪ, -trɪ) *n, pl* **signatories. 1** a person who has signed a document such as a treaty or an organization, state, etc., on whose behalf such a document has been signed. ◆ *adj* **2** having signed a document, treaty, etc. [C17: from L *signātōrius* concerning sealing, from *signāre* to seal, from *signum* a mark]

signature ('sɪgnɪtʃə) *n* **1** the name of a person or a mark or sign representing his name. **2** the act of signing one's name. **3** a distinctive mark, characteristic, etc., that identifies a person or thing. **4** *Music.* See **key signature, time signature. 5** *Printing.* **5a** a sheet of paper printed with several pages that upon folding will become a section or sections of a book. **5b** such a sheet so folded. **5c** a mark, esp. a letter, printed on the first page of a signature. [C16: from OF, from Med. L *signātura,* from L *signāre* to sign]

signature tune *n Brit.* a melody used to introduce or identify a television or radio programme, a performer, etc.

sign away ⓘ *vb (tr, adv)* to dispose of by or as if by signing a document.

signboard ('saɪn,bɔːd) *n* a board carrying a sign or notice, esp. one used to advertise a product, event, etc.

signet ('sɪgnɪt) *n* **1** a small seal, esp. one as part of a finger ring. **2** a seal used to stamp or authenticate documents. **3** the impression made by such a seal. [C14: from Med. L *signētum* a little seal, from L *signum* a sign]

signet ring *n* a finger ring bearing a signet.

significance ⓘ (sɪg'nɪfɪkəns) *n* **1** consequence or importance. **2** something expressed or intended. **3** the state or quality of being significant. **4** *Statistics.* a measure of the confidence that can be placed in a result as not being merely a matter of chance.

significant ⓘ (sɪg'nɪfɪkənt) *adj* **1** having or expressing a meaning. **2** having a covert or implied meaning. **3** important or momentous. **4** *Statistics.* of or relating to a difference between a result derived from a hypothesis and its observed value that is too large to be attributed to chance. [C16: from L *significāre* to SIGNIFY]
▸**sig'nificantly** *adv*

significant figures *pl n* **1** the figures of a number that express a magnitude to a specified degree of accuracy: *3.141 59 to four significant figures is 3.142.* **2** the number of such figures: *3.142 has four significant figures.*

significant other *n US inf.* a spouse or lover.

signification (,sɪgnɪfɪ'keɪʃən) *n* **1** meaning or sense. **2** the act of signifying.

signify ⓘ ('sɪgnɪ,faɪ) *vb* **signifies, signifying, signified.** (when *tr, may take a clause as object*) **1** *(tr)* to indicate or suggest. **2** *(tr)* to imply or portend: *the clouds signified the coming storm.* **3** *(tr)* to stand as a symbol, sign, etc. (for). **4** *(intr)* to be important. [C13: from OF, from L *significāre,* from *signum* a mark + *facere* to make]
▸**sig'nificative** *adj* ▸'**signi,fier** *n*

sign in *vb (adv)* **1** to sign or cause to sign a register, as at a hotel, club, etc. **2** to make or become a member, as of a club.

signing ('saɪnɪŋ) *n* a specific set of manual signs used to communicate with deaf people.

sign language *n* any system of communication by manual signs or gestures, such as one used by deaf people.

sign off *vb (adv)* **1** *(intr)* to announce the end of a radio or television programme, esp. at the end of a day. **2** *(tr)* (of a doctor) to declare (someone) unfit for work, because of illness. **3** *(intr) Brit.* to terminate one's claim to social security benefits.

sign of the zodiac *n* any of the 12 equal areas into which the zodiac can be divided, named after the 12 zodiacal constellations. In astrology, it is thought that a person's attitudes to life can be correlated with the sign in which the sun lay at the moment of their birth. Also called: **sign, star sign, sun sign.**

sign on *vb (adv)* **1** *(tr)* to hire or employ. **2** *(intr)* to commit oneself to a job, activity, etc. **3** *(intr) Brit.* to claim social security benefits.

signor *or* **signior** ('siːnjɔː; *Italian* siɲ'ɲor) *n, pl* **signors** *or* **signori** (*Italian* -'ɲori). an Italian man: usually used before a name as a title equivalent to *Mr.*

signora (siːn'jɔːrə; *Italian* siɲ'ɲora) *n, pl* **signoras** *or* **signore** (*Italian* -re). a married Italian woman: a title of address equivalent to *Mrs* when placed before a name or *madam* when used alone. [It., fem of SIGNORE]

signore (siːn'jɔːreɪ; *Italian* siɲ'ɲore) *n, pl* **signori** (-rɪ; *Italian* -ri). an Italian man: a title of respect equivalent to *sir* when used alone. [It., ult. from L *senior* an elder, from *senex* an old man]

signorina (,siːnjɔː'riːnə; *Italian* siɲɲo'rina) *n, pl* **signorinas** *or* **signorine** (*Italian* -ne). an unmarried Italian woman: a title of address equivalent to *Miss* when placed before a name or *madam* or *miss* when used alone. [It., dim. of SIGNORA]

signory ('siːnjərɪ) *n, pl* **signories.** a variant spelling of **seigniory.**

sign out *vb (adv)* to sign (one's name) to indicate that one is leaving a place: *he signed out for the evening.*

signpost ('saɪn,pəʊst) *n* **1** a post bearing a sign that shows the way, as at a roadside. **2** something that serves as a clue or indication. ◆ *vb (tr; usually passive)* **3** to mark with signposts. **4** to indicate direction towards.

sign up ⓘ *vb (adv)* to enlist or cause to enlist, as for military service.

sika ('siːkə) *n* a Japanese forest-dwelling deer, now introduced into Britain, having a brown coat and a large white patch on the rump. [from Japanese *shika*]

Sikh (siːk) *n* **1** a member of an Indian religion that separated from Hinduism and was founded in the 16th century, that teaches monotheism and rejects the authority of the Vedas. ◆ *adj* **2** of or relating to the Sikhs or their religious beliefs. [C18: from Hindi, lit.: disciple, from Sansk. *śiksati* he studies]
▸'**Sikh,ism** *n*

silage ('saɪlɪdʒ) *n* any crop harvested while green for fodder and kept succulent by partial fermentation in a silo. Also called: **ensilage.** [C19: alteration (infl. by SILO) of ENSILAGE]

sild (sɪld) *n* any of various small young herrings, esp. when prepared and canned in Norway. [Norwegian]

silence ⓘ ('saɪləns) *n* **1** the state or quality of being silent. **2** the absence of sound or noise. **3** refusal or failure to speak, etc., when expected: *his silence on their promotion was alarming.* **4** a period of time without noise. **5** oblivion or obscurity. ◆ *vb* **silences, silencing, silenced.** *(tr)* **6** to bring to silence. **7** to put a stop to: *to silence all complaint.*

silencer ('saɪlənsə) *n* **1** any device designed to reduce noise, esp. the device in the exhaust system of a motor vehicle. US and Canad. name: **muffler. 2** a device fitted to the muzzle of a firearm to deaden the report. **3** a person or thing that silences.

silene (saɪ'liːnɪ) *n* any of a genus of plants with pink or white flowers and slender leaves. [C18: NL, from L]

silent ⓘ ('saɪlənt) *adj* **1** characterized by an absence or near absence of noise or sound: *a silent house.* **2** tending to speak very little or not at all. **3** unable to speak. **4** failing to speak, communicate, etc., when expected: *the witness chose to remain silent.* **5** not spoken or expressed. **6** (of a letter) used in the orthography of a word but no longer pronounced in that word: *the "k" in "know" is silent.* **7** denoting a film that

THESAURUS

signal *n* **1** = **sign**, beacon, cue, flare, gesture, go-ahead (*inf.*), green light, indication, indicator, mark, token ◆ *adj* **4** = **significant**, conspicuous, distinguished, eminent, exceptional, extraordinary, famous, memorable, momentous, notable, noteworthy, outstanding, remarkable, serious (*inf.*), striking ◆ *vb* **6** = **gesture**, beckon, communicate, gesticulate, give a sign to, indicate, motion, nod, sign, wave

sign away *vb* = **give up**, abandon, dispose of, forgo, lose, relinquish, renounce, surrender, transfer, waive

significance *n* **1** = **importance**, consequence, consideration, impressiveness, matter, moment, relevance, weight **2** = **meaning**, force, implication(s), import, message, point, purport, sense, signification

significant *adj* **1, 2** = **meaningful**, denoting, eloquent, expressing, expressive, indicative, knowing, meaning, pregnant, suggestive **3** = **important**, critical, material, momentous, noteworthy, serious, vital, weighty
Antonyms *adj* ≠ **meaningful:** meaningless ≠ **important:** immaterial, inconsequential, insignificant, irrelevant, nit-picking, nugatory, of no consequence, paltry, petty, trivial, unimportant, worthless

signify *vb* **1-3** = **indicate**, announce, be a sign of, betoken, communicate, connote, convey, denote, evidence, exhibit, express, imply, intimate, matter, mean, portend, proclaim, represent, show, stand for, suggest, symbolize **4** *Informal* = **matter**, be important, carry weight, count

sign up *vb* = **enlist**, contract with, enrol, join, join up, register, volunteer

silence *n* **1** = **quiet**, calm, hush, lull, noiselessness, peace, quiescence, stillness **3** = **muteness**, dumbness, reticence, speechlessness, taciturnity, uncommunicativeness ◆ *vb* **6** = **quieten**, cut off, cut short, deaden, extinguish, gag, muffle, quell, quiet, stifle, still, strike dumb, subdue, suppress
Antonyms *n* ≠ **quiet:** cacophony, din, noise, racket, sound, tumult, uproar ≠ **muteness:** babble, bawling, chatter, clamour, garrulousness, hubbub, loquaciousness, murmuring, prattle, shouting, speech, talk, talking, verbosity, whispering, yelling ◆ *vb* ≠ **quieten:** amplify, broadcast, disseminate, encourage, foster, make louder, promote, promulgate, publicize, rouse, spread, support, ungag

silent *adj* **1** = **quiet**, hushed, muted, noiseless, soundless, still, stilly (*poetic*) **2-4** = **mute**, dumb, mum, nonvocal, not talkative, speechless, struck dumb, taciturn, tongue-tied, uncommunicative, unspeaking, voiceless, wordless **5** = **unspoken**, aphonic (*Phonetics*), implicit, im-

has no accompanying soundtrack. [C16: from L *silēns*, from *silēre* to be quiet]
▸'**silently** *adv* ▸'**silentness** *n*

silent cop *n Austral. sl.* a small raised hemispherical marker in the middle of a crossroads.

silent majority *n* a presumed moderate majority of the citizens who are too passive to make their views known.

Silenus (saɪ'liːnəs; 'silɛɪnəs) *n Greek myth.* **1** chief of the satyrs and foster father to Dionysus. **2** (*pl* **Sileni** (saɪ'liːnaɪ; 'silɛniː). (*often not cap.*) one of a class of woodland deities, closely similar to the satyrs.

silex ('saɪlɛks) *n* a type of heat-resistant glass made from fused quartz. [C16: from L: hard stone]

silhouette ❶ (ˌsɪluː'ɛt) *n* **1** the outline of a solid figure as cast by its shadow. **2** an outline drawing filled in with black, often a profile portrait cut out of black paper and mounted on a light ground. ◆ *vb* **silhouettes, silhouetting, silhouetted.** **3** (*tr*) to cause to appear in silhouette. [C18: after Étienne de *Silhouette* (1709–67), F politician]

silica ('sɪlɪkə) *n* the dioxide of silicon (SiO_2), occurring naturally as quartz. It is a refractory insoluble material used in the manufacture of glass, ceramics, and abrasives. [C19: NL, from L *silex* hard stone]

silica gel *n* an amorphous form of silica capable of absorbing large quantities of water: used esp. in drying gases and oils.

silicate ('sɪlɪkɪt, -ˌkeɪt) *n* a salt or ester that can be regarded as derived from silicic acid. Silicates constitute a large proportion of the earth's minerals and are present in cement and glass.

siliceous *or* **silicious** (sɪ'lɪʃəs) *adj* **1** of, relating to, or containing silica: *a siliceous clay.* **2** (of plants) growing in soil rich in silica.

silicic (sɪ'lɪsɪk) *adj* of or containing silicon or an acid obtained from silicon.

silicic acid *n* a white gelatinous substance obtained by adding an acid to a solution of sodium silicate. It is best regarded as hydrated silica.

silicify (sɪ'lɪsɪˌfaɪ) *vb* **silicifies, silicifying, silicified.** to convert or be converted into silica: *silicified wood.*
▸**siˌlicifi'cation** *n*

silicon ('sɪlɪkən) *n* **a** a brittle metalloid element that exists in two allotropic forms; occurs principally in sand, quartz, granite, feldspar, and clay. It is usually a grey crystalline solid but is also found as a brown amorphous powder. It is used in transistors, solar cells, and alloys. Its compounds are widely used in glass manufacture and the building industry. Symbol: Si; atomic no.: 14; atomic wt.: 28.09. **b** (*modifier; sometimes cap.*) denoting an area of a country that contains much high-technology industry. [C19: from SILICA, on the model of *boron, carbon*]

silicon carbide *n* an extremely hard bluish-black insoluble crystalline substance produced by heating carbon with sand at a high temperature and used as an abrasive and refractory material. Very pure crystals are used as semiconductors. Formula: SiC.

silicon chip *n* another term for **chip** (sense 7).

silicon-controlled rectifier *n* a semiconductor rectifier whose forward current between two electrodes, the anode and cathode, is initiated by means of a signal applied to a third electrode, the gate. The current subsequently becomes independent of the signal. Also called: **thyristor.**

silicone ('sɪlɪˌkəʊn) *n Chem.* **a** any of a large class of polymeric synthetic materials that usually have resistance to temperature, water, and chemicals, and good insulating and lubricating properties, making them suitable for wide use as oils, water repellents, resins, etc. **b** (*as modifier*): *silicone rubber.*

Silicon Valley *n* any area in which industries associated with information technology are concentrated.

silicosis (ˌsɪlɪ'kəʊsɪs) *n Pathol.* a form of pneumoconiosis caused by breathing in tiny particles of silica, quartz, or slate, and characterized by shortness of breath.

siliqua (sɪ'liːkwə, 'sɪlɪkwə) *or* **silique** (sɪ'liːk, 'sɪlɪk) *n, pl* **siliquae** (-'liːkwiː), **siliquas,** *or* **siliques.** the long dry dehiscent fruit of cruciferous plants, such as the wallflower. [C18: via F from L *siliqua* a pod]
▸**siliquose** ('sɪlɪˌkwəʊs) *or* **siliquous** ('sɪlɪkwəs) *adj*

silk (sɪlk) *n* **1** the very fine soft lustrous fibre produced by a silkworm to make its cocoon. **2a** thread or fabric made from this fibre. **2b** (*as modifier*): *a silk dress.* **3** a garment made of this. **4** a very fine fibre produced by a spider to build its web, nest, or cocoon. **5** the tuft of long fine styles on an ear of maize. **6** *Brit.* **6a** the gown worn by a Queen's (or King's) Counsel. **6b** *Inf.* a Queen's (or King's) Counsel. **6c take silk.** to become a Queen's (or King's) Counsel. [OE *sioluc;* ult. from Chinese *ssŭ* silk]
▸'**silkˌlike** *adj*

silk cotton *n* another name for **kapok.**

silk-cotton tree *n* any of a genus of tropical trees having seeds covered with silky hairs from which kapok is obtained. Also called: **kapok tree.**

silken ('sɪlkən) *adj* **1** made of silk. **2** resembling silk in smoothness or gloss. **3** dressed in silk. **4** soft and delicate.

silk hat *n* a man's top hat covered with silk.

silkworm ('sɪlkˌwɜːm) *n* **1** the larva of the Chinese moth that feeds on the leaves of the mulberry tree: widely cultivated as a source of silk. **2** any of various similar or related larvae.

silky ❶ ('sɪlkɪ) *adj* **silkier, silkiest.** **1** resembling silk in texture; glossy. **2** made of silk. **3** (of a voice, manner, etc.) suave; smooth. **4** *Bot.* covered with long fine soft hairs: *silky leaves.*
▸'**silkily** *adv* ▸'**silkiness** *n*

silky oak *n* any of an Australian genus of trees having divided leaves and showy clusters of orange, red, or white flowers: cultivated in the tropics as shade trees.

sill (sɪl) *n* **1** a shelf at the bottom of a window inside a room. **2** a horizontal piece along the outside lower member of a window, that throws water clear of the wall below. **3** the lower horizontal member of a window or door frame. **4** a horizontal member placed on top of a foundation wall in order to carry a timber framework. **5** a mass of igneous rock, situated between two layers of older sedimentary rock. [OE *syll*]

sillabub ('sɪləˌbʌb) *n* a variant spelling of **syllabub.**

silly ❶ ('sɪlɪ) *adj* **sillier, silliest.** **1** lacking in good sense; absurd. **2** frivolous, trivial, or superficial. **3** feeble-minded. **4** dazed, as from a blow. ◆ *n* **5** (*modifier*) *Cricket.* (of a fielding position) near the batsman's wicket: *silly mid-on.* **6** (*pl* **sillies**) Also called: **silly-billy.** *Inf.* a foolish person. [C15 (in the sense: pitiable, hence the later senses: foolish): from OE *sǣlig* (unattested) happy, from *sǣl* happiness]
▸'**silliness** *n*

silly season *n Brit.* a period, usually during the summer months, when journalists fill space reporting on frivolous events and activities.

silo ('saɪləʊ) *n, pl* **silos.** **1** a pit, trench, or tower, often cylindrical in shape, in which silage is made and stored. **2** an underground position in which missile systems are sited for protection. [C19: from Sp., ? of Celtic origin]

silt ❶ (sɪlt) *n* **1** a fine deposit of mud, clay, etc., esp. one in a river or lake. ◆ *vb* **2** (usually foll. by *up*) to fill or become filled with silt; choke. [C15: from ON]
▸**sil'tation** *n* ▸'**silty** *adj*

Silurian (saɪ'lʊərɪən) *adj* **1** of or formed in the third period of the Palaeozoic era, during which fishes first appeared. ◆ *n* **2 the.** the Silurian period or rock system. [C19: from *Silures,* a Welsh tribe who opposed the Romans]

silurid (saɪ'lʊərɪd) *n* **1** any freshwater teleost fish of the family Siluridae, such as the **European catfish,** which has an elongated body, naked skin, and a long anal fin. ◆ *adj* **2** of, relating to, or belonging to the family Siluridae. [C19: from L *silūrus,* from Gk *silouros* a river fish]

silva ('sɪlvə) *n* a variant spelling of **sylva.**

silvan ('sɪlvən) *adj, n* a variant spelling of **sylvan.**

silver ❶ ('sɪlvə) *n* **1a** a ductile malleable brilliant greyish-white element having the highest electrical and thermal conductivity of any metal. It occurs free and in argentite and other ores: used in jewellery, tableware, coinage, electrical contacts, and electroplating. Symbol: Ag; atomic no.: 47; atomic wt.: 107.870. **1b** (*as modifier*): *a silver coin.* Related adj: **argent.** **2** coin made of, or having the appearance of, this metal. **3** cutlery, whether made of silver or not. **4** any household articles made of silver. **5** short for **silver medal.** **6a** a brilliant or light greyish-white colour. **6b** (*as adj*): *silver hair.* ◆ *adj* **7** well-articulated: *silver speech.* **8** (*prenominal*) denoting the 25th in a series: *a silver wedding anniversary.* ◆ *vb* **9** (*tr*) to coat with silver or a silvery substance: *to silver a spoon.* **10** to become or cause to become silvery in colour. [OE *siolfor*]
▸'**silvering** *n*

silver age *n* **1** (in Greek and Roman mythology) the second of the world's major epochs, inferior to the preceding golden age. **2** the postclassical period of Latin literature, occupying the early part of the Roman imperial era.

silver beet *n* an Australian and New Zealand variety of beet, cultivated for its edible leaves with white stems.

silver bell *n* any of various deciduous trees of North America and China, having white bell-shaped flowers. Also called: **snowdrop tree.**

silver birch *n* a tree of N temperate regions of the Old World, having silvery-white peeling bark.

silver bromide *n* a yellowish powder that darkens when exposed to light: used in making photographic emulsions. Formula: AgBr.

silver chloride *n* a white powder that darkens on exposure to

THESAURUS

plied, tacit, understood, unexpressed, unpronounced

silently *adv* **1** = **quietly,** as quietly as a mouse (*inf.*), dumbly, inaudibly, in silence, mutely, noiselessly, soundlessly, speechlessly, without a sound, wordlessly

silhouette *n* **1** = **outline,** delineation, form, profile, shape ◆ *vb* **3** = **outline,** delineate, etch, stand out

silky *adj* **1** = **smooth,** silken, sleek, velvety

silly *adj* **1** = **foolish,** absurd, asinine, brainless, childish, daft, fatuous, foolhardy, frivolous, giddy, idiotic, immature, imprudent, inane, inappropriate, irresponsible, meaningless, pointless, preposterous, puerile, ridiculous, senseless, stupid, unwise, witless **4** = **dazed,** benumbed, groggy (*inf.*), in a daze, muzzy, stunned, stupefied ◆ *n* **6** *Informal* = **fool,** clot (*Brit. inf.*), duffer (*inf.*), goose (*inf.*), ignoramus, ninny, nitwit (*inf.*), silly-billy (*inf.*), simpleton, twit (*inf.*), wally (*sl.*)

Antonyms *adj* ≠ **foolish:** acute, aware, bright, clever, intelligent, mature, perceptive, profound, prudent, reasonable, sane, sensible, serious, smart, thoughtful, well-thought-out, wise

silt *n* **1** = **sediment,** alluvium, deposit, ooze, residue, sludge ◆ *vb* **2** *with* **up** = **clog,** choke, congest, dam

silver *modifier* **1b** = **silvery,** argent (*poetic*), pearly, silvered ◆ *n* **4** = **silverware,** silver plate

light: used in making photographic emulsions and papers. Formula: AgCl.

silver disc *n* (in Britain) an album certified to have sold 60 000 copies or a single certified to have sold 200 000 copies.

silver-eye *n Austral. & NZ.* another name for **waxeye** or **white-eye.**

silver fern *n NZ.* **1** another name for **ponga. 2** a formalized spray of fern leaf, silver on a black background: the symbol of New Zealand sporting teams.

silver fir *n* any of various fir trees the leaves of which have a silvery undersurface.

silverfish ('sɪlvəˌfɪʃ) *n, pl* **silverfish** *or* **silverfishes. 1** a silver variety of the goldfish. **2** any of various other silvery fishes, such as the moonfish. **3** any of various small primitive wingless insects that have long antennae and tail appendages and occur in buildings, feeding on food scraps, book-bindings, etc.

silver fox *n* **1** an American red fox in a colour phase in which the fur is black with long silver-tipped hairs. **2** the valuable fur or pelt of this animal.

silver-gilt *n* silver covered with a thin film of gold.

silver iodide *n* a yellow powder that darkens on exposure to light: used in photography and artificial rainmaking. Formula: AgI.

silver lining *n* a hopeful aspect of an otherwise desperate or unhappy situation (esp. in the phrase **every cloud has a silver lining**).

silver medal *n* a medal of silver awarded to a competitor who comes second in a contest or race.

silver nitrate *n* a white crystalline soluble poisonous substance used in making photographic emulsions and as a medical antiseptic and astringent. Formula: $AgNO_3$.

silver plate *n* **1** a thin layer of silver deposited on a base metal. **2** articles, esp. tableware, made of silver plate. ◆ *vb* **silver-plate, silver-plates, silver-plating, silver-plated. 3** (*tr*) to coat (a metal, object, etc.) with silver, as by electroplating.

silver screen *n* **the.** *Inf.* **1** films collectively or the film industry. **2** the screen onto which films are projected.

silver service *n* (in restaurants) a style of serving food using a spoon and fork in one hand like a pair of tongs.

silverside ('sɪlvəˌsaɪd) *n* **1** *Brit. & NZ.* a cut of beef below the aitchbone and above the leg. **2** a small marine or freshwater teleost fish related to the grey mullets.

silversmith ('sɪlvəˌsmɪθ) *n* a craftsman who makes or repairs articles of silver.
▸ **'silverˌsmithing** *n*

silverware ('sɪlvəˌwɛə) *n* articles, esp. tableware, made of or plated with silver.

silverweed ('sɪlvəˌwiːd) *n* **1** a rosaceous perennial creeping plant with silvery pinnate leaves and yellow flowers. **2** any of various twining shrubs of SE Asia and Australia, having silvery leaves and showy purple flowers.

silvery ('sɪlvərɪ) *adj* **1** of or having the appearance of silver: *the silvery moon.* **2** containing or covered with silver. **3** having a clear ringing sound.
▸ **'silveriness** *n*

silviculture ('sɪlvɪˌkʌltʃə) *n* the branch of forestry that is concerned with the cultivation of trees. [C20: *silvi-,* from L *silva* woodland + CULTURE]
▸ **ˌsilvi'cultural** *adj* ▸ **ˌsilvi'culturist** *n*

sima ('saɪmə) *n* **1** the silicon-rich and magnesium-rich rocks of the earth's oceanic crust. **2** the earth's continental lower crust. [C20: from SI(LICA) + MA(GNESIA)]

simian ('sɪmɪən) *adj* **1** of or resembling a monkey or ape. ◆ *n* **2** a monkey or ape. [C17: from L *sīmia* an ape, prob. from Gk *sīmos* flat-nosed]

similar ⓘ ('sɪmɪlə) *adj* **1** showing resemblance in qualities, characteristics, or appearance. **2** *Geom.* (of two or more figures) having corresponding angles equal and all corresponding sides in the same ratio. [C17: from OF, from L *similis*]
▸ **similarity** (ˌsɪmɪ'lærɪtɪ) *n* ▸ **'similarly** *adv*

> **USAGE NOTE** *As should not be used after similar: Wilson held a similar position to Jones* (not *a similar position as Jones*); *the system is similar to the one in France* (not *similar as in France*).

simile ('sɪmɪlɪ) *n* a figure of speech that expresses the resemblance of one thing to another of a different category, usually introduced by *as* or *like.* Cf. **metaphor.** [C14: from L *simile* something similar, from *similis* like]

similitude (sɪ'mɪlɪˌtjuːd) *n* **1** likeness. **2** a thing or sometimes a person that is like or the counterpart of another. **3** *Arch.* a simile or parable. [C14: from L *similitūdō,* from *similis* like]

simmer ⓘ ('sɪmə) *vb* **1** to cook (food) gently at or just below the boiling point. **2** (*intr*) to be about to break out in rage or excitement. ◆ *n* **3** the act, sound, or state of simmering. [C17: ? imit.]

simmer down ⓘ *vb* (*adv*) **1** (*intr*) *Inf.* to grow calmer, as after intense rage. **2** (*tr*) to reduce the volume of (a liquid) by boiling slowly.

simnel cake ('sɪmnᵊl) *n Brit.* a fruit cake covered with a layer of marzipan, traditionally eaten during Lent or at Easter. [C13 *simenel,* from OF, from L *simila* fine flour, prob. of Semitic origin]

simon-pure ('saɪmən-) *adj Rare.* real; authentic. [C19: from *the real Simon Pure,* a character in the play *A Bold Stroke for a Wife* (1717) by Susannah Centlivre (1669–1723), who is impersonated by another character in some scenes]

simony ('saɪmənɪ) *n Christianity.* the practice, now usually regarded as a sin, of buying or selling spiritual or Church benefits such as pardons, relics, etc. [C13: from OF *simonie,* from LL *simōnia,* from *Simon Magus,* a biblical sorcerer who tried to buy magical powers]
▸ **'simonist** *n*

simoom (sɪ'muːm) *or* **simoon** (sɪ'muːn) *n* a strong suffocating sand-laden wind of the deserts of Arabia and North Africa. [from Ar. *samūm* poisonous, from Aramaic *sammā* poison]

simpatico (sɪm'pɑːtɪˌkəʊ) *adj Inf.* **1** pleasant or congenial. **2** of similar mind or temperament. [It.: from *simpatia* SYMPATHY]

simper ⓘ ('sɪmpə) *vb* **1** (*intr*) to smile coyly, affectedly, or in a silly self-conscious way. **2** (*tr*) to utter (something) in such a manner. ◆ *n* **3** a simpering smile; smirk. [C16: prob. from Du. *simper* affected]
▸ **'simpering** *adj* ▸ **'simperingly** *adv*

simple ⓘ ('sɪmpᵊl) *adj* **1** easy to understand or do: *a simple problem.* **2** plain; unadorned: *a simple dress.* **3** not combined or complex: *a simple mechanism.* **4** unaffected or unpretentious: *despite his fame, he remained a simple man.* **5** sincere; frank: *her simple explanation was readily accepted.* **6** of humble condition or rank: *the peasant was of simple birth.* **7** feeble-minded. **8** (*prenominal*) without additions or modifications: *the witness told the simple truth.* **9** (*prenominal*) straightforward: *a simple case of mumps.* **10** *Chem.* (of a substance) consisting of only one chemical compound. **11** *Maths.* (of an equation) containing variables to the first power only. **12** *Biol.* **12a** not divided into parts: *a simple leaf.* **12b** formed from only one ovary: *simple fruit.* **13** *Music.* relating to or denoting a time where the number of beats per bar may be two, three, or four. ◆ *n Arch.* **14** a simpleton. **15** a plant having medicinal properties. [C13: via OF from L *simplex* plain]
▸ **simplicity** (sɪm'plɪsɪtɪ) *n*

simple fraction *n* a fraction in which the numerator and denominator are both integers. Also called: **common fraction, vulgar fraction.**

simple fracture *n* a fracture in which the broken bone does not pierce the skin.

simple harmonic motion *n* a form of periodic motion of a particle, etc., in which the acceleration is always directed towards some equilibrium point and is proportional to the displacement from this point. Abbrev.: **SHM.**

simple-hearted *adj* free from deceit; frank.

simple interest *n* interest paid on the principal alone. Cf. **compound interest.**

simple machine *n* a simple device for altering the magnitude or direction of a force. The six basic types are the lever, wheel and axle, pulley, screw, wedge, and inclined plane.

THESAURUS

similar *adj* **1** = **alike,** analogous, close, comparable, congruous, corresponding, cut from the same cloth, homogeneous, homogenous, in agreement, like, much the same, of a piece, resembling, uniform
Antonyms *adj* antithetical, clashing, contradictory, contrary, different, disparate, dissimilar, diverse, heterogeneous, irreconcilable, opposite, unalike, unrelated, various, varying

similarity *n* **1** = **resemblance,** affinity, agreement, analogy, closeness, comparability, concordance, congruence, correspondence, likeness, point of comparison, relation, sameness, similitude
Antonyms *n* antithesis, contradictoriness, difference, disagreement, discordance, discrepancy, disparity, dissimilarity, diversity, heterogeneity, incomparability, irreconcilability, unalikeness, variation, variety

similarly *adv* **1** = **in the same way,** by the same token, correspondingly, in like manner, likewise

simmer *vb* **2** = **fume,** be agitated, be angry, be tense, be uptight, boil, burn, rage, see red (*inf.*), seethe, smart, smoulder

simmer down *vb* **1** *Informal* = **calm down,** collect oneself, contain oneself, control oneself, cool off *or* down, get down off one's high horse (*inf.*), grow quieter, unwind (*inf.*)

simper *vb* **1** = **smile coyly,** grimace, smile affectedly, smile self-consciously, smirk

simpering *adj* **1** = **coy,** affected, self-conscious

simple *adj* **1** = **uncomplicated,** clear, easy, easy-peasy (*sl.*), elementary, intelligible, lucid, manageable, plain, straightforward, understandable, uninvolved **2** = **plain,** classic, clean, natural, severe, Spartan, unadorned, uncluttered, unembellished, unfussy **3** = **pure,** elementary, single, unalloyed, unblended, uncombined, undivided, unmixed **4** = **artless,** childlike, frank, green, guileless, ingenuous, innocent, naive, natural, simplistic, sincere, unaffected, unpretentious, unsophisticated **5** = **honest,** bald, basic, direct, frank, naked, plain, sincere, stark, undeniable, unvarnished **6** = **unpretentious,** homely, humble, lowly, modest, rustic **7** *Informal* = **feeble-minded,** brainless, credulous, dense, dumb (*inf.*), feeble, foolish, half-witted, moronic, obtuse, shallow, silly, slow, stupid, thick
Antonyms *adj* ≠ **uncomplicated:** advanced, complex, complicated, convoluted, difficult, elaborate, highly developed, intricate, involved, refined, sophisticated ≠ **plain:** contrived, elaborate, fussy, intricate, ornate ≠ **artless:** artful, smart, sophisticated, worldly, worldly-wise ≠ **unpretentious:** extravagant, fancy, flashy ≠ **feeble-minded:** astute, bright, clever, intelligent, knowing, on the ball, quick, quick on the uptake, quick-witted, sharp, smart, wise

simple-minded Ⓣ *adj* **1** stupid; foolish; feeble-minded. **2** unsophisticated; artless.
▸ˌ**simple-'mindedly** *adv* ▸ˌ**simple-'mindedness** *n*

simple sentence *n* a sentence consisting of a single main clause.

simpleton Ⓣ ('sɪmpᵊltən) *n* a foolish or ignorant person.

simplify Ⓣ ('sɪmplɪˌfaɪ) *vb* **simplifies, simplifying, simplified.** (*tr*) **1** to make less complicated or easier. **2** *Maths.* to reduce (an equation, fraction, etc.) to its simplest form. [C17: via F from Med. L *simplificāre*, from L *simplus* simple + *facere* to make]
▸ˌ**simplifi'cation** *n*

simplistic Ⓣ (sɪm'plɪstɪk) *adj* **1** characterized by extreme simplicity. **2** making unrealistically simple judgments or analyses.
▸'**simplism** *n* ▸**sim'plistically** *adv*

> **USAGE NOTE** Since *simplistic* already has *too* as part of its meaning, it is tautologous to talk about something being *too simplistic* or *over-simplistic.*

simply Ⓣ ('sɪmplɪ) *adv* **1** in a simple manner. **2** merely. **3** absolutely; altogether: *a simply wonderful holiday.* **4** (*sentence modifier*) frankly.

simulacrum (ˌsɪmjʊ'leɪkrəm) *n, pl* **simulacra** (-krə). *Arch.* **1** any image or representation of something. **2** a superficial likeness. [C16: from L: likeness, from *simulāre* to imitate, from *similis* like]

simulate Ⓣ *vb* ('sɪmjʊˌleɪt), **simulates, simulating, simulated.** (*tr*) **1** to make a pretence of: *to simulate anxiety.* **2** to reproduce the conditions of (a situation, etc.), as in carrying out an experiment: *to simulate weightlessness.* **3** to have the appearance of. ◆ *adj* ('sɪmjʊlɪt, -ˌleɪt). **4** *Arch.* assumed. [C17: from L *simulāre* to copy, from *similis* like]
▸ˌ**simu'lation** *n* ▸'**simulative** *adj*

simulated Ⓣ ('sɪmjʊˌleɪtɪd) *adj* **1** (of fur, leather, pearls, etc.) being an imitation of the genuine article, usually made from cheaper material. **2** (of actions, emotions, etc.) imitated; feigned.

simulator ('sɪmjʊˌleɪtə) *n* **1** any device that simulates specific conditions for the purposes of research or operator training: *space simulator.* **2** a person who simulates.

simulcast ('sɪməlˌkɑːst) *vb* **1** (*tr*) to broadcast (a programme, etc.) simultaneously on radio and television. ◆ *n* **2** a programme, etc., so broadcast. [C20: from SIMUL(TANEOUS) + (BROAD)CAST]

simultaneous Ⓣ (ˌsɪməl'teɪnɪəs) *adj* occurring, existing, or operating at the same time. [C17: on the model of INSTANTANEOUS from L *simul* at the same time]
▸ˌ**simul'taneously** *adv* ▸ˌ**simul'taneousness** *or* **simultaneity** (ˌsɪməltə'niːɪtɪ) *n*

> **USAGE NOTE** See at **unique.**

simultaneous equations *pl n* a set of equations that are all satisfied by the same values of the variables, the number of variables being equal to the number of equations.

sin[1] Ⓣ (sɪn) *n* **1a** transgression of God's known will or any principle or law regarded as embodying this. **1b** the condition of estrangement from God arising from such transgression. **2** any serious offence, as against a religious or moral principle. **3** any offence against a principle or standard. **4 live in sin.** *Inf.* (of an unmarried couple) to live together. ◆ *vb* **sins, sinning, sinned.** (*intr*) **5** to commit a sin. **6** (usually foll. by *against*) to commit an offence (against a person, etc.). [OE *synn*]
▸'**sinner** *n*

sin[2] (saɪn) *Maths. abbrev. for* sine.

SIN (in Canada) *abbrev. for* Social Insurance Number.

sinanthropus (sɪn'ænθrəpəs) *n* a primitive apelike man of the genus *Sinanthropus,* now considered a subspecies of *Homo erectus.* [C20: from NL, from LL *Sīnae* the Chinese + *-anthropus,* from Gk *anthrōpos* man]

sin bin *n* **1** *Sl.* (in ice hockey, etc.) an area off the field of play where a player who has committed a foul can be sent to sit for a specified period. **2** *Inf.* a separate unit for disruptive schoolchildren.

since (sɪns) *prep* **1** during or throughout the period of time after: *since May it has only rained once.* ◆ *conj* (*subordinating*) **2** (sometimes preceded by *ever*) continuously from or starting from the time when. **3** seeing that; because. ◆ *adv* **4** since that time: *I haven't seen him since.* [OE *sīththan,* lit.: after that]

> **USAGE NOTE** See at **ago.**

sincere Ⓣ (sɪn'sɪə) *adj* **1** not hypocritical or deceitful; genuine: *sincere regret.* **2** *Arch.* pure; unmixed. [C16: from L *sincērus*]
▸**sin'cerely** *adv* ▸**sincerity** (sɪn'serɪtɪ) *or* **sin'cereness** *n*

sinciput ('sɪnsɪˌpʌt) *n, pl* **sinciputs** *or* **sincipita** (sɪn'sɪpɪtə). *Anat.* the forward upper part of the skull. [C16: from L: half a head, from SEMI- + *caput* head]
▸**sin'cipital** *adj*

sine[1] (saɪn) *n* (of an angle) a trigonometric function that in a right-angled triangle is the ratio of the length of the opposite side to that of the hypotenuse. [C16: from L *sinus* a bend; in NL, *sinus* was mistaken as a translation of Ar. *jiba* sine (from Sansk. *jīva,* lit.: bowstring) because of confusion with Ar. *jaib* curve]

sine[2] ('saɪnɪ) *prep* (esp. in Latin phrases or legal terms) lacking; without.

sinecure Ⓣ ('saɪnɪˌkjʊə) *n* **1** a paid office or post involving minimal duties. **2** a Church benefice to which no spiritual charge is attached. [C17: from Med. L (*beneficium*) *sine cūrā* (benefice) without cure (of souls), from L *sine* without + *cūra* cure]
▸'**sineˌcurism** *n* ▸'**sineˌcurist** *n*

sine curve (saɪn) *n* a curve of the equation $y = \sin x$. Also called: **sinusoid.**

sine die *Latin.* ('saɪnɪ 'daɪɪ) *adv, adj* without a day fixed. [lit.: without a day]

sine qua non *Latin.* ('saɪnɪ kweɪ 'nɒn) *n* an essential requirement. [lit.: without which not]

sinew ('sɪnjuː) *n* **1** *Anat.* another name for **tendon. 2** (*often pl*) **2a** a source of strength or power. **2b** a literary word for **muscle.** [OE *sionu*]
▸'**sinewless** *adj*

sine wave (saɪn) *n* any oscillation, such as an alternating current, whose waveform is that of a sine curve.

sinewy Ⓣ ('sɪnjʊɪ) *adj* **1** consisting of or resembling a tendon or tendons. **2** muscular. **3** (esp. of language, style, etc.) forceful. **4** (of meat, etc.) tough.
▸'**sinewiness** *n*

sinfonia (ˌsɪnfə'nɪə) *n, pl* **sinfonie** (-'niːeɪ) *or* **sinfonias. 1** another word for **symphony** (senses 2, 3). **2** (*cap. when part of a name*) a symphony orchestra. [It.]

sinfonietta (ˌsɪnfən'jɛtə) *n* **1** a short or light symphony. **2** (*cap. when part of a name*) a small symphony orchestra. [It.: a little symphony]

sinful Ⓣ ('sɪnfʊl) *adj* **1** having committed or tending to commit sin: *a sinful person.* **2** characterized by or being a sin: *a sinful act.*
▸'**sinfully** *adv* ▸'**sinfulness** *n*

THESAURUS

simple-minded *adj* **1** = **feeble-minded**, a bit lacking (*inf.*), addle-brained, backward, brainless, dead from the neck up (*inf.*), dim-witted, foolish, idiot, idiotic, moronic, retarded, simple, stupid **2** = **unsophisticated**, artless, natural

simpleton *n* = **halfwit**, blockhead, booby, chump, coot, dolt, dope (*inf.*), dullard, dunce, fool, idiot, imbecile (*inf.*), jackass, moron, nincompoop, ninny, nitwit (*inf.*), numskull *or* numbskull, oaf, schmuck (*US sl.*), Simple Simon, stupid (*inf.*), twerp *or* twirp (*inf.*), twit (*inf., chiefly Brit.*)

simplicity *n* **1** = **ease**, absence of complications, clarity, clearness, easiness, elementariness, obviousness, straightforwardness **2** = **plainness**, clean lines, lack of adornment, modesty, naturalness, purity, restraint **4** = **artlessness**, candour, directness, guilelessness, innocence, lack of sophistication, naivety, openness
Antonyms *n* ≠ **ease:** complexity, complicatedness, difficulty, intricacy, lack of clarity ≠ **plainness:** decoration, elaborateness, embellishment, fanciness, fussiness, ornateness, ostentation ≠ **artlessness:** brains, craftiness, cunning, deviousness, guile, insincerity, knowingness, sharpness, slyness, smartness, sophistication, wariness, wisdom, worldliness

simplify *vb* **1** = **make simpler**, abridge, decipher, disentangle, dumb down, facilitate, make intelligible, reduce to essentials, streamline

simplistic *adj* **2** = **oversimplified**, naive

simply *adv* **1** = **plainly**, clearly, directly, easily, intelligibly, modestly, naturally, straightforwardly, unaffectedly, unpretentiously, without any elaboration **2** = **just**, merely, only, purely, solely **3** = **totally**, absolutely, altogether, completely, really, unreservedly, utterly, wholly

simulate *vb* **1** = **pretend**, act, affect, assume, counterfeit, fabricate, feign, imitate, make believe, put on, reproduce, sham

simulated *adj* **1** = **synthetic**, artificial, fake, imitation, man-made, mock, pseudo (*inf.*), sham, substitute **2** = **pretended**, artificial, assumed, feigned, insincere, make-believe, phoney *or* phony (*inf.*), put-on

simultaneous *adj* = **coinciding**, at the same time, coincident, concurrent, contemporaneous, synchronous

simultaneously *adv* = **at the same time**, all together, concurrently, in chorus, in concert, in the same breath, in unison, together

sin[1] *n* **1-3** = **wrongdoing**, crime, damnation, error, evil, guilt, iniquity, misdeed, offence, sinfulness, transgression, trespass, ungodliness, unrighteousness, wickedness, wrong ◆ *vb* **5** = **transgress**, err, fall, fall from grace, go astray, lapse, offend, trespass (*arch.*)

sincere *adj* **1** = **honest**, artless, bona fide, candid, earnest, frank, genuine, guileless, heartfelt, natural, no-nonsense, open, real, serious, straightforward, true, unaffected, unfeigned, upfront (*inf.*), wholehearted
Antonyms *adj* affected, artful, artificial, deceitful, deceptive, dishonest, false, feigned, hollow, insincere, phoney *or* phony (*inf.*), pretended, put on, synthetic, token, two-faced

sincerely *adv* **1** = **honestly**, earnestly, from the bottom of one's heart, genuinely, in all sincerity, in earnest, in good faith, really, seriously, truly, wholeheartedly

sincerity *n* **1** = **honesty**, artlessness, bona fides, candour, frankness, genuineness, good faith, guilelessness, probity, seriousness, straightforwardness, truth, wholeheartedness

sinecure *n* **1** = **cushy number** (*inf.*), gravy train (*sl.*), money for jam *or* old rope (*inf.*), soft job (*inf.*), soft option

sinewy *adj* **2** = **muscular**, athletic, brawny, lusty, powerful, robust, strong, sturdy, vigorous, wiry

sinful *adj* **1, 2** = **wicked**, bad, corrupt, criminal, depraved, erring, guilty, immoral, iniquitous, irreligious, morally wrong, ungodly, unholy, unrighteous
Antonyms *adj* beatified, blessed, chaste, decent, free from sin, godly, holy, honest, honourable, immaculate, moral, pure, righteous, sinless, spotless, squeaky-clean, unblemished, upright, virtuous, without sin

sing ❶ (sɪŋ) *vb* **sings, singing, sang, sung. 1** to produce or articulate (sounds, words, a song, etc.) with musical intonation. **2** (when *intr*, often foll. by *to*) to perform (a song) to the accompaniment (of): *to sing to a guitar*. **3** (*intr*; foll. by *of*) to tell a story in song (about): *I sing of a maiden*. **4** (*intr*) to perform songs for a living. **5** (*intr*) (esp. of certain birds and insects) to utter calls or sounds reminiscent of music. **6** (when *intr*, usually foll. by *of*) to tell (something), esp. in verse: *the poet who sings of the war*. **7** (*intr*) to make a whining, ringing, or whistling sound: *the arrow sang past his ear*. **8** (*intr*) (of the ears) to experience a continuous ringing. **9** (*tr*) to bring to a given state by singing: *to sing a child to sleep*. **10** (*intr*) *Sl., chiefly US.* to confess or act as an informer. ◆ *n* **11** *Inf.* an act or performance of singing. ◆ See also **sing out**. [OE *singan*]
▸ **'singable** *adj* ▸ **'singer** *n* ▸ **'singing** *adj, n*

USAGE NOTE See at **ring**².

sing. *abbrev. for* singular.
singe ❶ (sɪndʒ) *vb* **singes, singeing, singed. 1** to burn or be burnt superficially; scorch: *to singe one's clothes*. **2** (*tr*) to burn the ends of (hair, etc.). **3** (*tr*) to expose (a carcass) to flame to remove bristles or hair. ◆ *n* **4** a superficial burn. [OE *sengan*]
Singh (sɪŋ) *n* a title assumed by a Sikh when he becomes a full member of the community. [from Hindi, from Sansk. *sinhá* a lion]
Singhalese (ˌsɪŋəˈliːz) *n, pl* **Singhaleses** *or* **Singhalese**, *adj* a variant spelling of **Sinhalese**.
singing telegram *n* **a** a service by which a person is employed to present greetings or congratulations by singing. **b** the greetings or congratulations presented thus.
single ❶ (ˈsɪŋgᵊl) *adj* (*usually prenominal*) **1** existing alone; solitary: *upon the hill stood a single tower*. **2** distinct from other things. **3** composed of one part. **4** designed or sufficient for one user: *a single bed*. **5** (*also postpositive*) unmarried. **6** connected with the condition of being unmarried: *he led a single life*. **7** (esp. of combat) involving two individuals. **8** even one: *there wasn't a single person on the beach*. **9** (of a flower) having only one set or whorl of petals. **10** single-minded: *a single devotion to duty*. **11** *Rare.* honest or sincere. ◆ *n* **12** something forming one individual unit. **13** (*often pl*) **13a** an unmarried person. **13b** (*as modifier*): *singles bar*. **14** a gramophone record, CD, or cassette with a short recording, usually of pop music, on it. **15** *Cricket.* a hit from which one run is scored. **16a** *Brit.* a pound note. **16b** *US & Canad.* a dollar note. **17** See **single ticket**. ◆ *vb* **singles, singling, singled. 18** (*tr*; usually foll. by *out*) to select from a group of people or things: *he singled him out for special mention*. ◆ See also **singles**. [C14: from OF *sengle*, from L *singulus* individual]
▸ **'singleness** *n*
single-acting *adj* (of a reciprocating engine or pump) having a piston or pistons pressurized on one side only.
single-breasted *adj* (of a garment) having the fronts overlapping only slightly and with one row of fastenings.
single cream *n* cream having a low fat content that does not thicken with beating.
single-decker *n Brit. inf.* a bus with only one passenger deck.
single-end *n Scot.* a dwelling consisting of a single room.
single entry *n* **a** a book-keeping system in which transactions are entered in one account only. **b** (*as modifier*): *a single-entry account*.
single file *n* a line of persons, animals, or things ranged one behind the other.
single-foot *n* **1** a rapid showy gait of a horse in which each foot strikes the ground separately. ◆ *vb* **2** to move or cause to move at this gait.
single-handed ❶ *adj, adv* **1** unaided or working alone: *a single-handed crossing of the Atlantic*. **2** having or operated by one hand or one person only.
▸ **ˌsingle-'handedly** *adv* ▸ **ˌsingle-'handedness** *n*
single-lens reflex *n* See **reflex camera**.
single-minded ❶ *adj* having but one aim or purpose; dedicated.
▸ **ˌsingle-'mindedly** *adv* ▸ **ˌsingle-'mindedness** *n*
single-parent family *n* a household consisting of at least one dependent child and the mother or father, the other parent being dead or permanently absent. Also called: **one-parent family**.
singles (ˈsɪŋgᵊlz) *pl n Tennis, etc.* a match played with one person on each side.
singles bar *n* a bar or club that is a social meeting place for single people.
single-sex *adj* (of schools, etc.) admitting members of one sex only.
single sideband transmission *n* a method of transmitting radio waves in which either the upper or the lower sideband is transmitted, the carrier being either wholly or partially suppressed.
singlestick (ˈsɪŋgᵊlˌstɪk) *n* **1** a wooden stick used instead of a sword for fencing. **2** fencing with such a stick. **3** any short heavy stick.
singlet (ˈsɪŋglɪt) *n* **1** a sleeveless undergarment covering the body from the shoulders to the hips. **2** a garment worn with shorts by athletes, boxers, etc. [C18: from SINGLE, on the model of *doublet*]
single ticket *n Brit.* a ticket entitling a passenger to travel only to his destination, without returning.
singleton (ˈsɪŋgᵊltən) *n* **1** *Bridge, etc.* an original holding of one card only in a suit. **2** a single object, etc., distinguished from a pair or group. **3** *Maths.* a set containing only one member. [C19: from SINGLE, on the model of SIMPLETON]
single-track *adj* **1** (of a railway) having only a single pair of lines, so that trains can travel in only one direction at a time. **2** (of a road) only wide enough for one vehicle.
Single Transferable Vote *n* (*modifier*) of or relating to a system of voting in which voters list the candidates in order of preference. Abbrev.: **STV**. See **proportional representation**.
singletree (ˈsɪŋgᵊlˌtriː) *n US & Austral.* another word for **swingletree**.
singly ❶ (ˈsɪŋglɪ) *adv* **1** one at a time; one by one. **2** apart from others; separately; alone.
sing out ❶ *vb* (*tr, adv*) to call out in a loud voice; shout.
singsong (ˈsɪŋˌsɒŋ) *n* **1** an accent or intonation that is characterized by an alternately rising and falling rhythm, such as in a person's voice. **2** *Brit.* an informal session of singing, esp. of popular songs. ◆ *adj* **3** having a monotonous rhythm: *a singsong accent*.
singular ❶ (ˈsɪŋgjʊlə) *adj* **1** remarkable; extraordinary: *a singular feat*. **2** unusual; odd: *a singular character*. **3** unique. **4** denoting a word or an inflected form of a word indicating that one referent is being referred to or described. **5** *Logic.* (of a proposition) referring to a specific thing or person. ◆ *n* **6** *Grammar.* **6a** the singular number. **6b** a singular form of a word. [C14: from L *singulāris* single]
▸ **'singularly** *adv*
singularity ❶ (ˌsɪŋgjʊˈlærɪtɪ) *n, pl* **singularities. 1** the state or quality of being singular. **2** something distinguishing a person or thing from others. **3** something unusual. **4** *Maths.* a point at which a function is not differentiable although it is differentiable in a neighbourhood of that point. **5** *Astron.* a hypothetical point in space-time at which matter is infinitely compressed to infinitesimal volume.
singularize *or* **singularise** (ˈsɪŋgjʊləˌraɪz) *vb* **singularizes, singularizing, singularized** *or* **singularises, singularising, singularised.** (*tr*) **1** to make (a word, etc.) singular. **2** to make conspicuous.
▸ **ˌsingulari'zation** *or* **ˌsingulari'sation** *n*
singultus (sɪŋˈgʌltəs) *n, pl* **singultuses.** a technical name for **hiccup**. [C18: from L, lit.: a sob]
sinh (ʃaɪn, sɪnʃ) *n* hyperbolic sine. [C20: from SIN(E)¹ + H(YPERBOLIC)]
Sinhalese (ˌsɪnhəˈliːz) *or* **Singhalese** *n* **1** (*pl* **Sinhaleses** *or* **Sinhalese**) a member of a people living chiefly in Sri Lanka, where they constitute the majority of the population. **2** the language of this people: the official language of Sri Lanka. ◆ *adj* **3** of or relating to this people or their language.
sinister ❶ (ˈsɪnɪstə) *adj* **1** threatening or suggesting evil or harm: *a sinister glance*. **2** evil or treacherous. **3** (*usually postpositive*) *Heraldry.* of, on, or starting from the left side from the bearer's point of view. **4** *Arch.* located on the left side. [C15: from L *sinister* on the left-hand side, considered by Roman augurs to be the unlucky one]
▸ **'sinisterly** *adv* ▸ **'sinisterness** *n*

THESAURUS

sing *vb* **1, 5 = warble**, carol, chant, chirp, croon, make melody, pipe, trill, vocalize, yodel **7, 8 = hum**, buzz, purr, whine, whistle **10** *Slang, chiefly U.S.* **= inform (on)**, betray, blow the whistle (on), fink (on) (*sl., chiefly US*), grass (*Brit. sl.*), peach (*sl.*), rat (on) (*inf.*), shop (*sl., chiefly Brit.*), spill one's guts (*sl.*), spill the beans (*inf.*), squeal (*sl.*), tell all, turn in (*inf.*)
singe *vb* **1 = burn**, char, scorch, sear
singer *n* **2, 4 = vocalist**, balladeer, cantor, chanteuse (*fem.*), chorister, crooner, minstrel, soloist, songster *or* songstress, troubadour
single *adj* **1 = one**, distinct, individual, lone, only, particular, separate, singular, sole, solitary, unique **2 = individual**, exclusive, separate, undivided, unshared **3 = simple**, unblended, uncompounded, unmixed **5 = unmarried**, free, unattached, unwed ◆ *vb* **18** *with* **out = pick**, choose, cull, distinguish, fix on, pick on *or* out, put on one side, select, separate, set apart, winnow
single-handed *adv* **1 = unaided**, alone, by oneself, independently, on one's own, solo, unassisted, under one's own steam, without help
single-minded *adj* **= determined**, dedicated, dogged, fixed, hellbent (*inf.*), monomaniacal, steadfast, stubborn, tireless, undeviating, unswerving, unwavering
singly *adv* **1, 2 = one by one**, individually, one at a time, separately
sing out *vb* **= call (out)**, cooee, cry (out), halloo, holler (*inf.*), make oneself heard, shout, shout ahoy, yell
singular *adj* **1 = remarkable**, conspicuous, eminent, exceptional, extraordinary, notable, noteworthy, outstanding, prodigious, rare, uncommon, unique, unparalleled **2 = unusual**, atypical, curious, eccentric, extraordinary, odd, oddball (*inf.*), out-of-the-way, outré, peculiar, puzzling, queer, strange **3 = single**, individual, separate, sole
Antonyms *adj* ≠ **remarkable, unusual:** common, common or garden, commonplace, conventional, everyday, familiar, normal, routine, run-of-the-mill, unexceptional, unremarkable, usual
singularity *n* **1 = oddness**, abnormality, curiousness, extraordinariness, irregularity, peculiarity, queerness, strangeness **2, 3 = idiosyncrasy**, eccentricity, oddity, particularity, peculiarity, quirk, twist
singularly *adv* **1 = remarkably**, conspicuously, especially, exceptionally, extraordinarily, notably, outstandingly, particularly, prodigiously, seriously (*inf.*), surprisingly, uncommonly, unusually
sinister *adj* **1 = threatening**, baleful, dire, disquieting, evil, forbidding, injurious, malevolent, malign, malignant, menacing, ominous
Antonyms *adj* auspicious, benevolent, benign, calming, encouraging, good, heartening, heroic, honourable, just, noble, promising, propitious, reassuring, righteous, upright, worthy

sinistral ('sɪnɪstrəl) *adj* **1** of or located on the left side, esp. the left side of the body. **2** a technical term for **left-handed. 3** (of the shells of certain molluscs) coiling in a clockwise direction from the apex.
▸'**sinistrally** *adv*

sinistrorse ('sɪnɪˌstrɔːs, ˌsɪnɪ'strɔːs) *adj* (of some climbing plants) growing upwards in a spiral from right to left. [C19: from L *sinistrōrsus* turned towards the left, from *sinister* on the left + *vertere* to turn]
▸ˌ**sinis'trorsal** *adj*

Sinitic (sɪ'nɪtɪk) *n* **1** a branch of the Sino-Tibetan family of languages, consisting of the various dialects of Chinese. ◆ *adj* **2** belonging to this group of languages.

sink ❶ (sɪŋk) *vb* **sinks, sinking, sank; sunk** *or* **sunken. 1** to descend or cause to descend, esp. beneath the surface of a liquid. **2** (*intr*) to appear to move down towards or descend below the horizon. **3** (*intr*) to slope downwards. **4** (*intr;* often foll. by *in* or *into*) to pass into a specified lower state or condition: *to sink into apathy.* **5** to make or become lower in volume, pitch, etc. **6** to make or become lower in value, price, etc. **7** (*intr*) to become weaker in health, strength, etc. **8** (*intr*) to seep or penetrate. **9** (*tr*) to dig, cut, drill, bore, or excavate (a hole, shaft, etc.). **10** (*tr*) to drive into the ground: *to sink a stake.* **11** (*tr;* usually foll. by *in* or *into*) **11a** to invest (money). **11b** to lose (money) in an unwise investment. **12** (*tr*) to pay (a debt). **13** (*intr*) to become hollow: *his cheeks had sunk during his illness.* **14** (*tr*) to hit or propel (a ball) into a hole, pocket, etc.: *he sank a 15-foot putt.* **15** (*tr*) *Brit. inf.* to drink, esp. quickly: *he sank three pints in half an hour.* **16 sink or swim.** to take risks where the alternatives are loss or success. ◆ *n* **17** a fixed basin, esp. in a kitchen, made of stone, metal, etc., used for washing. **18** a place of vice or corruption. **19** an area of ground below that of the surrounding land, where water collects. **20** *Physics.* a device by which energy is removed from a system: *a heat sink.* ◆ *adj* **21** *Inf.* (of a housing estate or school) deprived or having low standards of achievement. [OE *sincan*]
▸'**sinkable** *adj*

sinker ('sɪŋkə) *n* **1** a weight attached to a fishing line, net, etc., to cause it to sink in water. **2** a person who sinks shafts, etc.

sinkhole ('sɪŋkˌhəʊl) *n* **1** Also called (esp. in Britain): **swallow hole.** a depression in the ground surface, esp. in limestone, where a surface stream disappears underground. **2** a place into which foul matter runs.

sink in ❶ *vb* (*intr, adv*) to enter or penetrate the mind: *eventually the news sank in.*

sinking ('sɪŋkɪŋ) *n* **a** a feeling in the stomach caused by hunger or uneasiness. **b** (*as modifier*): *a sinking feeling.*

sinking fund *n* a fund accumulated out of a business enterprise's earnings or a government's revenue and invested to repay a long-term debt.

sinless ❶ ('sɪnlɪs) *adj* free from sin or guilt; pure.
▸'**sinlessly** *adv* ▸'**sinlessness** *n*

Sinn Féin ('ʃɪn 'feːn) *n* an Irish republican political movement founded about 1905 and linked to the revolutionary Irish Republican Army. [C20: from Irish Gaelic: we ourselves]
▸'**Sinn 'Féiner** *n* ▸'**Sinn 'Féinism** *n*

Sino- *combining form.* Chinese: *Sino-Tibetan; Sinology.* [from F, from LL *Sīnae* the Chinese, from LGk, from Ar. *Sīn* China, prob. from Chinese *Ch'in*]

Sinology (saɪ'nɒlədʒɪ) *n* the study of Chinese history, language, culture, etc.
▸**Sinological** (ˌsaɪnə'lɒdʒɪkᵊl) *adj* ▸**Si'nologist** *n* ▸**Sinologue** ('saɪnəˌlɒg) *n*

Sino-Tibetan ('saɪnəʊ-) *n* **1** a family of languages that includes most of the languages of China, as well as Tibetan, Burmese, and possibly Thai. ◆ *adj* **2** belonging or relating to this family of languages.

sinsemilla (ˌsɪnsə'miːljə) *n* **1** a type of marijuana with a very high narcotic content. **2** the plant from which it is obtained, a strain of *Cannabis sativa.* [C20: from American Sp., lit.: without seed]

sinter ('sɪntə) *n* **1** a whitish porous incrustation, usually consisting of silica, that is deposited from hot springs. **2** the product of a sintering process. ◆ *vb* **3** (*tr*) to form large particles, lumps, or masses from (metal powders) by heating or pressure or both. [C18: from G *Sinter* CINDER]

sinuate ('sɪnjʊɪt, -ˌeɪt) *adj* **1** Also: **sinuous.** (of leaves) having a strongly waved margin. **2** another word for **sinuous.** [C17: from L *sinuātus* curved]
▸'**sinuately** *adv*

sinuous ❶ ('sɪnjʊəs) *adj* **1** full of turns or curves. **2** devious; not straightforward. **3** supple. [C16: from L *sinuōsus* winding, from *sinus* a curve]
▸'**sinuously** *adv* ▸**sinuosity** (ˌsɪnjʊ'ɒsɪtɪ) *n*

sinus ('saɪnəs) *n, pl* **sinuses. 1** *Anat.* **1a** any bodily cavity or hollow space. **1b** a large channel for venous blood, esp. between the brain and the skull. **1c** any of the air cavities in the cranial bones. **2** *Pathol.* a passage leading to a cavity containing pus. [C16: from L: a curve]

sinusitis (ˌsaɪnə'saɪtɪs) *n* inflammation of the membrane lining a sinus, esp. a nasal sinus.

sinusoid ('saɪnəˌsɔɪd) *n* **1** any of the irregular terminal blood vessels that replace capillaries in certain organs, such as the liver, heart, spleen, and pancreas. **2** another name for **sine curve.** ◆ *adj* **3** resembling a sinus. [C19: from F *sinusoïde.* See SINUS, -OID]

sinusoidal projection *n* an equal-area map projection on which all parallels are straight lines and all except the prime meridian are sine curves, often used to show tropical latitudes.

Siouan ('suːən) *n* a family of North American Indian languages, including Sioux.

Sioux (suː) *n* **1** (*pl* **Sioux** (suː, suːz)). a member of a group of North American Indian peoples. **2** any of the languages of the Sioux. [from F, shortened from *Nadowessioux*]

sip ❶ (sɪp) *vb* **sips, sipping, sipped. 1** to drink (a liquid) by taking small mouthfuls. ◆ *n* **2** a small quantity of a liquid taken into the mouth and swallowed. **3** an act of sipping. [C14: prob. from Low G *sippen*]
▸'**sipper** *n*

siphon *or* **syphon** ('saɪfᵊn) *n* **1** a tube placed with one end at a certain level in a vessel of liquid and the other end outside the vessel below this level, so that atmospheric pressure forces the liquid through the tube and out of the vessel. **2** See **soda siphon. 3** *Zool.* any of various tubular organs in different aquatic animals, such as molluscs, through which water passes. ◆ *vb* **4** (often foll. by *off*) to draw off through or as if through a siphon. [C17: from L *sīphō,* from Gk *siphōn*]
▸'**siphonal** *or* **siphonic** (saɪ'fɒnɪk) *adj*

siphon bottle *n* another name (esp. US) for **soda siphon.**

siphonophore ('saɪfənəˌfɔː) *n* any of an order of marine colonial hydrozoans, including the Portuguese man-of-war. [C19: from NL, from Gk *siphōnophoros* tube-bearing]

sippet ('sɪpɪt) *n* a small piece of something, esp. a piece of toast or fried bread eaten with soup or gravy. [C16: used as dim. of SOP]

sir (sɜː) *n* **1** a formal or polite term of address for a man. **2** *Arch.* a gentleman of high social status. [C13: var. of SIRE]

Sir (sɜː) *n* **1** a title of honour placed before the name of a knight or baronet: *Sir Walter Raleigh.* **2** *Arch.* a title placed before the name of a figure from ancient history.

sirdar ('sɜːdɑː) *n* **1** a general or military leader in Pakistan and India. **2** (formerly) the title of the British commander in chief of the Egyptian Army. **3** a variant of **sardar.** [from Hindi *sardār,* from Persian, from *sar* head + *dār* possession]

sire ('saɪə) *n* **1** a male parent, esp. of a horse or other domestic animal. **2** a respectful term of address, now used only in addressing a male monarch. ◆ *vb* **sires, siring, sired. 3** (*tr*) (esp. of a domestic animal) to father. [C13: from OF, from L *senior* an elder, from *senex* an old man]

siren ❶ ('saɪərən) *n* **1** a device for emitting a loud wailing sound, esp. as a warning or signal, consisting of a rotating perforated metal drum through which air or steam is passed under pressure. **2** (*sometimes cap.*) *Greek myth.* one of several sea nymphs whose singing was believed to lure sailors to destruction on the rocks the nymphs inhabited. **3** a woman considered to be dangerously alluring or seductive. **4** an aquatic eel-like salamander of North America, having external gills, no hind limbs, and reduced forelimbs. [C14: from OF *sereine,* from L *sīrēn,* from Gk *seirēn*]

sirenian (saɪ'riːnɪən) *adj* **1** of or belonging to the *Sirenia,* an order of aquatic herbivorous placental mammals having forelimbs modified as paddles and a horizontally flattened tail: contains only the dugong and manatees. ◆ *n* **2** an animal belonging to this order; sea cow.

Sirius ('sɪrɪəs) *n* the brightest star in the sky, lying in the constellation Canis Major. Also called: the **Dog Star.** [C14: via L from Gk *Seirios,* from ?]

sirloin ('sɜːˌlɔɪn) *n* a prime cut of beef from the loin, esp. the upper part. [C16 *surloyn,* from OF *surlonge,* from *sur* above + *longe,* from *loigne* LOIN]

sirocco (sɪ'rɒkəʊ) *n, pl* **siroccos.** a hot oppressive and often dusty wind usually occurring in spring, beginning in N Africa and reaching S Europe. [C17: from It., from Ar. *sharq* east wind]

sironize *or* **sironise** ('saɪrəˌnaɪz) *vb* **sironizes, sironizing, sironized** *or* **sironises, sironising, sironised.** (*tr*) *Austral.* to treat (a woollen fabric) chemically to prevent it wrinkling after being washed. [C20: from (C)SIRO + *-n-* + -IZE]

siroset ('saɪrəʊˌsɛt) *adj Austral.* of or relating to the chemical treatment of woollen fabrics to give a permanent-press effect, or a garment so treated.

THESAURUS

sink *vb* **1** = **descend,** cave in, decline, dip, disappear, droop, drop, drown, ebb, engulf, fall, founder, go down, go under, lower, merge, plummet, plunge, sag, slope, submerge, subside **4** = **fall,** abate, collapse, drop, lapse, relapse, retrogress, slip, slump, subside **7** = **decline,** decay, decrease, degenerate, depreciate, deteriorate, die, diminish, dwindle, fade, fail, flag, go downhill (*inf.*), lessen, weaken, worsen **9** = **dig,** bore, drill, drive, excavate, lay, put down

Antonyms *vb* ≠ **descend:** arise, ascend, climb, go up, move up, rise, rise up ≠ **decline:** enlarge, go up, grow, improve, increase, intensify, rise, rise up, swell, wax

sink in *vb* = **be understood,** get through to, make an impression, penetrate, register (*inf.*), take hold of

sinless *adj* = **innocent,** faultless, guiltless, immaculate, pure, squeaky-clean, unblemished, uncorrupted, undefiled, unsullied, virtuous, without fault, without sin

sinner *n* **5** = **wrongdoer,** evildoer, malefactor, miscreant, offender, reprobate, transgressor, trespasser (*arch.*)

sinuous *adj* **1** = **curving,** coiling, crooked, curvy, lithe, mazy, meandering, serpentine, tortuous, twisty, undulating, winding

sip *vb* **1** = **drink,** sample, sup, taste ◆ *n* **2** = **swallow,** drop, taste, thimbleful

siren *n* **3** = **seductress,** charmer, Circe, *femme fatale,* Lorelei, temptress, vamp (*inf.*), witch

sirrah ('sɪrə) *n Arch.* a contemptuous term used in addressing a man or boy. [C16: prob. var. of SIRE]

sirree (sə'ri:) *interj (sometimes cap.) US inf.* an exclamation used with *yes* or *no*.

sirup ('sɪrəp) *n US.* a less common spelling of **syrup.**

sis (sɪs) *n Inf.* short for **sister.**

SIS (in Britain) *abbrev. for* Secret Intelligence Service. Also called: **MI6.**

sisal ('saɪsᵊl) *n* **1** a Mexican agave plant cultivated for its large fleshy leaves, which yield a stiff fibre used for making rope. **2** the fibre of this plant. ◆ Also called: **sisal hemp.** [C19: from Mexican Sp., after *Sisal,* a port in Yucatán, Mexico]

siskin ('sɪskɪn) *n* **1** a yellow-and-black Eurasian finch. **2 pine siskin.** a North American finch, having a streaked yellowish-brown plumage. [C16: from MDu. *sīseken,* from MLow G *sīsek*]

sissy ❶ *or* **cissy** ('sɪsɪ) *n, pl* **sissies. 1** an effeminate, weak, or cowardly boy or man. ◆ *adj* **2** effeminate, weak, or cowardly.

sister ('sɪstə) *n* **1** a female person having the same parents as another person. **2** a female person who belongs to the same group, trade union, etc., as another or others. **3** a senior nurse. **4** *Chiefly RC Church.* a nun or a title given to a nun. **5** a woman fellow member of a religious body. **6** *(modifier)* belonging to the same class, fleet, etc., as another or others: *a sister ship.* **7** *(modifier) Biol.* denoting any of the cells or cell components formed by division of a parent cell or cell component: *sister nuclei.* [OE *sweostor*]

sisterhood ('sɪstə,hʊd) *n* **1** the state of being related as a sister or sisters. **2** a religious body or society of sisters.

sister-in-law *n, pl* **sisters-in-law. 1** the sister of one's husband or wife. **2** the wife of one's brother.

sisterly ('sɪstəlɪ) *adj* of or suitable to a sister, esp. in showing kindness.
▸ **'sisterliness** *n*

sistrum ('sɪstrəm) *n, pl* **sistra** (-trə). a musical instrument of ancient Egypt consisting of a metal rattle. [C14: via L from Gk *seistron,* from *seiein* to shake]

Sisyphean (,sɪsɪ'fi:ən) *adj* **1** relating to Sisyphus, in Greek myth doomed to roll a stone uphill eternally. **2** actually or seemingly endless and futile.

sit ❶ (sɪt) *vb* **sits, sitting, sat.** *(mainly intr)* **1** *(also tr;* when *intr,* often foll. by *down, in,* or *on)* to adopt a posture in which the body is supported on the buttocks and the torso is more or less upright: *to sit on a chair.* **2** *(tr)* to cause to adopt such a posture. **3** (of an animal) to adopt or rest in a posture with the hindquarters lowered to the ground. **4** (of a bird) to perch or roost. **5** (of a hen or other bird) to cover eggs to hatch them. **6** to be situated or located. **7** (of the wind) to blow from the direction specified. **8** to adopt and maintain a posture for one's portrait to be painted, etc. **9** to occupy or be entitled to a seat in some official capacity, as a judge, etc. **10** (of a deliberative body) to be in session. **11** to remain inactive or unused: *his car sat in the garage.* **12** (of a garment) to fit or hang as specified: *that dress sits well on you.* **13** to weigh, rest, or lie as specified: *greatness sits easily on him.* **14** *(tr) Chiefly Brit.* to take (an examination): *he's sitting his bar finals.* **15** (usually foll. by *for*) *Chiefly Brit.* to be a candidate (for a qualification): *he's sitting for a BA.* **16** *(intr; in combination)* to look after a specified person or thing for someone else: *granny-sit.* **17** *(tr)* to have seating capacity for. **18 sit tight.** *Inf.* **18a** to wait patiently. **18b** to maintain one's stand, opinion, etc., firmly. ◆ See also **sit back, sit down,** etc. [OE *sittan*]

sitar (sɪ'tɑ:) *n* a stringed musical instrument, esp. of India, having a long neck, a rounded body, and movable frets. [from Hindi *sitār,* lit.: three-stringed]
▸ **si'tarist** *n*

sit back *vb (intr, adv)* to relax, as when action should be taken: *many people just sit back and ignore the problems of today.*

sitcom ('sɪt,kɒm) *n* an informal term for **situation comedy.**

sit down *vb (adv)* **1** to adopt or cause (oneself or another) to adopt a sitting posture. **2** *(intr;* foll. by *under)* to suffer (insults, etc.) without protests or resistance. ◆ *n* **sit-down. 3** a form of civil disobedience in which demonstrators sit down in a public place. **4** See **sit-down strike.** ◆ *adj* **sit-down. 5** (of a meal, etc.) eaten while sitting down at a table.

sit-down strike *n* a strike in which workers refuse to leave their place of employment until a settlement is reached.

site ❶ (saɪt) *n* **1a** the piece of land where something was, is, or is intended to be located: *a building site.* **1b** *(as modifier): site office.* **2** *Computing.* an Internet location where information relating to a specific subject or group of subjects can be accessed. ◆ *vb* **sites, siting, sited. 3** *(tr)* to locate or install (something) in a specific place. [C14: from L *situs* situation, from *sinere* to be placed]

sith (sɪθ) *adv, conj, prep* an archaic word for **since.** [OE *siththa*]

sit-in *n* **1** a form of civil disobedience in which demonstrators occupy seats in a public place and refuse to move. **2** another term for **sit-down strike.** ◆ *vb* **sit in.** *(intr, adv)* **3** (often foll. by *for*) to deputize (for). **4** (foll. by *on*) to take part (in) as a visitor or guest. **5** to organize or take part in a sit-in.

sitkamer ('sɪt,kɑ:mə) *n S. African.* a sitting room. [from Afrik.]

sitka spruce ('sɪtkə) *n* a tall North American spruce tree having yellowish-green needle-like leaves. [from *Sitka,* a town in SE Alaska]

sit on *vb (intr, prep)* **1** to be a member of (a committee, etc.). **2** *Inf.* to suppress. **3** *Inf.* to check or rebuke.

sit out *vb (tr, adv)* **1** to endure to the end: *I sat out the play although it was terrible.* **2** to remain seated throughout (a dance, etc.).

sitter ('sɪtə) *n* **1** a person or animal that sits. **2** a person who is posing for his or her portrait to be painted, etc. **3** a broody hen that is sitting on its eggs to hatch them. **4** *(in combination)* a person who looks after a specified person or thing for someone else: *flat-sitter.* **5** *US.* short for **baby-sitter. 6** anyone, other than the medium, taking part in a seance. **7** anything that is extremely easy, such as an easy catch in cricket.

sitting ❶ ('sɪtɪŋ) *n* **1** a continuous period of being seated: *I read his novel at one sitting.* **2** such a period in a restaurant, canteen, etc.: *dinner will be served in two sittings.* **3** the act or period of posing for one's portrait to be painted, etc. **4** a meeting, esp. of an official body, to conduct business. **5** the incubation period of a bird's eggs during which the mother sits on them. ◆ *adj* **6** in office: *a sitting councillor.* **7** seated: *in a sitting position.*

sitting duck *n Inf.* a person or thing in a defenceless or vulnerable position. Also called: **sitting target.**

sitting room *n* a room in a private house or flat used for relaxation and entertainment of guests.

sitting tenant *n* a tenant occupying a house, flat, etc.

situate ('sɪtjʊ,eɪt) *vb* **situates, situating, situated. 1** *(tr; often passive)* to place. ◆ *adj* **2** (now used esp. in legal contexts) situated. [C16: from LL *situāre* to position, from L *situs* a SITE]

situation ❶ (,sɪtjʊ'eɪʃən) *n* **1** physical placement, esp. with regard to the surroundings. **2a** state of affairs. **2b** a complex or critical state of affairs in a novel, play, etc. **3** social or financial status, position, or circumstances. **4** a position of employment.
▸ **,situ'ational** *adj*

> **USAGE NOTE** *Situation* is often used in contexts in which it is redundant or imprecise. Typical examples are: *the company is in a crisis situation* or *people in a job situation.* In the first example, *situation* does not add to the meaning and should be omitted. In the second example, it would be clearer and more concise to substitute a phrase such as *people at work.*

situation comedy *n* (on television or radio) a comedy series involving the same characters in various day-to-day situations which are developed as separate stories for each episode. Also called: **sitcom.**

sit up *vb (adv)* **1** to raise (oneself or another) from a recumbent to an upright posture. **2** *(intr)* to remain out of bed and awake, esp. until a late hour. **3** *(intr) Inf.* to become suddenly interested: *devaluation of the dollar made the money market sit up.* ◆ *n* **sit-up. 4** a physical exercise in which the body is brought into a sitting position from one of lying on the back. Also called: **trunk curl.**

sitz bath (sɪts, zɪts) *n* a bath in which the buttocks and hips are immersed in hot water. [half translation of G *Sitzbad,* from *Sitz* seat + *Bad* bath]

SI unit *n* any of the units adopted for international use under the Système International d'Unités, now employed for all scientific and most technical purposes. There are seven fundamental units: the metre, kilogram, second, ampere, kelvin, candela, and mole; and two supplementary units: the radian and the steradian. All other units are derived by multiplication or division of these units.

Siva ('si:və) *n Hinduism.* the destroyer, one of the three chief divinities of the later Hindu pantheon. [from Sansk. *Śiva,* lit.: the auspicious (one)]
▸ **'Siva,ism** *n*

six (sɪks) *n* **1** the cardinal number that is the sum of five and one. **2** a numeral, 6, VI, etc., representing this number. **3** something representing, represented by, or consisting of six units, such as a playing card with six symbols on it. **4** Also: **six o'clock.** six hours after noon or midnight. **5** *Cricket.* **5a** a stroke from which the ball crosses the boundary without bouncing. **5b** the six runs scored for such a stroke. **6** a division of a Brownie Guide or Cub Scout pack. **7 at sixes and sevens. 7a** in disagreement. **7b** in a state of confusion. **8 knock (someone) for six.** *Inf.* to upset or overwhelm (someone) completely. **9 six of one and half a dozen of the other.** a situation in which the alternatives are considered equivalent. ◆ *determiner* **10a** amounting to six: *six nations.* **10b** *(as pron): set the table for six.* [OE *siex*]

Six Counties *pl n* the counties of Northern Ireland.

sixer ('sɪksə) *n* the leader of a group of six Cub Scouts or Brownie Guides.

sixfold ('sɪks,fəʊld) *adj* **1** equal to or having six times as many or as

THESAURUS

sissy *n* **1** = **wimp** *(inf.),* baby, coward, jessie *(Scot. sl.),* milksop, milquetoast *(US),* mollycoddle, mummy's boy, namby-pamby, pansy, softie *(inf.),* weakling, wet *(Brit. inf.)* ◆ *adj* **2** = **wimpish** *or* **wimpy** *(inf.),* cowardly, effeminate, feeble, namby-pamby, sissified *(inf.),* soft *(inf.),* unmanly, weak, wet *(Brit. inf.)*

sit *vb* **1** = **rest,** be seated, perch, settle, take a seat, take the weight off one's feet **9** = **preside,** officiate **10** = **convene,** assemble, be in session, deliberate, meet **17** = **hold,** accommodate, contain, have space for, seat

site *n* **1** = **location,** ground, place, plot, position, setting, spot ◆ *vb* **3** = **locate,** install, place, position, set, situate

sitting *n* **4** = **meeting,** congress, consultation, get-together *(inf.),* hearing, period, session

situation *n* **1** = **location,** locale, locality, place, position, seat, setting, site, spot **2** = **state of affairs,** ball game *(inf.),* case, circumstances, condition, equation, kettle of fish *(inf.),* lie of the land, plight, scenario, state, status quo, the picture *(inf.)* **3** = **status,** rank, sphere, station **4** = **job,** berth *(inf.),* employment, office, place, position, post

much. **2** composed of six parts. ◆ *adv* **3** by or up to six times as many or as much.

sixmo ('sɪksməʊ) *n, pl* **sixmos.** a book size resulting from folding a sheet of paper into six leaves or twelve pages, each one sixth the size of the sheet. Often written: **6mo, 6°.** Also called: **sexto.**

sixpence ('sɪkspəns) *n* (formerly) a small British cupronickel coin with a face value of six old pennies, worth 2½ pence.

six-shooter *n US inf.* a revolver with six chambers. Also called: **six-gun.**

sixte (sɪkst) *n* the sixth of eight basic positions from which a parry or attack can be made in fencing. [from F: (the) sixth (parrying position), from L *sextus* sixth]

sixteen ('sɪks'ti:n) *n* **1** the cardinal number that is the sum of ten and six. **2** a numeral, 16, XVI, etc., representing this number. **3** something represented by, representing, or consisting of 16 units. ◆ *determiner* **4a** amounting to sixteen: *sixteen tons.* **4b** (*as pron*): *sixteen are known to the police.* [OE *sextyne*]
▸ **'six'teenth** *adj, n*

sixteenmo ('sɪks'ti:nməʊ) *n, pl* **sixteenmos.** a book size resulting from folding a sheet of paper into 16 leaves or 32 pages. Often written: **16mo, 16°.** Also called: **sextodecimo.**

sixteenth note *n* the usual US and Canad. name for **semiquaver.**

sixth (sɪksθ) *adj* **1** (*usually prenominal*) **1a** coming after the fifth and before the seventh in numbering, position, time, etc.; being the ordinal number of *six:* often written 6th. **1b** (*as n*): *the sixth to go.* ◆ *n* **2a** one of six parts of an object, quantity, measurement, etc. **2b** (*as modifier*): *a sixth part.* **3** the fraction equal to one divided by six (1/6). **4** *Music.* **4a** the interval between one note and another six notes away from it in the diatonic scale. **4b** one of two notes constituting such an interval in relation to the other. ◆ *adv* **5** Also: **sixthly.** after the fifth person, position, etc. ◆ *sentence connector.* **6** Also: **sixthly.** as the sixth point.

sixth form *n* (in England and Wales) **a** the most senior level in a secondary school to which pupils, usually above the legal leaving age, may proceed to take A levels, retake GCSEs, etc. **b** (*as modifier*): *a sixth-form college.*
▸ **'sixth-,former** *n*

sixth sense 🅣 *n* any supposed means of perception, such as intuition, other than the five senses of sight, hearing, touch, taste, and smell.

sixty ('sɪkstɪ) *n, pl* **sixties.** **1** the cardinal number that is the product of ten and six. **2** a numeral, 60, LX, etc., representing sixty. **3** something represented by, representing, or consisting of 60 units. ◆ *determiner* **4a** amounting to sixty: *sixty soldiers.* **4b** (*as pron*): *sixty are dead.* [OE *sixtig*]
▸ **'sixtieth** *adj, n*

sixty-fourmo (,sɪkstɪ'fɔ:məʊ) *n, pl* **sixty-fourmos.** a book size resulting from folding a sheet of paper into 64 leaves or 128 pages, each one sixty-fourth the size of the sheet. Often written **64mo, 64°.**

sixty-fourth note *n* the usual US and Canad. name for **hemidemisemiquaver.**

sixty-nine *n* another term for **soixante-neuf.**

sizable 🅣 *or* **sizeable** ('saɪzəbᵊl) *adj* quite large.
▸ **'sizably** *or* **'sizeably** *adv*

size[1] 🅣 (saɪz) *n* **1** the dimensions, amount, or extent of something. **2** large dimensions, etc. **3** one of a series of graduated measurements, as of clothing: *she takes size 4 shoes.* **4** *Inf.* state of affairs as summarized: *he's bankrupt, that's the size of it.* ◆ *vb* **sizes, sizing, sized.** **5** to sort according to size. **6** (*tr*) to cut to a particular size or sizes. [C13: from OF *sise,* shortened from *assise* ASSIZE]
▸ **'sizer** *n*

> **USAGE NOTE** The use of *-size* and *-sized* after *large* or *small* is redundant, except when describing something which is made in specific sizes: *a large* (not *large-size*) *organization.* Similarly, *in size* is redundant in the expressions *large in size* and *small in size.*

size[2] (saɪz) *n* **1** Also called: **sizing.** a thin gelatinous mixture, made from glue, clay, or wax, that is used as a sealer on paper or plaster surfaces. ◆ *vb* **sizes, sizing, sized.** **2** (*tr*) to treat or coat (a surface) with size. [C15: ?from OF *sise;* see SIZE[1]]

sized (saɪzd) *adj* of a specified size: *medium-sized.*

> **USAGE NOTE** See at **size**[1].

size up 🅣 *vb* (*adv*) **1** (*tr*) *Inf.* to make an assessment of (a person, problem, etc.). **2** to conform to or make so as to conform to certain specifications of dimension.

sizzle 🅣 ('sɪzᵊl) *vb* **sizzles, sizzling, sizzled.** (*intr*) **1** to make the hissing sound characteristic of frying fat. **2** *Inf.* to be very hot. **3** *Inf.* to be very angry. ◆ *n* **4** a hissing sound. [C17: imit.]
▸ **'sizzler** *n* ▸ **'sizzling** *adj*

SJ *abbrev. for* Society of Jesus.

SJA *abbrev. for* Saint John's Ambulance (Brigade *or* Association).

sjambok ('ʃæmbʌk) *n* (in South Africa) a heavy whip of rhinoceros or hippopotamus hide. [C19: from Afrik., ult. from Urdu *chābuk* horsewhip]

ska (skɑ:) *n* a type of West Indian pop music: a precursor of reggae. [C20: from ?]

skaapsteker ('skɑ:p,stɪəkə) *n* any of several back-fanged venomous South African snakes. [from Afrik. *skaap* sheep + *steek* to pierce]

skald *or* **scald** (skɔ:ld) *n* (in ancient Scandinavia) a bard or minstrel. [from ON, from ?]
▸ **'skaldic** *or* **'scaldic** *adj*

skat (skæt) *n* a three-handed card game using 32 cards, popular in German-speaking communities. [C19: from G, from It. *scarto* played cards, from *scartare* to discard, from L *charta* CARD[1]]

skate[1] (skeɪt) *n* **1** See **roller skate, ice skate.** **2** the steel blade or runner of an ice skate. **3** such a blade fitted with straps for fastening to a shoe. **4** **get one's skates on.** to hurry. ◆ *vb* **skates, skating, skated.** (*intr*) **5** to glide swiftly on skates. **6** to slide smoothly over a surface. **7** **skate on thin ice.** to place oneself in a dangerous situation. [C17: via Du. from OF *éschasse* stilt, prob. of Gmc origin]
▸ **'skater** *n*

skate[2] (skeɪt) *n, pl* **skate** *or* **skates.** any of a family of large rays of temperate and tropical seas, having two dorsal fins, a short spineless tail, and a long snout. [C14: from ON *skata*]

skateboard ('skeɪt,bɔ:d) *n* **1** a board mounted on roller-skate wheels, usually ridden while standing up. ◆ *vb* **2** (*intr*) to ride on a skateboard.
▸ **'skate,boarder** *n* ▸ **'skate,boarding** *n*

skate over *vb* (*intr, prep*) **1** to cross on or as if on skates. **2** to avoid dealing with (a matter) fully.

skean-dhu (,ski:ən'du:) *n* a dirk worn in the stocking as part of Highland dress. [C19: from Gaelic *sgian dubh* black knife]

skedaddle 🅣 (skɪ'dædᵊl) *Inf.* ◆ *vb* **skedaddles, skedaddling, skedaddled.** **1** (*intr*) to run off hastily. ◆ *n* **2** a hasty retreat. [C19: from ?]

skeet (ski:t) *n* a form of clay-pigeon shooting in which targets are hurled from two traps at varying speeds and angles. [C20: changed from ON *skeyti* a thrown object, from *skjōta* to shoot]

skein (skeɪn) *n* **1** a length of yarn, etc., wound in a long coil. **2** something resembling this, such as a lock of hair. **3** a flock of geese flying. [C15: from OF *escaigne,* from ?]

skeleton 🅣 ('skelɪtən) *n* **1** a hard framework consisting of inorganic material that supports and protects the soft parts of an animal's body: may be internal, as in vertebrates, or external, as in arthropods. **2** *Inf.* a very thin emaciated person or animal. **3** the essential framework of any structure, such as a building or leaf. **4** an outline consisting of bare essentials: *the skeleton of a novel.* **5** (*modifier*) reduced to a minimum: *a skeleton staff.* **6** **skeleton in the cupboard** *or US & Canad.* **closet.** a scandalous fact or event in the past that is kept secret. [C16: via NL from Gk: something desiccated, from *skellein* to dry up]
▸ **'skeletal** *or* **'skeleton-,like** *adj*

skeletonize *or* **skeletonise** ('skelɪtə,naɪz) *vb* **skeletonizes, skeletonizing, skeletonized** *or* **skeletonises, skeletonising, skeletonised.** (*tr*) **1** to reduce to a minimum framework or outline. **2** to create the essential framework of.

skeleton key *n* a key with the serrated edge filed down so that it can open numerous locks. Also called: **passkey.**

skep (skep) *n* **1** a beehive, esp. one constructed of straw. **2** *Now chiefly dialect.* a large basket of wickerwork or straw. [OE *sceppe*]

skeptic ('skeptɪk) *n, adj* an archaic and the usual US spelling of **sceptic.**

skerrick ('skerɪk) *n US, Austral., & NZ.* a small fragment or amount (esp. in **not a skerrick**). [C20: N English dialect, prob. of Scand. origin]

skerry ('skerɪ) *n, pl* **skerries.** *Chiefly Scot.* **1** a small rocky island. **2** a reef. [C17: Orkney dialect, from ON *sker* scar (rock formation)]

sketch 🅣 (sketʃ) *n* **1** a rapid drawing or painting. **2** a brief usually descriptive essay or other literary composition. **3** a short play, often comic, forming part of a revue. **4** a short evocative piece of instrumental music. **5** any brief outline. ◆ *vb* **6** to make a rough drawing (of). **7** (*tr;* often foll. by *out*) to make a brief description of. [C17: from Du. *schets,* via It. from L *schedius* hastily made, from Gk *skhedios* unprepared]
▸ **'sketcher** *n*

sketchbook ('sketʃ,bʊk) *n* **1** a book of plain paper containing sketches or for making sketches in. **2** a book of literary sketches.

THESAURUS

sixth sense *n* = **intuition,** clairvoyance, feyness, second sight

sizable *adj* = **large,** considerable, decent, decent-sized, goodly, largish, respectable, substantial, tidy (*inf.*)

size[1] *n* **1, 2** = **dimensions,** amount, bigness, bulk, extent, greatness, hugeness, immensity, largeness, magnitude, mass, measurement(s), proportions, range, vastness, volume

size up *vb* **1** *Informal* = **assess,** appraise, evaluate, eye up, get (something) taped (*Brit. inf.*), get the measure of, take stock of

sizzle *vb* **1** = **hiss,** crackle, frizzle, fry, spit, sputter

skedaddle *vb* **1** *Informal* = **run away,** abscond, beat a hasty retreat, bolt, decamp, disappear, do a bunk (*Brit. sl.*), flee, scarper (*Brit. sl.*), scoot, scram (*inf.*), scurry away, scuttle away, vamoose (*sl., chiefly US*)

skeletal *adj* **2** = **emaciated,** cadaverous, fleshless, gaunt, hollow-cheeked, lantern-jawed, skin-and-bone (*inf.*), wasted, worn to a shadow

skeleton *n* **3** = **framework,** bare bones, bones, draft, frame, outline, sketch, structure

sketch *n* **1** = **drawing,** delineation, design, draft, outline, plan, skeleton ◆ *vb* **6** = **draw,** block out, delineate, depict, draft, outline, paint, plot, portray, represent, rough out

sketchy ● ('sketʃɪ) *adj* **sketchier, sketchiest. 1** existing only in outline. **2** superficial or slight.
▸ **'sketchily** *adv* ▸ **'sketchiness** *n*

skew (skju:) *adj* **1** placed in or turning into an oblique position or course. **2** *Machinery.* having a component that is at an angle to the main axis of an assembly: *a skew bevel gear.* **3** *Maths.* composed of or being elements that are neither parallel nor intersecting. **4** (of a statistical distribution) not having equal probabilities above and below the mean. **5** distorted or biased. ◆ *n* **6** an oblique, slanting, or indirect course or position. ◆ *vb* **7** to take or cause to take an oblique course or direction. **8** (*intr*) to look sideways. **9** (*tr*) to distort. [C14: from OF *escuer* to shun, of Gmc origin]
▸ **'skewness** *n*

skewback ('skju:,bæk) *n Archit.* the sloping surface on both sides of a segmental arch that takes the thrust.

skewbald ('skju:,bɔ:ld) *adj* **1** marked or spotted in white and any colour except black. ◆ *n* **2** a horse with this marking. [C17: see SKEW, PIEBALD]

skewer (skjʊə) *n* **1** a long pin for holding meat in position while being cooked, etc. **2** a similar pin having some other function. ◆ *vb* **3** (*tr*) to drive a skewer through or fasten with a skewer. [C17: prob. from dialect *skiver*]

skewwhiff ● ('skju:'wɪf) *adj* (*postpositive*) *Brit. inf.* not straight. [C18: prob. infl. by ASKEW]

ski (ski:) *n, pl* **skis** *or* **ski. 1a** one of a pair of wood, metal, or plastic runners that are used for gliding over snow. **1b** (*as modifier*): *a ski boot.* **2** a water-ski. ◆ *vb* **skis, skiing; skied** *or* **ski'd. 3** (*intr*) to travel on skis. [C19: from Norwegian, from ON *skith* snowshoes]
▸ **'skier** *n* ▸ **'skiing** *n*

skibob ('ski:bɒb) *n* a vehicle made of two short skis, the forward one having a steering handle and the rear one supporting a low seat, for gliding down snow slopes.
▸ **'skibobber** *n*

skid (skɪd) *vb* **skids, skidding, skidded. 1** to cause (a vehicle) to slide sideways or (of a vehicle) to slide sideways while in motion, esp. out of control. **2** (*intr*) to slide without revolving, as the wheel of a moving vehicle after sudden braking. ◆ *n* **3** an instance of sliding, esp. sideways. **4** a support on which heavy objects may be stored and moved short distances by sliding. **5** a shoe or drag used to apply pressure to the metal rim of a wheel to act as a brake. [C17: ? of Scand. origin]

Skidoo ('skɪdu:) *n Canad., trademark.* another name for **snowmobile.**

skid row (rəʊ) *or* **skid road** *n Sl., chiefly US & Canad.* a dilapidated section of a city inhabited by vagrants, etc.

skied[1] (skaɪd) *vb* the past tense and past participle of **sky.**

skied[2] (ski:d) *vb* a past tense and past participle of **ski.**

skiff (skɪf) *n* a small narrow boat. [C18: from F *esquif,* from OIt. *schifo* a boat, of Gmc origin]

skiffle ('skɪfᵊl) *n* a style of popular music of the 1950s, played chiefly on guitars and improvised percussion instruments. [C20: from ?]

skijoring (ski:'dʒɔ:rɪŋ, -'jɔ:rɪŋ) *n* a sport in which a skier is pulled over snow or ice, usually by a horse. [Norwegian *skikjöring,* lit.: ski-driving]
▸ **ski'jorer** *n*

ski jump *n* **1** a high ramp overhanging a slope from which skiers compete to make the longest jump. ◆ *vb* **ski-jump. 2** (*intr*) to perform a ski jump.
▸ **ski jumper** *n*

skilful ● *or US* **skillful** ('skɪlfʊl) *adj* **1** possessing or displaying accomplishment or skill. **2** involving or requiring accomplishment or skill.
▸ **'skilfully** *or US* **'skillfully** *adv*

ski lift *n* any device for carrying skiers up a slope, such as a chairlift.

skill ● (skɪl) *n* **1** special ability in a sport, etc., esp. ability acquired by training. **2** something, esp. a trade or technique, requiring special training or manual proficiency. [C12: from ON *skil* distinction]
▸ **'skill-less** *or* **'skilless** *adj*

skilled ● (skɪld) *adj* **1** demonstrating accomplishment or special training. **2** (*prenominal*) involving skill or special training: *a skilled job.*

skillet ('skɪlɪt) *n* **1** a small frying pan. **2** *Chiefly Brit.* a saucepan. [C15: prob. from *skele* bucket, from ON]

skilly ('skɪlɪ) *n Chiefly Brit.* a thin soup or gruel. [C19: from *skilligallee,* from ?]

skim ● (skɪm) *vb* **skims, skimming, skimmed. 1** (*tr*) to remove floating material from the surface of (a liquid), as with a spoon: *to skim milk.* **2** to glide smoothly or lightly over (a surface). **3** (*tr*) to throw (something) in a path over a surface, so as to bounce or ricochet: *to skim stones over water.* **4** (when *intr,* usually foll. by *through*) to read (a book) in a superficial manner. ◆ *n* **5** the act or process of skimming. **6** material skimmed off a liquid, esp. off milk. **7** any thin layer covering a surface. [C15 *skimmen,* prob. from *scumen* to skim]

skimmed milk *n* milk from which the cream has been removed. Also called: **skim milk.**

skimmer ('skɪmə) *n* **1** a person or thing that skims. **2** any of several mainly tropical coastal aquatic birds having a bill with an elongated lower mandible for skimming food from the surface of the water. **3** a flat perforated spoon used for skimming fat from liquids.

skimmia ('skɪmɪə) *n* any of a genus of rutaceous shrubs grown for their ornamental red berries and evergreen foliage. [C18: NL from Japanese (*mijama-*) *shikimi,* a native name of the plant]

skimp ● (skɪmp) *vb* **1** to be extremely sparing or supply (someone) sparingly. **2** to perform (work, etc.) carelessly or with inadequate materials. [C17: ? a combination of SCANT & SCRIMP]

skimpy ● ('skɪmpɪ) *adj* **skimpier, skimpiest. 1** made of too little material. **2** excessively thrifty; mean.
▸ **'skimpily** *adv* ▸ **'skimpiness** *n*

skin ● (skɪn) *n* **1** the tissue forming the outer covering of the vertebrate body: it consists of two layers, the outermost of which may be covered with hair, scales, feathers, etc. **2** a person's complexion: *a fair skin.* **3** any similar covering in a plant or lower animal. **4** any coating or film, such as one that forms on the surface of a liquid. **5** the outer covering of a fur-bearing animal, dressed and finished with the hair on. **6** a container made from animal skin. **7** the outer covering surface of a vessel, rocket, etc. **8** a person's skin regarded as his life: *to save one's skin.* **9** (*often pl*) *Inf.* (in jazz or pop use) a drum. **10** *Inf.* short for **skinhead. 11 by the skin of one's teeth.** only just. **12 get under one's skin.** *Inf.* to irritate. **13 no skin off one's nose.** *Inf.* not a matter that affects one adversely. **14 skin and bone.** extremely thin. **15 thick** (*or* **thin**) **skin.** an insensitive (or sensitive) nature. ◆ *vb* **skins, skinning, skinned. 16** (*tr*) to remove the outer covering from (fruit, etc.). **17** (*tr*) to scrape a small piece of skin from (a part of oneself) in falling, etc.: *he skinned his knee.* **18** (often foll. by *over*) to cover (something) with skin or a skinlike substance or (of something) to become covered in this way. **19** (*tr*) *Sl.* to swindle. ◆ *adj* **20** of or for the skin: *skin cream.* [OE *scinn*]
▸ **'skinless** *adj* ▸ **'skin,like** *adj*

skin-deep ● *adj* **1** superficial; shallow. ◆ *adv* **2** superficially.

skin diving *n* the sport or activity of diving and underwater swimming without wearing a diver's costume.
▸ **'skin-,diver** *n*

skin flick *n Sl.* a film containing much nudity and explicit sex for sensational purposes.

skinflint ● ('skɪn,flɪnt) *n* an ungenerous or niggardly person. [C18: referring to a person so avaricious that he would skin (swindle) a flint]

skinful ('skɪn,fʊl) *n, pl* **skinfuls.** *Sl.* sufficient alcoholic drink to make one drunk.

skin graft *n* a piece of skin removed from one part of the body and surgically grafted at the site of a severe burn or similar injury.

skinhead ('skɪn,hɛd) *n* **1** a member of a group of White youths, noted for their closely cropped hair, aggressive behaviour, and overt racism. **2** a closely cropped hairstyle.

skink (skɪŋk) *n* any of a family of lizards commonest in tropical Africa

THESAURUS

sketchily *adv* **2** = **incompletely**, cursorily, hastily, imperfectly, patchily, perfunctorily, roughly

sketchy *adj* **2** = **incomplete**, bitty, cobbled together, crude, cursory, inadequate, outline, perfunctory, rough, scrappy, skimpy, slight, superficial, unfinished, vague
Antonyms *adj* complete, detailed, full, thorough

skewwhiff *adj Brit. informal* = **crooked**, askew, aslant, cockeyed (*inf.*), out of true, squint (*inf.*), tilted

skilful *adj* **1** = **expert**, able, accomplished, adept, adroit, apt, clever, competent, dexterous, experienced, handy, masterly, practised, professional, proficient, quick, ready, skilled, trained
Antonyms *adj* amateurish, awkward, bungling, cack-handed, clumsy, cowboy (*inf.*), ham-fisted, incompetent, inept, inexperienced, inexpert, maladroit, slapdash, unaccomplished, unqualified, unskilful, unskilled

skill *n* **1** = **expertise**, ability, accomplishment, adroitness, aptitude, art, cleverness, competence, craft, dexterity, experience, expertness, facility, finesse, handiness, ingenuity, intelligence, knack, proficiency, quickness, readiness, skilfulness, talent, technique
Antonyms *n* awkwardness, brute force, cack-handedness, clumsiness, gaucheness, ham-fistedness, inability, incompetence, ineptitude, inexperience, lack of finesse, maladroitness, unhandiness

skilled *adj* **1** = **expert**, able, accomplished, a dab hand at (*Brit. inf.*), experienced, masterly, practised, professional, proficient, skilful, trained
Antonyms *adj* amateurish, cowboy (*inf.*), inexperienced, inexpert, uneducated, unprofessional, unqualified, unskilled, untalented, untrained

skim *vb* **1** = **separate**, cream **2** = **glide**, brush, coast, dart, float, fly, sail, soar **4** *usually with* **through** = **scan**, glance, run one's eye over, skip (*inf.*), thumb *or* leaf through

skimp *vb* **1** = **stint**, be mean with, be niggardly, be sparing with, cut corners, pinch, scamp, scant, scrimp, tighten one's belt, withhold
Antonyms *vb* act as if one had money to burn, be extravagant, be generous with, be prodigal, blow (*sl.*), fritter away, lavish, overspend, pour on, splurge, squander, throw money away

skimpy *adj* **1** = **inadequate**, exiguous, insufficient, meagre, miserly, niggardly, scant, scanty, short, sparse, thin, tight

skin *n* **3** = **hide**, fell, integument, pelt, tegument **4** = **coating**, casing, crust, film, husk, membrane, outside, peel, rind **11 by the skin of one's teeth** = **narrowly**, by a hair's-breadth, by a narrow margin, by a whisker (*inf.*), only just **12 get under one's skin** *Informal* = **annoy**, aggravate (*inf.*), get in one's hair (*inf.*), get on one's nerves (*inf.*), grate on, irk, irritate, needle (*inf.*), nettle, piss one off (*taboo sl.*), rub up the wrong way ◆ *vb* **16** = **peel**, abrade, bark, excoriate, flay **17** = **graze**, scrape

skin-deep *adj* **1** = **superficial**, artificial, external, meaningless, on the surface, shallow, surface

skinflint *n* = **miser**, meanie *or* meany (*inf., chiefly Brit.*), niggard, penny-pincher (*inf.*), Scrooge, tightwad (*US & Canad. sl.*)

and Asia, having an elongated body covered with smooth scales. [C16: from L *scincus* a lizard, from Gk *skinkos*]

skinned (skɪnd) *adj* **1** stripped of the skin. **2a** having a skin as specified. **2b** (*in combination*): *thick-skinned.*

skinny Ⓣ ('skɪnɪ) *adj* **skinnier, skinniest. 1** lacking in flesh; thin. **2** consisting of or resembling skin.

skint (skɪnt) *adj* (*usually postpositive*) *Brit. sl.* without money. [var. of *skinned,* p.p. of SKIN]

skin test *n Med.* any test to determine immunity to a disease or hypersensitivity by introducing a small amount of the test substance beneath the skin.

skintight ('skɪn'taɪt) *adj* (of garments) fitting tightly over the body; clinging.

skip[1] Ⓣ (skɪp) *vb* **skips, skipping, skipped. 1** (when *intr,* often foll. by *over, into,* etc.) to spring or move lightly, esp. to move by hopping from one foot to the other. **2** (*intr*) to jump over a skipping-rope. **3** to cause (a stone, etc.) to skim over a surface or (of a stone) to move in this way. **4** to omit (intervening matter): *he skipped a chapter of the book.* **5** (*intr;* foll. by *through*) *Inf.* to read or deal with quickly or superficially. **6 skip it!** *Inf.* it doesn't matter! **7** (*tr*) *Inf.* to miss deliberately: *to skip school.* **8** (*tr*) *Inf., chiefly US & Canad.* to leave (a place) in haste: *to skip town.* ◆ *n* **9** a skipping movement or gait. **10** the act of passing over or omitting. [C13: prob. from ON]

skip[2] (skɪp) *n, vb* **skips, skipping, skipped.** *Inf.* short for **skipper**[1].

skip[3] (skɪp) *n* **1** a large open container for transporting building materials, etc. **2** a cage used as a lift in mines, etc. [C19: var. of SKEP]

ski pants *pl n* stretch trousers, worn for skiing or as a fashion garment, kept taut by a strap under the foot.

skip distance *n* the shortest distance between a transmitter and a receiver that will permit reception of radio waves of a specified frequency by one reflection from the ionosphere.

skipjack ('skɪpˌdʒæk) *n, pl* **skipjack** *or* **skipjacks. 1** Also called: **skipjack tuna.** an important food fish that has a striped abdomen and occurs in all tropical seas. **2 black skipjack.** a small spotted tuna of Indo-Pacific seas.

skiplane ('skiːˌpleɪn) *n* an aircraft fitted with skis to enable it to land on and take off from snow.

skipper[1] ('skɪpə) *n* **1** the captain of any vessel. **2** the captain of an aircraft. **3** a leader, as of a sporting team. ◆ *vb* **4** to act as skipper (of). [C14: from MLow G, MDu. *schipper* shipper]

skipper[2] ('skɪpə) *n* **1** a person or thing that skips. **2** a small butterfly having a hairy mothlike body and erratic darting flight.

skipping ('skɪpɪŋ) *n* the act of jumping over a rope that is held either by the person jumping or by two other people, as a game or for exercise.

skipping-rope *n Brit.* a cord, usually having handles at each end, that is held in the hands and swung round and down so that the holder or others can jump over it.

skip-tooth saw *n* a saw with alternate teeth absent.

skip zone *n* a region surrounding a broadcasting station that cannot receive transmissions either directly or by reflection off the ionosphere.

skirl (skɜːl) *Scot. & N English dialect.* ◆ *vb* **1** (*intr*) (esp. of bagpipes) to emit a shrill sound. ◆ *n* **2** the sound of bagpipes. [C14: prob. from ON]

skirmish Ⓣ ('skɜːmɪʃ) *n* **1** a minor short-lived military engagement. **2** any brisk clash or encounter. ◆ *vb* **3** (*intr;* often foll. by *with*) to engage in a skirmish. [C14: from OF *eskirmir,* of Gmc origin]
▶ **'skirmisher** *n*

skirt Ⓣ (skɜːt) *n* **1** a garment hanging from the waist, worn chiefly by women and girls. **2** the part of a dress below the waist. **3** Also called: **apron.** a circular flap, as round the base of a hovercraft. **4** the flaps on a saddle. **5** *Brit.* a cut of beef from the flank. **6** (*often pl*) an outlying area. **7 bit of skirt.** *Sl.* a girl or woman. ◆ *vb* **8** (*tr*) to form the edge of. **9** (*tr*) to provide with a border. **10** (when *intr,* foll. by *around, along,* etc.) to pass (by) or be situated (near) the outer edge of (an area, etc.). **11** (*tr*) to avoid (a difficulty, etc.): *he skirted the issue.* **12** *Chiefly Austral. & NZ.* to trim the ragged edges from (a fleece). [C13: from ON *skyrta* shirt]
▶ **'skirted** *adj*

skirting ('skɜːtɪŋ) *n* **1** a border, esp. of wood or tiles, fixed round the base of an interior wall to protect it. **2** material used for skirts.

skirting board *n* a skirting made of wood.

skirtings ('skɜːtɪŋz) *pl n* ragged edges trimmed from the fleece of a sheep.

ski stick *or* **pole** *n* a stick, usually with a metal point, used by skiers to gain momentum and maintain balance.

skit Ⓣ (skɪt) *n* **1** a brief satirical theatrical sketch. **2** a short satirical piece of writing. [C18: rel. to earlier verb *skit* to move rapidly, hence to score a satirical hit, prob. of Scand. origin]

skite[1] (skaɪt) *Scot. dialect.* ◆ *vb* **skites, skiting, skited. 1** (*intr*) to slide or slip, as on ice. **2** (*tr*) to strike with a sharp blow. ◆ *n* **3** an instance of slipping or sliding. **4** a sharp blow. [C18: from ?]

skite[2] (skaɪt) *Austral. & NZ inf.* ◆ *vb* **skites, skiting, skited.** (*intr*) **1** to boast. ◆ *n* **2** boastful talk. **3** a person who boasts. [C19: from Scot. & N English dialect]

ski tow *n* a device for pulling skiers uphill, usually a motor-driven rope grasped by the skier while riding on his skis.

skitter ('skɪtə) *vb* **1** (*intr;* often foll. by *off*) to move or run rapidly or lightly. **2** to skim or cause to skim lightly and rapidly. **3** (*intr*) *Angling.* to draw a bait lightly over the surface of water. [C19: prob. from dialect *skite* to dash about]

skittish Ⓣ ('skɪtɪʃ) *adj* **1** playful, lively, or frivolous. **2** difficult to handle or predict. [C15: prob. from ON]
▶ **'skittishly** *adv* ▶ **'skittishness** *n*

skittle ('skɪt^{ə}l) *n* **1** a wooden or plastic pin, typically widest just above the base. **2** (*pl; functioning as sing*) Also called (esp. US): **ninepins.** a bowling game in which players knock over as many skittles as possible by rolling a wooden ball at them. [C17: from ?]

skive[1] (skaɪv) *vb* **skives, skiving, skived.** (*tr*) to shave or remove the surface of (leather). [C19: of Scand. origin, from *skifa*]
▶ **'skiver** *n*

skive[2] Ⓣ (skaɪv) *vb* **skives, skiving, skived.** (when *intr,* often foll. by *off*) *Brit. inf.* to evade (work or responsibility). [C20: from ?]
▶ **'skiver** *n*

skivvy[1] ('skɪvɪ) *n, pl* **skivvies. 1** *Chiefly Brit., often contemptuous.* a servant, esp. a female; drudge. ◆ *vb* **skivvies, skivvying, skivvied. 2** (*intr*) *Brit.* to work as a skivvy. [C20: from ?]

skivvy[2] ('skɪvɪ) *n, pl* **skivvies.** *Austral. & NZ.* a lightweight sweater-like garment with long sleeves and a polo neck. [from ?]

skol (skɒl) *or* **skoal** (skəʊl) *sentence substitute* good health! (a drinking toast). [C16: from Danish *skaal* bowl, of Scand. origin, from *skal*]

skookum ('skuːkəm) *adj W Canad.* large or big. [from Chinook Jargon]

Skt, Skt., Skr, *or* **Skr.** *abbrev. for* Sanskrit.

skua ('skjuːə) *n* any of various predatory aquatic gull-like birds having a dark plumage and long tail. [C17: from NL, from Faeroese *skūgvur,* of Scand. origin, from *skūfr*]

skulduggery Ⓣ *or US* **skullduggery** (skʌl'dʌgərɪ) *n Inf.* underhand dealing; trickery. [C18: from earlier Scot. *skulduddery,* from ?]

skulk Ⓣ (skʌlk) *vb* (*intr*) **1** to move stealthily so as to avoid notice. **2** to lie in hiding; lurk. **3** to shirk duty or evade responsibilities. ◆ *n* **4** a person who skulks. **5** *Obs.* a pack of foxes. [C13: from ON]
▶ **'skulker** *n*

skull (skʌl) *n* **1** the bony skeleton of the head of vertebrates. **2** *Often derog.* the head regarded as the mind or intelligence: *to have a dense skull.* **3** a picture of a skull used to represent death or danger. [C13: from ON]

skull and crossbones *n* a picture of the human skull above two crossed thighbones, formerly on the pirate flag, now used as a warning of danger or death.

skullcap ('skʌlˌkæp) *n* **1** a rounded brimless hat fitting the crown of the head. **2** the top part of the skull. **3** any of a genus of perennial plants, that have helmet-shaped flowers.

skunk (skʌŋk) *n, pl* **skunks** *or* **skunk. 1** any of various American mammals having a black-and-white coat and bushy tail: they eject an unpleasant-smelling fluid from the anal gland when attacked. **2** *Inf.* a despicable person. [C17: of Amerind origin]

skunk cabbage *n* a low-growing fetid aroid swamp plant of E North America, having broad leaves and minute flowers enclosed in a greenish spathe.

sky Ⓣ (skaɪ) *n, pl* **skies. 1** (*sometimes pl*) the apparently dome-shaped expanse extending upwards from the horizon that is blue or grey during the day and black at night. **2** outer space, as seen from the earth. **3** (*often pl*) weather, as described by the appearance of the upper air:

THESAURUS

skinny *adj* **1** = **thin**, emaciated, lean, scraggy, scrawny, skeletal, skin-and-bone (*inf.*), twiggy, undernourished
Antonyms *adj* beefy (*inf.*), broad in the beam (*inf.*), fat, fleshy, heavy, obese, plump, podgy, portly, stout, tubby

skip[1] *vb* **1** = **hop**, bob, bounce, caper, cavort, dance, flit, frisk, gambol, prance, trip **4** = **pass over**, eschew, give (something) a miss, leave out, miss out, omit, skim over **7** *Informal* = **miss**, bunk off (*sl.*), cut (*inf.*), dog it *or* dog off (*dialect*), play truant from, wag (*dialect*)

skirmish *n* **1, 2** = **fight**, affair, affray (*Law*), battle, brush, clash, combat, conflict, contest, dust-up (*inf.*), encounter, engagement, fracas, incident, scrap (*inf.*), scrimmage, set-to (*inf.*), spat, tussle ◆ *vb* **3** = **fight**, clash, collide, come to blows, scrap (*inf.*), tussle

skirt *n* **6** *often plural* = **outskirts**, edge, fringe, hem, margin, periphery, purlieus, rim ◆ *vb* **8** = **border**, edge, flank, lie alongside **11** = **avoid**, body-swerve (*Scot.*), bypass, circumvent, detour, evade, steer clear of

skit *n* **1, 2** = **parody**, burlesque, sketch, spoof (*inf.*), takeoff (*inf.*), travesty, turn

skittish *adj* **1** = **lively**, excitable, fickle, fidgety, frivolous, highly strung, jumpy, nervous, playful, restive
Antonyms *adj* calm, composed, demure, laid-back, placid, relaxed, sober, staid, steady, unexcitable, unfazed (*inf.*), unflappable, unruffled

skive[2] *vb Brit. informal* = **slack**, bob off (*Brit. sl.*), dodge, gold-brick (*US sl.*), idle, malinger, scrimshank (*Brit. military sl.*), shirk, skulk, swing the lead

skiver *n Brit. informal* = **slacker**, dodger, do-nothing, gold brick (*US sl.*), idler, loafer, scrimshanker (*Brit. military sl.*), shirker

skulduggery *n Informal* = **trickery**, double-dealing, duplicity, fraudulence, machinations, shenanigan(s) (*inf.*), swindling, underhandedness, unscrupulousness

skulk *vb* **1** = **sneak**, creep, pad, prowl, slink **2** = **lurk**, lie in wait, loiter

sky *n* **1** = **heavens**, azure (*poetic*), empyrean, firmament, upper atmosphere, vault of heaven, welkin (*arch.*) **6 to the skies** = **fulsomely**, excessively, extravagantly, highly, immoderately, inordinately, profusely

sunny skies. **4** heaven. **5** *Inf.* the highest level of attainment: *the sky's the limit.* **6 to the skies.** extravagantly. ◆ *vb* **skies, skying, skied. 7** *Rowing.* to lift (the blade of an oar) too high before a stroke. **8** (*tr*) *Inf.* to hit (a ball) high in the air. [C13: from ON *sky̅*]

sky blue *n, adj* (of) a light or pale blue colour.

skydiving ('skaɪˌdaɪvɪŋ) *n* the sport of parachute jumping, in which participants perform manoeuvres before opening the parachute. ▸**'sky,dive** *vb* **'sky,dives, 'sky,diving, 'sky,dived** *or US* **'sky,dove; 'sky-,dived** ▸**'sky,diver** *n*

Skye terrier *n* a short-legged long-bodied breed of terrier with long wiry hair and erect ears. [C19: after *Skye*, Scot. island]

sky-high *adj, adv* **1** at or to an unprecedented level: *prices rocketed sky-high.* ◆ *adv* **2** high into the air. **3 blow sky-high.** to destroy.

skyjack ('skaɪˌdʒæk) *vb* (*tr*) to hijack (an aircraft). [C20: from SKY + HIJACK]

skylark ('skaɪˌlɑːk) *n* **1** an Old World lark, noted for singing while hovering at a great height. ◆ *vb* **2** (*intr*) *Inf.* to romp or play jokes.

skylight ('skaɪˌlaɪt) *n* a window placed in a roof or ceiling to admit daylight. Also called: **fanlight.**

skyline ('skaɪˌlaɪn) *n* **1** the line at which the earth and sky appear to meet. **2** the outline of buildings, trees, etc., seen against the sky.

sky pilot *n Sl.* a clergyman, esp. a chaplain.

skyrocket ('skaɪˌrɒkɪt) *n* **1** another word for **rocket**[1] (sense 1). ◆ *vb* **2** (*intr*) *Inf.* to rise rapidly, as in price.

skysail ('skaɪˌseɪl) *n Naut.* a square sail set above the royal on a square-rigger.

skyscraper ('skaɪˌskreɪpə) *n* a tall multistorey building.

skyward ('skaɪwəd) *adj* **1** directed or moving towards the sky. ◆ *adv* **2** Also: **skywards.** towards the sky.

skywriting ('skaɪˌraɪtɪŋ) *n* **1** the forming of words in the sky by the release of smoke or vapour from an aircraft. **2** the words so formed. ▸**'sky,writer** *n*

slab ⓣ (slæb) *n* **1** a broad flat thick piece of wood, stone, or other material. **2** a thick slice of cake, etc. **3** any of the outside parts of a log that are sawn off while the log is being made into planks. **4** *Austral. & NZ.* **4a** a rough-hewn wooden plank. **4b** (*as modifier*): *a slab hut.* **5** *Inf., chiefly Brit.* an operating or mortuary table. ◆ *vb* **slabs, slabbing, slabbed.** (*tr*) **6** to cut or make into a slab or slabs. **7** to saw slabs from (a log). [C13: from ?]

slack[1] ⓣ (slæk) *adj* **1** not tight, tense, or taut. **2** negligent or careless. **3** (esp. of water, etc.) moving slowly. **4** (of trade, etc.) not busy. **5** *Phonetics.* another term for **lax** (sense 4). ◆ *adv* **6** in a slack manner. ◆ *n* **7** a part of a rope, etc., that is slack: *take in the slack.* **8** a period of decreased activity. ◆ *vb* **9** to neglect (one's duty, etc.). **10** (often foll. by *off*) to loosen. ◆ See also **slacks.** [OE *slæc, sleac*] ▸**'slackly** *adv* ▸**'slackness** *n*

slack[2] (slæk) *n* small pieces of coal with a high ash content. [C15: prob. from MLow G *slecke*]

slacken ⓣ ('slækən) *vb* (often foll. by *off*) **1** to make or become looser. **2** to make or become slower, less intense, etc.

slacker ⓣ ('slækə) *n* a person who evades work or duty; shirker.

slacks (slæks) *pl n* informal trousers worn by both sexes.

slack water *n* the period of still water around the turn of the tide, esp. at low tide.

slag ⓣ (slæg) *n* **1** Also called: **cinder.** the fused material formed during the smelting or refining of metals. It usually consists of a mixture of silicates with calcium, phosphorus, sulphur, etc. **2** the mass of rough fragments of rock derived from volcanic lava. **3** a mixture of shale, clay, coal dust, etc., produced during coal mining. **4** *Brit. sl.* a coarse or dissipated woman or girl. ◆ *vb* **slags, slagging, slagged. 5** to convert into or become slag. **6** (*tr;* sometimes foll. by *off*) *Sl.* to make disparaging comments about; slander. [C16: from MLow G *slagge,* ?from *slagen* to slay] ▸**'slagging** *n* ▸**'slaggy** *adj*

slag heap *n* a hillock of waste matter from coal mining, etc.

slain (sleɪn) *vb* the past participle of **slay.**

slake ⓣ (sleɪk) *vb* **slakes, slaking, slaked. 1** (*tr*) *Literary.* to satisfy (thirst, desire, etc.). **2** (*tr*) *Poetic.* to cool or refresh. **3** to undergo or cause to undergo the process in which lime reacts with water to produce calcium hydroxide. [OE *slacian,* from *slæc* SLACK[1]] ▸**'slakable** *or* **'slakeable** *adj*

slaked lime *n* another name for **calcium hydroxide.**

slalom ('slɑːləm) *n Skiing, canoeing, etc.* a race over a winding course marked by artificial obstacles. [Norwegian, from *slad* sloping + *lom* path]

slam[1] ⓣ (slæm) *vb* **slams, slamming, slammed. 1** to cause (a door or window) to close noisily or (of a door, etc.) to close in this way. **2** (*tr*) to throw (something) down violently. **3** (*tr*) *Sl.* to criticize harshly. **4** (*intr;* usually foll. by *into* or *out of*) *Inf.* to go (into or out of a room, etc.) in violent haste or anger. **5** (*tr*) to strike with violent force. **6** (*tr*) *Inf.* to defeat easily. ◆ *n* **7** the act or noise of slamming. [C17: of Scand. origin]

slam[2] (slæm) *n* **a** the winning of all (**grand slam**) or all but one (**little** *or* **small slam**) of the 13 tricks at bridge or whist. **b** the bid to do so in bridge. [C17: from ?]

slam-dance *vb* **slam-dances, slam-dancing, slam-danced.** (*intr*) to hurl oneself repeatedly into or through a crowd at a rock-music concert.

slammer ('slæmə) *n* **the.** *Sl.* prison.

slander ⓣ ('slɑːndə) *n* **1** *Law.* **1a** defamation in some transient form, as by spoken words, gestures, etc. **1b** a slanderous statement, etc. **2** any defamatory words spoken about a person. ◆ *vb* **3** to utter or circulate slander (about). [C13: via Anglo-F from OF *escandle,* from LL *scandalum* a cause of offence; see SCANDAL] ▸**'slanderer** *n* ▸**'slanderous** *adj*

slang ⓣ (slæŋ) *n* **1a** vocabulary, idiom, etc., that is not appropriate to the standard form of a language or to formal contexts and may be restricted as to social status or distribution. **1b** (*as modifier*): *a slang word.* ◆ *vb* **2** to abuse (someone) with vituperative language. [C18: from ?] ▸**'slangy** *adj* ▸**'slangily** *adv* ▸**'slanginess** *n*

slant ⓣ (slɑːnt) *vb* **1** to incline or be inclined at an oblique or sloping angle. **2** (*tr*) to write or present (news, etc.) with a bias. **3** (*intr;* foll. by *towards*) (of a person's opinions) to be biased. ◆ *n* **4** an inclined or oblique line or direction. **5** a way of looking at something. **6** a bias or opinion, as in an article. **7 on a** (*or* **the**) **slant.** sloping. ◆ *adj* **8** oblique; sloping. [C17: short for ASLANT, prob. of Scand. origin] ▸**'slanting** *adj*

slantwise ('slɑːntˌwaɪz) *or* **slantways** *adv, adj* (*prenominal*) in a slanting or oblique direction.

slap ⓣ (slæp) *n* **1** a sharp blow or smack, as with the open hand, something flat, etc. **2** the sound made by or as if by such a blow. **3** (**a bit of**) **slap and tickle.** *Brit. inf.* sexual play. **4 a slap in the face.** an insult or rebuff. **5 a slap on the back.** congratulation. ◆ *vb* **slaps, slapping, slapped. 6** (*tr*) to strike (a person or thing) sharply, as with the open hand or something flat. **7** (*tr*) to bring down (the hand, etc.) sharply. **8** (when *intr,* usually foll. by *against*) to strike (something) with or as if with a slap. **9** (*tr*) *Inf., chiefly Brit.* to apply in large quantities, haphazardly, etc.: *she slapped butter on the bread.* **10 slap on the back.** to congratulate. ◆ *adv Inf.* **11** exactly: *slap on time.* **12** forcibly or abruptly: *to fall slap on the floor.* [C17: from Low G *slapp,* G *Schlappe,* imit.]

slapdash ⓣ ('slæpˌdæʃ) *adv* **1** in a careless, hasty, or haphazard manner. ◆ *adj* **2** careless, hasty, or haphazard. ◆ *n* **3** slapdash activity or work.

slaphappy ⓣ ('slæpˌhæpɪ) *adj* **slaphappier, slaphappiest.** *Inf.* **1** cheerfully

THESAURUS

slab *n* **1, 2** = **piece**, chunk, hunk, lump, nugget, portion, slice, wedge, wodge (*Brit. inf.*)

slack[1] *adj* **1** = **loose**, baggy, easy, flaccid, flexible, lax, limp, not taut, relaxed **2** = **negligent**, asleep on the job (*inf.*), easy-going, idle, inactive, inattentive, lax, lazy, neglectful, remiss, slapdash, slipshod, tardy **3, 4** = **slow**, dull, inactive, quiet, slow-moving, sluggish ◆ *n* **7** = **room**, excess, give (*inf.*), leeway, looseness, play ◆ *vb* **9** = **shirk**, bob off (*Brit. sl.*), dodge, flag, idle, neglect, relax, skive (*Brit. sl.*), slacken
Antonyms *adj* ≠ **loose**: inflexible, rigid, stiff, strained, stretched, taut, tight ≠ **negligent**: concerned, diligent, exacting, hard, hard-working, meticulous, stern, strict ≠ **slow**: active, bustling, busy, fast-moving, hectic

slacken *vb, often with* **off 2** = **lessen**, abate, decrease, diminish, drop off, ease (off), let up, loosen, moderate, reduce, relax, release, slack off, slow down, tire

slacker *n* = **layabout**, dodger, do-nothing, gold brick (*US sl.*), good-for-nothing, idler, loafer, passenger, scrimshanker (*Brit. military sl.*), shirker, skiver (*Brit. sl.*)

slag *vb* **6** *sometimes with* **off** *Slang* = **criticize**, abuse, berate, deride, insult, lambast(e), malign, mock, slam, slander, slang, slate

slake *vb* **1** = **satisfy**, assuage, gratify, quench, sate, satiate

slam[1] *vb* **1** = **bang**, crash, smash, thump **2** = **throw**, dash, fling, hurl **3** *Slang* = **criticize**, attack, blast, castigate, damn, excoriate, lambast(e), pan (*inf.*), pillory, shoot down (*inf.*), slate (*inf.*), tear into (*inf.*), vilify

slander *n* **2** = **defamation**, aspersion, backbiting, calumny, detraction, libel, misrepresentation, muckraking, obloquy, scandal, smear ◆ *vb* **3** = **defame**, backbite, blacken (someone's) name, calumniate, decry, detract, disparage, libel, malign, muckrake, slur, smear, traduce, vilify
Antonyms *n* ≠ **defamation**: acclaim, acclamation, approval, laudation, praise, tribute ◆ *vb* ≠ **defame**: acclaim, applaud, approve, compliment, eulogize, laud, praise, sing the praises of

slanderous *adj* **2** = **defamatory**, abusive, calumnious, damaging, libellous, malicious

slang *vb* **2** = **insult**, abuse, berate, call names, hurl insults at, inveigh against, malign, rail against, revile, vilify, vituperate

slant *vb* **1** = **slope**, angle off, bend, bevel, cant, heel, incline, lean, list, shelve, skew, tilt **2** = **bias**, angle, colour, distort, twist, weight ◆ *n* **4** = **slope**, camber, declination, diagonal, gradient, incline, pitch, rake, ramp, tilt **5, 6** = **bias**, angle, attitude, emphasis, leaning, one-sidedness, point of view, prejudice, viewpoint

slanting *adj* **1** = **sloping**, angled, aslant, asymmetrical, at an angle, atilt, bent, canted, cater-cornered (*US inf.*), diagonal, inclined, oblique, on the bias, sideways, slanted, slantwise, tilted, tilting

slap *n* **1** = **smack**, bang, blow, chin (*sl.*), clout (*inf.*), cuff, deck (*sl.*), spank, swipe, wallop (*inf.*), whack **4 a slap in the face** = **insult**, affront, blow, humiliation, put-down, rebuff, rebuke, rejection, repulse, snub ◆ *vb* **6** = **smack**, bang, clap, clout (*inf.*), cuff, hit, spank, strike, swipe, whack **9** *Informal, chiefly Brit.* = **plaster**, daub, plonk, spread ◆ *adv* **11** *Informal* = **exactly**, bang, directly, plumb (*inf.*), precisely, slap-bang (*inf.*), smack (*inf.*)

slapdash *adj* **2** = **careless**, clumsy, disorderly, haphazard, hasty, hurried, last-minute, messy, negligent, perfunctory, slipshod, sloppy (*inf.*), slovenly, thoughtless, thrown-together, untidy
Antonyms *adj* careful, conscientious, fastidious, meticulous, ordered, orderly, painstaking, precise, punctilious, thoughtful, tidy

slaphappy *adj* **1** = **happy-go-lucky**, casual, haphazard, hit-or-miss (*inf.*), irresponsible,

irresponsible or careless. **2** dazed or giddy from or as if from repeated blows.

slapstick ('slæpˌstɪk) *n* **1a** comedy characterized by horseplay and physical action. **1b** *(as modifier): slapstick humour.* **2** a pair of paddles formerly used in pantomime to strike a blow with a loud sound but without injury.

slap-up *adj (prenominal) Brit. inf.* (esp. of meals) lavish; excellent; first-class.

slash (slæʃ) *vb (tr)* **1** to cut or lay about (a person or thing) with sharp sweeping strokes, as with a sword, etc. **2** to lash with a whip. **3** to make large gashes in: *to slash tyres.* **4** to reduce (prices, etc.) drastically. **5** to criticize harshly. **6** to slit (the outer fabric of a garment) so that the lining material is revealed. **7** to clear (scrub or undergrowth) by cutting. ◆ *n* **8** a sharp sweeping stroke, as with a sword or whip. **9** a cut or rent made by such a stroke. **10** a decorative slit in a garment revealing the lining material. **11** *US & Canad.* littered wood chips that remain after trees have been cut down. **12** another name for **solidus. 13** *Brit. sl.* the act of urinating. [C14 *slaschen,* ?from OF *esclachier* to break]

slasher ('slæʃə) *n* **1** a person or thing that slashes. **2** *Austral. & NZ.* a tool or machine used for cutting scrub or undergrowth in the bush.

slasher movie *n Sl.* a film in which victims, usually women, are slashed with knives, razors, etc. Also called: **stalk-and-slash movie.**

slashing ('slæʃɪŋ) *adj* aggressively or harshly critical (esp. in **slashing attack**).

slat (slæt) *n* **1** a narrow thin strip of wood or metal, as used in a Venetian blind, etc. **2** a movable or fixed aerofoil attached to the leading edge of an aircraft wing to increase lift. [C14: from OF *esclat* splinter, from *esclater* to shatter]

slate[1] (sleɪt) *n* **1a** a compact fine-grained metamorphic rock that can be split into thin layers and is used as a roofing and paving material. **1b** *(as modifier): a slate tile.* **2** a roofing tile of slate. **3** (formerly) a writing tablet of slate. **4** a dark grey colour. **5** *Chiefly US & Canad.* a list of candidates in an election. **6 clean slate.** a record without dishonour. **7 have a slate loose.** *Brit. & Irish inf.* to be eccentric or crazy. **8 on the slate.** *Brit. inf.* on credit. ◆ *vb* **slates, slating, slated.** *(tr)* **9** to cover (a roof) with slates. **10** *Chiefly US.* to enter (a person's name) on a list, esp. on a political slate. ◆ *adj* **11** of the colour slate. [C14: from OF *esclate,* from *esclat* a fragment]
▸ **'slaty** *adj*

slate[2] (sleɪt) *vb* **slates, slating, slated.** *(tr) Inf., chiefly Brit.* to criticize harshly. [C19: prob. from SLATE[1]]
▸ **'slating** *n*

slater ('sleɪtə) *n* **1** a person trained in laying roof slates. **2** another name for **woodlouse.**

slather ('slɑːðə) *n* **1** *(usually pl) Inf., chiefly US & Canad.* a large quantity. **2 open slather.** *Austral. & NZ sl.* a free-for-all. [C19: from ?]

slattern ('slætən) *n* a slovenly woman or girl. [C17: prob. from *slattering,* from dialect *slatter* to slop]
▸ **'slatternly** *adj* ▸ **'slatternliness** *n*

slaughter ('slɔːtə) *n* **1** the killing of animals, esp. for food. **2** the savage killing of a person. **3** the indiscriminate or brutal killing of large numbers of people, as in war. ◆ *vb (tr)* **4** to kill (animals), esp. for food. **5** to kill in a brutal manner. **6** to kill indiscriminately or in large numbers. [OE *sleaht*]
▸ **'slaughterer** *n* ▸ **'slaughterous** *adj*

slaughterhouse ('slɔːtəˌhaʊs) *n* a place where animals are butchered for food; abattoir.

Slav (slɑːv) *n* a member of any of the peoples of E Europe or NW Asia who speak a Slavonic language. [C14: from Med. L *Sclāvus* a captive Slav; see SLAVE]

slave (sleɪv) *n* **1** a person legally owned by another and having no freedom of action or right to property. **2** a person who is forced to work for another against his will. **3** a person under the domination of another person or some habit or influence. **4** a drudge. **5** a device that is controlled by or that duplicates the action of another similar device. ◆ *vb* **slaves, slaving, slaved. 6** *(intr;* often foll. by *away)* to work like a slave. [C13: via OF from Med. L *Sclāvus* a Slav, one held in bondage (the Slavonic races were frequently conquered in the Middle Ages), from LGk *Sklabos* a Slav]

slave cylinder *n* a small cylinder containing a piston that operates the brake shoes or pads in hydraulic brakes or the working part in any other hydraulically operated system.

slave-driver *n* **1** (esp. formerly) a person forcing slaves to work. **2** an employer who demands excessively hard work from his employees.

slaveholder ('sleɪvˌhəʊldə) *n* a person who owns slaves.
▸ **'slaveˌholding** *n*

slaver[1] ('sleɪvə) *n* **1** an owner of or dealer in slaves. **2** another name for **slave ship.**

slaver[2] ('slævə) *vb (intr)* **1** to dribble saliva. **2** (often foll. by *over)* **2a** to fawn or drool (over someone). **2b** to show great desire (for). ◆ *n* **3** saliva dribbling from the mouth. **4** *Inf.* drivel. [C14: prob. from Low Du.]
▸ **'slaverer** *n*

slavery ('sleɪvərɪ) *n* **1** the state or condition of being a slave. **2** the subjection of a person to another person, esp. in being forced into work. **3** the condition of being subject to some influence or habit. **4** work done in harsh conditions for low pay.

slave ship *n* a ship used to transport slaves, esp. formerly from Africa to the New World.

Slave State *n US history.* any of the 15 Southern states in which slavery was legal until the Civil War.

slave trade *n* the business of trading in slaves, esp. the transportation of Black Africans to America from the 16th to 19th centuries.
▸ **'slave-ˌtrader** *n* ▸ **'slave-ˌtrading** *n*

slavey ('sleɪvɪ) *n Brit. inf.* a female general servant.

Slavic ('slɑːvɪk) *n, adj* another word (esp. US) another word (esp. US) for **Slavonic.**

slavish ('sleɪvɪʃ) *adj* **1** of or befitting a slave. **2** being or resembling a slave. **3** unoriginal; imitative.
▸ **'slavishly** *adv*

Slavonic (slə'vɒnɪk) *or esp. US* **Slavic** *n* **1** a branch of the Indo-European family of languages, usually divided into three subbranches: **South Slavonic** (including Bulgarian), **East Slavonic** (including Russian), and **West Slavonic** (including Polish and Czech). ◆ *adj* **2** of or relating to this group of languages. **3** of or relating to the people who speak these languages.

slaw (slɔː) *n Chiefly US & Canad.* short for **coleslaw.** [C19: from Danish *sla,* short for *salade* SALAD]

slay (sleɪ) *vb* **slays, slaying, slew, slain.** *(tr)* **1** *Arch. or literary.* to kill, esp. violently. **2** *Sl.* to impress (someone of the opposite sex). [OE *slēan*]
▸ **'slayer** *n*

SLCM *abbrev. for* sea-launched cruise missile: a type of cruise missile that can be launched from either a submarine or a surface ship.

SLD *abbrev. for* Social and Liberal Democrats.

sleaze (sliːz) *n Inf.* **1** sleaziness. **2** dishonest, disreputable, or immoral behaviour, esp. of public officials or employees: *political sleaze.*

sleazy ('sliːzɪ) *adj* **sleazier, sleaziest. 1** disreputable: *a sleazy nightclub.* **2** flimsy, as cloth. [C17: from ?]
▸ **'sleazily** *adv* ▸ **'sleaziness** *n*

sledge[1] (slɛdʒ) *or esp. US & Canad.* **sled** (slɛd) *n* **1** Also called: **sleigh.** a vehicle mounted on runners, drawn by horses or dogs, for transporting people or goods, esp. over snow. **2** a light wooden frame used, esp. by children, for sliding over snow. ◆ *vb* **sledges, sledging, sledged. 3** to convey, travel, or go by sledge. [C17: from MDu. *sleedse;* C14 *sled,* from MLow G, from ON *slethi*]
▸ **'sledger** *n*

sledge[2] (slɛdʒ) *n* short for **sledgehammer.**

sledge[3] (slɛdʒ) *vb* **sledges, sledging, sledged.** *(tr) Austral.* to bait (an opponent, esp. a batsman in cricket) in order to upset his concentration. [from ?]

sledgehammer ('slɛdʒˌhæmə) *n* **1** a large heavy hammer with a long

THESAURUS

nonchalant **2** = **dazed**, giddy, punch-drunk, reeling, woozy *(inf.)*

slapstick *n* **1** = **knockabout comedy**, buffoonery, farce, horseplay

slap-up *adj Brit. informal* = **luxurious**, elaborate, excellent, first-rate, fit for a king, lavish, magnificent, no-expense-spared, princely, splendid, sumptuous, superb

slash *vb* **1** = **cut**, gash, hack, lacerate, rend, rip, score, slit **4** = **reduce**, cut, drop, lower ◆ *n* **9** = **cut**, gash, incision, laceration, rent, rip, slit

slashing *adj* = **savage**, aggressive, biting, brutal, ferocious, harsh, searing, vicious

slate[2] *vb Informal, chiefly Brit.* = **criticize**, berate, blame, blast, castigate, censure, excoriate, haul over the coals *(inf.)*, lambast(e), pan *(inf.)*, pitch into *(inf.)*, rail against, rap (someone's) knuckles, rebuke, roast *(inf.)*, scold, slam *(sl.)*, slang, take to task, tear into *(inf.)*, tear (someone) off a strip *(inf.)*

slattern *n* = **sloven**, drab *(arch.)*, slut, trollop

slatternly *adj* = **slovenly**, bedraggled, dirty, draggletailed, frowzy, slipshod, sloppy *(inf.)*, sluttish, unclean, unkempt, untidy

slaughter *n* **3** = **slaying**, blood bath, bloodshed, butchery, carnage, extermination, holocaust, killing, liquidation, massacre, murder ◆ *vb* **4-6** = **slay**, butcher, destroy, do to death, exterminate, kill, liquidate, massacre, murder, put to the sword, take out *(sl.)*

slaughterhouse *n* = **abattoir**, butchery, shambles

slave *n* **1-4** = **servant**, bondservant, bondsman, drudge, scullion *(arch.)*, serf, skivvy *(chiefly Brit.)*, slavey *(Brit. inf.)*, varlet *(arch.)*, vassal, villein ◆ *vb* **6** = **toil**, drudge, grind *(inf.)*, skivvy *(Brit.)*, slog, sweat, work one's fingers to the bone

slaver[2] *vb* **1** = **drool**, dribble, salivate, slobber

slavery *n* **1, 2** = **enslavement**, bondage, captivity, serfdom, servitude, subjugation, thraldom, thrall, vassalage
Antonyms *n* emancipation, freedom, liberty, manumission, release

slavish *adj* **1** = **servile**, abject, base, cringing, despicable, fawning, grovelling, low, mean, menial, obsequious, submissive, sycophantic **3** = **imitative**, conventional, second-hand, unimaginative, uninspired, unoriginal
Antonyms *adj* ≠ **servile:** assertive, domineering, masterful, rebellious, self-willed, wilful ≠ **imitative:** creative, imaginative, independent, inventive, original, radical, revolutionary

slay *vb* **1** *Archaic* = **kill**, annihilate, assassinate, butcher, destroy, dispatch, do away with, do in *(sl.)*, eliminate, exterminate, massacre, mow down, murder, rub out *(US sl.)*, slaughter **2** *Slang* = **impress**, amuse, be the death of *(inf.)*, make a hit with *(inf.)*, wow *(sl., chiefly US)*

sleaze *n* **2** *Informal* = **corruption**, bribery, crookedness *(inf.)*, dishonesty, extortion, fiddling *(inf.)*, fraud, shady dealings *(inf.)*, unscrupulousness, venality

sleazy *adj* **1** = **sordid**, crummy, disreputable, low, run-down, seedy, squalid, tacky *(inf.)*

handle used with both hands for heavy work such as breaking rocks, etc. **2** (*modifier*) resembling the action of a sledgehammer in power, etc.: *a sledgehammer blow*. [C15: *sledge*, from OE *slecg* a large hammer]

sleek ❶ (sliːk) *adj* **1** smooth and shiny. **2** polished in speech or behaviour. **3** (of an animal or bird) having a shiny healthy coat or feathers. **4** (of a person) having a prosperous appearance. ◆ *vb* (*tr*) **5** to make smooth and glossy, as by grooming, etc. **6** (usually foll. by *over*) to gloss (over). [C16: var. of SLICK]
▸**'sleekly** *adv* ▸**'sleekness** *n* ▸**'sleeky** *adj*

sleep ❶ (sliːp) *n* **1** a periodic state of physiological rest during which consciousness is suspended. **2** *Bot.* the nontechnical name for **nyctitropism. 3** a period spent sleeping. **4** a state of quiescence or dormancy. **5** a poetic word for **death.** ◆ *vb* **sleeps, sleeping, slept. 6** (*intr*) to be in or as in the state of sleep. **7** (*intr*) (of plants) to show nyctitropism. **8** (*intr*) to be inactive or quiescent. **9** (*tr*) to have sleeping accommodation for (a certain number): *the boat could sleep six*. **10** (*tr*; foll. by *away*) to pass (time) sleeping. **11** (*intr*) *Poetic*. to be dead. **12 sleep on it.** to give (something) extended consideration, esp. overnight. ◆ See also **sleep around, sleep in,** etc. [OE *slǣpan*]

sleep around *vb* (*intr, adv*) *Inf.* to be sexually promiscuous.

sleeper ('sliːpə) *n* **1** a person, animal, or thing that sleeps. **2** a railway sleeping car or compartment. **3** *Brit.* one of the blocks supporting the rails on a railway track. **4** a heavy timber beam, esp. one that is laid horizontally on the ground. **5** *Chiefly Brit.* a small plain gold circle worn in a pierced ear lobe to prevent the hole from closing up. **6** *Inf.* a person or thing that achieves unexpected success after an initial period of obscurity. **7** a spy planted in advance for future use.

sleep in *vb* (*intr, adv*) **1** *Brit.* to sleep longer than usual. **2** to sleep at the place of one's employment.

sleeping bag *n* a large well-padded bag designed for sleeping in, esp. outdoors.

sleeping car *n* a railway carriage fitted with compartments containing bunks for people to sleep in.

sleeping partner *n* a partner in a business who does not play an active role. Also called: **silent partner.**

sleeping pill *n* a pill or tablet containing a sedative drug, such as a barbiturate, used to induce sleep.

sleeping policeman *n* a bump built across a road to deter motorists from speeding. Official name: **road hump.**

sleeping sickness *n* **1** Also called: **African sleeping sickness.** an African disease transmitted by the bite of the tsetse fly, characterized by fever and sluggishness. **2** Also called: **sleepy sickness.** an epidemic viral form of encephalitis characterized by extreme drowsiness. Technical name: **encephalitis lethargica.**

sleepless ❶ ('sliːplɪs) *adj* **1** without sleep or rest: *a sleepless journey*. **2** unable to sleep. **3** always alert. **4** *Chiefly poetic.* always active or moving.
▸**'sleeplessly** *adv* ▸**'sleeplessness** *n*

sleep off *vb* (*tr, adv*) *Inf.* to lose by sleeping: *to sleep off a hangover*.

sleep out *vb* (*intr, adv*) **1** (esp. of a tramp) to sleep in the open air. **2** to sleep away from the place of one's employment. ◆ *n* **sleep-out. 3** *Austral. & NZ.* an area of a veranda partitioned off so that it may be used as a bedroom.

sleepwalk ❶ ('sliːpˌwɔːk) *vb* (*intr*) to walk while asleep.
▸**'sleepˌwalker** *n* ▸**'sleepˌwalking** *n, adj*

sleep with *vb* (*intr, prep*) to have sexual intercourse and (usually) spend the night with. Also: **sleep together.**

sleepy ❶ ('sliːpɪ) *adj* **sleepier, sleepiest. 1** inclined to or needing sleep. **2** characterized by or exhibiting drowsiness, etc. **3** conducive to sleep. **4** without activity or bustle: *a sleepy town*.
▸**'sleepily** *adv* ▸**'sleepiness** *n*

sleet (sliːt) *n* **1** partly melted falling snow or hail or (esp. US) partly frozen rain. **2** *Chiefly US.* the thin coat of ice that forms when sleet or rain freezes on cold surfaces. ◆ *vb* **3** (*intr*) to fall as sleet. [C13: of Gmc origin]
▸**'sleety** *adj*

sleeve (sliːv) *n* **1** the part of a garment covering the arm. **2** a tubular piece that is shrunk into a cylindrical bore to reduce its bore or to line it with a different material. **3** a tube fitted externally over two cylindrical parts in order to join them. **4** a flat cardboard container to protect a gramophone record. US name: **jacket. 5** (**have a few tricks**) **up one's sleeve.** (to have options, etc.) secretly ready. **6 roll up one's sleeves.** to prepare oneself for work, a fight, etc. ◆ *vb* **sleeves, sleeving, sleeved. 7** (*tr*) to provide with a sleeve or sleeves. [OE *slīf, slēf*]
▸**'sleeveless** *adj* ▸**'sleeveˌlike** *adj*

sleeve board *n* a small ironing board for pressing sleeves, fitted onto an ironing board or table.

sleeving ('sliːvɪŋ) *n Electronics, chiefly Brit.* tubular flexible insulation into which bare wire can be inserted.

sleigh (sleɪ) *n* **1** another name for **sledge**[1] (sense 1). ◆ *vb* **2** (*intr*) to travel by sleigh. [C18: from Du. *slee*, var. of *slede* SLEDGE[1]]

sleight (slaɪt) *n Arch.* **1** skill; dexterity. **2** a trick or stratagem. **3** cunning. [C14: from ON *slægth*, from *slǣgr* SLY]

sleight of hand ❶ *n* **1** manual dexterity used in performing conjuring tricks. **2** the performance of such tricks.

slender ❶ ('slɛndə) *adj* **1** of small width relative to length or height. **2** (esp. of a person's figure) slim and well-formed. **3** small or inadequate in amount, size, etc.: *slender resources*. **4** (of hopes, etc.) feeble. **5** very small: *a slender margin*. [C14 *slendre*, from ?]
▸**'slenderly** *adv* ▸**'slenderness** *n*

slenderize *or* **slenderise** ('slɛndəˌraɪz) *vb* **slenderizes, slenderizing, slenderized** *or* **slenderises, slenderising, slenderised.** *Chiefly US & Canad.* to make or become slender.

slept (slɛpt) *vb* the past tense and past participle of **sleep.**

sleuth ❶ (sluːθ) *n* **1** an informal word for **detective. 2** short for **sleuthhound** (sense 1). ◆ *vb* **3** (*tr*) to track or follow. [C19: short for *sleuthhound*, from C12 *sleuth* trail, from ON *sloth*]

sleuthhound ('sluːθˌhaʊnd) *n* **1** a dog trained to track people, esp. a bloodhound. **2** an informal word for **detective.**

S level *n Brit.* the Special level of a subject taken for the General Certificate of Education: usually taken at the same time as A levels as an additional qualification.

slew[1] (sluː) *vb* the past tense of **slay.**

slew[2] *or esp. US* **slue** (sluː) *vb* **1** to twist or be twisted sideways, esp. awkwardly. **2** *Naut.* to cause (a mast) to rotate in its step or (of a mast) to rotate in its step. ◆ *n* **3** the act of slewing. [C18: from ?]

slew[3] (sluː) *n* a variant spelling (esp. US) of **slough**[1] (sense 2).

slew[4] *or* **slue** (sluː) *n Inf., chiefly US & Canad.* a great number. [C20: from Irish Gaelic *sluagh*]

slice ❶ (slaɪs) *n* **1** a thin flat piece cut from something having bulk: *a slice of pork*. **2** a share or portion: *a slice of the company's revenue*. **3** any of various utensils having a broad flat blade and resembling a spatula. **4** (in golf, tennis, etc.) **4a** the flight of a ball that travels obliquely. **4b** the action of hitting such a shot. **4c** the shot so hit. ◆ *vb* **slices, slicing, sliced. 5** to divide or cut (something) into parts or slices. **6** (when *intr*, usually foll. by *through*) to cut in a clean and effortless manner. **7** (when *intr*, foll. by *into* or *through*) to move or go (through something) like a knife. **8** (usually foll. by *off, from, away,* etc.) to cut or be cut (from) a larger piece. **9** (*tr*) to remove by use of a slicing implement. **10** to hit (a ball) with a slice. [C14: from OF *esclice* a piece split off, from *esclicier* to splinter]
▸**'sliceable** *adj* ▸**'slicer** *n*

slick ❶ (slɪk) *adj* **1** flattering and glib: *a slick salesman*. **2** adroitly devised or executed: *a slick show*. **3** *Inf., chiefly US & Canad.* shrewd; sly. **4** *Inf.* superficially attractive: *a slick publication*. **5** *Chiefly US & Canad.* slippery. ◆ *n* **6** a slippery area, esp. a patch of oil floating on water. ◆ *vb* (*tr*) **7** *Chiefly US & Canad.* to make smooth or sleek. [C14: prob. from ON]
▸**'slickly** *adv* ▸**'slickness** *n*

slicker ('slɪkə) *n* **1** *Inf.* a sly or untrustworthy person (esp. in **city slicker**). **2** *US & Canad.* a shiny raincoat, esp. an oilskin.

slide ❶ (slaɪd) *vb* **slides, sliding, slid** (slɪd); **slid** *or* **slidden** ('slɪdᵊn). **1** to move or cause to move smoothly along a surface in continual contact

THESAURUS

sleek *adj* **1 = glossy**, lustrous, shiny, smooth **4 = well-groomed**, well-fed
Antonyms *adj* ≠ **glossy:** rough, shaggy ≠ **well-groomed:** badly groomed, bedraggled, dishevelled, frowzy, ill-nourished, in poor condition, ratty (*Brit. & NZ inf.*), sloppy, slovenly, unkempt

sleep *n* **1, 3 = slumber(s)**, beauty sleep (*inf.*), dormancy, doze, forty winks (*inf.*), hibernation, kip (*Brit. sl.*), nap, repose, rest, shuteye (*sl.*), siesta, snooze (*inf.*), zizz (*Brit. inf.*) ◆ *vb* **6 = slumber**, be in the land of Nod, catnap, doze, drop off (*inf.*), drowse, go out like a light, hibernate, kip (*Brit. sl.*), nod off (*inf.*), rest in the arms of Morpheus, snooze (*inf.*), snore, take a nap, take forty winks (*inf.*), zizz (*Brit. inf.*)

sleepiness *n* **2 = drowsiness**, doziness, heaviness, lethargy, somnolence, torpor

sleepless *adj* **2 = wakeful**, disturbed, insomniac, restless, unsleeping **3 = alert**, unsleeping, vigilant, watchful, wide awake

sleeplessness *n* **2 = insomnia**, wakefulness

sleepwalker *n* **= somnambulist**, noctambulist

sleepwalking *n* **= somnambulism**, noctambulation, noctambulism, somnambulation

sleepy *adj* **2 = drowsy**, dull, heavy, inactive, lethargic, sluggish, slumbersome, somnolent, torpid **3 = quiet**, dull, hypnotic, inactive, sleep-inducing, slow, slumberous, somnolent, soporific
Antonyms *adj* ≠ **drowsy:** active, alert, alive and kicking, animated, attentive, awake, boisterous, energetic, full of beans (*inf.*), lively, restless, wakeful, wide-awake ≠ **quiet:** active, bustling, busy, lively, thriving

sleight of hand *n* **1 = dexterity**, adroitness, artifice, legerdemain, manipulation, prestidigitation, skill

slender *adj* **1, 2 = slim**, lean, narrow, slight, svelte, sylphlike, willowy **3 = meagre**, inadequate, inconsiderable, insufficient, little, scant, scanty, small, spare **4 = faint**, feeble, flimsy, fragile, poor, remote, slight, slim, tenuous, thin, weak
Antonyms *adj* ≠ **slim:** bulky, chubby, fat, heavy, large, podgy, stout, tubby, well-built ≠ **meagre:** ample, appreciable, considerable, generous, large, substantial ≠ **faint:** good, solid, strong

sleuth *n* **1** *Informal* **= detective**, dick (*sl., chiefly US*), gumshoe (*US sl.*), private eye (*inf.*), (private) investigator, sleuthhound (*inf.*), tail (*inf.*)

slice *n* **1, 2 = piece**, cut, helping, portion, segment, share, sliver, wedge ◆ *vb* **5, 6 = cut**, carve, divide, sever

slick *adj* **1 = glib**, meretricious, plausible, polished, smooth, sophistical, specious **2 = skilful**, adroit, deft, dexterous, dextrous, polished, professional, sharp ◆ *vb* **7 = smooth**, make glossy, plaster down, sleek, smarm down (*Brit. inf.*)
Antonyms *adj* ≠ **skilful:** amateur, amateurish, clumsy, crude, inexpert, unaccomplished, unpolished, unprofessional, unskilful

slide *vb* **1 = slip**, coast, glide, glissade, skim, slither, toboggan, veer **6 let slide = neglect**, forget, gloss over, ignore, let ride, pass over, push to the back of one's mind, turn a blind eye to

with it: *doors that slide open.* **2** (*intr*) to lose grip or balance: *he slid on his back.* **3** (*intr;* usually foll. by *into, out of, away from,* etc.) to pass or move unobtrusively: *she slid into the room.* **4** (*intr;* usually foll. by *into*) to go (into a specified condition) by degrees, etc.: *he slid into loose living.* **5** (foll. by *in, into,* etc.) to move (an object) unobtrusively or (of an object) to move in this way: *he slid the gun into his pocket.* **6 let slide.** to allow to deteriorate: *to let things slide.* ◆ *n* **7** the act or an instance of sliding. **8** a smooth surface, as of ice or mud, for sliding on. **9** a construction incorporating an inclined smooth slope for sliding down in playgrounds, etc. **10** a small glass plate on which specimens are mounted for microscopical study. **11** Also called: **diapositive, transparency.** a positive photograph on a transparent base, mounted in a frame, that can be viewed by means of a slide projector. **12** Also called: **hair slide.** *Chiefly Brit.* an ornamental clip to hold hair in place. **13** *Machinery.* a sliding part or member. **14** *Music.* a portamento. **15** *Music.* the sliding curved tube of a trombone that is moved in or out. **16** *Music.* **16a** a tube placed over a finger held against the frets of a guitar to produce a portamento. **16b** the style of guitar playing using a slide. **17** *Geol.* **17a** the downward movement of a large mass of earth, rocks, etc. **17b** the mass of material involved in this descent. See also **landslide.** [OE *slīdan*]
▸'**slidable** *adj* ▸'**slider** *n*

slide over *vb* (*intr, prep*) **1** to cross as if by sliding. **2** to avoid dealing with (a matter) fully.

slide rule *n* a mechanical calculating device consisting of two strips, one sliding along a central groove in the other, each strip graduated in two or more logarithmic scales of numbers, trigonometric functions, etc.

sliding scale *n* a variable scale according to which specified wages, prices, etc., fluctuate in response to changes in some other factor.

slier ('slaɪə) *adj* a comparative of **sly.**

sliest ('slaɪɪst) *adj* a superlative of **sly.**

slight ❶ (slaɪt) *adj* **1** small in quantity or extent. **2** of small importance. **3** slim and delicate. **4** lacking in strength or substance. ◆ *vb* (*tr*) **5** to show disregard for (someone); snub. **6** to treat as unimportant or trifling. **7** *US.* to devote inadequate attention to (work, duties, etc.). ◆ *n* **8** an act or omission indicating supercilious neglect. [C13: from ON *slēttr* smooth]
▸'**slightingly** *adv* ▸'**slightly** *adv* ▸'**slightness** *n*

slily ('slaɪlɪ) *adv* a variant spelling of **slyly.**

slim ❶ (slɪm) *adj* **slimmer, slimmest. 1** small in width relative to height or length. **2** poor; meagre: *slim chances of success.* ◆ *vb* **3** to make or become slim, esp. by diets and exercise. **4** (*tr*) to reduce in size: *the workforce was slimmed.* [C17: from Du.: crafty, from MDu. *slimp* slanting]
▸'**slimmer** *n* ▸'**slimming** *n* ▸'**slimness** *n*

Slim (slɪm) *n* the E African name for **AIDS.** [from its wasting effects]

slim down *vb* (*adv*) **1** to make or become slim, esp. intentionally. **2** to make (an organization) more efficient or (of an organization) to become more efficient, esp. by cutting staff. ◆ *n* **slimdown. 3** an instance of an organization slimming down.

slime (slaɪm) *n* **1** soft thin runny mud or filth. **2** any moist viscous fluid, esp. when noxious or unpleasant. **3** a mucous substance produced by various organisms, such as fish, slugs, and fungi. ◆ *vb* **slimes, sliming, slimed.** (*tr*) **4** to cover with slime. [OE *slīm*]

slimline ('slɪm,laɪn) *adj* slim or conducive to slimness.

slimy ❶ ('slaɪmɪ) *adj* **slimier, slimiest. 1** characterized by, covered with, secreting, or resembling slime. **2** offensive or repulsive. **3** *Chiefly Brit.* characterized by servility.

sling[1] ❶ (slɪŋ) *n* **1** a simple weapon consisting of a loop of leather, etc., in which a stone is whirled and then let fly. **2** a rope or strap by which something may be secured or lifted. **3** *Med.* a wide piece of cloth suspended from the neck for supporting an injured hand or arm. **4** a loop or band attached to an object for carrying. **5** the act of slinging. ◆ *vb* **slings, slinging, slung. 6** (*tr*) to hurl with or as if with a sling. **7** to attach a sling or slings to (a load, etc.). **8** (*tr*) to carry or hang loosely from or as if from a sling: *to sling washing from the line.* **9** (*tr*) *Inf.* to throw. [C13: ?from ON]
▸'**slinger** *n*

sling[2] (slɪŋ) *n* a mixed drink with a spirit base, usually sweetened. [C19: from ?]

slingback ('slɪŋ,bæk) *n* a shoe with a strap instead of a full covering for the heel.

sling off *vb* (*intr, adv;* often foll. by *at*) *Austral. & NZ inf.* to mock; deride; jeer (at).

slingshot ('slɪŋ,ʃɒt) *n* **1** the US and Canad. name for **catapult** (sense 1). **2** another name for **sling**[1] (sense 1).

slink ❶ (slɪŋk) *vb* **slinks, slinking, slunk. 1** (*intr*) to move or act in a furtive manner from or as if from fear, guilt, etc. **2** (*intr*) to move in a sinuous alluring manner. **3** (*tr*) (of animals, esp. cows) to give birth to prematurely. ◆ *n* **4** an animal, esp. a calf, born prematurely. [OE *slincan*]

slinky ❶ ('slɪŋkɪ) *adj* **slinkier, slinkiest.** *Inf.* **1** moving in a sinuously graceful or provocative way. **2** (of clothes) figure-hugging.
▸'**slinkily** *adv* ▸'**slinkiness** *n*

slip[1] ❶ (slɪp) *vb* **slips, slipping, slipped. 1** to move or cause to move smoothly and easily. **2** (*tr*) to place, insert, or convey quickly or stealthily. **3** (*tr*) to put on or take off easily or quickly: *to slip on a sweater.* **4** (*intr*) to lose balance and slide unexpectedly: *he slipped on the ice.* **5** to let loose or be let loose. **6** to be released from (something). **7** (*tr*) to let go (mooring or anchor lines) over the side. **8** (when *intr,* often foll. by *from* or *out of*) to pass out of (the mind or memory). **9** (*intr*) to move or pass swiftly or unperceived: *to slip quietly out of the room.* **10** (*intr;* sometimes foll. by *up*) to make a mistake. **11** Also: **sideslip.** to cause (an aircraft) to slide sideways or (of an aircraft) to slide sideways. **12** (*intr*) to decline in health, mental ability, etc. **13** (*intr*) (of an intervertebral disc) to become displaced from the normal position. **14** (*tr*) to dislocate (a bone). **15** (of animals) to give birth to (offspring) prematurely. **16** (*tr*) to pass (a stitch) from one needle to another without knitting it. **17a** (*tr*) to operate (the clutch of a motor vehicle) so that it partially disengages. **17b** (*intr*) (of the clutch of a motor vehicle) to fail to engage, esp. as a result of wear. **18 let slip. 18a** to allow to escape. **18b** to say unintentionally. ◆ *n* **19** the act or an instance of slipping. **20** a mistake or oversight: *a slip of the pen.* **21** a moral lapse or failing. **22** a woman's sleeveless undergarment, worn as a lining for a dress. **23** a pillowcase. **24** See **slipway. 25** *Cricket.* **25a** the position of the fielder who stands a little way behind and to the offside of the wicketkeeper. **25b** the fielder himself. **26** the relative movement of rocks along a fault plane. **27** *Metallurgy, crystallog.* the deformation of a metallic crystal caused when one part glides over another part along a plane. **28** a landslide. **29** the deviation of a propeller from its helical path through a fluid. **30** another name for **sideslip** (sense 1). **31 give someone the slip.** to elude or escape from someone. ◆ See also **slip up.** [C13: from MLow G or Du. *slippen*]
▸'**slipless** *adj*

slip[2] ❶ (slɪp) *n* **1** a narrow piece; strip. **2** a small piece of paper: *a receipt slip.* **3** a part of a plant that, when detached from the parent, will grow into a new plant; cutting. **4** a young slender person: *a slip of a child.* **5** *Printing.* **5a** a long galley. **5b** a galley proof. ◆ *vb* **slips, slipping, slipped. 6** (*tr*) to detach (portions of stem, etc.) from (a plant) for propagation. [C15: prob. from MLow G, MDu. *slippe* to cut, strip]

slip[3] (slɪp) *n* clay mixed with water to a creamy consistency, used for decorating or patching a ceramic piece. [OE *slyppe* slime]

slipcase ('slɪp,keɪs) *n* a protective case for a book or set of books that is open at one end so that only the spines of the books are visible.

slipcover ('slɪp,kʌvə) *n US & Canad.* **1** a loose cover. **2** a book jacket; dust cover.

slipe (slaɪp) *n NZ.* **a** wool removed from the pelt of a slaughtered sheep by immersion in a chemical bath. **b** (*as modifier*): *slipe wool.* [C14 in England: from *slype* to strip, skin]

slipknot ('slɪp,nɒt) *n* **1** Also called: **running knot.** a nooselike knot tied so that it will slip along the rope round which it is made. **2** a knot that can be easily untied by pulling one free end.

slip-on *adj* **1** (of a garment or shoe) made so as to be easily and quickly put on or taken off. ◆ *n* **2** a slip-on garment or shoe.

slipover ('slɪp,əʊvə) *adj* **1** of or denoting a garment that can be put on easily over the head. ◆ *n* **2** such a garment, esp. a sleeveless pullover.

slippage ('slɪpɪdʒ) *n* **1** the act or an instance of slipping. **2** the amount

THESAURUS

slight *adj* **1, 2, 4 = small,** feeble, inconsiderable, insignificant, insubstantial, meagre, measly, minor, modest, negligible, paltry, scanty, superficial, trifling, trivial, unimportant, weak **3 = slim,** delicate, feeble, fragile, lightly-built, small, spare ◆ *vb* **5 = snub,** affront, cold-shoulder, despise, disdain, disparage, give offence *or* umbrage to, ignore, insult, neglect, put down, scorn, show disrespect for, treat with contempt ◆ *n* **8 = insult,** affront, contempt, discourtesy, disdain, disregard, disrespect, inattention, indifference, neglect, rebuff, slap in the face (*inf.*), snub, (the) cold shoulder
Antonyms *adj* ≠ **small:** appreciable, considerable, great, heavy, important, large, noticeable, obvious, significant, substantial ≠ **slim:** muscular, solid, strong, sturdy, well-built ◆ *vb* ≠ **snub:** compliment, flatter, praise, speak well of, treat considerately ◆ *n* ≠ **insult:** compliment, flattery, praise

slightly *adv* **1 = a little,** marginally, on a small scale, somewhat, to some extent *or* degree

slim *adj* **1 = slender,** lean, narrow, slight, svelte, sylphlike, thin, trim **2 = slight,** faint, poor, remote, slender ◆ *vb* **3 = lose weight,** diet, reduce, slenderize (*chiefly US*)
Antonyms *adj* ≠ **slender:** broad, bulky, chubby, fat, heavy, muscular, obese, overweight, sturdy, tubby, well-built, wide ≠ **slight:** good, strong ◆ *vb* ≠ **lose weight:** build oneself up, put on weight

slimy *adj* **1 = viscous,** clammy, gloopy, glutinous, miry, mucous, muddy, oozy **3** *Chiefly Brit.* **= obsequious,** creeping, grovelling, oily, servile, smarmy (*Brit. inf.*), soapy (*sl.*), sycophantic, toadying, unctuous

sling[1] *vb* **8 = hang,** dangle, suspend, swing **9** *Informal* **= throw,** cast, chuck, fling, heave, hurl, lob (*inf.*), shy, toss

slink *vb* **1 = creep,** prowl, pussyfoot (*inf.*), skulk, slip, sneak, steal

slinky *adj* **1 = sinuous,** feline **2 = figure-hugging,** clinging, close-fitting, skintight, sleek

slip[1] *vb* **1 = slide,** glide, skate, slither **4 = fall,** lose one's balance, miss *or* lose one's footing, skid, trip (over) **10** *sometimes with* **up = make a mistake,** blunder, boob (*Brit. sl.*), drop a brick *or* clanger (*inf.*), err, go wrong, miscalculate, misjudge, mistake **18b let slip = give away,** blurt out, come out with (*inf.*), disclose, divulge, leak, let out (*inf.*), let the cat out of the bag, reveal ◆ *n* **20 = mistake,** bloomer (*Brit. inf.*), blunder, boob (*Brit. sl.*), error, failure, fault, faux pas, imprudence, indiscretion, lapse, omission, oversight, slip of the tongue, slip-up (*inf.*) **31 give (someone) the slip = escape from,** dodge, elude, evade, get away from, lose (someone), outwit, shake (someone) off

slip[2] *n* **1 = strip,** piece, sliver **3 = cutting,** offshoot, runner, scion, shoot, sprig, sprout

of slipping or the extent to which slipping occurs. **3a** an instance of not reaching a target, etc. **3b** the extent of this.

slipped disc *n Pathol.* a herniated intervertebral disc, often resulting in pain because of pressure on the spinal nerves.

slipper ('slɪpə) *n* **1** a light shoe of some soft material, for wearing around the house. **2** a woman's evening shoe. ◆ *vb* **3** (*tr*) *Inf.* to hit or beat with a slipper.
▸'**slippered** *adj*

slipper bath *n* a bath in the shape of a slipper, with a covered end.

slipperwort ('slɪpəˌwɜːt) *n* another name for **calceolaria.**

slippery ⓣ ('slɪpərɪ, -prɪ) *adj* **1** causing or tending to cause objects to slip: *a slippery road.* **2** liable to slip from the grasp, etc. **3** not to be relied upon: *a slippery character.* **4** (esp. of a situation) unstable. [C16: prob. coined by Coverdale to translate G *schlipfferig* in Luther's Bible (Psalm 35:6)]
▸'**slipperiness** *n*

slippery elm *n* **1** a North American tree, having notched winged fruits and a mucilaginous inner bark. **2** the bark of this tree, used medicinally as a demulcent. ◆ Also called: **red elm.**

slippy ('slɪpɪ) *adj* **slippier, slippiest. 1** *Inf. or dialect.* another word for **slippery** (senses 1, 2). **2** *Brit. inf.* alert; quick.
▸'**slippiness** *n*

slip rail *n Austral. & NZ.* a rail in a fence that can be slipped out of place to make an opening.

slip road *n Brit.* a short road connecting a motorway to another road.

slipshod ⓣ ('slɪpˌʃɒd) *adj* **1** (of an action) negligent; careless. **2** (of a person's appearance) slovenly; down-at-heel. [C16: from SLIP[1] + SHOD]

slip-slop *n S. African.* the usual name for **flip-flop** (sense 5).

slipstream ('slɪpˌstriːm) *n* Also called: **airstream. a** the stream of air forced backwards by an aircraft propeller. **b** a stream of air behind any moving object.

slip up *Inf.* ◆ *vb* (*intr, adv*) **1** to make a blunder or mistake. ◆ *n* **slip-up. 2** a mistake or mishap.

slipware ('slɪpˌwɛə) *n* pottery that has been decorated with slip and glazed.

slipway ('slɪpˌweɪ) *n* **1** the sloping area in a shipyard, containing the ways. **2** the ways on which a vessel is launched.

slit ⓣ (slɪt) *vb* **slits, slitting, slit.** (*tr*) **1** to make a straight long incision in. **2** to cut into strips lengthwise. ◆ *n* **3** a long narrow cut. **4** a long narrow opening. [OE *slītan* to slice]
▸'**slitter** *n*

slither ⓣ ('slɪðə) *vb* **1** to move or slide or cause to move or slide unsteadily, as on a slippery surface. **2** (*intr*) to travel with a sliding motion. ◆ *n* **3** a slithering motion. [OE *slidrian*, from *slīdan* to slide]
▸'**slithery** *adj*

slit trench *n Mil.* a narrow trench dug for the protection of a small number of people.

sliver ⓣ ('slɪvə) *n* **1** a thin piece that is cut or broken off lengthwise. **2** a loose fibre obtained by carding. ◆ *vb* **3** to divide or be divided into splinters. **4** (*tr*) to form (wool, etc.) into slivers. [C14: from *sliven* to split]

Sloane Ranger (sləʊn) *n* (in Britain) *Inf.* a young upper-class person having a home in London and in the country, characterized as wearing expensive informal clothes. Also called: **Sloane.** [C20: pun on *Sloane* Square, London, and *Lone Ranger,* television cowboy character]

slob ⓣ (slɒb) *n* **1** *Inf.* a slovenly, unattractive, and lazy person. **2** *Irish.* mire. [C19: from Irish Gaelic *slab* mud]
▸'**slobbish** *adj*

slobber ⓣ ('slɒbə) *or* **slabber** *vb* **1** to dribble (saliva, food, etc.) from the mouth. **2** (*intr*) to speak or write mawkishly. **3** (*tr*) to smear with matter dribbling from the mouth. ◆ *n* **4** liquid or saliva spilt from the mouth. **5** maudlin language or behaviour. [C15: from MLow G, MDu. *slubberen*]
▸'**slobberer** *or* '**slabberer** *n* ▸'**slobbery** *or* '**slabbery** *adj*

sloe (sləʊ) *n* **1** the small sour blue-black fruit of the blackthorn. **2** another name for **blackthorn.** [OE *slāh*]

sloe-eyed *adj* having dark slanted or almond-shaped eyes.

sloe gin *n* gin flavoured with sloe juice.

slog ⓣ (slɒg) *vb* **slogs, slogging, slogged. 1** to hit with heavy blows, as in boxing. **2** (*intr*) to work hard; toil. **3** (*intr;* foll. by *down, up, along,* etc.) to move with difficulty. **4** *Cricket.* to take large swipes at the ball. ◆ *n* **5** a tiring walk. **6** long exhausting work. **7** a heavy blow or swipe. [C19: from ?]
▸'**slogger** *n*

slogan ⓣ ('sləʊgən) *n* **1** a distinctive or topical phrase used in politics, advertising, etc. **2** *Scot. history.* a Highland battle cry. [C16: from Gaelic *sluagh-ghairm* war cry]

sloop (sluːp) *n* a single-masted sailing vessel, rigged fore-and-aft. [C17: from Du. *sloep*]

sloot (sluːt) *n S. African.* a ditch for irrigation or drainage. [from Afrik., from Du. *sluit, sluis* SLUICE]

slop[1] ⓣ (slɒp) *vb* **slops, slopping, slopped. 1** (when *intr*, often foll. by *about*) to cause (liquid) to splash or spill or (of liquid) to splash or spill. **2** (*intr;* foll. by *along, through,* etc.) to tramp (through) mud or slush. **3** (*tr*) to feed slop or swill to: *to slop the pigs.* **4** (*tr*) to ladle or serve, esp. clumsily. **5** (*intr;* foll. by *over*) *Inf., chiefly US & Canad.* to be unpleasantly effusive. ◆ *n* **6** a puddle of spilt liquid. **7** (*pl*) wet feed, esp. for pigs, made from kitchen waste, etc. **8** (*pl*) waste food or liquid refuse. **9** (*often pl*) *Inf.* liquid or semiliquid food of low quality. **10** soft mud, snow, etc. [C14: prob. from OE *-sloppe* in *cūsloppe* COWSLIP]

slop[2] (slɒp) *n* **1** (*pl*) sailors' clothing and bedding issued from a ship's stores. **2** any loose article of clothing, esp. a smock. **3** (*pl*) shoddy manufactured clothing. [OE *oferslop* surplice]

slop basin *n* a bowl or basin into which the dregs from teacups are emptied at the table.

slope ⓣ (sləʊp) *vb* **slopes, sloping, sloped. 1** to lie or cause to lie at a slanting or oblique angle. **2** (*intr*) (esp. of natural features) to follow an inclined course: *many paths sloped down the hillside.* **3** (*intr;* foll. by *off, away,* etc.) to go furtively. **4** (*tr*) *Mil.* (formerly) to hold (a rifle) in the slope position. ◆ *n* **5** an inclined portion of ground. **6** (*pl*) hills or foothills. **7** any inclined surface or line. **8** the degree or amount of such inclination. **9** *Maths.* (of a line) the tangent of the angle between the line and another line parallel to the *x*-axis. **10** (formerly) the position adopted for military drill when the rifle is rested on the shoulder. [C15: short for *aslope,* ?from the p.p. of OE *āslūpan* to slip away]
▸'**sloper** *n* ▸'**sloping** *adj*

slop out *vb* (*intr, adv*) (of prisoners) to empty chamber pots and collect water for washing.

sloppy ⓣ ('slɒpɪ) *adj* **sloppier, sloppiest. 1** (esp. of the ground, etc.) wet; slushy. **2** *Inf.* careless; untidy. **3** *Inf.* mawkishly sentimental. **4** (of food or drink) watery and unappetizing. **5** splashed with slops. **6** (of clothes) loose; baggy.
▸'**sloppily** *adv* ▸'**sloppiness** *n*

slosh ⓣ (slɒʃ) *n* **1** watery mud, snow, etc. **2** *Brit. sl.* a heavy blow. **3** the sound of splashing liquid. ◆ *vb* **4** (*tr;* foll. by *around, on, in,* etc.) *Inf.* to throw or pour (liquid). **5** (when *intr,* often foll. by *about* or *around*) *Inf.* **5a** to shake or stir (something) in a liquid. **5b** (of a person) to splash (around) in water, etc. **6** (*tr*) *Brit. sl.* to deal a heavy blow to. **7** (usually foll. by *about* or *around*) *Inf.* to shake (a container of liquid) or (of liquid within a container) to be shaken. [C19: var. of SLUSH, infl. by SLOP[1]]
▸'**sloshy** *adj*

sloshed (slɒʃt) *adj Chiefly Brit. sl.* drunk.

slot[1] ⓣ (slɒt) *n* **1** an elongated aperture or groove, such as one in a vending machine for inserting a coin. **2** *Inf.* a place in a series or scheme. ◆ *vb* **slots, slotting, slotted. 3** (*tr*) to furnish with a slot or slots. **4** (usually foll. by *in* or *into*) to fit or adjust in a slot. **5** *Inf.* to situate or be situated in a series. [C13: from OF *esclot* the depression of the breastbone, from ?]
▸'**slotter** *n*

slot[2] (slɒt) *n* the trail of an animal, esp. a deer. [C16: from OF *esclot* horse's hoofprint, prob. of Scand. origin]

sloth ⓣ (sləʊθ) *n* **1** any of a family of shaggy-coated arboreal edentate mammals, such as the three-toed sloth or ai or the two-toed sloth or

THESAURUS

slippery *adj* **1 = smooth,** glassy, greasy, icy, lubricious (*rare*), perilous, skiddy (*inf.*), slippy (*inf. or dialect*), unsafe, unstable, unsteady **3 = untrustworthy,** crafty, cunning, devious, dishonest, duplicitous, evasive, false, foxy, shifty, sneaky, treacherous, tricky, two-faced, unpredictable, unreliable

slipshod *adj* **1 = careless,** casual, loose, slapdash, sloppy (*inf.*), slovenly, unsystematic, untidy

slit *vb* **1 = cut (open),** gash, impale, knife, lance, pierce, rip, slash, split open ◆ *n* **3, 4 = cut,** fissure, gash, incision, opening, rent, split, tear

slither *vb* **1, 2 = slide,** glide, skitter, slink, slip, snake, undulate

sliver *n* **1 = shred,** flake, fragment, paring, shaving, slip, splinter

slob *n* **1** *Informal* **= layabout,** couch potato (*sl.*), good-for-nothing, idler, loafer, lounger

slobber *vb* **1 = drool,** dribble, drivel, salivate, slabber (*dialect*), slaver, water at the mouth

slobbish *adj* **1 = messy,** slatternly, sloppy (*inf.*), slovenly, unclean, unkempt, untidy

slog *vb* **1 = hit,** hit for six, punch, slosh (*Brit. sl.*), slug, sock (*sl.*), strike, thump, wallop (*inf.*) **2 = work,** apply oneself to, keep one's nose to the grindstone, labour, peg away at, persevere, plod, plough through, slave, sweat blood (*inf.*), toil, work one's fingers to the bone **3 = trudge,** tramp, trek ◆ *n* **5 = trudge,** hike, tramp, trek **6 = labour,** blood, sweat, and tears (*inf.*), effort, exertion, struggle

slogan *n* **1 = catch phrase,** catchword, jingle, motto, rallying cry, tag-line

slop[1] *vb* **1 = spill,** overflow, slosh (*inf.*), spatter, splash, splatter

slope *vb* **1 = slant,** drop away, fall, incline, lean, pitch, rise, tilt **3** *with* **off** *or* **away = slink away,** creep away, make oneself scarce, skulk, slip away, steal ◆ *n* **5 = inclination,** brae (*Scot.*), declination, declivity, descent, downgrade (*chiefly US*), gradient, incline, ramp, rise, scarp, slant, tilt

sloping *adj* **1 = slanting,** atilt, bevelled, cant, inclined, inclining, leaning, oblique

sloppy *adj* **1 = wet,** sludgy, slushy, splashy, watery **2** *Informal* **= careless,** amateurish, clumsy, hit-or-miss (*inf.*), inattentive, messy, slipshod, slovenly, unkempt, untidy, weak **3** *Informal* **= sentimental,** banal, gushing, mawkish, mushy (*inf.*), overemotional, slushy (*inf.*), soppy (*Brit. inf.*), three-hankie (*inf.*), trite, wet (*Brit. inf.*)

slosh *vb Informal* **4 = pour,** shower, slap, spray **5 = splash,** flounder, plash, slop, swash, wade **6** *Brit. slang* **= hit,** bash (*inf.*), belt (*inf.*), biff (*sl.*), punch, slog, slug, sock (*sl.*), strike, swipe (*inf.*), thwack, wallop (*inf.*)

slot[1] *n* **1 = opening,** aperture, channel, groove, hole, slit, vent **2** *Informal* **= place,** niche, opening, position, space, time, vacancy ◆ *vb* **4 = fit in,** adjust, assign, fit, insert, pigeonhole

sloth *n* **2 = laziness,** idleness, inactivity, indolence, inertia, slackness, slothfulness, sluggishness, torpor

unau, of Central and South America. They are slow-moving, hanging upside down by their long arms and feeding on vegetation. **2** reluctance to exert oneself. [OE *slǣwth*, from *slǣw*, var. of *slāw* slow]

sloth bear *n* a bear of forests of S India and Sri Lanka, having an elongated snout specialized for feeding on termites.

slothful ➊ ('sləʊθfʊl) *adj* lazy; indolent.
▸ **'slothfully** *adv* ▸ **'slothfulness** *n*

slot machine *n* a machine, esp. one for gambling, activated by placing a coin in a slot.

slouch ➊ (slaʊtʃ) *vb* **1** (*intr*) to sit or stand with a drooping bearing. **2** (*intr*) to walk or move with an awkward slovenly gait. **3** (*tr*) to cause (the shoulders) to droop. ◆ *n* **4** a drooping carriage. **5** (*usually used in negative constructions*) *Inf.* an incompetent or slovenly person: *he's no slouch at football.* [C16: from ?]
▸ **'slouching** *adj*

slouch hat *n* any soft hat with a brim that can be pulled down over the ears, esp. an Australian army hat with the left side of the brim turned up.

slough[1] (slaʊ) *n* **1** a hollow filled with mud; bog. **2** (sluː) Also: **slew** (esp. US), **slue.** *North American.* a large hole where water collects or a marshy inlet. **3** despair or degradation. [OE *slōh*]
▸ **'sloughy** *adj*

slough[2] (slʌf) *n* **1** any outer covering that is shed, such as the dead outer layer of the skin of a snake, the cellular debris in a wound, etc. ◆ *vb* **2** (often foll. by *off*) to shed (a skin, etc.) or (of a skin, etc.) to be shed. [C13: of Gmc origin]
▸ **'sloughy** *adj*

slough off (slʌf) *vb* (*tr, adv*) to cast off (cares, etc.).

Slovak ('sləʊvæk) *adj* **1** of or characteristic of Slovakia in E Europe, its people, or their language. ◆ *n* **2** the official language of Slovakia. Slovak is closely related to Czech; they are mutually intelligible. **3** a native or inhabitant of Slovakia.

sloven ('slʌvᵊn) *n* a person who is habitually negligent in appearance, hygiene, or work. [C15: prob. rel. to Flemish *sloef* dirty, Du. *slof* negligent]

Slovene (sləʊ'viːn) *adj* **1** of or characteristic of Slovenia, in SE Europe, its people or their language. ◆ *n* **2** Also **Slovenian.** the official language of Slovenia. **3** a native or inhabitant of Slovenia.

slovenly ➊ ('slʌvənlɪ) *adj* **1** frequently or habitually unclean or untidy. **2** negligent and careless: *slovenly manners.* ◆ *adv* **3** in a negligent or slovenly manner.
▸ **'slovenliness** *n*

slow ➊ (sləʊ) *adj* **1** performed or occurring during a comparatively long interval of time. **2** lasting a comparatively long time: *a slow journey.* **3** characterized by lack of speed: *a slow walker.* **4** (*prenominal*) adapted to or productive of slow movement: *the slow lane of a motorway.* **5** (of a clock, etc.) indicating a time earlier than the correct time. **6** not readily responsive to stimulation: *a slow mind.* **7** dull or uninteresting: *the play was very slow.* **8** not easily aroused: *a slow temperament.* **9** lacking promptness or immediacy: *a slow answer.* **10** unwilling to perform an action or enter into a state: *slow to anger.* **11** behind the times. **12** (of trade, etc.) unproductive; slack. **13** (of a fire) burning weakly. **14** (of an oven) cool. **15** *Photog.* requiring a relatively long time of exposure to produce a given density: *a slow lens.* **16** *Sport.* (of a court, track, etc.) tending to reduce the speed of the ball or the competitors. **17** *Cricket.* (of a bowler, etc.) delivering the ball slowly, usually with spin. ◆ *adv* **18** in a manner characterized by lack of speed; slowly. ◆ *vb* **19** (often foll. by *up, down,* etc.) to decrease or cause to decrease in speed, efficiency, etc. [OE *slāw* sluggish]
▸ **'slowly** *adv* ▸ **'slowness** *n*

slowcoach ('sləʊˌkəʊtʃ) *n Brit. inf.* a person who moves or works slowly. US and Canad. equivalent: **slowpoke.**

slow handclap *n Brit.* slow rhythmic clapping, esp. used by an audience to indicate dissatisfaction or impatience.

slow march *n Mil.* a march in **slow time,** usually 65 or 75 paces to the minute.

slow match *or* **fuse** *n* a match or fuse that burns slowly without flame.

slow-mo *or* **slo-mo** ('sləʊˌməʊ) *n, adj Inf.* short for **slow motion** *or* **slow-motion.**

slow motion *n* **1** *Films, television, etc.* action that is made to appear slower than normal by passing the film through the camera at a faster rate or by replaying a video recording more slowly. ◆ *adj* **slow-motion. 2** of or relating to such action. **3** moving or functioning at considerably less than usual speed.

slow virus *n* a type of virus that is present in the body for a long time before it becomes active or infectious.

slowworm ('sləʊˌwɜːm) *n* a Eurasian legless lizard with a brownish-grey snakelike body. Also called: **blindworm.**

SLR *abbrev. for* single-lens reflex: see **reflex camera.**

SLSC *Austral. abbrev. for* Surf Life Saving Club.

slub (slʌb) *n* **1** a lump in yarn or fabric, often made intentionally to give a knobbly effect. **2** a loosely twisted roll of fibre prepared for spinning. ◆ *vb* **slubs, slubbing, slubbed. 3** (*tr*) to draw out and twist (a sliver of fibre). ◆ *adj* **4** (of material) having an irregular appearance. [C18: from ?]

sludge ➊ (slʌdʒ) *n* **1** soft mud, snow, etc. **2** any deposit or sediment. **3** a surface layer of ice that is not frozen solid but has a slushy appearance. **4** (in sewage disposal) the solid constituents of sewage that are removed for purification. [C17: prob. rel. to SLUSH]
▸ **'sludgy** *adj*

slue[1] (sluː) *n, vb* **slues, sluing, slued.** a variant spelling (esp. US) of **slew**[2].

slue[2] (sluː) *n* a variant spelling of **slough**[1] (sense 2).

slug[1] (slʌg) *n* **1** any of various terrestrial gastropod molluscs in which the body is elongated and the shell is absent or very much reduced. **2** any of various other invertebrates having a soft slimy body, esp. the larvae of certain sawflies. [C15 (in the sense: a slow person or animal): prob. from ON]

slug[2] (slʌg) *n* **1** an fps unit of mass; the mass that will acquire an acceleration of 1 foot per second per second when acted upon by a force of 1 pound. **2** *Metallurgy.* a metal blank from which small forgings are worked. **3** a bullet. **4** *Chiefly US & Canad.* a metal token for use in slot machines, etc. **5** *Printing.* **5a** a thick strip of type metal that is used for spacing. **5b** a metal strip containing a line of characters as produced by a Linotype machine. **6** a draught of a drink, esp. an alcoholic one. [C17 (bullet), C19 (printing): ?from SLUG[1], with allusion to the shape of the animal]

slug[3] (slʌg) *vb* **slugs, slugging, slugged. 1** *Chiefly US & Canad.* to hit very hard and solidly. **2** (*tr*) *Austral. & NZ inf.* to charge (someone) an exorbitant price. ◆ *n* **3** *US & Canad.* a heavy blow. **4** *Austral. & NZ inf.* an exorbitant price. [C19: ?from SLUG[2] (bullet)]

sluggard ('slʌgəd) *n* **1** a person who is habitually indolent. ◆ *adj* **2** lazy. [C14 *slogarde*]
▸ **'sluggardly** *adj*

sluggish ➊ ('slʌgɪʃ) *adj* **1** lacking energy; inactive. **2** functioning at below normal rate or level. **3** exhibiting poor response to stimulation.
▸ **'sluggishly** *adv* ▸ **'sluggishness** *n*

sluice ➊ (sluːs) *n* **1** Also called: **sluiceway.** a channel that carries a rapid current of water, esp. one that has a sluicegate to control the flow. **2** the body of water controlled by a sluicegate. **3** See **sluicegate. 4** *Mining.* an inclined trough for washing ore. **5** an artificial channel through which logs can be floated. ◆ *vb* **sluices, sluicing, sluiced. 6** (*tr*) to draw out or drain (water, etc.) from (a pond, etc.) by means of a sluice. **7** (*tr*) to wash or irrigate with a stream of water. **8** (*tr*) *Mining.* to wash in a sluice. **9** (*tr*) to send (logs, etc.) down a sluice. **10** (*intr;* often foll. by *away* or *out*) (of water, etc.) to run or flow from or as if from a sluice. **11** (*tr*) to provide with a sluice. [C14: from OF *escluse,* from LL *exclūsa aqua* water shut out, from L *exclūdere* to shut out]
▸ **'sluiceˌlike** *adj*

sluicegate ('sluːsˌgeɪt) *n* a valve or gate fitted to a sluice to control the rate of flow of water. See also **floodgate** (sense 1).

slum ➊ (slʌm) *n* **1** a squalid overcrowded house, etc. **2** (*often pl*) a

THESAURUS

slothful *adj* = **lazy,** do-nothing (*inf.*), good-for-nothing, idle, inactive, indolent, inert, skiving (*Brit. sl.*), slack, sluggish, torpid, workshy

slouch *vb* **1** = **slump,** droop, loll, stoop

slouching *adj* **2** = **shambling,** awkward, loutish, lumbering, uncouth, ungainly

slovenly *adj* **1** = **untidy,** disorderly, slatternly, unkempt **2** = **careless,** heedless, loose, negligent, slack, slapdash, slipshod, sloppy (*inf.*)
Antonyms *adj* ≠ **untidy:** clean, meticulous, neat, orderly, shipshape, smart, soigné *or* soignée, tidy, trim, well-groomed ≠ **careless:** careful, conscientious, disciplined, methodical, meticulous, well-ordered

slow *adj* **1, 2** = **prolonged,** gradual, lingering, long-drawn-out, protracted, time-consuming **3** = **unhurried,** creeping, dawdling, deliberate, easy, lackadaisical, laggard, lagging, lazy, leaden, leisurely, loitering, measured, plodding, ponderous, slow-moving, sluggardly, sluggish, tortoise-like **6** = **stupid,** blockish, bovine, braindead (*inf.*), dense, dim, dozy (*Brit. inf.*), dull, dull-witted, dumb (*inf.*), obtuse, retarded, slow on the uptake (*inf.*), slow-witted, thick, unresponsive **7** = **dull,** boring, conservative, dead, dead-and-alive (*Brit.*), inactive, one-horse (*inf.*), quiet, slack, sleepy, sluggish, stagnant, tame, tedious, uneventful, uninteresting, unproductive, unprogressive, wearisome **9** = **late,** backward, behind, behindhand, delayed, dilatory, long-delayed, tardy, unpunctual **10** = **unwilling,** averse, disinclined, hesitant, indisposed, loath, reluctant ◆ *vb* **19** *often with* **up** *or* **down** = **reduce speed,** brake, check, curb, decelerate, delay, detain, handicap, hold up, lag, rein in, relax, restrict, retard, slacken (off), spin out
Antonyms *adj* ≠ **unhurried:** brisk, eager, fast, hectic, hurried, precipitate, prompt, quick, quickie (*inf.*), quick-moving, sharp, speedy, swift ≠ **stupid:** bright, clever, intelligent, perceptive, quick, quick-witted, sharp, smart ≠ **dull:** action-packed, animated, exciting, interesting, lively, stimulating ◆ *vb* ≠ **reduce speed:** accelerate, advance, aid, boost, help, pick up speed, quicken, speed up

slowly *adv* **1-3** = **gradually,** at a snail's pace, at one's leisure, by degrees, inchmeal, in one's own (good) time, leisurely, ploddingly, steadily, taking one's time, unhurriedly, with leaden steps

sludge *n* **2** = **sediment,** dregs, gloop (*inf.*), mire, muck, mud, ooze, residue, silt, slime, slob (*Irish*), slop, slush

sluggish *adj* **1-3** = **inactive,** dull, heavy, indolent, inert, lethargic, lifeless, listless, phlegmatic, slothful, slow, slow-moving, torpid, unresponsive
Antonyms *adj* alive and kicking, animated, brisk, dynamic, energetic, enthusiastic, fast, free-flowing, full of beans (*inf.*), full of life, industrious, lively, swift, vigorous

sluggishness *n* **1-3** = **inactivity,** apathy, drowsiness, dullness, heaviness, indolence, inertia, languor, lassitude, lethargy, listlessness, slothfulness, somnolence, stagnation, torpor

sluice *vb* **6** = **drain,** flush **7** = **wash out,** cleanse, drench, irrigate, wash down

slum *n* **1, 2** = **hovel,** ghetto, rookery (*arch.*), warren

squalid section of a city, characterized by inferior living conditions. **3** (*modifier*) of or characteristic of slums: *slum conditions.* ◆ *vb* **slums, slumming, slummed.** (*intr*) **4** to visit slums, esp. for curiosity. **5** Also: **slum it.** to suffer conditions below those to which one is accustomed. [C19: orig. sl., from ?]
▸ **'slummy** *adj*

slumber ⓣ ('slʌmbə) *vb* **1** (*intr*) to sleep, esp. peacefully. **2** (*intr*) to be quiescent or dormant. **3** (*tr;* foll. by *away*) to spend (time) sleeping. ◆ *n* **4** (*sometimes pl*) sleep. **5** a dormant or quiescent state. [OE *slūma* sleep (n)]
▸ **'slumberer** *n* ▸ **'slumbering** *adj*

slumberous ('slʌmbərəs) *or* **slumbrous** *adj Chiefly poetic.* **1** sleepy; drowsy. **2** inducing sleep.
▸ **'slumberously** *adv* ▸ **'slumberousness** *n*

slump ⓣ (slʌmp) *vb* (*intr*) **1** to sink or fall heavily and suddenly. **2** to relax ungracefully. **3** (of business activity, etc.) to decline suddenly. **4** (of health, interest, etc.) to deteriorate or decline suddenly. ◆ *n* **5** a sudden or marked decline or failure, as in progress or achievement. **6** a decline in commercial activity, prices, etc.; depression. **7** the act of slumping. [C17: prob. of Scand. origin]

slung (slʌŋ) *vb* the past tense and past participle of **sling**[1].

slunk (slʌŋk) *vb* the past tense and past participle of **slink.**

slur ⓣ (slɜː) *vb* **slurs, slurring, slurred.** (*mainly tr*) **1** (often foll. by *over*) to treat superficially, hastily, or without due deliberation. **2** (*also intr*) to pronounce or utter (words, etc.) indistinctly. **3** to speak disparagingly of. **4** *Music.* to execute (a melodic interval of two or more notes) smoothly, as in legato performance. ◆ *n* **5** an indistinct sound or utterance. **6** a slighting remark. **7** a stain or disgrace, as upon one's reputation. **8** *Music.* **8a** a performance or execution of a melodic interval of two or more notes in a part. **8b** the curved line (⌒ or ⌣) indicating this. [C15: prob. from MLow G]

slurp (slɜːp) *Inf.* ◆ *vb* **1** to eat or drink (something) noisily. ◆ *n* **2** a sound produced in this way. [C17: from MDu. *slorpen* to sip]

slurry ('slʌrɪ) *n, pl* **slurries.** a suspension of solid particles in a liquid, as in a mixture of cement, coal dust, manure, meat, etc. with water. [C15 *slory*]

slush (slʌʃ) *n* **1** any watery muddy substance, esp. melting snow. **2** *Inf.* sloppily sentimental language. ◆ *vb* **3** (*intr;* often foll. by *along*) to make one's way through or as if through slush. [C17: rel. to Danish *slus* sleet, Norwegian *slusk* slops]
▸ **'slushy** *adj* ▸ **'slushiness** *n*

slush fund *n* a fund for financing political or commercial corruption.

slushy ('slʌʃɪ) *adj* **slushier, slushiest.** of, resembling, or consisting of slush.
▸ **'slushiness** *n*

slut ⓣ (slʌt) *n* **1** a dirty slatternly woman. **2** an immoral woman. [C14: from ?]
▸ **'sluttish** *adj* ▸ **'sluttishness** *n*

sly ⓣ (slaɪ) *adj* **slyer, slyest** *or* **slier, sliest. 1** crafty; artful: *a sly dodge.* **2** insidious; furtive: *a sly manner.* **3** roguish: *sly humour.* ◆ *n* **4 on the sly.** in a secretive manner. [C12: from ON *slægr* clever, lit.: able to strike, from *slā* to slay]
▸ **'slyly** *or* **'slily** *adv* ▸ **'slyness** *n*

slype (slaɪp) *n* a covered passage in a church that connects the transept to the chapterhouse. [C19: prob. from MFlemish *slijpen* to slip]

Sm *the chemical symbol for* samarium.

SM *abbrev. for* **1** sergeant major. **2** sadomasochism.

smack[1] ⓣ (smæk) *n* **1** a smell or flavour that is distinctive though faint. **2** a distinctive trace: *the smack of corruption.* **3** a small quantity, esp. a taste. **4** a slang word for **heroin.** ◆ *vb* (*intr;* foll. by *of*) **5** to have the characteristic smell or flavour (of something): *to smack of the sea.* **6** to have an element suggestive (of something): *his speeches smacked of bigotry.* [OE *smæc*]

smack[2] ⓣ (smæk) *vb* **1** (*tr*) to strike or slap smartly, with or as if with the open hand. **2** to strike or send forcibly or loudly or to be struck or sent forcibly or loudly. **3** to open and close (the lips) loudly, esp. to show pleasure. ◆ *n* **4** a sharp resounding slap or blow with something flat, or the sound of such a blow. **5** a loud kiss. **6** a sharp sound made by the lips, as in enjoyment. **7 have a smack at.** *Inf., chiefly Brit.* to attempt. **8 smack in the eye.** *Inf., chiefly Brit.* a snub or setback. ◆ *adv Inf.* **9** directly; squarely. **10** sharply and unexpectedly. [C16: from MLow G or MDu. *smacken,* prob. imit.]

smack[3] (smæk) *n* a sailing vessel, usually sloop-rigged, used in coasting and fishing along the British coast. [C17: from Low G *smack* or Du. *smak,* from ?]

smacker ('smækə) *n Sl.* **1** a loud kiss; smack. **2** a pound note or dollar bill.

small ⓣ (smɔːl) *adj* **1** limited in size, number, importance, etc. **2** of little importance or on a minor scale: *a small business.* **3** lacking in moral or mental breadth or depth: *a small mind.* **4** modest or humble: *small beginnings.* **5** of low or inferior status, esp. socially. **6 feel small.** to be humiliated. **7** (of a child or animal) young; not mature. **8** unimportant; trivial: *a small matter.* **9** of or designating the ordinary modern minuscule letter used in printing and cursive writing. **10** lacking great strength or force: *a small effort.* **11** in fine particles: *small gravel.* ◆ *adv* **12** into small pieces: *cut it small.* **13** in a small or soft manner. ◆ *n* **14** (often preceded by *the*) an object, person, or group considered to be small: *the small or the large?* **15** a small slender part, esp. of the back. **16** (*pl*) *Inf., chiefly Brit.* items of personal laundry, such as underwear. [OE *smæl*]
▸ **'smallish** *adj* ▸ **'smallness** *n*

small arms *pl n* portable firearms of relatively small calibre.

small beer *n Inf., chiefly Brit.* people or things of no importance.

small change *n* **1** coins, esp. those of low value. **2** a person or thing that is not outstanding or important.

small circle *n* a circular section of a sphere that does not contain the centre of the sphere.

small claims court *n Brit. & Canad.* a local court with jurisdiction to try civil actions involving small claims.

small fry *pl n* **1** people or things regarded as unimportant. **2** young children. **3** young or small fishes.

small goods *pl n Austral. & NZ.* meats bought from a delicatessen, such as sausages.

smallholding ('smɔːlˌhəʊldɪŋ) *n* a holding of agricultural land smaller than a small farm.
▸ **'smallˌholder** *n*

small hours *pl n* **the.** the early hours of the morning, after midnight and before dawn.

small intestine *n* the longest part of the alimentary canal, in which digestion is completed. Cf. **large intestine.**

small-minded ⓣ *adj* narrow-minded; intolerant.
▸ **ˌsmall-'mindedly** *adv* ▸ **ˌsmall-'mindedness** *n*

smallpox ('smɔːlˌpɒks) *n* a highly contagious viral disease characterized by high fever and a rash changing to pustules, which dry up and form scabs that are cast off, leaving pitted depressions. Technical name: **variola.**

small print *n* matter in a contract, etc., printed in small type, esp. when considered to be a trap for the unwary.

small-scale *adj* **1** of limited size or scope. **2** (of a map, model, etc.) giving a relatively small representation of something.

small screen *n* an informal name for **television.**

small slam *n Bridge.* another name for **little slam.**

small talk *n* light conversation for social occasions.

THESAURUS

slumber *vb* **1** = **sleep,** be inactive, doze, drowse, kip (*Brit. sl.*), lie dormant, nap, repose, snooze (*inf.*), zizz (*Brit. inf.*)

slummy *adj* **1, 2** = **squalid,** decayed, overcrowded, run-down, seedy, sleazy, sordid, wretched

slump *vb* **1, 3** = **fall,** collapse, crash, decline, deteriorate, fall off, go downhill (*inf.*), plummet, plunge, reach a new low, sink, slip **2** = **sag,** bend, droop, hunch, loll, slouch ◆ *n* **5** = **fall,** collapse, crash, decline, depreciation, downturn, drop, failure, falling-off, lapse, low, meltdown (*inf.*), reverse, stagnation, trough **6** = **recession,** depression
Antonyms *vb* ≠ **fall:** advance, boom, develop, expand, flourish, grow, increase, prosper, thrive ◆ *n* ≠ **fall:** advance, boom, boost, development, expansion, gain, growth, improvement, increase, upsurge, upswing, upturn

slur *n* **6, 7** = **insult,** affront, aspersion, blot, blot on one's escutcheon, brand, calumny, discredit, disgrace, innuendo, insinuation, reproach, smear, stain, stigma

slut *n* **2** = **tart,** drab (*arch.*), scrubber (*Brit. & Austral. sl.*), slag (*Brit. sl.*), slapper (*Brit. sl.*), slattern, sloven, trollop

sluttish *adj* **1** = **slovenly,** dirty, slatternly **2** = **promiscuous,** coarse, dissipated, immoral, tarty (*inf.*), trollopy, whorish

sly *adj* **1, 2** = **cunning,** artful, astute, clever, conniving, covert, crafty, devious, foxy, furtive, guileful, insidious, scheming, secret, shifty, stealthy, subtle, underhand, wily **3** = **roguish,** arch, impish, knowing, mischievous ◆ *n* **4 on the sly** = **secretly,** behind (someone's) back, covertly, like a thief in the night, on the q.t. (*inf.*), on the quiet, privately, surreptitiously, underhandedly, under the counter (*inf.*)
Antonyms *adj* ≠ **cunning:** above-board, artless, direct, frank, guileless, honest, ingenuous, open, straightforward, trustworthy

smack[1] *vb, with* **of 5** = **smell of,** be redolent of, reek of **6** = **be suggestive** *or* **indicative of,** bear the stamp of, betoken, have all the hallmarks of, suggest, testify to

smack[2] *vb* **1, 2** = **slap,** box, clap, cuff, hit, pat, sock (*sl.*), spank, strike, swipe, tap ◆ *n* **4** = **slap,** blow, crack, swipe **8 smack in the eye** *Informal, chiefly Brit.* = **snub,** blow, rebuff, repulse, setback, slap in the face ◆ *adv* **9** *Informal* = **directly,** exactly, plumb, point-blank, precisely, right, slap (*inf.*), squarely, straight

small *adj* **1** = **little,** diminutive, immature, Lilliputian, mini, miniature, minute, petite, pint-sized (*inf.*), pocket-sized, puny, pygmy *or* pigmy, slight, teeny, tiny, undersized, wee, young **2** = **minor,** lesser **3** = **petty,** base, grudging, illiberal, mean, narrow, selfish **4** = **modest,** humble, small-scale, unpretentious **6 make (someone) feel small** = **humiliate,** chagrin, disconcert, humble, make (someone) look foolish, mortify, put down (*sl.*), show up (*inf.*), take down a peg or two (*inf.*) **8** = **unimportant,** insignificant, negligible, paltry, petty, trifling, trivial **10** = **meagre,** inadequate, inconsiderable, insufficient, limited, measly, scant, scanty
Antonyms *adj* ≠ **little:** big, colossal, enormous, great, huge, immense, massive, mega (*sl.*), sizable *or* sizeable, stellar (*inf.*), vast ≠ **modest:** grand, large-scale ≠ **unimportant:** appreciable, important, major, powerful, serious, significant, urgent, vital, weighty ≠ **meagre:** ample, considerable, generous, substantial

small-minded *adj* = **petty,** bigoted, envious, grudging, hidebound, intolerant, mean, narrow-minded, rigid, ungenerous
Antonyms *adj* broad-minded, far-sighted, generous, liberal, open, open-minded, tolerant, unbigoted

small-time ⊕ *adj Inf.* insignificant; minor: *a small-time criminal.*
▸ **'small-'timer** *n*

smalt (smɔːlt) *n* **1** a type of silica glass coloured deep blue with cobalt oxide. **2** a pigment made by crushing this glass, used in colouring enamels. [C16: via F from It. *smalto* coloured glass, of Gmc origin]

smarm (smɑːm) *vb Brit. inf.* **1** (*tr;* often foll. by *down*) to flatten (the hair, etc.) with grease. **2** (when *intr,* foll. by *up to*) to ingratiate oneself (with). [C19: from ?]

smarmy ⊕ ('smɑːmɪ) *adj* **smarmier, smarmiest.** *Brit. inf.* obsequiously flattering or unpleasantly suave.
▸ **'smarmily** *adv* ▸ **'smarminess** *n*

smart ⊕ (smɑːt) *adj* **1** astute, as in business. **2** quick, witty, and often impertinent in speech: *a smart talker.* **3** fashionable; chic: *a smart hotel.* **4** well-kept; neat. **5** causing a sharp stinging pain. **6** vigorous or brisk. **7** (of systems) operating as if by human intelligence by using automatic computer control. **8** (of a weapon, etc.) containing a device which enables it to be guided to its target: *smart bombs.* ◆ *vb* (*mainly intr*) **9** to feel, cause, or be the source of a sharp stinging physical pain or keen mental distress: *he smarted under their abuse.* **10** (often foll. by *for*) to suffer a harsh penalty. ◆ *n* **11** a stinging pain or feeling. ◆ *adv* **12** in a smart manner. ◆ See also **smarts.** [OE *smeortan*]
▸ **'smartly** *adv* ▸ **'smartness** *n*

smart aleck ⊕ ('ælɪk) *n Inf.* **a** an irritatingly oversmart person. **b** (*as modifier*): *a smart-aleck remark.* [C19: from *Aleck, Alec,* short for *Alexander*]
▸ **'smart-ˌalecky** *adj*

smart card *n* a plastic card with integrated circuits used for storing and processing computer data. Also called: **laser card, intelligent card.**

smart drug *n* any of various drugs that are claimed to improve the intelligence or memory of the person taking them.

smarten ⊕ ('smɑːtᵊn) *vb* (usually foll. by *up*) **1** (*intr*) to make oneself neater. **2** (*tr*) to make quicker or livelier.

smart money *n* **1** money bet or invested by experienced gamblers or investors. **2** money paid in order to extricate oneself from an unpleasant situation or agreement, esp. from military service. **3** *Law.* damages awarded to a plaintiff where the wrong was aggravated by fraud, malice, etc.

smarts (smɑːts) *pl n Sl., chiefly US.* know-how, intelligence, or wits: *street smarts.*

smart set *n* (*functioning as sing or pl*) fashionable people considered as a group.

smash ⊕ (smæʃ) *vb* **1** to break into pieces violently and usually noisily. **2** (when *intr,* foll. by *against, through, into,* etc.) to throw or crash (against) vigorously, causing shattering: *he smashed the equipment.* **3** (*tr*) to hit forcefully and suddenly. **4** (*tr*) *Tennis, etc.* to hit (the ball) fast and powerfully, esp. with an overhead stroke. **5** (*tr*) to defeat (persons, theories, etc.). **6** to make or become bankrupt. **7** (*intr*) to collide violently; crash. ◆ *n* **8** an act, instance, or sound of smashing or the state of being smashed. **9** a violent collision, esp. of vehicles. **10** a total failure or collapse, as of a business. **11** *Tennis, etc.* a fast and powerful overhead stroke. **12** *Inf.* **12a** something having popular success. **12b** (*in combination*): *smash-hit.* ◆ *adv* **13** with a smash. ◆ See also **smash-up.** [C18: prob. from SM(ACK² + M)ASH]
▸ **'smashable** *adj*

smash-and-grab *adj Inf.* of or relating to a robbery in which a shop window is broken and the contents removed.

smashed (smæʃt) *adj Sl.* drunk or under the influence of a drug.

smasher ('smæʃə) *n Inf., chiefly Brit.* a person or thing that is very attractive or outstanding.

smashing ⊕ ('smæʃɪŋ) *adj Inf., chiefly Brit.* excellent or first-rate: *we had a smashing time.*

smash-up *Inf.* ◆ *n* **1** a bad collision, esp of cars. ◆ *vb* **smash up. 2** (*tr, adv*) to damage to the point of complete destruction: *they smashed the place up.*

smatter ('smætə) *n* **1** a smattering. ◆ *vb* **2** (*tr*) *Arch.* to dabble in. [C14 (in the sense: to prattle): from ?]
▸ **'smatterer** *n*

smattering ⊕ ('smætərɪŋ) *n* **1** a slight or superficial knowledge. **2** a small amount.

smear ⊕ (smɪə) *vb* (*mainly tr*) **1** to bedaub or cover with oil, grease, etc. **2** to rub over or apply thickly. **3** to rub so as to produce a smudge. **4** to slander. **5** (*intr*) to be or become smeared or dirtied. ◆ *n* **6** a dirty mark or smudge. **7a** a slanderous attack. **7b** (*as modifier*): *smear tactics.* **8** a preparation of blood, secretions, etc., smeared onto a glass slide for examination under a microscope. [OE *smeoru* (n)]
▸ **'smeary** *adj* ▸ **'smearily** *adv* ▸ **'smeariness** *n*

smear test *n Med.* another name for **Pap test.**

smectic ('smɛktɪk) *adj Chem.* (of a substance) existing in or having a mesomorphic state in which the molecules are oriented in layers. [C17: via L from Gk *smēktikos,* from *smēkhein* to wash; from the soaplike consistency of a smectic substance]

smegma ('smɛgmə) *n Physiol.* a whitish sebaceous secretion that accumulates beneath the prepuce. [C19: via L from Gk *smēgma* detergent, from *smekhein* to wash]

smell ⊕ (smɛl) *vb* **smells, smelling, smelt** *or* **smelled. 1** (*tr*) to perceive the scent of (a substance) by means of the olfactory nerves. **2** (*copula*) to have a specified smell: *the curry smells very spicy.* **3** (*intr;* often foll. by *of*) to emit an odour (of): *the park smells of flowers.* **4** (*intr*) to emit an unpleasant odour. **5** (*tr;* often foll. by *out*) to detect through shrewdness or instinct. **6** (*intr*) to have or use the sense of smell; sniff. **7** (*intr;* foll. by *of*) to give indications (of): *he smells of money.* **8** (*intr;* foll. by *around, about,* etc.) to search, investigate, or pry. **9** (*copula*) to be or seem to be untrustworthy. ◆ *n* **10** that sense (olfaction) by which scents or odours are perceived. Related adj: **olfactory. 11** anything detected by the sense of smell. **12** a trace or indication. **13** the act or an instance of smelling. [C12: from ?]
▸ **'smeller** *n*

smelling salts *pl n* a pungent preparation containing crystals of ammonium carbonate that has a stimulant action when sniffed in cases of faintness, headache, etc.

smelly ⊕ ('smɛlɪ) *adj* **smellier, smelliest.** having a strong or nasty smell.
▸ **'smelliness** *n*

smelt[1] (smɛlt) *vb* (*tr*) to extract (a metal) from (an ore) by heating. [C15: from MLow G, MDu. *smelten*]

smelt[2] (smɛlt) *n, pl* **smelt** *or* **smelts.** a marine or freshwater salmonoid food fish having a long silvery body and occurring in temperate and cold northern waters. [OE *smylt*]

smelt[3] (smɛlt) *vb* a past tense and past participle of **smell.**

smelter ('smɛltə) *n* **1** a person engaged in smelting. **2** Also called: **smeltery.** an industrial plant in which smelting is carried out.

smew (smjuː) *n* a merganser of N Europe and Asia, having a male plumage of white with black markings. [C17: from ?]

smidgen *or* **smidgin** ('smɪdʒən) *n Inf., chiefly US.* a very small amount. [C20: from ?]

smilax ('smaɪlæks) *n* **1** any of a genus of climbing shrubs having slightly lobed leaves, small greenish or yellow flowers, and berry-like fruits: includes the sarsaparilla plant and greenbrier. **2** a fragile, much branched vine of southern Africa: cultivated for its glossy green foliage. [C17: via L from Gk: bindweed]

smile ⊕ (smaɪl) *n* **1** a facial expression characterized by an upturning of the corners of the mouth, usually showing amusement, friendliness, etc. **2** favour or blessing: *the smile of fortune.* ◆ *vb* **smiles, smiling,**

THESAURUS

small-time *adj* = **minor**, insignificant, no-account (*US inf.*), of no account, of no consequence, petty, piddling (*inf.*), unimportant

smarmy *adj Brit. informal* = **obsequious**, bootlicking (*inf.*), bowing and scraping, crawling, fawning, fulsome, greasy, ingratiating, oily, servile, slimy, smooth, soapy (*sl.*), suave, sycophantic, toadying, unctuous

smart *adj* **1** = **clever**, acute, adept, agile, apt, astute, bright, brisk, canny, ingenious, intelligent, keen, nimble, quick, quick-witted, ready, sharp, shrewd **2** = **impertinent**, nimble-witted, pointed, ready, saucy, smart-alecky (*inf.*), witty **3** = **chic**, as fresh as a daisy, elegant, fashionable, fine, modish, natty (*inf.*), neat, snappy, spruce, stylish, trendy (*Brit. inf.*), trim, well turned-out **5** = **stinging**, hard, keen, painful, piercing, resounding, sharp **6** = **brisk**, cracking (*inf.*), jaunty, lively, quick, spanking, spirited, vigorous ◆ *vb* **9** = **sting**, burn, hurt, pain, throb, tingle ◆ *n* **11** = **sting**, burning sensation, pain, pang, smarting, soreness
Antonyms *adj* ≠ **clever**: daft (*inf.*), dense, dim-witted (*inf.*), dull, dumb (*inf.*), dumb-ass (*sl.*), foolish, idiotic, moronic, slow, stupid, thick, unintelligent ≠ **chic**: dowdy, dull, fogeyish, naff (*Brit. sl.*), old-fashioned, outmoded, out-of-date, passé, scruffy, sloppy, uncool, unfashionable, untrendy (*Brit. inf.*)

smart aleck *n Informal* = **know-all** (*inf.*), clever-clogs (*inf.*), clever Dick (*inf.*), smartarse (*sl.*), smarty boots (*inf.*), smarty pants (*inf.*), wise guy (*inf.*)

smarten *vb* **1** = **tidy**, beautify, groom, put in order, put to rights, spruce up

smash *vb* **1, 2** = **break**, crush, demolish, disintegrate, pulverize, shatter, shiver **5** = **destroy**, defeat, lay waste, overthrow, ruin, total (*sl.*), trash (*sl.*), wreck **7** = **collide**, crash ◆ *n* **9** = **collision**, accident, crash, pile-up (*inf.*), smash-up (*inf.*) **10** = **destruction**, collapse, defeat, disaster, downfall, failure, ruin, shattering

smashing *adj Informal, chiefly Brit.* = **excellent**, brilliant (*inf.*), cracking, exhilarating, fabulous (*inf.*), fantastic (*inf.*), first-class, first-rate, great (*inf.*), jim-dandy (*sl.*), magnificent, marvellous, out of this world (*inf.*), sensational (*inf.*), sovereign, stupendous, super (*inf.*), superb, superlative, terrific (*inf.*), wonderful, world-class
Antonyms *adj* abysmal, appalling, average, awful, bad, boring, disappointing, disgraceful, disgusting, dreadful, dreary, dull, hideous, horrible, mediocre, no great shakes (*inf.*), ordinary, rotten, run-of-the-mill, sickening, terrible, unexciting, uninspired, vile

smattering *n* **1, 2** = **modicum**, bit, dash, elements, nodding acquaintance, passing acquaintance, rudiments, smatter, sprinkling

smear *vb* **1** = **spread over**, bedaub, coat, cover, daub, plaster, rub on **3** = **dirty**, bedim, besmirch, blur, smirch, smudge, soil, stain, sully **4** = **slander**, asperse, besmirch, blacken, calumniate, drag (someone's) name through the mud, malign, sully, tarnish, traduce, vilify ◆ *n* **6** = **smudge**, blot, blotch, daub, smirch, splotch, streak **7** = **slander**, calumny, defamation, libel, mudslinging, vilification, whispering campaign

smell *vb* **1** = **sniff**, get a whiff of, nose, scent **4** = **stink**, be malodorous, hum (*sl.*), niff, pong (*Brit. inf.*), reek, stink to high heaven (*inf.*), whiff (*Brit. sl.*) ◆ *n* **11** = **odour**, aroma, bouquet, fragrance, niff (*Brit. sl.*), perfume, redolence, scent, stench, stink, whiff

smelly *adj* = **stinking**, evil-smelling, fetid, foul, foul-smelling, high, malodorous, mephitic, niffy (*Brit. sl.*), noisome, olid, pongy (*Brit. inf.*), putrid, reeking, stinky (*inf.*), strong, strong-smelling, whiffy (*Brit. sl.*)

smile *n* **1** = **grin**, beam ◆ *vb* **3** = **grin**, beam

smiled. 3 (*intr*) to wear or assume a smile. 4 (*intr;* foll. by *at*) 4a to look (at) with a kindly expression. 4b to look derisively (at). 4c to bear (troubles, etc.) patiently. 5 (*intr;* foll. by *on* or *upon*) to show approval. 6 (*tr*) to express by means of a smile: *she smiled a welcome.* 7 (*tr;* often foll. by *away*) to drive away or change by smiling. 8 **come up smiling.** to recover cheerfully from misfortune. [C13: prob. from ON]
▸'**smiler** *n* ▸'**smiling** *adj* ▸'**smilingly** *adv*

smiley ('smaılı) *adj* 1 given to smiling; cheerful. 2 depicting a smile: *a smiley badge.* ◆ *n* 3 any of a group of symbols depicting a smile, or other facial expression, used in electronic mail.

smirch (smɜːtʃ) *vb* (*tr*) 1 to dirty; soil. ◆ *n* 2 the act of smirching or state of being smirched. 3 a smear or stain. [C15 *smorchen,* from ?]

smirk ❶ (smɜːk) *n* 1 a smile expressing scorn, smugness, etc., rather than pleasure. ◆ *vb* 2 (*intr*) to give such a smile. 3 (*tr*) to express with such a smile. [OE *smearcian*]
▸'**smirker** *n* ▸'**smirking** *adj* ▸'**smirkingly** *adv*

smite (smaıt) *vb* **smites, smiting, smote; smitten** *or* **smit** (smıt). (*mainly tr*) *Now arch. in most senses.* 1 to strike with a heavy blow. 2 to damage with or as if with blows. 3 to affect severely: *smitten with flu.* 4 to afflict in order to punish. 5 (*intr;* foll. by *on*) to strike forcibly or abruptly: *the sun smote down on him.* [OE *smītan*]
▸'**smiter** *n*

smith (smıθ) *n* 1a a person who works in metal. 1b (*in combination*)*: a silversmith.* 2 See **blacksmith.** [OE]

smithereens (ˌsmıðə'riːnz) *pl n* little shattered pieces or fragments. [C19: from Irish Gaelic *smidirīn,* from *smiodar*]

smithery ('smıθərı) *n, pl* **smitheries.** 1 the trade or craft of a blacksmith. 2 a rare word for **smithy.**

smithy ('smıðı) *n, pl* **smithies.** a place in which metal, usually iron or steel, is worked by heating and hammering; forge. [OE *smiththe*]

smitten ❶ ('smıtᵊn) *vb* 1 a past participle of **smite.** ◆ *adj* 2 (*postpositive*) affected by love (for).

smock (smɒk) *n* 1 any loose protective garment, worn by artists, laboratory technicians, etc. 2 a woman's loose blouselike garment, reaching to below the waist, worn over slacks, etc. 3 Also called: **smock frock.** a loose protective overgarment decorated with smocking, worn formerly esp. by farm workers. 4 *Arch.* a woman's loose undergarment. ◆ *vb* 5 to ornament (a garment) with smocking. [OE *smocc*]
▸'**smock,like** *adj*

smocking ('smɒkıŋ) *n* ornamental needlework used to gather and stitch material in a honeycomb pattern so that the part below the gathers hangs in even folds.

smog (smɒg) *n* a mixture of smoke, fog, and chemical fumes. [C20: from SM(OKE + F)OG[1]]
▸'**smoggy** *adj*

smoke (sməʊk) *n* 1 the product of combustion, consisting of fine particles of carbon carried by hot gases and air. 2 any cloud of fine particles suspended in a gas. 3a the act of smoking tobacco, esp. as a cigarette. 3b the duration of smoking such substances. 4 *Inf.* a cigarette or cigar. 5 something with no concrete or lasting substance: *everything turned to smoke.* 6 a thing or condition that obscures. 7 **go** *or* **end up in smoke.** 7a to come to nothing. 7b to burn up vigorously. 7c to flare up in anger. ◆ *vb* **smokes, smoking, smoked.** 8 (*intr*) to emit smoke or the like, sometimes excessively or in the wrong place. 9 to draw in on (a burning cigarette, etc.) and exhale the smoke. 10 (*tr*) to bring (oneself) into a specified state by smoking. 11 (*tr*) to subject or expose to smoke. 12 (*tr*) to cure (meat, fish, etc.) by treating with smoke. 13 (*tr*) to fumigate or purify the air of (rooms, etc.). 14 (*tr*) to darken (glass, etc.) by exposure to smoke. ◆ See also **smoke out.** [OE *smoca* (n)]
▸'**smokable** *or* '**smokeable** *adj*

Smoke (sməʊk) *n* **the.** short for the **Big Smoke.**

smoke-dried *adj* (of fish, etc.) cured in smoke.

smoked rubber *n* a type of crude natural rubber in the form of brown sheets obtained by coagulating latex with an acid, rolling it into sheets, and drying over open wood fires. It is the main raw material for natural rubber products.

smokeho ('sməʊkəʊ) *n* a variant spelling of **smoko.**

smokehouse ('sməʊkˌhaʊs) *n* a building or special construction for curing meat, fish, etc., by smoking.

smokeless ('sməʊklıs) *adj* having or producing little or no smoke: *smokeless fuel.*

smokeless zone *n* an area where only smokeless fuels are permitted to be used.

smoke out *vb* (*tr, adv*) 1 to subject to smoke in order to drive out of hiding. 2 to bring into the open: *they smoked out the plot.*

smoker ('sməʊkə) *n* 1 a person who habitually smokes tobacco. 2 Also called: **smoking compartment.** a compartment of a train where smoking is permitted. 3 an informal social gathering, as at a club.

smoke screen *n* 1 *Mil.* a cloud of smoke produced to obscure movements. 2 something said or done in order to hide the truth.

smokestack ('sməʊkˌstæk) *n* a tall chimney that conveys smoke into the air.

smokestack industry *n Inf.* any of the traditional British industries, esp. heavy engineering or manufacturing, as opposed to such modern industries as electronics.

smoking jacket *n* (formerly) a man's comfortable jacket of velvet, etc., closed by a tie belt or fastenings, worn at home.

smoko *or* **smokeho** ('sməʊkəʊ) *n, pl* **smokos** *or* **smokehos.** *Austral. & NZ inf.* 1 a short break from work for tea, a cigarette, etc. 2 refreshment taken during this break.

smoky ❶ ('sməʊkı) *adj* **smokier, smokiest.** 1 emitting or resembling smoke. 2 emitting smoke excessively or in the wrong place: *a smoky fireplace.* 3 having the flavour of having been cured by smoking. 4 made dirty or hazy by smoke: *a smoky atmosphere.*
▸'**smokily** *adv* ▸'**smokiness** *n*

smolder ('sməʊldə) *vb, n* the US spelling of **smoulder.**

smolt (sməʊlt) *n* a young salmon at the stage when it migrates from fresh water to the sea. [C14: Scot., from ?]

smooch (smuːtʃ) *Sl.* ◆ *vb* (*intr*) 1 Also (Austral. and NZ): **smoodge, smooge.** (of two people) to kiss and cuddle. 2 *Brit.* to dance very slowly and amorously with one's arms around another person or (of two people) to dance together in such a way. ◆ *n* 3 the act of smooching. [C20: var. of dialect *smouch,* imit.]

smoodge *or* **smooge** (smuːdʒ) *vb* **smoodges, smoodging, smoodged** *or* **smooges, smooging, smooged.** (*intr*) *Austral. & NZ.* 1 another word for **smooch** (sense 1). 2 to seek to ingratiate oneself.

smooth ❶ (smuːð) *adj* 1 without bends or irregularities. 2 silky to the touch: *smooth velvet.* 3 lacking roughness of surface; flat. 4 tranquil or unruffled: *smooth temper.* 5 lacking obstructions or difficulties. 6a suave or persuasive, esp. as suggestive of insincerity. 6b (*in combination*)*: smooth-tongued.* 7 (of the skin) free from hair. 8 of uniform consistency: *smooth batter.* 9 free from jolts: *smooth driving.* 10 not harsh or astringent: *a smooth wine.* 11 having all projections worn away: *smooth tyres.* 12 *Phonetics.* without preliminary aspiration. 13 *Physics.* (of a plane, etc.) regarded as being frictionless. ◆ *adv* 14 in a calm or even manner. ◆ *vb* (*mainly tr*) 15 (*also intr;* often foll. by *down*) to make or become flattened or without roughness. 16 (often foll. by *out* or *away*) to take or rub (away) in order to make smooth: *she smoothed out the creases in her dress.* 17 to make calm; soothe. 18 to make easier: *smooth his path.* ◆ *n* 19 the smooth part of something. 20 the act of smoothing. 21 *Tennis, etc.* the side of a racket on which the binding strings form a continuous line. ◆ See also **smooth over.** [OE *smōth*]
▸'**smoother** *n* ▸'**smoothly** *adv* ▸'**smoothness** *n*

smoothbore ('smuːðˌbɔː) *n* (*modifier*) (of a firearm) having an unrifled bore: *a smoothbore shotgun.*
▸'**smooth,bored** *adj*

smooth breathing *n* (in Greek) the sign (') placed over an initial vowel, indicating that (in ancient Greek) it was not pronounced with an *h.*

smoothen ('smuːðən) *vb* to make or become smooth.

smooth hound *n* any of several small sharks of North Atlantic coastal regions.

smoothie *or* **smoothy** ('smuːðı) *n, pl* **smoothies.** *Sl., usually derog.* a person, esp. a man, who is suave or slick, esp. in speech, dress, or manner.

smoothing iron *n* a former name for **iron** (sense 3).

smooth muscle *n* muscle that is capable of slow rhythmic involuntary contractions: occurs in the walls of the blood vessels, etc.

smooth over *vb* (*tr*) to ease or gloss over: *to smooth over a difficulty.*

smooth snake *n* any of several slender nonvenomous European snakes having very smooth scales and a reddish-brown coloration.

smooth-spoken *adj* speaking or spoken in a gently persuasive or competent manner.

smooth-tongued *adj* suave or persuasive in speech.

smorgasbord ('smɔːgəsˌbɔːd) *n* a variety of cold or hot savoury dishes served in Scandinavia as hors d'oeuvres or as a buffet meal. [Swedish, from *smörgås* sandwich + *bord* table]

smote (sməʊt) *vb* the past tense of **smite.**

smother ❶ ('smʌðə) *vb* 1 to suffocate or stifle by cutting off or being cut off from the air. 2 (*tr*) to surround (with) or envelop (in): *he smothered her with love.* 3 (*tr*) to extinguish (a fire) by covering so as to cut it

THESAURUS

smirk *n* 1 = **smug look,** grin, leer, simper, sneer

smitten *adj* 1 = **afflicted,** beset, laid low, plagued, struck 2 = **infatuated,** beguiled, bewitched, bowled over (*inf.*), captivated, charmed, enamoured, swept off one's feet

smoky *adj* 4 = **black,** begrimed, caliginous (*arch.*), grey, grimy, hazy, murky, reeky, smoke-darkened, sooty, thick

smooth *adj* 2 = **sleek,** glassy, glossy, mirror-like, polished, shiny, silky, soft, velvety 3 = **even,** flat, flush, horizontal, level, plain, plane, unwrinkled 4 = **calm,** equable, peaceful, serene, tranquil, undisturbed, unruffled 5 = **easy,** effortless, untroubled, well-ordered 6 = **suave,** debonair, facile, glib, ingratiating, persuasive, silky, slick, smarmy (*Brit. inf.*), unctuous, urbane 9 = **flowing,** fluent, regular, rhythmic, steady, uniform 10 = **mellow,** agreeable, bland, mild, pleasant, soothing ◆ *vb* 15, 16 = **flatten,** iron, level, plane, polish, press 17 = **ease,** allay, alleviate, appease, assuage, calm, extenuate, mitigate, mollify, palliate, soften, soothe 18 = **facilitate,** ease, iron out the difficulties of, pave the way
Antonyms *adj* ≠ **sleek:** abrasive, coarse, jagged, rough, sharp ≠ **even:** bumpy, irregular, lumpy, rough, uneven ≠ **calm:** agitated, edgy, excitable, nervous, ruffled, troubled, troublesome, turbulent, uneasy ◆ *vb* ≠ **ease:** aggravate, exacerbate, hamper, hinder, intensify, make worse, roughen

smoothness *n* 2 = **sleekness,** silkiness, smooth texture, softness, velvetiness 3 = **evenness,** flushness, levelness, regularity, unbrokenness 4 = **calmness,** placidity, serenity, stillness 5 = **fluency,** ease, efficiency, effortlessness, felicity, finish, flow, polish, rhythm, slickness, smooth running 6 = **suavity,** glibness, oiliness, smarminess (*Brit. inf.*), urbanity

smother *vb* 1 = **suffocate,** choke, stifle, stran-

off from the air. **4** to be or cause to be suppressed or stifled: *smother a giggle.* **5** (*tr*) to cook or serve (food) thickly covered with sauce, etc. ◆ *n* **6** anything, such as a cloud of smoke, that stifles. **7** a profusion or turmoil. [OE *smorian* to suffocate]
▸ **'smothery** *adj*

smothered mate *n Chess.* checkmate given by a knight when the king is prevented from moving by surrounding men.

smoulder ❶ *or US* **smolder** ('sməʊldə) *vb* (*intr*) **1** to burn slowly without flame, usually emitting smoke. **2** (esp. of anger, etc.) to exist in a suppressed state. **3** to have strong repressed feelings, esp. anger. ◆ *n* **4** a smouldering fire. [C14: from *smolder* (n), from ?]

SMP *abbrev. for* statutory maternity pay.

smudge ❶ (smʌdʒ) *vb* **smudges, smudging, smudged. 1** to smear or soil or cause to do so. **2** (*tr*) *Chiefly US & Canad.* to fill (an area) with smoke in order to drive insects away. ◆ *n* **3** a smear or dirty mark. **4** a blurred form or area: *that smudge in the distance is a quarry.* **5** *Chiefly US & Canad.* a smoky fire for driving insects away or protecting plants from frost. [C15: from ?]
▸ **'smudgy** *adj* ▸ **'smudgily** *adv* ▸ **'smudginess** *n*

smug ❶ (smʌg) *adj* **smugger, smuggest.** excessively self-satisfied or complacent. [C16: of Gmc origin]
▸ **'smugly** *adv* ▸ **'smugness** *n*

smuggle ❶ ('smʌgᵊl) *vb* **smuggles, smuggling, smuggled. 1** to import or export (prohibited or dutiable goods) secretly. **2** (*tr; often foll. by into or out of*) to bring or take secretly, as against the law or rules. [C17: from Low G *smukkelen* & Du. *smokkelen,* ?from OE *smūgen* to creep]
▸ **'smuggler** *n* ▸ **'smuggling** *n*

smut ❶ (smʌt) *n* **1** a small dark smudge or stain, esp. one caused by soot. **2** a speck of soot or dirt. **3** something obscene or indecent. **4a** any of various fungal diseases of flowering plants, esp. cereals, in which black sooty masses of spores cover the affected parts. **4b** any parasitic fungus that causes such a disease. ◆ *vb* **smuts, smutting, smutted. 5** to mark or become marked or smudged, as with soot. **6** to affect (grain, etc.) or (of grain) to be affected with smut. [OE *smitte;* associated with SMUDGE, SMUTCH]
▸ **'smutty** *adj* ▸ **'smuttily** *adv* ▸ **'smuttiness** *n*

smutch (smʌtʃ) *vb* **1** (*tr*) to smudge; mark. ◆ *n* **2** a mark; smudge. **3** soot; dirt. [C16: prob. from MHG *smutzen* to soil]
▸ **'smutchy** *adj*

Sn *the chemical symbol for* tin. [from NL *stannum*]

snack ❶ (snæk) *n* **1** a light quick meal eaten between or in place of main meals. **2** a sip or bite. ◆ *vb* **3** (*intr*) to eat a snack. [C15: prob. from MDu. *snacken,* var. of *snappen* to snap]

snack bar *n* a place where light meals or snacks can be obtained, often with a self-service system.

snaffle ('snæfᵊl) *n* **1** Also called: **snaffle bit.** a simple jointed bit for a horse. ◆ *vb* **snaffles, snaffling, snaffled.** (*tr*) **2** *Brit. inf.* to steal or take for oneself. **3** to equip or control with a snaffle. [C16: from ?]

snafu (snæ'fuː) *Sl., chiefly mil.* ◆ *n* **1** confusion or chaos regarded as the normal state. ◆ *adj* **2** (*postpositive*) confused or muddled up, as usual. ◆ *vb* **snafus, snafuing, snafued. 3** (*tr*) *US & Canad.* to throw into chaos. [C20: from *s(ituation) n(ormal): a(ll) f(ucked) u(p)*]

snag[1] ❶ (snæg) *n* **1** a difficulty or disadvantage: *the snag is that I have nothing suitable to wear.* **2** a sharp protuberance, such as a tree stump. **3** a small loop or hole in a fabric caused by a sharp object. **4** *Chiefly US & Canad.* a tree stump in a riverbed that is dangerous to navigation. **5** *US & Canad.* a standing dead tree, esp. one used as a perch by an eagle. ◆ *vb* **snags, snagging, snagged. 6** (*tr*) to hinder or impede. **7** (*tr*) to tear or catch (fabric). **8** (*intr*) to develop a snag. **9** (*intr*) *Chiefly US & Canad.* (of a boat) to strike a snag. **10** (*tr*) *Chiefly US & Canad.* to clear (a stretch of water) of snags. **11** (*tr*) *US.* to seize (an opportunity, etc.). [C16: of Scand. origin]
▸ **'snaggy** *adj*

snag[2] (snæg) *n* (*usually pl*) *Austral. sl.* a sausage. [from ?]

snaggletooth ('snægᵊlˌtuːθ) *n, pl* **snaggleteeth.** a tooth that is broken or projecting.

snail (sneɪl) *n* **1** any of numerous terrestrial or freshwater gastropod molluscs with a spirally coiled shell, esp. the **garden snail. 2** any other gastropod with a spirally coiled shell, such as a whelk. **3** a slow-moving person or animal. [OE *snægl*]
▸ **'snail-ˌlike** *adj*

snail mail *Inf. n* **1** the conventional postal system, as opposed to electronic mail. ◆ *vb* **snail-mail. 2** (*tr*) to send by the conventional postal system, rather than by electronic mail. [C20: so named because of the relative slowness of the conventional postal system]

snail's pace *n* a very slow speed or rate.

snake (sneɪk) *n* **1** a reptile having a scaly cylindrical limbless body, fused eyelids, and a jaw modified for swallowing large prey: includes venomous forms such as cobras and rattlesnakes, large nonvenomous constrictors (boas and pythons), and small harmless types such as the grass snake. **2** Also: **snake in the grass.** a deceitful or treacherous person. **3** anything resembling a snake in appearance or action. **4** (in the European Union) a group of currencies, any one of which can only fluctuate within narrow limits, but each can fluctuate more against other currencies. **5** a tool in the form of a long flexible wire for unblocking drains. ◆ *vb* **snakes, snaking, snaked. 6** (*intr*) to glide or move like a snake. **7** (*tr*) to move in or follow (a sinuous course). [OE *snaca*]
▸ **'snakeˌlike** *adj*

snakebird ('sneɪkˌbɜːd) *n* another name for **darter** (the bird).

snakebite ('sneɪkˌbaɪt) *n* **1** a bite inflicted by a snake, esp. a venomous one. **2** a drink of cider and lager.

snake charmer *n* an entertainer, esp. in Asia, who charms or appears to charm snakes by playing music.

snakeroot ('sneɪkˌruːt) *n* **1** any of various North American plants the roots or rhizomes of which have been used as a remedy for snakebite. **2** the rhizome or root of any such plant.

snakes and ladders *n* (*functioning as sing*) a board game in which players move counters along a series of squares according to throws of a dice. A ladder provides a short cut to a square nearer the finish and a snake obliges a player to return to a square nearer the start.

snake's head *n* a European fritillary plant of damp meadows, having purple-and-white flowers.

snakeskin ('sneɪkˌskɪn) *n* the skin of a snake, esp. when made into a leather valued for handbags, shoes, etc.

snaky ❶ ('sneɪkɪ) *adj* **snakier, snakiest. 1** of or like a snake. **2** treacherous or insidious. **3** infested with snakes. **4** *Austral. & NZ sl.* angry or bad-tempered.
▸ **'snakily** *adv* ▸ **'snakiness** *n*

snap ❶ (snæp) *vb* **snaps, snapping, snapped. 1** to break or cause to break suddenly, esp. with a sharp sound. **2** to make or cause to make a sudden sharp cracking sound. **3** (*intr*) to give way or collapse suddenly, esp. from strain. **4** to move, close, etc., or cause to move, close, etc., with a sudden sharp sound. **5** to move or cause to move in a sudden or abrupt way. **6** (*intr; often foll. by at or up*) to seize something suddenly or quickly. **7** (when *intr,* often foll. by *at*) to bite at (something) bringing the jaws rapidly together. **8** to speak (words) sharply or abruptly. **9** to take a snapshot of (something). **10** (*tr*) *American football.* to put (the ball) into play by sending it back from the line of scrimmage. **11 snap one's fingers at.** *Inf.* **11a** to dismiss with contempt. **11b** to defy. **12 snap out of it.** *Inf.* to recover quickly, esp. from depression or anger. ◆ *n* **13** the act of breaking suddenly or the sound produced by a sudden breakage. **14** a sudden sharp sound, esp. of bursting, popping, or cracking. **15** a catch, clasp, or fastener that operates with a snapping sound. **16** a sudden grab or bite. **17** a thin crisp biscuit: *ginger snaps.* **18** *Inf.* See **snapshot. 19** *Inf.* vigour, liveliness, or energy. **20** *Inf.* a task or job that is easy or profitable to do. **21** a short spell or period, esp. of cold weather. **22** *Brit.* a card game in which the word *snap* is called when two cards of equal value are turned up on the separate piles dealt by each player. **23** *American football.* the start of each play when the centre passes the ball back from the line of scrimmage to a teammate. **24** (*modifier*) done on the spur of the moment: *a snap decision.* **25** (*modifier*) closed or fastened with a snap. ◆ *adv* **26** with a snap. ◆ *interj* **27a** *Cards.* the word called while playing snap. **27b** an exclamation used to draw attention to the similarity of two things. ◆ See also **snap up.** [C15: from MLow G or MDu. *snappen* to seize]
▸ **'snapless** *adj* ▸ **'snappingly** *adv*

snapdragon ('snæpˌdrægən) *n* any of several plants of the genus *Antirrhinum* having spikes of showy white, yellow, pink, red, or purplish flowers. Also called: **antirrhinum.**

snap fastener *n* another name for **press stud.**

snapper ('snæpə) *n, pl* **snapper** *or* **snappers. 1** any large sharp-toothed percoid food fish of warm and tropical coastal regions. See also **red snapper. 2** a food fish of Australia and New Zealand that has a pinkish body covered with blue spots. **3** another name for the **snapping turtle. 4** a person or thing that snaps. ◆ Also (for sense 1, 2): **schnapper.**

THESAURUS

gle **2** = **overwhelm**, cocoon, cover, envelop, heap, inundate, shower, shroud, surround **3** = **extinguish**, snuff **4** = **suppress**, conceal, hide, keep back, muffle, repress, stifle

smoulder *vb* **3** = **seethe**, be resentful, boil, burn, fester, fume, rage, simmer, smart under

smudge *vb* **1** = **smear**, blacken, blur, daub, dirty, mark, smirch, soil ◆ *n* **3** = **smear**, blemish, blot, blur, smut, smutch

smug *adj* = **self-satisfied**, complacent, conceited, holier-than-thou, priggish, self-opinionated, self-righteous, superior

smuggler *n* **1** = **trafficker**, bootlegger, contrabandist, gentleman, moonshiner (*US*), rum-runner, runner, wrecker

smutty *adj* **3** = **obscene**, bawdy, blue, coarse, crude, dirty, filthy, improper, indecent, indelicate, lewd, off colour, pornographic, prurient, racy, raunchy (*US sl.*), risqué, salacious, suggestive, vulgar, X-rated (*inf.*)

snack *n* **1** = **light meal**, bite, bite to eat, break, elevenses (*Brit. inf.*), nibble, refreshment(s), titbit

snag[1] *n* **1** = **difficulty**, catch, complication, disadvantage, downside, drawback, hazard, hitch, inconvenience, obstacle, problem, stumbling block, the rub ◆ *vb* **7** = **catch**, hole, rip, tear

snaky *adj* **1** = **twisting**, convoluted, serpentine, sinuous, tortuous, twisty, writhing **2** = **treacherous**, crafty, insidious, perfidious, sly, venomous

snap *vb* **1** = **break**, come apart, crack, give way, separate **2** = **crackle**, click, pop **7** = **bite at**, bite, catch, grip, nip, seize, snatch **8** = **speak sharply**, bark, flash, fly off the handle at (*inf.*), growl, jump down (someone's) throat (*inf.*), lash out at, retort, snarl **11 snap one's fingers at** *Informal* = **defy**, cock a snook at (*Brit.*), flout, pay no attention to, scorn, set at naught, wave two fingers at (*sl.*) **12 snap out of it** *Informal* = **get over**, cheer up, get a grip on oneself, liven up, perk up, pull oneself together (*inf.*), recover ◆ *n* **14** = **crackle**, pop **16** = **bite**, grab, nip **19** *Informal* = **liveliness**, energy, get-up-and-go (*inf.*), go (*inf.*), pep, pizzazz *or* pizazz (*inf.*), vigour, zip (*inf.*) **24** *modifier* = **instant**, abrupt, immediate, spur-of-the-moment, sudden, unpremeditated

snapping turtle *n* any large aggressive North American river turtle having powerful hooked jaws and a rough shell. Also called: **snapper.**
snappy Ⓣ (ˈsnæpɪ) *adj* **snappier, snappiest. 1** Also: **snappish.** apt to speak sharply or irritably. **2** Also: **snappish.** apt to snap or bite. **3** crackling in sound: *a snappy fire.* **4** brisk, sharp, or chilly: *a snappy pace.* **5** smart and fashionable: *a snappy dresser.* **6 make it snappy.** *Sl.* hurry up!
▸**ˈsnappily** *adv* ▸**ˈsnappiness** *n*
snap ring *n Mountaineering.* another name for **karabiner.**
snapshot (ˈsnæpˌʃɒt) *n* an informal photograph taken with a simple camera. Often shortened to **snap.**
snap shot *n Sport.* a sudden, fast shot at goal.
snap up Ⓣ *vb* (*tr, adv*) **1** to avail oneself of eagerly and quickly: *she snapped up the bargains.* **2** to interrupt abruptly.
snare[1] Ⓣ (snɛə) *n* **1** a device for trapping birds or small animals, esp. a flexible loop that is drawn tight around the prey. **2** a surgical instrument for removing certain tumours, consisting of a wire loop that may be drawn tight around their base to sever them. **3** anything that traps or entangles someone or something unawares. ◆ *vb* **snares, snaring, snared.** (*tr*) **4** to catch (birds or small animals) with a snare. **5** to catch or trap in or as if in a snare. [OE *sneare*]
▸**ˈsnarer** *n*
snare[2] (snɛə) *n Music.* a set of gut strings wound with wire fitted against the lower drumhead of a snare drum. They produce a rattling sound when the drum is beaten. [C17: from MDu. *snaer* or MLow G *snare* string]
snare drum *n Music.* a cylindrical drum with two drumheads, the upper of which is struck and the lower fitted with a snare. See **snare**[2].
snarl[1] Ⓣ (snɑːl) *vb* **1** (*intr*) (of an animal) to growl viciously, baring the teeth. **2** to speak or express (something) viciously. ◆ *n* **3** a vicious growl or facial expression. **4** the act of snarling. [C16: of Gmc origin]
▸**ˈsnarler** *n* ▸**ˈsnarling** *adj* ▸**ˈsnarly** *adj*
snarl[2] Ⓣ (snɑːl) *n* **1** a tangled mass of thread, hair, etc. **2** a complicated or confused state or situation. **3** a knot in wood. ◆ *vb* **4** (often foll. by *up*) to be, become, or make tangled or complicated. **5** (*tr;* often foll. by *up*) to confuse mentally. **6** (*tr*) to emboss (metal) by hammering on a tool held against the under surface. [C14: from ON]
▸**ˈsnarler** *n* ▸**ˈsnarly** *adj*
snarl-up Ⓣ *n Inf., chiefly Brit.* a confusion, obstruction, or tangle, esp. a traffic jam.
snatch Ⓣ (snætʃ) *vb* **1** (*tr*) to seize or grasp (something) suddenly or peremptorily: *he snatched the chocolate.* **2** (*intr;* usually foll. by *at*) to seize or attempt to seize suddenly. **3** (*tr*) to take hurriedly: *to snatch some sleep.* **4** (*tr*) to remove suddenly: *she snatched her hand away.* **5** (*tr*) to gain, win, or rescue, esp. narrowly: *they snatched victory in the closing seconds.* ◆ *n* **6** an act of snatching. **7** a fragment or incomplete part: *snatches of conversation.* **8** a brief spell: *snatches of time off.* **9** *Weightlifting.* a lift in which the weight is raised in one quick motion from the floor to an overhead position. **10** *Sl., chiefly US.* an act of kidnapping. **11** *Brit. sl.* a robbery: *a diamond snatch.* [C13 *snacchen*]
▸**ˈsnatcher** *n*
snatchy (ˈsnætʃɪ) *adj* **snatchier, snatchiest.** disconnected or spasmodic.
▸**ˈsnatchily** *adv*
snazzy Ⓣ (ˈsnæzɪ) *adj* **snazzier, snazziest.** *Inf.* (esp. of clothes) stylishly and often flashily attractive. [C20: ?from SN(APPY + J)AZZY]
▸**ˈsnazzily** *adv* ▸**ˈsnazziness** *n*
sneak Ⓣ (sniːk) *vb* **1** (*intr;* often foll. by *along, off, in,* etc.) to move furtively. **2** (*intr*) to behave in a cowardly or underhand manner. **3** (*tr*) to bring, take, or put stealthily. **4** (*intr*) *Inf., chiefly Brit.* to tell tales (esp. in schools). **5** (*tr*) *Inf.* to steal. **6** (*intr;* foll. by *off, out, away,* etc.) *Inf.* to leave unobtrusively. ◆ *n* **7** a person who acts in an underhand or cowardly manner, esp. as an informer. **8a** a stealthy act. **8b** (*as modifier*): *a sneak attack.* [OE *snīcan* to creep]
▸**ˈsneaky** *adj* ▸**ˈsneakily** *adv* ▸**ˈsneakiness** *n*
sneakers (ˈsniːkəz) *pl n Chiefly US & Canad.* canvas shoes with rubber soles worn informally.
sneaking Ⓣ (ˈsniːkɪŋ) *adj* **1** acting in a furtive or cowardly way. **2** secret: *a sneaking desire to marry a millionaire.* **3** slight but nagging (esp. in **a sneaking suspicion**).
▸**ˈsneakingly** *adv*
sneak thief *n* a person who steals paltry articles from premises, which he enters through open doors, windows, etc.
sneer Ⓣ (snɪə) *n* **1** a facial expression of scorn or contempt, typically with the upper lip curled. **2** a scornful or contemptuous remark or utterance. ◆ *vb* **3** (*intr*) to assume a facial expression of scorn or contempt. **4** to say or utter (something) in a scornful manner. [C16: ?from Low Du.]
▸**ˈsneerer** *n* ▸**ˈsneering** *adj, n*
sneeze Ⓣ (sniːz) *vb* **sneezes, sneezing, sneezed. 1** (*intr*) to expel air from the nose involuntarily, esp. as the result of irritation of the nasal mucous membrane. ◆ *n* **2** the act or sound of sneezing. [OE *fnēosan* (unattested)]
▸**ˈsneezer** *n* ▸**ˈsneezy** *adj*
sneeze at *vb* (*intr, prep;* usually with a negative) *Inf.* to dismiss lightly: *his offer is not to be sneezed at.*
sneezewood (ˈsniːzˌwʊd) *n* **1** a South African tree. **2** its exceptionally hard wood, used for furniture, gateposts and railway sleepers.
sneezewort (ˈsniːzˌwɜːt) *n* a Eurasian plant having daisy-like flowers and long grey-green leaves, which cause sneezing when powdered.
snick (snɪk) *n* **1** a small cut; notch. **2** *Cricket.* **2a** a glancing blow off the edge of the bat. **2b** the ball so hit. ◆ *vb* (*tr*) **3** to cut a small corner or notch in (material, etc.). **4** *Cricket.* to hit (the ball) with a snick. [C18: prob. of Scand. origin]
snicker (ˈsnɪkə) *n, vb* **1** another word (esp. US and Canad.) for **snigger.** ◆ *vb* **2** (*intr*) (of a horse) to whinny. [C17: prob. imit.]
snide Ⓣ (snaɪd) *adj* **1** Also: **snidey** (ˈsnaɪdɪ). (of a remark, etc.) maliciously derogatory. **2** counterfeit. ◆ *n* **3** *Sl.* sham jewellery. [C19: from ?]
▸**ˈsnidely** *adv* ▸**ˈsnideness** *n*
sniff Ⓣ (snɪf) *vb* **1** to inhale through the nose, usually in short rapid audible inspirations, as for clearing a congested nasal passage or for taking a drug. **2** (when *intr,* often foll. by *at*) to perceive or attempt to perceive (a smell) by inhaling through the nose. ◆ *n* **3** the act or sound of sniffing. **4** a smell perceived by sniffing, esp. a faint scent. ◆ See also **sniff at, sniff out.** [C14: prob. rel. to *snivelen* to snivel]
▸**ˈsniffer** *n* ▸**ˈsniffing** *n, adj*
sniff at *vb* (*intr, prep*) to express contempt or dislike for.
sniffer dog *n* a police dog trained to detect drugs or explosives by smell.
sniffle (ˈsnɪfᵊl) *vb* **sniffles, sniffling, sniffled. 1** (*intr*) to breathe audibly through the nose, as when the nasal passages are congested. ◆ *n* **2** the act, sound, or an instance of sniffling.
▸**ˈsniffler** *n* ▸**ˈsniffly** *adj*
sniffles (ˈsnɪfᵊlz) *or* **snuffles** *pl n Inf.* **the.** a cold in the head.
sniff out *vb* (*tr, adv*) to detect through shrewdness or instinct.
sniffy Ⓣ (ˈsnɪfɪ) *adj* **sniffier, sniffiest.** *Inf.* contemptuous or disdainful.
▸**ˈsniffily** *adv* ▸**ˈsniffiness** *n*
snifter (ˈsnɪftə) *n* **1** a pear-shaped glass with a bowl that narrows towards the top so that the aroma of brandy or a liqueur is retained. **2** *Inf.* a small quantity of alcoholic drink. [C19: ?from dialect *snifter* to sniff, ? of Scand. origin]
snig (snɪg) *vb* **snigs, snigging, snigged.** (*tr*) *NZ.* to drag (a felled log) by a chain or cable. [from E dialect]
snigger Ⓣ (ˈsnɪgə) *n* **1** a sly or disrespectful laugh, esp. one partly stifled. ◆ *vb* (*intr*) **2** to utter such a laugh. [C18: var. of SNICKER]
▸**ˈsniggering** *n, adj*
snigging chain *n Austral. & NZ.* a chain attached to a log when being hauled out of the bush.
snip Ⓣ (snɪp) *vb* **snips, snipping, snipped. 1** to cut or clip with a small quick stroke or a succession of small quick strokes, esp. with scissors or shears. ◆ *n* **2** the act of snipping. **3** the sound of scissors or shears closing. **4** Also called: **snipping.** a small piece of anything. **5** a small cut made by snipping. **6** *Chiefly Brit.* an informal word for **bargain. 7** *Inf.*

THESAURUS

snappy *adj* **1** = **irritable**, cross, edgy, hasty, impatient, like a bear with a sore head (*inf.*), quick-tempered, ratty (*Brit. & NZ inf.*), snappish, tart, testy, tetchy, touchy, waspish **5** = **smart**, chic, dapper, fashionable, modish, natty, stylish, trendy (*Brit. inf.*), up-to-the-minute, voguish **6 make it snappy** = **hurry (up)**, be quick, buck up (*inf.*), get a move on (*inf.*), get one's skates on, look lively, make haste
snap up *vb* **1** = **take advantage of**, avail oneself of, grab, grasp, nab (*inf.*), pounce upon, seize, swoop down on
snare[1] *n* **1** = **trap**, catch, gin, net, noose, pitfall, springe, wire ◆ *vb* **4** = **trap**, catch, entrap, net, seize, springe, trepan (*arch.*), wire
snarl[1] *vb* **1** = **growl**, show one's teeth (*of an animal*)
snarl[2] *vb* **4, 5** *often with* **up** = **tangle**, complicate, confuse, embroil, enmesh, entangle, entwine, muddle, ravel
snarl-up *n* = **tangle**, confusion, entanglement, muddle, (traffic) jam
snatch *vb* **1** = **seize**, catch up, clutch, gain, grab, grasp, grip, make off with, pluck, pull, rescue, take, win, wrench, wrest ◆ *n* **7, 8** = **bit**, fragment, part, piece, smattering, snippet, spell
snazzy *adj Informal* = **stylish**, attractive, dashing, flamboyant, flashy, jazzy (*inf.*), raffish, ritzy (*sl.*), showy, smart, sophisticated, sporty, swinging (*sl.*), with it (*inf.*)
sneak *vb* **1** = **slink**, cower, lurk, pad, sidle, skulk, slip, steal **3** = **slip**, smuggle, spirit **4** *Informal, chiefly Brit.* = **inform on**, grass on, peach (*sl.*), shop (*sl., chiefly Brit.*), sing (*sl., chiefly US*), spill one's guts (*sl.*), tell on (*inf.*), tell tales ◆ *n* **7** = **informer**, snake in the grass, telltale ◆ *modifier* **8b** = **surprise**, clandestine, furtive, quick, secret, stealthy
sneaking *adj* **1** = **underhand**, contemptible, furtive, mean, sly, sneaky, surreptitious, two-faced **2** = **secret**, hidden, private, suppressed, unavowed, unconfessed, undivulged, unexpressed, unvoiced **3** = **nagging**, intuitive, niggling, persistent, uncomfortable, worrying
sneaky *adj* **7** = **sly**, base, contemptible, cowardly, deceitful, devious, dishonest, disingenuous, double-dealing, furtive, low, malicious, mean, nasty, shifty, slippery, snide, unreliable, unscrupulous, untrustworthy
sneer *n* **2** = **scorn**, derision, disdain, gibe, jeer, mockery, ridicule, snigger ◆ *vb* **3** = **scorn**, curl one's lip, deride, disdain, gibe, hold in contempt, hold up to ridicule, jeer, laugh, look down on, mock, ridicule, scoff, sniff at, snigger, turn up one's nose (*inf.*)
sneeze *n* **2** = **sternutation**
snide *adj* **1** = **nasty**, cynical, disparaging, hurtful, ill-natured, insinuating, malicious, mean, sarcastic, scornful, shrewish, sneering, spiteful, unkind
sniff *vb* **1** = **inhale**, breathe, smell, snuff, snuffle
sniffy *adj Informal* = **contemptuous**, condescending, disdainful, haughty, scornful, supercilious, superior
snigger *n* **1** = **laugh**, giggle, smirk, sneer, snicker, titter ◆ *vb* **2** = **laugh**, giggle, smirk, sneer, snicker, titter
snip *vb* **1** = **cut**, clip, crop, dock, nick, nip off,

something easily done; cinch. ◆ See also **snips.** [C16: from Low G, Du. *snippen*]
snipe ⓘ (snaɪp) *n, pl* **snipe** *or* **snipes. 1** any of a genus of birds, such as the common snipe, of marshes and river banks, having a long straight bill. **2** a shot, esp. a gunshot, fired from a place of concealment. ◆ *vb* **snipes, sniping, sniped. 3** (when *intr,* often foll. by *at*) to attack (a person or persons) with a rifle from a place of concealment. **4** (*intr;* often foll. by *at*) to criticize a person or persons from a position of security. **5** (*intr*) to hunt or shoot snipe. [C14: from ON *snīpa*]
▸**'sniper** *n*
snipefish ('snaɪp,fɪʃ) *n, pl* **snipefish** *or* **snipefishes.** a teleost fish of tropical and temperate seas, having a deep body, long snout, and a single long dorsal fin. Also called: **bellows fish.**
snippet ⓘ ('snɪpɪt) *n* a small scrap or fragment of fabric, news, etc.
▸**'snippetiness** *n* ▸**'snippety** *adj*
snips (snɪps) *pl n* a small pair of shears used for cutting sheet metal.
snitch (snɪtʃ) *Sl.* ◆ *vb* **1** (*tr*) to steal; take, esp. in an underhand way. **2** (*intr*) to act as an informer. ◆ *n* **3** an informer. **4** the nose. [C17: from ?]
snitchy ('snɪtʃɪ) *adj* **snitchier, snitchiest.** *NZ inf.* bad-tempered or irritable.
snivel ⓘ ('snɪvᵊl) *vb* **snivels, snivelling, snivelled** *or US* **snivels, sniveling, sniveled. 1** (*intr*) to sniffle as a sign of distress. **2** to utter (something) tearfully; whine. **3** (*intr*) to have a runny nose. ◆ *n* **4** an instance of snivelling. [C14 *snivelen*]
▸**'sniveller** *n* ▸**'snivelling** *adj, n*
snob ⓘ (snɒb) *n* **1a** a person who strives to associate with those of higher social status and who behaves condescendingly to others. **1b** (*as modifier*): *snob appeal.* **2** a person having similar pretensions with regard to his tastes, etc.: *an intellectual snob.* [C18 (in the sense: shoemaker; hence, C19: a person who flatters those of higher station, etc.): from ?]
▸**'snobbery** *n* ▸**'snobbish** *adj* ▸**'snobbishly** *adv*
SNOBOL ('snəubɒl) *n* String Oriented Symbolic Language: a computer-programming language for handling strings of symbols.
Sno-Cat ('snəu,kæt) *n Trademark.* a type of snowmobile.
snoek (snuk) *n* a South African edible marine fish. [Afrik., from Du. *snoek* pike]
snog (snɒg) *Brit. sl.* ◆ *vb* **snogs, snogging, snogged. 1** to kiss and cuddle (someone). ◆ *n* **2** the act of kissing and cuddling. [from ?]
snood (snu:d) *n* **1** a pouchlike hat, often of net, loosely holding a woman's hair at the back. **2** a headband, esp. one formerly worn by young unmarried women in Scotland. [OE *snōd;* from ?]
snook[1] (snu:k) *n, pl* **snook** *or* **snooks. 1** any of a genus of large game fishes of tropical American marine and fresh waters. **2** *Austral.* the sea pike. [C17: from Du. *snoek* pike]
snook[2] (snu:k) *n Brit.* a rude gesture, made by putting one thumb to the nose with the fingers of the hand outstretched (esp. in **cock a snook**). [C19: from ?]
snooker ('snu:kə) *n* **1** a game played on a billiard table with 15 red balls, six balls of other colours, and a white cue ball. The object is to pot the balls in a certain order. **2** a shot in which the cue ball is left in a position such that another ball blocks the target ball. ◆ *vb* (*tr*) **3** to leave (an opponent) in an unfavourable position by playing a snooker. **4** to place (someone) in a difficult situation. **5** (*often passive*) to thwart; defeat. [C19: from ?]
snoop ⓘ (snu:p) *Inf.* ◆ *vb* **1** (*intr;* often foll. by *about* or *around*) to pry into the private business of others. ◆ *n* **2** a person who pries into the business of others. **3** an act or instance of snooping. [C19: from Du. *snoepen* to eat furtively]
▸**'snooper** *n* ▸**'snoopy** *adj*
snooperscope ('snu:pə,skəup) *n Mil., US.* an instrument that enables the user to see objects in the dark by illuminating the object with infrared radiation.
snoot (snu:t) *n Sl.* the nose. [C20: var. of SNOUT]
snooty ⓘ ('snu:tɪ) *adj* **snootier, snootiest.** *Inf.* **1** aloof or supercilious. **2** snobbish: *a snooty restaurant.*
▸**'snootily** *adv* ▸**'snootiness** *n*
snooze ⓘ (snu:z) *Inf.* ◆ *vb* **snoozes, snoozing, snoozed. 1** (*intr*) to take a brief light sleep. ◆ *n* **2** a nap. [C18: from ?]
▸**'snoozer** *n* ▸**'snoozy** *adj*
snore (snɔ:) *vb* **snores, snoring, snored. 1** (*intr*) to breathe through the mouth and nose while asleep with snorting sounds caused by the soft palate vibrating. ◆ *n* **2** the act or sound of snoring. [C14: imit.]
▸**'snorer** *n*
snorkel ('snɔ:kᵊl) *n* **1** a device allowing a swimmer to breathe while face down on the surface of the water, consisting of a bent tube fitting into the mouth and projecting above the surface. **2** (on a submarine) a retractable vertical device containing air-intake and exhaust pipes for the engines and general ventilation. ◆ *vb* **snorkels, snorkelling, snorkelled** *or US* **snorkels, snorkeling, snorkeled. 3** (*intr*) to swim with a snorkel. [C20: from G *Schnorchel*]
snort (snɔ:t) *vb* **1** (*intr*) to exhale forcibly through the nostrils, making a characteristic noise. **2** (*intr*) (of a person) to express contempt or annoyance by such an exhalation. **3** (*tr*) to utter in a contemptuous or annoyed manner. **4** *Sl.* to inhale (a powdered drug) through the nostrils. ◆ *n* **5** a forcible exhalation of air through the nostrils, esp. (of persons) as a noise of contempt. **6** *Sl.* an instance of snorting a drug. [C14 *snorten*]
▸**'snorting** *n, adj* ▸**'snortingly** *adv*
snorter ('snɔ:tə) *n* **1** a person or animal that snorts. **2** *Brit. sl.* something outstandingly impressive or difficult.
snot (snɒt) *n* (*usually considered vulgar*) **1** nasal mucus or discharge. **2** *Sl.* a contemptible person. [OE *gesnot*]
snotty ('snɒtɪ) *adj* **snottier, snottiest.** (*considered vulgar*) **1** dirty with nasal discharge. **2** *Sl.* contemptible; nasty. **3** snobbish; conceited.
▸**'snottily** *adv* ▸**'snottiness** *n*
snout (snaut) *n* **1** the part of the head of a vertebrate, esp. a mammal, consisting of the nose, jaws, and surrounding region. **2** the corresponding part of the head of such insects as weevils. **3** anything projecting like a snout, such as a nozzle. **4** *Sl.* a person's nose. **5** *Brit. sl.* a cigarette or tobacco. **6** *Sl.* an informer. [C13: of Gmc origin]
▸**'snouted** *adj* ▸**'snoutless** *adj* ▸**'snout,like** *adj*
snout beetle *n* another name for **weevil.**
snow (snəu) *n* **1** precipitation from clouds in the form of flakes of ice crystals formed in the upper atmosphere. **2** a layer of snowflakes on the ground. **3** a fall of such precipitation. **4** anything resembling snow in whiteness, softness, etc. **5** the random pattern of white spots on a television or radar screen, occurring when the signal is weak. **6** *Sl.* cocaine. ◆ *vb* **7** (*intr,* with *it* as subject) to be the case that snow is falling. **8** (*tr;* usually passive, foll. by *over, under, in,* or *up*) to cover or confine with a heavy fall of snow. **9** (often with *it* as subject) to fall or cause to fall as or like snow. **10** (*tr*) *US & Canad. sl.* to overwhelm with elaborate often insincere talk. **11 be snowed under.** to be overwhelmed, esp. with paperwork. [OE *snāw*]
▸**'snowless** *adj* ▸**'snow,like** *adj*
snowball ('snəu,bɔ:l) *n* **1** snow pressed into a ball for throwing, as in play. **2** a drink made of advocaat and lemonade. ◆ *vb* **3** (*intr*) to increase rapidly in size, importance, etc. **4** (*tr*) to throw snowballs at.
snowball tree *n* any of several shrubs of the genus *Viburnum,* with spherical clusters of white or pinkish flowers.
snowberry ('snəubərɪ) *n, pl* **snowberries. 1** a shrub cultivated for its small pink flowers and white berries. **2** Also called: **waxberry.** any of the berries of such a plant.
snow-blind *adj* having temporarily impaired vision because of the intense reflection of sunlight from snow.
▸**snow blindness** *n*
snowblower ('snəu,bləuə) *n* a snow-clearing machine that draws the snow in and blows it away.
snowboard ('snəu,bɔ:d) *n* a shaped board, resembling a skateboard without wheels, on which a person can stand to slide across snow. [C20: on the model of SURFBOARD]
▸**'snow,boarding** *n*
snowbound ('snəu,baund) *adj* confined to one place by heavy falls or drifts of snow; snowed in.
snow bunting *n* a bunting of northern and arctic regions, having a white plumage with dark markings on the wings, back, and tail.
snowcap ('snəu,kæp) *n* a cap of snow, as on top of a mountain.
▸**'snow,capped** *adj*
snowdrift ('snəu,drɪft) *n* a bank of deep snow driven together by the wind.
snowdrop ('snəu,drɒp) *n* a Eurasian plant having drooping white bell-shaped flowers that bloom in early spring.
snowfall ('snəu,fɔ:l) *n* **1** a fall of snow. **2** *Meteorol.* the amount of snow received in a specified place and time.
snow fence *n* a lath-and-wire fence put up in winter beside windy roads to prevent snowdrifts.
snowfield ('snəu,fi:ld) *n* a large area of permanent snow.
snowflake ('snəu,fleɪk) *n* **1** one of the mass of small thin delicate ar-

THESAURUS

notch, shave, trim ◆ *n* **4** = **bit**, clipping, fragment, piece, scrap, shred, snippet **6** *Informal, chiefly Brit.* = **bargain**, giveaway, good buy, steal (*inf.*)
snipe *vb* **4** = **criticize**, bitch, carp, denigrate, disparage, have a go (at) (*inf.*), jeer, knock (*inf.*), put down
snippet *n* = **piece**, fragment, part, particle, scrap, shred, snatch
snivel *vb* **1, 2** = **whine**, blubber, cry, gripe (*inf.*), grizzle (*inf., chiefly Brit.*), mewl, moan, sniffle, snuffle, weep, whimper, whinge (*inf.*)
snob *n* **1, 2** = **elitist**, highbrow, prig, social climber
snobbery *n* **1, 2** = **arrogance**, airs, condescension, pretension, pride, side (*Brit. sl.*), snobbishness, snootiness (*inf.*), uppishness (*Brit. inf.*)
snobbish *adj* **1, 2** = **superior**, arrogant, condescending, high and mighty (*inf.*), high-hat (*inf., chiefly US*), hoity-toity (*inf.*), patronizing, pretentious, snooty (*inf.*), stuck-up (*inf.*), toffee-nosed (*sl., chiefly Brit.*), uppish (*Brit. inf.*), uppity
Antonyms *adj* down to earth, humble, modest, natural, unassuming, unostentatious, unpretentious, without airs
snoop *vb* **1** = **pry**, interfere, poke one's nose in (*inf.*), spy
snooper *n* **1** = **nosy parker** (*inf.*), busybody, meddler, Paul Pry, pry, snoop (*inf.*), stickybeak (*Austral. inf.*)
snooty *adj* **1, 2** = **snobbish**, aloof, condescending, disdainful, haughty, high and mighty (*inf.*), high-hat (*inf., chiefly US*), hoity-toity (*inf.*), pretentious, proud, snotty, stuck-up (*inf.*), supercilious, superior, toffee-nosed (*sl., chiefly Brit*), toplofty (*inf.*), uppish (*Brit. inf.*), uppity
Antonyms *adj* down to earth, humble, modest, natural, unassuming, unpretentious, without airs
snooze *Informal vb* **1** = **doze**, catnap, drop off (*inf.*), drowse, kip (*Brit. sl.*), nap, nod off (*inf.*), take forty winks (*inf.*) ◆ *n* **2** = **doze**, catnap, forty winks (*inf.*), kip (*Brit. sl.*), nap, siesta

rangements of ice crystals that fall as snow. **2** any of various European plants that have white nodding bell-shaped flowers.

snow goose *n* a North American goose having a white plumage with black wing tips.

snow gum *n* any of several eucalypts of mountainous regions of SE Australia.

snow-in-summer *n* a plant of SE Europe and Asia having white flowers and downy stems and leaves: cultivated as a rock plant.

snow leopard *n* a large feline mammal of mountainous regions of central Asia, closely related to the leopard but having a long pale brown coat marked with black rosettes.

snow lily *n Canad.* another name for **dogtooth violet.**

snow line *n* the altitudinal or latitudinal limit of permanent snow.

snowman ('snəʊˌmæn) *n, pl* **snowmen.** a figure resembling a man, made of packed snow.

snowmobile ('snəʊməˌbiːl) *n* a motor vehicle for travelling on snow, esp. one with caterpillar tracks and front skis.

snowplough *or esp. US* **snowplow** ('snəʊˌplaʊ) *n* an implement or vehicle for clearing away snow.

snowshoe ('snəʊˌʃuː) *n* **1** a device to facilitate walking on snow, esp. a racket-shaped frame with a network of thongs stretched across it. ◆ *vb* **snowshoes, snowshoeing, snowshoed. 2** (*intr*) to walk or go using snowshoes.
▸ **'snowˌshoer** *n*

snowstorm ('snəʊˌstɔːm) *n* a storm with heavy snow.

snow tyre *n* a motor-vehicle tyre with deep treads to give improved grip on snow and ice.

snow-white *adj* **1** white as snow. **2** pure as white snow.

snowy ('snəʊɪ) *adj* **snowier, snowiest. 1** covered with or abounding in snow: *snowy hills.* **2** characterized by snow: *snowy weather.* **3** resembling snow in whiteness, purity, etc.
▸ **'snowily** *adv* ▸ **'snowiness** *n*

snowy owl *n* a large owl of tundra regions, having a white plumage flecked with brown.

SNP *abbrev. for* Scottish National Party.

Snr *or* **snr** *abbrev. for* senior.

snub ❶ (snʌb) *vb* **snubs, snubbing, snubbed.** (*tr*) **1** to insult (someone) deliberately. **2** to stop or check the motion of (a boat, horse, etc.) by taking turns of a rope around a post. ◆ *n* **3** a deliberately insulting act or remark. **4** *Naut.* an elastic shock absorber attached to a mooring line. ◆ *adj* **5** short and blunt. See also **snub-nosed.** [C14: from ON *snubba* to scold]
▸ **'snubber** *n* ▸ **'snubby** *adj*

snub-nosed *adj* **1** having a short turned-up nose. **2** (of a pistol) having an extremely short barrel.

snuff[1] (snʌf) *vb* **1** (*tr*) to inhale through the nose. **2** (when *intr,* often foll. by *at*) (esp. of an animal) to examine by sniffing. ◆ *n* **3** an act or the sound of snuffing. [C16: prob. from MDu. *snuffen* to snuffle, ult. imit.]
▸ **'snuffer** *n*

snuff[2] (snʌf) *n* **1** finely powdered tobacco, esp. for sniffing up the nostrils. **2** a small amount of this. **3 up to snuff.** *Inf.* **3a** in good health or in good condition. **3b** *Chiefly Brit.* not easily deceived. ◆ *vb* **4** (*intr*) to use or inhale snuff. [C17: from Du. *snuf,* shortened from *snuftabale,* lit.: tobacco for snuffing]

snuff[3] (snʌf) *vb* (*tr*) **1** (often foll. by *out*) to extinguish (a light from a candle). **2** to cut off the charred part of (the wick of a candle, etc.). **3** (usually foll. by *out*) *Inf.* to put an end to. **4 snuff it.** *Brit. inf.* to die. ◆ *n* **5** the burned portion of the wick of a candle. [C14 *snoffe,* from ?]

snuffbox ('snʌfˌbɒks) *n* a container, often of elaborate ornamental design, for holding small quantities of snuff.

snuff-dipping *n* the practice of absorbing nicotine by holding in one's mouth, between the cheek and the gum, a small amount of tobacco.

snuffer ('snʌfə) *n* **1** a cone-shaped implement for extinguishing candles. **2** (*pl*) an instrument resembling a pair of scissors for trimming the wick or extinguishing the flame of a candle.

snuffle ('snʌfᵊl) *vb* **snuffles, snuffling, snuffled. 1** (*intr*) to breathe noisily or with difficulty. **2** to say or speak in a nasal tone. **3** (*intr*) to snivel. ◆ *n* **4** an act or the sound of snuffling. **5** a nasal voice. **6 the snuffles.** a condition characterized by snuffling. [C16: from Low G or Du. *snuffelen*]
▸ **'snuffly** *adj*

snuff movie *or* **film** *n Sl.* a pornographic film in which an unsuspecting actress or actor is murdered as the climax of the film.

snuffy ('snʌfɪ) *adj* **snuffier, snuffiest. 1** of or resembling snuff. **2** covered with or smelling of snuff. **3** disagreeable.
▸ **'snuffiness** *n*

snug ❶ (snʌg) *adj* **snugger, snuggest. 1** comfortably warm and well protected; cosy: *the children were snug in bed.* **2** small but comfortable: *a snug cottage.* **3** well ordered; compact: *a snug boat.* **4** sheltered and secure: *a snug anchorage.* **5** fitting closely and comfortably. **6** offering safe concealment. ◆ *n* **7** (in Britain and Ireland) one of the bars in certain pubs, offering intimate seating for only a few persons. ◆ *vb* **snugs, snugging, snugged. 8** to make or become comfortable and warm. [C16 (in the sense: prepared for storms (used of a ship)) from O Icelandic *snöggr* short-haired, from Swedish *snygg* tidy]
▸ **'snugly** *adv* ▸ **'snugness** *n*

snuggery ('snʌgərɪ) *n, pl* **snuggeries. 1** a cosy and comfortable place or room. **2** another name for **snug** (sense 7).

snuggle ❶ ('snʌgᵊl) *vb* **snuggles, snuggling, snuggled. 1** (usually *intr;* usually foll. by *down, up,* or *together*) to nestle into or draw close to (somebody or something) for warmth or from affection. ◆ *n* **2** the act of snuggling. [C17: frequentative of SNUG (vb)]

so[1] (səʊ) *adv* **1** (foll. by an adjective or adverb and a correlative clause often introduced by *that*) to such an extent: *the river is so dirty that it smells.* **2** (*used with a negative;* it replaces the first *as* in an equative comparison) to the same extent as: *she is not so old as you.* **3** (intensifier): *it's so lovely.* **4** in the state or manner expressed or implied: *they're happy and will remain so.* **5** (*not used with a negative;* foll. by an auxiliary verb or *do, have,* or *be* used as main verbs) also: *I can speak Spanish and so can you.* **6** *Dialect.* indeed: used to contradict a negative statement: *"you didn't phone her." "I did so!"* **7** *Arch.* provided that. **8 and so on** *or* **forth.** and continuing similarly. **9 or so.** approximately: *fifty or so people came to see me.* **10 so be it.** used to express agreement or resignation. **11 so much. 11a** a certain degree or amount (of). **11b** a lot (of): *it's just so much nonsense.* **12 so much for. 12a** no more can or need be said about. **12b** used to express contempt for something that has failed. ◆ *conj* (*subordinating;* often foll. by *that*) **13** in order (that): *to die so that you might live.* **14** with the consequence (that): *he was late home, so that there was trouble.* **15 so as.** (*takes an infinitive*) in order (to): *to diet so as to lose weight.* ◆ *sentence connector.* **16** in consequence: *she wasn't needed, so she left.* **17** thereupon: *and so we ended up in France.* **18 so what!** *Inf.* what importance does that have? ◆ *pron* **19** used to substitute for a clause or sentence, which may be understood: *you'll stop because I said so.* ◆ *adj* **20** (used with *is, was,* etc.) factual: *it can't be so.* ◆ *interj* **21** an exclamation of surprise, etc. [OE *swā*]

so[2] (səʊ) *n Music.* a variant spelling of **soh.**

> **USAGE NOTE** In formal English, *so* is not used as a conjunction, to indicate either purpose (*he left by a back door so he could avoid photographers*) or result (*the project was abandoned so his services were no longer needed*). In the former case *to* or *in order to* should be used instead, and in the latter case *and so* or *and therefore.*

So. *abbrev. for* south(ern).

soak ❶ (səʊk) *vb* **1** to make, become, or be thoroughly wet or saturated, esp. by immersion in a liquid. **2** (when *intr,* usually foll. by *in* or *into*) (of a liquid) to penetrate or permeate. **3** (*tr;* usually foll. by *in* or *up*) (of a permeable solid) to take in (a liquid) by absorption: *the earth soaks up rainwater.* **4** (*tr;* foll. by *out* or *out of*) to remove by immersion in a liquid: *she soaked the stains out of the dress.* **5** *Inf.* to drink excessively or make or become drunk. **6** (*tr*) *Sl.* to overcharge. ◆ *n* **7** the act of immersing in a liquid or the period of immersion. **8** the liquid in which something may be soaked. **9** *Austral.* a natural depression holding rainwater, esp. just beneath the surface of the ground. **10** *Sl.* a person who drinks to excess. [OE *sōcian* to cook]
▸ **'soaker** *n* ▸ **'soaking** *n, adj* ▸ **'soakingly** *adv*

soakaway ('səʊkəˌweɪ) *n* a pit filled with rubble, etc., into which waste water drains.

so-and-so *n, pl* **so-and-sos.** *Inf.* **1** a person whose name is forgotten or ignored. **2** *Euphemistic.* a person or thing regarded as unpleasant: *which so-and-so broke my razor?*

soap (səʊp) *n* **1** a cleaning agent made by reacting animal or vegetable fats or oils with potassium or sodium hydroxide. Soaps act by emulsifying grease and lowering the surface tension of water, so that it more readily penetrates open materials such as textiles. **2** any metallic salt of a fatty acid, such as palmitic or stearic acid. **3** *Sl.* flattery or persuasive talk (esp. in **soft soap**). **4** *Inf.* short for **soap opera. 5 no soap.** *Sl.* not possible. ◆ *vb* (*tr*) **6** to apply soap to. **7** (often foll. by *up*) *Sl.* to flatter. [OE *sāpe*]
▸ **'soapless** *adj* ▸ **'soapˌlike** *adj*

soapberry ('səʊpˌberɪ) *n, pl* **soapberries. 1** any of various chiefly tropical American trees having pulpy fruit containing saponin. **2** the fruit of any of these trees.

soapbox ('səʊpˌbɒks) *n* **1** a box or crate for packing soap. **2** a crate used as a platform for speech-making. **3** a child's home-made racing cart.

soap opera *n* a serialized drama, usually dealing with domestic themes, broadcast on radio or television. Often shortened to **soap.** [C20: so called because manufacturers of soap were typical sponsors]

soapstone ('səʊpˌstəʊn) *n* a massive compact soft variety of talc, used for making table tops, hearths, ornaments, etc. Also called: **steatite.**

THESAURUS

snub *vb* **1** = **insult,** cold-shoulder, cut, cut dead (*inf.*), give (someone) the brush-off (*sl.*), give (someone) the cold shoulder, humble, humiliate, kick in the teeth (*sl.*), mortify, put down, rebuff, shame, slight ◆ *n* **3** = **insult,** affront, brush-off (*sl.*), bum's rush (*sl.*), humiliation, put-down, slap in the face

snug *adj* **1** = **cosy,** comfortable, comfy (*inf.*), homely, intimate, sheltered, warm **5** = **close,** compact, neat, trim

snuggle *vb* **1** = **nestle,** cuddle, nuzzle

soak *vb* **1** = **wet,** bathe, damp, drench, immerse, infuse, marinate (*Cookery*), moisten, saturate, steep **2** = **penetrate,** permeate, seep **3** with **up** = **absorb,** assimilate, drink in, take in *or* up

soaking *adj* **1** = **soaked,** drenched, dripping, droukit *or* drookit (*Scot.*), like a drowned rat, saturated, soaked to the skin, sodden, sopping, streaming, waterlogged, wet through, wringing wet

soapsuds ('səʊpˌsʌdz) *pl n* foam or lather made from soap.
▸**'soapˌsudsy** *adj*

soapwort ('səʊpˌwɜːt) *n* a Eurasian plant having rounded clusters of fragrant pink or white flowers and leaves that were formerly used as a soap substitute. Also called: **bouncing Bet.**

soapy ('səʊpɪ) *adj* **soapier, soapiest. 1** containing or covered with soap: *soapy water.* **2** resembling or characteristic of soap. **3** *Sl.* flattering.
▸**'soapily** *adv* ▸**'soapiness** *n*

soar Ⓣ (sɔː) *vb (intr)* **1** to rise or fly upwards into the air. **2** (of a bird, aircraft, etc.) to glide while maintaining altitude by the use of ascending air currents. **3** to rise or increase in volume, size, etc.: *soaring prices.* [C14: from OF *essorer,* from Vulgar L *exaurāre* (unattested) to expose to the breezes, from L EX-[1] + *aura* breeze]
▸**'soarer** *n* ▸**'soaring** *n, adj* ▸**'soaringly** *adv*

sob Ⓣ (sɒb) *vb* **sobs, sobbing, sobbed. 1** *(intr)* to weep with convulsive gasps. **2** *(tr)* to utter with sobs. **3** to cause (oneself) to be in a specified state by sobbing: *to sob oneself to sleep.* ◆ *n* **4** a convulsive gasp made in weeping. [C12: prob. from Low G]
▸**'sobbing** *n, adj*

sober Ⓣ ('səʊbə) *adj* **1** not drunk. **2** not given to excessive indulgence in drink or any other activity. **3** sedate and rational: *a sober attitude to a problem.* **4** (of colours) plain and dull or subdued. **5** free from exaggeration or speculation: *he told us the sober truth.* ◆ *vb* **6** (usually foll. by *up*) to make or become less intoxicated. [C14 *sobre,* from OF, from L *sōbrius*]
▸**'sobering** *n, adj* ▸**'soberly** *adv*

sobriety Ⓣ (səʊ'braɪətɪ) *n* **1** the state or quality of being sober. **2** the quality of refraining from excess. **3** the quality of being serious or sedate.

sobriquet *or* **soubriquet** ('səʊbrɪˌkeɪ) *n* a humorous epithet, assumed name, or nickname. [C17: from F *soubriquet,* from ?]

sob story *n* a tale of personal distress intended to arouse sympathy.

Soc. *or* **soc.** *abbrev. for:* **1** socialist. **2** society.

soca ('səʊkə) *n* a mixture of soul and calypso music typical of the E Caribbean. [C20: a blend of *soul* + *calypso*]

socage ('sɒkɪdʒ) *n English legal history.* the tenure of land by certain services, esp. of an agricultural nature. [C14: from Anglo-F, from *soc* SOKE]

so-called Ⓣ *adj* **a** *(prenominal)* designated or styled by the name or word mentioned, esp. (in the speaker's opinion) incorrectly: *a so-called genius.* **b** (also used parenthetically after a noun): *these experts, so-called, are no help.*

soccer ('sɒkə) *n* **a** a game in which two teams of eleven players try to kick or head a ball into their opponents' goal, only the goalkeeper on either side being allowed to touch the ball with his hands and arms, except in the case of throw-ins. **b** *(as modifier): a soccer player.* ◆ Also called: **Association Football.** [C19: from *Assoc(iation Football)* + -ER[1]]

socceroo (ˌsɒkə'ruː) *n, pl* **socceroos.** *Austral. sl.* a member of the Australian national soccer team. [C20: from SOCCER + (KANGAR)OO]

sociable Ⓣ ('səʊʃəbᵊl) *adj* **1** friendly or companionable. **2** (of an occasion) providing the opportunity for friendliness and conviviality. ◆ *n* **3** *Chiefly US.* a social. **4** a type of open carriage with two seats facing each other. [C16: via F from L, from *sociāre* to unite, from *socius* an associate]
▸**ˌsocia'bility** *n* ▸**'sociably** *adv*

social Ⓣ ('səʊʃəl) *adj* **1** living or preferring to live in a community rather than alone. **2** denoting or relating to human society or any of its subdivisions. **3** of or characteristic of the behaviour and interaction of persons forming groups. **4** relating to or having the purpose of promoting companionship, communal activities, etc.: *a social club.* **5** relating to or engaged in social services: *a social worker.* **6** relating to or considered appropriate to a certain class of society. **7** (esp. of certain species of insects) living together in organized colonies: *social bees.* **8** (of plant species) growing in clumps. ◆ *n* **9** an informal gathering, esp. of an organized group. [C16: from L *sociālis* companionable, from *socius* a comrade]
▸**'socially** *adv*

Social and Liberal Democrats *pl n* (in Britain) a political party formed in 1988 by the merging of the Liberal Party and part of the Social Democratic Party; in 1989 it changed its name to the Liberal Democrats.

social anthropology *n* the branch of anthropology that deals with cultural and social phenomena such as kinship systems or beliefs.

Social Chapter *n* the section of the **Maastricht Treaty** concerning working conditions, consultation of workers, employment rights, and social security.

Social Charter *n* a declaration of the rights, minimum wages, maximum hours, etc., of workers in the European Union, codified in the Maastricht Treaty (1992).

social climber *n* a person who seeks advancement to a higher social class, esp. by obsequious behaviour.
▸**social climbing** *n*

social contract *or* **compact** *n* (in the theories of Locke, Hobbes, Rousseau, and others) an agreement, entered into by individuals, that results in the formation of the state, the prime motive being the desire for protection, which entails the surrender of some personal liberties.

Social Credit *n* **1** (esp. in Canada) a right-wing Populist political party, movement, or doctrine. **2 Social Credit League.** (in New Zealand) a middle-of-the-road political party, in favour of free enterprise. **3 Social Credit Rally.** (in Canada) a political party formed in 1963 from a splinter group of the Social Credit Party.

social democrat *n* **1** any socialist who believes in the gradual transformation of capitalism into democratic socialism. **2** *(usually cap.)* a member of a Social Democratic Party.
▸**social democracy** *n*

Social Democratic and Labour Party *n* a Northern Irish political party, which advocates peaceful union with the Republic of Ireland. Abbrev.: **SDLP.**

Social Democratic Party *n* **1** (in Britain, 1981–90) a political party founded by ex-members of the Labour Party. It formed an alliance with the Liberal Party and continued in a reduced form after many members left to join the Social and Liberal Democrats in 1988. **2** one of the two major political parties in Germany, favouring gradual reform. **3** any of the parties in many other countries similar to that of Germany.

social engineering *n* the manipulation of the social position and function of individuals in order to manage change in a society.

social fund *n* (in Britain) a social security fund from which loans or payments may be made to people in cases of extreme need.

social insurance *n* government insurance providing coverage for the unemployed, the injured, the old, etc.: usually financed by contributions from employers and employees.

Social Insurance Number *n Canad.* an identification number issued to individuals by the government in connection with income tax and social insurance.

socialism ('səʊʃəˌlɪzəm) *n* **1** an economic theory or system in which the means of production, distribution, and exchange are owned by the community collectively, usually through the state. Cf. **capitalism. 2** any of various social or political theories or movements in which the common welfare is to be achieved through the establishment of a socialist economic system. **3** (in Leninist theory) a transitional stage in the development of a society from capitalism to communism: characterized by the distribution of income according to work rather than need.

socialist ('səʊʃəlɪst) *n* **1** a supporter or advocate of socialism or any party promoting socialism (**socialist party**). ◆ *adj* **2** of, implementing, or relating to socialism. **3** *(sometimes cap.)* of or relating to socialists or a socialist party.
▸**ˌsocia'listic** *adj*

Socialist International *n* an international association of largely anti-Communist Social Democratic Parties founded in Frankfurt in 1951.

socialist realism *n* (in Communist countries, esp. formerly) the doctrine that art, literature, etc., should present an idealized portrayal of reality, which glorifies the achievements of the Communist Party.

socialite ('səʊʃəˌlaɪt) *n* a person who is or seeks to be prominent in fashionable society.

sociality (ˌsəʊʃɪ'ælɪtɪ) *n, pl* **socialities. 1** the tendency of groups and persons to develop social links and live in communities. **2** the quality or state of being social.

socialize Ⓣ *or* **socialise** ('səʊʃəˌlaɪz) *vb* **socializes, socializing, socialized** *or* **socialises, socialising, socialised. 1** *(intr)* to behave in a friendly or socia-

THESAURUS

soar *vb* **1** = **ascend**, fly, mount, rise, tower, wing **3** = **rise**, climb, escalate, rocket, shoot up
Antonyms *vb* descend, dive, drop, fall, nose-dive, plummet, plunge, swoop

sob *vb* **1** = **cry**, bawl, blubber, boohoo, greet (*Scot. or arch.*), howl, shed tears, snivel, weep

sober *adj* **2** = **abstinent**, abstemious, moderate, on the wagon (*inf.*), temperate **3** = **serious**, calm, clear-headed, composed, cool, dispassionate, grave, level-headed, lucid, practical, rational, realistic, reasonable, sedate, solemn, sound, staid, steady, unexcited, unruffled **4** = **plain**, dark, drab, quiet, severe, sombre, subdued ◆ *vb* **6** *usually with* **up** = **clear one's head**, come *or* bring to one's senses
Antonyms *adj* ≠ **abstinent:** drunk, inebriated, intoxicated, merry (*Brit. inf.*), paralytic (*inf.*), pie-eyed (*sl.*), pissed (*taboo sl.*), plastered, smashed (*sl.*), tiddly (*sl., chiefly Brit.*), tight (*inf.*), tipsy, tired and emotional (*euphemistic*) ≠ **serious:** excessive, frivolous, happy, immoderate, imprudent, injudicious, irrational, light-hearted, sensational, unrealistic ≠ **plain:** bright, flamboyant, flashy, garish, gaudy, light ◆ *vb* ≠ **clear one's head:** become intoxicated, get drunk

sobriety *n* **2** = **abstinence**, abstemiousness, moderation, nonindulgence, self-restraint, soberness, temperance **3** = **seriousness**, calmness, composure, coolness, gravity, level-headedness, reasonableness, restraint, sedateness, solemnity, staidness, steadiness

so-called *adj* = **alleged**, ostensible, pretended, professed, self-styled, *soi-disant,* supposed

sociability *n* **1** = **friendliness**, affability, companionability, congeniality, conviviality, cordiality, gregariousness, neighbourliness

sociable *adj* **1** = **friendly**, accessible, affable, approachable, companionable, conversable, convivial, cordial, familiar, genial, gregarious, neighbourly, outgoing, social, warm
Antonyms *adj* antisocial, businesslike, cold, distant, formal, introverted, reclusive, standoffish, stiff, tense, uncommunicative, unfriendly, unsociable, uptight (*inf.*), withdrawn

social *adj* **1** = **sociable**, companionable, friendly, gregarious, neighbourly **2** = **communal**, collective, common, community, general, group, organized, public, societal ◆ *n* **9** = **get-together** (*inf.*), do (*inf.*), gathering, party

socialize *vb* **1** = **mix**, be a good mixer, break the ice, entertain, fraternize, get about *or* around, get together, go out

ble manner. **2** (*tr*) to prepare for life in society. **3** (*tr*) *Chiefly US.* to alter or create so as to be in accordance with socialist principles.

social market *n* **a** an economic system in which industry and commerce are run by private enterprise within limits set by the government to ensure equality of opportunity and social and environmental responsibility. **b** (*as modifier*): *a social-market economy.*

social realism *n* **1** the use of realist art, literature, etc., as a medium for social or political comment. **2** another name for **socialist realism.**

social science *n* **1** the study of society and of the relationship of individual members within society, including economics, history, political science, psychology, anthropology, and sociology. **2** any of these subjects studied individually.
▸**social scientist** *n*

social secretary *n* **1** a member of an organization who arranges its social events. **2** a personal secretary who deals with private correspondence, etc.

social security *n* **1** public provision for the economic welfare of the aged, unemployed, etc., esp. through pensions and other monetary assistance. **2** (*often cap.*) a government programme designed to provide such assistance.

social services *pl n* welfare activities organized by the state or a local authority and carried out by trained personnel.

social studies *n* (*functioning as sing*) the study of how people live and organize themselves in society, embracing geography, history, economics, and other subjects.

social welfare *n* **1** social services provided by a state for the benefit of its citizens. **2** (*caps.*) (in New Zealand) a government department concerned with pensions and benefits for the elderly, the sick, etc.

social work *n* any of various social services designed to alleviate the conditions of the poor and aged and to increase the welfare of children.
▸**social worker** *n*

societal (sə'saɪət^ə^l) *adj* of or relating to society, esp. human society.
▸**so'cietally** *adv*

societal marketing *n* **1** marketing that takes into account society's long-term welfare. **2** the marketing of a social or charitable cause, such as an anti-apartheid campaign.

society ❶ (sə'saɪətɪ) *n, pl* **societies. 1** the totality of social relationships among organized groups of human beings or animals. **2** a system of human organizations generating distinctive cultural patterns and institutions. **3** such a system with reference to its mode of social and economic organization or its dominant class: *middle-class society.* **4** those with whom one has companionship. **5** an organized group of people associated for some specific purpose or on account of some common interest: *a learned society.* **6a** the privileged class of people in a community, esp. as considered superior or fashionable. **6b** (*as modifier*): *a society woman.* **7** the social life and intercourse of such people: *to enter society.* **8** companionship: *I enjoy her society.* **9** *Ecology.* a small community of plants within a larger association. [C16: via OF *societé* from L *societās,* from *socius* a comrade]

Society of Jesus *n* the religious order of the Jesuits, founded by Ignatius Loyola.

socio- *combining form.* denoting social or society: *socioeconomic; sociopolitical; sociology.*

sociobiology (ˌsəʊsɪəʊbaɪ'ɒlədʒɪ) *n* the study of social behaviour in animals and humans.
▸ˌ**sociobi'ologist** *n*

socioeconomic (ˌsəʊsɪəʊˌiːkə'nɒmɪk, -ˌɛkə-) *adj* of, relating to, or involving both economic and social factors.
▸ˌ**socioˌeco'nomically** *adv*

sociolinguistics (ˌsəʊsɪəʊlɪŋ'gwɪstɪks) *n* (*functioning as sing*) the study of language in relation to its social context.
▸ˌ**socio'linguist** *n*

sociology (ˌsəʊsɪ'ɒlədʒɪ) *n* the study of the development, organization, functioning, and classification of human societies.
▸**sociological** (ˌsəʊsɪə'lɒdʒɪk^ə^l) *adj* ▸ˌ**soci'ologist** *n*

sociometry (ˌsəʊsɪ'ɒmɪtrɪ) *n* the study of sociological relationships within groups.
▸**sociometric** (ˌsəʊsɪə'mɛtrɪk) *adj* ▸ˌ**soci'ometrist** *n*

sociopath ('səʊsɪəˌpæθ) *n Psychiatry.* another term for **psychopath.**
▸ˌ**socio'pathic** *adj* ▸**sociopathy** (ˌsəʊsɪ'ɒpəθɪ) *n*

sociopolitical (ˌsəʊsɪəʊpə'lɪtɪk^ə^l) *adj* of or involving both political and social factors.

sock[1] (sɒk) *n* **1** a cloth covering for the foot, reaching to between the ankle and knee and worn inside a shoe. **2** an insole put in a shoe, as to make it fit better. **3** a light shoe worn by actors in ancient Greek and Roman comedy. **4 pull one's socks up.** *Brit. inf.* to make a determined effort, esp. to improve one's behaviour or performance. **5 put a sock in it.** *Brit. sl.* be quiet! [OE *socc* a light shoe, from L *soccus,* from Gk *sukkhos*]

sock[2] (sɒk) *Sl.* ◆ *vb* **1** (*usually tr*) to hit with force. **2 sock it to.** *Sl.* to make a forceful impression on. ◆ *n* **3** a forceful blow. [C17: from ?]

socket ('sɒkɪt) *n* **1** a device into which an electric plug can be inserted in order to make a connection in a circuit. **2** *Chiefly Brit.* such a device mounted on a wall and connected to the electricity supply; power point. **3** a part with an opening or hollow into which some other part can be fitted. **4** *Anat.* **4a** a bony hollow into which a part or structure fits: *an eye socket.* **4b** the receptacle of a ball-and-socket joint. ◆ *vb* **5** (*tr*) to furnish with or place into a socket. [C13: from Anglo-Norman *soket* a little ploughshare, from *soc,* of Celtic origin]

socket set *n* a set of tools consisting of a handle into which various interchangeable heads can be fitted.

sockeye ('sɒkˌaɪ) *n* a Pacific salmon having red flesh and valued as a food fish. Also called: **red salmon.** [by folk etymology from *sukkegh,* of Amerind origin]

socle ('səʊk^ə^l) *n* another name for **plinth** (sense 1). [C18: via F from It. *zoccolo,* from L *socculus* a little shoe, from *soccus* a SOCK[1]]

Socratic (sɒ'krætɪk) *adj* **1** of Socrates (?470–399 B.C.), the Greek philosopher, his methods, etc. ◆ *n* **2** a person who follows the teachings of Socrates.
▸**So'cratically** *adv* ▸**So'cratiˌcism** *n* ▸**Socratist** ('sɒkrətɪst) *n*

Socratic irony *n Philosophy.* a means by which the feigned ignorance of a questioner leads the person answering to expose his own ignorance.

Socratic method *n Philosophy.* the method of instruction by question and answer used by Socrates in order to elicit from his pupils truths he considered to be implicitly known by all rational beings.

sod[1] (sɒd) *n* **1** a piece of grass-covered surface soil held together by the roots of the grass; turf. **2** *Poetic.* the ground. ◆ *vb* **sods, sodding, sodded. 3** (*tr*) to cover with sods. [C15: from Low G]

sod[2] (sɒd) *Sl., chiefly Brit.* ◆ *n* **1** a person considered to be obnoxious. **2** a jocular word for a **person. 3 sod all.** *Sl.* nothing. ◆ *interj* **4 sod it.** a strong exclamation of annoyance. See also **sod off.** [C19: shortened from SODOMITE]
▸**'sodding** *adj*

soda ('səʊdə) *n* **1** any of a number of simple inorganic compounds of sodium, such as sodium carbonate (**washing soda**), sodium bicarbonate (**baking soda**), and sodium hydroxide (**caustic soda**). **2** See **soda water. 3** *US & Canad.* a fizzy drink. [C16: from Med. L, from *sodanum* barilla, a plant that was burned to obtain a type of sodium carbonate, ?from Ar.]

soda ash *n* the anhydrous commercial form of sodium carbonate.

soda bread *n* a type of bread leavened with sodium bicarbonate combined with milk and cream of tartar.

soda fountain *n US & Canad.* **1** a counter that serves drinks, snacks, etc. **2** an apparatus dispensing soda water.

sodality (səʊ'dælɪtɪ) *n, pl* **sodalities. 1** *RC Church.* a religious society. **2** fellowship. [C16: from L *sodālitās* fellowship, from *sodālis* a comrade]

sodamide ('səʊdəˌmaɪd) *n* a white crystalline compound used as a dehydrating agent and in making sodium cyanide. Formula: $NaNH_2$.

soda siphon *n* a sealed bottle containing and dispensing soda water. The water is forced up a tube reaching to the bottom of the bottle by the pressure of gas above the water.

soda water *n* an effervescent beverage made by charging water with carbon dioxide under pressure. Sometimes shortened to **soda.**

sodden ❶ ('sɒd^ə^n) *adj* **1** completely saturated. **2a** dulled, esp. by excessive drinking. **2b** (*in combination*): *a drink-sodden mind.* **3** doughy, as bread is when improperly cooked. ◆ *vb* **4** to make or become sodden. [C13 *soden,* p.p. of SEETHE]
▸**'soddenness** *n*

sodium ('səʊdɪəm) *n* **a** a very reactive soft silvery-white element of the alkali metal group occurring principally in common salt, Chile saltpetre, and cryolite. It is used in the production of chemicals, in metallurgy, and, alloyed with potassium, as a cooling medium in nuclear reactors. Symbol: Na; atomic no.: 11; atomic wt.: 22.99. **b** (*as modifier*): *sodium light.* [C19: NL, from SODA + -IUM]

sodium amytal *n* another name for **Amytal.**

sodium benzoate *n* a white crystalline soluble compound used in preserving food (**E 211**), as an antiseptic, and in making dyes.

sodium bicarbonate *n* a white crystalline soluble compound used in effervescent drinks, baking powders, fire-extinguishers, and in medicine as an antacid; sodium hydrogen carbonate. Formula: $NaHCO_3$. Systematic name: **sodium hydrogencarbonate.** Also called: **bicarbonate of soda, baking soda.**

sodium carbonate *n* a colourless or white odourless soluble crystalline compound used in the manufacture of glass, ceramics, soap, and paper, and as a cleansing agent. Formula: Na_2CO_3.

sodium chlorate *n* a colourless crystalline soluble compound used as a bleaching agent, antiseptic, and weedkiller. Formula: $NaClO_3$.

sodium chloride *n* common table salt; a soluble colourless crystalline compound widely used as a seasoning and preservative for food and in the manufacture of chemicals, glass, and soap. Formula: NaCl. Also called: **salt.**

sodium cyanide *n* a white odourless crystalline soluble poisonous

THESAURUS

society *n* **1 = civilization,** culture, humanity, mankind, people, population, social order, the community, the general public, the public, the world at large **5 = organization,** association, brotherhood *or* sisterhood, circle, club, corporation, fellowship, fraternity, group, guild, institute, league, order, union **6 = upper classes,** beau monde, elite, gentry, *haut monde,* high society, polite society, the country set, the nobs (*sl.*), the smart set, the swells (*inf.*), the toffs, the top drawer, upper crust (*inf.*) **8 = companionship,** camaraderie, company, fellowship, friendship

sodden *adj* **1 = soaked,** boggy, drenched, droukit *or* drookit (*Scot.*), marshy, miry, saturated, soggy, sopping, waterlogged

compound used for extracting gold and silver from their ores and for case-hardening steel. Formula: NaCN.

sodium glutamate (ˈgluːtəˌmeɪt) *n* another name for **monosodium glutamate.**

sodium hydrogencarbonate *n* the systematic name for **sodium bicarbonate.**

sodium hydroxide *n* a white strongly alkaline solid used in the manufacture of rayon, paper, aluminium, soap, and sodium compounds. Formula: NaOH. Also called: **caustic soda.**

sodium hyposulphite *n* another name (not in technical usage) for **sodium thiosulphate.**

sodium lamp *n* another name for **sodium-vapour lamp.**

sodium nitrate *n* a white crystalline soluble solid compound used in matches, explosives, and rocket propellants, as a fertilizer, and as a curing salt for preserving food (**E 251**). Formula: $NaNO_3$.

Sodium Pentothal *n Trademark.* another name for **thiopentone sodium.**

sodium silicate *n* **1** Also called: **soluble glass.** See **water glass. 2** any sodium salt of a silicic acid.

sodium sulphate *n* a solid white substance used in making glass, detergents, and pulp. Formula: Na_2SO_4. See **salt cake** and **Glauber's salt.**

sodium thiosulphate *n* a white soluble substance used in photography as a fixer to dissolve unchanged silver halides and also to remove excess chlorine from chlorinated water. Formula: $Na_2S_2O_3$. Also called (not in technical usage): **sodium hyposulphite, hypo.**

sodium-vapour lamp *n* a type of electric lamp consisting of a glass tube containing neon and sodium vapour at low pressure through which an electric current is passed to give an orange light: used in street lighting.

sod off *Brit. taboo sl.* ◆ *interj* **1** a forceful expression of dismissal. ◆ *vb* **sods, sodding, sodded. 2** (*intr, adv*) to go away.

Sodom (ˈsɒdəm) *n* **1** *Old Testament.* a city destroyed by God for its wickedness that, with Gomorrah, traditionally typifies depravity (Genesis 19:24). **2** this city as representing homosexuality. **3** any place notorious for depravity.

sodomite (ˈsɒdəˌmaɪt) *n* a person who practises sodomy.

sodomize *or* **sodomise** (ˈsɒdəˌmaɪz) *vb* **sodomizes, sodomizing, sodomized** *or* **sodomises, sodomising, sodomised.** (*tr*) to have anal intercourse with (a person).

sodomy **T** (ˈsɒdəmɪ) *n* anal intercourse committed by a man with another man or a woman. [C13: via OF *sodomie* from L (Vulgate) *Sodoma* Sodom]

Sod's law (sɒdz) *n Inf.* a facetious precept stating that if something can go wrong or turn out inconveniently it will.

soever (səʊˈɛvə) *adv* in any way at all: used to emphasize or make less precise a word or phrase, usually in combination with *what, where, when, how*, etc., or else separated by intervening words. Cf. **whatsoever.**

sofa **T** (ˈsəʊfə) *n* an upholstered seat with back and arms for two or more people. [C17 (in the sense: dais upholstered as a seat): from Ar. *suffah*]

soffit (ˈsɒfɪt) *n* the underside of a part of a building or a structural component, such as an arch, beam, stair, etc. [C17: via F from It. *soffitto*, from L *suffixus* something fixed underneath, from *suffigere*, from *sub-* under + *figere* to fasten]

S. of Sol. *Bible. abbrev. for* Song of Solomon.

soft **T** (sɒft) *adj* **1** easy to dent, work, or cut without shattering; malleable. **2** not hard; giving little or no resistance to pressure or weight. **3** fine, light, smooth, or fluffy to the touch. **4** gentle; tranquil. **5** (of music, sounds, etc.) low and pleasing. **6** (of light, colour, etc.) not excessively bright or harsh. **7** (of a breeze, climate, etc.) temperate, mild, or pleasant. **8** slightly blurred; not sharply outlined: *soft focus.* **9** (of a diet) consisting of easily digestible foods. **10** kind or lenient, often excessively so. **11** easy to influence or impose upon. **12** prepared to compromise; not doctrinaire: *the soft left.* **13** *Inf.* feeble or silly; simple (often in **soft in the head**). **14** unable to endure hardship, esp. through pampering. **15** physically out of condition; flabby: *soft muscles.* **16** loving; tender: *soft words.* **17** *Inf.* requiring little exertion; easy: *a soft job.* **18** *Chem.* (of water) relatively free of mineral salts and therefore easily able to make soap lather. **19** (of a drug such as cannabis) nonaddictive. **20** *Phonetics.* (not in technical usage) denoting the consonants *c* and *g* in English when they are pronounced as palatal or alveolar fricatives or affricates (s, dʒ, ʃ, ð, tʃ) before *e* and *i*, rather than as velar stops (k, g). **21** *Finance, chiefly US.* (of prices, a market, etc.) unstable and tending to decline. **22** (of currency) in relatively little demand, esp. because of a weak balance of payments situation. **23** (of radiation, such as X-rays and ultraviolet radiation) having low energy and not capable of deep penetration of materials. **24 soft on** *or* **about. 24a** gentle, sympathetic, or lenient towards. **24b** feeling affection or infatuation for. ◆ *adv* **25** in a soft manner: *to speak soft.* ◆ *n* **26** a soft object, part, or piece. **27** *Inf.* See **softie.** ◆ *sentence substitute. Arch.* **28** quiet! **29** wait! [OE *sōfte*]
► **ˈsoftly** *adv* ► **ˈsoftness** *n*

softa (ˈsɒftə) *n* a Muslim student of divinity and jurisprudence, esp. in Turkey. [C17: from Turkish, from Persian *sōkhtah* aflame (with love of learning)]

softball (ˈsɒftˌbɔːl) *n* a variation of baseball using a larger softer ball, pitched underhand.

soft ball *n Cookery.* a term used for sugar syrup boiled to a consistency at which it may be rubbed into balls after dipping in cold water.

soft-boiled *adj* (of an egg) boiled for a short time so that the yolk is still soft.

soft coal *n* another name for **bituminous coal.**

soft commodities *pl n* nonmetal commodities, such as cocoa, sugar, and grains, bought and sold on a futures market. Also called: **softs.**

soft-core *adj* (of pornography) suggestive and titillating through not being totally explicit.

soft-cover *adj* a less common word for **paperback.**

soft drink *n* a nonalcoholic drink.

soften **T** (ˈsɒfᵊn) *vb* **1** to make or become soft or softer. **2** to make or become more gentle.
► **ˈsoftener** *n*

softening of the brain *n* an abnormal softening of the tissues of the cerebrum characterized by mental impairment.

soft-focus lens *n Photog.* a lens designed to produce an image that is slightly out of focus: typically used for portrait work.

soft furnishings *pl n Brit.* curtains, hangings, rugs, etc.

soft goods *pl n* textile fabrics and related merchandise. Also called (US and Canad.): **dry goods.**

soft-headed *adj* **1** *Inf.* feeble-minded; stupid; simple. **2** (of a stick or hammer for playing a percussion instrument) having a soft head.
► **ˌsoft-ˈheadedness** *n*

softhearted **T** (ˌsɒftˈhɑːtɪd) *adj* easily moved to pity.
► **ˌsoftˈheartedly** *adv* ► **ˌsoftˈheartedness** *n*

softie *or* **softy** (ˈsɒftɪ) *n, pl* **softies.** *Inf.* a person who is sentimental, weakly foolish, or lacking in physical endurance.

soft landing *n* **1** a landing by a spacecraft on the moon or a planet at a sufficiently low velocity for the equipment or occupants to remain unharmed. **2** a painless resolution of a problem, esp. an economic problem. Cf. **hard landing.**

soft option *n* in a number of choices, the one involving the least difficulty or exertion.

soft palate *n* the posterior fleshy portion of the roof of the mouth.

soft paste *n* **a** artificial porcelain made from clay, bone ash, etc. **b** (*as modifier*): *softpaste porcelain.*

soft-pedal **T** *vb* **soft-pedals, soft-pedalling, soft-pedalled** *or US* **soft-pedals, soft-pedaling, soft-pedaled.** (*tr*) **1** to mute the tone of (a piano) by depressing the soft pedal. **2** *Inf.* to make (something, esp. something unpleasant) less obvious by deliberately failing to emphasize or allude to it. ◆ *n* **soft pedal. 3** a foot-operated lever on a piano, the left one of two, that either moves the whole action closer to the strings so that the hammers strike with less force or causes fewer of the strings to sound.

soft porn *n Inf.* soft-core pornography.

softs (sɒfts) *pl n* another name for **soft commodities.**

soft sell *n* a method of selling based on indirect suggestion or inducement.

soft shoulder *or* **verge** *n* a soft edge along the side of a road that is unsuitable for vehicles to drive on.

soft soap *n* **1** *Med.* Also called: **green soap.** a soft or liquid alkaline soap used in treating certain skin disorders. **2** *Inf.* flattering, persuasive, or cajoling talk. ◆ *vb* **soft-soap. 3** *Inf.* to use such talk on (a person).

soft-spoken *adj* **1** speaking or said with a soft gentle voice. **2** able to persuade or impress by glibness of tongue.

THESAURUS

sodomy *n* = **anal intercourse**, anal sex, buggery

sofa *n* = **couch**, chaise longue, chesterfield, divan, ottoman, settee

soft *adj* **1** = **pliable**, bendable, ductile (*of metals*), elastic, flexible, impressible, malleable, mouldable, plastic, supple, tensile **2** = **yielding**, cushioned, cushiony, doughy, elastic, gelatinous, pulpy, quaggy, spongy, squashy, swampy **3** = **velvety**, downy, feathery, fleecy, flowing, fluid, furry, like a baby's bottom (*inf.*), rounded, silky, smooth **5** = **quiet**, dulcet, gentle, low, mellifluous, mellow, melodious, murmured, muted, soft-toned, soothing, subdued, sweet, understated, whispered **6** = **pale**, bland, light, mellow, pastel, pleasing, subdued **7** = **mild**, balmy, caressing, delicate, shaded, temperate **8** = **dim**, diffuse, dimmed, faint, restful, twilight **10** = **lenient**, boneless, easy-going, indulgent, lax, liberal, overindulgent, permissive, spineless, weak **13** *Informal* = **feeble-minded**, a bit lacking (*inf.*), daft (*inf.*), foolish, silly, simple, soft in the head (*inf.*), soppy (*Brit. inf.*) **14, 15** = **out of condition**, effeminate, flabby, flaccid, limp, namby-pamby, out of training, overindulged, pampered, podgy, weak **16** = **kind**, compassionate, gentle, pitying, sensitive, sentimental, sympathetic, tender, tenderhearted, touchy-feely (*inf.*) **17** *Informal* = **easy**, comfortable, cushy (*inf.*), easy-peasy (*sl.*), undemanding
Antonyms *adj* ≠ **pliable, yielding:** firm, hard, inflexible, rigid, solid, stiff, tough, unyielding ≠ **velvety:** abrasive, coarse, grating, hard, rough ≠ **quiet:** harsh, loud, noisy, strident ≠ **pale:** bright, garish, gaudy, glaring, harsh ≠ **dim:** bright, glaring, harsh ≠ **lenient:** austere, harsh, no-nonsense, stern, strict

soften *vb* **2** = **lessen**, abate, allay, alleviate, appease, assuage, calm, cushion, diminish, ease, lighten, lower, melt, mitigate, moderate, modify, mollify, muffle, palliate, quell, relax, soothe, still, subdue, temper, tone down, turn down

softhearted *adj* = **kind**, charitable, compassionate, generous, indulgent, sentimental, sympathetic, tender, tenderhearted, warmhearted
Antonyms *adj* callous, cold, cruel, hard, hardhearted, heartless, insensitive, uncaring, unkind, unsympathetic

soft-pedal *vb* **2** = **play down**, de-emphasize, go easy (*inf.*), moderate, tone down

soft spot ⓣ *n* a sentimental fondness (esp. in **have a soft spot for**).
soft touch *n Inf.* a person easily persuaded or imposed on, esp. to lend money.
software ('sɒft,wɛə) *n Computing.* the programs that can be used with a particular computer system. Cf. **hardware** (sense 2).
softwood ('sɒft,wʊd) *n* **1** the open-grained wood of any of numerous coniferous trees, such as pine and cedar. **2** any tree yielding this wood.
SOGAT ('səʊgæt) *n* (formerly, in Britain) *acronym for* Society of Graphical and Allied Trades.
soggy ⓣ ('sɒgɪ) *adj* **soggier, soggiest. 1** soaked with liquid. **2** (of bread, pastry, etc.) moist and heavy. **3** *Inf.* lacking in spirit or positiveness. [C18: prob. from dialect *sog* marsh, from ?]
▸ **'soggily** *adv* ▸ **'sogginess** *n*
soh *or* **so** (səʊ) *n Music.* (in tonic sol-fa) the name used for the fifth note or dominant of any scale. [C14: later variant of *sol*; see GAMUT]
soi-disant *French.* (swadizɑ̃) *adj* so-called; self-styled. [lit.: calling oneself]
soigné *or* (*fem*) **soignée** ('swɑːnjeɪ) *adj* well-groomed; elegant. [F, from *soigner* to take good care of, of Gmc origin]
soil[1] ⓣ (sɔɪl) *n* **1** the top layer of the land surface of the earth that is composed of disintegrated rock particles, humus, water, and air. **2** a type of this material having specific characteristics: *loamy soil.* **3** land, country, or region: *one's native soil.* **4 the soil.** life and work on a farm; land: *he belonged to the soil.* **5** any place or thing encouraging growth or development. [C14: from Anglo-Norman, from L *solium* a seat, but confused with L *solum* the ground]
soil[2] ⓣ (sɔɪl) *vb* **1** to make or become dirty or stained. **2** (*tr*) to pollute with sin or disgrace; sully; defile. ◆ *n* **3** the state or result of soiling. **4** refuse, manure, or excrement. [C13: from OF *soillier* to defile, from *soil* pigsty, prob. from L *sūs* a swine]
soil[3] (sɔɪl) *vb* (*tr*) to feed (livestock) green fodder to fatten or purge them. [C17: ?from obs. vb (C16) *soil* to manure, from SOIL[2] (n)]
soil pipe *n* a pipe that conveys sewage or waste water from a toilet, etc., to a soil drain or sewer.
soiree ('swɑːreɪ) *n* an evening party or gathering, usually at a private house, esp. where guests listen to, play, or dance to music. [C19: from F, from OF *soir* evening, from L *sērum* a late time, from *sērus* late]
soixante-neuf *French.* (swasɑ̃tnœf) *n* a sexual activity in which two people simultaneously stimulate each other's genitalia with their mouths. Also called: **sixty-nine.** [lit.: sixty-nine, from the position adopted by the participants]
sojourn ⓣ ('sɒdʒɜːn, 'sʌdʒ-) *n* **1** a temporary stay. ◆ *vb* **2** (*intr*) to stay or reside temporarily. [C13: from OF *sojorner,* from Vulgar L *subdiurnāre* (unattested) to spend a day, from L *sub-* during + LL *diurnum* day]
▸ **'sojourner** *n*
soke (səʊk) *n English legal history.* **1** the right to hold a local court. **2** the territory under the jurisdiction of a particular court. [C14: from Med. L *sōca,* from OE *sōcn* a seeking]
sol[1] (sɒl) *n Music.* the syllable used in the fixed system of solmization for the note G. [C14: see GAMUT]
sol[2] (sɒl) *n* a colloid that has a continuous liquid phase, esp. one in which a solid is suspended in a liquid. [C20: shortened from SOLUTION]
Sol (sɒl) *n* **1** the Roman god personifying the sun. **2** a poetic word for the **sun.**
sol. *abbrev. for:* **1** soluble. **2** solution.
Sol. *abbrev. for:* **1** Also: **Solr.** solicitor. **2** *Bible.* Solomon.
sola *Latin.* ('səʊlə) *adj* the feminine form of ***solus.***
solace ⓣ ('sɒlɪs) *n* **1** comfort in misery, disappointment, etc. **2** something that gives comfort or consolation. ◆ *vb* **solaces, solacing, solaced.** (*tr*) **3** to give comfort or cheer to (a person) in time of sorrow, distress, etc. **4** to alleviate (sorrow, misery, etc.). [C13: from OF *solas,* from L *sōlātium* comfort, from *sōlārī* to console]
▸ **'solacer** *n*
solan *or* **solan goose** ('səʊlən) *n* an archaic name for the **gannet.** [C15 *soland,* from ON]
solanaceous (,sɒlə'neɪʃəs) *adj* of or relating to the Solanaceae, a family of plants having typically tubular flowers, protruding anthers, and often poisonous or narcotic properties: includes the potato, tobacco, and several nightshades. [C19: from NL *Sōlānāceae,* from L *sōlānum* nightshade]
solanum (səʊ'leɪnəm) *n* any tree, shrub, or herbaceous plant of the mainly tropical solanaceous genus *Solanum:* includes the potato and certain nightshades. [C16: from L: nightshade]
solar ('səʊlə) *adj* **1** of or relating to the sun. **2** operating by or utilizing the energy of the sun: *solar cell.* **3** *Astron.* determined from the motion of the earth relative to the sun: *solar year.* **4** *Astrol.* subject to the influence of the sun. [C15: from L *sōlāris,* from *sōl* the sun]
solar cell *n* a cell that produces electricity from the sun's rays, used esp. in spacecraft.
solar constant *n* the rate at which the sun's energy is received per unit area at the top of the earth's atmosphere when the sun is at its mean distance from the earth and atmospheric absorption has been corrected for.
solar day *n* See under **day** (sense 6).
solar energy *n* energy obtained from solar power.
solar flare *n* a brief powerful eruption of intense high-energy radiation from the sun's surface, associated with sunspots and causing radio and magnetic disturbances on earth.
solarium (səʊ'lɛərɪəm) *n, pl* **solariums** *or* **solaria** (-'lɛərɪə) **1** a room built largely of glass to afford exposure to the sun. **2** a bed equipped with ultraviolet lights used for acquiring an artificial suntan. **3** an establishment offering such facilities. [C19: from L: a terrace, from *sōl* sun]
solar month *n* See under **month** (sense 4).
solar plexus *n* **1** *Anat.* the network of nerves situated behind the stomach that supply the abdominal organs. **2** (not in technical usage) the part of the stomach beneath the diaphragm; pit of the stomach. [C18: referring to resemblance between the radial network of nerves & ganglia & the rays of the sun]
solar power *n* radiation from the sun used to heat a fluid or to generate electricity using solar cells.
solar system *n* the system containing the sun and the bodies held in its gravitational field, including the planets (Mercury, Venus, earth, Mars, Jupiter, Saturn, Uranus, Neptune, Pluto), the asteroids, and comets.
solar wind (wɪnd) *n* the stream of charged particles, such as protons, emitted by the sun at high velocities, its intensity increasing during periods of solar activity.
solar year *n* See under **year** (sense 4).
solatium (səʊ'leɪʃɪəm) *n, pl* **solatia** (-ʃɪə). *Law, chiefly US & Scot.* compensation awarded for injury to the feelings as distinct from physical suffering and pecuniary loss. [C19: from L: see SOLACE]
sold ⓣ (səʊld) *vb* **1** the past tense and past participle of **sell.** ◆ *adj* **2 sold on.** *Sl.* uncritically attached to or enthusiastic about.
solder ('sɒldə; *US* 'sɒdər) *n* **1** an alloy used for joining two metal surfaces by melting the alloy so that it forms a thin layer between the surfaces. **2** something that joins things together firmly; a bond. ◆ *vb* **3** to join or mend or be joined or mended with or as if with solder. [C14: via OF from L *solidāre* to strengthen, from *solidus* solid]
▸ **'solderable** *adj* ▸ **'solderer** *n*
soldering iron *n* a hand tool consisting of a handle fixed to a copper tip that is heated and used to melt and apply solder.
soldier ⓣ ('səʊldʒə) *n* **1a** a person who serves or has served in an army. **1b** Also called: **common soldier.** a noncommissioned member of an army as opposed to a commissioned officer. **2** a person who works diligently for a cause. **3** *Zool.* an individual in a colony of social insects, esp. ants, that has powerful jaws adapted for defending the colony, crushing food, etc. ◆ *vb* **4** (*intr*) to serve as a soldier. [C13: from OF *soudier,* from *soude* (army) pay, from LL *solidus* a gold coin, from L: firm]
▸ **'soldierly** *adj*
soldier of fortune *n* a man who seeks money or adventure as a soldier; mercenary.
soldier on *vb* (*intr, adv*) to persist in one's efforts in spite of difficulties, pressure, etc.
soldiery ('səʊldʒərɪ) *n, pl* **soldieries. 1** soldiers collectively. **2** a group of soldiers. **3** the profession of being a soldier.
sole[1] ⓣ (səʊl) *adj* **1** (*prenominal*) being the only one; only. **2** (*prenominal*) of or relating to one individual or group and no other: *sole rights.* **3** *Law.* having no wife or husband. **4** an archaic word for **solitary.** [C14: from OF *soule,* from L *sōlus* alone]
▸ **'soleness** *n*
sole[2] (səʊl) *n* **1** the underside of the foot. **2** the underside of a shoe. **3a** the bottom of a furrow. **3b** the bottom of a plough. **4** the underside of a golf-club head. ◆ *vb* **soles, soling, soled.** (*tr*) **5** to provide (a shoe) with a sole. [C14: via OF from L *solea* sandal]
sole[3] (səʊl) *n, pl* **sole** *or* **soles.** any of various tongue-shaped flatfishes, esp. the **European sole:** most common in warm seas and highly valued as food fishes. [C14: via OF from Vulgar L *sola* (unattested), from L *solea* a sandal (from the fish's shape)]
solecism ('sɒlɪ,sɪzəm) *n* **1a** the nonstandard use of a grammatical construction. **1b** any mistake, incongruity, or absurdity. **2** a violation of good manners. [C16: from L *soloecismus,* from Gk, from *soloikos* speaking incorrectly, from *Soloi* an Athenian colony of Cilicia where the inhabitants spoke a corrupt form of Greek]
▸ **'solecist** *n* ▸ **,sole'cistic** *adj* ▸ **,sole'cistically** *adv*

THESAURUS

soft spot *n* – **fondness**, liking, partiality, weakness
soggy *adj* **1** = **sodden**, dripping, heavy, moist, mushy, pulpy, saturated, soaked, sopping, spongy, waterlogged
soil[1] *n* **1** = **earth**, clay, dirt, dust, ground, loam **3** = **land**, country, region
soil[2] *vb* **1, 2** = **dirty**, bedraggle, befoul, begrime, besmirch, defile, foul, maculate (*literary*), muddy, pollute, smear, smirch, spatter, spot, stain, sully, tarnish
sojourn *n* **1** = **stay**, rest, stop, stopover, visit ◆ *vb* **2** = **stay**, abide, dwell, lodge, reside, rest, stop, tarry
solace *n* **1** = **comfort**, alleviation, assuagement, consolation, relief ◆ *vb* **3, 4** = **comfort**, allay, alleviate, console, mitigate, soften, soothe
sold *adj* **2 sold on** *Slang* = **convinced of**, converted to, hooked on, persuaded of, talked into, won over to
soldier *n* **1** = **fighter**, enlisted man (*US*), GI (*US inf.*), man-at-arms, military man, redcoat, serviceman, squaddie *or* squaddy (*Brit. sl.*), Tommy (*Brit. inf.*), trooper, warrior
sole[1] *adj* **1, 2** = **only**, alone, exclusive, individual, one, one and only, single, singular, solitary

solely ❶ ('səʊllɪ) *adv* **1** only; completely. **2** without others; singly. **3** for one thing only.

solemn ❶ ('sɒləm) *adj* **1** characterized or marked by seriousness or sincerity: *a solemn vow.* **2** characterized by pomp, ceremony, or formality. **3** serious, glum, or pompous. **4** inspiring awe: *a solemn occasion.* **5** performed with religious ceremony. **6** gloomy or sombre: *solemn colours.* [C14: from OF *solempne,* from L *sōllemnis* appointed, ?from *sollus* whole]
▸'**solemnly** *adv* ▸'**solemnness** *or* '**solemness** *n*

solemnify (sə'lɛmnɪˌfaɪ) *vb* **solemnifies, solemnifying, solemnified.** (*tr*) to make serious or grave.
▸**soˌlemnifi'cation** *n*

solemnity ❶ (sə'lɛmnɪtɪ) *n, pl* **solemnities. 1** the state or quality of being solemn. **2** (*often pl*) solemn ceremony, observance, etc. **3** *Law.* a formality necessary to validate a deed, contract, etc.

solemnize ❶ *or* **solemnise** ('sɒləmˌnaɪz) *vb* **solemnizes, solemnizing, solemnized** *or* **solemnises, solemnising, solemnised.** (*tr*) **1** to celebrate or observe with rites or formal ceremonies, as a religious occasion. **2** to celebrate or perform the ceremony of (marriage). **3** to make solemn or serious. **4** to perform or hold (ceremonies, etc.) in due manner.
▸ˌ**solemni'zation** *or* ˌ**solemni'sation** *n* ▸'**solemˌnizer** *or* '**solemˌniser** *n*

solenodon (sə'lɛnədən) *n* either of two rare shrewlike nocturnal mammals of the Caribbean having a long hairless tail and an elongated snout. [C19: from NL, from L *sōlēn* sea mussel (from Gk: pipe) + Gk *odōn* tooth]

solenoid ('səʊlɪˌnɔɪd) *n* **1** a coil of wire, usually cylindrical, in which a magnetic field is set up by passing a current through it. **2** a coil of wire, partially surrounding an iron core, that is made to move inside the coil by the magnetic field set up by a current: used to convert electrical to mechanical energy, as in the operation of a switch. [C19: from F *solénoïde,* from Gk *sōlēn* a tube]
▸ˌ**sole'noidal** *adj*

sol-fa ('sɒl'fɑː) *n* **1** short for **tonic sol-fa.** ◆ *vb* **sol-fas, sol-faing, sol-faed. 2** *US.* to use tonic sol-fa syllables in singing (a tune). [C16: see GAMUT]

solfatara (ˌsɒlfə'tɑːrə) *n* a volcanic vent emitting only sulphurous gases and water vapour or sometimes hot mud. [C18: from It.: a sulphurous volcano near Naples, from *solfo* sulphur]

solfeggio (sɒl'fɛdʒɪəʊ) *or* **solfège** (sɒl'fɛʒ) *n, pl* **solfeggi** (-'fɛdʒiː), **solfeggios,** *or* **solfèges.** *Music.* **1** a voice exercise in which runs, scales, etc., are sung to the same syllable or syllables. **2** solmization, esp. the French or Italian system, in which the names correspond to the notes of the scale of C major. [C18: from It. *solfeggiare* to use the syllables sol-fa; see GAMUT]

soli ('səʊlɪ) *adj, adv Music.* (of a piece or passage) (to be performed) by or with soloists.

solicit ❶ (sə'lɪsɪt) *vb* **solicits, soliciting, solicited. 1** (when *intr,* foll. by *for*) to make a request, application, etc., to (a person for business, support, etc.). **2** to accost (a person) with an offer of sexual relations in return for money. **3** to provoke or incite (a person) to do something wrong or illegal. [C15: from OF *solliciter* to disturb, from L *sollicitāre* to harass, from *sollus* whole + *ciēre* to excite]
▸**soˌlici'tation** *n*

solicitor (sə'lɪsɪtə) *n* **1** (in Britain) a lawyer who advises clients on matters of law, draws up legal documents, prepares cases for barristers, etc. **2** (in the US) an officer responsible for the legal affairs of a town, city, etc. **3** a person who solicits.
▸**so'licitorˌship** *n*

Solicitor General *n, pl* **Solicitors General. 1** (in Britain) the law officer of the Crown ranking next to the Attorney General (in Scotland to the Lord Advocate) and acting as his assistant. **2** (in New Zealand) the government's chief lawyer.

solicitous ❶ (sə'lɪsɪtəs) *adj* **1** showing consideration, concern, attention, etc. **2** keenly anxious or willing; eager. [C16: from L *sollicitus* anxious; see SOLICIT]
▸**so'licitousness** *n*

solicitude ❶ (sə'lɪsɪˌtjuːd) *n* **1** the state or quality of being solicitous. **2** (*often pl*) something that causes anxiety or concern. **3** anxiety or concern.

solid ❶ ('sɒlɪd) *adj* **1** of, concerned with, or being a substance in a physical state in which it resists changes in size and shape. Cf. **gas** (sense 1), **liquid** (sense 1). **2** consisting of matter all through. **3** of the same substance all through: *solid rock.* **4** sound; proved or provable: *solid facts.* **5** reliable or sensible; upstanding: *a solid citizen.* **6** firm, strong, compact, or substantial: *a solid table; solid ground.* **7** (of a meal or food) substantial. **8** (*often postpositive*) without interruption or respite: *solid bombardment.* **9** financially sound or solvent: *a solid institution.* **10** strongly linked or consolidated: *a solid relationship.* **11 solid for.** unanimously in favour of. **12** *Geom.* having or relating to three dimensions. **13** (of a word composed of two or more elements) written or printed as a single word without a hyphen. **14** *Printing.* with no space or leads between lines of type. **15** (of a writer, work, etc.) adequate; sensible. **16** of or having a single uniform colour or tone. **17** *Austral. & NZ inf.* excessively severe or unreasonable. ◆ *n* **18** *Geom.* **18a** a closed surface in three-dimensional space. **18b** such a surface together with the volume enclosed by it. **19** a solid substance, such as wood, iron, or diamond. [C14: from OF *solide,* from L *solidus* firm]
▸**solidity** (sə'lɪdɪtɪ) *n* ▸'**solidly** *adv* ▸'**solidness** *n*

solidago (ˌsɒlɪ'deɪgəʊ) *n, pl* **solidagos.** any plant of a chiefly American genus, which includes the goldenrods. [C18: via NL from Med. L *soldago* a plant reputed to have healing properties, from *soldāre* to strengthen, from L *solidāre,* from *solidus* solid]

solid angle *n* an area subtended in three dimensions by lines intersecting at a point on a sphere whose radius is the distance to the point. See also **steradian.**

solidarity ❶ (ˌsɒlɪ'dærɪtɪ) *n, pl* **solidarities.** unity of interests, sympathies, etc., as among members of the same class.

solid fuel *n* **1** a fuel, such as coal or coke, that is a solid rather than an oil or gas. **2** Also called: **solid propellant.** a rocket fuel that is a solid rather than a liquid or a gas.

solid geometry *n* the branch of geometry concerned with three-dimensional geometric figures.

solidify ❶ (sə'lɪdɪˌfaɪ) *vb* **solidifies, solidifying, solidified. 1** to make or become solid or hard. **2** to make or become strong, united, determined, etc.
▸**soˌlidifi'cation** *n* ▸**so'lidiˌfier** *n*

solid-state *n* (*modifier*) **1** (of an electronic device) activated by a semiconductor component in which current flow is through solid material rather than in a vacuum. **2** of, concerned with, characteristic of, or consisting of solid matter.

solid-state physics *n* (*functioning as sing*) the branch of physics concerned with the properties of solids, such as superconductivity, photoconductivity, and ferromagnetism.

solidus ('sɒlɪdəs) *n, pl* **solidi** (-ˌdaɪ). **1** Also called: **diagonal, oblique, separatrix, shilling mark, slash, stroke, virgule.** a short oblique stroke used in text to separate items of information, such as days, months, and years in dates (*18/7/80*), alternative words (*and/or*), numerator from denominator in fractions (*55/103*), etc. **2** a gold coin of the Byzantine empire. [C14: from LL *solidus* (*nummus*) a gold coin (from *solidus* solid); in Med. L, *solidus* referred to a shilling and was indicated by a long *s,* which ult. became the virgule]

solifluction *or* **solifluxion** ('sɒlɪˌflʌkʃən, 'səʊlɪ-) *n* slow downhill movement of soil, saturated with meltwater, over a permanently frozen subsoil in tundra regions. [C20: from L *solum* soil + *fluctio* act of flowing]

soliloquize *or* **soliloquise** (sə'lɪləˌkwaɪz) *vb* **soliloquizes, soliloquizing, soliloquized** *or* **soliloquises, soliloquising, soliloquised.** (*intr*) to utter a soliloquy.
▸**so'liloquist** *n* ▸**so'liloˌquizer** *or* **so'liloˌquiser** *n*

soliloquy (sə'lɪləkwɪ) *n, pl* **soliloquies. 1** the act of speaking alone or to oneself, esp. as a theatrical device. **2** a speech in a play that is spoken in soliloquy. [C17: via LL *sōliloquium,* from L *sōlus* sole + *loquī* to speak]

> **USAGE NOTE** *Soliloquy* is sometimes wrongly used where *monologue* is meant. Both words refer to a long speech by one person, but a *monologue* can be addressed to other people, whereas in a *soliloquy* the speaker is always talking to himself or herself.

solipsism ('sɒlɪpˌsɪzəm) *n Philosophy.* the extreme form of scepticism

THESAURUS

solely *adv* **1-3** = **only,** alone, completely, entirely, exclusively, merely, single-handedly, singly

solemn *adj* **1, 2** = **formal,** august, awe-inspiring, ceremonial, ceremonious, dignified, grand, grave, imposing, impressive, majestic, momentous, stately **3** = **serious,** earnest, glum, grave, portentous, sedate, sober, staid, thoughtful **5** = **sacred,** devotional, hallowed, holy, religious, reverential, ritual, sanctified, venerable
Antonyms *adj* ≠ **formal:** informal, relaxed, unceremonious ≠ **serious:** bright, cheerful, chirpy (*inf.*), comical, frivolous, genial, happy, jovial, light-hearted, merry ≠ **sacred:** irreligious, irreverent, unholy

solemnity *n* **1** = **formality,** earnestness, grandeur, gravitas, gravity, impressiveness, momentousness, portentousness, seriousness **2** *often plural* = **ritual,** celebration, ceremonial, ceremony, formalities, observance, proceedings, rite

solemnize *vb* **1, 2** = **celebrate,** commemorate, honour, keep, observe, perform

solicit *vb* **1** = **request,** ask, beg, beseech, canvass, crave, entreat, implore, importune, petition, plead for, pray, seek, supplicate

solicitous *adj* **1** = **concerned,** anxious, apprehensive, attentive, careful, caring, earnest, troubled, uneasy, worried **2** = **eager,** zealous

solicitude *n* **1** = **concern,** anxiety, attentiveness, care, considerateness, consideration, regard, worry

solid *adj* **1, 2** = **firm,** compact, concrete, dense, hard, massed **3** = **continuous,** complete, unalloyed, unanimous, unbroken, undivided, uninterrupted, united, unmixed **4** = **sound,** genuine, good, pure, real, reliable **5** = **reliable,** constant, decent, dependable, estimable, law-abiding, level-headed, sensible, serious, sober, trusty, upright, upstanding, worthy **6, 10** = **strong,** stable, sturdy, substantial, unshakable
Antonyms *adj* ≠ **firm:** gaseous, hollow, liquid, permeable, unsubstantial ≠ **sound:** impure, unreliable, unsound ≠ **reliable:** flighty, irresponsible, unreliable, unsound, unstable, unsteady ≠ **strong:** crumbling, decaying, flimsy, precarious, shaky, unstable, unsteady

solidarity *n* = **unity,** accord, camaraderie, cohesion, community of interest, concordance, esprit de corps, harmony, like-mindedness, singleness of purpose, soundness, stability, team spirit, unanimity, unification

solidify *vb* **1** = **harden,** cake, coagulate, cohere, congeal, jell, set

which denies the possibility of any knowledge other than of one's own existence. [C19: from L *sōlus* alone + *ipse* self]
▸ **'solipsist** *n, adj* ▸ **,solip'sistic** *adj*

solitaire ('sɒlɪˌtɛə, ˌsɒlɪ'tɛə) *n* **1** Also called: **pegboard.** a game played by one person, esp. one involving moving and taking pegs in a pegboard with the object of being left with only one. **2** the US name for **patience** (the card game). **3** a gem, esp. a diamond, set alone in a ring. **4** any of several extinct birds related to the dodo. **5** any of several dull grey North American songbirds. [C18: from OF: SOLITARY]

solitary ⓘ ('sɒlɪtərɪ, -trɪ) *adj* **1** following or enjoying a life of solitude: *a solitary disposition.* **2** experienced or performed alone: *a solitary walk.* **3** (of a place) unfrequented. **4** (*prenominal*) single; sole: *a solitary cloud.* **5** having few companions; lonely. **6** (of animals) not living in organized colonies or large groups: *solitary bees.* **7** (of flowers) growing singly. ◆ *n, pl* **solitaries. 8** a person who lives in seclusion; hermit. **9** *Inf.* short for **solitary confinement.** [C14: from L *sōlitārius,* from *sōlus* SOLE[1]]
▸ **'solitarily** *adv* ▸ **'solitariness** *n*

solitary confinement *n* isolation imposed on a prisoner, as by confinement in a special cell.

solitude ⓘ ('sɒlɪˌtju:d) *n* **1** the state of being solitary or secluded. **2** *Poetic.* a solitary place. [C14: from L *sōlitūdō,* from *sōlus* alone, SOLE[1]]
▸ **,soli'tudinous** *adj*

solmization *or* **solmisation** (ˌsɒlmɪ'zeɪʃən) *n Music.* a system of naming the notes of a scale by syllables instead of letters, which assigns the names *ut* (or *do*), *re, mi, fa, sol, la, si* (or *ti*) to the degrees of the major scale of C (**fixed system**) or (excluding the syllables *ut* and *si*) to the major scale in any key (**movable system**). See also **tonic sol-fa.** [C18: from F *solmisation,* from *solmiser* to use the sol-fa syllables, from SOL[1] + MI]

solo ('səʊləʊ) *n, pl* **solos. 1** (*pl* **solos** *or* **soli** (-li:)). a musical composition for one performer with or without accompaniment. **2** any of various card games in which each person plays on his own, such as solo whist. **3** a flight in which an aircraft pilot is unaccompanied. **4a** any performance carried out by an individual without assistance. **4b** (*as modifier*): *a solo attempt.* ◆ *adj* **5** *Music.* unaccompanied: *a sonata for cello solo.* ◆ *adv* **6** by oneself; alone: *to fly solo.* ◆ *vb* **7** (*intr*) to operate an aircraft alone. [C17: via It. from L *sōlus* alone]
▸ **soloist** ('səʊləʊɪst) *n*

Solomon ('sɒləmən) *n* any person credited with great wisdom. [after 10th-cent. B.C. king of Israel]
▸ **Solomonic** (ˌsɒlə'mɒnɪk) *adj*

Solomon's seal *n* **1** another name for **Star of David. 2** any of several plants of N temperate regions, having greenish or yellow paired flowers, long narrow waxy leaves, and prominent leaf scars. [C16: translation of Med. L *sigillum Solomonis,* ?from resemblance of the leaf scars to seals]

Solon ('səʊlən) *n* a wise lawmaker. [after Athenian statesman (?638–?559 B.C.), who introduced economic, political, and legal reforms]

so long *sentence substitute.* **1** *Inf.* farewell; goodbye. ◆ *adv* **2** *S. African sl.* for the time being; meanwhile.

solo whist *n* a version of whist for four players acting independently, each of whom may bid to win or lose a fixed number of tricks.

solstice ('sɒlstɪs) *n* **1** either the shortest day of the year (**winter solstice**) or the longest day of the year (**summer solstice**). **2** either of the two points on the ecliptic at which the sun is overhead at the tropic of Cancer or Capricorn at the summer and winter solstices. [C13: via OF from L *sōlstitium,* lit.: the (apparent) standing still of the sun, from *sōl* sun + *sistere* to stand still]
▸ **solstitial** (sɒl'stɪʃəl) *adj*

soluble ('sɒljʊbᵊl) *adj* **1** (of a substance) capable of being dissolved, esp. easily dissolved. **2** capable of being solved or answered. [C14: from LL *solūbilis,* from L *solvere* to dissolve]
▸ **,solu'bility** *n* ▸ **'solubly** *adv*

solus ('səʊləs) *adj* **1** alone; separate. **2** of or denoting the position of an advertising poster or press advertisement that is separated from competing advertisements: *a solus position.* **3** of or denoting a retail outlet, such as a petrol station, that sells the products of one company exclusively: *a solus site.* **4** (*fem* **sola**) alone; by oneself (formerly used in stage directions). [C17: from L *sōlus* alone]

solute ('sɒlju:t) *n* **1** the substance in a solution that is dissolved. ◆ *adj* **2** *Bot.* loose or unattached; free. [C16: from L *solūtus* free, from *solvere* to release]

solution ⓘ (sə'lu:ʃən) *n* **1** a homogeneous mixture of two or more substances in which the molecules or atoms of the substances are completely dispersed. **2** the act or process of forming a solution. **3** the state of being dissolved (esp. in **in solution**). **4** a mixture of substances in which one or more components are present as small particles with colloidal dimension: *a colloidal solution.* **5** a specific answer to or way of answering a problem. **6** the act or process of solving a problem. **7** *Maths.* **7a** the unique set of values that yield a true statement when substituted for the variables in an equation. **7b** a member of a set of assignments of values to variables under which a given statement is satisfied; a member of a solution set. [C14: from L *solūtiō* an unloosing, from *solūtus;* see SOLUTE]

solution set *n* another name for **truth set.**

Solutrean (sə'lu:trɪən) *adj* of or relating to an Upper Palaeolithic culture of Europe. [C19: after *Solutré,* village in central France where traces of this culture were orig. found]

solvation (sɒl'veɪʃən) *n* the process in which there is some chemical association between the molecules of a solute and those of the solvent.

Solvay process ('sɒlveɪ) *n* an industrial process for manufacturing sodium carbonate. Carbon dioxide is passed into a solution of sodium chloride saturated with ammonia. Sodium bicarbonate is precipitated and heated to form the carbonate. [C19: after Ernest *Solvay* (1838–1922), Belgian chemist who invented it]

solve ⓘ (sɒlv) *vb* **solves, solving, solved.** (*tr*) **1** to find the explanation for or solution to (a mystery, problem, etc.). **2** *Maths.* **2a** to work out the answer to (a problem). **2b** to obtain the roots of (an equation). [C15: from L *solvere* to loosen]
▸ **'solvable** *adj*

solvent ⓘ ('sɒlvənt) *adj* **1** capable of meeting financial obligations. **2** (of a substance, esp. a liquid) capable of dissolving another substance. ◆ *n* **3** a liquid capable of dissolving another substance. **4** something that solves. [C17: from L *solvēns* releasing, from *solvere* to free]
▸ **'solvency** *n*

solvent abuse *n* the deliberate inhaling of intoxicating fumes given off by certain solvents.

Som. *abbrev. for* Somerset.

soma[1] ('səʊmə) *n, pl* **somata** (-mətə) *or* **somas.** the body of an organism, as distinct from the germ cells. [C19: via NL from Gk *sōma* the body]

soma[2] ('səʊmə) *n* an intoxicating plant juice drink used in Vedic rituals. [from Sansk.]

Somali (səʊ'mɑ:lɪ) *n* **1** (*pl* **Somalis** *or* **Somali**) a member of a tall dark-skinned people inhabiting Somalia in NE Africa. **2** the Cushitic language of this people. ◆ *adj* **3** of, relating to, or characteristic of Somalia, the Somalis, or their language.

somatic (səʊ'mætɪk) *adj* **1** of or relating to the soma: *somatic cells.* **2** of or relating to an animal body or body wall as distinct from the viscera, limbs, and head. **3** of or relating to the human body as distinct from the mind: *a somatic disease.* [C18: from Gk *sōmatikos* concerning the body, from *sōma* the body]
▸ **so'matically** *adv*

somato- *or before a vowel* **somat-** *combining form.* body: *somatotype.* [from Gk *sōma, sōmat-* body]

somatogenic (səˌmætəʊ'dʒɛnɪk) *adj Med.* originating in the cells of the body: of organic, rather than mental, origin: *a somatogenic disorder.*

somatotype ('səʊmətəˌtaɪp) *n* a type or classification of physique or body build. See **endomorph, mesomorph, ectomorph.**

sombre ⓘ *or US* **somber** ('sɒmbə) *adj* **1** dismal; melancholy: *a sombre mood.* **2** dim, gloomy, or shadowy. **3** (of colour, clothes, etc.) sober, dull, or dark. [C18: from F, from Vulgar L *subumbrāre* (unattested) to shade, from L *sub* beneath + *umbra* shade]
▸ **'sombrely** *or US* **'somberly** *adv* ▸ **'sombreness** *or US* **'somberness** *n*
▸ **sombrous** ('sɒmbrəs) *adj*

sombrero (sɒm'brɛərəʊ) *n, pl* **sombreros.** a hat with a wide brim, as worn in Mexico. [C16: from Sp., from *sombrero de sol* shade from the sun]

some (sʌm; *unstressed* səm) *determiner* **1a** (a) certain unknown or unspecified: *some people never learn.* **1b** (*as pron; functioning as sing or pl*): *some can teach and others can't.* **2a** an unknown or unspecified quantity or amount of: *there's some rice on the table; he owns some horses.* **2b** (*as pron; functioning as sing or pl*): *we'll buy some.* **3a** a considerable number or amount of: *he lived some years afterwards.* **3b** a little: *show him some respect.* **4** (*usually stressed*) *Inf.* an impressive or remarkable: *that was some game!* ◆ *adv* **5** about; approximately: *some thirty pounds.* **6** a certain amount (more) (in **some more** and (*inf.*) **and then some**). **7** *US, not standard.* to a certain degree or extent: *I like him some.* [OE *sum*]

-some[1] *suffix forming adjectives.* characterized by; tending to: *awesome; tiresome.* [OE *-sum*]

-some[2] *suffix forming nouns.* indicating a group of a specified number of members: *threesome.* [OE *sum,* special use of SOME (determiner)]

-some[3] (-səʊm) *n combining form.* a body: *chromosome.* [from Gk *sōma* body]

THESAURUS

solitary *adj* **1 = unsociable,** cloistered, hermitical, isolated, reclusive, retired, unsocial **3 = isolated,** desolate, hidden, out-of-the-way, remote, sequestered, unfrequented, unvisited **4 = single,** alone, lone, sole **5 = lonely,** companionless, friendless, lonesome ◆ *n* **8 = hermit,** introvert, loner (*inf.*), lone wolf, recluse
Antonyms *adj* ≠ **unsociable:** companionable, convivial, cordial, gregarious, outgoing, sociable, social ≠ **isolated:** bustling, busy, frequented, public, well-frequented ◆ *n* ≠ **hermit:** extrovert, mixer, socialite

solitude *n* **1 = isolation,** ivory tower, loneliness, privacy, reclusiveness, retirement, seclusion **2** *Poetic* **= wilderness,** desert, emptiness, waste, wasteland

solution *n* **1 = mixture,** blend, compound, emulsion, mix, solvent, suspension **2 = dissolving,** disconnection, dissolution, liquefaction, melting **5, 6 = answer,** clarification, elucidation, explanation, explication, key, resolution, result, solving, unfolding, unravelling

solve *vb* **1 = answer,** clarify, clear up, crack, decipher, disentangle, elucidate, explain, expound, get to the bottom of, interpret, resolve, suss (out) (*sl.*), unfold, unravel, work out

solvent *adj* **1 = financially sound,** in the black, solid, unindebted **2 = resolvent,** dissolvent

sombre *adj* **1 = gloomy,** dismal, doleful, funereal, grave, joyless, lugubrious, melancholy, mournful, sad, sepulchral, sober **2 = dark,** dim, drab, dull, dusky, gloomy, obscure, shadowy, shady, sober
Antonyms *adj* ≠ **gloomy:** bright, cheerful, chirpy (*inf.*), effusive, full of beans, genial, happy, lively, sunny, upbeat (*inf.*) ≠ **dark:** bright, colourful, dazzling, garish, gaudy

somebody ⓣ ('sʌmbədɪ) *pron* **1** some person; someone. ◆ *n, pl* **somebodies. 2** a person of great importance: *he is somebody in this town.*

> **USAGE NOTE** See at **everyone.**

someday ⓣ ('sʌm,deɪ) *adv* at some unspecified time in the (distant) future.
somehow ⓣ ('sʌm,haʊ) *adv* **1** in some unspecified way. **2** Also: **somehow or other.** by any means that are necessary.
someone ('sʌm,wʌn, -wən) *pron* some person; somebody.

> **USAGE NOTE** See at **everyone.**

someplace ('sʌm,pleɪs) *adv US & Canad. inf.* in, at, or to some unspecified place or region.
somersault *or* **summersault** ('sʌmə,sɔːlt) *n* **1a** a forward roll in which the head is placed on the ground and the trunk and legs are turned over it. **1b** a similar roll in a backward direction. **2** an acrobatic feat in which either of these rolls is performed in midair, as in diving or gymnastics. **3** a complete reversal of opinion, policy, etc. ◆ *vb* **4** (*intr*) to perform a somersault. [C16: from OF *soubresault,* prob. from OProvençal *sobresaut,* from *sobre* over (from L *super*) + *saut* a jump, leap (from L *saltus*)]
something ('sʌmθɪŋ) *pron* **1** an unspecified or unknown thing; some thing: *take something warm with you.* **2 something or other.** one unspecified thing or an alternative thing. **3** an unspecified or unknown amount: *something less than a hundred.* **4** an impressive or important person, thing, or event: *isn't that something?* ◆ *adv* **5** to some degree; a little; somewhat: *to look something like me.* **6** (foll. by an *adj*) *Inf.* (intensifier): *it hurts something awful.* **7 something else.** *Sl., chiefly US.* a remarkable person or thing.
-something *n combining form.* **a** a person whose age can be approximately expressed by a specified decade. **b** (*as modifier*): *the thirty-something market.* [C20: from the US television series *thirtysomething*]
sometime ('sʌm,taɪm) *adv* **1** at some unspecified point of time. ◆ *adj* **2** (*prenominal*) having been at one time; former: *the sometime President.*

> **USAGE NOTE** The form *sometime* should not be used to refer to a fairly long period of time: *he has been away for some time* (not *for sometime*).

sometimes ⓣ ('sʌm,taɪmz) *adv* **1** now and then; from time to time. **2** *Obs.* formerly; sometime.
someway ('sʌm,weɪ) *adv* in some unspecified manner.
somewhat ('sʌm,wɒt) *adv* (*not used with a negative*) rather; a bit: *she found it somewhat odd.*
somewhere ('sʌm,wɛə) *adv* **1** in, to, or at some unknown or unspecified place or point: *somewhere in England; somewhere between 3 and 4 o'clock.* **2 get somewhere.** *Inf.* to make progress.
sommelier ('sʌməl,jeɪ) *n* a wine waiter. [F: butler, via OF from OProvençal *saumalier* pack-animal driver, from LL *sagma* a pack-saddle, from Gk]
somnambulate (sɒm'næmbjʊ,leɪt) *vb* **somnambulates, somnambulating, somnambulated.** (*intr*) to walk while asleep. [C19: from L *somnus* sleep + *ambulāre* to walk]
▸**som'nambulance** *n* ▸**som'nambulant** *adj, n* ▸**som,nambu'lation** *n* ▸**som'nambu,lator** *n*
somnambulism (sɒm'næmbjʊ,lɪzəm) *n* a condition characterized by walking while asleep or in a hypnotic trance. Also called: **noctambulism.**
▸**som'nambulist** *n*
somniferous (sɒm'nɪfərəs) *or* **somnific** *adj Rare.* tending to induce sleep.
somnolent ⓣ ('sɒmnələnt) *adj* **1** drowsy; sleepy. **2** causing drowsiness. [C15: from L *somnus* sleep]
▸**'somnolence** *or* **'somnolency** *n* ▸**'somnolently** *adv*
son (sʌn) *n* **1** a male offspring; a boy or man in relation to his parents. **2** a male descendant. **3** (*often cap.*) a familiar term of address for a boy or man. **4** a male from a certain country, environment, etc.: *a son of the circus.* ◆ Related adj: **filial.** [OE *sunu*]
▸**'sonless** *adj*
Son (sʌn) *n Christianity.* the second person of the Trinity, Jesus Christ.
sonant ('səʊnənt) *adj* **1** *Phonetics.* denoting a voiced sound capable of forming a syllable or syllable nucleus. **2** inherently possessing, exhibiting, or producing a sound. **3** *Rare.* resonant; sounding. ◆ *n* **4** *Phonetics.* a voiced sound belonging to the class of frictionless continuants or nasals (l, r, m, n, ŋ) considered from the point of view of being a vowel and, in this capacity, able to form a syllable or syllable nucleus. [C19: from L *sonāns* sounding, from *sonāre* to make a noise, resound]
▸**'sonance** *n*
sonar ('səʊnɑː) *n* a communication and position-finding device used in underwater navigation and target detection using echolocation. [C20: from *so(und) na(vigation and) r(anging)*]
sonata (sə'nɑːtə) *n* **1** an instrumental composition, usually in three or more movements, for piano alone (**piano sonata**) or for any other instrument with or without piano accompaniment (**violin sonata, cello sonata,** etc.). See also **sonata form. 2** a one-movement keyboard composition of the baroque period. [C17: from It., from *sonare* to sound, from L]
sonata form *n* a musical structure consisting of an expanded ternary form whose three sections (exposition, development, and recapitulation), followed by a coda, are characteristic of the first movement in a sonata, symphony, string quartet, concerto, etc.
sondage (sɒn'dɑːʒ) *n, pl* **sondages** (-'dɑːʒɪz, -'dɑːʒ). *Archaeol.* a deep trial trench for inspecting stratigraphy. [C20: from F: a sounding, from *sonder* to sound]
sonde (sɒnd) *n* a rocket, balloon, or probe used for observing in the upper atmosphere. [C20: from F: plummet, plumb line; see SOUND[3]]
sone (səʊn) *n* a unit of loudness equal to 40 phons. [C20: from L *sonus* a sound]
son et lumière ('sɒn eɪ 'luːmɪ,ɛə) *n* an entertainment staged at night at a famous building, historical site, etc., whereby the history of the location is presented by means of lighting effects, sound effects, and narration. [F, lit.: sound and light]
song ⓣ (sɒŋ) *n* **1a** a piece of music, usually employing a verbal text, composed for the voice, esp. one intended for performance by a soloist. **1b** the whole repertory of such pieces. **1c** (*as modifier*): *a song book.* **2** poetical composition; poetry. **3** the characteristic tuneful call or sound made by certain birds or insects. **4** the act or process of singing: *they raised their voices in song.* **5 for a song.** at a bargain price. **6 on song.** *Brit. inf.* performing at peak efficiency or ability. [OE *sang*]
song and dance ⓣ *n Inf.* **1** *Brit.* a fuss, esp. one that is unnecessary. **2** *US & Canad.* a long or elaborate story or explanation.
songbird ('sɒŋ,bɜːd) *n* **1** any of a suborder of passerine birds having highly developed vocal organs and, in most, a musical call. **2** any bird having a musical call.
song cycle *n* any of several groups of songs written during and after the Romantic period, each series relating a story or grouped around a central motif.
songololo (,sɒŋgɒ'lɒlɒ) *n, pl* **songololos.** *S. African.* a millipede. [from Nguni, from *ukusonga* to roll up]
songster ('sɒŋstə) *n* **1** a singer or poet. **2** a singing bird; songbird.
▸**'songstress** *fem n*
song thrush *n* a common Old World thrush with a spotted breast, noted for its song.
songwriter ('sɒŋ,raɪtə) *n* a person who composes songs in a popular idiom.
sonic ('sɒnɪk) *adj* **1** of, involving, or producing sound. **2** having a speed about equal to that of sound in air. [C20: from L *sonus* sound]
sonic barrier *n* another name for **sound barrier.**
sonic boom *n* a loud explosive sound caused by the shock wave of an aircraft, etc., travelling at supersonic speed.
sonic depth finder *n* an instrument for detecting the depth of water or of a submerged object by means of sound waves; Fathometer.
sonics ('sɒnɪks) *n* (*functioning as sing*) *Physics.* the study of mechanical vibrations in matter.
son-in-law *n, pl* **sons-in-law.** the husband of one's daughter.
sonnet ('sɒnɪt) *Prosody.* ◆ *n* **1** a verse form consisting of 14 lines in iambic pentameter with a fixed rhyme scheme, usually divided into octave and sestet or, in the English form, into three quatrains and a couplet. ◆ *vb* **2** (*intr*) to compose sonnets. **3** (*tr*) to celebrate in a sonnet. [C16: via It. from OProvençal *sonet* a little poem, from *son* song, from L *sonus* a sound]
sonneteer (,sɒnɪ'tɪə) *n* a writer of sonnets.
sonny ('sʌnɪ) *n, pl* **sonnies.** *Often patronizing.* a familiar term of address to a boy or man.
sonobuoy ('səʊnə,bɔɪ) *n* a buoy equipped to detect underwater noises and transmit them by radio. [SONIC + BUOY]
sonorant ('sɒnərənt) *n Phonetics.* **1** one of the frictionless continuants or nasals (l, r, m, n, ŋ) having consonantal or vocalic functions depending on its situation within the syllable. **2** either of the two con-

THESAURUS

somebody *n* **2** = **celebrity,** big hitter, big name, big noise (*inf.*), big shot (*inf.*), bigwig (*inf.*), dignitary, heavyweight (*inf.*), household name, luminary, megastar (*inf.*), name, notable, personage, public figure, star, superstar, V.I.P.
Antonyms *n* also-ran, cipher, lightweight (*inf.*), menial, nobody, nonentity, nothing (*inf.*)
someday *adv* = **eventually,** in the fullness of time, one day, one of these (fine) days, sooner or later, ultimately
somehow *adv* **2** = **one way or another,** by fair means or foul, by hook or (by) crook, by some means or other, come hell or high water (*inf.*), come what may
sometimes *adv* **1** = **occasionally,** at times, every now and then, every so often, from time to time, now and again, now and then, off and on, once in a while, on occasion
Antonyms *adv* always, consistently, constantly, continually, eternally, ever, everlastingly, evermore, forever, invariably, perpetually, unceasingly, without exception
somnolent *adj* **1** = **sleepy,** comatose, dozy, drowsy, half-awake, heavy-eyed, nodding off (*inf.*), soporific, torpid
song *n* **1** = **ballad,** air, anthem, canticle, canzonet, carol, chant, chorus, ditty, hymn, lay, lyric, melody, number, pop song, psalm, shanty, strain, tune
song and dance *n* **1** *Brit. informal* = **fuss,** ado, commotion, flap, hoo-ha, kerfuffle (*inf.*), pantomime (*inf.*), performance (*inf.*), pother, shindig (*inf.*), stir, to-do

sonants represented in English orthography by *w* or *y* and regarded as either consonantal or vocalic articulations of the vowels (iː) and (uː).

sonorous ❶ (səˈnɔːrəs, ˈsɒnərəs) *adj* **1** producing or capable of producing sound. **2** (of language, sound, etc.) deep or resonant. **3** (esp. of speech) high-flown; grandiloquent. [C17: from L *sonōrus* loud, from *sonor* a noise]
▸**sonority** (səˈnɒrɪtɪ) *n* ▸**soˈnorously** *adv* ▸**soˈnorousness** *n*

sonsy *or* **sonsie** (ˈsɒnsɪ) *adj* **sonsier, sonsiest.** *Scot., Irish, & English dialect.* **1** plump; buxom. **2** cheerful; good-natured. **3** lucky. [C16: from Gaelic *sonas* good fortune]

sook (sʊk) *n* **1** *SW English dialect.* a baby. **2** *Derog.* a coward. [?from OE *sūcan* to suck, infl. by Welsh *swci swead* tame]

sool (suːl) *vb* (*tr*) *Austral. & NZ sl.* **1** to incite (esp. a dog) to attack. **2** to attack.
▸ˈ**sooler** *n*

soon ❶ (suːn) *adv* **1** in or after a short time; in a little while; before long. **2 as soon as.** at the very moment that: *as soon as she saw him.* **3 as soon ... as.** used to indicate that the second alternative is not preferable to the first: *I'd just as soon go by train as drive.* [OE *sōna*]

sooner (ˈsuːnə) *adv* **1** the comparative of **soon**: *he came sooner than I thought.* **2** rather; in preference: *I'd sooner die than give up.* **3 no sooner ... than.** immediately after or when: *no sooner had he got home than the rain stopped.* **4 sooner or later.** eventually; inevitably.

> **USAGE NOTE** *When* is sometimes used instead of *than* after *no sooner*, but this use is generally regarded as incorrect: *no sooner had he arrived than* (not *when*) *the telephone rang.*

soot (sʊt) *n* **1** finely divided carbon deposited from flames during the incomplete combustion of organic substances such as coal. ◆ *vb* **2** (*tr*) to cover with soot. [OE *sōt*]

sooth (suːθ) *Arch. or poetic.* ◆ *n* **1** truth or reality (esp. in **in sooth**). ◆ *adj* **2** true or real. [OE *sōth*]

soothe ❶ (suːð) *vb* **soothes, soothing, soothed. 1** (*tr*) to make calm or tranquil. **2** (*tr*) to relieve or assuage (pain, longing, etc.). **3** (*intr*) to bring tranquillity or relief. [C16 (in the sense: to mollify): from OE *sōthian* to prove]
▸ˈ**soother** *n* ▸ˈ**soothing** *adj* ▸ˈ**soothingly** *adv* ▸ˈ**soothingness** *n*

soothsayer ❶ (ˈsuːθˌseɪə) *n* a seer or prophet.

sooty (ˈsʊtɪ) *adj* **sootier, sootiest. 1** covered with soot. **2** resembling or consisting of soot.
▸ˈ**sootily** *adv* ▸ˈ**sootiness** *n*

sop (sɒp) *n* **1** (*often pl*) food soaked in a liquid before being eaten. **2** a concession, bribe, etc., given to placate or mollify: *a sop to one's feelings.* **3** *Inf.* a stupid or weak person. ◆ *vb* **sops, sopping, sopped. 4** (*tr*) to dip or soak (food) in liquid. **5** (when *intr*, often foll. by *in*) to soak or be soaked. **6** (*tr*; often foll. by *up*) to mop or absorb (liquid) as with a sponge. [OE *sopp*]

SOP *abbrev. for* standard operating procedure.

sop. *abbrev. for* soprano.

sophism (ˈsɒfɪzəm) *n* an instance of sophistry. Cf. **paralogism.** [C14: from L *sophisma*, from Gk: ingenious trick, from *sophizesthai* to use clever deceit, from *sophos* wise]

sophist (ˈsɒfɪst) *n* **1** a person who uses clever or quibbling but unsound arguments. **2** one of the pre-Socratic philosophers who were prepared to enter into debate on any subject however specious. [C16: from L *sophista*, from Gk *sophistēs* a wise man, from *sophizesthai* to act craftily]

sophistic (səˈfɪstɪk) *or* **sophistical** *adj* **1** of or relating to sophists or sophistry. **2** consisting of sophisms or sophistry; specious.
▸**soˈphistically** *adv*

sophisticate ❶ *vb* (səˈfɪstɪˌkeɪt), **sophisticates, sophisticating, sophisticated. 1** (*tr*) to make (someone) less natural or innocent, as by education. **2** to pervert or corrupt (an argument, etc.) by sophistry. **3** (*tr*) to make more complex or refined. **4** *Rare.* to falsify (a text, etc.) by alterations. ◆ *n* (səˈfɪstɪˌkeɪt, -kɪt). **5** a sophisticated person. [C14: from Med. L *sophisticāre*, from L *sophisticus* sophistic]
▸**soˌphistiˈcation** *n* ▸**soˈphistiˌcator** *n*

sophisticated ❶ (səˈfɪstɪˌkeɪtɪd) *adj* **1** having refined or cultured tastes and habits. **2** appealing to sophisticates: *a sophisticated restaurant.* **3** unduly refined or cultured. **4** pretentiously or superficially wise. **5** (of machines, methods, etc.) complex and refined.

sophistry ❶ (ˈsɒfɪstrɪ) *n, pl* **sophistries. 1a** a method of argument that is seemingly plausible though actually invalid and misleading. **1b** the art of using such arguments. **2** subtle but unsound or fallacious reasoning. **3** an instance of this.

sophomore (ˈsɒfəˌmɔː) *n Chiefly US & Canad.* a second-year student at a secondary (high) school or college. [C17: ?from earlier *sophumer*, from *sophum*, var. of SOPHISM, + -ER¹]

Sophy *or* **Sophi** (ˈsəʊfɪ) *n, pl* **Sophies.** (formerly) a title of the Persian monarchs. [C16: from L *sophī* wise men, from Gk *sophos* wise]

-sophy *n combining form.* indicating knowledge or an intellectual system: *philosophy.* [from Gk, from *sophia* wisdom, from *sophos* wise]
▸**-sophic** *or* **-sophical** *adj combining form.*

soporific ❶ (ˌsɒpəˈrɪfɪk) *adj also* (*arch.*) ˌ**soporˈiferous. 1** inducing sleep. **2** drowsy; sleepy. ◆ *n* **3** a drug or other agent that induces sleep. [C17: from F, from L *sopor* sleep + -FIC]

sopping (ˈsɒpɪŋ) *adj* completely soaked; wet through. Also: **sopping wet.**

soppy ❶ (ˈsɒpɪ) *adj* **soppier, soppiest. 1** wet or soggy. **2** *Brit. inf.* silly or sentimental. **3 soppy on.** *Brit. inf.* foolishly charmed or affected by.
▸ˈ**soppily** *adv* ▸ˈ**soppiness** *n*

sopranino (ˌsɒprəˈniːnəʊ) *n, pl* **sopraninos. a** the instrument with the highest possible pitch in a family of instruments. **b** (*as modifier*): *a sopranino recorder.* [It., dim. of SOPRANO]

soprano (səˈprɑːnəʊ) *n, pl* **sopranos** *or* **soprani** (-ˈprɑːniː). **1** the highest adult female voice. **2** the voice of a young boy before puberty. **3** a singer with such a voice. **4** the highest part of a piece of harmony. **5a** the highest or second highest instrument in a family of instruments. **5b** (*as modifier*): *a soprano saxophone.* ◆ See also **treble.** [C18: from It., from *sopra* above, from L *suprā*]

soprano clef *n* the clef that establishes middle C as being on the bottom line of the staff.

sorb (sɔːb) *n* **1** another name for **service tree. 2** any of various related trees, esp. the mountain ash. **3** Also called: **sorb apple.** the fruit of any of these trees. [C16: from L *sorbus*]

sorbefacient (ˌsɔːbɪˈfeɪʃənt) *adj* **1** inducing absorption. ◆ *n* **2** a sorbefacient drug. [C19: from L *sorbē(re)* to absorb + -FACIENT]

sorbet (ˈsɔːbeɪ, -bɪt) *n* **1** a water ice made from fruit juice, egg whites, etc. **2** a US word for **sherbet** (sense 1). [C16: from F, from OIt. *sorbetto*, from Turkish *şerbet*, from Ar. *sharbah* a drink]

sorbic acid (ˈsɔːbɪk) *n* a white crystalline carboxylic acid found in berries of the mountain ash and used to inhibit the growth of moulds and as an additive (**E 200**) for certain synthetic coatings. [C19: from SORB (the tree), from its discovery in berries of the mountain ash]

sorbitol (ˈsɔːbɪˌtɒl) *n* a white crystalline alcohol, found in certain fruits and berries and manufactured by the catalytic hydrogenation of sucrose: used as a sweetener (**E 420**) and in the manufacture of ascorbic acid and synthetic resins. [C19: from SORB + -ITOL]

sorbo rubber (ˈsɔːbəʊ) *n Brit.* a spongy form of rubber. [C20: from ABSORB]

sorcerer ❶ (ˈsɔːsərə) *or* (*fem*) **sorceress** (ˈsɔːsərɪs) *n* a person who seeks to control and use magic powers; a wizard or magician. [C16: from OF *sorcier*, from Vulgar L *sortiārius* (unattested) caster of lots, from L *sors* lot]

sorcery ❶ (ˈsɔːsərɪ) *n, pl* **sorceries.** the art, practices, or spells of magic, esp. black magic. [C13: from OF *sorcerie*, from *sorcier* SORCERER]

sordid ❶ (ˈsɔːdɪd) *adj* **1** dirty, foul, or squalid. **2** degraded; vile; base. **3** selfish and grasping: *sordid avarice.* [C16: from L *sordidus*, from *sordēre* to be dirty]
▸ˈ**sordidly** *adv* ▸ˈ**sordidness** *n*

sordino (sɔːˈdiːnəʊ) *n, pl* **sordini** (-niː). **1** a mute for a stringed or brass musical instrument. **2** any of the dampers in a piano. **3 con sordino** *or* **sordini.** a musical direction to play with a mute. **4 senza sordino** *or* **sordini.** a musical direction to remove or play without the mute or (on the piano) with the sustaining pedal pressed down. [It.: from *sordo* deaf, from L *surdus*]

THESAURUS

sonorous *adj* **2 = rich**, deep, full, loud, plangent, resonant, resounding, ringing, rounded, sounding **3 = grandiloquent**, high-flown, high-sounding, orotund

soon *adv* **1 = before long**, anon, any minute now, betimes (*arch.*), erelong (*arch. or poetic*), in a couple of shakes, in a little while, in a minute, in a short time, in the near future, in two shakes of a lamb's tail, shortly

soothe *vb* **1 = calm**, allay, appease, calm down, compose, hush, lull, mitigate, mollify, pacify, quiet, settle, smooth down, soften, still, tranquillize **2 = relieve**, alleviate, assuage, ease
Antonyms *vb* ≠ **calm:** aggravate (*inf.*), agitate, annoy, disquiet, disturb, excite, get on one's nerves (*inf.*), hassle (*inf.*), inflame, irritate, rouse, upset, vex, worry ≠ **relieve:** exacerbate, increase, inflame, irritate, stimulate

soothing *adj* **1 = calming**, relaxing, restful **2 = emollient**, balsamic, demulcent, easeful, lenitive, palliative

soothsayer *n* **= prophet**, augur, diviner, fortune-teller, seer, sibyl

sophisticated *adj* **1-3 = cultured**, citified, cosmopolitan, cultivated, jet-set, refined, seasoned, urbane, worldly, worldly-wise, world-weary **5 = complex**, advanced, complicated, delicate, elaborate, highly-developed, intricate, multifaceted, refined, subtle
Antonyms *adj* ≠ **cultured:** naive, unrefined, unsophisticated, unworldly, wet behind the ears (*inf.*) ≠ **complex:** basic, old-fashioned, plain, primitive, simple, uncomplicated, unrefined, unsophisticated, unsubtle

sophistication *n* **1 = savoir-faire**, finesse, poise, *savoir-vivre*, urbanity, worldliness, worldly wisdom

sophistry *n* **1-3 = fallacy**, casuistry, quibble, sophism

soporific *adj* **1 = sleep-inducing**, hypnotic, sedative, sleepy, somniferous (*rare*), somnolent, tranquillizing ◆ *n* **3 = sedative**, anaesthetic, hypnotic, narcotic, opiate, tranquillizer

soppy *adj* **2** *Brit. informal* **= sentimental**, corny (*sl.*), daft (*inf.*), drippy, gushy (*inf.*), lovey-dovey, mawkish, overemotional, schmaltzy (*sl.*), silly, slushy (*inf.*), soft (*inf.*), weepy (*inf.*)

sorcerer *n* **= magician**, enchanter, mage (*arch.*), magus, necromancer, warlock, witch, wizard

sorcery *n* **= black magic**, black art, charm, divination, enchantment, incantation, magic, necromancy, spell, witchcraft, witchery, wizardry

sordid *adj* **1 = dirty**, filthy, foul, mean, seamy, seedy, sleazy, slovenly, slummy, squalid, unclean, wretched **2 = base**, debauched, degenerate, degraded, despicable, disreputable, low, shabby, shameful, vicious, vile **3 = mercenary**, avaricious, corrupt, covetous, grasping, miserly, niggardly, selfish, self-seeking, ungenerous, venal

sore Ⓣ (sɔː) *adj* **1** (esp. of a wound, injury, etc.) painfully sensitive; tender. **2** causing annoyance: *a sore point.* **3** resentful; irked. **4** urgent; pressing: *in sore need.* **5** (*postpositive*) grieved; distressed. **6** causing grief or sorrow. ◆ *n* **7** a painful or sensitive wound, injury, etc. **8** any cause of distress or vexation. ◆ *adv* **9** *Arch.* direly; sorely (now only in such phrases as **sore afraid**). [OE *sār*]
▸ **'soreness** *n*

sorehead ('sɔːˌhɛd) *n Inf., chiefly US & Canad.* a peevish or disgruntled person.

sorely ('sɔːlɪ) *adv* **1** painfully or grievously: *sorely wounded.* **2** pressingly or greatly: *to be sorely taxed.*

sorghum ('sɔːgəm) *n* any grass of the Old World genus *Sorghum,* having glossy seeds: cultivated for grain, hay, and as a source of syrup. [C16: from NL, from It. *sorgo,* prob. from Vulgar L *Syricum grānum* (unattested) Syrian grain]

soroptimist (sə'rɒptɪmɪst) *n* a member of Soroptimist International, an organization of clubs for professional and executive businesswomen.

sorority (sə'rɒrɪtɪ) *n, pl* **sororities.** *Chiefly US.* a social club or society for university women. [C16: from Med. L *sorōritās,* from L *soror* sister]

sorption ('sɔːpʃən) *n* the process in which one substance takes up or holds another; adsorption or absorption. [C20: back formation from ABSORPTION, ADSORPTION]

sorrel[1] ('sɒrəl) *n* **1a** a light brown to brownish-orange colour. **1b** (*as adj*)*: a sorrel carpet.* **2** a horse of this colour. [C15: from OF *sorel,* from *sor* a reddish brown, of Gmc origin]

sorrel[2] ('sɒrəl) *n* **1** any of several plants of Eurasia and North America, having acid-tasting leaves used in salads and sauces. **2** short for **wood sorrel.** [C14: from OF *surele,* from *sur* sour, of Gmc origin]

sorrow Ⓣ ('sɒrəʊ) *n* **1** the feeling of sadness, grief, or regret associated with loss, bereavement, sympathy for another's suffering, etc. **2** a particular cause or source of this. **3** Also called: **sorrowing.** the outward expression of grief or sadness. ◆ *vb* **4** (*intr*) to mourn or grieve. [OE *sorg*]
▸ **'sorrowful** *adj* ▸ **'sorrowfully** *adv* ▸ **'sorrowfulness** *n*

sorry Ⓣ ('sɒrɪ) *adj* **sorrier, sorriest. 1** (*usually postpositive;* often foll. by *for*) feeling or expressing pity, sympathy, grief, or regret: *I feel sorry for him.* **2** pitiful, wretched, or deplorable: *a sorry sight.* **3** poor; paltry: *a sorry excuse.* **4** affected by sorrow; sad. **5** causing sorrow or sadness. ◆ *interj* **6** an exclamation expressing apology. [OE *sārig*]
▸ **'sorrily** *adv* ▸ **'sorriness** *n*

sort Ⓣ (sɔːt) *n* **1** a class, group, kind, etc., as distinguished by some common quality or characteristic. **2** *Inf.* a type of character, nature, etc.: *he's a good sort.* **3** *Austral. sl.* a person, esp. a girl. **4** a more or less definable or adequate example: *it's a sort of review.* **5** (*often pl*) *Printing.* any of the individual characters making up a fount of type. **6** *Arch.* manner; way: *in this sort we struggled home.* **7 after a sort.** to some extent. **8 of sorts** *or* **of a sort. 8a** of an inferior kind. **8b** of an indefinite kind. **9 out of sorts.** not in normal good health, temper, etc. **10 sort of.** in some way or other; as it were; rather. ◆ *vb* **11** (*tr*) to arrange according to class, type, etc. **12** (*tr*) to put (something) into working order. **13** to arrange (computer information) by machine in an order convenient to the user. **14** (*intr*) *Arch.* to agree; accord. [C14: from OF, from Med. L *sors* kind, from L: fate]
▸ **'sortable** *adj* ▸ **'sorter** *n*

> **USAGE NOTE** See at **kind**[2].

sortie ('sɔːtɪ) *n* **1a** (of troops, etc.) the act of attacking from a contained or besieged position. **1b** the troops doing this. **2** an operational flight made by one aircraft. **3** a short or relatively short return trip. ◆ *vb* **sorties, sortieing, sortied. 4** (*intr*) to make a sortie. [C17: from F: a going out, from *sortir* to go out]

sortilege ('sɔːtɪlɪdʒ) *n* the act or practice of divination by drawing lots. [C14: via OF from Med. L *sortilegium,* from L *sortilegus* a soothsayer, from *sors* fate + *legere* to select]

sort out Ⓣ *vb* (*tr, adv*) **1** to find a solution to (a problem, etc.), esp. to make clear or tidy: *to sort out the mess.* **2** to take or separate, as from a larger group: *to sort out the likely ones.* **3** to organize into an orderly and disciplined group. **4** *Inf.* to beat or punish.

SOS *n* **1** an internationally recognized distress signal in which the letters SOS are repeatedly spelt out, as by radiotelegraphy: used esp. by ships and aircraft. **2** a message broadcast in an emergency for people otherwise unobtainable. **3** *Inf.* a call for help.

sosatie (sə'sɑːtɪ) *n S. African.* curried meat on skewers. [from Afrik., from Du.]

so-so Ⓣ *Inf.* ◆ *adj* **1** (*postpositive*) neither good nor bad. ◆ *adv* **2** in an average or indifferent manner.

sostenuto (ˌsɒstə'nuːtəʊ) *adj, adv Music.* to be performed in a smooth sustained manner. [C18: from It., from *sostenere* to sustain, from L *sustinēre*]

sot (sɒt) *n* **1** a habitual or chronic drunkard. **2** a person stupefied by or as if by drink. [OE, from Med. L *sottus*]
▸ **'sottish** *adj*

soteriology (sɒˌtɪərɪ'ɒlədʒɪ) *n Christian theol.* the doctrine of salvation. [C19: from Gk *sōtēria* deliverance (from *sōtēr* a saviour) + -LOGY]

sotto voce ('sɒtəʊ 'vəʊtʃɪ) *adv* in an undertone. [C18: from It.: under (one's) voice]

sou (suː) *n* **1** a former French coin of low denomination. **2** a very small amount of money: *I haven't a sou.* [C19: from F, from OF *sol,* from L: SOLIDUS]

soubrette (suː'brɛt) *n* **1** a minor female role in comedy, often that of a pert lady's maid. **2** any pert or flirtatious girl. [C18: from F: maidservant, from Provençal, from *soubret* conceited, from *soubra* to exceed, from L *superāre* to surmount]

soubriquet ('səʊbrɪˌkeɪ) *n* a variant spelling of **sobriquet.**

soufflé ('suːfleɪ) *n* **1** a light fluffy dish made with beaten egg whites combined with cheese, fish, etc. **2** a similar sweet or savoury cold dish, set with gelatine. ◆ *adj also* **souffléed. 3** made light and puffy, as by beating and cooking. [C19: from F, from *souffler* to blow, from L *sufflāre*]

sough (saʊ) *vb* **1** (*intr*) (esp. of the wind) to make a sighing sound. ◆ *n* **2** a soft continuous murmuring sound. [OE *swōgan* to resound]

sought (sɔːt) *vb* the past tense and past participle of **seek.**

souk (suːk) *n* an open-air marketplace in Muslim countries, esp. North Africa and the Middle East. [from Ar.]

soukous ('suːkʊs) *n* a style of African popular music that originated in Zaïre (now the Democratic Republic of the Congo), characterized by syncopated rhythms and intricate contrasting guitar melodies. [C20: ? from F *secouer* to shake]

soul Ⓣ (səʊl) *n* **1** the spirit or immaterial part of man, the seat of human personality, intellect, will, and emotions: regarded as an entity that survives the body after death. **2** *Christianity.* the spiritual part of a person, capable of redemption from sin through divine grace. **3** the essential part or fundamental nature of anything. **4** a person's feelings or moral nature. **5a** Also called: **soul music.** a type of Black music resulting from the addition of jazz, gospel, and pop elements to the urban blues style. **5b** (*as modifier*)*: a soul singer.* **6** (*modifier*) of or relating to Black Americans and their culture: *soul food.* **7** nobility of spirit or temperament: *a man of great soul.* **8** an inspiring or leading figure, as of a movement. **9** a person regarded as typifying some characteristic or quality: *the soul of discretion.* **10** a person; individual: *an honest soul.* **11 upon my soul!** an exclamation of surprise. [OE *sāwol*]

THESAURUS

Antonyms *adj* ≠ **dirty:** clean, fresh, pure, spotless, squeaky-clean, unblemished, undefiled, unsullied ≠ **base:** blameless, decent, honourable, noble, pure, upright

sore *adj* **1** = **painful,** angry, burning, chafed, inflamed, irritated, raw, reddened, sensitive, smarting, tender **2** = **annoying,** distressing, grievous, harrowing, severe, sharp, troublesome **3** = **annoyed,** afflicted, aggrieved, angry, cross, grieved, hurt, irked, irritated, pained, peeved (*inf.*), resentful, stung, upset, vexed **4** = **urgent,** acute, critical, desperate, dire, extreme, pressing ◆ *n* **7** = **abscess,** boil, chafe, gathering, inflammation, ulcer

sorrow *n* **1** = **grief,** affliction, anguish, distress, heartache, heartbreak, misery, mourning, regret, sadness, unhappiness, woe **2** = **affliction,** blow, bummer (*sl.*), hardship, misfortune, trial, tribulation, trouble, woe, worry ◆ *vb* **4** = **grieve,** agonize, bemoan, be sad, bewail, eat one's heart out, lament, moan, mourn, weep
Antonyms *n* ≠ **grief:** bliss, delight, elation, exaltation, exultation, gladness, happiness, joy, pleasure ≠ **affliction:** good fortune, lucky break ◆ *vb* ≠ **grieve:** celebrate, delight, exult, jump for joy, rejoice, revel

sorrowful *adj* **1** = **sad,** affecting, afflicted, dejected, depressed, disconsolate, dismal, distressing, doleful, down in the dumps (*inf.*), grieving, harrowing, heartbroken, heartrending, heavy-hearted, lamentable, lugubrious, melancholy, miserable, mournful, painful, piteous, rueful, sick at heart, sorry, tearful, unhappy, woebegone, woeful, wretched

sorry *adj* **1** = **regretful,** apologetic, commiserative, compassionate, conscience-stricken, contrite, guilt-ridden, in sackcloth and ashes, penitent, pitying, remorseful, repentant, self-reproachful, shamefaced, sympathetic **2, 3** = **wretched,** abject, base, deplorable, dismal, distressing, mean, miserable, paltry, pathetic, piteous, pitiable, pitiful, poor, sad, shabby, vile **4** = **sad,** disconsolate, distressed, grieved, melancholy, mournful, sorrowful, unhappy
Antonyms *adj* ≠ **regretful:** heartless, impenitent, indifferent, not contrite, shameless, unapologetic, unashamed, uncompassionate, unconcerned, unmoved, unpitying, unremorseful, unrepentant, unsympathetic ≠ **sad:** cheerful, delighted, elated, happy, joyful

sort *n* **1** = **kind,** brand, breed, category, character, class, denomination, description, family, genus, group, ilk, make, nature, order, quality, race, species, stamp, style, type, variety **9 out of sorts** = **in low spirits,** crotchety, down in the dumps (*inf.*), down in the mouth (*inf.*), grouchy (*inf.*), mopy, not up to par, not up to snuff (*inf.*), off colour, poorly (*inf.*), under the weather (*inf.*) **10 sort of** = **rather,** as it were, in part, moderately, reasonably, slightly, somewhat, to some extent ◆ *vb* **11** = **arrange,** assort, catalogue, categorize, choose, class, classify, distribute, divide, file, grade, group, order, put in order, rank, select, separate, sequence, systematize, tabulate

sort out *vb* **1** = **resolve,** clarify, clear up, put *or* get straight **2** = **separate,** pick out, put on one side, segregate, select, sift **3** = **organize,** tidy up

so-so *adj* **1** *Informal* = **average,** adequate, fair, fair to middling (*inf.*), indifferent, middling, moderate, not bad (*inf.*), O.K. *or* okay (*inf.*), ordinary, passable, respectable, run-of-the-mill, tolerable, undistinguished

soul *n* **1** = **spirit,** animating principle, essence, intellect, life, mind, psyche, reason, vital force **7** = **feeling,** animation, ardour, courage, energy, fervour, force, inspiration, vitality, vivacity **9** = **embodiment,** epitome, incarnation, personification, quintessence **10** = **person,** being, body, creature, individual, man *or* woman, mortal

soul-destroying ❶ *adj* (of an occupation, situation, etc.) unremittingly monotonous.

soul food *n Inf.* food, such as chitterlings, yams, etc., traditionally eaten by African-Americans.

soulful ❶ ('səʊlfʊl) *adj* expressing profound thoughts or feelings.
▸ **'soulfully** *adv* ▸ **'soulfulness** *n*

soulless ❶ ('səʊllɪs) *adj* **1** lacking humanizing qualities or influences; mechanical: *soulless work.* **2** (of a person) lacking in sensitivity or nobility.
▸ **'soullessness** *n*

soul mate *n* a person for whom one has a deep affinity, esp. a lover, wife, husband, etc.

soul-searching *n* **1** deep or critical examination of one's motives, actions, beliefs, etc. ◆ *adj* **2** displaying the characteristics of this.

sound[1] ❶ (saʊnd) *n* **1a** a periodic disturbance in the pressure or density of a fluid or in the elastic strain of a solid, produced by a vibrating object. It travels as longitudinal waves. **1b** (*as modifier*): *a sound wave.* **2** the sensation produced by such a periodic disturbance in the organs of hearing. **3** anything that can be heard. **4** (*modifier*) of or relating to radio as distinguished from television: *sound broadcasting.* **5** a particular instance or type of sound: *the sound of running water.* **6** volume or quality of sound: *a radio with poor sound.* **7** the area or distance over which something can be heard: *within the sound of Big Ben.* **8** impression or implication: *I don't like the sound of that.* **9** (*often pl*) *Sl.* music, esp. rock, jazz, or pop. ◆ *vb* **10** to cause (an instrument, etc.) to make a sound or (of an instrument, etc.) to emit a sound. **11** to announce or be announced by a sound: *to sound the alarm.* **12** (*intr*) (of a sound) to be heard. **13** (*intr*) to resonate with a certain quality or intensity: *to sound loud.* **14** (*copula*) to give the impression of being as specified: *to sound reasonable.* **15** (*tr*) to pronounce distinctly or audibly: *to sound one's consonants.* [C13: from OF *soner* to make a sound, from L *sonāre*, from *sonus* a sound]
▸ **'soundable** *adj*

sound[2] ❶ (saʊnd) *adj* **1** free from damage, injury, decay, etc. **2** firm; substantial: *a sound basis.* **3** financially safe or stable: *a sound investment.* **4** showing good judgment or reasoning; wise: *sound advice.* **5** valid, logical, or justifiable: *a sound argument.* **6** holding approved beliefs; ethically correct; honest. **7** (of sleep) deep; peaceful; unbroken. **8** thorough: *a sound examination.* ◆ *adv* **9** soundly; deeply: now archaic except when applied to sleep. [OE *sund*]
▸ **'soundly** *adv* ▸ **'soundness** *n*

sound[3] ❶ (saʊnd) *vb* **1** to measure the depth of (a well, the sea, etc.) by plumb line, sonar, etc. **2** to seek to discover (someone's views, etc.), as by questioning. **3** (*intr*) (of a whale, etc.) to dive downwards swiftly and deeply. **4** *Med.* **4a** to probe or explore (a bodily cavity or passage) by means of a sound. **4b** to examine (a patient) by means of percussion and auscultation. ◆ *n* **5** *Med.* an instrument for insertion into a bodily cavity or passage to dilate strictures, dislodge foreign material, etc. ◆ See also **sound out.** [C14: from OF *sonder*, from *sonde* sounding line, prob. of Gmc origin]
▸ **'sounder** *n*

sound[4] ❶ (saʊnd) *n* **1** a relatively narrow channel between two larger areas of sea or between an island and the mainland. **2** an inlet or deep bay of the sea. **3** the air bladder of a fish. [OE *sund* swimming, narrow sea]

soundalike ('saʊndəˌlaɪk) *n* **a** a person or thing that sounds like another, often well-known, person or thing. **b** (*as modifier*): *a soundalike band.*

sound barrier *n* (not in technical usage) a hypothetical barrier to flight at or above the speed of sound, when a sudden large increase in drag occurs. Also called: **sonic barrier.**

sound bite *n* a short pithy sentence or phrase extracted from a longer speech for use on radio or television.

soundbox ('saʊndˌbɒks) *n* the resonating chamber of the hollow body of a violin, guitar, etc.

sound effect *n* any sound artificially produced, reproduced from a recording, etc., to create a theatrical effect, as in plays, films, etc.

sounding[1] ('saʊndɪŋ) *adj* **1** resounding; resonant. **2** having an imposing sound and little content; pompous: *sounding phrases.*

sounding[2] ('saʊndɪŋ) *n* **1** (*sometimes pl*) the act or process of measuring depth of water or examining the bottom of a river, lake, etc., as with a sounding line. **2** an observation or measurement of atmospheric conditions, as made using a sonde. **3** (*often pl*) measurements taken by sounding. **4** (*pl*) a place where a sounding line will reach the bottom, esp. less than 100 fathoms in depth.

sounding board *n* **1** Also called: **soundboard.** a thin wooden board in a violin, piano, etc., serving to amplify the vibrations produced by the strings passing across it. **2** Also called: **soundboard.** a thin screen suspended over a pulpit, stage, etc., to reflect sound towards an audience. **3** a person, group, experiment, etc., used to test a new idea, policy, etc.

sounding line *n* a line marked off to indicate its length and having a **sounding lead** at one end. It is dropped over the side of a vessel to determine the depth of the water.

soundless ('saʊndlɪs) *adj* extremely still or silent.
▸ **'soundlessness** *n*

sound out ❶ *vb* (*tr, adv*) to question (someone) in order to discover (opinions, facts, etc.).

soundpost ('saʊndˌpəʊst) *n Music.* a small wooden post in guitars, violins, etc., that joins the front to the back and helps support the bridge.

soundproof ('saʊndˌpruːf) *adj* **1** not penetrable by sound. ◆ *vb* **2** (*tr*) to render soundproof.

sound spectrograph *n* an electronic instrument that produces a record (**sound spectrogram**) of the frequencies and intensities of the components of a sound.

sound system *n* **1** any system of sounds, as in the speech of a language. **2** integrated equipment for producing amplified sound, as in a hi-fi or mobile disco, or as a public-address system on stage.

soundtrack ('saʊndˌtræk) *n* **1** the recorded sound accompaniment to a film. **2** a narrow strip along the side of a spool of film, which carries the sound accompaniment.

sound wave *n* a wave that propagates sound.

soup (suːp) *n* **1** a liquid food made by boiling or simmering meat, fish, vegetables, etc. **2** *Inf.* a photographic developer. **3** *Inf.* anything resembling soup, esp. thick fog. **4** a slang name for **nitroglycerine. 5 in the soup.** *Sl.* in trouble or difficulties. [C17: from OF *soupe*, from LL *suppa*, of Gmc origin]
▸ **'soupy** *adj*

soupçon *French.* (supsõ) *n* a slight amount; dash. [C18: from F, ult. from L *suspicio* SUSPICION]

soup kitchen *n* **1** a place or mobile stall where food and drink, esp. soup, is served to destitute people. **2** *Mil.* a mobile kitchen.

soup plate *n* a deep plate with a wide rim, used esp. for drinking soup.

soup up *vb* (*tr, adv*) *Sl.* to modify the engine of (a car or motorcycle) in order to increase its power. Also: **hot up,** (esp. US and Canad.) **hop up.**

sour ❶ ('saʊə) *adj* **1** having or denoting a sharp biting taste like that of lemon juice or vinegar. **2** made acid or bad, as in the case of milk, by the action of microorganisms. **3** having a rancid or unwholesome smell. **4** (of a person's temperament) sullen, morose, or disagreeable. **5** (esp. of the weather) harsh and unpleasant. **6** disagreeable; distasteful: *a sour experience.* **7** (of land, etc.) lacking in fertility, esp. due to excessive acidity. **8** (of petrol, gas, etc.) containing a relatively large amount of sulphur compounds. **9 go** *or* **turn sour.** to become unfavourable or inharmonious: *his marriage went sour.* ◆ *n* **10** something sour. **11** *Chiefly US.* an iced drink usually made with spirits, lemon juice, and ice: *a whiskey sour.* **12** an acid used in bleaching clothes or in curing skins. ◆ *vb* **13** to make or become sour. [OE *sūr*]
▸ **'sourish** *adj* ▸ **'sourly** *adv* ▸ **'sourness** *n*

source ❶ (sɔːs) *n* **1** the point or place from which something originates. **2a** a spring that forms the starting point of a stream. **2b** the area where the headwaters of a river rise. **3** a person, group, etc., that creates, issues, or originates something: *the source of a complaint.* **4a** any person, book, organization, etc., from which information, evidence,

THESAURUS

soul-destroying *adj* = **mind-numbing**, dreary, dull, humdrum, monotonous, tedious, tiresome, treadmill, unvarying, wearisome

soulful *adj* = **expressive**, eloquent, heartfelt, meaningful, mournful, moving, profound, sensitive

soulless *adj* **1** = **spiritless**, dead, lifeless, mechanical, soul-destroying, uninteresting **2** = **unfeeling**, callous, cold, cruel, harsh, inhuman, unkind, unsympathetic

sound[1] *n* **2, 3, 5** = **noise**, din, report, resonance, reverberation, tone, voice **7** = **range**, earshot, hearing **8** = **impression**, drift, idea, implication(s), look, tenor ◆ *vb* **10, 12, 13** = **resound**, echo, resonate, reverberate **11** = **pronounce**, announce, articulate, declare, enunciate, express, signal, utter **14** = **seem**, appear, give the impression of, look, strike one as being

sound[2] *adj* **1, 2** = **perfect**, complete, entire, firm, fit, hale, hale and hearty, healthy, intact, robust, solid, sturdy, substantial, undamaged, unhurt, unimpaired, uninjured, vigorous, well-constructed, whole **3** = **safe**, established, proven, recognized, reliable, reputable, secure, solid, solvent, stable, tried-and-true **4-6** = **sensible**, correct, fair, just, level-headed, logical, orthodox, proper, prudent, rational, reasonable, reliable, responsible, right, right-thinking, true, trustworthy, valid, well-founded, well-grounded, wise **7** = **deep**, peaceful, unbroken, undisturbed, untroubled
Antonyms *adj* ≠ **perfect:** ailing, damaged, flimsy, frail, light, shaky, sketchy, superficial, unbalanced, unstable, weak ≠ **safe:** unreliable, unsound, unstable ≠ **sensible:** fallacious, faulty, flawed, irrational, irresponsible, specious ≠ **deep:** broken, fitful, shallow, troubled

sound[3] *vb* **1** = **fathom**, plumb, probe **2** = **examine**, inspect, investigate, test

sound[4] *n* **1** = **channel**, passage, strait **2** = **inlet**, arm of the sea, fjord, voe

sound out *vb* = **probe**, canvass, examine, pump, put out feelers to, question, see how the land lies, test the water

sour *adj* **1** = **sharp**, acetic, acid, acidulated, bitter, pungent, tart, unpleasant **2** = **gone off**, curdled, fermented, gone bad, rancid, turned, unsavoury, unwholesome **4** = **ill-natured**, acrid, acrimonious, churlish, crabbed, cynical, disagreeable, discontented, embittered, grouchy (*inf.*), grudging, ill-tempered, jaundiced, peevish, tart, ungenerous, waspish ◆ *vb* **13** = **embitter**, alienate, disenchant, envenom, exacerbate, exasperate, turn off (*inf.*)
Antonyms *adj* ≠ **sharp:** agreeable, bland, mild, pleasant, savoury, sugary, sweet ≠ **gone off:** fresh, unimpaired, unspoiled ≠ **ill-natured:** affable, amiable, congenial, friendly, genial, good-humoured, good-natured, good-tempered, pleasant, warm-hearted ◆ *vb* ≠ **embitter:** enhance, improve, strengthen

source *n* **1, 3** = **origin**, author, begetter, beginning, cause, commencement, derivation, fount, fountainhead, originator, rise, spring, wellspring **4** = **informant**, authority

etc., is obtained. **4b** (*as modifier*): *source material.* **5** anything, such as a story or work of art, that provides a model or inspiration for a later work. **6 at source.** at the point of origin. ◆ *vb* **sources, sourcing, sourced.** (*tr*) **7** to establish an originator or source of (a product, etc.). **8** (foll. by *from*) to originate from. [C14: from OF *sors*, from *sourdre* to spring forth, from L *surgere* to rise]

source program *n* an original computer program written by a programmer that is converted into the equivalent object program, written in machine language.

sour cherry *n* **1** a Eurasian tree with white flowers: cultivated for its tart red fruits. **2** the fruit.

sour cream *n* cream soured by lactic acid bacteria, used in making salads, dips, etc.

sourdough ('saʊəˌdəʊ) *Dialect.* ◆ *adj* **1** (of bread) made with fermented dough used as leaven. ◆ *n* **2** (in the Western US, Canada, and Alaska) an old-time prospector or pioneer.

sour gourd *n* **1** a large tree of N Australia, having gourdlike fruit. **2** the acid-tasting fruit. **3** the fruit of the baobab tree.

sour grapes *n* (*functioning as sing*) the attitude of affecting to despise something because one cannot have it oneself.

sourpuss **T** ('saʊəˌpʊs) *n Inf.* a person who is habitually gloomy or sullen.

sourveld ('saʊəˌfɛlt) *n* (in South Africa) a type of grazing characterized by long coarse grass. [from Afrik. *suur* sour + *veld* grassland]

sousaphone ('suːzəˌfəʊn) *n* a large tuba that encircles the player's body and has a bell facing forwards. [C20: after J. P. *Sousa* (1854–1932), US composer & bandmaster]
▸ **'sousaˌphonist** *n*

souse **T** (saʊs) *vb* **souses, sousing, soused.** **1** to plunge (something) into water or other liquid. **2** to drench or be drenched. **3** (*tr*) to pour or dash (liquid) over (a person or thing). **4** to steep or cook (food) in a marinade. **5** (*tr*) *Sl.* to make drunk. ◆ *n* **6** the liquid used in pickling. **7** the act or process of sousing. **8** *Sl.* a drunkard. [C14: from OF *sous*, of Gmc origin]

soutane (suː'tæn) *n RC Church.* a priest's cassock. [C19: from F, from OIt. *sottana*, from Med. L *subtanus* (adj) (worn) beneath, from L *subtus* below]

souterrain ('suːtəˌreɪn) *n Archaeol.* an underground chamber or passage. [C18: from F]

south (saʊθ) *n* **1** one of the four cardinal points of the compass, at 180° from north and 90° clockwise from east and anticlockwise from west. **2** the direction along a meridian towards the South Pole. **3 the south.** (*often cap.*) any area lying in or towards the south. **4** (*usually cap.*) *Cards.* the player or position corresponding to south on the compass. ◆ *adj* **5** in, towards, or facing the south. **6** (esp. of the wind) from the south. ◆ *adv* **7** in, to, or towards the south. [OE *sūth*]

South (saʊθ) *n* **the. 1** the southern part of England, generally regarded as lying to the south of an imaginary line between the Wash and the Severn. **2** (in the US) **2a** the states south of the Mason-Dixon Line that formed the Confederacy during the Civil War. **2b** the Confederacy itself. **3** the countries of the world that are not economically and technically advanced. ◆ *adj* **4** of or denoting the southern part of a specified country, area, etc.

southbound ('saʊθˌbaʊnd) *adj* going or leading towards the south.

south by east *n* **1** one point on the compass east of south. ◆ *adj, adv* **2** in, from, or towards this direction.

south by west *n* **1** one point on the compass west of south. ◆ *adj, adv* **2** in, from, or towards this direction.

Southdown ('saʊθˌdaʊn) *n* an English breed of sheep with short wool and a greyish-brown face and legs. [C18: so called because it was originally bred on the *South Downs* in SE England]

southeast (ˌsaʊθ'iːst; *Naut.* ˌsaʊ'iːst) *n* **1** the point of the compass or the direction midway between south and east. **2** (*often cap.*; usually preceded by *the*) any area lying in or towards this direction. ◆ *adj also* **southeastern. 3** (*sometimes cap.*) of or denoting the southeastern part of a specified country, area, etc. **4** in, towards, or facing the southeast. **5** (esp. of the wind) from the southeast. ◆ *adv* **6** in, to, or towards the southeast.
▸ **ˌsouth'easternmost** *adj*

Southeast (ˌsaʊθ'iːst) *n* (usually preceded by *the*) the southeastern part of Britain, esp. the London area.

southeast by east *n* **1** one point on the compass north of southeast. ◆ *adj, adv* **2** in, from, or towards this direction.

southeast by south *n* **1** one point on the compass south of southeast. ◆ *adj, adv* **2** in, from, or towards this direction.

southeaster (ˌsaʊθ'iːstə; *Naut.* ˌsaʊ'iːstə) *n* a strong wind or storm from the southeast.

southeasterly (ˌsaʊθ'iːstəlɪ; *Naut.* ˌsaʊ'iːstəlɪ) *adj, adv* **1** in, towards, or (esp. of the wind) from the southeast. ◆ *n, pl* **southeasterlies. 2** a strong wind or storm from the southeast.

southeastward (ˌsaʊθ'iːstwəd; *Naut.* ˌsaʊ'iːstwəd) *adj* **1** towards or (esp. of a wind) from the southeast. ◆ *n* **2** a direction towards or area in the southeast. ◆ *adv* **3** Also: **southeastwards.** towards the southeast.

souther ('saʊðə) *n* a strong wind or storm from the south.

southerly ('sʌðəlɪ) *adj* **1** of or situated in the south. ◆ *adv, adj* **2** towards the south. **3** from the south. ◆ *n, pl* **southerlies. 4** a wind from the south.
▸ **'southerliness** *n*

southern ('sʌðən) *adj* **1** in or towards the south. **2** (of a wind, etc.) coming from the south. **3** native to or inhabiting the south.
▸ **'southernˌmost** *adj*

Southern ('sʌðən) *adj* of, relating to, or characteristic of the south of a particular region or country.

Southern Cross *n* a small constellation in the S hemisphere whose four brightest stars form a cross. It is represented on the national flags of Australia and New Zealand.

Southerner ('sʌðənə) *n* (*sometimes not cap.*) a native or inhabitant of the south of any specified region, esp. the South of England or the Southern states of the US.

southern hemisphere *n* (*often caps.*) that half of the earth lying south of the equator.

southern lights *pl n* another name for **aurora australis.**

South Gloucestershire *n* a unitary authority of SW England, in Gloucestershire. Pop.: 220 000 (1996 est.). Area: 510 sq. km (197 sq. miles).

southing ('saʊðɪŋ) *n* **1** *Navigation.* movement, deviation, or distance covered in a southerly direction. **2** *Astron.* a south or negative declination.

southpaw ('saʊθˌpɔː) *Inf.* ◆ *n* **1** a left-handed boxer. **2** any left-handed person. ◆ *adj* **3** of or relating to a southpaw.

South Pole *n* **1** the southernmost point on the earth's axis, at the latitude of 90°S. **2** *Astron.* the point of intersection of the earth's extended axis and the southern half of the celestial sphere. **3** (*usually not caps.*) the south-seeking pole of a freely suspended magnet.

South Sea Bubble *n Brit. history.* the financial crash that occurred in 1720 after the **South Sea Company** had taken over the national debt in return for a monopoly of trade with the South Seas, causing feverish speculation in their stocks.

South Seas *pl n* the seas south of the equator.

south-southeast *n* **1** the point on the compass or the direction midway between southeast and south. ◆ *adj, adv* **2** in, from, or towards this direction.

south-southwest *n* **1** the point on the compass or the direction midway between south and southwest. ◆ *adj, adv* **2** in, from, or towards this direction.

southward ('saʊθwəd; *Naut.* 'sʌðəd) *adj* **1** situated, directed, or moving towards the south. ◆ *n* **2** the southward part, direction, etc. ◆ *adv* **3** Also: **southwards.** towards the south.

southwest (ˌsaʊθ'wɛst; *Naut.* ˌsaʊ'west) *n* **1** the point of the compass or the direction midway between west and south. **2** (*often cap.*; usually preceded by *the*) any area lying in or towards this direction. ◆ *adj also* **southwestern. 3** (*sometimes cap.*) of or denoting the southwestern part of a specified country, area, etc.: *southwest Italy.* **4** in or towards the southwest. **5** (esp. of the wind) from the southwest. ◆ *adv* **6** in, to, or towards the southwest.
▸ **ˌsouth'westernmost** *adj*

Southwest (ˌsaʊθ'wɛst) *n* (usually preceded by *the*) the southwestern part of Britain, esp. Cornwall, Devon, and Somerset.

southwest by south *n* **1** one point on the compass south of southwest. ◆ *adj, adv* **2** in, from, or towards this direction.

southwest by west *n* **1** one point on the compass north of southwest. ◆ *adj, adv* **2** in, from, or towards this direction.

southwester (ˌsaʊθ'wɛstə; *Naut.* ˌsaʊ'wɛstə) *n* a strong wind or storm from the southwest.

southwesterly (ˌsaʊθ'wɛstəlɪ; *Naut.* ˌsaʊ'wɛstəlɪ) *adj, adv* **1** in, towards, or (esp. of a wind) from the southwest. ◆ *n, pl* **southwesterlies. 2** a wind or storm from the southwest.

southwestward (ˌsaʊθ'wɛstwəd; *Naut.* ˌsaʊ'wɛstwəd) *adj* **1** from or towards the southwest. ◆ *adv* **2** Also: **southwestwards.** towards the southwest. ◆ *n* **3** a direction towards or area in the southwest.

souvenir **T** (ˌsuːvə'nɪə, 'suːvəˌnɪə) *n* **1** an object that recalls a certain place, occasion, or person; memento. **2** *Rare.* a thing recalled. ◆ *vb* **3** (*tr*) *Austral. & NZ. sl.* to steal or keep for one's own use; purloin. [C18: from F, from (*se*) *souvenir* to remember, from L *subvenīre* to come to mind]

sou'wester (saʊ'wɛstə) *n* a waterproof hat having a very broad rim behind, worn esp. by seamen. [C19: a contraction of SOUTHWESTER]

sovereign **T** ('sɒvrɪn) *n* **1** a person exercising supreme authority, esp. a monarch. **2** a former British gold coin worth one pound sterling. ◆ *adj* **3** supreme in rank or authority: *a sovereign lord.* **4** excellent or outstanding: *a sovereign remedy.* **5** of or relating to a sovereign. **6** independent of outside authority: *a sovereign state.* [C13: from OF *soverain*,

THESAURUS

sourpuss *n Informal* = **killjoy**, crosspatch (*inf.*), grouser, grump (*inf.*), misery (*Brit. inf.*), prophet of doom, shrew, wowser (*Austral. & NZ sl.*)

souse *vb* **1-4** = **steep**, drench, dunk, immerse, marinate (*Cookery*), pickle, soak

souvenir *n* **1** = **keepsake**, memento, relic, remembrancer (*arch.*), reminder, token

sovereign *n* **1** = **monarch**, chief, emperor *or* empress, king *or* queen, potentate, prince *or* princess, ruler, shah, supreme ruler, tsar *or* tsarina ◆ *adj* **3** = **supreme**, absolute, chief, dominant, imperial, kingly *or* queenly, monarchal, paramount, predominant, principal, regal, royal, ruling, unlimited **4** = **excellent**, effectual, efficacious, efficient

from Vulgar L *superānus* (unattested), from L *super* above; also infl. by REIGN]
▸ **'sovereignly** *adv*

sovereignty ❶ ('sɒvrəntɪ) *n, pl* **sovereignties. 1** supreme and unrestricted power, as of a state. **2** the position, dominion, or authority of a sovereign. **3** an independent state.

soviet ('səʊvɪət, 'sɒv-) *n* **1** (in the former Soviet Union) an elected government council at the local, regional, and national levels, culminating in the Supreme Soviet. ◆ *adj* **2** of or relating to a soviet. [C20: from Russian *sovyet* council, from ORussian sŭvětŭ]
▸ **'sovie,tism** *n*

Soviet ('səʊvɪət, 'sɒv-) *adj* of or relating to the former Soviet Union, its people, or its government.

sovietize *or* **sovietise** ('səʊvɪɪ,taɪz, 'sɒv-) *vb* **sovietizes, sovietizing, sovietized** *or* **sovietises, sovietising, sovietised.** (*tr*) (*often cap.*) **1** to bring (a country, person, etc.) under Soviet control or influence. **2** to cause (a country) to conform to the Soviet model in its social, political, and economic structure.
▸ **,sovieti'zation** *or* **,sovieti'sation** *n*

Soviets ('səʊvɪəts, 'sɒv-) *pl n* the people or government of the former Soviet Union.

sow[1] ❶ (səʊ) *vb* **sows, sowing, sowed; sown** *or* **sowed. 1** to scatter or place (seed, a crop, etc.) in or on (a piece of ground, field, etc.) so that it may grow: *to sow wheat; to sow a strip of land.* **2** (*tr*) to implant or introduce: *to sow a doubt in someone's mind.* [OE *sāwan*]
▸ **'sower** *n*

sow[2] (saʊ) *n* **1** a female adult pig. **2** the female of certain other animals, such as the mink. **3** *Metallurgy.* **3a** the channels for leading molten metal to the moulds in casting pig iron. **3b** iron that has solidified in these channels. [OE *sugu*]

sown (səʊn) *vb* a past participle of **sow**[1].

sow thistle (saʊ) *n* any of various plants of an Old World genus, having milky juice, prickly leaves, and heads of yellow flowers.

soya bean ('sɔɪə) *or US & Canad.* **soybean** ('sɔɪ,biːn) *n* **1** an Asian bean plant cultivated for its nutritious seeds, for forage, and to improve the soil. **2** the seed, used as food, forage, and as the source of an oil. [C17 *soya*, via Du. from Japanese *shōyu*, from Chinese *chiang yu*, from *chiang* paste + *yu* sauce]

soy sauce (sɔɪ) *n* a salty dark brown sauce made from fermented soya beans, used esp. in Chinese cookery. Also called: **soya sauce.**

sozzled ('sɒzəld) *adj* an informal word for **drunk.** [C19: ?from obs. *sozzle* stupor]

SP *abbrev. for* starting price.

sp. *abbrev. for:* **1** special. **2** (*pl* **spp.**) species. **3** specific. **4** specimen. **5** spelling.

Sp. *abbrev. for:* **1** Spain. **2** Spaniard. **3** Spanish.

spa (spɑː) *n* a mineral spring or a place or resort where such a spring is found. [C17: after *Spa*, a watering place in Belgium]

space ❶ (speɪs) *n* **1** the unlimited three-dimensional expanse in which all material objects are located. Related adj: **spatial. 2** an interval of distance or time between two points, objects, or events. **3** a blank portion or area. **4a** unoccupied area or room: *there is no space for a table.* **4b** (*in combination*): *space-saving.* Related adj: **spacious. 5a** the region beyond the earth's atmosphere containing other planets, stars, galaxies, etc.; universe. **5b** (*as modifier*): *a space probe.* **6** a seat or place, as on a train, aircraft, etc. **7** *Printing.* a piece of metal, less than type-high, used to separate letters or words. **8** *Music.* any of the gaps between the lines that make up the staff. **9** Also called: **spacing.** *Telegraphy.* the period of time that separates characters in Morse code. ◆ *vb* **spaces, spacing, spaced.** (*tr*) **10** to place or arrange at intervals or with spaces between. **11** to divide into or by spaces: *to space one's time evenly.* **12** *Printing.* to separate (letters, words, or lines) by the insertion of spaces. [C13: from OF *espace*, from L *spatium*]
▸ **'spacer** *n*

space age *n* **1** the period in which the exploration of space has become possible. ◆ *adj* **space-age. 2** (*usually prenominal*) futuristic or ultramodern.

space-bar *n* a horizontal bar on a typewriter that is depressed in order to leave a space between words, letters, etc.

space capsule *n* a vehicle, sometimes carrying people or animals, designed to obtain scientific information from space, planets, etc., and be recovered on returning to earth.

spacecraft ('speɪs,krɑːft) *n* a manned or unmanned vehicle designed to orbit the earth or travel to celestial objects.

spaced out *adj Sl.* intoxicated through or as if through taking a drug. Often shortened to **spaced.**

space heater *n* a heater used to warm the air in an enclosed area, such as a room.

Space Invaders *n Trademark.* a video or computer game, the object of which is to destroy attacking alien spacecraft.

spaceman ❶ ('speɪs,mæn) *or* (*fem*) **spacewoman** *n, pl* **spacemen** *or* (*fem*) **spacewomen.** a person who travels in outer space.

space platform *n* another name for **space station.**

spaceport ('speɪs,pɔːt) *n* a base equipped to launch, maintain, and test spacecraft.

space probe *n* a vehicle, such as a satellite, equipped to obtain scientific information, normally transmitted back to earth by radio, about a planet, conditions in space, etc.

spaceship ('speɪs,ʃɪp) *n* a manned spacecraft.

space shuttle *n* any of a series of reusable US space vehicles (*Columbia, Challenger* (exploded 1986), *Discovery, Atlantis, Endeavor*) that can be launched into earth orbit transporting astronauts and equipment for a period of observation, research, etc., before re-entry and an unpowered landing on a runway; the first operational flight was in 1982.

space station *n* any large manned artificial satellite designed to orbit the earth during a long period of time thus providing a base for scientific research in space and a construction site, launch pad, and docking arrangements for spacecraft.

spacesuit ('speɪs,suːt, -,sjuːt) *n* a sealed and pressurized suit worn by astronauts providing an artificial atmosphere, acceptable temperature, radiocommunication link, and protection from radiation.

space-time *or* **space-time continuum** *n Physics.* the four-dimensional continuum having three spatial coordinates and one time coordinate that together completely specify the location of a particle or an event.

spacewalk ('speɪs,wɔːk) *n* **1** the act or an instance of floating and manoeuvring in space, outside but attached by a lifeline to a spacecraft. Technical name: **extravehicular activity.** ◆ *vb* **2** (*intr*) to engage in this activity.

spacey ('speɪsɪ) *adj* **spacier, spaciest.** *Sl.* vague and dreamy, as if under the influence of drugs. [C20: SPACE + -EY]

spacial ('speɪʃəl) *adj* a variant spelling of **spatial.**

spacing ('speɪsɪŋ) *n* **1** the arrangement of letters, words, spaces, etc., on a page. **2** the arrangement of objects in a space.

spacious ❶ ('speɪʃəs) *adj* having a large capacity or area.
▸ **'spaciously** *adv* ▸ **'spaciousness** *n*

spade[1] (speɪd) *n* **1** a tool for digging, typically consisting of a flat rectangular steel blade attached to a long wooden handle. **2** something resembling a spade. **3** a cutting tool for stripping the blubber from a whale or skin from a carcass. **4 call a spade a spade.** to speak plainly and frankly. ◆ *vb* **spades, spading, spaded. 5** (*tr*) to use a spade on. [OE *spadu*]
▸ **'spader** *n*

spade[2] (speɪd) *n* **1a** the black symbol on a playing card resembling a heart-shaped leaf with a stem. **1b** a card with one or more of these symbols or (*when pl*) the suit of cards so marked, usually the highest ranking of the four. **2** a derogatory word for a **Black**[1]. **3 in spades.** *Inf.* in an extreme or emphatic way. [C16: from It. *spada* sword, used as an emblem on playing cards, from L *spatha*, from Gk *spathē* blade]

spadework ❶ ('speɪd,wɜːk) *n* dull or routine preparatory work.

spadix ('speɪdɪks) *n, pl* **spadices** (speɪ'daɪsiːz). a spike of small flowers on a fleshy stem, the whole being enclosed in a spathe. [C18: from L: pulled-off branch of a palm, with its fruit, from Gk: torn-off frond]

spaghetti (spə'getɪ) *n* pasta in the form of long strings. [C19: from It.: little cords, from *spago* a cord]

spaghetti junction *n* a junction, usually between motorways, in which there are a large number of intersecting roads used by a large volume of high-speed traffic. [C20: from the nickname given to the Gravelly Hill Interchange, Birmingham, where the M6, A38M, A38, and A5127 intersect]

spaghetti western *n* a cowboy film made in Europe, esp. by an Italian director.

spahi *or* **spahee** ('spɑːhiː, 'spɑːiː) *n, pl* **spahis** *or* **spahees. 1** (formerly) an irregular cavalryman in the Turkish army. **2** (formerly) a member of a body of native Algerian cavalry in the French army. [C16: from OF, from Turkish *sipahi*, from Persian *sipāhī* soldier]

spake (speɪk) *vb Arch.* a past tense of **speak.**

spam (spæm) *vb* **spams, spamming, spammed.** *Computing sl.* to send unsolicited electronic mail simultaneously to a number of newsgroups on the Internet. [C20: from the repeated use of the word *Spam* in a popular sketch from the Brit. television show *Monty Python's Flying Circus*, first broadcast in 1969]

Spam (spæm) *n Trademark.* a kind of tinned luncheon meat, made largely from pork.

span[1] ❶ (spæn) *n* **1** the interval, space, or distance between two points, such as the ends of a bridge or arch. **2** the complete duration or extent: *the span of his life.* **3** *Psychol.* the amount of material that can be processed in a single mental act: *span of attention.* **4** short for **wingspan. 5** a unit of length based on the width of an expanded hand, usually

THESAURUS

sovereignty *n* **1** = **supreme power,** ascendancy, domination, kingship, primacy, supremacy, suzerainty, sway

sow[1] *vb* **1** = **scatter,** broadcast, disseminate, implant, inseminate, lodge, plant, seed

space *n* **1** = **expanse,** amplitude, extension, extent, volume **2** = **interval,** capacity, duration, elbowroom, leeway, margin, period, play, room, scope, spaciousness, span, time, while **3** = **gap,** blank, distance, interval, lacuna, omission **6** = **place,** accommodation, berth, seat

spaceman *n* = **astronaut,** cosmonaut

spacious *adj* = **roomy,** ample, broad, capacious, comfortable, commodious, expansive, extensive, huge, large, sizable *or* sizeable, uncrowded, vast

Antonyms *adj* close, confined, cramped, crowded, limited, narrow, poky, restricted, small

spadework *n* = **preparation,** donkey-work, groundwork, labour

span[1] *n* **1** = **extent,** amount, distance, length, reach, spread, stretch **2** = **period,** duration, spell, term ◆ *vb* **6** = **extend across,** arch across, bridge, cover, cross, link, range over, traverse, vault

taken as nine inches. ◆ *vb* **spans, spanning, spanned.** (*tr*) **6** to stretch or extend across, over, or around. **7** to provide with something that spans: *to span a river with a bridge.* **8** to measure or cover, esp. with the extended hand. [OE *spann*]

span[2] (spæn) *n* a team of horses or oxen, esp. two matched animals. [C16 (in the sense: yoke): from MDu.: something stretched, from *spannen* to stretch]

span[3] (spæn) *vb Arch. or dialect.* a past tense of **spin.**

Span. *abbrev. for* Spanish.

spandrel *or* **spandril** ('spændrəl) *n Archit.* **1** an approximately triangular surface bounded by the outer curve of an arch and the adjacent wall. **2** the surface area between two adjacent arches and the horizontal cornice above them. [C15 *spaundrell,* from Anglo-F *spaundre,* from OF *spandre* to spread]

spangle ('spæŋgᵊl) *n* **1** a small thin piece of metal or other shiny material used as a decoration, esp. on clothes; sequin. **2** any glittering or shiny spot or object. ◆ *vb* **spangles, spangling, spangled. 3** (*intr*) to glitter or shine with or like spangles. **4** (*tr*) to cover with spangles. [C15: dim. of *spange,* ?from MDu.: clasp]
▸ **'spangly** *adj*

Spaniard ('spænjəd) *n* a native or inhabitant of Spain.

spaniel ('spænjəl) *n* **1** any of several breeds of gundog with long drooping ears and a silky coat. **2** an obsequiously devoted person. [C14: from OF *espaigneul* Spanish (dog), from OProvençal *espanhol,* ult. from L *Hispāniolus* Spanish]

Spanish ('spænɪʃ) *n* **1** the official language of Spain, Mexico, and most countries of South and Central America except Brazil. Spanish is an Indo-European language belonging to the Romance group. **2 the Spanish.** (*functioning as pl*) the natives, citizens, or inhabitants of Spain. ◆ *adj* **3** of or relating to the Spanish language or its speakers. **4** of or relating to Spain or Spaniards.

Spanish America *n* the parts of America colonized by Spaniards and now chiefly Spanish-speaking: includes most of South and Central America, Mexico, and much of the Caribbean.

Spanish-American *adj* **1** of or relating to any of the Spanish-speaking countries or peoples of the Americas. ◆ *n* **2** a native or inhabitant of Spanish America. **3** a Spanish-speaking person in the US.

Spanish customs *or* **practices** *pl n Inf.* irregular practices among a group of workers to gain increased financial allowances, reduced working hours, etc.

Spanish fly *n* **1** a European blister beetle, the dried body of which yields cantharides. **2** another name for **cantharides.**

Spanish guitar *n* the classic form of the guitar; a six-stringed instrument with a waisted body and a central sound hole.

Spanish Main *n* **1** the mainland of Spanish America, esp. the N coast of South America. **2** the Caribbean Sea, the S part of which in colonial times was the haunt of pirates.

Spanish moss *n* **1** an epiphytic plant growing in tropical and subtropical regions as long bluish-grey strands suspended from the branches of trees. **2** a tropical lichen growing as long trailing green threads from the branches of trees.

Spanish omelette *n* an omelette containing green peppers, onions, tomato, etc.

Spanish rice *n* rice cooked with tomatoes, onions, green peppers, etc.

spank[1] **T** (spæŋk) *vb* **1** (*tr*) to slap with the open hand, esp. on the buttocks. ◆ *n* **2** one or a series of these slaps. [C18: prob. imit.]

spank[2] (spæŋk) *vb* (*intr*) to go at a quick and lively pace. [C19: back formation from SPANKING[2]]

spanker ('spæŋkə) *n* **1** a person or thing that spanks. **2** *Naut.* a fore-and-aft sail or a mast that is aftermost in a sailing vessel. **3** *Inf.* something outstandingly fine or large.

spanking[1] ('spæŋkɪŋ) *n* a series of spanks, usually as a punishment for children.

spanking[2] **T** ('spæŋkɪŋ) *adj* (*prenominal*) **1** *Inf.* outstandingly fine, smart, large, etc. **2** quick and energetic. **3** (esp. of a breeze) fresh and brisk.

spanner ('spænə) *n* **1** a steel hand tool with jaws or a hole, designed to grip a nut or bolt head. **2 spanner in the works.** *Brit. inf.* an impediment or annoyance. [C17: from G, from *spannen* to stretch]

span roof *n* a roof consisting of two equal sloping sides.

spanspek ('spæn,spɛk) *n S. African.* the sweet melon. [C19: possibly from Afrik.: literally, Spanish bacon]

spar[1] (spɑː) *n* **1** any piece of nautical gear resembling a pole and used as a mast, boom, gaff, etc. **2** a principal supporting structural member of an aerofoil that runs from tip to tip or root to tip. [C13: from ON *sperra* beam]

spar[2] **T** (spɑː) *vb* **spars, sparring, sparred.** (*intr*) **1** *Boxing & martial arts.* to box using light blows, as in training. **2** to dispute or argue. **3** (of gamecocks, etc.) to fight with the feet or spurs. ◆ *n* **4** an unaggressive fight. **5** an argument or wrangle. [OE, ? from SPUR]

spar[3] (spɑː) *n* any of various minerals, such as feldspar, that are light-coloured, crystalline, and easily cleavable. [C16: from MLow G *spar*]

sparaxis (spəˈræksɪs) *n* a South African plant of the iris family, having lacerated spathes and showy flowers. [C19: NL, from Gk, from *sparassō* to tear]

spare T (spɛə) *vb* **spares, sparing, spared. 1** (*tr*) to refrain from killing, punishing, or injuring. **2** (*tr*) to release or relieve, as from pain, suffering, etc. **3** (*tr*) to refrain from using: *spare the rod, spoil the child.* **4** (*tr*) to be able to afford or give: *I can't spare the time.* **5** (*usually passive*) (esp. of Providence) to allow to survive: *I'll see you next year if we are spared.* **6** (*intr*) *Now rare.* to act or live frugally. **7 not spare oneself.** to exert oneself to the full. **8 to spare.** more than is required: *two minutes to spare.* ◆ *adj* **9** (*often immediately postpositive*) in excess of what is needed; additional. **10** able to be used when needed: *a spare part.* **11** (of a person) thin and lean. **12** scanty or meagre. **13** (*postpositive*) *Brit. sl.* upset, angry, or distracted (esp. in **go spare**). ◆ *n* **14** a duplicate kept as a replacement in case of damage or loss. **15** a spare tyre. **16** *Tenpin bowling.* **16a** the act of knocking down all the pins with the two bowls of a single frame. **16b** the score thus made. [OE *sparian* to refrain from injuring]
▸ **'sparely** *adv* ▸ **'spareness** *n* ▸ **'sparer** *n*

spare-part surgery *n* surgical replacement of defective or damaged organs by transplant or insertion of artficial devices.

sparerib (,spɛəˈrɪb) *n* a cut of pork ribs with most of the meat trimmed off.

spare tyre *n* **1** an additional tyre carried by a motor vehicle in case of puncture. **2** *Brit. sl.* a deposit of fat just above the waist.

sparing T ('spɛərɪŋ) *adj* **1** (sometimes foll. by *of*) economical or frugal (with). **2** scanty; meagre. **3** merciful or lenient.
▸ **'sparingly** *adv* ▸ **'sparingness** *n*

spark[1] **T** (spɑːk) *n* **1** a fiery particle thrown out or left by burning material or caused by the friction of two hard surfaces. **2a** a momentary flash of light accompanied by a sharp crackling noise, produced by a sudden electrical discharge through the air or some other insulating medium between two points. **2b** the electrical discharge itself. **2c** (*as modifier*): *a spark gap.* **3** anything that serves to animate or kindle. **4** a trace or hint: *a spark of interest.* **5** vivacity, enthusiasm, or humour. **6** a small piece of diamond, as used in cutting glass. ◆ *vb* **7** (*intr*) to give off sparks. **8** (*intr*) (of the sparking plug or ignition system of an internal-combustion engine) to produce a spark. **9** (*tr; often foll. by off*) to kindle or animate. ◆ See also **sparks.** [OE *spearca*]

spark[2] (spɑːk) *n* **1** *Rare.* a fashionable or gallant young man. **2 bright spark.** *Brit., usually ironic.* a person who appears clever or witty. [C16 (in the sense: beautiful or witty woman): ? of Scand. origin]
▸ **'sparkish** *adj*

spark gap *n* the space between two electrodes across which a spark can jump.

sparking plug *n* a device screwed into the cylinder head of an internal-combustion engine to ignite the explosive mixture by means of an electric spark. Also called: **spark plug.**

sparkle T ('spɑːkᵊl) *vb* **sparkles, sparkling, sparkled. 1** to issue or reflect or cause to issue or reflect bright points of light. **2** (*intr*) (of wine, mineral water, etc.) to effervesce. **3** (*intr*) to be vivacious or witty. ◆ *n* **4** a point of light, spark, or gleam. **5** vivacity or wit. [C12 *sparklen,* frequentative of *sparken* to SPARK[1]]

sparkler ('spɑːklə) *n* **1** a type of firework that throws out sparks. **2** *Inf.* a sparkling gem.

sparkling wine *n* a wine made effervescent by carbon dioxide gas added artificially or produced naturally by secondary fermentation.

THESAURUS

spank[1] *vb* **1** = **smack**, belt (*inf.*), cuff, give (someone) a hiding (*inf.*), put (someone) over one's knee, slap, slipper (*inf.*), tan (*sl.*), wallop (*inf.*), whack

spanking[2] *adj* **1** *Informal* = **smart**, brand-new, fine, gleaming **2** = **fast**, brisk, energetic, invigorating, lively, quick, smart, snappy, vigorous

spar[2] *vb* **2** = **argue**, bicker, dispute, fall out (*inf.*), have a tiff, row, scrap (*inf.*), skirmish, spat (*US*), squabble, wrangle

spare *vb* **1, 2** = **have mercy on**, be merciful to, deal leniently with, go easy on (*inf.*), leave, let off (*inf.*), pardon, refrain from, release, relieve from, save from **4** = **afford**, allow, bestow, dispense with, do without, give, grant, let (someone) have, manage without, part with, relinquish ◆ *adj* **9, 10** = **extra**, additional, emergency, free, going begging, in excess, in reserve, leftover, odd, over, superfluous, supernumerary, surplus, unoccupied, unused, unwanted **11** = **thin**, gaunt, lank, lean, meagre, slender, slight, slim, wiry **12** = **meagre**, economical, frugal, modest, scanty, sparing **13 go spare** *Brit. slang* = **become enraged**, become angry, become distracted, become distraught, become mad (*inf.*), become upset, blow one's top (*inf.*), do one's nut (*Brit. sl.*), go mental (*sl.*), go up the wall (*sl.*), have *or* throw a fit (*inf.*)
Antonyms *vb* ≠ **have mercy on:** afflict, condemn, damn, destroy, hurt, punish, show no mercy to ◆ *adj* ≠ **extra:** allocated, designated, earmarked, in use, necessary, needed, set aside, spoken for ≠ **thin:** corpulent, fat, flabby, fleshy, generous, heavy, large, plump

sparing *adj* **1** = **economical**, careful, chary, cost-conscious, frugal, money-conscious, prudent, saving, thrifty
Antonyms *adj* extravagant, lavish, liberal, open-handed, prodigal, spendthrift

spark[1] *n* **1** = **flicker**, flare, flash, gleam, glint, scintillation, spit **4** = **trace**, atom, hint, jot, scintilla, scrap, vestige ◆ *vb* **9** *often with* **off** = **start**, animate, excite, inspire, kick-start, kindle, precipitate, prod, provoke, rouse, set in motion, set off, stimulate, stir, touch off, trigger (off)

sparkle *vb* **1** = **glitter**, beam, coruscate, dance, flash, gleam, glint, glisten, glister (*arch.*), glow, scintillate, shimmer, shine, spark, twinkle, wink **2** = **fizz**, bubble, effervesce, fizzle ◆ *n* **4** = **glitter**, brilliance, coruscation, dazzle, flash, flicker, gleam, glint, radiance, spark, twinkle **5** = **vivacity**, animation, brio, dash, élan, gaiety, life, liveliness, panache, spirit, vim (*sl.*), vitality, zip (*inf.*)

spark plug *n* another name for **sparking plug.**

sparks (spɑːks) *n* (*functioning as sing*) *Inf.* **1** an electrician. **2** a radio officer, esp. on a ship.

sparky ('spɑːkɪ) *adj* **sparkier, sparkiest.** lively, vivacious, spirited.

sparring partner ('spɑːrɪŋ) *n* **1** a person who practises with a boxer during training. **2** a person with whom one has friendly arguments.

sparrow ('spærəʊ) *n* **1** any of various weaverbirds, esp. the house sparrow, having a brown or grey plumage and feeding on seeds or insects. **2** *US & Canad.* any of various North American finches, such as the chipping sparrow, that have a dullish streaked plumage. ◆ See also **hedge sparrow, tree sparrow.** [OE *spearwa*]

sparrowgrass ('spærəʊˌgrɑːs) *n* a dialect or popular name for **asparagus.**

sparrowhawk ('spærəʊˌhɔːk) *n* any of several small hawks of Eurasia and N Africa that prey on smaller birds.

sparrow hawk *n* a very small North American falcon, closely related to the kestrels.

sparse ❶ (spɑːs) *adj* scattered or scanty; not dense. [C18: from L *sparsus,* from *spargere* to scatter]
▸'**sparsely** *adv* ▸'**sparseness** *or* '**sparsity** *n*

Spartan ❶ ('spɑːtᵊn) *adj* **1** of or relating to the ancient Greek city of Sparta or its citizens. **2** (*sometimes not cap.*) very strict or austere: *a Spartan upbringing.* **3** (*sometimes not cap.*) possessing courage and resolve. ◆ *n* **4** a citizen of Sparta. **5** (*sometimes not cap.*) a disciplined or brave person.

spasm ❶ ('spæzəm) *n* **1** an involuntary muscular contraction, esp. one resulting in cramp or convulsion. **2** a sudden burst of activity, emotion, etc. [C14: from L *spasmus,* from Gk *spasmos* a cramp, from *span* to tear]

spasmodic ❶ (spæz'mɒdɪk) *or* (*rarely*) **spasmodical** *adj* **1** taking place in sudden brief spells. **2** of or characterized by spasms. [C17: NL, from Gk *spasmos* SPASM]
▸**spas'modically** *adv*

spastic ('spæstɪk) *n* **1** a person who is affected by spasms or convulsions, esp. one who has cerebral palsy. **2** *Offens. sl.* a clumsy, incapable, or incompetent person. ◆ *adj* **3** affected by or resembling spasms. **4** *Offens. sl.* clumsy, incapable, or incompetent. [C18: from L *spasticus,* from Gk, from *spasmos* SPASM]
▸'**spastically** *adv* ▸**spas'ticity** (spæs'tɪsɪtɪ) *n*

spat[1] ❶ (spæt) *n* **1** *Now rare.* a slap or smack. **2** a slight quarrel. ◆ *vb* **spats, spatting, spatted. 3** *Rare.* to slap (someone). **4** (*intr*) *US, Canad., & NZ.* to have a slight quarrel. [C19: prob. imit.]

spat[2] (spæt) *vb* a past tense and past participle of **spit**[1].

spat[3] (spæt) *n* another name for **gaiter** (sense 2). [C19: short for SPATTERDASH]

spat[4] (spæt) *n* **1** a larval oyster or similar bivalve mollusc. **2** such oysters or other molluscs collectively. [C17: from Anglo-Norman *spat*]

spatchcock ('spætʃˌkɒk) *n* **1** a chicken or game bird split down the back and grilled. ◆ *vb* (*tr*) **2** to interpolate (words, a story, etc.) into a sentence, narrative, etc., esp. inappropriately. [C18: ? var. of *spitchcock* eel when prepared & cooked]

spate ❶ (speɪt) *n* **1** a fast flow, rush, or outpouring: *a spate of words.* **2** *Chiefly Brit.* a sudden flood: *the rivers were in spate.* **3** *Chiefly Brit.* a sudden heavy downpour. [C15 (Scot. & N English): from ?]

spathe (speɪð) *n* a large bract that encloses the inflorescence of several members of the lily family. [C18: from L *spatha,* from Gk *spathē* a blade]
▸**spathaceous** (spə'θeɪʃəs) *adj*

spathic ('spæθɪk) *or* **spathose** ('spæθəʊs) *adj* (of minerals) resembling spar, esp. in having good cleavage. [C18: from G *Spat* SPAR[3]]

spatial *or* **spacial** ('speɪʃəl) *adj* **1** of or relating to space. **2** existing or happening in space.
▸**spatiality** (ˌspeɪʃɪ'ælɪtɪ) *n* ▸'**spatially** *adv*

spatiotemporal (ˌspeɪʃɪəʊ'tɛmpərəl) *adj* **1** of or existing in both space and time. **2** of or concerned with space-time.
▸ˌ**spatio'temporally** *adv*

spatter ❶ ('spætə) *vb* **1** to scatter or splash (a substance, esp. a liquid) or (of a substance) to splash (something) in scattered drops: *to spatter mud on the car; mud spattered in her face.* **2** (*tr*) to sprinkle, cover, or spot (with a liquid). **3** (*tr*) to slander or defame. **4** (*intr*) to shower or rain down: *bullets spattered around them.* ◆ *n* **5** the sound of spattering. **6** something spattered, such as a spot or splash. **7** the act or an instance of spattering. [C16: imit.]

spatterdash ('spætəˌdæʃ) *n* **1** *US.* another name for **roughcast. 2** (*pl*) long leather leggings worn in the 18th century, as to protect from mud when riding. [C17: see SPATTER, DASH[1]]

spatula ('spætjʊlə) *n* a utensil with a broad flat blade, used for lifting, spreading, or stirring foods, etc. [C16: from L: a broad piece, from *spatha* a flat wooden implement; see SPATHE]
▸'**spatular** *adj*

spatulate ('spætjʊlɪt) *adj* **1** shaped like a spatula; having thickened rounded ends: *spatulate fingers.* **2** Also: **spathulate.** *Bot.* having a narrow base and a broad rounded apex.

spavin ('spævɪn) *n* enlargement of the hock of a horse by a bony growth (**bony spavin**) or distension of the ligament (**bog spavin**), often resulting in lameness. [C15: from OF *espavin,* from ?]
▸'**spavined** *adj*

spawn ❶ (spɔːn) *n* **1** the mass of eggs deposited by fish, amphibians, or molluscs. **2** *Often derog.* offspring, product, or yield. **3** *Bot.* the nontechnical name for **mycelium.** ◆ *vb* **4** (of fish, amphibians, etc.) to produce or deposit (eggs). **5** *Often derog.* (of people) to produce (offspring). **6** (*tr*) to produce or engender. [C14: from Anglo-Norman *espaundre,* from OF *spandre* to spread out]
▸'**spawner** *n*

spay (speɪ) *vb* (*tr*) to remove the ovaries from (a female animal). [C15: from OF *espeer* to cut with the sword, from *espee* sword, from L *spatha*]

SPCK (in Britain) *abbrev. for* Society for Promoting Christian Knowledge.

speak ❶ (spiːk) *vb* **speaks, speaking, spoke, spoken. 1** to make (verbal utterances); utter (words). **2** to communicate or express (something) in or as if in words. **3** (*intr*) to deliver a speech, discourse, etc. **4** (*tr*) to know how to talk in (a language or dialect): *he does not speak German.* **5** (*intr*) to make a characteristic sound: *the clock spoke.* **6** (*intr*) (of hounds used in hunting) to give tongue; bark. **7** (*tr*) *Naut.* to hail and communicate with (another vessel) at sea. **8** (*intr*) (of a musical instrument) to produce a sound. **9 on speaking terms.** on good terms; friendly. **10 so to speak.** in a manner of speaking; as it were. **11 speak one's mind.** to express one's opinions frankly and plainly. **12 to speak of.** of a significant or worthwhile nature: *no support to speak of.* ◆ See also **speak for, speak out, speak to.** [OE *specan*]
▸'**speakable** *adj*

speakeasy ('spiːkˌiːzɪ) *n, pl* **speakeasies.** *US.* a place where alcoholic drink was sold illicitly during Prohibition.

speaker ❶ ('spiːkə) *n* **1** a person who speaks, esp. at a formal occasion. **2** See **loudspeaker.**
▸'**speakership** *n*

Speaker ('spiːkə) *n* the presiding officer in any of numerous legislative bodies.

speak for ❶ *vb* (*intr, prep*) **1** to speak as a representative of (other people). **2 speak for itself.** to be so evident that no further comment is necessary. **3 speak for yourself.** *Inf.* (used as an imperative) do not presume that other people agree with you.

speaking ❶ ('spiːkɪŋ) *adj* **1** (*prenominal*) eloquent, impressive, or striking. **2a** able to speak. **2b** (*in combination*) able to speak a particular language: *French-speaking.*

speaking clock *n Brit.* a telephone service that gives a verbal statement of the time.

speaking in tongues *n* another term for **gift of tongues.**

speaking tube *n* a tube for conveying a person's voice from one room or building to another.

speak out ❶ *or* **up** *vb* (*intr, adv*) **1** to state one's beliefs, objections, etc., bravely and firmly. **2** to speak more loudly and clearly.

speak to ❶ *vb* (*intr, prep*) **1** to address (a person). **2** to reprimand. **3** *Formal.* to give evidence of or comments on (a subject).

spear[1] (spɪə) *n* **1** a weapon consisting of a long shaft with a sharp pointed end of metal, stone, or wood that may be thrown or thrust. **2** a similar implement used to catch fish. **3** another name for **spearman.** ◆ *vb* **4** to pierce (something) with or as if with a spear. [OE *spere*]

spear[2] (spɪə) *n* a shoot, stalk, or blade, as of grass. [C16: prob. var. of SPIRE[1], infl. by SPEAR[1]]

spear grass *n* **1** Also called: **wild Spaniard.** a New Zealand grass with sharp leaves that grows on mountains. **2** any of various other grasses with sharp stiff blades or seeds.

spear gun *n* a device for shooting spears underwater.

spearhead ❶ ('spɪəˌhɛd) *n* **1** the pointed head of a spear. **2** the leading force in a military attack. **3** any person or thing that leads or initiates

THESAURUS

sparse *adj* = **scattered**, few and far between, meagre, scanty, scarce, sporadic
Antonyms *adj* crowded, dense, lavish, lush, luxuriant, numerous, plentiful, thick

Spartan *adj* **2** *sometimes not cap.* = **austere**, abstemious, ascetic, bleak, disciplined, extreme, frugal, plain, rigorous, self-denying, severe, stern, strict, stringent

spasm *n* **1** = **convulsion**, contraction, paroxysm, throe (*rare*), twitch **2** = **burst**, access, eruption, fit, frenzy, outburst, seizure

spasmodic *adj* **1** = **sporadic**, erratic, fitful, intermittent, irregular **2** = **convulsive**, jerky

spat[1] *n* **2** = **quarrel**, altercation, bicker, contention, controversy, dispute, squabble, tiff

spate *n* **1** = **flood**, deluge, flow, outpouring, rush, torrent

spatter *vb* **1** = **splash**, bespatter, bestrew, daub, dirty, scatter, soil, speckle, splodge, spray, sprinkle

spawn *n* **2** *Often derogatory* = **offspring**, issue, product, progeny, seed (*chiefly Biblical*), yield

speak *vb* **1, 2** = **talk**, articulate, communicate, converse, discourse, enunciate, express, make known, pronounce, say, state, tell, utter, voice **3** = **lecture**, address, argue, declaim, deliver an address, descant, discourse, harangue, hold forth, plead, speechify, spiel (*inf.*), spout

speaker *n* **1** = **orator**, lecturer, mouthpiece, public speaker, spokesman *or* spokeswoman, spokesperson, word-spinner

speak for *vb* **1** = **represent**, act for *or* on behalf of, appear for, hold a brief for, hold a mandate for

speaking *adj* **1** = **expressive**, eloquent, moving, noticeable, striking

speak out *vb* **1** = **speak one's mind**, have one's say, make one's position plain, sound off, stand up and be counted **2** = **speak loudly**, make oneself heard, say it loud and clear

speak to *vb* **1** = **address**, accost, apostrophize, direct one's words at, talk to **2** = **reprimand**, admonish, bring to book, dress down (*inf.*), lecture, rebuke, scold, tell off (*inf.*), tick off (*inf.*), warn

spearhead *vb* **4** = **lead**, be in the van, blaze the

an attack, campaign, etc. ◆ *vb* **4** (*tr*) to lead or initiate (an attack, campaign, etc.).
spearman ('spɪəmən) *n, pl* **spearmen.** a soldier armed with a spear.
spearmint ('spɪəmɪnt) *n* a purple-flowered mint plant of Europe, having leaves that yield an oil used for flavouring.
spec (spɛk) *n* **1 on spec.** *Inf.* as a speculation or gamble: *all the tickets were sold so I went to the theatre on spec.* ◆ *adj* **2** (*prenominal*) *Austral. & NZ inf.* speculative: *a spec developer.*
spec. *abbrev. for:* **1** special. **2** specification. **3** speculation.
special **T** ('spɛʃəl) *adj* **1** distinguished from, set apart from, or excelling others of its kind. **2** (*prenominal*) designed or reserved for a particular purpose. **3** not usual or commonplace. **4** (*prenominal*) particular or primary: *his special interest was music.* **5** of or relating to the education of handicapped children: *a special school.* ◆ *n* **6** a special person or thing, such as an extra edition of a newspaper or a train reserved for a particular purpose. **7** a dish or meal given prominence, esp. at a low price, in a café, etc. **8** short for **special constable. 9** *US, Canad., Austral., & NZ inf.* an item in a store advertised at a reduce price. ◆ *vb* **specials, specialling, specialled.** (*tr*) **10** (of a nurse) to give (a gravely ill patient) constant individual care. **11** *NZ inf.* to advertise and sell (an item) at a reduced price. [C13: from OF *especial,* from L *speciālis* individual, special, from *speciēs* appearance]
▸**'specially** *adv* ▸**'specialness** *n*

USAGE NOTE See at **especial.**

Special Branch *n* (in Britain) the department of the police force that is concerned with political security.
special clearing *n Banking.* (in Britain) the clearing of a cheque through a bank in less than the usual three days, for an additional charge.
special constable *n* a person recruited for temporary or occasional police duties, esp. in time of emergency.
special delivery *n* the delivery of a piece of mail outside the time of a scheduled delivery.
special drawing rights *pl n* (*sometimes caps.*) the reserve assets of the International Monetary Fund on which member nations may draw.
special effects *pl n Films.* techniques used in the production of scenes that cannot be achieved by normal techniques.
specialist **T** ('spɛʃəlɪst) *n* a person who specializes in a particular activity, field of research, etc.
▸**'special,ism** *n* ▸**,special'istic** *adj*
speciality **T** (,spɛʃɪ'ælɪtɪ) *or esp. US & Canad.* **specialty** *n, pl* **specialities** *or esp. US & Canad.* **specialties. 1** a special interest or skill. **2a** a service or product specialized in, as at a restaurant. **2b** (*as modifier*): *a speciality dish.* **3** a special feature or characteristic.
specialize *or* **specialise** ('spɛʃə,laɪz) *vb* **specializes, specializing, specialized** *or* **specialises, specialising, specialised. 1** (*intr*) to train in or devote oneself to a particular area of study, occupation, or activity. **2** (*usually passive*) to cause (organisms or parts) to develop in a way most suited to a particular environment or way of life or (of organisms, etc.) to develop in this way. **3** (*tr*) to modify for a special use or purpose.
▸**,speciali'zation** *or* **,speciali'sation** *n*
special licence *n Brit.* a licence permitting a marriage to take place by dispensing with the usual legal conditions.
special pleading *n Law.* **1** a pleading that alleges new facts that offset those put forward by the other side rather than directly admitting or denying those facts. **2** a pleading that emphasizes the favourable aspects of a case while omitting the unfavourable.
special school *n Brit.* a school for children who are unable to benefit from ordinary schooling because they have learning difficulties, physical or mental handicaps, etc.
special team *n American football.* any of several predetermined permutations of the players within a team that play in situations, such as kickoffs and attempts at field goals, where the standard offensive and defensive formations are not appropriate.
specialty ('spɛʃəltɪ) *n, pl* **specialties. 1** *Law.* a formal contract or obligation expressed in a deed. **2** a variant (esp. US and Canad.) of **speciality.**
speciation (,spiːʃɪ'eɪʃən) *n* the evolutionary development of a biological species.
specie ('spiːʃiː) *n* **1** coin money, as distinguished from bullion or paper money. **2 in specie. 2a** (of money) in coin. **2b** in kind. [C16: from L *in speciē* in kind]
species **T** ('spiːʃiːz; *Latin* 'spiːʃɪ,iːz) *n, pl* **species. 1** *Biol.* **1a** any of the taxonomic groups into which a genus is divided, the members of which are capable of interbreeding. Abbrev.: **sp. 1b** the animals of such a group. **1c** any group of related animals or plants not necessarily of this taxonomic rank. **2** (*modifier*) denoting a plant that is a natural member of a species rather than a hybrid or cultivar: *a species clematis.* **3** *Logic.* a group of objects or individuals, all sharing common attributes, that forms a subdivision of a genus. **4** a kind, sort, or variety: *a species of treachery.* **5** *Chiefly RC Church.* the outward form of the bread and wine in the Eucharist. **6** *Obs.* an outward appearance or form. [C16: from L: appearance, from *specere* to look]
specif. *abbrev. for* specifically.
specific **T** (spɪ'sɪfɪk) *adj* **1** explicit, particular, or definite. **2** relating to a specified or particular thing: *a specific treatment for arthritis.* **3** of or relating to a biological species. **4** (of a disease) caused by a particular pathogenic agent. **5** *Physics.* **5a** characteristic of a property of a substance, esp. in relation to the same property of a standard reference substance: *specific gravity.* **5b** characteristic of a property of a substance per unit mass, length, area, etc.: *specific heat.* **5c** (of an extensive physical quantity) divided by mass: *specific volume.* **6** denoting a tariff levied at a fixed sum per unit of weight, quantity, volume, etc., irrespective of value. ◆ *n* **7** (*sometimes pl*) a designated quality, thing, etc. **8** *Med.* any drug used to treat a particular disease. [C17: from Med. L *specificus,* from L SPECIES]
▸**spe'cifically** *adv* ▸**specificity** (,spɛsɪ'fɪsɪtɪ) *n*
specification **T** (,spɛsɪfɪ'keɪʃən) *n* **1** the act or an instance of specifying. **2** (in patent law) a written statement accompanying an application for a patent that describes the nature of an invention. **3** a detailed description of the criteria for the constituents, construction, appearance, performance, etc., of a material, apparatus, etc., or of the standard of workmanship required in its manufacture. **4** an item, detail, etc., specified.
specific charge *n Physics.* the charge-to-mass ratio of an elementary particle.
specific gravity *n* the ratio of the density of a substance to that of water.
specific heat capacity *n* the heat required to raise unit mass of a substance by unit temperature interval under specified conditions, such as constant pressure. Also called: **specific heat.**
specific humidity *n* the mass of water vapour in a sample of moist air divided by the mass of the sample.
specific volume *n Physics.* the volume of matter per unit mass.
specify **T** ('spɛsɪ,faɪ) *vb* **specifies, specifying, specified.** (*tr; may take a clause as object*) **1** to refer to or state specifically. **2** to state as a condition. **3** to state or include in the specification of. [C13: from Med. L *specificāre* to describe]
▸**'speci,fiable** *adj* ▸**specificative** ('spɛsɪfɪ,keɪtɪv) *adj*
specimen **T** ('spɛsɪmɪn) *n* **1a** an individual, object, or part regarded as typical of its group or class. **1b** (*as modifier*): *a specimen page.* **2** *Med.* a sample of tissue, blood, urine, etc., taken for diagnostic examination or evaluation. **3** the whole or a part of an organism, plant, rock, etc., collected and preserved as an example of its class, species, etc. **4** *Inf., often derog.* a person. [C17: from L: mark, proof, from *specere* to look at]
specious **T** ('spiːʃəs) *adj* **1** apparently correct or true, but actually wrong or false. **2** deceptively attractive in appearance. [C14 (orig.: fair): from L *speciōsus* plausible, from *speciēs* outward appearance, from *specere* to look at]
▸**'speciously** *adv* ▸**speciosity** (,spiːʃɪ'ɒsɪtɪ) *or* **'speciousness** *n*
speck **T** (spɛk) *n* **1** a very small mark or spot. **2** a small or tiny piece of something. ◆ *vb* **3** (*tr*) to mark with specks or spots. [OE *specca*]
speckle **T** ('spɛkᵊl) *n* **1** a small mark usually of a contrasting colour, as on the skin, eggs, etc. ◆ *vb* **speckles, speckling, speckled. 2** (*tr*) to mark with or as if with speckles. [C15: from MDu. *spekkel*]
▸**'speckled** *adj*
specs (spɛks) *pl n Inf.* short for **spectacles.**
spectacle **T** ('spɛktəkᵊl) *n* **1** a public display or performance, esp. a showy or ceremonial one. **2** a thing or person seen, esp. an unusual or

THESAURUS

trail, head, initiate, launch, lay the first stone, lead the way, pioneer, set in motion, set off
special *adj* **1, 3** = **exceptional**, distinguished, especial, extraordinary, festive, gala, important, memorable, momentous, one in a million, out of the ordinary, red-letter, significant, uncommon, unique, unusual **2** = **specific**, appropriate, certain, characteristic, distinctive, especial, individual, particular, peculiar, precise, specialized **4** = **particular**, chief, main, major, primary
Antonyms *adj* ≠ **exceptional:** common, everyday, humdrum, mediocre, no great shakes (*inf.*), normal, ordinary, routine, run-of-the-mill, undistinguished, unexceptional, usual ≠ **specific:** general, multi-purpose, undistinctive, unspecialized
specialist *n* = **expert**, authority, buff (*inf.*), connoisseur, consultant, guru, hotshot (*inf.*), master, maven (*US*), professional, whizz (*inf.*)
speciality *n* **1** = **forte**, bag (*sl.*), claim to fame, distinctive *or* distinguishing feature, métier, *pièce de résistance,* special, specialty
species *n* **4** = **kind**, breed, category, class, collection, description, genus, group, sort, type, variety
specific *adj* **1** = **precise**, clear-cut, definite, exact, explicit, express, limited, unambiguous, unequivocal **2** = **particular**, characteristic, definite, distinguishing, especial, peculiar, special
Antonyms *adj* ≠ **precise:** approximate, general, hazy, imprecise, non-specific, uncertain, unclear, vague, woolly ≠ **particular:** common, general
specification *n* **4** = **requirement**, condition, detail, item, particular, qualification, stipulation
specify *vb* **1, 2** = **state**, be specific about, cite, define, designate, detail, enumerate, indicate, individualize, itemize, mention, name, particularize, spell out, stipulate
specimen *n* **1** = **sample**, copy, embodiment, example, exemplar, exemplification, exhibit, individual, instance, model, pattern, proof, representative, type
specious *adj* **1** = **fallacious**, casuistic, deceptive, misleading, plausible, sophistic, sophistical, unsound
speck *n* **1** = **mark**, blemish, blot, defect, dot, fault, flaw, fleck, mote, speckle, spot, stain **2** = **particle**, atom, bit, dot, grain, iota, jot, mite, modicum, shred, tittle, whit
speckled *adj* **2** = **flecked**, brindled, dappled, dotted, freckled, mottled, speckledy, spotted, spotty, sprinkled, stippled
spectacle *n* **1** = **show**, display, event, exhibition, extravaganza, pageant, parade, perfor-

ridiculous one: *he makes a spectacle of himself.* **3** a strange or interesting object or phenomenon. [C14: via OF from L *spectaculum* a show, from *spectāre* to watch, from *specere* to look at]

spectacles ('spɛktək°lz) *pl n* a pair of glasses for correcting defective vision. Often (informal) shortened to **specs.**
▸ **'spectacled** *adj*

spectacular ❶ (spɛk'tækjʊlə) *adj* **1** of or resembling a spectacle; impressive, grand, or dramatic. **2** unusually marked or great: *a spectacular increase.* ◆ *n* **3** a lavishly produced performance.
▸ **spec'tacularly** *adv*

spectate (spɛk'teɪt) *vb* **spectates, spectating, spectated.** (*intr*) to be a spectator; watch. [C20: back formation from SPECTATOR]

spectator ❶ (spɛk'teɪtə) *n* a person viewing anything; onlooker; observer. [C16: from L, from *spectāre* to watch; see SPECTACLE]

spectator sport *n* a sport that attracts more people as spectators than as participants.

spectra ('spɛktrə) *n* the plural of **spectrum.**

spectral ❶ ('spɛktrəl) *adj* **1** of or like a spectre. **2** of or relating to a spectrum.
▸ **spectrality** (spɛk'trælɪtɪ) *n* ▸ **'spectrally** *adv*

spectral type *or* **class** *n* any of various groups into which stars are classified according to characteristic spectral lines and bands.

spectre ❶ *or US* **specter** ('spɛktə) *n* **1** a ghost; phantom; apparition. **2** an unpleasant or menacing mental image: *the spectre of redundancy.* [C17: from L *spectrum,* from *specere* to look at]

spectro- *combining form.* indicating a spectrum: *spectrogram.*

spectrograph ('spɛktrəʊˌgrɑːf) *n* a spectroscope or spectrometer that produces a photographic record (**spectrogram**) of a spectrum. See also **sound spectrograph.**
▸ **ˌspectro'graphic** *adj* ▸ **ˌspectro'graphically** *adv* ▸ **spectrography** (spɛk'trɒgrəfɪ) *n*

spectroheliograph (ˌspɛktrəʊ'hiːlɪəˌgrɑːf) *n* an instrument used to take a photograph (**spectroheliogram**) of the sun in light of a particular wavelength, usually that of calcium or hydrogen, to show the distribution of the element over the surface and in the atmosphere.
▸ **ˌspectroˌhelio'graphic** *adj*

spectrometer (spɛk'trɒmɪtə) *n* any instrument for producing a spectrum, esp. one in which wavelength, energy, intensity, etc., can be measured. See also **mass spectrometer.**
▸ **spectrometric** (ˌspɛktrəʊ'mɛtrɪk) *adj* ▸ **spec'trometry** *n*

spectrophotometer (ˌspɛktrəʊfəʊ'tɒmɪtə) *n* an instrument for producing or recording a spectrum and measuring the photometric intensity of each wavelength present.
▸ **spectrophotometric** (ˌspɛktrəʊˌfəʊtə'mɛtrɪk) *adj* ▸ **ˌspectropho'tometry** *n*

spectroscope ('spɛktrəˌskəʊp) *n* any of a number of instruments for dispersing electromagnetic radiation and thus forming or recording a spectrum.
▸ **spectroscopic** (ˌspɛktrə'skɒpɪk) *or* **ˌspectro'scopical** *adj*

spectroscopy (spɛk'trɒskəpɪ) *n* the science and practice of using spectrometers and spectroscopes and of analysing spectra.
▸ **spec'troscopist** *n*

spectrum ('spɛktrəm) *n, pl* **spectra. 1** the distribution of colours produced when white light is dispersed by a prism or diffraction grating. There is a continuous change in wavelength from red, the longest wavelength, to violet, the shortest. Seven colours are usually distinguished: violet, indigo, blue, green, yellow, orange, and red. **2** the whole range of electromagnetic radiation with respect to its wavelength or frequency. **3** any particular distribution of electromagnetic radiation often showing lines or bands characteristic of the substance emitting the radiation or absorbing it. **4** any similar distribution or record of the energies, velocities, masses, etc., of atoms, ions, electrons, etc.: *a mass spectrum.* **5** any range or scale, as of capabilities, emotions, or moods. **6** another name for an **afterimage.** [C17: from L: image, from *spectāre* to observe, from *specere* to look at]

spectrum analysis *n* the analysis of a spectrum to determine the properties of its source.

specular ('spɛkjʊlə) *adj* **1** of, relating to, or having the properties of a mirror. **2** of or relating to a speculum. [C16: from L *speculāris,* from *speculum* a mirror, from *specere* to look at]

speculate ❶ ('spɛkjʊˌleɪt) *vb* **speculates, speculating, speculated. 1** (when *tr, takes a clause as object*) to conjecture without knowing the complete facts. **2** (*intr*) to buy or sell securities, property, etc., in the hope of deriving capital gains. **3** (*intr*) to risk loss for the possibility of considerable gain. **4** (*intr*) *NZ.* in rugby football, to make an emergency undirected forward kick at the ball. [C16: from L *speculārī* to spy out, from *specula* a watchtower, from *specere* to look at]

speculation ❶ (ˌspɛkjʊ'leɪʃən) *n* **1** the act or an instance of speculating. **2** a supposition, theory, or opinion arrived at through speculating. **3** investment involving high risk but also possible high profits.
▸ **'speculative** *adj*

speculator ('spɛkjʊˌleɪtə) *n* **1** a person who speculates. **2** *NZ rugby.* an undirected kick of the ball.

speculum ('spɛkjʊləm) *n, pl* **specula** (-lə) *or* **speculums. 1** a mirror, esp. one made of polished metal for use in a telescope, etc. **2** *Med.* an instrument for dilating a bodily cavity or passage to permit examination of its interior. **3** a patch of distinctive colour on the wing of a bird. [C16: from L: mirror, from *specere* to look at]

sped (spɛd) *vb* a past tense and past participle of **speed.**

speech ❶ (spiːtʃ) *n* **1a** the act or faculty of speaking. **1b** (*as modifier*): *speech therapy.* **2** that which is spoken; utterance. **3** a talk or address delivered to an audience. **4** a person's characteristic manner of speaking. **5** a national or regional language or dialect. **6** *Linguistics.* another word for **parole.** [OE *spēc*]

speech day *n Brit.* (in schools) an annual day on which prizes are presented, speeches are made by guest speakers, etc.

speechify ('spiːtʃɪˌfaɪ) *vb* **speechifies, speechifying, speechified.** (*intr*) **1** to make a speech or speeches. **2** to talk pompously and boringly.
▸ **'speechiˌfier** *n*

speechless ❶ ('spiːtʃlɪs) *adj* **1** not able to speak. **2** temporarily deprived of speech. **3** not expressed or able to be expressed in words: *speechless fear.*
▸ **'speechlessly** *adv* ▸ **'speechlessness** *n*

speed ❶ (spiːd) *n* **1** the act or quality of acting or moving fast; rapidity. **2** the rate at which something moves, is done, or acts. **3** *Physics.* **3a** a scalar measure of the rate of movement of a body expressed either as the distance travelled divided by the time taken (**average speed**) or the rate of change of position with respect to time at a particular point (**instantaneous speed**). **3b** another word for **velocity** (sense 2). **4** a rate of rotation, usually expressed in revolutions per unit time. **5a** a gear ratio in a motor vehicle, bicycle, etc. **5b** (*in combination*): *a three-speed gear.* **6** *Photog.* a numerical expression of the sensitivity to light of a particular type of film, paper, or plate. See also **ISO rating. 7** *Photog.* a measure of the ability of a lens to pass light from an object to the image position. **8** a slang word for **amphetamine. 9** *Arch.* prosperity or success. **10 at speed.** quickly. ◆ *vb* **speeds, speeding; sped** *or* **speeded. 11** to move or go or cause to move or go quickly. **12** (*intr*) to drive (a motor vehicle) at a high speed, esp. above legal limits. **13** (*tr*) to help further the success or completion of. **14** (*intr*) *Sl.* to take or be under the influence of amphetamines. **15** (*intr*) to operate or run at a high speed. **16** *Arch.* **16a** (*intr*) to prosper or succeed. **16b** (*tr*) to wish success to. ◆ See also **speed up.** [OE *spēd* (orig. in the sense: success)]
▸ **'speeder** *n*

speedball ('spiːdˌbɔːl) *n Sl.* a mixture of heroin with amphetamine or cocaine.

speedboat ('spiːdˌbəʊt) *n* a high-speed motorboat.

speed chess *n* a form of chess in which each player's game is limited to a total stipulated time, usually half an hour; the first player to exceed the time limit loses.

speed limit *n* the maximum permitted speed at which a vehicle may travel on certain roads.

THESAURUS

mance, sight **3** = **sight**, curiosity, marvel, phenomenon, scene, wonder

spectacular *adj* **1** = **impressive**, breathtaking, daring, dazzling, dramatic, eye-catching, fantastic (*inf.*), grand, magnificent, marked, remarkable, sensational, splendid, staggering, striking, stunning (*inf.*) ◆ *n* **3** = **show**, display, extravaganza, spectacle
Antonyms *adj* ≠ **impressive:** everyday, modest, ordinary, plain, run-of-the-mill, simple, unimpressive, unostentatious, unspectacular

spectator *n* = **onlooker**, beholder, bystander, eyewitness, looker-on, observer, viewer, watcher, witness
Antonyms *n* contestant, contributor, partaker, participant, participator, party, player

spectral *adj* **1** = **ghostly**, eerie, incorporeal, insubstantial, phantom, shadowy, spooky (*inf.*), supernatural, uncanny, unearthly, weird, wraithlike

spectre *n* **1** = **ghost**, apparition, eidolon, phantom, presence, shade (*literary*), shadow, spirit, vision, wraith

speculate *vb* **1** = **conjecture**, cogitate, consider, contemplate, deliberate, guess, hypothesize, meditate, muse, scheme, suppose, surmise, theorize, wonder **2, 3** = **gamble**, have a flutter (*inf.*), hazard, play the market, risk, take a chance with, venture

speculation *n* **2** = **conjecture**, consideration, contemplation, deliberation, guess, guesswork, hypothesis, opinion, supposition, surmise, theory

speculative *adj* **1** = **risky**, chancy, dicey (*inf., chiefly Brit.*), hazardous, uncertain, unpredictable **2** = **hypothetical**, abstract, academic, conjectural, notional, suppositional, tentative, theoretical

speech *n* **1** = **communication**, conversation, dialogue, discussion, intercourse, talk **2, 4, 5** = **language**, articulation, dialect, diction, enunciation, idiom, jargon, lingo (*inf.*), parlance, tongue, utterance, voice **3** = **talk**, address, discourse, disquisition, harangue, homily, lecture, oration, spiel (*inf.*)

speechless *adj* **1** = **mute**, dumb, inarticulate, lost for words, mum, silent, tongue-tied, unable to get a word out (*inf.*), wordless **2** = **astounded**, aghast, amazed, dazed, dumbfounded, dumbstruck, shocked, thunderstruck

speed *n* **1, 2** = **swiftness**, acceleration, celerity, expedition, fleetness, haste, hurry, momentum, pace, precipitation, quickness, rapidity, rush, velocity ◆ *vb* **11** = **race**, bomb (along), bowl along, burn rubber (*inf.*), career, dispatch, flash, gallop, get a move on (*inf.*), go hell for leather (*inf.*), go like the wind, hasten, hurry, lose no time, make haste, press on, put one's foot down (*inf.*), quicken, rush, sprint, step on it (*inf.*), tear, urge, zoom **13** = **help**, advance, aid, assist, boost, expedite, facilitate, further, impel, promote
Antonyms *n* ≠ **swiftness:** delay, slowness, sluggishness, tardiness ◆ *vb* ≠ **race:** crawl, creep, dawdle, delay, take one's time, tarry ≠ **help:** delay, hamper, hinder, hold up, retard, slow

speedo ('spi:dəʊ) *n, pl* **speedos.** an informal name for **speedometer.**

speed of light *n* the speed at which electromagnetic radiation travels in a vacuum; 2.997 924 58 × 10^8 metres per second exactly. Symbol: *c* Also called (not in technical usage): **velocity of light.**

speedometer (spɪ'dɒmɪtə) *n* a device fitted to a vehicle to measure and display the speed of travel. See also **mileometer.**

speed up 🅣 *vb (adv)* **1** to increase or cause to increase in speed or rate; accelerate. ◆ *n* **speed-up. 2** an instance of this; acceleration.

> **USAGE NOTE** The past tense and past participle of *speed up* is *speeded up*, not *sped up*.

speedway ('spi:dˌweɪ) *n* **1** the sport of racing on light powerful motorcycles round cinder tracks. **2** the track or stadium where such races are held. **3** *US & Canad.* **3a** a racetrack for cars. **3b** a road on which fast driving is allowed.

speedwell ('spi:dˌwɛl) *n* any of various temperate plants, such as the **common speedwell** and the **germander speedwell,** having small blue or pinkish-white flowers.

speedy 🅣 ('spi:dɪ) *adj* **speedier, speediest. 1** characterized by speed. **2** done or decided without delay.
▸**'speedily** *adv* ▸**'speediness** *n*

spek (spɛk) *n S. African.* bacon. [from Afrik., from Du.]

speleology *or* **spelaeology** (ˌspi:lɪ'ɒlədʒɪ) *n* **1** the scientific study of caves. **2** the sport or pastime of exploring caves. [C19: from L *spēlaeum* cave]
▸**speleological** *or* **spelaeological** (ˌspi:lɪə'lɒdʒɪkᵊl) *adj* ▸**ˌspele'ologist** *or* **ˌspelae'ologist** *n*

spell[1] 🅣 (spɛl) *vb* **spells, spelling; spelt** *or* **spelled. 1** to write or name in correct order the letters that comprise the conventionally accepted form of (a word). **2** *(tr)* (of letters) to go to make up the conventionally established form of (a word) when arranged correctly: *d-o-g spells dog.* **3** *(tr)* to indicate or signify: *such actions spell disaster.* ◆ See also **spell out.** [C13: from OF *espeller,* of Gmc origin]
▸**'spellable** *adj*

spell[2] 🅣 (spɛl) *n* **1** a verbal formula considered as having magical force. **2** any influence that can control the mind or character; fascination. **3** a state induced as by the pronouncing of a spell; trance: *to break the spell.* **4 under a spell.** held in or as if in a spell. [OE *spell* speech]

spell[3] 🅣 (spɛl) *n* **1** an indeterminate, usually short, period of time: *a spell of cold weather.* **2** a period or tour of duty after which one person or group relieves another. **3** *Scot., Austral., & NZ.* a period or interval of rest. ◆ *vb* **4** *(tr)* to take over from (a person) for an interval of time; relieve temporarily. [OE *spelian* to take the place of, from ?]

spellbind ('spɛlˌbaɪnd) *vb* **spellbinds, spellbinding, spellbound.** *(tr)* to cause to be spellbound; entrance or enthral.
▸**'spellˌbinder** *n*

spellbound 🅣 ('spɛlˌbaʊnd) *adj* having one's attention held as though one is bound by a spell.

spellchecker ('spɛlˌtʃɛkə) *n Computing.* a program that highlights any word in a word-processed document that is not recognized as being correctly spelt.

speller ('spɛlə) *n* **1** a person who spells words in the manner specified: *a bad speller.* **2** a book designed to teach or improve spelling.

spelling 🅣 ('spɛlɪŋ) *n* **1** the act or process of writing words by using the letters conventionally accepted for their formation; orthography. **2** the art or study of orthography. **3** the way in which a word is spelt. **4** the ability of a person to spell.

spelling bee *n* a contest in which players are required to spell words.

spell out 🅣 *vb (tr, adv)* **1** to make clear, distinct, or explicit; clarify in detail: *let me spell out the implications.* **2** to read laboriously or with difficulty, working out each word letter by letter. **3** to discern by study; puzzle out.

spelt[1] (spɛlt) *vb* a past tense and past participle of **spell**[1].

spelt[2] (spɛlt) *n* a species of wheat that was formerly much cultivated and was used to develop present-day cultivated wheats. [OE]

spelter ('spɛltə) *n* impure zinc. [C17: prob. from MDu. *speauter,* from ?]

spelunker (spɪ'lʌŋkə) *n* a person whose hobby is the exploration of caves. [C20: from L *spēlunca,* from Gk *spēlunx* a cave]
▸**spe'lunking** *n*

spencer[1] ('spɛnsə) *n* **1** a short fitted coat or jacket. **2** a woman's knitted vest. [C18: after Earl *Spencer* (1758–1834)]

spencer[2] ('spɛnsə) *n Naut.* a large loose-footed gaffsail on a square-rigger or barque. [C19: ?from a proper name]

spend 🅣 (spɛnd) *vb* **spends, spending, spent. 1** to pay out (money, wealth, etc.). **2** *(tr)* to concentrate (time, effort, etc.) upon an object, activity, etc. **3** *(tr)* to pass (time) in a specific way, place, etc. **4** *(tr)* to use up completely: *the hurricane spent its force.* **5** *(tr)* to give up (one's blood, life, etc.) in a cause. [OE *spendan,* from L *expendere;* infl. also by OF *despendre* to spend; see EXPEND, DISPENSE]
▸**'spendable** *adj* ▸**'spender** *n*

spendthrift 🅣 ('spɛndˌθrɪft) *n* **1** a person who spends money in an extravagant manner. ◆ *adj* **2** *(usually prenominal)* of or like a spendthrift.

Spenserian (spɛn'sɪərɪən) *adj* **1** relating to or characteristic of the 16th-century English poet Edmund Spenser or his poetry. ◆ *n* **2** a student or imitator of Edmund Spenser.

Spenserian stanza *n Prosody.* the stanza form used by the poet Spenser in his poem *The Faerie Queene,* consisting of eight lines in iambic pentameter and a concluding Alexandrine, rhyming a b a b b c b c c.

spent 🅣 (spɛnt) *vb* **1** the past tense and past participle of **spend.** ◆ *adj* **2** used up or exhausted; consumed. **3** (of a fish) exhausted by spawning.

sperm[1] 🅣 (spɜ:m) *n, pl* **sperms** *or* **sperm. 1** another name for **semen. 2** a male reproductive cell; male gamete. [C14: from LL *sperma,* from Gk]

sperm[2] (spɜ:m) *n* short for **sperm whale, spermaceti,** or **sperm oil.**

-sperm *n combining form.* (in botany) a seed: *gymnosperm.*
▸**-spermous** *or* **-spermal** *adj combining form.*

spermaceti (ˌspɜ:mə'sɛtɪ, -'si:tɪ) *n* a white waxy substance obtained from oil from the head of the sperm whale. [C15: from Med. L *sperma cētī* whale's sperm, from *sperma* SPERM[1] + L *cētus* whale, from Gk *kētos*]

spermatic (spɜ:'mætɪk), **spermic** ('spɜ:mɪk), *or* **spermous** ('spɜ:məs) *adj* **1** of or relating to spermatozoa: *spermatic fluid.* **2** of or relating to the testis: *the spermatic artery.* [C16: from LL *spermaticus,* from Gk *spermatikos* concerning seed, from *sperma* seed]
▸**sper'matically** *adv*

spermatid ('spɜ:mətɪd) *n Zool.* any of four immature male gametes that are formed from a spermatocyte, each of which develops into a spermatozoon.

spermato-, spermo- *or before a vowel* **spermat-, sperm-** *combining form.* **1** indicating sperm: *spermatozoon.* **2** indicating seed: *spermatophyte.* [from Gk *sperma, spermat-* seed]

spermatocyte ('spɜ:mətəʊˌsaɪt) *n* an immature male germ cell.

spermatogenesis (ˌspɜ:mətəʊ'dʒɛnɪsɪs) *n* the formation and maturation of spermatozoa in the testis.
▸**spermatogenetic** (ˌspɜ:mətəʊdʒɪ'nɛtɪk) *adj*

spermatogonium (ˌspɜ:mətə'gəʊnɪəm) *n, pl* **spermatogonia** (-nɪə). *Zool.* an immature male germ cell that divides to form many spermatocytes.

spermatophyte ('spɜ:mətəʊˌfaɪt) *or* **spermophyte** *n* (in traditional classifications) any seed-bearing plant. Former name: **phanerogam.**
▸**spermatophytic** (ˌspɜ:mətəʊ'fɪtɪk) *adj*

spermatozoon (ˌspɜ:mətəʊ'zəʊɒn) *n, pl* **spermatozoa** (-zəʊə). any of the male reproductive cells released in the semen during ejaculation. Also called: **sperm, zoosperm.**
▸**ˌspermato'zoal, ˌspermato'zoan,** *or* **ˌspermato'zoic** *adj*

spermicide ('spɜ:mɪˌsaɪd) *n* any agent that kills spermatozoa.
▸**ˌspermi'cidal** *adj*

sperm oil *n* an oil obtained from the head of the sperm whale, used as a lubricant.

spermous ('spɜ:məs) *adj* **1** of or relating to the sperm whale or its products. **2** another word for **spermatic.**

sperm whale *n* a large toothed whale, having a square-shaped head

THESAURUS

speed up *vb* **1** = **accelerate**, gather momentum, get moving, get under way, increase, increase the tempo, open up the throttle, put one's foot down (*inf.*), put on speed
Antonyms *vb* brake, decelerate, reduce speed, rein in, slacken (off), slow down

speedy *adj* **1, 2** = **quick**, expeditious, express, fast, fleet, fleet of foot, hasty, headlong, hurried, immediate, nimble, precipitate, prompt, rapid, summary, swift, winged
Antonyms *adj* dead slow and stop, delayed, dilatory, late, leisurely, lingering, long-drawn-out, plodding, slow, sluggish, tardy, unhurried, unrushed

spell[1] *vb* **3** = **indicate**, amount to, augur, herald, imply, mean, point to, portend, presage, promise, signify, suggest

spell[2] *n* **1** = **incantation**, abracadabra, charm, conjuration, exorcism, sorcery, witchery **2, 3** = **enchantment**, allure, bewitchment, fascination, glamour, magic, trance

spell[3] *n* **1, 2** = **period**, bout, course, interval, patch, season, stint, stretch, term, time, turn

spellbound *adj* = **entranced**, bemused, bewitched, captivated, charmed, enthralled, fascinated, gripped, hooked, mesmerized, possessed, rapt, transfixed, transported, under a spell

spelling *n* **1-4** = **orthography**

spell out *vb* **1** = **make clear** *or* **plain**, clarify, elucidate, explicate, make explicit, specify **3** = **puzzle out**, discern, make out

spend *vb* **1** = **pay out**, disburse, expend, fork out, lay out, shell out (*inf.*), splash out (*Brit. inf.*) **2** = **apply**, bestow, concentrate, devote, employ, exert, invest, lavish, put in, use **3** = **pass**, fill, occupy, while away **4** = **use up**, blow (*sl.*), consume, deplete, dissipate, drain, empty, exhaust, fritter away, run through, squander, waste
Antonyms *vb* ≠ **pay out, use up:** hoard, invest, keep, put aside, put by, save, store

spendthrift *n* **1** = **squanderer**, big spender, prodigal, profligate, spender, waster, wastrel ◆ *adj* **2** = **wasteful**, extravagant, improvident, prodigal, profligate
Antonyms *n* ≠ **squanderer:** meanie *or* meany (*inf., chiefly Brit.*), miser, penny-pincher (*inf.*), Scrooge, skinflint, tightwad (*US & Canad. sl.*) ◆ *adj* ≠ **wasteful:** careful, economical, frugal, parsimonious, provident, prudent, sparing, thrifty

spent *adj* **2** = **used up**, consumed, expended, finished, gone **2** = **exhausted**, all in (*sl.*), burnt out, bushed (*inf.*), clapped out (*Austral. & NZ inf.*), dead beat (*inf.*), debilitated, dog-tired (*inf.*), done in *or* up (*inf.*), drained, effete, knackered (*sl.*), played out (*inf.*), prostrate, ready to drop (*inf.*), shattered (*inf.*), tired out, weakened, wearied, weary, whacked (*Brit. inf.*), wiped out (*inf.*), worn out

sperm[1] *n* **1** = **semen**, scum (*US sl.*), seed (*arch. or dialect*), spermatozoa **2** = **spermatozoon**, male gamete, reproductive cell

and hunted for sperm oil, spermaceti, and ambergris. Also called: **cachalot.** [C19: short for SPERMACETI *whale*]

spew ❶ (spju:) *vb* **1** to eject (the contents of the stomach) involuntarily through the mouth; vomit. **2** to spit (spittle, phlegm, etc.) out of the mouth. **3** (usually foll. by *out*) to send or be sent out in a stream: *flames spewed out.* ◆ *n* **4** something ejected from the mouth. ◆ Also (archaic): **spue.** [OE *spīwan*]
▸'**spewer** *n*

sp. gr. *abbrev. for* specific gravity.

sphagnum ('sfægnəm) *n* any moss of the genus *Sphagnum,* of temperate bogs: layers of these mosses decay to form peat. Also called: **peat moss, bog moss.** [C18: from NL, from Gk *sphagnos* a variety of moss]
▸'**sphagnous** *adj*

sphairee (sfaɪri:) *n Austral.* a game resembling tennis played with wooden bats and a perforated plastic ball. [from Gk *sphaira* a ball]

sphalerite ('sfæləˌraɪt, 'sfeɪlə-) *n* a yellow to brownish-black mineral consisting mainly of zinc sulphide in cubic crystalline form: the chief source of zinc. Formula: ZnS. Also called: **zinc blende.** [C19: from Gk *sphaleros* deceitful, from *sphallein* to cause to stumble]

sphene (sfi:n) *n* a brown, yellow, green, or grey lustrous mineral consisting of calcium titanium silicate in monoclinic crystalline form. Also called: **titanite.** [C19: from F *sphène,* from Gk *sphēn* a wedge, alluding to its crystals]

sphenoid ('sfi:nɔɪd) *adj also* **sphenoidal. 1** wedge-shaped. **2** of or relating to the sphenoid bone. ◆ *n* **3** See **sphenoid bone.**

sphenoid bone *n* the large butterfly-shaped compound bone at the base of the skull.

sphere ❶ (sfɪə) *n* **1** *Maths.* **1a** a three-dimensional closed surface such that every point on the surface is equidistant from a given point, the centre. **1b** the solid figure bounded by this surface or the space enclosed by it. **2** any object having approximately this shape; a globe. **3** the night sky considered as a vaulted roof; firmament. **4** any heavenly object such as a planet, natural satellite, or star. **5** (in the Ptolemaic or Copernican systems of astronomy) one of a series of revolving hollow globes, arranged concentrically, on whose transparent surfaces the sun, the moon, the planets, and fixed stars were thought to be set. **6** a particular field of activity; environment. **7** a social class or stratum of society. ◆ *vb* **spheres, sphering, sphered.** (*tr*) *Chiefly poetic.* **8** to surround or encircle. **9** to place aloft or in the heavens. [C14: from LL *sphēra,* from L *sphaera* globe, from Gk *sphaira*]
▸'**spheral** *adj*

-sphere *n combining form.* **1** having the shape or form of a sphere: *bathysphere.* **2** indicating a spherelike enveloping mass: *atmosphere.*
▸**-spheric** *adj combining form.*

spherical ❶ ('sferɪkᵊl) *or* **spheric** *adj* **1** shaped like a sphere. **2** of or relating to a sphere: *spherical geometry.* **3** *Geom.* formed on the surface of or inside a sphere: *a spherical triangle.* **4a** of or relating to heavenly bodies. **4b** of or relating to the spheres of the Ptolemaic or the Copernican system.
▸'**spherically** *adv* ▸'**sphericalness** *n*

spherical aberration *n Physics.* a defect of optical systems that arises when light striking a mirror or lens near its edge is focused at different points on the axis to the light striking near the centre. The effect occurs when the mirror or lens has spherical surfaces.

spherical angle *n* an angle formed at the intersection of two great circles of a sphere.

spherical coordinates *pl n* three coordinates that define the location of a point in space in terms of its radius vector, *r,* the angle, θ, which this vector makes with one axis, and the angle, ϕ, which the plane of this vector makes with a mutually perpendicular axis.

spherical trigonometry *n* the branch of trigonometry concerned with the measurement of the angles and sides of spherical triangles.

spheroid ('sfɪərɔɪd) *n* **1** another name for **ellipsoid of revolution.** ◆ *adj* **2** shaped like but not exactly a sphere.
▸**spher'oidal** *adj* ▸ˌ**spheroid'icity** *n*

spherometer (sfɪə'rɒmɪtə) *n* an instrument for measuring the curvature of a surface.

spherule ('sferu:l) *n* a very small sphere. [C17: from LL *sphaerula*]
▸'**spherular** *adj*

spherulite ('sferuˌlaɪt) *n* any of several spherical masses of radiating needle-like crystals of one or more minerals occurring in rocks such as obsidian.
▸**spherulitic** (ˌsferu'lɪtɪk) *adj*

sphincter ('sfɪŋktə) *n Anat.* a ring of muscle surrounding the opening of a hollow organ or body and contracting to close it. [C16: from LL, from Gk *sphinkter,* from *sphingein* to grip tightly]
▸'**sphincteral** *adj*

sphinx (sfɪŋks) *n, pl* **sphinxes** *or* **sphinges** ('sfɪndʒi:z). **1** any of a number of huge stone statues built by the ancient Egyptians, having the body of a lion and the head of a man. **2** an inscrutable person.

Sphinx (sfɪŋks) *n* **the. 1** *Greek myth.* a monster with a woman's head and a lion's body. She lay outside Thebes, asking travellers a riddle and killing them when they failed to answer it. Oedipus answered the riddle and the Sphinx then killed herself. **2** the huge statue of a sphinx near the pyramids at El Gîza in Egypt. [C16: via L from Gk, apparently from *sphingein* to hold fast]

sphragistics (sfrə'dʒɪstɪks) *n* (*functioning as sing*) the study of seals and signet rings. [C19: from Gk *sphragistikos,* from *sphragizein* to seal, from *sphragis* a seal]
▸**sphra'gistic** *adj*

sphygmo- *or before a vowel* **sphygm-** *combining form.* indicating the pulse: *sphygmograph.* [from Gk *sphugmos* pulsation, from *sphuzein* to throb]

sphygmograph ('sfɪgməʊˌgrɑ:f) *n Med.* an instrument for making a recording (**sphygmogram**) of variations in blood pressure and pulse.
▸**sphygmographic** (ˌsfɪgməʊ'græfɪk) *adj* ▸**sphygmography** (sfɪg'mɒgrəfɪ) *n*

sphygmomanometer (ˌsfɪgməʊmə'nɒmɪtə) *n Med.* an instrument for measuring arterial blood pressure.

spicate ('spaɪkeɪt) *adj Bot.* having, arranged in, or relating to spikes: *a spicate inflorescence.* [C17: from L *spīcātus* having spikes, from *spīca* a point]

spiccato (spɪ'kɑ:təʊ) *Music.* ◆ *n* **1** a style of playing a bowed stringed instrument in which the bow bounces lightly off the strings. ◆ *adj, adv* **2** (to be played) in this manner. [It.: detached]

spice ❶ (spaɪs) *n* **1a** any of a variety of aromatic vegetable substances, such as ginger, cinnamon, or nutmeg, used as flavourings. **1b** these substances collectively. **2** something that represents or introduces zest, charm, or gusto. **3** *Rare.* a small amount. ◆ *vb* **spices, spicing, spiced.** (*tr*) **4** to prepare or flavour (food) with spices. **5** to introduce charm or zest into. [C13: from OF *espice,* from LL *speciēs* (pl) spices, from L *speciēs* (sing) kind; also associated with LL *spīcea* (unattested) fragrant herb, from L *spīceus* having spikes of foliage]

spicebush ('spaɪsˌbʊʃ) *n* a North American shrub having aromatic leaves and bark.

spick-and-span ❶ *or* **spic-and-span** ('spɪkən'spæn) *adj* **1** extremely neat and clean. **2** new and fresh. [C17: shortened from *spick-and-span-new,* from obs. *spick* spike + *span-new,* from ON *spānnȳr* absolutely new]

spicule ('spɪkju:l) *n* **1** Also called: **spiculum.** a small slender pointed structure or crystal, esp. any of the calcareous or siliceous elements of the skeleton of sponges, corals, etc. **2** *Astron.* a spiked ejection of hot gas above the sun's surface. [C18: from L *spiculum* small, sharp point]
▸**spiculate** ('spɪkjuˌleɪt, -lɪt) *adj*

spicy ❶ ('spaɪsɪ) *adj* **spicier, spiciest. 1** seasoned with or containing spice. **2** highly flavoured; pungent. **3** *Inf.* suggestive of scandal or sensation.
▸'**spicily** *adv* ▸'**spiciness** *n*

spider ('spaɪdə) *n* **1** any of various predatory silk-producing arachnids, having four pairs of legs and a rounded unsegmented body. **2** any of various similar or related arachnids. **3** any implement or tool having the shape of a spider. **4** any part of a machine having a number of radiating spokes, tines, or arms. **5** Also called: **octopus.** *Brit.* a cluster of elastic straps fastened at a central point and used to hold a load on a car rack, motorcycle, etc. **6** *Snooker, etc.* a rest having long legs, used to raise the cue above the level of the height of the ball. [OE *spīthra*]
▸'**spidery** *adj*

spider crab *n* any of various crabs having a small triangular body and very long legs.

spiderman ('spaɪdəˌmæn) *n, pl* **spidermen.** *Inf., chiefly Brit.* a person who erects the steel structure of a building.

spider mite *n* any of various plant-feeding mites, esp. the **red spider mite,** which is a serious orchard pest.

spider monkey *n* **1** any of several arboreal New World monkeys of Central and South America, having very long legs, a long prehensile tail, and a small head. **2 woolly spider monkey.** a rare related monkey of SE Brazil.

spider plant *n* a house plant having long narrow leaves with a light central stripe.

spiderwort ('spaɪdəˌwɜ:t) *n* **1** any of various American plants having blue, purplish, or pink flowers and widely grown as house plants. See also **tradescantia. 2** any of various similar or related plants.

spiel ❶ (ʃpi:l) *n* **1** glib plausible talk, associated esp. with salesmen. ◆ *vb* **2** (*intr*) to deliver a prepared spiel. **3** (*tr;* usually foll. by *off*) to recite (a prepared oration). [C19: from G *Spiel* play]
▸'**spieler** *n*

spier ('spaɪə) *n Arch.* a person who spies or scouts.

THESAURUS

spew *vb* **1 = vomit,** barf (*US sl.*), belch forth, chuck (up) (*sl., chiefly US*), chunder (*sl., chiefly Austral.*), disgorge, do a technicolour yawn (*sl.*), puke (*sl.*), regurgitate, spit out, throw up (*inf.*), toss one's cookies (*US sl.*)

sphere *n* **2 = ball,** circle, globe, globule, orb **6 = field,** capacity, compass, department, domain, employment, function, patch, province, range, realm, scope, territory, turf (*US sl.*), walk of life **7 = rank,** station, stratum

spherical *adj* **1 = round,** globe-shaped, globular, orbicular, rotund

spice *n* **1 = seasoning,** relish, savour **2 = excitement,** colour, gusto, kick (*inf.*), pep, piquancy, tang, zest, zing (*inf.*), zip (*inf.*)

spick-and-span *adj* **1 = neat,** clean, fresh as paint, immaculate, impeccable, in apple-pie order (*inf.*), shipshape, spotless, spruce, tidy, trim

spicy *adj* **2 = hot,** aromatic, flavoursome, piquant, pungent, savoury, seasoned, tangy **3** *Informal* **= scandalous,** broad, hot (*inf.*), improper, indecorous, indelicate, off-colour, racy, ribald, risqué, sensational, suggestive, titillating, unseemly

spiel *n* **1 = patter,** harangue, pitch, recital, sales patter, sales talk, speech

spiffing ('spɪfɪŋ) *adj Brit. sl., old-fashioned.* excellent; splendid. [C19: prob. from dialect *spiff* spruce, smart]

spiffy ('spɪfɪ) *adj* **spiffier, spiffiest.** *US & Canad. sl.* smart; stylish. [C19: from dialect *spiff* smartly dressed]
▸'**spiffily** *adv*

spigot ('spɪgət) *n* **1** a stopper for the vent hole of a cask. **2** a tap, usually of wood, fitted to a cask. **3** a US name for **tap**[2] (sense 1). **4** a short projection on one component designed to fit into a hole on another, esp. the male part of a joint between two pipes. [C14: prob. from OProvençal *espiga* a head of grain, from L *spīca* a point]

spike[1] ❶ (spaɪk) *n* **1** a sharp point. **2** any sharp-pointed object, esp. one made of metal. **3** a long metal nail. **4** *(pl)* shoes with metal projections on the sole and heel for greater traction, as used by athletes. **5** *Brit. sl.* another word for **dosshouse.** ◆ *vb* **spikes, spiking, spiked.** *(tr)* **6** to secure or supply with or as with spikes. **7** to render ineffective or block the intentions of; thwart. **8** to impale on a spike. **9** to add alcohol to (a drink). **10** *Volleyball.* to hit (a ball) sharply downwards with an overarm motion from the front of one's own court into the opposing court. **11** (formerly) to render (a cannon) ineffective by blocking its vent with a spike. **12 spike (someone's) guns.** to thwart (someone's) purpose. [C13 *spyk*]
▸'**spiky** *adj*

spike[2] (spaɪk) *n Bot.* **1** an inflorescence consisting of a raceme of sessile flowers. **2** an ear of wheat, etc. [C14: from L *spīca* ear of corn]

spikelet ('spaɪklɪt) *n Bot.* a small spike, esp. the inflorescence of most grasses and sedges.

spikenard ('spaɪknɑːd, 'spaɪkəˌnɑːd) *n* **1** an aromatic Indian plant, having rose-purple flowers. **2** an aromatic ointment obtained from this plant. **3** any of various similar or related plants. **4** a North American plant having small green flowers and an aromatic root. ◆ Also called (for senses 1, 2): **nard.** [C14: from Med. L *spīca nardī*; see SPIKE[2], NARD]

spile (spaɪl) *n* **1** a heavy timber stake or pile. **2** *US.* a spout for tapping sap from the sugar maple tree. **3** a plug or spigot. ◆ *vb* **spiles, spiling, spiled.** *(tr)* **4** to provide or support with a spile. **5** *US.* to tap (a tree) with a spile. [C16: prob. from MDu. *spile* peg]

spill[1] ❶ (spɪl) *vb* **spills, spilling; spilt** *or* **spilled.** *(mainly tr)* **1** (when *intr*, usually foll. by *from, out of,* etc.) to fall or cause to fall from or as from a container, esp. unintentionally. **2** to disgorge (contents, occupants, etc.) or (of contents, occupants, etc.) to be disgorged. **3** to shed (blood). **4** Also: **spill the beans.** *Inf.* to divulge something confidential. **5** *Naut.* to let (wind) escape from a sail or (of the wind) to escape from a sail. ◆ *n* **6** *Inf.* a fall or tumble. **7** short for **spillway. 8** a spilling of liquid, etc., or the amount spilt. **9** *Austral.* the declaring of several political jobs vacant when one higher up becomes so. [OE *spillan* to destroy]
▸'**spillage** *n* ▸'**spiller** *n*

spill[2] (spɪl) *n* a splinter of wood or strip of twisted paper with which pipes, fires, etc., are lit. [C13: of Gmc origin]

spillikin, spilikin ('spɪlɪkɪn), *or* **spellican** ('spɛlɪkən) *n* a thin strip of wood, cardboard, or plastic, esp. one used in spillikins.

spillikins ('spɪlɪkɪnz) *n (functioning as sing) Brit.* a game in which players try to pick each spillikin from a heap without moving any of the others. Also called: **jackstraws.**

spill over *vb* **1** *(intr, adv)* to overflow or be forced out of an area, container, etc. ◆ *n* **spillover.** *Chiefly US & Canad.* **2** the act of spilling over. **3** the excess part of something.

spillway ('spɪlˌweɪ) *n* a channel that carries away surplus water, as from a dam.

spilt (spɪlt) *vb* a past tense and past participle of **spill**[1].

spin ❶ (spɪn) *vb* **spins, spinning, spun. 1** to rotate or cause to rotate rapidly, as on an axis. **2a** to draw out and twist (natural fibres, as of silk or cotton) into a long continuous thread. **2b** to make such a thread or filament from (synthetic resins, etc.), usually by forcing through a nozzle. **3** (of spiders, silkworms, etc.) to form (webs, cocoons, etc.) from a silky fibre exuded from the body. **4** *(tr)* to shape (metal) into a rounded form on a lathe. **5** *(tr) Inf.* to tell (a tale, story, etc.) by drawing it out at great length (esp. in **spin a yarn**). **6** to bowl, pitch, hit, or kick (a ball) so that it rotates in the air and changes direction or speed on bouncing, or (of a ball) to be projected in this way. **7** *(intr)* (of wheels) to revolve rapidly without causing propulsion. **8** to cause (an aircraft) to dive in a spiral descent or (of an aircraft) to dive in a spiral descent. **9** *(intr;* foll. by *along)* to drive or travel swiftly. **10** *(tr)* Also: **spin-dry.** to rotate (clothes) in a washing machine in order to extract surplus water. **11** *(intr)* to reel or grow dizzy, as from turning around: *my head is spinning.* **12** *(intr)* to fish by drawing a revolving lure through the water. **13** *(intr) Inf.* to present news or information in a way that creates a favourable impression. ◆ *n* **14** a swift rotating motion; instance of spinning. **15** *Physics.* **15a** the intrinsic angular momentum of an elementary particle or atomic nucleus. **15b** a quantum number determining values of this angular momentum. **16** a condition of loss of control of an aircraft or an intentional flight manoeuvre in which the aircraft performs a continuous spiral descent. **17** a spinning motion imparted to a ball, etc. **18** *Inf.* a short or fast drive, ride, etc., esp. in a car, for pleasure. **19 flat spin.** *Inf., chiefly Brit.* a state of agitation or confusion. **20** *Austral. & NZ inf.* a period of a specified kind of fortune: *a bad spin.* **21** *Inf.* the practice of presenting news or information in a way that creates a favourable impression. ◆ See also **spin out.** [OE *spinnan*]

spina bifida ('spaɪnə 'bɪfɪdə) *n* a congenital condition in which the meninges of the spinal cord protrude through a gap in the backbone, sometimes causing enlargement of the skull and paralysis. [NL; see SPINE, BIFID]

spinach ('spɪnɪdʒ, -ɪtʃ) *n* **1** an annual plant cultivated for its dark green edible leaves. **2** the leaves, eaten as a vegetable. [C16: from OF *espinache,* from OSp., from Ar. *isfānākh,* from Persian]

spinal ('spaɪnᵊl) *adj* **1** of or relating to the spine or the spinal cord. ◆ *n* **2** short for **spinal anaesthesia.**
▸'**spinally** *adv*

spinal anaesthesia *n* **1** anaesthesia of the lower half of the body produced by injecting an anaesthetic beneath the arachnoid membrane. Cf. **epidural** (sense 2). **2** loss of sensation in part of the body as the result of injury of the spinal cord.

spinal canal *n* the passage through the spinal column that contains the spinal cord.

spinal column *n* a series of contiguous or interconnecting bony or cartilaginous segments that surround and protect the spinal cord. Also called: **spine, vertebral column.** Nontechnical name: **backbone.**

spinal cord *n* the thick cord of nerve tissue within the spinal canal, which together with the brain forms the central nervous system.

spin bowler *n* another name for **spinner** (sense 2b).

spindle ('spɪndᵊl) *n* **1** a rod or stick that has a notch in the top, used to draw out natural fibres for spinning into thread, and a long narrow body around which the thread is wound when spun. **2** one of the thin rods or pins bearing bobbins upon which spun thread is wound in a spinning machine. **3** any of various parts in the form of a rod, esp. a rotating rod that acts as an axle, etc. **4** a piece of wood that has been turned, such as a table leg. **5** a small square metal shaft that passes through the lock of a door and to which the door knobs or handles are fixed. **6** *Biol.* a spindle-shaped structure formed in a cell during mitosis or meiosis which draws the duplicated chromosomes apart during cell division. **7** a device consisting of a sharp upright spike on a pedestal on which bills, order forms, etc., are impaled. ◆ *vb* **spindles, spindling, spindled. 8** *(tr)* to form into a spindle or equip with spindles. **9** *(intr) Rare.* (of a plant, stem, shoot, etc.) to grow rapidly and become elongated and thin. [OE *spinel*]

spindlelegs ('spɪndᵊlˌlegz) *or* **spindleshanks** *n* **1** *(functioning as pl)* long thin legs. **2** *(functioning as sing)* a person who has such legs.

spindle tree *n* any of various shrubs or trees of Europe and W Asia, typically having red fruits and yielding a hard wood formerly used in making spindles.

spindly ❶ ('spɪndlɪ) *adj* **spindlier, spindliest.** tall, slender, and frail; attenuated.

spin doctor *n Inf.* a person who provides a favourable slant to an item of news, potentially unpopular policy, etc., esp. on behalf of a political personality or party. [C20: from the spin given to a ball in various sports to make it go in the desired direction]

spindrift ('spɪnˌdrɪft) *n* spray blown up from the sea. Also: **spoondrift.** [C16: Scot. var. of *spoondrift,* from *spoon* to scud + DRIFT]

spin-dry *vb* **spin-dries, spin-drying, spin-dried.** *(tr)* to extract water from (wet washing) by spinning in a washing machine or spin-dryer.

spin-dryer *n* a device that extracts water from clothes, etc., by spinning them in a perforated drum.

spine ❶ (spaɪn) *n* **1** the spinal column. **2** the sharply pointed tip or outgrowth of a leaf, stem, etc. **3** *Zool.* a hard pointed process or structure, such as the quill of a porcupine. **4** the back of a book, record sleeve, etc. **5** a ridge, esp. of a hill. **6** strength of endurance, will, etc. **7** anything resembling the spinal column in function or importance; main support or feature. [C14: from OF *espine* spine, from L *spīna* thorn, backbone]
▸**spined** *adj*

spine-chiller ❶ *n* a book, film, etc., that arouses terror.
▸'**spine-ˌchilling** *adj*

spinel (spɪ'nɛl) *n* any of a group of hard glassy minerals of variable colour consisting of oxides of aluminium, magnesium, iron, zinc, or manganese: used as gemstones. [C16: from F *spinelle,* from It. *spinella,* dim. of *spina* a thorn, from L; so called from the shape of the crystals]

THESAURUS

spike[1] *n* **1, 2** = **point,** barb, prong, spine ◆ *vb* **8** = **impale,** spear, spit, stick

spill[1] *vb* **1, 2** = **pour,** discharge, disgorge, overflow, scatter, shed, slop over, spill *or* run over, teem, throw off, upset **4 spill the beans** *Informal* = **betray a secret,** blab, blow the gaff *(Brit. sl.)*, give the game away, grass *(Brit. sl.)*, inform, let the cat out of the bag, shop *(sl., chiefly Brit.)*, sing *(sl., chiefly US)*, spill one's guts *(sl.)*, split *(sl.)*, squeal *(sl.)*, talk out of turn, tattle, tell all ◆ *n* **6** *Informal* = **fall,** accident, cropper *(inf.)*, tumble

spin *vb* **1** = **revolve,** birl *(Scot.)*, gyrate, pirouette, reel, rotate, turn, twirl, twist, wheel, whirl **5** *As in* **spin a yarn** = **tell,** concoct, develop, invent, narrate, recount, relate, unfold **11** = **reel,** be giddy, be in a whirl, grow dizzy, swim, whirl ◆ *n* **14** = **revolution,** gyration, roll, twist, whirl **18** *Informal* = **drive,** hurl *(Scot.)*, joy ride *(inf.)*, ride, turn, whirl **19 flat spin** *Informal* = **panic,** agitation, commotion, flap *(inf.)*, state *(inf.)*, tizwoz *(inf.)*, tizzy *(inf.)*

spindly *adj* = **lanky,** attenuated, gangling, gangly, leggy, spidery, spindle-shanked, twiggy

spine *n* **1** = **backbone,** spinal column, vertebrae, vertebral column **3** = **barb,** needle, quill, rachis, ray, spike, spur

spine-chilling *adj* = **frightening,** bloodcurdling, eerie, hair-raising, horrifying, scary *(inf.)*, spooky *(inf.)*, terrifying

spineless Ⓣ ('spaɪnlɪs) *adj* **1** lacking a backbone. **2** having no spiny processes: *spineless stems.* **3** lacking character, resolution, or courage.
▸**'spinelessly** *adv* ▸**'spinelessness** *n*

spinet (spɪ'nɛt, 'spɪnɪt) *n* a small type of harpsichord having one manual. [C17: from It. *spinetta,* ? from Giovanni *Spinetti,* 16th-cent. It. maker of musical instruments & its supposed inventor]

spinifex ('spɪnɪˌfɛks) *n* **1** any of various Australian grasses having pointed leaves and spiny seed heads. **2** Also called: **porcupine grass.** *Austral.* any of various coarse spiny-leaved inland grasses. [C19: from NL, from L *spīna* a thorn + *-fex* maker, from *facere* to make]

spinnaker ('spɪnəkə; *Naut.* 'spæŋkə) *n* a large light triangular racing sail set from the foremast of a yacht. [C19: prob. from SPIN + (MO)NIKER, but traditionally from *Sphinx,* the yacht that first adopted this type of sail]

spinner ('spɪnə) *n* **1** a person or thing that spins. **2** *Cricket.* **2a** a ball that is bowled with a spinning motion. **2b** a bowler who specializes in bowling such balls. **3** a streamlined fairing that fits over the hub of an aircraft propeller. **4** a fishing lure with a fin or wing that revolves.

spinneret ('spɪnəˌrɛt) *n* **1** any of several organs in spiders and certain insects through which silk threads are exuded. **2** a finely perforated dispenser through which a liquid is extruded in the production of synthetic fibres.

spinney ('spɪnɪ) *n Chiefly Brit.* a small wood or copse. [C16: from OF *espinei,* from *espine* thorn, from L *spīna*]

spinning ('spɪnɪŋ) *n* **1** the act or process of spinning. **2** the act or technique of casting and drawing a revolving lure through the water so as to imitate a live fish, etc.

spinning jenny *n* an early type of spinning frame with several spindles, invented in 1764.

spinning wheel *n* a wheel-like machine for spinning at home, having one hand- or foot-operated spindle.

spin-off *n* **1** any product or development derived incidentally from the application of existing knowledge or enterprise. **2** a book, film, or television series derived from a similar successful book, film, or television series.

spinose ('spaɪnəʊs, spaɪ'nəʊs) *adj* (esp. of plants) bearing many spines. [C17: from L *spīnōsus* prickly, from *spīna* a thorn]

spin out Ⓣ *vb* (*tr, adv*) **1** to extend or protract (a story, etc.) by including superfluous detail. **2** to spend or pass (time). **3** to contrive to cause (money, etc.) to last as long as possible.

spinster ('spɪnstə) *n* **1** an unmarried woman. **2** a woman regarded as being beyond the age of marriage. **3** (formerly) a woman who spins thread for her living. [C14 (in the sense: a person, esp. a woman, whose occupation is spinning; C17: a woman still unmarried): from SPIN + -STER]
▸**'spinsterˌhood** *n* ▸**'spinsterish** *adj*

spiny ('spaɪnɪ) *adj* **spinier, spiniest. 1** (of animals) having or covered with quills or spines. **2** (of plants) covered with spines; thorny. **3** troublesome; puzzling.
▸**'spininess** *n*

spiny anteater *n* another name for **echidna.**

spiny-finned *adj* (of certain fishes) having fins that are supported by stiff bony spines.

spiny lobster *n* any of various large edible marine decapod crustaceans having a very tough spiny carapace. Also called: **rock lobster, crawfish, langouste.**

spiracle ('spaɪərəkᵊl, 'spaɪrə-) *n* **1** any of several paired apertures in the cuticle of an insect, by which air enters and leaves the trachea. **2** a small paired rudimentary gill slit in skates, rays, and related fishes. **3** any similar respiratory aperture, such as the blowhole in whales. [C14 (orig.: breath): from L *spīrāculum* vent, from *spīrāre* to breathe]
▸**spiracular** (spɪ'rækjʊlə) *adj* ▸**spi'raculate** *adj*

spiraea *or esp. US* **spirea** (spaɪ'rɪə) *n* any of various rosaceous plants having sprays of small white or pink flowers. See also **meadowsweet** (sense 2). [C17: via L from Gk *speiraia,* from *speira* SPIRE[2]]

spiral Ⓣ ('spaɪərəl) *n* **1** *Geom.* one of several plane curves formed by a point winding about a fixed point at an ever-increasing distance from it. **2** a curve that lies on a cylinder or cone, at a constant angle to the line segments making up the surface; helix. **3** something that pursues a winding, usually upward, course or that displays a twisting form or shape. **4** a flight manoeuvre in which an aircraft descends describing a helix of comparatively large radius with the angle of attack within the normal flight range. **5** *Econ.* a continuous upward or downward movement in economic activity or prices, caused by interaction between prices, wages, demand, and production. ◆ *adj* **6** having the shape of a spiral. ◆ *vb* **spirals, spiralling, spiralled** *or US* **spirals, spiraling, spiraled. 7** to assume or cause to assume a spiral course or shape. **8** (*intr*) to increase or decrease with steady acceleration: *prices continue to spiral.* [C16: via F from Med. L *spīrālis,* from L *spīra* a coil; see SPIRE[2]]
▸**'spirally** *adv*

spiral galaxy *n* a galaxy consisting of an ellipsoidal nucleus of old stars from opposite sides of which arms, containing younger stars, spiral outwards around the nucleus.

spirant ('spaɪrənt) *adj* **1** *Phonetics.* another word for **fricative.** ◆ *n* **2** a fricative consonant. [C19: from L *spīrāns* breathing, from *spīrāre* to breathe]

spire[1] ('spaɪə) *n* **1** Also called: **steeple.** a tall structure that tapers upwards to a point, esp. one on a tower or roof or one that forms the upper part of a steeple. **2** a slender tapering shoot or stem, such as a blade of grass. **3** the apical part of any tapering formation; summit. ◆ *vb* **spires, spiring, spired. 4** (*intr*) to assume the shape of a spire; point up. **5** (*tr*) to furnish with a spire or spires. [OE *spīr* blade]
▸**'spiry** *adj*

spire[2] ('spaɪə) *n* **1** any of the coils or turns in a spiral structure. **2** the apical part of a spiral shell. [C16: from L *spīra* a coil, from Gk *speira*]

spirillum (spaɪ'rɪləm) *n, pl* **spirilla** (-lə). **1** any bacterium having a curved or spirally twisted rodlike body. **2** any bacterium of the genus *Spirillum,* such as *S. minus,* which causes ratbite fever. [C19: from NL, lit.: a little coil, from *spīra* a coil]

spirit[1] Ⓣ ('spɪrɪt) *n* **1** the force or principle of life that animates the body of living things. **2** temperament or disposition: *truculent in spirit.* **3** liveliness; mettle: *they set to it with spirit.* **4** the fundamental, emotional, and activating principle of a person; will: *the experience broke his spirit.* **5** a sense of loyalty or dedication: *team spirit.* **6** the prevailing element; feeling: *a spirit of joy pervaded the atmosphere.* **7** state of mind or mood; attitude: *he did it in the wrong spirit.* **8** (*pl*) an emotional state, esp. with regard to exaltation or dejection: *in high spirits.* **9** a person characterized by some activity, quality, or disposition: *a leading spirit of the movement.* **10** the deeper more significant meaning as opposed to a pedantic interpretation: *the spirit of the law.* **11** a person's intangible being as contrasted with his physical presence: *I shall be with you in spirit.* **12a** an incorporeal being, esp. the soul of a dead person. **12b** (*as modifier*): *spirit world.* ◆ *vb* (*tr*) **13** (usually foll. by *away* or *off*) to carry off mysteriously or secretly. **14** (often foll. by *up*) to impart animation or determination to. [C13: from OF *esperit,* from L *spīritus* breath, spirit]
▸**'spiritless** *adj*

spirit[2] Ⓣ ('spɪrɪt) *n* **1** (*often pl*) any distilled alcoholic liquor, such as whisky or gin. **2** *Chem.* **2a** an aqueous solution of ethanol, esp. one obtained by distillation. **2b** the active principle or essence of a substance, extracted as a liquid, esp. by distillation. **3** *Pharmacol.* a solution of a volatile substance, esp. a volatile oil, in alcohol. **4** *Alchemy.* any of the four substances sulphur, mercury, sal ammoniac, or arsenic. [C14: special use of SPIRIT[1], name applied to alchemical substances (as in sense 4), hence extended to distilled liquids]

Spirit ('spɪrɪt) *n* **the. a** another name for the **Holy Spirit. b** God, esp. when regarded as transcending material limitations.

spirited Ⓣ ('spɪrɪtɪd) *adj* **1** displaying animation, vigour, or liveliness. **2** (*in combination*) characterized by mood, temper, or disposition as specified: *high-spirited; public-spirited.*
▸**'spiritedly** *adv* ▸**'spiritedness** *n*

spirit gum *n* a glue made from gum dissolved in ether used to affix a false beard, etc.

spiritism ('spɪrɪˌtɪzəm) *n* a less common word for **spiritualism.**
▸**'spiritist** *n* ▸**ˌspirit'istic** *adj*

spirit lamp *n* a lamp that burns methylated or other spirits instead of oil.

spirit level *n* a device for setting horizontal surfaces, consisting of a block of material in which a sealed tube partially filled with liquid is set so that the air bubble rests between two marks on the tube when the block is horizontal.

spiritous ('spɪrɪtəs) *adj* a variant of **spirituous.**

THESAURUS

spineless *adj* **3** = **weak,** boneless, cowardly, faint-hearted, feeble, gutless (*inf.*), inadequate, ineffective, irresolute, lily-livered, pathetic, soft, spiritless, squeamish, submissive, vacillating, weak-kneed (*inf.*), weak-willed, without a will of one's own, yellow (*inf.*)
Antonyms *adj* bold, brave, courageous, gritty, strong, strong-willed

spin out *vb* **1** = **prolong,** amplify, delay, drag out, draw out, extend, lengthen, pad out, prolongate, protract

spiral *n* **3** = **coil,** corkscrew, curlicue, gyre (*literary*), helix, screw, volute, whorl ◆ *adj* **6** = **coiled,** circular, cochlear, cochleate (*Biology*), corkscrew, helical, scrolled, voluted, whorled, winding

spirit[1] *n* **1** = **life force,** air, breath, life, psyche, soul, vital spark **2** = **temperament,** attitude, character, complexion, disposition, essence, humour, outlook, quality, temper **3** = **liveliness,** animation, ardour, brio, earnestness, energy, enterprise, enthusiasm, fire, force, life, mettle, resolution, sparkle, vigour, warmth, zest **4** = **will,** motivation, resolution, resolve, willpower **5** = **courage,** backbone, dauntlessness, gameness, grit, guts (*inf.*), spunk (*inf.*), stoutheartedness **6** = **feeling,** atmosphere, gist, humour, tenor, tone **8** *plural* = **mood,** feelings, frame of mind, humour, morale **10** = **intention,** essence, intent, meaning, purport, purpose, sense, substance **12** = **ghost,** apparition, eidolon, phantom, shade (*literary*), shadow, spectre, spook (*inf.*), sprite, vision ◆ *vb* **13** *with* **away** *or* **off** = **remove,** abduct, abstract, carry, convey, make away with, purloin, seize, snaffle (*Brit. inf.*), steal, whisk

spirit[2] *n, often plural* = **alcohol,** firewater, liquor, strong liquor, the hard stuff (*inf.*)

spirited *adj* **1** = **lively,** active, animated, ardent, bold, courageous, energetic, feisty (*inf., chiefly US & Canad.*), game, have-a-go (*inf.*), high-spirited, mettlesome, plucky, sparkling, sprightly, spunky (*inf.*), vigorous, vivacious
Antonyms *adj* apathetic, bland, calm, dispirited, dull, feeble, half-hearted, lacklustre, lifeless, low-key, spiritless, timid, token, unenthusiastic, weary

spiritless *adj* **3, 5** = **lifeless,** apathetic, dejected, depressed, despondent, dispirited, droopy, dull, lacklustre, languid, listless, low (*inf.*), melancholic, melancholy, mopy, torpid, unenthusiastic, unmoved

spirits of ammonia *n* (*functioning as sing or pl*) another name for **sal volatile.**

spirits of hartshorn *n* (*functioning as sing or pl*) a solution of ammonia gas in water. See **ammonium hydroxide.** Also called: **aqueous ammonia.**

spirits of salt *n* (*functioning as sing or pl*) a solution of hydrochloric acid in water.

spiritual ➊ ('spɪrɪtjʊəl) *adj* **1** relating to the spirit or soul and not to physical nature or matter; intangible. **2** of or relating to sacred things, the Church, religion, etc. **3** standing in a relationship based on communication between souls or minds: *a spiritual father.* **4** having a mind or emotions of a high and delicately refined quality. ◆ *n* **5** Also called: **Negro spiritual.** a type of religious song originating among Black slaves in the American South. **6** (*often pl*) the sphere of religious, spiritual, or ecclesiastical matters, or such matters in themselves.
▸ˌ**spiritu'ality** *n* ▸'**spiritually** *adv*

spiritualism ('spɪrɪtjʊəˌlɪzəm) *n* **1** the belief that the disembodied spirits of the dead, surviving in another world, can communicate with the living in this world, esp. through mediums. **2** the doctrines and practices associated with this belief. **3** *Philosophy.* the belief that because reality is to some extent immaterial it is therefore spiritual. **4** any doctrine that prefers the spiritual to the material.
▸'**spiritualist** *n*

spiritualize *or* **spiritualise** ('spɪrɪtjʊəˌlaɪz) *vb* **spiritualizes, spiritualizing, spiritualized** *or* **spiritualises, spiritualising, spiritualised.** (*tr*) to make spiritual or infuse with spiritual content.
▸ˌ**spirituali'zation** *or* ˌ**spirituali'sation** *n* ▸'**spiritualˌizer** *or* '**spiritualˌiser** *n*

spirituel (ˌspɪrɪtjʊ'ɛl) *adj* having a refined and lively mind or wit. Also (fem): **spirituelle.** [C17: from F]

spirituous ('spɪrɪtjʊəs) *adj* **1** characterized by or containing alcohol. **2** (of a drink) being a spirit.
▸**spirituosity** (ˌspɪrɪtjʊ'ɒsɪtɪ) *or* '**spirituousness** *n*

spirochaete *or US* **spirochete** ('spaɪrəʊˌkiːt) *n* any of a group of spirally coiled rodlike bacteria that includes the causative agent of syphilis. [C19: from NL, from *spiro-*, from L *spira*, from Gk *speira* a coil + *chaeta*, from Gk *khaitē* long hair]

spirograph ('spaɪrəˌgrɑːf) *n Med.* an instrument for recording the movements of breathing. [C20: NL, from *spiro-*, from L *spīrāre* to breathe + -GRAPH]
▸ˌ**spiro'graphic** *adj*

spirogyra (ˌspaɪrə'dʒaɪrə) *n* any of various green freshwater multicellular algae containing spirally coiled chloroplasts. [C20: from NL, from *spiro-*, from L *spīra*, from Gk *speira* a coil + Gk *guros* a circle]

spirt (spɜːt) *n* a variant spelling of **spurt.**

spiry ('spaɪərɪ) *adj Poetic.* of spiral form; helical.

spit[1] ➊ (spɪt) *vb* **spits, spitting, spat** *or* **spit. 1** (*intr*) to expel saliva from the mouth; expectorate. **2** (*intr*) *Inf.* to show disdain or hatred by spitting. **3** (of a fire, hot fat, etc.) to eject (sparks, etc.) violently and with an explosive sound. **4** (*intr*) to rain very lightly. **5** (*tr*; often foll. by *out*) to eject or discharge (something) from the mouth: *he spat the food out.* **6** (*tr*; often foll. by *out*) to utter (short sharp words or syllables), esp. in a violent manner. **7 spit it out!** *Brit. inf.* a command given to someone that he should speak forthwith. ◆ *n* **8** another name for **spittle. 9** a light or brief fall of rain, snow, etc. **10** the act or an instance of spitting. **11** *Inf., chiefly Brit.* another word for **spitting image.** [OE *spittan*]
▸'**spitter** *n*

spit[2] (spɪt) *n* **1** a pointed rod on which meat is skewered and roasted before or over an open fire. **2** Also called: **rotisserie, rotating spit.** a similar device fitted onto a cooker. **3** an elongated often hooked strip of sand or shingle projecting from a shore. ◆ *vb* **spits, spitting, spitted. 4** (*tr*) to impale on or transfix with or as if with a spit. [OE *spitu*]

spit and polish *n Inf.* punctilious attention to neatness, discipline, etc., esp. in the armed forces.

spite ➊ (spaɪt) *n* **1** maliciousness; venomous ill will. **2** an instance of such malice; grudge. **3 in spite of.** (*prep*) in defiance of; regardless of; notwithstanding. ◆ *vb* **spites, spiting, spited.** (*tr*) **4** to annoy in order to vent spite. [C13: var. of DESPITE]
▸'**spiteful** *adj*

spitfire ('spɪtˌfaɪə) *n* a person given to outbursts of spiteful temper, esp. a woman or girl.

spitting image ➊ *n Inf.* a person who bears a strong physical resemblance to another. Also called: **spit, spit and image.** [C19: modification of *spit and image*, from SPIT[1] (as in *the very spit of* the exact likeness of)]

spitting snake *n* another name for the **rinkhals.**

spittle ('spɪt^əl) *n* **1** the fluid secreted in the mouth; saliva. **2** Also called: **cuckoo spit, frog spit.** the frothy substance secreted on plants by the larvae of certain froghoppers. [OE *spǣtl* saliva]

spittoon (spɪ'tuːn) *n* a receptacle for spittle, usually in a public place.

spitz (spɪts) *n* any of various breeds of dog characterized by a stocky build, a pointed muzzle, erect ears, and a tightly-curled tail. [C19: from G *Spitz*, from *spitz* pointed]

spiv (spɪv) *n Brit. sl.* a person who makes a living by underhand dealings or swindling; black marketeer. [C20: back formation from dialect *spiving* smart]
▸'**spivvy** *adj*

splake (spleɪk) *n* a type of hybrid trout bred by Canadian zoologists. [from *sp(eckled)* + *lake (trout)*]

splanchnic ('splæŋknɪk) *adj* of or relating to the viscera: *a splanchnic nerve.* [C17: from NL *splanchnicus*, from Gk, from *splankhna* the entrails]

splash ➊ (splæʃ) *vb* **1** to scatter (liquid) about in blobs; spatter. **2** to descend or cause to descend upon in scattered blobs: *he splashed his jacket; rain splashed against the window.* **3** to make (one's way) by or as if by splashing: *he splashed through the puddle.* **4** (*tr*) to print (a story or photograph) prominently in a newspaper. ◆ *n* **5** an instance or sound of splashing. **6** an amount splashed. **7** a mark or patch created by or as if by splashing. **8** *Inf.* an extravagant display, usually for effect (esp. in **make a splash**). **9** a small amount of soda water, etc., added to an alcoholic drink. [C18: alteration of PLASH]
▸'**splashy** *adj*

splashdown ('splæʃˌdaʊn) *n* **1** the controlled landing of a spacecraft on water at the end of a space flight. **2** the time scheduled for this event. ◆ *vb* **splash down. 3** (*intr, adv*) (of a spacecraft) to make a splashdown.

splat[1] (splæt) *n* a wet slapping sound. [C19: imit.]

splat[2] (splæt) *n* a wide flat piece of wood, esp. one that is the upright central part of a chair back. [C19: ? rel. to OE *splātan* to split]

splatter ('splætə) *vb* **1** to splash with small blobs. ◆ *n* **2** a splash of liquid, mud, etc.

splatter movie *n Sl.* a film in which the main feature is the graphic and gory murder of numerous victims.

splay (spleɪ) *adj* **1** spread out; broad and flat. **2** turned outwards in an awkward manner. ◆ *vb* **3** to spread out; turn out or expand. ◆ *n* **4** a surface of a wall that forms an oblique angle to the main flat surfaces, esp. at a doorway or window opening. [C14: short for DISPLAY]

splayfoot ('spleɪˌfʊt) *n, pl* **splayfeet.** *Pathol.* another word for **flatfoot.**
▸'**splayˌfooted** *adj*

spleen ➊ (spliːn) *n* **1** a spongy highly vascular organ situated near the stomach in man. It forms lymphocytes, produces antibodies, and filters bacteria and foreign particles from the blood. **2** the corresponding organ in other animals. **3** spitefulness or ill humour: *to vent one's spleen.* **4** *Arch.* the organ in the human body considered to be the seat of the emotions. **5** *Arch.* another word for **melancholy.** [C13: from OF *esplen*, from L *splēn*, from Gk]
▸'**spleenish** *or* '**spleeny** *adj*

spleenwort ('spliːnˌwɜːt) *n* any of various ferns that often grow on walls.

splendent ('splɛndənt) *adj Arch.* **1** shining brightly; lustrous: *a splendent sun.* **2** famous; illustrious. [C15: from L *splendēns* brilliant, from *splendēre* to shine]

splendid ➊ ('splɛndɪd) *adj* **1** brilliant or fine, esp. in appearance. **2**

THESAURUS

spiritual *adj* **1 = nonmaterial**, ethereal, ghostly, immaterial, incorporeal **2 = sacred**, devotional, divine, holy, religious **4 = otherworldly**, pure
Antonyms *adj* ≠ **nonmaterial:** concrete, corporeal, material, nonspiritual, palpable, physical, substantial, tangible

spit[1] *vb* **1, 3, 5 = eject**, discharge, expectorate, hiss, spew, splutter, sputter, throw out ◆ *n* **8 = saliva**, dribble, drool, slaver, spittle, sputum

spite *n* **1 = malice**, animosity, bitchiness (*sl.*), gall, grudge, hate, hatred, ill will, malevolence, malignity, pique, rancour, spitefulness, spleen, venom **3 in spite of = despite**, (even) though, in defiance of, notwithstanding, regardless of ◆ *vb* **4 = annoy**, discomfit, gall, harm, hurt, injure, needle (*inf.*), nettle, offend, pique, provoke, put out, put (someone's) nose out of joint (*inf.*), vex
Antonyms *n* ≠ **malice:** benevolence, big-heartedness, charity, compassion, generosity of spirit, goodwill, kindliness, kindness, love, warm-heartedness ◆ *vb* ≠ **annoy:** aid, benefit, encourage, go along with, help, please, serve, support

spiteful *adj* **1 = malicious**, barbed, bitchy (*inf.*), catty (*inf.*), cruel, ill-disposed, ill-natured, malevolent, malignant, nasty, rancorous, shrewish, snide, splenetic, venomous, vindictive

spitting image *n* **= double**, clone, (dead) ringer (*sl.*), likeness, living image, lookalike, picture, replica, spit (*inf., chiefly Brit.*), spit and image (*inf.*)

splash *vb* **1 = scatter**, bespatter, shower, slop, slosh (*inf.*), spatter, splodge, spray, spread, sprinkle, squirt, strew, wet **2 = dash**, batter, break, buffet, plash, plop, smack, strike, surge, wash **3 = wade**, bathe, dabble, paddle, plunge, wallow **4 = publicize**, blazon, broadcast, flaunt, headline, plaster, tout, trumpet ◆ *n* **6, 7 = dash**, burst, patch, spattering, splodge, touch **8** *Informal* **= display**, effect, impact, sensation, splurge, stir **8 make a splash** *Informal* **= cause a stir**, be ostentatious, cut a dash, go overboard (*inf.*), go to town, splurge

spleen *n* **3 = spite**, acrimony, anger, animosity, animus, bad temper, bile, bitterness, gall, hatred, hostility, ill humour, ill will, malevolence, malice, malignity, peevishness, pique, rancour, resentment, spitefulness, venom, vindictiveness, wrath

splendid *adj* **2 = magnificent**, costly, dazzling, gorgeous, grand, imposing, impressive, lavish, luxurious, ornate, resplendent, rich, splendiferous (*facetious*), sumptuous, superb **3 = glorious**, admirable, brilliant, exceptional, grand, heroic, illustrious, magnificent, outstanding, rare, remarkable, renowned, sterling, sublime, superb, supreme **4 = radiant**, beaming, bright, brilliant, glittering, glowing, lustrous, refulgent **5 = excellent**, awesome (*sl.*), bodacious (*sl., chiefly US*), boffo (*sl.*), brill, chillin' (*US sl.*), cracking (*Brit. inf.*), crucial (*sl.*), def (*sl.*), fantastic (*inf.*), fine, first-class, glorious, great (*inf.*), marvellous, mean (*sl.*), mega (*sl.*), sovereign, topping (*Brit. sl.*), wonderful
Antonyms *adj* ≠ **magnificent:** beggarly, drab, dull, low, mean, plain, poor, poverty-stricken, sordid, squalid ≠ **glorious:** ignoble, ignominious ≠ **radiant:** tarnished ≠ **excellent:** depressing, disgusting, lacklustre, mediocre, miserable, no great shakes

characterized by magnificence. **3** glorious or illustrious: *a splendid reputation.* **4** brightly gleaming; radiant: *splendid colours.* **5** very good or satisfactory: *a splendid time.* [C17: from L *splendidus,* from *splendēre* to shine]
▸'**splendidly** *adv* ▸'**splendidness** *n*

splendiferous (splɛn'dɪfərəs) *adj Facetious.* grand; splendid: *a really splendiferous meal.* [C15: from Med. L *splendiferus,* from L *splendor* radiance + *ferre* to bring]

splendour ⓘ *or US* **splendor** ('splɛndə) *n* **1** the state or quality of being splendid. **2 sun in splendour.** *Heraldry.* a representation of the sun with rays and a human face.

splenetic ⓘ (splɪ'nɛtɪk) *adj* **1** of or relating to the spleen. **2** spiteful or irritable; peevish. ◆ *n* **3** a spiteful or irritable person.
▸**sple'netically** *adv*

splenic ('splɛnɪk, 'spli:-) *adj* **1** of, relating to, or in the spleen. **2** having a disease or disorder of the spleen.

splenius ('spli:nɪəs) *n, pl* **splenii** (-nɪˌaɪ). either of two muscles at the back of the neck that rotate, flex, and extend the head and neck. [C18: via NL from Gk *splēnion* a plaster]
▸'**splenial** *adj*

splenomegaly (ˌspli:nəʊ'mɛgəlɪ) *n* abnormal enlargement of the spleen. [C20: NL, from Gk *splēn* spleen + *megal-,* stem of *megas* big]

splice ⓘ (splaɪs) *vb* **splices, splicing, spliced.** (*tr*) **1** to join (two ropes) by intertwining the strands. **2** to join up the trimmed ends of (two pieces of wire, film, etc.) with solder or an adhesive material. **3** to join (timbers) by overlapping and binding or bolting the ends together. **4** (*passive*) *Inf.* to enter into marriage: *the couple got spliced.* **5 splice the mainbrace.** *Naut. hist.* to issue and partake of an extra allocation of alcoholic spirits. ◆ *n* **6** a join made by splicing. **7** the place where such a join occurs. **8** the wedge-shaped end of a cricket-bat handle that fits into the blade. [C16: prob. from MDu. *splissen*]
▸'**splicer** *n*

spline (splaɪn) *n* **1** any one of a series of narrow keys formed longitudinally around a shaft that fit into corresponding grooves in a mating part: used to prevent movement between two parts, esp. in transmitting torque. **2** a long narrow strip of wood, metal, etc.; slat. **3** a thin narrow strip made of wood, metal, or plastic fitted into a groove in the edge of a board, tile, etc., to connect it to another. ◆ *vb* **splines, splining, splined. 4** (*tr*) to provide (a shaft, part, etc.) with splines. [C18: East Anglian dialect; ? rel. to OE *splin* spindle]

splint (splɪnt) *n* **1** a rigid support for restricting movement of an injured part, esp. a broken bone. **2** a thin sliver of wood, esp. one used to light cigars, a fire, etc. **3** a thin strip of wood woven with others to form a chair seat, basket, etc. **4** *Vet. science.* a bony enlargement of the cannon bone of a horse. ◆ *vb* **5** to apply a splint to (a broken arm, etc.). [C13: from MLow G *splinte*]

splinter ⓘ ('splɪntə) *n* **1** a small thin sharp piece of wood, glass, etc., broken off from a whole. **2** a metal fragment from a shell, bomb, etc., thrown out during an explosion. ◆ *vb* **3** to reduce or be reduced to sharp fragments. **4** to break or be broken off in small sharp fragments. [C14: from MDu. *splinter;* see SPLINT]
▸'**splintery** *adj*

splinter group *n* a number of members of an organization, political party, etc., who split from the main body and form an independent association of their own.

split ⓘ (splɪt) *vb* **splits, splitting, split. 1** to break or cause to break, esp. forcibly, by cleaving into separate pieces, often into two roughly equal pieces. **2** to separate or be separated from a whole: *he split a piece of wood from the block.* **3** to separate or be separated into factions, usually through discord. **4** (often foll. by *up*) to separate or cause to separate through a disagreement. **5** (when *tr,* often foll. by *up*) to divide or be divided among two or more persons: *split up the pie among us.* **6** *Sl.* to depart; leave: *let's split.* **7** (*tr*) to separate (something) into its components by interposing something else: *to split a word with hyphens.* **8** (*intr;* usually foll. by *on*) *Sl.* to betray; inform: *he split on me to the cops.* **9** (*tr*) *US politics.* to mark (a ballot, etc.) so as to vote for the candidates of more than one party: *he split the ticket.* **10 split one's sides.** to laugh very heartily. ◆ *n* **11** the act or process of splitting. **12** a gap or rift caused or a piece removed by the process of splitting. **13** a breach or schism in a group or the faction resulting from such a breach. **14** a dessert of sliced fruit and ice cream, covered with whipped cream, nuts, etc.: *banana split.* **15** See **Devonshire split. 16** *Tenpin bowling.* a formation of the pins after the first bowl in which there is a large gap between two pins or groups of pins. **17** *Inf.* an arrangement or process of dividing up loot or money. ◆ *adj* **18** having been split; divided: *split logs.* **19** having a split or splits: *hair with split ends.* ◆ See also **splits, split up.** [C16: from MDu. *splitten* to cleave]
▸'**splitter** *n*

split infinitive *n* (in English grammar) an infinitive used with another word between *to* and the verb itself, as in *to really finish it.*

> **USAGE NOTE** The traditional rule against placing an adverb between *to* and its verb is gradually disappearing. Although it is true that a split infinitive may result in a clumsy sentence (*he decided to firmly and definitively deal with the problem*), this is not enough to justify the absolute condemnation that this practice has attracted. Indeed, very often the most natural position of the adverb is between *to* and the verb (*he decided to really try next time*) and to change it would result in an artificial and awkward construction (*he decided really to try next time*). The current view is therefore that the split infinitive is not a grammatical error. Nevertheless, many writers prefer to avoid splitting infinitives in formal written English, since readers with a more traditional point of view are likely to interpret this type of construction as incorrect.

split-level *adj* (of a house, room, etc.) having the floor level of one part about half a storey above the floor level of an adjoining part.

split pea *n* a pea dried and split and used in soups, pease pudding, or as a vegetable.

split personality *n* **1** the tendency to change rapidly in mood or temperament. **2** a nontechnical term for **multiple personality.**

split pin *n* a metal pin made by bending double a wire, often of hemispherical section, so that it can be passed through a hole in a nut, shaft, etc., to secure another part by bending back the ends of the wire.

split ring *n* a steel ring having two helical turns, often used as a key ring.

splits (splɪts) *n* (*functioning as sing*) (in gymnastics, etc.) the act of sinking to the floor to achieve a sitting position in which both legs are straight, pointing in opposite directions, and at right angles to the body.

split-screen technique *n* a cinematic device by which two or more complete images are projected simultaneously onto separate parts of the screen. Also called: **split screen.**

split second *n* **1** an extremely small period of time; instant. ◆ *adj* **split-second.** (*prenominal*) **2** made or arrived at in an extremely short time: *a split-second decision.* **3** depending upon minute precision: *split-second timing.*

split shift *n* a work period divided into two parts that are separated by an interval longer than a normal rest period.

splitting ('splɪtɪŋ) *adj* **1** (of a headache) intolerably painful; acute. **2** (of the head) assailed by an overpowering unbearable pain.

split up ⓘ *vb* (*adv*) **1** (*tr*) to separate out into parts; divide. **2** (*intr*) to become parted through disagreement: *they split up after years of marriage.* **3** to break down or be capable of being broken down into constituent parts. ◆ *n* **split-up. 4** the act or an instance of separating.

splodge (splɒdʒ) *n* **1** a large irregular spot or blot. ◆ *vb* **splodges, splodging, splodged. 2** (*tr*) to mark (something) with such a blot or blots. [C19: alteration of earlier SPLOTCH]
▸'**splodgy** *adj*

splotch (splɒtʃ) *n, vb* the usual US word for **splodge.** [C17: ? a blend of SPOT + BLOTCH]
▸'**splotchy** *adj*

splurge (splɜ:dʒ) *n* **1** an ostentatious display, esp. of wealth. **2** a bout of unrestrained extravagance. ◆ *vb* **splurges, splurging, splurged. 3** (often foll. by *out*) to spend (money) extravagantly. [C19: from ?]

splutter ('splʌtə) *vb* **1** to spit out (saliva, food particles, etc.) from the mouth in an explosive manner, as through choking or laughing. **2** to utter (words) with spitting sounds, as through rage or choking. **3** to eject or be ejected in an explosive manner: *sparks spluttered from the fire.* **4** (*tr*) to bespatter (a person) with tiny particles explosively ejected. ◆ *n* **5** the process or noise of spluttering. **6** spluttering incoherent speech. **7** anything ejected through spluttering. [C17: var. of SPUTTER, infl. by SPLASH]
▸'**splutterer** *n*

THESAURUS

(*inf.*), ordinary, pathetic, poor, rotten, run-of-the-mill, tawdry, undistinguished, unexceptional

splendour *n* **2 = magnificence,** ceremony, display, éclat, gorgeousness, grandeur, majesty, pomp, resplendence, richness, show, solemnity, spectacle, stateliness, sumptuousness
Antonyms *n* **≠ magnificence:** lacklustreness, meanness, ordinariness, plainness, poverty, simplicity, squalor, tawdriness

splenetic *adj* **2** *Literary* **= irritable,** acid, bad-tempered, bitchy (*inf.*), choleric, churlish, crabbed, crabby, cross, envenomed, fretful, irascible, morose, peevish, petulant, rancorous, ratty (*Brit. & NZ inf.*), sour, spiteful, sullen, testy, tetchy, touchy

splice *vb* **1-3 = join,** braid, entwine, graft, interlace, intertwine, intertwist, interweave, knit, marry, mesh, plait, unite, wed, yoke

splinter *n* **1, 2 = sliver,** chip, flake, fragment, needle, paring, shaving ◆ *vb* **3, 4 = shatter,** break into fragments, disintegrate, fracture, shiver, split

split *vb* **1 = break,** break up, burst, come apart, come undone, crack, gape, give way, open, rend, rip, slash, slit, snap, splinter **3 = separate,** bifurcate, branch, cleave, disband, disunite, diverge, fork, go separate ways, part, pull apart **5 = share out,** allocate, allot, apportion, carve up, distribute, divide, divvy up (*inf.*), dole out, halve, parcel out, partition, slice up **8** *foll. by* **on** *Slang* **= betray,** give away, grass (*Brit. sl.*), inform on, peach (*sl.*), shop (*sl., chiefly Brit.*), sing (*sl., chiefly US*), spill one's guts (*sl.*), squeal (*sl.*) ◆ *n* **11 = division,** breach, break, break-up, difference, discord, disruption, dissension, disunion, divergence, estrangement, partition, rift, rupture, schism **12 = crack,** breach, damage, division, fissure, gap, rent, rip, separation, slash, slit, tear ◆ *adj* **18, 19 = divided,** ambivalent, bisected, broken, cleft, cracked, dual, fractured, ruptured, twofold

split up *vb* **1, 2 = separate,** break up, disband, divorce, go separate ways, part, part company

spode (spəud) *n* (*sometimes cap.*) china or porcelain manufactured by Josiah Spode (1754–1827), English potter, or his company.

spoil ⓣ (spɔɪl) *vb* **spoils, spoiling, spoilt** *or* **spoiled. 1** (*tr*) to cause damage to (something), in regard to its value, beauty, usefulness, etc. **2** (*tr*) to weaken the character of (a child) by complying unrestrainedly with its desires. **3** (*intr*) (of perishable substances) to become unfit for consumption or use. **4** (*intr*) *Sport.* to disrupt the play or style of an opponent, as to prevent him from settling into a rhythm. **5** *Arch.* to strip (a person or place) of (property) by force. **6 be spoiling for.** to have an aggressive desire for (a fight, etc.). ◆ *n* **7** waste material thrown up by an excavation. **8** any treasure accumulated by a person. **9** *Obs.* the act of plundering. ◆ See also **spoils.** [C13: from OF *espoillier,* from L *spoliāre* to strip, from *spolium* booty]

spoilage ('spɔɪlɪdʒ) *n* **1** the act or an instance of spoiling or the state or condition of being spoilt. **2** an amount of material that has been wasted by being spoilt: *considerable spoilage.*

spoiler ('spɔɪlə) *n* **1** a plunderer or robber. **2** a person or thing that causes spoilage or corruption. **3** a device fitted to an aircraft wing to increase drag and reduce lift. **4** a similar device fitted to a car. **5** *Sport.* a competitor who adopts spoiling tactics. **6** a magazine, newspaper, etc., produced specifically to coincide with the production of a rival magazine, newspaper, etc., in order to divert public interest and reduce its sales.

spoils ⓣ (spɔɪlz) *pl n* **1** (*sometimes sing*) valuables seized by violence, esp. in war. **2** *Chiefly US.* the rewards and benefits of public office regarded as plunder for the winning party or candidate. See also **spoils system.**

spoilsport ⓣ ('spɔɪl,spɔːt) *n Inf.* a person who spoils the pleasure of other people.

spoils system *n Chiefly US.* the practice of filling appointive public offices with friends and supporters of the ruling political party.

spoilt (spɔɪlt) *vb* a past tense and past participle of **spoil.**

spoke[1] (spəuk) *vb* **1** the past tense of **speak. 2** *Arch. or dialect.* a past participle of **speak.**

spoke[2] (spəuk) *n* **1** a radial member of a wheel, joining the hub to the rim. **2** a radial projection from the rim of a wheel, as in a ship's wheel. **3** a rung of a ladder. **4 put a spoke in someone's wheel.** *Brit.* to thwart someone's plans. ◆ *vb* **spokes, spoking, spoked. 5** (*tr*) to equip with or as if with spokes. [OE *spaca*]

spoken ⓣ ('spəukən) *vb* **1** the past participle of **speak.** ◆ *adj* **2** uttered in speech. **3** (*in combination*) having speech as specified: *soft-spoken.* **4 spoken for.** engaged or reserved.

spokeshave ('spəuk,ʃeɪv) *n* a small plane with two handles, one on each side of its blade, used for shaping or smoothing cylindrical wooden surfaces, such as spokes.

spokesman ('spəuksmən), **spokesperson** ⓣ ('spəuks,pɜːsᵊn), *or* **spokeswoman** ('spəuks,wumən) *n, pl* **spokesmen, spokespersons** *or* **spokespeople,** *or* **spokeswomen.** a person authorized to speak on behalf of another person or group.

spoliation (,spəulɪ'eɪʃən) *n* **1** the act or an instance of despoiling or plundering. **2** the authorized plundering of neutral vessels on the seas by a belligerent state in time of war. **3** *Law.* the material alteration of a document so as to render it invalid. **4** *English ecclesiastical law.* the taking of the fruits of a benefice by a person not entitled to them. [C14: from L *spoliātiō,* from *spoliāre* to SPOIL]
▸**spoliatory** ('spəulɪətərɪ, -trɪ) *adj*

spondee ('spɒndiː) *n Prosody.* a metrical foot consisting of two long syllables (''). [C14: from OF *spondée,* from L *spondēus,* from Gk, from *spondē* ritual libation; from use of spondee in the music for such ceremonies]
▸**spondaic** (spɒn'deɪɪk) *adj*

spondylitis (,spɒndɪ'laɪtɪs) *n* inflammation of the vertebrae. [C19: from NL, from Gk *spondulos* vertebra; see -ITIS]

sponge ⓣ (spʌndʒ) *n* **1** any of various multicellular typically marine animals, usually occurring in complex sessile colonies, in which the porous body is supported by a fibrous, calcareous, or siliceous skeletal framework. **2** a piece of the light porous highly absorbent elastic skeleton of certain sponges, used in bathing, cleaning, etc. **3** any of a number of light porous elastic materials resembling a sponge. **4** another word for **sponger** (sense 1). **5** *Inf.* a person who indulges in heavy drinking. **6** leavened dough, esp. before kneading. **7** See **sponge cake. 8** Also called: **sponge pudding.** *Brit.* a light steamed or baked spongy pudding. **9** porous metal capable of absorbing large quantities of gas: *platinum sponge.* **10** a rub with a sponge. **11 throw in the sponge** (*or* **towel**). See **throw in** (sense 3). ◆ *vb* **sponges, sponging, sponged. 12** (*tr;* often foll. by *off* or *down*) to clean (something) by wiping or rubbing with a damp or wet sponge. **13** (*tr;* usually foll. by *off, away, out,* etc.) to remove (marks, etc.) by rubbing with a damp or wet sponge or cloth. **14** (when *tr,* often foll. by *up*) to absorb (liquids, esp. when spilt) in the manner of a sponge. **15** (*intr*) to go collecting sponges. **16** (foll. by *off*) to get (something) from someone by presuming on his generosity: *to sponge a meal off someone.* **17** (foll. by *off* or *on*) to obtain one's subsistence, etc., unjustifiably (from): *he sponges off his friends.* [OE, from L *spongia,* from Gk]
▸**'spongy** *adj*

sponge bag *n* a small waterproof bag made of plastic, etc., that holds toilet articles, used esp. when travelling.

sponge bath *n* a washing of the body with a wet sponge or cloth, without immersion in water.

sponge cake *n* a light porous cake, made of eggs, sugar, flour, and flavourings, without any fat.

sponger ⓣ ('spʌndʒə) *n* **1** *Inf.* a person who lives off other people by continually taking advantage of their generosity; parasite or scrounger. **2** a person or ship employed in collecting sponges.

spongiform ('spʌndʒɪ,fɔːm) *adj* **1** resembling a sponge in appearance, esp. in having many holes. **2** denoting diseases characterized by this appearance of affected tissues.

sponsion ('spɒnʃən) *n* **1** the act or process of becoming surety; sponsorship. **2** (*often pl*) *International law.* an unauthorized agreement made by a public officer, requiring ratification by his government. **3** any act or promise, esp. one made on behalf of someone else. [C17: from L *sponsiō,* from *spondēre* to pledge]

sponson ('spɒnsən) *n* **1** *Naval.* an outboard support for a gun, etc. **2** a structural projection from the side of a paddle steamer for supporting a paddle wheel. **3** a float or flotation chamber along the gunwale of a boat or ship. **4** a structural unit attached to a helicopter fuselage by struts, housing the landing gear and flotation bags. [C19: ?from EXPANSION]

sponsor ⓣ ('spɒnsə) *n* **1** a person or group that promotes either another person or group in an activity or the activity itself, either for profit or for charity. **2** *Chiefly US & Canad.* a person or business firm that pays the costs of a radio or television programme in return for advertising time. **3** a legislator who presents and supports a bill, motion, etc. **4** Also called: **godparent. 4a** an authorized witness who makes the required promises on behalf of a person to be baptized and thereafter assumes responsibility for his Christian upbringing. **4b** a person who presents a candidate for confirmation. ◆ *vb* **5** (*tr*) to act as a sponsor for. [C17: from L, from *spondēre* to promise solemnly]
▸**sponsorial** (spɒn'sɔːrɪəl) *adj* ▸**'sponsor,ship** *n*

sponsored ('spɒnsəd) *adj* denoting an activity organized to raise money for a charity in which sponsors agree to donate money on completion of the activity by participants.

spontaneity (,spɒntə'niːɪtɪ, -'neɪ-) *n, pl* **spontaneities. 1** the state or quality of being spontaneous. **2** (*often pl*) the exhibiting of spontaneous actions, impulses, or behaviour.

spontaneous ⓣ (spɒn'teɪnɪəs) *adj* **1** occurring, produced, or performed through natural processes without external influence. **2** arising from an unforced personal impulse; voluntary; unpremeditated. **3** (of plants) growing naturally; indigenous. [C17: from LL *spontāneus,* from L *sponte* voluntarily]
▸**spon'taneously** *adv* ▸**spon'taneousness** *n*

spontaneous combustion *n* the ignition of a substance or body as a result of internal oxidation processes, without the application of an external source of heat.

spontaneous generation *n* another name for **abiogenesis.**

spoof ⓣ (spuːf) *Inf.* ◆ *n* **1** a mildly satirical mockery or parody; lampoon. **2** a good-humoured deception or trick. ◆ *vb* **3** to indulge in a spoof of (a person or thing). [C19: coined by A. Roberts (1852–1933), E comedian]
▸**'spoofer** *n*

THESAURUS

spoil *vb* **1 = ruin,** blemish, blow (*sl.*), damage, debase, deface, destroy, disfigure, harm, impair, injure, mar, mess up, put a damper on, scar, total (*sl.*), trash (*sl.*), undo, upset, wreck **2 = overindulge,** baby, cocker (*rare*), coddle, cosset, indulge, kill with kindness, mollycoddle, pamper, spoon-feed **3 = go bad,** addle, become tainted, curdle, decay, decompose, go off (*Brit. inf.*), mildew, putrefy, rot, turn **6 be spoiling for = be eager for,** be bent upon, be desirous of, be enthusiastic about, be keen to, be looking for, be out to get (*inf.*), be raring to
Antonyms *vb* ≠ **ruin:** augment, conserve, enhance, improve, keep, preserve, save ≠ **overindulge:** be strict with, deprive, ignore, pay no attention to, treat harshly

spoils *pl n* **1 = booty,** boodle (*sl., chiefly US*), gain, loot, pickings, pillage, plunder, prey, prizes, rapine, swag (*sl.*)

spoilsport *n Informal* **= killjoy,** damper, dog in the manger, misery (*Brit. inf.*), party-pooper (*US sl.*), wet blanket (*inf.*)

spoken *adj* **2 = said,** by word of mouth, expressed, oral, phonetic, put into words, told, unwritten, uttered, verbal, viva voce, voiced

spokesperson *n* **= speaker,** mouthpiece, official, spin doctor (*inf.*), spokesman *or* spokeswoman, voice

sponger *n* **1** *Informal* **= scrounger** (*inf.*), bloodsucker (*inf.*), cadge, cadger, freeloader (*sl.*), hanger-on, leech, parasite

spongy *adj* **2, 3 = porous,** absorbent, cushioned, cushiony, elastic, light, springy

sponsor *n* **1, 3, 4a = backer,** angel (*inf.*), godparent, guarantor, patron, promoter ◆ *vb* **5 = back,** finance, fund, guarantee, lend one's name to, patronize, promote, put up the money for, subsidize

spontaneous *adj* **2 = unplanned,** extempore, free, impromptu, impulsive, instinctive, natural, unbidden, uncompelled, unconstrained, unforced, unpremeditated, unprompted, voluntary, willing
Antonyms *adj* arranged, calculated, contrived, deliberate, forced, mannered, orchestrated, planned, prearranged, premeditated, preplanned, stage-managed, studied

spontaneously *adv* **2 = of one's own accord,** extempore, freely, impromptu, impulsively, instinctively, in the heat of the moment, off one's own bat, off the cuff (*inf.*), on impulse, quite unprompted, voluntarily

spoof *n Informal* **1 = parody,** burlesque, caricature, lampoon, mockery, satire, send-up (*Brit. inf.*), take-off (*inf.*), travesty **2 = trick,** bluff, canard, deception, game, hoax, joke, leg-pull (*Brit. inf.*), prank

spook ❶ (spu:k) *Inf.* ◆ *n* **1** a ghost. **2** *US & Canad.* a spy. **3** a strange or frightening person. ◆ *vb* (*tr*) *US & Canad.* **4** to frighten: *to spook horses; to spook a person.* **5** (of a ghost) to haunt. [C19: Du. *spook,* from MLow G *spōk* ghost]
▸**'spooky** *adj*

spool (spu:l) *n* **1** a device around which magnetic tape, film, cotton, etc., can be wound, with plates at top and bottom to prevent it from slipping off. **2** anything round which other materials, esp. thread, are wound. ◆ *vb* **3** (sometimes foll. by *up*) to wind or be wound onto a spool. [C14: of Gmc origin]

spoon (spu:n) *n* **1** a utensil having a shallow concave part, usually elliptical in shape, attached to a handle, used in eating or serving food, stirring, etc. **2** Also called: **spoonbait.** an angling lure consisting of a bright piece of metal which swivels on a trace to which are attached a hook or hooks. **3** *Golf.* a former name for a No. 3 wood. **4 be born with a silver spoon in one's mouth.** to inherit wealth or social standing. **5** *Rowing.* a type of oar blade that is curved at the edges and tip. ◆ *vb* **6** (*tr*) to scoop up or transfer (food, liquid, etc.) from one container to another with or as if with a spoon. **7** (*intr*) *Old-fashioned sl.* to kiss and cuddle. **8** *Sport.* to hit (a ball) with a weak lifting motion, as in golf, cricket, etc. [OE *spōn* splinter]

spoonbill ('spu:n,bɪl) *n* any of several wading birds of warm regions, having a long horizontally flattened bill.

spoondrift ('spu:n,drɪft) *n* a less common spelling of **spindrift.**

spoonerism ('spu:nə,rɪzəm) *n* the transposition of the initial consonants or consonant clusters of a pair of words, often resulting in an amusing ambiguity, such as *hush my brat* for *brush my hat.* [C20: after W. A. *Spooner* (1844–1930), E clergyman renowned for this]

spoon-feed ❶ *vb* **spoon-feeds, spoon-feeding, spoon-fed.** (*tr*) **1** to feed with a spoon. **2** to overindulge or spoil. **3** to provide (a person) with ready-made opinions, judgments, etc.

spoonful ('spu:n,fʊl) *n, pl* **spoonfuls. 1** the amount that a spoon is able to hold. **2** a small quantity.

spoony *or* **spooney** ('spu:nɪ) *Inf., old-fashioned.* ◆ *adj* **spoonier, spooniest. 1** foolishly or stupidly amorous. ◆ *n, pl* **spoonies. 2** a fool or silly person, esp. one in love.

spoor (spʊə, spɔ:) *n* **1** the trail of an animal or person, esp. as discernible to the eye. ◆ *vb* **2** to track (an animal) by following its trail. [C19: from Afrik., from MDu. *spor;* rel. to OE *spor* track]

sporadic ❶ (spə'rædɪk) *adj* **1** occurring at irregular points in time; intermittent: *sporadic firing.* **2** scattered; isolated: *a sporadic disease.* [C17: from Med. L *sporadicus,* from Gk, from *sporas* scattered]
▸**spo'radically** *adv*

sporangium (spə'rændʒɪəm) *n, pl* **sporangia** (-dʒɪə). any organ, esp. in fungi, in which asexual spores are produced. [C19: from NL, from SPORO- + Gk *angeion* receptacle]
▸**spo'rangial** *adj*

spore (spɔ:) *n* **1** a reproductive body, produced by bacteria, fungi, some protozoans and many plants, that develops into a new individual. A **sexual spore** is formed after the fusion of gametes and an **asexual spore** is the result of asexual reproduction. **2** a germ cell, seed, dormant bacterium, or similar body. ◆ *vb* **spores, sporing, spored. 3** (*intr*) to produce, carry, or release spores. [C19: from NL *spora,* from Gk: a sowing; rel. to Gk *speirein* to sow]

spore case *n* the nontechnical name for **sporangium.**

sporo- *or before a vowel* **spor-** *combining form.* spore: *sporophyte.* [from NL *spora*]

sporogenesis (,spɔ:rəʊ'dʒɛnɪsɪs, ,spɒ-) *n* the process of spore formation in plants and animals.
▸**sporogenous** (spɔ:'rɒdʒɪnəs, spɒ-) *adj*

sporogonium (,spɔ:rəʊ'gəʊnɪəm, ,spɒ-) *n, pl* **sporogonia** (-nɪə). a structure in mosses and liverworts consisting of a spore-bearing capsule on a short stalk that arises from the parent plant.

sporophyll *or* **sporophyl** ('spɔ:rəʊfɪl, 'spɒ-) *n* a leaf in mosses, ferns, and related plants that bears the sporangia.

sporophyte ('spɔ:rəʊ,faɪt, 'spɒ-) *n* the diploid form of plants that have alternation of generations. It produces asexual spores.
▸**sporophytic** (,spɔ:rə'fɪtɪk, ,spɒ-) *adj*

-sporous *adj combining form.* (in botany) having a specified type or number of spores.

sporozoan (,spɔ:rə'zəʊən, ,spɒ-) *n* **1** any parasitic protozoan of a phylum that includes the malaria parasite. ◆ *adj* **2** of or relating to the sporozoans.

sporran ('spɒrən) *n* a large pouch, usually of fur, worn hanging from a belt in front of the kilt in Scottish Highland dress. [C19: from Scot. Gaelic *sporan* purse]

sport ❶ (spɔ:t) *n* **1** an individual or group activity pursued for exercise or pleasure, often taking a competitive form. **2** such activities considered collectively. **3** any pastime indulged in for pleasure. **4** the pleasure derived from a pastime, esp. hunting, shooting, or fishing. **5** playful or good-humoured joking: *to say a thing in sport.* **6** derisive mockery or the object of such mockery: *to make sport of someone.* **7** someone or something that is controlled by external influences: *the sport of fate.* **8** *Inf.* (sometimes qualified by *good, bad,* etc.) a person who reacts cheerfully in the face of adversity, esp. a good loser. **9** *Inf.* a person noted for being scrupulously fair and abiding by the rules of a game. **10** *Inf.* a person who leads a merry existence, esp. a gambler: *he's a bit of a sport.* **11** *Austral. & NZ inf.* a form of address used esp. between males. **12** *Biol.* **12a** an animal or plant that differs conspicuously from other organisms of the same species, usually because of a mutation. **12b** an anomalous characteristic of such an organism. ◆ *vb* **13** (*tr*) *Inf.* to wear or display in an ostentatious or proud manner: *she was sporting a new hat.* **14** (*intr*) to skip about or frolic happily. **15** to amuse (oneself), esp. in outdoor physical recreation. **16** (*intr;* often foll. by *with*) *Arch.* to make fun (of). **17** (*intr*) *Biol.* to produce or undergo a mutation. ◆ See also **sports.** [C15 *sporten,* var. of *disporten* to DISPORT]
▸**'sporter** *n* ▸**'sportful** *adj* ▸**'sportfully** *adv* ▸**'sportfulness** *n*

sporting ❶ ('spɔ:tɪŋ) *adj* **1** (*prenominal*) of, relating to, or used or engaged in a sport or sports. **2** relating or conforming to sportsmanship; fair. **3** of or relating to gambling. **4** willing to take a risk.
▸**'sportingly** *adv*

sportive ❶ ('spɔ:tɪv) *adj* **1** playful or joyous. **2** done in jest rather than seriously.
▸**'sportively** *adv* ▸**'sportiveness** *n*

sports (spɔ:ts) *n* **1** (*modifier*) relating to, concerned with, or used in sports: *sports equipment.* **2** Also called: **sports day.** *Brit.* a meeting held at a school or college for competitions in various athletic events.

sports car *n* a production car designed for speed and manoeuvrability, having a low body and usually seating only two persons.

sportscast ('spɔ:ts,kɑ:st) *n US.* a broadcast consisting of sports news.
▸**'sports,caster** *n*

sports jacket *n* a man's informal jacket, made esp. of tweed. Also called (US, Austral., and NZ): **sports coat.**

sportsman ('spɔ:tsmən) *n, pl* **sportsmen. 1** a man who takes part in sports, esp. of the outdoor type. **2** a person who exhibits fairness, generosity, observance of the rules, and good humour when losing.
▸**'sportsman-,like** *or* **'sportsmanly** *adj* ▸**'sportsman,ship** *n*

sports medicine *n* the branch of medicine concerned with injuries sustained through sport.

sportswear ('spɔ:ts,wɛə) *n* clothes worn for sport or outdoor leisure wear.

sportswoman ('spɔ:ts,wʊmən) *n, pl* **sportswomen.** a woman who takes part in sports, esp. of the outdoor type.

sporty ❶ ('spɔ:tɪ) *adj* **sportier, sportiest. 1** (of a person) fond of sport or outdoor activities. **2** (of clothes) having the appearance of sportswear. **3** (of a car) having the performance or appearance of a sports car.
▸**'sportily** *adv* ▸**'sportiness** *n*

sporule ('spɒru:l) *n* a very small spore. [C19: from NL *sporula*]

spot ❶ (spɒt) *n* **1** a small mark on a surface, such as a circular patch or stain, differing in colour or texture from its surroundings. **2** a location: *this is the exact spot.* **3** a blemish of the skin, esp. a pimple or one occurring through some disease. **4** a blemish on the character of a person; moral flaw. **5** *Inf.* a place of entertainment: *a night spot.* **6** *Inf., chiefly Brit.* a small quantity or amount: *a spot of lunch.* **7** *Inf.* an awkward situation: *that puts me in a spot.* **8** a short period between regular television or radio programmes that is used for advertising. **9** a position or length of time in a show assigned to a specific performer. **10** short for **spotlight. 11** (in billiards) **11a** Also called: **spot ball.** the white ball that is distinguished from the plain by a mark or spot. **11b** the player using this ball. **12** *Billiards, snooker, etc.* one of the marked places where the ball is placed. **13** (*modifier*) **13a** denoting or relating to goods, currencies, or securities available for immediate delivery and payment: *spot goods.* See also **spot price. 13b** involving immediate cash payment: *spot sales.* **14 change one's spots.** (*used mainly in negative constructions*) to reform one's character. **15 high spot.** an outstanding

THESAURUS

spooky *adj* **1** = **eerie,** chilling, creepy (*inf.*), frightening, ghostly, mysterious, scary (*inf.*), spine-chilling, supernatural, uncanny, unearthly, weird

spoon-feed *vb* **2** = **mollycoddle,** baby, cosset, featherbed, overindulge, overprotect, spoil, wrap up in cotton wool (*inf.*)

sporadic *adj* **1, 2** = **intermittent,** infrequent, irregular, isolated, occasional, on and off, random, scattered, spasmodic
Antonyms *adj* consistent, frequent, recurrent, regular, set, steady, systematic

sport *n* **1-3** = **game,** amusement, diversion, entertainment, exercise, pastime, physical activity, play, recreation **5** = **fun,** badinage, banter, frolic, jest, joking, josh (*sl., chiefly US & Canad.*), kidding (*inf.*), merriment, mirth, raillery, ridicule, teasing **6** = **mockery,** derision **6** = **butt,** buffoon, fair game, laughing stock, plaything ◆ *vb* **13** *Informal* = **wear,** display, exhibit, show off **14** = **frolic,** caper, disport, gambol, play, romp **16 sport with** *Archaic* = **make fun of,** amuse oneself with, dally with, flirt with, fool around with, play with, take advantage of, toy with, treat lightly *or* cavalierly, trifle with

sporting *adj* **2** = **fair,** game (*inf.*), gentlemanly, sportsmanlike
Antonyms *adj* unfair, unsporting, unsportsmanlike

sportive *adj* **1, 2** = **playful,** coltish, frisky, frolicsome, full of beans (*inf.*), full of fun, gamesome, gay, joyous, kittenish, lively, merry, prankish, rollicking, skittish, sprightly

sporty *adj* **1** = **athletic,** energetic, hearty, outdoor

spot *n* **1** = **mark,** blemish, blot, blotch, daub, discoloration, flaw, scar, smudge, speck, speckle, stain, taint **2** = **place,** locality, location, point, position, scene, site, situation **3** = **pimple,** plook (*Scot.*), pustule, zit (*sl.*) **6** *Informal, chiefly Brit.* = **bit,** little, morsel, splash **7** *Informal* = **predicament,** difficulty, hot water (*inf.*), mess, plight, quandary, tight spot, trouble ◆ *vb* **20** = **see,** behold (*arch. or literary*), catch sight of, descry, detect, discern, espy, identify, make out, observe, pick out, recognize, sight

event: *the high spot of the holiday.* **16 knock spots off.** to outstrip or outdo with ease. **17 on the spot. 17a** immediately. **17b** at the place in question. **17c** in the best position to deal with a situation. **17d** in an awkward predicament. **17e** (*as modifier*): *our on-the-spot reporter.* **18 tight spot.** a serious, difficult, or dangerous situation. **19 weak spot. 19a** some aspect of a character or situation that is susceptible to criticism. **19b** a flaw in a person's knowledge. ◆ *vb* **spots, spotting, spotted. 20** (*tr*) to observe or perceive suddenly; discern. **21** to put stains or spots upon (something). **22** (*intr*) (of some fabrics) to be susceptible to spotting by or as if by water: *silk spots easily.* **23** *Billiards.* to place (a ball) on one of the spots. **24** to look out for and note (trains, talent, etc.). **25** (*intr*) to rain slightly; spit. [C12 (in the sense: moral blemish): from G]
▸ **'spotless** *adj* ▸ **'spotlessly** *adv* ▸ **'spotlessness** *n*

spot check *n* **1** a quick random examination. **2** a check made without prior warning. ◆ *vb* **spot-check. 3** (*tr*) to perform a spot check on.

spot height *n* a mark on a map indicating the height of a hill, mountain, etc.

spotlight **T** ('spɒt,laɪt) *n* **1** a powerful light focused so as to illuminate a small area. **2 the.** the focus of attention. ◆ *vb* **spotlights, spotlighting, spotlit** *or* **spotlighted.** (*tr*) **3** to direct a spotlight on. **4** to focus attention on.

spot-on **T** *adj Brit. inf.* absolutely correct; very accurate.

spot price *n* the price of goods, currencies, or securities that are offered for immediate delivery and payment.

spotted **T** ('spɒtɪd) *adj* **1** characterized by spots or marks, esp. in having a pattern of spots. **2** stained or blemished; soiled or bespattered.

spotted dick *or* **dog** *n Brit.* a steamed or boiled suet pudding containing dried fruit and shaped into a roll.

spotted fever *n* any of various severe febrile diseases characterized by small irregular spots on the skin.

spotted gum *n* **1** an Australian eucalyptus tree. **2** the wood of this tree, used for shipbuilding, sleepers, etc.

spotter ('spɒtə) *n* **1a** a person or thing that watches or observes. **1b** (*as modifier*): *a spotter plane.* **2** a person who makes a hobby of watching for and noting numbers or types of trains, buses, etc.: *a train spotter.* **3** *Mil.* a person who advises adjustment of fire on a target by observations. **4** a person, esp. one engaged in civil defence, who watches for enemy aircraft.

spottie ('spɒtɪ) *n NZ.* a young deer of up to three months of age.

spotty **T** ('spɒtɪ) *adj* **spottier, spottiest. 1** abounding in or characterized by spots or marks, esp. on the skin. **2** not consistent or uniform; irregular or uneven.
▸ **'spottily** *adv* ▸ **'spottiness** *n*

spot-weld *vb* **1** (*tr*) to join (two pieces of metal) by small circular welds by means of heat, usually electrically generated, and pressure. ◆ *n* **2** a weld so formed.
▸ **'spot-,welder** *n*

spousal ('spaʊzᵊl) *n* **1** (*often pl*) **1a** the marriage ceremony. **1b** a wedding. ◆ *adj* **2** of or relating to marriage.
▸ **'spousally** *adv*

spouse **T** *n* (spaʊs, spaʊz). **1** a person's partner in marriage. Related adj: **spousal.** ◆ *vb* (spaʊz, spaʊs), **spouses, spousing, spoused. 2** (*tr*) *Obs.* to marry. [C12: from OF *spus* (masc), *spuse* (fem), from L *sponsus, sponsa* betrothed man or woman, from *spondēre* to promise solemnly]

spout **T** (spaʊt) *vb* **1** to discharge (a liquid) in a continuous jet or in spurts, esp. through a narrow gap or under pressure, or (of a liquid) to gush thus. **2** (of a whale, etc.) to discharge air through the blowhole in a spray at the surface of the water. **3** *Inf.* to utter (a stream of words) on a subject. ◆ *n* **4** a tube, pipe, chute, etc., allowing the passage or pouring of liquids, grain, etc. **5** a continuous stream or jet of liquid. **6** short for **waterspout. 7 up the spout.** *Sl.* **7a** ruined or lost: *any hope of rescue is right up the spout.* **7b** pregnant. [C14: ?from MDu. *spouten,* from ON *spyta* to spit]
▸ **'spouter** *n*

spouting ('spaʊtɪŋ) *n NZ.* **a** a rainwater downpipe on the exterior of a building. **b** such pipes collectively.

SPQR *abbrev. for* Senatus Populusque Romanus. [L: the Senate and People of Rome]

sprag (spræg) *n* **1** a chock or steel bar used to prevent a vehicle from running backwards on an incline. **2** a support or post used in mining. [C19: from ?]

sprain (spreɪn) *vb* **1** (*tr*) to injure (a joint) by a sudden twisting or wrenching of its ligaments. ◆ *n* **2** the injury, characterized by swelling and temporary disability. [C17: from ?]

sprang (spræŋ) *vb* a past tense of **spring.**

sprat (spræt) *n* **1** Also called: **brisling.** a small marine food fish of the herring family. **2** any of various small or young herrings. [C16: var. of OE *sprott*]

sprawl **T** (sprɔːl) *vb* **1** (*intr*) to sit or lie in an ungainly manner with one's limbs spread out. **2** to fall down or knock down with the limbs spread out in an ungainly way. **3** to spread out or cause to spread out in a straggling fashion: *his handwriting sprawled all over the paper.* ◆ *n* **4** the act or an instance of sprawling. **5** a sprawling posture or arrangement of items. **6a** the urban area formed by the expansion of a town or city into surrounding countryside: *the urban sprawl.* **6b** the process by which this has happened. [OE *spreawlian*]
▸ **'sprawling** *or* **'sprawly** *adj*

spray[1] **T** (spreɪ) *n* **1** fine particles of a liquid. **2a** a liquid, such as perfume, paint, etc., designed to be discharged from an aerosol or atomizer: *hair spray.* **2b** the aerosol or atomizer itself. **3** a quantity of small objects flying through the air: *a spray of bullets.* ◆ *vb* **4** to scatter (liquid) in the form of fine particles. **5** to discharge (a liquid) from an aerosol or atomizer. **6** (*tr*) to treat or bombard with a spray: *to spray the lawn.* [C17: from MDu. *spraien*]
▸ **'sprayer** *n*

spray[2] **T** (spreɪ) *n* **1** a single slender shoot, twig, or branch that bears buds, leaves, flowers, or berries. **2** an ornament or floral design like this. [C13: of Gmc origin]

spray gun *n* a device that sprays a fluid in a finely divided form by atomizing it in an air jet.

spread **T** (sprɛd) *vb* **spreads, spreading, spread. 1** to extend or unfold or be extended or unfolded to the fullest width: *she spread the map.* **2** to extend or cause to extend over a larger expanse: *the milk spread all over the floor; the political unrest spread over several years.* **3** to apply or be applied in a coating: *butter does not spread very well when cold.* **4** to distribute or be distributed over an area or region. **5** to display or be displayed in its fullest extent: *the landscape spread before us.* **6** (*tr*) to prepare (a table) for a meal. **7** (*tr*) to lay out (a meal) on a table. **8** to send or be sent out in all directions; disseminate or be disseminated: *someone was spreading rumours; the disease spread quickly.* **9** (of rails, wires, etc.) to force or be forced apart. **10** to increase the breadth of (a part), esp. to flatten the head of a rivet by pressing, hammering, or forging. **11** (*tr*) *Agriculture.* **11a** to lay out (hay) in a relatively thin layer to dry. **11b** to scatter (seed, manure, etc.) over an area. **12** (*tr;* often foll. by *around*) *Inf.* to make (oneself) agreeable to a large number of people. ◆ *n* **13** the act or process of spreading; diffusion, dispersion, expansion, etc. **14** *Inf.* the wingspan of an aircraft. **15** an extent of space or time; stretch: *a spread of 50 years.* **16** *Inf., chiefly US & Canad.* a ranch or large tract of land. **17** the limit of something fully extended: *the spread of a bird's wings.* **18** a covering for a table or bed. **19** *Inf.* a large meal or feast, esp. when it is laid out on a table. **20** a food which can be spread on bread, etc.: *salmon spread.* **21** two facing pages in a book or other publication. **22** a widening of the hips and waist: *middle-age spread.* ◆ *adj* **23** extended or stretched out, esp. to the fullest extent. [OE *sprǣdan*]
▸ **'spreadable** *adj* ▸ **'spreader** *n*

spread betting *n* a form of gambling in which stakes are placed not on the results of contests but on the number of points scored, etc. Winnings and losses are calculated according to the accuracy or inaccuracy of the prediction.

spread eagle *n* **1** the representation of an eagle with outstretched wings, used as an emblem of the US. **2** an acrobatic skating figure.

spread-eagle *adj also* **spread-eagled. 1** lying or standing with arms and legs outstretched. ◆ *vb* **spread-eagles, spread-eagling, spread-eagled. 2** to assume or cause to assume the shape of a spread eagle. **3** (*intr*) *Skating.* to execute a spread eagle.

spreadsheet ('sprɛd,ʃiːt) *n* a computer program that allows easy entry

THESAURUS

spotless *adj* **1** = **clean**, faultless, flawless, gleaming, immaculate, impeccable, pure, shining, snowy, unblemished, unstained, unsullied, untarnished, virgin, virginal, white **4** = **blameless**, above reproach, chaste, innocent, irreproachable, squeaky-clean, unimpeachable
Antonyms *adj* ≠ **clean:** besmirched, bespattered, blemished, defiled, dirty, filthy, flawed, impure, messy, soiled, spotted, stained, sullied, tainted, tarnished, unchaste ≠ **blameless:** notorious, reprehensible

spotlight *n* **2** = **attention**, fame, interest, limelight, notoriety, public attention, public eye ◆ *vb* **4** = **highlight**, accentuate, draw attention to, feature, focus attention on, give prominence to, illuminate, point up, throw into relief

spot-on *adj Informal* = **accurate**, correct, exact, hitting the nail on the head (*inf.*), on the bull's-eye (*inf.*), on the money (*US*), precise, punctual (to the minute), right, unerring

spotted *adj* **1** = **speckled**, dappled, dotted, flecked, mottled, pied, polka-dot, specked

spotty *adj* **1** = **pimply**, blotchy, pimpled, plooky-faced (*Scot.*), poor-complexioned **2** = **inconsistent**, erratic, fluctuating, irregular, patchy, sporadic, uneven

spouse *n* **1** = **partner**, better half (*humorous*), companion, consort, helpmate, her indoors (*Brit. sl.*), husband *or* wife, mate, significant other (*US inf.*)

spout *vb* **1** = **stream**, discharge, emit, erupt, gush, jet, shoot, spray, spurt, squirt, surge **3** *Informal* = **hold forth**, declaim, expatiate, go on (*inf.*), orate, pontificate, rabbit (on) (*Brit. inf.*), ramble (on), rant, speechify, spiel (*inf.*), talk

sprawl *vb* **1** = **loll**, flop, lounge, slouch, slump **3** = **spread**, ramble, straggle, trail

spray[1] *n* **1** = **droplets**, drizzle, fine mist, moisture, spindrift, spoondrift **2b** = **aerosol**, atomizer, sprinkler ◆ *vb* **4** = **scatter**, atomize, diffuse, shower, sprinkle

spray[2] *n* = **sprig**, bough, branch, corsage, floral arrangement, shoot

spread *vb* **1** = **open (out)**, be displayed, bloat, broaden, dilate, expand, extend, fan out, sprawl, stretch, swell, unfold, unfurl, unroll, widen **6, 7** = **lay out**, arrange, array, cover, furnish, prepare, set **8** = **circulate**, advertise, blazon, broadcast, bruit, cast, cover, diffuse, disseminate, distribute, make known, make public, proclaim, promulgate, propagate, publicize, publish, radiate, scatter, shed, strew, transmit ◆ *n* **13** = **increase**, advance, advancement, development, diffusion, dispersal, dissemination, escalation, expansion, proliferation, spreading, suffusion, transmission **15** = **extent**, compass, period, reach, span, stretch, sweep, term **19** *Informal* = **feast**, array, banquet, blowout (*sl.*), repast

and manipulation of figures, equations, and text: used esp. for financial planning.

sprechgesang (*German* 'ʃprɛçgəzaŋ) *n Music.* a type of vocalization between singing and recitation. [C20: from G *Sprechgesang,* lit.: speaking-song]

spree Ⓣ (spriː) *n* **1** a session of considerable overindulgence, esp. in drinking, squandering money, etc. **2** a romp. [C19: ? changed from Scot. *spreath* plundered cattle, ult. from L *praeda* booty]

sprig (sprɪg) *n* **1** a shoot, twig, or sprout of a tree, shrub, etc.; spray. **2** an ornamental device resembling a spray of leaves or flowers. **3** Also called: **dowel pin.** a small wire nail without a head. **4** *Inf., rare.* a youth. **5** *Inf., rare.* a person considered as the descendant of an established family, social class, etc. **6** *NZ.* another word for **stud**[1] (sense 5). ◆ *vb* **sprigs, sprigging, sprigged.** (*tr*) **7** to fasten or secure with sprigs. **8** to ornament (fabric, etc.) with a design of sprigs. [C15: prob. of Gmc origin]
▸**'sprigger** *n* ▸**'spriggy** *adj*

sprightly Ⓣ ('spraɪtlɪ) *adj* **sprightlier, sprightliest. 1** full of vitality; lively and active. ◆ *adv* **2** *Obs.* in an active or lively manner. [C16: from *spright,* var. of SPRITE + -LY[1]]
▸**'sprightliness** *n*

spring Ⓣ (sprɪŋ) *vb* **springs, springing, sprang** *or* **sprung; sprung. 1** to move or cause to move suddenly upwards or forwards in a single motion. **2** to release or be released from a forced position by elastic force: *the bolt sprang back.* **3** (*tr*) to leap or jump over. **4** (*intr*) to come or arise suddenly. **5** (*intr*) (of a part of a mechanism, etc.) to jump out of place. **6** to make (wood, etc.) warped or split or (of wood, etc.) to become warped or split. **7** to happen or cause to happen unexpectedly: *to spring a surprise.* **8** (*intr;* usually foll. by *from*) to originate; be descended: *the idea sprang from a chance meeting; he sprang from peasant stock.* **9** (*intr;* often foll. by *up*) to come into being or appear suddenly: *factories springing up.* **10** (*tr*) (of a gundog) to rouse (game) from cover. **11** (*intr*) (of game or quarry) to start or rise suddenly from cover. **12** to explode (a mine) or (of a mine) to explode. **13** (*tr*) to provide with a spring or springs. **14** (*tr*) *Inf.* to arrange the escape of (someone) from prison. **15** (*intr*) *Arch. or poetic.* (of daylight or dawn) to begin to appear. ◆ *n* **16** the act or an instance of springing. **17** a leap, jump, or bound. **18a** the quality of resilience; elasticity. **18b** (*as modifier*): *spring steel.* **19** the act or an instance of moving rapidly back from a position of tension. **20a** a natural outflow of ground water, as forming the source of a stream. **20b** (*as modifier*): *spring water.* **21a** a device, such as a coil or strip of steel, that stores potential energy when it is compressed, stretched, or bent and releases it when the restraining force is removed. **21b** (*as modifier*): *a spring mattress.* **22** a structural defect such as a warp or bend. **23a** (*sometimes cap.*) the season of the year between winter and summer, astronomically from the March equinox to the June solstice in the N hemisphere and from the September equinox to the December solstice in the S hemisphere. **23b** (*as modifier*): *spring showers.* Related adj: **vernal. 24** the earliest or freshest time of something. **25** a source or origin. **26** Also called: **spring line.** *Naut.* a mooring line, usually one of a pair that cross amidships. [OE *springan*]
▸**'springless** *adj* ▸**'spring,like** *adj*

spring balance *or esp. US* **spring scale** *n* a device in which an object to be weighed is attached to the end of a helical spring, the extension of which indicates the weight of the object on a calibrated scale.

springboard ('sprɪŋ,bɔːd) *n* **1** a flexible board, usually projecting low over the water, used for diving. **2** a similar board used for gaining height or momentum in gymnastics. **3** *Austral. & NZ.* a board inserted into the trunk of a tree at some height above the ground on which a lumberjack stands to chop down the tree. **4** anything that serves as a point of departure or initiation.

springbok ('sprɪŋ,bʌk) *n, pl* **springbok** *or* **springboks.** an antelope of semidesert regions of southern Africa, which moves in leaps. [C18: from Afrik., from Du. *springen* to spring + *bok* goat]

Springbok ('sprɪŋ,bʌk, -,bɒk) *n* a person who has represented South Africa in a national sports team.

spring chicken *n* **1** *Chiefly US.* a young chicken, tender for cooking, esp. one from two to ten months old. **2 he** *or* **she is no spring chicken.** *Inf.* he or she is no longer young.

spring-clean *vb* **1** to clean (a house) thoroughly: traditionally at the end of winter. ◆ *n* **2** an instance of this.
▸**,spring-'cleaning** *n*

springe (sprɪndʒ) *n* **1** a snare set to catch small wild animals or birds and consisting of a loop attached to a bent twig or branch under tension. ◆ *vb* **springes, springeing, springed. 2** (*tr*) to catch (animals or birds) with this. [C13: rel. to OE *springan* to spring]

springer ('sprɪŋə) *n* **1** a person or thing that springs. **2** short for **springer spaniel. 3** *Archit.* **3a** the first and lowest stone of an arch. **3b** the impost of an arch.

springer spaniel *n* either of two breeds of spaniel with a slightly domed head and ears of medium length.

springhaas ('sprɪŋ,hɑːs) *n, pl* **springhaas** *or* **springhase** (-,hɑːzə). a small S and E African nocturnal kangaroo-like rodent. [from Afrik.: spring hare]

springing ('sprɪŋɪŋ) *n Archit.* the level where an arch or vault rises from a support.

spring lock *n* a type of lock having a spring-loaded bolt, a key being required only to unlock it.

spring onion *n* an immature form of the onion, widely cultivated for its tiny bulb and long green leaves which are eaten in salads, etc. Also called: **scallion.**

spring roll *n* a Chinese dish consisting of a savoury mixture rolled up in a thin pancake and fried.

springtail ('sprɪŋ,teɪl) *n* any of various primitive wingless insects having a forked springing organ.

spring tide *n* **1** either of the two tides that occur at or just after new moon and full moon: the greatest rise and fall in tidal level. Cf. **neap tide. 2** any great rush or flood.

springtime ('sprɪŋ,taɪm) *n* **1** Also called: **springtide.** the season of spring. **2** the earliest, usually the most attractive, period of the existence of something.

springy Ⓣ ('sprɪŋɪ) *adj* **springier, springiest. 1** possessing or characterized by resilience or bounce. **2** (of a place) having many springs of water.
▸**'springily** *adv* ▸**'springiness** *n*

sprinkle Ⓣ ('sprɪŋkᵊl) *vb* **sprinkles, sprinkling, sprinkled. 1** to scatter (liquid, powder, etc.) in tiny particles or droplets over (something). **2** (*tr*) to distribute over (something): *the field was sprinkled with flowers.* **3** (*intr*) to drizzle slightly. ◆ *n* **4** the act or an instance of sprinkling or a quantity that is sprinkled. **5** a slight drizzle. [C14: prob. from MDu. *sprenkelen*]
▸**'sprinkler** *n*

sprinkler system *n* a fire-extinguishing system that releases water from overhead nozzles opened automatically by a temperature rise.

sprinkling Ⓣ ('sprɪŋklɪŋ) *n* a small quantity or amount: *a sprinkling of common sense.*

sprint Ⓣ (sprɪnt) *n* **1** *Athletics.* a short race run at top speed. **2** a fast finishing speed at the end of a longer race, as in running or cycling, etc. **3** any quick run. ◆ *vb* **4** (*intr*) to go at top speed, as in running, cycling, etc. [C16: of Scand. origin]
▸**'sprinter** *n*

sprit (sprɪt) *n Naut.* a light spar pivoted at the mast and crossing a fore-and-aft quadrilateral sail diagonally to the peak. [OE *spreot*]

sprite Ⓣ (spraɪt) *n* **1** (in folklore) a nimble elflike creature, esp. one associated with water. **2** a small dainty person. [C13: from OF *esprit,* from L *spīritus* SPIRIT[1]]

spritsail ('sprɪt,seɪl; *Naut.* 'sprɪtsəl) *n Naut.* a sail mounted on a sprit or bowsprit.

spritzer ('sprɪtsə) *n* a drink, usually white wine, with soda water added. [from G *spritzen* to splash]

sprocket ('sprɒkɪt) *n* **1** Also called: **sprocket wheel.** a relatively thin wheel having teeth projecting radially from the rim, esp. one that drives or is driven by a chain. **2** an individual tooth on such a wheel. **3** a cylindrical wheel with teeth on one or both rims for pulling film through a camera or projector. [C16: from ?]

sprout Ⓣ (spraʊt) *vb* **1** (of a plant, seed, etc.) to produce (new leaves, shoots, etc.). **2** (*intr;* often foll. by *up*) to begin to grow or develop. ◆ *n* **3** a new shoot or bud. **4** something that grows like a sprout. **5** See **Brussels sprout.** [OE *sprūtan*]

spruce[1] (spruːs) *n* **1** any coniferous tree of a N temperate genus, cultivated for timber and for ornament. They grow in a pyramidal shape and have needle-like leaves and light-coloured wood. See also **Norway spruce. 2** the wood of any of these trees. [C17: short for *Spruce fir,* from C14 *Spruce* Prussia, changed from *Pruce,* via OF from L *Prussia*]

spruce[2] Ⓣ (spruːs) *adj* neat, smart, and trim. [C16: ?from *Spruce leather,* a fashionable leather imported from Prussia; see SPRUCE[1]]
▸**'sprucely** *adv* ▸**'spruceness** *n*

THESAURUS

Antonyms *vb* ≠ **circulate:** contain, control, curb, hold back, hold in, repress, restrain, stifle

spree *n* **1** = **binge** (*inf.*), bacchanalia, beano (*Brit. sl.*), bender (*inf.*), carousal, carouse, debauch, fling, jag (*sl.*), junketing, orgy, revel, splurge

sprightly *adj* **1** = **lively,** active, agile, airy, alert, animated, blithe, bright-eyed and bushy-tailed, brisk, cheerful, energetic, frolicsome, gay, jaunty, joyous, nimble, perky, playful, spirited, sportive, spry, vivacious
Antonyms *adj* dull, inactive, lethargic, sedentary, sluggish, torpid, unenergetic

spring *vb* **1-3** = **jump,** bounce, bound, hop, leap, rebound, recoil, vault **8** *usually with* **from** = **originate,** arise, be derived, be descended, come, derive, descend, emanate, emerge, grow, issue, proceed, start, stem **9** *often with* **up** = **appear,** burgeon, come into existence *or* being, develop, mushroom, shoot up ◆ *n* **16, 17** = **jump,** bound, buck, hop, leap, saltation, vault **18a** = **elasticity,** bounce, bounciness, buoyancy, flexibility, give (*inf.*), recoil, resilience, springiness ◆ *modifier* **23b** = **vernal,** springlike ◆ *n* **25** = **source,** beginning, cause, fount, fountainhead, origin, root, well, wellspring

springy *adj* **1** = **elastic,** bouncy, buoyant, flexible, resilient, rubbery, spongy

sprinkle *vb* **1** = **scatter,** dredge, dust, pepper, powder, shower, spray, strew

sprinkling *n* = **scattering,** admixture, dash, dusting, few, handful, scatter, smattering, sprinkle

sprint *vb* **4** = **race,** barrel (along) (*inf., chiefly US & Canad.*), dart, dash, go at top speed, go like a bomb (*Brit. & NZ inf.*), hare (*Brit. inf.*), hotfoot, put on a burst of speed, scamper, shoot, tear, whizz (*inf.*)

sprite *n* **1** = **spirit,** apparition, brownie, dryad, elf, fairy, goblin, imp, leprechaun, naiad, nymph, Oceanid (*Greek myth*), peri, pixie, sylph

sprout *vb* **1, 2** = **grow,** bud, develop, germinate, push, shoot, spring, vegetate

spruce[2] *adj* = **smart,** as if one had just stepped out of a bandbox, dainty, dapper, elegant, natty (*inf.*), neat, soigné *or* soignée, trig (*arch. or dialect*), trim, well-groomed, well turned out

spruce beer *n* an alcoholic drink made of fermented molasses flavoured with spruce twigs and cones.

spruce up ❶ *vb* **spruces, sprucing, spruced.** (*adv*) to make (oneself, a person, or thing) smart and neat.

sprue[1] (spruː) *n* **1** a vertical channel in a mould through which plastic or molten metal is introduced or out of which it flows when the mould is filled. **2** plastic or metal that solidifies in a sprue. [C19: from ?]

sprue[2] (spruː) *n* a chronic disease, esp. of tropical climates, characterized by diarrhoea and emaciation. [C19: from Du. *spruw*]

spruik (ˈspruːɪk) *vb* (*intr*) *Austral. sl.* to describe or hold forth like a salesman; spiel or advertise loudly. [C20: from ?]
▸ˈ**spruiker** *n*

spruit (spreɪt) *n S. African.* a small tributary stream or watercourse. [Afrik. *sprint* offshoot, tributary]

sprung (sprʌŋ) *vb* a past tense and past participle of **spring.**

sprung rhythm *n Prosody.* a type of poetic rhythm characterized by metrical feet of irregular composition, each having one strongly stressed syllable, often the first, and an indefinite number of unstressed syllables.

spry ❶ (spraɪ) *adj* **spryer, spryest** *or* **sprier, spriest.** active and brisk; nimble. [C18: ? of Scand. origin]
▸ˈ**spryly** *adv* ▸ˈ**spryness** *n*

spud (spʌd) *n* **1** an informal word for **potato. 2** a narrow-bladed spade for cutting roots, digging up weeds, etc. ◆ *vb* **spuds, spudding, spudded. 3** (*tr*) to eradicate (weeds) with a spud. **4** (*intr*) to drill the first foot of an oil well. [C15 *spudde* short knife, from ?; applied later to a digging tool, & hence to a potato]

spue (spjuː) *vb* **spues, spuing, spued.** an archaic spelling of **spew.**
▸ˈ**spuer** *n*

spume (spjuːm) *n* **1** foam or surf, esp. on the sea; froth. ◆ *vb* **spumes, spuming, spumed. 2** (*intr*) to foam or froth. [C14: from OF *espume,* from L *spūma*]
▸ˈ**spumous** *or* ˈ**spumy** *adj*

spun (spʌn) *vb* **1** the past tense and past participle of **spin.** ◆ *adj* **2** formed or manufactured by spinning: *spun gold; spun glass.*

spunk ❶ (spʌŋk) *n* **1** *Inf.* courage or spirit. **2** *Brit. taboo sl.* semen. **3** touchwood or tinder. [C16 (in the sense: a spark): from Scot. Gaelic *spong* tinder, sponge, from L *spongia* sponge]
▸ˈ**spunky** *adj* ▸ˈ**spunkily** *adv*

spun silk *n* shiny yarn or fabric made from silk waste.

spur ❶ (spɜː) *n* **1** a pointed device or sharp spiked wheel fixed to the heel of a rider's boot to enable him to urge his horse on. **2** anything serving to urge or encourage. **3** a sharp horny projection from the leg in male birds, such as the domestic cock. **4** a pointed process in any of various animals. **5** a tubular extension at the base of the corolla in flowers such as larkspur. **6** a short or stunted branch of a tree. **7** a ridge projecting laterally from a mountain or mountain range. **8** another name for **groyne. 9** Also called: **spur track.** a railway branch line or siding. **10** a short side road leading off a main road. **11** a sharp cutting instrument attached to the leg of a gamecock. **12 on the spur of the moment.** on impulse. **13 win one's spurs. 13a** to prove one's ability; gain distinction. **13b** *History.* to earn knighthood. ◆ *vb* **spurs, spurring, spurred. 14** (*tr*) to goad or urge with or as if with spurs. **15** (*intr*) to go or ride quickly; press on. **16** (*tr*) to provide with a spur or spurs. [OE *spura*]

spurge (spɜːdʒ) *n* any of various plants that have milky sap and small flowers typically surrounded by conspicuous bracts. [C14: from OF *espurge,* from *espurgier* to purge, from L *expurgāre* to cleanse]

spur gear *or* **wheel** *n* a gear having involuted teeth either straight or helically cut on a cylindrical surface.

spurious ❶ (ˈspjʊərɪəs) *adj* **1** not genuine or real. **2** (of a plant part or organ) resembling another part in appearance only; false: *a spurious fruit.* **3** *Rare.* illegitimate. [C17: from L *spurius* of illegitimate birth]
▸ˈ**spuriously** *adv* ▸ˈ**spuriousness** *n*

spurn ❶ (spɜːn) *vb* **1** to reject (a person or thing) with contempt. **2** (when *intr,* often foll. by *against*) *Arch.* to kick (at). ◆ *n* **3** an instance of spurning. **4** *Arch.* a kick or thrust. [OE *spurnan*]
▸ˈ**spurner** *n*

spurt ❶ *or* **spirt** (spɜːt) *vb* **1** to gush or cause to gush forth in a sudden stream or jet. **2** (*intr*) to make a sudden effort. ◆ *n* **3** a sudden stream or jet. **4** a short burst of activity, speed, or energy. [C16: ? rel. to MHG *sprützen* to squirt]

Sputnik (ˈsputnɪk, ˈspʌt-) *n* any of a series of Soviet artificial satellites, **Sputnik 1** (launched in 1957) being the first man-made satellite to orbit the earth. [C20: from Russian, lit.: fellow traveller, from *s-* with + *put* path + *-nik,* suffix indicating agent]

sputter (ˈspʌtə) *vb* **1** another word for **splutter** (senses 1–3). **2** *Physics.* **2a** to undergo or cause to undergo a process in which atoms of a solid are removed from its surface by the impact of high-energy ions. **2b** to coat (a metal) onto (a solid surface) by this process. ◆ *n* **3** the process or noise of sputtering. **4** incoherent stammering speech. **5** something ejected while sputtering. [C16: from Du. *sputteren,* imit.]
▸ˈ**sputterer** *n*

sputum (ˈspjuːtəm) *n, pl* **sputa** (-tə). saliva ejected from the mouth, esp. mixed with mucus. [C17: from L: spittle, from *spuere* to spit out]

spy ❶ (spaɪ) *n, pl* **spies. 1** a person employed by a state or institution to obtain secret information from rival countries, organizations, companies, etc. **2** a person who keeps secret watch on others. **3** *Obs.* a close view. ◆ *vb* **spies, spying, spied. 4** (*intr;* usually foll. by *on*) to keep a secret or furtive watch (on). **5** (*intr*) to engage in espionage. **6** (*tr*) to catch sight of; descry. [C13 *spien,* from OF *espier,* of Gmc origin]

spyglass (ˈspaɪˌglɑːs) *n* a small telescope.

spy out *vb* (*tr, adv*) **1** to discover by careful observation. **2** to make a close scrutiny of.

sq. *abbrev. for:* **1** sequence. **2** square. **3** (*pl* **sqq.**) the following one. [from L *sequens*]

Sq. *abbrev. for:* **1** Squadron. **2** Square.

SQL *abbrev. for* structured query language: a computer programming language used for database management.

squab (skwɒb) *n, pl* **squabs** *or* **squab. 1** a young unfledged bird, esp. a pigeon. **2** a short fat person. **3a** a well-stuffed bolster or cushion. **3b** a sofa. ◆ *adj* **4** (of birds) unfledged. **5** short and fat. [C17: prob. of Gmc origin]
▸ˈ**squabby** *adj*

squabble ❶ (ˈskwɒbᵊl) *vb* **squabbles, squabbling, squabbled. 1** (*intr*) to quarrel over a small matter. ◆ *n* **2** a petty quarrel. [C17: prob. of Scand. origin]
▸ˈ**squabbler** *n*

squad ❶ (skwɒd) *n* **1** the smallest military formation, typically a dozen soldiers, esp. a drill formation. **2** any small group of people engaged in a common pursuit. **3** *Sport.* a number of players from which a team is to be selected. [C17: from OF *esquade,* from OSp. *escuadra,* from *escuadrar* to SQUARE, from the square formations used]

squaddie *or* **squaddy** (ˈskwɒdɪ) *n, pl* **squaddies.** *Brit. sl.* a private soldier. [C20: from SQUAD]

squadron (ˈskwɒdrən) *n* **1** a subdivision of a naval fleet detached for a particular task. **2** a cavalry unit comprising two or more troops. **3** the basic tactical and administrative air force unit comprising two or more flights. [C16: from It. *squadrone* soldiers drawn up in square formation, from *squadro* square]

squadron leader *n* an officer holding commissioned rank, between flight lieutenant and wing commander in the air forces of Britain and certain other countries.

squalene (ˈskweɪˌliːn) *n Biochemistry.* a terpene first found in the liver of sharks but also present in the livers of most higher animals. [C20: from NL *squalus,* genus name of the shark]

squalid ❶ (ˈskwɒlɪd) *adj* **1** dirty and repulsive, esp. as a result of neglect or poverty. **2** sordid. [C16: from L *squālidus,* from *squālēre* to be stiff with dirt]
▸**squaˈlidity** *or* ˈ**squalidness** *n* ▸ˈ**squalidly** *adv*

squall[1] ❶ (skwɔːl) *n* **1** a sudden strong wind or brief turbulent storm. **2**

THESAURUS

Antonyms *adj* bedraggled, disarrayed, dishevelled, frowsy, messy, rumpled, uncombed, unkempt, untidy

spruce up *vb* = **smarten up**, groom, have a wash and brush-up (*Brit.*), tidy, titivate

spry *adj* = **active**, agile, alert, brisk, nimble, nippy (*Brit. inf.*), quick, ready, sprightly, supple
Antonyms *adj* awkward, decrepit, doddering, inactive, lethargic, slow, sluggish, stiff

spunk *n* **1** *Old-fashioned, informal* = **courage**, backbone, balls (*taboo sl.*), ballsiness (*taboo sl.*), bottle (*Brit. sl.*), gameness, grit, gumption (*inf.*), guts (*inf.*), mettle, nerve, pluck, resolution, spirit, toughness

spur *n* **1** = **goad**, prick, rowel **2** = **stimulus**, impetus, impulse, incentive, incitement, inducement, kick up the backside (*inf.*), motive **12 on the spur of the moment** = **on impulse**, impetuously, impromptu, impulsively, on the spot, unpremeditatedly, unthinkingly, without planning, without thinking ◆ *vb* **14** = **incite**, animate, drive, goad, impel, press, prick, prod, prompt, put a bomb under (*inf.*), stimulate, urge

spurious *adj* **1** = **false**, artificial, bogus, contrived, counterfeit, deceitful, ersatz, fake, feigned, forged, imitation, mock, phoney *or* phony (*inf.*), pretended, pseudo (*inf.*), sham, simulated, specious, unauthentic
Antonyms *adj* authentic, bona fide, genuine, honest, kosher (*inf.*), legitimate, real, sound, unfeigned, valid

spurn *vb* **1** = **reject**, cold-shoulder, contemn, despise, disdain, disregard, kick in the teeth (*sl.*), put down, rebuff, repulse, scorn, slight, snub, turn one's nose up at (*inf.*)
Antonyms *vb* embrace, grasp, seize, take up, welcome

spurt *vb* **1** = **gush**, burst, erupt, jet, shoot, spew, squirt, surge ◆ *n* **4** = **burst**, access, fit, rush, spate, surge

spy *n* **1** = **undercover agent**, double agent, fifth columnist, foreign agent, mole, nark (*Brit., Austral., & NZ sl.*), secret agent, secret service agent ◆ *vb* **4** *usually with* **on** = **watch**, follow, keep under surveillance, keep watch on, shadow, tail (*inf.*), trail **6** = **catch sight of**, behold (*arch. or literary*), descry, espy, glimpse, notice, observe, set eyes on, spot

spying *n* **5** = **espionage**, secret service

squabble *vb* **1** = **quarrel**, argue, bicker, brawl, clash, dispute, fall out (*inf.*), fight, fight like cat and dog, go at it hammer and tongs, have words, row, scrap (*inf.*), spar, wrangle ◆ *n* **2** = **quarrel**, argument, barney (*inf.*), difference of opinion, disagreement, dispute, fight, row, scrap (*inf.*), set-to (*inf.*), spat, tiff

squad *n* **1-3** = **team**, band, company, crew, force, gang, group, troop

squalid *adj* **1, 2** = **dirty**, broken-down, decayed, disgusting, fetid, filthy, foul, low, nasty, poverty-stricken, repulsive, run-down, seedy, sleazy, slovenly, slummy, sordid, unclean, yucky *or* yukky (*sl.*)
Antonyms *adj* attractive, clean, hygienic, in good condition, pleasant, salubrious, spick-and-span, spotless, tidy, well-kempt, well looked-after

any sudden commotion. ◆ *vb* **3** (*intr*) to blow in a squall. [C18: ? a special use of SQUALL[2]]
▸ **'squally** *adj*

squall[2] (skwɔːl) *vb* **1** (*intr*) to cry noisily; yell. ◆ *n* **2** a shrill or noisy yell or howl. [C17: prob. of Scand. origin]
▸ **'squaller** *n*

squalor 🅣 ('skwɒlə) *n* the condition or quality of being squalid; disgusting filth. [C17: from L]

squama ('skweɪmə) *n, pl* **squamae** (-miː). *Biol.* a scale or scalelike structure. [C18: from L]
▸ **squamate** ('skweɪmeɪt) *adj* ▸ **squa'mation** *n* ▸ **'squamose** *or* **'squamous** *adj*

squander 🅣 ('skwɒndə) *vb* (*tr*) to spend wastefully or extravagantly; dissipate. [C16: from ?]
▸ **'squanderer** *n*

square 🅣 (skwɛə) *n* **1** a plane geometric figure having four equal sides and four right angles. **2** any object, part, or arrangement having this or a similar shape. **3** an open area in a town, sometimes including the surrounding buildings, which may form a square. **4** *Maths.* the product of two equal factors; the second power: *9 is the square of 3, written* 3^2. **5** an instrument having two strips of wood, metal, etc., set in the shape of a T or L, used for constructing or testing right angles. **6** *Cricket.* the closely-cut area in the middle of a ground on which wickets are prepared. **7** *Inf.* a person who is old-fashioned in views, customs, appearance, etc. **8** *Obs.* a standard, pattern, or rule. **9 back to square one.** indicating a return to the starting point because of failure, lack of progress, etc. **10 on the square. 10a** at right angles. **10b** *Inf.* honestly and openly. **11 out of square. 11a** not at right angles or not having a right angle. **11b** not in order or agreement. ◆ *adj* **12** being a square in shape or section. **13** having or forming one or more right angles or being at right angles to something. **14a** (*prenominal*) denoting a measure of area of any shape: *a circle of four square feet.* **14b** (*immediately postpositive*) denoting a square having a specified length on each side: *a board four feet square.* **15** fair and honest (esp. in **a square deal**). **16** straight, even, or level: *a square surface.* **17** *Cricket.* at right angles to the wicket: *square leg.* **18** *Soccer, hockey, etc.* in a straight line across the pitch: *a square pass.* **19** *Naut.* (of the sails of a square-rigged ship) set at right angles to the keel. **20** *Inf.* old-fashioned. **21** stocky or sturdy: *square shoulders.* **22** (*postpositive*) having no remaining debts or accounts to be settled. **23** (*prenominal*) unequivocal or straightforward: *a square contradiction.* **24** (*postpositive*) neat and tidy. **25** *Maths.* (of a matrix) having the same number of rows and columns. **26 all square.** on equal terms; even in score. **27 square peg** (**in a round hole**). *Inf.* a person or thing that is a misfit. ◆ *vb* **squares, squaring, squared.** (*mainly tr*) **28** to make into a square or similar shape. **29** *Maths.* to raise (a number or quantity) to the second power. **30** to test or adjust for deviation with respect to a right angle, plane surface, etc. **31** (sometimes foll. by *off*) to divide into squares. **32** to position so as to be rectangular, straight, or level: *to square the shoulders.* **33** (sometimes foll. by *up*) to settle (debts, accounts, etc.). **34** to level (the score) in a game, etc. **35** (*also intr;* often foll. by *with*) to agree or cause to agree: *your ideas don't square with mine.* **36** to arrange (something) or come to an arrangement with (someone) as by bribery. **37 square the circle.** to attempt the impossible (in reference to the insoluble problem of constructing a square having exactly the same area as a given circle). ◆ *adv* **38** in order to be square. **39** at right angles. **40** *Soccer, hockey, etc.* in a straight line across the pitch: *to pass the ball square.* **41** *Inf.* squarely. ◆ See also **square away, square off, square up.** [C13: from OF *esquare,* from Vulgar L *exquadra* (unattested), from L *quadrāre* to make square]
▸ **'squareness** *n* ▸ **'squarer** *n*

square away *vb* (*adv*) **1** to set the sails of (a square-rigged ship) at right angles to the keel. **2** (*tr*) *US & Canad.* to make neat and tidy.

square-bashing *n Brit. mil. sl.* drill on a barracks square.

square bracket *n* **1** either of a pair of characters [ ], used to enclose a section of writing or printing to separate it from the main text. **2** Also called: **bracket.** either of these characters used as a sign of aggregation in mathematical or logical expressions.

square dance *n* **1** any of various formation dances in which the couples form squares. ◆ *vb* **square-dance, square-dances, square-dancing, square-danced. 2** (*intr*) to perform such a dance.
▸ **'square-ˌdancer** *n*

square knot *n* another name for **reef knot.**

square leg *n Cricket.* **1** a fielding position on the on side approximately at right angles to the batsman. **2** a person who fields in this position.

squarely ('skwɛəlɪ) *adv* **1** in a direct way; straight: *he hit me squarely on the nose.* **2** in an honest, frank, and just manner. **3** at right angles.

square meal *n* a substantial meal consisting of enough to satisfy.

square measure *n* a unit or system of units for measuring areas.

square number *n* an integer, such as 1, 4, 9, or 16, that is the square of an integer.

square off *vb* (*intr, adv*) to assume a posture of offence or defence, as in boxing.

square of opposition *n Logic.* the diagrammatic representation of the relationships between the four types of proposition found in the syllogism.

square-rigged *adj Naut.* rigged with square sails. See **square sail.**

square root *n* a number or quantity that when multiplied by itself gives a given number or quantity: *the square roots of 4 are 2 and –2.*

square sail *n Naut.* a rectangular or square sail set on a horizontal yard rigged more or less at right angles to the keel.

square shooter *n Inf., chiefly US.* an honest or frank person.
▸ **square shooting** *adj*

square up *vb* (*adv*) **1** to pay or settle (bills, debts, etc.). **2** *Inf.* to arrange or be arranged satisfactorily. **3** (*intr;* foll. by *to*) to prepare to be confronted (with), esp. courageously. **4** (*tr;* foll. by *to*) to adopt a position of readiness to fight (an opponent). **5** *Scot.* to tidy up.

squarrose ('skwærəʊz, 'skwɒ-) *adj* **1** *Biol.* having a rough surface, caused by projecting hairs, scales, etc. **2** *Bot.* having or relating to overlapping parts that are pointed or recurved. [C18: from L *squarrōsus* scabby]

squash[1] 🅣 (skwɒʃ) *vb* **1** to press or squeeze or be pressed or squeezed in or down so as to crush, distort, or pulp. **2** (*tr*) to suppress or overcome. **3** (*tr*) to humiliate or crush (a person), esp. with a disconcerting retort. **4** (*intr*) to make a sucking, splashing, or squelching sound. **5** (often foll. by *in* or *into*) to enter or insert in a confined space. ◆ *n* **6** *Brit.* a still drink made from fruit juice or fruit syrup diluted with water. **7** a crush, esp. of people in a confined space. **8** something squashed. **9** the act or sound of squashing or the state of being squashed. **10** Also called: **squash rackets.** a game for two or four players played in an enclosed court with a small rubber ball and light long-handled rackets. **11** Also called: **squash tennis.** a similar game played with larger rackets and a larger pneumatic ball. [C16: from OF *esquasser,* from Vulgar L *exquassāre* (unattested), from L EX-[1] + *quassāre* to shatter]
▸ **'squasher** *n*

squash[2] (skwɒʃ) *n, pl* **squashes** *or* **squash.** *US & Canad.* **1** any of various marrow-like plants, the fruits of which have a hard rind surrounding edible flesh. **2** the fruit, eaten as a vegetable. [C17: of Amerind origin, from *askutasquash,* lit.: green vegetable eaten green]

squashy 🅣 ('skwɒʃɪ) *adj* **squashier, squashiest. 1** easily squashed; pulpy: *a squashy peach.* **2** soft and wet; marshy: *squashy ground.*
▸ **'squashily** *adv* ▸ **'squashiness** *n*

squat (skwɒt) *vb* **squats, squatting, squatted.** (*intr*) **1** to rest in a crouching position with the knees bent and the weight on the feet. **2** to crouch down, esp. in order to hide. **3** *Law.* to occupy land or property to which the occupant has no legal title. ◆ *adj* **4** Also: **squatty.** short and broad. ◆ *n* **5** a squatting position. **6** a house occupied by squatters. [C13: from OF *esquater,* from *es-* EX-[1] + *catir* to press together, from Vulgar L *coactīre* (unattested), from L *cōgere* to compress]
▸ **'squatly** *adv* ▸ **'squatness** *n*

squatter ('skwɒtə) *n* **1** a person who occupies property or land to which he has no legal title. **2** (in Australia) **2a** a grazier with extensive holdings. **2b** *History.* a person occupying land as tenant of the Crown. **3** (in New Zealand) a 19th-century settler who took up large acreage on a crown lease.

squat thrust *n* an exercise in which the hands are kept on the floor with the arms held straight while the legs are straightened out behind and quickly drawn in towards the body again.

squattocracy (skwɒ'tɒkrəsɪ) *n Austral.* squatters collectively, regarded as rich and influential. See **squatter** (sense 2a). [C19: from SQUATTER + -CRACY]

squaw (skwɔː) *n* **1** *Offens.* a North American Indian woman. **2** *Sl., usually facetious.* a woman or wife. [C17: of Amerind origin]

squawk 🅣 (skwɔːk) *n* **1** a loud raucous cry; screech. **2** *Inf.* a loud complaint. ◆ *vb* **3** to utter (with) a squawk. **4** (*intr*) *Inf.* to complain loudly. [C19: imit.]
▸ **'squawker** *n*

squaw man *n Derog.* a White man married to a North American Indian woman.

THESAURUS

squally[1] *adj* = **stormy**, blustery, gusty, inclement, rough, tempestuous, turbulent, wild, windy

squalor *n* = **filth**, decay, foulness, meanness, sleaziness, slumminess, squalidness, wretchedness
Antonyms *n* beauty, cleanliness, fine condition, luxury, neatness, order, pleasantness, splendour

squander *vb* = **waste**, be prodigal with, blow, consume, dissipate, expend, fritter away, frivol away, lavish, misspend, misuse, run through, scatter, spend, spend like water, throw away
Antonyms *vb* be frugal, be thrifty, economize, keep, put aside for a rainy day, save, store

square *n* **7** *Informal* = **(old) fogey**, antediluvian, back number (*inf.*), conservative, die-hard, dinosaur, fuddy-duddy (*inf.*), old buffer (*Brit. inf.*), stick-in-the-mud (*inf.*), traditionalist ◆ *adj* **15** = **honest**, above board, decent, equitable, ethical, fair, fair and square, genuine, just, kosher (*inf.*), on the level (*inf.*), on the up and up, straight, straightforward, upfront (*inf.*), upright **20** *Informal* = **old-fashioned**, behind the times, bourgeois, conservative, conventional, dated, out of date, out of the ark (*inf.*), Pooterish, straight (*sl.*), strait-laced, stuffy ◆ *vb* **32** = **even up**, accommodate, adapt, adjust, align, level, regulate, suit, tailor, true (up) **33** *sometimes with* **up** = **pay off**, balance, clear (up), discharge, liquidate, make even, quit, satisfy, settle **35** *often with* **with** = **agree**, accord, conform, correspond, fit, harmonize, match, reconcile, tally **36** *Slang* = **bribe**, buy off, corrupt, fix (*inf.*), rig, suborn
Antonyms *adj* ≠ **old-fashioned:** fashionable, in vogue, modern, modish, stylish, trendy (*Brit. inf.*), voguish

squash[1] *vb* **1** = **crush**, compress, distort, flatten, mash, pound, press, pulp, smash, stamp on, trample down **3** = **suppress**, annihilate, crush, humiliate, put down (*sl.*), put (someone) in his (*or* her) place, quash, quell, silence, sit on (*inf.*)

squashy *adj* **1, 2** = **soft**, mushy, pappy, pulpy, spongy, yielding

squawk *vb* **3** = **cry**, cackle, crow, hoot, screech, yelp **4** *Informal* = **complain**, kick up a fuss (*inf.*), protest, raise Cain (*sl.*), squeal (*inf., chiefly Brit.*)

squeak ⓘ (skwi:k) *n* **1** a short shrill cry or high-pitched sound. **2** *Inf.* an escape (esp. in **narrow squeak, near squeak**). **3** *Inf.* (*usually used with a negative*) a word; a slight sound. ◆ *vb* **4** to make or cause to make a squeak. **5** (*intr; usually foll. by through or by*) to pass with only a narrow margin: *to squeak through an examination.* **6** (*intr*) *Inf.* to confess information about oneself or another. **7** (*tr*) to utter with a squeak. [C17: prob. of Scand. origin]
▸ **'squeaky** *adj* ▸ **'squeakily** *adv* ▸ **'squeakiness** *n*

squeaky-clean *adj* **1** (of hair) washed so clean that wet strands squeak when rubbed. **2** completely clean. **3** *Inf., derog.* (of a person) cultivating a virtuous and wholesome image.

squeal ⓘ (skwi:l) *n* **1** a high shrill yelp, as of pain. **2** a screaming sound. ◆ *vb* **3** to utter (with) a squeal. **4** (*intr*) *Sl.* to confess information about another. **5** (*intr*) *Inf., chiefly Brit.* to complain loudly. [C13 *squelen,* imit.]
▸ **'squealer** *n*

squeamish ⓘ ('skwi:mɪʃ) *adj* **1** easily sickened or nauseated. **2** easily shocked; prudish. **3** easily frightened: *squeamish about spiders.* [C15: from Anglo-F *escoymous,* from ?]
▸ **'squeamishly** *adv* ▸ **'squeamishness** *n*

squeegee ('skwi:dʒi:) *n* **1** an implement with a rubber blade used for wiping away surplus water from a surface, such as a windowpane. **2** any of various similar devices used in photography for pressing water out of wet prints or negatives or for squeezing prints onto a glazing surface. ◆ *vb* **squeegees, squeegeeing, squeegeed. 3** to remove (liquid) from (something) by use of a squeegee. [C19: prob. imit., infl. by SQUEEZE]

squeeze ⓘ (skwi:z) *vb* **squeezes, squeezing, squeezed.** (*mainly tr*) **1** to grip or press firmly, esp. so as to crush or distort. **2** to crush or press (something) so as to extract (a liquid): *to squeeze juice from an orange; to squeeze an orange.* **3** to apply gentle pressure to, as in affection or reassurance: *he squeezed her hand.* **4** to push or force in a confined space: *to squeeze six lettuces into one box; to squeeze through a crowd.* **5** to hug closely. **6** to oppress with exacting demands, such as excessive taxes. **7** to exert pressure on (someone) in order to extort (something): *to squeeze money out of a victim by blackmail.* **8** *Bridge, whist.* to lead a card that forces (opponents) to discard potentially winning cards. ◆ *n* **9** the act or an instance of squeezing or of being squeezed. **10** a hug or handclasp. **11** a crush of people in a confined space. **12** *Chiefly Brit.* a condition of restricted credit imposed by a government to counteract price inflation. **13** an amount extracted by squeezing: *a squeeze of lemon juice.* **14** *Inf.* pressure brought to bear in order to extort something (esp. in **put the squeeze on**). **15** *Commerce.* any action taken by a trader or traders on a market that forces buyers to make purchases and prices to rise. **16** Also called: **squeeze play.** *Bridge, whist.* a manoeuvre that forces opponents to discard potentially winning cards. [C16: from ME *queysen* to press, from OE *cwȳsan*]
▸ **'squeezable** *adj* ▸ **'squeezer** *n*

squelch (skwɛltʃ) *vb* **1** (*intr*) to walk laboriously through soft wet material or with wet shoes, making a sucking noise. **2** (*intr*) to make such a noise. **3** (*tr*) to crush completely; squash. **4** (*tr*) *Inf.* to silence, as by a crushing retort. ◆ *n* **5** a squelching sound. **6** something that has been squelched. **7** *Inf.* a crushing remark. [C17: imit.]
▸ **'squelcher** *n* ▸ **'squelchy** *adj*

squib (skwɪb) *n* **1** a firework that burns with a hissing noise and culminates in a small explosion. **2** a short witty attack; lampoon. **3 damp squib.** something intended but failing to impress. ◆ *vb* **squibs, squibbing, squibbed. 4** (*intr*) to sound, move, or explode like a squib. **5** (*intr*) to let off or shoot a squib. **6** to write a squib against (someone). [C16: prob. imit. of a light explosion]

squid (skwɪd) *n, pl* **squid** *or* **squids.** any of various ten-limbed pelagic cephalopod molluscs of most seas, having a torpedo-shaped body ranging from about 10 centimetres to 16.5 metres long. See also **cuttlefish.** [C17: from ?]

squiffy ('skwɪfɪ) *adj* **squiffier, squiffiest.** *Brit. inf.* slightly drunk. [C19: from ?]

squiggle ('skwɪgᵊl) *n* **1** a mark or movement in the form of a wavy line; curlicue. **2** an illegible scrawl. ◆ *vb* **squiggles, squiggling, squiggled. 3** (*intr*) to wriggle. **4** (*intr*) to form or draw squiggles. **5** (*tr*) to make into squiggles. [C19: ? a blend of SQUIRM + WIGGLE]
▸ **'squiggler** *n* ▸ **'squiggly** *adj*

squilgee ('skwɪldʒi:) *n* a variant spelling of **squeegee.** [C19: ?from SQUEEGEE, infl. by SQUELCH]

squill (skwɪl) *n* **1** Also called: **sea squill.** a Mediterranean plant of the lily family. **2** any of various related Old World plants. **3** Also called: **scilla.** the bulb of the sea squill, which is sliced, dried, and used medicinally, as an expectorant. [C14: from L *squilla* sea onion, from Gk *skilla,* from ?]

squinch (skwɪntʃ) *n* a small arch, corbelling, etc., across an internal corner of a tower, used to support a spire, etc. Also called: **squinch arch.** [C15: from obs. *scunch,* from ME *sconcheon,* from OF *escoinson,* from *es-* EX-[1] + *coin* corner]

squint ⓘ (skwɪnt) *vb* **1** (*usually intr*) to cross or partly close (the eyes). **2** (*intr*) to have a squint. **3** (*intr*) to look or glance sideways or askance. ◆ *n* **4** the nontechnical name for **strabismus. 5** the act or an instance of squinting; glimpse. **6** a narrow oblique opening in a wall or pillar of a church to permit a view of the main altar from a side aisle or transept. **7** *Inf.* a quick look; glance. ◆ *adj* **8** having a squint. **9** *Inf.* askew; crooked. [C14: short for ASQUINT]
▸ **'squinter** *n* ▸ **'squinty** *adj*

squire ⓘ ('skwaɪə) *n* **1** a country gentleman in England, esp. the main landowner in a rural community. **2** *Feudal history.* a young man of noble birth, who attended upon a knight. **3** *Rare.* a man who courts or escorts a woman. **4** *Inf., chiefly Brit.* a term of address used by one man to another. ◆ *vb* **squires, squiring, squired. 5** (*tr*) (of a man) to escort (a woman). [C13: from OF *esquier;* see ESQUIRE]

squirearchy *or* **squirarchy** ('skwaɪəˌrɑ:kɪ) *n, pl* **squirearchies** *or* **squirarchies. 1** government by squires. **2** squires collectively, esp. as a political or social force.
▸ **squire'archal, squir'archal** *or* **squire'archical, squir'archical** *adj*

squireen (skwaɪ'ri:n) *or* **squireling** ('skwaɪəlɪŋ) *n Rare.* a petty squire. [C19: from SQUIRE + *-een,* Anglo-Irish dim. suffix]

squirm ⓘ (skwɜ:m) *vb* (*intr*) **1** to move with a wriggling motion; writhe. **2** to feel deep mental discomfort, guilt, embarrassment, etc. ◆ *n* **3** a squirming movement. [C17: imit. (? infl. by WORM)]
▸ **'squirmer** *n* ▸ **'squirmy** *adj*

squirrel ('skwɪrəl) *n, pl* **squirrels** *or* **squirrel. 1** any of various arboreal rodents having a bushy tail and feeding on nuts, seeds, etc. **2** any of various related rodents, such as a ground squirrel or a marmot. **3** the fur of such an animal. **4** *Inf.* a person who hoards things. ◆ *vb* **squirrels, squirrelling, squirrelled** *or US* **squirrels, squirreling, squirreled. 5** (*tr; usually foll. by away*) *Inf.* to store for future use; hoard. [C14: from OF *esquireul,* from LL *sciūrus,* from Gk *skiouros,* from *skia* shadow + *oura* tail]

squirrel cage *n* **1** a cage consisting of a cylindrical framework that is made to rotate by a small animal running inside the framework. **2** a repetitive purposeless task, way of life, etc. **3** Also called: **squirrel-cage motor.** *Electrical engineering.* the rotor of an induction motor with a cylindrical winding having copper bars around the periphery parallel to the axis.

squirt (skwɜ:t) *vb* **1** to force (a liquid) or (of a liquid) to be forced out of a narrow opening. **2** (*tr*) to cover or spatter with liquid so ejected. ◆ *n* **3** a jet or amount of liquid so ejected. **4** the act or an instance of squirting. **5** an instrument used for squirting. **6** *Inf.* **6a** a person regarded as insignificant or contemptible. **6b** a short person. [C15: imit.]
▸ **'squirter** *n*

squirting cucumber *n* a hairy plant of the Mediterranean region, having a fruit that discharges seeds explosively when ripe.

squish (skwɪʃ) *vb* **1** (*tr*) to crush, esp. so as to make a soft splashing noise. **2** (*intr*) (of mud, etc.) to make a splashing noise. ◆ *n* **3** a soft squashing sound. [C17: imit.]
▸ **'squishy** *adj*

squit (skwɪt) *n Brit. sl.* **1** an insignificant person. **2** nonsense. [C19: var. of SQUIRT]

squiz (skwɪz) *n, pl* **squizzes.** *Austral. & NZ sl.* a look or glance, esp. an inquisitive one. [C20: ? blend of SQUINT + QUIZ]

sr *Maths. abbrev. for* steradian.

Sr *abbrev. for:* **1** (after a name) senior. **2** Señor. **3** Sir. **4** Sister (religious). **5** *the chemical symbol for* strontium.

Sra *abbrev. for* Señora.

SRC (in Britain) *abbrev. for* Science Research Council.

Sri Lankan (srɪ'læŋkən) *adj* **1** of Sri Lanka, a republic in S Asia, or its inhabitants. ◆ *n* **2** an inhabitant of Sri Lanka.

SRN (formerly, in Britain) *abbrev. for* State Registered Nurse.

SRO *abbrev. for:* **1** standing room only. **2** (in Britain) Statutory Rules and Orders. **3** self-regulatory organization.

Srta *abbrev. for* Señorita.

SS *abbrev. for:* **1** Saints. **2** a paramilitary organization within the Nazi party that provided Hitler's bodyguard, security forces, concentration-camp guards, etc. [G *Schutzstaffel* protection squad] **3** steamship.

THESAURUS

squeak *vb* **4** = **peep**, pipe, shrill, squeal, whine, yelp

squeal *n, vb* **3** = **scream**, screech, shriek, wail, yell, yelp, yowl **4** *Slang* = **inform on**, betray, blab, blow the gaff (*Brit. sl.*), grass (*Brit. sl.*), peach (*sl.*), rat on (*inf.*), sell (someone) down the river (*inf.*), shop (*sl., chiefly Brit.*), sing (*sl., chiefly US*), snitch (*sl.*), spill one's guts (*sl.*), spill the beans (*inf.*), tell all **5** *Informal, chiefly Brit.* = **complain**, kick up a fuss (*inf.*), moan, protest, squawk (*inf.*)

squeamish *adj* **1** = **queasy**, nauseous, qualmish, queer, sick, sickish **2** = **fastidious**, delicate, finicky, nice (*rare*), particular, prissy (*inf.*), prudish, punctilious, scrupulous, strait-laced
Antonyms *adj* ≠ **queasy:** strong-stomached ≠ **fastidious:** bold, brassy, brazen, coarse, earthy, immodest, indifferent, tough, wanton

squeeze *vb* **1** = **press**, clutch, compress, crush, grip, nip, pinch, squash, wring **4** = **cram**, crowd, force, jam, jostle, pack, press, ram, stuff, thrust, wedge **5** = **hug**, clasp, cuddle, embrace, enfold, hold tight **7** = **extort**, bleed (*inf.*), bring pressure to bear on, lean on (*inf.*), milk, oppress, pressurize, put the screws on (*inf.*), put the squeeze on (*inf.*), wrest ◆ *n* **10** = **hug**, clasp, embrace, handclasp, hold **11** = **crush**, congestion, crowd, jam, press, squash

squint *adj* **9** *Informal* = **crooked**, askew, aslant, awry, cockeyed, oblique, off-centre, skew-whiff (*inf.*)
Antonyms *adj* aligned, even, horizontal, in line, level, perpendicular, plum, square, straight, true, vertical

squire *vb* **5** *Old-fashioned* = **escort**, accompany, attend, companion

squirm *vb* **1** = **wriggle**, fidget, flounder, shift, twist, wiggle, writhe

SSE *symbol for* south-southeast.
ssp. (*pl* **sspp.**) *Biol. abbrev. for* subspecies.
SSR (formerly) *abbrev. for* Soviet Socialist Republic.
SSRC (formerly in Britain) *abbrev. for* Social Science Research Council.
SST *abbrev. for* supersonic transport.
SSW *symbol for* south-southwest.
St *abbrev. for:* **1** Saint (all entries that are usually preceded by *St* are in this dictionary listed alphabetically under **Saint**). **2** statute. **3** Strait. **4** Street.
st. *abbrev. for:* **1** stanza. **2** statute. **3** stone. **4** *Cricket.* stumped by.
s.t. *abbrev. for* short ton.
-st *suffix.* a variant of **-est**[2].
Sta (in the names of places or churches) *abbrev. for* Saint (female). [It. *Santa*]
stab ⓣ (stæb) *vb* **stabs, stabbing, stabbed. 1** (*tr*) to pierce or injure with a sharp pointed instrument. **2** (*tr*) (of a sharp pointed instrument) to pierce or wound. **3** (when *intr*, often foll. by *at*) to make a thrust (at); jab. **4** (*tr*) to inflict with a sharp pain. **5 stab in the back. 5a** (*vb*) to damage the reputation of (a person, esp. a friend) in a surreptitious way. **5b** (*n*) a treacherous action or remark that causes the downfall of or injury to a person. ◆ *n* **6** the act or an instance of stabbing. **7** an injury or rift made by stabbing. **8** a sudden sensation, esp. an unpleasant one: *a stab of pity.* **9** *Inf.* an attempt (esp. in **make a stab at**). [C14: from *stabbe* stab wound]
► **'stabber** *n*
Stabat Mater ('stɑːbæt 'mɑːtə) *n* **1** *RC Church.* a Latin hymn commemorating the sorrows of the Virgin Mary at the crucifixion. **2** a musical setting of this hymn. [from opening words, lit.: the mother was standing]
stabile ('steɪbaɪl) *n* **1** *Arts.* a stationary abstract construction, usually of wire, metal, wood, etc. ◆ *adj* **2** fixed; stable. **3** resistant to chemical change. [C18: from L *stabilis*]
stability ⓣ (stə'bɪlɪtɪ) *n, pl* **stabilities. 1** the quality of being stable. **2** the ability of an aircraft to resume its original flight path after inadvertent displacement.
stabilize *or* **stabilise** ('steɪbɪˌlaɪz) *vb* **stabilizes, stabilizing, stabilized** *or* **stabilises, stabilising, stabilised. 1** to make or become stable or more stable. **2** to keep or be kept stable. **3** (*tr*) to put or keep (an aircraft, vessel, etc.) in equilibrium by one or more special devices or (of an aircraft, etc.) to become stable.
► **ˌstabili'zation** *or* **ˌstabili'sation** *n*
stabilizer *or* **stabiliser** ('steɪbɪˌlaɪzə) *n* **1** any device for stabilizing an aircraft. **2** a substance added to something to maintain it in a stable or unchanging state, such as an additive that preserves the texture of food. **3** *Naut.* **3a** a system of pairs of fins projecting from the hull of a ship and controllable to counteract roll. **3b** See **gyrostabilizer. 4** either of a pair of small wheels fitted to the back wheel of a bicycle to help a beginner to maintain balance. **5** *Econ.* a measure, such as progressive taxation, interest-rate control, or unemployment benefit, used to restrict swings in prices, employment, production, etc., in a free economy. **6** a person or thing that stabilizes.
stable[1] ('steɪbᵊl) *n* **1** a building, usually consisting of stalls, for the lodging of horses or other livestock. **2** the animals lodged in such a building, collectively. **3a** the racehorses belonging to a particular establishment or owner. **3b** the establishment itself. **3c** (*as modifier*): *stable companion.* **4** *Inf.* a source of training, such as a school, theatre, etc.: *the two athletes were out of the same stable.* **5** a number of people considered as a source of a particular talent: *a stable of writers.* **6** (*modifier*) of, relating to, or suitable for a stable: *stable door.* ◆ *vb* **stables, stabling, stabled. 7** to put, keep, or be kept in a stable. [C13: from OF *estable* cowshed, from L *stabulum* shed, from *stāre* to stand]
stable[2] ⓣ ('steɪbᵊl) *adj* **1** steady in position or balance; firm. **2** lasting: *a stable relationship.* **3** steadfast or firm of purpose. **4** (of an elementary particle, etc.) not undergoing decay; not radioactive. **5** (of a chemical compound) not readily partaking in a chemical change. [C13: from OF *estable*, from L *stabilis* steady, from *stāre* to stand]
► **'stableness** *n* ► **'stably** *adv*
stableboy ('steɪbᵊlˌbɔɪ), **stablegirl** ('steɪbᵊlˌgɜːl), *or* **stableman** ('steɪbᵊlˌmæn, -mən) *n, pl* **stableboys, stablegirls,** *or* **stablemen.** a boy, girl, or man who works in a stable.
stable door *n* a door with an upper and lower leaf that may be opened separately. US and Canad. equivalent: **Dutch door.**
Stableford ('steɪbᵊlfəd) *n Golf.* **a** a scoring system in which points are awarded according to the number of strokes taken at each hole, whereby a hole completed in one stroke over par counts as one point, a hole completed in level par counts as two points, etc. **b** (*as modifier*): *a Stableford competition.* ◆ Cf. **match play, stroke play.** [C20: after its inventor Dr Frank *Stableford* (1870–1959), E amateur golfer]
stable lad *n* a person who looks after the horses in a racing stable.
stabling ('steɪblɪŋ) *n* stable buildings or accommodation.
stablish ('stæblɪʃ) *vb* an archaic variant of **establish.**
staccato (stə'kɑːtəʊ) *adj* **1** *Music.* (of notes) short, clipped, and separate. **2** characterized by short abrupt sounds, as in speech: *a staccato command.* ◆ *adv* **3** (esp. used as a musical direction) in a staccato manner. [C18: from It., from *staccare* to detach, shortened from *distaccare*]
stachys ('stækɪs) *n* any plant of the herbaceous genus *Stachys.* See also **woundwort.** [C16: from L, from Gk: ear of corn]
stack ⓣ (stæk) *n* **1** an ordered pile or heap. **2** a large orderly pile of hay, straw, etc., for storage in the open air. **3** (*often pl*) compactly spaced bookshelves, used to house collections of books in an area usually prohibited to library users. **4** a number of aircraft circling an airport at different altitudes, awaiting their signal to land. **5** a large amount. **6** *Mil.* a pile of rifles or muskets in the shape of a cone. **7** *Brit.* a measure of coal or wood equal to 108 cubic feet. **8** See **chimney stack, smokestack. 9** a vertical pipe, such as the funnel of a ship or the soil pipe attached to the side of a building. **10** a high column of rock, esp. one isolated from the mainland by the erosive action of the sea. **11** an area in a computer memory for temporary storage. ◆ *vb* (*tr*) **12** to place in a stack; pile. **13** to load or fill up with piles of something: *to stack a lorry with bricks.* **14** to control a number of aircraft waiting to land at an airport so that each flies at a different altitude. **15 stack the cards.** to prearrange the order of a pack of cards secretly so as to cheat. [C13: from ON *stakkr* haystack, of Gmc origin]
► **'stackable** *adj* ► **'stacker** *n*
stacked (stækt) *adj Sl.* a variant of **well-stacked.**
stadholder *or* **stadtholder** ('stædˌhəʊldə) *n* **1** the chief magistrate of the former Dutch republic or any of its provinces (from about 1580 to 1802). **2** a viceroy or governor of a province. [C16: from Du. *stad houder,* from *stad* city + *houder* holder]
stadia[1] ('steɪdɪə) *n* **1** measurement of distance using a telescopic surveying instrument and a graduated staff calibrated to correspond with the distance from the observer. **2** the two parallel cross hairs or **stadia hairs** in the eyepiece of the instrument used. **3** the staff used. [C19: prob. from STADIA[2]]
stadia[2] ('steɪdɪə) *n* a plural of **stadium.**
stadium ('steɪdɪəm) *n, pl* **stadiums** *or* **stadia. 1** a sports arena with tiered seats for spectators. **2** (in ancient Greece) a course for races, usually located between two hills providing slopes for tiers of seats. **3** an ancient Greek measure of length equivalent to about 607 feet or 184 metres. [C16: via L from Gk *stadion,* changed from *spadion* racecourse, from *spān* to pull; infl. by Gk *stadios* steady]
staff[1] ⓣ (stɑːf) *n, pl* **staffs** *for senses 1–4;* **staffs** *or* **staves** *for senses 5–9.* **1** a group of people employed by a company, individual, etc., for executive, clerical, sales work, etc. **2** (*modifier*) attached to or provided for the staff of an establishment: *a staff doctor.* **3** the body of teachers or lecturers of an educational institution. **4** *Mil.* the officers appointed to assist a commander, service, or central headquarters organization. **5** a stick with some special use, such as a walking stick or an emblem of authority. **6** something that sustains or supports: *bread is the staff of life.* **7** a pole on which a flag is hung. **8** *Chiefly Brit.* a graduated rod used in surveying, esp. for sighting to with a levelling instrument. **9** Also called: **stave.** *Music.* **9a** the system of horizontal lines grouped into sets of five (four in plainsong) upon which music is written. The spaces between them are employed in conjunction with a clef in order to give a graphic indication of pitch. **9b** any set of five lines in this system together with its clef: *the treble staff.* ◆ *vb* **10** (*tr*) to provide with a staff. [OE *stæf*]
staff[2] (stɑːf) *n US.* a mixture of plaster and hair used to cover the external surface of temporary structures and for decoration. [C19: from ?]
staff corporal *n* a noncommissioned rank in the British Army above that of staff sergeant and below that of warrant officer.
staff nurse *n* a qualified nurse ranking immediately below a sister.
staff officer *n* a commissioned officer serving on the staff of a commander, service, or central headquarters.
Staffordshire bull terrier ('stæfədˌʃɪə, -ʃə) *n* a breed of smooth-coated terrier with a stocky frame and generally a pied or brindled coat.
Staffs. (stæfs) *abbrev. for* Staffordshire.
staff sergeant *n Mil.* **1** *Brit.* a noncommissioned officer holding a rank between sergeant and warrant officer and employed on administrative duties. **2** *US.* a noncommissioned officer who ranks: **2a** (in the Army) above sergeant and below sergeant first class. **2b** (in the Air

THESAURUS

stab *vb* **1, 2** = **pierce,** bayonet, cut, gore, impale, injure, jab, knife, puncture, run through, spear, spill blood, stick, thrust, transfix, wound **5a stab in the back** = **betray,** break faith with, deceive, do the dirty on (*Brit. sl.*), double-cross (*inf.*), give the Judas kiss to, inform on, let down, play false, sell, sell out (*inf.*), slander ◆ *n* **7** = **wound,** gash, incision, jab, puncture, rent, thrust **8** = **twinge,** ache, pang, prick **9** *Informal* = **attempt,** crack (*inf.*), endeavour, essay (*inf.*), go, shot (*inf.*), try
stability *n* **1** = **firmness,** constancy, durability, permanence, solidity, soundness, steadfastness, steadiness, strength
Antonyms *n* changeableness, fickleness, fragility, frailty, inconstancy, instability, unpredictability, unreliability, unsteadiness
stable[2] *adj* **1** = **firm,** abiding, constant, deep-rooted, durable, enduring, established, fast, fixed, immovable, immutable, invariable, lasting, permanent, secure, sound, strong, sturdy, unalterable, unchangeable, unwavering, well-founded **3** = **steady,** reliable, staunch, steadfast, sure
Antonyms *adj* ≠ **firm:** changeable, erratic, inconstant, insecure, irresolute, mercurial, mutable, shaky, shifting, temperamental, uncertain, unpredictable, unreliable, unstable, variable, volatile, wavering ≠ **steady:** unsteady, unsure
stack *n* **1, 2** = **pile,** clamp (*Brit. agriculture*), cock, heap, hoard, load, mass, mound, mountain, rick ◆ *vb* **12, 13** = **pile,** accumulate, amass, assemble, bank up, heap up, load, stockpile
staff[1] *n* **1** = **workers,** employees, lecturers, officers, organization, personnel, teachers, team, workforce **5** = **stick,** cane, crook, pole, prop, rod, sceptre, stave, wand

Force) above airman first class and below technical sergeant. **2c** (in the Marine Corps) above sergeant and below gunnery sergeant.

stag (stæg) *n* **1** the adult male of a deer. **2** a man unaccompanied by a woman at a social gathering. **3** *Stock Exchange, Brit.* a speculator who applies for shares in a new issue in anticipation of a rise in its price and thus a quick profit on resale. **4** (*modifier*) (of a social gathering) attended by men only. ◆ *adv* **5** without a female escort. ◆ *vb* **stags, stagging, stagged.** (*tr*) **6** *Stock Exchange.* to apply for (shares in a new issue) with the intention of selling them for a quick profit when trading commences. [OE *stagga* (unattested); rel. to ON *steggr* male bird]

stag beetle *n* any of various beetles, the males of which have large branched mandibles.

stage Ⓣ (steɪdʒ) *n* **1** a distinct step or period of development, growth, or progress. **2** a raised area or platform. **3** the platform in a theatre where actors perform. **4 the.** the theatre as a profession. **5** any scene regarded as a setting for an event or action. **6** a portion of a journey or a stopping place after such a portion. **7** short for **stagecoach. 8** *Brit.* a division of a bus route for which there is a fixed fare. **9** one of the separate propulsion units of a rocket that can be jettisoned when it has burnt out. **10** a small stratigraphical unit; a subdivision of a rock series or system. **11** the platform on a microscope on which the specimen is mounted for examination. **12** *Electronics.* a part of a complex circuit, esp. a transistor with the associated elements required to amplify a signal in an amplifier. **13 by** *or* **in easy stages.** not hurriedly: *he learned French by easy stages.* ◆ *vb* **stages, staging, staged.** (*tr*) **14** to perform (a play), esp. on a stage: *to stage "Hamlet".* **15** to set the action of (a play) in a particular time or place. **16** to plan, organize, and carry out (an event). [C13: from OF *estage* position, from Vulgar L *staticum* (unattested), from L *stāre* to stand]

stagecoach (ˈsteɪdʒˌkəʊtʃ) *n* a large four-wheeled horse-drawn vehicle formerly used to carry passengers, mail, etc., on a regular route.

stagecraft (ˈsteɪdʒˌkrɑːft) *n* skill in or the art of writing or staging plays.

stage direction *n* an instruction to an actor or director, written into the script of a play.

stage door *n* a door at a theatre leading backstage.

stage fright *n* nervousness or panic that may beset a person about to appear in front of an audience.

stagehand (ˈsteɪdʒˌhænd) *n* a person who sets the stage, moves props, etc., in a theatrical production.

stage left *n* the part of the stage to the left of a performer facing the audience.

stage-manage *vb* **stage-manages, stage-managing, stage-managed. 1** to work as stage manager (for a play, etc.). **2** (*tr*) to arrange, present, or supervise from behind the scenes.

stage manager *n* a person who supervises the stage arrangements of a theatrical production.

stager (ˈsteɪdʒə) *n* **1** a person of experience; veteran (esp. in **old stager**). **2** an archaic word for **actor.**

stage right *n* the part of the stage to the right of a performer facing the audience.

stage-struck *adj* infatuated with the glamour of theatrical life, esp. with the desire to act.

stage whisper *n* **1** a loud whisper from one actor to another onstage intended to be heard by the audience. **2** any loud whisper that is intended to be overheard.

stagflation (stægˈfleɪʃən) *n* a situation in which inflation is combined with stagnant or falling output and employment. [C20: blend of *stagnation* + *inflation*]

stagger Ⓣ (ˈstægə) *vb* **1** (*usually intr*) to walk or cause to walk unsteadily as if about to fall. **2** (*tr*) to astound or overwhelm, as with shock: *I am staggered by his ruthlessness.* **3** (*tr*) to place or arrange in alternating or overlapping positions or time periods to prevent confusion or congestion: *a staggered junction; to stagger holidays.* **4** (*intr*) to falter or hesitate: *his courage staggered in the face of the battle.* ◆ *n* **5** the act or an instance of staggering. [C13: from dialect *stacker,* from ON *staka* to push]
▸ˈ**staggerer** *n* ▸ˈ**staggering** *adj* ▸ˈ**staggeringly** *adv*

staggered directorships *pl n Business.* a defence against unwelcome takeover bids in which a company resolves that its directors should serve staggered terms of office and that no director can be removed from office without just cause, thus preventing a bidder from controlling the board for some years.

staggers (ˈstægəz) *n* (*functioning as sing or pl*) **1** a form of vertigo associated with decompression sickness. **2** Also called: **blind staggers.** a disease of horses and some other domestic animals characterized by a swaying unsteady gait, caused by infection or lesions of the central nervous system.

staging (ˈsteɪdʒɪŋ) *n* any temporary structure used in the process of building, esp. the horizontal platforms supported by scaffolding.

staging area *n* a checkpoint or regrouping area for military formations in transit.

staging post *n* a place where a journey is usually broken, esp. a stopover on a flight.

stagnant Ⓣ (ˈstægnənt) *adj* **1** (of water, etc.) standing still; without flow or current. **2** brackish and foul from standing still. **3** stale, sluggish, or dull from inaction. **4** not growing or developing; static. [C17: from L *stagnāns,* from *stagnāre* to be stagnant, from *stagnum* a pool]
▸ˈ**stagnancy** *n*

stagnate Ⓣ (stægˈneɪt) *vb* **stagnates, stagnating, stagnated.** (*intr*) to be or become stagnant.
▸**stagˈnation** *n*

stag night *or* **party** *n* a party for men only, esp. one held for a man just before he is married.

stagy *or US* **stagey** (ˈsteɪdʒɪ) *adj* **stagier, stagiest.** excessively theatrical or dramatic.
▸ˈ**stagily** *adv* ▸ˈ**staginess** *n*

staid Ⓣ (steɪd) *adj* of a settled, sedate, and steady character. [C16: obs. p.p. of STAY[1]]
▸ˈ**staidly** *adv* ▸ˈ**staidness** *n*

stain Ⓣ (steɪn) *vb* (*mainly tr*) **1** to mark or discolour with patches of something that dirties. **2** to dye with a penetrating dyestuff or pigment. **3** to bring disgrace or shame on: *to stain one's honour.* **4** to colour (specimens) for microscopic study by treatment with a dye or similar reagent. **5** (*intr*) to produce indelible marks or discoloration: *does ink stain?* ◆ *n* **6** a spot, mark, or discoloration. **7** a moral taint; blemish or slur. **8** a dye or similar reagent, used to colour specimens for microscopic study. **9** a solution or liquid used to penetrate the surface of a material, esp. wood, and impart a rich colour without covering up the surface or grain. **10** any dye used to colour textiles and hides. [C14 *steynen* (vb), shortened from *disteynen* to remove colour from, from OF *desteindre* to discolour, ult. from L *tingere* to tinge]
▸ˈ**stainable** *adj* ▸ˌ**stainaˈbility** *n* ▸ˈ**stainer** *n*

stained glass *n* **a** glass that has been coloured, as by fusing with a film of metallic oxide or burning pigment into the surface. **b** (*as modifier*): *a stained-glass window.*

stainless (ˈsteɪnlɪs) *adj* **1** resistant to discoloration, esp. that resulting from corrosion; rust-resistant: *stainless steel.* **2** having no blemish: *stainless reputation.*
▸ˈ**stainlessly** *adv*

stainless steel *n* **a** a type of steel resistant to corrosion as a result of the presence of large amounts of chromium. **b** (*as modifier*): *stainless-steel cutlery.*

stair (stɛə) *n* **1** one of a flight of stairs. **2** a series of steps: *a narrow stair.* ◆ See also **stairs.** [OE *stæger*]

staircase (ˈstɛəˌkeɪs) *n* a flight of stairs, its supporting framework, and, usually, a handrail or banisters.

stairs (stɛəz) *pl n* **1** a flight of steps leading from one storey or level to another, esp. indoors. **2 below stairs.** *Brit.* in the servants' quarters.

stairway (ˈstɛəˌweɪ) *n* a means of access consisting of stairs; staircase or flight of steps.

stairwell (ˈstɛəˌwɛl) *n* a vertical shaft or opening that contains a staircase.

stake[1] Ⓣ (steɪk) *n* **1** a stick or metal bar driven into the ground as a marker, part of a fence, support for a plant, etc. **2** one of a number of vertical posts that fit into sockets around a flat truck or railway wagon to hold the load in place. **3** a method or the practice of executing a person by binding him to a stake in the centre of a pile of wood that is then set on fire. **4 pull up stakes.** to leave one's home or resting place and move on. ◆ *vb* **stakes, staking, staked.** (*tr*) **5** to tie, fasten, or tether with or to a stake. **6** (often foll. by *out* or *off*) to fence or surround with stakes. **7** (often foll. by *out*) to lay (a claim) to land, rights, etc. **8** to support with a stake. [OE *staca* pin]

stake[2] Ⓣ (steɪk) *n* **1** the money or valuables that a player must hazard in order to buy into a gambling game or make a bet. **2** an interest, often financial, held in something: *a stake in the company's future.* **3** (*often pl*) the money that a player has available for gambling. **4** (*often pl*) a prize in a race, etc., esp. one made up of contributions from con-

THESAURUS

stage *n* **1** = **step,** division, juncture, lap, leg, length, level, period, phase, point ◆ *vb* **14** = **present,** do, give, perform, play, produce, put on **16** = **organize,** arrange, engineer, lay on, mount, orchestrate

stagger *vb* **1** = **totter,** falter, lurch, reel, sway, teeter, waver, wobble **2** = **astound,** amaze, astonish, bowl over (*inf.*), confound, dumbfound, flabbergast, give (someone) a shock, nonplus, overwhelm, shake, shock, strike (someone) dumb, stun, stupefy, surprise, take (someone) aback, take (someone's) breath away, throw off balance **3** = **alternate,** overlap, step, zigzag

stagnant *adj* **1, 2** = **stale,** brackish, motionless, quiet, sluggish, standing, still
Antonyms *adj* clear, flowing, fresh, moving, pure, running, unpolluted

stagnate *vb* = **vegetate,** decay, decline, deteriorate, fester, go to seed, idle, languish, lie fallow, rot, rust, stand still

staid *adj* = **sedate,** calm, composed, decorous, demure, grave, quiet, self-restrained, serious, set in one's ways, sober, solemn, steady
Antonyms *adj* adventurous, capricious, demonstrative, exuberant, flighty, giddy, indecorous, lively, rowdy, sportive, wild

stain *vb* **1** = **mark,** blemish, blot, dirty, discolour, smirch, soil, spot, tarnish, tinge **2** = **dye,** colour, tint **3** = **disgrace,** besmirch, blacken, contaminate, corrupt, defile, deprave, drag through the mud, sully, taint ◆ *n* **6** = **mark,** blemish, blot, discoloration, smirch, spot **7** = **stigma,** blemish, blot on the escutcheon, disgrace, dishonour, infamy, reproach, shame, slur **9, 10** = **dye,** colour, tint

stake[1] *n* **1** = **pole,** pale, paling, palisade, picket, post, spike, stave, stick ◆ *vb* **7** *often with* **out** = **lay claim to,** define, delimit, demarcate, mark out, outline, reserve **8** = **support,** brace, prop, secure, tether, tie up

stake[2] *n* **1** = **bet,** ante, chance, hazard, peril, pledge, risk, venture, wager **2** = **interest,** claim, concern, investment, involvement, share ◆ *vb* **9** = **bet,** chance, gamble, hazard, imperil, jeopardize, pledge, put on, risk, venture, wager

testants or owners. **5** (*pl*) a horse race in which all owners of competing horses contribute to the prize. **6** *US & Canad. inf.* short for **grubstake. 7 at stake.** at risk: *lives are at stake.* **8 raise the stakes. 8a** to increase the amount of money or valuables hazarded in a gambling game. **8b** to increase the costs, risks, or considerations involved in taking an action or reaching a conclusion. ◆ *vb* **stakes, staking, staked.** (*tr*) **9** to hazard (money, etc.) on a result. **10** to invest in or support with money, etc.: *to stake a business.* **[**C16: from ?**]**

stakeholder ('steɪkˌhaʊldə) *n* **1** a person or group owning a significant percentage of a company's shares. **2** a person or group not owning shares in an enterprise but affected by or having an interest in its operations, such as the employees, customers, local community, etc. ◆ *adj* **3** of or relating to policies intended to allow people to participate in and benefit from decisions made by enterprises in which they have a stake: *a stakeholder economy.*

stakeout ('steɪkaʊt) *Chiefly US & Canad. sl.* ◆ *n* **1** a police surveillance. **2** an area or house kept under such surveillance. ◆ *vb* **stake out. 3** (*tr, adv*) to keep under surveillance.

Stakhanovism (stæ'kænəˌvɪzəm) *n* (in the former Soviet Union) a system designed to raise production by offering incentives to efficient workers. **[**C20: after A. G. *Stakhanov* (1906–77), Soviet miner, the worker first awarded benefits under the system in 1935**]**
▸**Sta'khanovˌite** *n, adj*

stalactite ('stæləkˌtaɪt) *n* a cylindrical mass of calcium carbonate hanging from the roof of a limestone cave: formed by precipitation from continually dripping water. Cf. **stalagmite. [**C17: from NL *stalactites,* from Gk *stalaktos* dripping, from *stalassein* to drip**]**
▸**stalactiform** (stə'læktɪˌfɔːm) *adj* ▸**stalactitic** (ˌstæləkˈtɪtɪk) *or* **ˌstalac'titical** *adj*

stalag ('stælæg) *n* a German prisoner-of-war camp in World War II, esp. for men from the ranks. **[**short for *Stammlager* base camp**]**

stalagmite ('stæləgˌmaɪt) *n* a cylindrical mass of calcium carbonate projecting upwards from the floor of a limestone cave: formed by precipitation from continually dripping water. Cf. **stalactite. [**C17: from NL *stalagmites,* from Gk *stalagmos* dripping, from Gk *stalassein* to drip**]**
▸**stalagmitic** (ˌstæləg'mɪtɪk) *or* **ˌstalag'mitical** *adj*

stale[1] **T** (steɪl) *adj* **1** (esp. of food) hard, musty, or dry from being kept too long. **2** (of beer, etc.) flat and tasteless from being kept open too long. **3** (of air) stagnant; foul. **4** uninteresting from overuse: *stale clichés.* **5** no longer new: *stale news.* **6** lacking in energy or ideas through overwork or lack of variety. **7** *Banking.* (of a cheque) not negotiable by a bank as a result of not having been presented within six months of being written. **8** *Law.* (of a claim, etc.) having lost its effectiveness or force, as by failure to act or by the lapse of time. ◆ *vb* **stales, staling, staled. 9** to make or become stale. **[**C13 (orig. applied to liquor in the sense: well matured): prob. from OF *estale* (unattested) motionless, of Frankish origin**]**
▸**'staleness** *n*

stale[2] (steɪl) *vb* **stales, staling, staled. 1** (*intr*) (of livestock) to urinate. ◆ *n* **2** the urine of horses or cattle. **[**C15: ?from OF *estaler* to stand in one position**]**

stale bull *n Business.* a dealer or speculator who holds unsold commodities after a rise in market prices but who cannot trade because there are no buyers at the new levels and because his financial commitments prevent him from making further purchases.

stalemate T ('steɪlˌmeɪt) *n* **1** a chess position in which any of a player's possible moves would place his king in check: in this position the game ends in a draw. **2** a situation in which two opposing forces find that further action is impossible or futile; deadlock. ◆ *vb* **stalemates, stalemating, stalemated. 3** (*tr*) to subject to a stalemate. **[**C18: from obs. *stale,* from OF *estal* STALL[1] + (CHECK)MATE**]**

Stalinism ('stɑːlɪˌnɪzəm) *n* the theory and form of government associated with Joseph Stalin (1879–1953), general secretary of the Communist Party of the Soviet Union 1922–53: a variant of Marxism-Leninism characterized by totalitarianism, rigid bureaucracy, and loyalty to the state.

stalk[1] (stɔːk) *n* **1** the main stem of a herbaceous plant. **2** any of various subsidiary plant stems, such as a leafstalk or flower stalk. **3** a slender supporting structure in animals such as crinoids and barnacles. **4** any long slender supporting shaft or column. **[**C14: prob. dim. from OE *stalu* upright piece of wood**]**
▸**stalked** *adj* ▸**'stalkˌlike** *adj*

stalk[2] **T** (stɔːk) *vb* **1** to follow or approach (game, prey, etc.) stealthily and quietly. **2** to pursue persistently and, sometimes, attack (a person with whom one is obsessed, often a celebrity). **3** to spread over (a place) in a menacing or grim manner: *fever stalked the camp.* **4** (*intr*) to walk in a haughty, stiff, or threatening way. **5** to search (a piece of land) for prey. ◆ *n* **6** the act of stalking. **7** a stiff or threatening stride. **[**OE *bestealcian* to walk stealthily**]**
▸**'stalker** *n*

stalk-and-slash movie *n* another name for **slasher movie.**

stalking-horse *n* **1** a horse or an imitation one used by a hunter to hide behind while stalking. **2** something serving as a means of concealing plans; pretext. **3** a candidate put forward to divide the opposition or mask the candidacy of another person for whom the stalking-horse would then withdraw.

stalky ('stɔːkɪ) *adj* **stalkier, stalkiest. 1** like a stalk; slender and tall. **2** having or abounding in stalks.
▸**'stalkily** *adv* ▸**'stalkiness** *n*

stall[1] (stɔːl) *n* **1a** a compartment in a stable or shed for a single animal. **1b** another name for **stable**[1] (sense 1). **2** a small often temporary stand or booth for the sale of goods. **3** (in a church) **3a** one of a row of seats usually divided by armrests or a small screen, for the choir or clergy. **3b** a pen. **4** an instance of an engine stalling. **5** a condition of an aircraft in flight in which a reduction in speed or an increase in the aircraft's angle of attack causes a sudden loss of lift resulting in a downward plunge. **6** any small room or compartment. **7** *Brit.* **7a** a seat in a theatre or cinema, usually fixed to the floor. **7b** (*pl*) the area of seats on the ground floor of a theatre or cinema nearest to the stage or screen. **8** a tubelike covering for a finger. **9** (*pl*) short for **starting stalls.** ◆ *vb* **10** to cause (a motor vehicle or its engine) to stop, usually by incorrect use of the clutch or incorrect adjustment of the fuel mixture, or (of an engine or motor vehicle) to stop, usually for these reasons. **11** to cause (an aircraft) to go into a stall or (of an aircraft) to go into a stall. **12** to stick or cause to stick fast, as in mud or snow. **13** (*tr*) to confine (an animal) in a stall. **[**OE *steall* a place for standing**]**

stall[2] **T** (stɔːl) *vb* **1** to employ delaying tactics towards (someone); be evasive. ◆ *n* **2** an evasive move; pretext. **[**C16: from Anglo-F *estale* bird used as a decoy, infl. by STALL[1]**]**

stall-feed *vb* **stall-feeds, stall-feeding, stall-fed.** (*tr*) to keep and feed (an animal) in a stall, esp. as an intensive method of fattening it for slaughter.

stallholder ('stɔːlˌhəʊldə) *n* a person who sells goods at a market stall.

stallion ('stæljən) *n* an uncastrated male horse, esp. one used for breeding. **[**C14 *staloun,* from OF *estalon,* of Gmc origin**]**

stalwart T ('stɔːlwət) *adj* **1** strong and sturdy; robust. **2** solid, dependable, and courageous. **3** resolute and firm. ◆ *n* **4** a stalwart person, esp. a supporter. **[**OE *stǣlwirthe* serviceable, from *stǣl,* from *stathol* support + *wierthe* WORTH**]**
▸**'stalwartly** *adv* ▸**'stalwartness** *n*

stamen ('steɪmɛn) *n, pl* **stamens** *or* **stamina.** the male reproductive organ of a flower, consisting of a stalk (filament) bearing an anther in which pollen is produced. **[**C17: from L: the warp in an upright loom, from *stāre* to stand**]**
▸**staminiferous** (ˌstæmɪ'nɪfərəs) *adj*

stamina[1] **T** ('stæmɪnə) *n* enduring energy, strength, and resilience. **[**C19: identical with STAMINA[2], from L *stāmen* thread, hence the threads of life spun out by the Fates, hence energy, etc.**]**

stamina[2] ('stæmɪnə) *n* a plural of **stamen.**

staminate ('stæmɪnɪt, -ˌneɪt) *adj* (of plants) having stamens, esp. having stamens but no carpels; male.

stammer T ('stæmə) *vb* **1** to speak or say (something) in a hesitant way, esp. as a result of a speech disorder or through fear, stress, etc. ◆ *n* **2** a speech disorder characterized by involuntary repetitions and hesitations. **[**OE *stamerian***]**
▸**'stammerer** *n* ▸**'stammering** *n, adj*

stamp T (stæmp) *vb* **1** (when *intr,* often foll. by *on*) to bring (the foot) down heavily (on the ground, etc.). **2** (*intr*) to walk with heavy or noisy footsteps. **3** (*intr;* foll. by *on*) to repress or extinguish: *he stamped on criticism.* **4** (*tr*) to impress or mark (a device or sign) on (something). **5** to mark (something) with an official seal or device: *to stamp a passport.* **6** (*tr*) to fix or impress permanently: *the date was stamped on her memory.* **7** (*tr*) to affix a postage stamp to. **8** (*tr*) to distinguish or reveal: *that behaviour stamps him as a cheat.* **9** to pound or crush (ores, etc.). ◆ *n* **10** the act or an instance of stamping. **11a** See **postage stamp. 11b** a mark applied to postage stamps for cancellation. **12** a similar piece of gummed paper used for commercial or trading purposes. **13** a block, die, etc., used for imprinting a design or device. **14** a design, device, or mark that has been stamped. **15** a characteristic feature or trait; hallmark: *the stamp of authenticity.* **16** a piece of gummed paper or other mark applied to official documents to indicate payment, validity,

THESAURUS

stale[1] *adj* **1-3 = old,** decayed, dry, fetid, flat, fusty, hard, insipid, musty, sour, stagnant, tasteless **4 = unoriginal,** antiquated, banal, cliché-ridden, common, commonplace, drab, effete, flat, hackneyed, insipid, old hat, overused, platitudinous, repetitious, stereotyped, threadbare, trite, worn-out
Antonyms *adj* **≠ old:** crisp, fresh **≠ unoriginal:** different, imaginative, innovative, lively, new, novel, original, refreshing

stalemate *n* **2 = deadlock,** draw, impasse, standstill, tie

stalk[2] *vb* **1 = pursue,** creep up on, follow, haunt, hunt, shadow, tail (*inf.*), track **4 = strut,** flounce, march, pace, stride

stall[2] *vb* **1 = play for time,** beat about the bush (*inf.*), hedge, stonewall, temporize

stalwart *adj* **1 = strong,** athletic, beefy (*inf.*), brawny, hefty (*inf.*), husky (*inf.*), lusty, manly, muscular, robust, rugged, sinewy, stout, strapping, sturdy, vigorous **2, 3 = loyal,** courageous, daring, dependable, firm, indomitable, intrepid, redoubtable, reliable, resolute, staunch, valiant
Antonyms *adj* **≠ strong:** feeble, frail, infirm, namby-pamby, puny, shilpit (*Scot.*), sickly, weak **≠ courageous:** faint-hearted, timid

stamina[1] *n* **= staying power,** endurance, energy, force, grit, indefatigability, lustiness, power, power of endurance, resilience, resistance, strength, tenacity, vigour

stammer *vb* **1 = stutter,** falter, hem and haw, hesitate, pause, splutter, stumble

stamp *vb* **1 = trample,** beat, crush **4 = imprint,** engrave, fix, impress, inscribe, mark, mould, print **8 = identify,** betray, brand, categorize, exhibit, label, mark, pronounce, reveal, show to be, typecast ◆ *n* **13 = imprint,** brand, cast, earmark, hallmark, mark, mould, signature **18 = type,** breed, cast, character, cut, description, fashion, form, kind, sort

ownership, etc. **17** *Brit. inf.* a national insurance contribution, formerly recorded by means of a stamp on an official card. **18** type or class: *men of his stamp.* **19** an instrument or machine for crushing or pounding ores, etc., or the pestle in such a device. ◆ See also **stamp out.** [OE *stampe*]
▸ **'stamper** *n*

stamp duty *or* **tax** *n* a tax on legal documents, publications, etc., the payment of which is certified by the attaching or impressing of official stamps.

stampede ❶ (stæm'piːd) *n* **1** an impulsive headlong rush of startled cattle or horses. **2** headlong rush of a crowd. **3** any sudden large-scale action, such as a rush of people to support a candidate. **4** *W US & Canad.* a rodeo event featuring fairground and social elements. ◆ *vb* **stampedes, stampeding, stampeded. 5** to run away or cause to run away in a stampede. [C19: from American Sp. *estampida,* from Sp.: a din, from *estampar* to stamp, of Gmc origin]
▸ **stam'peder** *n*

stamping ground *n* a habitual or favourite meeting or gathering place.

stamp mill *n* a machine for crushing ore.

stamp out ❶ *vb* (*tr, adv*) **1** to put out or extinguish by stamping: *to stamp out a fire.* **2** to suppress by force: *to stamp out a rebellion.*

stance ❶ (stæns, stɑːns) *n* **1** the manner and position in which a person or animal stands. **2** *Sport.* the posture assumed when about to play the ball, as in golf, cricket, etc. **3** emotional or intellectual attitude: *a leftist stance.* **4** *Chiefly Scot.* a place where a vehicle waits: *taxi stance.* [C16: via F from It. *stanza* place for standing, from L *stāns,* from *stāre* to stand]

stanch ❶ (stɑːntʃ) *vb* a variant of **staunch**[2].

stanchion ('stɑːnʃən) *n* **1** any vertical pole, beam, rod, etc., used as a support. ◆ *vb* **2** (*tr*) to provide or support with a stanchion or stanchions. [C15: from OF *estanchon,* from *estance,* from Vulgar L *stantia* (unattested) a standing, from L *stāre* to stand]

stand ❶ (stænd) *vb* **stands, standing, stood.** (*mainly intr*) **1** (*also tr*) to be or cause to be in an erect or upright position. **2** to rise to, assume, or maintain an upright position. **3** (*copula*) to have a specified height when standing: *to stand six feet tall.* **4** to be situated or located: *the house stands in the square.* **5** to be in a specified state or condition: *to stand in awe of someone.* **6** to adopt or remain in a resolute position or attitude. **7** (*may take an infinitive*) to be in a specified position: *I stand to lose money in this venture.* **8** to remain in force or continue in effect: *my orders stand.* **9** to come to a stop or halt, esp. temporarily. **10** (of water, etc.) to collect and remain without flowing. **11** (often foll. by *at*) (of a score, account, etc.) to indicate the specified position: *the score stands at 20 to 1.* **12** (*also tr;* when *intr,* foll. by *for*) to tolerate or bear: *I won't stand for your nonsense; I can't stand spiders.* **13** (*tr*) to resist; survive: *to stand the test of time.* **14** (*tr*) to submit to: *to stand trial.* **15** (often foll. by *for*) *Chiefly Brit.* to be or become a candidate: *stand for Parliament.* **16** to navigate in a specified direction: *we were standing for Madeira.* **17** (of a gun dog) to point at game. **18** to halt, esp. to give action, repel attack, or disrupt an enemy advance when retreating. **19** (*tr*) *Inf.* to bear the cost of; pay for: *to stand someone a drink.* **20 stand a chance.** to have a hope or likelihood of winning, succeeding, etc. **21 stand fast.** to maintain one's position firmly. **22 stand one's ground.** to maintain a stance or position in the face of opposition. **23 stand still. 23a** to remain motionless. **23b** (foll. by *for*) *US.* to tolerate: *I won't stand still for your threats.* **24 stand to (someone).** *Irish inf.* to be useful to (someone): *your knowledge of English will stand to you.* ◆ *n* **25** the act or an instance of standing. **26** an opinion, esp. a resolutely held one: *he took a stand on capital punishment.* **27** a halt or standstill. **28** a place where a person or thing stands. **29** *Austral. & NZ.* **29a** a position on the floor of a shearing shed allocated to one shearer. **29b** the shearer's equipment. **30** a structure on which people can sit or stand. **31** a frame or rack on which such articles as coats and hats may be hung. **32** a small table or piece of furniture where articles may be placed or stored: *a music stand.* **33** a supporting framework, esp. for a tool or instrument. **34** a stall, booth, or counter from which goods may be sold. **35** a halt to give action, etc., esp. during a retreat and having some duration or success. **36** *Cricket.* an extended period at the wicket by two batsmen. **37** a growth of plants in a particular area, esp. trees in a forest or a crop in a field. **38** a stop made by a touring theatrical company, pop group, etc., to give a performance (esp. in **one-night stand**). **39** (of a gun dog) the act of pointing at game. ◆ See also **stand by, stand down,** etc. [OE *standan*]
▸ **'stander** *n*

standard ❶ ('stændəd) *n* **1** an accepted or approved example of something against which others are judged or measured. **2** (*often pl*) a principle of propriety, honesty, and integrity. **3** a level of excellence or quality. **4** any distinctive flag or device, etc., as of a nation, sovereign, or special cause, etc., or the colours of a cavalry regiment. **5** a flag or emblem formerly used to show the central or rallying point of an army in battle. **6** the commodity or commodities in which is stated the value of a basic monetary unit: *the gold standard; the silver standard.* **7** an authorized model of a unit of measure or weight. **8** a unit of board measure equal to 1980 board feet. **9** (in coinage) the prescribed proportion by weight of precious metal and base metal that each coin must contain. **10** an upright pole or beam, esp. one used as a support. **11a** a piece of furniture consisting of an upright pole or beam on a base or support. **11b** (*as modifier*): *a standard lamp.* **12a** a plant, esp. a fruit tree, that is trained so that it has an upright stem free of branches. **12b** (*as modifier*): *a standard cherry.* **13** a song or piece of music that has remained popular for many years. **14** a form or grade in an elementary school. ◆ *adj* **15** of the usual, regularized, medium, or accepted kind: *a standard size.* **16** of recognized authority, competence, or excellence: *the standard work on Greece.* **17** denoting or characterized by idiom, vocabulary, etc., that is regarded as correct and acceptable by educated native speakers. **18** *Brit.* (formerly) (of eggs) of a size that is smaller than *large* and larger than *medium.* [C12: from OF *estandart* gathering place, flag to mark such a place, prob. of Gmc origin]

standard assessment tasks *pl n Brit. education.* the formal name for assessment tests. Acronym: **SATs.**

standard-bearer *n* **1** a man who carries a standard. **2** a leader of a cause or party.

standard cell *n* a voltaic cell producing a constant and accurately known electromotive force that can be used to calibrate voltage-measuring instruments.

standard cost *n* the predetermined budgeted cost of a manufacturing process against which actual costs are compared.

standard deviation *n Statistics.* a measure of dispersion obtained by extracting the square root of the mean of the squared deviations of the observed values from their mean in a frequency distribution.

standard error of the mean *n Statistics.* the standard deviation of the distribution of means of samples chosen from a larger population; equal to the standard deviation of the whole population divided by the square root of the sample size.

standard function *n Computing.* a subprogram provided by a translator that carries out a task, for example the computation of a mathematical function, such as sine, square root, etc.

standard gauge *n* **1** a railway track with a distance of 4 ft. 8½ in. (1.435 m) between the lines; used on most railways. ◆ *adj* **standard-gauge** *or* **standard-gauged. 2** of, relating to, or denoting a railway with a standard gauge.

Standard Grade *n* (in Scotland) an examination designed to test skills and the application of knowledge, which is replaced O grade.

standardize ❶ *or* **standardise** ('stændəˌdaɪz) *vb* **standardizes, standardizing, standardized** *or* **standardises, standardising, standardised. 1** to make or become standard. **2** (*tr*) to test by or compare with a standard.
▸ **ˌstandardi'zation** *or* **ˌstandardi'sation** *n* ▸ **'standardˌizer** *or* **'standardˌiser** *n*

standard model *n Physics.* a theory of fundamental interactions in which the electromagnetic, weak, and strong interactions are described in terms of the exchange of virtual particles.

standard of living *n* a level of subsistence or material welfare of a community, class, or person.

standard time *n* the official local time of a region or country determined by the distance from Greenwich of a line of longitude passing through the area.

stand by ❶ *vb* (*intr*) **1** (*adv*) to be available and ready to act if needed. **2** (*adv*) to be present as an onlooker or without taking any action: *he stood by at the accident.* **3** (*prep*) to be faithful to: *to stand by one's principles.* ◆ *n* **stand-by. 4a** a person or thing that is ready for use or can be relied on in an emergency. **4b** (*as modifier*): *stand-by provisions.* **5 on stand-by.** in a state of readiness for action or use. ◆ *adj* **stand-by. 6** not booked in advance but awaiting or subject to availability: *a stand-by ticket.*

stand down *vb* (*adv*) **1** (*intr*) to resign or withdraw, esp. in favour of an-

THESAURUS

stampede *n* **1, 2** = **rush**, charge, flight, rout, scattering

stamp out *vb* **1, 2** = **eliminate**, crush, destroy, eradicate, extinguish, extirpate, put down, put out, quell, quench, scotch, suppress

stance *n* **1** = **posture**, bearing, carriage, deportment **3** = **attitude**, position, stand, standpoint, viewpoint

stanch *see* **staunch**[2]

stand *vb* **1, 2** = **be upright**, be erect, be vertical, rise **8** = **exist**, be in force, belong, be situated *or* located, be valid, continue, halt, hold, obtain, pause, prevail, remain, rest, stay, stop **12** = **tolerate**, abide, allow, bear, brook, cope with, countenance, endure, experience, hack (*sl.*), handle, put up with (*inf.*), stomach, submit to, suffer, support, sustain, take, thole (*dialect*), undergo, wear (*Brit. sl.*), weather, withstand ◆ *n* **26** = **position**, attitude, determination, firm stand, opinion, stance, standpoint **27** = **stop**, halt, rest, standstill, stay, stopover **30** = **grandstand 31** = **support**, base, bracket, dais, frame, place, platform, rack, rank, stage, staging, stance (*chiefly Scot.*), tripod, trivet **32** = **stall**, booth, table

standard *n* **1** = **criterion**, average, benchmark, example, guide, guideline, model, norm, par, pattern, sample, touchstone, yardstick **2** *often plural* = **principles**, canon, code of honour, ethics, ideals, moral principles, morals, rule **3** = **level**, gauge, grade, measure **5** = **flag**, banner, colours, ensign, pennant, pennon, streamer ◆ *adj* **15** = **usual**, average, basic, customary, normal, orthodox, popular, prevailing, regular, set, staple, stock, typical **16** = **accepted**, approved, authoritative, classic, definitive, established, official, recognized

Antonyms *adj* ≠ **usual:** abnormal, atypical, exceptional, extraordinary, irregular, singular, strange, uncommon, unusual ≠ **accepted:** unauthorised, unconventional, unofficial

standardize *vb* **1** = **bring into line**, assimilate, institutionalize, mass-produce, regiment, stereotype

stand by *vb* **1** = **be prepared**, wait, wait in the wings **3** = **support**, back, befriend, be loyal to, champion, defend, stick up for (*inf.*), take (someone's) part, uphold

other. **2** (*intr*) to leave the witness box in a court of law after giving evidence. **3** *Chiefly Brit.* to go or be taken off duty.

stand for ➊ *vb* (*intr, prep*) **1** to represent or mean. **2** *Chiefly Brit.* to be or become a candidate for. **3** to support or recommend. **4** *Inf.* to tolerate or bear: *he won't stand for it.*

stand in ➊ *vb* **1** (*intr, adv; usually foll. by for*) to act as a substitute. **2** **stand (someone) in good stead.** to be of benefit or advantage to (someone). ◆ *n* **stand-in. 3a** a person or thing that serves as a substitute. **3b** (*as modifier*): *a stand-in teacher.* **4** a person who substitutes for an actor during intervals of waiting or in dangerous stunts.

standing ➊ ('stændɪŋ) *n* **1** social or financial position, status, or reputation: *a man of some standing.* **2** length of existence, experience, etc. **3** (*modifier*) used to stand in or on: *standing room.* ◆ *adj* **4** *Athletics.* **4a** (of the start of a race) begun from a standing position. **4b** (of a jump, leap, etc.) performed from a stationary position without a run-up. **5** (*prenominal*) permanent, fixed, or lasting. **6** (*prenominal*) still or stagnant: *a standing pond.* **7** *Printing.* (of type) set and stored for future use.

standing army *n* a permanent army of paid soldiers maintained by a nation.

standing order *n* **1** Also called: **banker's order.** an instruction to a bank by a depositor to pay a stated sum at regular intervals. Cf. **direct debit. 2** a rule or order governing the procedure, conduct, etc., of an organization. **3** *Mil.* one of a number of orders which have long-term validity.

standing rigging *n* the stays, shrouds, and other more or less fixed, though adjustable, ropes that support the masts of a sailing vessel.

standing wave *n Physics.* a wave that has unchanging amplitude at each point along its axis. Also called: **stationary wave.**

standoff ('stænd,ɒf) *n* **1** *US & Canad.* the act or an instance of standing off or apart. **2** a deadlock or stalemate. **3** *Rugby.* short for **stand-off half.** ◆ *vb* **stand off.** (*adv*) **4** (*intr*) to navigate a vessel so as to avoid the shore, an obstruction, etc. **5** (*tr*) to keep or cause to keep at a distance. **6** (*intr*) to reach a deadlock or stalemate. **7** (*tr*) to dismiss (workers), esp. temporarily.

stand-off half *n Rugby.* **1** a player who acts as a link between his scrum half and three-quarter backs. **2** this position. ◆ Also called: **fly half.**

standoffish ➊ (,stænd'ɒfɪʃ) *adj* reserved, haughty, or aloof.
▸**,stand'offishness** *n*

stand on *vb* (*intr*) **1** (*adv*) to continue to navigate a vessel on the same heading. **2** (*prep*) to insist on: *to stand on ceremony.*

stand out ➊ *vb* (*intr, adv*) **1** to be distinctive or conspicuous. **2** to refuse to agree or comply: *they stood out for a better price.* **3** to protrude or project. **4** to navigate a vessel away from a port, harbour, etc. ◆ *n* **standout. 5** *Inf.* **5a** a person or thing that is distinctive or outstanding. **5b** (*as modifier*): *the standout track from the album.*

stand over *vb* (*tr, prep*) **1** to supervise closely. **2** *Austral. & NZ inf.* to threaten or intimidate.

standover man ('stænd,əʊvə) *n Austral.* a person who extorts money by intimidation.

standpipe ('stænd,paɪp) *n* **1** a vertical pipe, open at the upper end, attached to a pipeline or tank serving to limit the pressure head to that of the height of the pipe. **2** a temporary freshwater outlet installed in a street when household water supplies are cut off.

standpoint ➊ ('stænd,pɔɪnt) *n* a physical or mental position from which things are viewed.

standstill ('stænd,stɪl) *n* a complete cessation of movement; halt: *come to a standstill.*

stand to *vb* **1** (*adv*) *Mil.* to assume positions or cause to assume positions to resist a possible attack. **2** **stand to reason.** to conform with the dictates of reason: *it stands to reason.*

stand up ➊ *vb* (*adv*) **1** (*intr*) to rise to the feet. **2** (*intr*) to resist or withstand wear, criticism, etc. **3** (*tr*) *Inf.* to fail to keep an appointment with, esp. intentionally. **4** **stand up for.** to support, side with, or defend. **5** **stand up to. 5a** to confront or resist courageously. **5b** to withstand or endure (wear, criticism, etc.). ◆ *adj* **stand-up.** (*prenominal*) **6** having or being in an erect position: *a stand-up collar.* **7** done, taken, etc., while standing: *a stand-up meal.* **8** (of comedy or a comedian) performed or performing solo. ◆ *n* **stand-up. 9** a stand-up comedian. **10** stand-up comedy.

Stanford-Binet test (-bɪ'neɪ) *n Psychol.* a revision, esp. for US use, of the Binet-Simon scale designed to measure mental ability by comparing the performance of an individual with the average performance for his age group. See also **Binet-Simon scale, intelligence test.** [C20: after *Stanford University*, California, & Alfred *Binet* (1857–1911), F psychologist]

stanhope ('stænəp) *n* a light one-seater carriage with two or four wheels. [C18: after Fitzroy *Stanhope* (1787–1864), E clergyman for whom it was first built]

stank (stæŋk) *vb* a past tense of **stink.**

Stanley knife *n Trademark.* a type of knife used for carpet fitting, etc., consisting of a thick hollow metal handle with a short, very sharp, replaceable blade inserted in one end. [C19: after F. T. *Stanley*, US businessman and founder of the Stanley Rule and Level Company]

stann- *combining form.* denoting tin: *stannite.* [from LL *stannum* tin]

Stannaries ('stænərɪz) *n* (*sometimes functioning as sing*) **the.** a former tin-mining district of Devon and Cornwall, under the jurisdiction of special courts.

stannary ('stænərɪ) *n, pl* **stannaries.** a place or region where tin is mined or worked. [C15: from Med. L *stannāria*, from LL *stannum* tin]

stannic ('stænɪk) *adj* of or containing tin, esp. in the tetravalent state; designating a tin(IV) compound. [C18: from LL *stannum* tin]

stannite ('stænaɪt) *n* a grey metallic mineral that consists of a sulphide of tin, copper, and iron and is a source of tin. Formula: Cu_2FeSnS_4. [C19: from LL *stannum* tin + -ITE[1]]

stannous ('stænəs) *adj* of or containing tin, esp. in the divalent state; designating a tin(II) compound.

stanza ('stænzə) *n* **1** *Prosody.* a fixed number of verse lines arranged in a definite metrical pattern, forming a unit of a poem. **2** *US & Austral.* a half or a quarter in a football match. [C16: from It.: halting place, from Vulgar L *stantia* (unattested) station, from L *stāre* to stand]
▸**'stanzaed** *adj* ▸**stanzaic** (stæn'zeɪɪk) *adj*

stapelia (stə'piːlɪə) *n* any of various fleshy cactus-like leafless African plants having large fetid flowers. [C18: from NL, after J. B. van *Stapel* (died 1636), Du. botanist]

stapes ('steɪpiːz) *n, pl* **stapes** *or* **stapedes** (stæ'piːdiːz). the stirrup-shaped bone that is the innermost of three small bones in the middle ear of mammals. Nontechnical name: **stirrup bone.** Cf. **incus, malleus.** [C17: via NL from Med. L, ? var. of *stapeda* stirrup, infl. by L *stāre* to stand + *pēs* a foot]

staphylo- *combining form.* **1** uvula: *staphyloplasty.* **2** resembling a bunch of grapes: *staphylococcus.* [from Gk *staphulē* bunch of grapes, uvula]

staphylococcus (,stæfɪləʊ'kɒkəs) *n, pl* **staphylococci** (-'kɒkaɪ; *US* -'kɒksaɪ). any spherical Gram-positive bacterium of the genus *Staphylococcus*, typically occurring in clusters and causing boils, infection in wounds, and septicaemia. Often shortened to **staph.**
▸**,staphylo'coccal** *adj*

staphyloplasty ('stæfɪləʊ,plæstɪ) *n* plastic surgery or surgical repair involving the soft palate or the uvula.
▸**,staphylo'plastic** *adj*

staple[1] ('steɪpᵊl) *n* **1** a short length of thin wire bent into a square U-shape, used to fasten papers, cloth, etc. **2** a short length of stiff wire formed into a U-shape with pointed ends, used for holding a hasp to a post, securing electric cables, etc. ◆ *vb* **staples, stapling, stapled. 3** (*tr*) to secure (papers, wire, etc.) with staples. [OE *stapol* prop, of Gmc origin]
▸**'stapler** *n*

staple[2] ➊ ('steɪpᵊl) *adj* **1** of prime importance; principal: *staple foods.* **2** (of a commodity) forming a predominant element in the product, consumption, or trade of a nation, region, etc. ◆ *n* **3** a staple commodity. **4** a main constituent; integral part. **5** *Chiefly US & Canad.* a principal raw material produced or grown in a region. **6** the fibre of wool, cotton, etc., graded as to length and degree of fineness. ◆ *vb* **staples, stapling, stapled. 7** (*tr*) to arrange or sort (wool, cotton, etc.) according to length and fineness. [C15: from MDu. *stapel* warehouse]

staple gun *n* a mechanism that fixes staples to a surface.

star ➊ (stɑː) *n* **1** any of a vast number of celestial objects visible in the clear night sky as points of light. **2a** a hot gaseous mass, such as the sun, that radiates energy, esp. as light and infrared radiation, and in some cases as ultraviolet, radio waves, and X-rays. **2b** (*as modifier*): *a star catalogue.* Related adjs.: **astral, sidereal, stellar. 3** *Astrol.* **3a** a celestial body, esp. a planet, supposed to influence events, personalities, etc. **3b** (*pl*) another name for **horoscope** (sense 1). **4** an emblem shaped like a conventionalized star, often used as a symbol of rank, an award, etc. **5** a small white blaze on the forehead of an animal, esp. a horse. **6a** a distinguished or glamorous celebrity, often from the entertainment world. **6b** (*as modifier*): *star quality.* **7** another word for **asterisk. 8** **see stars.** to see or seem to see bright moving pinpoints of light, as from a blow on the head, increased blood pressure, etc. ◆ *vb* **stars, starring, starred. 9** (*tr*) to mark or decorate with a star or stars. **10** to feature or be

THESAURUS

stand for *vb* **1** = **represent**, betoken, denote, exemplify, indicate, mean, signify, symbolize **4** *Informal* = **tolerate**, bear, brook, endure, lie down under (*inf.*), put up with, suffer, wear (*Brit. inf.*)

stand in *vb* **1** *usually with* **for** = **be a substitute for**, cover for, deputize for, do duty for, hold the fort for, replace, represent, take the place of, understudy ◆ *n* **stand-in 3a** = **substitute**, deputy, locum, replacement, reserve, stopgap, surrogate, understudy

standing *n* **1** = **status**, condition, credit, eminence, estimation, footing, position, rank, reputation, repute, station **2** = **duration**, continuance, existence, experience ◆ *adj* **5** = **permanent**, fixed, lasting, perpetual, regular, repeated

standoffish *adj* = **reserved**, aloof, cold, distant, haughty, remote, unapproachable, unsociable
Antonyms *adj* affable, approachable, congenial, cordial, friendly, open, sociable, warm

stand out *vb* **1** = **be conspicuous**, attract attention, be distinct, be highlighted, be obvious, be prominent, be striking, be thrown into relief, bulk large, catch the eye, leap to the eye, project, stare one in the face (*inf.*), stick out a mile (*inf.*), stick out like a sore thumb (*inf.*)

standpoint *n* = **point of view**, angle, position, post, stance, station, vantage point, viewpoint

stand up for *vb* **4** = **support**, champion, come to the defence of, defend, side with, stick up for (*inf.*), uphold

stand up to *vb* **5a** = **resist**, brave, confront, defy, oppose, tackle **5b** = **withstand**, endure

staple[2] *adj* **1** = **principal**, basic, chief, essential, fundamental, key, main, predominant, primary

star *n* **1** = **heavenly body 6a** = **celebrity**, big name, celeb (*inf.*), draw, idol, lead, leading man *or* lady, luminary, main attraction, megastar (*inf.*), name ◆ *adj* **6b** = **leading**, brilliant, celebrated, illustrious, major, paramount, principal, prominent, talented, well-known

featured as a star: *"Greed" starred Erich von Stroheim; Olivier starred in "Hamlet"*. [OE *steorra*]
▸ **'starless** *adj* ▸ **'star,like** *adj*

starboard ('stɑːbəd, -ˌbɔːd) *n* **1** the right side of an aeroplane or vessel when facing the nose or bow. Cf. **port**[2] (sense 1). ◆ *adj* **2** relating to or on the starboard. ◆ *vb* **3** to turn or be turned towards the starboard. [OE *stēorbord,* lit.: steering side, from *stēor* steering paddle + *bord* side; from the fact that boats were formerly steered by a paddle held over the right-hand side]

starburst ('stɑːˌbɜːst) *n* **1** a pattern of rays or lines radiating from a light source. **2** *Photog.* a lens attachment which produces a starburst effect.

starch (stɑːtʃ) *n* **1** a polysaccharide composed of glucose units that occurs widely in plant tissues in the form of storage granules. **2** a starch obtained from potatoes and some grain: it is fine white powder that, in solution with water, is used to stiffen fabric. **3** any food containing a large amount of starch, such as rice and potatoes. **4** stiff or pompous formality. ◆ *vb* **5** (*tr*) to stiffen with or soak in starch. [OE *stercan* (unattested except by the p.p. *sterced*) to stiffen]
▸ **'starcher** *n*

Star Chamber *n* **1** *English history.* the Privy Council sitting as a court of equity; abolished 1641. **2** (*sometimes not caps.*) any arbitrary tribunal dispensing summary justice. **3** (*sometimes not caps.*) (in Britain, in a Conservative government) a group of senior ministers who make the final decision on the public spending of each government department.

starch-reduced *adj* (of food, esp. bread) having the starch content reduced, as in proprietary slimming products.

starchy ❶ ('stɑːtʃɪ) *adj* **starchier, starchiest. 1** of or containing starch. **2** extremely formal, stiff, or conventional: *a starchy manner.* **3** stiffened with starch.
▸ **'starchily** *adv* ▸ **'starchiness** *n*

star connection *n* a connection used in a polyphase electrical device or system of devices in which the windings each have one end connected to a common junction, the **star point**, and the other end to a separate terminal.

star-crossed *adj* dogged by ill luck; destined to misfortune.

stardom ('stɑːdəm) *n* **1** the fame and prestige of being a star in films, sport, etc. **2** the world of celebrities.

stardust ('stɑːˌdʌst) *n* **1** a large number of distant stars appearing to the observer as a cloud of dust. **2** a dreamy romantic or sentimental quality or feeling.

stare ❶ (stɛə) *vb* **stares, staring, stared. 1** (*intr*) (often foll. by *at*) to look or gaze fixedly, often with hostility or rudeness. **2** (*intr*) to stand out as obvious; glare. **3 stare one in the face.** to be glaringly obvious or imminent. ◆ *n* **4** the act or an instance of staring. [OE *starian*]
▸ **'starer** *n*

starfish ('stɑːˌfɪʃ) *n, pl* **starfish** *or* **starfishes.** any of various echinoderms, typically having a flattened body covered with a flexible test and five arms radiating from a central disc.

star fruit *n* another name for **carambola.**

stargaze ('stɑːˌgeɪz) *vb* **stargazes, stargazing, stargazed.** (*intr*) **1** to observe the stars. **2** to daydream.
▸ **'star,gazer** *n* ▸ **'star,gazing** *n, adj*

stark ❶ (stɑːk) *adj* **1** (*usually prenominal*) devoid of any elaboration; blunt: *the stark facts.* **2** grim; desolate: *a stark landscape.* **3** (*usually prenominal*) utter; absolute: *stark folly.* **4** *Arch.* severe; violent. **5** *Arch. or poetic.* rigid, as in death (esp. in **stiff and stark, stark dead**). **6** short for **stark-naked.** ◆ *adv* **7** completely: *stark mad.* **8** *Rare.* starkly. [OE *stearc* stiff]
▸ **'starkly** *adv* ▸ **'starkness** *n*

stark-naked ❶ *adj* completely naked. Informal word (*postpositive*): **starkers.** [C13 *stert naket,* lit.: tail naked; *stert,* from OE *steort* tail]

starlet ('stɑːlɪt) *n* **1** a young actress who is projected as a potential star. **2** a small star.

starlight ('stɑːˌlaɪt) *n* **1** the light emanating from the stars. ◆ *adj also* **starlighted. 2** of or like starlight. **3** Also: **starlit** ('stɑːˌlɪt). illuminated by starlight.

starling ('stɑːlɪŋ) *n* any gregarious passerine songbird of an Old World family, esp. the **common starling,** which has a blackish iridescent plumage and a short tail. [OE *stærlinc,* from *stær* starling + *-line* -LING[1]]

star-of-Bethlehem *n* **1** Also: **starflower.** a Eurasian liliaceous plant having narrow leaves and starlike white flowers. **2** any of several similar and related plants.

Star of David *n* an emblem symbolizing Judaism and consisting of a six-pointed star formed by superimposing one inverted equilateral triangle upon another of equal size.

starry ('stɑːrɪ) *adj* **starrier, starriest. 1** filled, covered with, or illuminated by stars. **2** of, like, or relating to a star or stars.
▸ **'starriness** *n*

starry-eyed *adj* given to naive wishes, judgments, etc.; full of unsophisticated optimism.

Stars and Stripes *n* (*functioning as sing*) **the.** the national flag of the United States of America, consisting of 50 white stars representing the present states on a blue field and seven red and six white horizontal stripes representing the original states. Also called: the **Star-Spangled Banner.**

star sapphire *n* a sapphire showing a starlike figure in reflected light because of its crystalline structure.

star sign *n* another name for **sign of the zodiac.**

Star-Spangled Banner *n* **the. 1** the national anthem of the United States of America. **2** another term for the **Stars and Stripes.**

star stream *n* one of two main streams of stars that, because of the rotation of the Milky Way, appear to move in opposite directions.

star-studded *adj* featuring a large proportion of well-known performers: *a star-studded cast.*

start ❶ (stɑːt) *vb* **1** to begin or cause to begin (something or to do something); come or cause to come into being, operation, etc.: *he started a quarrel; they started to work.* **2** (when *intr*, sometimes foll. by *on*) to make or cause to make a beginning of (a process, series of actions, etc.): *they started on the project.* **3** (sometimes foll. by *up*) to set or be set in motion: *he started up the machine.* **4** (*intr*) to make a sudden involuntary movement, as from fright; jump. **5** (*intr;* sometimes foll. by *up, away,* etc.) to spring or jump suddenly from a position or place. **6** to establish or be established; set up: *to start a business.* **7** (*tr*) to support (someone) in the first part of a venture, career, etc. **8** to work or cause to work loose. **9** to enter or be entered in a race. **10** (*intr*) to flow violently from a source: *wine started from a hole in the cask.* **11** (*tr*) to rouse (game) from a hiding place, lair, etc. **12** (*intr*) (esp. of eyes) to bulge; pop. **13** (*intr*) *Brit. inf.* to commence quarrelling or causing a disturbance. **14 to start with.** in the first place. ◆ *n* **15** the beginning or first part of a journey, series of actions or operations, etc. **16** the place or time of starting, as of a race or performance. **17** a signal to proceed, as in a race. **18** a lead or advantage, either in time or distance, in a competitive activity: *he had an hour's start on me.* **19** a slight involuntary movement, as through fright, surprise, etc.: *she gave a start as I entered.* **20** an opportunity to enter a career, undertake a project, etc. **21** *Inf.* a surprising incident. **22 for a start.** in the first place. ◆ See also **start in, start off,** etc. [OE *styrtan*]

starter ('stɑːtə) *n* **1** Also called: **self-starter.** a device for starting an internal-combustion engine, usually consisting of a powerful electric motor that engages with the flywheel. **2** a person who supervises and signals the start of a race. **3** a competitor who starts in a race or contest. **4** *Inf., chiefly Austral.* an acceptable or practicable proposition, plan, idea, etc. **5** *Chiefly Brit.* the first course of a meal. **6** (*modifier*) designed to be used by a novice: *a starter kit.* **7 for starters.** *Sl.* in the first place. **8 under starter's orders. 8a** (of horses in a race) awaiting the start signal. **8b** (of a person) eager or ready to begin.

starter home *n* a compact flat or house marketed by price and size specifications to suit the requirements of first-time home buyers.

start in *vb* (*adv*) to undertake (something or doing something); commence or begin.

starting block *n* one of a pair of adjustable devices with pads or blocks against which a sprinter braces his feet in crouch starts.

starting gate *n* **1** a movable barrier so placed on the starting line of a racecourse that the raising of it releases all the contestants simultaneously. **2** the US name for **starting stalls.**

starting grid *n Motor racing.* a marked section of the track at the start where the cars line up according to their times in practice, the fastest occupying the front position.

starting price *n* (esp. in horse racing) the latest odds offered by bookmakers at the start of a race.

starting stalls *pl n Brit.* a line of stalls in which horses are enclosed at

THESAURUS

starchy *adj* **2** = **formal**, ceremonious, conventional, precise, prim, punctilious, stiff, stuffy

stare *vb* **1** = **gaze**, eyeball (*sl.*), gape, gawk, gawp (*Brit. sl.*), goggle, look, ogle, rubberneck (*sl.*), watch

stark *adj* **1** = **absolute**, arrant, bald, bare, blunt, consummate, downright, entire, flagrant, out-and-out, palpable, patent, pure, sheer, simple, unalloyed, unmitigated, utter **2** = **harsh**, austere, bare, barren, bleak, cold, depressing, desolate, dreary, forsaken, godforsaken, grim, hard, plain, severe, solitary, unadorned ◆ *adv* **7** = **absolutely**, altogether, clean, completely, entirely, quite, utterly, wholly

stark-naked *adj* = **undressed**, buck naked, in a state of nature, in one's birthday suit (*inf.*), in the altogether (*inf.*), in the bare scud (*sl.*), in the buff (*inf.*), in the raw (*inf.*), naked, naked as the day one was born (*inf.*), nude, stark, starkers (*inf.*), stripped, unclad, without a stitch on (*inf.*)

start *vb* **1** = **begin**, appear, arise, come into being, come into existence, commence, first see the light of day, get under way, go ahead, issue, originate **2** = **set about**, embark upon, make a beginning, put one's hand to the plough, take the first step, take the plunge (*inf.*) **3** = **set in motion**, activate, engender, enter upon, get going, get (something) off the ground, get *or* set *or* start the ball rolling, initiate, instigate, kick off (*inf.*), kick-start, open, originate, trigger, turn on **4** = **jump**, blench, flinch, jerk, recoil, shy, twitch **6** = **establish**, begin, create, father, found, inaugurate, initiate, institute, introduce, launch, lay the foundations of, pioneer, set up ◆ *n* **15** = **beginning**, birth, commencement, dawn, first step(s), foundation, inauguration, inception, initiation, kickoff (*inf.*), onset, opening, opening move, outset **18** = **advantage**, edge, head start, lead **19** = **jump**, convulsion, jar, spasm, twitch **20** = **opportunity**, backing, break (*inf.*), chance, helping hand, introduction, opening, sponsorship

Antonyms *vb* ≠ **begin, set about, set in motion:** abandon, bring to an end, call it a day (*inf.*), cease, conclude, delay, desist, end, finish, give up, put aside, put off, quit, stop, switch off, terminate, turn off, wind up ◆ *n* ≠ **beginning:** cessation, conclusion, denouement, end, finale, finish, outcome, result, stop, termination, turning off, wind-up

the start of a race and from which they are released by the simultaneous springing open of retaining barriers at the front of each stall.

startle ❶ (ˈstɑːtᵊl) *vb* **startles, startling, startled.** to be or cause to be surprised or frightened, esp. so as to start involuntarily. [OE *steartlian* to stumble]
▸ **ˈstartler** *n* ▸ **ˈstartling** *adj*

start off *vb* (*adv*) **1** (*intr*) to set out on a journey. **2** to be or make the first step in (an activity); initiate: *he started the show off with a lively song.* **3** (*tr*) to cause (a person) to act or do something, such as to laugh, to tell stories, etc.

start on *vb* (*intr, prep*) *Brit. inf.* to pick a quarrel with; upbraid.

start out *vb* (*intr, adv*) **1** to set out on a journey. **2** to take the first steps, as in life, one's career, etc.: *he started out as a salesman.* **3** to take the first actions in an activity in a particular way or with a specified aim: *they started out wanting a house, but eventually bought a flat.*

start up *vb* (*adv*) **1** to come or cause to come into being for the first time; originate. **2** (*intr*) to spring or jump suddenly. **3** to set in or go into motion, activity, etc.: *he started up the engine.* ◆ *adj* **start-up. 4** of or relating to input, usually financial, made to establish a new project or business: *a start-up mortgage.*

starve ❶ (stɑːv) *vb* **starves, starving, starved. 1** to die or cause to die from lack of food. **2** to deprive (a person or animal) or (of a person, etc.) to be deprived of food. **3** (*intr*) *Inf.* to be very hungry. **4** (foll. by *of* or *for*) to deprive or be deprived (of something), esp. so as to cause suffering or malfunctioning: *the engine was starved of fuel.* **5** (*tr;* foll. by *into*) to bring (to) a specified condition by starving: *to starve someone into submission.* **6** *Arch. or dialect.* to be or cause to be extremely cold. [OE *steorfan* to die]
▸ **starˈvation** *n*

starveling (ˈstɑːvlɪŋ) *Arch.* ◆ *n* **1a** a starving or poorly fed person, animal, etc. **1b** (*as modifier*): *a starveling child.* ◆ *adj* **2** insufficient; meagre; scant.

Star Wars *n* (*functioning as sing*) (in the US) a proposed system of artificial satellites armed with lasers to destroy enemy missiles in space. [C20: popularly named after the science-fiction film *Star Wars* (1977)]

starwort (ˈstɑːˌwɜːt) *n* **1** any of several plants with star-shaped flowers, esp. the stitchwort. **2** any of several aquatic plants having a star-shaped rosette of floating leaves.

stash ❶ (stæʃ) *vb* **1** (*tr;* often foll. by *away*) *Inf.* to put or store (money, valuables, etc.) in a secret place, as for safekeeping. ◆ *n* **2** *Inf., chiefly US & Canad.* a secret store or the place where this is hidden. **3** *Sl.* drugs kept for personal consumption. [C20: from ?]

stasis (ˈsteɪsɪs) *n* **1** *Pathol.* a stagnation in the normal flow of bodily fluids, such as the blood or urine. **2** a state or condition in which there is no action or progress. [C18: via NL from Gk: a standing, from *histanai* to cause to stand]

-stat *n combining form.* indicating a device that causes something to remain stationary or constant: *thermostat.* [from Gk *-statēs,* from *histanai* to cause to stand]

state ❶ (steɪt) *n* **1** the condition of a person, thing, etc., with regard to main attributes. **2** the structure or form of something: *a solid state.* **3** any mode of existence. **4** position in life or society; estate. **5** ceremonious style, as befitting wealth or dignity: *to live in state.* **6** a sovereign political power or community. **7** the territory occupied by such a community. **8** the sphere of power in such a community: *affairs of state.* **9** (*often cap.*) one of a number of areas or communities having their own governments and forming a federation under a sovereign government, as in the US. **10** (*often cap.*) the body politic of a particular sovereign power, esp. as contrasted with a rival authority such as the Church. **11** *Obs.* a class or order; estate. **12** *Inf.* a nervous, upset, or excited condition (esp. in **in a state**). **13 lie in state.** (of a body) to be placed on public view before burial. **14 state of affairs.** a situation; circumstances or condition. ◆ *modifier.* **15** controlled or financed by a state: *state university.* **16** of, relating to, or concerning the State: *State trial.* **17** involving ceremony or concerned with a ceremonious occasion: *state visit.* ◆ *vb* **states, stating, stated.** (*tr; may take a clause as object*) **18** to articulate in words; utter. **19** to declare formally or publicly. [C13: from OF *estat,* from L *status* a standing, from *stāre* to stand]
▸ **ˈstatable** *or* **ˈstateable** *adj* ▸ **ˈstatehood** *n*

state bank *n* (in the US) a commercial bank incorporated under a State charter and not required to be a member of the Federal Reserve System.

statecraft (ˈsteɪtˌkrɑːft) *n* the art of conducting public affairs; statesmanship.

state duma *n* another name for **duma** (sense 3).

state house *n NZ.* a house built by the government and rented to a **state tenant.** Brit. equivalent: **council house.**

Statehouse (ˈsteɪtˌhaʊs) *n* (in the US) the building which houses a state legislature.

stateless (ˈsteɪtlɪs) *adj* **1** without nationality: *stateless persons.* **2** without a state or states.
▸ **ˈstatelessness** *n*

stately ❶ (ˈsteɪtlɪ) *adj* **statelier, stateliest. 1** characterized by a graceful, dignified, and imposing appearance or manner. ◆ *adv* **2** in a stately manner.
▸ **ˈstateliness** *n*

stately home *n Brit.* a large mansion, esp. one open to the public.

statement ❶ (ˈsteɪtmənt) *n* **1** the act of stating. **2** something that is stated, esp. a formal prepared announcement or reply. **3** *Law.* a declaration of matters of fact. **4** an account containing a summary of bills or invoices and displaying the total amount due. **5** an account prepared by a bank for a client, usually at regular intervals, to show all credits and debits and the balance at the end of the period. **6** a computer instruction written in a source language, such as FORTRAN, which is converted into one or more machine-code instructions by a compiler. **7** *Logic.* the content of a sentence that affirms or denies something and may be true or false. **8** *Brit. education.* a legally binding account of the provisions that will be made to meet the needs of a pupil with special educational needs.

statement of attainment *n Brit. education.* a programme of specific objectives that pupils should achieve within their own levels of attainment in a particular subject.

statement of claim *n Law.* (in England) the first pleading made by the plaintiff in a High Court action.

state of the art ❶ *n* **1** the level of knowledge and development achieved in a technique, science, etc., esp. at present. ◆ *adj* **state-of-the-art.** (*prenominal*) **2** the most recent and therefore considered the best; up-to-the-minute: *a state-of-the-art amplifier.*

State Registered Nurse *n* (formerly, in Britain) a nurse who had extensive training and was qualified to perform all nursing services. See **Registered General Nurse.**

stateroom (ˈsteɪtˌruːm, -ˌrʊm) *n* **1** a private cabin or room on a ship, train, etc. **2** *Chiefly Brit.* a large room in a palace or other building for use on state occasions.

States (steɪts) *n* (*functioning as sing or pl*) **the.** an informal name for the United States of America.

state school *n* any school maintained by the state, in which education is free.

stateside (ˈsteɪtˌsaɪd) *adj, adv* (*sometimes cap.*) *US.* of, in, to, or towards the US.

statesman (ˈsteɪtsmən) *n, pl* **statesmen. 1** a political leader whose wisdom, integrity, etc., win great respect. **2** a person active and influential in the formulation of high government policy.
▸ **ˈstatesman-ˌlike** *or* **ˈstatesmanly** *adj* ▸ **ˈstatesmanship** *n* ▸ **ˈstatesˌwoman** *fem n*

state socialism *n* a variant of socialism in which the power of the state is employed for the purpose of creating an egalitarian society by means of public control of major industries, banks, etc.
▸ **state socialist** *n*

state trooper *n US.* a state policeman.

static ❶ (ˈstætɪk) *adj also* **statical. 1** not active or moving; stationary. **2** (of a weight, force, or pressure) acting but causing no movement. **3** of or concerned with forces that do not produce movement. **4** relating to or causing stationary electric charges; electrostatic. **5** of or relating to interference in the reception of radio or television transmissions. **6** of or concerned with statics. **7** *Computing.* (of a memory) not needing its contents refreshed periodically. ◆ *n* **8** random hissing or crackling or a speckled picture caused by interference in the reception of radio or television transmissions. **9** electric sparks or crackling produced by friction. [C16: from NL *staticus,* from Gk *statikos* causing to stand, from *histanai* to stand]
▸ **ˈstatically** *adv*

statice (ˈstætɪsɪ) *n* another name for **sea lavender.**

THESAURUS

startle *vb* = **surprise**, agitate, alarm, amaze, astonish, astound, frighten, give (someone) a turn (*inf.*), make (someone) jump, scare, shock, take (someone) aback

startling *adj* = **surprising**, alarming, astonishing, astounding, extraordinary, jaw-dropping, shocking, staggering, sudden, unexpected, unforeseen

starving *adj* **3** = **hungry**, esurient, faint from lack of food, famished, hungering, ravenous, ready to eat a horse (*inf.*), sharp-set, starved

stash *vb* **1** *Informal* = **store**, cache, hide, hoard, lay up, put aside for a rainy day, salt away, save up, secrete, stockpile, stow

state *n* **1** = **condition**, case, category, circumstances, equation, mode, pass, plight, position, predicament, shape, situation, state of affairs **5** = **ceremony**, dignity, display, glory, grandeur, majesty, pomp, splendour, style **6, 7** = **country**, body politic, commonwealth, federation, government, kingdom, land, nation, republic, territory **12 in a state** *Informal* = **distressed**, agitated, all steamed up (*sl.*), anxious, disturbed, flustered, het up, panic-stricken, ruffled, upset, uptight (*inf.*) ◆ *vb* **18, 19** = **express**, affirm, articulate, assert, asseverate, aver, declare, enumerate, explain, expound, present, propound, put, report, say, specify, utter, voice

stately *adj* **1** = **grand**, august, ceremonious, deliberate, dignified, elegant, imperial, imposing, impressive, lofty, majestic, measured, noble, pompous, regal, royal, solemn
Antonyms *adj* common, humble, lowly, modest, simple, undignified, undistinguished, unimpressive

statement *n* **2** = **account**, announcement, communication, communiqué, declaration, explanation, proclamation, recital, relation, report, testimony, utterance

state-of-the-art *adj* **2** = **latest**, newest, up-to-date, up-to-the-minute
Antonyms *adj* obsolescent, obsolete, old-fashioned, outdated, outmoded, out of date, out of the ark (*inf.*)

static *adj* **1** = **stationary**, changeless, constant, fixed, immobile, inert, motionless, stagnant, still, stock-still, unmoving, unvarying
Antonyms *adj* active, dynamic, kinetic, lively, mobile, moving, travelling, varied

static electricity *n* electricity that is not dynamic or flowing as a current.

statics ('stætɪks) *n* (*functioning as sing*) the branch of mechanics concerned with the forces that produce a state of equilibrium in a system.

station ⓣ ('steɪʃən) *n* **1** the place or position at which a thing or person stands. **2a** a place along a route or line at which a bus, train, etc., stops for fuel or to pick up or let off passengers or goods, esp. one with ancillary buildings and services. **2b** (*as modifier*): *a station buffet.* **3a** the headquarters or local offices of an organization such as the police or fire services. **3b** (*as modifier*): *a station sergeant.* See **police station, fire station. 4** a building, depot, etc., with special equipment for some particular purpose: *power station; petrol station.* **5** *Mil.* a place of duty: *an action station.* **6** *Navy.* **6a** a location to which a ship or fleet is assigned for duty. **6b** an assigned location for a member of a ship's crew. **7** a television or radio channel. **8** a position or standing, as in a particular society or organization. **9** the type of one's occupation; calling. **10** (in British India) a place where the British district officials or garrison officers resided. **11** *Biol.* the habitat occupied by a particular animal or plant. **12** *Austral. & NZ.* a large sheep or cattle farm. **13** (*sometimes cap.*) *RC Church.* **13a** one of the stations of the Cross. **13b** any of the churches (**station churches**) in Rome used as points of assembly for religious processions and ceremonies on particular days (**station days**). ◆ *vb* **14** (*tr*) to place in or assign to a station. [C14: via OF from L *statiō* a standing still, from *stāre* to stand]

stationary ⓣ ('steɪʃənərɪ) *adj* **1** not moving; standing still. **2** not able to be moved. **3** showing no change: *the doctors said his condition was stationary.* **4** tending to remain in one place. [C15: from L *statiōnārius*, from *statiō* STATION]

> **USAGE NOTE** Avoid confusion with **stationery.**

stationary orbit *n Astronautics.* a synchronous orbit lying in or approximately in the plane of the equator.

stationary wave *n* another name for **standing wave.**

stationer ('steɪʃənə) *n* a person who sells stationery or a shop where stationery is sold. [C14: from Med. L *stationarius* a person having a regular station, hence a shopkeeper (esp. a bookseller) as distinguished from an itinerant tradesman; see STATION]

stationery ('steɪʃənərɪ) *n* any writing materials, such as paper, envelopes, pens, ink, rulers, etc.

> **USAGE NOTE** Avoid confusion with **stationary.**

station house *n Chiefly US.* a house that is situated by or serves as a station, esp. as a police or fire station.

stationmaster ('steɪʃən,mɑːstə) *n* the senior official in charge of a railway station.

Stations of the Cross *pl n RC Church.* **1** a series of 14 crosses, often accompanied by 14 pictures or carvings, arranged around the walls of a church, to commemorate 14 stages in Christ's journey to Calvary. **2** a devotion of 14 prayers relating to each of these stages.

station wagon *n* another name (less common in Britain) for **estate car.**

statism ('steɪtɪzəm) *n* the theory or practice of concentrating economic and political power in the state.
▸ **'statist** *n*

statistic (stə'tɪstɪk) *n* a datum capable of exact numerical representation, such as the correlation coefficient of two series or the standard deviation of a sample.
▸ **sta'tistical** *adj* ▸ **sta'tistically** *adv* ▸ **statistician** (,stætɪ'stɪʃən) *n*

statistical mechanics *n* (*functioning as sing*) the study of the properties of physical systems as predicted by the statistical behaviour of their constituent particles.

statistics (stə'tɪstɪks) *n* **1** (*functioning as sing*) a science concerned with the collection, classification, and interpretation of quantitative data and with the application of probability theory to the analysis and estimation of population parameters. **2** the quantitative data themselves. [C18 (orig. "science dealing with facts of a state"): via G *Statistik*, from NL *statisticus* concerning state affairs, from L *status* STATE]

stator ('steɪtə) *n* the stationary part of a rotary machine or device, esp. of a motor or generator. [C20: from L: one who stands (by), from *stāre* to stand]

statoscope ('stætə,skəʊp) *n* a very sensitive form of aneroid barometer used to detect and measure small variations in atmospheric pressure, such as one used in an aircraft to indicate small changes in altitude.

statuary ('stætjʊərɪ) *n* **1** statues collectively. **2** the art of making statues. ◆ *adj* **3** of or for statues. [C16: from L *statuārius*]

statue ('stætjuː) *n* a wooden, stone, metal, plaster, or other sculpture of a human or animal figure, usually life-size or larger. [C14: via OF from L *statua*, from *statuere* to set up; cf. STATUTE]

statuesque ⓣ (,stætjʊ'esk) *adj* like a statue, esp. in possessing great formal beauty or dignity.
▸ **,statu'esquely** *adv* ▸ **,statu'esqueness** *n*

statuette (,stætjʊ'ɛt) *n* a small statue.

stature ⓣ ('stætʃə) *n* **1** height, esp. of a person or animal when standing. **2** the degree of development of a person: *the stature of a champion.* **3** intellectual or moral greatness: *a man of stature.* [C13: via OF from L *statūra*, from *stāre* to stand]

status ⓣ ('steɪtəs) *n, pl* **statuses. 1** a social or professional position, condition, or standing. **2** the relative position or standing of a person or thing. **3** a high position or standing: *he has acquired a new status in that job.* **4** the legal standing or condition of a person. **5** a state of affairs. [C17: from L: posture, from *stāre* to stand]

status quo (kwəʊ) *n* (usually preceded by *the*) the existing state of affairs. [lit.: the state in which]

status symbol *n* a possession which is regarded as proof of the owner's social position, wealth, prestige, etc.

statute ⓣ ('stætjuːt) *n* **1a** an enactment of a legislative body expressed in a formal document. **1b** this document. **2** a permanent rule made by a body or institution. [C13: from OF *estatut*, from LL *statūtum*, from L *statuere* to set up, decree, ult. from *stāre* to stand]

statute book *n Chiefly Brit.* a register of enactments passed by the legislative body of a state: *not on the statute book.*

statute law *n* **1** a law enacted by a legislative body. **2** a particular example of this. ◆ Cf. **common law, equity.**

statute mile *n* a legal or formal name for **mile** (sense 1).

statute of limitations *n* a legislative enactment prescribing the period of time within which proceedings must be instituted to enforce a right or bring an action at law.

statutory ('stætjʊtərɪ, -trɪ) *adj* **1** of, relating to, or having the nature of a statute. **2** prescribed or authorized by statute. **3** (of an offence) **3a** recognized by statute. **3b** subject to a punishment or penalty prescribed by statute.
▸ **'statutorily** *adv*

statutory order *n* a statute that applies further legislation to an existing act.

staunch[1] ⓣ (stɔːntʃ) *adj* **1** loyal, firm, and dependable: *a staunch supporter.* **2** solid or substantial in construction. **3** *Rare.* (of a ship, etc.) watertight; seaworthy. [C15 (orig.: watertight): from OF *estanche*, from *estanchier* to STANCH]
▸ **'staunchly** *adv* ▸ **'staunchness** *n*

staunch[2] ⓣ (stɔːntʃ) *or* **stanch** (stɑːntʃ) *vb* **1** to stem the flow of (a liquid, esp. blood) or (of a liquid) to stop flowing. **2** to prevent the flow of a liquid, esp. blood, from (a hole, wound, etc.). [C14: from OF *estanchier*, from Vulgar L *stanticāre* (unattested) to cause to stand, from L *stāre* to halt]
▸ **'staunchable** *or* **'stanchable** *adj* ▸ **'stauncher** *or* **'stancher** *n*

stave (steɪv) *n* **1** any one of a number of long strips of wood joined together to form a barrel, bucket, boat hull, etc. **2** any of various bars, slats, or rods, usually of wood, such as a rung of a ladder. **3** any stick, staff, etc. **4** a stanza or verse of a poem. **5** *Music.* **5a** *Brit.* an individual group of five lines and four spaces used in staff notation. **5b** another word for **staff**[1] (sense 9). ◆ *vb* **staves, staving, staved** *or* **stove. 6** (often foll. by *in*) to break or crush (the staves of a boat, barrel, etc.) or (of the staves of a boat) to be broken or crushed. **7** (*tr;* usually foll. by *in*) to burst or force (a hole in something). **8** (*tr*) to provide (a ladder, chair, etc.) with staves. [C14: back formation from *staves*, pl. of STAFF[1]]

stave off ⓣ *vb* (*tr, adv*) to avert or hold off, esp. temporarily: *to stave off hunger.*

staves (steɪvz) *n* a plural of **staff**[1] or **stave.**

stavesacre ('steɪvz,eɪkə) *n* **1** a Eurasian ranunculaceous plant having poisonous seeds. **2** the seeds, which have strong emetic and cathartic properties. [C14 *staphisagre*, from L *staphis agria*, from Gk, from *staphis* raisin + *agria* wild]

stay[1] ⓣ (steɪ) *vb* **1** (*intr*) to continue or remain in a certain place, position, etc.: *to stay outside.* **2** (*copula*) to continue to be; remain: *to stay awake.* **3** (*intr;* often foll. by *at*) to reside temporarily: *to stay at a hotel.* **4** (*tr*) to remain for a specified period: *to stay the weekend.* **5** (*intr*) *Scot. & S.*

THESAURUS

station *n* **1** = **place**, location, position, post, seat, situation **3a** = **headquarters**, base, depot **8** = **position**, grade, post, rank, situation, sphere, standing, status **9** = **occupation**, appointment, business, calling, employment ◆ *vb* **14** = **assign**, establish, fix, garrison, install, locate, post, set

stationary *adj* **1** = **motionless**, at a standstill, fixed, inert, moored, parked, standing, static, stock-still, unmoving
Antonyms *adj* changeable, changing, inconstant, mobile, moving, shifting, travelling, unstable, variable, varying, volatile

statuesque *adj* = **well-proportioned**, dignified, imposing, Junoesque, majestic, regal, stately

stature *n* **1-3** = **importance**, consequence, eminence, high station, prestige, prominence, rank, size, standing

status *n* **1-3** = **position**, condition, consequence, degree, distinction, eminence, grade, prestige, rank, standing

statute *n* **1** = **law**, act, decree, edict, enactment, ordinance, regulation, rule

staunch[1] *adj* **1** = **loyal**, constant, dependable, faithful, firm, immovable, reliable, resolute, sound, stalwart, steadfast, stout, strong, sure, tried and true, true, true-blue, trustworthy, trusty

staunch[2] *vb* **1, 2** = **stop**, arrest, check, dam, halt, plug, stay, stem

stave off *vb* = **hold off**, avert, evade, fend off, foil, keep at arm's length, keep at bay, parry, ward off

stay[1] *vb* **1** = **remain**, abide, bide, continue, delay, establish oneself, halt, hang around (*inf.*), hang in the air, hover, linger, loiter, pause, put down roots, reside, settle, stand, stay put, stop, tarry, wait **3** *often with* **at** = **lodge**, be accommodated at, put up at, sojourn, visit **8** = **delay**, arrest, check, curb, detain, hinder,

African. to reside permanently or habitually; live. **6** *Arch.* to stop or cause to stop. **7** (*intr*) to wait, pause, or tarry. **8** (*tr*) to delay or hinder. **9** (*tr*) **9a** to discontinue or suspend (a judicial proceeding). **9b** to hold in abeyance or restrain from enforcing (an order, decree, etc.). **10** to endure (something testing or difficult, such as a race): *stay the course.* **11** (*tr*) to hold back or restrain: *to stay one's anger.* **12** (*tr*) to satisfy or appease (an appetite, etc.) temporarily. ◆ *n* **13** the act of staying or sojourning in a place or the period during which one stays. **14** the act of stopping or restraining or state of being stopped, etc. **15** the suspension of a judicial proceeding, etc.: *stay of execution.* [C15 *staien,* from Anglo-F *estaier* to stay, from OF *ester* to stay, from L *stāre* to stand]
▸ **'stayer** *n*

stay[2] ❶ (steɪ) *n* **1** anything that supports or steadies, such as a prop or buttress. **2** a thin strip of metal, plastic, bone, etc., used to stiffen corsets, etc. See also **stays** (sense 1). ◆ *vb* (*tr*) *Arch.* **3** (often foll. by *up*) to prop or hold. **4** (often foll. by *up*) to comfort or sustain. **5** (foll. by *on* or *upon*) to cause to rely or depend. [C16: from OF *estaye,* of Gmc origin]

stay[3] (steɪ) *n* a rope, cable, or chain, usually one of a set, used for bracing uprights, such as masts, funnels, flagpoles, chimneys, etc.; guy. ◆ See also **stays** (senses 2, 3). [OE *stæg*]

stay-at-home *adj* **1** (of a person) enjoying a quiet, settled, and unadventurous use of leisure. ◆ *n* **2** a stay-at-home person.

staying power ❶ *n* endurance; stamina.

stays (steɪz) *pl n* **1** old-fashioned corsets with bones in them. **2** a position of a sailing vessel relative to the wind so that the sails are luffing or aback. **3 miss** *or* **refuse stays.** (of a sailing vessel) to fail to come about.

staysail ('steɪˌseɪl; *Naut.* 'steɪsᵊl) *n* an auxiliary sail, often triangular, set on a stay.

STD *abbrev. for:* **1** Doctor of Sacred Theology. **2** sexually transmitted disease. **3** subscriber trunk dialling.

STD code *n Brit.* a code of four or more digits, other than those comprising a subscriber's local telephone number, that determines the routing of a call. [C20: *s(ubscriber) t(runk) d(ialling)*]

Ste *abbrev. for* Saint (female). [F *Sainte*]

stead (stɛd) *n* **1** (preceded by *in*) *Rare.* the place, function, or position that should be taken by another: *to come in someone's stead.* **2 stand (someone) in good stead.** to be useful or of good service to (someone). ◆ *vb* **3** (*tr*) *Arch.* to help or benefit. [OE *stede*]

steadfast ❶ *or* **stedfast** ('stɛdfəst, -ˌfɑːst) *adj* **1** (esp. of a person's gaze) fixed in intensity or direction; steady. **2** unwavering or determined in purpose, loyalty, etc.: *steadfast resolve.*
▸ **'steadfastly** *or* **'stedfastly** *adv* ▸ **'steadfastness** *or* **'stedfastness** *n*

steading ('stɛdɪŋ) *n* another name for **farmstead.**

steady ❶ ('stɛdɪ) *adj* **steadier, steadiest. 1** not able to be moved or disturbed easily; stable. **2** free from fluctuation. **3** not easily excited; imperturbable. **4** staid; sober. **5** regular; habitual: *a steady drinker.* **6** continuous: *a steady flow.* **7** *Naut.* (of a vessel) keeping upright, as in heavy seas. ◆ *vb* **steadies, steadying, steadied. 8** to make or become steady. ◆ *adv* **9** in a steady manner. **10 go steady.** *Inf.* to date one person regularly. ◆ *n, pl* **steadies. 11** *Inf.* one's regular boyfriend or girlfriend. ◆ *interj* **12** *Naut.* an order to the helmsman to stay on a steady course. **13** a warning to keep calm, be careful, etc. **14** *Brit.* a command to get set to start, as in a race: *ready, steady, go!* [C16: from STEAD + -Y[1]]
▸ **'steadily** *adv* ▸ **'steadiness** *n* ▸ **'steadying** *adj*

steady state *n Physics.* the condition of a system when some or all of the quantities describing it are independent of time but not necessarily in thermodynamic or chemical equilibrium.

steady-state theory *n* a theory postulating that the universe exists throughout time in a steady state such that the average density of matter does not vary with distance or time. Matter is continuously created in the space left by the receding stars and galaxies of the expanding universe. Cf. **big-bang theory.**

steak (steɪk) *n* **1** See **beefsteak. 2** any of various cuts of beef, for braising, stewing, etc. **3** a thick slice of pork, veal, cod, salmon, etc. **4** minced meat prepared in the same way as steak: *hamburger steak.* [C15: from ON *steik* roast]

steakhouse ('steɪkˌhaʊs) *n* a restaurant that has steaks as its speciality.

steak tartare (tɑː'tɑː) *or* **tartar** *n* raw minced steak, mixed with onion, seasonings, and raw egg. Also called: **tartare steak, tartar steak.**

steal ❶ (stiːl) *vb* **steals, stealing, stole, stolen. 1** to take (something) from someone, etc., without permission or unlawfully, esp. in a secret manner. **2** (*tr*) to obtain surreptitiously. **3** (*tr*) to appropriate (ideas, etc.) without acknowledgment, as in plagiarism. **4** to move or convey stealthily: *they stole along the corridor.* **5** (*intr*) to pass unnoticed: *the hours stole by.* **6** (*tr*) to win or gain by strategy or luck, as in various sports: *to steal a few yards.* ◆ *n Inf.* **7** the act of stealing. **8** something stolen or acquired easily or at little cost. [OE *stelan*]
▸ **'stealer** *n*

stealth ❶ (stɛlθ) *n* **1** the act or characteristic of moving with extreme care and quietness, esp. so as to avoid detection. **2** cunning or underhand procedure or dealing. [C13 *stelthe;* see STEAL, -TH[1]]
▸ **'stealthy** *adj*

Stealth (stɛlθ) *n* (*modifier*) *Inf.* denoting or referring to technology that aims to reduce the radar, thermal, and acoustic recognizability of aircraft and missiles.

Stealth bomber *or* **plane** *n* a type of US military aircraft using advanced technology to render it virtually undetectable to sight, radar, or infrared sensors. Also called: **B-2.**

steam (stiːm) *n* **1** the gas or vapour into which water is changed when boiled. **2** the mist formed when such gas or vapour condenses in the atmosphere. **3** any vaporous exhalation. **4** *Inf.* power, energy, or speed. **5 get up steam. 5a** (of a ship, etc.) to work up a sufficient head of steam in a boiler to drive an engine. **5b** *Inf.* to go quickly. **6 let off steam.** *Inf.* to release pent-up energy, feelings, etc. **7 under one's own steam.** without the assistance of others. **8** (*modifier*) driven, operated, heated, powered, etc., by steam: *a steam radiator.* **9** (*modifier*) treated by steam: *steam-ironed.* **10** (*modifier*) *Humorous.* old-fashioned; outmoded: *steam radio.* ◆ *vb* **11** to emit or be emitted as steam. **12** (*intr*) to generate steam, as a boiler, etc. **13** (*intr*) to move or travel by steam power, as a ship, etc. **14** (*intr*) *Inf.* to proceed quickly and sometimes forcefully. **15** to cook or be cooked in steam. **16** (*tr*) to treat with steam or apply steam to, as in cleaning, pressing clothes, etc. ◆ See also **steam up.** [OE]

steam bath *n* **1** a room or enclosure that can be filled with steam in which people bathe to induce sweating and refresh or cleanse themselves. **2** an act of taking such a bath.

steamboat ('stiːmˌbəʊt) *n* a boat powered by a steam engine.

steam boiler *n* a vessel in which water is boiled to generate steam.

steam engine *n* an engine that uses steam to produce mechanical work, esp. one in which steam from a boiler is expanded in a cylinder to drive a reciprocating piston.

steamer ('stiːmə) *n* **1** a boat or ship driven by steam engines. **2** a vessel used to cook food by steam. **3** *Austral. sl.* a rough clash between sports teams.

steaming ('stiːmɪŋ) *adj* **1** very hot. **2** *Inf.* angry. **3** *Sl.* drunk. ◆ *n* **4** *Inf.* robbery, esp. of passengers in a railway carriage or bus, by a large gang of armed youths.

steam iron *n* an electric iron that emits steam from channels in the iron face to facilitate pressing and ironing, the steam being produced from water contained within the iron.

steam jacket *n Engineering.* a jacket containing steam that surrounds and heats a cylinder.

steam organ *n* a type of organ powered by steam, once common at fairgrounds, played either by a keyboard or by a moving punched card. US name: **calliope.**

steam point *n* the temperature at which the maximum vapour pressure of water is equal to one atmosphere (1.01325×10^5 N/m^2). It has the value of 100° on the Celsius scale.

steam reforming *n Chem.* a process in which methane from natural gas is heated, with steam, usually with a catalyst, to produce a mixture of carbon monoxide and hydrogen used in organic synthesis and as a fuel.

steamroller ('stiːmˌrəʊlə) *n* **1a** a steam-powered vehicle with heavy rollers used for compressing road surfaces during road-making. **1b** another word for **roadroller. 2a** an overpowering force or person that

THESAURUS

hold, impede, obstruct, prevent **9** = **suspend**, adjourn, defer, discontinue, hold in abeyance, hold over, prorogue, put off ◆ *n* **13** = **visit**, holiday, sojourn, stop, stopover **14** = **postponement**, deferment, delay, halt, pause, remission, reprieve, stopping, suspension
Antonyms *vb* ≠ **remain:** abandon, depart, exit, go, leave, move on, pack one's bags (*inf.*), pass through, quit, withdraw

stay[2] *n* **1** = **support**, brace, buttress, prop, reinforcement, shoring, stanchion

staying power *n* = **endurance**, stamina, strength, toughness

steadfast *adj* **1, 2** = **firm**, constant, dedicated, dependable, established, faithful, fast, fixed, immovable, intent, loyal, persevering, reliable, resolute, single-minded, stable, stalwart, staunch, steady, unfaltering, unflinching, unswerving, unwavering
Antonyms *adj* capricious, faint-hearted, faltering, fickle, flagging, half-hearted, inconstant, irresolute, uncommitted, undependable, unreliable, unstable, vacillating, wavering

steady *adj* **1** = **firm**, fixed, immovable, on an even keel, safe, secure, stable, substantial, unchangeable, uniform **4** = **dependable**, balanced, calm, equable, having both feet on the ground, imperturbable, level-headed, reliable, sedate, sensible, serene, serious-minded, settled, sober, staid, staunch, steadfast **6** = **continuous**, ceaseless, confirmed, consistent, constant, even, habitual, incessant, nonstop, persistent, regular, rhythmic, unbroken, unfaltering, unfluctuating, uninterrupted, unremitting, unvarying, unwavering ◆ *vb* **8** = **stabilize**, balance, brace, secure, support
Antonyms *adj* ≠ **firm:** insecure, unsettled, unstable, unsteady ≠ **continuous:** changeable, faltering, fluctuating, inconsistent, infrequent, intermittent, irregular, occasional, sporadic ≠ **dependable:** careless, fickle, half-hearted, in two minds, uncommitted, unconscientious, undependable, unpredictable, unreliable, vacillating, wavering ◆ *vb* ≠ **stabilize:** agitate, shake, tilt, upset

steal *vb* **1-3** = **take**, appropriate, be light-fingered, blag (*sl.*), cabbage (*Brit. sl.*), embezzle, filch, half-inch (*old-fashioned sl.*), heist (*US sl.*), lift (*inf.*), misappropriate, nick (*sl., chiefly Brit.*), peculate, pilfer, pinch (*inf.*), pirate, plagiarize, poach, prig (*Brit. sl.*), purloin, shoplift, snitch (*sl.*), swipe (*sl.*), thieve, walk *or* make off with **4** = **sneak**, creep, flit, insinuate oneself, slink, slip, tiptoe

stealing *n* **1-3** = **theft**, embezzlement, larceny, misappropriation, pilferage, pilfering, plagiarism, robbery, shoplifting, thievery, thieving

stealth *n* **1, 2** = **secrecy**, furtiveness, slyness, sneakiness, stealthiness, surreptitiousness, unobtrusiveness

stealthy *adj* **1, 2** = **secret**, clandestine, covert, furtive, secretive, skulking, sly, sneaking, sneaky, surreptitious, underhand

overcomes all opposition. **2b** (*as modifier*): *steamroller tactics.* ◆ *vb* **3** (*tr*) to crush (opposition, etc.) by overpowering force.
steamship ('sti:m,ʃɪp) *n* a ship powered by one or more steam engines.
steam shovel *n* a steam-driven mechanical excavator.
steam turbine *n* a turbine driven by steam.
steam up *vb* (*adv*) **1** to cover (windows, etc.) or (of windows, etc.) to become covered with a film of condensed steam. **2** (*tr; usually passive*) *Sl.* to excite or make angry: *he's all steamed up about the delay.*
steamy ➊ ('sti:mɪ) *adj* **steamier, steamiest. 1** of, resembling, full of, or covered with steam. **2** *Inf.* lustful or erotic: *steamy nightlife.*
▸**'steaminess** *n*
steapsin (stɪ'æpsɪn) *n Biochem.* a pancreatic lipase. [C19: from Gk *stear* fat + PEPSIN]
stearic (stɪ'ærɪk) *adj* **1** of or relating to suet or fat. **2** of, consisting of, containing, or derived from stearic acid.
stearic acid *n* a colourless odourless insoluble waxy carboxylic acid used for making candles and suppositories. Formula: $CH_3(CH_2)_{16}COOH$. Systematic name: **octadecanoic acid.**
stearin *or* **stearine** ('stɪərɪn) *n* **1** Also called: **tristearin.** a colourless crystalline ester of glycerol and stearic acid, present in fats and used in soap and candles. **2** another name for **stearic acid. 3** fat in its solid form. [C19: from F *stéarine,* from Gk *stear* fat + -IN]
steatite ('stɪə,taɪt) *n* another name for **soapstone.** [C18: from L *steatītēs,* from Gk *stear* fat + -ITE[1]]
▸**steatitic** (,stɪə'tɪtɪk) *adj*
steato- *combining form.* denoting fat. [from Gk *stear, steat-* fat, tallow]
steatolysis (,stɪə'tɒlɪsɪs) *n Physiol.* **1** the digestive process whereby fats are emulsified and then hydrolysed to fatty acids and glycerine. **2** the breaking down of fat.
steatopygia (,stɪətəʊ'pɪdʒɪə, -'paɪ-) *or* **steatopyga** (,stɪətəʊ'paɪgə) *n* excessive fatness of the buttocks. [C19: from NL, from STEATO- + Gk *pugē* the buttocks]
▸**,steato'pygic** *or* **steatopygous** (,stɪə'tɒpɪgəs) *adj*
stedfast ('stɛdfəst, -,fɑ:st) *adj* a less common spelling of **steadfast.**
steed (sti:d) *n Arch. or literary.* a horse, esp. one that is spirited or swift. [OE *stēda* stallion]
steel ➊ (sti:l) *n* **1a** any of various alloys based on iron containing carbon and often small quantities of other elements such as sulphur, manganese, chromium, and nickel. Steels exhibit a variety of properties, such as strength, malleability, etc., depending on their composition and the way they have been treated. **1b** (*as modifier*): *steel girders.* See also **stainless steel. 2** something that is made of steel. **3** a steel stiffener in a corset, etc. **4** a ridged steel rod used for sharpening knives. **5** the quality of hardness, esp. with regard to a person's character or attitudes. **6** *Canad.* a railway track or line. **7 cold steel.** bladed weapons. ◆ *vb* (*tr*) **8** to fit, plate, edge, or point with steel. **9** to make hard and unfeeling: *he steeled his heart against her sorrow; he steeled himself for the blow.* [OE *stēli*]
▸**'steely** *adj* ▸**'steeliness** *n*
steel band *n Music.* a type of band, popular in the Caribbean Islands, consisting mainly of percussion instruments made from oil drums, hammered or embossed to obtain different notes.
steel blue *n* **a** a dark bluish-grey colour. **b** (*as adj*): *steel-blue eyes.*
steel engraving *n* **a** a method or art of engraving (letters, etc.) on a steel plate. **b** a print made from such a plate.
steel grey *n* **a** a dark grey colour, usually slightly purple. **b** (*as adj*): *a steel-grey suit.*
steelhead ('sti:l,hɛd) *n, pl* **steelheads** *or* **steelhead.** a silvery North Pacific variety of the rainbow trout.
steel wool *n* a tangled or woven mass of fine steel fibres, used for cleaning or polishing.
steelworks ('sti:l,wɜ:ks) *n* (*functioning as sing or pl*) a plant in which steel is made from iron ore and rolled or forged into bars, sheets, etc.
▸**'steel,worker** *n*
steelyard ('sti:l,jɑ:d) *n* a portable balance consisting of a pivoted bar with two unequal arms. The load is suspended from the shorter one and the bar is returned to the horizontal by sliding a weight along the longer, graduated arm.
steenbok ('sti:n,bɒk) *n, pl* **steenboks** *or* **steenbok.** a small antelope of central and southern Africa, having a reddish-brown coat and straight horns. [C18: from Afrik., from Du. *steen* stone + *bok* BUCK[1]]
steep[1] ➊ (sti:p) *adj* **1a** having or being a slope or gradient approaching the perpendicular. **1b** (*as n*): *the steep.* **2** *Inf.* (of a fee, price, demand, etc.) unduly high; unreasonable (esp. in **that's a bit steep**). **3** *Inf.* excessively demanding or ambitious: *a steep task.* **4** *Brit. inf.* (of a statement) extreme or far-fetched. [OE *steap*]
▸**'steeply** *adv* ▸**'steepness** *n*
steep[2] ➊ (sti:p) *vb* **1** to soak or be soaked in a liquid in order to soften, cleanse, extract an element, etc. **2** (*tr; usually passive*) to saturate; imbue: *steeped in ideology.* ◆ *n* **3** an instance or the process of steeping or the condition of being steeped. **4** a liquid or solution used for the purpose of steeping something. [OE *stēpan*]
▸**'steeper** *n*
steepen ('sti:pᵊn) *vb* to become or cause to become steep or steeper.
steeple ('sti:pᵊl) *n* **1** a tall ornamental tower that forms the superstructure of a church, temple, etc. **2** such a tower with the spire above it. **3** any spire or pointed structure. [OE *stēpel*]
▸**'steepled** *adj*
steeplechase ('sti:pᵊl,tʃeɪs) *n* **1** a horse race over a course equipped with obstacles to be jumped. **2** a track race in which the runners have to leap hurdles, a water jump, etc. **3** *Arch.* **3a** a horse race across a stretch of open countryside including obstacles to be jumped. **3b** a rare word for **point-to-point.** ◆ *vb* **steeplechases, steeplechasing, steeplechased. 4** (*intr*) to take part in a steeplechase.
▸**'steeple,chaser** *n* ▸**'steeple,chasing** *n*
steeplejack ('sti:pᵊl,dʒæk) *n* a person trained and skilled in the construction and repair of steeples, chimneys, etc.
steer[1] ➊ (stɪə) *vb* **1** to direct the course of (a vehicle or vessel) with a steering wheel, rudder, etc. **2** (*tr*) to guide with tuition: *his teachers steered him through his exams.* **3** (*tr*) to direct the movements or course of (a person, conversation, etc.). **4** to pursue (a specified course). **5** (*intr*) (of a vessel, vehicle, etc.) to admit of being guided in a specified fashion: *this boat does not steer properly.* **6 steer clear of.** to keep away from; shun. ◆ *n* **7** *Chiefly US.* guidance; information (esp. in **a bum steer**). [OE *stieran*]
▸**'steerable** *adj* ▸**'steerer** *n*
steer[2] (stɪə) *n* a castrated male ox or bull; bullock. [OE *stēor*]
steerage ('stɪərɪdʒ) *n* **1** the cheapest accommodation on a passenger ship, originally the compartments containing steering apparatus. **2** an instance or the practice of steering and its effect on a vessel or vehicle.
steerageway ('stɪərɪdʒ,weɪ) *n Naut.* enough forward movement to allow a vessel to be steered.
steering committee *n* a committee set up to prepare and arrange topics to be discussed, the order of business, etc., for a legislative assembly or other body.
steering wheel *n* a wheel turned by the driver of a motor vehicle, ship, etc., when he wishes to change direction.
steersman ➊ ('stɪəzmən) *n, pl* **steersmen.** the helmsman of a vessel.
stegosaur ('stɛgə,sɔ:) *or* **stegosaurus** (,stɛgə'sɔ:rəs) *n* any of various quadrupedal herbivorous dinosaurs of Jurassic and early Cretaceous times, having an armour of bony plates. [C19: from Gk *stegos* roof + -SAUR]
stein (staɪn) *n* an earthenware beer mug, esp. of a German design. [from G *Stein,* lit.: stone]
steinbok ('staɪn,bɒk) *n, pl* **steinboks** *or* **steinbok.** a variant of **steenbok.**
stele ('sti:lɪ, sti:l) *n, pl* **stelae** ('sti:li:) *or* **steles. 1** an upright stone slab or column decorated with figures or inscriptions, common in prehistoric times. **2** a prepared vertical surface that has a commemorative inscription or design, esp. one on the face of a building. **3** the conducting tissue of the stems and roots of plants, which is in the form of a cylinder. ◆ Also called (for senses 1, 2): **stela.** [C19: from Gk *stēlē*]
▸**'stelar** *adj*
stellar ('stɛlə) *adj* **1** of, relating to, or resembling a star or stars. **2** of or relating to star entertainers. **3** *Inf.* outstanding or immense: *companies are registering stellar profits.* [C17: from LL *stellāris,* from L *stella* star]
stellar evolution *n Astron.* the sequence of changes that occurs in a star as it ages.
stellate ('stɛlɪt, -eɪt) *or* **stellated** *adj* resembling a star in shape; radiating from the centre: *a stellate arrangement of petals.* [C16: from L *stellātus* starry, from *stellāre* to stud with stars, from *stella* a star]
▸**'stellately** *adv*
stellular ('stɛljʊlə) *adj* **1** displaying or abounding in small stars: *a stellular pattern.* **2** resembling a little star or little stars. [C18: from LL *stellula,* dim. of L *stella* star]
▸**'stellularly** *adv*
stem[1] ➊ (stɛm) *n* **1** the main axis of a plant, which bears the leaves, axillary buds, and flowers and contains a hollow cylinder of vascular tissue. **2** any similar subsidiary structure in such plants that bears a flower, fruit, or leaf. **3** a corresponding structure in algae and fungi. **4** any long slender part, such as the hollow part of a tobacco pipe between the bit and the bowl. **5** the main line of descent or branch of a family. **6** any shank or cylindrical pin or rod, such as the pin that carries the winding knob on a watch. **7** *Linguistics.* the form of a word that remains after removal of all inflectional affixes. **8** the main, usually vertical, stroke of a letter or of a musical note such as a minim. **9a**

THESAURUS

steamy *adj* **2** *Informal* = **erotic,** carnal, hot (*sl.*), lascivious, lewd, lubricious (*formal or literary*), lustful, prurient, raunchy (*sl.*), sensual, sexy (*inf.*), titillating
steel oneself *vb* **9** = **brace oneself,** fortify oneself, grit one's teeth, harden oneself, make up one's mind
steep[1] *adj* **1a** = **sheer,** abrupt, headlong, precipitous **2** *Informal* = **high,** excessive, exorbitant, extortionate, extreme, overpriced, stiff, uncalled-for, unreasonable
Antonyms *adj* ≠ **sheer:** easy, gentle, gradual, moderate, slight ≠ **high:** fair, moderate, reasonable
steep[2] *vb* **1** = **soak,** damp, drench, imbrue (*rare*), immerse, macerate, marinate (*Cookery*), moisten, souse, submerge **2** = **saturate,** fill, imbue, infuse, permeate, pervade, suffuse
steer[1] *vb* **1** = **drive,** control, direct, guide, handle, pilot **2, 3** = **direct,** administer, be in the driver's seat, conduct, control, govern **6 steer clear of** = **avoid,** body-swerve (*Scot.*), circumvent, eschew, evade, give a wide berth to, sheer off, shun
steersman *n* = **pilot,** cox, coxswain, helmsman
stem[1] *n* **1-3** = **stalk,** axis, branch, peduncle, shoot, stock, trunk ◆ *vb* **10 stem from** = **originate from,** arise from, be bred by, be brought about by, be caused by, be generated by, derive from, develop from, emanate from, flow from, issue forth from

the main upright timber or structure at the bow of a vessel. **9b** the very forward end of a vessel (esp. in **from stem to stern**). ◆ *vb* **stems, stemming, stemmed. 10** (*intr;* usually foll. by *from*) to be derived; originate. **11** (*tr*) to make headway against (a tide, wind, etc.). **12** (*tr*) to remove or disengage the stem or stems from. [OE *stemn*]
▸'**stem,like** *adj*

stem[2] ❶ (stɛm) *vb* **stems, stemming, stemmed. 1** (*tr*) to restrain or stop (the flow of something) by or as if by damming up. **2** (*tr*) to pack tightly or stop up. **3** *Skiing.* to manoeuvre (a ski or skis), as in performing a stem. ◆ *n* **4** *Skiing.* a technique in which the heel of one ski or both skis is forced outwards from the direction of movement in order to slow down or turn. [C15 *stemmen,* from ON *stemma*]

stem cell *n Histology.* an undifferentiated cell that gives rise to specialized cells, such as blood cells.

stem ginger *n* choice pieces of the underground stem of the ginger plant which are crystallized or preserved in syrup and eaten as a sweetmeat.

stemma ('stɛmə) *n* a family tree; pedigree. [C19: via L from Gk *stema* garland, wreath, from *stephein* to crown, wreathe]

stemmed (stɛmd) *adj* **1a** having a stem. **1b** (*in combination*): *a long-stemmed glass.* **2** having had the stem or stems removed.

stem turn *n Skiing.* a turn in which the heel of one ski is stemmed and the other ski is brought parallel. Also called: **stem.**

stench ❶ (stɛntʃ) *n* a strong and extremely offensive odour; stink. [OE *stenc*]

stencil ('stɛnsᵊl) *n* **1** a device for applying a design, characters, etc., to a surface, consisting of a thin sheet of plastic, metal, etc., in which the design or characters have been cut so that ink or paint can be applied through the incisions onto the surface. **2** a design or characters produced in this way. ◆ *vb* **stencils, stencilling, stencilled** *or US* **stencils, stenciling, stenciled.** (*tr*) **3** to mark (a surface) with a stencil. **4** to produce (characters or a design) with a stencil. [C14 *stanselen* to decorate with bright colours, from OF *estenceler,* from *estencele* a spark, from L *scintilla*]

Sten gun (stɛn) *n* a light 9mm sub-machine-gun formerly used in the British Army. [C20: from *S* & *T* (initials of Shepherd & Turpin, the inventors) + *-en,* as in BREN GUN]

steno- *or before a vowel* **sten-** *combining form.* indicating narrowness or contraction: *stenography; stenosis.* [from Gk *stenos* narrow]

stenograph ('stɛnə,grɑːf) *n* **1** any of various keyboard machines for writing in shorthand. **2** any character used in shorthand. ◆ *vb* **3** (*tr*) to record (minutes, letters, etc.) in shorthand.

stenographer (stə'nɒgrəfə) *n* the US & Canad. name for **shorthand typist.**

stenography (stə'nɒgrəfɪ) *n* **1** the act or process of writing in shorthand by hand or machine. **2** matter written in shorthand.
▸**stenographic** (,stɛnə'græfɪk) *adj*

stenosis (stɪ'nəʊsɪs) *n, pl* **stenoses** (-siːz). *Pathol.* an abnormal narrowing of a bodily canal or passage. [C19: via NL from Gk *stenōsis,* ult. from *stenos* narrow]
▸**stenotic** (stɪ'nɒtɪk) *adj*

Stenotype ('stɛnə,taɪp) *n* **1** *Trademark.* a machine with a keyboard for recording speeches, etc., in a phonetic shorthand. **2** any machine resembling this. **3** the phonetic symbol typed in one stroke of such a machine.

stenotypy ('stɛnə,taɪpɪ) *n* a form of shorthand in which alphabetic combinations are used to represent groups of sounds or short common words.
▸'**steno,typist** *n*

Stentor ('stɛntɔː) *n* **1** *Greek myth.* a Greek herald with a powerful voice who died after he lost a shouting contest with Hermes, herald of the gods. **2** (*not cap.*) any person with an unusually loud voice.

stentorian (stɛn'tɔːrɪən) *adj* (of the voice, etc.) uncommonly loud: *stentorian tones.* [C17: after STENTOR]

step ❶ (stɛp) *n* **1** the act of raising the foot and setting it down again in coordination with the transference of the weight of the body. **2** the distance or space covered by such a motion. **3** the sound made by such a movement. **4** the impression made by such movement of the foot; footprint. **5** the manner of walking or moving the feet; gait: *a proud step.* **6** a sequence of foot movements that make up a particular dance or part of a dance: *the steps of the waltz.* **7** any of several paces or rhythmic movements in marching, dancing, etc.: *the goose step.* **8** (*pl*) a course followed by a person in walking or as walking: *they followed in their leader's steps.* **9** one of a sequence of separate consecutive stages in the progression towards some goal. **10** a rank or grade in a series or scale. **11** an object or device that offers support for the foot when ascending or descending. **12** (*pl*) a flight of stairs, esp. out of doors. **13** (*pl*) another name for **stepladder. 14** a very short easily walked distance: *it is only a step.* **15** *Music.* a melodic interval of a second. **16** an offset or change in the level of a surface similar to the step of a stair. **17** a strong block or frame bolted onto the keel of a vessel and fitted to receive the base of a mast. **18** a ledge cut in mining or quarrying excavations. **19 break step.** to cease to march in step. **20 in step. 20a** marching, dancing, etc., in conformity with a specified pace or moving in unison with others. **20b** *Inf.* in agreement or harmony. **21 keep step.** to remain walking, marching, dancing, etc., in unison or in a specified rhythm. **22 out of step. 22a** not moving in conformity with a specified pace or in accordance with others. **22b** *Inf.* not in agreement; out of harmony. **23 step by step.** with care and deliberation; gradually. **24 take steps.** to undertake measures (to do something). **25 watch one's step. 25a** *Inf.* to conduct oneself with caution and good behaviour. **25b** to walk or move carefully. ◆ *vb* **steps, stepping, stepped. 26** (*intr*) to move by raising the foot and then setting it down in a different position, transferring the weight of the body to this foot and repeating the process with the other foot. **27** (*intr;* often foll. by *in, out,* etc.) to move or go on foot, esp. for a short distance: *step this way.* **28** (*intr*) *Inf., chiefly US.* to move, often in an attractive graceful manner, as in dancing: *he can really step around.* **29** (*intr;* usually foll. by *on* or *upon*) to place or press the foot; tread: *to step on the accelerator.* **30** (*intr;* usually foll. by *into*) to enter (into a situation) apparently with ease: *she stepped into a life of luxury.* **31** (*tr*) to walk or take (a number of paces, etc.): *to step ten paces.* **32** (*tr*) to perform the steps of: *they step the tango well.* **33** (*tr*) to set or place (the foot). **34** (*tr;* usually foll. by *off* or *out*) to measure (some distance of ground) by stepping. **35** (*tr*) to arrange in or supply with a series of steps so as to avoid coincidence or symmetry. **36** (*tr*) to raise (a mast) and fit it into its step. ◆ See also **step down, step in,** etc. [OE *stepe, stæpe*]
▸'**step,like** *adj*

Step (stɛp) *n* **a** a set of aerobic exercises designed to improve the cardiovascular system, which consists of stepping on and off a special box of adjustable height. **b** (*as modifer*): *Step aerobics.*

step- *combining form.* indicating relationship through the previous marriage of a spouse or parent: *stepson; stepfather.* [OE *stēop-*]

stepbrother ('stɛp,brʌðə) *n* a son of one's stepmother or stepfather by a union with someone other than one's father or mother.

stepchild ('stɛp,tʃaɪld) *n, pl* **stepchildren.** a stepson or stepdaughter.

stepdaughter ('stɛp,dɔːtə) *n* a daughter of one's husband or wife by a former union.

step down ❶ *vb* (*adv*) **1** (*tr*) to reduce gradually. **2** (*intr*) *Inf.* to resign or abdicate (from a position). **3** (*intr*) *Inf.* to assume an inferior or less senior position. ◆ *adj* **step-down.** (*prenominal*) **4** (of a transformer) reducing a high voltage to a lower voltage. Cf. **step-up** (sense 3). ◆ *n* **step-down. 5** *Inf.* a decrease in quantity or size.

stepfather ('stɛp,fɑːðə) *n* a man who has married one's mother after the death or divorce of one's father.

stephanotis (,stɛfə'nəʊtɪs) *n* any of various climbing shrubs of Madagascar and Malaya, cultivated for their fragrant white waxy flowers. [C19: via NL from Gk: fit for a crown, from *stephanos* a crown]

step in ❶ *vb* **1** (*intr, adv*) *Inf.* to intervene or involve oneself. ◆ *adj* **step-in. 2** (*prenominal*) (of garments, etc.) put on by being stepped into; without fastenings. **3** (of a ski binding) engaging automatically when the boot is positioned on the ski. ◆ *n* **step-in. 4** (*often pl*) a step-in garment, esp. underwear.

stepladder ('stɛp,lædə) *n* a folding portable ladder that is made of broad flat steps fixed to a supporting frame hinged at the top to another supporting frame.

stepmother ('stɛp,mʌðə) *n* a woman who has married one's father after the death or divorce of one's mother.

step on *vb* (*intr, prep*) **1** to place or press the foot on. **2** *Inf.* to behave harshly or contemptuously towards. **3 step on it.** *Inf.* to go more quickly; hurry up.

step out *vb* (*intr, adv*) **1** to go outside or leave a room, etc., esp. briefly. **2** to begin to walk more quickly and take longer strides. **3** *US & Canad. inf.* to withdraw from involvement.

step-parent ('stɛp,pɛərənt) *n* a stepfather or stepmother.
▸'**step-,parenting** *n*

steppe (stɛp) *n* (*often pl*) an extensive grassy plain usually without trees. [C17: from ORussian *step* lowland]

stepper ('stɛpə) *n* a person who or animal that steps, esp. a horse or a dancer.

stepping stone *n* **1** one of a series of stones acting as footrests for crossing streams, marshes, etc. **2** a circumstance that assists progress towards some goal.

stepsister ('stɛp,sɪstə) *n* a daughter of one's stepmother or stepfather by a union with someone other than one's father or mother.

stepson ('stɛp,sʌn) *n* a son of one's husband or wife by a former union.

THESAURUS

stem[2] *vb* **1** = **stop**, bring to a standstill, check, contain, curb, dam, hold back, oppose, resist, restrain, stanch, staunch, stay (*arch.*), withstand

stench *n* = **stink**, foul smell, malodour, mephitis, niff (*Brit. sl.*), noisomeness, pong (*Brit. inf.*), reek, whiff (*Brit. sl.*)

step *n* **1** = **footstep**, footfall, footprint, impression, pace, print, stride, trace, track **5** = **gait**, walk **9** = **stage**, advance, advancement, move, phase, point, process, progression **10** = **degree**, level, rank, remove **11** = **stair**, doorstep, round, rung, tread **20 in step** *Informal* = **in agreement**, coinciding, conforming, in conformity, in harmony, in line, in unison **22 out of step** *Informal* = **in disagreement**, erratic, incongruous, out of harmony, out of line, out of phase, pulling different ways **24 take steps** = **take action**, act, intervene, move in, prepare, take measures, take the initiative **25 watch one's step** *Informal* = **be careful**, be canny, be cautious, be discreet, be on one's guard, have one's wits about one, look out, mind how one goes, mind one's p's and q's, take care, take heed, tread carefully ◆ *vb* **26** = **walk**, move, pace, tread

step down *vb* **2** *Informal* = **resign**, abdicate, bow out, give up, hand over, leave, pull out, quit, retire

step in *vb* **1** *Informal* = **intervene**, become involved, chip in (*inf.*), intercede, take action, take a hand

step up ⓣ *vb (adv) Inf.* **1** *(tr)* to increase or raise by stages; accelerate. **2** *(intr)* to make progress or effect an advancement; be promoted. ◆ *adj* **step-up.** *(prenominal)* **3** (of a transformer) increasing a low voltage to a higher voltage. Cf. **step-down** (sense 4). ◆ *n* **step-up. 4** *Inf.* an increment in quantity, size, etc.

-ster *suffix forming nouns.* **1** indicating a person who is engaged in a certain activity: *prankster; songster.* **2** indicating a person associated with or being something specified: *mobster; youngster.* [OE *-estre*]

steradian (stəˈreɪdɪən) *n* an SI unit of solid angle; the angle that, having its vertex in the centre of a sphere, cuts off an area of the surface of the sphere equal to the square of the length of the radius. Symbol: sr [C19: from STEREO- + RADIAN]

stercoraceous (ˌstɜːkəˈreɪʃəs) *adj* of, relating to, or consisting of dung or excrement. [C18: from L *stercus* dung + -ACEOUS]

stere (stɪə) *n* a unit used to measure volumes of stacked timber equal to one cubic metre (35.315 cubic feet). [C18: from F *stère*, from Gk *stereos* solid]

stereo (ˈstɛrɪəʊ, ˈstɪər-) *adj* **1** short for **stereophonic** or **stereoscopic.** ◆ *n, pl* **stereos. 2** stereophonic sound: *to broadcast in stereo.* **3** a stereophonic record player, tape recorder, etc. **4** *Photog.* **4a** stereoscopic photography. **4b** a stereoscopic photograph. **5** *Printing.* short for **stereotype.** [C20: shortened form]

stereo- *or sometimes before a vowel* **stere-** *combining form.* indicating three-dimensional quality or solidity: *stereoscope.* [from Gk *stereos* solid]

stereochemistry (ˌstɛrɪəʊˈkɛmɪstrɪ, ˌstɪər-) *n* the study of the spatial arrangement of atoms in molecules and its effect on chemical properties.

stereograph (ˈstɛrɪəˌgrɑːf, ˈstɪər-) *n* two almost identical pictures, or one special picture, that when viewed through special glasses or a stereoscope form a single three-dimensional image. Also called: **stereogram.**

stereoisomer (ˌstɛrɪəʊˈaɪsəmə, ˌstɪər-) *n Chem.* an isomer that exhibits stereoisomerism.

stereoisomerism (ˌstɛrɪəʊaɪˈsɒməˌrɪzəm, ˌstɪər-) *n Chem.* isomerism caused by differences in the spatial arrangement of atoms in molecules.

stereophonic (ˌstɛrɪəˈfɒnɪk, ˌstɪər-) *adj* (of a system for recording, reproducing, or broadcasting sound) using two or more separate microphones to feed two or more loudspeakers through separate channels in order to give a spatial effect to the sound. Often shortened to **stereo.**
▸**ˌstereoˈphonically** *adv* ▸**stereophony** (ˌstɛrɪˈɒfənɪ, ˌstɪər-) *n*

stereoscope (ˈstɛrɪəˌskəʊp, ˈstɪər-) *n* an optical instrument for viewing two-dimensional pictures, giving an illusion of depth and relief. It has a binocular eyepiece through which two slightly different pictures of an object are viewed, one with each eye.
▸**stereoscopic** (ˌstɛrɪəˈskɒpɪk, ˌstɪər-) *adj*

stereoscopy (ˌstɛrɪˈɒskəpɪ, ˌstɪər-) *n* **1** the viewing or appearance of objects in or as if in three dimensions. **2** the study and use of the stereoscope.
▸**ˌstereˈoscopist** *n*

stereospecific (ˌstɛrɪəʊspɪˈsɪfɪk, ˌstɪər-) *adj Chem.* relating to or having fixed position in space, as in the spatial arrangements of atoms in certain polymers.

stereotype ⓣ (ˈstɛrɪəˌtaɪp, ˈstɪər-) *n* **1a** a method of producing cast-metal printing plates from a mould made from a forme of type. **1b** the plate so made. **2** another word for **stereotypy. 3** an idea, convention, etc., that has grown stale through fixed usage. **4** a standardized image or conception of a type of person, etc. ◆ *vb* **stereotypes, stereotyping, stereotyped.** *(tr)* **5a** to make a stereotype of. **5b** to print from a stereotype. **6** to impart a fixed usage or convention to.
▸**ˈstereoˌtyper** *or* **ˈstereoˌtypist** *n*

stereotyped ⓣ (ˈstɛrɪəˌtaɪpt, ˈstɪər-) *adj* **1** lacking originality or individuality; conventional; trite. **2** reproduced from or on a stereotype printing plate.

stereotypy (ˈstɛrɪəˌtaɪpɪ, ˈstɪər-) *n* **1** the act or process of making stereotype printing plates. **2** a tendency to think or act in rigid, repetitive, and often meaningless patterns.

stereovision (ˈstɛrɪəʊˌvɪʒən, ˈstɪər-) *n* the perception or exhibition of three-dimensional objects in three dimensions.

steric (ˈstɛrɪk, ˈstɪər-) *or* **sterical** *adj Chem.* of or caused by the spatial arrangement of atoms in a molecule. [C19: from STEREO- + -IC]

sterile ⓣ (ˈstɛraɪl) *adj* **1** unable to produce offspring; permanently infertile. **2** free from living, esp. pathogenic, microorganisms. **3** (of plants or their parts) not producing or bearing seeds, fruit, spores, stamens, or pistils. **4** lacking inspiration or vitality; fruitless. [C16: from L *sterilis*]
▸**ˈsterilely** *adv* ▸**sterility** (stɛˈrɪlɪtɪ) *n*

sterilize ⓣ *or* **sterilise** (ˈstɛrɪˌlaɪz) *vb* **sterilizes, sterilizing, sterilized** *or* **sterilises, sterilising, sterilised.** *(tr)* to render sterile; make infertile or barren.
▸**ˌsteriliˈzation** *or* **ˌsteriliˈsation** *n* ▸**ˈsteriˌlizer** *or* **ˈsteriˌliser** *n*

sterling ⓣ (ˈstɜːlɪŋ) *n* **1a** British money: *pound sterling.* **1b** *(as modifier): sterling reserves.* **2** the official standard of purity of British coins. **3a** short for **sterling silver. 3b** *(as modifier): a sterling bracelet.* **4** an article or articles manufactured from sterling silver. ◆ *adj* **5** *(prenominal)* genuine and reliable: first-class: *sterling quality.* [C13: prob. from OE *steorra* star + -LING[1]; referring to a small star on early Norman pennies]

sterling area *n* a group of countries that use sterling as a medium of international payments. Also called: **scheduled territories.**

sterling silver *n* **1** an alloy containing not less than 92.5 per cent of silver. **2** sterling-silver articles collectively.

stern[1] ⓣ (stɜːn) *adj* **1** showing uncompromising or inflexible resolve; firm or authoritarian. **2** lacking leniency or clemency. **3** relentless; unyielding: *the stern demands of parenthood.* **4** having an austere or forbidding appearance or nature. [OE *styrne*]
▸**ˈsternly** *adv* ▸**ˈsternness** *n*

stern[2] (stɜːn) *n* **1** the rear or after part of a vessel, opposite the bow or stem. **2** the rear part of any object. ◆ *adj* **3** relating to or located at the stern. [C13: from ON *stjōrn* steering]

sternforemost (ˈstɜːnˈfɔːməʊst) *adv Naut.* backwards.

sternmost (ˈstɜːnˌməʊst) *adj Naut.* **1** farthest to the stern; aftmost. **2** nearest the stern.

sternpost (ˈstɜːnˌpəʊst) *n Naut.* the main upright timber or structure at the stern of a vessel.

stern sheets *pl n Naut.* the part of an open boat near the stern.

sternum (ˈstɜːnəm) *n, pl* **sterna** (-nə) *or* **sternums. 1** (in man) a long flat vertical bone in front of the thorax, to which are attached the collarbone and the first seven pairs of ribs. Nontechnical name: **breastbone. 2** the corresponding part in many other vertebrates. [C17: via NL from Gk *sternon* breastbone]
▸**ˈsternal** *adj*

sternutation (ˌstɜːnjʊˈteɪʃən) *n* a sneeze or the act of sneezing. [C16: from LL *sternūtāre* to sneeze, from *sternuere* to sputter (of a light)]

sternutator (ˈstɜːnjʊˌteɪtə) *n* a substance that causes sneezing, coughing, and tears; used in chemical warfare.
▸**sternutatory** (stɜːˈnjuːtətərɪ, -trɪ) *adj, n*

sternwards (ˈstɜːnwədz) *or* **sternward** *adv Naut.* towards the stern; astern.

sternway (ˈstɜːnˌweɪ) *n Naut.* movement of a vessel sternforemost.

stern-wheeler *n* a vessel, esp. a river boat, propelled by a large paddle wheel at the stern.

steroid (ˈstɪərɔɪd, ˈstɛr-) *n Biochem.* any of a large group of organic compounds containing a characteristic chemical ring system, including sterols, bile acids, many hormones, and the D vitamins. [C20: from STEROL + -OID]
▸**steˈroidal** *adj*

sterol (ˈstɛrɒl) *n Biochem.* any of a group of natural steroid alcohols, such as cholesterol and ergosterol, that are waxy insoluble substances. [C20: shortened from CHOLESTEROL, ERGOSTEROL, etc.]

stertorous (ˈstɜːtərəs) *adj* **1** marked by heavy snoring. **2** breathing in this way. [C19: from L *stertere* to snore]
▸**ˈstertorously** *adv* ▸**ˈstertorousness** *n*

stet (stɛt) *n* **1** a word or mark indicating that certain deleted typeset or written matter is to be retained. ◆ *vb* **stets, stetting, stetted. 2** *(tr)* to mark (matter) thus. [L, lit.: let it stand]

stethoscope (ˈstɛθəˌskəʊp) *n Med.* an instrument for listening to the sounds made within the body, typically consisting of a hollow disc that transmits the sound through hollow tubes to earpieces. [C19: from F, from Gk *stēthos* breast + -SCOPE]
▸**stethoscopic** (ˌstɛθəˈskɒpɪk) *adj* ▸**stethoscopy** (stɛˈθɒskəpɪ) *n*

Stetson (ˈstɛtsᵊn) *n Trademark.* a type of felt hat with a broad brim and high crown, worn mainly by cowboys. [C20: after John *Stetson* (1830–1906), US hat-maker]

stevedore (ˈstiːvɪˌdɔː) *n* **1** a person employed to load or unload ships. ◆ *vb* **stevedores, stevedoring, stevedored. 2** to load or unload (a ship, ship's cargo, etc.). [C18: from Sp. *estibador* a packer, from *estibar* to load (a ship), from L *stīpāre* to pack full]

stew[1] ⓣ (stjuː) *n* **1a** a dish of meat, fish, or other food, cooked by stewing. **1b** *(as modifier): stew pot.* **2** *Inf.* a difficult or worrying situation or a troubled state (esp. in **in a stew**). **3** a heterogeneous mixture: *a stew of*

THESAURUS

step up *vb* **1** *Informal* = **increase**, accelerate, augment, boost, escalate, intensify, raise, speed up, up

stereotype *n* **3** = **formula**, mould, pattern, received idea ◆ *vb* **6** = **categorize**, conventionalize, dub, ghettoize, pigeonhole, standardize, take to be, typecast

stereotyped *adj* **1** = **unoriginal**, banal, cliché-ridden, conventional, corny (*sl.*), hackneyed, mass-produced, overused, platitudinous, played out, stale, standard, standardized, stock, threadbare, tired, trite

sterile *adj* **1** = **barren**, abortive, bare, dry, empty, fruitless, infecund, unfruitful, unproductive, unprofitable, unprolific **2** = **germ-free**, antiseptic, aseptic, disinfected, sterilized
Antonyms *adj* ≠ **barren:** fecund, fertile, fruitful, productive, prolific ≠ **germ-free:** contaminated, dirty, germ-ridden, infected, insanitary, unhygienic, unsterile

sterilize *vb* = **disinfect**, autoclave, fumigate, purify

sterling *adj* **5** = **excellent**, authentic, fine, first-class, genuine, pure, real, sound, standard, substantial, superlative, true

stern[1] *adj* **1-3** = **strict**, austere, authoritarian, cruel, drastic, grim, hard, harsh, inflexible, relentless, rigid, rigorous, unrelenting, unsparing, unyielding **4** = **severe**, flinty, forbidding, frowning, serious, steely
Antonyms *adj* ≠ **strict:** compassionate, flexible, gentle, kind, lenient, liberal, permissive, soft, sympathetic, tolerant ≠ **severe:** amused, approachable, friendly, warm

stew[1] *n* **1b** = **hash**, goulash, olio, olla, olla podrida, potpourri, ragout **2 in a stew** *Informal* = **troubled**, anxious, concerned, fretting, in a lather (*inf.*), in a panic, worrying **3** = **mixture**, blend, hash, hodgepodge (*US & Canad.*), hotchpotch, medley, miscellany, mix, olio, olla, potpourri

people of every race. **4** (*usually pl*) *Arch.* a brothel. ◆ *vb* **5** to cook or cause to cook by long slow simmering. **6** (*intr*) *Inf.* to be troubled or agitated. **7** (*intr*) *Inf.* to be oppressed with heat or crowding. **8** to cause (tea) to become bitter or (of tea) to become bitter through infusing for too long. **9 stew in one's own juice.** to suffer unaided the consequences of one's actions. [C14 *stuen* to take a very hot bath, from OF *estuver,* from Vulgar L *extūfāre* (unattested), from EX-[1] + (unattested) *tūfus* vapour, from Gk *tuphos*]

stew[2] (stju:) *n Brit.* **1** a fishpond or fishtank. **2** an artificial oyster bed. [C14: from OF *estui,* from *estoier* to confine, ult. from L *studium* STUDY]

steward (ˈstjʊəd) *n* **1** a person who administers the property, house, finances, etc., of another. **2** a person who manages the eating arrangements, staff, or service at a club, hotel, etc. **3** a waiter on a ship or aircraft. **4** a mess attendant in a naval mess. **5** a person who helps to supervise some event or proceedings in an official capacity. **6** short for **shop steward.** ◆ *vb* **7** to act or serve as a steward (of something). [OE *stigweard,* from *stig* hall + *weard* WARD]

▸ˈ**stewardship** *n*

stewardess (ˈstjʊədɪs, ˌstjʊəˈdɛs) *n* a woman steward on an aircraft or ship.

stewed (stju:d) *adj* **1** (of meat, fish, etc.) cooked by stewing. **2** *Brit.* (of tea) bitter through having been left to infuse for too long. **3** a slang word for **drunk** (sense 1).

stg *abbrev. for* sterling.

sthenic (ˈsθɛnɪk) *adj* abounding in energy or bodily strength; active or strong. [C18: from NL *sthenicus,* from Gk *sthenos* force, on the model of *asthenic*]

stibine (ˈstɪbaɪn) *n* **1** a colourless poisonous gas with an offensive odour: made by the action of hydrochloric acid on an alloy of antimony and zinc. **2** any one of a class of stibine derivatives in which one or more hydrogen atoms have been replaced by organic groups. [C19: from L *stibium* antimony + -INE[2]]

stibnite (ˈstɪbnaɪt) *n* a soft greyish mineral consisting of antimony sulphide in crystalline form: the chief ore of antimony. [C19: from obs. *stibine* stibnite + -ITE[1]]

-stichous *adj combining form.* having a certain number of rows. [from LL *-stichus,* from Gk *-stikhos,* from *stikhos* row]

stick[1] **T** (stɪk) *n* **1** a small thin branch of a tree. **2a** any long thin piece of wood. **2b** such a piece of wood having a characteristic shape for a special purpose: *a walking stick; a hockey stick.* **2c** a baton, wand, staff, or rod. **3** an object or piece shaped like a stick: *a stick of celery.* **4** In full: **control stick.** the lever by which a pilot controls the movements of an aircraft. **5** *Inf.* the lever used to change gear in a motor vehicle. **6** *Naut.* a mast or yard. **7a** a group of bombs arranged to fall at intervals across a target. **7b** a number of paratroops jumping in sequence. **8** *Sl.* **8a** verbal abuse, criticism: *I got some stick for that blunder.* **8b** physical power, force (esp. in **give it some stick**). **9** (*usually pl*) a piece of furniture: *these few sticks are all I have.* **10** (*pl*) *Inf.* a rural area considered remote or backward (esp. in **in the sticks**). **11** (*pl*) *Hockey.* a declaration made by the umpire if a player's stick is above the shoulders. **12** (*pl*) goalposts. **13** *Inf.* a dull boring person. **14** (usually preceded by *old*) *Inf.* a familiar name for a person: *not a bad old stick.* **15** punishment; beating. **16 in a cleft stick.** in a difficult position. **17 wrong end of the stick.** a complete misunderstanding of a situation, explanation, etc. ◆ *vb* **sticks, sticking, sticked. 18** to support (a plant) with sticks; stake. [OE *sticca*]

stick[2] **T** (stɪk) *vb* **sticks, sticking, stuck. 1** (*tr*) to pierce or stab with or as if with something pointed. **2** to thrust or push (a sharp or pointed object) or (of a sharp or pointed object) to be pushed into or through another object. **3** (*tr*) to fasten in position by pushing or forcing a point into something: *to stick a peg in a hole.* **4** (*tr*) to fasten in position by or as if by pins, nails, etc.: *to stick a picture on the wall.* **5** (*tr*) to transfix or impale on a pointed object. **6** (*tr*) to cover with objects piercing or set in the surface. **7** (when *intr,* foll. by *out, up, through,* etc.) to put forward or be put forward; protrude or cause to protrude: *to stick one's head out.* **8** (*tr*) *Inf.* to place or put in a specified position: *stick your coat on this chair.* **9** to fasten or be fastened by or as if by an adhesive substance: *stick the pages together; they won't stick.* **10** (*tr*) *Inf.* to cause to become sticky. **11** (when *tr, usually passive*) to come or cause to come to a standstill: *stuck in a traffic jam; the wheels stuck.* **12** (*intr*) to remain for a long time: *the memory sticks in my mind.* **13** (*tr*) *Sl., chiefly Brit.* to tolerate; abide: *I can't stick that man.* **14** (*intr*) to be reluctant. **15** (*tr; usually passive*) *Inf.* to cause to be at a loss; baffle or puzzle: *I was totally stuck for an answer.* **16** (*tr*) *Sl.* to force or impose something unpleasant on: *they stuck me with the bill.* **17** (*tr*) to kill by piercing or stabbing. **18 stick to the ribs.** *Inf.* (of food) to be hearty and satisfying. ◆ *n* **19** the state or condition of adhering. **20** *Inf.* a substance causing adhesion. **21** *Obs.* something that causes delay or stoppage. ◆ See also **stick around, stick by,** etc. [OE *stician*]

stick around *or* **about** *vb* (*intr, adv*) *Inf.* to remain in a place, esp. awaiting something.

stick by *vb* (*intr, prep*) to remain faithful to; adhere to.

sticker (ˈstɪkə) *n* **1** an adhesive label, poster, or paper. **2** a person or thing that sticks. **3** a persevering or industrious person. **4** something prickly, such as a thorn, that clings to one's clothing, etc. **5** *Inf.* something that perplexes. **6** *Inf.* a knife used for stabbing or piercing.

stickhandle (ˈstɪkˌhændᵊl) *vb* **stickhandles, stickhandling, stickhandled.** *Ice hockey.* to manoeuvre (the puck) deftly.

sticking plaster *n* a thin cloth with an adhesive substance on one side, used for covering slight or superficial wounds.

stick insect *n* any of various mostly tropical insects that have an elongated cylindrical body and long legs and resemble twigs.

stick-in-the-mud **T** *n Inf.* a conservative person who lacks initiative or imagination.

stickle (ˈstɪkᵊl) *vb* **stickles, stickling, stickled.** (*intr*) **1** to dispute stubbornly, esp. about minor points. **2** to refuse to agree or concur, esp. by making petty stipulations. [C16 *stightle* (in the sense: to arbitrate): frequentative of OE *stihtan* to arrange]

stickleback (ˈstɪkᵊlˌbæk) *n* any of various small fishes that have a series of spines along the back and occur in cold and temperate northern regions. [C15: from OE *stickel* prick, sting + BACK]

stickler **T** (ˈstɪklə) *n* **1** (usually foll. by *for*) a person who makes insistent demands: *a stickler for accuracy.* **2** a problem or puzzle.

stick out **T** *vb* (*adv*) **1** to project or cause to project. **2** (*tr*) *Inf.* to endure (something disagreeable) (esp. in **stick it out**). **3 stick out a mile** *or* **like a sore thumb.** *Inf.* to be extremely obvious. **4 stick out for.** to insist on (a demand), refusing to yield until it is met.

stick shift *n US & Canad.* **1a** a manually operated transmission system in a motor vehicle. **1b** a motor vehicle having manual transmission. **2** a gear lever.

stick to **T** *vb* (*prep, mainly intr*) **1** (*also tr*) to adhere or cause to adhere to. **2** to continue constantly at. **3** to remain faithful to. **4** not to move or digress from: *the speaker stuck closely to his subject.* **5 stick to someone's fingers.** *Inf.* to be stolen by someone.

stick-up **T** *n* **1** *Sl., chiefly US.* a robbery at gunpoint; hold-up. ◆ *vb* **stick up.** (*adv*) **2** (*tr*) *Sl., chiefly US.* to rob, esp. at gunpoint. **3** (*intr;* foll. by *for*) *Inf.* to support or defend: *stick up for oneself.*

sticky **T** (ˈstɪkɪ) *adj* **stickier, stickiest. 1** covered or daubed with an adhesive or viscous substance: *sticky fingers.* **2** having the property of sticking to a surface. **3** (of weather or atmosphere) warm and humid; muggy. **4** *Inf.* difficult, awkward, or painful: *a sticky business.* ◆ *vb* **stickies, stickying, stickied. 5** (*tr*) *Inf.* to make sticky.

▸ˈ**stickily** *adv* ▸ˈ**stickiness** *n*

stickybeak (ˈstɪkɪˌbi:k) *Austral. & NZ inf.* ◆ *n* **1** an inquisitive person. ◆ *vb* **2** (*intr*) to pry.

sticky end *n Inf.* an unpleasant finish or death (esp. in **come to** *or* **meet a sticky end**).

sticky wicket *n* **1** a cricket pitch that is rapidly being dried by the sun after rain and is particularly conducive to spin. **2** *Inf.* a difficult or awkward situation.

stiff **T** (stɪf) *adj* **1** not easily bent; rigid; inflexible. **2** not working or moving easily or smoothly: *a stiff handle.* **3** difficult to accept in its severity or harshness: *a stiff punishment.* **4** moving with pain or difficulty; not supple: *a stiff neck.* **5** difficult; arduous: *a stiff climb.* **6** unrelaxed or awkward; formal. **7** firmer than liquid in consistency; thick or viscous. **8** powerful; strong: *a stiff breeze; a stiff drink.* **9** exces-

THESAURUS

stick[1] *n* **1-3** = **cane**, baton, birch, crook, pole, rod, sceptre, staff, stake, switch, twig, wand **8a** *Slang* = **abuse**, blame, criticism, flak (*inf.*), hostility, punishment **13** *Informal* = **(old) fogey**, dinosaur, fuddy-duddy (*inf.*), pain (*inf.*), prig, stick-in-the-mud (*inf.*)

stick[2] *vb* **1** = **poke**, dig, gore, insert, jab, penetrate, pierce, pin, prod, puncture, spear, stab, thrust, transfix **7** *with* **out, up, through** *etc.* = **protrude**, bulge, extend, jut, obtrude, poke, project, show **8** *Informal* = **put**, deposit, drop, fix, install, lay, place, plant, plonk, position, set, store, stuff **9** = **fasten**, adhere, affix, attach, bind, bond, cement, cleave, cling, fix, fuse, glue, hold, hold on, join, paste, weld **11** = **catch**, be bogged down, become immobilized, be embedded, clog, come to a standstill, jam, lodge, snag, stop **12** = **stay**, linger, persist, remain **13** *Slang* = **tolerate**, abide, bear up under, endure, get on with, hack (*sl.*), stand, stomach, take

stick-in-the-mud *n Informal* = **(old) fogey**, Colonel Blimp, conservative, die-hard, dinosaur, fuddy-duddy (*inf.*), reactionary, sobersides, stick (*inf.*)

stickler *n* **1** = **fanatic**, fusspot (*Brit. inf.*), hard taskmaster, maniac (*inf.*), martinet, nut (*sl.*), pedant, perfectionist, purist

stick out *vb* **2** *Informal* = **endure**, bear, grin and bear it (*inf.*), last out, put up with (*inf.*), see through, soldier on, take it (*inf.*), weather

stick to *vb* **1-4** = **remain faithful**, adhere to, cleave to, continue in, honour, keep, persevere in, remain loyal, remain true, stick at

stick up for *vb* **3** *Informal* = **defend**, champion, stand up for, support, take the part *or* side of, uphold

sticky *adj* **1** = **tacky**, adhesive, claggy, clinging, gluey, glutinous, gooey (*inf.*), gummy, syrupy, tenacious, viscid, viscous **3** = **humid**, clammy, close, muggy, oppressive, sultry, sweltering **4** *Informal* = **difficult**, awkward, delicate, discomforting, embarrassing, hairy (*sl.*), nasty, painful, thorny, tricky, unpleasant

stiff *adj* **1** = **inflexible**, brittle, firm, hard, hardened, inelastic, rigid, solid, solidified, taut, tense, tight, unbending, unyielding **3** = **severe**, austere, cruel, drastic, extreme, great, hard, harsh, heavy, inexorable, oppressive, pitiless, rigorous, sharp, strict, stringent **4** = **unsupple**, arthritic, creaky (*inf.*), rheumaticky **5** = **difficult**, arduous, exacting, fatiguing, formidable, hard, laborious, tough, trying, uphill **6** = **unrelaxed**, artificial, austere, ceremonious, chilly, cold, constrained, forced, formal, laboured, mannered, pompous, priggish, prim, punctilious, standoffish, starchy (*inf.*), stilted, uneasy, unnatural, wooden **8** = **powerful**, brisk, fresh, strong, vigorous **10** = **awkward**, clumsy, crude, graceless, inelegant, jerky (*inf.*), ungainly, ungraceful

Antonyms *adj* ≠ **inflexible:** bendable, ductile, elastic, flexible, pliable, pliant, yielding ≠ **unsupple:** flexible, limber, lissom(e), lithe, supple ≠ **unrelaxed:** casual, easy, informal, laid-back, natural, relaxed, spontaneous, unceremonious, unofficial

sively high: *a stiff price.* **10** lacking grace or attractiveness. **11** stubborn or stubbornly maintained: *a stiff fight.* **12** *Obs.* tightly stretched; taut. **13** *Sl.* intoxicated. **14 stiff with.** *Inf.* amply provided with. ◆ *n* **15** *Sl.* a corpse. **16** *Sl.* anything thought to be a loser or a failure; flop. ◆ *adv* **17** completely or utterly: *bored stiff; frozen stiff.* ◆ *vb* **18** (*intr*) *Sl.* to fail: *the film stiffed.* **19** (*tr*) *Sl., chiefly US.* to cheat or swindle. [OE *stīf*]
▸ **'stiffish** *adj* ▸ **'stiffly** *adv* ▸ **'stiffness** *n*

stiffen 🅣 ('stɪfᵊn) *vb* **1** to make or become stiff or stiffer. **2** (*intr*) to become suddenly tense or unyielding.
▸ **'stiffener** *n*

stiff-necked 🅣 *adj* haughtily stubborn or obstinate.

stifle 🅣 ('staɪfᵊl) *vb* **stifles, stifling, stifled. 1** (*tr*) to smother or suppress: *stifle a cough.* **2** to feel or cause to feel discomfort and difficulty in breathing. **3** to prevent or be prevented from breathing so as to cause death. **4** (*tr*) to crush or stamp out. [C14: var. of *stuflen,* prob. from OF *estouffer* to smother]

stigma 🅣 ('stɪgmə) *n, pl* **stigmas** *or* **stigmata** ('stɪgmətə, stɪg'mɑːtə). **1** a distinguishing mark of social disgrace: *the stigma of having been in prison.* **2** a small scar or mark such as a birthmark. **3** *Pathol.* any mark on the skin, such as one characteristic of a specific disease. **4** *Bot.* the terminal part of the ovary, at the end of the style, where deposited pollen enters the gynoecium. **5** *Zool.* **5a** a pigmented eyespot in some invertebrates. **5b** the spiracle of an insect. **6** *Arch.* a mark branded on the skin. **7** (*pl*) *Christianity.* marks resembling the wounds of the crucified Christ, believed to appear on the bodies of certain individuals. [C16: via L from Gk: brand, from *stizein* to tattoo]

stigmatic (stɪg'mætɪk) *adj* **1** relating to or having a stigma or stigmata. **2** another word for **anastigmatic.** ◆ *n also* **stigmatist** ('stɪgmətɪst). **3** *Chiefly RC Church.* a person marked with the stigmata.

stigmatism ('stɪgməˌtɪzəm) *n* **1** *Physics.* the state or condition of being anastigmatic. **2** *Pathol.* the condition resulting from or characterized by stigmata.

stigmatize 🅣 *or* **stigmatise** ('stɪgməˌtaɪz) *vb* **stigmatizes, stigmatizing, stigmatized** *or* **stigmatises, stigmatising, stigmatised.** (*tr*) **1** to mark out or describe (as something bad). **2** to mark with a stigma or stigmata.
▸ **ˌstigmati'zation** *or* **ˌstigmati'sation** *n* ▸ **'stigmaˌtizer** *or* **'stigmaˌtiser** *n*

stilbene ('stɪlbiːn) *n* a colourless or slightly yellow crystalline unsaturated hydrocarbon used in the manufacture of dyes. [C19: from Gk *stilbos* glittering + -ENE]

stilboestrol *or US* **stilbestrol** (stɪl'biːstrəl) *n* a synthetic hormone having derivatives with oestrogenic properties. Also called: **diethylstilboestrol.** [C20: from STILBENE + OESTRUS + -OL[1]]

stile[1] (staɪl) *n* **1** a set of steps or rungs in a wall or fence to allow people, but not animals, to pass over. **2** short for **turnstile.** [OE *stigel*]

stile[2] (staɪl) *n* a vertical framing member in a door, window frame, etc. [C17: prob. from Du. *stijl* pillar, ult. from L *stilus* writing instrument]

stiletto (stɪ'letəʊ) *n, pl* **stilettos. 1** a small dagger with a slender tapered blade. **2** a sharply pointed tool used to make holes in leather, cloth, etc. **3** Also called: **spike heel, stiletto heel.** a very high heel on a woman's shoe, tapering to a very narrow tip. ◆ *vb* **stilettoes, stilettoeing, stilettoed. 4** (*tr*) to stab with a stiletto. [C17: from It., from *stilo* a dagger, from L *stilus* a stake, pen]

still[1] 🅣 (stɪl) *adj* **1** (*usually predicative*) motionless; stationary. **2** undisturbed or tranquil; silent and calm. **3** not sparkling or effervescent. **4** gentle or quiet; subdued. **5** *Obs.* (of a child) dead at birth. ◆ *adv* **6** continuing now or in the future as in the past: *do you still love me?* **7** up to this or that time; yet: *I still don't know your name.* **8** (often used with a comparative) even or yet: *still more insults.* **9** quietly or without movement: *sit still.* **10** *Poetic & dialect.* always. ◆ *n* **11** *Poetic.* silence or tranquillity: *the still of the night.* **12a** a still photograph, esp. of a scene from a film. **12b** (*as modifier*): *a still camera.* ◆ *vb* **13** to make or become still, quiet, or calm. **14** (*tr*) to allay or relieve: *her fears were stilled.* ◆ *sentence connector.* **15** even then; nevertheless: *the child has some new toys and still cries.* [OE *stille*]
▸ **'stillness** *n*

still[2] (stɪl) *n* an apparatus for carrying out distillation, used esp. in the manufacture of spirits. [C16: from OF *stiller* to drip, from L *stillāre,* from *stilla* a drip]

stillage ('stɪlɪdʒ) *n* **1** a frame or stand for keeping things off the ground, such as casks in a brewery. **2** a container in which goods, machinery, etc., are transported. [C16: prob. from Du. *stillagie* frame, scaffold, from *stellen* to stand; see -AGE]

stillborn ('stɪlˌbɔːn) *adj* **1** (of a fetus) dead at birth. **2** (of an idea, plan, etc.) fruitless; abortive; unsuccessful.
▸ **'stillˌbirth** *n*

still life *n, pl* **still lifes. 1a** a painting or drawing of inanimate objects, such as fruit, flowers, etc. **1b** (*as modifier*): *a still-life painting.* **2** the genre of such paintings.

still room *n Brit.* **1** a room in which distilling is carried out. **2** a pantry or storeroom, as in a large house.

Stillson wrench ('stɪlsᵊn) *n Trademark.* a large wrench having adjustable jaws that tighten as the pressure on the handle is increased.

stilly *adv* ('stɪllɪ). **1** *Arch. or literary.* quietly or calmly. ◆ *adj* ('stɪlɪ). **2** *Poetic.* still, quiet, or calm.

stilt (stɪlt) *n* **1** either of a pair of two long poles with footrests on which a person stands and walks, as used by circus clowns. **2** a long post or column that is used with others to support a building above ground level. **3** any of several shore birds similar to the avocets but having a straight bill. ◆ *vb* **4** (*tr*) to raise or place on or as if on stilts. [C14 (in the sense: crutch, handle of a plough): rel. to Low G *stilte* pole]

stilted 🅣 ('stɪltɪd) *adj* **1** (of speech, writing, etc.) formal, pompous, or bombastic. **2** not flowing continuously or naturally: *stilted conversation.* **3** *Archit.* (of an arch) having vertical piers between the impost and the springing.
▸ **'stiltedly** *adv* ▸ **'stiltedness** *n*

Stilton ('stɪltən) *n Trademark.* either of two rich cheeses, blue-veined (**blue Stilton**) or white (**white Stilton**), both very strong in flavour. [C18: named after *Stilton,* Cambridgeshire, where it was orig. sold]

stimulant 🅣 ('stɪmjʊlənt) *n* **1** a drug or similar substance that increases physiological activity, esp. of a particular organ. **2** any stimulating agent or thing. ◆ *adj* **3** stimulating. [C18: from L *stimulāns* goading, from *stimulāre* to urge on]

stimulate 🅣 ('stɪmjʊˌleɪt) *vb* **stimulates, stimulating, stimulated. 1** (*tr*) to arouse or quicken the activity or senses of. **2** (*tr*) *Physiol.* to excite (a nerve, organ, etc.) with a stimulus. **3** (*intr*) to act as a stimulant or stimulus. [C16: from L *stimulāre*]
▸ **'stimuˌlating** *adj* ▸ **ˌstimu'lation** *n* ▸ **'stimulative** *adj, n* ▸ **'stimuˌlator** *n*

stimulus 🅣 ('stɪmjʊləs) *n, pl* **stimuli** (-ˌlaɪ, -ˌliː). **1** something that stimulates or acts as an incentive. **2** any drug, agent, electrical impulse, or other factor able to cause a response in an organism. [C17: from L: a cattle goad]

sting 🅣 (stɪŋ) *vb* **stings, stinging, stung. 1** (of certain animals and plants) to inflict a wound on (an organism) by the injection of poison. **2** to feel or cause to feel a sharp mental or physical pain. **3** (*tr*) to goad or incite (esp. in **sting into action**). **4** (*tr*) *Inf.* to cheat, esp. by overcharging. ◆ *n* **5** a skin wound caused by the poison injected by certain insects or plants. **6** pain caused by or as if by the sting of a plant or animal. **7** a mental pain or pang: *a sting of conscience.* **8** a sharp pointed organ, such as the ovipositor of a wasp, by which poison can be injected. **9** the ability to sting: *a sharp sting in his criticism.* **10** something as painful or swift of action as a sting: *the sting of death.* **11** a sharp stimulus or incitement. **12** *Sl.* a swindle or fraud. **13** *Sl.* a police trap, esp. one whereby a person is enticed into committing a crime for which he is then arrested. [OE *stingan*]
▸ **'stinger** *n* ▸ **'stinging** *adj*

stinging nettle *n* See **nettle** (sense 1).

stingray ('stɪŋˌreɪ) *n* any of various rays having a whiplike tail bearing a serrated venomous spine capable of inflicting painful weals.

stingy[1] 🅣 ('stɪndʒɪ) *adj* **stingier, stingiest. 1** unwilling to spend or give. **2** insufficient or scanty. [C17 (? in the sense: ill-tempered): ?from *stinge,* dialect var. of STING]
▸ **'stingily** *adv* ▸ **'stinginess** *n*

THESAURUS

stiffen *vb* **1** = **brace**, reinforce, starch, tauten, tense **2** = **set**, coagulate, congeal, crystallize, harden, jell, solidify, thicken

stiff-necked *adj* = **stubborn**, boneheaded (*sl.*), contumacious, haughty, obstinate, opinionated, uncompromising, unreceptive

stifle *vb* **1** = **suppress**, check, choke back, cover up, curb, extinguish, gag, hush, muffle, prevent, repress, restrain, silence, smother, stop **3** = **suffocate**, asphyxiate, choke, smother, strangle

stigma *n* **1** = **disgrace**, blot, brand, dishonour, imputation, mark, reproach, shame, slur, smirch, spot, stain

stigmatize *vb* **1** = **brand**, cast a slur upon, defame, denounce, discredit, label, mark, pillory

still[1] *adj* **1** = **motionless**, at rest, calm, inert, lifeless, pacific, peaceful, placid, restful, serene, smooth, stationary, tranquil, undisturbed, unruffled, unstirring **2** = **silent**, hushed, noiseless, quiet, stilly (*poetic*) ◆ *n* **11** *Poetic* = **stillness**, hush, peace, quiet, silence, tranquillity ◆ *vb* **12** = **quieten**, allay, alleviate, appease, calm, hush, lull, pacify, quiet, settle, silence, smooth, smooth over, soothe, subdue, tranquillize ◆ *sentence connector* **15** = **however**, but, for all that, nevertheless, notwithstanding, yet

Antonyms *adj* ≠ **motionless:** active, agitated, astir, bustling, busy, humming, lively, moving, restless, turbulent ≠ **silent:** noisy ◆ *n* ≠ **stillness:** bustle, clamour, hubbub, noise, uproar ◆ *vb* ≠ **quieten:** aggravate, agitate, exacerbate, increase, inflame, rouse, stir up

stilted *adj* **1, 2** = **stiff**, artificial, arty-farty (*inf.*), bombastic, constrained, forced, fustian, grandiloquent, high-flown, high-sounding, inflated, laboured, pedantic, pompous, pretentious, unnatural, wooden

Antonyms *adj* flowing, fluid, free, natural, spontaneous, unaffected, unpretentious

stimulant *n* **1** = **pick-me-up** (*inf.*), analeptic, bracer (*inf.*), energizer, excitant, pep pill (*inf.*), restorative, reviver, tonic, upper (*sl.*)

Antonyms *n* depressant, downer (*sl.*), sedative, tranquilliser

stimulate *vb* **1, 3** = **encourage**, animate, arouse, fan, fire, foment, gee up, goad, impel, incite, inflame, inspire, instigate, prod, prompt, provoke, quicken, rouse, spur, turn on (*sl.*), urge, whet

stimulating *adj* **1, 3** = **exciting**, exhilarating, galvanic, inspiring, intriguing, provocative, provoking, rousing, stirring, thought-provoking

Antonyms *adj* as dry as dust, boring, dull, mind-numbing, unexciting, unimaginative, uninspiring, uninteresting, unstimulating

stimulus *n* **1** = **incentive**, clarion call, encouragement, fillip, geeing-up, goad, impetus, incitement, inducement, provocation, shot in the arm (*inf.*), spur

sting *vb* **1** = **hurt**, burn, pain, smart, tingle, wound **2** = **anger**, gall, incense, inflame, infuriate, nettle, pique, provoke, rile **4** *Informal* = **cheat**, defraud, do (*sl.*), fleece, overcharge, rip off (*sl.*), skin (*sl.*), stiff (*sl.*), swindle, take for a ride (*inf.*)

stingy[1] *adj* **1** = **mean**, avaricious, cheeseparing, close-fisted, covetous, illiberal, mingy (*Brit.*

stingy[2] ('stɪŋɪ) *adj* **stingier, stingiest.** *Inf.* stinging or capable of stinging.

stink ❶ (stɪŋk) *n* **1** a strong foul smell; stench. **2** *Sl.* a great deal of trouble (esp. in **make** *or* **raise a stink**). **3 like stink.** intensely; furiously. ◆ *vb* **stinks, stinking, stank** *or* **stunk; stunk.** (*mainly intr*) **4** to emit a foul smell. **5** *Sl.* to be thoroughly bad or abhorrent: *this town stinks.* **6** *Inf.* to have a very bad reputation: *his name stinks.* **7** to be of poor quality. **8** (foll. by *of* or *with*) *Sl.* to have or appear to have an excessive amount (of money). **9** (*tr;* usually foll. by *up*) *Inf.* to cause to stink. ◆ See also **stink out.** [OE *stincan*]
▸ **'stinky** *adj*

stink bomb *n* a small glass globe used by practical jokers: it releases a liquid with an offensive smell when broken.

stinker ❶ ('stɪŋkə) *n* **1** a person or thing that stinks. **2** *Sl.* a difficult or very unpleasant person or thing. **3** *Sl.* something of very poor quality. **4** *Inf.* any of several fulmars or related birds that feed on carrion.

stinkhorn ('stɪŋk,hɔːn) *n* any of various fungi having an unpleasant odour.

stinking ❶ ('stɪŋkɪŋ) *adj* **1** having a foul smell. **2** *Inf.* unpleasant or disgusting. **3** (*postpositive*) *Sl.* very drunk. **4 cry stinking fish.** to decry something, esp. one's own products. ◆ *adv* **5** *Inf.* (intensifier, expressing contempt): *stinking rich.*
▸ **'stinkingly** *adv* ▸ **'stinkingness** *n*

stinko ('stɪŋkəʊ) *adj* (*postpositive*) *Sl.* drunk.

stink out *vb* (*tr, adv*) **1** to drive out or away by a foul smell. **2** *Brit.* to cause to stink: *the smell of orange peel stinks out the room.*

stinkweed ('stɪŋk,wiːd) *n* **1** Also called: **wall mustard.** a cruciferous plant, naturalized in Britain and S and central Europe, having pale yellow flowers and a disagreeable smell when bruised. **2** any of various other ill-smelling plants.

stinkwood ('stɪŋk,wʊd) *n* **1** any of various trees having offensive-smelling wood, esp. a southern African lauraceous tree yielding a hard wood used for furniture. **2** the heavy durable wood of any of these trees.

stint[1] ❶ (stɪnt) *vb* **1** to be frugal or miserly towards (someone) with (something). **2** *Arch.* to stop or check (something). ◆ *n* **3** an allotted or fixed amount of work. **4** a limitation or check. [OE *styntan* to blunt]
▸ **'stinter** *n*

stint[2] (stɪnt) *n* any of various small sandpipers of a chiefly northern genus. [OE]

stipe (staɪp) *n* **1** a stalk in plants that bears reproductive structures, esp. the stalk bearing the cap of a mushroom. **2** the stalk that bears the leaflets of a fern or the thallus of a seaweed. **3** *Zool.* any stalklike part; stipes. [C18: via F from L *stīpes* tree trunk]

stipel ('staɪpᵊl) *n* a small paired leaflike structure at the base of certain leaflets; secondary stipule. [C19: via NL from L *stipula,* dim. of *stīpes* a log]
▸ **stipellate** (staɪ'pelɪt, -eɪt) *adj*

stipend ('staɪpend) *n* a fixed or regular amount of money paid as a salary or allowance, as to a clergyman. [C15: from OF *stipende,* from L *stīpendium* tax, from *stips* a contribution + *pendere* to pay out]

stipendiary (staɪ'pendɪərɪ) *adj* **1** receiving or working for regular pay: *a stipendiary magistrate.* **2** paid for by a stipend. ◆ *n, pl* **stipendiaries. 3** a person who receives regular payment. [C16: from L *stīpendiārius* concerning tribute, from *stīpendium* STIPEND]

stipes ('staɪpiːz) *n, pl* **stipites** ('stɪpɪ,tiːz). *Zool.* **1** the second maxillary segment in insects and crustaceans. **2** the eyestalk of a crab or similar crustacean. **3** any similar stemlike structure. [C18: from L; see STIPE]
▸ **stipiform** ('staɪpɪ,fɔːm) *or* **stipitiform** ('stɪpɪtɪ,fɔːm) *adj*

stipple ('stɪpᵊl) *vb* **stipples, stippling, stippled.** (*tr*) **1** to draw, engrave, or paint using dots or flecks. **2** to apply paint, powder, etc., to (something) with many light dabs. ◆ *n also* **stippling. 3** the technique of stippling or a picture produced by or using stippling. [C18: from Du. *stippelen,* from *stippen* to prick, from *stip* point]
▸ **'stippler** *n*

stipulate ❶ ('stɪpjʊ,leɪt) *vb* **stipulates, stipulating, stipulated. 1** (*tr; may take a clause as object*) to specify, often as a condition of an agreement. **2** (*intr;* foll. by *for*) to insist (on) as a term of an agreement. **3** (*tr; may take a clause as object*) to guarantee or promise. [C17: from L *stipulārī,* prob. from OL *stipulus* firm]
▸ **,stipu'lation** *n* ▸ **'stipu,lator** *n*

stipule ('stɪpjuːl) *n* a small paired usually leaflike outgrowth occurring at the base of a leaf or its stalk. [C18: from L; see STIPE]
▸ **stipular** ('stɪpjʊlə) *adj*

stir[1] ❶ (stɜː) *vb* **stirs, stirring, stirred. 1** to move an implement such as a spoon around in (a liquid) so as to mix up the constituents. **2** to change or cause to change position; disturb or be disturbed. **3** (*intr;* often foll. by *from*) to venture or depart (from one's usual or preferred place). **4** (*intr*) to be active after a rest; be up and about. **5** (*tr*) to excite or stimulate, esp. emotionally. **6** to move (oneself) briskly or vigorously; exert (oneself). **7** (*tr*) to rouse or awaken: *to stir someone from sleep; to stir memories.* **8** (when *tr,* foll. by *up*) to cause or incite others to cause (trouble, arguments, etc.). **9 stir one's stumps.** to move or become active. ◆ *n* **10** the act or an instance of stirring or the state of being stirred. **11** a strong reaction, esp. of excitement: *his publication caused a stir.* **12** a slight movement. **13** *NZ inf.* a noisy party. ◆ See also **stir up.** [OE *styrian*]

stir[2] (stɜː) *n* **1** a slang word for **prison:** *in stir.* **2 stir-crazy.** *Sl., chiefly US & Canad.* mentally disturbed as a result of being in prison. [C19: from ?]

stir-fry *vb* **stir-fries, stir-frying, stir-fried. 1** to cook (chopped meat, vegetables, etc.) rapidly by stirring them in a wok or frying pan over a high heat. ◆ *n, pl* **stir-fries. 2** a dish cooked in this way.

stirk (stɜːk) *n* **1** a heifer of 6 to 12 months old. **2** a yearling heifer or bullock. [OE *stierc*]

stirps (stɜːps) *n, pl* **stirpes** ('stɜːpiːz). **1** *Genealogy.* a line of descendants from an ancestor. **2** *Bot.* a race or variety. [C17: from L: root, family origin]

stirrer ('stɜːrə) *n* **1** a person or thing that stirs. **2** *Inf.* a person who deliberately causes trouble. **3** *Austral. & NZ inf.* a political activist or agitator.

stirring ❶ ('stɜːrɪŋ) *adj* **1** exciting the emotions; stimulating. **2** active, lively, or busy.
▸ **'stirringly** *adv*

stirrup ('stɪrəp) *n* **1** Also called: **stirrup iron.** either of two metal loops on a riding saddle, with a flat footpiece through which a rider puts his foot for support. They are attached to the saddle by **stirrup leathers. 2** a U-shaped support or clamp. **3** *Naut.* one of a set of ropes fastened to a yard at one end and having a thimble at the other through which a footrope is reeved for support. [OE *stigrāp,* from *stīg* step + *rāp* rope]

stirrup cup *n* a cup containing an alcoholic drink offered to a horseman ready to ride away.

stirrup pump *n* a hand-operated pump, the base of the cylinder of which is placed in a bucket of water: used in fighting fires.

stir up *vb* (*tr, adv*) to set in motion; instigate: *he stirred up trouble.*

stitch (stɪtʃ) *n* **1** a link made by drawing a thread through material by means of a needle. **2** a loop of yarn formed around an implement used in knitting, crocheting, etc. **3** a particular method of stitching or shape of stitch. **4** a sharp spasmodic pain in the side resulting from running or exercising. **5** (*usually used with a negative*) *Inf.* the least fragment of clothing: *he wasn't wearing a stitch.* **6** *Agriculture.* the ridge between two furrows. **7 drop a stitch.** to allow a loop of wool to fall off a knitting needle accidentally while knitting. **8 in stitches.** *Inf.* laughing uncontrollably. ◆ *vb* **9** (*tr*) to sew, fasten, etc., with stitches. **10** (*intr*) to be engaged in sewing. **11** (*tr*) to bind together (the leaves of a book, pamphlet, etc.) with wire staples or thread. ◆ *n, vb* **12** an informal word for **suture** (senses 1b, 5). [OE *stice* sting]
▸ **'stitcher** *n*

stitch up *vb* (*tr, adv*) **1** to join or mend by means of stitches or sutures. **2** *Sl.* **2a** to incriminate (someone) on a false charge by manufacturing evidence. **2b** to betray, cheat, or defraud. **3** *Sl.* to prearrange (some-

THESAURUS

inf.), miserly, near, niggardly, parsimonious, penny-pinching (*inf.*), penurious, scrimping, tight-arse (*taboo sl.*), tight-arsed (*taboo sl.*), tight as a duck's arse (*taboo sl.*), tight-ass (*US taboo sl.*), tight-assed (*US taboo sl.*), tightfisted, ungenerous **2** = **insufficient**, inadequate, meagre, measly (*inf.*), on the small side, pathetic, scant, scanty, skimpy, small

stink *n* **1** = **stench**, fetor, foulness, foul smell, malodour, noisomeness, pong (*Brit. inf.*) **2** *Slang As in* **make, create** *or* **kick up a stink** = **fuss**, brouhaha, commotion, deal of trouble (*inf.*), disturbance, hubbub, row, rumpus, scandal, stir, to-do, uproar, upset ◆ *vb* **4** = **reek**, offend the nostrils, pong (*Brit. inf.*), stink to high heaven (*inf.*), whiff (*Brit. sl.*) **5** *Slang* = **be bad**, be abhorrent, be detestable, be held in disrepute, be no good, be offensive, be rotten, have a bad name

stinker *n Slang* **2** = **scoundrel**, bounder (*old-fashioned Brit. sl.*), cad (*Brit. inf.*), cur, dastard (*arch.*), heel, nasty piece of work (*inf.*), rotter (*sl., chiefly Brit.*), scab, sod (*sl.*), swine **2** = **problem**, affliction, beast, difficulty, fine how-do-you-do (*inf.*), horror, impediment, plight, poser, predicament, shocker

stinking *adj* **1** = **foul-smelling**, fetid, ill-smelling, malodorous, mephitic, niffy (*Brit. sl.*), noisome, olid, pongy (*Brit. inf.*), reeking, smelly, whiffy (*Brit. sl.*) **2** *Informal* = **rotten**, contemptible, disgusting, low, low-down (*inf.*), mean, shitty (*taboo sl.*), unpleasant, vile, wretched

stint[1] *vb* **1** = **be mean**, be frugal, begrudge, be mingy (*Brit. inf.*), be parsimonious, be sparing, economize, hold back, save, scrimp, skimp on, spoil the ship for a ha'porth of tar, withhold ◆ *n* **3** = **share**, assignment, bit, period, quota, shift, spell, stretch, term, time, tour, turn

stipulate *vb* **1** = **specify**, agree, contract, covenant, engage, guarantee, insist upon, lay down, lay down *or* impose conditions, make a point of, pledge, postulate, promise, require, settle

stipulation *n* **1** = **condition**, agreement, clause, contract, engagement, precondition, prerequisite, provision, proviso, qualification, requirement, restriction, rider, settlement, *sine qua non,* specification, term

stir[1] *vb* **1** = **mix**, agitate, beat, disturb, flutter, move, quiver, rustle, shake, tremble **4** = **get moving**, bestir oneself, be up and about (*inf.*), budge, exert oneself, get a move on (*inf.*), hasten, look lively (*inf.*), make an effort, mill about, move, shake a leg (*inf.*) **5** = **stimulate**, affect, animate, arouse, awaken, electrify, excite, fire, incite, inflame, inspire, instigate, kindle, move, prod, prompt, provoke, quicken, raise, rouse, spur, thrill, touch, urge ◆ *n* **11** = **commotion**, activity, ado, agitation, bustle, disorder, disturbance, excitement, ferment, flurry, fuss, movement, to-do, tumult, uproar
Antonyms *vb* ≠ **stimulate:** check, curb, dampen, inhibit, restrain, stifle, suppress, throw cold water on (*inf.*)

stirring *adj* **1** = **exciting**, animating, dramatic, emotive, exhilarating, heady, impassioned, inspiring, intoxicating, lively, moving, rousing, spirited, stimulating, thrilling

thing) in a clandestine manner. ◆ *n* **stitch-up.** **4** *Sl.* a matter that has been prearranged clandestinely.

stitchwort ('stɪtʃˌwɜːt) *n* any of several low-growing N temperate herbaceous plants having small white star-shaped flowers.

stiver ('staɪvə) *n* **1** a former Dutch coin worth one twentieth of a guilder. **2** a small amount, esp. of money. [C16: from Du. *stuiver*]

stoa ('stəʊə) *n, pl* **stoae** ('stəʊiː) *or* **stoas.** a covered walk that has a colonnade on one or both sides, esp. as in ancient Greece. [C17: from Gk]

stoat (stəʊt) *n* a small Eurasian mammal, closely related to the weasels, having a brown coat and a black-tipped tail: in the northern parts of its range it has a white winter coat and is then known as an ermine. [C15: from ?]

stochastic (stɒ'kæstɪk) *adj* **1** *Statistics.* **1a** (of a random variable) having a probability distribution, usually with finite variance. **1b** (of a process) involving a random variable the successive values of which are not independent. **1c** (of a matrix) square with non-negative elements that add to unity in each row. **2** *Rare.* involving conjecture. [C17: from Gk *stokhastikos* capable of guessing, from *stokhazesthai* to aim at, conjecture, from *stokhos* a target]

stock ❶ (stɒk) *n* **1a** (*sometimes pl*) the total goods or raw material kept on the premises of a shop or business. **1b** (*as modifier*): *a stock book.* **2** a supply of something stored for future use. **3** *Finance.* **3a** the capital raised by a company through the issue and subscription of shares entitling their holders to dividends, partial ownership, and usually voting rights. **3b** the proportion of such capital held by an individual shareholder. **3c** the shares of a specified company or industry. **4** standing or status. **5a** farm animals, such as cattle and sheep, bred and kept for their meat, skins, etc. **5b** (*as modifier*): *stock farming.* **6** the trunk or main stem of a tree or other plant. **7** *Horticulture.* **7a** a rooted plant into which a scion is inserted during grafting. **7b** a plant or stem from which cuttings are taken. **8** the original type from which a particular race, family, group, etc., is derived. **9** a race, breed, or variety of animals or plants. **10** (*often pl*) a small pen in which a single animal can be confined. **11** a line of descent. **12** any of the major subdivisions of the human species; race or ethnic group. **13** the part of a rifle, etc., into which the barrel is set: held by the firer against the shoulder. **14** the handle of something, such as a whip or fishing rod. **15** the main body of a tool, such as the block of a plane. **16** short for **diestock, gunstock,** or **rolling stock.** **17** (formerly) the part of a plough to which the irons and handles were attached. **18** the main upright part of a supporting structure. **19** a liquid or broth in which meat, fish, bones, or vegetables have been simmered for a long time. **20** film material before exposure and processing. **21** Also called: **gillyflower.** any of several cruciferous plants such as **evening** or **night-scented stock,** of the Mediterranean region: cultivated for their brightly coloured flowers. **22** **Virginian stock.** a similar and related North American plant. **23** a long usually white neckcloth wrapped around the neck, worn in the 18th century and as part of modern riding dress. **24a** the repertoire of plays available to a repertory company. **24b** (*as modifier*): *a stock play.* **25** a log or block of wood. **26** See **laughing stock.** **27** **in stock.** **27a** stored on the premises or available for sale or use. **27b** supplied with goods of a specified kind. **28** **out of stock.** **28a** not immediately available for sale or use. **28b** not having goods of a specified kind immediately available. **29** **take stock.** **29a** to make an inventory. **29b** to make a general appraisal, esp. of prospects, resources, etc. **30** **take stock in.** to attach importance to. ◆ *adj* **31** staple; standard: *stock sizes in clothes.* **32** (*prenominal*) being a cliché; hackneyed: *a stock phrase.* ◆ *vb* **33** (*tr*) to keep (goods) for sale. **34** (*intr;* usually foll. by *up* or *up on*) to obtain a store of (something) for future use or sale: *to stock up on beer.* **35** (*tr*) to supply with live animals, fish, etc.: *to stock a farm.* **36** (*intr*) (of a plant) to put forth new shoots. **37** (*tr*) *Obs.* to punish by putting in the stocks. ◆ See also **stocks.** [OE *stocc* trunk (of a tree), stem, stick (the various senses developed from these meanings, as trunk of a tree, hence line of descent; structures made of timber; a store of timber or other goods for future use, hence an aggregate of goods, animals, etc.)]
▸ **'stocker** *n*

stockade (stɒ'keɪd) *n* **1** an enclosure or barrier of stakes and timbers. ◆ *vb* **stockades, stockading, stockaded.** **2** (*tr*) to surround with a stockade. [C17: from Sp. *estacada,* from *estaca* a stake, of Gmc origin]

stockbreeder ('stɒkˌbriːdə) *n* a person who breeds or rears livestock as an occupation.
▸ **'stockˌbreeding** *n*

stockbroker ('stɒkˌbrəʊkə) *n* a person who buys and sells securities on a commission basis for customers.
▸ **'stockˌbrokerage** *or* **'stockˌbroking** *n*

stockbroker belt *n Brit. inf.* the area outside a city, esp. London, in which rich commuters live.

stock car *n* **1** a car, usually a production saloon, strengthened and modified for a form of racing in which the cars often collide. **2** *US & Canad.* a railway wagon for carrying livestock.

stock dove *n* a European dove, smaller than the wood pigeon and having a grey plumage.

stock exchange *n* **1a** a highly organized market facilitating the purchase and sale of securities and operated by professional stockbrokers and market makers according to fixed rules. **1b** a place where securities are regularly traded. **1c** (*as modifier*): *a stock-exchange operator; stock-exchange prices.* **2** the prices or trading activity of a stock exchange: *the stock exchange fell heavily today.* ◆ Also called: **stock market.**

stockfish ('stɒkˌfɪʃ) *n, pl* **stockfish** *or* **stockfishes.** fish cured by splitting and drying in the air.

stockholder ('stɒkˌhəʊldə) *n* **1** an owner of corporate capital stock. **2** *Austral.* a person who keeps livestock.
▸ **'stockˌholding** *n*

stockhorse ('stɒkˌhɔːs) *n Austral.* a stockman's horse.

stockinet (ˌstɒkɪ'nɛt) *n* a machine-knitted elastic fabric used, esp. formerly, for stockings, underwear, etc. [C19: ?from earlier *stocking-net*]

stocking ('stɒkɪŋ) *n* **1** one of a pair of close-fitting garments made of knitted yarn to cover the foot and part or all of the leg. **2** something resembling this in position, function, etc. **3** **in (one's) stocking** *or* **stockinged feet.** wearing stockings or socks but no shoes. [C16: from dialect *stock* stocking + -ING[1]]
▸ **'stockinged** *adj*

stocking cap *n* a conical knitted cap, often with a tassel.

stocking filler *n Brit.* a present of a size suitable for inclusion in a Christmas stocking.

stock in trade *n* **1** goods in stock necessary for carrying on a business. **2** anything constantly used by someone as a part of his profession, occupation, or trade: *friendliness is the salesman's stock in trade.*

stockist ('stɒkɪst) *n Commerce, Brit.* a dealer who undertakes to maintain stocks of a specified product at or above a certain minimum in return for favourable buying terms granted by the manufacturer of the product.

stockjobber ('stɒkˌdʒɒbə) *n* **1** *Brit.* (formerly) a wholesale dealer on a stock exchange who sold securities to brokers without transacting directly with the public. See **market maker.** **2** *US, disparaging.* a stockbroker, esp. one dealing in worthless securities.
▸ **'stockˌjobbery** *or* **'stockˌjobbing** *n*

stockman ('stɒkmən, -ˌmæn) *n, pl* **stockmen.** **1a** a man engaged in the rearing or care of farm livestock, esp. cattle. **1b** an owner of cattle or other livestock. **2** *US & Canad.* a man employed in a warehouse or stockroom.

stock market *n* another name for **stock exchange.**

stockpile ('stɒkˌpaɪl) *vb* **stockpiles, stockpiling, stockpiled.** **1** to acquire and store a large quantity of (something). ◆ *n* **2** a large store or supply accumulated for future use.
▸ **'stockˌpiler** *n*

stockpot ('stɒkˌpɒt) *n Chiefly Brit.* a pot in which stock for soup, etc., is made or kept.

stockroom ('stɒkˌruːm, -ˌrʊm) *n* a room in which a stock of goods is kept, as in a shop or factory.

stock route *n Austral. & NZ.* a route designated for droving sheep or cattle.

stocks (stɒks) *pl n* **1** *History.* an instrument of punishment consisting of a heavy wooden frame with holes in which the feet, hands, or head of an offender were locked. **2** a frame used to support a boat while under construction. **3** *Naut.* a vertical post or shaft at the forward edge of a rudder, extended upwards for attachment to the steering controls. **4** **on the stocks.** in preparation or under construction.

stock-still *adv* absolutely still; motionless.

stocktaking ('stɒkˌteɪkɪŋ) *n* **1** the examination, counting, and valuing of goods on hand in a shop or business. **2** a reassessment of one's current situation, progress, prospects, etc.

stock watering *n Business.* the creation of more new shares in a company than is justified by its assets.

stock whip *n* a whip with a long lash and a short handle, used to herd cattle, etc.

stocky ❶ ('stɒkɪ) *adj* **stockier, stockiest.** (usually of a person) thickset; sturdy.
▸ **'stockily** *adv* ▸ **'stockiness** *n*

stockyard ('stɒkˌjɑːd) *n* a large yard with pens or covered buildings where farm animals are assembled, sold, etc.

stodge (stɒdʒ) *Inf.* ◆ *n* **1** heavy filling starchy food. **2** a dull person or subject. ◆ *vb* **stodges, stodging, stodged.** **3** to stuff (oneself or another) with food. [C17: ? blend of STUFF + *podge,* from *podgy* fat]

stodgy ❶ ('stɒdʒɪ) *adj* **stodgier, stodgiest.** **1** (of food) heavy or uninteresting. **2** excessively formal and conventional. [C19: from STODGE]
▸ **'stodgily** *adv* ▸ **'stodginess** *n*

THESAURUS

stock *n* **1** = **goods**, array, assortment, cache, choice, commodities, inventory, merchandise, range, selection, variety, wares **2** = **supply**, fund, hoard, reserve, reservoir, stockpile, store **3a** = **property**, assets, capital, funds, investment **5a** = **livestock**, beasts, cattle, domestic animals **11** = **lineage**, ancestry, background, breed, descent, extraction, family, forebears, house, line, line of descent, parentage, pedigree, race, strain, type, variety **29b** **take stock** = **review the situation**, appraise, estimate, see how the land lies, size up (*inf.*), weigh up ◆ *adj* **31** = **standard**, basic, commonplace, conventional, customary, formal, ordinary, regular, routine, run-of-the-mill, set, staple, traditional, usual **32** = **hackneyed**, banal, overused, stereotyped, trite, worn-out ◆ *vb* **33** = **sell**, deal in, handle, keep, supply, trade in **34** *foll. by* **up, up on** = **store (up)**, accumulate, amass, buy up, gather, hoard, lay in, put away, replenish, save, supply **35** = **provide with**, equip, fill, fit out, furnish, kit out, provision, supply

stocky *adj* = **thickset**, chunky, dumpy, mesomorphic, solid, stubby, stumpy, sturdy

stodgy *adj* **1** = **heavy**, filling, leaden, starchy, substantial **2** = **dull**, boring, dull as ditchwater, formal, fuddy-duddy (*inf.*), heavy going, ho-hum, laboured, staid, stuffy, tedious, tiresome, turgid, unexciting, unimaginative, uninspired
Antonyms *adj* ≠ **heavy:** appetizing, fluffy, insub-

stoep (stu:p) *n S. African.* a veranda. [from Afrik., from Du.]

stoic ('stəʊɪk) *n* **1** a person who maintains stoical qualities. ◆ *adj* **2** a variant of **stoical.**

Stoic ('stəʊɪk) *n* **1** a member of the ancient Greek school of philosophy founded by Zeno of Citium (?336–?264 B.C.), holding that virtue and happiness can be attained only by submission to destiny and the natural law. ◆ *adj* **2** of or relating to the doctrines of the Stoics. [C16: via L from Gk *stōikos,* from *stoa,* the porch in Athens where Zeno taught]

stoical Ⓣ ('stəʊɪkᵊl) *adj* characterized by impassivity or resignation.
► **'stoically** *adv*

stoichiometry *or* **stoicheiometry** (ˌstɔɪkɪ'ɒmɪtrɪ) *n* the branch of chemistry concerned with the proportions in which elements are combined in compounds and the quantitative relationships between reactants and products in chemical reactions. [C19: from Gk *stoikheion* element + -METRY]
► **ˌstoichio'metric** *or* **ˌstoicheio'metric** *adj*

stoicism Ⓣ ('stəʊɪˌsɪzəm) *n* **1** indifference to pleasure and pain. **2** (*cap.*) the philosophy of the Stoics.

stoke (stəʊk) *vb* **stokes, stoking, stoked. 1** to feed, stir, and tend (a fire, furnace, etc.). **2** (*tr*) to tend the furnace of; act as a stoker for. [C17: back formation from STOKER]

stokehold ('stəʊkˌhəʊld) *n Naut.* **1** a coal bunker for a ship's furnace. **2** the hold for a ship's boilers; fire room.

stokehole ('stəʊkˌhəʊl) *n* **1** another word for **stokehold. 2** a hole in a furnace through which it is stoked.

stoker ('stəʊkə) *n* a person employed to tend a furnace, as on a steamship. [C17: from Du., from *stoken* to stoke]

stoke up *vb* (*adv*) **1** to feed and tend (a fire, etc.) with fuel. **2** (*intr*) to fill oneself with food.

STOL (stɒl) *n* **1** a system in which an aircraft can take off and land in a short distance. **2** an aircraft using this system. Cf. **VTOL** [C20: *s(hort) t(ake)o(ff and) l(anding)*]

stole[1] (stəʊl) *vb* the past tense of **steal.**

stole[2] (stəʊl) *n* **1** a long scarf or shawl, worn by women. **2** a long narrow scarf worn by various officiating clergymen. [OE *stole,* from L *stola,* from Gk *stolē* clothing]

stolen Ⓣ ('stəʊlən) *vb* the past participle of **steal.**

stolid Ⓣ ('stɒlɪd) *adj* showing little or no emotion or interest. [C17: from L *stolidus* dull]
► **stolidity** (stɒ'lɪdɪtɪ) *or* **'stolidness** *n* ► **'stolidly** *adv*

stolon ('stəʊlən) *n* **1** another name for **runner** (sense 9). **2** a branching structure in lower animals, esp. the anchoring rootlike part of colonial organisms. [C17: from L *stolō* shoot]
► **stoloniferous** (ˌstəʊlə'nɪfərəs) *adj*

stoma ('stəʊmə) *n, pl* **stomata. 1** *Bot.* an epidermal pore in plant leaves, that controls the passage of gases into and out of a plant. **2** *Zool., anat.* a mouth or mouthlike part. **3** *Surgery.* an artificial opening made in a tubular organ, esp. the colon or ileum. See **colostomy, ileostomy.** [C17: via NL from Gk: mouth]

stomach Ⓣ ('stʌmək) *n* **1** (in vertebrates) the enlarged muscular saclike part of the alimentary canal in which food is stored until it has been partially digested. Related adj: **gastric. 2** the corresponding organ in invertebrates. **3** the abdominal region. **4** desire, appetite, or inclination: *I have no stomach for arguments.* ◆ *vb* (*tr; used mainly in negative constructions*) **5** to tolerate; bear: *I can't stomach his bragging.* **6** to eat or digest: *he cannot stomach oysters.* [C14: from OF *stomaque,* from L *stomachus,* from Gk *stomakhos,* from *stoma* mouth]

stomachache ('stʌməkˌeɪk) *n* pain in the stomach, as from acute indigestion. Also called: **stomach upset, upset stomach.**

stomacher ('stʌməkə) *n* a decorative V-shaped panel of stiff material worn over the chest and stomach by men and women in the 16th century, later only by women.

stomachic (stə'mækɪk) *adj also* **stomachical. 1** stimulating gastric activity. **2** of or relating to the stomach. ◆ *n* **3** a stomachic medicine.

stomach pump *n Med.* a suction device for removing stomach contents by a tube inserted through the mouth.

stomata ('stəʊmətə, 'stɒm-, stəʊ'mɑːtə) *n* the plural of **stoma.**

stomatitis (ˌstəʊmə'taɪtɪs, ˌstɒm-) *n* inflammation of the mouth.
► **stomatitic** (ˌstəʊmə'tɪtɪk, ˌstɒm-) *adj*

stomato- *or before a vowel* **stomat-** *combining form.* indicating the mouth or a mouthlike part: *stomatology.* [from Gk *stoma, stomat-*]

stomatology (ˌstəʊmə'tɒlədʒɪ) *n* the branch of medicine concerned with the mouth.
► **stomatological** (ˌstəʊmətə'lɒdʒɪkᵊl) *adj*

-stome *n combining form.* indicating a mouth or opening resembling a mouth: *peristome.* [from Gk *stoma* mouth, & *stomion* little mouth]

-stomous *adj combining form.* having a specified type of mouth.

stomp (stɒmp) *vb* **1** (*intr*) to tread or stamp heavily. ◆ *n* **2** a rhythmic stamping jazz dance. [var. of STAMP]
► **'stomper** *n*

-stomy *n combining form.* indicating a surgical operation performed to make an artificial opening into or for a specified part: *cytostomy.* [from Gk *-stomia,* from *stoma* mouth]

stone (stəʊn) *n* **1** the hard compact nonmetallic material of which rocks are made. **2** a small lump of rock; pebble. **3** short for **gemstone. 4a** a piece of rock designed or shaped for some particular purpose. **4b** (*in combination*): *gravestone; millstone.* **5a** something that resembles a stone. **5b** (*in combination*): *hailstone.* **6** the woody central part of such fruits as the peach and plum, that contains the seed; endocarp. **7** any similar hard part of a fruit, such as the stony seed of a date. **8** (*pl* **stone**) *Brit.* a unit of weight, used esp. to express human body weight, equal to 14 pounds or 6.350 kilograms. **9** Also called: **granite.** the rounded heavy mass of granite or iron used in the game of curling. **10** *Pathol.* a nontechnical name for **calculus. 11** *Printing.* a table with a very flat iron or stone surface upon which pages are composed. **12** (*modifier*) relating to or made of stone: *a stone house.* **13** (*modifier*) made of stoneware: *a stone jar.* **14 cast a stone** (**at**). cast aspersions (upon). **15 heart of stone.** an obdurate or unemotional nature. **16 leave no stone unturned.** to do everything possible to achieve an end. ◆ *vb* **stones, stoning, stoned.** (*tr*) **17** to throw stones at, esp. to kill. **18** to remove the stones from. **19** to furnish or provide with stones. [OE *stān*]
► **'stoner** *n*

stone- *prefix* very, completely: *stone-blind, stone-cold.* [from STONE in sense of "like a stone"]

Stone Age *n* **1** a period in human culture identified by the use of stone implements. ◆ *modifier.* **Stone-Age. 2** (*sometimes not caps.*) of or relating to this period.

stone-blind *adj* completely blind. Cf. **sand-blind.**

stonechat ('stəʊnˌtʃæt) *n* an Old World songbird having a black plumage with a reddish-brown breast. [C18: from its cry, which sounds like clattering pebbles]

stone-cold *adj* **1** completely cold. **2 stone-cold sober.** completely sober.

stonecrop ('stəʊnˌkrɒp) *n* any of various N temperate plants having fleshy leaves and typically red, yellow, or white flowers.

stone curlew *n* any of several brownish shore birds having a large head and eyes. Also called: **thick-knee.**

stonecutter ('stəʊnˌkʌtə) *n* **1** a person who is skilled in cutting and carving stone. **2** a machine used to dress stone.
► **'stoneˌcutting** *n*

stoned (stəʊnd) *adj Sl.* under the influence of drugs or alcohol.

stone-deaf *adj* completely deaf.

stonefish ('stəʊnˌfɪʃ) *n, pl* **stonefish** *or* **stonefishes.** a venomous tropical marine fish that resembles a piece of rock on the seabed.

stonefly ('stəʊnˌflaɪ) *n, pl* **stoneflies.** any of various insects, in which the larvae are aquatic, living beneath stones.

stone fruit *n* the nontechnical name for **drupe.**

stonemason ('stəʊnˌmeɪsᵊn) *n* a person who is skilled in preparing stone for building.
► **'stoneˌmasonry** *n*

stone pine *n* a pine tree with a short bole and radiating branches forming an umbrella shape.

stone's throw *n* a short distance.

stonewall (ˌstəʊn'wɔːl) *vb* **1** (*intr*) *Cricket.* (of a batsman) to play defensively. **2** to obstruct (an investigation, etc.), esp. by giving uncommunicative answers to questioning. **3** to obstruct or hinder (parliamentary business).
► **ˌstone'waller** *n*

stoneware ('stəʊnˌwɛə) *n* **1** a hard opaque pottery, fired at a very high temperature. ◆ *adj* **2** made of stoneware.

stonewashed ('stəʊnˌwɒʃt) *adj* (of clothes or fabric) given a worn faded look by being subjected to the abrasive action of many small pieces of pumice.

stonework ('stəʊnˌwɜːk) *n* **1** any structure or part of a building made of stone. **2** the process of dressing or setting stones.
► **'stoneˌworker** *n*

stonkered ('stɒŋkəd) *adj Sl.* completely exhausted or beaten. [C20: from *stonker* to beat, from ?]

stony Ⓣ *or* **stoney** ('stəʊnɪ) *adj* **stonier, stoniest. 1** of or resembling stone. **2** abounding in stone or stones. **3** unfeeling or obdurate. **4** short for **stony-broke.**
► **'stonily** *adv* ► **'stoniness** *n*

stony-broke *adj Brit. sl.* completely without money; penniless.

stony-hearted *adj* unfeeling; hardhearted.
► **ˌstony-'heartedness** *n*

stood (stʊd) *vb* the past tense and past participle of **stand.**

THESAURUS

stantial, light ≠ **dull:** animated, exciting, fashionable, fresh, interesting, light, lively, readable, stimulating, trendy (*Brit. inf.*), up-to-date

stoical *adj* **2** = **resigned,** calm, cool, dispassionate, impassive, imperturbable, indifferent, long-suffering, philosophic, phlegmatic, stoic, stolid

stoicism *n* **1** = **resignation,** acceptance, calmness, dispassion, fatalism, forbearance, fortitude, impassivity, imperturbability, indifference, long-suffering, patience, stolidity

stolen *adj* = **hot** (*sl.*), bent (*sl.*), hooky (*sl.*)

stolid *adj* = **apathetic,** bovine, doltish, dozy (*Brit. inf.*), dull, heavy, lumpish, obtuse, slow, stupid, unemotional, wooden
Antonyms *adj* acute, animated, bright, emotional, energetic, excitable, intelligent, interested, lively, passionate, sharp, smart

stomach *n* **1** = **belly,** abdomen, breadbasket (*sl.*), gut (*inf.*), inside(s) (*inf.*), paunch, pot, potbelly, spare tyre (*inf.*), tummy (*inf.*) **4** = **inclination,** appetite, desire, mind, relish, taste ◆ *vb* **5** = **bear,** abide, endure, hack (*sl.*), put up with (*inf.*), reconcile *or* resign oneself to, submit to, suffer, swallow, take, tolerate

stony *adj* **3** = **cold,** adamant, blank, callous, chilly, expressionless, frigid, hard, harsh, heartless, hostile, icy, indifferent, inexorable, merciless, obdurate, pitiless, unfeeling, unforgiving, unresponsive

DICTIONARY

stooge 🅣 (stu:dʒ) *n* **1** an actor who feeds lines to a comedian or acts as his butt. **2** *Sl.* someone who is taken advantage of by another. ◆ *vb* **stooges, stooging, stooged. 3** (*intr*) *Sl.* to act as a stooge. [C20: from ?]

stook (stu:k) *n* **1** a number of sheaves set upright in a field to dry with their heads together. ◆ *vb* **2** (*tr*) to set up (sheaves) in stooks. [C15: var. of *stouk*, of Gmc origin]
▸ **'stooker** *n*

stool (stu:l) *n* **1** a backless seat or footrest consisting of a small flat piece of wood, etc., resting on three or four legs, a pedestal, etc. **2** a rootstock or base of a plant from which shoots, etc., are produced. **3** a cluster of shoots growing from such a base. **4** *Chiefly US.* a decoy used in hunting. **5** waste matter evacuated from the bowels. **6** a lavatory seat. **7** (in W Africa, esp. Ghana) a chief's throne. **8 fall between two stools. 8a** to fail through vacillation between two alternatives. **8b** to be in an unsatisfactory situation through not belonging to either of two categories or groups. ◆ *vb* (*intr*) **9** (of a plant) to send up shoots from the base of the stem, rootstock, etc. **10** to lure wildfowl with a decoy. [OE *stōl*]

stool ball *n* a game resembling cricket, still played by girls and women in Sussex, England.

stool pigeon *n* **1** an informer for the police. **2** *Sl.* a person acting as a decoy. [C19: from use of pigeon fixed to a stool as a decoy]

stoop[1] 🅣 (stu:p) *vb* (*mainly intr*) **1** (*also tr*) to bend (the body) forward and downward. **2** to carry oneself with head and shoulders habitually bent forward. **3** (often foll. by *to*) to abase or degrade oneself. **4** (often foll. by *to*) to condescend; deign. **5** (of a bird of prey) to swoop down. ◆ *n* **6** the act, position, or characteristic of stooping. **7** a lowering from a position of dignity or superiority. **8** a downward swoop, esp. of a bird of prey. [OE *stūpan*]
▸ **'stooping** *adj*

stoop[2] (stu:p) *n US.* an open porch or small platform with steps leading up to it at the entrance to a building. [C18: from Du. *stoep*, of Gmc origin]

stop 🅣 (stɒp) *vb* **stops, stopping, stopped. 1** to cease from doing or being (something); discontinue. **2** to cause (something moving) to halt or (of something moving) to come to a halt. **3** (*tr*) to prevent the continuance or completion of. **4** (*tr;* often foll. by *from*) to prevent or restrain: *to stop George from fighting.* **5** (*tr*) to keep back: *to stop supplies.* **6** (*tr*) to intercept or hinder in transit: *to stop a letter.* **7** (*tr;* often foll. by *up*) to block or plug, esp. so as to close: *to stop up a pipe.* **8** (*tr;* often foll. by *up*) to fill a hole or opening in: *to stop up a wall.* **9** (*tr*) to staunch or stem: *to stop a wound.* **10** (*tr*) to instruct a bank not to honour (a cheque). **11** (*tr*) to deduct (money) from pay. **12** (*tr*) *Brit.* to provide with punctuation. **13** (*tr*) *Boxing.* to beat (an opponent) by a knockout. **14** (*tr*) *Inf.* to receive (a blow, hit, etc.). **15** (*intr*) to stay or rest: *we stopped at the Robinsons'.* **16** (*tr*) *Rare.* to defeat, beat, or kill. **17** (*tr*) *Music.* **17a** to alter the vibrating length of (a string on a violin, guitar, etc.) by pressing down on it at some point with the finger. **17b** to alter the vibrating length of an air column in a wind instrument by closing (a finger hole, etc.). **17c** to produce (a note) in this manner. **18** *Bridge.* to have a protecting card or winner in (a suit in which one's opponents are strong). **19 stop at nothing.** to be prepared to do anything; be unscrupulous or ruthless. ◆ *n* **20** an arrest of movement or progress. **21** the act of stopping or the state of being stopped. **22** a place where something halts or pauses: *a bus stop.* **23** a stay in or as if in the course of a journey. **24** the act or an instance of blocking or obstructing. **25** a plug or stopper. **26** a block, screw, etc., that prevents, limits, or terminates the motion of a mechanism or moving part. **27** *Brit.* a punctuation mark, esp. a full stop. **28** *Music.* **28a** the act of stopping the string, finger hole, etc., of an instrument. **28b** a set of organ pipes or harpsichord strings that may be allowed to sound as a group by muffling or silencing all other such sets. **28c** a knob, lever, or handle on an organ, etc., that is operated to allow sets of pipes to sound. **28d** an analogous device on a harpsichord or other instrument with variable registers, such as an electronic instrument. **29 pull out all the stops. 29a** to play at full volume. **29b** to spare no effort. **30** Also called: **stop consonant.** *Phonetics.* any of a class of consonants articulated by first making a complete closure at some point of the vocal tract and then releasing it abruptly with audible plosion. **31** Also called: **f-stop.** *Photog.* **31a** a setting of the aperture of a camera lens, calibrated to the corresponding f-number. **31b** another name for **diaphragm** (sense 4). **32** Also called: **stopper.** *Bridge.* a protecting card or winner in a suit in which one's opponents are strong. ◆ See also **stop off, stop out, stopover.** [C14: from OE *stoppian* (unattested), as in *forstoppian* to plug the ear, ult. from LL *stuppāre* to stop with tow, from L *stuppa* tow, from Gk *stuppē*]
▸ **'stoppable** *adj*

stopbank ('stɒpbæŋk) *n NZ.* an embankment to prevent flooding.

stop bath *n* a weakly acidic solution used to stop the action of a developer on a film, plate, or paper before the material is immersed in fixer.

stopcock ('stɒp,kɒk) *n* a valve used to control or stop the flow of a fluid in a pipe.

stope (stəup) *n* **1** a steplike excavation made in a mine to extract ore. ◆ *vb* **stopes, stoping, stoped. 2** to mine (ore, etc.) in stopes. [C18: prob. from Low G *stope*]

stopgap 🅣 ('stɒp,gæp) *n* **a** a temporary substitute. **b** (*as modifier*): *a stopgap programme.*

stop-go *adj Brit.* (of economic policy) characterized by deliberate alternate expansion and contraction of aggregate demand in an effort to curb inflation and eliminate balance-of-payments deficits, and yet maintain full employment.

stoplight ('stɒp,laɪt) *n* **1** a red light on a traffic signal indicating that vehicles or pedestrians coming towards it should stop. **2** another word for **brake light.**

stop-loss *adj Business.* of or relating to an order to a broker in a commodity or security market to close an open position at a specified price in order to limit any loss.

stop off *vb also* **stop in,** (esp. US) **stop by. 1** (*intr, adv;* often foll. by *at*) to halt and call somewhere, as on a visit or errand, esp. en route to another place. ◆ *n* **stopoff. 2a** a break in a journey. **2b** (*as modifier*): *stopoff point.*

stop out *vb* (*adv*) **1** (*tr*) to cover (part of the area) of a piece of cloth, printing plate, etc., to prevent it from being dyed, etched, etc. **2** (*intr*) to remain out of a house, esp. overnight.

stopover ('stɒp,əuvə) *n* **1** a stopping place on a journey. ◆ *vb* **stop over. 2** (*intr, adv*) to make a stopover.

stoppage 🅣 ('stɒpɪdʒ) *n* **1** the act of stopping or the state of being stopped. **2** something that stops or blocks. **3** a deduction of money, as from pay. **4** an organized cessation of work, as during a strike.

stoppage time *n Soccer, rugby, etc.* another name for **injury time.**

stopped (stɒpt) *adj* (of a pipe, esp. an organ pipe) closed at one end and thus sounding an octave lower than an open pipe of the same length.

stopper ('stɒpə) *n* **1** Also called: **stopple.** a plug or bung for closing a bottle, pipe, duct, etc. **2** a person or thing that stops or puts an end to something. **3** *Bridge.* another name for **stop** (sense 32). ◆ *vb* **4** (*tr*) Also: **stopple.** to close or fit with a stopper.

stopping ('stɒpɪŋ) *n* **1** *Brit. inf.* a dental filling. ◆ *adj* **2** *Chiefly Brit.* making many stops in a journey: *a stopping train.*

stop press *n Brit.* **1** news items inserted into a newspaper after the printing has been started. **2** the space regularly left blank for this.

stopwatch ('stɒp,wɒtʃ) *n* a type of watch used for timing sporting events, etc., accurately, having a device for stopping the hands instantly.

storage ('stɔ:rɪdʒ) *n* **1** the act of storing or the state of being stored. **2** space or an area reserved for storing. **3** a charge made for storing. **4** *Computing.* **4a** the act or process of storing information in a computer memory or on a disk, etc. **4b** (*as modifier*): *storage capacity.*

storage battery *n* another name (esp. US) for **accumulator** (sense 1).

storage capacity *n* the maximum number of bits, bytes, words, etc., that can be held in a memory system such as that of a computer or of the brain.

storage device *n* a piece of computer equipment, such as a magnetic tape, disk, drum, etc., in or on which information can be stored.

storage heater *n* an electric device capable of accumulating and radiating heat generated by off-peak electricity.

storax ('stɔ:ræks) *n* **1** any of numerous trees or shrubs of tropical and subtropical regions, having drooping showy white flowers. **2** a vanilla-scented solid resin obtained from one of these trees, formerly used as incense and in perfumery and medicine. **3** a liquid aromatic balsam obtained from liquidambar trees and used in perfumery and medicine. [C14: via LL from Gk *sturax*]

store 🅣 (stɔ:) *vb* **stores, storing, stored. 1** (*tr*) to keep, set aside, or accumulate for future use. **2** (*tr*) to place in a warehouse, depository, etc., for safekeeping. **3** (*tr*) to supply, provide, or stock. **4** (*intr*) to be put into

THESAURUS

stooge *n* **1, 2 = pawn,** butt, dupe, fall guy (*inf.*), foil, henchman, lackey, patsy (*sl., chiefly US & Canad.*), puppet

stoop[1] *vb* **1 = bend,** be bowed *or* round-shouldered, bow, crouch, descend, duck, hunch, incline, kneel, lean, squat **3, 4** *foll. by* **to = lower oneself by,** condescend to, deign to, demean oneself by, descend to, resort to, sink to ◆ *n* **6 = slouch,** bad posture, droop, round-shoulderedness, sag, slump

stop *vb* **1 = halt,** axe (*inf.*), belay (*Nautical*), be over, break off, bring *or* come to a halt *or* standstill, call it a day (*inf.*), cease, come to an end, conclude, cut out (*inf.*), cut short, desist, discontinue, draw up, end, finish, leave off, pack in (*Brit. inf.*), pause, peter out, pull up, put an end to, quit, refrain, run down, run its course, shut down, stall, terminate **3 = prevent,** arrest, bar, break, check, close, forestall, frustrate, hinder, hold back, impede, intercept, interrupt, nip (something) in the bud, rein in, repress, restrain, silence, suspend **7 = plug,** block, bung, obstruct, seal, staunch, stem **15 = stay,** break one's journey, lodge, put up, rest, sojourn, tarry ◆ *n* **20 = block,** bar, break, check, control, hindrance, impediment, plug, stoppage **21 = end,** cessation, conclusion, discontinuation, finish, halt, standstill **22 = station,** depot, destination, halt, stage, termination, terminus **23 = stay,** break, rest, sojourn, stopover, visit
Antonyms *vb* ≠ **halt:** advance, begin, commence, continue, get going, get under way, give the go ahead, go, institute, keep going, keep on, kick off (*inf.*), proceed, set in motion, set off, start ≠ **prevent:** assist, boost, encourage, expedite, facilitate, further, gee up, hasten, promote, push ◆ *n* ≠ **end:** beginning, commencement, kick-off (*inf.*), start ≠ **block:** boost, encouragement, geeing-up, incitement

stopgap *n* **a = makeshift,** improvisation, resort, shift, substitute, temporary expedient ◆ *modifier* **b = makeshift,** emergency, impromptu, improvised, provisional, rough-and-ready, temporary

stoppage *n* **1 = stopping,** abeyance, arrest, close, closure, cutoff, deduction, discontinuance, halt, hindrance, lay-off, shutdown, standstill **2 = blockage,** check, curtailment, interruption, obstruction, occlusion, stopping up

store *vb* **1 = put by,** accumulate, deposit, garner, hoard, husband, keep, keep in reserve, lay by *or*

storage. **5** *Computing.* to enter or retain (information) in a storage device. ◆ *n* **6a** an establishment for the retail sale of goods and services. **6b** (*in combination*): *storefront.* **7** a large supply or stock kept for future use. **8** short for **department store. 9a** a storage place such as a warehouse or depository. **9b** (*in combination*): *storeman.* **10** the state of being stored (esp. in **in store**). **11** a large amount or quantity. **12** *Computers, chiefly Brit.* another name for **memory** (sense 7). **13 in store.** forthcoming or imminent. **14 lay, put,** *or* **set store by.** to value or reckon as important. ◆ *adj* **15** (of cattle, sheep, etc.) bought lean to be fattened up for market. ◆ See also **stores.** [C13: from OF *estor,* from *estorer* to restore, from L *instaurāre* to refresh]
▸**'storable** *adj*

store card *n* another name for **charge card.**

storehouse ('stɔːˌhaʊs) *n* a place where things are stored.

storekeeper ('stɔːˌkiːpə) *n* a manager, owner, or keeper of a store.
▸**'storeˌkeeping** *n*

store of value *n Econ.* the function of money that enables goods and services to be paid for a considerable time after they have been acquired.

storeroom ('stɔːˌruːm, -ˌrʊm) *n* **1** a room in which things are stored. **2** room for storing.

stores (stɔːz) *pl n* supply or stock of something, esp. essentials, for a specific purpose.

storey *or esp. US* **story** ('stɔːrɪ) *n, pl* **storeys** *or* **stories. 1** a floor or level of a building. **2** a set of rooms on one level. [C14: from Anglo-L *historia,* picture, from L: narrative, prob. from the pictures on medieval windows]

storeyed *or US* **storied** ('stɔːrɪd) *adj* **a** having a storey or storeys. **b** (*in combination*): *a two-storeyed house.*

storied ('stɔːrɪd) *adj* **1** recorded in history or in a story. **2** decorated with narrative scenes.

stork (stɔːk) *n* any of a family of large wading birds, chiefly of warm regions of the Old World, having very long legs and a long stout pointed bill, and typically having a white-and-black plumage. [OE *storc*]

storksbill ('stɔːksˌbɪl) *n* a plant related to the geranium, having pink or reddish-purple flowers and fruits with a beaklike process.

storm 🅣 (stɔːm) *n* **1a** a violent weather condition of strong winds, rain, hail, thunder, lightning, blowing sand, snow, etc. **1b** (*as modifier*): *storm cloud.* **1c** (*in combination*): *stormproof.* **2** *Meteorol.* a wind of force 10 on the Beaufort scale, reaching speeds of 55 to 63 mph. **3** a strong or violent reaction: *a storm of protest.* **4** a direct assault on a stronghold. **5** a heavy discharge or rain, as of bullets or missiles. **6** short for **storm window. 7 storm in a teacup.** *Brit.* a violent fuss or disturbance over a trivial matter. **8 take by storm. 8a** to capture or overrun by a violent assault. **8b** to overwhelm and enthral. ◆ *vb* **9** to attack or capture (something) suddenly and violently. **10** (*intr*) to be vociferously angry. **11** (*intr*) to move or rush violently or angrily. **12** (*intr;* with *it* as subject) to rain, hail, or snow hard and be very windy, often with thunder and lightning. [OE]

stormbound ('stɔːmˌbaʊnd) *adj* detained or harassed by storms.

storm centre *n* **1** the centre of a cyclonic storm, etc., where pressure is lowest. **2** the centre of any disturbance or trouble.

storm cloud *n* **1** a heavy dark cloud presaging rain or a storm. **2** a herald of disturbance, anger, etc.: *the storm clouds of war.*

storm-cock *n* another name for **mistle thrush.**

storm cone *n Brit.* a canvas cone hoisted as a warning of high winds.

storm door *n* an additional door outside an ordinary door, providing extra insulation against wind, cold, rain, etc.

storming ('stɔːmɪŋ) *adj Inf.* characterized by or displaying dynamism, speed, and energy: *a storming performance.*

storm lantern *n* another name for **hurricane lamp.**

storm trooper *n* **1** a member of the Nazi SA. **2** a member of a force of shock troops.

storm window *n* **1** an additional window fitted outside an ordinary window to provide insulation against wind, cold, rain, etc. **2** a type of dormer window.

stormy 🅣 ('stɔːmɪ) *adj* **stormier, stormiest. 1** characterized by storms. **2** involving or characterized by violent disturbance or emotional outburst.
▸**'stormily** *adv* ▸**'storminess** *n*

stormy petrel *n* **1** Also called: **storm petrel.** any of various small petrels typically having dark plumage and paler underparts. **2** a person who brings or portends trouble.

Storting *or* **Storthing** ('stɔːtɪŋ) *n* the parliament of Norway. [C19: Norwegian, from *stor* great + *thing* assembly]

story[1] 🅣 ('stɔːrɪ) *n, pl* **stories. 1** a narration of a chain of events told or written in prose or verse. **2** Also called: **short story.** a piece of fiction, briefer and usually less detailed than a novel. **3** Also called: **story line.** the plot of a book, film, etc. **4** an event that could be the subject of a narrative. **5** a report or statement on a matter or event. **6** the event or material for such a report. **7** *Inf.* a lie, fib, or untruth. **8 cut** (*or* **make**) **a long story short.** to leave out details in a narration. **9 the same old story.** *Inf.* the familiar or regular course of events. **10 the story goes.** it is commonly said or believed. ◆ *vb* **stories, storying, storied.** (*tr*) **11** to decorate (a pot, wall, etc.) with scenes from history or legends. [C13: from Anglo-F *estorie,* from L *historia;* see HISTORY]

story[2] ('stɔːrɪ) *n, pl* **stories.** another spelling (esp. US) of **storey.**

storyboard ('stɔːrɪˌbɔːd) *n* (in films, television, etc.) a series of sketches or photographs showing the sequence of shots or images planned for a film.

storybook ('stɔːrɪˌbʊk) *n* **1** a book containing stories, esp. for children. ◆ *adj* **2** unreal or fantastic: *a storybook world.*

storyteller 🅣 ('stɔːrɪˌtɛlə) *n* **1** a person who tells stories. **2** *Inf.* a liar.
▸**'storyˌtelling** *n*

Stoss (*German* ʃtoːs) *n* **Veit** (faɪət). ?1445–1533, German Gothic sculptor and woodcarver. His masterpiece is the high altar in the Church of St Mary, Cracow (1477–89).

stoup *or* **stoop** (stuːp) *n* **1** a small basin for holy water. **2** *Dialect.* a bucket or cup. [C14 (in the sense: bucket): from ON]

stoush (staʊʃ) *Austral. & NZ sl.* ◆ *vb* **1** (*tr*) to hit or punch. ◆ *n* **2** fighting, violence, or a fight. [C19: from ?]

stout 🅣 (staʊt) *adj* **1** solidly built or corpulent. **2** (*prenominal*) resolute or valiant: *stout fellow.* **3** strong, substantial, and robust. **4 a stout heart.** courage; resolution. ◆ *n* **5** strong porter highly flavoured with malt. [C14: from OF *estout* bold, of Gmc origin]
▸**'stoutly** *adv* ▸**'stoutness** *n*

stouthearted 🅣 (ˌstaʊt'hɑːtɪd) *adj* valiant; brave.
▸**ˌstout'heartedly** *adv* ▸**ˌstout'heartedness** *n*

stove[1] (stəʊv) *n* **1** another word for **cooker** (sense 1). **2** any heating apparatus, such as a kiln. [OE *stofa* bathroom]

stove[2] (stəʊv) *vb* a past tense and past participle of **stave.**

stove enamel *n* a type of enamel made heatproof by treatment in a stove.

stovepipe ('stəʊvˌpaɪp) *n* **1** a pipe that serves as a flue to a stove. **2** Also called: **stovepipe hat.** a man's tall silk hat.

stow 🅣 (stəʊ) *vb* (*tr*) **1** (often foll. by *away*) to pack or store. **2** to fill by packing. **3** *Naut.* to pack or put away (cargo, sails, etc.). **4** to have enough room for. **5** (*usually imperative*) *Brit. sl.* to cease from: *stow your noise!* [OE *stōwian* to keep, from *stōw* a place]

Stow (stəʊ) *n* **John.** 1525–1605, English antiquary, noted for his *Survey of London and Westminster* (1598; 1603).

stowage ('stəʊɪdʒ) *n* **1** space, room, or a charge for stowing goods. **2** the act or an instance of stowing or the state of being stowed. **3** something that is stowed.

stowaway ('stəʊəˌweɪ) *n* **1** a person who hides aboard a vehicle, ship, or aircraft in order to gain free passage. ◆ *vb* **stow away. 2** (*intr, adv*) to travel in such a way.

STP *abbrev. for:* **1** Professor of Sacred Theology. [from L: *Sanctae Theologiae Professor*] **2** *Trademark.* scientifically treated petroleum: an oil substitute promising renewed power for an internal-combustion engine. **3** standard temperature and pressure. ◆ *n* **4** a synthetic hallucinogenic drug related to mescaline. [from humorous reference to the extra power resulting from scientifically treated petroleum]

THESAURUS

in, lock away, put aside, put aside for a rainy day, put in storage, reserve, salt away, save, stash (*inf.*), stock, stockpile ◆ *n* **6a** = **shop,** chain store, department store, emporium, hypermarket, market, mart, outlet, supermarket **7** = **supply,** abundance, accumulation, cache, fund, hoard, lot, mine, plenty, plethora, provision, quantity, reserve, reservoir, stock, stockpile, wealth **9a** = **repository,** depository, depot, storehouse, storeroom, warehouse **14 lay store by** = **value,** appreciate, esteem, hold in high regard, prize, think highly of

storm *n* **1a** = **tempest,** blast, blizzard, cyclone, gale, gust, hurricane, squall, tornado, whirlwind **3** = **outburst,** agitation, anger, clamour, commotion, disturbance, furore, hubbub, outbreak, outcry, passion, roar, row, rumpus, stir, strife, tumult, turmoil, violence **4** = **attack,** assault, blitz, blitzkrieg, offensive, onset, onslaught, rush ◆ *vb* **9** = **attack,** assail, assault, beset, charge, rush, take by storm **10** = **rage,** bluster, complain, fly off the handle, fume, go ballistic (*sl., chiefly US*), rant, rave, scold, thunder, wig out (*sl.*) **11** = **rush,** flounce, fly, stalk, stamp, stomp (*inf.*)

stormy *adj* **1** = **wild,** blustering, blustery, dirty, foul, gusty, inclement, raging, rough, squally, tempestuous, turbulent, windy

story[1] *n* **1** = **tale,** account, anecdote, chronicle, fictional account, history, legend, narration, narrative, novel, recital, record, relation, romance, urban legend, urban myth, version, yarn **5** = **report,** article, feature, news, news item, scoop **7** *Informal* = **lie,** falsehood, fib, fiction, pork pie (*Brit. sl.*), porky (*Brit. sl.*), untruth, white lie

storyteller *n* **1** = **raconteur,** anecdotist, author, bard, chronicler, fabulist, narrator, novelist, romancer, spinner of yarns

stout *adj* **1** = **fat,** big, bulky, burly, corpulent, fleshy, heavy, obese, on the large *or* heavy side, overweight, plump, portly, rotund, substantial, tubby **2** = **brave,** bold, courageous, dauntless, doughty, fearless, gallant, indomitable, intrepid, lion-hearted, manly, plucky, resolute, valiant, valorous **3** = **strong,** able-bodied, athletic, beefy (*inf.*), brawny, hardy, hulking, husky (*inf.*), lusty, muscular, robust, stalwart, strapping, sturdy, substantial, thickset, tough, vigorous

Antonyms *adj* ≠ **fat:** insubstantial, lanky, lean, skin-and-bones (*inf.*), skinny, slender, slight, slim ≠ **strong:** feeble, flimsy, frail, insubstantial, puny ≠ **brave:** cowardly, faint-hearted, fearful, irresolute, shrinking, soft, spineless, timid, weak

stouthearted *adj Old-fashioned* = **brave,** ballsy (*taboo sl.*), bold, courageous, dauntless, doughty, fearless, great-hearted, gutsy (*sl.*), heroic, indomitable, intrepid, lion-hearted, plucky, spirited, stalwart, valiant, valorous

stow *vb* **1, 2** = **pack,** bundle, cram, deposit, jam, load, put away, secrete, stash (*inf.*), store, stuff, tuck

strabismus (strəˈbɪzməs) *n* abnormal alignment of one or both eyes, characterized by a turning inwards or outwards from the nose: caused by paralysis of an eye muscle, etc. Also called: **squint.** [C17: via NL from Gk *strabismos*, from *strabizein* to squint, from *strabos* cross-eyed] ▸**straˈbismal, straˈbismic,** *or* **straˈbismical** *adj*

straddle (ˈstrædᵊl) *vb* **straddles, straddling, straddled. 1** (*tr*) to have one leg, part, or support on each side of. **2** (*tr*) *US & Canad. inf.* to be in favour of both sides of (something). **3** (*intr*) to stand, walk, or sit with the legs apart. **4** (*tr*) to spread (the legs) apart. **5** *Gunnery.* to fire a number of shots slightly beyond and slightly short of (a target) to determine the correct range. **6** (*intr*) (in poker, of the second player after the dealer) to double the ante before looking at one's cards. ◆ *n* **7** the act or position of straddling. **8** a noncommittal attitude or stand. **9** *Business.* a contract or option permitting its purchaser either to sell or buy securities or commodities within a specified period of time at specified prices. **10** *Athletics.* a high-jumping technique in which the body is parallel with the bar and the legs straddle it at the highest point of the jump. **11** (in poker) the stake put up after the ante in poker by the second player after the dealer. [C16: from obs. *strad-* (OE *strode*), past stem of STRIDE] ▸ˈ**straddler** *n*

Stradivarius (ˌstrædɪˈvɛərɪəs) *n* any of a number of violins manufactured in Italy by Antonio Stradivari (?1644–1737) or his family. Often shortened to (informal): **Strad.**

strafe (streɪf, strɑːf) *vb* **strafes, strafing, strafed.** (*tr*) **1** to machine-gun (troops, etc.) from the air. **2** *Sl.* to punish harshly. ◆ *n* **3** an act or instance of strafing. [C20: from G *strafen* to punish] ▸ˈ**strafer** *n*

straggle ❶ (ˈstrægᵊl) *vb* **straggles, straggling, straggled.** (*intr*) **1** to go, come, or spread in a rambling or irregular way. **2** to linger behind or wander from a main line or part. [C14: from ?] ▸ˈ**straggler** *n* ▸ˈ**straggly** *adj*

straight ❶ (streɪt) *adj* **1** not curved or crooked; continuing in the same direction without deviating. **2** straightforward, outright, or candid: *a straight rejection.* **3** even, level, or upright. **4** in keeping with the facts; accurate. **5** honest, respectable, or reliable. **6** accurate or logical: *straight reasoning.* **7** continuous; uninterrupted. **8** (esp. of an alcoholic drink) undiluted; neat. **9** not crisp, kinked, or curly: *straight hair.* **10** correctly arranged; orderly. **11** (of a play, acting style, etc.) straightforward or serious. **12** *Boxing.* (of a blow) delivered with an unbent arm: *a straight left.* **13** (of the cylinders of an internal-combustion engine) in line, rather than in a V-formation or in some other arrangement: *a straight eight.* **14** a slang word for **heterosexual. 15** *Inf.* no longer owing or being owed something: *if you buy the next round we'll be straight.* **16** *Sl.* conventional in views, customs, appearance, etc. **17** *Sl.* not using narcotics. ◆ *adv* **18** in a straight line or direct course. **19** immediately; at once: *he came straight back.* **20** in an even, level, or upright position. **21** without cheating, lying, or unreliability: *tell it to me straight.* **22** continuously; uninterruptedly. **23** (often foll. by *out*) frankly; candidly: *he told me straight out.* **24 go straight.** *Inf.* to reform after having been dishonest or a criminal. ◆ *n* **25** the state of being straight. **26** a straight line, form, part, or position. **27** *Brit.* a straight part of a racetrack. **28** *Poker.* **28a** five cards that are in sequence irrespective of suit. **28b** a hand containing such a sequence. **28c** (*as modifier*): *a straight flush.* **29** *Sl.* a conventional person. **30** a slang word for a **heterosexual. 31** *Sl.* a cigarette containing only tobacco, without marijuana, etc. [C14: from p.p. of OE *streccan* to stretch] ▸ˈ**straightly** *adv* ▸ˈ**straightness** *n*

straight and narrow *n Inf.* the proper, honest, and moral path of behaviour.

straight angle *n* an angle of 180°.

straightaway ❶ *adv* (ˌstreɪtəˈweɪ). *also* **straight away. 1** at once. ◆ *n* (ˈstreɪtəˌweɪ). **2** the US word for **straight** (sense 27).

straight chair *n* a straight-backed side chair.

straightedge (ˈstreɪtˌedʒ) *n* a stiff strip of wood or metal with one edge straight, used for ruling and testing straight lines.

straighten ❶ (ˈstreɪtᵊn) *vb* (sometimes foll. by *up* or *out*) **1** to make or become straight. **2** (*tr*) to make neat or tidy. ▸ˈ**straightener** *n*

straighten out ❶ *vb* (*adv*) **1** to make or become less complicated or confused. **2** *US & Canad.* to reform or become reformed.

straight face *n* a serious facial expression, esp. one that conceals the impulse to laugh. ▸ˈ**straight-ˈfaced** *adj*

straight fight *n* a contest between two candidates only.

straight flush *n* (in poker) five consecutive cards of the same suit.

straightforward ❶ (ˌstreɪtˈfɔːwəd) *adj* **1** (of a person) honest, frank, or simple. **2** *Chiefly Brit.* (of a task, etc.) simple; easy. ◆ *adv, adj* **3** in a straight course. ▸ˌ**straightˈforwardly** *adv* ▸ˌ**straightˈforwardness** *n*

straightjacket (ˈstreɪtˌdʒækɪt) *n* a less common spelling of **straitjacket.**

straight-laced *adj* a variant spelling of **strait-laced.**

straight man *n* a subsidiary actor who acts as stooge to a comedian.

straight-out *adj US inf.* **1** complete; thoroughgoing. **2** frank or honest.

straight razor *n* another name for **cut-throat** (sense 2).

straightway (ˈstreɪtˌweɪ) *adv Arch.* at once.

strain[1] ❶ (streɪn) *vb* **1** to draw or be drawn taut; stretch tight. **2** to exert, tax, or use (resources) to the utmost extent. **3** to injure or damage or be injured or damaged by overexertion: *he strained himself.* **4** to deform or be deformed as a result of a stress. **5** (*intr*) to make intense or violent efforts; strive. **6** to subject or be subjected to mental tension or stress. **7** to pour or pass (a substance) or (of a substance) to be poured or passed through a sieve, filter, or strainer. **8** (*tr*) to draw off or remove (one part of a substance or mixture from another) by or as if by filtering. **9** (*tr*) to clasp tightly; hug. **10** (*intr;* foll. by *at*) to push, pull, or work with violent exertion (upon). ◆ *n* **11** the act or an instance of straining. **12** the damage resulting from excessive exertion. **13** an intense physical or mental effort. **14** (*often pl*) *Music.* a theme, melody, or tune. **15** a great demand on the emotions, resources, etc. **16** a way of speaking; tone of voice: *don't go on in that strain.* **17** tension or tiredness resulting from overwork, worry, etc.; stress. **18** *Physics.* the change in dimension of a body under load expressed as the ratio of the total deflection or change in dimension to the original unloaded dimension. [C13: from OF *estreindre* to press together, from L *stringere* to bind tightly]

strain[2] ❶ (streɪn) *n* **1** the main body of descendants from one ancestor. **2** a group of organisms within a species or variety, distinguished by one or more minor characteristics. **3** a variety of bacterium or fungus, esp. one used for a culture. **4** a streak; trace. **5** *Arch.* a kind, type, or sort. [OE *strēon*]

strained ❶ (streɪnd) *adj* **1** (of an action, expression, etc.) not natural or spontaneous. **2** (of an atmosphere, relationship, etc.) not relaxed; tense.

strainer (ˈstreɪnə) *n* **1** a sieve used for straining sauces, vegetables, tea, etc. **2** a gauze or simple filter used to strain liquids.

THESAURUS

straggle *vb* **1** = **spread**, drift, lag, loiter, ramble, range, roam, rove, stray, string out, trail, wander

straggly *adj* **1** = **spread out**, aimless, disorganized, drifting, irregular, loose, rambling, random, spreading, straggling, straying, untidy

straight *adj* **1** = **direct**, near, short, undeviating, unswerving **2** = **frank**, blunt, bold, candid, downright, forthright, honest, outright, plain, point-blank, straightforward, unqualified, upfront (*inf.*) **3** = **level**, aligned, even, horizontal, in line, perpendicular, plumb, right, smooth, square, true, upright, vertical **4** = **accurate**, authentic, fair, honest, reliable, trustworthy **5** = **honest**, above board, decent, equitable, fair, fair and square, honourable, just, law-abiding, reliable, respectable, trustworthy, upright **7** = **successive**, consecutive, continuous, nonstop, running, solid, sustained, through, uninterrupted, unrelieved **8** = **undiluted**, neat, pure, unadulterated, unmixed **10** = **orderly**, arranged, in order, neat, organized, put to rights, shipshape, sorted out, tidy **16** *Slang* = **conventional**, bourgeois, conservative, orthodox, Pooterish, square (*inf.*), traditional ◆ *adv* **18** = **directly**, as the crow flies, at once, immediately, instantly **23** = **frankly**, candidly, honestly, in plain English, point-blank, pulling no punches (*inf.*), with no holds barred
Antonyms *adj* ≠ **direct:** circuitous, indirect, roundabout, winding, zigzag ≠ **level:** askew, bent, crooked, curved, skewwhiff (*Brit. inf.*), twisted, uneven ≠ **frank:** ambiguous, cryptic, equivocal, evasive, indirect, vague ≠ **successive:** broken, discontinuous, interrupted, non-consecutive ≠ **orderly:** confused, disorderly, disorganized, in disarray, messy, untidy ≠ **honest:** bent (*sl.*), crooked (*inf.*), dishonest, dishonourable, shady (*inf.*), unlawful ≠ **conventional:** cool, fashionable, trendy (*Brit. inf.*), voguish

straight away *adv* **1** = **immediately**, at once, directly, instantly, now, on the spot, right away, straightway (*arch.*), there and then, this minute, without any delay, without more ado

straighten *vb* **2** = **neaten**, arrange, order, put in order, set *or* put to rights, smarten up, spruce up, tidy (up)

straighten out *vb* **1** = **make clear**, clear up, correct, disentangle, put right, rectify, regularize, resolve, settle, sort out, unsnarl, work out

straightforward *adj* **1** = **honest**, above board, candid, direct, forthright, genuine, guileless, open, sincere, truthful, upfront (*inf.*) **2** *Chiefly Brit.* = **simple**, clear-cut, easy, easy-peasy (*sl.*), elementary, routine, uncomplicated, undemanding
Antonyms *adj* ≠ **honest:** devious, disingenuous, roundabout, shady, sharp, unscrupulous ≠ **simple:** complex, complicated, confused, convoluted, unclear

strain[1] *vb* **1** = **stretch**, distend, draw tight, extend, tauten, tighten **2** = **strive**, bend over backwards (*inf.*), break one's back *or* neck (*inf.*), bust a gut (*inf.*), do one's damnedest (*inf.*), endeavour, give it one's all (*inf.*), give it one's best shot (*inf.*), go all out for (*inf.*), go for broke (*sl.*), go for it (*inf.*), knock oneself out (*inf.*), labour, make an all-out effort (*inf.*), rupture oneself (*inf.*), struggle **3** = **overexert**, drive, exert, fatigue, injure, overtax, overwork, pull, push to the limit, sprain, tax, tear, test, tire, twist, weaken, wrench **7** = **sieve**, filter, percolate, purify, riddle, screen, seep, separate, sift ◆ *n* **12** = **injury**, pull, sprain, tautness, tension, tensity (*rare*), wrench **13** = **exertion**, effort, force, struggle **14** *often plural* = **tune**, air, lay, measure (*poetic*), melody, song, theme **15** = **stress**, anxiety, burden, pressure, tension
Antonyms *n* ≠ **stress, exertion:** ease, effortlessness, lack of tension, relaxation ◆ *vb* ≠ **strive, overexert:** idle, loose, pamper, relax, rest, slacken, take it easy, yield

strain[2] *n* **1** = **breed**, ancestry, blood, descent, extraction, family, lineage, pedigree, race, stock **4** = **trace**, streak, suggestion, suspicion, tendency, trait

strained *adj* **1** = **forced**, artificial, false, laboured, put on, unnatural **2** = **tense**, awkward, constrained, difficult, embarrassed, self-conscious, stiff, uncomfortable, uneasy, unrelaxed
Antonyms *adj* ≠ **forced:** natural ≠ **tense:** comfortable, relaxed

strait ❶ (streɪt) *n* **1** (*often pl*) a narrow channel of the sea linking two larger areas of sea. **2** (*often pl*) a position of acute difficulty (often in **in dire** *or* **desperate straits**). **3** *Arch.* a narrow place or passage. ◆ *adj* **4** *Arch.* (of spaces, etc.) affording little room. [C13: from OF *estreit* narrow, from L *strictus* constricted, from *stringere* to bind tightly]
▸ **'straitly** *adv* ▸ **'straitness** *n*

straiten ('streɪtᵊn) *vb* **1** (*tr; usually passive*) to embarrass or distress, esp. financially. **2** (*tr*) to limit, confine, or restrict. **3** *Arch.* to make or become narrow.

straitjacket ('streɪtˌdʒækɪt) *n* **1** Also: **straightjacket.** a jacket made of strong canvas material with long sleeves for binding the arms of violent prisoners or mental patients. **2** a restriction or limitation. ◆ *vb* **3** (*tr*) to confine in or as if in a straitjacket.

strait-laced ❶ *or* **straight-laced** *adj* prudish or puritanical.

strake (streɪk) *n* **1a** a curved metal plate forming part of the metal rim on a wooden wheel. **1b** any metal plate let into a rubber tyre. **2** Also called: **streak.** *Naut.* one of a continuous range of planks or plates forming the side of a vessel. [C14: rel. to OE *streccan* to stretch]

stramonium (strəˈməʊnɪəm) *n* **1** a preparation of the dried leaves and flowers of the thorn apple, containing hyoscyamine and used as a drug to treat nervous disorders. **2** another name for **thorn apple** (sense 1). [C17: from NL, from ?]

strand[1] ❶ (strænd) *vb* **1** to leave or drive (ships, fish, etc.) aground or ashore or (of ships, etc.) to be left or driven ashore. **2** (*tr; usually passive*) to leave helpless, as without transport, money, etc. ◆ *n* **3** *Chiefly poetic.* a shore or beach. [OE]

strand[2] ❶ (strænd) *n* **1** a set of or one of the individual fibres or threads of string, wire, etc., that form a rope, cable, etc. **2** a single length of string, hair, wool, wire, etc. **3** a string of pearls or beads. **4** a constituent element of something. ◆ *vb* **5** (*tr*) to form (a rope, cable, etc.) by winding strands together. [C15: from ?]

strange ❶ (streɪndʒ) *adj* **1** odd, unusual, or extraordinary; peculiar. **2** not known, seen, or experienced before; unfamiliar. **3** not easily explained. **4** (usually foll. by *to*) inexperienced (in) or unaccustomed (to): *strange to a task.* **5** not of one's own kind, locality, etc.; alien; foreign. **6** shy; distant; reserved. **7 strange to say.** it is unusual or surprising (that). **8** *Physics.* **8a** denoting a particular flavour of quark. **8b** denoting or relating to a hypothetical form of matter composed of such quarks: *strange matter; a strange star.* ◆ *adv* **9** *Not standard.* in a strange manner. [C13: from OF *estrange,* from L *extrāneus* foreign; see EXTRANEOUS]
▸ **'strangely** *adv*

strangeness ('streɪndʒnɪs) *n* **1** the state or quality of being strange. **2** *Physics.* a property of certain elementary particles characterized by a quantum number (**strangeness number**) conserved in strong but not in weak interactions.

stranger ❶ ('streɪndʒə) *n* **1** any person whom one does not know. **2** a person who is new to a particular locality, from another region, town, etc. **3** a guest or visitor. **4** (foll. by *to*) a person who is unfamiliar (with) or new (to) something: *he is no stranger to computing.*

strangle ❶ ('strængᵊl) *vb* **strangles, strangling, strangled.** (*tr*) **1** to kill by compressing the windpipe; throttle. **2** to prevent or inhibit the growth or development of: *to strangle originality.* **3** to suppress (an utterance) by or as if by swallowing suddenly: *to strangle a cry.* ◆ See also **strangles.** [C13: via OF, ult. from Gk *strangalē* a halter]
▸ **'strangler** *n*

stranglehold ('strængᵊlˌhəʊld) *n* **1** a wrestling hold in which a wrestler's arms are pressed against his opponent's windpipe. **2** complete power or control over a person or situation.

strangles ('strængᵊlz) *n* (*functioning as sing*) an acute infectious bacterial disease of horses, characterized by inflammation of the respiratory tract. Also called: **equine distemper.**

strangulate ('strængjʊˌleɪt) *vb* **strangulates, strangulating, strangulated.** (*tr*) **1** to constrict (a hollow organ, vessel, etc.) so as to stop the flow of air, blood, etc., through it. **2** another word for **strangle.**
▸ **ˌstranguˈlation** *n*

strangury ('strængjʊrɪ) *n Pathol.* painful excretion of urine, drop by drop. [C14: from L *strangūria,* from Gk, from *stranx* a drop squeezed out + *ouron* urine]

strap ❶ (stræp) *n* **1** a long strip of leather or similar material, for binding trunks, baggage, etc. **2** a strip of leather or similar material used for carrying, lifting, or holding. **3** a loop of leather, rubber, etc., suspended from the roof in a bus or train for standing passengers to hold on to. **4** a razor strop. **5** short for **shoulder strap. 6** *Business.* a triple option on a security or commodity consisting of one put option and two call options at the same price and for the same period. Cf. **strip**[2] (sense 4). **7** *Irish, derog. sl.* a shameless or promiscuous woman. **8 the strap.** a beating with a strap as a punishment. ◆ *vb* **straps, strapping, strapped.** (*tr*) **9** to tie or bind with a strap. **10** to beat with a strap. **11** to sharpen with a strap or strop. [C16: var. of STROP]

straphanger ('stræpˌhæŋə) *n Inf.* a passenger in a bus, train, etc., who has to travel standing, esp. holding on to a strap.
▸ **'strapˌhanging** *n*

strapping ❶ ('stræpɪŋ) *adj* (*prenominal*) tall and sturdy. [C17: from STRAP (in the arch. sense: to work vigorously)]

strapwork ('stræpˌwɜːk) *n Archit.* decorative work resembling interlacing straps.

strata ('strɑːtə) *n* a plural of **stratum.**

> **USAGE NOTE** *Strata* is sometimes wrongly used as a singular noun: *this stratum* (not *strata*) *of society is often disregarded.*

stratagem ❶ ('strætɪdʒəm) *n* a plan or trick, esp. to deceive an enemy. [C15: ult. from Gk *stratēgos* a general, from *stratos* an army + *agein* to lead]

strategic ❶ (strəˈtiːdʒɪk) *or* **strategical** *adj* **1** of or characteristic of strategy. **2** important to strategy. **3** (of weapons, esp. missiles) directed against an enemy's homeland rather than used on a battlefield. Cf. **tactical.**
▸ **straˈtegically** *adv*

strategics (strəˈtiːdʒɪks) *n* (*functioning as sing*) strategy, esp. in a military sense.

strategist ('strætɪdʒɪst) *n* a specialist or expert in strategy.

strategy ❶ ('strætɪdʒɪ) *n, pl* **strategies. 1** the art or science of the planning and conduct of a war. **2** a particular long-term plan for success, esp. in politics, business, etc. **3** a plan or stratagem. [C17: from F *stratégie,* from Gk *stratēgia* function of a general; see STRATAGEM]

strath (stræθ) *n Scot.* a flat river valley. [C16: from Scot. & Irish Gaelic *srath*]

strathspey (stræθˈspeɪ) *n* **1** a Scottish dance with gliding steps, slower than a reel. **2** a piece of music composed for or in the rhythm of this dance. [after *Strathspey,* valley of the river Spey]

strati- *combining form.* indicating stratum or strata: *stratigraphy.*

straticulate (strəˈtɪkjʊlɪt, -ˌleɪt) *adj* (of a rock formation) composed of very thin even strata. [C19: from NL *strāticulum* (unattested), dim. of L *strātum* something strewn; see STRATUS]
▸ **straˌticuˈlation** *n*

stratify ('strætɪˌfaɪ) *vb* **stratifies, stratifying, stratified. 1** to form or be formed in layers or strata. **2** *Sociol.* to divide (a society) into status groups or (of a society) to develop such groups. [C17: from F *stratifier,* from NL *stratificāre,* from L STRATUM]
▸ **ˌstratifiˈcation** *n* ▸ **'stratiˌfied** *adj*

stratigraphy (strəˈtɪgrəfɪ) *n* **1** the study of the composition, relative positions, etc., of rock strata in order to determine their geological history. **2** *Archaeol.* a vertical section through the earth showing the relative positions of the human artefacts and therefore the chronology of successive levels of occupation.
▸ **stratigraphic** (ˌstrætɪˈgræfɪk) *or* **ˌstratiˈgraphical** *adj*

stratocumulus (ˌstrætəʊˈkjuːmjʊləs) *n, pl* **stratocumuli** (-ˌlaɪ). *Meteorol.* a uniform stretch of cloud containing dark grey globular masses.

stratopause ('strætəˌpɔːz) *n Meteorol.* the transitional zone of maximum temperature between the stratosphere and the mesosphere.

stratosphere ('strætəˌsfɪə) *n* the atmospheric layer lying between the troposphere and the mesosphere, in which temperature generally increases with height.
▸ **stratospheric** (ˌstrætəˈsfɛrɪk) *or* **ˌstratoˈspherical** *adj*

stratum ❶ ('strɑːtəm) *n, pl* **strata** *or* **stratums. 1** (*usually pl*) any of the dis-

THESAURUS

strait *n* **1** *often plural* = **channel,** narrows, sound **2** *often plural* = **difficulty,** crisis, dilemma, distress, embarrassment, emergency, extremity, hardship, hole (*sl.*), mess, panic stations (*inf.*), pass, perplexity, plight, predicament, pretty *or* fine kettle of fish (*inf.*)

strait-laced *adj* = **puritanical,** moralistic, narrow, narrow-minded, niminy-piminy, of the old school, old-maidish (*inf.*), overscrupulous, prim, proper, prudish, strict, Victorian
Antonyms *adj* broad-minded, earthy, immoral, loose, relaxed, uninhibited, unreserved

strand[2] *n* **1, 2** = **filament,** fibre, length, lock, rope, string, thread, tress, twist, wisp

stranded *adj* **1** = **beached,** aground, ashore, cast away, grounded, marooned, shipwrecked **2** = **helpless,** abandoned, high and dry, homeless, left in the lurch, penniless

strange *adj* **1** = **odd,** abnormal, astonishing, bizarre, curious, curiouser and curiouser, eccentric, exceptional, extraordinary, fantastic, funny, irregular, left-field (*inf.*), marvellous, mystifying, oddball (*inf.*), off-the-wall (*sl.*), out-of-the-way, outré, peculiar, perplexing, queer, rare, remarkable, rum (*Brit. sl.*), singular, unaccountable, uncanny, uncommon, unheard-of, weird, wonderful **2** = **unfamiliar,** alien, exotic, foreign, new, novel, outside one's experience, remote, unexplored, unknown, untried **4 strange to** = **unaccustomed to,** a stranger to, ignorant of, inexperienced in, new to, unpractised in, unseasoned in, unused to, unversed in
Antonyms *adj* ≠ **odd:** accustomed, bog-standard (*Brit. & Irish sl.*), common, commonplace, conventional, familiar, habitual, ordinary, regular, routine, run-of-the-mill, standard, typical, unexceptional, usual, well-known ≠ **unfamiliar:** accustomed, familiar, habitual

stranger *n* **1-3** = **newcomer,** alien, foreigner, guest, incomer, new arrival, outlander, unknown, visitor

strangle *vb* **1** = **throttle,** asphyxiate, choke, garrotte, smother, strangulate, suffocate **3** = **suppress,** gag, inhibit, repress, stifle

strap *n* **1** = **belt,** leash, thong, tie ◆ *vb* **2** = **fasten,** bind, buckle, lash, secure, tie, truss **10** = **beat,** belt (*inf.*), flog, lash, scourge, whip

strapping *adj* = **well-built,** beefy, big, brawny, burly, hefty (*inf.*), hulking, husky (*inf.*), powerful, robust, stalwart, sturdy, well set-up

stratagem *n* = **trick,** artifice, device, dodge, feint, intrigue, manoeuvre, plan, plot, ploy, ruse, scheme, subterfuge, wile

strategic *adj* **1** = **tactical,** calculated, deliberate, diplomatic, planned, politic **2** = **crucial,** cardinal, critical, decisive, important, key, vital

strategy *n* **2, 3** = **plan,** approach, grand design, manoeuvring, planning, policy, procedure, programme, scheme

stratum *n* **1, 3, 4** = **layer,** bed, level, lode, seam, stratification, table, tier, vein **5** = **class,** bracket, caste, category, estate, grade, group, level, rank, station

tinct layers into which sedimentary rocks are divided. **2** *Biol.* a single layer of tissue or cells. **3** a layer of any material, esp. one of several parallel layers. **4** a layer of ocean or atmosphere either naturally or arbitrarily demarcated. **5** a level of a social hierarchy. [C16: via NL from L: something strewn, from *sternere* to scatter]
▸ **'stratal** *adj*

stratus ('streɪtəs) *n, pl* **strati** (-taɪ). a grey layer cloud. [C19: via NL from L: strewn, from *sternere* to extend]

straw (strɔː) *n* **1a** stalks of threshed grain, esp. of wheat, rye, oats, or barley, used in plaiting hats, baskets, etc., or as fodder. **1b** (*as modifier*): *a straw hat.* **2** a single dry or ripened stalk, esp. of a grass. **3** a long thin hollow paper or plastic tube, used for sucking up liquids into the mouth. **4** (*usually used with a negative*) anything of little value or importance: *I wouldn't give a straw for our chances.* **5** a measure or remedy that one turns to in desperation (esp. in **clutch** *or* **grasp at a straw** *or* **straws**). **6a** a pale yellow colour. **6b** (*as adj*): *straw hair.* **7 draw the short straw.** to be the person to whom an unpleasant task falls. **8 straw in the wind.** a hint or indication. **9 the last straw.** a small incident, setback, etc., that coming after others proves insufferable. [OE *streaw*]
▸ **'strawy** *adj*

strawberry ('strɔːbərɪ, -brɪ) *n, pl* **strawberries. 1** any of various low-growing rosaceous plants which have red edible fruits and spread by runners. **2a** the fruit of any of these plants, consisting of a sweet fleshy receptacle bearing small seedlike parts (the true fruits). **2b** (*as modifier*): *strawberry ice cream.* **3a** a purplish-red colour. **3b** (*as adj*): *strawberry shoes.* [OE *streawberige;* ?from the strawlike appearance of the runners]

strawberry blonde *adj* **1** (of hair) reddish blonde. ◆ *n* **2** a woman with such hair.

strawberry mark *n* a soft vascular red birthmark. Also called: **strawberry.**

strawberry tomato *n* **1** a tropical annual plant having bell-shaped whitish-yellow flowers and small edible round yellow berries. **2** the fruit of this plant, eaten fresh or made into preserves or pickles. ◆ Also called: **Cape gooseberry.**

strawberry tree *n* a S European evergreen tree having white or pink flowers and red strawberry-like berries. See also **arbutus.**

strawboard ('strɔːˌbɔːd) *n* a board made of compressed straw and adhesive.

strawflower ('strɔːˌflaʊə) *n* an Australian plant in which the coloured bracts retain their colour when the plant is dried. See also **immortelle.**

straw man *n Chiefly US.* **1** a figure of a man made from straw. **2** a person of little substance. **3** a person used as a cover for some dubious plan or enterprise.

straw poll *or esp. US, Canad., & NZ.* **vote** *n* an unofficial poll or vote taken to determine the opinion of a group or the public on some issue.

strawweight ('strɔːˌweɪt) *n* **a** a professional boxer weighing not more than 47.6 kg (105 pounds). **b** (*as modifier*): *the strawweight title.* ◆ Also called: **mini-flyweight.**

stray ⓘ (streɪ) *vb* (*intr*) **1** to wander away, as from the correct path or from a given area. **2** to wander haphazardly. **3** to digress from the point, lose concentration, etc. **4** to deviate from certain moral standards. ◆ *n* **5a** a domestic animal, fowl, etc., that has wandered away from its place of keeping and is lost. **5b** (*as modifier*): *stray dogs.* **6** a lost or homeless person, esp. a child: *waifs and strays.* **7** an occurrence, specimen, etc., that is out of place or outside the usual pattern. ◆ *adj* **8** scattered, random, or haphazard. [C14: from OF *estraier,* from Vulgar L *estragāre* (unattested), from L *extrā-* outside + *vagārī* to roam]
▸ **'strayer** *n*

strays (streɪz) *pl n* **1** Also called: **stray capacitance.** *Electronics.* undesired capacitance in equipment. **2** another word for **static** (sense 8).

streak ⓘ (striːk) *n* **1** a long thin mark, stripe, or trace of some contrasting colour. **2** (of lightning) a sudden flash. **3** an element or trace, as of some quality or characteristic. **4** a strip, vein, or layer. **5** a short stretch or run, esp. of good or bad luck. **6** *Inf.* an act or the practice of running naked through a public place. ◆ *vb* **7** (*tr*) to mark or daub with a streak or streaks. **8** (*intr*) to form streaks or become streaked. **9** (*intr*) to move rapidly in a straight line. **10** (*intr*) *Inf.* to run naked through a public place in order to shock or to amuse. [OE *strica*]
▸ **streaked** *adj* ▸ **'streaker** *n* ▸ **'streakˌlike** *adj*

streaky ('striːkɪ) *adj* **streakier, streakiest. 1** marked with streaks. **2** occurring in streaks. **3** (of bacon) having alternate layers of meat and fat. **4** of varying or uneven quality.
▸ **'streakiness** *n*

stream ⓘ (striːm) *n* **1** a small river; brook. **2** any steady flow of water or other fluid. **3** something that resembles a stream in moving continuously in a line or particular direction. **4** a rapid or unbroken flow of speech, etc.: *a stream of abuse.* **5** *Brit., Austral., & NZ.* any of several parallel classes of schoolchildren, or divisions of children within a class, grouped together because of similar ability. **6 go** (*or* **drift**) **with the stream.** to conform to the accepted standards. **7 on** (*or* **off**) **stream.** (of an industrial plant, manufacturing process, etc.) in (*or* not in) operation or production. ◆ *vb* **8** to emit or be emitted in a continuous flow: *his nose streamed blood.* **9** (*intr*) to move in unbroken succession, as a crowd of people, vehicles, etc. **10** (*intr*) to float freely or with a waving motion: *bunting streamed in the wind.* **11** (*tr*) to unfurl (a flag, etc.). **12** *Brit. education.* to group or divide (children) in streams. [OE]
▸ **'streamlet** *n*

streamer ⓘ ('striːmə) *n* **1** a long narrow flag or part of a flag. **2** a long narrow coiled ribbon of coloured paper that becomes unrolled when tossed. **3** a stream of light, esp. one appearing in some forms of the aurora. **4** *Journalism.* a large heavy headline printed across the width of a page. **5** *Computing.* another word for **tape streamer.**

streamline ('striːmˌlaɪn) *n* **1** a contour on a body that offers the minimum resistance to a gas or liquid flowing around it. ◆ *vb* **streamlines, streamlining, streamlined. 2** (*tr*) to make streamlined.

streamlined ⓘ ('striːmˌlaɪnd) *adj* **1** offering or designed to offer the minimum resistance to the flow of a gas or liquid. **2** made more efficient, esp. by simplifying.

stream of consciousness *n* **1** *Psychol.* the continuous flow of ideas, thoughts, and feelings forming the content of an individual's consciousness. **2** a literary technique that reveals the flow of thoughts and feelings of characters through long passages of soliloquy.

streamy ('striːmɪ) *adj* **streamier, streamiest.** *Chiefly poetic.* **1** (of an area, land, etc.) having many streams. **2** flowing or streaming.

street ⓘ (striːt) *n* **1a** a public road that is usually lined with buildings, esp. in a town: *Oxford Street.* **1b** (*as modifier*): *a street directory.* **2** the buildings lining a street. **3** the part of the road between the pavements, used by vehicles. **4** the people living, working, etc., in a particular street. **5** (*modifier*) of or relating to the urban counterculture. **6 on the streets. 6a** earning a living as a prostitute. **6b** homeless. **7** (**right**) **up one's street.** *Inf.* (just) what one knows or likes best. **8 streets ahead of.** *Inf.* superior to, more advanced than, etc. **9 streets apart.** *Inf.* markedly different. [OE *strǣt,* from L *via strāta* paved way (*strāta,* from *strātus,* p.p. of *sternere* to stretch out)]

street Arab *n Literary & old-fashioned.* a homeless child, esp. one who survives by begging and stealing; urchin.

streetcar ('striːtˌkɑː) *n* the usual US and Canad. name for **tram** (sense 1).

street credibility *n* a command of the style, knowledge, etc., associated with urban counter-culture. Often shortened to **street cred.**
▸ **ˌstreet-'credible** *adj*

street cry *n* (*often pl*) the cry of a street hawker.

street furniture *n* pieces of equipment, such as street lights and pillar boxes, placed in the street for the benefit of the public.

street value *n* the monetary worth of a commodity, usually an illicit one, considered as the price it would fetch when sold to the ultimate user.

streetwalker ('striːtˌwɔːkə) *n* a prostitute who solicits on the streets.
▸ **'streetˌwalking** *n, adj*

streetwise ('striːtˌwaɪz) *adj* adept at surviving in an urban, poor, and often criminal environment.

strelitzia (streˈlɪtsɪə) *n* any of various southern African perennial herbaceous plants, cultivated for their showy flowers: includes the bird-of-paradise flower. [C18: after Charlotte of Mecklenburg-*Strelitz* (1744–1818), queen of Great Britain & Ireland]

strength ⓘ (streŋθ) *n* **1** the state or quality of being physically or mentally strong. **2** the ability to withstand or exert great force, stress, or pressure. **3** something regarded as beneficial or a source of power: *their chief strength is technology.* **4** potency, as of a drink, drug, etc. **5** power to convince; cogency: *the strength of an argument.* **6** degree of intensity or concentration of colour, light, sound, flavour, etc. **7** the full or part of the full complement as specified: *at full strength; below strength.* **8 from strength to strength.** with ever-increasing success. **9 in strength.** in large numbers. **10 on the strength of.** on the basis of or relying

THESAURUS

stray *vb* **1 = wander,** be abandoned *or* lost, drift, err, go astray, lose one's way, meander, range, roam, rove, straggle **2 = digress,** deviate, diverge, get off the point, get sidetracked, go off at a tangent, ramble ◆ *modifier* **5b = lost,** abandoned, homeless, roaming, vagrant ◆ *adj* **8 = random,** accidental, chance, erratic, freak, odd, scattered

streak *n* **1 = band,** layer, line, slash, smear, strip, stripe, stroke, vein **3 = trace,** dash, element, strain, touch, vein ◆ *vb* **7 = band,** daub, fleck, slash, smear, striate, stripe **9 = speed,** barrel (along), burn rubber (*inf.*), dart, flash, fly, hurtle, move like greased lightning (*inf.*), sprint, sweep, tear, whistle, whizz (*inf.*), zoom

stream *n* **1 = river,** bayou, beck, brook, burn (*Scot.*), creek (*US*), freshet, rill, rivulet, tributary, undertow **2 = flow,** course, current, drift, outpouring, run, rush, surge, tide, tideway, torrent ◆ *vb* **9 = flow,** cascade, course, emit, flood, glide, gush, issue, pour, run, shed, spill, spout

streamer *n* **1 = banner,** colours, ensign, flag, gonfalon, pennant, pennon, ribbon, standard

streamlined *adj* **2 = efficient,** modernized, organized, rationalized, sleek, slick, smooth, smooth-running, time-saving, well-run

street *n* **1 = road,** avenue, boulevard, lane, roadway, row, terrace, thoroughfare **7** (**right**) **up one's street** *Informal* **= to one's liking,** acceptable, compatible, congenial, familiar, one's cup of tea (*inf.*), pleasing, suitable, to one's taste

strength *n* **1 = might,** backbone, brawn, brawniness, courage, firmness, fortitude, health, lustiness, muscle, robustness, sinew, stamina, stoutness, sturdiness, toughness, wellness **3 = strong point,** advantage, anchor, asset, mainstay, security, succour, tower of strength **5 = power,** cogency, concentration, effectiveness, efficacy, energy, force, intensity, potency, resolution, spirit, vehemence, vigour, virtue (*arch.*)
Antonyms *n* ≠ **might:** debility, feebleness, frailty, infirmity, powerlessness, weakness ≠ **strong point:** Achilles heel, chink in one's armour, defect, failing, flaw, shortcoming, weakness ≠ **power:** feebleness, impotence, powerlessness, weakness

upon. **11 the strength of.** *Austral. & NZ inf.* the essential facts about. [OE *strengthu*]

strengthen ➊ ('strɛŋθən) *vb* to make or become stronger.
▸**'strengthener** *n*

strenuous ➊ ('strɛnjʊəs) *adj* **1** requiring or involving the use of great energy or effort. **2** characterized by great activity, effort, or endeavour. [C16: from L *strēnuus* brisk]
▸**'strenuously** *adv* ▸**'strenuousness** *n*

strep (strɛp) *n Inf.* short for **streptococcus.**

strepitoso (ˌstrɛpɪ'təʊsəʊ) *adv Music.* boisterously. [It.]

strepto- *combining form.* **1** indicating a shape resembling a twisted chain: *streptococcus.* **2** indicating streptococcus. [from Gk *streptos* twisted, from *strephein* to twist]

streptocarpus (ˌstrɛptəʊ'kɑːpəs) *n* any of various mostly African plants having spirally-twisted capsules. [C19: from NL, from Gk *streptos* twisted + *karpos* fruit]

streptococcus (ˌstrɛptəʊ'kɒkəs) *n, pl* **streptococci** (-'kɒkaɪ; *US* -'kɒksaɪ). any spherical bacterium of the genus *Streptococcus,* typically occurring in chains and including many pathogenic species. Often shortened to **strep.**
▸**streptococcal** (ˌstrɛptəʊ'kɒkᵊl) *or* **streptococcic** (ˌstrɛptəʊ'kɒksɪk) *adj*

streptomycin (ˌstrɛptəʊ'maɪsɪn) *n* an antibiotic obtained from the bacterium *Streptomyces griseus:* used in the treatment of tuberculosis and other bacterial infections.

streptothricin (ˌstrɛptəʊ'θraɪsɪn) *n* an antibiotic produced by the bacterium *Streptomyces lavendulae.*

stress ➊ (strɛs) *n* **1** special emphasis or significance. **2** mental, emotional, or physical strain or tension. **3** emphasis placed upon a syllable by pronouncing it more loudly than those that surround it. **4** such emphasis as part of a rhythm in music or poetry. **5** a syllable so emphasized. **6** *Physics.* **6a** force or a system of forces producing deformation or strain. **6b** the force acting per unit area. ◆ *vb (tr)* **7** to give emphasis or prominence to. **8** to pronounce (a word or syllable) more loudly than those that surround it. **9** to subject to stress. [C14 *stresse,* shortened from DISTRESS]
▸**'stressful** *adj*

-stress *suffix forming nouns.* indicating a woman who performs or is engaged in a certain activity: *songstress; seamstress.* [from -ST(E)R + -ESS]

stretch ➊ (strɛtʃ) *vb* **1** to draw out or extend or be drawn out or extended in length, area, etc. **2** to extend or be extended to an undue degree, esp. so as to distort or lengthen permanently. **3** to extend (the limbs, body, etc.). **4** *(tr)* to reach or suspend (a rope, etc.) from one place to another. **5** *(tr)* to draw tight; tighten. **6** (often foll. by *out, forward,* etc.) to reach or hold (out); extend. **7** *(intr;* usually foll. by *over)* to extend in time: *the course stretched over three months.* **8** *(intr;* foll. by *for, over,* etc.) (of a region, etc.) to extend in length or area. **9** *(intr)* (esp. of a garment) to be capable of expanding, as to a larger size: *socks that will stretch.* **10** *(tr)* to put a great strain upon or extend to the limit. **11** to injure (a muscle, tendon, etc.) by means of a strain or sprain. **12** *(tr;* often foll. by *out)* to make do with (limited resources): *to stretch one's budget.* **13** *(tr) Inf.* to expand or elaborate (a story, etc.) beyond what is credible or acceptable. **14** *(tr; often passive)* to extend, as to the limit of one's abilities or talents. **15** *Arch. or sl.* to hang or be hanged by the neck. **16 stretch a point. 16a** to make a concession or exception not usually made. **16b** to exaggerate. ◆ *n* **17** the act of stretching or state of being stretched. **18** a large or continuous expanse or distance: *a stretch of water.* **19** extent in time, length, area, etc. **20a** capacity for being stretched, as in some garments. **20b** *(as modifier): stretch pants.* **21** the section or sections of a racecourse that are straight, esp. the final section leading to the finishing line. **22** *Sl.* a term of imprisonment. **23 at a stretch.** *Chiefly Brit.* **23a** with some difficulty; by making a special effort. **23b** if really necessary or in extreme circumstances. **23c** at one time: *he sometimes read for hours at a stretch.* [OE *streccan*]
▸**'stretchable** *adj* ▸ˌ**stretcha'bility** *n*

stretcher ('strɛtʃə) *n* **1** a device for transporting the ill, wounded, or dead, consisting of a frame covered by canvas or other material. **2** a strengthening often decorative member joining the legs of a chair, table, etc. **3** the wooden frame on which canvas is stretched and fixed for oil painting. **4** a tie beam or brace used in a structural framework. **5** a brick or stone laid horizontally with its length parallel to the length of a wall. **6** *Rowing.* a fixed board across a boat on which an oarsman braces his feet. **7** *Austral. & NZ.* a camp bed. ◆ *vb (tr)* **8** to transport (a sick or injured person) on a stretcher.

stretcher-bearer *n* a person who helps to carry a stretcher, esp. in wartime.

stretch limo *n Inf.* a limousine that has been lengthened to provide extra seating accommodation and more legroom. In full: **stretch limousine.**

stretchmarks ('strɛtʃˌmɑːks) *pl n* marks that remain visible on the abdomen after its distension in pregnancy.

stretchy ('strɛtʃɪ) *adj* **stretchier, stretchiest.** characterized by elasticity.
▸**'stretchiness** *n*

stretto ('strɛtəʊ) *n, pl* **strettos** *or* **stretti** (-tiː). **1** (in a fugue) the close overlapping of two parts or voices, the second one entering before the first has completed its statement. **2** Also called: **stretta.** a concluding passage, played at a faster speed than earlier material. [C17: from It., from L *strictus* tightly bound; see STRICT]

strew ➊ (struː) *vb* **strews, strewing, strewed; strewn** *or* **strewed.** to spread or scatter or be spread or scattered, as over a surface or area. [OE *streowian*]
▸**'strewer** *n*

strewth (struːθ) *interj* an expression of surprise or dismay. [C19: alteration of *God's truth*]

stria ('straɪə) *n, pl* **striae** ('straɪiː). *(often pl)* **1** Also called: **striation.** *Geol.* any of the parallel scratches or grooves on the surface of a rock over which a glacier has flowed or on the surface of a crystal. **2** *Biol., anat.* a narrow band of colour or a ridge, groove, or similar linear mark. **3** *Archit.* a narrow channel, such as a flute on the shaft of a column. [C16: from L: a groove]

striate *adj* ('straɪɪt), *also* **striated. 1** marked with striae; striped. ◆ *vb* ('straɪeɪt), **striates, striating, striated. 2** *(tr)* to mark with striae. [C17: from L *striāre* to make grooves]

striation (straɪ'eɪʃən) *n* **1** an arrangement or pattern of striae. **2** the condition of being striate. **3** another word for **stria** (sense 1).

stricken ➊ ('strɪkən) *adj* **1** laid low, as by disease or sickness. **2** deeply affected, as by grief, love, etc. **3** *Arch.* wounded or injured. **4 stricken in years.** made feeble by age. [C14: p.p. of STRIKE]
▸**'strickenly** *adv*

strict ➊ (strɪkt) *adj* **1** adhering closely to specified rules, ordinances, etc. **2** complied with or enforced stringently; rigorous: *a strict code of conduct.* **3** severely correct in attention to conduct or morality: *a strict teacher.* **4** (of a punishment, etc.) harsh; severe. **5** *(prenominal)* complete; absolute: *strict secrecy.* [C16: from L *strictus,* from *stringere* to draw tight]
▸**'strictly** *adv* ▸**'strictness** *n*

strict implication *n Logic.* a form of implication in which the proposition "if A then B" is true only when B is deducible from A.

stricture ➊ ('strɪktʃə) *n* **1** a severe criticism; censure. **2** *Pathol.* an abnormal constriction of a tubular organ or part. [C14: from L *strictūra* contraction; see STRICT]
▸**'strictured** *adj*

stride (straɪd) *n* **1** a long step or pace. **2** the space measured by such a step. **3** a striding gait. **4** an act of forward movement by an animal. **5** progress or development (esp. in **make rapid strides**). **6** a regular pace or rate of progress: *to get into one's stride; to be put off one's stride.* **7** Also: **stride piano.** *Jazz.* a piano style characterized by single bass notes on the first and third beats and chords on the second and fourth. **8** *(pl) Inf., chiefly Austral. & NZ.* men's trousers. **9 take (something) in one's stride.** to do (something) without difficulty or effort. ◆ *vb* **strides, striding, strode, stridden** ('strɪdᵊn). **10** *(intr)* to walk with long regular or measured paces, as in haste, etc. **11** *(tr)* to cover or traverse by striding: *he strode thirty miles.* **12** (often foll. by *over, across,* etc.) to cross (over a space, obstacle, etc.) with a stride. **13** *Arch. or poetic.* to straddle or bestride. [OE *strīdan*]
▸**'strider** *n*

strident ➊ ('straɪdᵊnt) *adj* **1** (of a shout, voice, etc.) loud or harsh. **2** urgent, clamorous, or vociferous: *strident demands.* [C17: from L *strīdēns,* from *strīdēre* to make a grating sound]
▸**'stridence** *or* **'stridency** *n* ▸**'stridently** *adv*

stridor ('straɪdɔː) *n* **1** *Pathol.* a high-pitched whistling sound made dur-

THESAURUS

strengthen *vb* = **fortify,** animate, brace up, consolidate, encourage, gee up, give new energy to, harden, hearten, invigorate, nerve, nourish, rejuvenate, restore, stiffen, toughen
Antonyms *vb* crush, debilitate, destroy, dilute, enervate, render impotent, sap, subvert, undermine, weaken

strenuous *adj* **1** = **demanding,** arduous, exhausting, hard, Herculean, laborious, taxing, toilsome, tough, tough going, unrelaxing, uphill **2** = **tireless,** active, bold, determined, eager, earnest, energetic, persistent, resolute, spirited, strong, vigorous, zealous
Antonyms *adj* ≠ **demanding:** easy, effortless, relaxing, undemanding, untaxing ≠ **tireless:** relaxed, unenergetic

stress *n* **1** = **emphasis,** force, importance, significance, urgency, weight **2** = **strain,** anxiety, burden, hassle *(inf.),* nervous tension, oppression, pressure, tension, trauma, worry **3-5** = **accent,** accentuation, beat, emphasis, ictus ◆ *vb* **7** = **emphasize,** accentuate, belabour, dwell on, harp on, lay emphasis upon, point up, repeat, rub in, underline, underscore

stressful *adj* **2** = **worrying,** agitating, anxious, tense, traumatic

stretch *vb* **1** = **extend,** cover, put forth, reach, spread, unfold, unroll **2** = **pull,** distend, draw out, elongate, expand, inflate, lengthen, pull out of shape, rack, strain, swell, tighten ◆ *n* **18** = **expanse,** area, distance, extent, spread, sweep, tract **19** = **period,** bit, run, space, spell, stint, term, time

strew *vb* = **scatter,** bestrew, disperse, litter, spread, sprinkle, toss

stricken *adj* **1** = **affected,** afflicted, hit, injured, laid low, smitten, struck, struck down

strict *adj* **1** = **exact,** accurate, close, faithful, meticulous, particular, precise, religious, scrupulous, true **3, 4** = **severe,** austere, authoritarian, firm, harsh, no-nonsense, rigid, rigorous, stern, stringent **5** = **absolute,** complete, perfect, total, utter
Antonyms *adj* ≠ **severe:** easy-going, easy-oasy *(sl.),* flexible, laid-back *(inf.),* lax, mild, moderate, soft, tolerant

stricture *n* **1** *Formal* = **criticism,** animadversion, bad press, blame, censure, flak *(inf.),* rebuke, stick *(sl.)*

strident *adj* **1** = **harsh,** clamorous, clashing, discordant, grating, jangling, jarring, rasping, raucous, screeching, shrill, stridulant, stridulous, unmusical

ing respiration, caused by obstruction of the air passages. **2** *Chiefly literary.* a harsh or shrill sound. [C17: from L; see STRIDENT]

stridulate ('strɪdjʊˌleɪt) *vb* **stridulates, stridulating, stridulated.** (*intr*) (of insects such as the cricket) to produce sounds by rubbing one part of the body against another. [C19: back formation from *stridulation,* from L *strīdulus* creaking, from *strīdēre* to make a harsh noise]
▸ˌ**striduˈlation** *n* ▸ˈ**striduˌlator** *n*

stridulous ('strɪdjʊləs) *or* **stridulant** *adj* **1** making a harsh, shrill, or grating noise. **2** *Pathol.* of, relating to, or characterized by stridor.
▸ˈ**stridulousness** *or* ˈ**stridulance** *n*

strife ⓣ (straɪf) *n* **1** angry or violent struggle; conflict. **2** rivalry or contention, esp. of a bitter kind. **3** *Austral. & NZ inf.* trouble or discord of any kind. **4** *Arch.* striving. [C13: from OF *estrif,* prob. from *estriver* to STRIVE]

strigil ('strɪdʒɪl) *n* a curved blade used by the ancient Romans and Greeks to scrape the body after bathing. [C16: from L *strigilis,* from *stringere* to graze]

strigose ('straɪgəʊs) *adj* **1** *Bot.* bearing stiff hairs or bristles. **2** *Zool.* marked with fine closely set grooves or ridges. [C18: via NL *strigōsus,* from *striga* a bristle, from L: grain cut down]

strike ⓣ (straɪk) *vb* **strikes, striking, struck. 1** to deliver (a blow or stroke) to (a person). **2** to come or cause to come into sudden or violent contact (with). **3** (*tr*) to make an attack on. **4** to produce (fire, sparks, etc.) or (of fire, sparks, etc.) to be produced by ignition. **5** to cause (a match) to light by friction or (of a match) to be lighted. **6** to press (the key of a piano, organ, etc.) or to sound (a specific note) in this or a similar way. **7** to indicate (a specific time) by the sound of a hammer striking a bell or by any other percussive sound. **8** (of a venomous snake) to cause injury by biting. **9** (*tr*) to affect or cause to affect deeply, suddenly, or radically: *her appearance struck him as strange.* **10** (*past participle* **struck** *or* **stricken**) (*tr; passive;* usually foll. by *with*) to render incapable or nearly so: *stricken with grief.* **11** (*tr*) to enter the mind of: *it struck me that he had become very quiet.* **12** (*past participle* **struck** *or* **stricken**) to render: *struck dumb.* **13** (*tr*) to be perceived by; catch: *the glint of metal struck his eye.* **14** to arrive at or come upon (something), esp. suddenly or unexpectedly: *to strike the path for home; to strike upon a solution.* **15** (*intr; sometimes* foll. by *out*) to set (out) or proceed, esp. upon a new course: *to strike out for the coast.* **16** (*tr; usually passive*) to afflict with a disease, esp. unexpectedly: *he was struck with polio.* **17** (*tr*) to discover or come upon a source of (ore, petroleum, etc.). **18** (*tr*) (of a plant) to produce or send down (a root or roots). **19** (*tr*) to take apart or pack up; break (esp. in **strike camp**). **20** (*tr*) to take down or dismantle (a stage set, etc.). **21** (*tr*) *Naut.* **21a** to lower or remove (a specified piece of gear). **21b** to haul down or dip (a flag, sail, etc.) in salute or in surrender. **22** to attack (an objective). **23** to impale the hook in the mouth of (a fish) by suddenly tightening or jerking the line after the bait has been taken. **24** (*tr*) to form or impress (a coin, metal, etc.) by or as if by stamping. **25** to level (a surface) by use of a flat board. **26** (*tr*) to assume or take up (an attitude, posture, etc.). **27** (*intr*) (of workers in a factory, etc.) to cease work collectively as a protest against working conditions, low pay, etc. **28** (*tr*) to reach by agreement: *to strike a bargain.* **29** (*tr*) to form (a jury, esp. a special jury) by cancelling certain names among those nominated for jury service until only the requisite number remains. **30 strike home. 30a** to deliver an effective blow. **30b** to achieve the intended effect. **31 strike it rich.** *Inf.* **31a** to discover an extensive deposit of a mineral, petroleum, etc. **31b** to have an unexpected financial success. ◆ *n* **32** an act or instance of striking. **33** a cessation of work, as a protest against working conditions or low pay: *on strike.* **34** a military attack, esp. an air attack on a surface target: *air strike.* **35** *Baseball.* a pitched ball judged good but missed or not swung at, three of which cause a batter to be out. **36** Also called: **ten-strike.** *Tenpin bowling.* **36a** the act or an instance of knocking down all the pins with the first bowl of a single frame. **36b** the score thus made. **37** a sound made by striking. **38** the mechanism that makes a clock strike. **39** the discovery of a source of ore, petroleum, etc. **40** the horizontal direction of a fault, rock stratum, etc. **41** *Angling.* the act or an instance of striking. **42** *Inf.* an unexpected or complete success, esp. one that brings financial gain. **43 take strike.** *Cricket.* (of a batsman) to prepare to play a ball delivered by the bowler. ◆ See also **strike down, strike off,** etc. [OE *strīcan*]

strikebound ('straɪkˌbaʊnd) *adj* (of a factory, etc.) closed or made inoperative by a strike.

strikebreaker ('straɪkˌbreɪkə) *n* a person who tries to make a strike ineffectual by working or by taking the place of those on strike.
▸ˈ**strikeˌbreaking** *n, adj*

strike down ⓣ *vb* (*tr, adv*) to cause to die, esp. suddenly: *he was struck down in his prime.*

strike off *vb* (*tr*) **1** to remove or erase from (a list, record, etc.) by or as if by a stroke of the pen. **2** (*adv*) to cut off or separate by or as if by a blow: *she was struck off from the inheritance.*

strike out ⓣ *vb* (*adv*) **1** (*tr*) to remove or erase. **2** (*intr*) to start out or begin: *to strike out on one's own.* **3** *Baseball.* to put out or be put out on strikes. **4** (*intr*) *US inf.* to fail utterly.

strike pay *n* money paid to strikers from the funds of a trade union.

striker ('straɪkə) *n* **1** a person who is on strike. **2** the hammer in a timepiece that rings a bell or alarm. **3** any part in a mechanical device that strikes something, such as the firing pin of a gun. **4** *Soccer, inf.* an attacking player, esp. one who generally positions himself near his opponent's goal in the hope of scoring. **5** *Cricket.* the batsman who is about to play a ball.

strike up *vb* (*adv*) **1** (of a band, orchestra, etc.) to begin to play or sing. **2** (*tr*) to bring about; cause to begin: *to strike up a friendship.*

striking ⓣ ('straɪkɪŋ) *adj* **1** attracting attention; fine; impressive: *a striking beauty.* **2** conspicuous; noticeable: *a striking difference.*
▸ˈ**strikingly** *adv* ▸ˈ**strikingness** *n*

striking circle *n Hockey.* the semicircular area in front of each goal, which an attacking player must have entered before scoring a goal.

Strimmer ('strɪmə) *n Trademark.* an electrical tool for trimming the edges of lawns.

Strine (straɪn) *n* a humorous transliteration of Australian pronunciation, as in *Gloria Soame* for *glorious home.* [C20: a jocular rendering of the Australian pronunciation of *Australian*]

string ⓣ (strɪŋ) *n* **1** a thin length of cord, twine, fibre, or similar material used for tying, hanging, binding, etc. **2** a group of objects threaded on a single strand: *a string of beads.* **3** a series or succession of things, events, etc.: *a string of oaths.* **4** a number, chain, or group of similar things, animals, etc., owned by or associated with one person or body: *a string of girlfriends.* **5** a tough fibre or cord in a plant. **6** *Music.* a tightly stretched wire, cord, etc., found on stringed instruments, such as the violin, guitar, and piano. **7** short for **bowstring. 8** *Archit.* short for **string course** or **stringer** (sense 1). **9** (*pl; usually preceded by the*) **9a** violins, violas, cellos, and double basses collectively. **9b** the section of a symphony orchestra constituted by such instruments. **10** a group of characters that can be treated as a unit by a computer program. **11** *Physics.* a one-dimensional entity postulated to be a fundamental component of matter in some theories of particle physics. See also **cosmic string. 12** (*pl*) complications or conditions (esp. in **no strings attached**). **13** (*modifier*) composed of stringlike strands woven in a large mesh: *a string bag; a string vest.* **14 first (second,** etc.) **string.** a person or thing regarded as a primary (secondary, etc.) source of strength. **15 keep on a string.** to have control or a hold over (a person), esp. emotionally. **16 pull strings.** *Inf.* to exert power or influence, esp. secretly or unofficially. **17 pull the strings.** to have real or ultimate control of something. ◆ *vb* **strings, stringing, strung. 18** (*tr*) to provide with a string or strings. **19** (*tr*) to suspend or stretch from one point to another. **20** (*tr*) to thread on a string. **21** (*tr*) to form or extend in a line or series. **22** (foll. by *out*) to space or spread out at intervals. **23** (*tr; usually* foll. by *up*) *Inf.* to kill (a person) by hanging. **24** (*tr*) to remove the stringy parts from (vegetables, esp. beans). **25** (*intr*) (esp. of viscous liquids) to become stringy or ropey. **26** (*tr; often* foll. by *up*) to cause to be tense or nervous. [OE *streng*]
▸ˈ**stringˌlike** *adj*

string along ⓣ *vb* (*adv*) *Inf.* **1** (*intr; often* foll. by *with*) to agree or appear to be in agreement (with). **2** (*intr; often* foll. by *with*) to accompany. **3** to deceive or hoax, esp. in order to gain time.

stringboard ('strɪŋˌbɔːd) *n* a skirting that covers the ends of the steps in a staircase. Also called: **stringer.**

string course *n Archit.* an ornamental projecting band or continuous moulding along a wall. Also called: **cordon.**

stringed (strɪŋd) *adj* (of musical instruments) having or provided with strings.

stringendo (strɪn'dʒendəʊ) *adj, adv Music.* to be performed with increasing speed. [It., from *stringere* to compress, from L: to draw tight]

THESAURUS

Antonyms *adj* dulcet, gentle, harmonious, mellifluous, mellow, quiet, soft, soothing, sweet

strife *n* **1, 2 = conflict,** animosity, battle, bickering, clash, clashes, combat, contention, contest, controversy, discord, dissension, friction, quarrel, rivalry, row, squabbling, struggle, warfare, wrangling

strike *vb* **1 = hit,** bang, beat, box, buffet, chastise, chin (*sl.*), clobber (*sl.*), clout (*inf.*), clump (*sl.*), cuff, deck (*sl.*), hammer, knock, lambast(e), lay a finger on (*inf.*), lay one on (*sl.*), pound, punch, punish, slap, smack, smite, sock (*sl.*), swipe, thump, wallop (*inf.*) **2 = collide with,** be in collision with, bump into, clash, come into contact with, dash, hit, knock into, run into, smash into, touch **9 = affect,** hit, make an impact on, reach, register (*inf.*) **11 = occur to,** come to, come to the mind of, dawn on *or* upon, hit, register (*inf.*), seem **14** *sometimes with* **upon = discover,** arrive at, come upon *or* across, encounter, find, happen *or* chance upon, hit upon, light upon, reach, stumble upon *or* across, turn up, uncover, unearth **22 = attack,** affect, assail, assault, deal a blow to, devastate, fall upon, hit, invade, set upon, smite **27 = walk out,** down tools, mutiny, revolt

strike down *vb* **= kill,** afflict, bring low, deal a deathblow to, destroy, ruin, slay, smite

strike out *vb* **1 = score out,** cancel, cross out, delete, efface, erase, excise, expunge, remove **2 = begin,** get under way, set out, start out

striking *adj* **1, 2 = impressive,** astonishing, conspicuous, dazzling, dramatic, drop-dead (*sl.*), extraordinary, forcible, jaw-dropping, memorable, noticeable, out of the ordinary, outstanding, stunning (*inf.*), wonderful
Antonyms *adj* average, dull, indifferent, undistinguished, unexceptional, unextraordinary, unimpressive, uninteresting, vanilla (*inf.*)

string *n* **1 = cord,** fibre, twine **3 = series,** chain, file, line, procession, queue, row, sequence, strand, succession **12** *plural* **= conditions,** catches (*inf.*), complications, obligations, prerequisites, provisos, qualifications, requirements, riders, stipulations ◆ *vb* **19 = hang,** festoon, link, loop, sling, stretch, suspend, thread **22 = spread out,** disperse, extend, fan out, lengthen, protract, space out, straggle

string along *vb* **2** *often with* **with = accompany,** go along with **3 = deceive,** bluff, dupe, fool, hoax, kid (*inf.*), play fast and loose with (someone) (*inf.*), play (someone) false, put one

stringent ❶ (ˈstrɪndʒənt) *adj* **1** requiring strict attention to rules, procedure, detail, etc. **2** *Finance.* characterized by or causing a shortage of credit, loan capital, etc. [C17: from L *stringere* to bind]
▸**ˈstringency** *n* ▸**ˈstringently** *adv*

stringer (ˈstrɪŋə) *n* **1** *Archit.* **1a** a long horizontal beam that is used for structural purposes. **1b** another name for **stringboard. 2** *Naut.* a longitudinal structural brace for strengthening the hull of a vessel. **3** a journalist retained by a newspaper or news service on a part-time basis to cover a particular town or area.

stringhalt (ˈstrɪŋˌhɔːlt) *n Vet. science.* a sudden spasmodic lifting of the hind leg of a horse. Also called: **springhalt.** [C16: prob. STRING + HALT[2]]

stringpiece (ˈstrɪŋˌpiːs) *n* a long horizontal timber beam used to strengthen or support a framework.

string quartet *n Music.* **1** an instrumental ensemble consisting of two violins, one viola, and one cello. **2** a piece of music for such a group.

string tie *n* a very narrow tie.

stringy ❶ (ˈstrɪŋɪ) *adj* **stringier, stringiest. 1** made of strings or resembling strings. **2** (of meat, etc.) fibrous. **3** (of a person's build) wiry; sinewy. **4** (of liquids) forming in strings.
▸**ˈstringily** *adv* ▸**ˈstringiness** *n*

stringy-bark *n Austral.* any of several eucalyptus trees having fibrous bark.

strip[1] ❶ (strɪp) *vb* **strips, stripping, stripped. 1** to take or pull (the covering, clothes, etc.) off (oneself, another person, or thing). **2** (*intr*) **2a** to remove all one's clothes. **2b** to perform a striptease. **3** (*tr*) to denude or empty completely. **4** (*tr*) to deprive: *he was stripped of his pride.* **5** (*tr*) to rob or plunder. **6** (*tr*) to remove (paint, etc.) from (a surface, furniture, etc.): *stripped pine.* **7** (*tr*) to pull out the old coat of hair from (dogs of certain long- and wire-haired breeds). **8a** to remove the leaves from the stalks of (tobacco, etc.). **8b** to separate the leaves from the stems of (tobacco, etc.). **9** (*tr*) *Agriculture.* to draw the last milk from (a cow). **10** to dismantle (an engine, mechanism, etc.). **11** to tear off or break (the thread) from (a screw, bolt, etc.) or (the teeth) from (a gear). **12** (often foll. by *down*) to remove the accessories from (a motor vehicle): *his car was stripped down.* ◆ *n* **13** the act or an instance of undressing or of performing a striptease. [OE *bestriepan* to plunder]

strip[2] ❶ (strɪp) *n* **1** a relatively long, flat, narrow piece of something. **2** short for **airstrip. 3** the clothes worn by the members of a team, esp. a football team. **4** *Business.* a triple option on a security or commodity consisting of one call option and two put options at the same price and for the same period. Cf. **strap** (sense 6). **5 tear (someone) off a strip.** *Inf.* to rebuke (someone) angrily. ◆ *vb* **strips, stripping, stripped. 6** to cut or divide into strips. [C15: from MDu. *strīpe* STRIPE[1]]

strip cartoon *n* a sequence of drawings in a newspaper, magazine, etc., relating a humorous story or an adventure. Also called: **comic strip.**

strip club *n* a small club in which striptease performances take place.

stripe[1] (straɪp) *n* **1** a relatively long band of colour or texture that differs from the surrounding material or background. **2** a fabric having such bands. **3** a strip, band, or chevron worn on a uniform, etc., esp. to indicate rank. **4** *Chiefly US & Canad.* kind; type: *a man of a certain stripe.* ◆ *vb* **stripes, striping, striped. 5** (*tr*) to mark with stripes. [C17: prob. from MDu. *strīpe*]
▸**striped** *adj*

stripe[2] (straɪp) *n* a stroke from a whip, rod, cane, etc. [C15: ?from MLow G *strippe*]

striped muscle *n* a type of contractile tissue that is marked by transverse striations. Also called: **striated muscle.**

strip lighting *n* electric lighting by means of long glass tubes that are fluorescent lamps or that contain long filaments.

stripling ❶ (ˈstrɪplɪŋ) *n* a lad. [C13: from STRIP[2] + -LING[1]]

strip mining *n* another term (esp. US) for **opencast mining.**

stripper (ˈstrɪpə) *n* **1** a striptease artiste. **2** a person or thing that strips. **3** a device or substance for removing paint, varnish, etc.

strip-search *vb* **1** (*tr*) (of police, customs officials, etc.) to strip (a prisoner or suspect) naked to search him or her for contraband, narcotics, etc. ◆ *n* **2** a search that involves stripping a person naked.
▸**ˈstrip-ˌsearching** *n*

striptease (ˈstrɪpˌtiːz) *n* **a** a form of erotic entertainment in which a person gradually undresses to music. **b** (*as modifier*): *a striptease club.*
▸**ˈstripˌteaser** *n*

stripy *or* **stripey** (ˈstraɪpɪ) *adj* **stripier, stripiest.** marked by or with stripes; striped.

strive ❶ (straɪv) *vb* **strives, striving, strove, striven** (ˈstrɪvᵊn). **1** (*may take a clause as object or an infinitive*) to make a great and tenacious effort. **2** (*intr*) to fight; contend. [C13: from OF *estriver,* of Gmc origin]
▸**ˈstriver** *n*

strobe (strəʊb) *n* short for **strobe lighting** or **stroboscope.**

strobe lighting *n* **1** a high-intensity flashing beam of light produced by rapid electrical discharges in a tube or by a perforated disc rotating in front of an intense light source. **2** the use of or the apparatus for producing such light. Sometimes shortened to **strobe.**

strobilus (ˈstrəʊbɪləs) *or* **strobile** (ˈstrəʊbaɪl) *n, pl* **strobiluses, strobili** (-bɪlaɪ), *or* **strobiles.** *Bot.* the technical name for **cone** (sense 3). [C18: via LL from Gk *strobilos* a fir cone]

stroboscope (ˈstrəʊbəˌskəʊp) *n* **1** an instrument producing an intense flashing light, the frequency of which can be synchronized with some multiple of the frequency of rotation, vibration, or operation of an object, etc., making it appear stationary. Sometimes shortened to **strobe. 2** a similar device synchronized with the shutter of a camera so that a series of still photographs can be taken of a moving object. [C19: from *strobo-,* from Gk *strobos* a whirling + -SCOPE]
▸**stroboscopic** (ˌstrəʊbəˈskɒpɪk) *or* **ˌstroboˈscopical** *adj* ▸**ˌstroboˈscopically** *adv*

strode (strəʊd) *vb* the past tense of **stride.**

stroganoff (ˈstrɒgəˌnɒf) *n* a dish of sliced beef cooked with onions and mushrooms, served in a sour-cream sauce. Also called: **beef stroganoff.** [C19: after Count *Stroganoff,* 19th-century Russian diplomat]

stroke ❶ (strəʊk) *n* **1** the act or an instance of striking; a blow, knock, or hit. **2** a sudden action, movement, or occurrence: *a stroke of luck.* **3** a brilliant or inspired act or feat: *a stroke of genius.* **4** *Pathol.* apoplexy; rupture of a blood vessel in the brain resulting in loss of consciousness, often followed by paralysis, or embolism or thrombosis affecting a cerebral vessel. **5a** the striking of a clock. **5b** the hour registered by this: *on the stroke of three.* **6** a mark made by a writing implement. **7** another name for **solidus** (sense 1), used esp. when dictating or reading aloud. **8** a light touch or caress, as with the fingers. **9** a pulsation, esp. of the heart. **10** a single complete movement or one of a series of complete movements. **11** *Sport.* the act or manner of striking the ball with a club, bat, etc. **12** any one of the repeated movements used by a swimmer. **13** a manner of swimming, esp. one of several named styles such as the crawl. **14a** any one of a series of linear movements of a reciprocating part, such as a piston. **14b** the distance travelled by such a part from one end of its movement to the other. **15** a single pull on an oar or oars in rowing. **16** manner or style of rowing. **17** the oarsman who sits nearest the stern of a shell, facing the cox, and sets the rate of rowing. **18 a stroke (of work).** (*usually used with a negative*) a small amount of work. **19 at a stroke.** with one action. **20 off one's stroke.** performing or working less well than usual. **21 on the stroke.** punctually. ◆ *vb* **strokes, stroking, stroked. 22** (*tr*) to touch, brush, etc. lightly or gently. **23** (*tr*) to mark a line or a stroke on or through. **24** to act as the stroke of (a racing shell). **25** (*tr*) *Sport.* to strike (a ball) with a smooth swinging blow. [OE *strācian*]

stroke play *n Golf.* **a** scoring by counting the strokes taken. **b** (*as modifier*): *a strokeplay tournament.* ◆ Also called: **medal play.** Cf. **match play, Stableford.**

stroll ❶ (strəʊl) *vb* **1** to walk about in a leisurely manner. **2** (*intr*) to wander about. ◆ *n* **3** a leisurely walk. [C17: prob. from dialect G *strollen,* from ?]

stroller (ˈstrəʊlə) *n* the usual US, Canad., and Austral. word for **pushchair.**

stroma (ˈstrəʊmə) *n, pl* **stromata** (-mətə). *Biol.* **1** the dense colourless framework of a chloroplast and certain cells. **2** the fibrous connective tissue forming the matrix of the mammalian ovary and testis. **3** a dense mass of hyphae that is produced by certain fungi and gives rise to spore-producing bodies. [C19: via NL from LL: a mattress, from Gk]
▸**stromatic** (strəʊˈmætɪk) *or* **ˈstromatous** *adj*

Strombolian (strɒmˈbəʊlɪən) *adj* relating to or denoting a type of volcanic eruption characterized by repeated small explosions caused by gas escaping through lava. [from *Stromboli,* island with a famous active volcano, off the N coast of Sicily]

strong ❶ (strɒŋ) *adj* **stronger** (ˈstrɒŋgə), **strongest** (ˈstrɒŋgɪst). **1** involving or possessing strength. **2** solid or robust; not easily broken or injured. **3** resolute or morally firm. **4** intense in quality; not faint or feeble: *a strong voice; a strong smell.* **5** easily defensible; incontestable or formidable. **6** concentrated; not weak or diluted. **7a** (*postpositive*) containing or having a specified number: *a navy 40 000 strong.* **7b** (*in combination*): *a 40 000-strong navy.* **8** having an unpleasantly powerful taste or smell. **9**

THESAURUS

over on (someone) (*inf.*), take (someone) for a ride (*inf.*)

stringent *adj* **1** = **strict**, binding, demanding, exacting, inflexible, rigid, rigorous, severe, tight, tough
Antonyms *adj* equivocal, flexible, inconclusive, lax, loose, relaxed, slack, unrigorous, vague

stringy *adj* = **fibrous**, chewy, gristly, sinewy, tough, wiry

strip[1] *vb* **1, 2a** = **undress**, disrobe, unclothe, uncover **3, 4, 5** = **plunder**, bare, denude, deprive, despoil, dismantle, divest, empty, gut, lay bare, loot, peel, pillage, ransack, rob, sack, skin, spoil

strip[2] *n* **1** = **piece**, band, belt, bit, fillet, ribbon, shred, slip, swathe, tongue

stripling *n* = **boy**, adolescent, fledgling, hobbledehoy (*arch.*), lad, shaver (*inf.*), young fellow, youngster, youth

strive *vb* **1, 2** = **try**, attempt, bend over backwards, bust a gut (*inf.*), compete, contend, do all one can, do one's best, do one's damnedest (*inf.*), do one's utmost, endeavour, exert oneself, fight, give it one's all (*inf.*), give it one's best shot (*inf.*), go all out (*inf.*), go for broke (*sl.*), go for it (*inf.*), jump through hoops (*inf.*), knock oneself out (*inf.*), labour, make an all-out effort (*inf.*), make every effort, strain, struggle, toil, try hard

stroke *n* **1** = **blow**, hit, knock, pat, rap, swipe, thump **3** = **feat**, accomplishment, achievement, flourish, move, movement **4** = **apoplexy**, attack, collapse, fit, seizure, shock ◆ *vb* **8** = **caress**, fondle, pat, pet, rub

stroll *vb* **1, 2** = **walk**, amble, make one's way, mooch (*sl.*), mosey (*inf.*), promenade, ramble, saunter, stooge (*sl.*), stretch one's legs, take a turn, toddle, wander ◆ *n* **3** = **walk**, airing, breath of air, constitutional, excursion, promenade, ramble, turn

strong *adj* **1** = **powerful**, athletic, beefy (*inf.*),

having an extreme or drastic effect: *strong discipline.* **10** emphatic or immoderate: *strong language.* **11** convincing, effective, or cogent. **12** (of a colour) having a high degree of saturation or purity; produced by a concentrated quantity of colouring agent. **13** *Grammar.* **13a** of or denoting a class of verbs, in certain languages including the Germanic languages, whose conjugation shows vowel gradation, as *sing, sang, sung.* **13b** belonging to any part-of-speech class, in various languages, whose inflections follow the less regular of two possible patterns. Cf. **weak** (sense 10). **14** (of a wind, current, etc.) moving fast. **15** (of a syllable) accented or stressed. **16** (of an industry, etc.) firm in price or characterized by firm or increasing prices. **17** (of certain acids and bases) producing high concentrations of hydrogen or hydroxide ions in aqueous solution. **18 have a strong stomach.** not to be prone to nausea. ◆ *adv* **19** *Inf.* in a strong way; effectively: *going strong.* **20 come on strong.** to make a forceful or exaggerated impression. [OE *strang*]
▸**'strongly** *adv* ▸**'strongness** *n*

strong-arm ⓘ *Inf.* ◆ *n* **1** (*modifier*) of or involving physical force or violence: *strong-arm tactics.* ◆ *vb* **2** (*tr*) to show violence towards.

strongbox ('strɒŋ,bɒks) *n* a box or safe in which valuables are locked for safety.

strong breeze *n Meteorol.* a wind of force 6 on the Beaufort scale, reaching speeds of 25 to 31 mph.

strong drink *n* alcoholic drink.

strong-eye dog *n NZ.* See **eye dog.**

strong gale *n Meteorol.* a wind of force 9 on the Beaufort scale, reaching speeds of 47 to 54 mph.

stronghold ⓘ ('strɒŋ,həʊld) *n* **1** a defensible place; fortress. **2** a major centre or area of predominance.

strong interaction *or* **force** *n Physics.* an interaction between elementary particles responsible for the forces between nucleons in the nucleus. Also called: **strong nuclear interaction** *or* **force.** See **interaction** (sense 2). Cf. **weak interaction.**

strong-minded ⓘ *adj* having strength of mind; firm, resolute, and determined.
▸**,strong-'mindedly** *adv* ▸**,strong-'mindedness** *n*

strong point ⓘ *n* something at which one excels; forte.

strongroom ('strɒŋ,ru:m, -,rʊm) *n* a specially designed room in which valuables are locked for safety.

strong-willed *adj* having strength of will.

strontium ('strɒntɪəm) *n* a soft silvery-white element of the alkaline earth group of metals. The radioisotope **strontium-90,** with a half-life of 28.1 years, is used in nuclear power sources and is a hazardous nuclear fallout product. Symbol: Sr; atomic no.: 38; atomic wt.: 87.62. [C19: from NL, after *Strontian,* in the Highlands of Scotland, where discovered]

strontium unit *n* a unit expressing the concentration of strontium-90 in an organic medium, such as soil, bone, etc., relative to the concentration of calcium in the medium.

strop (strɒp) *n* **1** a leather strap or an abrasive strip for sharpening razors. **2** a rope or metal band around a block or deadeye for support. ◆ *vb* **strops, stropping, stropped. 3** (*tr*) to sharpen (a razor, etc.) on a strop. [C14 (in nautical use: a strip of rope): via MLow G or MDu. *strop,* ult. from L *stroppus,* from Gk *strophos* cord]

strophanthin (strəʊ'fænθɪn) *n* a toxic glycoside or mixture of glycosides obtained from the ripe seeds of certain species of strophanthus. [C19: NL, from STROPHANTH(US) + -IN]

strophanthus (strəʊ'fænθəs) *n* **1** any of various small trees or shrubs of tropical Africa and Asia, having strap-shaped twisted petals. **2** the seeds of any of these plants. [C19: NL, from Gk *strophos* twisted cord + *anthos* flower]

strophe ('strəʊfɪ) *n Prosody.* (in ancient Greek drama) **a** the first of two movements made by a chorus during the performance of a choral ode. **b** the first part of a choral ode sung during this movement. ◆ See **antistrophe, epode.** [C17: from Gk: a verse, lit.: a turning, from *strephein* to twist]
▸**strophic** ('strɒfɪk, 'strəʊ-) *adj*

stroppy ⓘ ('strɒpɪ) *adj* **stroppier, stroppiest.** *Brit. inf.* angry or awkward. [C20: changed & shortened from OBSTREPEROUS]
▸**'stroppily** *adv* ▸**'stroppiness** *n*

strove (strəʊv) *vb* the past tense of **strive.**

strow (strəʊ) *vb* **strows, strowing, strowed; strown** *or* **strowed.** an archaic variant of **strew.**

struck (strʌk) *vb* **1** the past tense and past participle of **strike.** ◆ *adj* **2** *Chiefly US & Canad.* (of an industry, factory, etc.) shut down or otherwise affected by a labour strike.

structural ('strʌktʃərəl) *adj* **1** of, relating to, or having structure or a structure. **2** of, relating to, or forming part of the structure of a building. **3** of or relating to the structure of the earth's crust. **4** of or relating to the structure of organisms. **5** *Chem.* of or involving the arrangement of atoms in molecules.
▸**'structurally** *adv*

structural formula *n* a chemical formula showing the composition and structure of a molecule.

structuralism ('strʌktʃərə,lɪzəm) *n* **1** an approach to social sciences and to literature in terms of oppositions, contrasts, and hierarchical structures, esp. as they might reflect universal mental characteristics or organizing principles. **2** an approach to linguistics that analyses and describes the structure of language, as distinguished from its comparative and historical aspects.
▸**'structuralist** *n, adj*

structural linguistics *n* (*functioning as sing*) a descriptive approach to an analysis of language on the basis of its structure as reflected by irreducible units of phonological, morphological, and semantic features.

structural unemployment *n Econ.* unemployment resulting from changes in the structure of an industry as a result of changes in either technology or taste.

structure ⓘ ('strʌktʃə) *n* **1** a complex construction or entity. **2** the arrangement and interrelationship of parts in a construction. **3** the manner of construction or organization. **4** *Chem.* the arrangement of atoms in a molecule of a chemical compound. **5** *Geol.* the way in which a mineral, rock, etc., is made up of its component parts. ◆ *vb* **structures, structuring, structured.** (*tr*) **6** to impart a structure to. [C15: from L *structūra,* from *struere* to build]

structured interview *n Marketing.* an interview in which the respondent answers only "yes", "no", or "don't know".

strudel ('stru:dəl) *n* a thin sheet of filled dough rolled up and baked: *apple strudel.* [G, from MHG *strodel* whirlpool, from the way the pastry is rolled]

struggle ⓘ ('strʌgᵊl) *vb* **struggles, struggling, struggled.** (*intr*) **1** (usually foll. by *for* or *against; may take an infinitive*) to exert strength, energy, and force; work or strive. **2** to move about strenuously so as to escape from something confining. **3** to contend, battle, or fight. **4** to go or progress with difficulty. ◆ *n* **5** a laboured or strenuous exertion or effort. **6** a fight or battle. **7** the act of struggling. [C14: from ?]
▸**'struggling** *adj*

strum (strʌm) *vb* **strums, strumming, strummed. 1** to sound (the strings of a guitar, etc.) with a downward or upward sweep of the thumb or of a plectrum. **2** to play (chords, a tune, etc.) in this way. [C18: prob. imit.]
▸**'strummer** *n*

struma ('stru:mə) *n, pl* **strumae** (-mi:). **1** an abnormal enlargement of the thyroid gland; goitre. **2** *Bot.* a swelling, esp. at the base of a moss capsule. **3** another word for **scrofula.** [C16: from L: scrofulous tumour, from *struere* to heap up]
▸**strumous** ('stru:məs) *or* **strumose** ('stru:məʊs) *adj*

strumpet ('strʌmpɪt) *n Arch.* a prostitute or promiscuous woman. [C14: from ?]

strung (strʌŋ) *vb* **1** a past tense and past participle of **string.** ◆ *adj* **2a** (of a piano, etc.) provided with strings. **2b** (*in combination*): *gut-strung.* **3 highly strung.** very nervous or volatile in character.

THESAURUS

brawny, burly, capable, fighting fit, fit, fit as a fiddle, hale, hardy, healthy, Herculean, lusty, muscular, robust, sinewy, sound, stalwart, stout, strapping, sturdy, tough, virile **2** = **durable**, hard-wearing, heavy-duty, on a firm foundation, reinforced, sturdy, substantial, well-armed, well-built, well-protected **3** = **self-confident**, aggressive, brave, courageous, determined, feisty (*inf., chiefly US & Canad.*), firm in spirit, forceful, hard as nails, hard-nosed (*inf.*), high-powered, plucky, resilient, resolute, resourceful, self-assertive, steadfast, stout-hearted, tenacious, tough, unyielding **4** = **distinct**, clear, marked, overpowering, unmistakable **6, 8** = **pungent**, biting, concentrated, heady, highly-flavoured, highly-seasoned, hot, intoxicating, piquant, powerful, pure, sharp, spicy, undiluted **9** = **extreme**, Draconian, drastic, forceful, severe **11** = **persuasive**, clear, clear-cut, cogent, compelling, convincing, effective, formidable, great, overpowering, potent, redoubtable, sound, telling, trenchant, urgent, weighty, well-established, well-founded **12** = **bright**, bold, brilliant, dazzling, glaring, loud, stark

Antonyms *adj* ≠ **powerful:** delicate, feeble, frail, ineffectual, namby-pamby, puny, weak ≠ **self-confident:** characterless, faint-hearted, lacking drive, spineless, timid, unassertive, uncommitted, unimpassioned ≠ **distinct:** delicate, faint, slight ≠ **pungent:** bland, mild, tasteless, vapid, weak ≠ **bright:** dull, insipid, pale, pastel, washed-out

strong-arm *adj* **1** *Informal* = **bullying**, aggressive, coercive, forceful, high-pressure, terror, terrorizing, threatening, thuggish, violent

stronghold *n* **1** = **fortress**, bastion, bulwark, castle, citadel, fastness, fort, keep, refuge

strong-minded *adj* = **determined**, firm, independent, iron-willed, resolute, strong-willed, unbending, uncompromising

strong point *n* = **forte**, advantage, asset, long suit (*inf.*), métier, speciality, strength, strong suit

stroppy *adj Brit. informal* = **awkward**, bloody-minded (*Brit. inf.*), cantankerous, destructive, difficult, litigious, obstreperous, perverse, quarrelsome, uncooperative, unhelpful

structure *n* **1** = **building**, construction, edifice, erection, pile **2** = **arrangement**, configuration, conformation, construction, design, fabric, form, formation, interrelation of parts, make, make-up, organization ◆ *vb* **6** = **arrange**, assemble, build up, design, organize, put together, shape

struggle *vb* **1** = **strive**, bend over backwards, break one's neck (*inf.*), bust a gut (*inf.*), do one's damnedest (*inf.*), exert oneself, give it one's all (*inf.*), give it one's best shot (*inf.*), go all out (*inf.*), go for broke (*sl.*), go for it (*inf.*), knock oneself out (*inf.*), labour, make an all-out effort (*inf.*), make every effort, rupture oneself (*inf.*), strain, toil, work, work like a Trojan **3** = **fight**, battle, compete, contend, grapple, lock horns, scuffle, wrestle ◆ *n* **5** = **effort**, exertion, grind (*inf.*), labour, long haul, pains, scramble, toil, work **6** = **fight**, battle, brush, clash, combat, conflict, contest, encounter, hostilities, skirmish, strife, tussle

strung up ❶ *adj* (*postpositive*) *Inf.* tense or nervous.

strut ❶ (strʌt) *vb* **struts, strutting, strutted.** **1** (*intr*) to walk in a pompous manner; swagger. **2** (*tr*) to support or provide with struts. ◆ *n* **3** a structural member, esp. as part of a framework. **4** an affected, proud, or stiff walk. [C14 *strouten* (in the sense: swell, stand out; C16: to walk stiffly), from OE *strūtian* to stand stiffly]
▸ **'strutter** *n* ▸ **'strutting** *adj* ▸ **'struttingly** *adv*

struthious ('struːθɪəs) *adj* **1** (of birds) related to or resembling the ostrich. **2** of, relating to, or designating all flightless birds. [C18: from LL *strūthiō*, from Gk *strouthiōn*, from *strouthos* ostrich]

strychnine ('strɪkniːn) *n* a white crystalline very poisonous alkaloid, obtained from the plant nux vomica: formerly used in small quantities as a stimulant. [C19: via F from NL *Strychnos*, from Gk *strukhnos* nightshade]

Stuart ('stjʊət) *adj* of or relating to the royal house that ruled Scotland from 1371 to 1714 and England from 1603 to 1714.

stub ❶ (stʌb) *n* **1** a short piece remaining after something has been cut, removed, etc.: *a cigar stub.* **2** the residual piece or section of a receipt, ticket, cheque, etc. **3** the usual US and Canad. word for **counterfoil.** **4** any short projection or blunted end. **5** the stump of a tree or plant. ◆ *vb* **stubs, stubbing, stubbed.** (*tr*) **6** to strike (one's toe, foot, etc.) painfully against a hard surface. **7** (usually foll. by *out*) to put (out a cigarette or cigar) by pressing the end against a surface. **8** to clear (land) of stubs. **9** to dig up (the roots) of (a tree or bush). [OE *stubb*]

stub axle *n* a short axle that carries one of the front steered wheels of a motor vehicle.

stubble ('stʌbᵊl) *n* **1a** the stubs of stalks left in a field where a crop has been harvested. **1b** (*as modifier*): *a stubble field.* **2** any bristly growth. [C13: from OF *estuble*, from L *stupula*, var. of *stipula* stalk]
▸ **'stubbled** *or* **'stubbly** *adj*

stubble-jumper *n Canad. sl.* a prairie grain farmer.

stubborn ❶ ('stʌbᵊn) *adj* **1** refusing to comply, agree, or give in. **2** difficult to handle, treat, or overcome. **3** persistent and dogged. [C14 *stoborne*, from ?]
▸ **'stubbornly** *adv* ▸ **'stubbornness** *n*

stubby ❶ ('stʌbɪ) *adj* **stubbier, stubbiest.** **1** short and broad; stumpy or thickset. **2** bristling and stiff. ◆ *n* **3** *Austral. sl.* Also: **stubbie.** a small bottle of beer.
▸ **'stubbily** *adv* ▸ **'stubbiness** *n*

stucco ('stʌkəʊ) *n, pl* **stuccoes** *or* **stuccos.** **1** a weather-resistant mixture of dehydrated lime, powdered marble, and glue, used in decorative mouldings on buildings. **2** any of various types of cement or plaster used for coating outside walls. **3** Also called: **stuccowork.** decorative work moulded in stucco. ◆ *vb* **stuccoes** *or* **stuccos, stuccoing, stuccoed.** **4** (*tr*) to apply stucco to. [C16: from It., of Gmc origin]

stuck ❶ (stʌk) *vb* **1** the past tense and past participle of **stick**². ◆ *adj* **2** *Inf.* baffled or nonplussed. **3** (foll. by *on*) *Sl.* keen (on) or infatuated (with). **4** **get stuck in** *or* **into.** *Inf.* **4a** to perform (a task) with determination. **4b** to attack (a person).

stuck-up ❶ *adj Inf.* conceited, arrogant, or snobbish.
▸ **'stuck-'upness** *n*

stud¹ ❶ (stʌd) *n* **1** a large-headed nail or other projection protruding from a surface, usually as decoration. **2** a type of fastener consisting of two discs at either end of a short shank, used to fasten shirtfronts, collars, etc. **3** a vertical member used with others to construct the framework of a wall. **4** the crossbar in the centre of a link of a heavy chain. **5** one of a number of rounded projections on the sole of a boot or shoe to give better grip, as on a football boot. ◆ *vb* **studs, studding, studded.** (*tr*) **6** to provide, ornament, or make with studs. **7** to dot or cover (with): *the park was studded with daisies.* **8** to provide or support (a wall, partition, etc.) with studs. [OE *studu*]

stud² (stʌd) *n* **1** a group of pedigree animals, esp. horses, kept for breeding purposes. **2** any male animal kept principally for breeding purposes, esp. a stallion. **3** a farm or stable where a stud is kept. **4** the state or condition of being kept for breeding purposes: *at stud; put to stud.* **5** (*modifier*) of or relating to such animals or the place where they are kept: *a stud farm; a stud horse.* **6** *Sl.* a virile or sexually active man. **7** short for **stud poker.** [OE *stōd*]

studbook ('stʌdˌbʊk) *n* a written record of the pedigree of a purebred stock, esp. of racehorses.

studding ('stʌdɪŋ) *n* **1** studs collectively, esp. as used to form a wall or partition. **2** material used to form or serve as studs.

studdingsail ('stʌdɪŋˌseɪl; *Naut.* 'stʌnsᵊl) *n Naut.* a light auxiliary sail set outboard on spars on either side of a square sail. Also called: **stunsail, stuns'l.** [C16: *studding*, ?from MLow G, MDu. *stōtinge*, from *stōten* to thrust]

student ❶ ('stjuːdᵊnt) *n* **1a** a person following a course of study, as in a school, college, university, etc. **1b** (*as modifier*): *student teacher.* **2** a person who makes a thorough study of a subject. [C15: from L *studēns* diligent, from *studēre* to be zealous]

Student's t *n* a statistic often used to test the hypothesis that a random sample of normally distributed observations has a given mean. [after *Student*, pen name of W. S. Gosset (1876–1937), Brit. mathematician]

studhorse ('stʌdˌhɔːs) *n* another word for **stallion.**

studied ❶ ('stʌdɪd) *adj* carefully practised, designed, or premeditated: *a studied reply.*
▸ **'studiedly** *adv* ▸ **'studiedness** *n*

studio ❶ ('stjuːdɪəʊ) *n, pl* **studios.** **1** a room in which an artist, photographer, or musician works. **2** a room used to record television or radio programmes, make films, etc. **3** (*pl*) the premises of a radio, television, or film company. [C19: from It., lit.: study, from L *studium* diligence]

studio couch *n* an upholstered couch, usually backless, convertible into a double bed.

studio flat *n* a flat with one main room.

studious ❶ ('stjuːdɪəs) *adj* **1** given to study. **2** of a serious, thoughtful, and hard-working character. **3** showing deliberation, care, or precision. [C14: from L *studiōsus* devoted to, from *studium* assiduity]
▸ **'studiously** *adv* ▸ **'studiousness** *n*

stud poker *n* a variety of poker in which the first card is dealt face down before each player and the next four are dealt face up (**five-card stud**) or in which the first two cards and the last card are dealt face down and the intervening four cards are dealt face up (**seven-card stud**).

study ❶ ('stʌdɪ) *vb* **studies, studying, studied.** **1** to apply the mind to the learning or understanding of (a subject), esp. by reading. **2** (*tr*) to investigate or examine, as by observation, research, etc. **3** (*tr*) to look at minutely; scrutinize. **4** (*tr*) to give much careful or critical thought to. **5** to take a course in (a subject), as at a college. **6** (*tr*) to try to memorize: *to study a part for a play.* **7** (*intr*) to meditate or contemplate; reflect. ◆ *n, pl* **studies.** **8a** the act or process of studying. **8b** (*as modifier*): *study group.* **9** a room used for studying, reading, writing, etc. **10** (*often pl*) work relating to a particular discipline: *environmental studies.* **11** an investigation and analysis of a subject, institution etc. **12** a product of studying, such as a written paper or book. **13** a drawing, sculpture, etc., executed for practice or in preparation for another work. **14** a musical composition intended to develop one aspect of performing technique. **15** *Inf.* **in a brown study.** in a reverie or daydream. [C13: from OF *estudie*, from L *studium* zeal, from *studēre* to be diligent]

stuff ❶ (stʌf) *vb* (*mainly tr*) **1** to pack or fill completely; cram. **2** (*intr*) to eat large quantities. **3** to force, shove, or squeeze: *to stuff money into a pocket.* **4** to fill (food such as poultry or tomatoes) with a stuffing. **5** to fill (an animal's skin) with material so as to restore the shape of the live animal. **6** *Taboo sl.* to have sexual intercourse with (a woman). **7** *US & Canad.* to fill (a ballot box) with fraudulent votes. **8** *Sl.* to ruin, frustrate, or defeat. ◆ *n* **9** the raw material or fabric of something. **10**

THESAURUS

strung up *adj Informal* = **tense**, a bundle of nerves (*inf.*), edgy, jittery (*inf.*), keyed up, nervous, on edge, on tenterhooks, twitchy (*inf.*), under a strain, uptight (*inf.*), wired (*sl.*)

strut *vb* **1** = **swagger**, parade, peacock, prance, stalk

stub *n* **1** = **butt**, dog-end (*inf.*), end, fag end (*inf.*), remnant, stump, tail, tail end **2** = **counterfoil**

stubborn *adj* **1, 3** = **obstinate**, bull-headed, contumacious, cross-grained, dogged, dour, fixed, headstrong, inflexible, intractable, mulish, obdurate, opinionated, persistent, pigheaded, recalcitrant, refractory, self-willed, stiff-necked, tenacious, unbending, unmanageable, unshakable, unyielding, wilful
Antonyms *adj* biddable, compliant, docile, flexible, half-hearted, irresolute, malleable, manageable, pliable, pliant, tractable, vacillating, wavering, yielding

stubby *adj* **1** = **stocky**, chunky, dumpy, fubsy (*arch. or dialect*), short, squat, stumpy, thickset

stuck *adj* **1** = **fastened**, cemented, fast, firm, fixed, glued, joined **2** *Informal* = **baffled**, at a loss, at a standstill, at one's wits' end, beaten, bereft of ideas, nonplussed, stumped, up against a brick wall (*inf.*) **3** *Slang foll. by* **on** = **infatuated with**, crazy about, for, *or* over (*inf.*), enthusiastic about, hung up on, keen on, mad about, obsessed with, wild about (*inf.*) **4** **get stuck in** *Informal* = **set about**, get down to, make a start on, tackle, take the bit between one's teeth

stuck-up *adj Informal* = **snobbish**, arrogant, bigheaded (*inf.*), conceited, condescending, haughty, high and mighty (*inf.*), hoity-toity (*inf.*), patronizing, proud, snooty (*inf.*), swollen-headed, toffee-nosed (*sl., chiefly Brit.*), uppish (*Brit. inf.*), uppity (*inf.*)

stud¹ *vb* **6, 7** = **ornament**, bejewel, bespangle, dot, fleck, spangle, speckle, spot, sprinkle

student *n* **1a, 2** = **learner**, apprentice, disciple, observer, pupil, scholar, trainee, undergraduate

studied *adj* = **planned**, calculated, conscious, deliberate, intentional, premeditated, purposeful, well-considered, wilful
Antonyms *adj* impulsive, natural, spontaneous, spur-of-the-moment, unplanned, unpremeditated

studio *n* **1** = **workshop**, atelier

studious *adj* **1, 2** = **scholarly**, academic, assiduous, bookish, diligent, eager, earnest, hard-working, intellectual, meditative, reflective, sedulous, serious, thoughtful **3** = **careful**, attentive, deliberate, precise
Antonyms *adj* ≠ **scholarly**: frivolous, idle, lazy, loafing, unacademic, unintellectual, unscholarly ≠ **careful**: careless, inattentive, indifferent, negligent

study *vb* **1** = **learn**, bone up on (*inf.*), burn the midnight oil, cram (*inf.*), hammer away at, lucubrate (*rare*), mug up (*Brit. sl.*), read up, swot (up) (*Brit. inf.*) **2** = **contemplate**, apply oneself (to), cogitate, con (*arch.*), consider, examine, go into, meditate, ponder, pore over, read **3** = **examine**, analyse, deliberate, investigate, look into, peruse, research, scrutinize, survey, work over ◆ *n* **8a** = **learning**, academic work, application, book work, cramming (*inf.*), lessons, reading, research, school work, swotting (*Brit. inf.*), thought **11** = **examination**, analysis, attention, cogitation, consideration, contemplation, inquiry, inspection, investigation, perusal, review, scrutiny, survey

stuff *vb* **1** = **cram**, compress, crowd, fill, force, jam, load, pack, pad, push, ram, shove, squeeze, stow, wedge **2** = **gorge**, gobble, gor-

woollen cloth or fabric. **11** any general or unspecified substance or accumulation of objects. **12** stupid or worthless actions, speech, etc. **13** subject matter, skill, etc.: *he knows his stuff.* **14** a slang word for **money. 15** *Sl.* a drug, esp. cannabis. **16** *Inf.* **do one's stuff.** to do what is expected of one. **17 that's the stuff.** that is what is needed. **18** *Brit. sl.* a girl or woman considered sexually (esp. in **bit of stuff**). [C14: from OF *estoffe,* from *estoffer* to furnish, of Gmc origin]
▸**'stuffer** *n*

stuffed (stʌft) *adj* **1** filled with something, esp. (of poultry and other food) filled with stuffing. **2** (foll. by *up*) having the nasal passages blocked with mucus. **3 get stuffed!** *Brit. taboo sl.* an exclamation of contemptuous anger or annoyance against another person.

stuffed shirt *n Inf.* a pompous person.

stuff gown *n Brit.* a woollen gown worn by a barrister who has not taken silk.

stuffing ➊ ('stʌfɪŋ) *n* **1** the material with which something is stuffed. **2** a mixture of ingredients with which poultry, meat, etc., is stuffed before cooking. **3 knock the stuffing out of (someone).** to defeat (someone) utterly.

stuffing box *n* a small chamber in which packing is compressed around a reciprocating or rotating rod or shaft to form a seal.

stuffy ➊ ('stʌfɪ) *adj* **stuffier, stuffiest. 1** lacking fresh air. **2** excessively dull, staid, or conventional. **3** (of the nasal passages) blocked with mucus.
▸**'stuffily** *adv* ▸**'stuffiness** *n*

stultify ('stʌltɪˌfaɪ) *vb* **stultifies, stultifying, stultified.** (*tr*) **1** to make useless, futile, or ineffectual, esp. by routine. **2** to cause to appear absurd or inconsistent. [C18: from L *stultus* stupid + *facere* to make]
▸ˌ**stultifi'cation** *n* ▸**'stultiˌfier** *n*

stum (stʌm) (in wine-making) ◆ *n* **1** a less common word for **must**[2]. **2** partly fermented wine added to fermented wine as a preservative. ◆ *vb* **stums, stumming, stummed. 3** to preserve (wine) by adding stum. [C17: from Du. *stom* dumb]

stumble ➊ ('stʌmbᵊl) *vb* **stumbles, stumbling, stumbled.** (*intr*) **1** to trip or fall while walking or running. **2** to walk in an awkward, unsteady, or unsure way. **3** to make mistakes or hesitate in speech or actions. **4** (foll. by *across* or *upon*) to come (across) by accident. ◆ *n* **5** a false step, trip, or blunder. **6** the act of stumbling. [C14: rel. to Norwegian *stumla,* Danish dialect *stumle*]
▸**'stumbler** *n* ▸**'stumbling** *adj* ▸**'stumblingly** *adv*

stumbling block ➊ *n* any impediment or obstacle.

stumer ('stju:mə) *n* **1** *Sl.* a forgery or cheat. **2** *Irish dialect.* a poor bargain. **3** *Scot.* a stupid person. **4 come a stumer.** *Austral. sl.* to crash financially. [from ?]

stump ➊ (stʌmp) *n* **1** the base of a tree trunk left standing after the tree has been felled or has fallen. **2** the part of something, such as a tooth, limb, or blade, that remains after a larger part has been removed. **3** (*often pl*) *Inf., facetious.* a leg (esp. in **stir one's stumps**). **4** *Cricket.* any of three upright wooden sticks that, with two bails laid across them, form a wicket (the **stumps**). **5** Also called: **tortillon.** a short sharply-pointed stick of cork or rolled paper or leather, used in drawing and shading. **6** a heavy tread or the sound of heavy footsteps. **7** a platform used by an orator when addressing a meeting. ◆ *vb* **8** (*tr*) to stop, confuse, or puzzle. **9** (*intr*) to plod or trudge heavily. **10** (*tr*) *Cricket.* to dismiss (a batsman) by breaking his wicket with the ball or with the ball in the hand while he is out of his crease. **11** *Chiefly US & Canad.* to campaign or canvass (an area), esp. by political speech- making. [C14: from MLow G *stump*]
▸**'stumper** *n*

stump up ➊ *vb* (*adv*) *Brit. inf.* to give (the money required).

stumpy ➊ ('stʌmpɪ) *adj* **stumpier, stumpiest. 1** short and thickset like a stump; stubby. **2** full of stumps.
▸**'stumpiness** *n*

stun ➊ (stʌn) *vb* **stuns, stunning, stunned.** (*tr*) **1** to render unconscious, as by a heavy blow or fall. **2** to shock or overwhelm. **3** to surprise or astound. ◆ *n* **4** the state or effect of being stunned. [C13 *stunen,* from OF *estoner* to daze, ult. from L EX-[1] + *tonāre* to thunder]

stung ➊ (stʌŋ) *vb* the past tense and past participle of **sting.**

stunk (stʌŋk) *vb* a past tense and past participle of **stink.**

stunner ➊ ('stʌnə) *n Inf.* a person or thing of great beauty, quality, size, etc.

stunning ➊ ('stʌnɪŋ) *adj Inf.* very attractive, impressive, astonishing, etc.
▸**'stunningly** *adv*

stunsail *or* **stuns'l** ('stʌnsᵊl) *n* another word for **studdingsail.**

stunt[1] ➊ (stʌnt) *vb* **1** (*tr*) to prevent or impede (the growth or development) of (a plant, animal, etc.). ◆ *n* **2** the act or an instance of stunting. **3** a person, animal, or plant that has been stunted. [C17 (as vb: to check the growth of): ?from C15 *stont* of short duration, from OE *stunt* foolish; sense prob. infl. by ON *stuttr* dwarfed]
▸**'stunted** *adj* ▸**'stuntedness** *n*

stunt[2] ➊ (stʌnt) *n* **1** a feat of daring or skill. **2a** an acrobatic or dangerous piece of action in a film, etc. **2b** (*as modifier*): *a stunt man.* **3** anything spectacular or unusual done for attention. ◆ *vb* **4** (*intr*) to perform a stunt or stunts. [C19: US student slang, from ?]

stupa ('stu:pə) *n* a domed edifice housing Buddhist or Jain relics. [C19: from Sansk.: dome]

stupe (stju:p) *n Med.* a hot damp cloth, usually sprinkled with an irritant, applied to the body to relieve pain by counterirritation. [C14: from L *stuppa* flax, from Gk *stuppē*]

stupefacient (ˌstju:pɪ'feɪʃɪənt) *n* **1** a drug that causes stupor. ◆ *adj* **2** of, relating to, or designating this type of drug. [C17: from L *stupefaciēns,* from *stupēre* to be stunned + *facere* to make]

stupefaction ➊ (ˌstju:pɪ'fækʃən) *n* **1** astonishment. **2** the act of stupefying or the state of being stupefied.

stupefy ➊ ('stju:pɪˌfaɪ) *vb* **stupefies, stupefying, stupefied.** (*tr*) **1** to render insensitive or lethargic. **2** to confuse or astound. [C16: from OF *stupefier,* from L *stupefacere;* see STUPEFACIENT]
▸**'stupeˌfying** *adj*

stupendous ➊ (stju:'pɛndəs) *adj* astounding, wonderful, huge, etc. [C17: from L *stupēre* to be amazed]
▸**stu'pendously** *adv* ▸**stu'pendousness** *n*

stupid ➊ ('stju:pɪd) *adj* **1** lacking in common sense, perception, or intelligence. **2** (*usually postpositive*) dazed or stupefied: *stupid from lack of sleep.* **3** slow-witted. **4** trivial, silly, or frivolous. ◆ *n* **5** *Inf.* a stupid person. [C16: from F *stupide,* from L *stupidus* silly, from *stupēre* to be amazed]
▸**stu'pidity** *or* **'stupidness** *n*

THESAURUS

mandize, guzzle, make a pig of oneself (*inf.*), overindulge, pig out (*sl.*), sate, satiate ◆ *n* **9** = **substance**, essence, matter, pith, quintessence, staple **10** = **material**, cloth, fabric, raw material, textile **11** = **things**, belongings, bits and pieces, clobber, effects, equipment, gear, goods and chattels, impedimenta, junk, kit, luggage, materials, objects, paraphernalia, possessions, tackle, trappings **12** = **nonsense**, balderdash, baloney (*inf.*), bosh (*inf.*), bunk (*inf.*), bunkum, claptrap (*inf.*), foolishness, humbug, poppycock (*inf.*), rot, rubbish, stuff and nonsense, tommyrot, trash, tripe (*inf.*), twaddle, verbiage

stuffing *n* **1** = **filling**, kapok, packing, quilting, wadding **2** = **forcemeat**, farce, farcemeat

stuffy *adj* **1** = **airless**, close, fetid, frowsty, fuggy, heavy, muggy, oppressive, stale, stifling, suffocating, sultry, unventilated **2** *Informal* = **staid**, as dry as dust, conventional, deadly, dreary, dull, fusty, humourless, musty, niminy-piminy, old-fashioned, old-fogeyish, pompous, priggish, prim, prim and proper, stilted, stodgy, strait-laced, uninteresting
Antonyms *adj* ≠ **airless:** airy, breezy, cool, draughty, fresh, gusty, pleasant, well-ventilated

stumble *vb* **1** = **trip**, blunder about, come a cropper (*inf.*), fall, falter, flounder, lose one's balance, lurch, reel, slip, stagger **3** = **falter**, fluff (*inf.*), hesitate, stammer, stutter **4** *with* **across, on** *or* **upon** = **discover**, blunder upon, chance upon, come across, encounter, find, happen upon, light upon, run across, turn up

stumbling block *n* = **obstacle**, bar, barrier, difficulty, hazard, hindrance, hurdle, impediment, obstruction, snag

stump *vb* **8** = **baffle**, bewilder, bring (someone) up short, confound, confuse, dumbfound, flummox, foil, mystify, nonplus, outwit, perplex, puzzle, snooker, stop, stymie **9** = **stamp**, clomp, clump, lumber, plod, stomp (*inf.*), trudge

stumped *adj* = **baffled**, at a loss, at one's wits' end, at sea, brought to a standstill, floored (*inf.*), flummoxed, in despair, nonplussed, perplexed, stymied, uncertain which way to turn

stump up *vb Brit. informal* = **pay**, chip in (*inf.*), come across with (*inf.*), contribute, cough up (*inf.*), donate, fork out (*sl.*), hand over, shell out (*inf.*)

stumpy *adj* **1** = **stocky**, chunky, dumpy, fubsy (*arch. or dialect*), heavy, short, squat, stubby, thick, thickset

stun *vb* **1** = **knock out**, daze **2, 3** = **overcome**, amaze, astonish, astound, bewilder, confound, confuse, dumbfound, flabbergast (*inf.*), hit (someone) like a ton of bricks (*inf.*), knock (someone) for six (*inf.*), overpower, shock, stagger, strike (someone) dumb, stupefy, take (someone's) breath away

stung *adj* = **goaded**, angered, exasperated, hurt, incensed, nettled, piqued, resentful, roused, wounded

stunner *n Informal* = **beauty**, charmer, dazzler, dish (*inf.*), dolly (*sl.*), eyeful (*inf.*), glamour puss, good-looker, heart-throb, honey (*inf.*), humdinger (*sl.*), knockout (*inf.*), looker (*inf., chiefly US*), lovely (*sl.*), peach (*inf.*), sensation, smasher (*inf.*), wow (*sl., chiefly US*)

stunning *adj Informal* = **wonderful**, beautiful, brilliant, dazzling, devastating (*inf.*), dramatic, drop-dead (*sl.*), gorgeous, great (*inf.*), heavenly, impressive, jaw-dropping, lovely, marvellous, out of this world (*inf.*), ravishing, remarkable, sensational (*inf.*), smashing (*inf.*), spectacular, striking
Antonyms *adj* average, dreadful, horrible, mediocre, no great shakes (*inf.*), ordinary, plain, poor, rotten, run-of-the-mill, ugly, unattractive, unimpressive, uninspiring, unremarkable

stunt[2] *n* **1** = **feat**, act, deed, exploit, feature, gest (*arch.*), *tour de force*, trick

stunted *adj* **1** = **undersized**, diminutive, dwarfed, dwarfish, little, small, tiny

stupefaction *n* **1** = **astonishment**, amazement, awe, wonder, wonderment

stupefy *vb* **1, 2** = **astound**, amaze, bewilder, confound, daze, dumbfound, knock senseless, numb, shock, stagger, stun

stupendous *adj* = **wonderful**, amazing, astounding, breathtaking, brilliant, colossal, enormous, fabulous (*inf.*), fantastic (*inf.*), gigantic, jaw-dropping, marvellous, mega (*sl.*), mind-blowing (*inf.*), mind-boggling (*inf.*), out of this world (*inf.*), overwhelming, phenomenal, prodigious, sensational (*inf.*), staggering, stunning (*inf.*), superb, surpassing belief, surprising, tremendous (*inf.*), vast, wondrous (*arch. or literary*)
Antonyms *adj* ≠ **wonderful:** average, mediocre, modest, no great shakes (*inf.*), ordinary, petty, unexciting, unimpressive, unremarkable, unsurprising ≠ **huge:** diminutive, puny, tiny

stupid *adj* **1, 3** = **unintelligent**, Boeotian, brain-dead (*inf.*), brainless, crass, cretinous, dead from the neck up, deficient, dense, dim, dolt-

stupor ➊ ('stju:pə) *n* **1** a state of unconsciousness. **2** mental dullness; torpor. [C17: from L, from *stupēre* to be aghast]
▸'**stuporous** *adj*

sturdy ➊ ('stɜ:dɪ) *adj* **sturdier, sturdiest. 1** healthy, strong, and vigorous. **2** strongly built; stalwart. [C13 (in the sense: rash, harsh): from OF *estordi* dazed, from *estordir* to stun]
▸'**sturdily** *adv* ▸'**sturdiness** *n*

sturgeon ('stɜ:dʒən) *n* any of various primitive bony fishes of temperate waters of the N hemisphere, having an elongated snout and rows of spines along the body. [C13: from OF *estourgeon*, of Gmc origin]

Sturt's desert pea (stɜ:ts) *n* another name for **desert pea.**

stutter ➊ ('stʌtə) *vb* **1** to speak (a word, phrase, etc.) with recurring repetition of consonants, esp. initial ones. **2** to make (an abrupt sound) repeatedly: *the gun stuttered.* ◆ *n* **3** the act or habit of stuttering. **4** a stuttering sound. [C16]
▸'**stutterer** *n* ▸'**stuttering** *n, adj* ▸'**stutteringly** *adv*

sty (staɪ) *n, pl* **sties. 1** a pen in which pigs are housed. **2** any filthy or corrupt place. ◆ *vb* **sties, stying, stied. 3** to enclose or be enclosed in a sty. [OE *stig*]

stye *or* **sty** (staɪ) *n, pl* **styes** *or* **sties.** inflammation of a sebaceous gland of the eyelid. [C15 *styanye* (mistaken as *sty on eye*), from OE *stīgend* rising, hence swelling, + *ye* eye]

Stygian ('stɪdʒɪən) *adj* **1** of or relating to the Styx, a river in Hades. **2** *Chiefly literary.* dark, gloomy, or hellish. [C16: from L *Stygius*, from Gk *Stugios*, from *Stux* Styx]

style ➊ (staɪl) *n* **1** a form of appearance, design, or production; type or make. **2** the way in which something is done: *good style.* **3** the manner in which something is expressed or performed, considered as separate from its intrinsic content, meaning, etc. **4** a distinctive, formal, or characteristic manner of expression in words, music, painting, etc. **5** elegance or refinement of manners, dress, etc. **6** prevailing fashion in dress, looks, etc. **7** a fashionable or ostentatious mode of existence: *to live in style.* **8** the particular mode of orthography, punctuation, design, etc., followed in a book, journal, etc., or in a printing or publishing house. **9** *Chiefly Brit.* the distinguishing title or form of address of a person or firm. **10** *Bot.* the long slender extension of the ovary, bearing the stigma. **11** a method of expressing or calculating dates. See **Old Style, New Style. 12** another word for **stylus** (sense 1). **13** the arm of a sundial. ◆ *vb* **styles, styling, styled.** (*mainly tr*) **14** to design, shape, or tailor: *to style hair.* **15** to adapt or make suitable for. **16** to make consistent or correct according to a printing or publishing style. **17** to name or call; designate: *to style a man a fool.* [C13: from L *stylus, stilus* writing implement, hence characteristics of the writing, style]
▸'**stylar** *adj* ▸'**styler** *n*

stylebook ('staɪl,bʊk) *n* a book containing rules and examples of punctuation, typography, etc., for the use of writers, editors, and printers.

stylet ('staɪlɪt) *n Surgery.* **1** a wire for insertion into a catheter, etc., to maintain its rigidity during passage. **2** a slender probe. [C17: from F *stilet*, from OIt. STILETTO; infl. by L *stylus* style]

styling mousse *n* a light foamy substance applied to the hair before styling in order to retain the style.

stylish ➊ ('staɪlɪʃ) *adj* having style; smart; fashionable.
▸'**stylishly** *adv* ▸'**stylishness** *n*

stylist ('staɪlɪst) *n* **1** a person who performs, writes, or acts with attention to style. **2** a designer of clothes, décor, etc. **3** a hairdresser who styles hair.

stylistic (staɪ'lɪstɪk) *adj* of or relating to style, esp. artistic or literary style.
▸**sty'listically** *adv*

stylite ('staɪlaɪt) *n Christianity.* one of a class of recluses who in ancient times lived on the top of high pillars. [C17: from LGk *stulitēs*, from Gk *stulos* a pillar]
▸**stylitic** (staɪ'lɪtɪk) *adj*

stylize *or* **stylise** ('staɪlaɪz) *vb* **stylizes, stylizing, stylized** *or* **stylises, stylising, stylised.** (*tr*) to give a conventional or established stylistic form to.
▸,**styli'zation** *or* ,**styli'sation** *n*

stylo- *or before a vowel* **styl-** *combining form.* **1** (in biology) a style. **2** indicating a column or point: *stylobate; stylograph.* [from Gk *stulos* column]

stylobate ('staɪlə,beɪt) *n* a continuous horizontal course of masonry that supports a colonnade. [C17: from L *stylobatēs*, from Gk *stulos* pillar + *-batēs*, from *bainein* to walk]

stylograph ('staɪlə,grɑ:f) *n* a fountain pen having a fine hollow tube as the writing point instead of a nib. [C19: from STYL(US) + -GRAPH]

styloid ('staɪlɔɪd) *adj* **1** resembling a stylus. **2** *Anat.* of or relating to a projecting process of the temporal bone. [C18: from NL *styloides*, from Gk *stuloeidēs* like a stylus; infl. by Gk *stulos* pillar]

stylops ('staɪlɒps) *n, pl* **stylopes** (-lə,pi:z). any of various insects living as a parasite in other insects, esp. bees and wasps. [C19: NL, from Gk, from *stulos* a pillar + *ōps* an eye, from the fact that the male has stalked eyes]

stylus ('staɪləs) *n, pl* **styli** (-laɪ) *or* **styluses. 1** Also called: **style.** a pointed instrument for engraving, drawing, or writing. **2** a tool used in ancient times for writing on wax tablets, which was pointed at one end and blunt at the other for erasing. **3** Also called: **needle.** a device attached to the cartridge in the pick-up arm of a record player that rests in the groove in the record, transmitting the vibrations to the sensing device in the cartridge. [C18: from L, var. of *stilus* writing implement]

stymie ➊ *or* **stymy** ('staɪmɪ) *vb* **stymies, stymieing** *or* **stymying, stymied.** (*tr; often passive*) **1** to hinder or thwart. **2** *Golf.* (formerly) to impede with a stymie. ◆ *n, pl* **stymies. 3** *Golf.* (formerly) a situation in which an opponent's ball is blocking the line between the hole and the ball about to be played. **4** a situation of obstruction. [C19: from ?]

styptic ('stɪptɪk) *adj* **1** contracting the blood vessels or tissues. ◆ *n* **2** a styptic drug. [C14: via LL, from Gk *stuptikos* capable of contracting, from *stuphein* to contract]

styrene ('staɪri:n) *n* a colourless oily volatile flammable liquid made from ethylene and benzene. It readily polymerizes and is used in making synthetic plastics and rubbers. Formula: $C_6H_5CH{:}CH_2$. Systematic name: **phenylethene.** [C20: from Gk *sturax* tree of the genus *Styrax* + -ENE]

suable ('sju:əbᵊl) *adj* liable to be sued in a court.
▸,**sua'bility** *n*

suasion ('sweɪʒən) *n* a rare word for **persuasion.** [C14: from L *suāsiō*, from *suādēre* to PERSUADE]
▸'**suasive** *adj*

suave ➊ (swɑ:v) *adj* (esp. of a man) displaying smoothness and sophistication in manner; urbane. [C16: from L *suāvis* sweet]
▸'**suavely** *adv* ▸**suavity** ('swɑ:vɪtɪ) *or* '**suaveness** *n*

sub (sʌb) *n* **1** short for several words beginning with *sub-*, such as **subeditor, submarine, subordinate, subscription,** and **substitute. 2** *Brit. inf.* an advance payment of wages or salary. Formal term: **subsistence allowance.** ◆ *vb* **subs, subbing, subbed. 3** (*intr*) to serve or act as a substitute. **4** *Brit. inf.* to grant or receive (an advance payment of wages or salary). **5** (*tr*) *Inf.* short for **subedit.**

sub. *abbrev. for:* **1** subeditor. **2** *Music.* subito. **3** subscription. **4** substitute.

sub- *prefix* **1** situated under or beneath: *subterranean.* **2** secondary in rank; subordinate: *subeditor.* **3** falling short of; less than or imperfectly: *subarctic; subhuman.* **4** forming a subdivision or subordinate part: *subcommittee.* **5** (in chemistry) **5a** indicating that a compound contains a relatively small proportion of a specified element: *suboxide.* **5b** indicating that a salt is basic salt: *subacetate.* [from L *sub*]

subacid (sʌb'æsɪd) *adj* (esp. of some fruits) moderately acid or sour.
▸**subacidity** (,sʌbə'sɪdɪtɪ) *or* **sub'acidness** *n*

subadar *or* **subahdar** ('su:bə,dɑ:) *n* (formerly) the chief native officer

THESAURUS

ish, dopey (*inf.*), dozy (*Brit. inf.*), dull, dumb (*inf.*), dumb-ass (*sl.*), gullible, half-witted, moronic, naive, obtuse, simple, simple-minded, slow, slow on the uptake (*inf.*), slow-witted, sluggish, stolid, thick, thick as mince (*Scot. inf.*), thickheaded, witless, woodenheaded (*inf.*) **2** = **dazed**, groggy, in a daze, insensate, punch-drunk, semiconscious, senseless, stunned, stupefied **4** = **silly**, asinine, crackbrained, crackpot (*inf.*), daft (*inf.*), foolish, futile, half-baked (*inf.*), idiotic, ill-advised, imbecilic, inane, irresponsible, laughable, ludicrous, meaningless, mindless, nonsensical, pointless, puerile, rash, senseless, short-sighted, trivial, unintelligent, unthinking
Antonyms *adj* ≠ **unintelligent:** astute, brainy, bright, brilliant, clear-headed, clever, intelligent, lucid, on the ball (*inf.*), quick, quick on the uptake, quick-witted, sensible, sharp, shrewd, smart, wise ≠ **silly:** astute, prudent, realistic, reasonable, sensible, shrewd, thoughtful, well-thought-out, wise

stupidity *n* **1** = **lack of intelligence**, asininity, brainlessness, denseness, dimness, dopiness (*sl.*), doziness (*Brit. inf.*), dullness, dumbness (*inf.*), feeble-mindedness, imbecility, lack of brain, naivety, obtuseness, simplicity, slowness, thickheadedness, thickness **4** = **silliness**, absurdity, fatuity, fatuousness, folly, foolhardiness, foolishness, futility, idiocy, impracticality, inanity, irresponsibility, ludicrousness, lunacy, madness, pointlessness, puerility, rashness, senselessness

stupor *n* **1, 2** = **daze**, coma, inertia, insensibility, lethargy, numbness, stupefaction, torpor, trance, unconsciousness

sturdy *adj* **1** = **robust**, athletic, brawny, firm, hardy, hearty, lusty, muscular, powerful, stalwart, staunch, thickset, vigorous **2** = **substantial**, built to last, durable, secure, solid, well-built, well-made
Antonyms *adj* ≠ **robust:** feeble, infirm, puny, skinny, weak, weakly ≠ **substantial:** flimsy, frail, rickety, unsubstantial

stutter *vb* **1** = **stammer**, falter, hesitate, speak haltingly, splutter, stumble

style *n* **1** = **design**, appearance, category, characteristic, cut, form, genre, kind, manner, pattern, sort, spirit, strain, tenor, tone, type, variety **2, 3** = **manner**, approach, custom, method, mode, technique, way **4** = **mode of expression**, diction, expression, phraseology, phrasing, treatment, turn of phrase, vein, wording **5** = **elegance**, *bon ton*, chic, cosmopolitanism, dash, dressiness (*inf.*), élan, fashionableness, flair, grace, panache, polish, refinement, savoir-faire, smartness, sophistication, stylishness, taste, urbanity **6** = **fashion**, mode, rage, trend, vogue **7** = **luxury**, affluence, comfort, ease, elegance, gracious living, grandeur ◆ *vb* **14** = **design**, adapt, arrange, cut, dress, fashion, shape, tailor **17** = **call**, address, christen, denominate, designate, dub, entitle, label, name, term

stylish *adj* = **smart**, à la mode, chic, classy (*sl.*), dapper, dressy (*inf.*), fashionable, in fashion, in vogue, modish, natty (*inf.*), polished, snappy, snazzy (*inf.*), trendy (*Brit. inf.*), urbane, voguish, well turned-out
Antonyms *adj* badly-tailored, naff (*Brit. sl.*), old-fashioned, outmoded, out-of-date, passé, scruffy, shabby, slovenly, tacky, tawdry, unfashionable, unstylish, untrendy (*Brit. inf.*)

stymie *vb* **1** = **frustrate**, balk, confound, defeat, flummox, foil, hinder, mystify, nonplus, puzzle, snooker, spike (someone's) guns, stump, throw a spanner in the works (*Brit. inf.*), thwart

suave *adj* = **smooth**, affable, agreeable, bland, charming, civilized, cool, courteous, debonair, diplomatic, gracious, obliging, pleasing, polite,

of a company of Indian soldiers in the British service. [C17: via Urdu from Persian, from *sūba* province + *-dār* holding]

subalpine (sʌbˈælpaɪn) *adj* **1** situated in or relating to the regions at the foot of mountains. **2** (of plants) growing below the tree line in mountainous regions.

subaltern (ˈsʌbəltən) *n* **1** a commissioned officer below the rank of captain in certain armies, esp. the British. ◆ *adj* **2** of inferior position or rank. **3** *Logic.* (of a proposition) particular, esp. in relation to a universal of the same quality. [C16: from LL *subalternus,* from L SUB- + *alternus* alternate, from *alter* the other]

subalternation (ˌsʌbɔːltəˈneɪʃən) *n Logic.* the relation between a universal and a particular proposition of the same quality where the universal proposition implies the particular proposition.

subantarctic (ˌsʌbæntˈɑːktɪk) *adj* of or relating to latitudes immediately north of the Antarctic Circle.

subaqua (ˌsʌbˈækwə) *adj* of or relating to underwater sport: *subaqua swimming.*

subaqueous (sʌbˈeɪkwɪəs, -ˈækwɪ-) *adj* occurring, formed, or used under water.

subarctic (sʌbˈɑːktɪk) *adj* of or relating to latitudes immediately south of the Arctic Circle.

subatomic (ˌsʌbəˈtɒmɪk) *adj* **1** of, relating to, or being a particle making up an atom or a process occurring within atoms. **2** having dimensions smaller than atomic dimensions.

subbasement (ˈsʌbˌbeɪsmənt) *n* a storey of a building beneath the main basement.

subclass (ˈsʌbˌklɑːs) *n* **1** a principal subdivision of a class. **2** *Biol.* a taxonomic group that is a subdivision of a class. **3** *Maths.* another name for **subset.**

subclavian (sʌbˈkleɪvɪən) *adj Anat.* (of an artery, vein, etc.) below the clavicle. [C17: from NL *subclāvius,* from L SUB- + *clavis* key]

subclinical (sʌbˈklɪnɪkəl) *adj Med.* of or relating to the stage in the course of a disease before the symptoms are first noted.
▸**subˈclinically** *adv*

subconscious ➊ (sʌbˈkɒnʃəs) *adj* **1** acting or existing without one's awareness. ◆ *n* **2** *Psychol.* that part of the mind on the fringe of consciousness which contains material it is possible to become aware of by redirecting attention.
▸**subˈconsciously** *adv* ▸**subˈconsciousness** *n*

subcontinent (sʌbˈkɒntɪnənt) *n* a large land mass that is a distinct part of a continent, such as India is of Asia.
▸**subcontinental** (ˌsʌbkɒntɪˈnentəl) *adj*

subcontract *n* (sʌbˈkɒntrækt). **1** a subordinate contract under which the supply of materials, labour, etc., is let out to someone other than a party to the main contract. ◆ *vb* (ˌsʌbkənˈtrækt). **2** (*intr;* often foll. by *for*) to enter into or make a subcontract. **3** (*tr*) to let out (work) on a subcontract.
▸ˌ**subconˈtractor** *n*

subcontrary (sʌbˈkɒntrərɪ) *Logic.* ◆ *adj* **1** (of a pair of propositions) related such that they cannot both be false at once, although they may be true together. ◆ *n, pl* **subcontraries. 2** a statement which cannot be false when a given statement is false.

subcritical (sʌbˈkrɪtɪkəl) *adj Physics.* (of a nuclear reaction, power station, etc.) having or involving a chain reaction that is not self- sustaining; not yet critical.

subculture (ˈsʌbˌkʌltʃə) *n* a subdivision of a national culture or an enclave within it with a distinct integrated network of behaviour, beliefs, and attitudes.
▸**subˈcultural** *adj*

subcutaneous (ˌsʌbkjuːˈteɪnɪəs) *adj Med.* situated, used, or introduced beneath the skin.
▸ˌ**subcuˈtaneously** *adv*

subdeacon (ˌsʌbˈdiːkən) *n Chiefly RC Church.* **1** a cleric who assists at High Mass. **2** (formerly) a person ordained to the lowest of the major orders.
▸**subdeaconate** (sʌbˈdiːkənɪt) *n*

subdivide (ˌsʌbdɪˈvaɪd, ˈsʌbdɪˌvaɪd) *vb* **subdivides, subdividing, subdivided.** to divide (something) resulting from an earlier division.
▸ˈ**subdiˌvision** *n*

subdominant (sʌbˈdɒmɪnənt) *Music.* ◆ *n* **1** the fourth degree of a major or minor scale. **2** a key or chord based on this. ◆ *adj* **3** of or relating to the subdominant.

subdue ➊ (səbˈdjuː) *vb* **subdues, subduing, subdued.** (*tr*) **1** to establish ascendancy over by force. **2** to overcome and bring under control, as by intimidation or persuasion. **3** to hold in check or repress (feelings, etc.). **4** to render less intense or less conspicuous. [C14 *sobdue,* from OF *soduire* to mislead, from L *subdūcere* to remove; infl. by L *subdere* to subject]
▸**subˈduable** *adj* ▸**subˈdual** *n*

subdued ➊ (səbˈdjuːd) *adj* **1** cowed, passive, or shy. **2** gentle or quiet: *a subdued whisper.* **3** (of colours, lighting, etc.) not harsh or bright.

subdural (sʌbˈdjʊərəl) *adj Anat.* between the dura mater and the arachnoid: *subdural haematoma.*

subedit (sʌbˈɛdɪt) *vb* **subedits, subediting, subedited.** to edit and correct (written or printed material).

subeditor (sʌbˈɛdɪtə) *n* a person who checks and edits copy, esp. on a newspaper.

subequatorial (sʌbˌɛkwəˈtɔːrɪəl) *adj* in or characteristic of regions immediately north or south of equatorial regions.

suberose (ˈsjuːbəˌrəʊs), **subereous** (sjuːˈbɛrɪəs), *or* **suberic** (sjuːˈbɛrɪk) *adj Bot.* relating to, resembling, or consisting of cork; corky. [C19: from L *sūber* cork + -OSE[1]]

subfamily (ˈsʌbˌfæmɪlɪ) *n, pl* **subfamilies. 1** *Biol.* a taxonomic group that is a subdivision of a family. **2** a subdivision of a family of languages.

subfusc (ˈsʌbfʌsk) *adj* **1** devoid of brightness or appeal; drab, dull, or dark. ◆ *n* **2** (at Oxford University) formal academic dress. [C18: from L *subfuscus* dusky, from *fuscus* dark]

subgenus (ˈsʌbˌdʒiːnəs, -ˌdʒɛn-) *n, pl* **subgenera** (-ˈdʒɛnərə) *or* **subgenuses.** *Biol.* a subdivision of a genus that is of higher rank than a species.
▸**subgeneric** (ˌsʌbdʒəˈnɛrɪk) *adj*

subheading (ˈsʌbˌhɛdɪŋ) *or* **subhead** *n* **1** the heading or title of a subdivision or subsection of a printed work. **2** a division subordinate to a main heading or title.

subhuman (sʌbˈhjuːmən) *adj* **1** of or designating animals below man (*Homo sapiens*) in evolutionary development. **2** less than human.

subindex (sʌbˈɪndɛks) *n, pl* **subindices** (-dɪˌsiːz) *or* **subindexes.** another word for **subscript** (sense 2).

subitize *or* **subitise** (ˈsʌbɪˌtaɪz) *vb* **subitizes, subitizing, subitized** *or* **subitises, subitising, subitised.** *Psychol.* to perceive the number of (a group of items) at a glance and without counting: *the maximum number of items that can be subitized is about five.* [C20: from L *subitus* sudden + -IZE]

subito (ˈsuːbɪˌtəʊ) *adv Music.* suddenly; immediately. [C18: via It. from L: suddenly, from *subitus* sudden, from *subīre* to approach]

subj. *abbrev. for:* **1** subject. **2** subjective(ly). **3** subjunctive.

subjacent (sʌbˈdʒeɪsənt) *adj* **1** forming a foundation; underlying. **2** lower than. [C16: from L *subjacēre* to lie close, be under]
▸**subˈjacency** *n* ▸**subˈjacently** *adv*

subject ➊ *n* (ˈsʌbdʒɪkt). **1** the predominant theme or topic, as of a book, discussion, etc. **2** any branch of learning considered as a course of study. **3** *Grammar, logic.* a word, phrase, etc., about which something is predicated or stated in a sentence; for example, *the cat* in the sentence *The cat catches mice.* **4** a person or thing that undergoes experiment, treatment, etc. **5** a person under the rule of a monarch, government, etc. **6** an object, figure, scene, etc., as portrayed by an artist or photographer. **7** *Philosophy.* **7a** that which thinks or feels as opposed to the object of thinking and feeling; the self or the mind. **7b** a substance as opposed to its attributes. **8** Also called: **theme.** *Music.* the principal motif of a fugue, the basis from which the musical material is derived in a sonata-form movement, or the recurrent figure in a rondo. **9** *Logic.* the term of a proposition about which something is asserted. **10** an originating motive. **11 change the subject.** to select a new topic of conversation. ◆ *adj* (ˈsʌbdʒɪkt). (*usually postpositive;* foll. by *to*) **12** being under the power or sovereignty of a ruler, government, etc.: *subject peoples.* **13** showing a tendency (towards): *a child subject to indiscipline.* **14** exposed or vulnerable: *subject to ribaldry.* **15** conditional upon: *the results are subject to correction.* ◆ *adv* (ˈsʌbdʒɪkt). **16 subject to.** (*prep*) under the condition that: *we accept, subject to her agreement.* ◆ *vb* (səbˈdʒɛkt). (*tr*) **17** (foll. by *to*) to cause to undergo: *they subjected him to torture.* **18** (*often passive;* foll. by *to*) to expose or render vulnerable or liable (to some experience): *he was subjected to great danger.* **19** (foll. by *to*) to bring under the control or authority (of): *to subject a soldier to discipline.* **20** *Rare.* to present for consideration; submit. [C14: from L *subjectus* brought under, from *subicere* to place under, from SUB- + *jacere* to throw]
▸**subˈjectable** *adj* ▸**subˈjection** *n*

subjective ➊ (səbˈdʒɛktɪv) *adj* **1** of, proceeding from, or relating to the

THESAURUS

smooth-tongued, sophisticated, svelte, urbane, worldly

subconscious *adj* **1** = **hidden,** inner, innermost, intuitive, latent, repressed, subliminal, suppressed
Antonyms *adj* aware, conscious, knowing, sensible, sentient

subdue *vb* **1, 2** = **overcome,** beat down, break, conquer, control, crush, defeat, discipline, gain ascendancy over, get the better of, get the upper hand over, get under control, humble, master, overpower, overrun, put down, quell, tame, trample, triumph over, vanquish **3, 4** = **moderate,** check, control, mellow, quieten down, repress, soften, suppress, tone down
Antonyms *vb* ≠ **moderate:** agitate, arouse, awaken, incite, provoke, stir up, waken, whip up

subdued *adj* **1** = **quiet,** chastened, crestfallen, dejected, downcast, down in the mouth, grave, out of spirits, repentant, repressed, restrained, sad, sadder and wiser, serious, sobered, solemn **3** = **soft,** dim, hushed, low-key, muted, quiet, shaded, sober, subtle, toned down, unobtrusive
Antonyms *adj* ≠ **quiet:** cheerful, enthusiastic, full of beans (*inf.*), happy, lively, vivacious ≠ **soft:** bright, loud, strident

subject *n* **1** = **topic,** affair, business, field of inquiry *or* reference, issue, matter, object, point, question, subject matter, substance, theme **4** = **participant,** case, client, guinea pig (*inf.*), patient, victim **5** = **citizen,** dependant, liegeman, national, subordinate, vassal ◆ *adj* **12** = **subordinate,** captive, dependent, enslaved, inferior, obedient, satellite, subjugated, submissive, subservient **13** = **liable to,** disposed to, prone to **14** = **vulnerable,** exposed, in danger, open, susceptible **16 subject to** = **conditional on,** contingent on, dependent on ◆ *vb* **17, 18** = **put through,** expose, lay open, make liable, submit, treat

subjective *adj* **2** = **personal,** biased, emotional, idiosyncratic, instinctive, intuitive, nonobjective, prejudiced
Antonyms *adj* concrete, detached, disinterested,

mind of the thinking subject and not the nature of the object being considered. **2** of, relating to, or emanating from a person's emotions, prejudices, etc. **3** relating to the inherent nature of a person or thing; essential. **4** existing only as perceived and not as a thing in itself. **5** *Med.* (of a symptom, condition, etc.) experienced only by the patient and incapable of being recognized or studied by anyone else. **6** *Grammar.* denoting a case of nouns and pronouns, esp. in languages having only two cases, that identifies the subject of a finite verb and (in formal use in English) is selected for predicate complements, as in *It is I.* ◆ *n* **7** *Grammar.* **7a** the subjective case. **7b** a subjective word or speech element. Cf. **objective.**
▸**sub'jectively** *adv* ▸ˌ**subjec'tivity** *or* **sub'jectiveness** *n*

subjectivism (səb'dʒɛktɪˌvɪzəm) *n Philosophy.* the doctrine that there are no absolute moral values but that these are variable in the same way that taste is.
▸**sub'jectivist** *n*

subjoin (sʌb'dʒɔɪn) *vb* (*tr*) to add or attach at the end of something spoken, written, etc. [C16: from F *subjoindre,* from L *subjungere* to add to, from *sub-* in addition + *jungere* to join]
▸**sub'joinder** *n*

sub judice ('dʒuːdɪsɪ) *adj* (*usually postpositive*) before a court of law or a judge; under judicial consideration. [L]

subjugate ❶ ('sʌbdʒʊˌgeɪt) *vb* **subjugates, subjugating, subjugated.** (*tr*) **1** to bring into subjection. **2** to make subservient or submissive. [C15: from LL *subjugāre* to subdue, from L SUB- + *jugum* yoke]
▸**'subjugable** *adj* ▸ˌ**subju'gation** *n* ▸**'subjuˌgator** *n*

subjunctive (səb'dʒʌŋktɪv) *Grammar.* ◆ *adj* **1** denoting a mood of verbs used when the content of the clause is being doubted, supposed, feared true, etc., rather than being asserted. In the following sentence, *were* is in the subjunctive: *I'd think seriously about it if I were you.* Cf. **indicative.** ◆ *n* **2a** the subjunctive mood. **2b** a verb in this mood. [C16: via LL *subjunctīvus,* from L *subjungere* to SUBJOIN]
▸**sub'junctively** *adv*

sublease *n* ('sʌbˌliːs). **1** a lease of property made by a lessee or tenant of that property. ◆ *vb* (sʌb'liːs), **subleases, subleasing, subleased. 2** to grant a sublease of (property); sublet. **3** (*tr*) to obtain or hold by sublease.
▸**sublessee** (ˌsʌblɛ'siː) *n* ▸**sublessor** (ˌsʌblɛ'sɔː) *n*

sublet (sʌb'lɛt) *vb* **sublets, subletting, sublet. 1** to grant a sublease of (property). **2** to let out (work, etc.) under a subcontract.

sublieutenant (ˌsʌblə'tɛnənt) *n* the most junior commissioned officer in the Royal Navy and certain other navies.
▸ˌ**sublieu'tenancy** *n*

sublimate ❶ ('sʌblɪˌmeɪt) *vb* **sublimates, sublimating, sublimated. 1** *Psychol.* to direct the energy of (a primitive impulse) into activities that are socially more acceptable. **2** (*tr*) to make purer; refine. ◆ *n* **3** *Chem.* the material obtained when a substance is sublimed. [C16: from L *sublīmāre* to elevate, from *sublīmis* lofty; see SUBLIME]
▸ˌ**subli'mation** *n*

sublime ❶ (sə'blaɪm) *adj* **1** of high moral, intellectual, or spiritual value; noble; exalted. **2** inspiring deep veneration or awe. **3** unparalleled; supreme. **4** *Poetic.* of proud bearing or aspect. **5** *Arch.* raised up. ◆ *n* **the sublime. 6** something that is sublime. **7** the ultimate degree or perfect example: *the sublime of folly.* ◆ *vb* **sublimes, subliming, sublimed. 8** (*tr*) to make higher or purer. **9** to change or cause to change directly from a solid to a vapour or gas without first melting. **10** to undergo or cause to undergo this process followed by a reverse change directly from a vapour to a solid: *to sublime iodine onto glass.* [C14: from L *sublīmis* lofty, ?from *sub-* up to + *līmen* lintel]
▸**sub'limely** *adv* ▸**sublimity** (sə'blɪmɪtɪ) *n*

subliminal ❶ (sʌb'lɪmɪnᵊl) *adj* **1** resulting from processes of which the individual is not aware. **2** (of stimuli) less than the minimum intensity or duration required to elicit a response. [C19: from L *sub-* below + *līmen* threshold]
▸**sub'liminally** *adv*

subliminal advertising *n* advertising on film or television that employs subliminal images to influence the viewer unconsciously.

sublingual (sʌb'lɪŋgwəl) *adj Anat.* situated beneath the tongue.

sublunary (sʌb'luːnərɪ) *adj* **1** between the moon and the earth. **2** of or relating to the earth. [C16: via LL, from L SUB- + *lūna* moon]

sub-machine-gun *n* a portable automatic or semiautomatic light gun with a short barrel, designed to be fired from the hip or shoulder.

submarginal (sʌb'mɑːdʒɪnᵊl) *adj* **1** below the minimum requirements. **2** (of land) infertile and unprofitable.
▸**sub'marginally** *adv*

submarine ('sʌbməˌriːn, ˌsʌbmə'riːn) *n* **1** a vessel, esp. a warship, capable of operating below the surface of the sea. **2** (*modifier*) **2a** of or relating to a submarine: *a submarine captain.* **2b** below the surface of the sea: *a submarine cable.*
▸**submariner** (sʌb'mærɪnə) *n*

submaxillary gland (ˌsʌbmæk'sɪlərɪ) *n* (in mammals) either of a pair of salivary glands situated on each side behind the lower jaw.

submediant (sʌb'miːdɪənt) *Music.* ◆ *n* **1** the sixth degree of a major or minor scale. **2** a key or chord based on this. ◆ *adj* **3** of or relating to the submediant.

submerge ❶ (səb'mɜːdʒ) *or* **submerse** (səb'mɜːs) *vb* **submerges, submerging, submerged** *or* **submerses, submersing, submersed. 1** to plunge, sink, or dive or cause to plunge, sink, or dive below the surface of water, etc. **2** (*tr*) to cover with water or other liquid. **3** (*tr*) to hide; suppress. **4** (*tr*) to overwhelm, as with work, etc. [C17: from L *submergere*]
▸**sub'mergence** *or* **sub'mersion** *n*

submersible (səb'mɜːsɪbᵊl) *or* **submergible** (səb'mɜːdʒɪbᵊl) *adj* **1** able to be submerged. **2** capable of operating under water, etc. ◆ *n* **3** a vessel designed to operate under water for short periods. **4** a submarine designed and equipped to carry out work below the level that divers can work.
▸**subˌmersi'bility** *or* **subˌmergi'bility** *n*

subminiature (sʌb'mɪnɪətʃə) *adj* smaller than miniature.

subminiature camera *n* a pocket-sized camera, usually using 16 millimetre film.

submission ❶ (səb'mɪʃən) *n* **1** an act or instance of submitting. **2** something submitted; a proposal, etc. **3** the quality or condition of being submissive. **4** the act of referring a document, etc., for the consideration of someone else.

submissive ❶ (səb'mɪsɪv) *adj* of, tending towards, or indicating submission, humility, or servility.
▸**sub'missively** *adv* ▸**sub'missiveness** *n*

submit ❶ (səb'mɪt) *vb* **submits, submitting, submitted. 1** (often foll. by *to*) to yield (oneself), as to the will of another person, a superior force, etc. **2** (foll. by *to*) to subject or be voluntarily subjected (to analysis, treatment, etc.). **3** (*tr;* often foll. by *to*) to refer (something to someone) for judgment or consideration. **4** (*tr; may take a clause as object*) to state, contend, or propose deferentially. **5** (*intr;* often foll. by *to*) to defer or accede (to the decision, etc., of another). [C14: from L *submittere* to place under]
▸**sub'mittable** *or* **sub'missible** *adj* ▸**sub'mittal** *n* ▸**sub'mitter** *n*

submultiple (sʌb'mʌltɪpᵊl) *n* **1** a number that can be divided into another number an integral number of times without a remainder: *three is a submultiple of nine.* ◆ *adj* **2** being a submultiple of a quantity or number.

subnormal ❶ (sʌb'nɔːməl) *adj* **1** less than the normal. **2** having a low intelligence. ◆ *n* **3** a subnormal person.
▸**subnormality** (ˌsʌbnɔː'mælɪtɪ) *n*

subnuclear (sʌb'njuːklɪə) *adj* in or smaller than the nucleus of an atom.

suborbital (sʌb'ɔːbɪtᵊl) *adj* **1** (of a rocket, missile, etc.) having a flight path that is less than an orbit of the earth or other celestial body. **2** *Anat.* situated beneath the orbit of the eye.

suborder ('sʌbˌɔːdə) *n Biol.* a subdivision of an order.
▸**sub'ordinal** *adj*

subordinate ❶ *adj* (sə'bɔːdɪnɪt). **1** of lesser order or importance. **2** under the authority or control of another: *a subordinate functionary.* ◆ *n* (sə'bɔːdɪnɪt). **3** a person or thing that is subordinate. ◆ *vb* (sə'bɔːdɪˌneɪt), **subordinates, subordinating, subordinated.** (*tr;* usually foll. by *to*) **4** to put in a lower rank or position (than). **5** to make subservient: *to subordinate mind to heart.* [C15: from Med. L *subordināre,* from L SUB- + *ordō* rank]
▸**sub'ordinately** *adv* ▸**subˌordi'nation** *n* ▸**sub'ordinative** *adj*

THESAURUS

dispassionate, impartial, impersonal, objective, open-minded, unbiased

subjugate *vb* **1, 2** = **conquer**, bring (someone) to his knees, bring to heel, bring under the yoke, crush, defeat, enslave, hold sway over, lick (*inf.*), master, overcome, overpower, overthrow, put down, quell, reduce, rule over, subdue, suppress, tame, vanquish

sublimate *vb* **1** = **channel**, divert, redirect, transfer, turn

sublime *adj* **1** = **noble**, elevated, eminent, exalted, glorious, grand, great, high, imposing, lofty, magnificent, majestic, transcendent
Antonyms *adj* bad, commonplace, lowly, mundane, ordinary, poor, ridiculous, worldly

subliminal *adj* **1** = **subconscious**, unconscious

submerge *vb* **1, 2** = **immerse**, deluge, dip, drown, duck, dunk, engulf, flood, inundate, overflow, overwhelm, plunge, sink, swamp

submission *n* **1** = **surrender**, acquiescence, assent, capitulation, cave-in (*inf.*), giving in, yielding **2** = **proposal**, argument, contention **3** = **meekness**, compliance, deference, docility, obedience, passivity, resignation, submissiveness, tractability, unassertiveness **4** = **presentation**, entry, handing in, submitting, tendering

submissive *adj* = **meek**, abject, accommodating, acquiescent, amenable, biddable, bootlicking (*inf.*), compliant, deferential, docile, dutiful, humble, ingratiating, lowly, malleable, obedient, obeisant, obsequious, passive, patient, pliant, resigned, subdued, tractable, uncomplaining, unresisting, yielding
Antonyms *adj* awkward, difficult, disobedient, headstrong, intractable, obstinate, stubborn, uncooperative, unyielding

submit *vb* **1** = **surrender**, accede, acquiesce, agree, bend, bow, capitulate, cave in (*inf.*), comply, defer, endure, give in, hoist the white flag, knuckle under, lay down arms, put up with, resign oneself, stoop, succumb, throw in the sponge, toe the line, tolerate, yield **3** = **present**, commit, hand in, proffer, put forward, refer, table, tender **4** = **suggest**, advance, argue, assert, claim, contend, move, propose, propound, put, state, volunteer

subnormal *adj* **2** = **retarded**, cretinous, E.S.N., feeble-minded, imbecilic, mentally defective, moronic, simple, slow

subordinate *adj* **1** = **lesser**, dependent, inferior, junior, lower, minor, secondary, subject, subservient **2** = **auxiliary**, ancillary, subsidiary, supplementary ◆ *n* **3** = **inferior**, aide, assistant, attendant, dependant, junior, second, subaltern, underling
Antonyms *adj* ≠ **lesser:** central, essential, greater, higher, key, main, necessary, predominant, senior, superior, vital ◆ *n* ≠ **inferior:** boss (*inf.*), captain, chief, commander, head, leader, master, principal, senior, superior

subordinate clause *n Grammar.* a clause with an adjectival, adverbial, or nominal function, rather than one that functions as a separate sentence in its own right.

subordinating conjunction *n* a conjunction that introduces subordinate clauses, such as *if, because, although,* and *until.*

suborn (sə'bɔ:n) *vb (tr)* **1** to bribe, incite, or instigate (a person) to commit a wrongful act. **2** *Law.* to induce (a witness) to commit perjury. [C16: from L *subornāre,* from *sub-* secretly + *ornāre* to furnish]
▸**subornation** (ˌsʌbɔ:'neɪʃən) *n* ▸**subornative** (sʌ'bɔ:nətɪv) *adj* ▸**sub'orner** *n*

suboxide (sʌb'ɒksaɪd) *n* an oxide of an element containing less oxygen than the common oxide formed by the element: *carbon suboxide,* C_3O_2.

subplot ('sʌbˌplɒt) *n* a subordinate or auxiliary plot in a novel, play, film, etc.

subpoena (səb'pi:nə) *n* **1** a writ issued by a court of justice requiring a person to appear before the court at a specified time. ◆ *vb* **subpoenas, subpoenaing, subpoenaed. 2** *(tr)* to serve with a subpoena. [C15: from L: under penalty]

subrogate ('sʌbrəˌgeɪt) *vb* **subrogates, subrogating, subrogated.** *(tr) Law.* to put (one person or thing) in the place of another in respect of a right or claim. [C16: from L *subrogāre,* from *sub-* in place of + *rogāre* to ask]
▸ˌ**subro'gation** *n*

sub rosa ('rəuzə) *adv* in secret. [L, lit.: under the rose; from use of the rose in ancient times as a token of secrecy]

subroutine ('sʌbru:ˌti:n) *n* a section of a computer program that is stored only once but can be used at several different points in the program. Also called: **procedure.**

sub-Saharan *adj* in, of, or relating to Africa south of the Sahara desert.

subscribe Ⓣ (səb'skraɪb) *vb* **subscribes, subscribing, subscribed. 1** (usually foll. by *to*) to pay or promise to pay (money) as a contribution (to a fund, for a magazine, etc.), esp. at regular intervals. **2** to sign (one's name, etc.) at the end of a document. **3** *(intr; foll. by to)* to give support or approval: *to subscribe to the theory of reincarnation.* [C15: from L *subscrībere* to write underneath]
▸**sub'scriber** *n*

subscriber trunk dialling *n Brit.* a service by which telephone subscribers can obtain trunk calls by dialling direct without the aid of an operator. Abbrev.: **STD.**

subscript ('sʌbskrɪpt) *Printing.* ◆ *adj* **1** (of a character) written or printed below the base line. Cf. **superscript.** ◆ *n* **2** Also called: **subindex.** a subscript character.

subscription Ⓣ (səb'skrɪpʃən) *n* **1** a payment or promise of payment for consecutive issues of a magazine, newspaper, book, etc., over a specified period of time. **2a** the advance purchase of tickets for a series of concerts, etc. **2b** *(as modifier): a subscription concert.* **3** money paid or promised, as to a charity, or the fund raised in this way. **4** an offer to buy shares or bonds issued by a company. **5** the act of signing one's name to a document, etc. **6** a signature or other appendage attached to the bottom of a document, etc. **7** agreement or acceptance expressed by or as if by signing one's name. **8** a signed document, statement, etc. **9** *Chiefly Brit.* the membership dues or fees paid to a society or club. **10** an advance order for a new product. **11a** the sale of books, etc., prior to publishing. **11b** *(as modifier): a subscription edition.*
▸**sub'scriptive** *adj* ▸**sub'scriptively** *adv*

subsequence ('sʌbsɪkwəns) *n* **1** the fact or state of being subsequent. **2** a subsequent incident or occurrence.

subsequent Ⓣ ('sʌbsɪkwənt) *adj* occurring after; succeeding. [C15: from L *subsequēns* following on, from *subsequī,* from *sub-* near + *sequī* to follow]
▸**'subsequently** *adv* ▸**'subsequentness** *n*

subserve (səb'sɜ:v) *vb* **subserves, subserving, subserved.** *(tr)* to be helpful or useful to. [C17: from L *subservīre* to be subject to, from SUB- + *servīre* to serve]

subservient Ⓣ (səb'sɜ:vɪənt) *adj* **1** obsequious. **2** serving as a means to an end. **3** a less common word for **subordinate** (sense 2). [C17: from L *subserviēns* complying with, from *subservīre* to SUBSERVE]
▸**sub'serviently** *adv* ▸**sub'servience** *or* **sub'serviency** *n*

subset ('sʌbˌset) *n* a mathematical set contained within a larger set.

subshrub ('sʌbˌʃrʌb) *n* a small bushy plant that is woody except for the tips of the branches.

subside Ⓣ (səb'saɪd) *vb* **subsides, subsiding, subsided.** *(intr)* **1** to become less loud, excited, violent, etc.; abate. **2** to sink or fall to a lower level. **3** (of the surface of the earth, etc.) to cave in; collapse. **4** (of sediment, etc.) to sink or descend to the bottom; settle. [C17: from L *subsīdere* to settle down]
▸**sub'sider** *n*

subsidence Ⓣ (səb'saɪdᵊns, 'sʌbsɪdᵊns) *n* **1** the act or process of subsiding or the condition of having subsided. **2** *Geol.* the gradual sinking of landforms to a lower level.

subsidiarity (səbˌsɪdɪ'ærɪtɪ) *n* the principle of devolving political decisions to the lowest practical level.

subsidiary Ⓣ (səb'sɪdɪərɪ) *adj* **1** serving to aid or supplement; auxiliary. **2** of lesser importance; subordinate. ◆ *n, pl* **subsidiaries. 3** a subsidiary person or thing. **4** Also called: **subsidiary company.** a company with at least half of its capital stock owned by another company. [C16: from L *subsidiārius* supporting, from *subsidium* SUBSIDY]
▸**sub'sidiarily** *adv* ▸**sub'sidiariness** *n*

subsidize Ⓣ *or* **subsidise** ('sʌbsɪˌdaɪz) *vb* **subsidizes, subsidizing, subsidized** *or* **subsidises, subsidising, subsidised.** *(tr)* **1** to aid or support with a subsidy. **2** to obtain the aid of by means of a subsidy.
▸ˌ**subsidi'zation** *or* ˌ**subsidi'sation** *n* ▸**'subsiˌdizer** *or* **'subsiˌdiser** *n*

subsidy Ⓣ ('sʌbsɪdɪ) *n, pl* **subsidies. 1** a financial aid supplied by a government, as to industry, for public welfare, the balance of payments, etc. **2** *English history.* a financial grant made originally for special purposes by Parliament to the Crown. **3** any monetary aid, grant, or contribution. [C14: from Anglo-Norman *subsidie,* from L *subsidium* assistance, from *subsidēre* to remain, from *sub-* down + *sedēre* to sit]

subsist Ⓣ (səb'sɪst) *vb (mainly intr)* **1** (often foll. by *on*) to be sustained; manage to live: *to subsist on milk.* **2** to continue in existence. **3** (foll. by *in*) to lie or reside by virtue (of); consist. **4** *(tr) Obs.* to provide with support. [C16: from L *subsistere* to stand firm]
▸**sub'sistent** *adj*

subsistence Ⓣ (səb'sɪstəns) *n* **1** the means by which one maintains life. **2** the act or condition of subsisting.

subsistence farming *n* a type of farming in which most of the produce (**subsistence crop**) is consumed by the farmer and his family.

subsistence level *n* a standard of living barely adequate to support life.

subsistence wage *n* the lowest wage upon which a worker and his family can survive.

subsoil ('sʌbˌsɔɪl) *n* **1** Also called: **undersoil.** the layer of soil beneath the surface soil and overlying the bedrock. ◆ *vb* **2** *(tr)* to plough (land) to a depth so as to break up the subsoil.

subsonic (sʌb'sɒnɪk) *adj* being, having, or travelling at a velocity below that of sound.

subspecies ('sʌbˌspi:ʃi:z) *n, pl* **subspecies.** *Biol.* a subdivision of a species: usually occurs because of isolation within a species.

substance Ⓣ ('sʌbstəns) *n* **1** the tangible basic matter of which a thing consists. **2** a specific type of matter, esp. a homogeneous material with definite or fairly definite chemical composition. **3** the essence, meaning, etc., of a discourse, thought, or written article. **4** solid or meaningful quality: *an education of substance.* **5** material density or body: *free space has no substance.* **6** material possessions or wealth: *a man of substance.* **7** *Philosophy.* the supposed immaterial substratum of anything that can receive modifications and in which attributes and accidents inhere. **8 in substance.** with regard to the salient points. [C13: via OF from L *substantia,* from *substāre,* from SUB- + *stāre* to stand]

substandard Ⓣ (sʌb'stændəd) *adj* **1** below an established or required standard. **2** another word for **nonstandard.**

substantial Ⓣ (səb'stænʃəl) *adj* **1** of a considerable size or value: *sub-*

THESAURUS

subordination *n* **4, 5** = **inferiority**, inferior *or* secondary status, servitude, subjection

subscribe *vb* **1** = **contribute**, chip in, donate, give, offer, pledge, promise **3** = **support**, acquiesce, advocate, agree, consent, countenance, endorse

subscription *n* **1** *Chiefly Brit.* = **membership fee**, annual payment, dues **3** = **contribution**, donation, gift, offering

subsequent *adj* = **following**, after, consequent, consequential, ensuing, later, succeeding, successive
Antonyms *adj* antecedent, earlier, erstwhile, former, one-time, past, preceding, previous, prior

subsequently *adv* = **later**, afterwards, at a later date, consequently, in the aftermath (of), in the end

subservient *adj* **1** = **servile**, abject, bootlicking (*inf.*), deferential, inferior, obsequious, slavish, subject, submissive, sycophantic, truckling **2** = **subordinate**, accessory, ancillary, auxiliary, conducive, subsidiary
Antonyms *adj* ≠ **servile:** bolshie, bossy, disobedient, domineering, overbearing, overriding, rebellious, superior, wilful

subside *vb* **1** = **decrease**, abate, de-escalate, diminish, dwindle, ease, ebb, lessen, let up, level off, melt away, moderate, peter out, quieten, recede, slacken, wane **2** = **drop**, decline, descend, ebb, fall **3, 4** = **collapse**, cave in, drop, lower, settle, sink
Antonyms *vb* ≠ **decrease, drop:** escalate, grow, heighten, increase, inflate, intensify, mount, rise, soar, swell, tumefy, wax

subsidence *n* **1** = **decrease**, abatement, de-escalation, diminution, easing off, lessening, slackening **1** = **drop**, decline, descent, ebb **2** = **sinking**, collapse, settlement, settling

subsidiary *adj* **1, 2** = **lesser**, aiding, ancillary, assistant, auxiliary, contributory, cooperative, helpful, minor, secondary, subordinate, subservient, supplemental, supplementary, useful
Antonyms *adj* central, chief, head, key, leading, main, major, primary, principal, vital

subsidize *vb* **1** = **fund**, finance, promote, put up the money for, sponsor, support, underwrite

subsidy *n* **3** = **aid**, allowance, assistance, contribution, financial aid, grant, help, stipend, subvention, support

subsist *vb* **1, 2** = **stay alive**, be, continue, eke out an existence, endure, exist, keep going, keep one's head above water, last, live, make ends meet, remain, survive, sustain oneself

subsistence *n* **1** = **food**, aliment, provision, rations, sustenance, victuals **2** = **living**, existence, keep, livelihood, maintenance, support, survival, upkeep

substance *n* **1** = **material**, body, element, fabric, stuff, texture **3** = **meaning**, burden, essence, gist, gravamen, import, main point, matter, pith, significance, subject, sum and substance, theme **5** = **reality**, actuality, concreteness, entity, force **6** = **wealth**, affluence, assets, estate, means, property, resources

substandard *adj* **1** = **inferior**, damaged, imperfect, inadequate, second-rate, shoddy, unacceptable

substantial *adj* **1** = **big**, ample, considerable, generous, goodly, important, large, significant,

stantial funds. **2** worthwhile; important; telling: *a substantial reform.* **3** having wealth or importance: *a substantial member of the community.* **4** (of food or a meal) sufficient and nourishing. **5** solid or strong: *a substantial door.* **6** real; actual; true: *substantial evidence.* **7** of or relating to the basic or fundamental substance or aspects of a thing. ◆ *n* **8** (*often pl*) *Rare.* an essential or important element.
▸**substantiality** (səbˌstænʃɪˈælɪtɪ) *or* **sub'stantialness** *n* ▸**sub'stantially** *adv*

substantialism (səbˈstænʃəˌlɪzəm) *n Philosophy.* the doctrine that a substantial reality underlies phenomena.
▸**sub'stantialist** *n*

substantiate ❶ (səbˈstænʃɪˌeɪt) *vb* **substantiates, substantiating, substantiated.** (*tr*) **1** to establish as valid or genuine. **2** to give form or real existence to. [C17: from NL *substantiāre,* from L *substantia* SUBSTANCE]
▸**subˌstanti'ation** *n*

substantive (ˈsʌbstəntɪv) *n* **1** *Grammar.* a noun or pronoun used in place of a noun. ◆ *adj* **2** of, relating to, containing, or being the essential element of a thing. **3** having independent function, resources, or existence. **4** of substantial quantity. **5** solid in foundation or basis. **6** *Grammar.* denoting, relating to, or standing in place of a noun. **7** (səbˈstæntɪv). (of a dye or colour) staining the material directly without use of a mordant. [C15: from LL *substantīvus,* from L *substāre* to stand beneath]
▸**substantival** (ˌsʌbstənˈtaɪvᵊl) *adj* ▸**ˌsubstan'tivally** *adv* ▸**'substantively** *adv*

substantive rank *n* a permanent rank in the armed services.

substation (ˈsʌbˌsteɪʃən) *n* **1** a subsidiary station. **2** an installation at which electrical energy is received from one or more power stations for conversion from alternating to direct current, stepping down the voltage, or switching before distribution by a low-tension network.

substituent (sʌbˈstɪtjʊənt) *n* **1** *Chem.* an atom or group that replaces another atom or group in a molecule or can be regarded as replacing an atom in a parent compound. ◆ *adj* **2** substituted or substitutable. [C19: from L *substituere* to SUBSTITUTE]

substitute ❶ (ˈsʌbstɪˌtjuːt) *vb* **substitutes, substituting, substituted. 1** (often foll. by *for*) to serve or cause to serve in place of another person or thing. **2** *Chem.* to replace (an atom or group in a molecule) with (another atom or group). ◆ *n* **3a** a person or thing that serves in place of another, such as a player in a game who takes the place of an injured colleague. **3b** (*as modifier*): *a substitute goalkeeper.* [C16: from L *substituere,* from *sub-* in place of + *statuere* to set up]
▸**ˌsubsti'tutable** *adj* ▸**'substiˌtutive** *adj*

> **USAGE NOTE** *Substitute* is sometimes wrongly used where *replace* is meant: *he replaced* (not *substituted*) *the worn tyre with a new one.*

substitution ❶ (ˌsʌbstɪˈtjuːʃən) *n* **1** the act of substituting or state of being substituted. **2** something or someone substituted.

substrate (ˈsʌbstreɪt) *n* **1** *Biochem.* the substance upon which an enzyme acts. **2** another word for **substratum.**

substratum (sʌbˈstrɑːtəm, -ˈstreɪ-) *n, pl* **substrata** (-ˈstrɑːtə, -ˈstreɪtə). **1** any layer or stratum lying underneath another. **2** a basis or foundation; groundwork. [C17: from NL, from L *substrātus* strewn beneath, from *substernere* to spread under]
▸**sub'strative** *or* **sub'stratal** *adj*

substructure (ˈsʌbˌstrʌktʃə) *n* **1** a structure, pattern, etc., that forms the basis of anything. **2** a structure forming a foundation or framework for a building or other construction.
▸**sub'structural** *adj*

subsume (səbˈsjuːm) *vb* **subsumes, subsuming, subsumed.** (*tr*) **1** to incorporate (an idea, case, etc.) under a comprehensive or inclusive classification. **2** to consider (an instance of something) as part of a general rule. [C16: from NL *subsumere,* from L SUB- + *sumere* to take]
▸**sub'sumable** *adj* ▸**subsumption** (səbˈsʌmpʃən) *n*

subtemperate (sʌbˈtɛmpərɪt) *adj* of or relating to the colder temperate regions.

subtenant (sʌbˈtɛnənt) *n* a person who rents or leases property from a tenant.
▸**sub'tenancy** *n*

subtend (səbˈtɛnd) *vb* (*tr*) **1** *Geom.* to be opposite to and delimit (an angle or side). **2** (of a bract, stem, etc.) to have (a bud or similar part) growing in its axil. [C16: from L *subtendere* to extend beneath]

subterfuge ❶ (ˈsʌbtəˌfjuːdʒ) *n* a stratagem employed to conceal something, evade an argument, etc. [C16: from LL *subterfugium,* from L *subterfugere* to escape by stealth, from *subter* secretly + *fugere* to flee]

subterminal (sʌbˈtɜːmɪnᵊl) *adj* almost at an end.

subterranean (ˌsʌbtəˈreɪnɪən) *adj* **1** Also: **subterraneous, subterrestrial.** situated, living, or operating below the surface of the earth. **2** existing or operating in concealment. [C17: from L *subterrāneus,* from SUB- + *terra* earth]
▸**ˌsubter'raneanly** *or* **ˌsubter'raneously** *adv*

subtext (ˈsʌbˌtɛkst) *n* **1** an underlying theme in a piece of writing. **2** a message which is not stated directly but can be inferred.

subtile (ˈsʌtᵊl) *adj* a rare spelling of **subtle.**
▸**'subtilely** *adv* ▸**subtility** (sʌbˈtɪlɪtɪ) *or* **'subtileness** *n* ▸**'subtilty** *n*

subtilize *or* **subtilise** (ˈsʌtɪˌlaɪz) *vb* **subtilizes, subtilizing, subtilized** *or* **subtilises, subtilising, subtilised. 1** (*tr*) to bring to a purer state; refine. **2** to debate subtly. **3** (*tr*) to make (the mind, etc.) keener.
▸**ˌsubtili'zation** *or* **ˌsubtili'sation** *n*

subtitle (ˈsʌbˌtaɪtᵊl) *n* **1** an additional subordinate title given to a literary or other work. **2** (*often pl*) **2a** text superimposed on a film or television broadcast, either a translation of foreign dialogue or as an aid for the hard of hearing. **2b** Also called: **caption.** explanatory text on a silent film. ◆ *vb* **subtitles, subtitling, subtitled. 3** (*tr; usually passive*) to provide a subtitle for.

subtle ❶ (ˈsʌtᵊl) *adj* **1** not immediately obvious or comprehensible. **2** difficult to detect or analyse, often through being delicate or highly refined: *a subtle scent.* **3** showing or making or capable of showing or making fine distinctions of meaning. **4** marked by or requiring mental acuteness or ingenuity; discriminating. **5** delicate or faint: *a subtle shade.* **6** cunning or wily: *a subtle rogue.* **7** operating or executed in secret: *a subtle intrigue.* [C14: from OF *soutil,* from L *subtīlis* finely woven]
▸**'subtleness** *n* ▸**'subtly** *adv*

subtlety ❶ (ˈsʌtᵊltɪ) *n, pl* **subtleties. 1** the state or quality of being subtle; delicacy. **2** a fine distinction. **3** something subtle.

subtonic (sʌbˈtɒnɪk) *n Music.* the seventh degree of a major or minor scale.

subtotal (sʌbˈtəʊtᵊl, ˈsʌbˌtəʊtᵊl) *n* **1** the total made up by a column of figures, etc., forming part of the total made up by a larger column. ◆ *vb* **subtotals, subtotalling, subtotalled** *or US* **subtotals, subtotaling, subtotaled. 2** to work out a subtotal for (a column, etc.).

subtract ❶ (səbˈtrækt) *vb* **1** to calculate the difference between (two numbers or quantities) by subtraction. **2** to remove (a part of a thing, quantity, etc.) from the whole. [C16: from L *subtractus* withdrawn, from *subtrahere* to draw away from beneath]
▸**sub'tracter** *n* ▸**sub'tractive** *adj*

subtraction (səbˈtrækʃən) *n* **1** the act or process of subtracting. **2** a mathematical operation in which the difference between two numbers or quantities is calculated.

subtrahend (ˈsʌbtrəˌhɛnd) *n* the number to be subtracted from another number (the **minuend**). [C17: from L *subtrahendus,* from *subtrahere* to SUBTRACT]

subtropics (sʌbˈtrɒpɪks) *pl n* the region lying between the tropics and temperate lands.
▸**sub'tropical** *adj*

subulate (ˈsuːbjʊlɪt, -ˌleɪt) *adj* (esp. of plant parts) tapering to a point; awl-shaped. [C18: from NL *subulatus* like an awl, from L *sūbula* awl]

suburb ❶ (ˈsʌbɜːb) *n* a residential district situated on the outskirts of a city or town. [C14: from L *suburbium,* from *sub-* close to + *urbs* a city]

suburban (səˈbɜːbᵊn) *adj* **1** of, in, or inhabiting a suburb or the suburbs. **2** characteristic of a suburb or the suburbs. **3** *Mildly derog.* narrow or unadventurous in outlook.
▸**su'burbanˌite** *n* ▸**su'burbanˌize** *or* **su'burbanˌise** *vb* (*tr*)

THESAURUS

sizable *or* sizeable, tidy (*inf.*), worthwhile **5** = **solid**, bulky, durable, firm, hefty, massive, sound, stout, strong, sturdy, well-built **6** *Formal* = **real**, actual, existent, material, positive, true, valid, weighty
Antonyms *adj* ≠ **big:** inadequate, inconsiderable, insignificant, insubstantial, meagre, niggardly, pathetic, poor, skimpy, small ≠ **solid:** feeble, frail, infirm, insubstantial, jerry-built, light-weight, rickety, weak ≠ **real:** fictitious, imaginary, imagined, insubstantial, nonexistent, unreal

substantially *adv* **7** = **essentially**, in essence, in essentials, in substance, in the main, largely, materially, to a large extent

substantiate *vb* **1** = **support**, affirm, attest to, authenticate, bear out, confirm, corroborate, establish, prove, validate, verify
Antonyms *vb* confute, contradict, controvert, disprove, expose, invalidate, make a nonsense of, negate, prove false, rebut, refute

substitute *vb* **1** *often foll. by* **for** = **stand in for**, act for, be in place of, cover for, deputize for, double for, fill in for, hold the fort for, relieve, take over from ◆ *n* **3a** = **replacement**, agent, depute (*Scot.*), deputy, equivalent, expedient, locum, locum tenens, makeshift, proxy, relief, representative, reserve, stand-by, stopgap, sub, supply, surrogate, temp (*inf.*), temporary ◆ *modifier* **3b** = **replacement**, acting, additional, alternative, fall-back, proxy, reserve, second, surrogate, temporary

substitution *n* **1, 2** = **replacement**, change, exchange, interchange, swap, switch

subterfuge *n* = **trick**, artifice, deception, deviousness, dodge, duplicity, evasion, excuse, machination, manoeuvre, ploy, pretence, pretext, quibble, ruse, shift, stall, stratagem

subtle *adj* **1, 2** = **faint**, delicate, implied, indirect, insinuated, slight, understated **3, 4** = **sophisticated**, delicate, discriminating, nice, refined **6** = **crafty**, artful, astute, cunning, designing, devious, ingenious, intriguing, keen, Machiavellian, scheming, shrewd, sly, wily
Antonyms *adj* ≠ **faint:** overwhelming, strong ≠ **crafty:** artless, blunt, direct, downright, guileless, obvious, simple, straightforward ≠ **sophisticated:** crass, heavy-handed, lacking finesse, tactless, unsophisticated, unsubtle

subtlety *n* **1** = **discrimination**, delicacy, discernment, finesse, refinement, sophistication **1** = **cunning**, acumen, acuteness, artfulness, astuteness, cleverness, craftiness, deviousness, guile, ingenuity, sagacity, skill, slyness, wiliness **2** = **fine point**, intricacy, nicety

subtract *vb* **2** = **take away**, deduct, detract, diminish, remove, take from, take off, withdraw
Antonyms *vb* add, add to, append, increase by, supplement

suburb *n* = **residential area**, dormitory area (*Brit.*), environs, faubourgs, neighbourhood, outskirts, precincts, purlieus, suburbia

suburbia (səˈbɜːbɪə) *n* **1** suburbs or the people living in them considered as an identifiable community or class in society. **2** the life, customs, etc., of suburbanites.

subvention (səbˈvɛnʃən) *n* **1** a grant, aid, or subsidy, as from a government. **2** *Sport.* a fee paid indirectly to a supposedly amateur athlete for appearing at a meeting. [C15: from LL *subventiō* assistance, from L *subvenīre,* from *sub-* under + *venīre* to come]

subversion (səbˈvɜːʃən) *n* **1** the act or an instance of subverting a legally constituted government, institution, etc. **2** the state of being subverted; destruction or ruin. [C14: from LL *subversiō* destruction, from L *subvertere* to overturn]

subversive ⓣ (səbˈvɜːsɪv) *adj* **1** liable to subvert or overthrow a government, legally constituted institution, etc. ◆ *n* **2** a person engaged in subversive activities, etc.
▸**subˈversively** *adv* ▸**subˈversiveness** *n*

subvert ⓣ (səbˈvɜːt) *vb* (*tr*) **1** to bring about the complete downfall or ruin of (something existing by a system of law, etc.). **2** to undermine the moral principles of (a person, etc.). [C14: from L *subvertere* to overturn]
▸**subˈverter** *n*

subway (ˈsʌbˌweɪ) *n* **1** *Brit.* an underground tunnel enabling pedestrians to cross a road, railway, etc. **2** an underground tunnel for traffic, power supplies, etc. **3** an underground railway.

succedaneum (ˌsʌksɪˈdeɪnɪəm) *n, pl* **succedanea** (-nɪə). something that is used as a substitute, esp. any medical drug or agent that may be taken or prescribed in place of another. [C17: from L *succēdāneus* following after; see SUCCEED]
▸ˌ**succeˈdaneous** *adj*

succeed ⓣ (səkˈsiːd) *vb* **1** (*intr*) to accomplish an aim, esp. in the manner desired. **2** (*intr*) to happen in the manner desired: *the plan succeeded.* **3** (*intr*) to acquit oneself satisfactorily or do well, as in a specified field. **4** (when *intr,* often foll. by *to*) to come next in order (after someone or something). **5** (when *intr,* often foll. by *to*) to take over an office, post, etc. (from a person). **6** (*intr;* usually foll. by *to*) to come into possession (of property, etc.); inherit. **7** (*intr*) to have a result according to a specified manner: *the plan succeeded badly.* [C15: from L *succēdere* to follow after]
▸**sucˈceeder** *n* ▸**sucˈceedingly** *adv*

success ⓣ (səkˈsɛs) *n* **1** the favourable outcome of something attempted. **2** the attainment of wealth, fame, etc. **3** an action, performance, etc., that is characterized by success. **4** a person or thing that is successful. [C16: from L *successus* an outcome; see SUCCEED]

successful ⓣ (səkˈsɛsful) *adj* **1** having succeeded in one's endeavours. **2** marked by a favourable outcome. **3** having obtained fame, wealth, etc.
▸**sucˈcessfully** *adv* ▸**sucˈcessfulness** *n*

succession ⓣ (səkˈsɛʃən) *n* **1** the act or an instance of one person or thing following another. **2** a number of people or things following one another in order. **3** the act, process, or right by which one person succeeds to the office, etc., of another. **4** the order that determines how one person or thing follows another. **5** a line of descent to a title, etc. **6 in succession.** in a manner such that one thing is followed uninterruptedly by another. [C14: from L *successio;* see SUCCEED]
▸**sucˈcessional** *adj*

successive ⓣ (səkˈsɛsɪv) *adj* **1** following another without interruption. **2** of or involving succession: *a successive process.*
▸**sucˈcessively** *adv* ▸**sucˈcessiveness** *n*

successor (səkˈsɛsə) *n* a person or thing that follows, esp. a person who succeeds another.

succinct ⓣ (səkˈsɪŋkt) *adj* marked by brevity and clarity; concise. [C15: from L *succinctus* girt about, from *succingere* to gird from below]
▸**sucˈcinctly** *adv* ▸**sucˈcinctness** *n*

succinic acid (sʌkˈsɪnɪk) *n* a colourless odourless water-soluble acid found in plant and animal tissues, deriving from amber. Formula: $HOOC(CH_2)_2COOH$. Systematic name: **butanedioic acid.** [C19: from L *succinum* amber]

succotash (ˈsʌkəˌtæʃ) *n US & Canad.* a mixture of cooked sweet corn kernels and lima beans, served as a vegetable. [C18: of Amerind origin, from *msiquatash,* lit.: broken pieces]

succour ⓣ *or US* **succor** (ˈsʌkə) *n* **1** help or assistance, esp. in time of difficulty. **2** a person or thing that provides help. ◆ *vb* **3** (*tr*) to give aid to. [C13: from OF *sucurir,* from L *succurrere* to hurry to help]

succubus (ˈsʌkjubəs) *n, pl* **succubi** (-ˌbaɪ). **1** Also called: **succuba.** a female demon fabled to have sexual intercourse with sleeping men. Cf. **incubus. 2** any evil demon. [C16: from Med. L, from LL *succuba* harlot, from L *succubāre* to lie beneath]

succulent ⓣ (ˈsʌkjulənt) *adj* **1** juicy. **2** (of plants) having thick fleshy leaves or stems. ◆ *n* **3** a plant that can exist in arid conditions by using water stored in its fleshy tissues. [C17: from L *succulentus,* from *sūcus* juice]
▸ˈ**succulence** *or* ˈ**succulency** *n* ▸ˈ**succulently** *adv*

succumb ⓣ (səˈkʌm) *vb* (*intr;* often foll. by *to*) **1** to give way to the force (of) or desire (for). **2** to be fatally overwhelmed (by disease, etc.); die (of). [C15: from L *succumbere* to be overcome, from SUB- + *-cumbere,* from *cubāre* to lie down]

succursal (sʌˈkɜːsᵊl) *adj* **1** (esp. of a religious establishment) subsidiary. ◆ *n* **2** a subsidiary establishment. [C19: from F, from Med. L *succursus,* from L *succurrere* to SUCCOUR]

such (sʌtʃ) (often foll. by a corresponding subordinate clause introduced by *that* or *as*) ◆ *determiner* **1a** of the sort specified or understood: *such books.* **1b** (*as pronoun*): *such is life; robbers, rapists, and such.* **2** so great; so much: *such a help.* **3 as such. 3a** in the capacity previously specified or understood: *a judge as such hasn't so much power.* **3b** in itself or themselves: *intelligence as such can't guarantee success.* **4 such and such.** specific, but not known or named: *at such and such a time.* **5 such as. 5a** for example: *animals, such as tigers.* **5b** of a similar kind as; like: *people such as your friend.* **5c** of the (usually small) amount, etc.: *the food, such as there was, was excellent.* **6 such that.** so that: used to express purpose or result: *power such that it was effortless.* ◆ *adv* **7** (intensifier): *such a nice person.* [OE *swilc*]

suchlike (ˈsʌtʃˌlaɪk) *adj* **1** (*prenominal*) of such a kind; similar: *John, Ken, and other suchlike idiots.* ◆ *n* **2** such or similar persons or things: *hyenas, jackals, and suchlike.*

suck (sʌk) *vb* **1** to draw (a liquid or other substance) into the mouth by creating a partial vacuum in the mouth. **2** to draw in (fluid, etc.) by or as if by a similar action: *plants suck moisture from the soil.* **3** to drink milk from (a mother's breast); suckle. **4** (*tr*) to extract fluid content from (a solid food): *to suck a lemon.* **5** (*tr*) to take into the mouth and moisten, dissolve, or roll around with the tongue: *to suck one's thumb.* **6** (*tr;* often foll. by *down, in,* etc.) to draw by using irresistible force. **7** (*intr*) (of a pump) to draw in air because of a low supply level or leaking valves, etc. **8** (*tr*) to assimilate or acquire (knowledge, comfort, etc.). **9** (*intr*) *Sl.* to be contemptible or disgusting. ◆ *n* **10** the act or an instance of sucking. **11** something that is sucked, esp. milk from the mother's breast. **12 give suck to.** to give (a baby or young animal) milk from the breast or udder. **13** an attracting or sucking force. **14** a sound caused by sucking. ◆ See also **suck in, sucks, suck up to.** [OE *sūcan*]

sucker ⓣ (ˈsʌkə) *n* **1** a person or thing that sucks. **2** *Sl.* a person who is

THESAURUS

subversive *adj* **1** = **seditious,** destructive, incendiary, inflammatory, insurrectionary, overthrowing, perversive, riotous, treasonous, underground, undermining ◆ *n* **2** = **dissident,** deviationist, fifth columnist, insurrectionary, quisling, saboteur, seditionary, seditionist, terrorist, traitor

subvert *vb* **1** = **overturn,** demolish, destroy, invalidate, raze, ruin, sabotage, undermine, upset, wreck **2** = **corrupt,** confound, contaminate, debase, demoralize, deprave, pervert, poison, vitiate

succeed *vb* **1-3** = **make it** (*inf.*), arrive (*inf.*), be successful, bring home the bacon (*inf.*), carry all before one, come off (*inf.*), crack it (*inf.*), cut it (*inf.*), do all right for oneself (*inf.*), do the trick (*inf.*), do well, flourish, gain one's end, get to the top, go down a bomb (*inf., chiefly Brit.*), go like a bomb (*Brit. & NZ inf.*), hit the jackpot (*inf.*), make good, make one's mark (*inf.*), make the grade (*inf.*), prosper, thrive, triumph, turn out well, work **4** = **follow,** be subsequent, come next, ensue, result, supervene **6** = **take over,** accede, assume the office of, come into, come into possession of, enter upon, fill (someone's) boots, inherit, replace, step into (someone's) boots

Antonyms *vb* ≠ **make it:** be unsuccessful, collapse, come a cropper (*inf.*), fail, fall by the wayside, fall flat, fall short, flop (*inf.*), go belly up (*inf.*), go by the board, not make the grade, not manage ≠ **follow:** be a precursor of, come before, go ahead of, go before, pave the way, precede

success *n* **1, 2** = **favourable outcome,** ascendancy, eminence, fame, fortune, happiness, luck, prosperity, triumph **4** = **hit** (*inf.*), best seller, big name, celebrity, market leader, megastar (*inf.*), sensation, smash (*inf.*), smash hit (*inf.*), somebody, star, V.I.P., winner, wow (*sl.*)

Antonyms *n* ≠ **favourable outcome:** collapse, disaster, downfall, failure, misfortune ≠ **hit:** dead duck (*sl.*), fiasco, flop (*inf.*), loser, nobody, no-hoper, washout

successful *adj* **2** = **thriving,** acknowledged, best-selling, booming, efficacious, favourable, flourishing, fortunate, fruitful, going places, home and dry (*Brit. inf.*), lucky, lucrative, moneymaking, on a roll, out in front (*inf.*), paying, profitable, rewarding, top, unbeaten, victorious **3** = **prosperous,** at the top of the tree, wealthy

Antonyms *adj* ≠ **thriving:** defeated, failed, ineffective, losing, luckless, uneconomic, unprofitable, unsuccessful, useless

successfully *adv* **2** = **well,** famously (*inf.*), favourably, in triumph, swimmingly, victoriously, with flying colours

succession *n* **2** = **series,** chain, continuation, course, cycle, flow, order, procession, progression, run, sequence, train **3** = **taking over,** accession, assumption, elevation, entering upon, inheritance **5** = **lineage,** descendants, descent, line, race **6 in succession** = **one after the other,** consecutively, one behind the other, on the trot (*inf.*), running, successively

successive *adj* **1** = **consecutive,** following, in a row, in succession, sequent, succeeding

succinct *adj* = **brief,** compact, compendious, concise, condensed, gnomic, in a few well-chosen words, laconic, pithy, summary, terse, to the point

Antonyms *adj* circuitous, circumlocutory, diffuse, discursive, long-winded, prolix, rambling, verbose, wordy

succour *n* **1** = **help,** aid, assistance, comfort, relief, support ◆ *vb* **3** = **help,** aid, assist, befriend, comfort, encourage, foster, give aid and encouragement to, minister to, nurse, relieve, render assistance to, support

succulent *adj* **1** = **juicy,** luscious, lush, mellow, moist, mouthwatering, rich

succumb *vb* **1** = **surrender,** capitulate, cave in (*inf.*), give in, give way, go under, knuckle under, submit, yield **2** = **die,** fall, fall victim to

Antonyms *vb* ≠ **surrender:** beat, conquer, get the better of, master, overcome, rise above, surmount, triumph over

sucker *n* **2** *Slang* = **fool,** butt, cat's paw, dupe, easy game *or* mark (*inf.*), mug (*Brit. sl.*), nerd *or*

easily deceived or swindled. **3** *Sl.* a person who cannot resist the attractions of a particular type of person or thing: *he's a sucker for blondes.* **4** a young animal that is not yet weaned. **5** *Zool.* an organ specialized for sucking or adhering. **6** a cup-shaped device, generally made of rubber, that may be attached to articles allowing them to adhere to a surface by suction. **7** *Bot.* **7a** a strong shoot that arises in a mature plant from a root, rhizome, or the base of the main stem. **7b** a short branch of a parasitic plant that absorbs nutrients from the host. **8** a pipe or tube through which a fluid is drawn by suction. **9** any of various small mainly North American cyprinoid fishes having a large sucking mouth. **10** any of certain fishes that have sucking discs, esp. the sea snail. **11** a piston in a suction pump or the valve in such a piston. ◆ *vb* **12** (*tr*) to strip the suckers from (a plant). **13** (*intr*) (of a plant) to produce suckers.

suck in *vb* (*adv*) **1** (*tr*) to attract by using an inexorable force, inducement, etc. **2** to draw in (one's breath) sharply.

suckle ('sʌkᵊl) *vb* **suckles, suckling, suckled. 1** to give (a baby or young animal) milk from the breast or (of a baby, etc.) to suck milk from the breast. **2** (*tr*) to bring up; nurture. [C15: prob. back formation from SUCKLING]
▸**'suckler** *n*

suckling ('sʌklɪŋ) *n* **1** an infant or young animal that is still taking milk from the mother. **2** a very young child. [C15: see SUCK, -LING[1]]

sucks (sʌks) *interj Sl.* **1** an expression of disappointment. **2** an exclamation of defiance or derision (esp. in **yah boo sucks to you**).

suck up to ❶ *vb* (*intr, adv + prep*) *Inf.* to flatter for one's own profit; toady.

sucrase ('sju:kreɪz) *n* another name for **invertase.** [C19: from F *sucre* sugar + -ASE]

sucre (*Spanish* 'sukre) *n* the standard monetary unit of Ecuador. [C19: after Antonio José de *Sucre* (1795–1830), S American liberator]

sucrose ('sju:krəʊz, -krəʊs) *n* the technical name for **sugar** (sense 1). [C19: F *sucre* sugar + -OSE[2]]

suction ('sʌkʃən) *n* **1** the act or process of sucking. **2** the force produced by a pressure difference, as the force holding a sucker onto a surface. **3** the act or process of producing such a force. [C17: from LL *suctiō* a sucking, from L *sūgere* to suck]
▸**'suctional** *adj*

suction pump *n* a pump for raising water or a similar fluid by suction. It usually consists of a cylinder containing a piston fitted with a flap valve.

suctorial (sʌk'tɔ:rɪəl) *adj* **1** specialized for sucking or adhering. **2** relating to or possessing suckers or suction. [C19: from NL *suctōrius,* from L *sūgere* to suck]

Sudanese (ˌsu:dᵊ'ni:z) *adj* **1** of or relating to the Sudan, in NE Africa. ◆ *n* **2** a native or inhabitant of the Sudan.

sudarium (sju'dɛərɪəm) *n, pl* **sudaria** (-'dɛərɪə). another word for **sudatorium.** [C17: from L, from *sūdāre* to sweat]

sudatorium (ˌsju:də'tɔ:rɪəm) *or* **sudatory** *n, pl* **sudatoria** (-'tɔ:rɪə) *or* **sudatories.** a room, esp. in a Roman bathhouse, where sweating is induced by heat. [C18: from L, from *sūdāre* to sweat]

sudatory ('sju:dətərɪ, -trɪ) *adj* **1** relating to or producing sweating. ◆ *n, pl* **sudatories. 2** a sudatory agent. **3** another word for **sudatorium.**

sudd (sʌd) *n* floating masses of reeds and weeds that occur on the White Nile and obstruct navigation. [C19: from Ar., lit.: obstruction]

sudden ❶ ('sʌdᵊn) *adj* **1** occurring or performed quickly and without warning. **2** marked by haste; abrupt. **3** *Rare.* rash; precipitate. ◆ *n* **4** *Arch.* an abrupt occurrence (in **on a sudden**). **5 all of a sudden.** without warning; unexpectedly. [C13: via F from LL *subitāneus,* from L *subitus* unexpected, from *subīre* to happen unexpectedly, from *sub-* secretly + *īre* to go]
▸**'suddenly** *adv* ▸**'suddenness** *n*

sudden death *n* **1** (in sports, etc.) an extra game or contest to decide the winner of a tied competition. **2** an unexpected or quick death.

sudden infant death syndrome *n* a technical name for **cot death.** Abbrev.: **SIDS.**

sudor ('sju:dɔ:) *n* a technical name for **sweat.** [L]
▸**sudoral** ('sju:dərəl) *adj*

sudoriferous (ˌsju:də'rɪfərəs) *adj* producing or conveying sweat. Also: ˌ**sudo'riparous.** [C16: via NL from SUDOR + L *ferre* to bear]
▸ˌ**sudor'iferousness** *n*

sudorific (ˌsju:də'rɪfɪk) *adj* **1** producing or causing sweating. ◆ *n* **2** a sudorific agent. [C17: from NL *sūdōrificus,* from SUDOR + L *facere* to make]

suds (sʌdz) *pl n* **1** the bubbles on the surface of water in which soap, detergents, etc., have been dissolved; lather. **2** soapy water. [C16: prob. from MDu. *sudse* marsh]
▸**'sudsy** *adj*

sue ❶ (sju:, su:) *vb* **sues, suing, sued. 1** to institute legal proceedings (against). **2** to make suppliant requests of (someone for something). [C13: from OF *sivre,* from L *sequī* to follow]
▸**'suer** *n*

suede (sweɪd) *n* **a** a leather with a fine velvet-like nap on the flesh side, produced by abrasive action. **b** (*as modifier*): *a suede coat.* [C19: from F *gants de Suède,* lit.: gloves from Sweden]

suet ('su:ɪt, 'sju:ɪt) *n* a hard waxy fat around the kidneys and loins in sheep, cattle, etc., used in cooking and making tallow. [C14: from OF *seu,* from L *sēbum*]
▸**'suety** *adj*

suet pudding *n Brit.* any of a variety of puddings made with suet and steamed or boiled.

suffer ❶ ('sʌfə) *vb* **1** to undergo or be subjected to (pain, punishment, etc.). **2** (*tr*) to undergo or experience (anything): *to suffer a change of management.* **3** (*intr*) to be set at a disadvantage: *this author suffers in translation.* **4** (*tr*) *Arch.* to tolerate; permit (someone to do something): *suffer the little children to come unto me.* **5 suffer from. 5a** to be ill with, esp. recurrently. **5b** to be given to: *he suffers from a tendency to exaggerate.* [C13: from OF *soffrir,* from L *sufferre,* from SUB- + *ferre* to bear]
▸**'sufferer** *n* ▸**'suffering** *n*

sufferable ('sʌfərəbᵊl, 'sʌfrə-) *adj* able to be tolerated or suffered; endurable.

sufferance ('sʌfərəns, 'sʌfrəns) *n* **1** tolerance arising from failure to prohibit; tacit permission. **2** capacity to endure pain, injury, etc. **3** the state or condition of suffering. **4 on sufferance.** tolerated with reluctance. [C13: via OF from LL *sufferentia* endurance, from L *sufferre* to SUFFER]

suffice ❶ (sə'faɪs) *vb* **suffices, sufficing, sufficed. 1** to be adequate or satisfactory for (something). **2 suffice it to say that.** (*takes a clause as object*) let us say no more than that; I shall just say that. [C14: from OF *suffire,* from L *sufficere* from *sub-* below + *facere* to make]

sufficiency (sə'fɪʃənsɪ) *n, pl* **sufficiencies. 1** the quality or condition of being sufficient. **2** an adequate amount. **3** *Arch.* efficiency.

sufficient ❶ (sə'fɪʃənt) *adj* **1** enough to meet a need or purpose; adequate. **2** *Logic.* (of a condition) assuring the truth of a statement; requiring but not necessarily caused by some other state of affairs. Cf. **necessary** (sense 3b). **3** *Arch.* competent; capable. ◆ *n* **4** a sufficient quantity. [C14: from L *sufficiens* supplying the needs of, from *sufficere* to SUFFICE]
▸**suf'ficiently** *adv*

suffix *n* ('sʌfɪks). **1** *Grammar.* an affix that follows the stem to which it is attached, as for example *-s* and *-ness* in *dogs* and *softness.* Cf. **prefix** (sense 1). **2** anything added at the end of something else. ◆ *vb* ('sʌfɪks, sə'fɪks). **3** (*tr*) *Grammar.* to add (a morpheme) as a suffix to a word. [C18: from NL *suffixum,* from L *suffixus* fastened below, from *suffigere* to fasten below]

suffocate ❶ ('sʌfəˌkeɪt) *vb* **suffocates, suffocating, suffocated. 1** to kill or be killed by the deprivation of oxygen, as by obstruction of the air passage. **2** to block the air passages or have the air passages blocked. **3** to feel or cause to feel discomfort from heat and lack of air. [C16: from L *suffōcāre,* from SUB- + *faucēs* throat]
▸**'suffoˌcating** *adj* ▸ˌ**suffo'cation** *n*

Suffolk punch ('sʌfək) *n* a breed of draught horse with a chestnut coat and short legs.

suffragan ('sʌfrəgən) *adj* **1a** (of any bishop of a diocese) subordinate to and assisting his superior archbishop or metropolitan. **1b** (of any assistant bishop) assisting the bishop of his diocese but having no ordinary jurisdiction in that diocese. ◆ *n* **2** a suffragan bishop. [C14: from Med. L *suffrāgāneus,* from *suffrāgium* assistance, from L: suffrage]
▸**'suffraganship** *n*

suffrage ('sʌfrɪdʒ) *n* **1** the right to vote, esp. in public elections; franchise. **2** the exercise of such a right; casting a vote. **3** a short intercessory prayer. [C14: from L *suffrāgium*]

suffragette (ˌsʌfrə'dʒet) *n* a female advocate of the extension of the franchise to women, esp. a militant one, as in Britain at the beginning of the 20th century. [C20: from SUFFRAG(E) + -ETTE]

THESAURUS

nurd (*sl.*), pushover (*sl.*), sap (*sl.*), sitting duck (*inf.*), sitting target, victim

suck up to *vb Informal* = **ingratiate oneself with**, brown-nose (*taboo sl.*), butter up, curry favour with, dance attendance on, fawn on, flatter, get on the right side of, keep in with (*inf.*), kiss (someone's) ass (*US & Canad. taboo sl.*), lick (someone's) boots, pander to, play up to (*inf.*), toady, truckle, worm oneself into (someone's) favour

sudden *adj* **1, 2** = **quick**, abrupt, hasty, hurried, impulsive, rapid, rash, swift, unexpected, unforeseen, unusual
Antonyms *adj* anticipated, deliberate, expected, foreseen, gentle, gradual, slow, unhasty

suddenly *adv* **1, 2** = **abruptly**, all at once, all of a sudden, on the spur of the moment, out of the blue (*inf.*), unexpectedly, without warning

sue *vb* **1** *Law* = **take (someone) to court**, bring an action against (someone), charge, have the law on (someone) (*inf.*), indict, institute legal proceedings against (someone), prefer charges against (someone), prosecute, summon **2** = **appeal for**, beg, beseech, entreat, petition, plead, solicit, supplicate

suffer *vb* **1** = **be affected**, ache, agonize, be in pain, be racked, feel wretched, go through a lot (*inf.*), go through the mill (*inf.*), grieve, have a bad time, hurt **2** = **undergo**, bear, endure, experience, feel, go through, sustain **3** = **be shown to disadvantage**, appear in a poor light, be handicapped **4** *Archaic* = **tolerate**, allow, let, permit, put up with (*inf.*), support

suffering *n* **1** = **pain**, affliction, agony, anguish, discomfort, distress, hardship, martyrdom, misery, ordeal, torment, torture

suffice *vb* **1** = **be enough**, answer, be adequate, be sufficient, content, do, fill the bill (*inf.*), meet requirements, satisfy, serve

sufficient *adj* **1** = **adequate**, competent, enough, enow (*arch.*), satisfactory
Antonyms *adj* deficient, inadequate, insufficient, meagre, not enough, poor, scant, short, sparse

suffocate *vb* **1, 2** = **choke**, asphyxiate, smother, stifle, strangle

suffragist ('sʌfrədʒɪst) *n* an advocate of the extension of the franchise, esp. to women.
▸**'suffragism** *n*

suffruticose (sə'fruːtɪˌkəʊz) *adj* (of a plant) having a permanent woody base and herbaceous branches. [C18: from NL *suffruticōsus*, from L SUB- + *frutex* shrub]

suffuse ❶ (sə'fjuːz) *vb* **suffuses, suffusing, suffused.** (*tr; usually passive*) to spread or flood through or over (something). [C16: from L *suffūsus* overspread with, from *suffundere*, from SUB- + *fundere* to pour]
▸**suffusion** (sə'fjuːʒən) *n* ▸**suf'fusive** *adj*

Sufi ('suːfɪ) *n, pl* **Sufis.** an adherent of any of various Muslim mystical orders or teachings, which emphasize the direct personal experience of God. [C17: from Ar. *sūfiy*, lit.: (man) of wool; prob. from the ascetic's woollen garments]
▸**'Sufic** *adj* ▸**'Sufism** *n*

sugar ('ʃʊgə) *n* **1** Also called: **sucrose, saccharose.** a white crystalline sweet carbohydrate, a disaccharide, found in many plants: used esp. as a sweetening agent in food and drinks. Related adj: **saccharine. 2** any of a class of simple water-soluble carbohydrates, such as sucrose, lactose, and fructose. **3** *Inf., chiefly US & Canad.* a term of affection, esp. for one's sweetheart. ◆ *vb* **4** (*tr*) to add sugar to; make sweet. **5** (*tr*) to cover or sprinkle with sugar. **6** (*intr*) to produce sugar. **7 sugar the pill** *or* **medicine.** to make something unpleasant more agreeable by adding something pleasant. [C13 *suker*, from OF *çucre*, from Med. L *zuccārum*, ult. from Sansk. *śarkarā*]
▸**'sugared** *adj*

sugar beet *n* a variety of beet cultivated for its white roots from which sugar is obtained.

sugar candy *n* **1** Also called: **rock candy.** large crystals of sugar formed by suspending strings in a strong sugar solution that hardens on the strings, used chiefly for sweetening coffee. **2** *Chiefly US.* confectionery; sweets.

sugar cane *n* a coarse perennial grass of Old World tropical regions, having tall stout canes that yield sugar: cultivated chiefly in the Caribbean and the southern US.

sugar-coat *vb* (*tr*) **1** to coat or cover with sugar. **2** to cause to appear more attractive.

sugar diabetes *n* an informal name for **diabetes mellitus** (see **diabetes**).

sugar glider *n* a common Australian phalanger that glides from tree to tree feeding on insects and nectar.

sugaring off *n Canad.* the boiling down of maple sap to produce sugar, traditionally a social event in early spring.

sugar loaf *n* **1** a large conical mass of hard refined sugar. **2** something resembling this.

sugar maple *n* a North American maple tree, grown as a source of sugar, which is extracted from the sap, and for its hard wood.

sugar of lead (lɛd) *n* another name for **lead acetate.**

sugarplum ('ʃʊgəˌplʌm) *n* a crystallized plum.

sugary ('ʃʊgərɪ) *adj* **1** of, like, or containing sugar. **2** excessively sweet. **3** deceptively pleasant; insincere.
▸**'sugariness** *n*

suggest ❶ (sə'dʒɛst) *vb* (*tr; may take a clause as object*) **1** to put forward (a plan, idea, etc.) for consideration: *I suggest Smith for the post; a plan suggested itself.* **2** to evoke (a person, thing, etc.) in the mind by the association of ideas: *that painting suggests home to me.* **3** to give an indirect or vague hint of: *his face always suggests his peace of mind.* [C16: from L *suggerere* to bring up]
▸**sug'gester** *n*

suggestible ❶ (sə'dʒɛstɪbᵊl) *adj* **1** easily influenced by ideas provided by other persons. **2** characteristic of something that can be suggested.
▸**sugˌgesti'bility** *n*

suggestion ❶ (sə'dʒɛstʃən) *n* **1** something that is suggested. **2** a hint or indication: *a suggestion of the odour of violets.* **3** *Psychol.* the process whereby the mere presentation of an idea to a receptive individual leads to the acceptance of that idea. See also **autosuggestion.**

suggestive ❶ (sə'dʒɛstɪv) *adj* **1** (*postpositive; foll. by of*) conveying a hint (of something). **2** tending to suggest something improper or indecent.
▸**sug'gestively** *adv* ▸**sug'gestiveness** *n*

suicidal (ˌsuːɪ'saɪdᵊl, ˌsjuː-) *adj* **1** involving, indicating, or tending towards suicide. **2** liable to result in suicide: *a suicidal attempt.* **3** liable to destroy one's own interests or prospects; dangerously rash.
▸**ˌsui'cidally** *adv*

suicide ('suːɪˌsaɪd, 'sjuː-) *n* **1** the act or an instance of killing oneself intentionally. **2** the self-inflicted ruin of one's own prospects or interests: *a merger would be financial suicide.* **3** a person who kills himself intentionally. **4** (*modifier*) reckless; extremely dangerous: *a suicide mission.* **5** (*modifier*) (of an action) undertaken or (of a person) undertaking an action in the knowledge that it will result in the death of the person performing it in order that maximum damage may be inflicted: *suicide bomber.* [C17: from NL *suīcīdium*, from L *suī* of oneself + *-cīdium*, from *caedere* to kill]

sui generis (ˌsuːaɪ 'dʒɛnərɪs) *adj* unique. [L, lit.: of its own kind]

suint ('suːɪnt, swɪnt) *n* a water-soluble substance found in the fleece of sheep, formed from dried perspiration. [C18: from F *suer* to sweat, from L *sūdāre*]

suit ❶ (suːt, sjuːt) *n* **1** any set of clothes of the same or similar material designed to be worn together, now usually (for men) a jacket with matching trousers or (for women) a jacket with matching or contrasting skirt or trousers. **2** (*in combination*) any outfit worn for a specific purpose: *a spacesuit.* **3** any set of items, such as parts of personal armour. **4** any of the four sets of 13 cards in a pack of playing cards, being spades, hearts, diamonds, and clubs. **5** a civil proceeding; lawsuit. **6** the act or process of suing in a court of law. **7** a petition or appeal made to a person of superior rank or status or the act of making such a petition. **8** a man's courting of a woman. **9** *Sl.* an executive, manager, or bureaucrat, esp. one considered faceless or dull. **10 follow suit. 10a** to play a card of the same suit as the card played immediately before it. **10b** to act in the same way as someone else. **11 strong** *or* **strongest suit.** something that one excels in. ◆ *vb* **12** to make or be fit or appropriate for: *that dress suits your figure.* **13** to meet the requirements or standards (of). **14** to be agreeable or acceptable to (someone). **15 suit oneself.** to pursue one's own intentions without reference to others. [C13: from OF *sieute* set of things, from *sivre* to follow]

suitable ❶ ('suːtəbᵊl, 'sjuːt-) *adj* appropriate; proper; fit.
▸**ˌsuita'bility** *or* **'suitableness** *n* ▸**'suitably** *adv*

suitcase ('suːtˌkeɪs, 'sjuːt-) *n* a portable rectangular travelling case for clothing, etc.

suite ❶ (swiːt) *n* **1** a series of items intended to be used together; set. **2** a set of connected rooms in a hotel. **3** a matching set of furniture, esp. of two armchairs and a settee. **4** a number of attendants or followers. **5** *Music.* **5a** an instrumental composition consisting of several movements in the same key based on or derived from dance rhythms, esp. in the baroque period. **5b** an instrumental composition in several movements less closely connected than a sonata. [C17: from F, from OF *sieute*; see SUIT]

suiting ('suːtɪŋ, 'sjuːt-) *n* a fabric used for suits.

suitor ❶ ('suːtə, 'sjuːt-) *n* **1** a man who courts a woman; wooer. **2** *Law.* a person who brings a suit in a court of law; plaintiff. [C13: from Anglo-Norman *suter*, from L *secūtor* follower, from *sequī* to follow]

sukiyaki (ˌsuːkɪ'jɑːkɪ) *n* a Japanese dish consisting of very thinly sliced beef or other meat, vegetables, and seasonings cooked together quickly, usually at the table. [from Japanese]

Sukkoth *or* **Succoth** ('sʊkəʊt, -kəʊθ; *Hebrew* suː'kɔt) *n* an eight-day Jewish harvest festival beginning on Tishri 15, which commemorates the period when the Israelites lived in the wilderness. Also called: **Feast of Tabernacles.** [from Heb., lit.: tabernacles]

sulcate ('sʌlkeɪt) *adj Biol.* marked with longitudinal parallel grooves. [C18: via L *sulcātus* from *sulcāre* to plough, from *sulcus* a furrow]

sulcus ('sʌlkəs) *n, pl* **sulci** (-saɪ). **1** a linear groove, furrow, or slight depression. **2** any of the narrow grooves on the surface of the brain that mark the cerebral convolutions. [C17: from L]

sulf- *combining form.* a US variant of **sulph-.**

sulfur ('sʌlfə) *n* the US spelling of **sulphur.**

sulk ❶ (sʌlk) *vb* **1** (*intr*) to be silent and resentful because of a wrong done to one; brood sullenly: *the child sulked after being slapped.* ◆ *n* **2** (*often pl*) a state or mood of feeling resentful or sullen: *he's in a sulk; he's got the sulks.* **3** Also: **sulker.** a person who sulks. [C18: ? back formation from SULKY[1]]

sulky[1] ❶ ('sʌlkɪ) *adj* **sulkier, sulkiest. 1** sullen, withdrawn, or moody,

THESAURUS

suffuse *vb* = **spread through** *or* **over**, bathe, cover, flood, imbue, infuse, mantle, overspread, permeate, pervade, steep, transfuse

suggest *vb* **1** = **recommend**, advise, advocate, move, offer a suggestion, prescribe, propose, put forward **2** = **bring to mind**, connote, evoke, put one in mind of **3** = **hint**, imply, indicate, insinuate, intimate, lead one to believe

suggestible *adj* **1** = **impressionable**, accessible, amenable, influencable, malleable, open, open-minded, persuadable, pervious, pliant, receptive, susceptible, tractable
Antonyms *adj* firm, headstrong, impervious, obdurate, single-minded, unwavering

suggestion *n* **1** = **recommendation**, motion, plan, proposal, proposition **2** = **hint**, breath, indication, insinuation, intimation, suspicion, trace, whisper

suggestive *adj* **1** *foll. by* **of** = **evocative of**, expressing, indicative of, redolent of, reminiscent of **2** = **smutty**, bawdy, blue, immodest, improper, indecent, indelicate, off colour, provocative, prurient, racy, ribald, risqué, rude, spicy (*inf.*), titillating, unseemly

suit *n* **1** = **outfit**, clothing, costume, dress, ensemble, habit **5** = **lawsuit**, action, case, cause, industrial tribunal, proceeding, prosecution, trial **7** = **appeal**, addresses, entreaty, invocation, petition, prayer, request **8** = **courtship**, attentions **10b follow suit** = **copy**, accord with, emulate, run with the herd, take one's cue from ◆ *vb* **12** = **befit**, agree, agree with, become, be seemly, conform to, correspond, go with, harmonize, match, tally **12** = **fit**, accommodate, adapt, adjust, customize, fashion, modify, proportion, tailor **14** = **be acceptable to**, answer, do, gratify, please, satisfy

suitability *n* = **appropriateness**, aptness, fitness, opportuneness, rightness, timeliness

suitable *adj* = **appropriate**, acceptable, applicable, apposite, apt, becoming, befitting, convenient, cut out for, due, fit, fitting, in character, in keeping, opportune, pertinent, proper, relevant, right, satisfactory, seemly, suited
Antonyms *adj* discordant, inapposite, inappropriate, incorrect, inopportune, jarring, out of character, out of keeping, unbecoming, unfitting, unseemly, unsuitable, unsuited

suite *n* **1** = **set**, collection, series **2** = **rooms**, apartment **3** = **furniture 4** = **attendants**, entourage, escort, followers, retainers, retinue, train

suitor *n* **1** *Old-fashioned* = **admirer**, beau, follower (*obs.*), swain (*arch.*), wooer, young man

sulk *vb* **1** = **be sullen**, be in a huff, be put out, brood, have the hump (*Brit. inf.*), pout

sulky[1] *adj* **1** = **huffy**, aloof, churlish, cross, dis-

through or as if through resentment. **2** dull or dismal: *sulky weather.* [C18: ?from obs. *sulke* sluggish]
▸**'sulkily** *adv* ▸**'sulkiness** *n*

sulky[2] ('sʌlkɪ) *n, pl* **sulkies.** a light two-wheeled vehicle for one person, usually drawn by one horse. [C18: from SULKY[1]]

sullage ('sʌlɪdʒ) *n* **1** filth or waste, esp. sewage. **2** sediment deposited by running water. [C16: ?from F *souiller* to sully]

sullen ❶ ('sʌlən) *adj* **1** unwilling to talk or be sociable; sulky; morose. **2** sombre; gloomy: *a sullen day.* ◆ *n* **3** *(pl) Arch.* a sullen mood. [C16: ?from Anglo-F *solain* (unattested), ult. rel. to L *sōlus* alone]
▸**'sullenly** *adv* ▸**'sullenness** *n*

sully ❶ ('sʌlɪ) *vb* **sullies, sullying, sullied.** *(tr)* to stain or tarnish (a reputation, etc.) or (of a reputation) to become stained or tarnished. [C16: prob. from F *souiller* to soil]

sulph- *or US* **sulf-** *combining form.* containing sulphur: *sulphate.*

sulpha *or US* **sulfa drug** ('sʌlfə) *n* any of a group of sulphonamides that inhibit the activity of bacteria and are used to treat bacterial infections.

sulphadiazine *or US* **sulfadiazine** (ˌsʌlfə'daɪəˌziːn) *n* an important sulpha drug used chiefly in combination with an antibiotic. [from SULPH- + DIAZ(O) + -INE[2]]

sulphanilamide *or US* **sulfanilamide** (ˌsʌlfə'nɪləˌmaɪd) *n* a white crystalline compound formerly used in the treatment of bacterial infections. [from SULPH- + ANIL(INE) + AMIDE]

sulphate *or US* **sulfate** ('sʌlfeɪt) *n* **1** any salt or ester of sulphuric acid. ◆ *vb* **sulphates, sulphating, sulphated** *or US* **sulfates, sulfating, sulfated.** **2** *(tr)* to treat with a sulphate or convert into a sulphate. **3** to undergo or cause to undergo the formation of a layer of lead sulphate on the plates of an accumulator. [C18: from NL *sulfātum*]
▸**sul'phation** *or US* **sul'fation** *n*

sulphide *or US* **sulfide** ('sʌlfaɪd) *n* a compound of sulphur with a more electropositive element.

sulphite *or US* **sulfite** ('sʌlfaɪt) *n* any salt or ester of sulphurous acid.
▸**sulphitic** *or US* **sulfitic** (sʌl'fɪtɪk) *adj*

sulphonamide *or US* **sulfonamide** (sʌl'fɒnəˌmaɪd) *n* any of a class of organic compounds that are amides of sulphonic acids containing the group $-SO_2NH_2$ or a group derived from this. An important class of sulphonamides are the sulpha drugs.

sulphone *or US* **sulfone** ('sʌlfəʊn) *n* any of a class of organic compounds containing the divalent group SO_2 linked to two other organic groups.

sulphonic *or US* **sulfonic acid** (sʌl'fɒnɪk) *n* any of a large group of strong organic acids that contain the group $-SO_2OH$ and are used in the manufacture of dyes and drugs.

sulphonmethane *or US* **sulfonmethane** (ˌsʌlfɒn'miːθeɪn) *n* a colourless crystalline compound used medicinally as a hypnotic. Formula: $C_7H_{16}O_4S_2$.

sulphur *or US* **sulfur** ('sʌlfə) *n* **a** an allotropic nonmetallic element, occurring free in volcanic regions and in combined state in gypsum, pyrite, and galena. It is used in the production of sulphuric acid, in the vulcanization of rubber, and in fungicides. Symbol: S; atomic no.: 16; atomic wt.: 32.066. **b** *(as modifier)*: *sulphur springs.* [C14 *soufre,* from OF, from L *sulfur*]
▸**sulphuric** *or US* **sulfuric** (sʌl'fjʊərɪk) *adj*

sulphurate *or US* **sulfurate** ('sʌlfjʊˌreɪt) *vb* **sulphurates, sulphurating, sulphurated.** *(tr)* to combine or treat with sulphur or a sulphur compound.
▸**ˌsulphu'ration** *or US* **ˌsulfu'ration** *n*

sulphur-bottom *n* another name for **blue whale.**

sulphur dioxide *n* a colourless soluble pungent gas. It is both an oxidizing and a reducing agent and is used in the manufacture of sulphuric acid, the preservation of foodstuffs (**E 220**), bleaching, and disinfecting. Formula: SO_2. Systematic name: **sulphur(IV) oxide.**

sulphureous *or US* **sulfureous** (sʌl'fjʊərɪəs) *adj* **1** another word for **sulphurous** (sense 1). **2** of the yellow colour of sulphur.

sulphuretted *or US* **sulfureted hydrogen** ('sʌlfjʊˌretɪd) *n* another name for **hydrogen sulphide.**

sulphuric acid *n* a colourless dense oily corrosive liquid used in accumulators and in the manufacture of fertilizers, dyes, and explosives. Formula: H_2SO_4. Systematic name: **tetraoxosulphuric(VI) acid.**

sulphurize, sulphurise, *or US* **sulfurize** ('sʌlfjʊˌraɪz) *vb* **sulphurizes, sulphurizing, sulphurized, sulphurises, sulphurising, sulphurised** *or US* **sulfurizes, sulfurizing, sulfurized.** *(tr)* to combine or treat with sulphur or a sulphur compound.
▸**ˌsulphuri'zation, ˌsulphuri'sation,** *or US* **ˌsulfuri'zation** *n*

sulphurous *or US* **sulfurous** ('sʌlfərəs) *adj* **1** Also: **sulphureous.** of, relating to, or resembling sulphur: *a sulphurous colour.* **2** (sʌl'fjʊərəs). of or containing sulphur with an oxidation state of 4: *sulphurous acid.* **3** of or relating to hellfire. **4** hot-tempered.
▸**'sulphurously** *or US* **'sulfurously** *adv* ▸**'sulphurousness** *or US* **'sulfurousness** *n*

sulphurous acid *n* an unstable acid produced when sulphur dioxide dissolves in water: used as a preservative for food and a bleaching agent. Formula: H_2SO_3. Systematic name: **sulphuric(IV) acid.**

sulphur trioxide *n* a colourless reactive fuming solid that forms sulphuric acid with water. Formula: SO_3. Systematic name: **sulphur(VI) oxide.**

sultan ('sʌltən) *n* **1** the sovereign of a Muslim country, esp. of the former Ottoman Empire. **2** a small domestic fowl with a white crest and heavily feathered legs and feet: originated in Turkey. [C16: from Med. L *sultānus,* from Ar. *sultān* rule, from Aramaic *salita* to rule]

sultana (sʌl'tɑːnə) *n* **1a** the dried fruit of a small white seedless grape, originally produced in SW Asia; seedless raisin. **1b** the grape itself. **2** Also called: **sultaness.** a wife, concubine, or female relative of a sultan. **3** a mistress; concubine. [C16: from It., fem of *sultano* SULTAN]

sultanate ('sʌltəˌneɪt) *n* **1** the territory or a country ruled by a sultan. **2** the office, rank, or jurisdiction of a sultan.

sultry ❶ ('sʌltrɪ) *adj* **sultrier, sultriest.** **1** (of weather or climate) oppressively hot and humid. **2** characterized by or emitting oppressive heat. **3** displaying or suggesting passion; sensual: *sultry eyes.* [C16: from obs. *sulter* to swelter + -Y[1]]
▸**'sultrily** *adv* ▸**'sultriness** *n*

sum ❶ (sʌm) *n* **1** the result of the addition of numbers, quantities, objects, etc. **2** one or more columns or rows of numbers to be added, subtracted, multiplied, or divided. **3** *Maths.* the limit of the first *n* terms of a converging infinite series as *n* tends to infinity. **4** a quantity, esp. of money: *he borrows enormous sums.* **5** the essence or gist of a matter (esp. in **in sum, in sum and substance**). **6** a less common word for **summary.** **7** *(modifier)* complete or final (esp. in **sum total**). ◆ *vb* **sums, summing, summed.** **8** (often foll. by *up*) to add or form a total of (something). **9** *(tr)* to calculate the sum of (the terms in a sequence). ◆ See also **sum up.** [C13 *summe,* from OF, from L *summa* the top, sum, from *summus* highest, from *super* above]

sumach *or US* **sumac** ('suːmæk, 'ʃuː-) *n* **1** any of various temperate or subtropical shrubs or small trees, having compound leaves and red hairy fruits. See also **poison sumach.** **2** a preparation of powdered leaves of certain species of sumach, used in dyeing and tanning. **3** the wood of any of these plants. [C14: via OF from Ar. *summāq*]

Sumerian (suː'mɪərɪən, -'mɛər-) *n* **1** a member of a people who established a civilization in Sumer, in W Asia, during the 4th millennium B.C. **2** the extinct language of this people. ◆ *adj* **3** of or relating to ancient Sumer, its inhabitants, or their language or civilization.

summa cum laude ('sʊmɑː kʊm 'laʊdeɪ) *adv, adj Chiefly US.* with the utmost praise: the highest designation for achievement in examinations. In Britain it is sometimes used to designate a first-class honours degree. [from L]

summarize ❶ *or* **summarise** ('sʌməˌraɪz) *vb* **summarizes, summarizing, summarized** *or* **summarises, summarising, summarised.** *(tr)* to make or be a summary of; express concisely.
▸**ˌsummari'zation** *or* **ˌsummari'sation** *n* ▸**'summaˌrizer, 'summaˌriser,** *or* **'summarist** *n*

summary ❶ ('sʌmərɪ) *n, pl* **summaries.** **1** a brief account giving the main points of something. ◆ *adj (usually prenominal).* **2** performed arbitrarily and quickly, without formality: *a summary execution.* **3** (of legal proceedings) short and free from the complexities and delays of a full trial. **4 summary jurisdiction.** the right a court has to adjudicate immediately upon some matter. **5** giving the gist or essence. [C15: from L *summārium,* from *summa* SUM]
▸**'summarily** *adv* ▸**'summariness** *n*

summary offence *n* an offence that is triable in a magistrates' court.

summation (sʌ'meɪʃən) *n* **1** the act or process of determining a sum; addition. **2** the result of such an act or process. **3** a summary. **4** *US law.* the concluding statements made by opposing counsel in a case before a court. [C18: from Med. L *summātiō,* from *summāre* to total, from L *summa* SUM]
▸**sum'mational** *adj* ▸**'summative** *adj*

summative assessment *n Brit. education.* general assessment of a pupil's achievements over a range of subjects by means of a combined appraisal of formative assessments.

summer ('sʌmə) *n* **1** *(sometimes cap.)* **1a** the warmest season of the year, between spring and autumn, astronomically from the June solstice to

THESAURUS

gruntled, ill-humoured, in the sulks, moody, morose, perverse, petulant, put out, querulous, resentful, sullen, vexed

sullen *adj* **1 = morose,** brooding, cheerless, cross, dismal, dour, gloomy, glowering, moody, obstinate, out of humour, perverse, silent, sour, stubborn, sulky, surly, unsociable **2 = dull,** gloomy, heavy, sombre
Antonyms *adj ≠* **morose:** amiable, bright, cheerful, cheery, chirpy *(inf.)*, genial, good-humoured, good-natured, pleasant, sociable, sunny, warm, warm-hearted

sullenness *n* **1 = moroseness,** glumness, ill humour, moodiness, sourness, sulkiness, sulks

sully *vb* **= dishonour,** besmirch, disgrace, ruin, smirch, tarnish

sultry *adj* **1 = humid,** close, hot, muggy, oppressive, sticky, stifling, stuffy, sweltering **3 = seductive,** amorous, come-hither *(inf.)*, erotic, passionate, provocative, sensual, sexy *(inf.)*, voluptuous
Antonyms *adj ≠* **humid:** cool, fresh, invigorating, refreshing

sum *n* **1 = total,** aggregate, amount, entirety, quantity, reckoning, score, sum total, tally, totality, whole

summarily *adv* **2 = immediately,** arbitrarily, at short notice, expeditiously, forthwith, on the spot, peremptorily, promptly, speedily, swiftly, without delay, without wasting words

summarize *vb* **= sum up,** abridge, condense, encapsulate, epitomize, give a rundown of, give the main points of, outline, précis, put in a nutshell, recap, recapitulate, review

summary *n* **1 = synopsis,** abridgment, abstract, compendium, digest, epitome, essence, extract, outline, précis, recapitulation, résumé, review, rundown, summing-up ◆ *adj* **2 = hasty,** arbitrary, cursory, perfunctory **5 = succinct,** brief, compact, compendious, concise, condensed, laconic, pithy

the September equinox in the N hemisphere and at the opposite time of year in the S hemisphere. **1b** (*as modifier*): *summer flowers*. Related adj: **aestival.** **2** the period of hot weather associated with the summer. **3** a time of blossoming, greatest happiness, etc. **4** *Chiefly poetic.* a year represented by this season: *a child of nine summers.* ◆ *vb* **5** (*intr*) to spend the summer (at a place). **6** (*tr*) to keep or feed (farm animals) during the summer: *they summered their cattle on the mountain slopes.* [OE *sumor*]
► **'summerly** *adj* ► **'summery** *adj*

summerhouse ('sʌmə,haus) *n* a small building in a garden or park, used for shade or recreation in the summer.

summer pudding *n Brit.* a pudding made by filling a bread-lined basin with a purée of fruit.

summersault ('sʌmə,sɔ:lt) *n, vb* a variant spelling of **somersault.**

summer school *n* a school, academic course, etc., held during the summer.

summer solstice *n* **1** the time at which the sun is at its northernmost point in the sky (southernmost point in the S hemisphere). It occurs about June 21 (December 22 in the S hemisphere). **2** *Astron.* the point on the celestial sphere, opposite the **winter solstice,** at which the ecliptic is furthest north from the celestial equator.

summertime ('sʌmə,taɪm) *n* the period or season of summer.

summer time *n Brit.* any daylight-saving time, esp. British Summer Time.

summerweight ('sʌmə,weɪt) *adj* (of clothes) suitable in weight for wear in the summer.

summing-up *n* **1** a review or summary of the main points of an argument, speech, etc. **2** concluding statements made by a judge to the jury before they retire to consider their verdict.

summit ❶ ('sʌmɪt) *n* **1** the highest point or part, esp. of a mountain; top. **2** the highest possible degree or state; peak or climax: *the summit of ambition.* **3** the highest level, importance, or rank: *a meeting at the summit.* **4a** a meeting of chiefs of governments or other high officials. **4b** (*as modifier*): *a summit conference.* [C15: from OF *somet,* dim. of *som,* from L *summum;* see SUM]

summon ❶ ('sʌmən) *vb* (*tr*) **1** to order to come; send for, esp. to attend court, by issuing a summons. **2** to order or instruct (to do something) or call (to something): *the bell summoned them to their work.* **3** to call upon to meet or convene. **4** (often foll. by *up*) to muster or gather (one's strength, courage, etc.). **5** *Arch.* to call upon to surrender. [C13: from L *summonēre* to give a discreet reminder, from *monēre* to advise]

summons ('sʌmənz) *n, pl* **summonses.** **1** a call, signal, or order to do something, esp. to attend at a specified place or time. **2a** an official order requiring a person to attend court, either to answer a charge or to give evidence. **2b** the writ making such an order. **3** a call or command given to the members of an assembly to convene a meeting. ◆ *vb* **4** to take out a summons against (a person). [C13: from OF *somonse,* from *somondre* to SUMMON]

summum bonum *Latin.* ('sumum 'bɒnum) *n* the principle of goodness in which all moral values are included or from which they are derived; highest or supreme good.

sumo ('su:məu) *n* the national style of wrestling of Japan, in which two contestants of great height and weight attempt to force each other to touch the ground with any part of the body except the soles of the feet or to step out of the ring. [from Japanese *sumō*]

sump (sʌmp) *n* **1** a receptacle, as in the crankcase of an internal-combustion engine, into which liquids, esp. lubricants, can drain to form a reservoir. **2** another name for **cesspool** (sense 1). **3** *Mining.* a depression at the bottom of a shaft where water collects. [C17: from MDu. *somp* marsh]

sumpter ('sʌmptə) *n Arch.* a packhorse, mule, or other beast of burden. [C14: from OF *sometier* driver of a baggage horse, from Vulgar L *sagmatārius* (unattested), from LL *sagma* packsaddle]

sumptuary ('sʌmptjuərɪ) *adj* relating to or controlling expenditure or extravagance. [C17: from L *sumptuārius* concerning expense, from *sumptus* expense, from *sūmere* to spend]

sumptuous ❶ ('sʌmptjuəs) *adj* **1** expensive or extravagant: *sumptuous costumes.* **2** magnificent; splendid: *a sumptuous scene.* [C16: from OF *somptueux,* from L *sumptuōsus* costly, from *sumptus;* see SUMPTUARY]
► **'sumptuously** *adv* ► **'sumptuousness** *n*

sum up ❶ *vb* (*adv*) **1** to summarize (the main points of an argument, etc.). **2** (*tr*) to form a quick opinion of: *I summed him up in five minutes.*

sun ❶ (sʌn) *n* **1** the star that is the source of heat and light for the planets in the solar system. Related adj: **solar.** **2** any star around which a planetary system revolves. **3** the sun as it appears at a particular time or place: *the winter sun.* **4** the radiant energy, esp. heat and light, received from the sun; sunshine. **5** a person or thing considered as a source of radiant warmth, glory, etc. **6** a pictorial representation of the sun, often depicted with a human face. **7** *Poetic.* a year or a day. **8** *Poetic.* a climate. **9** *Arch.* sunrise or sunset (esp. in **from sun to sun**). **10** **catch the sun.** to become slightly sunburnt. **11** **place in the sun.** a prominent or favourable position. **12** **take** *or* **shoot the sun.** *Naut.* to measure the altitude of the sun in order to determine latitude. **13** **touch of the sun.** slight sunstroke. **14** **under** *or* **beneath the sun.** on earth; at all: *nobody under the sun eats more than you.* ◆ *vb* **suns, sunning, sunned.** **15** to expose (oneself) to the sunshine. **16** (*tr*) to expose to the sunshine in order to warm, etc. [OE *sunne*]

Sun. *abbrev. for* Sunday.

sunbaked ('sʌn,beɪkt) *adj* **1** (esp. of roads, etc.) dried or cracked by the sun's heat. **2** baked hard by the heat of the sun: *sunbaked bricks.*

sun bath *n* the exposure of the body to the rays of the sun or a sun lamp, esp. in order to get a suntan.

sunbathe ('sʌn,beɪð) *vb* **sunbathes, sunbathing, sunbathed.** (*intr*) to bask in the sunshine, esp. in order to get a suntan.
► **'sun,bather** *n*

sunbeam ('sʌn,bi:m) *n* a beam, ray, or stream of sunlight.
► **'sun,beamed** *or* **'sun,beamy** *adj*

sunbird ('sʌn,bɜ:d) *n* any of various small songbirds of tropical regions of the Old World, esp. Africa, having a long slender curved bill and a bright plumage in the males.

sunbonnet ('sʌn,bɒnɪt) *n* a hat that shades the face and neck from the sun, esp. one of cotton with a projecting brim, now worn esp. by babies.

sunburn ❶ ('sʌn,bɜ:n) *n* **1** inflammation of the skin caused by overexposure to the sun. **2** another word for **suntan.**
► **'sun,burnt** *or* **'sun,burned** *adj*

sunburst ('sʌn,bɜ:st) *n* **1** a burst of sunshine, as through a break in the clouds. **2** a pattern or design resembling that of the sun. **3** a jewelled brooch with this pattern.

sun-cured *adj* cured or preserved by exposure to the sun.

sundae ('sʌndɪ, -deɪ) *n* ice cream topped with a sweet sauce, nuts, whipped cream, etc. [C20: from ?]

Sunday ('sʌndɪ) *n* the first day of the week and the Christian day of worship. [OE *sunnandæg,* translation of L *diēs sōlis* day of the sun, translation of Gk *hēmera hēliou*]

Sunday best *n* one's best clothes, esp. regarded as those most suitable for churchgoing.

Sunday school *n* **1a** a school for the religious instruction of children on Sundays, usually held in a church hall. **1b** (*as modifier*): *a Sunday-school outing.* **2** the members of such a school.

sunder ('sʌndə) *Arch. or literary.* ◆ *vb* **1** to break or cause to break apart or in pieces. ◆ *n* **2** **in sunder.** into pieces; apart. [OE *sundrian*]

sundew ('sʌn,dju:) *n* any of several bog plants having leaves covered with sticky hairs that trap and digest insects. [C16: translation of L *ros solis*]

sundial ('sʌn,daɪəl) *n* a device indicating the time during the hours of sunlight by means of a stationary arm (the **gnomon**) that casts a shadow onto a plate or surface marked in hours.

sun disc *n* a disc symbolizing the sun, esp. one flanked by two serpents and the extended wings of a vulture: a religious figure in ancient Egypt.

sundog ('sʌn,dɒg) *n* another word for **parhelion.**

sundown ('sʌn,daun) *n* another name for **sunset.**

sundowner ('sʌn,daunə) *n* **1** *Austral. sl.* a tramp, esp. one who seeks food and lodging at sundown when it is too late to work. **2** *Inf., chiefly Brit.* an alcoholic drink taken at sunset.

sundress ('sʌn,drɛs) *n* a dress for hot weather that exposes the shoulders, arms, and back.

sun-dried *adj* dried or preserved by exposure to the sun.

sundry ❶ ('sʌndrɪ) *determiner* **1** several or various; miscellaneous. ◆ *pron* **2** **all and sundry.** everybody, individually and collectively. ◆ *n, pl* **sundries.** **3** (*pl*) miscellaneous unspecified items. **4** the Austral. term for **extra** (sense 6). [OE *syndrig* separate]

sunfast ('sʌn,fa:st) *adj Chiefly US & Canad.* not fading in sunlight.

sunfish ('sʌn,fɪʃ) *n, pl* **sunfish** *or* **sunfishes.** **1** any of various large fishes of temperate and tropical seas, esp. one which has a large rounded compressed body, long pointed dorsal and anal fins, and a fringelike tail fin. **2** any of various small predatory North American freshwater percoid fishes, typically having a compressed brightly coloured body.

sunflower ('sʌn,flauə) *n* **1** any of several American plants having very tall thick stems, large flower heads with yellow rays, and seeds used as food, esp. for poultry. See also **Jerusalem artichoke.** **2** **sunflower seed oil.** the oil extracted from sunflower seeds, used as a salad oil, in margarine, etc.

THESAURUS

summit *n* **2** = **peak,** acme, apex, crest, crown, crowning point, culmination, head, height, pinnacle, top, zenith
Antonyms *n* base, bottom, depths, foot, lowest point, nadir

summon *vb* **3** = **send for,** arouse, assemble, bid, call, call together, cite, convene, convoke, invite, rally, rouse **4** *often with* **up** = **gather,** call into action, draw on, invoke, mobilize, muster

sumptuous *adj* **1, 2** = **luxurious,** costly, dear, de luxe, expensive, extravagant, gorgeous, grand, lavish, magnificent, opulent, palatial, plush (*inf.*), posh (*inf., chiefly Brit.*), rich, ritzy (*sl.*), splendid, splendiferous (*facetious*), superb
Antonyms *adj* austere, basic, cheap, frugal, inexpensive, meagre, mean, miserly, plain, shabby, wretched

sum up *vb* **1** = **summarize,** close, conclude, put in a nutshell, recapitulate, review **2** = **form an opinion of,** estimate, get the measure of, size up (*inf.*)

sun *n* **1** = **Sol** (*Roman myth*), daystar (*poetic*), eye of heaven, Helios (*Greek myth*), Phoebus (*Greek myth*), Phoebus Apollo (*Greek myth*) ◆ *vb* **15** **sun oneself** = **sunbathe,** bake, bask, tan

sunburnt *adj* **1** = **tanned,** bronzed, brown, brown as a berry, burnt, burnt to a crisp, like a lobster, peeling, red, ruddy, scarlet

sundry *determiner* **1** = **various,** assorted, different, divers (*arch.*), miscellaneous, several, some, varied

sung (sʌŋ) *vb* **1** the past participle of **sing.** ◆ *adj* **2** produced by singing: *a sung syllable.*

USAGE NOTE See at **ring**².

sunglass ('sʌn,glɑːs) *n* another name for **burning glass.**
sunglasses ('sʌn,glɑːsɪz) *pl n* glasses with darkened or polarizing lenses that protect the eyes from the sun's glare.
sun-god *n* **1** the sun considered as a personal deity. **2** a deity associated with the sun or controlling its movements.
sunk ❶ (sʌŋk) *vb* **1** a past participle of **sink.** ◆ *adj* **2** *Inf.* with all hopes dashed; ruined.
sunken ❶ ('sʌŋkən) *vb* **1** a past participle of **sink.** ◆ *adj* **2** unhealthily hollow: *sunken cheeks.* **3** situated at a lower level than the surrounding or usual one: *a sunken bath.* **4** situated under water; submerged. **5** depressed; low: *sunken spirits.*
sunk fence *n* another name for **ha-ha**².
sun lamp *n* **1** a lamp that generates ultraviolet rays, used for obtaining an artificial suntan, for muscular therapy, etc. **2** a lamp used in film studios, etc., to give an intense beam of light by means of parabolic mirrors.
sunless ❶ ('sʌnlɪs) *adj* **1** without sun or sunshine. **2** gloomy; depressing.
▸**'sunlessly** *adv*
sunlight ('sʌnlaɪt) *n* **1** the light emanating from the sun. **2** an area or the time characterized by sunshine.
▸**'sunlit** *adj*
sun lounge *or US* **sun parlor** *n* a room with large windows positioned to receive as much sunlight as possible.
Sunna ('sʌnə) *n* the body of traditional Islamic law accepted by most orthodox Muslims as based on the words and acts of Mohammed. [C18: from Ar. *sunnah* rule]
Sunni ('sʌnɪ) *n* **1** one of the two main branches of orthodox Islam (the other being the Shiah), consisting of those who acknowledge the authority of the Sunna. **2** (*pl* **Sunni**) a less common word for **Sunnite.**
Sunnite ('sʌnaɪt) *n* an adherent of the Sunni.
sunny ❶ ('sʌnɪ) *adj* **sunnier, sunniest. 1** full of or exposed to sunlight. **2** radiating good humour. **3** of or resembling the sun.
▸**'sunnily** *adv* ▸**'sunniness** *n*
sunrise ❶ ('sʌn,raɪz) *n* **1** the daily appearance of the sun above the horizon. **2** the atmospheric phenomena accompanying this appearance. **3** Also called (esp. US): **sunup.** the time at which the sun rises at a particular locality.
sunrise industry *n* any of the high-technology industries, such as electronics, that hold promise of future development.
sunroof ('sʌn,ruːf) *or* **sunshine roof** *n* a panel, often translucent, that may be opened in the roof of a car.
sunset ❶ ('sʌn,sɛt) *n* **1** the daily disappearance of the sun below the horizon. **2** the atmospheric phenomena accompanying this disappearance. **3** Also called: **sundown.** the time at which the sun sets at a particular locality. **4** the final stage or closing period, as of a person's life.
sunshade ('sʌn,ʃeɪd) *n* a device, esp. a parasol or awning, serving to shade from the sun.
sunshine ('sʌn,ʃaɪn) *n* **1** the light received directly from the sun. **2** the warmth from the sun. **3** a sunny area. **4** a light-hearted or ironic term of address.
▸**'sun,shiny** *adj*
sun sign *n* another name for **sign of the zodiac.**
sunspot ('sʌn,spɒt) *n* **1** any of the dark cool patches that appear on the surface of the sun and last about a week. **2** *Inf.* a sunny holiday resort. **3** *Austral.* a small cancerous spot produced by overexposure to the sun.
sunstroke ('sʌn,strəʊk) *n* heatstroke caused by prolonged exposure to intensely hot sunlight.
sunsuit ('sʌn,suːt, -,sjuːt) *n* a child's outfit consisting of a brief top and shorts or skirt.
suntan ('sʌn,tæn) *n* **a** a brownish colouring of the skin caused by the formation of the pigment melanin within the skin on exposure to the ultraviolet rays of the sun or a sun lamp. Often shortened to **tan. b** (*as modifier*): *suntan oil.*
▸**'sun,tanned** *adj*
suntrap ('sʌn,træp) *n* a very sunny sheltered place.
sunward ('sʌnwəd) *adj* **1** directed or moving towards the sun. ◆ *adv* **2** Also: **sunwards.** towards the sun.
sup¹ (sʌp) *vb* **sups, supping, supped.** (*intr*) *Arch.* to have supper. [C13: from OF *soper*]
sup² (sʌp) *vb* **sups, supping, supped. 1** to partake of (liquid) by swallowing a little at a time. **2** *Scot. & N English dialect.* to drink. ◆ *n* **3** a sip. [OE *sūpan*]
sup. *abbrev. for:* **1** above. [from L *supra*] **2** superior. **3** *Grammar.* superlative. **4** supplement. **5** supplementary. **6** supply.
super ❶ (suːpə) *adj* **1** *Inf.* outstanding; exceptional. ◆ *n* **2** petrol with a high octane rating. **3** *Inf.* a supervisor. **4** *Austral. & NZ inf.* superannuation benefits. **5** *Austral & NZ inf.* superphosphate. ◆ *interj* **6** *Brit. inf.* an enthusiastic expression of approval. [from L: above]
super. *abbrev. for:* **1** superfine. **2** superior.
super- *prefix* **1** placed above or over: *superscript.* **2** surpassing others; outstanding: *superstar.* **3** of greater size, extent, quality, etc.: *supermarket.* **4** beyond a standard or norm: *supersonic.* **5** indicating that a chemical compound contains a specified element in a higher proportion than usual: *superphosphate.* [from L *super* above]
superable ('suːpərəbᵊl) *adj* able to be surmounted or overcome. [C17: from L *superābilis,* from *superāre* to overcome]
▸**,supera'bility** *or* **'superableness** *n* ▸**'superably** *adv*
superannuate (,suːpər'ænjʊ,eɪt) *vb* **superannuates, superannuating, superannuated.** (*tr*) **1** to pension off. **2** to discard as obsolete or old-fashioned.
superannuated ❶ (,suːpər'ænjʊ,eɪtɪd) *adj* **1** discharged, esp. with a pension, owing to age or illness. **2** too old to serve usefully. **3** obsolete. [C17: from Med. L *superannātus* aged more than one year, from L SUPER- + *annus* a year]
superannuation (,suːpər,ænjʊ'eɪʃən) *n* **1a** the amount deducted regularly from employees' incomes in a contributory pension scheme. **1b** the pension finally paid. **2** the act or process of superannuating or the condition of being superannuated.
superb ❶ (sʊ'pɜːb, sjʊ-) *adj* **1** surpassingly good; excellent. **2** majestic or imposing. **3** magnificently rich; luxurious. [C16: from OF *superbe,* from L *superbus* distinguished, from *super* above]
▸**su'perbly** *adv* ▸**su'perbness** *n*
Super Bowl *n American football.* the championship game held annually between the best team of the American Football Conference and that of the National Football Conference.
supercalender (,suːpə'kæləndə) *n* **1** a calender that gives a high gloss to paper. ◆ *vb* **2** (*tr*) to finish (paper) in this way.
▸**,super'calendered** *adj*
supercargo (,suːpə'kɑːgəʊ) *n, pl* **supercargoes.** an officer on a merchant ship who supervises commercial matters and is in charge of the cargo. [C17: changed from Sp. *sobrecargo,* from *sobre* over + *cargo* CARGO]
supercharge ('suːpə,tʃɑːdʒ) *vb* **supercharges, supercharging, supercharged.** (*tr*) **1** to increase the intake pressure of (an internal-combustion engine) with a supercharger; boost. **2** to charge (the atmosphere, a remark, etc.) with an excess amount of (tension, emotion, etc.). **3** to apply pressure to (a fluid); pressurize.
supercharger ('suːpə,tʃɑːdʒə) *n* a device that increases the mass of air drawn into an internal-combustion engine by raising the intake pressure. Also called: **blower, booster.**
superciliary (,suːpə'sɪlɪərɪ) *adj* over the eyebrow or a corresponding region in lower animals. [C18: from NL *superciliaris,* from L, from SUPER- + *cilium* eyelid]
supercilious ❶ (,suːpə'sɪlɪəs) *adj* displaying arrogant pride, scorn, or indifference. [C16: from L, from *supercilium* eyebrow]
▸**,super'ciliously** *adv* ▸**,super'ciliousness** *n*
superclass ('suːpə,klɑːs) *n* a taxonomic group that is a subdivision of a subphylum.
supercolumnar (,suːpəkə'lʌmnə) *adj Archit.* **1** having one colonnade above another. **2** placed above a colonnade or a column.
▸**,supercol,umni'ation** *n*
superconductivity (,suːpə,kɒndʌk'tɪvɪtɪ) *n Physics.* the property of

THESAURUS

sunk *adj* **2** = **ruined**, all washed up (*inf.*), done for (*inf.*), finished, lost, on the rocks, up the creek without a paddle (*inf.*)
sunken *adj* **2** = **hollow**, concave, drawn, haggard, hollowed **3** = **lower**, at a lower level, below ground, buried, depressed, immersed, recessed, submerged
sunless *adj* **1** = **cloudy**, dark, gloomy, grey, hazy, overcast **2** = **depressing**, bleak, cheerless, gloomy, sombre
sunny *adj* **1** = **bright**, brilliant, clear, fine, luminous, radiant, summery, sunlit, sunshiny, unclouded, without a cloud in the sky **2** = **cheerful**, beaming, blithe, buoyant, cheery, chirpy (*inf.*), genial, happy, joyful, light- hearted, optimistic, pleasant, smiling
Antonyms *adj* ≠ **bright:** cloudy, depressing, dreary, dreich (*Scot.*), dull, gloomy, murky, overcast, rainy, shaded, shadowy, sunless, wet, wintry ≠ **cheerful:** doleful, down in the dumps (*inf.*), gloomy, miserable, morbid, unsmiling
sunrise *n* **1** = **dawn**, aurora (*poetic*), break of day, cockcrow, daybreak, daylight, dayspring (*poetic*), sunup
sunset *n* **1** = **nightfall**, close of (the) day, dusk, eventide, gloaming (*Scot. or poetic*), sundown
super *adj* **1** *Informal* = **excellent**, awesome (*sl.*), brill (*inf.*), cracking (*Brit. inf.*), glorious, incomparable, magnificent, marvellous, matchless, mega (*sl.*), out of this world (*inf.*), outstanding, peerless, sensational (*inf.*), smashing (*inf.*), sovereign, superb, terrific (*inf.*), top-notch (*inf.*), wonderful
superannuated *adj* **1** = **retired**, discharged, pensioned off, put out to grass (*inf.*) **2, 3** = **obsolete**, aged, antiquated, decrepit, old, past it (*inf.*), senile, unfit
superb *adj* **1** = **splendid**, awesome (*sl.*), brill (*inf.*), choice, divine, excellent, exquisite, fine, first-rate, gorgeous, marvellous, mega (*sl.*), of the first water, superior, superlative, topping (*Brit. sl.*), unrivalled, world-class
Antonyms *adj* abysmal, awful, bad, disappointing, dreadful, inferior, mediocre, no great shakes (*inf.*), pathetic, poor quality, run-of-the-mill, terrible, third-rate, uninspired, woeful
supercilious *adj* = **scornful**, arrogant, condescending, contemptuous, disdainful, haughty, high and mighty (*inf.*), hoity-toity (*inf.*), imperious, insolent, lofty, lordly, overbearing, patronizing, proud, snooty (*inf.*), stuck-up (*inf.*), toffee-nosed (*sl., chiefly Brit.*), uppish (*Brit. inf.*), vainglorious
Antonyms *adj* deferential, generous, humble, meek, modest, obsequious, self-effacing, submissive, unassuming, unpretentious, warm-hearted

certain substances that have no electrical resistance. In metals it occurs at very low temperatures; higher-temperature superconductivity occurs in some ceramic materials.
▸**superconduction** (ˌsuːpəkənˈdʌkʃən) *n* ▸ˌ**superconˈductive** *or* ˌ**superconˈducting** *adj* ▸ˌ**superconˈductor** *n*

supercontinent (ˈsuːpəˌkɒntɪnənt) *n* a great landmass thought to have existed in the geological past and to have split into smaller landmasses, which drifted and formed the present continents.

supercool (ˌsuːpəˈkuːl) *vb Chem.* to cool or be cooled without freezing or crystallization to a temperature below that at which freezing or crystallization should occur.

supercritical (ˌsuːpəˈkrɪtɪkəl) *adj* **1** *Physics.* (of a fluid) brought to a temperature and pressure higher than its critical temperature and pressure, so that its physical and chemical properties change. **2** *Nuclear physics.* of or containing more than the critical mass.

superdense theory (ˌsuːpəˈdɛns) *n Astron.* another name for the **big-bang theory.**

super-duper (ˈsuːpəˈduːpə) *adj Inf.* extremely pleasing, impressive, etc.: often used as an exclamation.

superego (ˌsuːpərˈiːgəʊ, -ˈɛgəʊ) *n, pl* **superegos.** *Psychoanal.* that part of the unconscious mind that acts as a conscience for the ego.

superelevation (ˌsuːpərˌɛlɪˈveɪʃən) *n* **1** another name for **bank**[2] (sense 8). **2** the difference between the heights of the sides of a road or railway track on a bend.

supereminent (ˌsuːpərˈɛmɪnənt) *adj* of distinction, dignity, or rank superior to that of others; pre-eminent.
▸ˌ**superˈeminence** *n* ▸ˌ**superˈeminently** *adv*

supererogation (ˌsuːpərˌɛrəˈgeɪʃən) *n* **1** the performance of work in excess of that required or expected. **2** *RC Church.* supererogatory prayers, devotions, etc.

supererogatory (ˌsuːpərɛˈrɒgətərɪ, -trɪ) *adj* **1** performed to an extent exceeding that required or expected. **2** exceeding what is needed; superfluous. **3** *RC Church.* of or relating to prayers, good works, etc., performed over and above those prescribed as obligatory. [C16: from Med. L *superērogātōrius,* from L *supererogāre* to spend over and above]

superfamily (ˈsuːpəˌfæmɪlɪ) *n, pl* **superfamilies. 1** *Biol.* a subdivision of a suborder. **2** any analogous group, such as a group of related languages.

superfecundation (ˌsuːpəˌfiːkənˈdeɪʃən) *n Physiol.* the fertilization of two or more ova, produced during the same menstrual cycle, by sperm ejaculated during two or more acts of sexual intercourse.

superfetation (ˌsuːpəfiːˈteɪʃən) *n Physiol.* the presence in the uterus of two fetuses developing from ova fertilized at different times. [C17 *superfetate,* from L *superfētāre* to fertilize when already pregnant, from *fētus* offspring]

superficial Ⓣ (ˌsuːpəˈfɪʃəl) *adj* **1** of, near, or forming the surface: *superficial bruising.* **2** displaying a lack of thoroughness or care: *a superficial inspection.* **3** only outwardly apparent rather than genuine or actual: *the similarity was merely superficial.* **4** of little substance or significance: *superficial differences.* **5** lacking profundity: *the film's plot was quite superficial.* **6** (of measurements) involving only the surface area. [C14: from LL *superficiālis* of the surface, from L SUPERFICIES]
▸**superficiality** (ˌsuːpəˌfɪʃɪˈælɪtɪ) *n* ▸ˌ**superˈficially** *adv*

superficies (ˌsuːpəˈfɪʃiːz) *n, pl* **superficies. 1** a surface or outer face. **2** the outward form of a thing. [C16: from L: upper side]

superfine (ˌsuːpəˈfaɪn) *adj* **1** of exceptional fineness or quality. **2** excessively refined.
▸ˌ**superˈfineness** *n*

superfix (ˈsuːpəˌfɪks) *n Linguistics.* a type of feature distinguishing the meaning or grammatical function of one word or phrase from that of another, as stress does for example between the noun *conduct* and the verb *conduct.*

superfluid (ˌsuːpəˈfluːɪd) *n* **1** *Physics.* a fluid in a state characterized by a very low viscosity, high thermal conductivity, high capillarity, etc. The only known example is that of liquid helium at temperatures close to absolute zero. ◆ *adj* **2** being or relating to a superfluid.
▸ˌ**superfluˈidity** *n*

superfluity Ⓣ (ˌsuːpəˈfluːɪtɪ) *n* **1** the condition of being superfluous. **2** a quantity or thing that is in excess of what is needed. **3** a thing that is not needed. [C14: from OF *superfluité,* via LL from L *superfluus* SUPERFLUOUS]

superfluous Ⓣ (suːˈpɜːfluəs) *adj* **1** exceeding what is sufficient or required. **2** not necessary or relevant; uncalled for. [C15: from L *superfluus* overflowing, from *fluere* to flow]
▸**suˈperfluously** *adv* ▸**suˈperfluousness** *n*

Super-G *n Skiing.* a type of slalom in which the course is shorter than in a standard slalom and the obstacles are farther apart than in a giant slalom. [C20: from SUPER- + G(IANT)]

supergiant (ˈsuːpəˌdʒaɪənt) *n* any of a class of extremely bright stars which have expanded to a large diameter and are eventually likely to explode as supernovas.

superglue (ˈsuːpəˌgluː) *n* any of various adhesives that quickly make an exceptionally strong bond.

supergrass (ˈsuːpəˌgrɑːs) *n* an informer whose information implicates a large number of people.

supergravity (ˌsuːpəˈgrævɪtɪ) *n Physics.* any of various theories in which supersymmetry is applied to the theory of gravitation.

superheat (ˌsuːpəˈhiːt) *vb (tr)* **1** to heat (a vapour, esp. steam) to a temperature above its saturation point for a given pressure. **2** to heat (a liquid) to a temperature above its boiling point without boiling occurring. **3** to heat excessively; overheat.
▸ˌ**superˈheater** *n*

superheavy (ˌsuːpəˈhɛvɪ) *adj Physics.* denoting or relating to elements of high atomic number (above 109) postulated to exist with special stability as a consequence of the shell model of the nucleus.

superheterodyne receiver (ˌsuːpəˈhɛtərəˌdaɪn) *n* a radio receiver that combines two radio-frequency signals by heterodyne action, to produce a signal above the audible frequency limit. Sometimes shortened to **superhet.** [C20: from SUPER(SONIC) + HETERODYNE]

superhigh frequency (ˈsuːpəˌhaɪ) *n* a radio-frequency band or radio frequency lying between 30 000 and 3000 megahertz.

superhuman Ⓣ (ˌsuːpəˈhjuːmən) *adj* **1** having powers above and beyond those of mankind. **2** exceeding normal human ability or experience.
▸ˌ**superˈhumanly** *adv*

superimpose (ˌsuːpərɪmˈpəʊz) *vb* **superimposes, superimposing, superimposed.** *(tr)* **1** to set or place on or over something else. **2** (usually foll. by *on* or *upon*) to add (to).
▸ˌ**superˌimpoˈsition** *n*

superinduce (ˌsuːpərɪnˈdjuːs) *vb* **superinduces, superinducing, superinduced.** *(tr)* to introduce as an additional feature, factor, etc.
▸**superinduction** (ˌsuːpərɪnˈdʌkʃən) *n*

superintend Ⓣ (ˌsuːpərɪnˈtɛnd) *vb* to undertake the direction or supervision (of); manage. [C17: from Church L *superintendere,* from L SUPER- + *intendere* to give attention to]
▸ˌ**superinˈtendence** *n*

superintendent Ⓣ (ˌsuːpərɪnˈtɛndənt) *n* **1** a person who directs and manages an organization, office, etc. **2** (in Britain) a senior police officer higher in rank than an inspector but lower than a chief superintendent. **3** (in the US) the head of a police department. **4** *Chiefly US & Canad.* a caretaker, esp. of a block of apartments. ◆ *adj* **5** of or relating to supervision; superintending. [C16: from Church L *superintendens* overseeing]
▸ˌ**superinˈtendency** *n*

superior Ⓣ (suːˈpɪərɪə) *adj* **1** greater in quality, quantity, etc. **2** of high or extraordinary worth, merit, etc. **3** higher in rank or status. **4** displaying a conscious sense of being above or better than others; supercilious. **5** *(often postpositive;* foll. by *to)* not susceptible (to) or influenced (by). **6** placed higher up; further from the base. **7** *Astron.* (of a planet) having an orbit further from the sun than the orbit of the earth. **8** (of a plant ovary) situated above the calyx and other floral parts. **9** *Printing.* (of a character) written or printed above the line; superscript. ◆ *n* **10** a person or thing of greater rank or quality. **11** *Printing.* a character set in a superior position. **12** *(often cap.)* the head of a community in a religious order. [C14: from L, from *superus* placed above, from *super* above]
▸**suˈperioress** *fem n* ▸**superiority** (suːˌpɪərɪˈɒrɪtɪ) *n*

> **USAGE NOTE** *Superior* should not be used with *than: he is a better* (not *a superior*) *poet than his brother; his poetry is superior to* (not *superior than*) *his brother's.*

THESAURUS

superficial *adj* **1** = **surface,** cosmetic, exterior, external, on the surface, peripheral, skin-deep, slight **2** = **hasty,** casual, cursory, desultory, facile, hurried, inattentive, nodding, passing, perfunctory, sketchy, slapdash **3** = **outward,** apparent, evident, ostensible, seeming **5** = **shallow,** empty, empty-headed, frivolous, lightweight, silly, trivial
Antonyms ≠ **surface:** deep, profound *adj* ≠ **hasty:** complete, comprehensive, detailed, exhaustive, in depth, major, penetrating, probing, substantial, thorough ≠ **shallow:** earnest, serious

superficiality *n* **4, 5** = **shallowness,** emptiness, lack of depth, lack of substance, triviality

superficially *adv* **3** = **at first glance,** apparently, at face value, externally, on the surface, ostensibly, to the casual eye

superfluity *n* **1** = **excess,** exuberance, glut, plethora, redundancy, superabundance, surfeit, surplus

superfluous *adj* **1** = **excess,** excessive, extra, in excess, left over, needless, on one's hands, pleonastic (*Rhetoric*), redundant, remaining, residuary, spare, superabundant, supererogatory, supernumerary, surplus, surplus to requirements, uncalled-for, unnecessary, unneeded, unrequired
Antonyms *adj* called for, essential, imperative, indispensable, necessary, needed, requisite, vital, wanted

superhuman *adj* **1** = **heroic,** herculean, phenomenal, prodigious, stupendous, valiant **2** = **supernatural,** divine, paranormal, preternatural

superintend *vb* = **supervise,** administer, control, direct, handle, inspect, look after, manage, overlook, oversee, run

superintendence *n* = **supervision,** care, charge, control, direction, government, guidance, inspection, management, surveillance

superintendent *n* **1** = **supervisor,** administrator, chief, conductor, controller, director, governor, inspector, manager, overseer

superior *adj* **1** = **better,** grander, greater, higher, more advanced, more expert, more extensive, more skilful, paramount, predominant, preferred, prevailing, surpassing, unrivalled **2** = **first-class,** a cut above, admirable, choice, de luxe, distinguished, excellent, exceptional, exclusive, fine, first-rate, good, good quality, high calibre, high-class, of the first order, running rings around (*inf.*), streets ahead (*inf.*), world-class **4** = **supercilious,** airy, condescending, disdainful, haughty, lofty, lordly, on one's high horse (*inf.*), patronizing, pretentious, snobbish,

superior court *n* **1** (in England) a higher court not subject to control by any other court except by way of appeal. See also **Supreme Court of Judicature. 2** (in several states of the US) a court of general jurisdiction ranking above the inferior courts and below courts of last resort.
superiority complex *n Inf.* an inflated estimate of one's own merit, usually manifested in arrogance.
superior planet *n* any of the six planets (Mars, Jupiter, Saturn, Uranus, Neptune, and Pluto) whose orbit lies outside that of the earth.
superl. *abbrev. for* superlative.
superlative ❶ (suː'pɜːlətɪv) *adj* **1** of outstanding quality, degree, etc.; supreme. **2** *Grammar.* denoting the form of an adjective or adverb that expresses the highest or a very high degree of quality. In English this is usually marked by the suffix *-est* or the word *most,* as in *loudest* or *most loudly.* **3** (of language or style) excessive; exaggerated. ◆ *n* **4** a thing that excels all others or is of the highest quality. **5** *Grammar.* the superlative form of an adjective or adverb. **6** the highest degree; peak. [C14: from OF *superlatif,* via LL from L *superlātus* extravagant, from *superferre* to carry beyond]
▸**su'perlatively** *adv* ▸**su'perlativeness** *n*
superlunar (ˌsuːpə'luːnə) *adj* beyond the moon; celestial.
▸**ˌsuper'lunary** *adj*
superman ('suːpəˌmæn) *n, pl* **supermen. 1** (in the philosophy of Nietzsche) an ideal man who would rise above good and evil and who represents the goal of human evolution. **2** any man of apparently superhuman powers.
supermarket ('suːpəˌmɑːkɪt) *n* a large self-service store selling food and household supplies.
supermembrane (ˌsuːpə'mɛmbreɪn) *n Physics.* a type of membrane postulated in certain theories of elementary particles that involve supersymmetry.
supermundane (ˌsuːpə'mʌndeɪn) *adj* elevated above earthly things.
supernal (suː'pɜːnᵊl, sjuː-) *adj Literary.* **1** divine; celestial. **2** of, from above, or from the sky. [C15: from Med. L *supernālis,* from L *supernus* that is on high, from *super* above]
▸**su'pernally** *adv*
supernatant (ˌsuːpə'neɪtᵊnt) *adj* **1** floating on the surface or over something. **2** *Chem.* (of a liquid) lying above a sediment or precipitate. [C17: from L *supernatāre* to float, from SUPER- + *natāre* to swim]
▸**ˌsuperna'tation** *n*
supernatural ❶ (ˌsuːpə'nætʃərəl) *adj* **1** of or relating to things that cannot be explained according to natural laws. **2** of or caused as if by a god; miraculous. **3** of or involving occult beings. **4** exceeding the ordinary; abnormal. ◆ *n* **5 the supernatural.** supernatural forces, occurrences, and beings collectively.
▸**ˌsuper'naturally** *adv* ▸**ˌsuper'naturalness** *n*
supernaturalism (ˌsuːpə'nætʃərəlɪzəm) *n* **1** the quality or condition of being supernatural. **2** belief in supernatural forces or agencies as producing effects in this world.
▸**ˌsuper'naturalist** *n, adj* ▸**ˌsuperˌnatural'istic** *adj*
supernormal (ˌsuːpə'nɔːməl) *adj* greatly exceeding the normal.
▸**supernormality** (ˌsuːpənɔː'mælɪtɪ) *n* ▸**ˌsuper'normally** *adv*
supernova (ˌsuːpə'nəʊvə) *n, pl* **supernovae** (-viː) *or* **supernovas.** a star that explodes owing to instabilities following the exhaustion of its nuclear fuel, becoming for a few days up to one hundred million times brighter than the sun. Cf. **nova.**
supernumerary ❶ (ˌsuːpə'njuːmərərɪ) *adj* **1** exceeding a regular or proper number; extra. **2** functioning as a substitute or assistant with regard to a regular body or staff. ◆ *n, pl* **supernumeraries. 3** a person or thing that exceeds the required or regular number. **4** a substitute or assistant. **5** an actor who has no lines, esp. a nonprofessional one. [C17: from LL *supernumerārius,* from L SUPER- + *numerus* number]
superorder ('suːpərˌɔːdə) *n Biol.* a subdivision of a subclass.
superordinate (ˌsuːpər'ɔːdɪnɪt) *adj* **1** of higher status or condition. ◆ *n* **2** a person or thing that is superordinate. **3** a word the meaning of which includes the meaning of another word or words: *"red" is the superordinate of "scarlet" and "crimson".*
superphosphate (ˌsuːpə'fɒsfeɪt) *n* **1** a mixture of the diacid calcium salt of orthophosphoric acid with calcium sulphate and small quantities of other phosphates: used as a fertilizer. **2** a salt of phosphoric acid formed by incompletely replacing its acidic hydrogen atoms.
superpose (ˌsuːpə'pəʊz) *vb* **superposes, superposing, superposed.** (*tr*) *Geom.* to transpose (the coordinates of one geometric figure) to coincide with those of another. [C19: from F *superposer,* from L *superpōnere,* from *pōnere* to place]
superposition (ˌsuːpəpə'zɪʃən) *n* **1** the act of superposing or state of being superposed. **2** *Geol.* the principle that in any sequence of sedimentary rocks that has not been disturbed the lowest strata are the oldest.
superpower ('suːpəˌpaʊə) *n* **1** an extremely powerful state, such as the US. **2** extremely high power, esp. electrical or mechanical.
▸**'superˌpowered** *adj*
supersaturated (ˌsuːpə'sætʃəˌreɪtɪd) *adj* **1** (of a solution) containing more solute than a saturated solution. **2** (of a vapour) containing more material than a saturated vapour.
▸**ˌsuperˌsatu'ration** *n*
superscribe (ˌsuːpə'skraɪb) *vb* **superscribes, superscribing, superscribed.** (*tr*) to write (an inscription, name, etc.) above, on top of, or outside. [C16: from L *superscrībere,* from *scrībere* to write]
▸**superscription** (ˌsuːpə'skrɪpʃən) *n*
superscript ('suːpəˌskrɪpt) *Printing.* ◆ *adj* **1** (of a character) written or printed above the line; superior. Cf. **subscript.** ◆ *n* **2** a superscript or superior character. [C16: from L *superscriptus*]
supersede ❶ (ˌsuːpə'siːd) *vb* **supersedes, superseding, superseded.** (*tr*) **1** to take the place of (something old-fashioned or less appropriate); supplant. **2** to replace in function, office, etc.; succeed. **3** to discard or set aside or cause to be set aside as obsolete or inferior. [C15: via OF from L *supersedēre* to sit above]
▸**ˌsuper'sedence** *n* ▸**supersedure** (ˌsuːpə'siːdʒə) *n* ▸**supersession** (ˌsuːpə'sɛʃən) *n*
supersex ('suːpəˌsɛks) *n Genetics.* a sterile organism in which the ratio between the sex chromosomes is disturbed.
supersonic (ˌsuːpə'sɒnɪk) *adj* being, having, or capable of a velocity in excess of the velocity of sound.
▸**ˌsuper'sonically** *adv*
supersonics (ˌsuːpə'sɒnɪks) *n* (*functioning as sing*) **1** the study of supersonic motion. **2** a less common name for **ultrasonics.**
superstar ('suːpəˌstɑː) *n* an extremely popular film star, pop star, etc.
▸**'superˌstardom** *n*
superstition (ˌsuːpə'stɪʃən) *n* **1** irrational belief usually founded on ignorance or fear and characterized by obsessive reverence for omens, charms, etc. **2** a notion, act, or ritual that derives from such belief. **3** any irrational belief, esp. with regard to the unknown. [C15: from L *superstitiō,* from *superstāre* to stand still by something (as in amazement)]
superstitious (ˌsuːpə'stɪʃəs) *adj* **1** disposed to believe in superstition. **2** of or relating to superstition.
▸**ˌsuper'stitiously** *adv* ▸**ˌsuper'stitiousness** *n*
superstore ('suːpəˌstɔː) *n* a large supermarket.
superstratum (ˌsuːpə'strɑːtəm, -'streɪ-) *n, pl* **superstrata** (-tə) *or* **superstratums.** *Geol.* a layer or stratum overlying another layer or similar structure.
superstring ('suːpəˌstrɪŋ) *n Physics.* a type of string postulated in certain theories of elementary particles that involve supersymmetry.
superstructure ('suːpəˌstrʌktʃə) *n* **1** the part of a building above its foundation. **2** any structure or concept erected on something else. **3** *Naut.* any structure above the main deck of a ship with sides flush with the sides of the hull. **4** the part of a bridge supported by the piers and abutments.
▸**'superˌstructural** *adj*
supersymmetry (ˌsuːpə'sɪmɪtrɪ) *n Physics.* a symmetry of elementary particles having a higher order than that in the standard model, postulated to encompass the behaviour of both bosons and fermions.
supertanker ('suːpəˌtæŋkə) *n* a large fast tanker of more than 275 000 tons capacity.
supertax ('suːpəˌtæks) *n* a tax levied in addition to the basic tax, esp. on incomes above a certain level.
supertonic (ˌsuːpə'tɒnɪk) *n Music.* **1** the second degree of a major or minor scale. **2** a key or chord based on this.
supervene (ˌsuːpə'viːn) *vb* **supervenes, supervening, supervened.** (*intr*) **1** to follow closely; ensue. **2** to occur as an unexpected or extraneous development. [C17: from L *supervenīre* to come upon]
▸**ˌsuper'venience** *or* **supervention** (ˌsuːpə'vɛnʃən) *n* ▸**ˌsuper'venient** *adj*
supervise ❶ ('suːpəˌvaɪz) *vb* **supervises, supervising, supervised.** (*tr*) **1** to direct or oversee the performance or operation of. **2** to watch over so as to maintain order, etc. [C16: from Med. L *supervidēre,* from L SUPER- + *vidēre* to see]
▸**supervision** (ˌsuːpə'vɪʒən) *n*
supervisor ❶ ('suːpəˌvaɪzə) *n* **1** a person who manages or supervises. **2**

THESAURUS

stuck-up (*inf.*) ◆ *n* **10** = **boss** (*inf.*), chief, director, manager, principal, senior, supervisor
Antonyms *adj* ≠ **better:** inferior, less, lesser, lower, not as good, poorer, worse ≠ **first-class:** average, inferior, mediocre, no great shakes (*inf.*), ordinary, second-class, second-rate, substandard, unremarkable ◆ *n* ≠ **boss:** assistant, cohort (*chiefly US*), dogsbody, inferior, junior, lackey, minion, subordinate, underling
superiority *n* **1** = **supremacy,** advantage, ascendancy, excellence, lead, predominance, pre-eminence, preponderance, prevalence
superlative *adj* **1** = **supreme,** consummate, crack (*sl.*), excellent, greatest, highest, magnificent, matchless, of the first water, of the highest order, outstanding, peerless, stellar (*inf.*), surpassing, transcendent, unparalleled, unrivalled, unsurpassed
Antonyms *adj* abysmal, appalling, average, dreadful, easily outclassed, inferior, ordinary, poor, rotten, run-of-the-mill, undistinguished, unexceptional, uninspired, unspectacular
supernatural *adj* **1-4** = **paranormal,** abnormal, dark, ghostly, hidden, miraculous, mysterious, mystic, occult, phantom, preternatural, psychic, spectral, uncanny, unearthly, unnatural
supernumerary *adj* **1** = **extra,** excess, excessive, in excess, odd, redundant, spare, superfluous, surplus, unrequired
supersede *vb* **1, 2** = **replace,** displace, fill *or* step into (someone's) boots, oust, remove, supplant, take over, take the place of, usurp **3** = **set aside,** annul, overrule
supervise *vb* **1, 2** = **oversee,** administer, be on duty at, be responsible for, conduct, control, direct, handle, have *or* be in charge of, inspect, keep an eye on, look after, manage, preside over, run, superintend
supervision *n* **1, 2** = **superintendence,** administration, auspices, care, charge, control, direction, guidance, instruction, management, oversight, stewardship, surveillance
supervisor *n* **1, 2** = **boss** (*inf.*), administrator, chief, foreman, gaffer (*inf., chiefly Brit.*), inspec-

a foreman or forewoman. **3** (in some British universities) a tutor supervising the work, esp. research work, of a student. **4** (in some US schools) an administrator running a department of teachers.
▸ **ˌsuperˈvisorship** *n* ▸ **ˌsuperˈvisory** *adj*

supinate (ˈsuːpɪˌneɪt, ˈsjuː-) *vb* **supinates, supinating, supinated.** to turn (the hand and forearm) so that the palm faces up or forwards. [C19: from L *supīnāre* to lay on the back, from *supīnus* supine]
▸ **ˌsupiˈnation** *n*

supine Ⓣ *adj* (suːˈpaɪn, sjuː-; ˈsuːpaɪn, ˈsjuː-). **1** lying or resting on the back with the face, palm, etc., upwards. **2** displaying no interest or animation; lethargic. ◆ *n* (ˈsuːpaɪn, ˈsjuː-). **3** *Grammar.* a noun form derived from a verb in Latin, often used to express purpose with verbs of motion. [C15: from L *supīnus* rel. to *sub* under, up; (in grammatical sense) from L *verbum supīnum* supine word (from ?)]
▸ **suˈpinely** *adv* ▸ **suˈpineness** *n*

supp. *or* **suppl.** *abbrev. for* supplement(ary).

supper (ˈsʌpə) *n* **1** an evening meal, esp. a light one. **2** an evening social event featuring a supper. **3 sing for one's supper.** to obtain something by performing a service. [C13: from OF *soper*]
▸ **ˈsupperless** *adj*

supplant Ⓣ (səˈplɑːnt) *vb* (*tr*) to take the place of, often by trickery or force. [C13: via OF from L *supplantāre* to trip up, from *sub-* from below + *planta* sole of the foot]
▸ **supˈplanter** *n*

supple Ⓣ (ˈsʌpᵊl) *adj* **1** bending easily without damage. **2** capable of or showing easy or graceful movement; lithe. **3** mentally flexible; responding readily. **4** disposed to agree, sometimes to the point of servility. ◆ *vb* **supples, suppling, suppled. 5** *Rare.* to make or become supple. [C13: from OF *souple,* from L *supplex* bowed]
▸ **ˈsuppleness** *n*

supplejack (ˈsʌpᵊlˌdʒæk) *n* **1** a North American twining woody vine that has greenish-white flowers and purple fruits. **2** a bush plant of New Zealand having tough climbing vines. **3** a tropical American woody vine having strong supple wood. **4** any of various other vines with strong supple stems. **5** *US.* a walking stick made from the wood of the tropical supplejack.

supplement Ⓣ *n* (ˈsʌplɪmənt). **1** an addition designed to complete, make up for a deficiency, etc. **2** a section appended to a publication to supply further information, correct errors, etc. **3** a magazine or section inserted into a newspaper or periodical, such as one issued every week. **4** *Geom.* **4a** either of a pair of angles whose sum is 180°. **4b** an arc of a circle that when added to another arc forms a semicircle. ◆ *vb* (ˈsʌplɪˌmɛnt). **5** (*tr*) to provide a supplement to, esp. in order to remedy a deficiency. [C14: from L *supplēmentum,* from *supplēre* to SUPPLY]
▸ **ˌsupplemenˈtation** *n*

supplementary Ⓣ (ˌsʌplɪˈmɛntərɪ) *adj* **1** Also (*less commonly*): **supplemental** (ˌsʌpləˈmɛntᵊl). forming or acting as a supplement. ◆ *n, pl* **supplementaries. 2** a person or thing that is a supplement.
▸ **ˌsuppleˈmentarily** *or* (*less commonly*) **ˌsuppleˈmentally** *adv*

supplementary angle *n* either of two angles whose sum is 180°. Cf. **complementary angle.**

suppliant (ˈsʌplɪənt) *adj* **1** expressing entreaty or supplication. ◆ *n, adj* **2** another word for **supplicant.** [C15: from F *supplier* to beseech, from L *supplicāre* to kneel in entreaty]
▸ **ˈsuppliantly** *adv*

supplicant Ⓣ (ˈsʌplɪkənt) *or* **suppliant** *n* **1** a person who supplicates. ◆ *adj* **2** entreating humbly; supplicating. [C16: from L *supplicāns* beseeching]

supplicate Ⓣ (ˈsʌplɪˌkeɪt) *vb* **supplicates, supplicating, supplicated. 1** to make a humble request to (someone); plead. **2** (*tr*) to ask for or seek humbly. [C15: from L *supplicāre* to beg on one's knees]
▸ **ˌsuppliˈcation** *n* ▸ **ˈsuppliˌcatory** *adj*

supply[1] Ⓣ (səˈplaɪ) *vb* **supplies, supplying, supplied. 1** (*tr;* often foll. by *with*) to furnish with something required. **2** (*tr;* often foll. by *to* or *for*) to make available or provide (something desired or lacking): *to supply books to the library.* **3** (*tr*) to provide for adequately; satisfy: *who will supply their needs?* **4** to serve as a substitute, usually temporary, in (another's position, etc.): *there are no clergymen to supply the pulpit.* **5** (*tr*) *Brit.* to fill (a vacancy, position, etc.). ◆ *n, pl* **supplies. 6a** the act of providing or something provided. **6b** (*as modifier*): *a supply dump.* **7** (*often pl*) an amount available for use; stock. **8** (*pl*) food, equipment, etc., needed for a campaign or trip. **9** *Econ.* **9a** willingness and ability to offer goods and services for sale. **9b** the amount of a commodity that producers are willing and able to offer for sale at a specified price. Cf. **demand** (sense 9). **10** *Mil.* **10a** the management and disposal of food and equipment. **10b** (*as modifier*): *supply routes.* **11** (*often pl*) a grant of money voted by a legislature for government expenses. **12** (in Parliament and similar legislatures) the money voted annually for the expenses of the civil service and armed forces. **13a** a person who acts as a temporary substitute. **13b** (*as modifier*): *a supply vicar.* **14** a source of electricity, gas, etc. [C14: from OF *souppleier,* from L *supplēre* to complete, from *sub-* up + *plēre* to fill]
▸ **supˈpliable** *adj* ▸ **supˈplier** *n*

supply[2] (ˈsʌplɪ) *or* **supplely** (ˈsʌpᵊlɪ) *adv* in a supple manner.

supply-side economics (səˈplaɪ-) *n* (*functioning as sing*) a school of economic thought that emphasizes the importance to a strong economy of policies that remove impediments to supply.

support Ⓣ (səˈpɔːt) *vb* (*tr*) **1** to carry the weight of. **2** to bear (pressure, weight, etc.). **3** to provide the necessities of life for (a family, person, etc.). **4** to tend to establish (a theory, statement, etc.) by providing new facts. **5** to speak in favour of (a motion). **6** to give aid or courage to. **7** to give approval to (a cause, principle, etc.); subscribe to. **8** to endure with forbearance: *I will no longer support bad behaviour.* **9** to give strength to; maintain: *to support a business.* **10** (in a concert) to perform earlier than (the main attraction). **11** *Films, theatre.* **11a** to play a subordinate role to. **11b** to accompany (the feature) in a film programme. **12** to act or perform (a role or character). ◆ *n* **13** the act of supporting or the condition of being supported. **14** a thing that bears the weight or part of the weight of a construction. **15** a person who or thing that furnishes aid. **16** the means of maintenance of a family, person, etc. **17** a band or entertainer not topping the bill. **18** (often preceded by *the*) an actor or group of actors playing subordinate roles. **19** *Med.* an appliance worn to ease the strain on an injured bodily structure or part. **20** Also: **athletic support.** a more formal term for **jockstrap.** [C14: from OF *supporter,* from L *supportāre* to bring, from *sub-* up + *portāre* to carry]
▸ **supˈportable** *adj* ▸ **supˈportive** *adj*

supporter Ⓣ (səˈpɔːtə) *n* **1** a person who or thing that acts as a support. **2** a person who backs a sports team, politician, etc. **3** a garment or device worn to ease the strain on or restrict the movement of a bodily structure or part. **4** *Heraldry.* a figure or beast in a coat of arms depicted as holding up the shield.

supporting (səˈpɔːtɪŋ) *adj* **1** (of a role) being a fairly important but not leading part. **2** (of an actor or actress) playing a supporting role.

suppose Ⓣ (səˈpəʊz) *vb* **supposes, supposing, supposed.** (*tr; may take a clause as object*) **1** to presume (something) to be true without certain knowledge: *I suppose he meant to kill her.* **2** to consider as a possible sug-

THESAURUS

tor, manager, overseer, steward, superintendent

supervisory *adj* **1** = **managerial**, administrative, executive, overseeing, superintendent

supine *adj* **1** = **flat on one's back**, flat, horizontal, recumbent **2** = **lethargic**, apathetic, careless, heedless, idle, incurious, indifferent, indolent, inert, languid, lazy, listless, lymphatic, negligent, passive, slothful, sluggish, spineless, spiritless, torpid, uninterested
Antonyms *adj* ≠ **flat on one's back:** lying on one's face, prone, prostrate

supplant *vb* = **replace**, displace, oust, overthrow, remove, supersede, take over, take the place of, undermine, unseat

supple *adj* **1** = **pliant**, bending, elastic, plastic, pliable **2** = **flexible**, limber, lissom(e), lithe, loose-limbed
Antonyms ≠ **pliant:** firm, inflexible, rigid, stiff, taut, unbending, unyielding *adj* ≠ **flexible:** awkward, creaky (*inf.*), graceless, inflexible, stiff, unsupple

supplement *n* **1** = **addition**, added feature, addendum, add-on, appendix, codicil, complement, extra, insert, postscript, pull-out, sequel ◆ *vb* **5** = **add**, augment, complement, extend, fill out, reinforce, supply, top up

supplementary *adj* **1** = **additional**, accompanying, add-on, ancillary, auxiliary, complementary, extra, secondary, supplemental

supplicant *n* **1** = **petitioner**, applicant, suitor, suppliant ◆ *adj* **2** = **imploring**, begging, beseeching, craving, entreating, importunate, on bended knee

supplication *n* **1** = **plea**, appeal, entreaty, invocation, petition, pleading, prayer, request, solicitation, suit

supply[1] *vb* **1-3** = **provide**, afford, cater to *or* for, come up with, contribute, endow, equip, fill, furnish, give, grant, minister, outfit, produce, purvey, replenish, satisfy, stock, store, victual, yield ◆ *n* **7** = **store**, cache, fund, hoard, quantity, reserve, reservoir, source, stock, stockpile **8** *plural* = **provisions**, equipment, food, foodstuff, items, materials, necessities, provender, rations, stores

support *vb* **1, 2** = **bear**, bolster, brace, buttress, carry, hold, hold up, prop, reinforce, shore up, sustain, underpin, uphold **3** = **provide for**, cherish, finance, foster, fund, keep, look after, maintain, nourish, subsidize, sustain, take care of, underwrite **4** = **bear out**, attest to, authenticate, confirm, corroborate, document, endorse, lend credence to, substantiate, verify **5-7** = **help**, advocate, aid, assist, back, be a source of strength to, boost (someone's) morale, buoy up, champion, defend, encourage, espouse, forward, go along with, hold (someone's) hand, promote, second, side with, stand behind, stand up for, stick up for (*inf.*), strengthen, succour, take (someone's) part, take up the cudgels for, uphold **8** = **tolerate**, bear, brook, countenance, endure, put up with (*inf.*), stand (for), stomach, submit, suffer, thole (*dialect*), undergo ◆ *n* **13** = **help**, aid, approval, assistance, backing, blessing, championship, comfort, encouragement, espousal, friendship, furtherance, loyalty, moral support, patronage, promotion, protection, relief, succour, sustenance **14** = **prop**, abutment, back, brace, foundation, lining, pillar, post, shore, stanchion, stay, stiffener, underpinning **15** = **supporter**, backbone, backer, comforter, mainstay, prop, second, stay, tower of strength **16** = **upkeep**, keep, livelihood, maintenance, subsistence, sustenance
Antonyms *vb* ≠ **provide for:** live off, sponge off ≠ **bear out:** challenge, contradict, deny, refute ≠ **help:** go against, hinder, hold out against, oppose, reject, stab in the back, turn one's back on, undermine, walk away from ◆ *n* ≠ **help:** burden, denial, encumbrance, hindrance, impediment, opposition, refutation, rejection, undermining ≠ **supporter:** antagonist

supporter *n* **2** = **follower**, adherent, advocate, ally, apologist, champion, co-worker, defender, fan, friend, helper, henchman, patron, protagonist, sponsor, upholder, well-wisher
Antonyms *n* adversary, antagonist, challenger, competitor, foe, opponent, rival

supportive *adj* **6** = **helpful**, caring, encouraging, reassuring, sympathetic, understanding

suppose *vb* **1** = **presume**, assume, calculate (*US dialect*), conjecture, dare say, expect, guess

gestion for the sake of discussion, etc.: *suppose that he wins.* **3** (of theories, etc.) to imply the inference or assumption (of): *your policy supposes full employment.* [C14: from OF *supposer,* from Med. L *suppōnere,* from L: to substitute, from SUB- + *pōnere* to put]
▸**sup'posable** *adj* ▸**sup'poser** *n*

supposed ❶ (sə'pəʊzd, -'pəʊzɪd) *adj* **1** (*prenominal*) presumed to be true without certain knowledge. **2** (*prenominal*) believed to be true on slight grounds; highly doubtful. **3** (sə'pəʊzd). (*postpositive;* foll. by *to*) expected or obliged (to): *I'm supposed to be there.* **4** (sə'pəʊzd). (*postpositive; used in negative;* foll. by *to*) expected or obliged not (to): *you're not supposed to walk on the grass.*
▸**supposedly** (sə'pəʊzɪdlɪ) *adv*

supposition ❶ (ˌsʌpə'zɪʃən) *n* **1** the act of supposing. **2** a fact, theory, etc., that is supposed.
▸ˌ**suppo'sitional** *adj* ▸ˌ**suppo'sitionally** *adv*

suppositious (ˌsʌpə'zɪʃəs) *adj* deduced from supposition; hypothetical.
▸ˌ**suppo'sitiously** *adv* ▸ˌ**suppo'sitiousness** *n*

supposititious (səˌpɒzɪ'tɪʃəs) *adj* substituted with intent to mislead or deceive.
▸**supˌposi'titiously** *adv* ▸**supˌposi'titiousness** *n*

suppositive (sə'pɒzɪtɪv) *adj* **1** of, involving, or arising out of supposition. **2** *Grammar.* denoting a conjunction introducing a clause expressing a supposition, as for example *if, supposing,* or *provided that.* ◆ *n* **3** *Grammar.* a suppositive conjunction.
▸**sup'positively** *adv*

suppository (sə'pɒzɪtərɪ, -trɪ) *n, pl* **suppositories.** *Med.* a solid medication for insertion into the vagina, rectum, or urethra, where it melts and releases the active substance. [C14: from Med. L *suppositōrium,* from L *suppositus* placed beneath]

suppress ❶ (sə'prɛs) *vb* (*tr*) **1** to put an end to; prohibit. **2** to hold in check; restrain: *I was obliged to suppress a smile.* **3** to withhold from circulation or publication: *to suppress seditious pamphlets.* **4** to stop the activities of; crush: *to suppress a rebellion.* **5** *Electronics.* **5a** to reduce or eliminate (unwanted oscillations) in a circuit. **5b** to eliminate (a particular frequency or frequencies) in a signal. **6** *Psychiatry.* to resist consciously (an idea or a desire entering one's mind). [C14: from L *suppressus* held down, from *supprimere* to restrain, from *sub-* down + *premere* to press]
▸**sup'pressible** *adj* ▸**sup'pressive** *adj* ▸**sup'presser** *n*

suppressant (sə'prɛsənt) *adj* **1** tending to suppress or restrain an action or condition. ◆ *n* **2** a suppressant drug or agent: *a cough suppressant.*

suppression ❶ (sə'prɛʃən) *n* **1** the act or process of suppressing or the condition of being suppressed. **2** *Psychiatry.* the conscious avoidance of unpleasant thoughts.

suppressor (sə'prɛsə) *n* **1** a person or thing that suppresses. **2** a device fitted to an electrical appliance to suppress unwanted electrical interference to audiovisual signals.

suppurate ❶ ('sʌpjʊˌreɪt) *vb* **suppurates, suppurating, suppurated.** (*intr*) *Pathol.* (of a wound, sore, etc.) to discharge pus; fester. [C16: from L *suppūrāre,* from SUB- + *pūs* pus]
▸ˌ**suppu'ration** *n* ▸'**suppurative** *adj*

supra- *prefix* over, above, beyond, or greater than: *supranational.* [from L *suprā* above]

supraliminal (ˌsuːprə'lɪmɪnᵊl, ˌsjuː-) *adj* of or relating to any stimulus that is above the threshold of sensory awareness.
▸ˌ**supra'liminally** *adv*

supramolecular (ˌsuːprəmə'lɛkjʊlə, ˌsjuː-) *adj* **1** more complex than a molecule. **2** consisting of more than one molecule.

supranational (ˌsuːprə'næʃənᵊl, ˌsjuː-) *adj* beyond the authority or jurisdiction of one national government: *the supranational institutions of the EU.*
▸ˌ**supra'nationalism** *n*

supraorbital (ˌsuːprə'ɔːbɪtᵊl, ˌsjuː-) *adj Anat.* situated above the orbit.

suprarenal (ˌsuːprə'riːnᵊl, ˌsjuː-) *adj Anat.* situated above a kidney.

suprarenal gland *n* another name for **adrenal gland.**

supremacist (sʊ'prɛməsɪst, sjʊ-) *n* **1** a person who promotes or advocates the supremacy of any particular group. ◆ *adj* **2** characterized by belief in the supremacy of any particular group.
▸**su'prematism** *n*

supremacy ❶ (sʊ'prɛməsɪ, sjʊ-) *n* **1** supreme power; authority. **2** the quality or condition of being supreme.

supreme ❶ (sʊ'priːm, sjʊ-) *adj* **1** of highest status or power. **2** (*usually prenominal*) of highest quality, importance, etc. **3** greatest in degree; extreme: *supreme folly.* **4** (*prenominal*) final or last, ultimate: *the supreme judgment.* [C16: from L *suprēmus* highest, from *superus* that is above, from *super* above]
▸**su'premely** *adv*

Supreme Being *n* God.

Supreme Court *n* (in the US) **1** the highest Federal court. **2** (in many states) the highest state court.

Supreme Court of Judicature *n* (in England) a court formed in 1873 by the amalgamation of several superior courts into two divisions, the High Court of Justice and the Court of Appeal.

supreme sacrifice *n* **the.** the sacrifice of one's life.

Supreme Soviet *n* (in the former Soviet Union) **1** the bicameral legislature, comprising the **Soviet of the Union** and the **Soviet of the Nationalities. 2** a similar legislature in each former Soviet republic.

supremo ❶ (sʊ'priːməʊ, sjʊ-) *n, pl* **supremos.** *Brit. inf.* a person in overall authority. [C20: from SUPREME]

Supt *or* **supt** *abbrev. for* superintendent.

sur-[1] *prefix* over; above; beyond: *surcharge; surrealism.* Cf. **super-.** [from OF, from L SUPER-]

sur-[2] *prefix* a variant of **sub-** before *r: surrogate.*

sura ('sʊərə) *n* any of the 114 chapters of the Koran. [C17: from Ar. *sūrah* section]

surah ('sʊərə) *n* a twill-weave fabric of silk or rayon. [C19: from F pronunciation of *Surat,* a port in W India where orig. made]

sural ('sjʊərəl) *adj Anat.* of or relating to the calf of the leg. [C17: via NL from L *sūra* calf]

surbase ('sɜːˌbeɪs) *n* the uppermost part, such as a moulding, of a pedestal, base, or skirting.

surcease (sɜː'siːs) *Arch.* ◆ *n* **1** cessation or intermission. ◆ *vb* **surceases, surceasing, surceased. 2** to desist from (some action). **3** to cease or cause to cease. [C16: from earlier *sursesen,* from OF *surseoir,* from L *supersedēre* to sit above]

surcharge *n* ('sɜːˌtʃɑːdʒ). **1** a charge in addition to the usual payment, tax, etc. **2** an excessive sum charged, esp. when unlawful. **3** an extra and usually excessive burden or supply. **4** an overprint that alters the face value of a postage stamp. ◆ *vb* (sɜː'tʃɑːdʒ, 'sɜːˌtʃɑːdʒ), **surcharges, surcharging, surcharged.** (*tr*) **5** to charge an additional sum, tax, etc. **6** to overcharge (a person) for something. **7** to put an extra physical burden upon; overload. **8** to fill to excess; overwhelm. **9** *Law.* to insert credits that have been omitted in (an account). **10** to overprint a surcharge on (a stamp).

surcingle ('sɜːˌsɪŋgᵊl) *n* a girth for a horse which goes around the body, used esp. with a racing saddle. [C14: from OF *surcengle,* from *sur-* over + *cengle* a belt, from L *cingulum*]

surcoat ('sɜːˌkəʊt) *n* **1** a tunic, often embroidered with heraldic arms, worn by a knight over his armour during the Middle Ages. **2** (formerly) an outer coat or other garment.

surculose ('sɜːkjʊˌləʊs) *adj* (of a plant) bearing suckers. [C19: from L *surculōsus* woody, from *surculus* twig, from *sūrus* a branch]

surd (sɜːd) *n* **1** *Maths.* a number containing an irrational root, such as $2\sqrt{3}$; irrational number. **2** *Phonetics.* a voiceless consonant, such as (t). ◆ *adj* **3** of or relating to a surd. [C16: from L *surdus* muffled]

sure ❶ (ʃʊə, ʃɔː) *adj* **1** (sometimes foll. by *of*) free from hesitancy or uncertainty (with regard to a belief, conviction, etc.): *we are sure of the accuracy of the data; I am sure that he is lying.* **2** (foll. by *of*) having no

THESAURUS

(*inf., chiefly US & Canad.*), imagine, infer, judge, opine, presuppose, surmise, take as read, take for granted, think **2** = **imagine**, believe, conceive, conclude, conjecture, consider, fancy, hypothesize, postulate, pretend

supposed *adj* **1** = **presumed**, accepted, alleged, assumed, hypothetical, presupposed, professed, putative, reputed, rumoured **3** *usually with* **to** = **meant**, expected, obliged, required

supposedly *adv* **1** = **presumably**, allegedly, at a guess, avowedly, by all accounts, hypothetically, ostensibly, professedly, purportedly, theoretically
Antonyms *adv* absolutely, actually, certainly, in actuality, in fact, really, surely, truly, undoubtedly, without a doubt

supposition *n* **1** = **guess**, conjecture, doubt, guesswork, hypothesis, idea, notion, postulate, presumption, speculation, surmise, theory

suppress *vb* **2** = **restrain**, conceal, contain, cover up, curb, hold in *or* back, hold in check, keep secret, muffle, muzzle, repress, silence, smother, stifle, sweep under the carpet (*inf.*), withhold **4** = **stop**, beat down, check, clamp down on, conquer, crack down on, crush, drive underground, extinguish, overpower, overthrow, put an end to, quash, quell, quench, snuff out, stamp out, subdue, trample on
Antonyms *vb* encourage, foster, further, gee up, incite, inflame, promote, rouse, spread, stimulate, stir up, whip up

suppression *n* **1** = **elimination**, check, clampdown, crackdown, crushing, dissolution, extinction, prohibition, quashing, termination **2** = **inhibition**, smothering

suppurate *vb Pathology* = **discharge**, fester, gather, maturate, ooze, weep

supremacy *n* **2** = **domination**, absolute rule, ascendancy, dominance, dominion, lordship, mastery, paramountcy, predominance, pre-eminence, primacy, sovereignty, supreme power, sway

supreme *adj* **1-4** = **highest**, cardinal, chief, crowning, culminating, extreme, final, first, foremost, greatest, head, incomparable, leading, matchless, mother of all (*inf.*), paramount, peerless, predominant, pre-eminent, prevailing, prime, principal, sovereign, superlative, surpassing, top, ultimate, unsurpassed, utmost
Antonyms *adj* least, least successful, lowest, most inferior, most minor, most subordinate, most trivial, poorest, worst

supremo *n Brit. informal* = **head**, boss (*inf.*), commander, director, governor, leader, master, principal, ruler

sure *adj* **1** = **certain**, assured, clear, confident, convinced, decided, definite, free from doubt, persuaded, positive, satisfied **3-6** = **reliable**, accurate, dependable, effective, foolproof, honest, indisputable, infallible, never-failing, precise, sure-fire (*inf.*), tried and true, trustworthy, trusty, undeniable, undoubted, unerring, unfailing, unmistakable, well-proven **8** = **inevitable**, assured, bound, guaranteed, ineluctable, inescapable, in the bag (*sl.*), irrevocable **10** = **secure**, fast, firm, fixed, safe, solid, stable, staunch, steady
Antonyms *adj* ≠ **certain**: distrustful, doubtful, dubious, sceptical, unassured, uncertain, unconvinced, uneasy, unsure ≠ **reliable**: dodgy (*Brit., Austral., & NZ inf.*), dubious, fallible, iffy (*inf.*), un-

doubt, as of the occurrence of a future state or event: *sure of success.* **3** always effective; unfailing: *a sure remedy.* **4** reliable in indication or accuracy: *a sure criterion.* **5** (of persons) worthy of trust or confidence: *a sure friend.* **6** not open to doubt: *sure proof.* **7** admitting of no vacillation or doubt: *he is sure in his beliefs.* **8** bound to be or occur; inevitable: *victory is sure.* **9** (*postpositive*) bound inevitably (to be or do something); certain: *she is sure to be there.* **10** physically secure or dependable: *a sure footing.* **11 be sure.** (*usually imperative or dependent imperative; takes a clause as object or an infinitive,* sometimes with *to* replaced by *and*) to be careful or certain: *be sure and shut the door; be sure to shut the door.* **12 for sure.** without a doubt; surely. **13 make sure. 13a** (*takes a clause as object*) to make certain; ensure. **13b** (foll. by *of*) to establish or confirm power or possession (over). **14 sure enough.** *Inf.* as might have been confidently expected; definitely: often used as a sentence substitute. **15 to be sure. 15a** without doubt; certainly. **15b** it has to be acknowledged; admittedly. ◆ *adv* **16** (*sentence modifier*) *US & Canad. inf.* without question; certainly. ◆ *sentence substitute.* **17** *US & Canad. inf.* willingly; yes. [C14: from OF *seur,* from L *sēcūrus* SECURE]
▸ **'sureness** *n*

sure-fire *adj* (*usually prenominal*) *Inf.* certain to succeed or meet expectations; assured.

sure-footed *adj* **1** unlikely to fall, slip, or stumble. **2** not likely to err or fail.
▸ **,sure-'footedly** *adv* ▸ **,sure-'footedness** *n*

surely ⓘ ('ʃʊəlɪ, 'ʃɔː-) *adv* **1** without doubt; assuredly. **2** without fail; inexorably (esp. in **slowly but surely**). **3** (*sentence modifier*) am I not right in thinking that?; I am sure that: *surely you don't mean it?* **4** *Rare.* in a sure manner. **5** *Arch.* safely; securely. ◆ *sentence substitute.* **6** *Chiefly US & Canad.* willingly; yes.

sure thing *Inf.* ◆ *sentence substitute.* **1** *Chiefly US.* used to express enthusiastic assent. ◆ *n* **2** something guaranteed to be successful.

surety ⓘ ('ʃʊətɪ, 'ʃʊərɪtɪ) *n, pl* **sureties. 1** a person who assumes legal responsibility for another's debt or obligation and himself becomes liable if the other defaults. **2** security given against loss or damage or as a guarantee that an obligation will be met. **3** *Obs.* the quality or condition of being sure. **4 stand surety.** to act as a surety. [C14: from OF *seurte,* from L *sēcūritās* security]
▸ **'suretyship** *n*

surf (sɜːf) *n* **1** waves breaking on the shore or on a reef. **2** foam caused by the breaking of waves. ◆ *vb* (*intr*) **3** to take part in surfing. **4** to move rapidly and easily through a particular medium: *surfing the Internet.* **5** *Inf.* to be carried on top of something: *that guy's surfing the audience.* [C17: prob. var. of SOUGH]

surface ⓘ ('sɜːfɪs) *n* **1a** the exterior face of an object or one such face. **1b** (*as modifier*): *surface gloss.* **2** the area or size of such a face. **3** material resembling such a face, with length and width but without depth. **4a** the superficial appearance as opposed to the real nature. **4b** (*as modifier*): *a surface resemblance.* **5** *Geom.* **5a** the complete boundary of a solid figure. **5b** a continuous two-dimensional configuration. **6a** the uppermost level of the land or sea. **6b** (*as modifier*): *surface transportation.* **7 come to the surface.** to emerge; become apparent. **8 on the surface.** to all appearances. ◆ *vb* **surfaces, surfacing, surfaced. 9** to rise or cause to rise to or as if to the surface (of water, etc.). **10** (*tr*) to treat the surface of, as by polishing, smoothing, etc. **11** (*tr*) to furnish with a surface. **12** (*intr*) to become apparent; emerge. **13** (*intr*) *Inf.* **13a** to wake up. **13b** to get up. [C17: from F, from *sur* on + *face* FACE]
▸ **'surfacer** *n*

surface-active *adj* (of a substance, esp. a detergent) capable of lowering the surface tension of a liquid. See also **surfactant.**

surface mail *n* mail transported by land or sea. Cf. **airmail.**

surface structure *n Generative grammar.* a representation of a string of words or morphemes as they occur in a sentence, together with labels and brackets that represent syntactic structure. Cf. **deep structure.**

surface tension *n* **1** a property of liquids caused by intermolecular forces near the surface leading to the apparent presence of a surface film and to capillarity, etc. **2** a measure of this.

surface-to-air *adj* of or relating to a missile launched from the surface of the earth against airborne targets.

surfactant (sɜː'fæktənt) *n* **1** Also called: **surface-active agent.** a substance, such as a detergent, that can reduce the surface tension of a liquid and thus allow it to foam or penetrate solids; a wetting agent. ◆ *adj* **2** having the properties of a surfactant. [C20: *surf(ace)-act(ive) a(ge)nt*]

surfboard ('sɜːf,bɔːd) *n* a long narrow board used in surfing.

surfboat ('sɜːf,bəʊt) *n* a boat with a high bow and stern and flotation chambers, equipped for use in rough surf.

surfcasting ('sɜːf,kɑːstɪŋ) *n* fishing from the shore by casting into the surf.
▸ **'surf,caster** *n*

surfeit ⓘ ('sɜːfɪt) *n* **1** (usually foll. by *of*) an excessive amount. **2** overindulgence, esp. in eating or drinking. **3** disgust, nausea, etc., caused by such overindulgence. ◆ *vb* **4** (*tr*) to supply or feed excessively; satiate. **5** (*intr*) *Arch.* to eat, drink, or be supplied to excess. [C13: from F *sourfait,* from *sourfaire* to overdo, from SUR-[1] + *faire,* from L *facere* to do]

surfie ('sɜːfɪ) *n Austral. & NZ sl.* a young person whose main interest in life is surfing.

surfing ('sɜːfɪŋ) *n* the sport of riding towards shore on the crest of a wave by standing or lying on a surfboard.
▸ **'surfer** *or* **'surf,rider** *n*

surf mat *n Austral. inf.* a small inflatable rubber mattress used to ride on waves.

surg. *abbrev. for:* **1** surgeon. **2** surgery. **3** surgical.

surge ⓘ (sɜːdʒ) *n* **1** a strong rush or sweep; sudden increase: *a surge of anger.* **2** the rolling swell of the sea. **3** a heavy rolling motion or sound: *the surge of the trumpets.* **4** an undulating rolling surface, as of hills. **5** a billowing cloud or volume. **6** *Naut.* a temporary release or slackening of a rope or cable. **7** a large momentary increase in the voltage or current in an electric circuit. **8** an instability or unevenness in the power output of an engine. ◆ *vb* **surges, surging, surged. 9** (*intr*) (of waves, the sea, etc.) to rise or roll with a heavy swelling motion. **10** (*intr*) to move like a heavy sea. **11** *Naut.* to slacken or temporarily release (a rope or cable) from a capstan or (of a rope, etc.) to be slackened or released and slip back. **12** (*intr*) (of an electric current or voltage) to undergo a large momentary increase. **13** (*tr*) *Rare.* to cause to move in or as if in a wave or waves. [C15: from L *surgere* to rise, from *sub-* up + *regere* to lead]
▸ **'surger** *n*

surgeon ('sɜːdʒən) *n* **1** a medical practitioner who specializes in surgery. **2** a medical officer in the Royal Navy. [C14: from Anglo-Norman *surgien,* from OF *cirurgien;* see SURGERY]

surgeonfish ('sɜːdʒən,fɪʃ) *n, pl* **surgeonfish** *or* **surgeonfishes.** any of various tropical marine spiny-finned fishes, having a compressed brightly coloured body with knifelike spines at the base of the tail.

surgeon general *n, pl* **surgeons general. 1** (esp. in the British and US armies and navies) the senior officer of the medical service. **2** the head of the US public health service.

surgery ('sɜːdʒərɪ) *n, pl* **surgeries. 1** the branch of medicine concerned with manual or operative procedures, esp. incision into the body. **2** the performance of such procedures by a surgeon. **3** *Brit.* a place where, or time when, a doctor, dentist, etc., can be consulted. **4** *Brit.* an occasion when an MP, lawyer, etc., is available for consultation. **5** *US & Canad.* an operating theatre. [C14: via OF from L *chirurgia,* from Gk *kheirurgia,* from *kheir* hand + *ergon* work]

surgical ('sɜːdʒɪkᵊl) *adj* of, relating to, involving, or used in surgery.
▸ **'surgically** *adv*

surgical boot *n* a specially designed boot or shoe that compensates for deformities of the foot or leg.

surgical spirit *n* methylated spirit used medically for sterilizing.

suricate ('sjʊərɪ,keɪt) *n* another name for **slender-tailed meerkat** (see **meerkat**). [C18: from F *surikate,* prob. from a native South African word]

surly ⓘ ('sɜːlɪ) *adj* **surlier, surliest. 1** sullenly ill-tempered or rude. **2** (of an animal) ill-tempered or refractory. [C16: from obs. *sirly* haughty]
▸ **'surlily** *adv* ▸ **'surliness** *n*

surmise ⓘ *vb* (sɜː'maɪz), **surmises, surmising, surmised. 1** (when *tr, may take a clause as object*) to infer (something) from incomplete or uncertain evidence. ◆ *n* (sɜː'maɪz, 'sɜːmaɪz). **2** an idea inferred from inconclusive evidence. [C15: from OF, from *surmettre* to accuse, from L *supermittere* to throw over]
▸ **surmisedly** (sɜː'maɪzɪdlɪ) *adv*

surmount ⓘ (sɜː'maʊnt) *vb* (*tr*) **1** to prevail over; overcome. **2** to ascend and cross to the opposite side of. **3** to lie on top of or rise above. **4** to put something on top of or above. [C14: from OF *surmonter,* from SUR-[1] + *monter* to mount]
▸ **sur'mountable** *adj*

surname ('sɜː,neɪm) *n* **1** Also called: **last name, second name.** a family name as opposed to a first or Christian name. **2** (formerly) a descrip-

THESAURUS

dependable, unreliable, untrustworthy, vague ≠ **inevitable:** touch-and-go, unsure ≠ **secure:** insecure

surely *adv* **1, 2** = **undoubtedly,** assuredly, beyond the shadow of a doubt, certainly, come what may, definitely, doubtlessly, for certain, indubitably, inevitably, inexorably, unquestionably, without doubt, without fail

surety *n* **1** = **guarantor,** bondsman, hostage, mortgagor, sponsor **2** = **security,** bail, bond, deposit, guarantee, indemnity, insurance, pledge, safety, warranty

surface *n* **1a** = **outside,** covering, exterior, façade, face, facet, plane, side, skin, superficies (*rare*), top, veneer ◆ *modifier* **4b** = **outward,** apparent, exterior, external, superficial ◆ *n* **8 on the surface** = **at first glance,** apparently, ostensibly, outwardly, seemingly, superficially, to all appearances, to the casual eye ◆ *vb* **12** = **appear,** arise, come to light, come up, crop up (*inf.*), emerge, materialize, transpire

surfeit *n* **1, 2** = **excess,** glut, overindulgence, plethora, satiety, superabundance, superfluity ◆ *vb* **4** = **glut,** cram, fill, gorge, overfeed, overfill, satiate, stuff
Antonyms *n* ≠ **excess:** dearth, deficiency, insufficiency, lack, scarcity, shortage, shortness, want

surge *n* **1** = **rush,** flood, flow, gush, outpouring, uprush, upsurge **2** = **wave,** billow, breaker, efflux, roller, swell ◆ *vb* **9** = **rush,** gush, rise, swell, tower, well forth **10** = **roll,** billow, eddy, heave, swirl, undulate

surly *adj* **1** = **ill-tempered,** bearish, brusque, churlish, crabbed, cross, crusty, curmudgeonly, grouchy (*inf.*), gruff, morose, perverse, shrewish, sulky, sullen, testy, uncivil, ungracious
Antonyms *adj* agreeable, cheerful, cheery, genial, good-natured, happy, pleasant, sunny

surmise *vb* **1** = **guess,** come to the conclusion, conclude, conjecture, consider, deduce, fancy, hazard a guess, imagine, infer, opine, presume, speculate, suppose, suspect ◆ *n* **2** = **guess,** assumption, conclusion, conjecture, deduction, hypothesis, idea, inference, notion, possibility, presumption, speculation, supposition, suspicion, thought

surmount *vb* **1** = **overcome,** conquer, exceed,

tive epithet attached to a person's name to denote a personal characteristic, profession, etc.; nickname. ◆ *vb* **surnames, surnaming, surnamed. 3** (*tr*) to furnish with or call by a surname.
▸**'sur,namer** *n*

surpass ⓘ (sɜː'pɑːs) *vb* (*tr*) **1** to be greater than in degree, extent, etc. **2** to be superior to in achievement or excellence. **3** to overstep the limit or range of: *the theory surpasses my comprehension.* [C16: from F *surpasser,* from SUR-[1] + *passer* to PASS]
▸**sur'passable** *adj*

surpassing ⓘ (sɜː'pɑːsɪŋ) *adj* **1** exceptional; extraordinary. ◆ *adv* **2** *Obs. or poetic.* (intensifier): *surpassing fair.*
▸**sur'passingly** *adv*

surplice ('sɜːplɪs) *n* a loose wide-sleeved liturgical vestment of linen, reaching to the knees, worn over the cassock by clergymen, choristers, and acolytes. [C13: from OF *sourpelis,* from Med. L *superpellīcium,* from SUPER- + *pellīcium* coat made of skins, from L *pellis* a skin]

surplus ⓘ ('sɜːpləs) *n, pl* **surpluses. 1** a quantity or amount in excess of what is required. **2** *Accounting.* **2a** an excess of total assets over total liabilities. **2b** an excess of actual net assets over the nominal value of capital stock. **2c** an excess of revenues over expenditures. **3** *Econ.* **3a** an excess of government revenues over expenditures. **3b** an excess of receipts over payments on the balance of payments. ◆ *adj* **4** being in excess; extra. [C14: from OF, from Med. L *superplūs,* from L SUPER- + *plūs* more]

surprise ⓘ (sə'praɪz) *vb* **surprises, surprising, surprised.** (*tr*) **1** to cause to feel amazement or wonder. **2** to encounter or discover unexpectedly or suddenly. **3** to capture or assault suddenly and without warning. **4** to present with something unexpected, such as a gift. **5** (foll. by *into*) to provoke (someone) to unintended action by a trick, etc. **6** (often foll. by *from*) to elicit by unexpected behaviour or by a trick: *to surprise information from a prisoner.* ◆ *n* **7** the act or an instance of surprising; the act of taking unawares. **8** a sudden or unexpected event, gift, etc. **9** the feeling or condition of being surprised; astonishment. **10** (*modifier*) causing, characterized by, or relying upon surprise: *a surprise move.* **11 take by surprise. 11a** to come upon suddenly and without warning. **11b** to capture unexpectedly or catch unprepared. **11c** to astonish; amaze. [C15: from OF, from *surprendre* to overtake, from SUR-[1] + L *prehendere* to grasp]
▸**sur'prisal** *n* ▸**sur'prised** *adj* ▸**surprisedly** (sə'praɪzɪdlɪ) *adv*

surprising ⓘ (sə'praɪzɪŋ) *adj* causing surprise; unexpected or amazing.
▸**sur'prisingly** *adv*

surra ('sʊərə) *n* a tropical febrile disease of cattle, horses, camels, and dogs. [from Marathi, a language of India]

surrealism (sə'rɪə,lɪzəm) *n* (*sometimes cap.*) a movement in art and literature in the 1920s, which developed esp. from Dada, characterized by the evocative juxtaposition of incongruous images in order to include unconscious and dream elements. [C20: from F *surréalisme,* from SUR-[1] + *réalisme* realism]
▸**sur'real** *adj* ▸**sur'realist** *n, adj* ▸**sur,real'istic** *adj*

surrebutter (,sɜːrɪ'bʌtə) *n Law.* (in pleading) the plaintiff's reply to the defendant's rebutter.
▸**,surre'buttal** *n*

surrejoinder (,sɜːrɪ'dʒɔɪndə) *n Law.* (in pleading) the plaintiff's reply to the defendant's rejoinder.

surrender ⓘ (sə'rendə) *vb* **1** (*tr*) to relinquish to another under duress or on demand: *to surrender a city.* **2** (*tr*) to relinquish or forego (an office, position, etc.), esp. as a voluntary concession to another: *he surrendered his place to a lady.* **3** to give (oneself) up physically, as to an enemy. **4** to allow (oneself) to yield, as to a temptation, influence, etc. **5** (*tr*) to give up (hope, etc.). **6** (*tr*) *Law.* to give up or restore (an estate), esp. to give up a lease before expiration of the term. **7 surrender to bail.** to present oneself at court at the appointed time after having been on bail. ◆ *n* **8** the act or instance of surrendering. **9** *Insurance.* the voluntary discontinuation of a life policy by its holder in return for a consideration (the **surrender value**). **10** *Law.* **10a** the yielding up or restoring of an estate, esp. the giving up of a lease before its term has expired. **10b** the giving up to the appropriate authority of a fugitive from justice. **10c** the act of surrendering or being surrendered to bail. **10d** the deed by which a legal surrender is effected. [C15: from OF *surrendre* to yield]

surreptitious ⓘ (,sʌrəp'tɪʃəs) *adj* **1** done, acquired, etc., in secret or by improper means. **2** operating by stealth. [C15: from L *surreptīcius* furtive, from *surripere* to steal, from *sub-* secretly + *rapere* to snatch]
▸**,surrep'titiously** *adv* ▸**,surrep'titiousness** *n*

surrey ('sʌrɪ) *n* a light four-wheeled horse-drawn carriage having two or four seats. [C19: from *Surrey cart,* after *Surrey* where orig. made]

surrogate ⓘ *n* ('sʌrəgɪt). **1** a person or thing acting as a substitute. **2** *Chiefly Brit.* a deputy, such as a clergyman appointed to deputize for a bishop in granting marriage licences. **3** (in some US states) a judge with jurisdiction over the probate of wills, etc. **4** (*modifier*) of, relating to, or acting as a surrogate: *a surrogate pleasure.* ◆ *vb* ('sʌrə,geɪt), **surrogates, surrogating, surrogated.** (*tr*) **5** to put in another's position as a deputy, substitute, etc. [C17: from L *surrogāre* to substitute]
▸**'surrogateship** *n* ▸**,surro'gation** *n*

surrogate motherhood *or* **surrogacy** ('sʌrəgəsɪ) *n* the role of a woman who bears a child on behalf of a childless couple, either by artificial insemination or implantation of an embryo.
▸**surrogate mother** *n*

surround ⓘ (sə'raʊnd) *vb* (*tr*) **1** to encircle or enclose or cause to be encircled or enclosed. **2** to deploy forces on all sides of (a place or military formation), so preventing access or retreat. **3** to exist around: *the people who surround her.* ◆ *n* **4** *Chiefly Brit.* a border, esp. the area of uncovered floor between the walls of a room and the carpet or around an opening or panel. **5** *Chiefly US.* **5a** a method of capturing wild beasts by encircling the area in which they are believed to be. **5b** the area so encircled. [C15 *surrounden* to overflow, from OF *suronder,* from LL, from L SUPER- + *undāre* to abound, from *unda* a wave]
▸**sur'rounding** *adj*

surroundings ⓘ (sə'raʊndɪŋz) *pl n* the conditions, scenery, etc., around a person, place, or thing; environment.

sursum corda ('sɜːsəm 'kɔːdə) *n* **1** *RC Church.* a Latin versicle meaning *Lift up your hearts,* said by the priest at Mass. **2** a cry of exhortation, hope, etc.

surtax ('sɜː,tæks) *n* **1** a tax, usually highly progressive, levied on the amount by which a person's income exceeds a specific level. **2** an additional tax on something that has already been taxed. ◆ *vb* **3** (*tr*) to assess for liability to surtax; charge with an extra tax.

surtitles ('sɜː,taɪtᵊlz) *pl n* brief translations of the text of an opera or play that is being sung or spoken in a foreign language, projected above the stage.

surtout ('sɜːtuː) *n* a man's overcoat resembling a frock coat, popular in the late 19th century. [C17: from F, from *sur* over + *tout* all]

surveillance ⓘ (sɜː'veɪləns) *n* close observation or supervision over a person, group, etc., esp. one in custody or under suspicion. [C19: from F, from *surveiller* to watch over, from SUR-[1] + *veiller* to keep watch (from L *vigilāre;* see VIGIL)]
▸**sur'veillant** *adj, n*

survey ⓘ *vb* (sɜː'veɪ, 'sɜːveɪ). **1** (*tr*) to view or consider in a comprehensive or general way. **2** (*tr*) to examine carefully, in order to or as if to appraise condition and value. **3** to plot a detailed map of (an area of land) by measuring or calculating distances and height. **4** *Brit.* to inspect a building to determine its condition and value. **5** to examine a vessel thoroughly in order to determine its seaworthiness. **6** (*tr*) to run a statistical survey on (incomes, opinions, etc.). ◆ *n* ('sɜːveɪ). **7** a comprehensive or general view. **8** a critical, detailed, and formal inspec-

THESAURUS

master, overpower, pass, prevail over, surpass, triumph over, vanquish

surpass *vb* **2** = **outdo**, beat, best, cap (*inf.*), eclipse, exceed, excel, go one better than (*inf.*), outshine, outstrip, override, overshadow, put in the shade, top, tower above, transcend

surpassing *adj* **1** = **supreme**, exceptional, extraordinary, incomparable, matchless, outstanding, phenomenal, rare, stellar (*inf.*), transcendent, unrivalled

surplus *n* **1** = **excess**, balance, remainder, residue, superabundance, superfluity, surfeit ◆ *adj* **4** = **extra**, excess, in excess, left over, odd, remaining, spare, superfluous, unused
Antonyms *n* ≠ **excess:** dearth, deficiency, deficit, insufficiency, lack, paucity, shortage, shortfall ◆ *adj* ≠ **extra:** deficient, falling short, inadequate, insufficient, lacking, limited, scant, scanty, scarce

surprise *vb* **1** = **amaze**, astonish, astound, bewilder, bowl over (*inf.*), confuse, disconcert, flabbergast (*inf.*), leave open-mouthed, nonplus, stagger, stun, take aback, take (someone's) breath away **2** = **catch unawares** *or* **off-guard**, burst in on, catch in the act *or* red-handed, catch napping, catch on the hop (*inf.*), come down on like a bolt from the blue, discover, spring upon, startle ◆ *n* **8** = **shock**, bolt from the blue, bombshell, eye-opener (*inf.*), jolt, revelation, start (*inf.*), turn-up for the books (*inf.*) **9** = **amazement**, astonishment, bewilderment, incredulity, stupefaction, wonder

surprised *adj* **1** = **amazed**, astonished, at a loss, disconcerted, incredulous, nonplussed, open-mouthed, speechless, startled, taken aback, thunderstruck, unable to believe one's eyes **2** = **taken by surprise**, caught on the hop, caught on the wrong foot (*inf.*)

surprising *adj* = **amazing**, astonishing, astounding, bewildering, extraordinary, incredible, jaw-dropping, marvellous, remarkable, staggering, startling, unexpected, unlooked-for, unusual, wonderful

surrender *vb* **1** = **give up**, abandon, cede, concede, deliver up, forego, part with, relinquish, renounce, resign, waive, yield **3** = **give in**, capitulate, cave in (*inf.*), give oneself up, give way, lay down arms, quit, show the white flag, submit, succumb, throw in the towel, yield ◆ *n* **8** = **submission**, capitulation, cave-in (*inf.*), relinquishment, renunciation, resignation, yielding
Antonyms *vb* ≠ **give in:** defy, fight (on), make a stand against, oppose, resist, stand up to, withstand

surreptitious *adj* **1, 2** = **secret**, clandestine, covert, fraudulent, furtive, sly, sneaking, stealthy, unauthorized, underhand, veiled
Antonyms *adj* blatant, conspicuous, frank, honest, manifest, obvious, open, overt, unconcealed, undisguised

surrogate *n* **1, 2** = **substitute**, deputy, proxy, representative, stand-in

surround *vb* **1** = **enclose**, close in on, encircle, encompass, envelop, environ, enwreath, fence in, girdle, hem in, ring **2** *Military* = **besiege**, beset, invest (*rare*), lay siege to

surrounding *adj* **3** = **nearby**, neighbouring

surroundings *pl n* = **environment**, background, environs, location, milieu, neighbourhood, setting

surveillance *n* = **observation**, care, control, direction, inspection, scrutiny, superintendence, supervision, vigilance, watch

survey *vb* **1** = **look over**, contemplate, examine, eyeball (*sl.*), eye up, inspect, observe, recce (*sl.*), reconnoitre, scan, scrutinize, supervise, view **2** = **estimate**, appraise, assess, eye up, measure, plan, plot, prospect, size up, take stock of, triangulate ◆ *n* **8** = **examination**, inspection, once-over (*inf.*), overview, perusal, scrutiny

tion. **9** *Brit.* an inspection of a building to determine its condition and value. **10** a report incorporating the results of such an inspection. **11a** a body of surveyors. **11b** an area surveyed. [C15: from F *surveoir*, from SUR-[1] + *veoir* to see, from L *vidēre*]

surveying (sɜːˈveɪɪŋ) *n* **1** the study or practice of making surveys of land. **2** the setting out on the ground of the positions of proposed construction or engineering works.

surveyor (sɜːˈveɪə) *n* **1** a person whose occupation is to survey land or buildings. See also **quantity surveyor. 2** *Chiefly Brit.* a person concerned with the official inspection of something for purposes of measurement and valuation. **3** a person who carries out surveys, esp. of ships (**marine surveyor**) to determine seaworthiness, etc. **4** a customs official. **5** *Arch.* a supervisor.
▸**surˈveyorship** *n*

surveyor's measure *n* the system of measurement based on the **surveyor's chain** (66 feet) as a unit.

survival (səˈvaɪvᵊl) *n* **1** a person or thing that survives, such as a custom. **2a** the act or fact of surviving or condition of having survived. **2b** (*as modifier*): *survival kit.*

survival bag *n* a large plastic bag carried by climbers for use in an emergency as protection against exposure.

survivalist (səˈvaɪvəlɪst) *n Chiefly US.* **a** a person who believes in ensuring his personal survival of a catastrophic event by arming himself and often by living in the wild. **b** (*as modifier*): *survivalist weapons.*
▸**surˈvivalˌism** *n*

survival of the fittest *n* a popular term for **natural selection.**

survive ❶ (səˈvaɪv) *vb* **survives, surviving, survived. 1** (*tr*) to live after the death of (another). **2** to continue in existence or use after (a passage of time, adversity, etc.). **3** *Inf.* to endure (something): *I don't know how I survive such an awful job.* [C15: from OF *sourvivre*, from L *supervīvere*, from SUPER- + *vīvere* to live]
▸**surˈvivor** *n*

sus (sʌs) *Brit. sl.* ◆ *n* **1** short for **suspicion,** with reference to former police powers (**sus laws**) of detaining for questioning, searching, etc., any person suspected of criminal intent: *he was picked up on sus.* ◆ *vb* **susses, sussing, sussed. 2** a variant spelling of **suss** (sense 2).

susceptance (səˈsɛptəns) *n Physics.* the imaginary component of the admittance. [C19: from *suscept(ibility)* + -ANCE]

susceptibility ❶ (səˌsɛptəˈbɪlɪtɪ) *n, pl* **susceptibilities. 1** the quality or condition of being susceptible. **2** the ability or tendency to be impressed by emotional feelings. **3** (*pl*) emotional sensibilities; feelings. **4** *Physics.* **4a** Also called: **electric susceptibility.** (of a dielectric) the amount by which the relative permittivity differs from unity. **4b** Also called: **magnetic susceptibility.** (of a magnetic medium) the amount by which the relative permeability differs from unity.

susceptible ❶ (səˈsɛptəbᵊl) *adj* **1** (*postpositive;* foll. by *of* or *to*) yielding readily (to); capable (of): *hypotheses susceptible of refutation; susceptible to control.* **2** (*postpositive;* foll. by *to*) liable to be afflicted (by): *susceptible to colds.* **3** easily impressed emotionally. [C17: from LL *susceptibilis*, from L *suscipere* to take up]
▸**susˈceptibly** *adv*

sushi (ˈsuːʃɪ) *n* a Japanese dish consisting of small cakes of cold rice with a topping, esp. of raw fish. [Japanese]

suslik (ˈsʌslɪk) *or* **souslik** *n* a central Eurasian ground squirrel having large eyes and small ears. [from Russian]

suspect ❶ *vb* (səˈspɛkt). **1** (*tr*) to believe guilty of a specified offence without proof. **2** (*tr*) to think false, questionable, etc.: *she suspected his sincerity.* **3** (*tr; may take a clause as object*) to surmise to be the case; think probable: *to suspect fraud.* **4** (*intr*) to have suspicion. ◆ *n* (ˈsʌspɛkt). **5** a person under suspicion. ◆ *adj* (ˈsʌspɛkt). **6** causing or open to suspicion. [C14: from L *suspicere* to mistrust, from SUB- + *specere* to look]

suspend ❶ (səˈspɛnd) *vb* **1** (*tr*) to hang from above. **2** (*tr; passive*) to cause to remain floating or hanging: *a cloud of smoke was suspended over the town.* **3** (*tr*) to render inoperative or cause to cease, esp. temporarily. **4** (*tr*) to hold in abeyance; postpone action on. **5** (*tr*) to debar temporarily from privilege, office, etc., as a punishment. **6** (*tr*) *Chem.* to cause (particles) to be held in suspension in a fluid. **7** (*tr*) *Music.* to continue (a note) until the next chord is sounded, with which it usually forms a dissonance. See **suspension** (sense 11). **8** (*intr*) to cease payment, as from incapacity to meet financial obligations. [C13: from L *suspendere* from SUB- + *pendere* to hang]
▸**susˈpendible** *or* **susˈpensible** *adj* ▸**susˌpendiˈbility** *n*

suspended animation *n* a temporary cessation of the vital functions, as by freezing an organism.

suspended sentence *n* a sentence of imprisonment that is not served by an offender unless he commits a further offence during its currency.

suspender (səˈspɛndə) *n* **1** (*often pl*) *Brit.* **1a** an elastic strap attached to a belt or corset having a fastener at the end, for holding up women's stockings. **1b** a similar fastener attached to a garter worn by men in order to support socks. **2** (*pl*) the US and Canad. name for **braces. 3** a person or thing that suspends, such as one of the vertical cables in a suspension bridge.

suspender belt *n* a belt with suspenders hanging from it to hold up women's stockings.

suspense ❶ (səˈspɛns) *n* **1** the condition of being insecure or uncertain. **2** mental uncertainty; anxiety: *their father's illness kept them in a state of suspense.* **3** excitement felt at the approach of the climax: *a play of terrifying suspense.* **4** the condition of being suspended. [C15: from Med. L *suspensum* delay, from L *suspendere* to hang up]
▸**susˈpenseful** *adj*

suspense account *n Book-keeping.* an account in which entries are made until determination of their proper disposition.

suspension ❶ (səˈspɛnʃən) *n* **1** an interruption or temporary revocation: *the suspension of a law.* **2** a temporary debarment, as from position, privilege, etc. **3** a deferment, esp. of a decision, judgment, etc. **4** *Law.* a postponement of execution of a sentence or the deferring of a judgment, etc. **5** cessation of payment of business debts, esp. as a result of insolvency. **6** the act of suspending or the state of being suspended. **7** a system of springs, shock absorbers, etc., that supports the body of a wheeled or tracked vehicle and insulates it from shocks transmitted by the wheels. **8** a device or structure, usually a wire or spring, that serves to suspend or support something, such as the pendulum of a clock. **9** *Chem.* a dispersion of fine solid or liquid particles in a fluid, the particles being supported by buoyancy. See also **colloid. 10** the process by which eroded particles of rock are transported in a river. **11** *Music.* one or more notes of a chord that are prolonged until a subsequent chord is sounded, usually to form a dissonance.

suspension bridge *n* a bridge suspended from cables or chains that hang between two towers and are anchored at both ends.

suspensive (səˈspɛnsɪv) *adj* **1** having the power of deferment; effecting suspension. **2** causing, characterized by, or relating to suspense.
▸**susˈpensively** *adv* ▸**susˈpensiveness** *n*

suspensory (səˈspɛnsərɪ) *n, pl* **suspensories. 1** Also called: **suspensor.** *Anat.* a ligament or muscle that holds a structure or part in position. **2** *Med.* a bandage, sling, etc., for supporting a dependent part. ◆ *adj* **3** suspending or supporting. **4** *Anat.* (of a ligament or muscle) supporting or holding a structure or part in position.

suspicion ❶ (səˈspɪʃən) *n* **1** the act or an instance of suspecting; belief without sure proof, esp. that something is wrong. **2** the feeling of mistrust of a person who suspects. **3** the state of being suspected: *to be shielded from suspicion.* **4** a slight trace. **5 above suspicion.** in such a position that no guilt may be thought or implied, esp. through having an unblemished reputation. **6 on suspicion.** as a suspect. **7 under suspicion.** regarded with distrust. [C14: from OF *sospeçon*, from L *suspīciō* distrust, from *suspicere;* see SUSPECT]
▸**susˈpicional** *adj*

suspicious ❶ (səˈspɪʃəs) *adj* **1** exciting or liable to excite suspicion;

THESAURUS

survive *vb* **1-3** = **remain alive**, be extant, endure, exist, fight for one's life, hold out, keep body and soul together (*inf.*), keep one's head above water, last, live, live on, outlast, outlive, pull through, subsist

susceptibility *n* **1, 2** = **vulnerability**, liability, predisposition, proneness, propensity, responsiveness, sensitivity, suggestibility, weakness

susceptible *adj* **1, 2** *usually with* **to** = **liable**, disposed, given, inclined, open, predisposed, prone, subject, vulnerable **3** = **impressionable**, alive to, easily moved, receptive, responsive, sensitive, suggestible, tender
Antonyms *adj* ≠ **liable:** immune, insusceptible, invulnerable, resistant, unaffected by ≠ **impressionable:** insensitive, unaffected by, unmoved by, unresponsive

suspect *vb* **2** = **distrust**, doubt, harbour suspicions about, have one's doubts about, mistrust, smell a rat (*inf.*) **3** = **believe**, conclude, conjecture, consider, fancy, feel, guess, have a sneaking suspicion, hazard a guess, speculate, suppose, surmise, think probable ◆ *adj* **6** = **dubious**, dodgy, doubtful, fishy (*inf.*), iffy (*inf.*), open to suspicion, questionable
Antonyms ≠ **distrust:** have faith in, think innocent, trust *vb* ≠ **believe:** accept, be certain, be confident of, believe, buy (*sl.*), know, swallow (*inf.*) ◆ *adj* ≠ **dubious:** above suspicion, innocent, reliable, straightforward, trustworthy, trusty

suspend *vb* **1** = **hang**, append, attach, dangle, swing **3-5** = **postpone**, adjourn, arrest, cease, cut short, debar, defer, delay, discontinue, hold off, interrupt, lay aside, pigeonhole, put in cold storage, put off, shelve, stay, withhold
Antonyms *vb* ≠ **postpone:** carry on, continue, re-establish, reinstate, restore, resume, return

suspense *n* **1, 2** = **uncertainty**, anticipation, anxiety, apprehension, doubt, expectancy, expectation, indecision, insecurity, irresolution, tension, wavering

suspenseful *adj* **3** = **thrilling**, cliffhanging, exciting, gripping, hair-raising, spine-chilling

suspension *n* **1-3** = **postponement**, abeyance, adjournment, break, breaking off, deferment, delay, disbarment, discontinuation, interruption, moratorium, remission, respite, stay

suspicion *n* **1** = **idea**, conjecture, guess, gut feeling (*inf.*), hunch, impression, notion, supposition, surmise **2** = **distrust**, bad vibes (*sl.*), chariness, doubt, dubiety, funny feeling (*inf.*), jealousy, lack of confidence, misgiving, mistrust, qualm, scepticism, wariness **4** = **trace**, glimmer, hint, shade, shadow, *soupçon*, strain, streak, suggestion, tinge, touch **5 above suspicion** = **blameless**, above reproach, honourable, like Caesar's wife, pure, sinless, unimpeachable, virtuous

suspicious *adj* **1** = **suspect**, dodgy (*Brit., Austral., & NZ inf.*), doubtful, dubious, fishy (*inf.*), funny, irregular, of doubtful honesty, open to doubt or misconstruction, queer, questionable, shady (*inf.*) **2** = **distrustful**, apprehensive, doubtful, jealous, leery (*sl.*), mistrustful, sceptical, suspecting, unbelieving, wary
Antonyms *adj* ≠ **suspect:** above board, beyond suspicion, not open to question, open, straight, straightforward, unquestionable, upright ≠ **dis-**

questionable. **2** disposed to suspect something wrong. **3** indicative or expressive of suspicion.
▸**sus'piciously** *adv* ▸**sus'piciousness** *n*

suss ❶ (sʌs) *Sl.* ◆ *vb* (*tr*) **1** (often foll. by *out*) to attempt to work out (a situation, person's character, etc.), esp. using one's intuition. **2** Also: **sus.** to become aware of; suspect (esp. in **suss it**). ◆ *n* **3** sharpness of mind; social astuteness. [C20: shortened from SUSPECT]

sustain ❶ (sə'steɪn) *vb* (*tr*) **1** to hold up under; withstand: *to sustain great provocation.* **2** to undergo (an injury, loss, etc.); suffer: *to sustain a broken arm.* **3** to maintain or prolong: *to sustain a discussion.* **4** to support physically from below. **5** to provide for or give support to, esp. by supplying necessities: *to sustain one's family.* **6** to keep up the vitality or courage of. **7** to uphold or affirm the justice or validity of: *to sustain a decision.* **8** to establish the truth of; confirm. ◆ *n* **9** *Music.* the prolongation of a note, by playing technique or electronics. [C13: via OF from L *sustinēre* to hold up]
▸**sus'tained** *adj* ▸**sustainedly** (sə'steɪnɪdlɪ) *adv* ▸**sus'tainer** *n* ▸**sus'taining** *adj* ▸**sus'tainment** *n*

sustainable (sə'steɪnəbᵊl) *adj* **1** capable of being sustained. **2** (of economic development, energy sources, etc.) capable of being maintained at a steady level without exhausting natural resources or causing severe ecological damage: *sustainable development.*

sustaining pedal *n Music.* a foot-operated lever on a piano that keeps the dampers raised from the strings when keys are released, allowing them to continue to vibrate.

sustenance ❶ ('sʌstənəns) *n* **1** means of sustaining health or life; nourishment. **2** means of maintenance; livelihood. **3** Also: **sustention** (sə'stenʃən). the act or process of sustaining or the quality of being sustained. [C13: from OF *sostenance,* from *sustenir* to SUSTAIN]

sustentation (ˌsʌsten'teɪʃən) *n* a less common word for **sustenance.** [C14: from L *sustentātio,* from *sustentāre,* frequentative of *sustinēre* to SUSTAIN]

susurrate ('sjuːsəˌreɪt) *vb* **susurrates, susurrating, susurrated.** (*intr*) *Literary.* to make a soft rustling sound; whisper; murmur. [C17: from L *susurrāre* to whisper]
▸ˌ**susur'ration** *or* **susurrus** (sjuː'sʌrəs) *n*

sutler ('sʌtlə) *n* (formerly) a merchant who accompanied an army in order to sell provisions to the soldiers. [C16: from obs. Du. *soeteler,* ult. from MHG *sudelen* to do dirty work]

sutra ('suːtrə) *n* **1** *Hinduism.* Sanskrit sayings or collections of sayings on Vedic doctrine dating from about 200 A.D. onwards. **2** (*modifier*) *Hinduism.* **2a** of or relating to the last of the Vedic literary periods, from about 500 to 100 B.C.: *the sutra period.* **2b** of or relating to the sutras or compilations of sutras of about 200 A.D. onwards. **3** *Buddhism.* collections of dialogues and discourses of classic Mahayana Buddhism dating from the 2nd to the 6th century A.D. [C19: from Sansk.: list of rules]

suttee (sʌ'tiː, 'sʌtiː) *n* **1** the former Hindu custom whereby a widow burnt herself to death on her husband's funeral pyre. **2** a widow performing this. [C18: from Sansk. *satī* virtuous woman, from *sat* good]
▸**sut'teeism** *n*

suture ('suːtʃə) *n* **1** *Surgery.* **1a** catgut, silk thread, or wire used to stitch together two bodily surfaces. **1b** the surgical seam formed after stitching. **2** *Anat.* a type of immovable joint, esp. between the bones of the skull (**cranial suture**). **3** a seam or joining, as in sewing. **4** *Zool.* a line of junction in a mollusc shell. ◆ *vb* **sutures, suturing, sutured. 5** (*tr*) *Surgery.* to join (the edges of a wound, etc.) by means of sutures. [C16: from L *sūtūra,* from *suere* to sew]
▸**'sutural** *adj*

suzerain ('suːzəˌreɪn) *n* **1a** a state or sovereign exercising some degree of dominion over a dependent state, usually controlling its foreign affairs. **1b** (*as modifier*): *a suzerain power.* **2a** a feudal overlord. **2b** (*as modifier*): *suzerain lord.* [C19: from F, from *sus* above (from L *sursum* turned upwards) + *-erain,* as in *souverain* sovereign]

suzerainty ('suːzərəntɪ) *n, pl* **suzerainties. 1** the position, power, or dignity of a suzerain. **2** the relationship between suzerain and subject.

sv *abbrev. for:* **1** sailing vessel. **2** side valve. **3** sub verbo *or* voce. [L: under the word *or* voice]

svelte ❶ (svelt, sfelt) *adj* attractively or gracefully slim; slender. [C19: from F, from It. *svelto,* from *svellere* to pull out, from L *ēvellere*]

Svengali (sven'gɑːlɪ) *n* a person who controls another's mind, usually with sinister intentions. [after a character in George Du Maurier's novel *Trilby* (1894)]

SW 1 *symbol for* southwest(ern). **2** *abbrev. for* short wave.

Sw. *abbrev. for:* **1** Sweden. **2** Swedish.

swab (swɒb) *n* **1** *Med.* **1a** a small piece of cotton, gauze, etc., for use in applying medication, cleansing a wound, or obtaining a specimen of a secretion, etc. **1b** the specimen so obtained. **2** a mop for cleaning floors, decks, etc. **3** a brush used to clean a firearm's bore. **4** *Sl.* an uncouth or worthless fellow. ◆ *vb* **swabs, swabbing, swabbed. 5** (*tr*) to clean or medicate with or as if with a swab. **6** (*tr;* foll. by *up*) to take up with a swab. [C16: prob. from MDu. *swabbe* mop]
▸**'swabber** *n*

swaddle ('swɒdᵊl) *vb* **swaddles, swaddling, swaddled.** (*tr*) **1** to wind a bandage round. **2** to wrap (a baby) in swaddling clothes. **3** to restrain as if by wrapping with bandages; smother. ◆ *n* **4** *Chiefly US.* swaddling clothes. [C15: from OE *swæthel* swaddling clothes]

swaddling clothes *pl n* **1** long strips of linen or other cloth formerly wrapped round a newly born baby. **2** restrictions or supervision imposed on the immature.

swaddy *or* **swaddie** ('swɒdɪ) *n Brit. sl., old-fashioned.* a soldier. [C19: from E dialect *swad* country bumpkin, soldier]

swag (swæg) *n* **1** *Sl.* property obtained by theft or other illicit means. **2** *Sl.* goods; valuables. **3** an ornamental festoon of fruit, flowers, or drapery or a representation of this. **4** a swaying movement; lurch. **5** *Austral. & NZ inf.* a swagman's pack containing personal belongings, etc. **6 swags of.** *Austral. & NZ inf.* lots of. ◆ *vb* **swags, swagging, swagged. 7** *Chiefly Brit.* to lurch or sag or cause to lurch or sag. **8** (*tr*) to adorn or arrange with swags. [C17: ? of Scand. origin]

swage (sweɪdʒ) *n* **1** a shaped tool or die used in forming cold metal by hammering, pressing, etc. ◆ *vb* **swages, swaging, swaged. 2** (*tr*) to form (metal) with a swage. [C19: from F *souage,* from ?]
▸**'swager** *n*

swage block *n* an iron block with holes, grooves, etc., to assist in the cold-working of metal.

swagger ❶ ('swægə) *vb* **1** (*intr*) to walk or behave in an arrogant manner. **2** (*intr;* often foll. by *about*) to brag loudly. ◆ *n* **3** an arrogant gait or manner. ◆ *adj* **4** *Brit. inf., rare.* elegantly fashionable. [C16: prob. from SWAG]
▸**'swaggerer** *n* ▸**'swaggering** *adj* ▸**'swaggeringly** *adv*

swagger stick *or esp. Brit.* **swagger cane** *n* a short cane or stick carried on occasion mainly by army officers.

swaggie ('swægɪ) *n Austral. sl.* short for **swagman.**

swagman ('swægˌmæn, -mən) *n, pl* **swagmen.** *Austral. & NZ inf.* a tramp or vagrant worker who carries his possessions on his back. Also called: **swaggie.**

Swahili (swɑː'hiːlɪ) *n* **1** a language of E Africa that is an official language of Kenya and Tanzania and is widely used as a lingua franca throughout E and central Africa. Also called: **Kiswahili. 2** (*pl* **Swahilis** *or* **Swahili**) a member of a people speaking this language, living chiefly in Zanzibar. Also called: **Mswahili** (*pl* **Waswahili**). ◆ *adj* **3** of or relating to the Swahilis or their language. [C19: from Ar. *sawāhil* coasts]
▸**Swa'hilian** *adj*

swain (sweɪn) *n Arch. or poetic.* **1** a male lover or admirer. **2** a country youth. [OE *swān* swineherd]

swallow[1] ❶ ('swɒləʊ) *vb* (*mainly tr*) **1** to pass (food, drink, etc.) through the mouth to the stomach by means of the muscular action of the oesophagus. **2** (often foll. by *up*) to engulf or destroy as if by ingestion. **3** *Inf.* to believe gullibly: *he will never swallow such an excuse.* **4** to refrain from uttering or manifesting: *to swallow one's disappointment.* **5** to endure without retaliation. **6** to enunciate (words, etc.) indistinctly; mutter. **7** (often foll. by *down*) to eat or drink reluctantly. **8** (*intr*) to perform or simulate the act of swallowing, as in gulping. ◆ *n* **9** the act of swallowing. **10** the amount swallowed at any single time; mouthful. **11** *Rare.* another word for **throat** or **gullet.** [OE *swelgan*]
▸**'swallowable** *adj* ▸**'swallower** *n*

swallow[2] ('swɒləʊ) *n* any of various passerine songbirds having long pointed wings, a forked tail, short legs, and a rapid flight. [OE *swealwe*]

swallow dive *n* a type of dive in which the diver arches back while in the air, keeping his legs straight and together and his arms outstretched, finally entering the water headfirst. US and Canad. equivalent: **swan dive.**

swallow hole *n Chiefly Brit.* another word for **sinkhole** (sense 1).

swallowtail ('swɒləʊˌteɪl) *n* **1** any of various butterflies of Europe, having a tail-like extension of each hind wing. **2** the forked tail of a swallow or similar bird. **3** short for **swallow-tailed coat.**
▸**'swallow-ˌtailed** *adj*

swallow-tailed coat *n* another name for **tail coat.**

THESAURUS

trustful: believing, credulous, gullible, trustful, trusting, unsuspecting, unsuspicious

suss *vb* **1** *often foll. by* **out** *Brit. & NZ slang* = **work out**, calculate, clear up, figure out, find out, puzzle out, resolve, solve

sustain *vb* **1, 2** = **suffer**, bear, bear up under, endure, experience, feel, undergo, withstand **3** = **maintain**, continue, keep alive, keep going, keep up, prolong, protract **4** = **support**, bear, carry, keep from falling, keep up, uphold **5** = **keep alive**, aid, assist, comfort, foster, help, nourish, nurture, provide for, relieve **7, 8** = **uphold**, approve, confirm, endorse, ratify, validate, verify

sustained *adj* **3** = **continuous**, constant, nonstop, perpetual, prolonged, steady, unremitting
Antonyms *adj* broken, discontinuous, intermittent, irregular, periodic, spasmodic, sporadic

sustenance *n* **1** = **nourishment**, aliment, comestibles, daily bread, eatables, edibles, food, provender, provisions, rations, refection, refreshments, victuals **2** = **livelihood**, maintenance, subsistence, support

svelte *adj* = **slender**, graceful, lissom(e), lithe, slinky, sylphlike, willowy

swagger *vb* **1, 2** = **show off** (*inf.*), bluster, boast, brag, bully, gasconade (*rare*), hector, hot-dog (*chiefly US*), parade, prance, strut, swank (*inf.*) ◆ *n* **3** = **ostentation**, arrogance, bluster, braggadocio, display, gasconade (*rare*), pomposity, show, showing off (*inf.*), swank (*inf.*), swashbuckling

swallow[1] *vb* **1** = **gulp**, absorb, consume, devour, down (*inf.*), drink, eat, ingest, swig (*inf.*), swill, wash down **2** *often foll. by* **up** = **absorb**, assimilate, consume, engulf, envelop, overrun, overwhelm, use up **3** *Informal* = **believe**, accept, buy (*sl.*), fall for, take (something) as gospel **4** = **hold in**, choke back, repress

swam (swæm) *vb* the past tense of **swim.**

swami (ˈswɑːmɪ) *n, pl* **swamies** *or* **swamis.** (in India) a title of respect for a Hindu saint or religious teacher. [C18: from Hindi *svāmī*, from Sansk. *svāmin* master, from *sva* one's own]

swamp ❶ (swɒmp) *n* **1** permanently waterlogged ground that is usually overgrown and sometimes partly forested. Cf. **marsh.** ◆ *vb* **2** to drench or submerge or be drenched or submerged. **3** *Naut.* to cause (a boat) to sink or fill with water or (of a boat) to sink or fill with water. **4** to overburden or overwhelm or be overburdened or overwhelmed, as by excess work or great numbers. **5** (*tr*) to render helpless. [C17: prob. from MDu. *somp*]
▸ˈ**swampy** *adj*

swamp boat *n* a shallow-draught boat powered by an aeroplane engine mounted on a raised structure for use in swamps. Also called: **airboat.**

swamp cypress *n* a North American deciduous coniferous tree that grows in swamps. Also called: **bald cypress.**

swamp fever *n* **1** Also called: **equine infectious anaemia.** a viral disease of horses. **2** *US.* another name for **malaria.**

swampland (ˈswɒmpˌlænd) *n* a permanently waterlogged area; marshland.

swan (swɒn) *n* **1** any of various large aquatic birds having a long neck and usually a white plumage. **2** *Rare, literary.* **2a** a poet. **2b** (*cap. when part of a title or epithet*): *the Swan of Avon* (Shakespeare). ◆ *vb* **swans, swanning, swanned. 3** (*intr; usually foll. by around or about*) *Inf.* to wander idly. [OE]
▸ˈ**swanˌlike** *adj*

swan dive *n* the US and Canad. name for **swallow dive.**

swank ❶ (swæŋk) *Inf.* ◆ *vb* **1** (*intr*) to show off or swagger. ◆ *n* **2** Also called: **swankpot.** *Brit.* a swaggering or conceited person. **3** *Chiefly US.* showy elegance or style. **4** swagger; ostentation. ◆ *adj* **5** another word (esp. US) for **swanky.** [C19: ?from MHG *swanken* to sway]

swanky ❶ (ˈswæŋkɪ) *adj* **swankier, swankiest.** *Inf.* **1** expensive and showy; stylish: *a swanky hotel.* **2** boastful or conceited.
▸ˈ**swankily** *adv* ▸ˈ**swankiness** *n*

swan neck *n* a tube, rail, etc., curved like a swan's neck.

swannery (ˈswɒnərɪ) *n, pl* **swanneries.** a place where swans are kept and bred.

swan's-down *n* **1** the fine soft down feathers of a swan, used to trim powder puffs, clothes, etc. **2** a thick soft fabric of wool with silk, cotton, or rayon, used for infants' clothing, etc. **3** a cotton fabric with a heavy nap.

swan song *n* **1** the last act, publication, etc., of a person before retirement or death. **2** the song that a dying swan is said to sing.

swan-upping *n Brit.* **1** the practice or action of marking nicks in swans' beaks as a sign of ownership. **2** the annual swan-upping of royal cygnets on the River Thames.

swap ❶ *or* **swop** (swɒp) *vb* **swaps, swapping, swapped** *or* **swops, swopping, swopped. 1** to trade or exchange (something or someone) for another. ◆ *n* **2** an exchange. **3** something that is exchanged. **4** *Finance.* Also called: **swap option, swaption.** a contract in which the parties to it exchange liabilities on outstanding debts, often exchanging fixed-interest-rate for floating-rate debts (**debt swap**), either as a means of debt management or in trading (**swap trading**). [C14 (in the sense: to shake hands on a bargain, strike): prob. imit.]
▸ˈ**swapper** *or* ˈ**swopper** *n*

SWAPO *or* **Swapo** (ˈswɑːpəʊ) *n acronym for* South-West Africa People's Organization.

swaption (ˈswɒpʃən) *n* another name for **swap** (sense 4).

swaraj (swəˈrɑːdʒ) *n* (in British India) self-government; independence. [C20: from Sansk. *svarāj*, from *sva* self + *rājya* rule]
▸**swaˈrajism** *n* ▸**swaˈrajist** *n, adj*

sward (swɔːd) *n* **1** turf or grass or a stretch of turf or grass. ◆ *vb* **2** to cover or become covered with grass. [OE *sweard* skin]

swarf (swɔːf, swɑːf) *n* material removed by cutting or grinding tools in the machining of metals, stone, etc. [C16: of Scand. origin]

swarm[1] ❶ (swɔːm) *n* **1** a group of bees, led by a queen, that has left the parent hive to start a new colony. **2** a large mass of small animals, esp. insects. **3** a throng or mass, esp. when moving or in turmoil. ◆ *vb* **4** (*intr*) (of small animals, esp. bees) to move in or form a swarm. **5** (*intr*) to congregate, move about or proceed in large numbers. **6** (when *intr*, often foll. by *with*) to overrun or be overrun (with): *swarming with rats.* **7** (*tr*) to cause to swarm. [OE *swearm*]

swarm[2] (swɔːm) *vb* (when *intr*, usually foll. by *up*) to climb (a ladder, etc.) by gripping with the hands and feet: *the boys swarmed up the rigging.* [C16: from ?]

swart (swɔːt) *or* **swarth** (swɔːθ) *adj Arch. or dialect.* swarthy. [OE *sweart*]

swarthy ❶ (ˈswɔːðɪ) *adj* **swarthier, swarthiest.** dark-hued or dark-complexioned. [C16: from obs. *swarty*]
▸ˈ**swarthily** *adv* ▸ˈ**swarthiness** *n*

swash (swɒʃ) *vb* **1** (*intr*) (esp. of water or things in water) to wash or move with noisy splashing. **2** (*tr*) to dash (a liquid, esp. water) against or upon. **3** (*intr*) *Arch.* to swagger. ◆ *n* **4** Also called: **send.** the dashing movement or sound of water, as of waves on a beach. **5** Also called: **swash channel.** a channel of moving water cutting through or running behind a sandbank. **6** *Arch.* swagger or bluster. [C16: prob. imit.]

swashbuckler ❶ (ˈswɒʃˌbʌklə) *n* **1** a swaggering or flamboyant adventurer. **2** a film, book, play, etc., depicting excitement and adventure, esp. in a historical setting. [C16: from SWASH (in archaic sense: to make the noise of a sword striking a shield) + BUCKLER]
▸ˈ**swashˌbuckling** *adj*

swash letter *n Printing.* a decorative letter, esp. an ornamental italic capital. [C17: from *aswash* aslant]

swastika ❶ (ˈswɒstɪkə) *n* **1** a primitive religious symbol or ornament in the shape of a Greek cross, usually having the ends of the arms bent at right angles. **2** this symbol with clockwise arms, the emblem of Nazi Germany. [C19: from Sansk. *svastika*, from *svasti* prosperity; from belief that it brings good luck]

swat (swɒt) *vb* **swats, swatting, swatted.** (*tr*) **1** to strike or hit sharply: *to swat a fly.* ◆ *n* **2** a sharp or violent blow. ◆ Also: **swot.** [C17: N English dialect & US var. of SQUAT]
▸ˈ**swatter** *n*

swatch (swɒtʃ) *n* **1** a sample of cloth or other material. **2** a number of such samples, usually fastened together in book form. [C16: Scot. & N English, from ?]

swath (swɔːθ) *or* **swathe** (sweɪð) *n, pl* **swaths** (swɔːðz) *or* **swathes. 1** the width of one sweep of a scythe or of the blade of a mowing machine. **2** the strip cut by these in one course. **3** the quantity of cut grass, hay, etc., left in one such course. **4** a long narrow strip or belt. [OE *swæth*]

swathe ❶ (sweɪð) *vb* **swathes, swathing, swathed.** (*tr*) **1** to bandage (a wound, limb, etc.), esp. completely. **2** to wrap a band, garment, etc., around, esp. so as to cover completely; swaddle. **3** to envelop. ◆ *n* **4** a bandage or wrapping. **5** a variant spelling of **swath.** [OE *swathian*]

sway ❶ (sweɪ) *vb* **1** (*usually intr*) to swing or cause to swing to and fro: *the door swayed in the wind.* **2** (*usually intr*) to lean or incline or cause to lean or incline to one side or in different directions in turn. **3** (*usually intr*) to vacillate or cause to vacillate between two or more opinions. **4** to be influenced or swerve or influence or cause to swerve to or from a purpose or opinion. **5** *Arch. or poetic.* to rule or wield power (over). ◆ *n* **6** control; power. **7** a swinging or leaning movement. **8** *Arch.* dominion; governing authority. **9 hold sway.** to be master; reign. [C16: prob. from ON *sveigja* to bend]

sway-back *n* an abnormal sagging or concavity of the spine in horses. ▸ˈ**sway-ˌbacked** *adj*

swear ❶ (swɛə) *vb* **swears, swearing, swore, sworn. 1** to declare or affirm (a statement) as true, esp. by invoking a deity, etc., as witness. **2** (foll. by *by*) **2a** to invoke (a deity, etc.) by name as a witness or guarantee to an oath. **2b** to trust implicitly; have complete confidence (in). **3** (*intr*; often foll. by *at*) to curse, blaspheme, or use swearwords. **4** (when *tr*, *may take a clause as object or an infinitive*) to promise solemnly on oath; vow. **5** (*tr*) to assert or affirm with great emphasis or earnestness. **6**

THESAURUS

swamp *n* **1** = **bog**, everglade(s) (*US*), fen, marsh, mire, morass, moss (*Scot. & N English dialect*), quagmire, slough ◆ *vb* **3** *Nautical* = **flood**, capsize, drench, engulf, inundate, overwhelm, sink, submerge, swallow up, upset, wash over, waterlog **4** = **overwhelm**, beset, besiege, deluge, engulf, flood, inundate, overload, snow under, submerge

swampy *adj* **1** = **boggy**, fenny, marish (*obs.*), marshy, miry, quaggy, waterlogged, wet

swank *Informal* ◆ *vb* **1** = **show off** (*inf.*), give oneself airs, hot-dog (*chiefly US*), posture, put on side (*Brit. sl.*), swagger ◆ *n* **2** = **show-off** (*inf.*), attitudinizer, braggadocio, hot dog (*chiefly US*), poser, poseur, swankpot (*inf.*), swashbuckler **4** = **boastfulness**, display, ostentation, show, swagger, vainglory

swanky *adj* **1** *Informal* = **ostentatious**, de luxe, exclusive, expensive, fancy, fashionable, flash, flashy, glamorous, glitzy (*sl.*), gorgeous, grand, lavish, luxurious, plush (*inf.*), posh (*inf., chiefly Brit.*), rich, ritzy (*sl.*), showy, smart, stylish, sumptuous, swish (*inf., chiefly Brit.*)
Antonyms *adj* discreet, humble, inconspicuous, low-key, low-profile, modest, subdued, unassuming, unostentatious, unpretentious

swap *vb* **1** = **exchange**, bandy, barter, interchange, switch, trade, traffic

swarm[1] *n* **3** = **multitude**, army, bevy, concourse, crowd, drove, flock, herd, horde, host, mass, myriad, shoal, throng ◆ *vb* **5** = **crowd**, congregate, flock, mass, stream, throng **6** = **teem**, abound, be alive, be infested, be overrun, bristle, crawl

swarthy *adj* = **dark-skinned**, black, brown, dark, dark-complexioned, dusky, swart (*arch.*), tawny

swashbuckling *adj* **1** = **dashing**, bold, daredevil, flamboyant, gallant, mettlesome, roisterous, spirited, swaggering

swastika *n* **1** = **crooked cross**, fylfot

swathe *vb* **1-3** = **wrap**, bandage, bind, bundle up, cloak, drape, envelop, enwrap, fold, furl, lap, muffle up, sheathe, shroud, swaddle

sway *vb* **1** = **bend**, fluctuate, incline, lean, lurch, oscillate, rock, roll, swing, wave **4** = **influence**, affect, control, direct, dominate, govern, guide, induce, persuade, prevail on, win over ◆ *n* **6** = **power**, ascendency, authority, clout (*inf.*), command, control, dominion, government, influence, jurisdiction, predominance, rule, sovereignty **9 hold sway** = **prevail**, predominate, reign, rule, run

swear *vb* **2b** *with* **by** = **trust**, depend on, have confidence in, rely on **3** = **curse**, be foul-mouthed, blaspheme, cuss (*inf.*), imprecate, take the Lord's name in vain, turn the air blue (*inf.*), utter profanities **4** = **vow**, attest, avow, depose, give one's word, pledge oneself, promise, state under oath, take an oath, testify, warrant **5** = **declare**, affirm, assert, asseverate, swear blind

(*intr*) to give evidence or make any statement or solemn declaration on oath. **7** to take an oath in order to add force or solemnity to (a statement or declaration). ◆ *n* **8** a period of swearing. [OE *swerian*]
▸**'swearer** *n*

swear in *vb* (*tr, adv*) to administer an oath to (a person) on his assuming office, entering the witness box to give evidence, etc.

swear off *vb* (*intr, prep*) to promise to abstain from something: *to swear off drink.*

swearword ❶ ('swɛə,wɜ:d) *n* a socially taboo word of a profane, obscene, or insulting character.

sweat ❶ (swɛt) *n* **1** the secretion from the sweat glands, esp. when profuse and visible, as during strenuous activity, from excessive heat, etc.; perspiration. **2** the act or process of secreting this fluid. **3** the act of inducing the exudation of moisture. **4** drops of moisture given forth or gathered on the surface of something. **5** *Inf.* a state or condition of worry or eagerness (esp. in **in a sweat**). **6** *Sl.* drudgery or hard labour: *mowing lawns is a real sweat!* **7** *Sl., chiefly Brit.* a soldier, esp. one who is old and experienced. **8 no sweat!** *Sl.* an expression conveying consent or assurance. ◆ *vb* **sweats, sweating, sweat** *or* **sweated. 9** to secrete (sweat) through the pores of the skin, esp. profusely; perspire. **10** (*tr*) to make wet or stain with perspiration. **11** to give forth or cause to give forth (moisture) in droplets: *the maple sweats sap.* **12** (*intr*) to collect and condense moisture on an outer surface: *a glass of beer sweating.* **13** (*intr*) (of a liquid) to pass through a porous surface in droplets. **14** (of tobacco leaves, hay, etc.) to exude moisture and, sometimes, begin to ferment or to cause (tobacco leaves, etc.) to exude moisture. **15** (*tr*) to heat (food, esp. vegetables) slowly in butter in a tightly closed saucepan. **16** (*tr*) to join (pieces of metal) by pressing together and heating. **17** (*tr*) to heat (solder) until it melts. **18** (*tr*) to heat (partially fused metal) to extract an easily fusible constituent. **19** *Inf.* to suffer anxiety, impatience, or distress. **20** *Inf.* to overwork or be overworked. **21** (*tr*) *Inf.* to employ at very low wages and under bad conditions. **22** (*tr*) *Inf.* to extort, esp. by torture: *to sweat information out of a captive.* **23** (*intr*) *Inf.* to suffer punishment: *you'll sweat for this!* **24 sweat blood.** *Inf.* **24a** to work very hard. **24b** to be filled with anxiety or impatience. ◆ See also **sweat off, sweat out, sweats.** [OE *swǣtan* to sweat, from *swāt* sweat]

sweatband ('swɛt,bænd) *n* **1** a band of material set in a hat or cap to protect it from sweat. **2** a piece of cloth tied around the forehead to keep sweat out of the eyes or around the wrist to keep the hands dry, as in sports.

sweated ('swɛtɪd) *adj* **1** made by exploited labour: *sweated goods.* **2** (of workers, etc.) forced to work in poor conditions for low pay.

sweater ('swɛtə) *n* **1** a garment made of knitted or crocheted material covering the upper part of the body, esp. a heavy one worn for warmth. **2** a person or thing that sweats. **3** an employer who overworks and underpays his employees.

sweat gland *n* any of the coiled tubular subcutaneous glands that secrete sweat.

sweating sickness *n* an acute infectious febrile disease that was widespread in Europe during the late 15th century, characterized by profuse sweating.

sweat off *or* **away** *vb* (*tr, adv*) *Inf.* to get rid of (weight) by strenuous exercise or sweating.

sweat out ❶ *vb* (*tr, adv*) **1** to cure or lessen the effects of (a cold, respiratory infection, etc.) by sweating. **2** *Inf.* to endure (hardships) for a time (often in **sweat it out**). **3 sweat one's guts out.** *Inf.* to work extremely hard.

sweats (swɛts) *pl n* sweatshirts and sweat-suit trousers: *jeans and sweats.*

sweatshirt ('swɛt,ʃɜ:t) *n* a long-sleeved knitted cotton sweater worn by athletes, etc.

sweatshop ('swɛt,ʃɒp) *n* a workshop where employees work long hours under bad conditions for low wages.

sweat suit *n* a suit worn by athletes for training comprising knitted cotton trousers and a light cotton sweater.

sweaty ❶ ('swɛtɪ) *adj* **sweatier, sweatiest. 1** covered with perspiration; sweating. **2** smelling of or like sweat. **3** causing sweat.
▸**'sweatily** *adv* ▸**'sweatiness** *n*

swede (swi:d) *n* **1** a Eurasian plant cultivated for its bulbous edible root, which is used as a vegetable and as cattle fodder. **2** the root of this plant. ◆ Also called: **Swedish turnip.** [C19: so called after being introduced into Scotland from Sweden in the 18th century]

Swede (swi:d) *n* a native, citizen, or inhabitant of Sweden, a kingdom in NW Europe.

Swedish ('swi:dɪʃ) *adj* **1** of, relating to, or characteristic of Sweden, its people, or their language. ◆ *n* **2** the official language of Sweden.

sweep ❶ (swi:p) *vb* **sweeps, sweeping, swept. 1** to clean or clear (a space, chimney, etc.) with a brush, broom, etc. **2** (often foll. by *up*) to remove or collect (dirt, rubbish, etc.) with a brush, broom, etc. **3** to move in a smooth or continuous manner, esp. quickly or forcibly: *cars swept along the road.* **4** to move in a proud or dignified fashion: *she swept past.* **5** to spread or pass rapidly across, through, or along (a region, area, etc.): *the news swept through the town.* **6** (*tr*) to direct (the gaze, line of fire, etc.) over; survey. **7** (*tr;* foll. by *away* or *off*) to overwhelm emotionally: *she was swept away by his charm.* **8** to brush or lightly touch (a surface, etc.): *the dress swept along the ground.* **9** (*tr;* often foll. by *away*) to convey, clear, or abolish, esp. with strong or continuous movements: *the sea swept the sandcastle away; secondary modern schools were swept away.* **10** (*intr*) to extend gracefully or majestically, esp. in a wide circle: *the plains sweep down to the sea.* **11** to search (a body of water) for mines, etc., by dragging. **12** (*tr*) to win overwhelmingly, esp. in an election: *Labour swept the country.* **13** (*tr*) to propel (a boat) with sweeps. **14 sweep the board. 14a** (in gambling) to win all the cards or money. **14b** to win every event or prize in a contest. **15 sweep (something) under the carpet.** to conceal (something, esp. a problem) in the hope that it will be overlooked by others. ◆ *n* **16** the act or an instance of sweeping; removal by or as if by a brush or broom. **17** a swift or steady movement, esp. in an arc. **18** the distance, arc, etc., through which something, such as a pendulum, moves. **19** a wide expanse or scope: *the sweep of the plains.* **20** any curving line or contour. **21** short for **sweepstake. 22a** a long oar used on an open boat. **22b** *Austral.* a person steering a surf boat with such an oar at the stern. **23** any of the sails of a windmill. **24** *Electronics.* a steady horizontal or circular movement of an electron beam across or around the fluorescent screen of a cathode-ray tube. **25** a curving driveway. **26** *Chiefly Brit.* See **chimney sweep. 27** another name for **swipe** (sense 6). **28 clean sweep. 28a** an overwhelming victory or success. **28b** a complete change; purge: *to make a clean sweep.* [C13 *swepen*]
▸**'sweepy** *adj*

sweeper ('swi:pə) *n* **1** a person employed to sweep, such as a roadsweeper. **2** any device for sweeping: *a carpet sweeper.* **3** *Inf., soccer.* a player who supports the main defenders, as by intercepting loose balls, etc.

sweep hand *n Horology.* a long hand that registers seconds or fractions of seconds on the perimeter of the dial.

sweeping ❶ ('swi:pɪŋ) *adj* **1** comprehensive and wide-ranging: *sweeping reforms.* **2** indiscriminate or without reservations: *sweeping statements.* **3** decisive or overwhelming: *a sweeping victory.* **4** taking in a wide area: *a sweeping glance.* **5** driving steadily onwards, esp. over a large area: *a sweeping attack.*
▸**'sweepingly** *adv* ▸**'sweepingness** *n*

sweep-saw *n* a saw with a thin blade that can be used for cutting curved shapes.

sweepstake ('swi:p,steɪk) *or esp. US* **sweepstakes** *n* **1a** a lottery in which the stakes of the participants constitute the prize. **1b** the prize itself. **2** any event involving such a lottery, esp. a horse race. ◆ Often shortened to **sweep.** [C15: orig. referring to someone who *sweeps* or takes all the stakes in a game]

sweet ❶ (swi:t) *adj* **1** having or denoting a pleasant taste like that of sugar. **2** agreeable to the senses or the mind: *sweet music.* **3** having pleasant manners; gentle: *a sweet child.* **4** (of wine, etc.) having a relatively high sugar content; not dry. **5** (of foods) not decaying or rancid: *sweet milk.* **6** not salty: *sweet water.* **7** free from unpleasant odours: *sweet air.* **8** containing no corrosive substances: *sweet soil.* **9** (of petrol) containing no sulphur compounds. **10** sentimental or unrealistic. **11** *Jazz.* performed with a regular beat, with the emphasis on clearly outlined melody and little improvisation. **12** *Arch.* respected; dear (used in polite forms of address): *sweet sir.* **13** smooth and precise; perfectly executed: *a sweet shot.* **14 at one's own sweet will.** as it suits oneself alone. **15 keep (someone) sweet.** to ingratiate oneself in order to ensure cooperation. **16 sweet on.** fond of or infatuated with. ◆ *adv* **17** *Inf.* in a sweet manner. ◆ *n* **18** a sweet taste or smell; sweetness in general. **19** (*often pl*) *Brit.* any of numerous kinds of confectionery consisting

THESAURUS

swearword *n* = **oath**, curse, cuss (*inf.*), expletive, four-letter word, obscenity, profanity

sweat *n* **1** = **perspiration**, diaphoresis (*Medical*), exudation, sudor (*Medical*) **5** *Informal* = **worry**, agitation, anxiety, distress, flap, panic, strain **6** *Slang* = **labour**, backbreaking task, chore, drudgery, effort, toil ◆ *vb* **9** = **perspire**, break out in a sweat, exude moisture, glow **19** *Informal* = **worry**, agonize, be on pins and needles (*inf.*), be on tenterhooks, chafe, fret, lose sleep over, suffer, torture oneself

sweat out *vb* **2** *Informal, as in* **sweat it out** = **endure**, see (something) through, stay the course, stick it out (*inf.*)

sweaty *adj* **1** = **perspiring**, bathed *or* drenched *or* soaked in perspiration, clammy, glowing, sticky, sweating

sweep *vb* **1, 2** = **clear**, brush, clean, remove **3, 4** = **sail**, flounce, fly, glide, hurtle, pass, scud, skim, tear, zoom ◆ *n* **17** = **arc**, bend, curve, gesture, move, movement, stroke, swing **18, 19** = **extent**, compass, range, scope, span, stretch, vista **21** = **lottery**, draw, raffle, sweepstake

sweeping *adj* **1** = **wide-ranging**, all-embracing, all-inclusive, broad, comprehensive, extensive, global, overarching, radical, thoroughgoing, wide **2** = **indiscriminate**, across-the-board, blanket, exaggerated, overdrawn, overstated, unqualified, wholesale
Antonyms *adj* ≠ **wide-ranging:** constrained, limited, minor, modest, narrow, restricted, token, unimportant

sweet *adj* **1** = **sugary**, cloying, honeyed, luscious, melting, saccharine, sweetened, syrupy, toothsome, treacly **2** = **delightful**, appealing, attractive, beautiful, cute, engaging, fair, likable *or* likeable, lovable, taking, winning, winsome **2** = **melodious**, dulcet, euphonic, euphonious, harmonious, mellow, musical, silver-toned, silvery, soft, sweet-sounding, tuneful **3** = **charming**, affectionate, agreeable, amiable, gentle, kind, sweet-tempered, tender, unselfish **7** = **fragrant**, aromatic, balmy, clean, fresh, new, perfumed, pure, redolent, sweet-smelling, wholesome **12** = **beloved**, cherished, darling, dear, dearest, pet, precious, treasured **16 sweet on** = **in love with**, enamoured of, fond of, gone on (*sl.*), head over heels in love with, infatuated with, keen on, obsessed *or* bewitched by, taken

wholly or partly of sugar, esp. of sugar boiled and crystallized (**boiled sweets**). **20** *Brit.* any sweet dish served as a dessert. **21** dear; sweetheart (used as a form of address). **22** anything that is sweet. **23** (*often pl*) a pleasurable experience, state, etc.: *the sweets of success.* [OE *swēte*] ▸**'sweetish** *adj* ▸**'sweetly** *adv* ▸**'sweetness** *n*

sweet alyssum *n* a Mediterranean plant having clusters of small fragrant white or violet flowers. See also **alyssum.**

sweet-and-sour *adj* (of food) cooked in a sauce made from sugar and vinegar and other ingredients.

sweet bay *n* a small tree of SE North America, belonging to the magnolia family and having large fragrant white flowers. Sometimes shortened to **bay.**

sweetbread ('swiːtˌbrɛd) *n* the pancreas or the thymus gland of an animal, used for food. [C16: SWEET + BREAD, ? from OE *brǣd* meat]

sweetbrier ('swiːtˌbraɪə) *n* a Eurasian rose having a tall bristly stem, fragrant leaves, and single pink flowers. Also called: **eglantine.**

sweet cherry *n* either of two types of cherry tree that are cultivated for their edible sweet fruit.

sweet chestnut *n* See **chestnut** (sense 1).

sweet cicely ('sɪsəlɪ) *n* **1** Also called: **myrrh.** an aromatic European plant, having compound leaves and clusters of small white flowers. **2** the leaves, formerly used in cookery for their flavour of aniseed. **3** any of various related plants of Asia and America, having aromatic roots.

sweet corn *n* **1** a variety of maize whose kernels are rich in sugar and eaten as a vegetable when young. **2** the unripe ears of maize, esp. the sweet kernels removed from the cob, cooked as a vegetable.

sweeten ❶ ('swiːtᵊn) *vb* (*mainly tr*) **1** (*also intr*) to make or become sweet or sweeter. **2** to mollify or soften (a person). **3** to make more agreeable. **4** (*also intr*) *Chem.* to free or be freed from unpleasant odours, acidic or corrosive substances, or the like.

sweetener ('swiːtᵊnə) *n* **1** a sweetening agent, esp. one that does not contain sugar. **2** *Inf.* a bribe. **3** *Inf.* a financial inducement.

sweetening ('swiːtᵊnɪŋ) *n* something that sweetens.

sweet flag *n* an aroid marsh plant, having swordlike leaves, small greenish flowers, and aromatic roots. Also called: **calamus.**

sweet gale *n* a shrub of northern swamp regions, having yellow catkin-like flowers and aromatic leaves. Also called: **bog myrtle.** Often shortened to **gale.**

sweet gum *n* **1** a North American liquidambar tree, having prickly spherical fruit clusters and fragrant sap: the wood (called **satin walnut**) is used to make furniture. **2** the sap of this tree. ◆ Also called: **red gum.**

sweetheart ❶ ('swiːtˌhɑːt) *n* **1** a person loved by another. **2** *Inf.* a lovable, generous, or obliging person. **3** a term of endearment.

sweetheart agreement *n Austral. inf.* an industrial agreement on pay and conditions concluded without resort to arbitration.

sweetie ('swiːtɪ) *n Inf.* **1** sweetheart; darling: used as a term of endearment. **2** *Brit.* another word for **sweet** (sense 19). **3** *Chiefly Brit.* an endearing person. **4** a large seedless variety of grapefruit that has a green-to-yellow rind and juicy sweet pulp.

sweeting ('swiːtɪŋ) *n* **1** a variety of sweet apple. **2** an archaic word for **sweetheart.**

sweet marjoram *n* another name for **marjoram** (sense 1).

sweetmeat ('swiːtˌmiːt) *n* a sweetened delicacy, such as a preserve, sweet, or, formerly, a cake or pastry.

sweet pea *n* a climbing plant of S Europe, widely cultivated for its butterfly-shaped fragrant flowers of delicate pastel colours.

sweet pepper *n* **1** a pepper plant with large bell-shaped fruits that are eaten unripe (**green pepper**) or ripe (**red pepper**). **2** the fruit of this plant.

sweet potato *n* **1** a twining plant of tropical America, cultivated in the tropics for its edible fleshy yellow root. **2** the root of this plant.

sweet shop *n Chiefly Brit.* a shop solely or largely selling sweets, esp. boiled sweets.

sweetsop ('swiːtˌsɒp) *n* **1** a small West Indian tree, having yellowish-green fruit. **2** the fruit, which has a sweet edible pulp. ◆ Also called: **custard apple.**

sweet spot *n Sport.* the centre area of a racket, golf club, etc., from which the cleanest shots are made.

sweet-talk ❶ *Inf.* ◆ *vb* **1** to coax, flatter, or cajole (someone). ◆ *n* **sweet talk. 2** cajolery; coaxing.

sweet tooth *n* a strong liking for sweet foods.

sweetveld ('swiːtˌfɛlt) *n* (in South Africa) a type of grazing characterized by high-quality grass. [pron. from Afrik. *soetveld*]

sweet william ('wɪljəm) *n* a widely cultivated Eurasian plant with flat clusters of white, pink, red, or purple flowers.

swell ❶ (swɛl) *vb* **swells, swelling, swelled; swollen** *or* **swelled. 1** to grow or cause to grow in size, esp. as a result of internal pressure. **2** to expand or cause to expand at a particular point or above the surrounding level; protrude. **3** to grow or cause to grow in size, amount, intensity, or degree: *the party is swelling with new recruits.* **4** to puff or be puffed up with pride or another emotion. **5** (*intr*) (of seas or lakes) to rise in waves. **6** (*intr*) to well up or overflow. **7** (*tr*) to make (a musical phrase) increase gradually in volume and then diminish. ◆ *n* **8a** the undulating movement of the surface of the open sea. **8b** a succession of waves or a single large wave. **9** a swelling or being swollen; expansion. **10** an increase in quantity or degree; inflation. **11** a bulge; protuberance. **12** a gentle hill. **13** *Inf.* a person very fashionably dressed. **14** *Inf.* a man of high social or political standing. **15** *Music.* a crescendo followed by an immediate diminuendo. **16** Also called: **swell organ.** *Music.* **16a** a set of pipes on an organ housed in a box (**swell box**) fitted with a shutter operated by a pedal, which can be opened or closed to control the volume. **16b** the manual on an organ controlling this. ◆ *adj* **17** *Inf.* stylish or grand. **18** *Sl.* excellent; first-class. [OE *swellan*]

swelled head *or* **swollen head** *Inf.* ◆ *n* **1** an inflated view of one's own worth, often caused by sudden success. ◆ *adj* **swelled-headed, swell-headed,** *or* **swollen-headed. 2** conceited.

swelling ❶ ('swɛlɪŋ) *n* **1** the act of expansion or inflation. **2** the state of being or becoming swollen. **3** a swollen or inflated part or area. **4** an abnormal enlargement of a bodily structure or part, esp. as the result of injury. ◆ Related adj: **tumescent.**

swelter ('swɛltə) *vb* **1** (*intr*) to suffer under oppressive heat, esp. to perspire and feel faint. **2** (*tr*) *Rare.* to cause to suffer under oppressive heat. ◆ *n* **3** a sweltering condition (esp. in **in a swelter**). **4** oppressive humid heat. [C15 *swelten,* from OE *sweltan* to die]

sweltering ❶ ('swɛltərɪŋ) *adj* oppressively hot and humid: *a sweltering day.*
▸**'swelteringly** *adv*

swept (swɛpt) *vb* the past tense and past participle of **sweep.**

sweptback ('swɛptˌbæk) *adj* (of an aircraft wing) inclined backwards towards the rear of the fuselage.

sweptwing ('swɛptˌwɪŋ) *adj* (of an aircraft, etc.) having wings swept (usually) backwards.

swerve ❶ (swɜːv) *vb* **swerves, swerving, swerved. 1** to turn or cause to turn aside, usually sharply or suddenly, from a course. ◆ *n* **2** the act, instance, or degree of swerving. [OE *sweorfan* to scour] ▸**'swervable** *adj* ▸**'swerver** *n* ▸**'swerving** *adj*

SWG *abbrev. for* Standard Wire Gauge; a notation for the diameters of metal rods or thickness of metal sheet ranging from 16 mm to 0.02 mm or from 0.5 inch to 0.001 inch.

swift ❶ (swɪft) *adj* **1** moving or able to move quickly; fast. **2** occurring or performed quickly or suddenly; instant. **3** (*postpositive;* foll. by *to*) prompt to act or respond: *swift to take revenge.* ◆ *adv* **4a** swiftly or quickly. **4b** (*in combination*): *swift-moving.* ◆ *n* **5** any of various insectivorous birds of the Old World. They have long narrow wings and spend most of the time on the wing. **6** any of certain North American

THESAURUS

with, wild *or* mad about (*inf.*) ◆ *n* **19** *usually plural* = **confectionery**, bonbon, candy (*US*), sweetie, sweetmeats **20** *Brit.* = **dessert**, afters (*Brit. inf.*), pudding, sweet course
Antonyms *adj* ≠ **sugary:** acerbic, acetic, acid, bitter, savoury, sharp, sour, tart, vinegary ≠ **delightful:** hated, loathsome, nasty, objectionable, obnoxious, unappealing, unattractive, unlovable, unpleasant, unwanted ≠ **melodious:** cacophonous, discordant, grating, harsh, shrill, strident, unharmonious, unmusical, unpleasant ≠ **charming:** bad-tempered, disagreeable, grouchy (*inf.*), grumpy, ill-tempered, nasty, obnoxious ≠ **fragrant:** fetid, foul, noisome, rank, stinking

sweeten *vb* **1** = **sugar**, honey, sugar-coat **2, 3** = **mollify**, alleviate, appease, pacify, soften up, soothe, sugar the pill

sweetheart *n* **1** = **love**, admirer, beau, beloved, boyfriend *or* girlfriend, darling, dear, flame (*inf.*), follower (*obs.*), inamorata *or* inamorato, leman (*arch.*), lover, steady (*inf.*), suitor, swain (*arch.*), sweetie (*inf.*), truelove, valentine

sweet-talk *vb* **1** *Informal* = **flatter**, beguile, blandish, cajole, chat up, coax, dupe, entice, inveigle, manoeuvre, mislead, palaver, persuade, seduce, soft-soap (*inf.*), tempt, wheedle

swell *vb* **1** = **expand**, balloon, become bloated *or* distended, become larger, be inflated, belly, billow, bloat, bulge, dilate, distend, enlarge, extend, fatten, grow, increase, protrude, puff up, rise, round out, tumefy, well up **3** = **increase**, add to, aggravate, augment, enhance, heighten, intensify, mount, surge ◆ *n* **8** = **wave**, billow, rise, surge, undulation **13, 14** *Old-fashioned, informal* = **dandy**, beau, blade (*arch.*), cockscomb (*inf.*), fashion plate, fop, nob (*sl.*), toff (*Brit. sl.*) ◆ *adj* **18** *Slang* = **grand**, de luxe, exclusive, fashionable, plush *or* plushy (*inf.*), posh (*inf., chiefly Brit.*), ritzy (*sl.*), smart, stylish
Antonyms *vb* ≠ **expand:** become smaller, contract, deflate, shrink ≠ **increase:** decrease, diminish, ebb, fall, go down, lessen, reduce, wane ◆ *adj* ≠ **grand:** common, grotty (*sl.*), ordinary, plebeian, poor, run down, seedy, shabby, sordid, tatty, unimpressive, vulgar

swelling *n* **4** = **enlargement**, blister, bruise, bulge, bump, dilation, distension, inflammation, lump, protuberance, puffiness, tumescence

sweltering *adj* = **hot**, airless, baking, boiling, burning, humid, oppressive, roasting, scorching, steaming, stifling, sultry, torrid

swerve *vb* **1** = **veer**, bend, deflect, depart from, deviate, diverge, incline, sheer off, shift, skew, stray, swing, turn, turn aside, wander, wind

swift *adj* **1-3** = **quick**, abrupt, expeditious, express, fast, fleet, fleet-footed, flying, hurried, nimble, nippy (*Brit. inf.*), prompt, quickie (*inf.*), rapid, ready, short, short-lived, spanking, speedy, sudden, winged
Antonyms *adj* lead-footed, lingering, plodding, ponderous, slow, sluggish, tardy, tortoise-like, unhurried

swiftly *adv* **1** = **quickly**, apace, as fast as one's legs can carry one, (at) full tilt, double-quick, fast, hell for leather, hotfoot, hurriedly, in less than no time, like greased lightning (*inf.*), like lightning, like the clappers, nippily (*Brit. inf.*), posthaste, promptly, pronto (*inf.*), rapidly, speedily, without losing time

swiftness *n* **1** = **speed**, alacrity, celerity,

lizards of the iguana family that can run very rapidly. **7** the main cylinder in a carding machine. **8** an expanding circular frame used to hold skeins of silk, wool, etc. [OE, from *swīfan* to turn]
▸ '**swiftly** *adv* ▸ '**swiftness** *n*

swiftlet ('swɪftlɪt) *n* any of various small swifts of an Asian genus that often live in caves and use echolocation.

swig (swɪg) *Inf.* ◆ *n* **1** a large swallow or deep drink, esp. from a bottle. ◆ *vb* **swigs, swigging, swigged. 2** to drink (some liquid) deeply, esp. from a bottle. [C16: from ?]
▸ '**swigger** *n*

swill Ⓣ (swɪl) *vb* **1** to drink large quantities of (liquid, esp. alcoholic drink); guzzle. **2** (*tr*; often foll. by *out*) *Chiefly Brit.* to drench or rinse in large amounts of water. **3** (*tr*) to feed swill to (pigs, etc.). ◆ *n* **4** wet feed, esp. for pigs, consisting of kitchen waste, skimmed milk, etc. **5** refuse, esp. from a kitchen. **6** a deep drink, esp. beer. **7** any liquid mess. **8** the act of swilling. [OE *swilian* to wash out]
▸ '**swiller** *n*

swim (swɪm) *vb* **swims, swimming, swam, swum. 1** (*intr*) to move along in water by means of movements of the body, esp. the arms and legs, or (in the case of fish) tail and fins. **2** (*tr*) to cover (a distance or stretch of water) in this way. **3** (*tr*) to compete in (a race) in this way. **4** (*intr*) to be supported by and on a liquid; float. **5** (*tr*) to use (a particular stroke) in swimming. **6** (*intr*) to move smoothly, usually through air or over a surface. **7** (*intr*) to reel or seem to reel: *my head swam; the room swam around me.* **8** (*intr*; often foll. by *in* or *with*) to be covered or flooded with water or other liquid. **9** (*intr*; often foll. by *in*) to be liberally supplied (with): *he's swimming in money.* **10** (*tr*) to cause to float or swim. **11 swim with** (*or* **against**) **the stream** *or* **tide.** to conform to (or resist) prevailing opinion. ◆ *n* **12** the act, an instance, or period of swimming. **13** any graceful gliding motion. **14** a condition of dizziness; swoon. **15** a pool in a river good for fishing. **16 in the swim.** *Inf.* fashionable or active in social or political activities. [OE *swimman*]
▸ '**swimmable** *adj* ▸ '**swimmer** *n* ▸ '**swimming** *n, adj*

swim bladder *n Ichthyol.* another name for **air bladder** (sense 1).

swimmeret ('swɪmə,rɛt) *n* any of the small paired appendages on the abdomen of crustaceans, used chiefly in locomotion.

swimming bath *n* (*often pl*) an indoor swimming pool.

swimming costume *or* **bathing costume** *n Chiefly Brit.* any garment worn for swimming or sunbathing, such as a woman's one-piece garment covering most of the torso but not the limbs.

swimmingly Ⓣ ('swɪmɪŋlɪ) *adv* successfully, effortlessly, or well (esp. in **go swimmingly**).

swimming pool *n* an artificial pool for swimming.

swimsuit ('swɪm,suːt, -,sjuːt) *n* a woman's one-piece swimming garment that leaves the arms and legs bare.

swindle Ⓣ ('swɪndᵊl) *vb* **swindles, swindling, swindled. 1** to cheat (someone) of money, etc.; defraud. **2** (*tr*) to obtain (money, etc.) by fraud. ◆ *n* **3** a fraudulent scheme or transaction. [C18: back formation from G *Schwindler*, from *schwindeln*, from OHG *swintilōn*, from *swintan* to disappear]
▸ '**swindler** *n*

swindle sheet *n* a slang term for **expense account.**

swine (swaɪn) *n* **1** (*pl* **swine** *or* **swines**). a coarse or contemptible person. **2** (*pl* **swine**). another name for a **pig.** [OE *swīn*]
▸ '**swinish** *adj* ▸ '**swinishly** *adv* ▸ '**swinishness** *n*

swine fever *n* an infectious viral disease of pigs, characterized by fever and diarrhoea.

swineherd ('swaɪn,hɜːd) *n Arch.* a person who looks after pigs.

swing Ⓣ (swɪŋ) *vb* **swings, swinging, swung. 1** to move or cause to move rhythmically to and fro, as a free-hanging object; sway. **2** (*intr*) to move, walk, etc., with a relaxed and swaying motion. **3** to pivot or cause to pivot, as on a hinge. **4** to move or cause to move in a curve: *the car swung around the bend.* **5** to move or cause to move by suspending or being suspended. **6** to hang or be hung so as to be able to turn freely. **7** (*intr*) *Sl.* to be hanged: *he'll swing for it.* **8** to alter or cause to alter habits, a course, etc. **9** (*tr*) *Inf.* to influence or manipulate successfully: *I hope he can swing the deal.* **10** (*tr*; foll. by *up*) to raise or hoist, esp. in a sweeping motion. **11** (*intr*; often foll. by *at*) to hit out or strike (at), esp. with a sweeping motion. **12** (*tr*) to wave (a weapon, etc.) in a sweeping motion; flourish. **13** to arrange or play (music) with the rhythmically flexible and compulsive quality associated with jazz. **14** (*intr*) (of popular music, esp. jazz, or of the musicians who play it) to have this quality. **15** *Sl.* to be lively and modern. **16** (*intr*) *Cricket.* to bowl (a ball) with swing or (of a ball) to move with a swing. **17 swing the lead.** *Inf.* to malinger or make up excuses. ◆ *n* **18** the act or manner of swinging or the distance covered while swinging: *a wide swing.* **19** a sweeping stroke or blow. **20** *Boxing.* a wide punch from the side similar to but longer than a hook. **21** *Cricket.* the lateral movement of a bowled ball through the air. **22** any free-swaying motion. **23** any curving movement; sweep. **24** something that swings or is swung, esp. a suspended seat on which a person may swing back and forth. **25** a kind of popular dance music influenced by jazz, usually played by big bands and originating in the 1930s. **26** *Prosody.* a steady distinct rhythm or cadence in prose or verse. **27** *Inf.* the normal round or pace: *the swing of things.* **28a** a fluctuation, as in some business activity, voting pattern, etc. **28b** (*modifier*) able to bring about a swing in a voting pattern. **29** *Canad.* (in the North) a train of freight sleighs or canoes. **30** *Chiefly US.* a circular tour. **31 go with a swing.** to go well; be successful. **32 in full swing.** at the height of activity. **33 swings and roundabouts.** equal advantages and disadvantages. [OE *swingan*]

swingboat ('swɪŋ,bəʊt) *n* a piece of fairground equipment consisting of a boat-shaped carriage for swinging in.

swing bridge *n* a low bridge that can be rotated about a vertical axis to permit the passage of ships, etc.

swinge (swɪndʒ) *vb* **swinges, swingeing** *or* **swinging, swinged.** (*tr*) *Arch.* to beat, flog, or punish. [OE *swengan*]

swingeing Ⓣ ('swɪndʒɪŋ) *adj Chiefly Brit.* punishing; severe.

swinger ('swɪŋə) *n Sl.* **1** a person regarded as being modern and lively. **2** a person who swaps sexual partners in a group, esp. habitually.
▸ '**swinging** *adj* ▸ '**swingingly** *adv*

swingle ('swɪŋgᵊl) *n* **1** a flat-bladed wooden instrument used for beating and scraping flax or hemp to remove coarse matter from it. ◆ *vb* **swingles, swingling, swingled. 2** (*tr*) to use a swingle on. [OE *swingel* stroke]

swingletree ('swɪŋgᵊl,triː) *n* a crossbar in a horse's harness to which the ends of the traces are attached. Also called: **whippletree.**

swing shift *n US & Canad. inf.* the usual US and Canad. term for **back shift.**

swing-wing *adj* **1** of or relating to a variable-geometry aircraft. ◆ *n* **2a** such an aircraft. **2b** either of the two wings of such an aircraft.

swipe Ⓣ (swaɪp) *vb* **swipes, swiping, swiped. 1** (when *intr*, usually foll. by *at*) *Inf.* to hit hard with a sweeping blow. **2** (*tr*) *Sl.* to steal. **3** (*tr*) to pass a machine-readable card, such as a credit card, debit card, etc., through a machine that electronically interprets the information encoded on it, usu. in a magnetic strip. ◆ *n* **4** *Inf.* a hard blow. **5** an unexpected criticism of someone or something while discussing another subject. **6** Also called: **sweep.** a type of lever for raising and lowering a weight, such as a bucket in a well. [C19: ? rel. to SWEEP]

swirl Ⓣ (swɜːl) *vb* **1** to turn or cause to turn in a twisting spinning fashion. **2** (*intr*) to be dizzy; swim: *my head was swirling.* ◆ *n* **3** a whirling or spinning motion, esp. in water. **4** a whorl; curl. **5** the act of swirling or stirring. **6** dizzy confusion or disorder. [C15: prob. from Du. *zwirrelen*]
▸ '**swirling** *adj* ▸ '**swirly** *adj*

swish Ⓣ (swɪʃ) *vb* **1** to move with or make or cause to move with or make a whistling or hissing sound. **2** (*intr*) (esp. of fabrics) to rustle. **3** (*tr*) *Sl., now rare.* to whip; flog. **4** (*tr*; foll. by *off*) to cut with a swishing blow. ◆ *n* **5** a hissing or rustling sound or movement. **6** a rod for flogging or a blow from this. ◆ *adj* **7** *Inf., chiefly Brit.* fashionable; smart. [C18: imit.]
▸ '**swishy** *adj*

Swiss (swɪs) *adj* **1** of, relating to, or characteristic of Switzerland, a republic in W central Europe, its inhabitants, or their dialects of German, French, and Italian. ◆ *n, pl* **Swiss. 2** a native, inhabitant, or citizen of Switzerland.

Swiss chard *n* another name for **chard.**

Swiss cheese plant *n* See **monstera.**

THESAURUS

dispatch, expedition, fleetness, promptness, quickness, rapidity, speediness, velocity

swill *vb* **1** = **drink**, bend the elbow (*inf.*), bevvy (*dialect*), consume, drain, gulp, guzzle, imbibe, pour down one's gullet, quaff, swallow, swig (*inf.*), toss off **2** *Chiefly Brit. often with* **out** = **rinse**, drench, flush, sluice, wash down, wash out ◆ *n* **4** = **waste**, hogwash, mash, mush, pigswill, scourings, slops

swimmingly *adv* = **successfully**, as planned, cosily, effortlessly, like a dream, like clockwork, smoothly, very well, with no trouble, without a hitch

swindle *vb* **1** = **cheat**, bamboozle (*inf.*), bilk (of), con, cozen, deceive, defraud, diddle (*inf.*), do (*sl.*), dupe, fleece, overcharge, pull a fast one (on someone) (*inf.*), put one over on (someone) (*inf.*), rip (someone) off (*sl.*), rook (*sl.*), skin (*sl.*), stiff (*sl.*), sting (*inf.*), take (someone) for a ride (*inf.*), take to the cleaners (*inf.*), trick ◆ *n* **3** = **fraud**, con trick (*inf.*), deceit, deception, double-dealing, fiddle (*Brit. inf.*), imposition, knavery, racket, rip-off (*sl.*), roguery, scam (*sl.*), sharp practice, sting (*inf.*), swizz (*Brit. inf.*), swizzle (*Brit. inf.*), trickery

swindler *n* **1** = **cheat**, charlatan, chiseller (*inf.*), confidence trickster, con man (*inf.*), fraud, fraudster, hustler (*US inf.*), impostor, knave (*arch.*), mountebank, rascal, rogue, rook (*sl.*), shark, sharper, trickster

swing *vb* **1** = **sway**, fluctuate, oscillate, rock, vary, veer, vibrate, wave **3, 4** *usually with* **round** = **turn**, curve, pivot, rotate, swivel, turn on one's heel, wheel **5, 6** = **hang**, be pendent, be suspended, dangle, move back and forth, suspend ◆ *n* **18** = **swaying**, fluctuation, oscillation, stroke, sway, vibration **32 in full swing** = **at its height**, animated, lively, on the go (*inf.*), under way

swingeing *adj Chiefly Brit.* = **severe**, daunting, Draconian, drastic, excessive, exorbitant, harsh, heavy, huge, oppressive, punishing, stringent

swipe *vb* **1** *Informal* = **hit**, chin (*sl.*), clip (*inf.*), deck (*sl.*), fetch (someone) a blow, lash out at, lay one on (*sl.*), slap, slosh (*Brit. sl.*), sock (*sl.*), strike, wallop (*inf.*) **2** *Slang* = **steal**, appropriate, cabbage (*Brit. sl.*), filch, lift (*inf.*), make off with, nick, pilfer, pinch (*inf.*), purloin, snaffle (*Brit. inf.*) ◆ *n* **4** = **blow**, clip (*inf.*), clout (*inf.*), clump (*sl.*), cuff, slap, smack, thump, wallop (*inf.*)

swirl *vb* **1** = **whirl**, agitate, boil, churn, eddy, spin, surge, twirl, twist

swish *adj* **7** *Informal, chiefly Brit.* = **smart**, de luxe, elegant, exclusive, fashionable, grand, plush *or* plushy (*inf.*), posh (*inf., chiefly Brit.*), ritzy (*sl.*), sumptuous, swell (*inf.*)

swiss roll *n* a sponge cake spread with jam, cream, or some other filling, and rolled up.

switch Ⓣ (swɪtʃ) *n* **1** a mechanical, electrical, or electronic device for opening or closing a circuit or for diverting a current from one part of a circuit to another. **2** a swift and usually sudden shift or change. **3** an exchange or swap. **4** a flexible rod or twig, used esp. for punishment. **5** the sharp movement or blow of such an instrument. **6** a tress of false hair used to give added length or bulk to a woman's own hair-style. **7** the tassel-like tip of the tail of cattle and certain other animals. **8** any of various card games in which the suit is changed during play. **9** *US & Canad.* a railway siding. **10** *US & Canad.* a railway point. **11** *Austral. inf.* short for **switchboard** (sense 1). ◆ *vb* **12** to shift, change, turn aside, or change the direction of (something). **13** to exchange (places); replace (something by something else). **14** *Chiefly US & Canad.* to transfer (rolling stock) from one railway track to another. **15** *(tr)* to cause (an electric current) to start or stop flowing or to change its path by operating a switch. **16** *(tr)* to lash or whip with or as if with a switch. ◆ See also **switch off, switch on.** [C16: ?from MDu. *swijch* twig]
▸**'switcher** *n*

switchback ('swɪtʃ,bæk) *n* **1** a mountain road, railway, or track which rises and falls sharply many times or a sharp rise and fall on such a road, railway, or track. **2** another word (esp. Brit.) for **big dipper.**

switchblade *or* **switchblade knife** ('swɪtʃ,bleɪd) *n* another name (esp. US and Canad.) for **flick knife.**

switchboard ('swɪtʃ,bɔːd) *n* **1** an installation in a telephone exchange, office, etc., at which the interconnection of telephone lines is manually controlled. **2** an assembly of switchgear for the control of power supplies in an installation or building.

switchgear ('swɪtʃ,gɪə) *n Electrical engineering.* any of several devices used for opening and closing electric circuits, esp. those that pass high currents.

switchman ('swɪtʃmən) *n, pl* **switchmen.** the US and Canad. name for **pointsman.**

switch off *vb (adv)* **1** to cause (a device) to stop operating as by moving a switch, knob, etc. **2** *Inf.* to cease to interest or be interested; make or become bored, alienated, etc.

switch on *vb (adv)* **1** to cause (a device) to operate as by moving a switch, knob, or lever. **2** *(tr) Inf.* to produce (charm, tears, etc.) suddenly or automatically. **3** *(tr) Inf.* (now dated) to make up-to-date, esp. in outlook, dress, etc.

swither ('swɪðə) *Scot.* ◆ *vb (intr)* **1** to hesitate; vacillate; be perplexed. ◆ *n* **2** hesitation; perplexity; agitation. [C16: from ?]

Switzer ('swɪtsə) *n* a less common word for **Swiss.** [C16: from MHG, from *Swīz* Switzerland]

swivel Ⓣ ('swɪv^{ə}l) *n* **1** a coupling device which allows an attached object to turn freely. **2** such a device made of two parts which turn independently, such as a compound link of a chain. **3a** a pivot on which is mounted a gun that may be swung horizontally from side to side. **3b** Also called: **swivel gun.** the gun itself. ◆ *vb* **swivels, swivelling, swivelled** *or US* **swivels, swiveling, swiveled. 4** to turn or swing on or as if on a pivot. **5** *(tr)* to provide with, secure by, or support with a swivel. [C14: from OE *swīfan* to turn]

swivel chair *n* a chair, the seat of which is joined to the legs by a swivel and which thus may be spun round.

swivel pin *n* another name for **kingpin** (sense 2).

swiz *or* **swizz** (swɪz) *n Brit. inf.* a swindle or disappointment; swizzle.

swizzle ('swɪz^{ə}l) *n* **1** an alcoholic drink containing gin or rum. **2** *Brit. inf.* a swiz. ◆ *vb* **swizzles, swizzling, swizzled. 3** *(tr)* to stir a swizzle stick in (a drink). **4** *Brit. inf.* to swindle; cheat. [C19: from ?]

swizzle stick *n* a small rod used to agitate an effervescent drink to facilitate the escape of carbon dioxide.

swob (swɒb) *n, vb* **swobs, swobbing, swobbed.** a less common word for **swab.**

swollen Ⓣ ('swəʊlən) *vb* **1** a past participle of **swell.** ◆ *adj* **2** tumid or enlarged as by swelling. **3** turgid or bombastic.
▸**'swollenness** *n*

swoon (swuːn) *vb (intr)* **1** a literary word for **faint. 2** to become ecstatic. ◆ *n* **3** an instance of fainting. ◆ Also (archaic or dialect): **swound** (swaʊnd). [OE *geswōgen* insensible, p.p. of *swōgan* (unattested except in compounds) suffocate]
▸**'swooning** *adj*

swoop Ⓣ (swuːp) *vb* **1** *(intr; usually foll. by down, on,* or *upon)* to sweep or pounce suddenly. **2** *(tr; often foll. by up, away,* or *off)* to seize or scoop suddenly. ◆ *n* **3** the act of swooping. **4** a swift descent. [OE *swāpan* to sweep]

swoosh (swuʃ) *vb* **1** to make or cause to make a rustling or swirling sound, esp. when moving or pouring out. ◆ *n* **2** a swirling or rustling sound or movement. [C20: imit.]

swop (swɒp) *vb* **swops, swopping, swopped,** *n* a variant spelling of **swap.**

sword Ⓣ (sɔːd) *n* **1** a thrusting, striking, or cutting weapon with a long blade having one or two cutting edges, a hilt, and usually a crosspiece or guard. **2** such a weapon worn on ceremonial occasions as a symbol of authority. **3** something resembling a sword, such as the snout of a swordfish. **4 the sword. 4a** violence or power, esp. military power. **4b** death; destruction: *to put to the sword.* [OE *sweord*]

swordbearer ('sɔːd,beərə) *n* an official who carries a ceremonial sword.

sword dance *n* a dance in which the performers dance nimbly over swords on the ground or brandish them in the air.
▸**sword dancer** *n* ▸**sword dancing** *n*

swordfish ('sɔːd,fɪʃ) *n, pl* **swordfish** *or* **swordfishes.** a large fish with a very long upper jaw: valued as a food and game fish.

sword grass *n* any of various grasses and other plants having sword-shaped sharp leaves.

sword knot *n* a loop on the hilt of a sword by which it was attached to the wrist, now purely decorative.

sword lily *n* another name for **gladiolus.**

Sword of Damocles ('dæmə,kliːz) *n* a closely impending disaster. [after a sycophant forced by Dionysius, tyrant of ancient Syracuse, to sit under a sword suspended by a hair]

swordplay ('sɔːd,pleɪ) *n* **1** the action or art of fighting with a sword. **2** verbal sparring.

swordsman ('sɔːdzmən) *n, pl* **swordsmen.** one who uses or is skilled in the use of a sword.
▸**'swordsmanship** *n*

swordstick ('sɔːd,stɪk) *n* a hollow walking stick containing a short sword or dagger.

swordtail ('sɔːd,teɪl) *n* any of several small freshwater fishes of Central America having a long swordlike tail.

swore (swɔː) *vb* the past tense of **swear.**

sworn (swɔːn) *vb* **1** the past participle of **swear.** ◆ *adj* **2** bound, pledged, or made inveterate, by or as if by an oath: *a sworn statement; he was sworn to God.*

swot[1] Ⓣ (swɒt) *Brit. inf.* ◆ *vb* **swots, swotting, swotted. 1** (often foll. by *up*) to study (a subject) intensively, as for an examination; cram. ◆ *n* **2** Also called: **swotter.** a person who works or studies hard. **3** hard work or grind. ◆ Also: **swat.** [C19: var. of SWEAT (n)]

swot[2] (swɒt) *vb* **swots, swotting, swotted,** *n* a variant of **swat.**

SWOT (swɒt) *n acronym for* strengths, weaknesses, opportunities, and threats: an analysis of a product made before it is marketed.

swounds *or* **'swounds** (zwaʊndz, zaʊndz) *interj Arch.* less common spellings of **zounds.**

swum (swʌm) *vb* the past participle of **swim.**

swung (swʌŋ) *vb* the past tense and past participle of **swing.**

swy (swaɪ) *n Austral.* another name for **two-up.** [C20: from G *zwei* two]

sybarite Ⓣ ('sɪbə,raɪt) *n* **1** *(sometimes cap.)* a devotee of luxury and the sensual vices. ◆ *adj* **2** luxurious; sensuous. [C16: from L *Sybarīta*, from Gk *Subaritēs* inhabitant of *Sybaris*, Gk colony in S Italy, famed for its luxury]
▸**sybaritic** (,sɪbə'rɪtɪk) *adj* ▸**,syba'ritically** *adv* ▸**'sybaritism** *n*

sycamore ('sɪkə,mɔː) *n* **1** a Eurasian maple tree, naturalized in Britain and North America, having five-lobed leaves and two-winged fruits. **2** *US & Canad.* an American plane tree. See **plane tree. 3** a tree of N Africa and W Asia, having an edible figlike fruit. [C14: from OF *sicamor*, from L *sȳcomorus*, from Gk, from *sukon* fig + *moron* mulberry]

syconium (saɪ'kəʊnɪəm) *n, pl* **syconia** (-nɪə). *Bot.* the fleshy fruit of the fig, consisting of an enlarged receptacle. [C19: from NL, from Gk *sukon* fig]

sycophant Ⓣ ('sɪkəfənt) *n* a person who uses flattery to win favour from individuals wielding influence; toady. [C16: from L *sȳcophanta*, from Gk *sukophantēs*, lit.: person showing a fig, apparently referring to the fig sign used in accusation, from *sukon* fig + *phainein* to show; sense prob. developed from "accuser" to "informer, flatterer"]
▸**'sycophancy** *n* ▸**sycophantic** (,sɪkə'fæntɪk) *adj* ▸**,syco'phantically** *adv*

THESAURUS

switch *n* **2 = change**, about-turn, alteration, change of direction, reversal, shift **3 = exchange**, substitution, swap ◆ *vb* **12 = change**, change course, deflect, deviate, divert, shift, turn aside **13 = exchange**, interchange, rearrange, replace by, substitute, swap, trade

swivel *vb* **4 = turn**, pirouette, pivot, revolve, rotate, spin, swing round

swollen *adj* **2 = enlarged**, bloated, distended, dropsical, edematous, inflamed, oedematous, puffed up, puffy, tumescent, tumid

swoop *vb* **1 = pounce**, descend, dive, rush, stoop, sweep ◆ *n* **3, 4 = pounce**, descent, drop, lunge, plunge, rush, stoop, sweep

sword *n* **1 = blade**, brand *(arch.)*, trusty steel **4 the sword: a = military power**, aggression, arms, war **b = death**, butchery, massacre, murder, slaying, violence

swot[1] *vb* **1** *Informal* **= study**, apply oneself to, bone up on *(inf.)*, burn the midnight oil, cram *(inf.)*, get up *(inf.)*, lucubrate *(rare)*, mug up *(Brit. sl.)*, pore over, revise, toil over, work

sybarite *n* **1 = hedonist**, epicure, epicurean, playboy, sensualist, voluptuary

sybaritic *adj* **1 = pleasure-loving**, bacchanalian, epicurean, hedonistic, Lucullan, luxurious, luxury-loving, self-indulgent, sensual, voluptuous

sycophancy *n* **= obsequiousness**, adulation, bootlicking *(inf.)*, cringing, fawning, flattery, grovelling, kowtowing, servility, slavishness, toadyism, truckling

sycophant *n* **= crawler**, apple polisher *(US sl.)*, ass-kisser *(US & Canad. taboo sl.)*, bootlicker *(inf.)*, brown-noser *(taboo sl.)*, cringer, fawner, flatterer, hanger-on, lickspittle, parasite, slave, sponger, toadeater *(rare)*, toady, truckler, yes man

sycophantic *adj* **= obsequious**, all over (some-one) *(inf.)*, arse-licking *(taboo sl.)*, bootlicking *(inf.)*, crawling, cringing, fawning, flattering, grovelling, ingratiating, parasitical,

sycosis (saɪ'kəʊsɪs) *n* chronic inflammation of the hair follicles, esp. those of the beard. [C16: via NL from Gk *sukōsis,* from *sukon* fig]

Sydenham's chorea ('sɪdᵊnəmz) *n* a form of chorea affecting children, often associated with rheumatic fever. Nontechnical name: **Saint Vitus's dance.** [after T. *Sydenham* (1624–89), E physician]

syenite ('saɪəˌnaɪt) *n* a light-coloured coarse-grained igneous rock consisting of feldspars with hornblende. [C18: from F, from L *syēnītēs lapis* stone from *Syene* (Aswan), Egypt, where orig. quarried]
▸**syenitic** (ˌsaɪə'nɪtɪk) *adj*

syllabary ('sɪləbərɪ) *n, pl* **syllabaries. 1** a table or list of syllables. **2** a set of symbols used in certain writing systems, such as one used for Japanese, in which each symbol represents a spoken syllable. [C16: from NL *syllabārium,* from L *syllaba* SYLLABLE]

syllabi ('sɪləˌbaɪ) *n* a plural of **syllabus.**

syllabic (sɪ'læbɪk) *adj* **1** of or relating to syllables or the division of a word into syllables. **2** denoting a kind of verse line based on a specific number of syllables rather than being regulated by stresses or quantities. **3** (of a consonant) constituting a syllable. ◆ *n* **4** a syllabic consonant.
▸**syl'labically** *adv*

syllabify (sɪ'læbɪˌfaɪ) *or* **syllabicate** *vb* **syllabifies, syllabifying, syllabified** *or* **syllabicates, syllabicating, syllabicated.** (*tr*) to divide (a word) into its constituent syllables.
▸**sylˌlabifi'cation** *or* **sylˌlabi'cation** *n*

syllable ('sɪləbᵊl) *n* **1** a combination or set of one or more units of sound in a language that must consist of a sonorous element (a sonant or vowel) and may or may not contain less sonorous elements (consonants or semivowels) flanking it: for example "paper" has two syllables. **2** (in the writing systems of certain languages, esp. ancient ones) a symbol or set of symbols standing for a syllable. **3** the least mention: *don't breathe a syllable of it.* **4 in words of one syllable.** simply; bluntly. ◆ *vb* **syllables, syllabling, syllabled. 5** to pronounce syllables of (a text); articulate. **6** (*tr*) to write down in syllables. [C14: via OF from L *syllaba,* from Gk *sullabē,* from *sullambanein* to collect together]

syllabub *or* **sillabub** ('sɪləˌbʌb) *n* **1** a spiced drink made of milk with rum, port, brandy, or wine, often hot. **2** *Brit.* a cold dessert made from milk or cream beaten with sugar, wine, and lemon juice. [C16: from ?]

syllabus ❶ ('sɪləbəs) *n, pl* **syllabuses** *or* **syllabi** (-ˌbaɪ). **1** an outline of a course of studies, text, etc. **2** *Brit., Austral., & NZ.* **2a** the subjects studied for a particular course. **2b** a list of these subjects. [C17: from LL, erroneously from L *sittybus* parchment strip giving title and author, from Gk *sittuba*]

syllepsis (sɪ'lɛpsɪs) *n, pl* **syllepses** (-siːz). **1** (in grammar or rhetoric) the use of a single sentence construction in which a verb, adjective, etc., is made to cover two syntactical functions, as *have* in *she and they have promised to come.* **2** another word for **zeugma.** [C16: from LL, from Gk *sullēpsis,* from *sul-* SYN- + *lēpsis,* from *lambanein* to take]
▸**syl'leptic** *adj* ▸**syl'leptically** *adv*

syllogism ('sɪləˌdʒɪzəm) *n* **1** a deductive inference consisting of two premises and a conclusion, all of which are categorical propositions. The subject of the conclusion is the **minor term** and its predicate the **major term;** the **middle term** occurs in both premises but not the conclusion. There are 256 such arguments but only 24 are valid. *Some men are mortal; some men are angelic; so some mortals are angelic* is invalid, while *some temples are in ruins; all ruins are fascinating; so some temples are fascinating* is valid. Here *fascinating, in ruins,* and *temples* are respectively major, middle, and minor terms. **2** a piece of deductive reasoning from the general to the particular. [C14: via L from Gk *sullogismos,* from *sullogizesthai* to reckon together, from *logos* a discourse]
▸ˌ**syllo'gistic** *adj* ▸**'sylloˌgize** *or* **'sylloˌgise** *vb*

sylph ❶ (sɪlf) *n* **1** a slender graceful girl or young woman. **2** any of a class of imaginary beings assumed to inhabit the air. [C17: from NL *sylphus,* prob. coined from L *silva* wood + Gk *numphē* nymph]
▸**'sylphˌlike** *adj*

sylva *or* **silva** ('sɪlvə) *n, pl* **sylvas** *or* **sylvae** (-viː). the trees growing in a particular region. [C17: from L *silva* a wood]

sylvan *or* **silvan** ('sɪlvən) *Chiefly poetic.* ◆ *adj* **1** of or consisting of woods or forests. **2** in woods or forests. **3** idyllically rural or rustic. ◆ *n* **4** an inhabitant of the woods, esp. a spirit. [C16: from L *silvānus,* from *silva* forest]

sylvanite ('sɪlvəˌnaɪt) *n* a silver-white mineral consisting of a compound of tellurium with gold and silver in the form of elongated crystals. [C18: from *(Tran)sylvan(ia),* Romania, + -ITE[1], with reference to the region where first found]

sylviculture ('sɪlvɪˌkʌltʃə) *n* a variant spelling of **silviculture.**

sym- *prefix* a variant of **syn-** before *b, p,* and *m.*

symbiont ('sɪmbɪˌɒnt) *n* an organism living in a state of symbiosis. [C19: from Gk *sumbioun* to live together, from *bioun* to live]
▸ˌ**symbi'ontic** *adj* ▸ˌ**symbi'ontically** *adv*

symbiosis (ˌsɪmbɪ'əʊsɪs) *n* **1** a close association of two interdependent animal or plant species. **2** a similar relationship between persons or groups. [C19: via NL from Gk: a living together]
▸ˌ**symbi'otic** *adj*

symbol ❶ ('sɪmbᵊl) *n* **1** something that represents or stands for something else, usually by convention or association, esp. a material object used to represent something abstract. **2** an object, person, etc., used in a literary work, film, etc., to stand for or suggest something else with which it is associated. **3** a letter, figure, or sign used in mathematics, music, etc., to represent a quantity, phenomenon, operation, function, etc. ◆ *vb* **symbols, symbolling, symbolled** *or US* **symbols, symboling, symboled. 4** (*tr*) another word for **symbolize.** [C15: from Church L *symbolum,* from Gk *sumbolon* sign, from *sumballein* to throw together, from SYN- + *ballein* to throw]

symbolic ❶ (sɪm'bɒlɪk) *or* **symbolical** *adj* **1** of or relating to a symbol or symbols. **2** serving as a symbol. **3** characterized by the use of symbols or symbolism.
▸**sym'bolically** *adv*

symbolic logic *n* another name for **formal logic.**

symbolism ('sɪmbəˌlɪzəm) *n* **1** the representation of something in symbolic form or the attribution of symbolic character to something. **2** a system of symbols or symbolic representation. **3** a symbolic significance or quality. **4** (*often cap.*) a late 19th-century movement in art that sought to express mystical or abstract ideas through the symbolic use of images.

symbolist ('sɪmbəlɪst) *n* **1** a person who uses or can interpret symbols, esp. as a means to revealing aspects of truth and reality. **2** an artist or writer who practises symbolism in his work. **3** (*usually cap.*) a writer associated with the symbolist movement. **4** (*often cap.*) an artist associated with the symbolist movement. ◆ *adj* **5** of, relating to, or characterizing symbolism or symbolists.
▸ˌ**symbol'istic** *adj* ▸ˌ**symbol'istically** *adv*

symbolist movement *n* (*usually cap.*) a movement beginning in French and Belgian poetry towards the end of the 19th century with Mallarmé, Valéry, Verlaine, Rimbaud, and others, and seeking to express states of mind rather than objective reality by the power of words and images to suggest as well as denote.

symbolize ❶ *or* **symbolise** ('sɪmbəˌlaɪz) *vb* **symbolizes, symbolizing, symolized** *or* **symbolises, symbolising, symbolised. 1** (*tr*) to serve as or be a symbol of. **2** (*tr;* usually foll. by *by*) to represent by a symbol or symbols. **3** (*intr*) to use symbols. **4** (*tr*) to treat or regard as symbolic.
▸ˌ**symboli'zation** *or* ˌ**symboli'sation** *n*

symbol retailer *n* any member of a voluntary group of independent retailers, often using a common name or symbol, formed to obtain better prices from wholesalers or manufacturers in competition with supermarket chains. Also called: **voluntary retailer.**

symmetrical ❶ (sɪ'mɛtrɪkᵊl) *adj* possessing or displaying symmetry.

symmetry ❶ ('sɪmɪtrɪ) *n, pl* **symmetries. 1** similarity, correspondence, or balance among systems or parts of a system. **2** *Maths.* an exact correspondence in position or form about a given point, line, or plane. **3** beauty or harmony of form based on a proportionate arrangement of parts. [C16: from L *symmetria,* from Gk *summetria* proportion, from SYN- + *metron* measure]

sympathectomy (ˌsɪmpə'θɛktəmɪ) *n, pl* **sympathectomies.** the surgical excision or chemical destruction (**chemical sympathectomy**) of one or more parts of the sympathetic nervous system. [C20: from SYMPATHETIC + -ECTOMY]

sympathetic ❶ (ˌsɪmpə'θɛtɪk) *adj* **1** characterized by, feeling, or showing sympathy; understanding. **2** in accord with the subject's personality or mood; congenial: *a sympathetic atmosphere.* **3** (when *postpositive,* often foll. by *to* or *towards*) showing agreement (with) or favour (towards). **4** *Anat., physiol.* of or relating to the division of the autonomic nervous system that acts in opposition to the parasympathetic system accelerating the heartbeat, dilating the bronchi, inhib-

THESAURUS

servile, slavish, slimy, smarmy (*Brit. inf.*), time-serving, toadying, unctuous

syllabus *n* **1** = **course of study**, curriculum

sylphlike *adj* **1** = **slender**, graceful, lithe, svelte, willowy

symbol *n* **1-3** = **sign**, badge, emblem, figure, glyph, image, logo, mark, representation, token, type

symbolic *adj* **2, 3** = **representative**, allegorical, emblematic, figurative, significant, token, typical

symbolize *vb* **1** = **represent**, betoken, body forth, connote, denote, exemplify, mean, personify, signify, stand for, typify

symmetrical *adj* = **balanced**, in proportion, proportional, regular, well-proportioned
Antonyms *adj* asymmetrical, disorderly, irregular, lopsided, unbalanced, unequal, unsymmetrical

symmetry *n* **1** = **balance**, agreement, correspondence, evenness, form, harmony, order, proportion, regularity

sympathetic *adj* **1** = **caring**, affectionate, commiserating, compassionate, concerned, condoling, feeling, interested, kind, kindly, pitying, responsive, supportive, tender, understanding, warm, warm-hearted **2** = **like-minded**, agreeable, appreciative, companionable, compatible, congenial, friendly, responsive, well-intentioned **3** *often foll. by* **to** = **favourably disposed towards**, agreeable with, approving of, encouraging, friendly to, in sympathy with, pro, well-disposed towards
Antonyms *adj* ≠ **caring:** apathetic, callous, cold, cold-hearted, disinterested, indifferent, inhumane, insensitive, steely, uncaring, uncompassionate, unfeeling, uninterested, unmoved, unsympathetic ≠ **like-minded:** uncongenial, unresponsive

sympathetically *adv* **1** = **feelingly**, appreciatively, kindly, perceptively, responsively, sensitively, understandingly, warm-heartedly, warmly, with compassion, with feeling, with interest

iting the smooth muscles of the digestive tract, etc. Cf. **parasympathetic.** 5 relating to vibrations occurring as a result of similar vibrations in a neighbouring body: *sympathetic strings on a sitar.*
▸ ,**sympa'thetically** *adv*

sympathetic magic *n* a type of magic in which it is sought to produce a large-scale effect, often at a distance, by performing some small-scale ceremony resembling it, such as the pouring of water on an altar to induce rainfall.

sympathize ➊ *or* **sympathise** ('sɪmpəˌθaɪz) *vb* **sympathizes, sympathizing, sympathized** *or* **sympathises, sympathising, sympathised.** (*intr;* often foll. by *with*) **1** to feel or express compassion or sympathy (for); commiserate: *he sympathized with my troubles.* **2** to share or understand the sentiments or ideas (of); be in sympathy (with).
▸ '**sympa,thizer** *or* '**sympa,thiser** *n*

sympatholytic (ˌsɪmpəθəʊ'lɪtɪk) *Med.* ◆ *adj* **1a** inhibiting or antagonistic to nerve impulses of the sympathetic nervous system. **1b** of or relating to such inhibition. ◆ *n* **2** a sympatholytic drug. Cf. **sympathomimetic.** [C20: from SYMPATH(ETIC) + -LYTIC]

sympathomimetic (ˌsɪmpəθəʊmɪ'mɛtɪk) *Med.* ◆ *adj* **1** causing a physiological effect similar to that produced by stimulation of the sympathetic nervous system. ◆ *n* **2** a sympathomimetic drug. Cf. **sympatholytic.** [C20: from SYMPATH(ETIC) + MIMETIC]

sympathy ➊ ('sɪmpəθɪ) *n, pl* **sympathies. 1** the sharing of another's emotions, esp. of sorrow or anguish; compassion. **2** affinity or harmony, usually of feelings or interests, between persons or things: *to be in sympathy with someone.* **3** mutual affection or understanding arising from such a relationship. **4** the condition of a physical system or body when its behaviour is similar or corresponds to that of a different system that influences it, such as the vibration of sympathetic strings. **5** (*sometimes pl*) a feeling of loyalty, support, or accord, as for an idea, cause, etc. **6** *Physiol.* the relationship between two organs or parts whereby a change in one affects the other. [C16: from L *sympathīa,* from Gk, from *sumpathēs,* from SYN- + *pathos* suffering]

sympathy strike *n* a strike organized in support of another strike or cause. Also called: **sympathetic strike.**

symphonic poem *n Music.* an extended orchestral composition, originated by Liszt (1811–86), Hungarian composer, based on nonmusical material, such as a work of literature or folk tale. Also called: **tone poem.**

symphony ('sɪmfənɪ) *n, pl* **symphonies. 1** an extended large-scale orchestral composition, usually with several movements, at least one of which is in sonata form. **2** a piece of instrumental music in up to three very short movements, used as an overture to or interlude in a baroque opera. **3** any purely orchestral movement in a vocal work, such as a cantata or oratorio. **4** short for **symphony orchestra. 5** anything distinguished by a harmonious composition: *the picture was a symphony of green.* **6** *Arch.* harmony in general; concord. [C13: from OF *symphonie,* from L *symphōnia* concord, from Gk, from SYN- + *phōnē* sound]
▸**symphonic** (sɪm'fɒnɪk) *adj* ▸**sym'phonically** *adv*

symphony orchestra *n Music.* an orchestra capable of performing symphonies, esp. a large orchestra comprising strings, brass, woodwind, harp and percussion.

symphysis ('sɪmfɪsɪs) *n, pl* **symphyses** (-ˌsiːz). **1** *Anat., bot.* a growing together of parts or structures, such as two bony surfaces joined by an intermediate layer of fibrous cartilage. **2** a line marking this growing together. **3** *Pathol.* an abnormal adhesion of two or more parts or structures. [C16: via NL from Gk *sumphusis,* from *sumphuein,* from SYN- + *phuein* to grow]
▸**symphysial** *or* **symphyseal** (sɪm'fɪzɪəl) *adj*

sympodium (sɪm'pəʊdɪəm) *n, pl* **sympodia** (-dɪə). the main axis of growth in the grapevine and similar plants: a number of lateral branches that arise from just behind the apex of the main stem, which ceases to grow. [C19: from NL, from SYN- + Gk *podion* a little foot]
▸**sym'podial** *adj* ▸**sym'podially** *adv*

symposium (sɪm'pəʊzɪəm) *n, pl* **symposiums** *or* **symposia** (-zɪə). **1** a conference or meeting for the discussion of some subject, esp. an academic topic or social problem. **2** a collection of scholarly contributions on a given subject. **3** (in classical Greece) a drinking party with intellectual conversation, music, etc. [C16: via L from Gk *sumposion,* from *sumpinein* to drink together]

symptom ➊ ('sɪmptəm) *n* **1** *Med.* any sensation or change in bodily function experienced by a patient that is associated with a particular disease. **2** any phenomenon or circumstance accompanying something and regarded as evidence of its existence; indication. [C16: from LL *symptōma,* from Gk *sumptōma* chance, from *sumpiptein* to occur, from SYN- + *piptein* to fall]

symptomatic ➊ (ˌsɪmptə'mætɪk) *adj* **1** (often foll. by *of*) being a symptom; indicative: *symptomatic of insanity.* **2** of, relating to, or according to symptoms: *a symptomatic analysis.*
▸ ,**sympto'matically** *adv*

symptomatology (ˌsɪmptəmə'tɒlədʒɪ) *n* the branch of medicine concerned with the study and classification of the symptoms of disease.

syn. *abbrev. for* synonym(ous).

syn- *prefix* **1** with or together: *synecology.* **2** fusion: *syngamy.* [from Gk *sun* together]

synaeresis (sɪ'nɪərɪsɪs) *n* a variant spelling of **syneresis.**

synaesthesia *or US* **synesthesia** (ˌsɪniːs'θiːzɪə) *n* **1** *Physiol.* a sensation experienced in a part of the body other than the part stimulated. **2** *Psychol.* the subjective sensation of a sense other than the one being stimulated. [C19: from NL, from SYN- + *-esthesia,* from Gk *aisthēsis* sensation]
▸**synaesthetic** *or US* **synesthetic** (ˌsɪniːs'θɛtɪk) *adj*

synagogue ('sɪnəˌɡɒɡ) *n* **1a** a building for Jewish religious services and religious instruction. **1b** (*as modifier*): *synagogue services.* **2** a congregation of Jews who assemble for worship or religious study. **3** the religion of Judaism as organized in such congregations. [C12: from OF, from LL *synagōga,* from Gk *sunagōgē* a gathering, from *sunagein* to bring together]
▸**synagogical** (ˌsɪnə'ɡɒdʒɪkᵊl) *or* **synagogal** ('sɪnəˌɡɒɡᵊl) *adj*

synapse ('saɪnæps) *n* the point at which a nerve impulse is relayed from the terminal portion of an axon to the dendrites of an adjacent neuron.

synapsis (sɪ'næpsɪs) *n, pl* **synapses** (-siːz). **1** *Cytology.* the association in pairs of homologous chromosomes at the start of meiosis. **2** another word for **synapse.** [C19: from NL, from Gk *sunapsis* junction, from *sunaptein* to join together]
▸**synaptic** (sɪ'næptɪk) *adj* ▸**syn'aptically** *adv*

synarthrosis (ˌsɪnɑː'θrəʊsɪs) *n, pl* **synarthroses** (-siːz). *Anat.* any of various joints which lack a synovial cavity and are virtually immovable; a fixed joint. [C16: via NL from Gk *sunarthrōsis,* from *sunarthrousthai* to be connected by joints, from *sun-* SYN- + *arthron* a joint]
▸ ,**synar'throdial** *adj*

sync *or* **synch** (sɪŋk) *Films, television, computing.* ◆ *vb* **1** an informal word for **synchronize.** ◆ *n* **2** an informal word for **synchronization** (esp. in **in** *or* **out of sync**).

syncarp ('sɪnkɑːp) *n Bot.* a fleshy multiple fruit, formed from two or more carpels of one flower or the aggregated fruits of several flowers. [C19: from NL *syncarpium,* from SYN- + Gk *karpos* fruit]

syncarpous (sɪn'kɑːpəs) *adj* **1** (of the ovaries of certain flowering plants) consisting of united carpels. **2** of or relating to a syncarp.

synchro ('sɪŋkrəʊ) *n, pl* **synchros. 1** Also called: **selsyn.** any of a number of electrical devices in which the angular position of a rotating part is transformed into a voltage, or vice versa. **2** short for **synchronized swimming.**

synchro- *combining form.* indicating synchronization: *synchromesh.*

synchrocyclotron (ˌsɪŋkrəʊ'saɪkləˌtrɒn) *n* a cyclotron in which the frequency of the electric field is modulated to allow for relativistic effects at high velocities and thus produce higher energies.

synchromesh ('sɪŋkrəʊˌmɛʃ) *adj* **1** (of a gearbox, etc.) having a system of clutches that synchronizes the speeds of the driving and driven members before engagement to avoid shock in gear changing and to reduce noise and wear. ◆ *n* **2** a gear system having these features. [C20: shortened from *synchronized mesh*]

synchronic (sɪn'krɒnɪk) *adj* **1** concerned with the events or phenomena at a particular period without considering historical antecedents: *synchronic linguistics.* Cf. **diachronic. 2** synchronous.
▸**syn'chronically** *adv* ▸**synchronicity** (ˌsɪnkrə'nɪsɪtɪ) *n*

synchronicity (ˌsɪŋkrə'nɪsɪtɪ) *n* an apparently meaningful coincidence in time of two or more similar or identical events that are causally unrelated. [C20: coined by Carl *Jung* (1875–1961), Swiss psychologist, from SYNCHRONIC + -ITY]

synchronism ('sɪŋkrəˌnɪzəm) *n* **1** the quality or condition of being synchronous. **2** a chronological list of historical persons and events, arranged to show parallel or synchronous occurrence. **3** the representation in a work of art of one or more incidents that occurred at separate times. [C16: from Gk *sunkhronismos*]
▸ ,**synchro'nistic** *or* ,**synchro'nistical** *adj* ▸ ,**synchro'nistically** *adv*

synchronize *or* **synchronise** ('sɪŋkrəˌnaɪz) *vb* **synchronizes, synchronizing, synchronized** *or* **synchronises, synchronising, synchronised. 1** (when *intr,* usually foll. by *with*) to occur or recur or cause to occur or recur at the same time or in unison. **2** to indicate or cause to indicate the same time: *synchronize your watches.* **3** (*tr*) *Films.* to establish (the picture and soundtrack records) in their correct relative position. **4** (*tr*) to designate (events) as simultaneous.
▸ ,**synchroni'zation** *or* ,**synchroni'sation** *n* ▸'**synchro,nizer** *or* '**synchro,niser** *n*

THESAURUS

sympathize *vb* **1** = **feel for,** bleed for, commiserate, condole, empathize, feel one's heart go out to, grieve with, have compassion, offer consolation, pity, share another's sorrow **2** = **agree,** be in accord, be in sympathy, go along with, identify with, side with, understand
Antonyms *vb* ≠ **feel for:** disdain, disregard, have no feelings for, mock, scorn ≠ **agree:** disagree, fail to understand, misunderstand, oppose, reject

sympathizer *n* **2** = **supporter,** fellow traveller, partisan, protagonist, well-wisher

sympathy *n* **1** = **compassion,** commiseration, condolence(s), empathy, pity, tenderness, thoughtfulness, understanding **2** = **affinity,** agreement, congeniality, correspondence, fellow feeling, harmony, rapport, union, warmth
Antonyms *n* ≠ **compassion:** callousness, coldness, disdain, hard-heartedness, indifference, insensitivity, lack of feeling *or* understanding *or* sympathy, pitilessness, scorn ≠ **affinity:** antagonism, disapproval, hostility, opposition, resistance, unfriendliness

synchronized swimming *n* a sport in which swimmers move in patterns in time to music. Sometimes shortened to **synchro** *or* **synchro swimming.**

synchronous ('sɪŋkrənəs) *adj* **1** occurring at the same time. **2** *Physics.* (of periodic phenomena, such as voltages) having the same frequency and phase. **3** occurring or recurring exactly together and at the same rate. [C17: from LL *synchronus*, from Gk *sunkhronos*, from SYN- + *khronos* time]
▸'**synchronously** *adv* ▸'**synchronousness** *n*

synchronous machine *n* an electrical machine whose rotating speed is proportional to the frequency of the alternating-current supply and independent of the load.

synchronous motor *n* an alternating-current motor that runs at a speed that is equal to or is a multiple of the frequency of the supply.

synchrony ('sɪŋkrənɪ) *n* the state of being synchronous; simultaneity.

synchrotron ('sɪŋkrəˌtrɒn) *n* a particle accelerator having an electric field of fixed frequency and a changing magnetic field. [C20: from SYNCHRO- + (ELEC)TRON]

syncline ('sɪŋklaɪn) *n* a downward fold of stratified rock in which the strata slope towards a vertical axis. [C19: from SYN- + Gk *klīnein* to lean]
▸**syn'clinal** *adj*

Syncom ('sɪnˌkɒm) *n* a communications satellite in stationary orbit. [C20: from *syn(chronous) com(munication)*]

syncopate ('sɪŋkəˌpeɪt) *vb* **syncopates, syncopating, syncopated.** (*tr*) **1** *Music.* to modify or treat (a beat, rhythm, note, etc.) by syncopation. **2** to shorten (a word) by omitting sounds or letters from the middle. [C17: from Med. L *syncopāre* to omit a letter or syllable, from LL *syncopa* SYNCOPE]
▸'**syncoˌpator** *n*

syncopation (ˌsɪŋkə'peɪʃən) *n* **1** *Music.* **1a** the displacement of the usual rhythmic accent away from a strong beat onto a weak beat. **1b** a note, beat, rhythm, etc., produced by syncopation. **2** another word for **syncope** (sense 2).

syncope ('sɪŋkəpɪ) *n* **1** a technical word for a **faint. 2** the omission of sounds or letters from the middle of a word. [C16: from LL *syncopa*, from Gk *sunkopē* a cutting off, from SYN- + *koptein* to cut]
▸**syncopic** (sɪŋ'kɒpɪk) *or* '**syncopal** *adj*

syncretism ('sɪŋkrɪˌtɪzəm) *n* **1** the tendency to syncretize. **2** the historical tendency of languages to reduce their use of inflection, as in the development of Old English into Modern English. [C17: from NL *syncrētismus*, from Gk *sunkrētismos* alliance of Cretans, from *sunkrētizein* to join forces (in the manner of the Cretan towns), from SYN- + *Krēs* a Cretan]
▸**syncretic** (sɪŋ'kretɪk) *or* ˌ**syncre'tistic** *adj* ▸'**syncretist** *n*

syncretize *or* **syncretise** ('sɪŋkrɪˌtaɪz) *vb* **syncretizes, syncretizing, syncretized** *or* **syncretises, syncretising, syncretised.** to attempt to combine the characteristic teachings, beliefs, or practices of (differing systems of religion or philosophy).
▸ˌ**syncreti'zation** *or* ˌ**syncreti'sation** *n*

syndactyl (sɪn'dæktɪl) *adj* **1** (of certain animals) having two or more digits growing fused together. ◆ *n* **2** an animal with this arrangement of digits.
▸**syn'dactylism** *n*

syndesmosis (ˌsɪndɛs'məʊsɪs) *n, pl* **syndesmoses** (-siːz). *Anat.* a type of joint in which the articulating bones are held together by a ligament of connective tissue. [C18: NL, from Gk *sundein* to bind together]
▸**syndesmotic** (ˌsɪndɛs'mɒtɪk) *adj*

syndetic (sɪn'dɛtɪk) *adj* denoting a grammatical construction in which two clauses are connected by a conjunction. [C17: from Gk *sundetikos*, from *sundetos* bound together]
▸**syndesis** (sɪn'diːsɪs) *n* ▸**syn'detically** *adv*

syndic ('sɪndɪk) *n* **1** *Brit.* a business agent of some universities or other bodies. **2** (in several countries) a government administrator or magistrate with varying powers. [C17: via OF from LL *syndicus*, from Gk *sundikos* defendant's advocate, from SYN- + *dikē* justice]
▸'**syndical** *adj*

syndicalism ('sɪndɪkəˌlɪzəm) *n* **1** a revolutionary movement and theory advocating seizure of the means of production and distribution by syndicates of workers, esp. by a general strike. **2** an economic system resulting from such action.
▸'**syndical** *adj* ▸'**syndicalist** *adj, n* ▸ˌ**syndical'istic** *adj*

syndicate *n* ('sɪndɪkɪt). **1** an association of business enterprises or individuals organized to undertake a joint project. **2** a news agency that sells articles, photographs, etc., to a number of newspapers for simultaneous publication. **3** any association formed to carry out an enterprise of common interest to its members. **4** a board of syndics or the office of syndic. ◆ *vb* ('sɪndɪˌkeɪt) **syndicates, syndicating, syndicated. 5** (*tr*) to sell (articles, photographs, etc.) to several newspapers for simultaneous publication. **6** (*tr*) *US.* to sell (a programme or programmes) to several local commercial stations. **7** to form a syndicate of (people). [C17: from OF *syndicat* office of a SYNDIC]
▸ˌ**syndi'cation** *n*

syndicated research *n Marketing.* a large-scale marketing research project undertaken without being commissioned and subsequently offered to interested parties.

syndrome ('sɪndrəʊm) *n* **1** *Med.* any combination of signs and symptoms that are indicative of a particular disease or disorder. **2** a symptom, characteristic, or set of symptoms or characteristics indicating the existence of a condition, problem, etc. [C16: via NL from Gk *sundromē*, lit.: a running together, from SYN- + *dramein* to run]
▸**syndromic** (sɪn'drɒmɪk) *adj*

syne *or* **syn** (saɪn) *adv, prep, conj* a Scottish word for **since.** [C14: prob. rel. to OE *sīth* since]

synecdoche (sɪn'ɛkdəkɪ) *n* a figure of speech in which a part is substituted for a whole or a whole for a part, as in *50 head of cattle* for *50 cows*, or *the army* for *a soldier.* [C14: via L from Gk *sunekdokhē*, from SYN- + *ekdokhē* interpretation, from *dekhesthai* to accept]
▸**synecdochic** (ˌsɪnɛk'dɒkɪk) *or* ˌ**synec'dochical** *adj*

synecious (sɪ'niːʃəs) *adj* a variant spelling of **synoecious.**

synecology (ˌsɪnɪ'kɒlədʒɪ) *n* the ecological study of communities of plants and animals.
▸**synecologic** (sɪnˌɛkə'lɒdʒɪk) *or* **synˌeco'logical** *adj* ▸**synˌeco'logically** *adv*

syneresis *or* **synaeresis** (sɪ'nɪərɪsɪs) *n* **1** *Chem.* the process in which a gel contracts on standing and exudes liquid, as in the separation of whey in cheese-making. **2** the contraction of two vowels into a diphthong. [C16: via LL from Gk *sunairesis* a shortening, from *sunairein* to draw together, from SYN- + *hairein* to take]

synergism ('sɪnəˌdʒɪzəm, sɪ'nɜː-) *n* **1** Also called: **synergy.** the working together of two or more drugs, muscles, etc., to produce an effect greater than the sum of their individual effects. **2** another name for **synergy** (sense 1). [C18: from NL *synergismus*, from Gk *sunergos*, from SYN- + *ergon* work]
▸ˌ**syner'getic** *adj* ▸'**synergist** *n, adj*

synergy ('sɪnədʒɪ) *n, pl* **synergies. 1** Also called: **synergism.** the potential ability of individual organizations or groups to be more successful or productive as a result of a merger. **2** another name for **synergism** (sense 1). [C19: from NL *synergia*, from Gk *sunergos*; see SYNERGISM]
▸**sy'nergic** *adj*

synesis ('sɪnɪsɪs) *n* a grammatical construction in which the inflection or form of a word is conditioned by the meaning rather than the syntax, as for example the plural form *have* with the singular noun *group* in the sentence *the group have already assembled.* [via NL from Gk *sunesis* union, from *sunienai* to bring together, from SYN- + *hienai* to send]

synesthesia (ˌsɪniːs'θiːzɪə) *n* the usual US spelling of **synaesthesia.**

syngamy ('sɪŋgəmɪ) *or* **syngenesis** (sɪn'dʒɛnɪsɪs) *n* reproduction involving the fusion of a male and female haploid gamete. Also called: **sexual reproduction.**
▸**syngamic** (sɪŋ'gæmɪk) *or* **syngamous** ('sɪŋgəməs) *adj*

synod ('sɪnəd, 'sɪnɒd) *n* **1** a special ecclesiastical council, esp. of a diocese, formally convened to discuss ecclesiastical affairs. **2** *Rare.* any council, esp. for discussion. [C14: from LL *synodus*, from Gk SYN- + *hodos* a way]
▸'**synodal** *adj*

synodic (sɪ'nɒdɪk) *adj* relating to or involving a conjunction or two successive conjunctions of the same star, planet, or satellite.

synodic month *n* See **month** (sense 6).

synoecious *or* **synecious** (sɪ'niːʃəs) *adj* (of plants) having male and female organs on the same flower or structure. [C19: SYN- + *-oecious*, from Gk *oikion* dim. of *oikos* house]

synonym ('sɪnənɪm) *n* **1** a word that means the same or nearly the same as another word, such as *bucket* and *pail.* **2** a word or phrase used as another name for something, such as *Hellene* for a *Greek.*
▸ˌ**syno'nymic** *or* ˌ**syno'nymical** *adj* ▸ˌ**syno'nymity** *n*

synonymous ❶ (sɪ'nɒnɪməs) *adj* **1** (often foll. by *with*) being a synonym (of). **2** (*postpositive;* foll. by *with*) closely associated (with) or suggestive (of): *his name was synonymous with greed.*
▸**syn'onymously** *adv* ▸**syn'onymousness** *n*

synonymy (sɪ'nɒnɪmɪ) *n, pl* **synonymies. 1** the study of synonyms. **2** the character of being synonymous; equivalence. **3** a list or collection of synonyms, esp. one in which their meanings are discriminated.

synopsis ❶ (sɪ'nɒpsɪs) *n, pl* **synopses** (-siːz). a brief review of a subject; summary. [C17: via LL from Gk *sunopsis*, from SYN- + *opsis* view]

synopsize *or* **synopsise** (sɪ'nɒpsaɪz) *vb* **synopsizes, synopsizing, synopsized** *or* **synopsises, synopsising, synopsised.** (*tr*) **1** *US.* variants of **epitomize. 2** *US & Canad.* to make a synopsis of.

synoptic (sɪ'nɒptɪk) *adj* **1** of or relating to a synopsis. **2** (*often cap.*) *Bible.* **2a** (of the Gospels of Matthew, Mark, and Luke) presenting the narrative of Christ's life, ministry, etc., from a point of view held in common by all three, and with close similarities in content, order, etc. **2b**

THESAURUS

symptom *n* **2** = **sign**, expression, indication, mark, note, syndrome, token, warning

symptomatic *adj* **1** = **indicative**, characteristic, suggestive

synonymous *adj* **1** = **equivalent**, equal, identical, identified, interchangeable, one and the same, similar, tantamount, the same

synopsis *n* = **summary**, abridgment, abstract, *aperçu*, compendium, condensation, conspectus, digest, epitome, outline, outline sketch, précis, résumé, review, rundown

of or relating to these three Gospels. **3** *Meteorol.* concerned with the distribution of meteorological conditions over a wide area at a given time: *a synoptic chart.* ◆ *n* **4** (*often cap.*) *Bible.* **4a** any of the three synoptic Gospels. **4b** any of the authors of these. [C18: from Gk *sunoptikos*]
▸**syn'optically** *adv* ▸**syn'optist** *n*

synovia (saɪ'nəuvɪə, sɪ-) *n* a transparent viscid lubricating fluid, secreted by the membrane lining joints, tendon sheaths, etc. [C17: from NL, prob. from SYN- + L *ōvum* egg]
▸**syn'ovial** *adj*

synovitis (ˌsaɪnəu'vaɪtɪs, ˌsɪn-) *n* inflammation of the membrane surrounding a joint.
▸**synovitic** (ˌsaɪnəu'vɪtɪk, ˌsɪn-) *adj*

synroc ('sɪnˌrɒk) *n* a titanium-ceramic substance that can incorporate nuclear waste in its crystals. [from *syn(thetic)* + *roc(k)*]

syntactics (sɪn'tæktɪks) *n* (*functioning as sing*) the branch of semiotics that deals with the formal properties of symbol systems; proof theory.

syntagma (sɪn'tægmə) *or* **syntagm** ('sɪnˌtæm) *n, pl* **syntagmata** (-'tægmətə) *or* **syntagms. 1** a word or phrase forming a syntactic unit. **2** a systematic collection of statements or propositions. [C17: from LL, from Gk, from *suntassein* to put in order; see SYNTAX]
▸ˌ**syntag'matic** *adj*

syntax ('sɪntæks) *n* **1** the branch of linguistics that deals with the grammatical arrangement of words and morphemes in sentences. **2** the totality of facts about the grammatical arrangement of words in a language. **3** a systematic statement of the rules governing the grammatical arrangement of words and morphemes in a language. **4** a systematic statement of the rules governing the properly formed formulas of a logical system. [C17: from LL *syntaxis,* from Gk *suntaxis,* from *suntassein* to put in order, from SYN- + *tassein* to arrange]
▸**syn'tactic** *or* **syn'tactical** *adj* ▸**syn'tactically** *adv*

synth (sɪnθ) *n* short for **synthesizer.**

synthesis ❶ ('sɪnθɪsɪs) *n, pl* **syntheses** (-ˌsi:z). **1** the process of combining objects or ideas into a complex whole. **2** the combination or whole produced by such a process. **3** the process of producing a compound by a chemical reaction or series of reactions, usually from simpler starting materials. **4** *Linguistics.* the use of inflections rather than word order and function words to express the syntactic relations in a language. [C17: via L from Gk *sunthesis,* from *suntithenai* to put together, from SYN- + *tithenai* to place]
▸**'synthesist** *n*

synthesis gas *n Chem.* **1** a mixture of carbon dioxide, carbon monoxide, and hydrogen formerly made by reacting water gas with steam to enrich the proportion of hydrogen in the synthesis of ammonia. **2** a similar mixture of gases made by steam reforming natural gas, used for synthesizing organic chemicals and as a fuel.

synthesize ('sɪnθɪˌsaɪz), **synthetize,** *or* **synthesise, synthetise** *vb* **synthesizes, synthesizing, synthesized; synthetizes, synthetizing, synthetized** *or* **synthesises, synthesising, synthesised; synthetises, synthetising, synthetised. 1** to combine or cause to combine into a whole. **2** (*tr*) to produce by synthesis.
▸ˌ**synthesi'zation,** ˌ**syntheti'zation** *or* ˌ**synthesi'sation,** ˌ**syntheti'sation** *n*

synthesizer ('sɪnθɪˌsaɪzə) *n* **1** an electronic musical instrument, usually operated by means of a keyboard, in which sounds are produced by oscillators, filters, and amplifiers. **2** a person or thing that synthesizes.

synthetic ❶ (sɪn'θɛtɪk) *adj also* **synthetical. 1** (of a substance or material) made artificially by chemical reaction. **2** not genuine; insincere: *synthetic compassion.* **3** denoting languages, such as Latin, whose morphology is characterized by synthesis. **4** *Philosophy.* **4a** (of a proposition) having a truth-value that is not determined solely by virtue of the meanings of the words, as in *all men are arrogant.* **4b** contingent. ◆ *n* **5** a synthetic substance or material. [C17: from NL *syntheticus,* from Gk *sunthetikos* expert in putting together, from *suntithenai* to put together; see SYNTHESIS]
▸**syn'thetically** *adv*

syphilis ('sɪfɪlɪs) *n* a sexually transmitted disease caused by infection with the microorganism *Treponema pallidum:* characterized by an ulcerating chancre, usually on the genitals and progressing through the lymphatic system to nearly all tissues of the body, producing serious clinical manifestations. [C18: from NL *Syphilis* (*sive Morbus Gallicus*) "Syphilis (or the French disease)", title of a poem (1530) by G. Fracastoro, It. physician and poet, in which a shepherd *Syphilus* is portrayed as the first victim of the disease]
▸**syphilitic** (ˌsɪfɪ'lɪtɪk) *adj* ▸**'syphiˌloid** *adj*

syphon ('saɪfᵊn) *n, vb* a variant spelling of **siphon.**

Syriac ('sɪrɪˌæk) *n* a dialect of Aramaic spoken in Syria until about the 13th century A.D.

Syrian ('sɪrɪən) *adj* **1** of or relating to Syria, a republic in W Asia, its people, or their dialect of Arabic. ◆ *n* **2** a native or inhabitant of Syria.

syringa (sɪ'rɪŋgə) *n* another name for **mock orange** (sense 1) or **lilac** (sense 1). [C17: from NL, from Gk *surinx* tube, from use of its hollow stems for pipes]

syringe ('sɪrɪndʒ, sɪ'rɪndʒ) *n* **1** *Med.* a hypodermic syringe or a rubber ball with a slender nozzle, for use in withdrawing or injecting fluids, cleaning wounds, etc. **2** any similar device for injecting, spraying, or extracting liquids by means of pressure or suction. ◆ *vb* **syringes, syringing, syringed. 3** (*tr*) to cleanse, inject, or spray with a syringe. [C15: from LL, from L: SYRINX]

syringomyelia (səˌrɪŋgəumaɪ'i:lɪə) *n* a chronic progressive disease of the spinal cord in which cavities form in the grey matter: characterized by loss of the sense of pain and temperature. [C19: *syringo-,* from Gk: SYRINX + *-myelia* from Gk *muelos* marrow]
▸**syringomyelic** (səˌrɪŋgəumaɪ'ɛlɪk) *adj*

syrinx ('sɪrɪŋks) *n, pl* **syringes** (sɪ'rɪndʒi:z) *or* **syrinxes. 1** the vocal organ of a bird, situated in the lower part of the trachea. **2** (in classical Greek music) a panpipe or set of panpipes. [C17: via L from Gk *surinx* pipe]
▸**syringeal** (sɪ'rɪndʒɪəl) *adj*

syrup ('sɪrəp) *n* **1** a solution of sugar dissolved in water and often flavoured with fruit juice: used for sweetening fruit, etc. **2** any of various thick sweet liquids prepared for cooking or table use from molasses, sugars, etc. **3** *Inf.* cloying sentimentality. **4** a liquid medicine containing a sugar solution for flavouring or preservation. ◆ Also: **sirup.** [C15: from Med. L *syrupus,* from Ar. *sharāb* a drink, from *shariba* to drink]
▸**'syrupy** *adj*

syssarcosis (ˌsɪsɑ:'kəusɪs) *n, pl* **syssarcoses** (-si:z). *Anat.* the union or articulation of bones by muscle. [C17: from NL, from Gk *sussarkōsis,* from *sus-* SYN- + *sarkoun* to become fleshy, from *sarx* flesh]
▸**syssarcotic** (ˌsɪsɑ:'kɒtɪk) *adj*

systaltic (sɪ'stæltɪk) *adj* (esp. of the action of the heart) of, relating to, or characterized by alternate contractions and dilations; pulsating. [C17: from LL *systalticus,* from Gk, from *sustellein* to contract, from SYN- + *stellein* to place]

system ❶ ('sɪstəm) *n* **1** a group or combination of interrelated, interdependent, or interacting elements forming a collective entity; a methodical or coordinated assemblage of parts, facts, etc. **2** any scheme of classification or arrangement. **3** a network of communications, transportation, or distribution. **4** a method or complex of methods: *he has a perfect system at roulette.* **5** orderliness; an ordered manner. **6 the system.** (*often cap.*) society seen as an environment exploiting, restricting, and repressing individuals. **7** an organism considered as a functioning entity. **8** any of various bodily parts or structures that are anatomically or physiologically related: *the digestive system.* **9** one's physiological or psychological constitution: *get it out of your system.* **10** any assembly of electronic, mechanical, etc., components with interdependent functions, usually forming a self-contained unit: *a brake system.* **11** a group of celestial bodies that are associated as a result of natural laws, esp. gravitational attraction: *the solar system.* **12** a point of view or doctrine used to interpret a branch of knowledge. **13** *Mineralogy.* one of a group of divisions into which crystals may be placed on the basis of the lengths and inclinations of their axes. **14** *Geol.* a stratigraphical unit for the rock strata formed during a period of geological time. [C17: from F, from LL *systēma,* from Gk *sustēma,* from SYN- + *histanai* to cause to stand]

systematic ❶ (ˌsɪstɪ'mætɪk) *adj* **1** characterized by the use of order and planning; methodical: *a systematic administrator.* **2** comprising or resembling a system: *systematic theology.* **3** Also: **systematical.** *Biol.* of or relating to taxonomic classification.
▸ˌ**system'atically** *adv* ▸**'systemaˌtism** *n* ▸**'systematist** *n*

systematics (ˌsɪstɪ'mætɪks) *n* (*functioning as sing*) the study of systems and the principles of classification and nomenclature.

systematize ❶ ('sɪstɪməˌtaɪz), **systemize** *or* **systematise, system-**

THESAURUS

synthesis *n* **1 = combining,** amalgamation, coalescence, integration, unification, welding **2 = combination,** amalgam, blend, composite, compound, fusion, meld, union

synthetic *adj* **1 = artificial,** ersatz, fake, man-made, manufactured, mock, pseudo (*inf.*), sham, simulated
Antonyms *adj* authentic, genuine, kosher (*inf.*), natural, pure, real

system *n* **1 = method,** fixed order, frame of reference, methodology, modus operandi, practice, procedure, routine, technique, theory, usage **2 = arrangement,** classification, combination, coordination, organization, scheme, set-up (*inf.*), structure **5 = orderliness,** definite plan, logical process, method, methodicalness, regularity, systematization

systematic *adj* **1 = methodical,** businesslike, efficient, orderly, organized, precise, standardized, systematized, well-ordered
Antonyms *adj* arbitrary, cursory, disorderly, disorganized, haphazard, indiscriminate, random, slapdash, unbusinesslike, unmethodical, unpremeditated, unsystematic

systematize *vb* **= arrange,** classify, dispose, make uniform, methodize, organize, put in order, rationalize, regulate, schematize, sequence, standardize, tabulate

ise *vb* **systematizes, systematizing, systematized; systemizes, systemizing, systemized** *or* **systematises, systematising, systematised; systemises, systemising, systemised.** (*tr*) to arrange in a system.
▸**ˌsystematiˈzation, ˌsystematiˈsation** *or* **ˌsystemiˈzation, ˌsystemiˈsation** *n* ▸**ˈsystemaˌtizer, ˈsystemaˌtiser** *or* **ˈsysteˌmizer, ˈsysteˌmiser** *n*

system building *n* a method of building in which prefabricated components are used to speed the construction of buildings.
▸**ˌsystem ˈbuilt** *adj*

Système International d'Unités (*French* sistɛm ɛ̃tɛrnasjɔnal dynite) *n* the International System of units. See **SI unit.**

systemic (sɪˈstɛmɪk, -ˈstiː-) *adj* **1** another word for **systematic** (senses 1, 2). **2** *Physiol.* (of a poison, disease, etc.) affecting the entire body. **3** (of an insecticide, fungicide, etc.) designed to be absorbed by a plant into its tissues. ◆ *n* **4** a systemic insecticide, fungicide, etc.
▸**sysˈtemically** *adv*

systems analysis *n* the analysis of the requirements of a task and the expression of these in a form that permits the assembly of computer hardware and software to perform the task.
▸**systems analyst** *n*

systems engineering *n* the branch of engineering, based on systems analysis and information theory, concerned with the design of integrated systems.

systole (ˈsɪstəlɪ) *n* contraction of the heart, during which blood is pumped into the aorta and the arteries. Cf. **diastole.** [C16: via LL from Gk *sustolē*, from *sustellein* to contract; see SYSTALTIC]
▸**systolic** (sɪˈstɒlɪk) *adj*

syzygy (ˈsɪzɪdʒɪ) *n, pl* **syzygies. 1** either of the two positions (conjunction or opposition) of a celestial body when sun, earth, and the body lie in a straight line: *the moon is at syzygy when full.* **2** *Rare.* any pair, usually of opposites. [C17: from LL, from Gk *suzugia*, from *suzugos* yoked together, from SYN- + *zugon* a yoke]
▸**syzygial** (sɪˈzɪdʒɪəl), **syzygetic** (ˌsɪzɪˈdʒɛtɪk), *or* **syzygal** (ˈsɪzɪgᵊl) *adj* ▸**ˌsyzyˈgetically** *adv*

Tt

t *or* **T**(ti:) *n, pl* **t's, T's,** *or* **Ts. 1** the 20th letter of the English alphabet. **2** a speech sound represented by this letter. **3** something shaped like a T. **4 to a T.** in every detail; perfectly.

t *symbol for:* **1** *Statistics.* distribution. **2** tonne(s). **3** troy (weight).

T *symbol for:* **1** absolute temperature. **2** surface tension. **3** tera-. **4** tesla. **5** *Chem.* tritium. **6** *Biochem.* thymine.

t. *abbrev. for:* **1** *Commerce.* tare. **2** teaspoon(ful). **3** temperature. **4** *Music.* tempo. **5** *Music.* Also: **T.** tenor. **6** *Grammar.* tense. **7** ton(s). **8** transitive.

't *contraction of* it.

ta (tɑ:) *interj Brit. inf.* thank you. [C18: imit. of baby talk]

Ta *the chemical symbol for* tantalum.

TA (in Britain) *abbrev. for* Territorial Army (now superseded by **TAVR**).

taal (tɑ:l) *n S. African* language: usually, by implication, Afrikaans. [Afrik. from Du.]

tab[1] Ⓣ (tæb) *n* **1** a small flap of material, esp. one on a garment for decoration or for fastening to a button. **2** any similar flap, such as a piece of paper attached to a file for identification. **3** *Brit. mil.* the insignia on the collar of a staff officer. **4** *Chiefly US & Canad.* a bill, esp. for a meal or drinks. **5 keep tabs on.** *Inf.* to keep a watchful eye on. ◆ *vb* **tabs, tabbing, tabbed. 6** *(tr)* to supply with a tab or tabs. [C17: from ?]

tab[2] (tæb) *n* short for **tabulator** or **tablet.**

TAB *abbrev. for:* **1** *Austral. & NZ.* Totalizator Agency Board. **2** typhoid-paratyphoid A and B (vaccine).

tabard ('tæbəd) *n* a sleeveless or short-sleeved jacket, esp. one worn by a herald, bearing a coat of arms, or by a knight over his armour. [C13: from OF *tabart,* from ?]

tabaret ('tæbərɪt) *n* a hard-wearing fabric of silk or similar cloth with stripes of satin or moire, used esp. for upholstery. [C19: ? from TABBY[1]]

Tabasco (tə'bæskəʊ) *n Trademark.* a very hot red sauce made from matured capsicums.

tabby[1] ('tæbɪ) *n* a fabric with a watered pattern, esp. silk or taffeta. [C17: from OF *tabis* silk cloth, from Ar. *al-'attabiya,* lit.: the quarter of (Prince) 'Attab, the part of Baghdad where the fabric was first made]

tabby[2] Ⓣ ('tæbɪ) *adj* **1** (esp. of cats) brindled with dark stripes or wavy markings on a lighter background. **2** having a wavy or striped pattern, particularly in colours of grey and brown. ◆ *n, pl* **tabbies. 3** a tabby cat. **4** any female domestic cat. [C17: from *Tabby,* pet form of the girl's name *Tabitha,* prob. infl. by TABBY[1]]

tabernacle ('tæbə,nækᵊl) *n* **1** *(often cap.) Old Testament.* **1a** the portable sanctuary in which the ancient Israelites carried the Ark of the Covenant. **1b** the Jewish Temple. **2** any place of worship that is not called a church. **3** *RC Church.* a receptacle in which the Blessed Sacrament is kept. **4** *Chiefly RC Church.* a canopied niche. **5** *Naut.* a strong framework for holding the foot of a mast, allowing it to be swung down to pass under low bridges, etc. [C13: from L *tabernāculum* a tent, from *taberna* a hut]
▸ **,taber'nacular** *adj*

tabes ('teɪbi:z) *n, pl* **tabes. 1** a wasting of a bodily organ or part. **2** short for **tabes dorsalis.** [C17: from L: a wasting away]
▸ **tabetic** (tə'bɛtɪk) *adj*

tabescent (tə'bɛsᵊnt) *adj* **1** progressively emaciating; wasting away. **2** of, relating to, or having tabes. [C19: from L *tābēscere,* from TABES]
▸ **ta'bescence** *n*

tabes dorsalis (dɔ:'sɑ:lɪs) *n* a form of late syphilis that attacks the spinal cord causing degeneration of the nerve fibres, paralysis of the leg muscles, acute abdominal pain, etc. [NL, lit.: tabes of the back]

tabla ('tʌblə, 'tɑ:blɑ:) *n* a musical instrument of India consisting of a pair of drums whose pitches can be varied. [Hindu, from Ar. *tabla* drum]

tablature ('tæblətʃə) *n Music.* any of a number of forms of musical notation, esp. for playing the lute, consisting of letters and signs indicating rhythm and fingering. [C16: from F, ult. from L *tabulātum* wooden floor, from *tabula* a plank]

table Ⓣ ('teɪbᵊl) *n* **1** a flat horizontal slab or board, usually supported by one or more legs. **2a** such a slab or board on which food is served. **2b** *(as modifier): table linen.* **3** food as served in a particular household, etc.: *a good table.* **4** such a piece of furniture specially designed for any of various purposes: *a bird table.* **5a** a company of persons assembled for a meal, game, etc. **5b** *(as modifier): table talk.* **6** any flat or level area, such as a plateau. **7** a rectangular panel set below or above the face of a wall. **8** *Archit.* another name for **string course. 9** any of various flat surfaces, as an upper horizontal facet of a cut gem. **10** *Music.* the sounding board of a violin, guitar, etc. **11a** an arrangement of words, numbers, or signs, usually in parallel columns. **11b** See **multiplication table. 12** a tablet on which laws were inscribed by the ancient Romans, the Hebrews, etc. **13 turn the tables.** to cause a complete reversal of circumstances. **14 under the table. 14a** (**under-the-table** *when prenominal*) done illicitly and secretly. **14b** *Sl.* drunk. ◆ *vb* **tables, tabling, tabled.** *(tr)* **15** to place on a table. **16** *Brit.* to submit (a bill, etc.) for consideration by a legislative body. **17** *US.* to suspend discussion of (a bill, etc.) indefinitely. **18** to enter in or form into a list. [C12: via OF from L *tabula* a writing tablet]

tableau Ⓣ ('tæbləʊ) *n, pl* **tableaux** (-ləʊ, -ləʊz) *or* **tableaus. 1** See ***tableau vivant.*** **2** a pause on stage when all the performers briefly freeze in position. **3** any dramatic group or scene. [C17: from F, from OF *tablel* a picture, dim. of TABLE]

tableau vivant *French.* (tablo vivɑ̃) *n, pl* ***tableaux vivants*** (tablo vivɑ̃). a representation of a scene by a person or group posed silent and motionless. [C19, lit.: living picture]

tablecloth ('teɪbᵊl,klɒθ) *n* a cloth for covering the top of a table, esp. during meals.

table d'hôte ('tɑ:bᵊl 'dəʊt) *adj* **1** (of a meal) consisting of a set number of courses with limited choice of dishes offered at a fixed price. Cf. **à la carte.** ◆ *n, pl* **tables d'hôte** ('tɑ:bᵊlz 'dəʊt). **2** a table d'hôte meal or menu. [C17: from F, lit.: the host's table]

tableland Ⓣ ('teɪbᵊl,lænd) *n* flat elevated land.

table licence *n* a licence authorizing the sale of alcoholic drinks with meals only.

tablespoon ('teɪbᵊl,spu:n) *n* **1** a spoon, larger than a dessertspoon, used for serving food, etc. **2** Also called: **tablespoonful.** the amount contained in such a spoon. **3** a unit of capacity used in cooking, etc., equal to half a fluid ounce.

tablet ('tæblɪt) *n* **1** a pill made of a compressed medicinal substance. **2** a flattish cake of some substance, such as soap. **3** a slab of stone, wood, etc., esp. one used for inscriptions. **4a** a rigid sheet, as of bark, etc., used for similar purposes. **4b** *(often pl)* a set of these fastened together. **5** a pad of writing paper. **6** *Scot.* a sweet made from butter, sugar, and condensed milk, usually shaped into flat oblong cakes. [C14: from OF *tablete* a little table, from L *tabula* a board]

table tennis *n* a miniature form of tennis played on a table with bats and a hollow ball.

table-turning *n* the movement of a table attributed by spiritualists to the power of spirits.

tableware ('teɪbᵊl,wɛə) *n* articles such as dishes, plates, knives, forks, etc., used at meals.

tabloid ('tæblɔɪd) *n* **1** a newspaper with pages about 30 cm (12 inches) by 40 cm (16 inches), usually with many photographs and a concise and often sensational style. **2** *(modifier)* designed to appeal to a mass audience or readership; sensationalist: *the tabloid press; tabloid television.* [C20: from earlier *Tabloid,* a trademark for a medicine in tablet form]

taboo Ⓣ *or* **tabu** (tə'bu:) *adj* **1** forbidden or disapproved of: *taboo words.* **2** (in Polynesia) marked off as sacred and forbidden. ◆ *n, pl* **taboos** *or* **tabus. 3** any prohibition resulting from social or other conventions. **4** ritual restriction or prohibition, esp. of something that is considered holy or unclean. ◆ *vb* **5** *(tr)* to place under a taboo. [C18: from Tongan *tapu*]

tabor *or* **tabour** ('teɪbə) *n* a small drum used esp. in the Middle Ages, struck with one hand while the other held a pipe. [C13: from OF *tabour,* ?from Persian *tabīr*]

taboret *or* **tabouret** ('tæbərɪt) *n* **1** a low stool. **2** a frame for stretching out cloth while it is being embroidered. **3** a small tabor. [C17: from F *tabouret,* dim. of TABOR]

tabular ('tæbjʊlə) *adj* **1** arranged in systematic or table form. **2** calculated from or by means of a table. **3** like a table in form; flat. [C17: from L *tabulāris* concerning boards, from *tabula* a board]
▸ **'tabularly** *adv*

tabula rasa ('tæbjʊlə 'rɑ:sə) *n, pl* **tabulae rasae** ('tæbjʊli: 'rɑ:si:). **1** the mind in its uninformed original state. **2** an opportunity for a fresh start; clean slate. [L: a scraped tablet]

tabulate Ⓣ *vb* ('tæbjʊ,leɪt), **tabulates, tabulating, tabulated.** *(tr)* **1** to set out, arrange, or write in tabular form. **2** to form or cut with a flat surface.

THESAURUS

tab[1] *n* **1, 2** = **flap**, flag, label, marker, sticker, tag, ticket

tabby[2] *adj* **2** = **striped**, banded, brindled, streaked, stripy, wavy

table *n* **1** = **counter**, bench, board, slab, stand **3** *Formal* = **food**, board, diet, fare, spread *(inf.)*, victuals **6** = **plateau**, flat, flatland, mesa, plain, tableland **11a** = **list**, agenda, catalogue, chart, diagram, digest, graph, index, inventory, plan, record, register, roll, schedule, synopsis, tabulation ◆ *vb* **16** *Brit.* = **submit**, enter, move, propose, put forward, suggest

tableau *n* **3** = **picture**, representation, scene, spectacle

tableland *n* = **plateau**, flat, flatland, mesa, plain, table

taboo *adj* **1** = **forbidden**, anathema, banned, beyond the pale, disapproved of, frowned on, not allowed, not permitted, off limits, outlawed, prohibited, proscribed, ruled out, unacceptable, unmentionable, unthinkable ◆ *n* **3** = **prohibition**, anathema, ban, disapproval, interdict, proscription, restriction
Antonyms *adj* ≠ **forbidden**: acceptable, allowed, permitted, sanctioned

tabulate *vb* **1** = **arrange**, catalogue, categorize, chart, classify, codify, index, list, order, range, systematize, tabularize

◆ *adj* ('tæbjʊlɪt, -ˌleɪt). **3** having a flat surface. [C18: from L *tabula* a board]
▸ **'tabulable** *adj* ▸ **ˌtabu'lation** *n*

tabulator ('tæbjʊˌleɪtə) *n* **1** a device for setting the stops that locate the column margins on a typewriter. **2** *Computing.* a machine that reads data from one medium, such as punched cards, producing lists, tabulations, or totals.

tacamahac ('tækəməˌhæk) *or* **tacmahack** *n* **1** any of several strong-smelling resinous gums used in ointments, incense, etc. **2** any tree yielding this resin. [C16: from Sp. *tacamahaca,* from Nahuatl *tecomahca* aromatic resin]

tacet ('teɪset, 'tæs-) *vb* (*intr*) (on a musical score) a direction indicating that a particular instrument or singer does not take part. [C18: from L: it is silent, from *tacēre* to be quiet]

tacheometer (ˌtækɪ'ɒmɪtə) *or* **tachymeter** *n Surveying.* a type of theodolite designed for the rapid measurement of distances, elevations, and directions.
▸ **ˌtache'ometry** *n*

tachisme ('tɑːʃɪzəm) *n* a type of action painting in which haphazard dabs and blots of colour are treated as a means of unconscious expression. [C20: F, from *tache* stain]

tachistoscope (tæ'kɪstəˌskəʊp) *n* an instrument for displaying visual images for very brief intervals, usually a fraction of a second. [C20: from Gk *takhistos* swiftest + -SCOPE]
▸ **tachistoscopic** (tæˌkɪstə'skɒpɪk) *adj*

tacho- *combining form.* speed: *tachograph; tachometer.* [from Gk *takhos*]

tachograph ('tækəˌgrɑːf) *n* a tachometer that produces a record (**tachogram**) of its readings, esp. a device for recording the speed of and distance covered by a vehicle. Often shortened to **tacho.**

tachometer (tæ'kɒmɪtə) *n* any device for measuring speed, esp. the rate of revolution of a shaft. Tachometers are often fitted to cars to indicate the number of revolutions per minute of the engine.
▸ **ta'chometry** *n*

tachy- *or* **tacheo-** *combining form.* swift or accelerated: *tachyon.* [from Gk *takhus* swift]

tachycardia (ˌtækɪ'kɑːdɪə) *n* abnormally rapid beating of the heart.

tachygraphy (tæ'kɪgrəfɪ) *n* shorthand, esp. as used in ancient Rome or Greece.

tachymeter (tæ'kɪmɪtə) *n* another name for **tacheometer.**

tachyon ('tækɪˌɒn) *n Physics.* a hypothetical elementary particle capable of travelling faster than the velocity of light. [C20: from TACHY- + -ON]

tachyphylaxis (ˌtækɪfɪ'læksɪs) *n* very rapid development of tolerance or immunity to the effects of a drug. [NL, from TACHY- + *phylaxis* on the model of *prophylaxis;* see PROPHYLACTIC]

tacit ⓣ ('tæsɪt) *adj* implied or inferred without direct expression; understood: *a tacit agreement.* [C17: from L *tacitus,* p.p. of *tacēre* to be silent]
▸ **'tacitly** *adv*

taciturn ⓣ ('tæsɪˌtɜːn) *adj* habitually silent, reserved, or uncommunicative. [C18: from L *taciturnus,* from *tacēre* to be silent]
▸ **ˌtaci'turnity** *n* ▸ **'taciˌturnly** *adv*

tack[1] ⓣ (tæk) *n* **1** a short sharp-pointed nail, with a large flat head. **2** *Brit.* a long loose temporary stitch used in dressmaking, etc. **3** See **tailor's-tack. 4** a temporary fastening. **5** stickiness. **6** *Naut.* the heading of a vessel sailing to windward, stated in terms of the side of the sail against which the wind is pressing. **7** *Naut.* **7a** a course sailed with the wind blowing from forward of the beam. **7b** one such course or a zigzag pattern of such courses. **8** *Naut.* **8a** a sheet for controlling the weather clew of a course. **8b** the weather clew itself. **9** *Naut.* the forward lower clew of a fore-and-aft sail. **10** a course of action or policy. **11 on the wrong tack.** under a false impression. ◆ *vb* **12** (*tr*) to secure by a tack or tacks. **13** *Brit.* to sew (something) with long loose temporary stitches. **14** (*tr*) to attach or append. **15** *Naut.* to change the heading of (a sailing vessel) to the opposite tack. **16** *Naut.* to steer (a sailing vessel) on alternate tacks. **17** (*intr*) *Naut.* (of a sailing vessel) to proceed on a different tack or to alternate tacks. **18** (*intr*) to follow a zigzag route; keep changing one's course of action. [C14 *tak* fastening, nail]
▸ **'tacker** *n*

tack[2] (tæk) *n* riding harness for horses, such as saddles, bridles, etc. [C20: shortened from TACKLE]

tack hammer *n* a light hammer for driving tacks.

tackies *or* **takkies** ('tækɪz) *pl n, sing* **tacky.** *S. African inf.* tennis shoes or plimsolls. [C20: prob. from TACKY[1], from their nonslip rubber soles]

tackle ⓣ ('tæk^{ə}l) *n* **1** an arrangement of ropes and pulleys designed to lift heavy weights. **2** the equipment required for a particular occupation, etc. **3** *Naut.* the halyards and other running rigging aboard a vessel. **4** *Sport.* a physical challenge to an opponent, as to prevent his progress with the ball. **5** *American football.* a defensive lineman. ◆ *vb* **tackles, tackling, tackled. 6** (*tr*) to undertake (a task, etc.). **7** (*tr*) to confront (esp. an opponent) with a difficult proposition. **8** *Sport.* to challenge (an opponent) with a tackle. [C13: rel. to MLow G *takel* ship's rigging]
▸ **'tackler** *n*

tack rag *n Building trades.* a cotton cloth impregnated with an oil, used to remove dust from a surface prior to painting.

tacky[1] ⓣ ('tækɪ) *adj* **tackier, tackiest.** slightly sticky or adhesive. [C18: from TACK[1] (in the sense: stickiness)]
▸ **'tackily** *adv* ▸ **'tackiness** *n*

tacky[2] ⓣ ('tækɪ) *adj* **tackier, tackiest.** *Inf.* **1** shabby or shoddy. **2** ostentatious and vulgar. **3** *US.* (of a person) dowdy; seedy. [C19: from dialect *tacky* an inferior horse, from ?]
▸ **'tackiness** *n*

tacnode ('tækˌnəʊd) *n* another name for **osculation** (sense 1). [C19: from L *tactus* touch (from *tangere* to touch) + NODE]

tact ⓣ (tækt) *n* **1** a sense of what is fitting and considerate in dealing with others, so as to avoid giving offence. **2** skill in handling difficult situations; diplomacy. [C17: from L *tactus* a touching, from *tangere* to touch]
▸ **'tactful** *adj* ▸ **'tactfulness** *n* ▸ **'tactless** *adj* ▸ **'tactlessness** *n*

tactic ⓣ ('tæktɪk) *n* a piece of tactics; tactical move. See also **tactics.**

-tactic *adj combining form.* having a specified kind of pattern or arrangement or having an orientation determined by a specified force: *syndiotactic; phototactic.* [from Gk *taktikos* relating to order; see TACTICS]

tactical ⓣ ('tæktɪk^{ə}l) *adj* **1** of, relating to, or employing tactics: *a tactical error.* **2** (of missiles, bombing, etc.) for use in or supporting limited military operations; short-range. **3** skilful, adroit, or diplomatic.
▸ **'tactically** *adv*

tactical voting *n* (in an election) the practice of casting one's vote not for the party of one's choice but for the second strongest contender in a constituency in order to defeat the likeliest winner.

tactics ⓣ ('tæktɪks) *pl n* **1** (*functioning as sing*) *Mil.* the art and science of the detailed direction and control of movement of forces in battle to achieve an aim or task. **2** the manoeuvres used to achieve an aim or task. **3** plans followed to achieve a particular short-term aim. [C17: from NL *tactica,* from Gk, from *taktikos* concerning arrangement, from *taktos* arranged (for battle), from *tassein* to arrange]
▸ **tac'tician** *n*

tactile ('tæktaɪl) *adj* **1** of, relating to, affecting, or having a sense of touch. **2** *Now rare.* tangible. [C17: from L *tactilis,* from *tangere* to touch]
▸ **tactility** (tæk'tɪlɪtɪ) *n*

tadpole ('tædˌpəʊl) *n* the aquatic larva of frogs, toads, etc., which develops from a limbless tailed form with external gills into a form with internal gills, limbs, and a reduced tail. [C15 *taddepol,* from *tadde* toad + *pol* head]

taedium vitae ('tiːdɪəm 'viːtaɪ, 'vaɪtiː) *n* the feeling that life is boring and dull. [L, lit.: weariness of life]

tae kwon do ('taɪ 'kwɒn 'dəʊ, 'teɪ) *n* a Korean martial art that resembles karate. [C20: Korean *tae* kick + *kwon* fist + *do* way, method]

tael (teɪl) *n* **1** a unit of weight, used in the Far East. **2** (formerly) a Chi-

THESAURUS

tacit *adj* = **implied**, implicit, inferred, silent, taken for granted, undeclared, understood, unexpressed, unspoken, unstated, wordless
Antonyms *adj* explicit, express, spelled-out, spoken, stated

taciturn *adj* = **uncommunicative**, aloof, antisocial, close-lipped, cold, distant, dumb, mute, quiet, reserved, reticent, silent, tight-lipped, unforthcoming, withdrawn
Antonyms *adj* blethering, chatty, communicative, forthcoming, garrulous, loquacious, open, outgoing, prattling, sociable, talkative, unreserved, verbose, voluble, wordy

tack[1] *n* **1** = **nail**, drawing pin, pin, staple, thumbtack (*US*), tintack ◆ *vb* **12** = **fasten**, affix, attach, fix, nail, pin, staple **13** *Brit.* = **stitch**, baste, sew **14 tack on** = **append**, add, annex, attach, tag

tackle *n* **2** = **equipment**, accoutrements, apparatus, gear, implements, outfit, paraphernalia, rig, rigging, tools, trappings **4** = **challenge**, block, stop ◆ *vb* **6** = **deal with**, apply oneself to, attempt, begin, come *or* get to grips with, embark upon, engage in, essay, get stuck into (*inf.*), have a go *or* stab at (*inf.*), set about, sink one's teeth into, take on, take the bit between one's teeth, try, turn one's hand to, undertake, wade into **7** = **confront**, block, bring down, challenge, clutch, grab, grasp, halt, intercept, seize, stop, take hold of, throw

tacky[1] *adj* = **sticky**, adhesive, gluey, gummy, wet

tacky[2] *adj* **1** = **shabby**, seedy, shoddy, tatty **2** = **vulgar**, naff (*Brit. sl.*), nasty, sleazy, tasteless

tact *n* **1, 2** = **diplomacy**, address, adroitness, consideration, delicacy, discretion, finesse, judgment, perception, savoir-faire, sensitivity, skill, thoughtfulness, understanding
Antonyms *n* awkwardness, clumsiness, gaucherie, heavy-handedness, indiscretion, insensitivity, lack of consideration, lack of discretion, tactlessness

tactful *adj* **1, 2** = **diplomatic**, careful, considerate, delicate, discreet, judicious, perceptive, polished, polite, politic, prudent, sensitive, subtle, thoughtful, treating with kid gloves, understanding
Antonyms *adj* awkward, clumsy, gauche, inconsiderate, indiscreet, insensitive, tactless, tasteless, thoughtless, undiplomatic, unsubtle, untoward

tactic *n* = **policy**, approach, course, device, line, manoeuvre, means, method, move, ploy, scheme, stratagem, tack, trick, way

tactical *adj* **3** = **strategic**, adroit, artful, clever, cunning, diplomatic, foxy, politic, shrewd, skilful, smart
Antonyms *adj* blundering, clumsy, gauche, impolitic, inept

tactics *n* **1-3** = **strategy**, campaigning, generalship, manoeuvres, plans

tactless *adj* **1, 2** = **insensitive**, blundering, boorish, careless, clumsy, discourteous, gauche, harsh, impolite, impolitic, imprudent, inconsiderate, indelicate, indiscreet, inept, injudicious, maladroit, rough, rude, sharp, thoughtless, uncivil, undiplomatic, unfeeling, unkind, unsubtle

nese monetary unit. [C16: from Port., from Malay *tahil* weight, ?from Sansk.]

ta'en (teɪn) *vb* a Scot. or poetic contraction of **taken.**

taenia *or US* **tenia** ('tiːnɪə) *n, pl* **taeniae** *or US* **teniae** (-nɪ,iː). **1** (in ancient Greece) a headband. **2** *Archit.* the fillet between the architrave and frieze of a Doric entablature. **3** *Anat.* any bandlike structure or part. **4** any of a genus of tapeworms. [C16: via L from Gk *tainia* narrow strip]

taeniasis *or US* **teniasis** (tiː'naɪəsɪs) *n Pathol.* infestation with tapeworms of the genus *Taenia.*

taffeta ('tæfɪtə) *n* a thin crisp lustrous plain-weave fabric of silk, etc., used esp. for women's clothes. [C14: from Med. L *taffata,* from Persian *tāftah* spun, from *tāftan* to spin]

taffrail ('tæf,reɪl) *n Naut.* a rail at the stern of a vessel. [C19: changed from earlier *tafferel,* from Du. *tafereel* panel (hence applied to the part of a vessel decorated with carved panels), from *tafel* table]

Taffy ('tæfɪ) *n, pl* **Taffies.** a slang word or nickname for a **Welshman.** [C17: from the supposed Welsh pronunciation of *Davy* (from *David,* Welsh *Dafydd*), a common Welsh Christian name]

tafia *or* **taffia** ('tæfɪə) *n* a type of rum, esp. from Guyana or the Caribbean. [C18: from F, from West Indian Creole, prob. from RATAFIA]

tag[1] Ⓣ (tæg) *n* **1** a piece of paper, leather, etc., for attaching to something as a mark or label: *a price tag.* **2** Also called: **electronic tag.** an electronic device worn by an offender serving a noncustodial sentence, which monitors the offender's whereabouts by means of a link to a central computer through the telephone system. **3** a small piece of material hanging from a part or piece. **4** a point of metal, etc., at the end of a cord or lace. **5** an epithet or verbal appendage, the refrain of a song, the moral of a fable, etc. **6** a brief quotation. **7** an ornamental flourish. **8** the tip of an animal's tail. **9** a matted lock of wool or hair. **10** *Sl.* a graffito consisting of a nickname or personal symbol. ◆ *vb* **tags, tagging, tagged.** (*mainly tr*) **11** to mark with a tag. **12** to monitor the whereabouts of (an offender) by means of an electronic tag. **13** to add or append as a tag. **14** to supply (prose or blank verse) with rhymes. **15** (*intr;* usually foll. by *on* or *along*) to trail (behind). **16** to name or call (someone something). **17** to cut the tags of wool or hair from (an animal). [C15: from ?]

tag[2] (tæg) *n* **1** Also called: **tig.** a children's game in which one player chases the others in an attempt to catch one of them who will then become the chaser. **2** the act of tagging one's partner in tag wrestling. **3** (*modifier*) denoting a wrestling contest between two teams of two wrestlers, in which only one from each team may be in the ring at one time. The contestant outside the ring may change places with his team-mate inside the ring after touching his hand. ◆ *vb* **tags, tagging, tagged.** (*tr*) **4** to catch (another child) in the game of tag. **5** (in tag wrestling) to touch the hand of (one's partner). [C18: ?from TAG[1]]

Tagalog (tə'gɑːlɒg) *n* **1** (*pl* **Tagalogs** *or* **Tagalog**) a member of a people of the Philippines. **2** the language of this people. ◆ *adj* **3** of or relating to this people or their language.

tag end *n* **1** the last part of something. **2** a loose end of cloth, thread, etc.

tagetes (tæ'dʒiːtiːz) *n, pl* **tagetes.** any of a genus of plants with yellow or orange flowers, including the French and African marigolds. [from NL, from *Tages,* an Etruscan god]

tagliatelle (,tæljə'telɪ) *n* a form of pasta made in narrow strips. [It., from *tagliare* to cut]

tag line *n* **1** an amusing or memorable phrase designed to catch attention in an advert. **2** another name for **punch line.**

tahr *or* **thar** (tɑː) *n* any of several goatlike mammals of S and SW Asia, having a shaggy coat and curved horns. [from Nepali *thār*]

tahsil (tə'siːl) *n* an administrative division in certain states in India. [Urdu, from Ar.: collection]

Tai (taɪ) *adj, n* a variant spelling of **Thai.**

taiaha ('taɪə,hɑː) *n NZ.* a carved weapon in the form of a staff, now used in Maori ceremonial oratory. [from Maori]

t'ai chi ch'uan ('taɪ dʒiː 'tʃwɑːn) *n* a Chinese system of callisthenics characterized by coordinated and rhythmic movements. Often shortened to **t'ai chi** ('taɪ 'dʒiː). [Chinese, lit.: great art of boxing]

taiga ('taɪgɑː) *n* the coniferous forests extending across much of subarctic North America and Eurasia. [from Russian, of Turkic origin]

taihoa ('taɪhəʊə) *sentence substitute. NZ.* hold on! no hurry! [Maori]

tail[1] Ⓣ (teɪl) *n* **1** the rear part of the vertebrate body that contains an elongation of the vertebral column, esp. forming a flexible appendage. **2** anything resembling such an appendage; the bottom, lowest, or rear part. **3** the last part or parts: *the tail of the storm.* **4** the rear part of an aircraft including the fin, tailplane, and control surfaces. **5** *Astron.* the luminous stream of gas and dust particles driven from the head of a comet when close to the sun. **6** the rear portion of a bomb, rocket, missile, etc., usually fitted with guiding or stabilizing vanes. **7** a line of people or things. **8** a long braid or tress of hair: *a pigtail.* **9** a final short line in a stanza. **10** *Inf.* a person employed to follow and spy upon another. **11** an informal word for **buttocks. 12** *Taboo sl.* **12a** the female genitals. **12b** a woman considered sexually (esp. in **piece of tail, bit of tail**). **13** the foot of a page. **14** the lower end of a pool or part of a stream. **15** *Inf.* the course or track of a fleeing person or animal. **16** (*modifier*) coming from or situated in the rear: *a tail wind.* **17 turn tail.** to run away; escape. **18 with one's tail between one's legs.** in a state of utter defeat or confusion. ◆ *vb* **19** to form or cause to form the tail. **20** to remove the tail of (an animal). **21** (*tr*) to remove the stalk of. **22** (*tr*) to connect (objects, ideas, etc.) together by or as if by the tail. **23** (*tr*) *Inf.* to follow stealthily. **24** (*intr*) (of a vessel) to assume a specified position, as when at a mooring. **25** to build the end of (a brick, joist, etc.) into a wall or (of a brick, etc.) to have one end built into a wall. ◆ See also **tail off, tail out, tails.** [OE *tægel*]
▸ **'tailless** *adj*

tail[2] (teɪl) *Law.* ◆ *n* **1** the limitation of an estate or interest to a person and the heirs of his body. ◆ *adj* **2** (*immediately postpositive*) limited in this way. [C15: from OF *taille* a division; see TAILOR]
▸ **'tailless** *adj*

tailback ('teɪl,bæk) *n* a queue of traffic stretching back from an obstruction.

tailboard ('teɪl,bɔːd) *n* a board at the rear of a lorry, etc., that can be removed or let down.

tail coat *n* **1** a man's black coat having a horizontal cut over the hips and a tapering tail with a vertical slit up to the waist. **2** a cutaway frock coat, part of morning dress.

tail covert *n* any of the covert feathers of a bird covering the bases of the tail feathers.

tail end *n* the last, endmost, or final part.

tailgate ('teɪl,geɪt) *n* **1** another name for **tailboard. 2** a door at the rear of a hatchback vehicle. ◆ *vb* **tailgates, tailgating, tailgated. 3** to drive very close behind (a vehicle).
▸ **'tail,gater** *n*

tail gate *n* a gate that is used to control the flow of water at the lower end of a lock.

tailing ('teɪlɪŋ) *n* the part of a beam, rafter, projecting brick, etc., embedded in a wall.

tailings ('teɪlɪŋz) *pl n* waste left over after certain processes, such as from an ore-crushing plant or in milling grain.

tail-light ('teɪl,laɪt) *or* **tail lamp** *n* other names for **rear light.**

tail off Ⓣ *or* **away** *vb* (*adv; usually intr*) to decrease or cause to decrease in quantity, degree, etc., esp. gradually.

tailor Ⓣ ('teɪlə) *n* **1** a person who makes, repairs, or alters outer garments, esp. menswear. Related adj: **sartorial. 2** a voracious and active marine food fish of Australia. ◆ *vb* **3** to cut or style (material, etc.) to satisfy certain requirements. **4** (*tr*) to adapt so as to make suitable. **5** (*intr*) to work as a tailor. [C13: from Anglo-Norman *taillour,* from OF *taillier* to cut, from L *tālea* a cutting]
▸ **'tailored** *adj*

tailorbird ('teɪlə,bɜːd) *n* any of several tropical Asian warblers that build nests by sewing together large leaves using plant fibres.

tailor-made Ⓣ *adj* **1** made by a tailor to fit exactly. **2** perfectly meeting a particular purpose. ◆ *n* **3** a tailor-made garment. **4** *Inf.* a factory-made cigarette.

tailor's chalk *n* pipeclay used by tailors and dressmakers to mark seams, darts, etc., on material.

tailor's-tack *n* one of a series of loose looped stitches used to transfer markings for seams, darts, etc., from a paper pattern to material.

tail out *vb* (*tr, adv*) *NZ.* to guide (timber) as it emerges from a circular saw.

tailpiece ('teɪl,piːs) *n* **1** an extension or appendage that lengthens or completes something. **2** a decorative design at the foot of a page or end of a chapter. **3** *Music.* a piece of wood to which the strings of a violin, etc., are attached at their lower end. **4** a short beam or rafter that has one end embedded in a wall.

tailpipe ('teɪl,paɪp) *n* a pipe from which exhaust gases are discharged, esp. the terminal pipe of the exhaust system of a motor vehicle.

tailplane ('teɪl,pleɪn) *n* a small horizontal wing at the tail of an aircraft to provide longitudinal stability. Also called (esp. US): **horizontal stabilizer.**

tailrace ('teɪl,reɪs) *n* a channel that carries water away from a water wheel, turbine, etc.

tail rotor *n* a small propeller fitted to the rear of a helicopter to coun-

THESAURUS

Antonyms *adj* considerate, diplomatic, discreet, polite, subtle, tactful

tag[1] *n* **1** = **label,** docket, flag, flap, identification, mark, marker, note, slip, sticker, tab, ticket ◆ *vb* **11** = **label,** earmark, flag, identify, mark, ticket **13** *with* **on** = **add,** adjoin, affix, annex, append, fasten, tack **15** *with* **along** *or* **on** = **accompany,** attend, dog, follow, shadow, tail (*inf.*), trail **16** = **name,** call, christen, dub, label, nickname, style, term

tail[1] *n* **2** = **extremity,** appendage, conclusion, empennage, end, rear end, tailpiece, train **7** = **line,** file, queue, tailback, train **8** = **braid,** pigtail, plait, ponytail, tress **11** *Informal* = **buttocks,** arse, ass (*US & Canad. taboo sl.*), backside (*inf.*), behind (*inf.*), bottom, bum (*Brit. sl.*), buns (*US sl.*), butt (*US & Canad. inf.*), croup, derrière (*euphemistic*), jacksy (*Brit. sl.*), posterior, rear (*inf.*), rear end, rump **17 turn tail** = **run away,** cut and run, escape, flee, hook it (*sl.*), make off, retreat, run for it (*inf.*), run off, scarper (*Brit. sl.*), show a clean pair of heels, skedaddle (*inf.*), take off (*inf.*), take to one's heels ◆ *vb* **23** *Informal* = **follow,** dog the footsteps of, keep an eye on, shadow, stalk, track, trail

tail off *vb* = **decrease,** die out, drop, dwindle, fade, fall away, peter out, wane
Antonyms *vb* grow, increase, intensify, wax

tailor *n* **1** = **outfitter,** clothier, costumier, couturier, dressmaker, garment maker, seamstress ◆ *vb* **4** = **adapt,** accommodate, adjust, alter, convert, customize, cut, fashion, fit, modify, mould, shape, style, suit

tailor-made *adj* **1** = **made-to-measure,** cut to fit, fitted, made to order **2** = **perfect,** custom-made, ideal, just right, right, right up one's street (*inf.*), suitable, up one's alley

DICTIONARY

teract the torque reaction of the main rotor and thus prevent the body of the helicopter from rotating in an opposite direction.

tails (teɪlz) *pl n* **1** an informal name for **tail coat.** ◆ *interj, adv* **2** with the reverse side of a coin uppermost.

tailskid ('teɪlˌskɪd) *n* **1** a runner under the tail of an aircraft. **2** a rear-wheel skid of a motor vehicle.

tailspin ('teɪlˌspɪn) *n* **1** *Aeronautics.* another name for **spin** (sense 16). **2** *Inf.* a state of confusion or panic.

tailstock ('teɪlˌstɒk) *n* a casting that slides on the bed of a lathe and is locked in position to support the free end of a workpiece.

tailwind ('teɪlˌwɪnd) *n* a wind blowing in the same direction as the course of an aircraft or ship.

Taino ('taɪnəʊ) *n* **1** (*pl* **Tainos** *or* **Taino**) a member of an extinct American Indian people of the West Indies. **2** the language of this people.

taint ➊ (teɪnt) *vb* **1** to affect or be affected by pollution or contamination. **2** to tarnish (someone's reputation, etc.). ◆ *n* **3** a defect or flaw. **4** a trace of contamination or infection. [C14: (infl. by *attaint* infected, from ATTAIN) from OF *teindre* to dye, from L *tingere*]
▸ **'taintless** *adj*

taipan ('taɪˌpæn) *n* a large highly venomous Australian snake. [C20: from Abor.]

Taisho (taɪ'ʃəʊ) *n* **1** the period of Japanese history and artistic style associated with the reign of Emperor Yoshihito (1912–26). **2** the throne name of Yoshihito (1879–1926), emperor of Japan (1912–26).

taj (tɑːdʒ) *n* a tall conical cap worn as a mark of distinction by Muslims. [via Ar. from Persian: crown]

takahe ('tɑːkəˌhiː) *n* a rare flightless New Zealand rail. Also called: **notornis.** [from Maori]

take ➊ (teɪk) *vb* **takes, taking, took, taken.** (*mainly tr*) **1** (*also intr*) to gain possession of (something) by force or effort. **2** to appropriate or steal. **3** to receive or accept into a relationship with oneself: *to take a wife.* **4** to pay for or buy. **5** to rent or lease. **6** to obtain by regular payment. **7** to win. **8** to obtain or derive from a source. **9** to assume the obligations of: *to take office.* **10** to endure, esp. with fortitude: *to take punishment.* **11** to adopt as a symbol of duty, etc.: *to take the veil.* **12** to receive in a specified way: *she took the news very well.* **13** to adopt as one's own: *to take someone's part in a quarrel.* **14** to receive and make use of: *to take advice.* **15** to receive into the body, as by eating, inhaling, etc. **16** to eat, drink, etc., esp. habitually. **17** to have or be engaged in for one's benefit or use: *to take a rest.* **18** to work at or study: *to take economics at college.* **19** to make, do, or perform (an action). **20** to make use of: *to take an opportunity.* **21** to put into effect: *to take measures.* **22** (*also intr*) to make a photograph of or admit of being photographed. **23** to act or perform. **24** to write down or copy: *to take notes.* **25** to experience or feel: *to take offence.* **26** to consider or regard: *I take him to be honest.* **27** to accept as valid: *I take your point.* **28** to hold or maintain in the mind: *his father took a dim view of his career.* **29** to deal or contend with. **30** to use as a particular case: *take hotels for example.* **31** (*intr;* often foll. by *from*) to diminish or detract: *the actor's bad performance took from the effect of the play.* **32** to confront successfully: *the horse took the jump at the third attempt.* **33** (*intr*) to have or produce the intended effect: *her vaccination took.* **34** (*intr*) (of plants, etc.) to start growing successfully. **35** to aim or direct: *he took a swipe at his opponent.* **36** to deal a blow to in a specified place. **37** *Arch.* to have sexual intercourse with (a woman). **38** to remove from a place. **39** to carry along or have in one's possession. **40** to convey or transport. **41** to use as a means of transport: *I shall take the bus.* **42** to conduct or lead. **43** to escort or accompany. **44** to bring or deliver to a state, position, etc.: *his ability took him to the forefront.* **45** to seek: *to take cover.* **46** to ascertain by measuring, etc.: *to take a pulse.* **47** (*intr*) (of a mechanism) to catch or engage (a part). **48** to put an end to: *she took her own life.* **49** to come upon unexpectedly. **50** to contract: *he took a chill.* **51** to affect or attack: *the fever took him one night.* **52** (*copula*) to become suddenly or be rendered (ill): *he was taken sick.* **53** (*also intr*) to absorb or become absorbed by something: *to take a polish.* **54** (*usually passive*) to charm: *she was very taken with the puppy.* **55** (*intr*) to be or become popular; win favour. **56** to require: *that task will take all your time.* **57** to subtract or deduct. **58** to hold: *the suitcase won't take all your clothes.* **59** to quote or copy. **60** to proceed to occupy: *to take a seat.* **61** (often foll. by *to*) to use or employ: *to take steps to ascertain the answer.* **62** to win or capture (a trick, piece, etc.). **63** *Sl.* to cheat, deceive, or victimize. **64 take five** (*or* **ten**). *Inf., chiefly US & Canad.* to take a break of five (or ten) minutes. **65 take it. 65a** to assume; believe. **65b** *Inf.* to stand up to or endure criticism, harsh treatment, etc. **66 take one's time.** to use as much time as is needed. **67 take (someone's) name in vain. 67a** to use a name, esp. of God, disrespectfully or irreverently. **67b** *Jocular.* to say (someone's) name. **68 take upon oneself.** to assume the right to do or responsibility for something. ◆ *n* **69** the act of taking. **70** the number of quarry killed or captured. **71** *Inf., chiefly US.* the amount of anything taken, esp. money. **72** *Films, music.* **72a** one of a series of recordings from which the best will be selected. **72b** the process of taking one such recording. **72c** a scene photographed without interruption. **73** *Inf., chiefly US.* a version or interpretation: *Cronenberg's harsh take on the sci-fi story.* ◆ See also **take after, take against,** etc. [OE *tacan*]
▸ **'takable** *or* **'takeable** *adj* ▸ **'taker** *n*

take after *vb* (*intr, prep*) to resemble in appearance, character, behaviour, etc.

take against *vb* (*intr, prep*) to start to dislike, esp. without good reason.

take apart *vb* (*tr, adv*) **1** to separate (something) into component parts. **2** to criticize severely.

take away *vb* (*tr, adv*) **1** to subtract: *take away four from nine to leave five.* ◆ *prep* **2** minus: *nine take away four is five.* ◆ *adj* **takeaway.** *Brit., Austral., & NZ.* **3** sold for consumption away from the premises: *a takeaway meal.* **4** selling food for consumption away from the premises: *a takeaway Indian restaurant.* ◆ *n* **takeaway.** *Brit., Austral., & NZ.* **5** a shop or restaurant that sells such food. **6** a meal bought at such a shop or restaurant: *we'll have a Chinese takeaway tonight.* ◆ Scot. word (for senses 3–6): **carry out.** US and Canad. word (for senses 3–6): **takeout.**

take back ➊ *vb* (*adv, mainly tr*) **1** to retract or withdraw (something said, promised, etc.). **2** to regain possession of. **3** to return for exchange. **4** to accept (someone) back (into one's home, affections, etc.). **5** to remind one of the past: *that tune really takes me back.* **6** (*also intr*) *Printing.* to move (copy) to the previous line.

take down ➊ *vb* (*tr, adv*) **1** to record in writing. **2** to dismantle or tear down. **3** to lower or reduce in power, arrogance, etc. (esp. in **take down a peg**). ◆ *adj* **take-down. 4** made or intended to be disassembled.

take for *vb* (*tr, prep*) *Inf.* to consider or suppose to be, esp. mistakenly: *the fake coins were taken for genuine; who do you take me for?*

take-home pay *n* the remainder of one's pay after all income tax and other compulsory deductions have been made.

take in ➊ *vb* (*tr, adv*) **1** to understand. **2** to include. **3** to receive into one's house in exchange for payment: *to take in lodgers.* **4** to make (clothing, etc.) smaller by altering seams. **5** *Inf.* to cheat or deceive. **6** *US.* to go to: *let's take in a movie tonight.*

taken ('teɪkən) *vb* **1** the past participle of **take.** ◆ *adj* **2** (*postpositive;* foll. by *with*) enthusiastically impressed (by); infatuated (with).

take off ➊ *vb* (*adv*) **1** (*tr*) to remove (a garment). **2** (*intr*) (of an aircraft) to become airborne. **3** *Inf.* to set out or cause to set out on a journey: *they took off for Spain.* **4** (*tr*) (of a disease) to kill. **5** (*tr*) *Inf.* to mimic. **6** (*intr*) *Inf.* to become successful or popular. ◆ *n* **takeoff. 7** the act or process of making an aircraft airborne. **8** the stage of a country's eco-

THESAURUS

taint *vb* **1** = **spoil**, adulterate, besmirch, blemish, blight, blot, contaminate, corrupt, damage, defile, dirty, foul, infect, muddy, poison, pollute, ruin, smear, smirch, soil, stain, sully, tarnish, vitiate **2** = **disgrace**, blacken, brand, dishonour, ruin, shame, stigmatize ◆ *n* **3** = **stain**, black mark, blemish, blot, defect, demerit, fault, flaw, smear, smirch, spot **4** = **contamination**, contagion, infection, pollution
Antonyms *vb* ≠ **spoil:** clean, cleanse, decontaminate, disinfect, purify

take *vb* **1** = **obtain**, acquire, capture, carry off, cart off (*sl.*), catch, clutch, gain possession of, get, get hold of, grasp, grip, have, help oneself to, lay hold of, receive, secure, seize, win **2** = **steal**, abstract, appropriate, blag (*sl.*), cabbage (*Brit. sl.*), carry off, filch, misappropriate, nick (*sl., chiefly Brit.*), pinch (*inf.*), pocket, purloin, run off with, swipe (*sl.*), walk off with **4, 5** = **choose**, book, buy, engage, hire, lease, pay for, pick, purchase, rent, reserve, select **9** = **accept**, adopt, assume, enter upon, undertake **10** = **tolerate**, abide, bear, brave, brook, endure, go through, hack (*sl.*), pocket, put up with (*inf.*), stand, stomach, submit to, suffer, swallow, thole (*Scot.*), undergo, weather, withstand **15, 16** = **consume**, drink, eat, imbibe, ingest, inhale, swallow **17, 21** = **perform**, do, effect, execute, have, make **26** = **assume**, believe, consider, deem, hold, interpret as, perceive, presume, receive, regard, see as, think of as, understand **33** = **work**, be efficacious, do the trick (*inf.*), have effect, operate, succeed **40** = **carry**, bear, bring, cart, convey, ferry, fetch, haul, tote (*inf.*), transport **42, 43** = **accompany**, bring, conduct, convoy, escort, guide, hold (someone's) hand, lead, usher **54, 55** = **charm**, attract, become popular, captivate, delight, enchant, fascinate, please, win favour **56** = **require**, call for, demand, necessitate, need **57** = **subtract**, deduct, eliminate, remove **58** = **have room for**, accept, accommodate, contain, hold **63** *Slang* = **cheat**, bilk, con (*inf.*), deceive, defraud, do (*sl.*), dupe, fiddle (*inf.*), gull (*arch.*), pull a fast one on (*inf.*), stiff (*sl.*), swindle ◆ *n* **71** = **takings**, gate, haul, proceeds, profits, receipts, return, revenue, yield
Antonyms *vb* ≠ **capture:** free, let go, release ≠ **steal:** give, give back, hand over, restore, return, surrender, yield ≠ **accept:** decline, dismiss, eschew, ignore, refuse, reject, scorn, spurn ≠ **tolerate:** avoid, dodge, give in, give way ≠ **work:** fail, flop (*inf.*) ≠ **carry:** send ≠ **subtract:** add, put

take back *vb* **1** = **retract**, disavow, disclaim, recant, renege, renounce, unsay, withdraw **2** = **regain**, get back, recapture, reclaim, reconquer, repossess, retake **3** = **give one a refund for**, accept back, exchange

take down *vb* **1** = **make a note of**, minute, note, put on record, record, set down, transcribe, write down **2** = **dismantle**, demolish, disassemble, level, raze, take apart, take to pieces, tear down **3** = **humble**, deflate, humiliate, mortify, put down (*sl.*)

take in *vb* **1** = **understand**, absorb, assimilate, comprehend, digest, get the hang of (*inf.*), grasp **2** = **include**, comprise, contain, cover, embrace, encompass **3** = **let in**, accommodate, admit, receive **5** = **deceive**, bilk, cheat, con, cozen, do (*sl.*), dupe, fool, gull (*arch.*), hoodwink, mislead, pull the wool over (someone's) eyes (*inf.*), stiff (*sl.*), swindle, trick

take off *vb* **1** = **remove**, discard, divest oneself of, doff, drop, peel off, strip off **2** = **lift off**, become airborne, leave the ground, take to the air **3** *Informal* = **depart**, abscond, beat it (*sl.*), decamp, disappear, go, hit the road (*sl.*), hook it (*sl.*), leave, pack one's bags (*inf.*), set out, slope off, split (*sl.*), strike out **5** *Informal* = **parody**, caricature, hit off, imitate, lampoon, mimic, mock, satirize, send up (*Brit. inf.*), spoof (*inf.*), take the piss (out of) (*taboo sl.*), travesty ◆ *n* **takeoff 7** = **departure**, launch, liftoff **9** *Informal* = **parody**, caricature, imitation, lampoon, mocking, satire, send-up (*Brit. inf.*), spoof (*inf.*), travesty

nomic development when rapid and sustained economic growth is first achieved. **9** *Inf.* an act of mimicry.

take on Ⓣ *vb* (*adv, mainly tr*) **1** to employ or hire. **2** to assume or acquire: *his voice took on a plaintive note.* **3** to agree to do; undertake. **4** to compete against; fight. **5** (*intr*) *Inf.* to exhibit great emotion, esp. grief.

take out *vb* (*tr, adv*) **1** to extract or remove. **2** to obtain or secure (a licence, patent, etc.). **3** to go out with; escort. **4** *Bridge.* to bid a different suit from (one's partner) in order to rescue him from a difficult contract. **5** *Sl.* to kill or destroy. **6** *Austral. inf.* to win, esp. in sport. **7** **take it** *or* **a lot out of.** *Inf.* to sap the energy or vitality of. **8** **take out on.** *Inf.* to vent (anger, etc.) on. **9** **take someone out of himself.** *Inf.* to make someone forget his anxieties, problems, etc. ◆ *adj* **takeout. 10** *Bridge.* of or designating a conventional informatory bid, asking one's partner to bid another suit. ◆ *adj, n* **takeout. 11** the US and Canad. word for **takeaway** (senses 3–6).

take over Ⓣ *vb* (*adv*) **1** to assume the control or management of. **2** *Printing.* to move (copy) to the next line. ◆ *n* **takeover. 3** the act of seizing or assuming power, control, etc.

take to Ⓣ *vb* (*intr, prep*) **1** to make for; flee to: *to take to the hills.* **2** to form a liking for. **3** to have recourse to: *to take to the bottle.*

take up Ⓣ *vb* (*adv, mainly tr*) **1** to adopt the study, practice, or activity of: *to take up gardening.* **2** to shorten (a garment). **3** to pay off (a note, mortgage, etc.). **4** to agree to or accept (an invitation, etc.). **5** to pursue further or resume (something): *he took up French where he left off.* **6** to absorb (a liquid). **7** to act as a patron to. **8** to occupy or fill (space or time). **9** to interrupt, esp. in order to contradict or criticize. **10** *Austral. & NZ.* to occupy and break in (uncultivated land): *he took up some hundreds of acres in the back country.* **11 take up on. 11a** to argue with (someone): *can I take you up on two points in your talk?* **11b** to accept what is offered by (someone): *let me take you up on your invitation.* **12 take up with. 12a** to discuss with (someone); refer to. **12b** (*intr*) to begin to keep company or associate with. ◆ *n* **take-up. 13a** the claiming of something, esp. a state benefit. **13b** (*as modifier*): *take-up rate.*

takin ('tɑːkiːn) *n* a massive bovid mammal of S Asia, having a shaggy coat, short legs, and horns. [C19: from Tibetan native name]

taking Ⓣ ('teɪkɪŋ) *adj* **1** charming, fascinating, or intriguing. **2** *Inf.* infectious; catching. ◆ *n* **3** something taken. **4** (*pl*) receipts; earnings. ▸ **'takingly** *adv* ▸ **'takingness** *n*

talapoin ('tælə,pɔɪn) *n* **1** a small W African monkey. **2** (in Myanmar and Thailand) a Buddhist monk. [C16: from F, lit.: Buddhist monk, from Port. *talapão;* orig. jocular, from the appearance of the monkey]

talaria (tə'lɛərɪə) *pl n Greek myth.* winged sandals. [C16: from L, from *tālāris* belonging to the ankle, from *tālus* ankle]

talc (tælk) *n also* **talcum. 1** See **talcum powder. 2** a soft mineral, consisting of magnesium silicate, used in the manufacture of ceramics and paints and as a filler in talcum powder, etc. ◆ *vb* **talcs, talcking, talcked** *or* **talcs, talcing, talced. 3** (*tr*) to apply talc to. [C16: from Med. L *talcum,* from Ar. *talq* mica, from Persian *talk*] ▸ **'talcose** *or* **'talcous** *adj*

talcum powder ('tælkəm) *n* a powder made of purified talc, usually scented, used for perfuming the body and for absorbing excess moisture. Often shortened to **talcum** or **talc.**

tale Ⓣ (teɪl) *n* **1** a report, narrative, or story. **2** one of a group of short stories. **3a** a malicious or meddlesome rumour or piece of gossip. **3b** (*in combination*): *talebearer; taleteller.* **4** a fictitious or false statement. **5 tell tales. 5a** to tell fanciful lies. **5b** to report malicious stories, trivial complaints, etc., esp. to someone in authority. **6 tell a tale.** to reveal something important. **7 tell its own tale.** to be self-evident. **8** *Arch.* a number; amount. [OE *talu* list]

talent Ⓣ ('tælənt) *n* **1** innate ability, aptitude, or faculty; above average ability: *a talent for cooking; a child with talent.* **2** a person or persons possessing such ability. **3** any of various ancient units of weight and money. **4** *Inf.* members of the opposite sex collectively: *the local talent.* [OE *talente,* from L *talenta,* pl. of *talentum* sum of money, from Gk *talanton* unit of money; in Med. L the sense was extended to ability through the infl. of the parable of the talents (Matthew 25:14–30)] ▸ **'talented** *adj*

talent scout *n* a person whose occupation is the search for talented sportsmen, performers, etc., for engagements as professionals.

tales ('teɪliːz) *n Law.* **1** (*functioning as pl*) a group of persons summoned to fill vacancies on a jury panel. **2** (*functioning as sing*) the writ summoning such jurors. [C15: from Med. L *tālēs dē circumstantibus* such men from among the bystanders, from L *tālis* such] ▸ **'talesman** *n*

Taliban *or* **Taleban** ('tælɪ,bæn) *n* a militant Islamic organization in Afghanistan. [C20: from Ar. *tāliban* seekers]

taligrade ('tælɪ,greɪd) *adj* (of mammals) walking on the outer side of the foot. [C20: from NL, from L *tālus* ankle, heel + -GRADE]

talion ('tælɪən) *n* the system or legal principle of making the punishment correspond to the crime; retaliation. [C15: via OF from L *tāliō,* from *tālis* such]

talipes ('tælɪ,piːz) *n* **1** a congenital deformity of the foot by which it is twisted in any of various positions. **2** a technical name for **club foot.** [C19: NL, from L *tālus* ankle + *pēs* foot]

talipot *or* **talipot palm** ('tælɪ,pɒt) *n* a palm tree of the East Indies, having large leaves that are used for fans, thatching houses, etc. [C17: from Bengali: palm leaf, from Sansk. *tālī* fan palm + *pattra* leaf]

talisman Ⓣ ('tælɪzmən) *n, pl* **talismans. 1** a stone or other small object, usually inscribed or carved, believed to protect the wearer from evil influences. **2** anything thought to have magical or protective powers. [C17: via F or Sp. from Ar. *tilsam,* from Med. Gk *telesma* ritual, from Gk: consecration, from *telein* to perform a rite, complete] ▸ **talismanic** (,tælɪz'mænɪk) *adj*

talk Ⓣ (tɔːk) *vb* **1** (*intr; often foll. by to or with*) to express one's thoughts, feelings, or desires by means of words (to). **2** (*intr*) to communicate by other means: *lovers talk with their eyes.* **3** (*intr; usually foll. by about*) to exchange ideas or opinions (about). **4** (*intr*) to articulate words. **5** (*tr*) to give voice to; utter: *to talk rubbish.* **6** (*tr*) to discuss: *to talk business.* **7** (*intr*) to reveal information. **8** (*tr*) to know how to communicate in (a language or idiom): *he talks English.* **9** (*intr*) to spread rumours or gossip. **10** (*intr*) to make sounds suggestive of talking. **11** (*intr*) to be effective or persuasive: *money talks.* **12 now you're talking.** *Inf.* at last you're saying something agreeable. **13 talk big.** to boast. **14 you can talk.** *Inf.* **14a** you don't have to worry about doing a particular thing yourself. **14b** Also: **you can't talk.** you yourself are guilty of offending in the very matter you are upholding or decrying. ◆ *n* **15** a speech or lecture. **16** an exchange of ideas or thoughts. **17** idle chatter, gossip, or rumour. **18** a subject of conversation; theme. **19** (*often pl*) a conference, discussion, or negotiation. **20** a specific manner of speaking: *children's talk.* ◆ See also **talk about, talk back,** etc. [C13 *talkien*] ▸ **'talker** *n*

talk about *vb* (*intr, prep*) **1** to discuss. **2** used informally and often ironically to add emphasis to a statement: *all his plays have such ridiculous plots – talk about good drama!*

talkative Ⓣ ('tɔːkətɪv) *adj* given to talking a great deal. ▸ **'talkatively** *adv* ▸ **'talkativeness** *n*

talk back *vb* (*intr, adv*) **1** to answer boldly or impudently. **2** *NZ.* to conduct a telephone dialogue for immediate transmission over the air. ◆ *n* **talkback. 3** *Television, radio.* a system of telephone links enabling spoken directions to be given during the production of a programme. **4** *NZ.* a broadcast telephone dialogue.

talk down *vb* (*adv*) **1** (*intr; often foll. by to*) to behave (towards) in a superior manner. **2** (*tr*) to override (a person) by continuous or loud

THESAURUS

take on *vb* **1** = **engage,** employ, enlist, enrol, hire, retain **2** = **acquire,** assume, come to have **3** = **accept,** address oneself to, agree to do, have a go at (*inf.*), tackle, undertake **4** = **compete against,** contend with, enter the lists against, face, fight, match oneself against, oppose, pit oneself against, vie with **5** *Informal* = **get upset,** break down, get excited, give way, make a fuss

take over *vb* **1** = **gain control of,** assume control of, become leader of, come to power, take command of ◆ *n* **takeover 3** = **merger,** change of leadership, coup, incorporation

take to *vb* **1** = **head for,** flee to, make for, run for **2** = **like,** become friendly with, be pleased by, be taken with, conceive an affection for, get on with, warm to **3** = **start,** have recourse to, make a habit of, resort to

take up *vb* **1** = **start,** adopt, assume, become involved in, engage in **5** = **resume,** begin again, carry on, continue, follow on, go on, pick up, proceed, recommence, restart **8** = **occupy,** absorb, consume, cover, extend over, fill, use up

taking *adj* **1** = **charming,** attractive, beguiling, captivating, compelling, cute, delightful, enchanting, engaging, fascinating, fetching (*inf.*), intriguing, likable *or* likeable, pleasing, prepossessing, winning **2** *Informal* = **infectious,** catching, contagious ◆ *n* **4** *plural* = **revenue,** earnings, gain, gate, income, pickings, proceeds, profits, receipts, returns, take, yield
Antonyms *adj* ≠ **charming:** abhorrent, loathsome, offensive, repulsive, unattractive, unpleasant

tale *n* **1** = **story,** account, anecdote, *conte,* fable, fiction, legend, narration, narrative, novel, relation, report, romance, saga, short story, spiel (*inf.*), urban legend, urban myth, yarn (*inf.*) **3a** = **lie,** cock-and-bull story (*inf.*), fabrication, falsehood, fib, gossip, rigmarole, rumour, spiel (*inf.*), tall story (*inf.*), untruth

talent *n* **1** = **ability,** aptitude, bent, capacity, endowment, faculty, flair, forte, genius, gift, knack, parts, power

talented *adj* **1** = **gifted,** able, artistic, brilliant, well-endowed

talisman *n* **1, 2** = **charm,** amulet, fetish, juju, lucky charm, mascot, periapt (*rare*)

talk *vb* **1, 4** = **speak,** articulate, chat, chatter, communicate, converse, crack (*Scot. & Irish*), express oneself, gab (*inf.*), give voice to, gossip, natter, prate, prattle, rap (*sl.*), run off at the mouth (*sl.*), say, shoot the breeze (*US sl.*), spout, utter, verbalize, witter (*inf.*) **3** = **discuss,** chew the rag *or* fat (*sl.*), confabulate, confer, have a confab (*inf.*), hold discussions, negotiate, palaver, parley **7** = **inform,** blab, crack, give the game away, grass (*Brit. sl.*), let the cat out of the bag, reveal information, shop (*sl., chiefly Brit.*), sing (*sl., chiefly US*), spill one's guts (*sl.*), spill the beans (*inf.*), squeak (*inf.*), squeal (*sl.*), tell all **13 talk big** = **boast,** blow one's own trumpet, bluster, brag, crow, exaggerate, vaunt ◆ *n* **15** = **speech,** address, discourse, disquisition, dissertation, harangue, lecture, oration, sermon **16** = **discussion,** confab (*inf.*), confabulation, conference, consultation, dialogue **17** = **conversation,** blather, blether, chat, chatter, chitchat, crack (*Scot. & Irish*), gossip, hearsay, rumour, tittle-tattle **19** = **meeting,** colloquy, conclave, conference, congress, negotiation, palaver, parley, seminar, symposium **20** = **language,** argot, dialect, jargon, lingo (*inf.*), patois, slang, speech, words

talkative *adj* = **loquacious,** big-mouthed (*sl.*), chatty, effusive, gabby (*inf.*), garrulous, gossipy, long-winded, mouthy, prolix, verbose, voluble, wordy
Antonyms *adj* quiet, reserved, reticent, silent, taciturn, tight-lipped, uncommunicative, un- forthcoming

talker *n* **15, 17** = **speaker,** chatterbox, conversationalist, lecturer, orator, speechmaker

talking. **3** (*tr*) to give instructions to (an aircraft) by radio to enable it to land.

talkie ('tɔːkɪ) *n Inf.* an early film with a soundtrack. Full name: **talking picture.**

Talking Book *n Trademark.* a recording of a book, designed to be used by blind people.

talking head *n* (on television) a person, shown only from the shoulders up, who speaks without illustrative material.

talking-to *n Inf.* a session of criticism, as of a subordinate by a person in authority.

talk into *vb* (*tr, prep*) to persuade to by talking: *I talked him into buying the house.*

talk out *vb* (*tr, adv*) **1** to resolve or eliminate by talking. **2** *Brit.* to block (a bill, etc.) in a legislative body by lengthy discussion. **3 talk out of.** to dissuade from by talking.

talk round *vb* **1** (*tr, adv*) Also: **talk over.** to persuade to one's opinion. **2** (*intr, prep*) to discuss (a subject), esp. without coming to a conclusion.

talk shop *vb* to talk about one's profession, esp. at a social occasion.

talk show *n* another name for **chat show.**

tall (tɔːl) *adj* **1** of more than average height. **2** (*postpositive*) having a specified height: *five feet tall.* [C14 (in the sense: big, comely, valiant)]
▸'**tallness** *n*

tallage ('tælɪdʒ) *n English history.* **a** a tax levied by kings on Crown lands and royal towns. **b** a toll levied by a lord upon his tenants or by a feudal lord upon his vassals. [C13: from OF *taillage,* from *taillier* to cut; see TAILOR]

tallboy ('tɔːlˌbɔɪ) *n* **1** a high chest of drawers made in two sections placed one on top of the other. **2** a fitting on the top of a chimney to prevent downdraughts.

tallith ('tælɪθ) *n* a shawl with fringed corners worn by Jewish males, esp. during religious services. [C17: from Heb. *tallīt*]

tall order *n Inf.* a difficult or unreasonable request.

tallow ('tæləʊ) *n* **1** a fatty substance extracted chiefly from the suet of sheep and cattle: used for making soap, candles, food, etc. ◆ *vb* **2** (*tr*) to cover or smear with tallow. [OE *tælg,* a dye]
▸'**tallowy** *adj*

tallowwood ('tæləʊˌwʊd) *n Austral.* a tall eucalyptus tree having soft fibrous bark and a greasy timber.

tall poppy *n Austral. inf.* a prominent or highly paid person.

tall poppy syndrome *n Austral. inf.* a tendency to disparage any person who has achieved great prominence or wealth.

tall ship *n* any square-rigged sailing ship.

tall story *n Inf.* an exaggerated or incredible account.

tally ('tælɪ) *vb* **tallies, tallying, tallied. 1** (*intr*) to correspond one with the other: *the two stories don't tally.* **2** (*tr*) to supply with an identifying tag. **3** (*intr*) to keep score. **4** (*tr*) *Obs.* to record or mark. ◆ *n, pl* **tallies. 5** any record of debit, credit, the score in a game, etc. **6** *Austral. & NZ.* the number of sheep shorn in a specified period. **7** an identifying label or mark. **8** a counterpart or duplicate of something. **9** a stick used (esp. formerly) as a record of the amount of a debt according to the notches cut in it. **10** a notch or mark made on such a stick. **11** a mark used to represent a certain number in counting. [C15: from Med. L *tālea,* from L: cutting]

tally clerk *n Austral. & NZ.* a person, esp. on a wharf or in an airport, who checks the count of goods being loaded or unloaded.

tally-ho (ˌtælɪ'həʊ) *interj* **1** the cry of a participant at a hunt when the quarry is sighted. ◆ *n, pl* **tally-hos. 2** an instance of crying tally-ho. **3** another name for a **four-in-hand** (sense 1). ◆ *vb* **tally-hos, tally-hoing, tally-hoed** *or* **tally-ho'd. 4** (*intr*) to make the cry of tally-ho. [C18: ?from F *taïaut* cry used in hunting]

tallyman ('tælɪmən) *n, pl* **tallymen. 1** a scorekeeper or recorder. **2** *Dialect.* a travelling salesman for a firm specializing in hire-purchase.
▸'**tallyˌwoman** *fem n*

Talmud ('tælmʊd) *n Judaism.* the primary source of Jewish religious law, consisting of the Mishnah and the Gemara. [C16: from Heb. *talmūdh,* lit.: instruction, from *lāmadh* to learn]
▸**Tal'mudic** *or* **Tal'mudical** *adj* ▸'**Talmudism** *n* ▸'**Talmudist** *n*

talon ('tælən) *n* **1** a sharply hooked claw, esp. of a bird of prey. **2** anything resembling this. **3** the part of a lock that the key presses on when it is turned. **4** *Piquet, etc.* the pile of cards left after the deal. **5** *Archit.* another name for **ogee. 6** *Stock Exchange.* a printed slip attached to some bearer bonds to enable the holder to apply for a new sheet of coupons. [C14: from OF: heel, from L *tālus*]
▸'**taloned** *adj*

talus[1] ('teɪləs) *n, pl* **tali** (-laɪ). the bone of the ankle that articulates with the leg bones to form the ankle joint; anklebone. [C18: from L: ankle]

talus[2] ('teɪləs) *n, pl* **taluses. 1** *Geol.* another name for **scree. 2** *Fortifications.* the sloping side of a wall. [C17: from F, from L *talūtium* slope, ? of Iberian origin]

tam (tæm) *n* short for **tam-o'-shanter.**

tamale (tə'mɑːlɪ) *n* a Mexican dish made of minced meat mixed with crushed maize and seasonings, wrapped in maize husks and steamed. [C19: erroneously for *tamal,* from Mexican Sp., from Nahuatl *tamalli*]

tamandua (ˌtæmən'dʊə) *n* a small arboreal mammal of Central and South America, having a tubular mouth specialized for feeding on termites. Also called: **lesser anteater.** [C17: via Port. from Tupi: ant trapper, from *taixi* ant + *mondê* to catch]

tamarack ('tæməˌræk) *n* **1** any of several North American larches. **2** the wood of any of these trees. [C19: of Amerind origin]

tamari (tə'mɑːrɪ) *n* a Japanese variety of soy sauce. [Japanese]

tamarillo (ˌtæmə'rɪləʊ) *n, pl* **tamarillos.** another name for **tree tomato.**

tamarin ('tæmərɪn) *n* any of numerous small monkeys of South and Central American forests; similar to the marmosets. [C18: via F, of Amerind origin]

tamarind ('tæmərɪnd) *n* **1** a tropical evergreen tree having yellow flowers and brown pods. **2** the fruit of this tree, used as a food and to make beverages and medicines. **3** the wood of this tree. [C16: from Med. L *tamarindus,* ult. from Ar. *tamr hindī* Indian date]

tamarisk ('tæmərɪsk) *n* any of a genus of trees and shrubs of the Mediterranean region and S and SE Asia, having scalelike leaves, slender branches, and feathery flower clusters. [C15: from LL *tamariscus,* from L *tamarix*]

tambour ('tæmbʊə) *n* **1** *Real Tennis.* the sloping buttress on one side of the receiver's end of the court. **2** a small embroidery frame, consisting of two hoops over which the fabric is stretched while being worked. **3** embroidered work done on such a frame. **4** a sliding door on desks, cabinets, etc., made of thin strips of wood glued onto a canvas backing. **5** *Archit.* a wall that is circular in plan, esp. one that supports a dome or one that is surrounded by a colonnade. **6** a drum. ◆ *vb* **7** to embroider on a tambour. [C15: from F, from *tabour* TABOR]

tamboura (tæm'bʊərə) *n* a stringed instrument with a long neck used in Indian music to provide a drone. [from Persian *tanbūr,* from Ar. *tunbūr*]

tambourin ('tæmbʊrɪn) *n* **1** an 18th-century Provençal folk dance. **2** a piece of music composed for or in the rhythm of this dance. **3** a small drum. [C18: from F: a little drum]

tambourine (ˌtæmbə'riːn) *n Music.* a percussion instrument consisting of a single drumhead of skin stretched over a circular wooden frame hung with pairs of metal discs that jingle when it is struck or shaken. [C16: from MFlemish *tamborijn* a little drum, from OF: TAMBOURIN]
▸ˌ**tambou'rinist** *n*

tame (teɪm) *adj* **1** changed by man from a wild state into a domesticated or cultivated condition. **2** (of animals) not fearful of human contact. **3** meek or submissive. **4** flat, insipid, or uninspiring. ◆ *vb* **tames, taming, tamed.** (*tr*) **5** to make tame; domesticate. **6** to break the spirit of, subdue, or curb. **7** to tone down, soften, or mitigate. [OE *tam*]
▸'**tamable** *or* '**tameable** *adj* ▸'**tamely** *adv* ▸'**tameness** *n* ▸'**tamer** *n*

Tamil ('tæmɪl) *n* **1** (*pl* **Tamils** *or* **Tamil**) a member of a mixed Dravidian and Caucasoid people of S India and Sri Lanka. **2** the language of this people. ◆ *adj* **3** of or relating to this people or their language.

tammy[1] ('tæmɪ) *n, pl* **tammies.** another word for **tam-o'-shanter.**

tammy[2] ('tæmɪ) *n, pl* **tammies.** (esp. formerly) a woollen cloth used for straining sauces, soups, etc. [C18: changed from F *tamis,* ? of Celtic origin]

tam-o'-shanter (ˌtæmə'ʃæntə) *n* a Scottish brimless wool or cloth cap with a bobble in the centre. [C19: after the hero of Burns's poem *Tam o' Shanter* (1790)]

tamoxifen (tə'mɒksɪˌfɛn) *n* a drug that antagonizes the action of oestrogen and is used to treat breast cancer and some types of infertility in women. [C20: from T(RANS-) + AM(INE) + OXY-[2] + PHEN(OL)]

tamp (tæmp) *vb* (*tr*) **1** to force or pack down firmly by repeated blows. **2** to pack sand, earth, etc., into (a drill hole) over an explosive. [C17: prob. back formation from *tampin* (obs. var. of TAMPION), taken as a present participle *tamping*]

THESAURUS

talking-to *n Informal* = **reprimand**, criticism, dressing-down (*inf.*), lecture, rap on the knuckles, rebuke, reproach, reproof, row, scolding, telling-off (*inf.*), ticking-off (*inf.*), wigging (*Brit. sl.*)
Antonyms *n* acclaim, approbation, commendation, encouragement, praise

talk into *vb* = **persuade**, bring round (*inf.*), convince, prevail on *or* upon, sway, win over

tall *adj* **1** = **high**, big, elevated, giant, lanky, lofty, soaring, towering
Antonyms *adj* ≠ **high:** fubsy (*arch. or dialect*), short, small, squat, stumpy, tiny, wee ≠ **implausible:** accurate, believable, plausible, realistic, reasonable, true, unexaggerated

tally *vb* **1** = **agree**, accord, coincide, concur, conform, correspond, fit, harmonize, jibe (*inf.*), match, parallel, square, suit **3** = **keep score**, compute, count up, total **4** = **record**, mark, reckon, register ◆ *n* **5** = **record**, count, mark, reckoning, running total, score, total **8** = **counterpart**, counterfoil, duplicate, match, mate, stub
Antonyms *vb* ≠ **agree:** clash, conflict, contradict, differ, disagree

tame *adj* **1** = **domesticated**, amenable, broken, cultivated, disciplined, docile, gentle, obedient, tractable **2** = **unafraid**, fearless, used to human contact **3** = **submissive**, compliant, docile, manageable, meek, obedient, spiritless, subdued, unresisting **4** = **unexciting**, bland, boring, dull, flat, humdrum, insipid, lifeless, prosaic, tedious, tiresome, uninspiring, uninteresting, vapid, wearisome ◆ *vb* **5** = **domesticate**, break in, gentle, house-train, make tame, pacify, train **6** = **subdue**, break the spirit of, bridle, bring to heel, conquer, curb, discipline, enslave, humble, master, repress, subjugate, suppress
Antonyms *adj* ≠ **domesticated:** aggressive, feral, ferocious, savage, undomesticated, untamed, wild ≠ **submissive:** aggressive, argumentative, obdurate, strong-willed, stubborn, unmanageable ≠ **unexciting:** exciting, frenzied, hot, interesting, lively, stimulating ◆ *vb* ≠ **domesticate:** make fiercer ≠ **subdue:** arouse, incite, intensify

DICTIONARY

tamper[1] Ⓣ ('tæmpə) *vb (intr)* **1** (usually foll. by *with*) to interfere or meddle. **2** to use bribery or blackmail. **3** (usually foll. by *with*) to attempt to influence, esp. by bribery. [C16: alteration of TEMPER (vb)] ▸**'tamperer** *n*

tamper[2] ('tæmpə) *n* **1** a person or thing that tamps, esp. an instrument for packing down tobacco in a pipe. **2** a casing around the core of a nuclear weapon to increase its efficiency by reflecting neutrons and delaying the expansion.

tampion ('tæmpɪən) *or* **tompion** *n* a plug placed in a gun's muzzle when the gun is not in use. [C15: from F: TAMPON]

tampon ('tæmpɒn) *n* **1** a plug of lint, cotton wool, etc., inserted into a wound or body cavity to stop the flow of blood, absorb secretions, etc. ◆ *vb* **2** *(tr)* to plug (a wound, etc.) with a tampon. [C19: via F from OF *tapon* a little plug, of Gmc origin] ▸**tamponage** ('tæmpənɪdʒ) *n*

tam-tam *n* another name for **gong** (sense 1). [from Hindi; see TOM-TOM]

tan[1] (tæn) *n* **1** the brown colour produced by the skin after exposure to ultraviolet rays, esp. those of the sun. **2** a yellowish-brown colour. **3** short for **tanbark**. ◆ *vb* **tans, tanning, tanned. 4** to go brown or cause to go brown after exposure to ultraviolet rays. **5** to convert (a skin or hide) into leather by treating it with a tanning agent. **6** *(tr) Sl.* to beat or flog. ◆ *adj* **tanner, tannest. 7** of the colour tan. [OE *tannian* (unattested as infinitive, attested as *getanned,* p.p.), from Med. L *tannāre,* from *tannum* tanbark, ? of Celtic origin] ▸**'tannable** *adj* ▸**'tannish** *adj*

tan[2] (tæn) *abbrev. for* tangent (sense 2).

tanager ('tænədʒə) *n* any of a family of American songbirds having a short thick bill and, in the male, a brilliantly coloured plumage. [C19: from NL *tanagra,* based on Amerind *tangara*]

tanbark ('tænˌbɑːk) *n* the bark of certain trees, esp. the oak, used as a source of tannin.

tandem ('tændəm) *n* **1** a bicycle with two sets of pedals and two saddles, arranged one behind the other for two riders. **2** a two-wheeled carriage drawn by two horses harnessed one behind the other. **3** a team of two horses so harnessed. **4** any arrangement of two things in which one is placed behind the other. **5 in tandem.** together or in conjunction. ◆ *adj* **6** *Brit.* used as, used in, or routed through an intermediate automatic telephone exchange. ◆ *adv* **7** one behind the other. [C18: whimsical use of L *tandem* at length, to indicate a long vehicle]

tandoori (tæn'dʊərɪ) *n* an Indian method of cooking meat or vegetables on a spit in a clay oven. [from Urdu, from *tandoor* an oven]

tang Ⓣ (tæŋ) *n* **1** a strong taste or flavour. **2** a pungent or characteristic smell. **3** a trace, touch, or hint of something. **4** the pointed end of a tool, such as a chisel, file, knife, etc., which is fitted into a handle, shaft, or stock. [C14: from ON *tangi* point]

tangent ('tændʒənt) *n* **1** a geometric line, curve, plane, or curved surface that touches another curve or surface at one point but does not intersect it. **2** (of an angle) a trigonometric function that in a right-angled triangle is the ratio of the length of the opposite side to that of the adjacent side; the ratio of sine to cosine. Abbrev.: **tan. 3** *Music.* a small piece of metal that strikes the string of a clavichord. **4 on** *or* **at a tangent.** on a completely different or divergent course, esp. of thought. ◆ *adj* **5a** of or involving a tangent. **5b** touching at a single point. **6** touching. [C16: from L *līnea tangēns* the touching line, from *tangere* to touch] ▸**'tangency** *n*

tangent galvanometer *n* a galvanometer having a vertical coil of wire with a horizontal magnetic needle at its centre. The current to be measured is passed through the coil and produces a proportional magnetic field which deflects the needle.

tangential (tæn'dʒɛnʃəl) *adj* **1** of, being, or in the direction of a tangent. **2** *Astron.* (of velocity) in a direction perpendicular to the line of sight of a celestial object. **3** of superficial relevance only; digressive. ▸**tanˌgenti'ality** *n* ▸**tan'gentially** *adv*

tangerine (ˌtændʒə'riːn) *n* **1** an Asian citrus tree cultivated for its small orange-like fruits. **2** the fruit of this tree, having sweet spicy flesh. **3a** a reddish-orange colour. **3b** *(as adj)*: *a tangerine door.* [C19: from *Tangier,* a port in N Morocco]

tangi ('tæŋiː) *n NZ.* **1** a Maori funeral ceremony. **2** *Inf.* a lamentation.

tangible Ⓣ ('tændʒɪbᵊl) *adj* **1** capable of being touched or felt. **2** capable of being clearly grasped by the mind. **3** having a physical existence: *tangible assets.* [C16: from LL *tangibilis,* from L *tangere* to touch] ▸**ˌtangi'bility** *or* **'tangibleness** *n* ▸**'tangibly** *adv*

tangle Ⓣ ('tæŋgᵊl) *n* **1** a confused or complicated mass of hairs, lines, fibres, etc., knotted or coiled together. **2** a complicated problem, condition, or situation. ◆ *vb* **tangles, tangling, tangled. 3** to become or cause to become twisted together in a confused mass. **4** *(intr; often foll. by with)* to come into conflict; contend. **5** *(tr)* to involve in matters which hinder or confuse. **6** *(tr)* to ensnare or trap, as in a net. [C14 *tangilen,* var. of *tagilen,* prob. from ON] ▸**'tangled** *or* **'tangly** *adj*

tango ('tæŋgəʊ) *n, pl* **tangos. 1** a Latin-American dance characterized by long gliding steps and sudden pauses. **2** a piece of music composed for or in the rhythm of this dance. ◆ *vb* **tangoes, tangoing, tangoed. 3** *(intr)* to perform this dance. [C20: from American Sp., prob. of Niger-Congo origin]

tangram ('tæŋgræm) *n* a Chinese puzzle in which a square, cut into a parallelogram, a square, and five triangles, is formed into figures. [C19: ?from Chinese *t'ang* Chinese + -GRAM]

tangy Ⓣ ('tæŋɪ) *adj* **tangier, tangiest.** having a pungent, fresh, or briny flavour or aroma.

tanh (θæn, tænʃ) *n* hyperbolic tangent; a hyperbolic function that is the ratio of sinh to cosh. [C20: from TAN(GENT) + H(YPERBOLIC)]

tank (tæŋk) *n* **1** a large container or reservoir for liquids or gases. **2** an armoured combat vehicle moving on tracks and armed with guns, etc. **3** *Brit. or US dialect.* a reservoir, lake, or pond. **4** *Sl., chiefly US.* a jail. **5** Also called: **tankful.** the quantity contained in a tank. **6** *Austral.* a reservoir formed by excavation and damming. ◆ *vb* **7** *(tr)* to put or keep in a tank. **8** *Sl.* to defeat heavily. ◆ See also **tank up.** [C17: from Gujarati (a language of W India) *tānkh* artificial lake, but infl. also by Port. *tanque,* from *estanque* pond, ult. from Vulgar L *stanticāre* (unattested) to block]

tanka ('tɑːŋkə) *n, pl* **tankas** *or* **tanka.** a Japanese verse form consisting of five lines, the first and third having five syllables, the others seven. [C19: from Japanese, from *tan* short + *ka* verse]

tankage ('tæŋkɪdʒ) *n* **1** the capacity or contents of a tank or tanks. **2** the act of storing in a tank or tanks, or a fee charged for this. **3** *Agriculture.* **3a** fertilizer consisting of the dried and ground residues of animal carcasses. **3b** a protein supplement feed for livestock.

tankard ('tæŋkəd) *n* a large one-handled drinking vessel sometimes fitted with a hinged lid. [C14]

tank engine *or* **locomotive** *n* a steam locomotive that carries its water supply in tanks mounted around its boiler.

tanker ('tæŋkə) *n* a ship, lorry, or aeroplane designed to carry liquid in bulk, such as oil.

tank farming *n* another name for **hydroponics.** ▸**tank farmer** *n*

tank top *n* a sleeveless upper garment with wide shoulder straps and a low neck. [C20: after *tank suits,* one-piece bathing costumes of the 1920s worn in tanks or swimming pools]

tank up *vb (adv) Chiefly Brit.* **1** to fill the tank of (a vehicle) with petrol. **2** *Sl.* to imbibe or cause to imbibe a large quantity of alcoholic drink.

tank wagon *or esp. US & Canad.* **tank car** *n* a form of railway wagon carrying a tank for the transport of liquids.

tanner[1] ('tænə) *n* a person who tans skins and hides.

tanner[2] ('tænə) *n Brit.* an informal word for **sixpence.** [C19: from ?]

tannery ('tænərɪ) *n, pl* **tanneries.** a place or building where skins and hides are tanned.

tannic ('tænɪk) *adj* of, relating to, containing, or produced from tan, tannin, or tannic acid.

tannin ('tænɪn) *n* any of a class of yellowish compounds found in many plants and used as tanning agents, mordants, medical astringents, etc. Also called: **tannic acid.** [C19: from F *tanin,* from TAN[1]]

Tannoy ('tænɔɪ) *n Trademark.* a type of public-address system.

Tans (tænz) *pl n* **the.** *Irish inf.* short for the **Black and Tans.**

tansy ('tænzɪ) *n, pl* **tansies.** any of numerous plants having yellow flowers in flat-topped clusters and formerly used in medicine and for seasoning. [C15: from OF *tanesie,* from Med. L *athanasia* (from its alleged power to prolong life) from Gk: immortality]

tantalite ('tæntəˌlaɪt) *n* a heavy brownish mineral: it occurs in coarse granite and is an ore of tantalum. [C19: from TANTALUM + -ITE[1]]

tantalize Ⓣ *or* **tantalise** ('tæntəˌlaɪz) *vb* **tantalizes, tantalizing, tantalized** *or* **tantalises, tantalising, tantalised.** *(tr)* to tease or make frustrated, as by tormenting with the sight of something desired but inaccessible. [C16: from *Tantalus,* a king in Gk mythology condemned to stand in water that receded when he tried to drink it and under fruit that moved away when he tried to reach for it]

THESAURUS

tamper[1] *vb* **1 = interfere,** alter, damage, fiddle (*inf.*), fool about (*inf.*), intrude, meddle, mess about, monkey around, muck about (*Brit. sl.*), poke one's nose into (*inf.*), tinker **2, 3 = influence,** bribe, corrupt, fix (*inf.*), get at, manipulate, rig

tang *n* **1, 2 = taste,** aroma, bite, flavour, odour, piquancy, reek, savour, scent, smack, smell **3 = trace,** hint, suggestion, tinge, touch, whiff

tangible *adj* **1-3 = definite,** actual, concrete, corporeal, discernible, evident, manifest, material, objective, palpable, perceptible, physical, positive, real, solid, substantial, tactile, touchable

Antonyms *adj* abstract, disembodied, ethereal, immaterial, impalpable, imperceptible, indiscernible, insubstantial, intangible, theoretical, unreal

tangle *n* **1 = knot,** coil, entanglement, jungle, mass, mat, mesh, ravel, snarl, twist, web **2 = confusion,** complication, entanglement, fix (*inf.*), imbroglio, jam, labyrinth, maze, mess, mix-up ◆ *vb* **3 = twist,** coil, confuse, entangle, interlace, interlock, intertwist, interweave, jam, kink, knot, mat, mesh, ravel, snarl **4** *often with* **with = come into conflict,** come up against, contend, contest, cross swords, dispute, lock horns **5 = involve,** drag into, embroil, implicate **6 = catch,** enmesh, ensnare, entangle, entrap

Antonyms *vb* ≠ **twist:** disentangle, extricate, free, straighten out, unravel, untangle

tangled *adj* **1 = twisted,** entangled, jumbled, knotted, knotty, matted, messy, scrambled, snarled, tousled **2 = complicated,** complex, confused, convoluted, involved, knotty, messy, mixed-up

tangy *adj* **= sharp,** biting, briny, fresh, piquant, pungent, spicy, tart

tantalize *vb* **= torment,** baffle, balk, disappoint, entice, frustrate, keep (someone) hanging on, lead on, make (someone's) mouth water, provoke, taunt, tease, thwart, titillate, torture

▸ ˌtantaliˈzation *or* ˌtantaliˈsation *n* ▸ ˈtantaˌlizing *or* ˈtantaˌlising *adj* ▸ ˈtantaˌlizingly *or* ˈtantaˌlisingly *adv*

tantalum (ˈtæntələm) *n* a hard greyish-white metallic element: used in electrolytic rectifiers and in alloys to increase hardness and chemical resistance, esp. in surgical instruments. Symbol: Ta; atomic no.: 73; atomic wt.: 180.95. [C19: after *Tantalus* (see TANTALIZE), from the metal's incapacity to absorb acids]

tantalus (ˈtæntələs) *n Brit.* a case in which bottles may be locked with their contents tantalizingly visible.

tantamount ❶ (ˈtæntəˌmaʊnt) *adj* (*postpositive;* foll. by *to*) as good (as); equivalent in effect (to). [C17: from Anglo-F *tant amunter* to amount to as much]

tantara (ˈtæntərə, tænˈtɑːrə) *n* a fanfare or blast, as on a trumpet or horn. [C16: from L *taratantara*, imit. of the sound of the tuba]

tantivy (tænˈtɪvɪ) *adv* **1** at full speed; rapidly. ◆ *n, pl* **tantivies**, *sentence substitute.* **2** a hunting cry, esp. at full gallop. [C17: ? imit. of galloping hooves]

tant mieux *French.* (tɑ̃ mjø) so much the better.

tanto (ˈtæntəʊ) *adv Music.* too much; excessively. [It.]

tant pis *French.* (tɑ̃ pi) so much the worse.

Tantrism (ˈtæntrɪzəm) *n* **1** a movement within Hinduism combining magical and mystical elements and with sacred writings of its own (**the Tantra**). **2** a similar movement within Buddhism. [C18: from Sansk. *tantra*, lit.: warp, hence doctrine]

▸ ˈ**Tantric** *adj* ▸ ˈ**Tantrist** *n*

tantrum ❶ (ˈtæntrəm) *n* (*often pl*) a childish fit of rage; outburst of bad temper. [C18: from ?]

Tao (taʊ) *n* (in the philosophy of Taoism) **1** that in virtue of which all things happen or exist. **2** the rational basis of human conduct. **3** the course of life and its relation to eternal truth. [Chinese, lit.: path, way]

Taoiseach (ˈtiːʃæx) *n* the prime mininster of the Irish Republic. [from Irish, lit.: leader]

Taoism (ˈtaʊɪzəm) *n* a system of religion and philosophy based on the teachings of Lao Zi, 6th-century B.C. Chinese philosopher, and advocating a simple honest life and noninterference with the course of natural events.

▸ ˈ**Taoist** *n, adj* ▸ ˌ**Taoˈistic** *adj*

taonga (tɑˈɔŋgə) *n NZ.* anything highly prized. [Maori]

tap[1] ❶ (tæp) *vb* **taps, tapping, tapped. 1** to strike (something) lightly and usually repeatedly. **2** (*tr*) to produce by striking in this way: *to tap a rhythm.* **3** (*tr*) to strike lightly with (something): *to tap one's finger on the desk.* **4** (*intr*) to walk with a tapping sound. **5** (*tr*) to attach reinforcing pieces to (the toe or heel of a shoe). ◆ *n* **6** a light blow or knock, or the sound made by it. **7** the metal piece attached to the toe or heel of a shoe used for tap-dancing. **8** short for **tap-dancing.** ◆ See also **taps.** [C13 *tappen*, prob. from OF *taper*, of Gmc origin]

tap[2] ❶ (tæp) *n* **1** a valve by which a fluid flow from a pipe can be controlled. US names: **faucet, spigot. 2** a stopper to plug a cask or barrel. **3** a particular quality of alcoholic drink, esp. when contained in casks: *an excellent tap.* **4** *Brit.* short for **taproom. 5** the withdrawal of fluid from a bodily cavity. **6** a tool for cutting female screw threads. **7** *Electronics, chiefly US & Canad.* a connection made at some point between the end terminals of an inductor, resistor, etc. Usual Brit. name: **tapping. 8** *Stock Exchange.* **8a** an issue of a government security released slowly onto the market when its market price reaches a predetermined level. **8b** (*as modifier*): *tap stock; tap issue.* **9** a concealed listening or recording device connected to a telephone or telegraph wire. **10 on tap. 10a** *Inf.* ready for use. **10b** (of drinks) on draught. ◆ *vb* **taps, tapping, tapped.** (*tr*) **11** to furnish with a tap. **12** to draw off with or as if with a tap. **13** to cut into (a tree) and draw off sap from it. **14** *Brit. inf.* **14a** to ask (someone) for money: *he tapped me for a fiver.* **14b** to obtain (money) from someone. **15** to connect a tap to (a telephone or telegraph wire). **16** to make a connection to (a pipe, drain, etc.). **17** to cut a female screw thread in (an object or material) by use of a tap. **18** *Inf.* (of a sports team or an employer) to make an illicit attempt to recruit (a player or employee bound by an existing contract). [OE *tæppa*]

▸ ˈ**tapper** *n*

tapa (ˈtɑːpə) *n* **1** the inner bark of the paper mulberry. **2** a cloth made from this in the Pacific islands. [C19: from native Polynesian name]

tapas (ˈtæpəs) *pl n* **a** light snacks or appetizers, usually eaten with drinks. **b** (*as modifier*): *a tapas bar.* [from Sp. *tapa* cover, lid]

tap dance *n* **1** a step dance in which the performer wears shoes equipped with taps that make a rhythmic sound on the stage as he dances. ◆ *vb* **tap-dance, tap-dances, tap-dancing, tap-danced.** (*intr*) **2** to perform a tap dance.

▸ ˈ**tap-ˌdancer** *n* ▸ ˈ**tap-ˌdancing** *n*

tape ❶ (teɪp) *n* **1** a long thin strip of cotton, linen, etc., used for binding, fastening, etc. **2** a long narrow strip of paper, metal, etc. **3** a string stretched across the track at the end of a race course. **4** See **magnetic tape, ticker tape, paper tape, tape recording.** ◆ *vb* **tapes, taping, taped.** (*mainly tr*) **5** (*also intr*) Also: **tape record.** to record (speech, music, etc.). **6** to furnish with tapes. **7** to bind, measure, secure, or wrap with tape. **8** (*usually passive*) *Brit. inf.* to take stock of (a person or situation). [OE *tæppe*]

▸ ˈ**tapeˌlike** *adj* ▸ ˈ**taper** *n*

tape deck *n* **1** a tape recording unit in a hi-fi system. **2** the platform supporting the spools, cassettes, or cartridges of a tape recorder, incorporating the motor and the playback, recording, and erasing heads.

tape machine *n* **1** another word for **tape recorder. 2** a telegraphic device that records current stock quotations electronically or on ticker tape. US equivalent: **ticker.**

tape measure *n* a tape or length of metal marked off in inches, centimetres, etc., used for measuring. Also called (esp. US): **tapeline.**

tapenade (ˈtæpənɑːd) *n* a savoury paste made from capers, olives, and anchovies, with olive oil and lemon juice. [C20: F, from Provençal *tapéo* capers]

taper ❶ (ˈteɪpə) *vb* **1** to become or cause to become narrower towards one end. **2** (often foll. by *off*) to become or cause to become smaller or less significant. ◆ *n* **3** a thin candle. **4** a thin wooden or waxed strip for transferring a flame; spill. **5** a narrowing. **6** any feeble light. [OE *tapor*, prob. from L *papȳrus* papyrus (from its use as a wick)]

▸ ˈ**taperer** *n* ▸ ˈ**tapering** *adj*

tape recorder *n* an electrical device used for recording sounds on magnetic tape and usually also for reproducing them.

tape recording *n* **1** the act of recording on magnetic tape. **2** the magnetized tape used for this. **3** the speech, music, etc., so recorded.

tape streamer *n Computing.* an electromechanical device that enables data to be copied byte by byte from a hard disk onto magnetic tape for security or storage.

tapestry (ˈtæpɪstrɪ) *n, pl* **tapestries. 1** a heavy woven fabric, often in the form of a picture, used for wall hangings, furnishings, etc. **2** another word for **needlepoint** (sense 1). **3** a colourful and complicated situation: *the rich tapestry of life.* [C15: from OF *tapisserie* carpeting, from OF *tapiz;* see TAPIS]

▸ ˈ**tapestried** *adj*

tapeworm (ˈteɪpˌwɜːm) *n* any of a class of parasitic ribbon-like flatworms. The adults inhabit the intestines of vertebrates.

taphole (ˈtæpˌhəʊl) *n* a hole in a furnace for running off molten metal or slag.

taphouse (ˈtæpˌhaʊs) *n Now rare.* an inn.

tapioca (ˌtæpɪˈəʊkə) *n* a beadlike starch obtained from cassava root, used in cooking as a thickening agent, esp. in puddings. [C18: via Port. from Tupi *tipioca* pressed-out juice, from *tipi* residue + *ok* to squeeze out]

tapir (ˈteɪpə) *n, pl* **tapirs** *or* **tapir.** any of various mammals of South and Central America and SE Asia, having an elongated snout, three-toed hind legs, and four-toed forelegs. [C18: from Tupi *tapiira*]

tapis (ˈtæpiː) *n, pl* **tapis. 1** tapestry or carpeting, esp. as formerly used to cover a table. **2 on the tapis.** currently under consideration. [C17: from F, from OF *tapiz*, from Gk *tapētion* rug, from *tapēs* carpet]

tappet (ˈtæpɪt) *n* a mechanical part that reciprocates to receive or transmit intermittent motion. [C18: from TAP[1] + -ET]

taproom (ˈtæpˌruːm, -ˌrʊm) *n* a bar, as in a hotel or pub.

taproot (ˈtæpˌruːt) *n* the main root of plants such as the dandelion, which grows vertically downwards and bears smaller lateral roots.

taps (tæps) *n* (*functioning as sing*) **1** *Chiefly US.* **1a** (in army camps, etc.) a signal given on a bugle, drum, etc., indicating that lights are to be put out. **1b** any similar signal, as at a military funeral. **2** (in the Guide movement) a closing song sung at an evening camp fire or at the end of a meeting.

tapster (ˈtæpstə) *n* **1** *Rare.* a barman. **2** (in W Africa) a man who taps palm trees. [OE *tæppestre*, fem. of *tæppere*, from *tappian* to TAP[2]]

tap water *n* water drawn off through taps from pipes in a house, as distinguished from distilled water, mineral water, etc.

tar[1] (tɑː) *n* **1** any of various dark viscid substances obtained by the destructive distillation of organic matter such as coal, wood, or peat. **2** another name for **coal tar.** ◆ *vb* **tars, tarring, tarred.** (*tr*) **3** to coat with tar. **4 tar and feather.** to punish by smearing tar and feathers over (someone). **5 tarred with the same brush.** regarded as having the same faults. [OE *teoru*]

▸ ˈ**tarry** *adj* ▸ ˈ**tarriness** *n*

tar[2] (tɑː) *n* an informal word for **seaman.** [C17: short for TARPAULIN]

taradiddle (ˈtærəˌdɪdᵊl) *n* a variant spelling of **tarradiddle.**

tarakihi *or* **terakihi** (ˈtærəˌkiːhiː) *n, pl* **tarakihis.** a common edible sea fish of New Zealand waters. [from Maori]

taramasalata (ˌtærəməsəˈlɑːtə) *n* a creamy pale pink paté, made from

THESAURUS

tantamount *adj, foll. by* **to** = **equivalent to**, as good as, commensurate with, equal to, synonymous with, the same as

tantrum *n* = **outburst**, bate (*Brit. sl.*), fit, flare-up, hysterics, ill humour, paddy (*Brit. inf.*), paroxysm, storm, temper, wax (*inf., chiefly Brit.*)

tap[1] *vb* **1** = **knock**, beat, drum, pat, rap, strike, touch ◆ *n* **6** = **knock**, beat, light blow, pat, rap, touch

tap[2] *n* **1** = **valve**, faucet (*US*), spigot, spout, stopcock **2** = **stopper**, bung, plug, spile **9** = **bug** (*inf.*), listening device **10 on tap: a** *Informal* = **ready**, at hand, in reserve, on hand **b** = **on draught** ◆ *vb* **12** = **draw off**, bleed, broach, drain, open, pierce, siphon off

tape *n* **1, 2** = **strip**, band, ribbon ◆ *vb* **5** = **record**, tape-record, video **7** = **bind**, seal, secure, stick, wrap

taper *vb* **1** = **narrow**, come to a point, thin **2** *often foll. by* **off** = **decrease**, die away, die out, dwindle, fade, lessen, reduce, subside, thin out, wane, weaken, wind down

Antonyms *vb* ≠ **decrease:** grow, increase, intensify, step up, strengthen, swell, widen

the roe of grey mullet or smoked cod and served as an hors d'oeuvre. [C20: from Mod. Gk, from *tarama* cod's roe]

tarantass (ˌtɑːrən'tæs) *n* a four-wheeled Russian carriage without springs. [C19: from Russian *tarantas*]

tarantella (ˌtærən'tɛlə) *n* **1** a peasant dance from S Italy. **2** a piece of music composed for or in the rhythm of this dance. [C18: from It., from *Taranto,* port in SE Italy]

tarantism ('tærənˌtɪzəm) *n* a nervous disorder marked by uncontrollable bodily movement, widespread in S Italy during the 15th to 17th centuries: popularly thought to be caused by the bite of a tarantula. [C17: from NL *tarantismus,* from *Taranto;* see TARANTULA, TARANTELLA]

tarantula (tə'ræntjʊlə) *n, pl* **tarantulas** *or* **tarantulae** (-ˌliː). **1** any of various large hairy spiders of tropical America. **2** a large hairy spider of S Europe. [C16: from Med. L, from OIt. *tarantola,* from *Taranto;* see TARANTELLA]

taraxacum (tə'ræksəkəm) *n* **1** any of a genus of perennial plants of the composite family, such as the dandelion. **2** the dried root of the dandelion, used as a laxative, diuretic, and tonic. [C18: from Med. L, from Ar. *tarakhshaqūn* wild chicory, ? of Persian origin]

tarboosh (tɑː'buːʃ) *n* a felt or cloth brimless cap, usually red and often with a silk tassel, worn by Muslim men. [C18: from Ar. *tarbūsh*]

tarboy ('tɑːˌbɔɪ) *n Austral. & NZ inf.* a boy who applies tar to the skin of sheep cut during shearing.

Tardenoisian (ˌtɑːdə'nɔɪzɪən) *adj* of or referring to a Mesolithic culture characterized by small flint instruments. [C20: after *Tardenois,* France, where implements were found]

tardigrade ('tɑːdɪˌgreɪd) *n* any of various minute aquatic segmented eight-legged invertebrates occurring in soil, ditches, etc. Popular name: **water bear.** [C17: via L *tardigradus,* from *tardus* sluggish + *gradī* to walk]

tardy ❶ ('tɑːdɪ) *adj* **tardier, tardiest. 1** occurring later than expected. **2** slow in progress, growth, etc. [C15: from OF *tardif,* from L *tardus* slow]
▸ **'tardily** *adv* ▸ **'tardiness** *n*

tare[1] (tɛə) *n* **1** any of various vetch plants of Eurasia and N Africa. **2** the seed of any of these plants. **3** *Bible.* a weed, thought to be the darnel. [C14: from ?]

tare[2] (tɛə) *n* **1** the weight of the wrapping or container in which goods are packed. **2** a deduction from gross weight to compensate for this. **3** the weight of an unladen vehicle. ◆ *vb* **tares, taring, tared. 4** *(tr)* to weigh (a package, etc.) in order to calculate the amount of tare. [C15: from OF: waste, from Med. L *tara,* from Ar. *tarhah* something discarded, from *taraha* to reject]

targe (tɑːdʒ) *n* an archaic word for **shield.** [C13: from OF, of Gmc origin]

target ❶ ('tɑːgɪt) *n* **1a** an object or area at which an archer or marksman aims, usually a round flat surface marked with concentric rings. **1b** *(as modifier): target practice.* **2a** any point or area aimed at. **2b** *(as modifier): target area; target company.* **3** a fixed goal or objective. **4** a person or thing at which an action or remark is directed or the object of a person's feelings. **5** a joint of lamb consisting of the breast and neck. **6** (formerly) a small round shield. **7** *Physics, electronics.* **7a** a substance subjected to bombardment by electrons or other particles, or to irradiation. **7b** an electrode in a television camera tube whose surface is scanned by the electron beam. **8** *Electronics.* an object detected by the reflection of a radar or sonar signal, etc. ◆ *vb* **targets, targeting, targeted.** *(tr)* **9** to make a target of. **10** to direct or aim: *to target benefits at those most in need.* [C14: from OF *targette* a little shield, from OF TARGE]

tariff ❶ ('tærɪf) *n* **1a** a tax levied by a government on imports or occasionally exports. **1b** a system or list of such taxes. **2** any schedule of prices, fees, fares, etc. **3** *Chiefly Brit.* **3a** a method of charging for the supply of services such as gas and electricity. **3b** a schedule of such charges. **4** *Chiefly Brit.* a bill of fare with prices listed; menu. ◆ *vb (tr)* **5** to set a tariff on. **6** to price according to a schedule of tariffs. [C16: from It. *tariffa,* from Ar. *ta'rīfa* to inform]

tariff office *n Insurance.* a company whose premiums are based on a tariff agreed with other insurance companies.

tarlatan ('tɑːlətən) *n* an open-weave cotton fabric, used for stiffening garments. [C18: from F *tarlatane,* var. of *tarnatane* type of muslin, ? of Indian origin]

Tarmac ('tɑːmæk) *n* **1** *Trademark.* *(often not cap.)* a paving material that consists of crushed stone rolled and bound with a mixture of tar and bitumen, esp. as used for a road, airport runway, etc. Full name: **Tarmacadam** (ˌtɑːmə'kædəm). See also **macadam.** ◆ *vb* **Tarmacs, Tarmacking, Tarmacked.** *(tr)* **2** *(usually not cap.)* to apply Tarmac to.

tarn (tɑːn) *n* a small mountain lake or pool. [C14: from ON]

tarnation (tɑː'neɪʃən) *n* a euphemism for **damnation.**

tarnish ❶ ('tɑːnɪʃ) *vb* **1** to lose or cause to lose the shine, esp. by exposure to air or moisture resulting in surface oxidation; discolour. **2** to stain or become stained; taint. ◆ *n* **3** a tarnished condition, surface, or film. [C16: from OF *ternir* to make dull, from *terne* lustreless of Gmc origin]
▸ **'tarnishable** *adj*

taro ('tɑːrəʊ) *n, pl* **taros. 1** a plant cultivated in the tropics for its large edible rootstock. **2** the rootstock of this plant. ◆ Also called: **eddo.** [C18: from Tahitian & Maori]

tarot ('tærəʊ) *n* **1** one of a special pack of cards, now used mainly for fortune-telling. **2** a card in a tarot pack with distinctive symbolic design. ◆ *adj* **3** relating to tarot cards. [C16: from F, from OIt. *tarocco,* from ?]

tarpan ('tɑːpæn) *n* a European wild horse, now extinct. [from Tatar]

tarpaulin (tɑː'pɔːlɪn) *n* **1** a heavy waterproof fabric made of canvas or similar material coated with tar, wax, or paint. **2** a sheet of this fabric. **3** a hat made of or covered with this fabric, esp. a sailor's hat. **4** a rare word for **seaman.** [C17: prob. from TAR[1] + PALL[1] + -ING[1]]

tarpon ('tɑːpən) *n, pl* **tarpons** *or* **tarpon.** a large silvery game fish of warm oceans. [C17: ?from Du. *tarpoen,* from ?]

tarradiddle ('tærəˌdɪdᵊl) *n* **1** a trifling lie. **2** nonsense; twaddle. [C18: from ?]

tarragon ('tærəgən) *n* **1** an aromatic plant of the Old World, having leaves which are used as seasoning. **2** the leaves of this plant. [C16: from OF *targon,* from Med. L *tarcon,* ? ult. from Gk *drakontion* adderwort]

tarry ❶ ('tærɪ) *vb* **tarries, tarrying, tarried. 1** *(intr)* to delay; linger. **2** *(intr)* to remain temporarily or briefly. **3** *(intr)* to wait or stay. **4** *(tr) Arch. or poetic.* to await. [C14 *tarien,* from ?]
▸ **'tarrier** *n*

tarsal ('tɑːsᵊl) *adj* **1** of the tarsus or tarsi. ◆ *n* **2** a tarsal bone.

tarseal ('tɑːˌsiːl) *n NZ.* **1** the bitumen surface of a road. **2 the tarseal.** the main highway.

tarsia ('tɑːsɪə) *n* another term for **intarsia.** [C17: from It., from Ar. *tarsī'*]

tarsier ('tɑːsɪə) *n* any of several nocturnal arboreal primates of Indonesia and the Philippines, having huge eyes, long hind legs, and digits ending in pads to facilitate climbing. [C18: from F, from *tarse* the flat of the foot; see TARSUS]

tarsus ('tɑːsəs) *n, pl* **tarsi** (-saɪ). **1** the bones of the ankle and heel, collectively. **2** the corresponding part in other mammals and in amphibians and reptiles. **3** the connective tissue supporting the free edge of each eyelid. **4** the part of an insect's leg that lies distal to the tibia. [C17: from NL, from Gk *tarsos* flat surface, instep]

tart[1] ❶ (tɑːt) *n* a pastry case often having no top crust, with a filling of fruit, custard, etc. [C14: from OF *tarte,* from ?]

tart[2] ❶ (tɑːt) *adj* **1** (of a flavour, etc.) sour; acid. **2** cutting; sharp: *a tart remark.* [OE *teart* rough]
▸ **'tartly** *adv* ▸ **'tartness** *n*

tart[3] ❶ (tɑːt) *n Inf.* a promiscuous woman, esp. a prostitute. See also **tart up.** [C19: shortened from SWEETHEART]
▸ **'tarty** *adj*

tartan ('tɑːtᵊn) *n* **1a** a design of straight lines, crossing at right angles to give a chequered appearance, esp. the distinctive design or designs associated with each Scottish clan. **1b** *(as modifier): a tartan kilt.* **2** a fabric or garment with this design. [C16: ?from OF *tertaine* linsey-woolsey, from OSp. *tiritaña* a fine silk fabric, from *tiritar* to rustle]
▸ **'tartaned** *adj*

tartar[1] ('tɑːtə) *n* **1** a hard deposit on the teeth, consisting of food, cellular debris, and mineral salts. **2** a brownish-red substance consisting mainly of potassium hydrogen tartrate, deposited during the fermentation of wine. [C14: from Med. L *tartarum,* from Med. Gk *tartaron*]

tartar[2] ('tɑːtə) *n* *(sometimes cap.)* a fearsome or formidable person. [C16: special use of TARTAR]

Tartar ('tɑːtə) *n, adj* a variant spelling of **Tatar.**

Tartarean (tɑː'tɛərɪən) *adj Literary.* of or relating to Tartarus, in Greek mythology an abyss below Hades; infernal.

tartar emetic *n* antimony potassium tartrate, a poisonous, crystalline salt used as a mordant and in medicine.

tartaric (tɑː'tærɪk) *adj* of, containing, or derived from tartar or tartaric acid.

THESAURUS

tardiness *n* **1, 2 = lateness,** belatedness, delay, dilatoriness, procrastination, slowness, unpunctuality

tardy *adj* **1 = late,** behindhand, belated, overdue **2 = slow,** backward, dawdling, dilatory, loitering, procrastinating, retarded, slack, sluggish, unpunctual

target *n* **1a, 2a, 3 = goal,** aim, ambition, bull's-eye, end, Holy Grail *(inf.)*, intention, mark, object, objective **4 = victim,** butt, quarry, scapegoat

tariff *n* **1 = tax,** assessment, duty, excise, impost, levy, rate, toll **2 = price list,** bill of fare, charges, menu, schedule

tarnish *vb* **1 = stain,** befoul, blemish, blot, darken, dim, discolour, dull, lose lustre *or* shine, rust, soil, spot **2 = damage,** blacken, drag through the mud, smirch, sully, taint ◆ *n* **3 = stain,** blemish, blot, discoloration, rust, spot, taint
Antonyms *vb* ≠ **stain:** brighten, enhance, polish up, shine ≠ **damage:** enhance

tarry *vb Old-fashioned* **1, 3 = linger,** bide, dally, dawdle, delay, drag one's feet *or* heels, hang around, loiter, lose time, pause, remain, take one's time, wait **2 = stay,** abide, dwell, lodge, rest, sojourn
Antonyms *vb* ≠ **linger:** hasten, hurry, move on, rush, scoot, step on it *(inf.)*

tart[1] *n* **= pie,** pastry, tartlet

tart[2] *adj* **1 = sharp,** acid, acidulous, astringent, bitter, piquant, pungent, sour, tangy, vinegary **2 = cutting,** acrimonious, astringent, barbed, biting, caustic, crusty, harsh, hurtful, mordacious, mordant, nasty, scathing, sharp, short, snappish, testy, trenchant, vitriolic, wounding
Antonyms *adj* ≠ **sharp:** honeyed, sugary, sweet, syrupy, toothsome ≠ **cutting:** agreeable, delightful, gentle, kind, pleasant

tart[3] *n* **= slut,** call girl, fallen woman, *fille de joie,* floozy *(sl.)*, harlot, hooker, loose woman, prostitute, scrubber *(Brit. & Austral. sl.)*, slag *(Brit. sl.)*, streetwalker, strumpet, trollop, whore, woman of easy virtue, working girl *(facetious sl.)*

tartaric acid *n* a colourless crystalline acid which is found in many fruits: used as a food additive (**E334**) in soft drinks, confectionery, and baking powders, and in tanning and photography. Formula: $(CHOH)_2(COOH)_2$. Systematic name: **2,3-dihydroxybutanedioic acid.**

tartar sauce *n* a mayonnaise sauce mixed with hard-boiled egg yolks, chopped herbs, capers, etc. [from F *sauce tartare,* from TARTAR]

tartlet ('tɑːtlɪt) *n Brit.* an individual pastry case with a sweet or savoury filling.

tartrate ('tɑːtreɪt) *n* any salt or ester of tartaric acid.

tartrated ('tɑːtreɪtɪd) *adj* being in the form of a tartrate.

tartrazine ('tɑːtrəˌziːn, -zɪn) *n* an azo dye that produces a yellow colour: used as a food additive (**E102**), in drugs, and to dye textiles.

tart up *vb (tr; adv) Brit. inf.* **1** to dress and make (oneself) up in a provocative or promiscuous way. **2** to decorate or improve the appearance of: *to tart up a bar.*

tarwhine ('tɑːˌwaɪn) *n* any of various Australian marine food fishes, esp. the sea bream. [?from Abor.]

Tarzan ('tɑːzən) *n (sometimes not cap.) Inf., often ironical.* a man with great physical strength, agility, and virility. [C20: after the hero of a series of stories by E. R. *Burroughs* 1875–1950]

Tas. *abbrev. for* Tasmania.

tasimeter (tə'sɪmɪtə) *n* a device for measuring small temperature changes. It depends on the changes of pressure resulting from expanding or contracting solids. [C19 *tasi-,* from Gk *tasis* tension + -METER]
► **tasimetric** (ˌtæsɪ'metrɪk) *adj* ► **ta'simetry** *n*

task ⓣ (tɑːsk) *n* **1** a specific piece of work required to be done. **2** an unpleasant or difficult job or duty. **3** any piece of work. **4 take to task.** to criticize or reprove. ◆ *vb (tr)* **5** to assign a task to. **6** to subject to severe strain; tax. [C13: from OF *tasche,* from Med. L *tasca,* from *taxa* tax, from L *taxāre* to TAX]

task force *n* **1** a temporary grouping of military units formed to undertake a specific mission. **2** any organization set up to carry out a continuing task.

taskmaster ('tɑːskˌmɑːstə) *n* a person, discipline, etc., that enforces work, esp. hard or continuous work.
► **'taskˌmistress** *fem n*

taskwork ('tɑːskˌwɜːk) *n* **1** hard or unpleasant work. **2** a rare word for **piecework.**

Tasmanian devil (tæz'meɪnɪən) *n* a small ferocious carnivorous marsupial of Tasmania.

Tasmanian wolf *or* **tiger** *n* other names for **thylacine.**

tass (tæs) *or* **tassie** ('tæsɪ) *n Scot. & N English dialect.* **1** a cup or glass. **2** its contents. [C15: from OF *tasse* cup, from Ar. *tassah* basin, from Persian *tast*]

Tass (tæs) *n* (formerly) the principal news agency of the Soviet Union: replaced in 1992 by Itar Tass. [*T(elegrafnoye) a(gentstvo) S(ovetskogo) S(oyuza)* Telegraphic Agency of the Soviet Union]

tassel ('tæsᵊl) *n* **1** a tuft of loose threads secured by a knot or knob, used to decorate soft furnishings, clothes, etc. **2** anything resembling this, esp. the tuft of stamens at the tip of a maize inflorescence. ◆ *vb* **tassels, tasselling, tasselled** *or US* **tassels, tasseling, tasseled. 3** *(tr)* to adorn with tassels. **4** *(intr)* (of maize) to produce stamens in a tuft. [C13: from OF, from Vulgar L *tassellus* (unattested), changed from L *taxillus* a small die]

Tassie *or* **Tassy** ('tæzɪ) *n, Austral. inf.* **1** Tasmania. **2** *(pl* **Tassies***)* a native or inhabitant of Tasmania.

taste ⓣ (teɪst) *n* **1** the sense by which the qualities and flavour of a substance are distinguished by the taste buds. **2** the sensation experienced by means of the taste buds. **3** the act of tasting. **4** a small amount eaten, drunk, or tried on the tongue. **5** a brief experience of something: *a taste of the whip.* **6** a preference or liking for something. **7** the ability to make discerning judgments about aesthetic, artistic, and intellectual matters. **8** judgment of aesthetic or social matters according to a generally accepted standard: *bad taste.* **9** discretion; delicacy: *that remark lacks taste.* ◆ *vb* **tastes, tasting, tasted. 10** to distinguish the taste of (a substance) by means of the taste buds. **11** *(usually tr)* to take a small amount of (a food, liquid, etc.) into the mouth, esp. in order to test the quality. **12** (often foll. by *of*) to have a specific flavour or taste. **13** (when *intr,* usually foll. by *of*) to have an experience of (something): *to taste success.* **14** *(tr)* an archaic word for **enjoy.** [C13: from OF *taster,* ult. from L *taxāre* to appraise]
► **'tastable** *adj*

taste bud *n* any of the elevated sensory organs on the surface of the tongue, by means of which the sensation of taste is experienced.

tasteful ⓣ ('teɪstfʊl) *adj* indicating good taste: *a tasteful design.*
► **'tastefully** *adv* ► **'tastefulness** *n*

tasteless ⓣ ('teɪstlɪs) *adj* **1** lacking in flavour; insipid. **2** lacking social or aesthetic taste.
► **'tastelessly** *adv* ► **'tastelessness** *n*

taster ('teɪstə) *n* **1** a person who samples food or drink for quality. **2** any device used in tasting or sampling. **3** a person employed, esp. formerly, to taste food and drink prepared for a king, etc., to test for poison. **4** a sample or preview of a product, experience, etc., intended to stimulate interest in the product, experience, etc., itself: *the single serves as a taster for the band's new album.*

tasty ⓣ ('teɪstɪ) *adj* **tastier, tastiest.** having a pleasant flavour.
► **'tastily** *adv* ► **'tastiness** *n*

tat[1] (tæt) *vb* **tats, tatting, tatted.** to make (something) by tatting. [C19: from ?]

tat[2] (tæt) *n* **1** tatty articles or a tatty condition. **2** tasteless articles. **3** a tangled mass. [C20: back formation from TATTY]

tat[3] (tæt) *n* See **tit for tat.**

ta-ta (tæ'tɑː) *sentence substitute. Brit. inf.* goodbye; farewell. [C19: from ?]

Tatar *or* **Tartar** ('tɑːtə) *n* **1a** a member of a Mongoloid people who established a powerful state in central Asia in the 13th century. **1b** a descendant of this people, now scattered throughout Russia and N central Asia. **2** any of the Turkic languages spoken by the present-day Tatars. ◆ *adj* **3** of or relating to the Tatars. [C14: from OF *Tartare,* from Med. L *Tartarus* (associated with L *Tartarus* the underworld), from Persian *Tātār*]
► **Tatarian** (tɑː'teərɪən), **Tar'tarian** *or* **Tataric** (tɑː'tærɪk), **Tar'taric** *adj*

tater ('teɪtə) *n* a dialect word for **potato.**

tatouay ('tætuˌeɪ) *n* a large armadillo of South America. [C16: from Sp. *tatuay,* from Guarani, from *tatu* armadillo + *ai* worthless (because inedible)]

tatter ⓣ ('tætə) *vb* **1** to make or become ragged or worn to shreds. ◆ *n* **2** a torn or ragged piece, esp. of material. [C14: from ON]

tatterdemalion (ˌtætədɪ'meɪljən) *n Rare.* a person dressed in ragged clothes. [C17: from TATTER + *-demalion,* from ?]

tattersall ('tætəˌsɔːl) *n* a fabric having stripes or bars in a checked or squared pattern. [C19: after *Tattersall's,* a horse market in London founded by Richard *Tattersall* (died 1795), Brit. horseman; the horse blankets at the market orig. had this pattern]

Tattersall's ('tætəˌsɔːlz) *n Austral.* **1** Also called (inf.): **Tatt's.** a lottery now based in Melbourne. **2** a name used for sportsmen's clubs. [after *Tattersall's* horse market; see TATTERSALL]

tatting ('tætɪŋ) *n* **1** an intricate type of lace made by looping a thread of cotton or linen by means of a hand shuttle. **2** the act or work of producing this. [C19: from ?]

tattle ⓣ ('tætᵊl) *vb* **tattles, tattling, tattled. 1** *(intr)* to gossip about another's personal matters. **2** *(tr)* to reveal by gossiping. **3** *(intr)* to talk idly; chat. ◆ *n* **4** the act or an instance of tattling. **5** a scandalmonger; gossip. [C15 (in the sense: to stammer, hesitate): from MDu. *tatelen* to prate, imit.]
► **'tattler** *n*

THESAURUS

task *n* **1-3** = **job**, assignment, business, charge, chore, duty, employment, enterprise, exercise, labour, mission, occupation, toil, undertaking, work **4 take to task** = **criticize**, bawl out (*inf.*), blame, blast, carpet (*inf.*), censure, lambast(e), lecture, read the riot act, rebuke, reprimand, reproach, reprove, scold, tear into (*inf.*), tear (someone) off a strip (*Brit. inf.*), tell off (*inf.*), upbraid ◆ *vb* **5** = **assign to**, charge, entrust **6** = **strain**, burden, exhaust, load, lumber (*Brit. inf.*), oppress, overload, push, saddle, tax, test, weary

taste *n* **2** = **flavour**, relish, savour, smack, tang **4** = **bit**, bite, dash, drop, morsel, mouthful, nip, sample, sip, *soupçon,* spoonful, swallow, titbit, touch **6** = **liking**, appetite, bent, desire, fancy, fondness, inclination, leaning, palate, partiality, penchant, predilection, preference, relish **7** = **refinement**, appreciation, cultivation, culture, discernment, discrimination, elegance, grace, judgment, perception, polish, sophistication, style **8, 9** = **propriety**, correctness, decorum, delicacy, discretion, nicety, politeness, restraint, tact, tactfulness ◆ *vb* **10** = **distinguish**, differentiate, discern, perceive **11** = **sample**, assay, nibble, relish, savour, sip, test, try **12** = **have a flavour of**, savour of, smack of **13** = **experience**, come up against, encounter, feel, have knowledge of, know, meet with, partake of, undergo
Antonyms *n* ≠ **flavour**: blandness, insipidity, tastelessness ≠ **liking**: disinclination, dislike, distaste, hatred, loathing ≠ **refinement**: lack of discernment, lack of judgment, mawkishness, tackiness, tastelessness ≠ **propriety**: bawdiness, blueness, coarseness, crudeness, impropriety, indelicacy, obscenity (*inf.*), tactlessness, unsubtlety ◆ *vb* ≠ **distinguish**: fail to discern ≠ **experience**: fail to achieve, miss, remain ignorant of

tasteful *adj* = **refined**, aesthetically pleasing, artistic, beautiful, charming, cultivated, cultured, delicate, discriminating, elegant, exquisite, fastidious, graceful, handsome, harmonious, in good taste, polished, restrained, smart, stylish, urbane
Antonyms *adj* brash, flashy, garish, gaudy, inelegant, loud, objectionable, offensive, showy, sick, tacky (*inf.*), tasteless, tawdry, twee, uncultured, unrefined, vulgar

tasteless *adj* **1** = **insipid**, bland, boring, dull, flat, flavourless, mild, stale, tame, thin, uninspired, uninteresting, vapid, watered-down, weak **2** = **vulgar**, cheap, coarse, crass, crude, flashy, garish, gaudy, graceless, gross, impolite, improper, indecorous, indelicate, indiscreet, inelegant, low, naff (*Brit. sl.*), rude, tacky (*inf.*), tactless, tawdry, uncouth, unseemly
Antonyms *adj* ≠ **insipid**: appetizing, delectable, delicious, flavoursome, savoury, scrumptious (*inf.*), tasty ≠ **vulgar**: elegant, graceful, refined, tasteful

tasty *adj* = **delicious**, appetizing, delectable, flavourful, flavoursome, full-flavoured, good-tasting, luscious, palatable, sapid, savoury, scrumptious (*inf.*), toothsome, yummy (*sl.*)
Antonyms *adj* bland, flavourless, insipid, tasteless, unappetizing, unsavoury

tatter *n* **2** = **rag**, bit, piece, scrap, shred

tattle *vb* **1, 3** = **gossip**, babble, blab, blather, blether, chat, chatter, jabber, natter, prate, prattle, run off at the mouth (*sl.*), spread rumours, talk idly, tell tales, tittle-tattle, yak (*sl.*) ◆ *n* **4** = **gossip**, babble, blather, blether, chat, chatter, chitchat, hearsay, idle talk, jabber, prattle, small talk, tittle-tattle, yak (*sl.*), yap (*sl.*)

tattler *n* **1** = **gossip**, bigmouth (*sl.*), quidnunc,

tattletale ('tæt^{a}l,teɪl) *Chiefly US & Canad.* *n* **1** a scandalmonger or gossip. **2** another word for **telltale** (sense 1).

tattoo[1] (tæ'tuː) *n, pl* **tattoos. 1** (formerly) a signal by drum or bugle ordering the military to return to their quarters. **2** a military display or pageant. **3** any similar beating on a drum, etc. [C17: from Du. *taptoe,* from *tap toe!* turn off the taps! from *tap* tap of a barrel + *toe* to shut]

tattoo[2] (tæ'tuː) *vb* **tattoos, tattooing, tattooed. 1** to make (pictures or designs) on (the skin) by pricking and staining with indelible colours. ◆ *n, pl* **tattoos. 2** a design made by this process. **3** the practice of tattooing. [C18: from Tahitian *tatau*]
▸**tat'tooer** *or* **tat'tooist** *n*

tatty ❶ ('tætɪ) *adj* **tattier, tattiest.** *Chiefly Brit.* worn out, shabby, or unkempt. [C16: of Scot. origin]
▸**'tattily** *adv* ▸**'tattiness** *n*

tau (tɔː, taʊ) *n* the 19th letter in the Greek alphabet (Τ or τ). [C13: from Gk]

tau cross *n* a cross shaped like the Greek letter tau. Also called: **Saint Anthony's cross.**

taught (tɔːt) *vb* the past tense and past participle of **teach.**

taunt ❶ (tɔːnt) *vb* (*tr*) **1** to provoke or deride with mockery, contempt, or criticism. **2** to tease; tantalize. ◆ *n* **3** a jeering remark. [C16: from F *tant pour tant* like for like]
▸**'taunting** *adj*

tau particle *n Physics.* a type of elementary particle classified as a lepton.

taupe (təʊp) *n* **a** a brownish-grey colour. **b** (*as adj*): *a taupe coat.* [C20: from F, lit.: mole, from L *talpa*]

taurine ('tɔːraɪn) *adj* of or resembling a bull. [C17: from L *taurīnus,* from *taurus* a bull]

tauromachy (tɔː'rɒməkɪ) *n* the art or act of bullfighting. [C19: Gk *tauromakhia,* from *tauros* bull + *makhē* fight]

Taurus ('tɔːrəs) *n* **1** *Astron.* a constellation in the N hemisphere. **2** *Astrol.* Also called: the **Bull.** the second sign of the zodiac. The sun is in this sign between about April 20 and May 20. [C14: from L: bull]

taut ❶ (tɔːt) *adj* **1** tightly stretched; tense. **2** showing nervous strain; stressed. **3** *Chiefly naut.* in good order; neat. [C14 *tought*]
▸**'tautly** *adv* ▸**'tautness** *n*

tauten ('tɔːt^{a}n) *vb* to make or become taut.

tauto- *or before a vowel* **taut-** *combining form.* identical or same: *tautology.* [from Gk *tauto,* from *to auto*]

tautog (tɔː'tɒg) *n* a large dark-coloured food fish of the North American coast of the Atlantic Ocean. [C17: from Narraganset *tautauog,* pl. of *tautau* sheepshead]

tautology ❶ (tɔː'tɒlədʒɪ) *n, pl* **tautologies. 1** the use of words that merely repeat elements of the meaning already conveyed, as in *Will these supplies be adequate enough?* in place of *Will these supplies be adequate?* **2** *Logic.* a statement that is always true, as in *either the sun is out or the sun is not out.* [C16: from LL *tautologia,* from Gk, from *tautologos*]
▸**tautological** (,tɔːt^{a}'lɒdʒɪk^{a}l) *or* **tau'tologous** *adj*

tautomerism (tɔː'tɒmə,rɪzəm) *n* the ability of certain chemical compounds to exist as a mixture of two interconvertible isomers in equilibrium. [C19: from TAUTO- + ISOMERISM]
▸**tautomer** ('tɔːtəmə) *n* ▸**tautomeric** (,tɔːtə'mɛrɪk) *adj*

tautonym ('tɔːtənɪm) *n Biol.* a taxonomic name in which the generic and specific components are the same, as in *Rattus rattus* (black rat).
▸,**tauto'nymic** *or* **tautonymous** (tɔː'tɒnəməs) *adj* ▸**tau'tonymy** *n*

tavern ❶ ('tævən) *n* **1** a less common word for **pub. 2** *US, E Canad., & NZ.* a place licensed for the sale and consumption of alcoholic drink. [C13: from OF *taverne,* from L *taberna* hut]

taverna (tə'vɜːnə) *n* **1** (in Greece) a guesthouse that has its own bar. **2** a Greek restaurant. [C20: Mod. Gk, from L *taberna*]

TAVR *abbrev. for* Territorial and Army Volunteer Reserve.

taw[1] (tɔː) *n* **1** a large marble used for shooting. **2** a game of marbles. **3** the line from which the players shoot in marbles. **4 back to taws.** *Austral. inf.* back to the beginning. [C18: from ?]

taw[2] (tɔː) *vb* (*tr*) to convert (skins) into leather by treatment with alum and salt rather than by normal tanning processes. [OE *tawian*]
▸**'tawer** *n*

tawa ('tɑːwə) *n* a New Zealand timber tree with edible berries. [from Maori]

tawdry ❶ ('tɔːdrɪ) *adj* **tawdrier, tawdriest.** cheap, showy, and of poor quality: *tawdry jewellery.* [C16 *tawdry lace,* shortened & altered from *Seynt Audries lace,* finery sold at the fair of St *Audrey* (Etheldrida), 7th-century queen of Northumbria]
▸**'tawdrily** *adv* ▸**'tawdriness** *n*

tawny ('tɔːnɪ) *n* **a** a light brown to brownish-orange colour. **b** (*as adj*): *tawny port.* [C14: from OF *tané,* from *taner* to tan]
▸**'tawniness** *n*

tawny owl *n* a European owl having a reddish-brown plumage and a round head.

tawse *or* **taws** (tɔːz) *n Chiefly Scot.* a leather strap having one end cut into thongs, formerly used as an instrument of punishment by a schoolteacher. [C16: prob. pl of obs. *taw* strip of leather; see TAW[2]]

tax ❶ (tæks) *n* **1** a compulsory financial contribution imposed by a government to raise revenue, levied on income or property, on the prices of goods and services, etc. **2** a heavy demand on something; strain. ◆ *vb* (*tr*) **3** to levy a tax on (persons, companies, etc.). **4** to make heavy demands on; strain. **5** to accuse or blame. **6** *Law.* to determine (the amount legally chargeable or allowable to a party to a legal action): *to tax costs.* **7** *Sl.* to demand money or goods from (someone) with menaces. [C13: from OF *taxer,* from L *taxāre* to appraise, from *tangere* to touch]
▸**'taxable** *adj* ▸**'taxer** *n*

taxation (tæk'seɪʃən) *n* **1** the act or principle of levying taxes or the condition of being taxed. **2a** an amount assessed as tax. **2b** a tax rate. **3** revenue from taxes.
▸**tax'ational** *adj*

tax avoidance *n* reduction or minimization of tax liability by lawful methods.

tax-deductible *adj* legally deductible from income or wealth before tax assessment.

tax disc *n* a paper disc displayed on the windscreen of a motor vehicle showing that the tax due on it has been paid.

taxeme ('tæksiːm) *n Linguistics.* any element of speech that may differentiate one utterance from another with a different meaning, such as the occurrence of a particular phoneme, the presence of a certain intonation, or a distinctive word order. [C20: from Gk *taxis* order, arrangement + -EME]
▸**tax'emic** *adj*

tax evasion *n* reduction or minimization of tax liability by illegal methods.

tax exile *n* a person having a high income who chooses to live abroad so as to avoid paying high taxes.

tax haven *n* a country or state having a lower rate of taxation than elsewhere.

tax holiday *n* a period during which tax concessions are made for some reason; examples include an export incentive or an incentive to start a new business given by some governments, in which a company is excused all or part of its tax liability.

taxi ('tæksɪ) *n, pl* **taxis** *or* **taxies. 1** Also called: **cab, taxicab.** a car, usually fitted with a taximeter, that may be hired, along with its driver, to carry passengers to any specified destination. ◆ *vb* **taxis** *or* **taxies, taxiing** *or* **taxying, taxied. 2** to cause (an aircraft) to move along the ground, esp. before takeoff and after landing, or (of an aircraft) to move along the ground in this way. **3** (*intr*) to travel in a taxi. [C20: shortened from *taximeter cab*]

taxidermy ('tæksɪ,dɜːmɪ) *n* the art or process of preparing, stuffing, and mounting animal skins so that they have a lifelike appearance. [C19: from Gk *taxis* arrangement + *-dermy,* from Gk *derma* skin]
▸,**taxi'dermal** *or* ,**taxi'dermic** *adj* ▸**'taxi,dermist** *n*

taximeter ('tæksɪ,miːtə) *n* a meter fitted to a taxi to register the fare, based on the length of the journey. [C19: from F *taximètre;* see TAX, -METER]

taxing ❶ ('tæksɪŋ) *adj* demanding, onerous, and wearing.
▸**'taxingly** *adv*

taxi rank *n* a place where taxis wait to be hired.

taxis ('tæksɪs) *n* **1** the movement of an organism in response to an ex-

THESAURUS

rumourmonger, scandalmonger, talebearer, taleteller, telltale

tatty *adj Chiefly Brit.* = **shabby,** bedraggled, dilapidated, down at heel, frayed, having seen better days, neglected, poor, ragged, rumpled, run-down, scruffy, seedy, tattered, tawdry, the worse for wear, threadbare, unkempt, worn, worn out
Antonyms *adj* good, new, smart, well-preserved

taunt *vb* **1** = **jeer,** deride, flout, gibe, guy (*inf.*), insult, mock, provoke, revile, ridicule, sneer, take the piss (out of) (*taboo sl.*), tease, torment, twit ◆ *n* **3** = **jeer,** barb, cut, derision, dig, gibe, insult, provocation, ridicule, sarcasm, teasing

taut *adj* **1** = **tight,** flexed, rigid, strained, stressed, stretched, tense **3** *Nautical* = **neat,** in good order, orderly, shipshape, spruce, tidy, tight, trim, well-ordered, well-regulated
Antonyms *adj* ≠ **tight:** loose, relaxed, slack

tautological *adj* **1** = **repetitive,** iterative, pleonastic, prolix, redundant, repetitious, verbose

tautology *n* **1** = **repetition,** iteration, pleonasm, prolixity, redundancy, repetitiousness, repetitiveness, verbiage, verbosity

tavern *n* **1, 2** = **inn,** alehouse (*arch.*), bar, boozer (*Brit., Austral., & NZ inf.*), hostelry, pub (*inf., chiefly Brit.*), public house, taproom, watering hole (*facetious sl.*)

tawdry *adj* = **vulgar,** brummagem, cheap, cheap-jack (*inf.*), flashy, gaudy, gimcrack, glittering, meretricious, naff (*Brit. sl.*), plastic (*sl.*), raffish, showy, tacky (*inf.*), tasteless, tatty, tinsel, tinselly
Antonyms *adj* elegant, graceful, plain, refined, simple, stylish, tasteful, unflashy, unostentatious, well-tailored

tax *n* **1** = **charge,** assessment, contribution, customs, duty, excise, imposition, impost, levy, rate, tariff, tithe, toll, tribute **2** = **strain,** burden, demand, drain, load, pressure, weight ◆ *vb* **3** = **charge,** assess, demand, exact, extract, impose, levy a tax on, rate, tithe **4** = **strain,** burden, drain, enervate, exhaust, load, make heavy demands on, overburden, push, put pressure on, sap, stretch, task, test, try, weaken, wear out, weary, weigh heavily on **5** = **accuse,** arraign, blame, charge, impeach, impugn, incriminate, lay at one's door
Antonyms *vb* ≠ **accuse:** acquit, clear, exculpate, exonerate, vindicate

taxing *adj* = **demanding,** burdensome, enervating, exacting, heavy, onerous, punishing, sapping, stressful, tiring, tough, trying, wearing, wearisome
Antonyms *adj* easy, easy-peasy (*sl.*), effortless, light, unburdensome, undemanding

ternal stimulus. **2** *Surgery.* the repositioning of a displaced part by manual manipulation only. [C18: via NL from Gk: arrangement, from *tassein* to place in order]

-taxis *or* **-taxy** *n combining form.* **1** indicating movement towards or away from a specified stimulus: *thermotaxis.* **2** order or arrangement: *phyllotaxis.* [from NL, from Gk *taxis* order]
▸**-tactic** *or* **-taxic** *adj combining form.*

taxiway ('tæksɪˌweɪ) *n* a marked path along which aircraft taxi to or from a runway, parking area, etc.

tax loss *n* a loss sustained by a company that can be set against future profits for tax purposes.

taxman ('tæksˌmæn) *n, pl* **-men. 1** a collector of taxes. **2** *Inf.* a tax-collecting body personified: *he was convicted of conspiring to cheat the taxman of five million pounds.*

taxon ('tæksɒn) *n, pl* **taxa** ('tæksə). *Biol.* any taxonomic group or rank. [C20: back formation from TAXONOMY]

taxonomy (tæk'sɒnəmɪ) *n* **1** the branch of biology concerned with the classification of organisms into groups based on similarities of structure, origin, etc. **2** the science or practice of classification. [C19: from F *taxonomie,* from Gk *taxis* order + -NOMY]
▸**taxonomic** (ˌtæksə'nɒmɪk) *or* ˌ**taxo'nomical** *adj* ▸ˌ**taxo'nomically** *adv*
▸**tax'onomist** *n*

taxpayer ('tæksˌpeɪə) *n* a person or organization that pays taxes.

tax relief *n* remission of income tax due on a proportion of income earned.

tax return *n* a declaration of personal income used as a basis for assessing an individual's liability for taxation.

tax shelter *n* a form into which business activities may be organized to minimize taxation.

-taxy *n combining form.* a variant of **-taxis.**

Tay-Sachs disease (ˌteɪ'sæks) *n* an inherited disorder, caused by a faulty recessive gene, in which lipids accumulate in the brain, leading to mental retardation and blindness. [C20: after W. *Tay* (1843–1927), Brit. physician, and B. *Sachs* (1858–1944), US neurologist]

tazza ('tætsə) *n* a wine cup with a shallow bowl and a circular foot. [C19: from It., prob. from Ar. *tassah* bowl]

Tb *the chemical symbol for* terbium.

TB *abbrev. for:* **1** torpedo boat. **2** Also: **tb.** tuberculosis.

T-bar *n* **1** a T-shaped wrench for use with a socket. **2** a T-shaped bar on a ski tow which skiers hold on to while being pulled up slopes.

T-bone steak *n* a large choice steak cut from the sirloin of beef, containing a T-shaped bone.

tbs. *or* **tbsp.** *abbrev. for* tablespoon(ful).

TBT *abbrev. for* tri-*n*-butyl tin: a biocide used in marine paints to prevent fouling.

Tc *the chemical symbol for* technetium.

T-cell *n* a type of lymphocyte that matures in the thymus gland and is responsible for killing cells infected by a virus. Also called: **T-lymphocyte.**

t.d.c. *abbrev. for* top dead-centre.

t distribution *n* See **Student's t.**

te *or* **ti** (tiː) *n Music.* (in tonic sol-fa) the syllable used for the seventh note or subtonic of any scale. [later variant of *si;* see GAMUT]

Te *the chemical symbol for* tellurium.

tea (tiː) *n* **1** an evergreen shrub of tropical and subtropical Asia, having white fragrant flowers: family *Theaceae.* **2a** the dried leaves of this shrub, used to make a beverage by infusion in boiling water. **2b** such a beverage, served hot or iced. **3a** any of various similar plants or any plants that are used to make a tealike beverage. **3b** any such beverage. **4** *Chiefly Brit.* **4a** Also called: **afternoon tea.** a light meal eaten in mid-afternoon, usually consisting of tea and cakes, etc. **4b** Also called: **high tea.** afternoon tea that also includes a light cooked dish. **5** *Brit., Austral., & NZ.* the main evening meal. **6** *US & Canad. dated sl.* marijuana. **7 tea and sympathy.** *Inf.* a caring attitude, esp. to someone in trouble. [C17: from Chinese (Amoy) *t'e,* from Ancient Chinese *d'a*]

tea bag *n* a small bag containing tea leaves, infused in boiling water to make tea.

tea ball *n Chiefly US.* a perforated metal ball filled with tea leaves and used to make tea.

tea break *n* a short rest period during working hours during which tea, coffee, etc., is drunk.

teacake ('tiːˌkeɪk) *n Brit.* a flat bun, usually eaten toasted and buttered.

teach Ⓣ (tiːtʃ) *vb* **teaches, teaching, taught. 1** *(tr; may take a clause as object or an infinitive;* often foll. by *how)* to help to learn; tell or show (how). **2** to give instruction or lessons in (a subject) to (a person or animal). **3** *(tr; may take a clause as object or an infinitive)* to cause to learn or understand: *experience taught him that he could not be a journalist.* [OE *tǣcan*]
▸**'teachable** *adj*

teacher Ⓣ ('tiːtʃə) *n* a person whose occupation is teaching others, esp. children.

teach-in *n* an informal conference, esp. on a topical subject, usually held at a university or college and involving a panel of visiting speakers, lecturers, students, etc.

teaching ('tiːtʃɪŋ) *n* **1** the art or profession of a teacher. **2** *(sometimes pl)* something taught; precept. **3** *(modifier)* denoting a person or institution that teaches: *a teaching hospital.* **4** *(modifier)* used in teaching: *teaching aids.*

teaching machine *n* a machine that presents information and questions to the user, registers the answers, and indicates whether these are correct or acceptable.

tea cloth *n* another name for **tea towel.**

tea cosy *n* a covering for a teapot to keep the contents hot.

teacup ('tiːˌkʌp) *n* **1** a cup out of which tea may be drunk. **2** Also called: **teacupful.** the amount a teacup will hold, about four fluid ounces.

tea dance *n* a dance held in the afternoon at which tea is served.

teahouse ('tiːˌhaʊs) *n* a restaurant, esp. in Japan or China, where tea and light refreshments are served.

teak (tiːk) *n* **1** a large tree of the East Indies. **2** the hard resinous yellowish-brown wood of this tree, used for furniture making, etc. [C17: from Port. *teca,* from Malayalam *tēkka*]

teakettle ('tiːˌketᵊl) *n* a kettle for boiling water to make tea.

teal (tiːl) *n, pl* **teals** *or* **teal. 1** any of various small freshwater ducks that are related to the mallard. **2** a greenish-blue colour. [C14]

tea lady *n* a woman employed in a factory, office, etc., to make tea during a tea break.

tea leaf *n* **1** the dried leaf of the tea shrub, used to make tea. **2** *(usually pl)* shredded parts of these leaves, esp. after infusion.

team Ⓣ (tiːm) *n (sometimes functioning as pl)* **1** a group of people organized to work together. **2** a group of players forming one of the sides in a sporting contest. **3** two or more animals working together, as to pull a vehicle. **4** such animals and the vehicle. ◆ *vb* **5** (when *intr,* often foll. by *up)* to make or cause to make a team. **6** *(tr) US & Canad.* to drag or transport in or by a team. **7** *(intr) US & Canad.* to drive a team. [OE *team* offspring]

tea-maker *n* a spoon with a perforated cover used to infuse tea in a cup of boiling water.

team-mate *n* a fellow member of a team.

team spirit *n* willingness to cooperate as part of a team.

teamster ('tiːmstə) *n* **1** a driver of a team of horses. **2** *US & Canad.* the driver of a lorry.

team teaching *n* a system whereby two or more teachers pool their skills, knowledge, etc., to teach combined classes.

teamwork Ⓣ ('tiːmˌwɜːk) *n* **1** the cooperative work done by a team. **2** the ability to work efficiently as a team.

teapot ('tiːˌpɒt) *n* a container with a lid, spout, and handle, in which tea is made and from which it is served.

teapoy ('tiːpɔɪ) *n* a small table with a tripod base. [C19: from Hindi *tipāī,* from Sansk. *tri* three + *pāda* foot]

tear[1] (tɪə) *n* **1** a drop of the secretion of the lacrimal glands. See **tears. 2** something shaped like a hanging drop: *a tear of amber.* ◆ Also called: **teardrop.** [OE *tēar*]
▸**'tearless** *adj*

tear[2] Ⓣ (tɛə) *vb* **tears, tearing, tore, torn. 1** to cause to come apart or to come apart; rip. **2** *(tr)* to make (a hole or split) in (something). **3** *(intr;* often foll. by *along)* to hurry or rush. **4** *(tr;* usually foll. by *away* or *from)* to remove or take by force. **5** (when *intr,* often foll. by *at)* to cause pain, distress, or anguish (to). **6 tear one's hair.** *Inf.* to be angry, frustrated, very worried, etc. ◆ *n* **7** a hole, cut, or split. **8** the act of tearing. ◆ See also **tear away, tear down,** etc. [OE *teran*]
▸**'tearable** *adj* ▸**'tearer** *n*

tear away Ⓣ (tɛə) *vb* **1** *(tr, adv)* to persuade (oneself or someone else) to leave. ◆ *n* **tearaway. 2** *Brit.* a reckless impetuous unruly person.

tear down (tɛə) *vb (tr, adv)* to destroy or demolish: *to tear down an argument.*

tear duct (tɪə) *n* a short tube in the inner corner of the eyelid through which tears drain into the nose. Technical name: **lacrimal duct.**

tearful Ⓣ ('tɪəfʊl) *adj* **1** crying or about to cry. **2** tending to produce tears; sad.
▸**'tearfully** *adv* ▸**'tearfulness** *n*

tear gas (tɪə) *n* a gas that makes the eyes smart and water, causing temporary blindness; used in warfare and to control riots.

THESAURUS

teach *vb* **1-3** = **instruct**, advise, coach, demonstrate, direct, discipline, drill, edify, educate, enlighten, give lessons in, guide, impart, implant, inculcate, inform, instil, school, show, train, tutor

teacher *n* = **instructor**, coach, dominie (*Scot.*), don, educator, guide, guru, handler, lecturer, master *or* mistress, mentor, pedagogue, professor, schoolmaster *or* schoolmistress, schoolteacher, trainer, tutor

team *n* **1** = **group**, band, body, bunch, company, crew, gang, line-up, posse (*inf.*), set, side, squad, troupe **3** = **pair**, span, yoke ◆ *vb* **5** *often with* **up** = **join**, band together, cooperate, couple, get together, link, unite, work together, yoke

teamwork *n* **1** = **cooperation**, collaboration, concert, coordination, esprit de corps, fellowship, harmony, joint action, unity

tear[2] *vb* **1** = **rip**, divide, rend, rive, run, rupture, scratch, shred, split, sunder **3** = **rush**, barrel (along) (*inf., chiefly US & Canad.*), belt, bolt, burn rubber (*inf.*), career, charge, dart, dash, fly, gallop, hurry, race, run, shoot, speed, sprint, zoom **4** = **seize**, grab, pluck, pull, rip, snatch, wrench, wrest, yank ◆ *n* **7** = **hole**, laceration, rent, rip, run, rupture, scratch, split

tear away *n* **tearaway 2** *Brit.* = **hooligan**, daredevil, delinquent, good-for-nothing, madcap, rough (*inf.*), roughneck (*sl.*), rowdy, ruffian, tough

tearful *adj* **1** = **weeping**, blubbering, crying, in tears, lachrymose, sobbing, weepy (*inf.*), whimpering **2** = **sad**, distressing, dolorous, harrowing, lamentable, mournful, pathetic, pitiable, pitiful, poignant, sorrowful, upsetting, woeful

tearing ('tɛərɪŋ) *adj* violent or furious (esp. in **tearing hurry** *or* **rush**).
tear into (tɛə) *vb (intr, prep) Inf.* to attack vigorously and damagingly.
tear-jerker ('tɪəˌdʒɜːkə) *n Inf.* an excessively sentimental film, play, book, etc.
tearoom ('tiːˌruːm, -ˌrʊm) *n Brit.* a restaurant where tea and light refreshments are served. Also called: **teashop.**
tea rose *n* any of several varieties of hybrid rose that have pink or yellow flowers with a scent resembling that of tea.
tears ⊕ (tɪəz) *pl n* **1** the clear salty solution secreted by the lacrimal glands that lubricates and cleanses the surface of the eyeball. **2** a state of intense frustration (esp. in **bored to tears**). **3 in tears.** weeping.
tear sheet (tɛə) *n* a page in a newspaper or periodical that is cut or perforated so that it can be easily torn out.
tease ⊕ (tiːz) *vb* **teases, teasing, teased. 1** to annoy (someone) by deliberately offering something with the intention of delaying or withdrawing the offer. **2** to vex (someone) maliciously or playfully. **3** *(tr)* to separate the fibres of; comb; card. **4** *(tr)* to raise the nap of (a fabric) with a teasel. **5** another word (esp. US and Canad.) for **backcomb. 6** *(tr)* to loosen or pull apart (biological tissues, etc.). ◆ *n* **7** a person or thing that teases. **8** the act of teasing. ◆ See also **tease out.** [OE *tǣsan*]
▸ **'teasing** *adj* ▸ **'teasingly** *adv*
teasel, teazel, *or* **teazle** ('tiːzᵊl) *n* **1** any of various plants (esp. the **fuller's teasel**) of Eurasia and N Africa, having prickly leaves and prickly heads of yellow or purple flowers. **2a** the dried flower head of the fuller's teasel, used for teasing. **2b** any implement used for the same purpose. ◆ *vb* **teasels, teaselling, teaselled** *or US* **teasels, teaseling, teaseled. 3** *(tr)* to tease (a fabric). [OE *tǣsel*]
▸ **'teaseller** *n*
tease out *vb (tr, adv)* to extract (information) with difficulty.
teaser ('tiːzə) *n* **1** a person who teases. **2** a difficult question. **3** a preliminary advertisement in a campaign that attracts attention by making people curious to know what product is being advertised.
tea service *or* **set** *n* the china or pottery articles used in serving tea, including a teapot, cups, saucers, etc.
teashop ('tiːˌʃɒp) *n Brit.* another name for **tearoom.**
teaspoon ('tiːˌspuːn) *n* **1** a small spoon used for stirring tea, etc. **2** Also called: **teaspoonful** the amount contained in such a spoon. **3** a unit of capacity used in cooking, medicine, etc., equal to about 5 ml.
teat (tiːt) *n* **1a** the nipple of a mammary gland. **1b** (in cows, etc.) any of the projections from the udder. **2** something resembling a teat such as the rubber mouthpiece of a feeding bottle. [C13: from OF *tete*, of Gmc origin]
tea towel *or* **cloth** *n* a towel for drying dishes, etc. US name: **dishtowel.**
tea tree *n* any of various trees of Australia and New Zealand that yield an oil used as an antiseptic.
tea trolley *n Brit.* a trolley from which tea is served.
TEC (tɛk) *n acronym for* Training and Enterprise Council. See **Training Agency.**
tech (tɛk) *n Inf.* a technical college.
tech. *abbrev. for:* **1** technical. **2** technology.
technetium (tɛk'niːʃɪəm) *n* a silvery-grey metallic element, artificially produced by bombardment of molybdenum by deuterons. The radioisotope **technetium-99m** is used in radiotherapy. Symbol: Tc; atomic no.: 43; half-life of most stable isotope, ^{97}Tc: 2.6×10^6 years. [C20: NL, from Gk *tekhnētos* manmade, from *tekhnasthai* to devise artificially, from *tekhnē* skill]
technic *n* **1** (tɛk'niːk). another word for **technique. 2** ('tɛknɪk). another word for **technics.** [C17: from L *technicus*, from Gk *tekhnikos*, from *tekhnē* skill]
technical ⊕ ('tɛknɪkᵊl) *adj* **1** of or specializing in industrial, practical, or mechanical arts and applied sciences. **2** skilled in practical arts rather than abstract thinking. **3** relating to a particular field of activity: *the technical jargon of linguistics.* **4** existing by virtue of a strict application of the rules or a strict interpretation of the wording: *a technical loophole in the law.* **5** of or showing technique: *technical brilliance.*
▸ **'technically** *adv* ▸ **'technicalness** *n*
technical college *n Brit.* an institution for further education that provides courses in technology, art, secretarial skills, agriculture, etc.
technical drawing *n* the study and practice of the basic techniques of draughtsmanship, as employed in mechanical drawing, architecture, etc.
technicality (ˌtɛknɪ'kælɪtɪ) *n, pl* **technicalities. 1** a petty formal point arising from a strict interpretation of rules, etc. **2** the state or quality of being technical. **3** technical methods and vocabulary.
technical knockout *n Boxing.* a judgment of a knockout given when a boxer is in the referee's opinion too badly beaten to continue without risk of serious injury.
technician (tɛk'nɪʃən) *n* **1** a person skilled in mechanical or industrial techniques or in a particular technical field. **2** a person employed in a laboratory, etc., to do mechanical and practical work. **3** a person having specific artistic or mechanical skill, esp. if lacking flair.
Technicolor ('tɛknɪˌkʌlə) *n Trademark.* the process of producing colour film by means of superimposing synchronized films of the same scene, each of which has a different colour filter.
technics ('tɛknɪks) *n (functioning as sing)* the study or theory of industry and industrial arts; technology.
technique ⊕ (tɛk'niːk) *n* **1** a practical method, skill, or art applied to a particular task. **2** proficiency in a practical or mechanical skill. **3** special facility; knack. [C19: from F, from *technique* (adj): see TECHNIC]
techno ('tɛknəʊ) *n* a type of fast disco music, using electronic sounds and having a strong technological influence.
techno- *combining form.* **1** craft or art: *technology; technography.* **2** technological or technical: *technocracy.* [from Gk *tekhnē* skill]
technocracy (tɛk'nɒkrəsɪ) *n, pl* **technocracies.** government by scientists, engineers, and other such experts.
▸ **technocrat** ('tɛknəˌkræt) *n* ▸ **ˌtechno'cratic** *adj*
technology (tɛk'nɒlədʒɪ) *n, pl* **technologies. 1** the application of practical or mechanical sciences to industry or commerce. **2** the methods, theory, and practices governing such application. **3** the total knowledge and skills available to any human society. [C17: from Gk *tekhnologia* systematic treatment, from *tekhnē* skill]
▸ **technological** (ˌtɛknə'lɒdʒɪkᵊl) *adj* ▸ **tech'nologist** *n*
technophile ('tɛknəʊˌfaɪl) *n* **1** a person who is enthusiastic about technology. ◆ *adj* **2** enthusiastic about technology.
technophobe (ˌtɛknəʊ'fəʊb) *n* **1** someone who fears the effects of technological development on society or the environment. **2** someone who is afraid of using technological devices, such as computing.
techy ('tɛtʃɪ) *adj* **techier, techiest.** a variant spelling of **tetchy.**
▸ **'techily** *adv* ▸ **'techiness** *n*
tectonic (tɛk'tɒnɪk) *adj* **1** denoting or relating to building. **2** *Geol.* **2a** (of landforms, etc.) resulting from distortion of the earth's crust due to forces within it. **2b** (of processes, movements, etc.) occurring within the earth's crust and causing structural deformation. [C17: from LL *tectonicus*, from Gk *tektonikos* belonging to carpentry, from *tektōn* a builder]
tectonics (tɛk'tɒnɪks) *n (functioning as sing)* **1** the art and science of construction or building. **2** the study of the processes by which the earth's surface has attained its present structure.
tectrix ('tɛktrɪks) *n, pl* **tectrices** ('tɛktrɪˌsiːz). *(usually pl) Ornithol.* another name for **covert** (sense 5). [C19: NL, from L *tector* plasterer, from *tegere* to cover]
▸ **tectricial** (tɛk'trɪʃəl) *adj*
ted[1] (tɛd) *vb* **teds, tedding, tedded.** to shake out (hay), so as to dry it. [C15: from ON *tethja*]
ted[2] (tɛd) *n Inf.* short for **teddy boy.**
tedder ('tɛdə) *n* **1** a machine equipped with a series of small rotating forks for tedding hay. **2** a person who teds.
teddy ('tɛdɪ) *n, pl* **teddies.** a woman's one-piece undergarment, incorporating a chemise top and panties.
teddy bear *n* a stuffed toy bear. Often shortened to **teddy.** [C20: from *Teddy*, from *Theodore*, after Theodore Roosevelt (1858–1919), US president, well known as a hunter of bears]
teddy boy *n* **1** (in Britain, esp. in the mid-1950s) one of a cult of youths who wore mock Edwardian fashions. **2** any tough or delinquent youth. [C20: from *Teddy*, from *Edward*, referring to the Edwardian dress]
Te Deum (ˌtiː 'diːəm) *n* **1** an ancient Latin hymn in rhythmic prose. **2** a musical setting of this hymn. **3** a service of thanksgiving in which the recital of this hymn forms a central part. [from the L canticle beginning *Tē Deum laudāmus*, lit.: Thee, God, we praise]
tedious ⊕ ('tiːdɪəs) *adj* causing fatigue or tedium; monotonous.
▸ **'tediousness** *n*
tedium ⊕ ('tiːdɪəm) *n* the state of being bored or the quality of being boring; monotony. [C17: from L *taedium*, from *taedēre* to weary]
tee[1] (tiː) *n* **1** a pipe fitting in the form of a letter T, used to join three pipes. **2** a metal section with a cross section in the form of a letter T.
tee[2] (tiː) *Golf.* ◆ *n* **1** an area from which the first stroke of a hole is made. **2** a support for a golf ball, usually a small wooden or plastic peg, used when teeing off or in long grass, etc. ◆ *vb* **tees, teeing, teed. 3** (when *intr*, often foll. by *up*) to position (the ball) ready for striking, on or as if on a tee. ◆ See also **tee off.** [C17 *teaz*, from ?]

THESAURUS

tears *pl n* **3 in tears = weeping**, blubbering, crying, distressed, sobbing, visibly moved, whimpering
tease *vb* **1 = tantalize**, lead on **2 = mock**, aggravate (*inf.*), annoy, badger, bait, bedevil, bother, chaff, gibe, goad, guy (*inf.*), needle (*inf.*), pester, plague (*inf.*), provoke, pull someone's leg (*inf.*), rag, rib (*inf.*), ridicule, take the mickey (*inf.*), take the piss (out of) (*taboo sl.*), taunt, torment, twit, vex, wind up (*Brit. sl.*), worry
technical *adj* **1 = scientific**, hi-tech *or* high-tech, skilled, specialist, specialized, technological
technique *n* **1 = method**, approach, course, fashion, manner, means, mode, modus operandi, procedure, style, system, way **2, 3 = skill**, address, adroitness, art, artistry, craft, craftsmanship, delivery, execution, facility, knack, know-how (*inf.*), performance, proficiency, touch
tedious *adj* **= boring**, annoying, banal, deadly dull, drab, dreary, dreich (*Scot.*), dull, fatiguing, ho-hum (*inf.*), humdrum, irksome, laborious, lifeless, long-drawn-out, mind-numbing, monotonous, prosaic, prosy, soporific, tiresome, tiring, unexciting, uninteresting, vapid, wearisome
Antonyms *adj* enjoyable, enthralling, exciting, exhilarating, imaginative, inspiring, interesting, quickly finished, short, stimulating
tedium *n* **= boredom**, banality, deadness, drabness, dreariness, dullness, ennui, lifelessness, monotony, routine, sameness, tediousness, the doldrums
Antonyms *n* challenge, excitement, exhilaration, fascination, interest, liveliness, stimulation

tee[3] (tiː) *n* a mark used as a target in certain games such as curling and quoits. [C18: ?from T-shaped marks, which may have orig. been used in curling]

tee-hee *or* **te-hee** (ˈtiːˈhiː) *interj* **1** an exclamation of laughter, esp. when mocking. ◆ *n* **2** a chuckle. ◆ *vb* **tee-hees, tee-heeing, tee-heed** *or* **te-hees, te-heeing, te-heed. 3** (*intr*) to snigger or laugh, esp. derisively. [C14: imit.]

teem[1] ⓣ (tiːm) *vb* (*intr;* usually foll. by *with*) to be prolific or abundant (in). [OE *tēman* to produce offspring; rel. to West Saxon *tīeman;* see TEAM]

teem[2] ⓣ (tiːm) *vb* **1** (*intr;* often foll. by *down* or *with rain*) to pour in torrents. **2** (*tr*) to pour or empty out. [C15 *temen* to empty, from ON *tœma*]

teen (tiːn) *adj Inf.* another word for **teenage.**

teenage ⓣ (ˈtiːnˌeɪdʒ) *adj* (*prenominal*) of or relating to the time in a person's life between the ages of 13 and 19. Also: **teenaged.**

teenager ⓣ (ˈtiːnˌeɪdʒə) *n* a person between the ages of 13 and 19 inclusive.

teens (tiːnz) *pl n* **1** the years of a person's life between the ages of 13 and 19 inclusive. **2** all the numbers that end in *-teen.*

teeny ⓣ (ˈtiːnɪ) *adj* **teenier, teeniest.** *Inf.* extremely small; tiny. Also: **teeny-weeny** (ˈtiːnɪˈwiːnɪ) *or* **teensy-weensy** (ˈtiːnzɪˈwiːnzɪ). [C19: var. of TINY]

teenybopper (ˈtiːnɪˌbɒpə) *n Sl.* a young teenager, usually a girl, who avidly follows fashions in clothes and pop music. [C20: *teeny,* from teenage + *-bopper;* see BOP]

tee off *vb* (*adv*) **1** *Golf.* to strike (the ball) from a tee. **2** *Inf.* to begin; start.

teepee (ˈtiːpiː) *n* a variant spelling of **tepee.**

tee shirt *n* a variant of **T-shirt.**

teeter ⓣ (ˈtiːtə) *vb* **1** to move or cause to move unsteadily; wobble. ◆ *n, vb* **2** another word for **seesaw.** [C19: from ME *titeren*]

teeth (tiːθ) *n* **1** the plural of **tooth. 2** the most violent part: *the teeth of the gale.* **3** the power to produce a desired effect: *that law has no teeth.* **4 get one's teeth into.** to become engrossed in. **5 in the teeth of.** in direct opposition to; against. **6 to the teeth.** to the greatest possible degree: *armed to the teeth.* **7 show one's teeth.** to threaten.

teethe (tiːð) *vb* **teethes, teething, teethed.** (*intr*) to cut one's baby (deciduous) teeth.

teething ring *n* a hard ring on which babies may bite while teething.

teething troubles *pl n* the problems that arise during the initial stages of a project, etc.

teetotal ⓣ (tiːˈtəʊtᵊl) *adj* **1** of or practising abstinence from alcoholic drink. **2** *Dialect.* complete. [C19: allegedly coined in 1833 by Richard Turner, E advocate of total abstinence from alcohol; prob. from TOTAL, with emphatic reduplication]
▸**teeˈtotaller** *n* ▸**teeˈtotalism** *n*

teetotum (tiːˈtəʊtəm) *n Arch.* a spinning top bearing letters of the alphabet on its four sides. [C18: from *T totum,* from *T* initial on one of the faces + *totum* the name of the toy, from L *tōtum* the whole]

teff (tɛf) *n* an annual grass of NE Africa, grown for its grain. [C18: from Amharic *tēf*]

TEFL (ˈtɛfᵊl) *acronym for* Teaching (of) English as a Foreign Language.

Teflon (ˈtɛflɒn) *n* a trademark for **polytetrafluoroethylene.**

teg (tɛg) *n* **1** a two-year-old sheep. **2** the fleece of a two-year-old sheep. [C16: from ?]

tegmen (ˈtɛgmən) *n, pl* **tegmina** (-mɪnə). **1** either of the leathery forewings of the cockroach and related insects. **2** the delicate inner covering of a seed. **3** any similar covering or layer. [C19: from L: a cover, from *tegere* to cover]
▸**ˈtegminal** *adj*

tegument (ˈtɛgjʊmənt) *n* a less common word for **integument.** [C15: from L *tegumentum* a covering, from *tegere* to cover]

te-hee (tiːˈhiː) *interj, n, vb* a variant of **tee-hee.**

te igitur *Latin.* (teɪ ˈɪgɪˌtʊə; *English* teɪ ˈɪdʒɪtʊə) *n RC Church.* the first prayer of the canon of the Mass, which begins *Te igitur clementissime Pater* (Thee, therefore, most merciful Father).

tektite (ˈtɛktaɪt) *n* a small dark glassy object found in several areas around the world, thought to be a product of meteorite impact. [C20: from Gk *tēktos* molten]

tel. *abbrev. for:* **1** telegram. **2** telegraph(ic). **3** telephone.

tel- *combining form.* a variant of **tele-** and **telo-** before a vowel.

telaesthesia *or US* **telesthesia** (ˌtɛlɪsˈθiːzɪə) *n* the alleged perception of events that are beyond the normal range of perceptual processes.
▸**telaesthetic** *or US* **telesthetic** (ˌtɛlɪsˈθɛtɪk) *adj*

telamon (ˈtɛləmən) *n, pl* **telamones** (ˌtɛləˈməʊniːz) *or* **telamons.** a column in the form of a male figure, used to support an entablature. [C18: via L from Gk, from *tlēnai* to bear]

telangiectasis (tɪˌlændʒɪˈɛktəsɪs) *or* **telangiectasia** (tɪˌlændʒɪɛkˈteɪzɪə) *n, pl* **telangiectases** (-ˌsiːz). *Pathol.* an abnormal dilation of the capillaries or terminal arteries producing blotched red spots, esp. on the face or thighs. [C19: NL, from Gk *telos* end + *angeion* vessel + *ektasis* dilation]
▸**telangiectatic** (tɪˌlændʒɪɛkˈtætɪk) *adj*

tele- *combining form.* **1** at or over a distance; distant: *telescope; telekinesis.* **2** television: *telecast.* **3** by means of or via telephone or television: *telesales.* [from Gk *tele* far]

telecast (ˈtɛləˌkɑːst) *vb* **telecasts, telecasting, telecast** *or* **telecasted. 1** to broadcast by television. ◆ *n* **2** a television broadcast.
▸**ˈteleˌcaster** *n*

telecom (ˈtɛlɪˌkɒm) *or* **telecoms** (ˈtɛlɪˌkɒmz) *n* (*functioning as sing*) short for **telecommunications.**

telecommunications (ˌtɛlɪkəˌmjuːnɪˈkeɪʃənz) *n* (*functioning as sing*) the science and technology of communications by telephony, radio, television, etc.

telecommuting (ˌtɛlɪkəˈmjuːtɪŋ) *n* another name for **teleworking.**
▸**ˌtelecomˈmuter** *n*

teledu (ˈtɛlɪˌduː) *n* a badger of SE Asia and Indonesia, having dark brown hair with a white stripe along the back and producing a fetid secretion when attacked. [C19: from Malay]

telegenic (ˌtɛlɪˈdʒɛnɪk) *adj* having or showing a pleasant television image. [C20: from TELE(VISION) + (PHOTO)GENIC]
▸**ˌteleˈgenically** *adv*

telegnosis (ˌtɛləˈnəʊsɪs, ˌtɛləg-) *n* knowledge about distant events alleged to have been obtained without the use of any normal sensory mechanism. [C20: from TELE- + *-gnosis,* from Gk *gnōsis* knowledge]

telegony (tɪˈlɛgənɪ) *n Genetics.* the supposed influence of a previous sire on offspring borne by a female to other sires.
▸**telegonic** (ˌtɛlɪˈgɒnɪk) *or* **teˈlegonous** *adj*

telegram ⓣ (ˈtɛlɪˌgræm) *n* a communication transmitted by telegraph.

telegraph ⓣ (ˈtɛlɪˌgrɑːf) *n* **1a** a device, system, or process by which information can be transmitted over a distance, esp. using radio signals or coded electrical signals sent along a transmission line. **1b** (*as modifier*): *telegraph pole.* ◆ *vb* **2** to send a telegram to (a person or place); wire. **3** (*tr*) to transmit or send by telegraph. **4** (*tr*) to give advance notice of (anything), esp. unintentionally. **5** (*tr*) *Canad. inf.* to cast (votes) illegally by impersonating registered voters.
▸**telegraphist** (tɪˈlɛgrəˌfɪst) *or* **telegrapher** (tɪˈlɛgrəfə) *n* ▸**ˌteleˈgraphic** *adj*

telegraph plant *n* a small tropical Asian shrub having small leaflets that turn in various directions during the day and droop at night.

telegraphy (tɪˈlɛgrəfɪ) *n* **1** a system of telecommunications involving any process providing reproduction at a distance of written, printed, or pictorial matter. **2** the skill or process of operating a telegraph.

Telegu (ˈtɛləˌguː) *n, adj* a variant spelling of **Telugu.**

telekinesis (ˌtɛlɪkaɪˈniːsɪs) *n* **1** the movement of a body caused by thought or willpower without the application of a physical force. **2** the ability to cause such movement.
▸**telekinetic** (ˌtɛlɪkɪˈnɛtɪk) *adj*

telemark (ˈtɛlɪˌmɑːk) *n Skiing.* a turn in which one ski is placed far forward of the other and turned gradually inwards. [C20: after *Telemark,* county in Norway]

telemarketing (ˈtɛlɪˌmɑːkɪtɪŋ) *n* another name for **telesales.**
▸**ˈteleˌmarketer** *n*

telemedicine (ˈtɛlɪˌmɛdɪsɪn, -ˌmɛdsɪn) *n* the treatment of disease or injury by consultation with a specialist in a distant place, esp. by means of a computer or satellite link.

Telemessage (ˈtɛlɪˌmɛsɪdʒ) *n Trademark.* a message sent by telephone or telex and delivered in printed form.

telemeter (tɪˈlɛmɪtə) *n* **1** any device for recording or measuring a distant event and transmitting the data to a receiver. **2** any device used to measure a distance without directly comparing it with a measuring rod, etc. ◆ *vb* **3** (*tr*) to obtain and transmit (data) from a distant source.
▸**telemetric** (ˌtɛlɪˈmɛtrɪk) *adj*

telemetry (tɪˈlɛmɪtrɪ) *n* **1** the use of radio waves, telephone lines, etc., to transmit the readings of measuring instruments to a device on which the readings can be indicated or recorded. **2** the measurement of linear distance using a tellurometer.

telencephalon (ˌtɛlɛnˈsɛfəˌlɒn) *n* the cerebrum together with related parts of the hypothalamus and the third ventricle.
▸**telencephalic** (ˈtɛlɛnsɪˈfælɪk) *adj*

teleology (ˌtɛlɪˈɒlədʒɪ, ˌtiːlɪ-) *n* **1** *Philosophy.* **1a** the doctrine that there is evidence of purpose or design in the universe, and esp. that this provides proof of the existence of a Designer. **1b** the belief that certain phenomena are best explained in terms of purpose rather than cause. **2** *Biol.* the belief that natural phenomena have a predetermined purpose and are not determined by mechanical laws. [C18: from NL *teleologia,* from Gk *telos* end + -LOGY]
▸**teleological** (ˌtɛlɪəˈlɒdʒɪkᵊl, ˌtiːlɪ-) *adj* ▸**ˌteleˈologist** *n*

teleost (ˈtɛlɪˌɒst, ˈtiːlɪ-) *n* any of a subclass of bony fishes having rayed fins and a swim bladder, as herrings, carps, eels, cod, perches, etc.

THESAURUS

teem[1] *vb* = **be full of,** abound, be abundant, bear, be crawling with, be prolific, brim, bristle, burst at the seams, overflow, produce, pullulate, swarm

teem[2] *vb* **1** = **pour,** belt (*sl.*), bucket down (*inf.*), lash, pelt (down), rain cats and dogs (*inf.*), stream

teenage *adj* = **youthful,** adolescent, immature, juvenile

teenager *n* = **youth,** adolescent, boy, girl, juvenile, minor

teeny *adj Informal* = **tiny,** diminutive, microscopic, miniature, minuscule, minute, teensy-weensy, teeny-weeny, wee

teeter *vb* **1, 2** = **wobble,** balance, pivot, rock, seesaw, stagger, sway, totter, tremble, waver

teetotaller *n* **1** = **abstainer,** nondrinker, Rechabite

telegram *n* = **cable,** radiogram, telegraph, telex, wire (*inf.*)

telegraph *n* **1** = **cable,** radiogram, telegram,

[C19: from NL *teleosteī* (pl) creatures having complete skeletons, from Gk *teleos* complete + *osteon* bone]

telepathy ❶ (tɪ'lɛpəθɪ) *n* the communication between people of thoughts, feelings, etc., involving mechanisms that cannot be understood in terms of known scientific laws.
▸**telepathic** (ˌtɛlɪ'pæθɪk) *adj* ▸**te'lepathist** *n* ▸**te'lepaˌthize** *or* ▸**te'lepaˌthise** *vb (intr)*

telephone ❶ ('tɛlɪˌfəʊn) *n* **1** an electrical device for transmitting speech, consisting of a microphone and receiver mounted on a handset. **2a** a worldwide system of communications using telephones. The microphone in one telephone converts sound waves into electrical signals that are transmitted along a telephone wire or by radio to one or more distant sets. **2b** *(as modifier)*: *a telephone exchange.* ◆ *vb* **3** to call or talk to (a person) by telephone. **4** to transmit (a message, etc.) by telephone.
▸**'teleˌphoner** *n* ▸**telephonic** (ˌtɛlɪ'fɒnɪk) *adj*

telephone banking *n* a facility enabling customers to make use of banking services, such as oral payment instructions, account movements, raising loans, etc., over the telephone rather than by personal visit.

telephone box *n* an enclosure from which a paid telephone call can be made. Also called: **telephone kiosk, telephone booth.**

telephone directory *n* a book listing the names, addresses, and telephone numbers of subscribers in a particular area.

telephone number *n* **1** a set of figures identifying the telephone of a particular subscriber, and used in making connections to that telephone. **2** *(pl)* extremely large numbers, esp. in reference to salaries or prices.

telephone selling *n* another name for **telesales.**

telephonist (tɪ'lɛfənɪst) *n Brit.* a person who operates a telephone switchboard. Also called (esp. US): **telephone operator.**

telephony (tɪ'lɛfənɪ) *n* a system of telecommunications for the transmission of speech or other sounds.

telephotography (ˌtɛlɪfə'tɒgrəfɪ) *n* the process or technique of photographing distant objects using a telephoto lens.

telephoto lens ('tɛlɪˌfəʊtəʊ) *n* a compound camera lens in which the focal length is greater than that of a simple lens and thus produces a magnified image of a distant object.

teleprinter ('tɛlɪˌprɪntə) *n* **1** a telegraph apparatus consisting of a keyboard transmitter, which converts a typed message into coded pulses for transmission along a wire or cable, and a printing receiver, which converts incoming signals and prints out the message. US name: **teletypewriter. 2** a network of such devices: no longer widely used. **3** a similar device used for direct input/output of data into a computer at a distant location.

Teleprompter ('tɛlɪˌprɒmptə) *n Trademark.* a device for displaying a television script so that the speaker can read it while appearing to look at the camera.

Teleran ('tɛləˌræn) *n Trademark.* an electronic navigational aid in which the image of a ground-based radar system is televised to aircraft. [C20: from *Tele(vision) R(adar) A(ir) N(avigation)*]

telesales ('tɛlɪˌseɪlz) *n (functioning as sing)* the selling or attempted selling of a particular commodity or service by a salesman who makes his initial approach by telephone. Also called: **telemarketing, telephone selling.**

telescope ❶ ('tɛlɪˌskəʊp) *n* **1** an optical instrument for making distant objects appear closer by use of a combination of lenses (**refracting telescope**) or lenses and curved mirrors (**reflecting telescope**). **2** any instrument, such as a radio telescope, for collecting, focusing, and detecting electromagnetic radiation from space. ◆ *vb* **telescopes, telescoping, telescoped. 3** to crush together or be crushed together, as in a collision. **4** to fit together like a set of cylinders that slide into one another, thus allowing extension and shortening. **5** to make or become smaller or shorter. [C17: from It. *telescopio* or NL *telescopium,* lit.: far-seeing instrument]

telescopic (ˌtɛlɪ'skɒpɪk) *adj* **1** of or relating to a telescope. **2** seen through or obtained by means of a telescope. **3** visible only with a telescope. **4** able to see far. **5** having parts that telescope.
▸**ˌtele'scopically** *adv*

telescopic sight *n* a telescope mounted on a rifle, etc., used for sighting.

telescopy (tɪ'lɛskəpɪ) *n* the branch of astronomy concerned with the use and design of telescopes.

telespectroscope (ˌtɛlɪ'spɛktrəˌskəʊp) *n* a combination of a telescope and a spectroscope, used for spectroscopic analysis of radiation from stars and other celestial bodies.

telestereoscope (ˌtɛlɪ'stɪərɪəˌskəʊp, -'stɛrɪə-) *n* an optical instrument for obtaining stereoscopic images of distant objects.

telestich (tɪ'lɛstɪk, 'tɛlɪˌstɪk) *n* a short poem in which the last letters of each successive line form a word. [C17: from Gk *telos* end + *stikhos* row]

Teletext ('tɛlɪˌtɛkst) *n Trademark.* a form of Videotex in which information is broadcast by a television station and received on an adapted television set. **Ceefax** is provided by the BBC and **Oracle** by ITV.

telethon ('tɛlɪˌθɒn) *n* a lengthy television programme to raise charity funds, etc. [C20: from TELE- + MARATHON]

Teletype ('tɛlɪˌtaɪp) *n* **1** *Trademark.* a type of teleprinter. **2** *(sometimes not cap.)* a network of such devices. ◆ *vb* **Teletypes, Teletyping, Teletyped. 3** *(sometimes not cap.)* to transmit (a message) by Teletype.

teletypewriter (ˌtɛlɪ'taɪpˌraɪtə, 'tɛlɪˌtaɪp-) *n* a US name for **teleprinter.**

televangelist (ˌtɛlɪ'vændʒəlɪst) *n US.* an evangelical preacher who appears regularly on television, preaching the gospel and appealing for donations from viewers. [C20: from TELE(VISION + E)VANGELIST]

televise ('tɛlɪˌvaɪz) *vb* **televises, televising, televised. 1** to put on television. **2** *(tr)* to transmit by television.

television ❶ ('tɛlɪˌvɪʒən) *n* **1** the system or process of producing on a distant screen a series of transient visible images, usually with an accompanying sound signal. Electrical signals, converted from optical images by a camera tube, are transmitted by radio waves or by cable and reconverted into optical images by means of a television tube inside a television set. **2** Also called: **television set.** a device designed to receive and convert incoming electrical signals into a series of visible images on a screen together with accompanying sound. **3** the content, etc., of television programmes. **4** the occupation or profession concerned with any aspect of the broadcasting of television programmes. **5** *(modifier)* of, relating to, or used in the transmission or reception of video and audio UHF or VHF radio signals: *a television transmitter.* ◆ Abbrev.: **TV.**

television tube *n* a cathode-ray tube designed for the reproduction of television pictures. Sometimes shortened to **tube.**

televisual (ˌtɛlɪ'vɪʒʊəl, -zjʊ-) *adj* relating to or suitable for production on television.
▸**ˌtele'visually** *adv*

teleworking ('tɛlɪˌwɜːkɪŋ) *n* the use of home computers, telephones, etc., to enable a person to work from home while maintaining contact with colleagues, customers, or a central office. Also called: **telecommuting.**
▸**'teleˌworker** *n*

telex ('tɛlɛks) *n* **1** an international telegraph service in which teleprinters are rented out to subscribers. **2** a teleprinter used in such a service. **3** a message transmitted or received by telex. ◆ *vb* **4** to transmit (a message) to (a person, etc.) by telex. [C20: from *tel(eprinter) ex(change)*]

Telidon ('tɛlɪˌdɒn) *n Trademark.* a Canadian interactive viewdata service.

tell[1] ❶ (tɛl) *vb* **tells, telling, told. 1** (when *tr, may take a clause as object*) to let know or notify. **2** *(tr)* to order or instruct. **3** (when *intr,* usually foll. by *of*) to give an account or narration (of). **4** *(tr)* to communicate by words: *tell lies.* **5** *(tr)* to make known: *to tell fortunes.* **6** *(intr;* often foll. by *of)* to serve as an indication: *her blush told of her embarrassment.* **7** *(tr;* used with *can,* etc.; *may take a clause as object)* to discover or discern: *I can tell what is wrong.* **8** *(tr;* used with *can,* etc.) to distinguish or discriminate: *he couldn't tell chalk from cheese.* **9** *(intr)* to have or produce an impact, effect, or strain: *every step told on his bruised feet.* **10** *(intr;* sometimes foll. by *on) Inf.* to reveal secrets or gossip (about). **11** *(tr)* to assure: *I tell you, I've had enough!* **12** *(tr)* to count (votes). **13 tell the time.** to read the time from a clock. **14 you're telling me.** *Sl.* I know that very well. ◆ See also **tell apart, tell off.** [OE *tellan*]
▸**'tellable** *adj*

tell[2] (tɛl) *n* a large mound resulting from the accumulation of rubbish on a long-settled site, esp. in the Middle East. [C19: from Ar. *tall*]

tell apart *vb (tr, adv)* to distinguish between.

teller ('tɛlə) *n* **1** a bank cashier. **2** a person appointed to count votes. **3** a person who tells; narrator.

telling ❶ ('tɛlɪŋ) *adj* **1** having a marked effect or impact. **2** revealing.
▸**'tellingly** *adv*

THESAURUS

telex, wire (*inf.*) ◆ *vb* **2** = **cable**, send, telex, transmit, wire (*inf.*)

telepathy *n* = **mind-reading**, sixth sense, thought transference

telephone *n* **1** = **phone**, blower, dog and bone (*sl.*), handset, line, mobile (phone) ◆ *vb* **3** = **call**, buzz (*inf.*), call up, dial, get on the blower (*inf.*), give (someone) a bell (*Brit. sl.*), give (someone) a buzz (*inf.*), give (someone) a call, give (someone) a ring (*inf., chiefly Brit.*), give someone a tinkle (*Brit. inf.*), phone, ring (*chiefly Brit.*)

telescope *n* **1** = **glass**, spyglass ◆ *vb* **3** = **crush**, concertina, squash **5** = **shorten**, abbreviate, abridge, capsulize, compress, condense, consolidate, contract, curtail, cut, shrink, tighten, trim, truncate
Antonyms *vb* ≠ **shorten:** amplify, draw out, elongate, extend, flesh out, lengthen, protract, spread out

television *n* **2** = **TV**, gogglebox (*Brit. sl.*), idiot box (*sl.*), receiver, small screen (*inf.*), telly (*Brit. inf.*), the box, the tube (*sl.*), TV set

tell[1] *vb* **1** = **inform**, acquaint, announce, apprise, communicate, confess, disclose, divulge, express, get off one's chest (*inf.*), impart, let know, make known, mention, notify, proclaim, reveal, say, speak, state, utter **2** = **instruct**, authorize, bid, call upon, command, direct, enjoin, order, require, summon **3** = **describe**, chronicle, depict, give an account of, narrate, portray, recount, rehearse, relate, report **7** = **see**, comprehend, discern, discover, make out, understand **8** = **distinguish**, differentiate, discern, discriminate, identify **9** = **have** *or* **take effect**, carry weight, count, have force, make its presence felt, register, take its toll, weigh **12** = **count**, calculate, compute, enumerate, number, reckon, tally

telling *adj* **1** = **effective**, considerable, decisive, effectual, forceful, forcible, impressive, influential, marked, potent, powerful, significant, solid, striking, trenchant, weighty
Antonyms *adj* easily ignored, inconsequential, indecisive, ineffectual, insignificant, lightweight, minor, negligible, slight, trivial, unimportant

DICTIONARY

tell off Ⓣ *vb* (*tr, adv*) **1** *Inf.* to reprimand; scold. **2** to count and select for duty.

telltale ('tɛlˌteɪl) *n* **1** a person who tells tales about others. **2a** an outward indication of something concealed. **2b** (*as modifier*): *a telltale paw mark.* **3** a device used to monitor a process, machine, etc.

tellurian (tɛ'lʊərɪən) *adj* **1** of the earth. ◆ *n* **2** (esp. in science fiction) an inhabitant of the earth. [C19: from L *tellūs* the earth]

telluric[1] (tɛ'lʊərɪk) *adj* of or originating on or in the earth or soil; terrestrial. [C19: from L *tellūs* the earth]

telluric[2] (tɛ'lʊərɪk) *adj* of or containing tellurium, esp. in a high valence state. [C20: from TELLUR(IUM) + -IC]

tellurion *or* **tellurian** (tɛ'lʊərɪən) *n* an instrument that shows how day and night, etc., result from the earth's rotation on its axis, etc. [C19: from L *tellūs* the earth]

tellurium (tɛ'lʊərɪəm) *n* a brittle silvery-white nonmetallic element. Symbol: Te; atomic no.: 52; atomic wt.: 127.60. [C19: NL, from L *tellūs* the earth, by analogy with URANIUM]

tellurometer (ˌtɛljʊ'rɒmɪtə) *n Surveying.* an electronic instrument for measuring distances by the transmission of radio waves. [C20: from L *tellūs* the earth + -METER]

telly ('tɛlɪ) *n, pl* **tellies.** *Inf., chiefly Brit.* short for **television.**

telo- *or before a vowel* **tel-** *combining form.* **1** complete; final; perfect. **2** end; at the end. [from Gk *telos* end]

telpherage ('tɛlfərɪdʒ) *n* an overhead transport system in which an electrically driven truck runs along a rail or cable, the load being suspended in a car beneath. Also called: **telpher.** [C19: changed from *telephore,* from TELE- + -PHORE + -AGE]

telson ('tɛlsən) *n* the last segment or an appendage on the last segment of the body of crustaceans and arachnids. [C19: from Gk: a boundary]

Telugu *or* **Telegu** ('tɛləˌguː) *n* **1** a language of SE India, belonging to the Dravidian family of languages. **2** (*pl* **Telugus** *or* **Telugu**) a member of the people who speak this language. ◆ *adj* **3** of or relating to this people or their language.

temazepam (tə'mæzəˌpæm) *n* a sedative in the form of a gel-like capsule, which is taken orally or melted and injected by drug users.

temblor ('tɛmblə, -blɔː) *n, pl* **temblors** *or* **temblores** (tɛm'blɔːreɪz). *Chiefly US.* an earthquake or earth tremor. [C19: American Sp., from Sp. *temblar* to shake, tremble]

temerity Ⓣ (tɪ'mɛrɪtɪ) *n* rashness or boldness. [C15: from L *temeritās* accident, from *temere* at random]
▸**temerarious** (ˌtɛmə'rɛərɪəs) *adj*

temp (tɛmp) *Inf.* ◆ *n* **1** a person, esp. a typist or other office worker, employed on a temporary basis. ◆ *vb* (*intr*) **2** to work as a temp.

temp. *abbrev. for:* **1** temperature. **2** temporary. **3** tempore. [L: in the time of]

temper Ⓣ ('tɛmpə) *n* **1** a frame of mind; mood or humour. **2** a sudden outburst of anger. **3** a tendency to exhibit anger; irritability. **4** a mental condition of moderation and calm (esp. in **keep one's temper** *or* **lose one's temper**). **5** the degree of hardness, elasticity, etc., of a metal. ◆ *vb* (*tr*) **6** to make more acceptable or suitable by adding something else; moderate: *he tempered his criticism with sympathy.* **7** to reduce the brittleness of (a hardened metal) by reheating it and allowing it to cool. **8** *Music.* **8a** to adjust the frequency differences between the notes of a scale on (a keyboard instrument). **8b** to make such an adjustment to the pitches of notes in (a scale). [OE *temprian* to mingle, from L *temperāre* to mix, prob. from *tempus* time]
▸**'temperable** *adj* ▸**'temperer** *n*

tempera ('tɛmpərə) *n* **1** a painting medium for powdered pigments, consisting usually of egg yolk and water. **2a** any emulsion used as a painting medium, with casein, glue, wax, etc., as a base. **2b** the paint made from this. **3** the technique of painting with tempera. [C19: from It. *pingere a tempera* painting in tempera, from *temperare* to mingle; see TEMPER]

temperament Ⓣ ('tɛmpərəmənt) *n* **1** a person's character, disposition, and tendencies. **2** excitability, moodiness, or anger. **3** the characteristic way an individual behaves, esp. towards other people. **4a** an adjustment made to the frequency differences between notes on a keyboard instrument to allow modulation to other keys. **4b** any of several systems of such adjustment, esp. **equal temperament,** a system giving a scale based on an octave divided into twelve exactly equal semitones. **5** *Obs.* the characteristic way an individual behaves, viewed as the result of the influence of the four humours. [C15: from L *temperāmentum* a mixing in proportion, from *temperāre* to TEMPER]

temperamental Ⓣ (ˌtɛmpərə'mɛntᵊl) *adj* **1** easily upset or irritated; excitable. **2** of or caused by temperament. **3** *Inf.* working erratically and inconsistently; unreliable.
▸**ˌtempera'mentally** *adv*

temperance Ⓣ ('tɛmpərəns) *n* **1** restraint or moderation, esp. in yielding to one's appetites or desires. **2** abstinence from alcoholic drink. [C14: from L *temperantia,* from *temperāre* to regulate]

temperate Ⓣ ('tɛmpərɪt) *adj* **1** having a climate intermediate between tropical and polar; moderate or mild in temperature. **2** mild in quality or character; exhibiting temperance. [C14: from L *temperātus*]
▸**'temperately** *adv* ▸**'temperateness** *n*

Temperate Zone *n* those parts of the earth's surface lying between the Arctic Circle and the tropic of Cancer and between the Antarctic Circle and the tropic of Capricorn.

temperature ('tɛmprɪtʃə) *n* **1** the degree of hotness of a body, substance, or medium, esp. as measured on a scale that has one or more fixed reference points. **2** *Inf.* a body temperature in excess of the normal. [C16 (orig.: a mingling): from L *temperātūra* proportion, from *temperāre* to TEMPER]

temperature gradient *n* the rate of change in temperature in a given direction.

temperature-humidity index *n* an index of the effect on human comfort of temperature and humidity levels, 65 being the highest comfortable level.

tempered ('tɛmpəd) *adj* **1** *Music.* adjusted in accordance with a system of temperament. **2** (*in combination*) having a temper or temperament as specified: *ill-tempered.*

tempest Ⓣ ('tɛmpɪst) *n* **1** *Chiefly literary.* a violent wind or storm. **2** a violent commotion, uproar, or disturbance. [C13: from OF *tempeste,* from L *tempestās* storm, from *tempus* time]

tempestuous Ⓣ (tɛm'pɛstjʊəs) *adj* **1** of or relating to a tempest. **2** violent or stormy.
▸**tem'pestuously** *adv* ▸**tem'pestuousness** *n*

tempi ('tɛmpiː) *n* (in musical senses) the plural of **tempo.**

Templar ('tɛmplə) *n* **1** a member of a military order (**Knights of the Temple of Solomon**) founded by Crusaders in Jerusalem around 1118; suppressed in 1312. **2** (*sometimes not cap.*) *Brit.* a lawyer who has chambers in the Temple in London. [C13: from Med. L *templārius* of the TEMPLE; applied to the order because their house adjoined the site of the Temple of Solomon]

template *or* **templet** ('tɛmplɪt) *n* **1** a gauge or pattern, cut out in wood or metal, used in woodwork, etc., to help shape something accurately. **2** a pattern cut out in card or plastic, used to reproduce shapes. **3** a short beam that is used to spread a load, as over a doorway. **4** *Biochem.* the molecular structure of a compound that serves as a pattern for the production of another compound. [C17 *templet* (later spelling infl. by PLATE), prob. from F, dim. of TEMPLE[3]]

temple[1] Ⓣ ('tɛmpᵊl) *n* **1** a building or place dedicated to the worship of

THESAURUS

tell off *vb* **1** = **reprimand,** berate, carpet (*inf.*), censure, chide, give (someone) a piece of one's mind, haul over the coals (*inf.*), lecture, read the riot act, rebuke, reproach, reprove, scold, take to task, tear (someone) off a strip (*Brit. inf.*), tick off (*inf.*), upbraid

temerity *n* = **audacity,** assurance, boldness, brass neck (*Brit. inf.*), cheek, chutzpah (*US & Canad. inf.*), effrontery, foolhardiness, forwardness, front, gall (*inf.*), heedlessness, impudence, impulsiveness, intrepidity, nerve (*inf.*), pluck, rashness, recklessness, sassiness (*US inf.*)

temper *n* **1** = **frame of mind,** attitude, character, constitution, disposition, humour, mind, mood, nature, temperament, tenor, vein **2** = **rage,** bate (*Brit. sl.*), fit of pique, fury, gall, paddy (*Brit. inf.*), passion, tantrum, wax (*inf., chiefly Brit.*) **3** = **irritability,** anger, annoyance, heat, hot-headedness, ill humour, irascibility, irritation, passion, peevishness, petulance, resentment, surliness **4** = **self-control,** calm, calmness, composure, cool (*sl.*), coolness, equanimity, good humour, moderation, tranquillity ◆ *vb* **6** = **moderate,** abate, admix, allay, assuage, calm, lessen, mitigate, mollify, palliate, restrain, soften, soft-pedal (*inf.*), soothe, tone down **7** = **strengthen,** anneal, harden, toughen
Antonyms *n* ≠ **irritability:** contentment, goodwill ≠ **self-control:** agitation, anger, bad mood, excitability, foul humour, fury, grumpiness, indignation, irascibility, irritation, pique, vexation, wrath ◆ *vb* ≠ **moderate:** aggravate, arouse, excite, heighten, intensify, provoke, stir ≠ **strengthen:** soften

temperament *n* **1** = **nature,** bent, cast of mind, character, complexion, constitution, disposition, frame of mind, humour, make-up, mettle, outlook, personality, quality, soul, spirit, stamp, temper, tendencies, tendency **2** = **excitability,** anger, explosiveness, hot-headedness, impatience, mercurialness, moodiness, moods, petulance, volatility

temperamental *adj* **1** = **moody,** capricious, easily upset, emotional, erratic, excitable, explosive, fiery, highly strung, hot-headed, hypersensitive, impatient, irritable, mercurial, neurotic, passionate, petulant, sensitive, touchy, volatile **2** = **natural,** congenital, constitutional, inborn, ingrained, inherent, innate **3** *Informal* = **unreliable,** erratic, inconsistent, inconstant, undependable, unpredictable
Antonyms *adj* ≠ **moody:** calm, cool-headed, easy-going, even-tempered, level-headed, phlegmatic, unexcitable, unflappable, unperturbable ≠ **unreliable:** constant, dependable, reliable, stable, steady

temperance *n* **1** = **moderation,** continence, discretion, forbearance, restraint, self-control, self-discipline, self-restraint **2** = **teetotalism,** abstemiousness, abstinence, prohibition, sobriety
Antonyms *n* ≠ **moderation:** excess, immoderation, intemperance, overindulgence, prodigality

temperate *adj* **1** = **mild,** agreeable, balmy, calm, clement, cool, fair, gentle, moderate, pleasant, soft **2** = **moderate,** calm, composed, dispassionate, equable, even-tempered, mild, reasonable, self-controlled, self-restrained, sensible, stable
Antonyms *adj* ≠ **mild:** extreme, harsh, inclement, intemperate, severe, torrid ≠ **moderate:** intemperate, uncontrolled, undisciplined, unreasonable, unrestrained, wild

tempest *n* **1** *Literary* = **storm,** cyclone, gale, hurricane, squall, tornado, typhoon **2** = **uproar,** commotion, disturbance, ferment, furore, storm, tumult, upheaval
Antonyms *n* ≠ **uproar:** calm, peace, quiet, serenity, stillness, tranquillity

tempestuous *adj* **2** = **stormy,** agitated, blustery, boisterous, breezy, furious, gusty, inclement, intense, raging, squally, turbulent, uncontrolled, violent, wild, windy
Antonyms *adj* ≠ **passionate:** calm, peaceful, quiet, serene, still, tranquil, undisturbed, unruffled

temple[1] *n* **1** = **shrine,** church, holy place, place of worship, sanctuary

a deity or deities. **2** a Mormon church. **3** *US.* another name for a **synagogue.** **4** a Christian church. **5** any place or object regarded as a shrine where God makes himself present. **6** a building regarded as the focus of an activity, interest, or practice: *a temple of the arts.* [OE *tempel,* from L *templum*]

temple[2] ('tɛmpᵊl) *n* the region on each side of the head in front of the ear and above the cheek bone. [C14: from OF *temple,* from L *tempora* the temples, from *tempus* temple of the head]

temple[3] ('tɛmpᵊl) *n* the part of a loom that keeps the cloth being woven stretched to the correct width. [C15: from F, from L *templum* a small timber]

Temple ('tɛmpəl) *n* **1** a building in London that belonged to the Templars: it now houses two law societies. **2** any of three buildings erected by the Jews in ancient Jerusalem for the worship of Jehovah.

tempo Ⓣ ('tɛmpəʊ) *n, pl* **tempos** *or* **tempi** (-piː). **1** the speed at which a piece of music is meant to be played. **2** rate or pace. [C18: from It., from L *tempus* time]

temporal[1] Ⓣ ('tɛmpərəl) *adj* **1** of or relating to time. **2** of secular as opposed to spiritual or religious affairs. **3** lasting for a relatively short time. **4** *Grammar.* of or relating to tense or the linguistic expression of time. [C14: from L *temporālis,* from *tempus* time]
►**'temporally** *adv*

temporal[2] ('tɛmpərəl) *adj Anat.* of or near the temple or temples. [C16: from LL *temporālis* belonging to the temples; see TEMPLE[2]]

temporal bone *n* either of two compound bones forming the sides of the skull.

temporality (ˌtɛmpə'rælɪtɪ) *n, pl* **temporalities.** **1** the state or quality of being temporal. **2** something temporal. **3** (*often pl*) a secular possession or revenue belonging to a Church.

temporal lobe *n* the laterally protruding portion of each cerebral hemisphere, situated below the parietal lobe and associated with sound perception and interpretation.

temporary Ⓣ ('tɛmpərərɪ) *adj* **1** not permanent; provisional. **2** lasting only a short time. ◆ *n, pl* **temporaries.** **3** a person employed on a temporary basis. [C16: from L *temporārius,* from *tempus* time]
►**'temporarily** *adv* ►**'temporariness** *n*

temporize Ⓣ *or* **temporise** ('tɛmpəˌraɪz) *vb* **temporizes, temporizing, temporized** *or* **temporises, temporising, temporised.** (*intr*) **1** to delay, act evasively, or protract a negotiation, etc., esp. in order to gain time or effect a compromise. **2** to adapt oneself to the circumstances, as by temporary or apparent agreement. [C16: from F *temporiser,* from Med. L *temporizāre,* from L *tempus* time]
►ˌ**tempori'zation** *or* ˌ**tempori'sation** *n* ►**'tempoˌrizer** *or* **'tempoˌriser** *n*

tempt Ⓣ (tɛmpt) *vb* (*tr*) **1** to entice to do something, esp. something morally wrong or unwise. **2** to allure or attract. **3** to give rise to a desire in (someone) to do something; dispose. **4** to risk provoking (esp. in **tempt fate**). [C13: from OF *tempter,* from L *temptāre* to test]
►**'temptable** *adj* ►**'tempter** *n* ►**'temptress** *fem n*

temptation Ⓣ (tɛmp'teɪʃən) *n* **1** the act of tempting or the state of being tempted. **2** a person or thing that tempts.

tempting Ⓣ ('tɛmptɪŋ) *adj* attractive or inviting: *a tempting meal.*
►**'temptingly** *adv*

tempus fugit *Latin.* ('tɛmpəs 'fjuːdʒɪt) time flies.

ten (tɛn) *n* **1** the cardinal number that is the sum of nine and one. It is the base of the decimal number system and the base of the common logarithm. **2** a numeral, 10, X, etc., representing this number. **3** something representing or consisting of ten units. **4** Also called: **ten o'clock.** ten hours after noon or midnight. ◆ *determiner* **5** amounting to ten. ◆ Related adj: **decimal.** [OE *tēn*]

ten. *Music. abbrev. for:* **1** tenor. **2** tenuto.

tenable Ⓣ ('tɛnəbᵊl) *adj* able to be upheld, believed, maintained, or defended. [C16: from OF, from *tenir* to hold, from L *tenēre*]
►ˌ**tena'bility** *or* **'tenableness** *n* ►**'tenably** *adv*

tenace ('tɛneɪs) *n Bridge, whist.* a holding of two nonconsecutive high cards of a suit, such as the ace and queen. [C17: from F, from Sp. *tenaza* forceps, ult. from L *tenāx* holding fast, from *tenēre* to hold]

tenacious Ⓣ (tɪ'neɪʃəs) *adj* **1** holding firmly: *a tenacious grip.* **2** retentive: *a tenacious memory.* **3** stubborn or persistent. **4** holding together firmly; cohesive. **5** tending to stick or adhere. [C16: from L *tenāx,* from *tenēre* to hold]
►**te'naciously** *adv* ►**te'naciousness** *or* **tenacity** (tɪ'næsɪtɪ) *n*

tenaculum (tɪ'nækjʊləm) *n, pl* **tenacula** (-lə). a hooked surgical instrument for grasping and holding parts. [C17: from LL, from L *tenēre* to hold]

tenancy Ⓣ ('tɛnənsɪ) *n, pl* **tenancies.** **1** the temporary possession or holding by a tenant of lands or property owned by another. **2** the period of holding or occupying such property. **3** the period of holding office, a position, etc.

tenant Ⓣ ('tɛnənt) *n* **1** a person who holds, occupies, or possesses land or property, esp. from a landlord. **2** a person who has the use of a house, etc., subject to the payment of rent. **3** any holder or occupant. ◆ *vb* **4** (*tr*) to hold as a tenant. [C14: from OF, lit.: (one who is) holding, from *tenir* to hold, from L *tenēre*]
►**'tenantable** *adj* ►**'tenantless** *adj*

tenant farmer *n* a person who farms land rented from another, the rent usually taking the form of crops or livestock.

tenantry ('tɛnəntrɪ) *n* **1** tenants collectively. **2** the status or condition of being a tenant.

tench (tɛntʃ) *n* a European freshwater game fish of the carp family. [C14: from OF *tenche,* from LL *tinca*]

Ten Commandments *pl n* **the.** *Old Testament.* the commandments summarizing the basic obligations of man towards God and his fellow men, delivered to Moses on Mount Sinai engraved on two tables of stone (Exodus 20:1–17).

tend[1] Ⓣ (tɛnd) *vb* (when *intr,* usually foll. by *to* or *towards*) **1** (when *tr, takes an infinitive*) to have a general disposition (to do something); be inclined: *children tend to prefer sweets to meat.* **2** (*intr*) to have or be an influence (towards a specific result). **3** (*intr*) to go or move (in a particular direction): *to tend to the south.* [C14: from OF *tendre,* from L *tendere* to stretch]

tend[2] Ⓣ (tɛnd) *vb* **1** (*tr*) to care for. **2** (when *intr,* often foll. by *on* or *to*) to attend (to). **3** (*tr*) to handle or control. **4** (*intr;* often foll. by *to*) *Inf., chiefly US & Canad.* to pay attention. [C14: var. of ATTEND]

tendency Ⓣ ('tɛndənsɪ) *n, pl* **tendencies.** **1** (often foll. by *to*) an inclination, predisposition, propensity, or leaning. **2** the general course, purport, or drift of something, esp. a written work. [C17: from Med. L *tendentia,* from L *tendere* to TEND[1]]

tendentious *or* **tendencious** (tɛn'dɛnʃəs) *adj* having or showing an intentional tendency or bias, esp. a controversial one. [C20: from TENDENCY]
►**ten'dentiously** *or* **ten'denciously** *adv* ►**ten'dentiousness** *or* **ten'denciousness** *n*

THESAURUS

tempo *n* **1, 2** = **pace**, beat, cadence, measure (*Prosody*), metre, pulse, rate, rhythm, speed, time

temporal[1] *adj* **2** = **secular**, carnal, civil, earthly, fleshly, lay, material, mortal, mundane, profane, sublunary, terrestrial, worldly **3** = **temporary**, evanescent, fleeting, fugacious, fugitive, impermanent, momentary, passing, short-lived, transient, transitory

temporarily *adv* **2** = **briefly**, fleetingly, for a little while, for a moment, for a short time, for a short while, for the moment, for the nonce, for the time being, momentarily, pro tem

temporary *adj* **1, 2** = **impermanent**, brief, ephemeral, evanescent, fleeting, fugacious, fugitive, here today and gone tomorrow, interim, momentary, passing, pro tem, *pro tempore,* provisional, short-lived, transient, transitory
Antonyms *adj* durable, enduring, eternal, everlasting, long-lasting, long-term, permanent

temporize *vb* **1** = **play for time**, beat about the bush, be evasive, delay, equivocate, gain time, hum and haw, play a waiting game, procrastinate, stall, tergiversate

tempt *vb* **1** = **entice**, coax, decoy, inveigle, invite, lead on, lure, seduce, tantalize, woo **2** = **attract**, allure, appeal to, draw, make one's mouth water, whet the appetite of **4** = **provoke**, bait, dare, fly in the face of, risk, test, try
Antonyms *vb* ≠ **entice:** deter, discourage, dissuade, hinder, inhibit, put off

temptation *n* **1, 2** = **enticement**, allurement, appeal, attraction, attractiveness, bait, coaxing, come-on (*inf.*), decoy, draw, inducement, invitation, lure, pull, seduction, snare, tantalization

tempting *adj* = **inviting**, alluring, appetizing, attractive, enticing, mouthwatering, seductive, tantalizing
Antonyms *adj* off-putting (*Brit. inf.*), unappetizing, unattractive, undesirable, uninviting, untempting

tenable *adj* = **sound**, arguable, believable, defendable, defensible, justifiable, maintainable, plausible, rational, reasonable, viable
Antonyms *adj* indefensible, insupportable, unjustifiable, untenable

tenacious *adj* **1** = **firm**, clinging, fast, forceful, immovable, iron, strong, tight, unshakable **2** = **retentive**, unforgetful **3** = **stubborn**, adamant, determined, dogged, firm, immovable, inflexible, intransigent, obdurate, obstinate, persistent, pertinacious, resolute, staunch, steadfast, stiff-necked, strong-willed, sure, unswerving, unyielding **4** = **cohesive**, coherent, solid, strong, tough **5** = **adhesive**, clinging, gluey, glutinous, mucilaginous, sticky
Antonyms *adj* ≠ **stubborn:** changeable, flexible, irresolute, vacillating, wavering, yielding

tenacity *n* **1** = **firmness**, fastness, force, forcefulness, power, strength **2** = **retentiveness**, firm grasp, retention **3** = **perseverance**, application, determination, diligence, doggedness, firmness, inflexibility, intransigence, obduracy, obstinacy, persistence, pertinacity, resoluteness, resolution, resolve, staunchness, steadfastness, strength of purpose, strength of will, stubbornness **4** = **cohesiveness**, coherence, solidity, solidness, strength, toughness **5** = **adhesiveness**, clingingness, stickiness
Antonyms *n* ≠ **firmness:** looseness, powerlessness, slackness, weakness

tenancy *n* **1** = **lease**, holding, occupancy, occupation, possession, renting, residence **3** = **period of office**, incumbency, tenure, time in office

tenant *n* **1-3** = **leaseholder**, holder, inhabitant, lessee, occupant, occupier, renter, resident

tend[1] *vb* **1** = **be inclined**, be apt, be biased, be disposed, be liable, be likely, gravitate, have a leaning, have an inclination, have a tendency, incline, lean, trend **2** = **influence**, be conducive, conduce, contribute **3** = **go**, aim, bear, head, lead, make for, move, point

tend[2] *vb* **1-3** = **take care of**, attend, care for, cater for, control, cultivate, feed, guard, handle, keep, keep an eye on, look after, maintain, manage, minister to, nurse, nurture, protect, see to, serve, wait on, watch, watch over
Antonyms *vb* disregard, ignore, neglect, overlook, shirk

tendency *n* **1** = **inclination**, bent, disposition, leaning, liability, partiality, penchant, predilection, predisposition, proclivity, proneness, propensity, readiness, susceptibility **2** = **course**, bearing, bias, direction, drift, drive, heading, movement, purport, tenor, trend, turning

tender[1] ⓣ (ˈtɛndə) *adj* **1** easily broken, cut, or crushed; soft. **2** easily damaged; vulnerable or sensitive: *at a tender age.* **3** having or expressing warm feelings. **4** kind or sympathetic: *a tender heart.* **5** arousing warm feelings; touching. **6** gentle and delicate: *a tender breeze.* **7** requiring care in handling: *a tender question.* **8** painful or sore. **9** sensitive to moral or spiritual feelings. **10** (*postpositive;* foll. by *of*) protective: *tender of one's emotions.* [C13: from OF *tendre,* from L *tener* delicate]
▸ **ˈtenderly** *adv* ▸ **ˈtenderness** *n*

tender[2] ⓣ (ˈtɛndə) *vb* **1** (*tr*) to give, present, or offer: *to tender a bid.* **2** (*intr;* foll. by *for*) to make a formal offer or estimate (for a job or contract). **3** (*tr*) *Law.* to offer (money or goods) in settlement of a debt or claim. ◆ *n* **4** the act or an instance of tendering; offer. **5** a formal offer to supply specified goods or services at a stated cost or rate. **6** something, esp. money, used as an official medium of payment: *legal tender.* [C16: from Anglo-F *tendre,* from L *tendere* to extend]
▸ **ˈtenderer** *n*

tender[3] (ˈtɛndə) *n* **1** a small boat towed or carried by a ship. **2** a vehicle drawn behind a steam locomotive to carry the fuel and water. **3** a person who tends. [C15: var. of *attender*]

tenderfoot (ˈtɛndəˌfʊt) *n, pl* **tenderfoots** *or* **tenderfeet. 1** a newcomer, esp. to the mines or ranches of the southwestern US. **2** (formerly) a beginner in the Scouts or Guides.

tenderhearted ⓣ (ˌtɛndəˈhɑːtɪd) *adj* having a compassionate, kindly, or sensitive disposition.

tenderize *or* **tenderise** (ˈtɛndəˌraɪz) *vb* **tenderizes, tenderizing, tenderized** *or* **tenderises, tenderising, tenderised.** (*tr*) to make (meat) tender, as by pounding it or adding a substance to break down the fibres.
▸ **ˌtenderiˈzation** *or* **ˌtenderiˈsation** *n* ▸ **ˈtenderˌizer** *or* **ˈtenderˌiser** *n*

tenderloin (ˈtɛndəˌlɔɪn) *n* a tender cut of pork or other meat from between the sirloin and ribs.

tendon (ˈtɛndən) *n* a cord or band of tough tissue that attaches a muscle to a bone or some other part; sinew. [C16: from Med. L *tendō,* from L *tendere* to stretch]

tendril (ˈtɛndrɪl) *n* a threadlike leaf or stem that attaches climbing plants to a support by twining or adhering. [C16: ?from OF *tendron* tendril (confused with OF *tendron* bud), from Med. L *tendō* TENDON]

tenebrism (ˈtɛnəˌbrɪzəm) *n* (*sometimes cap.*) a school, style, or method of painting, adopted chiefly by 17th-century Spanish and Neapolitan painters, characterized by large areas of dark colours, usually relieved with a shaft of light.
▸ **ˈtenebrist** *n, adj*

tenebrous (ˈtɛnəbrəs) *or* **tenebrious** (təˈnɛbrɪəs) *adj* gloomy, shadowy, or dark. [C15: from L *tenebrōsus* from *tenebrae* darkness]

tenement (ˈtɛnəmənt) *n* **1** Also called: **tenement building.** a large building divided into rooms or flats. **2** a dwelling place or residence. **3** *Chiefly Brit.* a room or flat for rent. **4** *Property law.* any form of permanent property, such as land, dwellings, offices, etc. [C14: from Med. L *tenementum,* from L *tenēre* to hold]
▸ **tenemental** (ˌtɛnəˈmɛntˡl) *adj*

tenesmus (tɪˈnɛzməs) *n* an ineffective painful straining to empty the bowels or bladder. [C16: from Med. L, from L *tēnesmos,* from Gk, from *teinein* to strain]
▸ **teˈnesmic** *adj*

tenet ⓣ (ˈtɛnɪt, ˈtiːnɪt) *n* a belief, opinion, or dogma. [C17: from L, lit.: he (it) holds, from *tenēre* to hold]

tenfold (ˈtɛnˌfəʊld) *adj* **1** equal to or having 10 times as many or as much. **2** composed of 10 parts. ◆ *adv* **3** by or up to 10 times as many or as much.

ten-gallon hat *n* (in the US) a cowboy's broad-brimmed felt hat with a very high crown.

Ten Gurus *pl n* the ten leaders of the Sikh religion, from its founder Guru Nanak (1469–1539) to Guru Govind Singh (1666–1708).

tenner (ˈtɛnə) *n Inf.* **1** *Brit.* **1a** a ten-pound note. **1b** the sum of ten pounds. **2** *US.* a ten-dollar bill.

tennis (ˈtɛnɪs) *n* **a** a racket game played between two players or pairs of players who hit a ball to and fro over a net on a rectangular court of grass, asphalt, clay, etc. See also **lawn tennis, real tennis, table tennis. b** (*as modifier*): *tennis court; tennis racket.* [C14: prob. from Anglo-F *tenetz* hold (imperative), from OF *tenir* to hold, from L *tenēre*]

tennis elbow *n* inflammation of the elbow caused by exertion in playing tennis, etc.

tennis shoe *n* a rubber-soled canvas shoe tied with laces.

Tennysonian (ˌtɛnɪˈsəʊnɪən) *adj* of or in the style of Alfred, Lord Tennyson (1809–92), British poet.

teno- *or before a vowel* **ten-** *combining form.* tendon: *tenosynovitis.* [from Gk *tenōn*]

tenon (ˈtɛnən) *n* **1** the projecting end of a piece of wood formed to fit into a corresponding mortise in another piece. ◆ *vb* (*tr*) **2** to form a tenon on (a piece of wood). **3** to join with a tenon and mortise. [C15: from OF, from *tenir* to hold, from L *tenēre*]
▸ **ˈtenoner** *n*

tenon saw *n* a small fine-toothed saw with a strong back, used esp. for cutting tenons.

tenor ⓣ (ˈtɛnə) *n* **1** *Music.* **1a** the male voice intermediate between alto and baritone. **1b** a singer with such a voice. **1c** a saxophone, horn, etc., intermediate between the alto and baritone or bass. **2** general drift of thought; purpose. **3** a settled course of progress. **4** *Arch.* general tendency. **5** *Finance.* the time required for a bill of exchange or promissory note to become due for payment. **6** *Law.* **6a** the exact words of a deed, etc. **6b** an exact copy. [C13 (orig.: general sense): from OF *tenour,* from L *tenor* a holding to a course, from *tenēre* to hold; musical sense via It. *tenore,* referring to the voice part that was continuous, that is, to which the melody was assigned]

tenor clef *n* the clef that establishes middle C as being on the fourth line of the staff.

tenorrhaphy (tɪˈnɒrəfɪ) *n, pl* **tenorrhaphies.** *Surgery.* the union of torn or divided tendons by means of sutures. [C19: from TENO- + Gk *raphē* a sewing]

tenosynovitis (ˈtɛnəʊˌsaɪnəʊˈvaɪtɪs) *n* painful swelling and inflammation of tendons, usually of the wrist, often the result of repetitive movements such as typing.

tenotomy (təˈnɒtəmɪ) *n, pl* **tenotomies.** surgical division of a tendon.
▸ **teˈnotomist** *n*

tenpin bowling (ˈtɛnˌpɪn) *n* a bowling game in which bowls are rolled down a lane to knock over the ten target pins. Also called (esp. US and Canad.): **tenpins.**

tenrec (ˈtɛnrɛk) *n* any of a family of small mammals of Madagascar resembling hedgehogs or shrews. [C18: via F from Malagasy *tràndraka*]

tense[1] ⓣ (tɛns) *adj* **1** stretched or stressed tightly; taut or rigid. **2** under mental or emotional strain. **3** producing mental or emotional strain: *a tense day.* **4** *Phonetics.* Also: **narrow.** pronounced with considerable muscular effort, as the vowel (iː) in "beam". ◆ *vb* **tenses, tensing, tensed.** (often foll. by *up*) **5** to make or become tense. [C17: from L *tensus* taut, from *tendere* to stretch]
▸ **ˈtensely** *adv* ▸ **ˈtenseness** *n*

tense[2] (tɛns) *n Grammar.* a category of the verb or verbal inflections, such as present, past, and future, that expresses the temporal relations between what is reported in a sentence and the time of its utterance. [C14: from OF *tens* time, from L *tempus*]
▸ **ˈtenseless** *adj*

tense logic *n Logic.* the study of temporal relations between propositions, usually pursued by considering the logical properties of symbols representing the tenses of natural languages.

tensile (ˈtɛnsaɪl) *adj* **1** of or relating to tension. **2** sufficiently ductile to be stretched or drawn out. [C17: from NL *tensilis,* from L *tendere* to stretch]
▸ **tensility** (tɛnˈsɪlɪtɪ) *or* **ˈtensileness** *n*

tensile strength *n* a measure of the ability of a material to withstand a longitudinal stress, expressed as the greatest stress that the material can stand without breaking.

tensimeter (tɛnˈsɪmɪtə) *n* a device that measures differences in vapour pressures. [C20: from TENSI(ON) + -METER]

THESAURUS

tender[1] *adj* **1** = **fragile**, breakable, delicate, feeble, frail, soft, weak **2** = **vulnerable**, impressionable, raw, sensitive **3, 4** = **gentle**, affectionate, amorous, benevolent, caring, compassionate, considerate, fond, humane, kind, loving, merciful, pitiful, sentimental, softhearted, sympathetic, tenderhearted, touchy-feely (*inf.*), warm, warm-hearted **5** = **touching**, emotional, evocative, moving, poignant, romantic **7** = **difficult**, complicated, dangerous, risky, sensitive, ticklish, touchy, tricky **8** = **sensitive**, aching, acute, bruised, inflamed, irritated, painful, raw, smarting, sore
Antonyms *adj* ≠ **fragile:** hard, leathery, strong, tough ≠ **vulnerable:** sophisticated, worldly, worldly-wise ≠ **gentle:** brutal, cold-hearted, cruel, hard, hard-hearted, inhuman, insensitive, pitiless, tough, uncaring, unkind, unsympathetic

tender[2] *vb* **1** = **offer**, extend, give, hand in, proffer, propose, put forward, submit, suggest, volunteer ◆ *n* **4** = **offer**, bid, estimate, proffer, proposal, submission, suggestion

tenderhearted *adj* = **kind**, affectionate, benevolent, benign, caring, compassionate, considerate, fond, gentle, humane, kind-hearted, kindly, loving, merciful, mild, responsive, sensitive, sentimental, softhearted, sympathetic, touchy-feely (*inf.*), warm, warm-hearted

tenderness *n* **1** = **fragility**, delicateness, feebleness, frailness, sensitiveness, sensitivity, softness, vulnerability, weakness **2** = **vulnerability**, impressionableness, rawness, sensitivity **3, 4** = **gentleness**, affection, amorousness, attachment, benevolence, care, compassion, consideration, devotion, fondness, humaneness, humanity, kindness, liking, love, mercy, pity, sentimentality, softheartedness, sympathy, tender-heartedness, warm-heartedness, warmth **8** = **soreness**, ache, aching, bruising, inflammation, irritation, pain, painfulness, rawness, sensitiveness, sensitivity, smart
Antonyms *n* ≠ **gentleness:** cruelty, hardness, harshness, indifference, insensitivity, unkindness

tenet *n* = **principle**, article of faith, belief, canon, conviction, creed, doctrine, dogma, maxim, opinion, precept, rule, teaching, thesis, view

tenor *n* **2, 3** = **direction**, aim, burden, course, drift, evolution, intent, meaning, path, purport, purpose, sense, substance, tendency, theme, trend, way

tense[1] *adj* **1** = **tight**, rigid, strained, stretched, taut **2** = **nervous**, anxious, apprehensive, edgy, fidgety, jittery, jumpy, keyed up, on edge, on tenterhooks, overwrought, restless, strained, strung up (*inf.*), twitchy (*inf.*), under pressure, uptight (*inf.*), wired (*sl.*), wound up (*inf.*), wrought up **3** = **exciting**, moving, nerve-racking, stressful, worrying ◆ *vb* **5** = **tighten**, brace, flex, strain, stretch, tauten
Antonyms *adj* ≠ **tight:** flaccid, flexible, limp, loose, pliant, relaxed ≠ **nervous:** calm, collected, cool-headed, easy-going, self-possessed, serene, unconcerned, unruffled, unworried ≠ **exciting:** boring, dull, uninteresting ◆ *vb* ≠ **tighten:** loosen, relax, slacken

tensiometer (ˌtɛnsɪˈɒmɪtə) *n* **1** an instrument for measuring the tensile strength of a wire, beam, etc. **2** an instrument used to compare the vapour pressures of two liquids. **3** an instrument for measuring the surface tension of a liquid. **4** an instrument for measuring the moisture content of soil.

tension ➊ (ˈtɛnʃən) *n* **1** the act of stretching or the state or degree of being stretched. **2** mental or emotional strain; stress. **3** a situation or condition of hostility, suspense, or uneasiness. **4** *Physics.* a force that tends to produce an elongation of a body or structure. **5** *Physics.* voltage, electromotive force, or potential difference. **6** a device for regulating the tension in a part, string, thread, etc., as in a sewing machine. **7** the degree of tightness or looseness with which a person knits. [C16: from L *tensiō*, from *tendere* to strain]
▸ **ˈtensional** *adj* ▸ **ˈtensionless** *adj*

tensor (ˈtɛnsə, -sɔː) *n* **1** *Anat.* any muscle that can cause a part to become firm or tense. **2** *Maths.* a set of components, functions of the coordinates of any point in space, that transform linearly between coordinate systems. [C18: from NL, lit.: a stretcher]
▸ **tensorial** (tɛnˈsɔːrɪəl) *adj*

tent (tɛnt) *n* **1** a portable shelter of canvas, plastic, etc., supported on poles and fastened to the ground by pegs and ropes. **2** something resembling this in function or shape. ◆ *vb* **3** (*intr*) to camp in a tent. **4** (*tr*) to cover with or as if with a tent or tents. **5** (*tr*) to provide with a tent as shelter. [C13: from OF *tente*, from L *tentōrium* something stretched out, from *tendere* to stretch]
▸ **ˈtentage** *n* ▸ **ˈtented** *adj*

tentacle (ˈtɛntəkᵊl) *n* **1** any of various elongated flexible organs that occur near the mouth in many invertebrates and are used for feeding, grasping, etc. **2** any of the hairs on the leaf of an insectivorous plant that are used to capture prey. **3** something resembling a tentacle, esp. in its ability to reach out or grasp. [C18: from NL *tentāculum*, from L *tentāre*, var. of *temptāre* to feel]
▸ **ˈtentacled** *adj* ▸ **tentacular** (tɛnˈtækjʊlə) *adj*

tentation (tɛnˈteɪʃən) *n* a method of achieving the correct adjustment of a mechanical device by a series of trials. [C14: from L *tentātiō*, variant of *temptātiō* TEMPTATION]

tentative ➊ (ˈtɛntətɪv) *adj* **1** provisional or experimental. **2** hesitant, uncertain, or cautious. [C16: from Med. L *tentātīvus*, from L *tentāre* to test]
▸ **ˈtentatively** *adv* ▸ **ˈtentativeness** *n*

tenter (ˈtɛntə) *n* **1** a frame on which cloth is stretched in order that it may retain its shape while drying. **2** a person who stretches cloth on a tenter. ◆ *vb* **3** (*tr*) to stretch (cloth) on a tenter. [C14: from Med. L *tentōrium*, from L *tentus* stretched, from *tendere* to stretch]

tenterhook (ˈtɛntəˌhʊk) *n* **1** one of a series of hooks used to hold cloth on a tenter. **2** **on tenterhooks.** in a state of tension or suspense.

tenth (tɛnθ) *adj* **1** (*usually prenominal*) **1a** coming after the ninth in numbering, position, etc.; being the ordinal number of *ten:* often written 10th. **1b** (*as n*): *see you on the tenth.* ◆ *n* **2a** one of 10 equal parts of something. **2b** (*as modifier*): *a tenth part.* **3** the fraction equal to one divided by ten (1/10). ◆ *adv* **4** Also: **tenthly.** after the ninth person, position, event, etc. [C12 *tenthe*, from OE *tēotha*]

tent stitch *n* another term for **petit point.** [C17: from ?]

tenuis (ˈtɛnjʊɪs) *n, pl* **tenues** (ˈtɛnjʊˌiːz). (in classical Greek) a voiceless stop (k, p, t). [C17: from L: thin]

tenuous ➊ (ˈtɛnjʊəs) *adj* **1** insignificant or flimsy: *a tenuous argument.* **2** slim, fine, or delicate: *a tenuous thread.* **3** diluted or rarefied in consistency or density: *a tenuous fluid.* [C16: from L *tenuis*]
▸ **tenuity** (tɛˈnjuːɪtɪ) *or* **ˈtenuousness** *n* ▸ **ˈtenuously** *adv*

tenure ➊ (ˈtɛnjʊə, ˈtɛnjə) *n* **1** the possession or holding of an office or position. **2** the length of time an office, position, etc., lasts. **3** *Chiefly US & Canad.* the improved security status of a person after having been in the employ of the same company or institution for a specified period. **4** the right to permanent employment until retirement, esp. for teachers, etc. **5a** the holding of property, esp. realty, in return for services rendered, etc. **5b** the duration of such holding. [C15: from OF, from Med. L *tenitūra*, ult. from L *tenēre* to hold]
▸ **tenˈurial** *adj*

tenuto (tɪˈnjuːtəʊ) *adj, adv Music.* (of a note) to be held for or beyond its full time value. [from It., lit.: held, from *tenere* to hold, from L *tenēre*]

teocalli (ˌtiːəʊˈkælɪ) *n, pl* **teocallis.** any of various truncated pyramids built by the Aztecs as bases for their temples. [C17: from Nahuatl, from *teotl* god + *calli* house]

tepee *or* **teepee** (ˈtiːpiː) *n* a cone-shaped tent of animal skins used by American Indians. [C19: from Siouan *tīpī*, from *ti* to dwell + *pi* used for]

tephra (ˈtɛfrə) *n Chiefly US.* solid matter ejected during a volcanic eruption. [C20: Gk, lit.: ashes]

tepid ➊ (ˈtɛpɪd) *adj* **1** slightly warm; lukewarm. **2** relatively unenthusiastic or apathetic. [C14: from L *tepidus*, from *tepēre* to be lukewarm]
▸ **tepidity** (tɛˈpɪdɪtɪ) *or* **ˈtepidness** *n* ▸ **ˈtepidly** *adv*

tequila (tɪˈkiːlə) *n* **1** a spirit that is distilled in Mexico from an agave plant and forms the basis of many mixed drinks. **2** the plant from which this drink is made. [C19: from Mexican Sp., from *Tequila*, region of Mexico]

ter. *abbrev. for:* **1** terrace. **2** territory.

ter- *combining form.* three, third, or three times. [from L *ter* thrice]

tera- *prefix* denoting 10^{12}: *terameter.* Symbol: T [from Gk *teras* monster]

terat- *or* **terato-** *combining form.* indicating a monster or something abnormal: *teratism.* [from Gk *terat-*, *teras* monster, prodigy]

teratism (ˈtɛrəˌtɪzəm) *n* a malformed animal or human, esp. in the fetal stage; monster.

teratogen (ˈtɛrətədʒən, tɪˈrætə-) *n* any substance, organism, or process that causes malformations in a fetus. Teratogens include certain drugs (such as thalidomide), infections (such as German measles), and ionizing radiation.
▸ **ˌteratoˈgenic** *adj*

teratoid (ˈtɛrəˌtɔɪd) *adj Biol.* resembling a monster.

teratology (ˌtɛrəˈtɒlədʒɪ) *n* **1** the branch of medical science concerned with the development of physical abnormalities during the fetal or early embryonic stage. **2** the branch of biology concerned with the structure, development, etc., of monsters. **3** a collection of tales about mythical or fantastic creatures, monsters, etc.
▸ **ˌteraˈtologist** *n*

teratoma (ˌtɛrəˈtəʊmə) *n, pl* **teratomata** (-mətə) *or* **teratomas.** a tumour composed of tissue foreign to the site of growth.

terbium (ˈtɜːbɪəm) *n* a soft malleable silvery-grey element of the lanthanide series of metals. Symbol: Tb; atomic no.: 65; atomic wt.: 158.925. [C19: from NL, after *Ytterby*, Sweden, village where discovered]
▸ **ˈterbic** *adj*

terbium metal *n Chem.* any of a group of related lanthanides, including terbium, europium, and gadolinium.

terce (tɜːs) *or* **tierce** *n Chiefly RC Church.* the third of the seven canonical hours, originally fixed at the third hour of the day, about 9 a.m. [C14: var. of TIERCE]

tercel (ˈtɜːsᵊl) *or* **tiercel** *n* a male falcon or hawk, esp. as used in falconry. [C14: from OF, from Vulgar L *tertiolus* (unattested), from L *tertius* third, from the tradition that only one egg in three hatched a male chick]

tercentenary (ˌtɜːsɛnˈtiːnərɪ) *or* **tercentennial** *adj* **1** of a period of 300 years. **2** of a 300th anniversary. ◆ *n, pl* **tercentenaries** *or* **tercentennials. 3** an anniversary of 300 years.

tercet (ˈtɜːsɪt, tɜːˈsɛt) *n* a group of three lines of verse that rhyme together or are connected by rhyme with adjacent groups of three lines. [C16: from F, from It. *terzetto*, dim. of *terzo* third, from L *tertius*]

terebene (ˈtɛrəˌbiːn) *n* a mixture of hydrocarbons prepared from oil of turpentine and sulphuric acid, used to make paints and varnishes and medicinally as an expectorant and antiseptic. [C19: from TEREB(INTH) + -ENE]

terebinth (ˈtɛrɪbɪnθ) *n* a small Mediterranean tree that yields a turpentine. [C14: from L *terebinthus*, from Gk *terebinthos* turpentine tree]

terebinthine (ˌtɛrɪˈbɪnθaɪn) *adj* **1** of or relating to terebinth or related plants. **2** of, consisting of, or resembling turpentine.

teredo (tɛˈriːdəʊ) *n, pl* **teredos** *or* **teredines** (-dɪˌniːz). any of a genus of marine bivalve molluscs. See **shipworm.** [C17: via L from Gk *terēdōn* wood-boring worm]

terete (ˈtɛriːt) *adj* (esp. of plant parts) cylindrical and tapering. [C17: from L *teres* smooth, from *terere* to rub]

tergiversate (ˈtɜːdʒɪvəˌseɪt) *vb* **tergiversates, tergiversating, tergiversated.** (*intr*) **1** to change sides or loyalties. **2** to be evasive or ambiguous. [C17: from L *tergiversārī* to turn one's back, from *tergum* back + *vertere* to turn]
▸ **ˌtergiverˈsation** *n* ▸ **ˈtergiverˌsator** *n*

tergum (ˈtɜːgəm) *n, pl* **terga** (-gə). a cuticular plate covering the dorsal surface of a body segment of an arthropod. [C19: from L: the back]
▸ **ˈtergal** *adj*

term ➊ (tɜːm) *n* **1** a name, expression, or word used for some particular thing, esp. in a specialized field of knowledge: *a medical term.* **2** any

THESAURUS

tension *n* **1** = **tightness**, pressure, rigidity, stiffness, straining, stress, stretching, tautness **2, 3** = **strain**, anxiety, apprehension, edginess, hostility, ill feeling, nervousness, pressure, restlessness, stress, suspense, the jitters (*inf.*), unease
Antonyms *n* ≠ **strain:** calmness, peacefulness, relaxation, restfulness, serenity, tranquillity

tentative *adj* **1** = **unconfirmed**, conjectural, experimental, indefinite, provisional, speculative, unsettled **2** = **hesitant**, backward, cautious, diffident, doubtful, faltering, timid, uncertain, undecided, unsure
Antonyms *adj* ≠ **unconfirmed:** conclusive, confirmed, decisive, definite, final, fixed, resolved, settled ≠ **hesitant:** assured, bold, certain, confident, unhesitating

tenuous *adj* **1** = **slight**, doubtful, dubious, flimsy, insignificant, insubstantial, nebulous, questionable, shaky, sketchy, weak **2** = **fine**, attenuated, delicate, gossamer, slim
Antonyms *adj* ≠ **slight:** significant, solid, sound, strong, substantial

tenure *n* **1, 2** = **holding**, incumbency, occupancy, occupation, possession, proprietorship, residence, tenancy, term, time

tepid *adj* **1** = **lukewarm**, slightly warm, warmish **2** = **half-hearted**, apathetic, cool, half-arsed (*Brit. sl.*), half-assed (*US & Canad. sl.*), indifferent, lukewarm, unenthusiastic
Antonyms *adj* ≠ **half-hearted:** animated, eager, enthusiastic, excited, keen, passionate, vibrant, zealous

term *n* **1, 2** = **word**, appellation, denomination, designation, expression, locution, name, phrase, title **3** = **period**, duration, interval, season, space, span, spell, time, while **4** = **session**, course **5** = **end**, bound, boundary, close, conclusion, confine, culmination, finish, fruition, limit, terminus ◆ *vb* **11** = **call**, denominate, designate, dub, entitle, label, name, style

word or expression. **3** a limited period of time: *a prison term.* **4** any of the divisions of the academic year during which a school, college, etc., is in session. **5** a point in time determined for an event or for the end of a period. **6** the period at which childbirth is imminent. **7** *Law.* **7a** an estate or interest in land limited to run for a specified period. **7b** the duration of an estate, etc. **7c** (formerly) a period of time during which sessions of courts of law are held. **7d** time allowed to a debtor to settle. **8** *Maths.* any distinct quantity making up a fraction or proportion, or contained in a polynominal, sequence, series, etc. **9** *Logic.* **9a** the word or phrase that forms either the subject or predicate of a proposition. **9b** a name or variable, as opposed to a predicate. **9c** any of the three subjects or predicates occurring in a syllogism. **10** *Archit.* a sculptured post, esp. one in the form of an armless bust or an animal on the top of a square pillar. ◆ *vb* **11** (*tr*) to designate; call: *he was termed a thief.* ◆ See also **terms.** [C13: from OF *terme,* from L *terminus* end]
▸**'termly** *adj, adv*

termagant ('tɜːməgənt) *n* a shrewish woman; scold. [C13: from earlier *Tervagaunt,* from OF *Tervagan,* from It. *Trivigante;* after an arrogant character in medieval mystery plays who was supposed to be a Muslim deity]

-termer *n* (*in combination*) a person serving a specified length of time in prison: *a short-termer.*

terminable ('tɜːmɪnəb^{ə}l) *adj* **1** able to be terminated. **2** terminating after a specific period or event.
▸**ˌtermina'bility** *or* **'terminableness** *n* ▸**'terminably** *adv*

terminal ⓘ ('tɜːmɪn^{ə}l) *adj* **1** of, being, or situated at an end, terminus, or boundary. **2** of or occurring after or in a term: *terminal examinations.* **3** (of a disease) terminating in death. **4** *Inf.* extreme: *terminal boredom.* **5** of or relating to the storage or delivery of freight at a warehouse. ◆ *n* **6** a terminating point, part, or place. **7a** a point at which current enters or leaves an electrical device, such as a battery or a circuit. **7b** a conductor by which current enters or leaves at such a point. **8** *Computing.* a device having input/output links with a computer. **9** *Archit.* **9a** an ornamental carving at the end of a structure. **9b** another name for **term** (sense 10). **10a** a point or station at the end of the line of a railway or at an airport, serving as an important access point for passengers or freight. **10b** a less common name for **terminus** (sense 2). **11** a reception and departure building at the terminus of a bus, sea, or air transport route. **12** a site where raw material is unloaded and processed, esp. an onshore installation designed to receive offshore oil or gas. [C15: from L *terminālis,* from *terminus* end]
▸**'terminally** *adv*

terminal market *n* a commodity market in a trading centre rather than at a producing centre.

terminal velocity *n* **1** the constant maximum velocity reached by a body falling under gravity through a fluid, esp. the atmosphere. **2** the velocity of a missile or projectile when it reaches its target. **3** the maximum velocity attained by a rocket, missile, or shell flying in a parabolic flight path. **4** the maximum velocity that an aircraft can attain.

terminate ⓘ ('tɜːmɪˌneɪt) *vb* **terminates, terminating, terminated.** (when *intr,* often foll. by *in* or *with*) to form, be, or put an end (to); conclude. [C16: from L *terminātus* limited, from *termināre* to set boundaries, from *terminus* end]
▸**'terminative** *adj* ▸**'termiˌnator** *n*

termination ⓘ (ˌtɜːmɪ'neɪʃən) *n* **1** the act of terminating or the state of being terminated. **2** something that terminates. **3** a final result.

terminology ⓘ (ˌtɜːmɪ'nɒlədʒɪ) *n, pl* **terminologies. 1** the body of specialized words relating to a particular subject. **2** the study of terms. [C19: from Med. L *terminus* term from L: end]
▸**terminological** (ˌtɜːmɪnə'lɒdʒɪk^{ə}l) *adj* ▸**ˌtermi'nologist** *n*

term insurance *n* life assurance, usually low in cost and offering no cash value, that provides for the payment of a specified sum of money only if the insured dies within a stipulated time.

terminus ⓘ ('tɜːmɪnəs) *n, pl* **termini** (-naɪ) *or* **terminuses. 1** the last or final part or point. **2** either end of a railway, bus route, etc., or a station or town at such a point. **3** a goal aimed for. **4** a boundary or boundary marker. **5** *Archit.* another name for **term** (sense 10). [C16: from L: end]

terminus ad quem *Latin.* ('tɜːmɪˌnʊs æd 'kwɛm) *n* the aim or terminal point. [lit.: the end to which]

terminus a quo *Latin.* ('tɜːmɪˌnʊs ɑː 'kwəʊ) *n* the starting point; beginning. [lit.: the end from which]

termitarium (ˌtɜːmɪ'tɛərɪəm) *n, pl* **termitaria** (-ɪə). the nest of a termite colony. [C20: from TERMITE + -ARIUM]

termite ('tɜːmaɪt) *n* any of an order of whitish antlike social insects of warm and tropical regions. Some species feed on wood, causing damage to buildings, trees, etc. [C18: from NL *termitēs* white ants, pl of *termes,* from L: a woodworm]
▸**termitic** (tɜː'mɪtɪk) *adj*

termless ('tɜːmlɪs) *adj* **1** without limit or boundary. **2** unconditional. **3** an archaic word for **indescribable.**

termor *or* **termer** ('tɜːmə) *n Property law.* a person who holds an estate for a term of years or until he dies.

terms ⓘ (tɜːmz) *pl n* **1** (usually specified prenominally) the actual language or mode of presentation used: *he described the project in loose terms.* **2** conditions of an agreement. **3** a sum of money paid for a service. **4** (usually preceded by *on*) mutual relationship or standing: *they are on affectionate terms.* **5 bring to terms.** to cause to agree or submit. **6 come to terms.** to reach acceptance or agreement. **7 in terms of.** as expressed by; regarding: *in terms of money he was no better off.*

terms of trade *pl n Economics, Brit.* the ratio of export prices to import prices.

tern (tɜːn) *n* any of several aquatic birds related to the gulls, having a forked tail, long narrow wings, and a typically black-and-white plumage. [C18: from ON *therna*]

ternary ('tɜːnərɪ) *adj* **1** consisting of three or groups of three. **2** *Maths.* (of a number system) to the base three. [C14: from L *ternārius,* from *ternī* three each]

ternary form *n* a musical structure consisting of two contrasting sections followed by a repetition of the first; the form *aba.*

ternate ('tɜːnɪt, -neɪt) *adj* **1** (esp. of a leaf) consisting of three leaflets or other parts. **2** (esp. of plants) having groups of three members. [C18: from NL *ternātus,* from Med. L *ternāre* to increase threefold]
▸**'ternately** *adv*

terne (tɜːn) *n* **1** an alloy of lead containing tin and antimony. **2** Also called: **terne plate.** steel plate coated with this alloy. [C16: ?from F *terne* dull, from OF *ternir* to TARNISH]

terotechnology (ˌtɪərəʊtɛk'nɒlədʒɪ, tɛr-) *n* a branch of technology that utilizes management, financial, and engineering expertise in the installation, efficient operation, and maintenance of equipment and machinery. [C20: from Gk *tērein* to care for + TECHNOLOGY]

terpene ('tɜːpiːn) *n* any one of a class of unsaturated hydrocarbons, such as pinene and the carotenes, that are found in the essential oils of many plants, esp. conifers. [C19: *terp-* from obs. *terpentine* turpentine + -ENE]

terpineol (tɜː'pɪnɪˌɒl) *n* a terpene alcohol with an odour of lilac, existing in three isomeric forms that occur in several essential oils. [C20: from TERPENE + -INE^{2} + -OL^{1}]

Terpsichore (tɜːp'sɪkərɪ) *n* the Muse of the dance and of choral song. [C18: via L from Gk, from *terpsikhoros* delighting in the dance, from *terpein* to delight + *khoros* dance]

Terpsichorean (ˌtɜːpsɪkə'rɪən, -'kɔːrɪən) *Often used facetiously.* ◆ *adj also* **Terpsichoreal. 1** of or relating to dancing. ◆ *n* **2** a dancer.

terra ('tɛrə) *n* (in legal contexts) earth or land. [from L]

terra alba ('ælbə) *n* **1** a white finely powdered form of gypsum, used to make paints, paper, etc. **2** any of various other white earthy substances, such as kaolin, pipeclay, and magnesia. [from L, lit.: white earth]

terrace ('tɛrəs) *n* **1** a horizontal flat area of ground, often one of a series in a slope. **2a** a row of houses, usually identical and having common dividing walls, or the street onto which they face. **2b** (*cap. when part of a street name*): *Grosvenor Terrace.* **3** a paved area alongside a building, serving partly as a garden. **4** a balcony or patio. **5** the flat roof of a house built in a Spanish or Oriental style. **6** a flat area bounded by a short steep slope formed by the down-cutting of a river or by erosion. **7** (*usually pl*) unroofed tiers around a football pitch on which the spectators stand. ◆ *vb* **terraces, terracing, terraced. 8** (*tr*) to make into or provide with a terrace or terraces. [C16: from OF *terrasse,* from OProvençal *terrassa* pile of earth, from *terra* earth, from L]

terraced house *n Brit.* a house that is part of a terrace. US and Canad. name: **row house.**

terracing ('tɛrəsɪŋ) *n* **1** a series of terraces, esp. one dividing a slope into a steplike system of flat narrow fields. **2** the act of making a terrace or terraces. **3** another name for **terrace** (sense 7).

terra cotta ('kɒtə) *n* **1** a hard unglazed brownish-red earthenware, or the clay from which it is made. **2** something made of terra cotta, such as a sculpture. **3** a strong reddish-brown to brownish-orange colour. [C18: from It., lit.: baked earth]
▸**'terra-'cotta** *adj*

terra firma ('fɜːmə) *n* the solid earth; firm ground. [C17: from L]

THESAURUS

terminal *adj* **1** = **final,** bounding, concluding, extreme, last, limiting, ultimate, utmost **3** = **fatal,** deadly, incurable, killing, lethal, mortal ◆ *n* **6** = **end,** boundary, extremity, limit, termination, terminus **10** = **terminus,** depot, end of the line, station
Antonyms *adj* ≠ **final:** beginning, commencing, first, initial, introductory, opening

terminate *vb* = **end,** abort, axe (*inf.*), belay, bring *or* come to an end, cease, close, complete, conclude, cut off, discontinue, expire, finish, issue, lapse, pull the plug on (*inf.*), put an end to, result, run out, stop, wind up
Antonyms *vb* begin, commence, inaugurate, initiate, instigate, introduce, open, start

termination *n* **1-3** = **ending,** abortion, cessation, close, completion, conclusion, consequence, cut-off point, discontinuation, effect, end, expiry, finale, finis, finish, issue, result, wind-up
Antonyms *n* beginning, commencement, inauguration, initiation, opening, start

terminology *n* **1** = **language,** argot, cant, jargon, lingo (*inf.*), nomenclature, patois, phraseology, terms, vocabulary

terminus *n* **1, 3, 4** = **end,** boundary, close, extremity, final point, goal, limit, target, termination **2** = **end of the line,** depot, garage, last stop, station

terms *pl n* **1** = **language,** manner of speaking, phraseology, terminology **2** = **conditions,** particulars, premises (*Law*), provisions, provisos, qualifications, specifications, stipulations **3** = **price,** charges, fee, payment, rates **4** = **relationship,** footing, position, relations, standing, status **6 come to terms** = **learn to live with,** be reconciled, come to accept, come to an understanding, conclude agreement, reach acceptance, reach agreement

terrain ❶ (tə'reɪn) *n* a piece of ground, esp. with reference to its physical character or military potential: *a rocky terrain*. [C18: from F, ult. from L *terrēnum* ground, from *terra* earth]

terra incognita *Latin*. ('tɛrə ɪn'kɒgnɪtə) *n* an unexplored or unknown land, region, or area.

Terramycin (ˌtɛrə'maɪsɪn) *n Trademark*. a broad-spectrum antibiotic used in treating various infections.

terrapin ('tɛrəpɪn) *n* any of various web-footed reptiles that live on land and in fresh water and feed on small aquatic animals. Also called: **water tortoise**. [C17: of Amerind origin]

terrarium (tɛ'rɛərɪəm) *n, pl* **terrariums** *or* **terraria** (-'rɛərɪə). **1** an enclosure for small land animals. **2** a glass container, often a globe, in which plants are grown. [C19: NL, from L *terra* earth]

terra sigillata (ˌsɪdʒɪ'lɑːtə) *n* **1** a reddish-brown clayey earth found on the Aegean island of Lemnos: formerly used as an astringent and in the making of earthenware pottery. **2** any similar earth resembling this. **3** earthenware pottery made from this or a similar earth, esp. Samian ware. [from L: sealed earth]

terrazzo (tɛ'rætsəʊ) *n, pl* **terrazzos**. a floor made by setting marble chips into a layer of mortar and polishing the surface. [C20: from It.: TERRACE]

terrene (tɛ'riːn) *adj* **1** of the earth; worldly; mundane. **2** *Rare*. of earth; earthy. ◆ *n* **3** a land. **4** a rare word for **earth**. [C14: from Anglo-Norman, from L *terrēnus*, from *terra* earth]

terreplein ('tɛəˌpleɪn) *n* the top of a rampart where guns are placed behind the parapet. [C16: from F, from Med. L *terrā plēnus* filled with earth]

terrestrial ❶ (tə'rɛstrɪəl) *adj* **1** of the earth. **2** of the land as opposed to the sea or air. **3** (of animals and plants) living or growing on the land. **4** earthly, worldly, or mundane. **5** *Television*. denoting or using signals sent over the earth's surface from a transmitter on land, rather than by satellite. ◆ *n* **6** an inhabitant of the earth. [C15: from L *terrestris*, from *terra* earth]
► **ter'restrially** *adv* ► **ter'restrialness** *n*

terrestrial telescope *n* a telescope for use on earth rather than for making astronomical observations. Such telescopes contain an additional lens or prism system to produce an erect image.

terret ('tɛrɪt) *n* **1** either of the two rings on a harness through which the reins are passed. **2** the ring on a dog's collar for attaching the lead. [C15: var. of *toret*, from OF, dim. of *tor* loop]

terre-verte ('tɛəˌvɜːt) *n* **1** a greyish-green pigment used in paints. It is made from a mineral found in greensand and similar rocks. ◆ *adj* **2** of a greyish-green colour. [C17: from F, lit.: green earth]

terrible ❶ ('tɛrəbəl) *adj* **1** very serious or extreme. **2** *Inf*. of poor quality; unpleasant or bad. **3** causing terror. **4** causing awe. [C15: from L *terribilis*, from *terrēre* to terrify]
► **'terribleness** *n* ► **'terribly** *adv*

terricolous (tɛ'rɪkələs) *adj* living on or in the soil. [C19: from L *terricola*, from *terra* earth + *colere* to inhabit]

terrier[1] ('tɛrɪə) *n* any of several usually small, active, and short-bodied breeds of dog, originally trained to hunt animals living underground. [C15: from OF *chien terrier* earth dog, from Med. L *terrārius* belonging to the earth, from L *terra* earth]

terrier[2] ('tɛrɪə) *n English legal history*. a register or survey of land. [C15: from OF, from Med. L *terrārius* of the land, from L *terra* land]

terrific ❶ (tə'rɪfɪk) *adj* **1** very great or intense. **2** *Inf*. very good; excellent. **3** very frightening. [C17: from L *terrificus*, from *terrēre* to frighten]
► **ter'rifically** *adv*

terrify ❶ ('tɛrɪˌfaɪ) *vb* **terrifies, terrifying, terrified**. (*tr*) to inspire fear or dread in; frighten greatly. [C16: from L *terrificāre*, from *terrēre* to alarm + *facere* to cause]
► **'terriˌfying** *adj* ► **'terriˌfyingly** *adv*

terrigenous (tɛ'rɪdʒɪnəs) *adj* **1** of or produced by the earth. **2** (of geological deposits) formed in the sea from material derived from the land by erosion. [C17: from L *terrigenus*, from *terra* earth + *gignere* to beget]

terrine (tɛ'riːn) *n* **1** an oval earthenware cooking dish with a tightly fitting lid used for pâtés, etc. **2** the food cooked or served in such a dish, esp. pâté. [C18: earlier form of TUREEN]

territorial (ˌtɛrɪ'tɔːrɪəl) *adj* **1** of or relating to a territory or territories. **2** restricted to or owned by a particular territory. **3** local or regional. **4** *Zool*. establishing and defending a territory. **5** pertaining to a territorial army, providing a reserve of trained men for use in emergency.
► **ˌterriˌtori'ality** *n* ► **ˌterri'torially** *adv*

Territorial (ˌtɛrɪ'tɔːrɪəl) *n* a member of a Territorial Army.

Territorial Army *n* (in Britain) a standing reserve army originally organized between 1907 and 1908. Full name: **Territorial and Volunteer Reserve**.

Territorial Council *n* (in Canada) an elected body responsible for local government in the Northwest Territories or the Yukon.

territorial waters *pl n* the waters over which a nation exercises jurisdiction and control.

territory ❶ ('tɛrɪtərɪ) *n, pl* **territories**. **1** any tract of land; district. **2** the geographical domain under the jurisdiction of a political unit, esp. of a sovereign state. **3** the district for which an agent, etc., is responsible. **4** an area inhabited and defended by an animal or a pair of animals. **5** an area of knowledge. **6** (in football, hockey, etc.) the area defended by a team. **7** (*often cap*.) a region of a country, esp. of a federal state, that enjoys less autonomy and a lower status than most constituent parts of the state. **8** (*often cap*.) a protectorate or other dependency of a country. [C15: from L *territōrium* land surrounding a town, from *terra* land]

terror ❶ ('tɛrə) *n* **1** great fear, panic, or dread. **2** a person or thing that inspires great dread. **3** *Inf*. a troublesome person or thing, esp. a child. **4** terrorism. [C14: from OF *terreur*, from L *terror*, from *terrēre* to frighten]
► **'terrorful** *adj* ► **'terrorless** *adj*

terrorism ('tɛrəˌrɪzəm) *n* **1** the systematic use of violence and intimidation to achieve some goal. **2** the act of terrorizing. **3** the state of being terrorized.
► **'terrorist** *n, adj*

terrorize ❶ *or* **terrorise** ('tɛrəˌraɪz) *vb* **terrorizes, terrorizing, terrorized** *or* **terrorises, terrorising, terrorised**. (*tr*) **1** to coerce or control by violence, fear, threats, etc. **2** to inspire with dread; terrify.
► **ˌterrori'zation** *or* **ˌterrori'sation** *n* ► **'terrorˌizer** *or* **'terrorˌiser** *n*

terror-stricken *or* **terror-struck** *adj* in a state of terror.

terry ('tɛrɪ) *n, pl* **terries**. **1** an uncut loop in the pile of towelling or a similar fabric. **2** a fabric with such a pile. [C18: ? var. of TERRET]

terse ❶ (tɜːs) *adj* **1** neatly brief and concise. **2** curt; abrupt. [C17: from L *tersus* precise, from *tergēre* to polish]
► **'tersely** *adv* ► **'terseness** *n*

tertial ('tɜːʃəl) *adj, n* another word for **tertiary** (senses 5, 6). [C19: from L *tertius* third, from *ter* thrice, from *trēs* three]

tertian ('tɜːʃən) *adj* **1** (of a fever) occurring every other day. ◆ *n* **2** a tertian fever. [C14: from L *febris tertiāna* fever occurring every third day, from *tertius* third]

tertiary ('tɜːʃərɪ) *adj* **1** third in degree, order, etc. **2** (of an industry) involving services as opposed to extraction or manufacture, such as transport, finance, etc. **3** *RC Church*. of or relating to a Third Order. **4** *Chem*. **4a** (of an organic compound) having a functional group attached to a carbon atom that is attached to three other groups. **4b** (of an amine) having three organic groups attached to a nitrogen atom. **4c** (of a salt) derived from a tribasic acid by replacement of all its acidic hydrogen atoms with metal atoms or electropositive groups. **5** *Ornithol*., *rare*. of or designating any of the small flight feathers at-

THESAURUS

terrain *n* = **ground**, country, going, land, landscape, topography

terrestrial *adj* **1, 4** = **earthly**, global, mundane, sublunary, tellurian, terrene, worldly ◆ *n* **6** = **earthling**, earthman, earthwoman, human

terrible *adj* **1** = **serious**, bad, dangerous, desperate, extreme, severe **2** *Informal* = **bad**, abhorrent, abysmal, awful, beastly (*inf.*), dire, dreadful, duff (*Brit. inf.*), foul, frightful, from hell (*inf.*), hateful, hideous, loathsome, obnoxious, obscene, odious, offensive, poor, repulsive, revolting, rotten (*inf.*), shitty (*taboo sl.*), unpleasant, vile **3** = **fearful**, appalling, awful, dread, dreaded, dreadful, frightful, gruesome, harrowing, hellacious (*US sl.*), horrendous, horrible, horrid, horrifying, monstrous, shocking, terrifying, unspeakable
Antonyms *adj* ≠ **serious**: harmless, insignificant, mild, moderate, paltry, small ≠ **bad**: admirable, brilliant, delightful, excellent, fine, great, magic, noteworthy, pleasant, remarkable, super, superb, terrific, very good, wonderful ≠ **fearful**: calming, comforting, encouraging, reassuring, settling, soothing

terribly *adv* **1** = **extremely**, awfully (*inf.*), decidedly, desperately, exceedingly, gravely, greatly, much, seriously, thoroughly, very

terrific *adj* **1** = **great**, awesome, awful, dreadful, enormous, excessive, extreme, fearful, fierce, gigantic, harsh, horrific, huge, intense, monstrous, severe, terrible, tremendous **2** *Informal* = **excellent**, ace (*inf.*), amazing, awesome (*sl.*), breathtaking, brill (*inf.*), brilliant, cracking, fabulous (*inf.*), fantastic (*inf.*), fine, great (*inf.*), jim-dandy (*sl.*), magnificent, marvellous, outstanding, sensational (*inf.*), smashing (*inf.*), stupendous, super (*inf.*), superb, very good, wonderful
Antonyms *adj* ≠ **great**: insignificant, mild, moderate, paltry ≠ **excellent**: appalling, awful, bad, dreadful, terrible

terrified *adj* = **frightened**, alarmed, appalled, awed, dismayed, frightened out of one's wits, horrified, horror-struck, intimidated, panic-stricken, petrified, scared, scared shitless (*taboo sl.*), scared stiff, scared to death, shit-scared (*taboo sl.*), shocked, terror-stricken

terrify *vb* = **frighten**, alarm, appal, awe, dismay, fill with terror, frighten out of one's wits, horrify, intimidate, make one's blood run cold, make one's flesh creep, make one's hair stand on end, petrify, put the fear of God into, scare, scare to death, shock, terrorize

territory *n* **1-3** = **district**, area, bailiwick, country, domain, land, patch, province, region, sector, state, terrain, tract, turf (*US sl.*), zone

terror *n* **1** = **fear**, alarm, anxiety, awe, consternation, dismay, dread, fear and trembling, fright, horror, intimidation, panic, shock **2** = **scourge**, bogeyman, bugbear, devil, fiend, monster

terrorize *vb* **1** = **oppress**, browbeat, bully, coerce, intimidate, menace, strong-arm (*inf.*), threaten **2** = **terrify**, alarm, appal, awe, dismay, fill with terror, frighten, frighten out of one's wits, horrify, inspire panic in, intimidate, make one's blood run cold, make one's flesh creep, make one's hair stand on end, petrify, put the fear of God into, scare, scare to death, shock, strike terror into

terse *adj* **1** = **concise**, aphoristic, brief, clipped, compact, condensed, crisp, elliptical, epigrammatic, gnomic, incisive, laconic, monosyllabic, neat, pithy, sententious, short, succinct, summary, to the point **2** = **curt**, abrupt, brusque, short, snappy
Antonyms *adj* ≠ **concise**: circumlocutory, confused, discursive, lengthy, long-winded, rambling, roundabout, vague, verbose, wordy ≠ **curt**: chatty, polite

tached to the part of the humerus nearest to the body. ◆ *n, pl* **tertiaries.** **6** *Ornithol., rare.* any of the tertiary feathers. **7** *RC Church.* a member of a Third Order. [C16: from L *tertiārius* containing one third, from *tertius* third]

Tertiary ('tɜːʃərɪ) *adj* **1** of, denoting, or formed in the first period of the Cenozoic era. ◆ *n* **2 the.** the Tertiary period or rock system.

tertiary college *n Brit.* a college system incorporating the secondary school sixth form and vocational courses.

tertiary colour *n* a colour formed by mixing two secondary colours.

tertium quid ('tɜːtɪəm) *n* an unknown or indefinite thing related in some way to two known or definite things, but distinct from both. [C18: from LL, rendering Gk *triton ti* some third thing]

tervalent (tɜː'veɪlənt) *adj Chem.* another word for **trivalent.**
▸**ter'valency** *n*

Terylene ('terɪˌliːn) *n Trademark.* a synthetic polyester fibre or fabric. US name (trademark): **Dacron.**

terza rima ('teətsə 'riːmə) *n, pl* **terze rime** ('teətseɪ 'riːmeɪ). a verse form consisting of a series of tercets in which the middle line of one tercet rhymes with the first and third lines of the next. [C19: from It., lit.: third rhyme]

TESL ('tesᵊl) *acronym for* Teaching (of) English as a Second Language.

tesla ('teslə) *n* the derived SI unit of magnetic flux density equal to a flux of 1 weber in an area of 1 square metre. Symbol: T [C20: after Nikola *Tesla* (1857–1943), US electrical engineer & inventor]

tesla coil *n* a step-up transformer with an air core, used for producing high voltages at high frequencies.

Tessa ('tesə) *n* (in Britain) *acronym for* Tax Exempt Special Savings Account; a savings scheme introduced in 1991 enabling interest on up to £1800 p.a. to be paid tax free if the capital remains intact for five years.

tessellate ('tesɪˌleɪt) *vb* **tessellates, tessellating, tessellated. 1** (*tr*) to construct, pave, or inlay with a mosaic of small tiles. **2** (*intr*) (of identical shapes) to fit together exactly. [C18: from L *tessellātus* checked, from *tessella* small stone cube, from TESSERA]

tessera ('tesərə) *n, pl* **tesserae** (-səˌriː). **1** a small square tile of stone, glass, etc., used in mosaics. **2** a die, tally, etc., used in classical times, made of bone or wood. [C17: from L, from Ionic Gk *tesseres* four]
▸**'tesseral** *adj*

tessitura (ˌtesɪ'tʊərə) *n Music.* the general pitch level of a piece of vocal music. [It.: texture, from L *textura;* see TEXTURE]

test[1] ❶ (test) *vb* **1** to ascertain (the worth, capability, or endurance) of (a person or thing) by subjection to certain examinations, etc.; try. **2** (often foll. by *for*) to carry out an examination on (a substance, material, or system) to indicate the presence of a substance or the possession of a property: *to test food for arsenic.* **3** (*tr*) to put under severe strain: *the long delay tested my patience.* **4** (*intr*) to achieve a specified result in a test: *he tested positive for the AIDS virus.* ◆ *n* **5** a method, practice, or examination designed to test a person or thing. **6** a series of questions or problems designed to test a specific skill or knowledge. **7** a standard of judgment; criterion. **8a** a chemical reaction or physical procedure for testing a substance, material, etc. **8b** a chemical reagent used in such a procedure. **8c** the result of the procedure or the evidence gained from it. **9** *Sport.* See **test match. 10** *Arch.* a declaration of truth, loyalty, etc. **11** (*modifier*) performed as a test: *test drive.* [C14 (in the sense: vessel used in treating metals): from L *testum* earthen vessel]
▸**'testable** *adj* ▸**'testing** *adj*

test[2] (test) *n* the hard outer covering of certain invertebrates and tunicates. [C19: from L *testa* shell]

testa ('testə) *n, pl* **testae** (-tiː). the hard outer layer of a seed. [C18: from L: shell]

testaceous (te'steɪʃəs) *adj Biol.* **1** of or possessing a test or testa. **2** of the reddish-brown colour of terra cotta. [C17: from L *testācens,* from TESTA]

testament ❶ ('testəmənt) *n* **1** *Law.* a will (esp. in **last will and testament**). **2** a proof, attestation, or tribute. **3a** a covenant instituted between God and man. **3b** a copy of either the Old or the New Testament, or of the complete Bible. [C14: from L *testamentum* a will, from *testārī* to bear witness, from *testis* a witness]
▸ˌ**testa'mental** *adj* ▸ˌ**testa'mentary** *adj*

Testament ('testəmənt) *n* **1** either of the two main parts of the Bible; the Old Testament or the New Testament. **2** the New Testament as distinct from the Old.

testate ('testeɪt, 'testɪt) *adj* **1** having left a legally valid will at death. ◆ *n* **2** a person who dies testate. [C15: from L *testārī* to make a will; see TESTAMENT]
▸**testacy** ('testəsɪ) *n*

testator (te'steɪtə) *or* (*fem*) **testatrix** (te'steɪtrɪks) *n* a person who makes a will, esp. one who dies testate. [C15: from Anglo-F *testatour,* from LL *testātor,* from L *testārī* to make a will]

test ban *n* an agreement among nations to forgo tests of nuclear weapons.

test-bed *n Engineering.* an area used for testing machinery, etc., under working conditions.

test card *or* **pattern** *n* a complex pattern used to test the characteristics of a television transmission system.

test case *n* a legal action that serves as a precedent in deciding similar succeeding cases.

test-drive *vb* **test-drives, test-driving, test-drove, test-driven.** (*tr*) to drive (a car or other motor vehicle) for a limited period in order to assess it.

tester[1] ('testə) *n* a person or thing that tests.

tester[2] ('testə) *n* a canopy over a bed. [C14: from Med. L *testerium,* from LL *testa* a skull, from L: shell]

testes ('testiːz) *n* the plural of **testis.**

testicle ('testɪkᵊl) *n* either of the two male reproductive glands, in most mammals enclosed within the scrotum, that produce spermatozoa. [C15: from L *testiculus,* dim. of *testis*]
▸**testicular** (te'stɪkjʊlə) *adj*

testiculate (te'stɪkjʊlɪt) *adj Bot.* having an oval shape: *the testiculate tubers of certain orchids.* [C18: from LL *testiculātus;* see TESTICLE]

testify ❶ ('testɪˌfaɪ) *vb* **testifies, testifying, testified. 1** (when *tr, may take a clause as object*) to state (something) formally as a declaration of fact. **2** *Law.* to declare or give (evidence) under oath, esp. in court. **3** (when *intr,* often foll. by *to*) to be evidence (of); serve as witness (to). **4** (*tr*) to declare or acknowledge openly. [C14: from L *testificārī,* from *testis* witness]
▸ˌ**testifi'cation** *n* ▸**'testiˌfier** *n*

testimonial ❶ (ˌtestɪ'məʊnɪəl) *n* **1a** a recommendation of the character, ability, etc., of a person or of the quality of a product or service. **1b** (*as modifier*): *testimonial advertising.* **2** a formal statement of truth or fact. **3** a tribute given for services or achievements. **4** a sports match to raise money for a particular player. ◆ *adj* **5** of or relating to a testimony or testimonial.

> **USAGE NOTE** *Testimonial* is sometimes wrongly used where *testimony* is meant: *his re-election is a testimony* (not *a testimonial*) *to his popularity with his constituents.*

testimony ❶ ('testɪmənɪ) *n, pl* **testimonies. 1** a declaration of truth or fact. **2** *Law.* evidence given by a witness, esp. in court under oath. **3** evidence testifying to something: *her success was a testimony to her good luck.* **4** *Old Testament.* the Ten Commandments. [C15: from L *testimōnium,* from *testis* witness]

testis ('testɪs) *n, pl* **testes.** another word for **testicle.** [C17: from L, lit.: witness (to masculinity)]

test match *n* (in various sports, esp. cricket) an international match, esp. one of a series.

testosterone (te'stɒstəˌrəʊn) *n* a potent steroid hormone secreted mainly by the testes. [C20: from TESTIS + STEROL + -ONE]

test paper *n* **1** *Chem.* paper impregnated with an indicator for use in chemical tests. **2a** the question sheet of a test. **2b** the paper completed by a test candidate.

test pilot *n* a pilot who flies aircraft of new design to test their performance in the air.

test tube *n* **1** a cylindrical round-bottomed glass tube open at one end: used in scientific experiments. **2** (*modifier*) made synthetically in, or as if in, a test tube: *a test-tube product.*

test-tube baby *n* **1** a fetus that has developed from an ovum fertilized in an artificial womb. **2** a baby conceived by artificial insemination.

testudinal (te'stjuːdɪnᵊl) *adj* of or resembling a tortoise. [C19: from L TESTUDO]

testudo (te'stjuːdəʊ) *n, pl* **testudines** (-dɪˌniːz). a form of shelter used by the ancient Roman Army as protection against attack from above, consisting of a mobile arched structure or of overlapping shields held by the soldiers over their heads. [C17: from L: a tortoise, from *testa* a shell]

testy ('testɪ) *adj* **testier, testiest.** irritable or touchy. [C14: from Anglo-Norman *testif* headstrong, from OF *teste* head, from LL *testa* skull, from L: shell]
▸**'testily** *adv* ▸**'testiness** *n*

tetanus ('tetənəs) *n* **1** Also called: **lockjaw.** an acute infectious disease in which sustained muscular spasm, contraction, and convulsion are caused by the release of toxins from a bacterium. **2** *Physiol.* any tense contraction of a muscle. [C16: via L from Gk *tetanos,* ult. from *teinein* to stretch]
▸**'tetanal** *adj* ▸**'tetaˌnoid** *adj*

THESAURUS

test *vb* **1** = **check,** analyse, assay, assess, examine, experiment, investigate, prove, put through their paces, put to the proof, put to the test, research, try, try out, verify, work over ◆ *n* **5** = **examination,** acid test, analysis, assessment, attempt, catechism, check, evaluation, investigation, ordeal, probation, proof, research, trial

testament *n* **1** = **will,** last wishes **2** = **proof,** attestation, demonstration, earnest, evidence, exemplification, testimony, tribute, witness

testify *vb* **1** = **bear witness,** affirm, assert, asseverate, attest, certify, corroborate, declare, depone (*Scots Law*), depose (*Law*), evince, give testimony, show, state, swear, vouch, witness
Antonyms *vb* belie, contradict, controvert, disprove, dispute, gainsay (*arch. or literary*), oppose

testimonial *n* **1a, 3** = **tribute,** certificate, character, commendation, credential, endorsement, recommendation, reference

testimony *n* **2** = **evidence,** affidavit, affirmation, attestation, avowal, confirmation, corroboration, declaration, deposition, information, profession, statement, submission, witness **3** = **proof,** corroboration, demonstration, evidence, indication, manifestation, support, verification

testing *adj* **3** = **difficult,** arduous, challenging, demanding, exacting, formidable, rigorous, searching, strenuous, taxing, tough, trying
Antonyms *adj* easy, friendly, gentle, mild, simple, straightforward, undemanding

tetany ('tɛtənɪ) *n* an abnormal increase in the excitability of nerves and muscles caused by a deficiency of parathyroid secretion. [C19: from F; see TETANUS]

tetchy ⓣ ('tɛtʃɪ) *adj* **tetchier, tetchiest.** being or inclined to be cross, irritable, or touchy. [C16: prob. from obs. *tetch* defect, from OF *tache* spot, of Gmc origin]
▸'**tetchily** *adv* ▸'**tetchiness** *n*

tête-à-tête ⓣ (ˌteɪtə'teɪt) *n, pl* **tête-à-têtes** *or* **tête-à-tête. 1a** a private conversation between two people. **1b** (*as modifier*): *a tête-à-tête conversation.* **2** a small sofa for two people, esp. one that is S-shaped in plan so that the sitters are almost face to face. ◆ *adv* **3** intimately; in private. [C17: from F, lit.: head to head]

tête-bêche (tɛt'bɛʃ) *adj Philately.* (of an unseparated pair of stamps) printed so that one is inverted in relation to the other. [C19: from F, from *tête* head + *bêche,* from obs. *béchevet* double-headed (orig. of a bed)]

tether ⓣ ('tɛðə) *n* **1** a rope, chain, etc., by which an animal is tied to a particular spot. **2** the range of one's endurance, etc. **3 at the end of one's tether.** distressed or exasperated to the limit of one's endurance. ◆ *vb* **4** (*tr*) to tie with or as if with a tether. [C14: from ON *tjothr*]

Tethys ('ti:θɪs, 'tɛθ-) *n* the sea that lay between the two ancient supercontinents, Laurasia and Gondwanaland, and which can be regarded as the predecessor of today's smaller Mediterranean.

tetra- *or before a vowel* **tetr-** *combining form.* four: *tetrameter.* [from Gk]

tetrabasic (ˌtɛtrə'beɪsɪk) *adj* (of an acid) containing four replaceable hydrogen atoms.
▸**tetrabasicity** (ˌtɛtrəbeɪ'sɪsɪtɪ) *n*

tetrachloromethane ('tɛtrəklɔ:rəʊˌmi:θeɪn) *n* the systematic name for **carbon tetrachloride.**

tetrachord ('tɛtrəˌkɔ:d) *n Music.* any of several groups of four notes in descending order, in which the first and last notes form a perfect fourth. [C17: from Gk *tetrakhordos* four-stringed]
▸ˌ**tetra'chordal** *adj*

tetracyclic (ˌtɛtrə'saɪklɪk) *adj Chem.* containing four rings in its molecular structure.

tetracycline (ˌtɛtrə'saɪklaɪn, -klɪn) *n* an antibiotic synthesized from chlortetracycline or derived from a bacterium. [C20: from TETRA- + CYCL(IC) + -INE[2]]

tetrad ('tɛtræd) *n* a group or series of four. [C17: from Gk *tetras,* from *tettares* four]

tetraethyl lead (ˌtɛtrə'i:θaɪl lɛd) *n* a colourless oily insoluble liquid used in petrol to prevent knocking. Systematic name: **lead tetraethyl.**

tetrafluoroethene ('tɛtrəˌfluərəʊ'ɛθi:n) *n Chem.* a dense colourless gas that is polymerized to make polytetrafluorethene (PTFE). Formula: $F_2C{:}CF_2$. Also called: **tetrafluoroethylene.** [C20: from TETRA- + FLUORO- + ETHENE]

tetragon ('tɛtrəˌgɒn) *n* a less common name for **quadrilateral** (sense 2). [C17: from Gk *tetragōnon*]

tetragonal (tɛ'trægən°l) *adj* **1** *Crystallog.* relating or belonging to the crystal system characterized by three mutually perpendicular axes of which only two are equal. **2** of or shaped like a quadrilateral.
▸**te'tragonally** *adv*

Tetragrammaton (ˌtɛtrə'græmət°n) *n Bible.* the Hebrew name for God consisting of the four consonants Y H V H (or Y H W H). It is usually transliterated as *Jehovah* or *Yahweh.* Sometimes shortened to **Tetragram.** [C14: from Gk, from *tetragrammatos* having four letters]

tetrahedron (ˌtɛtrə'hi:drən) *n, pl* **tetrahedrons** *or* **tetrahedra** (-drə). a solid figure having four triangular plane faces. A **regular tetrahedron** has faces that are equilateral triangles. [C16: from NL, from LGk *tetraedron*]
▸ˌ**tetra'hedral** *adj*

tetralogy (tɛ'trælədʒɪ) *n, pl* **tetralogies.** a series of four related works, as in drama or opera. [C17: from Gk *tetralogia*]

tetramerous (tɛ'træmərəs) *adj Biol.* having or consisting of four parts. [C19: from NL *tetramerus,* from Gk *tetramerēs*]

tetrameter (tɛ'træmɪtə) *n Prosody.* **1** a line of verse consisting of four metrical feet. **2** a verse composed of such lines.

tetraplegia (ˌtɛtrə'pli:dʒɪə) *n* another name for **quadriplegia.**
▸ˌ**tetra'plegic** *adj*

tetraploid ('tɛtrəˌplɔɪd) *Genetics.* ◆ *adj* **1** having four times the haploid number of chromosomes in the nucleus. ◆ *n* **2** a tetraploid organism, nucleus, or cell.

tetrapod ('tɛtrəˌpɒd) *n* **1** any vertebrate that has four limbs. **2** a device consisting of four arms radiating from a central point: three arms form a supporting tripod and the fourth is vertical.

tetrapterous (tɛ'træptərəs) *adj* having four wings. [C19: from NL *tetrapterus,* from Gk *tetrapteros,* from TETRA- + *pteron* wing]

tetrarch ('tɛtrɑ:k) *n* **1** the ruler of one fourth of a country. **2** a subordinate ruler. **3** any of four joint rulers. [C14: from Gk *tetrarkhēs;* see TETRA-, -ARCH]
▸**tetrarchate** (tɛ'trɑ:ˌkeɪt, -kɪt) *n* ▸**te'trarchic** *adj* ▸'**tetrarchy** *n*

tetrastich ('tɛtrəˌstɪk) *n* a poem, stanza, or strophe that consists of four lines. [C16: via L from Gk *tetrastikhon,* from TETRA- + *stikhos* row]
▸**tetrastichic** (ˌtɛtrə'stɪkɪk) *or* **tetrastichal** (tɛ'træstɪk°l) *adj*

tetravalent (ˌtɛtrə'veɪlənt) *adj Chem.* **1** having a valency of four. **2** Also: **quadrivalent.** having four valencies.
▸ˌ**tetra'valency** *n*

tetrode ('tɛtrəʊd) *n* an electronic valve having four electrodes.

tetroxide (tɛ'trɒksaɪd) *n* any oxide that contains four oxygen atoms per molecule.

tetryl ('tɛtrɪl) *n* a yellow crystalline explosive solid, trinitrophenylmethylnitramine, used in detonators.

Teucrian ('tju:krɪən) *n, adj* another word for **Trojan.**

Teut. *abbrev. for* Teuton(ic).

Teuton ('tju:tən) *n* **1** a member of an ancient Germanic people from Jutland who migrated to S Gaul in the 2nd century B.C. **2** a member of any people speaking a Germanic language, esp. a German. ◆ *adj* **3** Teutonic. [C18: from L *Teutonī* the Teutons, of Gmc origin]

Teutonic (tju:'tɒnɪk) *adj* **1** characteristic of or relating to the German people. **2** of the ancient Teutons. **3** (not used in linguistics) of or relating to the Germanic languages.

Tex-Mex ('tɛksˌmɛks) *adj* of, relating to, or denoting the Texan version of something Mexican, such as music, food, or language.

text ⓣ (tɛkst) *n* **1** the main body of a printed or written work as distinct from commentary, notes, illustrations, etc. **2** the words of something printed, written, or displayed on a visual display unit. **3** the original exact wording of a work as distinct from a revision or translation. **4** a short passage of the Bible used as a starting point for a sermon. **5** the topic or subject of a discussion or work. **6** short for **textbook. 7** any novel, play, etc., prescribed as part of a course of study. [C14: from Med. L *textus* version, from L *textus* texture, from *texere* to compose]

textbook ('tɛkstˌbʊk) *n* a book used as a standard source of information on a particular subject.
▸'**textˌbookish** *adj*

textile ('tɛkstaɪl) *n* **1** any fabric or cloth, esp. woven. **2** raw material suitable to be made into cloth. ◆ *adj* **3** of or relating to fabrics. [C17: from L *textilis* woven, from *texere* to weave]

textual ('tɛkstjʊəl) *adj* **1** of or relating to a text or texts. **2** based on a text.
▸'**textually** *adv*

textual criticism *n* **1** the scholarly study of manuscripts, esp. of the Bible, in an effort to establish the original text. **2** literary criticism emphasizing a close analysis of the text.

textualism ('tɛkstjʊəˌlɪzəm) *n* **1** doctrinaire adherence to a text, esp. of the Bible. **2** textual criticism, esp. of the Bible.
▸'**textualist** *n, adj*

texture ⓣ ('tɛkstʃə) *n* **1** the surface of a material, esp. as perceived by the sense of touch. **2** the structure, appearance, and feel of a woven fabric. **3** the general structure and disposition of the constituent parts of something: *the texture of a cake.* **4** the distinctive character or quality of something: *the texture of life in America.* ◆ *vb* **textures, texturing, textured. 5** (*tr*) to give a distinctive texture to. [C15: from L *textūra* web, from *texere* to weave]
▸'**textural** *adj* ▸'**texturally** *adv*

TGAT ('ti:gæt) *n* (in Britain) *acronym for* Task Group on Assessment and Testing: a group that advises on assessment and testing within the National Curriculum.

TGV (ˌti:dʒi:'vi:, *French* teʒeve) (in France) *abbrev. for* train à grande vitesse: a high-speed passenger train.

TGWU (in Britain) *abbrev. for* Transport and General Workers' Union.

Th *the chemical symbol for* thorium.

Th. *abbrev. for* Thursday.

-th[1] *suffix forming nouns.* **1** (*from verbs*) indicating an action or its consequence: *growth.* **2** (*from adjectives*) indicating a quality: *width.* [from OE *-thu, -tho*]

-th[2] *or* **-eth** *suffix.* forming ordinal numbers: *fourth; thousandth.* [from OE *-(o)tha, -(o)the*]

Thai (taɪ) *adj* **1** of Thailand, its people, or their language. ◆ *n* **2** (*pl* **Thais** *or* **Thai**) a native or inhabitant of Thailand. **3** the language of Thailand, sometimes classified as belonging to the Sino-Tibetan family.

thalamus ('θæləməs) *n, pl* **thalami** (-ˌmaɪ). **1** either of the two contiguous egg-shaped masses of grey matter at the base of the brain. **2** both of these masses considered as a functional unit. **3** the receptacle or torus of a flower. [C18: from L, from Gk *thalamos* inner room]
▸**thalamic** (θə'læmɪk) *adj*

thalassaemia *or US* **thalassemia** (ˌθælə'si:mɪə) *n* a hereditary disease resulting from defects in the synthesis of the red blood pigment haemoglobin. [NL, from Gk *thalassa* sea + -AEMIA, it being esp. prevalent round the eastern Mediterranean]

thalassic (θə'læsɪk) *adj* of or relating to the sea, esp. to small or inland seas. [C19: from F *thalassique,* from Gk *thalassa* sea]

THESAURUS

tetchy *adj* = **irritable**, bad-tempered, cantankerous, captious, crabbed, cross, fretful, grumpy, impatient, irascible, liverish, peevish, peppery, petulant, quarrelsome, quick-tempered, ratty (*Brit. & NZ inf.*), short-tempered, snappish, snappy, splenetic, sullen, testy, touchy, waspish

tête-à-tête *n* **1a** = **private conversation**, chat, confab (*inf.*), cosy chat, parley, private word, talk ◆ *adv* **3** = **in private**, intimately, privately

tether *n* **1** = **rope**, bond, chain, fastening, fetter, halter, lead, leash, restraint, shackle **3 at the end of one's tether** = **exasperated**, at one's wits' end, at the limit of one's endurance, exhausted, finished, out of patience ◆ *vb* **4** = **tie**, bind, chain, fasten, fetter, leash, manacle, picket, restrain, rope, secure, shackle

text *n* **1** = **contents**, body, main body, matter **2** = **words**, wording **4** = **passage**, paragraph, sentence, verse **5** = **subject**, argument, matter, motif, theme, topic **6** = **reference book**, reader, source, textbook

texture *n* **1-4** = **feel**, character, composition, consistency, constitution, fabric, grain, make, quality, structure, surface, tissue, weave

thaler (ˈtɑːlə) *n, pl* **thaler** *or* **thalers.** a former German, Austrian, or Swiss silver coin. [from G; see DOLLAR]

Thalia (θəˈlaɪə) *n Greek myth.* **1** the Muse of comedy and pastoral poetry. **2** one of the three Graces, the others are Aglaia and Euphrosyne. [C17: via L from Gk, from *thaleia* blooming]

thalidomide (θəˈlɪdəˌmaɪd) *n* **a** a drug formerly used as a sedative and hypnotic but withdrawn from use when found to cause abnormalities in developing fetuses. **b** (*as modifier*): *a thalidomide baby.* [C20: from *thali(mi)do(glutari)mide*]

thallium (ˈθælɪəm) *n* a soft malleable highly toxic white metallic element. Symbol: Tl; atomic no.: 81; atomic wt.: 204.37. [C19: from NL, from Gk *thallos* a green shoot; from the green line in its spectrum]

thallus (ˈθæləs) *n, pl* **thalli** (ˈθælaɪ) *or* **thalluses.** the undifferentiated vegetative body of algae, fungi, and lichens. [C19: from L, from Gk *thallos* green shoot, from *thallein* to bloom]
▸ **ˈthalloid** *adj*

thalweg *or* **talweg** (ˈtɑːlvɛg) *n Geog., rare.* **1** the longitudinal outline of a riverbed from source to mouth. **2** the line of steepest descent from any point on the land surface. [C19: from G *Thal* or *Tal* valley + *Weg* way]

than (ðæn; *unstressed* ðən) *conj* (*coordinating*), *prep* **1** used to introduce the second element of a comparison, the first element of which expresses difference: *shorter than you.* **2** used after adverbs such as *rather* or *sooner* to introduce a rejected alternative in an expression of preference: *rather than be imprisoned, I shall die.* [OE *thanne*]

> **USAGE NOTE** In formal English, *than* is usually regarded as a conjunction governing an unexpressed verb: *he does it far better than I (do).* The case of any pronoun therefore depends on whether it is the subject or object of the unexpressed verb: *she likes him more than I (like him); she likes him more than (she likes) me.* However in ordinary speech and writing *than* is usually treated as a preposition and is followed by the object form of a pronoun: *my brother is younger than me.*

thanatology (ˌθænəˈtɒlədʒɪ) *n* the scientific study of death and its related phenomena. [C19: from Gk *thanatos* death + -LOGY]

thanatopsis (ˌθænəˈtɒpsɪs) *n* a meditation on death, as in a poem. [C19: from Gk *thanatos* death + *opsis* a view]

thane *or* (*less commonly*) **thegn** (θeɪn) *n* **1** (in Anglo-Saxon England) a member of an aristocratic class who held land from the king or from another nobleman in return for certain services. **2** (in medieval Scotland) a person of rank holding land from the king. [OE *thegn*]
▸ **thanage** (ˈθeɪnɪdʒ) *n*

thank Ⓣ (θæŋk) *vb* (*tr*) **1** to convey feelings of gratitude to. **2** to hold responsible: *he has his creditors to thank for his bankruptcy.* [OE *thancian*]

thankful Ⓣ (ˈθæŋkful) *adj* grateful and appreciative.
▸ **ˈthankfully** *adv* ▸ **ˈthankfulness** *n*

> **USAGE NOTE** The use of *thankfully* to mean *fortunately* was formerly considered incorrect by many people, but has now become acceptable in informal contexts.

thankless Ⓣ (ˈθæŋklɪs) *adj* **1** receiving no thanks or appreciation. **2** ungrateful.
▸ **ˈthanklessly** *adv* ▸ **ˈthanklessness** *n*

thanks Ⓣ (θæŋks) *pl n* **1** an expression of appreciation or gratitude. **2** **thanks to.** because of: *thanks to him we lost the match.* ◆ *interj* **3** *Inf.* an exclamation expressing gratitude.

thanksgiving (ˈθæŋksˌgɪvɪŋ; *US* θæŋksˈgɪv-) *n* **1** the act of giving thanks. **2** a formal public expression of thanks to God.

Thanksgiving Day *n* an annual day of holiday celebrated in thanksgiving to God on the fourth Thursday of November in the United States, and on the second Monday of October in Canada. Often shortened to **Thanksgiving.**

thar (tɑː) *n* a variant spelling of **tahr.**

that (ðæt; *unstressed* ðət) *determiner* (*used before a sing n*) **1a** used preceding a noun that has been mentioned or is understood: *that idea of yours.* **1b** (*as pronoun*): *don't eat that.* **2a** used preceding a noun that denotes something more remote or removed: *that building over there is for sale.* **2b** (*as pronoun*): *that is John and this is his wife.* **3** used to refer to something that is familiar: *that old chap from across the street.* **4** **and (all) that.** *Inf.* everything connected with the subject mentioned: *he knows a lot about building and that.* **5** **at that.** (*completive-intensive*) additionally, all things considered, or nevertheless: *I might decide to go at that.* **6** **like that. 6a** effortlessly: *he gave me the answer just like that.* **6b** of such a nature, character, etc.: *he paid for all our tickets — he's like that.* **7** **that is. 7a** to be precise. **7b** in other words. **7c** for example. **8** **that's that.** there is no more to be done, discussed, etc. ◆ *conj* (*subordinating*) **9** used to introduce a noun clause: *I believe that you'll come.* **10** used to introduce: **10a** a clause of purpose: *they fought that others might have peace.* **10b** a clause of result: *he laughed so hard that he cried.* **10c** a clause after an understood sentence expressing desire, indignation, or amazement: *oh, that I had never lived!* ◆ *adv* **11** used to reinforce the specification of a precise degree already mentioned: *go just that fast and you should be safe.* **12** Also: **all that.** (*usually used with a negative*) *Inf.* (intensifier): *he wasn't that upset at the news.* **13** *Dialect.* (intensifier): *the cat was that weak after the fight.* ◆ *pron* **14** used to introduce a restrictive relative clause: *the book that we want.* **15** used to introduce a clause with the verb *to be* to emphasize the extent to which the preceding noun is applicable: *genius that she is, she outwitted the computer.* [OE *thæt*]

> **USAGE NOTE** Precise stylists maintain a distinction between *that* and *which: that* is used as a relative pronoun in restrictive clauses and *which* in nonrestrictive clauses. In *the book that is on the table is mine,* the clause *that is on the table* is used to distinguish one particular book (the one on the table) from another or others (which may be anywhere, but not on the table). In *the book, which is on the table, is mine,* the *which* clause is merely descriptive or incidental. The more formal the level of language, the more important it is to preserve the distinction between the two relative pronouns; but in informal or colloquial usage, the words are often used interchangeably.

thatch (θætʃ) *n* **1a** Also called: **thatching.** a roofing material that consists of straw, reed, etc. **1b** a roof made of such a material. **2** anything resembling this, such as the hair of the head. **3** Also called: **thatch palm.** any of various palms with leaves suitable for thatching. ◆ *vb* **4** to cover with thatch. [OE *theccan* to cover]
▸ **ˈthatcher** *n*

Thatcherism (ˈθætʃəˌrɪzəm) *n* the policies of monetarism, privatization, and self-help promoted by Margaret Thatcher, British prime minister (1979–90).
▸ **ˈThatcherˌite** *n, adj*

thaumatology (ˌθɔːməˈtɒlədʒɪ) *n* the study of or a treatise on miracles. [C19: from Gk *thaumato-* combining form of *thauma* a wonder, marvel + -LOGY]

thaumatrope (ˈθɔːməˌtrəʊp) *n* a toy in which partial pictures on the two sides of a card appear to merge when the card is twirled rapidly. [C19: from Gk *thaumato-* (see THAUMATOLOGY) + -TROPE]
▸ **thaumatropical** (ˌθɔːməˈtrɒpɪkᵊl) *adj*

thaumaturge (ˈθɔːməˌtɜːdʒ) *n Rare.* a performer of miracles; magician. [C18: from Med. L *thaumaturgus,* from Gk *thaumatourgos* miracle-working]
▸ **ˌthaumaˈturgic** *adj* ▸ **ˈthaumaˌturgy** *n*

thaw Ⓣ (θɔː) *vb* **1** to melt or cause to melt: *the snow thawed.* **2** to become or cause to become unfrozen; defrost. **3** (*intr*) to be the case that the ice or snow is melting: *it's thawing fast.* **4** (*intr*) to become more relaxed or friendly. ◆ *n* **5** the act or process of thawing. **6** a spell of relatively warm weather, causing snow or ice to melt. **7** an increase in relaxation or friendliness. [OE *thawian*]

ThD *abbrev. for* Doctor of Theology.

the[1] (*stressed or emphatic* ðiː; *unstressed before a consonant* ðə; *unstressed before a vowel* ðɪ) *determiner* (*article*) **1** used preceding a noun that has been previously specified: *the pain should disappear soon.* Cf. **a**[1]. **2** used to indicate a particular person, object, etc.: *ask the man standing outside.* Cf. **a**[1]. **3** used preceding certain nouns associated with one's culture, society, or community: *to go to the doctor; to listen to the news.* **4** used preceding present participles and adjectives when they function as nouns: *the singing is awful.* **5** used preceding titles and certain uniquely specific or proper nouns: *the United States; the Chairman.* **6** used preceding a qualifying adjective or noun in certain names or titles: *Edward the First.* **7** used preceding a noun to make it refer to its class generically: *the white seal is hunted for its fur.* **8** used instead of *my, your, her,* etc., with parts of the body: *take me by the hand.* **9** (usually stressed) the best, only, or most remarkable: *Harry's is the club in this town.* **10** used with proper nouns when qualified: *written by the young Hardy.* **11** another word for **per:** *fifty pence the pound.* **12** *Often facetious or derog.* my; our: *the wife goes out on Thursdays.* **13** used preceding a unit of time in phrases or titles indicating an outstanding person, event, etc.: *housewife of the year.* [ME, from OE *thē,* a demonstrative adjective that later superseded *sē* (masculine singular) and *sēo, sio* (feminine singular)]

the[2] (ðə, ðɪ) *adv* **1** (often foll. by *for*) used before comparative adjectives or adverbs for emphasis: *she looks the happier for her trip.* **2** used correlatively before each of two comparative adjectives or adverbs to indicate equality: *the sooner you come, the better; the more I see you, the more I love you.* [OE *thī, thȳ*]

theanthropism (θiːˈænθrəˌpɪzəm) *n* **1** the ascription of human traits or characteristics to a god or gods. **2** *Christian theol.* the doctrine of the union of the divine and human natures in the single person of Christ. [C19: from Ecclesiastical Gk *theanthrōpos* (from *theos* god + *anthrōpos* man) + -ISM]
▸ **theanthropic** (ˌθiːænˈθrɒpɪk) *adj*

THESAURUS

thank *vb* **1 = say thank you,** express gratitude, show gratitude, show one's appreciation

thankful *adj* **= grateful,** appreciative, beholden, indebted, in (someone's) debt, obliged, pleased, relieved
Antonyms *adj* thankless, unappreciative, ungrateful

thankless *adj* **1 = unrewarding,** fruitless, unappreciated, unprofitable, unrequited, useless
Antonyms *adj* fruitful, productive, profitable, rewarding, useful, worthwhile

thanks *pl n* **1 = gratitude,** acknowledgment, appreciation, Brownie points, credit, gratefulness, recognition, thanksgiving **2 thanks to = because of,** as a result of, by reason of, due to, owing to, through

thaw *vb* **1, 2 = melt,** defrost, dissolve, liquefy, soften, unfreeze, warm
Antonyms *vb* chill, congeal, freeze, harden, solidify, stiffen

thearchy ('θiːɑːkɪ) *n, pl* **thearchies.** rule or government by God or gods; theocracy. [C17: from Church Gk *thearkhia;* see THEO-, -ARCHY]

theatre *or US* **theater** ('θɪətə) *n* **1** a building designed for the performance of plays, operas, etc. **2** a large room or hall, usually with a raised platform and tiered seats for an audience. **3** a room in a hospital equipped for surgical operations. **4** plays regarded collectively as a form of art. **5 the theatre.** the world of actors, theatrical companies, etc. **6** a setting for dramatic or important events. **7** writing that is suitable for dramatic presentation: *a good piece of theatre.* **8** *US, Austral., & NZ.* the usual word for **cinema** (sense 1). **9** a major area of military activity. **10** a circular or semicircular open-air building with tiers of seats. [C14: from L *theātrum,* from Gk *theatron* place for viewing, from *theasthai* to look at]

theatre-in-the-round *n, pl* **theatres-in-the-round.** a theatre with seats arranged around a central acting area.

theatre of cruelty *n* a type of theatre that seeks to communicate a sense of pain, suffering, and evil, using gesture, movement, sound, and symbolism rather than language.

theatre of the absurd *n* drama in which normal conventions and dramatic structure are modified in order to present life as irrational.

theatrical ➊ (θɪ'ætrɪkᵊl) *adj* **1** of or relating to the theatre or dramatic performances. **2** exaggerated and affected in manner or behaviour; histrionic.
▸**the,atri'cality** *or* **the'atricalness** *n* ▸**the'atrically** *adv*

theatricals (θɪ'ætrɪkᵊlz) *pl n* dramatic performances, esp. as given by amateurs.

theatrics (θɪ'ætrɪks) *n* (*functioning as sing*) **1** the art of staging plays. **2** exaggerated mannerisms or displays of emotions.

thebaine ('θiːbə,iːn) *n* a poisonous white crystalline alkaloid, extracted from opium. [C19: from NL *thebaia* opium of Thebes (with reference to Egypt as a chief source of opium) + -INE²]

Theban ('θiːbən) *adj* **1** of or relating to Thebes, (in ancient Greece) the chief city of Boeotia, or (in ancient Egypt) a city on the Nile, at various times the capital. ◆ *n* **2** a native or inhabitant of either of these cities.

theca ('θiːkə) *n, pl* **thecae** (-siː). **1** *Bot.* an enclosing organ, cell, or spore case. **2** *Zool.* a hard outer covering, such as the container of a coral polyp. [C17: from L *thēca,* from Gk *thēkē* case]
▸**'thecate** *adj*

thecodont ('θiːkə,dɒnt) *adj* **1** (of mammals and certain reptiles) having teeth that grow in sockets. **2** of or relating to teeth of this type. ◆ *n* **3** any of various extinct reptiles of Triassic times, having teeth set in sockets: they gave rise to the dinosaurs, crocodiles, pterodactyls, and birds. [C20: NL *Thecodontia,* from Gk *thēkē* case + -ODONT]

thé dansant *French.* (te dɑ̃sɑ̃) *n, pl* ***thés dansant*** (te dɑ̃sɑ̃). a dance held while afternoon tea is served, popular in the 1920s and 1930s. [lit.: dancing tea]

thee (ðiː) *pron* **1** the objective form of **thou**¹. **2** (*subjective*) *Rare.* refers to the person addressed: used mainly by members of the Society of Friends. [OE *thē*]

theft ➊ (θɛft) *n* **1** the dishonest taking of property belonging to another person with the intention of depriving the owner permanently of its possession. **2** *Rare.* something stolen. [OE *thēofth*]

thegn (θeɪn) *n* a less common variant of **thane.**

theine ('θiːiːn, -ɪn) *n* caffeine, esp. when present in tea. [C19: from NL *thea* tea + -INE²]

their (ðɛə) *determiner* **1** of or associated in some way with them: *their own clothes; she tried to combat their mocking her.* **2** belonging to or associated with people in general: *in many countries they wash their clothes in the river.* **3** belonging to or associated with an indefinite antecedent such as *one, whoever,* or *anybody: everyone should bring their own lunch.* [C12: from ON *theira*]

> **USAGE NOTE** See at **they.**

theirs (ðɛəz) *pron* **1** something or someone belonging to or associated with them: *theirs is difficult.* **2** something or someone belonging to or associated with an indefinite antecedent such as *one, whoever,* or *anybody: everyone thinks theirs is best.* **3 of theirs.** belonging to or associated with them.

theism ('θiːɪzəm) *n* **1** the belief in one God as the creator and ruler of the universe. **2** the belief in the existence of a God or gods. [C17: from Gk *theos* god + -ISM]
▸**'theist** *n, adj* ▸**the'istic** *or* **the'istical** *adj*

them (ðɛm; *unstressed* ðəm) *pron* **1** (*objective*) refers to things or people other than the speaker or people addressed: *I'll kill them; what happened to them?* ◆ *determiner* **2** a nonstandard word for **those:** *three of them oranges.* [OE *thǣm,* infl. by ON *theim*]

> **USAGE NOTE** See at **me**¹, **they.**

thematic apperception test *n Psychol.* a projective test in which drawings of interacting people are shown and the person being tested is asked to make up a story about them.

theme ➊ (θiːm) *n* **1** an idea or topic expanded in a discourse, discussion, etc. **2** (in literature, music, art, etc.) a unifying idea, image, or motif, repeated or developed throughout a work. **3** *Music.* a group of notes forming a recognizable melodic unit, often used as the basis of the musical material in a composition. **4** a short essay, esp. one set as an exercise for a student. **5** *Grammar.* another word for **root**¹ (sense 8) or **stem**¹ (sense 7). **6** (*modifier*) planned or designed round one unifying subject, image, etc.: *a theme holiday.* ◆ *vb* **themes, theming, themed.** (*tr*) **7** to design, decorate, etc., in accordance with a theme. [C13: from L *thema,* from Gk: deposit, from *tithenai* to lay down]
▸**thematic** (θɪ'mætɪk) *adj*

theme park *n* an area planned as a leisure attraction, in which all the displays, buildings, activities, etc., are based on one subject.

theme song *n* **1** a melody used, esp. in a film score, to set a mood, introduce a character, etc. **2** another term for **signature tune.**

themselves (ðəm'sɛlvz) *pron* **1a** the reflexive form of *they* or *them.* **1b** (intensifier): *the team themselves voted on it.* **2** (*preceded by a copula*) their normal or usual selves: *they don't seem themselves any more.* **3** Also: **themself.** *Not standard.* a reflexive form of an indefinite antecedent such as *one, whoever,* or *anybody: everyone has to look after themselves.*

then (ðɛn) *adv* **1** at that time; over that period of time. **2** (*sentence modifier*) in that case; that being so: *then why don't you ask her? go on then, take it.* ◆ *sentence connector.* **3** after that; with that: *then John left the room.* ◆ *n* **4** that time: *from then on.* ◆ *adj* **5** (*prenominal*) existing, functioning, etc., at that time: *the then prime minister.* [OE *thenne*]

thenar ('θiːnɑː) *n* **1** the palm of the hand. **2** the fleshy area of the palm at the base of the thumb. [C17: via NL from Gk]

thence (ðɛns) *adv* **1** from that place. **2** Also: **thenceforth** ('ðɛns'fɔːθ). from that time or event; thereafter. **3** therefore. [C13 *thannes,* from *thanne,* from OE *thanon*]

thenceforward ('ðɛns'fɔːwəd) *or* **thenceforwards** *adv* from that time or place on.

theo- *or before a vowel* **the-** *combining form.* indicating God or gods: *theology.* [from Gk *theos* god]

theobromine (,θiːəʊ'brəʊmiːn, -mɪn) *n* a white crystalline alkaloid that occurs in tea and cacao: used to treat coronary heart disease and headaches. [C18: from NL *theobroma* genus of trees, lit.: food of the gods]

theocentric (,θɪə'sɛntrɪk) *adj Theol.* having God as the focal point of attention.

theocracy (θɪ'ɒkrəsɪ) *n, pl* **theocracies. 1** government by a deity or by a priesthood. **2** a community under such government.
▸**'theo,crat** *n* ▸**,theo'cratic** *adj*

theocrasy (θɪ'ɒkrəsɪ) *n* **1** a mingling into one of deities or divine attributes previously regarded as distinct. **2** the union of the soul with God in mysticism. [C19: from Gk *theokrasia,* from THEO- + *-krasia* from *krasis* a blending]

theodicy (θɪ'ɒdɪsɪ) *n, pl* **theodicies.** the branch of theology concerned with defending the attributes of God against objections resulting from the existence of physical and moral evil. [C18: coined by Leibnitz in F as *théodicée,* from THEO- + Gk *dikē* justice]
▸**the,odi'cean** *adj*

theodolite (θɪ'ɒdə,laɪt) *n* a surveying instrument for measuring horizontal and vertical angles, consisting of a small tripod-mounted telescope. Also called (in the US and Canada): **transit.** [C16: from NL *theodolitus,* from ?]
▸**theodolitic** (θɪ,ɒdə'lɪtɪk) *adj*

theogony (θɪ'ɒgənɪ) *n, pl* **theogonies. 1** the origin and descent of the gods. **2** an account of this. [C17: from Gk *theogonia*]
▸**theogonic** (,θɪə'gɒnɪk) *adj* ▸**the'ogonist** *n*

theol. *abbrev. for:* **1** theologian. **2** theological. **3** theology.

theologian (,θɪə'ləʊdʒɪən) *n* a person versed in or engaged in the study of theology.

theological ➊ (,θɪə'lɒdʒɪkᵊl) *adj* of, relating to, or based on theology.
▸**,theo'logically** *adv*

theological virtues *pl n* those virtues that are infused into man by a special grace of God, specifically faith, hope, and charity.

theologize *or* **theologise** (θɪ'ɒlə,dʒaɪz) *vb* **theologizes, theologizing, theologized** *or* **theologises, theologising, theologised. 1** (*intr*) to speculate upon theological subjects or engage in theological study or discussion. **2** (*tr*) to render theological or treat from a theological point of view.
▸**the,ologi'zation** *or* **the,ologi'sation** *n* ▸**the'olo,gizer** *or* **the'olo,giser** *n*

theology (θɪ'ɒlədʒɪ) *n, pl* **theologies. 1** the systematic study of the existence and nature of the divine and its relationship to other beings. **2** the systematic study of Christian revelation concerning God's nature and purpose. **3** a specific system, form, or branch of this study. [C14: from LL *theologia,* from L]
▸**the'ologist** *n*

THESAURUS

theatrical *adj* **1 = dramatic,** dramaturgic, scenic, Thespian **2 = exaggerated,** actorly *or* actressy, affected, artificial, camp (*inf.*), ceremonious, dramatic, hammy (*inf.*), histrionic, mannered, melodramatic, ostentatious, overdone, pompous, showy, stagy, stilted, unreal

Antonyms *adj* ≠ **exaggerated:** natural, plain, simple, straightforward, unaffected, unassuming, unexaggerated, unpretentious, unsophisticated

theft *n* **1 = stealing,** embezzlement, fraud, larceny, pilfering, purloining, rip-off (*sl.*), robbery, swindling, thievery, thieving

theme *n* **1 = subject,** argument, burden, idea, keynote, matter, subject matter, text, thesis, topic **2 = motif,** leitmotif, recurrent image, unifying idea **4 = essay,** composition, dissertation, exercise, paper

theological *adj* **= religious,** divine, doctrinal, ecclesiastical

theomachy (θɪ'ɒməkɪ) *n, pl* **theomachies.** a battle among the gods or against them. [C16: from Gk *theomakhia,* from THEO- + *makhē* battle]

theomancy ('θiːəʊˌmænsɪ) *n* divination or prophecy by an oracle or by people directly inspired by a god.

theomania (ˌθɪə'meɪnɪə) *n* religious madness, esp. when it takes the form of believing oneself to be a god.
▸ˌ**theo'maniˌac** *n*

theophany (θɪ'ɒfənɪ) *n, pl* **theophanies.** a visible manifestation of a deity to man. [C17: from LL *theophania,* from LGk, from THEO- + *phainein* to show]
▸**theophanic** (ˌθɪə'fænɪk) *adj*

theophylline (ˌθɪə'fɪliːn, -ɪn) *n* a white crystalline alkaloid that is an isomer of theobromine: it occurs in plants such as tea. [C19: from THEO(BROMINE) + PHYLLO- + -INE[2]]

theorem ❶ ('θɪərəm) *n* a statement or formula that can be deduced from the axioms of a formal system by means of its rules of inference. [C16: from LL *theōrēma,* from Gk: something to be viewed, from *theōrein* to view]
▸**theorematic** (ˌθɪərə'mætɪk) *or* **theoremic** (ˌθɪə'rɛmɪk) *adj*

theoretical ❶ (ˌθɪə'rɛtɪkᵊl) *or* **theoretic** *adj* **1** of or based on theory. **2** lacking practical application or actual existence; hypothetical. **3** using or dealing in theory; impractical.
▸ˌ**theo'retically** *adv*

theoretician (ˌθɪərɪ'tɪʃən) *n* a student or user of the theory rather than the practical aspects of a subject.

theoretics (ˌθɪə'rɛtɪks) *n* (*functioning as sing or pl*) the theory of a particular subject.

theorize ❶ *or* **theorise** ('θɪəˌraɪz) *vb* **theorizes, theorizing, theorized** *or* **theorises, theorising, theorised.** (*intr*) to produce or use theories; speculate.
▸**'theorist** *n* ▸ˌ**theori'zation** *or* ˌ**theori'sation** *n* ▸**'theoˌrizer** *or* **'theoˌriser** *n*

theory ❶ ('θɪərɪ) *n, pl* **theories. 1** a system of rules, procedures, and assumptions used to produce a result. **2** abstract knowledge or reasoning. **3** a conjectural view or idea: *I have a theory about that.* **4** an ideal or hypothetical situation (esp. in **in theory**). **5** a set of hypotheses related by logical or mathematical arguments to explain a wide variety of connected phenomena in general terms: *the theory of relativity.* **6** a nontechnical name for **hypothesis.** [C16: from LL *theōria,* from Gk: a sight, from *theōrein* to gaze upon]

theory of games *n* a mathematical theory concerned with the optimum choice of strategy in situations involving a conflict of interest. Also called: **game theory.**

theosophy (θɪ'ɒsəfɪ) *n* **1** any of various religious or philosophical systems claiming to be based on or to express an intuitive insight into the divine nature. **2** the system of beliefs of the Theosophical Society founded in 1875, claiming to be derived from the sacred writings of Brahmanism and Buddhism. [C17: from Med. L *theosophia,* from LGk; see THEO-, -SOPHY]
▸**theosophical** (ˌθɪə'sɒfɪkᵊl) *or* ˌ**theo'sophic** *adj* ▸**the'osophist** *n*

therapeutic ❶ (ˌθɛrə'pjuːtɪk) *adj* **1** of or relating to the treatment of disease; curative. **2** serving or performed to maintain health: *therapeutic abortion.* [C17: from NL *therapeuticus,* from Gk, from *therapeuein* to minister to, from *theraps* an attendant]
▸ˌ**thera'peutically** *adv*

therapeutics (ˌθɛrə'pjuːtɪks) *n* (*functioning as sing*) the branch of medicine concerned with the treatment of disease.

therapy ❶ ('θɛrəpɪ) *n, pl* **therapies. a** the treatment of physical, mental, or social disorders or disease. **b** (*in combination*): *physiotherapy.* [C19: from NL *therapia,* from Gk *therapeia* attendance; see THERAPEUTIC]
▸**'therapist** *n*

Theravada (ˌθɛrə'vɑːdə) *n* the southern school of Buddhism, the name preferred by Hinayana Buddhists. [from Pali: doctrine of the elders]

there (ðɛə) *adv* **1** in, at, or to that place, point, case, or respect: *we never go there; I agree with you there.* ◆ *pron* **2** used as a grammatical subject with some verbs, esp. *be,* when the true subject follows the verb: *there is a girl in that office.* ◆ *adj* **3** (*postpositive*) who or which is in that place or position: *that boy there did it.* **4 all there.** (*predicative*) of normal intelligence. **5 so there.** an exclamation that usually follows a declaration of refusal or defiance. **6 there you are. 6a** an expression used when handing a person something requested or desired. **6b** an exclamation of triumph. ◆ *n* **7** that place: *near there.* ◆ *interj* **8** an expression of sympathy, as in consoling a child: *there, there, dear.* [OE *thǣr*]

USAGE NOTE In correct usage, the verb should agree with the number of the subject in such constructions as *there is a man waiting* and *there are several people waiting.* However, where the subject is compound, it is common in speech to use the singular as in *there's a police car and an ambulance outside.*

thereabouts ('ðɛərəˌbaʊts) *or US* **thereabout** *adv* near that place, time, amount, etc.

thereafter (ˌðɛər'ɑːftə) *adv* from that time on or after that time.

thereat (ˌðɛər'æt) *adv Rare.* **1** at that point or time. **2** for that reason.

thereby (ˌðɛə'baɪ, 'ðɛəˌbaɪ) *adv* **1** by that means; because of that. **2** *Arch.* thereabouts.

therefor (ˌðɛə'fɔː) *adv Arch.* for this, that, or it.

therefore ❶ ('ðɛəˌfɔː) *sentence connector.* **1** thus; hence: *those people have their umbrellas up; therefore, it must be raining.* **2** consequently; as a result.

therefrom (ˌðɛə'frɒm) *adv Arch.* from that or there: *the roads that lead therefrom.*

therein (ˌðɛər'ɪn) *adv Formal or law.* in or into that place, thing, etc.

thereinto (ˌðɛər'ɪntuː) *adv Formal or law.* into that place, circumstance, etc.

thereof (ˌðɛər'ɒv) *adv Formal or law.* **1** of or concerning that or it. **2** from or because of that.

thereon (ˌðɛər'ɒn) *adv Arch.* thereupon.

thereto (ˌðɛə'tuː) *adv* **1** *Formal or law.* to that or it. **2** *Obs.* in addition to that.

theretofore (ˌðɛətʊ'fɔː) *adv Formal or law.* before that time; previous to that.

thereunder (ˌðɛər'ʌndə) *adv Formal or law.* **1** (in documents, etc.) below that or it; subsequently in that; thereafter. **2** under the terms or authority of that.

thereupon (ˌðɛərə'pɒn) *adv* **1** immediately after that; at that point. **2** *Formal or law.* upon that thing, point, subject, etc.

therewith (ˌðɛə'wɪθ, -'wɪð) *or* **therewithal** *adv* **1** *Formal or law.* with or in addition to that. **2** a less common word for **thereupon** (sense 1). **3** *Arch.* by means of or on account of that.

therianthropic (ˌθɪərɪən'θrɒpɪk) *adj* **1** (of certain mythical creatures or deities) having a partly animal, partly human form. **2** of or relating to such creatures or deities. [C19: from Gk *thērion* wild animal + *anthrōpos* man]
▸**therianthropism** (ˌθɪərɪ'ænθrəˌpɪzəm) *n*

theriomorphic (ˌθɪərɪəʊ'mɔːfɪk) *adj* (esp. of a deity) possessing or depicted in the form of a beast. [C19: from Gk *thēriomorphos,* from *thērion* wild animal + *morphē* shape]

therm (θɜːm) *n Brit.* a unit of heat equal to 100 000 British thermal units. One therm is equal to $1.055\ 056 \times 10^8$ joules. [C19: from Gk *thermē* heat]

thermae ('θɜːmiː) *pl n* public baths or hot springs, esp. in ancient Greece or Rome. [C17: from L, from Gk *thermai,* pl. of *thermē* heat]

thermal ('θɜːməl) *adj* **1** Also: **thermic.** of, caused by, or generating heat. **2** hot or warm: *thermal baths.* **3** (of garments) specially made so as to have exceptional heat-retaining qualities: *thermal underwear.* ◆ *n* **4** a column of rising air caused by local unequal heating of the land surface, and used by gliders and birds to gain height. **5** (*pl*) thermal garments, esp. underclothes.
▸**'thermally** *adv*

thermal barrier *n* an obstacle to flight at very high speeds as a result of the heating effect of air friction. Also called: **heat barrier.**

thermal conductivity *n* a measure of the ability of a substance to conduct heat.

thermal efficiency *n* the ratio of the work done by a heat engine to the energy supplied to it.

thermal equator *n* an imaginary line round the earth running through the point on each meridian with the highest average temperature.

thermal imaging *n* the use of heat-sensitive equipment to detect or provide images of people or things.

thermalize *or* **thermalise** ('θɜːməˌlaɪz) *vb* **thermalizes, thermalizing, thermalized** *or* **thermalises, thermalising, thermalised.** *Physics.* to undergo or cause to undergo a process in which neutrons lose energy in a moderator and become thermal neutrons.
▸ˌ**thermali'zation** *or* ˌ**thermali'sation** *n*

thermal neutrons *pl n* slow neutrons that are approximately in thermal equilibrium with a moderator.

thermal reactor *n* a nuclear reactor in which most of the fission is caused by thermal neutrons.

thermal shock *n* a fluctuation in temperature causing stress in a material. It often results in fracture, esp. in brittle materials such as ceramics.

thermion ('θɜːmɪən) *n Physics.* an electron or ion emitted by a body at high temperature.

thermionic (ˌθɜːmɪ'ɒnɪk) *adj* of, relating to, or operated by electrons emitted from materials at high temperatures: *a thermionic valve.*

THESAURUS

theorem *n* = **proposition,** deduction, dictum, formula, hypothesis, principle, rule, statement

theoretical *adj* **1-3** = **abstract,** academic, conjectural, hypothetical, ideal, impractical, notional, pure, speculative
Antonyms *adj* applied, experiential, factual, practical, realistic

theorize *vb* = **speculate,** conjecture, formulate, guess, hypothesize, project, propound, suppose

theory *n* **1** = **system,** philosophy, plan, proposal, scheme **2** = **hypothesis,** assumption, conjecture, guess, presumption, speculation, supposition, surmise, thesis
Antonyms *n* ≠ **hypothesis:** certainty, experience, fact, practice, reality

therapeutic *adj* **1-2** = **beneficial,** ameliorative, analeptic, corrective, curative, good, healing, remedial, restorative, salubrious, salutary, sanative
Antonyms *adj* adverse, damaging, destructive, detrimental, harmful

therapist *n* = **healer,** physician

therapy *n* = **remedy,** cure, healing, remedial treatment, treatment

therefore *sentence connector* **1, 2** = **consequently,** accordingly, as a result, ergo, for that reason, hence, so, then, thence, thus, whence

thermionic current *n* an electric current produced between two electrodes as a result of electrons emitted by thermionic emission.

thermionic emission *n* the emission of electrons from very hot solids or liquids.

thermionics (ˌθɜːmɪˈɒnɪks) *n* (*functioning as sing*) the branch of electronics concerned with the emission of electrons by hot bodies and with devices based on this effect.

thermionic valve *or esp. US & Canad.* **tube** *n* an electronic valve in which electrons are emitted from a heated rather than a cold cathode.

thermistor (θɜːˈmɪstə) *n* a semiconductor device having a resistance that decreases rapidly with an increase in temperature. It is used for temperature measurement and control. [C20: from THERMO- + (RES)ISTOR]

Thermit (ˈθɜːmɪt) *or* **Thermite** (ˈθɜːmaɪt) *n Trademark.* a mixture of aluminium powder and a metal oxide, which when ignited produces great heat: used for welding and in incendiary bombs.

thermo- *or before a vowel* **therm-** *combining form.* related to, caused by, or measuring heat: *thermodynamics; thermophile.* [from Gk *thermos* hot, *thermē* heat]

thermobarograph (ˌθɜːməʊˈbærəˌgrɑːf) *n* a device that simultaneously records the temperature and pressure of the atmosphere.

thermobarometer (ˌθɜːməʊbəˈrɒmɪtə) *n* an apparatus that provides an accurate measurement of pressure by observation of the change in the boiling point of a fluid.

thermochemistry (ˌθɜːməʊˈkɛmɪstrɪ) *n* the branch of chemistry concerned with the study and measurement of the heat evolved or absorbed during chemical reactions.
▸ˌ**thermoˈchemical** *adj* ▸ˌ**thermoˈchemist** *n*

thermocline (ˈθɜːməʊˌklaɪn) *n* a temperature gradient in a thermally stratified body of water, such as a lake.

thermocouple (ˈθɜːməʊˌkʌpᵊl) *n* **1** a device for measuring temperature consisting of a pair of wires of different metals or semiconductors joined at both ends. One junction is at the temperature to be measured, the second at a fixed temperature. The electromotive force generated depends upon the temperature difference. **2** a similar device with only one junction between two dissimilar metals or semiconductors.

thermodynamic (ˌθɜːməʊdaɪˈnæmɪk) *or* **thermodynamical** *adj* **1** of or concerned with thermodynamics. **2** determined by or obeying the laws of thermodynamics.

thermodynamic equilibrium *n* the condition of a system in which the quantities that specify its properties, such as pressure, temperature, etc., all remain unchanged.

thermodynamics (ˌθɜːməʊdaɪˈnæmɪks) *n* (*functioning as sing*) the branch of physical science concerned with the interrelationship and interconversion of different forms of energy.

thermodynamic temperature *n* temperature defined in terms of the laws of thermodynamics rather than of the properties of a real material: expressed in kelvins.

thermoelectric (ˌθɜːməʊɪˈlɛktrɪk) *or* **thermoelectrical** *adj* **1** of, relating to, used in, or operated by the conversion of heat energy to electrical energy. **2** of, relating to, used in, or operated by the conversion of electrical energy.

thermoelectric effect *n* another name for the **Seebeck effect.**

thermoelectricity (ˌθɜːməʊɪlɛkˈtrɪsɪtɪ) *n* **1** electricity generated by a thermocouple. **2** the study of the relationship between heat and electrical energy.

thermoelectron (ˌθɜːməʊɪˈlɛktrɒn) *n* an electron emitted at high temperature, as in a thermionic valve.

thermogenesis (ˌθɜːməʊˈdʒɛnɪsɪs) *n* the production of heat by metabolic processes.

thermogram (ˈθɜːməʊˌgræm) *n* **1** *Med.* a picture produced by thermography, using film sensitive to infrared radiation. **2** the record produced by a thermograph.

thermograph (ˈθɜːməʊˌgrɑːf, -ˌgræf) *n* a type of thermometer that produces a continuous record of a fluctuating temperature.

thermography (θɜːˈmɒgrəfɪ) *n* **1** any writing, printing, or recording process involving the use of heat. **2** *Med.* the measurement and recording of heat produced by a part of the body: used in the diagnosis of tumours, esp. of the breast (**mammothermography**), which have increased blood supply and therefore generate more heat than normal tissue. See also **thermogram.**
▸**therˈmographer** *n* ▸**thermographic** (ˌθɜːməʊˈgræfɪk) *adj*

thermojunction (ˌθɜːməʊˈdʒʌŋkʃən) *n* a point of electrical contact between two dissimilar metals across which a voltage appears, the magnitude of which depends on the temperature of the contact and the nature of the metals.

thermolabile (ˌθɜːməʊˈleɪbɪl) *adj* easily decomposed or subject to a loss of characteristic properties by the action of heat.

thermoluminescence (ˌθɜːməʊˌluːmɪˈnɛsəns) *n* phosphorescence of certain materials or objects as a result of heating.

thermolysis (θɜːˈmɒlɪsɪs) *n* **1** *Physiol.* loss of heat from the body. **2** the dissociation of a substance as a result of heating.
▸**thermolytic** (ˌθɜːməʊˈlɪtɪk) *adj*

thermomagnetic (ˌθɜːməʊmægˈnɛtɪk) *adj* of or concerned with the relationship between heat and magnetism, esp. the change in temperature of a body when it is magnetized or demagnetized.

thermometer (θəˈmɒmɪtə) *n* an instrument used to measure temperature, esp. one in which a thin column of liquid, such as mercury, expands and contracts within a graduated sealed tube.
▸**therˈmometry** *n*

thermonuclear (ˌθɜːməʊˈnjuːklɪə) *adj* **1** involving nuclear fusion. **2** involving thermonuclear weapons.

thermonuclear reaction *n* a nuclear fusion reaction occurring at a very high temperature: responsible for the energy produced in the sun, nuclear weapons, and fusion reactors.

thermophile (ˈθɜːməʊˌfaɪl) *or* **thermophil** (ˈθɜːməʊˌfɪl) *n* **1** an organism, esp. a bacterium or plant, that thrives under warm conditions. ◆ *adj* **2** thriving under warm conditions.
▸ˌ**thermoˈphilic** *adj*

thermopile (ˈθɜːməʊˌpaɪl) *n* an instrument for detecting and measuring heat radiation or for generating a thermoelectric current. It consists of a number of thermocouple junctions.

thermoplastic (ˌθɜːməʊˈplæstɪk) *adj* **1** (of a material, esp. a synthetic plastic) becoming soft when heated and rehardening on cooling without appreciable change of properties. ◆ *n* **2** a synthetic plastic or resin, such as polystyrene, with these properties.

Thermos *or* **Thermos flask** (ˈθɜːməs) *n Trademark.* a type of stoppered vacuum flask used to preserve the temperature of its contents.

thermosetting (ˌθɜːməʊˈsɛtɪŋ) *adj* (of a material, esp. a synthetic plastic) hardening permanently after one application of heat and pressure.

thermosiphon (ˌθɜːməʊˈsaɪfən) *n* a system in which a coolant is circulated by convection caused by a difference in density between the hot and cold portions of the liquid.

thermosphere (ˈθɜːməˌsfɪə) *n* an atmospheric layer lying between the mesosphere and the exosphere.

thermostable (ˌθɜːməʊˈsteɪbᵊl) *adj* capable of withstanding moderate heat without loss of characteristic properties.

thermostat (ˈθɜːməˌstæt) *n* **1** a device that maintains a system at a constant temperature. **2** a device that sets off a sprinkler, etc., at a certain temperature.
▸ˌ**thermoˈstatic** *adj* ▸ˌ**thermoˈstatically** *adv*

thermostatics (ˌθɜːməˈstætɪks) *n* (*functioning as sing*) the branch of science concerned with thermal equilibrium.

thermotaxis (ˌθɜːməʊˈtæksɪs) *n* the directional movement of an organism in response to the stimulus of heat.
▸ˌ**thermoˈtaxic** *adj*

thermotropism (ˌθɜːməʊˈtrəʊpɪzəm) *n* the directional growth of a plant in response to the stimulus of heat.
▸ˌ**thermoˈtropic** *adj*

-thermy *n combining form.* indicating heat: *diathermy.* [from NL *-thermia,* from Gk *thermē*]
▸**-thermic** *or* **-thermal** *adj combining form.*

theroid (ˈθɪərɔɪd) *adj* of, relating to, or resembling a beast. [C19: from Gk *thēroeidēs,* from *thēr* wild animal; see -OID]

thesaurus ❶ (θɪˈsɔːrəs) *n, pl* **thesauruses** *or* **thesauri** (-raɪ). **1** a book containing systematized lists of synonyms and related words. **2** a dictionary of selected words or topics. **3** *Rare.* a treasury. [C18: from L, Gk: TREASURE]

these (ðiːz) *determiner* **a** the form of **this** used before a plural noun: *these men.* **b** (*as pronoun*): *I don't much care for these.*

thesis ❶ (ˈθiːsɪs) *n, pl* **theses** (-siːz). **1** a dissertation resulting from original research, esp. when submitted for a degree or diploma. **2** a doctrine maintained in argument. **3** a subject for a discussion or essay. **4** an unproved statement put forward as a premise in an argument. [C16: via LL from Gk: a placing, from *tithenai* to place]

Thespian (ˈθɛspɪən) *adj* **1** of or relating to Thespis, 6th-century B.C. Greek poet. **2** (*usually not cap.*) of or relating to drama and the theatre; dramatic. ◆ *n* (*usually not cap.*) **3** *Often facetious.* an actor or actress.

Thess. *Bible. abbrev. for* Thessalonians.

theta (ˈθiːtə) *n* the eighth letter of the Greek alphabet (Θ, θ). [C17: from Gk]

theurgy (ˈθiːˌɜːdʒɪ) *n, pl* **theurgies. 1** the intervention of a divine or supernatural agency in the affairs of man. **2** beneficent magic as taught by Egyptian Neoplatonists. [C16: from LL *theūrgia,* from LGk *theourgia* the practice of magic, from *theo-* THEO- + *-urgia,* from *ergon* work]
▸**theˈurgic** *or* **theˈurgical** *adj* ▸ˈ**theurgist** *n*

thew (θjuː) *n* **1** muscle, esp. if strong or well-developed. **2** (*pl*) muscular strength. [OE *thēaw*]
▸ˈ**thewless** *adj* ▸ˈ**thewy** *adj*

they (ðeɪ) *pron* (*subjective*) **1** refers to people or things other than the speaker or people addressed: *they fight among themselves.* **2** refers to people in general: *in Australia they have Christmas in the summer.* **3** refers to an indefinite antecedent such as *one, whoever,* or *anybody: if anyone objects, they can go.* [C12 *thei* from ON *their,* masc. nominative pl, equivalent to OE *thā*]

THESAURUS

thesaurus *n* **1-3** = **wordbook**, dictionary, encyclopedia, repository, storehouse, treasury, wordfinder

thesis *n* **1** = **dissertation**, composition, disquisition, essay, monograph, paper, treatise **2** = **proposition**, contention, hypothesis, idea, line of argument, opinion, proposal, theory, view **3** = **subject**, area, theme, topic **4** *Logic* = **premise**, assumption, postulate, proposition, statement, supposition, surmise

USAGE NOTE It was formerly considered correct to use *he, him,* or *his* after pronouns such as *everyone, no-one, anyone,* or *someone* as in *everyone did his best,* but it is now more common to use *they, them,* or *their,* and this use has become acceptable in all but the most formal contexts: *everyone did their best.*

they'd (ðeɪd) *contraction of* they would *or* they had.
they'll (ðeɪl) *contraction of* they will *or* they shall.
they're (ðɛə, 'ðeɪə) *contraction of* they are.
they've (ðeɪv) *contraction of* they have.
thi- *combining form.* a variant of **thio-**.
thiamine ('θaɪəˌmiːn, -mɪn) *or* **thiamin** ('θaɪəmɪn) *n* a white crystalline vitamin that occurs in the outer coat of rice and other grains. It forms part of the vitamin B complex: deficiency leads to nervous disorders and to the disease beriberi. Also called: **vitamin B_1, aneurin.** [C20: THIO- + (VIT)AMIN]
thiazine ('θaɪəˌziːn, -ˌzaɪn) *n* any of a group of organic compounds containing a ring system composed of four carbon atoms, a sulphur atom, and a nitrogen atom.
thiazole ('θaɪəˌzəʊl) *n* **1** a colourless liquid that contains a ring system composed of three carbon atoms, a sulphur atom, and a nitrogen atom. **2** any of a group of compounds derived from this substance that are used in dyes.
thick ➊ (θɪk) *adj* **1** of relatively great extent from one surface to the other: *a thick slice of bread.* **2a** (*postpositive*) of specific fatness: *ten centimetres thick.* **2b** (*in combination*): *a six-inch-thick wall.* **3** having a dense consistency: *thick soup.* **4** abundantly covered or filled: *a piano thick with dust.* **5** impenetrable; dense: *a thick fog.* **6** stupid, slow, or insensitive. **7** throaty or badly articulated: *a voice thick with emotion.* **8** (of accents, etc.) pronounced. **9** *Inf.* very friendly (esp. in **thick as thieves**). **10 a bit thick.** *Brit.* unfair or excessive. ◆ *adv* **11** in order to produce something thick: *to slice bread thick.* **12** profusely; in quick succession (esp. in **thick and fast**). **13 lay it on thick.** *Inf.* **13a** to exaggerate a story, etc. **13b** to flatter excessively. ◆ *n* **14** a thick piece or part. **15 the thick.** the busiest or most intense part. **16 through thick and thin.** in good times and bad. [OE *thicce*]
▸ '**thickish** *adj* ▸ '**thickly** *adv*
thicken ➊ ('θɪkən) *vb* **1** to make or become thick or thicker. **2** (*intr*) to become more involved: *the plot thickened.*
▸ '**thickener** *n*
thickening ('θɪkənɪŋ) *n* **1** something added to a liquid to thicken it. **2** a thickened part or piece.
thicket ➊ ('θɪkɪt) *n* a dense growth of small trees, shrubs, and similar plants. [OE *thiccet*]
thickhead ➊ ('θɪkˌhɛd) *n* **1** a stupid or ignorant person; fool. **2** any of a family of Australian and SE Asian songbirds.
▸ ˌ**thick'headed** *adj*
thickie *or* **thicky** ('θɪkɪ) *n, pl* **thickies.** *Brit. sl.* a variant of **thicko.**
thick-knee *n* another name for **stone curlew.**
thickness ('θɪknɪs) *n* **1** the state or quality of being thick. **2** the dimension through an object, as opposed to length or width. **3** a layer.
thicko ('θɪkəʊ) *n, pl* **thickos** *or* **thickoes.** *Brit. sl.* a slow-witted unintelligent person. Also: **thickie, thicky.**
thickset ➊ (ˌθɪk'sɛt) *adj* **1** stocky in build; sturdy. **2** densely planted or placed. ◆ *n* **3** a rare word for **thicket.**
thick-skinned ➊ *adj* insensitive to criticism or hints; not easily upset or affected.
thick-witted *or* **thick-skulled** *adj* stupid, dull, or slow to learn.
▸ ˌ**thick-'wittedly** *adv* ▸ ˌ**thick-'wittedness** *n*
thief ➊ (θiːf) *n, pl* **thieves** (θiːvz). a person who steals something from another. [OE *thēof*]
▸ '**thievish** *adj*
thieve ➊ (θiːv) *vb* **thieves, thieving, thieved.** to steal (someone's possessions). [OE *thēofian,* from *thēof* thief]
▸ '**thievery** *n* ▸ '**thieving** *adj*
thigh (θaɪ) *n* **1** the part of the leg between the hip and the knee in man. **2** the corresponding part in other vertebrates and insects. ◆ Related adj: **femoral.** [OE *thēh*]
thighbone ('θaɪˌbəʊn) *n* a nontechnical name for the **femur.**
thimble ('θɪmbᵊl) *n* **1** a cap of metal, plastic, etc., used to protect the end of the finger when sewing. **2** any small metal cap resembling this. **3** *Naut.* a loop of metal having a groove at its outer edge for a rope or cable. [OE *thȳmel* thumbstall, from *thūma* thumb]
thimbleful ➊ ('θɪmbᵊlˌfʊl) *n* a very small amount, esp. of a liquid.
thimblerig ('θɪmbᵊlˌrɪg) *n* a game in which the operator rapidly moves about three inverted thimbles, often with sleight of hand, one of which conceals a token, the other player betting on which thimble the token is under. [C19: from THIMBLE + RIG (in obs. sense meaning a trick, scheme)]
▸ '**thimbleˌrigger** *n*
thin ➊ (θɪn) *adj* **thinner, thinnest. 1** of relatively small extent from one side or surface to the other. **2** slim or lean. **3** sparsely placed; meagre: *thin hair.* **4** of low density: *a thin liquid.* **5** weak; poor: *a thin disguise.* **6 thin on the ground.** few in number; scarce. ◆ *adv* **7** in order to produce something thin: *to cut bread thin.* ◆ *vb* **thins, thinning, thinned. 8** to make or become thin or sparse. [OE *thynne*]
▸ '**thinly** *adv* ▸ '**thinness** *n*
thine (ðaɪn) *determiner Arch.* **a** (*preceding a vowel*) of or associated with you (thou): *thine eyes.* **b** (*as pronoun*): *thine is the greatest burden.* [OE *thīn*]
thin-film *adj* (of an electronic component, etc.) composed of one or more extremely thin layers of metal, semiconductor, etc.
thing ➊ (θɪŋ) *n* **1** an object, fact, affair, circumstance, or concept considered as being a separate entity. **2** any inanimate object. **3** an object or entity that cannot or need not be precisely named. **4** *Inf.* a person or animal: *you poor thing.* **5** an event or act. **6** a thought or statement. **7** *Law.* property. **8** a device, means, or instrument. **9** (*often pl*) a posses-

THESAURUS

thick *adj* **1** = **wide,** broad, bulky, deep, fat, solid, substantial **3, 5** = **dense,** close, clotted, coagulated, compact, concentrated, condensed, crowded, deep, heavy, impenetrable, opaque **4** = **full,** abundant, brimming, bristling, bursting, chock-a-block, chock-full, covered, crawling, frequent, numerous, packed, replete, swarming, teeming **6** *Informal* = **stupid,** blockheaded, braindead (*inf.*), brainless, dense, dim-witted (*inf.*), dopey (*inf.*), dozy, dull, insensitive, moronic, obtuse, slow, slow-witted, thickheaded **7** = **hoarse,** distorted, guttural, husky, inarticulate, indistinct, throaty **8** = **strong,** broad, decided, distinct, marked, pronounced, rich **9** *As in* **thick as thieves** *Informal* = **friendly,** buddy-buddy (*sl., chiefly US & Canad.*), chummy (*inf.*), close, confidential, devoted, familiar, hand in glove, inseparable, intimate, matey *or* maty (*Brit. inf.*), on good terms, pally (*inf.*), palsy-walsy (*inf.*), well in (*inf.*) **10 a bit thick** *Brit. informal* = **unreasonable,** excessive, over the score (*inf.*), too much, unfair, unjust
Antonyms *adj* ≠ **wide:** narrow, slight, slim, thin ≠ **dense:** clear, diluted, runny, thin, watery, weak ≠ **full:** bare, clear, devoid of, empty, free from, sparse, thin ≠ **stupid:** articulate, brainy, bright, clever, intellectual, intelligent, quick-witted, sharp, smart ≠ **hoarse:** articulate, clear, distinct, sharp, shrill, thin ≠ **strong:** faint, slight, vague, weak ≠ **friendly:** antagonistic, distant, hostile, unfriendly
thicken *vb* **1** = **set,** cake, clot, coagulate, condense, congeal, deepen, gel, inspissate (*arch.*), jell
Antonyms *vb* dilute, thin, water down, weaken
thicket *n* = **wood,** brake, clump, coppice, copse, covert, grove, hurst (*arch.*), spinney (*Brit.*), woodland
thickhead *n* **1** *Slang* = **idiot,** berk (*Brit. sl.*), blockhead, bonehead (*sl.*), chump, clot (*Brit. inf.*), dimwit (*inf.*), dipstick, divvy (*Brit. sl.*), dolt, dope (*inf.*), dummy (*sl.*), dunce, dunderhead, fathead (*inf.*), fool, imbecile, lamebrain (*inf.*), moron, numbskull *or* numskull, pillock (*Brit. sl.*), pinhead (*sl.*), plank (*Brit. sl.*)
thickheaded *adj* **1** = **idiotic,** blockheaded, braindead (*inf.*), brainless, dense, dim-witted (*inf.*), doltish, dopey (*inf.*), dozy (*Brit. inf.*), moronic, obtuse, slow, slow-witted, stupid, thick
thickset *adj* **1** = **stocky,** beefy (*inf.*), brawny, bulky, burly, heavy, muscular, powerfully built, strong, stubby, sturdy, well-built **2** = **dense,** closely packed, densely planted, solid, thick
Antonyms *adj* ≠ **stocky:** angular, bony, gangling, gaunt, lanky, rawboned, scraggy, scrawny, weedy (*inf.*)
thick-skinned *adj* = **insensitive,** callous, case-hardened, hard-boiled (*inf.*), hardened, impervious, stolid, tough, unfeeling, unsusceptible
Antonyms *adj* concerned, feeling, sensitive, tender, thin-skinned, touchy
thief *n* = **robber,** bandit, burglar, cheat, cracksman (*sl.*), crook (*inf.*), embezzler, footpad (*arch.*), housebreaker, larcenist, mugger (*inf.*), pickpocket, pilferer, plunderer, purloiner, shoplifter, stealer, swindler
thieve *vb* = **steal,** blag (*sl.*), filch, knock off (*sl.*), lift (*inf.*), misappropriate, nick (*sl., chiefly Brit.*), peculate, pilfer, pinch (*inf.*), plunder, poach, purloin, rob, run off with, snitch (*sl.*), swipe (*sl.*)
thievery *n* = **stealing,** banditry, burglary (*inf.*), larceny, pilfering, plundering, robbery, shoplifting, theft, thieving
thieving *adj* = **thievish,** larcenous, light-fingered, predatory, rapacious, sticky-fingered (*inf.*)
thimbleful *n* = **drop,** capful, dab, dash, dram, jot, modicum, nip, pinch, sip, *soupçon,* spoonful, spot, taste, toothful
thin *adj* **1** = **narrow,** attenuate, attenuated, fine, threadlike **2** = **slim,** bony, emaciated, lank, lanky, lean, light, meagre, scraggy, scrawny, skeletal, skin and bone, skinny, slender, slight, spare, spindly, thin as a rake, undernourished, underweight **3** = **meagre,** deficient, scanty, scarce, scattered, skimpy, sparse, wispy **4** = **fine,** delicate, diaphanous, filmy, flimsy, gossamer, see-through, sheer, translucent, transparent, unsubstantial **4** = **watery,** dilute, diluted, rarefied, runny, weak, wishy-washy (*inf.*) **5** = **unconvincing,** feeble, flimsy, inadequate, insufficient, lame, poor, scant, scanty, shallow, slight, superficial, unsubstantial, weak ◆ *vb* **8** = **reduce,** attenuate, cut back, dilute, diminish, emaciate, prune, rarefy, refine, trim, water down, weaken, weed out
Antonyms *adj* ≠ **narrow:** heavy, thick ≠ **slim:** bulky, corpulent, fat, heavy, obese, stout ≠ **meagre:** abundant, adequate, plentiful, profuse ≠ **fine:** bulky, dense, heavy, strong, substantial, thick ≠ **watery:** concentrated, dense, strong, thick, viscous ≠ **unconvincing:** adequate, convincing, strong, substantial
thing *n* **1** = **object,** affair, article, being, body, circumstance, concept, entity, fact, matter, part, portion, something, substance **5** = **happening,** act, deed, event, eventuality, feat, incident, occurrence, phenomenon, proceeding **8** = **device,** apparatus, contrivance, gadget, implement, instrument, machine, means, mechanism, tool **9** *often plural* = **possessions,** baggage, belongings, bits and pieces, clobber (*Brit. sl.*), clothes, effects, equipment, gear, goods, impedimenta, luggage, odds and ends, paraphernalia, stuff **10** *Informal* = **obsession,** attitude, bee in one's bonnet, fetish, fixation, hang-up (*inf.*), *idée fixe,* mania, phobia, preoccupation, quirk

sion, article of clothing, etc. **10** *Inf.* a preoccupation or obsession (esp. in **have a thing about**). **11** an activity or mode of behaviour satisfying to one's personality (esp. in **do one's (own) thing**). **12 make a thing of.** exaggerate the importance of. **13 the thing.** the latest fashion. [OE *thing* assembly]

thing-in-itself *n* (in the philosophy of Immanuel Kant (1724–1804), German idealist philosopher) reality regarded apart from human knowledge and perception.

thingumabob *or* **thingamabob** ('θɪŋəmə,bɒb) *n Inf.* a person or thing the name of which is unknown, temporarily forgotten, or deliberately overlooked. Also: **thingumajig, thingamajig,** *or* **thingummy.** [C18: from THING, with humorous suffix]

think ❶ (θɪŋk) *vb* **thinks, thinking, thought. 1** (*tr; may take a clause as object*) to consider, judge, or believe: *he thinks my ideas impractical.* **2** (*intr;* often foll. by *about*) to exercise the mind as in order to make a decision; ponder. **3** (*intr*) to be capable of conscious thought: *man is the only animal that thinks.* **4** to remember; recollect. **5** (*intr;* foll. by *of*) to make the mental choice (of): *think of a number.* **6** (*may take a clause as object or an infinitive*) **6a** to expect; suppose. **6b** to be considerate enough (to do something): *he did not think to thank them.* **7** (*intr*) to focus the attention on being: *think big.* **8 think twice.** to consider carefully before deciding. ◆ *n* **9** *Inf.* a careful, open-minded assessment. **10** (*modifier*) *Inf.* characterized by or involving thinkers, thinking, or thought. ◆ See also **think over, think up.** [OE *thencan*]
▸ **'thinkable** *adj* ▸ **'thinker** *n*

thinking ❶ ('θɪŋkɪŋ) *n* **1** opinion or judgment. **2** the process of thought. ◆ *adj* **3** (*prenominal*) using or capable of using intelligent thought: *thinking people.* **4 put on one's thinking cap.** to ponder a matter or problem.

think over ❶ *vb* (*tr, adv*) to ponder or consider.

think-tank *n Inf.* a group of specialists commissioned to undertake intensive study and research into specified problems.

think up ❶ *vb* (*tr, adv*) to invent or devise.

thinner ('θɪnə) *n* (*often pl, functioning as sing*) a solvent, such as turpentine, added to paint or varnish to dilute it, reduce its opacity or viscosity, or increase its penetration.

thin-skinned ❶ *adj* sensitive to criticism or hints; easily upset or affected.

thio- *or before a vowel* **thi-** *combining form.* sulphur, esp. denoting the replacement of an oxygen atom with a sulphur atom: *thiol; thiosulphate.* [from Gk *theion* sulphur]

thiol ('θaɪɒl) *n* any of a class of sulphur-containing organic compounds with the formula RSH, where R is an organic group.

thionine ('θaɪəʊ,niːn, -,naɪn) *or* **thionin** ('θaɪənɪn) *n* **1** a crystalline derivative of thiazine used as a violet dye to stain microscope specimens. **2** any of a class of related dyes. [C19: by shortening, from *ergothioneine*]

thiopentone sodium (,θaɪəʊ'pɛntəʊn) *or* **thiopental sodium** (,θaɪəʊ'pɛntæl) *n* a barbiturate drug used as an intravenous general anaesthetic. Also called: **Sodium Pentothal.**

thiophen ('θaɪəʊ,fɛn) *or* **thiophene** ('θaɪəʊ,fiːn) *n* a colourless liquid heterocyclic compound found in the benzene fraction of coal tar and manufactured from butane and sulphur.

thiosulphate (,θaɪəʊ'sʌlfeɪt) *n* any salt of thiosulphuric acid.

thiosulphuric acid (,θaɪəʊsʌl'fjʊərɪk) *n* an unstable acid known only in solutions and in the form of its salts. Formula: $H_2S_2O_3$.

thiouracil (,θaɪəʊ'jʊərəsɪl) *n* a white crystalline water-insoluble substance with an intensely bitter taste, used in medicine to treat hyperthyroidism. [from THIO- + *uracil* (URO- + AC(ETIC) + -IL(E))]

thiourea (,θaɪəʊ'jʊərɪə) *n* a white crystalline substance used in photographic fixing, rubber vulcanization, and the manufacture of synthetic resins.

third (θɜːd) *adj* (*usually prenominal*) **1a** coming after the second in numbering, position, etc.; being the ordinal number of *three:* often written 3rd. **1b** (*as n*): *the third got a prize.* **2** rated, graded, or ranked below the second level. **3** denoting the third from lowest forward ratio of a gearbox in a motor vehicle. ◆ *n* **4a** one of three equal parts of an object, quantity, etc. **4b** (*as modifier*): *a third part.* **5** the fraction equal to one divided by three (1/3). **6** the forward ratio above second of a gearbox in a motor vehicle. **7a** the interval between one note and another three notes away from it counting inclusively along the diatonic scale. **7b** one of two notes constituting such an interval in relation to the other. **8** *Brit.* an honours degree of the third and usually the lowest class. Full term: **third class honours degree.** ◆ *adv* **9** Also: **thirdly.** in the third place. [OE *thirda,* var. of *thridda;* rel. to OFrisian *thredda,* OSaxon *thriddio*]
▸ **'thirdly** *adv*

Third Age *n* **the.** old age, esp. when viewed as a period of opportunity for learning something new or for other new developments: *University of the Third Age.*

third class *n* **1** the class or grade next in value, quality, etc., to the second. ◆ *adj* (**third-class** *when prenominal*). **2** of the class or grade next in value, quality, etc., to the second. ◆ *adv* **3** by third-class transport, etc.

third degree *n Inf.* torture or bullying, esp. used to extort confessions or information.

third-degree burn *n Pathol.* the most severe type of burn, involving the destruction of both epidermis and dermis.

third dimension *n* the dimension of depth by which a solid object may be distinguished from a two-dimensional drawing or picture of it.

third eyelid *n* another name for **nictitating membrane.**

Third International *n* another name for **Comintern.**

third-line forcing *n* the deprecated practice of forcing a buyer to purchase a supply of a product that he does not want as a condition of supplying him with the product he does want.

third man *n Cricket.* **a** a fielding position on the off side near the boundary behind the batsman's wicket. **b** a fielder in this position.

Third Market *n Stock Exchange.* a new small market designed to meet the needs of young growing British companies for raising capital.

Third Order *n RC Church.* a religious society of laymen affiliated to one of the religious orders and following a mitigated form of religious rule.

third party *n* **1** a person who is involved by chance or only incidentally in a legal proceeding, agreement, or other transaction. ◆ *adj* **2** *Insurance.* providing protection against liability caused by accidental injury or death of other persons.

third person *n* a grammatical category of pronouns and verbs used when referring to objects or individuals other than the speaker or his addressee or addressees.

third-rate ❶ *adj* mediocre or inferior.

third reading *n* (in a legislative assembly) **1** *Brit.* the process of discussing the committee's report on a bill. **2** *US.* the final consideration of a bill.

Third World *n* the less economically and industrially advanced countries of Africa, Asia, and Latin America collectively. Also called: **developing world.**

thirst ❶ (θɜːst) *n* **1** a craving to drink, accompanied by a feeling of dryness in the mouth and throat. **2** an eager longing, craving, or yearning. ◆ *vb* (*intr*) **3** to feel a thirst. [OE *thyrstan,* from *thurst*]

thirsty ❶ ('θɜːstɪ) *adj* **thirstier, thirstiest. 1** feeling a desire to drink. **2** dry; arid. **3** (foll. by *for*) feeling an eager desire. **4** causing thirst.
▸ **'thirstily** *adv* ▸ **'thirstiness** *n*

thirteen ('θɜː'tiːn) *n* **1** the cardinal number that is the sum of ten and three and is a prime number. **2** a numeral, 13, XIII, etc., representing this number. **3** something representing or consisting of 13 units. ◆ *determiner* **4a** amounting to thirteen. **4b** (*as pronoun*): *thirteen of them fell.* [OE *threotēne*]
▸ **'thir'teenth** *adj, n*

thirteenth chord *n* a chord much used in jazz and pop, consisting of a major or minor triad upon which are superimposed the seventh, ninth, eleventh, and thirteenth above the root. Often shortened to **thirteenth.**

thirty ('θɜːtɪ) *n, pl* **thirties. 1** the cardinal number that is the product of ten and three. **2** a numeral, 30, XXX, etc., representing this number. **3** (*pl*) the numbers 30-39, esp. the 30th to the 39th year of a person's life or of a century. **4** the amount or quantity that is three times as big as ten. **5** something representing or consisting of 30 units. ◆ *determiner* **6a** amounting to thirty. **6b** (*as pronoun*): *thirty are broken.* [OE *thrītig*]
▸ **'thirtieth** *adj, n*

Thirty-nine Articles *pl n* a set of formulas defining the doctrinal position of the Church of England, drawn up in the 16th century.

THESAURUS

think *vb* **1** = **believe,** conceive, conclude, consider, deem, determine, esteem, estimate, guess (*inf., chiefly US & Canad.*), hold, imagine, judge, reckon, regard, suppose, surmise **2** = **ponder,** brood, cerebrate, chew over (*inf.*), cogitate, consider, contemplate, deliberate, have in mind, meditate, mull over, muse, obsess, rack one's brains, reason, reflect, revolve, ruminate, turn over in one's mind, weigh up **4** = **remember,** call to mind, recall, recollect **6a** = **anticipate,** envisage, expect, foresee, imagine, plan for, presume, suppose ◆ *n* **9** *Informal* = **consideration,** assessment, contemplation, deliberation, look, reflection

thinkable *adj* **2** = **possible,** conceivable, feasible, imaginable, likely, reasonable, within the bounds of possibility
Antonyms *adj* absurd, impossible, inconceivable, not on (*inf.*), out of the question, unlikely, unreasonable, unthinkable

thinking *n* **1** = **reasoning,** assessment, conclusions, conjecture, idea, judgment, opinion, outlook, philosophy, position, theory, thoughts, view ◆ *adj* **3** = **thoughtful,** contemplative, cultured, intelligent, meditative, philosophical, ratiocinative, rational, reasoning, reflective, sophisticated

think over *vb* = **consider,** chew over (*inf.*), consider the pros and cons of, contemplate, give thought to, mull over, ponder, rack one's brains, reflect upon, turn over in one's mind, weigh up

think up *vb* = **devise,** come up with, concoct, contrive, create, dream up, imagine, improvise, invent, manufacture, trump up, visualize

thin-skinned *adj* = **easily hurt,** hypersensitive, quick to take offence, sensitive, soft, susceptible, tender, touchy, vulnerable
Antonyms *adj* callous, hard, heartless, insensitive, obdurate, stolid, thick-skinned, tough, unfeeling

third-rate *adj* = **mediocre,** bad, cheap-jack, duff (*Brit. inf.*), indifferent, inferior, low-grade, no great shakes (*inf.*), not much cop (*inf.*), poor, poor-quality, ropey *or* ropy (*Brit. inf.*), shoddy

thirst *n* **1** = **thirstiness,** craving to drink, drought, dryness **2** = **craving,** ache, appetite, desire, eagerness, hankering, hunger, keenness, longing, lust, passion, yearning, yen (*inf.*)
Antonyms *n* ≠ **craving:** apathy, aversion, disinclination, dislike, distaste, loathing, revulsion

thirsty *adj* **2** = **parched,** arid, dehydrated, dry **3** *with* **for** = **eager,** athirst, avid, burning, craving, desirous, dying, greedy, hankering, hungry, itching, longing, lusting, thirsting, yearning

thirty-second note *n* the usual US and Canad. name for **demisemiquaver.**

thirty-twomo (ˌθɜːtɪˈtuːməʊ) *n, pl* **thirty-twomos.** a book size resulting from folding a sheet of paper into 32 leaves or 64 pages.

this (ðɪs) *determiner (used before a sing n)* **1a** used preceding a noun referring to something or someone that is closer: *look at this picture.* **1b** *(as pronoun): take this.* **2a** used preceding a noun that has just been mentioned or is understood: *this plan of yours won't work.* **2b** *(as pronoun): I first saw this on Sunday.* **3a** used to refer to something about to be said, read, etc.: *consider this argument.* **3b** *(as pronoun): listen to this.* **4a** the present or immediate: *this time you'll know better.* **4b** *(as pronoun): before this, I was mistaken.* **5** *Inf.* an emphatic form of **a** or **the**[1]: *I saw this big brown bear.* **6 this and that.** various unspecified and trivial actions, matters, objects, etc. **7 with** *(or* **at***)* **this.** after this. ◆ *adv* **8** used with adjectives and adverbs to specify a precise degree that is about to be mentioned: *go just this fast and you'll be safe.* [OE *thēs, thēos, this* (masc, fem, neuter sing)]

thistle (ˈθɪsᵊl) *n* **1** any of a genus of plants of the composite family, having prickly-edged leaves, dense flower heads, and feathery hairs on the seeds: the national emblem of Scotland. **2** any of various similar or related plants. [OE *thīstel*]
▸ **ˈthistly** *adj*

thistledown (ˈθɪsᵊlˌdaʊn) *n* the mass of feathery plumed seeds produced by a thistle.

thither (ˈðɪðə) *or* **thitherward** *adv Obs. or formal.* to or towards that place; in that direction. [OE *thider*, var. of *thæder*, infl. by *hider* hither]

thitherto (ˌðɪðəˈtuː, ˈðɪðəˌtuː) *adv Obs. or formal.* until that time.

thixotropic (ˌθɪksəˈtrɒpɪk) *adj* (of fluids and gels) having a reduced viscosity when stress is applied, as when stirred: *thixotropic paints.* [C20: from Gk *thixis* the act of touching + -TROPIC]
▸ **thixotropy** (θɪkˈsɒtrəpɪ) *n* ▸ **thixotrope** (ˈθɪksəˌtrəʊp) *n*

tho' *or* **tho** (ðəʊ) *conj, adv US or poetic.* a variant spelling of **though.**

thole[1] (θəʊl) *or* **tholepin** (ˈθəʊlˌpɪn) *n* a wooden pin or one of a pair, set upright in the gunwales of a rowing boat to serve as a fulcrum in rowing. [OE *tholl*]

thole[2] (θəʊl) *vb* **tholes, tholing, tholed. 1** *(tr) Scot. & N English dialect.* to put up with; bear. **2** an archaic word for **suffer.** [OE *tholian*]

tholos (ˈθəʊlɒs) *n, pl* **tholoi** (-lɔɪ). a dry-stone beehive-shaped tomb associated with the Mycenaean culture of Greece from the 16th to the 12th centuries B.C. [C17: from Gk]

Thomism (ˈtəʊmɪzəm) *n* the system of philosophy and theology developed by Saint Thomas Aquinas in the 13th century.

Thompson sub-machine-gun (ˈtɒmsən) *n Trademark.* a .45 calibre sub-machine-gun. [C20: after John T. *Thompson* (1860–1940), US Army officer, its co-inventor]

-thon *suffix forming nouns.* indicating a large-scale event or operation of a specified kind: *telethon.* [C20: on the pattern of MARATHON]

thong (θɒŋ) *n* **1** a thin strip of leather or other material. **2** a whip or whiplash, esp. one made of leather. **3** *US, Canad., Austral., & NZ.* the usual name for **flip-flop** (sense 5). [OE *thwang*]

thoracic (θɔːˈræsɪk) *adj* of, near, or relating to the thorax.

thoracic duct *n* the major duct of the lymphatic system, beginning below the diaphragm and ascending in front of the spinal column to the base of the neck.

thoraco- *or before a vowel* **thorac-** *combining form.* thorax: *thoracotomy.*

thoracoplasty (ˈθɔːrəkəʊˌplæstɪ) *n, pl* **thoracoplasties. 1** plastic surgery of the thorax. **2** surgical removal of several ribs or a part of them to permit the collapse of a diseased lung.

thorax (ˈθɔːræks) *n, pl* **thoraxes** *or* **thoraces** (ˈθɔːrəˌsiːz, θɔːˈreɪsiːz). **1** the part of the human body enclosed by the ribs. **2** the corresponding part in other vertebrates. **3** the part of an insect's body between the head and abdomen. [C16: via L from Gk *thōrax* breastplate, chest]

thorium (ˈθɔːrɪəm) *n* a silvery-white radioactive metallic element. It is used in electronic equipment and as a nuclear power source. Symbol: Th; atomic no.: 90; atomic wt.: 232.04. [C19: NL, *Thor* Norse god of thunder + -IUM]
▸ **ˈthoric** *adj*

thorium dioxide *n* a white powder used in incandescent mantles. Also called: **thoria.**

thorium series *n* a radioactive series that starts with thorium–232 and ends with lead–208.

thorn Ⓣ (θɔːn) *n* **1** a sharp pointed woody extension of a stem or leaf. Cf. **prickle** (sense 1). **2** any of various trees or shrubs having thorns, esp. the hawthorn. **3** a Germanic character of runic originus (þ) used in Icelandic to represent the sound of *th*, as in *thin, bath.* **4** this same character as used in Old and Middle English to represent this sound. **5** a source of irritation (esp. in **a thorn in one's side** *or* **flesh**). [OE]
▸ **ˈthornless** *adj*

thorn apple *n* **1** a poisonous plant of the N hemisphere, having white funnel-shaped flowers and spiny fruits. US name: **jimson weed. 2** the fruit of certain types of hawthorn.

thornbill (ˈθɔːnˌbɪl) *n* **1** any of various South American hummingbirds having a thornlike bill. **2** Also called: **thornbill warbler.** any of various Australasian wrens. **3** any of various other birds with thornlike bills.

thorny Ⓣ (ˈθɔːnɪ) *adj* **thornier, thorniest. 1** bearing or covered with thorns. **2** difficult or unpleasant. **3** sharp.
▸ **ˈthornily** *adv* ▸ **ˈthorniness** *n*

thoron (ˈθɔːrɒn) *n* a radioisotope of radon that is a decay product of thorium. Symbol: Tn or ^{220}Rn; atomic no.: 86; half-life: 54.5s. [C20: from THORIUM + -ON]

thorough Ⓣ (ˈθʌrə) *adj* **1** carried out completely and carefully. **2** *(prenominal)* utter: *a thorough bore.* **3** painstakingly careful. [OE *thurh*]
▸ **ˈthoroughly** *adv* ▸ **ˈthoroughness** *n*

thorough bass (beɪs) *n* a bass part underlying a piece of concerted music. Also called: **basso continuo, continuo.** See also **figured bass.**

thoroughbred Ⓣ (ˈθʌrəˌbrɛd) *adj* **1** purebred. ◆ *n* **2** a pedigree animal; purebred. **3** a person regarded as being of good breeding.

Thoroughbred (ˈθʌrəˌbrɛd) *n* a British breed of horse the ancestry of which can be traced to English mares and Arab sires.

thoroughfare Ⓣ (ˈθʌrəˌfɛə) *n* **1** a road from one place to another, esp. a main road. **2** way through, access, or passage: *no thoroughfare.*

thoroughgoing (ˈθʌrəˌgəʊɪŋ) *adj* **1** extremely thorough. **2** *(usually prenominal)* absolute; complete: *thoroughgoing incompetence.*

thoroughpaced (ˈθʌrəˌpeɪst) *adj* **1** (of a horse) showing performing ability in all paces. **2** thoroughgoing.

thorp *or* **thorpe** (θɔːp) *n Obs. except in place names.* a small village. [OE]

those (ðəʊz) *determiner* the form of **that** used before a plural noun. [OE *thās*, pl. of THIS]

thou[1] (ðaʊ) *pron (subjective)* **1** *Arch. or dialect.* refers to the person addressed: used mainly in familiar address. **2** *(usually cap.)* refers to God when addressed in prayer, etc. [OE *thū*]

thou[2] (θaʊ) *n, pl* **thous** *or* **thou. 1** one thousandth of an inch. **2** *Inf.* short for **thousand.**

though Ⓣ (ðəʊ) *conj (subordinating)* **1** (sometimes preceded by *even*) despite the fact that: *though he tries hard, he always fails.* ◆ *adv* **2** nevertheless; however: *he can't dance; he sings well, though.* [OE *theah*]

thought Ⓣ (θɔːt) *vb* **1** the past tense and past participle of **think.** ◆ *n* **2** the act or process of thinking. **3** a concept, opinion, or idea. **4** ideas typical of a particular time or place: *German thought in the 19th century.* **5** application of mental attention; consideration. **6** purpose or intention: *I have no thought of giving up.* **7** expectation: *no thought of reward.* **8** a small amount; trifle: *you could be a thought more enthusiastic.* **9** kindness or regard. [OE *thōht*]

thoughtful Ⓣ (ˈθɔːtfʊl) *adj* **1** considerate in the treatment of other people. **2** showing careful thought. **3** pensive; reflective.
▸ **ˈthoughtfully** *adv* ▸ **ˈthoughtfulness** *n*

THESAURUS

thorn *n* **1** = **prickle**, barb, spike, spine **5** *As in* **thorn in one's side** *or* **flesh** = **irritation**, affliction, annoyance, bane, bother, curse, hassle *(inf.)*, irritant, nuisance, pest, plague, scourge, torment, torture, trouble

thorny *adj* **1** = **prickly**, barbed, bristling with thorns, bristly, pointed, sharp, spiky, spinous, spiny **2** = **troublesome**, awkward, difficult, harassing, hard, irksome, problematic(al), sticky *(inf.)*, ticklish, tough, trying, unpleasant, upsetting, vexatious, worrying

thorough *adj* **1** = **careful**, all-embracing, all-inclusive, assiduous, complete, comprehensive, conscientious, efficient, exhaustive, full, in-depth, intensive, leaving no stone unturned, meticulous, painstaking, scrupulous, sweeping **2** = **complete**, absolute, arrant, deep-dyed *(usually derogatory)*, downright, entire, out-and-out, outright, perfect, pure, sheer, total, unmitigated, unqualified, utter
Antonyms *adj* ≠ **careful:** careless, cursory, half-hearted, haphazard, lackadaisical, sloppy ≠ **complete:** imperfect, incomplete, partial, superficial

thoroughbred *adj* **1** = **purebred**, blood, full-blooded, of unmixed stock, pedigree, pure-blooded
Antonyms *adj* crossbred, crossed, half-breed, hybrid, mongrel, of mixed breed

thoroughfare *n* **1. 2** = **road**, access, avenue, highway, passage, passageway, roadway, street, way

thoroughly *adv* **1** = **carefully**, assiduously, completely, comprehensively, conscientiously, efficiently, exhaustively, from top to bottom, fully, inside out, intensively, leaving no stone unturned, meticulously, painstakingly, scrupulously, sweepingly, through and through, throughout **2** = **completely**, absolutely, downright, entirely, perfectly, quite, totally, to the full, to the hilt, utterly, without reservation
Antonyms *adv* ≠ **carefully:** carelessly, cursorily, half-heartedly, haphazardly, lackadaisically, sloppily ≠ **completely:** imperfectly, incompletely, in part, partly, somewhat, superficially

though *conj* **1** = **although**, albeit, allowing, despite the fact that, even if, even supposing, even though, granted, notwithstanding, tho' *(US or poetic)*, while ◆ *adv* **2** = **nevertheless**, all the same, for all that, however, nonetheless, notwithstanding, still, yet

thought *n* **2** = **thinking**, brainwork, cerebration, cogitation, consideration, contemplation, deliberation, introspection, meditation, musing, navel-gazing *(sl.)*, reflection, regard, rumination **3** = **idea**, assessment, belief, concept, conception, conclusion, conjecture, conviction, estimation, judgment, notion, opinion, thinking, view **5** = **consideration**, attention, heed, regard, scrutiny, study **6** = **intention**, aim, design, idea, notion, object, plan, purpose **7** = **expectation**, anticipation, aspiration, dream, hope, prospect **8** = **little**, dash, jot, small amount, *soupçon*, touch, trifle, whisker *(inf.)* **9** = **kindness**, anxiety, attentiveness, care, compassion, concern, regard, solicitude, sympathy, thoughtfulness

thoughtful *adj* **1** = **considerate**, attentive, caring, helpful, kind, kindly, solicitous, unselfish **2** = **well-thought-out**, astute, canny, careful, cautious, circumspect, deliberate, discreet, heedful, mindful, prudent, wary **3** = **reflective**, contemplative, deliberative, in a brown study, introspective, lost in thought, meditative, musing, pensive, rapt, ruminative, serious, studious, thinking, wistful
Antonyms *adj* ≠ **considerate:** cold-hearted, impolite, inconsiderate, insensitive, neglectful, selfish, uncaring ≠ **well-thought-out:** flippant, heedless,

thoughtless ❶ ('θɔːtlɪs) *adj* **1** inconsiderate. **2** having or showing lack of thought.
▸**'thoughtlessly** *adv* ▸**'thoughtlessness** *n*

thought-out *adj* conceived and developed by careful thought: *a well thought-out scheme.*

thought transference *n Psychol.* another name for **telepathy.**

thousand ('θaʊzənd) *n* **1** the cardinal number that is the product of 10 and 100. **2** a numeral, 1000, 10^3, M, etc., representing this number. **3** (*often pl*) a very large but unspecified number, amount, or quantity. **4** something representing or consisting of 1000 units. ◆ *determiner* **5a** amounting to a thousand. **5b** (*as pronoun*): *a thousand is hardly enough.* ◆ Related adj: **millenary.** [OE *thūsend*]
▸**'thousandth** *adj, n*

Thousand Guineas *n* (*functioning as sing*), usually written **1,000 Guineas.** an annual horse race, restricted to fillies, run at Newmarket in England since 1814.

Thousand Island dressing *n* a salad dressing made from mayonnaise with ketchup, chopped gherkins, etc.

Thracian ('θreɪʃɪən) *n* **1** a member of an ancient Indo-European people who lived in Thrace, an ancient country in the SE corner of the Balkan Peninsula. **2** the ancient language spoken by this people. ◆ *adj* **3** of or relating to Thrace, its inhabitants, or the extinct Thracian language.

thrall ❶ (θrɔːl) *n* **1** Also: **thraldom** *or US* **thralldom** ('θrɔːldəm). the state or condition of being in the power of another person. **2** a person who is in such a state. **3** a person totally subject to some need, desire, appetite, etc. ◆ *vb* **4** (*tr*) to enslave or dominate. [OE *thrǣl* slave]

thrash ❶ (θræʃ) *vb* **1** (*tr*) to beat soundly, as with a whip or stick. **2** (*tr*) to defeat totally; overwhelm. **3** (*intr*) to beat or plunge about in a wild manner. **4** to sail (a boat) against the wind or tide or (of a boat) to sail in this way. **5** another word for **thresh.** ◆ *n* **6** the act of thrashing; beating. **7** *Inf.* a party. ◆ See also **thrash out.** [OE *threscan*]

thrasher[1] ('θræʃə) *n* another name for **thresher** (the shark).

thrasher[2] ('θræʃə) *n* any of various brown thrushlike American songbirds.

thrashing ❶ ('θræʃɪŋ) *n* a physical assault; flogging.

thrash metal *n* a type of very fast very loud rock music that combines elements of heavy metal and punk rock. Often shortened to **thrash.**

thrash out ❶ *vb* (*tr, adv*) to discuss fully or vehemently, esp. in order to come to an agreement.

thrasonical (θrə'sɒnɪkᵊl) *adj Rare.* bragging; boastful. [C16: from L *Thrasō* name of boastful soldier in *Eunuchus,* a play by Terence, from Gk *Thrasōn,* from *thrasus* forceful]
▸**thra'sonically** *adv*

thrawn (θrɔːn) *adj Scot. & N English dialect.* **1** crooked or twisted. **2** stubborn; perverse. [N English dialect, var. of *thrown,* from OE *thrāwan* to twist about, throw]

thread ❶ (θrɛd) *n* **1** a fine strand, filament, or fibre of some material. **2** a fine cord of twisted filaments, esp. of cotton, used in sewing, etc. **3** any of the filaments of which a spider's web is made. **4** any fine line, stream, mark, or piece. **5** the helical ridge on a screw, bolt, nut, etc. **6** a very thin seam of coal or vein of ore. **7** something acting as the continuous link or theme of a whole: *the thread of the story.* **8** the course of an individual's life believed in Greek mythology to be spun, measured, and cut by the Fates. ◆ *vb* **9** (*tr*) to pass (thread, film, tape, etc.) through (something). **10** (*tr*) to string on a thread: *she threaded the beads.* **11** to make (one's way) through or over (something). **12** (*tr*) to produce a screw thread. **13** (*tr*) to pervade: *hysteria threaded his account.* **14** (*intr*) (of boiling syrup) to form a fine thread when poured from a spoon. ◆ See also **threads.** [OE *thrǣd*]
▸**'threader** *n* ▸**'thread,like** *adj*

threadbare ❶ ('θrɛd,bɛə) *adj* **1** (of cloth, clothing, etc.) having the nap worn off so that the threads are exposed; worn out. **2** meagre or poor. **3** hackneyed: *a threadbare argument.* **4** wearing threadbare clothes; shabby.

thread mark *n* a mark put into paper money to prevent counterfeiting, consisting of a pattern of silk fibres.

threads (θrɛdz) *pl n Sl.* clothes.

threadworm ('θrɛd,wɜːm) *n* any of various nematodes, esp. the pinworm.

thready ('θrɛdɪ) *adj* **threadier, threadiest. 1** of or resembling a thread. **2** (of the pulse) barely perceptible; weak. **3** sounding thin, weak, or reedy.
▸**'threadiness** *n*

threat ❶ (θrɛt) *n* **1** a declaration of the intention to inflict harm, pain, or misery. **2** an indication of imminent harm, danger, or pain. **3** a person or thing that is regarded as dangerous or likely to inflict pain or misery. [OE]

threaten ❶ ('θrɛtᵊn) *vb* **1** (*tr*) to be a threat to. **2** to be a menacing indication of (something); portend. **3** (when *tr, may take a clause as object*) to express a threat to (a person or people).
▸**'threatening** *adj* ▸**'threateningly** *adv*

three (θriː) *n* **1** the cardinal number that is the sum of two and one and is a prime number. **2** a numeral, 3, III, (iii), representing this number. **3** something representing or consisting of three units. **4** Also called: **three o'clock.** three hours after noon or midnight. ◆ *determiner* **5a** amounting to three. **5b** (*as pronoun*): *three were killed.* ◆ Related adjs.: **ternary, tertiary, treble, triple.** [OE *thrēo*]

three-card trick *n* a game in which players bet on which of three playing cards is the queen.

three-colour *adj* of or comprising a colour print or a photomechanical process in which a picture is reproduced by superimposing three prints from half-tone plates in inks corresponding to the three primary colours.

three-D *or* **3-D** *n* a three-dimensional effect.

three-decker *n* **1a** anything having three levels or layers. **1b** (*as modifier*): *a three-decker sandwich.* **2** a warship with guns on three decks.

three-dimensional *adj* **1** of, having, or relating to three dimensions. **2** simulating the effect of depth. **3** having volume. **4** lifelike.

threefold ('θriː,fəʊld) *adj* **1** equal to or having three times as many or as much; triple. **2** composed of three parts. ◆ *adv* **3** by or up to three times as many or as much.

three-legged race *n* a race in which pairs of competitors run with their adjacent legs tied together.

threepenny bit *or* **thrupenny bit** ('θrʌpnɪ, -ənɪ, 'θrɛp-) *n* a twelve-sided British coin valued at three old pence, obsolete since 1971.

three-phase *adj* (of an electrical circuit, etc.) having or using three alternating voltages of the same frequency, displaced in phase by 120°.

three-ply *adj* **1** having three layers or thicknesses. **2** (of wool, etc.) three-stranded.

three-point landing *n* an aircraft landing in which the main wheels and the nose or tail wheel touch the ground simultaneously.

three-point turn *n* a complete turn of a motor vehicle using forward and reverse gears alternately, and completed after only three movements.

three-quarter *adj* **1** being three quarters of something. **2** being of three quarters the normal length. ◆ *n* **3** *Rugby.* any of the four players between the fullback and the halfbacks.

three-ring circus *n US.* **1** a circus with three rings for simultaneous performances. **2** a situation of confusion, characterized by a bewildering variety of events or activities.

three Rs *pl n* **the.** the three skills regarded as the fundamentals of education; reading, writing, and arithmetic. [from the humorous spelling *reading, 'riting,* and *'rithmetic*]

threescore ('θriː'skɔː) *determiner* an archaic word for **sixty.**

threesome ❶ ('θriːsəm) *n* **1** a group of three. **2** *Golf.* a match in which a

THESAURUS

irresponsible, rash, thoughtless, unthinking ≠ **reflective:** extrovert, shallow, superficial

thoughtless *adj* **1** = **inconsiderate,** impolite, indiscreet, insensitive, rude, selfish, tactless, uncaring, undiplomatic, unkind **2** = **unthinking,** absent-minded, careless, ditsy *or* ditzy (*sl.*), foolish, heedless, ill-considered, imprudent, inadvertent, inattentive, injudicious, mindless, neglectful, negligent, rash, reckless, regardless, remiss, silly, slapdash, slipshod, stupid, unmindful, unobservant
Antonyms *adj* ≠ **inconsiderate:** attentive, considerate, diplomatic, tactful, thoughtful, unselfish ≠ **unthinking:** considered, intelligent, prudent, smart, well-advised, well-thought-out, wise

thrall *n* **1** = **slavery,** bondage, enslavement, serfdom, servitude, subjection, subjugation, thraldom, vassalage **2** = **slave,** bondservant, bondsman, serf, subject, varlet (*arch.*), vassal

thrash *vb* **1** = **beat,** belt (*inf.*), birch, cane, chastise, clobber (*sl.*), drub, flagellate, flog, give (someone) a (good) hiding (*inf.*), hide (*inf.*), horsewhip, lambast(e), leather, lick (*inf.*), paste (*sl.*), punish, scourge, spank, take a stick to, tan (*sl.*), whip **2** = **defeat,** beat, beat (someone) hollow (*Brit. inf.*), blow out of the water (*sl.*), clobber (*sl.*), crush, drub, hammer (*inf.*), lick (*inf.*), make mincemeat of (*inf.*), maul, overwhelm, paste (*sl.*), rout, run rings around (*inf.*), slaughter (*inf.*), stuff (*sl.*), tank (*sl.*), trounce, wipe the floor with (*inf.*) **3** = **thresh,** flail, heave, jerk, plunge, squirm, toss, toss and turn, writhe

thrashing *n* = **beating,** belting (*inf.*), caning, chastisement, drubbing, flogging, hiding (*inf.*), lashing, pasting (*sl.*), punishment, tanning (*sl.*), whipping

thrash out *vb* = **settle,** argue out, debate, discuss, have out, resolve, solve, talk over

thread *n* **1, 2** = **strand,** cotton, fibre, filament, line, string, yarn **7** = **theme,** course, direction, drift, motif, plot, story line, strain, tenor, train of thought ◆ *vb* **10** = **string 11** = **pass,** ease, inch, loop, meander, pick (one's way), squeeze through

threadbare *adj* **1** = **shabby,** down at heel, frayed, old, ragged, scruffy, tattered, tatty, used, worn, worn-out **3** = **hackneyed,** clichéd, cliché-ridden, common, commonplace, conventional, corny, familiar, overused, stale, stereotyped, stock, tired, trite, well-worn
Antonyms *adj* ≠ **shabby:** brand-new, good, new, smart, unused, well-preserved ≠ **hackneyed:** different, fresh, new, novel, original, unconventional, unfamiliar, unusual

threat *n* **1** = **menace,** commination, intimidatory remark, threatening remark **2** = **warning,** foreboding, foreshadowing, omen, portent, presage, writing on the wall **3** = **danger,** hazard, menace, peril, risk

threaten *vb* **1** = **endanger,** imperil, jeopardize, put at risk, put in jeopardy, put on the line **2** = **foreshadow,** be imminent, be in the air, be in the offing, forebode, hang over, hang over (someone's) head, impend, loom over, portend, presage, warn **3** = **intimidate,** browbeat, bully, cow, lean on (*sl.*), make threats to, menace, pressurize, terrorize, warn
Antonyms *vb* ≠ **intimidate, endanger:** defend, guard, protect, safeguard, shelter, shield

threatening *adj* **2** = **ominous,** baleful, forbidding, grim, inauspicious, sinister **3** = **menacing,** bullying, comminatory, intimidatory, minatory, terrorizing
Antonyms *adj* ≠ **ominous:** auspicious, bright, comforting, encouraging, favourable, promising, propitious, reassuring

threesome *n* **1** = **trio,** triad, trilogy, trine, trinity, triple, triplet, triplex, triptych, triumvirate, triune, troika

single player playing his own ball competes against two others playing on the same ball. **3** any game, etc., for three people. **4** (*modifier*) performed by three.

thremmatology (ˌθrɛməˈtɒlədʒɪ) *n* the science of breeding domesticated animals and plants. [C19: from Gk *thremma* nursling + -LOGY]

threnody (ˈθrɛnədɪ, ˈθriː-) *or* **threnode** (ˈθriːnəʊd, ˈθrɛn-) *n, pl* **threnodies** *or* **threnodes.** an ode, song, or speech of lamentation, esp. for the dead. [C17: from Gk *thrēnōidia,* from *thrēnos* dirge + *ōidē* song]
▸**threnodic** (θrɪˈnɒdɪk) *adj* ▸**threnodist** (ˈθrɛnədɪst, ˈθriː-) *n*

thresh (θrɛʃ) *vb* **1** to beat stalks of ripe corn, etc., either with a hand implement or a machine to separate the grain from the husks and straw. **2** (*tr*) to beat or strike. **3** (*intr;* often foll. by *about*) to toss and turn; thrash. [OE *threscan*]

thresher (ˈθrɛʃə) *n* **1** a person who threshes. **2** short for **threshing machine. 3** any of a genus of large sharks occurring in tropical and temperate seas. They have a very long whiplike tail.

threshing machine *n* a machine for threshing crops.

threshold Ⓣ (ˈθrɛʃəʊld, ˈθrɛʃˌhəʊld) *n* **1** a sill, esp. one made of stone or hardwood, placed at a doorway. **2** any doorway or entrance. **3** the starting point of an experience, event, or venture. **4** *Psychol.* the strength at which a stimulus is just perceived: *the threshold of consciousness.* **5a** a point at which something would stop, take effect, etc. **5b** (*as modifier*): *threshold price; threshold effect.* **6** the minimum intensity or value of a signal, etc., that will produce a response or specified effect. **7** (*modifier*) of a pay agreement, clause, etc., that raises wages to compensate for increases in the cost of living. ◆ Related adj: **liminal.** [OE *therscold*]

threshold agreement *n* an agreement between an employer and employees or their union to increase wages by a specified sum if inflation exceeds a specified level in a specified time.

threw (θruː) *vb* the past tense of **throw.**

thrice (θraɪs) *adv* **1** three times. **2** threefold. **3** *Arch.* greatly. [OE *thrīwa, thrīga*]

thrift Ⓣ (θrɪft) *n* **1** wisdom and caution in the management of money. **2** Also called: **sea pink.** any of a genus of perennial low-growing plants of Europe, W Asia, and North America, having narrow leaves and round heads of pink or white flowers. [C13: from ON: success; see THRIVE]
▸ˈ**thriftless** *adj* ▸ˈ**thriftlessly** *adv*

thrifty Ⓣ (ˈθrɪftɪ) *adj* **thriftier, thriftiest. 1** showing thrift; economical or frugal. **2** *Rare.* thriving or prospering.
▸ˈ**thriftily** *adv* ▸ˈ**thriftiness** *n*

thrill Ⓣ (θrɪl) *n* **1** a sudden sensation of excitement and pleasure. **2** a situation producing such a sensation. **3** a trembling sensation caused by fear or emotional shock. **4** *Pathol.* an abnormal slight tremor. ◆ *vb* **5** to feel or cause to feel a thrill. **6** to tremble or cause to tremble; vibrate or quiver. [OE *thӯrlian* to pierce, from *thyrel* hole]
▸ˈ**thrilling** *adj*

thriller (ˈθrɪlə) *n* a book, film, play, etc., depicting crime, mystery, or espionage in an atmosphere of excitement and suspense.

thrips (θrɪps) *n, pl* **thrips.** any of various small slender-bodied insects typically having piercing mouthparts and feeding on plant sap. [C18: via NL from Gk: woodworm]

thrive Ⓣ (θraɪv) *vb* **thrives, thriving; thrived** *or* **throve; thrived** *or* **thriven** (ˈθrɪvᵊn). (*intr*) **1** to grow strongly and vigorously. **2** to do well; prosper. [C13: from ON *thrīfask* to grasp for oneself, from ?]

thro' *or* **thro** (θruː) *prep, adv Inf. or poetic.* variant spellings of **through.**

throat (θrəʊt) *n* **1a** that part of the alimentary and respiratory tracts extending from the back of the mouth to just below the larynx. **1b** the front part of the neck. **2** something resembling a throat, esp. in shape or function: *the throat of a chimney.* **3 cut one's (own) throat.** to bring about one's own ruin. **4 ram** *or* **force (something) down someone's throat.** to insist that someone listen to or accept (something). ◆ Related adjs.: **guttural, laryngeal.** [OE *throtu*]

throaty Ⓣ (ˈθrəʊtɪ) *adj* **throatier, throatiest. 1** indicating a sore throat; hoarse: *a throaty cough.* **2** of or produced in the throat. **3** deep, husky, or guttural.
▸ˈ**throatily** *adv*

throb Ⓣ (θrɒb) *vb* **throbs, throbbing, throbbed.** (*intr*) **1** to pulsate or beat repeatedly, esp. with increased force. **2** (of engines, drums, etc.) to have a strong rhythmic vibration or beat. ◆ *n* **3** a throbbing, esp. a rapid pulsation as of the heart: *a throb of pleasure.* [C14: ? imit.]

throes Ⓣ (θrəʊz) *pl n* **1** a condition of violent pangs, pain, or convulsions: *death throes.* **2 in the throes of.** struggling with great effort with. [OE *thrāwu* threat]

thrombin (ˈθrɒmbɪn) *n Biochem.* an enzyme that acts on fibrinogen in blood causing it to clot. [C19: from THROMB(US) + -IN]

thrombocyte (ˈθrɒmbəˌsaɪt) *n* another name for **platelet.**
▸**thrombocytic** (ˌθrɒmbəˈsɪtɪk) *adj*

thromboembolism (ˌθrɒmbəʊˈɛmbəˌlɪzəm) *n* the obstruction of a blood vessel by a thrombus that has become detached from its original site.

thrombose (ˈθrɒmbəʊz) *vb* **thromboses, thrombosing, thrombosed.** to become or affect with a thrombus. [C19: back formation from THROMBOSIS]

thrombosis (θrɒmˈbəʊsɪs) *n, pl* **thromboses** (-siːz). **1** the formation or presence of a thrombus. **2** *Inf.* short for **coronary thrombosis.** [C18: from NL, from Gk: curdling, from *thrombousthai* to clot, from *thrombos* THROMBUS]
▸**thrombotic** (θrɒmˈbɒtɪk) *adj*

thrombus (ˈθrɒmbəs) *n, pl* **thrombi** (-baɪ). a clot of coagulated blood that forms within a blood vessel or inside the heart, often impeding the flow of blood. [C17: from NL, from Gk *thrombos* lump, from ?]

throne (θrəʊn) *n* **1** the ceremonial seat occupied by a monarch, bishop, etc., on occasions of state. **2** the power or rank ascribed to a royal person. **3** a person holding royal rank. **4** (*pl; often cap.*) the third of the nine orders into which the angels are divided in medieval angelology. ◆ *vb* **thrones, throning, throned. 5** to place or be placed on a throne. [C13: from OF *trone,* from L *thronus,* from Gk *thronos*]

throng Ⓣ (θrɒŋ) *n* **1** a great number of people or things crowded together. ◆ *vb* **2** to gather in or fill (a place) in large numbers; crowd. **3** (*tr*) to hem in (a person); jostle. [OE *gethrang*]

throstle (ˈθrɒsᵊl) *n* **1** a poetic name for the **song thrush. 2** a spinning machine for wool or cotton in which the fibres are twisted and wound continuously. [OE]

throttle Ⓣ (ˈθrɒtᵊl) *n* **1** Also called: **throttle valve.** any device that controls the quantity of fuel or fuel and air mixture entering an engine. **2** an informal or dialect word for **throat.** ◆ *vb* **throttles, throttling, throttled.** (*tr*) **3** to kill or injure by squeezing the throat. **4** to suppress. **5** to control or restrict (a flow of fluid) by means of a throttle valve. [C14: *throtelen,* from *throte* THROAT]
▸ˈ**throttler** *n*

through Ⓣ (θruː) *prep* **1** going in at one side and coming out at the other side of: *a path through the wood.* **2** occupying or visiting several points scattered around in (an area). **3** as a result of; by means of. **4** *Chiefly US.* up to and including: *Monday through Friday.* **5** during: *through the night.* **6** at the end of; having completed. **7 through with.** having finished with (esp. when dissatisfied with). ◆ *adj* **8** (*postpositive*) having successfully completed some specified activity. **9** (on a telephone line) connected. **10** (*postpositive*) no longer able to function successfully in some specified capacity: *as a journalist, you're through.* **11** (*prenominal*) (of a route, journey, etc.) continuous or unbroken: *a through train.* ◆ *adv* **12** through some specified thing, place, or period of time. **13 through and through.** thoroughly; completely. [OE *thurh*]

through bridge *n Civil engineering.* a bridge in which the track is carried by the lower horizontal members.

throughout Ⓣ (θruːˈaʊt) *prep* **1** right through; through the whole of (a

THESAURUS

threshold *n* **1, 2** = **entrance**, door, doorsill, doorstep, doorway, sill **3** = **start**, beginning, brink, dawn, inception, opening, outset, starting point, verge **5a** = **minimum**, lower limit
Antonyms *n* ≠ **start:** close, decline, end, finish, twilight

thrift *n* **1** = **economy**, carefulness, frugality, good husbandry, parsimony, prudence, saving, thriftiness
Antonyms *n* carelessness, extravagance, prodigality, profligacy, recklessness, squandering, waste

thriftless *adj* **1** = **spendthrift**, extravagant, improvident, imprudent, lavish, prodigal, profligate, unthrifty, wasteful
Antonyms *adj* careful, economical, frugal, provident, prudent, sparing, thrifty

thrifty *adj* **1** = **economical**, careful, frugal, parsimonious, provident, prudent, saving, sparing
Antonyms *adj* extravagant, free-spending, generous, improvident, prodigal, spendthrift, wasteful

thrill *n* **1** = **pleasure**, buzz (*sl.*), charge (*sl.*), flush of excitement, glow, kick (*inf.*), sensation, stimulation, tingle, titillation **3** = **trembling**, flutter, fluttering, quiver, shudder, throb, tremor, vibration ◆ *vb* **5** = **excite**, arouse, electrify, flush, get a charge (*sl.*), get a kick (*inf.*), move, send (*sl.*), stimulate, stir, tingle, titillate **6** = **tremble**, flutter, quake, quiver, shake, shudder, throb, vibrate
Antonyms *n* ≠ **pleasure:** boredom, dreariness, dullness, ennui, monotony, tedium

thrilling *adj* **1** = **exciting**, electrifying, gripping, hair-raising, rip-roaring (*inf.*), riveting, rousing, sensational, sexy (*inf.*), stimulating, stirring
Antonyms *adj* ≠ **exciting:** boring, dreary, dull, monotonous, quiet, staid, tedious, tiresome, uninteresting, unmoving

thrive *vb* **1, 2** = **prosper**, advance, bloom, boom, burgeon, develop, do well, flourish, get on, grow, grow rich, increase, succeed, wax
Antonyms *vb* decline, droop, fail, languish, perish, shrivel, stagnate, wane, wilt, wither

throaty *adj* **3** = **hoarse**, deep, gruff, guttural, husky, low, thick

throb *vb* **1** = **pulsate**, beat, palpitate, pound, pulse, thump, vibrate ◆ *n* **3** = **pulse**, beat, palpitation, pounding, pulsating, thump, thumping, vibration

throes *pl n* **1** = **pains**, convulsions, fit, pangs, paroxysm, spasms, stabs **2 in the throes of** = **struggling with**, agonized by, anguished by, in the midst of, in the pangs of, in the process of, suffering from, toiling with, wrestling with

throng *n* **1** = **crowd**, assemblage, concourse, congregation, crush, horde, host, jam, mass, mob, multitude, pack, press, swarm ◆ *vb* **2** = **crowd**, bunch, congregate, converge, cram, fill, flock, hem in, herd, jam, mill around, pack, press, swarm around, troop
Antonyms *vb* ≠ **crowd:** break up, disband, dispel, disperse, scatter, separate, spread out

throttle *vb* **3** = **strangle**, choke, garrotte, strangulate **4** = **suppress**, control, gag, inhibit, silence, stifle

through *prep* **1** = **from one side to the other of**, between, by, from end to end of, in and out of, past **3** = **because of**, as a consequence *or* result of, by means of, by virtue of, by way of, using, via, with the help of **5** = **during**, in, in the middle of, throughout ◆ *adj* **7 through with** = **finished**, done, having had enough of **8** = **completed**, done, ended, finished, terminated ◆ *adv* **13 through and through** = **completely**, altogether, entirely, fully, thoroughly, totally, to the core, unreservedly, utterly, wholly

throughout *prep* **1** = **through the whole of**, all over, all through, during the whole of, every-

place or a period of time): *throughout the day.* ◆ *adv* **2** through the whole of some specified period or area.

throughput ('θruːˌpʊt) *n* the quantity of raw material or information processed or communicated in a given period, esp. by a computer.

throughway ('θruːˌweɪ) *n US.* a thoroughfare, esp. a motorway.

throve (θrəʊv) *vb* a past tense of **thrive.**

throw ❶ (θrəʊ) *vb* **throws, throwing, threw, thrown.** (*mainly tr*) **1** (*also intr*) to project (something) through the air, esp. with a rapid motion of the arm. **2** (foll. by *in, on, onto,* etc.) to put or move suddenly, carelessly, or violently. **3** to bring to or cause to be in a specified state or condition, esp. suddenly: *the news threw them into a panic.* **4** to direct or cast (a shadow, light, etc.). **5** to project (the voice) so as to make it appear to come from other than its source. **6** to give or hold (a party). **7** to cause to fall or be upset: *the horse threw his rider.* **8a** to tip (dice) out onto a flat surface. **8b** to obtain (a specified number) in this way. **9** to shape (clay) on a potter's wheel. **10** to move (a switch or lever) to engage or disengage a mechanism. **11** to be subjected to (a fit). **12** to turn (wood, etc.) on a lathe. **13** *Inf.* to baffle or astonish; confuse: *the question threw me.* **14** *Boxing.* to deliver (a punch). **15** *Wrestling.* to hurl (an opponent) to the ground. **16** *Inf.* to lose (a contest, etc.) deliberately. **17a** to play (a card). **17b** to discard (a card). **18** (of an animal) to give birth to (young). **19** to twist or spin (filaments) into thread. **20** *Austral. inf.* (often foll. by *at*) to mock or poke fun. **21 throw oneself at.** to strive actively to attract the attention or affection of. **22 throw oneself into.** to involve oneself enthusiastically in. **23 throw oneself on.** to rely entirely upon. ◆ *n* **24** the act or an instance of throwing. **25** the distance over which anything may be thrown: *a stone's throw.* **26** *Inf.* a chance or try. **27** an act or result of throwing dice. **28a** the eccentricity of a cam. **28b** the radial distance between the central axis of a crankshaft and the axis of a crankpin forming part of the shaft. **29** a decorative blanket or cover. **30** *Geol.* the vertical displacement of rock strata at a fault. **31** *Physics.* the deflection of a measuring instrument as a result of a fluctuation. ◆ See also **throwaway, throwback, throw in,** etc. [OE *thrāwan* to turn, torment]

▸ **'thrower** *n*

throwaway ❶ ('θrəʊəˌweɪ) *adj* (*prenominal*) **1** said or done incidentally, esp. for rhetorical effect; casual: *a throwaway remark.* **2** designed to be discarded after use rather than reused, refilled, etc.: *a throwaway carton.* ◆ *n* **3** *Chiefly US & Canad.* a handbill. ◆ *vb* **throw away.** (*tr, adv*) **4** to get rid of; discard. **5** to fail to make good use of; waste.

throwback ('θrəʊˌbæk) *n* **1a** a person, animal, or plant that has the characteristics of an earlier or more primitive type. **1b** a reversion to such an organism. ◆ *vb* **throw back.** (*adv*) **2** (*intr*) to revert to an earlier or more primitive type. **3** (*tr;* foll. by *on*) to force to depend (on): *the crisis threw her back on her faith in God.*

throw in *vb* (*tr, adv*) **1** to add at no additional cost. **2** to contribute or interpose (a remark, argument, etc.). **3 throw in the sponge** (*or* **towel**). to give in; accept defeat. ◆ *n* **throw-in. 4** *Soccer, etc.* the method of putting the ball into play after it has gone into touch by throwing it to a team-mate.

thrown (θrəʊn) *vb* the past participle of **throw.**

throw off ❶ *vb* (*mainly tr, adv*) **1** to free oneself of; discard. **2** to produce or utter in a casual manner. **3** to escape from or elude. **4** to confuse or disconcert. **5** (*intr;* often foll. by **at**) *Austral. & NZ inf.* to deride or ridicule.

throw out ❶ *vb* (*tr, adv*) **1** to discard or reject. **2** to expel or dismiss, esp. forcibly. **3** to construct (something projecting or prominent). **4** to put forward or offer. **5** to utter in a casual or indirect manner. **6** to confuse or disconcert. **7** to give off or emit. **8** *Cricket.* (of a fielder) to put (the batsman) out by throwing the ball to hit the wicket. **9** *Baseball.* to make a throw to a team-mate who in turn puts out (a base runner).

throw over ❶ *vb* (*tr, adv*) to forsake or abandon; jilt.

throw together *vb* (*tr, adv*) **1** to assemble hurriedly. **2** to cause to become casually acquainted.

throw up ❶ *vb* (*adv, mainly tr*) **1** to give up; abandon. **2** to construct hastily. **3** to reveal; produce. **4** (*also intr*) *Inf.* to vomit.

thru (θruː) *prep, adv, adj Chiefly US.* a variant spelling of **through.**

thrum[1] (θrʌm) *vb* **thrums, thrumming, thrummed. 1** to strum rhythmically but without expression on (a musical instrument). **2** (*intr*) to drum incessantly: *rain thrummed on the roof.* ◆ *n* **3** a repetitive strumming. [C16: imit.]

thrum[2] (θrʌm) *n* **1a** any of the unwoven ends of warp thread remaining on the loom when the web has been removed. **1b** such ends of thread collectively. **2** a fringe or tassel of short unwoven threads. ◆ *vb* **thrums, thrumming, thrummed. 3** (*tr*) to trim with thrums. [C14: from OE]

thrush[1] (θrʌʃ) *n* any of a subfamily of songbirds, esp. those having a brown plumage with a spotted breast, such as the mistle thrush and song thrush. [OE *thrȳsce*]

thrush[2] (θrʌʃ) *n* **1** a fungal disease, esp. of infants, characterized by the formation of whitish spots. **2** a genital infection caused by the same fungus. **3** a softening of the frog of a horse's hoof characterized by inflammation and a thick foul discharge. [C17: from ?]

thrust ❶ (θrʌst) *vb* **thrusts, thrusting, thrust. 1** (*tr*) to push (someone or something) with force. **2** (*tr*) to force upon (someone) or into (some condition or situation): *they thrust responsibilities upon her.* **3** (*tr;* foll. by *through*) to pierce; stab. **4** (*intr;* usually foll. by *through* or *into*) to force a passage. **5** to make a stab or lunge at. ◆ *n* **6** a forceful drive, push, stab, or lunge. **7** a force, esp. one that produces motion. **8a** a propulsive force produced by the fluid pressure or the change of momentum of the fluid in a jet engine, rocket engine, etc. **8b** a similar force produced by a propeller. **9** a continuous pressure exerted by one part of an object, structure, etc., against another. **10** force, impetus, or drive. **11** the essential or most forceful part: *the thrust of the argument.* [C12: from ON *thrysta*]

thruster ('θrʌstə) *n* **1** a person or thing that thrusts. **2** a small rocket engine, esp. one used to correct the altitude or course of a spacecraft.

thrust fault *n* a fault in which the rocks on the lower side of an inclined fault plane have been displaced downwards; a reverse fault.

thud ❶ (θʌd) *n* **1** a dull heavy sound. **2** a blow or fall that causes such a sound. ◆ *vb* **thuds, thudding, thudded. 3** to make or cause to make such a sound. [OE *thyddan* to strike]

thug ❶ (θʌg) *n* **1** a tough and violent man, esp. a criminal. **2** (*sometimes cap.*) (formerly) a member of an organization of robbers and assassins in India. [C19: from Hindi *thag* thief, from Sansk. *sthaga* scoundrel, from *sthagati* to conceal]

▸ **'thuggery** *n* ▸ **'thuggish** *adj*

thuja *or* **thuya** ('θuːjə) *n* any of a genus of coniferous trees of North America and East Asia, having scalelike leaves, small cones, and an aromatic wood. [C18: from NL, from Med. L *thuia*, ult. from Gk *thua* an African tree]

thulium ('θjuːlɪəm) *n* a malleable ductile silvery-grey element. The radioisotope **thulium-170** is used as an electron source in portable X-ray units. Symbol: Tm; atomic no.: 69; atomic wt.: 168.93. [C19: NL, from *Thule* a region thought, by ancient geographers, to be northernmost in the world + -IUM]

thumb ❶ (θʌm) *n* **1** the first and usually shortest and thickest of the digits of the hand. **2** the corresponding digit in other vertebrates. **3** the part of a glove shaped to fit the thumb. **4 all thumbs.** clumsy. **5 thumbs down.** an indication of refusal or disapproval. **6 thumbs up.** an indication of encouragement or approval. **7 under someone's thumb.** at

THESAURUS

where in, for the duration of, from end to end of, over the length and breadth of, right through ◆ *adv* **2** = **from start to finish**, all the time, all through, from beginning to end, from the start, in every nook and cranny, right through, the whole time

throw *vb* **1** = **hurl**, cast, chuck (*inf.*), fling, heave, launch, lob (*inf.*), pitch, project, propel, put, send, shy, sling, toss **7** = **bring down**, dislodge, fell, floor, hurl to the ground, overturn, unseat, upset **13** *Informal* = **confuse**, astonish, baffle, confound, disconcert, dumbfound, faze, put one off one's stroke, throw off, throw one off one's stride, throw out ◆ *n* **24** = **toss**, cast, fling, heave, lob, pitch, projection, put, shy, sling **26** *Informal* = **try**, attempt, chance, essay, gamble, hazard, venture, wager

throwaway *adj* **1** = **casual**, careless, offhand, passing, understated ◆ *vb* **throw away 4** = **discard**, axe (*inf.*), bin (*inf.*), cast off, chuck (*inf.*), dispense with, dispose of, ditch (*sl.*), dump (*inf.*), get rid of, jettison, junk (*inf.*), reject, scrap, throw out **5** = **waste**, blow (*sl.*), fail to make use of, fritter away, lose, make poor use of, squander

Antonyms *vb* ≠ **discard**: conserve, keep, preserve, rescue, retain, retrieve, salvage, save

throw off *vb* **1** *Literary* = **free oneself of**, abandon, cast off, discard, drop, rid oneself of, shake off **3** = **escape from**, elude, evade, get away from, give (someone) the slip, leave behind, lose, outdistance, outrun, shake off, show a clean pair of heels to **4** = **disconcert**, confuse, disturb, faze, put one off one's stroke, throw (*inf.*), throw one off one's stride, unsettle, upset

throw out *vb* **1** = **discard**, bin (*inf.*), cast off, chuck (*inf.*), dispense with, ditch (*sl.*), dump (*inf.*), jettison, junk (*inf.*), reject, relegate, scrap, throw away, turn down **2** = **expel**, dismiss, eject, evict, get rid of, give the bum's rush (*sl.*), kick out (*inf.*), oust, show one the door, turf out (*Brit. inf.*) **6** = **disconcert**, confuse, disturb, put one off one's stroke, throw (*inf.*), throw one off one's stride, unsettle, upset **7** = **emit**, diffuse, disseminate, give off, put forth, radiate

throw over *vb Old-fashioned* = **abandon**, break with, chuck (*inf.*), desert, discard, drop (*inf.*), finish with, forsake, jilt, leave, quit, split up with, walk out on (*inf.*)

throw up *vb* **1** = **give up**, abandon, chuck (*inf.*), jack in, leave, quit, relinquish, renounce, resign from, step down from (*inf.*) **2** = **throw together**, jerry-build, run up, slap together **3** = **produce**, bring forward, bring to light, bring to notice, bring to the surface, reveal **4** *Informal* = **vomit**, barf (*US sl.*), be sick, bring up, chuck (up), chunder (*sl., chiefly Austral.*), disgorge, heave, puke (*sl.*), regurgitate, retch, spew

thrust *vb* **1** = **push**, butt, drive, force, impel, jam, plunge, poke, press, prod, propel, ram, shove, urge **3** = **stab**, jab, lunge, pierce, stick **4** = **shove**, elbow *or* shoulder one's way, push ◆ *n* **6** = **push**, drive, lunge, poke, prod, shove, stab **7** = **momentum**, impetus, motive force, motive power, propulsive force

thud *n, vb* **1-3** = **thump**, clonk, clump, clunk, crash, knock, smack, wallop (*inf.*)

thug *n* **1** = **ruffian**, assassin, bandit, bruiser (*inf.*), bully boy, cut-throat, gangster, heavy (*sl.*), hooligan, killer, mugger (*inf.*), murderer, robber, tough, tsotsi (*S. Afr.*)

thumb *n* **1** = **pollex 4 all thumbs** = **clumsy**, butterfingered, cack-handed (*inf.*), ham-fisted (*inf.*), inept, maladroit **5 thumbs down** = **disapproval**, negation, no, rebuff, refusal, rejection **6 thumbs up** = **approval**, acceptance, affirmation, encouragement, go-ahead (*inf.*), green light, O.K. *or* okay (*inf.*), yes ◆ *vb* **8** = **handle**, dog-ear, finger, mark **9** = **hitch** (*inf.*), hitchhike **10** *often foll. by* **through** = **flick through**, browse through, flip through, glance at, leaf through, riffle through, run one's eye over, scan the pages of, skim through, turn over **11 thumb one's nose at** = **show contempt for**, be contemptuous of, cock a snook at, deride, flout, jeer at, laugh at, laugh in the face of, mock, ridicule, show disrespect to

someone's mercy or command. ◆ *vb* **8** (*tr*) to touch, mark, or move with the thumb. **9** to attempt to obtain (a lift or ride) by signalling with the thumb. **10** (when *intr*, often foll. by *through*) to flip the pages of (a book, etc.) in order to glance at the contents. **11 thumb one's nose at.** to deride or mock, esp. by placing the thumb on the nose with fingers extended. [OE *thūma*]

thumb index *n* **1** a series of indentations cut into the fore-edge of a book to facilitate quick reference. ◆ *vb* **thumb-index. 2** (*tr*) to furnish with a thumb index.

thumbnail ❶ ('θʌmˌneɪl) *n* **1** the nail of the thumb. **2** (*modifier*) concise and brief: *a thumbnail sketch.*

thumbnut ('θʌmˌnʌt) *n* a wing nut.

thumb piano *n* another name for **mbira.**

thumbscrew ('θʌmˌskruː) *n* **1** an instrument of torture that pinches or crushes the thumbs. **2** a screw with projections on its head enabling it to be turned by the thumb and forefinger.

thumbtack ('θʌmˌtæk) *n* the US and Canad. name for **drawing pin.**

thump ❶ (θʌmp) *n* **1** the sound of a heavy solid body hitting a comparatively soft surface. **2** a heavy blow with the hand. ◆ *vb* **3** (*tr*) to strike or beat heavily; pound. **4** (*intr*) to throb, beat, or pound violently. [C16]

▸ **'thumper** *n*

thumping ❶ ('θʌmpɪŋ) *adj* (*prenominal*) *Sl.* huge or excessive: *a thumping loss.*

thunbergia (θʌnˈbɜːdʒɪə) *n* any of various climbing or dwarf plants of tropical and subtropical Africa and Asia. [C19: after K. P. *Thunberg* (1743-1822), Swedish botanist]

thunder ❶ ('θʌndə) *n* **1** a loud cracking or deep rumbling noise caused by the rapid expansion of atmospheric gases which are suddenly heated by lightning. **2** any loud booming sound. **3** *Rare.* a violent threat or denunciation. **4 steal someone's thunder.** to lessen the effect of someone's idea or action by anticipating it. ◆ *vb* **5** to make (a loud sound) or utter (words) in a manner suggesting thunder. **6** (*intr;* with *it* as subject) to be the case that thunder is being heard. **7** (*intr*) to move fast and heavily: *the bus thundered downhill.* **8** (*intr*) to utter vehement threats or denunciation; rail. [OE *thunor*]

▸ **'thundery** *adj* ▸ **'thunderer** *n*

thunderbolt ('θʌndəˌbəʊlt) *n* **1** a flash of lightning accompanying thunder. **2** the imagined agency of destruction produced by a flash of lightning. **3** (in mythology) the destructive weapon wielded by several gods, esp. the Greek god Zeus. **4** something very startling.

thunderclap ('θʌndəˌklæp) *n* **1** a loud outburst of thunder. **2** something as violent or unexpected as a clap of thunder.

thundercloud ('θʌndəˌklaʊd) *n* a towering electrically charged cumulonimbus cloud associated with thunderstorms.

thunderhead ('θʌndəˌhɛd) *n Chiefly US.* the anvil-shaped top of a cumulonimbus cloud.

thundering ❶ ('θʌndərɪŋ) *adj* (*prenominal*) *Sl.* very great or excessive: *a thundering idiot.*

thunderous ❶ ('θʌndərəs) *adj* **1** threatening; angry. **2** resembling thunder, esp. in loudness.

thunderstorm ('θʌndəˌstɔːm) *n* a storm with thunder and lightning and usually heavy rain or hail.

thunderstruck ❶ ('θʌndəˌstrʌk) *or* **thunderstricken** ('θʌndəˌstrɪkən) *adj* **1** completely taken aback; amazed or shocked. **2** *Rare.* struck by lightning.

thurible ('θjʊərɪbᵊl) *n* another word for **censer.** [C15: from L *tūribulum* censer, from *tūs* incense]

Thurs. *abbrev. for* Thursday.

Thursday ('θɜːzdɪ) *n* the fifth day of the week; fourth day of the working week. [OE *Thursdæg,* lit.: Thor's day]

thus ❶ (ðʌs) *adv* **1** in this manner: *do it thus.* **2** to such a degree: *thus far and no further.* ◆ *sentence connector.* **3** therefore: *We have failed. Thus we have to take the consequences.* [OE]

thuya ('θuːjə) *n* a variant spelling of **thuja.**

thwack ❶ (θwæk) *vb* **1** to beat, esp. with something flat. ◆ *n* **2a** a blow with something flat. **2b** the sound made by it. [C16: imit.]

thwart ❶ (θwɔːt) *vb* **1** to oppose successfully or prevent; frustrate. **2** *Obs.* to be or move across. ◆ *n* **3** an oarsman's seat lying across a boat. ◆ *adj* **4** passing or being situated across. ◆ *prep, adv* **5** *Obs.* across. [C13: from ON *thvert,* from *thverr* transverse]

thy (ðaɪ) *determiner* (*usually preceding a consonant*) *Arch. or Brit. dialect.* belonging to or associated in some way with you (thou): *thy goodness.* [C12: var. of THINE]

thylacine ('θaɪləˌsaɪn) *n* an extinct or rare doglike carnivorous marsupial of Tasmania. Also called: **Tasmanian wolf.** [C19: from NL *thȳlacīnus,* from Gk *thulakos* pouch]

thyme (taɪm) *n* any of various small shrubs having a strong odour, small leaves, and white, pink, or red flowers. [C14: from OF *thym,* from L *thymum,* from Gk, from *thuein* to make a burnt offering]

▸ **'thymy** *adj*

-thymia *n combining form.* indicating a certain emotional condition, mood, or state of mind: *cyclothymia.* [NL, from Gk *thumos* temper]

thymine ('θaɪmiːn) *n* a white crystalline base found in DNA. [C19: from THYMIC (see THYMUS) + -INE[2]]

thymol ('θaɪmɒl) *n* a white crystalline substance obtained from thyme and used as a fungicide, antiseptic, etc. [C19: from THYME + -OL[2]]

thymus ('θaɪməs) *n, pl* **thymuses** *or* **thymi** (-maɪ). a glandular organ of vertebrates, consisting in man of two lobes situated below the thyroid. It atrophies with age and is almost nonexistent in the adult. [C17: from NL, from Gk *thumos* sweetbread]

▸ **'thymic** *adj*

thyratron ('θaɪrəˌtrɒn) *n Electronics.* a gas-filled tube that has three electrodes and can be switched between an 'off' state and an 'on' state. It has been superseded by the thyristor. [C20: orig. a trademark, from Gk *thura* door, valve + -TRON]

thyristor (θaɪˈrɪstə) *n* any of a group of semiconductor devices, such as the silicon-controlled rectifier, that can be switched between two states. [C20: from THYR(ATRON) + (TRANS)ISTOR]

thyroid ('θaɪrɔɪd) *adj* **1** of or relating to the thyroid gland. **2** of or relating to the largest cartilage of the larynx. ◆ *n* **3** See **thyroid gland. 4** a preparation of the thyroid gland of certain animals, used to treat hypothyroidism. [C18: from NL *thyroidēs,* from Gk *thureoeidēs,* from *thureos* oblong (lit.: door-shaped), from *thura* door]

thyroid gland *n* an endocrine gland of vertebrates, consisting in man of two lobes near the base of the neck. It secretes hormones that control metabolism and growth.

thyrotropin (ˌθaɪrəʊˈtrəʊpɪn) *or* **thyrotrophin** *n* a hormone secreted by the pituitary gland: it stimulates the activity of the thyroid gland. [C20: from *thyro-* thyroid + -TROPE + -IN]

thyroxine (θaɪˈrɒksiːn, -sɪn) *or* **thyroxin** (θaɪˈrɒksɪn) *n* the principal hormone produced by the thyroid gland. [C19: from *thyro-* thyroid + OXY-[2] + -INE[2]]

thyrse (θɜːs) *or* **thyrsus** ('θɜːsəs) *n, pl* **thyrses** *or* **thyrsi** ('θɜːsaɪ). *Bot.* a type of inflorescence, occurring in the lilac and grape, in which the main branch is racemose and the lateral branches cymose. [C17: from F: THYRSUS]

thyrsus ('θɜːsəs) *n, pl* **thyrsi** (-saɪ). **1** *Greek myth.* a staff, usually one tipped with a pine cone, borne by Dionysus (Bacchus) and his followers. **2** a variant spelling of **thyrse.** [C18: from L, from Gk *thursos* stalk]

thyself (ðaɪˈsɛlf) *pron Arch.* **a** the reflexive form of *thou* or *thee.* **b** (intensifier): *thou, thyself, wouldst know.*

ti (tiː) *n Music.* a variant spelling of **te.**

Ti *the chemical symbol for* titanium.

tiara (tɪˈɑːrə) *n* **1** a woman's semicircular jewelled headdress for formal occasions. **2** a high headdress worn by Persian kings in ancient times. **3** a headdress worn by the pope, consisting of a beehive-shaped diadem surrounded by three coronets. [C16: via L from Gk, of Oriental origin]

▸ **ti'araed** *adj*

Tibetan (tɪˈbɛtᵊn) *adj* **1** of or characteristic of Tibet, its people, or their language. ◆ *n* **2** a native or inhabitant of Tibet. **3** the language of Tibet.

tibia ('tɪbɪə) *n, pl* **tibiae** ('tɪbɪˌiː) *or* **tibias. 1** the inner and thicker of the two bones of the human leg below the knee; shinbone. **2** the corresponding bone in other vertebrates. **3** the fourth segment of an insect's leg. [C16: from L: leg, pipe]

▸ **'tibial** *adj*

THESAURUS

thumbnail *modifier* **2** = **brief**, compact, concise, pithy, quick, short, succinct

thump *n* **1** = **thud**, bang, clunk, crash, thwack **2** = **blow**, clout (*inf.*), knock, punch, rap, smack, swipe, wallop (*inf.*), whack ◆ *vb* **3** = **strike**, batter, beat, belabour, chin (*sl.*), clobber (*sl.*), clout (*inf.*), deck (*sl.*), hit, knock, lambast(e), lay one on (*sl.*), pound, punch, rap, smack, swipe, thrash, wallop (*inf.*), whack **4** = **throb**, beat

thumping *adj Slang* = **huge**, colossal, elephantine, enormous, excessive, exorbitant, gargantuan, gigantic, great, humongous *or* humungous (*US sl.*), impressive, mammoth, massive, monumental, stellar (*inf.*), terrific, thundering (*sl.*), titanic, tremendous, whopping (*inf.*)
Antonyms *adj* inconsequential, insignificant, meagre, measly (*inf.*), negligible, paltry, petty, piddling (*inf.*), trifling, trivial

thunder *n* **1, 2** = **rumble**, boom, booming, cracking, crash, crashing, detonation, explosion, pealing, rumbling ◆ *vb* **5** = **rumble**, bark, bellow, blast, boom, clap, crack, crash, detonate, explode, peal, resound, reverberate, roar, shout, yell **8** = **rail**, curse, denounce, fulminate, threaten, utter threats

thundering *adj Old-fashioned slang* = **great**, decided, enormous, excessive, monumental, remarkable, unmitigated, utter

thunderous *adj* **2** = **loud**, booming, deafening, ear-splitting, noisy, resounding, roaring, tumultuous

thunderstruck *adj* **1** = **amazed**, aghast, astonished, astounded, bowled over (*inf.*), dazed, dumbfounded, flabbergasted (*inf.*), floored (*inf.*), flummoxed, gobsmacked (*Brit. sl.*), knocked for six (*inf.*), left speechless, nonplussed, open-mouthed, paralysed, petrified, rooted to the spot, shocked, staggered, struck dumb, stunned, taken aback

thus *adv* **1, 2** = **in this way**, as follows, in this fashion, in this manner, like so, like this, so, to such a degree ◆ *sentence connector* **3** = **therefore**, accordingly, consequently, ergo, for this reason, hence, on that account, so, then

thwack *vb* **1** = **smack**, bash (*inf.*), beat, chin (*sl.*), clout (*inf.*), deck (*sl.*), flog, hit, lambast(e), lay one on (*sl.*), swipe, thump, wallop (*inf.*), whack ◆ *n* **2** = **smack**, bash (*inf.*), blow, clout (*inf.*), swipe, thump, wallop (*inf.*), whack

thwart *vb* **1** = **frustrate**, baffle, balk, check, cook (someone's) goose (*inf.*), defeat, foil, hinder, impede, obstruct, oppose, outwit, prevent, put a spoke in someone's wheel (*inf.*), snooker, stop, stymie
Antonyms *vb* aggravate, aid, assist, encourage, exacerbate, facilitate, hasten, help, intensify, support

tic ❶ (tɪk) *n* spasmodic twitching of a particular group of muscles. [C19: from F, from ?]
tic douloureux ('tɪk ˌduːlə'ruː) *n* a condition of momentary stabbing pain along the trigeminal nerve. [C19: from F, lit.: painful tic]
tick[1] ❶ (tɪk) *n* **1** a recurrent metallic tapping or clicking sound, such as that made by a clock. **2** *Brit. inf.* a moment or instant. **3** a mark (✓) used to check off or indicate the correctness of something. **4** *Commerce.* the smallest increment by which a price can fluctuate in a commodity or financial futures market. ◆ *vb* **5** to produce a recurrent tapping sound or indicate by such a sound: *the clock ticked the minutes away.* **6** (when *tr*, often foll. by *off*) to mark or check with a tick. **7 what makes someone tick.** *Inf.* the basic drive or motivation of a person. ◆ See also **tick off, tick over.** [C13: from Low G *tikk* touch]
tick[2] (tɪk) *n* any of a large group of small parasitic arachnids typically living on the skin of warm-blooded animals and feeding on the blood, etc., of their hosts. [OE *ticca*]
tick[3] (tɪk) *n* **1** the strong covering of a pillow, mattress, etc. **2** *Inf.* short for **ticking.** [C15: prob. from MDu. *tīke*]
tick[4] ❶ (tɪk) *n Brit. inf.* account or credit (esp. in **on tick**). [C17: shortened from TICKET]
tick bird *n* another name for **oxpecker.**
ticker ('tɪkə) *n* **1** *Sl.* **1a** the heart. **1b** a watch. **2** a person or thing that ticks. **3** the US word for **tape machine.**
ticker tape *n* a continuous paper ribbon on which a tape machine prints current stock quotations.
ticket ❶ ('tɪkɪt) *n* **1a** a piece of paper, cardboard, etc., showing that the holder is entitled to certain rights, such as travel on a train or bus, entry to a place of public entertainment, etc. **1b** (*modifier*) concerned with the issue, sale, or checking of tickets: *a ticket collector.* **2** a piece of card, cloth, etc., attached to an article showing information such as its price, size, etc. **3** a summons served for a parking or traffic offence. **4** *Inf.* the certificate of competence issued to a ship's captain or an aircraft pilot. **5** *Chiefly US & NZ.* the group of candidates nominated by one party in an election; slate. **6** *Chiefly US.* the declared policy of a political party at an election. **7** *Brit. inf.* a certificate of discharge from the armed forces. **8** *Inf.* the right or appropriate thing: *that's the ticket.* **9 have (got) tickets on oneself.** *Austral. inf.* to be conceited. ◆ *vb* **tickets, ticketing, ticketed.** (*tr*) **10** to issue or attach a ticket or tickets to. [C17: from OF *etiquet*, from *estiquier* to stick on, from MDu. *steken* to stick]
ticket day *n Stock Exchange.* the day before settling day, when the stockbrokers are given the names of the purchasers.
ticket of leave *n* (formerly, in Britain) a permit allowing a convict (**ticket-of-leave man**) to leave prison, after serving only part of his sentence, with certain restrictions placed on him.
tick fever *n* any acute infectious febrile disease caused by the bite of an infected tick.
ticking ('tɪkɪŋ) *n* a strong cotton fabric, often striped, used esp. for mattress and pillow covers. [C17: from TICK[3]]
tickle ❶ ('tɪkəl) *vb* **tickles, tickling, tickled. 1** to touch or stroke, so as to produce pleasure, laughter, or a twitching sensation. **2** (*tr*) to excite pleasurably; gratify. **3** (*tr*) to delight or entertain (often in **tickle one's fancy**). **4** (*intr*) to itch or tingle. **5** (*tr*) to catch (a fish, esp. a trout) with the hands. **6 tickle pink** *or* **to death.** *Inf.* to please greatly. ◆ *n* **7** a sensation of light stroking or itching. **8** the act of tickling. **9** *Canad.* (in the Atlantic Provinces) a narrow strait. [C14]
tickler ('tɪklə) *n* **1** *Inf., chiefly Brit.* a difficult problem. **2** Also called: **tickler file.** *US.* a memorandum book. **3** a person or thing that tickles.
ticklish ❶ ('tɪklɪʃ) *adj* **1** sensitive to being tickled. **2** delicate or difficult. **3** easily upset or offended.
▸ **'ticklishly** *adv* ▸ **'ticklishness** *n*
tick off ❶ *vb* (*tr, adv*) **1** to mark with a tick. **2** *Inf., chiefly Brit.* to scold; reprimand.
tick over *vb* (*intr, adv*) **1** Also: **idle.** *Brit.* (of an engine) to run at low speed with the throttle control closed and the transmission disengaged. **2** to run smoothly without any major changes.
ticktack ('tɪkˌtæk) *n* **1** *Brit.* a system of sign language, mainly using the hands, by which bookmakers transmit their odds to each other at race courses. **2** *US.* a ticking sound. [from TICK[1]]
ticktock ('tɪkˌtɒk) *n* **1** a ticking sound as made by a clock. ◆ *vb* **2** (*intr*) to make a ticking sound.
tidal ('taɪdəl) *adj* **1** relating to, characterized by, or affected by tides. **2** dependent on the tide: *a tidal ferry.*
▸ **'tidally** *adv*
tidal energy *n* energy obtained by harnessing tidal power.
tidal volume *n* **1** the volume of water associated with a rising tide. **2** *Physiol.* the amount of air passing into and out of the lungs during normal breathing.
tidal wave *n* **1** a name (not in technical usage) for **tsunami. 2** an unusually large incoming wave, often caused by high winds and spring tides. **3** a forceful and widespread movement in public opinion, action, etc.
tidbit ('tɪdˌbɪt) *n* the usual US spelling of **titbit.**
tiddler ('tɪdlə) *n Brit. inf.* **1** a very small fish, esp. a stickleback. **2** a small child. [C19: from *tittlebat*, childish var. of STICKLEBACK, infl. by TIDDLY[1]]
tiddly[1] ('tɪdlɪ) *adj* **tiddlier, tiddliest.** *Brit.* small; tiny. [C19: childish var. of LITTLE]
tiddly[2] ('tɪdlɪ) *adj Sl., chiefly Brit.* slightly drunk. [C19 (meaning: a drink): from ?]
tiddlywinks ('tɪdlɪˌwɪŋks) *n* (*functioning as sing*) a game in which players try to flick discs of plastic into a cup by pressing them with other larger discs. [C19: prob. from TIDDLY[1] + dialect *wink*, var. of WINCH[1]]
tide ❶ (taɪd) *n* **1** the cyclic rise and fall of sea level caused by the gravitational pull of the sun and moon. There are usually two high tides and two low tides in each lunar day. **2** the current, ebb, or flow of water at a specified place resulting from these changes in level. **3** See **ebb** (sense 3) and **flood** (sense 3). **4** a widespread tendency or movement. **5** a critical point in time; turning point. **6** *Arch. except in combination.* a season or time: *Christmastide.* **7** *Arch.* a favourable opportunity. **8 the tide is in** (*or* **out**). the sea has reached its highest (*or* lowest) level. ◆ *vb* **tides, tiding, tided. 9** to carry or be carried with or as if with the tide. **10** (*intr*) to ebb and flow like the tide. [OE *tīd* time]
▸ **'tideless** *adj*
tideland ('taɪdˌlænd) *n US.* land between high-water and low-water marks.
tideline ('taɪdˌlaɪn) *n* the mark or line left by the tide when it retreats from its highest point.
tidemark ('taɪdˌmɑːk) *n* **1** a mark left by the highest or lowest point of a tide. **2** *Chiefly Brit.* a mark showing a level reached by a liquid: *a tidemark on the bath.* **3** *Inf., chiefly Brit.* a dirty mark on the skin, indicating the extent to which someone has washed.
tide over ❶ *vb* (*tr, adv*) to help to get through (a period of difficulty, distress, etc.).
tide-rip *n* another word for **riptide** (sense 1).
tidewaiter ('taɪdˌweɪtə) *n* (formerly) a customs officer who boarded and inspected incoming ships.
tidewater ('taɪdˌwɔːtə) *n* **1** water that advances and recedes with the tide. **2** *US.* coastal land drained by tidal streams.
tideway ('taɪdˌweɪ) *n* a strong tidal current or its channel, esp. the tidal part of a river.
tidings ❶ ('taɪdɪŋz) *pl n* information or news. [OE *tīdung*]
tidy ❶ ('taɪdɪ) *adj* **tidier, tidiest. 1** characterized by or indicating neatness and order. **2** *Inf.* considerable: *a tidy sum of money.* ◆ *vb* **tidies, tidying, tidied. 3** (when *intr*, usually foll. by *up*) to put (things) in order; neaten. ◆ *n, pl* **tidies. 4a** a small container for odds and ends. **4b sink tidy.** a container to retain rubbish that might clog the plughole. **5** *Chiefly US & Canad.* an ornamental protective covering for the back or arms of a chair. [C13 (in the sense: timely, excellent): from TIDE + -Y[1]]
▸ **'tidily** *adv* ▸ **'tidiness** *n*
tie ❶ (taɪ) *vb* **ties, tying, tied. 1** (when *tr*, often foll. by *up*) to fasten or be fastened with string, thread, etc. **2** to make (a knot or bow) in (something). **3** (*tr*) to restrict or secure. **4** to equal (the score) of a competitor, etc. **5** (*tr*) *Inf.* to unite in marriage. **6** *Music.* **6a** to execute (two

THESAURUS

tic *n* = **twitch**, jerk, spasm
tick[1] *n* **1** = **tapping**, clack, click, clicking, tap, ticktock **2** *Brit. informal* = **moment**, flash, half a mo (*Brit. inf.*), instant, jiffy, minute, sec (*inf.*), second, shake (*inf.*), split second, trice, twinkling, two shakes of a lamb's tail (*inf.*) **3** = **mark**, dash, stroke ◆ *vb* **5** = **tap**, clack, click, ticktock **6** = **mark**, check off, choose, indicate, mark off, select **7 what makes someone tick** *Informal* = **motivation**, drive, motive, *raison d'être*
tick[4] *n Brit. informal* = **credit**, account, deferred payment, the slate (*Brit. inf.*)
ticket *n* **1a** = **voucher**, card, certificate, coupon, pass, slip, token **2** = **label**, card, docket, marker, slip, sticker, tab, tag
tickle *vb* **2** = **amuse**, delight, divert, entertain, excite, gratify, please, thrill, titillate
Antonyms *vb* annoy, bore, bother, irritate, pester, trouble, vex, weary
ticklish *adj* **2** = **difficult**, awkward, critical, delicate, nice, risky, sensitive, thorny, touchy, tricky, uncertain, unstable, unsteady
tick off *vb* **1** = **mark off**, check off, put a tick at **2** *Informal* = **scold**, carpet (*inf.*), censure, chide, lecture, read the riot act, rebuke, reprimand, reproach, reprove, take to task, tell off (*inf.*), upbraid
tide *n* **2** = **current**, course, ebb, flow, stream, tideway, undertow **4** = **tendency**, course, current, direction, drift, movement, trend
tide over *vb* = **keep one going**, aid, assist, bridge the gap, help, keep one's head above water, keep the wolf from the door, see one through
tidings *pl n* = **news**, advice, bulletin, communication, gen (*Brit. inf.*), information, intelligence, latest (*inf.*), message, report, word
tidy *adj* **1** = **neat**, businesslike, clean, cleanly, in apple-pie order (*inf.*), methodical, ordered, orderly, shipshape, spick-and-span, spruce, systematic, trig (*arch. or dialect*), trim, well-groomed, well-kept, well-ordered **2** *Informal* = **considerable**, ample, fair, generous, good, goodly, handsome, healthy, large, largish, respectable, sizable *or* sizeable, substantial ◆ *vb* **3** = **neaten**, clean, groom, order, put in order, put in trim, put to rights, spruce up, straighten
Antonyms *adj* ≠ **neat:** careless, dirty, dishevelled, disordered, disorderly, filthy, in disarray, messy, scruffy, sloppy, slovenly, unbusinesslike, unkempt, unmethodical, unsystematic, untidy ≠ **considerable:** inconsiderable, insignificant, little, small, tiny ◆ *vb* ≠ **neaten:** dirty, dishevel, disorder, mess, mess up
tie *vb* **1** = **fasten**, attach, bind, connect, interlace, join, knot, lash, link, make fast, moor, rope, secure, tether, truss, unite **3** = **restrict**, bind, confine, hamper, hinder, hold, limit, restrain **4** = **draw**, be even, be neck and neck, equal, match ◆ *n* **7, 9** = **fastening**, band, bond, connection, cord, fetter, joint, knot, ligature, link, rope, string **8** = **encumbrance**, hindrance, limitation, restraint, restriction **11** = **draw**, dead heat, deadlock, stalemate **13** *Brit.* = **match**, contest, fixture, game
Antonyms *vb* ≠ **fasten:** free, loose, release, separate, undo, unfasten, unhitch, unknot, untie ≠ **restrict:** free, release

successive notes) as though they formed one note. **6b** to connect (two printed notes) with a tie. ◆ *n* **7** a bond, link, or fastening. **8** a restriction or restraint. **9** a string, wire, etc., with which something is tied. **10** a long narrow piece of material worn, esp. by men, under the collar of a shirt, tied in a knot close to the throat with the ends hanging down the front. US name: **necktie. 11a** an equality in score, attainment, etc., in a contest. **11b** the match or competition in which such a result is attained. **12** a structural member such as a tie beam or tie rod. **13** *Sport, Brit.* a match or game in an eliminating competition: *a cup tie.* **14** (*usually pl*) a shoe fastened by means of laces. **15** the US and Canad. name for **sleeper** (on a railway track). **16** *Music.* a slur connecting two notes of the same pitch indicating that the sound is to be prolonged for their joint time value. ◆ See also **tie in, tie up.** [OE *tīgan* to tie]

tie beam *n* a horizontal beam that serves to prevent two other structural members from separating, esp. one that connects two corresponding rafters in a roof or roof truss.

tie-break *or* **tie-breaker** *n* **1** *Tennis.* an extra game played to decide the result of a set when the score is 6–6. **2** any method of deciding quickly the result of a drawn contest, esp. an extra game, question, etc.

tie clasp *n* a clip which holds a tie in place against a shirt. Also called: **tie clip.**

tied (taɪd) *adj Brit.* **1** (of a public house, retail shop, etc.) obliged to sell only the beer, products, etc. of a particular producer: *a tied house; tied outlet.* **2** (of a house) rented out to the tenant for as long as he is employed by the owner. **3** (of a loan) made by one nation to another on condition that the money is spent on goods or services provided by the lending nation.

tie-dyeing, tie-dye *or* **tie and dye** *n* a method of dyeing textiles to produce patterns by tying sections of the cloth together so that they will not absorb the dye.
▸ **'tie-ˌdyed** *adj*

tie in ❶ *vb* (*adv*) **1** to come or bring into a certain relationship; coordinate. ◆ *n* **tie-in. 2** a link, relationship, or coordination. **3** publicity material, a book, etc., linked to a film, etc. **4** *US.* **4a** a sale or advertisement offering products of which a purchaser must buy one or more in addition to his purchase. **4b** an item sold or advertised in this way. **4c** (*as modifier*): *a tie-in sale.*

tie line *n* a telephone line between two private branch exchanges or private exchanges that may or may not pass through a main exchange.

tiepin ('taɪˌpɪn) *n* an ornamental pin of various shapes used to pin the two ends of a tie to a shirt.

tier[1] ❶ (tɪə) *n* **1** one of a set of rows placed one above and behind the other, such as theatre seats. **2a** a layer or level. **2b** (*in combination*): *a three-tier cake.* ◆ *vb* **3** to be or arrange in tiers. [C16: from OF *tire* rank, of Gmc origin]

tier[2] ('taɪə) *n* a person or thing that ties.

tierce (tɪəs) *n* **1** a variant of **terce. 2** the third of eight positions from which a parry or attack can be made in fencing. **3** (tɜːs). a sequence of three cards. **4** an obsolete measure of capacity equal to 42 wine gallons. [C15: from OF, fem of *tiers* third, from L *tertius*]

tiercel ('tɪəsᵊl) *n* a variant of **tercel.**

tie up ❶ *vb* (*adv*) **1** (*tr*) to bind securely with or as if with string, rope, etc. **2** to moor (a vessel). **3** (*tr; often passive*) to engage the attentions of. **4** (*tr; often passive*) to conclude (the organization of something). **5** to come or bring to a complete standstill. **6** (*tr*) to commit (funds, etc.) and so make unavailable for other uses. **7** (*tr*) to subject (property) to conditions that prevent sale, alienation, etc. ◆ *n* **tie-up. 8** a link or connection. **9** *Chiefly US & Canad.* a standstill. **10** *Chiefly US & Canad.* an informal term for **traffic jam.**

tiff ❶ (tɪf) *n* **1** a petty quarrel. **2** a fit of ill humour. ◆ *vb* **3** (*intr*) to have or be in a tiff. [C18: from ?]

tiffany ('tɪfənɪ) *n, pl* **tiffanies.** a sheer fine gauzy fabric. [C17 (in the sense: a fine dress worn on Twelfth Night): from OF *tifanie,* from ecclesiastical L *theophania* Epiphany]

tiffin ('tɪfɪn) *n* (in India) a light meal, esp. at midday. [C18: prob. from obs. *tiffing,* from *tiff* to sip]

tig (tɪg) *n, vb* **tigs, tigging, tigged.** another word for **tag**[2] (senses 1, 4).

tiger ('taɪgə) *n* **1** a large feline mammal of forests in most of Asia, having a tawny yellow coat with black stripes. **2** a dynamic, forceful, or cruel person. **3a** a country, esp. in E Asia, that is achieving rapid economic growth. **3b** (*as modifier*): *a tiger economy.* [C13: from OF *tigre,* from L *tigris,* from Gk, of Iranian origin]
▸ **'tigerish** *or* **'tigrish** *adj*

Tiger ('taɪgə) *n* a variant of **TIGR.**

tiger beetle *n* any of a family of active predatory beetles, chiefly of warm dry regions, having powerful mandibles and long legs.

tiger cat *n* a medium-sized feline mammal of Central and South America, having a dark-striped coat.

tiger lily *n* a lily plant of China and Japan cultivated for its flowers, which have black-spotted orange petals.

tiger moth *n* any of various moths having wings that are conspicuously marked with stripes and spots.

tiger's-eye *or* **tigereye** ('taɪgərˌaɪ) *n* a semiprecious golden-brown stone.

tiger shark *n* a voracious omnivorous requiem shark of tropical waters, having a striped or spotted body.

tiger snake *n* a highly venomous and aggressive Australian snake, usually with dark bands on the back.

tight ❶ (taɪt) *adj* **1** stretched or drawn so as not to be loose; taut. **2** fitting in a close manner. **3** held, made, fixed, or closed firmly and securely: *a tight knot.* **4a** of close and compact construction or organization, esp. so as to be impervious to water, air, etc. **4b** (*in combination*): *airtight.* **5** unyielding or stringent. **6** cramped or constricted: *a tight fit.* **7** mean or miserly. **8** difficult and problematic: *a tight situation.* **9** hardly profitable: *a tight bargain.* **10** *Econ.* **10a** (of a commodity) difficult to obtain. **10b** (of funds, money, etc.) difficult and expensive to borrow. **10c** (of markets) characterized by excess demand or scarcity. **11** (of a match or game) very close or even. **12** (of a team or group, esp. of a pop group) playing well together, in a disciplined coordinated way. **13** *Inf.* drunk. **14** *Inf.* (of a person) showing tension. ◆ *adv* **15** in a close, firm, or secure way. [C14: prob. var. of *thight,* from ON *thēttr* close]
▸ **'tightly** *adv* ▸ **'tightness** *n*

tightass ('taɪtˌæs) *n Sl., chiefly US.* an inhibited or excessively self-controlled person.
▸ **'tightˌassed** *adj*

tighten ❶ ('taɪtᵊn) *vb* to make or become tight or tighter.

tightfisted ❶ (ˌtaɪt'fɪstɪd) *adj* mean; miserly.

tight head *n Rugby.* the prop on the hooker's right in the front row of a scrum. Cf. **loose head.**

tightknit (ˌtaɪt'nɪt) *adj* **1** closely integrated: *a tightknit community.* **2** organized carefully.

tight-lipped ❶ *adj* **1** secretive or taciturn. **2** with the lips pressed tightly together, as through anger.

tightrope ('taɪtˌrəʊp) *n* a rope stretched taut on which acrobats walk or perform balancing feats.
▸ **tightrope walker** *n*

tights (taɪts) *pl n* **1a** Also called: (US) **panty hose,** (Canad. and NZ) **panty-hose,** (Austral. and NZ) **pantihose.** a one-piece clinging garment covering the body from the waist to the feet, worn by women and also by acrobats, dancers, etc. **1b** *US & Canad.* Also called: **leotards.** a similar, tight-fitting garment worn instead of trousers by either sex. **2** a similar garment formerly worn by men, as in the 16th century with a doublet.

tiglic acid ('tɪglɪk) *n* a syrupy liquid or crystalline unsaturated carboxylic acid, found in croton oil and used in perfumery. [C19 *tiglic,* from NL *Croton tiglium* (the croton plant), from ?]

tigon ('taɪgən) *or* **tiglon** ('tɪglɒn) *n* the hybrid offspring of a male tiger and a female lion.

TIGR *abbrev. for* Treasury Investment Growth Receipts: a bond denominated in dollars and linked to US treasury bonds, the yield on which is taxed in the UK as income when it is cashed or redeemed. Also called: **Tiger.**

THESAURUS

tie in *vb* **1** = **link**, be relevant, come in, connect, coordinate, fit in, have bearing, relate ◆ *n* **tie-in 2** = **link**, association, connection, coordination, hook-up, liaison, relation, relationship, tie-up

tier[1] *n* **1, 2a** = **row**, bank, echelon, file, layer, level, line, order, rank, series, storey, stratum

tie up *vb* **1** = **bind**, attach, pinion, restrain, tether, truss **2** = **moor**, lash, make fast, rope, secure **3** = **occupy**, engage, engross, keep busy **4** = **conclude**, bring to a close, end, finish off, settle, terminate, wind up, wrap up (*inf.*) ◆ *n* **tie-up 8** = **link**, association, connection, coordination, hook-up, liaison, linkup, relation, relationship, tie-in

tiff *n* **1** = **quarrel**, difference, disagreement, dispute, falling-out (*inf.*), petty quarrel, row, scrap (*inf.*), squabble, words **2** = **temper**, bad mood, fit of ill humour, fit of pique, huff, ill humour, pet, sulk, tantrum, wax (*inf., chiefly Brit.*)

tight *adj* **1** = **taut**, rigid, stiff, stretched, tense **2** = **close-fitting**, close, compact, constricted, cramped, narrow, snug **3** = **secure**, fast, firm, fixed **4a** = **sealed**, hermetic, impervious, proof, sound, watertight **5** = **strict**, harsh, inflexible, rigid, rigorous, severe, stern, stringent, tough, uncompromising, unyielding **7** *Informal* = **miserly**, close, grasping, mean, niggardly, parsimonious, penurious, sparing, stingy, tight-arsed (*taboo sl.*), tightfisted **8** = **difficult**, dangerous, hazardous, perilous, precarious, problematic, sticky (*inf.*), ticklish, tough, tricky, troublesome, worrisome **11** = **close**, even, evenly-balanced, near, well-matched **13** *Informal* = **drunk**, blotto, Brahms and Liszt (*sl.*), half cut (*Brit. sl.*), inebriated, in one's cups, intoxicated, legless (*inf.*), out of it (*sl.*), out to it (*Austral. & NZ sl.*), pickled (*inf.*), pie-eyed (*sl.*), pissed (*taboo sl.*), plastered (*sl.*), rat-arsed (*taboo sl.*), smashed (*sl.*), sozzled (*inf.*), three sheets in the wind (*sl.*), tiddly (*sl., chiefly Brit.*), tipsy, under the influence (*inf.*)
Antonyms *adj* ≠ **taut:** relaxed, slack ≠ **close-fitting:** loose, spacious ≠ **sealed:** loose, open, porous ≠ **strict:** easy, easy-going, generous, lax, lenient, liberal, relaxed, soft, undemanding ≠ **miserly:** abundant, extravagant, generous, lavish, munificent, open, prodigal, profuse, spendthrift ≠ **difficult:** easy ≠ **close:** easy, landslide, overwhelming, runaway, uneven ≠ **drunk:** sober

tighten *vb* = **stretch**, rigidify, stiffen, tauten, tense = **squeeze**, close, constrict, cramp, narrow = **fasten**, fix, screw, secure
Antonyms *vb* ≠ **stretch:** loosen, relax, slacken, weaken ≠ **squeeze:** ease off, let out, slacken ≠ **fasten:** unbind, unfasten, unscrew

tightfisted *adj* = **miserly**, close, close-fisted, grasping, mean, mingy (*Brit. inf.*), niggardly, parsimonious, penurious, sparing, stingy, tight, tight-arsed (*taboo sl.*)

tight-lipped *adj* **1** = **secretive**, close-lipped, close-mouthed, mum, mute, quiet, reserved, reticent, silent, taciturn, uncommunicative, unforthcoming

tigress (ˈtaɪgrɪs) *n* **1** a female tiger. **2** a fierce, cruel, or wildly passionate woman.

tigridia (taɪˈgrɪdɪə) *n* any of various bulbous plants of Mexico, Central America, and tropical S America. [C19: from Mod. L, from Gk *tigris* tiger (alluding to the spotted flowers of these plants)]

tike (taɪk) *n* a variant spelling of **tyke**.

tiki (ˈtiːkiː) *n* a Maori greenstone neck ornament in the form of a fetus. Also called: **heitiki**. [from Maori *heitiki* figure worn round neck]

tikka (ˈtiːkə) *adj* (*immediately postpositive*) *Indian cookery*. (of meat, esp. chicken or lamb) marinated in spices and then dry-roasted, usually in a clay oven.

tilak (ˈtɪlək) *n, pl* **tilak** *or* **tilaks**. a coloured spot or mark worn by Hindus, esp. on the forehead, often indicating membership of a religious sect, caste, etc., or (in the case of a woman) marital status. [from Sansk. *tilaka*]

tilbury (ˈtɪlbərɪ, -brɪ) *n, pl* **tilburies**. a light two-wheeled horse-drawn open carriage, seating two people. [C19: prob. after the inventor]

tilde (ˈtɪldə) *n* the diacritical mark (˜) placed over a letter to indicate a nasal sound, as in Spanish *señor*. [C19: from Sp., from L *titulus* title]

tile (taɪl) *n* **1** a thin slab of fired clay, rubber, linoleum, etc., used with others to cover a roof, floor, wall, etc. **2** a short pipe made of earthenware, plastic, etc., used with others to form a drain. **3** tiles collectively. **4** a rectangular block used as a playing piece in mah jong and other games. **5 on the tiles**. *Inf.* on a spree, esp. of drinking or debauchery. ◆ *vb* **tiles, tiling, tiled**. **6** (*tr*) to cover with tiles. [OE *tīgele*, from L *tēgula*]
▸ˈ**tiler** *n*

tiling (ˈtaɪlɪŋ) *n* **1** tiles collectively. **2** something made of or surfaced with tiles.

till[1] (tɪl) *conj, prep* short for **until**. Also (not standard): **'til**. [OE *til*]

> **USAGE NOTE** *Till* is a variant of *until* that is acceptable at all levels of language. *Until* is, however, often preferred at the beginning of a sentence in formal writing: *until his behaviour improves, he cannot become a member*.

till[2] Ⓣ (tɪl) *vb* (*tr*) **1** to cultivate and work (land) for the raising of crops. **2** to plough. [OE *tilian* to try, obtain]
▸ˈ**tillable** *adj* ▸ˈ**tiller** *n*

till[3] Ⓣ (tɪl) *n* a box, case, or drawer into which money taken from customers is put, now usually part of a cash register. [C15 *tylle*, from ?]

till[4] (tɪl) *n* a glacial deposit consisting of rock fragments of various sizes. The most common is boulder clay. [C17: from ?]

tillage (ˈtɪlɪdʒ) *n* **1** the act, process, or art of tilling. **2** tilled land.

tiller[1] (ˈtɪlə) *n Naut.* a handle fixed to the top of a rudderpost to serve as a lever in steering it. [C14: from Anglo-F *teiler* beam of a loom, from Med. L *tēlārium*, from L *tēla* web]
▸ˈ**tillerless** *adj*

tiller[2] (ˈtɪlə) *n* **1** a shoot that arises from the base of the stem in grasses. **2** a less common name for **sapling**. ◆ *vb* **3** (*intr*) (of a plant) to produce tillers. [OE *telgor* twig]

tilt Ⓣ (tɪlt) *vb* **1** to incline or cause to incline at an angle. **2** (*usually intr*) to attack or overthrow (a person) in a tilt or joust. **3** (when *intr*, often foll. by *at*) to aim or thrust: *to tilt a lance*. **4** (*tr*) to forge with a tilt hammer. ◆ *n* **5** a slope or angle: *at a tilt*. **6** the act of tilting. **7** (esp. in medieval Europe) **7a** a jousting contest. **7b** a thrust with a lance or pole delivered during a tournament. **8** an attempt to win a contest. **9** See **tilt hammer**. **10** **(at) full tilt**. at full speed or force. [OE *tealtian*]
▸ˈ**tilter** *n*

tilth (tɪlθ) *n* **1** the act or process of tilling land. **2** the condition of soil or land that has been tilled. [OE *tilthe*]

tilt hammer *n* a drop hammer with a heavy head; used in forging.

tiltyard (ˈtɪlt,jɑːd) *n* (formerly) an enclosed area for tilting.

Tim. *Bible. abbrev. for* Timothy.

timbal *or* **tymbal** (ˈtɪmbᵊl) *n Music.* a type of kettledrum. [C17: from F *timbale*, from OF *tamballe*, (associated also with *cymbale* cymbal), from OSp. *atabal*, from Ar. *at-tabl* the drum]

timbale (tæmˈbɑːl) *n* **1** a mixture of meat, fish, etc., cooked in a mould lined with potato or pastry. **2** a straight-sided mould in which such a dish is prepared. [C19: from F: kettledrum]

timber Ⓣ (ˈtɪmbə) *n* **1a** wood, esp. when regarded as a construction material. Usual US and Canad. word: **lumber**. **1b** (*as modifier*): *a timber cottage*. **2a** trees collectively. **2b** *Chiefly US.* woodland. **3** a piece of wood used in a structure. **4** *Naut.* a frame in a wooden vessel. ◆ *vb* **5** (*tr*) to provide with timbers. ◆ *sentence substitute*. **6** a lumberjack's shouted warning when a tree is about to fall. [OE]
▸ˈ**timbered** *adj* ▸ˈ**timbering** *n*

timber hitch *n* a knot used for tying a rope round a spar, log, etc., for haulage.

timber limit *n Canad.* **1** the area to which rights of cutting timber, granted by a government licence, are limited. **2** another term for **timber line**.

timber line *n* the altitudinal or latitudinal limit of normal tree growth. See also **tree line**.

timber wolf *n* a wolf with a grey brindled coat found in forested northern regions, esp. of North America.

timberyard (ˈtɪmbə,jɑːd) *n Brit., Austral., & NZ.* an establishment where timber, etc., is stored or sold. US and Canad. word: **lumberyard**.

timbre Ⓣ (ˈtɪmbə, ˈtæmbə) *n* **1** *Phonetics.* the distinctive tone quality differentiating one vowel or sonant from another. **2** *Music.* tone colour or quality of sound. [C19: from F: note of a bell, from OF: drum, from Med. Gk *timbanon*, from Gk *tumpanon*]

timbrel (ˈtɪmbrəl) *n Chiefly biblical.* a tambourine. [C16: from OF; see TIMBRE]

Timbuktu (,tɪmbʌkˈtuː) *n* any distant or outlandish place: *from here to Timbuktu*. [from *Timbuktu*, town in Africa: terminus of a trans-Saharan caravan route]

time Ⓣ (taɪm) *n* **1** the continuous passage of existence in which events pass from a state of potentiality in the future, through the present, to a state of finality in the past. Related adj: **temporal**. **2** *Physics.* a quantity measuring duration, usually with reference to a periodic process such as the rotation of the earth or the vibration of electromagnetic radiation emitted from certain atoms. Time is considered as a fourth coordinate required to specify an event. See **space-time continuum**. **3** a specific point on this continuum expressed in hours and minutes: *the time is four o'clock*. **4** a system of reckoning for expressing time: *Greenwich Mean Time*. **5a** a definite and measurable portion of this continuum. **5b** (*as modifier*): *time limit*. **6a** an accepted period such as a day, season, etc. **6b** (*in combination*): *springtime*. **7** an unspecified interval; a while. **8** (*often pl*) a period or point marked by specific attributes or events: *the Victorian times*. **9** a sufficient interval or period: *have you got time to help me?* **10** an instance or occasion: *I called you three times*. **11** an occasion or period of specified quality: *have a good time*. **12** the duration of human existence. **13** the heyday of human life: *in her time she was a great star*. **14** a suitable moment: *it's time I told you*. **15** the expected interval in which something is done. **16** a particularly important moment, esp. childbirth or death: *her time had come*. **17** (*pl*) indicating a degree or amount calculated by multiplication with the number specified: *ten times three is thirty*. **18** (*often pl*) the fashions, thought, etc., of the present age (esp. in **ahead of one's time, behind the times**). **19** *Brit.* Also: **closing time**. the time at which bars, pubs, etc., are legally obliged to stop selling alcoholic drinks. **20** *Inf.* a term in jail (esp. in **do time**). **21a** a customary or full period of work. **21b** the rate of pay for this period. **22** Also (esp. US): **metre**. **22a** the system of combining beats or pulses in music into successive groupings by which the rhythm of the music is established. **22b** a specific system having a specific number of beats in each grouping or bar: *duple time*. **23** *Music.* short for **time value**. **24 against time**. in an effort to complete something in a limited period. **25 ahead of time**. before the deadline. **26 at one time**. **26a** once; formerly. **26b** simultaneously. **27 at the same time**. **27a** simultaneously. **27b** nevertheless; however. **28 at times**. sometimes. **29 beat time**. to indicate the tempo of a piece of music by waving a baton, hand, etc. **30 for the time being**. for the moment; temporarily. **31 from time to time**. at intervals; occasionally. **32 have no time for**. to have no patience with; not tolerate. **33 in good time**. **33a** early. **33b** quickly. **34 in no time**. very quickly. **35 in one's own time**. **35a** outside paid working hours. **35b** at one's own rate. **36 in time**. **36a** early or at the appointed time. **36b** eventually. **36c** *Music.* at a correct metrical or rhythmic pulse. **37 keep time**. to observe correctly the accent or rhythmic pulse of a piece of music in relation to tempo. **38 make time**. **38a** to find an opportunity. **38b** (often foll. by *with*) *US inf.* to succeed in seducing. **39 on time**.

THESAURUS

till[2] *vb* **1, 2** = **cultivate**, dig, plough, turn over, work

till[3] *n* = **cash register**, cash box, cash drawer

tilt *vb* **1** = **slant**, cant, heel, incline, lean, list, slope, tip **2** = **joust**, attack, break a lance, clash, contend, cross swords, duel, encounter, fight, lock horns, spar ◆ *n* **5** = **slope**, angle, cant, inclination, incline, list, pitch, slant **7a** *Medieval history* = **joust**, clash, combat, duel, encounter, fight, lists, set-to (*inf.*), tournament, tourney **10** **(at) full tilt** = **full speed**, for dear life, full force, headlong, like a bat out of hell (*sl.*), like the clappers (*Brit. inf.*)

timber *n* **1a** = **wood**, beams, boards, logs, planks **2a** = **trees**, forest

timbre *n* **2** = **tone**, colour, quality of sound, resonance, ring, tonality, tone colour

time *n* **5a, 7** = **period**, age, chronology, date, duration, epoch, era, generation, hour, interval, season, space, span, spell, stretch, term, while **10** = **occasion**, instance, juncture, point, stage **12** = **lifetime**, allotted span, day, duration, life, life span, season **13** = **heyday**, hour, peak **22** = **tempo**, beat, measure, metre, rhythm **26 at one time: a** = **once**, for a while, formerly, hitherto, once upon a time, previously **b** = **simultaneously**, all at once, at the same time, together **28 at times** = **sometimes**, every now and then, every so often, from time to time, now and then, occasionally, once in a while, on occasion **30 for the time being** = **for now**, for the moment, for the nonce, for the present, in the meantime, meantime, meanwhile, pro tem, temporarily **31 from time to time** = **occasionally**, at times, every now and then, every so often, now and then, once in a while, on occasion, sometimes **33 in good time: a** = **on time**, early, with time to spare **b** = **quickly**, rapidly, speedily, swiftly, with dispatch **34 in no time** = **quickly**, apace, before one knows it, before you can say Jack Robinson, in a flash, in a jiffy (*inf.*), in a moment, in an instant, in a trice, in two shakes of a lamb's tail (*inf.*), rapidly, speedily, swiftly **36 in time: a** = **on time**, at the appointed time, early, in good time, on schedule, with time to spare **b** = **eventually**, by and by, in the fullness of time, one day, someday, sooner or later, ultimately **39a on time** = **punctually**, in good time, on the dot **41 time and again** = **frequently**, many times, often, on many occasions, over and over again, repeatedly, time after time ◆ *vb* **46** = **measure**, clock, count, judge **47** = **schedule**, set **48** = **regulate**, control

39a at the expected or scheduled time. **39b** *US.* payable in instalments. **40 pass the time of day.** to exchange casual greetings (with an acquaintance). **41 time and again.** frequently. **42 time off.** a period when one is absent from work for a holiday, through sickness, etc. **43 time of one's life.** a memorably enjoyable time. **44 time out of mind.** from time immemorial. **45** (*modifier*) operating automatically at or for a set time: *time lock; time switch.* ◆ *vb* **times, timing, timed.** (*tr*) **46** to ascertain the duration or speed of. **47** to set a time for. **48** to adjust to keep accurate time. **49** to pick a suitable time for. **50** *Sport.* to control the execution or speed of (an action). ◆ *sentence substitute.* **51** the word called out by a publican signalling that it is closing time. [OE *tīma*]

time and a half *n* the rate of pay equalling one and a half times the normal rate, often offered for overtime work.

time and motion study *n* the analysis of industrial or work procedures to determine the most efficient methods of operation. Also: **time and motion, time study, motion study.**

time bomb *n* a bomb containing a timing mechanism that determines the time at which it will detonate.

time capsule *n* a container holding articles, documents, etc., representative of the current age, buried for discovery in the future.

time charter *n* the hire of a ship or aircraft for a specified period. Cf. **voyage charter.**

time clock *n* a clock which records, by punching or stamping **timecards** inserted into it, the time of arrival or departure of people, such as employees in a factory.

time-consuming *adj* taking up or involving a great deal of time.

time exposure *n* **1** an exposure of a photographic film for a relatively long period, usually a few seconds. **2** a photograph produced by such an exposure.

time-honoured ❶ *adj* having been observed for a long time and sanctioned by custom.

time immemorial *n* the distant past beyond memory or record.

timekeeper ('taɪm,kiːpə) *n* **1** a person or thing that keeps or records time. **2** an employee who maintains a record of the hours worked by the other employees. **3** an employee whose record of punctuality is of a specified nature: *a bad timekeeper.*
▸ **'time,keeping** *n*

time-lag *n* an interval between two connected events.

time-lapse photography *n* the technique of recording a very slow process on film by exposing single frames at regular intervals. The film is then projected at normal speed.

timeless ❶ ('taɪmlɪs) *adj* **1** unaffected or unchanged by time; ageless. **2** eternal.
▸ **'timelessly** *adv* ▸ **'timelessness** *n*

timely ❶ ('taɪmlɪ) *adj* **timelier, timeliest,** *adv* at the right or an opportune or appropriate time.

time machine *n* (in science fiction) a machine in which people or objects can be transported into the past or the future.

time-out *n Chiefly US & Canad.* **1** *Sport.* an interruption in play during which players rest, discuss tactics, etc. **2** a period of rest; break. **3** *Computing.* a condition that occurs when the amount of time a computer has been instructed to wait for another device to perform a task has expired, usually indicated by an error message. ◆ *vb* **time out. 4** (of a computer) to stop operating because of a time-out.

timepiece ('taɪm,piːs) *n* any of various devices, such as a clock, watch, or chronometer, which measure and indicate time.

timer ('taɪmə) *n* **1** a device for measuring, recording, or indicating time. **2** a switch or regulator that causes a mechanism to operate at a specific time. **3** a person or thing that times.

time-saving *adj* shortening the length of time required for an operation, activity, etc.
▸ **time-saver** *n*

timescale ('taɪm,skeɪl) *n* the span of time within which certain events occur or are scheduled in relation to any broader period of time.

time-served *adj* (of a craftsman or tradesman) having completed an apprenticeship; fully trained and competent.

timeserver ❶ ('taɪm,sɜːvə) *n* a person who compromises and changes his opinions, way of life, etc., to suit the current fashions.

time sharing *n* **1** a system of part ownership of a property for use as a holiday home whereby each participant owns the property for a particular period every year. **2** a system by which users at different terminals of a computer can, because of its high speed, apparently communicate with it at the same time.

time signal *n* an announcement of the correct time, esp. on radio or television.

time signature *n Music.* a sign usually consisting of two figures, one above the other, the upper figure representing the number of beats per bar and the lower one the time value of each beat: it is placed after the key signature.

timetable ❶ ('taɪm,teɪbᵊl) *n* **1** a list or table of events arranged according to the time when they take place; schedule. ◆ *vb* **timetables, timetabling, timetabled.** (*tr*) **2** to include in or arrange according to a timetable.

time value *n Music.* the duration of a note relative to other notes in a composition and considered in relation to the basic tempo.

time warp *n* an imagined distortion of the progress of time so that, for instance, events from the past may appear to be happening in the present.

timeworn ❶ ('taɪm,wɔːn) *adj* **1** showing the adverse effects of overlong use or of old age. **2** hackneyed; trite.

time zone *n* a region throughout which the same standard time is used. There are 24 time zones in the world, demarcated approximately by meridians at 15° intervals, an hour apart.

timid ❶ ('tɪmɪd) *adj* **1** easily frightened or upset, esp. by human contact; shy. **2** indicating shyness or fear. [C16: from L *timidus,* from *timēre* to fear]
▸ **ti'midity** *or* **'timidness** *n* ▸ **'timidly** *adv*

timing ('taɪmɪŋ) *n* the regulation of actions or remarks in relation to others to produce the best effect, as in music, the theatre, etc.

timocracy (taɪ'mɒkrəsɪ) *n, pl* **timocracies. 1** a political system in which possession of property is a requirement for participation in government. **2** a political system in which love of honour is deemed the guiding principle of government. [C16: from OF *tymocracie,* ult. from Gk *timokratia,* from *timē* worth, honour, + -CRACY]

timorous ❶ ('tɪmərəs) *adj* **1** fearful or timid. **2** indicating fear or timidity. [C15: from OF *temoros,* from Med. L, from L *timor* fear, from *timēre* to be afraid]
▸ **'timorously** *adv* ▸ **'timorousness** *n*

timothy grass *or* **timothy** ('tɪməθɪ) *n* a perennial grass of temperate regions having erect stiff stems: grown for hay and pasture. [C18: apparently after a *Timothy Hanson,* who brought it to colonial Carolina]

timpani *or* **tympani** ('tɪmpənɪ) *pl n* (*sometimes functioning as sing*) a set of kettledrums. [from It., pl of *timpano* kettledrum, from L: TYMPANUM]
▸ **'timpanist** *or* **'tympanist** *n*

tin (tɪn) *n* **1** a malleable silvery-white metallic element. It is used extensively in alloys, esp. bronze and pewter, and as a noncorroding coating for steel. Symbol: Sn; atomic no.: 50; atomic wt.: 118.69. Related adjs.: **stannic, stannous. 2** Also called (esp. US and Canad.): **can.** an airtight sealed container of thin sheet metal coated with tin, used for preserving and storing food or drink. **3** any container made of metallic tin. **4** Also called: **tinful.** the contents of a tin. **5** *Brit., Austral., & NZ.* galvanized iron: *a tin roof.* **6** any metal regarded as cheap or flimsy. **7** *Brit.* a loaf of bread with a rectangular shape. **8** *NZ.* a receptacle for home-baked biscuits, etc. (esp. in **fill her tins** to bake a supply of biscuits, etc.). ◆ *vb* **tins, tinning, tinned.** (*tr*) **9** to put (food, etc.) into a tin or tins; preserve in a tin. **10** to plate or coat with tin. **11** to prepare (a metal) for soldering or brazing by applying a thin layer of solder to the surface. [OE]

tinamou ('tɪnə,muː) *n* any of various birds of Central and South America, having small wings and a heavy body. [C18: via F from Carib *tinamu*]

tin can *n* a metal food container, esp. when empty.

tinctorial (tɪŋk'tɔːrɪəl) *adj* of or relating to colouring, staining, or dyeing. [C17: from L *tinctōrius,* from *tingere* to tinge]

tincture ❶ ('tɪŋktʃə) *n* **1** a medicinal extract in a solution of alcohol. **2** a tint, colour, or tinge. **3** a slight flavour, aroma, or trace. **4** a colour or metal used on heraldic arms. **5** *Obs.* a dye. ◆ *vb* **tinctures, tincturing, tinctured. 6** (*tr*) to give a tint or colour to. [C14: from L *tinctūra* a dyeing, from *tingere* to dye]

tinder ('tɪndə) *n* **1** dry wood or other easily combustible material used for lighting a fire. **2** anything inflammatory or dangerous. [OE *tynder*]
▸ **'tindery** *adj*

THESAURUS

time-honoured *adj* = **long-established**, age-old, ancient, conventional, customary, established, fixed, old, traditional, usual, venerable

timeless *adj* **1, 2** = **eternal**, abiding, ageless, ceaseless, changeless, deathless, endless, enduring, everlasting, immortal, immutable, imperishable, indestructible, lasting, permanent, persistent, undying
Antonyms *adj* ephemeral, evanescent, momentary, mortal, passing, temporal, temporary, transitory

timely *adj* = **opportune**, appropriate, at the right time, convenient, judicious, prompt, propitious, punctual, seasonable, suitable, well-timed
Antonyms *adj* ill-timed, inconvenient, inopportune, late, tardy, unseasonable, untimely

timeserver *n* = **opportunist**, hypocrite, self-seeker, trimmer, Vicar of Bray, weathercock

timetable *n* **1** = **schedule**, agenda, calendar, curriculum, diary, list, order of the day, programme

timeworn *adj* **1** = **decrepit**, aged, ancient, broken-down, dog-eared, lined, ragged, rundown, shabby, the worse for wear, weathered, worn, wrinkled **2** = **hackneyed**, ancient, clichéd, dated, hoary, old hat, out of date, outworn, passé, stale, stock, threadbare, tired, trite, well-worn

timid *adj* **1** = **fearful**, afraid, apprehensive, bashful, cowardly, coy, diffident, faint-hearted, irresolute, modest, mousy, nervous, pusillanimous, retiring, shrinking, shy, timorous
Antonyms *adj* aggressive, arrogant, ballsy (*taboo sl.*), bold, brave, confident, daring, fearless, fierce, forceful, forward, presumptuous, self-assured, self-confident, shameless, unabashed

timorous *adj* **1** *Literary* = **timid**, afraid, apprehensive, bashful, cowardly, coy, diffident, faint-hearted, fearful, frightened, irresolute, mousy, nervous, pusillanimous, retiring, shrinking, shy, trembling
Antonyms *adj* assertive, assured, audacious, bold, confident, courageous, daring, fearless

tincture *n* **2, 3** = **tinge**, aroma, colour, dash, flavour, hint, hue, seasoning, shade, smack, *soupçon,* stain, suggestion, tint, touch, trace ◆ *vb* **6** = **tinge**, colour, dye, flavour, scent, season, stain, tint

tinderbox ('tɪndəˌbɒks) *n* **1** a box used formerly for holding tinder, esp. one fitted with a flint and steel. **2** a person or thing that is particularly touchy or explosive.

tine (taɪn) *n* **1** a slender prong, esp. of a fork. **2** any of the sharp terminal branches of a deer's antler. [OE *tind*]
▸**tined** *adj*

tinea ('tɪnɪə) *n* any fungal skin disease, esp. ringworm. [C17: from L: worm]
▸'**tineal** *adj*

tinfoil ('tɪnˌfɔɪl) *n* **1** thin foil made of tin or an alloy of tin and lead. **2** thin foil made of aluminium; used for wrapping foodstuffs.

ting (tɪŋ) *n* **1** a high metallic sound such as that made by a small bell. ◆ *vb* **2** to make or cause to make such a sound. [C15: imit.]

ting-a-ling ('tɪŋə'lɪŋ) *n* the sound of a small bell.

tinge ❶ (tɪndʒ) *n* **1** a slight tint or colouring. **2** any slight addition. ◆ *vb* **tinges, tingeing** *or* **tinging, tinged.** (*tr*) **3** to colour or tint faintly. **4** to impart a slight trace to: *her thoughts were tinged with nostalgia.* [C15: from L *tingere* to colour]

tingle ❶ ('tɪŋgᵊl) *vb* **tingles, tingling, tingled. 1** (*usually intr*) to feel or cause to feel a prickling, itching, or stinging sensation of the flesh, as from a cold plunge. ◆ *n* **2** a sensation of tingling. [C14: ? a var. of TINKLE]
▸'**tingler** *n* ▸'**tingling** *adj* ▸'**tingly** *adj*

tin god *n* **1** a self-important person. **2** a person erroneously regarded as holy or venerable.

tin hat *n Inf.* a steel helmet worn by military personnel.

tinker ❶ ('tɪŋkə) *n* **1** (esp. formerly) a travelling mender of pots and pans. **2** a clumsy worker. **3** the act of tinkering. **4** *Scot. & Irish.* a Gypsy. ◆ *vb* **5** (*intr; foll. by with*) to play, fiddle, or meddle (with machinery, etc.), esp. while undertaking repairs. **6** to mend (pots and pans) as a tinker. [C13 *tinkere*, ?from *tink* tinkle, imit.]
▸'**tinkerer** *n*

tinker's damn *or* **cuss** *n Sl.* the slightest heed (esp. in **not give a tinker's damn** *or* **cuss**).

tinkle ('tɪŋkᵊl) *vb* **tinkles, tinkling, tinkled. 1** to ring with a high tinny sound like a small bell. **2** (*tr*) to announce or summon by such a ringing. **3** (*intr*) *Brit. inf.* to urinate. ◆ *n* **4** a high clear ringing sound. **5** the act of tinkling. **6** *Brit. inf.* a telephone call. [C14: imit.]
▸'**tinkly** *adj*

tin lizzie ('lɪzɪ) *n Inf.* an old or decrepit car.

tinned (tɪnd) *adj* **1** plated, coated, or treated with tin. **2** *Chiefly Brit.* preserved or stored in airtight tins. **3** coated with a layer of solder.

tinnitus (tɪ'naɪtəs) *n Pathol.* a ringing, hissing, or booming sensation in one or both ears, caused by infection of the ear, a side effect of certain drugs, etc. [C19: from L, from *tinnīre* to ring]

tinny ('tɪnɪ) *adj* **tinnier, tinniest. 1** of or resembling tin. **2** cheap or shoddy. **3** (of a sound) high, thin, and metallic. **4** (of food or drink) flavoured with metal, as from a container. **5** *Austral. & NZ sl.* lucky. ◆ *n, pl* **tinnies. 6** *Austral. sl.* a can of beer.
▸'**tinnily** *adv* ▸'**tinniness** *n*

tin-opener *n* a small tool for opening tins.

Tin Pan Alley *n* **1** originally, a district in New York concerned with the production of popular music. **2** the commercial side of show business and pop music.

tin plate *n* **1** thin steel sheet coated with a layer of tin that protects the steel from corrosion. ◆ *vb* **tin-plate, tin-plates, tin-plating, tin-plated. 2** (*tr*) to coat with a layer of tin.

tinpot ❶ ('tɪnˌpɒt) *adj* (*prenominal*) *Brit. inf.* **1** inferior, cheap, or worthless. **2** petty; unimportant.

tinsel ❶ ('tɪnsəl) *n* **1** a decoration consisting of a piece of string with thin strips of metal foil attached along its length. **2** a yarn or fabric interwoven with strands of glittering thread. **3** anything cheap, showy, and gaudy. ◆ *vb* **tinsels, tinselling, tinselled** *or US* **tinsels, tinseling, tinseled.** (*tr*) **4** to decorate with or as if with tinsel: *snow tinsels the trees.* **5** to give a gaudy appearance to. ◆ *adj* **6** made of or decorated with tinsel. **7** showily but cheaply attractive; gaudy. [C16: from OF *estincele* a spark, from L *scintilla*]
▸'**tinselly** *adj*

Tinseltown ('tɪnsəlˌtaʊn) *n* an informal name for **Hollywood**, esp. as the home of the film industry. [C20: from the insubstantial glitter of the film world]

tinsmith ('tɪnˌsmɪθ) *n* a person who works with tin or tin plate.

tin soldier *n* a miniature toy soldier, usually made of lead.

tinstone ('tɪnˌstəʊn) *n* another name for **cassiterite.**

tint ❶ (tɪnt) *n* **1** a shade of a colour, esp. a pale one. **2** a colour that is softened by the addition of white. **3** a tinge. **4** a dye for the hair. **5** a trace or hint. **6** *Engraving.* uniform shading, produced esp. by hatching. ◆ *vb* **7** (*tr*) to colour or tinge. **8** (*intr*) to acquire a tint. [C18: from earlier *tinct*, from L *tingere* to colour]
▸'**tinter** *n*

tintinnabulation (ˌtɪntɪˌnæbjʊ'leɪʃən) *n* the act or an instance of the ringing or pealing of bells. [from L, from *tintinnāre* to tinkle, from *tinnīre* to ring]

tinware ('tɪnˌwɛə) *n* objects made of tin plate.

tin whistle *n* another name for **penny whistle.**

tinworks ('tɪnˌwɜːks) *n* (*functioning as sing or pl*) a place where tin is mined, smelted, or rolled.

tiny ❶ ('taɪnɪ) *adj* **tinier, tiniest.** very small. [C16 *tine*, from ?]
▸'**tinily** *adv* ▸'**tininess** *n*

-tion *suffix forming nouns.* indicating state, condition, action, process, or result: *election; prohibition.* [from OF, from L *-tiō, -tiōn-*]

tip[1] ❶ (tɪp) *n* **1** a narrow or pointed end of something. **2** the top or summit. **3** a small piece forming an end: *a metal tip on a cane.* ◆ *vb* **tips, tipping, tipped.** (*tr*) **4** to adorn or mark the tip of. **5** to cause to form a tip. [C15: from ON *typpa*]
▸'**tipless** *adj*

tip[2] ❶ (tɪp) *vb* **tips, tipping, tipped. 1** to tilt or cause to tilt. **2** (usually foll. by *over* or *up*) to tilt or cause to tilt, so as to overturn or fall. **3** *Brit.* to dump (rubbish, etc.). **4 tip one's hat.** to raise one's hat in salutation. ◆ *n* **5** a tipping or being tipped. **6** *Brit.* a dump for refuse, etc. [C14: from ?]
▸'**tipper** *n*

tip[3] ❶ (tɪp) *n* **1** a payment given for services in excess of the standard charge; gratuity. **2** a helpful hint or warning. **3** a piece of inside information, esp. in betting or investing. ◆ *vb* **tips, tipping, tipped. 4** to give a tip to. [C18: ?from TIP[4]]
▸'**tipper** *n*

tip[4] (tɪp) *vb* **tips, tipping, tipped.** (*tr*) **1** to hit or strike lightly. ◆ *n* **2** a light blow. [C13: ?from Low G *tippen*]

tip-off ❶ *n* **1** a warning or hint, esp. given confidentially and based on inside information. **2** *Basketball.* the act or an instance of putting the ball in play by the referee throwing it high between two opposing players. ◆ *vb* **tip off. 3** (*tr, adv*) to give a hint or warning to.

tipper truck *or* **lorry** *n* a truck or lorry the rear platform of which can be raised at the front end to enable the load to be discharged.

tippet ('tɪpɪt) *n* **1** a woman's fur cape for the shoulders. **2** the long stole of Anglican clergy worn during a service. **3** a long streamer-like part to a sleeve, hood, etc., esp. in the 16th century. [C14: ?from TIP[1]]

tipple ❶ ('tɪpᵊl) *vb* **tipples, tippling, tippled. 1** to make a habit of taking (alcoholic drink), esp. in small quantities. ◆ *n* **2** alcoholic drink. [C15: back formation from obs. *tippler* tapster, from ?]
▸'**tippler** *n*

tipstaff ('tɪpˌstɑːf) *n* **1** a court official. **2** a metal-tipped staff formerly used as a symbol of office. [C16 *tipped staff*]

tipster ('tɪpstə) *n* a person who sells tips on horse racing, the stock market, etc.

tipsy ❶ ('tɪpsɪ) *adj* **tipsier, tipsiest. 1** slightly drunk. **2** slightly tilted or tipped; askew. [C16: from TIP[2]]
▸'**tipsily** *adv* ▸'**tipsiness** *n*

tipsy cake *n Brit.* a kind of trifle made from a sponge cake soaked with wine or sherry and decorated with almonds and crystallized fruit.

tiptoe ('tɪpˌtəʊ) *vb* **tiptoes, tiptoeing, tiptoed.** (*intr*) **1** to walk with the heels off the ground. **2** to walk silently or stealthily. ◆ *n* **3 on tiptoe. 3a** on the tips of the toes or on the ball of the foot and the toes. **3b** eagerly

THESAURUS

tinge *n* **1** = **tint**, cast, colour, dye, shade, stain, tincture, wash **2** = **bit**, dash, drop, pinch, smack, smattering, *soupçon*, sprinkling, suggestion, touch, trace ◆ *vb* **3** = **tint**, colour, dye, imbue, shade, stain, suffuse

tingle *vb* **1** = **prickle**, have goose pimples, itch, sting, tickle ◆ *n* **2** = **quiver**, goose pimples, itch, itching, pins and needles (*inf.*), prickling, shiver, stinging, thrill, tickle, tickling

tinker *vb* **5** = **meddle**, dabble, fiddle (*inf.*), mess about, monkey, muck about (*Brit. sl.*), play, potter, toy

tinpot *adj* **1** *Brit. informal* = **worthless**, inferior, Mickey Mouse (*sl.*), miserable, paltry, pathetic, poxy (*sl.*), second-class, second-rate, two-bit (*US & Canad. sl.*), twopenny-halfpenny, unimportant, wretched

tinsel *adj* **7** = **showy**, brummagem, cheap, flashy, gaudy, gimcrack, meretricious, ostentatious, pinchbeck, plastic (*sl.*), sham, specious, superficial, tawdry, trashy

tint *n* **1** = **shade**, cast, colour, hue, tone **3, 5** = hint, shade, suggestion, tinge, touch, trace **4** = **dye**, rinse, stain, tincture, tinge, wash ◆ *vb* **7** = **dye**, colour, rinse, stain, tincture, tinge

tiny *adj* = **small**, diminutive, dwarfish, infinitesimal, insignificant, Lilliputian, little, microscopic, mini, miniature, minute, negligible, petite, pint-sized (*inf.*), puny, pygmy *or* pigmy, slight, teensy-weensy, teeny-weeny, trifling, wee
Antonyms *adj* colossal, enormous, extra-large, gargantuan, giant, gigantic, great, huge, immense, mammoth, massive, monstrous, titanic, vast

tip[1] *n* **2** = **end**, apex, cap, crown, extremity, head, peak, pinnacle, point, summit, top ◆ *vb* **4** = **cap**, crown, finish, surmount, top

tip[2] *vb* **1** = **tilt**, cant, capsize, incline, lean, list, overturn, slant, spill, topple over, upend, upset **3** *Brit.* = **dump**, ditch (*sl.*), empty, pour out, unload ◆ *n* **6** *Brit.* = **dump**, midden (*dialect*), refuse heap, rubbish heap

tip[3] *n* **1** = **gratuity**, baksheesh, gift, perquisite, *pourboire* **2** = **hint**, gen (*Brit. inf.*), information, inside information, pointer, suggestion ◆ *vb* **4** = **reward**, remunerate **4** = **advise**, give a clue, give a hint, suggest, tip (someone) the wink (*Brit. inf.*)

tip-off *n* **1** = **hint**, clue, forecast, gen (*Brit. inf.*), information, inside information, pointer, suggestion, warning, word, word of advice ◆ *vb* **tip off 3** = **advise**, caution, forewarn, give a clue, give a hint, suggest, tip (someone) the wink (*Brit. inf.*), warn

tipple *vb* **1** = **drink**, bend the elbow, bevvy (*dialect*), imbibe, indulge (*inf.*), quaff, swig, take a drink, tope ◆ *n* **2** = **alcohol**, booze (*inf.*), drink, John Barleycorn, liquor, poison (*inf.*)

tippler *n* **1** = **drinker**, bibber, boozer (*inf.*), drunk, drunkard, inebriate, soak (*sl.*), sot, sponge (*inf.*), toper

tipsy *adj* **1** = **tiddly** (*sl., chiefly Brit.*), babalas (*S. Afr.*), elevated (*inf.*), fuddled, happy (*inf.*), mellow, merry (*Brit. inf.*), slightly drunk, woozy (*inf.*)

anticipating something. **3c** stealthily or silently. ◆ *adv* **4** on tiptoe. ◆ *adj* **5** walking or standing on tiptoe.

tiptop (ˌtɪpˈtɒp) *adj, adv* **1** at the highest point of health, excellence, etc. **2** at the topmost point. ◆ *n* **3** the best in quality. **4** the topmost point.

tip-up *adj (prenominal)* able to be turned upwards around a hinge or pivot: *a tip-up seat.*

TIR *abbrev. for* Transports Internationaux Routiers. [F: International Road Transport]

tirade ⓣ (taɪˈreɪd) *n* a long angry speech or denunciation. [C19: from F, lit.: a pulling, from It. *tirata,* from *tirare* to pull, from ?]

tire[1] ⓣ (ˈtaɪə) *vb* **tires, tiring, tired. 1** *(tr)* to reduce the energy of, esp. by exertion; weary. **2** *(tr; often passive)* to reduce the tolerance of; bore or irritate: *I'm tired of the children's chatter.* **3** *(intr)* to become wearied or bored; flag. [OE *tēorian,* from ?]
▸ **ˈtiring** *adj*

tire[2] (ˈtaɪə) *n, vb* the US spelling of **tyre.**

tired ⓣ (ˈtaɪəd) *adj* **1** weary; fatigued. **2** no longer fresh; hackneyed. **3 tired and emotional.** *Euphemistic.* drunk.
▸ **ˈtiredness** *n*

tireless ⓣ (ˈtaɪəlɪs) *adj* unable to be tired.
▸ **ˈtirelessly** *adv* ▸ **ˈtirelessness** *n*

tiresome ⓣ (ˈtaɪəsəm) *adj* boring and irritating.
▸ **ˈtiresomely** *adv* ▸ **ˈtiresomeness** *n*

tirewoman (ˈtaɪəˌwʊmən) *n, pl* **tirewomen.** an obsolete term for a lady's maid. [C17: from *tire* (obs.) to ATTIRE]

tiring room (ˈtaɪərɪŋ) *n Arch.* a dressing room.

tiro (ˈtaɪrəʊ) *n, pl* **tiros.** a variant spelling of **tyro.**

'tis (tɪz) *Poetic or dialect. contraction of* it is.

tisane (tɪˈzæn) *n* an infusion of leaves or flowers. [C19: from F, from L *ptisana* barley water]

Tishri *Hebrew.* (tɪʃˈriː) *n* (in the Jewish calendar) the seventh month of the year according to biblical reckoning and the first month of the civil year, falling in September and October. [C19: from Heb.]

tissue ⓣ (ˈtɪsjuː, ˈtɪʃuː) *n* **1** a part of an organism consisting of a large number of cells having a similar structure and function: nerve tissue. **2** a thin piece of soft absorbent paper used as a disposable handkerchief, towel, etc. **3** See **tissue paper. 4** an interwoven series: *a tissue of lies.* **5** a woven cloth, esp. of a light gauzy nature. ◆ *vb* **tissues, tissuing, tissued.** *(tr)* **6** to decorate or clothe with tissue or tissue paper. [C14: from OF *tissu* woven cloth, from *tistre* to weave, from L *texere*]

tissue culture *n* **1** the growth of small pieces of animal or plant tissue in a sterile controlled medium. **2** the tissue produced.

tissue paper *n* very thin soft delicate paper used to wrap breakable goods, as decoration, etc.

tit[1] (tɪt) *n* any of numerous small active Old World songbirds, esp. the bluetit, great tit, etc. They have a short bill and feed on insects and seeds. [C16: ? imit., applied to small animate or inanimate objects]

tit[2] (tɪt) *n* **1** *Sl.* a female breast. **2** a teat or nipple. **3** *Derog.* a young woman. **4** *Taboo sl.* a despicable or unpleasant person. [OE *titt*]

Tit. *Bible. abbrev. for* Titus.

titan ⓣ (ˈtaɪtᵊn) *n* a person of great strength or size. [after *Titans,* a family of gods in Gk myth]

titanic ⓣ (taɪˈtænɪk) *adj* possessing or requiring colossal strength: *a titanic battle.*

titanium (taɪˈteɪnɪəm) *n* a strong malleable white metallic element, which is very corrosion-resistant. It is used in the manufacture of strong lightweight alloys, esp. aircraft parts. Symbol: Ti; atomic no.: 22; atomic wt.: 47.88. [C18: NL; see TITAN, -IUM]

titanium dioxide *n* a white powder used chiefly as a pigment. Formula: TiO_2. Also called: **titanium oxide, titanic oxide, titania.**

titbit ⓣ (ˈtɪtˌbɪt) *or esp. US* **tidbit** *n* **1** a tasty small piece of food; dainty. **2** a pleasing scrap of anything, such as scandal. [C17: ?from dialect *tid* tender, from ?]

titchy *or* **tichy** (ˈtɪtʃɪ) *adj* **titchier, titchiest** *or* **tichier, tichiest.** *Brit. sl.* very small; tiny. [C20: from *tich* or *titch* a small person, from *Little Tich,* stage name of Harry Relph (1867–1928), E actor noted for his small stature]

titfer (ˈtɪtfə) *n Brit. sl.* a hat. [from rhyming slang *tit for tat*]

tit for tat ⓣ *n* an equivalent given in return or retaliation; blow for blow. [C16: from earlier *tip for tap*]

tithe ⓣ (taɪð) *n* **1** *(often pl)* a tenth part of produce, income, or profits, contributed for the support of the church or clergy. **2** any levy, esp. of one tenth. **3** a tenth or a very small part of anything. ◆ *vb* **tithes, tithing, tithed. 4** *(tr)* **4a** to exact or demand a tithe from. **4b** to levy a tithe upon. **5** *(intr)* to pay a tithe or tithes. [OE *teogoth*]
▸ **ˈtithable** *adj*

tithe barn *n* a large barn where, formerly, the agricultural tithe of a parish was stored.

titi (ˈtiːtiː) *n, pl* **titis.** any of a genus of small New World monkeys of South America, having beautifully coloured fur and a long nonprehensile tail. [via Sp. from Aymara, lit.: little cat]

Titian red (ˈtɪʃən) *n* a reddish-yellow colour, as in the hair colour in many of the works of Titian (?1490–1576), Italian painter.

titillate ⓣ (ˈtɪtɪˌleɪt) *vb* **titillates, titillating, titillated.** *(tr)* **1** to arouse or excite pleasurably. **2** to cause a tickling or tingling sensation in, esp. by touching. [C17: from L *tītillāre*]
▸ **ˈtitilˌlating** *adj* ▸ **ˌtitilˈlation** *n*

titivate ⓣ *or* **tittivate** (ˈtɪtɪˌveɪt) *vb* **titivates, titivating, titivated** *or* **tittivates, tittivating, tittivated.** to smarten up; spruce up. [C19: earlier *tidivate,* ? based on TIDY & CULTIVATE]
▸ **ˌtitiˈvation** *or* **ˌtittiˈvation** *n*

titlark (ˈtɪtˌlɑːk) *n* another name for **pipit,** esp. the meadow pipit. [C17: from TIT[1] + LARK[1]]

title ⓣ (ˈtaɪtᵊl) *n* **1** the distinctive name of a work of art, musical or literary composition, etc. **2** a descriptive name or heading of a section of a book, speech, etc. **3** See **title page. 4** a name or epithet signifying rank, office, or function. **5** a formal designation, such as *Mr.* **6** an appellation designating nobility. **7** *Films.* **7a** short for **subtitle. 7b** written material giving credits in a film or television programme. **8** *Sport.* a championship. **9** *Law.* **9a** the legal right to possession of property, esp. real property. **9b** the basis of such right. **9c** the documentary evidence of such right: *title deeds.* **10a** any customary or established right. **10b** a claim based on such a right. **11** a definite spiritual charge or office in the church as a prerequisite for ordination. **12** *RC Church.* a titular church. ◆ *vb* **titles, titling, titled. 13** *(tr)* to give a title to. [C13: from OF, from L *titulus*]

title deed *n* a document evidencing a person's legal right or title to property, esp. real property.

titleholder (ˈtaɪtᵊlˌhəʊldə) *n* a person who holds a title, esp. a sporting championship.

title page *n* the page in a book that gives the title, author, publisher, etc.

title role *n* the role of the character after whom a play, etc., is named.

titmouse (ˈtɪtˌmaʊs) *n, pl* **titmice.** another name for **tit**[1]. [C14 *titemous,* from *tite* (see TIT[1]) + MOUSE]

titrate (ˈtaɪtreɪt) *vb* **titrates, titrating, titrated.** *(tr)* to measure the volume or

THESAURUS

tirade *n* = **outburst**, abuse, denunciation, diatribe, fulmination, harangue, invective, lecture, philippic

tire[1] *vb* **1** = **exhaust**, drain, enervate, fag *(inf.)*, fatigue, knacker *(sl.)*, take it out of *(inf.)*, wear down, wear out, weary, whack *(Brit. inf.)* **2** *usually passive* = **bore**, aggravate *(inf.)*, annoy, exasperate, get on one's nerves *(inf.)*, harass, hassle *(inf.)*, irk, irritate, piss one off *(taboo sl.)*, weary **3** = **flag**, droop, fail
Antonyms *vb* ≠ **exhaust:** energize, enliven, exhilarate, invigorate, liven up, pep up, refresh, restore, revive

tired *adj* **1** = **exhausted**, all in *(sl.)*, asleep *or* dead on one's feet, clapped out *(Austral. & NZ inf.)*, dead beat *(inf.)*, dog-tired *(inf.)*, done in *(inf.)*, drained, drooping, drowsy, enervated, fagged *(inf.)*, fatigued, flagging, knackered *(sl.)*, ready to drop, sleepy, spent, weary, whacked *(Brit. inf.)*, worn out, zonked *(sl.)* **2** = **hackneyed**, clichéd, conventional, corny *(sl.)*, familiar, old, outworn, stale, stock, threadbare, trite, well-worn
Antonyms *adj* ≠ **exhausted:** alive and kicking, energetic, fresh, full of beans *(inf.)*, lively, refreshed, rested, wide-awake ≠ **hackneyed:** innovative, original

tireless *adj* = **energetic**, determined, indefatigable, industrious, resolute, unflagging, untiring, unwearied, vigorous
Antonyms *adj* drained, exhausted, fatigued, flagging, tired, weak, weary, worn out

tiresome *adj* = **boring**, annoying, dull, exasperating, flat, irksome, irritating, laborious, monotonous, tedious, trying, uninteresting, vexatious, wearing, wearisome
Antonyms *adj* exhilarating, inspiring, interesting, refreshing, rousing, stimulating

tiring *adj* **1** = **exhausting**, arduous, demanding, enervative, exacting, fatiguing, laborious, strenuous, tough, wearing, wearying

tissue *n* **2** = **paper**, paper handkerchief, wrapping paper **4** = **series**, accumulation, chain, collection, combination, concatenation, conglomeration, fabrication, mass, network, pack, web **5** = **fabric**, gauze, mesh, structure, stuff, texture, web

titan *n* = **giant**, colossus, leviathan, ogre, superman

titanic *adj* = **gigantic**, Brobdingnagian, colossal, elephantine, enormous, giant, herculean, huge, humongous *or* humungous *(US sl.)*, immense, jumbo *(inf.)*, mammoth, massive, mighty, monstrous, mountainous, prodigious, stellar *(inf.)*, stupendous, towering, vast

titbit *n* **1** = **delicacy**, *bonne bouche,* choice item, dainty, goody, juicy bit, morsel, scrap, snack, treat

tit for tat *n* = **retaliation**, an eye for an eye, as good as one gets, a tooth for a tooth, blow for blow, like for like, measure for measure

tithe *n* **2** = **tax**, assessment, duty, impost, levy, tariff, tenth, toll, tribute ◆ *vb* **4b** = **tax**, assess, charge, levy, rate **5** = **pay a tithe on**, give up, pay, render, surrender, turn over

titillate *vb* **1** = **excite**, arouse, interest, provoke, stimulate, tantalize, tease, thrill, tickle, turn on *(sl.)*

titillating *adj* **1** = **exciting**, arousing, interesting, lewd, lurid, provocative, sensational, stimulating, suggestive, teasing, thrilling

titivate *vb* = **smarten up**, doll up *(sl.)*, do up *(inf.)*, make up, prank, preen, primp, prink, refurbish, tart up *(Brit. sl.)*, touch up

title *n* **1** = **name**, appellation, denomination, designation, epithet, handle *(sl.)*, moniker *or* monicker *(sl.)*, nickname, nom de plume, pseudonym, sobriquet, term **2** = **heading**, caption, inscription, label, legend, name, style **8** *Sport* = **championship**, crown, laurels **9a** *Law* = **ownership**, claim, entitlement, prerogative, privilege, right ◆ *vb* **13** = **name**, call, designate, label, style, term

the concentration of (a solution) by titration. [C19: from F *titrer;* see TITRE]
▸**ti'tratable** *adj*

titration (taɪ'treɪʃən) *n* an operation in which a measured amount of one solution is added to a known quantity of another solution until the reaction between the two is complete. If the concentration of one solution is known, that of the other can be calculated.

titre *or US* **titer** ('taɪtə) *n* the concentration of a solution as determined by titration. [C19: from F *titre* proportion of gold or silver in an alloy, from OF *title* TITLE]

titter Ⓣ ('tɪtə) *vb* (*intr*) **1** to snigger, esp. derisively or in a suppressed way. ◆ *n* **2** a suppressed laugh, chuckle, or snigger. [C17: imit.]
▸**'titterer** *n* ▸**'tittering** *adj*

tittle Ⓣ ('tɪtᵊl) *n* **1** a small mark in printing or writing, esp. a diacritic. **2** a jot; particle. [C14: from Med. L *titulus* label, from L: title]

tittle-tattle Ⓣ *n* **1** idle chat or gossip. ◆ *vb* **tittle-tattles, tittle-tattling, tittle-tattled. 2** (*intr*) to chatter or gossip.
▸**'tittle-ˌtattler** *n*

tittup ('tɪtəp) *vb* **tittups, tittupping, tittupped** *or US* **tittups, tittuping, tittuped. 1** (*intr*) to prance or frolic. ◆ *n* **2** a caper. [C18 (in the sense: a horse's gallop): prob. imit.]

titubation (ˌtɪtju'beɪʃən) *n Pathol.* a disordered gait characterized by stumbling or staggering, often caused by a lesion of the cerebellum. [C17: from L *titubātiō,* from *titubāre* to reel]

titular Ⓣ ('tɪtjʊlə) *adj* **1** of, relating to, or of the nature of a title. **2** in name only. **3** bearing a title. **4** *RC Church.* designating any of certain churches in Rome to whom cardinals or bishops are attached as their nominal incumbents. ◆ *n* **5** the bearer of a title. **6** the bearer of a nominal office. [C18: from F *titulaire,* from L *titulus* title]

tizzy ('tɪzɪ) *n, pl* **tizzies.** *Inf.* a state of confusion or excitement. Also called: **tizz, tiz-woz.** [C19: from ?]

T-junction *n* a road junction in which one road joins another at right angles but does not cross it.

TKO *Boxing. abbrev. for* technical knockout.

Tl *the chemical symbol for* thallium.

Tm *the chemical symbol for* thulium.

TM *abbrev. for* transcendental meditation.

tmesis (tə'mi:sɪs) *n* interpolation of a word or words between the parts of a compound word, as in *every-blooming-where.* [C16: via L from Gk, lit.: a cutting, from *temnein* to cut]

TNT *n* 2,4,6-trinitrotoluene; a yellow solid: used chiefly as a high explosive.

T-number *or* **T number** *n Photog.* a function of the f-number of a lens that takes into account the light transmitted by the lens. [from *T(otal Light Transmission) Number*]

to (tu:; *unstressed* tʊ, tə) *prep* **1** used to indicate the destination of the subject or object of an action: *he climbed to the top.* **2** used to mark the indirect object of a verb: *telling stories to children.* **3** used to mark the infinitive of a verb: *he wanted to go.* **4** as far as; until: *working from Monday to Friday.* **5** used to indicate equality: *16 ounces to the pound.* **6** against; upon; onto: *put your ear to the wall.* **7** before the hour of: *five minutes to four.* **8** accompanied by: *dancing to loud music.* **9** as compared with, as against: *the score was eight to three.* **10** used to indicate a resulting condition: *they starved to death.* ◆ *adv* **11** towards a fixed position, esp. (of a door) closed. [OE *tō*]

toad (təʊd) *n* **1** any of a group of amphibians similar to frogs but more terrestrial, having a drier warty skin. **2** a loathsome person. [OE *tādige,* from ?]
▸**'toadish** *adj*

toadfish ('təʊdˌfɪʃ) *n, pl* **toadfish** *or* **toadfishes.** any of various spiny-finned marine fishes of tropical and temperate seas.

toadflax ('təʊdˌflæks) *n* a perennial plant having narrow leaves and spurred two-lipped yellow-orange flowers. Also called: **butter-and-eggs.**

toad-in-the-hole *n Brit. & Austral.* a dish made of sausages baked in a batter.

toadstone ('təʊdˌstəʊn) *n* an intrusive volcanic rock occurring in limestone. [C18: ?from a supposed resemblance to a toad's spotted skin]

toadstool ('təʊdˌstu:l) *n* (*not in technical use*) any basidiomycetous fungus with a capped spore-producing body that is poisonous. Cf. **mushroom.**

toady Ⓣ ('təʊdɪ) *n, pl* **toadies. 1** Also: **toadeater.** a person who flatters and ingratiates himself in a servile way; sycophant. ◆ *vb* **toadies, toadying, toadied. 2** to fawn on and flatter (someone). [C19: shortened from *toadeater,* orig. a quack's assistant who pretended to eat toads, hence a flatterer]
▸**'toadyish** *adj* ▸**'toadyism** *n*

to and fro *adv,* **to-and-fro** *adj* **1** back and forth. **2** here and there.
▸**'toing and 'froing** *n*

toast[1] Ⓣ (təʊst) *n* **1a** sliced bread browned by exposure to heat. **1b** (*as modifier*): *a toast rack.* ◆ *vb* **2** (*tr*) to brown under a grill or over a fire: *to toast cheese.* **3** to warm or be warmed: *to toast one's hands by the fire.* [C14: from OF *toster,* from L *tōstus* parched, from *torrēre* to dry with heat]

toast[2] Ⓣ (təʊst) *n* **1** a tribute or proposal of health, success, etc., given to a person or thing and marked by people raising glasses and drinking together. **2** a person or thing honoured by such a tribute or proposal. **3** (esp. formerly) an attractive woman to whom such tributes are frequently made. ◆ *vb* **4** to propose or drink a toast to (a person or thing). **5** (*intr*) to add vocal effects to a prerecorded track: a disc-jockey technique. [C17 (in the sense: a lady to whom the company is asked to drink): from TOAST[1], from the idea that the name of the lady would flavour the drink like a piece of spiced toast]
▸**'toaster** *n*

toaster ('təʊstə) *n* a device, esp. an electrical device, for toasting bread.

toastmaster ('təʊstˌmɑ:stə) *n* a person who introduces speakers, proposes toasts, etc., at public dinners.
▸**'toastˌmistress** *fem n*

toasty *or* **toastie** ('təʊstɪ) *n, pl* **toasties.** a toasted sandwich.

Tob. *abbrev. for* Tobit.

tobacco (tə'bækəʊ) *n, pl* **tobaccos** *or* **tobaccoes. 1** any of a genus of plants having mildly narcotic properties, one species of which is cultivated as the chief source of commercial tobacco. **2** the leaves of certain of these plants dried and prepared for snuff, chewing, or smoking. [C16: from Sp. *tabaco,* ?from Taino: leaves rolled for smoking, assumed by the Spaniards to be the name of the plant]

tobacco mosaic virus *n* the virus that causes mosaic disease in tobacco and related plants: its discovery provided the first evidence of the existence of viruses. Abbrev.: **TMV.**

tobacconist (tə'bækənɪst) *n Chiefly Brit.* a person or shop that sells tobacco, cigarettes, pipes, etc.

-to-be *adj* (*in combination*) about to be; future: *a mother-to-be; the bride-to-be.*

toboggan (tə'bɒgən) *n* **1** a light wooden frame on runners used for sliding over snow and ice. **2** a long narrow sledge made of a thin board curved upwards at the front. ◆ *vb* **toboggans, tobogganing, tobogganed.** (*intr*) **3** to ride on a toboggan. [C19: from Canad. F, of Amerind origin]
▸**to'bogganer** *or* **to'bogganist** *n*

toby ('təʊbɪ) *n, pl* **tobies.** *NZ.* a water stopcock at the boundary of a street and house section.

toby jug ('təʊbɪ) *n* a beer mug or jug in the form of a stout seated man wearing a three-cornered hat and smoking a pipe. Also called: **toby.** [C19: from the familiar form of the name *Tobias*]

toccata (tə'kɑ:tə) *n* a rapid keyboard composition for organ, harpsichord, etc., usually in a rhythmically free style. [C18: from It., lit.: touched, from *toccare* to play (an instrument)]

Toc H ('tɒk 'eɪtʃ) *n* a society formed after World War I to encourage Christian comradeship. [C20: from the obs. telegraphic code for *T.H.,* initials of *Talbot House,* Poperinge, Belgium, the original headquarters of the society]

Tocharian *or* **Tokharian** (tɒ'kɑ:rɪən) *n* **1** a member of an Asian people who lived in the Tarim Basin until around 800 A.D. **2** the language of this people, known from records in a N Indian script of the 7th and 8th centuries A.D. [C20: ult. from Gk *Tokharoi,* from ?]

tocopherol (tɒ'kɒfəˌrɒl) *n* any of a group of fat-soluble alcohols that occur in wheat-germ oil, lettuce, egg yolk, etc. Also called: **vitamin E.** [C20: from *toco-,* from Gk *tokos* offspring + *-pher-,* from *pherein* to bear + -OL[1]]

tocsin ('tɒksɪn) *n* **1** an alarm or warning signal, esp. one sounded on a bell. **2** an alarm bell. [C16: from F, from OF *toquassen,* from OProvençal, from *tocar* to touch + *senh* bell, from L *signum*]

tod (tɒd) *n* **on one's tod.** *Brit. sl.* on one's own. [C19: rhyming sl. *Tod Sloan/alone,* after *Tod* Sloan, a jockey]

today (tə'deɪ) *n* **1** this day, as distinct from yesterday or tomorrow. **2** the present age. ◆ *adv* **3** during or on this day. **4** nowadays. [OE *tō dæge,* lit.: on this day]

toddle ('tɒdᵊl) *vb* **toddles, toddling, toddled.** (*intr*) **1** to walk with short unsteady steps, as a child. **2** (foll. by *off*) *Jocular.* to depart. **3** (foll. by *round, over,* etc.) *Jocular.* to visit. ◆ *n* **4** the act or an instance of toddling. [C16 (Scot. & N English): from ?]

toddler ('tɒdlə) *n* a young child, usually between the ages of one and two and a half.

toddy ('tɒdɪ) *n, pl* **toddies. 1** a drink made from spirits, esp. whisky, hot

THESAURUS

titter *vb* **1** = **snigger,** chortle (*inf.*), chuckle, giggle, laugh, tee-hee, te-hee

tittle *n* **2** = **bit,** atom, dash, drop, grain, iota, jot, mite, particle, scrap, shred, speck, whit

tittle-tattle *n* **1** = **gossip,** babble, blather, blether, cackle, chatter, chitchat, clishmaclaver (*Scot.*), dirt (*US sl.*), hearsay, idle chat, jaw (*sl.*), natter, prattle, rumour, twaddle, yackety-yak (*sl.*), yatter (*inf.*) ◆ *vb* **2** = **gossip,** babble, blather, blether, cackle, chat, chatter, chitchat, jaw (*sl.*), natter, prattle, run off at the mouth (*sl.*), witter (*inf.*), yak (*sl.*), yatter (*inf.*)

titular *adj* **2** = **in name only,** honorary, nominal, puppet, putative, so-called, theoretical, token
Antonyms *adj* actual, effective, functioning, real, true

toady *n* **1** = **sycophant,** apple polisher (*US sl.*), ass-kisser (*US & Canad. taboo sl.*), bootlicker (*inf.*), brown-noser (*taboo sl.*), crawler (*sl.*), creep (*sl.*), fawner, flatterer, flunkey, groveller, hanger-on, jackal, lackey, lickspittle, minion, parasite, spaniel, truckler, yes man ◆ *vb* **2** = **fawn on,** be obsequious to, bow and scrape, brown-nose (*taboo sl.*), butter up, crawl, creep, cringe, curry favour with, flatter, grovel, kiss the feet of, kowtow to, lick (someone's) boots, pander to, suck up to (*inf.*)
Antonyms *vb* ≠ **fawn on:** confront, defy, oppose, rebel, resist, stand against, withstand

toast[1] *vb* **2** = **brown,** grill, roast **3** = **warm,** heat

toast[2] *n* **1** = **tribute,** compliment, drink, health, pledge, salutation, salute **2, 3** = **favourite,** darling, hero *or* heroine ◆ *vb* **4** = **drink to,** drink (to) the health of, pledge, salute

water, sugar, and usually lemon juice. **2** the sap of various palm trees used as a beverage. **[**C17: from Hindi *tārī* juice of the palmyra palm, from *tār* palmyra palm, from Sansk. *tāra***]**

to-do Ⓣ (tə'duː) *n, pl* **to-dos.** a commotion, fuss, or quarrel.

toe Ⓣ (təʊ) *n* **1** any one of the digits of the foot. **2** the corresponding part in other vertebrates. **3** the part of a shoe, etc., covering the toes. **4** anything resembling a toe in shape or position. **5 on one's toes.** alert. **6 tread on someone's toes.** to offend a person, esp. by trespassing on his field of responsibility. ◆ *vb* **toes, toeing, toed. 7** (*tr*) to touch, kick, or mark with the toe. **8** (*tr*) to drive (a nail, etc.) obliquely. **9** (*intr*) to walk with the toes pointing in a specified direction: *to toe inwards.* **10 toe the line** *or* **mark.** to conform to expected attitudes, standards, etc. **[**OE *tā***]**

toe and heel *n* a technique used by racing drivers on sharp bends, in which the brake and accelerator are operated simultaneously by the toe and heel of the right foot.

toecap ('təʊˌkæp) *n* a reinforced covering for the toe of a boot or shoe.

toed (təʊd) *adj* **1** having a part resembling a toe. **2** fixed by nails driven in at the foot. **3** (*in combination*) having a toe or toes as specified: *five-toed; thick-toed.*

toehold ('təʊˌhəʊld) *n* **1** a small foothold to facilitate climbing. **2** any means of gaining access, support, etc. **3** a wrestling hold in which the opponent's toe is held and his leg twisted.

toe-in *n* a slight forward convergence given to the wheels of motor vehicles to improve steering.

toenail ('təʊˌneɪl) *n* **1** a thin horny translucent plate covering part of the surface of the end joint of each toe. **2** *Carpentry.* a nail driven obliquely. ◆ *vb* **3** (*tr*) *Carpentry.* to join (beams) by driving nails obliquely.

toerag ('təʊˌræg) *n Brit. sl.* a contemptible or despicable person. **[**C20: orig., a beggar, tramp: from the rags wrapped round their feet**]**

toey ('təʊɪ) *adj Austral. sl.* nervous and restless; anxious.

toff (tɒf) *n Brit. sl.* a well-dressed or upper-class person, esp. a man. **[**C19: ? var. of TUFT, nickname for a titled student at Oxford University, wearing a cap with a gold tassel**]**

toffee *or* **toffy** ('tɒfɪ) *n, pl* **toffees** *or* **toffies. 1** a sweet made from sugar or treacle boiled with butter, nuts, etc. **2 for toffee.** (preceded by *can't*) *Inf.* to be incompetent at: *he can't sing for toffee.* **[**C19: var. of earlier *taffy***]**

toffee-apple *n* an apple fixed on a stick and coated with a thin layer of toffee.

toffee-nosed *adj Sl., chiefly Brit.* pretentious or supercilious; used esp. of snobbish people.

toft (tɒft) *n Brit. history.* **1** a homestead. **2** a homestead and its arable land. **[**OE**]**

tofu ('təʊˌfuː) *n* unfermented soya-bean curd, a food with a soft cheese-like consistency. **[**from Japanese**]**

tog[1] (tɒg) *Inf.* ◆ *vb* **togs, togging, togged. 1** (often foll. by *up* or *out*) to dress oneself, esp. in smart clothes. ◆ *n* **2** See **togs. [**C18: ?from obs. cant *togemans* coat, from L *toga* TOGA + *-mans*, from ?**]**

tog[2] (tɒg) *n* **a** a unit of thermal resistance used to measure the power of insulation of a fabric, garment, quilt, etc. **b** (*as modifier*): *tog-rating.* **[**C20: arbitrary coinage from TOG[1] (n)**]**

toga ('təʊgə) *n* **1** a garment worn by citizens of ancient Rome, consisting of a piece of cloth draped around the body. **2** a robe of office. **[**C16: from L**]**
 ▸**togaed** ('təʊgəd) *adj*

together Ⓣ (tə'geðə) *adv* **1** with cooperation and interchange between constituent elements, members, etc.: *we worked together.* **2** in or into contact with each other: *to stick papers together.* **3** in or into one place; with each other: *the people are gathered together.* **4** at the same time. **5** considered collectively: *all our wages put together couldn't buy that car.* **6** continuously: *working for eight hours together.* **7** closely or compactly united or held: *water will hold the dough together.* **8** mutually or reciprocally: *to multiply seven and eight together.* **9** *Inf.* organized: *to get things together.* ◆ *adj* **10** *Sl.* self-possessed, competent, and well-organized. **11 together with.** (*prep*) in addition to. **[**OE *tōgædre***]**

> **USAGE NOTE** See at **plus.**

togetherness (tə'geðənɪs) *n* a feeling of closeness or affection from being united with other people.

toggery ('tɒgərɪ) *n Inf.* clothes; togs.

toggle ('tɒg^əl) *n* **1** a peg or rod at the end of a rope, chain, or cable, for fastening by insertion through an eye in another rope, chain, etc. **2** a bar-shaped button inserted through a loop for fastening. **3** a toggle joint or a device having such a joint. ◆ *vb* **toggles, toggling, toggled. 4** (*tr*) to supply or fasten with a toggle. **[**C18: from ?**]**

toggle joint *n* a device consisting of two arms pivoted at a common joint and at their outer ends and used to apply pressure by straightening the angle between the two arms.

toggle switch *n* **1** an electric switch having a projecting lever that is manipulated in a particular way to open or close a circuit. **2** a computer device used to turn a feature on or off.

togs (tɒgz) *pl n Inf.* **1** clothes. **2** *Austral., NZ, & Irish.* a swimming costume. **[**from TOG[1]**]**

toheroa (ˌtəʊə'rəʊə) *n* a large edible bivalve mollusc of New Zealand with a distinctive flavour. **[**from Maori**]**

tohunga ('tɒhʊŋə) *n NZ.* a Maori priest, the repository of traditional lore.

toil[1] Ⓣ (tɔɪl) *n* **1** hard or exhausting work. ◆ *vb* (*intr*) **2** to labour. **3** to progress with slow painful movements. **[**C13: from Anglo-F *toiler* to struggle, from OF *toeillier* to confuse, from L *tudiculāre* to stir, ult. from *tundere* to beat**]**
 ▸'**toiler** *n*

toil[2] (tɔɪl) *n* **1** (*often pl*) a net or snare. **2** *Arch.* a trap for wild beasts. **[**C16: from OF *toile*, from L *tēla* loom**]**

toile (twɑːl) *n* **1** a transparent linen or cotton fabric. **2** a garment of exclusive design made up in cheap cloth so that alterations can be made. **[**C19: from F, from L *tēla* a loom**]**

toilet Ⓣ ('tɔɪlɪt) *n* **1** another word for **lavatory. 2** *Old-fashioned.* the act of dressing and preparing oneself. **3** *Old-fashioned.* a dressing table. **4** *Rare.* costume. **5** the cleansing of a wound, etc., after an operation or childbirth. **[**C16: from F *toilette* dress, from TOILE**]**

toilet paper *or* **tissue** *n* thin absorbent paper, often wound in a roll round a cardboard cylinder (**toilet roll**), used for cleaning oneself after defecation or urination.

toiletry ('tɔɪlɪtrɪ) *n, pl* **toiletries.** an object or cosmetic used in making up, dressing, etc.

toilet set *n* a matching set consisting of a hairbrush, comb, mirror, and clothes brush.

toilette (twɑː'lɛt) *n* another word for **toilet** (sense 2). **[**C16: from F; see TOILET**]**

toilet water *n* a form of liquid perfume lighter than cologne.

toilsome Ⓣ ('tɔɪlsəm) *or* **toilful** *adj* laborious.
 ▸'**toilsomely** *adv* ▸'**toilsomeness** *n*

toitoi ('tɔɪtɔɪ) *n* a tall New Zealand grass with feathery seed-heads. **[**from Maori**]**

tokamak ('təʊkəˌmæk) *n Physics.* a toroidal reactor used in thermonuclear experiments, in which strong axial magnetic fields keep the plasma from contacting the external walls. **[**C20: from Russian acronym, from *to(roidál'naya) kám(era s) ak(siál'nym magnitnym pólem)*, toroidal chamber with magnetic field**]**

Tokay (təʊ'keɪ) *n* **1** a sweet wine made near Tokaj, Hungary. **2** a variety of grape used to make this. **3** a similar wine made elsewhere.

token Ⓣ ('təʊkən) *n* **1** an indication, warning, or sign of something. **2** a symbol or visible representation of something. **3** something that indicates authority, proof, etc. **4** a metal or plastic disc, such as a substitute for currency for use in slot machines. **5** a memento. **6** a gift voucher that can be used as payment for goods of a specified value. **7** (*modifier*) as a matter of form only; nominal: *a token increase in salary.* ◆ *vb* **8** (*tr*) to act or serve as a warning or symbol of; betoken. **[**OE *tācen***]**

tokenism ('təʊkəˌnɪzəm) *n* the practice of making only a token effort or doing no more than the minimum, esp. in order to comply with a law.
 ▸'**tokeˌnist** *adj*

token money *n* coins having greater face value than the value of their metal content.

token strike *n* a brief strike intended to convey strength of feeling on a disputed issue.

token vote *n* a Parliamentary vote of money in which the amount quoted is not binding.

THESAURUS

to-do *n* = **fuss**, agitation, bother, brouhaha, bustle, commotion, disturbance, excitement, flap (*inf.*), furore, hoo-ha, hue and cry, performance (*inf.*), quarrel, ruction (*inf.*), rumpus, stir, tumult, turmoil, unrest, upheaval, uproar

toe *n* **6 tread on someone's toes** = **offend**, affront, annoy, bruise, disgruntle, get someone's back up, hurt, hurt someone's feelings, infringe, injure, irk, vex

together *adv* **1** = **collectively**, as a group, as one, cheek by jowl, closely, hand in glove, hand in hand, in a body, in concert, in cooperation, in unison, jointly, mutually, shoulder to shoulder, side by side **4** = **at the same time**, all at once, as one, at one fell swoop, concurrently, contemporaneously, en masse, in unison, simultaneously, with one accord **6** *Old-fashioned* = **in succession**, consecutively, continuously, in a row, one after the other, on end, successively, without a break, without interruption **9** *Informal* = **organized**, arranged, fixed, ordered, settled, sorted out, straight, to rights ◆ *adj* **10** *Slang* = **self-possessed**, calm, composed, cool, stable, well-adjusted, well-balanced, well-organized
Antonyms *adv* ≠ **collectively**: alone, apart, independently, individually, one at a time, one by one, separately, singly

toil[1] *n* **1** = **hard work**, application, blood, sweat, and tears (*inf.*), donkey-work, drudgery, effort, elbow grease (*inf.*), exertion, graft (*inf.*), industry, labour, pains, slog, sweat, travail ◆ *vb* **2** = **labour**, bust a gut (*inf.*), graft (*inf.*), grind (*inf.*), grub, knock oneself out (*inf.*), make an all-out effort (*inf.*), push oneself, slave, slog, strive, struggle, sweat (*inf.*), work, work like a dog, work like a Trojan, work one's fingers to the bone
Antonyms *n* ≠ **hard work**: idleness, inactivity, indolence, inertia, laziness, sloth, torpor

toilet *n* **1** = **lavatory**, ablutions (*Military inf.*), bathroom, bog (*sl.*), can (*US & Canad. sl.*), closet, convenience, gents *or* ladies, john (*sl., chiefly US & Canad.*), ladies' room, latrine, little boy's *or* little girl's room (*inf.*), loo (*Brit. inf.*), outhouse, powder room, privy, throne (*inf.*), urinal, washroom, water closet, W.C. **2** *Old-fashioned* = **dressing**, ablutions, bathing, grooming, toilette

toilsome *adj Literary* = **laborious**, arduous, backbreaking, difficult, fatiguing, hard, herculean, painful, severe, strenuous, taxing, tedious, tiresome, tough, wearisome

token *n* **1-3** = **symbol**, badge, clue, demonstra-

tokoloshe (ˌtɒkɒˈlɒʃ, -ˈlɒʃɪ) *n* (in Bantu folklore) a malevolent mythical manlike animal. Also called: **tikoloshe.** [from Xhosa *uthikoloshe*]

toktokkie (ˈtɒkˌtɒkɪ) *n* a large S. African beetle. [from Afrik., from Du. *tokken* to tap]

tolbooth (ˈtəʊlˌbuːθ, -ˌbuːð, ˈtɒl-) *n* **1** *Chiefly Scot.* a town hall. **2** a variant spelling of **tollbooth.**

tolbutamide (tɒlˈbjuːtəˌmaɪd) *n* a synthetic crystalline compound used in the treatment of diabetes to lower blood glucose levels. [C20: from TOL(UENE) + BUT(YRIC ACID) + AMIDE]

told (təʊld) *vb* **1** the past tense and past participle of **tell**[1]. ◆ *adj* **2** See **all told.**

tole (təʊl) *n* enamelled or lacquered metal ware, popular in the 18th century. [from F *tôle* sheet metal, from F (dialect): table, from L *tabula* table]

Toledo (tɒˈleɪdəʊ) *n* a fine-tapered sword or sword blade. [C16: from *Toledo,* city in Spain]

tolerable ➊ (ˈtɒlərəbᵊl) *adj* **1** able to be tolerated; endurable. **2** permissible. **3** *Inf.* fairly good.
▸ˌtoleraˈbility *n* ▸ˈtolerably *adv*

tolerance ➊ (ˈtɒlərəns) *n* **1** the state or quality of being tolerant. **2** capacity to endure something, esp. pain or hardship. **3** the permitted variation in some characteristic of an object or workpiece. **4** the capacity to endure the effects of a poison or other substance, esp. after it has been taken over a prolonged period.

tolerant ➊ (ˈtɒlərənt) *adj* **1** able to tolerate the beliefs, actions, etc., of others. **2** permissive. **3** able to withstand extremes. **4** exhibiting tolerance to a drug.
▸ˈtolerantly *adv*

tolerate ➊ (ˈtɒləˌreɪt) *vb* **tolerates, tolerating, tolerated.** (*tr*) **1** to treat with indulgence or forbearance. **2** to permit. **3** to be able to bear; put up with. **4** to have tolerance for (a drug, etc.). [C16: from L *tolerāre* to sustain]

toleration ➊ (ˌtɒləˈreɪʃən) *n* **1** the act or practice of tolerating. **2** freedom to hold religious opinions that differ from the established religion of a country.
▸ˌtolerˈationist *n*

toll[1] ➊ (təʊl) *vb* **1** to ring slowly and recurrently. **2** (*tr*) to summon or announce by tolling. **3** *US & Canad.* to decoy (game, esp. ducks). ◆ *n* **4** the act or sound of tolling. [C15: ? rel. to OE *-tyllan,* as in *fortyllan* to attract]

toll[2] ➊ (təʊl, tɒl) *n* **1a** an amount of money levied, esp. for the use of certain roads, bridges, etc. **1b** (*as modifier*): *toll road; toll bridge.* **2** loss or damage incurred through a disaster, etc.: *the war took its toll of the inhabitants.* **3** (formerly) the right to levy a toll. [OE *toln*]

tollbooth *or* **tolbooth** (ˈtəʊlˌbuːθ, -ˌbuːð, ˈtɒl-) *n* a booth or kiosk at which a toll is collected.

tollgate (ˈtəʊlˌgeɪt, ˈtɒl-) *n* a gate across a toll road or bridge at which travellers must pay.

tollhouse (ˈtəʊlˌhaʊs, ˈtɒl-) *n* a small house at a tollgate occupied by a toll collector.

tollie (ˈtɒlɪ) *n, pl* **tollies.** *S. African.* a castrated calf. [C19: from Xhosa *ithole* calf on which the horns have begun to appear]

Toltec (ˈtɒltɛk) *n, pl* **Toltecs** *or* **Toltec. 1** a member of a Central American Indian people who dominated the valley of Mexico until they were overrun by the Aztecs. ◆ *adj also* **Toltecan. 2** of or relating to this people.

tolu (tɒˈluː) *n* an aromatic balsam obtained from a South American tree. [C17: after *Santiago de Tolu,* Colombia, from which it was exported]

toluene (ˈtɒljuˌiːn) *n* a colourless volatile flammable liquid obtained from petroleum and coal tar and used as a solvent and in the manufacture of many organic chemicals. [C19: from TOLU + -ENE, since it was previously obtained from tolu]

toluic acid (tɒˈluːɪk) *n* a white crystalline derivative of toluene used in synthetic resins and as an insect repellent. [C19: from TOLU(ENE) + -IC]

toluidine (tɒˈljuːɪˌdiːn) *n* an amine derived from toluene, used in making dyes. [C19: from TOLU(ENE) + -IDE + -INE[2]]

tom (tɒm) *n* **a** the male of various animals, esp. the cat. **b** (*as modifier*): *a tom turkey.* **c** (*in combination*): *a tomcat.* [C16: special use of the short form of *Thomas,* applied to any male, often implying a common or ordinary type of person, etc.]

tomahawk (ˈtɒməˌhɔːk) *n* a fighting axe with a stone or iron head, used by the North American Indians. [C17: from Algonquian *tamahaac*]

tomato (təˈmɑːtəʊ) *n, pl* **tomatoes. 1** a South American plant widely cultivated for its red fleshy many-seeded fruits. **2** the fruit of this plant, eaten in salads, as a vegetable, etc. [C17 *tomate,* from Sp., from Nahuatl *tomatl*]

tomb ➊ (tuːm) *n* **1** a place, esp. a vault beneath the ground, for the burial of a corpse. **2** a monument to the dead. **3 the tomb.** a poetic term for death. [C13: from OF *tombe,* from LL *tumba* burial mound, from Gk *tumbos*]

tombac (ˈtɒmbæk) *n* any of various alloys containing copper and zinc: used for making cheap jewellery, etc. [C17: from F, from Du. *tombak,* from Malay *tambâga* copper, apparently from Sansk. *tāmraka,* from *tāmra* dark coppery red]

tombola (tɒmˈbəʊlə) *n Brit.* a type of lottery, esp. at a fête, in which tickets are drawn from a revolving drum. [C19: from It., from *tombolare* to somersault]

tomboy (ˈtɒmˌbɔɪ) *n* a girl who acts or dresses in a boyish way, liking rough outdoor activities.
▸ˈtomˌboyish *adj* ▸ˈtomˌboyishly *adv*

tombstone ➊ (ˈtuːmˌstəʊn) *n* another word for **gravestone.**

Tom Collins *n* a long drink consisting of gin, lime or lemon juice, sugar, and soda water.

Tom, Dick, and (**or**) **Harry** *n* an ordinary, undistinguished, or common person (esp. in **every Tom, Dick, and Harry; any Tom, Dick, or Harry**).

tome ➊ (təʊm) *n* **1** a large weighty book. **2** one of the several volumes of a work. [C16: from F, from L *tomus* section of larger work, from Gk *tomos* a slice, from *temnein* to cut]

-tome *n combining form.* indicating an instrument for cutting: *osteotome.* [from Gk *tomē* a cutting, *tomos* a slice, from *temnein* to cut]

tomentum (təˈmɛntəm) *n, pl* **tomenta** (-tə). **1** a covering of downy hairs on leaves and other plant parts. **2** a network of minute blood vessels occurring in the human brain. [C17: NL, from L: stuffing for cushions]
▸toˈmentose *adj*

tomfool ➊ (ˌtɒmˈfuːl) *n* **a** a fool. **b** (*as modifier*): *tomfool ideas.*
▸ˌtomˈfoolishness *n*

tomfoolery ➊ (ˌtɒmˈfuːlərɪ) *n, pl* **tomfooleries. 1** foolish behaviour. **2** utter nonsense; rubbish.

tommy (ˈtɒmɪ) *n, pl* **tommies.** (*often cap.*) *Brit. inf.* a private in the British Army. [C19: orig. *Thomas Atkins,* name representing typical private in specimen forms]

Tommy gun *n* an informal name for **Thompson sub-machine-gun.**

tommyrot (ˈtɒmɪˌrɒt) *n* utter nonsense.

tomography (təˈmɒgrəfɪ) *n* a technique used to obtain an X-ray pho-

THESAURUS

tion, earnest, evidence, expression, index, indication, manifestation, mark, note, proof, representation, sign, warning **5** = **memento,** keepsake, memorial, remembrance, reminder, souvenir ◆ *modifier* **7** = **nominal,** hollow, minimal, perfunctory, superficial, symbolic

tolerable *adj* **1** = **bearable,** acceptable, allowable, endurable, sufferable, supportable **3** *Informal* = **fair,** acceptable, adequate, all right, average, fairly good, fair to middling, good enough, indifferent, middling, not bad (*inf.*), O.K. *or* okay (*inf.*), ordinary, passable, run-of-the-mill, so-so (*inf.*), unexceptional
Antonyms *adj* ≠ **bearable:** insufferable, intolerable, unacceptable, unbearable, unendurable ≠ **fair:** awful, bad, dreadful, rotten

tolerance *n* **1** = **broad-mindedness,** charity, forbearance, indulgence, lenity, magnanimity, open-mindedness, patience, permissiveness, sufferance, sympathy **2** = **endurance,** fortitude, hardiness, hardness, resilience, resistance, stamina, staying power, toughness **3** = **variation,** fluctuation, play, swing
Antonyms *n* ≠ **broad-mindedness:** bigotry, discrimination, intolerance, narrow-mindedness, prejudice, sectarianism

tolerant *adj* **1** = **broad-minded,** catholic, charitable, fair, forbearing, latitudinarian, liberal, long-suffering, magnanimous, open-minded, patient, sympathetic, unbigoted, understanding, unprejudiced **2** = **permissive,** complaisant, easy-going, easy-oasy (*sl.*), free and easy, indulgent, kind-hearted, lax, lenient, soft
Antonyms *adj* ≠ **broad-minded:** biased, bigoted, dogmatic, illiberal, intolerant, narrow-minded, prejudiced, sectarian, uncharitable ≠ **permissive:** authoritarian, despotic, dictatorial, intolerant, repressive, rigid, stern, strict, tyrannical

tolerate *vb* **1, 2** = **allow,** accept, admit, brook, condone, countenance, indulge, permit, pocket, put up with (*inf.*), receive, sanction, take, turn a blind eye to, wink at **3** = **endure,** abide, bear, hack (*sl.*), put up with (*inf.*), stand, stomach, submit to, suffer, swallow, take, thole (*Scot.*), undergo
Antonyms *vb* ≠ **allow:** ban, disallow, disapprove, forbid, outlaw, preclude, prohibit, veto

toleration *n* **1** = **acceptance,** allowance, condonation, endurance, indulgence, permissiveness, sanction, sufferance **2** = **religious freedom,** freedom of conscience, freedom of worship

toll[1] *vb* **1** = **ring,** chime, clang, knell, peal, sound, strike **2** = **announce,** call, signal, summon, warn ◆ *n* **4** = **ringing,** chime, clang, knell, peal, ring, tolling

toll[2] *n* **1a** = **charge,** assessment, customs, demand, duty, fee, impost, levy, payment, rate, tariff, tax, tribute **2** = **damage,** cost, inroad, loss, penalty

tomb *n* **1** = **grave,** burial chamber, catacomb, crypt, mausoleum, sarcophagus, sepulchre, vault

tombstone *n* = **gravestone,** headstone, marker, memorial, monument

tome *n* **1, 2** = **book,** title, volume, work

tomfool *n* **a** = **fool,** ass, berk (*Brit. sl.*), blockhead, chump (*inf.*), clown, dipstick (*Brit. sl.*), divvy (*Brit. sl.*), dolt, dork (*sl.*), idiot, nincompoop, ninny, nitwit (*inf.*), numbskull *or* numskull, pillock (*Brit. sl.*), plank (*Brit. sl.*), plonker (*sl.*), simpleton, twit (*inf., chiefly Brit.*), wally (*sl.*) ◆ *modifier* **b** = **idiotic,** asinine, crackbrained, crazy, daft (*inf.*), dumb-ass (*sl.*), foolish, half-witted, harebrained, inane, rash, senseless, silly, stupid

tomfoolery *n* **1** = **foolishness,** buffoonery, childishness, clowning, fooling around (*inf.*), horseplay, idiocy, larks (*inf.*), messing around (*inf.*), shenanigans (*inf.*), silliness, skylarking (*inf.*), stupidity **2** = **nonsense,** balderdash, baloney (*inf.*), bilge (*inf.*), bosh, bunk (*inf.*), bunkum *or* buncombe (*chiefly US*), claptrap (*inf.*), hogwash, hooey (*sl.*), inanity, poppycock (*inf.*), rot, rubbish, stuff and nonsense, tommyrot, tosh (*sl., chiefly Brit.*), trash, twaddle
Antonyms *n* ≠ **foolishness:** demureness, gravity, heaviness, reserve, sedateness, seriousness, sobriety, solemnity, sternness

tograph of a plane section of the human body or some other object. [C20: from Gk *tomē* a cutting + -GRAPHY]

tomorrow (tə'mɒrəʊ) *n* **1** the day after today. **2** the future. ◆ *adv* **3** on the day after today. **4** at some time in the future. [OE *tō morgenne,* from *to* on + *morgenne,* dative of *morgen* morning]

Tom Thumb *n* a dwarf; midget. [after *Tom Thumb,* the tiny hero of several E folk tales]

tomtit ('tɒm,tɪt) *n Brit.* any of various tits, esp. the bluetit.

tom-tom *n* a drum usually beaten with the hands as a signalling instrument. [C17: from Hindi *tamtam,* imit.]

-tomy *n combining form.* indicating a surgical cutting of a specified part or tissue: *lobotomy.* [from Gk *-tomia*]

ton[1] (tʌn) *n* **1** Also called: **long ton.** *Brit.* a unit of weight equal to 2240 pounds or 1016.046 909 kilograms. **2** Also called: **short ton, net ton.** *US & Canad.* a unit of weight equal to 2000 pounds or 907.184 kilograms. **3** See **metric ton, tonne.** a unit of weight equal to 1000 kilograms. **4** Also called: **freight ton, measurement ton.** a unit of volume or weight used for charging or measuring freight in shipping. It is usually equal to 40 cubic feet, 1 cubic metre, or 1000 kilograms. **5** Also called: **displacement ton.** a unit used for measuring the displacement of a ship, equal to 35 cubic feet of sea water or 2240 pounds. **6** Also called: **register ton.** a unit of internal capacity of ships equal to 100 cubic feet. ◆ *adv* **7** **tons.** (intensifier): *the new flat is tons better than the old one.* [C14: var. of TUN]

ton[2] (tʌn) *n Sl., chiefly Brit.* a score or achievement of a hundred, esp. a hundred miles per hour, as on a motorcycle. [C20: special use of TON[1] applied to quantities of one hundred]

tonal ('təʊnᵊl) *adj* **1** of or relating to tone. **2** of or utilizing the diatonic system; having an established key. **3** (of an answer in a fugue) not having the same melodic intervals as the subject, so as to remain in the original key.
▸'**tonally** *adv*

tonality (təʊ'nælɪtɪ) *n, pl* **tonalities. 1** *Music.* **1a** the presence of a musical key in a composition. **1b** the system of major and minor keys prevalent in Western music. **2** the overall scheme of colours and tones in a painting.

tondo ('tɒndəʊ) *n, pl* **tondi** (-diː). a circular easel painting or relief carving. [C19: from It.: a circle, shortened from *rotondo* round]

tone 🅣 (təʊn) *n* **1** sound with reference to quality, pitch, or volume. **2** short for **tone colour. 3** *US & Canad.* another word for **note** (sense 10). **4** an interval of a major second; whole tone. **5** Also called: **Gregorian tone.** any of several plainsong melodies or other chants used in the singing of psalms. **6** *Linguistics.* any of the pitch levels or pitch contours at which a syllable may be pronounced, such as high tone, falling tone, etc. **7** the quality or character of a sound: *a nervous tone of voice.* **8** general aspect, quality, or style. **9** high quality or style: *to lower the tone of a place.* **10** the quality of a given colour, as modified by mixture with white or black; shade; tint. **11** *Physiol.* **11a** the normal tension of a muscle at rest. **11b** the natural firmness of the tissues and normal functioning of bodily organs in health. **12** the overall effect of the colour values and gradations of light and dark in a picture. **13** *Photog.* a colour of a particular area on a negative or positive that can be distinguished from surrounding areas. ◆ *vb* **tones, toning, toned. 14** (*intr;* often foll. by *with*) to be of a matching or similar tone (to). **15** (*tr*) to give a tone to or correct the tone of. **16** (*tr*) *Photog.* to soften or change the colour of the tones of (a photographic image). ◆ See also **tone down, tone up.** [C14: from L *tonus,* from Gk *tonos* tension, tone, from *teinein* to stretch]
▸'**toneless** *adj* ▸'**tonelessly** *adv*

tone arm *n* another name for **pick-up.**

tone colour *n* the quality of a musical sound that is conditioned or distinguished by the upper partials or overtones present in it.

tone-deaf *adj* unable to distinguish subtle differences in musical pitch.
▸**tone deafness** *n*

tone down 🅣 *vb* (*adv*) to moderate or become moderated in tone: *to tone down an argument.*

tone language *n* a language, such as Chinese, in which differences in tone may make differences in meaning.

toneme ('təʊniːm) *n Linguistics.* a phoneme that is distinguished from another phoneme only by its tone. [C20]
▸**to'nemic** *adj*

tone poem *n* another term for **symphonic poem.**

toner ('təʊnə) *n* **1** a person or thing that tones. **2** a cosmetic preparation that is applied to produce a desired effect, such as to reduce the oiliness of the skin. **3** *Photog.* a chemical solution that softens or alters the tones of a photographic image. **4** a powdered chemical used in photocopying machines, which adheres to electrostatically charged areas of a plate or roller and is then transferred onto the paper to form the copy.

tone row *or* **series** *n Music.* a group of notes having a characteristic pattern that forms the basis of the musical material in a serial composition, esp. one consisting of the twelve notes of the chromatic scale.

tone up 🅣 *vb* (*adv*) to make or become more vigorous, healthy, etc.

tong (tɒŋ) *n* (formerly) a secret society of Chinese Americans. [C20: from Chinese (Cantonese) *t'ong* meeting place]

tonga ('tɒŋgə) *n* a light two-wheeled vehicle used in rural areas of India. [C19: from Hindi *tāṅgā*]

Tongan ('tɒŋgən) *adj* **1** of or relating to Tonga, a kingdom occupying an archipelago in the SW Pacific. ◆ *n* **2** a native or inhabitant of Tonga. **3** the Polynesian language of the Tongans.

Tongchak (,tɒŋ'tʃæk) *n* the former name for **Chondokyo.**

tongs (tɒŋz) *pl n* a tool for grasping or lifting, consisting of a hinged, sprung, or pivoted pair of arms or levers, joined at one end. Also called: **pair of tongs.** [pl. of OE *tange*]

tongue 🅣 (tʌŋ) *n* **1** a movable mass of muscular tissue attached to the floor of the mouth in most vertebrates. It is used in tasting, eating, and (in man) speaking. Related adj: **lingual. 2** an analogous organ in invertebrates. **3** the tongue of certain animals used as food. **4** a language, dialect, or idiom: *the English tongue.* **5** the ability to speak: *to lose one's tongue.* **6** a manner of speaking: *a glib tongue.* **7** utterance or voice (esp. in **give tongue**). **8** anything which resembles a tongue in shape or function. **9** a promontory or spit of land. **10** a flap of leather on a shoe. **11** *Music.* the reed of an oboe or similar instrument. **12** the clapper of a bell. **13** the harnessing pole of a horse-drawn vehicle. **14** a projection on a machine part that serves as a guide for assembly, etc. **15** a projecting strip along an edge of a board that is made to fit a groove in another board. **16 hold one's tongue.** to keep quiet. **17 on the tip of one's tongue.** about to come to mind. **18 with (one's) tongue in (one's) cheek.** Also: **tongue in cheek.** with insincere or ironical intent. ◆ *vb* **tongues, tonguing, tongued. 19** to articulate (notes on a wind instrument) by tonguing. **20** (*tr*) to lick, feel, or touch with the tongue. **21** (*tr*) to provide (a board) with a tongue. **22** (*intr*) (of a piece of land) to project into a body of water. [OE *tunge*]
▸'**tongueless** *adj* ▸'**tongue,like** *adj*

tongue-and-groove joint *n* a joint made between two boards by means of a tongue along the edge of one board that fits into a groove along the edge of the other board.

tongued (tʌŋd) *adj* **1** having a tongue or tongues. **2** (*in combination*) having a manner of speech as specified: *sharp-tongued.*

tongue-lash 🅣 *vb* (*tr*) to reprimand severely; scold.
▸'**tongue-,lashing** *n, adj*

tongue-tie *n* a congenital condition in which the tongue has restricted mobility as the result of an abnormally short fraenum.

tongue-tied 🅣 *adj* **1** speechless, esp. with embarrassment or shyness. **2** having a condition of tongue-tie.

tongue twister *n* a sentence or phrase that is difficult to articulate clearly and quickly, such as *Peter Piper picked a peck of pickled pepper.*

tonguing ('tʌŋɪŋ) *n* a technique of playing (any nonlegato passage) on a wind instrument by obstructing and uncovering the air passage through the lips with the tongue.

tonic 🅣 ('tɒnɪk) *n* **1** a medicinal preparation that improves the functioning of the body or increases the feeling of wellbeing. **2** anything that enlivens or strengthens. **3** Also called: **tonic water.** a mineral water, usually carbonated and containing quinine and often mixed with gin or other alcoholic drinks. **4** *Music.* **4a** the first degree of a major or minor scale and the tonal centre of a piece composed in a particular key. **4b** a key or chord based on this. ◆ *adj* **5** serving to enliven and invigorate: *a tonic wine.* **6** of or relating to a tone or tones. **7** *Music.* of the first degree of a major or minor scale. **8** of or denoting the general effect of colour and light and shade in a picture. **9** *Physiol.* of or affecting normal muscular or bodily tone: *a tonic spasm.* [C17: from NL *tonicus,* from Gk *tonikos* concerning tone, from *tonos* TONE]
▸'**tonically** *adv*

tonic accent *n* **1** emphasis imparted to a note by virtue of its having a higher pitch. **2** (in some languages) an accent in which emphatic syllables are pronounced on a higher musical pitch.

tonicity (təʊ'nɪsɪtɪ) *n* **1** the condition or quality of being tonic. **2** another name for **tonus.**

tonic sol-fa *n* a method of teaching music, by which syllables are used as names for the notes of the major scale in any key.

tonight (tə'naɪt) *n* **1** the night or evening of this present day. ◆ *adv* **2** in or during the night or evening of this day. **3** *Obs.* last night. [OE *tōniht*]

toning table *n* an exercise table, parts of which move mechanically

THESAURUS

tone *n* **1** = **pitch,** accent, emphasis, force, inflection, intonation, modulation, strength, stress, timbre, tonality, volume **8** = **character,** air, approach, aspect, attitude, drift, effect, feel, frame, grain, manner, mood, note, quality, spirit, style, temper, tenor, vein **10** = **colour,** cast, hue, shade, tinge, tint ◆ *vb* **14** = **harmonize,** blend, go well with, match, suit

tone down *vb* = **moderate,** dampen, dim, mitigate, modulate, play down, reduce, restrain, soften, soft-pedal (*inf.*), subdue, temper

tone up *vb* = **get into condition,** freshen, get in shape, invigorate, limber up, shape up, sharpen up, trim, tune up

tongue *n* **4** = **language,** argot, dialect, idiom, lingo (*inf.*), parlance, patois, speech, talk, vernacular **7** *As in* **give tongue** = **utterance,** articulation, speech, verbal expression, voice

tongue-lashing *n* = **scolding,** dressing-down (*inf.*), lecture, rebuke, reprimand, reproach, reproof, slating (*inf.*), talking-to (*inf.*), telling-off (*inf.*), ticking-off (*inf.*), wigging (*Brit. sl.*)

tongue-tied *adj* **1** = **speechless,** at a loss for words, dumb, dumbstruck, inarticulate, mute, struck dumb
Antonyms *adj* articulate, chatty, effusive, garrulous, loquacious, talkative, verbose, voluble, wordy

tonic *n* **2** = **stimulant,** analeptic, boost, bracer (*inf.*), cordial, fillip, livener, pick-me-up (*inf.*), refresher, restorative, roborant, shot in the arm (*inf.*)

for a set time in order to exercise specific parts of the body of the person lying on it.

tonka bean ('tɒŋkə) *n* **1** a tall tree of tropical America. **2** the seeds of this tree, used in the manufacture of perfumes, snuff, etc. [C18: prob. from Tupi *tonka*]

tonnage *or* **tunnage** ('tʌnɪdʒ) *n* **1** the capacity of a merchant ship expressed in tons. **2** the weight of the cargo of a merchant ship. **3** the total amount of shipping of a port or nation. **4** a duty on ships based either on their capacity or their register tonnage. [C15: from OF, from *tonne* barrel]

tonne (tʌn) *n* a unit of mass equal to 1000 kg or 2204.6 pounds. Also called (not in technical use): **metric ton.** [from F]

tonneau ('tɒnəʊ) *n, pl* **tonneaus** *or* **tonneaux** (-nəʊ, -nəʊz). **1** a detachable cover to protect empty passenger seats in an open vehicle. **2** *Rare.* the part of an open car in which the rear passengers sit. [C20: from F: special type of vehicle body, from OF *tonnel* cask, from *tonne* tun]

tonometer (təʊ'nɒmɪtə) *n* **1** an instrument for measuring the pitch of a sound, esp. one consisting of a set of tuning forks. **2** any of various types of instrument for measuring pressure or tension, such as the blood pressure, vapour pressure, etc. [C18: from Gk *tonos* TONE + -METER]
▸**tonometric** (ˌtɒnə'metrɪk, ˌtəʊ-) *adj*

tonsil ('tɒnsəl) *n* either of two small masses of lymphatic tissue situated one on each side of the back of the mouth. [C17: from L *tōnsillae* (pl) tonsils, from ?]
▸'**tonsillar** *adj*

tonsillectomy (ˌtɒnsɪ'lektəmɪ) *n, pl* **tonsillectomies.** surgical removal of the tonsils.

tonsillitis (ˌtɒnsɪ'laɪtɪs) *n* inflammation of the tonsils.
▸**tonsillitic** (ˌtɒnsɪ'lɪtɪk) *adj*

tonsorial (tɒn'sɔːrɪəl) *adj Often facetious.* of barbering or hairdressing. [C19: from L *tōnsōrius* concerning shaving, from *tondēre* to shave]

tonsure ('tɒnʃə) *n* **1** (in certain religions and monastic orders) **1a** the shaving of the head or the crown of the head only. **1b** the part of the head left bare by shaving. ◆ *vb* **tonsures, tonsuring, tonsured. 2** (*tr*) to shave the head of. [C14: from L *tōnsūra* a clipping, from *tondēre* to shave]
▸'**tonsured** *adj*

tontine ('tɒntiːn, tɒn'tiːn) *n* an annuity scheme by which several subscribers accumulate and invest a common fund out of which they receive an annuity that increases as subscribers die until the last survivor takes the whole. [C18: from F, after Lorenzo *Tonti,* Neapolitan banker who devised the scheme]

ton-up *Brit. inf.* ◆ *adj* (*prenominal*) **1** (esp. of a motorcycle) capable of speeds of a hundred miles per hour or more. **2** liking to travel at such speeds: *a ton-up boy.* ◆ *n* **3** a person who habitually rides at such speeds.

tonus ('təʊnəs) *n* the normal tension of a muscle at rest; tone. [C19: from L, from Gk *tonos* TONE]

too ⓘ (tuː) *adv* **1** as well; in addition; also: *can I come too?* **2** in or to an excessive degree: *I have too many things to do.* **3** extremely: *you're too kind.* **4** *US & Canad. inf.* indeed: used to reinforce a command: *you will too do it!* [OE *tō*]

USAGE NOTE See at **very.**

took (tʊk) *vb* the past tense of **take.**

tool ⓘ (tuːl) *n* **1a** an implement, such as a hammer, saw, or spade, that is used by hand. **1b** a power-driven instrument; machine tool. **1c** (*in combination*): *a toolkit.* **2** the cutting part of such an instrument. **3** any of the instruments used by a bookbinder to impress a design on a book cover. **4** anything used as a means of achieving an end. **5** a person used to perform dishonourable or unpleasant tasks for another. **6** a necessary medium for or adjunct to one's profession: *numbers are the tools of the mathematician's trade.* ◆ *vb* **7** to work, cut, or form (something) with a tool. **8** (*tr*) to decorate (a book cover) with a bookbinder's tool. **9** (*tr;* often foll. by *up*) to furnish with tools. [OE *tōl*]
▸'**tooler** *n*

tooling ('tuːlɪŋ) *n* **1** any decorative work done with a tool, esp. a design stamped onto a book cover, etc. **2** the selection, provision, and setting up of tools for a machining operation.

tool-maker *n* a person who specializes in the production or reconditioning of precision tools, cutters, etc.
▸'**tool-**ˌ**making** *n*

tool pusher *n* a foreman who supervises drilling operations on an oil rig.

toolroom ('tuːlruːm, -rʊm) *n* a room, such as in a machine shop, where tools are made, stored, etc.

toot (tuːt) *vb* **1** to give or cause to give (a short blast, hoot, or whistle). ◆ *n* **2** the sound made by or as if by a horn, whistle, etc. **3** *Sl.* any drug for snorting, esp. cocaine. **4** *US & Canad. sl.* a drinking spree. **5** *Austral. sl.* a lavatory. [C16: from MLow G *tuten,* imit.]
▸'**tooter** *n*

tooth (tuːθ) *n, pl* **teeth** (tiːθ). **1** any of various bonelike structures set in the jaws of most vertebrates and used for biting, tearing, or chewing. Related adj: **dental. 2** any of various similar structures in invertebrates. **3** anything resembling a tooth in shape, prominence, or function: *the tooth of a comb.* **4** any of the indentations on the margin of a leaf, petal, etc. **5** any of the projections on a gear, sprocket, rack, etc. **6** taste or appetite (esp. in **sweet tooth**). **7 long in the tooth.** old or ageing. **8 tooth and nail.** with ferocity and force. ◆ *vb* (tuːð, tuːθ). **9** (*tr*) to provide with a tooth or teeth. **10** (*intr*) (of two gearwheels) to engage. [OE *tōth*]
▸'**toothless** *adj* ▸'**tooth**ˌ**like** *adj*

toothache ('tuːθˌeɪk) *n* a pain in or about a tooth. Technical name: **odontalgia.**

toothbrush ('tuːθˌbrʌʃ) *n* a small brush, usually with a long handle, for cleaning the teeth.

toothed (tuːθt) *adj* **a** having a tooth or teeth. **b** (*in combination*): *sabre-toothed; six-toothed.*

toothed whale *n* any of a suborder of whales having simple teeth and feeding on fish, smaller mammals, etc.: includes dolphins and porpoises.

toothpaste ('tuːθˌpeɪst) *n* a paste used for cleaning the teeth, applied with a toothbrush.

toothpick ('tuːθˌpɪk) *n* a small sharp sliver of wood, plastic, etc., used for extracting pieces of food from between the teeth.

tooth powder *n* a powder used for cleaning the teeth, applied with a toothbrush.

tooth shell *n* another name for the **tusk shell.**

toothsome ⓘ ('tuːθsəm) *adj* of delicious or appetizing appearance, flavour, or smell.

toothwort ('tuːθˌwɜːt) *n* **1** a European plant having scaly stems and pinkish flowers and a rhizome covered with toothlike scales. **2** any of a genus of North American or Eurasian plants having rhizomes covered with toothlike projections.

toothy ('tuːθɪ) *adj* **toothier, toothiest.** having or showing numerous, large, or projecting teeth: *a toothy grin.*
▸'**toothily** *adv* ▸'**toothiness** *n*

tootle ('tuːtəl) *vb* **tootles, tootling, tootled. 1** to toot or hoot softly or repeatedly. ◆ *n* **2** a soft hoot or series of hoots. [C19: from TOOT]
▸'**tootler** *n*

top[1] ⓘ (tɒp) *n* **1** the highest or uppermost part of anything: *the top of a hill.* **2** the most important or successful position: *the top of the class.* **3** the part of a plant that is above ground: *carrot tops.* **4** a thing that forms or covers the uppermost part of anything, esp. a lid or cap. **5** the highest degree or point: *at the top of his career.* **6** the most important person. **7** the best part of anything. **8** the loudest or highest pitch (esp. in **top of one's voice**). **9** another name for **top gear** (sense 1). **10** *Cards.* the highest card of a suit in a player's hand. **11** *Sport.* **11a** a stroke that hits the ball above its centre. **11b** short for **topspin. 12** a platform around the head of a lower mast of a sailing vessel. **13** a garment, esp. for a woman, that extends from the shoulders to the waist or hips. **14 off the top of one's head.** with no previous preparation; extempore. **15 on top of. 15a** in addition to. **15b** *Inf.* in complete control of (a difficult situation, etc.). **16 over the top. 16a** over the parapet or leading edge of a trench. **16b** over the limit; lacking restraint or a sense of proportion. **17 the top of the morning.** a morning greeting regarded as characteristic of Irishmen. ◆ *adj* **18** of, relating to, serving as, or situated on the top. ◆ *vb* **tops, topping, topped.** (*mainly tr*) **19** to form a top on (something): *to top a cake with cream.* **20** to remove the top of or from. **21** to reach or pass the top of. **22** to be at the top of: *he tops the team.* **23** to exceed or surpass. **24** *Sl.* to kill, esp. by hanging. **25** (*also intr*) *Sport.* **25a** to hit (a ball) above the centre. **25b** to make (a stroke) by hitting the ball in this way. **26 top and tail. 26a** to trim off the ends of (fruit or vegetables) before cooking them. **26b** to wash a baby's face and bottom without immersion in a bath. ◆ See also **top off, top out, tops, top up.** [OE *topp*]

top[2] (tɒp) *n* **1** a toy that is spun on its pointed base. **2 sleep like a top.** to sleep very soundly. [OE, from ?]

THESAURUS

too *adv* **1** = **also**, as well, besides, further, in addition, into the bargain, likewise, moreover, to boot **2, 3** = **excessively**, exorbitantly, extremely, immoderately, inordinately, over-, overly, unduly, unreasonably, very

tool *n* **1a** = **implement**, apparatus, appliance, contraption, contrivance, device, gadget, instrument, machine, utensil **4** = **means**, agency, agent, intermediary, medium, vehicle, wherewithal **5** = **puppet**, cat's-paw, creature, dupe, flunkey, hireling, jackal, lackey, minion, pawn, stooge (*sl.*) ◆ *vb* **7** = **make**, chase, cut, decorate, ornament, shape, work

toothsome *adj* = **appetizing**, agreeable, dainty, delectable, delicious, luscious, mouthwatering, nice, palatable, savoury, scrumptious (*inf.*), sweet, tasty, tempting, yummy (*sl.*)

top[1] *n* **1** = **peak**, acme, apex, apogee, crest, crown, culmination, head, height, high point, meridian, pinnacle, summit, vertex, zenith **2** = **first place**, head, highest rank, lead **4** = **lid**, cap, cork, cover, stopper **16b over the top** = **excessive**, a bit much (*inf.*), going too far, immoderate, inordinate, over the limit, too much, uncalled-for ◆ *adj* **18** = **leading**, best, chief, crack, crowning, culminating, dominant, elite, finest, first, foremost, greatest, head, highest, lead, pre-eminent, prime, principal, ruling, sovereign, superior, topmost, upper, uppermost ◆ *vb* **19** = **cover**, cap, crown, finish, garnish, roof, tip **21** = **reach the top of**, ascend, climb, crest, scale, surmount **22** = **lead**, be first, be in charge of, command, head, rule **23** = **surpass**, beat, best, better, eclipse, exceed, excel, go beyond, outdo, outshine, outstrip, transcend

Antonyms *n* ≠ **peak:** base, bottom, foot, nadir, underneath, underside ◆ *adj* ≠ **leading:** amateurish, bottom, incompetent, inept, inferior, least, lower, lowest, second-rate, unknown, unranked, worst ◆ *vb* ≠ **surpass:** fail to equal, fall short of, not be as good as

topaz ('təʊpæz) *n* **1** a hard glassy mineral consisting of a silicate of aluminium and fluorine in crystalline form. It is yellow, pink, or colourless, and is a valuable gemstone. **2 oriental topaz.** a yellowish-brown variety of sapphire. **3 false topaz.** another name for **citrine. 4a** a yellowish-brown colour, as in some varieties of topaz. **4b** (*as adj*): *topaz eyes.* **5** either of two South American hummingbirds. [C13: from OF *topaze,* from L *topazus,* from Gk *topazos*]

top boot *n* a high boot, often with a decorative or contrasting upper section.

top brass *n* (*functioning as pl*) *Inf.* the most important or high-ranking officials or leaders.

topcoat ('tɒp,kəʊt) *n* an outdoor coat worn over a suit, etc.

top dog *n Inf.* the leader or chief of a group.

top dollar *n Inf.* the highest level of payment.

top drawer *n* people of the highest standing, esp. socially (esp. in **out of the top drawer**).

top dressing *n* a surface application of some material, such as fertilizer.
▸**'top-,dress** *vb* (*tr*)

tope[1] (təʊp) *vb* **topes, toping, toped.** to consume (alcoholic drink) as a regular habit, usually in large quantities. [C17: from F *toper* to keep an agreement, from Sp. *topar* to take a bet; prob. because a wager was generally followed by a drink]
▸**'toper** *n*

tope[2] (təʊp) *n* a small grey shark of European coastal waters. [C17: from ?]

topee *or* **topi** ('təʊpiː, -pɪ) *n, pl* **topees** *or* **topis.** another name for **pith helmet.** [C19: from Hindi *topī* hat]

top-flight *adj* of superior or excellent quality.

topgallant (,tɒp'gælənt; *Naut.* tə'gælənt) *n* **1** a mast on a square-rigger above a topmast or an extension of a topmast. **2** a sail set on a yard of a topgallant mast. **3** (*modifier*) of or relating to a topgallant.

top gear *n* **1** Also called: **top.** the highest forward ratio of a gearbox in a motor vehicle. **2** the highest speed, greatest energy, etc.

top hat *n* a man's hat with a tall cylindrical crown and narrow brim, often made of silk, now worn for some formal occasions.

top-hat scheme *n Inf.* a pension scheme for the senior executives of an organization.

top-heavy *adj* **1** unstable through being overloaded at the top. **2** *Finance.* characterized by too much debt capital in relation to revenue or profit; overcapitalized.

tophus ('təʊfəs) *n, pl* **tophi** (-faɪ). a deposit of sodium urate in the ear or surrounding a joint: a diagnostic of gout. [C16: from L, var. of *tōfus* TUFA, TUFF]

topi[1] ('təʊpiː, -pɪ) *n, pl* **topis.** another name for **pith helmet.** [C19: from Hindi: hat]

topi[2] ('təʊpɪ) *n, pl* **topi** *or* **topis.** a glossy brown African antelope. [C19: from Swahili]

topiary ('təʊpɪərɪ) *adj* **1** of, relating to, or characterized by the trimming or training of trees or bushes into artificial decorative shapes. ◆ *n, pl* **topiaries. 2a** topiary work. **2b** a topiary garden. **3** the art of topiary. [C16: from F *topiaire,* from L *topia* decorative garden work, from Gk *topion* little place, from *topos* place]
▸**'topiarist** *n*

topic ❶ ('tɒpɪk) *n* **1** a subject or theme of a speech, book, etc. **2** a subject of conversation. [C16: from L *topica* translating Gk *ta topika,* lit.: matters relating to commonplaces, title of a treatise by Aristotle, from *topoi,* pl. of *topos* place]

topical ❶ ('tɒpɪkəl) *adj* **1** of, relating to, or constituting current affairs. **2** relating to a particular place; local. **3** of or relating to a topic or topics. **4** (of a drug, ointment, etc.) for application to the body surface; local.
▸**topicality** (,tɒpɪ'kælɪtɪ) *n* ▸**'topically** *adv*

topknot ('tɒp,nɒt) *n* **1** a crest, tuft, chignon, etc., on top of the head. **2** any of several European flatfishes.

topless ('tɒplɪs) *adj* **1** having no top. **2a** denoting a costume which has no covering for the breasts. **2b** wearing such a costume.

top-level *n* (*modifier*) of, involving, or by those on the highest level of influence or authority: *top-level talks.*

toplofty ('tɒp,lɒftɪ) *adj Inf.* haughty or pretentious.
▸**'top,loftiness** *n*

topmast ('tɒp,mɑːst; *Naut.* 'tɒpməst) *n* the mast next above a lower mast on a sailing vessel.

topmost ❶ ('tɒp,məʊst) *adj* at or nearest the top.

top-notch ('tɒp'nɒtʃ) *adj Inf.* excellent; superb.
▸**'top-'notcher** *n*

topo- *or before a vowel* **top-** *combining form.* indicating place or region: *topography.* [from Gk *topos* a place]

top off *vb* (*tr, adv*) to finish or complete, esp. with some decisive action.

topography (tə'pɒgrəfɪ) *n, pl* **topographies. 1** the study or detailed description of the surface features of a region. **2** the detailed mapping of the configuration of a region. **3** the land forms or surface configuration of a region. **4** the surveying of a region's surface features. **5** the study or description of the configuration of any object.
▸**to'pographer** *n* ▸**topographic** (,tɒpə'græfɪk) *or* **,topo'graphical** *adj*

topological group *n Maths.* a group, such as the set of all real numbers, that constitutes a topological space and in which multiplication and inversion are continuous.

topological space *n Maths.* a set *S* with an associated family of subsets τ that is closed under set union and finite intersection.

topology (tə'pɒlədʒɪ) *n* **1** the branch of mathematics concerned with generalization of the concepts of continuity, limit, etc. **2** a branch of geometry describing the properties of a figure that are unaffected by continuous distortion. **3** *Maths.* a family of subsets of a given set *S,* such that *S* is a topological space. **4** the study of the topography of a given place. **5** the anatomy of any specific bodily area, structure, or part.
▸**topologic** (,tɒpə'lɒdʒɪk) *or* **,topo'logical** *adj* ▸**,topo'logically** *adv* ▸**to'pologist** *n*

top out *vb* (*adv*) to place the highest part of a building in position.

topper ('tɒpə) *n* **1** an informal name for **top hat. 2** a person or thing that tops or excels.

topping ('tɒpɪŋ) *n* **1** something that tops something else, esp. a sauce or garnish for food. ◆ *adj* **2** high or superior in rank, degree, etc. **3** *Brit. sl.* excellent; splendid.

topple ❶ ('tɒpəl) *vb* **topples, toppling, toppled. 1** to tip over or cause to tip over, esp. from a height. **2** (*intr*) to lean precariously or totter. [C16: frequentative of TOP[1] (vb)]

tops (tɒps) *Sl.* ◆ *n* **1 the tops.** a person or thing of top quality. ◆ *adj* **2** (*postpositive*) excellent.

topsail ('tɒp,seɪl; *Naut.* 'tɒpsəl) *n* a square sail carried on a yard set on a topmast.

top-secret *adj* classified as needing the highest level of secrecy and security.

topside ('tɒp,saɪd) *n* **1** the uppermost side of anything. **2** *Brit. & NZ.* a lean cut of beef from the thigh containing no bone. **3** (*often pl*) **3a** the part of a ship's sides above the water line. **3b** the parts of a ship above decks.

topsoil ('tɒp,sɔɪl) *n* the surface layer of soil.

topspin ('tɒp,spɪn) *n Tennis, etc.* a spin imparted to make a ball bounce or travel exceptionally far, high, or quickly.

topsy-turvy ❶ ('tɒpsɪ'tɜːvɪ) *adj* **1** upside down. **2** in a state of confusion. ◆ *adv* **3** in a topsy-turvy manner. ◆ *n* **4** a topsy-turvy state. [C16: prob. from *tops,* pl. of TOP[1] + obs. *tervy* to turn upside down]

top up ❶ *vb* (*tr, adv*) *Brit.* **1** to raise the level of (a liquid, powder, etc.) in (a container), usually bringing it to the brim of the container. **2a** to increase the benefits from (an insurance scheme), esp. to increase a pension when a salary rise enables higher premiums to be paid. **2b** to add money to (a loan, bank account, etc.) in order to keep it at a constant or acceptable level. ◆ *n* **top-up. 3a** an amount added to something in order to raise it to or maintain it at a desired level. **3b** (*as modifier*): *a top-up loan; a top-up policy.*

toque (təʊk) *n* **1** a woman's small round brimless hat. **2** a chef's tall white hat. **3** *Canad.* a variant spelling of **tuque** (sense 2). **4** a small plumed hat popular in the 16th century. [C16: from F, from OSp. *toca* headdress, prob. from Basque *tauka* hat]

tor (tɔː) *n* a high hill, esp. a bare rocky one. [OE *torr*]

Torah ('təʊrə) *n* **1a** the Pentateuch. **1b** the scroll on which this is written. **2** the whole body of traditional Jewish teaching, including the Oral Law. [C16: from Heb.: precept, from *yārāh* to instruct]

torc (tɔːk) *n* a variant of **torque** (sense 1).

torch (tɔːtʃ) *n* **1** a small portable electric lamp powered by batteries. US and Canad. word: **flashlight. 2** a wooden or tow shaft dipped in wax or tallow and set alight. **3** anything regarded as a source of enlightenment, guidance, etc. **4** any apparatus with a hot flame for welding, brazing, etc. **5 carry a torch for.** to be in love with, esp. unrequitedly. ◆ *vb* **6** (*tr*) to set fire to, esp. deliberately as an act of arson. [C13: from OF *torche* handful of twisted straw, from Vulgar L *torca* (unattested), from L *torquēre* to twist]

torchbearer ('tɔːtʃ,bɛərə) *n* **1** a person or thing that carries a torch. **2** a person who leads or inspires.

torchère (tɔː'ʃɛə) *n* a tall stand for holding a candelabrum. [C20: from F, from *torche* TORCH]

torchier *or* **torchiere** ('tɔːtʃɪə) *n* a standing lamp with a bowl for casting light upwards. [C20: from TORCHÈRE]

torch song *n* a sentimental song, usually sung by a woman. [C20: from *to carry a torch for* (*someone*)]
▸**torch singer** *n*

tore (tɔː) *vb* the past tense of **tear**[2].

toreador ('tɒrɪə,dɔː) *n* a bullfighter. [C17: from Sp., from *torear* to take part in bullfighting, from *toro* a bull, from L *taurus*]

torero (tɒ'rɛərəʊ) *n, pl* **toreros.** a bullfighter, esp. one who fights on foot. [C18: from Sp., from LL *taurārius,* from L *taurus* a bull]

toric lens ('tɒrɪk) *n* a lens used to correct astigmatism, having one of its

THESAURUS

topic *n* **1** = **subject**, issue, matter, point, question, subject matter, text, theme, thesis

topical *adj* **1** = **current**, contemporary, newsworthy, popular, up-to-date, up-to-the-minute

topmost *adj* = **highest**, dominant, foremost, leading, loftiest, paramount, principal, supreme, top, upper, uppermost
Antonyms *adj* base, basic, bottom, bottommost, last, lowest, undermost

topple *vb* **1** = **fall over**, capsize, collapse, fall, fall headlong, keel over, knock down, knock over, overbalance, overturn, tip over, totter, tumble, upset

topsy-turvy *adj* **2** = **confused**, chaotic, disarranged, disorderly, disorganized, inside-out, jumbled, messy, mixed-up, untidy, upside-down
Antonyms *adj* neat, ordered, orderly, organized, shipshape, systematic, tidy

top up *vb* **2** = **supplement**, add to, augment, boost, enhance, fill out *or* up

surfaces shaped like part of a torus so that its focal lengths are different in different meridians.

torii ('tɔːrɪ,iː) *n, pl* **torii.** a gateway at the entrance to a Shinto temple. [C19: from Japanese, lit.: a perch for birds]

torment ⓣ *vb* (tɔː'mɛnt). (*tr*) **1** to afflict with great pain, suffering, or anguish; torture. **2** to tease or pester in an annoying way. ◆ *n* ('tɔːmɛnt). **3** physical or mental pain. **4** a source of pain, worry, annoyance, etc. [C13: from OF, from L *tormentum*, from *torquēre*] ▸**tor'mented** *adj* ▸**tor'menting** *adj, n* ▸**tor'mentor** *n*

tormentil ('tɔːməntɪl) *n* a perennial plant of Europe and W Asia, having yellow flowers, and an astringent root used in medicine, tanning, and dyeing. [C15: from OF *tormentille*, from Med. L *tormentilla*, from L *tormentum* agony; from its use in relieving pain]

torn ⓣ (tɔːn) *vb* **1** the past participle of **tear**[2]. **2 that's torn it.** *Brit. sl.* an unexpected event or circumstance has upset one's plans. ◆ *adj* **3** split or cut. **4** divided or undecided, as in preference: *torn between staying and leaving.*

tornado ⓣ (tɔː'neɪdəʊ) *n, pl* **tornadoes** *or* **tornados. 1** a violent storm with winds whirling around a small area of extremely low pressure, usually characterized by a dark funnel-shaped cloud causing damage along its path. **2** a small but violent squall or whirlwind. **3** any violently active or destructive person or thing. [C16: prob. alteration of Sp. *tronada* thunderstorm (from *tronar* to thunder, from L *tonāre*) through infl. of *tornar* to turn, from L *tornāre* to turn in a lathe] ▸**tornadic** (tɔː'nædɪk) *adj*

toroid ('tɔːrɔɪd) *n* **1** *Geom.* a surface generated by rotating a closed plane curve about a coplanar line that does not intersect the curve. **2** the solid enclosed by such a surface. See also **torus.** ▸**to'roidal** *adj*

torpedo (tɔː'piːdəʊ) *n, pl* **torpedoes. 1** a cylindrical self-propelled weapon carrying explosives that is launched from aircraft, ships, or submarines and follows an underwater path to hit its target. **2** *Obs.* a submarine mine. **3** *US & Canad.* a firework with a percussion cap. **4** an electric ray. ◆ *vb* **torpedoes, torpedoing, torpedoed.** (*tr*) **5** to attack or hit (a ship, etc.) with one or a number of torpedoes. **6** to destroy or wreck: *to torpedo the administration's plan.* [C16: from L: crampfish (whose electric discharges can cause numbness), from *torpēre* to be inactive] ▸**tor'pedo-,like** *adj*

torpedo boat *n* (formerly) a small high-speed warship designed to carry out torpedo attacks.

torpedo tube *n* the tube from which a torpedo is discharged from submarines or ships.

torpid ⓣ ('tɔːpɪd) *adj* **1** apathetic; sluggish. **2** (of a hibernating animal) dormant. **3** unable to move or feel. [C17: from L *torpidus*, from *torpēre* to be numb] ▸**tor'pidity** *n* ▸**'torpidly** *adv*

torpor ⓣ ('tɔːpə) *n* a state of torpidity. [C17: from L: inactivity, from *torpēre* to be motionless]

torque (tɔːk) *n* **1** a necklace or armband made of twisted metal. **2** any force that causes rotation. [C19: from L *torquēs* necklace & *torquēre* to twist]

torque converter *n* a device for the transmission of power in which an engine-driven impeller transmits its momentum to a fluid held in a sealed container, which in turn drives a rotor. Also called: **hydraulic coupling.**

torques ('tɔːkwiːz) *n* a distinctive band of hair, feathers, skin, or colour around the neck of an animal; a collar. [C17: from L: necklace, from *torquēre* to twist] ▸**torquate** ('tɔːkwɪt, -kweɪt) *adj*

torque wrench *n* a type of wrench with a gauge attached to indicate the torque applied.

torr (tɔː) *n, pl* **torr.** a unit of pressure equal to one millimetre of mercury (133.322 newtons per square metre). [C20: after E. *Torricelli* (1608–47), It. physicist]

torrefy ('tɒrɪ,faɪ) *vb* **torrefies, torrefying, torrefied.** (*tr*) to dry (drugs, ores, etc.) by heat. [C17: from F *torréfier*, from L *torrefacere*, from *torrēre* to parch + *facere* to make] ▸**torrefaction** (,tɒrɪ'fækʃən) *n*

Torrens title ('tɒrənz) *n Austral.* legal title to land based on record of registration rather than on title deeds. [from Sir Robert Richard *Torrens* (1814–84), who introduced the system as premier of South Australia in 1857]

torrent ⓣ ('tɒrənt) *n* **1** a fast or violent stream, esp. of water. **2** an overwhelming flow of thoughts, words, sound, etc. [C17: from F, from L *torrēns* (n), from *torrēns* (adj) burning, from *torrēre* to burn] ▸**torrential** (tɒ'rɛnʃəl) *adj*

Torricellian tube (,tɒrɪ'sɛlɪən) *n* a vertical glass tube partly evacuated and partly filled with mercury, used to measure atmospheric pressure. [C17: after E. *Torricelli*; see TORR]

torrid ⓣ ('tɒrɪd) *adj* **1** so hot and dry as to parch or scorch. **2** arid or parched. **3** highly charged emotionally: *a torrid love scene.* [C16: from L *torridus*, from *torrēre* to scorch] ▸**tor'ridity** *or* **'torridness** *n* ▸**'torridly** *adv*

Torrid Zone *n Rare.* that part of the earth's surface lying between the tropics of Cancer and Capricorn.

torsion ('tɔːʃən) *n* **1a** the twisting of a part by application of equal and opposite torques. **1b** the condition of twist and shear stress produced by a torque on a part or component. **2** a twisting or being twisted. [C15: from OF, from Medical L *torsiō* griping pains, from L *torquēre* to twist, torture] ▸**'torsional** *adj* ▸**'torsionally** *adv*

torsion balance *n* an instrument used to measure small forces, esp. electric or magnetic forces, by the torsion they produce in a thin wire.

torsion bar *n* a metal bar acting as a torsional spring.

torsk (tɔːsk) *n, pl* **torsks** *or* **torsk.** a food fish of northern coastal waters. Usual US name: **cusk.** [C17: of Scand. origin]

torso ('tɔːsəʊ) *n, pl* **torsos** *or* **torsi** (-sɪ). **1** the trunk of the human body. **2** a statue of a nude human trunk, esp. without the head or limbs. [C18: from It.: stalk, stump, from L: THYRSUS]

tort (tɔːt) *n Law.* a civil wrong or injury arising out of an act or failure to act, independently of any contract, for which an action for damages may be brought. [C14: from OF, from Med. L *tortum*, lit.: something twisted, from L *torquēre* to twist]

torte (tɔːt) *n* a rich cake usually decorated or filled with cream, fruit, etc. [C16: ult. ?from LL *tōrta* a round loaf, from ?]

torticollis (,tɔːtɪ'kɒlɪs) *n Pathol.* an abnormal position of the head, usually with the neck bent to one side. [C19: NL, from L *tortus* twisted (from *torquēre* to twist) + *collum* neck]

tortilla (tɔː'tiːə) *n Mexican cookery.* a kind of thin pancake made from corn meal. [C17: from Sp.: a little cake, from *torta* a round cake, from LL]

tortoise ('tɔːtəs) *n* **1** any of a family of herbivorous reptiles having a heavy dome-shaped shell and clawed limbs. **2** a slow-moving person. **3** another word for **testudo.** [C15: prob. from OF *tortue* (infl. by L *tortus* twisted), from Med. L *tortūca*, from LL *tartarūcha* coming from Tartarus (in the underworld), from Gk *tartaroukhos*; from belief that the tortoise originated in the underworld]

tortoiseshell ('tɔːtəs,ʃɛl) *n* **1** the horny yellow-and-brown mottled shell of the hawksbill turtle: used for making ornaments, jewellery, etc. **2** a similar synthetic substance. **3** a breed of domestic cat having black, cream, and brownish markings. **4** any of several butterflies having orange-brown wings with black markings. **5a** a yellowish-brown mottled colour. **5b** (*as adj*): *a tortoiseshell décor.* **6** (*modifier*) made of tortoiseshell.

tortricid ('tɔːtrɪsɪd) *n* any of a family of moths, the larvae of which live in leaves, which they roll or tie together. [C19: from NL *Tortrīcidae*, from *tortrix*, fem. of *tortor*, lit.: twister, from the leaf-rolling of the larvae, from *torquēre* to twist]

tortuous ⓣ ('tɔːtjʊəs) *adj* **1** twisted or winding. **2** devious or cunning. **3** intricate. ▸**tortuosity** (,tɔːtjʊ'ɒsɪtɪ) *n* ▸**'tortuously** *adv* ▸**'tortuousness** *n*

torture ⓣ ('tɔːtʃə) *vb* **tortures, torturing, tortured.** (*tr*) **1** to cause extreme physical pain to, esp. to extract information, etc.: *to torture prisoners.* **2** to give mental anguish to. **3** to twist into a grotesque form. ◆ *n* **4** physical or mental anguish. **5** the practice of torturing a person. **6** a

THESAURUS

torment *vb* **1** = **torture**, afflict, agonize, crucify, distress, excruciate, harrow, pain, rack **2** = **tease**, aggravate (*inf.*), annoy, bedevil, bother, chivvy, devil (*inf.*), harass, harry, hassle (*inf.*), hound, irritate, lead (someone) a merry dance (*Brit. inf.*), nag, persecute, pester, plague, provoke, trouble, vex, worry ◆ *n* **3** = **suffering**, agony, anguish, distress, hell, misery, pain, torture **4** = **trouble**, affliction, annoyance, bane, bother, harassment, hassle (*inf.*), irritation, nag, nagging, nuisance, pain in the neck (*inf.*), persecution, pest, plague, provocation, scourge, thorn in one's flesh *or* side, vexation, worry
Antonyms *vb* ≠ **torture**: comfort, delight, ease, encourage, make happy, put at ease, reassure, soothe ◆ *n* ≠ **suffering**: bliss, comfort, ease, ecstasy, encouragement, happiness, joy, reassurance, rest

torn *adj* **3** = **cut**, lacerated, ragged, rent, ripped, slit, split **4** = **undecided**, divided, in two minds (*inf.*), irresolute, split, uncertain, unsure, vacillating, wavering

tornado *n* **1, 2** = **whirlwind**, cyclone, gale, hurricane, squall, storm, tempest, twister, typhoon, windstorm

torpid *adj* **1** = **inactive**, apathetic, benumbed, drowsy, dull, indolent, inert, lackadaisical, languid, languorous, lazy, lethargic, listless, lymphatic, motionless, numb, passive, slothful, slow, slow-moving, sluggish, somnolent, stagnant

torpor *n* = **inactivity**, accidie, acedia, apathy, drowsiness, dullness, inanition, indolence, inertia, inertness, languor, laziness, lethargy, listlessness, numbness, passivity, sloth, sluggishness, somnolence, stagnancy, stupor, torpidity
Antonyms *n* animation, energy, get-up-and-go (*inf.*), go, liveliness, pep, vigour

torrent *n* **1** = **stream**, cascade, deluge, downpour, effusion, flood, flow, gush, outburst, rush, spate, tide

torrid *adj* **1** = **hot**, blistering, boiling, broiling, burning, dry, fiery, flaming, parching, scorching, sizzling, stifling, sultry, sweltering, tropical **2** = **arid**, dried, parched, scorched **3** = **passionate**, ardent, erotic, fervent, flaming, hot, intense, sexy (*inf.*), steamy (*inf.*)

tortuous *adj* **1** = **winding**, bent, circuitous, convoluted, crooked, curved, indirect, mazy, meandering, serpentine, sinuous, twisted, twisting, twisty, zigzag **2** = **complicated**, ambiguous, convoluted, cunning, deceptive, devious, indirect, involved, mazy, misleading, roundabout, tricky
Antonyms *adj* ≠ **complicated**: candid, direct, honest, ingenuous, open, reliable, straightforward, upright

torture *vb* **1, 2** = **torment**, afflict, agonize, crucify, distress, excruciate, harrow, lacerate, martyr, pain, persecute, put on the rack, rack ◆ *n* **4, 5** = **agony**, affliction, anguish, distress, hell, laceration, martyrdom, misery, pain, pang(s), persecution, rack, suffering, torment
Antonyms *vb* ≠ **torment**: alleviate, comfort, con-

cause of mental agony. [C16: from LL *tortūra* a twisting, from *torquēre* to twist]
▸**'torturer** *n* ▸**'torturous** *adj* ▸**'torturously** *adv*

USAGE NOTE The adjective *torturous* is sometimes confused with *tortuous*. One speaks of a *torturous* experience, i.e. one that involves pain or suffering, but of a *tortuous* road, i.e. one that winds or twists.

torus ('tɔːrəs) *n, pl* **tori** (-raɪ). **1** a large convex moulding semicircular in cross section, esp. one used on the base of a column. **2** *Geom.* a ring-shaped surface generated by rotating a circle about a coplanar line that does not intersect the circle. **3** *Bot.* another name for **receptacle** (sense 2). [C16: from L: a swelling, from ?]
▸**toric** ('tɒrɪk) *adj*

Tory ('tɔːrɪ) *n, pl* **Tories. 1** a member or supporter of the Conservative Party in Great Britain or Canada. **2** a member of the English political party that opposed the exclusion of James, Duke of York from the royal succession (1679–80). Tory remained the label for conservative interests until they gave birth to the Conservative Party in the 1830s. **3** an American supporter of the British cause; loyalist. Cf. **Whig. 4** (*sometimes not cap.*) an ultraconservative or reactionary. ◆ *adj* **5** of, characteristic of, or relating to Tories. **6** (*sometimes not cap.*) ultraconservative or reactionary. [C17: from Irish *tōraidhe* outlaw, from MIrish *tōir* pursuit]
▸**'Toryish** *adj* ▸**'Toryism** *n*

tosa ('təʊsə) *n* a large dog, usually red in colour, that is a cross between a mastiff and a Great Dane: originally developed for dog-fighting; it is not recognized as a breed by kennel clubs outside Japan. [C20: from the name of a province of Japan]

tosh (tɒʃ) *n Sl., chiefly Brit.* nonsense; rubbish. [C19: from ?]

toss ❶ (tɒs) *vb* **1** (*tr*) to throw lightly, esp. with the palm of the hand upwards. **2** to fling or be flung about, esp. in an agitated or violent way: *a ship tosses in a storm.* **3** to discuss or put forward for discussion in an informal way. **4** (*tr*) (of a horse, etc.) to throw (its rider). **5** (*tr*) (of an animal) to butt with the head or the horns and throw into the air. **6** (*tr*) to shake or disturb. **7** to toss up a coin with (someone) in order to decide something. **8** (*intr*) to move away angrily or impatiently. ◆ *n* **9** an abrupt movement. **10** a rolling or pitching motion. **11** the act or an instance of tossing. **12** the act of tossing up a coin. See **toss up. 13** a fall from a horse. [C16: of Scand. origin]

tosser ('tɒsə) *n Brit. sl.* a stupid or despicable person. [C20: probably from TOSS OFF (to masturbate)]

toss off *vb* (*adv*) **1** (*tr*) to perform, write, etc., quickly and easily. **2** (*tr*) to drink at one draught. **3** (*intr*) *Brit. taboo.* to masturbate.

toss up *vb* (*adv*) **1** to spin (a coin) in the air in order to decide between alternatives by guessing which side will fall uppermost. ◆ *n* **toss-up. 2** an instance of tossing up a coin. **3** *Inf.* an even chance or risk.

tot[1] ❶ (tɒt) *n* **1** a young child; toddler. **2** *Chiefly Brit.* a small amount of anything. **3** a small measure of spirits. [C18: ? short for *totterer;* see TOTTER]

tot[2] ❶ (tɒt) *vb* **tots, totting, totted.** (usually foll. by *up*) *Chiefly Brit.* to total; add. [C17: shortened from TOTAL or from L *totum* all]

total ❶ ('təʊtᵊl) *n* **1** the whole, esp. regarded as the complete sum of a number of parts. ◆ *adj* **2** complete; absolute. **3** (*prenominal*) being or related to a total. ◆ *vb* **totals, totalling, totalled** *or US* **totals, totaling, totaled. 4** (when *intr,* sometimes foll. by *to*) to amount: *to total six pounds.* **5** (*tr*) to add up. **6** (*tr*) *Sl.* to kill or destroy. [C14: from OF, from Med. L *tōtālis,* from L *tōtus* all]
▸**'totally** *adv*

total football *n* an attacking style of play, popularized by the Dutch national team of the 1970s, in which there are no fixed positions and every outfield player can join in the attack.

total internal reflection *n Physics.* the complete reflection of a light ray at the boundary of two media, when the ray is in the medium with greater refractive index.

totalitarian ❶ (təʊˌtælɪ'tɛərɪən) *adj* **1** of, denoting, relating to, or characteristic of a dictatorial one-party state that regulates every realm of life. ◆ *n* **2** a person who advocates or practises totalitarian policies.
▸**toˌtali'tarianism** *n*

totality ❶ (təʊ'tælɪtɪ) *n, pl* **totalities. 1** the whole amount. **2** the state of being total.

totalizator ('təʊtᵊlaɪˌzeɪtə), **totalizer** *or* **totalisator, totaliser** *n* **1** a system of betting on horse races in which the aggregate stake, less tax, etc., is paid out to winners in proportion to their stake. **2** the machine that records bets in this system and works out odds, pays out winnings, etc. ◆ US and Canad. term: **pari-mutuel.**

total quality management *n* an approach to the management of an organization that integrates the needs of customers with a deep understanding of the technical details, costs, and human-resource relationships of the organization. Abbrev.: **TQM.**

totaquine ('təʊtəˌkwiːn, -kwɪn) *n* a mixture of quinine and other alkaloids derived from cinchona bark, used as a substitute for quinine in treating malaria. [C20: from NL *tōtaquīna,* from TOTA(L) + Sp. *quina* cinchona bark; see QUININE]

totara ('təʊtərə) *n* a tall coniferous forest tree of New Zealand with durable wood.

tote[1] (təʊt) *Inf.* ◆ *vb* **totes, toting, toted. 1** (*tr*) to carry, convey, or drag. ◆ *n* **2** the act of or an instance of toting. **3** something toted. [C17: from ?]
▸**'toter** *n*

tote[2] (təʊt) *n* (usually preceded by *the*) *Inf.* short for **totalizator.**

tote bag *n* a large handbag or shopping bag.

totem ('təʊtəm) *n* **1** (in some societies, esp. among North American Indians) an object, animal, plant, etc., symbolizing a clan, family, etc., often having ritual associations. **2** a representation of such an object. [C18: from Ojibwa *nintōtēm* mark of my family]
▸**totemic** (təʊ'tɛmɪk) *adj* ▸**'totemˌism** *n*

totem pole *n* a pole carved or painted with totemic figures set up by certain North American Indians as a tribal symbol, etc.

tother *or* **t'other** ('tʌðə) *adj, n Arch. or dialect.* the other. [C13 *the tother,* by mistaken division from *thet other* (*thet,* from OE *thæt,* neuter of THE[1])]

totipalmate (ˌtəʊtɪ'pælmɪt, -ˌmeɪt) *adj* (of certain birds) having all four toes webbed. [C19: from L *tōtus* entire + *palmate,* from *palmātus* shaped like a hand, from *palma* PALM[1]]

totter ❶ ('tɒtə) *vb* (*intr*) **1** to move in an unsteady manner. **2** to sway or shake as if about to fall. **3** to be failing, unstable, or precarious. ◆ *n* **4** the act or an instance of tottering. [C12: ?from OE *tealtrian* to waver, & MDu. *touteren* to stagger]
▸**'totterer** *n* ▸**'tottery** *adj*

totting ('tɒtɪŋ) *n Brit.* the practice of searching through rubbish for usable or saleable items. [C19: from ?]

toucan ('tuːkən) *n* any of a family of tropical American fruit-eating birds having a large brightly coloured bill and a bright plumage. [C16: from F, from Port. *tucano,* from Tupi *tucana,* prob. imit. of its cry]

touch ❶ (tʌtʃ) *n* **1** the sense by which the texture and other qualities of objects can be experienced when they come in contact with a part of the body surface, esp. the tips of the fingers. Related adj: **tactile. 2** the quality of an object as perceived by this sense; feel; feeling. **3** the act or an instance of something coming into contact with the body. **4** a gentle push, tap, or caress. **5** a small amount; hint: *a touch of sarcasm.* **6** a noticeable effect; influence: *the house needed a woman's touch.* **7** any slight stroke or mark. **8** characteristic manner or style. **9** a detail of some work: *she added a few finishing touches to the book.* **10** a slight attack, as of a disease. **11** a specific ability or facility. **12** the state of being aware of a situation or in contact with someone. **13** the state of being in physical contact. **14** a trial or test (esp. in **put to the touch**). **15** *Rugby, soccer, etc.* the area outside the touchlines, beyond which the ball is out of play (esp. in **in touch**). **16** a scoring hit in fencing. **17** an estimate of the amount of gold in an alloy as obtained by use of a touchstone. **18** the technique of fingering a keyboard instrument. **19** the quality of the

THESAURUS

sole, ease, mollify, relieve, salve, solace, soothe ◆ *n* ≠ **agony:** amusement, bliss, delight, enjoyment, happiness, joy, pleasure, well-being

toss *vb* **1** = **throw**, cast, chuck, fling, flip, hurl, launch, lob (*inf.*), pitch, project, propel, shy, sling **2** = **heave**, labour, lurch, pitch, roll, wallow **6** = **thrash**, agitate, disturb, jiggle, joggle, jolt, rock, roll, shake, tumble, wriggle, writhe ◆ *n* **11** = **throw**, cast, fling, lob (*inf.*), pitch, shy

tot[1] *n* **1** = **infant**, ankle-biter (*Austral. sl.*), baby, child, little one, mite, rug rat (*sl.*), sprog (*sl.*), toddler, wean (*Scot.*) **3** = **measure**, dram, finger, nip, shot (*inf.*), slug, snifter (*inf.*), toothful

tot[2] *vb, usually foll. by* **up** = **add up**, calculate, count up, reckon, sum (up), tally, total

total *n* **1** = **whole**, aggregate, all, amount, entirety, full amount, mass, sum, totality ◆ *adj* **2** = **complete**, absolute, all-out, arrant, comprehensive, consummate, deep-dyed (*usually derogatory*), downright, entire, full, gross, integral, out-and-out, outright, overarching, perfect, sheer, sweeping, thorough, thoroughgoing, unconditional, undisputed, undivided, unmitigated, unqualified, utter, whole ◆ *vb* **4** = **amount to**, come to, mount up to, reach **5** = **add up**, reckon, sum up, tot up
Antonyms *n* ≠ **whole:** individual amount, part, subtotal ◆ *adj* ≠ **complete:** conditional, fragmentary, incomplete, limited, mixed, part, partial, qualified, restricted, uncombined ◆ *vb* ≠ **add up:** deduct, subtract

totalitarian *adj* **1** = **dictatorial**, authoritarian, despotic, monolithic, one-party, oppressive, tyrannous, undemocratic
Antonyms *adj* autonomous, democratic, egalitarian, popular, self-governing

totality *n* **1** = **whole**, aggregate, all, entirety, everything, sum, total **2** = **completeness**, entireness, fullness, wholeness

totally *adv* **2** = **completely**, absolutely, comprehensively, consummately, entirely, fully, one hundred per cent, perfectly, quite, thoroughly, to the hilt, unconditionally, unmitigatedly, utterly, wholeheartedly, wholly
Antonyms *adv* incompletely, in part, partially, partly, somewhat, to a certain extent

totter *vb* **1, 2** = **stagger**, falter, lurch, quiver, reel, rock, shake, stumble, sway, teeter, tremble, walk unsteadily, waver, wobble

touch *n* **2** = **feeling**, feel, handling, palpation, physical contact, tactility **4** = **tap**, brush, caress, fondling, pat, stroke **5** = **bit**, dash, detail, drop, hint, intimation, jot, pinch, smack, small amount, smattering, *soupçon*, speck, spot, suggestion, suspicion, taste, tincture, tinge, trace, whiff **6** = **influence**, direction, effect, hand **8** = **style**, approach, characteristic, handiwork, manner, method, technique, trademark, way **11** = **skill**, ability, adroitness, art, artistry, command, craft, deftness, facility, flair, knack, mastery, virtuosity **12** = **communication**, acquaintance, awareness, contact, correspondence, familiarity, understanding ◆ *vb* **21** = **handle**, brush, caress, contact, feel, finger, fondle, graze, lay a finger on, palpate, stroke **22** = **tap**, hit, pat, push, strike **23, 24** = **come into con-**

action of a keyboard instrument with regard to the ease with which the keys may be depressed. **20** *Sl.* **20a** the act of asking for money, often by devious means. **20b** the money received. **20c** a person asked for money in this way. ◆ *vb* **21** (*tr*) to cause or permit a part of the body to come into contact with. **22** (*tr*) to tap, feel, or strike. **23** to come or cause to come into contact with. **24** (*intr*) to be in contact. **25** (*tr; usually used with a negative*) to take hold of (a person or thing), esp. in violence. **26** to be adjacent to (each other). **27** (*tr*) to move or disturb by handling. **28** (*tr*) to have an effect on. **29** (*tr*) to produce an emotional response in. **30** (*tr*) to affect; concern. **31** (*tr; usually used with a negative*) to partake of, eat, or drink. **32** (*tr; usually used with a negative*) to handle or deal with: *I wouldn't touch that business.* **33** (when *intr*, often foll. by *on*) to allude (to) briefly or in passing. **34** (*tr*) to tinge or tint slightly: *brown hair touched with gold.* **35** (*tr*) to spoil slightly: *blackfly touched the flowers.* **36** (*tr*) to mark, as with a brush or pen. **37** (*tr*) to compare to in quality or attainment. **38** (*tr*) to reach or attain: *he touched the high point in his career.* **39** (*intr*) to dock or stop briefly: *the ship touches at Tenerife.* **40** (*tr*) *Sl.* to ask for a loan or gift of money from. ◆ See also **touchdown, touch off, touch up.** [C13: from OF *tochier,* from Vulgar L *toccāre* (unattested) to strike, prob. imit. of a tapping sound]
▸ **'touchable** *adj* ▸ **'toucher** *n*

touch and go ❶ *adj* (**touch-and-go** *when prenominal*) risky or critical.

touchdown ('tʌtʃ,daʊn) *n* **1** the moment at which a landing aircraft or spacecraft comes into contact with the landing surface. **2** *Rugby.* the act of placing or touching the ball on the ground behind the goal line, as in scoring a try. **3** *American football.* a scoring play worth six points, achieved by being in possession of the ball in the opposing team's end zone. Abbrev.: **TD.** ◆ *vb* **touch down.** (*intr, adv*) **4** (of an aircraft, etc.) to land. **5** *Rugby.* to place the ball behind the goal line, as when scoring a try.

touché (tu:'ʃeɪ) *interj* **1** an acknowledgment of a scoring hit in fencing. **2** an acknowledgment of the striking home of a remark, witty reply, etc. [from F, lit.: touched]

touched ❶ (tʌtʃt) *adj* (*postpositive*) **1** moved to sympathy or emotion. **2** showing slight insanity.

touchhole ('tʌtʃ,həʊl) *n* a hole in the breech of early cannon and firearms through which the charge was ignited.

touching ❶ ('tʌtʃɪŋ) *adj* **1** evoking or eliciting tender feelings. ◆ *prep* **2** on the subject of; relating to.
▸ **'touchingly** *adv*

touch judge *n* one of the two linesmen in rugby.

touchline ('tʌtʃ,laɪn) *n* either of the lines marking the side of the playing area in certain games, such as rugby.

touchmark ('tʌtʃ,mɑ:k) *n* a maker's mark stamped on pewter objects.

touch-me-not *n* an impatiens with yellow spurred flowers and seed pods that burst open at a touch when ripe. Also called: **noli-me-tangere.**

touch off ❶ *vb* (*tr, adv*) **1** to cause to explode, as by touching with a match. **2** to cause (a disturbance, violence, etc.) to begin.

touchpaper ('tʌtʃ,peɪpə) *n* paper soaked in saltpetre for lighting fireworks or firing gunpowder.

touchstone ❶ ('tʌtʃ,stəʊn) *n* **1** a criterion or standard. **2** a hard dark stone that is used to test gold and silver from the streak they produce on it.

touch-tone *adj* of or relating to a telephone dialling system in which each dialling button pressed generates a different pitch, which is transmitted to the exchange.

touch-type *vb* **touch-types, touch-typing, touch-typed.** (*intr*) to type without looking at the keyboard.
▸ **'touch-,typist** *n*

touch up ❶ *vb* (*tr, adv*) **1** to put extra or finishing touches to. **2** to enhance, renovate, or falsify by putting extra touches to. **3** *Brit. sl.* to touch or caress (someone).

touchwood ('tʌtʃ,wʊd) *n* something, esp. dry wood or fungus material, used as tinder. [C16: TOUCH (in the sense: to kindle) + WOOD]

touchy ❶ ('tʌtʃɪ) *adj* **touchier, touchiest. 1** easily upset or irritated. **2** extremely risky. **3** easily ignited.
▸ **'touchily** *adv* ▸ **'touchiness** *n*

touchy-feely ('tʌtʃɪ,fi:lɪ) *adj Inf., sometimes derog.* sensitive and caring.

tough ❶ (tʌf) *adj* **1** strong or resilient; durable. **2** not tender. **3** hardy and fit. **4** rough or pugnacious. **5** resolute or intractable. **6** difficult or troublesome to do or deal with: *a tough problem.* **7** *Inf.* unfortunate or unlucky: *it's tough on him.* ◆ *n* **8** a rough, vicious, or pugnacious person. ◆ *adv* **9** *Inf.* violently, aggressively, or intractably: *to treat someone tough.* ◆ *vb* (*tr*) **10** *Sl.* to stand firm, hold out against (a difficulty or difficult situation) (esp. in **tough it out**). [OE *tōh*]
▸ **'toughly** *adv* ▸ **'toughness** *n*

toughen ('tʌfən) *vb* to make or become tough or tougher.
▸ **'toughener** *n*

tough love *n* the practice of taking a stern attitude towards a relative or friend suffering from an addiction, etc., to help the addict overcome the problem.

tough-minded *adj* practical, unsentimental, or intractable.
▸ **,tough-'mindedness** *n*

toupee ('tu:peɪ) *n* a hairpiece worn by men to cover a bald place. [C18: apparently from F *toupet* forelock, from OF *toup* top, of Gmc origin]

tour ❶ (tʊə) *n* **1** an extended journey visiting places of interest along the route. **2** *Mil.* a period of service, esp. in one place. **3** a short trip, as for inspection. **4** a trip made by a theatre company, orchestra, etc., to perform in several places. **5** an overseas trip made by a cricket or rugby team, etc., to play in several places. ◆ *vb* **6** to make a tour of (a place). [C14: from OF: a turn, from L *tornus* a lathe, from Gk *tornos*]

touraco *or* **turaco** ('tʊərə,kəʊ) *n, pl* **touracos** *or* **turacos.** any of a family of brightly coloured crested African birds. [C18: of West African origin]

tour de force *French.* (tur də fɔrs) *n, pl* ***tours de force*** (tur). a masterly or brilliant stroke, creation, effect, or accomplishment. [lit.: feat of skill or strength]

tourer ('tʊərə) *n* a large open car with a folding top, usually seating a driver and four passengers. Also called (esp. US): **touring car.**

tourism ('tʊərɪzəm) *n* tourist travel, esp. when regarded as an industry.

tourist ❶ ('tʊərɪst) *n* **1a** a person who travels for pleasure, usually sightseeing and staying in hotels. **1b** (*as modifier*): *tourist attractions.* **2** a person on an excursion or sightseeing tour. **3** a member of a touring team. **4** Also called: **tourist class.** the lowest class of accommodation on a passenger ship or aircraft. ◆ *adj* **5** of or relating to tourist accommodation.
▸ **tour'istic** *adj*

touristy ('tʊərɪstɪ) *adj Inf., often derog.* abounding in or designed for tourists.

tourmaline ('tʊəmə,li:n) *n* any of a group of hard glassy minerals of variable colour consisting of a complex silicate of boron and aluminium in crystalline form: used in jewellery and optical and electrical equipment. [C18: from G *Turmalin,* from Sinhalese *toramalli* carnelian]

tournament ❶ ('tʊənəmənt) *n* **1** a sporting competition in which contestants play a series of games to determine an overall winner. **2** a meeting for athletic or other sporting contestants: *an archery tournament.* **3** *Medieval history.* a martial sport or contest in which mounted combatants fought for a prize. [C13: from OF *torneiement,* from

THESAURUS

tact, abut, adjoin, be in contact, border, brush, come together, contact, converge, graze, impinge upon, meet **28** = **affect**, get through to, get to (*inf.*), have an effect on, impress, influence, inspire, make an impression on, mark, strike **29** = **move**, disturb, melt, soften, stir, tug at (someone's) heartstrings (*often facetious*), upset **30** = **concern**, bear upon, have to do with, interest, pertain to, regard **31** = **consume**, drink, eat, partake of **32** = **get involved in**, be a party to, concern oneself with, deal with, handle, have to do with, use, utilize **33** *often foll. by* **on** = **refer to**, allude to, bring in, cover, deal with, mention, speak of **37** = **match**, be a match for, be in the same league as, be on a par with, come near, come up to, compare with, equal, hold a candle to (*inf.*), parallel, rival **38** = **reach**, arrive at, attain, come to

touch and go *adj* = **risky**, close, critical, dangerous, hairy, hazardous, near, nerve-racking, parlous, perilous, precarious, sticky (*inf.*), tricky

touched *adj* **1** = **moved**, affected, disturbed, impressed, melted, softened, stirred, swayed, upset **2** = **moved**, daft (*inf.*), loopy (*inf.*), not all there, not right in the head, out to lunch (*inf.*), soft in the head (*inf.*)

touchiness *n* **1** = **irritability**, bad temper, crabbedness, fretfulness, grouchiness (*inf.*), irascibility, peevishness, pettishness, petulance, surliness, testiness, tetchiness, ticklishness

touching *adj* **1** = **moving**, affecting, emotive, heartbreaking, melting, pathetic, piteous, pitiable, pitiful, poignant, sad, stirring, tender

touch off *vb* **1** = **ignite**, fire, light, put a match to, set off **2** = **trigger (off)**, arouse, begin, cause, foment, give rise to, initiate, provoke, set in motion, spark off

touchstone *n* **1** = **standard**, criterion, gauge, measure, norm, par, yardstick

touch up *vb* **1** = **finish off**, perfect, put the finishing touches to, round off **2** = **enhance**, brush up, fake (up), falsify, give a face-lift to, gloss over, improve, patch up, polish up, renovate, retouch, revamp, titivate, whitewash (*inf.*)

touchy *adj* **1** = **oversensitive**, bad-tempered, captious, crabbed, cross, easily offended, grouchy (*inf.*), grumpy, irascible, irritable, peevish, pettish, petulant, querulous, quick-tempered, ratty (*Brit. & NZ inf.*), splenetic, surly, testy, tetchy, thin-skinned, ticklish
Antonyms *adj* affable, cheerful, easy-going, genial, good-humoured, imperious, indifferent, insensitive, light-hearted, pleasant, sunny, sweet, thick-skinned, unconcerned

tough *adj* **1** = **resilient**, cohesive, durable, firm, hard, inflexible, leathery, resistant, rigid, rugged, solid, stiff, strong, sturdy, tenacious **3** = **strong**, brawny, fit, hard as nails, hardened, hardy, resilient, seasoned, stalwart, stout, strapping, sturdy, vigorous **4** = **rough**, hard-bitten, pugnacious, ruffianly, ruthless, vicious, violent **5** = **strict**, adamant, exacting, firm, hard, inflexible, intractable, merciless, resolute, severe, stern, unbending, unforgiving, unyielding **6** = **difficult**, arduous, baffling, exacting, exhausting, hard, irksome, knotty, laborious, perplexing, puzzling, strenuous, thorny, troublesome, uphill **7** *Informal* = **unlucky**, bad, lamentable, regrettable, too bad (*inf.*), unfortunate ◆ *n* **8** = **ruffian**, bravo, bruiser (*inf.*), brute, bully, bully boy, heavy, hooligan, rough (*inf.*), roughneck (*sl.*), rowdy, thug, tsotsi (*S. Afr.*)
Antonyms *adj* ≠ **resilient:** delicate, flexible, flimsy, fragile, soft, tender, weak ≠ **strong:** delicate, soft, weak ≠ **rough:** civilized, gentle, humane, soft, tender ≠ **strict:** accommodating, benign, compassionate, considerate, easy, flexible, gentle, humane, indulgent, kind, lenient, merciful, mild, soft, sympathetic, tender, unexacting ≠ **difficult:** easy, easy-peasy (*sl.*), unexacting

tour *n* **1** = **journey**, excursion, expedition, jaunt, outing, peregrination, progress, trip ◆ *vb* **6** = **visit**, explore, go on the road, go round, holiday in, journey, sightsee, travel round, travel through

tourist *n* **1a, 2** = **traveller**, excursionist, globetrotter, holiday-maker, journeyer, sightseer, tripper, voyager

tournament *n* **1, 2** = **competition**, contest, event, match, meeting, series **3** *Medieval* = **joust**, the lists, tourney

torneier to fight on horseback, lit.: to turn, from the constant wheeling round of the combatants; see TOURNEY]

tournedos ('tʊənəˌdəʊ) *n, pl* **tournedos** (-ˌdəʊz). a thick round steak of beef. [from F, from *tourner* to TURN + *dos* back]

tourney ('tʊənɪ, 'tɔː-) *Medieval history.* ◆ *n* **1** a knightly tournament. ◆ *vb* **2** (*intr*) to engage in a tourney. [C13: from OF *torneier,* from Vulgar L *tornidiāre* (unattested) to turn constantly, from L *tornāre* to TURN (in a lathe); see TOURNAMENT].

tourniquet ('tʊənɪˌkeɪ) *n Med.* any device for constricting an artery of the arm or leg to control bleeding. [C17: from F: device that operates by turning, from *tourner* to TURN]

tour operator *n* a person or company that specializes in providing package holidays.

tousle ❶ ('taʊzᵊl) *vb* **tousles, tousling, tousled.** (*tr*) **1** to tangle, ruffle, or disarrange. **2** to treat roughly. ◆ *n* **3** a disorderly, tangled, or rumpled state. **4** a dishevelled or disordered mass, esp. of hair. [C15: from Low G *tūsen* to shake]

tout ❶ (taʊt) *vb* **1** to solicit (business, customers, etc.) or hawk (merchandise), esp. in a brazen way. **2** (*intr*) **2a** to spy on racehorses being trained in order to obtain information for betting purposes. **2b** to sell such information or to take bets, esp. in public places. ◆ *n* **3** a person who touts. **4** Also: **ticket tout.** a person who sells tickets for a heavily booked event at inflated prices. [C14 (in the sense: to peer, look out): rel. to OE *tȳtan* to peep out]
▸ **'touter** *n*

tout à fait *French.* (tut a fɛ) *adv* completely.

tout de suite *French.* (tud sɥit) *adv* at once.

tout le monde *French.* (tu lə mɔ̃d) *n* all the world; everyone.

tovarisch, tovarich, *or* **tovarish** (tə'vɑːrɪʃ) *n* comrade: a term of address. [from Russian]

tow[1] ❶ (təʊ) *vb* **1** (*tr*) to pull or drag (a vehicle, boat, etc.), esp. by means of a rope or cable. ◆ *n* **2** the act or an instance of towing. **3** the state of being towed (esp. in **in tow, on tow**). **4** something towed. **5** something used for towing. **6 in tow.** in one's charge or under one's influence. **7** short for **ski tow.** [OE *togian*]
▸ **'towable** *adj* ▸ **'towage** *n*

tow[2] (təʊ) *n* the coarse and broken fibres of hemp, flax, jute, etc., prepared for spinning. [OE *tōw*]
▸ **'towy** *adj*

toward *adj* ('təʊəd). **1** *Now rare.* in progress; afoot. **2** *Obs.* about to happen; imminent. **3** *Obs.* promising or favourable. ◆ *prep* (tə'wɔːd, tɔːd). **4** a variant of **towards.** [OE *tōweard*]

towards ❶ (tə'wɔːdz, tɔːdz) *prep* **1** in the direction or vicinity of: *towards London.* **2** with regard to: *her feelings towards me.* **3** as a contribution or help to: *money towards a new car.* **4** just before: *towards noon.* ◆ Also: **toward.**

towbar ('təʊˌbɑː) *n* a rigid metal bar or frame used for towing vehicles.

towboat ('təʊˌbəʊt) *n* another word for **tug** (sense 4).

tow-coloured *adj* pale yellow; flaxen.

towel ('taʊəl) *n* **1** a piece of absorbent cloth or paper used for drying things. **2 throw in the towel.** See **throw in** (sense 3). ◆ *vb* **towels, towelling, towelled** *or US* **towels, toweling, toweled. 3** (*tr*) to dry or wipe with a towel. **4** (*tr*; often foll. by *up*) *Austral. sl.* to assault or beat (a person). [C13: from OF *toaille,* of Gmc origin]

towelling ('taʊəlɪŋ) *n* an absorbent fabric used for making towels, bathrobes, etc.

tower ❶ ('taʊə) *n* **1** a tall, usually square or circular structure, sometimes part of a larger building and usually built for a specific purpose. **2** a place of defence or retreat. **3 tower of strength.** a person who gives support, comfort, etc. ◆ *vb* **4** (*intr*) to be or rise like a tower; loom. [C12: from OF *tur,* from L *turris,* from Gk]

towering ❶ ('taʊərɪŋ) *adj* **1** very tall; lofty. **2** outstanding, as in importance or stature. **3** (*prenominal*) very intense: *a towering rage.*

towhead ('təʊˌhɛd) *n* **1** a person with blond or yellowish hair. **2** a head of such hair. [from TOW[2] (flax)]
▸ **ˌtow'headed** *adj*

towhee ('taʊˌhiː, 'təʊ-) *n* any of various North American brownish-coloured sparrows. [C18: imit.]

towline ('təʊˌlaɪn) *n* another name for **towrope.**

town (taʊn) *n* **1** a densely populated urban area, typically smaller than a city and larger than a village. **2** a city, borough, or other urban area. **3** (in the US) a territorial unit of local government that is smaller than a county; township. **4** the nearest town or commercial district. **5** London or the chief city of an area. **6** the inhabitants of a town. **7 go to town. 7a** to make a supreme or unrestricted effort. **7b** *Austral. & NZ inf.* to lose one's temper. **8 on the town.** seeking out entertainments and amusements. [OE *tūn* village]
▸ **'townish** *adj*

town clerk *n* **1** (in Britain until 1974) the secretary and chief administrative officer of a town or city. **2** (in the US) the official who keeps the records of a town.

town crier *n* (formerly) a person employed to make public announcements in the streets.

town gas *n* coal gas manufactured for domestic and industrial use.

town hall *n* the chief building in which municipal business is transacted, often with a hall for public meetings.

town house *n* **1** a terraced house in an urban area, esp. a fashionable one. **2** a person's town residence as distinct from his country residence.

townie ('taʊnɪ) *or* **townee** (taʊ'niː) *n Inf., often disparaging.* a permanent resident in a town, esp. as distinct from country dwellers or students.

townland ('taʊnlænd) *n Irish.* a division of land of various sizes.

town planning *n* the comprehensive planning of the physical and social development of a town. US term: **city planning.**

townscape ('taʊnskeɪp) *n* **1** a view of an urban scene. **2** an extensive area of urban development.

township ('taʊnʃɪp) *n* **1** a small town. **2** (in the Scottish Highlands) a small crofting community. **3** (in the US and Canada) a territorial area, esp. a subdivision of a county: often organized as a unit of local government. **4** (in Canada) a land-survey area, usually 36 square miles (93 square kilometres). **5** (formerly, in South Africa) a planned urban settlement of Black Africans or Coloured people. **6** *English history.* **6a** any of the local districts of a large parish. **6b** the parish itself.

townsman ('taʊnzmən) *n, pl* **townsmen. 1** an inhabitant of a town. **2** a person from the same town as oneself.
▸ **'towns,woman** *fem n*

townspeople ('taʊnzˌpiːpᵊl) *or* **townsfolk** ('taʊnzˌfəʊk) *pl n* the inhabitants of a town; citizens.

towpath ('təʊˌpɑːθ) *n* a path beside a canal or river, used by people or animals towing boats. Also called: **towing path.**

towrope ('təʊˌrəʊp) *n* a rope or cable used for towing a vehicle or vessel. Also called: **towline.**

tox-, toxic- *or before a consonant* **toxo-, toxico-** *combining form.* indicating poison: *toxaemia.* [from L *toxicum*]

toxaemia *or US* **toxemia** (tɒk'siːmɪə) *n* **1** a condition characterized by the presence of bacterial toxins in the blood. **2** the condition in pregnancy of pre-eclampsia or eclampsia.
▸ **tox'aemic** *or US* **tox'emic** *adj*

toxic ❶ ('tɒksɪk) *adj* **1** of or caused by a toxin or poison. **2** harmful or deadly. [C17: from Medical L *toxicus,* from L *toxicum* poison, from Gk *toxikon* (*pharmakon*) (poison) used on arrows, from *toxon* arrow]
▸ **'toxically** *adv* ▸ **toxicity** (tɒk'sɪsɪtɪ) *n*

toxicant ('tɒksɪkənt) *n* **1** a toxic substance; poison. ◆ *adj* **2** poisonous; toxic. [C19: from Med. L *toxicāre* to poison]

toxicology (ˌtɒksɪ'kɒlədʒɪ) *n* the branch of science concerned with poisons, their effects, antidotes, etc.
▸ **toxicological** (ˌtɒksɪkə'lɒdʒɪkᵊl) *or* **ˌtoxico'logic** *adj* ▸ **ˌtoxi'cologist** *n*

toxic shock syndrome *n* a potentially fatal condition in women, characterized by fever, stomachache, a painful rash, and a drop in blood pressure, that is caused by staphylococcal blood poisoning, commonly from a retained tampon.

toxin ('tɒksɪn) *n* **1** any of various poisonous substances produced by microorganisms that stimulate the production of neutralizing substances (antitoxins) in the body. **2** any other poisonous substance of plant or animal origin.

toxin-antitoxin *n* a mixture of a toxin and antitoxin. The diphtheria toxin-antitoxin was formerly used for immunization.

toxocariasis (ˌtɒksəkə'raɪəsɪs) *n* the infection of humans with the larvae of a genus of roundworms, *Toxocara,* of dogs and cats.

toxoid ('tɒksɔɪd) *n* a toxin that has been treated to reduce its toxicity and is used in immunization to stimulate production of antitoxins.

toxophilite (tɒk'sɒfɪˌlaɪt) *Formal.* ◆ *n* **1** an archer. ◆ *adj* **2** of archery. [C18: from *Toxophilus,* the title of a book (1545) by Ascham, designed to mean: a lover of the bow, from Gk *toxon* bow + *philos* loving]
▸ **tox'ophily** *n*

toxoplasmosis (ˌtɒksəʊplæz'məʊsɪs) *n* a protozoal disease characterized by jaundice and convulsions.
▸ **ˌtoxo'plasmic** *adj*

toy ❶ (tɔɪ) *n* **1** an object designed to be played with. **2a** something that is a nonfunctioning replica of something else, esp. a miniature one.

THESAURUS

tousle *vb* **1 = dishevel,** disarrange, disarray, disorder, mess up, ruffle, rumple, tangle

tout *vb* **1 = solicit,** bark (*US inf.*), canvass, drum up, spiel ◆ *n* **3 = seller,** barker, canvasser, solicitor

tow[1] *vb* **1 = drag,** draw, hale, haul, lug, pull, trail, trawl, tug, yank

towards *prep* **1 = in the direction of,** en route for, for, in the vicinity of, on the road to, on the way to, to **2 = regarding,** about, concerning, for, with regard to, with respect to **4 = just before,** almost, close to, coming up to, getting on for, nearing, nearly, not quite, shortly before

tower *n* **1 = column,** belfry, obelisk, pillar, skyscraper, steeple, turret **2 = stronghold,** castle, citadel, fort, fortification, fortress, keep, refuge ◆ *vb* **4 = rise,** ascend, dominate, loom, mount, overlook, overtop, rear, soar, surpass, top, transcend

towering *adj* **1 = tall,** colossal, elevated, gigantic, great, high, lofty, soaring **2 = impressive,** extraordinary, imposing, magnificent, outstanding, paramount, prodigious, stellar (*inf.*), striking, sublime, superior, supreme, surpassing, transcendent **3 = intense,** burning, excessive, extreme, fiery, immoderate, inordinate, intemperate, mighty, passionate, vehement, violent

toxic *adj* **2 = poisonous,** baneful (*arch.*), deadly, harmful, lethal, noxious, pernicious, pestilential, septic
Antonyms *adj* harmless, invigorating, nonpoisonous, nontoxic, safe, salubrious

toy *n* **1 = plaything,** doll, game **3 = trinket,** bauble, gewgaw, knick-knack, trifle ◆ *vb* **5** *usually foll. by* **with = play,** amuse oneself with, dally with, fiddle (*inf.*), flirt with, fool (about *or* around) with, play fast and loose (*inf.*), sport, trifle, wanton

2b (*as modifier*): *a toy guitar.* **3** any small thing of little value; trifle. **4a** something small or miniature, esp. a miniature variety of a breed of dog. **4b** (*as modifier*): *a toy poodle.* ◆ *vb* **5** (*intr; usually foll. by with*) to play, fiddle, or flirt. [C16 (in the sense: amorous dalliance): from ?]

toy boy *n* the much younger male lover of an older woman.

TPI *abbrev. for* tax and price index: a measure of the increase in taxable income needed to compensate for an increase in retail prices.

TQM *abbrev. for* total quality management.

tr *abbrev. for* treasurer.

tr. *abbrev. for:* **1** transitive. **2** translated. **3** translator. **4** *Music.* trill. **5** trustee.

trabeated ('treɪbɪˌeɪtɪd) *or* **trabeate** ('treɪbɪɪt, -ˌeɪt) *adj Archit.* constructed with horizontal beams as opposed to arches. [C19: back formation from *trabeation,* from L *trabs* a beam]

trabecula (trə'bɛkjʊlə) *n, pl* **trabeculae** (-ˌliː). *Anat., bot.* any of various rod-shaped structures that support other organs. [C19: via NL from L: a little beam, from *trabs* a beam]
▸**tra'becular** *or* **tra'beculate** *adj*

trace[1] Ⓣ (treɪs) *n* **1** a mark or other sign that something has been in a place. **2** a scarcely detectable amount or characteristic. **3** a footprint or other indication of the passage of an animal or person. **4** any line drawn by a recording instrument or a record consisting of a number of such lines. **5** something drawn, such as a tracing. **6** *Chiefly US.* a beaten track or path. ◆ *vb* **traces, tracing, traced. 7** (*tr*) to follow, discover, or ascertain the course or development of (something). **8** (*tr*) to track down and find, as by following a trail. **9** to copy (a design, map, etc.) by drawing over the lines visible through a superimposed sheet of transparent paper. **10** (*tr; often foll. by out*) **10a** to draw or delineate a plan or diagram of. **10b** to outline or sketch (an idea, etc.). **11** (*tr*) to decorate with tracery. **12** (usually foll. by *back*) to follow or be followed to source; date back: *his ancestors trace back to the 16th century.* [C13: from F *tracier,* from Vulgar L *tractiāre* (unattested) to drag, from L *tractus,* from *trahere*]
▸**'traceable** *adj* ▸**ˌtracea'bility** *or* **'traceableness** *n* ▸**'traceably** *adv*

trace[2] (treɪs) *n* **1** either of the two side straps that connect a horse's harness to the swingletree. **2** *Angling.* a length of nylon or, formerly, gut attaching a hook or fly to a line. **3 kick over the traces.** to escape or defy control. [C14 *trais,* from OF *trait,* ult. from L *trahere* to drag]

trace element *n* any of various chemical elements, such as iron, manganese, zinc, copper, and iodine, that occur in very small amounts in organisms and are essential for many physiological and biochemical processes.

trace fossil *n* the fossilized remains of a track, trail, footprint, burrow, etc., of an organism.

tracer ('treɪsə) *n* **1** a person or thing that traces. **2** a projectile that can be observed when in flight by the burning of chemical substances in its base. **3** *Med.* any radioactive isotope introduced into the body to study metabolic processes, etc., by following its progress with a gamma counter or other detector. **4** an investigation to trace missing cargo, mail, etc.

tracer bullet *n* a round of small arms ammunition containing a tracer.

tracery ('treɪsərɪ) *n, pl* **traceries. 1** a pattern of interlacing ribs, esp. as used in the upper part of a Gothic window, etc. **2** any fine pattern resembling this.
▸**'traceried** *adj*

trachea (trə'kiːə) *n, pl* **tracheae** (-'kiːiː). **1** *Anat., zool.* the tube that conveys inhaled air from the larynx to the bronchi. **2** any of the tubes in insects and related animals that convey air from the spiracles to the tissues. [C16: from Med. L, from Gk *trakheia,* shortened from (*artēria*) *trakheia* rough (artery), from *trakhus* rough]
▸**tra'cheal** *or* **tra'cheate** *adj*

tracheitis (ˌtreɪkɪ'aɪtɪs) *n* inflammation of the trachea.

tracheo- *or before a vowel* **trache-** *combining form.* denoting the trachea.

tracheotomy (ˌtrækɪ'ɒtəmɪ) *n, pl* **tracheotomies.** surgical incision into the trachea, as performed when the air passage has been blocked.

trachoma (trə'kəʊmə) *n* a chronic contagious disease of the eye caused by a species of chlamydia: a severe form of conjunctivitis that can result in scarring and blindness. [C17: from NL, from Gk *trakhōma* roughness, from *trakhus* rough]
▸**trachomatous** (trə'kɒmətəs) *adj*

trachyte ('treɪkaɪt, 'træ-) *n* a light-coloured fine-grained volcanic rock. [C19: from F, from Gk *trakhutēs,* from *trakhus* rough]

tracing ('treɪsɪŋ) *n* **1** a copy made by tracing. **2** the act of making a trace. **3** a record made by an instrument.

track Ⓣ (træk) *n* **1** the mark or trail left by something that has passed by. **2** any road or path, esp. a rough one. **3** a rail or pair of parallel rails on which a vehicle, such as a locomotive, runs. **4** a course of action, thought, etc.: *don't start on that track again!* **5** a line of motion or travel, such as flight. **6** an endless band on the wheels of a tank, tractor, etc., to enable it to move across rough ground. **7a** a course for running or racing. **7b** (*as modifier*): *track events.* **8** *US & Canad.* **8a** sports performed on a track. **8b** track and field events as a whole. **9** a path on a magnetic recording medium, esp. magnetic tape, on which music or speech is recorded. **10** any of a number of separate sections in the recording on a record, CD, or cassette. **11** the distance between the points of contact with the ground of a pair of wheels, as of a motor vehicle. **12 keep** (*or* **lose**) **track of.** to follow (or fail to follow) the passage, course, or progress of. **13 off the track.** away from what is correct or true. **14 on the track of.** on the scent or trail of; pursuing. ◆ *vb* **15** to follow the trail of (a person, animal, etc.). **16** to follow the flight path of (a satellite, etc.) by picking up signals transmitted or reflected by it. **17** *US railways.* **17a** to provide with a track. **17b** to run on a track of (a certain width). **18** (of a camera or camera-operator) to follow (a moving object) while operating. **19** to follow a track through (a place): *to track the jungles.* **20** (*intr*) (of the pick-up, stylus, etc., of a record player) to follow the groove of a record. ◆ See also **tracks.** [C15: from OF *trac,* prob. of Gmc origin]
▸**'tracker** *n*

track down Ⓣ *vb* (*tr, adv*) to find by tracking or pursuing.

tracker dog *n* a dog specially trained to search for missing people.

track event *n* a competition in athletics, such as relay running or sprinting, that takes place on a running track.

tracking ('trækɪŋ) *n* **1** the act or process of following something or someone. **2** *Electrical engineering.* a leakage of electric current between two insulated points caused by dirt, carbon particles, moisture, etc.

tracking shot *n* a camera shot in which the cameraman follows a specific person or event in the action.

tracking station *n* a station that can use a radio or radar beam to follow the path of an object in space or in the atmosphere.

tracklaying ('trækˌleɪɪŋ) *adj also* **tracked.** (of a vehicle) having an endless jointed metal band around the wheels.

track record *n Inf.* the past record of the accomplishments and failures of a person, business, etc.

track rod *n* the rod connecting the two front wheels of a motor vehicle.

tracks Ⓣ (træks) *pl n* **1** (*sometimes sing*) marks, such as footprints, etc., left by someone or something that has passed. **2 in one's tracks.** on the very spot where one is standing. **3 make tracks.** to leave or depart. **4 make tracks for.** to go or head towards.

track shoe *n* either of a pair of light running shoes fitted with steel spikes for better grip.

tracksuit ('trækˌsuːt) *n* a warm suit worn by athletes, etc., esp. during training.

tract[1] Ⓣ (trækt) *n* **1** an extended area, as of land. **2** *Anat.* a system of organs, glands, etc., that has a particular function: *the digestive tract.* **3** *Arch.* an extended period of time. [C15: from L *tractus* a stretching out, from *trahere* to drag]

tract[2] Ⓣ (trækt) *n* a treatise or pamphlet, esp. a religious or moralistic one. [C15: from L *tractātus* TRACTATE]

tractable Ⓣ ('træktəbᵊl) *adj* **1** easily controlled or persuaded. **2** readily worked; malleable. [C16: from L *tractābilis,* from *tractāre* to manage, from *trahere* to draw]
▸**ˌtracta'bility** *or* **'tractableness** *n* ▸**'tractably** *adv*

Tractarianism (træk'tɛərɪəˌnɪzəm) *n* another name for the **Oxford Movement.** [after the series of tracts, *Tracts for the Times* published between 1833 and 1841, in which the principles of the movement were presented]
▸**Trac'tarian** *n, adj*

tractate ('trækteɪt) *n* a treatise. [C15: from L *tractātus,* from *tractāre* to handle; see TRACTABLE]

traction Ⓣ ('trækʃən) *n* **1** the act of drawing or pulling, esp. by motive power. **2** the state of being drawn or pulled. **3** *Med.* the application of a steady pull on a limb, etc., using a system of weights and pulleys or splints. **4** adhesive friction, as between a wheel of a motor vehicle and

THESAURUS

trace[1] *n* **1** = **remnant**, evidence, indication, mark, record, relic, remains, sign, survival, token, vestige **2** = **bit**, dash, drop, hint, iota, jot, shadow, *soupçon,* suggestion, suspicion, tincture, tinge, touch, trifle, whiff **3** = **track**, footmark, footprint, footstep, path, slot, spoor, trail ◆ *vb* **7** = **find**, ascertain, detect, determine, discover, ferret out, follow, hunt down, pursue, search for, seek, shadow, stalk, track, trail, unearth **9** = **copy 10** *often foll. by* **out** = **outline**, chart, delineate, depict, draw, map, mark out, show, sketch

track *n* **1** = **trail**, footmark, footprint, footstep, mark, path, scent, slipstream, slot, spoor, trace, wake **3** = **line**, permanent way, rail, rails **5** = **path**, course, flight path, line, orbit, pathway, road, trajectory, way **12 keep track of** = **keep up with**, follow, keep an eye on, keep in sight, keep in touch with, keep up to date with, monitor, oversee, watch **12 lose track of** = **lose**, lose sight of, misplace ◆ *vb* **15** = **follow**, chase, dog, follow the trail of, hunt down, pursue, shadow, stalk, tail (*inf.*), trace, trail

track down *vb* = **find**, apprehend, bring to light, capture, catch, dig up, discover, expose, ferret out, hunt down, run to earth *or* ground, sniff out, trace, unearth

tracks *pl n* **1** = **trail**, footprints, impressions, imprints, tyre marks, tyre prints, wheel marks **4 make tracks** = **leave**, beat it (*sl.*), depart, disappear, get going, get moving, go, head off, hit the road (*sl.*), pack one's bags (*inf.*), set out, split (*sl.*), take off (*inf.*)

tract[1] *n* **1** = **area**, district, estate, expanse, extent, lot, plot, quarter, region, stretch, territory, zone

tract[2] *n* = **treatise**, booklet, brochure, disquisition, dissertation, essay, homily, leaflet, monograph, pamphlet, tractate

tractable *adj Formal* **1** = **manageable**, amenable, biddable, compliant, controllable, docile, governable, obedient, persuadable, submissive, tame, willing, yielding **2** = **malleable**, ductile, fictile, plastic, pliable, pliant, tensile, tractile, workable
Antonyms *adj* ≠ **manageable:** defiant, headstrong, obstinate, refractory, stiff-necked, stubborn, unruly, wilful

traction *n* **1** = **pulling**, drag, draught, drawing, haulage, pull **4** = **grip**, adhesion, friction, purchase, resistance

the road. [C17: from Med. L *tractiō*, from L *tractus* dragged, from *trahere* to drag]
▸'**tractional** *adj* ▸**tractive** ('træktɪv) *adj*

traction engine *n* a steam-powered locomotive used, esp. formerly, for drawing heavy loads along roads or over rough ground.

traction load *n Geol.* the solid material that is carried along the bed of a river.

tractor ('træktə) *n* **1** a motor vehicle with large rear wheels or endless belt treads, used to pull heavy loads, esp. farm machinery. **2** a short vehicle with a driver's cab, used to pull a trailer, as in an articulated lorry. [C18: from LL: one who pulls, from *trahere* to drag]

trad (træd) *n* **1** *Chiefly Brit.* traditional jazz. ◆ *adj* **2** short for **traditional**.

trade ⓘ (treɪd) *n* **1** the act or an instance of buying and selling goods and services. **2** a personal occupation, esp. a craft requiring skill. **3** the people and practices of an industry, craft, or business. **4** exchange of one thing for something else. **5** the regular clientele of a firm or industry. **6** amount of custom or commercial dealings; business. **7** a specified market or business: *the tailoring trade*. **8** an occupation in commerce, as opposed to a profession. ◆ *vb* **trades, trading, traded. 9** (*tr*) to buy and sell (merchandise). **10** to exchange (one thing) for another. **11** (*intr*) to engage in trade. **12** (*intr*) to deal or do business (with). ◆ See also **trade-in, trade on.** [C14 (in the sense: track, hence, a regular business)]
▸'**tradable** *or* '**tradeable** *adj*

trade agreement *n* a commercial treaty between two or more nations.

trade association *n* an association of organizations in the same trade formed to further their collective interests, esp. in negotiating with governments, trade unions, etc.

trade cycle *n* the recurrent fluctuation between boom and depression in the economic activity of a capitalist country.

trade discount *n* a sum or percentage deducted from the list price of a commodity allowed to a retailer or by one enterprise to another in the same trade.

traded option *n Stock Exchange.* an option that can itself be bought and sold on a stock exchange. Cf. **traditional option.**

trade down *vb* (*intr, adv*) to sell a large or relatively expensive house, car, etc., and replace it with a smaller or less expensive one.

trade gap *n* the amount by which the value of a country's visible imports exceeds that of visible exports; an unfavourable balance of trade.

trade-in *n* **1a** a used article given in part payment for the purchase of a new article. **1b** a transaction involving such part payment. **1c** the valuation put on the article traded in. ◆ *vb* **trade in. 2** (*tr, adv*) to give (a used article) as part payment for a new article.

trademark ('treɪdˌmɑːk) *n* **1a** the name or other symbol used by a manufacturer or dealer to distinguish his products from those of competitors. **1b Registered Trademark.** one that is officially registered and legally protected. **2** any distinctive sign or mark of the presence of a person or animal. ◆ *vb* (*tr*) **3** to label with a trademark. **4** to register as a trademark.

trade name *n* **1** the name used by a trade to refer to a commodity, service, etc. **2** the name under which a commercial enterprise operates in business.

trade-off *n* an exchange, esp. as a compromise.

trade on *vb* (*intr, prep*) to exploit or take advantage of: *he traded on her endless patience.*

trade plate *n* a numberplate attached temporarily to a vehicle by a dealer, etc., before the vehicle has been registered.

trader ⓘ ('treɪdə) *n* **1** a person who engages in trade. **2** a vessel regularly employed in trade. **3** *Stock Exchange, US.* a member who operates mainly on his own account.

trade reference *n* a reference in which one trader gives his opinion as to the credit worthiness of another trader in the same trade, esp. to a supplier.

tradescantia (ˌtrædɛs'kænʃɪə) *n* any of a genus of plants widely cultivated for their striped variegated leaves. [C18: NL, after John *Tradescant* (1608–62), E botanist]

Trades Council *n* (in Britain) an association of the different trade unions in one town or area.

trade secret *n* a secret formula, technique, process, etc., known and used to advantage by only one manufacturer.

tradesman ⓘ ('treɪdzmən) *n, pl* **tradesmen. 1** a man engaged in trade, esp. a retail dealer. **2** a skilled worker.
▸'**tradesˌwoman** *fem n*

tradespeople ('treɪdzˌpiːpᵊl) *or* **tradesfolk** ('treɪdzˌfəʊk) *pl n Chiefly Brit.* people engaged in trade, esp. shopkeepers.

Trades Union Congress *n* the major association of British trade unions, which includes all the larger unions. Abbrev.: **TUC**

trade union *or* **trades union** *n* an association of employees formed to improve their incomes and working conditions by collective bargaining.
▸**trade unionism** *or* **trades unionism** *n* ▸**trade unionist** *or* **trades unionist** *n*

trade up *vb* (*intr, adv*) to sell a small or relatively inexpensive house, car, etc., and replace it with a larger or more expensive one.

trade wind (wɪnd) *n* a wind blowing obliquely towards the equator either from the northeast in the N hemisphere or the southeast in the S hemisphere, between latitudes 30° N and S. [C17: from *to blow trade* to blow steadily in one direction, from *trade* in the obs. sense: a track]

trading estate *n Chiefly Brit.* a large area in which a number of commercial or industrial firms are situated. Also called: **industrial estate.**

trading post *n* a general store in an unsettled or thinly populated region.

tradition ⓘ (trə'dɪʃən) *n* **1** the handing down from generation to generation of customs, beliefs, etc. **2** the body of customs, thought, etc., belonging to a particular country, people, family, or institution over a long period. **3** a specific custom or practice of long standing. **4** *Christianity.* a doctrine regarded as having been established by Christ or the apostles though not contained in Scripture. **5** (*often cap.*) *Judaism.* a body of laws regarded as having been handed down from Moses orally. **6** the beliefs and customs of Islam supplementing the Koran. **7** *Law, chiefly Roman & Scots.* the act of formally transferring ownership of movable property. [C14: from L *trāditiō* a handing down, surrender, from *trādere* to give up, transmit, from TRANS- + *dāre* to give]
▸**tra'ditionless** *adj*

traditional ⓘ (trə'dɪʃənᵊl) *adj* **1** of, relating to, or being a tradition. **2** of the style of jazz originating in New Orleans, characterized by collective improvisation by a front line of trumpet, trombone, and clarinet.
▸**tra'ditionally** *adv*

traditionalism (trə'dɪʃənᵊˌlɪzəm) *n* **1** the doctrine that all knowledge originates in divine revelation and is perpetuated by tradition. **2** adherence to tradition, esp. in religion.
▸**tra'ditionalist** *n, adj* ▸**traˌditional'istic** *adj*

traditional logic *n* the logic of the late Middle Ages, derived from Aristotelian logic, and concerned esp. with the study of the syllogism.

traditional option *n Stock Exchange.* an option that once purchased cannot be resold. Cf. **traded option.**

traduce ⓘ (trə'djuːs) *vb* **traduces, traducing, traduced.** (*tr*) to speak badly or maliciously of. [C16: from L *trādūcere* to lead over, disgrace]
▸**tra'ducement** *n* ▸**tra'ducer** *n*

traffic ⓘ ('træfɪk) *n* **1a** the vehicles coming and going in a street, town, etc. **1b** (*as modifier*): *traffic lights.* **2** the movement of vehicles, people, etc., in a particular place or for a particular purpose: *sea traffic.* **3** (usually foll. by *with*) dealings or business. **4** trade, esp. of an illicit kind: *drug traffic.* **5** the aggregate volume of messages transmitted through a communications system in a given period. **6** *Chiefly US.* the number of customers patronizing a commercial establishment in a given time period. ◆ *vb* **traffics, trafficking, trafficked.** (*intr*) **7** (often foll. by *in*) to carry on trade or business, esp. of an illicit kind. **8** (usually foll. by *with*) to have dealings. [C16: from OF *trafique*, from OIt. *traffico*, from *trafficare* to engage in trade]
▸'**trafficker** *n*

trafficator ('træfɪˌkeɪtə) *n* (formerly) an illuminated arm on a motor vehicle raised to indicate a left or right turn.

traffic calming *n* the use of a series of devices, such as bends and humps in the road, to slow down traffic, esp. in residential areas.

traffic island *n* a raised area in the middle of a road designed as a guide for traffic flow and to provide a stopping place for pedestrians crossing.

traffic jam *n* a number of vehicles so obstructed that they can scarcely move.

traffic light *or* **signal** *n* one of a set of coloured lights at crossroads or junctions, to control the flow of traffic.

traffic pattern *n* a pattern of permitted lanes in the air around an airport to which an aircraft is restricted.

traffic warden *n Brit.* a person who is appointed to supervise road traffic and report traffic offences.

tragacanth ('trægəˌkænθ) *n* **1** any of various spiny plants that yield a

THESAURUS

trade *n* **1** = **commerce**, barter, business, buying and selling, dealing, exchange, traffic, transactions, truck **2** = **job**, avocation, business, calling, craft, employment, line, line of work, métier, occupation, profession, pursuit, skill **4** = **exchange**, deal, interchange, swap **5** = **customers**, clientele, custom, market, patrons, public ◆ *vb* **9, 12** = **deal**, bargain, barter, buy and sell, cut a deal, do business, exchange, have dealings, peddle, traffic, transact, truck **10** = **exchange**, barter, swap, switch

trader *n* **1** = **dealer**, broker, buyer, marketer, merchandiser, merchant, purveyor, seller, supplier

tradesman *n* **1** = **shopkeeper**, dealer, merchant, purveyor, retailer, seller, supplier, vendor **2** = **craftsman**, artisan, journeyman, skilled worker, workman

tradition *n* **1, 2** = **custom**, convention, customs, established practice, folklore, habit, institution, lore, praxis, ritual, unwritten law, usage

traditional *adj* **1** = **customary**, accustomed, ancestral, conventional, established, fixed, folk, historic, long-established, old, oral, time-honoured, transmitted, unwritten, usual
Antonyms *adj* avant-garde, contemporary, ground-breaking, innovative, modern, new, novel, off-the-wall (*sl.*), original, revolutionary, unconventional, unusual

traduce *vb Formal* = **malign**, abuse, asperse, bad-mouth (*sl., chiefly US & Canad.*), blacken, calumniate, decry, defame, denigrate, deprecate, depreciate, detract, disparage, drag through the mud, knock (*inf.*), misrepresent, revile, rubbish (*inf.*), run down, slag (off) (*sl.*), slander, smear, speak ill of, vilify

traffic *n* **2** = **transport**, coming and going, freight, movement, passengers, transportation, vehicles **3, 4** = **trade**, barter, business, buying and selling, commerce, communication, dealing, dealings, doings, exchange, intercourse, peddling, relations, truck ◆ *vb* **7, 8** = **trade**, bargain, barter, buy and sell, cut a deal, deal, do business, exchange, have dealings, have transactions, market, peddle, truck

substance that is made into a gum. **2** the gum obtained from these plants, used in the manufacture of pills and lozenges and in calico printing. [C16: from F *tragacante,* from L *tragacantha* goat's thorn, from Gk, from *tragos* goat + *akantha* thorn]

tragedian (trəˈdʒiːdɪən) *or (fem)* **tragedienne** (trəˌdʒiːdɪˈɛn) *n* **1** an actor who specializes in tragic roles. **2** a writer of tragedy.

tragedy Ⓣ (ˈtrædʒɪdɪ) *n, pl* **tragedies. 1** a play in which the protagonist falls to disaster through the combination of a personal failing and circumstances with which he cannot deal. **2** any dramatic or literary composition dealing with serious or sombre themes and ending with disaster. **3** the branch of drama dealing with such themes. **4** the unfortunate aspect of something. **5** a shocking or sad event; disaster. [C14: from OF *tragédie,* from L *tragoedia,* from Gk, from *tragos* goat + *ōidē* song; ?from the goat-satyrs of Peloponnesian plays]

tragic Ⓣ (ˈtrædʒɪk) *or (less commonly)* **tragical** *adj* **1** of, relating to, or characteristic of tragedy. **2** mournful or pitiable.
▸ **ˈtragically** *adv*

tragic flaw *n* the failing of character in a tragic hero.

tragic irony *n* the use of dramatic irony in a tragedy so that the audience is aware that a character's words or actions will bring about a tragic or fatal result, while the character himself is not.

tragicomedy (ˌtrædʒɪˈkɒmɪdɪ) *n, pl* **tragicomedies. 1** a drama in which aspects of both tragedy and comedy are found. **2** an event or incident having both comic and tragic aspects. [C16: from F, ult. from LL *tragicōmoedia*]
▸ **ˌtragiˈcomic** *or* **ˌtragiˈcomical** *adj*

tragopan (ˈtrægəˌpæn) *n* any of a genus of pheasants of S and SE Asia, having brightly coloured fleshy processes on the head. [C19: via L from Gk, from *tragos* goat + *Pan,* ancient Gk god, represented as a man with goat's legs, horns, and ears]

tragus (ˈtreɪgəs) *n, pl* **tragi** (-dʒaɪ). the fleshy projection that partially covers the entrance to the external ear. [C17: from LL, from Gk *tragos* hairy projection of the ear, lit.: goat]

trail Ⓣ (treɪl) *vb* **1** to drag, stream, or permit to drag or stream along a surface, esp. the ground. **2** to make (a track) through (a place). **3** to follow or hunt (an animal or person) by following marks or tracks. **4** (when *intr,* often foll. by *behind*) to lag or linger behind (a person or thing). **5** (*intr*) (esp. of plants) to extend or droop over or along a surface. **6** (*intr*) to be falling behind in a race: *the favourite is trailing at the last fence.* **7** (*tr*) to tow (a caravan, etc.) behind a motor vehicle. **8** (*tr*) to carry (a rifle) at the full length of the right arm in a horizontal position, with the muzzle to the fore. **9** (*intr*) to move wearily or slowly. **10** (*tr*) (on television or radio) to advertise (a future programme) with short extracts. ◆ *n* **11** a print, mark, or scent made by a person, animal, or object. **12** the act or an instance of trailing. **13** a path, track, or road, esp. one roughly blazed. **14** something that trails behind or trails in loops or strands. **15** the part of a towed gun carriage and limber that connects the two when in movement and rests on the ground as a partial support when unlimbered. [C14: from OF *trailler* to tow, from Vulgar L *tragulāre* (unattested), from L *trāgula* dragnet, from *trahere* to drag]

trail away Ⓣ *or* **off** *vb* (*intr, adv*) to make or become fainter, quieter, or weaker.

trailblazer (ˈtreɪlˌbleɪzə) *n* **1** a leader or pioneer in a particular field. **2** a person who blazes a trail.
▸ **ˈtrailˌblazing** *adj, n*

trailer (ˈtreɪlə) *n* **1** a road vehicle, usually two-wheeled, towed by a motor vehicle: used for transporting boats, etc. **2** the rear section of an articulated lorry. **3** a series of short extracts from a film, used to advertise it in a cinema or on television. **4** a person or thing that trails. **5** the US and Canad. name for **caravan** (sense 1).

trailing edge *n* the rear edge of a propeller blade or aerofoil. Cf. **leading edge.**

train Ⓣ (treɪn) *vb* **1** (*tr*) to guide or teach (to do something), as by subjecting to various exercises or experiences. **2** (*tr*) to control or guide towards a specific goal: *to train a plant up a wall.* **3** (*intr*) to do exercises and prepare for a specific purpose. **4** (*tr*) to improve or curb by subjecting to discipline: *to train the mind.* **5** (*tr*) to focus or bring to bear (on something): *to train a telescope on the moon.* ◆ *n* **6** a line of coaches or wagons coupled together and drawn by a railway locomotive. **7** a sequence or series: *a train of disasters.* **8** a procession of people, vehicles, etc., travelling together, such as one carrying equipment in support of a military operation. **9** a series of interacting parts through which motion is transmitted: *a train of gears.* **10** a fuse or line of gunpowder to an explosive charge, etc. **11** something drawn along, such as the long back section of a dress that trails along the floor. **12** a retinue or suite. [C14: from OF *trahiner,* from Vulgar L *tragīnāre* (unattested) to draw]
▸ **ˈtrainable** *adj*

trainband (ˈtreɪnˌbænd) *n* a company of English militia from the 16th to the 18th century. [C17: altered from *trained band*]

trainbearer (ˈtreɪnˌbeərə) *n* an attendant who holds up the train of a dignitary's robe or bride's gown.

trainee (treɪˈniː) *n* **a** a person undergoing training. **b** (*as modifier*): *a trainee journalist.*

trainer Ⓣ (ˈtreɪnə) *n* **1** a person who trains athletes. **2** a piece of equipment employed in training, such as a simulated aircraft cockpit. **3** a person who schools racehorses. **4** (*pl*) another name for **training shoes.**

training Ⓣ (ˈtreɪnɪŋ) *n* **1a** the process of bringing a person, etc., to an agreed standard of proficiency, etc., by practice and instruction. **1b** (*as modifier*): *training college.* **2 in training. 2a** undergoing physical training. **2b** physically fit. **3 out of training.** physically unfit.

Training Agency *n* (in Britain) an organization established in 1989 to replace the **Training Commission**; it provides training and retraining for adult workers and operates the Youth Training Scheme, in England and Wales working through the local **Training and Enterprise Councils** (TECs) and in Scotland through the **Local Enterprise Companies** (LECs) set up in 1990.

training shoes *pl n* **1** running shoes for sports training, esp. in contrast to studded or spiked shoes worn for the sport itself. **2** shoes in the style of those used for sports training. ◆ Also called: **trainers.**

train oil *n* whale oil obtained from blubber. [C16: from earlier *train* or *trane,* from MLow G *trān,* or MDu. *traen* tear, drop]

train spotter *n* **1** a person who collects the numbers of railway locomotives. **2** *Inf.* a person who is obsessed with trivial details, esp. of a subject generally considered uninteresting.

traipse Ⓣ *or* **trapes** (treɪps) *Inf.* ◆ *vb* **traipses, traipsing, traipsed** *or* **trapeses, trapesing, trapesed. 1** (*intr*) to walk heavily or tiredly. ◆ *n* **2** a long or tiring walk; trudge. [C16: from ?]

trait Ⓣ (treɪt, treɪ) *n* **1** a characteristic feature or quality distinguishing a particular person or thing. **2** *Rare.* a touch or stroke. [C16: from F, from OF: a pulling, from L *tractus,* from *trahere* to drag]

traitor Ⓣ (ˈtreɪtə) *n* a person who is guilty of treason or treachery, in betraying friends, country, a cause, etc. [C13: from OF *traitour,* from L *trāditor,* from *trādere* to hand over]
▸ **ˈtraitorous** *adj* ▸ **ˈtraitress** *fem n*

trajectory Ⓣ (trəˈdʒɛktərɪ) *n, pl* **trajectories. 1** the path described by an object moving in air or space, esp. the curved path of a projectile. **2** *Geom.* a curve that cuts a family of curves or surfaces at a constant angle. [C17: from L *trājectus* cast over, from *trāicere* to throw across]

tram (træm) *n* **1** Also called: **tramcar.** an electrically driven public transport vehicle that runs on rails let into the surface of the road. US and Canad. names: **streetcar, trolley car. 2** a small vehicle on rails for carrying loads in a mine; tub. [C16 (in the sense: shaft of a cart): prob. from Low G *traam* beam]
▸ **ˈtramless** *adj*

tramline (ˈtræmˌlaɪn) *n* **1** (*often pl*) Also called: **tramway.** the tracks on which a tram runs. **2** the route taken by a tram. **3** (*often pl*) the outer markings along the sides of a tennis or badminton court.

trammel Ⓣ (ˈtræməl) *n* **1** (*often pl*) a hindrance to free action or move-

THESAURUS

tragedy *n* **5** = **disaster**, adversity, affliction, calamity, catastrophe, grievous blow, misfortune, whammy (*inf., chiefly US*)
Antonyms *n* fortune, happiness, joy, prosperity, success

tragic *adj* **1** = **distressing**, appalling, awful, calamitous, catastrophic, deadly, dire, disastrous, dreadful, fatal, grievous, ill-fated, ill-starred, lamentable, ruinous, sad, shocking, unfortunate, woeful, wretched **2** = **sad**, anguished, dismal, doleful, heartbreaking, heart-rending, miserable, mournful, pathetic, pitiable, sorrowful
Antonyms *adj* ≠ **distressing:** beneficial, fortunate, lucky, satisfying, worthwhile ≠ **sad:** cheerful, comic, happy, joyful

trail *vb* **1** = **drag**, dangle, draw, hang down, haul, pull, stream, tow **3** = **follow**, chase, hunt, pursue, shadow, stalk, tail (*inf.*), trace, track **4** = **lag**, bring up the rear, dawdle, drag oneself, fall behind, follow, hang back, linger, loiter, straggle, traipse (*inf.*) ◆ *n* **11** = **tracks**, footprints, footsteps, mark, marks, path, scent, slipstream, spoor, trace, wake **13** = **path**, beaten track, footpath, road, route, track, way **14** = **stream**, appendage, tail, train

trail away *vb* = **fade away** *or* **out**, decrease, die away, diminish, dwindle, fall away, grow faint, grow weak, lessen, peter out, shrink, sink, subside, tail off, taper off, weaken

train *vb* **1** = **instruct**, coach, discipline, drill, educate, guide, improve, prepare, rear, rehearse, school, teach, tutor **3** = **exercise**, prepare, work out **5** = **aim**, bring to bear, direct, focus, level, line up, point ◆ *n* **6** = **convoy**, caravan, column, file, procession **7** = **sequence**, chain, concatenation, course, order, progression, series, set, string, succession **11** = **tail**, appendage, trail **12** = **retinue**, attendants, cortege, court, entourage, followers, following, household, staff, suite

trainer *n* **1, 3** = **coach**, handler

training *n* **1a** = **instruction**, coaching, discipline, education, grounding, guidance, schooling, teaching, tuition, tutelage, upbringing

traipse *vb Informal* **1** = **trudge**, drag oneself, footslog, slouch, trail, tramp ◆ *n Informal* **2** = **trudge**, long walk, slog, tramp, trek

trait *n* **1** = **characteristic**, attribute, feature, idiosyncrasy, lineament, mannerism, peculiarity, quality, quirk

traitor *n* = **betrayer**, apostate, back-stabber, deceiver, defector, deserter, double-crosser (*inf.*), fifth columnist, informer, Judas, miscreant, quisling, rebel, renegade, snake in the grass (*inf.*), turncoat
Antonyms *n* defender, loyalist, patriot, supporter

traitorous *adj* = **treacherous**, apostate, disloyal, double-crossing, double-dealing, faithless, false, perfidious, renegade, seditious, treasonable, unfaithful, untrue
Antonyms *adj* constant, faithful, loyal, patriotic, staunch, steadfast, true, trusty

trajectory *n* **1** = **path**, course, flight, flight path, line, route, track

trammel *n* **1** *often pl* = **restrictions**, bars, blocks, bonds, chains, checks, curbs, fetters, handicaps, hazards, hindrances, impediments, obstacles, reins, shackles, stumbling blocks ◆ *vb* **8, 9** = **hinder**, bar, block, capture, catch, check, clog, curb, enmesh, ensnare, entrap, fetter,

ment. **2** Also called: **trammel net.** a fishing net in three sections, the two outer nets having a large mesh and the middle one a fine mesh. **3** *Rare.* a fowling net. **4** *US.* a shackle for a horse. **5** a device for drawing ellipses consisting of a flat sheet having a cruciform slot in which run two pegs attached to a beam. **6** (*sometimes pl*) a beam compass. **7** a device set in a fireplace to support cooking pots. ◆ *vb* **trammels, trammelling, trammelled** *or US* **trammels, trammeling, trammeled.** (*tr*) **8** to hinder or restrain. **9** to catch or ensnare. [C14: from OF *tramail* three-mesh net, from LL *trēmaculum,* from L *trēs* three + *macula* mesh in a net]

tramontane (trəˈmɒnteɪn) *adj* **1** being or coming from the far side of the mountains, esp. from the other side of the Alps as seen from Italy. ◆ *n* **2** an inhabitant of a tramontane country. **3** Also called: **tramontana.** a cold dry wind blowing south or southwest from the mountains in Italy and the W Mediterranean. [C16: from It. *tramontano,* from L *trānsmontānus,* from TRANS- + *montānus,* from *mōns* mountain]

tramp **T** (træmp) *vb* **1** (*intr*) to walk long and far; hike. **2** to walk heavily or firmly across or through (a place). **3** (*intr*) to wander about as a vagabond or tramp. **4** (*tr*) to traverse on foot, esp. laboriously or wearily. **5** (*intr*) to tread or trample. ◆ *n* **6** a person who travels about on foot, living by begging or doing casual work. **7** a long hard walk; hike. **8** a heavy or rhythmic tread. **9** the sound of heavy treading. **10** a merchant ship that does not run on a regular schedule but carries cargo wherever the shippers desire. **11** *Sl., chiefly US & Canad.* a prostitute or promiscuous girl or woman. [C14: prob. from MLow G *trampen*]
▸ **ˈtrampish** *adj*

tramper (ˈtræmpə) *n NZ.* a person who tramps, or walks long distances, in the bush.

tramping (ˈtræmpɪŋ) *n NZ.* **1** the leisure activity of walking in the bush. **2** (*as modifier*): *tramping boots.*

trample **T** (ˈtræmpᵊl) *vb* **tramples, trampling, trampled.** (when *intr,* usually foll. by *on, upon,* or *over*) **1** to stamp or walk roughly (on). **2** to encroach (upon) so as to violate or hurt. ◆ *n* **3** the action or sound of trampling. [C14: frequentative of TRAMP]
▸ **ˈtrampler** *n*

trampoline (ˈtræmpəlɪn, -ˌliːn) *n* **1** a tough canvas sheet suspended by springs or cords from a frame, used by acrobats, gymnasts, etc. ◆ *vb* **trampolines, trampolining, trampolined. 2** (*intr*) to exercise on a trampoline. [C18: via Sp. from It. *trampolino,* from *trampoli* stilts, of Gmc origin]
▸ **ˈtrampoliner** *or* **ˈtrampolinist** *n*

trance **T** (trɑːns) *n* **1** a hypnotic state resembling sleep. **2** any mental state in which a person is unaware of the environment, characterized by loss of voluntary movement, rigidity, and lack of sensitivity to external stimuli. **3** a dazed or stunned state. **4** a state of ecstasy or mystic absorption so intense as to cause a temporary loss of consciousness at the earthly level. **5** *Spiritualism.* a state in which a medium can supposedly be controlled by an intelligence from without as a means of communication with the dead. ◆ *vb* **trances, trancing, tranced. 6** (*tr*) to put into or as into a trance. [C14: from OF *transe,* from *transir* to faint, from L *trānsīre* to go over]
▸ **ˈtranceˌlike** *adj*

tranche (trɑːnʃ) *n* an instalment or portion, esp. of a loan or share issue. [F, lit.: slice]

trannie *or* **tranny** (ˈtrænɪ) *n, pl* **trannies.** *Inf., chiefly Brit.* a transistor radio.

tranquil **T** (ˈtræŋkwɪl) *adj* calm, peaceful, or quiet. [C17: from L *tranquillus*]
▸ **ˈtranquilly** *adv*

tranquillity **T** *or US* (*sometimes*) **tranquility** (træŋˈkwɪlɪtɪ) *n* a state of calm or quietude.

tranquillize **T**, **tranquillise,** *or US* **tranquilize** (ˈtræŋkwɪˌlaɪz) *vb* **tranquillizes, tranquillizing; tranquillized, tranquillises, tranquillising, tranquillised,** *or US* **tranquilizes, tranquilizing, tranquilized.** to make or become calm or calmer.
▸ **ˌtranquilliˈzation, ˌtranquilliˈsation,** *or US* **ˌtranquiliˈzation** *n*

tranquillizer **T**, **tranquilliser,** *or US* **tranquilizer** (ˈtræŋkwɪˌlaɪzə) *n* **1** a drug that calms a person. **2** anything that tranquillizes.

tranquillo (ˌtræŋˈkwiːləʊ) *adj Music.* calm; tranquil. [It.]

trans. *abbrev. for:* **1** transaction. **2** transferred. **3** transitive. **4** translated. **5** translator. **6** transport(ation). **7** transverse.

trans- *prefix* **1** across, beyond, crossing, on the other side: *transatlantic.* **2** changing thoroughly: *transliterate.* **3** transcending: *transubstantiation.* **4** transversely: *transect.* **5** (*often in italics*) indicating that a chemical compound has a molecular structure in which two identical groups or atoms are on opposite sides of a double bond: *trans-butadiene.* [from L *trāns* across, through, beyond]

transact **T** (trænˈzækt) *vb* to do, conduct, or negotiate (business, a deal, etc.). [C16: from L *trānsactus,* from *trānsigere,* lit.: to drive through]
▸ **transˈactor** *n*

transactinide (trænsˈæktɪˌnaɪd) *n* any artificially produced element with an atomic number greater than 103. [C20]

transaction **T** (trænˈzækʃən) *n* **1** something that is transacted, esp. a business deal. **2** a transacting or being transacted. **3** (*pl*) the records of the proceedings of a society, etc.
▸ **transˈactional** *adj*

transalpine (trænzˈælpaɪn) *adj* (*prenominal*) **1** situated in or relating to places beyond the Alps, esp. from Italy. **2** passing over the Alps.

transaminase (trænzˈæmɪˌneɪz, -ˌneɪs) *n Biochem.* an enzyme that catalyses the transfer of an amino group from one molecule, esp. an amino acid, to another, esp. a keto acid, in the process of **transamination.**

transatlantic (ˌtrænzətˈlæntɪk) *adj* **1** on or from the other side of the Atlantic. **2** crossing the Atlantic.

transceiver (trænˈsiːvə) *n* a device which transmits and receives radio or electronic signals. [C20: from TRANS(MITTER) + (RE)CEIVER]

transcend **T** (trænˈsɛnd) *vb* **1** to go above or beyond (a limit, expectation, etc.), as in degree or excellence. **2** (*tr*) to be superior to. [C14: from L *trānscendere* to climb over]

transcendent **T** (trænˈsɛndənt) *adj* **1** exceeding or surpassing in degree or excellence. **2** (in the philosophy of Kant) beyond or before experience. **3** *Theol.* (of God) having existence outside the created world. **4** free from the limitations inherent in matter. ◆ *n* **5** *Philosophy.* a transcendent thing.
▸ **tranˈscendence** *or* **tranˈscendency** *n* ▸ **tranˈscendently** *adv*

transcendental (ˌtrænsɛnˈdɛntᵊl) *adj* **1** transcendent, superior, or surpassing. **2** (in the philosophy of Kant) **2a** (of a judgment or logical deduction) being both synthetic and a priori. **2b** of or relating to knowledge of the presuppositions of thought. **3** *Philosophy.* beyond our experience of phenomena, although not beyond potential knowledge. **4** *Theol.* supernatural or mystical. **5** *Maths.* **5a** (of a number or quantity) not being a root of any polynomial with rational coefficients. **5b** (of a function) not capable of expression in terms of a finite number of arithmetical operations.
▸ **ˌtranscenˈdentally** *adv*

transcendentalism (ˌtrænsɛnˈdɛntəˌlɪzəm) *n* **1a** any system of philosophy, esp. that of Kant, holding that the key to knowledge of the nature of reality lies in the critical examination of the processes of reason on which depends the nature of experience. **1b** any system of philosophy, esp. that of Emerson, that emphasizes intuition as a means to knowledge or the importance of the search for the divine. **2** vague philosophical speculation. **3** the state of being transcendental. **4** something, such as thought or language, that is transcendental.
▸ **ˌtranscenˈdentalist** *n, adj*

transcendental meditation *n* a technique, based on Hindu traditions, for relaxing and refreshing the mind and body through the silent repetition of a mantra.

transcontinental (ˌtrænzkɒntɪˈnɛntᵊl) *adj* **1** crossing a continent. **2** on or from the far side of a continent.
▸ **ˌtranscontiˈnentally** *adv*

transcribe **T** (trænˈskraɪb) *vb* **transcribes, transcribing, transcribed.** (*tr*) **1** to write, type, or print out fully from speech, notes, etc. **2** to transliterate or translate. **3** to make an electrical recording of (a programme or speech) for a later broadcast. **4** *Music.* to rewrite (a piece of music)

THESAURUS

hamper, handicap, impede, net, restrain, restrict, snag, tie
Antonyms *vb* ≠ **hinder:** advance, assist, expedite, facilitate, foster, further, promote, support

tramp *vb* **1 = hike,** footslog, march, ramble, range, roam, rove, slog, trek, walk, yomp **2 = trudge,** march, plod, stamp, stump, toil, traipse (*inf.*), walk heavily **5 = trample,** crush, stamp, stomp (*inf.*), tread, walk over ◆ *n* **6 = vagrant,** bag lady (*chiefly US*), bum (*inf.*), derelict, dosser (*Brit. sl.*), down-and-out, drifter, hobo (*chiefly US*), vagabond **7 = hike,** march, ramble, slog, trek **8 = tread,** footfall, footstep, stamp

trample *vb* **1** *often with* **on = crush,** flatten, run over, squash, stamp, tread, walk over **2** *usually with* **on = show no consideration for,** hurt, ride roughshod over

trance *n* **1-4 = daze,** abstraction, dream, ecstasy, hypnotic state, muse, rapture, reverie, spell, stupor, unconsciousness

tranquil *adj* **= calm,** at peace, composed, cool, pacific, peaceful, placid, quiet, restful, sedate, serene, still, undisturbed, unexcited, unperturbed, unruffled, untroubled
Antonyms *adj* agitated, busy, confused, disturbed, excited, hectic, restless, troubled

tranquillity *n* **= calm,** ataraxia, calmness, composure, coolness, equanimity, hush, imperturbability, peace, peacefulness, placidity, quiet, quietness, quietude, repose, rest, restfulness, sedateness, serenity, stillness
Antonyms *n* agitation, commotion, confusion, disturbance, excitement, noise, restlessness, turmoil, upset

tranquillize *vb* **= calm,** compose, lull, pacify, quell, quiet, relax, sedate, settle one's nerves, soothe
Antonyms *vb* agitate, confuse, distress, disturb, harass, perturb, ruffle, trouble, upset

tranquillizer *n* **1 = sedative,** barbiturate, bromide, downer (*sl.*), opiate, red (*sl.*)

transact *vb* **= carry out,** accomplish, carry on, conclude, conduct, discharge, do, enact, execute, handle, manage, negotiate, perform, prosecute, see to, settle, take care of

transaction *n* **1 = deal,** action, affair, bargain, business, coup, deed, enterprise, event, matter, negotiation, occurrence, proceeding, undertaking **3** *plural* **= records,** affairs, annals, doings, goings-on (*inf.*), minutes, proceedings

transcend *vb* **1 = surpass,** eclipse, exceed, excel, go above, go beyond, leave behind, leave in the shade (*inf.*), outdo, outrival, outshine, outstrip, overstep, rise above

transcendence *n* **1 = greatness,** ascendancy, excellence, incomparability, matchlessness, paramountcy, pre-eminence, sublimity, superiority, supremacy

transcendent *adj* **1 = unparalleled,** consummate, exceeding, extraordinary, incomparable, matchless, peerless, pre-eminent, second to none, sublime, superior, transcendental, unequalled, unique, unrivalled

transcribe *vb* **1 = write out,** copy out, engross, note, reproduce, rewrite, set out, take down,

for an instrument or medium other than that originally intended; arrange. **5** *Computing.* **5a** to transfer (information) from one storage device to another. **5b** to transfer (information) from a computer to an external storage device. [C16: from L *trānscrībere*]
▸**tran'scribable** *adj* ▸**tran'scriber** *n*

transcript ⓣ ('trænskrɪpt) *n* **1** a written, typed, or printed copy or manuscript made by transcribing. **2** *Chiefly US & Canad.* an official record of a student's school progress. **3** any reproduction or copy. [C13: from L *trānscriptum,* from *trānscrībere* to transcribe]

transcriptase (træn'skrɪpteɪz) *n* See **reverse transcriptase.**

transcription (træn'skrɪpʃən) *n* **1** the act or an instance of transcribing or the state of being transcribed. **2** something transcribed. **3** a representation in writing of the actual pronunciation of a speech sound, word, etc., using phonetic symbols.
▸**tran'scriptional** *or* **tran'scriptive** *adj*

transducer (trænz'djuːsə) *n* any device, such as a microphone or electric motor, that converts one form of energy into another. [C20: from L *trānsdūcere* to lead across]

transect *vb* (træn'sɛkt). (*tr*) **1** to cut or divide crossways. ◆ *n* ('trænsɛkt). **2** a sample strip of land used to monitor plant distribution, animal populations, or some other feature, within a given area. [C17: from L TRANS- + *secāre* to cut]
▸**tran'section** *n*

transept ('trænsept) *n* either of the two wings of a cruciform church at right angles to the nave. [C16: from Anglo-L *trānseptum,* from L TRANS- + *saeptum* enclosure]
▸**tran'septal** *adj*

trans-fatty acid *n* a polyunsaturated fatty acid that has been converted from the cis-form by hydrogenation: used in the manufacture of margarine.

transfer ⓣ *vb* (træns'fɜː), **transfers, transferring, transferred.** **1** to change or go or cause to change or go from one thing, person, or point to another. **2** to change (buses, trains, etc.). **3** *Law.* to make over (property, etc.) to another; convey. **4** to displace (a drawing, design, etc.) from one surface to another. **5** (of a football player) to change clubs or (of a club, manager, etc.) to sell or release (a player) to another club. **6** to leave one school, college, etc., and enrol at another. **7** to change (the meaning of a word, etc.), esp. by metaphorical extension. ◆ *n* ('trænsfɜː). **8** the act, process, or system of transferring, or the state of being transferred. **9** a person or thing that transfers or is transferred. **10** a design or drawing that is transferred from one surface to another. **11** *Law.* the passing of title to property or other right from one person to another; conveyance. **12** any document or form effecting or regulating a transfer. **13** *Chiefly US & Canad.* a ticket that allows a passenger to change routes. [C14: from L *trānsferre,* from TRANS- + *ferre* to carry]
▸**trans'ferable** *or* **trans'ferrable** *adj* ▸**transference** ('trænsfərəns) *n*

transferable vote *n* a vote that is transferred to a second candidate indicated by the voter if the first is eliminated from the ballot.

transferee (ˌtrænsfə'riː) *n* **1** *Property law.* a person to whom property is transferred. **2** a person who is transferred.

transfer fee *n* a sum of money paid by one football club to another for a transferred player.

transferrin (træns'fɜːrɪn) *n Biochem.* any of a group of blood proteins that transport iron. [C20: from TRANS- + FERRO- + -IN]

transfer RNA *n Biochem.* any of several soluble forms of RNA of low molecular weight, each of which transports a specific amino acid to a ribosome during protein synthesis.

transfiguration (ˌtrænsfɪgjʊ'reɪʃən) *n* a transfiguring or being transfigured.

Transfiguration (ˌtrænsfɪgjʊ'reɪʃən) *n* **1** *New Testament.* the change in the appearance of Christ that took place before three disciples (Matthew 17:1–9). **2** the Church festival held in commemoration of this on Aug. 6.

transfigure ⓣ (træns'fɪgə) *vb* **transfigures, transfiguring, transfigured.** (*usually tr*) **1** to change or cause to change in appearance. **2** to become or cause to become more exalted. [C13: from L *trānsfigūrāre,* from TRANS- + *figūra* appearance]
▸**trans'figurement** *n*

transfinite number (træns'faɪnaɪt) *n* a cardinal or ordinal number used in the comparison of infinite sets for which several types of infinity can be classified.

transfix ⓣ (træns'fɪks) *vb* **transfixes, transfixing, transfixed** *or* **transfixt.** (*tr*) **1** to render motionless, esp. with horror or shock. **2** to impale or fix with a sharp weapon or other device. [C16: from L *trānsfīgere* to pierce through]
▸**transfixion** (træns'fɪkʃən) *n*

transform ⓣ *vb* (træns'fɔːm). **1** to alter or be altered in form, function, etc. **2** (*tr*) to convert (one form of energy) to another form. **3** (*tr*) *Maths.* to change the form of (an equation, etc.) by a mathematical transformation. **4** (*tr*) to change (an alternating current or voltage) using a transformer. ◆ *n* ('træns,fɔːm). **5** *Maths.* the result of a mathematical transformation. [C14: from L *trānsfōrmāre*]
▸**trans'formable** *adj* ▸**trans'formative** *adj*

transformation ⓣ (ˌtrænsfə'meɪʃən) *n* **1** a change or alteration, esp. a radical one. **2** a transforming or being transformed. **3** *Maths.* **3a** a change in position or direction of the reference axes in a coordinate system without an alteration in their relative angle. **3b** an equivalent change in an expression or equation resulting from the substitution of one set of variables by another. **4** *Physics.* a change in an atomic nucleus to a different nuclide as the result of the emission of either an alpha-particle or a beta-particle. **5** *Linguistics.* another word for **transformational rule.** **6** an apparently miraculous change in the appearance of a stage set.
▸ˌ**transfor'mational** *adj*

transformational grammar *n* a grammatical description of a language making essential use of transformational rules.

transformational rule *n Generative grammar.* a rule that converts one phrase marker into another. Taken together, these rules convert the deep structures of sentences into their surface structures.

transformer (træns'fɔːmə) *n* **1** a device that transfers an alternating current from one circuit to one or more other circuits, usually with a change of voltage. **2** a person or thing that transforms.

transfuse ⓣ (træns'fjuːz) *vb* **transfuses, transfusing, transfused.** (*tr*) **1** to permeate or infuse. **2a** to inject (blood, etc.) into a blood vessel. **2b** to give a transfusion to (a patient). [C15: from L *trānsfundere* to pour out]
▸**trans'fuser** *n* ▸**trans'fusible** *or* **trans'fusable** *adj* ▸**trans'fusive** *adj*

transfusion (træns'fjuːʒən) *n* **1** a transfusing. **2** the injection of blood, blood plasma, etc., into the blood vessels of a patient.

transgenic (trænz'dʒɛnɪk) *adj* (of an animal or plant) containing genetic material artificially transferred from another species.

transgress ⓣ (trænz'grɛs) *vb* **1** to break (a law, etc.). **2** to go beyond or overstep (a limit). [C16: from L *trānsgredī,* from TRANS- + *gradī* to step]
▸**trans'gressive** *adj* ▸**trans'gressor** *n*

transgression ⓣ (trænz'grɛʃən) *n* **1** a breach of a law, etc.; sin or crime. **2** a transgressing.

tranship (træn'ʃɪp) *vb* **tranships, transhipping, transhipped.** a variant spelling of **transship.**

transhumance (træns'hjuːməns) *n* the seasonal migration of livestock to suitable grazing grounds. [C20: from F, from *transhumer* to change one's pastures, from Sp. *trashumar,* from L TRANS- + *humus* ground]
▸**trans'humant** *adj*

transient ⓣ ('trænzɪənt) *adj* **1** for a short time only; temporary or transitory. ◆ *n* **2** a transient person or thing. [C17: from L *trānsiēns* going over, from *trānsīre* to pass over]
▸**'transiently** *adv* ▸**'transience** *or* **'transiency** *n*

transistor (træn'zɪstə) *n* **1** a semiconductor device, having three or more terminals attached to electrode regions, in which current flowing between two electrodes is controlled by a voltage or current applied to one or more specified electrodes. The device has replaced the valve in most circuits since it is much smaller and works at a much lower voltage. **2** *Inf.* a transistor radio. [C20: orig. a trademark, from TRANSFER + RESISTOR, from the transfer of electric signals across a resistor]

transistorize *or* **transistorise** (træn'zɪstəˌraɪz) *vb* **transistorizes, transistorizing, transistorized** *or* **transistorises, transistorising, transistorised.** **1** to

THESAURUS

transfer **2** = **translate**, interpret, render, transliterate **3** = **record**, tape, tape-record

transcript *n* **1** = **copy**, carbon, carbon copy, duplicate, manuscript, note, notes, record, reproduction, transcription, translation, transliteration, version

transfer *vb* **1** = **move**, carry, change, consign, convey, displace, hand over, make over, pass on, relocate, remove, shift, translate, transmit, transplant, transport, transpose, turn over ◆ *n* **8** = **move**, change, displacement, handover, relocation, removal, shift, transference, translation, transmission, transposition

transfigure *vb* **1** = **change**, alter, convert, metamorphose, transform, transmute **2** = **exalt**, apotheosize, glorify, idealize

transfix *vb* **1** = **stun**, engross, fascinate, halt *or* stop in one's tracks, hold, hypnotize, mesmerize, paralyse, petrify, rivet the attention of, root to the spot, spellbind, stop dead **2** = **pierce**, fix, impale, puncture, run through, skewer, spear, spit, transpierce
Antonyms *vb* ≠ **stun:** bore, fatigue, tire, weary

transform *vb* **1** = **change**, alter, convert, make over, metamorphose, reconstruct, remodel, renew, revolutionize, transfigure, translate, transmogrify (*jocular*), transmute

transformation *n* **1** = **change**, alteration, conversion, metamorphosis, radical change, renewal, revolution, revolutionary change, sea change, transfiguration, transmogrification (*jocular*), transmutation

transfuse *vb* **1** = **permeate**, instil, pervade, spread over, suffuse

transgress *vb Formal* **1** = **break**, be out of order, break the law, contravene, defy, disobey, do *or* go wrong, err, fall from grace, go astray, infringe, lapse, misbehave, offend, sin, trespass, violate **2** = **go beyond**, encroach, exceed, overstep

transgression *n* **1** = **crime**, breach, contravention, encroachment, error, fault, infraction, infringement, iniquity, lapse, misbehaviour, misdeed, misdemeanour, offence, peccadillo, sin, trespass, violation, wrong, wrongdoing

transgressor *n* **1** = **criminal**, culprit, delinquent, evildoer, felon, lawbreaker, malefactor, miscreant, offender, sinner, trespasser, villain, wrongdoer

transience *n* **1** = **briefness**, brevity, ephemerality, evanescence, fleetingness, fugacity, fugitiveness, impermanence, momentariness, shortness, transitoriness

transient *adj* **1** = **brief**, ephemeral, evanescent, fleeting, flying, fugacious, fugitive, here today and gone tomorrow, impermanent, momentary, passing, short, short-lived, short-term, temporary, transitory
Antonyms *adj* abiding, constant, durable, enduring, eternal, imperishable, long-lasting, long-term, permanent, perpetual, persistent, undying

convert to the use or manufacture of transistors and other solid-state components. **2** (*tr*) to equip with transistors and other solid-state components.

transit ('trænsɪt, 'trænz-) *n* **1a** the passage or conveyance of goods or people. **1b** (*as modifier*): *a transit visa.* **2** a change or transition. **3** a route. **4** *Astron.* **4a** the passage of a celestial body or satellite across the face of a larger body as seen from the earth. **4b** the apparent passage of a celestial body across the meridian. **5 in transit.** while being conveyed; during passage. ◆ *vb* **6** to make a transit through or over (something). [C15: from L *trānsitus* a going over, from *trānsīre* to pass over]

transit camp *n* a camp in which refugees, soldiers, etc., live temporarily.

transit instrument *n* an astronomical instrument used to time the transit of a star, etc., across the meridian.

transition (træn'zɪʃən) *n* **1** change or passage from one state or stage to another. **2** the period of time during which something changes. **3** *Music.* **3a** a movement from one key to another; modulation. **3b** a linking passage between two divisions in a composition; bridge. **4** a style of architecture in the late 11th and early 12th centuries, characterized by late Romanesque forms combined with early Gothic details. **5** *Physics.* a change in the configuration of an atomic nucleus, involving either a change in energy level or a transformation to another element or isotope. **6** a sentence, passage, etc., that links sections of a written work. [C16: from L *transitio*; see TRANSIENT]
▸**tran'sitional** *adj* ▸**tran'sitionally** *adv*

transition element *or* **metal** *n Chem.* any element belonging to one of three series of elements with atomic numbers between 21 and 30, 39 and 48, and 57 and 80. They have an incomplete penultimate electron shell and tend to form complexes.

transition temperature *n* the temperature at which a sudden change of physical properties occurs.

transitive ('trænsɪtɪv) *adj* **1** *Grammar.* **1a** denoting an occurrence of a verb when it requires a direct object or denoting a verb that customarily requires a direct object: *"to find" is a transitive verb.* **1b** (*as n*): *these verbs are transitives.* **2** *Logic, maths.* having the property that if one object bears a relationship to a second object that also bears the same relationship to a third object, then the first object bears this relationship to the third object: *if* $x = y$ *and* $y = z$ *then* $x = z$. ◆ Cf. **intransitive.** [C16: from LL *trānsitīvus*, from L *trānsitus* a going over; see TRANSIENT]
▸**'transitively** *adv* ▸**ˌtransi'tivity** *or* **'transitiveness** *n*

transitory ('trænsɪtərɪ, -trɪ) *adj* of short duration; transient or ephemeral. [C14: from Church L *trānsitōrius* passing, from L *trānsitus* a crossing over]
▸**'transitoriness** *n*

transit theodolite *n* a theodolite the telescope of which can be rotated completely about its horizontal axis.

transl. *abbrev. for:* **1** translated. **2** translator.

translate (træns'leɪt, trænz-) *vb* **translates, translating, translated. 1** to express or be capable of being expressed in another language. **2** (*intr*) to act as translator. **3** (*tr*) to express or explain in simple or less technical language. **4** (*tr*) to interpret or infer the significance of (gestures, symbols, etc.). **5** (*tr*) to transform or convert: *to translate hope into reality.* **6** to transfer from one place or position to another. **7** (*tr*) *Theol.* to transfer (a person) from one place or plane of existence to another, as from earth to heaven. **8** (*tr*) *Maths, physics.* to move (a figure or body) laterally, without rotation, dilation, or angular displacement. [C13: from L *trānslātus* carried over, from *trānsferre* to TRANSFER]
▸**trans'latable** *adj* ▸**trans'lator** *n*

translation (træns'leɪʃən, trænz-) *n* **1** something that is or has been translated. **2** a translating or being translated. **3** *Maths.* a transformation in which the origin of a coordinate system is moved to another position so that each axis retains the same direction.
▸**trans'lational** *adj*

transliterate (trænz'lɪtəˌreɪt) *vb* **transliterates, transliterating, transliterated.** (*tr*) to transcribe (a word, etc.) into corresponding letters of another alphabet. [C19: TRANS- + *-literate*, from L *līttera* letter]
▸**ˌtransliter'ation** *n* ▸**trans'literˌator** *n*

translocation (ˌtrænzləʊ'keɪʃən) *n* **1** *Genetics.* the transfer of one part of a chromosome to another part of the same or a different chromosome. **2** *Bot.* the transport of minerals, sugars, etc., in solution within a plant. **3** a movement from one position or place to another.

translucent (trænz'lu:sᵊnt) *adj* allowing light to pass through partially or diffusely; semitransparent. [C16: from L *trānslūcēre* to shine through]
▸**trans'lucence** *or* **trans'lucency** *n* ▸**trans'lucently** *adv*

translunar (trænz'lu:nə) *or* **translunary** (trænz'lu:nərɪ) *adj* **1** lying beyond the moon. **2** unworldly or ethereal.

transmigrate (ˌtrænzmaɪ'greɪt) *vb* **transmigrates, transmigrating, transmigrated.** (*intr*) **1** to move from one place, state, or stage to another. **2** (of souls) to pass from one body into another at death.
▸**ˌtransmi'gration** *n* ▸**trans'migratory** *adj*

transmission (trænz'mɪʃən) *n* **1** the act or process of transmitting. **2** something that is transmitted. **3** the extent to which a body or medium transmits light, sound, etc. **4** the transference of motive force or power. **5** a system of shafts, gears, etc., that transmits power, esp. the arrangement of such parts that transmits the power of the engine to the driving wheels of a motor vehicle. **6** the act or process of sending a message, picture, or other information by means of radio waves, electrical signals, light signals, etc. **7** a radio or television broadcast. [C17: from L *trānsmissiō* a sending across]
▸**trans'missible** *adj* ▸**trans'missive** *adj*

transmission density *n Physics.* a measure of the extent to which a substance transmits light or other electromagnetic radiation.

transmission line *n* a coaxial cable, waveguide, etc., that transfers electrical signals from one location to another.

transmissivity (ˌtrænzmɪ'sɪvɪtɪ) *n Physics.* a measure of the ability of a material to transmit radiation.

transmit (trænz'mɪt) *vb* **transmits, transmitting, transmitted. 1** (*tr*) to pass or cause to go from one place or person to another; transfer. **2** (*tr*) to pass on or impart (a disease, etc.). **3** (*tr*) to hand down to posterity. **4** (*tr; usually passive*) to pass (an inheritable characteristic) from parent to offspring. **5** to allow the passage of (particles, energy, etc.): *radio waves are transmitted through the atmosphere.* **6a** to send out (signals) by means of radio waves or along a transmission line. **6b** to broadcast (a radio or television programme). **7** (*tr*) to transfer (a force, motion, etc.) from one part of a mechanical system to another. [C14: from L *trānsmittere* to send across]
▸**trans'mittable** *adj* ▸**trans'mittal** *n*

transmittance (trænz'mɪtᵊns) *n* **1** the act of transmitting. **2** Also called: **transmission factor.** *Physics.* a measure of the ability of anything to transmit radiation, equal to the ratio of the transmitted flux to the incident flux.

transmitter (trænz'mɪtə) *n* **1** a person or thing that transmits. **2** the equipment used for generating and amplifying a radio-frequency carrier, modulating the carrier with information, and feeding it to an aerial for transmission. **3** the microphone in a telephone that converts sound waves into audio-frequency electrical signals. **4** a device that converts mechanical movements into coded electrical signals transmitted along a telegraph circuit. **5** a substance released by nerve endings that transmits impulses across synapses.

transmogrify (trænz'mɒgrɪˌfaɪ) *vb* **transmogrifies, transmogrifying, transmogrified.** (*tr*) *Jocular.* to change or transform into a different shape, esp. a grotesque or bizarre one. [C17: from ?]
▸**transˌmogrifi'cation** *n*

transmontane (ˌtrænzmɒn'teɪn) *adj, n* another word for **tramontane.**

transmutation (ˌtrænzmju:'teɪʃən) *n* **1** the act or an instance of transmuting. **2** the change of one chemical element into another by a nuclear reaction. **3** the attempted conversion, by alchemists, of base metals into gold or silver.
▸**ˌtransmu'tational** *or* **trans'mutative** *adj*

transmute (trænz'mju:t) *vb* **transmutes, transmuting, transmuted.** (*tr*) **1** to change the form, character, or substance of. **2** to alter (an element, metal, etc.) by alchemy. [C15: via OF from L *trānsmūtāre* to shift; from TRANS- + *mūtāre* to change]
▸**transˌmuta'bility** *n* ▸**trans'mutable** *adj*

transnational (trænz'næʃənəl) *adj* extending beyond the boundaries, etc., of a single nation.

transoceanic (trænzˌəʊʃɪ'ænɪk) *adj* **1** on or from the other side of an ocean. **2** crossing an ocean.

transom ('trænsəm) *n* **1** a horizontal member across a window. **2** a hori-

THESAURUS

transit *n* **1a** = **movement**, carriage, conveyance, crossing, motion, passage, portage, shipment, transfer, transport, transportation, travel, traverse **2** = **change**, alteration, changeover, conversion, shift, transition **5 in transit** = **en route**, during passage, on the journey, on the move, on the road, on the way, while travelling ◆ *vb* **6** = **move**, cross, journey, pass, travel, traverse

transition *n* **1** = **change**, alteration, changeover, conversion, development, evolution, flux, metamorphosis, metastasis, passage, passing, progression, shift, transit, transmutation, upheaval

transitional *adj* **1** = **changing**, developmental, fluid, intermediate, passing, provisional, temporary, transitionary, unsettled

transitory *adj* = **short-lived**, brief, ephemeral, evanescent, fleeting, flying, fugacious, here today and gone tomorrow, impermanent, momentary, passing, short, short-term, temporary, transient
Antonyms *adj* abiding, enduring, eternal, everlasting, lasting, long-lived, long-term, permanent, perpetual, persistent, undying

translate *vb* **1** = **interpret**, construe, convert, decipher, decode, paraphrase, render, transcribe, transliterate **3** = **put in plain English**, elucidate, explain, make clear, paraphrase, simplify, spell out, state in layman's language **5** = **convert**, alter, change, metamorphose, transfigure, transform, transmute, turn **6** = **transfer**, carry, convey, move, remove, send, transplant, transport, transpose

translator *n* **1** = **interpreter**, linguist

translucent *adj* = **semitransparent**, clear, diaphanous, limpid, lucent, pellucid

transmigration *n* **1, 2** = **reincarnation**, journey, metempsychosis, migration, movement, passage, rebirth, travel

transmission *n* **1** = **transfer**, carriage, communication, conveyance, diffusion, dispatch, dissemination, remission, sending, shipment, spread, transference, transport **6** = **broadcasting**, dissemination, putting out, relaying, sending, showing **7** = **programme**, broadcast, show

transmit *vb* **1-5** = **pass on**, bear, carry, communicate, convey, diffuse, dispatch, disseminate, forward, hand down, hand on, impart, remit, send, spread, take, transfer, transport **6b** = **broadcast**, disseminate, put on the air, radio, relay, send, send out

transmute *vb* **1, 2** = **transform**, alchemize, alter, change, convert, metamorphose, remake, transfigure

zontal member that separates a door from a window over it. **3** the usual US name for **fanlight. 4** *Naut.* **4a** a surface forming the stern of a vessel. **4b** any of several transverse beams used for strengthening the stern of a vessel. [C14: earlier *traversayn,* from OF *traversin,* from TRAVERSE]
▸ˈ**transomed** *adj*

transonic (trænˈsɒnɪk) *adj* of or relating to conditions when travelling at or near the speed of sound.

transparency Ⓣ (trænsˈpærənsɪ) *n, pl* **transparencies. 1** Also called: **transparence.** the state of being transparent. **2** Also called: **slide.** a positive photograph on a transparent base, usually mounted in a frame or between glass plates. It can be viewed by means of a slide projector.

transparent Ⓣ (trænsˈpærənt) *adj* **1** permitting the uninterrupted passage of light; clear. **2** easy to see through, understand, or recognize; obvious. **3** permitting the free passage of electromagnetic radiation. **4** candid, open, or frank. [C15: from Med. L *trānspārēre* to show through, from L TRANS- + *pārēre* to appear]
▸**transˈparently** *adv* ▸**transˈparentness** *n*

transpire Ⓣ (trænˈspaɪə) *vb* **transpires, transpiring, transpired. 1** (*intr*) to come to light; be known. **2** (*intr*) *Inf.* to happen or occur. **3** *Physiol.* to give off or exhale (water or vapour) through the skin, a mucous membrane, etc. **4** (of plants) to lose (water), esp. through the stomata of the leaves. [C16: from Med. L *trānspīrāre,* from L TRANS- + *spīrāre* to breathe]
▸**transpiration** (ˌtrænspəˈreɪʃən) *n* ▸**tranˈspiratory** *adj*

> **USAGE NOTE** It is often maintained that *transpire* should not be used to mean happen or occur, as in *the event transpired late in the evening,* and that the word is properly used to mean become known, as in *it transpired later that the thief had been caught.* The word is, however, widely used in the former sense, esp. in spoken English.

transplant Ⓣ *vb* (trænsˈplɑːnt). **1** (*tr*) to remove or transfer (esp. a plant) from one place to another. **2** (*intr*) to be capable of being transplanted. **3** *Surgery.* to transfer (an organ or tissue) from one part of the body or from one person to another. ◆ *n* (ˈtrænsˌplɑːnt). **4** *Surgery.* **4a** the procedure involved in such a transfer. **4b** the organ or tissue transplanted.
▸**transˈplantable** *adj* ▸ˌ**transplanˈtation** *n*

transponder (trænˈspɒndə) *n* **1** a type of radio or radar transmitter-receiver that transmits signals automatically when it receives predetermined signals. **2** the receiver and transmitter in a communications satellite, relaying signals back to earth. [C20: from TRANSMITTER + RESPONDER]

transport Ⓣ *vb* (trænsˈpɔːt). (*tr*) **1** to carry or cause to go from one place to another, esp. over some distance. **2** to deport or exile to a penal colony. **3** (*usually passive*) to have a strong emotional effect on. ◆ *n* (ˈtrænsˌpɔːt). **4a** the business or system of transporting goods or people. **4b** (*as modifier*): *a modernized transport system.* **5** *Brit.* freight vehicles generally. **6a** a vehicle used to transport goods or people, esp. troops. **6b** (*as modifier*): *a transport plane.* **7** a transporting or being transported. **8** ecstasy, rapture, or any powerful emotion. **9** a convict sentenced to be transported. [C14: from L *trānsportāre,* from TRANS- + *portāre* to carry]
▸**transˈportable** *adj* ▸**transˈporter** *n*

transportation (ˌtrænspɔːˈteɪʃən) *n* **1** a means or system of transporting. **2** the act of transporting or the state of being transported. **3** (esp. formerly) deportation to a penal colony.

transport café (ˈtrænsˌpɔːt) *n Brit.* an inexpensive eating place on a main route, used mainly by long-distance lorry drivers.

transpose Ⓣ (trænsˈpəʊz) *vb* **transposes, transposing, transposed. 1** (*tr*) to alter the positions of; interchange, as words in a sentence. **2** *Music.* to play (notes, music, etc.) in a different key from that originally intended. **3** (*tr*) *Maths.* to move (a term) from one side of an equation to the other with a corresponding reversal in sign. [C14: from OF *transposer,* from L *trānspōnere* to remove]
▸**transˈposable** *adj* ▸**transˈposal** *n* ▸**transˈposer** *n* ▸**transposition** (ˌtrænspəˈzɪʃən) *n*

transposing instrument *n* a musical instrument, esp. a horn or clarinet, pitched in a key other than C major, but whose music is written down as if its basic scale were C major.

transposon (trænsˈpəʊzɒn) *n Genetics.* a fragment of bacterial nucleic acid that can move from one site in a chromosome to another site in the same or a different chromosome and thus alter the genetic constitution of the bacterium. [C20: TRANSPOS(E) + -ON]

transputer (trænzˈpjuːtə) *n Computing.* a type of fast powerful microchip that is the equivalent of a 32-bit microprocessor with its own RAM facility. [C20: from TRANS(ISTOR) + (COM)PUTER]

transsexual *or* **transexual** (trænzˈseksjʊəl) *n* **1** a person who completely identifies with the opposite sex. **2** a person who has undergone medical procedures to alter sexual characteristics to those of the opposite sex.

transship (trænsˈʃɪp) *or* **tranship** *vb* **transships, transshipping, transshipped** *or* **tranships, transhipping, transhipped.** to transfer or be transferred from one vessel or vehicle to another.
▸**transˈshipment** *or* **tranˈshipment** *n*

transubstantiation (ˌtrænsəbˌstænʃɪˈeɪʃən) *n* **1** (esp. in Roman Catholic theology) **1a** the doctrine that the whole substance of the bread and wine changes into the substance of the body and blood of Christ when consecrated in the Eucharist. **1b** the mystical process by which this is believed to take place during consecration. Cf. **consubstantiation. 2** a substantial change; transmutation.
▸ˌ**transubˌstantiˈationalist** *n*

transude (trænˈsjuːd) *vb* **transudes, transuding, transuded.** (of a fluid) to ooze or pass through interstices, pores, or small holes. [C17: from NL *trānsūdāre,* from L TRANS- + *sūdāre* to sweat]
▸**transudation** (ˌtrænsjʊˈdeɪʃən) *n*

transuranic (ˌtrænzjʊˈrænɪk), **transuranian** (ˌtrænzjʊˈreɪnɪən), *or* **transuranium** *adj* **1** (of an element) having an atomic number greater than that of uranium. **2** of or having the behaviour of transuranic elements. [C20]

transversal (trænzˈvɜːsᵊl) *n* **1** *Geom.* a line intersecting two or more other lines. ◆ *adj* **2** a less common word for **transverse.**
▸**transˈversally** *adv*

transverse Ⓣ (trænzˈvɜːs) *adj* **1** crossing from side to side; athwart; crossways. ◆ *n* **2** a transverse piece or object. [C16: from L *trānsversus,* from *trānsvertere* to turn across]
▸**transˈversely** *adv*

transverse colon *n Anat.* the part of the large intestine passing transversely in front of the liver and stomach.

transverse wave *n* a wave, such as an electromagnetic wave, that is propagated in a direction perpendicular to the displacement of the transmitting field or medium.

transvestite (trænzˈvestaɪt) *n* a person who seeks sexual pleasure from wearing clothes of the opposite sex. [C19: from G *Transvestit,* from TRANS- + L *vestītus* clothed, from *vestīre* to clothe]
▸**transˈvestism** *or* **transˈvestitism** *n*

trap[1] Ⓣ (træp) *n* **1** a mechanical device or enclosed place or pit in which something, esp. an animal, is caught or penned. **2** any device or plan for tricking a person or thing into being caught unawares. **3** anything resembling a trap or prison. **4** a fitting for a pipe in the form of a U-shaped or S-shaped bend that contains standing water to prevent the passage of gases. **5** any similar device. **6** a device that hurls clay pigeons into the air to be fired at by trapshooters. **7** *Greyhound racing.* any one of a line of boxlike stalls in which greyhounds are enclosed before the start of a race. **8** See **trap door. 9** a light two-wheeled carriage. **10** a slang word for **mouth. 11** *Golf.* an obstacle or hazard, esp. a bunker. **12** (*pl*) *Jazz sl.* percussion instruments. **13** (*usually pl*) *Austral. sl.* a policeman. ◆ *vb* **traps, trapping, trapped. 14** to catch, take, or pen in or as if in a trap. **15** (*tr*) to ensnare by trickery; trick. **16** (*tr*) to provide (a pipe) with a trap. **17** to set traps in (a place), esp. for animals. [OE *træppe*]
▸ˈ**trapˌlike** *adj*

trap[2] (træp) *vb* **traps, trapping, trapped.** (*tr;* often foll. by *out*) to dress or adorn. ◆ See also **traps.** [C11: prob. from OF *drap* cloth]

trap[3] (træp) *or* **traprock** (ˈtræpˌrɒk) *n* **1** any fine-grained often columnar dark igneous rock, esp. basalt. **2** any rock in which oil or gas has

THESAURUS

transparency *n* **1** = **clarity,** clearness, diaphaneity, diaphanousness, filminess, gauziness, limpidity, limpidness, pellucidity, pellucidness, sheerness, translucence, translucency, transparence **1** = **obviousness,** apparentness, distinctness, explicitness, patentness, perspicuousness, plainness, unambiguousness **1** = **frankness,** candour, directness, forthrightness, openness, straightforwardness **2** = **photograph,** slide
Antonyms *n* ≠ **clarity:** cloudiness, murkiness, opacity, unclearness ≠ **obviousness:** obscurity, unclearness, vagueness ≠ **frankness:** ambiguity, vagueness

transparent *adj* **1** = **clear,** crystal clear, crystalline, diaphanous, filmy, gauzy, limpid, lucent, lucid, pellucid, see-through, sheer, translucent, transpicuous **2** = **obvious,** apparent, as plain as the nose on one's face (*inf.*), bold, distinct, easy, evident, explicit, manifest, patent, perspicuous, plain, recognizable, unambiguous, understandable, undisguised, visible **4** = **frank,** candid, direct, forthright, open, plain-spoken, straight, straightforward, unambiguous, unequivocal
Antonyms *adj* ≠ **clear:** cloudy, muddy, opaque, thick, turbid, unclear ≠ **obvious:** hidden, mysterious, opaque, uncertain, unclear, vague ≠ **frank:** ambiguous, deceptive, disingenuous, mysterious, unclear, vague

transpire *vb* **1** = **become known,** be disclosed, be discovered, be made public, come out, come to light, emerge **2** = **happen,** arise, befall, chance, come about, come to pass (*arch.*), occur, take place, turn up

transplant *vb* **1** = **transfer,** displace, relocate, remove, resettle, shift, uproot

transport *vb* **1** = **convey,** bear, bring, carry, fetch, haul, move, remove, run, ship, take, transfer **2** *History* = **exile,** banish, deport, sentence to transportation **3** = **enrapture,** captivate, carry away, delight, electrify, enchant, entrance, move, ravish, spellbind ◆ *n* **4a** = **transference,** carriage, conveyance, removal, shipment, shipping, transportation **6a** = **vehicle,** conveyance, transportation, wheels (*inf.*) **8** = **ecstasy,** bliss, cloud nine (*inf.*), delight, enchantment, euphoria, happiness, heaven, rapture, ravishment, seventh heaven
Antonyms *n* ≠ **ecstasy:** blues (*inf.*), depression, despondency, doldrums, dumps (*inf.*), melancholy

transpose *vb* **1** = **interchange,** alter, change, exchange, move, rearrange, relocate, reorder, shift, substitute, swap, switch, transfer

transverse *adj* **1** = **crossways,** athwart, crosswise, diagonal, oblique

trap[1] *n* **1** = **snare,** ambush, gin, net, noose, pitfall, springe, toils **2** = **trick,** ambush, artifice, deception, device, ruse, stratagem, subterfuge, wile ◆ *vb* **14** = **catch,** corner, enmesh, ensnare, entrap, snare, take **15** = **trick,** ambush, beguile, deceive, dupe, ensnare, inveigle

accumulated. [C18: from Swedish *trappa* stair (from its steplike formation)]

trap door *n* a door or flap flush with and covering an opening, esp. in a ceiling.

trap-door spider *n* any of various spiders that construct a silk-lined hole in the ground closed by a hinged door of earth and silk.

trapes (treɪps) *vb, n* a less common spelling of **traipse.**

trapeze (trəˈpiːz) *n* a free-swinging bar attached to two ropes, used by circus acrobats, etc. [C19: from F *trapèze,* from NL; see TRAPEZIUM]

trapezium (trəˈpiːzɪəm) *n, pl* **trapeziums** *or* **trapezia** (-zɪə). **1** *Chiefly Brit.* a quadrilateral having two parallel sides of unequal length. Usual US and Canad. name: **trapezoid. 2** *Chiefly US & Canad.* a quadrilateral having neither pair of sides parallel. [C16: via LL from Gk *trapezion,* from *trapeza* table]
▸**traˈpezial** *adj*

trapezius (trəˈpiːzɪəs) *n, pl* **trapeziuses.** either of two flat triangular muscles that rotate the shoulder blades. [C18: from NL *trapezius* (*musculus*) trapezium-shaped (muscle)]

trapezoid (ˈtræpɪˌzɔɪd) *n* **1** a quadrilateral having neither pair of sides parallel. **2** the usual US and Canad. name for **trapezium.** [C18: from NL *trapezoidēs,* from LGk *trapezoeidēs* trapezium-shaped, from *trapeza* table]

trapper (ˈtræpə) *n* a person who traps animals, esp. for their furs or skins.

trappings ❶ (ˈtræpɪŋz) *pl n* **1** the accessories and adornments that symbolize a condition, office, etc.: *the trappings of success.* **2** ceremonial harness for a horse or other animal. [C16: from TRAP[2]]

Trappist (ˈtræpɪst) *n* **a** a member of a branch of the Cistercian order of Christian monks, which originated at La Trappe in France in 1664. They are noted for their rule of silence. **b** (*as modifier*): *a Trappist monk.*

traps (træps) *pl n* belongings; luggage. [C19: prob. shortened from TRAPPINGS]

trapshooting (ˈtræpˌʃuːtɪŋ) *n* the sport of shooting at clay pigeons thrown up by a trap.
▸**ˈtrapˌshooter** *n*

trash ❶ (træʃ) *n* **1** foolish ideas or talk; nonsense. **2** *Chiefly US & Canad.* useless or unwanted matter or objects; rubbish. **3** a literary or artistic production of poor quality. **4** *Chiefly US & Canad.* a poor or worthless person or a group of such people. **5** bits that are broken or lopped off, esp. the trimmings from trees or plants. **6** the dry remains of sugar cane after the juice has been extracted. ◆ *vb* **7** to remove the outer leaves and branches from (growing plants, esp. sugar cane). **8** *Sl.* to attack or destroy (someone or something) wilfully or maliciously. [C16: from ?]

trashy ❶ (ˈtræʃɪ) *adj* **trashier, trashiest.** cheap, worthless, or badly made.
▸**ˈtrashily** *adv* ▸**ˈtrashiness** *n*

trass (træs) *n* a volcanic rock used to make a hydraulic cement. [C18: from Du. *tras, tarasse,* from It. *terrazza* worthless earth; see TERRACE]

trattoria (ˌtrætəˈrɪə) *n* an Italian restaurant. [C19: from It., from *trattore* innkeeper, from F *traiteur,* from OF *tretier* to TREAT]

trauma ❶ (ˈtrɔːmə) *n, pl* **traumata** (-mətə) *or* **traumas. 1** *Psychol.* a powerful shock that may have long-lasting effects. **2** *Pathol.* any bodily injury or wound. [C18: from Gk: a wound]
▸**traumatic** (trɔːˈmætɪk) *adj* ▸**trauˈmatically** *adv*

traumatize *or* **traumatise** (ˈtrɔːməˌtaɪz) *vb* **traumatizes, traumatizing, traumatized** *or* **traumatises, traumatising, traumatised. 1** (*tr*) to wound or injure (the body). **2** to subject or be subjected to mental trauma.
▸**ˌtraumatiˈzation** *or* **ˌtraumatiˈsation** *n*

travail ❶ (ˈtræveɪl) *Literary.* ◆ *n* **1** painful or excessive labour or exertion. **2** the pangs of childbirth; labour. ◆ *vb* **3** (*intr*) to suffer or labour painfully, esp. in childbirth. [C13: from OF *travaillier,* from Vulgar L *tripaliāre* (unattested) to torture, from LL *trepālium* instrument of torture, from L *tripālis* having three stakes]

travel ❶ (ˈtræv[ə]l) *vb* **travels, travelling, travelled** *or US* **travels, traveling, traveled.** (*mainly intr*) **1** to go, move, or journey from one place to another. **2** (*tr*) to go, move, or journey through or across (an area, region, etc.). **3** to go, move, or cover a distance. **4** to go from place to place as a salesman. **5** (esp. of perishable goods) to withstand a journey. **6** (of light, sound, etc.) to be transmitted or move. **7** to progress or advance. **8** *Basketball.* to take an excessive number of steps while holding the ball. **9** (of part of a mechanism) to move in a fixed path. **10** *Inf.* to move rapidly. ◆ *n* **11a** the act of travelling. **11b** (*as modifier*): *a travel brochure.* Related adj: **itinerant. 12** (*usually pl*) a tour or journey. **13** the distance moved by a mechanical part, such as the stroke of a piston. **14** movement or passage. [C14 *travaillen* to make a journey, from OF *travaillier* to TRAVAIL]

travel agency *or* **bureau** *n* an agency that arranges and negotiates flights, holidays, etc., for travellers.
▸**travel agent** *n*

travelled *or US* **traveled** (ˈtr[ə]vəld) *adj* having experienced or undergone much travelling.

traveller ❶ (ˈtrævələ, ˈtrævlə) *n* **1** a person who travels, esp. habitually. **2** See **travelling salesman. 3** a part of a mechanism that moves in a fixed course. **4** *Austral.* a swagman.

traveller's cheque *n* a cheque sold by a bank, etc., to the bearer, who signs it on purchase and can cash it abroad by signing it again.

traveller's joy *n* a ranunculaceous Old World climbing plant having white flowers and heads of feathery plumed fruits; wild clematis.

travelling people *or* **folk** *pl n* (*sometimes caps.*) *Brit.* Gypsies or other itinerant people: a term used esp. by such people of themselves.

travelling salesman *n* a salesman who travels within an assigned territory in order to sell merchandise or to solicit orders for the commercial enterprise he represents by direct personal contact with customers.

travelling wave *n* **a** a wave carrying energy away from its source. **b** (*as modifier*): *a travelling-wave aerial.*

travelogue *or US* (*sometimes*) **travelog** (ˈtræv[ə]lɒg) *n* a film, lecture, or brochure on travels and travelling.

traverse ❶ (ˈtrævɜːs, trəˈvɜːs) *vb* **traverses, traversing, traversed. 1** to pass or go over or back and forth over (something); cross. **2** (*tr*) to go against; oppose. **3** to move sideways or crosswise. **4** (*tr*) to extend or reach across. **5** to turn (an artillery gun) laterally or (of an artillery gun) to turn laterally. **6** (*tr*) to examine carefully. **7** (*tr*) *Law.* to deny (an allegation). **8** *Mountaineering.* to move across (a face) horizontally. ◆ *n* **9** something being or lying across, such as a transom. **10** a gallery or loft inside a building that crosses it. **11** an obstruction. **12** a protective bank or other barrier across a trench or rampart. **13** a railing, screen, or curtain. **14** the act or an instance of traversing or crossing. **15** *Mountaineering.* the act or an instance of moving horizontally across a face. **16** a path or road across. **17** *Naut.* the zigzag course of a vessel tacking frequently. **18** *Law.* the formal denial of a fact alleged in the opposite party's pleading. **19** *Surveying.* a survey consisting of a series of straight lines, the length of each and the angle between them being measured. ◆ *adj* **20** being or lying across; transverse. [C14: from OF *traverser,* from LL *trānsversāre,* from L *trānsversus* TRANSVERSE]
▸**traˈversal** *n* ▸**ˈtraverser** *n*

travertine (ˈtrævətɪn) *n* a porous rock consisting of calcium carbonate, used for building. [C18: from It. *travertino* (infl. by *tra-* TRANS-), from L *lapis Tīburtīnus* Tiburtine stone, from *Tībur*s the district around Tibur (now Tivoli)]

travesty ❶ (ˈtrævɪstɪ) *n, pl* **travesties. 1** a farcical or grotesque imitation; mockery. ◆ *vb* **travesties, travestying, travestied.** (*tr*) **2** to make or be a travesty of. [C17: from F *travesti* disguised, from *travestir* to disguise, from It. *travestire,* from *tra-* TRANS- + *vestire* to clothe]

travois (trəˈvɔɪ) *n, pl* **travois** (-ˈvɔɪz). **1** *History.* a sled formerly used by the Plains Indians of North America, consisting of two poles joined by a frame and pulled by an animal. **2** *Canad.* a similar sled used for dragging logs. [from Canad. F, from F *travail* beam, from L *trabs*]

THESAURUS

trappings *pl n* **1** = **accessories,** accoutrements, adornments, bells and whistles, decorations, dress, equipment, finery, fittings, fixtures, fripperies, furnishings, gear, livery, ornaments, panoply, paraphernalia, raiment (*arch. or poetic*), things, trimmings

trash *n* **1** = **nonsense,** balderdash, balls (*taboo sl.*), bilge (*inf.*), bosh (*inf.*), bull (*sl.*), bullshit (*taboo sl.*), bunkum *or* buncombe (*chiefly US*), cobblers (*Brit. taboo sl.*), crap (*sl.*), drivel, eyewash (*inf.*), foolish talk, garbage (*inf.*), guff (*sl.*), hogwash, hokum (*sl., chiefly US & Canad.*), hot air (*inf.*), moonshine, pap, piffle (*inf.*), poppycock (*inf.*), rot, rubbish, tommyrot, tosh (*sl., chiefly Brit.*), tripe (*inf.*), trumpery, twaddle **2** *Chiefly U.S. & Canad.* = **litter,** dreck (*sl., chiefly US*), dregs, dross, garbage, junk (*inf.*), offscourings, refuse, rubbish, sweepings, waste
Antonyms *n* ≠ **nonsense:** logic, reason, sense, significance

trashy *adj* = **worthless,** brummagem, catchpenny, cheap, cheap-jack (*inf.*), crappy (*sl.*), flimsy, inferior, meretricious, of a sort *or* of sorts, poxy (*sl.*), rubbishy, shabby, shoddy, tawdry, thrown together, tinsel
Antonyms *adj* A1 *or* A-one (*inf.*), excellent, exceptional, first-class, first-rate, outstanding, superlative

trauma *n* **1** = **shock,** anguish, disturbance, jolt, ordeal, pain, strain, suffering, torture, upheaval, upset **2** = **injury,** agony, damage, hurt, wound

traumatic *adj* **1** = **shocking,** disturbing, painful, scarring, upsetting **2** = **wounding,** agonizing, damaging, hurtful, injurious
Antonyms *adj* ≠ **shocking:** calming, relaxing, therapeutic ≠ **wounding:** healing, helpful, therapeutic, wholesome

travail *n Literary* **1** = **toil,** distress, drudgery, effort, exertion, grind, hardship, hard work, labour, pain, slavery, slog, strain, stress, suffering, sweat, tears **2** = **labour pains,** birth pangs, childbirth, labour ◆ *vb* **3** = **toil,** drudge, grind (*inf.*), labour, slave, slog, suffer, sweat

travel *vb* **1, 2** = **go,** cross, journey, make a journey, make one's way, move, proceed, progress, ramble, roam, rove, take a trip, tour, traverse, trek, voyage, walk, wander, wend **6** = **be transmitted,** carry, get through, move ◆ *n* **12** *usually plural* = **journey,** excursion, expedition, globetrotting, movement, passage, peregrination, ramble, tour, touring, trip, voyage, walk, wandering

traveller *n* **1** = **voyager,** excursionist, explorer, globetrotter, gypsy, hiker, holiday-maker, journeyer, migrant, nomad, passenger, tourist, tripper, wanderer, wayfarer **2** = **travelling salesman,** agent, commercial traveller, rep, representative, salesman, sales rep

traverse *vb* **1** = **cross,** bridge, cover, cut across, go across, go over, make one's way across, negotiate, pass over, ply, range, roam, span, travel over, wander **2** = **oppose,** balk, contravene, counter, counteract, deny, frustrate, go against, hinder, impede, obstruct, thwart **6** = **examine,** check, consider, eye, inspect, investigate, look into, look over, pore over, range over, review, scan, scrutinize, study

travesty *n* **1** = **mockery,** burlesque, caricature, distortion, lampoon, parody, perversion, send-up (*Brit. inf.*), sham, spoof (*inf.*), takeoff (*inf.*) ◆ *vb* **2** = **mock,** burlesque, caricature, deride, distort, lampoon, make a mockery of, make fun of, parody, pervert, ridicule, send up (*Brit. inf.*), sham, spoof (*inf.*), take off (*inf.*)

trawl (trɔːl) *n* **1** Also called: **trawl net.** a large net, usually in the shape of a sock or bag, drawn at deep levels behind special boats (trawlers). **2** Also called: **trawl line.** a long line to which numerous shorter hooked lines are attached, suspended between buoys. **3** the act of trawling. ◆ *vb* **4** to catch (fish) with a trawl net or trawl line. **5** (*intr;* foll. by *for*) to seek or gather (information, etc.) from a wide variety of sources. [C17: from MDu. *traghelen* to drag, from L *trāgula* dragnet; see TRAIL]

trawler ('trɔːlə) *n* **1** a vessel used for trawling. **2** a person who trawls.

tray (treɪ) *n* **1** a thin flat board or plate of metal, plastic, etc., usually with a raised edge, on which things can be carried. **2** a shallow receptacle for papers, etc., sometimes forming a drawer in a cabinet or box. [OE *trieg*]

treacherous ❶ ('tretʃərəs) *adj* **1** betraying or likely to betray faith or confidence. **2** unstable, unreliable, or dangerous.
▸ **'treacherously** *adv* ▸ **'treacherousness** *n*

treachery ❶ ('tretʃərɪ) *n, pl* **treacheries. 1** the act or an instance of wilful betrayal. **2** the disposition to betray. [C13: from OF *trecherie,* from *trechier* to cheat]

treacle ('triːk^əl) *n* **1** Also called: **black treacle,** (US and Canad.) **molasses.** *Brit.* a dark viscous syrup obtained during the refining of sugar. **2** *Brit.* another name for **golden syrup. 3** anything sweet and cloying. [C14: from OF *triacle,* from L *thēriaca* antidote to poison]
▸ **'treacly** *adj*

tread ❶ (tred) *vb* **treads, treading, trod; trodden** *or* **trod. 1** to walk or trample in, on, over, or across (something). **2** (when *intr,* foll. by *on*) to crush or squash by or as if by treading. **3** (*intr;* sometimes foll. by *on*) to subdue or repress. **4** (*tr*) to do by walking or dancing: *to tread a measure.* **5** (*tr*) (of a male bird) to copulate with (a female bird). **6 tread lightly.** to proceed with delicacy or tact. **7 tread water.** to stay afloat in an upright position by moving the legs in a walking motion. ◆ *n* **8** a manner or style of walking, dancing, etc.: *a light tread.* **9** the act of treading. **10** the top surface of a step in a staircase. **11** the outer part of a tyre or wheel that makes contact with the road, esp. the grooved surface of a pneumatic tyre. **12** the part of a rail that wheels touch. **13** the part of a shoe that is generally in contact with the ground. [OE *tredan*]
▸ **'treader** *n*

treadle ('tred^əl) *n* **1** a lever operated by the foot to drive a machine. ◆ *vb* **treadles, treadling, treadled. 2** to work (a machine) with a treadle. [OE *tredel,* from *trǣde* something firm, from *tredan* to tread]

treadmill ('tred,mɪl) *n* **1** Also called: **treadwheel.** (formerly) an apparatus turned by the weight of men or animals climbing steps on the periphery of a cylinder or wheel. **2** a dreary round or routine. **3** an exercise machine that consists of a continuous moving belt on which to walk or jog.

treas. *abbrev. for:* **1** treasurer. **2** treasury.

treason ❶ ('triːz^ən) *n* **1** betrayal of one's sovereign or country, esp. by attempting to overthrow the government. **2** any treachery or betrayal. [C13: from OF *traïson,* from L *trāditiō* a handing over; see TRADITION]
▸ **'treasonable** *or* **'treasonous** *adj* ▸ **'treasonably** *adv*

treasure ❶ ('treʒə) *n* **1** wealth and riches, usually hoarded, esp. in the form of money, precious metals, or gems. **2** a thing or person that is highly prized or valued. ◆ *vb* **treasures, treasuring, treasured.** (*tr*) **3** to prize highly as valuable, rare, or costly. **4** to store up and save; hoard. [C12: from OF *tresor,* from L *thēsaurus* anything hoarded, from Gk *thēsauros*]

treasure hunt *n* a game in which players act upon successive clues to find a hidden prize.

treasurer ('treʒərə) *n* a person appointed to look after the funds of a society, company, city, or other governing body.
▸ **'treasurership** *n*

Treasurer ('treʒərə) *n* (in Australia) the minister of finance.

treasure-trove *n* **1** *Brit. Law.* valuable articles, such as coins, etc., found hidden and of unknown ownership. **2** any valuable discovery. [C16: from Anglo-F *tresor trové* treasure found, from OF *tresor* TREASURE + *trover* to find]

treasury ❶ ('treʒərɪ) *n, pl* **treasuries. 1** a storage place for treasure. **2** the revenues or funds of a government, private organization, or individual. **3** a place where funds are kept and disbursed. **4** a person or thing regarded as a valuable source of information. **5** a collection of highly valued poems, etc.; anthology. **6** Also: **treasure house.** a source of valuable items: *a treasury of information.* [C13: from OF *tresorie,* from *tresor* TREASURE]

Treasury ('treʒərɪ) *n* (in various countries) the government department in charge of finance.

Treasury Bench *n* (in Britain) the front bench to the right of the Speaker in the House of Commons, traditionally reserved for members of the Government.

treasury note *n* a note issued by a government treasury and generally receivable as legal tender for any debt.

treat ❶ (triːt) *n* **1** a celebration, entertainment, gift, or feast given for or to someone and paid for by another. **2** any delightful surprise or specially pleasant occasion. **3** the act of treating. ◆ *vb* **4** (*tr*) to deal with or regard in a certain manner: *she treats school as a joke.* **5** (*tr*) to apply treatment to. **6** (*tr*) to subject to a process or to the application of a substance. **7** (often foll. by *to*) to provide (someone) (with) as a treat. **8** (*intr;* usually foll. by *of*) to deal (with), as in writing or speaking. **9** (*intr*) to discuss settlement; negotiate. [C13: from OF *tretier,* from L *tractāre* to manage, from *trahere* to drag]
▸ **'treatable** *adj* ▸ **'treater** *n*

treatise ❶ ('triːtɪz) *n* a formal work on a subject, esp. one that deals systematically with its principles and conclusions. [C14: from Anglo-F *tretiz,* from OF *tretier* to TREAT]

treatment ❶ ('triːtmənt) *n* **1** the application of medicines, surgery, etc., to a patient. **2** the manner of handling a person or thing, as in a literary or artistic work. **3** the act, practice, or manner of treating. **4 the treatment.** *Sl.* the usual manner of dealing with a particular type of person (esp. in **give someone the (full) treatment**).

treaty ❶ ('triːtɪ) *n, pl* **treaties. 1a** a formal agreement between two or more states, such as an alliance or trade arrangement. **1b** the document in which such a contract is written. **2** any pact or agreement. **3** an agreement between two parties concerning the purchase of property at a price privately agreed between them. [C14: from OF *traité,* from Med. L *tractātus,* from L: discussion, from *tractāre* to manage; see TREAT]

treaty port *n History.* (in China, Japan, and Korea) a city, esp. a port, in which foreigners, esp. Westerners, were allowed by treaty to conduct trade.

treble ('treb^əl) *adj* **1** threefold; triple. **2** of or denoting a soprano voice or part or a high-pitched instrument. ◆ *n* **3** treble the amount, size, etc. **4** a soprano voice or part or a high-pitched instrument. **5** the highest register of a musical instrument. **6** the high-frequency response of an audio amplifier, esp. in a record player or tape recorder. **7a** the narrow inner ring on a dartboard. **7b** a hit on this ring. ◆ *vb* **trebles, trebling, trebled. 8** to make or become three times as much. [C14: from OF, from L *triplus* threefold]
▸ **'trebly** *adv, adj*

treble chance *n* a method of betting in football pools in which the chances of winning are related to the number of draws and the number of home and away wins forecast by the competitor.

treble clef *n Music.* the clef that establishes G a fifth above middle C as being on the second line of the staff. Symbol: 𝄞

trebuchet ('trebjʊ,ʃet) *or* **trebucket** ('triː,bʌkɪt) *n* a large medieval siege engine consisting of a sling on a pivoted wooden arm set in motion by the fall of a weight. [C13: from OF, from *trebuchier* to stumble, from *tre-* TRANS- + *-buchier,* from *buc* trunk of the body, of Gmc origin]

trecento (treɪ'tʃentəʊ) *n* the 14th century, esp. with reference to Italian art and literature. [C19: shortened from It. *mille trecento* one thousand three hundred]
▸ **tre'centist** *n*

tree (triː) *n* **1** any large woody perennial plant with a distinct trunk giv-

THESAURUS

treacherous *adj* **1 = disloyal,** deceitful, double-crossing (*inf.*), double-dealing, duplicitous, faithless, false, perfidious, recreant (*arch.*), traitorous, treasonable, unfaithful, unreliable, untrue, untrustworthy **2 = dangerous,** deceptive, hazardous, icy, perilous, precarious, risky, slippery, slippy (*inf. or dialect*), tricky, unreliable, unsafe, unstable
Antonyms *adj* ≠ **disloyal:** dependable, faithful, loyal, reliable, true, trustworthy ≠ **dangerous:** reliable, safe

treachery *n* **1, 2 = betrayal,** disloyalty, double-cross (*inf.*), double-dealing, duplicity, faithlessness, infidelity, perfidiousness, perfidy, stab in the back, treason
Antonyms *n* allegiance, dependability, faithfulness, fealty, fidelity, loyalty, reliability

tread *vb* **1 = step,** hike, march, pace, plod, stamp, stride, tramp, trudge, walk **2 = crush underfoot,** squash, trample **3 = repress,** bear down, crush, oppress, quell, ride roughshod over, subdue, subjugate, suppress ◆ *n* **8 = step,** footfall, footstep, gait, pace, stride, walk

treason *n* **1, 2 = disloyalty,** disaffection, duplicity, lese-majesty, mutiny, perfidy, sedition, subversion, traitorousness, treachery
Antonyms *n* allegiance, faithfulness, fealty, fidelity, loyalty, patriotism

treasonable *adj* **1, 2 = disloyal,** false, mutinous, perfidious, seditious, subversive, traitorous, treacherous, treasonous
Antonyms *adj* dependable, faithful, loyal, patriotic, reliable, trustworthy

treasure *n* **1 = riches,** cash, fortune, funds, gold, jewels, money, valuables, wealth **2** *Informal* **= darling,** apple of one's eye, gem, jewel, nonpareil, paragon, pearl, precious, pride and joy, prize ◆ *vb* **3 = prize,** adore, cherish, dote upon, esteem, hold dear, idolize, love, revere, value, venerate, worship **4 = hoard,** accumulate, cache, collect, garner, husband, lay up, salt away, save, stash (away) (*inf.*), store up

treasury *n* **1 = storehouse,** bank, cache, hoard, repository, store, vault **2 = funds,** assets, capital, coffers, exchequer, finances, money, resources, revenues

treat *n* **1 = entertainment,** banquet, celebration, feast, gift, party, refreshment **2 = pleasure,** delight, enjoyment, fun, gratification, joy, satisfaction, surprise, thrill ◆ *vb* **4 = behave towards,** act towards, consider, deal with, handle, look upon, manage, regard, use **5 = take care of,** apply treatment to, attend to, care for, doctor, medicate, nurse **7 = provide,** buy for, entertain, feast, foot *or* pay the bill, give, lay on, pay for, regale, stand (*inf.*), take out, wine and dine **8** *usually foll. by* **of = deal with,** be concerned with, contain, discourse upon, discuss, go into, touch upon **9 = negotiate,** bargain, come to terms, confer, have talks, make terms, parley

treatise *n* **= paper,** disquisition, dissertation, essay, exposition, monograph, pamphlet, study, thesis, tract, work, writing

treatment *n* **1 = care,** cure, healing, medication, medicine, remedy, surgery, therapy **2 = handling,** action, behaviour, conduct, dealing, management, manipulation, reception, usage

treaty *n* **1a, 2 = agreement,** alliance, bargain, bond, compact, concordat, contract, convention, covenant, entente, pact

ing rise to branches. Related adj: **arboreal.** **2** any plant that resembles this. **3** a wooden post, bar, etc. **4** See **family tree, shoetree, saddletree.** **5** *Chem.* a treelike crystal growth. **6** a branching diagrammatic representation of something. **7 at the top of the tree.** in the highest position of a profession, etc. **8 up a tree.** *US & Canad. inf.* in a difficult situation; trapped or stumped. ◆ *vb* **trees, treeing, treed.** (*tr*) **9** to drive or force up a tree. **10** to stretch on a shoetree. [OE *treo*]
▸ **'treeless** *adj* ▸ **'treelessness** *n* ▸ **'tree,like** *adj*

tree creeper *n* any of a family of small songbirds of the N hemisphere, having a slender downward-curving bill. They creep up trees to feed on insects.

tree diagram *n* a diagram in which relationships are represented by lines and nodes having other lines branching off from them.

tree fern *n* any of numerous large tropical ferns having a trunklike stem.

tree frog *n* any of various arboreal frogs of SE Asia, Australia, and America.

treehopper ('triː,hɒpə) *n* any of a family of insects which live among trees and have a large hoodlike thoracic process curving backwards over the body.

tree kangaroo *n* any of several arboreal kangaroos of New Guinea and N Australia, having hind legs and forelegs of a similar length.

tree line *n* the zone, at high altitudes or high latitudes, beyond which no trees grow. Trees growing between the timber line and the tree line are typically stunted.

treen ('triːən) *adj* **1** made of wood; wooden. ◆ *n* **2** dishes and other utensils made of wood. [OE *trēowen*, from *trēow* tree]
▸ **'treen,ware** *n*

treenail *or* **trenail** ('triːneɪl, 'trɛnᵊl) *n* a dowel used for pinning planks or timbers together.

tree of heaven *n* another name for **ailanthus.**

tree shrew *n* any of a family of small arboreal mammals of SE Asia having large eyes and resembling squirrels.

tree sparrow *n* **1** a small European weaverbird similar to the house sparrow but having a brown head. **2** a small North American finch.

tree surgery *n* the treatment of damaged trees by filling cavities, applying braces, etc.
▸ **tree surgeon** *n*

tree toad *n* a less common name for **tree frog.**

tree tomato *n* **1** an arborescent shrub of South America bearing red egg-shaped edible fruit. **2** the fruit of this plant. ◆ Also called: **tamarillo.**

tref (treɪf) *adj Judaism.* ritually unfit to be eaten. [Yiddish, from Heb. *terēphāh*, lit.: torn (i.e., animal meat torn by beasts), from *tāraf* to tear]

trefoil ('trɛfɔɪl) *n* **1** any of a genus of leguminous plants having leaves divided into three leaflets. **2** any of various related plants having similar leaves. **3** a flower or leaf having three lobes. **4** *Archit.* an ornament in the form of three arcs arranged in a circle. [C14: from Anglo-F *trifoil*, from L *trifolium* three-leaved herb]
▸ **'trefoiled** *adj*

trek ❶ (trɛk) *n* **1** a long and often difficult journey. **2** *S. African.* a journey or stage of a journey, esp. a migration by ox wagon. ◆ *vb* **treks, trekking, trekked.** **3** (*intr*) to make a trek. [C19: from Afrik., from MDu. *trekken* to travel]

trellis ('trɛlɪs) *n* **1** a structure of latticework, esp. one used to support climbing plants. ◆ *vb* (*tr*) **2** to interweave (strips of wood, etc.) to make a trellis. **3** to provide or support with a trellis. [C14: from OF *treliz* fabric of open texture, from LL *trilīcius* woven with three threads, from L TRI- + *līcium* thread]
▸ **'trellis,work** *n*

trematode ('trɛmə,təʊd, 'triː-) *n* any of a class of parasitic flatworms, which includes the flukes. [C19: from NL *Trematoda*, from Gk *trēmatōdēs* full of holes, from *trēma* hole]

tremble ❶ ('trɛmbᵊl) *vb* **trembles, trembling, trembled.** (*intr*) **1** to vibrate with short slight movements; quiver. **2** to shake involuntarily, as with cold or fear; shiver. **3** to experience fear or anxiety. ◆ *n* **4** the act or an instance of trembling. [C14: from OF *trembler*, from Med. L *tremulāre*, from L *tremulus* quivering, from *tremere* to quake]
▸ **'trembling** *adj* ▸ **'trembly** *adj*

trembler ('trɛmblə) *n* a device that vibrates to make or break an electrical circuit.

trembles ('trɛmbᵊlz) *n* (*functioning as sing*) a disease of cattle and sheep characterized by trembling.

trembling poplar *n* another name for **aspen.**

tremendous ❶ (trɪ'mɛndəs) *adj* **1** vast; huge. **2** *Inf.* very exciting or unusual. **3** *Inf.* (intensifier): *a tremendous help.* **4** *Arch.* terrible or dreadful. [C17: from L *tremendus* terrible, lit.: that is to be trembled at, from *tremere* to quake]
▸ **tre'mendously** *adv* ▸ **tre'mendousness** *n*

tremolo ('trɛmə,ləʊ) *n, pl* **tremolos.** *Music.* **1** (in playing the violin, cello, etc.) the rapid reiteration of a note or notes to produce a trembling effect. **2** (in singing) a fluctuation in pitch. **3** a device, as on an organ, that produces a tremolo effect. [C19: from It.: quavering, from Med. L *tremulāre* to TREMBLE]

tremor ❶ ('trɛmə) *n* **1** an involuntary shudder or vibration. **2** any trembling movement. **3** a vibrating or trembling effect, as of sound or light. **4** a minor earthquake. ◆ *vb* **5** (*intr*) to tremble. [C14: from L: a shaking, from *tremere* to tremble]
▸ **'tremorous** *adj*

tremulous ❶ ('trɛmjʊləs) *adj* **1** vibrating slightly; quavering; trembling. **2** showing or characterized by fear, anxiety, excitement, etc. [C17: from L *tremulus*, from *tremere* to shake]
▸ **'tremulously** *adv* ▸ **'tremulousness** *n*

trenail ('triːneɪl, 'trɛnᵊl) *n* a variant spelling of **treenail.**

trench ❶ (trɛntʃ) *n* **1** a deep ditch. **2** a ditch dug as a fortification, having a parapet of earth. ◆ *vb* **3** to make a trench in (a place). **4** (*tr*) to fortify with a trench. **5** to slash or be slashed. **6** (*intr*; foll. by *on* or *upon*) to encroach or verge. [C14: from OF *trenche* something cut, from *trenchier* to cut, from L *truncāre* to cut off]

trenchant ❶ ('trɛntʃənt) *adj* **1** keen or incisive: *trenchant criticism.* **2** vigorous and effective: *a trenchant foreign policy.* **3** distinctly defined. **4** *Arch. or poetic.* sharp. [C14: from OF *trenchant* cutting, from *trenchier* to cut; see TRENCH]
▸ **'trenchancy** *n* ▸ **'trenchantly** *adv*

trench coat *n* a belted waterproof coat resembling a military officer's coat.

trencher ('trɛntʃə) *n* **1** (esp. formerly) a wooden board on which food was served or cut. **2** Also called: **trencher cap.** a mortarboard. [C14 *trenchour* knife, plate for carving on, from OF *trencheoir*, from *trenchier* to cut; see TRENCH]

trencherman ('trɛntʃəmən) *n, pl* **trenchermen.** a person who enjoys food; hearty eater.

trench fever *n* an acute infectious disease characterized by fever and muscular aches and pains and transmitted by lice.

trench foot *n* a form of frostbite affecting persons standing for long periods in cold water.

trench mortar *or* **gun** *n* a portable mortar used in trench warfare to shoot projectiles at a high trajectory over a short range.

trench warfare *n* a type of warfare in which opposing armies face each other in entrenched positions.

trend ❶ (trɛnd) *n* **1** general tendency or direction. **2** fashion; mode. ◆ *vb* **3** (*intr*) to take a certain trend. [OE *trendan* to turn]

trendsetter ❶ ('trɛnd,sɛtə) *n* a person or thing that creates, or may create, a new fashion.
▸ **'trend,setting** *adj*

trendy ❶ ('trɛndɪ) *Brit. inf.* ◆ *adj* **trendier, trendiest.** **1** consciously fashionable. ◆ *n, pl* **trendies.** **2** a trendy person.
▸ **'trendily** *adv* ▸ **'trendiness** *n*

trente et quarante (*French* trɑ̃t e karɑ̃t) *n Cards.* another name for **rouge et noir.** [C17: F, lit.: thirty and forty; from the rule that forty is the maximum number that may be dealt and the winning colour is the one closest to thirty-one]

trepan (trɪ'pæn) *n* **1** *Surgery.* an instrument resembling a carpenter's

THESAURUS

trek *n* **1 = journey**, expedition, footslog, hike, long haul, march, odyssey, safari, slog, tramp ◆ *vb* **3 = journey**, footslog, hike, march, plod, range, roam, rove, slog, traipse (*inf.*), tramp, trudge, yomp

tremble *vb* **1, 2 = shake**, oscillate, quake, quake in one's boots, quiver, rock, shake in one's boots *or* shoes, shiver, shudder, teeter, totter, vibrate, wobble ◆ *n* **4 = shake**, oscillation, quake, quiver, shiver, shudder, tremor, vibration, wobble

tremendous *adj* **1 = huge**, awesome, colossal, enormous, formidable, gargantuan, gigantic, great, immense, mammoth, monstrous, prodigious, stellar (*inf.*), stupendous, terrific, titanic, towering, vast, whopping (*inf.*) **2 = excellent**, amazing, awesome (*sl.*), exceptional, extraordinary, fabulous (*inf.*), fantastic (*inf.*), great, incredible, marvellous, sensational (*inf.*), terrific (*inf.*), wonderful **4** *Archaic* **= dreadful**, appalling, awful, fearful, frightful, terrible
Antonyms *adj* ≠ **huge:** diminutive, little, minuscule, minute, small, tiny ≠ **excellent:** abysmal, appalling, average, awful, dreadful, mediocre, no great shakes (*inf.*), ordinary, rotten, run-of-the-mill, so-so, terrible

tremor *n* **1, 2 = shake**, agitation, quaking, quaver, quiver, quivering, shaking, shiver, tremble, trembling, vibration, wobble **4 = earthquake**, quake (*inf.*), shock

tremulous *adj* **1, 2 = trembling**, aflutter, afraid, agitated, agog, anxious, aquiver, excited, fearful, frightened, jittery (*inf.*), jumpy, nervous, quavering, quivering, quivery, scared, shaking, shivering, timid, vibrating, wavering

trench *n* **1 = ditch**, channel, cut, drain, earthwork, entrenchment, excavation, fosse, furrow, gutter, pit, trough, waterway

trenchant *adj* **1 = scathing**, acerbic, acid, acidulous, acute, astringent, biting, caustic, cutting, hurtful, incisive, keen, mordacious, mordant, penetrating, piquant, pointed, pungent, sarcastic, severe, sharp, tart, vitriolic **2 = effective**, driving, effectual, emphatic, energetic, forceful, potent, powerful, strong, vigorous **3 = clear**, clear-cut, crisp, distinct, distinctly defined, explicit, salient, unequivocal, well-defined
Antonyms *adj* ≠ **scathing:** appeasing, kind, mollifying, soothing ≠ **clear:** ill-defined, indistinct, nebulous, obscure, unclear, vague, woolly

trend *n* **1 = tendency**, bias, course, current, direction, drift, flow, inclination, leaning **2 = fashion**, craze, fad (*inf.*), look, mode, rage, style, thing, vogue ◆ *vb* **3 = tend**, bend, flow, head, incline, lean, run, stretch, swing, turn, veer

trendsetter *n* **= leader of fashion**, arbiter of taste, avant-gardist, pacemaker, pacesetter

trendy *adj Brit. informal* **1 = fashionable**, flash (*inf.*), in (*sl.*), in fashion, in vogue, latest, modish, now (*inf.*), stylish, up to the minute, voguish, with it (*inf.*) ◆ *n Brit. informal* **2 = poser** (*inf.*), pseud (*inf.*)

brace and bit formerly used to remove circular sections of bone from the skull. **2** a tool for cutting out circular blanks or for making grooves around a fixed centre. ◆ *vb* **trepans, trepanning, trepanned.** (*tr*) **3** to cut (a hole or groove) with a trepan. **4** *Surgery.* another word for **trephine.** [C14: from Med. L *trepanum* rotary saw, from Gk *trupanon* auger, from *trupan* to bore, from *trupa* a hole]
▸**trepanation** (ˌtrɛpəˈneɪʃən) *n*

trepang (trɪˈpæŋ) *n* any of various large sea cucumbers of tropical Oriental seas, the body walls of which are used as food by the Japanese and Chinese. [C18: from Malay *tĕripang*]

trephine (trɪˈfiːn) *n* **1** a surgical sawlike instrument for removing circular sections of bone esp. from the skull. ◆ *vb* **trephines, trephining, trephined.** **2** (*tr*) to remove a circular section of bone from (esp. the skull). [C17: from F *tréphine,* from obs. E *trefine* TREPAN, allegedly from L *trēs fīnēs,* lit.: three ends]
▸**trephination** (ˌtrɛfɪˈneɪʃən) *n*

trepidation ⓣ (ˌtrɛpɪˈdeɪʃən) *n* **1** a state of fear or anxiety. **2** a condition of quaking or palpitation, esp. one caused by anxiety. [C17: from L *trepidātiō,* from *trepidāre* to be in a state of alarm]

trespass ⓣ (ˈtrɛspəs) *vb* (*intr*) **1** (often foll. by *on* or *upon*) to go or intrude (on the property, privacy, or preserves of another) with no right or permission. **2** *Law.* to commit trespass. **3** *Arch.* (often foll. by *against*) to sin or transgress. ◆ *n* **4** *Law.* **4a** any unlawful act committed with force, which causes injury to another person, his property or his rights. **4b** a wrongful entry upon another's land. **5** an intrusion on another's privacy or preserves. **6** a sin or offence. [C13: from OF *trespas* a passage, from *trespasser* to pass through, ult. from L *passus* a PACE[1]]
▸ˈ**trespasser** *n*

tress ⓣ (trɛs) *n* **1** (*often pl*) a lock of hair, esp. a long lock of woman's hair. **2** a plait or braid of hair. ◆ *vb* (*tr*) **3** to arrange in tresses. [C13: from OF *trece,* from ?]
▸ˈ**tressy** *adj*

trestle (ˈtrɛsᵊl) *n* **1** a framework in the form of a horizontal member supported at each end by a pair of splayed legs, used to carry scaffold boards, a table top, etc. **2a** a framework of timber, metal, or reinforced concrete that is used to support a bridge or ropeway. **2b** a bridge constructed of such frameworks. [C14: from OF *trestel,* ult. from L *trānstrum* transom]

trestlework (ˈtrɛsᵊlˌwɜːk) *n* an arrangement of trestles, esp. one that supports a bridge.

trevally (trɪˈvælɪ) *n, pl* **trevallies.** *Austral. & NZ.* any of various food and game fishes of the genus *Caranx.* [C19: prob. alteration of *cavally,* from *cavalla* species of tropical fish, from Sp. *caballa* horse]

trews (truːz) *pl n Chiefly Brit.* close-fitting trousers of tartan cloth. [C16: from Scot. Gaelic *triubhas,* from OF *trebus*]

trey (treɪ) *n* any card or dice throw with three spots. [C14: from OF *treis* three, from L *trēs*]

tri- *prefix* **1** three or thrice: *triaxial; trigon; trisect.* **2** occurring every three: *trimonthly.* [from L *trēs,* Gk *treis*]

triable (ˈtraɪəbᵊl) *adj* **1** subject to trial in a court of law. **2** *Rare.* able to be tested.

triacid (traɪˈæsɪd) *adj* capable of reacting with three molecules of a monobasic acid.

triad ⓣ (ˈtraɪæd) *n* **1** a group of three; trio. **2** *Chem.* an atom, element, group, or ion that has a valency of three. **3** *Music.* a three-note chord consisting of a note and the third and fifth above it. **4** an aphoristic literary form used in medieval Welsh and Irish literature. [C16: from LL *trias,* from Gk]
▸**triˈadic** *adj* ▸ˈ**triadism** *n*

Triad (ˈtraɪæd) *n* any of several Chinese secret societies, esp. one involved in criminal activities, such as drug trafficking.

triage (ˈtraɪɪdʒ) *n* **1** the action of sorting casualties, patients, etc. according to priority. **2** the allocating of limited resources on a basis of expediency rather than moral principles. [C18: from F; see TRY, -AGE]

trial ⓣ (ˈtraɪəl, traɪl) *n* **1a** the act or an instance of trying or proving; test or experiment. **1b** (*as modifier*): *a trial run.* **2** *Law.* **2a** the judicial examination and determination of the issues in a civil or criminal cause by a competent tribunal. **2b** the determination of an accused person's guilt or innocence after hearing evidence and the judicial examination of the issues involved. **2c** (*as modifier*): *trial proceedings.* **3** an effort or attempt to do something. **4** trouble or grief. **5** an annoying or frustrating person or thing. **6** (*often pl*) a competition for individuals: *sheepdog trials.* **7** a motorcycling competition in which the skills of the riders are tested over rough ground. **8 on trial. 8a** undergoing trial, esp. before a court of law. **8b** being tested, as before a commitment to purchase. ◆ *vb* **trials, trialling, trialled.** **9** to test or make experimental use of (something): *the idea has been trialled in several schools.* [C16: from Anglo-F, from *trier* to TRY]
▸ˈ**trialling** *n*

trial and error *n* a method of discovery, solving problems, etc., based on practical experiment and experience rather than on theory: *he learned to cook by trial and error.*

trial balance *n Book-keeping.* a statement of all the debit and credit balances in the ledger of a double-entry system, drawn up to test their equality.

triallist *or* **trialist** (ˈtraɪəlɪst, ˈtraɪlɪst) *n* **1** a person who takes part in a competition, esp. a motorcycle trial. **2** *Sport.* a person who takes part in a preliminary match or heat held to determine selection for an event, a team, etc.

triangle (ˈtraɪˌæŋgᵊl) *n* **1** *Geom.* a three-sided polygon that can be classified by angle, as in an acute triangle, or by side, as in an equilateral triangle. **2** any object shaped like a triangle. **3** any situation involving three parties or points of view. **4** *Music.* a percussion instrument consisting of a sonorous metal bar bent into a triangular shape, beaten with a metal stick. **5** a group of three. [C14: from L *triangulum* (n), from *triangulus* (adj), from TRI- + *angulus* corner]
▸**triangular** (traɪˈæŋgjʊlə) *adj*

triangle of forces *n Physics.* a triangle whose sides represent the magnitudes and directions of three forces in equilibrium.

triangulate *vb* (traɪˈæŋgjʊˌleɪt), **triangulates, triangulating, triangulated.** (*tr*) **1a** to survey by the method of triangulation. **1b** to calculate trigonometrically. **2** to divide into triangles. **3** to make triangular. ◆ *adj* (traɪˈæŋgjʊlɪt, -ˌleɪt). **4** marked with or composed of triangles.
▸**triˈangulately** *adv*

triangulation (traɪˌæŋgjʊˈleɪʃən) *n* a method of surveying in which an area is divided into triangles, one side (the base line) and all angles of which are measured and the lengths of the other lines calculated trigonometrically.

triangulation station *n* a point on a hilltop, etc., used for triangulation by a surveyor.

Triassic (traɪˈæsɪk) *adj* **1** of or formed in the first period of the Mesozoic era. ◆ *n* **2 the.** Also called: **Trias.** the Triassic period or rock system. [C19: from L *trias* triad, from the three subdivisions]

triathlon (traɪˈæθlɒn) *n* an athletic contest in which each athlete competes in three different events, swimming, cycling, and running. [C20: from TRI- + Gk *athlon* contest]
▸ˌ**triˈathlete** *n*

triatomic (ˌtraɪəˈtɒmɪk) *adj Chem.* having three atoms in the molecule.

tribade (ˈtrɪbɑːd) *n* a lesbian who practises tribadism. [C17: from L *tribas,* from Gk *tribein* to rub]

tribadism (ˈtrɪbədɪzəm) *n* a lesbian practice in which one partner lies on top of the other and simulates the male role in heterosexual intercourse.

tribalism (ˈtraɪbəˌlɪzəm) *n* **1** the state of existing as a tribe. **2** the customs and beliefs of a tribal society. **3** loyalty to a tribe.
▸ˈ**tribalist** *n, adj* ▸ˌ**tribalˈistic** *adj*

tribasic (traɪˈbeɪsɪk) *adj* **1** (of an acid) containing three replaceable hydrogen atoms in the molecule. **2** (of a molecule) containing three monovalent basic atoms or groups.

tribe ⓣ (traɪb) *n* **1** a social division of a people, esp. of a preliterate people, defined in terms of common descent, territory, culture, etc. **2** an ethnic or ancestral division of ancient cultures, esp.: **2a** one of the political divisions of the Roman people. **2b** any of the 12 divisions of ancient Israel, each of which was believed to be descended from one of the 12 patriarchs. **3** *Inf.* **3a** a large number of persons, animals, etc. **3b** a specific class or group of persons. **3c** a family, esp. a large one. **4** *Biol.* a taxonomic group that is a subdivision of a subfamily. [C13: from L *tribus*]
▸ˈ**tribal** *adj*

tribesman (ˈtraɪbzmən) *n, pl* **tribesmen.** a member of a tribe.

tribo- *combining form.* indicating friction: *triboelectricity.* [from Gk *tribein* to rub]

triboelectricity (ˌtraɪbəʊɪlɛkˈtrɪsɪtɪ, -ˌiːlɛk-) *n* electricity generated by friction.

THESAURUS

trepidation *n* **1, 2** *Formal* = **anxiety**, agitation, alarm, apprehension, blue funk (*inf.*), butterflies (*inf.*), cold feet (*inf.*), consternation, dismay, disquiet, disturbance, dread, emotion, excitement, fear, fright, jitters (*inf.*), nervousness, palpitation, perturbation, quivering, shaking, the heebie-jeebies (*sl.*), trembling, tremor, uneasiness, worry
Antonyms *n* aplomb, calm, composure, confidence, coolness, equanimity, self-assurance

trespass *vb* **1** = **intrude**, encroach, infringe, invade, obtrude, poach **3** *Archaic* = **sin**, offend, transgress, violate, wrong ◆ *n* **5** = **intrusion**, encroachment, infringement, invasion, poaching, unlawful entry, wrongful entry **6** *Old-fashioned* = **sin**, breach, crime, delinquency, error, evildoing, fault, infraction, iniquity, injury, misbehaviour, misconduct, misdeed, misdemeanour, offence, transgression, wrongdoing

trespasser *n* **5** = **intruder**, infringer, interloper, invader, poacher, unwelcome visitor **6** *Archaic* = **sinner**, criminal, delinquent, evildoer, malefactor, offender, transgressor, wrongdoer

tress *n* **1, 2** = **hair**, braid, curl, lock, pigtail, plait, ringlet

triad *n* **1** = **threesome**, trilogy, trine, trinity, trio, triple, triplet, triptych, triumvirate, triune

trial *n* **1a** = **test**, assay, audition, check, dry run (*inf.*), examination, experience, experiment, probation, proof, testing, test-run ◆ *modifier* **1b** = **experimental**, exploratory, pilot, probationary, provisional, testing ◆ *n* **2a** *Law* = **hearing**, contest, industrial tribunal, judicial examination, litigation, tribunal **3** = **attempt**, crack (*inf.*), effort, endeavour, go (*inf.*), shot (*inf.*), stab (*inf.*), try, venture, whack (*inf.*) **4** = **hardship**, adversity, affliction, burden, cross to bear, distress, grief, hard times, load, misery, ordeal, pain, suffering, tribulation, trouble, unhappiness, vexation, woe, wretchedness **5** = **nuisance**, bane, bother, drag (*inf.*), hassle (*inf.*), irritation, pain in the arse (*taboo sl.*), pain in the neck (*inf.*), pest, plague (*inf.*), thorn in one's flesh *or* side, vexation

tribe *n* **1** = **race**, blood, caste, clan, class, division, dynasty, ethnic group, family, gens, house, people, seed (*chiefly Biblical*), sept, stock

tribology (traɪˈbɒlədʒɪ) *n* the study of friction, lubrication, and wear between moving surfaces.

triboluminescence (ˌtraɪbəʊˌluːmɪˈnɛsəns) *n* luminescence produced by friction, such as the emission of light when certain crystals are crushed.
▸ˌ**triboˌlumiˈnescent** *adj*

tribrach (ˈtraɪbræk, ˈtrɪb-) *n* a metrical foot of three short syllables. [C16: from L *tribrachys,* from Gk, from TRI- + *brakhus* short]

tribromoethanol (traɪˌbrəʊməʊˈɛθəˌnɒl) *n* a soluble white crystalline compound with a slight aromatic odour, used as a general anaesthetic.

tribulation ❶ (ˌtrɪbjʊˈleɪʃən) *n* **1** a cause of distress. **2** a state of suffering or distress. [C13: from OF, from Church L *trībulātiō,* from L *trībulāre* to afflict, from *trībulum* a threshing board, from *terere* to rub]

tribunal ❶ (traɪˈbjuːnᵊl, trɪ-) *n* **1** a court of justice. **2** (in England) a special court, convened by the government to inquire into a specific matter. **3** a raised platform containing the seat of a judge. [C16: from L *tribūnus* TRIBUNE[1]]

tribune[1] (ˈtrɪbjuːn) *n* **1** (in ancient Rome) **1a** an officer elected by the plebs to protect their interests. **1b** a senior military officer. **2** a person who upholds public rights. [C14: from L *tribunus,* prob. from *tribus* tribe]
▸**tribunate** (ˈtrɪbjʊnɪt) *or* ˈ**tribuneship** *n*

tribune[2] (ˈtrɪbjuːn) *n* **1a** the apse of a Christian basilica that contains the bishop's throne. **1b** the throne itself. **2** a gallery or raised area in a church. **3** *Rare.* a raised platform; dais. [C17: via F from It. *tribuna,* from Med. L *tribūna,* var. of L *tribūnal* TRIBUNAL]

tributary (ˈtrɪbjʊtərɪ) *n, pl* **tributaries. 1** a stream, river, or glacier that feeds another larger one. **2** a person, nation, or people that pays tribute. ◆ *adj* **3** (of a stream, etc.) feeding a larger stream. **4** given or owed as a tribute. **5** paying tribute.
▸ˈ**tributarily** *adv*

tribute ❶ (ˈtrɪbjuːt) *n* **1** a gift or statement made in acknowledgment, gratitude, or admiration. **2** a payment by one ruler or state to another, usually as an acknowledgment of submission. **3** the obligation to pay tribute. [C14: from L *tribūtum,* from *tribuere* to grant (orig.: to distribute among the tribes), from *tribus* tribe]

trice ❶ (traɪs) *n* a moment; instant (esp. in **in a trice**). [C15 (in *at* or *in a trice,* in the sense: at one tug): apparent substantive use of *trice* to haul up, from MDu. *trīse* pulley]

tricentenary (ˌtraɪsɛnˈtiːnərɪ) *or* **tricentennial** (ˌtraɪsɛnˈtɛnɪəl) *adj* **1** of a period of 300 years. **2** of a 300th anniversary. ◆ *n, pl* **tricentenaries** *or* **tricentennials. 3** an anniversary of 300 years.

triceps (ˈtraɪsɛps) *n, pl* **tricepses** (-sɛpsɪz) *or* **triceps.** any muscle having three heads, esp. the one that extends the forearm. [C16: from L, from TRI- + *caput* head]

trichiasis (trɪˈkaɪəsɪs) *n Pathol.* an abnormal position of the eyelashes that causes irritation when they rub against the eyeball. [C17: via LL from Gk *trikhiasis,* from *thrix* a hair]

trichina (trɪˈkaɪnə) *n, pl* **trichinae** (-niː). a parasitic nematode worm occurring in the intestines of pigs, rats, and man and producing larvae that form cysts in skeletal muscle. [C19: from NL, from Gk *trikhinos* relating to hair, from *thrix* a hair]
▸**trichinous** (ˈtrɪkɪnəs) *adj*

trichinosis (ˌtrɪkɪˈnəʊsɪs) *n* a disease characterized by nausea, fever, diarrhoea, and swelling of the muscles, caused by ingestion of pork infected with trichina larvae. [C19: from NL TRICHINA]

trichloride (traɪˈklɔːraɪd) *n* any compound that contains three chlorine atoms per molecule.

tricho- *or before a vowel* **trich-** *combining form.* indicating hair or a part resembling hair: *trichocyst.* [from Gk *thrix* (genitive *trikhos*) hair]

trichology (trɪˈkɒlədʒɪ) *n* the branch of medicine concerned with the hair and its diseases.
▸**triˈchologist** *n*

trichomoniasis (ˌtrɪkəʊməˈnaɪəsɪs) *n* inflammation of the vagina caused by infection with parasitic protozoa. [C19: NL]

trichopteran (traɪˈkɒptərən) *n* **1** any insect of the order *Trichoptera,* which comprises the caddis flies. ◆ *adj* **2** Also: **trichopterous** (trɪˈkɒptərəs). of or belonging to the order *Trichoptera.* [C19: from NL *Trichoptera,* lit.: having hairy wings, from Gk *thrix* a hair + *pteron* wing]

trichosis (trɪˈkəʊsɪs) *n* any abnormal condition or disease of the hair. [C19: via NL from Gk *trikhōsis* growth of hair]

trichotomy (traɪˈkɒtəmɪ) *n, pl* **trichotomies. 1** division into three categories. **2** *Theol.* the division of man into body, spirit, and soul. [C17: prob. from NL *trichotomia,* from Gk *trikhotomein* to divide into three]
▸**trichotomic** (ˌtrɪkəˈtɒmɪk) *or* **triˈchotomous** *adj*

trichroism (ˈtraɪkrəʊˌɪzəm) *n* a property of biaxial crystals as a result of which they show a difference in colour when viewed along three different axes. [C19: from Gk *trikhroos* three-coloured, from TRI- + *khrōma* colour]

trichromatic (ˌtraɪkrəʊˈmætɪk) *or* **trichromic** (traɪˈkrəʊmɪk) *adj* **1** involving the combination of three primary colours. **2** of or having normal colour vision. **3** having or involving three colours.
▸**triˈchromaˌtism** *n*

trick ❶ (trɪk) *n* **1** a deceitful or cunning action or plan. **2a** a mischievous, malicious, or humorous action or plan; joke. **2b** (*as modifier*): *a trick spider.* **3** an illusory or magical feat. **4** a simple feat learned by an animal or person. **5** an adroit or ingenious device; knack: *a trick of the trade.* **6** a habit or mannerism. **7** a turn of duty. **8** *Cards.* a batch of cards containing one from each player, usually played in turn and won by the player or side that plays the card with the highest value. **9 can't take a trick.** *Austral. sl.* to be consistently unsuccessful or unlucky. **10 do the trick.** *Inf.* to produce the desired result. **11 how's tricks?** *Sl.* how are you? **12 turn a trick.** *Sl.* (of a prostitute) to gain a customer. ◆ *vb* **13** (*tr*) to defraud, deceive, or cheat (someone). ◆ See also **trick out.** [C15: from OF *trique,* from *trikier* to deceive, ult. from L *trīcārī* to play tricks]

trick cyclist *n* **1** a cyclist who performs tricks, such as in a circus. **2** a slang term for **psychiatrist.**

trickery ❶ (ˈtrɪkərɪ) *n, pl* **trickeries.** the practice or an instance of using tricks.

trickle ❶ (ˈtrɪkᵊl) *vb* **trickles, trickling, trickled. 1** to run or cause to run in thin or slow streams. **2** (*intr*) to move gradually: *the crowd trickled away.* ◆ *n* **3** a thin, irregular, or slow flow of something. **4** the act of trickling. [C14: ? imit.]
▸ˈ**trickling** *adj*

trickle charger *n* a small mains-operated battery charger, esp. one used by car owners.

trickle-down *adj* of or concerning the theory that granting concessions such as tax cuts to the rich will benefit all levels of society by stimulating the economy.

trick or treat *sentence substitute. Chiefly US & Canad.* a customary cry used by children at Halloween when they call at houses in disguise, indicating that they want a present of sweets, apples, or money and, if refused, will play a trick on the householder.

trick out ❶ *or* **up** *vb* (*tr, adv*) to dress up; deck out: *tricked out in frilly dresses.*

trickster ❶ (ˈtrɪkstə) *n* a person who deceives or plays tricks.

tricksy (ˈtrɪksɪ) *adj* **tricksier, tricksiest. 1** playing tricks habitually; mischievous. **2** crafty or difficult to deal with.
▸ˈ**tricksiness** *n*

tricky ❶ (ˈtrɪkɪ) *adj* **trickier, trickiest. 1** involving snags or difficulties. **2** needing careful handling. **3** sly; wily: *a tricky dealer.*
▸ˈ**trickily** *adv* ▸ˈ**trickiness** *n*

THESAURUS

tribulation *n* **1, 2** = **trouble**, adversity, affliction, bad luck, blow, bummer (*sl.*), burden, care, cross to bear, curse, distress, grief, hardship, hassle (*inf.*), heartache, ill fortune, misery, misfortune, ordeal, pain, reverse, sorrow, suffering, trial, unhappiness, vexation, woe, worry, wretchedness
Antonyms *n* blessing, bliss, ease, good fortune, happiness, joy, pleasure, rest

tribunal *n* **1** = **hearing**, bar, bench, court, industrial tribunal, judgment seat, judicial examination, trial

tribute *n* **1** = **accolade**, acknowledgment, applause, commendation, compliment, encomium, esteem, eulogy, gift, gratitude, honour, laudation, panegyric, praise, recognition, respect, testimonial **2** = **tax**, charge, contribution, customs, duty, excise, homage, impost, offering, payment, ransom, subsidy, toll
Antonyms *n* ≠ **accolade:** blame, complaint, condemnation, criticism, disapproval, reproach, reproof

trice *n As in* **in a trice** = **moment**, bat of an eye (*inf.*), flash, instant, jiffy (*inf.*), minute, second, shake (*inf.*), split second, tick (*Brit. inf.*), twinkling, twinkling of an eye, two shakes of a lamb's tail (*inf.*)

trick *n* **1** = **deception**, artifice, canard, con (*sl.*), deceit, device, dodge, feint, fraud, gimmick, hoax, imposition, imposture, manoeuvre, ploy, ruse, scam (*sl.*), sting (*inf.*), stratagem, subterfuge, swindle, trap, wile **2a** = **joke**, antic, cantrip (*Scot.*), caper, frolic, gag, gambol, jape, leg-pull (*Brit. inf.*), practical joke, prank, put-on (*sl.*), stunt **3** = **sleight of hand**, device, feat, juggle, legerdemain **5** = **secret**, art, command, craft, device, expertise, gift, hang (*inf.*), knack, know-how (*inf.*), skill, technique **6** = **mannerism**, characteristic, crotchet, foible, habit, idiosyncrasy, peculiarity, practice, quirk, trait **10 do the trick** *Informal* = **work**, be effective *or* effectual, have effect, produce the desired result ◆ *vb* **13** = **deceive**, bamboozle (*inf.*), cheat, con, defraud, delude, dupe, fool, gull (*arch.*), have (someone) on, hoax, hoodwink, impose upon, kid (*inf.*), mislead, pull a fast one on (*inf.*), pull the wool over (someone's) eyes, put one over on (someone) (*inf.*), stiff (*sl.*), sting (*inf.*), swindle, take in (*inf.*), trap

trickery *n* = **deception**, cheating, chicanery, con (*inf.*), deceit, dishonesty, double-dealing, fraud, funny business, guile, hanky-panky (*inf.*), hoax, hokum (*sl., chiefly US & Canad.*), imposture, jiggery-pokery (*inf., chiefly Brit.*), monkey business (*inf.*), pretence, skulduggery (*inf.*), swindling
Antonyms *n* artlessness, candour, directness, frankness, honesty, openness, straightforwardness, uprightness

trickle *vb* **1** = **dribble**, crawl, creep, drip, drop, exude, ooze, percolate, run, seep, stream ◆ *n* **3** = **dribble**, drip, seepage

trick out *vb* = **dress up**, adorn, array, attire, bedeck, deck out, doll up (*sl.*), do up (*inf.*), get up (*inf.*), ornament, prank, prink

trickster *n* = **deceiver**, cheat, chiseller (*inf.*), con man (*inf.*), fraud, fraudster, hoaxer, hustler (*US inf.*), impostor, joker, practical joker, pretender, swindler

tricky *adj* **1, 2** = **difficult**, complicated, delicate, knotty, problematic, risky, sticky (*inf.*), thorny, ticklish, touch-and-go **3** = **crafty**, artful, cunning, deceitful, deceptive, devious, foxy, scheming, slippery, sly, subtle, wily
Antonyms *adj* ≠ **difficult:** clear, easy, obvious, simple, straightforward, uncomplicated ≠ **crafty:** above board, artless, direct, genuine, honest, ingenuous, open, sincere, truthful

triclinic (traɪˈklɪnɪk) *adj* of the crystal system characterized by three unequal axes, no pair of which are perpendicular.

triclinium (traɪˈklɪnɪəm) *n, pl* **triclinia** (-ɪə). (in ancient Rome) **1** an arrangement of three couches around a table for reclining upon while dining. **2** a dining room. [C17: from L, from Gk *triklinion,* from TRI- + *klinē* a couch]

tricolour *or US* **tricolor** (ˈtrɪkələ, ˈtraɪˌkʌlə) *adj also* **tricoloured** *or US* **tricolored** (ˈtraɪˌkʌləd). **1** having or involving three colours. ◆ *n* **2** (*often cap.*) the French flag, having three stripes in blue, white, and red. **3** any flag, badge, etc., with three colours.

tricorn (ˈtraɪˌkɔːn) *n also* **tricorne. 1** a cocked hat with the brim turned up on three sides. ◆ *adj also* **tricornered. 2** having three horns or corners. [C18: from L *tricornis,* from TRI- + *cornu* horn]

tricot (ˈtrɪkəʊ, ˈtriː-) *n* **1** a thin rayon or nylon fabric knitted or resembling knitting, used for dresses, etc. **2** a type of ribbed dress fabric. [C19: from F, from *tricoter* to knit, from ?]

tricuspid (traɪˈkʌspɪd) *Anat.* ◆ *adj also* **tricuspidal. 1** having three points, cusps, or segments: *a tricuspid tooth; a tricuspid valve.* ◆ *n* **2** a tooth having three cusps.

tricycle (ˈtraɪsɪkᵊl) *n* a three-wheeled cycle, esp. one driven by pedals.
▸ˈ**tricyclist** *n*

trident (ˈtraɪdᵊnt) *n* a three-pronged spear. [C16: from L *tridēns* three-pronged, from TRI- + *dēns* tooth]

Trident (ˈtraɪdᵊnt) *n* a type of US submarine-launched ballistic missile with independently targetable warheads.

tridentate (traɪˈdɛnteɪt) *or* **tridental** *adj* having three prongs, teeth, or points.

Tridentine (traɪˈdɛntaɪn) *adj* **1a** *History.* of the Council of Trent in the 16th century. **1b** in accord with Tridentine doctrine: *Tridentine mass.* ◆ *n* **2** an orthodox Roman Catholic. [C16: from Med. L *Tridentīnus,* from *Tridentum* Trent]

tried (traɪd) *vb* the past tense and past participle of **try.**

triella (traɪˈɛlə) *n* a cumulative bet on horses in three specified races.

triennial (traɪˈɛnɪəl) *adj* **1** relating to, lasting for, or occurring every three years. ◆ *n* **2** a third anniversary. **3** a triennial period, thing, or occurrence. [C17: from L TRIENNIUM]
▸**triˈennially** *adv*

triennium (traɪˈɛnɪəm) *n, pl* **trienniums** *or* **triennia** (-nɪə). a period or cycle of three years. [C19: from L, from TRI- + *annus* a year]

trier (ˈtraɪə) *n* a person or thing that tries.

trifacial (traɪˈfeɪʃəl) *adj* another word for **trigeminal.**

trifecta (traɪˈfɛktə) *n Austral.* a form of betting in which punters select first-, second-, and third-place winners in the correct order.

trifid (ˈtraɪfɪd) *adj* divided or split into three parts or lobes. [C18: from L *trifidus,* from TRI- + *findere* to split]

trifle ❶ (ˈtraɪfᵊl) *n* **1** a thing of little or no value or significance. **2** a small amount; bit: *a trifle more enthusiasm.* **3** *Brit.* a cold dessert made with sponge cake spread with jam or fruit, soaked in sherry, covered with custard and cream. ◆ *vb* **trifles, trifling, trifled. 4** (*intr;* usually foll. by *with*) to deal (with) as if worthless; dally: *to trifle with a person's affections.* **5** to waste (time) frivolously. [C13: from OF *trufle* mockery, from *trufler* to cheat]
▸ˈ**trifler** *n*

trifling ❶ (ˈtraɪflɪŋ) *adj* **1** insignificant or petty. **2** frivolous or idle.
▸ˈ**triflingly** *adv*

trifocal *adj* (traɪˈfəʊkᵊl). **1** having three focuses. **2** having three focal lengths. ◆ *n* (traɪˈfəʊkᵊl, ˈtraɪˌfəʊkᵊl). **3** (*pl*) glasses that have trifocal lenses.

triforium (traɪˈfɔːrɪəm) *n, pl* **triforia** (-rɪə). an arcade above the arches of the nave, choir, or transept of a church. [C18: from Anglo-L, apparently from L TRI- + *foris* a doorway; from the fact that each bay had three openings]

trifurcate (ˈtraɪfɜːkɪt, -ˌkeɪt) *or* **trifurcated** *adj* having three branches or forks. [C19: from L *trifurcus,* from TRI- + *furca* a fork]

trig (trɪg) *Arch. or dialect.* ◆ *adj* **1** neat or spruce. ◆ *vb* **trigs, trigging, trigged. 2** to make or become trim or spruce. [C12 (orig.: trusty): from ON]
▸ˈ**trigly** *adv* ▸ˈ**trigness** *n*

trig. *abbrev. for:* **1** trigonometrical. **2** trigonometry.

trigeminal (traɪˈdʒɛmɪnᵊl) *adj Anat.* of or relating to the trigeminal nerve. [C19: from L *trigeminus* triplet, from TRI- + *geminus* twin]

trigeminal nerve *n* either one of the fifth pair of cranial nerves, which supply the muscles of the mandible and maxilla. Their ophthalmic branches supply the area around the orbit of the eye, the nasal cavity, and the forehead.

trigeminal neuralgia *n Pathol.* another name for **tic douloureux.**

trigger ❶ (ˈtrɪgə) *n* **1** a small lever that activates the firing mechanism of a firearm. **2** a device that releases a spring-loaded mechanism. **3** any event that sets a course of action in motion. ◆ *vb* (*tr*) **4** (usually foll. by *off*) to give rise (to); set off. **5** to fire or set in motion by or as by pulling a trigger. [C17 *tricker,* from Du. *trekker,* from *trekken* to pull]

triggerfish (ˈtrɪgəˌfɪʃ) *n, pl* **triggerfish** *or* **triggerfishes.** any of a family of fishes of tropical and temperate seas. They have erectile spines in the first dorsal fin.

trigger-happy *adj Inf.* **1** tending to resort to the use of firearms or violence irresponsibly. **2** tending to act rashly.

triglyceride (traɪˈglɪsəˌraɪd) *n* any ester of glycerol and one or more carboxylic acids, in which each glycerol molecule has combined with three carboxylic acid molecules.

triglyph (ˈtraɪˌglɪf) *n Archit.* a stone block in a Doric frieze, having three vertical channels. [C16: via L from Gk *trigluphos,* from TRI- + *gluphē* carving]

trigonal (ˈtrɪgənᵊl) *adj* **1** triangular. **2** of the crystal system characterized by three equal axes that are equally inclined and not perpendicular to each other. [C16: via L from Gk *trigōnon* triangle]

trigonometric function *n* any of a group of functions of an angle expressed as a ratio of two of the sides of a right-angled triangle containing the angle. The group includes sine, cosine, tangent, etc.

trigonometry (ˌtrɪgəˈnɒmɪtrɪ) *n* the branch of mathematics concerned with the properties of trigonometric functions and their application to the determination of the angles and sides of triangles: used in surveying, navigation, etc. [C17: from NL *trigōnometria,* from Gk *trigōnon* triangle]
▸**trigonometric** (ˌtrɪgənəˈmɛtrɪk) *or* ˌ**trigonoˈmetrical** *adj*

trig point *n* an informal name for **triangulation station.** [from *trigonometric*]

trigraph (ˈtraɪˌgrɑːf) *n* a combination of three letters used to represent a single speech sound or phoneme, such as *eau* in French *beau.*

trihedral (traɪˈhiːdrəl) *adj* **1** having three plane faces. ◆ *n* **2** a figure formed by the intersection of three lines in different planes.

trihedron (traɪˈhiːdrən) *n, pl* **trihedrons** *or* **trihedra** (-drə). a figure determined by the intersection of three planes.

trike (traɪk) *n* short for **tricycle.**

trilateral (traɪˈlætərəl) *adj* having three sides.

trilby (ˈtrɪlbɪ) *n, pl* **trilbies.** a man's soft felt hat with an indented crown. [C19: after *Trilby,* the heroine of a dramatized novel (1893) of that title by George Du Maurier]

trilingual (traɪˈlɪŋgwəl) *adj* **1** able to speak three languages fluently. **2** expressed or written in three languages.
▸**triˈlingualism** *n*

trilithon (traɪˈlɪθɒn) *or* **trilith** (ˈtraɪlɪθ) *n* a structure consisting of two upright stones with a third placed across the top, as at Stonehenge. [C18: from Gk]
▸**trilithic** (traɪˈlɪθɪk) *adj*

trill (trɪl) *n* **1** *Music.* a rapid alternation between a principal note and the note above it. **2** a shrill warbling sound, esp. as made by some birds. **3** the articulation of an (r) sound produced by the rapid vibration of the tongue or the uvula. ◆ *vb* **4** to sound, sing, or play (a trill or with a trill). **5** (*tr*) to pronounce (an (r) sound) by the production of a trill. [C17: from It. *trillo,* from *trillare,* apparently from MDu. *trillen* to vibrate]

trillion (ˈtrɪljən) *n* **1** the number represented as one followed by twelve zeros (10^{12}); a million million. **2** (formerly, in Britain) the number represented as one followed by eighteen zeros (10^{18}); a million million million. ◆ *determiner* **3** (preceded by *a* or a numeral) amounting to a trillion. [C17: from F, on the model of *million*]
▸ˈ**trillionth** *n, adj*

trillium (ˈtrɪljəm) *n* any of a genus of herbaceous plants of Asia and North America, having a whorl of three leaves at the top of the stem with a single white, pink, or purple three-petalled flower. [C18: from NL, modification by Linnaeus of Swedish *trilling* triplet]

trilobate (traɪˈləʊbeɪt, ˈtraɪləˌbeɪt) *adj* (esp. of a leaf) consisting of or having three lobes or parts.

trilobite (ˈtraɪləˌbaɪt) *n* any of various extinct marine arthropods abundant in Palaeozoic times, having a segmented exoskeleton divided into three parts. [C19: from NL *Trilobītēs,* from Gk *trilobos* having three lobes]
▸**trilobitic** (ˌtraɪləˈbɪtɪk) *adj*

trilogy (ˈtrɪlədʒɪ) *n, pl* **trilogies. 1** a series of three related works, esp. in literature, etc. **2** (in ancient Greece) a series of three tragedies performed together. [C19: from Gk *trilogia*]

trim ❶ (trɪm) *adj* **trimmer, trimmest. 1** neat and spruce in appearance. **2** slim; slender. **3** in good condition. ◆ *vb* **trims, trimming, trimmed.** (*mainly tr*) **4** to put in good order, esp. by cutting or pruning. **5** to shape and finish (timber). **6** to adorn or decorate. **7** (sometimes foll. by *off* or *away*) to cut so as to remove: *to trim off a branch.* **8** to cut down to the desired size or shape. **9** *Naut.* **9a** (*also intr*) to adjust the balance of (a vessel) or (of a vessel) to maintain an even balance, by distribu-

THESAURUS

trifle *n* **1 = knick-knack,** bagatelle, bauble, child's play (*inf.*), gewgaw, nothing, plaything, toy, triviality **2 = little,** bit, dash, drop, jot, pinch, spot, touch, trace ◆ *vb* **4** *usually foll. by* **with = toy,** amuse oneself, coquet, dally, flirt, mess about, palter, play, play fast and loose (*inf.*), wanton **5 = waste time,** dawdle, fritter, idle, waste

trifler *n* **5 = idler,** dilettante, good-for-nothing, layabout, loafer, ne'er-do-well, skiver (*Brit. sl.*), waster

trifling *adj* **1, 2 = insignificant,** empty, footling (*inf.*), frivolous, idle, inconsiderable, measly, minuscule, negligible, nickel-and-dime (*US sl.*), paltry, petty, piddling (*inf.*), puny, shallow, silly, slight, small, tiny, trivial, unimportant, valueless, worthless
Antonyms *adj* considerable, crucial, important, large, major, serious, significant, vital, weighty

trigger *vb* **4 = set off,** activate, bring about, cause, elicit, generate, give rise to, produce, prompt, provoke, set in motion, spark off, start
Antonyms *vb* bar, block, hinder, impede, inhibit, obstruct, prevent, repress, stop

trim *adj* **1 = neat,** compact, dapper, natty (*inf.*), nice, orderly, shipshape, smart, soigné *or* soignée, spick-and-span, spruce, tidy, trig (*arch. or dialect*), well-groomed, well-ordered, well turned-out **2 = slender,** fit, shapely, sleek,

tion of ballast, cargo, etc. **9b** (*also intr*) to adjust (a vessel's sails) to take advantage of the wind. **10** to balance (an aircraft) before flight by adjusting the position of the load or in flight by the use of trim tabs, fuel transfer, etc. **11** (*also intr*) to modify (one's opinions, etc.) for expediency. **12** *Inf.* to thrash or beat. **13** *Inf.* to rebuke. ◆ *n* **14** a decoration or adornment. **15** the upholstery and decorative facings of a car's interior. **16** proper order or fitness; good shape. **17** a haircut that neatens but does not alter the existing hairstyle. **18** *Naut.* **18a** the general set and appearance of a vessel. **18b** the difference between the draught of a vessel at the bow and at the stern. **18c** the fitness of a vessel. **18d** the position of a vessel's sails relative to the wind. **19** dress or equipment. **20** *US.* window-dressing. **21** the attitude of an aircraft in flight when the pilot allows the main control surfaces to take up their own positions. **22** material that is trimmed off. **23** decorative mouldings, such as architraves, picture rails, etc. [OE *trymman* to strengthen]
▸**'trimly** *adv* ▸**'trimness** *n*

trimaran ('traɪmə,ræn) *n* a vessel, usually of shallow draught, with two hulls flanking the main hull. [C20: from TRI- + (CATA)MARAN]

trimer ('traɪmə) *n* a polymer or a molecule of a polymer consisting of three identical monomers.

trimerous ('trɪmərəs) *adj* **1** having parts in groups of three. **2** having three parts.

trimester (traɪ'mɛstə) *n* **1** a period of three months. **2** (in some US and Canad. universities or schools) any of the three academic sessions. [C19: from F *trimestre,* from L *trimēstris* of three months]
▸**tri'mestral** *or* **tri'mestrial** *adj*

trimeter ('trɪmɪtə) *Prosody.* ◆ *n* **1** a verse line consisting of three metrical feet. ◆ *adj* **2** designating such a line.

trimethadione (,traɪmɛθə'daɪəʊn) *n* a crystalline compound with a camphor-like odour, used in the treatment of epilepsy.

trimetric projection (traɪ'mɛtrɪk) *n* a geometric projection, used in mechanical drawing, in which the three axes are at arbitrary angles, often using different linear scales.

trimmer ('trɪmə) *n* **1** a beam attached to truncated joists in order to leave an opening for a staircase, chimney, etc. **2** a machine for trimming timber. **3** a variable capacitor of small capacitance used for making fine adjustments, etc. **4** a person who alters his opinions on the grounds of expediency. **5** a person who fits out motor vehicles.

trimming ❶ ('trɪmɪŋ) *n* **1** an extra piece used to decorate or complete. **2** (*pl*) usual or traditional accompaniments: *roast turkey with all the trimmings.* **3** (*pl*) parts that are cut off.

trimolecular (,traɪmə'lɛkjʊlə) *adj Chem.* of, formed from, or involving three molecules.

trimonthly (traɪ'mʌnθlɪ) *adj, adv* every three months.

trimorphism (traɪ'mɔːfɪzəm) *n* **1** *Biol.* the property exhibited by certain species of having or occurring in three different forms. **2** the property of certain minerals of existing in three crystalline forms.

trinary ('traɪnərɪ) *adj* **1** made up of three parts; ternary. **2** going in threes. [C15: from LL *trīnārius* of three sorts, from L *trīnī* three each, from *trēs* three]

trine (traɪn) *n* **1** *Astrol.* an aspect of 120° between two planets. **2** anything comprising three parts. ◆ *adj* **3** of or relating to a trine. **4** threefold; triple. [C14: from OF *trin,* from L *trīnus* triple, from *trēs* three]
▸**'trinal** *adj*

Trinitarian (,trɪnɪ'tɛərɪən) *n* **1** a person who believes in the doctrine of the Trinity. ◆ *adj* **2** of or relating to the doctrine of the Trinity or those who uphold it.
▸**,Trini'tarian,ism** *n*

trinitroglycerine (traɪ,naɪtrəʊ'glɪsərɪn) *n* the full name for **nitroglycerine.**

trinitrotoluene (traɪ,naɪtrəʊ'tɒljʊ,iːn) *or* **trinitrotoluol** (traɪ,naɪtrəʊ'tɒljʊ,ɒl) *n* the full name for **TNT.**

trinity ❶ ('trɪnɪtɪ) *n, pl* **trinities. 1** a group of three. **2** the state of being threefold. [C13: from OF *trinite,* from LL *trīnitās,* from L *trīnus* triple]

Trinity ('trɪnɪtɪ) *n Christian theol.* the union of three persons, the Father, Son, and Holy Spirit, in one Godhead.

Trinity Brethren *pl n* the members of Trinity House.

Trinity House *n* an association that provides lighthouses, buoys, etc., around the British coast.

Trinity Sunday *n* the Sunday after Whit Sunday.

Trinity term *n* the summer term at the Inns of Court and certain universities.

trinket ❶ ('trɪŋkɪt) *n* **1** a small or worthless ornament or piece of jewellery. **2** a trivial object; trifle. [C16: ? from earlier *trenket* little knife, via OF, from L *truncāre* to lop]

trinomial (traɪ'nəʊmɪəl) *adj* **1** consisting of three terms. ◆ *n* **2** *Maths.* a polynomial consisting of three terms, such as $ax^2 + bx + c$. **3** *Biol.* the three-part name of an organism that incorporates its genus, species, and subspecies. [C18: TRI- + *-nomial* on the model of *binomial*]

trio ❶ ('triːəʊ) *n, pl* **trios. 1** a group of three. **2** *Music.* **2a** a group of three singers or instrumentalists or a piece of music composed for such a group. **2b** a subordinate section in a scherzo, minuet, etc. [C18: from It., ult. from L *trēs* three]

triode ('traɪəʊd) *n* **1** an electronic valve having three electrodes, a cathode, an anode, and a grid. **2** any electronic device having three electrodes. [C20: TRI- + ELECTRODE]

trioecious *or* **triecious** (traɪ'iːʃəs) *adj* (of a plant species) having male, female, and hermaphrodite flowers in three different plants. [C18: from NL *trioecia,* from Gk TRI- + *oikos* house]

triolein (traɪ'əʊlɪɪn) *n* a naturally occurring glyceride of oleic acid, found in fats and oils.

triolet ('triːəʊ,lɛt) *n* a verse form of eight lines, having the first line repeated as the fourth and seventh and the second line as the eighth, rhyming a b a a a b a b. [C17: from F: a little TRIO]

trioxide (traɪ'ɒksaɪd) *n* any oxide that contains three oxygen atoms per molecule.

trip ❶ (trɪp) *n* **1** an outward and return journey, often for a specific purpose. **2** any journey. **3** a false step; stumble. **4** any slip or blunder. **5** a light step or tread. **6** a manoeuvre or device to cause someone to trip. **7** Also called: **tripper.** any catch on a mechanism that acts as a switch. **8** *Inf.* a hallucinogenic drug experience. **9** *Inf.* any stimulating, profound, etc., experience. ◆ *vb* **trips, tripping, tripped. 10** (often foll. by *up,* or when *intr,* by *on* or *over*) to stumble or cause to stumble. **11** to make or cause to make a mistake. **12** (*tr;* often foll. by *up*) to trap or catch in a mistake. **13** (*intr*) to go on a short journey. **14** (*intr*) to move or tread lightly. **15** (*intr*) *Inf.* to experience the effects of a hallucinogenic drug. **16** (*tr*) to activate a mechanical trip. [C14: from OF *triper* to tread, of Gmc origin]

tripartite (traɪ'pɑːtaɪt) *adj* **1** divided into or composed of three parts. **2** involving three participants. **3** (esp. of leaves) consisting of three parts formed by divisions extending almost to the base.
▸**tri'partitely** *adv*

tripe ❶ (traɪp) *n* **1** the stomach lining of an ox, cow, etc., prepared for cooking. **2** *Inf.* something silly; rubbish. [C13: from OF, from ?]

triphammer ('trɪp,hæmə) *n* a power hammer that is raised or tilted by a cam and allowed to fall under gravity.

triphibious (traɪ'fɪbɪəs) *adj* (esp. of military operations) occurring on land, at sea, and in the air. [C20: from TRI- + (AM)PHIBIOUS]

triphthong ('trɪfθɒŋ, 'trɪp-) *n* **1** a composite vowel sound during the articulation of which the vocal organs move from one position through a second, ending in a third, as in *fire.* **2** a trigraph representing such a composite vowel sound. [C16: via NL from Med. Gk *triphthongos,* from TRI- + *phthongos* sound]
▸**triph'thongal** *adj*

tripinnate (traɪ'pɪnɪt, -eɪt) *adj* (of a leaf) having pinnate leaflets that are bipinnately arranged.

triplane ('traɪ,pleɪn) *n* an aeroplane having three wings arranged one above the other.

triple ❶ ('trɪpᵊl) *adj* **1** consisting of three parts; threefold. **2** (of musical time or rhythm) having three beats in each bar. **3** three times as great or as much. ◆ *n* **4** a threefold amount. **5** a group of three. ◆ *vb* **triples, tripling, tripled. 6** to increase threefold; treble. [C16: from L *triplus*]
▸**'triply** *adv*

triple A *n Mil.* anti-aircraft artillery. [referring to the abbrev. AAA]

triple jump *n* an athletic event in which the competitor has to per-

THESAURUS

slim, streamlined, svelte, willowy ◆ *vb* **4** = **cut,** barber, clip, crop, curtail, cut back, dock, even up, lop, pare, prune, shave, shear, tidy **6** = **decorate,** adorn, array, beautify, bedeck, deck out, dress, embellish, embroider, garnish, ornament, trick out **9** = **adjust,** arrange, balance, distribute, order, prepare, settle ◆ *n* **14** = **decoration,** adornment, border, edging, embellishment, frill, fringe, garnish, ornamentation, piping, trimming **16** = **condition,** fettle, fitness, form, health, order, repair, shape (*inf.*), situation, state, wellness **17** = **cut,** clipping, crop, pruning, shave, shearing, tidying up, trimming
Antonyms *adj* ≠ **neat:** disarrayed, disorderly, messy, scruffy, shabby, sloppy, ungroomed, unkempt, untidy

trimming *n* **1** = **decoration,** adornment, border, braid, edging, embellishment, festoon, frill, fringe, garnish, ornamentation, piping **2** *pl* = **extras,** accessories, accompaniments, appurtenances, frills, garnish, ornaments, paraphernalia, trappings **3** *pl* = **clippings,** brash, cuttings, ends, parings, shavings

trinity *n* **1** = **threesome,** triad, trilogy, trine, trio, triple, triplet, triptych, triumvirate, triune

trinket *n* **1, 2** = **ornament,** bagatelle, bauble, bibelot, gewgaw, gimcrack, kickshaw, knick-knack, nothing, piece of bric-a-brac, toy, trifle

trio *n* **1** = **threesome,** triad, trilogy, trine, trinity, triple, triplet, triptych, triumvirate, triune

trip *n* **1, 2** = **journey,** errand, excursion, expedition, foray, jaunt, outing, ramble, run, tour, travel, voyage **3** = **stumble,** blunder, fall, false move, false step, misstep, slip **4** = **blunder,** bloomer (*Brit. inf.*), boob (*Brit. sl.*), error, faux pas, indiscretion, lapse, slip ◆ *vb* **10** = **stumble,** fall, lose one's balance, lose one's footing, make a false move, misstep, slip, tumble **11** = **blunder,** boob (*Brit. sl.*), err, go wrong, lapse, make a faux pas, miscalculate, slip up (*inf.*) **12** = **catch out,** confuse, disconcert, put off one's stride, throw off, trap, unsettle **13** = **journey,** go, ramble, tour, travel, voyage **14** = **skip,** caper, dance, flit, frisk, gambol, hop, spring, tread lightly **15** *Informal* = **take drugs,** get high (*inf.*), get stoned (*sl.*), turn on (*sl.*) **16** = **activate,** engage, flip, pull, release, set off, switch on, throw, turn on

tripe 2 *n Informal* = **nonsense,** balderdash, bollocks (*Brit. taboo sl.*), bull (*sl.*), bullshit (*taboo sl.*), bunkum *or* buncombe (*chiefly US*), claptrap (*inf.*), cobblers (*Brit. taboo sl.*), crap (*sl.*), drivel, eyewash (*inf.*), garbage (*inf.*), guff (*sl.*), hogwash, hokum (*sl., chiefly US & Canad.*), inanity, moonshine, pap, piffle (*inf.*), poppycock (*inf.*), rot, rubbish, tommyrot, tosh (*sl., chiefly Brit.*), trash, trumpery, twaddle

triple *adj* **1** = **threefold,** three times as much, three-way, tripartite ◆ *n* **5** = **threesome,** triad, trilogy, trine, trinity, trio, triplet, triumvirate, triune ◆ *vb* **6** = **treble,** increase threefold, triplicate

form successively a hop, a step, and a jump in continuous movement.

triple point *n Chem.* the temperature and pressure at which the three phases of a substance are in equilibrium.

triplet ➊ ('trɪplɪt) *n* **1** a group or set of three similar things. **2** one of three offspring born at one birth. **3** *Music.* a group of three notes played in a time value of two, four, etc. **4** *Chem.* a state of a molecule or free radical in which there are two unpaired electrons. [C17: from TRIPLE, on the model of *doublet*]

Triplex ('trɪplɛks) *n Brit. trademark.* a laminated safety glass, as used in car windows.

triplicate *adj* ('trɪplɪkɪt). **1** triple. ◆ *vb* ('trɪplɪˌkeɪt), **triplicates, triplicating, triplicated. 2** to multiply or be multiplied by three. ◆ *n* ('trɪplɪkɪt). **3a** a group of three things. **3b** one of such a group. **4 in triplicate.** written out three times. [C15: from L *triplicāre* to triple]
▸ˌ**tripli'cation** *n*

triploid ('trɪplɔɪd) *adj* **1** having or relating to three times the haploid number of chromosomes: *a triploid organism.* ◆ *n* **2** a triploid organism. [C19: from Gk *tripl(oos)* triple + (HAPL)OID]

tripod ('traɪpɒd) *n* **1** a three-legged stand to which a camera, etc., can be attached to hold it steady. **2** a stand or table having three legs.
▸**tripodal** ('trɪpəd^əl) *adj*

tripoli ('trɪpəlɪ) *n* a lightweight porous siliceous rock used in a powdered form as a polish. [C17: after *Tripoli*, in Libya or in Lebanon]

tripos ('traɪpɒs) *n Brit.* the final honours degree examinations at Cambridge University. [C16: from L *tripūs*, infl. by Gk noun ending *-os*]

tripper ➊ ('trɪpə) *n* **1** *Chiefly Brit.* a tourist. **2** another word for **trip** (sense 7). **3** any device that causes a trip to operate.

trippy ('trɪpɪ) *adj* **trippier, trippiest.** *Inf.* suggestive of or resembling the effect produced by a hallucinogenic drug.

triptane ('trɪpteɪn) *n* a liquid hydrocarbon used in aviation fuel. [C20: shortened & altered from *trimethylbutane*]

triptych ('trɪptɪk) *n* **1** a set of three pictures or panels, usually hinged so that the two wing panels fold over the larger central one: often used as an altarpiece. **2** a set of three hinged writing tablets. [C18: from Gk *triptukhos*, from TRI- + *ptux* plate]

triptyque (trɪp'tiːk) *n* a customs permit for the temporary importation of a motor vehicle. [C20: from F: TRIPTYCH (from its three sections)]

tripwire ('trɪpˌwaɪə) *n* a wire that activates a trap, mine, etc., when tripped over.

trireme ('traɪriːm) *n* an ancient Greek galley with three banks of oars on each side. [C17: from L *trirēmis*, from TRI- + *rēmus* oar]

trisect (traɪ'sɛkt) *vb (tr)* to divide into three parts, esp. three equal parts. [C17: TRI- + *-sect* from L *secāre* to cut]
▸**trisection** (traɪ'sɛkʃən) *n*

trishaw ('traɪˌʃɔː) *n* another name for **rickshaw** (sense 2). [C20: from TRI- + RICKSHAW]

triskelion (trɪ'skɛlɪˌɒn) *n, pl* **triskelia** (trɪ'skɛlɪə). a symbol consisting of three bent limbs or lines radiating from a centre. [C19: from Gk *triskelēs* three-legged]

trismus ('trɪzməs) *n Pathol.* the state of being unable to open the mouth because of sustained contractions of the jaw muscles, caused by tetanus. Nontechnical name: **lockjaw.** [C17: from NL, from Gk *trismos* a grinding]

triste (triːst) *adj* an archaic word for **sad.** [from F]

trisyllable (traɪ'sɪləb^əl) *n* a word of three syllables.
▸**trisyllabic** (ˌtraɪsɪ'læbɪk) *adj*

trite ➊ (traɪt) *adj* hackneyed; dull: *a trite comment.* [C16: from L *trītus* worn down, from *terere* to rub]
▸'**tritely** *adv* ▸'**triteness** *n*

tritheism ('traɪθɪˌɪzəm) *n Theol.* belief in three gods, esp. in the Trinity as consisting of three distinct gods.
▸'**tritheist** *n, adj*

triticum ('trɪtɪkəm) *n* any of a genus of cereal grasses which includes the wheats. [C19: L, lit.: wheat, prob. from *tritum*, supine of *terere* to grind]

tritium ('trɪtɪəm) *n* a radioactive isotope of hydrogen. Symbol: T or ^{3}H; half-life: 12.5 years. [C20: NL, from Gk *tritos* third]

triton[1] ('traɪt^ən) *n* any of various chiefly tropical marine gastropod molluscs having large spiral shells. [C16: via L from Gk *tritōn*]

triton[2] ('traɪtɒn) *n Physics.* a nucleus of an atom of tritium, containing two neutrons and one proton. [C20: from TRIT(IUM) + -ON]

Triton ('traɪt^ən) *n Greek myth.* a sea god depicted as having the upper parts of a man with a fish's tail.

tritone ('traɪˌtəʊn) *n* a musical interval consisting of three whole tones.

triturate ('trɪtjʊˌreɪt) *vb* **triturates, triturating, triturated. 1** *(tr)* to grind or rub into a fine powder or pulp. ◆ *n* **2** the powder or pulp resulting from this. [C17: from LL *trītūrāre* to thresh, from L *trītūra* a threshing, from *terere* to grind]
▸ˌ**tritu'ration** *n*

triumph ➊ ('traɪəmf) *n* **1** the feeling of exultation and happiness derived from a victory or major achievement. **2** the act or condition of being victorious; victory. **3** (in ancient Rome) a procession held in honour of a victorious general. ◆ *vb (intr)* **4** (often foll. by *over*) to win a victory or control: *to triumph over one's weaknesses.* **5** to rejoice over a victory. **6** to celebrate a Roman triumph. [C14: from OF *triumphe*, from L *triumphus*, from OL *triumpus*]
▸**triumphal** (traɪ'ʌmfəl) *adj*

triumphant ➊ (traɪ'ʌmfənt) *adj* **1** experiencing or displaying triumph. **2** exultant through triumph.
▸**tri'umphantly** *adv*

triumvir (traɪ'ʌmvə) *n, pl* **triumvirs** *or* **triumviri** (-vɪˌriː). (esp. in ancient Rome) a member of a triumvirate. [C16: from L: one of three administrators, from *trium virōrum* of three men, from *trēs* three + *vir* man]
▸**tri'umviral** *adj*

triumvirate (traɪ'ʌmvɪrɪt) *n* **1** (in ancient Rome) a board of three officials jointly responsible for some task. **2** joint rule by three men. **3** any group of three men associated in some way. **4** the office of a triumvir.

triune ('traɪjuːn) *adj* constituting three in one, esp. the three persons in one God of the Trinity. [C17: TRI- + *-une*, from L *ūnus* one]
▸**tri'unity** *n*

trivalent (traɪ'veɪlənt, 'trɪvələnt) *adj Chem.* **1** having a valency of three. **2** having three valencies. ◆ Also: **tervalent.**
▸**tri'valency** *n*

trivet ('trɪvɪt) *n* **1** a stand, usually three-legged and metal, on which cooking vessels are placed over a fire. **2** a short metal stand on which hot dishes are placed on a table. **3 as right as a trivet.** in perfect health. [OE *trefet* (infl. by OE *thrifēte* having three feet), from L *tripēs* having three feet]

trivia ➊ ('trɪvɪə) *n (functioning as sing or pl)* petty details or considerations; trifles; trivialities. [from NL, pl of L *trivium* junction of three roads]

trivial ➊ ('trɪvɪəl) *adj* **1** of little importance; petty or frivolous: *trivial complaints.* **2** ordinary or commonplace; trite: *trivial conversation.* **3** *Biol., chem.* denoting the common name of an organism or substance. **4** *Biol.* denoting the specific name of an organism in binomial nomenclature. [C15: from L *triviālis* belonging to the public streets, common, from *trivium* junction of three roads]
▸'**trivially** *adv* ▸'**trivialness** *n*

triviality ➊ (ˌtrɪvɪ'ælɪtɪ) *n, pl* **trivialities. 1** the state or quality of being trivial. **2** something, such as a remark, that is trivial.

trivialize ➊ *or* **trivialise** ('trɪvɪəˌlaɪz) *vb* **trivializes, trivializing, trivialized** *or* **trivialises, trivialising, trivialised.** *(tr)* to cause to seem trivial or more trivial; minimize.
▸ˌ**triviali'zation** *or* ˌ**triviali'sation** *n*

trivium ('trɪvɪəm) *n, pl* **trivia** (-ɪə). (in medieval learning) the arts of grammar, rhetoric, and logic. Cf. **quadrivium.** [C19: from Med. L, from L: crossroads]

-trix *suffix forming nouns.* indicating a feminine agent, corresponding to nouns ending in *-tor: executrix.* [from L]

t-RNA *abbrev. for* transfer RNA.

trocar ('trəʊkɑː) *n* a surgical instrument for removing fluid from bodily cavities. [C18: from F *trocart*, lit.: with three sides, from *trois* three + *carre* side]

trochal ('trəʊk^əl) *adj Zool.* shaped like a wheel. [C19: from Gk *trokhos* wheel]

THESAURUS

triplet *n* **1 = threesome,** triad, trilogy, trine, trinity, trio, triple, triumvirate, triune

tripper *n* **1** *Chiefly Brit.* **= tourist,** excursionist, holiday-maker, journeyer, sightseer, voyager

trite *adj* **= unoriginal,** banal, bromidic, clichéd, common, commonplace, corny (*sl.*), dull, hack, hackneyed, ordinary, pedestrian, routine, run-of-the-mill, stale, stereotyped, stock, threadbare, tired, uninspired, worn
Antonyms *adj* exciting, fresh, interesting, new, novel, original, out-of-the-ordinary, uncommon, unexpected, unfamiliar

triumph *n* **1 = joy,** elation, exultation, happiness, jubilation, pride, rejoicing **2 = success,** accomplishment, achievement, attainment, conquest, coup, feat, feather in one's cap, hit (*inf.*), mastery, sensation, smash (*inf.*), smash hit (*inf.*), *tour de force*, victory, walkover (*inf.*) ◆ *vb* **4** *often with* **over = succeed,** best, carry the day, come out on top (*inf.*), dominate, flourish, get the better of, overcome, overwhelm, prevail, prosper, subdue, take the honours, thrive, vanquish, win **5 = rejoice,** celebrate, crow, drool, exult, gloat, glory, jubilate, revel, swagger
Antonyms *n* ≠ **success:** catastrophe, defeat, disaster, failure, fiasco, flop (*inf.*), washout (*inf.*) ◆ *vb* ≠ **succeed:** come a cropper (*inf.*), fail, fall, flop (*inf.*), lose

triumphant *adj* **1 = victorious,** boastful, cock-a-hoop, conquering, dominant, elated, exultant, glorious, proud, successful, swaggering, undefeated, winning **2 = celebratory,** jubilant, rejoicing, triumphal
Antonyms *adj* ≠ **victorious:** beaten, defeated, embarrassed, humbled, humiliated, shamed, unsuccessful

trivia *n* **= minutiae,** details, petty details, trifles, trivialities
Antonyms *n* basics, brass tacks (*inf.*), core, essentials, fundamentals, nitty-gritty (*inf.*), rudiments

trivial *adj* **1, 2 = unimportant,** commonplace, everyday, frivolous, incidental, inconsequential, inconsiderable, insignificant, little, meaningless, minor, negligible, nickel-and-dime (*US sl.*), paltry, petty, puny, slight, small, trifling, trite, valueless, worthless
Antonyms *adj* considerable, crucial, essential, important, profound, serious, significant, uncommon, unusual, vital, weighty, worthwhile

triviality *n* **1 = insignificance,** frivolity, inconsequentiality, littleness, meaninglessness, much ado about nothing, negligibility, paltriness, pettiness, slightness, smallness, triteness, unimportance, valuelessness, worthlessness **2 = trifle,** detail, no big thing, no great matter, nothing, petty detail, technicality
Antonyms *n* ≠ **insignificance:** consequence, importance, significance, value, worth ≠ **trifle:** essential, rudiment

trivialize *vb* **= undervalue,** belittle, laugh off, make light of, minimize, play down, scoff at, underestimate, underplay

trochanter (trəʊ'kæntə) *n* **1** any of several processes on the upper part of the vertebrate femur, to which muscles are attached. **2** the third segment of an insect's leg. [C17: via F from Gk *trokhantēr,* from *trekhein* to run]

troche (trəʊʃ) *n Med.* another name for **lozenge** (sense 1). [C16: from F *trochisque,* from LL *trochiscus,* from Gk *trokhiskos* little wheel, from *trokhos* wheel]

trochee ('trəʊki:) *n* a metrical foot of two syllables, the first long and the second short. [C16: via L from Gk *trokhaios pous,* lit.: a running foot, from *trekhein* to run]
▸**trochaic** (trəʊ'keɪɪk) *adj*

trochlea ('trɒklɪə) *n, pl* **trochleae** (-lɪˌi:). any bony or cartilaginous part with a grooved surface over which a bone, etc., may slide or articulate. [C17: from L, from Gk *trokhileia* a sheaf of pulleys]

trochlear nerve ('trɒklɪə) *n* either one of the fourth pair of cranial nerves, which supply the superior oblique muscle of the eye.

trochoid ('trəʊkɔɪd) *n* **1** the curve described by a fixed point on the radius of a circle as the circle rolls along a straight line. ◆ *adj also* **trochoidal. 2** rotating about a central axis. **3** *Anat.* (of a structure or part) resembling or functioning as a pivot or pulley. [C18: from Gk *trokhoeidēs* circular, from *trokhos* wheel]

trod (trɒd) *vb* the past tense and a past participle of **tread.**

trodden ('trɒdᵊn) *vb* a past participle of **tread.**

trode (trəʊd) *vb Arch.* a past tense of **tread.**

troglodyte ('trɒgləˌdaɪt) *n* **1** a cave dweller, esp. of prehistoric times. **2** *Inf.* a person who lives alone and appears eccentric. [C16: via L from Gk *trōglodutēs* one who enters caves, from *trōglē* hole + *duein* to enter]
▸**troglodytic** (ˌtrɒglə'dɪtɪk) *adj*

trogon ('trəʊgɒn) *n* any of an order of birds of tropical regions of America, Africa, and Asia, having a brilliant plumage and long tail. See also **quetzal** (sense 1). [C18: from NL, from Gk *trōgōn,* from *trōgein* to gnaw]

troika ('trɔɪkə) *n* **1** a Russian vehicle drawn by three horses abreast. **2** three horses harnessed abreast. **3** a triumvirate. [C19: from Russian, from *troe* three]

Trojan ('trəʊdʒən) *n* **1** a native or inhabitant of ancient Troy. **2** a person who is hard-working and determined. ◆ *adj* **3** of or relating to ancient Troy or its inhabitants.

Trojan Horse *n* **1** *Greek myth.* the huge wooden hollow figure of a horse left outside Troy by the Greeks and dragged inside by the Trojans. The men concealed inside it opened the city to the final Greek assault. **2** a trap intended to undermine an enemy. **3** *Computing.* a bug inserted into a program or system designed to be activated after a certain time or a certain number of operations.

troll[1] (trəʊl) *vb* **1** *Angling.* **1a** to draw (a baited line, etc.) through the water. **1b** to fish (a stretch of water) by trolling. **1c** to fish (for) by trolling. **2** to roll or cause to roll. **3** *Arch.* to sing (a refrain, chorus, etc.) in a loud hearty voice. **4** (*intr*) *Brit. inf.* to walk or stroll. ◆ *n* **5** a trolling. **6** *Angling.* a bait or lure used in trolling. [C14: from OF *troller* to run about]
▸**'troller** *n*

troll[2] (trəʊl) *n* (in Scandinavian folklore) one of a class of supernatural creatures that dwell in caves or mountains and are depicted either as dwarfs or as giants. [C19: from ON: demon]

trolley ('trɒlɪ) *n* **1** a small table on casters used for conveying food, etc. **2** *Chiefly Brit.* a wheeled cart or stand used for moving heavy items, such as shopping in a supermarket or luggage at a railway station. **3** *Brit.* (in a hospital) a bed mounted on casters and used for moving patients who are unconscious, etc. **4** *Brit.* See **trolleybus. 5** *US & Canad.* See **trolley car. 6** a device that collects the current from an overhead wire, third rail, etc., to drive the motor of an electric vehicle. **7** a pulley or truck that travels along an overhead wire in order to support a suspended load. **8** *Chiefly Brit.* a low truck running on rails, used in factories, mines, etc. **9** a truck, cage, or basket suspended from an overhead track or cable for carrying loads in a mine, etc. [C19: prob. from TROLL[1]]

trolleybus ('trɒlɪˌbʌs) *n* an electrically driven public-transport vehicle that does not run on rails but takes its power from two overhead wires.

trolley car *n* a US and Canad. name for **tram** (sense 1).

trollius ('trəʊlɪəs) *n* another name for **globeflower.** [from G *Trollblume* globeflower]

trollop ● ('trɒləp) *n* **1** a promiscuous woman, esp. a prostitute. **2** an untidy woman; slattern. [C17: ?from G dialect *Trolle* prostitute]
▸**'trollopy** *adj*

trombone (trɒm'bəʊn) *n* a brass instrument, a low-pitched counterpart of the trumpet, consisting of a tube the effective length of which is varied by means of a U-shaped slide. [C18: from It., from *tromba* a trumpet, from OHG *trumba*]
▸**trom'bonist** *n*

trommel ('trɒməl) *n* a revolving cylindrical sieve used to screen crushed ore. [C19: from G: a drum]

trompe (trɒmp) *n* an apparatus for supplying the blast of air in a forge, consisting of a thin column down which water falls, drawing in air through side openings. [C19: from F, lit.: trumpet]

trompe l'oeil (*French* trɔ̃p lœj) *n, pl* **trompe l'oeils** (trɔ̃p lœj). **1** a painting, etc., giving a convincing illusion of reality. **2** an effect of this kind. [from F, lit.: deception of the eye]

-tron *suffix forming nouns.* **1** indicating a vacuum tube. **2** indicating an instrument for accelerating atomic particles. [from Gk, suffix indicating instrument]

tronc (trɒŋk) *n* a pool into which waiters, etc., pay their tips for later distribution to staff by a **tronc master,** according to agreed percentages. [C20: from F: collecting box]

tronk (trɒŋk) *n S. African inf.* a prison. [Afrik.]

troop ● (tru:p) *n* **1** a large group or assembly. **2** a subdivision of a cavalry squadron or artillery battery of about platoon size. **3** (*pl*) armed forces; soldiers. **4** a large group of Scouts comprising several patrols. ◆ *vb* **5** (*intr*) to gather, move, or march in or as if in a crowd. **6** (*tr*) *Mil., chiefly Brit.* to parade (the colour or flag) ceremonially. [C16: from F *troupe,* from *troupeau* flock, of Gmc origin]

trooper ('tru:pə) *n* **1** a soldier in a cavalry regiment. **2** *US & Austral.* a mounted policeman. **3** *US.* a state policeman. **4** a cavalry horse. **5** *Inf., chiefly Brit.* a troopship.

troopship ('tru:pˌʃɪp) *n* a ship used to transport military personnel.

tropaeolum (trəʊ'pi:ələm) *n, pl* **tropaeolums** *or* **tropaeola** (-lə). any of a genus of garden plants, esp. the nasturtium. [C18: from NL, from L *tropaeum* TROPHY; from the shield-shaped leaves and helmet-shaped flowers]

trope (trəʊp) *n* a word or expression used in a figurative sense. [C16: from L *tropus* figurative use of a word, from Gk *tropos* style, turn]

-trope *n combining form.* indicating a turning towards, development in the direction of, or affinity to: *heliotrope.* [from Gk *tropos* a turn]

trophic ('trɒfɪk) *adj* of nutrition. [C19: from Gk *trophikos,* from *trophē* food, from *trephein* to feed]

tropho- *or before a vowel* **troph-** *combining form.* indicating nourishment or nutrition: *trophozoite.* [from Gk *trophē* food, from *trephein* to feed]

trophoblast ('trɒfəˌblæst) *n* a membrane that encloses the embryo of mammals and absorbs nourishment from the uterine fluids.

trophozoite (ˌtrɒfə'zəʊaɪt) *n* the form of a sporozoan protozoan, esp. of certain parasites, in the feeding stage.

trophy ● ('trəʊfɪ) *n, pl* **trophies. 1** an object such as a silver cup that is symbolic of victory in a contest, esp. a sporting contest; prize. **2** a memento of success, esp. one taken in war or hunting. **3** (in ancient Greece and Rome) a memorial to a victory, usually consisting of captured arms raised on the battlefield or in a public place. **4** an ornamental carving that represents a group of weapons, etc. [C16: from F *trophée,* from L *tropaeum,* from Gk *tropaion,* from *tropē* a turning, defeat of the enemy]

-trophy *n combining form.* indicating a certain type of nourishment or growth: *dystrophy.* [from Gk *-trophia,* from *trophē* nourishment]
▸**-trophic** *adj combining form.*

tropic ('trɒpɪk) *n* **1** (*sometimes cap.*) either of the parallel lines of latitude at about 23½°N (**tropic of Cancer**) and 23½°S (**tropic of Capricorn**) of the equator. **2 the tropics.** (*often cap.*) that part of the earth's surface between the tropics of Cancer and Capricorn. **3** *Astron.* either of the two parallel circles on the celestial sphere having the same latitudes and names as the lines on the earth. ◆ *adj* **4** tropical. [C14: from LL *tropicus* belonging to a turn, from Gk *tropikos,* from *tropos* a turn; from the belief that the sun turned back at the solstices]

-tropic *adj combining form.* turning or developing in response to a certain stimulus: *heliotropic.* [from Gk *tropos* a turn]

tropical ● ('trɒpɪkᵊl) *adj* **1** situated in, used in, characteristic of, or relating to the tropics. **2** (of weather) very hot, esp. when humid. **3** of a trope.
▸ˌ**tropi'cality** *n* ▸**'tropically** *adv*

tropicbird ('trɒpɪkˌbɜ:d) *n* any of various tropical aquatic birds having long tail feathers and a white plumage with black markings.

tropism ('trəʊpɪzəm) *n* the response of an organism, esp. a plant, to an external stimulus by growth in a direction determined by the stimulus. [from Gk *tropos* a turn]
▸ˌ**tropis'matic** *adj*

-tropism *or* **-tropy** *n combining form.* indicating a tendency to turn or develop in response to a stimulus: *phototropism.* [from Gk *tropos* a turn]

tropo- *combining form.* indicating change or a turning: *tropophyte.* [from Gk *tropos* a turn]

tropopause ('trɒpəˌpɔ:z) *n Meteorol.* the plane of discontinuity between the troposphere and the stratosphere, characterized by a sharp change in the lapse rate.

troposphere ('trɒpəˌsfɪə) *n* the lowest atmospheric layer, about 18 kilometres (11 miles) thick at the equator to about 6 km (4 miles) at the Poles, in which air temperature decreases normally with height at about 6.5°C per km.
▸**tropospheric** (ˌtrɒpə'sferɪk) *adj*

THESAURUS

trollop *n* **1** *Derogatory* = **slut,** fallen woman, floozy (*sl.*), harlot, hussy, loose woman, prostitute, scrubber (*Brit. & Austral. sl.*), slag (*Brit. sl.*), streetwalker, strumpet, tart (*inf.*), wanton, whore, working girl (*facetious sl.*)

troop *n* **1** = **group,** assemblage, band, bevy, body, bunch (*inf.*), company, contingent, crew (*inf.*), crowd, drove, flock, gang, gathering, herd, horde, multitude, pack, posse (*inf.*), squad, swarm, team, throng, unit **3** *pl* = **soldiers,** armed forces, army, fighting men, men, military, servicemen, soldiery ◆ *vb* **5** = **flock,** crowd, march, parade, stream, swarm, throng, traipse (*inf.*)

trophy *n* **1, 2** = **prize,** award, bays, booty, cup, laurels, memento, souvenir, spoils

tropical *adj* **2** = **hot,** humid, lush, steamy, stifling, sultry, sweltering, torrid
Antonyms *adj* arctic, chilly, cold, cool, freezing, frosty, frozen, parky (*Brit. inf.*)

-tropous *adj combining form.* indicating a turning away: *anatropous.* [from Gk *-tropos* concerning a turn]

troppo[1] ('trɒpəʊ) *adv Music.* too much; excessively. See **non troppo.** [It.]

troppo[2] ('trɒpəʊ) *adj Austral. sl.* mentally affected by a tropical climate.

trot ● (trɒt) *vb* **trots, trotting, trotted. 1** to move or cause to move at a trot. ◆ *n* **2** a gait of a horse in which diagonally opposite legs come down together. **3** a steady brisk pace. **4** (in harness racing) a race for horses that have been trained to trot fast. **5** *Chiefly Brit.* a small child. **6** *US sl.* a student's crib. **7 on the trot.** *Inf.* **7a** one after the other: *to read two books on the trot.* **7b** busy, esp. on one's feet. **8 the trots.** *Inf.* **8a** diarrhoea. **8b** *NZ.* trotting races. ◆ See also **trot out.** [C13: from OF *trot,* from *troter* to trot, of Gmc origin]

Trot (trɒt) *n Inf.* a follower of Trotsky; Trotskyist.

troth (trəʊθ) *n Arch.* **1** a pledge of fidelity, esp. a betrothal. **2** truth (esp. in **in troth**). **3** loyalty; fidelity. [OE *trēowth*]

trotline ('trɒt,laɪn) *n Angling.* a long line suspended across a stream, river, etc., to which shorter hooked and baited lines are attached.

trot out ● *vb* (*tr, adv*) *Inf.* to bring forward, as for approbation or admiration, esp. repeatedly.

Trotskyism ('trɒtskɪ,ɪzəm) *n* the theory of communism of Leon Trotsky (1879–1940), Russian revolutionary and writer, in which he called for immediate worldwide revolution by the proletariat.
► **'Trotsky,ite** *or* **'Trotskyist** *n, adj*

trotter ('trɒtə) *n* **1** a horse that is specially trained to trot fast. **2** (*usually pl*) the foot of certain animals, esp. of pigs.

troubadour ● ('tru:bə,dʊə) *n* any of a class of lyric poets who flourished principally in Provence and N Italy from the 11th to the 13th century, writing chiefly on courtly love. [C18: from F, from OProvençal *trobador,* from *trobar* to write verses, ? ult. from L *tropus* TROPE]

trouble ● ('trʌbᵊl) *n* **1** a state of mental distress or anxiety. **2** a state of disorder or unrest: *industrial trouble.* **3** a condition of disease, pain, or malfunctioning: *liver trouble.* **4** a cause of distress, disturbance, or pain. **5** effort or exertion taken to do something. **6** liability to suffer punishment or misfortune (esp. in **be in trouble**): *he's in trouble with the police.* **7** a personal weakness or cause of annoyance: *his trouble is he's too soft.* **8** political unrest. **9** the condition of an unmarried girl who becomes pregnant (esp. in **in trouble**). ◆ *vb* **troubles, troubling, troubled. 10** (*tr*) to cause trouble to. **11** (*intr;* usually with a negative and foll. by *about*) to put oneself to inconvenience; be concerned: *don't trouble about me.* **12** (*intr;* usually with a negative) to take pains; exert oneself. **13** (*tr*) to cause inconvenience or discomfort to. **14** (*tr; usually passive*) to agitate or make rough: *the seas were troubled.* **15** (*tr*) *Caribbean.* to interfere with. [C13: from OF *troubler,* from Vulgar L *turbulāre* (unattested), from LL *turbidāre,* ult. from *turba* commotion]
► **'troubler** *n*

troublemaker ● ('trʌbᵊl,meɪkə) *n* a person who makes trouble, esp. between people.
► **'trouble,making** *adj, n*

troubleshooter ('trʌbᵊl,ʃu:tə) *n* a person who locates the cause of trouble and removes or treats it.
► **'trouble,shooting** *n, adj*

troublesome ● ('trʌbᵊlsəm) *adj* **1** causing trouble. **2** characterized by violence; turbulent.
► **'troublesomeness** *n*

troublous ('trʌbləs) *adj Arch. or literary.* unsettled; agitated.
► **'troublously** *adv*

trough ● (trɒf) *n* **1** a narrow open container, esp. one in which food or water for animals is put. **2** a narrow channel, gutter, or gulley. **3** a narrow depression, as between two waves. **4** *Meteorol.* an elongated area of low pressure. **5** a single or temporary low point; depression. **6** *Physics.* the portion of a wave in which the amplitude lies below its average value. **7** *Econ.* the lowest point of the trade cycle. [OE *trōh*]

trounce ● (traʊns) *vb* **trounces, trouncing, trounced.** (*tr*) to beat or defeat utterly; thrash. [C16: from ?]

troupe ● (tru:p) *n* **1** a company of actors or other performers, esp. one that travels. ◆ *vb* **troupes, trouping, trouped. 2** (*intr*) (esp. of actors) to move or travel in a group. [C19: from F; see TROOP]

trouper ● ('tru:pə) *n* **1** a member of a troupe. **2** a dependable worker or associate.

trouser ('traʊzə) *n* (*modifier*) of or relating to trousers: *trouser buttons.*

trousers ('traʊzəz) *pl n* a garment shaped to cover the body from the waist to the ankles or knees with separate tube-shaped sections for both legs. [C17: from earlier *trouse,* var. of TREWS, infl. by DRAWERS]

trousseau ('tru:səʊ) *n, pl* **trousseaux** *or* **trousseaus** (-səʊz). the clothes, linen, etc., collected by a bride for her marriage. [C19: from OF, lit.: a little bundle; see TRUSS]

trout (traʊt) *n, pl* **trout** *or* **trouts.** any of various game fishes, mostly of fresh water in northern regions. They are related to the salmon but are smaller and spotted. [OE *trūht,* from LL *tructa,* from Gk *troktēs* sharp-toothed fish]

trouvère (tru:'vɛə) *n* any of a group of poets of N France during the 12th and 13th centuries who composed chiefly narrative works. [C19: from F, from OF *troveor,* from *trover* to compose]

trove (trəʊv) *n* See **treasure-trove.**

trow (trəʊ) *vb Arch.* to think, believe, or trust. [OE *treow*]

trowel ('traʊəl) *n* **1** any of various small hand tools having a flat metal blade attached to a handle, used for scooping or spreading plaster or similar materials. **2** a similar tool with a curved blade used by gardeners for lifting plants, etc. ◆ *vb* **trowels, trowelling, trowelled** *or US* **trowels, troweling, troweled. 3** (*tr*) to use a trowel on. [C14: from OF *truele,* from L *trulla* a scoop, from *trua* a stirring spoon]

troy weight *or* **troy** (trɔɪ) *n* a system of weights used for precious metals and gemstones, based on the grain. 24 grains = 1 pennyweight; 20 pennyweights = 1 (troy) ounce; 12 ounces = 1 (troy) pound. [C14: after the city of *Troyes,* France, where first used]

trs *Printing. abbrev. for* transpose.

truant ● ('tru:ənt) *n* **1** a person who is absent without leave, esp. from school. ◆ *adj* **2** being or relating to a truant. ◆ *vb* **3** (*intr*) to play truant. [C13: from OF: vagabond, prob. of Celtic origin]
► **'truancy** *n*

truce ● (tru:s) *n* **1** an agreement to stop fighting, esp. temporarily. **2** temporary cessation of something unpleasant. [C13: from pl of OE *treow* trow]

truck[1] (trʌk) *n* **1** *Brit.* a vehicle for carrying freight on a railway; wagon. **2** another name (esp. US, Canad., Austral., and NZ) for **lorry. 3** Also called: **truckload.** the amount carried by a truck. **4** a frame carrying two or more pairs of wheels attached under an end of a railway coach, etc. **5** *Naut.* a disc-shaped block fixed to the head of a mast having holes for receiving halyards. **6** any wheeled vehicle used to move goods. ◆ *vb* **7** to convey (goods) in a truck. **8** (*intr*) *Chiefly US & Canad.* to drive a truck. [C17: ? shortened from *truckle* a small wheel]

truck[2] ● (trʌk) *n* **1** commercial goods. **2** dealings (esp. in **have no truck with**). **3** commercial exchange. **4** *Arch.* payment of wages in kind. **5**

THESAURUS

trot *vb* **1** = **run**, canter, go briskly, jog, lope, scamper ◆ *n* **3** = **run**, brisk pace, canter, jog, lope **7a on the trot** *Informal* = **one after the other**, consecutively, in a row, in succession, without break, without interruption

trot out *vb Informal* = **repeat**, bring forward, bring up, come out with, drag up, exhibit, recite, rehearse, reiterate, relate

troubadour *n* = **minstrel**, balladeer, jongleur, lyric poet, poet, singer

trouble *n* **1** = **distress**, agitation, annoyance, anxiety, bummer, disquiet, grief, hardship, hassle (*inf.*), heartache, irritation, misfortune, pain, sorrow, suffering, torment, tribulation, vexation, woe, worry **2** = **disorder**, agitation, bother (*inf.*), commotion, discontent, discord, dissatisfaction, disturbance, hassle (*inf.*), Pandora's box, row, strife, tumult, unrest **3** = **ailment**, complaint, defect, disability, disease, disorder, failure, illness, malfunction, upset **5** = **effort**, attention, bother, care, exertion, inconvenience, labour, pains, struggle, thought, work **6** = **difficulty**, bother, concern, danger, deep water, dilemma, dire straits, hassle (*inf.*), hot water (*inf.*), mess, nuisance, pest, pickle (*inf.*), predicament, problem, scrape (*inf.*), spot (*inf.*), tight spot ◆ *vb* **10** = **bother**, afflict, agitate, annoy, discompose, disconcert, disquiet, distress, disturb, faze, fret, grieve, harass, hassle (*inf.*), pain, perplex, perturb, pester, plague, put *or* get someone's back up, sadden, torment, upset, vex, worry **12** = **take pains**, exert oneself, go to the effort of, make an effort, take the time **13** = **inconvenience**, bother, burden, cause discomfort, discommode, disturb, impose upon, incommode, put out

Antonyms *n* ≠ **distress:** comfort, contentment, good fortune, happiness, pleasure, tranquillity ≠ **disorder:** agreement, contentment, harmony, peace, tranquillity, unity ≠ **effort:** convenience, ease, facility ◆ *vb* ≠ **bother:** appease, calm, mollify, please, relieve, soothe ≠ **take pains:** avoid, dodge ≠ **inconvenience:** relieve

troublemaker *n* = **mischief-maker**, *agent provocateur,* agitator, bad apple (*US inf.*), firebrand, incendiary, instigator, meddler, rabble-rouser, rotten apple (*Brit. inf.*), stirrer (*inf.*), stormy petrel

Antonyms *n* appeaser, arbitrator, conciliator, pacifier, peace-maker

troublesome *adj* **1** = **bothersome**, annoying, arduous, burdensome, demanding, difficult, harassing, hard, importunate, inconvenient, irksome, irritating, laborious, oppressive, pestilential, plaguy (*inf.*), taxing, tiresome, tricky, trying, upsetting, vexatious, wearisome, worrisome, worrying **2** = **disorderly**, insubordinate, rebellious, recalcitrant, refractory, rowdy, turbulent, uncooperative, undisciplined, unruly, violent

Antonyms *adj* ≠ **bothersome:** agreeable, calming, congenial, easy, pleasant, simple, soothing, undemanding ≠ **disorderly:** disciplined, eager-to-please, obedient, well-behaved

trough *n* **1** = **manger**, crib, water trough **2** = **channel**, canal, depression, ditch, duct, flume, furrow, gully, gutter, trench, watercourse

trounce *vb* = **defeat heavily** *or* **utterly**, beat, blow out of the water, clobber (*sl.*), crush, drub, give a hiding (*inf.*), hammer (*inf.*), lick (*inf.*), make mincemeat of, overwhelm, paste (*sl.*), rout, slaughter (*inf.*), stuff (*sl.*), tank (*sl.*), thrash, walk over (*inf.*), wipe the floor with (*inf.*)

troupe *n* **1** = **company**, band, cast

trouper *n* **1** = **performer**, actor, artiste, entertainer, player, theatrical, thespian

truancy *n* **2** = **absence**, absence without leave, malingering, shirking, skiving (*Brit. sl.*)

truant *n* **1** = **absentee**, delinquent, deserter, dodger, malingerer, runaway, shirker, skiver (*Brit. sl.*), straggler ◆ *adj* **2** = **absent**, absent without leave, A.W.O.L., missing, skiving (*Brit. sl.*) ◆ *vb* **3** = **absent oneself**, bob off (*Brit. sl.*), bunk off (*sl.*), desert, dodge, go missing, malinger, play truant, run away, shirk, skive (*Brit. sl.*), wag (*dialect*)

truce *n* **1, 2** = **ceasefire**, armistice, break, cessation, cessation of hostilities, intermission, interval, let-up (*inf.*), lull, moratorium, peace, respite, rest, stay, treaty

truck[2] *n* **1** = **commercial goods**, commodities, goods, merchandise, stock, stuff, wares **2, 3** = **dealings**, barter, business, buying and selling, commerce, communication, connection, contact, exchange, relations, trade, traffic ◆ *vb* **8, 9** = **buy and sell**, bargain, barter, cut a deal, deal,

miscellaneous articles. **6** *Inf.* rubbish. **7** *US & Canad.* vegetables grown for market. ◆ *vb* **8** *Arch.* to exchange (goods); barter. **9** (*intr*) to traffic or negotiate. [C13: from OF *troquer* (unattested) to barter, equivalent to Med. L *trocare*, from ?]

trucker ('trʌkə) *n Chiefly US & Canad.* **1** a lorry driver. **2** a person who arranges for the transport of goods by lorry.

truck farm *n US & Canad.* a market garden.
▸**truck farmer** *n* ▸**truck farming** *n*

truckie ('trʌkɪ) *n Austral. & NZ inf.* a truck driver.

trucking ('trʌkɪŋ) *n Chiefly US & Canad.* the transportation of goods by lorry.

truckle ❶ ('trʌkᵊl) *vb* **truckles, truckling, truckled.** (*intr;* usually foll. by *to*) to yield weakly; give in. [C17: from obs. *truckle* to sleep in a truckle bed]
▸'**truckler** *n*

truckle bed *n* a low bed on wheels, stored under a larger bed. [C17: from *truckle* small wheel, ult. from L *trochlea* sheaf of a pulley]

truck system *n* a system during the early years of the Industrial Revolution of forcing workers to accept payment of wages in kind.

truculent ❶ ('trʌkjʊlənt) *adj* **1** defiantly aggressive, sullen, or obstreperous. **2** *Arch.* savage, fierce, or harsh. [C16: from L *truculentus*, from *trux* fierce]
▸'**truculence** *or* '**truculency** *n* ▸'**truculently** *adv*

trudge ❶ (trʌdʒ) *vb* **trudges, trudging, trudged. 1** (*intr*) to walk or plod heavily or wearily. **2** (*tr*) to pass through or over by trudging. ◆ *n* **3** a long tiring walk. [C16: from ?]
▸'**trudger** *n*

trudgen ('trʌdʒən) *n* a type of swimming stroke that uses overarm action, as in the crawl, and a scissors kick. [C19: after John *Trudgen*, E swimmer, who introduced it]

true ❶ (truː) *adj* **truer, truest. 1** not false, fictional, or illusory; factual; conforming with reality. **2** (*prenominal*) real; not synthetic. **3** faithful and loyal. **4** conforming to a required standard, law, or pattern: *a true aim.* **5** exactly in tune. **6** (of a compass bearing) according to the earth's geographical rather than magnetic poles: *true north.* **7** *Biol.* conforming to the typical structure of a designated type. **8** *Physics.* not apparent or relative. ◆ *n* **9** correct alignment (esp. in **in true, out of true**). ◆ *adv* **10** truthfully; rightly. **11** precisely or unswervingly. ◆ *vb* **trues, truing, trued. 12** (*tr*) to adjust so as to make true. [OE *triewe*]
▸'**trueness** *n*

true bill *n* (formerly in Britain; now US) the endorsement made on a bill of indictment by a grand jury certifying it to be supported by sufficient evidence to warrant a trial.

true-blue ❶ *adj* **1** unwaveringly or staunchly loyal. ◆ *n* **true blue. 2** *Chiefly Brit.* a staunch royalist or Conservative.

true-life *adj* directly comparable to reality: *a true-life story.*

truelove ('truːˌlʌv) *n* **1** someone truly loved; sweetheart. **2** another name for **herb Paris.**

truelove knot *or* **true-lovers' knot** *n* a complicated bowknot that is hard to untie, symbolizing ties of love.

true north *n* the direction from any point along a meridian towards the North Pole. Also called: **geographic north.** Cf. **magnetic north.**

true rib *n* any of the upper seven pairs of ribs in man.

true time *n* the time shown by a sundial.

truffle ('trʌfᵊl) *n* **1** any of various edible subterranean European fungi. They have a tuberous appearance and are regarded as a delicacy. **2** Also called: **rum truffle.** *Chiefly Brit.* a sweet resembling this fungus in shape, flavoured with chocolate or rum. [C16: from F *truffe*, from OProvençal *trufa*, ult. from L *tūber*]

trug (trʌg) *n* a long shallow basket for carrying flowers, fruit, etc. [C16: ? var. of TROUGH]

trugo ('truːgəʊ) *n Austral.* a game similar to croquet, originally improvised in Victoria from the rubber discs used as buffers on railway carriages. [from *true go,* when the wheel is hit between the goalposts]

truism ❶ ('truːɪzəm) *n* an obvious truth; platitude.
▸**tru'istic** *adj*

trull (trʌl) *n Arch.* a prostitute; harlot. [C16: from G *Trulle*]

truly ❶ ('truːlɪ) *adv* **1** in a true, just, or faithful manner. **2** (intensifier): *a truly great man.* **3** indeed; really.

trumeau (truː'məʊ) *n, pl* **trumeaux** (-məʊz). *Archit.* a section of a wall or pillar between two openings. [from F]

trump[1] ❶ (trʌmp) *n* **1** Also called: **trump card. 1a** any card from the suit chosen as trumps. **1b** this suit itself; trumps. **2** a decisive or advantageous move, resource, action, etc. **3** *Inf.* a fine or reliable person. ◆ *vb* **4** to play a trump card on (a suit, or a particular card of a suit, that is not trumps). **5** (*tr*) to outdo or surpass. ◆ See also **trumps, trump up.** [C16: var. of TRIUMPH]

trump[2] (trʌmp) *n Arch. or literary.* **1** a trumpet or the sound produced by one. **2 the last trump.** the final trumpet call on the Day of Judgment. [C13: from OF *trompe*, from OHG *trumpa* trumpet]

trumpery ❶ ('trʌmpərɪ) *n, pl* **trumperies. 1** foolish talk or actions. **2** a useless or worthless article; trinket. ◆ *adj* **3** useless or worthless. [C15: from OF *tromperie* deceit, from *tromper* to cheat]

trumpet ❶ ('trʌmpɪt) *n* **1** a valved brass instrument of brilliant tone consisting of a narrow tube ending in a flared bell. **2** any similar instrument, esp. a straight instrument used for fanfares, signals, etc. **3** a loud sound such as that of a trumpet, esp. when made by an animal. **4** an eight-foot reed stop on an organ. **5** something resembling a trumpet in shape. **6** short for **ear trumpet. 7 blow one's own trumpet.** to boast about one's own skills or good qualities. ◆ *vb* **trumpets, trumpeting, trumpeted. 8** to proclaim or sound loudly. [C13: from OF *trompette* a little TRUMP[2]]

trumpeter ('trʌmpɪtə) *n* **1** a person who plays the trumpet, esp. one whose duty it is to play fanfares, signals, etc. **2** any of three birds of South America, having a rounded body, long legs, and a glossy blackish plumage. **3** (*sometimes cap.*) a breed of domestic fancy pigeon with a long ruff. **4** a large silvery-grey Australian marine food and game fish that grunts when taken from the water.

trumpeter swan *n* a large swan of W North America, having a white plumage and black bill.

trumps (trʌmps) *pl n* **1** (*sometimes sing*) *Cards.* any one of the four suits that outranks all the other suits for the duration of a deal or game. **2 turn up trumps.** (of a person) to bring about a happy or successful conclusion, esp. unexpectedly.

trump up ❶ *vb* (*tr, adv*) to invent (a charge, accusation, etc.) so as to deceive.

truncate ❶ *vb* (trʌŋ'keɪt, 'trʌŋkeɪt), **truncates, truncating, truncated. 1** (*tr*) to shorten by cutting. ◆ *adj* ('trʌŋkeɪt). **2** cut short; truncated. **3** *Biol.* having a blunt end. [C15: from L *truncāre* to lop]
▸**trun'cation** *n*

truncated (trʌŋ'keɪtɪd) *adj* **1** (of a cone, prism, etc.) having an apex or end removed by a plane intersection. **2** shortened by or as if by cutting off; truncate.

THESAURUS

do business, exchange, have dealings, negotiate, swap, trade, traffic, transact business

truckle *vb* = **give in**, bend the knee, bow and scrape, concede, cringe, crouch, defer, fawn, give way, knuckle under, kowtow, lick (someone's) boots, pander to, stoop, submit, toady, yield

truculent *adj* **1** = **hostile**, aggressive, antagonistic, bad-tempered, bellicose, belligerent, combative, contentious, cross, defiant, ill-tempered, itching *or* spoiling for a fight (*inf.*), obstreperous, pugnacious, scrappy (*inf.*), sullen
Antonyms *adj* agreeable, amiable, civil, co-operative, gentle, good-natured, peaceable, placid

trudge *vb* **1** = **plod**, clump, drag oneself, footslog, hike, lumber, march, slog, stump, traipse (*inf.*), tramp, trek, walk heavily, yomp ◆ *n* **3** = **tramp**, footslog, haul, hike, march, slog, traipse (*inf.*), trek, yomp

true *adj* **1, 2** = **correct**, accurate, actual, authentic, bona fide, exact, factual, genuine, legitimate, natural, precise, pure, real, right, truthful, valid, veracious, veritable **3** = **faithful**, confirmed, constant, dedicated, devoted, dutiful, fast, firm, honest, honourable, loyal, pure, reliable, sincere, staunch, steady, true-blue, trustworthy, trusty, unswerving, upright **4** = **exact**, accurate, correct, on target, perfect, precise, proper, spot-on (*Brit. inf.*), unerring ◆ *adv* **10** = **truthfully**, honestly, rightly, veraciously, veritably **11** = **precisely**, accurately, correctly, on target, perfectly, properly, unerringly
Antonyms *adj* ≠ **correct**: abnormal, artificial, atypical, bogus, counterfeit, erroneous, fake, false, fictional, fictitious, illegitimate, imaginary, inaccurate, incorrect, made-up, make-believe, phoney *or* phony (*inf.*), pretended, self-styled, spurious, unofficial, untrue, untruthful ≠ **faithful**: deceitful, disloyal, faithless, false, treacherous, unreliable, untrue, untrustworthy ≠ **exact**: askew, awry, inaccurate, incorrect

true-blue *adj* **1** = **staunch**, confirmed, constant, dedicated, devoted, dyed-in-the-wool, faithful, loyal, orthodox, trusty, uncompromising, unwavering

truism *n* = **cliché**, axiom, bromide, commonplace, platitude, stock phrase, trite saying

truly *adv* **1** = **correctly**, accurately, authentically, beyond doubt, beyond question, confirmedly, exactly, factually, firmly, genuinely, honestly, in actuality, in fact, in reality, in truth, legitimately, precisely, really, rightly, sincerely, truthfully, veraciously, veritably, without a doubt **3** = **really**, exceptionally, extremely, greatly, indeed, of course, seriously (*inf.*), to be sure, verily, very
Antonyms *adv* ≠ **correctly**: doubtfully, falsely, fraudulently, inaccurately, incorrectly, mistakenly

trump[1] *vb* **5** = **outdo**, cap, excel, score points off, surpass, top

trumpery *n* **1** = **nonsense**, balderdash, bilge (*inf.*), bosh (*inf.*), bullshit (*taboo sl.*), bunkum *or* buncombe (*chiefly US*), claptrap (*inf.*), cobblers (*Brit. taboo sl.*), drivel, eyewash (*inf.*), foolishness, foolish talk, garbage (*inf.*), guff (*sl.*), hogwash, hokum (*sl., chiefly US & Canad.*), hot air (*inf.*), idiocy, inanity, moonshine, pap, piffle (*inf.*), poppycock (*inf.*), stuff, tommyrot, tosh (*sl., chiefly Brit.*), tripe (*inf.*), twaddle **2** = **trifle**, bagatelle, bauble, gewgaw, kickshaw, knick-knack, toy, trinket ◆ *adj* **3** = **trifle**, brummagem, cheap, flashy, meretricious, nasty, rubbishy, shabby, shoddy, tawdry, trashy, trifling, useless, valueless, worthless

trumpet *n* **2** = **horn**, bugle, clarion **3** = **roar**, bay, bellow, call, cry **7 blow one's own trumpet** = **boast**, brag, crow, sing one's own praises, vaunt ◆ *vb* **8** = **proclaim**, advertise, announce, broadcast, crack up (*inf.*), extol, noise abroad, publish, shout from the rooftops, sound loudly, tout (*inf.*)
Antonyms *vb* ≠ **proclaim**: conceal, hide, hush up, keep secret, make light of, play down, soft pedal (*inf.*)

trump up *vb* = **invent**, concoct, contrive, cook up (*inf.*), create, fabricate, fake, make up, manufacture

truncate *vb* **1** = **shorten**, abbreviate, clip, crop, curtail, cut, cut short, dock, lop, pare, prune, trim
Antonyms *vb* drag out, draw out, extend, lengthen, prolong, protract, spin out, stretch

truncheon ➊ ('trʌntʃən) *n* **1** *Chiefly Brit.* a club or cudgel carried by a policeman. **2** a baton of office. [C16: from OF *tronchon* stump, from L *truncus* trunk; see TRUNCATE]

trundle ('trʌndᵊl) *vb* **trundles, trundling, trundled. 1** to move heavily on or as if on wheels: *the bus trundled by.* ◆ *n* **2** a trundling. **3** a small wheel or roller. [OE *tryndel*]

trundle bed *n* a less common word for **truckle bed.**

trundler ('trʌndlə) *n NZ.* **1** a trolley for shopping or one for golf clubs. **2** a child's pushchair.

trunk ➊ (trʌŋk) *n* **1** the main stem of a tree. **2** a large strong case or box used to contain clothes, etc., when travelling and for storage. **3** the body excluding the head, neck, and limbs; torso. **4** the elongated nasal part of an elephant. **5** the US and Canad. name for **boot**[1] (sense 2). **6** the main stem of a nerve, blood vessel, etc. **7** *Naut.* a watertight boxlike cover within a vessel, such as one used to enclose a centreboard. **8** an enclosed duct or passageway for ventilation, etc. **9** (*modifier*) of a main road, railway, etc., in a network: *a trunk line.* ◆ See also **trunks.** [C15: from OF *tronc,* from L *truncus,* from *truncus* (adj) lopped]

trunk call *n Chiefly Brit.* a long-distance telephone call.

trunk curl *n* another name for **sit-up.**

trunkfish ('trʌŋk,fɪʃ) *n, pl* **trunkfish** *or* **trunkfishes.** any of a family of fishes having the body encased in bony plates.

trunk hose *n* a man's puffed-out breeches reaching to the thighs and worn with tights in the 16th century.

trunking ('trʌŋkɪŋ) *n* **1** *Telecomm.* the cables that take a common route through a telephone exchange building. **2** plastic housing used to conceal wires, etc.; casing. **3** the delivery of goods over long distances, esp. by road vehicles to local distribution centres.

trunk line *n* **1** a direct link between two telephone exchanges or switchboards that are a considerable distance apart. **2** the main route or routes on a railway.

trunk road *n Brit.* a main road, esp. one that is suitable for heavy vehicles.

trunks (trʌŋks) *pl n* **1** a man's garment worn for swimming, extending from the waist to the thigh. **2** shorts worn for some sports. **3** *Chiefly Brit.* men's underpants with legs that reach midthigh.

trunnion ('trʌnjən) *n* one of a pair of coaxial projections attached to opposite sides of a container, cannon, etc., to provide a support about which it can turn. [C17: from OF *trognon* trunk]

truss ➊ (trʌs) *vb* (*tr*) **1** (sometimes foll. by *up*) to tie, bind, or bundle. **2** to bind the wings and legs of (a fowl) before cooking. **3** to support or stiffen (a roof, bridge, etc.) with structural members. **4** *Med.* to supply or support with a truss. ◆ *n* **5** a structural framework of wood or metal used to support a roof, bridge, etc. **6** *Med.* a device for holding a hernia in place, typically consisting of a pad held in position by a belt. **7** a cluster of flowers or fruit growing at the end of a single stalk. **8** *Naut.* a metal fitting fixed to a yard at its centre for holding it to a mast. **9** another name for **corbel. 10** a bundle or pack. **11** *Chiefly Brit.* a bundle of hay or straw, esp. one having a fixed weight of 36, 56, or 60 pounds. [C13: from OF *trousse,* from *trousser,* apparently from Vulgar L *torciāre* (unattested), from *torca* (unattested) a bundle]

trust ➊ (trʌst) *n* **1** reliance on and confidence in the truth, worth, reliability, etc., of a person or thing; faith. Related adj: **fiducial. 2** a group of commercial enterprises combined to control the market for any commodity. **3** the obligation of someone in a responsible position. **4** custody, charge, or care. **5** a person or thing in which confidence or faith is placed. **6** commercial credit. **7a** an arrangement whereby a person to whom the legal title to property is conveyed (the trustee) holds such property for the benefit of those entitled to the beneficial interest. **7b** property that is the subject of such an arrangement. Related adj: **fiduciary. 8** (in the British National Health Service) a self-governing hospital, group of hospitals, or other body providing health-care services, which operates as an independent commercial unit within the NHS. **9** (*modifier*) of or relating to a trust or trusts. ◆ *vb* **10** (*tr; may take a clause as object*) to expect, hope, or suppose. **11** (when *tr, may take an infinitive;* when *intr,* often foll. by *in* or *to*) to place confidence in (someone to do something); rely (upon). **12** (*tr*) to consign for care. **13** (*tr*) to allow (someone to do something) with confidence in his or her good sense or honesty. **14** (*tr*) to extend business credit to. [C13: from ON *traust*]

▸'**trustable** *adj* ▸'**truster** *n*

trust account *n* **1** Also called: **trustee account.** a savings account deposited in the name of a trustee who controls it during his lifetime, after which the balance is payable to a prenominated beneficiary. **2** property under the control of a trustee or trustees.

trustee (trʌ'sti:) *n* **1** a person to whom the legal title to property is entrusted. **2** a member of a board that manages the affairs of an institution or organization.

trustee in bankruptcy *n* a person entrusted with the administration of a bankrupt's affairs and with realizing his assets for the benefit of the creditors.

trustee investment *n Stock Exchange.* an investment in which trustees are authorized to invest money belonging to a trust fund.

trusteeship (trʌ'sti:ʃɪp) *n* **1** the office or function of a trustee. **2a** the administration or government of a territory by a foreign country under the supervision of the **Trusteeship Council** of the United Nations. **2b** (*often cap.*) any such dependent territory; trust territory.

trustful ➊ ('trʌstfʊl) *or* **trusting** *adj* characterized by a tendency or readiness to trust others.

▸'**trustfully** *or* '**trustingly** *adv*

trust fund *n* money, securities, etc., held in trust.

trust territory *n* (*sometimes cap.*) another name for a **trusteeship** (sense 2b).

trustworthy ➊ ('trʌst,wɜ:ðɪ) *adj* worthy of being trusted; honest, reliable, or dependable.

▸'**trust,worthily** *adv* ▸'**trust,worthiness** *n*

trusty ➊ ('trʌstɪ) *adj* **trustier, trustiest. 1** faithful or reliable. ◆ *n, pl* **trusties. 2** a trustworthy convict given special privileges.

▸'**trustily** *adv* ▸'**trustiness** *n*

truth ➊ (tru:θ) *n* **1** the quality of being true, genuine, actual, or factual. **2** something that is true as opposed to false. **3** a proven or verified fact, principle, etc.: *the truths of astronomy.* **4** (*usually pl*) a system of concepts purporting to represent some aspect of the world: *the truths of religion.* **5** fidelity to a standard or law. **6** faithful reproduction or portrayal. **7** honesty. **8** accuracy, as in the setting of a mechanical instrument. **9** loyalty. ◆ Related adjs.: **veritable, veracious.** [OE *triewth*]

▸'**truthless** *adj*

truth drug *or* **serum** *n Inf.* any of various drugs supposed to have the property of making people tell the truth, as by relaxing them.

truthful ➊ ('tru:θfʊl) *adj* **1** telling the truth; honest. **2** realistic: *a truthful portrayal of the king.*

▸'**truthfully** *adv* ▸'**truthfulness** *n*

truth-function *n Logic.* a function that determines the truth-value of a complex sentence solely in terms of the truth-values of the component sentences without reference to their meaning.

truth set *n Logic, maths.* the set of values that satisfy an open sentence, equation, inequality, etc., having no unique solution. Also called: **solution set.**

truth table *n* **1** a table, used in logic, indicating the truth-value of a compound statement for every truth-value of its component propositions. **2** a similar table, used in transistor technology, to indicate the value of the output signal of a logic circuit for every value of input signal.

truth-value *n Logic.* either of the values, true or false, that may be taken by a statement.

THESAURUS

truncheon *n* **1** *Chiefly Brit.* = **club**, baton, cudgel, staff

trunk *n* **1** = **stem**, bole, stalk, stock **2** = **chest**, bin, box, case, casket, coffer, crate, kist (*Scot. & N English dialect*), locker, portmanteau **3** = **body**, torso **4** = **snout**, proboscis

truss *vb* **1** = **tie**, bind, bundle, fasten, make fast, pack, pinion, secure, strap, tether **4** *Medical* = **support**, bandage ◆ *n* **5** = **joist**, beam, brace, buttress, prop, shore, stanchion, stay, strut, support

trust *n* **1** = **confidence**, assurance, belief, certainty, certitude, conviction, credence, credit, expectation, faith, hope, reliance **3** = **responsibility**, duty, obligation **4** = **custody**, care, charge, guard, guardianship, protection, safekeeping, trusteeship ◆ *vb* **10** = **expect**, assume, believe, hope, presume, suppose, surmise, think likely **11** = **believe in**, bank on, count on, depend on, have faith in, lean on, pin one's faith on, place confidence in, place one's trust in, place reliance on, rely upon, swear by, take as gospel, take at face value **12** = **entrust**, assign, command, commit, confide, consign, delegate, give, put into the hands of, sign over, turn over

Antonyms *n* ≠ **confidence:** distrust, doubt, fear, incredulity, lack of faith, mistrust, scepticism, suspicion, uncertainty, wariness ◆ *vb* ≠ **believe in:** be sceptical of, beware, disbelieve, discredit, distrust, doubt, lack confidence in, lack faith in, mistrust, suspect

trustful *adj* = **unsuspecting**, confiding, credulous, gullible, innocent, naive, optimistic, simple, unguarded, unsuspicious, unwary

Antonyms *adj* cagey (*inf.*), cautious, chary, distrustful, guarded, on one's guard, suspicious, wary

trustworthy *adj* = **dependable**, ethical, honest, honourable, level-headed, mature, principled, reliable, reputable, responsible, righteous, sensible, staunch, steadfast, to be trusted, true, trusty, truthful, upright

Antonyms *adj* deceitful, dishonest, disloyal, irresponsible, treacherous, undependable, unethical, unprincipled, unreliable, untrustworthy

trusty *adj* **1** = **reliable**, dependable, faithful, firm, honest, responsible, solid, staunch, steady, straightforward, strong, true, trustworthy, upright

Antonyms *adj* dishonest, irresolute, irresponsible, undependable, unfaithful, unreliable

truth *n* **1** = **truthfulness**, accuracy, actuality, exactness, fact, factuality, factualness, genuineness, legitimacy, naturalism, precision, reality, validity, veracity, verity **3** = **fact**, axiom, certainty, law, maxim, proven principle, reality, truism, verity **7** = **honesty**, candour, frankness, integrity, realism, uprightness **9** = **loyalty**, constancy, dedication, devotion, dutifulness, faith, faithfulness, fidelity

Antonyms *n* ≠ **truthfulness:** error, falsity, inaccuracy ≠ **fact:** delusion, fabrication, falsehood, fiction, invention, legend, lie, make-believe, myth, old wives' tale, untruth ≠ **honesty:** deceit, deception, dishonesty

truthful *adj* **1** = **honest**, candid, faithful, forthright, frank, plain-spoken, reliable, sincere, straight, straightforward, true, trustworthy, upfront (*inf.*), veracious **2** = **true**, accurate, correct, exact, literal, naturalistic, precise, realistic, veritable

Antonyms *adj* ≠ **honest:** deceptive, dishonest, false, insincere, lying, untruthful ≠ **true:** fabricated, false, fictional, fictitious, inaccurate, incorrect, made-up, untrue, untruthful

truthless *adj* **1** = **untrue**, deceitful, deceptive, dishonest, faithless, false, fraudulent, insincere, lying, mendacious, perjured, treacherous, untrustworthy

try ❶ (traɪ) *vb* **tries, trying, tried. 1** (when *tr, may take an infinitive,* sometimes with *to* replaced by *and*) to make an effort or attempt. **2** (*tr; often* foll. by *out*) to sample, test, or give experimental use to (something). **3** (*tr*) to put strain or stress on: *he tries my patience.* **4** (*tr; often passive*) to give pain, affliction, or vexation to. **5a** to examine and determine the issues involved in (a cause) in a court of law. **5b** to hear evidence in order to determine the guilt or innocence of (an accused). **6** (*tr*) to melt (fat, lard, etc.) in order to separate out impurities. ◆ *n, pl* **tries. 7** an experiment or trial. **8** an attempt or effort. **9** *Rugby.* the act of an attacking player touching the ball down behind the opposing team's goal line. **10** *American football.* an attempt made after a touchdown to score an extra point, as by kicking a goal. ◆ See also **try on, try out.** [C13: from OF *trier* to sort, from ?]

> **USAGE NOTE** The use of *and* instead of *to* after *try* is very common, but should be avoided in formal writing: *we must try to prevent* (not *try and prevent*) *this happening.*

trying ❶ ('traɪɪŋ) *adj* upsetting, difficult, or annoying.
▸ **'tryingly** *adv*

trying plane *n* a plane with a long body for planing the edges of long boards. Also called: **try plane.**

try on *vb* (*tr, adv*) **1** to put on (a garment) to find out whether it fits, etc. **2 try it on.** *Inf.* to attempt to deceive or fool someone. ◆ *n* **try-on. 3** *Brit. inf.* something done to test out a person's tolerance, etc.

try out ❶ *vb* (*adv*) **1** (*tr*) to test or put to experimental use. **2** (when *intr,* usually foll. by *for*) *US & Canad.* (of an athlete, actor, etc.) to undergo a test or to submit (an athlete, actor, etc.) to a test in order to determine suitability for a place in a team, an acting role, etc. ◆ *n* **tryout. 3** *Chiefly US & Canad.* a trial or test, as of an athlete or actor.

trypanosome ('trɪpənəˌsəʊm) *n* any parasitic flagellate protozoan that lives in the blood of vertebrates and causes sleeping sickness and certain other diseases. [C19: from NL *Trypanosoma,* from Gk *trupanon* borer + *sōma* body]

trypanosomiasis (ˌtrɪpənəsə'maɪəsɪs) *n* any infection of an animal or human with a trypanosome.

trypsin ('trɪpsɪn) *n* a digestive enzyme in the pancreatic juice: it catalyses the hydrolysis of proteins to peptides. [C19 *tryp-,* from Gk *tripsis* a rubbing, from *tribein* to rub + -IN; from the fact that it was orig. produced by rubbing the pancreas with glycerine]
▸ **tryptic** ('trɪptɪk) *adj*

tryptophan ('trɪptəˌfæn) *n* an essential amino acid; a component of proteins necessary for growth. [C20: from *trypt(ic),* from TRYPSIN + *-o-* + *-phan,* var. of -PHANE]

trysail ('traɪˌseɪl; *Naut.* 'traɪsᵊl) *n* a small fore-and-aft sail set on a sailing vessel in foul weather to help keep her head to the wind.

try square *n* a device for testing or laying out right angles, usually consisting of a metal blade fixed at right angles to a wooden handle.

tryst (trɪst, traɪst) *n Arch. or literary.* **1** an appointment to meet, esp. secretly. **2** the place of such a meeting or the meeting itself. [C14: from OF *triste* lookout post, apparently from ON]

tsar ❶ *or* **czar** (zɑː) *n* **1** (until 1917) the emperor of Russia. **2** a tyrant; autocrat. **3** *Inf.* a person in authority. [C17: from Russian *tsar,* via Gothic *kaisar* from L: CAESAR]
▸ **'tsardom** *or* **'czardom** *n*

tsarevitch *or* **czarevitch** ('zɑːrəvɪtʃ) *n* a son of a Russian tsar, esp. the eldest son. [from Russian *tsarevich,* from TSAR + *-evich,* masc. patronymic suffix]

tsarevna *or* **czarevna** (zɑː'rɛvnə) *n* **1** a daughter of a Russian tsar. **2** the wife of a Russian tsarevitch. [from Russian, from TSAR + *-evna,* fem. patronymic suffix]

tsarina, czarina (zɑː'riːnə) *or* **tsaritsa, czaritza** (zɑː'rɪtsə) *n* the wife of a Russian tsar; Russian empress. [from It., Sp. *czarina,* from G *Czarin*]

tsarism *or* **czarism** ('zɑːrɪzəm) *n* a system of government by a tsar.
▸ **'tsarist** *or* **'czarist** *n, adj*

TSE (in Canada) *abbrev. for* Toronto Stock Exchange.

tsetse fly *or* **tzetze fly** ('tsɛtsɪ) *n* any of various bloodsucking African dipterous flies which transmit various diseases, esp. sleeping sickness. [C19: via Afrik. from Tswana]

T-shirt *or* **tee-shirt** *n* a lightweight simple garment for the upper body, usually short-sleeved. [from T-shape formed when laid out flat]

tsotsi ('tsɒtsɪ) *n, pl* **tsotsis.** *S. African inf.* a Black street thug or gang member; wide boy. [C20: ?from Nguni *tsotsa* to dress flashily]

tsp. *abbrev. for* teaspoon.

T-square *n* a T-shaped ruler used for drawing horizontal lines and to support set squares when drawing vertical and inclined lines.

T-stop *n* a setting of the lens aperture on a camera calibrated photometrically and assigned a T-number.

tsunami (tsʊ'nɑːmɪ) *n, pl* **tsunamis** *or* **tsunami.** a large, often destructive sea wave produced by a submarine earthquake, subsidence, or volcanic eruption. [from Japanese, from *tsu* port + *nami* wave]

tsutsugamushi disease (ˌtsʊtsʊgə'mʊʃɪ) *n* one of the five major groups of acute infectious rickettsial diseases affecting man, common in Asia. It is transmitted by the bite of mites. [from Japanese, from *tsutsuga* disease + *mushi* insect]

Tswana ('tswɑːnə) *n* **1** (*pl* **Tswana** *or* **Tswanas**) a member of a mixed Negroid and Bushman people of southern Africa, living chiefly in Botswana. **2** the language of this people.

TT *abbrev. for:* **1** teetotal. **2** teetotaller. **3** telegraphic transfer: a method of sending money abroad by cabled transfer between banks. **4** Tourist Trophy (annual motorcycle races held in the Isle of Man). **5** tuberculin-tested.

TTL *abbrev. for:* **1** transistor transistor logic: a method of constructing electronic logic circuits. **2** through-the-lens: denoting a system of light metering in cameras.

TU *abbrev. for* trade union.

Tu. *abbrev. for* Tuesday.

tuatara (ˌtuːə'tɑːrə) *n* a lizard-like reptile occurring on certain islands near New Zealand. [C19: from Maori, from *tua* back + *tara* spine]

tub (tʌb) *n* **1** a low wide open container, typically round: used in a variety of domestic and industrial situations. **2** a small plastic or cardboard container of similar shape for ice cream, margarine, etc. **3** another word (esp. US) for **bath** (sense 1). **4** Also called: **tubful.** the amount a tub will hold. **5** a clumsy slow boat or ship. **6a** a small vehicle on rails for carrying loads in a mine. **6b** a container for lifting coal or ore up a mine shaft. ◆ *vb* **tubs, tubbing, tubbed. 7** *Brit. inf.* to wash (oneself) in a tub. **8** (*tr*) to keep or put in a tub. [C14: from MDu. *tubbe*]
▸ **'tubbable** *adj* ▸ **'tubber** *n*

tuba ('tjuːbə) *n, pl* **tubas** *or* **tubae** (-biː). **1** a valved brass instrument of bass pitch, in which the bell points upwards and the mouthpiece projects at right angles. **2** a powerful reed stop on an organ. [L]

tubal ('tjuːbᵊl) *adj* **1** of or relating to a tube. **2** of, relating to, or developing in a Fallopian tube.

tubby ❶ ('tʌbɪ) *adj* **tubbier, tubbiest. 1** plump. **2** shaped like a tub.
▸ **'tubbiness** *n*

tube (tjuːb) *n* **1** a long hollow cylindrical object, used for the passage of fluids or as a container. **2** a collapsible cylindrical container of soft metal or plastic closed with a cap, used to hold viscous liquids or pastes. **3** *Anat.* **3a** short for **Eustachian tube** or **Fallopian tube. 3b** any hollow cylindrical structure. **4** (*sometimes cap.*) *Brit.* **4a the tube.** an underground railway system, esp. that in London. US and Canad. equivalent: **subway. 4b** the tunnels through which the railway runs. **5** *Electronics.* **5a** another name for **valve** (sense 3). **5b** See **electron tube, cathode-ray tube, television tube. 6** *Sl., chiefly US.* a television set. **7** *Austral. sl.* a bottle or can of beer. **8** *Surfing.* the cylindrical passage formed when a wave breaks and the crest tips forward. ◆ *vb* **tubes, tubing, tubed.** (*tr*) **9** to supply with a tube. **10** to convey in a tube. **11** to shape like a tube. [C17: from L *tubus*]
▸ **'tubeless** *adj*

tube foot *n* any of numerous tubular outgrowths of most echinoderms that are used for locomotion, to aid ingestion of food, etc.

tubeless tyre *n* a pneumatic tyre in which the outer casing makes an airtight seal with the rim of the wheel so that an inner tube is unnecessary.

tuber ('tjuːbə) *n* **1** a fleshy underground stem or root. **2** *Anat.* a raised area; swelling. [C17: from L *tūber* hump]

tubercle ('tjuːbəkᵊl) *n* **1** any small rounded nodule or elevation, esp. on the skin, on a bone, or on a plant. **2** any small rounded pathological lesion, esp. one characteristic of tuberculosis. [C16: from L *tūberculum* a little swelling]

tubercle bacillus *n* a rodlike bacterium that causes tuberculosis.

tubercular (tjʊ'bɜːkjʊlə) *adj also* **tuberculous. 1** of or symptomatic of tuberculosis. **2** of or relating to a tubercle. **3** characterized by the presence of tubercles. ◆ *n* **4** a person with tuberculosis.

tuberculate (tjʊ'bɜːkjʊlɪt) *adj* covered with tubercles.
▸ **tuˌbercu'lation** *n*

tuberculin (tjʊ'bɜːkjʊlɪn) *n* a sterile liquid prepared from cultures of attenuated tubercle bacillus and used in the diagnosis of tuberculosis.

tuberculin-tested *adj* (of milk) produced by cows that have been certified as free of tuberculosis.

tuberculosis (tjʊˌbɜːkjʊ'ləʊsɪs) *n* a communicable disease caused by infection with the tubercle bacillus, most frequently affecting the lungs. [C19: from NL]

THESAURUS

try *vb* **1 = attempt,** aim, do one's best, do one's damnedest (*inf.*), endeavour, essay, exert oneself, give it one's best shot (*inf.*), have a crack (*inf.*), have a go, have a shot (*inf.*), have a stab (*inf.*), make an all-out effort (*inf.*), make an attempt, make an effort, move heaven and earth, seek, strive, struggle, undertake **2 = test,** appraise, check out, evaluate, examine, experiment, inspect, investigate, prove, put to the test, sample, taste **3, 4 = strain,** afflict, annoy, inconvenience, irk, irritate, pain, plague, stress, tax, tire, trouble, upset, vex, weary **5a = judge,** adjudge, adjudicate, examine, hear ◆ *n* **7 = test,** appraisal, evaluation, experiment, inspection, sample, taste, trial **8 = attempt,** crack (*inf.*), effort, endeavour, essay, go (*inf.*), shot (*inf.*), stab (*inf.*)

trying *adj* **= annoying,** aggravating, arduous, bothersome, difficult, exasperating, fatiguing, hard, irksome, irritating, stressful, taxing, tiresome, tough, troublesome, upsetting, vexing, wearisome

Antonyms *adj* calming, easy, no bother, no trouble, painless, simple, straightforward, undemanding

try out *vb* **1 = test,** appraise, check out, evaluate, experiment with, inspect, put into practice, put to the test, sample, taste

tsar *n* **2, 3** *Informal* **= head,** autocrat, despot, emperor, leader, overlord, ruler, sovereign, tyrant

tubby *adj* **1 = fat,** chubby, corpulent, obese, overweight, paunchy, plump, podgy, portly, roly-poly, stout

tuberose ('tju:bə,rəuz) *n* a perennial Mexican agave plant having a tuberous root and fragrant white flowers. [C17: from L *tūberōsus* full of lumps; from its root]

tuberous ('tju:bərəs) *or* **tuberose** ('tju:bə,rəus) *adj* **1** (of plants) forming, bearing, or resembling a tuber or tubers. **2** *Anat.* of or having warty protuberances or tubers. [C17: from L *tūberōsus* full of knobs]

tube worm *n* any of various worms that construct and live in a tube of sand, lime, etc.

tubifex ('tju:bɪ,fɛks) *n, pl* **tubifex** *or* **tubifexes.** any of a genus of small reddish freshwater worms. [C19: from NL, from L *tubus* tube + *facere* to make]

tubing ('tju:bɪŋ) *n* **1** tubes collectively. **2** a length of tube. **3** a system of tubes. **4** fabric in the form of a tube.

tub-thumper *n* a noisy, violent, or ranting public speaker.
▸**'tub-,thumping** *adj, n*

tubular ('tju:bjulə) *adj* **1** Also: **tubiform** ('tju:bɪ,fɔ:m). having the form of a tube or tubes. **2** of or relating to a tube or tubing.

tubular bells *pl n* a set of long tubes of brass tuned for use in an orchestra and struck with a mallet to simulate the sound of bells.

tubule ('tju:bju:l) *n* any small tubular structure, esp. in an animal body. [C17: from L *tubulus* a little TUBE]

TUC (in Britain) *abbrev. for* Trades Union Congress.

tuck ❶ (tʌk) *vb* **1** (*tr*) to push or fold into a small confined space or concealed place or between two surfaces. **2** (*tr*) to thrust the loose ends or sides of (something) into a confining space, so as to make neat and secure. **3** to make a tuck or tucks in (a garment). **4** (*usually tr*) to draw together, contract, or pucker. ◆ *n* **5** a tucked object or part. **6** a pleat or fold in a part of a garment, usually stitched down. **7** the part of a vessel where the planks meet at the sternpost. **8** *Brit. inf.* **8a** food, esp. cakes and sweets. **8b** (*as modifier*): *a tuck box.* **9** a position of the body, as in certain dives, in which the legs are bent with the knees drawn up against the chest and tightly clasped. ◆ See also **tuck away, tuck in.** [C14: from OE *tūcian* to torment]

tuck away *vb* (*tr, adv*) *Inf.* **1** to eat (a large amount of food). **2** to store, esp. in a place difficult to find.

tucker[1] ('tʌkə) *n* **1** a person or thing that tucks. **2** a detachable yoke of lace, linen, etc., often white, worn over the breast, as of a low-cut dress. **3** *Austral. & NZ. old-fashioned* an informal word for **food.**

tucker[2] ('tʌkə) *vb* (*tr; often passive;* usually foll. by *out*) *Inf., chiefly US & Canad.* to weary or tire.

tucker-bag *or* **tuckerbox** ('tʌkə,bɒks) *n Austral. old-fashioned sl.* a bag or box in which food is carried or stored.

tucket ('tʌkɪt) *n Arch.* a flourish on a trumpet. [C16: from OF *toquer* to sound (on a drum)]

tuck in ❶ *vb* (*adv*) **1** (*tr*) Also: **tuck into.** to put to bed and make snug. **2** (*tr*) to thrust the loose ends or sides of (something) into a confining space: *tuck the blankets in.* **3** (*intr*) Also: **tuck into.** *Inf.* to eat, esp. heartily. ◆ *n* **tuck-in. 4** *Brit. inf.* a meal, esp. a large one.

tuck shop *n Chiefly Brit.* a shop, esp. one near a school, where cakes and sweets are sold.

-tude *suffix forming nouns.* indicating state or condition: *plenitude.* [from L *-tūdō*]

Tudor ('tju:də) *adj* **1** of or relating to the English royal house ruling from 1485 to 1603. **2** characteristic of or happening in this period. **3** denoting a style of architecture characterized by half-timbered houses.

Tues. *abbrev. for* Tuesday.

Tuesday ('tju:zdɪ) *n* the third day of the week; second day of the working week. [OE *tīwesdæg*]

tufa ('tju:fə) *n* a porous rock formed of calcium carbonate deposited from springs. [C18: from It. *tufo,* from LL *tōfus*]
▸**tufaceous** (tju:'feɪʃəs) *adj*

tuff (tʌf) *n* a hard volcanic rock consisting of consolidated fragments of lava. [C16: from OF *tuf,* from It. *tufo;* see TUFA]
▸**tuffaceous** (tʌ'feɪʃəs) *adj*

tuffet ('tʌfɪt) *n* a small mound or low seat. [C16: alteration of TUFT]

tuft ❶ (tʌft) *n* **1** a bunch of feathers, grass, hair, etc., held together at the base. **2** a cluster of threads drawn tightly through upholstery, a quilt, etc., to secure the padding. **3** a small clump of trees or bushes. **4** (formerly) a gold tassel on the cap worn by titled undergraduates at English universities. ◆ *vb* **5** (*tr*) to provide or decorate with a tuft or tufts. **6** to form or be formed into tufts. **7** to secure with tufts. [C14: ?from OF *tufe,* of Gmc origin]
▸**'tufted** *adj* ▸**'tufty** *adj*

tufted duck *n* a European lake-dwelling duck, the male of which has a black plumage with white underparts and a long black drooping crest.

tug ❶ (tʌg) *vb* **tugs, tugging, tugged. 1** (when *intr,* sometimes foll. by *at*) to pull or drag with sharp or powerful movements. **2** (*tr*) to tow (a vessel) by means of a tug. ◆ *n* **3** a strong pull or jerk. **4** Also called: **tugboat.** a boat with a powerful engine, used for towing barges, ships, etc. **5** a hard struggle or fight. [C13: rel. to OE *tēon* to TOW[1]]
▸**'tugger** *n*

tug-of-love *n* a conflict over custody of a child between divorced parents or between natural parents and foster or adoptive parents.

tug-of-war *n* **1** a contest in which two people or teams pull opposite ends of a rope in an attempt to drag the opposition over a central line. **2** any hard struggle between two factions.

tui ('tu:i:) *n, pl* **tuis.** a New Zealand songbird with white feathers at the throat. Also called: **parson bird.** [from Maori]

tuition ❶ (tju:'ɪʃən) *n* **1** instruction, esp. that received individually or in a small group. **2** the payment for instruction, esp. in colleges or universities. [C15: from OF *tuicion,* from L *tuitiō* a guarding, from *tuērī* to watch over]
▸**tu'itional** *adj*

tularaemia *or US* **tularemia** (,tu:lə'ri:mɪə) *n* an infectious disease of rodents, transmitted to man by infected ticks or flies or by handling contaminated flesh. [C19/20: from NL, from *Tulare,* county in California where first observed]
▸**,tula'raemic** *or US* **,tula'remic** *adj*

tulip ('tju:lɪp) *n* **1** any of various spring-blooming bulb plants having long broad pointed leaves and single showy bell-shaped flowers. **2** the flower or bulb. [C17: from NL *tulipa,* from Turkish *tülbend* turban, which the opened bloom was thought to resemble]

tulip tree *n* **1** Also called: **tulip poplar.** a North American tree having tulip-shaped greenish-yellow flowers and long conelike fruits. **2** any of various other trees with tulip-shaped flowers, such as the magnolia.

tulipwood ('tju:lɪp,wud) *n* **1** the light soft wood of the tulip tree, used in making furniture and veneer. **2** any of several woods having streaks of colour.

tulle (tju:l) *n* a fine net fabric of silk, rayon, etc. [C19: from F, from *Tulle,* city in S central France, where first manufactured]

tumble ❶ ('tʌmbᵊl) *vb* **tumbles, tumbling, tumbled. 1** to fall or cause to fall, esp. awkwardly, precipitately, or violently. **2** (*intr;* usually foll. by *about*) to roll or twist, esp. in playing. **3** (*intr*) to perform leaps, somersaults, etc. **4** to move in a heedless or hasty way. **5** (*tr*) to polish (gemstones) in a tumbler. **6** (*tr*) to disturb, rumple, or toss around. ◆ *n* **7** a tumbling. **8** a fall or toss. **9** an acrobatic feat, esp. a somersault. **10** a state of confusion. **11** a confused heap or pile. ◆ See also **tumble to.** [OE *tumbian*]

tumbledown ❶ ('tʌmbᵊl,daun) *adj* falling to pieces; dilapidated; crumbling.

tumble dryer *or* **tumble drier** *n* a machine that dries wet laundry by rotating it in warmed air inside a metal drum. Also called: **tumbler dryer, tumbler.**

tumbler ('tʌmblə) *n* **1a** a flat-bottomed drinking glass with no handle or stem. **1b** Also called: **tumblerful.** its contents. **2** a person who performs somersaults and other acrobatic feats. **3** another name for **tumble dryer. 4** a box or drum rotated so that the contents (usually gemstones) become smooth and polished. **5** the part of a lock that retains or releases the bolt and is moved by the action of a key. **6** a lever in a gunlock that receives the action of the mainspring when the trigger is pressed and thus forces the hammer forwards. **7** a part that moves a gear in a train of gears into and out of engagement.

tumbler switch *n* a small electrical switch incorporating a spring, widely used in lighting.

tumble to *vb* (*intr, prep*) *Inf.* to understand; become aware of: *she tumbled to his plan quickly.*

tumbleweed ('tʌmbᵊl,wi:d) *n* any of various densely branched American and Australian plants that break off near the ground on withering and are rolled about by the wind.

tumbrel *or* **tumbril** ('tʌmbrəl) *n* **1** a farm cart, esp. one that tilts backwards to deposit its load. A cart of this type was used to take condemned prisoners to the guillotine during the French Revolution. **2** (formerly) a covered cart used to carry ammunition, tools, etc. [C14 *tumberell* ducking stool, from Med. L *tumbrellum,* from OF *tumberel* dump cart, ult. of Gmc origin]

tumefacient (,tju:mɪ'feɪʃɪənt) *adj* producing or capable of producing swelling: *a tumefacient drug.* [C16: from L *tumefacere* to cause to swell]

tumefy ('tju:mɪ,faɪ) *vb* **tumefies, tumefying, tumefied.** to make or become tumid; swell or puff up. [C16: from F *tuméfier,* from L *tumefacere*]
▸**,tume'faction** *n*

tumescent (tju:'mɛsənt) *adj* swollen or becoming swollen. [C19: from L *tumescere* to begin to swell, from *tumēre*]
▸**tu'mescence** *n*

tumid ❶ ('tju:mɪd) *adj* **1** enlarged or swollen. **2** bulging. **3** pompous or fulsome in style. [C16: from L *tumidus,* from *tumēre* to swell]
▸**tu'midity** *or* **'tumidness** *n* ▸**'tumidly** *adv*

THESAURUS

tuck *vb* **1 = push**, fold, gather, insert ◆ *n* **6 = fold**, gather, pinch, pleat **8a** *Brit. informal* **= food**, comestibles, eats (*sl.*), grub (*sl.*), nosebag (*sl.*), nosh (*sl.*), scoff (*sl.*), tack (*inf.*), victuals, vittles (*obs. or dialect*)

tuck in *vb* **1 = make snug**, bed down, enfold, fold under, put to bed, swaddle, wrap up **3** *Informal* **= eat up**, chow down (*sl.*), eat heartily, fall to, get stuck in (*inf.*)

tuft *n* **1-3 = clump**, bunch, cluster, collection, knot, shock, topknot, tussock

tug *vb* **1 = pull**, drag, draw, haul, heave, jerk, lug, tow, wrench, yank ◆ *n* **3 = pull**, drag, haul, heave, jerk, tow, traction, wrench, yank

tuition *n* **1 = training**, education, instruction, lessons, schooling, teaching, tutelage, tutoring

tumble *vb* **1 = fall**, drop, fall end over end, fall headlong, fall head over heels, flop, lose one's footing, pitch, plummet, roll, stumble, topple, toss, trip up ◆ *n* **8 = fall**, collapse, drop, flop, headlong fall, plunge, roll, spill, stumble, toss, trip

tumbledown *adj* **= dilapidated**, crumbling, decrepit, disintegrating, falling to pieces, ramshackle, rickety, ruined, shaky, tottering
Antonyms *adj* durable, firm, solid, sound, stable, sturdy, substantial, well-kept

tumid *adj* **1, 2 = swollen**, bloated, bulging, distended, enlarged, inflated, protuberant, puffed

tummy ❶ ('tʌmɪ) *n, pl* **tummies.** an informal or childish word for **stomach.** Also called: **tum.**

tummy tuck *n Inf.* the surgical removal of abdominal fat and skin for cosmetic purposes.

tumour ❶ *or US* **tumor** ('tju:mə) *n Pathol.* **a** any abnormal swelling. **b** a mass of tissue formed by a new growth of cells. [C16: from L, from *tumēre* to swell]
▸**'tumorous** *adj*

tumult ❶ ('tju:mʌlt) *n* **1** a loud confused noise, as of a crowd; commotion. **2** violent agitation or disturbance. **3** great emotional agitation. [C15: from L *tumultus,* from *tumēre* to swell up]

tumultuous ❶ (tju:'mʌltjuəs) *adj* **1** uproarious, riotous, or turbulent. **2** greatly agitated, confused, or disturbed. **3** making a loud or unruly disturbance.
▸**tu'multuously** *adv* ▸**tu'multuousness** *n*

tumulus ('tju:mjʊləs) *n, pl* **tumuli** (-li:). *Archaeol. (no longer in technical usage)* another word for **barrow**[2]. [C17: from L: a hillock, from *tumēre* to swell up]

tun (tʌn) *n* **1** a large beer cask. **2** a measure of capacity, usually equal to 252 wine gallons. ◆ *vb* **tuns, tunning, tunned. 3** *(tr)* to put into or keep in tuns. [OE *tunne*]

tuna[1] ('tju:nə) *n, pl* **tuna** *or* **tunas.** another name for **tunny** (sense 1). [C20: from American Sp., from Sp. *atún,* from Ar. *tūn,* from L *thunnus* tunny, from Gk]

tuna[2] ('tju:nə) *n* any of various tropical American prickly pear cacti. [C16: via Sp. from Taino]

tunable *or* **tuneable** ('tju:nəbᵊl) *adj* able to be tuned.

tundra ('tʌndrə) *n* a vast treeless zone lying between the ice cap and the timber line of North America and Eurasia and having a permanently frozen subsoil. [C19: from Russian, from Lapp *tundar* hill]

tune ❶ (tju:n) *n* **1** a melody, esp. one for which harmony is not essential. **2** the condition of producing accurately pitched notes, intervals, etc. (esp. in **in tune, out of tune**). **3** accurate correspondence of pitch and intonation between instruments (esp. in **in tune, out of tune**). **4** the correct adjustment of a radio, television, etc., with respect to the required frequency. **5** a frame of mind; mood. **6 call the tune.** to be in control of the proceedings. **7 change one's tune.** to alter one's attitude or tone of speech. **8 to the tune of.** *Inf.* to the amount or extent of. ◆ *vb* **tunes, tuning, tuned. 9** to adjust (a musical instrument) to a certain pitch. **10** to adjust (a note, etc.) so as to bring it into harmony or concord. **11** *(tr)* to adapt or adjust (oneself); attune. **12** *(tr; often foll. by up)* to make fine adjustments to (an engine, machine, etc.) to obtain optimum performance. **13** *Electronics.* to adjust (one or more circuits) for resonance at a desired frequency. ◆ See also **tune in, tune up.** [C14: var. of TONE]
▸**'tuner** *n*

tuneful ❶ ('tju:nfʊl) *adj* **1** having a pleasant tune; melodious. **2** producing a melody or music.
▸**'tunefully** *adv* ▸**'tunefulness** *n*

tune in *vb (adv; often foll. by to)* **1** to adjust (a radio or television) to receive (a station or programme). **2** *Sl.* to make or become more aware, knowledgeable, etc. (about).

tuneless ❶ ('tju:nlɪs) *adj* having no melody or tune.
▸**'tunelessly** *adv* ▸**'tunelessness** *n*

tune up *vb (adv)* **1** to adjust (a musical instrument) to a particular pitch. **2** to tune (instruments) to a common pitch. **3** *(tr)* to adjust (an engine) in (a car, etc.) to improve performance. ◆ *n* **tune-up. 4** adjustments made to an engine to improve its performance.

tung oil (tʌŋ) *n* a fast-drying oil obtained from the seeds of an Asian tree, used in paints, varnishes, etc. [partial translation of Chinese *yu t'ung* tung tree oil, from *yu* oil + *t'ung* tung tree]

tungsten ('tʌŋstən) *n* a hard malleable ductile greyish-white element. It is used in lamp filaments, electrical contact points, X-ray targets, and, alloyed with steel, in high-speed cutting tools. Symbol: W; atomic no.: 74; atomic wt.: 183.85. Also called: **wolfram.** [C18: from Swedish *tung* heavy + *sten* stone]

tungsten lamp *n* a lamp in which light is produced by a tungsten filament heated to incandescence by an electric current. Sometimes small amounts of a halogen, such as iodine, are added to improve the intensity (**tungsten-halogen lamp**).

tungsten steel *n* any of various hard steels containing tungsten and traces of carbon.

Tungusic (tʊŋ'gʊsɪk) *n* a branch or subfamily of the Altaic family of languages, some of which are spoken in NE Asia.

tunic ('tju:nɪk) *n* **1** any of various hip-length or knee-length garments, such as the loose sleeveless garb worn in ancient Greece or Rome, the jacket of some soldiers, or a woman's hip-length garment, worn with a skirt or trousers. **2** a covering, lining, or enveloping membrane of an organ or part. **3** Also called: **tunicle.** a short vestment worn by a bishop or subdeacon. [OE *tunice* (unattested except in the accusative case), from L *tunica*]

tunicate ('tju:nɪkɪt, -ˌkeɪt) *n* **1** any of various minute primitive marine animals having a saclike unsegmented body enclosed in a cellulose-like outer covering. ◆ *adj also* **tunicated. 2** (esp. of a bulb) having concentric layers of tissue. [C18: from L *tunicātus* clad in a TUNIC]

tuning ('tju:nɪŋ) *n Music.* **1** a set of pitches to which the open strings of a guitar, violin, etc., are tuned. **2** the accurate pitching of notes and intervals by a choir, orchestra, etc.; intonation.

tuning fork *n* a two-pronged metal fork that when struck produces a pure note of constant specified pitch. It is used to tune musical instruments and in acoustics.

tunnage ('tʌnɪdʒ) *n* a variant spelling of **tonnage.**

tunnel ❶ ('tʌnᵊl) *n* **1** an underground passageway, esp. one for trains or cars. **2** any passage or channel through or under something. ◆ *vb* **tunnels, tunnelling, tunnelled** *or US* **tunnels, tunneling, tunneled. 3** *(tr)* to make or force (a way) through or under (something). **4** *(intr; foll. by through, under, etc.)* to make or force a way (through or under something). [C15: from OF *tonel* cask, from *tonne* tun, from Med. L *tonna* barrel, of Celtic origin]
▸**'tunneller** *or US* **'tunneler** *n*

tunnel diode *n* an extremely stable semiconductor diode, having a very narrow highly doped p-n junction, in which electrons travel across the junction by means of the tunnel effect. Also called: **Esaki diode.**

tunnel effect *n Physics.* the phenomenon in which an object, usually an elementary particle, tunnels through a potential barrier even though it does not have sufficient energy to surmount it.

tunnel vision *n* **1** a condition in which peripheral vision is greatly restricted. **2** narrowness of viewpoint resulting from concentration on a single idea, opinion, etc.

tunny ('tʌnɪ) *n, pl* **tunnies** *or* **tunny. 1** Also called: **tuna.** any of a genus of large marine spiny-finned fishes, chiefly of warm waters. They are important food fishes. **2** any of various similar and related fishes. [C16: from OF *thon,* from OProvençal *ton,* from L *thunnus,* from Gk]

tup (tʌp) *n* **1** *Chiefly Brit.* a male sheep; ram. **2** the head of a pile-driver or steam hammer. ◆ *vb* **tups, tupping, tupped. 3** *(tr)* (of a ram) to mate with (a ewe). [C14: from ?]

Tupamaro (ˌtu:pə'mɑ:rəʊ) *n, pl* **Tupamaros.** any of a group of Marxist urban guerrillas in Uruguay. [C20: after *Tupac Amaru,* 18th-century Peruvian Indian who led a rebellion against the Spaniards]

tupelo ('tju:pɪˌləʊ) *n, pl* **tupelos. 1** any of several gum trees of the southern US. **2** the light strong wood of any of these trees. [C18: from Creek *ito opilwa,* from *ito* tree + *opilwa* swamp]

Tupi (tu:'pi:) *n* **1** *(pl* **Tupis** *or* **Tupi)** a member of a South American Indian people of Brazil and Paraguay. **2** their language.
▸**Tu'pian** *adj*

tupik ('tu:pək) *n Canad.* a tent of seal or caribou skin used for shelter by the Inuit in summer. [from Eskimo]

tuppence ('tʌpəns) *n Brit.* a variant spelling of **twopence.**
▸**'tuppenny** *adj*

Tupperware ('tʌpəweə) *n Trademark.* a range of plastic containers used for storing food. [C20: *Tupper,* US manufacturing company + WARE[1]]

tuque (tu:k) *n Canad.* **1** a knitted cap with a long tapering end. **2** Also called: **toque.** a close-fitting knitted hat often with a tassel or pompom. [C19: from Canad. F, from F: TOQUE]

turaco ('tʊərəˌkəʊ) *n, pl* **turacos.** a variant spelling of **touraco.**

THESAURUS

up, puffy, tumescent **3** = **pompous,** arty-farty *(inf.)*, bombastic, flowery, fulsome, fustian, grandiloquent, grandiose, high-flown, inflated, magniloquent, orotund, overblown, pretentious, sesquipedalian, stilted, turgid

tummy *n Informal* = **stomach,** abdomen, belly, breadbasket *(sl.)*, corporation *(inf.)*, gut *(inf.)*, inside(s) *(inf.)*, paunch, pot, potbelly, spare tyre, tum *(inf.)*

tumour *n* **a** = **growth,** cancer, carcinoma *(Pathology)*, lump, neoplasm *(Medical)*, sarcoma *(Medical)*, swelling

tumult *n* **1-3** = **commotion,** ado, affray *(Law)*, agitation, altercation, bedlam, brawl, brouhaha, clamour, din, disorder, disturbance, excitement, fracas, hubbub, hullabaloo, outbreak, pandemonium, quarrel, racket, riot, row, ruction *(inf.)*, stir, stramash *(Scot.)*, strife, turmoil, unrest, upheaval, uproar
Antonyms *n* calm, hush, peace, quiet, repose, serenity, silence, stillness

tumultuous *adj* **1-3** = **turbulent,** agitated, boisterous, clamorous, confused, disorderly, disturbed, excited, fierce, full-on *(inf.)*, hectic, irregular, lawless, noisy, obstreperous, passionate, raging, restless, riotous, rowdy, rumbustious, stormy, unrestrained, unruly, uproarious, violent, vociferous, wild
Antonyms *adj* calm, hushed, peaceful, quiet, restful, serene, still, tranquil

tune *n* **1** = **melody,** air, melody line, motif, song, strain, theme **3** = **concord,** agreement, concert, consonance, euphony, harmony, pitch, sympathy, unison **5** = **frame of mind,** attitude, demeanour, disposition, mood **6 call the tune** = **be in control,** be in charge, be in command, call the shots *(sl.)*, command, dictate, govern, lead, rule, rule the roost **7 change one's tune** = **change one's attitude,** change one's mind, do an about-face, have a change of heart, reconsider, take a different tack, think again ◆ *vb* **9-11** = **adjust,** adapt, attune, bring into harmony, harmonize, pitch, regulate
Antonyms *n* ≠ **concord:** clashing, conflict, contention, disagreement, discord, discordance, disharmony, disunity, friction

tuneful *adj* **1** = **melodious,** catchy, consonant, easy on the ear *(inf.)*, euphonic, euphonious, harmonious, mellifluous, melodic, musical, pleasant, symphonic
Antonyms *adj* cacophonous, clashing, discordant, dissonant, harsh, jangly, tuneless, unmelodious

tuneless *adj* = **discordant,** atonal, cacophonous, clashing, dissonant, harsh, unmelodic, unmelodious, unmusical
Antonyms *adj* harmonious, melodious, musical, pleasing, sonorous, symphonic, tuneful

tunnel *n* **1** = **passage,** burrow, channel, hole, passageway, shaft, subway, underpass ◆ *vb* **3, 4** = **dig,** burrow, dig one's way, excavate, mine, penetrate, scoop out, undermine

Turanian (tjʊˈreɪnɪən) *n, adj* another name for **Ural-Altaic.**
turban (ˈtɜːbᵊn) *n* **1** a man's headdress, worn esp. by Muslims, Hindus, and Sikhs, made by swathing a length of linen, silk, etc., around the head or around a caplike base. **2** a woman's brimless hat resembling this. **3** any headdress resembling this. [C16: from Turkish *tülbend,* from Persian *dulband*]
▸ˈ**turbaned** *adj*
turbary (ˈtɜːbərɪ) *n, pl* **turbaries. 1** land where peat or turf is cut. **2** the legal right to cut peat for fuel on a common. [C14: from OF *turbarie,* from Med. L *turbāria,* from *turba* peat]
turbellarian (ˌtɜːbɪˈlɛərɪən) *n* **1** any of a class of flatworms having a ciliated epidermis and a simple life cycle. ◆ *adj* **2** of or belonging to this class of flatworms. [C19: from NL *Turbellāria,* from L *turbellae* (pl) bustle, from *turba* brawl, referring to the swirling motion created in the water]
turbid (ˈtɜːbɪd) *adj* **1** muddy or opaque, as a liquid clouded with a suspension of particles. **2** dense, thick, or cloudy: *turbid fog.* **3** in turmoil or confusion. [C17: from L *turbidus,* from *turbāre* to agitate, from *turba* crowd]
▸**turˈbidity** *or* ˈ**turbidness** *n* ▸ˈ**turbidly** *adv*
turbinate (ˈtɜːbɪnɪt, -ˌneɪt) *or* **turbinal** (ˈtɜːbɪnᵊl) *adj also* **turbinated. 1** *Anat.* of any of the scroll-shaped bones on the walls of the nasal passages. **2** shaped like a spiral or scroll. **3** shaped like an inverted cone. ◆ *n* **4** a turbinate bone. **5** a turbinate shell. [C17: from L *turbō* spinning top]
▸ˌ**turbiˈnation** *n*
turbine (ˈtɜːbɪn, -baɪn) *n* any of various types of machine in which the kinetic energy of a moving fluid, as water, steam, air, etc., is converted into mechanical energy by causing a bladed rotor to rotate. [C19: from F, from L *turbō* whirlwind, from *turbāre* to throw into confusion]
turbine blade *n* any of a number of bladelike vanes assembled around the periphery of a turbine rotor to guide the steam or gas flow.
turbit (ˈtɜːbɪt) *n* a crested breed of domestic pigeon. [C17: from L *turbō* spinning top, from the bird's shape]
turbo- *combining form.* of, relating to, or driven by a turbine: *turbofan.*
turbocharger (ˈtɜːbəʊˌtʃɑːdʒə) *n* a centrifugal compressor which boosts the intake pressure of an internal-combustion engine, driven by an exhaust-gas turbine fitted to the engine's exhaust manifold.
turbofan (ˌtɜːbəʊˈfæn) *n* **1** a type of bypass engine in which a large fan driven by a turbine forces air rearwards around the exhaust gases in order to increase the propulsive thrust. **2** an aircraft driven by turbofans. **3** the fan in such an engine.
turbogenerator (ˌtɜːbəʊˈdʒɛnəˌreɪtə) *n* an electrical generator driven by a steam turbine.
turbojet (ˌtɜːbəʊˈdʒɛt) *n* **1** a turbojet engine. **2** an aircraft powered by turbojet engines.
turbojet engine *n* a gas turbine in which the exhaust gases provide the propulsive thrust to drive an aircraft.
turboprop (ˌtɜːbəʊˈprɒp) *n* **1** an aircraft propulsion unit where a propeller is driven by a gas turbine. **2** an aircraft powered by turboprops.
turbosupercharger (ˌtɜːbəʊˈsuːpəˌtʃɑːdʒə) *n Obs.* a supercharging device for an internal-combustion engine, consisting of a turbine driven by the exhaust gases.
turbot (ˈtɜːbət) *n, pl* **turbot** *or* **turbots. 1** a European flatfish having a speckled scaleless body covered with tubercles. It is highly valued as a food fish. **2** any of various similar or related fishes. [C13: from OF *tourbot,* from Med. L *turbō,* from L: spinning top, from a fancied similarity in shape]
turbulence ❶ (ˈtɜːbjʊləns) *n* **1** a state or condition of confusion, movement, or agitation. **2** *Meteorol.* instability in the atmosphere causing gusty air currents and cumulonimbus clouds.
turbulent ❶ (ˈtɜːbjʊlənt) *adj* **1** being in a state of turbulence. **2** wild or insubordinate; unruly. [C16: from L *turbulentus,* from *turba* confusion]
▸ˈ**turbulently** *adv*
turd (tɜːd) *n Taboo.* **1** a piece of excrement. **2** *Sl.* a contemptible person or thing. [OE *tord*]
tureen (təˈriːn) *n* a large deep usually rounded dish with a cover, used for serving soups, stews, etc. [C18: from F *terrine* earthenware vessel, from *terrin* made of earthenware, from Vulgar L *terrīnus* (unattested), from L *terra* earth]
turf ❶ (tɜːf) *n, pl* **turfs** *or* **turves. 1** the surface layer of fields and pastures, consisting of earth containing a dense growth of grasses with their roots; sod. **2** a piece cut from this layer. **3 the turf. 3a** a track where horse races are run. **3b** horse racing as a sport or industry. **4** an area of knowledge or influence: *he's on home turf when it comes to music.* **5** another word for **peat.** ◆ *vb* **6** (*tr*) to cover with pieces of turf. ◆ See also **turf out.** [OE]
turf accountant *n Brit.* a formal name for a **bookmaker.**
turfman (ˈtɜːfmən) *n, pl* **turfmen.** *Chiefly US.* a person devoted to horse racing.
turf out ❶ *vb* (*tr, adv*) *Brit. inf.* to throw out or dismiss; eject.
turgescent (tɜːˈdʒɛsᵊnt) *adj* becoming or being swollen; inflated; tumid.
▸**turˈgescence** *n*
turgid ❶ (ˈtɜːdʒɪd) *adj* **1** swollen and distended. **2** (of language) pompous; bombastic. [C17: from L *turgidus,* from *turgēre* to swell]
▸**turˈgidity** *or* ˈ**turgidness** *n* ▸ˈ**turgidly** *adv*
turgor (ˈtɜːgə) *n* the normal rigid state of a cell, caused by pressure of the cell contents against the cell wall or membrane. [C19: from LL: a swelling, from L *turgēre* to swell]
Turing machine (ˈtjʊərɪŋ) *n* a hypothetical universal computing machine able to modify its original instructions by reading, erasing, or writing a new symbol on a moving tape that acts as its program. [C20: after Alan Mathison *Turing* (1912–54), Brit. mathematician]
turion (ˈtʊərɪən) *n* a scaly shoot produced by many aquatic plants: it detaches from the parent plant and remains dormant until the following spring. [C17: from F *turion,* from L *turio* shoot]
Turk (tɜːk) *n* **1** a native, inhabitant, or citizen of Turkey. **2** a native speaker of any Turkic language. **3** *Obs., derog.* a brutal or domineering person. See also **Young Turk.**
Turk. *abbrev. for:* **1** Turkey. **2** Turkish.
turkey (ˈtɜːkɪ) *n, pl* **turkeys** *or* **turkey. 1** a large bird of North America, having a bare wattled head and neck and a brownish plumage. The male has a fan-shaped tail. A domesticated variety is bred for its flesh. **2** *Inf.* something, esp. a film or theatrical production, that fails. **3** See **cold turkey. 4 talk turkey.** *Sl., chiefly US & Canad.* to discuss frankly and practically. [C16: shortened from *Turkey cock (hen),* used at first to designate the African guinea fowl (apparently because the bird was brought through Turkish territory), later applied by mistake to the American bird]
turkey buzzard *or* **vulture** *n* a New World vulture having a naked red head.
turkey cock *n* **1** a male turkey. **2** an arrogant person.
turkey nest *n Austral.* a small earth dam adjacent to, and higher than, a larger earth dam, to feed water by gravity to a cattle trough, etc.
Turkey red *n* **1a** a moderate or bright red colour. **1b** (*as adj*): *a Turkey-red fabric.* **2** a cotton fabric of a bright red colour.
Turki (ˈtɜːkɪ) *adj* **1** of or relating to the Turkic languages. **2** of or relating to speakers of these languages. ◆ *n* **3** these languages collectively.
Turkic (ˈtɜːkɪk) *n* a branch of the Altaic family of languages, including Turkish, Tatar, etc., members of which are found from Turkey to NE China, esp. in Soviet central Asia.
Turkish (ˈtɜːkɪʃ) *adj* **1** of Turkey, its people, or their language. ◆ *n* **2** the official language of Turkey, belonging to the Turkic branch of the Altaic family.
Turkish bath *n* **1** a type of bath in which the bather sweats freely in hot dry air, is then washed, often massaged, and has a cold plunge or shower. **2** (*sometimes pl*) an establishment where such a bath is obtainable.
Turkish coffee *n* very strong black coffee.
Turkish delight *n* a jelly-like sweet flavoured with flower essences, usually cut into cubes and covered in icing sugar.
Turkish towel *n* a rough loose-piled towel.
Turk's-cap lily *n* any of several cultivated lilies that have brightly coloured flowers with reflexed petals.
Turk's-head *n* an ornamental turban-like knot.
turmeric (ˈtɜːmərɪk) *n* **1** a tropical Asian plant, *Curcuma longa,* having yellow flowers and an aromatic underground stem. **2** the powdered stem of this plant, used as a condiment and as a yellow dye. [C16: from OF *terre merite,* from Med. L *terra merita,* lit.: meritorious earth, name applied for obscure reasons to curcuma]
turmeric paper *n Chem.* paper impregnated with turmeric used as a test for alkalis and for boric acid.
turmoil ❶ (ˈtɜːmɔɪl) *n* violent or confused movement; agitation; tumult. [C16: ?from TURN + MOIL]
turn ❶ (tɜːn) *vb* **1** to move around an axis: *to turn a knob.* **2** (sometimes

THESAURUS

turbulence *n* **1 = confusion,** agitation, boiling, commotion, disorder, instability, pandemonium, roughness, storm, tumult, turmoil, unrest, upheaval
Antonyms *n* calm, peace, quiet, repose, rest, stillness
turbulent *adj* **1 = agitated,** blustery, boiling, choppy, confused, disordered, foaming, furious, raging, rough, tempestuous, tumultuous, unsettled, unstable **2 = wild,** agitated, anarchic, boisterous, disorderly, insubordinate, lawless, mutinous, obstreperous, rebellious, refractory, riotous, rowdy, seditious, tumultuous, unbridled, undisciplined, ungovernable, unruly, uproarious, violent
Antonyms *adj* ≠ **agitated:** calm, glassy, peaceful, quiet, smooth, still, unruffled
turf *n* **1 = grass,** clod, divot, green, sod, sward **3 the turf = horse-racing,** racecourse, racetrack, racing, the flat
turf out *vb Brit. informal* **= throw out,** banish, bounce (*sl.*), cast out, chuck out (*inf.*), discharge, dismiss, dispossess, eject, evict, expel, fire (*inf.*), fling out, give one the bum's rush (*sl.*), give one the sack (*inf.*), kick out (*inf.*), kiss off (*sl., chiefly US & Canad.*), oust, relegate, sack (*inf.*), show one the door
turgid *adj* **1 = swollen,** bloated, bulging, congested, distended, inflated, protuberant, puffed up, puffy, tumescent, tumid **2 = pompous,** arty-farty (*inf.*), bombastic, flowery, fulsome, fustian, grandiloquent, grandiose, high-flown, inflated, magniloquent, orotund, ostentatious, overblown, pretentious, sesquipedalian, stilted, tumid, windy
turmoil *n* **= confusion,** agitation, bedlam, brouhaha, bustle, chaos, commotion, disarray, disorder, disturbance, ferment, flurry, hubbub, noise, pandemonium, row, stir, strife, trouble, tumult, turbulence, upheaval, uproar, violence
Antonyms *n* calm, peace, quiet, repose, rest, serenity, stillness, tranquillity
turn *vb* **2 = rotate,** circle, go round, gyrate, move in a circle, pivot, revolve, roll, spin, swivel, twirl, twist, wheel, whirl **3 = change**

foll. by *round*) to change or cause to change positions by moving through an arc of a circle: *he turned the chair to face the light.* **3** to change or cause to change in course, direction, etc. **4** to go or pass to the other side of (a corner, etc.). **5** to assume or cause to assume a rounded, curved, or folded form: *the road turns here.* **6** to reverse or cause to reverse position. **7** (*tr*) to perform or do by a rotating movement: *to turn a somersault.* **8** (*tr*) to shape or cut a thread in (a workpiece) by rotating it on a lathe against a cutting tool. **9** (when *intr,* foll. by *into* or *to*) to change or convert or be changed or converted. **10** (foll. by *into*) to change or cause to change in nature, character, etc.: *the frog turned into a prince.* **11** (*copula*) to change so as to become: *he turned nasty.* **12** to cause (foliage, etc.) to change colour or (of foliage, etc.) to change colour. **13** to cause (milk, etc.) to become rancid or sour or (of milk, etc.) to become rancid or sour. **14** to change or cause to change in subject, trend, etc.: *the conversation turned to fishing.* **15** to direct or apply or be directed or applied: *he turned his attention to the problem.* **16** (*intr;* usually foll. by *to*) to appeal or apply (to) for help, advice, etc. **17** to reach, pass, or progress beyond in age, time, etc.: *she has just turned twenty.* **18** (*tr*) to cause or allow to go: *to turn an animal loose.* **19** to affect or be affected with nausea. **20** to affect or be affected with giddiness: *my head is turning.* **21** (*tr*) to affect the mental or emotional stability of (esp. in **turn (someone's) head**). **22** (*tr*) to release from a container. **23** (*tr*) to render into another language. **24** (usually foll. by *against* or *from*) to transfer or reverse (one's loyalties, affections, etc.). **25** (*tr*) to cause (an enemy agent) to become a double agent working for one's own side. **26** (*tr*) to bring (soil) from lower layers to the surface. **27** to blunt (an edge) or (of an edge) to become blunted. **28** (*tr*) to give a graceful form to: *to turn a compliment.* **29** (*tr*) to reverse (a cuff, collar, etc.). **30** (*intr*) *US.* to be merchandised as specified: *shirts are turning well this week.* **31** *Cricket.* to spin (the ball) or (of the ball) to spin. **32 turn a trick.** *Sl.* (of a prostitute) to gain a customer. **33 turn one's hand to.** to undertake (something practical). ◆ *n* **34** a turning or being turned. **35** a movement of complete or partial rotation. **36** a change of direction or position. **37** direction or drift: *his thoughts took a new turn.* **38** a deviation from a course or tendency. **39** the place, point, or time at which a deviation or change occurs. **40** another word for **turning** (sense 1). **41** the right or opportunity to do something in an agreed order or succession: *now it's George's turn.* **42** a change in nature, condition, etc.: *his illness took a turn for the worse.* **43** a period of action, work, etc. **44** a short walk, ride, or excursion. **45** natural inclination: *a speculative turn of mind.* **46** distinctive form or style: *a neat turn of phrase.* **47** requirement, need, or advantage: *to serve someone's turn.* **48** a deed that helps or hinders someone. **49** a twist, bend, or distortion in shape. **50** *Music.* a melodic ornament that makes a turn around a note, beginning with the note above, in a variety of sequences. **51** a short theatrical act. **52** *Stock Exchange, Brit.* the difference between a market maker's bid and offer prices, representing the market maker's profit. **53** *Inf.* a shock or surprise. **54 by turns.** one after another; alternately. **55 turn and turn about.** one after another; alternately. **56 to a turn.** to the proper amount; perfectly. ◆ See also **turn down, turn in,** etc. [OE *tyrnian,* from OF *torner,* from L *tornāre* to turn in a lathe, from *tornus* lathe, from Gk *tornos* dividers]
▸ '**turner** *n*

turnabout ('tɜːnəˌbaʊt) *n* **1** the act of turning so as to face a different direction. **2** a change or reversal of opinion, attitude, etc.

turnaround ('tɜːnəˌraʊnd) *n* **1a** the act or process in which a ship, aircraft, etc., unloads at the end of a trip and reloads for the next trip. **1b** the time taken for this. **2** the total time taken by a vehicle in a round trip. **3** a complete reversal of a situation.

turnbuckle ('tɜːnˌbʌkᵊl) *n* an open mechanical sleeve usually having a swivel at one end and a thread at the other to enable a threaded wire or rope to be tightened.

turncoat **T** ('tɜːnˌkəʊt) *n* a person who deserts one cause or party for the opposite faction.

turncock ('tɜːnˌkɒk) *n* (formerly) an official employed to turn on the water for the mains supply.

turn down **T** *vb* (*tr, adv*) **1** to reduce (the volume or brightness) of (something). **2** to reject or refuse. **3** to fold down (a collar, sheets, etc.). ◆ *adj* **turndown. 4** (*prenominal*) designed to be folded down.

turn in **T** *vb* (*adv*) *Inf.* **1** (*intr*) to go to bed for the night. **2** (*tr*) to hand in; deliver. **3** (*tr*) to give up or conclude (something). **4** (*tr*) to record (a score, etc.). **5 turn in on oneself.** to become preoccupied with one's own problems.

turning **T** ('tɜːnɪŋ) *n* **1** a road, river, or path that turns off the main way. **2** the point where such a way turns off. **3** a bend in a straight course. **4** an object made on a lathe. **5** the process or skill of turning objects on a lathe. **6** (*pl*) the waste produced in turning on a lathe.

turning circle *n* the smallest circle in which a vehicle can turn.

turning point **T** *n* **1** a moment when the course of events is changed. **2** a point at which there is a change in direction or motion.

turnip ('tɜːnɪp) *n* **1** a widely cultivated plant of the cabbage family with a large yellow or white edible root. **2** the root of this plant, which is eaten as a vegetable. [C16: from earlier *turnepe,* ?from TURN (indicating its rounded shape) + *nepe,* from L *nāpus* turnip]

turnkey ('tɜːnˌkiː) *n* **1** *Arch.* a keeper of the keys, esp. in a prison; warder or jailer. ◆ *adj* **2** denoting a project, as in civil engineering, in which a single contractor has responsibility for the complete job from the start to the time of installation or occupancy.

turn off **T** *vb* **1** (*intr*) to leave (a road, etc.). **2** (*intr*) (of a road, etc.) to deviate from (another road, etc.). **3** (*tr, adv*) to cause (something) to cease operating by turning a knob, pushing a button, etc. **4** (*tr*) *Inf.* to cause (a person, etc.) to feel dislike or distaste for (something): *this music turns me off.* **5** (*tr, adv*) *Brit. inf.* to dismiss from employment. ◆ *n* **turn-off. 6** a road or other way branching off from the main thoroughfare. **7** *Inf.* a person or thing that elicits dislike or distaste.

turn on **T** *vb* **1** (*tr, adv*) to cause (something) to operate by turning a knob, etc. **2** (*intr, prep*) to depend or hinge on: *the success of the party turns on you.* **3** (*prep*) to become hostile or to retaliate: *the dog turned on the children.* **4** (*tr, adv*) *Inf.* to produce (charm, tears, etc.) suddenly or automatically. **5** (*tr, adv*) *Sl.* to arouse emotionally or sexually. **6** (*intr, adv*) *Sl.* to take or become intoxicated by drugs. **7** (*tr, adv*) *Sl.* to introduce (someone) to drugs. ◆ *n* **turn-on. 8** *Sl.* a person or thing that causes emotional or sexual arousal.

turn out **T** *vb* (*adv*) **1** (*tr*) to cause (something, esp. a light) to cease operating by or as if by turning a knob, etc. **2** (*tr*) to produce by an effort or process. **3** (*tr*) to dismiss, discharge, or expel. **4** (*tr*) to empty the contents of, esp. in order to clean, tidy, or rearrange. **5** (*copula*) to prove to be as specified. **6** to end up; result: *it all turned out well.* **7** (*tr*) to fit as with clothes: *that woman turns her children out well.* **8** (*intr*) to assemble or gather. **9** (of a soldier) to parade or to call (a soldier) to pa-

THESAURUS

course, change position, go back, move, return, reverse, shift, swerve, switch, veer, wheel **4 = go round,** arc, come round, corner, negotiate, pass, pass around, take a bend **7, 8 = shape,** construct, execute, fashion, frame, make, mould, perform **9, 10 = change,** adapt, alter, become, convert, divert, fashion, fit, form, metamorphose, mould, mutate, remodel, shape, transfigure, transform, transmute **13 = go bad,** become rancid, curdle, go off (*Brit. inf.*), go sour, make rancid, sour, spoil, taint **16** *usually foll. by* **to = appeal,** apply, approach, go, have recourse, look, resort **19 = sicken,** nauseate, upset **24 = change sides,** apostatize, change one's mind, defect, desert, go over, renege, retract ◆ *n* **35 = rotation,** bend, change, circle, curve, cycle, gyration, pivot, reversal, revolution, spin, swing, turning, twist, whirl **36 = change of direction,** bend, change of course, curve, departure, deviation, shift **37 = direction,** bias, drift, heading, tendency, trend **41 = opportunity,** chance, crack, fling, go, period, round, shift, shot (*inf.*), spell, stint, succession, time, try, whack (*inf.*) **44 = excursion,** airing, circuit, constitutional, drive, jaunt, outing, promenade, ride, saunter, spin (*inf.*), stroll, walk **45 = inclination,** affinity, aptitude, bent, bias, flair, gift, knack, leaning, propensity, talent **46 = style,** cast, fashion, form, format, guise, make-up, manner, mode, mould, shape, way **48 = act,** action, deed, favour, gesture, service **49 = twist,** bend, distortion, warp **53** *Informal* **= shock,** fright, scare, start, surprise **54 by turns = alternately,** in succession, one after another, reciprocally, turn and turn about **56 to a turn** *Informal* **= perfectly,** correctly, exactly, just right, precisely

turncoat *n* **= traitor,** apostate, backslider, defector, deserter, rat (*inf.*), recreant (*arch.*), renegade, seceder, tergiversator

turn down *vb* **1 = lower,** diminish, lessen, muffle, mute, quieten, reduce the volume of, soften **2 = refuse,** abstain from, decline, rebuff, reject, repudiate, say no to, spurn, throw out
Antonyms *vb* ≠ **lower:** amplify, augment, boost, increase, raise, strengthen, swell, turn up ≠ **refuse:** accede, accept, acquiesce, agree, receive, take

turn in *vb Informal* **1 = go to bed,** go to sleep, hit the hay (*sl.*), hit the sack (*sl.*), retire for the night **2 = hand in,** deliver, give back, give up, hand over, return, submit, surrender, tender

turning *n* **1, 2 = turn-off,** bend, crossroads, curve, junction, side road, turn

turning point *n* **1 = crossroads,** change, climacteric, crisis, critical moment, crux, decisive moment, moment of decision, moment of truth, point of no return

turn off *vb* **1 = branch off,** change direction, depart from, deviate, leave, quit, take another road, take a side road **3 = stop,** cut out, kill, put out, shut down, switch off, turn out, unplug **4** *Informal* **= put off,** alienate, bore, disenchant, disgust, displease, gross out (*US sl.*), irritate, lose one's interest, nauseate, offend, repel, sicken ◆ *n* **turn-off 6 = turning,** branch, exit, side road, turn

turn on *vb* **1 = start,** activate, energize, ignite, kick-start, put on, set in motion, start up, switch on **2 = depend on,** balance on, be contingent on, be decided by, hang on, hinge on, pivot on, rest on **3 = attack,** assail, assault, fall on, lose one's temper with, round on **5** *Informal* **= arouse,** arouse one's desire, attract, excite, please, press one's buttons (*sl.*), ring (someone's) bell (*US sl.*), stimulate, thrill, titillate, work up **7** *Slang* **= introduce,** expose, get one started with, inform, initiate, show
Antonyms *vb* ≠ **start:** cut out, put out, shut off, stop, switch off, turn off

turn out *vb* **1 = turn off,** put out, switch off, unplug **2 = produce,** bring out, fabricate, finish, make, manufacture, process, put out **3 = expel,** banish, cashier, cast out, deport, discharge, dismiss, dispossess, drive out, drum out, evict, kick out (*inf.*), kiss off (*sl., chiefly US & Canad.*), oust, put out, show one the door, throw out, turf out (*Brit. inf.*), unseat **4 = empty,** clean out, clear, discharge, take out the contents of **5 = prove to be,** come to light, crop up (*inf.*), develop, emerge, happen **6 = end up,** become, come about, come to be, eventuate, evolve, result, transpire (*inf.*), work out **7 = dress,** accoutre, apparel (*arch.*), attire, clothe, fit, outfit, rig out **8 = come,** appear, assemble, attend, be present, gather, go, put in an appearance, show up (*inf.*), turn up ◆ *n* **turnout 12 = attendance,** assemblage, assembly, audience, congregation, crowd, gate, number, throng **13 = output,** amount produced, outturn (*rare*), production, production quota, productivity, turnover, volume, yield **14 = outfit,** array, attire, costume, dress, equipage, equipment, gear (*inf.*), get-up (*inf.*), rigout (*inf.*)

rade. **10** (*intr*) *Inf.* to get out of bed. **11** (*intr;* foll. by *for*) *Inf.* to make an appearance, esp. in a sporting competition: *he was asked to turn out for Liverpool.* ◆ *n* **turnout. 12** the body of people appearing together at a gathering. **13** the quantity or amount produced. **14** an array of clothing or equipment.

turn over ❶ *vb* (*adv*) **1** to change or cause to change position, esp. so as to reverse top and bottom. **2** to start (an engine), esp. with a starting handle, or (of an engine) to start or function correctly. **3** to shift or cause to shift position, as by rolling from side to side. **4** (*tr*) to deliver; transfer. **5** (*tr*) to consider carefully. **6** (*tr*) **6a** to sell and replenish (stock in trade). **6b** to transact business and so generate gross revenue of (a specified sum). **7** (*tr*) to invest and recover (capital). **8** (*tr*) *Sl.* to rob. ◆ *n* **turnover. 9a** the amount of business transacted during a specified period. **9b** (*as modifier*): *a turnover tax.* **10** the rate at which stock in trade is sold and replenished. **11** a change or reversal of position. **12** a small pastry case filled with fruit, jam, etc. **13a** the number of workers employed by a firm in a given period to replace those who have left. **13b** the ratio between this number and the average number of employees during the same period. **14** *Banking.* the amount of capital funds loaned on call during a specified period. ◆ *adj* **turnover. 15** (*prenominal*) designed to be turned over.

turnpike ('tɜːnˌpaɪk) *n* **1** *History.* **1a** a barrier set across a road to prevent passage until a toll had been paid. **1b** a road on which a turnpike was operated. **2** an obsolete word for **turnstile. 3** *US.* a motorway for use of which a toll is charged. [C15: from TURN + PIKE[2]]

turnround ('tɜːnˌraʊnd) *n* another word for **turnaround.**

turnspit ('tɜːnˌspɪt) *n* **1** (formerly) a servant or small dog whose job was to turn a spit. **2** a spit that can be so turned.

turnstile ('tɜːnˌstaɪl) *n* a mechanical barrier with arms that are turned to admit one person at a time.

turnstone ('tɜːnˌstəʊn) *n* a shore bird, related to the plovers and sandpipers, that lifts up stones in search of food.

turntable ('tɜːnˌteɪbᵊl) *n* **1** the circular platform that rotates a gramophone record while it is being played. **2** a circular platform used for turning locomotives and cars. **3** the revolvable platform on a microscope on which specimens are examined.

turntable ladder *n Brit.* a power-operated extending ladder mounted on a fire engine. US and Canad. name: **aerial ladder.**

turn to *vb* (*intr, adv*) to set about a task.

turn up ❶ *vb* (*adv*) **1** (*intr*) to arrive or appear. **2** to find or be found, esp. by accident. **3** (*tr*) to increase the flow, volume, etc., of. ◆ *n* **turn-up. 4** (*often pl*) *Brit.* the turned-up fold at the bottom of some trouser legs. US, Canad. and Austral. name: **cuff. 5** *Inf.* an unexpected or chance occurrence.

turpentine ('tɜːpᵊnˌtaɪn) *n* **1** Also called: **gum turpentine.** any of various oleoresins obtained from various coniferous trees and used as the main source of commercial turpentine. **2** a sticky oleoresin that exudes from the terebinth tree. **3** Also called: **oil of turpentine, spirits of turpentine.** a colourless volatile oil distilled from turpentine oleoresin. It is used as a solvent for paints and in medicine. **4** Also called: **turpentine substitute, white spirit.** (*not in technical usage*) any one of a number of thinners for paints and varnishes, consisting of fractions of petroleum. Related adj: **terebinthine.** ◆ *vb* **turpentines, turpentining, turpentined.** (*tr*) **5** to treat or saturate with turpentine. [C14 *terebentyne,* from Med. L, from L *terebinthīna* turpentine, from *terebinthus* the turpentine tree]

turpentine tree *n* **1** a tropical African tree yielding a hard dark wood and a useful resin. **2** either of two Australian evergreen trees that yield resin.

turpeth ('tɜːpɪθ) *n* **1** an East Indian plant having roots with purgative properties. **2** the root of this plant or the drug obtained from it. [C14: from Med. L *turbithum,* ult. from Ar. *turbid*]

turpitude ❶ ('tɜːpɪˌtjuːd) *n* base character or action; depravity. [C15: from L *turpitūdō* ugliness, from *turpis* base]

turps (tɜːps) *n* (*functioning as sing*) *Brit.* short for **turpentine** (sense 3).

turquoise ('tɜːkwɔɪz, -kwɑːz) *n* **1** a greenish-blue fine-grained mineral consisting of hydrated copper aluminium phosphate. It is used as a gemstone. **2a** the colour of turquoise. **2b** (*as adj*): *a turquoise dress.* [C14: from OF *turqueise* Turkish (stone)]

turret ('tʌrɪt) *n* **1** a small tower that projects from the wall of a building, esp. a castle. **2a** a self-contained structure, capable of rotation, in which weapons are mounted, esp. in tanks and warships. **2b** a similar structure on an aircraft. **3** (on a machine tool) a turret-like steel structure with tools projecting radially that can be indexed round to bring each tool to bear on the work. [C14: from OF *torete,* from *tor* tower, from L *turris*]
▸ **'turreted** *adj*

turret lathe *n* another name for **capstan lathe.**

turtle[1] ('tɜːtᵊl) *n* **1** any of various aquatic reptiles, esp. those having a flattened shell enclosing the body and flipper-like limbs adapted for swimming. **2 turn turtle.** to capsize. [C17: from F *tortue* TORTOISE (infl. by TURTLE[2])]

turtle[2] ('tɜːtᵊl) *n* an archaic name for **turtledove.** [OE *turtla,* from L *turtur,* imit.]

turtleback ('tɜːtᵊlˌbæk) *n* an arched projection over the upper deck of a ship for protection in heavy seas.

turtledove ('tɜːtᵊlˌdʌv) *n* **1** any of several Old World doves having a brown plumage with speckled wings and a long dark tail. **2** a gentle or loving person. [see TURTLE[2]]

turtleneck ('tɜːtᵊlˌnɛk) *n* a round high close-fitting neck on a sweater or the sweater itself.

turves (tɜːvz) *n* a plural of **turf.**

Tuscan ('tʌskən) *adj* **1** of or relating to Tuscany, a region of central Italy, its inhabitants, or their dialect of Italian. **2** of or denoting one of the five classical orders of architecture: characterized by a column with an unfluted shaft and a capital and base with mouldings but no decoration. ◆ *n* **3** a native or inhabitant of Tuscany. **4** any of the dialects of Italian spoken in Tuscany.

tusche (tʊʃ) *n* a substance used in lithography for drawing the design and as a resist in silk-screen printing and lithography. [from G, from *tuschen* to touch up with colour, from F *toucher* to touch]

tush (tʌʃ) *interj Arch.* an exclamation of disapproval or contempt. [C15: imit.]

tusk (tʌsk) *n* **1** a pointed elongated usually paired tooth in the elephant, walrus, and certain other mammals. **2** a tusklike tooth or part. **3** a sharp pointed projection. ◆ *vb* **4** to stab, tear, or gore with the tusks. [OE *tūsc*]
▸ **tusked** *adj*

tusker ('tʌskə) *n* any animal with long tusks.

tusk shell *n* any of various burrowing seashore molluscs that have a long narrow tubular shell open at both ends.

tussis ('tʌsɪs) *n* the technical name for a **cough.** See **pertussis.** [L: cough]
▸ **'tussive** *adj*

tussle ❶ ('tʌsᵊl) *vb* **tussles, tussling, tussled. 1** (*intr*) to fight or wrestle in a vigorous way. ◆ *n* **2** a vigorous fight; scuffle; struggle. [C15]

tussock ('tʌsək) *n* **1** a dense tuft of vegetation, esp. of grass. **2** *Austral. & NZ.* **2a** short for **tussock grass. 2b the.** country where tussock grass grows. [C16: from ?]
▸ **'tussocky** *adj*

tussock grass *n* any of several pasture grasses.

tussore (tʊ'sɔː, 'tʌsɔː), **tusser** ('tʌsə), *or* (*Chiefly US*) **tussah** ('tʌsə) *n* **1** Also called: **wild silk.** a coarse silk obtained from an oriental silkworm. **2** the silkworm producing this. [C17: from Hindi *tasar* shuttle, from Sansk. *tasara* a wild silkworm]

tut (tʌt) *interj, n, vb* **tuts, tutting, tutted.** short for **tut-tut.**

tutelage ❶ ('tjuːtɪlɪdʒ) *n* **1** the act or office of a guardian or tutor. **2** instruction or guidance, esp. by a tutor. **3** the condition of being under the supervision of a guardian or tutor. [C17: from L *tūtēla* a caring for, from *tuērī* to watch over]

tutelary ('tjuːtɪlərɪ) *or* **tutelar** ('tjuːtɪlə) *adj* **1** invested with the role of guardian or protector. **2** of or relating to a guardian. ◆ *n, pl* **tutelaries** *or* **tutelars. 3** a tutelary person, deity, etc.

tutor ❶ ('tjuːtə) *n* **1** a teacher, usually instructing individual pupils. **2** (at universities, colleges, etc.) a member of staff responsible for the teaching and supervision of a certain number of students. ◆ *vb* **3** to act as a tutor to (someone). **4** (*tr*) to act as guardian to. [C14: from L: a watcher, from *tuērī* to watch over]
▸ **'tutorage** *or* **'tutorship** *n*

tutorial ❶ (tjuː'tɔːrɪəl) *n* **1** a period of intensive tuition given by a tutor to an individual student or to a small group of students. ◆ *adj* **2** of or relating to a tutor.

tutsan ('tʌtsən) *n* a woodland shrub of Europe and W Asia, having yel-

THESAURUS

turn over *vb* **1** = **overturn**, capsize, flip over, keel over, reverse, tip over, upend, upset **2** = **start up**, activate, crank, press the starter button, set going, set in motion, switch on, switch on the ignition, warm up **4** = **hand over**, assign, commend, commit, deliver, give over, give up, pass on, render, surrender, transfer, yield **5** = **consider**, contemplate, deliberate, give thought to, mull over, ponder, reflect on, revolve, ruminate about, think about, think over, wonder about ◆ *n* **turnover 9a** = **output**, business, flow, outturn (*rare*), production, productivity, volume, yield **13a** = **movement**, change, coming and going, replacement

turn up *vb* **1** = **arrive**, appear, attend, come, put in an appearance, show (*inf.*), show one's face, show up (*inf.*) **2** = **find**, bring to light, come up with, dig up, disclose, discover, expose, reveal, unearth **2** = **come to light**, appear, become known, be found, come to pass, crop up (*inf.*), pop up, transpire **3** = **increase**, amplify, boost, enhance, increase the volume of, intensify, make louder, raise
Antonyms *vb* ≠ **find:** hide ≠ **come to light:** disappear, evaporate, fade, vanish ≠ **increase:** diminish, lessen, lower, reduce, soften, turn down

turpitude *n Formal* = **wickedness**, badness, baseness, corruption, criminality, degeneracy, depravity, evil, foulness, immorality, iniquity, nefariousness, sinfulness, viciousness, vileness, villainy

tussle *vb* **1** = **fight**, battle, brawl, contend, grapple, scrap (*inf.*), scuffle, struggle, vie, wrestle ◆ *n* **2** = **fight**, battle, bout, brawl, competition, conflict, contention, contest, fracas, fray, punch-up (*Brit. inf.*), scrap (*inf.*), scrimmage, scuffle, set-to (*inf.*), shindig (*inf.*), shindy (*inf.*), struggle

tutelage *n Formal* **1, 2** = **guidance**, care, charge, custody, dependence, education, guardianship, instruction, patronage, preparation, protection, schooling, teaching, tuition, wardship

tutor *n* **1, 2** = **teacher**, coach, educator, governor, guardian, guide, guru, instructor, lecturer, master *or* mistress, mentor, preceptor, schoolmaster *or* schoolmistress ◆ *vb* **3** = **teach**, coach, direct, discipline, drill, edify, educate, guide, instruct, lecture, school, train

tutorial *n* **1** = **seminar**, individual instruction, lesson ◆ *adj* **2** = **teaching**, coaching, guiding, instructional

low flowers and reddish-purple fruits. [C15: from OF *toute-saine* (unattested), lit.: all healthy]

tutti ('tʊtɪ) *adj, adv Music.* to be performed by the whole orchestra, choir, etc. [C18: from It., pl of *tutto* all, from L *tōtus*]

tutti-frutti ('tu:tɪ'fru:tɪ) *n* **1** (*pl* **tutti-fruttis**) an ice cream or a confection containing small pieces of candied or fresh fruits. **2** a preserve of chopped mixed fruits. **3** a flavour like that of many fruits combined. [from It., lit.: all the fruits]

tut-tut ('tʌt'tʌt) *interj* **1** an exclamation of mild reprimand, disapproval, or surprise. ◆ *vb* **tut-tuts, tut-tutting, tut-tutted.** **2** (*intr*) to express disapproval by the exclamation of "tut-tut". ◆ *n* **3** the act of tut-tutting.

tutty ('tʌtɪ) *n* impure zinc oxide used as a polishing powder. [C14: from OF *tutie,* from Ar. *tūtiyā,* prob. from Persian, from Sansk. *tuttha*]

tutu ('tu:tu:) *n* a very short skirt worn by ballerinas, made of projecting layers of stiffened material. [from F, changed from the nursery word *cucu* backside, from L *cūlus* the buttocks]

tu-whit tu-whoo (tə'wɪt tə'wu:) *interj* an imitation of the sound made by an owl.

tuxedo (tʌk'si:dəʊ) *n, pl* **tuxedos.** the usual US and Canad. name for **dinner jacket.** [C19: after a country club in *Tuxedo Park,* New York]

tuyère ('twi:ɛə, 'twaɪə) *or* **twyer** ('twaɪə) *n* a water-cooled nozzle through which air is blown into a cupola, blast furnace, or forge. [C18: from F, from *tuyau* pipe, from OF *tuel,* prob. of Gmc origin]

TV ➊ *abbrev. for* television.

TVEI (in Britain) *abbrev. for* technical and vocational educational initiative: a national educational scheme in which pupils gain practical experience in technology and industry often through work placement.

TVP *abbrev. for* textured vegetable protein: protein from soya beans or other vegetables spun into fibres and flavoured: used esp. as a substitute for meat.

TVR *abbrev. for* television rating: a measurement of the popularity of a TV programme based on a survey.

TVRO *abbrev. for* television receive only: an antenna and associated apparatus for reception from a broadcasting satellite.

twaddle ➊ ('twɒdᵊl) *n* **1** silly, trivial, or pretentious talk or writing. ◆ *vb* **twaddles, twaddling, twaddled.** **2** (*intr*) to talk or write in a silly or pretentious way. [C16 *twattle,* var. of *twittle* or *tittle*]
▸ **'twaddler** *n*

twain (tweɪn) *determiner, n* an archaic word for **two.** [OE *twēgen*]

twang (twæŋ) *n* **1** a sharp ringing sound produced by or as if by the plucking of a taut string. **2** the act of plucking a string to produce such a sound. **3** a strongly nasal quality in a person's speech. ◆ *vb* **4** to make or cause to make a twang. **5** to strum (music, a tune, etc.). **6** to speak with a nasal voice. **7** (*intr*) to be released or move with a twang: *the arrow twanged away.* [C16: imit.]
▸ **'twangy** *adj*

'twas (twɒz; *unstressed* twəz) *Poetic or dialect. contraction of* it was.

twat (twæt, twɒt) *n Taboo sl.* **1** the female genitals. **2** a foolish person. [from ?]

twayblade ('tweɪˌbleɪd) *n* any of various orchids having a basal pair of unstalked leaves arranged opposite each other. [C16: translation of Med. L *bifolium* having two leaves, from obs. *tway* two + BLADE]

tweak ➊ (twi:k) *vb* (*tr*) **1** to twist or pinch with a sharp or sudden movement. **2** *Inf.* to make a minor alteration. ◆ *n* **3** a tweaking. **4** *Inf.* a minor alteration. [OE *twiccian*]

twee ➊ (twi:) *adj Brit. inf.* excessively sentimental, sweet, or pretty. [C19: from *tweet,* mincing or affected pronunciation of *sweet*]
▸ **'tweely** *adv*

tweed (twi:d) *n* **1** a thick woollen cloth produced originally in Scotland. **2** (*pl*) clothes made of this. **3** (*pl*) *Austral. inf.* trousers. [C19: prob. from *tweel,* Scot. var. of TWILL, infl. by *Tweed,* a Scot. river]

Tweedledum and Tweedledee (ˌtwi:dᵊl'dʌm; ˌtwi:dᵊl'di:) *n* any two persons or things that differ only slightly from each other; two of a kind. [C19: from the proverbial names of Handel and the rival musician Buonocini. The names were popularized by Lewis Carroll's use of them in *Through the Looking Glass* (1872)]

tweedy ('twi:dɪ) *adj* **tweedier, tweediest.** **1** of, made of, or resembling tweed. **2** showing a fondness for a hearty outdoor life, usually associated with wearers of tweeds.

'tween (twi:n) *Poetic or dialect. contraction of* between.

'tween deck *or* **decks** *n Naut.* a space between two continuous decks of a vessel.

tweet (twi:t) *interj* **1** an imitation of the thin chirping sound made by small birds. ◆ *vb* **2** (*intr*) to make this sound. [C19: imit.]

tweeter ('twi:tə) *n* a loudspeaker used in high-fidelity systems for the reproduction of high audio frequencies. It is usually employed in conjunction with a woofer. [C20: from TWEET]

tweezers ('twi:zəz) *pl n* a small pincer-like instrument for handling small objects, plucking out hairs, etc. Also called: **pair of tweezers, tweezer** (esp. US). [C17: pl of *tweezer* (on the model of *scissors,* etc.), from *tweeze* case of instruments, from F *étuis,* from OF *estuier* to preserve, ult. from L *studēre* to care about]

Twelfth Day *n* Jan. 6, the twelfth day after Christmas and the feast of the Epiphany.

twelfth man *n* a reserve player in a cricket team.

Twelfth Night *n* **a** the evening of Jan. 5, the eve of Twelfth Day. **b** the evening of Twelfth Day itself.

twelve (twɛlv) *n* **1** the cardinal number that is the sum of ten and two. **2** a numeral, 12, XII, etc., representing this number. **3** something representing or consisting of 12 units. **4** Also called: **twelve o'clock.** noon or midnight. ◆ *determiner* **5a** amounting to twelve. **5b** (*as pronoun*): *twelve have arrived.* ◆ Related adj: **duodecimal.** [OE *twelf*]
▸ **twelfth** *adj, n*

twelve-inch *n* a gramophone record 12 inches in diameter and played at 45 revolutions per minute, usually containing an extended remix of a single.

twelvemo ('twɛlvməʊ) *n, pl* **twelvemos.** *Bookbinding.* another word for **duodecimo.**

twelvemonth ('twɛlvˌmʌnθ) *n Chiefly Brit.* an archaic or dialect word for a **year.**

twelve-tone *adj* of or denoting the type of serial music which uses as musical material a tone row formed by the 12 semitones of the chromatic scale. See **serialism.**

twenty ('twɛntɪ) *n, pl* **twenties.** **1** the cardinal number that is the product of ten and two. **2** a numeral, 20, XX, etc., representing this number. **3** something representing or consisting of 20 units. ◆ *determiner* **4a** amounting to twenty: *twenty questions.* **4b** (*as pronoun*): *to order twenty.*
▸ **'twentieth** *adj, n* [OE *twēntig*]

twenty-six counties *pl n* the counties of the Republic of Ireland.

twenty-twenty *adj Med.* (of vision) being of normal acuity: usually written 20/20.

'twere (twɜ:; *unstressed* twə) *Poetic or dialect. contraction of* it were.

twerp *or* **twirp** (twɜ:p) *n Inf.* a silly, weak-minded, or contemptible person. [C20: from ?]

twibill *or* **twibil** ('twaɪˌbɪl) *n* **1** a mattock with a blade shaped like an adze at one end and like an axe at the other. **2** *Arch.* a double-bladed battle-axe. [OE, from *twi-* double + *bill* sword]

twice (twaɪs) *adv* **1** two times; on two occasions or in two cases. **2** double in degree or quantity: *twice as long.* [OE *twiwa*]

twiddle ➊ ('twɪdᵊl) *vb* **twiddles, twiddling, twiddled.** **1** (when *intr,* often foll. by *with*) to twirl or fiddle (with), often in an idle way. **2 twiddle one's thumbs.** to do nothing; be unoccupied. **3** (*intr*) to turn, twirl, or rotate. **4** (*intr*) *Rare.* to be occupied with trifles. ◆ *n* **5** an act or instance of twiddling. [C16: prob. a blend of TWIRL + FIDDLE]
▸ **'twiddler** *n*

twig[1] ➊ (twɪg) *n* **1** any small branch or shoot of a tree. **2** something resembling this, esp. a minute branch of a blood vessel. [OE *twigge*]
▸ **'twiggy** *adj*

twig[2] ➊ (twɪg) *vb* **twigs, twigging, twigged.** *Brit. inf.* **1** to understand (something). **2** to find out or suddenly comprehend (something): *he hasn't twigged yet.* [C18: ?from Scot. Gaelic *tuig* I understand]

twilight ➊ ('twaɪˌlaɪt) *n* **1** the soft diffused light occurring when the sun is just below the horizon, esp. following sunset. **2** the period in which this light occurs. **3** any faint light. **4** a period in which strength, importance, etc., are waning. **5** (*modifier*) **5a** of or relating to the period towards the end of the day: *the twilight shift.* **5b** of or relating to the final phase of a particular era: *the twilight days of the Bush presidency.* **5c** denoting irregularity and obscurity: *a twilight existence.* [C15: lit.: half light (between day and night), from OE *twi-* half + LIGHT[1]]
▸ **twilit** ('twaɪˌlɪt) *adj*

Twilight of the Gods *n* another term for **Götterdämmerung.**

twilight sleep *n Med.* a state of partial anaesthesia in which the patient retains a slight degree of consciousness.

twilight zone *n* **1** any indefinite or transitional condition or area. **2** an inner-city area where houses have become dilapidated.

THESAURUS

TV *n* = **television,** gogglebox (*Brit. sl.*), idiot box (*sl.*), receiver, small screen (*inf.*), television set, telly (*Brit. inf.*), the box (*Brit. inf.*), the tube (*sl.*), TV set

twaddle *n* **1** = **nonsense,** balderdash, blather, bull (*sl.*), bullshit (*taboo sl.*), bunkum *or* buncombe (*chiefly US*), chatter, claptrap (*inf.*), cobblers (*Brit. taboo sl.*), crap (*sl.*), drivel, eyewash (*inf.*), foolish talk, gabble, garbage (*inf.*), gossip, guff (*sl.*), hogwash, hokum (*sl., chiefly US & Canad.*), hot air (*inf.*), inanity, moonshine, pap, piffle (*inf.*), poppycock (*inf.*), rigmarole, rot, rubbish, tattle, tommyrot, tosh (*sl., chiefly Brit.*), trash, tripe (*inf.*), trumpery, verbiage, waffle (*inf., chiefly Brit.*) ◆ *vb* **2** = **talk nonsense,** blather, chatter, gabble, gossip, prattle, rattle on, talk through one's hat, tattle, waffle (*inf., chiefly Brit.*)

tweak *vb, n* **1, 3** = **twist,** jerk, nip, pinch, pull, squeeze, twitch

twee *adj Informal* = **sweet,** bijou, cute, dainty, precious, pretty, quaint, sentimental

twiddle *vb* **1** = **fiddle** (*inf.*), adjust, finger, jiggle, juggle, monkey with (*inf.*), play with, twirl, wiggle **2 twiddle one's thumbs** = **be idle,** be unoccupied, do nothing, have nothing to do, malinger, mark time, sit around

twig[1] *n* = **branch,** offshoot, shoot, spray, sprig, stick, withe

twig[2] *vb* **1, 2** *Brit. informal* = **understand,** catch on, comprehend, fathom, find out, get, grasp, make out, rumble (*Brit. inf.*), see, tumble to (*inf.*)

twilight *n* **1** = **dusk,** dimness, evening, gloaming (*Scot. or poetic*), gloom, half-light, sundown, sunset **4** = **decline,** ebb, last phase ◆ *modifier* **5a** = **evening,** crepuscular, darkening, dim ◆ *adj* **5b** = **declining,** dying, ebbing, final, last

Antonyms *n* ≠ **dusk:** dawn, daybreak, morning,

twill (twɪl) *adj* **1** (in textiles) of a weave in which the yarns are worked to produce an effect of parallel diagonal lines or ribs. ◆ *n* **2** any fabric so woven. ◆ *vb* **3** (*tr*) to weave in this fashion. [OE *twilic* having a double thread]

'twill (twɪl) *Poetic or dialect. contraction of* it will.

twin ❶ (twɪn) *n* **1a** either of two persons or animals conceived at the same time. **1b** (*as modifier*): *a twin brother.* See also **identical** (sense 3), **fraternal** (sense 3). **2a** either of two persons or things that are identical or very similar. **2b** (*as modifier*): *twin carburettors.* **3** Also called: **macle.** a crystal consisting of two parts each of which has a definite orientation to the other. ◆ *vb* **twins, twinning, twinned. 4** to pair or be paired together; couple. **5** (*intr*) to bear twins. **6** (*intr*) (of a crystal) to form into a twin. **7a** (*tr*) to create a reciprocal relation between (two towns in different countries); pair (a town) with another in a different country. **7b** (*intr*) (of a town) to be paired in a town in a different country. [OE *twinn*]
▸ **'twinning** *n*

twin bed *n* one of a pair of matching single beds.

twine ❶ (twaɪn) *n* **1** string made by twisting together fibres of hemp, cotton, etc. **2** a twining. **3** something produced or characterized by twining. **4** a twist, coil, or convolution. **5** a knot or tangle. ◆ *vb* **twines, twining, twined. 6** (*tr*) to twist together; interweave. **7** (*tr*) to form by or as if by twining. **8** (when *intr*, often foll. by *around*) to wind or cause to wind, esp. in spirals. [OE *twīn*]
▸ **'twiner** *n*

twin-engined *adj* (of an aeroplane) having two engines.

twinge ❶ (twɪndʒ) *n* **1** a sudden brief darting or stabbing pain. **2** a sharp emotional pang. ◆ *vb* **twinges, twinging, twinged. 3** to have or cause to have a twinge. [OE *twengan* to pinch]

twinkle ❶ ('twɪŋkᵊl) *vb* **twinkles, twinkling, twinkled.** (*mainly intr*) **1** to emit or reflect light in a flickering manner; shine brightly and intermittently; sparkle. **2** (of the eyes) to sparkle, esp. with amusement or delight. **3** *Rare.* to move about quickly. ◆ *n* **4** a flickering brightness; sparkle. **5** an instant. [OE *twinclian*]
▸ **'twinkler** *n*

twinkling ❶ ('twɪŋklɪŋ) *or* **twink** (twɪŋk) *n* a very short time; instant; moment. Also called: **twinkling of an eye.**

Twins (twɪnz) *pl n* **the.** the constellation Gemini, the third sign of the zodiac.

twin-screw *adj* (of a vessel) having two propellers.

twinset ('twɪn,sɛt) *n Brit.* a matching jumper and cardigan.

twin town *n* a town that has civic associations, such as reciprocal visits and cultural exchanges, with a foreign town.

twin-tub *n* a type of washing machine that has two revolving drums, one for washing and the other for spin-drying.

twirl ❶ (twɜːl) *vb* **1** to move around rapidly and repeatedly in a circle. **2** (*tr*) to twist, wind, or twiddle, often idly: *she twirled her hair around her finger.* **3** (*intr;* often foll. by *around* or *about*) to turn suddenly to face another way. ◆ *n* **4** a rotating or being rotated; whirl or twist. **5** something wound around or twirled; coil. **6** a written flourish. [C16: ? a blend of TWIST + WHIRL]
▸ **'twirler** *n*

twirp (twɜːp) *n* a variant spelling of **twerp.**

twist ❶ (twɪst) *vb* **1** to cause (one end or part) to turn or (of one end or part) to turn in the opposite direction from another; coil or spin. **2** to distort or be distorted. **3** to wind or twine. **4** to force or be forced out of the natural form or position. **5** to change for the worse in character, meaning, etc.; pervert: *she twisted the statement.* **6** to revolve; rotate. **7** (*tr*) to wrench with a turning action. **8** (*intr*) to follow a winding course. **9** (*intr*) to squirm, as with pain. **10** (*intr*) to dance the twist. **11** (*tr*) *Brit. inf.* to cheat; swindle. **12 twist someone's arm.** to persuade or coerce someone. ◆ *n* **13** a twisting. **14** something formed by or as if by twisting. **15** a decisive change of direction, aim, meaning, or character. **16** (in a novel, play, etc.) an unexpected event, revelation, etc. **17** a bend: *a twist in the road.* **18** a distortion of the original shape or form. **19** a jerky pull, wrench, or turn. **20** a strange personal characteristic, esp. a bad one. **21** a confused tangle made by twisting. **22** a twisted thread used in sewing where extra strength is needed. **23 the twist.** a dance popular in the 1960s, in which dancers vigorously twist the hips. **24** a loaf or roll made of pieces of twisted dough. **25** a thin sliver of peel from a lemon, lime, etc., twisted and added to a drink. **26a** a cigar made by twisting three cigars around one another. **26b** chewing tobacco made in the form of a roll by twisting the leaves together. **27** *Physics.* torsional deformation or shear stress or strain. **28** *Sport, chiefly US & Canad.* spin given to a ball in various games. **29 round the twist.** *Brit. sl.* mad; eccentric. [OE]
▸ **'twisty** *adj*

twist drill *n* a drill bit having two helical grooves running from the point along the shank to clear swarf and cuttings.

twister ❶ ('twɪstə) *n* **1** *Brit.* a swindling or dishonest person. **2** a person or thing that twists. **3** *US & Canad.* an informal name for **tornado. 4** a ball moving with a twisting motion.

twist grip *n* a handlebar control in the form of a ratchet-controlled rotating grip.

twit[1] ❶ (twɪt) *vb* **twits, twitting, twitted. 1** (*tr*) to tease, taunt, or reproach, often in jest. ◆ *n* **2** *US & Canad. inf.* a nervous or excitable state. **3** *Rare.* a reproach; taunt. [OE *ætwītan,* from *æt* against + *wītan* to accuse]

twit[2] ❶ (twɪt) *n Inf., chiefly Brit.* a foolish or stupid person; idiot. [C19: from TWIT[1] (orig. in the sense: a person given to twitting)]

twitch ❶ (twɪtʃ) *vb* **1** to move in a jerky spasmodic way. **2** (*tr*) to pull (something) with a quick jerky movement. **3** (*intr*) to hurt with a sharp spasmodic pain. ◆ *n* **4** a sharp jerking movement. **5** a mental or physical twinge. **6** a sudden muscular spasm, esp. one caused by a nervous condition. **7** a loop of cord used to control a horse by drawing it tight about its upper lip. [OE *twiccian* to pluck]

twitcher ('twɪtʃə) *n* **1** a person or thing that twitches. **2** *Inf.* a birdwatcher who tries to spot as many rare varieties as possible.

twitch grass *n* another name for **couch grass.** Sometimes shortened to **twitch.** [C16: var. of QUITCH GRASS]

twite (twaɪt) *n* a N European finch with a brown streaked plumage. [C16: imit. of its cry]

twitter ❶ ('twɪtə) *vb* **1** (*intr*) (esp. of a bird) to utter a succession of chirping sounds. **2** (*intr*) to talk or move rapidly and tremulously. **3** (*intr*) to giggle. **4** (*tr*) to utter in a chirping way. ◆ *n* **5** a twittering sound. **6** the act of twittering. **7** a state of nervous excitement (esp. in **in a twitter**). [C14: imit.]
▸ **'twitterer** *n* ▸ **'twittery** *adj*

'twixt *or* **twixt** (twɪkst) *Poetic or dialect. contraction of* betwixt.

two (tuː) *n* **1** the cardinal number that is the sum of one and one. **2** a numeral, 2, II, (ii), etc., representing this number. **3** something representing or consisting of two units. **4** Also called: **two o'clock.** two hours after noon or midnight. **5 in two.** in or into two parts. **6 put two and two together.** to make an inference from available evidence, esp. an obvious inference. **7 that makes two of us.** the same applies to me. ◆ *determiner* **8a** amounting to two: *two nails.* **8b** (*as pronoun*): *he bought two.* ◆ Related adjs.: **binary, double, dual.** [OE *twā* (fem)]

THESAURUS

sunrise, sunup ≠ **decline:** climax, crowning moment, height, peak

twin *n* **2a** = **double**, clone, corollary, counterpart, duplicate, fellow, likeness, lookalike, match, mate, ringer (*sl.*) ◆ *modifier* **2b** = **identical**, corresponding, double, dual, duplicate, geminate, matched, matching, paired, parallel, twofold ◆ *vb* **4** = **pair**, couple, join, link, match, yoke

twine *n* **1** = **string**, cord, yarn **4** = **coil**, convolution, interlacing, twist, whorl **5** = **tangle**, knot, snarl ◆ *vb* **6** = **twist together**, braid, entwine, interlace, interweave, knit, plait, splice, twist, weave **8** = **coil**, bend, curl, encircle, loop, meander, spiral, surround, twist, wind, wrap, wreathe

twinge *n* **1** = **pain**, bite, gripe, pang, pinch, prick, sharp pain, spasm, stab, stitch, throb, throe (*rare*), tic, tweak, twist, twitch

twinkle *vb* **1** = **sparkle**, blink, coruscate, flash, flicker, gleam, glint, glisten, glitter, scintillate, shimmer, shine, wink ◆ *n* **4** = **sparkle**, blink, coruscation, flash, flicker, gleam, glimmer, glistening, glittering, light, scintillation, shimmer, shine, spark, wink **5** = **moment**, flash, instant, jiffy (*inf.*), second, shake (*inf.*), split second, tick (*Brit. inf.*), trice, twinkling, two shakes of a lamb's tail (*inf.*)

twinkling *n* = **moment**, bat of an eye (*inf.*), flash, instant, jiffy, second, shake (*inf.*), split second, tick (*Brit. inf.*), trice, twinkle, two shakes of a lamb's tail (*inf.*)

twirl *vb* **1** = **turn**, gyrate, pirouette, pivot, revolve, rotate, spin, turn on one's heel, twiddle, twist, wheel, whirl, wind ◆ *n* **4** = **turn**, gyration, pirouette, revolution, rotation, spin, twist, wheel, whirl **5** = **coil**, spiral, twist

twist *vb* **1, 3** = **wind**, coil, corkscrew, curl, encircle, entwine, intertwine, screw, spin, swivel, twine, weave, wrap, wreathe, wring **2** = **distort**, contort, screw up **5** = **misrepresent**, alter, change, distort, falsify, garble, misquote, pervert, warp **7** = **sprain**, rick, turn, wrench **9** = **squirm**, wriggle, writhe **12 twist someone's arm** = **force**, bully, coerce, persuade, pressurize, talk into ◆ *n* **13** = **wind**, coil, curl, spin, swivel, twine **14** = **coil**, braid, curl, hank, plug, quid, roll **16** = **development**, change, revelation, slant, surprise, turn, variation **17** = **curve**, arc, bend, convolution, meander, turn, undulation, zigzag **18** = **distortion**, defect, deformation, flaw, imperfection, kink, warp **19** = **jerk**, pull, sprain, turn, wrench **20** = **trait**, aberration, bent, characteristic, crotchet, eccentricity, fault, foible, idiosyncrasy, oddity, peculiarity, proclivity, quirk **21** = **tangle**, confusion, entanglement, kink, knot, mess, mix-up, ravel, snarl **29 round the twist** *Brit. slang* = **mad**, barmy (*sl.*), batty (*sl.*), bonkers (*sl., chiefly Brit.*), crazy, cuckoo (*inf.*), daft (*inf.*), insane, loopy (*inf.*), not all there, not right in the head, nuts (*sl.*), nutty (*sl.*), off one's rocker (*sl.*), off one's trolley (*sl.*), out to lunch (*inf.*)
Antonyms *vb* ≠ **distort:** straighten, untwist ≠ **wind:** straighten, uncoil, unravel, unroll, untwist, unwind

twister *n* **1** *Brit.* = **swindler**, cheat, chiseller (*inf.*), con man (*inf.*), crook (*inf.*), deceiver, fraud, fraudster, hustler (*US inf.*), rogue, trickster

twit[1] *vb* **1** = **make fun of**, banter, deride, jeer, poke fun at, scorn, taunt, tease **1** = **reproach**, berate, blame, censure, upbraid

twit[2] *n Informal, chiefly Brit.* = **fool**, airhead (*sl.*), ass, berk, blockhead, charlie (*Brit. inf.*), chump (*inf.*), clown, divvy (*Brit. sl.*), dope (*inf.*), dork (*sl.*), dumb-ass (*sl.*), geek (*sl.*), halfwit, idiot, nincompoop, ninny, nitwit (*inf.*), numbskull *or* numskull, pillock (*Brit. sl.*), plank (*Brit. sl.*), plonker (*sl.*), schmuck (*US sl.*), silly-billy (*inf.*), simpleton, wally (*sl.*)

twitch *vb* **1** = **jerk**, blink, flutter, jump, squirm **2** = **pull**, pluck, snatch, tug, yank ◆ *n* **4, 5** = **jerk**, blink, flutter, jump, spasm, tic, tremor, twinge

twitter *vb* **1** = **chirrup**, chatter, cheep, chirp, trill, tweet, warble, whistle **2** = **chatter**, prattle **3** = **giggle**, simper, snigger, titter ◆ *n* **5** = **chirrup**, call, chatter, cheep, chirp, cry, song, trill, tweet, warble, whistle **7** *As in* **in a twitter** = **nervousness**, agitation, anxiety, bustle, dither (*chiefly Brit.*), excitement, flurry, fluster, flutter, tizzy (*inf.*), whirl

two-by-four *n* **1** a length of untrimmed timber with a cross section that measures 2 inches by 4 inches. **2** a trimmed timber joist with a cross section that measures 1½ inches by 3½ inches.

twoccing *or* **twocking** ('twɒkɪŋ) *n Brit. sl.* the act of breaking into a motor vehicle and driving it away. [C20: from *T(aking) W(ithout) O(wner's) C(onsent),* the legal offence with which car thieves may be charged]
▸**'twoccer** *or* **'twocker** *n*

two-dimensional *adj* **1** of or having two dimensions. **2** having an area but not enclosing any volume. **3** lacking in depth.

two-edged ❶ *adj* **1** having two cutting edges. **2** (esp. of a remark) having two interpretations, such as *she looks nice when she smiles.*

two-faced ❶ *adj* deceitful; hypocritical.

twofold ('tuːˌfəʊld) *adj* **1** equal to twice as many or twice as much. **2** composed of two parts. ◆ *adv* **3** doubly.

two-handed *adj* **1** requiring the use of both hands. **2** ambidextrous. **3** requiring the participation or cooperation of two people.

two-pack *adj* (of a paint, filler, etc.) supplied as two separate components, for example a base and a catalyst, that are mixed together immediately before use.

twopence *or* **tuppence** ('tʌpəns) *n Brit.* **1** the sum of two pennies. **2** (*used with a negative*) something of little value (in **not care** *or* **give twopence**). **3** a former British silver coin.

twopenny *or* **tuppenny** ('tʌpənɪ) *adj Chiefly Brit.* **1** Also: **twopenny-halfpenny.** cheap or tawdry. **2** (intensifier): *a twopenny damn.* **3** worth two pence.

two-phase *adj* (of an electrical circuit, device, etc.) generating or using two alternating voltages of the same frequency, displaced in phase by 90°.

two-piece *adj* **1** consisting of two separate parts, usually matching, as of a garment. ◆ *n* **2** such an outfit.

two-ply *adj* **1** made of two thicknesses, layers, or strands. ◆ *n, pl* **two-plies. 2** a two-ply wood, knitting yarn, etc.

two-sided *adj* **1** having two sides or aspects. **2** controversial; debatable.

twosome ('tuːsəm) *n* **1** two together, esp. two people. **2** a match between two people.

two-step *n* **1** an old-time dance in duple time. **2** a piece of music composed for or in the rhythm of this dance.

two-stroke *adj* of an internal-combustion engine whose piston makes two strokes for every explosion. US and Canad. word: **two-cycle.**

Two Thousand Guineas *n* (*functioning as sing*), *usually written* **2000 Guineas. the.** an annual horse race run at Newmarket since 1809.

two-time *vb* **two-times, two-timing, two-timed.** *Inf.* to deceive (someone, esp. a lover) by carrying on a relationship with another.
▸**ˌtwo-'timer** *n*

two-tone *adj* **1** of two colours or two shades of the same colour. **2** (esp. of sirens, car horns, etc.) producing or consisting of two notes.

'twould (twʊd) *Poetic or dialect. contraction of* it would.

two-up *n Chiefly Austral.* a illegal gambling game in which two coins are tossed or spun.

two-way *adj* **1** moving, permitting movement, or operating in either of two opposite directions. **2** involving two participants. **3** involving reciprocal obligation or mutual action. **4** (of a radio, telephone, etc.) allowing communications in two directions using both transmitting and receiving equipment.

two-way mirror *n* a half-silvered sheet of glass that functions as a mirror when viewed from one side but is translucent from the other.

-ty[1] *suffix of numerals.* denoting a multiple of ten: *sixty; seventy.* [from OE *-tig*]

-ty[2] *suffix forming nouns.* indicating state, condition, or quality: *cruelty.* [from OF *-te, -tet,* from L *-tās, -tāt-*]

Tyburn ('taɪbɜːn) *n* (formerly) a place of execution in London, on the River Tyburn.

tychism ('taɪkɪzəm) *n Philosophy.* the theory that chance is an objective reality at work in the universe. [from Gk *tukhē* chance]

tycoon ❶ (taɪ'kuːn) *n* **1** a businessman of great wealth and power. **2** an archaic name for a **shogun.** [C19: from Japanese *taikun,* from Chinese *ta* great + *chün* ruler]

tyke *or* **tike** (taɪk) *n* **1** a dog, esp. a mongrel. **2** *Inf.* a small or cheeky child. **3** *Brit. dialect.* a rough ill-mannered person. **4** *Brit. sl. often offens.* a person from Yorkshire. **5** *Austral. sl., offens.* a Roman Catholic. [C14: from ON *tīk* bitch]

tylopod ('taɪləʊˌpɒd) *n* a mammal having padded, rather than hoofed, digits, such as camels and llamas. [C19: from NL, from Gk *tulos* knob or *tulē* cushion + -POD]

tympan ('tɪmpən) *n* **1** a membrane stretched over a frame or cylinder. **2** *Printing.* packing interposed between the platen and the paper to be printed in order to provide an even impression. **3** *Archit.* another name for **tympanum.** [OE *timpana,* from L; see TYMPANUM]

tympani ('tɪmpənɪ) *pl n* a variant spelling of **timpani.**

tympanic bone (tɪm'pænɪk) *n* the part of the temporal bone that surrounds the auditory canal.

tympanic membrane *n* the thin membrane separating the external ear from the middle ear. It transmits vibrations, produced by sound waves, to the cochlea. Nontechnical name: **eardrum.**

tympanites (ˌtɪmpə'naɪtiːz) *n* distension of the abdomen caused by an accumulation of gas in the intestinal or peritoneal cavity. Also called: **meteorism, tympany.** [C14: from LL, from Gk *tumpanitēs* concerning a drum, from *tumpanon* drum]
▸**tympanitic** (ˌtɪmpə'nɪtɪk) *adj*

tympanitis (ˌtɪmpə'naɪtɪs) *n* inflammation of the eardrum.

tympanum ('tɪmpənəm) *n, pl* **tympanums** *or* **tympana** (-nə). **1a** the cavity of the middle ear. **1b** another name for **tympanic membrane. 2** any diaphragm resembling that in the middle ear in function. **3** *Archit.* **3a** the recessed space bounded by the cornices of a pediment, esp. one that is triangular in shape. **3b** the recessed space bounded by an arch and the lintel of a doorway or window below it. **4** *Music.* a tympan or drum. **5** a scoop wheel for raising water. [C17: from L, from Gk *tumpanon* drum]
▸**tympanic** (tɪm'pænɪk) *adj*

Tyndall effect *n* the phenomenon in which light is scattered by particles of matter in its path. [C19: after John *Tyndall* (1820–93), Irish physicist]

Tynwald ('tɪnwəld, 'taɪn-) *n* **the.** the Parliament of the Isle of Man. [C15: from ON *thingvollr,* from *thing* assembly + *vollr* field]

typ., typo., *or* **typog.** *abbrev. for:* **1** typographer. **2** typographic(al). **3** typography.

typal ('taɪpᵊl) *adj* a rare word for **typical.**

type ❶ (taɪp) *n* **1** a kind, class, or category, the constituents of which share similar characteristics. **2** a subdivision of a particular class; sort: *what type of shampoo do you use?* **3** the general form, plan, or design distinguishing a particular group. **4** *Inf.* a person who typifies a particular quality: *he's the administrative type.* **5** *Inf.* a person, esp. of a specified kind: *he's a strange type.* **6a** a small block of metal or more rarely wood bearing a letter or character in relief for use in printing. **6b** such pieces collectively. **7** characters printed from type; print. **8** *Biol.* **8a** the taxonomic group the characteristics of which are used for defining the next highest group. **8b** (*as modifier*): *a type genus.* **9** See **type specimen. 10** the characteristic device on a coin. **11** *Chiefly Christian theol.* a figure, episode, or symbolic factor resembling some future reality in such a way as to foreshadow or prefigure it. ◆ *vb* **types, typing, typed. 12** to write (copy) on a typewriter. **13** (*tr*) to be a symbol of; typify. **14** (*tr*) to decide the type of. **15** (*tr*) *Med.* to determine the blood group of (a blood sample). **16** (*tr*) *Chiefly Christian theol.* to foreshadow or serve as a symbol of (some future reality). [C15: from L *typus* figure, from Gk *tupos* image, from *tuptein* to strike]

-type *n combining form.* **1** type or form: *archetype.* **2** printing type or photographic process: *collotype.* [from L *-typus,* from Gk *-typos,* from *tupos* TYPE]

typecast ('taɪpˌkɑːst) *vb* **typecasts, typecasting, typecast.** (*tr*) to cast (an actor) in the same kind of role continually, esp. because of his physical appearance or previous success in such roles.

typeface ('taɪpˌfeɪs) *n* another name for **face** (sense 14).

type founder *n* a person who casts metallic printer's type.
▸**type foundry** *n*

type metal *n Printing.* an alloy of tin, lead, and antimony, from which type is cast.

typescript ('taɪpˌskrɪpt) *n* **1** a typed copy of a document, etc. **2** any typewritten material.

typeset ('taɪpˌsɛt) *vb* **typesets, typesetting, typeset.** (*tr*) *Printing.* to set (textual matter) in type.

typesetter ('taɪpˌsɛtə) *n* **1** a person who sets type; compositor. **2** a typesetting machine.

type specimen *n Biol.* the original specimen from which a description of a new species is made.

typewrite ('taɪpˌraɪt) *vb* **typewrites, typewriting, typewrote, typewritten.** to write by means of a typewriter; type.
▸**'typeˌwriting** *n*

typewriter ('taɪpˌraɪtə) *n* a keyboard machine for writing mechanically in characters resembling print.

typhlitis (tɪf'laɪtɪs) *n* inflammation of the caecum. [C19: from NL, from Gk *tuphlon* the caecum, from *tuphlos* blind]
▸**typhlitic** (tɪf'lɪtɪk) *adj*

typhoid ('taɪfɔɪd) *Pathol.* ◆ *adj also* **typhoidal. 1** resembling typhus. ◆ *n* **2** short for **typhoid fever.** [C19: from TYPHUS + -OID]

typhoid fever *n* an acute infectious disease characterized by high fever, spots, abdominal pain, etc. It is caused by a bacillus ingested with food or water.

typhoon ❶ (taɪ'fuːn) *n* a violent tropical storm or cyclone, esp. in the China Seas and W Pacific. [C16: from Chinese *tai fung* great wind; infl. by Gk *tuphōn* whirlwind]
▸**typhonic** (taɪ'fɒnɪk) *adj*

THESAURUS

two-edged *adj* **2** = **ambiguous**, ambivalent, backhanded, double-edged, equivocal

two-faced *adj* = **hypocritical**, deceitful, deceiving, dissembling, double-dealing, duplicitous, false, insincere, Janus-faced, perfidious, treacherous, untrustworthy
Antonyms *adj* artless, candid, frank, genuine, honest, ingenuous, sincere, trustworthy

tycoon *n* **1** = **magnate**, baron, big cheese (*sl., old-fashioned*), big noise (*inf.*), capitalist, captain of industry, fat cat (*sl., chiefly US*), financier, industrialist, merchant prince, mogul, plutocrat, potentate, wealthy businessman

type *n* **1, 2** = **kind**, breed, category, class, classification, form, genre, group, ilk, kidney, order, sort, species, stamp, strain, style, subdivision, variety **4** = **epitome**, archetype, essence, example, exemplar, model, norm, original, paradigm, pattern, personification, prototype, quintessence, specimen, standard **7** = **print**, case, characters, face, font, fount, printing

typhoon *n* = **storm**, cyclone, squall, tempest, tornado, tropical storm

typhus ('taɪfəs) *n* any one of a group of acute infectious rickettsial diseases characterized by high fever, skin rash, and severe headache. Also called: **typhus fever.** [C18: from NL *tȳphus,* from Gk *tuphos* fever]
► **'typhous** *adj*

typical ⓘ ('tɪpɪkəl) *adj* **1** being or serving as a representative example of a particular type; characteristic. **2** considered to be an example of some undesirable trait: *that is typical of you!* **3** of or relating to a representative specimen or type. **4** conforming to a type. **5** *Biol.* having most of the characteristics of a particular taxonomic group. [C17: from Med. L *typicālis,* from LL *typicus* figurative, from Gk *tupikos,* from *tupos* TYPE]
► **'typically** *adv* ► **'typicalness** *or* **,typi'cality** *n*

typify ⓘ ('tɪpɪ,faɪ) *vb* **typifies, typifying, typified.** (*tr*) **1** to be typical of; characterize. **2** to symbolize or represent completely, by or as if by a type. [C17: from L *typus* TYPE]
► **,typifi'cation** *n*

typist ('taɪpɪst) *n* a person who types, esp. for a living.

typo ('taɪpəʊ) *n, pl* **typos.** *Inf.* a typographical error. Also called (Brit.): **literal.**

typographer (taɪ'pɒgrəfə) *n* **1** a person skilled in typography. **2** a compositor.

typography (taɪ'pɒgrəfɪ) *n* **1** the art, craft, or process of composing type and printing from it. **2** the planning, selection, and setting of type for a printed work.
► **typographical** (,taɪpə'græfɪkəl) *or* **,typo'graphic** *adj* ► **,typo'graphically** *adv*

typology (taɪ'pɒlədʒɪ) *n* **1** the study of types in archaeology, biology, etc. **2** *Christian theol.* the doctrine that symbols for events, figures, etc., in the New Testament can be found in the Old Testament.
► **typological** (,taɪpə'lɒdʒɪkəl) *adj* ► **ty'pologist** *n*

tyrannical ⓘ (tɪ'rænɪkəl) *or* **tyrannic** *adj* characteristic of or relating to a tyrant or to tyranny; oppressive.
► **ty'rannically** *adv*

tyrannicide (tɪ'rænɪ,saɪd) *n* **1** the killing of a tyrant. **2** a person who kills a tyrant.

tyrannize ⓘ *or* **tyrannise** ('tɪrə,naɪz) *vb* **tyrannizes, tyrannizing, tyrannized** or **tyrannises, tyrannising, tyrannised.** (when *intr,* often foll. by *over*) to rule or exercise power (over) in a cruel or oppressive manner.
► **'tyran,nizer** *or* **'tyran,niser** *n*

tyrannosaurus (tɪ,rænə'sɔːrəs) *or* **tyrannosaur** (tɪ'rænə,sɔː) *n* any of various large carnivorous two-footed dinosaurs common in North America in Upper Jurassic and Cretaceous times. [C19: from NL, from Gk *turannos* tyrant + -SAUR]

tyranny ⓘ ('tɪrənɪ) *n, pl* **tyrannies. 1a** government by a tyrant; despotism. **1b** oppressive and unjust government by more than one person. **2** arbitrary, unreasonable, or despotic behaviour or use of authority. **3** a tyrannical act. [C14: from OF *tyrannie,* from Med. L *tyrannia,* from L *tyrannus* TYRANT]
► **'tyrannous** *adj*

tyrant ⓘ ('taɪrənt) *n* **1** a person who governs oppressively, unjustly, and arbitrarily; despot. **2** any person who exercises authority in a tyrannical manner. [C13: from OF *tyrant,* from L *tyrannus,* from Gk *turannos*]

tyre *or US* **tire** ('taɪə) *n* **1** a rubber ring placed over the rim of a wheel of a road vehicle to provide traction and reduce road shocks, esp. a hollow inflated ring (**pneumatic tyre**) consisting of a reinforced outer casing enclosing an inner tube. **2** a metal band or hoop attached to the rim of a wooden cartwheel. [C18: var. of C15 *tire,* prob. from archaic var. of ATTIRE]

Tyrian ('tɪrɪən) *n* **1** a native or inhabitant of ancient Tyre, a port in S Lebanon and centre of ancient Phoenician culture. ◆ *adj* **2** of or relating to ancient Tyre.

Tyrian purple *n* **1** a deep purple dye obtained from certain molluscs and highly prized in antiquity. **2a** a vivid purplish-red colour. **2b** (*as adj*): *a Tyrian-purple robe.*

tyro ⓘ *or* **tiro** ('taɪrəʊ) *n, pl* **tyros** *or* **tiros.** a novice or beginner. [C17: from L *tīrō* recruit]

tyrosinase (,taɪrəʊsɪ'neɪz) *n* an enzyme that is a catalyst in the conversion of tyrosine to the pigment melanin.

tyrosine ('taɪrə,siːn, -sɪn, 'tɪrə-) *n* an amino acid that is a precursor of the hormones adrenaline and thyroxine and of the pigment melanin. [C19: from Gk *turos* cheese + -INE[2]]

tyrothricin (,taɪrəʊ'θraɪsɪn) *n* an antibiotic, obtained from a soil bacterium: applied locally for the treatment of ulcers and abscesses. [C20: from NL *Tyrothrix* (genus name), from Gk *turos* cheese + *thrix* hair]

tzar (zɑː) *n* a less common spelling of **tsar.**

tzatziki (tsæt'sɪkɪ) *n* a Greek dip made from yogurt, chopped cucumber, and mint. [C20: from Mod. Gk]

tzetze fly ('tsetsɪ) *n* a variant spelling of **tsetse fly.**

Tzigane (tsɪ'gɑːn, sɪ-) *n* **a** a Gypsy, esp. a Hungarian one. **b** (*as modifier*): *Tzigane music.* [C19: via F from Hungarian *czigány* Gypsy, from ?]

THESAURUS

typical *adj* **1** = **characteristic**, archetypal, average, bog-standard, classic, conventional, essential, illustrative, in character, indicative, in keeping, model, normal, orthodox, representative, standard, stock, true to type, usual
Antonyms *adj* atypical, exceptional, out of keeping, out of the ordinary, singular, uncharacteristic, unconventional, unexpected, unique, unrepresentative, unusual

typify *vb* **1, 2** = **represent**, characterize, embody, epitomize, exemplify, illustrate, incarnate, personify, sum up, symbolize

tyrannical *adj* = **oppressive**, absolute, arbitrary, authoritarian, autocratic, coercive, cruel, despotic, dictatorial, domineering, high-handed, imperious, inhuman, magisterial, overbearing, overweening, peremptory, severe, tyrannous, unjust, unreasonable
Antonyms *adj* democratic, easy-going, lax, lenient, liberal, reasonable, tolerant, understanding

tyrannize *vb* = **oppress**, browbeat, bully, coerce, dictate, domineer, enslave, have (someone) under one's thumb, intimidate, ride roughshod over, rule with an iron hand, subjugate, terrorize

tyranny *n* **1, 2** = **oppression**, absolutism, authoritarianism, autocracy, coercion, cruelty, despotism, dictatorship, harsh discipline, high-handedness, imperiousness, peremptoriness, reign of terror, unreasonableness
Antonyms *n* democracy, ease, laxity, leniency, liberality, mercy, relaxation, tolerance, understanding

tyrant *n* **1, 2** = **dictator**, absolutist, authoritarian, autocrat, bully, despot, Hitler, martinet, oppressor, slave-driver

tyro *n* = **beginner**, apprentice, catechumen, greenhorn (*inf.*), initiate, learner, neophyte, novice, novitiate, pupil, student, trainee

Uu

u *or* **U** (juː) *n, pl* **u's, U's,** *or* **Us. 1** the 21st letter and fifth vowel of the English alphabet. **2** any of several speech sounds represented by this letter, as in *mute, cut,* or *minus.* **3a** something shaped like a U. **3b** (*in combination*): *a U-bolt.*

U *symbol for:* **1** united. **2** unionist. **3** university. **4** (in Britain) **4a** universal (used to describe a category of film certified as suitable for viewing by anyone). **4b** (*as modifier*): *a U certificate film.* **5** *Chem.* uranium. **6** *Biochem.* uracil. ◆ *adj* **7** *Brit. inf.* (esp. of language habits) characteristic of or appropriate to the upper class.

U. *abbrev. for:* **1** *Maths.* union. **2** unit. **3** united. **4** university. **5** upper.

UAE *abbrev. for* United Arab Emirates.

UB40 *n* (in Britain) **1** a registration card issued by the Department of Employment to a person registering as unemployed. **2** *Inf.* a person registered as unemployed.

U-bend *n* a U-shaped bend in a pipe that traps water in the lower part of the U and prevents the escape of noxious fumes; trap.

uberrima fides (juˈberɪmə ˈfaɪdiːz) *n* another name for **utmost good faith.** [L: utmost good faith]

ubiety (juːˈbaɪɪtɪ) *n* the condition of being in a particular place. [C17: from L *ubī* where + *-ety,* on the model of *society*]

ubiquitarian (juːˌbɪkwɪˈtɛərɪən) *n* **1** a member of the Lutheran church who holds that Christ is no more present in the elements of the Eucharist than elsewhere, as he is present in all places at all times. ◆ *adj* **2** denoting or holding this belief. [C17: from L *ubīque* everywhere]
▸**uˌbiquiˈtarianˌism** *n*

ubiquitous ⓣ (juːˈbɪkwɪtəs) *adj* having or seeming to have the ability to be everywhere at once. [C14: from L *ubīque* everywhere, from *ubī* where]
▸**uˈbiquitously** *adv* ▸**uˈbiquity** *n*

U-boat *n* a German submarine, esp. in World Wars I and II. [from G *U-Boot,* short for *Unterseeboot,* lit.: undersea boat]

UBR *abbrev. for* uniform business rate.

u.c. *Printing. abbrev. for* upper case.

UCATT (in Britain) *abbrev. for* Union of Construction, Allied Trades and Technicians.

UCCA (ˈʌkə) *n* (formerly, in Britain) *acronym for* Universities Central Council on Admissions.

UDA *abbrev. for* Ulster Defence Association.

udal (ˈjuːdᵊl) *n Law.* a form of freehold possession of land existing in northern Europe before the introduction of the feudal system and still used in Orkney and Shetland. [C16: Orkney & Shetland dialect, from ON *othal*]

UDC (in Britain) *abbrev. for* Urban District Council.

udder (ˈʌdə) *n* the large baglike mammary gland of cows, sheep, etc., having two or more teats. [OE *ūder*]

UDI *abbrev. for* Unilateral Declaration of Independence.

UDM (in Britain) *abbrev. for* Union of Democratic Mineworkers.

udometer (juːˈdɒmɪtə) *n* another term for **rain gauge.** [C19: from F, from L *ūdus* damp]

UDR *abbrev. for* Ulster Defence Regiment.

UEFA (juːˈeɪfə, ˈjuːfə) *n acronym for* Union of European Football Associations.

uey (ˈjuːɪ) *n, pl* **ueys.** *Austral. sl.* a U-turn.

UFO (*sometimes* ˈjuːfəʊ) *abbrev. for* unidentified flying object.

ufology (ˌjuːˈfɒlədʒɪ) *n* the study of UFOs.
▸**uˈfologist** *n*

Ugaritic (ˌuːgəˈrɪtɪk) *n* **1** an extinct Semitic language of N Syria. ◆ *adj* **2** of or relating to this language. [C19: after *Ugarit* (modern name: Ras Shamra), an ancient Syrian city-state]

UGC (in Britain) *abbrev. for* University Grants Committee.

ugh (ʊx, ʊh, ʌx) *interj* an exclamation of disgust, annoyance, or dislike.

UGLI (ˈʌglɪ) *n, pl* **UGLIS** *or* **UGLIES.** *Trademark.* a large juicy yellow-skinned citrus fruit of the Caribbean: a cross between a tangerine, grapefruit, and orange. Also called: **UGLI fruit.** [C20: prob. an alteration of UGLY, from its wrinkled skin]

uglify (ˈʌglɪˌfaɪ) *vb* **uglifies, uglifying, uglified.** to make or become ugly or more ugly.
▸**ˌuglifiˈcation** *n*

ugly ⓣ (ˈʌglɪ) *adj* **uglier, ugliest. 1** of unpleasant or unsightly appearance. **2** repulsive or displeasing: *war is ugly.* **3** ominous or menacing: *an ugly situation.* **4** bad-tempered or sullen: *an ugly mood.* [C13: from ON *uggligr* dreadful, from *ugga* fear]
▸**ˈuglily** *adv* ▸**ˈugliness** *n*

ugly duckling *n* a person or thing, initially ugly or unpromising, that changes into something beautiful or admirable. [from *The Ugly Duckling* by Hans Christian Andersen]

Ugrian (ˈuːgrɪən, ˈjuː-) *adj* **1** of or relating to a subdivision of the Turanian people, who include the Samoyeds and Magyars. ◆ *n* **2** a member of this group. **3** another word for **Ugric.** [C19: from ORussian *Ugre* Hungarians]

Ugric (ˈuːgrɪk, ˈjuː-) *n* **1** one of the two branches of the Finno-Ugric family of languages, including Hungarian and some languages of NW Siberia. ◆ *adj* **2** of or relating to this group of languages or their speakers.

UHF *Radio. abbrev. for* ultrahigh frequency.

uh-huh (ˈʌhʌ) *sentence substitute. Inf.* a less emphatic variant of **yes.**

uhlan (ˈuːlɑːn) *n History.* a member of a body of lancers first employed in the Polish army and later in W European armies. [C18: via G from Polish *ulan,* from Turkish *ōlan* young man]

UHT *abbrev. for* ultra-heat-treated (milk or cream).

uhuru (uːˈhuːruː) *n* (esp. in E Africa) **1** national independence. **2** freedom. [C20: from Swahili]

uillean pipes (ˈuːlɪən) *pl n* bagpipes developed in Ireland and operated by squeezing bellows under the arm. Also called: **Irish pipes, union pipes.** [C19: Irish *píob uilleann,* from *píob* pipe + *uilleann* genitive sing of *uille* elbow]

uitlander (ˈeɪtˌlandə, -ˌlæn-) *n* (*sometimes cap.*) *S. African.* a foreigner. [C19: Afrik.: outlander]

UK *abbrev. for* United Kingdom.

ukase (juːˈkeɪz) *n* **1** (in imperial Russia) an edict of the tsar. **2** a rare word for **edict.** [C18: from Russian *ukaz,* from *ukazat* to command]

UKCC *abbrev. for* United Kingdom Central Council for Nursing, Midwifery, and Health Visiting.

Ukrainian (juːˈkreɪnɪən) *adj* **1** of or relating to the Ukraine, its people, or their language. ◆ *n* **2** the official language of the Ukraine: an East Slavonic language closely related to Russian. **3** a native or inhabitant of the Ukraine.

ukulele *or* **ukelele** (ˌjuːkəˈleɪlɪ) *n* a small four-stringed guitar, esp. of Hawaii. [C19: from Hawaiian, lit.: jumping flea]

ulcer ⓣ (ˈʌlsə) *n* **1** a disintegration of the surface of the skin or a mucous membrane resulting in an open sore that heals very slowly. **2** a source or element of corruption or evil. [C14: from L *ulcus*]

ulcerate (ˈʌlsəˌreɪt) *vb* **ulcerates, ulcerating, ulcerated.** to make or become ulcerous.
▸**ˌulceˈration** *n* ▸**ˈulcerative** *adj*

ulcerous ⓣ (ˈʌlsərəs) *adj* **1** relating to or characterized by ulcers. **2** being or having a corrupting influence.
▸**ˈulcerously** *adv*

-ule *suffix forming nouns.* indicating smallness: *globule.* [from L *-ulus,* dim. suffix]

ulema (ˈuːlɪmə) *n* **1** a body of Muslim scholars or religious leaders. **2** a member of this body. [C17: from Ar. *'ulamā* scholars, from *'alama* to know]

-ulent *suffix forming adjectives.* abundant or full of: *fraudulent.* [from L *-ulentus*]

ullage (ˈʌlɪdʒ) *n* **1** the volume by which a liquid container falls short of being full. **2a** the quantity of liquid lost from a container due to leakage or evaporation. **2b** (in customs terminology) the amount of liquid remaining in a container after such loss. [C15: from OF *ouillage* filling of a cask, from *ouil* eye, from L *oculus* eye]

ulna (ˈʌlnə) *n, pl* **ulnae** (-niː) *or* **ulnas. 1** the inner and longer of the two bones of the human forearm. **2** the corresponding bone in other vertebrates. [C16: from L: elbow]
▸**ˈulnar** *adj*

ulnar nerve *n* a nerve situated along the inner side of the arm and passing close to the surface of the skin near the elbow.

ulotrichous (juːˈlɒtrɪkəs) *adj* having woolly or curly hair. [C19: from NL *Ulotrichī* (classification applied to humans having this type of hair), from Gk *oulothrix,* from *oulos* curly + *thrix* hair]

ulster (ˈʌlstə) *n* a man's heavy double-breasted overcoat with a belt or half-belt. [C19: from *Ulster,* the northernmost province of Ireland]

Ulster Defence Association *n* (in Northern Ireland) a Loyalist paramilitary organization. Abbrev.: **UDA.**

Ulster Democratic Unionist Party *n* a Northern Irish political party advocating the maintenance of the Union with Great Britain.

Ulsterman (ˈʌlstəmən) *n, pl* **Ulstermen.** a native or inhabitant of Ulster.
▸**ˈUlsterˌwoman** *fem n*

THESAURUS

ubiquitous *adj* = **everywhere,** all-over, ever-present, omnipresent, pervasive, universal

ugly *adj* **1** = **unattractive,** hard-favoured, hard-featured, homely, ill-favoured, misshapen, no oil painting (*inf.*), not much to look at, plain, unlovely, unprepossessing, unsightly **2** = **unpleasant,** disagreeable, disgusting, distasteful, frightful, hideous, horrid, monstrous, objectionable, obscene, offensive, repugnant, repulsive, revolting, shocking, terrible, vile **3** = **ominous,** baleful, dangerous, forbidding, menacing, sinister, threatening **4** = **bad-tempered,** angry, dark, evil, malevolent, nasty, spiteful, sullen, surly
Antonyms *adj* ≠ **unattractive:** attractive, beautiful, cute, good-looking, gorgeous, handsome, lovely, pretty ≠ **unpleasant:** agreeable, pleasant ≠ **ominous:** auspicious, promising ≠ **bad-tempered:** friendly, good-humoured, good-natured, peaceful

ulcer *n* **1** = **sore,** abscess, boil, fester, gathering, gumboil, peptic ulcer, pustule

ulcerous *adj* **1** = **festering,** cankered, cankerous, suppurative, ulcerative

Ulster Unionist Council *n* a Northern Irish political party advocating the maintenance of the Union with Great Britain.

ult. *abbrev. for:* **1** ultimate(ly). **2** ultimo.

ulterior ➊ (ʌlˈtɪərɪə) *adj* **1** lying beneath or beyond what is revealed or supposed: *ulterior motives.* **2** succeeding, subsequent, or later. **3** lying beyond a certain line or point. [C17: from L: further, from *ulter* beyond]
▸**ulˈteriorly** *adv*

ultima (ˈʌltɪmə) *n* the final syllable of a word. [from L: the last]

ultimate ➊ (ˈʌltɪmɪt) *adj* **1** conclusive in a series or process; final: *an ultimate question.* **2** the highest or most significant: *the ultimate goal.* **3** elemental, fundamental, or essential. **4** most extreme: *the ultimate abuse of human rights.* **5** final or total: *the ultimate cost.* ◆ *n* **6** the most significant, highest, or greatest thing. [C17: from LL *ultimāre* to come to an end, from L *ultimus* last, from *ulter* distant]
▸ˈ**ultimately** *adv* ▸ˈ**ultimateness** *n*

ultima Thule (ˈθjuːlɪ) *n* **1** a region believed by ancient geographers to be the northernmost land. **2** any distant or unknown region. **3** a remote goal or aim. [L: the most distant Thule]

ultimatum (ˌʌltɪˈmeɪtəm) *n, pl* **ultimatums** *or* **ultimata** (-tə). **1** a final communication by a party setting forth conditions on which it insists, as during negotiations on some topic. **2** any final or peremptory demand or proposal. [C18: from NL, neuter of *ultimatus* ULTIMATE]

ultimo (ˈʌltɪˌməʊ) *adv Now rare except when abbreviated in formal correspondence.* in or during the previous month: *a letter of the 7th ultimo.* Abbrev.: **ult.** [C16: from L *ultimō* on the last]

ultimogeniture (ˌʌltɪməʊˈdʒenɪtʃə) *n Law.* a principle of inheritance whereby the youngest son succeeds to the estate of his ancestor. [C19: *ultimo-* from L *ultimus* last + LL *genitūra* a birth]

ultra (ˈʌltrə) *adj* **1** extreme or immoderate, esp. in beliefs or opinions. ◆ *n* **2** an extremist. [C19: from L: beyond, from *ulter* distant]

ultra- ➊ *prefix* **1** beyond or surpassing a specified extent, range, or limit: *ultramicroscopic.* **2** extreme or extremely: *ultramodern.* [from L *ultrā* beyond]

ultracentrifuge (ˌʌltrəˈsɛntrɪˌfjuːdʒ) *n Chem.* a high-speed centrifuge used to separate colloidal solutions.

ultraconservative (ˌʌltrəkənˈsɜːvətɪv) *adj* **1** highly reactionary. ◆ *n* **2** a reactionary person.

ultra-distance *n* (*modifier*) *Athletics.* covering a distance in excess of 30 miles, often as part of a longer race or competition: *an ultra-distance runner.*

ultrafiche (ˈʌltrəˌfiːʃ) *n* a sheet of film, usually the size of a filing card, that is similar to a microfiche but has a much larger number of microcopies. [C20: from ULTRA- + F *fiche* small card]

ultrahigh frequency (ˈʌltrəˌhaɪ) *n* a radio-frequency band or radio frequency lying between 3000 and 300 megahertz. Abbrev.: **UHF.**

ultraism (ˈʌltrəˌɪzəm) *n* extreme philosophy, belief, or action.
▸ˈ**ultraist** *n, adj*

ultramarine (ˌʌltrəməˈriːn) *n* **1** a blue pigment obtained by powdering natural lapis lazuli or made synthetically: used in paints, printing ink, plastics, etc. **2** a vivid blue colour. ◆ *adj* **3** of the colour ultramarine. **4** from across the seas. [C17: from Med. L *ultramarinus,* from *ultrā* beyond + *mare* sea; so called because the lapis lazuli from which the pigment was made was imported from Asia]

ultramicroscope (ˌʌltrəˈmaɪkrəˌskəʊp) *n* a microscope used for studying colloids, in which the sample is illuminated from the side and colloidal particles are seen as bright points on a dark background.

ultramicroscopic (ˌʌltrəˌmaɪkrəˈskɒpɪk) *adj* **1** too small to be seen with an optical microscope. **2** of or relating to an ultramicroscope.

ultramodern ➊ (ˌʌltrəˈmɒdən) *adj* extremely modern.
▸ˌ**ultraˈmodernism** *n* ▸ˌ**ultraˈmodernist** *n* ▸ˌ**ultraˌmodernˈistic** *adj*

ultramontane (ˌʌltrəmɒnˈteɪn) *adj* **1** on the other side of the mountains, esp. the Alps, from the speaker or writer. **2** of or relating to a movement in the Roman Catholic Church which favours the centralized authority and influence of the pope as opposed to local independence. ◆ *n* **3** a person from beyond the mountains, esp. the Alps. **4** a member of the ultramontane party of the Roman Catholic Church.

ultramundane (ˌʌltrəˈmʌndeɪn) *adj* extending beyond the world, this life, or the universe.

ultranationalism (ˌʌltrəˈnæʃnəˌlɪzəm) *n* extreme devotion to one's own nation.
▸ˌ**ultraˈnational** *adj* ▸ˌ**ultraˈnationalist** *adj, n*

ultrashort (ˌʌltrəˈʃɔːt) *adj* (of a radio wave) having a wavelength shorter than 10 metres.

ultrasonic (ˌʌltrəˈsɒnɪk) *adj* of, concerned with, or producing waves with the same nature as sound waves but frequencies above audio frequencies.
▸ˌ**ultraˈsonically** *adv*

ultrasonics (ˌʌltrəˈsɒnɪks) *n* (*functioning as sing*) the branch of physics concerned with ultrasonic waves. Also called: **supersonics.**

ultrasound (ˈʌltrəˌsaʊnd) *n* ultrasonic waves at frequencies above the audible range (above about 20 kHz), used in cleaning metallic parts, echo sounding, medical diagnosis and therapy, etc.

ultrasound scanner *n* a device used to examine an internal bodily structure by the use of ultrasonic waves, esp. for the diagnosis of abnormality in a fetus.

ultrastructure (ˈʌltrəˌstrʌktʃə) *n* the minute structure of an organ, tissue, or cell, as revealed by microscopy.

ultraviolet (ˌʌltrəˈvaɪəlɪt) *n* **1** the part of the electromagnetic spectrum with wavelengths shorter than light but longer than X-rays; in the range 0.4×10^{-6} and 1×10^{-8} metres. ◆ *adj* **2** of, relating to, or consisting of radiation lying in the ultraviolet: *ultraviolet radiation; ultraviolet spectroscopy.* Abbrev.: **UV.**

ultraviolet astronomy *n* the study of radiation from celestial sources in the wavelength range 91.2 to 320 nanometres.

ultra vires (ˈvaɪriːz) *adv, adj* (*predicative*) *Law.* beyond the legal power of a person, corporation, agent, etc. [L, lit.: beyond strength]

ultravirus (ˌʌltrəˈvaɪrəs) *n* a virus small enough to pass through the finest filter.

ululate (ˈjuːljʊˌleɪt) *vb* **ululates, ululating, ululated.** (*intr*) to howl or wail, as with grief. [C17: from L *ululāre* to howl, from *ulula* screech owl]
▸ˈ**ululant** *adj* ▸ˌ**uluˈlation** *n*

Uluru (ˌuːləˈruː) *n* the world's largest monolith, in the Northern Territory of Australia. Height: 330 m (1100 ft). Base circumference: 9 km (5.6 miles). Former name: **Ayers Rock.**

umbel (ˈʌmbᵊl) *n* a racemose inflorescence, characteristic of umbelliferous plants, in which the flowers arise from the same point in the main stem and have stalks of the same length, to give a cluster with the youngest flowers at the centre. [C16: from L *umbella* a sunshade, from *umbra* shade]
▸**umbellate** (ˈʌmbɪlɪt, -ˌleɪt) *or* **umbellar** (ʌmˈbɛlə) *adj* ▸**umbellule** (ʌmˈbɛljuːl) *n*

umbelliferous (ˌʌmbɪˈlɪfərəs) *adj* of or belonging to a family of herbaceous plants and shrubs, typically having hollow stems, divided or compound leaves, and flowers in umbels: includes fennel, parsley, carrot, and parsnip. [C17: from NL, from L *umbella* sunshade + *ferre* to bear]
▸**umˈbellifer** *n*

umber (ˈʌmbə) *n* **1** any of various natural brown earths containing ferric oxide together with lime and oxides of aluminium, manganese, and silicon. **2** any of the dark brown to greenish-brown colours produced by this pigment. **3** *Obs.* shade. ◆ *adj* **4** of, relating to, or stained with umber. [C16: from F (*terre d'*)*ombre* or It. (*terra di*) *ombra* shadow (earth), from L *umbra* shade]

umbilical (ʌmˈbɪlɪkᵊl, ˌʌmbɪˈlaɪkᵊl) *adj* **1** of, relating to, or resembling the umbilicus or the umbilical cord. **2** in the region of the umbilicus: *an umbilical hernia.*

umbilical cord *n* **1** the long flexible tubelike structure connecting a fetus with the placenta. **2** any flexible cord, tube, or cable, as between an astronaut walking in space and his spacecraft.

umbilicate (ʌmˈbɪlɪkɪt, -ˌkeɪt) *adj* **1** having an umbilicus. **2** having a central depression: *an umbilicate leaf.* **3** shaped like a navel, as some bacterial colonies.
▸**umˌbiliˈcation** *n*

umbilicus (ʌmˈbɪlɪkəs, ˌʌmbɪˈlaɪkəs) *n, pl* **umbilici** (-ˈbɪlɪˌsaɪ, -bɪˈlaɪsaɪ). **1** *Biol.* a hollow or navel-like structure, such as the cavity at the base of a gastropod shell. **2** *Anat.* a technical name for the **navel.** [C18: from L: navel, centre]

umble pie (ˈʌmbᵊl) *n* See **humble pie** (sense 1).

umbles (ˈʌmbᵊlz) *pl n* See **numbles.**

umbo (ˈʌmbəʊ) *n, pl* **umbones** (ʌmˈbəʊniːz) *or* **umbos. 1** *Bot., anat.* a small hump, prominence, or convex area, as in certain mushrooms, bivalve molluscs, and the outer surface of the eardrum. **2** a large projecting central boss on a shield, esp. on a Saxon shield. [C18: from L: projecting piece]
▸**umbonate** (ˈʌmbənɪt, -ˌneɪt), **umbonal** (ˈʌmbənᵊl), *or* **umbonic** (ʌmˈbɒnɪk) *adj*

umbra (ˈʌmbrə) *n, pl* **umbrae** (-briː) *or* **umbras. 1** a region of complete shadow resulting from the obstruction of light by an opaque object, esp. the shadow cast by the moon onto the earth during a solar eclipse. **2** the darker inner region of a sunspot. [C16: from L: shade]
▸ˈ**umbral** *adj*

umbrage ➊ (ˈʌmbrɪdʒ) *n* **1** displeasure or resentment; offence (in **give** *or* **take umbrage**). **2** the foliage of trees, considered as providing shade. **3** *Rare.* shadow or shade. [C15: from OF, from L *umbrāticus* relating to shade, from *umbra* shade]

THESAURUS

ulterior *adj* **1** = **hidden,** concealed, covert, personal, secondary, secret, selfish, undisclosed, unexpressed
Antonyms *adj* apparent, declared, manifest, obvious, overt, plain

ultimate *adj* **1** = **final,** conclusive, decisive, end, eventual, extreme, furthest, last, terminal **2** = **supreme,** extreme, greatest, highest, maximum, most significant, paramount, superlative, topmost, utmost **3** = **fundamental,** basic, elemental, primary, radical ◆ *n* **6** = **epitome,** culmination, extreme, greatest, height, mother of all (*inf.*), peak, perfection, summit, the last word

ultimately *adv* **1** = **finally,** after all, at last, at the end of the day, eventually, in due time, in the end, in the fullness of time, sooner or later **3** = **fundamentally,** basically

ultra- *prefix* **2** = **extremely,** excessively, fanatically, immoderately, rabidly, radically

ultramodern *adj* = **advanced,** ahead of its time, avant-garde, futuristic, modernistic, neoteric (*rare*), progressive, way-out (*inf.*)

umbrage *n* **1** *As in* **take umbrage** = **offence,** anger, chagrin, displeasure, grudge, high dudgeon, huff, indignation, pique, resentment, sense of injury
Antonyms *n* amity, cordiality, goodwill, harmony, pleasure, understanding

umbrageous (ʌm'breɪdʒəs) *adj* **1** shady or shading. **2** *Rare.* easily offended.

umbrella Ⓣ (ʌm'brɛlə) *n* **1** a portable device used for protection against rain, snow, etc., and consisting of a light canopy supported on a collapsible metal frame mounted on a central rod. **2** the flattened cone-shaped body of a jellyfish. **3** a protective shield or screen, esp. of aircraft or gunfire. **4** anything that has the effect of a protective screen, general cover, or organizing agency. [C17: from It. *ombrella*, dim. of *ombra* shade; see UMBRA]
►**um'brella-ˌlike** *adj*

umbrella pine *n* another name for **stone pine.**

umbrella stand *n* an upright rack or stand for umbrellas.

umbrella tree *n* **1** a North American magnolia having long leaves clustered into an umbrella formation at the ends of the branches and having unpleasant-smelling white flowers. **2** Also called: **umbrella bush.** any of various trees or shrubs having umbrella-shaped leaves or growing in an umbrella-like cluster.

Umbrian ('ʌmbrɪən) *adj* **1** of or relating to Umbria, in Italy, its inhabitants, or the ancient language once spoken there. **2** of or relating to a Renaissance school of painting that included Raphael. ◆ *n* **3** a native or inhabitant of Umbria. **4** an extinct language of ancient S Italy.

umfazi (ˌʊm'fɑːʒɪ) *n S. African.* a Black married woman. [from Bantu]

umiak *or* **oomiak** ('uːmɪˌæk) *n* a large open boat made of stretched skins, used by Eskimos. [C18: from Eskimo: boat for the use of women]

umlaut ('ʊmlaʊt) *n* **1** the mark (¨) placed over a vowel in some languages, such as German, indicating modification in the quality of the vowel. **2** (esp. in Germanic languages) the change of a vowel within a word brought about by the assimilating influence of a vowel or semivowel in a preceding or following syllable. [C19: G, from *um* around (in the sense of changing places) + *Laut* sound]

umlungu (ˌʊm'lʊŋgʊ) *n S. African.* a White man: used esp. as a term of address. [from Bantu]

umpire Ⓣ ('ʌmpaɪə) *n* **1** an official who rules on the playing of a game, as in cricket. **2** a person who rules on or judges disputes between contesting parties. ◆ *vb* **umpires, umpiring, umpired. 3** to act as umpire in (a game, dispute, or controversy). [C15: by mistaken division from *a noumpere*, from OF *nomper* not one of a pair, from *nom-, non-* not + *per* equal]

umpteen Ⓣ (ˌʌmp'tiːn) *determiner Inf.* **a** very many: *umpteen things to do.* **b** (*as pronoun*): *umpteen of them came.* [C20: from *umpty* a great deal (?from *-enty* as in *twenty*) + *-teen* ten]
►ˌ**ump'teenth** *n, adj*

UN *abbrev. for* United Nations.

un-[1] *prefix (freely used with adjectives, participles, and their derivative adverbs and nouns: less frequently used with certain other nouns)* not; contrary to; opposite of: *uncertain; untidiness; unbelief; untruth.* [from OE *on-, un-*]

un-[2] *prefix forming verbs.* **1** denoting reversal of an action or state: *uncover; untangle.* **2** denoting removal from, release, or deprivation: *unharness; unthrone.* **3** (intensifier): *unloose.* [from OE *un-, on-*]

'un *or* **un** (ən) *pron* a spelling of **one** intended to reflect a dialectal or informal pronunciation: *that's a big 'un.*

unable Ⓣ (ʌn'eɪbᵊl) *adj* (*postpositive;* foll. by *to*) lacking the necessary power, ability, or authority (to do something); not able.

unaccented (ˌʌnæk'sɛntɪd) *adj* not stressed or emphasized in pronunciation.

unaccountable Ⓣ (ˌʌnə'kaʊntəbᵊl) *adj* **1** allowing of no explanation; inexplicable. **2** extraordinary: *an unaccountable fear of heights.* **3** not accountable or answerable to.
►ˌ**unacˌcounta'bility** *n* ►ˌ**unac'countably** *adv*

unaccustomed Ⓣ (ˌʌnə'kʌstəmd) *adj* **1** (foll. by *to*) not used (to): *unaccustomed to pain.* **2** not familiar.
►ˌ**unac'customedness** *n*

una corda ('uːnə 'kɔːdə) *adj, adv Music.* (of the piano) to be played with the soft pedal depressed. [It., lit.: one string; the pedal moves the mechanism so that only one string of the three tuned to each note is struck by the hammer]

unadopted (ˌʌnə'dɒptɪd) *adj* **1** (of a child) not adopted. **2** *Brit.* (of a road, etc.) not maintained by a local authority.

unadvised Ⓣ (ˌʌnəd'vaɪzd) *adj* **1** rash or unwise. **2** not having received advice.
►**unadvisedly** (ˌʌnəd'vaɪzɪdlɪ) *adv* ►ˌ**unad'visedness** *n*

unaffected[1] Ⓣ (ˌʌnə'fɛktɪd) *adj* unpretentious, natural, or sincere.
►ˌ**unaf'fectedly** *adv* ►ˌ**unaf'fectedness** *n*

unaffected[2] Ⓣ (ˌʌnə'fɛktɪd) *adj* not affected.

unalienable (ʌn'eɪljənəbᵊl) *adj Law.* a variant of **inalienable.**

un-American *adj* **1** not in accordance with the aims, ideals, customs, etc., of the US. **2** against the interests of the US.
►ˌ**un-A'mericanism** *n*

unanimous Ⓣ (juː'nænɪməs) *adj* **1** in complete agreement. **2** characterized by complete agreement: *a unanimous decision.* [C17: from L, from *ūnus* one + *animus* mind]
►**u'nanimously** *adv* ►**unanimity** (ˌjuːnə'nɪmɪtɪ) *n*

unapproachable Ⓣ (ˌʌnə'prəʊtʃəbᵊl) *adj* **1** discouraging intimacy, friendliness, etc.; aloof. **2** inaccessible. **3** not to be rivalled.
►ˌ**unap'proachableness** *n* ►ˌ**unap'proachably** *adv*

unappropriated (ˌʌnə'prəʊprɪˌeɪtɪd) *adj* **1** not set aside for specific use. **2** *Accounting.* designating that portion of the profits of a business enterprise that is retained in the business and not withdrawn by the proprietor. **3** (of property) not having been taken into any person's possession or control.

unapt (ʌn'æpt) *adj* **1** (*usually postpositive;* often foll. by *for*) not suitable or qualified; unfitted. **2** mentally slow. **3** (*postpositive; may take an infinitive*) not disposed or likely (to).
►**un'aptly** *adv* ►**un'aptness** *n*

unarm (ʌn'ɑːm) *vb* a less common word for **disarm.**

unarmed Ⓣ (ʌn'ɑːmd) *adj* **1** without weapons. **2** (of animals and plants) having no claws, prickles, spines, thorns, or similar structures.

unassailable Ⓣ (ˌʌnə'seɪləbᵊl) *adj* **1** not able to be attacked. **2** undeniable or irrefutable.
►ˌ**unas'sailableness** *n* ►ˌ**unas'sailably** *adv*

unassuming Ⓣ (ˌʌnə'sjuːmɪŋ) *adj* modest or unpretentious.
►ˌ**unas'sumingly** *adv* ►ˌ**unas'sumingness** *n*

unattached Ⓣ (ˌʌnə'tætʃt) *adj* **1** not connected with any specific thing, body, group, etc. **2** not engaged or married. **3** (of property) not seized or held as security.

THESAURUS

umbrella *n* **1 = brolly** (*Brit. inf.*), gamp (*Brit. inf.*) **4 = cover**, aegis, agency, patronage, protection

umpire *n* **1, 2 = referee**, adjudicator, arbiter, arbitrator, judge, moderator, ref (*inf.*) ◆ *vb* **3 = referee**, adjudicate, arbitrate, call (*Sport*), judge, mediate, moderate

umpteen *determiner* **a** *Informal* **= very many**, a good many, a thousand and one, considerable, countless, ever so many, millions, n, numerous

unable *adj* **= incapable**, impotent, inadequate, ineffectual, no good, not able, not equal to, not up to, powerless, unfit, unfitted, unqualified
Antonyms *adj* able, adept, adequate, capable, competent, effective, potent, powerful

unaccountable *adj* **1 = inexplicable**, baffling, incomprehensible, inscrutable, mysterious, odd, peculiar, puzzling, strange, unexplainable, unfathomable, unintelligible **3 = not answerable**, clear, exempt, free, not responsible, unliable
Antonyms *adj* ≠ **inexplicable:** accountable, comprehensible, explicable, intelligible, understandable

unaccustomed *adj* **1 unaccustomed to = not used to**, a newcomer to, a novice at, green, inexperienced at, not given to, unfamiliar with, unpractised in, unused to, unversed in **2 = unfamiliar**, new, out of the ordinary, remarkable, special, strange, surprising, uncommon, unexpected, unprecedented, unusual, unwonted
Antonyms *adj* ≠ **unfamiliar:** accustomed, familiar, ordinary, regular, usual ≠ **not used to:** experienced at, given to, practised in, used to, well-versed in

unadvised *adj* **1 = rash**, careless, hasty, heedless, ill-advised, imprudent, inadvisable, indiscreet, injudicious, reckless, unwary, unwise **2 = uninformed**, ignorant, in the dark, not in the loop (*inf.*), unaware, unknowing, unsuspecting, unwarned

unaffected[1] *adj* **= natural**, artless, genuine, honest, ingenuous, naive, plain, simple, sincere, straightforward, unassuming, unpretentious, unsophisticated, unspoilt, unstudied, without airs
Antonyms *adj* affected, assumed, designing, devious, insincere, mannered, pretentious, put-on, snobbish, sophisticated

unaffected[2] *adj* **= impervious**, aloof, not influenced, proof, unaltered, unchanged, unimpressed, unmoved, unresponsive, unstirred, untouched
Antonyms *adj* affected, changed, concerned, disrupted, hard-hit, influenced, interested, responsive, sympathetic, touched

unanimity *n* **1, 2 = agreement**, accord, assent, chorus, concert, concord, concurrence, consensus, harmony, like-mindedness, one mind, unison, unity
Antonyms *n* difference, disagreement, discord, disunity, division, variance

unanimous *adj* **1 = agreed**, agreeing, at one, common, concerted, concordant, harmonious, in agreement, in complete accord, like-minded, of one mind, united
Antonyms *adj* differing, discordant, dissident, disunited, divided, schismatic, split

unanimously *adv* **2 = without exception**, by common consent, nem. con., unitedly, unopposed, with one accord, without opposition

unapproachable *adj* **1 = unfriendly**, aloof, chilly, cool, distant, frigid, offish, remote, reserved, standoffish, unsociable, withdrawn **2 = inaccessible**, out of reach, out-of-the-way, remote, un-get-at-able (*inf.*), unreachable
Antonyms *adj* ≠ **unfriendly:** affable, approachable, congenial, cordial, friendly, sociable

unarmed *adj* **1, 2 = defenceless**, assailable, exposed, helpless, open, open to attack, unarmoured, unprotected, weak, weaponless, without arms
Antonyms *adj* armed, equipped, fortified, protected, ready, strengthened

unassailable *adj* **1 = impregnable**, invincible, invulnerable, secure, well-defended **2 = undeniable**, absolute, conclusive, incontestable, incontrovertible, indisputable, irrefutable, positive, proven, sound
Antonyms *adj* ≠ **undeniable:** debatable, doubtful, dubious, inconclusive, uncertain, unfounded, unproven, unsound

unassuming *adj* **= modest**, diffident, humble, meek, quiet, reserved, retiring, self-effacing, simple, unassertive, unobtrusive, unostentatious, unpretentious
Antonyms *adj* assuming, audacious, conceited, ostentatious, overconfident, presumptuous, pretentious

unattached *adj* **1 = free**, autonomous, independent, nonaligned, unaffiliated, uncommitted **2 = single**, a free agent, available, by oneself, footloose and fancy-free, left on the shelf, not spoken for, on one's own, unengaged, unmarried
Antonyms *adj* ≠ **free:** affiliated, aligned, attached, committed, dependent, implicated, involved

unavailing Ⓣ (ˌʌnəˈveɪlɪŋ) *adj* useless or futile.
▸ˌ**unaˈvailingly** *adv*

unavoidable Ⓣ (ˌʌnəˈvɔɪdəbᵊl) *adj* **1** unable to be avoided. **2** *Law.* not capable of being declared null and void.
▸ˌ**unaˌvoidaˈbility** *or* ˌ**unaˈvoidableness** *n* ▸ˌ**unaˈvoidably** *adv*

unaware Ⓣ (ˌʌnəˈwɛə) *adj* **1** (*postpositive*) not aware or conscious (of): *unaware of the danger he ran across the road.* ◆ *adv* **2** a variant of **unawares.**
▸ˌ**unaˈwareness** *n*

unawares Ⓣ (ˌʌnəˈwɛəz) *adv* **1** without prior warning or plan: *she caught him unawares.* **2** without knowing: *he lost it unawares.*

unbacked (ʌnˈbækt) *adj* **1** (of a book, chair, etc.) not having a back. **2** bereft of support, esp. on a financial basis. **3** not supported by bets.

unbalance (ʌnˈbæləns) *vb* **unbalances, unbalancing, unbalanced.** (*tr*) **1** to upset the equilibrium or balance of. **2** to disturb the mental stability of (a person or his mind). ◆ *n* **3** imbalance or instability.

unbalanced Ⓣ (ʌnˈbælənst) *adj* **1** lacking balance. **2** irrational or unsound; erratic. **3** mentally disordered or deranged. **4** biased; one-sided: *unbalanced reporting.* **5** (in double-entry book-keeping) not having total debit balances equal to total credit balances.

unbar (ʌnˈbɑː) *vb* **unbars, unbarring, unbarred.** (*tr*) **1** to take away a bar or bars from. **2** to unfasten bars, locks, etc., from (a door); open.

unbearable Ⓣ (ʌnˈbɛərəbᵊl) *adj* not able to be borne or endured.
▸**unˈbearably** *adv*

unbeatable Ⓣ (ʌnˈbiːtəbᵊl) *adj* unable to be defeated or outclassed; surpassingly excellent.

unbeaten Ⓣ (ʌnˈbiːtᵊn) *adj* **1** having suffered no defeat. **2** not worn down; untrodden. **3** not mixed or stirred by beating: *unbeaten eggs.*

unbecoming Ⓣ (ˌʌnbɪˈkʌmɪŋ) *adj* **1** unsuitable or inappropriate, esp. through being unattractive: *an unbecoming hat.* **2** (when *postpositive,* usually foll. by *of* or an object) not proper or seemly (for): *manners unbecoming a lady.*
▸ˌ**unbeˈcomingly** *adv* ▸ˌ**unbeˈcomingness** *n*

unbeknown (ˌʌnbɪˈnəʊn) *adv* (*sentence modifier;* foll. by *to*) without the knowledge (of a person): *unbeknown to him she had left the country.* Also (esp. Brit.): **unbeknownst.** [C17: from arch. *beknown* known]

unbelief Ⓣ (ˌʌnbɪˈliːf) *n* disbelief or rejection of belief.

unbelievable Ⓣ (ˌʌnbɪˈliːvəbᵊl) *adj* unable to be believed; incredible.
▸ˌ**unbeˌlievaˈbility** *n* ▸ˌ**unbeˈlievably** *adv*

unbeliever Ⓣ (ˌʌnbɪˈliːvə) *n* a person who does not believe, esp. in religious matters.

unbelieving Ⓣ (ˌʌnbɪˈliːvɪŋ) *adj* **1** not believing; sceptical. **2** proceeding from or characterized by scepticism.
▸ˌ**unbeˈlievingly** *adv*

unbend Ⓣ (ʌnˈbɛnd) *vb* **unbends, unbending, unbent. 1** to release or be released from the restraints of formality and ceremony. **2** *Inf.* to relax (the mind) or (of the mind) to become relaxed. **3** to straighten out from an originally bent shape. **4** (*tr*) *Naut.* **4a** to remove (a sail) from a stay, mast, etc. **4b** to untie (a rope, etc.) or cast (a cable) loose.

unbending Ⓣ (ʌnˈbɛndɪŋ) *adj* **1** rigid or inflexible. **2** characterized by sternness or severity: *an unbending rule.*
▸**unˈbendingly** *adv* ▸**unˈbendingness** *n*

unbent (ʌnˈbɛnt) *vb* **1** the past tense and past participle of **unbend.** ◆ *adj* **2** not bent or bowed. **3** not compelled to give way by force.

unbidden Ⓣ (ʌnˈbɪdᵊn) *adj* **1** not ordered or commanded; voluntary or spontaneous. **2** not invited or asked.

unbind Ⓣ (ʌnˈbaɪnd) *vb* **unbinds, unbinding, unbound.** (*tr*) **1** to set free from restraining bonds or chains. **2** to unfasten or make loose (a bond, etc.).

unblessed (ʌnˈblɛst) *adj* **1** deprived of blessing. **2** cursed or evil. **3** unhappy or wretched.
▸**unblessedness** (ʌnˈblɛsɪdnɪs) *n*

unblushing Ⓣ (ʌnˈblʌʃɪŋ) *adj* immodest or shameless.
▸**unˈblushingly** *adv*

unbolt (ʌnˈbəʊlt) *vb* (*tr*) **1** to unfasten a bolt of (a door). **2** to undo (the nut) on a bolt.

unbolted (ʌnˈbəʊltɪd) *adj* (of grain, meal, or flour) not sifted.

unborn Ⓣ (ʌnˈbɔːn) *adj* **1** not yet born or brought to birth. **2** still to come in the future: *the unborn world.*

unbosom Ⓣ (ʌnˈbʊzəm) *vb* (*tr*) to relieve (oneself) of (secrets, etc.) by telling someone. [C16: from UN-[2] + BOSOM (in the sense: seat of the emotions)]

unbounded Ⓣ (ʌnˈbaʊndɪd) *adj* having no boundaries or limits.
▸**unˈboundedly** *adv* ▸**unˈboundedness** *n*

unbowed (ʌnˈbaʊd) *adj* **1** not bowed or bent. **2** free or unconquered.

unbridled Ⓣ (ʌnˈbraɪdᵊld) *adj* **1** with all restraints removed. **2** (of a horse) wearing no bridle.
▸**unˈbridledly** *adv* ▸**unˈbridledness** *n*

unbroken Ⓣ (ʌnˈbrəʊkən) *adj* **1** complete or whole. **2** continuous or incessant. **3** undaunted in spirit. **4** (of animals, esp. horses) not tamed; wild. **5** not disturbed or upset: *the unbroken quiet of the afternoon.* **6** (of a record, esp. at sport) not improved upon.
▸**unˈbrokenly** *adv* ▸**unˈbrokenness** *n*

unbundling (ʌnˈbʌndlɪŋ) *n Commerce.* the takeover of a large conglomerate with a view to retaining the core business and selling off some of the subsidiaries to help finance the takeover.

unburden Ⓣ (ʌnˈbɜːdᵊn) *vb* (*tr*) **1** to remove a load or burden from. **2** to

THESAURUS

unavailing *adj* = **useless**, abortive, bootless, fruitless, futile, idle, ineffective, ineffectual, of no avail, pointless, to no purpose, unproductive, unsuccessful, vain
Antonyms *adj* effective, fruitful, productive, rewarding, successful, useful, worthwhile

unavoidable *adj* **1** = **inevitable**, bound to happen, certain, compulsory, fated, ineluctable, inescapable, inexorable, necessary, obligatory, sure

unaware *adj* **1** = **ignorant**, heedless, incognizant, not in the loop (*inf.*), oblivious, unconscious, unenlightened, uninformed, unknowing, unmindful, unsuspecting
Antonyms *adj* attentive, aware, conscious, informed, in the loop (*inf.*), knowing, mindful

unawares *adv* **1** = **by surprise**, aback, abruptly, caught napping, off guard, on the hop (*Brit. inf.*), suddenly, unexpectedly, unprepared, without warning **2** = **unknowingly**, accidentally, by accident, by mistake, inadvertently, mistakenly, unconsciously, unintentionally, unwittingly
Antonyms *adv* ≠ **by surprise:** forewarned, on the lookout, prepared ≠ **unknowingly:** deliberately, knowingly, on purpose, wittingly

unbalanced *adj* **1** = **shaky**, asymmetrical, irregular, lopsided, not balanced, unequal, uneven, unstable, unsymmetrical, wobbly **3** = **deranged**, barking (*sl.*), barking mad (*sl.*), crazy, demented, disturbed, doolally (*sl.*), eccentric, erratic, insane, irrational, loopy (*inf.*), lunatic, mad, *non compos mentis,* not all there, not the full shilling (*inf.*), off one's trolley (*sl.*), out to lunch (*inf.*), touched, unhinged, unsound, unstable, up the pole (*inf.*) **4** = **biased**, inequitable, one-sided, partial, partisan, prejudiced, unfair, unjust
Antonyms *adj* ≠ **shaky:** balanced, equal, even, stable, symmetrical

unbearable *adj* = **intolerable**, insufferable, insupportable, oppressive, too much (*inf.*), unacceptable, unendurable
Antonyms *adj* acceptable, bearable, endurable, supportable, tolerable

unbeatable *adj* = **invincible**, indomitable, more than a match for, unconquerable, unstoppable, unsurpassable

unbeaten *adj* **1** = **undefeated**, triumphant, unbowed, unsubdued, unsurpassed, unvanquished, victorious, winning

unbecoming *adj* **1** = **unattractive**, ill-suited, inappropriate, incongruous, unbefitting, unfit, unflattering, unsightly, unsuitable, unsuited **2** = **unseemly**, discreditable, improper, indecorous, indelicate, offensive, tasteless
Antonyms *adj* ≠ **unseemly:** becoming, decent, decorous, delicate, proper, seemly

unbelief *n* = **scepticism**, atheism, disbelief, distrust, doubt, incredulity
Antonyms *n* belief, credence, credulity, faith, trust

unbelievable *adj* = **incredible**, astonishing, beyond belief, cock-and-bull (*inf.*), far-fetched, implausible, impossible, improbable, inconceivable, jaw-dropping, outlandish, preposterous, questionable, staggering, unconvincing, unimaginable, unthinkable
Antonyms *adj* ≠ **incredible:** authentic, believable, credible, likely, plausible, possible, probable, trustworthy

unbeliever *n* = **atheist**, agnostic, disbeliever, doubting Thomas, infidel, sceptic

unbelieving *adj* **1** = **sceptical**, disbelieving, distrustful, doubtful, doubting, dubious, incredulous, suspicious, unconvinced
Antonyms *adj* believing, convinced, credulous, trustful, undoubting, unsuspicious

unbend *vb* **1** = **relax**, be informal, calm down, chill out (*sl., chiefly US*), cool it (*sl.*), ease up, let it all hang out (*sl.*), let oneself go, let up, lighten up (*sl.*), loosen up, slacken, slow down, take it easy, unbutton (*inf.*), unwind **3** = **straighten**, put straight, uncoil, uncurl

unbending *adj* **1, 2** = **inflexible**, firm, hardline, intractable, resolute, rigid, severe, strict, stubborn, tough, uncompromising, unyielding

unbidden *adj* **1** = **voluntary**, free, spontaneous, unforced, unprompted, willing **2** = **uninvited**, unasked, unwanted, unwelcome

unbind *vb* **1, 2** = **free**, loosen, release, set free, unbridle, unchain, unclasp, undo, unfasten, unfetter, unloose, unshackle, unstrap, untie, unyoke
Antonyms *vb* bind, chain, fasten, fetter, restrain, shackle, tie, yoke

unblushing *adj* = **shameless**, amoral, bold, brazen, forward, immodest, unabashed, unashamed, unembarrassed

unborn *adj* **1, 2** = **expected**, awaited, embryonic, *in utero*

unbosom *vb* = **confide**, admit, confess, disburden, disclose, divulge, get (something) off one's chest (*inf.*), get (something) out of one's system, lay bare, let out, reveal, spill one's guts about (*sl.*), tell, unburden
Antonyms *vb* conceal, cover up, guard, hold back, suppress, withhold

unbounded *adj* = **unlimited**, absolute, boundless, endless, immeasurable, infinite, lavish, limitless, unbridled, unchecked, unconstrained, uncontrolled, unrestrained, vast
Antonyms *adj* bounded, confined, constrained, curbed, limited, restricted

unbridled *adj* **1** = **unrestrained**, excessive, full-on (*inf.*), intemperate, licentious, rampant, riotous, unchecked, unconstrained, uncontrolled, uncurbed, ungovernable, ungoverned, unruly, violent, wanton

unbroken *adj* **1** = **intact**, complete, entire, solid, total, unimpaired, whole **2** = **continuous**, ceaseless, constant, endless, incessant, progressive, serried, successive, uninterrupted, unremitting **5** = **undisturbed**, deep, fast, profound, sound, unruffled, untroubled **4** = **untamed**, unbowed, unsubdued
Antonyms *adj* ≠ **intact:** broken, cracked, damaged, fragmented, in pieces, shattered ≠ **continuous:** erratic, fitful, intermittent, interrupted, irregular, occasional, off-and-on, uneven

unburden *vb* **1** = **unload**, disburden, discharge, disencumber, ease the load, empty, lighten, relieve **2** = **confess**, come clean (*inf.*), confide, disclose, get (something) off one's chest (*inf.*), lay bare, make a clean breast of, re-

relieve or make free (one's mind, oneself, etc.) of a worry, trouble, etc., by revelation or confession.

unbutton (ʌn'bʌtᵊn) *vb* to undo by unfastening (the buttons) of (a garment).

unbuttoned (ʌn'bʌtᵊnd) *adj* **1** with buttons not fastened. **2** *Inf.* uninhibited; unrestrained: *hours of unbuttoned self-revelation.*

uncalled-for ⓣ (ˌʌn'kɔːldfɔː) *adj* unnecessary or unwarranted.

uncanny ⓣ (ʌn'kænɪ) *adj* **1** characterized by apparently supernatural wonder, horror, etc. **2** beyond what is normal: *uncanny accuracy.*
▸**un'cannily** *adv* ▸**un'canniness** *n*

uncap (ʌn'kæp) *vb* **uncaps, uncapping, uncapped. 1** (*tr*) to remove a cap or top from (a container): *to uncap a bottle.* **2** to remove a cap from (the head).

uncared-for (ˌʌn'kɛədfɔː) *adj* not cared for; neglected.

unceremonious (ˌʌnsɛrɪ'məʊnɪəs) *adj* without ceremony; informal, abrupt, rude, or undignified.
▸ˌ**uncere'moniously** *adv* ▸ˌ**uncere'moniousness** *n*

uncertain ⓣ (ʌn'sɜːtᵊn) *adj* **1** not able to be accurately known or predicted: *the issue is uncertain.* **2** (when *postpositive,* often foll. by *of*) not sure or confident (about): *he was uncertain of the date.* **3** not precisely determined or decided: *uncertain plans.* **4** not to be depended upon: *an uncertain vote.* **5** liable to variation; changeable: *the weather is uncertain.* **6 in no uncertain terms. 6a** unambiguously. **6b** forcefully.
▸**un'certainly** *adv*

uncertainty ⓣ (ʌn'sɜːtᵊntɪ) *n, pl* **uncertainties. 1** Also: **uncertainness.** the state or condition of being uncertain. **2** an uncertain matter, contingency, etc.

uncertainty principle *n* **the.** the principle that energy and time or position and momentum, cannot both be accurately measured simultaneously. Also called: **Heisenberg uncertainty principle, indeterminacy principle.**

uncharted ⓣ (ʌn'tʃɑːtɪd) *adj* (of a physical or nonphysical region or area) not yet mapped, surveyed, or investigated: *uncharted waters; the uncharted depths of the mind.*

unchartered (ʌn'tʃɑːtəd) *adj* **1** not authorized by charter; unregulated. **2** unauthorized, lawless, or irregular.

> **USAGE NOTE** Care should be taken not to use *unchartered* where *uncharted* is meant: *uncharted* (not *unchartered*) *territory.*

unchristian (ʌn'krɪstʃən) *adj* **1** not in accordance with the principles or ethics of Christianity. **2** non-Christian or pagan.
▸**un'christianly** *adv*

unchurch (ʌn'tʃɜːtʃ) *vb* (*tr*) **1** to excommunicate. **2** to remove church status from (a building).

uncial ('ʌnsɪəl) *adj* **1** of, relating to, or written in majuscule letters, as used in Greek and Latin manuscripts of the third to ninth centuries, that resemble modern capitals, but are characterized by much greater curvature. ◆ *n* **2** an uncial letter or manuscript. [C17: from LL *unciāles litterae* letters an inch long, from L *unciālis,* from *uncia* one twelfth, inch]
▸'**uncially** *adv*

uncinate ('ʌnsɪnɪt, -ˌneɪt) *adj Biol.* shaped like a hook: *the uncinate process of the ribs of certain vertebrates.* [C18: from L *uncīnātus,* from *uncīnus* a hook, from *uncus*]

uncircumcised (ʌn'sɜːkəmˌsaɪzd) *adj* **1** not circumcised. **2** not Jewish; gentile. **3** spiritually unpurified.
▸ˌ**uncircum'cision** *n*

uncivil ⓣ (ʌn'sɪvəl) *adj* **1** lacking civility or good manners. **2** an obsolete word for **uncivilized.**
▸**uncivility** (ˌʌnsɪ'vɪlɪtɪ) *n* ▸**un'civilly** *adv*

uncivilized ⓣ *or* **uncivilised** (ʌn'sɪvɪˌlaɪzd) *adj* **1** (of a tribe or people) not yet civilized, esp. not having developed a written language. **2** lacking culture or sophistication.
▸**un'civilˌizedness** *or* **un'civilˌisedness** *n*

unclad ⓣ (ʌn'klæd) *adj* having no clothes on; naked.

unclasp (ʌn'klɑːsp) *vb* **1** (*tr*) to unfasten the clasp of (something). **2** to release one's grip (upon an object).

uncle ('ʌŋkᵊl) *n* **1** a brother of one's father or mother. **2** the husband of one's aunt. **3** a term of address sometimes used by children for a male friend of their parents. **4** *Sl.* a pawnbroker. ◆ Related adj: **avuncular.** [C13: from OF *oncle,* from L *avunculus*]

unclean ⓣ (ʌn'kliːn) *adj* lacking moral, spiritual, or physical cleanliness.
▸**un'cleanness** *n*

uncleanly[1] (ʌn'kliːnlɪ) *adv* in an unclean manner.

uncleanly[2] (ʌn'klɛnlɪ) *adj* characterized by an absence of cleanliness.
▸**un'cleanliness** *n*

Uncle Sam (sæm) *n* a personification of the government of the United States. [C19: apparently a humorous interpretation of the letters stamped on army supply boxes during the War of 1812: *US*]

Uncle Tom (tɒm) *n Inf., derog.* a Black person whose behaviour towards White people is regarded as servile. [C20: after the main character of H. B. Stowe's novel *Uncle Tom's Cabin* (1852)]
▸'**Uncle 'Tom**ˌ**ism** *n*

unclose (ʌn'kləʊz) *vb* **uncloses, unclosing, unclosed. 1** to open or cause to open. **2** to come or bring to light.

unclothe (ʌn'kləʊð) *vb* **unclothes, unclothing, unclothed** *or* **unclad.** (*tr*) **1** to take off garments from; strip. **2** to uncover or lay bare.

uncoil (ʌn'kɔɪl) *vb* to unwind or become unwound; untwist.

uncomfortable ⓣ (ʌn'kʌmftəbᵊl) *adj* **1** not comfortable. **2** feeling or causing discomfort or unease; disquieting.
▸**un'comfortableness** *n* ▸**un'comfortably** *adv*

uncommitted ⓣ (ˌʌnkə'mɪtɪd) *adj* not bound or pledged to a specific opinion, course of action, or cause.

uncommon ⓣ (ʌn'kɒmən) *adj* **1** outside or beyond normal experience, etc. **2** in excess of what is normal: *an uncommon liking for honey.* ◆ *adv* **3** an archaic word for **uncommonly** (sense 2).
▸**un'commonness** *n*

uncommonly ⓣ (ʌn'kɒmənlɪ) *adv* **1** in an uncommon or unusual manner or degree; rarely. **2** (intensifier): *you're uncommonly friendly.*

uncommunicative ⓣ (ˌʌnkə'mjuːnɪkətɪv) *adj* disinclined to talk or give information or opinions.
▸ˌ**uncom'municatively** *adv* ▸ˌ**uncom'municativeness** *n*

THESAURUS

veal, spill one's guts about (*sl.*), tell all, unbosom

uncalled-for *adj* = **unnecessary**, gratuitous, inappropriate, needless, undeserved, unjust, unjustified, unprovoked, unwarranted, unwelcome
Antonyms *adj* appropriate, deserved, just, justified, necessary, needed, provoked, warranted

uncanny *adj* **1** = **weird**, creepy (*inf.*), eerie, eldritch (*poetic*), mysterious, preternatural, queer, spooky (*inf.*), strange, supernatural, unearthly, unnatural **2** = **extraordinary**, astonishing, astounding, exceptional, fantastic, incredible, inspired, miraculous, prodigious, remarkable, singular, unheard-of, unusual

uncertain *adj* **1** = **unpredictable**, ambiguous, chancy, conjectural, doubtful, iffy (*inf.*), incalculable, indefinite, indeterminate, indistinct, questionable, risky, speculative, undetermined, unforeseeable **2** = **unsure**, ambivalent, at a loss, doubtful, dubious, hazy, in the balance, in two minds, irresolute, unclear, unconfirmed, undecided, undetermined, unfixed, unresolved, unsettled, up in the air, vacillating, vague **5** = **changeable**, erratic, fitful, hesitant, iffy (*inf.*), inconstant, insecure, irregular, precarious, unpredictable, unreliable, vacillating, variable, wavering
Antonyms *adj* ≠ **unpredictable:** certain, clear, clear-cut, decided, definite, firm, fixed, known, predictable, unambiguous ≠ **unsure:** certain, positive, resolute, settled, sure, unhesitating ≠ **changeable:** certain, reliable, unvarying, unwavering

uncertainty *n* = **doubt**, bewilderment, confusion, dilemma, dubiety, hesitancy, hesitation, indecision, irresolution, lack of confidence, misgiving, mystification, perplexity, puzzlement, qualm, quandary, scepticism, vagueness
Antonyms ≠ **doubt:** assurance, certainty, confidence, decision, resolution, sureness, trust

uncharted *adj* = **unexplored**, not mapped, strange, undiscovered, unfamiliar, unknown, unplumbed, virgin

uncivil *adj* **1** = **impolite**, bad-mannered, bearish, boorish, brusque, churlish, discourteous, disrespectful, gruff, ill-bred, ill-mannered, rude, surly, uncouth, unmannerly
Antonyms *adj* civil, courteous, mannerly, polished, polite, refined, respectful, well-bred, well-mannered

uncivilized *adj* **1** = **primitive**, barbarian, barbaric, barbarous, illiterate, savage, wild **2** = **uncouth**, beyond the pale, boorish, brutish, churlish, coarse, gross, philistine, uncultivated, uncultured, uneducated, unmannered, unpolished, unsophisticated, vulgar

unclad *adj* = **naked**, bare, buck naked (*sl.*), in one's birthday suit (*inf.*), in the altogether (*inf.*), in the bare scud, in the buff (*inf.*), in the raw (*inf.*), naked as the day one was born (*inf.*), nude, starkers (*inf.*), stripped, unclothed, undressed, with nothing on, without a stitch on (*inf.*)

unclean *adj* = **dirty**, contaminated, corrupt, defiled, evil, filthy, foul, impure, nasty, polluted, scuzzy (*sl., chiefly US*), soiled, spotted, stained, sullied, tainted
Antonyms *adj* clean, faultless, flawless, pure, spotless, unblemished, unstained, unsullied

uncomfortable *adj* **1** = **painful**, awkward, causing discomfort, cramped, disagreeable, hard, ill-fitting, incommodious, irritating, rough, troublesome **2** = **uneasy**, awkward, confused, discomfited, disquieted, distressed, disturbed, embarrassed, ill at ease, like a fish out of water, out of place, self-conscious, troubled
Antonyms *adj* ≠ **uneasy:** at ease, at home, comfortable, easy, relaxed, serene, untroubled

uncommitted *adj* = **uninvolved**, floating, free, free-floating, neutral, nonaligned, nonpartisan, not involved, (sitting) on the fence, unattached

uncommon *adj* **1** = **rare**, bizarre, curious, few and far between, infrequent, novel, odd, out of the ordinary, peculiar, queer, scarce, singular, strange, thin on the ground, unfamiliar, unusual **2** = **extraordinary**, distinctive, exceptional, incomparable, inimitable, notable, noteworthy, outstanding, rare, remarkable, singular, special, superior, unparalleled, unprecedented
Antonyms *adj* ≠ **rare:** common, familiar, frequent, regular, routine, usual ≠ **extraordinary:** average, banal, commonplace, everyday, humdrum, mundane, ordinary, run-of-the-mill

uncommonly *adv* **1** = **rarely**, hardly ever, infrequently, not often, occasionally, only now and then, scarcely ever, seldom **2** = **exceptionally**, extremely, particularly, peculiarly, remarkably, seriously (*inf.*), strangely, to the nth degree, unusually, very

uncommunicative *adj* = **reticent**, close, curt, guarded, reserved, retiring, secretive, short, shy, silent, taciturn, tight-lipped, unforthcoming, unresponsive, unsociable, withdrawn
Antonyms *adj* chatty, communicative, forthcom-

uncompromising ⓣ (ʌn'kɒmprəˌmaɪzɪŋ) *adj* not prepared to give ground or to compromise.
►**un'compro,misingly** *adv*
unconcern ⓣ (ˌʌnkən'sɜːn) *n* apathy or indifference.
unconcerned ⓣ (ˌʌnkən'sɜːnd) *adj* **1** lacking in concern or involvement. **2** untroubled.
►**unconcernedly** (ˌʌnkən'sɜːnɪdlɪ) *adv*
unconditional ⓣ (ˌʌnkən'dɪʃənᵊl) *adj* without conditions or limitations; total: *unconditional surrender.*
►**ˌuncon'ditionally** *adv*
unconditioned (ˌʌnkən'dɪʃənd) *adj* **1** *Psychol.* characterizing an innate reflex and the stimulus and response that form parts of it. **2** *Metaphysics.* unrestricted by conditions; absolute. **3** without limitations.
►**ˌuncon'ditionedness** *n*
unconformable (ˌʌnkən'fɔːməbᵊl) *adj* **1** not conformable or conforming. **2** (of rock strata) consisting of a series of recent strata resting on different, much older rocks.
►**ˌuncon,forma'bility** *or* **ˌuncon'formableness** *n* ►**ˌuncon'formably** *adv* ►**ˌuncon'formity** *n*
unconscionable ⓣ (ʌn'kɒnʃənəbᵊl) *adj* **1** unscrupulous or unprincipled: *an unconscionable liar.* **2** immoderate or excessive: *unconscionable demands.*
►**un'conscionably** *adv*
unconscious ⓣ (ʌn'kɒnʃəs) *adj* **1** lacking normal sensory awareness of the environment; insensible. **2** not aware of one's actions, behaviour, etc.: *unconscious of his bad manners.* **3** characterized by lack of awareness or intention: *an unconscious blunder.* **4** coming from or produced by the unconscious: *unconscious resentment.* ◆ *n* **5** *Psychoanal.* the part of the mind containing instincts, impulses, images, and ideas that are not available for direct examination.
►**un'consciously** *adv*
unconstitutional (ˌʌnkɒnstɪ'tjuːʃənᵊl) *adj* at variance with or not permitted by a constitution.
►**ˌunconsti,tution'ality** *n*
unconventional ⓣ (ˌʌnkən'vɛnʃənᵊl) *adj* not conforming to accepted rules or standards.
►**ˌuncon,vention'ality** *n* ►**ˌuncon'ventionally** *adv*
uncool (ʌn'kuːl) *adj Sl.* **1** unsophisticated; unfashionable. **2** excitable; tense; not cool.
uncork (ʌn'kɔːk) *vb* (*tr*) **1** to draw the cork from (a bottle, etc.). **2** to release or unleash (emotions, etc.).
uncountable (ʌn'kaʊntəbᵊl) *adj* **1** too many to be counted; innumerable. **2** *Linguistics.* denoting a noun that does not refer to an isolable object. See **mass noun.**
uncounted ⓣ (ʌn'kaʊntɪd) *adj* **1** unable to be counted; innumerable. **2** not counted.
uncouple (ʌn'kʌpᵊl) *vb* **uncouples, uncoupling, uncoupled. 1** to disconnect or unfasten or become disconnected or unfastened. **2** (*tr*) to set loose; release.
uncouth ⓣ (ʌn'kuːθ) *adj* lacking in good manners, refinement, or grace. [OE *uncūth*, from UN-[1] + *cūth* familiar]
►**un'couthly** *adv* ►**un'couthness** *n*
uncover ⓣ (ʌn'kʌvə) *vb* **1** (*tr*) to remove the cover, cap, top, etc., from. **2** (*tr*) to reveal or disclose: *to uncover a plot.* **3** to take off (one's head covering), esp. as a mark of respect.
uncovered (ʌn'kʌvəd) *adj* **1** not covered; revealed or bare. **2** not protected by insurance, security, etc. **3** with hat off, as a mark of respect.
UNCTAD *abbrev. for* United Nations Conference on Trade and Development.
unction ('ʌŋkʃən) *n* **1** *Chiefly RC & Eastern Churches.* the act of anointing with oil in sacramental ceremonies, in the conferring of holy orders. **2** excessive suavity or affected charm. **3** an ointment or unguent. **4** anything soothing. [C14: from L *unctiō* an anointing, from *ungere* to anoint]
►**'unctionless** *adj*
unctuous ⓣ ('ʌŋktjʊəs) *adj* **1** slippery or greasy. **2** affecting an oily charm. [C14: from Med. L *unctuōsus*, from L *unctum* ointment, from *ungere* to anoint]
►**unctuosity** (ˌʌŋktjʊ'ɒsɪtɪ) *or* **'unctuousness** *n* ►**'unctuously** *adv*
uncut (ʌn'kʌt) *adj* **1** (of a book) not having the edges of its pages trimmed or slit. **2** (of a gemstone) not cut and faceted. **3** not abridged.
undamped (ʌn'dæmpt) *adj* **1** (of an oscillating system) having unrestricted motion; not damped. **2** not repressed, discouraged, or subdued.
undaunted ⓣ (ʌn'dɔːntɪd) *adj* not put off, discouraged, or beaten.
►**un'dauntedly** *adv* ►**un'dauntedness** *n*
undecagon (ʌn'dɛkəˌgɒn) *n* a polygon having eleven sides. [C18: from L *undecim* eleven + -GON]
undeceive ⓣ (ˌʌndɪ'siːv) *vb* **undeceives, undeceiving, undeceived.** (*tr*) to reveal the truth to (someone previously misled or deceived).
►**ˌunde'ceivable** *adj* ►**ˌunde'ceiver** *n*
undecidability (ˌʌndɪˌsaɪdə'bɪlɪtɪ) *n, pl* **undecidabilities.** *Maths, logic.* the condition of not being open to formal proof or disproof by logical deduction from the axioms of a system.
undecided ⓣ (ˌʌndɪ'saɪdɪd) *adj* **1** not having made up one's mind. **2** (of an issue, problem, etc.) not agreed or decided upon.
►**ˌunde'cidedly** *adv* ►**ˌunde'cidedness** *n*
undeniable(ˌʌndɪ'naɪəbᵊl) *adj* **1** unquestionably or obviously true. **2** of unquestionable excellence: *a man of undeniable character.* **3** unable to be resisted or denied.
►**ˌunde'niableness** *n* ►**ˌunde'niably** *adv*
under ⓣ ('ʌndə) *prep* **1** directly below; on, to, or beneath the underside or base of: *under one's feet.* **2** less than: *under forty years.* **3** lower in rank than: *under a corporal.* **4** subject to the supervision, jurisdiction, control, or influence of. **5** subject to (conditions); in (certain circumstances). **6** within a classification of: *a book under theology.* **7** known by: *under an assumed name.* **8** planted with: *a field under corn.* **9** powered by: *under sail.* **10** *Astrol.* during the period that the sun is in (a sign of the zodiac): *born under Aries.* ◆ *adv* **11** below; to a position underneath something. [OE]
under- *prefix* **1** below or beneath: *underarm; underground.* **2** of lesser importance or lower rank: *undersecretary.* **3** insufficient or insufficiently: *underemployed.* **4** indicating secrecy or deception: *underhand.*
underachieve (ˌʌndərə'tʃiːv) *vb* **underachieves, underachieving, under-**

THESAURUS

ing, garrulous, loquacious, responsive, talkative, voluble

uncompromising *adj* = **inflexible**, decided, die-hard, firm, hardline, inexorable, intransigent, obdurate, obstinate, rigid, steadfast, stiff-necked, strict, stubborn, tough, unbending, unyielding

unconcern *n* = **indifference**, aloofness, apathy, detachment, insouciance, lack of interest, nonchalance, remoteness, uninterestedness

unconcerned *adj* **1** = **indifferent**, aloof, apathetic, cool, detached, dispassionate, distant, incurious, oblivious, uninterested, uninvolved, unmoved, unsympathetic **2** = **untroubled**, blithe, callous, carefree, careless, easy, insouciant, nonchalant, not bothered, not giving a toss (*inf.*), relaxed, serene, unperturbed, unruffled, unworried
Antonyms *adj* ≠ **indifferent:** avid, curious, eager, interested, involved ≠ **untroubled:** agitated, anxious, concerned, distressed, perturbed, uneasy, worried

unconditional *adj* = **absolute**, arrant, categorical, complete, downright, entire, explicit, full, out-and-out, outright, plenary, positive, thoroughgoing, total, unlimited, unqualified, unreserved, unrestricted, utter
Antonyms *adj* conditional, limited, partial, qualified, reserved, restricted

unconscionable *adj* **1** = **unscrupulous**, amoral, criminal, unethical, unfair, unjust, unprincipled **2** = **excessive**, exorbitant, extravagant, extreme, immoderate, inordinate, outrageous, preposterous, unreasonable

unconscious *adj* **1** = **senseless**, blacked out, comatose, dead to the world (*inf.*), insensible, knocked out, numb, out, out cold, out for the count (*Boxing*), stunned **2** = **unaware**, blind to, deaf to, heedless, ignorant, in ignorance, lost to, oblivious, unknowing, unmindful, unsuspecting **3** = **unintentional**, accidental, inadvertent, unintended, unpremeditated, unwitting **4** = **subconscious**, automatic, gut (*inf.*), inherent, innate, instinctive, involuntary, latent, reflex, repressed, subliminal, suppressed, unrealized
Antonyms *adj* ≠ **senseless:** awake, conscious, sensible ≠ **unaware:** alert, aware, conscious, sensible ≠ **unintentional:** calculated, conscious, deliberate, intentional, planned, studied, wilful

unconventional *adj* = **unusual**, atypical, bizarre, bohemian, different, eccentric, far-out (*sl.*), freakish, idiosyncratic, individual, individualistic, informal, irregular, left-field (*inf.*), nonconformist, odd, oddball (*inf.*), offbeat, off-the-wall (*sl.*), original, out of the ordinary, outré, uncustomary, unorthodox, way-out (*inf.*)
Antonyms *adj* conventional, normal, ordinary, orthodox, proper, regular, typical, usual

uncounted *adj* = **innumerable**, countless, infinite, legion, multitudinous, myriad, numberless, unnumbered, untold

uncouth *adj* = **coarse**, awkward, barbaric, boorish, clownish, clumsy, crude, gawky, graceless, gross, ill-mannered, loutish, lubberly, oafish, rough, rude, rustic, uncivilized, uncultivated, ungainly, unrefined, unseemly, vulgar
Antonyms *adj* civilized, courteous, cultivated, elegant, graceful, refined, seemly, well-mannered

uncover *vb* **1** = **open**, bare, lay open, lift the lid, show, strip, unwrap **2** = **reveal**, blow wide open (*sl.*), bring to light, disclose, discover, divulge, expose, lay bare, make known, take the wraps off, unearth, unmask
Antonyms *vb* ≠ **reveal:** conceal, cover, cover up, hide, keep under wraps, suppress

unctuous *adj* **1** = **greasy**, oily, oleaginous, slippery, slithery **2** = **obsequious**, fawning, glib, gushing, ingratiating, insincere, oily, plausible, slick, smarmy (*Brit. inf.*), smooth, suave, sycophantic

undaunted *adj* = **undeterred**, bold, brave, courageous, dauntless, fearless, gallant, gritty, indomitable, intrepid, not discouraged, nothing daunted, not put off, resolute, steadfast, undiscouraged, undismayed, unfaltering, unflinching, unshrinking

undeceive *vb* = **enlighten**, be honest with, correct, disabuse, disillusion, open (someone's) eyes (to), put (someone) right, set (someone) straight, shatter (someone's) illusions

undecided *adj* **1** = **unsure**, ambivalent, dithering (*chiefly Brit.*), doubtful, dubious, hesitant, in two minds, irresolute, swithering (*Scot.*), torn, uncertain, uncommitted, wavering **2** = **unsettled**, debatable, iffy (*inf.*), indefinite, in the balance, moot, open, pending, tentative, unconcluded, undetermined, up in the air, vague
Antonyms *adj* ≠ **unsure:** certain, committed, decided, resolute, sure ≠ **unsettled:** decided, definite, determined, resolved, settled

undeniable *adj* **1** = **certain**, beyond (a) doubt, beyond question, clear, evident, incontestable, incontrovertible, indisputable, indubitable, irrefutable, manifest, obvious, patent, proven, sound, sure, unassailable, undoubted, unquestionable
Antonyms *adj* debatable, deniable, doubtful, dubious, questionable, uncertain, unproven

under *prep* **1** = **below**, beneath, on the bottom

achieved. (*intr*) to fail to achieve a performance appropriate to one's age or talents.
▸ **,undera'chievement** *n* ▸ **,undera'chiever** *n*

underact (ˌʌndər'ækt) *vb Theatre.* to play (a role) without adequate emphasis.

underage (ˌʌndər'eɪdʒ) *adj* below the required or standard age, esp. below the legal age for voting or drinking.

underarm ('ʌndərˌɑːm) *adj* **1** (of a measurement) extending along the arm from wrist to armpit. **2** *Cricket, tennis, etc.* denoting a style of throwing, bowling, or serving in which the hand is swung below shoulder level. **3** below the arm. ◆ *adv* **4** in an underarm style.

underbelly ('ʌndəˌbelɪ) *n, pl* **underbellies. 1** the part of an animal's belly nearest to the ground. **2** a vulnerable or unprotected part, aspect, or region.

underbid (ˌʌndə'bɪd) *vb* **underbids, underbidding, underbid. 1** (*tr*) to submit a bid lower than that of (others). **2** (*tr*) to submit an excessively low bid for. **3** *Bridge.* to bid (one's hand) at a lower level than the strength of the hand warrants: *he underbid his hand.*

underbidder ('ʌndəˌbɪdə) *n* **1** the person who makes the highest bid below the top bidder, esp. in an auction. **2** a person who underbids.

underbody ('ʌndəˌbɒdɪ) *n, pl* **underbodies.** the underpart of a body, as of an animal or motor vehicle.

underbred (ˌʌndə'brɛd) *adj* of impure stock; not thoroughbred.
▸ **,under'breeding** *n*

underbuy (ˌʌndə'baɪ) *vb* **underbuys, underbuying, underbought. 1** to buy (stock in trade) in amounts lower than required. **2** (*tr*) to buy at a price below that paid by (others). **3** (*tr*) to pay a price less than the true value for.

undercapitalize *or* **undercapitalise** (ˌʌndə'kæpɪtəˌlaɪz) *vb* **undercapitalizes, undercapitalizing, undercapitalized** *or* **undercapitalises, undercapitalising, undercapitalised.** to provide or issue capital for (a commercial enterprise) in an amount insufficient for efficient operation.

undercarriage ('ʌndəˌkærɪdʒ) *n* **1** Also called: **landing gear.** the assembly of wheels, shock absorbers, struts, etc., that supports an aircraft on the ground and enables it to take off and land. **2** the framework that supports the body of a vehicle, carriage, etc.

undercharge (ˌʌndə'tʃɑːdʒ) *vb* **undercharges, undercharging, undercharged. 1** to charge too little for something. **2** (*tr*) to load (a gun, cannon, etc.) with an inadequate charge.

underclass ('ʌndəˌklɑːs) *n* a class beneath the usual social scale consisting of the most disadvantaged people, such as the long-term unemployed.

underclothes Ⓣ ('ʌndəˌkləʊðz) *pl n* a variant of **underwear.** Also called: **underclothing.**

undercoat ('ʌndəˌkəʊt) *n* **1** a coat of paint or other substance applied before the top coat. **2** a coat worn under an overcoat. **3** *Zool.* another name for **underfur.** ◆ *vb* **4** (*tr*) to apply an undercoat to (a surface).

undercover Ⓣ (ˌʌndə'kʌvə) *adj* done or acting in secret: *undercover operations.*

undercroft ('ʌndəˌkrɒft) *n* an underground chamber, such as a church crypt, often with a vaulted ceiling. [C14: from *croft* a vault, cavern, ult. from L *crypta* CRYPT]

undercurrent Ⓣ ('ʌndəˌkʌrənt) *n* **1** a current that is not apparent at the surface or lies beneath another current. **2** an opinion, emotion, etc., lying beneath apparent feeling or meaning. ◆ Also called: **underflow.**

undercut Ⓣ *vb* (ˌʌndə'kʌt), **undercuts, undercutting, undercut. 1** to charge less than (a competitor) in order to obtain trade. **2** to cut away the under part of (something). **3** *Golf, tennis, etc.* to hit (a ball) in such a way as to impart backspin. ◆ *n* ('ʌndəˌkʌt). **4** the act of cutting underneath. **5** a part that is cut away underneath. **6** a tenderloin of beef. **7** *Forestry, chiefly US & Canad.* a notch cut in a tree trunk, to ensure a clean break in felling. **8** *Tennis, golf, etc.* a stroke that imparts backspin to the ball.

underdevelop (ˌʌndədɪ'vɛləp) *vb* (*tr*) *Photog.* to process (a film, plate, or paper) in developer for less than the required time, or at too low a temperature, or in an exhausted solution.

underdeveloped (ˌʌndədɪ'vɛləpt) *adj* **1** immature or undersized. **2** relating to societies in which both the surplus capital and the social organization necessary to advance are lacking. **3** *Photog.* (of a film, etc.) processed in developer for less than the required time.

underdog Ⓣ ('ʌndəˌdɒg) *n* **1** the losing competitor in a fight or contest. **2** a person in adversity or a position of inferiority.

underdone (ˌʌndə'dʌn) *adj* insufficiently or lightly cooked.

underdressed (ˌʌndə'drɛst) *adj* wearing clothes that are not elaborate or formal enough for a particular occasion.

underemployed (ˌʌndərɪm'plɔɪd) *adj* not fully or adequately employed.

underestimate Ⓣ *vb* (ˌʌndər'ɛstɪˌmeɪt), **underestimates, underestimating, underestimated.** (*tr*) **1** to make too low an estimate of: *he underestimated the cost.* **2** to think insufficiently highly of: *to underestimate a person.* ◆ *n* (ˌʌndər'ɛstɪmɪt). **3** too low an estimate.
▸ **,under,esti'mation** *n*

> **USAGE NOTE** *Underestimate* is sometimes wrongly used where *overestimate* is meant: *the importance of his work cannot be overestimated* (not *cannot be underestimated*).

underexpose (ˌʌndərɪk'spəʊz) *vb* **underexposes, underexposing, underexposed.** (*tr*) **1** *Photog.* to expose (a film, plate, or paper) for too short a period or with insufficient light so as not to produce the required effect. **2** (*often passive*) to fail to subject to appropriate or expected publicity.
▸ **,underex'posure** *n*

underfeed (ˌʌndə'fiːd) *vb* **underfeeds, underfeeding, underfed.** (*tr*) **1** to give too little food to. **2** to supply (a furnace, engine, etc.) with fuel from beneath.

underfelt ('ʌndəˌfɛlt) *n* thick felt laid between floorboards and carpet to increase insulation.

underfloor ('ʌndəˌflɔː) *adj* situated beneath the floor: *underfloor heating.*

underfoot (ˌʌndə'fʊt) *adv* **1** underneath the feet; on the ground. **2** in a position of subjugation. **3** in the way.

underfur ('ʌndəˌfɜː) *n* the layer of dense soft fur occurring beneath the outer coarser fur in certain mammals, such as the otter and seal. Also called: **undercoat.**

undergarment ('ʌndəˌgɑːmənt) *n* any garment worn under the visible outer clothes, usually next to the skin.

undergird (ˌʌndə'gɜːd) *vb* **undergirds, undergirding, undergirded** *or* **undergirt.** (*tr*) to strengthen or reinforce by passing a rope, cable, or chain around the underside of (an object, load, etc.). [C16: from UNDER- + GIRD[1]]

underglaze ('ʌndəˌgleɪz) *adj* **1** *Ceramics.* applied to pottery or porcelain before the application of glaze. ◆ *n* **2** a pigment, etc., applied in this way.

undergo Ⓣ (ˌʌndə'gəʊ) *vb* **undergoes, undergoing, underwent, undergone.** (*tr*) to experience, endure, or sustain: *to undergo a change of feelings.* [OE]
▸ **'under,goer** *n*

undergraduate (ˌʌndə'grædjʊɪt) *n* a person studying in a university for a first degree. Sometimes shortened to **undergrad.**

underground Ⓣ *adj* ('ʌndəˌgraʊnd), *adv* (ˌʌndə'graʊnd). **1** occurring, situated, used, or going below ground level: *an underground explosion.* **2** secret; hidden: *underground activities.* ◆ *n* ('ʌndəˌgraʊnd). **3** a space or region below ground level. **4a** a movement dedicated to overthrowing a government or occupation forces, as in the European countries occupied by the German army in World War II. **4b** (*as modifier*): *an underground group.* **5** (often preceded by *the*) an electric passenger railway operated in underground tunnels. US and Canad. equivalent: **subway. 6** (usually preceded by *the*) **6a** any avant-garde, experimental, or subversive movement in popular art, films, music, etc. **6b** (*as modifier*): *the underground press.*

underground railroad *n* (*often cap.*) (in the pre-Civil War US) the system established by abolitionists to aid escaping slaves.

undergrowth Ⓣ ('ʌndəˌgrəʊθ) *n* small trees, bushes, ferns, etc., growing beneath taller trees in a wood or forest.

underhand Ⓣ ('ʌndəˌhænd) *adj also* **underhanded. 1** clandestine, deceptive, or secretive. **2** *Sport.* another word for **underarm.** ◆ *adv* **3** in an underhand manner or style.

THESAURUS

of, underneath **3, 4** = **subject to,** directed by, governed by, inferior to, junior to, reporting to, secondary to, subordinate to, subservient to **6** = **included in,** belonging to, comprised in, subsumed under ◆ *adv* **11** = **below,** beneath, down, downward, lower, to the bottom
Antonyms *prep* ≠ **below:** above, over, up, upper, upward ◆ *adv* ≠ **below:** above, over, up, upward

underclothes *pl n* = **underwear,** lingerie, smalls (*inf.*), underclothing, undergarments, underlinen, underthings, undies (*inf.*), unmentionables (*humorous*)

undercover *adj* = **secret,** clandestine, concealed, confidential, covert, hidden, hush-hush (*inf.*), intelligence, private, spy, surreptitious, underground
Antonyms *adj* manifest, open, overt, plain, unconcealed, visible

undercurrent *n* **1** = **undertow,** crosscurrent, rip, rip current, riptide, tideway, underflow **2** = **undertone,** atmosphere, aura, drift, feeling, flavour, hidden feeling, hint, murmur, overtone, sense, suggestion, tendency, tenor, tinge, trend, vibes (*sl.*), vibrations

undercut *vb* **1** = **underprice,** sacrifice, sell at a loss, sell cheaply, undercharge, undersell **2** = **cut away,** cut out, excavate, gouge out, hollow out, mine, undermine

underdog *n* **1, 2** = **weaker party,** fall guy, little fellow (*inf.*), loser, outsider, victim

underestimate *vb* **2** = **underrate,** belittle, hold cheap, minimize, miscalculate, misprize, not do justice to, rate too low, sell short, set no store by, think too little of, undervalue
Antonyms *vb* exaggerate, inflate, overdo, overestimate, overrate, overstate

undergo *vb* = **experience,** bear, be subjected to, endure, go through, stand, submit to, suffer, sustain, weather, withstand

underground *adj* **1** = **subterranean,** below ground, below the surface, buried, covered **2** = **secret,** clandestine, concealed, covert, hidden, surreptitious, undercover ◆ *n* **4a** = **the Resistance,** partisans, the Maquis **5 the underground** = **the tube** (*Brit.*), the metro, the subway ◆ *modifier* **6b** = **avant-garde,** alternative, experimental, radical, revolutionary, subversive

undergrowth *n* = **scrub,** bracken, brambles, briars, brush, brushwood, underbrush, underbush, underwood

underhand *adj* **1** = **sly,** below the belt (*inf.*), clandestine, crafty, crooked (*inf.*), deceitful, deceptive, devious, dishonest, dishonourable, fraudulent, furtive, secret, secretive, sneaky, stealthy, surreptitious, treacherous, underhanded, unethical, unscrupulous

underhanded (ˌʌndəˈhændɪd) *adj* another word for **underhand** or **shorthanded.**

underhung (ˌʌndəˈhʌŋ) *adj* **1** (of the lower jaw) projecting beyond the upper jaw; undershot. **2** (of a sliding door, etc.) supported at its lower edge by a track or rail.

underlay *vb* (ˌʌndəˈleɪ), **underlays, underlaying, underlaid.** (*tr*) **1** to place (something) under or beneath. **2** to support by something laid beneath. **3** to achieve the correct printing pressure all over (a forme block) or to bring (a block) up to type height by adding material, such as paper, beneath it. ◆ *n* (ˈʌndəˌleɪ). **4** a lining, support, etc., laid underneath something else. **5** *Printing.* material, such as paper, used to underlay a forme or block. **6** felt, rubber, etc., laid beneath a carpet to increase insulation and resilience.

underlie (ˌʌndəˈlaɪ) *vb* **underlies, underlying, underlay, underlain.** (*tr*) **1** to lie or be placed under or beneath. **2** to be the foundation, cause, or basis of: *careful planning underlies all our decisions.* **3** to be the root or stem from which (a word) is derived: *"happy" underlies "happiest".*
►**ˈunderˌlier** *n*

underline ➊ (ˌʌndəˈlaɪn) *vb* **underlines, underlining, underlined.** (*tr*) **1** to put a line under. **2** to state forcibly; emphasize.

underlinen (ˈʌndəˌlɪnən) *n* underclothes, esp. when made of linen.

underling ➊ (ˈʌndəlɪŋ) *n* a subordinate or lackey.

underlying ➊ (ˌʌndəˈlaɪɪŋ) *adj* **1** concealed but detectable: *underlying guilt.* **2** fundamental; basic. **3** lying under. **4** *Finance.* (of a claim, liability, etc.) taking precedence; prior.

undermentioned (ˈʌndəˌmɛnʃənd) *adj* mentioned below or subsequently.

undermine ➊ (ˌʌndəˈmaɪn) *vb* **undermines, undermining, undermined.** (*tr*) **1** (of the sea, wind, etc.) to wear away the bottom or base of (land, cliffs, etc.). **2** to weaken gradually or insidiously: *insults undermined her confidence.* **3** to tunnel or dig beneath.
►ˌ**underˈminer** *n*

undermost (ˈʌndəˌməʊst) *adj* **1** being the furthest under; lowest. ◆ *adv* **2** in the lowest place.

underneath (ˌʌndəˈniːθ) *prep, adv* **1** under; beneath. ◆ *adj* **2** lower. ◆ *n* **3** a lower part, surface, etc. [OE *underneothan,* from UNDER + *neothan* below]

undernourish (ˌʌndəˈnʌrɪʃ) *vb* (*tr*) to deprive of or fail to provide with nutrients essential for health and growth.
►ˌ**underˈnourishment** *n*

underpants (ˈʌndəˌpænts) *pl n* a man's undergarment covering the body from the waist or hips to the thighs or ankles. Often shortened to **pants.**

underpass (ˈʌndəˌpɑːs) *n* **1** a section of a road that passes under another road, railway line, etc. **2** another word for **subway** (sense 1).

underpay (ˌʌndəˈpeɪ) *vb* **underpays, underpaying, underpaid.** to pay (someone) insufficiently.
►ˌ**underˈpayment** *n*

underpin (ˌʌndəˈpɪn) *vb* **underpins, underpinning, underpinned.** (*tr*) **1** to support from beneath, esp. by a prop, while avoiding damaging or weakening the superstructure: *to underpin a wall.* **2** to give corroboration, strength, or support to.

underpinning ➊ (ˈʌndəˌpɪnɪŋ) *n* a structure of masonry, concrete, etc., placed beneath a wall to provide support.

underplay (ˌʌndəˈpleɪ) *vb* **1** to play (a role) with restraint or subtlety. **2** to achieve (an effect) by deliberate lack of emphasis. **3** (*intr*) *Cards.* to lead or follow suit with a lower card when holding a higher one.

underprivileged ➊ (ˌʌndəˈprɪvɪlɪdʒd) *adj* lacking the rights and advantages of other members of society; deprived.

underproduction (ˌʌndəprəˈdʌkʃən) *n Commerce.* production below full capacity or below demand.

underproof (ˌʌndəˈpruːf) *adj* (of a spirit) containing less than 57.1 per cent alcohol by volume.

underquote (ˌʌndəˈkwəʊt) *vb* **underquotes, underquoting, underquoted. 1** to offer for sale (securities, goods, or services) at a price lower than the market price. **2** (*tr*) to quote a price lower than that quoted by (another).

underrate ➊ (ˌʌndəˈreɪt) *vb* **underrates, underrating, underrated.** (*tr*) to underestimate.

underscore (ˌʌndəˈskɔː) *vb* **underscores, underscoring, underscored.** (*tr*) **1** to draw or score a line or mark under. **2** to stress or reinforce.

undersea (ˈʌndəˌsiː) *adj, adv also* **underseas** (ˌʌndəˈsiːz). below the surface of the sea.

underseal (ˈʌndəˌsiːl) *Brit.* ◆ *n* **1** a coating of a tar, etc., applied to the underside of a motor vehicle to retard corrosion. ◆ *vb* **2** (*tr*) to apply a coating of underseal to (a vehicle).

undersecretary (ˌʌndəˈsɛkrətrɪ) *n, pl* **undersecretaries. 1** (in Britain) **1a** any of various senior civil servants in certain government departments. **1b** short for **undersecretary of state:** any of various high officials subordinate only to the minister in charge of a department. **2** (in the US) a high government official subordinate only to the secretary in charge of a department.

undersell ➊ (ˌʌndəˈsɛl) *vb* **undersells, underselling, undersold. 1** to sell for less than the usual price. **2** (*tr*) to sell at a price lower than that of (another seller). **3** (*tr*) to advertise (merchandise) with moderation or restraint.
►ˌ**underˈseller** *n*

undersexed (ˌʌndəˈsɛkst) *adj* having weaker sex urges or responses than is considered normal.

undershirt (ˈʌndəˌʃɜːt) *n* the US and Canad. name for **vest** (sense 1).

undershoot (ˌʌndəˈʃuːt) *vb* **undershoots, undershooting, undershot. 1** (of a pilot) to cause (an aircraft) to land short of (a runway) or (of an aircraft) to land in this way. **2** to shoot a projectile so that it falls short of (a target).

undershorts (ˈʌndəˌʃɔːts) *pl n* another word for **shorts** (sense 2).

undershot (ˈʌndəˌʃɒt) *adj* **1** (of the lower jaw) projecting beyond the upper jaw; underhung. **2** (of a water wheel) driven by a flow of water that passes under the wheel rather than over it.

underside (ˈʌndəˌsaɪd) *n* the bottom or lower surface.

undersigned (ˈʌndəˌsaɪnd) *n* **1 the.** the person or persons who have signed at the foot of a document, statement, etc. ◆ *adj* **2** having signed one's name at the foot of a document, statement, etc.

undersized ➊ (ˌʌndəˈsaɪzd) *adj* of less than usual size.

underskirt (ˈʌndəˌskɜːt) *n* any skirtlike garment worn under a skirt or dress; petticoat.

underslung (ˌʌndəˈslʌŋ) *adj* suspended below a supporting member, esp. (of a motor vehicle chassis) suspended below the axles.

understand ➊ (ˌʌndəˈstænd) *vb* **understands, understanding, understood. 1** (*may take a clause as object*) to know and comprehend the nature or meaning of: *I understand you.* **2** (*may take a clause as object*) to realize or grasp (something): *he understands your position.* **3** (*tr; may take a clause as object*) to assume, infer, or believe: *I understand you are thinking of marrying.* **4** (*tr*) to know how to translate or read: *can you understand Spanish?* **5** (*tr; may take a clause as object; often passive*) to accept as a condition or proviso: *it is understood that children must be kept quiet.* **6** (*tr*) to be sympathetic to or compatible with: *we understand each other.* [OE *understandan*]
►ˌ**underˈstandable** *adj* ►ˌ**underˈstandably** *adv*

understanding ➊ (ˌʌndəˈstændɪŋ) *n* **1** the ability to learn, judge, make decisions, etc. **2** personal opinion or interpretation of a subject: *my understanding of your predicament.* **3** a mutual agreement or compact, esp. an informal or private one. **4** *Chiefly Brit.* an unofficial engagement to be married. **5 on the understanding that.** providing. ◆ *adj* **6** sym-

THESAURUS

Antonyms *adj* above board, frank, honest, honourable, legal, open, outright, principled, scrupulous

underline *vb* **1** = **underscore**, italicize, mark, rule a line under **2** = **emphasize**, accentuate, bring home, call *or* draw attention to, give emphasis to, highlight, point up, stress
Antonyms *vb* ≠ **emphasize:** gloss over, make light of, minimize, play down, soft-pedal (*inf.*)

underling *n Derogatory* = **subordinate**, cohort (*chiefly US*), flunky, hireling, inferior, lackey, menial, minion, nonentity, retainer, servant, slave, understrapper

underlying *adj* **1** = **hidden**, concealed, latent, lurking, veiled **2** = **fundamental**, basal, basic, elementary, essential, intrinsic, primary, prime, radical, root

undermine *vb* **1** = **wear away**, dig out, eat away at, erode, excavate, mine, tunnel, undercut **2** = **weaken**, debilitate, disable, impair, sabotage, sap, subvert, threaten
Antonyms *vb* ≠ **weaken:** fortify, promote, reinforce, strengthen, sustain ≠ **wear away:** buttress, fortify, reinforce, strengthen, sustain

underpinning *n* = **support**, base, footing, foundation, groundwork, substructure

underprivileged *adj* = **disadvantaged**, badly off, deprived, destitute, impoverished, in need, in want, needy, on the breadline, poor

underrate *vb* = **underestimate**, belittle, discount, disparage, fail to appreciate, misprize, not do justice to, set (too) little store by, undervalue
Antonyms *vb* exaggerate, overestimate, overprize, overrate, overvalue

undersell *vb* **1, 2** = **undercut**, cut, mark down, reduce, slash, undercharge **3** = **understate**, play down

undersized *adj* = **stunted**, atrophied, dwarfish, miniature, pygmy *or* pigmy, runtish, runty, small, squat, teensy-weensy, teeny-weeny, tiny, underdeveloped, underweight
Antonyms *adj* big, colossal, giant, huge, massive, oversized, overweight

understand *vb* **1** = **comprehend**, appreciate, apprehend, be aware, catch on (*inf.*), conceive, cotton on (*inf.*), discern, fathom, follow, get, get one's head round, get the hang of (*inf.*), get to the bottom of, grasp, know, make head or tail of (*inf.*), make out, penetrate, perceive, realize, recognize, savvy (*sl.*), see, see the light, take in, tumble to (*inf.*), twig (*Brit. inf.*) **3** = **believe**, assume, be informed, conclude, gather, hear, learn, presume, suppose, take it, think **6** = **sympathize with**, accept, appreciate, be able to see, commiserate, empathize with, show compassion for, tolerate

understandable *adj* **2** = **reasonable**, justifiable, legitimate, logical, natural, normal, to be expected

understanding *n* **1** = **perception**, appreciation, awareness, comprehension, discernment, grasp, insight, intelligence, judgment, knowledge, penetration, sense **2** = **interpretation**, belief, conclusion, estimation, idea, judgment, notion, opinion, perception, view, viewpoint **3** = **agreement**, accord, common view, gentlemen's agreement, pact ◆ *adj* **6** = **sympathetic**, accepting, compassionate, considerate, discerning, forbearing, forgiving, kind, kindly, patient, perceptive, responsive, sensitive, tolerant
Antonyms *n* ≠ **perception:** ignorance, incomprehension, insensitivity, misapprehension, misunderstanding, obtuseness ≠ **agreement:** disagreement, dispute ◆ *adj* ≠ **sympathetic:** inconsiderate, insensitive, intolerant, strict, unfeeling, unsympathetic

pathetic, tolerant, or wise towards people. **7** possessing judgment and intelligence.
►ˌ**under'standingly** *adv*

understate (ˌʌndəˈsteɪt) *vb* **understates, understating, understated. 1** to state (something) in restrained terms, often to obtain an ironic effect. **2** to state that (something, such as a number) is less than it is.
►ˌ**under'statement** *n*

understeer (ˌʌndəˈstɪə) *vb* (*intr*) (of a vehicle) to turn less sharply, for a particular movement of the steering wheel, than anticipated.

understood ➊ (ˌʌndəˈstʊd) *vb* **1** the past tense and past participle of **understand.** ◆ *adj* **2** implied or inferred. **3** taken for granted.

understudy ➊ (ˈʌndəˌstʌdɪ) *vb* **understudies, understudying, understudied. 1** (*tr*) to study (a role or part) so as to be able to replace the usual actor or actress if necessary. **2** to act as understudy to (an actor or actress). ◆ *n, pl* **understudies. 3** an actor or actress who studies a part so as to be able to replace the usual actor or actress if necessary. **4** anyone who is trained to take the place of another in case of need.

undertake ➊ (ˌʌndəˈteɪk) *vb* **undertakes, undertaking, undertook, undertaken.** (*tr*) **1** to contract to or commit oneself to (something) or (to do something): *to undertake a job.* **2** to attempt to; agree to start. **3** to take (someone) in charge. **4** to promise.

undertaker ➊ (ˈʌndəˌteɪkə) *n* a person whose profession is the preparation of the dead for burial or cremation and the management of funerals; funeral director.

undertaking ➊ (ˈʌndəˌteɪkɪŋ) *n* **1** a task, venture, or enterprise. **2** an agreement to do something. **3** the business of an undertaker.

underthings (ˈʌndəˌθɪŋz) *pl n* girls' or women's underwear.

underthrust (ˈʌndəˌθrʌst) *n Geol.* a reverse fault in which the rocks on the lower surface of a fault plane have moved under the relatively static rocks on the upper surface.

undertone ➊ (ˈʌndəˌtəʊn) *n* **1** a quiet or hushed tone of voice. **2** an underlying suggestion in words or actions: *his offer has undertones of dishonesty.*

undertow (ˈʌndəˌtəʊ) *n* **1** the seaward undercurrent following the breaking of a wave on the beach. **2** any strong undercurrent flowing in a different direction from the surface current.

undertrick (ˈʌndəˌtrɪk) *n Bridge.* a trick by which a declarer falls short of making his or her contract.

undervalue ➊ (ˌʌndəˈvæljuː) *vb* **undervalues, undervaluing, undervalued.** (*tr*) to value at too low a level or price.
►ˌ**underˌvalu'ation** *n* ►ˌ**under'valuer** *n*

undervest (ˈʌndəˌvest) *n Brit.* another name for **vest** (sense 1).

underwater ➊ (ˈʌndəˈwɔːtə) *adj* **1** being, occurring, or going under the surface of the water, esp. the sea: *underwater exploration.* **2** *Naut.* below the water line of a vessel. ◆ *adv* **3** beneath the surface of the water.

under way ➊ *adj* (*postpositive*) **1** in progress; in operation: *the show was under way.* **2** *Naut.* in motion.

underwear ➊ (ˈʌndəˌwɛə) *n* clothing worn under the outer garments, usually next to the skin.

underweight ➊ (ˌʌndəˈweɪt) *adj* weighing less than is average, expected, or healthy.

underwent (ˌʌndəˈwɛnt) *vb* the past tense of **undergo.**

underwhelm (ˌʌndəˈwɛlm) *vb* (*tr*) to make no positive impact on; disappoint. [C20: orig. a humorous coinage based on *overwhelm*]
►ˌ**under'whelming** *adj*

underwing (ˈʌndəˌwɪŋ) *n* **1** the hind wing of an insect. **2** See **red underwing, yellow underwing.**

underwood (ˈʌndəˌwʊd) *n* a less common word for **undergrowth.**

underworld ➊ (ˈʌndəˌwɜːld) *n* **1a** criminals and their associates. **1b** (*as modifier*): *underworld connections.* **2** *Greek & Roman myth.* the regions below the earth's surface regarded as the abode of the dead. **3** the antipodes.

underwrite ➊ (ˈʌndəˌraɪt, ˌʌndəˈraɪt) *vb* **underwrites, underwriting, underwrote, underwritten.** (*tr*) **1** *Finance.* to undertake to purchase at an agreed price any unsold portion of (a public issue of shares, etc.). **2** to accept financial responsibility for (a commercial project or enterprise). **3** *Insurance.* **3a** to sign and issue (an insurance policy) thus accepting liability. **3b** to insure (a property or risk). **3c** to accept liability up to (a specified amount) in an insurance policy. **4** to write (words, a signature, etc.) beneath (other written matter). **5** to support.

underwriter (ˈʌndəˌraɪtə) *n* **1** a person or enterprise that underwrites public issues of shares, bonds, etc. **2a** a person or enterprise that underwrites insurance policies. **2b** an employee or agent of an insurance company who determines the premiums payable.

undesirable ➊ (ˌʌndɪˈzaɪərəbᵊl) *adj* **1** not desirable or pleasant; objectionable. ◆ *n* **2** a person or thing considered undesirable.
►ˌ**undeˌsira'bility** *or* ˌ**unde'sirableness** *n* ►ˌ**unde'sirably** *adv*

undetermined (ˌʌndɪˈtɜːmɪnd) *adj* **1** not yet resolved; undecided. **2** not known or discovered.

undies (ˈʌndɪz) *pl n Inf.* women's underwear.

undine (ˈʌndiːn) *n* any of various female water spirits. [C17: from NL *undina,* from L *unda* a wave]

undisputed world champion *n Boxing.* a boxer who holds the World Boxing Association and the World Boxing Council world championship titles simultaneously.

undistributed (ˌʌndɪˈstrɪbjʊtɪd) *adj* **1** *Logic.* (of a term) referring only to some members of the class designated by the term, as *doctors* in *some doctors are overworked.* **2** *Business.* (of a profit) not paid in dividends to the shareholders of a company but retained to help finance its trading.

undo ➊ (ʌnˈduː) *vb* **undoes, undoing, undid, undone.** (*mainly tr*) **1** (*also intr*) to untie, unwrap, or open or become untied, unwrapped, etc. **2** to reverse the effects of. **3** to cause the downfall of.

undoing ➊ (ʌnˈduːɪŋ) *n* **1** ruin; downfall. **2** the cause of downfall: *drink was his undoing.*

undone[1] ➊ (ʌnˈdʌn) *adj* not done or completed; unfinished.

undone[2] ➊ (ʌnˈdʌn) *adj* **1** ruined; destroyed. **2** unfastened; untied.

undoubted ➊ (ʌnˈdaʊtɪd) *adj* beyond doubt; certain or indisputable.
►**un'doubtedly** *adv*

undreamed (ʌnˈdriːmd) *or* **undreamt** (ʌnˈdrɛmt) *adj* (often foll. by *of*) not thought of, conceived, or imagined.

undress ➊ (ʌnˈdrɛs) *vb* **1** to take off clothes from (oneself or another). **2** (*tr*) to strip of ornamentation. **3** (*tr*) to remove the dressing from (a wound). ◆ *n* **4** partial or complete nakedness. **5** informal or normal working clothes or uniform.

undressed (ʌnˈdrɛst) *adj* **1** partially or completely naked. **2** (of an animal hide) not fully processed. **3** (of food, esp. salad) not prepared with sauce or dressing.

undue ➊ (ʌnˈdjuː) *adj* **1** excessive or unwarranted. **2** unjust, improper, or illegal. **3** (of a debt, bond, etc.) not yet payable.

> **USAGE NOTE** The use of *undue* in sentences such as *there is no cause for undue alarm* is redundant and should be avoided.

THESAURUS

understood *adj* **2** = **implied**, implicit, inferred, tacit, unspoken, unstated **3** = **assumed**, accepted, axiomatic, presumed, taken for granted

understudy *n* **3, 4** = **stand-in**, double, fill-in, replacement, reserve, sub, substitute

undertake *vb* **1** = **agree**, bargain, commit oneself, contract, covenant, engage, guarantee, pledge, promise, stipulate, take upon oneself **2** = **take on**, attempt, begin, commence, embark on, endeavour, enter upon, set about, tackle, try

undertaker *n* = **funeral director**, mortician (*US*)

undertaking *n* **1** = **task**, affair, attempt, business, effort, endeavour, enterprise, game, operation, project, venture **2** = **promise**, assurance, commitment, pledge, solemn word, vow, word, word of honour

undertone *n* **1** = **murmur**, low tone, subdued voice, whisper **2** = **undercurrent**, atmosphere, feeling, flavour, hint, suggestion, tinge, touch, trace, vibes (*sl.*)

undervalue *vb* = **underrate**, depreciate, hold cheap, look down on, make light of, minimize, misjudge, misprize, set no store by, underestimate

Antonyms *vb* exaggerate, overestimate, overrate, overvalue

underwater *adj* **1** = **submerged**, submarine, sunken, undersea

under way *adj* **1** = **in progress**, afoot, begun, going on, in business, in motion, in operation, started

underwear *n* = **underclothes**, lingerie, smalls (*inf.*), underclothing, undergarments, underlinen, underthings, undies (*inf.*), unmentionables (*humorous*)

underweight *adj* = **skinny**, emaciated, half-starved, puny, skin and bone, undernourished, undersized

underworld *n* **1a** = **criminals**, criminal element, gangland (*inf.*), gangsters, organized crime **2** = **nether world**, abode of the dead, Hades, hell, infernal region, nether regions, the inferno

underwrite *vb* **1** = **finance**, back, fund, guarantee, insure, provide security, sponsor, subsidize **3a** = **sign**, countersign, endorse, initial, subscribe **5** = **support**, agree to, approve, consent, O.K. *or* okay, sanction

undesirable *adj* **1** = **objectionable**, disagreeable, disliked, distasteful, dreaded, for the birds (*inf.*), obnoxious, offensive, out of place, repugnant, strictly for the birds (*inf.*), (to be) avoided, unacceptable, unattractive, unpleasing, unpopular, unsavoury, unsuitable, unwanted, unwelcome, unwished-for

Antonyms *adj* acceptable, agreeable, appealing, attractive, desirable, inviting, pleasing, popular, welcome

undo *vb* **1** = **open**, disengage, disentangle, loose, loosen, unbutton, unclasp, unfasten, unlock, unstrap, untie, unwrap **2** = **reverse**, annul, cancel, invalidate, neutralize, nullify, offset, wipe out **3** = **ruin**, bring to naught, defeat, destroy, impoverish, mar, overturn, quash, shatter, subvert, undermine, upset, wreck

undoing *n* **1** = **ruin**, collapse, defeat, destruction, disgrace, downfall, humiliation, overthrow, overturn, reversal, ruination, shame **2** = **downfall**, affliction, blight, curse, fatal flaw, misfortune, the last straw, trial, trouble, weakness

undone[1] *adj* = **unfinished**, incomplete, left, neglected, not completed, not done, omitted, outstanding, passed over, unattended to, unfulfilled, unperformed

Antonyms *adj* accomplished, attended to, complete, done, finished, fulfilled, performed

undone[2] *adj* = **ruined**, betrayed, destroyed, forlorn, hapless, overcome, prostrate, wretched

undoubted *adj* = **certain**, acknowledged, definite, evident, incontrovertible, indisputable, indubitable, obvious, sure, undisputed, unquestionable, unquestioned

undoubtedly *adv* = **certainly**, assuredly, beyond a shadow of (a) doubt, beyond question, come hell or high water (*inf.*), definitely, doubtless, of course, surely, undeniably, unmistakably, unquestionably, without doubt

undress *vb* **1** = **strip**, disrobe, divest oneself of, peel off (*sl.*), shed, take off one's clothes ◆ *n* **4** = **nakedness**, deshabille, disarray, nudity

undue *adj* **1** = **excessive**, disproportionate, extravagant, extreme, immoderate, improper, in-

undulant (ˈʌndjʊlənt) *adj Rare.* resembling waves; undulating.
▸**ˈundulance** *n*

undulant fever *n* another name for **brucellosis**. [C19: so called because the fever symptoms are intermittent]

undulate Ⓣ *vb* (ˈʌndjʊˌleɪt), **undulates, undulating, undulated. 1** to move or cause to move in waves or as if in waves. **2** to have or provide with a wavy form or appearance. ◆ *adj* (ˈʌndjʊlɪt, -ˌleɪt). **3** having a wavy or rippled appearance, margin, or form: *an undulate leaf.* [C17: from L *unda* a wave]
▸**ˈunduˌlator** *n* ▸**ˈundulatory** *adj*

undulation (ˌʌndjʊˈleɪʃən) *n* **1** the act or an instance of undulating. **2** any wave or wavelike form, line, etc.

unduly Ⓣ (ʌnˈdjuːlɪ) *adv* excessively.

undying Ⓣ (ʌnˈdaɪɪŋ) *adj* unending; eternal.
▸**unˈdyingly** *adv*

unearned (ʌnˈɜːnd) *adj* **1** not deserved. **2** not yet earned.

unearned income *n* income from property, investment, etc., comprising rent, interest, and dividends.

unearth Ⓣ (ʌnˈɜːθ) *vb (tr)* **1** to dig up out of the earth. **2** to reveal or discover, esp. by exhaustive searching.

unearthly Ⓣ (ʌnˈɜːθlɪ) *adj* **1** ghostly; eerie: *unearthly screams.* **2** heavenly; sublime: *unearthly music.* **3** ridiculous or unreasonable (esp. in **unearthly hour**).
▸**unˈearthliness** *n*

uneasy Ⓣ (ʌnˈiːzɪ) *adj* **1** (of a person) anxious; apprehensive. **2** (of a condition) precarious: *an uneasy truce.* **3** (of a thought, etc.) disquieting.
▸**unˈease** *n* ▸**unˈeasily** *adv* ▸**unˈeasiness** *n*

uneatable (ʌnˈiːtəbᵊl) *adj* (of food) not fit or suitable for eating, esp. because it is rotten or unattractive.

uneconomic Ⓣ (ˌʌniːkəˈnɒmɪk, ˌʌnɛkə-) *adj* not economic; not profitable.

uneconomical (ˌʌniːkəˈnɒmɪkᵊl, -ɛkə-) *adj* not economical; wasteful.

unemployable (ˌʌnɪmˈplɔɪəbᵊl) *adj* unable or unfit to keep a job.
▸**ˌunemˌployaˈbility** *n*

unemployed Ⓣ (ˌʌnɪmˈplɔɪd) *adj* **1a** without remunerative employment; out of work. **1b** (*as collective n; preceded by the*): *the unemployed.* **2** not being used; idle.

unemployment (ˌʌnɪmˈplɔɪmənt) *n* **1** the condition of being unemployed. **2** the number of unemployed workers, often as a percentage of the total labour force.

unemployment benefit *n* (in Britain, formerly) a regular payment to a person who is out of work: replaced by jobseeker's allowance in 1996. Informal term: **dole.**

unequal Ⓣ (ʌnˈiːkwəl) *adj* **1** not equal in quantity, size, rank, value, etc. **2** (foll. by *to*) inadequate; insufficient. **3** not evenly balanced. **4** (of character, quality, etc.) irregular; inconsistent. **5** (of a contest, etc.) having competitors of different ability.

unequalled Ⓣ *or US* **unequaled** (ʌnˈiːkwəld) *adj* not equalled; unrivalled; supreme.

unequivocal Ⓣ (ˌʌnɪˈkwɪvəkᵊl) *adj* not ambiguous; plain.
▸**ˌuneˈquivocally** *adv* ▸**ˌuneˈquivocalness** *n*

unerring Ⓣ (ʌnˈɜːrɪŋ) *adj* **1** not missing the mark or target. **2** consistently accurate; certain.
▸**unˈerringly** *adv* ▸**unˈerringness** *n*

UNESCO (juːˈnɛskəʊ) *n acronym for* United Nations Educational, Scientific, and Cultural Organization.

uneven Ⓣ (ʌnˈiːvən) *adj* **1** (of a surface, etc.) not level or flat. **2** spasmodic or variable. **3** not parallel, straight, or horizontal. **4** not fairly matched: *an uneven race.* **5** *Arch.* not equal.
▸**unˈevenly** *adv* ▸**unˈevenness** *n*

uneventful Ⓣ (ˌʌnɪˈvɛntfʊl) *adj* ordinary, routine, or quiet.
▸**ˌuneˈventfully** *adv* ▸**ˌuneˈventfulness** *n*

unexampled Ⓣ (ˌʌnɪgˈzɑːmpᵊld) *adj* without precedent or parallel.

unexceptionable (ˌʌnɪkˈsɛpʃənəbᵊl) *adj* beyond criticism or objection.
▸**ˌunexˈceptionably** *adv*

unexceptional Ⓣ (ˌʌnɪkˈsɛpʃənᵊl) *adj* **1** usual, ordinary, or normal. **2** subject to or allowing no exceptions.
▸**ˌunexˈceptionally** *adv*

unexcited (ˌʌnɪkˈsaɪtɪd) *adj* **1** not aroused to pleasure, interest, agitation, etc. **2** (of an atom, molecule, etc.) remaining in its ground state.

unexpected Ⓣ (ˌʌnɪkˈspɛktɪd) *adj* surprising or unforeseen.
▸**ˌunexˈpectedly** *adv* ▸**ˌunexˈpectedness** *n*

unfailing Ⓣ (ʌnˈfeɪlɪŋ) *adj* **1** not failing; unflagging. **2** continuous. **3** sure; certain.
▸**unˈfailingly** *adv* ▸**unˈfailingness** *n*

unfair Ⓣ (ʌnˈfɛə) *adj* **1** characterized by inequality or injustice. **2** dishonest or unethical.
▸**unˈfairly** *adv* ▸**unˈfairness** *n*

unfaithful Ⓣ (ʌnˈfeɪθfʊl) *adj* **1** not true to a promise, vow, etc. **2** not true to a wife, husband, lover, etc., esp. in having sexual intercourse

THESAURUS

appropriate, inordinate, intemperate, needless, overmuch, too great, too much, uncalled-for, undeserved, unjustified, unnecessary, unseemly, unsuitable, unwarranted
Antonyms *adj* appropriate, due, fitting, justified, necessary, proper, suitable, well-considered

undulate *vb* **1** = **wave**, billow, heave, ripple, rise and fall, roll, surge, swell

unduly *adv* = **excessively**, disproportionately, extravagantly, immoderately, improperly, inordinately, out of all proportion, overly, overmuch, unjustifiably, unnecessarily, unreasonably
Antonyms *adv* duly, justifiably, moderately, ordinately, properly, proportionately, reasonably

undying *adj* = **eternal**, constant, continuing, deathless, everlasting, imperishable, indestructible, inextinguishable, infinite, perennial, permanent, perpetual, sempiternal (*literary*), undiminished, unending, unfading
Antonyms *adj* ephemeral, finite, fleeting, impermanent, inconstant, momentary, mortal, perishable, short-lived

unearth *vb* **1** = **dig up**, disinter, dredge up, excavate, exhume **2** = **discover**, bring to light, expose, ferret out, find, reveal, root up, turn up, uncover

unearthly *adj* **1** = **eerie**, eldritch (*poetic*), ghostly, haunted, nightmarish, phantom, preternatural, spectral, spooky (*inf.*), strange, supernatural, uncanny, weird **3** = **unreasonable**, abnormal, absurd, extraordinary, ridiculous, strange, ungodly (*inf.*), unholy (*inf.*)

uneasiness *n* **1-3** = **anxiety**, agitation, alarm, apprehension, apprehensiveness, disquiet, doubt, dubiety, misgiving, nervousness, perturbation, qualms, suspicion, trepidation, worry
Antonyms *n* calm, composure, cool, ease, peace, quiet, serenity

uneasy *adj* **1** = **anxious**, agitated, apprehensive, discomposed, disturbed, edgy, ill at ease, impatient, jittery (*inf.*), like a fish out of water, nervous, on edge, perturbed, restive, restless, troubled, twitchy (*inf.*), uncomfortable, unsettled, upset, wired (*sl.*), worried **2** = **precarious**, awkward, constrained, insecure, shaky, strained, tense, uncomfortable, unstable **3** = **disturbing**, bothering, dismaying, disquieting, troubling, upsetting, worrying
Antonyms *adj* ≠ **anxious:** at ease, calm, comfortable, relaxed, tranquil, unfazed (*inf.*), unflustered, unperturbed, unruffled

uneconomic *adj* = **unprofitable**, loss-making, nonpaying, non-profit-making, nonviable
Antonyms *adj* economic, money-making, productive, profitable, remunerative, viable

unemployed *adj* **1a** = **out of work**, idle, jobless, laid off, on the dole (*Brit. inf.*), out of a job, redundant, resting (*of an actor*), workless

unequal *adj* **1** = **different**, differing, disparate, dissimilar, not uniform, unlike, unmatched, variable, varying **2** *with* **to** = **inadequate for**, found wanting, insufficient for, not up to **3** = **disproportionate**, asymmetrical, ill-matched, irregular, unbalanced, uneven
Antonyms *adj* ≠ **different:** equal, equivalent, identical, like, matched, similar, uniform

unequalled *adj* = **incomparable**, beyond compare, inimitable, matchless, nonpareil, paramount, peerless, pre-eminent, second to none, supreme, transcendent, unmatched, unparalleled, unrivalled, unsurpassed, without equal

unequivocal *adj* = **clear**, absolute, black-and-white, certain, clear-cut, cut-and-dried (*inf.*), decisive, definite, direct, evident, explicit, incontrovertible, indubitable, manifest, plain, positive, straight, unambiguous, uncontestable, unmistakable
Antonyms *adj* ambiguous, doubtful, equivocal, evasive, indecisive, noncommittal, vague

unerring *adj* = **accurate**, certain, exact, faultless, impeccable, infallible, perfect, sure, unfailing

uneven *adj* **1** = **rough**, bumpy, not flat, not level, not smooth **2** = **variable**, broken, changeable, fitful, fluctuating, intermittent, irregular, jerky, patchy, spasmodic, unsteady **3** = **unbalanced**, asymmetrical, lopsided, not parallel, odd, out of true **4** = **unequal**, disparate, ill-matched, one-sided, unfair
Antonyms *adj* ≠ **rough:** even, flat, level, plane, smooth

uneventful *adj* = **humdrum**, boring, commonplace, dull, ho-hum, monotonous, ordinary, quiet, routine, tedious, unexceptional, unexciting, uninteresting, unmemorable, unremarkable, unvaried
Antonyms *adj* eventful, exceptional, exciting, interesting, memorable, momentous, remarkable

unexampled *adj* = **unprecedented**, unequalled, unheard-of, unique, unmatched, unparalleled

unexceptional *adj* **1** = **ordinary**, bog-standard (*Brit. & Irish sl.*), common or garden (*inf.*), commonplace, conventional, insignificant, mediocre, no great shakes (*inf.*), normal, nothing to write home about (*inf.*), pedestrian, run-of-the-mill, undistinguished, unimpressive, unremarkable, usual
Antonyms *adj* distinguished, exceptional, impressive, notable, noteworthy, outstanding, remarkable, significant, unusual

unexpected *adj* = **unforeseen**, abrupt, accidental, astonishing, chance, fortuitous, not bargained for, out of the blue, startling, sudden, surprising, unanticipated, unlooked-for, unpredictable
Antonyms *adj* anticipated, awaited, expected, foreseen, normal, planned, predictable

unfailing *adj* **1, 2** = **continuous**, bottomless, boundless, ceaseless, continual, endless, inexhaustible, never-failing, persistent, unflagging, unlimited **3** = **reliable**, certain, constant, dependable, faithful, infallible, loyal, staunch, steadfast, sure, tried and true, true
Antonyms *adj* ≠ **reliable:** disloyal, fallible, inconstant, uncertain, unfaithful, unreliable, unsure, untrustworthy

unfair *adj* **1** = **biased**, arbitrary, bigoted, discriminatory, inequitable, one-sided, partial, partisan, prejudiced, unjust **2** = **unscrupulous**, crooked (*inf.*), dishonest, dishonourable, uncalled-for, unethical, unprincipled, unsporting, unwarranted, wrongful
Antonyms *adj* ≠ **unscrupulous:** ethical, fair, honest, just, principled, scrupulous

unfaithful *adj* **1** = **disloyal**, deceitful, faithless, false, false-hearted, perfidious, recreant (*arch.*), traitorous, treacherous, treasonable, unreliable, untrustworthy **2** = **faithless**, adulterous, fickle, inconstant, two-timing (*inf.*), unchaste, untrue

with someone else. **3** inaccurate; untrustworthy: *unfaithful copy*. **4** *Obs.* not having religious faith.
▶**un'faithfully** *adv* ▶**un'faithfulness** *n*

unfamiliar ⓣ (ˌʌnfə'mɪljə) *adj* **1** not known or experienced; strange. **2** (*postpositive;* foll. by *with*) not familiar.
▶**unfamiliarity** (ˌʌnfəˌmɪlɪ'ærɪtɪ) *n* ▶**unˌfa'miliarly** *adv*

unfasten ⓣ (ʌn'fɑːsᵊn) *vb* to undo, untie, or open or become undone, untied, or opened.

unfathered (ʌn'fɑːðəd) *adj* **1** having no known father. **2** of unknown or uncertain origin.

unfathomable ⓣ (ʌn'fæðəməbᵊl) *adj* **1** incapable of being fathomed; immeasurable. **2** incomprehensible.
▶**un'fathomableness** *n* ▶**un'fathomably** *adv*

unfavourable ⓣ *or US* **unfavorable** (ʌn'feɪvərəbᵊl) *adj* not favourable; adverse or inauspicious.
▶**un'favourably** *or US* **un'favorably** *adv*

unfazed (ʌn'feɪzd) *adj Inf.* not disconcerted; unperturbed.

unfeeling ⓣ (ʌn'fiːlɪŋ) *adj* **1** without sympathy; callous. **2** without physical feeling or sensation.
▶**un'feelingly** *adv* ▶**un'feelingness** *n*

unfinished ⓣ (ʌn'fɪnɪʃt) *adj* **1** incomplete or imperfect. **2** (of paint, polish, varnish, etc.) without an applied finish; rough. **3** (of fabric) unbleached or not processed.

unfit ⓣ (ʌn'fɪt) *adj* **1** (*postpositive;* often foll. by *for*) unqualified, incapable, or incompetent: *unfit for military service*. **2** (*postpositive;* often foll. by *for*) unsuitable or inappropriate: *the ground was unfit for football*. **3** in poor physical condition. ◆ *vb* **unfits, unfitting, unfitted. 4** (*tr*) *Rare.* to render unfit.
▶**un'fitly** *adv* ▶**un'fitness** *n*

unfix (ʌn'fɪks) *vb* (*tr*) **1** to unfasten, detach, or loosen. **2** to unsettle or disturb.

unflappable ⓣ (ʌn'flæpəbᵊl) *adj Inf.* hard to upset; calm; composed.
▶**unˌflappa'bility** *n* ▶**un'flappably** *adv*

unfledged ⓣ (ʌn'flɛdʒd) *adj* **1** (of a young bird) not having developed adult feathers. **2** immature and undeveloped.

unflinching ⓣ (ʌn'flɪntʃɪŋ) *adj* not shrinking from danger, difficulty, etc.
▶**un'flinchingly** *adv*

unfold ⓣ (ʌn'fəʊld) *vb* **1** to open or spread out or be opened or spread out from a folded state. **2** to reveal or be revealed: *the truth unfolds*. **3** to develop or expand or be developed or expanded.
▶**un'folder** *n*

unfortunate ⓣ (ʌn'fɔːtʃənɪt) *adj* **1** causing or attended by misfortune. **2** unlucky or unhappy: *an unfortunate character*. **3** regrettable or unsuitable: *an unfortunate speech*. ◆ *n* **4** an unlucky person.
▶**un'fortunately** *adv*

unfounded ⓣ (ʌn'faʊndɪd) *adj* **1** (of ideas, allegations, etc.) baseless; groundless. **2** not yet founded or established.
▶**un'foundedly** *adv* ▶**un'foundedness** *n*

unfranked income (ʌn'fræŋkt) *n* any income from an investment that does not qualify as franked investment income.

unfreeze (ʌn'friːz) *vb* **unfreezes, unfreezing, unfroze, unfrozen. 1** to thaw or cause to thaw. **2** (*tr*) to relax governmental restrictions on (wages, prices, credit, etc.) or on the manufacture or sale of (goods, etc.).

unfriended (ʌn'frɛndɪd) *adj Now rare.* without a friend or friends; friendless.

unfriendly ⓣ (ʌn'frɛndlɪ) *adj* **unfriendlier, unfriendliest. 1** not friendly; hostile. **2** unfavourable or disagreeable. ◆ *adv* **3** *Rare.* in an unfriendly manner.
▶**un'friendliness** *n*

unfrock (ʌn'frɒk) *vb* (*tr*) to deprive (a person in holy orders) of ecclesiastical status.

unfunded debt (ʌn'fʌndɪd) *n* a short-term floating debt not represented by bonds.

unfurl (ʌn'fɜːl) *vb* to unroll, unfold, or spread out or be unrolled, unfolded, or spread out from a furled state.

ungainly ⓣ (ʌn'geɪnlɪ) *adj* **ungainlier, ungainliest. 1** lacking grace when moving. **2** difficult to move or use; unwieldy. [C17: from UN-[1] + obs. or dialect *gainly* graceful]
▶**un'gainliness** *n*

ungodly ⓣ (ʌn'gɒdlɪ) *adj* **ungodlier, ungodliest. 1a** wicked, sinful. **1b** (*as collective n;* preceded by *the*): *the ungodly*. **2** *Inf.* unseemly; outrageous (esp. in **an ungodly hour**).
▶**un'godliness** *n*

ungovernable ⓣ (ʌn'gʌvənəbᵊl) *adj* not able to be disciplined, restrained, etc.: *an ungovernable temper*.
▶**un'governableness** *n* ▶**un'governably** *adv*

ungual ('ʌŋgwəl) *adj* **1** of, relating to, or affecting the fingernails or toenails. **2** of or relating to an unguis. [C19: from L *unguis* nail]

unguarded ⓣ (ʌn'gɑːdɪd) *adj* **1** unprotected; vulnerable. **2** open; frank. **3** incautious.
▶**un'guardedly** *adv* ▶**un'guardedness** *n*

unguent ('ʌŋgwənt) *n* a less common name for an **ointment.** [C15: from L, from *unguere* to anoint]

unguiculate (ʌŋ'gwɪkjʊlɪt, -ˌleɪt) *adj* **1** (of mammals) having claws or

THESAURUS

3 = **inaccurate**, distorted, erroneous, imperfect, imprecise, inexact, unreliable, untrustworthy
Antonyms *adj* ≠ **faithless:** constant, faithful ≠ **disloyal:** faithful, loyal, steadfast, true, trustworthy ≠ **inaccurate:** accurate, exact, perfect, precise, reliable

unfamiliar *adj* **1** = **strange**, alien, beyond one's ken, curious, different, little known, new, novel, out-of-the-way, unaccustomed, uncommon, unknown, unusual **2** **unfamiliar with** = **unacquainted with**, a stranger to, inexperienced in, unaccustomed to, unconversant with, uninformed about, uninitiated in, unpractised in, unskilled at, unversed in
Antonyms *adj* ≠ **strange:** accustomed, average, common, commonplace, everyday, familiar, normal, unexceptional, usual, well-known ≠ **unacquainted with:** accustomed to, acquainted with, conversant with, experienced in, familiar with, knowledgeable about, well-versed in

unfasten *vb* = **undo**, detach, disconnect, let go, loosen, open, separate, unclasp, uncouple, unlace, unlock, unstrap, untie

unfathomable *adj* **1** = **immeasurable**, bottomless, unmeasured, unplumbed, unsounded **2** = **baffling**, abstruse, deep, esoteric, impenetrable, incomprehensible, indecipherable, inexplicable, profound, unknowable

unfavourable *adj* = **adverse**, bad, contrary, disadvantageous, ill-suited, inauspicious, infelicitous, inopportune, ominous, threatening, unfortunate, unlucky, unpromising, unpropitious, unseasonable, unsuited, untimely, untoward

unfeeling *adj* **1** = **callous**, apathetic, cold, cruel, hardened, hardhearted, heartless, inhuman, insensitive, pitiless, stony, uncaring, unsympathetic **2** = **numb**, insensate, insensible, sensationless
Antonyms *adj* ≠ **callous:** benevolent, caring, concerned, feeling, gentle, humane, kind, sensitive, sympathetic

unfinished *adj* **1** = **incomplete**, deficient, half-done, imperfect, in the making, lacking, unaccomplished, uncompleted, undone, unfulfilled, wanting **2** = **rough**, bare, crude, natural, raw, sketchy, unpolished, unrefined, unvarnished
Antonyms *adj* ≠ **rough:** finished, flawless, perfected, polished, refined, smooth, varnished

unfit *adj* **1** = **incapable**, ill-equipped, inadequate, incompetent, ineligible, no good, not cut out for, not equal to, not up to, unprepared, unqualified, untrained, useless **2** = **unsuitable**, ill-adapted, inadequate, inappropriate, ineffective, not designed, not fit, unsuited, useless **3** = **out of shape**, debilitated, decrepit, feeble, flabby, in poor condition, out of kelter, out of trim, unhealthy
Antonyms *adj* ≠ **incapable:** able, capable, competent, equipped, qualified, ready ≠ **unsuitable:** acceptable, adequate, appropriate, suitable ≠ **out of shape:** fit, healthy, in good condition, strong, sturdy, well

unflappable *adj Informal* = **imperturbable**, calm, collected, composed, cool, impassive, level-headed, not given to worry, self-possessed, unfazed (*inf.*), unruffled
Antonyms *adj* excitable, flappable, hot-headed, nervous, temperamental, twitchy (*inf.*), volatile

unfledged *adj* **2** = **inexperienced**, callow, green, immature, raw, undeveloped, untried, young

unflinching *adj* = **determined**, bold, constant, firm, immovable, resolute, stalwart, staunch, steadfast, steady, unfaltering, unshaken, unshrinking, unswerving, unwavering
Antonyms *adj* cowed, faltering, scared, shaken, shrinking, wavering

unfold *vb* **1** = **open**, disentangle, expand, flatten, spread out, straighten, stretch out, undo, unfurl, unravel, unroll, unwrap **2** = **reveal**, clarify, describe, disclose, divulge, explain, illustrate, make known, present, show, uncover **3** = **develop**, bear fruit, blossom, evolve, expand, grow, mature

unfortunate *adj* **1** = **disastrous**, adverse, calamitous, ill-fated, ill-starred, infelicitous, inopportune, ruinous, unfavourable, untimely, untoward **2** = **unlucky**, cursed, doomed, hapless, hopeless, luckless, out of luck, poor, star-crossed, unhappy, unprosperous, unsuccessful, wretched **3** = **regrettable**, deplorable, ill-advised, inappropriate, lamentable, unbecoming, unsuitable
Antonyms *adj* ≠ **disastrous:** auspicious, felicitous, fortuitous, fortunate, opportune, timely ≠ **unlucky:** fortunate, happy, lucky, successful ≠ **regrettable:** appropriate, becoming, unsuitable

unfounded *adj* **1** = **groundless**, baseless, fabricated, false, idle, spurious, trumped up, unjustified, unproven, unsubstantiated, vain, without basis, without foundation
Antonyms *adj* attested, confirmed, factual, justified, proven, substantiated, verified

unfriendly *adj* **1** = **hostile**, aloof, antagonistic, chilly, cold, disagreeable, distant, ill-disposed, inhospitable, not on speaking terms, quarrelsome, sour, surly, uncongenial, unneighbourly, unsociable **2** = **unfavourable**, alien, hostile, inauspicious, inhospitable, inimical, unpropitious
Antonyms *adj* ≠ **hostile:** affable, amiable, convivial, friendly, hospitable, sociable, warm ≠ **unfavourable:** auspicious, congenial, hospitable, propitious

ungainly *adj* **1** = **awkward**, clumsy, gangling, gawky, inelegant, loutish, lubberly, lumbering, slouching, uncoordinated, uncouth, ungraceful
Antonyms *adj* attractive, comely, elegant, graceful, pleasing

ungodly *adj* **1a** = **wicked**, blasphemous, corrupt, depraved, godless, immoral, impious, irreligious, profane, sinful, vile **2** *Informal* = **unreasonable**, dreadful, horrendous, intolerable, outrageous, unearthly, unholy (*inf.*), unseemly

ungovernable *adj* = **uncontrollable**, unmanageable, unruly, wild

unguarded *adj* **1** = **unprotected**, defenceless, open to attack, undefended, unpatrolled, vulnerable **2** = **frank**, artless, candid, direct, guileless, open, straightforward **3** = **careless**, foolhardy, heedless, ill-considered, impolitic, imprudent, incautious, indiscreet, rash, thoughtless, uncircumspect, undiplomatic, unthinking, unwary
Antonyms *adj* ≠ **careless:** cagey (*inf.*), careful, cautious, diplomatic, discreet, guarded, prudent, wary

nails. **2** (of petals) having a clawlike base. ◆ *n* **3** an unguiculate mammal. [C19: from NL *unguiculātus*, from L *unguiculus*, dim. of *unguis* nail]

unguis (ˈʌŋgwɪs) *n, pl* **ungues** (-gwiːz). **1** a nail, claw, or hoof, or the part of the digit giving rise to it. **2** the clawlike base of a petal. [C18: from L]

ungulate (ˈʌŋgjʊlɪt, -ˌleɪt) *n* any of a large group of mammals all of which have hooves: divided into odd-toed ungulates (see **perissodactyl**) and even-toed ungulates (see **artiodactyl**). [C19: from LL *ungulātus* having hooves, from *ungula* hoof]

unhallowed ⓣ (ʌnˈhæləʊd) *adj* **1** not consecrated or holy: *unhallowed ground.* **2** sinful.

unhand (ʌnˈhænd) *vb (tr) Arch. or literary.* to release from the grasp.

unhappy ⓣ (ʌnˈhæpɪ) *adj* **unhappier, unhappiest. 1** not joyful; sad or depressed. **2** unfortunate or wretched: *an unhappy fellow.* **3** tactless or inappropriate: *an unhappy remark.*
▸**unˈhappily** *adv* ▸**unˈhappiness** *n*

UNHCR *abbrev. for* United Nations High Commissioner for Refugees.

unhealthy ⓣ (ʌnˈhɛlθɪ) *adj* **unhealthier, unhealthiest. 1** characterized by ill health; sick. **2** characteristic of, conducive to, or resulting from ill health: *an unhealthy complexion.* **3** morbid or unwholesome. **4** *Inf.* dangerous; risky.
▸**unˈhealthily** *adv* ▸**unˈhealthiness** *n*

unheard (ʌnˈhɜːd) *adj* **1** not heard; not perceived by the ear. **2** not listened to: *his warning went unheard.* **3** *Arch.* unheard-of.

unheard-of ⓣ *adj* **1** previously unknown: *an unheard-of actress.* **2** without precedent: *an unheard-of treatment.* **3** highly offensive: *unheard-of behaviour.*

unhinge ⓣ (ʌnˈhɪndʒ) *vb* **unhinges, unhinging, unhinged.** *(tr)* **1** to remove (a door, etc.) from its hinges. **2** to derange or unbalance (a person, his mind, etc.). **3** to disrupt or unsettle (a process or state of affairs).

unholy ⓣ (ʌnˈhəʊlɪ) *adj* **unholier, unholiest. 1** not holy or sacred. **2** immoral or depraved. **3** *Inf.* outrageous or unnatural: *an unholy alliance.*
▸**unˈholiness** *n*

unhook (ʌnˈhʊk) *vb* **1** *(tr)* to remove (something) from a hook. **2** *(tr)* to unfasten the hook of (a dress, etc.). **3** *(intr)* to become unfastened or be capable of unfastening: *the dress wouldn't unhook.*

unhorse (ʌnˈhɔːs) *vb* **unhorses, unhorsing, unhorsed.** *(tr)* **1** *(usually passive)* to knock or throw from a horse. **2** to overthrow or dislodge, as from a powerful position.

unhouseled (ʌnˈhaʊzəld) *adj Arch.* not having received the Eucharist. [C16: from *un-* + obs. *housel* to administer the sacrament, from OE *hūsl* (n), *hūslian* (vb), from ?]

uni (ˈjuːnɪ) *n Inf.* short for **university.**

uni- *combining form.* consisting of, relating to, or having only one: *unilateral.* [from L *ūnus* one]

Uniat (ˈjuːnɪˌæt) *or* **Uniate** (ˈjuːnɪɪt, -ˌeɪt) *adj* **1** designating any of the Eastern Churches that retain their own liturgy but submit to papal authority. ◆ *n* **2** a member of one of these Churches. [C19: from Russian *uniyat*, from Polish *unja* union, from LL *ūniō*; see UNION]
▸**ˈUniˌatism** *n*

uniaxial (ˌjuːnɪˈæksɪəl) *adj* **1** (esp. of plants) having an unbranched main axis. **2** (of a crystal) having only one direction along which double refraction of light does not occur.

unicameral (ˌjuːnɪˈkæmərəl) *adj* of or characterized by a single legislative chamber.
▸**ˌuniˈcameralism** *n* ▸**ˌuniˈcameralist** *n* ▸**ˌuniˈcamerally** *adv*

UNICEF (ˈjuːnɪˌsɛf) *n acronym for* United Nations Children's Fund (formerly, United Nations International Children's Emergency Fund).

unicellular (ˌjuːnɪˈsɛljʊlə) *adj* (of organisms, such as protozoans and certain algae) consisting of a single cell.
▸**ˌuniˌcelluˈlarity** *n*

unicorn (ˈjuːnɪˌkɔːn) *n* **1** an imaginary creature usually depicted as a white horse with one long spiralled horn growing from its forehead. **2** *Old Testament.* a two-horned animal: mistranslation in the Authorized Version of the original Hebrew. [C13: from OF, from L *ūnicornis* one-horned, from *ūnus* one + *cornu* a horn]

unicycle (ˈjuːnɪˌsaɪkᵊl) *n* a one-wheeled vehicle driven by pedals, esp. one used in a circus, etc. Also called: **monocycle.** [from UNI- + CYCLE, on the model of TRICYCLE]
▸**ˈuniˌcyclist** *n*

unidirectional (ˌjuːnɪdɪˈrɛkʃənᵊl) *adj* having, moving in, or operating in only one direction.

UNIDO (juːˈniːdəʊ) *n acronym for* United Nations Industrial Development Organization.

Unification Church *n* a religious sect founded in 1954 by Sun Myung Moon (born 1920), S Korean industrialist and religious leader.

unified field theory *n* any theory capable of describing in one set of equations the properties of gravitational fields, electromagnetic fields, and strong and weak nuclear interactions. No satisfactory theory has yet been found. See also **grand unified theory.**

uniform ⓣ (ˈjuːnɪˌfɔːm) *n* **1** a prescribed identifying set of clothes for the members of an organization, such as soldiers or schoolchildren. **2** a single set of such clothes. **3** a characteristic feature of some class or group. ◆ *adj* **4** unchanging in form, quality, etc.: *a uniform surface.* **5** alike or like: *a line of uniform toys.* ◆ *vb (tr)* **6** to fit out (a body of soldiers, etc.) with uniforms. **7** to make uniform. [C16: from L *ūniformis*, from *ūnus* one + *forma* shape]
▸**ˈuniˌformly** *adv* ▸**ˈuniˌformness** *n*

Uniform Business Rate *n* a local tax in the UK paid by businesses, based on a local valuation of their premises and a rate fixed by central government that applies throughout the country. Abbrev.: **UBR.**

uniformitarianism (ˌjuːnɪˌfɔːmɪˈtɛərɪəˌnɪzəm) *n* the concept that the earth's surface was shaped in the past by gradual processes, such as erosion, and by small sudden changes, such as earthquakes, rather than by sudden divine acts, such as Noah's flood.
▸**ˌuniˌformiˈtarian** *n, adj*

uniformity ⓣ (ˌjuːnɪˈfɔːmɪtɪ) *n, pl* **uniformities. 1** a state or condition in which everything is regular, homogeneous, or unvarying. **2** lack of diversity or variation.

unify ⓣ (ˈjuːnɪˌfaɪ) *vb* **unifies, unifying, unified.** to make or become one; unite. [C16: from Med. L *ūnificāre*, from L *ūnus* one + *facere* to make]
▸**ˈuniˌfiable** *adj* ▸**ˌunifiˈcation** *n* ▸**ˈuniˌfier** *n*

unilateral (ˌjuːnɪˈlætərəl) *adj* **1** of, having, affecting, or occurring on only one side. **2** involving or performed by only one party of several: *unilateral disarmament.* **3** *Law.* (of contracts, obligations, etc.) made by, affecting, or binding one party only. **4** *Bot.* having or designating parts situated or turned to one side of an axis.
▸**ˌuniˈlateralism** *n* ▸**ˌuniˈlaterally** *adv*

Unilateral Declaration of Independence *n* a declaration of independence made by a dependent state without the assent of the protecting state. Abbrev.: **UDI.**

unimpeachable ⓣ (ˌʌnɪmˈpiːtʃəbᵊl) *adj* unquestionable as to honesty, truth, etc.
▸**ˌunimˈpeachably** *adv*

unimproved (ˌʌnɪmˈpruːvd) *adj* **1** not improved or made better. **2** (of land) not cleared, drained, cultivated, etc. **3** neglected; unused: *unimproved resources.*

THESAURUS

unhallowed *adj* **1** = **unconsecrated**, not sacred, unblessed, unholy, unsanctified **2** = **wicked**, damnable, evil, godless, irreverent, profane, sinful

unhappiness *n* **1, 2** = **sadness**, blues, dejection, depression, despondency, discontent, dissatisfaction, gloom, heartache, low spirits, melancholy, misery, sorrow, wretchedness

unhappy *adj* **1** = **sad**, blue, crestfallen, dejected, depressed, despondent, disconsolate, dispirited, down, downcast, down in the dumps (*inf.*), gloomy, long-faced, low, melancholy, miserable, mournful, sorrowful **2** = **unlucky**, cursed, hapless, ill-fated, ill-omened, luckless, unfortunate, wretched **3** = **inappropriate**, awkward, clumsy, gauche, ill-advised, ill-timed, inept, infelicitous, injudicious, malapropos, tactless, unsuitable, untactful
Antonyms *adj* ≠ **sad**: cheerful, chirpy (*inf.*), content, exuberant, genial, good-humoured, happy, joyful, light-hearted, overjoyed, over the moon (*inf.*), satisfied ≠ **unlucky**: fortunate, lucky ≠ **inappropriate**: apt, becoming, prudent, suitable, tactful

unhealthy *adj* **1** = **sick**, ailing, delicate, feeble, frail, infirm, in poor health, invalid, poorly (*inf.*), sickly, unsound, unwell, weak **2** = **harmful**, deleterious, detrimental, insalubrious, insanitary, noisome, noxious, unwholesome **3** = **unwholesome**, bad, baneful (*arch.*), corrupt, corrupting, degrading, demoralizing, morbid, negative, undesirable
Antonyms ≠ **sick**: fit, healthy, robust, well *adj* ≠ **unwholesome**: desirable, moral, positive ≠ **harmful**: beneficial, good, healthy, salubrious, salutary, wholesome

unheard-of *adj* **1** = **obscure**, little known, undiscovered, unfamiliar, unknown, unregarded, unremarked, unsung **2** = **unprecedented**, ground-breaking, inconceivable, never before encountered, new, novel, singular, unbelievable, undreamed of, unexampled, unique, unusual **3** = **shocking**, disgraceful, extreme, offensive, outlandish, outrageous, preposterous, unacceptable, unthinkable

unhinge *vb* **1** = **detach**, disconnect, disjoint, dislodge, remove **2** = **unbalance**, confound, confuse, craze, dement, derange, disorder, distemper (*arch.*), drive out of one's mind, madden, unsettle

unholy *adj* **2** = **evil**, base, corrupt, depraved, dishonest, heinous, immoral, iniquitous, irreligious, profane, sinful, ungodly, vile, wicked **3** *Informal* = **outrageous**, appalling, awful, dreadful, horrendous, shocking, unearthly, ungodly (*inf.*), unnatural, unreasonable
Antonyms *adj* ≠ **evil**: devout, faithful, godly, holy, pious, religious, saintly, virtuous

unification *n* = **union**, alliance, amalgamation, coalescence, coalition, combination, confederation, federation, fusion, merger, uniting

uniform *n* **1** = **outfit**, costume, dress, garb, habit, livery, regalia, regimentals, suit ◆ *adj* **4** = **unvarying**, consistent, constant, equable, even, regular, smooth, unbroken, unchanging, undeviating **5** = **alike**, equal, identical, like, same, selfsame, similar
Antonyms *adj* ≠ **unvarying**: changeable, changing, deviating, inconsistent, irregular, uneven, varying

uniformity *n* **1** = **regularity**, constancy, evenness, homogeneity, invariability, sameness, similarity **2** = **monotony**, drabness, dullness, flatness, lack of diversity, sameness, tedium

unify *vb* = **unite**, amalgamate, bind, bring together, combine, confederate, consolidate, federate, fuse, join, merge
Antonyms *vb* alienate, disconnect, disjoin, disunite, divide, separate, sever, split

unimpeachable *adj* = **beyond question**, above reproach, beyond criticism, blameless, faultless, impeccable, irreproachable, perfect, squeaky-clean, unassailable, unblemished, unchallengeable, unexceptionable, unquestionable
Antonyms *adj* blameworthy, faulty, imperfect, reprehensible, reproachable, shameful

unincorporated business (ˌʌnɪnˈkɔːpəreɪtɪd) *n* a privately owned business, often owned by one person who has unlimited liability as the business is not legally registered as a company.

uninterested ❶ (ʌnˈɪntrɪstɪd) *adj* indifferent.
▸**unˈinterestedly** *adv* ▸**unˈinterestedness** *n*

USAGE NOTE See at **disinterested.**

union ❶ (ˈjuːnjən) *n* **1** the condition of being united, the act of uniting, or a conjunction formed by such an act. **2** an association, alliance, or confederation of individuals or groups for a common purpose, esp. political. **3** agreement or harmony. **4** short for **trade union. 5** the act or state of marriage or sexual intercourse. **6** a device on a flag representing union, such as another flag depicted in the top left corner. **7** a device for coupling pipes. **8** (*often cap.*) **8a** an association of students at a university or college formed to look after the students' interests. **8b** the building or buildings housing the facilities of such an organization. **9** *Maths.* a set containing all members of two given sets. Symbol: ∪ **10** (in 19th-century England) a number of parishes united for the administration of poor relief. **11** *Textiles.* a piece of cloth or fabric consisting of two different kinds of yarn. **12** (*modifier*) of or related to a union, esp. a trade union. [C15: from Church L *ūniō* oneness, from L *ūnus* one]

Union (ˈjuːnjən) *n* **the. 1** *Brit.* **1a** the union of England and Wales from 1543. **1b** the union of the English and Scottish crowns (1603–1707). **1c** the union of England and Scotland from 1707. **1d** the political union of Great Britain and Ireland (1801–1920). **1e** the union of Great Britain and Northern Ireland from 1921. **2** *US.* **2a** the United States of America. **2b** the northern states of the US during the Civil War. **2c** (*as modifier*): *Union supporters.*

union catalogue *n* a catalogue listing every publication held at cooperating libraries.

Union flag *n* the national flag of the United Kingdom, being a composite design composed of Saint George's Cross (England), Saint Andrew's Cross (Scotland), and Saint Patrick's Cross (Ireland). Often called: **Union Jack.**

unionism (ˈjuːnjəˌnɪzəm) *n* **1** the principles of trade unions. **2** adherence to the principles of trade unions. **3** the principle or theory of any union.
▸**ˈunionist** *n, adj*

Unionist (ˈjuːnjənɪst) *n* **1** (*sometimes not cap.*) **1a** (before 1920) a supporter of the Union of all Ireland and Great Britain. **1b** (since 1920) a supporter of Union between Britain and Northern Ireland. **2** a supporter of the US federal Union, esp. during the Civil War. ◆ *adj* **3** of, resembling, or relating to Unionists.
▸**ˈUnionˌism** *n*

Unionist Party *n* (formerly, in Northern Ireland) the major Protestant political party, closely identified with the Union with Britain. See also **Ulster Democratic Unionist Party, Ulster Unionist Council.**

unionize *or* **unionise** (ˈjuːnjəˌnaɪz) *vb* **unionizes, unionizing, unionized** *or* **unionises, unionising, unionised. 1** to organize (workers) into a trade union. **2** to join or cause to join a trade union. **3** (*tr*) to subject to the rules or codes of a trade union.
▸ˌ**unioniˈzation** *or* ˌ**unioniˈsation** *n*

Union Jack *n* a common name for **Union flag.**

union pipes *pl n* another name for **uillean pipes.**

union shop *n* (formerly) an establishment whose employment policy is governed by a contract between employer and a trade union permitting the employment of nonunion labour only on the condition that such labour joins the union within a specified time period.

unipolar (ˌjuːnɪˈpəʊlə) *adj* **1** of, concerned with, or having a single magnetic or electric pole. **2** (of a nerve cell) having a single process. **3** (of a transistor) utilizing charge carriers of one polarity only, as in a field-effect transistor.
▸**unipolarity** (ˌjuːnɪpəʊˈlærɪtɪ) *n*

unique ❶ (juːˈniːk) *adj* **1** being the only one of a particular type. **2** without equal or like. **3** *Inf.* very remarkable. **4** *Maths.* **4a** leading to only one result: *the sum of two integers is unique.* **4b** having precisely one value: *the unique positive square root of 4 is 2.* [C17: via F from L *ūnicus* unparalleled, from *ūnus* one]
▸**uˈniquely** *adv* ▸**uˈniqueness** *n*

USAGE NOTE *Unique* is normally taken to describe an absolute state, i.e. one that cannot be qualified; thus something is either *unique* or *not unique*; it cannot be *rather unique* or *very unique.* However, *unique* is sometimes used informally to mean very remarkable or unusual and this makes it possible to use comparatives or intensifiers with it, although many people object to this use.

unisex (ˈjuːnɪˌsɛks) *adj* of or relating to clothing, a hairstyle, hairdressers, etc., that can be worn or used by either sex. [C20: from UNI- + SEX]

unisexual (ˌjuːnɪˈsɛksjʊəl) *adj* **1** of one sex only. **2** (of some organisms) having either male or female reproductive organs but not both.
▸ˌ**uniˌsexuˈality** *n* ▸ˌ**uniˈsexually** *adv*

unison ❶ (ˈjuːnɪsᵊn) *n* **1** *Music.* **1a** the interval between two sounds of identical pitch. **1b** (*modifier*) played or sung at the same pitch: *unison singing.* **2** complete agreement (esp. in **in unison**). [C16: from LL *ūnisonus,* from UNI- + *sonus* sound]
▸**uˈnisonous, uˈnisonal,** *or* **uˈnisonant** *adj*

unit ❶ (ˈjuːnɪt) *n* **1** a single undivided entity or whole. **2** any group or individual, esp. when regarded as a basic element of a larger whole. **3** a mechanical part or assembly of parts that performs a subsidiary function: *a filter unit.* **4** a complete system or establishment that performs a specific function: *a production unit.* **5** a subdivision of a larger military formation. **6** a standard amount of a physical quantity, such as length, mass, etc., multiples of which are used to express magnitudes of that physical quantity: *the second is a unit of time.* **7** the amount of a drug, vaccine, etc., needed to produce a particular effect. **8** a standard measure used in calculating alcohol intake and its effect. **9** the digit or position immediately to the left of the decimal point. **10** (*modifier*) having or relating to a value of one: *a unit vector.* **11** *NZ.* a self-propelled railcar. **12** *Austral. & NZ.* short for **home unit.** [C16: back formation from UNITY, ? on the model of *digit*]

unitarian (ˌjuːnɪˈtɛərɪən) *n* **1** a supporter of unity or centralization in politics. ◆ *adj* **2** of or relating to unity or centralization.

Unitarian (ˌjuːnɪˈtɛərɪən) *n* **1** a person who believes that God is one being and rejects the doctrine of the Trinity. **2** a member of the Church (**Unitarian Church**) that embodies this system of belief. ◆ *adj* **3** of or relating to Unitarians or Unitarianism.
▸ˌ**Uniˈtariaˌnism** *n*

unitary (ˈjuːnɪtərɪ, -trɪ) *adj* **1** of a unit or units. **2** based on or characterized by unity. **3** individual; whole.

unitary authority *n* (in Britain) a district administered by a single tier of local government.

unit character *n Genetics.* a character inherited as a single unit and dependent on a single gene.

unit cost *n* the actual cost of producing one article.

unite[1] ❶ (juːˈnaɪt) *vb* **unites, uniting, united. 1** to make or become an integrated whole or a unity. **2** to join, unify or be unified in purpose, action, beliefs, etc. **3** to enter or cause to enter into an association or alliance. **4** to adhere or cause to adhere; fuse. **5** (*tr*) to possess (qualities) in combination or at the same time: *he united charm with severity.* [C15: from LL *ūnīre,* from *ūnus* one]

unite[2] (ˈjuːnaɪt, juːˈnaɪt) *n* an English gold coin of the Stuart period, originally worth 20 shillings. [C17: from obs. *unite* joined, from the union of England & Scotland (1603)]

united ❶ (juːˈnaɪtɪd) *adj* **1** produced by two or more persons or things in combination or from their union or amalgamation: *a united effort.* **2** in agreement. **3** in association or alliance.
▸**uˈnitedly** *adv* ▸**uˈnitedness** *n*

United Empire Loyalist *n Canad. history.* an American colonist who settled in Canada during or after the War of American Independence because of loyalty to the British Crown.

United Kingdom overseas territory *n* any of the territories that are governed by the UK but lie outside the British Isles; many were formerly British **crown colonies**: includes Bermuda, Falkland Islands, Gibraltar, and Montserrat.

United Nations *n* (*functioning as sing or pl*) an international organization of independent states, with its headquarters in New York City, that was formed in 1945 to promote peace and international cooperation and security. Abbrev.: **UN.**

unitive (ˈjuːnɪtɪv) *adj* **1** tending to unite or capable of uniting. **2** characterized by unity.

unitize *or* **unitise** (ˈjuːnɪˌtaɪz) *vb* **unitizes, unitizing, unitized** *or* **unitises, uni-**

THESAURUS

uninterested *adj* = **indifferent**, apathetic, blasé, bored, distant, impassive, incurious, listless, unconcerned, uninvolved, unresponsive
Antonyms *adj* alert, concerned, curious, enthusiastic, interested, involved, keen, responsive

union *n* **1** = **joining**, amalgam, amalgamation, blend, combination, conjunction, fusion, mixture, synthesis, uniting **2** = **alliance**, association, Bund, coalition, confederacy, confederation, federation, league **3** = **agreement**, accord, concord, concurrence, harmony, unanimity, unison, unity **5** = **intercourse**, coition, coitus, copulation, coupling, marriage, matrimony, nookie (*sl.*), rumpy-pumpy (*sl.*), the other (*inf.*), wedlock

unique *adj* **1** = **single**, lone, one and only, only, solitary, sui generis **2** = **unparalleled**, incomparable, inimitable, matchless, nonpareil, peerless, unequalled, unexampled, unmatched, unrivalled, without equal

unison *n* **2** = **agreement**, accord, accordance, concert, concord, cooperation, harmony, unanimity, unity
Antonyms *n* disagreement, discord, disharmony, dissension, dissidence, dissonance

unit *n* **1** = **item**, entity, module, piece, portion, whole **2** = **part**, component, constituent, element, member, section, segment **4** = **system**, assembly **5** = **section**, detachment, group **6** = **measure**, measurement, quantity

unite[1] *vb* **1** = **join**, amalgamate, blend, coalesce, combine, consolidate, couple, fuse, incorporate, link, marry, meld, merge, unify, wed **2** = **cooperate**, ally, associate, band, close ranks, club together, collaborate, confederate, join forces, join together, league, pool, pull together
Antonyms *vb* ≠ **join**: break, detach, disunite, divide, part, separate, sever, split ≠ **cooperate**: break, divorce, part, separate, split

united *adj* **1** = **combined**, affiliated, allied, banded together, collective, concerted, in partnership, leagued, pooled, unified **2** = **in agreement**, agreed, in accord, like-minded, of like

tising, unitised. (*tr*) *Finance.* to convert (an investment trust) into a unit trust.
▸ **ˌunitiˈzation** *or* **ˌunitiˈsation** *n*
unit-linked policy *n* a life-assurance policy the benefits of which are directly in proportion to the number of units purchased on the policyholder's behalf.
unit of account *n* **1** *Econ.* the function of money that enables the user to keep accounts, value transactions, etc. **2** a monetary denomination used for accounting purposes, etc., but not necessarily corresponding to any real currency: *the ECU is the unit of account of the European Monetary Fund.* **3** the unit of currency of a country.
unit price *n* a price for foodstuffs, etc., stated or shown as the cost per unit, as per pound, per kilogram, per dozen, etc.
unit pricing *n* a system of pricing foodstuffs, etc., in which the cost of a single unit is shown to enable shoppers to see the advantage of buying multipacks.
unit trust *n Brit.* an investment trust that issues units for public sale, the holders of which are creditors and not shareholders with their interests represented by a trust company independent of the issuing agency. US and Canad. equivalent: **mutual fund.**
unity ❶ (ˈjuːnɪtɪ) *n, pl* **unities. 1** the state or quality of being one; oneness. **2** the act, state, or quality of forming a whole from separate parts. **3** something whole or complete that is composed of separate parts. **4** mutual agreement; harmony or concord: *the participants were no longer in unity.* **5** uniformity or constancy: *unity of purpose.* **6** *Maths.* **6a** the number or numeral one. **6b** a quantity assuming the value of one: *the area of the triangle was regarded as unity.* **6c** the element of a set producing no change in a number following multiplication. **7** any one of the three principles of dramatic structure by which the action of a play should be limited to a single plot (unity of action), a single location (unity of place), and a single day (unity of time). [C13: from OF *unité*, from L *ūnitās*, from *ūnus* one]
Univ. *abbrev. for* University.
univalent (ˌjuːnɪˈveɪlənt, juːˈnɪvələnt) *adj* **1** (of a chromosome during meiosis) not paired with its homologue. **2** *Chem.* another word for **monovalent.**
▸ **ˌuniˈvalency** *n*
univalve (ˈjuːnɪˌvælv) *Zool.* ◆ *adj* **1** relating to or possessing a mollusc shell that consists of a single piece (valve). ◆ *n* **2** a gastropod mollusc.
universal ❶ (ˌjuːnɪˈvɜːsᵊl) *adj* **1** of or typical of the whole of mankind or of nature. **2** common to or proceeding from all in a particular group. **3** applicable to or affecting many individuals, conditions, or cases. **4** existing or prevailing everywhere. **5** applicable or occurring throughout or relating to the universe: *a universal constant.* **6** (esp. of a language) capable of being used and understood by all. **7** embracing or versed in many fields of knowledge, activity, interest, etc. **8** *Machinery.* designed or adapted for a range of sizes, fittings, or uses. **9** *Logic.* (of a statement or proposition) affirming or denying something about every member of a class, as in *all men are wicked.* Cf. **particular** (sense 6). **10** *Arch.* entire; whole. ◆ *n* **11** *Philosophy.* a general term or concept or the type such a term signifies. **12** *Logic.* a universal proposition, statement, or formula. **13** a characteristic common to every member of a particular culture or to every human being.

> **USAGE NOTE** The use of *more universal* as in *his writings have long been admired by fellow scientists, but his latest book should have more universal appeal* is acceptable in modern English usage.

universal class *or* **set** *n* (in Boolean algebra) the class containing all points and including all other classes.
universal gas constant *n* another name for **gas constant.**
universalism (ˌjuːnɪˈvɜːsəˌlɪzəm) *n* **1** a universal feature or characteristic. **2** another word for **universality.**
Universalism (ˌjuːnɪˈvɜːsəˌlɪzəm) *n* a system of religious beliefs maintaining that all men are predestined for salvation.
▸ **ˌUniˈversalist** *n, adj*
universality ❶ (ˌjuːnɪvɜːˈsælɪtɪ) *n* the state or quality of being universal.
universalize *or* **universalise** (ˌjuːnɪˈvɜːsəˌlaɪz) *vb* **universalizes, universalizing, universalized** *or* **universalises, universalising, universalised.** (*tr*) to make universal.
▸ **ˌuniˌversaliˈzation** *or* **ˌuniˌversaliˈsation** *n*
universal joint *or* **coupling** *n* a form of coupling between two rotating shafts allowing freedom of movement in all directions.
universally ❶ (ˌjuːnɪˈvɜːsəlɪ) *adv* everywhere or in every case: *this principle applies universally.*
universal motor *n* an electric motor capable of working on either direct current or single-phase alternating current at approximately the same speed and output.
universal time *n* **1** (from 1928) name adopted internationally for Greenwich Mean Time (measured from Greenwich midnight), now split into several slightly different scales, one of which (UT1) is used by astronomers. Abbrev.: **UT. 2** Also called: **universal coordinated time.** an internationally agreed system for civil timekeeping introduced in 1960 and redefined in 1972 as an atomic timescale. Available from broadcast signals, it has a second equal to the International Atomic Time (TAI) second, the difference between UTC and TAI being an integral number of seconds with leap seconds inserted when necessary to keep it within 0.9 seconds of UT1. Abbrev.: **UTC.**
universe ❶ (ˈjuːnɪˌvɜːs) *n* **1** *Astron.* the aggregate of all existing matter, energy, and space. **2** human beings collectively. **3** a province or sphere of thought or activity. [C16: from F, from L *ūniversum* the whole world, from *ūniversus* all together, from UNI- + *vertere* to turn]
universe of discourse *n Logic.* the complete range of objects, relations, ideas, etc., that are expressed or implied in a discussion.
university (ˌjuːnɪˈvɜːsɪtɪ) *n, pl* **universities. 1** an institution of higher education having authority to award bachelors' and higher degrees, usually having research facilities. **2** the buildings, members, staff, or campus of a university. [C14: from OF, from Med. L *universitās* group of scholars, from LL: guild, body of men, from L: whole]
UNIX (ˈjuːnɪks) *n Trademark.* a multi-user operating system found on many types of computer.
unjust ❶ (ʌnˈdʒʌst) *adj* not in accordance with accepted standards of fairness or justice; unfair.
▸ **unˈjustly** *adv* ▸ **unˈjustness** *n*
unkempt ❶ (ʌnˈkɛmpt) *adj* **1** (of the hair) uncombed; dishevelled. **2** ungroomed; slovenly: *unkempt appearance.* [OE *uncembed;* from UN-[1] + *cembed,* p.p. of *cemban* to comb]
▸ **unˈkemptly** *adv* ▸ **unˈkemptness** *n*
unkind ❶ (ʌnˈkaɪnd) *adj* lacking kindness; unsympathetic or cruel.
▸ **unˈkindly** *adv* ▸ **unˈkindness** *n*
unknowing (ʌnˈnəʊɪŋ) *adj* **1** not knowing; ignorant. **2** (*postpositive;* often foll. by *of*) unaware (of).
▸ **unˈknowingly** *adv*
unknown ❶ (ʌnˈnəʊn) *adj* **1** not known, understood, or recognized. **2** not established, identified, or discovered: *an unknown island.* **3** not famous: *some unknown artist.* ◆ *n* **4** an unknown person, quantity, or thing. **5** *Maths.* a variable the value of which is to be discovered by solving an equation; a variable in a conditional equation.
▸ **unˈknownness** *n*
Unknown Soldier *or* **Warrior** *n* (in various countries) an unidentified soldier who has died in battle and for whom a tomb is established as a memorial to the other unidentified dead of the nation's armed forces.
unlace (ʌnˈleɪs) *vb* **unlaces, unlacing, unlaced.** (*tr*) **1** to loosen or undo the lacing of (shoes, etc.). **2** to unfasten or remove garments, etc., of (oneself or another) by or as if by undoing lacing.
unlawful assembly (ʌnˈlɔːfʊl) *n Law.* a meeting of three or more people with the intent of carrying out any unlawful purpose.
unlay (ʌnˈleɪ) *vb* **unlays, unlaying, unlaid.** (*tr*) to untwist (a rope or cable) to separate its strands.
unleaded (ʌnˈlɛdɪd) *adj* **1** (of petrol) containing a reduced amount of tetraethyl lead, in order to reduce environmental pollution. ◆ *n* **2** petrol containing a reduced amount of tetraethyl lead.
unlearn (ʌnˈlɜːn) *vb* **unlearns, unlearning, unlearnt** *or* **unlearned** (-ˈlɜːnd). to try to forget (something learnt) or to discard (accumulated knowledge).

THESAURUS

mind, of one mind, of the same opinion, one, unanimous
unity *n* **1, 2** = **wholeness**, entity, integrity, oneness, singleness, undividedness, unification, union **4** = **agreement**, accord, assent, concord, concurrence, consensus, harmony, peace, solidarity, unanimity, unison
Antonyms *n* ≠ **wholeness:** disunity, division, heterogeneity, multiplicity, separation ≠ **agreement:** disagreement, discord, disunity, division, factionalism, ill will, independence, individuality, infighting, strife
universal *adj* **1-7** = **widespread**, all-embracing, catholic, common, ecumenical, entire, general, omnipresent, overarching, total, unlimited, whole, worldwide
universality *n* = **comprehensiveness**, all-inclusiveness, completeness, entirety, generality, generalization, totality, ubiquity
universally *adv* = **everywhere**, across the board, always, in all cases, in every instance, invariably, uniformly, without exception
universe *n* **1** = **cosmos**, creation, everything, macrocosm, nature, the natural world
unjust *adj* = **unfair**, biased, inequitable, one-sided, partial, partisan, prejudiced, undeserved, unjustified, unmerited, wrong, wrongful
Antonyms *adj* equitable, ethical, fair, impartial, just, justified, right, unbiased
unkempt *adj* **1** = **uncombed**, shaggy, tousled **2** = **untidy**, bedraggled, blowsy, disarranged, disarrayed, dishevelled, disordered, frowzy, messy, rumpled, scruffy, shabby, slatternly, sloppy (*inf.*), slovenly, sluttish, ungroomed
Antonyms *adj* ≠ **untidy:** neat, presentable, soigné *or* soignée, spruce, tidy, trim, well-groomed
unkind *adj* = **cruel**, hardhearted, harsh, inconsiderate, inhuman, insensitive, malicious, mean, nasty, spiteful, thoughtless, uncaring, uncharitable, unchristian, unfeeling, unfriendly, unsympathetic
Antonyms *adj* benevolent, caring, charitable, considerate, generous, kind, soft-hearted, sympathetic, thoughtful
unkindness *n* = **cruelty**, hardheartedness, harshness, ill will, inhumanity, insensitivity, malevolence, malice, maliciousness, meanness, spite, spitefulness, unfeeling
Antonyms *n* benevolence, charity, friendliness, generosity, goodwill, kindness, sympathy, thoughtfulness
unknown *adj* **1** = **hidden**, concealed, dark, mysterious, secret, unrecognized, unrevealed, untold **2** = **unidentified**, anonymous, beyond one's ken, nameless, uncharted, undiscovered, unexplored, unnamed **3** = **obscure**, humble, little known, undistinguished, unfamiliar, unheard-of, unrenowned, unsung
Antonyms *adj* ≠ **obscure:** celebrated, distin-

unlearned (ʌnˈlɜːnɪd) *adj* ignorant or untaught.
▸**unˈlearnedly** *adv*

unlearnt *or* **unlearned** (ʌnˈlɜːnt) *or* (ʌnˈlɜːnd) *adj* **1** denoting knowledge or skills innately present and therefore not learnt. **2** not learnt or taken notice of: *unlearnt lessons.*

unleash ⓘ (ʌnˈliːʃ) *vb* (*tr*) **1** to release from or as if from a leash. **2** to free from restraint.

unleavened (ʌnˈlɛvənd) *adj* (of bread, etc.) made from a dough containing no yeast or leavening.

unless (ʌnˈlɛs) *conj* (*subordinating*) except under the circumstances that; except on the condition that: *they'll sell it unless he hears otherwise.* [C14 *onlesse,* from *on* ON + *lesse* LESS]

unlettered (ʌnˈlɛtəd) *adj* uneducated; illiterate.

unlike ⓘ (ʌnˈlaɪk) *adj* **1** not alike; dissimilar or unequal; different. ◆ *prep* **2** not like; not typical of: *unlike his father he lacks intelligence.*
▸**unˈlikeness** *n*

unlikely ⓘ (ʌnˈlaɪklɪ) *adj* not likely; improbable.
▸**unˈlikeliness** *or* **unˈlikeliˌhood** *n*

unlimber (ʌnˈlɪmbə) *vb* **1** (*tr*) to disengage (a gun) from its limber. **2** to prepare (something) for use.

unlimited ⓘ (ʌnˈlɪmɪtɪd) *adj* **1** without limits or bounds: *unlimited knowledge.* **2** not restricted, limited, or qualified: *unlimited power.*
▸**unˈlimitedly** *adv* ▸**unˈlimitedness** *n*

unlisted (ʌnˈlɪstɪd) *adj* **1** not entered on a list. **2** the US and Canad. word for **ex-directory**.

Unlisted Securities Market *n* a market on the London Stock Exchange for trading in shares of smaller companies, who do not wish to comply with the requirements for a full listing. Abbrev.: **USM**.

unload ⓘ (ʌnˈləʊd) *vb* **1** to remove a load or cargo from (a ship, lorry, etc.). **2** to discharge (cargo, freight, etc.). **3** (*tr*) to relieve of a burden or troubles. **4** (*tr*) to give vent to (anxiety, troubles, etc.). **5** (*tr*) to get rid of or dispose of (esp. surplus goods). **6** (*tr*) to remove the charge of ammunition from (a firearm).
▸**unˈloader** *n*

unlock ⓘ (ʌnˈlɒk) *vb* **1** (*tr*) to unfasten (a lock, door, etc.). **2** (*tr*) to release or let loose. **3** (*tr*) to provide the key to: *unlock a puzzle.* **4** (*intr*) to become unlocked.
▸**unˈlockable** *adj*

unlooked-for ⓘ (ˌʌnˈlʊktfɔː) *adj* unexpected; unforeseen.

unloose (ʌnˈluːs) *or* **unloosen** *vb* **unlooses, unloosing, unloosed** *or* **unloosens, unloosening, unloosened.** (*tr*) **1** to set free; release. **2** to loosen or relax (a hold, grip, etc.). **3** to unfasten or untie.

unlovely (ʌnˈlʌvlɪ) *adj* unpleasant in appearance or character.
▸**unˈloveliness** *n*

unlucky ⓘ (ʌnˈlʌkɪ) *adj* **1** characterized by misfortune or failure: *an unlucky chance.* **2** ill-omened; inauspicious: *an unlucky date.* **3** regrettable; disappointing.
▸**unˈluckily** *adv* ▸**unˈluckiness** *n*

unmake (ʌnˈmeɪk) *vb* **unmakes, unmaking, unmade.** (*tr*) **1** to undo or destroy. **2** to depose from office or authority. **3** to alter the nature of.

unman ⓘ (ʌnˈmæn) *vb* **unmans, unmanning, unmanned.** (*tr*) **1** to cause to lose courage or nerve. **2** to make effeminate. **3** to remove the men from.

unmanly ⓘ (ʌnˈmænlɪ) *adj* **1** not masculine or virile. **2** ignoble, cowardly, or dishonourable. ◆ *adv* **3** *Arch.* in an unmanly manner.
▸**unˈmanliness** *n*

unmanned (ʌnˈmænd) *adj* **1** lacking personnel or crew: *an unmanned ship.* **2** (of aircraft, spacecraft, etc.) operated by automatic or remote control. **3** uninhabited.

unmannered (ʌnˈmænəd) *adj* **1** without good manners; rude. **2** without mannerisms.

unmannerly ⓘ (ʌnˈmænəlɪ) *adj* **1** lacking manners; discourteous. ◆ *adv* **2** *Arch.* rudely; discourteously.
▸**unˈmannerliness** *n*

unmask ⓘ (ʌnˈmɑːsk) *vb* **1** to remove (the mask or disguise) from (someone or oneself). **2** to appear or cause to appear in true character.
▸**unˈmasker** *n*

unmeaning (ʌnˈmiːnɪŋ) *adj* **1** having no meaning. **2** showing no intelligence; vacant: *an unmeaning face.*
▸**unˈmeaningly** *adv* ▸**unˈmeaningness** *n*

unmeet (ʌnˈmiːt) *adj Literary or arch.* unsuitable.
▸**unˈmeetly** *adv* ▸**unˈmeetness** *n*

unmentionable ⓘ (ʌnˈmɛnʃənəbᵊl) *adj* **a** unsuitable or forbidden as a topic of conversation. **b** (*as n*): *the unmentionable.*
▸**unˈmentionableness** *n* ▸**unˈmentionably** *adv*

unmentionables (ʌnˈmɛnʃənəbᵊlz) *pl n Chiefly humorous.* underwear.

unmerciful ⓘ (ʌnˈmɜːsɪfʊl) *adj* **1** showing no mercy; relentless. **2** extreme or excessive.
▸**unˈmercifully** *adv* ▸**unˈmercifulness** *n*

unmindful ⓘ (ʌnˈmaɪndfʊl) *adj* (*usually postpositive* and foll. by *of*) careless or forgetful.
▸**unˈmindfully** *adv* ▸**unˈmindfulness** *n*

unmissable (ʌnˈmɪsəbᵊl) *adj* (of a film, television programme, etc.) so good that it should not be missed.

unmistakable ⓘ *or* **unmistakeable** (ˌʌnmɪsˈteɪkəbᵊl) *adj* not mistakable; clear or unambiguous.
▸ˌ**unmisˈtakably** *or* ˌ**unmisˈtakeably** *adv*

unmitigated ⓘ (ʌnˈmɪtɪˌgeɪtɪd) *adj* **1** not diminished in intensity, severity, etc. **2** (*prenominal*) (intensifier): *an unmitigated disaster.*
▸**unˈmitiˌgatedly** *adv*

unmoral (ʌnˈmɒrəl) *adj* outside morality; amoral.
▸**unmorality** (ˌʌnməˈrælɪtɪ) *n* ▸**unˈmorally** *adv*

unmurmuring (ʌnˈmɜːmərɪŋ) *adj* not complaining.

unmuzzle (ʌnˈmʌzᵊl) *vb* **unmuzzles, unmuzzling, unmuzzled.** (*tr*) **1** to take the muzzle off (a dog, etc.). **2** to free from control or censorship.

unnatural ⓘ (ʌnˈnætʃərəl) *adj* **1** contrary to nature; abnormal. **2** not in accordance with accepted standards of behaviour or right and wrong: *unnatural love.* **3** uncanny; supernatural: *unnatural phenomena.* **4** affected or forced: *an unnatural manner.* **5** inhuman or monstrous: *an unnatural crime.*
▸**unˈnaturally** *adv* ▸**unˈnaturalness** *n*

unnecessary ⓘ (ʌnˈnɛsɪsərɪ) *adj* not necessary.
▸**unˈnecessarily** *adv* ▸**unˈnecessariness** *n*

THESAURUS

guished, familiar, known, recognized, renowned, well-known

unleash *vb* **1, 2** = **release**, free, let go, let loose, unbridle, unloose, untie

unlike *adj* = **different**, as different as chalk and cheese (*inf.*), contrasted, dissimilar, distinct, divergent, diverse, ill-matched, incompatible, not alike, opposite, unequal, unrelated
Antonyms *adj* compatible, equal, like, matched, related, similar

unlikely *adj* = **improbable**, doubtful, faint, not likely, remote, slight, unimaginable

unlimited *adj* **1** = **infinite**, boundless, countless, endless, extensive, great, illimitable, immeasurable, immense, incalculable, limitless, stellar (*inf.*), unbounded, vast **2** = **total**, absolute, all-encompassing, complete, full, unconditional, unconstrained, unfettered, unqualified, unrestricted
Antonyms *adj* ≠ **infinite:** bounded, confined, finite, limited ≠ **total:** circumscribed, constrained, limited, restricted

unload *vb* **1, 2** = **empty**, disburden, discharge, dump, lighten, off-load, relieve, unburden, unlade, unpack

unlock *vb* **1, 2** = **open**, free, let loose, release, unbar, unbolt, undo, unfasten, unlatch

unlooked-for *adj* = **unexpected**, chance, fortuitous, out of the blue, surprise, surprising, unanticipated, undreamed of, unforeseen, unhoped-for, unpredicted, unthought-of

unlucky *adj* **1** = **unfortunate**, cursed, disastrous, hapless, luckless, miserable, unhappy, unsuccessful, wretched **2** = **ill-fated**, doomed, ill-omened, ill-starred, inauspicious, ominous, unfavourable, untimely
Antonyms *adj* ≠ **unfortunate:** blessed, favoured, fortunate, happy, lucky, prosperous

unman *vb* **1** = **unnerve**, daunt, demoralize, discourage, dispirit, enervate, enfeeble, intimidate, psych out (*inf.*), weaken **2** = **emasculate**

unmanly *adj* **1** = **effeminate**, camp, feeble, sissy, soft (*inf.*), weak, womanish **2** = **cowardly**, abject, chicken-hearted, craven, dishonourable, ignoble, weak-kneed (*inf.*), yellow (*inf.*)

unmannerly *adj* **1** = **bad-mannered**, badly behaved, discourteous, disrespectful, ill-bred, ill-mannered, impolite, misbehaved, rude, uncivil, uncouth
Antonyms *adj* civil, courteous, mannerly, polite, respectful, well-behaved, well-bred, well-mannered

unmask *vb* **1, 2** = **reveal**, bare, bring to light, disclose, discover, expose, lay bare, show up, uncloak, uncover, unveil

unmentionable *adj* **a** = **taboo**, disgraceful, disreputable, forbidden, frowned on, immodest, indecent, obscene, scandalous, shameful, shocking, unspeakable, unutterable, X-rated (*inf.*)

unmerciful *adj* **1** = **merciless**, brutal, cruel, hard, heartless, implacable, inhumane, pitiless, relentless, remorseless, ruthless, uncaring, unfeeling, unsparing
Antonyms *adj* beneficent, caring, feeling, humane, merciful, pitying, sparing, tender-hearted

unmindful *adj* = **careless**, forgetful, heedless, inattentive, indifferent, lax, neglectful, negligent, oblivious, remiss, slack, unheeding
Antonyms *adj* alert, attentive, aware, careful, heedful, mindful, regardful, watchful

unmistakable *adj* = **clear**, blatant, certain, conspicuous, decided, distinct, evident, glaring, indisputable, manifest, obvious, palpable, patent, plain, positive, pronounced, sure, unambiguous, unequivocal
Antonyms *adj* ambiguous, dim, doubtful, equivocal, hidden, mistakable, obscure, uncertain, unclear, unsure

unmitigated *adj* **1** = **unrelieved**, grim, harsh, intense, oppressive, persistent, relentless, unabated, unalleviated, unbroken, undiminished, unmodified, unqualified, unredeemed **2** = **complete**, absolute, arrant, consummate, deep-dyed (*usually derogatory*), downright, out-and-out, outright, perfect, rank, sheer, thorough, thoroughgoing, utter

unnatural *adj* **1** = **abnormal**, aberrant, anomalous, irregular, odd, perverse, perverted, unusual **3** = **strange**, bizarre, extraordinary, freakish, outlandish, queer, supernatural, unaccountable, uncanny **4** = **false**, affected, artificial, assumed, contrived, factitious, feigned, forced, insincere, laboured, mannered, phoney *or* phony (*inf.*), self-conscious, stagy, stiff, stilted, strained, studied, theatrical **5** = **inhuman**, brutal, callous, cold-blooded, evil, fiendish, heartless, monstrous, ruthless, savage, unfeeling, wicked
Antonyms *adj* ≠ **strange, abnormal:** normal, ordinary, typical ≠ **false:** genuine, honest, natural, sincere, unaffected, unfeigned, unpretentious ≠ **inhuman:** caring, humane, loving, warm

unnecessary *adj* = **needless**, dispensable, expendable, inessential, nonessential, redundant, supererogatory, superfluous, surplus to requirements, uncalled-for, unneeded, unrequired, useless
Antonyms *adj* essential, indispensable, necessary, needed, required, vital

DICTIONARY

unnerve Ⓣ (ʌnˈnɜːv) *vb* **unnerves, unnerving, unnerved.** (*tr*) to cause to lose courage, strength, confidence, self-control, etc.
unnumbered (ʌnˈnʌmbəd) *adj* **1** countless; innumerable. **2** not counted or assigned a number.
UNO *abbrev. for* United Nations Organization.
unoccupied Ⓣ (ʌnˈɒkjʊˌpaɪd) *adj* **1** (of a building) without occupants. **2** unemployed or idle. **3** (of an area or country) not overrun by foreign troops.
unofficial Ⓣ (ˌʌnəˈfɪʃəl) *adj* **1** not official or formal: *an unofficial engagement.* **2** not confirmed officially: *an unofficial report.* **3** (of a strike) not approved by the strikers' trade union.
►ˌ**unofˈficially** *adv*
unorganized *or* **unorganised** (ʌnˈɔːgəˌnaɪzd) *adj* **1** not arranged into an organized system, structure, or unity. **2** (of workers) not unionized. **3** nonliving; inorganic.
unowned (ʌnˈəʊnd) *adj* **1** unacknowledged. **2** without an owner.
unpack (ʌnˈpæk) *vb* **1** to remove the packed contents of (a case, trunk, etc.). **2** (*tr*) to take (something) out of a packed container. **3** (*tr*) to unload: *to unpack a mule.*
►**unˈpacker** *n*
unpaged (ʌnˈpeɪdʒd) *adj* (of a book) having no page numbers.
unparalleled Ⓣ (ʌnˈpærəˌlɛld) *adj* unmatched; unequalled.
unparliamentary (ˌʌnpɑːləˈmɛntərɪ) *adj* not consistent with parliamentary procedure or practice.
►ˌ**unparliaˈmentarily** *adv* ►ˌ**unparliaˈmentariness** *n*
unpeg (ʌnˈpɛg) *vb* **unpegs, unpegging, unpegged.** (*tr*) **1** to remove the peg from, esp. to unfasten. **2** to allow (prices, etc.) to rise and fall freely.
unpeople (ʌnˈpiːpᵊl) *vb* **unpeoples, unpeopling, unpeopled.** (*tr*) to empty of people.
unperson (ˈʌnpɜːsᵊn) *n* a person whose existence is officially denied or ignored.
unpick (ʌnˈpɪk) *vb* (*tr*) **1** to undo (the stitches) of (a piece of sewing). **2** to unravel or undo (a garment, etc.).
unpin (ʌnˈpɪn) *vb* **unpins, unpinning, unpinned.** (*tr*) **1** to remove a pin or pins from. **2** to unfasten by removing pins.
unpleasant Ⓣ (ʌnˈplɛzᵊnt) *adj* not pleasant or agreeable.
►**unˈpleasantly** *adv* ►**unˈpleasantness** *n*
unplugged (ʌnˈplʌgd) *adj* (of a performer or performance of popular music) using acoustic rather than electric instruments: *Eric Clapton unplugged; an unplugged version of the song.*
unplumbed (ʌnˈplʌmd) *adj* **1** unfathomed; unsounded. **2** not understood in depth. **3** (of a building) having no plumbing.
unpolled (ʌnˈpəʊld) *adj* **1** not included in an opinion poll. **2** not having voted. **3** *Arch.* unshorn.
unpopular Ⓣ (ʌnˈpɒpjʊlə) *adj* not popular with an individual or group of people.
►**unpopularity** (ˌʌnpɒpjʊˈlærɪtɪ) *n* ►**unˈpopularly** *adv*
unpractical (ʌnˈpræktɪkᵊl) *adj* another word for **impractical.**
►ˌ**unpractiˈcality** *n* ►**unˈpractically** *adv*
unpractised *or US* **unpracticed** (ʌnˈpræktɪst) *adj* **1** without skill, training, or experience. **2** not used or done often or repeatedly. **3** not yet tested.
unprecedented Ⓣ (ʌnˈprɛsɪˌdɛntɪd) *adj* having no precedent; unparalleled.
►**unˈpreceˌdentedly** *adv*
unprejudiced Ⓣ (ʌnˈprɛdʒʊdɪst) *adj* not prejudiced or biased; impartial.
►**unˈprejudicedly** *adv*
unprincipled Ⓣ (ʌnˈprɪnsɪpᵊld) *adj* lacking moral principles; unscrupulous.
►**unˈprincipledness** *n*
unprintable (ʌnˈprɪntəbᵊl) *adj* unsuitable for printing for reasons of obscenity, libel, etc.
►**unˈprintableness** *n* ►**unˈprintably** *adv*
unprofessional Ⓣ (ˌʌnprəˈfɛʃənᵊl) *adj* **1** contrary to the accepted code of conduct of a profession. **2** amateur. **3** not belonging to or having the required qualifications for a profession.
►ˌ**unproˈfessionally** *adv*
unprotected sex *n* an act of sexual intercourse or sodomy performed without the use of a condom thus involving the risk of sexually transmitted diseases.
unputdownable (ˌʌnpʊtˈdaʊnəbᵊl) *adj* (esp. of a novel) so gripping as to be read at one sitting.
unqualified Ⓣ (ʌnˈkwɒlɪˌfaɪd) *adj* **1** lacking the necessary qualifications. **2** not restricted or modified: *an unqualified criticism.* **3** (*usually prenominal*) (intensifier): *an unqualified success.*
►**unˈqualiˌfiable** *adj*
unquestionable Ⓣ (ʌnˈkwɛstʃənəbᵊl) *adj* **1** indubitable or indisputable. **2** not admitting of exception: *an unquestionable ruling.*
►**unˌquestionaˈbility** *n* ►**unˈquestionably** *adv*
unquestioned (ʌnˈkwɛstʃənd) *adj* **1** accepted without question. **2** not admitting of doubt or question: *unquestioned power.* **3** not questioned or interrogated.
unquiet (ʌnˈkwaɪət) *Chiefly literary.* ◆ *adj* **1** characterized by disorder or tumult: *unquiet times.* **2** anxious; uneasy. ◆ *n* **3** a state of unrest.
►**unˈquietly** *adv* ►**unˈquietness** *n*
unquote (ʌnˈkwəʊt) *interj* **1** an expression used parenthetically to indicate that the preceding quotation is finished. ◆ *vb* **unquotes, unquoting, unquoted. 2** to close (a quotation), esp. in printing.
unravel Ⓣ (ʌnˈrævᵊl) *vb* **unravels, unravelling, unravelled** *or US* **unravels, unraveling, unraveled. 1** (*tr*) to reduce (something knitted or woven) to separate strands. **2** (*tr*) to explain or solve: *the mystery was unravelled.* **3** (*intr*) to become unravelled.
unreactive (ˌʌnrɪˈæktɪv) *adj* (of a substance) not readily partaking in chemical reactions.
unread (ʌnˈrɛd) *adj* **1** (of a book, etc.) not yet read. **2** (of a person) having read little.
unreadable Ⓣ (ʌnˈriːdəbᵊl) *adj* **1** illegible; undecipherable. **2** difficult or tedious to read.
►**unˌreadaˈbility** *or* **unˈreadableness** *n*
unready (ʌnˈrɛdɪ) *adj* **1** not ready or prepared. **2** slow or hesitant to see or act.
►**unˈreadily** *adv* ►**unˈreadiness** *n*
unreal Ⓣ (ʌnˈrɪəl) *adj* **1** imaginary or fanciful or seemingly so: *an unreal*

THESAURUS

unnerve *vb* = **intimidate**, confound, daunt, demoralize, disarm, disconcert, discourage, dishearten, dismay, dispirit, faze, fluster, frighten, psych out (*inf.*), rattle (*inf.*), shake, throw off balance, unhinge, unman, upset
Antonyms *vb* arm, brace, encourage, gee up, hearten, nerve, steel, strengthen, support
unoccupied *adj* **1** = **empty**, tenantless, uninhabited, untenanted, vacant **2** = **idle**, at a loose end, at leisure, disengaged, inactive, unemployed
unofficial *adj* = **unauthorized**, informal, off the record, personal, private, unconfirmed, wildcat
unparalleled *adj* = **unequalled**, beyond compare, consummate, exceptional, incomparable, matchless, peerless, rare, singular, superlative, unique, unmatched, unprecedented, unrivalled, unsurpassed, without equal
unpleasant *adj* = **nasty**, abhorrent, bad, disagreeable, displeasing, distasteful, horrid, ill-natured, irksome, objectionable, obnoxious, repulsive, troublesome, unattractive, unlikable *or* unlikeable, unlovely, unpalatable
Antonyms *adj* agreeable, congenial, delicious, good-natured, likable *or* likeable, lovely, nice, pleasant
unpleasantness *n* = **nastiness**, awfulness, disagreeableness, displeasure, dreadfulness, grimness, horridness, misery, trouble, ugliness, unacceptability, woe = **hostility**, abrasiveness, animosity, antagonism, argumentativeness, bad feeling, ill humour *or* will, malice, offensiveness, quarrelsomeness, rudeness, unfriendliness
Antonyms *n* ≠ **nastiness:** acceptability, agreeableness, amusement, congeniality, delectation, delight, enjoyment, pleasantness, pleasure ≠ **hostility:** friendliness, good humour *or* will, pleasantness
unpopular *adj* = **disliked**, avoided, detested, not sought out, out in the cold, out of favour, rejected, shunned, unattractive, undesirable, unloved, unwanted, unwelcome
Antonyms *adj* desirable, favoured, liked, loved, popular, wanted, welcome
unprecedented *adj* = **extraordinary**, abnormal, exceptional, freakish, ground-breaking, new, novel, original, remarkable, singular, unexampled, unheard-of, unparalleled, unrivalled, unusual
unprejudiced *adj* = **impartial**, balanced, even-handed, fair, fair-minded, just, nonpartisan, objective, open-minded, unbiased, uninfluenced
Antonyms *adj* biased, bigoted, influenced, narrow-minded, partial, prejudiced, unfair, unjust
unprincipled *adj* = **dishonest**, amoral, corrupt, crooked, deceitful, devious, dishonourable, immoral, sink, tricky, unconscionable, underhand, unethical, unprofessional, unscrupulous
Antonyms *adj* decent, ethical, honest, honourable, moral, righteous, scrupulous, upright, virtuous
unprofessional *adj* **1** = **unethical**, improper, lax, negligent, unfitting, unprincipled, unseemly, unworthy **3** = **amateurish**, amateur, cowboy (*inf.*), incompetent, inefficient, inexperienced, inexpert, slapdash, slipshod, untrained
Antonyms *adj* ≠ **amateurish:** adept, competent, efficient, experienced, expert, professional, skilful
unqualified *adj* **1** = **unfit**, ill-equipped, incapable, incompetent, ineligible, not equal to, not up to, unprepared **2** = **unconditional**, categorical, downright, outright, unmitigated, unreserved, unrestricted, without reservation **3** = **total**, absolute, arrant, complete, consummate, deep-dyed (*usually derogatory*), downright, out-and-out, outright, thorough, thoroughgoing, utter
unquestionable *adj* **1** = **certain**, absolute, beyond a shadow of doubt, clear, conclusive, definite, faultless, flawless, incontestable, incontrovertible, indisputable, indubitable, irrefutable, manifest, patent, perfect, self-evident, sure, undeniable, unequivocal, unmistakable
Antonyms *adj* ambiguous, doubtful, dubious, inconclusive, questionable, uncertain, unclear
unravel *vb* **1** = **undo**, disentangle, extricate, free, separate, straighten out, unknot, untangle, unwind **2** = **solve**, clear up, explain, figure out (*inf.*), get straight, get to the bottom of, interpret, make out, puzzle out, resolve, suss (out) (*sl.*), work out
unreadable *adj* **1** = **illegible**, crabbed, undecipherable **2** = **turgid**, badly written, dry as dust, heavy going
unreal *adj* **1** = **imaginary**, chimerical, dreamlike, fabulous, fanciful, fictitious, hypothetical, illusory, make-believe, mythical, phantasmagoric, storybook, visionary **2** = **insubstantial**, immaterial, impalpable, intangible, nebulous **3** = **fake**, artificial, false, insincere, mock, ostensible, pretended, seeming, sham
Antonyms *adj* ≠ **fake:** authentic, bona fide, genuine, real, realistic, sincere, true, veritable

situation. **2** having no actual existence or substance. **3** insincere or artificial.
▸**unreality** (ˌʌnrɪˈælɪtɪ) *n* ▸**unˈreally** *adv*

unreason (ʌnˈriːzᵊn) *n* **1** irrationality or madness. **2** something that lacks or is contrary to reason. **3** lack of order; chaos.

unreasonable ⓣ (ʌnˈriːznəbᵊl) *adj* **1** immoderate: *unreasonable demands.* **2** refusing to listen to reason. **3** lacking judgment.
▸**unˈreasonableness** *n* ▸**unˈreasonably** *adv*

unreasoning (ʌnˈriːzənɪŋ) *adj* not controlled by reason; irrational.
▸**unˈreasoningly** *adv*

unregenerate ⓣ (ˌʌnrɪˈdʒɛnərɪt) *adj also* **unregenerated. 1** unrepentant; unreformed. **2** obstinately adhering to one's own views. ◆ *n* **3** an unregenerate person.
▸**ˌunreˈgeneracy** *n* ▸**ˌunreˈgenerately** *adv*

unrelenting ⓣ (ˌʌnrɪˈlɛntɪŋ) *adj* **1** refusing to relent or take pity. **2** not diminishing in determination, speed, effort, force, etc.
▸**ˌunreˈlentingly** *adv* ▸**ˌunreˈlentingness** *n*

unreligious (ˌʌnrɪˈlɪdʒəs) *adj* **1** another word for **irreligious. 2** secular.
▸**ˌunreˈligiously** *adv*

unremitting ⓣ (ˌʌnrɪˈmɪtɪŋ) *adj* never slackening or stopping; unceasing; constant.
▸**ˌunreˈmittingly** *adv* ▸**ˌunreˈmittingness** *n*

unreserved ⓣ (ˌʌnrɪˈzɜːvd) *adj* **1** without reserve; having an open manner. **2** without reservation. **3** not booked or bookable.
▸**unreservedly** (ˌʌnrɪˈzɜːvɪdlɪ) *adv* ▸**ˌunreˈservedness** *n*

unrest ⓣ (ʌnˈrɛst) *n* **1** a troubled or rebellious state of discontent. **2** an uneasy or troubled state.

unriddle (ʌnˈrɪdᵊl) *vb* **unriddles, unriddling, unriddled.** (*tr*) to solve or puzzle out. [C16: from UN-[2] + RIDDLE[1]]
▸**unˈriddler** *n*

unrig (ʌnˈrɪg) *vb* **unrigs, unrigging, unrigged. 1** (*tr*) to strip (a vessel) of standing and running rigging. **2** *Arch. or dialect.* to undress (someone or oneself).

unrighteous (ʌnˈraɪtʃəs) *adj* **1a** sinful; wicked. **1b** (*as collective n; preceded by the*): *the unrighteous.* **2** not fair or right; unjust.
▸**unˈrighteously** *adv* ▸**unˈrighteousness** *n*

unrip (ʌnˈrɪp) *vb* **unrips, unripping, unripped.** (*tr*) **1** to rip open. **2** *Obs.* to reveal; disclose.

unripe (ʌnˈraɪp) *or* **unripened** *adj* **1** not fully matured. **2** not fully prepared or developed; not ready.
▸**unˈripeness** *n*

unrivalled ⓣ *or US* **unrivaled** (ʌnˈraɪvᵊld) *adj* having no equal; matchless.

unroll (ʌnˈrəʊl) *vb* **1** to open out or unwind (something rolled, folded, or coiled) or (of something rolled, etc.) to become opened out or unwound. **2** to make or become visible or apparent, esp. gradually; unfold.

unruffled ⓣ (ʌnˈrʌfᵊld) *adj* **1** unmoved; calm. **2** still: *the unruffled seas.*
▸**unˈruffledness** *n*

unruly ⓣ (ʌnˈruːlɪ) *adj* **unrulier, unruliest.** disposed to disobedience or indiscipline.
▸**unˈruliness** *n*

UNRWA (ˈʌnrə) *n acronym for* United Nations Relief and Works Agency.

unsaddle (ʌnˈsædᵊl) *vb* **unsaddles, unsaddling, unsaddled. 1** to remove the saddle from (a horse, mule, etc.). **2** (*tr*) to unhorse.

unsaddling enclosure *n* the area at a racecourse where horses are unsaddled after a race and often where awards are given to owners, trainers, and jockeys.

unsafe ⓣ (ʌnˈseɪf) *adj* **1** not safe; perilous. **2** (of a criminal conviction) based on inadequate or false evidence.

unsaid ⓣ (ʌnˈsɛd) *adj* not said or expressed; unspoken.

unsaturated (ʌnˈsætʃəˌreɪtɪd) *adj* **1** not saturated. **2** (of a chemical compound, esp. an organic compound) containing one or more double or triple bonds and thus capable of undergoing addition reactions. **3** (of a fat, esp. a vegetable fat) containing a high proportion of fatty acids having double bonds.
▸**ˌunsatuˈration** *n*

unsavoury ⓣ *or US* **unsavory** (ʌnˈseɪvərɪ) *adj* **1** objectionable or distasteful: *an unsavoury character.* **2** disagreeable in odour or taste.
▸**unˈsavourily** *or US* **unˈsavorily** *adv* ▸**unˈsavouriness** *or US* **unˈsavoriness** *n*

unsay (ʌnˈseɪ) *vb* **unsays, unsaying, unsaid.** (*tr*) to retract or withdraw (something said or written).

unscathed ⓣ (ʌnˈskeɪðd) *adj* not harmed or injured.

unscramble (ʌnˈskræmbᵊl) *vb* **unscrambles, unscrambling, unscrambled.** (*tr*) **1** to resolve from confusion or disorderliness. **2** to restore (a scrambled message) to an intelligible form.
▸**unˈscrambler** *n*

unscrew (ʌnˈskruː) *vb* **1** (*tr*) to remove a screw from (an object). **2** (*tr*) to loosen (a screw, lid, etc.) by rotating, usually in an anticlockwise direction. **3** (*intr*) (esp. of an engaged threaded part) to become loosened or separated.

unscripted (ʌnˈskrɪptɪd) *adj* (of a speech, play, etc.) not using or based on a script.

unscrupulous ⓣ (ʌnˈskruːpjʊləs) *adj* without scruples; unprincipled.
▸**unˈscrupulously** *adv* ▸**unˈscrupulousness** *n*

unseal (ʌnˈsiːl) *vb* (*tr*) **1** to remove or break the seal of. **2** to free (something concealed or closed as if sealed): *to unseal one's lips.*

unsealed (ʌnˈsiːld) *adj Austral. & NZ.* (of a road) surfaced with road metal not bound by bitumen or other sealant.

unseam (ʌnˈsiːm) *vb* (*tr*) to open or undo the seam of.

unseasonable ⓣ (ʌnˈsiːzənəbᵊl) *adj* **1** (esp. of the weather) inappropriate for the season. **2** untimely; inopportune.
▸**unˈseasonableness** *n* ▸**unˈseasonably** *adv*

unseat ⓣ (ʌnˈsiːt) *vb* (*tr*) **1** to throw or displace from a seat, saddle, etc. **2** to depose from office or position.

unseeded (ʌnˈsiːdɪd) *adj* (of players in various sports) not assigned to a preferential position in the preliminary rounds of a tournament.

unseemly ⓣ (ʌnˈsiːmlɪ) *adj* **1** not in good style or taste. **2** *Obs.* unattractive. ◆ *adv* **3** *Rare.* in an unseemly manner.
▸**unˈseemliness** *n*

unseen ⓣ (ʌnˈsiːn) *adj* **1** not observed or perceived; invisible. **2** (of passages of writing) not previously seen or prepared. ◆ *n* **3** *Chiefly Brit.* a

THESAURUS

unreasonable *adj* **1** = **excessive**, absurd, exorbitant, extortionate, extravagant, far-fetched, immoderate, irrational, preposterous, steep (*inf.*), too great, uncalled-for, undue, unfair, unjust, unwarranted **2** = **biased**, arbitrary, blinkered, capricious, erratic, headstrong, illogical, inconsistent, opinionated, quirky
Antonyms *adj* ≠ **excessive:** fair, just, justified, moderate, reasonable, temperate, warranted ≠ **biased:** fair-minded, flexible, open-minded

unregenerate *adj* **1, 2** = **unrepentant**, hardened, intractable, obdurate, obstinate, recalcitrant, refractory, self-willed, stubborn, unconverted, unreformed
Antonyms *adj* converted, reformed, regenerate, repentant

unrelenting *adj* **1** = **merciless**, cruel, implacable, inexorable, intransigent, pitiless, relentless, remorseless, ruthless, stern, tough, unsparing **2** = **steady**, ceaseless, constant, continual, continuous, endless, incessant, perpetual, unabated, unbroken, unremitting, unwavering

unremitting *adj* = **constant**, assiduous, continual, continuous, diligent, incessant, indefatigable, perpetual, relentless, remorseless, sedulous, unabated, unbroken, unceasing, unwavering, unwearied

unreserved *adj* **1** = **uninhibited**, demonstrative, extrovert, forthright, frank, free, open, open-hearted, outgoing, outspoken, unrestrained, unreticent **2** = **total**, absolute, complete, entire, full, unconditional, unlimited, unqualified, wholehearted, without reservation
Antonyms *adj* ≠ **uninhibited:** demure, inhibited, modest, reserved, restrained, reticent, shy, undemonstrative

unrest *n* **1** = **discontent**, agitation, disaffection, discord, dissatisfaction, dissension, protest, rebellion, sedition, strife, tumult, turmoil, upheaval **2** = **uneasiness**, agitation, anxiety, disquiet, distress, perturbation, restlessness, trepidation, worry
Antonyms *n* calm, contentment, peace, relaxation, rest, stillness, tranquillity

unrivalled *adj* = **unparalleled**, beyond compare, incomparable, matchless, nonpareil, peerless, supreme, unequalled, unexcelled, unmatched, unsurpassed, without equal

unruffled *adj* **1** = **calm**, collected, composed, cool, peaceful, placid, sedate, serene, tranquil, undisturbed, unfazed (*inf.*), unflustered, unmoved, unperturbed **2** = **smooth**, even, flat, level, unbroken

unruly *adj* = **uncontrollable**, disobedient, disorderly, fractious, headstrong, insubordinate, intractable, lawless, mutinous, obstreperous, rebellious, refractory, riotous, rowdy, turbulent, ungovernable, unmanageable, wayward, wild, wilful
Antonyms *adj* amenable, biddable, docile, governable, manageable, obedient, orderly, tractable

unsafe *adj* **1** = **dangerous**, hazardous, insecure, perilous, precarious, risky, threatening, treacherous, uncertain, unreliable, unsound, unstable
Antonyms *adj* certain, harmless, reliable, safe, secure, sound, stable, sure

unsaid *adj* = **unspoken**, left to the imagination, tacit, undeclared, unexpressed, unstated, unuttered, unvoiced

unsavoury *adj* **1** = **unpleasant**, distasteful, nasty, objectionable, obnoxious, offensive, repellent, repugnant, repulsive, revolting **2** = **unappetizing**, disagreeable, distasteful, nauseating, sickening, unpalatable
Antonyms *adj* ≠ **unappetizing:** agreeable, appetizing, palatable, pleasant, savoury, tasteful, tasty, toothsome

unscathed *adj* = **unharmed**, in one piece, safe, sound, unhurt, uninjured, unmarked, unscarred, unscratched, untouched, whole

unscrupulous *adj* = **unprincipled**, conscienceless, corrupt, crooked (*inf.*), dishonest, dishonourable, exploitative, immoral, improper, knavish, roguish, ruthless, sink, unconscientious, unconscionable, unethical
Antonyms *adj* ethical, honest, honourable, moral, principled, proper, scrupulous, upright

unseasonable *adj* **2** = **untimely**, ill-timed, inappropriate, inopportune, mistimed, out of keeping, unsuitable

unseat *vb* **1** = **throw**, unhorse, unsaddle **2** = **depose**, dethrone, discharge, dismiss, displace, oust, overthrow, remove

unseemly *adj* **1** = **improper**, discreditable, disreputable, inappropriate, indecorous, indelicate, in poor taste, out of keeping, out of place, unbecoming, unbefitting, undignified, unrefined, unsuitable
Antonyms *adj* acceptable, appropriate, becoming, decorous, fitting, proper, refined, seemly, suitable

unseen *adj* **1** = **hidden**, concealed, invisible, obscure, undetected, unnoticed, unobserved, unobtrusive, unperceived, veiled

passage, not previously seen, that is presented to students for translation.

unselfish Ⓣ (ʌnˈsɛlfɪʃ) *adj* not selfish; generous.
▸**unˈselfishly** *adv* ▸**unˈselfishness** *n*

unsettle Ⓣ (ʌnˈsɛtᵊl) *vb* **unsettles, unsettling, unsettled. 1** (*usually tr*) to change or become changed from a fixed or settled condition. **2** (*tr*) to confuse or agitate (emotions, the mind, etc.).
▸**unˈsettlement** *n*

unsettled Ⓣ (ʌnˈsɛtᵊld) *adj* **1** lacking order or stability: *an unsettled era.* **2** unpredictable: *an unsettled climate.* **3** constantly changing or moving from place to place: *an unsettled life.* **4** (of controversy, etc.) not brought to an agreed conclusion. **5** (of debts, law cases, etc.) not disposed of.
▸**unˈsettledness** *n*

unsex (ʌnˈsɛks) *vb* (*tr*) *Chiefly literary.* to deprive (a person) of the attributes of his or her sex, esp. to make a woman more callous.

unshapen (ʌnˈʃeɪpᵊn) *adj* **1** having no definite shape; shapeless. **2** deformed; misshapen.

unsheathe (ʌnˈʃiːð) *vb* **unsheathes, unsheathing, unsheathed.** (*tr*) to draw or pull out (something, esp. a weapon) from a sheath.

unship (ʌnˈʃɪp) *vb* **unships, unshipping, unshipped. 1** to be or cause to be unloaded, discharged, or disembarked from a ship. **2** (*tr*) *Naut.* to remove from a regular place: *to unship oars.*

unsighted (ʌnˈsaɪtɪd) *adj* **1** not sighted. **2** not having a clear view. **3** (of a gun) not equipped with a sight.
▸**unˈsightedly** *adv*

unsightly Ⓣ (ʌnˈsaɪtlɪ) *adj* unpleasant or unattractive to look at; ugly.
▸**unˈsightliness** *n*

unskilful Ⓣ *or US* **unskillful** (ʌnˈskɪlfʊl) *adj* lacking dexterity or proficiency.
▸**unˈskilfully** *or US* **unˈskillfully** *adv* ▸**unˈskilfulness** *or US* **unˈskillfulness** *n*

unskilled Ⓣ (ʌnˈskɪld) *adj* **1** not having or requiring any special skill or training: *an unskilled job.* **2** having no skill; inexpert.

unsling (ʌnˈslɪŋ) *vb* **unslings, unslinging, unslung.** (*tr*) **1** to remove or release from a slung position. **2** to remove slings from.

unsnap (ʌnˈsnæp) *vb* **unsnaps, unsnapping, unsnapped.** (*tr*) to unfasten (the snap or catch) of (something).

unsnarl (ʌnˈsnɑːl) *vb* (*tr*) to free from a snarl or tangle.

unsociable Ⓣ (ʌnˈsəʊʃəbᵊl) *adj* **1** (of a person) disinclined to associate or fraternize with others. **2** unconducive to social intercourse: *an unsociable neighbourhood.*
▸**unˌsociaˈbility** *or* **unˈsociableness** *n*

unsocial (ʌnˈsəʊʃəl) *adj* **1** not social; antisocial. **2** (of the hours of work of certain jobs) falling outside the normal working day.

unsophisticated Ⓣ (ˌʌnsəˈfɪstɪˌkeɪtɪd) *adj* **1** lacking experience or worldly wisdom. **2** marked by a lack of refinement or complexity: *an unsophisticated machine.* **3** unadulterated or genuine.
▸**ˌunsoˈphistiˌcatedly** *adv* ▸**ˌunsoˈphistiˌcatedness** *or* **ˌunsoˌphistiˈcation** *n*

unsound Ⓣ (ʌnˈsaʊnd) *adj* **1** diseased or unstable: *of unsound mind.* **2** unreliable or fallacious: *unsound advice.* **3** lacking strength or firmness: *unsound foundations.* **4** of doubtful financial or commercial viability: *an unsound enterprise.*
▸**unˈsoundly** *adv* ▸**unˈsoundness** *n*

unsparing Ⓣ (ʌnˈspɛərɪŋ) *adj* **1** not sparing or frugal; lavish. **2** showing harshness or severity.
▸**unˈsparingly** *adv* ▸**unˈsparingness** *n*

unspeakable Ⓣ (ʌnˈspiːkəbᵊl) *adj* **1** incapable of expression in words: *unspeakable ecstasy.* **2** indescribably bad or evil. **3** not to be uttered: *unspeakable thoughts.*
▸**unˈspeakableness** *n* ▸**unˈspeakably** *adv*

unstable Ⓣ (ʌnˈsteɪbᵊl) *adj* **1** lacking stability, fixity, or firmness. **2** disposed to temperamental or psychological variability. **3** (of a chemical compound) readily decomposing. **4** *Physics.* **4a** (of an elementary particle) having a very short lifetime. **4b** spontaneously decomposing by nuclear decay: *an unstable nuclide.* **5** *Electronics.* (of an electrical circuit, etc.) having a tendency to self-oscillation.
▸**unˈstableness** *n* ▸**unˈstably** *adv*

unsteady Ⓣ (ʌnˈstɛdɪ) *adj* **1** not securely fixed: *an unsteady foothold.* **2** (of behaviour, etc.) erratic. **3** without regularity: *an unsteady rhythm.* **4** (of a manner of walking, etc.) precarious or staggering, as from intoxication.
▸**unˈsteadily** *adv* ▸**unˈsteadiness** *n*

unstep (ʌnˈstɛp) *vb* **unsteps, unstepping, unstepped.** (*tr*) *Naut.* to remove (a mast) from its step.

unstick (ʌnˈstɪk) *vb* **unsticks, unsticking, unstuck.** (*tr*) to free or loosen (something stuck).

unstop (ʌnˈstɒp) *vb* **unstops, unstopping, unstopped.** (*tr*) **1** to remove the stop or stopper from. **2** to free from any stoppage or obstruction. **3** to draw out the stops on (an organ).
▸**unˈstoppable** *adj* ▸**unˈstoppably** *adv*

unstopped (ʌnˈstɒpt) *adj* **1** not obstructed or stopped up. **2** *Phonetics.* denoting a speech sound for whose articulation the closure is not complete. **3** *Prosody.* (of verse) having the sense of the line carried over into the next. **4** (of an organ pipe or a string on a musical instrument) not stopped.

unstriated (ʌnˈstraɪˌeɪtɪd) *adj* (of muscle) composed of elongated cells that do not have striations; smooth.

unstring (ʌnˈstrɪŋ) *vb* **unstrings, unstringing, unstrung.** (*tr*) **1** to remove the strings of. **2** (of beads, etc.) to remove from a string. **3** to weaken emotionally (a person or his nerves).

unstriped (ʌnˈstraɪpt) *adj* (esp. of smooth muscle) not having stripes; unstriated.

unstructured (ʌnˈstrʌktʃəd) *adj* **1** without formal structure or systematic organization. **2** without a preformed shape; (esp. of clothes) loose; untailored.

unstrung (ʌnˈstrʌŋ) *adj* **1** emotionally distressed; unnerved. **2** (of a stringed instrument) with the strings detached.

unstuck (ʌnˈstʌk) *adj* **1** freed from being stuck, glued, fastened, etc. **2** **come unstuck.** to suffer failure or disaster.

unstudied (ʌnˈstʌdɪd) *adj* **1** natural. **2** (foll. by *in*) without knowledge or training.

unsubstantial Ⓣ (ˌʌnsəbˈstænʃəl) *adj* **1** lacking weight or firmness. **2** (of an argument) of doubtful validity. **3** of no material existence.
▸**ˌunsubˌstantiˈality** *n* ▸**ˌunsubˈstantially** *adv*

unsung Ⓣ (ʌnˈsʌŋ) *adj* **1** not acclaimed or honoured: *unsung deeds.* **2** not yet sung.

THESAURUS

unselfish *adj* = **generous**, altruistic, charitable, devoted, disinterested, humanitarian, kind, liberal, magnanimous, noble, self-denying, selfless, self-sacrificing

unsettle *vb* **2** = **disturb**, agitate, bother, confuse, discompose, disconcert, disorder, faze, fluster, perturb, rattle (*inf.*), ruffle, throw (*inf.*), throw into confusion, throw into disorder, throw into uproar, throw off balance, trouble, unbalance, unnerve, upset

unsettled *adj* **1** = **unstable**, disorderly, insecure, shaky, unsteady **1** = **restless**, agitated, anxious, confused, disturbed, flustered, on edge, perturbed, restive, shaken, tense, troubled, uneasy, unnerved, wired (*sl.*) **2** = **inconstant**, changeable, changing, uncertain, unpredictable, variable **4** = **unresolved**, debatable, doubtful, moot, open, undecided, undetermined, up in the air **5** = **owing**, due, in arrears, outstanding, payable, pending

unsightly *adj* = **ugly**, disagreeable, hideous, horrid, repulsive, revolting (*inf.*), unattractive, unpleasant, unprepossessing
Antonyms *adj* agreeable, attractive, beautiful, comely, cute, handsome, pleasing, prepossessing, pretty

unskilful *adj* = **clumsy**, awkward, bungling, cowboy (*inf.*), fumbling, incompetent, inept, inexpert, maladroit, unhandy, unpractised, unworkmanlike

unskilled *adj* **2** = **unprofessional**, amateurish, cowboy (*inf.*), inexperienced, uneducated, unqualified, untalented, untrained
Antonyms *adj* adept, expert, masterly, professional, qualified, skilled, talented

unsociable *adj* **1** = **unfriendly**, chilly, cold, convivial, distant, hostile, inhospitable, introverted, reclusive, retiring, standoffish, uncongenial, unforthcoming, unneighbourly, unsocial, withdrawn
Antonyms *adj* congenial, convivial, friendly, gregarious, hospitable, neighbourly, outgoing, sociable

unsophisticated *adj* **1** = **natural**, artless, childlike, guileless, inexperienced, ingenuous, innocent, naive, unaffected, untutored, unworldly **2** = **simple**, plain, straightforward, uncomplex, uncomplicated, uninvolved, unrefined, unspecialized
Antonyms *adj* ≠ **simple:** advanced, complex, complicated, elegant, esoteric, intricate, sophisticated

unsound *adj* **1** = **unhealthy**, ailing, defective, delicate, deranged, diseased, frail, ill, in poor health, unbalanced, unhinged, unstable, unwell, weak **2** = **invalid**, defective, erroneous, fallacious, false, faulty, flawed, ill-founded, illogical, shaky, specious, unreliable, weak **3** = **unstable**, flimsy, insecure, not solid, rickety, shaky, tottering, unreliable, unsafe, unsteady, wobbly
Antonyms *adj* ≠ **unstable:** reliable, safe, solid, sound, stable, steady, strong, sturdy

unsparing *adj* **1** = **lavish**, abundant, bountiful, generous, liberal, munificent, open-handed, plenteous, prodigal, profuse, ungrudging, unstinting **2** = **severe**, cold-blooded, hard, harsh, implacable, inexorable, relentless, rigorous, ruthless, stern, stringent, uncompromising, unforgiving, unmerciful

unspeakable *adj* **1** = **indescribable**, beyond description, beyond words, inconceivable, ineffable, inexpressible, overwhelming, unbelievable, unimaginable, unutterable, wonderful **2** = **dreadful**, abominable, abysmal, appalling, awful, bad, evil, execrable, frightful, from hell (*inf.*), heinous, hellacious (*US sl.*), horrible, loathsome, monstrous, odious, repellent, shocking, too horrible for words

unstable *adj* **1** = **insecure**, not fixed, precarious, rickety, risky, shaky, tottering, unsettled, unsteady, wobbly **1** = **changeable**, fitful, fluctuating, inconstant, unpredictable, unsteady, variable, volatile **2** = **unpredictable**, capricious, changeable, erratic, inconsistent, irrational, temperamental, unreliable, untrustworthy, vacillating
Antonyms *adj* ≠ **changeable:** constant, predictable, stable, steady ≠ **unpredictable:** consistent, level-headed, rational, reliable, stable, trustworthy

unsteady *adj* **1** = **unstable**, infirm, insecure, precarious, reeling, rickety, shaky, tottering, treacherous, unsafe, wobbly **3** = **erratic**, changeable, flickering, flighty, fluctuating, inconstant, irregular, temperamental, unreliable, unsettled, vacillating, variable, volatile, wavering

unsubstantial *adj* **1** = **flimsy**, airy, fragile, frail, inadequate, light, slight, thin **2** = **unsound**, erroneous, full of holes, ill-founded, superficial, tenuous, unsupported, weak **3** = **immaterial**, dreamlike, fanciful, illusory, imaginary, impalpable, visionary

unsung *adj* **1** = **unacknowledged**, anonymous,

unsuspected (ˌʌnsəˈspɛktɪd) *adj* **1** not under suspicion. **2** not known to exist.
▸ˌ**unsusˈpectedly** *adv* ▸ˌ**unsusˈpectedness** *n*

unswerving ❶ (ʌnˈswɜːvɪŋ) *adj* not turning aside; constant.

untangle ❶ (ʌnˈtæŋgᵊl) *vb* **untangles, untangling, untangled.** (*tr*) **1** to free from a tangled condition. **2** to free from confusion.

untaught (ʌnˈtɔːt) *adj* **1** without training or education. **2** attained or achieved without instruction.

untenable ❶ (ʌnˈtɛnəbᵊl) *adj* **1** (of theories, etc.) incapable of being maintained or vindicated. **2** unable to be maintained against attack.
▸**unˌtenaˈbility** *or* **unˈtenableness** *n* ▸**unˈtenably** *adv*

unthinkable ❶ (ʌnˈθɪŋkəbᵊl) *adj* **1** not to be contemplated; out of the question. **2** unimaginable; inconceivable. **3** unreasonable; improbable.
▸**unˈthinkably** *adv*

unthinking ❶ (ʌnˈθɪŋkɪŋ) *adj* **1** lacking thoughtfulness; inconsiderate. **2** heedless; inadvertent. **3** not thinking or able to think.
▸**unˈthinkingly** *adv* ▸**unˈthinkingness** *n*

unthread (ʌnˈθrɛd) *vb* (*tr*) **1** to draw out the thread or threads from (a needle, etc.). **2** to disentangle.

unthrone (ʌnˈθrəʊn) *vb* **unthrones, unthroning, unthroned.** (*tr*) a less common word for **dethrone.**

untidy ❶ (ʌnˈtaɪdɪ) *adj* **untidier, untidiest. 1** not neat; slovenly. ◆ *vb* **untidies, untidying, untidied. 2** (*tr*) to make untidy.
▸**unˈtidily** *adv* ▸**unˈtidiness** *n*

untie ❶ (ʌnˈtaɪ) *vb* **unties, untying, untied. 1** to unfasten or free (a knot or something that is tied) or (of a knot, etc.) to become unfastened. **2** (*tr*) to free from constraint or restriction.

until (ʌnˈtɪl) *conj* (*subordinating*) **1** up to (a time) that: *he laughed until he cried.* **2** (*used with a negative*) before (a time or event): *until you change, you can't go out.* ◆ *prep* **3** (often preceded by *up*) in or throughout the period before: *he waited until six.* **4** (*used with a negative*) earlier than; before: *he won't come until tomorrow.* [C13 *untill;* see TILL[1]]

> **USAGE NOTE** The use of *until such time as* (as in *industrial action will continue until such time as our demands are met*) is unnecessary and should be avoided: *industrial action will continue until our demands are met.* See also **till**[1].

untimely ❶ (ʌnˈtaɪmlɪ) *adj* **1** occurring before the expected, normal, or proper time: *an untimely death.* **2** inappropriate to the occasion, time, or season: *his joking at the funeral was most untimely.* ◆ *adv* **3** prematurely or inopportunely.
▸**unˈtimeliness** *n*

unto (ˈʌntuː) *prep Arch.* to. [C13: from ON]

untogether (ˌʌntəˈgɛðə) *adj Sl.* incompetent or badly organized; mentally or emotionally unstable.

untold ❶ (ʌnˈtəʊld) *adj* **1** incapable of description: *untold suffering.* **2** incalculably great in number or quantity: *untold thousands.* **3** not told.

untouchable (ʌnˈtʌtʃəbᵊl) *adj* **1** lying beyond reach. **2** above reproach, suspicion, or impeachment. **3** unable to be touched. ◆ *n* **4** a member of the lowest class in India, whom those of the four main castes were formerly forbidden to touch.
▸**unˌtouchaˈbility** *n*

untoward ❶ (ˌʌntəˈwɔːd) *adj* **1** characterized by misfortune or annoyance. **2** not auspicious; unfavourable. **3** unseemly. **4** out of the ordinary; out of the way. **5** *Arch.* perverse. **6** *Obs.* awkward.
▸ˌ**untoˈwardly** *adv* ▸ˌ**untoˈwardness** *n*

untrue ❶ (ʌnˈtruː) *adj* **1** incorrect or false. **2** disloyal. **3** diverging from a rule, standard, or measure; inaccurate.
▸**unˈtruly** *adv*

untruss (ʌnˈtrʌs) *vb* **1** (*tr*) to release from or as if from a truss; unfasten. **2** *Obs.* to undress.

untruth ❶ (ʌnˈtruːθ) *n* **1** the state or quality of being untrue. **2** a statement, etc., that is not true.

untruthful ❶ (ʌnˈtruːθfʊl) *adj* **1** (of a person) given to lying. **2** diverging from the truth.
▸**unˈtruthfully** *adv* ▸**unˈtruthfulness** *n*

untuck (ʌnˈtʌk) *vb* to become or cause to become loose or not tucked in: *to untuck the blankets.*

untutored ❶ (ʌnˈtjuːtəd) *adj* **1** without formal education. **2** lacking sophistication or refinement.

unused ❶ *adj* **1** (ʌnˈjuːzd). not being or never having been made use of. **2** (ʌnˈjuːst). (*postpositive;* foll. by *to*) not accustomed or used (to something).

unusual ❶ (ʌnˈjuːʒʊəl) *adj* uncommon; extraordinary: *an unusual design.*
▸**unˈusually** *adv*

unutterable ❶ (ʌnˈʌtərəbᵊl) *adj* incapable of being expressed in words.
▸**unˈutterableness** *n* ▸**unˈutterably** *adv*

unvarnished ❶ (ʌnˈvɑːnɪʃt) *adj* not elaborated upon or glossed; plain and direct: *the unvarnished truth.*

unveil ❶ (ʌnˈveɪl) *vb* **1** (*tr*) to remove the cover from, esp. in the ceremonial unveiling of a monument, etc. **2** to remove the veil from (one's own or another person's face). **3** (*tr*) to make (something concealed) known or public.

unveiling (ʌnˈveɪlɪŋ) *n* **1** a ceremony involving the removal of a veil covering a statue, etc., for the first time. **2** the presentation of something, esp. for the first time.

unvoice (ʌnˈvɔɪs) *vb* **unvoices, unvoicing, unvoiced.** (*tr*) *Phonetics.* **1** to pronounce without vibration of the vocal cords. **2** Also: **devoice.** to make (a voiced speech sound) voiceless.

unvoiced (ʌnˈvɔɪst) *adj* **1** not expressed or spoken. **2** articulated without vibration of the vocal cords; voiceless.

THESAURUS

disregarded, neglected, unacclaimed, unappreciated, uncelebrated, unhailed, unhonoured, unknown, unnamed, unrecognized

unswerving *adj* = **constant**, dedicated, devoted, direct, firm, resolute, single-minded, staunch, steadfast, steady, true, undeviating, unfaltering, unflagging, untiring, unwavering

untangle *vb* **1** = **disentangle**, extricate, unravel, unsnarl **2** = **solve**, clear up, explain, straighten out
Antonyms *vb* ≠ **disentangle:** enmesh, entangle, jumble, muddle, snarl, tangle ≠ **solve:** complicate, confuse, muddle, puzzle

untenable *adj* **1** = **unsustainable**, fallacious, flawed, groundless, illogical, indefensible, insupportable, shaky, unreasonable, unsound, weak
Antonyms *adj* defensible, justified, logical, rational, reasonable, sensible, sound, supportable, unarguable, uncontestable, valid, verifiable, well-grounded

unthinkable *adj* **1, 3** = **impossible**, absurd, illogical, improbable, not on (*inf.*), out of the question, preposterous, unlikely, unreasonable **2** = **inconceivable**, beyond belief, beyond the bounds of possibility, implausible, incredible, insupportable, unbelievable, unimaginable

unthinking *adj* **1** = **thoughtless**, blundering, inconsiderate, insensitive, rude, selfish, tactless, undiplomatic **2** = **unconscious**, careless, heedless, impulsive, inadvertent, instinctive, mechanical, negligent, oblivious, unmindful, unwitting
Antonyms *adj* ≠ **unconscious:** careful, conscious, deliberate, heedful, mindful, sensible, witting

untidy *adj* **1** = **messy**, bedraggled, chaotic, cluttered, disarrayed, disordered, higgledy-piggledy (*inf.*), jumbled, littered, muddled, muddly, mussy (*US inf.*), rumpled, shambolic, slatternly, slipshod, sloppy (*inf.*), slovenly, topsy-turvy, unkempt
Antonyms *adj* methodical, neat, orderly, presentable, ship-shape, spruce, systematic, tidy, well-kept

untie *vb* **1, 2** = **undo**, free, loosen, release, unbind, unbridle, unclasp, unfasten, unknot, unlace, unstrap

untimely *adj* **1** = **early**, premature, unseasonable **2** = **ill-timed**, awkward, badly timed, inappropriate, inauspicious, inconvenient, inopportune, mistimed, unfortunate, unsuitable
Antonyms *adj* ≠ **early:** seasonable, timely ≠ **ill-timed:** appropriate, auspicious, convenient, fortunate, opportune, suitable, welcome, well-timed

untold *adj* **1** = **indescribable**, inexpressible, undreamed of, unimaginable, unspeakable, unthinkable, unutterable **2** = **countless**, incalculable, innumerable, measureless, myriad, numberless, uncountable, uncounted, unnumbered **3** = **undisclosed**, hidden, private, secret, unknown, unpublished, unrecounted, unrevealed

untoward *adj* **1** = **troublesome**, annoying, awkward, disastrous, ill-timed, inconvenient, inimical, irritating, unfortunate, vexatious **2** = **unfavourable**, adverse, contrary, inauspicious, inopportune, unlucky, untimely **3** = **unseemly**, improper, inappropriate, indecorous, out of place, unbecoming, unfitting, unsuitable

untrue *adj* **1** = **false**, deceptive, dishonest, erroneous, fallacious, inaccurate, incorrect, lying, misleading, mistaken, sham, spurious, untruthful, wrong **2** = **unfaithful**, deceitful, disloyal, faithless, false, forsworn, inconstant, perfidious, traitorous, treacherous, two-faced, untrustworthy
Antonyms *adj* ≠ **false:** accurate, correct, factual, right, true ≠ **unfaithful:** constant, dependable, faithful, honest, honourable, loyal

untruth *n* **1** = **untruthfulness**, deceitfulness, duplicity, falsity, inveracity (*rare*), lying, mendacity, perjury, truthlessness **2** = **lie**, deceit, fabrication, falsehood, falsification, fib, fiction, pork pie (*Brit. sl.*), porky (*Brit. sl.*), prevarication, story, tale, trick, whopper (*inf.*)

untruthful *adj* **1** = **dishonest**, crooked (*inf.*), deceitful, deceptive, dissembling, false, fibbing, hypocritical, lying, mendacious
Antonyms *adj* candid, honest, sincere, true, truthful, veracious

untutored *adj* **1** = **uneducated**, ignorant, illiterate, unlearned, unschooled, untrained, unversed **2** = **unsophisticated**, artless, inexperienced, simple, unpractised, unrefined

unused *adj* **1** = **unutilized**, available, extra, fresh, intact, left, leftover, new, pristine, remaining, unconsumed, unexhausted **2** *with* **to** = **unaccustomed to**, a stranger to, inexperienced in, new to, not ready for, not up to, unfamiliar with, unhabituated to

unusual *adj* = **extraordinary**, abnormal, atypical, bizarre, curious, different, exceptional, left-field (*inf.*), notable, odd, out of the ordinary, phenomenal, queer, rare, remarkable, singular, strange, surprising, uncommon, unconventional, unexpected, unfamiliar, unwonted
Antonyms *adj* average, banal, commonplace, conventional, everyday, familiar, normal, routine, traditional, typical, unremarkable, usual

unutterable *adj* = **indescribable**, beyond words, extreme, ineffable, overwhelming, unimaginable, unspeakable

unvarnished *adj* = **plain**, bare, candid, frank, honest, naked, pure, pure and simple, simple, sincere, stark, straightforward, unadorned, unembellished

unveil *vb* **3** = **reveal**, bare, bring to light, disclose, divulge, expose, lay bare, lay open, make known, make public, uncover
Antonyms *vb* cloak, conceal, cover, disguise, hide, mask, obscure, veil

DICTIONARY

unwaged (ʌnˈweɪdʒd) *adj* of or denoting a person who is not receiving pay because of being unemployed or working in the home.

unwarrantable (ʌnˈwɒrəntəbᵊl) *adj* incapable of vindication or justification.
▸**unˈwarrantableness** *n* ▸**unˈwarrantably** *adv*

unwarranted ❶ (ʌnˈwɒrəntɪd) *adj* **1** lacking justification or authorization. **2** another word for **unwarrantable.**

unwary ❶ (ʌnˈwɛərɪ) *adj* lacking caution or prudence.
▸**unˈwarily** *adv* ▸**unˈwariness** *n*

unwearied (ʌnˈwɪərɪd) *adj* **1** not abating or tiring. **2** not fatigued; fresh.
▸**unˈweariedly** *adv* ▸**unˈweariedness** *n*

unweighed (ʌnˈweɪd) *adj* **1** (of quantities purchased, etc.) not measured for weight. **2** (of statements, etc.) not carefully considered.

unwell ❶ (ʌnˈwɛl) *adj* (*postpositive*) not well; ill.

unwept (ʌnˈwɛpt) *adj* **1** not wept for or lamented. **2** *Rare.* (of tears) not shed.

unwholesome ❶ (ʌnˈhəʊlsəm) *adj* **1** detrimental to physical or mental health: *an unwholesome climate.* **2** morally harmful: *unwholesome practices.* **3** indicative of illness, esp. in appearance. **4** (esp. of food) of inferior quality.
▸**unˈwholesomeness** *n*

unwieldy ❶ (ʌnˈwiːldɪ) *adj* **1** too heavy, large, or awkwardly shaped to be easily handled. **2** ungainly; clumsy.
▸**unˈwieldily** *adv* ▸**unˈwieldiness** *n*

unwilled (ʌnˈwɪld) *adj* not intentional; involuntary.

unwilling ❶ (ʌnˈwɪlɪŋ) *adj* **1** reluctant. **2** performed or said with reluctance.
▸**unˈwillingly** *adv* ▸**unˈwillingness** *n*

unwind ❶ (ʌnˈwaɪnd) *vb* **unwinds, unwinding, unwound. 1** to slacken, undo, or unravel or cause to slacken, undo, or unravel. **2** (*tr*) to disentangle. **3** to make or become relaxed: *he finds it hard to unwind.*
▸**unˈwindable** *adj*

unwise ❶ (ʌnˈwaɪz) *adj* lacking wisdom or prudence.
▸**unˈwisely** *adv* ▸**unˈwiseness** *n*

unwish (ʌnˈwɪʃ) *vb* (*tr*) **1** to retract or revoke (a wish). **2** to desire (something) not to be or take place.

unwitting ❶ (ʌnˈwɪtɪŋ) *adj* (*usually prenominal*) **1** not knowing or conscious. **2** not intentional; inadvertent. [OE *unwitende,* from UN-[1] + *witting,* present participle of *witan* to know]
▸**unˈwittingly** *adv* ▸**unˈwittingness** *n*

unwonted ❶ (ʌnˈwəʊntɪd) *adj* **1** out of the ordinary; unusual. **2** (usually foll. by *to*) *Arch.* unaccustomed; unused.
▸**unˈwontedly** *adv*

unworldly ❶ (ʌnˈwɜːldlɪ) *adj* **1** not concerned with material values or pursuits. **2** lacking sophistication; naive. **3** not of this earth or world.
▸**unˈworldliness** *n*

unworthy ❶ (ʌnˈwɜːðɪ) *adj* **1** (often foll. by *of*) not deserving or worthy. **2** (often foll. by *of*) beneath the level considered befitting (to): *that remark is unworthy of you.* **3** lacking merit or value. **4** (of treatment) not warranted.
▸**unˈworthily** *adv* ▸**unˈworthiness** *n*

unwound (ʌnˈwaʊnd) *vb* the past tense and past participle of **unwind.**

unwrap (ʌnˈræp) *vb* **unwraps, unwrapping, unwrapped.** to remove the covering or wrapping from (something) or (of something wrapped) to have the covering come off.

unwritten ❶ (ʌnˈrɪtᵊn) *adj* **1** not printed or in writing. **2** effective only through custom.

unwritten law *n* the law based upon custom, usage, and judicial decisions, as distinguished from the enactments of a legislature, orders or decrees in writing, etc.

unyoke (ʌnˈjəʊk) *vb* **unyokes, unyoking, unyoked. 1** to release (an animal, etc.) from a yoke. **2** (*tr*) to set free; liberate. **3** (*tr*) to disconnect or separate.

unzip (ʌnˈzɪp) *vb* **unzips, unzipping, unzipped.** to unfasten the zip of (a garment, etc.) or (of a zip or garment with a zip) to become unfastened: *her skirt unzipped as she sat down.*

up (ʌp) *prep* **1** indicating movement from a lower to a higher position: *climbing up a mountain.* **2** at a higher or further level or position in or on: *a shop up the road.* ◆ *adv* **3** (*often particle*) to an upward, higher, or erect position, esp. indicating readiness for an activity: *up and doing something.* **4** (*particle*) indicating intensity or completion of an action: *he tore up the cheque.* **5** to the place referred to or where the speaker is: *the man came up and asked the way.* **6a** to a more important place: *up to London.* **6b** to a more northerly place: *up to Scotland.* **6c** (of a member of some British universities) to or at university. **6d** in a particular part of the country: *up north.* **7** above the horizon: *the sun is up.* **8** appearing for trial: *up before the magistrate.* **9** having gained: *ten pounds up on the deal.* **10** higher in price: *coffee is up again.* **11** raised (for discussion, etc.): *the plan was up for consideration.* **12** taught: *well up in physics.* **13** (*functioning as imperative*) get, stand, etc., up: *up with you!* **14 all up with.** *Inf.* **14a** over; finished. **14b** doomed to die. **15 up with.** (*functioning as imperative*) wanting the beginning or continuation of: *up with the monarchy!* **16 something's up.** *Inf.* something strange is happening. **17 up against. 17a** touching. **17b** having to cope with: *look what we're up against now.* **18 up for.** as a candidate or applicant for: *he's up for re-election again.* **19 up to. 19a** devising or scheming: *she's up to no good.* **19b** dependent or incumbent upon: *the decision is up to you.* **19c** equal to (a challenge, etc.) or capable of (doing, etc.): *are you up to playing in the final?* **19d** as far as: *up to his waist in mud.* **19e** as many as: *up to two years' waiting time.* **f.** comparable with: *not up to your normal standard.* **20 up top.** *Inf.* in the head or mind. **21 up yours.** *Sl.* a vulgar expression of contempt or refusal. **22 what's up?** *Inf.* **22a** what is the matter? **22b** what is happening? ◆ *adj* **23** (*predicative*) of a high or higher position. **24** (*predicative*) out of bed: *the children aren't up yet.* **25** (*prenominal*) of or relating to a train or trains to a more important place or one regarded as higher: *the up platform.* **26** (*predicative*) over or completed: *their time was up.* **27** (*predicative*) beating one's opponent by a specified amount: *a goal up.* ◆ *vb* **ups, upping, upped. 28** (*tr*) to increase or raise. **29** (*intr;* foll. by *and* with a verb) *Inf.* to do (something) suddenly, etc.: *she upped and married someone else.* ◆ *n* **30** a high point (esp. in **ups and downs**). **31** *Sl.* another word (esp. US) for **upper** (sense 8). **32 on the up and up. 32a** trustworthy or honest. **32b** *Brit.* on the upward trend or movement: *our firm's on the up and up.* [OE *upp*]

> **USAGE NOTE** The use of *up* before *until* is redundant and should be avoided: *the talks will continue until* (not *up until*) *23rd March.*

up- *prefix* up, upper, or upwards: *uproot; upmost; upthrust; upgrade; uplift.*

up-anchor *vb* (*intr*) *Naut.* to weigh anchor.

up-and-coming ❶ *adj* promising continued or future success; enterprising.

up-and-down *adj* **1** moving or formed alternately upwards and downwards. ◆ *adv, prep* **up and down. 2** backwards and forwards (along).

up-and-over *adj* (of a door, etc.) opened by being lifted and moved into a horizontal position.

THESAURUS

unwarranted *adj* **1** = **unnecessary**, gratuitous, groundless, indefensible, inexcusable, uncalled-for, unjust, unjustified, unprovoked, unreasonable, wrong

unwary *adj* = **careless**, hasty, heedless, imprudent, incautious, indiscreet, rash, reckless, thoughtless, uncircumspect, unguarded, unwatchful
Antonyms *adj* cautious, chary, circumspect, discreet, guarded, prudent, wary, watchful

unwell *adj* = **ill**, ailing, at death's door, green about the gills, indisposed, in poor health, off colour, out of sorts, poorly (*inf.*), sick, sickly, under the weather (*inf.*), unhealthy
Antonyms *adj* fine, healthy, robust, sound, well

unwholesome *adj* **1** = **harmful**, deleterious, insalubrious, insanitary, junk (*inf.*), noxious, poisonous, tainted, unhealthy, unnourishing **2** = **wicked**, bad, corrupting, degrading, demoralizing, depraving, evil, immoral, maleficent, perverting **3** = **sickly**, anaemic, pale, pallid, pasty, wan
Antonyms *adj* ≠ **harmful:** beneficial, germ-free, healthy, hygienic, salubrious, sanitary, wholesome ≠ **wicked:** edifying, moral

unwieldy *adj* **1** = **awkward**, burdensome, cumbersome, inconvenient, unhandy, unmanageable **2** = **bulky**, clumsy, clunky (*inf.*), hefty, massive, ponderous, ungainly, weighty

unwilling *adj* **1** = **reluctant**, averse, demurring, disinclined, grudging, indisposed, laggard (*rare*), loath, not in the mood, opposed, resistant, unenthusiastic
Antonyms *adj* amenable, compliant, disposed, eager, enthusiastic, inclined, voluntary, willing

unwind *vb* **1, 2** = **unravel**, disentangle, slacken, uncoil, undo, unreel, unroll, untwine, untwist **3** = **relax**, calm down, let oneself go, loosen up, make oneself at home, mellow out, quieten down, sit back, slow down, take a break, take it easy, wind down

unwise *adj* = **foolish**, asinine, foolhardy, ill-advised, ill-considered, ill-judged, impolitic, improvident, imprudent, inadvisable, inane, indiscreet, injudicious, irresponsible, rash, reckless, senseless, short-sighted, silly, stupid
Antonyms *adj* discreet, judicious, politic, prudent, responsible, sensible, shrewd, wise

unwitting *adj* **1** = **unknowing**, ignorant, innocent, unaware, unconscious, unsuspecting **2** = **unintentional**, accidental, chance, inadvertent, involuntary, undesigned, unintended, unmeant, unplanned
Antonyms *adj* ≠ **unknowing:** conscious, deliberate, knowing, witting ≠ **unintentional:** deliberate, designed, intended, intentional, meant, planned

unwonted *adj* **1** = **unusual**, atypical, extraordinary, infrequent, out of the ordinary, peculiar, rare, seldom seen, singular, unaccustomed, uncommon, uncustomary, unexpected, unfamiliar, unheard-of

unworldly *adj* **1** = **spiritual**, abstract, celestial, metaphysical, nonmaterialistic, religious, transcendental **2** = **naive**, as green as grass, green, idealistic, inexperienced, innocent, raw, trusting, unsophisticated, wet behind the ears (*inf.*) **3** = **otherworldly**, ethereal, extraterrestrial, unearthly

unworthy *adj* **1** = **undeserving**, ineligible, not deserving of, not fit for, not good enough, not worth **2** *often foll. by* **of** = **unbefitting**, beneath, improper, inappropriate, out of character, out of place, unbecoming, unfitting, unseemly, unsuitable **3** = **dishonourable**, base, contemptible, degrading, discreditable, disgraceful, disreputable, ignoble, shameful
Antonyms *adj* ≠ **undeserving:** deserving, eligible, fit, meritorious, worthy ≠ **dishonourable:** commendable, creditable, honourable

unwritten *adj* **1** = **oral**, unrecorded, vocal, word-of-mouth **2** = **customary**, accepted, conventional, tacit, traditional, understood, unformulated

up-and-coming *adj* = **promising**, ambitious, eager, go-getting, on the make (*sl.*), pushing

up-and-under *n Rugby League.* a high kick forwards followed by a charge to the place where the ball lands.

Upanishad (uːˈpʌnɪʃəd) *n Hinduism.* any of a class of the Sanskrit sacred books probably composed between 400 and 200 B.C. and embodying the mystical and esoteric doctrines of ancient Hindu philosophy. [C19: from Sansk. *upanisad* a sitting down near something]

upas (ˈjuːpəs) *n* **1** a large tree of Java having whitish bark and poisonous milky sap. **2** the sap of this tree, used as an arrow poison. ◆ Also called: **antiar.** [C19: from Malay: poison]

upbeat ❶ (ˈʌpˌbiːt) *n* **1** *Music.* **1a** a usually unaccented beat, esp. the last in a bar. **1b** the upward gesture of a conductor's baton indicating this. ◆ *adj* **2** *Inf.* marked by cheerfulness or optimism.

upbraid ❶ (ʌpˈbreɪd) *vb (tr)* **1** to reprove or reproach angrily. **2** to find fault with. [OE *upbregdan*]
▸**upˈbraider** *n* ▸**upˈbraiding** *n*

upbringing ❶ (ˈʌpˌbrɪŋɪŋ) *n* the education of a person during his formative years.

upcast (ˈʌpˌkɑːst) *n* **1** material cast or thrown up. **2** a ventilation shaft through which air leaves a mine. **3** *Geol.* (in a fault) the section of strata that has been displaced upwards. ◆ *adj* **4** directed or thrown upwards. ◆ *vb* **upcasts, upcasting, upcast. 5** *(tr)* to throw or cast up.

upcountry (ʌpˈkʌntrɪ) *adj* **1** of or coming from the interior of a country or region. ◆ *n* **2** the interior part of a region or country. ◆ *adv* **3** towards, in, or into the interior part of a country or region.

update ❶ *vb* (ʌpˈdeɪt), **updates, updating, updated.** *(tr)* **1** to bring up to date. ◆ *n* (ˈʌpˌdeɪt). **2** the act of updating or something that is updated.
▸**upˈdateable** *adj* ▸**upˈdater** *n*

updraught *or US* **updraft** (ˈʌpˌdrɑːft) *n* an upward movement of air or other gas.

upend (ʌpˈɛnd) *vb* **1** to turn or set or become turned or set on end. **2** *(tr)* to affect or upset drastically.

upfront (ˈʌpˈfrʌnt) *adj* **1** open and frank. ◆ *adv, adj* **2** (of money) paid out at the beginning of a business arrangement.

upgrade ❶ *vb* (ʌpˈgreɪd), **upgrades, upgrading, upgraded.** *(tr)* **1** to assign or promote (a person or job) to a higher professional rank or position. **2** to raise in value, importance, esteem, etc. **3** to improve (a breed of livestock) by crossing with a better strain. ◆ *n* (ˈʌpˌgreɪd). **4** *US & Canad.* an upward slope. **5 on the upgrade.** improving or progressing, as in importance, status, health, etc.
▸**upˈgrader** *n*

upheaval ❶ (ʌpˈhiːvᵊl) *n* **1** a strong, sudden, or violent disturbance, as in politics. **2** *Geol.* another word for **uplift** (sense 7).

upheave (ʌpˈhiːv) *vb* **upheaves, upheaving, upheaved** *or* **uphove. 1** to heave or rise upwards. **2** *Geol.* to thrust (land) upwards or (of land) to be thrust upwards. **3** *(tr)* to throw into disorder.

upheld (ʌpˈhɛld) *vb* the past tense and past participle of **uphold.**

uphill ❶ (ˈʌpˈhɪl) *adj* **1** inclining, sloping, or leading upwards. **2** requiring protracted effort: *an uphill task.* ◆ *adv* **3** up an incline or slope. **4** against difficulties. ◆ *n* **5** a rising incline.

uphold ❶ (ʌpˈhəʊld) *vb* **upholds, upholding, upheld.** *(tr)* **1** to maintain or defend against opposition. **2** to give moral support to. **3** *Rare.* to support physically. **4** to lift up.
▸**upˈholder** *n*

upholster (ʌpˈhəʊlstə) *vb (tr)* to fit (chairs, sofas, etc.) with padding, springs, webbing, and covering.
▸**upˈholstery** *n*

upholsterer (ʌpˈhəʊlstərə) *n* a person who upholsters furniture as a profession. [C17: from *upholster* small furniture dealer]

upkeep ❶ (ˈʌpˌkiːp) *n* **1** the act or process of keeping something in good repair, esp. over a long period. **2** the cost of maintenance.

upland (ˈʌplənd) *n* **1** an area of high or relatively high ground. ◆ *adj* **2** relating to or situated in an upland.

uplift ❶ *vb* (ʌpˈlɪft). *(tr)* **1** to raise; lift up. **2** to raise morally, spiritually, etc. **3** *Scot. & NZ.* to collect; pick up (goods, documents, etc.). ◆ *n* (ˈʌpˌlɪft). **4** the act, process, or result of lifting up. **5** the act or process of bettering moral, social, or cultural conditions, etc. **6** *(modifier)* designating a brassiere for lifting and supporting the breasts: *an uplift bra.* **7** the process or result of land being raised to a higher level, as during a period of mountain building.
▸**upˈlifter** *n* ▸**upˈlifting** *adj*

uplighter (ˈʌpˌlaɪtə) *n* a lamp or wall light designed or positioned to cast its light upwards.

up-market *adj* relating to commercial products, services, etc., that are relatively expensive and of superior quality.

upmost (ˈʌpˌməʊst) *adj* another word for **uppermost.**

upon (əˈpɒn) *prep* **1** another word for **on. 2** indicating a position reached by going up: *climb upon my knee.* **3** imminent for: *the weekend was upon us again.* [C13: from UP + ON]

upper ❶ (ˈʌpə) *adj* **1** higher or highest in relation to physical position, wealth, rank, status, etc. **2** *(cap. when part of a name)* lying farther upstream, inland, or farther north: *the upper valley of the Loire.* **3** *(cap. when part of a name) Geol., archaeol.* denoting the late part or division of a period, system, etc.: *Upper Palaeolithic.* **4** *Maths.* (of a limit or bound) greater than or equal to one or more numbers or variables. ◆ *n* **5** the higher of two objects, people, etc. **6** the part of a shoe above the sole, covering the upper surface of the foot. **7 on one's uppers.** destitute. **8** *Sl.* any of various drugs having a stimulant effect.

upper atmosphere *n Meteorol.* that part of the atmosphere above the troposphere, esp. at heights that cannot be reached by balloon.

upper case *Printing.* ◆ *n* **1** the top half of a compositor's type case in which capital letters, reference marks, and accents are kept. ◆ *adj* (**upper-case** *when prenominal*). **2** of or relating to capital letters kept in this case and used in the setting or production of printed or typed matter.

upper chamber *n* another name for an **upper house.**

upper class ❶ *n* **1** the class occupying the highest position in the social hierarchy, esp. the aristocracy. ◆ *adj* (**upper-class** *when prenominal*). **2** of or relating to the upper class.

upper crust *n Inf.* the upper class.

uppercut (ˈʌpəˌkʌt) *n* **1** a short swinging upward blow with the fist delivered at an opponent's chin. ◆ *vb* **uppercuts, uppercutting, uppercut. 2** to hit (an opponent) with an uppercut.

upper hand ❶ *n* **the.** the position of control (esp. in **have** *or* **get the upper hand**).

upper house *n (often cap.)* one of the two houses of a bicameral legislature.

uppermost ❶ (ˈʌpəˌməʊst) *adj also* **upmost. 1** highest in position, power, importance, etc. ◆ *adv* **2** in or into the highest position, etc.

upper regions *pl n* **the.** *Chiefly literary.* the sky; heavens.

upper works *pl n Naut.* the parts of a vessel above the water line when fully laden.

uppish ❶ (ˈʌpɪʃ) *adj Brit. inf.* another word for **uppity** (sense 1). [C18: from UP + -ISH]
▸ˈ**uppishly** *adv* ▸ˈ**uppishness** *n*

uppity ❶ (ˈʌpɪtɪ) *adj Inf.* **1** snobbish, arrogant, or presumptuous. **2** offensively self-assertive. [from UP + fanciful ending, ? infl. by -ITY]

upraise (ʌpˈreɪz) *vb* **upraises, upraising, upraised.** *(tr) Chiefly literary.* to lift up; elevate.
▸**upˈraiser** *n*

uprear (ʌpˈrɪə) *vb (tr)* to lift up; raise.

upright ❶ (ˈʌpˌraɪt) *adj* **1** vertical or erect. **2** honest or just. ◆ *adv* **3** ver-

THESAURUS

upbeat *adj* **2** *Informal* = **cheerful,** buoyant, cheery, encouraging, favourable, forward-looking, heartening, hopeful, looking up, optimistic, positive, promising, rosy

upbraid *vb* **1** = **scold,** admonish, bawl out, berate, blame, carpet (*inf.*), castigate, censure, chew out (*US & Canad. inf.*), chide, condemn, dress down (*inf.*), excoriate, give (someone) a rocket (*Brit. & NZ inf.*), lecture, rap (someone) over the knuckles, read the riot act, rebuke, reprimand, reproach, reprove, slap on the wrist, take to task, tear into (*inf.*), tear (someone) off a strip (*Brit. inf.*), tell off (*inf.*), tick off (*inf.*)

upbringing *n* = **education,** breeding, bringing-up, care, cultivation, nurture, raising, rearing, tending, training

update *vb* **1** = **bring up to date,** amend, modernize, rebrand, renew, revise

upgrade *vb* **1, 2** = **promote,** advance, ameliorate, better, elevate, enhance, improve, raise
Antonyms *vb* degrade, demote, downgrade, lower

upheaval *n* **1** = **disturbance,** cataclysm, disorder, disruption, eruption, overthrow, revolution, turmoil, violent change

uphill *adj* **1** = **ascending,** climbing, mounting, rising **2** = **arduous,** difficult, exhausting, gruelling, hard, laborious, punishing, Sisyphean, strenuous, taxing, tough, wearisome
Antonyms *adj* ≠ **ascending:** descending, downhill, lowering

uphold *vb* **2** = **support,** advocate, aid, back, champion, defend, encourage, endorse, hold to, justify, maintain, promote, stand by, stick up for (*inf.*), sustain, vindicate

upkeep *n* **1** = **maintenance,** conservation, keep, preservation, repair, running, subsistence, support, sustenance **2** = **running costs,** expenditure, expenses, oncosts, operating costs, outlay, overheads

uplift *vb* **1** = **raise,** elevate, heave, hoist, lift up **2** = **improve,** advance, ameliorate, better, civilize, cultivate, edify, inspire, raise, refine, upgrade ◆ *n* **5** = **improvement,** advancement, betterment, cultivation, edification, enhancement, enlightenment, enrichment, refinement

upper *adj* **1** = **higher,** elevated, eminent, greater, high, important, loftier, superior, top, topmost
Antonyms *adj* ≠ **higher:** bottom, inferior, junior, low, lower

upper class *adj* **upper-class 2** = **aristocratic,** blue-blooded, highborn, high-class, noble, patrician, top-drawer, well-bred

upper hand *n* = **control,** advantage, ascendancy, dominion, edge, mastery, superiority, supremacy, sway, whip hand

uppermost *adj* **1** = **top,** chief, dominant, foremost, greatest, highest, leading, loftiest, main, most elevated, paramount, predominant, pre-eminent, primary, principal, supreme, topmost, upmost
Antonyms *adj* ≠ **top:** bottom, bottommost, humblest, least, lowermost, lowest, lowliest

uppish *adj Brit. informal* = **conceited,** affected, arrogant, cocky, high and mighty (*inf.*), hoity-toity (*inf.*), overweening, presumptuous, putting on airs, self-important, snobbish, stuck-up (*inf.*), supercilious, toffee-nosed (*sl., chiefly Brit.*), uppity (*inf.*)
Antonyms *adj* diffident, humble, lowly, meek, obsequious, servile, unaffected, unassertive

uppity *adj* **1, 2** *Informal* = **conceited,** bigheaded (*inf.*), bumptious, cocky, full of oneself, impertinent, on one's high horse (*inf.*), overweening, self-important, swanky (*inf.*), too big for one's boots *or* breeches (*inf.*), uppish (*Brit. inf.*)

upright *adj* **1** = **vertical,** erect, on end, per-

tically. ◆ *n* **4** a vertical support, such as a stake or post. **5** short for **upright piano. 6** the state of being vertical.
▸**'up,rightly** *adv* ▸**'up,rightness** *n*

upright piano *n* a piano which has a rectangular vertical case.

uprise *vb* (ʌp'raɪz), **uprises, uprising, uprose, uprisen. 1** (*tr*) to rise up. ◆ *n* ('ʌp,raɪz). **2** another word for **rise** (senses 23, 24).
▸**up'riser** *n*

uprising 🅣 ('ʌp,raɪzɪŋ, ʌp'raɪzɪŋ) *n* **1** a revolt or rebellion. **2** *Arch.* an ascent.

uproar 🅣 ('ʌp,rɔ:) *n* a commotion or disturbance characterized by loud noise and confusion.

uproarious 🅣 (ʌp'rɔ:rɪəs) *adj* **1** causing or characterized by an uproar. **2** extremely funny. **3** (of laughter, etc.) loud and boisterous.
▸**up'roariously** *adv* ▸**up'roariousness** *n*

uproot 🅣 (ʌp'ru:t) *vb* (*tr*) **1** to pull up by or as if by the roots. **2** to displace (a person or persons) from native or habitual surroundings. **3** to remove or destroy utterly.
▸**up'rooter** *n*

uprush ('ʌp,rʌʃ) *n* an upward rush, as of consciousness.

upsadaisy ('ʌpsə'deɪzɪ) *interj* a variant spelling of **upsy-daisy.**

ups and downs 🅣 *pl n* alternating periods of good and bad fortune, high and low spirits, etc.

upscale ('ʌp'skeɪl) *adj Inf.* of or for the upper end of an economic or social scale; up-market.

upset 🅣 *vb* (ʌp'sɛt), **upsets, upsetting, upset.** (*mainly tr*) **1** (*also intr*) to tip or be tipped over; overturn or spill. **2** to disturb the normal state or stability of: *to upset the balance of nature.* **3** to disturb mentally or emotionally. **4** to defeat or overthrow, usually unexpectedly. **5** to make physically ill: *seafood always upsets my stomach.* **6** to thicken or spread (the end of a bar, etc.) by hammering. ◆ *n* ('ʌp,sɛt). **7** an unexpected defeat or reversal, as in a contest or plans. **8** a disturbance or disorder of the emotions, body, etc. ◆ *adj* (ʌp'sɛt). **9** overturned or capsized. **10** emotionally or physically disturbed or distressed. **11** disordered; confused. **12** defeated or overthrown. [C14 (in the sense: to erect; C19 in the sense: to overthrow)]
▸**up'setter** *n* ▸**up'setting** *adj* ▸**up'settingly** *adv*

upset price *n Chiefly Scot., US, & Canad.* the lowest price acceptable for something that is for sale, esp. a house. Cf. **reserve price.**

upshot 🅣 ('ʌp,ʃɒt) *n* **1** the final result; conclusion; outcome. **2** *Archery.* the final shot in a match. [C16: from UP + SHOT[1]]

upside ('ʌp,saɪd) *n* the upper surface or part.

upside down 🅣 *adj* **1** (*usually postpositive;* **upside-down** *when prenominal*) turned over completely; inverted. **2** (**upside-down** *when prenominal*) *Inf.* confused; topsy-turvy: *an upside-down world.* ◆ *adv* **3** in an inverted fashion. **4** in a chaotic manner. [C16: var., by folk etymology, of earlier *upsodown*]

upside-down cake *n* a sponge cake baked with fruit at the bottom, and inverted before serving.

upsides (,ʌp'saɪdz) *adv Inf., chiefly Brit.* (foll. by *with*) equal or level (with), as through revenge.

upsilon ('ʌpsɪ,lɒn) *n* **1** the 20th letter in the Greek alphabet (Υ or υ), a vowel transliterated as *y* or *u.* **2** a heavy short-lived subatomic particle produced by bombarding beryllium nuclei with high-energy protons. [C17: from Med. Gk *u psilon* simple *u,* name adopted for graphic *u* to avoid confusion with graphic *oi,* since pronunciation was the same for both in LGk]

upskill ('ʌp,skɪl) *vb* (*tr*) *NZ.* to improve a person's aptitude for work by additional training.

upstage ('ʌp'steɪdʒ) *adv* **1** on, at, or to the rear of the stage. ◆ *adj* **2** of or relating to the back half of the stage. **3** *Inf.* haughty. ◆ *vb* **upstages, upstaging, upstaged.** (*tr*) **4** to move upstage of (another actor), thus forcing him to turn away from the audience. **5** *Inf.* to draw attention to oneself from (someone else). **6** *Inf.* to treat haughtily.

upstairs ('ʌp'stɛəz) *adv* **1** up the stairs; to or on an upper floor. **2** *Inf.* to or into a higher rank or office. ◆ *n* (*functioning as sing or pl*) **3a** an upper floor. **3b** (*as modifier*): *an upstairs room.* **4** *Brit. inf., old-fashioned.* the masters and mistresses of a household collectively, esp. of a large house.

upstanding 🅣 (ʌp'stændɪŋ) *adj* **1** of good character. **2** upright and vigorous in build. **3 be upstanding. 3a** (in a court of law) a direction to all persons present to rise to their feet before the judge enters or leaves the court. **3b** (at a formal dinner) a direction to all persons present to rise to their feet for a toast.

upstart 🅣 ('ʌp,stɑ:t) *n* **1a** a person, group, etc., that has risen suddenly to a position of power. **1b** (*as modifier*): *an upstart family.* **2a** an arrogant person. **2b** (*as modifier*): *his upstart ambition.*

upstate ('ʌp'steɪt) *US.* ◆ *adj, adv* **1** towards, in, or relating to the outlying or northern sections of a state. ◆ *n* **2** the outlying, esp. northern, sections of a state.
▸**'up'stater** *n*

upstream ('ʌp'stri:m) *adv, adj* **1** in or towards the higher part of a stream; against the current. Cf. **downstream. 2** (in the oil industry) of or for any of the stages prior to oil production, such as exploration or research.

upstretched (ʌp'strɛtʃt) *adj* (esp. of the arms) stretched or raised up.

upstroke ('ʌp,strəuk) *n* **1a** an upward stroke or movement, as of a pen or brush. **1b** the mark produced by such a stroke. **2** the upward movement of a piston in a reciprocating engine.

upsurge *vb* (ʌp'sɜ:dʒ), **upsurges, upsurging, upsurged. 1** (*intr*) *Chiefly literary.* to surge up. ◆ *n* ('ʌp,sɜ:dʒ). **2** a rapid rise or swell.

upsweep *n* ('ʌp,swi:p). **1** a curve or sweep upwards. ◆ *vb* (ʌp'swi:p), **upsweeps, upsweeping, upswept. 2** to sweep, curve, or brush or be swept, curved, or brushed upwards.

upswing ('ʌp,swɪŋ) *n* **1** *Econ.* a recovery period in the trade cycle. **2** an upward swing or movement or any increase or improvement.

upsy-daisy ('ʌpsɪ'deɪzɪ) *or* **upsadaisy** *interj* an expression, usually of reassurance, uttered as when someone, esp. a child, stumbles or is being lifted up. [C18 *up-a-daisy,* irregularly formed from UP (adv)]

uptake ('ʌp,teɪk) *n* **1** a pipe, shaft, etc., that is used to convey smoke or gases, esp. one that connects a furnace to a chimney. **2** lifting up. **3** the act of accepting something on offer. **4 quick** (*or* **slow**) **on the uptake.** *Inf.* quick (or slow) to understand or learn.

upthrow ('ʌp,θrəu) *n Geol.* the upward movement of rocks on one side of a fault plane relative to rocks on the other side.

upthrust ('ʌp,θrʌst) *n* **1** an upward push or thrust. **2** *Geol.* a violent upheaval of the earth's surface.

uptight 🅣 (ʌp'taɪt) *adj Inf.* **1** displaying tense repressed nervousness, irritability, or anger. **2** unable to give expression to one's feelings.

uptime ('ʌp,taɪm) *n Commerce.* time during which a machine, such as a computer, actually operates.

up-to-date 🅣 *adj* **a** modern or fashionable: *an up-to-date magazine.* **b** (*predicative*): *the magazine is up to date.*
▸**'up-to-'dateness** *n*

THESAURUS

pendicular, straight **2** = **honest**, above board, conscientious, ethical, faithful, good, high-minded, honourable, incorruptible, just, principled, righteous, straightforward, true, trustworthy, unimpeachable, virtuous
Antonyms *adj* ≠ **vertical:** flat, horizontal, lying, prone, prostrate, supine ≠ **honest:** corrupt, devious, dishonest, dishonourable, unethical, unjust, untrustworthy, wicked

uprightness *n* **2** = **honesty**, fairness, faithfulness, goodness, high-mindedness, incorruptibility, integrity, justice, probity, rectitude, righteousness, straightforwardness, trustworthiness, virtue

uprising *n* **1** = **rebellion**, disturbance, insurgence, insurrection, mutiny, outbreak, putsch, revolt, revolution, rising, upheaval

uproar *n* = **commotion**, brawl, brouhaha, clamour, confusion, din, furore, hubbub, hullabaloo, hurly-burly, mayhem, noise, outcry, pandemonium, racket, riot, ruckus (*inf.*), ruction (*inf.*), rumpus, turbulence, turmoil

uproarious *adj* **1** = **riotous**, clamorous, confused, disorderly, loud, noisy, rowdy, tempestuous, tumultuous, turbulent, wild **2** = **hilarious**, convulsive (*inf.*), hysterical, killing (*inf.*), rib-tickling, rip-roaring (*inf.*), screamingly funny, side-splitting, very funny **3** = **boisterous**, gleeful, loud, rollicking, unrestrained
Antonyms ≠ **riotous:** inaudible, low-key, orderly, quiet, still *adj* ≠ **hilarious:** morose, mournful, sad, serious, sorrowful, tragic ≠ **boisterous:** peaceful, quiet

uproot *vb* **1** = **pull up**, deracinate, dig up, extirpate, grub up, pull out by the roots, rip up, root out, weed out **2** = **displace**, deracinate, disorient, exile **3** = **destroy**, do away with, eliminate, eradicate, extirpate, remove, wipe out

ups and downs *pl n* = **fluctuations**, changes, ebb and flow, moods, vicissitudes, wheel of fortune

upset *vb* **1** = **tip over**, capsize, knock over, overturn, spill, topple over **2** = **mess up**, change, disorder, disorganize, disturb, mix up, put out of order, spoil, turn topsy-turvy **3** = **distress**, agitate, bother, discompose, disconcert, dismay, disquiet, disturb, faze, fluster, grieve, hassle (*inf.*), perturb, ruffle, throw (someone) off balance, trouble, unnerve **4** = **defeat**, be victorious over, conquer, get the better of, overcome, overthrow, triumph over, win against the odds ◆ *n* **7** = **reversal**, defeat, shake-up (*inf.*), sudden change, surprise **8** = **distress**, agitation, bother, discomposure, disquiet, disturbance, hassle (*inf.*), shock, trouble, worry **8** = **illness**, bug (*inf.*), complaint, disorder, disturbance, indisposition, malady, queasiness, sickness ◆ *adj* **9** = **overturned**, capsized, spilled, tipped over, toppled, tumbled, upside down **10** = **distressed**, agitated, bothered, confused, disconcerted, dismayed, disquieted, disturbed, frantic, grieved, hassled (*inf.*), hurt, overwrought, put out, ruffled, troubled, worried **10** = **sick**, disordered, disturbed, gippy (*sl.*), ill, poorly (*inf.*), queasy **11** = **disordered**, at sixes and sevens, chaotic, confused, disarrayed, in disarray, in disorder, messed up, muddled, topsy-turvy **12** = **conquered**, beaten, defeated, overcome, overthrown, vanquished

upshot *n* **1** = **result**, conclusion, consequence, culmination, end, end result, event, finale, issue, outcome, payoff (*inf.*), sequel

upside down *adj* **1** = **inverted**, bottom up, on its head, overturned, upturned, wrong side up **2** *Informal* = **confused**, chaotic, disordered, higgledy-piggledy (*inf.*), in chaos, in confusion, in disarray, in disorder, jumbled, muddled, topsy-turvy

upstanding *adj* **1** = **honest**, ethical, good, honourable, incorruptible, moral, principled, true, trustworthy, upright **2** = **sturdy**, firm, hale and hearty, hardy, healthy, robust, stalwart, strong, upright, vigorous
Antonyms *adj* ≠ **honest:** bad, corrupt, dishonest, false, immoral, unethical, unprincipled, untrustworthy ≠ **sturdy:** delicate, feeble, frail, infirm, puny, unhealthy, weak

upstart *n* **1a** = **social climber**, arriviste, nobody, *nouveau riche*, parvenu, status seeker

uptight *adj* **1** *Informal* = **tense**, anxious, edgy, nervy (*Brit. inf.*), neurotic, on edge, on the defensive, prickly, uneasy, wired (*sl.*), withdrawn

up-to-date *adj* **a** = **modern**, à la mode, all the rage, contemporary, current, fashionable, happening (*inf.*), having one's finger on the pulse,

uptown (ˈʌpˈtaʊn) *US & Canad.* ◆ *adj, adv* **1** towards, in, or relating to some part of a town that is away from the centre. ◆ *n* **2** such a part of a town, esp. a residential part.
▸ **ˈupˈtowner** *n*

upturn ➊ *vb* (ʌpˈtɜːn). **1** to turn or cause to turn over or upside down. **2** (*tr*) to create disorder. **3** (*tr*) to direct upwards. ◆ *n* (ˈʌpˌtɜːn). **4** an upward trend or improvement. **5** an upheaval.

UPVC *abbrev. for* unplasticized polyvinyl chloride. See also **PVC**.

upward (ˈʌpwəd) *adj* **1** directed or moving towards a higher point or level. ◆ *adv* **2** a variant of **upwards**.
▸ **ˈupwardly** *adv* ▸ **ˈupwardness** *n*

upwardly mobile *adj* (of a person or social group) moving or aspiring to move to a higher social class or status.

upward mobility *n* movement from a lower to a higher economic and social status.

upwards (ˈʌpwədz) *or* **upward** *adv* **1** from a lower to a higher place, level, condition, etc. **2** towards a higher level, standing, etc.

upwind (ˈʌpˈwɪnd) *adv* **1** into or against the wind. **2** towards or on the side where the wind is blowing; windward. ◆ *adj* **3** going against the wind: *the upwind leg of the course.* **4** on the windward side.

uracil (ˈjʊərəsɪl) *n Biochem.* a pyrimidine present in all living cells, usually in a combined form, as in RNA. [C20: from URO- + ACETIC + -ILE]

uraemia *or US* **uremia** (jʊˈriːmɪə) *n Pathol.* the accumulation of waste products, normally excreted in the urine, in the blood. [C19: from NL, from Gk *ouron* urine + *haima* blood]
▸ **uˈraemic** *or US* **uˈremic** *adj*

uraeus (jʊˈriːəs) *n, pl* **uraeuses.** the sacred serpent represented on the headdresses of ancient Egyptian kings and gods. [C19: from NL, from Gk *ouraios,* from Egyptian *uro* asp]

Ural-Altaic (ˈjʊərəl-) *n* **1** a postulated group of related languages consisting of the Uralic and Altaic families of languages. ◆ *adj* **2** of or relating to this group of languages, characterized by agglutination and vowel harmony.

Uralic (jʊˈrælɪk) *or* **Uralian** (jʊˈreɪlɪən) *n* **1** a superfamily of languages consisting of the Finno-Ugric family together with Samoyed. See also **Ural-Altaic.** ◆ *adj* **2** of or relating to these languages.

uranalysis (ˌjʊərəˈnælɪsɪs) *n, pl* **uranalyses** (-ˌsiːz). *Med.* a variant spelling of **urinalysis.**

uranide (ˈjʊərəˌnaɪd) *n* any element having an atomic number greater than that of protactinium.

uranism (ˈjʊərænɪzəm) *n Rare.* homosexuality (esp. male homosexuality). [C20: from G *Uranismus,* from Gk *ouranios* heavenly, i.e. spiritual]

uranium (jʊˈreɪnɪəm) *n* a radioactive silvery-white metallic element of the actinide series. It occurs in several minerals including pitchblende and is used chiefly as a source of nuclear energy by fission of the radioisotope **uranium-235.** Symbol: U; atomic no.: 92; atomic wt.: 238.03; half-life of most stable isotope, ^{238}U: 4.51×10^9 years. [C18: from NL, from URANUS[2]; from the fact that the element was discovered soon after the planet]

uranium series *n Physics.* a radioactive series that starts with uranium-238 and proceeds by radioactive decay to lead-206.

urano- *combining form.* denoting the heavens: *uranography.* [from Gk *ouranos*]

uranography (ˌjʊərəˈnɒgrəfɪ) *n* the branch of astronomy concerned with the description and mapping of the stars, galaxies, etc.
▸ **ˌuraˈnographer** *n* ▸ **uranographic** (ˌjʊərənəˈgræfɪk) *adj*

Uranus[1] (jʊˈreɪnəs, ˈjʊərənəs) *n Greek myth.* the personification of the sky, who, as a god, ruled the universe and fathered the Titans and Cyclopes; overthrown by his son Cronus.

Uranus[2] (jʊˈreɪnəs, ˈjʊərənəs) *n* the seventh planet from the sun, sometimes visible to the naked eye. [C19: from L *Ūranus,* from Gk *Ouranos* heaven]

urate (ˈjʊəreɪt) *n* any salt or ester of uric acid.
▸ **uratic** (jʊˈrætɪk) *adj*

urban ➊ (ˈɜːbᵊn) *adj* **1** of, relating to, or constituting a city or town. **2** living in a city or town. ◆ Cf. **rural.** [C17: from L *urbānus,* from *urbs* city]

urban area *n* (in population censuses) a city area considered as the inner city plus built-up environs, irrespective of local body administrative boundaries.

urban district *n* **1** (in England and Wales from 1888 to 1974 and Northern Ireland from 1898 to 1973) an urban division of an administrative county with an elected council in charge of housing and environmental services. **2** (in the Republic of Ireland) any of 49 medium-sized towns with their own elected councils.

urbane ➊ (ɜːˈbeɪn) *adj* characterized by elegance or sophistication. [C16: from L *urbānus* of the town; see URBAN]
▸ **urˈbanely** *adv* ▸ **urˈbaneness** *n*

urban guerrilla *n* a guerrilla who operates in a town or city, engaging in terrorism, kidnapping, etc.

urbanism (ˈɜːbəˌnɪzəm) *n Chiefly US.* **a** the character of city life. **b** the study of this.

urbanite (ˈɜːbəˌnaɪt) *n* a resident of an urban community; city dweller.

urbanity ➊ (ɜːˈbænɪtɪ) *n, pl* **urbanities.** **1** the quality of being urbane. **2** (*usually pl*) civilities or courtesies.

urbanize *or* **urbanise** (ˈɜːbəˌnaɪz) *vb* **urbanizes, urbanizing, urbanized** *or* **urbanises, urbanising, urbanised.** (*tr*) (*usually passive*) **a** to make (esp. a predominantly rural area or country) more industrialized and urban. **b** to cause the migration of an increasing proportion of (rural dwellers) into cities.
▸ **ˌurbaniˈzation** *or* **ˌurbaniˈsation** *n*

urban myth *or* **legend** *n* a story, esp. one with a shocking or amusing ending, related as having actually happened, usually to someone vaguely connected with the teller.

urban renewal *n* the process of redeveloping dilapidated or no longer functional urban areas.

urbi et orbi *Latin.* (ˈɜːbɪ ɛt ˈɔːbɪ) *adv RC Church.* to the city and the world: a phrase qualifying the solemn papal blessing.

urceolate (ˈɜːsɪəlɪt, -ˌleɪt) *adj Biol.* shaped like an urn or pitcher: *an urceolate corolla.* [C18: via NL from L *urceolus,* dim. of *urceus* a pitcher]

urchin ➊ (ˈɜːtʃɪn) *n* **1** a mischievous roguish child, esp. one who is young, small, or raggedly dressed. **2** See **sea urchin.** **3** *Arch., dialect.* a hedgehog. **4** *Obs.* an elf or sprite. [C13 *urchon,* from OF *heriçon,* from L *ēricius* hedgehog]

Urdu (ˈʊəduː, ˈɜː-) *n* an official language of Pakistan, also spoken in India. The script derives primarily from Persia. It belongs to the Indic branch of the Indo-European family of languages, being closely related to Hindi. [C18: from Hindustani (*zabānī*) *urdū* (language of the) camp, from Persian *urdū* camp, from Turkish *ordū*]

-ure *suffix forming nouns.* **1** indicating act, process, or result: *seizure.* **2** indicating function or office: *legislature; prefecture.* [from F, from L *-ūra*]

urea (ˈjʊərɪə) *n* a white water-soluble crystalline compound, produced by protein metabolism and excreted in urine. A synthetic form is used as a fertilizer and animal feed. Formula: $CO(NH_2)_2$. [C19: from NL, from F *urée,* from Gk *ouron* urine]
▸ **uˈreal** *or* **uˈreic** *adj*

urea-formaldehyde resin *n* any one of a class of rigid odourless synthetic materials that are made from urea and formaldehyde and are used in electrical fittings, adhesives, laminates, and finishes for textiles.

ureide (ˈjʊərɪˌaɪd) *n Chem.* **1** any of a class of organic compounds derived from urea by replacing one or more of its hydrogen atoms by organic groups. **2** any of a class of derivatives of urea and carboxylic acids, in which one or more of the hydrogen atoms have been replaced by acid radical groups.

-uret *suffix of nouns.* formerly used to form the names of binary chemical compounds. [from NL *-uretum*]

ureter (jʊˈriːtə) *n* the tube that conveys urine from the kidney to the urinary bladder or cloaca. [C16: via NL from Gk *ourētēr,* from *ourein* to urinate]
▸ **uˈreteral** *or* **ureteric** (ˌjʊərɪˈtɛrɪk) *adj*

urethane (ˈjʊərɪˌθeɪn) *or* **urethan** (ˈjʊərɪˌθæn) *n* short for **polyurethane.** [C19: from URO- + ETHYL + -ANE]

urethra (jʊˈriːθrə) *n, pl* **urethrae** (-θriː) *or* **urethras.** the canal that in most mammals conveys urine from the bladder out of the body. In human males it also conveys semen. [C17: via LL from Gk *ourēthra,* from *ourein* to urinate]
▸ **uˈrethral** *adj*

urethritis (ˌjʊərɪˈθraɪtɪs) *n* inflammation of the urethra. [C19: from NL, from LL URETHRA]
▸ **urethritic** (ˌjʊərɪˈθrɪtɪk) *adj*

urethroscope (jʊˈriːθrəˌskəʊp) *n* a medical instrument for examining the urethra. [C20: see URETHRA, -SCOPE]
▸ **urethroscopic** (jʊˌriːθrəˈskɒpɪk) *adj* ▸ **urethroscopy** (ˌjʊərɪˈθrɒskəpɪ) *n*

uretic (jʊˈrɛtɪk) *adj* of or relating to the urine. [C19: via LL from Gk *ourētikos,* from *ouron* urine]

urge ➊ (ɜːdʒ) *vb* **urges, urging, urged.** (*tr*) **1** to plead, press, or move (someone to do something): *we urged him to surrender.* **2** (*may take a clause as object*) to advocate or recommend earnestly and persistently: *to urge the need for safety.* **3** to impel, drive, or hasten onwards: *he urged the horses on.* ◆ *n* **4** a strong impulse, inner drive, or yearning. [C16: from L *urgēre*]

THESAURUS

in, in vogue, newest, now (*inf.*), stylish, trendy (*Brit. inf.*), up-to-the-minute, with it (*inf.*)
Antonyms *adj* antiquated, dated, *démodé,* obsolete, old fashioned, outmoded, out of date, out of the ark (*inf.*), passé

upturn *n* **4** = **rise,** advancement, boost, improvement, increase, recovery, revival, upsurge, upswing

urban *adj* **1** = **civic,** city, inner-city, metropolitan, municipal, oppidan (*rare*), town

urbane *adj* = **sophisticated,** civil, civilized, cosmopolitan, courteous, cultivated, cultured, debonair, elegant, mannerly, polished, refined, smooth, suave, well-bred, well-mannered
Antonyms *adj* boorish, clownish, discourteous, gauche, impolite, rude, uncivilized, uncouth, uncultured

urbanity *n* **1** = **sophistication,** charm, civility, courtesy, culture, elegance, grace, mannerliness, polish, refinement, suavity, worldliness

urchin *n* **1** = **ragamuffin,** brat, gamin, guttersnipe, mudlark (*sl.*), street Arab (*offens.*), waif, young rogue

urge *vb* **1** = **beg,** appeal to, beseech, entreat, exhort, implore, plead, press, solicit **2** = **advocate,** advise, champion, counsel, insist on, push for, recommend, support **3** = **drive,** compel, constrain, egg on, encourage, force, gee up, goad, hasten, impel, incite, induce, instigate, press, prompt, propel, push, spur, stimulate ◆ *n* **4** = **impulse,** compulsion, desire, drive, fancy, itch, longing, thirst, wish, yearning, yen (*inf.*)
Antonyms *vb* ≠ **advocate, drive:** caution, deter, discourage, dissuade, warn ◆ *n* ≠ **impulse:** aversion, disinclination, distaste, indisposition, reluctance, repugnance

urgent Ⓣ ('ɜːdʒənt) *adj* **1** requiring or compelling speedy action or attention: *the matter is urgent.* **2** earnest and persistent. [C15: via F from L *urgent-, urgens,* present participle of *urgēre* to URGE]
▸**urgency** ('ɜːdʒənsɪ) *n* ▸'**urgently** *adv*

-urgy *n combining form.* indicating technology concerned with a specified material: *metallurgy.* [from Gk *-urgia,* from *ergon* work]

-uria *n combining form.* indicating a diseased or abnormal condition of the urine: *pyuria.* [from Gk *-ouria,* from *ouron* urine]
▸**-uric** *adj combining form.*

uric ('jʊərɪk) *adj* of, concerning, or derived from urine. [C18: from URO- + -IC]

uric acid *n* a white odourless tasteless crystalline product of protein metabolism, present in the blood and urine. Formula: $C_5H_4N_4O_3$.

uridine ('jʊərɪˌdiːn) *n Biochem.* a nucleoside present in all living cells in a combined form, esp. in RNA. [C20: from URO- + -IDE + -INE[2]]

urinal (jʊ'raɪnᵊl, 'jʊərɪ-) *n* **1** a sanitary fitting, esp. one fixed to a wall, used by men for urination. **2** a room containing urinals. **3** any vessel for holding urine prior to its disposal.

urinalysis (ˌjʊərɪ'nælɪsɪs) *n, pl* **urinalyses** (-ˌsiːz). *Med.* chemical analysis of the urine to test for the presence of disease.

urinary ('jʊərɪnərɪ) *adj* **1** *Anat.* of or relating to urine or to the organs and structures that secrete and pass urine. ◆ *n, pl* **urinaries. 2** a reservoir for urine.

urinary bladder *n* a distensible membranous sac in which the urine excreted from the kidneys is stored.

urinate Ⓣ ('jʊərɪˌneɪt) *vb* **urinates, urinating, urinated.** (*intr*) to excrete or void urine.
▸ˌ**uri'nation** *n* ▸'**urinative** *adj*

urine ('jʊərɪn) *n* the pale yellow slightly acid fluid excreted by the kidneys, containing waste products removed from the blood. It is stored in the urinary bladder and discharged through the urethra. [C14: via OF from L *ūrīna*]

urinogenital (ˌjʊərɪnəʊ'dʒɛnɪtᵊl) *adj* another word for **urogenital.**

URL *abbrev. for* uniform resource locator: a standardized address of a location on the Internet.

urn (ɜːn) *n* **1** a vaselike receptacle or vessel, esp. a large bulbous one with a foot. **2** a vase used as a receptacle for the ashes of the dead. **3** a large vessel, usually of metal, with a tap, used for making and holding tea, coffee, etc. [C14: from L *ūrna*]
▸'**urn**ˌ**like** *adj*

urnfield ('ɜːnˌfiːld) *n* **1** a cemetery full of individual cremation urns. ◆ *adj* **2** (of a number of Bronze Age cultures) characterized by cremation in urns, which began in E Europe about the second millennium B.C.

uro- *or before a vowel* **ur-** *combining form.* indicating urine or the urinary tract: *urogenital; urology.* [from Gk *ouron* urine]

urogenital (ˌjʊərəʊ'dʒɛnɪtᵊl) *or* **urinogenital** *adj* of or relating to the urinary and genital organs and their functions. Also: **genitourinary. urogenital system**

urogenital system *or* **tract** *n Anat.* the urinary tract and reproductive organs.

urolith ('jʊərəʊlɪθ) *n Pathol.* a calculus in the urinary tract.
▸ˌ**uro'lithic** *adj*

urology (jʊ'rɒlədʒɪ) *n* the branch of medicine concerned with the study and treatment of diseases of the urogenital tract.
▸**urologic** (ˌjʊərə'lɒdʒɪk) *adj* ▸**u'rologist** *n*

uropygial gland (ˌjʊərə'pɪdʒɪəl) *n* a gland, situated at the base of the tail in most birds, that secretes oil used in preening.

uropygium (ˌjʊərə'pɪdʒɪəm) *n* the hindmost part of a bird's body, from which the tail feathers grow. [C19: via NL from Gk *ouropugion,* from *oura* tail + *pugē* rump]
▸ˌ**uro'pygial** *adj*

uroscopy (jʊ'rɒskəpɪ) *n Med.* examination of the urine. See also **urinalysis.**
▸**uroscopic** (ˌjʊərə'skɒpɪk) *adj* ▸**u'roscopist** *n*

Ursa Major ('ɜːsə 'meɪdʒə) *n, Latin genitive* **Ursae Majoris** ('ɜːsiː mə'dʒɔːrɪs). an extensive conspicuous constellation in the N hemisphere. The seven brightest stars form the **Plough.** Also called: the **Great Bear,** the **Bear.** [L: greater bear]

Ursa Minor ('ɜːsə 'maɪnə) *n, Latin genitive* **Ursae Minoris** ('ɜːsiː mɪ'nɔːrɪs). a small faint constellation, the brightest star of which is the Pole Star. Also called: the **Little Bear,** the **Bear.** [L: lesser bear]

ursine ('ɜːsaɪn) *adj* of, relating to, or resembling a bear or bears. [C16: from L *ursus* a bear]

Ursprache *German.* ('uːrʃpraːxə) *n* any hypothetical extinct and unrecorded language reconstructed from groups of related recorded languages. For example, Indo-European is an Ursprache reconstructed by comparison of the Germanic group, Latin, Sanskrit, etc. [from *ur-* primeval + *Sprache* language]

Ursuline ('ɜːsjʊˌlaɪn) *n* **1** a member of an order of nuns devoted to teaching in the Roman Catholic Church: founded in 1537 at Brescia. ◆ *adj* **2** of or relating to this order. [C16: after St *Ursula,* patron saint of St Angela Merici, who founded the order]

Urtext *German.* ('uːrtɛkst) *n* **1** the earliest form of a text as established by linguistic scholars as a basis for variants in later texts still in existence. **2** an edition of a musical score showing the composer's intentions without later editorial interpolation. [from *ur-* original + TEXT]

urticaceous (ˌɜːtɪ'keɪʃəs) *adj* of or belonging to a family of plants having small flowers and, in many species, stinging hairs: includes the nettles and pellitory. [C18: via NL from L *urtīca* nettle, from *ūrere* to burn]

urticaria (ˌɜːtɪ'kɛərɪə) *n* a skin condition characterized by the formation of itchy red or whitish raised patches, usually caused by an allergy. Nontechnical names: **hives, nettle rash.** [C18: from NL, from L *urtīca* nettle]

urtication (ˌɜːtɪ'keɪʃən) *n* **1** a burning or itching sensation. **2** another name for **urticaria.**

urus ('jʊərəs) *n, pl* **uruses.** another name for the **aurochs.** [C17: from *ūrus,* of Gmc origin]

urushiol ('uːrʊʃɪˌɒl, uː'ruː-) *n* a poisonous pale yellow liquid occurring in poison ivy and the lacquer tree. [from Japanese *urushi* lacquer + -OL[2]]

us (ʌs) *pron* (*objective*) **1** refers to the speaker or writer and another person or other people: *don't hurt us.* **2** refers to all people or people in general: *this table shows us the tides.* **3** an informal word for **me:** *give us a kiss!* **4** a formal word for **me** used by editors, monarchs, etc. [OE *ūs*]

> **USAGE NOTE** See at **me**[1].

US *or* **U.S.** *abbrev. for* United States.

USA *abbrev. for:* **1.** Also: **U.S.A.** United States of America. **2** United States Army.

usable Ⓣ *or* **useable** ('juːzəbᵊl) *adj* able to be used.
▸ˌ**usa'bility** *or* ˌ**usea'bility** *n*

USAF *abbrev. for* United States Air Force.

usage Ⓣ ('juːsɪdʒ, -zɪdʒ) *n* **1** the act or a manner of using; use; employment. **2** constant use, custom, or habit. **3** something permitted or established by custom or practice. **4** what is actually said in a language, esp. as contrasted with what is prescribed. [C14: via OF from L *ūsus* USE (n)]

usance ('juːzəns) *n Commerce.* the period of time permitted by commercial usage for the redemption of foreign bills of exchange. [C14: from OF, from Med. L *ūsantia,* from *ūsāre* to USE]

USDAW ('ʌsdɔː) *n* (in Britain) *acronym for* Union of Shop, Distributive, and Allied Workers.

use Ⓣ *vb* (juːz), **uses, using, used.** (*tr*) **1** to put into service or action; employ for a given purpose: *to use a spoon to stir with.* **2** to make a practice or habit of employing; exercise: *he uses his brain.* **3** to behave towards in a particular way, esp. for one's own ends: *he uses people.* **4** to consume, expend, or exhaust: *the engine uses very little oil.* **5** to partake of (alcoholic drink, drugs, etc.) or smoke (tobacco, marijuana, etc.). ◆ *n* (juːs). **6** the act of using or the state of being used: *the carpet wore out through constant use.* **7** the ability or permission to use. **8** the occasion to use: *I have no use for this paper.* **9** an instance or manner of using. **10** usefulness; advantage: *it is of no use to complain.* **11** custom; habit: *long use has inured him to it.* **12** the purpose for which something is used; end. **13** *Christianity.* a distinctive form of liturgical or ritual observance, esp. one that is traditional. **14** the enjoyment of property, land, etc., by occupation or by deriving revenue from it. **15** *Law.* the beneficial enjoyment of property the legal title to which is held by another person as trustee. **16 have no use for. 16a** to have no need of. **16b** to have a contemptuous dislike for. **17 make use of. 17a** to employ; use. **17b** to exploit (a person). ◆ See also **use up.** [C13: from OF *user,* from L *ūsus* having used, from *ūtī* to use]

THESAURUS

urgency *n* **1** = **importance,** exigency, extremity, gravity, hurry, imperativeness, necessity, need, pressure, seriousness, stress

urgent *adj* **1** = **crucial,** compelling, critical, exigent, immediate, imperative, important, instant, not to be delayed, now or never, pressing, top-priority **2** = **insistent,** clamorous, earnest, importunate, intense, persistent, persuasive
Antonyms *adj* ≠ **crucial:** low-priority, minor, trivial, unimportant ≠ **insistent:** apathetic, casual, feeble, half-hearted, lackadaisical, perfunctory, weak

urinate *vb* = **pee** (*sl.*), leak (*sl.*), make water, micturate, pass water, piddle (*inf.*), piss (*taboo sl.*), spend a penny (*Brit. inf.*), tinkle (*Brit. inf.*), wee (*inf.*), wee-wee (*inf.*)

usable *adj* = **serviceable,** at one's disposal, available, current, fit for use, functional, in running order, practical, ready for use, utilizable, valid, working

usage *n* **1** = **use,** control, employment, handling, management, operation, regulation, running, treatment **2, 3** = **practice,** convention, custom, form, habit, matter of course, method, mode, procedure, regime, routine, rule, tradition, wont

use *vb* **1, 2** = **employ,** apply, avail oneself of, bring into play, exercise, exert, find a use for, make use of, operate, ply, practise, profit by, put to use, turn to account, utilize, wield, work **3** = **take advantage of,** act towards, behave towards, deal with, exploit, handle, manipulate, misuse, treat **4** = **consume,** exhaust, expend, run through, spend, waste ◆ *n* **6** = **usage,** application, employment, exercise, handling, operation, practice, service, treatment, wear and tear **10** = **good,** advantage, application, avail, benefit, help, mileage (*inf.*), point, profit, service, usefulness, utility, value, worth **11** = **custom,** habit, practice, usage, way, wont **12** = **purpose,** call, cause, end, necessity, need, object, occasion, point, reason

used Ⓣ (juːzd) *adj* second-hand: *used cars.*

used to Ⓣ (juːst) *adj* **1** accustomed to: *I am used to hitchhiking.* ◆ *vb (tr)* **2** (*takes an infinitive or implied infinitive*) used as an auxiliary to express habitual or accustomed actions, states, etc., taking place in the past but not continuing into the present: *I used to fish here every day.*

> **USAGE NOTE** The most common negative form of *used to* is *didn't used to* (or *didn't use to*), but in formal contexts *used not to* is preferred.

useful Ⓣ (ˈjuːsfʊl) *adj* **1** able to be used advantageously, beneficially, or for several purposes. **2** *Inf.* commendable or capable: *a useful term's work.*
▸ˈ**usefully** *adv* ▸ˈ**usefulness** *n*

useless Ⓣ (ˈjuːslɪs) *adj* **1** having no practical use or advantage. **2** *Inf.* ineffectual, weak, or stupid: *he's useless at history.*
▸ˈ**uselessly** *adv* ▸ˈ**uselessness** *n*

user (ˈjuːzə) *n* **1** *Law.* **1a** the continued exercise, use, or enjoyment of a right, esp. in property. **1b** a presumptive right based on long-continued use: *right of user.* **2** (*often in combination*) a person or thing that uses: *a road-user.* **3** *Inf.* a drug addict.

user-friendly *adj* (**user friendly** *when postpositive*) easy to familiarize oneself with, understand, or use.

use up Ⓣ *vb (tr, adv)* **1** to finish (a supply); consume completely. **2** to exhaust; wear out.

usher Ⓣ (ˈʌʃə) *n* **1** an official who shows people to their seats, as in a church or theatre. **2** a person who acts as doorkeeper, esp. in a court of law. **3** (in England) a minor official charged with maintaining order in a court of law. **4** an officer responsible for preceding persons of rank in a procession. **5** *Brit., obs.* a teacher. ◆ *vb (tr)* **6** to conduct or escort, esp. in a courteous or obsequious way. **7** (usually foll. by *in*) to be a precursor or herald (of). [C14: from OF *huissier* doorkeeper, from Vulgar L *ustiārius* (unattested), from L *ostium* door]

usherette (ˌʌʃəˈrɛt) *n* a woman assistant in a cinema, etc., who shows people to their seats.

USM *Stock Exchange. abbrev. for* unlisted securities market.

USN *abbrev. for* United States Navy.

USP *abbrev. for* unique selling proposition: a characteristic of a product that can be used in advertising to differentiate it from its competitors.

usquebaugh (ˈʌskwɪˌbɔː) *n* **1** *Irish.* the former name for **whiskey**. **2** *Scot.* the former name for **whisky**. [C16: from Irish Gaelic *uisce beathadh* or Scot. Gaelic *uisge beatha* water of life]

USS *abbrev. for:* **1** United States Senate. **2** United States Ship.

USSR *abbrev. for* (the former) Union of Soviet Socialist Republics.

usual Ⓣ (ˈjuːʒʊəl) *adj* **1** of the most normal, frequent, or regular type: *that's the usual sort of application to send.* ◆ *n* **2** ordinary or commonplace events (esp. in **out of the usual**). **3 the usual.** *Inf.* the habitual or usual drink, etc. [C14: from LL *ūsuālis* ordinary, from L *ūsus* USE]
▸ˈ**usually** *adv* ▸ˈ**usualness** *n*

usufruct (ˈjuːsjʊˌfrʌkt) *n* the right to use and derive profit from a piece of property belonging to another, provided the property itself remains undiminished and uninjured in any way. [C17: from LL *ūsūfrūctus*, from L *ūsus* use + *frūctus* enjoyment]
▸ˌ**usuˈfructuary** *n, adj*

usurer (ˈjuːʒərə) *n* a person who lends funds at an exorbitant rate of interest.

usurp Ⓣ (juːˈzɜːp) *vb* to seize or appropriate (land, a throne, etc.) without authority. [C14: from OF, from L *ūsūrpāre* to take into use, prob. from *ūsus* use + *rapere* to seize]
▸ˌ**usurˈpation** *n* ▸**uˈsurper** *n*

usury (ˈjuːʒərɪ) *n, pl* **usuries. 1** the practice of loaning money at an exorbitant rate of interest. **2** an unlawfully high rate of interest. **3** *Obs.* moneylending. [C14: from Med. L, from L *ūsūra* usage, from *ūsus* USE]
▸**usurious** (juːˈʒʊərɪəs) *adj*

USW *Radio. abbrev. for* ultrashort wave.

ut (ʌt, uːt) *n Music.* the syllable used in the fixed system of solmization for the note C. [C14: from L *ut*; see GAMUT]

UT *abbrev. for:* **1** universal time. **2** Utah.

UTC *abbrev. for* universal time coordinated. See **universal time.**

ute (juːt) *n Austral. & NZ inf.* short for **utility truck.**

utensil (juːˈtɛnsəl) *n* an implement, tool, or container for practical use: *writing utensils.* [C14 *utensele*, via OF from L *ūtēnsilia* necessaries, from *ūtēnsilis* available for use, from *ūtī* to use]

uterine (ˈjuːtəˌraɪn) *adj* **1** of, relating to, or affecting the uterus. **2** (of offspring) born of the same mother but not the same father.

uterus (ˈjuːtərəs) *n, pl* **uteri** (ˈjuːtəˌraɪ). **1** *Anat.* a hollow muscular organ lying within the pelvic cavity of female mammals. It houses the developing fetus. Nontechnical name: **womb. 2** the corresponding organ in other animals. [C17: from L]

utilidor (juːˈtɪlədɔ; *Canad.* -ˌdɒr) *n Canad.* above-ground insulated casing for pipes carrying water, etc., in permafrost regions.

utilitarian (juːˌtɪlɪˈtɛərɪən) *adj* **1** of or relating to utilitarianism. **2** designed for use rather than beauty. ◆ *n* **3** a person who believes in utilitarianism.

utilitarianism (juːˌtɪlɪˈtɛərɪəˌnɪzəm) *n Ethics.* **1** the doctrine that the morally correct course of action consists in the greatest good for the greatest number, that is, in maximizing the total benefit resulting, without regard to the distribution of benefits and burdens. **2** the theory that the criterion of virtue is utility.

utility Ⓣ (juːˈtɪlɪtɪ) *n, pl* **utilities. 1a** the quality of practical use; usefulness. **1b** (*as modifier*): *a utility fabric.* **2** something useful. **3a** a public service, such as the bus system. **3b** (*as modifier*): *utility vehicle.* **4** *Econ.* the ability of a commodity to satisfy human wants. Cf. **disutility. 5** *Austral.* short for **utility truck. 6** *Computing.* a piece of software that performs a routine task. [C14: from OF *utelite*, from L *ūtilitās* usefulness, from *ūtī* to use]

utility function *n Econ.* a function relating specific goods and services in an economy to individual preferences.

utility player *n Sport.* a player who is capable of playing competently in any of several positions.

utility room *n* a room with equipment for domestic work like washing and ironing.

utility truck *n Austral. & NZ.* a small truck with an open body and low sides, often with a removable tarpaulin cover; pick-up truck.

utilize Ⓣ *or* **utilise** (ˈjuːtɪˌlaɪz) *vb* **utilizes, utilizing, utilized** *or* **utilises, utilising, utilised.** (*tr*) to make practical or worthwhile use of.
▸ˈ**utiˌlizable** *or* ˈ**utiˌlisable** *adj* ▸ˌ**utiliˈzation** *or* ˌ**utiliˈsation** *n* ▸ˈ**utiˌlizer** *or* ˈ**utiˌliser** *n*

utmost Ⓣ (ˈʌtˌməʊst) *or* **uttermost** *adj* (*prenominal*) **1** of the greatest possible degree or amount: *the utmost degree.* **2** at the furthest limit: *the utmost town on the peninsula.* ◆ *n* **3** the greatest possible degree, extent, or amount: *he tried his utmost.* [OE *ūtemest*, from *ūte* out + *-mest* MOST]

utmost good faith *n* a principle used in insurance contracts, legally obliging all parties to reveal to the others any information that might influence the others' decision to enter into the contract. [from L *uberrima fides*]

Utopia Ⓣ (juːˈtəʊpɪə) *n* (*sometimes not cap.*) any real or imaginary society, place, state, etc., considered to be perfect or ideal. [C16: from NL *Utopia* (coined by Sir Thomas More in 1516 as the title of his book that described an imaginary island representing the perfect society), lit.: no place, from Gk *ou* not + *topos* a place]

Utopian Ⓣ (juːˈtəʊpɪən) (*sometimes not cap.*) ◆ *adj* **1** of or relating to a perfect or ideal existence. ◆ *n* **2** an idealistic social reformer.
▸**Uˈtopianism** *n*

THESAURUS

used *adj* = **second-hand**, cast-off, hand-me-down (*inf.*), nearly new, not new, reach-me-down (*inf.*), shopsoiled, worn
Antonyms *adj* brand-new, fresh, intact, new, pristine, unused

used to *adj* **1** = **accustomed to**, at home in, attuned to, familiar with, given to, habituated to, hardened to, in the habit of, inured to, tolerant of, wont to

useful *adj* **1** = **helpful**, advantageous, all-purpose, beneficial, effective, fruitful, general-purpose, of help, of service, of use, practical, profitable, salutary, serviceable, valuable, worthwhile
Antonyms *adj* inadequate, ineffective, unbeneficial, unhelpful, unproductive, useless, vain, worthless

usefulness *n* **1** = **helpfulness**, benefit, convenience, effectiveness, efficacy, help, practicality, profit, service, use, utility, value, worth

useless *adj* **1** = **worthless**, bootless, disadvantageous, fruitless, futile, hopeless, idle, impractical, ineffective, ineffectual, of no use, pointless, profitless, unavailing, unproductive, unworkable, vain, valueless **2** *Informal* = **inept**, hopeless, incompetent, ineffectual, no good, stupid, weak
Antonyms *adj* ≠ **worthless:** advantageous, effective, fruitful, practical, productive, profitable, useful, valuable, workable, worthwhile

use up *vb* **1, 2** = **consume**, absorb, burn up, deplete, devour, drain, exhaust, finish, fritter away, run through, squander, swallow up, waste

usher *n* **1** = **attendant**, doorkeeper, doorman, escort, guide, usherette ◆ *vb* **6** = **escort**, conduct, direct, guide, lead, pilot, show in *or* out, steer **7** *usually with* **in** = **introduce**, bring in, herald, inaugurate, initiate, launch, open the door to, pave the way for, precede, ring in

usual *adj* **1** = **normal**, accustomed, bog-standard (*Brit. & Irish sl.*), common, constant, customary, everyday, expected, familiar, fixed, general, habitual, ordinary, regular, routine, standard, stock, typical, wonted
Antonyms *adj* exceptional, extraordinary, new, novel, off-beat, out of the ordinary, peculiar, rare, singular, strange, uncommon, unexpected, unhackneyed, unique, unorthodox, unusual

usually *adv* **1** = **normally**, as a rule, as is the custom, as is usual, by and large, commonly, for the most part, generally, habitually, in the main, mainly, mostly, most often, on the whole, ordinarily, regularly, routinely

usurp *vb* = **seize**, appropriate, arrogate, assume, commandeer, infringe upon, lay hold of, take, take over, wrest

utility *n* **1a** = **usefulness**, advantageousness, avail, benefit, convenience, efficacy, fitness, mileage, point, practicality, profit, service, serviceableness, use

utilize *vb* = **use**, appropriate, avail oneself of, employ, have recourse to, make the most of, make use of, profit by, put to use, resort to, take advantage of, turn to account

utmost *adj* **1** = **greatest**, chief, extreme, highest, maximum, paramount, pre-eminent, supreme **2** = **farthest**, extreme, final, last, most distant, outermost, remotest, uttermost ◆ *n* **3** = **greatest**, best, hardest, highest, most

Utopia *n* = **paradise**, bliss, Eden, Garden of Eden, Happy Valley, heaven, ideal life, perfect place, seventh heaven, Shangri-la

Utopian *adj* **1** = **perfect**, airy, chimerical, dream, fanciful, fantasy, ideal, idealistic, illusory, imaginary, impractical, romantic, visionary ◆ *n* **2** = **dreamer**, Don Quixote, idealist, romanticist, visionary

utricle ('ju:trɪkᵊl) *n* **1** *Anat.* the larger of the two parts of the membranous labyrinth of the internal ear. Cf. **saccule. 2** *Bot.* the bladder-like one-seeded indehiscent fruit of certain plants. **[**C18: from L *ūtriculus,* dim. of *ūter* bag**]**
▸u'tricular *adj*

utriculitis (ju:ˌtrɪkju'laɪtɪs) *n* inflammation of the inner ear.

utter[1] ❶ ('ʌtə) *vb* **1** to give audible expression to (something): *to utter a growl.* **2** *Criminal law.* to put into circulation (counterfeit coin, forged banknotes, etc.). **3** (*tr*) to make publicly known; publish: *to utter slander.* **[**C14: prob. orig. a commercial term, from MDu. *ūteren* (modern Du. *uiteren*) to make known**]**
▸'utterable *adj* ▸'utterableness *n* ▸'utterer *n*

utter[2] ❶ ('ʌtə) *adj* (*prenominal*) (intensifier): *an utter fool; the utter limit.* **[**C15: from OE *utera* outer, comp. of *ūte* out (adv)**]**
▸'utterly *adv*

utterance ❶ ('ʌtərəns) *n* **1** something uttered, such as a statement. **2** the act or power of uttering or ability to utter.

utter barrister *n Law.* the full title of a barrister who is not a Queen's Counsel.

uttermost ❶ ('ʌtəˌməʊst) *adj, n* a variant of **utmost.**

U-turn *n* **1** a turn made by a vehicle in the shape of a U, resulting in a reversal of direction. **2** a complete change in direction of political policy, etc.

UV *abbrev. for* ultraviolet.

UV-A *or* **UVA** *abbrev. for* ultraviolet radiation with a range of 320-380 nanometres.

uvarovite (u:'vɑ:rəˌvaɪt) *n* an emerald-green garnet found in chromium deposits. **[**C19: from G *Uvarovit;* after Count Sergei *Uvarov* (1785–1855), Russian author & statesman**]**

UV-B *or* **UVB** *abbrev. for* ultraviolet radiation with a range of 280-320 nanometres.

uvea ('ju:vɪə) *n* the part of the eyeball consisting of the iris, ciliary body, and choroid. **[**C16: from Med. L *ūvea,* from L *ūva* grape**]**
▸'uveal *adj*

UVF *abbrev. for* Ulster Volunteer Force.

uvula ('ju:vjʊlə) *n, pl* **uvulas** *or* **uvulae** (-ˌli:). a small fleshy flap of tissue that hangs in the back of the throat and is an extension of the soft palate. **[**C14: from Med. L, lit.: a little grape, from L *ūva* a grape**]**

uvular ('ju:vjʊlə) *adj* **1** of or relating to the uvula. **2** *Phonetics.* articulated with the uvula and the back of the tongue, such as the (r) sound of Parisian French. ◆ *n* **3** a uvular consonant.

uxorial (ʌk'sɔ:rɪəl) *adj* of or relating to a wife: *uxorial influence.* **[**C19: from L *uxor* wife**]**
▸ux'orially *adv*

uxoricide (ʌk'sɔ:rɪˌsaɪd) *n* **1** the act of killing one's wife. **2** a man who kills his wife. **[**C19: from L *uxor* wife + -CIDE**]**
▸uxˌori'cidal *adj*

uxorious (ʌk'sɔ:rɪəs) *adj* excessively attached to or dependent on one's wife. **[**C16: from L *uxōrius* concerning a wife, from *uxor* wife**]**
▸ux'oriously *adv* ▸ux'oriousness *n*

Uzbek ('ʊzbɛk, 'ʌz-) *n* **1** (*pl* **Uzbeks** *or* **Uzbek**) a member of a Mongoloid people of Uzbekistan in central Asia. **2** the language of this people.

THESAURUS

utter[1] *vb* **1** = **express**, articulate, enunciate, pronounce, put into words, say, speak, verbalize, vocalize, voice **3** = **publish**, declare, divulge, give expression to, make known, proclaim, promulgate, reveal, state

utter[2] *adj* = **absolute**, arrant, complete, consummate, deep-dyed (*usually derogatory*), downright, entire, out-and-out, outright, perfect, sheer, stark, thorough, thoroughgoing, total, unmitigated, unqualified

utterance *n* **1** = **speech**, announcement, declaration, expression, opinion, remark, statement, words **2** = **expression**, articulation, delivery, ejaculation, verbalization, vocalization, vociferation

utterly *adv* = **totally**, absolutely, completely, entirely, extremely, fully, one hundred per cent, perfectly, thoroughly, to the core, to the nth degree, wholly

uttermost *adj* = **farthest**, extreme, final, last, outermost, remotest, utmost

Vv

v *or* **V** (viː) *n, pl* **v's, V's,** *or* **Vs. 1** the 22nd letter of the English alphabet. **2** a speech sound represented by this letter, usually a voiced fricative, as in *vote.* **3a** something shaped like a V. **3b** (*in combination*): *a V neck.*
v *symbol. for:* **1** *Physics.* velocity. **2** specific volume (of a gas).
V *symbol for:* **1** *Chem.* vanadium. **2** (in transformational grammar) verb. **3** volume (capacity). **4** volt. **5** victory. **6** *the Roman numeral for* five.
v. *abbrev. for:* **1** ventral. **2** verb. **3** verse. **4** verso. **5** (*usually italic*) versus. **6** very. **7** vide [L: see]. **8** volume.
V. *abbrev. for:* **1** Venerable. **2** (in titles) Very. **3** (in titles) Vice. **4** Viscount.
V-1 *n* a robot bomb invented by the Germans in World War II: used esp. to bombard London. Also called: **doodlebug, buzz bomb, flying bomb.** [from G *Vergeltungswaffe* revenge weapon]
V-2 *n* a rocket-powered ballistic missile invented by the Germans in World War II: used esp. to bombard London. [see V-1]
V6 *n* a car or internal-combustion engine having six cylinders arranged in the form of a V.
V8 *n* a car or internal-combustion engine having eight cylinders arranged in the form of a V.
VA *abbrev. for:* **1** Vicar Apostolic. **2** (Order of) Victoria and Albert. **3** volt-ampere. **4** Virginia.
vac (væk) *n Brit. inf.* short for **vacation.**
vacancy **T** (ˈveɪkənsɪ) *n, pl* **vacancies. 1** the state or condition of being vacant or unoccupied; emptiness. **2** an unoccupied post or office: *we have a vacancy in the accounts department.* **3** an unoccupied room in a hotel, etc.: *the manager put up the "No Vacancies" sign.* **4** lack of thought or intelligent awareness. **5** *Obs.* idleness or a period spent in idleness.
vacant **T** (ˈveɪkənt) *adj* **1** without any contents; empty. **2** (*postpositive;* foll. by *of*) devoid (of something specified). **3** having no incumbent: *a vacant post.* **4** having no tenant or occupant: *a vacant house.* **5** characterized by or resulting from lack of thought or intelligent awareness. **6** (of time, etc.) not allocated to any activity: *it is pleasant to have a vacant hour in one's day.* **7** spent in idleness or inactivity: *a vacant life.* [C13: from L *vacāre* to be empty]
► **ˈvacantly** *adv*
vacant possession *n* ownership of an unoccupied house or property, any previous owner or tenant having departed.
vacate **T** (vəˈkeɪt) *vb* **vacates, vacating, vacated.** (*mainly tr*) **1** to cause (something) to be empty, esp. by departing from or abandoning it: *to vacate a room.* **2** (*also intr*) to give up the tenure, possession, or occupancy of (a place, post, etc.). **3** *Law.* **3a** to cancel. **3b** to annul.
► **vaˈcatable** *adj*
vacation (vəˈkeɪʃən) *n* **1** *Chiefly Brit.* a period of the year when the law courts or universities are closed. **2** another word (esp. US. and Canad.) for **holiday** (sense 1). **3** the act of departing from or abandoning property, etc. ◆ *vb* **4** (*intr*) *US. & Canad.* to take a holiday. [C14: from L *vacātiō* freedom, from *vacāre* to be empty]
► **vaˈcationer** *or* **vaˈcationist** *n*
vaccinate (ˈvæksɪˌneɪt) *vb* **vaccinates, vaccinating, vaccinated.** to inoculate (a person) with vaccine so as to produce immunity against a specific disease.
► **ˈvacciˌnator** *n*
vaccination (ˌvæksɪˈneɪʃən) *n* **1** the act of vaccinating. **2** the scar left following inoculation with a vaccine.
vaccine (ˈvæksiːn) *n Med.* **1** a suspension of dead, attenuated, or otherwise modified microorganisms for inoculation to produce immunity to a disease by stimulating the production of antibodies. **2** a preparation of the virus of cowpox inoculated in humans to produce immunity to smallpox. **3** (*modifier*) of or relating to vaccination or vaccinia. **4** *Computing.* software designed to detect and remove computer viruses from a system. [C18: from NL *variolae vaccīnae* cowpox, title of medical treatise (1798) by Edward Jenner, from L *vacca* a cow]
► **ˈvaccinal** *adj*
vaccinia (vækˈsɪnɪə) *n* a technical name for **cowpox.** [C19: NL, from L *vaccīnus* of cows]
vacherin *French.* (vaʃrɛ̃) *n* a dessert consisting of a meringue shell filled with whipped cream, ice cream, fruit, etc. [also in France a kind of cheese, from F *vache* cow, from L *vacca*]
vacillate **T** (ˈvæsɪˌleɪt) *vb* **vacillates, vacillating, vacillated.** (*intr*) **1** to fluctuate in one's opinions. **2** to sway from side to side physically. [C16: from L *vacillāre* to sway, from ?]
► **ˌvacilˈlation** *n* ► **ˈvacilˌlator** *n*
vacua (ˈvækjʊə) *n* a plural of **vacuum.**
vacuity **T** (væˈkjuːɪtɪ) *n, pl* **vacuities. 1** the state or quality of being vacuous. **2** an empty space or void. **3** a lack or absence of something specified: *a vacuity of wind.* **4** lack of normal intelligence or awareness. **5** a statement, saying, etc., that is inane or pointless. **6** (in customs terminology) the difference in volume between the actual contents of a container and its full capacity. [C16: from L *vacuitās* empty space, from *vacuus* empty]
vacuole (ˈvækjʊˌəʊl) *n Biol.* a fluid-filled cavity in a cell. [C19: from F, lit.: little vacuum, from L VACUUM]
► **vacuolar** (ˌvækjʊˈəʊlə) *adj*
vacuous **T** (ˈvækjʊəs) *adj* **1** empty. **2** bereft of ideas or intelligence. **3** characterized by or resulting from vacancy of mind: *a vacuous gaze.* **4** indulging in no useful mental or physical activity. [C17: from L *vacuus* empty]
► **ˈvacuously** *adv*
vacuum **T** (ˈvækjʊəm) *n, pl* **vacuums** *or* **vacua. 1** a region containing no free matter; in technical contexts now often called: **free space. 2** a region in which gas is present at a low pressure. **3** the degree of exhaustion of gas within an enclosed space: *a perfect vacuum.* **4** a feeling of emptiness: *his death left a vacuum in her life.* **5** short for **vacuum cleaner. 6** (*modifier*) of, containing, producing, or operated by a low gas pressure: *a vacuum brake.* ◆ *vb* **7** to clean (something) with a vacuum cleaner. [C16: from L: empty space, from *vacuus* empty]
vacuum cleaner *n* an electrical household appliance used for cleaning floors, carpets, etc., by suction.
► **vacuum cleaning** *n*
vacuum distillation *n* distillation in which the liquid distilled is enclosed at a low pressure in order to reduce its boiling point.
vacuum flask *n* an insulating flask that has double walls, usually of silvered glass, with an evacuated space between them. It is used for maintaining substances at high or low temperatures. Also called: **Thermos.**
vacuum gauge *n* any of a number of instruments for measuring pressures below atmospheric pressure.
vacuum-packed *adj* packed in an airtight container or packet under low pressure in order to maintain freshness, prevent corrosion, etc.
vacuum pump *n* a pump for producing a low gas pressure.
vacuum tube *or* **valve** *n* the US. and Canad. name for **valve** (sense 3).
VAD *abbrev. for* **1** Voluntary Aid Detachment. ◆ *n* **2** a member of this organization.
vade mecum (ˈvɑːdɪ ˈmeɪkʊm) *n* a handbook or other aid carried on the person for immediate use when needed. [C17: from L, lit.: go with me]
vadose (ˈveɪdəʊs) *adj* of, designating, or derived from water occurring above the water table: *vadose deposits.* [C19: from L *vadōsus* full of shallows, from *vadum* a ford]
vagabond **T** (ˈvægəˌbɒnd) *n* **1** a person with no fixed home. **2** an idle wandering beggar or thief. **3** (*modifier*) of or like a vagabond. [C15: from L *vagābundus* wandering, from *vagārī* to roam, from *vagus* VAGUE]
► **ˈvagaˌbondage** *n*
vagal (ˈveɪgᵊl) *adj Anat.* of, relating to, or affecting the vagus nerve: *vagal inhibition.*
vagary **T** (ˈveɪgərɪ, vəˈgeərɪ) *n, pl* **vagaries.** an erratic notion or action. [C16: prob. from L *vagārī* to roam; cf. L *vagus* VAGUE]

THESAURUS

vacancy *n* **1 = emptiness,** gap, space, vacuum, void **2 = job,** opening, opportunity, position, post, room, situation **4 = blankness,** absent-mindedness, abstraction, inanity, inattentiveness, incomprehension, incuriousness, lack of interest, vacuousness
vacant *adj* **1, 3, 4 = unoccupied,** available, disengaged, empty, free, idle, not in use, to let, unemployed, unengaged, unfilled, untenanted, void **5 = blank,** absent-minded, abstracted, ditzy *or* ditsy (*sl.*), dreaming, dreamy, expressionless, idle, inane, incurious, thoughtless, unthinking, vacuous, vague
Antonyms *adj* ≠ **unoccupied:** busy, engaged, full, inhabited, in use, occupied, taken ≠ **blank:** animated, engrossed, expressive, lively, reflective, thoughtful
vacate *vb* **1 = leave,** depart, evacuate, give up, go away, leave empty, move out of, quit, relinquish possession of, withdraw
vacillate *vb* **1, 2 = keep changing one's mind,** be irresolute *or* indecisive, blow hot and cold (*inf.*), chop and change, dither, fluctuate, haver, hesitate, oscillate, reel, rock, shillyshally (*inf.*), sway, swither (*Scot.*), waver
vacillating *adj* **1 = irresolute,** hesitant, in two minds (*inf.*), oscillating, shillyshallying (*inf.*), uncertain, unresolved, wavering
vacillation *n* **1 = indecisiveness,** dithering (*chiefly Brit.*), fluctuation, hesitation, inconstancy, irresoluteness, irresolution, shillyshallying (*inf.*), unsteadiness, wavering
vacuity *n* **1, 4 = unintelligence,** blankness, emptiness, inanity, incognizance, incomprehension, vacuousness **2 = emptiness,** nothingness, space, vacuum, void
vacuous *adj* **1 = emptiness,** empty, unfilled, vacant, void **2, 3 = unintelligent,** blank, inane, stupid, uncomprehending, vacant
vacuum *n* **1 = emptiness,** free space, gap, nothingness, space, vacuity, void
vagabond *n* **1 = vagrant,** bag lady, beggar, bum (*inf.*), down-and-out, hobo (*US*), itinerant, knight of the road, migrant, nomad, outcast, rascal, rover, tramp, wanderer, wayfarer ◆ *modifier* **3 = vagrant,** destitute, down and out, drifting, fly-by-night (*inf.*), footloose, homeless, idle, itinerant, journeying, nomadic, rootless, roving, shiftless, wandering
vagary *n* **= whim,** caprice, crotchet, fancy, humour, megrim (*arch.*), notion, whimsy

vagina ⓘ (vəˈdʒaɪnə) *n, pl* **vaginas** *or* **vaginae** (-niː). **1** the canal in most female mammals that extends from the cervix of the uterus to an external opening between the labia minora. **2** *Anat., biol.* any sheath or sheathlike structure. [C17: from L: sheath]
▸**vagˈinal** *adj*

vaginate (ˈvædʒɪnɪt, -ˌneɪt) *adj* (esp. of plant parts) sheathed: *a vaginate leaf.*

vaginectomy (ˌvædʒɪˈnɛktəmɪ) *n, pl* **vaginectomies. 1** surgical removal of all or part of the vagina. **2** surgical removal of part of the serous sheath surrounding the testis and epididymis.

vaginismus (ˌvædʒɪˈnɪzməs) *n* painful spasm of the vagina. [C19: from NL, from VAGINA, + *-ismus;* see -ISM]

vaginitis (ˌvædʒɪˈnaɪtɪs) *n* inflammation of the vagina.

vagotomy (væˈgɒtəmɪ) *n, pl* **vagotomies.** surgical division of the vagus nerve, performed to limit gastric secretion in patients with severe peptic ulcers. [C19: from VAG(US) + -TOMY]

vagotonia (ˌveɪgəˈtəʊnɪə) *n* pathological overactivity of the vagus nerve, affecting various bodily functions controlled by this nerve. [C19: from VAG(US) + *-tonia,* from L *tonus* tension, TONE]

vagrancy (ˈveɪgrənsɪ) *n, pl* **vagrancies. 1** the state or condition of being a vagrant. **2** the conduct or mode of living of a vagrant.

vagrant ⓘ (ˈveɪgrənt) *n* **1** a person of no settled abode, income, or job; tramp. ◆ *adj* **2** wandering about. **3** of or characteristic of a vagrant or vagabond. **4** moving in an erratic fashion; wayward. **5** (of plants) showing straggling growth. [C15: prob. from OF *waucrant* (from *wancrer* to roam, of Gmc origin), but also infl. by OF *vagant* vagabond, from L *vagārī* to wander]
▸ˈ**vagrantly** *adv*

vague ⓘ (veɪg) *adj* **1** (of statements, meaning, etc.) imprecise: *vague promises.* **2** not clearly perceptible or discernible: *a vague idea.* **3** not clearly established or known: *a vague rumour.* **4** (of a person or his expression) absent-minded. [C16: via F from L *vagus* wandering, from ?]
▸ˈ**vaguely** *adv* ▸ˈ**vagueness** *n*

vagus *or* **vagus nerve** (ˈveɪgəs) *n, pl* **vagi** (ˈveɪdʒaɪ) *or* **vagus nerves.** the tenth cranial nerve, which supplies the heart, lungs, and viscera. [C19: from L *vagus* wandering]
▸ˈ**vagal** *adj*

vail (veɪl) *Obs.* ◆ *vb* (*tr*) **1** to lower (something, such as a weapon), esp. as a sign of deference. **2** to remove (the hat, etc.) as a mark of respect. ◆ *n* **3** a tip. [C14 *valen,* from obs. *avalen,* from OF *avaler* to let fall, from L *ad vallem,* lit.: to the valley, i.e., down]

vain ⓘ (veɪn) *adj* **1** inordinately proud of one's appearance, possessions, or achievements. **2** given to ostentatious display. **3** worthless. **4** senseless or futile. ◆ *n* **5 in vain.** fruitlessly. [C13: via OF from L *vānus*]
▸ˈ**vainly** *adv* ▸ˈ**vainness** *n*

vainglory (ˌveɪnˈglɔːrɪ) *n* **1** boastfulness or vanity. **2** ostentation.
▸ˌ**vainˈglorious** *adj*

vair (vɛə) *n* **1** a fur, probably Russian squirrel, used to trim robes in the Middle Ages. **2** a fur used on heraldic shields, conventionally represented by white and blue skins in alternate lines. [C13: from OF: of more than one colour, from L *varius* variegated]

Vaisya (ˈvaɪsjə, ˈvaɪʃjə) *n* the third of the four main Hindu castes, the traders. [C18: from Sansk., lit.: settler, from *viś* settlement]

valance (ˈvæləns) *n* a short piece of drapery hung along a shelf or bed to hide structural detail. [C15: ? after *Valence,* SE France, town noted for its textiles]
▸ˈ**valanced** *adj*

vale[1] (veɪl) *n* a literary word for **valley.** [C13: from OF *val,* from L *vallis* valley]

vale[2] *Latin.* (ˈvɑːleɪ) *sentence substitute.* farewell; goodbye.

valediction ⓘ (ˌvælɪˈdɪkʃən) *n* **1** the act or an instance of saying goodbye. **2** any valedictory statement, etc. [C17: from L *valedīcere,* from *valē* farewell + *dīcere* to say]

valedictory ⓘ (ˌvælɪˈdɪktərɪ) *adj* **1** saying goodbye. **2** of or relating to a farewell or an occasion of farewell. ◆ *n, pl* **valedictories. 3** a farewell address or speech.

valence (ˈveɪləns) *n Chem.* **1** another name (esp. US. and Canad.) for **valency. 2** the phenomenon of forming chemical bonds.

Valenciennes (ˌvælənsɪˈɛn) *n* a flat bobbin lace typically having scroll and floral designs and originally made of linen. [after *Valenciennes,* N France, where orig. made]

valency (ˈveɪlənsɪ) *or esp. US. & Canad.* **valence** *n, pl* **valencies** *or* **valences.** *Chem.* a property of atoms or groups equal to the number of atoms of hydrogen that the atom or group could combine with or displace in forming compounds. [C19: from L *valentia* strength, from *valēre* to be strong]

valency electron *n Chem.* an electron in the outer shell of an atom, responsible for forming chemical bonds.

valentine (ˈvælənˌtaɪn) *n* **1** a card or gift expressing love or affection, sent, often anonymously, on Saint Valentine's Day. **2** a sweetheart selected for such a greeting. [C15: after *St Valentine,* 3rd-century A.D. Christian martyr]

valerian (vəˈlɪərɪən) *n* **1** Also called: **allheal.** a Eurasian plant having small white or pinkish flowers and a medicinal root. **2** a sedative drug made from the dried roots of this plant. [C14: via OF from Med. L *valeriana* (*herba*) (herb) of *Valerius,* unexplained L personal name]

valeric (vəˈlɛrɪk, -ˈlɪərɪk) *adj* of, relating to, or derived from valerian.

valeric acid *n* another name for **pentanoic acid.**

valet (ˈvælɪt, ˈvæleɪ) *n* **1** a manservant who acts as personal attendant to his employer, looking after his clothing, serving his meals, etc. **2** a manservant who attends to the requirements of patrons in a hotel, etc.; steward. ◆ *vb* **valets, valeting, valeted. 3** to act as a valet for (a person). **4** (*tr*) to clean the bodywork and interior of (a car) as a professional service. [C16: from OF *vaslet* page, from Med. L *vassus* servant]

valeta *or* **veleta** (vəˈliːtə) *n* a ballroom dance in triple time. [from Sp.: weather vane]

valet de chambre *French.* (valɛ də ʃɑ̃brə) *n, pl* ***valets de chambre*** (valɛ də ʃɑ̃brə). the full French term for **valet** (sense 1).

valet parking *n* a system at hotels, airports, etc., in which patrons' cars are parked by a steward.

valetudinarian (ˌvælɪˌtjuːdɪˈnɛərɪən) *or* **valetudinary** (ˌvælɪˈtjuːdɪnərɪ) *n, pl* **valetudinarians** *or* **valetudinaries. 1** a person who is chronically sick. **2** a hypochondriac. ◆ *adj* **3** relating to or resulting from poor health. **4** being a valetudinarian. [C18: from L *valētūdō* state of health, from *valēre* to be well]
▸ˌ**valeˌtudiˈnarianism** *n*

valgus (ˈvælgəs) *adj Pathol.* twisted away from the midline of the body. [C19: from L: bow-legged]

Valhalla (vælˈhælə), **Walhalla, Valhall** (vælˈhæl, ˈvælhæl), *or* **Walhall** *n Norse myth.* the great hall of Odin where warriors who die as heroes in battle dwell eternally. [C18: from ON, from *valr* slain warriors + *höll* HALL]

valiant ⓘ (ˈvæljənt) *adj* **1** courageous or intrepid. **2** marked by bravery or courage: *a valiant deed.* [C14: from OF, from *valoir* to be of value, from L *valēre* to be strong]
▸ˈ**valiantly** *adv*

valid ⓘ (ˈvælɪd) *adj* **1** having some foundation; based on truth. **2** legally acceptable: *a valid licence.* **3a** having legal force. **3b** having legal authority. **4** having some force or cogency: *a valid point in a debate.* **5** *Logic.* (of an inference or argument) having premises and a conclusion so related that if the premises are true, the conclusion must be true. [C16: from L *validus* robust, from *valēre* to be strong]
▸**validity** (vəˈlɪdɪtɪ) *n* ▸ˈ**validly** *adv*

THESAURUS

vagina *n* **1** = **vulva**, beaver (*taboo sl.*), box (*taboo sl.*), crack (*taboo sl.*), cunt (*taboo*), fanny (*Brit. taboo sl.*), hole (*taboo sl.*), minge (*Brit. taboo*), muff (*taboo sl.*), pussy (*taboo sl.*), quim (*Brit. taboo*), snatch (*taboo sl.*), twat (*taboo sl.*), yoni

vagrant *n* **1** = **tramp**, bag lady (*chiefly US*), beggar, bird of passage, bum (*inf.*), drifter, hobo (*US*), itinerant, person of no fixed address, rolling stone, wanderer ◆ *adj* **2** = **itinerant**, nomadic, roaming, rootless, roving, unsettled, vagabond
Antonyms *adj* ≠ **itinerant**: established, fixed, purposeful, rooted, settled

vague *adj* **1** = **unclear**, doubtful, generalized, hazy, imprecise, indefinite, loose, uncertain, unspecified, woolly **2** = **indistinct**, amorphous, blurred, dim, fuzzy, hazy, ill-defined, indeterminate, nebulous, obscure, shadowy, unclear, unknown
Antonyms *adj* ≠ **unclear**: clear, clear-cut, definite, distinct, exact, explicit, precise, specific ≠ **indistinct**: clear, distinct, lucid, well-defined

vaguely *adv* **1** = **imprecisely**, dimly, evasively, in a general way, obscurely, slightly **4** = **absent-mindedly**, vacantly

vagueness *n* **1** = **impreciseness**, ambiguity, inexactitude, lack of preciseness, looseness, obscurity, undecidedness, woolliness
Antonyms *n* clarity, clearness, definition, exactness, obviousness, preciseness, precision

vain *adj* **1, 2** = **proud**, arrogant, bigheaded, cocky, conceited, egotistical, inflated, narcissistic, ostentatious, overweening, peacockish, pleased with oneself, self-important, stuck-up (*inf.*), swaggering, swanky (*inf.*), swollen-headed (*inf.*), vainglorious **3, 4** = **futile**, abortive, empty, fruitless, hollow, idle, nugatory, pointless, senseless, time-wasting, trifling, trivial, unavailing, unimportant, unproductive, unprofitable, useless, worthless ◆ *n* **5 in vain** = **to no avail**, bootless(ly), fruitless(ly), ineffectual(ly), to no purpose, unsuccessful(ly), useless(ly), vain(ly), wasted, without success
Antonyms *adj* ≠ **proud**: bashful, humble, meek, modest, self-deprecating ≠ **futile**: fruitful, profitable, serious, successful, useful, valid, worthwhile, worthy

valediction *n* **1, 2** = **farewell**, adieu, goodbye, leave-taking, sendoff (*inf.*), vale

valedictory *adj* **1** = **farewell**, final, parting

valiant *adj* **1, 2** = **brave**, bold, courageous, dauntless, doughty, fearless, gallant, heroic, indomitable, intrepid, lion-hearted, plucky, redoubtable, stouthearted, valorous, worthy
Antonyms *adj* cowardly, craven, fearful, shrinking, spineless, timid, weak

valid *adj* **1, 4** = **sound**, acceptable, binding, cogent, conclusive, convincing, efficacious, efficient, good, just, logical, powerful, sensible, substantial, telling, weighty, well-founded, well-grounded **2, 3** = **legal**, authentic, bona fide, genuine, in force, lawful, legally binding, legitimate, official, signed and sealed
Antonyms *adj* ≠ **sound**: baseless, bogus, fallacious, false, illogical, sham, spurious, unacceptable, unfounded, unrealistic, unrecognized, untrue, weak ≠ **legal**: illegal, inoperative, invalid, unlawful, unofficial

validate *vb* **1** = **confirm**, certify, corroborate, prove, substantiate **2** = **authorize**, authenticate, endorse, legalize, make legally binding, ratify, set one's seal on *or* to

validity *n* **3** = **legality**, authority, lawfulness, legitimacy, right **4** = **soundness**, cogency, force, foundation, grounds, point, power, strength, substance, weight

validate ❶ ('vælɪˌdeɪt) *vb* **validates, validating, validated.** (*tr*) **1** to confirm or corroborate. **2** to give legal force or official confirmation to.
▸ **ˌvaliˈdation** *n*

valine ('veɪliːn) *n* an essential amino acid: a component of proteins. [C19: from VAL(ERIC ACID) + -INE[2]]

valise (və'liːz) *n* a small overnight travelling case. [C17: via F from It. *valigia*, from ?]

Valium ('vælɪəm) *n Trademark.* a preparation of the drug diazepam used as a tranquillizer.

Valkyrie, Walkyrie (væl'kɪərɪ, 'vælkɪərɪ), *or* **Valkyr** ('vælkɪə) *n Norse myth.* any of the beautiful maidens who serve Odin and ride over battlefields to claim the dead heroes and take them to Valhalla. [C18: from ON *Valkyrja*, from *valr* slain warriors + *köri* to CHOOSE]
▸ **Valˈkyrian** *adj*

vallation (və'leɪʃən) *n* **1** the act or process of building fortifications. **2** a wall or rampart. [C17: from LL *vallātiō*, from L *vallum* rampart]

vallecula (və'lɛkjʊlə) *n, pl* **valleculae** (-ˌliː). **1** *Anat.* any of various natural depressions or crevices. **2** *Bot.* a groove or furrow. [C19: from LL: little valley, from L *vallis* valley]

valley ❶ ('vælɪ) *n* **1** a long depression in the land surface, usually containing a river, formed by erosion or by movements in the earth's crust. **2** the broad area drained by a single river system: *the Thames valley*. **3** any elongated depression resembling a valley. [C13: from OF *valee*, from L *vallis*]

vallum ('væləm) *n Archaeol.* a Roman rampart or earthwork.

valonia (və'ləʊnɪə) *n* the acorn cups and unripe acorns of the Eurasian oak, used in tanning, dyeing, and making ink. [C18: from It. *vallonia*, ult. from Gk *balanos* acorn]

valorize *or* **valorise** ('væləˌraɪz) *vb* **valorizes, valorizing, valorized** *or* **valorises, valorising, valorised.** (*tr*) to fix an artificial price for (a commodity) by governmental action. [C20: back formation from *valorization*; see VALOUR]
▸ **ˌvaloriˈzation** *or* **ˌvaloriˈsation** *n*

valour ❶ *or US* **valor** ('vælə) *n* courage or bravery, esp. in battle. [C15: from LL *valor*, from *valēre* to be strong]
▸ **ˈvalorous** *adj*

valse *French.* (vals) *n* another word for **waltz.**

valuable ❶ ('væljuəbᵊl) *adj* **1** having considerable monetary worth. **2** of considerable importance or quality: *valuable information.* **3** able to be valued. ◆ *n* **4** (*usually pl*) a valuable article of personal property, esp. jewellery.
▸ **ˈvaluably** *adv*

valuate ('væljuˌeɪt) *vb* **valuates, valuating, valuated.** *US.* another word for **value** (senses 10, 12) or **evaluate.**
▸ **ˈvaluˌator** *n*

valuation (ˌvælju'eɪʃən) *n* **1** the act of valuing, esp. a formal assessment of the worth of property, jewellery, etc. **2** the price arrived at by the process of valuing: *I set a high valuation on technical ability.*
▸ **ˌvaluˈational** *adj*

value ❶ ('væljuː) *n* **1** the desirability of a thing, often in respect of some property such as usefulness or exchangeability. **2** an amount, esp. a material or monetary one, considered to be a fair exchange in return for a thing: *the value of the picture is £10 000.* **3** satisfaction: *value for money.* **4** precise meaning or significance. **5** (*pl*) the moral principles or accepted standards of a person or group. **6** *Maths.* a particular magnitude, number, or amount: *the value of the variable was 7.* **7** *Music.* short for **time value. 8** (in painting, drawing, etc.) **8a** a gradation of tone from light to dark. **8b** the relation of one of these elements to another or to the whole picture. **9** *Phonetics.* the quality of the speech sound associated with a written character representing it: *"g" has the value* (dʒ) *in English "gem".* ◆ *vb* **values, valuing, valued.** (*tr*) **10** to assess or estimate the worth, merit, or desirability of. **11** to have a high regard for, esp. in respect of worth, usefulness, merit, etc. **12** (foll. by *at*) to fix the financial or material worth of (a unit of currency, work of art, etc.). [C14: from OF, from *valoir*, from L *valēre* to be worth]
▸ **ˈvalued** *adj* ▸ **ˈvalueless** *adj* ▸ **ˈvaluer** *n*

value added *n* the difference between the total revenues of a firm, industry, etc., and its total purchases from other firms, industries, etc.

value-added tax *n* (in Britain) the full name for **VAT.**

valued policy *n* an insurance policy in which the amount payable in the event of a valid claim is agreed upon between the company and the policyholder when the policy is issued and is not related to the actual value of a loss.

value judgment *n* a subjective assessment based on one's own values or those of one's class.

Valuer General *n Austral.* a state official who values properties for rating purposes.

valuta (və'luːtə) *n Rare.* the value of one currency in terms of its exchange rate with another. [C20: from It., lit.: VALUE]

valvate ('vælveɪt) *adj* **1** furnished with a valve or valves. **2** *Bot.* **2a** taking place by means of valves: *valvate dehiscence.* **2b** (of petals) having the margins touching but not overlapping.

valve (vælv) *n* **1** any device that shuts off, starts, regulates, or controls the flow of a fluid. **2** *Anat.* a flaplike structure in a hollow organ, such as the heart, that controls the one-way passage of fluid through that organ. **3** Also called: **tube.** an evacuated electron tube containing a cathode, anode, and, usually, one or more additional control electrodes. When a positive potential is applied to the anode, it produces a one-way flow of current. **4** *Zool.* any of the separable pieces that make up the shell of a mollusc. **5** *Music.* a device on some brass instruments by which the effective length of the tube may be varied to enable a chromatic scale to be produced. **6** *Bot.* any of the several parts that make up a dry dehiscent fruit, esp. a capsule. [C14: from L *valva* a folding door]
▸ **ˈvalveless** *adj* ▸ **ˈvalveˌlike** *adj*

valve-in-head engine *n* the US name for **overhead-valve engine.**

valvular ('vælvjʊlə) *adj* **1** of, relating to, operated by, or having a valve or valves. **2** having the shape or function of a valve.

valvulitis (ˌvælvjʊ'laɪtɪs) *n* inflammation of a bodily valve, esp. a heart valve. [C19: from NL *valvula* dim. of VALVE + -ITIS]

vamoose ❶ (və'muːs) *vb* **vamooses, vamoosing, vamoosed.** (*intr*) *Sl., chiefly US.* to leave a place hurriedly; decamp. [C19: from Sp. *vamos* let us go, from L *vādere* to go, walk rapidly]

vamp[1] (væmp) *Inf.* ◆ *n* **1** a seductive woman who exploits men by use of her sexual charms. ◆ *vb* **2** to exploit (a man) in the fashion of a vamp. [C20: short for VAMPIRE]

vamp[2] (væmp) *n* **1** something patched up to make it look new. **2** the reworking of a story, etc. **3** an improvised accompaniment. **4** the front part of the upper of a shoe. ◆ *vb* **5** (*tr*; often foll. by *up*) to make a renovation of. **6** to improvise (an accompaniment) to (a tune). [C13: from OF *avantpié* the front part of a shoe (hence, something patched), from *avant-* fore- + *pié* foot, from L *pēs*]

vampire ('væmpaɪə) *n* **1** (in European folklore) a corpse that rises nightly from its grave to drink the blood of the living. **2** See **vampire bat. 3** a person who preys mercilessly upon others. [C18: from F, from G, from Magyar]
▸ **vampiric** (væm'pɪrɪk) *adj* ▸ **ˈvampirism** *n*

vampire bat *n* a bat of tropical regions of Central and South America, having sharp incisor and canine teeth and feeding on the blood of birds and mammals.

van[1] (væn) *n* **1** short for **caravan** (sense 1). **2** a motor vehicle for transporting goods, etc., by road. **3** *Brit.* a closed railway wagon in which the guard travels, for transporting goods, etc.

van[2] (væn) *n* short for **vanguard.**

van[3] (væn) *n Tennis, chiefly Brit.* short for **advantage** (sense 3).

van[4] (væn) *n* **1** any device for winnowing corn. **2** *Arch.* a wing. [C17: var. of FAN[1]]

vanadium (və'neɪdɪəm) *n* a toxic silvery-white metallic element used in steel alloys and as a catalyst. Symbol: V; atomic no.: 23; atomic wt.: 50.94. [C19: NL, from ON *Vanadis*, epithet of the goddess Freya + -IUM]

Van Allen belt *n* either of two regions of charged particles above the earth, the inner one extending from 2400 to 5600 kilometres above the earth and the outer one from 13 000 to 19 000 kilometres. [C20: after J. A. *Van Allen* (born 1914), US physicist]

V and A (in Britain) *abbrev. for* Victoria and Albert Museum.

vandal ❶ ('vændᵊl) *n* a person who deliberately causes damage to personal or public property. [C17: from VANDAL, from L *Vandallus*, of Gmc origin]

Vandal ('vændᵊl) *n* a member of a Germanic people that raided Roman provinces in the 3rd and 4th centuries A.D. before devastating Gaul, conquering Spain and N Africa, and sacking Rome.
▸ **Vandalic** (væn'dælɪk) *adj*

THESAURUS

valley *n* **1** = **hollow**, coomb, cwm (*Welsh*), dale, dell, depression, dingle, glen, strath (*Scot.*), vale

valorous *adj* = **brave**, bold, courageous, dauntless, doughty, fearless, gallant, heroic, intrepid, lion-hearted, plucky, valiant

valour *n* = **bravery**, boldness, courage, derring-do (*arch.*), doughtiness, fearlessness, gallantry, heroism, intrepidity, lion-heartedness, spirit
Antonyms *n* cowardice, dread, fear, timidity, trepidation, weakness

valuable *adj* **1** = **precious**, costly, dear, expensive, high-priced **2** = **useful**, beneficial, cherished, esteemed, estimable, held dear, helpful, important, prized, profitable, serviceable, treasured, valued, worthwhile, worthy ◆ *n* **4** *usually plural* = **treasures**, heirlooms, jewellery
Antonyms *adj* ≠ **precious:** cheap, cheapo (*inf.*), inexpensive, worthless ≠ **useful:** insignificant, pointless, silly, trifling, trivial, unimportant, useless, worthless

value *n* **1** = **importance**, advantage, benefit, desirability, help, merit, mileage (*inf.*), profit, serviceableness, significance, use, usefulness, utility, worth **2** = **cost**, equivalent, market price, monetary worth, rate **5** *plural* = **principles**, code of behaviour, ethics, (moral) standards ◆ *vb* **10, 12** = **evaluate**, account, appraise, assess, compute, estimate, price, put a price on, rate, set at, survey **11** = **regard highly**, appreciate, cherish, esteem, hold dear, hold in high regard *or* esteem, prize, respect, set store by, treasure
Antonyms *n* ≠ **importance:** insignificance, unimportance, uselessness, worthlessness ◆ *vb* ≠ **regard highly:** disregard, have no time for, hold a low opinion of, underestimate, undervalue

valued *adj* **11** = **highly regarded**, cherished, dear, esteemed, loved, prized, treasured

valueless *adj* **1** = **worthless**, miserable, no good, of no earthly use, of no value, unsaleable, useless

vamoose *vb Slang, chiefly U.S.* = **go away**, clear off (*inf.*), decamp, do a bunk (*Brit. sl.*), hook it (*sl.*), make off, make oneself scarce (*inf.*), run away, scarper (*Brit. sl.*), scram (*inf.*), skedaddle (*inf.*), take flight, take oneself off

vandal *n* = **hooligan**, delinquent, graffiti artist, lager lout, rowdy, yob *or* yobbo (*Brit. sl.*)

vandalism ('vændə,lɪzəm) *n* the deliberate destruction caused by a vandal or an instance of such destruction.
▸,**vandal'istic** *adj*

vandalize *or* **vandalise** ('vændə,laɪz) *vb* **vandalizes, vandalizing, vandalized** *or* **vandalises, vandalising, vandalised.** (*tr*) to destroy or damage (something) by an act of vandalism.

Van de Graaff generator ('væn də ,grɑːf) *n* a device for producing high electrostatic potentials, consisting of a hollow metal sphere on which a charge is accumulated from a continuous moving belt of insulating material: used in particle accelerators. [C20: after R. J. *Van de Graaff* (1901–67), US physicist]

Vandyke beard ('vændaɪk) *n* a short pointed beard. Often shortened to **Vandyke.** [C18: after Sir Anthony *Van Dyck* (1599–1641), Flemish painter]

Vandyke collar *or* **cape** *n* a large white collar with several very deep points. Often shortened to **Vandyke.**

vane (veɪn) *n* **1** Also called: **weather vane.** a flat plate or blade of metal mounted on a vertical axis in an exposed position to indicate wind direction. **2** any one of the flat blades or sails forming part of the wheel of a windmill. **3** any flat or shaped plate used to direct fluid flow, esp. in a turbine, etc. **4** a fin or plate fitted to a projectile or missile to provide stabilization or guidance. **5** *Ornithol.* the flat part of a feather. **6** *Surveying.* **6a** a sight on a quadrant or compass. **6b** the movable marker on a levelling staff. [OE *fana*]
▸**vaned** *adj*

vanguard ● ('væn,gɑːd) *n* **1** the leading division or units of a military force. **2** the leading position in any movement or field, or the people who occupy such a position. [C15: from OF *avant-garde*, from *avant-* fore- + *garde* GUARD]

vanilla (və'nɪlə) *n* **1** any of a genus of tropical climbing orchids having spikes of large fragrant flowers and long fleshy pods containing the seeds (beans). **2** the pod or bean of certain of these plants, used to flavour food, etc. **3** a flavouring extract prepared from vanilla beans and used in cooking. ◆ *adj* **4** flavoured with or as with vanilla: *vanilla ice cream.* **5** *Sl.* ordinary or conventional: *a vanilla kind of guy.* [C17: from NL, from Sp. *vainilla* pod, from *vaina*, from L *vāgīna* sheath]
▸**va'nillic** *adj*

vanillin ('vænɪlɪn, və'nɪlɪn) *n* a white crystalline aldehyde found in vanilla and many natural balsams and resins. It is a by-product of paper manufacture and is used as a flavouring and in perfumes.

vanish ● ('vænɪʃ) *vb* (*intr*) **1** to disappear, esp. suddenly or mysteriously. **2** to cease to exist. **3** *Maths.* to become zero. [C14 *vanissen*, from OF *esvanir*, from L *ēvānēscere* to evaporate, from *ē-* EX-[1] + *vānēscere*, from *vānus* empty]
▸**'vanisher** *n*

vanishing cream *n* a cosmetic cream that is colourless once applied, used as a foundation for powder or as a cleansing cream.

vanishing point *n* **1** the point to which parallel lines appear to converge in the rendering of perspective, usually on the horizon. **2** a point at which something disappears.

vanity ● ('vænɪtɪ) *n, pl* **vanities. 1** the state or quality of being vain. **2** ostentation occasioned by ambition or pride. **3** an instance of being vain or something about which one is vain. **4** the state or quality of being valueless or futile. [C13: from OF, from L *vānitās* emptiness, from *vānus* empty]

vanity bag, case, *or* **box** *n* a woman's small bag or hand case used to carry cosmetics, etc.

vanity unit *n* a hand basin built into a wooden Formica-covered or tiled top, usually with a built-in cupboard below it. Also called (trademark): **Vanitory unit.**

vanquish ● ('væŋkwɪʃ) *vb* (*tr*) **1** to defeat or overcome in a battle, contest, etc. **2** to defeat in argument or debate. **3** to conquer (an emotion). [C14 *vanquisshen*, from OF *venquis*, from *veintre* to overcome, from L *vincere*]
▸**'vanquishable** *adj* ▸**'vanquisher** *n*

vantage ('vɑːntɪdʒ) *n* **1** a state, position, or opportunity affording superiority or advantage. **2** superiority or benefit accruing from such a position, etc. **3** *Tennis.* short for **advantage** (sense 3). [C13: from OF *avantage* ADVANTAGE]

vantage point *n* a position or place that allows one an overall view of a scene or situation.

vanward ('vænwəd) *adj, adv* in or towards the front.

vapid ● ('væpɪd) *adj* **1** bereft of strength, sharpness, flavour, etc. **2** boring or dull. [C17: from L *vapidus*]
▸**va'pidity** *n* ▸**'vapidly** *adv*

vapor ('veɪpə) *n* the US spelling of **vapour.**

vaporescence (,veɪpə'rɛsəns) *n* the production or formation of vapour.
▸,**vapor'escent** *adj*

vaporetto (,veɪpə'rɛtəʊ) *n, pl* **vaporetti** (-tɪ) *or* **vaporettos.** a steam-powered passenger boat, as used on the canals in Venice. [It., from *vapore* a steamboat]

vaporific (,veɪpə'rɪfɪk) *adj* **1** producing, causing, or tending to produce vapour. **2** of, concerned with, or having the nature of vapour. **3** tending to become vapour; volatile. [C18: from NL *vaporificus*, from L *vapor* steam + *facere* to make]

vaporimeter (,veɪpə'rɪmɪtə) *n* an instrument for measuring vapour pressure, used to determine the volatility of oils.

vaporize *or* **vaporise** ('veɪpə,raɪz) *vb* **vaporizes, vaporizing, vaporized** *or* **vaporises, vaporising, vaporised. 1** to change or cause to change into vapour or into the gaseous state. **2** to evaporate or disappear or cause to evaporate or disappear, esp. suddenly. **3** to destroy or be destroyed by turning into a gas as a result of the extreme heat generated by a nuclear explosion.
▸,**vapori'zation** *or* ,**vapori'sation** *n*

vaporizer *or* **vaporiser** ('veɪpə,raɪzə) *n* **1** a substance that vaporizes or a device that causes vaporization. **2** *Med.* a device that produces steam or atomizes medication for inhalation.

vaporous ('veɪpərəs) *adj* **1** resembling or full of vapour. **2** lacking permanence or substance. **3** given to foolish imaginings.
▸**vaporosity** (,veɪpə'rɒsɪtɪ) *n* ▸**'vaporously** *adv*

vapour ● *or US* **vapor** ('veɪpə) *n* **1** particles of moisture or other substance suspended in air and visible as clouds, smoke, etc. **2** a gaseous substance at a temperature below its critical temperature. **3** a substance that is in a gaseous state at a temperature below its boiling point. **4 the vapours.** *Arch.* a depressed mental condition believed originally to be the result of vaporous exhalations from the stomach. ◆ *vb* **5** to evaporate or cause to evaporate. **6** (*intr*) to make vain empty boasts. [C14: from L *vapor*]
▸**'vapourer** *or US* **'vaporer** *n* ▸**'vapourish** *or US* **'vaporish** *adj* ▸**'vapour-,like** *or US* **'vapor-,like** *adj* ▸**'vapoury** *or US* **'vapory** *adj*

vapour density *n* the ratio of the density of a gas or vapour to that of hydrogen at the same temperature and pressure.

vapour lock *n* a stoppage in a pipe carrying a liquid caused by a bubble of gas, esp. in the pipe feeding the carburettor of an internal-combustion engine.

vapour pressure *n Physics.* the pressure exerted by a vapour in equilibrium with its solid or liquid phase at a particular temperature.

vapour trail *n* a visible trail left by an aircraft flying at high altitude or through supercold air caused by the deposition of water vapour in the engine exhaust as minute ice crystals.

var. *abbrev. for:* **1** variable. **2** variant. **3** variation. **4** variety. **5** various.

varactor ('vɛə,ræktə) *n* a semiconductor diode that acts as a voltage-dependent capacitor, being operated with a reverse bias. [C20: prob. a blend of *variable reactor*]

varec ('værɛk) *n* **1** another name for **kelp. 2** the ash obtained from kelp. [C17: from F, from ON *wrek* (unattested); see WRECK]

variable ● ('vɛərɪəbᵊl) *adj* **1** liable to or capable of change: *variable weather.* **2** (of behaviour, emotions, etc.) lacking constancy. **3** *Maths.* having a range of possible values. **4** (of a species, etc.) liable to deviate from the established type. **5** (of a wind) varying in direction and intensity. **6** (of an electrical component or device) designed so that a characteristic property, such as resistance, can be varied. ◆ *n* **7** something that is subject to variation. **8** *Maths.* **8a** an expression that can be assigned any of a set of values. **8b** a symbol, esp. *x, y,* or *z,* representing an unspecified member of a class of objects, numbers, etc. **9** *Logic.* a symbol, esp. *x, y,* or *z,* representing any member of a class of entities. **10** *Computing.* a named unit of storage that can be changed to any of a set of specified values during execution of a program. **11** *Astron.* See **variable star. 12** a variable wind. **13** (*pl*) a region where variable winds occur. [C14: from L *variābilis* changeable, from *variāre* to diversify]
▸,**varia'bility** *or* **'variableness** *n* ▸**'variably** *adv*

variable cost *n* a cost that varies directly with output.

variable-geometry *or* **variable-sweep** *adj* denoting an aircraft in which the wings are hinged to give the variable aspect ratio colloquially known as a **swing-wing.**

variable star *n* any star that varies considerably in brightness, either irregularly or in regular periods. **Intrinsic variables,** in which the variation is a result of internal changes, include novae and pulsating stars.

THESAURUS

vanguard *n* **1, 2 = forefront,** advance guard, cutting edge, forerunners, front, front line, front rank, leaders, spearhead, trailblazers, trendsetters, van
Antonyms *n* back, rear, rearguard, stern, tail, tail end

vanish *vb* **1, 2 = disappear,** become invisible, be lost to sight, die out, dissolve, evanesce, evaporate, exit, fade (away), melt (away), vanish off the face of the earth
Antonyms *vb* appear, arrive, become visible, come into view, materialize, pop up

vanity *n* **2, 3 = pride,** affected ways, airs, arrogance, bigheadedness, conceit, conceitedness, egotism, narcissism, ostentation, pretension, self-admiration, self-love, showing off (*inf.*), swollen-headedness (*inf.*), vainglory **4 = futility,** emptiness, frivolity, fruitlessness, hollowness, inanity, pointlessness, profitlessness, triviality, unproductiveness, unreality, unsubstantiality, uselessness, worthlessness
Antonyms *n* ≠ **pride:** humility, meekness, modesty, self-abasement, self-deprecation ≠ **futility:** importance, value, worth

vanquish *vb* **1, 2 = defeat,** beat, blow out of the water (*sl.*), clobber, conquer, crush, get the upper hand over, master, overcome, overpower, overwhelm, put down, put to flight, put to rout, quell, reduce, repress, rout, run rings around (*inf.*), stuff (*sl.*), subdue, subjugate, triumph over, undo

vapid *adj* **1, 2 = dull,** bland, boring, colourless, flat, insipid, limp, tame, uninspiring, uninteresting, weak, wishy-washy (*inf.*)

vapour *n* **1 = mist,** breath, dampness, exhalation, fog, fumes, haze, miasma, smoke, steam

variable *adj* **1, 2 = changeable,** capricious, chameleonic, fickle, fitful, flexible, fluctuating, inconstant, mercurial, mutable, protean, shifting, temperamental, uneven, unstable, unsteady, vacillating, wavering

variance ⓘ ('vɛərɪəns) *n* **1** the act of varying or the quality, state, or degree of being divergent. **2** an instance of diverging; dissension. **3 at variance. 3a** (often foll. by *with*) (of facts, etc.) not in accord. **3b** (of persons) in a state of dissension. **4** *Statistics.* a measure of dispersion; the square of the standard deviations. **5** a difference or discrepancy between two steps in a legal proceeding, esp. between a statement and the evidence given to support it. **6** *Chem.* the number of degrees of freedom of a system, used in the phase rule.

variant ⓘ ('vɛərɪənt) *adj* **1** liable to or displaying variation. **2** differing from a standard or type: *a variant spelling.* ◆ *n* **3** something that differs from a standard or type. **4** *Statistics.* another word for **variate.** [C14: via OF from L, from *variāre* to diversify, from *varius* VARIOUS]

variate ('vɛərɪɪt) *n Statistics.* a random variable or a numerical value taken by it. [C16: from L *variāre* to VARY]

variation ⓘ (ˌvɛərɪ'eɪʃən) *n* **1** the act, process, condition, or result of changing or varying. **2** an instance of varying or the amount, rate, or degree of such change. **3** something that differs from a standard or convention. **4** *Music.* a repetition of a musical theme in which the rhythm, harmony, or melody is altered or embellished. **5** *Biol.* a marked deviation from the typical form or function. **6** *Astron.* any deviation from the mean motion or orbit of a planet, satellite, etc. **7** another word for **magnetic declination. 8** *Ballet.* a solo dance.
▸ **ˌvari'ational** *adj*

varicella (ˌværɪ'sɛlə) *n* the technical name for **chickenpox.** [C18: NL, irregular dim. of VARIOLA]
▸ **ˌvari'cellar** *adj*

varices ('værɪˌsiːz) *n* the plural of **varix.**

varico- *or before a vowel* **varic-** *combining form.* indicating a varix or varicose veins: *varicotomy.* [from L *varix, varic-* distended vein]

varicoloured *or US* **varicolored** ('vɛərɪˌkʌləd) *adj* having many colours.

varicose ('værɪˌkəʊs) *adj* of or resulting from varicose veins: *a varicose ulcer.* [C18: from L *varicōsus,* from VARIX]

varicose veins *pl n* a condition in which the superficial veins, esp. of the legs, become knotted and swollen.

varicosis (ˌværɪ'kəʊsɪs) *n Pathol.* any condition characterized by distension of the veins. [C18: from NL, from L: VARIX]

varicosity (ˌværɪ'kɒsɪtɪ) *n, pl* **varicosities.** *Pathol.* **1** the state, condition, or quality of being varicose. **2** an abnormally distended vein.

varicotomy (ˌværɪ'kɒtəmɪ) *n, pl* **varicotomies.** surgical excision of a varicose vein.

varied ⓘ ('vɛərɪd) *adj* **1** displaying or characterized by variety; diverse. **2** modified or altered: *the amount may be varied.* **3** varicoloured; variegated.
▸ **'variedly** *adv*

variegate ('vɛərɪˌgeɪt) *vb* **variegates, variegating, variegated.** (*tr*) to alter the appearance of, esp. by adding different colours. [C17: from LL, from L *varius* diverse, VARIOUS + *agere* to make]
▸ **ˌvarie'gation** *n*

variegated ⓘ ('vɛərɪˌgeɪtɪd) *adj* **1** displaying differently coloured spots., streaks, etc. **2** (of foliage) having pale patches.

varietal (və'raɪɪtᵊl) *adj* **1** of, characteristic of, designating, or forming a variety, esp. a biological variety. ◆ *n* **2** a wine labelled with the name of the grape from which it is pressed.
▸ **va'rietally** *adv*

variety ⓘ (və'raɪɪtɪ) *n, pl* **varieties. 1** the quality or condition of being diversified or various. **2** a collection of unlike things, esp. of the same general group. **3** a different form or kind within a general category: *varieties of behaviour.* **4a** *Taxonomy.* a race whose distinct characters do not justify classification as a separate species. **4b** *Horticulture, stockbreeding.* a strain of animal or plant produced by artificial breeding. **5a** entertainment consisting of a series of short unrelated acts, such as comedy turns, songs, etc. **5b** (*as modifier*): *a variety show.* [C16: from L *varietās,* from VARIOUS]

variform ('vɛərɪˌfɔːm) *adj* varying in form or shape.
▸ **'variˌformly** *adv*

variola (və'raɪələ) *n* the technical name for **smallpox.** [C18: from Med. L: disease marked by little spots, from L *varius* spotted]
▸ **va'riolar** *adj*

variole ('vɛərɪˌəʊl) *n* any of the rounded masses that make up the rock variolite. [C19: from F, from Med. L; see VARIOLA]

variolite ('vɛərɪəˌlaɪt) *n* any basic igneous rock containing rounded bodies (varioles). [C18: from VARIOLA, referring to the pockmarked appearance of the rock]
▸ **variolitic** (ˌvɛərɪə'lɪtɪk) *adj*

variometer (ˌvɛərɪ'ɒmɪtə) *n* **1** an instrument for measuring variations in a magnetic field. **2** *Electronics.* a variable inductor consisting of a movable coil mounted inside and connected in series with a fixed coil.

variorum (ˌvɛərɪ'ɔːrəm) *adj* **1** containing notes by various scholars or various versions of the text. ◆ *n* **2** an edition or text of this kind. [C18: from L *ēditiō cum notīs variōrum* edition with the notes of various commentators]

various ⓘ ('vɛərɪəs) *determiner* **1** several different: *he is an authority on various subjects.* ◆ *adj* **2** of different kinds, though often within the same general category: *his disguises are many and various.* **3** (*prenominal*) relating to a collection of separate persons or things: *the various members of the club.* **4** displaying variety; many-sided: *his various achievements.* [C16: from L *varius* changing]
▸ **'variously** *adv* ▸ **'variousness** *n*

> **USAGE NOTE** The use of *different* after *various* should be avoided: *the disease exists in various forms* (not *in various different forms*).

varistor (və'rɪstə) *n* a two-electrode semiconductor device having a voltage-dependent nonlinear resistance. [C20: a blend of *variable resistor*]

Varityper ('vɛərɪˌtaɪpə) *n Trademark.* a justifying typewriter used to produce copy in various type styles.

varix ('vɛərɪks) *n, pl* **varices.** *Pathol.* **a** a tortuous dilated vein. **b** a similar condition affecting an artery or lymphatic vessel. [C15: from L]

varlet ('vɑːlɪt) *n Arch.* **1** a menial servant. **2** a knight's page. **3** a rascal. [C15: from OF, var. of *vallet* VALET]
▸ **'varletry** *n*

varmint ('vɑːmɪnt) *n Inf.* an irritating or obnoxious person or animal. [C16: dialect var. of *varmin* VERMIN]

varna ('vɑːnə) *n* any of the four Hindu castes; Brahman, Kshatriya, Vaisya, or Sudra. [from Sansk.: class]

varnish ⓘ ('vɑːnɪʃ) *n* **1** a preparation consisting of a solvent, a drying oil, and usually resin, rubber, etc., for application to a surface where it yields a hard glossy, usually transparent, coating. **2** a similar preparation consisting of a substance, such as shellac, dissolved in a volatile solvent, such as alcohol. It hardens to a film on evaporation of the solvent. **3** the sap of certain trees used to produce such a coating. **4** a smooth surface, coated with or as with varnish. **5** an artificial, superficial, or deceptively pleasing manner, covering, etc. **6** *Chiefly Brit.* another word for **nail polish.** ◆ *vb* (*tr*) **7** to cover with varnish. **8** to give a smooth surface to, as if by painting with varnish. **9** to impart a more attractive appearance to. [C14: from OF, from Med. L *veronix* sandarac, resin, from Med. Gk *berenikē,* ?from Gk *Berenikē,* city in Cyrenaica, Libya where varnishes were used]
▸ **'varnisher** *n*

varnish tree *n* any of various trees, such as the lacquer tree, yielding substances used to make varnish or lacquer.

varsity ('vɑːsɪtɪ) *n, pl* **varsities.** *Brit., S. African, & NZ inf.* short for **university.**

varus ('vɛərəs) *adj Pathol.* turned inwards towards the midline of the body. [C19: from L: crooked, bent]

varve (vɑːv) *n Geol.* a band of sediment deposited in glacial lakes, consisting of a light layer and a dark layer deposited at different seasons. [C20: from Swedish *varv* layer, from *varva,* from ON *hverfa* to turn]

vary ⓘ ('vɛərɪ) *vb* **varies, varying, varied. 1** to undergo or cause to undergo change or modification in appearance, character, form, etc. **2** to be different or cause to be different; be subject to change. **3** (*tr*) to give variety to. **4** (*intr;* foll. by *from*) to differ, as from a convention, standard, etc. **5** (*intr*) to change in accordance with another variable: *her mood varies with the weather.* [C14: from L, from *varius* VARIOUS]
▸ **'varying** *adj*

THESAURUS

Antonyms *adj* constant, firm, fixed, settled, stable, steady, unalterable, unchanging

variance *n* **1, 2** = **disagreement**, difference, difference of opinion, discord, discrepancy, dissension, dissent, divergence, inconsistency, lack of harmony, strife, variation **3 at variance** = **in disagreement**, at loggerheads, at odds, at sixes and sevens, conflicting, in opposition, out of harmony, out of line
Antonyms *n* ≠ **disagreement**: accord, agreement, congruity, correspondence, harmony, similarity, unison

variant *adj* **2** = **different**, alternative, derived, divergent, exceptional, modified

variation *n* **1-3** = **difference**, alteration, break in routine, change, departure, departure from the norm, deviation, discrepancy, diversification, diversity, innovation, modification, novelty, variety

Antonyms *n* dullness, monotony, sameness, tedium, uniformity

varied *adj* **1** = **different**, assorted, diverse, heterogeneous, manifold, miscellaneous, mixed, motley, sundry, various
Antonyms *adj* homogeneous, repetitive, similar, standardized, uniform, unvarying

variegated *adj* **1** = **mottled**, diversified, many-coloured, motley, parti-coloured, pied, streaked, varicoloured

variety *n* **1** = **diversity**, change, difference, discrepancy, diversification, many-sidedness, multifariousness, variation **2** = **range**, array, assortment, collection, cross section, intermixture, medley, miscellany, mixed bag (*inf.*), mixture, multiplicity **3** = **type**, brand, breed, category, class, kind, make, order, sort, species, strain

Antonyms *n* ≠ **diversity**: homogeneity, invariability, monotony, similarity, similitude, uniformity

various *adj* **2-4** = **different**, assorted, differing, disparate, distinct, divers (*arch.*), diverse, diversified, heterogeneous, manifold, many, many-sided, miscellaneous, several, sundry, varied, variegated
Antonyms *adj* alike, equivalent, matching, same, similar, uniform

varnish *n, vb* **1, 2, 7** = **lacquer**, glaze, gloss, japan, polish, shellac ◆ *vb* **9** = **adorn**, decorate, embellish, gild

vary *vb* **1** = **change**, alter, fluctuate, transform **2** = **differ**, be unlike, depart, disagree, diverge **3** = **alternate**, diversify, intermix, permutate, reorder

varying *adj* **1** = **changing**, fluctuating, inconsistent **2** = **different**, distinct, distinguishable, diverse

vas (væs) *n, pl* **vasa** ('veɪsə). *Anat., zool.* a vessel or tube that carries a fluid. [C17: from L: vessel]

vascular ('væskjulə) *adj Biol., anat.* of, relating to, or having vessels that conduct and circulate liquids: *a vascular bundle.* [C17: from NL *vāsculāris,* from L *vāsculum,* dim. of *vās* vessel]
►**vascularity** (ˌvæskjuˈlærɪtɪ) *n* ►'**vascularly** *adv*

vascular bundle *n* a longitudinal strand of vascular tissue in the stems and leaves of higher plants.

vascular tissue *n* tissue of plants occurring as a continuous system throughout the plant: it conducts water, mineral salts, and synthesized food, and provides mechanical support. Also called: **conducting tissue.**

vas deferens ('væs 'dɛfəˌrɛnz) *n, pl* **vasa deferentia** ('veɪsə ˌdɛfə'rɛnʃɪə). *Anat.* the duct that conveys spermatozoa from the epididymis to the urethra. [C16: from NL, from L *vās* vessel + *deferēns,* present participle of *deferre* to bear away]

vase (vɑːz) *n* a vessel used as an ornament or for holding cut flowers. [C17: via F from L *vās* vessel]

vasectomy (væ'sɛktəmɪ) *n, pl* **vasectomies.** surgical removal of all or part of the vas deferens, esp. as a method of contraception.

Vaseline ('væsɪˌliːn) *n* a trademark for **petrolatum.**

vaso- *or before a vowel* **vas-** *combining form.* **1** indicating a blood vessel: *vasodilator.* **2** indicating the vas deferens: *vasectomy.* [from L *vās* vessel]

vasoactive (ˌveɪzəu'æktɪv) *adj* affecting the diameter of blood vessels: *vasoactive peptides.*

vasoconstrictor (ˌveɪzəukən'strɪktə) *n* a drug, agent, or nerve that causes narrowing of the walls of blood vessels.

vasodilator (ˌveɪzəudaɪ'leɪtə) *n* a drug, agent, or nerve that can cause dilation of the walls of blood vessels.

vasoinhibitor (ˌveɪzəuɪn'hɪbɪtə) *n* any of a group of drugs that reduce or inhibit the action of the vasomotor nerves.

vasomotor (ˌveɪzəu'məutə) *adj* (of a drug, nerve, etc.) relating to or affecting the diameter of blood vessels.

vasopressin (ˌveɪzəu'prɛsɪn) *n* a hormone secreted by the pituitary gland. It increases the reabsorption of water by the kidney tubules and increases blood pressure by constricting the arteries. Also called: **antidiuretic hormone.** [from *Vasopressin,* a trademark]

vasopressor ('veɪzəuˌprɛsə) *Med.* ◆ *adj* **1** causing an increase in blood pressure by constricting the arteries. ◆ *n* **2** a substance that has such an effect.

vassal ⓘ ('væsᵊl) *n* **1** (in feudal society) a man who entered into a relationship with a lord to whom he paid homage and fealty in return for protection and often a fief. **2a** a person, nation, etc., in a subordinate or dependent position relative to another. **2b** (*as modifier*): *vassal status.* ◆ *adj* **3** of or relating to a vassal. [C14: via OF from Med. L *vassallus,* from *vassus* servant, of Celtic origin]
►'**vassalage** *n*

vast ⓘ (vɑːst) *adj* **1** unusually large in size, degree, or number. **2** (*prenominal*) (intensifier): *in vast haste.* ◆ *n* **3 the vast.** *Chiefly poetic.* immense or boundless space. [C16: from L *vastus* deserted]
►'**vastly** *adv* ►'**vastness** *n*

vasty ('vɑːstɪ) *adj* **vastier, vastiest.** an archaic or poetic word for **vast.**

vat (væt) *n* **1** a large container for holding or storing liquids. **2** *Chem.* a preparation of reduced vat dye. ◆ *vb* **vats, vatting, vatted. 3** (*tr*) to place, store, or treat in a vat. [OE *fæt*]

VAT (*sometimes* væt) (in Britain) *abbrev. for* value-added tax: a tax levied on the difference between the cost of materials and the selling price of a commodity or service.

vat dye *n* a dye, such as indigo, that is applied by first reducing it to its base, which is soluble in alkali, and then regenerating the insoluble dye by oxidation in the fibres of the material.
►'**vat-ˌdyed** *adj*

vatic ('vætɪk) *adj Rare.* of, relating to, or characteristic of a prophet; oracular. [C16: from L *vātēs* prophet]

Vatican ('vætɪkən) *n* **1a** the palace of the popes in Rome, which includes administrative offices and is attached to the basilica of St Peter's. **1b** (*as modifier*): *the Vatican Council.* **2a** the authority of the Pope and the papal curia. **2b** (*as modifier*): *a Vatican edict.* [C16: from L *Vāticānus mons* Vatican hill, on the western bank of the Tiber, of Etruscan origin]

vaudeville ('vəudəvɪl, 'vɔː-) *n* **1** *Chiefly US & Canad.* variety entertainment consisting of short acts such as acrobatic turns, song-and-dance routines, etc. Brit. name: **music hall. 2** a light or comic theatrical piece interspersed with songs and dances. [C18: from F, from *vaudevire* satirical folk song, shortened from *chanson du vau de Vire* song of the valley of Vire, a district in Normandy]
►ˌ**vaude'villian** *n, adj*

Vaudois ('vəudwɑː) *pl n, sing* **Vaudois. 1** another name for the **Waldenses. 2** the inhabitants of Vaud, in Switzerland.

vault[1] ⓘ (vɔːlt) *n* **1** an arched structure that forms a roof or ceiling. **2** a room, esp. a cellar, having an arched roof down to floor level. **3** a burial chamber, esp. when underground. **4** a strongroom for the storage of valuables. **5** an underground room used for the storage of wine, food, etc. **6** *Anat.* any arched or domed bodily cavity or space: *the cranial vault.* **7** something suggestive of an arched structure, as the sky. ◆ *vb* **8** (*tr*) to furnish with or as if with an arched roof. **9** (*tr*) to construct in the shape of a vault. **10** (*intr*) to curve in the shape of a vault. [C14 *vaute,* from OF, from Vulgar L *volvita* (unattested) a turn, prob. from L *volvere* to roll]

vault[2] ⓘ (vɔːlt) *vb* **1** to spring over (an object), esp. with the aid of a long pole or with the hands resting on the object. **2** (*intr*) to do, achieve, or attain something as if by a leap: *he vaulted to fame.* ◆ *n* **3** the act of vaulting. [C16: from OF *voulter* to turn from It. *voltare,* from Vulgar L *volvitāre* (unattested) to turn, leap; see VAULT[1]]
►'**vaulter** *n*

vaulting[1] ('vɔːltɪŋ) *n* one or more vaults in a building or such structures considered collectively.

vaulting[2] ('vɔːltɪŋ) *adj* (*prenominal*) **1** excessively confident: *vaulting arrogance.* **2** used to vault: *a vaulting pole.*

vaunt ⓘ (vɔːnt) *vb* **1** (*tr*) to describe, praise, or display (one's success, possessions, etc.) boastfully. **2** (*intr*) *Rare or literary.* to brag. ◆ *n* **3** a boast. [C14: from OF, from LL *vānitāre,* from L *vānus* VAIN]
►'**vaunter** *n*

vavasor ('vævəˌsɔː) *or* **vavasour** ('vævəˌsuə) *n* (in feudal society) the noble or knightly vassal of a baron or great lord who also has vassals himself. [C13: from OF *vavasour,* ?from Med. L *vassus vassōrum* vassal of vassals]

vb *abbrev. for* verb.

VC *abbrev. for:* **1** Vice-chairman. **2** Vice Chancellor. **3** Vice Consul. **4** Victoria Cross.

V-chip *n* a device within a television set that allows the set to be programmed not to receive transmissions that have been classified as containing sex, violence, or obscene language.

VCR *abbrev. for* video cassette recorder.

VD *abbrev. for* venereal disease.

V-Day *n* a day nominated to celebrate victory, as in V-E Day or V-J Day in World War II.

VDQS *abbrev. for* vins délimités de qualité supérieure: on a bottle of French wine, indicates that it contains high-quality wine from an approved regional vineyard: the second highest French wine classification. Cf. **AOC, *vin de pays.***

VDU *Computing. abbrev. for* visual display unit.

've *contraction of* have: *I've; you've.*

veal (viːl) *n* the flesh of the calf used as food. [C14: from OF *veel,* from L *vitellus,* dim. of *vitulus* calf]

vealer ('viːlə) *n US, Canad., & Austral.* a calf bred for veal.

vector ('vɛktə) *n* **1** *Maths.* a variable quantity, such as force, that has magnitude and direction and can be resolved into components that are odd functions of the coordinates. **2** *Maths.* an element of a vector space. **3** Also called: **carrier.** *Pathol.* an organism, esp. an insect, that carries a disease-producing microorganism from one host to another. **4** Also called: **cloning vector.** *Genetics.* an agent, such as a bacteriophage or a plasmid, by means of which a fragment of foreign DNA is inserted into a host cell to produce a gene clone in genetic engineering. **5** the course or compass direction of an aircraft. ◆ *vb* (*tr*) **6** to direct or guide (a pilot, aircraft, etc.) by directions transmitted by radio. **7** to alter the direction of (the thrust of a jet engine) as a means of steering an aircraft. [C18: from L: carrier, from *vehere* to convey]
►**vectorial** (vɛk'tɔːrɪəl) *adj*

vector field *n* a region of space under the influence of some vector quantity, such as magnetic field strength, in which each point can be described by a vector.

vector product *n* the product of two vectors that is a pseudovector, whose magnitude is the product of the magnitudes of the given vectors and the sine of the angle between them. Its axis is perpendicular to the plane of the given vectors.

vector sum *n* a vector whose length and direction are represented by the diagonal of a parallelogram whose sides represent the given vectors.

Veda ('veɪdə) *n* any or all of the most ancient sacred writings of Hinduism, esp. the Rig-Veda, Yajur-Veda, Sama-Veda, and Atharva-Veda. [C18: from Sansk.: knowledge]

vedalia (vɪ'deɪlɪə) *n* an Australian ladybird introduced elsewhere to control the scale insect, which is a pest of citrus fruits. [C20: from NL]

Vedanta (vɪ'dɑːntə) *n* one of the six main philosophical schools of

THESAURUS

Antonyms *adj* ≠ **changing:** consistent, fixed, monotonous, regular, settled, unchanging, unvarying

vassal *n* **1, 2** = **serf,** bondservant, bondsman, liegeman, retainer, slave, subject, thrall, varlet (*arch.*)

vassalage *n* **1, 2** = **serfdom,** bondage, dependence, servitude, slavery, subjection, thraldom

vast *adj* **1** = **huge,** astronomical, boundless, colossal, elephantine, enormous, extensive, gigantic, great, illimitable, immeasurable, immense, limitless, mammoth, massive, measureless, mega (*sl.*), monstrous, monumental, never-ending, prodigious, sweeping, tremendous, unbounded, unlimited, voluminous, wide

Antonyms *adj* bounded, limited, microscopic, narrow, negligible, paltry, puny, small, tiny, trifling

vault[1] *n* **1** = **arch,** ceiling, roof, span **3** = **crypt,** catacomb, cellar, charnel house, mausoleum, tomb, undercroft **4** = **strongroom,** depository, repository ◆ *vb* **10** = **arch,** bend, bow, curve, overarch, span

vault[2] *vb* **1** = **jump,** bound, clear, hurdle, leap, spring

vaunt *vb* **1** = **boast about,** brag about, crow about, exult in, flaunt, give oneself airs about, make a display of, make much of, parade, prate about, show off, talk big about (*inf.*)

Hinduism, expounding the monism regarded as implicit in the Veda in accordance with the doctrines of the Upanishads. [C19: from Sansk., from VEDA + *ánta* end]
▸**Ve'dantic** *adj* ▸**Ve'dantist** *n*

V-E Day *n* the day marking the Allied victory in Europe in World War II (May 8, 1945).

vedette (vɪ'dɛt) *n* **1** *Naval.* a small patrol vessel. **2** *Mil.* a mounted sentry posted forward of a formation's position. [C17: from F, from It. *vedetta* (infl. by *vedere* to see), from earlier *veletta,* ?from Sp., from L *vigilāre*]

Vedic ('veɪdɪk) *adj* **1** of or relating to the Vedas or the ancient form of Sanskrit in which they are written. ◆ *n* **2** the classical form of Sanskrit; the language of the Vedas.

veer ➊ (vɪə) *vb* **1** to alter direction (of). **2** (*intr*) to change from one position, opinion, etc., to another. **3** (*intr*) (of the wind) to change direction clockwise in the northern hemisphere and anticlockwise in the southern. ◆ *n* **4** a change of course or direction. [C16: from OF *virer,* prob. of Celtic origin]

veg (vɛdʒ) *n Inf.* a vegetable or vegetables.

Vega ('vi:gə) *n* the brightest star in the constellation Lyra and one of the most conspicuous in the N hemisphere. [C17: from Med. L, from Ar. *(al nasr) al wāqi,* lit.: the falling (vulture), i.e. the constellation Lyra]

vegan ('vi:gən) *n* a person who uses no animal products.

vegeburger *or* **veggieburger** ('vɛdʒɪ,bɜ:gə) *n* a flat cake of chopped seasoned vegetables and pulses that is grilled or fried and often served in a bread roll.

Vegemite ('vɛdʒɪ,maɪt) *n Austral. & NZ trademark.* a yeast extract used as a spread, flavouring for stews, etc.

vegetable ('vɛdʒtəbᵊl, 'vɛdʒətəbᵊl) *n* **1** any of various herbaceous plants having parts that are used as food, such as peas, potatoes, cauliflower, and onions. **2** *Inf.* a person who has lost control of his mental faculties, limbs, etc., as from an injury, mental disease, etc. **3** a dull inactive person. **4** (*modifier*) consisting of or made from edible vegetables: *a vegetable diet.* **5** (*modifier*) of, characteristic of, derived from, or consisting of plants or plant material: *the vegetable kingdom.* **6** *Rare.* any member of the plant kingdom. [C14 (adj): from LL *vegetābilis,* from *vegetāre* to enliven, from L *vegēre* to excite]

vegetable butter *n* any of a group of vegetable fats having the consistency of butter.

vegetable ivory *n* the hard whitish material obtained from the endosperm of the ivory nut: used to make buttons, ornaments, etc.

vegetable marrow *n* **1** a plant, probably native to America but widely cultivated for its oblong green striped fruit which is eaten as a vegetable. **2** the fruit of this plant. Often shortened to **marrow.**

vegetable oil *n* any of a group of oils that are obtained from plants.

vegetable oyster *n* another name for **salsify** (sense 1).

vegetable silk *n* any of various silky fibres obtained from the seed pods of certain plants.

vegetable wax *n* any of various waxes that occur on parts of certain plants, esp. the trunks of certain palms, and prevent loss of water.

vegetal ('vɛdʒɪtᵊl) *adj* **1** of or characteristic of vegetables or plant life. **2** vegetative. [C15: from LL *vegetāre* to quicken]

vegetarian (,vɛdʒɪ'tɛərɪən) *n* **1** a person who advocates or practises the exclusion of meat and fish, and sometimes eggs, milk, and cheese from the diet. ◆ *adj* **2** *Cookery.* strictly, consisting of vegetables and fruit only, but often including milk, cheese, eggs, etc.
▸,**vege'tarianism** *n*

vegetate ➊ ('vɛdʒɪ,teɪt) *vb* **vegetates, vegetating, vegetated.** (*intr*) **1** to grow like a plant. **2** to lead a life characterized by monotony, passivity, or mental inactivity. [C17: from LL *vegetāre* to invigorate]

vegetation (,vɛdʒɪ'teɪʃən) *n* **1** plant life as a whole, esp. the plant life of a particular region. **2** the process of vegetating.
▸,**vege'tational** *adj*

vegetative ('vɛdʒɪtətɪv) *adj* **1** of or concerned with plant life or plant growth. **2** (of reproduction) characterized by asexual processes. **3** of or relating to functions such as digestion and circulation rather than sexual reproduction. **4** (of a style of living, etc.) unthinking or passive.
▸'**vegetatively** *adv*

veggie ('vɛdʒɪ) *n, adj* an informal word for **vegetarian.**

veg out *vb* **vegges, vegging, vegged.** (*intr, adv*) *Sl., chiefly US.* to relax in an inert, passive way; vegetate: *vegging out in front of the television.*

vehement ➊ ('vi:ɪmənt) *adj* **1** marked by intensity of feeling or conviction. **2** (of actions, gestures, etc.) characterized by great energy, vigour, or force. [C15: from L *vehemēns* ardent]
▸'**vehemence** *n* ▸'**vehemently** *adv*

vehicle ➊ ('vi:ɪkᵊl) *n* **1** any conveyance in or by which people or objects are transported, esp. one fitted with wheels. **2** a medium for the expression or communication of ideas, power, etc. **3** *Pharmacol.* a therapeutically inactive substance mixed with the active ingredient to give bulk to a medicine. **4** Also called: **base.** a painting medium, such as oil, in which pigments are suspended. **5** (in the performing arts) a play, etc., that enables a particular performer to display his talents. [C17: from L *vehiculum,* from *vehere* to carry]
▸**vehicular** (vɪ'hɪkjʊlə) *adj*

veil ➊ (veɪl) *n* **1** a piece of more or less transparent material, usually attached to a hat or headdress, used to conceal or protect a woman's face and head. **2** part of a nun's headdress falling round the face onto the shoulders. **3** something that covers, conceals, or separates: *a veil of reticence.* **4 the veil.** the life of a nun in a religious order. **5 take the veil.** to become a nun. **6** Also called: **velum.** *Bot.* a membranous structure, esp. the thin layer of cells covering a young mushroom. ◆ *vb* **7** (*tr*) to cover, conceal, or separate with or as if with a veil. **8** (*intr*) to wear or put on a veil. [C13: from Norman F *veile,* from L *vēla,* pl of *vēlum* a covering]
▸'**veiler** *n* ▸'**veil-,like** *adj*

veiled ➊ (veɪld) *adj* **1** disguised: *a veiled insult.* **2** (of sound, tone, the voice, etc.) not distinct.
▸**veiledly** ('veɪlɪdlɪ) *adv*

veiling ('veɪlɪŋ) *n* a veil or the fabric used for veils.

vein ➊ (veɪn) *n* **1** any of the tubular vessels that convey oxygen-depleted blood to the heart. Cf. **pulmonary vein, artery** (sense 1). **2** any of the hollow branching tubes that form the supporting framework of an insect's wing. **3** any of the vascular bundles of a leaf. **4** a clearly defined mass of ore, mineral, etc. **5** an irregular streak of colour or alien substance in marble, wood, or other material. **6** a distinctive trait or quality in speech, writing, character, etc.: *a vein of humour.* **7** a temporary attitude or temper: *the debate entered a frivolous vein.* ◆ *vb* (*tr*) **8** to diffuse over or cause to diffuse over in streaked patterns. **9** to fill, furnish, or mark with or as if with veins. [C13: from OF, from L *vēna*]
▸'**veinless** *adj* ▸'**vein,like** *adj* ▸'**veiny** *adj*

veining ('veɪnɪŋ) *n* a pattern or network of veins or streaks.

veinlet ('veɪnlɪt) *n* any small vein or venule.

velamen (və'leɪmɛn) *n, pl* **velamina** (-'læmɪnə). **1** the thick layer of dead cells that covers the aerial roots of certain orchids. **2** *Anat.* another word for **velum.** [C19: from L: veil, from *vēlāre* to cover]

velar ('vi:lə) *adj* **1** of or attached to a velum: *velar tentacles.* **2** *Phonetics.* articulated with the soft palate and the back of the tongue, as in (k) or (ŋ). [C18: from L, from *vēlum* VEIL]

Velcro ('vɛlkrəʊ) *n Trademark.* a fastening consisting of two strips of nylon fabric, one having tiny hooked threads and the other a coarse surface, that form a strong bond when pressed together.

veld *or* **veldt** (fɛlt, vɛlt) *n* elevated open grassland in Southern Africa. See also **bushveld, highveld.** [C19: from Afrik., from earlier Du. *veldt* FIELD]

veldskoen ('fɛlt,skʊn, 'vɛlt-) *n* an ankle-length boot of soft but strong rawhide. [from Afrik., lit.: field shoe]

veleta (və'li:tə) *n* a variant spelling of **valeta.**

veliger ('vɛlɪdʒə) *n* the free-swimming larva of many molluscs, having a rudimentary shell and a ciliated velum used for feeding and locomotion. [C19: from NL, from VEL(UM) + -GER(OUS)]

vellum ('vɛləm) *n* **1** a fine parchment prepared from the skin of a calf, kid, or lamb. **2** a work printed or written on vellum. **3** a creamy coloured heavy paper resembling vellum. ◆ *adj* **4** made of or resembling vellum. [C15: from OF, from *velin* of a calf, from *veel* VEAL]

veloce (vɪ'ləʊtʃɪ) *adj, adv Music.* to be played rapidly. [from It., from L *vēlōx* quick]

velocipede (vɪ'lɒsɪ,pi:d) *n* an early form of bicycle, esp. one propelled by pushing along the ground with the feet. [C19: from F, from L *vēlōx* swift + *pēs* foot]
▸**ve'loci,pedist** *n*

velocity ➊ (vɪ'lɒsɪtɪ) *n, pl* **velocities. 1** speed of motion or operation; swiftness. **2** *Physics.* a measure of the rate of motion of a body expressed as the rate of change of its position in a particular direction with time. **3** *Physics.* (not in technical usage) another word for **speed** (sense 3). [C16: from L *vēlōcitās,* from *vēlōx* swift]

velocity of circulation *n Econ.* the average number of times a unit of

THESAURUS

veer *vb* **1-3** = **change direction**, be deflected, change, change course, sheer, shift, swerve, tack, turn

vegetate *vb* **1** = **grow**, burgeon, germinate, shoot, spring, sprout, swell **2** = **stagnate**, be inert, deteriorate, exist, go to seed, idle, languish, loaf, moulder, veg out (*sl., chiefly US*)
Antonyms *vb* ≠ **stagnate:** accomplish, develop, grow, participate, perform, react, respond

vehemence *n* **1, 2** = **forcefulness**, ardour, eagerness, earnestness, emphasis, energy, enthusiasm, fervency, fervour, fire, force, heat, intensity, keenness, passion, verve, vigour, violence, warmth, zeal
Antonyms *n* apathy, coolness, indifference, inertia, lethargy, listlessness, passivity, stoicism, torpor

vehement *adj* **1, 2** = **strong**, ablaze, ardent, eager, earnest, emphatic, enthusiastic, fervent, fervid, fierce, flaming, forceful, forcible, impassioned, intense, passionate, powerful, violent, zealous
Antonyms *adj* apathetic, calm, cool, dispassionate, half-hearted, impassive, lukewarm, moderate

vehicle *n* **1** = **transport**, conveyance, means of transport, transportation **2** = **medium**, apparatus, channel, means, means of expression, mechanism, organ

veil *n* **1, 3** = **cover**, blind, cloak, curtain, disguise, film, mask, screen, shade, shroud ◆ *vb* **7** = **cover**, cloak, conceal, dim, disguise, hide, mantle, mask, obscure, screen, shield
Antonyms *vb* ≠ **cover:** disclose, display, divulge, expose, lay bare, reveal, uncover, unveil

veiled *adj* **1** = **disguised**, concealed, covert, hinted at, implied, masked, suppressed

vein *n* **1** = **blood vessel 4** = **seam**, course, current, lode, stratum, streak, stripe **6** = **trait**, dash, hint, strain, streak, thread **7** = **mood**, attitude, bent, character, faculty, humour, mode, note, style, temper, tenor, tone, turn

velocity *n* **1** = **speed**, celerity, fleetness, impetus, pace, quickness, rapidity, swiftness

money is used in a given time, esp. calculated as the ratio of the total money spent in that time to the total amount of money in circulation.

velocity of light *n* a nontechnical name for **speed of light.**

velodrome ('viːləˌdrəʊm, 'vɛl-) *n* an arena with a banked track for cycle racing. [C20: from F *vélodrome,* from *vélo-* (from L *vēlōx* swift) + -DROME]

velour *or* **velours** (vɛ'lʊə) *n* any of various fabrics with a velvet-like finish, used for upholstery, clothing, etc. [C18: from OF, from OProvençal *velos* velvet, from L, from *villus* shaggy hair]

velouté (və'luːteɪ) *n* a rich white sauce or soup made from stock, egg yolks, and cream. [from F, lit.: velvety, from OF *velous;* see VELOUR]

velum ('viːləm) *n, pl* **vela** (-lə). **1** *Zool.* any of various membranous structures. **2** *Anat.* any of various veil-like bodily structures, esp. the soft palate. **3** *Bot.* another word for **veil** (sense 6). [C18: from L: veil]

velure (və'lʊə) *n* velvet or a similar fabric. [C16: from OF, from *velous;* see VELOUR]

velutinous (və'luːtɪnəs) *adj* covered with short dense soft hairs. [C19: from NL *velūtīnus* like velvet]

velvet ❶ ('vɛlvɪt) *n* **1a** a fabric of silk, cotton, nylon, etc., with a thick close soft pile. **1b** *(as modifier): velvet curtains.* **2** anything with a smooth soft surface. **3a** smoothness. **3b** *(as modifier): a velvet night.* **4** the furry covering of the newly formed antlers of a deer. **5** *Sl., chiefly US.* **5a** gambling winnings. **5b** a gain. **6 on velvet.** *Sl.* in a condition of ease, advantage, or wealth. **7 velvet glove.** gentleness, often concealing strength or determination (esp. in **an iron hand in a velvet glove**). [C14 *veluet,* from OF, from *velu* hairy, from Vulgar L *villutus* (unattested), from L *villus* shaggy hair]

▸'**velvet-ˌlike** *adj* ▸'**velvety** *adj*

velveteen (ˌvɛlvɪ'tiːn) *n* **1** a cotton fabric resembling velvet with a short thick pile, used for clothing, etc. **2** *(pl)* trousers made of velveteen.

Ven. *abbrev. for* Venerable.

vena ('viːnə) *n, pl* **venae** (-niː). *Anat.* a technical word for **vein.** [C15: from L *vēna* VEIN]

vena cava ('keɪvə) *n, pl* **venae cavae** ('keɪviː). either one of two large veins that convey oxygen-depleted blood to the heart. [L: hollow vein]

venal ❶ ('viːnᵊl) *adj* **1** easily bribed or corrupted: *a venal magistrate.* **2** characterized by corruption or bribery. [C17: from L *vēnālis,* from *vēnum* sale]

▸**ve'nality** *n* ▸'**venally** *adv*

venation (viː'neɪʃən) *n* **1** the arrangement of the veins in a leaf or in the wing of an insect. **2** such veins collectively.

▸**ve'national** *adj*

vend (vɛnd) *vb* **1** to sell or be sold. **2** to sell (goods) for a living. [C17: from L *vendere,* from *vēnum dare* to offer for sale]

vendace ('vɛndeɪs) *n, pl* **vendaces** *or* **vendace.** either of two small whitefish occurring in lakes in Scotland and NW England. [C18: from NL *vandēsius,* from OF *vandoise,* prob. of Celtic origin]

vendee (vɛn'diː) *n Chiefly law.* a person to whom something, esp. real property, is sold.

vendetta ❶ (vɛn'dɛtə) *n* **1** a private feud, originally between Corsican or Sicilian families, in which the relatives of a murdered person seek vengeance by killing the murderer or some member of his family. **2** any prolonged feud. [C19: from It., from L *vindicta,* from *vindicāre* to avenge]

▸**ven'dettist** *n*

vendible ('vɛndəbᵊl) *adj* **1** saleable or marketable. ◆ *n* **2** *(usually pl) Rare.* a saleable object.

▸ˌ**vendi'bility** *n*

vending machine *n* a machine that automatically dispenses consumer goods such as cigarettes or food, when money is inserted.

vendor ('vɛndɔː) *or* **vender** ('vɛndə) *n* **1** *Chiefly law.* a person who sells something, esp. real property. **2** another name for **vending machine.**

vendor placing *n Finance.* a method of financing the purchase of one company by another in which the purchasing company pays for the target company in its own shares, on condition that the vendor places these shares with investors for cash payment.

veneer ❶ (vɪ'nɪə) *n* **1** a thin layer of wood, plastic, etc., with a decorative or fine finish that is bonded to the surface of a less expensive material, usually wood. **2** a superficial appearance: *a veneer of gentility.* **3** any facing material that is applied to a different backing material. ◆ *vb (tr)* **4** to cover (a surface) with a veneer. **5** to conceal (something) under a superficially pleasant surface. [C17: from G *furnieren* to veneer, from OF *fournir* to FURNISH]

▸**ve'neerer** *n*

veneering (vɪ'nɪərɪŋ) *n* material used as veneer or a veneered surface.

venepuncture ('vɛnɪˌpʌŋktʃə) *n* a variant spelling of **venipuncture.**

venerable ❶ ('vɛnərəbᵊl) *adj* **1** (esp. of a person) worthy of reverence on account of great age, religious associations, character, etc. **2** (of inanimate objects) hallowed on account of age or historical or religious association. **3** *RC Church.* a title bestowed on a deceased person when the first stage of his canonization has been accomplished. **4** *Church of England.* a title given to an archdeacon. [C15: from L *venerābilis,* from *venerārī* to venerate]

▸ˌ**venera'bility** *or* '**venerableness** *n* ▸'**venerably** *adv*

venerate ❶ ('vɛnəˌreɪt) *vb* **venerates, venerating, venerated.** *(tr)* **1** to hold in deep respect. **2** to honour in recognition of qualities of holiness, excellence, etc. [C17: from L *venerārī,* from *venus* love]

▸'**venerˌator** *n*

veneration ❶ (ˌvɛnə'reɪʃən) *n* **1** a feeling or expression of awe or reverence. **2** the act of venerating or the state of being venerated.

venereal (vɪ'nɪərɪəl) *adj* **1** of or infected with venereal disease. **2** (of a disease) transmitted by sexual intercourse. **3** of or involving the genitals. **4** of or relating to sexual intercourse or erotic desire. [C15: from L *venereus,* from *venus* sexual love, from VENUS[1]]

venereal disease *n* another name for **sexually transmitted disease.** Abbrev.: **VD.**

venereology (vɪˌnɪərɪ'ɒlədʒɪ) *n* the branch of medicine concerned with the study and treatment of venereal disease.

▸**veˌnere'ologist** *n*

venery[1] ('vɛnərɪ, 'viː-) *n Arch.* the pursuit of sexual gratification. [C15: from Med. L *veneria,* from L *venus* love, VENUS[1]]

venery[2] ('vɛnərɪ, 'viː-) *n* the art, sport, lore, or practice of hunting, esp. with hounds; the chase. [C14: from OF *venerie,* from *vener* to hunt, from L *vēnārī*]

venesection ('vɛnɪˌsɛkʃən) *n* surgical incision into a vein. [C17: from NL *vēnae sectiō;* see VEIN, SECTION]

Venetian (vɪ'niːʃən) *adj* **1** of, relating to, or characteristic of Venice, a port in NE Italy, or its inhabitants. ◆ *n* **2** a native or inhabitant of Venice. **3** See **Venetian blind.**

Venetian blind *n* a window blind consisting of a number of horizontal slats whose angle may be altered to let in more or less light.

Venetian red *n* **1** natural or synthetic ferric oxide used as a red pigment. **2a** a moderate to strong reddish-brown colour. **2b** *(as adj): a Venetian-red coat.*

vengeance ❶ ('vɛndʒəns) *n* **1** the act of or desire for taking revenge. **2 with a vengeance.** (intensifier): *he's a coward with a vengeance.* [C13: from OF, from *venger* to avenge, from L *vindicāre* to punish]

vengeful ❶ ('vɛndʒfʊl) *adj* **1** desiring revenge. **2** characterized by or indicating a desire for revenge. **3** inflicting or taking revenge: *with vengeful blows.*

▸'**vengefully** *adv*

venial ❶ ('viːnɪəl) *adj* easily excused or forgiven: *a venial error.* [C13: via OF from LL *veniālis,* from L *venia* forgiveness]

▸ˌ**veni'ality** *n* ▸'**venially** *adv*

venial sin *n Christian theol.* a sin regarded as involving only a partial loss of grace.

venin ('vɛnɪn) *n* any of the poisonous constituents of animal venoms. [C20: from F *ven(in)* poison + -IN]

venipuncture *or* **venepuncture** ('vɛnɪˌpʌŋktʃə) *n Med.* the puncturing of a vein, esp. to take a sample of venous blood or inject a drug.

venison ('vɛnɪzᵊn, -sᵊn) *n* the flesh of a deer, used as food. [C13: from OF *venaison,* from L *vēnātiō* hunting, from *vēnārī* to hunt]

Venite (vɪ'naɪtɪ) *n* **1** the opening word of the 95th psalm, an invitatory prayer at matins. **2** a musical setting of this. [L: come ye]

Venn diagram (vɛn) *n Maths, logic.* a diagram in which mathematical sets or terms of a categorial statement are represented by overlapping circles within a boundary representing the universal set, so that all possible combinations of the relevant properties are represented by the various distinct areas in the diagram. [C19: after John *Venn* (1834–1923), Brit. logician]

venom ❶ ('vɛnəm) *n* **1** a poisonous fluid secreted by such animals as certain snakes and scorpions and usually transmitted by a bite or

THESAURUS

velvety *adj* **2** = **soft**, delicate, downy, mossy, smooth, velutinous, velvet-like

venal *adj* **1** = **corrupt**, bent *(sl.)*, corruptible, crooked *(inf.)*, dishonourable, grafting *(inf.)*, mercenary, prostituted, purchasable, rapacious, simoniacal, sordid, unprincipled
Antonyms *adj* honest, honourable, incorruptible, law-abiding, principled, upright

vendetta *n* **1, 2** = **feud**, bad blood, blood feud, quarrel

veneer *n* **1** = **layer**, finish, gloss **2** = **mask**, appearance, façade, false front, front, guise, pretence, semblance, show

venerable *adj* **1** = **respected**, august, esteemed, grave, honoured, revered, reverenced, sage, sedate, wise, worshipped
Antonyms *adj* discredited, disdained, disgraced, dishonourable, disreputable, ignominious, inglorious, scorned

venerate *vb* **1, 2** = **respect**, adore, esteem, hold in awe, honour, look up to, revere, reverence, worship
Antonyms *vb* deride, dishonour, disregard, execrate, mock, scorn, spurn

veneration *n* **1, 2** = **respect**, adoration, awe, deference, esteem, reverence, worship

vengeance *n* **1** = **revenge**, an eye for an eye, avenging, lex talionis, reprisal, requital, retaliation, retribution, settling of scores **2 with a vengeance** = **to the utmost**, and no mistake, extremely, greatly, to the full, to the nth degree, with no holds barred
Antonyms *n* ≠ **revenge**: absolution, acquittal, exoneration, forbearance, forgiveness, mercy, pardon, remission

vengeful *adj* **1** = **unforgiving**, avenging, implacable, punitive, rancorous, relentless, retaliatory, revengeful, spiteful, thirsting for revenge, vindictive

venial *adj* = **forgivable**, allowable, excusable, insignificant, minor, pardonable, slight, trivial

venom *n* **1** = **poison**, bane, toxin **2** = **malice**, acidity, acrimony, bitterness, gall, grudge, hate, ill will, malevolence, maliciousness, ma-

sting. **2** malice; spite. [C13: from OF, from L *venēnum* poison, love potion]
▸**'venomous** *adj* ▸**'venomously** *adv* ▸**'venomousness** *n*

venose ('vi:nəʊs) *adj* **1** having veins; venous. **2** (of a plant) covered with veins or similar ridges. [C17: via L *vēnōsus*, from *vēna* a VEIN]

venosity (vɪ'nɒsɪtɪ) *n* **1** an excessive quantity of blood in the venous system or in an organ or part. **2** an unusually large number of blood vessels in an organ or part.

venous ('vi:nəs) *adj* **1** *Physiol.* of or relating to the blood circulating in the veins. **2** of or relating to the veins. [C17: see VENOSE]

vent[1] Ⓣ (vɛnt) *n* **1** a small opening for the escape of fumes, liquids, etc. **2** the shaft of a volcano through which lava and gases erupt. **3** the external opening of the urinary or genital systems of lower vertebrates. **4** a small aperture at the breech of old guns through which the charge was ignited. **5 give vent to.** to release (an emotion, idea, etc.) in an outburst. ◆ *vb (mainly tr)* **6** to release or give expression or utterance to (an emotion, etc.): *he vents his anger on his wife.* **7** to provide a vent for or make vents in. **8** to let out (steam, etc.) through a vent. [C14: from OF *esventer* to blow out, from EX-[1] + *venter*, from Vulgar L *ventāre* (unattested), from L *ventus* wind]

vent[2] (vɛnt) *n* **1** a vertical slit at the back or both sides of a jacket. ◆ *vb* **2** *(tr)* to make a vent or vents in (a jacket). [C15: from OF *fente* slit, from *fendre* to split, from L *findere* to cleave]

venter ('vɛntə) *n* **1** *Anat., zool.* **1a** the belly or abdomen of vertebrates. **1b** a protuberant structure or part, such as the belly of a muscle. **2** *Bot.* the swollen basal region of an archegonium. **3** *Law.* the womb. [C16: from L]

ventilate Ⓣ ('vɛntɪˌleɪt) *vb* **ventilates, ventilating, ventilated.** *(tr)* **1** to drive foul air out of (an enclosed area). **2** to provide with a means of airing. **3** to expose (a question, grievance, etc.) to public discussion. **4** *Physiol.* to oxygenate (the blood). [C15: from L *ventilāre* to fan, from *ventulus*, dim. of *ventus* wind]
▸**'ventilable** *adj* ▸**ˌventi'lation** *n*

ventilator ('vɛntɪˌleɪtə) *n* **1** an opening or device, such as a fan, used to ventilate a room, building, etc. **2** *Med.* a machine that maintains a flow of air into and out of the lungs of a patient unable to breathe normally.

ventral ('vɛntrəl) *adj* **1** relating to the front part of the body. **2** of or situated on the upper or inner side of a plant organ, esp. a leaf, that is facing the axis. [C18: from L *ventrālis*, from *venter* abdomen]
▸**'ventrally** *adv*

ventral fin *n* **1** another name for **pelvic fin. 2** any unpaired median fin situated on the undersurface of fishes.

ventricle ('vɛntrɪkᵊl) *n Anat.* **1** a chamber of the heart that receives blood from the atrium and pumps it to the arteries. **2** any one of the four main cavities of the vertebrate brain. **3** any of various other small cavities in the body. [C14: from L *ventriculus*, dim. of *venter* belly]
▸**ven'tricular** *adj*

ventricose ('vɛntrɪˌkəʊs) *adj* **1** *Bot., zool., anat.* having a swelling on one side: *the ventricose corolla of many labiate plants.* **2** another word for **corpulent.** [C18: from NL, from L *venter* belly]

ventriculus (vɛn'trɪkjʊləs) *n, pl* **ventriculi** (-ˌlaɪ). **1** *Zool.* **1a** the midgut of an insect, where digestion takes place. **1b** the gizzard of a bird. **2** another word for **ventricle.** [C18: from L, dim. of *venter* belly]

ventriloquism (vɛn'trɪləˌkwɪzəm) *or* **ventriloquy** *n* the art of producing vocal sounds that appear to come from another source. [C18: from L *venter* belly + *loquī* to speak]
▸**ventriloquial** (ˌvɛntrɪ'ləʊkwɪəl) *adj* ▸**ˌventri'loquially** *adv* ▸**ven'triloquist** *n* ▸**ven'triloˌquize** *or* **ven'triloˌquise** *vb*

venture Ⓣ ('vɛntʃə) *vb* **ventures, venturing, ventured. 1** *(tr)* to expose to danger: *he ventured his life.* **2** *(tr)* to brave the dangers of (something): *I'll venture the seas.* **3** *(tr)* to dare (to do something): *does he venture to object?* **4** *(tr; may take a clause as object)* to express in spite of possible criticism: *I venture that he is not that honest.* **5** *(intr;* often foll. by *out, forth,* etc.) to embark on a possibly hazardous journey, etc.: *to venture forth upon the high seas.* ◆ *n* **6** an undertaking that is risky or of uncertain outcome. **7** a commercial undertaking characterized by risk of loss as well as opportunity for profit. **8** something hazarded or risked in an adventure. **9 at a venture.** at random. [C15: var. of *aventure* ADVENTURE]
▸**'venturer** *n*

venture capital *n* another name for **risk capital.**

Venture Scout *or* **Venturer** *n Brit.* a person aged 16–20 who is a member of the senior branch of the Scouts.

venturesome Ⓣ ('vɛntʃəsəm) *or* **venturous** ('vɛntʃərəs) *adj* **1** willing to take risks; daring. **2** hazardous.

Venturi tube (vɛn'tjʊərɪ) *n Physics.* a device for measuring or controlling fluid flow, consisting of a tube so constricted that the pressure differential produced by fluid flowing through the constriction gives a measure of the rate of flow. [C19: after G. B. *Venturi* (1746–1822), It. physicist]

venue ('vɛnju:) *n* **1** *Law.* **1a** the place in which a cause of action arises. **1b** the place fixed for the trial of a cause. **1c** the locality from which the jurors must be summoned. **2** a meeting place. **3** any place where an organized gathering, such as a rock concert, is held. [C14: from OF, from *venir* to come, from L *venīre*]

venule ('vɛnju:l) *n* **1** *Anat.* any of the small branches of a vein that receives oxygen-depleted blood from the capillaries and returns it to the heart via the venous system. **2** any of the branches of a vein in an insect's wing. [C19: from L *vēnula*, dim. of *vēna* VEIN]

Venus[1] ('vi:nəs) *n* the Roman goddess of love. Greek counterpart: **Aphrodite.**

Venus[2] ('vi:nəs) *n* one of the inferior planets and the second nearest to the sun, visible as a bright morning or evening star.
▸**Venusian** (vɪ'nju:zɪən) *n, adj*

Venus's-flytrap *or* **Venus flytrap** *n* an insectivorous plant having hinged two-lobed leaves that snap closed when the sensitive hairs on the surface are touched.

Venus's looking glass *n* a purple-flowered plant of Europe, W Asia, and N Africa.

veracious Ⓣ (vɛ'reɪʃəs) *adj* **1** habitually truthful or honest. **2** accurate. [C17: from L *vērax*, from *vērus* true]
▸**ve'raciously** *adv* ▸**ve'raciousness** *n*

veracity Ⓣ (vɛ'ræsɪtɪ) *n, pl* **veracities. 1** truthfulness or honesty, esp. when consistent or habitual. **2** accuracy. **3** a truth. [C17: from Med. L *vērācitās*, from L *vērax;* see VERACIOUS]

veranda *or* **verandah** (və'rændə) *n* **1** a porch or portico, sometimes partly enclosed, along the outside of a building. **2** *NZ.* a continuous overhead canopy that gives shelter to pedestrians. [C18: from Port. *varanda* railing]

veratrine ('vɛrəˌtri:n) *or* **veratrin** ('vɛrətrɪn) *n* a white poisonous mixture obtained from sabadilla, consisting of various alkaloids: formerly used in medicine as a counterirritant. [C19: from L *vērātrum* hellebore + -INE[2]]

verb (vɜ:b) *n* **1** (in traditional grammar) any of a large class of words that serve to indicate the occurrence or performance of an action, the existence of a state, etc. Such words as *run, make, do,* etc., are verbs. **2** (in modern descriptive linguistic analysis) **2a** a word or group of words that functions as the predicate of a sentence or introduces the predicate. **2b** *(as modifier): a verb phrase.* ◆ Abbrev.: **vb, v.** [C14: from L *verbum* word]

verbal Ⓣ ('vɜ:bᵊl) *adj* **1** of, relating to, or using words: *merely verbal concessions.* **2** oral rather than written: *a verbal agreement.* **3** verbatim; literal: *an almost verbal copy.* **4** *Grammar.* of or relating to verbs or a verb. ◆ See also **verbals.**
▸**'verbally** *adv*

verbalism ('vɜ:bəˌlɪzəm) *n* **1** a verbal expression; phrase or word. **2** an exaggerated emphasis on the importance of words. **3** a statement lacking real content.

verbalist ('vɜ:bəlɪst) *n* **1** a person who deals with words alone, rather than facts, ideas, etc. **2** a person skilled in the use of words.

verbalize *or* **verbalise** ('vɜ:bəˌlaɪz) *vb* **verbalizes, verbalizing, verbalized** *or* **verbalises, verbalising, verbalised. 1** to express (an idea, etc.) in words. **2** to change (any word) into a verb or derive a verb from (any word). **3** *(intr)* to be verbose.
▸**ˌverbali'zation** *or* **ˌverbali'sation** *n*

verbal noun *n* a noun derived from a verb, such as *smoking* in the sentence *smoking is bad for you.*

verbals ('vɜ:bᵊlz) *pl n Sl.* a criminal's admission of guilt on arrest.

verbascum (vɜ:'bæskəm) *n* any of a genus of hairy plants, mostly biennial, having spikes of yellow, purple, or red flowers. [L: mullein]

verbatim Ⓣ (vɜ:'beɪtɪm) *adv, adj* using exactly the same words; word for word. [C15: from Med. L: word by word, from L *verbum* word]

verbena (vɜ:'bi:nə) *n* **1** any of a genus of plants of tropical and temperate America, having red, white, or purple fragrant flowers: much cultivated as garden plants. **2** any of various similar plants, esp. the lemon verbena. [C16: via Med. L, from L: sacred bough used by the priest in religious acts]

THESAURUS

lignity, pungency, rancour, spite, spitefulness, spleen, virulence
Antonyms *n* ≠ **malice:** benevolence, charity, compassion, favour, goodwill, kindness, love, mercy

venomous *adj* **1** = **poisonous,** baneful *(arch.)*, envenomed, mephitic, noxious, poison, toxic, virulent **2** = **malicious,** baleful, hostile, malignant, rancorous, savage, spiteful, vicious, vindictive, virulent
Antonyms *adj* ≠ **poisonous:** harmless, nonpoisonous, nontoxic, nonvenomous ≠ **malicious:** affectionate, benevolent, compassionate, forgiving, harmless, loving, magnanimous

vent[1] *n* **1** = **outlet,** aperture, duct, hole, opening, orifice, split ◆ *vb* **6** = **express,** air, come out with, discharge, emit, empty, give expression to, give vent to, pour out, release, utter, voice
Antonyms *vb* ≠ **express:** bottle up, curb, hold back, inhibit, quash, quell, repress, stifle, subdue

ventilate *vb* **3** = **discuss,** air, bring out into the open, broadcast, debate, examine, make known, scrutinize, sift, talk about

venture *vb* **1** = **risk,** chance, endanger, hazard, imperil, jeopardize, put in jeopardy, speculate, stake, wager **4** = **dare,** advance, dare say, hazard, make bold, presume, stick one's neck out *(inf.)*, take the liberty, volunteer **5** = **go,** embark on, plunge into, set out ◆ *n* **6** = **undertaking,** adventure, chance, endeavour, enterprise, fling, gamble, hazard, jeopardy, project, risk, speculation

venturesome *adj* **1** = **daring,** adventurous, bold, courageous, daredevil, doughty, enterprising, fearless, intrepid, plucky, spirited

veracious *adj* **1** = **truthful,** ethical, frank, high-principled, honest, trustworthy, veridical **2** = **accurate,** credible, dependable, factual, faithful, genuine, reliable, straightforward, true

veracity *n* **1** = **truthfulness,** candour, frankness, honesty, integrity, probity, rectitude, trustworthiness, uprightness **2** = **accuracy,** credibility, exactitude, precision, truth

verbal *adj* **2, 3** = **spoken,** literal, oral, unwritten, verbatim, word-of-mouth

verbally *adv* **2** = **orally,** by word of mouth

verbatim *adv* = **word for word,** exactly, precisely, to the letter

verbiage ⓘ ('vɜːbɪɪdʒ) *n* the excessive and often meaningless use of words. [C18: from F, from OF *verbier* to chatter, from *verbe* word, from L *verbum*]

verbose ⓘ (vɜː'bəʊs) *adj* using or containing an excess of words, so as to be pedantic or boring. [C17: from L, from *verbum* word]
▸**ver'bosely** *adv* ▸**verbosity** (vɜː'bɒsɪtɪ) *n*

verboten *German.* (fɛr'boːtən) *adj* forbidden.

verb phrase *n Grammar.* a constituent of a sentence that contains the verb and any direct and indirect objects but not the subject.

verdant ⓘ ('vɜːdᵊnt) *adj* **1** covered with green vegetation. **2** (of plants, etc.) green in colour. **3** unsophisticated; green. [C16: from OF, from *verdoyer* to become green, from OF *verd* green, from L *viridis*]
▸**'verdancy** *n* ▸**'verdantly** *adv*

verd antique (vɜːd) *n* **1** a dark green mottled impure variety of serpentine marble. **2** any of various similar marbles or stones. [C18: from F, from It. *verde antico* ancient green]

verdict ⓘ ('vɜːdɪkt) *n* **1** the findings of a jury on the issues of fact submitted to it for examination and trial. **2** any decision or conclusion. [C13: from Med. L *vērdictum*, from L *vērē dictum* truly spoken, from *vērus* true + *dīcere* to say]

verdigris ('vɜːdɪgrɪs) *n* **1** a green or bluish patina formed on copper, brass, or bronze. **2** a green or blue crystalline substance obtained by the action of acetic acid on copper and used as a fungicide and pigment. [C14: from OF *vert de Grice* green of Greece]

verdure ('vɜːdʒə) *n* **1** flourishing green vegetation or its colour. **2** a condition of freshness or healthy growth. [C14: from OF *verd* green, from L *viridis*]
▸**'verdured** *adj*

verge[1] ⓘ (vɜːdʒ) *n* **1** an edge or rim; margin. **2** a limit beyond which something occurs: *on the verge of ecstasy*. **3** *Brit.* a grass border along a road. **4** *Archit.* the edge of the roof tiles projecting over a gable. **5** *English legal history.* **5a** the area encompassing the royal court that is subject to the jurisdiction of the Lord High Steward. **5b** a rod or wand carried as a symbol of office or emblem of authority, as in the Church. ◆ *vb* **verges, verging, verged. 6** (*intr;* foll. by *on*) to be near (to): *to verge on chaos*. **7** (when *intr*, sometimes foll. by *on*) to serve as the edge of (something): *this narrow strip verges the road.* [C15: from OF, from L *virga* rod]

verge[2] (vɜːdʒ) *vb* **verges, verging, verged.** (*intr;* foll. by *to* or *towards*) to move or incline in a certain direction. [C17: from L *vergere*]

verger ('vɜːdʒə) *n Chiefly Church of England.* **1** a church official who acts as caretaker and attendant. **2** an official who carries the verge or rod of office before a bishop or dean in ceremonies and processions. [C15: from OF, from *verge*, from L *virga* rod, twig]

verglas ('vɛəglɑː) *n, pl* **verglases** (-glɑː, -glɑːz). a thin film of ice on rock. [from OF *verre-glaz*, from *verre* glass + *glaz* ice]

veridical (vɪ'rɪdɪkᵊl) *adj* **1** truthful. **2** *Psychol.* of revelations in dreams, etc., that appear to be confirmed by subsequent events. [C17: from L, from *vērus* true + *dīcere* to say]
▸**ve,ridi'cality** *n* ▸**ve'ridically** *adv*

veriest ('vɛrɪɪst) *adj Arch.* (intensifier): *the veriest coward.*

verification ⓘ (,vɛrɪfɪ'keɪʃən) *n* **1** establishment of the correctness of a theory, fact, etc. **2** evidence that provides proof of an assertion, theory, etc.
▸**'verifi,catory** *adj*

verify ⓘ ('vɛrɪ,faɪ) *vb* **verifies, verifying, verified.** (*tr*) **1** to prove to be true; confirm. **2** to check or determine the correctness or truth of by investigation, etc. **3** *Law.* to substantiate or confirm (an oath). [C14: from OF, from Med. L *vērificāre*, from L *vērus* true + *facere* to make]
▸**'veri,fiable** *adj* ▸**'veri,fiably** *adv* ▸**'veri,fier** *n*

verily ('vɛrɪlɪ) *adv* (*sentence modifier*) *Arch.* in truth; truly: *verily, thou art a man of God.* [C13: from VERY + -LY[2]]

verisimilar (,vɛrɪ'sɪmɪlə) *adj* probable; likely. [C17: from L, from *vērus* true + *similis* like]

verisimilitude ⓘ (,vɛrɪsɪ'mɪlɪ,tjuːd) *n* **1** the appearance or semblance of truth or reality. **2** something that merely seems to be true or real, such as a doubtful statement. [C17: from L, from *vērus* true + *similitūdō* SIMILITUDE]

verism ('vɪərɪzəm) *n* extreme naturalism in art or literature. [C19: from It. *verismo*, from *vero* true, from L *vērus*]
▸**'verist** *n, adj* ▸**ve'ristic** *adj*

verismo (ve'rɪzməʊ) *n Music.* a school of composition that originated in Italian opera towards the end of the 19th century, drawing its themes from real life. [C19: from It.; see VERISM]

veritable ('vɛrɪtəbᵊl) *adj* (*prenominal*) (intensifier; *usually qualifying a word used metaphorically*): *he's a veritable swine!* [C15: from OF, from *vérité* truth; see VERITY]
▸**'veritableness** *n* ▸**'veritably** *adv*

vérité ('veɪriː,teɪ; *French* verite) *adj* involving a high degree of realism or naturalism: *a vérité look at David Bowie.* See also **cinéma vérité.** [F, lit.: truth]

verity ('vɛrɪtɪ) *n, pl* **verities. 1** the quality or state of being true, real, or correct. **2** a true statement, idea, etc. [C14: from OF from L *vēritās*, from *vērus* true]

verjuice ('vɜː,dʒuːs) *n* **1** the acid juice of unripe grapes, apples, or crab apples, formerly much used in making sauces, etc. **2** *Rare.* sourness or sharpness of temper, looks, etc. [C14: from OF *vert jus* green (unripe) juice]

verkrampte (fə'kramtə) *n* (in South Africa during apartheid) **a** an Afrikaner Nationalist violently opposed to the end of apartheid and to liberalism in general. **b** (*as modifier*): *verkrampte politics.* [C20: from Afrik. (adj), lit.: restricted]

verligte (fə'ləxtə) *n* (in South Africa during apartheid) **a** a follower of any liberal White political party. **b** (*as modifier*): *verligte politics.* [C20: from Afrik. (adj), lit.: enlightened]

vermeil ('vɜːmeɪl) *n* **1** gilded silver, bronze, or other metal, used esp. in the 19th century. **2a** vermilion. **2b** (*as adj*): *vermeil shoes.* [C15: from OF, from LL *vermiculus* insect (of the genus *Kermes*) or the red dye prepared from it, from L: little worm]

vermi- *combining form.* worm: *vermicide; vermiform; vermifuge.* [from L *vermis* worm]

vermicelli (,vɜːmɪ'sɛlɪ, -'tʃɛlɪ) *n* **1** very fine strands of pasta, used in soups. **2** tiny chocolate strands used to coat cakes, etc. [C17: from It.: little worms, from *verme*, from L *vermis*]

vermicide ('vɜːmɪ,saɪd) *n* any substance used to kill worms.
▸**,vermi'cidal** *adj*

vermicular (vɜː'mɪkjʊlə) *adj* **1** resembling the form, motion, or tracks of worms. **2** of worms or wormlike animals. [C17: from Med. L, from L *vermiculus*, dim. of *vermis* worm]
▸**ver'miculate** *adj* ▸**ver,micu'lation** *n*

vermiculite (vɜː'mɪkjʊ,laɪt) *n* any of a group of micaceous minerals consisting mainly of hydrated silicate of magnesium, aluminium, and iron: on heating they expand and in this form are used in heat and sound insulation. [C19: from VERMICUL(AR) + -ITE[1]]

vermiform ('vɜːmɪ,fɔːm) *adj* resembling a worm.

vermiform appendix *n* a wormlike pouch extending from the lower end of the caecum in some mammals. Also called: **appendix.**

vermifuge ('vɜːmɪ,fjuːdʒ) *n* any drug or agent able to destroy or expel intestinal worms.
▸**vermifugal** (,vɜːmɪ'fjuːgᵊl) *adj*

vermilion (və'mɪljən) *n* **1a** a bright red to reddish-orange colour. **1b** (*as adj*): *a vermilion car.* **2** mercuric sulphide, esp. when used as a bright red pigment; cinnabar. [C13: from OF *vermeillon*, from *vermeil*, from L *vermiculus*, dim. of *vermis* worm]

vermin ⓘ ('vɜːmɪn) *n* **1** (*functioning as pl*) small animals collectively, esp. insects and rodents, that are troublesome to man, domestic animals, etc. **2** (*pl* **vermin**) an unpleasant person. [C13: from OF, from L *vermis* worm]
▸**'verminous** *adj*

vermis ('vɜːmɪs) *n, pl* **vermes** (-miːz). *Anat.* the middle lobe connecting the two halves of the cerebellum. [C19: via NL from L: worm]

vermouth ('vɜːməθ) *n* any of several wines containing aromatic herbs. [C19: from F, from G *Wermut* WORMWOOD (absinthe)]

vernacular ⓘ (və'nækjʊlə) *n* **1 the.** the commonly spoken language or dialect of a particular people or place. **2** a local style of architecture, in which ordinary houses are built: *a true English vernacular.* ◆ *adj* **3** relating to or in the vernacular. **4** designating or relating to the common name of an animal or plant. **5** built in the local style of ordinary houses. [C17: from L *vernāculus* belonging to a household slave, from *verna* household slave]
▸**ver'nacularly** *adv*

vernal ('vɜːnᵊl) *adj* **1** of or occurring in spring. **2** *Poetic.* of or characteristic of youth. [C16: from L, from *vēr* spring]
▸**'vernally** *adv*

vernal equinox *n* See at **equinox.**

vernal grass *n* any of a genus of Eurasian grasses, such as **sweet vernal grass**, having the fragrant scent of coumarin.

vernalize *or* **vernalise** ('vɜːnə,laɪz) *vb* **vernalizes, vernalizing, vernalized** *or* **vernalises, vernalising, vernalised.** to shorten the period between sowing

THESAURUS

verbiage *n* = **verbosity**, circumlocution, periphrasis, pleonasm, prolixity, redundancy, repetition, tautology

verbose *adj* = **long-winded**, circumlocutory, diffuse, garrulous, periphrastic, pleonastic, prolix, tautological, windy, wordy
Antonyms *adj* brief, brusque, concise, curt, quiet, reticent, short, succinct, terse, untalkative

verbosely *adv* = **at great length**, at undue length, long-windedly, wordily

verbosity *n* = **long-windedness**, garrulity, logorrhoea, loquaciousness, prolixity, rambling, verbiage, verboseness, windiness, wordiness

verdant *adj* **1** = **green**, flourishing, fresh, grassy, leafy, lush

verdict *n* **1, 2** = **decision**, adjudication, conclusion, finding, judgment, opinion, sentence

verge[1] *n* **1, 2** = **border**, boundary, brim, brink, edge, extreme, limit, lip, margin, roadside, threshold ◆ *vb* **6** *foll. by* **on** = **come near to**, approach, border

verification *n* **1** = **proof**, authentication, confirmation, corroboration, substantiation, validation

verify *vb* **1** = **prove**, attest, attest to, authenticate, bear out, confirm, corroborate, substantiate, support, validate **2** = **check**
Antonyms *vb* ≠ **prove**: deny, discount, discredit, dispute, invalidate, nullify, undermine, weaken

verisimilitude *n* **1** = **realism**, authenticity, colour, credibility, likeliness, likeness, plausibility, resemblance, semblance, show of

verminous *adj* **1** = **lousy**, alive, crawling, flea-ridden

vernacular *n* **1** = **dialect**, argot, cant, idiom, jargon, native language, parlance, patois, speech, vulgar tongue ◆ *adj* **3** = **colloquial**, common, indigenous, informal, local, mother, native, popular, vulgar

and flowering in (plants), esp. by subjection of the seeds to low temperatures before planting.
▸ **ˌvernaliˈzation** *or* **ˌvernaliˈsation** *n*

vernation (vɜːˈneɪʃən) *n* the way in which leaves are arranged in the bud. [C18: from NL, from L *vernāre* to be springlike, from *vēr* spring]

vernier (ˈvɜːnɪə) *n* **1** a small movable scale running parallel to the main graduated scale in certain measuring instruments, such as theodolites, used to obtain a fractional reading of one of the divisions on the main scale. **2** (*modifier*) relating to or fitted with a vernier: *a vernier scale*. [C18: after Paul *Vernier* (1580–1637), F mathematician, who described the scale]

vernissage (ˌvɜːnɪˈsɑːʒ) *n* a preview or the opening or the first day of an exhibition of paintings. [F, from *vernis* VARNISH]

Veronal (ˈvɛrənᵊl) *n* a trademark for **barbitone.**

veronica[1] (vəˈrɒnɪkə) *n* any plant of a genus, including the speedwells, of temperate and cold regions, having small blue, pink, or white flowers and flattened notched fruits. [C16: from Med. L, ?from the name *Veronica*]

veronica[2] (vəˈrɒnɪkə) *n Bullfighting*. a pass in which the matador slowly swings the cape away from the charging bull. [from Sp., from the name *Veronica*]

verruca (vɛˈruːkə) *n, pl* **verrucae** (-siː) *or* **verrucas. 1** *Pathol*. a wart, esp. one growing on the hand or foot. **2** *Biol*. a wartlike outgrowth. [C16: from L: wart]

verrucose (ˈvɛrʊˌkəʊs) *or* **verrucous** (ˈvɛrʊkəs, vɛˈruːkəs) *adj Bot*. covered with warty processes. [C17: from L *verrūcōsus* full of warts, from *verrūca* a wart]
▸ **verrucosity** (ˌvɛrʊˈkɒsɪtɪ) *n*

versant (ˈvɜːsᵊnt) *n* **1** the side or slope of a mountain or mountain range. **2** the slope of a region. [C19: from F, from *verser* to turn, from L *versāre*]

versatile ❶ (ˈvɜːsəˌtaɪl) *adj* **1** capable of or adapted for many different uses, skills, etc. **2** variable. **3** *Bot*. (of an anther) attached to the filament by a small area so that it moves freely in the wind. **4** *Zool*. able to turn forwards and backwards. [C17: from L *versātilis* moving around, from *versāre* to turn]
▸ **ˈversaˌtilely** *adv* ▸**versatility** (ˌvɜːsəˈtɪlɪtɪ) *n*

verse (vɜːs) *n* **1** (not in technical usage) a stanza of a poem. **2** poetry as distinct from prose. **3a** a series of metrical feet forming a rhythmic unit of one line. **3b** (*as modifier*): *verse line*. **4** a specified type of metre or metrical structure: *iambic verse*. **5** one of the series of short subsections into which most of the writings in the Bible are divided. **6** a poem. ◆ *vb* **verses, versing, versed. 7** a rare word for **versify.** [OE *vers*, from L *versus* furrow, lit.: a turning (of the plough), from *vertere* to turn]

versed ❶ (vɜːst) *adj* (*postpositive*; foll. by *in*) thoroughly knowledgeable (about), acquainted (with), or skilled (in).

versed sine *n* a trigonometric function equal to one minus the cosine of the specified angle. [C16: from NL, from SINE[1] + *versus*, from *vertere* to turn]

versicle (ˈvɜːsɪkᵊl) *n* **1** a short verse. **2** a short sentence recited or sung by a minister and responded to by his congregation. [C14: from L *versiculus* a little line, from *versus* VERSE]

versicolour *or US* **versicolor** (ˈvɜːsɪˌkʌlə) *adj* of variable or various colours. [C18: from L *versicolor*, from *versāre* to turn + *color* COLOUR]

versification (ˌvɜːsɪfɪˈkeɪʃən) *n* **1** the technique or art of versifying. **2** the form or metrical composition of a poem. **3** a metrical version of a prose text.

versify (ˈvɜːsɪˌfaɪ) *vb* **versifies, versifying, versified. 1** (*tr*) to render (something) into verse. **2** (*intr*) to write in verse. [C14: from OF, from L, from *versus* VERSE + *facere* to make]
▸ **ˈversiˌfier** *n*

version ❶ (ˈvɜːʃən) *n* **1** an account of a matter from a certain point of view, as contrasted with others: *his version of the accident is different from the policeman's*. **2** a translation, esp. of the Bible, from one language into another. **3** a variant form of something. **4** an adaptation, as of a book or play into a film. **5** *Med*. manual turning of a fetus to correct an irregular position within the uterus. [C16: from Med. L *versiō* a turning, from L *vertere* to turn]
▸ **ˈversional** *adj*

vers libre *French*. (vɛr librə) *n* (in French poetry) another term for **free verse.**

verso (ˈvɜːsəʊ) *n, pl* **versos. 1a** the back of a sheet of printed paper. **1b** the left-hand pages of a book, bearing the even numbers. Cf. **recto** (sense 2). **2** the side of a coin opposite to the obverse. [C19: from NL *versō foliō* the leaf having been turned, from L *vertere* to turn + *folium* leaf]

verst (vɛəst, vɜːst) *n* a unit of length, used in Russia, equal to 1.067 kilometres (0.6629 miles). [C16: from F or G, from Russian *versta* line]

versus (ˈvɜːsəs) *prep* **1** (esp. in a competition or lawsuit) against. Abbrev.: **v.,** (esp. US) **vs. 2** in contrast with. [C15: from L: turned (in the direction of), opposite, from *vertere* to turn]

vertebra (ˈvɜːtɪbrə) *n, pl* **vertebrae** (-briː) *or* **vertebras.** one of the bony segments of the spinal column. [C17: from L: joint of the spine, from *vertere* to turn]
▸ **ˈvertebral** *adj* ▸ **ˈvertebrally** *adv*

vertebral column *n* another name for **spinal column.**

vertebrate (ˈvɜːtɪˌbreɪt, -brɪt) *n* **1** any animal of a subphylum characterized by a bony skeleton and a well-developed brain: the group contains fishes, amphibians, reptiles, birds, and mammals. ◆ *adj* **2** of or belonging to this subphylum.

vertebration (ˌvɜːtɪˈbreɪʃən) *n* the formation of vertebrae or segmentation resembling vertebrae.

vertex ❶ (ˈvɜːtɛks) *n, pl* **vertexes** *or* **vertices. 1** the highest point. **2** *Maths*. **2a** the point opposite the base of a figure. **2b** the point of intersection of two sides of a plane figure or angle. **2c** the point of intersection of a pencil of lines or three or more planes of a solid figure. **3** *Anat*. the crown of the head. [C16: from L: highest point, from *vertere* to turn]

vertical ❶ (ˈvɜːtɪkᵊl) *adj* **1** at right angles to the horizon; upright: *a vertical wall*. **2** extending in a perpendicular direction. **3** directly overhead. **4** *Econ*. of or relating to associated or consecutive, though not identical, stages of industrial activity: *vertical integration*. **5** of or relating to the vertex. **6** *Anat*. of or situated at the top of the head (vertex). ◆ *n* **7** a vertical plane, position, or line. **8** a vertical post, pillar, etc. [C16: from LL *verticālis*, from L VERTEX]
▸ **ˌvertiˈcality** *n* ▸ **ˈvertically** *adv*

vertical angles *pl n Geom*. the pair of equal angles between a pair of intersecting lines.

vertical mobility *n Sociol*. the movement of individuals or groups to positions in society that involve a change in class, status, and power.

vertices (ˈvɜːtɪˌsiːz) *n* a plural of **vertex** (in technical and scientific senses only).

verticil (ˈvɜːtɪsɪl) *n Biol*. a circular arrangement of parts about an axis, esp. leaves around a stem. [C18: from L *verticillus* whorl (of a spindle), from VERTEX]
▸**verˈticillate** *adj*

vertiginous (vɜːˈtɪdʒɪnəs) *adj* **1** of, relating to, or having vertigo. **2** producing dizziness. **3** whirling. **4** changeable; unstable. [C17: from L *vertīginōsus*, from VERTIGO]
▸**verˈtiginously** *adv*

vertigo ❶ (ˈvɜːtɪgəʊ) *n, pl* **vertigoes** *or* **vertigines** (vɜːˈtɪdʒɪˌniːz). *Pathol*. a sensation of dizziness resulting from a disorder of the sense of balance. [C16: from L: a whirling round, from *vertere* to turn]

vertu (vɜːˈtuː) *n* a variant spelling of **virtu.**

vervain (ˈvɜːveɪn) *n* any of several plants of the genus *Verbena*, having square stems and long slender spikes of purple, blue, or white flowers. [C14: from OF *verveine*, from L *verbēna* sacred bough]

verve ❶ (vɜːv) *n* great vitality and liveliness. [C17: from OF: garrulity, from L *verba* words, chatter]

vervet (ˈvɜːvɪt) *n* a variety of a South African guenon monkey having dark hair on the hands and feet and a reddish patch beneath the tail. [C19: from F, from *vert* green]

very ❶ (ˈvɛrɪ) *adv* **1** (intensifier) used to add emphasis to adjectives that are able to be graded: *very good; very tall*. ◆ *adj* (*prenominal*) **2** (intensifier) used with nouns preceded by a definite article or possessive determiner, in order to give emphasis to the significance or relevance of a noun in a particular context, or to give exaggerated intensity to certain nouns: *the very man I want to see; the very back of the room*. **3** (intensifier) used in metaphors to emphasize the applicability of the image to the situation described: *he was a very lion in the fight*. **4** *Arch*. genuine: *the very living God*. [C13: from OF *verai* true, from L *vērax*, from *vērus*]

USAGE NOTE In strict usage adverbs of degree such as *very, too, quite, really,* and *extremely* are used only to qualify adjectives: *he is very happy; she is too sad*. By this rule, these words should not be used to qualify past participles that follow the verb *to be*, since they would then be technically qualifying verbs. With the exception of certain participles, such as *tired* or *disappointed*, that have come to be regarded as adjectives, all other past participles are qualified by adverbs such as *much, greatly, seriously,* or *excessively*: *he has been much* (not *very*) *inconvenienced; she has been excessively* (not *too*) *criticized*.

THESAURUS

versatile *adj* **1, 2** = **adaptable**, adjustable, all-purpose, all-round, all-singing, all-dancing, flexible, functional, handy, many-sided, multifaceted, protean, resourceful, variable
Antonyms *adj* fixed, inflexible, invariable, limited, one-sided, unadaptable

versed *adj* = **knowledgeable**, accomplished, acquainted, competent, conversant, experienced, familiar, practised, proficient, qualified, seasoned, skilled, well informed, well up in (*inf.*)
Antonyms *adj* callow, green, ignorant, inexperienced, new, raw, unacquainted, unfledged, unpractised, unschooled, unskilled, unversed

version *n* **1** = **account**, interpretation, side, take (*inf., chiefly US*) **2, 4** = **adaptation**, exercise, portrayal, reading, rendering, translation **3** = **form**, design, kind, model, style, type, variant

vertex *n* **1** = **top**, acme, apex, apogee, crest, crown, culmination, extremity, height, pinnacle, summit, zenith

vertical *adj* **1, 2** = **upright**, erect, on end, perpendicular
Antonyms *adj* flat, horizontal, level, plane, prone

vertigo *n* = **dizziness**, giddiness, light-headedness, loss of equilibrium, swimming of the head

verve *n* = **enthusiasm**, animation, brio, dash, élan, energy, force, get-up-and-go (*inf.*), gusto, life, liveliness, pep, punch (*inf.*), sparkle, spirit, vigour, vim (*sl.*), vitality, vivacity, zeal, zip (*inf.*)
Antonyms *n* apathy, disdain, half-heartedness, indifference, inertia, lack of enthusiasm, languor, lethargy, lifelessness, reluctance, torpor

very *adv* **1** = **extremely**, absolutely, acutely, awfully (*inf.*), decidedly, deeply, eminently,

very high frequency *n* a radio-frequency band or radio frequency lying between 30 and 300 megahertz. Abbrev.: **VHF.**

Very light ('vɛrɪ) *n* a coloured flare fired from a special pistol (**Very pistol**) for signalling at night, esp. at sea. [C19: after Edward W. *Very* (1852–1910), US naval ordnance officer]

very low frequency *n* a radio-frequency band or radio frequency lying between 3 and 30 kilohertz. Abbrev.: **VLF.**

vesica ('vɛsɪkə) *n, pl* **vesicae** (-ˌsiː). *Anat.* a technical name for **bladder** (sense 1). [C17: from L: bladder, sac, blister]
▸ **'vesical** *adj* ▸ **vesiculate** (vɛ'sɪkjʊˌleɪt, -lɪt) *vb, adj*

vesicant ('vɛsɪkənt) *or* **vesicatory** ('vɛsɪˌkeɪtərɪ) *n, pl* **vesicants** *or* **vesicatories. 1** any substance that causes blisters. ◆ *adj* **2** acting as a vesicant. [C19: see VESICA]

vesicate ('vɛsɪˌkeɪt) *vb* **vesicates, vesicating, vesicated.** to blister. [C17: from NL *vēsīcāre* to blister; see VESICA]
▸ **ˌvesi'cation** *n*

vesicle ('vɛsɪkᵊl) *n* **1** *Pathol.* **1a** any small sac or cavity, esp. one containing serous fluid. **1b** a blister. **2** *Geol.* a rounded cavity within a rock. **3** *Bot.* a small bladder-like cavity occurring in certain seaweeds. **4** any small cavity or cell. [C16: from L *vēsīcula*, dim. of VESICA]
▸ **vesicular** (vɛ'sɪkjʊlə) *adj*

vesper ('vɛspə) *n* **1** an evening prayer, service, or hymn. **2** *Arch.* evening. **3** (*modifier*) of or relating to vespers. ◆ See also **vespers.** [C14: from L: evening, the evening star]

vespers ('vɛspəz) *n* (*functioning as sing*) **1** *Chiefly RC Church.* the sixth of the seven canonical hours of the divine office. **2** another word for **evensong** (sense 1).

vespertine ('vɛspəˌtaɪn) *adj* **1** *Bot., zool.* appearing, opening, or active in the evening: *vespertine flowers.* **2** occurring in the evening or (esp. of stars) setting in the evening.

vespiary ('vɛspɪərɪ) *n, pl* **vespiaries.** a nest or colony of social wasps or hornets. [C19: from L *vespa* a wasp, on the model of *apiary*]

vespid ('vɛspɪd) *n* **1** any of a family of hymenopterous insects, including the common wasp. ◆ *adj* **2** of or belonging to this family. [C19: from NL, from L *vespa* a wasp]
▸ **'vespine** *adj*

vessel Ⓣ ('vɛsᵊl) *n* **1** any object used as a container, esp. for a liquid. **2** a passenger or freight-carrying ship, boat, etc. **3** *Anat.* a tubular structure that transports such body fluids as blood and lymph. **4** *Bot.* a tubular element of xylem tissue transporting water. **5** *Rare.* a person regarded as a vehicle for some purpose or quality. [C13: from OF, from LL *vascellum* urn, from L *vās* vessel]

vest Ⓣ (vɛst) *n* **1** an undergarment covering the body from the shoulders to the hips, made of cotton, nylon, etc. Austral. equivalent: **singlet.** US and Canad. equivalent: **undershirt. 2** *US, Canad., & Austral.* a waistcoat. **3** *Obs.* any form of dress. ◆ *vb* **4** (*tr;* foll. by *in*) to place or settle (power, rights, etc., in): *power was vested in the committee.* **5** (*tr;* foll. by *with*) to bestow or confer (on): *the company was vested with authority.* **6** (usually foll. by *in*) to confer (a right, title, etc., upon) or (of a right, title, etc.) to pass (to) or devolve (upon). **7** (*tr*) to clothe. **8** (*intr*) to put on clothes, ecclesiastical vestments, etc. [C15: from OF *vestir* to clothe, from L *vestīre*, from *vestis* clothing]

vesta ('vɛstə) *n* a short friction match, usually of wood. [C19: after *Vesta*, Roman goddess of the hearth]

vestal ('vɛstᵊl) *adj* **1** chaste or pure. **2** of or relating to the Roman goddess Vesta. ◆ *n* **3** a chaste woman, esp. a nun.

vestal virgin *n* (in ancient Rome) one of the virgin priestesses whose lives were dedicated to Vesta and to maintaining the sacred fire in her temple.

vested ('vɛstɪd) *adj Property law.* having a present right to the immediate or future possession and enjoyment of property.

vested interest *n* **1** *Property law.* an existing right to the immediate or future possession and enjoyment of property. **2** a strong personal concern in a state of affairs, etc. **3** a person or group that has such an interest.

vestiary ('vɛstɪərɪ) *n, pl* **vestiaries.** *Obs.* a room for storing clothes or dressing in, such as a vestry. [C17: from LL *vestiārius*, from *vestis* clothing]

vestibule Ⓣ ('vɛstɪˌbjuːl) *n* **1** a small entrance hall or anteroom. **2** any small bodily cavity at the entrance to a passage or canal. [C17: from L *vestibulum*]

vestige Ⓣ ('vɛstɪdʒ) *n* **1** a small trace; hint: *a vestige of truth.* **2** *Biol.* an organ or part of an organism that is a small nonfunctioning remnant of a functional organ in an ancestor. [C17: via F from L *vestīgium* track]
▸ **ves'tigial** *adj*

vestment ('vɛstmənt) *n* **1** a garment or robe, esp. one denoting office, authority, or rank. **2** any of various ceremonial garments worn by the clergy at religious services, etc. [C13: from OF *vestiment*, from L *vestīmentum*, from *vestīre* to clothe]
▸ **vestmental** (vɛst'mɛntᵊl) *adj*

vest-pocket *n* (*modifier*) *Chiefly US.* small enough to fit into a waistcoat pocket.

vestry ('vɛstrɪ) *n, pl* **vestries. 1** a room in or attached to a church in which vestments, sacred vessels, etc., are kept. **2** a room in or attached to some churches, used for Sunday school, etc. **3a** *Church of England.* a meeting of all the members of a parish or their representatives, to transact the official and administrative business of the parish. **3b** the parish council. [C14: prob. from OF *vestiarie;* see VEST]
▸ **'vestral** *adj*

vestryman ('vɛstrɪmən) *n, pl* **vestrymen.** a member of a church vestry.

vesture ('vɛstʃə) *Arch.* ◆ *n* **1** a garment or something that seems like a garment: *a vesture of cloud.* ◆ *vb* **vestures, vesturing, vestured. 2** (*tr*) to clothe. [C14: from OF, from *vestir*, from L *vestīre*, from *vestis* clothing]
▸ **'vestural** *adj*

vet[1] Ⓣ (vɛt) *n* **1** short for **veterinary surgeon.** ◆ *vb* **vets, vetting, vetted. 2** (*tr*) *Chiefly Brit.* to make a prior examination and critical appraisal of (a person, document, etc.): *the candidates were well vetted.* **3** to examine or treat (an animal).

vet[2] (vɛt) *n US & Canad.* short for **veteran** (senses 2, 3).

vet. *abbrev. for:* **1** veteran. **2** veterinarian. **3** veterinary. ◆ Also (for senses 2, 3): **veter.**

vetch (vɛtʃ) *n* **1** any of various climbing plants having pinnate leaves, blue or purple flowers, and tendrils on the stems. **2** any of various similar and related plants, such as the kidney vetch. **3** the beanlike fruit of any of these plants. [C14 *fecche*, from OF *veche*, from L *vicia*]

vetchling ('vɛtʃlɪŋ) *n* any of various tendril-climbing plants, mainly of N temperate regions, having winged or angled stems and showy flowers. See also **sweet pea.**

veteran Ⓣ ('vɛtərən) *n* **1a** a person or thing that has given long service in some capacity. **1b** (*as modifier*): *veteran firemen.* **2** a soldier who has seen considerable active service. **3** *US & Canad.* a person who has served in the military forces. [C16: from L, from *vetus* old]

veteran car *n Brit.* a car constructed before 1919, esp. one constructed before 1905. Cf. **classic car, vintage car.**

veterinary ('vɛtərɪnərɪ) *adj* of or relating to veterinary medicine. [C18: from L *veterīnārius*, from *veterīnae* draught animals]

veterinary medicine *or* **science** *n* the branch of medicine concerned with the health of animals and the treatment of injuries or diseases that affect them.

veterinary surgeon *n Brit.* a person qualified to practise veterinary medicine. US and Canad. term: **veterinarian.**

veto Ⓣ ('viːtəʊ) *n, pl* **vetoes. 1** the power to prevent legislation or action proposed by others: *the presidential veto.* **2** the exercise of this power. ◆ *vb* **vetoes, vetoing, vetoed.** (*tr*) **3** to refuse consent to (a proposal, esp. a government bill). **4** to prohibit, ban, or forbid: *her parents vetoed her trip.* [C17: from L: I forbid, from *vetāre* to forbid]
▸ **'vetoer** *n*

vex Ⓣ (vɛks) *vb* (*tr*) **1** to anger or annoy. **2** to confuse; worry. **3** *Arch.* to agitate. [C15: from OF *vexer*, from L *vexāre* to jolt (in carrying), from *vehere* to convey]
▸ **'vexer** *n* ▸ **'vexing** *adj*

vexation Ⓣ (vɛk'seɪʃən) *n* **1** the act of vexing or the state of being vexed. **2** something that vexes.

vexatious Ⓣ (vɛk'seɪʃəs) *adj* **1** vexing or tending to vex. **2** vexed. **3** *Law.* (of a legal action or proceeding) instituted without sufficient grounds, esp. so as to cause annoyance to the defendant.
▸ **vex'atiously** *adv*

THESAURUS

exceedingly, excessively, greatly, highly, jolly (*Brit.*), noticeably, particularly, profoundly, really, remarkably, seriously (*inf.*), superlatively, surpassingly, terribly, truly, uncommonly, unusually, wonderfully ◆ *adj* **2** = **exact**, actual, appropriate, express, identical, perfect, precise, real, same, selfsame, unqualified

vessel *n* **1** = **container**, pot, receptacle, utensil **2** = **ship**, barque, boat, craft

vest *vb* **4, 5** *with* **in** *or* **with** = **place**, authorize, be devolved upon, bestow, confer, consign, empower, endow, entrust, furnish, invest, lodge, put in the hands of, settle

vestibule *n* **1** = **hall**, anteroom, entrance hall, foyer, lobby, porch, portico

vestige *n* **1** = **trace**, evidence, glimmer, hint, indication, relic, remainder, remains, remnant, residue, scrap, sign, suspicion, token, track

vestigial *adj* **2** = **rudimentary**, imperfect, incomplete, nonfunctional, surviving, undeveloped

Antonyms *adj* complete, developed, functional, perfect, practical, useful

vet[1] *vb* **2** = **check**, appraise, check out, examine, investigate, look over, pass under review, review, scan, scrutinize, size up (*inf.*)

veteran *n* **1a, 2** = **old hand**, master, old stager, old-timer, past master, pro (*inf.*), trouper, warhorse (*inf.*) ◆ *modifier* **1b** = **long-serving**, adept, battle-scarred, expert, old, proficient, seasoned
Antonyms *n* ≠ **old hand:** apprentice, beginner, freshman, initiate, neophyte, novice, recruit, tyro

veto *n* **2** = **ban**, boycott, embargo, interdict, nonconsent, prohibition ◆ *vb* **3, 4** = **ban**, boycott, disallow, forbid, give the thumbs down to, interdict, kill (*inf.*), negative, prohibit, put the kibosh on (*sl.*), refuse permission, reject, rule out, turn down
Antonyms *n* ≠ **ban:** approval, endorsement, go-ahead (*inf.*), ratification ◆ *vb* ≠ **ban:** approve, endorse, O.K. *or* okay (*inf.*), pass, ratify

vex *vb* **1, 2** = **annoy**, afflict, aggravate (*inf.*), agitate, bother, bug (*inf.*), confuse, displease, distress, disturb, exasperate, fret, gall, grate on, harass, hassle (*inf.*), irritate, molest, needle (*inf.*), nettle, offend, peeve (*inf.*), perplex, pester, pique, plague, provoke, put out, rile, tease, torment, trouble, upset, worry
Antonyms *vb* allay, appease, comfort, console, gratify, hush, mollify, please, quiet, soothe

vexation *n* **1** = **annoyance**, aggravation (*inf.*), chagrin, displeasure, dissatisfaction, exasperation, frustration, irritation, pique **2** = **problem**, bother, difficulty, hassle, headache (*inf.*), irritant, misfortune, nuisance, thorn in one's flesh, trouble, upset, worry

vexatious *adj* **1** = **annoying**, afflicting, aggravating (*inf.*), bothersome, burdensome,

vexed ➊ (vɛkst) *adj* **1** annoyed, confused, or agitated. **2** much debated (esp. in **a vexed question**).
▶**vexedly** (ˈvɛksɪdlɪ) *adv*

vexillology (ˌvɛksɪˈlɒlədʒɪ) *n* the study and collection of information about flags. [C20: from L *vexillum* flag + -LOGY]
▶ˌ**vexilˈlologist** *n*

vexillum (vɛkˈsɪləm) *n, pl* **vexilla** (-lə). **1** *Ornithol.* the vane of a feather. **2** Also called: **standard.** *Bot.* the largest petal of a papilionaceous flower. [C18: from L: banner, ?from *vēlum* sail]
▶ˈ**vexillate** *adj*

VF *abbrev. for* video frequency.

VFA (in Australia) *abbrev. for* Victorian Football Association.

vg *abbrev. for* very good.

VG *abbrev. for* Vicar General.

VGA *abbrev. for* video graphics array: a computing standard for spatial and colour resolution.

VHF *or* **vhf** *Radio. abbrev. for* very high frequency.

VHS *Trademark. abbrev. for* video home system: a video cassette recording system using ½″ magnetic tape.

VI *abbrev. for:* **1** Vancouver Island. **2** Virgin Islands.

v.i. *abbrev. for* vide infra (see **vide**).

via (ˈvaɪə) *prep* by way of; by means of; through: *to London via Paris.* [C18: from L *viā*, from *via* way]

viable ➊ (ˈvaɪəb^{ə}l) *adj* **1** capable of becoming actual, etc.: *a viable proposition.* **2** (of seeds, eggs, etc.) capable of normal growth and development. **3** (of a fetus) having reached a stage of development at which further development can occur independently of the mother. [C19: from F, from *vie* life, from L *vīta*]
▶ˌ**viaˈbility** *n*

Via Dolorosa (ˈviːə ˌdɒləˈrəʊsə) *n* the route followed by Christ from the place of his condemnation to Calvary for his crucifixion. [L, lit.: sorrowful road]

viaduct (ˈvaɪəˌdʌkt) *n* a bridge, esp. for carrying a road or railway across a valley, etc. [C19: from L *via* way + *dūcere* to bring, on the model of *aqueduct*]

Viagra (vaɪˈægrə, viː-) *n Trademark.* a drug that allows increased blood flow to the penis; used to treat impotence in men.

vial (ˈvaɪəl) *n* a less common variant of **phial.** [C14 *fiole*, from OF, ult. from Gk *phialē*; see PHIAL]

via media *Latin.* (ˈvaɪə ˈmiːdɪə) *n* a compromise between two extremes.

viand (ˈviːənd) *n* **1** a type of food, esp. a delicacy. **2** (*pl*) provisions. [C14: from OF, ult. from L *vīvenda* things to be lived on, from *vīvere* to live]

viatical (vaɪˈætɪk^{ə}l) *adj* **1** of or denoting a road or a journey. **2** *Bot.* (of a plant) growing by the side of a road. [C19: from L *viāticus* belonging to a journey + -AL]

viatical settlement *n* the purchase by a charity of a life assurance policy owned by a person with only a short time to live, to enable that person to use the proceeds during his or her lifetime. See also **death futures.**

viaticum (vaɪˈætɪkəm) *n, pl* **viatica** (-kə) *or* **viaticums. 1** *Christianity.* Holy Communion as administered to a person dying or in danger of death. **2** *Rare.* provisions or a travel allowance for a journey. [C16: from L, from *viāticus* belonging to a journey, from *via* way]

vibes ➊ (vaɪbz) *pl n* **1** *Inf.* short for **vibraphone. 2** *Sl.* short for **vibrations.**

vibraculum (vaɪˈbrækjʊləm) *n, pl* **vibracula** (-lə). *Zool.* any of the specialized bristle-like polyps in certain bryozoans, the actions of which prevent parasites from settling on the colony. [C19: from NL, from L *vibrāre* to brandish]

vibrant ➊ (ˈvaɪbrənt) *adj* **1** characterized by or exhibiting vibration. **2** giving an impression of vigour and activity. **3** caused by vibration; resonant. [C16: from L *vibrāre* to agitate]
▶ˈ**vibrancy** *n* ▶ˈ**vibrantly** *adv*

vibraphone (ˈvaɪbrəˌfəʊn) *n* a percussion instrument consisting of a set of metal bars placed over tubular metal resonators, which are made to vibrate electronically.
▶ˈ**vibraˌphonist** *n*

vibrate ➊ (vaɪˈbreɪt) *vb* **vibrates, vibrating, vibrated. 1** to move or cause to move back and forth rapidly. **2** (*intr*) to oscillate. **3** to resonate or cause to resonate. **4** (*intr*) to waver. **5** *Physics.* to undergo or cause to undergo an oscillatory process, as of an alternating current. **6** (*intr*) *Rare.* to respond emotionally; thrill. [C17: from L *vibrāre*]
▶**vibratile** (ˈvaɪbrəˌtaɪl) *adj* ▶**viˈbrating** *adj* ▶**vibratory** (ˈvaɪbrətərɪ) *adj*

vibration ➊ (vaɪˈbreɪʃən) *n* **1** the act or an instance of vibrating. **2** *Physics.* **2a** a periodic motion about an equilibrium position, such as in the propagation of sound. **2b** a single cycle of such a motion. **3** the process or state of vibrating or being vibrated.
▶**viˈbrational** *adj*

vibrations (vaɪˈbreɪʃənz) *pl n Sl.* **1** instinctive feelings supposedly influencing human communication. **2** a characteristic atmosphere felt to be emanating from places or objects.

vibrato (vɪˈbrɑːtəʊ) *n, pl* **vibratos.** *Music.* **1** a slight, rapid, and regular fluctuation in the pitch of a note produced on a stringed instrument by a shaking movement of the hand stopping the strings. **2** an oscillatory effect produced in singing by fluctuation in breath pressure or pitch. [C19: from It., from L *vibrāre* to VIBRATE]

vibrator (vaɪˈbreɪtə) *n* **a** a device for producing a vibratory motion, such as one used in massage. **b** such a device with a vibrating part or tip, used as a dildo.

vibrissa (vaɪˈbrɪsə) *n, pl* **vibrissae** (-siː). (*usually pl*) **1** any of the bristle-like sensitive hairs on the face of many mammals; a whisker. **2** any of the specialized bristle-like feathers around the beak in certain insectivorous birds. [C17: from L, prob. from *vibrāre* to shake]
▶**viˈbrissal** *adj*

viburnum (vaɪˈbɜːnəm) *n* **1** any of various temperate and subtropical shrubs or trees having small white flowers and berry-like red or black fruits. **2** the dried bark of several species of this tree, sometimes used in medicine. [C18: from L: wayfaring tree]

Vic. *Austral. abbrev. for* Victoria (the state).

vicar (ˈvɪkə) *n* **1** *Church of England.* **1a** (in Britain) a clergyman appointed to act as priest of a parish from which, formerly, he did not receive tithes but a stipend. **1b** a clergyman who acts as assistant to or substitute for the rector of a parish at Communion. **2** *RC Church.* a bishop or priest representing the pope and exercising a limited jurisdiction. **3** Also called: **lay vicar, vicar choral.** *Church of England.* a member of a cathedral choir appointed to sing certain parts of the services. [C13: from OF, from L *vicārius* (n) a deputy, from *vicārius* (adj) VICARIOUS]
▶**vicarial** (vɪˈkeərɪəl) *adj* ▶**viˈcariate** *n* ▶ˈ**vicarly** *adj*

vicarage (ˈvɪkərɪdʒ) *n* the residence or benefice of a vicar.

vicar apostolic *n RC Church.* a titular bishop having jurisdiction in missionary countries.

vicar general *n, pl* **vicars general.** an official, usually a layman, appointed to assist the bishop of a diocese in discharging his administrative or judicial duties.

vicarious ➊ (vɪˈkeərɪəs, vaɪ-) *adj* **1** undergone at second hand through sympathetic participation in another's experiences. **2** undergone or done as the substitute for another: *vicarious punishment.* **3** delegated: *vicarious authority.* **4** taking the place of another. [C17: from L *vicārius* substituted, from *vicis* interchange]
▶**viˈcariously** *adv* ▶**viˈcariousness** *n*

Vicar of Christ *n RC Church.* the pope when regarded as Christ's earthly representative.

vice[1] ➊ (vaɪs) *n* **1** an immoral, wicked, or evil habit, action, or trait. **2** frequent indulgence in immoral or degrading practices. **3** a specific form of pernicious conduct, esp. prostitution or sexual perversion. **4** an imperfection in character, conduct, etc.: *smoking is his only vice.* **5** a bad trick or disposition, as of horses, dogs, etc. [C13: via OF from L *vitium* a defect]

vice[2] *or US* (*often*) **vise** (vaɪs) *n* **1** an appliance for holding an object while work is done on it, usually having a pair of jaws. ◆ *vb* **2** (*tr*) to grip (something) with or as if with a vice. [C15: from OF *vis* a screw, from L *vītis* vine, plant with spiralling tendrils (hence the later meaning)]

vice[3] (vaɪs) *adj* **1a** (*prenominal*) serving in the place of. **1b** (*in combination*): *viceroy.* ◆ *n* **2** *Inf.* a person who serves as a deputy to another. [C18: from L, from *vicis* interchange]

vice[4] (ˈvaɪsɪ) *prep* instead of; as a substitute for. [C16: from L, ablative of *vicis* change]

vice admiral *n* a commissioned officer of flag rank in certain navies, junior to an admiral and senior to a rear admiral.

vice-chairman *n, pl* **vice-chairmen.** a person who deputizes for a chairman and serves in his place during his absence.
▶ˌ**vice-ˈchairmanship** *n*

vice chancellor *n* **1** the chief executive or administrator at some British universities. **2** (in the US) a judge in courts of equity subordinate to the chancellor. **3** (formerly in England) a senior judge of the court

THESAURUS

disagreeable, disappointing, distressing, exasperating, harassing, irksome, irritating, nagging, plaguy (*arch.*), provoking, teasing, tormenting, troublesome, trying, unpleasant, upsetting, worrisome, worrying
Antonyms *adj* agreeable, balmy, calming, comforting, pleasant, reassuring, relaxing, soothing

vexed *adj* **1 = annoyed**, afflicted, aggravated (*inf.*), agitated, bothered, confused, displeased, distressed, disturbed, exasperated, fed up, harassed, irritated, miffed (*inf.*), nettled, out of countenance, peeved (*inf.*), perplexed, provoked, put out, riled, ruffled, tormented, troubled, upset, worried **2 = controversial**, contested, disputed, moot, much debated

viable *adj* **1 = workable**, applicable, feasible, operable, practicable, usable, within the bounds of possibility
Antonyms *adj* hopeless, impossible, impracticable, inconceivable, out of the question, unthinkable, unworkable

vibes *pl n Slang* **2 = feelings**, emotions, reaction, response **2 = atmosphere**, aura, emanation, vibrations

vibrant *adj* **2 = energetic**, alive, animated, colourful, dynamic, electrifying, full of pep (*inf.*), responsive, sensitive, sparkling, spirited, storming, vigorous, vivacious, vivid

vibrate *vb* **1-3 = shake**, fluctuate, judder (*inf.*), oscillate, pulsate, pulse, quiver, resonate, reverberate, shiver, sway, swing, throb, tremble, undulate

vibration *n* **1 = shake**, judder (*inf.*), oscillation, pulsation, pulse, quiver, resonance, reverberation, throb, throbbing, trembling, tremor

vicarious *adj* **1 = indirect**, at one remove, empathetic **2 = substituted**, surrogate **3, 4 = delegated**, acting, commissioned, deputed

vice[1] *n* **1 = wickedness**, corruption, degeneracy, depravity, evil, evildoing, immorality, iniquity, profligacy, sin, turpitude, venality **4 = fault**, blemish, defect, failing, imperfection, shortcoming, weakness
Antonyms *n* ≠ **wickedness:** honour, morality, virtue ≠ **fault:** gift, good point, strong point, talent

of chancery who acted as assistant to the Lord Chancellor. **4** a person serving as the deputy of a chancellor.
▸ **ˌvice-'chancellorship** *n*

vicegerent (ˌvaɪs'dʒɛrənt) *n* **1** a person appointed to exercise all or some of the authority of another. **2** *RC Church.* the pope or any other representative of God or Christ on earth, such as a bishop. ◆ *adj* **3** invested with or characterized by delegated authority. [C16: from NL, from VICE^3 + L *gerere* to manage]
▸ **ˌvice'gerency** *n*

vicennial (vɪ'sɛnɪəl) *adj* **1** occurring every 20 years. **2** lasting for a period of 20 years. [C18: from LL *vīcennium* period of twenty years, from L *vīciēs* twenty times + *-ennium,* from *annus* year]

vice president *n* an officer ranking immediately below a president and serving as his deputy. A vice president takes the president's place during his absence or incapacity, after his death, and in certain other circumstances. Abbrev.: **VP.**
▸ **ˌvice-'presidency** *n*

viceregal (ˌvaɪs'riːg^{ə}l) *adj* **1** of or relating to a viceroy. **2** *Chiefly Austral. & NZ.* of or relating to a governor or governor general.
▸ **ˌvice'regally** *adv*

vicereine (ˌvaɪs'reɪn) *n* **1** the wife of a viceroy. **2** a female viceroy. [C19: from F, from VICE^3 + *reine* queen, from L *rēgīna*]

viceroy ('vaɪsrɔɪ) *n* a governor of a colony, country, or province who acts for and rules in the name of his sovereign or government. Related adj: **viceregal.** [C16: from F, from VICE^3 + *roy* king, from L *rex*]
▸ **'viceroyship** *or* **ˌvice'royalty** *n*

vice squad *n* a police division to which is assigned the enforcement of gaming and prostitution laws.

vice versa Ⓣ ('vaɪsɪ 'vɜːsə) *adv* the other way around. [C17: from L: relations being reversed, from *vicis* change + *vertere* to turn]

vichyssoise (*French* viʃiswaz) *n* a thick soup made from leeks, potatoes, chicken stock, and cream, usually served chilled. [F, from (*crème*) *vichyssoise* (*glacée*) (ice-cold cream) from Vichy]

vichy water ('viːʃiː) *n* **1** (*sometimes cap.*) a mineral water from springs at Vichy in France, reputed to be beneficial to health. **2** any sparkling mineral water resembling this.

vicinage ('vɪsnɪdʒ) *n Now rare.* **1** the residents of a particular neighbourhood. **2** a less common word for **vicinity.** [C14: from OF *vicenage,* from *vicin* neighbouring, from L *vīcīnus*]

vicinal ('vɪsɪn^{ə}l) *adj* **1** neighbouring. **2** (esp. of roads) of or relating to a locality. [C17: from L *vīcīnālis* nearby, from *vīcīnus,* from *vīcus* a neighbourhood]

vicinity Ⓣ (vɪ'sɪnɪtɪ) *n, pl* **vicinities.** **1** a surrounding area; neighbourhood. **2** the fact or condition of being close in space or relationship. [C16: from L, from *vīcīnus* neighbouring, from *vīcus* village]

vicious Ⓣ ('vɪʃəs) *adj* **1** wicked or cruel: *a vicious thug.* **2** characterized by violence or ferocity: *a vicious blow.* **3** *Inf.* unpleasantly severe; harsh: *a vicious wind.* **4** characterized by malice: *vicious lies.* **5** (esp. of dogs, horses, etc.) ferocious. **6** characterized by or leading to vice. **7** invalidated by defects; unsound: *a vicious inference.* [C14: from OF, from L *vitiōsus* full of faults, from *vitium* defect]
▸ **'viciously** *adv* ▸ **'viciousness** *n*

vicious circle *n* **1** Also: **vicious cycle.** a situation in which an attempt to resolve one problem creates new problems that lead back to the original situation. **2** *Logic.* **2a** a form of reasoning in which a conclusion is inferred from premises the truth of which cannot be established independently of that conclusion. **2b** an explanation given in terms that cannot be understood independently of that which was to be explained.

vicissitude Ⓣ (vɪ'sɪsɪˌtjuːd) *n* **1** variation or mutability in nature or life, esp. successive alternation from one condition or thing to another. **2** a variation in circumstance, fortune, etc. [C16: from L *vicissitūdō,* from *vicis* change]
▸ **viˌcissi'tudinous** *adj*

victim Ⓣ ('vɪktɪm) *n* **1** a person or thing that suffers harm, death, etc.: *victims of tyranny.* **2** a person who is tricked or swindled. **3** a living person or animal sacrificed in a religious rite. [C15: from L *victima*]

victimize Ⓣ *or* **victimise** ('vɪktɪˌmaɪz) *vb* **victimizes, victimizing, victimized** *or* **victimises, victimising, victimised.** (*tr*) **1** to punish or discriminate against unfairly. **2** to make a victim of.
▸ **ˌvictimi'zation** *or* **ˌvictimi'sation** *n* ▸ **'victimˌizer** *or* **'victimˌiser** *n*

victor Ⓣ ('vɪktə) *n* **1a** a person, nation, etc., that has defeated an adversary in war, etc. **1b** (*as modifier*): *the victor army.* **2** the winner of any contest, conflict, or struggle. [C14: from L, from *vincere* to conquer]

victoria (vɪk'tɔːrɪə) *n* **1** a light four-wheeled horse-drawn carriage with a folding hood, two passenger seats, and a seat in front for the driver. **2** Also called: **victoria plum.** *Brit.* a large sweet variety of plum, red and yellow in colour. [C19: both after Queen *Victoria,* (1819–1901), queen of the United Kingdom]

Victoria and Albert Museum *n* a museum of the fine and applied arts in London, originating from 1856 and given its present name and site in 1899. Abbrev.: **V and A.**

Victoria Cross *n* the highest decoration for gallantry in the face of the enemy awarded to the British and Commonwealth armed forces: instituted in 1856 by Queen Victoria.

Victoria Day *n* the Monday preceding May 24: observed in Canada as a national holiday in commemoration of the birthday of Queen Victoria.

Victorian (vɪk'tɔːrɪən) *adj* **1** of or characteristic of Victoria (1819–1901), queen of the United Kingdom, or the period of her reign. **2** exhibiting the characteristics popularly attributed to the Victorians, esp. prudery, bigotry, or hypocrisy. Cf. **Victorian values.** **3** of or relating to Victoria (the state in Australia or any of the cities). ◆ *n* **4** a person who lived during the reign of Queen Victoria. **5** an inhabitant of Victoria (the state or any of the cities).
▸ **Vic'torianˌism** *n*

Victoriana (vɪkˌtɔːrɪ'ɑːnə) *pl n* objects, ornaments, etc., of the Victorian period.

Victorian values *pl n* the qualities of enterprise and initiative, the importance of the family, and the development of charitable voluntary work considered to characterize the Victorian period. Cf. **Victorian** (sense 2).

victorious Ⓣ (vɪk'tɔːrɪəs) *adj* **1** having defeated an adversary: *the victorious nations.* **2** of, indicative of, or characterized by victory: *a victorious conclusion.*
▸ **vic'toriously** *adv*

victory Ⓣ ('vɪktərɪ) *n, pl* **victories.** **1** final and complete superiority in a war. **2** a successful military engagement. **3** a success attained in a contest or struggle or over an opponent, obstacle, or problem. **4** the act of triumphing or state of having triumphed. [C14: from OF *victorie,* from L *victōria,* from *vincere* to subdue]

victory roll *n* a rolling aircraft manoeuvre made by a pilot to announce or celebrate the shooting down of an enemy plane.

victual ('vɪt^{ə}l) *vb* **victuals, victualling, victualled** *or US* **victuals, victualing, victualed.** to supply with or obtain victuals. See also **victuals.** [C14: from OF *vitaille,* from LL *victuālia* provisions, from L *victus* sustenance, from *vīvere* to live]
▸ **'victual-less** *adj*

victualler ('vɪtələ) *n* **1** a supplier of victuals, as to an army. **2** *Brit.* a licensed purveyor of spirits. **3** a supply ship, esp. one carrying foodstuffs.

victuals Ⓣ ('vɪt^{ə}lz) *pl n* (*sometimes sing*) food or provisions.

vicuña (vɪ'kuːnjə) *or* **vicuna** (vɪ'kjuːnə, -'kuːnjə) *n* **1** a tawny-coloured cud-chewing Andean mammal similar to the llama. **2** the fine light cloth made from the wool obtained from this animal. [C17: from Sp., from Quechuan *wikúña*]

vid (vɪd) *n Inf.* short for **video** (sense 4).

vide ('vaɪdɪ) (used to direct a reader to a specified place in a text, another book, etc.) refer to, see (often in **vide ante** (see before), **vide infra** (see below), **vide supra** (see above), etc.). Abbrev.: **v., vid.** [C16: from L]

videlicet (vɪ'diːlɪˌsɛt) *adv* namely: used to specify items, etc. Abbrev.: **viz.** [C15: from L]

video ('vɪdɪəʊ) *adj* **1** relating to or employed in the transmission or reception of a televised image. **2** of, concerned with, or operating at video frequencies. ◆ *n, pl* **videos.** **3** the visual elements of a television broadcast. **4** a film recorded on a video cassette. **5** short for **video cassette, video cassette recorder.** **6** *US.* an informal name for **television.** ◆ *vb*

THESAURUS

vice versa *adv* = **conversely**, contrariwise, in reverse, the other way round

vicinity *n* **1** = **neighbourhood**, area, district, environs, locality, neck of the woods (*inf.*), precincts, propinquity, proximity, purlieus

vicious *adj* **1, 2** = **savage**, abhorrent, atrocious, bad, barbarous, cruel, dangerous, diabolical, ferocious, fiendish, foul, heinous, monstrous, vile, violent **4** = **malicious**, backbiting, bitchy (*inf.*), cruel, defamatory, mean, rancorous, slanderous, spiteful, venomous, vindictive **6** = **depraved**, abandoned, corrupt, debased, degenerate, degraded, immoral, infamous, profligate, sinful, unprincipled, wicked, worthless, wrong
Antonyms *adj* ≠ **savage:** docile, friendly, gentle, good, honourable, kind, playful, tame, upright, virtuous ≠ **malicious:** appreciative, complimentary, congratulatory

viciousness *n* **1, 2** = **savagery**, cruelty, ferocity **4** = **malice**, bitchiness (*sl.*), rancour, spite, spitefulness, venom **6** = **depravity**, badness, corruption, immorality, profligacy, wickedness
Antonyms *n* ≠ **malice:** gentleness, goodness, goodwill, graciousness, kindness, mercy, virtue

vicissitude *n* **1** = **change of fortune**, alteration, life's ups and downs (*inf.*), shift **2** = **variation**, alternation, mutation

victim *n* **1** = **casualty**, fatality, injured party, martyr, sacrifice, scapegoat, sufferer **2** = **prey**, dupe, fall guy (*inf.*), gull (*arch.*), innocent, patsy (*sl., chiefly US & Canad.*), sitting duck (*inf.*), sitting target, sucker (*sl.*)
Antonyms *n* ≠ **casualty:** survivor ≠ **prey:** assailant, attacker, culprit, guilty party, offender

victimize *vb* **1** = **persecute**, demonize, discriminate against, have a down on (someone) (*inf.*), have it in for (someone) (*inf.*), have one's knife into (someone), pick on

victor *n* **1, 2** = **winner**, champ (*inf.*), champion, conquering hero, conqueror, first, prizewinner, top dog, vanquisher
Antonyms *n* also-ran, dud (*inf.*), failure, flop (*inf.*), loser, vanquished

victorious *adj* **1, 2** = **winning**, champion, conquering, first, prizewinning, successful, triumphant, vanquishing
Antonyms *adj* beaten, conquered, defeated, failed, losing, overcome, unsuccessful, vanquished

victory *n* **1, 3** = **win**, conquest, laurels, mastery, success, superiority, the palm, the prize, triumph
Antonyms *n* defeat, failure, loss

victuals *pl n* = **food**, bread, comestibles, eatables, eats (*sl.*), edibles, grub (*sl.*), meat, nosebag (*sl.*), nosh (*sl.*), provisions, rations, stores, supplies, tack (*inf.*), viands, vittles (*obs.*)

videos, videoing, videoed. **7** to record (a television programme, etc.) on a video cassette recorder. [C20: from L *vidēre* to see, on the model of AUDIO]

video cassette *n* a cassette containing video tape.

video cassette recorder *n* a tape recorder for vision and sound signals using magnetic tape in closed plastic cassettes: used for recording and playing back television programmes and films. Often shortened to **video** or **video recorder.**

videodisc ('vɪdɪəʊˌdɪsk) *n* another name for **optical disc.**

video frequency *n* the frequency of a signal conveying the image and synchronizing pulses in a television broadcasting system. It lies in the range from about 50 hertz to 8 megahertz.

video game *n* any of various games that can be played by using an electronic control to move graphical symbols on the screen of a visual display unit.

video jockey *n* a person who introduces and plays videos, esp. of pop songs, on a television programme.

video nasty *n, pl* **nasties.** a film, usually specially made for video, that is explicitly horrific and pornographic.

videophone ('vɪdɪəˌfəʊn) *n* a telephonic device through which there is both verbal and visual communication.

video recorder *n* short for **video cassette recorder.**

video tape *n* **1** magnetic tape used mainly for recording the sound and vision signals of a television programme or film for subsequent transmission. ◆ *vb* **video-tape, video-tapes, video-taping, video-taped.** **2** to record (a programme, etc.) on video tape.

video tape recorder *n* a tape recorder for visual signals and usually accompanying sound, using magnetic tape on open spools: used in television broadcasting.

Videotex ('vɪdɪəʊˌtɛks) *n Trademark.* an information system that displays information from a distant computer on a television screen. See also **Teletext, Viewdata.**

videotext ('vɪdɪəʊˌtɛkst) *n* a means of providing a written or graphical representation of computerized information on a television screen.

vidicon ('vɪdɪˌkɒn) *n* a small television camera tube, used in closed-circuit television and outside broadcasts, in which incident light forms an electric charge pattern on a photoconductive surface. [C20: from VID(EO) + ICON(OSCOPE)]

vie ➊ (vaɪ) *vb* **vies, vying, vied.** (*intr;* foll. by *with* or *for*) to contend for superiority or victory (with) or strive in competition (for). [C15: prob. from OF *envier* to challenge, from L *invītāre* to INVITE]
▸'**vier** *n* ▸'**vying** *adj, n*

Viennese (ˌvɪəˈniːz) *adj* **1** of or relating to Vienna, capital of Austria. ◆ *n, pl* **Viennese.** **2** a native or inhabitant of Vienna.

vies (fɪs) *adj S. African sl.* angry, furious, or disgusted. [Afrik.]

Vietnamese (ˌvjɛtnəˈmiːz) *adj* **1** of or characteristic of Vietnam, in SE Asia, its people, or their language. ◆ *n* **2** (*pl* **Vietnamese**) a native or inhabitant of Vietnam. **3** the language of Vietnam.

vieux jeu *French.* (vjø ʒø) *adj* old-fashioned. [lit.: old game]

view ➊ (vjuː) *n* **1** the act of seeing or observing. **2** vision or sight, esp. range of vision: *the church is out of view.* **3** a scene, esp. of a fine tract of countryside: *the view from the top was superb.* **4** a pictorial representation of a scene, such as a photograph. **5** (*sometimes pl*) opinion: *my own view on the matter differs from yours.* **6** (foll. by *to*) a desired end or intention: *he has a view to securing further qualifications.* **7** a general survey of a topic, subject, etc. **8** visual aspect or appearance: *they look the same in outward view.* **9** a sight of a hunted animal before or during the chase. **10 in view of.** taking into consideration. **11 on view.** exhibited to the public gaze. **12 take a dim** *or* **poor view of.** to regard (something) with disfavour. **13 with a view to. 13a** with the intention of. **13b** in anticipation or hope of. ◆ *vb* **14** (*tr*) to look at. **15** (*tr*) to consider in a specified manner: *they view Communism with horror.* **16** (*tr*) to examine or inspect carefully: *to view the accounts.* **17** (*tr*) to contemplate: *to view the difficulties.* **18** to watch (television). **19** (*tr*) to sight (a hunted animal) before or during the chase. [C15: from OF, from *veoir* to see, from L *vidēre*]
▸'**viewable** *adj*

Viewdata ('vjuːˌdeɪtə) *n Trademark.* an interactive form of Videotext that sends information from a distant computer along telephone lines, enabling shopping, booking theatre and airline tickets, and banking transactions to be conducted from the home.

viewer ➊ ('vjuːə) *n* **1** a person who views something, esp. television. **2** any optical device by means of which something is viewed, esp. one used for viewing photographic transparencies.

viewfinder ('vjuːˌfaɪndə) *n* a device on a camera, consisting of a lens system, enabling the user to see what will be included in his photograph.

view halloo *interj* a huntsman's cry uttered when the quarry is seen breaking cover or shortly afterwards.

viewing ('vjuːɪŋ) *n* **1** the act of watching television. **2** television programmes collectively: *late-night viewing.*

viewless ('vjuːlɪs) *adj* **1** (of windows, etc.) not affording a view. **2** having no opinions. **3** *Poetic.* invisible.

viewpoint ➊ ('vjuːˌpɔɪnt) *n* **1** the mental attitude that determines a person's judgments. **2** a place from which something can be viewed.

vigesimal (vaɪˈdʒɛsɪməl) *adj* **1** relating to or based on the number 20. **2** taking place or proceeding in intervals of 20. **3** twentieth. [C17: from L *vīgēsimus,* var. (infl. by *vīgintī* twenty) of *vīcēsimus* twentieth]

vigia ('vɪdʒɪə) *n Naut.* a navigational hazard marked on a chart although its existence and nature has not been confirmed. [C19: from Sp. *vigía* reef, from L *vigilāre* to keep watch]

vigil ('vɪdʒɪl) *n* **1** a purposeful watch maintained, esp. at night, to guard, observe, pray, etc. **2** the period of such a watch. **3** *RC Church, Church of England.* the eve of certain major festivals, formerly observed as a night spent in prayer. [C13: from OF, from Med. L *vigilia* watch preceding a religious festival, from L, from *vigil* alert, from *vigēre* to be lively]

vigilance ➊ ('vɪdʒɪləns) *n* **1** the fact, quality, or condition of being vigilant. **2** the abnormal state or condition of being unable to sleep.

vigilance committee *n* (in the US) a self-appointed body of citizens organized to maintain order, etc., where an efficient system of courts does not exist.

vigilant ➊ ('vɪdʒɪlənt) *adj* keenly alert to or heedful of trouble or danger. [C15: from L *vigilāns,* from *vigilāre* to be watchful; see VIGIL]
▸'**vigilantly** *adv*

vigilante (ˌvɪdʒɪˈlæntɪ) *n* **1** a self-appointed protector of public order. **2** *US.* a member of a vigilance committee. [C19: from Sp., from L *vigilāre* to keep watch]

vigilantism (ˌvɪdʒɪˈlæntɪzəm) *n US.* the methods, conduct, attitudes, etc., associated with vigilantes, esp. militancy or bigotry.

Vigil Mass *n RC Church.* a Mass held on Saturday evening, attendance at which fulfils one's obligation to attend Mass on Sunday.

vigneron ('viːnjərɒn; *French* viɲrɔ̃) *n* a person who grows grapes for winemaking. [F, from *vigne* vine]

vignette (vɪˈnjɛt) *n* **1** a small illustration placed at the beginning or end of a book or chapter. **2** a short graceful literary essay or sketch. **3** a photograph, drawing, etc., with edges that are shaded off. **4** any small endearing scene, view, etc. ◆ *vb* **vignettes, vignetting, vignetted.** (*tr*) **5** to finish (a photograph, etc.) with a fading border in the form of a vignette. **6** to portray in or as in a vignette. [C18: from F, lit.: little vine; with reference to the vine motif frequently used in embellishments to a text]
▸**vi'gnettist** *n*

vigoro ('vɪgəˌrəʊ) *n Austral.* a ball game combining elements of cricket and baseball. [C20: from VIGOUR]

vigorous ➊ ('vɪgərəs) *adj* **1** endowed with bodily or mental strength or vitality. **2** displaying, characterized by, or performed with vigour: *vigorous growth.*
▸'**vigorously** *adv*

vigour ➊ *or US* **vigor** ('vɪgə) *n* **1** exuberant and resilient strength of body or mind. **2** substantial effective energy or force: *the vigour of the tempest.* **3** forcefulness: *I was surprised by the vigour of her complaints.* **4** the capacity for survival or strong healthy growth in a plant or animal. **5** the most active period or stage of life, manhood, etc. [C14: from OF, from L *vigor,* from *vigēre* to be lively]

THESAURUS

vie *vb* = **compete,** be rivals, contend, contest, match oneself against, strive, struggle

view *n* **1** = **look,** contemplation, display, examination, inspection, recce (*sl.*), scan, scrutiny, sight, survey, viewing **2** = **vision,** range *or* field of vision, sight **3** = **scene,** aspect, landscape, outlook, panorama, perspective, picture, prospect, spectacle, vista **5** *sometimes plural* = **opinion,** attitude, belief, conviction, feeling, impression, judgment, notion, point of view, sentiment, thought, way of thinking **13 with a view to** = **with the aim** *or* **intention of,** in order to, in the hope of, so as to ◆ *vb* **14, 16** = **look at,** behold, check, check out (*inf.*), clock (*Brit. sl.*), contemplate, examine, explore, eye, eyeball (*sl.*), gaze at, get a load of (*inf.*), inspect, observe, recce (*sl.*), regard, scan, spectate, stare at, survey, take a dekko at (*Brit. sl.*), watch, witness **15** = **regard,** consider, deem, judge, look on, think about

viewer *n* **1** = **watcher,** observer, one of an audience, onlooker, spectator, TV watcher

viewpoint *n* **1** = **attitude,** angle, frame of reference, perspective, point of view, position, slant, stance, standpoint, vantage point, way of thinking

vigilance *n* **1** = **watchfulness,** alertness, attentiveness, carefulness, caution, circumspection, observance

vigilant *adj* = **watchful,** alert, attentive, careful, cautious, circumspect, on one's guard, on one's toes, on the alert, on the lookout, sleepless, unsleeping, wakeful, wide awake
Antonyms *adj* careless, inattentive, lax, neglectful, negligent, remiss, slack

vigorous *adj* **1, 2** = **energetic,** active, alive and kicking, brisk, dynamic, effective, efficient, enterprising, fighting fit, fit as a fiddle (*inf.*), flourishing, forceful, forcible, full of beans (*inf.*), hale, hale and hearty, hardy, healthy, intense, lively, lusty, powerful, red-blooded, robust, sound, spanking, spirited, strenuous, strong, virile, vital, zippy (*inf.*)
Antonyms *adj* apathetic, effete, enervated, feeble, frail, inactive, indolent, lethargic, lifeless, spiritless, torpid, weak, weedy (*inf.*), wimpish *or* wimpy (*inf.*), wishy-washy

vigorously *adv* **1, 2** = **energetically,** all out, eagerly, forcefully, hammer and tongs, hard, like mad (*sl.*), lustily, strenuously, strongly, with a vengeance, with might and main

vigour *n* **1-3** = **energy,** activity, animation, brio, dash, dynamism, force, forcefulness, gusto, health, liveliness, might, oomph (*inf.*), pep, power, punch (*inf.*), robustness, snap (*inf.*), soundness, spirit, strength, verve, vim (*sl.*), virility, vitality, wellness, zip (*inf.*)
Antonyms *n* apathy, feebleness, fragility, frailty, impotence, inactivity, inertia, infirmity, lethargy, sluggishness, weakness

Viking ('vaɪkɪŋ) *n* (*sometimes not cap.*) **1** Also called: **Norseman, Northman.** any of the Danes, Norwegians, and Swedes who raided by sea most of N and W Europe from the 8th to the 11th centuries. **2** (*modifier*) of, relating to, or characteristic of a Viking or Vikings: *a Viking ship.* [C19: from ON *víkingr,* prob. from *vík* creek, sea inlet + *-ingr* (see -ING[3])]

vile ❶ (vaɪl) *adj* **1** abominably wicked; shameful or evil. **2** morally despicable; ignoble: *vile accusations.* **3** disgusting to the senses or emotions; foul: *a vile smell.* **4** tending to humiliate or degrade: *only slaves would perform such vile tasks.* **5** unpleasant or bad: *vile weather.* [C13: from OF *vil,* from L *vīlis* cheap]
▸**'vilely** *adv* ▸**'vileness** *n*

vilify ❶ ('vɪlɪˌfaɪ) *vb* **vilifies, vilifying, vilified.** (*tr*) to revile with abusive language; malign. [C15: from LL, from L *vīlis* worthless + *facere* to make]
▸**vilification** (ˌvɪlɪfɪ'keɪʃən) *n* ▸**'viliˌfier** *n*

vilipend ('vɪlɪˌpɛnd) *vb* (*tr*) *Rare.* **1** to treat or regard with contempt. **2** to speak slanderously of. [C15: from LL, from L *vīlis* worthless + *pendere* to esteem]
▸**'viliˌpender** *n*

villa ('vɪlə) *n* **1** (in ancient Rome) a country house, usually consisting of farm buildings and residential quarters around a courtyard. **2** a large country residence. **3** *Brit.* a detached or semidetached suburban house. [C17: via It. from L]

village ('vɪlɪdʒ) *n* **1** a small group of houses in a country area, larger than a hamlet. **2** the inhabitants of such a community collectively. **3** an incorporated municipality smaller than a town in various parts of the US and Canada. **4** (*modifier*) of or characteristic of a village: *a village green.* [C15: from OF, from *ville* farm, from L: VILLA]
▸**'villager** *n*

villain ❶ ('vɪlən) *n* **1** a wicked or malevolent person. **2** (in a novel, play, etc.) the main evil character and antagonist to the hero. **3** *Often jocular.* a rogue. **4** *Obs.* an uncouth person; boor. [C14: from OF *vilein* serf, from LL *vīllānus* worker on a country estate, from L: VILLA]
▸**'villainess** *fem n*

villainous ❶ ('vɪlənəs) *adj* **1** of, like, or appropriate to a villain. **2** very bad or disagreeable: *a villainous climate.*
▸**'villainously** *adv* ▸**'villainousness** *n*

villainy ❶ ('vɪlənɪ) *n, pl* **villainies. 1** vicious behaviour or action. **2** an evil or criminal act or deed. **3** the fact or condition of being villainous.

villanelle (ˌvɪlə'nɛl) *n* a verse form of French origin consisting of 19 lines arranged in five tercets and a quatrain. [C16: from F, from It. *villanella,* from *villano* rustic]

-ville *n and adj combining form. Sl., chiefly US.* (denoting) a place, condition, or quality with a character as specified: *dragsville; squaresville.*

villein ('vɪlən) *n* (in medieval Europe) a peasant bound to his lord, to whom he paid dues and services in return for his land. [C14: from OF *vilein* serf; see VILLAIN]
▸**'villeinage** *n*

villiform ('vɪlɪˌfɔːm) *adj* having the form of a villus or a series of villi. [C19: from NL *villiformis,* from L *villus* shaggy hair + -FORM]

villus ('vɪləs) *n, pl* **villi** ('vɪlaɪ). (*usually pl*) **1** *Zool., anat.* any of the numerous finger-like projections of the mucous membrane lining the small intestine of many vertebrates. **2** any similar membranous process. **3** *Bot.* any of various hairlike outgrowths. [C18: from L: shaggy hair]
▸**villosity** (vɪ'lɒsɪtɪ) *n* ▸**'villous** *adj*

vim (vɪm) *n Sl.* exuberant vigour and energy. [C19: from L, from *vīs;* rel. to Gk *is* strength]

vimineous (vɪ'mɪnɪəs) *adj Bot.* having, producing, or resembling long flexible shoots. [C17: from L *vīmineus* made of osiers, from *vīmen* flexible shoot]

vina ('viːnə) *n* a stringed musical instrument, esp. of India, related to the sitar. [C18: from Hindi *bīnā,* from Sansk. *vīṇā*]

vinaceous (vaɪ'neɪʃəs) *adj* **1** of, relating to, or containing wine. **2** having a colour suggestive of red wine. [C17: from LL *vīnāceus,* from L *vīnum* wine]

vinaigrette (ˌvɪneɪ'grɛt) *n* **1** Also called: **vinaigrette sauce.** a salad dressing made from oil and vinegar with seasonings; French dressing. **2** Also called: **vinegarette.** a small decorative bottle or box with a perforated top, used for holding smelling salts, etc. [C17: from F, from *vinaigre* VINEGAR]

Vincent's angina *or* **disease** ('vɪnsənts) *n* an ulcerative bacterial infection of the mouth, esp. involving the throat and tonsils. [C20: after J. H. *Vincent* (died 1950), F bacteriologist]

vincible ('vɪnsɪbᵊl) *adj Rare.* capable of being defeated. [C16: from L *vincibilis,* from *vincere* to conquer]
▸**ˌvinci'bility** *n*

vincristine (vɪn'krɪstiːn) *n* an alkaloid used to treat leukaemia, derived from the tropical shrub Madagascar periwinkle. [C20: from NL *Vinca* genus name of the plant + L *crista* crest + -INE[2]]

vinculum ('vɪŋkjʊləm) *n, pl* **vincula** (-lə). **1** a horizontal line drawn above a group of mathematical terms, used as an alternative to parentheses in mathematical expressions, as in $x + \overline{y - z}$, which is equivalent to $x + (y - z)$. **2** *Anat.* any bandlike structure, esp. one uniting two or more parts. [C17: from L: bond, from *vincīre* to bind]

vindaloo (ˌvɪndə'luː) *n, pl* **vindaloos.** a type of very hot Indian curry. [C20: ? from Port. *vin d'alho* wine and garlic sauce]

vin de pays *French.* (vɛ̃ də pei) *n, pl* ***vins de pays*** (vɛ̃ də pei). the third highest French wine classification: indicates that the wine meets certain requirements concerning area of production, strength, etc. Also called: ***vin du pays.*** Abbrev.: **VDP.** Cf. **AOC, VDQS.** [lit.: local wine]

vindicable ('vɪndɪkəbᵊl) *adj* capable of being vindicated; justifiable.
▸**ˌvindica'bility** *n*

vindicate ❶ ('vɪndɪˌkeɪt) *vb* **vindicates, vindicating, vindicated.** (*tr*) **1** to clear from guilt, blame, etc., as by evidence or argument. **2** to provide justification for: *his promotion vindicated his unconventional attitude.* **3** to uphold or defend (a cause, etc.): *to vindicate a claim.* [C17: from L *vindicāre,* from *vindex* claimant]
▸**'vindiˌcator** *n* ▸**'vindiˌcatory** *adj*

vindication ❶ (ˌvɪndɪ'keɪʃən) *n* **1** the act of vindicating or the condition of being vindicated. **2** a fact, evidence, etc., that serves to vindicate a claim.

vindictive ❶ (vɪn'dɪktɪv) *adj* **1** disposed to seek vengeance. **2** characterized by spite or rancour. **3** *English law.* (of damages) in excess of the compensation due to the plaintiff and imposed in punishment of the defendant. [C17: from L *vindicta* revenge, from *vindicāre* to VINDICATE]
▸**vin'dictively** *adv* ▸**vin'dictiveness** *n*

vin du pays *French.* (vɛ̃ du pei) *n, pl* ***vins du pays.*** a variant of ***vin de pays.***

vine (vaɪn) *n* **1** any of various plants, esp. the grapevine, having long flexible stems that creep along the ground or climb by clinging to a support by means of tendrils, leafstalks, etc. **2** the stem of such a plant. [C13: from OF, from L *vīnea* vineyard, from *vīnum* wine]
▸**'viny** *adj*

vinedresser ('vaɪnˌdrɛsə) *n* a person who prunes, tends, or cultivates grapevines.

vinegar ('vɪnɪgə) *n* **1** a sour-tasting liquid consisting of impure dilute acetic acid, made by fermentation of beer, wine, or cider. It is used as a condiment or preservative. **2** sourness or peevishness of temper, speech, etc. [C13: from OF, from *vin* WINE + *aigre* sour, from L *acer*]
▸**'vinegarish** *adj* ▸**'vinegary** *adj*

vinery ('vaɪnərɪ) *n, pl* **vineries. 1** a hothouse for growing grapes. **2** another name for a **vineyard. 3** vines collectively.

vineyard ('vɪnjəd) *n* a plantation of grapevines, esp. where wine grapes are produced. [OE *wīngeard;* see VINE, YARD[2]]

vingt-et-un *French.* (vɛ̃teœ̃) *n* another name for **pontoon**[2]. [lit.: twenty-one]

vinho verde (ˌviːnjəʊ 'vɜːdɪ) *n* any of a variety of light sharp-tasting wines made from early-picked grapes of NW Portugal. [Port., lit.: green (or young) wine]

vini- *or before a vowel* **vin-** *combining form.* indicating wine: *viniculture.* [from L *vīnum*]

viniculture ('vɪnɪˌkʌltʃə) *n* the process or business of growing grapes and making wine.
▸**ˌvini'cultural** *adj* ▸**ˌvini'culturist** *n*

viniferous (vɪ'nɪfərəs) *adj* wine-producing.

THESAURUS

vile *adj* **1, 2, 4** = **wicked**, abandoned, abject, appalling, bad, base, coarse, contemptible, corrupt, debased, degenerate, degrading, depraved, despicable, disgraceful, evil, humiliating, ignoble, impure, loathsome, low, mean, miserable, nefarious, perverted, shocking, sinful, ugly, vicious, vulgar, worthless, wretched **3** = **disgusting**, foul, horrid, loathsome, nasty, nauseating, noxious, obscene, offensive, repellent, repugnant, repulsive, revolting, sickening, yucky *or* yukky (*sl.*)
Antonyms *adj* ≠ **wicked:** chaste, cultured, genteel, honourable, noble, polite, pure, refined, righteous, upright, worthy ≠ **disgusting:** agreeable, delicate, lovely, marvellous, pleasant, splendid, sublime

vileness *n* **1, 2** = **wickedness**, coarseness, corruption, degeneracy, depravity, dreadfulness, enormity, evil, heinousness, outrage, profanity, turpitude, ugliness **3** = **foulness**, noxiousness, offensiveness

vilification *n* = **denigration**, abuse, aspersion, calumniation, calumny, contumely, defamation, disparagement, invective, mudslinging, scurrility, vituperation

vilify *vb* = **malign**, abuse, asperse, berate, calumniate, debase, decry, defame, denigrate, disparage, knock (*inf.*), revile, rubbish (*inf.*), run down, slag (off) (*sl.*), slander, smear, speak ill of, traduce, vituperate
Antonyms *vb* adore, commend, esteem, exalt, glorify, honour, praise, revere, venerate

villain *n* **1** = **evildoer**, blackguard, caitiff (*arch.*), criminal, knave (*arch.*), libertine, malefactor, miscreant, profligate, rapscallion, reprobate, rogue, scoundrel, wretch **2** = **antihero**, baddy (*inf.*) **3** *Often jocular* = **scamp**, devil, monkey, rascal, rogue, scallywag (*inf.*)
Antonyms *n* ≠ **antihero:** goody, hero, heroine

villainous *adj* **1, 2** = **wicked**, atrocious, bad, base, blackguardly, criminal, cruel, debased, degenerate, depraved, detestable, diabolical, evil, fiendish, hateful, heinous, ignoble, infamous, inhuman, mean, nefarious, outrageous, ruffianly, scoundrelly, sinful, terrible, thievish, vicious, vile
Antonyms *adj* angelic, good, heroic, humane, moral, noble, righteous, saintly, virtuous

villainy *n* **1-3** = **wickedness**, atrocity, baseness, crime, criminality, delinquency, depravity, devilry, iniquity, knavery, rascality, sin, turpitude, vice

vindicate *vb* **1** = **clear**, absolve, acquit, exculpate, exonerate, free from blame, rehabilitate **2** = **justify**, defend, excuse **3** = **support**, advocate, assert, establish, maintain, uphold
Antonyms *vb* ≠ **clear:** accuse, blame, condemn, convict, incriminate, punish, reproach

vindication *n* **1** = **exoneration**, exculpating, exculpation **2** = **justification**, apology, defence, excuse

vindictive *adj* **1, 2** = **vengeful**, full of spleen, implacable, malicious, malignant, rancorous, relentless, resentful, revengeful, spiteful, unforgiving, unrelenting, venomous

vino ('viːnəʊ) *n, pl* **vinos.** an informal word for **wine.** [jocular use of It. or Sp. *vino*]

vin ordinaire *French.* (vɛ̃n ɔrdinɛr) *n, pl* ***vins ordinaires*** (vɛ̃z ɔrdinɛr). cheap table wine, esp. French.

vinosity (vɪ'nɒsɪtɪ) *n* the distinctive and essential quality and flavour of wine. [C17: from LL *vīnōsitas,* from L *vīnōsus* VINOUS]

vinous ('vaɪnəs) *adj* **1** of or characteristic of wine. **2** indulging in or indicative of indulgence in wine. [C17: from L, from *vīnum* WINE]

vintage ❶ ('vɪntɪdʒ) *n* **1** the wine obtained from a harvest of grapes, esp. in an outstandingly good year. **2** the harvest from which such a wine is obtained. **3a** the harvesting of wine grapes. **3b** the season of harvesting these grapes or for making wine. **4** a time of origin: *a car of Edwardian vintage.* **5** *Inf.* a group of people or objects of the same period: *a fashion of last season's vintage.* ◆ *adj* **6** (of wine) of an outstandingly good year. **7** representative of the best and most typical: *vintage Shakespeare.* **8** of lasting interest and importance; classic: *vintage films.* **9** old-fashioned; dated. [C15: from OF *vendage* (infl. by *vintener* VINTNER), from L *vindēmia,* from *vīnum* WINE, grape + *dēmere* to take away]

vintage car *n Chiefly Brit.* an old car, esp. one constructed between 1919 and 1930. Cf. **classic car, veteran car.**

vintager ('vɪntɪdʒə) *n* a grape harvester.

vintner ('vɪntnə) *n* a wine merchant. [C15: from OF *vinetier,* from Med. L, from L *vīnētum* vineyard]

vinyl ('vaɪnɪl) *n* **1** (*modifier*) of or containing the monovalent group of atoms CH_2:CH–: *vinyl chloride.* **2** (*modifier*) of or made of a vinyl resin: *a vinyl raincoat.* **3** any vinyl resin or plastic, esp. PVC. **4** (collectively) conventional records made of vinyl as opposed to compact discs. [C19: from VINI- + -YL]

vinyl acetate *n* a colourless volatile liquid unsaturated ester that polymerizes readily in light and is used for making polyvinyl acetate.

vinyl chloride *n* a colourless flammable gaseous unsaturated compound made by the chlorination of ethylene and used as a refrigerant and in the manufacture of PVC.

vinyl resin *or* **polymer** *n* any one of a class of thermoplastic materials, esp. PVC and polyvinyl acetate, made by polymerizing vinyl compounds.

viol ('vaɪəl) *n* any of a family of stringed musical instruments that preceded the violin family, consisting of a fretted fingerboard, a body like that of a violin but having a flat back and six strings, played with a curved bow. [C15: from OF *viole,* from OProvençal *viola;* see VIOLA[1]]

viola[1] (vɪ'əʊlə) *n* **1** a bowed stringed instrument, the alto of the violin family; held beneath the chin when played. **2** any of various instruments of the viol family, such as the viola da gamba. [C18: from It., prob. from O Provençal]

viola[2] ('vaɪələ, vaɪ'əʊ-) *n* any of various temperate perennial herbaceous plants, the flowers of which have showy irregular petals, white, yellow, blue, or mauve in colour. [C15: from L: violet]

viola clef (vɪ'əʊlə) *n* another term for **alto clef.**

viola da gamba (vɪ'əʊlə də 'gæmbə) *n* the second largest and lowest member of the viol family. [C18: from It., lit.: viol for the leg]

viola d'amore (vɪ'əʊlə dæ'mɔːrɪ) *n* an instrument of the viol family having no frets, seven strings, and a set of sympathetic strings. [C18: from It., lit.: viol of love]

violate ❶ ('vaɪə,leɪt) *vb* **violates, violating, violated.** (*tr*) **1** to break, disregard, or infringe (a law, agreement, etc.). **2** to rape or otherwise sexually assault. **3** to disturb rudely or improperly. **4** to treat irreverently or disrespectfully: *he violated a sanctuary.* [C15: from L *violāre* to do violence to, from *vīs* strength]
▸**'violable** *adj* ▸**,vio'lation** *n* ▸**'vio,lator** *or* **'vio,later** *n*

violence ❶ ('vaɪələns) *n* **1** the exercise or an instance of physical force, usually effecting or intended to effect injuries, destruction, etc. **2** powerful, untamed, or devastating force: *the violence of the sea.* **3** great strength of feeling, as in language, etc. **4** an unjust, unwarranted, or unlawful display of force. **5 do violence to. 5a** to inflict harm upon: *they did violence to the prisoners.* **5b** to distort the sense or intention of: *the reporters did violence to my speech.* [C13: via OF from L *violentia* impetuosity, from *violentus* VIOLENT]

violent ❶ ('vaɪələnt) *adj* **1** marked or caused by great physical force or violence: *a violent stab.* **2** (of a person) tending to the use of violence, esp. in order to injure or intimidate others. **3** marked by intensity of any kind: *a violent clash of colours.* **4** characterized by an undue use of force. **5** caused by or displaying strong or undue mental or emotional force. [C14: from L *violentus,* prob. from *vīs* strength]
▸**'violently** *adv*

violent storm *n* a wind of force 11 on the Beaufort scale, reaching speeds of 64 to 72 mph.

violet ('vaɪəlɪt) *n* **1** any of various temperate perennial herbaceous plants of the genus *Viola,* such as the **sweet** (or **garden**) **violet,** having mauve or bluish flowers with irregular showy petals. **2** any other plant of the genus *Viola,* such as the wild pansy. **3** any of various similar but unrelated plants, such as the African violet. **4a** any of a group of colours that have a purplish-blue hue. They lie at one end of the visible spectrum. **4b** (*as adj*): *a violet dress.* **5** a dye or pigment of or producing these colours. **6** violet clothing: *dressed in violet.* [C14: from OF *violete* a little violet, from L *viola* violet]

violin (,vaɪə'lɪn) *n* a bowed stringed instrument, the highest member of the violin family, consisting of a fingerboard, a hollow wooden body with waisted sides, and a sounding board connected to the back by means of a soundpost that also supports the bridge. It has two f-shaped sound holes cut in the belly. [C16: from It. *violino* a little viola, from VIOLA[1]]

violinist (,vaɪə'lɪnɪst) *n* a person who plays the violin.

violist[1] (vɪ'əʊlɪst) *n* a person who plays the viola.

violist[2] ('vaɪəlɪst) *n* a person who plays the viol.

violoncello (,vaɪələn'tʃɛləʊ) *n, pl* **violoncellos.** the full name for **cello.** [C18: from It., from *violone* large viol + *-cello,* dim. suffix]
▸**,violon'cellist** *n*

VIP ❶ *abbrev. for* very important person.

viper ('vaɪpə) *n* **1** any of a family of venomous Old World snakes having hollow fangs in the upper jaw that are used to inject venom. **2** any of various other snakes, such as the horned viper. **3** a malicious or treacherous person. [C16: from L *vīpera,* ?from *vīvus* living + *parere* to bear, referring to a tradition that the viper was viviparous]

viperous ('vaɪpərəs) *or* **viperish** *adj* **1** Also: **viperine** ('vaɪpə,raɪn). of or resembling a viper. **2** malicious.

viper's bugloss *n* **1** Also called (US): **blueweed.** a Eurasian weed, having blue flowers and pink buds. **2** a related plant that has purple flowers and is naturalized in Australia and New Zealand. Also called: (Austral.) **Paterson's curse, Salvation Jane.**

virago ❶ (vɪ'rɑːgəʊ) *n, pl* **viragoes** *or* **viragos. 1** a loud, violent, and ill-tempered woman. **2** *Arch.* a strong or warlike woman. [OE, from L: a manlike maiden, from *vir* a man]
▸**vi'rago-,like** *adj*

viral ('vaɪrəl) *adj* of or caused by a virus.

virelay ('vɪrɪ,leɪ) *n* an old French verse form, rarely used in English, having stanzas of short lines with two rhymes throughout and two opening lines recurring at intervals. [C14: from OF *virelai,* prob. from *vireli* (associated with *lai* LAY[4]), word used as a refrain]

vireo ('vɪrɪəʊ) *n, pl* **vireos.** any of a family of insectivorous American songbirds having an olive-grey back with pale underparts. [C19: from L: a bird, prob. a greenfinch; cf. *virēre* to be green]

vires ('vaɪriːz) *n* the plural of ***vis.***

virescent (vɪ'rɛsᵊnt) *adj* greenish or becoming green. [C19: from L *virescere,* from *virēre* to be green]
▸**vi'rescence** *n*

virgate[1] ('vɜːgɪt, -geɪt) *adj* long, straight, and thin; rod-shaped: *virgate stems.* [C19: from L *virgātus* made of twigs, from *virga* a rod]

virgate[2] ('vɜːgɪt, -geɪt) *n Brit.* an obsolete measure of land area, usually taken as 30 acres. [C17: from Med. L *virgāta* (*terrae*) a rod's measurement (of land), from L *virga* rod; translation of OE *gierd landes* a yard of land]

Virgilian *or* **Vergilian** (vɜː'dʒɪlɪən) *adj* of, relating to, or characteristic of Virgil (70–19 B.C.), Roman poet, or his style.

virgin ❶ ('vɜːdʒɪn) *n* **1** a person, esp. a woman, who has never had sexual intercourse. **2** an unmarried woman who has taken a religious vow of chastity. **3** any female animal that has never mated. **4** a female insect that produces offspring by parthenogenesis. ◆ *adj* (*usually prenominal*) **5** of, suitable for, or characteristic of a virgin or virgins. **6**

THESAURUS

Antonyms *adj* forgiving, generous, magnanimous, merciful, relenting, unvindictive

vintage *n* **2** = **harvest,** crop **4** = **era,** epoch, generation, time of origin, year ◆ *adj* **6-8** = **best,** choice, classic, mature, prime, rare, ripe, select, superior

violate *vb* **1** = **break,** contravene, disobey, disregard, encroach upon, infract, infringe, transgress **2** = **rape,** abuse, assault, debauch, ravish **4** = **desecrate,** abuse, befoul, defile, dishonour, invade, outrage, pollute, profane
Antonyms *vb* ≠ **break:** honour, obey, respect, uphold ≠ **desecrate:** defend, honour, protect, respect, revere, set on a pedestal

violation *n* **1** = **infringement,** abuse, breach, contravention, encroachment, infraction, transgression, trespass **4** = **desecration,** defilement, profanation, sacrilege, spoliation

violence *n* **1** = **force,** bestiality, bloodshed, bloodthirstiness, brutality, brute force, cruelty, destructiveness, ferocity, fierceness, fighting, frenzy, fury, murderousness, passion, rough handling, savagery, strong-arm tactics (*inf.*), terrorism, thuggery, vehemence, wildness **2** = **power,** boisterousness, raging, roughness, storminess, tumult, turbulence, wildness **3** = **intensity,** abandon, acuteness, fervour, force, harshness, severity, sharpness, vehemence

violent *adj* **1, 2** = **destructive,** berserk, bloodthirsty, brutal, cruel, fiery, flaming, forcible, furious, headstrong, homicidal, hot-headed, impetuous, intemperate, maddened, maniacal, murderous, passionate, powerful, raging, riotous, rough, savage, strong, tempestuous, uncontrollable, ungovernable, unrestrained, vehement, vicious, wild **3** = **intense,** acute, agonizing, biting, excruciating, extreme, harsh, inordinate, outrageous, painful, severe, sharp **4** = **powerful,** blustery, boisterous, devastating, full of force, gale force, raging, ruinous, storming, strong, tempestuous, tumultuous, turbulent, wild
Antonyms *adj* ≠ **destructive:** calm, composed, gentle, mild, peaceful, placid, quiet, rational, sane, serene, unruffled, well-behaved ≠ **powerful:** calm, gentle, mild, placid, serene

VIP *n* = **celebrity,** big hitter (*inf.*), big name, big noise (*inf.*), big shot, bigwig (*inf.*), heavy hitter (*inf.*), leading light (*inf.*), lion, luminary, notable, personage, public figure, somebody, star

virago *n* **1** = **harridan,** ballbreaker (*sl.*), battleaxe (*inf.*), fury, scold, shrew, termagant (*rare*), vixen, Xanthippe

virgin *n* **1, 2** = **maiden** (*arch.*), damsel (*arch.*), girl, maid (*arch.*), vestal, virgo intacta ◆ *adj* **6** = **pure,** chaste, immaculate, maidenly, modest, uncorrupted, undefiled, unsullied, vestal, virginal **7** = **fresh,** new, pristine, unsullied, untouched, unused
Antonyms *adj* ≠ **pure:** corrupted, defiled, impure ≠

pure and natural, uncorrupted or untouched: *virgin purity*. **7** not yet cultivated, explored, exploited, etc., by man: *virgin territories*. **8** being the first or happening for the first time. **9** (of a metal) made from an ore rather than from scrap. **10** occurring naturally in a pure and uncombined form: *virgin silver*. [C13: from OF *virgine*, from L *virgō* virgin]

Virgin[1] ('vɜːdʒɪn) *n* **1 the.** See **Virgin Mary. 2** a statue or other artistic representation of the Virgin Mary.

Virgin[2] ('vɜːdʒɪn) *n* **the.** the constellation Virgo, the sixth sign of the zodiac.

virginal[1] ⓣ ('vɜːdʒɪnᵊl) *adj* **1** of, characterized by, or maintaining a state of virginity; chaste. **2** extremely pure or fresh. [C15: from L *virginālis* maidenly, from *virgō* virgin]

▸ **'virginally** *adv*

virginal[2] ('vɜːdʒɪnᵊl) *n* (*often pl*) a smaller version of the harpsichord, but oblong in shape, having one manual and no pedals. [C16: prob. from L *virginālis* VIRGINAL[1], ? because it was played largely by young ladies]

▸ **'virginalist** *n*

Virgin Birth *n* the doctrine that Jesus Christ was conceived by the intervention of the Holy Spirit so that Mary remained a virgin.

virgin forest *n* a forest in its natural state, before it has been explored or exploited by man.

Virginia creeper (və'dʒɪnɪə) *n* a woody vine of North America, having tendrils with adhesive tips, bluish-black berry-like fruits, and compound leaves that turn red in autumn: widely planted for ornament.

Virginia stock *n* a Mediterranean plant cultivated for its white and pink flowers.

virginity ⓣ (və'dʒɪnɪtɪ) *n* **1** the condition or fact of being a virgin. **2** the condition of being untouched, unused, etc.

virginium (və'dʒɪnɪəm) *n Chem.* a former name for **francium.**

Virgin Mary *n* Mary, the mother of Christ. Also called: the **Virgin.**

virgin's-bower *n* any of several American varieties of clematis.

virgin soil *n* **1** soil that has not been cultivated before. **2** a person or thing that is as yet undeveloped.

virgin wool *n* wool that is being processed or woven for the first time.

Virgo ('vɜːgəʊ) *n, Latin genitive* **Virginis** ('vɜːdʒɪnɪs). **1** *Astron.* a large constellation on the celestial equator. **2** *Astrol.* Also called: **the Virgin.** the sixth sign of the zodiac. The sun is in this sign between about Aug. 23 and Sept. 22. [C14: from L]

virgo intacta ('vɜːgəʊ ɪn'tæktə) *n* a girl or woman whose hymen is unbroken. [L, lit.: untouched virgin]

virgule ('vɜːgjuːl) *n Printing.* another name for **solidus.** [C19: from F: comma, from L *virgula* dim. of *virga* rod]

viridescent (ˌvɪrɪ'desᵊnt) *adj* greenish or tending to become green. [C19: from LL *viridescere*, from L *viridis* green]

▸ **ˌviri'descence** *n*

viridian (vɪ'rɪdɪən) *n* a green pigment comprising a hydrated form of chromic oxide. [C19: from L *viridis* green]

viridity (vɪ'rɪdɪtɪ) *n* **1** the quality or state of being green. **2** innocence, youth, or freshness. [C15: from L *viriditās*, from *viridis* green]

virile ⓣ ('vɪraɪl) *adj* **1** of or having the characteristics of an adult male. **2** (of a male) possessing high sexual drive and capacity for sexual intercourse. **3** of or capable of copulation or procreation. **4** strong, forceful, or vigorous. [C15: from L *virīlis* manly, from *vir* a man; rel. to OE *wer* man]

▸ **virility** (vɪ'rɪlɪtɪ) *n*

virilism ('vɪrɪˌlɪzəm) *n Med.* the abnormal development in a woman of male secondary sex characteristics.

virology (vaɪ'rɒlədʒɪ) *n* the branch of medicine concerned with the study of viruses.

▸ **virological** (ˌvaɪrə'lɒdʒɪkᵊl) *adj*

virtu *or* **vertu** (vɜː'tuː) *n* **1** a taste or love for curios or works of fine art. **2** such objects collectively. **3** the quality of being appealing to a connoisseur (esp. in **articles of virtu; objects of virtu**). [C18: from It. *virtù*; see VIRTUE]

virtual ⓣ ('vɜːtʃʊəl) *adj* **1** having the essence or effect but not the appearance or form of: *a virtual revolution*. **2** *Physics.* being or involving a virtual image: *a virtual focus*. **3** *Computing.* of or relating to virtual storage: *virtual memory*. **4** of or relating to a computer technique by which a person, wearing a headset or mask, has the experience of being in an environment created by the computer, and of interacting with and causing changes within it. [C14: from Med. L *virtuālis* effective, from L *virtūs* VIRTUE]

▸ **ˌvirtu'ality** *n*

virtual image *n* an optical image formed by the apparent divergence of rays from a point, rather than their actual divergence from a point.

virtually ⓣ ('vɜːtʃʊəlɪ) *adv* in effect though not in fact; practically; nearly.

virtual reality *n* a computer-generated environment that, to the person experiencing it, closely resembles reality. Abbrev.: **VR.** See also **virtual** (sense 4).

virtual storage *or* **memory** *n* a computer system in which the size of the memory is increased by transferring sections of a program from a large capacity backing store, such as a disk, into the smaller core memory as they are required.

virtue ⓣ ('vɜːtjuː) *n* **1** the quality or practice of moral excellence or righteousness. **2** a particular moral excellence: *the virtue of tolerance*. **3** any of the cardinal virtues (prudence, justice, fortitude, and temperance) or theological virtues (faith, hope, and charity). **4** any admirable quality or trait. **5** chastity, esp. in women. **6** *Arch.* an effective, active, or inherent power. **7 by** *or* **in virtue of.** by reason of. **8 make a virtue of necessity.** to acquiesce in doing something unpleasant with a show of grace because one must do it in any case. [C13 *vertu*, from OF, from L *virtūs* manliness, courage]

virtuoso ⓣ (ˌvɜːtjʊ'əʊzəʊ, -səʊ) *n, pl* **virtuosos** *or* **virtuosi** (-siː). **1** a consummate master of musical technique and artistry. **2** a person who has a masterly or dazzling skill or technique in any field of activity. **3** a connoisseur or collector of art objects. **4** (*modifier*) showing masterly skill or brilliance: *a virtuoso performance*. [C17: from It.: skilled, from LL *virtuōsus* good, virtuous]

▸ **virtuosic** (ˌvɜːtjʊ'ɒsɪk) *adj* ▸ **ˌvirtu'osity** *n*

virtuous ⓣ ('vɜːtʃʊəs) *adj* **1** characterized by or possessing virtue or moral excellence. **2** (of women) chaste.

▸ **'virtuously** *adv*

virulent ⓣ ('vɪrʊlənt) *adj* **1a** (of a microorganism) extremely infective. **1b** (of a disease) having a violent effect. **2** extremely poisonous, injurious, etc. **3** extremely bitter, hostile, etc. [C14: from L *vīrulentus* full of poison, from *vīrus* poison]

▸ **'virulence** *or* **'virulency** *n* ▸ **'virulently** *adv*

virus ('vaɪrəs) *n, pl* **viruses. 1** any of a group of submicroscopic entities consisting of a single nucleic acid surrounded by a protein coat and capable of replication only within the cells of animals and plants. **2** *Inf.* a disease caused by a virus. **3** any corrupting or infecting influence. **4** *Computing.* an unauthorized program that inserts itself into a computer system, and then propagates itself to other computers via networks or disks; when activated it interferes with the operation of the computer. [C16: from L: slime, poisonous liquid]

vis *Latin.* (vɪs) *n, pl* **vires.** power, force, or strength.

visa ('viːzə) *n, pl* **visas. 1** an endorsement in a passport or similar document, signifying that the document is in order and permitting its bearer to travel into or through the country of the government issuing it. ◆ *vb* **visas, visaing, visaed. 2** (*tr*) to enter a visa into (a passport). [C19: via F from L: things seen, from *vīsus*, p.p. of *vidēre* to see]

visage ('vɪzɪdʒ) *n Chiefly literary.* **1** face or countenance. **2** appearance. [C13: from OF: aspect, from *vis* face, from L *vīsus* appearance]

-visaged *adj* (*in combination*) having a visage as specified: *flat-visaged*.

vis-à-vis (ˌviːzɑː'viː) *prep* **1** in relation to. **2** face to face with. ◆ *adv, adj* **3**

THESAURUS

fresh: contaminated, dirty, impure, polluted, spoiled, used

virginal[1] *adj* **1 = pure,** celibate, chaste, immaculate, maidenly, uncorrupted, undefiled, virgin **2 = fresh,** immaculate, pristine, pure, snowy, spotless, undisturbed, untouched, white

virginity *n* **1 = chastity,** maidenhead, maidenhood

virile *adj* **1-4 = manly,** forceful, lusty, macho, male, manlike, masculine, potent, red-blooded, robust, strong, vigorous

Antonyms *adj* camp (*inf.*), effeminate, emasculate, feminine, girlie, impotent, unmanly, weak, weedy (*inf.*), wimpish *or* wimpy (*inf.*)

virility *n* **1-4 = masculinity,** machismo, manhood, potency, vigour

Antonyms *n* effeminacy, femininity, impotence, softness, unmanliness, weakness

virtual *adj* **1 = practical,** essential, implicit, implied, in all but name, indirect, tacit, unacknowledged

virtually *adv* **= practically,** almost, as good as, effectually, for all practical purposes, in all but name, in effect, in essence, nearly, to all intents and purposes

virtue *n* **1 = goodness,** ethicalness, excellence, high-mindedness, incorruptibility, integrity, justice, morality, probity, quality, rectitude, righteousness, uprightness, worth, worthiness **4 = merit,** advantage, asset, attribute, credit, good point, good quality, plus (*inf.*), strength **5 = chastity,** honour, innocence, purity, virginity **7 by virtue of = because of,** as a result of, by dint of, by reason of, in view of, on account of, owing to, thanks to

Antonyms *n* ≠ **goodness:** corruption, debauchery, depravity, dishonesty, dishonour, evil, immorality, sin, sinfulness, turpitude, vice ≠ **merit:** drawback, failing, frailty, shortcoming, weak point ≠ **chastity:** promiscuity, unchastity

virtuosity *n* **2 = mastery,** brilliance, craft, éclat, expertise, finish, flair, panache, polish, skill

virtuoso *n* **1, 2 = master,** artist, genius, grandmaster, maestro, magician, master hand, maven (*US*) ◆ *modifier* **4 = masterly,** bravura (*Music*), brilliant, dazzling

virtuous *adj* **1 = good,** blameless, ethical, excellent, exemplary, high-principled, honest, honourable, incorruptible, just, moral, praiseworthy, pure, righteous, squeaky-clean, upright, worthy **2 = chaste,** celibate, clean-living, innocent, pure, spotless, virginal

Antonyms *adj* ≠ **good:** corrupt, debauched, depraved, dishonest, evil, immoral, sinful, unrighteous, vicious, wicked ≠ **chaste:** impure, loose, promiscuous, unchaste

virulence *n* **1, 2 = deadliness,** harmfulness, hurtfulness, infectiousness, injuriousness, malignancy, noxiousness, poisonousness, toxicity, virulency **3 = bitterness,** acrimony, antagonism, hatred, hostility, ill will, malevolence, malice, poison, pungency, rancour, resentment, spite, spleen, venom, viciousness, vindictiveness

virulent *adj* **1, 2 = deadly,** baneful (*arch.*), infective, injurious, lethal, malignant, pernicious, poisonous, septic, toxic, venomous **3 = bitter,** acrimonious, envenomed, hostile, malevolent, malicious, rancorous, resentful, spiteful, splenetic, venomous, vicious, vindictive

Antonyms *adj* ≠ **deadly:** harmless, innocuous, nonpoisonous, nontoxic ≠ **bitter:** amiable, benign, compassionate, kind, magnanimous, sympathetic, warm

face to face; opposite. ◆ *n, pl* **vis-à-vis. 4** a person or thing that is situated opposite to another. **5** a person who corresponds to another in office, capacity, etc. [C18: F, from *vis* face]

Visc. *abbrev. for* Viscount *or* Viscountess.

viscacha (vɪsˈkætʃə) *n* a gregarious burrowing rodent of southern South America, similar to but larger than the chinchillas. [C17: from Sp., from Quechuan *wiskácha*]

viscera (ˈvɪsərə) *pl n, sing* **viscus. 1** *Anat.* the large internal organs of the body collectively, esp. those in the abdominal cavity. **2** (less formally) the intestines; guts. [C17: from L: entrails, pl of *viscus* internal organ]

visceral (ˈvɪsərəl) *adj* **1** of or affecting the viscera. **2** characterized by instinct rather than intellect.
▸ **ˈviscerally** *adv*

viscid (ˈvɪsɪd) *adj* **1** cohesive and sticky. **2** (esp. of a leaf) covered with a sticky substance. [C17: from LL *viscidus* sticky, from L *viscum* mistletoe, birdlime]
▸ **visˈcidity** *n*

viscose (ˈvɪskəʊs) *n* **1a** a viscous orange-brown solution obtained by dissolving cellulose in sodium hydroxide and carbon disulphide. It can be converted back to cellulose by an acid, as in the manufacture of rayon and Cellophane. **1b** (*as modifier*): *viscose rayon.* **2** rayon made from this material. [C19: from LL *viscōsus* full of birdlime, sticky, from *viscum* birdlime]

viscosity (vɪsˈkɒsɪtɪ) *n, pl* **viscosities. 1** the state or property of being viscous. **2** *Physics.* **2a** the extent to which a fluid resists a tendency to flow. **2b** Also called: **absolute viscosity.** a measure of this resistance, measured in newton seconds per metre squared. Symbol: η

viscount (ˈvaɪkaʊnt) *n* **1** (in the British Isles) a nobleman ranking below an earl and above a baron. **2** (in various countries) a son or younger brother of a count. **3** (in medieval Europe) the deputy of a count. [C14: from OF, from Med. L, from LL *vice-* VICE[3] + *comes* COUNT[2]]
▸ **ˈviscountcy** *or* **ˈviscounty** *n*

viscountess (ˈvaɪkaʊntɪs) *n* **1** the wife or widow of a viscount. **2** a woman who holds the rank of viscount in her own right.

viscous ⓣ (ˈvɪskəs) *adj* **1** (of liquids) thick and sticky. **2** having viscosity. [C14: from LL *viscōsus;* see VISCOSE]
▸ **ˈviscously** *adv*

viscus (ˈvɪskəs) *n* the singular of **viscera.**

vise (vaɪs) *n, vb* **vises, vising, vised.** *US.* a variant spelling of **vice**[2].

Vishnu (ˈvɪʃnuː) *n Hinduism.* the Pervader or Sustainer, originally a solar deity occupying a secondary place in the Hindu pantheon, later the saviour appearing in many incarnations. [C17: from Sansk. *Viṣṇu,* lit.: the one who works everywhere]
▸ **ˈVishnuism** *n*

visibility (ˌvɪzɪˈbɪlɪtɪ) *n* **1** the condition or fact of being visible. **2** clarity of vision or relative possibility of seeing. **3** the range of vision: *visibility is 500 yards.*

visible ⓣ (ˈvɪzɪbəl) *adj* **1** capable of being perceived by the eye. **2** capable of being perceived by the mind: *no visible dangers.* **3** available: *the visible resources.* **4** of or relating to the balance of trade: *visible transactions.* [C14: from L *vīsibilis,* from *vidēre* to see]
▸ **ˈvisibly** *adv*

visible balance *n* another name for **balance of trade.**

visible radiation *n* electromagnetic radiation that causes the sensation of sight; light.

vision ⓣ (ˈvɪʒən) *n* **1** the act, faculty, or manner of perceiving with the eye; sight. **2a** the image on a television screen. **2b** (*as modifier*): *vision control.* **3** the ability or an instance of great perception, esp. of future developments: *a man of vision.* **4** mystical or religious experience of seeing some supernatural event, person, etc.: *the vision of St John of the Cross.* **5** that which is seen, esp. in such a mystical experience. **6** (*sometimes pl*) a vivid mental image produced by the imagination: *he had visions of becoming famous.* **7** a person or thing of extraordinary beauty. [C13: from L *vīsiō* sight, from *vidēre* to see]

visionary ⓣ (ˈvɪʒənərɪ) *adj* **1** marked by vision or foresight: *a visionary leader.* **2** incapable of being realized or effected. **3** (of people) characterized by idealistic or radical ideas, esp. impractical ones. **4** given to having visions. **5** of, of the nature of, or seen in visions. ◆ *n, pl* **visionaries. 6** a visionary person.

vision mixer *n Television.* **1** the person who selects and manipulates the television signals from cameras, film, etc., to make the composite programme. **2** the equipment used for vision mixing.

visit ⓣ (ˈvɪzɪt) *vb* **visits, visiting, visited. 1** to go or come to see (a person, place, etc.). **2** to stay with (someone) as a guest. **3** to go or come to (an institution, place, etc.) for the purpose of inspecting or examining. **4** (*tr*) (of a disease, disaster, etc.) to afflict. **5** (*tr;* foll. by *upon* or *on*) to inflict (punishment, etc.). **6** (often foll. by *with*) *US & Canad. inf.* to chat (with someone). ◆ *n* **7** the act or an instance of visiting. **8** a stay as a guest. **9** a professional or official call. **10** a formal call for the purpose of inspection or examination. **11** *International law.* the right of an officer of a belligerent state to stop and search neutral ships in war to verify their nationality and ascertain whether they carry contraband. **12** *US & Canad. inf.* a chat. [C13: from L *vīsitāre* to go to see, from *vīsere* to examine, from *vidēre* to see]
▸ **ˈvisitable** *adj*

visitant (ˈvɪzɪtənt) *n* **1** a ghost; apparition. **2** a visitor or guest, usually from far away. **3** Also called: **visitor.** a migratory bird that is present in a particular region only at certain times: *a summer visitant.* [C16: from L *vīsitāns,* from *vīsitāre;* see VISIT]

visitation ⓣ (ˌvɪzɪˈteɪʃən) *n* **1** an official call or visit for the purpose of inspecting or examining an institution. **2** a visiting of punishment or reward from heaven. **3** any disaster or catastrophe: *a visitation of the plague.* **4** an appearance or arrival of a supernatural being. **5** *Inf.* an unduly prolonged social call.

Visitation (ˌvɪzɪˈteɪʃən) *n* **1a** the visit made by the Virgin Mary to her cousin Elizabeth (Luke 1:39–56). **1b** the Church festival commemorating this, held on July 2. **2** a religious order of nuns, the **Order of the Visitation,** founded in 1610 and dedicated to contemplation.

visiting card *n Brit.* a small card bearing the name and usually the address of a person, esp. for giving to business or social acquaintances.

visiting fireman *n US inf.* a visitor whose presence is noticed because he is important, impressive, etc.

visitor ⓣ (ˈvɪzɪtə) *n* **1** a person who pays a visit. **2** another name for **visitant** (sense 3).

visitor centre *n* another term for **interpretive centre.**

visitor's passport *n* (in Britain) a passport, valid for one year, that can be purchased from post offices. It grants entry to certain countries, usually for a restricted period of time. Also called: **British Visitor's Passport.**

visor *or* **vizor** (ˈvaɪzə) *n* **1** a transparent flap on a helmet that can be pulled down to protect the face. **2** a piece of armour fixed or hinged to the helmet to protect the face. **3** another name for **peak** (on a cap). **4** a small movable screen used as protection against glare from the sun, esp. one attached above the windscreen of a motor vehicle. **5** *Arch. or literary.* a mask or any other means of disguise. [C14: from Anglo-F *viser,* from OF *visiere,* from *vis* face; see VISAGE]
▸ **ˈvisored** *or* **ˈvizored** *adj*

vista ⓣ (ˈvɪstə) *n* **1** a view, esp. through a long narrow avenue of trees, buildings, etc., or such a passage or avenue itself. **2** a comprehensive mental view of a distant time or a lengthy series of events. [C17: from It., from *vedere* to see, from L *vidēre*]
▸ **ˈvistaed** *adj*

visual ⓣ (ˈvɪʒʊəl, -zjʊ-) *adj* **1** of, done by, or used in seeing: *visual powers.* **2** another word for **optical. 3** capable of being seen; visible. **4** of, occurring as, or induced by a mental image. ◆ *n* **5** a sketch to show the proposed layout of an advertisement, as in a newspaper. **6** (*often pl*) a photograph, film, or other display material. [C15: from LL *vīsuālis,* from L *vīsus* sight, from *vidēre* to see]
▸ **ˈvisually** *adv*

visual aids *pl n* devices, such as films, videos, slides, models, and blackboards, that display in visual form material to be understood or remembered.

visual display unit *n Computing.* a device that displays characters or graphics representing data in a computer memory. It usually has a keyboard for the input of information or inquiries. Abbrev.: **VDU.**

THESAURUS

viscous *adj* **1** = **thick**, adhesive, clammy, gelatinous, gluey, glutinous, gooey (*inf.*), gummy, mucilaginous, sticky, syrupy, tenacious, treacly, viscid

visible *adj* **1** = **apparent**, anywhere to be seen, bold, clear, conspicuous, detectable, discernible, discoverable, distinguishable, evident, in sight, in view, manifest, not hidden, noticeable, observable, obvious, palpable, patent, perceivable, perceptible, plain, salient, to be seen, unconcealed, unmistakable
Antonyms *adj* concealed, hidden, imperceptible, invisible, obscured, unnoticeable, unseen

vision *n* **1** = **sight**, eyes, eyesight, perception, seeing, view **3** = **foresight**, breadth of view, discernment, farsightedness, imagination, insight, intuition, penetration, prescience **4, 5** = **hallucination**, apparition, chimera, delusion, eidolon, ghost, illusion, mirage, phantasm, phantom, revelation, spectre, wraith **6** *sometimes plural* = **image**, castle in the air, concept, conception, daydream, dream, fantasy, idea, ideal, imago (*Psychoanalysis*), mental picture, pipe dream **7** = **picture**, dream, feast for the eyes, perfect picture, sight, sight for sore eyes, spectacle

visionary *adj* **3** = **idealistic**, dreaming, dreamy, impractical, quixotic, romantic, speculative, starry-eyed, unrealistic, unworkable, utopian, with one's head in the clouds **5** = **imaginary**, chimerical, delusory, fanciful, fantastic, ideal, idealized, illusory, imaginal (*Psychoanal.*), unreal **5** = **prophetic**, mystical ◆ *n* **6** = **idealist**, daydreamer, Don Quixote, dreamer, romantic, theorist, utopian, zealot **6** = **prophet**, mystic, seer
Antonyms *adj* ≠ **idealistic:** pragmatic, realistic ≠ **imaginary:** actual, mundane, real, unimaginary ◆ *n* ≠ **idealist:** cynic, pessimist, pragmatist, realist

visit *vb* **1, 2** = **call on**, be the guest of, call in, drop in on (*inf.*), go to see, inspect, look (someone) up, pay a call on, pop in (*inf.*), stay at, stay with, stop by, take in (*inf.*) **4** = **afflict**, assail, attack, befall, descend upon, haunt, smite, trouble **5** *foll. by* **on** *or* **upon** = **inflict**, bring down upon, execute, impose, wreak ◆ *n* **7, 8** = **call**, sojourn, stay, stop

visitation *n* **1** = **inspection**, examination, visit **2, 3** = **catastrophe**, bane, blight, calamity, cataclysm, disaster, infliction, ordeal, punishment, scourge, trial

visitor *n* **1** = **guest**, caller, company, visitant

vista *n* **1** = **view**, panorama, perspective, prospect

visual *adj* **1, 2** = **optical**, ocular, optic **3** = **observable**, discernible, perceptible, visible
Antonyms *adj* ≠ **observable:** imperceptible, indiscernible, invisible, out of sight, unnoticeable, unperceivable

visual field *n* the whole extent of the image falling on the retina when the eye is fixed on a given point.

visualize ❶ *or* **visualise** ('vɪʒʊəˌlaɪz) *vb* **visualizes, visualizing, visualized** *or* **visualises, visualising, visualised.** to form a mental image of (something incapable of being viewed or not at that moment visible).
▸ **ˌvisualiˈzation** *or* **ˌvisualiˈsation** *n*

visual magnitude *n Astron.* the magnitude of a star as determined by visual observation.

visual purple *n* another name for **rhodopsin.**

visual violet *n* another name for **iodopsin.**

visual yellow *n* another name for **retinene.**

vital ❶ ('vaɪtᵊl) *adj* **1** essential to maintain life: *the lungs perform a vital function.* **2** forceful, energetic, or lively: *a vital person.* **3** of, having, or displaying life: *a vital organism.* **4** indispensable or essential: *books vital to this study.* **5** of great importance: *a vital game.* ◆ *n* **6** *(pl)* the bodily organs, such as the brain, liver, heart, lungs, etc., that are necessary to maintain life. **7** *(pl)* the essential elements of anything. [C14: via OF from L *vītālis*, from *vīta* life]
▸ **ˈvitally** *adv*

vital capacity *n Physiol.* the volume of air that can be exhaled from the lungs after the deepest possible breath has been taken.

vital force *n* (esp. in early biological theory) a hypothetical force, independent of physical and chemical forces, regarded as being the causative factor of the evolution of living organisms.

vitalism ('vaɪtəˌlɪzəm) *n* the philosophical doctrine that the phenomena of life cannot be explained in purely mechanical terms because there is something immaterial which distinguishes living from inanimate matter.
▸ **ˈvitalist** *n, adj* ▸ **ˌvitalˈistic** *adj*

vitality ❶ (vaɪˈtælɪtɪ) *n, pl* **vitalities. 1** physical or mental vigour, energy, etc. **2** the power or ability to continue in existence, live, or grow: *the vitality of a movement.*

vitalize *or* **vitalise** ('vaɪtəˌlaɪz) *vb* **vitalizes, vitalizing, vitalized** *or* **vitalises, vitalising, vitalised.** *(tr)* to make vital, living, or alive.
▸ **ˌvitaliˈzation** *or* **ˌvitaliˈsation** *n*

vital staining *n* the technique of treating living cells and tissues with dyes that do not immediately kill them, facilitating observation under a microscope.

vital statistics *pl n* **1** quantitative data concerning human life or the conditions affecting it, such as the death rate. **2** *Inf.* the measurements of a woman's bust, waist, and hips.

vitamin ('vɪtəmɪn, 'vaɪ-) *n* any of a group of substances that are essential, in small quantities, for the normal functioning of metabolism in the body. They cannot usually be synthesized in the body but they occur naturally in certain foods. [C20: *vit-* from L *vīta* life + *-amin* from AMINE; so named by Casimir *Funk* (1884–1967), US biochemist, who believed the substances to be amines]
▸ **ˌvitaˈminic** *adj*

vitamin A *n* **1** Also called: **vitamin** A_1, **retinol.** a fat-soluble yellow unsaturated alcohol occurring in green and yellow vegetables, butter, egg yolk, and fish-liver oil. It is essential for the prevention of night blindness and the protection of epithelial tissue. **2** Also called: **vitamin** A_2. a vitamin that occurs in the tissues of freshwater fish and has a function similar to that of vitamin A_1.

vitamin B *n, pl* **B vitamins.** any of the vitamins in the vitamin B complex.

vitamin B complex *n* a large group of water-soluble vitamins occurring esp. in liver and yeast: includes thiamine (**vitamin** B_1), riboflavin (**vitamin** B_2), nicotinic acid, pyridoxine (**vitamin** B_6), pantothenic acid, biotin, choline, folic acid, and cyanocobalamin (**vitamin** B_{12}). Sometimes shortened to **B complex.**

vitamin C *n* another name for **ascorbic acid.**

vitamin D *n, pl* **D vitamins.** any of the fat-soluble vitamins, including calciferol (**vitamin** D_2) and cholecalciferol (**vitamin** D_3), occurring in fish-liver oils, milk, butter, and eggs: used in the treatment of rickets.

vitamin E *n* another name for **tocopherol.**

vitamin G *n* another name (esp. US and Canad.) for **riboflavin.**

vitamin H *n* another name (esp. US and Canad.) for **biotin.**

vitamin K *n, pl* **K vitamins.** any of the fat-soluble vitamins, including phylloquinone (**vitamin** K_1) and the menaquinones (**vitamin** K_2), which are essential for the normal clotting of blood.

vitamin P *n, pl* **P vitamins.** any of a group of water-soluble crystalline substances occurring mainly in citrus fruits, blackcurrants, and rosehips: they regulate the permeability of the blood capillaries.

vitellin (vɪˈtɛlɪn) *n Biochem.* a phosphoprotein that is the major protein in egg yolk. [C19: from VITELLUS + -IN]

vitelline membrane (vɪˈtɛlɪn) *n Zool.* a membrane that surrounds a fertilized ovum and prevents the entry of other spermatozoa.

vitellus (vɪˈtɛləs) *n, pl* **vitelluses** *or* **vitelli** (-laɪ). *Zool., rare.* the yolk of an egg. [C18: from L, lit.: little calf, later: yolk of an egg, from *vitulus* calf]

vitiate ('vɪʃɪˌeɪt) *vb* **vitiates, vitiating, vitiated.** *(tr)* **1** to make faulty or imperfect. **2** to debase or corrupt. **3** to destroy the force or legal effect of (a deed, etc.). [C16: from L *vitiāre* to injure, from *vitium* a fault]
▸ **ˌvitiˈation** *n* ▸ **ˈvitiˌator** *n*

viticulture ('vɪtɪˌkʌltʃə) *n* **1** the science, art, or process of cultivating grapevines. **2** the study of grapes and the growing of grapes. [C19: *viti-*, from L *vītis* vine]
▸ **ˌvitiˈculturist** *n*

vitreous ('vɪtrɪəs) *adj* **1** of or resembling glass. **2** made of or containing glass. **3** of or relating to the vitreous humour or vitreous body. [C17: from L *vitreus* made of glass, from *vitrum* glass]
▸ **ˈvitreously** *adv*

vitreous humour *or* **body** *n* a transparent gelatinous substance that fills the interior of the eyeball between the lens and the retina.

vitrescence (vɪˈtrɛsəns) *n* **1** the quality or condition of being or becoming vitreous. **2** the process of producing a glass or turning a crystalline material into glass.
▸ **viˈtrescent** *adj*

vitrify ('vɪtrɪˌfaɪ) *vb* **vitrifies, vitrifying, vitrified.** to convert or be converted into glass or a glassy substance. [C16: from F, from L *vitrum* glass]
▸ **ˈvitriˌfiable** *adj* ▸ **vitrification** (ˌvɪtrɪfɪˈkeɪʃən) *n*

vitrine ('vɪtri:n) *n* a glass display case or cabinet for works of art, curios, etc. [C19: from F, from *vitre* pane of glass, from L *vitrum* glass]

vitriol ('vɪtrɪˌɒl) *n* **1** another name for **sulphuric acid. 2** any one of a number of sulphate salts, such as ferrous sulphate (iron(II) sulphate; **green vitriol**), copper sulphate (**blue vitriol**), or zinc sulphate (**white vitriol**). **3** speech, writing, etc., displaying vituperation or bitterness. [C14: from Med. L *vitriolum*, from LL, from L *vitrum* glass, referring to the glossy appearance of the sulphates]

vitriolic ❶ (ˌvɪtrɪˈɒlɪk) *adj* **1** (of a strong acid) highly corrosive. **2** severely bitter or caustic.

vitriolize *or* **vitriolise** ('vɪtrɪəˌlaɪz) *vb* **vitriolizes, vitriolizing, vitriolized** *or* **vitriolises, vitriolising, vitriolised.** *(tr)* **1** to convert into or treat with vitriol. **2** to injure with vitriol.
▸ **ˌvitrioliˈzation** *or* **ˌvitrioliˈsation** *n*

vittle ('vɪtᵊl) *n, vb* **vittles, vittling, vittled.** an obsolete or dialect spelling of **victual.**

vituperate (vɪˈtju:pəˌreɪt) *vb* **vituperates, vituperating, vituperated.** to berate or rail (against) abusively; revile. [C16: from L *vituperāre* to blame, from *vitium* a defect + *parāre* to make]
▸ **viˌtuperˈation** *n* ▸ **viˈtuperˌator** *n*

viva[1] ('vi:və) *interj* long live; up with (a specified person or thing). [C17: from It., lit.: may (he) live! from *vivere* to live, from L *vīvere*]

viva[2] ('vaɪvə) *Brit.* ◆ *n* **1** an oral examination. ◆ *vb* **vivas, vivaing, vivaed.** *(tr)* **2** to examine orally. [shortened from VIVA VOCE]

vivace (vɪˈvɑ:tʃɪ) *adj, adv Music.* to be performed in a brisk lively manner. [C17: from It., from L *vīvax* vigorous, from *vīvere* to live]

vivacious ❶ (vɪˈveɪʃəs) *adj* full of high spirits and animation. [C17: from L *vīvax* lively; see VIVACE]
▸ **viˈvaciously** *adv* ▸ **viˈvaciousness** *n*

vivacity ❶ (vɪˈvæsɪtɪ) *n, pl* **vivacities.** the quality or condition of being vivacious.

vivarium (vaɪˈvɛərɪəm) *n, pl* **vivariums** *or* **vivaria** (-ɪə). a place where live animals are kept under natural conditions for study, etc. [C16: from L: enclosure where live fish or game are kept, from *vīvus* alive]

viva voce ('vaɪvə 'vəʊtʃɪ) *adv, adj* **1** by word of mouth. ◆ *n, vb* **viva-voce, viva-voces, viva-voceing, viva-voced. 2** the full form of **viva**[2]. [C16: from Med. L, lit.: with living voice]

vive (vi:v) *interj* long live; up with (a specified person or thing). [from F]

vivid ❶ ('vɪvɪd) *adj* **1** (of a colour) very bright; intense. **2** brilliantly coloured: *vivid plumage.* **3** conveying to the mind striking realism, freshness, or trueness to life: *a vivid account.* **4** (of a memory, etc.) remaining distinct in the mind. **5** (of the imagination, etc.) prolific in

THESAURUS

visualize *vb* = **picture**, conceive of, conjure up a mental picture of, envisage, imagine, see in the mind's eye

vital *adj* **1, 3** = **living**, alive, alive and kicking, animate, generative, invigorative, life-giving, live, quickening **2** = **lively**, animated, dynamic, energetic, forceful, full of beans (*inf.*), full of the joy of living, sparky, spirited, vibrant, vigorous, vivacious, zestful **4** = **essential**, basic, cardinal, fundamental, imperative, indispensable, necessary, radical, requisite **5** = **important**, critical, crucial, decisive, key, life-or-death, significant, urgent
Antonyms *adj* ≠ **living:** dead, dying, inanimate, moribund ≠ **lively:** apathetic, lethargic, listless, uninvolved ≠ **essential:** dispensable, inessential, nonessential, unnecessary ≠ **important:** minor, trivial, unimportant

vitality *n* **1** = **energy**, animation, brio, exuberance, go (*inf.*), life, liveliness, lustiness, pep, robustness, sparkle, stamina, strength, vigour, vim (*sl.*), vivaciousness, vivacity
Antonyms *n* apathy, inertia, lethargy, listlessness, sluggishness, weakness

vitriolic *adj* **2** = **bitter**, acerbic, acid, bitchy, caustic, destructive, dripping with malice, envenomed, sardonic, scathing, venomous, virulent, withering

vivacious *adj* = **lively**, animated, bubbling, cheerful, chirpy (*inf.*), ebullient, effervescent, frolicsome, full of beans (*inf.*), full of life, gay, high-spirited, jolly, light-hearted, merry, scintillating, sparkling, sparky, spirited, sportive, sprightly, upbeat (*inf.*), vital
Antonyms *adj* boring, dull, languid, lifeless, listless, melancholy, spiritless, unenthusiastic

vivacity *n* = **liveliness**, animation, brio, ebullience, effervescence, energy, gaiety, high spirits, life, pep, quickness, sparkle, spirit, sprightliness
Antonyms *n* apathy, ennui, fatigue, heaviness, inertia, languor, lethargy, listlessness, weariness

vivid *adj* **1** = **bright**, brilliant, clear, colourful, glowing, highly-coloured, intense, rich **3, 4** = **clear**, distinct, dramatic, graphic, lifelike, memorable, powerful, realistic, sharp, sharply-etched, stirring, strong, telling, true to life **6, 7** = **lively**, active, animated, dynamic, energetic,

the formation of lifelike images. **6** uttered, operating, or acting with vigour. **7** full of life or vitality: *a vivid personality*. [C17: from L *vīvidus* animated, from *vīvere* to live]
▸'**vividly** *adv* ▸'**vividness** *n*

vivify ('vɪvɪˌfaɪ) *vb* **vivifies, vivifying, vivified.** (*tr*) **1** to bring to life; animate. **2** to make more vivid or striking. [C16: from LL *vīvificāre*, from L *vīvus* alive + *facere* to make]
▸ˌ**vivifiˈcation** *n*

viviparous (vɪ'vɪpərəs) *adj* **1** (of most mammals) giving birth to living offspring that develop within the uterus of the mother. **2** (of seeds) germinating before separating from the parent plant. **3** (of plants) producing bulbils or young plants instead of flowers. [C17: from L, from *vīvus* alive + *parere* to bring forth]
▸**viviparity** (ˌvɪvɪ'pærɪtɪ) *or* **vi'viparousness** *n* ▸**vi'viparously** *adv*

vivisect ('vɪvɪˌsɛkt, ˌvɪvɪ'sɛkt) *vb* to subject (an animal) to vivisection. [C19: back formation from VIVISECTION]
▸'**viviˌsector** *n*

vivisection (ˌvɪvɪ'sɛkʃən) *n* the act or practice of performing experiments on living animals, involving cutting into or dissecting the body. [C18: from *vivi-*, from L *vīvus* living + SECTION, as in DISSECTION]
▸ˌ**viviˈsectional** *adj*

vivisectionist (ˌvɪvɪ'sɛkʃənɪst) *n* a person who practises or advocates vivisection as being useful to science.

vivo ('viːvəʊ) *adj, adv Music.* (*in combination*) with life and vigour: *allegro vivo*. [It.: lively]

vixen ❶ ('vɪksən) *n* **1** a female fox. **2** a quarrelsome or spiteful woman. [C15 *fixen*; rel. to OE *fyxe*, fem. of FOX]
▸'**vixenish** *adj* ▸'**vixenly** *adv, adj*

Viyella (vaɪ'ɛlə) *n Trademark.* a soft fabric made of wool and cotton.

viz ❶ *abbrev. for* videlicet.

vizard ('vɪzəd) *n Arch. or literary.* a means of disguise. [C16: var. of VISOR]
▸'**vizarded** *adj*

vizier (vɪ'zɪə) *n* a high official in certain Muslim countries, esp. in the former Ottoman Empire. [C16: from Turkish *vezīr*, from Ar. *wazīr* porter, from *wazara* to bear a burden]
▸**vi'zierate** *n* ▸**vi'zierial** *adj* ▸**vi'ziership** *n*

vizor ('vaɪzə) *n* a variant spelling of **visor.**

vizsla ('vɪʒlə) *n* a breed of Hungarian hunting dog with a smooth rusty-gold coat. [C20: after *Vizsla*, town in Hungary]

VJ *abbrev. for* video jockey.

V-J Day *n* the day marking the Allied victory over Japan in World War II (Aug. 15, 1945).

VL *abbrev. for* Vulgar Latin.

vlei (fleɪ, vleɪ) *n S. African.* an area of low marshy ground, esp. one that feeds a stream. [C19: from Afrik.]

VLF *or* **vlf** *Radio. abbrev. for* very low frequency.

V neck *n* **a** a neck on a garment that comes down to a point, resembling the shape of the letter V. **b** a sweater with such a neck.
▸'**V-ˌneck** *or* '**V-ˌnecked** *adj*

voc. *or* **vocat.** *abbrev. for* vocative.

vocab ('vəʊkæb) *n* short for **vocabulary.**

vocable ('vəʊkəbᵊl) *n* any word, either written or spoken, regarded simply as a sequence of letters or spoken sounds. [C16: from L *vocābulum* a designation, from *vocāre* to call]
▸'**vocably** *adv*

vocabulary ❶ (və'kæbjʊlərɪ) *n, pl* **vocabularies. 1** a listing, either selective or exhaustive, containing the words and phrases of a language, with meanings or translations into another language. **2** the aggregate of words in the use or comprehension of a specified person, class, etc. **3** all the words contained in a language. **4** a range or system of symbols or techniques constituting a means of communication or expression, as any of the arts or crafts: *a wide vocabulary of textures and colours*. [C16: from Med. L *vocābulārium*, from L *vocābulum* VOCABLE]

vocal ❶ ('vəʊkᵊl) *adj* **1** of or designed for the voice: *vocal music*. **2** produced or delivered by the voice: *vocal noises*. **3** connected with the production of the voice: *vocal organs*. **4** frequently disposed to outspoken speech, criticism, etc.: *a vocal minority*. **5** full of sound or voices: *a vocal assembly*. **6** endowed with a voice. **7** *Phonetics.* **7a** of or relating to a speech sound. **7b** of or relating to a voiced speech sound, esp. a vowel. ◆ *n* **8** a piece of jazz or pop music that is sung. **9** a performance of such a piece of music. [C14: from L *vōcālis* possessed of a voice, from *vōx* voice]
▸**vocality** (vəʊ'kælɪtɪ) *n* ▸'**vocally** *adv*

vocal cords *pl n* either of two pairs of membranous folds in the larynx. The upper pair (**false vocal cords**) are not concerned with vocal production; the lower pair (**true vocal cords**) can be made to vibrate and produce sound when air from the lungs is forced over them.

vocalic (vəʊ'kælɪk) *adj Phonetics.* of, relating to, or containing a vowel or vowels.

vocalise (ˌvəʊkə'liːz) *n* a musical passage sung upon one vowel usually as an exercise to develop flexibility and control of pitch and tone.

vocalism ('vəʊkəˌlɪzəm) *n* **1** the exercise of the voice, as in singing or speaking. **2** *Phonetics.* **2a** a voiced speech sound, esp. a vowel. **2b** a system of vowels as used in a language.

vocalist ('vəʊkəlɪst) *n* a singer, esp. one who regularly appears with a jazz band or pop group.

vocalize *or* **vocalise** ('vəʊkəˌlaɪz) *vb* **vocalizes, vocalizing, vocalized** *or* **vocalises, vocalising, vocalised. 1** to express with or use the voice. **2** (*tr*) to make vocal or articulate. **3** (*tr*) *Phonetics.* to articulate (a speech sound) with voice. **4** another word for **vowelize. 5** (*intr*) to sing a melody on a vowel, etc.
▸ˌ**vocaliˈzation** *or* ˌ**vocaliˈsation** *n* ▸'**vocalˌizer** *or* '**vocalˌiser** *n*

vocal score *n* a musical score with voice parts in full and orchestral parts in the form of a piano transcription.

vocation ❶ (vəʊ'keɪʃən) *n* **1** a specified profession or trade. **2a** a special urge or predisposition to a particular calling or career, esp. a religious one. **2b** such a calling or career. [C15: from L *vocātiō*, from *vocāre* to call]

vocational (vəʊ'keɪʃənᵊl) *adj* **1** of or relating to a vocation or vocations. **2** of or relating to applied educational courses concerned with skills needed for an occupation, trade, or profession.

vocational guidance *n* a guidance service based on psychological tests and interviews to find out what career may best suit a person.

vocative ('vɒkətɪv) *Grammar.* ◆ *adj* **1** denoting a case of nouns, in some inflected languages, used when the referent of the noun is being addressed. ◆ *n* **2a** the vocative case. **2b** a vocative noun or speech element. [C15: from L *vocātīvus cāsus* the calling case, from *vocāre* to call]

voces ('vəʊsiːz) *n* the plural of **vox.**

vociferate (vəʊ'sɪfəˌreɪt) *vb* **vociferates, vociferating, vociferated.** to exclaim or cry out about (something) clamorously or insistently. [C17: from L *vōciferārī*, from *vōx* voice + *ferre* to bear]
▸**voˌciferˈation** *n*

vociferous ❶ (vəʊ'sɪfərəs) *adj* **1** characterized by vehemence or noisiness: *vociferous protests*. **2** making an outcry: *a vociferous mob*.
▸**vo'ciferously** *adv* ▸**vo'ciferousness** *n*

vocoder ('vəʊˌkəʊdə) *n Music.* a type of synthesizer that uses the human voice as an oscillator.

vodka ('vɒdkə) *n* an alcoholic drink originating in Russia, made from grain, potatoes, etc., usually consisting only of rectified spirit and water. [C19: from Russian, dim. of *voda* water]

voe (vəʊ) *n* (in Orkney and Shetland) a small bay or narrow creek. [C17: from ON *vagr*]

voetsek ('futsɛk, 'vʊt-) *interj S. African sl.* an expression of dismissal or rejection. [C19: Afrik., from Du. *voort se ek* forward, I say, commonly applied to animals]

voetstoets *or* **voetstoots** ('futstʊts, 'vʊt-) *S. African.* ◆ *adj* **1** denoting a sale in which the vendor is freed from all responsibility for the condition of the goods being sold. ◆ *adv* **2** without responsibility for the condition of the goods sold. [from Afrik. *voetstoots* as it is]

vogue ❶ (vəʊg) *n* **1** the popular style at a specified time (esp. in **in vogue**). **2** a period of general or popular usage or favour: *the vogue for such dances is over*. ◆ *adj* **3** (*usually prenominal*) fashionable: *a vogue word*. [C16: from F: a rowing fashion, from OIt., from *vogare* to row, from ?]
▸'**voguish** *adj*

vogueing ('vəʊgɪŋ) *n* a dance style of the late 1980s, in which a fashion model's movements and postures are imitated in a highly stylized manner. [C20: from *Vogue* magazine]

voice ❶ (vɔɪs) *n* **1** the sound made by the vibration of the vocal cords, esp. when modified by the tongue and mouth. **2** the natural and distinctive tone of the speech sounds characteristic of a particular person. **3** the condition, quality, or tone of such sounds: *a hysterical voice*. **4** the musical sound of a singing voice, with respect to its quality or tone: *she has a lovely voice*. **5** the ability to speak, sing, etc.: *he has lost his voice*. **6** a sound resembling or suggestive of vocal utterance: *the*

THESAURUS

expressive, flamboyant, quick, spirited, storming, striking, strong, vigorous
Antonyms *adj* ≠ **bright:** colourless, cool, drab, dull, pale, pastel, sombre ≠ **clear:** unclear, unmemorable, vague ≠ **lively:** lifeless, nondescript, ordinary, quiet, routine, run-of-the-mill, unremarkable

vividness *n* **1** = **brightness**, brilliancy, glow, radiance, resplendence **3, 4** = **clarity**, distinctness, graphicness, immediacy, intensity, realism, sharpness, strength **6, 7** = **liveliness**

vixen *n* **2** = **shrew**, ballbreaker, fury, harpy, harridan, hellcat, scold, spitfire, termagant (*rare*), virago, Xanthippe

viz *adv* = **namely**, that is to say, to wit, videlicet

vocabulary *n* **1, 3** = **words**, dictionary, glossary, language, lexicon, wordbook, word hoard, word stock

vocal *adj* **2** = **spoken**, articulate, articulated, oral, put into words, said, uttered, voiced **4** = **outspoken**, articulate, blunt, clamorous, eloquent, expressive, forthright, frank, free-spoken, noisy, plain-spoken, strident, vociferous
Antonyms *adj* ≠ **outspoken:** inarticulate, quiet, reserved, reticent, retiring, shy, silent, uncommunicative

vocation *n* **1, 2** = **profession**, business, calling, career, employment, job, life's work, life work, métier, mission, office, post, pursuit, role, trade

vociferous *adj* **1, 2** = **noisy**, clamant, clamorous, loud, loudmouthed (*inf.*), obstreperous, outspoken, ranting, shouting, strident, uproarious, vehement, vocal
Antonyms *adj* hushed, muted, noiseless, quiet, silent, still

vogue *n* **1** = **fashion**, craze, custom, *dernier cri*, last word, mode, style, the latest, the rage, the thing (*inf.*), trend, way **2** = **popularity**, acceptance, currency, fashionableness, favour, prevalence, usage, use ◆ *adj* **3** = **fashionable**, in, modish, now (*inf.*), popular, prevalent, trendy (*Brit. inf.*), up-to-the-minute, voguish, with it (*inf.*)

voice *n* **1, 2, 5** = **sound**, articulation, language, power of speech, tone, utterance, words **7** = **say**, decision, expression, part, view, vote, will, wish **9** = **instrument**, agency, medium, mouth-

voice of hard experience. **7** written or spoken expression, as of feeling, opinion, etc. (esp. in **give voice to**). **8** a stated choice, wish, or opinion: *to give someone a voice in a decision.* **9** an agency through which is communicated another's purpose, etc.: *such groups are the voice of our enemies.* **10** *Music.* **10a** musical notes produced by vibrations of the vocal chords at various frequencies and in certain registers: *a tenor voice.* **10b** (in harmony) an independent melodic line or part: *a fugue in five voices.* **11** *Phonetics.* the sound characterizing the articulation of several speech sounds, including all vowels or sonants, that is produced when the vocal cords are set in vibration by the breath. **12** *Grammar.* a category of the verb that expresses whether the relation between the subject and the verb is that of agent and action, action and recipient, or some other relation. **13 in voice.** in a condition to sing or speak well. **14 with one voice.** unanimously. ◆ *vb* **voices, voicing, voiced.** (*tr*) **15** to give expression to: *to voice a complaint.* **16** to articulate (a speech sound) with voice. **17** *Music.* to adjust (a wind instrument or organ pipe) so that it conforms to the correct standards of tone colour, pitch, etc. [C13: from OF *voiz,* from L *vōx*]
▸ **'voicer** *n*

voice box *n* **1** another word for the **larynx. 2** Also called: **talkbox.** an electronic guitar attachment with a tube into the player's mouth to modulate the sound vocally.

voiced (vɔɪst) *adj* **1** declared or expressed by the voice. **2** (*in combination*) having a voice as specified: *loud-voiced.* **3** *Phonetics.* articulated with accompanying vibration of the vocal cords: *in English* (b) *is a voiced consonant.*

voice input *n* the control and operation of computer systems by spoken commands.

voiceless ('vɔɪslɪs) *adj* **1** without a voice. **2** not articulated: *voiceless misery.* **3** silent. **4** *Phonetics.* articulated without accompanying vibration of the vocal cords: *in English* (p) *is a voiceless consonant.*
▸ **'voicelessly** *adv*

voice mail *n* an electronic system for the transfer and storage of telephone messages, which can then be dealt with by the user at his or her convenience.

voice-over *n* the voice of an unseen commentator heard during a film, etc.

voiceprint ('vɔɪsˌprɪnt) *n* a graphic representation of a person's voice recorded electronically, usually having time plotted along the horizontal axis and the frequency of the speech on the vertical axis.

void ❶ (vɔɪd) *adj* **1** without contents. **2** not legally binding: *null and void.* **3** (of an office, house, etc.) unoccupied. **4** (*postpositive;* foll. by *of*) destitute or devoid: *void of resources.* **5** useless: *all his efforts were rendered void.* **6** (of a card suit or player) having no cards in a particular suit: *his spades were void.* ◆ *n* **7** an empty space or area: *the huge desert voids of Asia.* **8** a feeling or condition of loneliness or deprivation. **9** a lack of any cards in one suit: *to have a void in spades.* ◆ *vb* (*mainly tr*) **10** to make ineffective or invalid. **11** to empty (contents, etc.) or make empty of contents. **12** (*also intr*) to discharge the contents of (the bowels or urinary bladder). [C13: from OF, from Vulgar L *vocītus* (untested), from L *vacuus,* from *vacāre* to be empty]
▸ **'voidable** *adj* ▸ **'voider** *n*

voidance ('vɔɪdᵊns) *n* **1** an annulment, as of a contract. **2** the condition of being vacant, as an office, benefice, etc. **3** the act of voiding or evacuating. [C14: var. of AVOIDANCE]

voile (vɔɪl) *n* a light semitransparent fabric of silk, rayon, cotton, etc., used for dresses, scarves, shirts, etc. [C19: from F: VEIL]

vol. *abbrev. for:* **1** volcano. **2** volume. **3** volunteer.

volant ('vəulənt) *adj* **1** (*usually postpositive*) *Heraldry.* in a flying position. **2** *Rare.* flying or capable of flight. [C16: from F, from *voler* to fly, from L *volāre*]

volar ('vəulə) *adj Anat.* of or relating to the palm of the hand or the sole of the foot. [C19: from L *vola* hollow of the hand, palm, sole of the foot]

volatile ❶ ('vɒləˌtaɪl) *adj* **1** (of a substance) capable of readily changing from a solid or liquid form to a vapour. **2** (of persons) disposed to caprice or inconstancy. **3** (of circumstances) liable to sudden change. **4** lasting only a short time: *volatile business interests.* **5** *Computing.* (of a memory) not retaining stored information when the power supply is cut off. ◆ *n* **6** a volatile substance. [C17: from L *volātilis* flying, from *volāre* to fly]
▸ **'volatileness** *or* **volatility** (ˌvɒlə'tɪlɪtɪ) *n*

volatilize *or* **volatilise** (vɒ'lætɪˌlaɪz) *vb* **volatilizes, volatilizing, volatilized** *or* **volatilises, volatilising, volatilised.** to change or cause to change from a solid or liquid to a vapour.
▸ **vo'latiˌlizable** *or* **vo'latiˌlisable** *adj* ▸ **voˌlatiliz'ation** *or* **voˌlatilis'ation** *n*

vol-au-vent (*French* vɔlovɑ̃) *n* a very light puff pastry case filled with a savoury mixture in a sauce. [C19: from F, lit.: flight in the wind]

volcanic (vɒl'kænɪk) *adj* **1** of, produced by, or characterized by the presence of volcanoes: *a volcanic region.* **2** suggestive of or resembling an erupting volcano: *a volcanic era.*
▸ **vol'canically** *adv* ▸ **volcanicity** (ˌvɒlkə'nɪsɪtɪ) *n*

volcanic glass *n* any of several glassy volcanic igneous rocks, such as obsidian.

volcanism ('vɒlkəˌnɪzəm) *or* **vulcanism** *n* those processes collectively that result in the formation of volcanoes and their products.

volcano (vɒl'keɪnəu) *n, pl* **volcanoes** *or* **volcanos. 1** an opening in the earth's crust from which molten lava, rock fragments, ashes, dust, and gases are ejected from below the earth's surface. **2** a mountain formed from volcanic material ejected from a vent in a central crater. [C17: from It., from L *Volcānus* Vulcan, Roman god of fire and metal-working, whose forges were believed to be responsible for volcanic rumblings]

volcanology (ˌvɒlkə'nɒlədʒɪ) *or* **vulcanology** *n* the study of volcanoes and volcanic phenomena.
▸ **volcanological** (ˌvɒlkənə'lɒdʒɪkᵊl) *or* **ˌvulcano'logical** *adj*

vole (vəul) *n* any of various small rodents, mostly of Eurasia and North America, having a stocky body, short tail, and inconspicuous ears. [C19: short for *volemouse,* from ON *vollr* field + *mus* MOUSE]

volitant ('vɒlɪtənt) *adj* **1** flying or moving about rapidly. **2** capable of flying. [C19: from L *volitāre* to flit, from *volāre* to fly]

volition ❶ (və'lɪʃən) *n* **1** the act of exercising the will: *of one's own volition.* **2** the faculty of conscious choice, decision, and intention. **3** the resulting choice or resolution. [C17: from Med. L *volitiō,* from L *vol-* as in *volō* I will, present stem of *velle* to wish]
▸ **vo'litional** *adj*

volitive ('vɒlɪtɪv) *adj* of, relating to, or emanating from the will.

Volk (fɒlk) *n S. African.* the Afrikaner people. [from Afrik., from Du.]

Volksraad ('fɒlksˌrɑːt) *n* (formerly, in South Africa) the Legislative Assemblies of the Transvaal and Orange Free State republics. [from Afrik., from Du. *volks* people's + *raad* council]

volley ❶ ('vɒlɪ) *n* **1** the simultaneous discharge of several weapons, esp. firearms. **2** the projectiles or missiles so discharged. **3** a burst of oaths, protests, etc., occurring simultaneously or in rapid succession. **4** *Sport.* a stroke, shot, or kick at a moving ball before it hits the ground. **5** *Cricket.* the flight of such a ball or the ball itself. ◆ *vb* **6** to discharge (weapons, etc.) in or as if in a volley or (of weapons, etc.) to be discharged. **7** (*tr*) to utter vehemently. **8** (*tr*) *Sport.* to strike or kick (a moving ball) before it hits the ground. [C16: from F *volée* a flight, from *voler* to fly, from L *volāre*]
▸ **'volleyer** *n*

volleyball ('vɒlɪˌbɔːl) *n* **1** a game in which two teams hit a large ball back and forth over a high net with their hands. **2** the ball used in this game.

volplane ('vɒlˌpleɪn) *vb* **volplanes, volplaning, volplaned. 1** (*intr*) (of an aircraft) to glide without engine power. ◆ *n* **2** a glide by an aircraft. [C20: from F *vol plané* a gliding flight]

vols. *abbrev. for* volumes.

volt[1] (vəult) *n* the derived SI unit of electric potential; the potential difference between two points on a conductor carrying a current of 1 ampere, when the power dissipated between these points is 1 watt. Symbol: V [C19: after Count Alessandro *Volta* (1745–1827), It. physicist]

volt[2] *or* **volte** (vɒlt) *n* **1** a circle executed in dressage. **2** a leap made in fencing to avoid an opponent's thrust. [C17: from F, from It. *volta,* ult. from L *volvere* to turn]

volta ('vɒltə; *Italian* 'vɔlta) *n, pl* **volte** (*Italian* -te). **1** an Italian dance popular during the 16th and 17th centuries. **2** a piece of music for or in the rhythm of this dance. [C17: from It.: turn; see VOLT[2]]

voltage ('vəultɪdʒ) *n* an electromotive force or potential difference expressed in volts.

voltaic (vɒl'teɪɪk) *adj* another word for **galvanic** (sense 1).

voltaic cell *n* another name for **primary cell.**

voltaic couple *n Physics.* a pair of dissimilar metals in an electrolyte with a potential difference between the metals resulting from chemical action.

voltaic pile *n* an early form of battery consisting of a pile of paired plates of dissimilar metals, such as zinc and copper, each pair being separated from the next by a pad moistened with an electrolyte.

voltameter (vɒl'tæmɪtə) *n* a device for measuring electric charge.
▸ **voltametric** (ˌvɒltə'mɛtrɪk) *adj*

voltammeter (ˌvəult'æmˌmiːtə) *n* a dual-purpose instrument that can measure both potential difference and electric current, usually in volts and amperes respectively.

THESAURUS

piece, organ, spokesman, spokesperson, spokeswoman, vehicle ◆ *vb* **15, 16** = **express,** air, articulate, assert, come out with (*inf.*), declare, divulge, enunciate, give expression *or* utterance to, put into words, say, utter, ventilate

void *adj* **2, 5** = **invalid,** dead, ineffective, ineffectual, inoperative, nonviable, nugatory, null and void, unenforceable, useless, vain, worthless **3** = **empty,** bare, clear, drained, emptied, free, tenantless, unfilled, unoccupied, vacant **4** *foll. by* **of** = **devoid,** destitute, lacking, without ◆ *n* **7** = **emptiness,** blank, blankness, gap, lack, opening, space, vacuity, vacuum, want ◆ *vb* **10** = **invalidate,** abnegate, cancel, nullify, rescind **11, 12** = **empty,** discharge, drain, eject, eliminate (*Physiology*), emit, evacuate
Antonyms *adj* ≠ **empty:** abounding, complete, filled, full, occupied, replete, tenanted

volatile *adj* **1** = **changeable,** explosive, inconstant, unsettled, unstable, unsteady, variable **2** = **temperamental,** airy, erratic, fickle, flighty, gay, giddy, inconstant, lively, mercurial, sprightly, up and down (*inf.*), whimsical
Antonyms *adj* ≠ **changeable:** constant, inert, settled, stable, steady ≠ **temperamental:** calm, consistent, cool-headed, dependable, reliable, self-controlled, sober

volition *n* **1** = **free will,** choice, choosing, determination, discretion, election, option, preference, purpose, resolution, will

volley *n* **1, 3** = **barrage,** blast, bombardment, burst, cannonade, discharge, explosion, fusillade, hail, salvo, shower

volt-ampere ('vəʊlt'æmpɛə) *n* the product of the potential in volts across an electrical circuit and the resultant current in amperes.

volte-face ('vɒlt'fɑːs) *n, pl* **volte-face.** **1** a reversal, as in opinion. **2** a change of position so as to look, lie, etc., in the opposite direction. [C19: from F, from It., from *volta* turn + *faccia* face]

voltmeter ('vəʊlt,miːtə) *n* an instrument for measuring potential difference or electromotive force.

voluble ➊ ('vɒljub°l) *adj* **1** talking easily and at length. **2** *Arch.* easily turning or rotating. **3** *Rare.* (of a plant) twining or twisting. [C16: from L *volūbilis* turning readily, from *volvere* to turn]
▸ **,volu'bility** *or* **'volubleness** *n* ▸ **'volubly** *adv*

volume ➊ ('vɒljuːm) *n* **1** the magnitude of the three-dimensional space enclosed within or occupied by an object, geometric solid, etc. **2** a large mass or quantity: *the volume of protest.* **3** an amount or total: *the volume of exports.* **4** fullness of sound. **5** the control on a radio, etc., for adjusting the intensity of sound. **6** a bound collection of printed or written pages; book. **7** any of several books either bound in an identical format or part of a series. **8** the complete set of issues of a periodical over a specified period, esp. one year. **9** *History.* a roll of parchment, etc. **10 speak volumes.** to convey much significant information. [C14: from OF, from L *volūmen* a roll, from *volvere* to roll up]

volumetric (,vɒlju'mɛtrɪk) *adj* of, concerning, or using measurement by volume: *volumetric analysis.*
▸ **,volu'metrically** *adv*

volumetric analysis *n Chem.* quantitative analysis of liquids or solutions by comparing the volumes that react with known volumes of standard reagents, usually by titration.

voluminous ➊ (və'luːmɪnəs) *adj* **1** of great size, quantity, or extent. **2** (of writing) consisting of or sufficient to fill volumes. [C17: from LL *volūminōsus* full of windings, from *volūmen* VOLUME]
▸ **voluminosity** (və,luːmɪ'nɒsɪtɪ) *n* ▸ **vo'luminously** *adv*

voluntarism ('vɒləntə,rɪzəm) *n* **1** *Philosophy.* the theory that the will rather than the intellect is the ultimate principle of reality. **2** a doctrine or system based on voluntary participation in a course of action. **3** another name for **voluntaryism.**
▸ **'voluntarist** *n, adj*

voluntary ➊ ('vɒləntərɪ) *adj* **1** performed, undertaken, or brought about by free choice or willingly: *a voluntary donation.* **2** (of persons) serving or acting in a specified function without compulsion or promise of remuneration: *a voluntary social worker.* **3** done by, composed of, or functioning with the aid of volunteers: *a voluntary association.* **4** exercising or having the faculty of willing: *a voluntary agent.* **5** spontaneous: *voluntary laughter.* **6** *Law.* **6a** acting or done without legal obligation, compulsion, or persuasion. **6b** made without payment or recompense: *a voluntary conveyance.* **7** (of the muscles of the limbs, neck, etc.) having their action controlled by the will. **8** maintained by the voluntary actions or contributions of individuals and not by the state: *voluntary schools.* ◆ *n, pl* **voluntaries.** **9** *Music.* a composition or improvisation, usually for organ, played at the beginning or end of a church service. [C14: from L *voluntārius,* from *voluntās* will, from *velle* to wish]
▸ **'voluntarily** *adv*

voluntary arrangement *n Law.* a procedure enabling an insolvent company to come to an arrangement with its creditors and resolve its financial problems, often in compliance with a court order.

voluntaryism ('vɒləntərɪ,ɪzəm) *or* **voluntarism** *n* the principle of supporting churches, schools, and various other institutions by voluntary contributions rather than with state funds.
▸ **'voluntaryist** *or* **'voluntarist** *n*

voluntary retailer *n* another name for **symbol retailer.**

volunteer ➊ (,vɒlən'tɪə) *n* **1a** a person who performs or offers to perform voluntary service. **1b** (*as modifier*): *a volunteer system.* **2** a person who freely undertakes military service. **3a** a plant that grows from seed that has not been deliberately sown. **3b** (*as modifier*): *a volunteer plant.* ◆ *vb* **4** to offer (oneself or one's services) for an undertaking by choice and without request or obligation. **5** (*tr*) to perform, give, or communicate voluntarily: *to volunteer help.* **6** (*intr*) to enlist voluntarily for military service. [C17: from F, from L *voluntārius;* see VOLUNTARY]

voluptuary ➊ (və'lʌptjuərɪ) *n, pl* **voluptuaries.** **1** a person devoted to luxury and sensual pleasures. ◆ *adj* **2** of or furthering sensual gratification or luxury. [C17: from LL *voluptuārius* delightful, from L *voluptās* pleasure]

voluptuous ➊ (və'lʌptjuəs) *adj* **1** relating to, characterized by, or consisting of pleasures of the body or senses. **2** devoted or addicted to sensual indulgence or luxurious pleasures. **3** sexually alluring, esp. through shapeliness or fullness: *a voluptuous woman.* [C14: from L *voluptuōsus* full of gratification, from *voluptās* pleasure]
▸ **vo'luptuously** *adv* ▸ **vo'luptuousness** *n*

volute ('vɒljuːt, və'luːt) *n* **1** a spiral or twisting turn, form, or object. **2** Also called: **helix.** a carved ornament, esp. as used on an Ionic capital, that has the form of a spiral scroll. **3** any of the whorls of the spirally coiled shell of a snail or similar gastropod mollusc. **4** any of a family of tropical marine gastropod molluscs having a spiral shell with beautiful markings. ◆ *adj also* **voluted** (və'luːtɪd). **5** having the form of a volute; spiral. [C17: from L *volūta* spiral decoration, from *volūtus,* from *volvere* to roll up]
▸ **vo'lution** *n*

vomer ('vəʊmə) *n* the thin flat bone forming part of the separation between the nasal passages in mammals. [C18: from L: ploughshare]

vomit ➊ ('vɒmɪt) *vb* **vomits, vomiting, vomited.** **1** to eject (the contents of the stomach) through the mouth as the result of involuntary muscular spasms of the stomach and oesophagus. **2** to eject or be ejected forcefully. ◆ *n* **3** the matter ejected in vomiting. **4** the act of vomiting. **5** an emetic. [C14: from L *vomitāre* to vomit repeatedly, from *vomere* to vomit]
▸ **'vomiter** *n*

vomitory ('vɒmɪtərɪ) *adj* **1** Also: **vomitive** ('vɒmɪtɪv). causing vomiting; emetic. ◆ *n, pl* **vomitories.** **2** a vomitory agent. **3** Also called: **vomitorium** (,vɒmɪ'tɔːrɪəm). a passageway in an ancient Roman amphitheatre that connects an outside entrance to a tier of seats.

voodoo ('vuːduː) *n, pl* **voodoos.** **1** Also called: **voodooism.** a religious cult involving witchcraft, common in Haiti and other Caribbean islands. **2** a person who practises voodoo. **3** a charm, spell, or fetish involved in voodoo worship. ◆ *adj* **4** relating to or associated with voodoo. ◆ *vb* **voodoos, voodooing, voodooed.** **5** (*tr*) to affect by or as if by the power of voodoo. [C19: from Louisiana F *voudou,* ult. of West African origin]
▸ **'voodooist** *n*

voorkamer ('fʊə,kɑːmə) *n S. African.* the front room of a house. [Afrik., from Du. *voor* fore + *kamer* chamber]

voorskot ('fʊə,skɒt) *n S. African.* advance payment made to a farmer for crops. Cf. **agterskot.** [C20: Afrik., from *voor* before + *skot* shot, payment]

Voortrekker ('fʊə,trɛkə) *n* (in South Africa) **1** one of the original Afrikaner settlers of the Transvaal and the Orange Free State who migrated from the Cape Colony in the 1830s. **2** a member of the Afrikaner youth movement founded in 1931. [C19: from Du., from *voor-* FORE- + *trekken* to TREK]

voracious ➊ (vɒ'reɪʃəs) *adj* **1** devouring or craving food in great quantities. **2** very eager or unremitting in some activity: *voracious reading.* [C17: from L *vorāx,* from *vorāre* to devour]
▸ **voracity** (vɒ'ræsɪtɪ) *or* **vo'raciousness** *n*

-vorous *adj combining form.* feeding on or devouring: *carnivorous.* [from L *-vorus;* rel. to *vorāre* to swallow up]
▸ **-vore** *n combining form.*

vortex ➊ ('vɔːtɛks) *n, pl* **vortexes** *or* **vortices** (-tɪ,siːz). **1** a whirling mass or motion of liquid, gas, flame, etc., such as the spiralling movement of water around a whirlpool. **2** any activity or way of life regarded as irresistibly engulfing. [C17: from L: a whirlpool]
▸ **vortical** ('vɔːtɪk°l) *adj*

vorticella (,vɔːtɪ'sɛlə) *n, pl* **vorticellae** (-liː). any of a genus of protozoans consisting of a goblet-shaped ciliated cell attached to the substratum

THESAURUS

volubility *n* **1** = **talkativeness**, fluency, garrulity, gift of the gab, glibness, loquaciousness, loquacity

voluble *adj* **1** = **talkative**, articulate, blessed with the gift of the gab, fluent, forthcoming, glib, loquacious
Antonyms *adj* hesitant, inarticulate, reticent, succinct, taciturn, terse, tongue-tied, unforthcoming

volume *n* **1** = **capacity**, compass, cubic content, dimensions **3** = **amount**, aggregate, body, bulk, mass, quantity, total **6** = **book**, publication, title, tome, treatise

voluminous *adj* **1** = **large**, ample, big, billowing, bulky, capacious, cavernous, full, massive, roomy, vast **2** = **copious**, prolific
Antonyms *adj* ≠ **large:** skimpy, slight, small, tiny ≠ **copious:** inadequate, insufficient, scanty

voluntarily *adv* **1** = **willingly**, by choice, freely, lief (*rare*), off one's own bat, of one's own accord, of one's own free will, on one's own initiative, without being asked, without prompting

voluntary *adj* **1, 2** = **unforced**, discretional, discretionary, free, gratuitous, honorary, intended, intentional, optional, spontaneous, uncompelled, unconstrained, unpaid, volunteer, willing
Antonyms *adj* automatic, conscripted, forced, instinctive, involuntary, obligatory, unintentional

volunteer *vb* **4** = **offer**, let oneself in for (*inf.*), need no invitation, offer one's services, present, proffer, propose, put oneself at (someone's) disposal, step forward **5** = **suggest**, advance, put forward, tender
Antonyms *vb* ≠ **offer:** begrudge, deny, keep, refuse, retain, withdraw, withhold

voluptuary *n* **1** = **sensualist**, *bon vivant,* epicurean, hedonist, luxury-lover, playboy, pleasure seeker, profligate, sybarite

voluptuous *adj* **1, 2** = **sensual**, bacchanalian, epicurean, hedonistic, licentious, luxurious, pleasure-loving, self-indulgent, sybaritic **3** = **buxom**, ample, curvaceous (*inf.*), enticing, erotic, full-bosomed, provocative, seductive, shapely
Antonyms *adj* ≠ **sensual:** abstemious, ascetic, celibate, rigorous, self-denying, Spartan

voluptuousness *n* **1, 2** = **sensuality**, carnality, licentiousness, opulence **3** = **curvaceousness** (*inf.*), seductiveness, shapeliness

vomit *vb* **1** = **be sick**, barf, belch forth, bring up, chuck (up) (*sl., chiefly US*), disgorge, eject, emit, heave, puke (*sl.*), regurgitate, retch, sick up (*inf.*), spew out *or* up, throw up (*inf.*)

voracious *adj* **1** = **gluttonous**, devouring, edacious, esurient, greedy, hungry, insatiable, omnivorous, ravening, ravenous **2** = **avid**, hungry, insatiable, prodigious, rapacious, uncontrolled, unquenchable
Antonyms *adj* ≠ **avid:** moderate, sated, satisfied, self-controlled, temperate

voracity *n* **1** = **greed**, edacity, hunger, ravenousness **2** = **avidity**, eagerness, hunger, rapacity

vortex *n* **1** = **whirlpool**, eddy, maelstrom

by a long contractile stalk. [C18: from NL, lit.: a little eddy, from VORTEX]
vorticism ('vɔːtɪˌsɪzəm) *n* an art movement in England combining the techniques of cubism with the concern for the problems of the machine age evinced in futurism. [C20: referring to the "vortices" of modern life on which the movement was based]
▸**'vorticist** *n*
vostro account ('vɒstrəʊ) *n* a bank account held by a foreign bank with a British bank, usually in sterling. Cf. **nostro account**.
votary Ⓣ ('vəʊtərɪ) *n, pl* **votaries**, *also* **votarist**. **1** *RC Church, Eastern Churches*. a person, such as a monk or nun, who has dedicated himself or herself to religion by taking vows. **2** a devoted adherent of a religion, cause, etc. ◆ *adj* **3** ardently devoted to the worship of God or a saint. [C16: from L *vōtum* a vow, from *vovēre* to vow]
▸**'votaress** *fem n*
vote Ⓣ (vəʊt) *n* **1** an indication of choice, opinion, or will on a question, such as the choosing of a candidate: *10 votes for Jones*. **2** the opinion of a group of persons as determined by voting: *it was put to the vote*. **3** a body of votes or voters collectively: *the Jewish vote*. **4** the total number of votes cast. **5** the ticket, ballot, etc., by which a vote is expressed. **6a** the right to vote; franchise. **6b** a person regarded as the embodiment of this right. **7** a means of voting, such as a ballot. **8** *Chiefly Brit*. a grant or other proposition to be voted upon. ◆ *vb* **votes, voting, voted. 9** (when *tr, takes a clause as object or an infinitive*) to express or signify (one's preference or will) (for or against some question, etc.): *to vote by ballot*. **10** (*intr*) to declare oneself as being (something or in favour of something) by exercising one's vote: *to vote socialist*. **11** (*tr*; foll. by *into* or *out of*, etc.) to appoint or elect (a person to or from a particular post): *he was voted out of office*. **12** (*tr*) to determine the condition of in a specified way by voting: *the court voted itself out of existence*. **13** (*tr*) to authorize or allow by voting: *vote us a rise*. **14** (*tr*) *Inf*. to declare by common opinion: *the party was voted a failure*. [C15: from L *vōtum* a solemn promise, from *vovēre* to vow]
▸**'votable** *or* **'voteable** *adj*
vote down *vb* (*tr, adv*) to decide against or defeat in a vote: *the bill was voted down*.
vote of no confidence *n Parliament*. a vote on a motion put by the Opposition censuring an aspect of the Government's policy; if the motion is carried the Government is obliged to resign. Also called: **vote of censure**.
voter ('vəʊtə) *n* a person who can or does vote.
voting machine *n* (esp. in the US) a machine at a polling station that voters operate to register their votes and that mechanically or electronically counts all votes cast.
votive ('vəʊtɪv) *adj* **1** given or dedicated in fulfilment of or in accordance with a vow. **2** *RC Church*. having the nature of a voluntary offering: *a votive Mass*. [C16: from L *vōtīvus* promised by a vow, from *vōtum* a vow]
vouch Ⓣ (vaʊtʃ) *vb* **1** (*intr*; usually foll. by *for*) to give personal assurance: *I'll vouch for his safety*. **2** (when *tr, usually takes a clause as object*; when *intr*, usually foll. by *for*) to furnish supporting evidence (for) or function as proof (of). **3** (*tr*) *Arch*. to cite (authors, principles, etc.) in support of something. [C14: from OF *vocher* to summon, ult. from L *vocāre* to call]
voucher Ⓣ ('vaʊtʃə) *n* **1** a document serving as evidence for some claimed transaction, as the receipt or expenditure of money. **2** *Brit*. a ticket or card serving as a substitute for cash: *a gift voucher*. **3** a person or thing that vouches for the truth of some statement, etc. [C16: from Anglo-F, noun use of OF *voucher* to summon; see VOUCH]
vouchsafe Ⓣ (ˌvaʊtʃ'seɪf) *vb* **vouchsafes, vouchsafing, vouchsafed**. (*tr*) **1** to give or grant or condescend to give or grant: *she vouchsafed no reply*. **2** (*may take a clause as object or an infinitive*) to agree, promise, or permit, often graciously or condescendingly: *he vouchsafed to come yesterday*. [C14 *vouchen sauf*; see VOUCH, SAFE]
voussoir (vuː'swɑː) *n* a wedge-shaped stone or brick that is used with others to construct an arch or vault. [C18: from F, from Vulgar L *volsōrium* (unattested), ult. from L *volvere* to turn, roll]
vow Ⓣ (vaʊ) *n* **1** a solemn or earnest pledge or promise binding the person making it to perform a specified act or behave in a certain way. **2** a solemn promise made to a deity or saint, by which the promiser pledges himself to some future act or way of life. **3 take vows**. to enter a religious order and commit oneself to its rule of life by the vows of poverty, chastity, and obedience. ◆ *vb* **4** (*tr; may take a clause as object or an infinitive*) to pledge, promise, or undertake solemnly: *he vowed to return*. **5** (*tr*) to dedicate or consecrate to God or a saint. **6** (*tr; usually takes a clause as object*) to assert or swear emphatically. **7** (*intr*) *Arch*. to declare solemnly. [C13: from OF *vou*, from L *vōtum*; see VOTE]
▸**'vower** *n*
vowel ('vaʊəl) *n* **1** *Phonetics*. a voiced speech sound whose articulation is characterized by the absence of obstruction in the vocal tract, allowing the breath stream free passage. The timbre of a vowel is chiefly determined by the position of the tongue and the lips. **2** a letter or character representing a vowel. [C14: from OF, from L *vocālis littera* vowel, from *vocālis*, from *vox* voice]
▸**'vowel-ˌlike** *adj*
vowel gradation *n* another name for **ablaut**. See **gradation** (sense 5).
vowelize *or* **vowelise** ('vaʊəˌlaɪz) *vb* **vowelizes, vowelizing, vowelized** *or* **vowelises, vowelising, vowelised**. (*tr*) to mark the vowel points in (a Hebrew word or text).
▸**ˌvoweli'zation** *or* **ˌvoweli'sation** *n*
vowel mutation *n* another name for **umlaut**.
vowel point *n* any of several marks or points placed above or below consonants, esp. those evolved for Hebrew or Arabic, in order to indicate vowel sounds.
vox (vɒks) *n, pl* **voces**. a voice or sound. [L: voice]
vox pop *n* interviews with members of the public on a radio or television programme. [C20: shortened from VOX POPULI]
vox populi ('pɒpjʊˌlaɪ) *n* the voice of the people; popular or public opinion. [L]
voyage Ⓣ ('vɔɪɪdʒ) *n* **1** a journey, travel, or passage, esp. one to a distant land or by sea or air. ◆ *vb* **voyages, voyaging, voyaged. 2** to travel over or traverse (something): *we will voyage to Africa*. [C13: from OF *veiage*, from L *viāticum* provision for travelling, from *via* way]
▸**'voyager** *n*
voyage charter *n* the hire of a ship or aircraft for a specific number of voyages. Cf. **time charter**.
voyageur (ˌvɔɪə'dʒɜː) *n* (in Canada) a woodsman, guide, trapper, boatman, or explorer, esp. in the North. [C19: F: traveller, from *voyager* to VOYAGE]
voyeur (vwaɪ'ɜː) *n* a person who obtains sexual pleasure from the observation of people undressing, having intercourse, etc. [C20: F, lit.: one who sees, from *voir* to see, from L *vidēre*]
▸**vo'yeurism** *n* ▸**ˌvoyeur'istic** *adj*
VP *abbrev. for*: **1** verb phrase. **2** Vice President.
VPL *Jocular abbrev. for* visible panty line.
VR *abbrev. for*: **1** variant reading. **2** Victoria Regina. [L: Queen Victoria] **3** virtual reality.
V. Rev. *abbrev. for* Very Reverend.
vrou (frəʊ) *n S. African*. an Afrikaner woman, esp. a married woman. [from Afrik., from Du.]
vrystater ('freɪˌstɑːtə) *n S. African*. a native inhabitant of the Free State, esp. one who is White. [from Afrik., from Du. *vrij* free + *staat* state]
vs *abbrev. for* versus.
VS *abbrev. for* Veterinary Surgeon.
v.s. *abbrev. for* vide supra (see **vide**).
V-sign *n* **1** (in Britain) an offensive gesture made by sticking up the index and middle fingers with the palm of the hand inwards. **2** a similar gesture with the palm outwards meaning victory or peace.
VSO *abbrev. for*: **1** very superior old: used to indicate that a brandy, port, etc., is between 12 and 17 years old. **2** (in Britain) Voluntary Service Overseas: an organization that sends young volunteers to use and teach their skills in developing countries.
VSOP *abbrev. for* very special (*or* superior) old pale: used to indicate that a brandy, port, etc., is between 20 and 25 years old.
VTOL ('viːtɒl) *n* vertical takeoff and landing; a system in which an aircraft can take off and land vertically. Cf. **STOL**.
VTR *abbrev. for* video tape recorder.
V-type engine *n* a type of internal-combustion engine having two cylinder blocks attached to a single crankcase, the angle between the two blocks forming a V.
vug (vʌg) *n Mining*. a small cavity in a rock or vein, usually lined with crystals. [C19: from Cornish *vooga* cave]
▸**'vuggy** *adj*
vulcanian (vʌl'keɪnɪən) *adj Geol*. of or relating to a volcanic eruption characterized by the explosive discharge of gases, fine ash, and viscous lava that hardens in the crater. [C17: after *Vulcan*, Roman god of fire and metalworking]
vulcanism ('vʌlkəˌnɪzəm) *n* a variant spelling of **volcanism**.
vulcanite ('vʌlkəˌnaɪt) *n* a hard usually black rubber produced by vulcanizing natural rubber with sulphur. It is used for electrical insulators, etc. Also called: **ebonite**.
vulcanize *or* **vulcanise** ('vʌlkəˌnaɪz) *vb* **vulcanizes, vulcanizing, vulcanized** *or* **vulcanises, vulcanising, vulcanised**. (*tr*) **1** to treat (rubber) with sulphur under heat and pressure to improve elasticity and strength or to produce a hard substance such as vulcanite. **2** to treat (substances other than rubber) by a similar process in order to improve their properties.
▸**ˌvulcani'zation** *or* **ˌvulcani'sation** *n*
vulcanology (ˌvʌlkə'nɒlədʒɪ) *n* a variant spelling of **volcanology**.
Vulg. *abbrev. for* Vulgate.
vulgar Ⓣ ('vʌlgə) *adj* **1** marked by lack of taste, culture, delicacy, man-

THESAURUS

votary *n* **2** = **devotee**, adherent, aficionado, believer, disciple, follower
vote *n* **1** = **poll**, ballot, franchise, plebiscite, referendum, show of hands **6a** = **right to vote**, suffrage ◆ *vb* **9** = **cast one's vote**, ballot, elect, go to the polls, opt, return **14** *Informal* = **declare**, judge, pronounce, propose, recommend, suggest
vouch *vb* **1** *usually foll. by* **for** = **guarantee**, answer for, asseverate, back, certify, give assurance of, go bail for, stand witness, swear to **2** *usually foll. by* **for** = **confirm**, affirm, assert, attest to, support, uphold
voucher *n* **2** = **ticket**, coupon, token
vouchsafe *vb* **1** = **grant**, accord, cede, condescend to give, confer, deign, favour (someone) with, yield
vow *n* **1** = **promise**, oath, pledge, troth (*arch.*) ◆ *vb* **4, 6** = **promise**, affirm, consecrate, dedicate, devote, pledge, swear, undertake solemnly
voyage *n* **1** = **journey**, crossing, cruise, passage, travels, trip
vulgar *adj* **1** = **crude**, blue, boorish, cheap and nasty, coarse, common, common as muck, dirty, flashy, gaudy, gross, ill-bred, impolite, improper, indecent, indecorous, indelicate, low, nasty, naughty, off colour, ribald, risqué,

ners, etc.: *vulgar language.* **2** (*often cap.; usually prenominal*) denoting a form of a language, esp. of Latin, current among common people, esp. at a period when the formal language is archaic. **3** *Arch.* of or current among the great mass of common people. [C14: from L *vulgāris*, from *vulgus* the common people]
▸'**vulgarly** *adv*

vulgar fraction *n* another name for **simple fraction.**

vulgarian ❶ (vʌl'gɛərɪən) *n* a vulgar person, esp. one who is rich or has pretensions to good taste.

vulgarism ('vʌlgəˌrɪzəm) *n* **1** a coarse, crude, or obscene expression. **2** a word or phrase found only in the vulgar form of a language.

vulgarity ❶ (vʌl'gærɪtɪ) *n, pl* **vulgarities. 1** the condition of being vulgar; lack of good manners. **2** a vulgar action, phrase, etc.

vulgarize *or* **vulgarise** ('vʌlgəˌraɪz) *vb* **vulgarizes, vulgarizing, vulgarized** *or* **vulgarises, vulgarising, vulgarised.** (*tr*) **1** to make commonplace or vulgar. **2** to make (something little known or difficult to understand) widely known or popular among the public.
▸ˌ**vulgari'zation** *or* ˌ**vulgari'sation** *n*

Vulgar Latin *n* any of the dialects of Latin spoken in the Roman Empire other than classical Latin.

vulgate ('vʌlgeɪt, -gɪt) *n Rare.* **1** a commonly recognized text or version. **2** the vernacular.

Vulgate ('vʌlgeɪt, -gɪt) *n* **a** (from the 13th century onwards) the fourth-century Latin version of the Bible produced by Jerome. **b** (*as modifier*): *the Vulgate version.* [C17: from Med. L, from LL *vulgāta editiō* popular version (of the Bible), from L *vulgāre* to make common]

vulnerable ❶ ('vʌlnərəbᵊl) *adj* **1** capable of being physically or emotionally wounded or hurt. **2** open to temptation, censure, etc. **3** *Mil.* exposed to attack. **4** *Bridge.* (of a side who have won one game towards rubber) subject to increased bonuses or penalties. [C17: from LL, from L *vulnerāre* to wound, from *vulnus* a wound]
▸ˌ**vulnera'bility** *n* ▸'**vulnerably** *adv*

vulnerary ('vʌlnərərɪ) *Med.* ◆ *adj* **1** of or used to heal a wound. ◆ *n, pl* **vulneraries. 2** a vulnerary drug or agent. [C16: from L *vulnerārius* from *vulnus* wound]

vulpine ('vʌlpaɪn) *adj* **1** of, relating to, or resembling a fox. **2** crafty, clever, etc. [C17: from L *vulpīnus* foxlike, from *vulpēs* fox]

vulture ('vʌltʃə) *n* **1** any of various very large diurnal birds of prey of Africa, Asia, and warm parts of Europe, typically having broad wings and soaring flight and feeding on carrion. **2** any similar bird of North, Central, and South America. **3** a person or thing that preys greedily and ruthlessly on others, esp. the helpless. [C14: from OF *voltour*, from L *vultur*]
▸**vulturine** ('vʌltʃəˌraɪn) *or* '**vulturous** *adj*

vulva ('vʌlvə) *n, pl* **vulvae** (-viː) *or* **vulvas.** the external genitals of human females, including the labia, mons veneris, clitoris, and the vaginal orifice. [C16: from L: covering, womb, matrix]
▸'**vulvar** *adj*

vulvitis (vʌl'vaɪtɪs) *n* inflammation of the vulva.

vv *abbrev. for* vice versa.

vv. *abbrev. for:* **1** versus. **2** *Music.* volumes.

THESAURUS

rude, suggestive, tasteless, tawdry, uncouth, unmannerly, unrefined **2** = **vernacular**, general, native, ordinary, unrefined
Antonyms *adj* ≠ **crude:** aristocratic, classical, decorous, elegant, genteel, high-brow, polite, refined, sophisticated, tasteful, upper-class, urbane, well-mannered

vulgarian *n* = **upstart**, arriviste, boor, churl, *nouveau riche,* parvenu, philistine

vulgarity *n* **1** = **crudeness**, bad taste, coarseness, crudity, gaudiness, grossness, indecorum, indelicacy, lack of refinement, ribaldry, rudeness, suggestiveness, tastelessness, tawdriness
Antonyms *n* decorum, gentility, good breeding, good manners, good taste, refinement, sensitivity, sophistication, tastefulness

vulnerable *adj* **1** = **susceptible**, sensitive, tender, thin-skinned, weak **3** *Military* = **exposed**, accessible, assailable, defenceless, open to attack, unprotected, wide open
Antonyms *adj* ≠ **susceptible:** immune, impervious, insensitive, thick-skinned ≠ **exposed:** guarded, invulnerable, unassailable, well-protected

w *or* **W** ('dʌbᵊl,juː) *n, pl* **w's, W's,** *or* **Ws. 1** the 23rd letter of the English alphabet. **2** a speech sound represented by this letter, usually a bilabial semivowel, as in *web.*

W *symbol for:* **1** *Chem.* tungsten. [from NL *wolframium,* from G *Wolfram*] **2** watt. **3** West. **4** women's (size). **5** *Physics.* work.

w. *abbrev. for:* **1** week. **2** weight. **3** *Cricket.* **3a** wide. **3b** wicket. **4** width. **5** wife. **6** with.

W. *abbrev. for:* **1** Wales. **2** Welsh.

WA *abbrev. for:* **1** Washington (state). **2** Western Australia.

WAAAF (formerly) *abbrev. for* Women's Auxiliary Australian Air Force.

WAAC (wæk) *n* (formerly) **1** *acronym for* Women's Army Auxiliary Corps. **2** Also called: **Waac.** a member of this corps.

WAAF (wæf) *n* (formerly) **1** *acronym for* Women's Auxiliary Air Force. **2** Also called: **Waaf.** a member of this force.

wabble ('wɒbᵊl) *vb* **wabbles, wabbling, wabbled,** *n* a variant spelling of **wobble.**

wacke ('wækə) *n Obs.* any of various soft earthy rocks derived from basalt. [C18: from G: rock, gravel, basalt]

wacko ('wækəʊ) *Inf.* ◆ *adj* **1** mad or eccentric. ◆ *n, pl* **wackos. 2** a mad or eccentric person. [C20: back formation from WACKY]

wacky Ⓣ ('wækɪ) *adj* **wackier, wackiest.** *Sl.* eccentric or unpredictable. [C19 (in dialect sense: a fool): from WHACK (hence, a *whacky,* a person who behaves as if he had been whacked on the head)]
► '**wackily** *adv* ► '**wackiness** *n*

wad Ⓣ (wɒd) *n* **1** a small mass or ball of fibrous or soft material, such as cotton wool, used esp. for packing or stuffing. **2a** a plug of paper, cloth, leather, etc., pressed against a charge to hold it in place in a muzzle-loading cannon. **2b** a disc of paper, felt, etc., used to hold in place the powder and shot in a shotgun cartridge. **3** a roll or bundle of something, esp. of banknotes. ◆ *vb* **wads, wadding, wadded. 4** to form (something) into a wad. **5** (*tr*) to roll into a wad or bundle. **6** (*tr*) **6a** to hold (a charge) in place with a wad. **6b** to insert a wad into (a gun). **7** (*tr*) to pack or stuff with wadding. [C14: from LL *wadda*]

wadding Ⓣ ('wɒdɪŋ) *n* **1a** any fibrous or soft substance used as padding, stuffing, etc. **1b** a piece of this. **2** material for wads used in cartridges or guns.

waddle Ⓣ ('wɒdᵊl) *vb* **waddles, waddling, waddled.** (*intr*) **1** to walk with short steps, rocking slightly from side to side. ◆ *n* **2** a swaying gait or motion. [C16: prob. frequentative of WADE]
► '**waddler** *n* ► '**waddling** *adj*

waddy ('wɒdɪ) *n, pl* **waddies. 1** a heavy wooden club used as a weapon by native Australians. ◆ *vb* **waddies, waddying, waddied. 2** (*tr*) to hit with a waddy. [C19: from Abor., ? based on E WOOD]

wade Ⓣ (weɪd) *vb* **wades, wading, waded. 1** to walk with the feet immersed in (water, a stream, etc.). **2** (*intr;* often foll. by *through*) to proceed with difficulty: *to wade through a book.* **3** (*intr;* foll. by *in* or *into*) to attack energetically. ◆ *n* **4** the act or an instance of wading. [OE *wadan*]
► '**wadable** *or* '**wadeable** *adj*

wader ('weɪdə) *n* **1** a person or thing that wades. **2** Also called: **wading bird.** any of various long-legged birds, esp. herons, storks, etc., that live near water and feed on fish, etc. **3** a Brit. name for **shore bird.**

waders ('weɪdəz) *pl n* long waterproof boots, sometimes extending to the chest like trousers, worn by anglers.

wadi *or* **wady** ('wɒdɪ) *n, pl* **wadies.** a watercourse in N Africa and Arabia, dry except in the rainy season. [C19: from Ar.]

wafer ('weɪfə) *n* **1** a thin crisp sweetened biscuit, served with ice cream, etc. **2** *Christianity.* a thin disc of unleavened bread used in the Eucharist. **3** *Pharmacol.* an envelope of rice paper enclosing a medicament. **4** *Electronics.* a large single crystal of semiconductor material, such as silicon, on which numerous integrated circuits are manufactured and then separated. **5** a small thin disc of adhesive material used to seal letters, etc. ◆ *vb* **6** (*tr*) to seal or fasten with a wafer. [C14: from OF *waufre,* from MLow G *wāfel*]
► '**wafery** *adj*

waffle[1] ('wɒfᵊl) *n* **a** a crisp golden-brown pancake with deep indentations on both sides. **b** (*as modifier*): *waffle iron.* [C19: from Du. *wafel* (earlier *wæfel*), of Gmc origin]

waffle[2] Ⓣ ('wɒfᵊl) *Inf., chiefly Brit.* ◆ *vb* **waffles, waffling, waffled. 1** (*intr;* often foll. by *on*) to speak or write in a vague and wordy manner. ◆ *n* **2** vague and wordy speech or writing. [C19: from ?]
► '**waffling** *adj, n*

waft Ⓣ (wɑːft, wɒft) *vb* **1** to carry or be carried gently on or as if on the air or water. ◆ *n* **2** the act or an instance of wafting. **3** something, such as a scent, carried on the air. **4** *Naut.* (formerly) a signal flag hoisted furled to signify various messages depending on where it was flown. [C16 (in obs. sense: to convey by ship): back formation from C15 *wafter* a convoy vessel, from MDu. *wachter* guard]

wag[1] Ⓣ (wæg) *vb* **wags, wagging, wagged. 1** to move or cause to move rapidly and repeatedly from side to side or up and down. **2** to move (the tongue) or (of the tongue) to be moved rapidly in talking, esp. in gossip. **3** to move (the finger) or (of the finger) to be moved from side to side, in or as in admonition. **4** *Sl.* to play truant (esp. in **wag it**). ◆ *n* **5** the act or an instance of wagging. [C13: from OE *wagian* to shake]

wag[2] Ⓣ (wæg) *n* a humorous or jocular person; wit. [C16: from ?]
► '**waggish** *adj*

wage Ⓣ (weɪdʒ) *n* **1** (*often pl*) payment in return for work or services, esp. that made to workers on a daily, hourly, weekly, or piecework basis. Cf. **salary. 2** (*pl*) *Econ.* the portion of the national income accruing to labour as earned income, as contrasted with the unearned income accruing to capital in the form of rent, interest, and dividends. **3** (*often pl*) recompense, return, or yield. ◆ *vb* **wages, waging, waged.** (*tr*) **4** to engage in. [C14: from OF *wagier* to pledge, from *wage,* of Gmc origin]
► '**wageless** *adj*

wage differential *n* the difference in wages between workers with different skills in the same industry or between those with comparable skills in different industries or localities.

wage earner *n* **1** a person who works for wages. **2** the person who earns money to support a household by working.

wage freeze *n* a statutory restriction on wage increases.

wage indexation *n* a linking of wage rises to increases in the cost of living usually in order to maintain real wages during periods of high inflation.

wager Ⓣ ('weɪdʒə) *n* **1** an agreement to pay an amount of money as a result of the outcome of an unsettled matter. **2** an amount staked on the outcome of such an event. **3 wager of battle.** (in medieval Britain) a pledge to do battle to decide guilt or innocence by single combat. **4 wager of law.** *English legal history.* a form of trial in which the accused offered to make oath of his innocence, supported by the oaths of 11 of his neighbours declaring their belief in his statements. ◆ *vb* **5** (when *tr, may take a clause as object*) to risk or bet (something) on the outcome of an unsettled matter. [C14: from Anglo-F *wageure* a pledge, from OF *wagier* to pledge; see WAGE]
► '**wagerer** *n*

wages council *n* (formerly, in Britain) a statutory body empowered to fix minimum wages in an industry; abolished in 1994.

wage slave *n Ironical.* a person dependent on a wage or salary.

wagga ('wɒgə) *n Austral.* a blanket or bed covering of sacks stitched together. [C19: after *Wagga Wagga,* a city in SE Australia]

waggle Ⓣ ('wægᵊl) *vb* **waggles, waggling, waggled. 1** to move or cause to move with a rapid shaking or wobbling motion. ◆ *n* **2** a rapid shaking or wobbling motion. [C16: from WAG[1]]
► '**waggly** *adj*

waggon ('wægən) *n* a variant spelling (esp. Brit.) of **wagon.**

wag-n-bietjie ('vɑːxᵊn,bɪkɪ) *n S. African.* any of various thorn bushes or trees. [from Afrik. *wag* wait + *n* a + *bietjie* bit]

Wagnerian (vɑːg'nɪərɪən) *adj* **1** of or suggestive of the dramatic musical compositions of Richard Wagner (1813–83), German composer, their massive scale, dramatic and emotional intensity, etc. ◆ *n also* **Wagnerite** ('vɑːgnə,raɪt). **2** a follower or disciple of the music or theories of Richard Wagner.

THESAURUS

wacky *adj Slang* = **eccentric**, crazy, daft (*inf.*), erratic, irrational, loony (*sl.*), nutty (*sl.*), odd, oddball (*inf.*), off-the-wall (*sl.*), outré, screwy (*inf.*), silly, unpredictable, wild, zany

wad *n* **1-3** = **mass**, ball, block, bundle, chunk, hunk, lump, plug, roll

wadding *n* **1** = **padding**, filler, lining, packing, stuffing

waddle *vb* **1** = **shuffle**, rock, sway, toddle, totter, wobble

wade *vb* **1** = **walk through**, ford, paddle, splash **2** *often foll. by* **through** = **plough through**, drudge at, labour at, peg away at, toil at, work one's way through **3** *foll. by* **in** *or* **into** = **launch oneself at**, assail, attack, get stuck in (*inf.*), go for, light into (*inf.*), set about, tackle, tear into (*inf.*)

waffle[2] *vb* **1** = **prattle**, blather, jabber, prate, rabbit (on) (*Brit. inf.*), verbalize, witter on (*inf.*) ◆ *n* **2** = **verbosity**, blather, jabber, padding, prating, prattle, prolixity, verbiage, wordiness

waft *vb* **1** = **carry**, bear, be carried, convey, drift, float, ride, transmit, transport ◆ *n* **2** = **current**, breath, breeze, draught, puff, whiff

wag[1] *vb* **1** = **wave**, bob, flutter, nod, oscillate, quiver, rock, shake, stir, vibrate, waggle, wiggle ◆ *n* **5** = **wave**, bob, flutter, nod, oscillation, quiver, shake, toss, vibration, waggle, wiggle

wag[2] *n* = **joker**, card (*inf.*), clown, comedian, comic, humorist, jester, wit

wage *n* **1** = **payment**, allowance, compensation, earnings, emolument, fee, hire, pay, recompense, remuneration, reward, stipend ◆ *vb* **4** = **engage in**, carry on, conduct, practise, proceed with, prosecute, pursue, undertake

wager *n* **1, 2** = **bet**, flutter (*Brit. inf.*), gamble, pledge, punt (*chiefly Brit.*), stake, venture ◆ *vb* **5** = **bet**, chance, gamble, hazard, lay, pledge, punt (*chiefly Brit.*), put on, risk, speculate, stake, venture

waggish *adj* = **humorous**, amusing, comical, droll, facetious, funny, impish, jesting, jocose, jocular, merry, mischievous, playful, puckish, risible, sportive, witty

waggle *vb* **1** = **wag**, flutter, oscillate, shake, wave, wiggle, wobble

wagon *or* **waggon** (ˈwægən) *n* **1** any of various types of wheeled vehicles, ranging from carts to lorries, esp. a vehicle with four wheels drawn by a horse, tractor, etc., and used for carrying heavy loads. **2** *Brit.* a railway freight truck, esp. an open one. **3** an obsolete word for **chariot. 4 on** (*or* **off**) **the wagon.** *Inf.* abstaining (*or* no longer abstaining) from alcohol. [C16: from Du. *wagen* WAIN]
▸ˈ**wagonless** *or* ˈ**waggonless** *adj*

wagoner *or* **waggoner** (ˈwægənə) *n* a person who drives a wagon.

wagonette *or* **waggonette** (ˌwægəˈnɛt) *n* a light four-wheeled horse-drawn vehicle with two lengthwise seats facing each other behind a crosswise driver's seat.

wagon-lit (*French* vagõli) *n, pl* **wagons-lits** (vagõli). **1** a sleeping car on a European railway. **2** a compartment on such a car. [C19: from F, from *wagon* railway coach + *lit* bed]

wagonload *or* **waggonload** (ˈwægənˌləʊd) *n* the load that is or can be carried by a wagon.

wagon train *n* a supply train of horses and wagons, esp. one going over rough terrain.

wagon vault *n* another name for **barrel vault.**

wagtail (ˈwægˌteɪl) *n* any of various passerine songbirds of Eurasia and Africa, having a very long tail that wags when the bird walks.

Wahhabi *or* **Wahabi** (wəˈhɑːbɪ) *n, pl* **Wahhabis** *or* **Wahabis.** a member of a strictly conservative Muslim sect founded in the 18th century.
▸**Wahˈhabism** *or* **Waˈhabism** *n*

wahine (wɑːˈhiːnɪ) *n* **1** *NZ.* a Maori woman. **2** a Polynesian woman. [from Maori & Hawaiian]

wahoo (wɑːˈhuː, ˈwɑːhuː) *n, pl* **wahoos.** a large fast-moving food and game fish of tropical seas. [from ?]

wah-wah (ˈwɑːˌwɑː) *n* **1** the sound made by a trumpet, cornet, etc., when the bell is alternately covered and uncovered. **2** an electronic attachment for an electric guitar, etc., that simulates this effect. [C20: imit.]

waif ➊ (weɪf) *n* **1** a person, esp. a child, who is homeless, friendless, or neglected. **2** anything found and not claimed, the owner being unknown. [C14: from Anglo-Norman, var. of OF *gaif,* from ON]
▸ˈ**waifˌlike** *adj*

wail ➊ (weɪl) *vb* **1** (*intr*) to utter a prolonged high-pitched cry, as of grief or misery. **2** (*intr*) to make a sound resembling such a cry: *the wind wailed in the trees.* **3** (*tr*) to lament, esp. with mournful sounds. ◆ *n* **4** a prolonged high-pitched mournful cry or sound. [C14: from ON]
▸ˈ**wailer** *n*

wain (weɪn) *n Chiefly poetic.* a farm wagon or cart. [OE *wægn*]

wainscot (ˈweɪnskət) *n* **1** Also called: **wainscoting** *or* **wainscotting.** a lining applied to the walls of a room, esp. one of wood panelling. **2** the lower part of the walls of a room, esp. when finished in a material different from the upper part. **3** fine-quality oak used as wainscot. ◆ *vb* **4** (*tr*) to line (a wall of a room) with a wainscot. [C14: from MLow G *wagenschot,* ?from *wagen* WAGON + *schot* planking]

wainwright (ˈweɪnˌraɪt) *n* a person who makes wagons.

waist (weɪst) *n* **1** *Anat.* the constricted part of the trunk between the ribs and hips. **2** the part of a garment covering the waist. **3** the middle part of an object that resembles the waist in narrowness or position. **4** the middle part of a ship. **5** the middle section of an aircraft fuselage. **6** the constriction between the thorax and abdomen in wasps and similar insects. [C14: from ?]
▸ˈ**waistless** *adj*

waistband (ˈweɪstˌbænd) *n* an encircling band of material to finish and strengthen a skirt or trousers at the waist.

waistcoat (ˈweɪsˌkəʊt) *n* **1** a man's sleeveless waistlength garment worn under a suit jacket, usually buttoning up the front. **2** a similar garment worn by women. ◆ US and Canad. name: **vest.**
▸ˈ**waistˌcoated** *adj*

waistline (ˈweɪstˌlaɪn) *n* **1** a line around the body at the narrowest part of the waist. **2** the intersection of the bodice and the skirt of a dress, etc., or the level of this.

wait ➊ (weɪt) *vb* **1** (when *intr,* often foll. by *for, until,* or *to*) to stay in one place or remain inactive in expectation (of something). **2** to delay temporarily or be temporarily delayed: *that work can wait.* **3** (when *intr,* usually foll. by *for*) (of things) to be ready or at hand; be in store (for a person): *supper was waiting for them when they got home.* **4** (*intr*) to act as a waiter or waitress. ◆ *n* **5** the act or an instance of waiting. **6** a period of waiting. **7** (*pl*) *Rare.* a band of musicians who go around the streets, esp. at Christmas, singing and playing carols. **8 lie in wait.** to prepare an ambush (for someone). ◆ See also **wait on, wait up.** [C12: from OF *waitier*]

wait-a-bit *n* any of various mainly tropical plants having sharp hooked thorns.

Waitangi Day (waɪˈtʌŋiː) *n* the national day of New Zealand (Feb. 6), commemorating the signing of the **Treaty of Waitangi** (1840) by Maori chiefs and a representative of the British Government. The treaty provided the basis for the British annexation of New Zealand.

waiter ➊ (ˈweɪtə) *n* **1** a man whose occupation is to serve at table, as in a restaurant. **2** an attendant at the London stock exchange or Lloyd's who carries messages: the modern equivalent of waiters who performed these duties in the 17th-century London coffee houses in which these institutions originated. **3** a person who waits. **4** a tray or salver.

waiting game *n* the postponement of action or decision in order to gain the advantage.

waiting list *n* a list of people waiting to obtain some object, treatment, status, etc.

waiting room *n* a room in which people may wait, as at a railway station, doctor's or dentist's surgery, etc.

wait on ➊ *vb* (*intr, prep*) **1** to serve at the table of. **2** to act as an attendant to. ◆ *sentence substitute.* **3** *Austral.* & *NZ.* stop! hold on! ◆ Also (for senses 1, 2): **wait upon.**

waitress (ˈweɪtrɪs) *n* **1** a woman who serves at table, as in a restaurant. ◆ *vb* (*intr*) **2** to act as a waitress.

wait up *vb* (*intr, adv*) to delay going to bed in order to await some event.

waive ➊ (weɪv) *vb* **waives, waiving, waived.** (*tr*) **1** to set aside or relinquish: *to waive one's rights.* **2** to refrain from enforcing or applying (a law, penalty, etc.). **3** to defer. [C13: from OF *weyver,* from *waif* abandoned; see WAIF]

waiver ➊ (ˈweɪvə) *n* **1** the voluntary relinquishment, expressly or by implication, of some claim or right. **2** the act or an instance of relinquishing a claim or right. **3** a formal statement in writing of such relinquishment. [C17: from OF *weyver* to relinquish]

wake[1] ➊ (weɪk) *vb* **wakes, waking, woke, woken. 1** (often foll. by *up*) to rouse or become roused from sleep. **2** (often foll. by *up*) to rouse or become roused from inactivity. **3** (*intr;* often foll. by *to* or *up to*) to become conscious or aware: *at last he woke up to the situation.* **4** (*intr*) to be or remain awake. ◆ *n* **5** a watch or vigil held over the body of a dead person during the night before burial. **6** (in Ireland) festivities held after a funeral. **7** the patronal or dedication festival of English parish churches. **8** a solemn or ceremonial vigil. **9** (*usually pl*) an annual holiday in various towns in Northern England, when the local factories close. [OE *wacian*]
▸ˈ**waker** *n*

> **USAGE NOTE** Where there is an object and the sense is the literal one *wake* (*up*) and *waken* are the commonest forms: *I wakened him; I woke him* (*up*). Both verbs are also commonly used without an object: *I woke up. Awake* and *awaken* are preferred to other forms of *wake* where the sense is a figurative one: *he awoke to the danger.*

wake[2] ➊ (weɪk) *n* **1** the waves or track left by a vessel or other object moving through water. **2** the track or path left by anything that has passed: *wrecked houses in the wake of the hurricane.* [C16: of Scand. origin]

wakeful ➊ (ˈweɪkfʊl) *adj* **1** unable or unwilling to sleep. **2** sleepless. **3** alert.
▸ˈ**wakefully** *adv* ▸ˈ**wakefulness** *n*

wakeless (ˈweɪklɪs) *adj* (of sleep) unbroken.

waken ➊ (ˈweɪkən) *vb* to rouse or be roused from sleep or some other inactive state.

> **USAGE NOTE** See at **wake**[1].

THESAURUS

waif *n* **1** = **stray**, foundling, orphan

wail *vb* **1, 3** = **cry**, bawl, bemoan, bewail, deplore, grieve, howl, keen, lament, ululate, weep, yowl ◆ *n* **3** = **cry**, complaint, grief, howl, keen, lament, lamentation, moan, ululation, weeping, yowl

wait *vb* **1, 2** = **remain**, abide, bide one's time, cool one's heels, dally, delay, hang fire, hold back, hold on (*inf.*), kick one's heels, linger, mark time, pause, rest, stand by, stay, tarry ◆ *n* **5, 6** = **delay**, entr'acte, halt, hold-up, interval, pause, rest, stay
Antonyms *vb* ≠ **remain:** depart, go, go away, leave, move off, quit, set off, take off (*inf.*)

waiter *n* **1** = **attendant**, server, steward *or* stewardess

wait on *vb* **1, 2** = **serve**, attend, minister to, tend

waive *vb* **1, 2** = **set aside**, abandon, defer, dispense with, forgo, give up, postpone, put off, refrain from, relinquish, remit, renounce, resign, surrender
Antonyms *vb* claim, demand, insist, maintain, press, profess, pursue, uphold

waiver *n* **1** = **renunciation**, abandonment, abdication, disclaimer, giving up, relinquishment, remission, resignation, setting aside, surrender

wake[1] *vb* **1** = **awaken**, arise, awake, bestir, come to, get up, rouse, rouse from sleep, stir **2** = **activate**, animate, arouse, awaken, enliven, excite, fire, galvanize, kindle, provoke, quicken, rouse, stimulate, stir up ◆ *n* **5** = **vigil**, deathwatch, funeral, watch
Antonyms *vb* ≠ **awaken:** catnap, doze, drop off (*inf.*), hibernate, nod off (*inf.*), sleep, snooze (*inf.*), take a nap

wake[2] *n* **1, 2** = **slipstream**, aftermath, backwash, path, track, trail, train, wash, waves

wakeful *adj* **1, 2** = **sleepless**, insomniac, restless, unsleeping **3** = **watchful**, alert, alive, attentive, heedful, observant, on guard, on the alert, on the lookout, on the qui vive, unsleeping, vigilant, wary
Antonyms *adj* ≠ **sleepless:** asleep, dormant, dozing ≠ **watchful:** dreamy, drowsy, heedless, inattentive, off guard, sleepy

waken *vb* = **awaken**, activate, animate, arouse, awake, be roused, come awake, come to, enliven, fire, galvanize, get up, kindle, quicken, rouse, stimulate, stir
Antonyms *vb* be inactive, doze, lie dormant, nap, repose, sleep, slumber, snooze (*inf.*)

wake-robin *n* any of a genus of North American herbaceous plants having a whorl of three leaves and three-petalled solitary flowers.

wake-up *n* **a wake-up to.** *Austral. sl.* fully alert to (a person, thing, action, etc.).

Waldenses (wɒlˈdɛnsiːz) *pl n* the members of a small sect founded as a reform movement within the Roman Catholic Church by Peter Waldo, a merchant of Lyons, in the late 12th century.
▸**Walˈdensian** *n, adj*

waldo (ˈwɔːldəʊ) *n, pl* **waldos, waldoes.** a gadget for manipulating objects by remote control. [C20: after *Waldo* F. Jones, an inventor, in a science-fiction story by Robert Heinlein]

Waldorf salad (ˈwɔːldɔːf) *n* a salad of diced apples, celery, and walnuts mixed with mayonnaise.

waldsterben (ˈwɔːldˌstɜːbən) *n Ecology.* the symptoms of tree decline in central Europe from the 1970s, considered to be caused by atmospheric pollution. [C20: from G *Wald* forest + *sterben* to die]

wale Ⓣ (weɪl) *n* **1** the raised mark left on the skin after the stroke of a rod or whip. **2** the weave or texture of a fabric, such as the ribs in corduroy. **3** *Naut.* a ridge of planking along the rail of a ship. ◆ *vb* **wales, waling, waled. 4** (*tr*) to raise a wale or wales on by striking. **5** to weave with a wale. [OE *walu* weal]

walk Ⓣ (wɔːk) *vb* **1** (*intr*) to move along or travel on foot at a moderate rate; advance in such a manner that at least one foot is always on the ground. **2** (*tr*) to pass through, on, or over on foot, esp. habitually. **3** (*tr*) to cause, assist, or force to move along at a moderate rate: *to walk a dog.* **4** (*tr*) to escort or conduct by walking: *to walk someone home.* **5** (*intr*) (of ghosts, spirits, etc.) to appear or move about in visible form. **6** (*intr*) to follow a certain course or way of life: *to walk in misery.* **7** (*tr*) to bring into a certain condition by walking: *I walked my shoes to shreds.* **8** to disappear or be stolen: *Where's my pencil? It seems to have walked.* **9 walk it.** to win easily. **10 walk on air.** to be delighted or exhilarated. **11 walk tall.** *Inf.* to have self-respect or pride. **12 walk the streets. 12a** to be a prostitute. **12b** to wander round a town, esp. when looking for work or when homeless. ◆ *n* **13** the act or an instance of walking. **14** the distance or extent walked. **15** a manner of walking; gait. **16** a place set aside for walking; promenade. **17** a chosen profession or sphere of activity (esp. in **walk of life**). **18a** an arrangement of trees or shrubs in widely separated rows. **18b** the space between such rows. **19** an enclosed ground for the exercise or feeding of domestic animals, esp. horses. **20** *Chiefly Brit.* the route covered in the course of work, as by a tradesman or postman. **21** a procession; march: *Orange walk.* **22** *Obs.* the section of a forest controlled by a keeper. ◆ See also **walk away, walk into,** etc. [OE *wealcan*]
▸**ˈwalkable** *adj*

walkabout (ˈwɔːkəˌbaʊt) *n* **1** a periodic nomadic excursion into the Australian bush made by a native Australian. **2** an occasion when celebrities, royalty, etc., walk among and meet the public. **3 go walkabout.** *Austral.* **3a** to wander through the bush. **3b** *Inf.* to be lost or misplaced. **3c** *Inf.* to lose one's concentration.

walk away *vb* (*intr, adv*) **1** to leave, esp. disregarding someone else's distress. **2 walk away with.** to achieve or win easily.

walker Ⓣ (ˈwɔːkə) *n* **1** a person who walks. **2** Also called: **baby walker.** a tubular frame on wheels or casters to support a baby learning to walk. **3** a similar support for walking, often with rubber feet, for use by disabled or infirm people.

walkie-talkie *or* **walky-talky** (ˌwɔːkɪˈtɔːkɪ) *n, pl* **walkie-talkies.** a small combined radio transmitter and receiver that can be carried around by one person: widely used by the police, medical services, etc.

walk-in *adj* **1** (of a cupboard) large enough to allow a person to enter and move about in. **2** (of a flat or house) in a suitable condition for immediate occupation.

walking papers *pl n Sl., chiefly US & Canad.* notice of dismissal.

walking stick *n* **1** a stick or cane carried in the hand to assist walking. **2** the usual US name for **stick insect.**

walk into *vb* (*intr, prep*) to meet with unwittingly: *to walk into a trap.*

Walkman (ˈwɔːkmən) *n Trademark.* a small portable cassette player with headphones.

walk off *vb* **1** (*intr*) to depart suddenly. **2** (*tr, adv*) to get rid of by walking: *to walk off an attack of depression.* **3 walk (a person) off his** *or* **her feet.** to make (a person) walk so fast or far that he or she is exhausted. **4 walk off with. 4a** to steal. **4b** to win, esp. easily.

walk-on *n* **a** a small part in a play or theatrical entertainment, esp. one without any lines. **b** (*as modifier*): *a walk-on part.*

walk out Ⓣ *vb* (*intr, adv*) **1** to leave without explanation, esp. in anger. **2** to go on strike. **3 walk out on.** *Inf.* to abandon or desert. **4 walk out with.** *Brit., obs. or dialect.* to court or be courted by. ◆ *n* **walkout. 5** a strike by workers. **6** the act of leaving a meeting, conference, etc., as a protest.

walkover Ⓣ (ˈwɔːkˌəʊvə) *n* **1** *Inf.* an easy or unopposed victory. **2** *Horse racing.* **2a** the running or walking over the course by the only contestant entered in a race at the time of starting. **2b** a race won in this way. ◆ *vb* **walk over.** (*intr, mainly prep*) **3** (*also adv*) to win a race by a walkover. **4** *Inf.* to beat (an opponent) conclusively or easily.

walk socks *pl n NZ.* knee-length, usually woollen, stockings.

walk through *Theatre.* ◆ *vb* **1** (*tr*) to act or recite (a part) in a perfunctory manner, as at a first rehearsal. ◆ *n* **walk-through. 2** a rehearsal of a part.

walkway (ˈwɔːkˌweɪ) *n* **1** a path designed and sometimes landscaped for pedestrian use. **2** a passage or path, esp. one for walking over machinery, connecting buildings, etc.

wall Ⓣ (wɔːl) *n* **1a** a vertical construction made of stone, brick, wood, etc., with a length and height much greater than its thickness, used to enclose, divide, or support. **1b** (*as modifier*): *wall hangings.* Related adj: **mural. 2** (*often pl*) a structure or rampart built to protect and surround a position or place for defensive purposes. **3** *Anat.* any lining, membrane, or investing part that encloses or bounds a bodily cavity or structure: *abdominal wall.* Technical name: **paries.** Related adj: **parietal. 4** anything that suggests a wall in function or effect: *a wall of fire.* **5 drive** (*or* **push**) **to the wall.** to force into an awkward situation. **6 go to the wall.** *Inf.* to be ruined. **7 go** (*or* **drive**) **up the wall.** *Sl.* to become (*or* cause to become) crazy or furious. **8 have one's back to the wall.** to be in a difficult situation. ◆ *vb* (*tr*) **9** to protect, provide, or confine with or as if with a wall. **10** (often foll. by *up*) to block (an opening) with a wall. **11** (often foll. by *in* or *up*) to seal by or within a wall or walls. [OE *weall,* from L *vallum* palisade, from *vallus* stake]
▸**walled** *adj* ▸**ˈwall-less** *adj*

wallaby (ˈwɒləbɪ) *n, pl* **wallabies** *or* **wallaby.** any of various herbivorous marsupials of Australia and New Guinea, similar to but smaller than kangaroos. [C19: from Abor. *wolabā*]

Wallaby (ˈwɒləbɪ) *n, pl* **Wallabies.** a member of the international rugby union football team of Australia.

Wallace's line (ˈwɒlɪsɪz) *n* the hypothetical boundary between the Oriental and Australasian zoogeographical regions, which runs through Indonesia and SE of the Philippines. [C20: after A. R. *Wallace* (1823–1913), Brit. naturalist]

wallah *or* **walla** (ˈwɒlə) *n* (*usually in combination*) *Inf.* a person involved with or in charge of (a specified thing): *the book wallah.* [C18: from Hindi *-wālā* from Sansk. *pāla* protector]

wallaroo (ˌwɒləˈruː) *n, pl* **wallaroos** *or* **wallaroo.** a large stocky Australian kangaroo of rocky or mountainous regions. [C19: from Abor. *wolarū*]

wall bars *pl n* a series of horizontal bars attached to a wall and used in gymnastics.

wallboard (ˈwɔːlˌbɔːd) *n* a thin board made of materials, such as compressed wood fibres or gypsum plaster, between stiff paper, and used to cover walls, partitions, etc.

wall creeper *n* a pink-and-grey woodpecker-like songbird of Eurasian mountain regions.

walled plain *n* any of the largest of the lunar craters, having diameters between 50 and 300 kilometres.

wallet Ⓣ (ˈwɒlɪt) *n* **1** a small folding case, usually of leather, for holding paper money, documents, etc. **2** *Arch., chiefly Brit.* a rucksack or knapsack. [C14: of Gmc origin]

walleye (ˈwɔːlˌaɪ) *n, pl* **walleyes** *or* **walleye. 1** a divergent squint. **2** opacity of the cornea. **3** an eye having a white or light-coloured iris. **4** Also called: **walleyed pike.** a North American pikeperch valued as a food and game fish. [back formation from earlier *walleyed,* from ON *vagleygr,* from *vage* ? a film over the eye + *-eygr* -eyed, from *auga* eye; infl. by WALL]
▸**ˈwallˌeyed** *adj*

wallflower (ˈwɔːlˌflaʊə) *n* **1** Also called: **gillyflower.** a cruciferous plant of S Europe, grown for its clusters of yellow, orange, brown, red, or purple fragrant flowers and naturalized on old walls, cliffs, etc. **2** *Inf.* a person who stays on the fringes of a dance or party on account of lacking a partner or being shy.

THESAURUS

wale *n* **1** = **mark,** contusion, scar, streak, stripe, weal, welt, wheal

walk *vb* **1, 2** = **go,** advance, amble, foot it, go by shanks's pony (*inf.*), go on foot, hike, hoof it (*sl.*), march, move, pace, perambulate, promenade, saunter, step, stride, stroll, traipse (*inf.*), tramp, travel on foot, tread, trek, trudge **4** = **escort,** accompany, convoy, take ◆ *n* **13** = **stroll,** constitutional, hike, march, perambulation, promenade, ramble, saunter, traipse (*inf.*), tramp, trek, trudge, turn **15** = **gait,** carriage, manner of walking, pace, step, stride **16** = **path,** aisle, alley, avenue, esplanade, footpath, lane, pathway, pavement, promenade, sidewalk, trail **17** *As in* **walk of life** = **profession,** area, arena, calling, career, course, field, line, métier, sphere, trade, vocation

walker *n* **1** = **pedestrian,** footslogger, hiker, rambler, wayfarer

walk out *vb* **1** = **leave suddenly,** flounce out, get up and go, storm out, take off (*inf.*), vote with one's feet **2** = **go on strike,** down tools, stop work, strike, take industrial action, withdraw one's labour **3 walk out on** *Informal* = **abandon,** chuck (*inf.*), desert, forsake, jilt, leave, leave in the lurch, pack in (*inf.*), run away from, strand, throw over ◆ *n* **walkout 5** = **strike,** industrial action, protest, stoppage
Antonyms *vb* ≠ **abandon:** be loyal to, defend, remain, stand by, stay, stick with, support, uphold

walkover *n* **1** *Informal* = **pushover** (*sl.*), breeze (*US & Canad. inf.*), cakewalk (*inf.*), child's play (*inf.*), cinch (*sl.*), doddle (*Brit. sl.*), easy victory, picnic (*inf.*), piece of cake (*inf.*), snap (*inf.*)
Antonyms *n* effort, grind (*inf.*), labour, ordeal, strain, struggle, trial

wall *n* **1** = **partition,** divider, enclosure, panel, screen **2** = **barricade,** breastwork, bulwark, embankment, fortification, palisade, parapet, rampart, stockade **6 go to the wall** *Informal* = **fail,** be ruined, collapse, fall, go bust (*inf.*), go under **7 drive up the wall** *Slang* = **infuriate,** aggravate (*inf.*), annoy, dement, derange, drive crazy (*inf.*), drive insane, exasperate, get on one's nerves (*inf.*), irritate, madden, send off one's head (*sl.*), try

wallet *n* **1** = **holder,** case, notecase, pocketbook, pouch, purse

wall of death *n* (at a fairground) a giant cylinder round the inside vertical walls of which a motorcyclist rides.

Walloon (wɒ'lu:n) *n* **1** a member of a French-speaking people living chiefly in S Belgium and adjacent parts of France. **2** the French dialect of Belgium. ◆ *adj* **3** of or characteristic of the Walloons or their dialect. [C16: from OF *Wallon,* from Med. L: foreigner, of Gmc origin]

wallop ⓣ ('wɒləp) *vb* **wallops, walloping, walloped. 1** (*tr*) *Inf.* to beat soundly; strike hard. **2** (*tr*) *Inf.* to defeat utterly. **3** (*intr*) (of liquids) to boil violently. ◆ *n* **4** *Inf.* a hard blow. **5** *Inf.* the ability to hit powerfully, as of a boxer. **6** *Inf.* a forceful impression. **7** *Brit. sl.* beer. [C14: from OF *waloper* to gallop, from OF *galoper,* from ?]

walloper ('wɒləpə) *n* **1** a person or thing that wallops. **2** *Austral. sl.* a policeman.

walloping ('wɒləpɪŋ) *Inf.* ◆ *n* **1** a thrashing. ◆ *adj* **2** (intensifier): *a walloping drop in sales.*

wallow ⓣ ('wɒləʊ) *vb* (*intr*) **1** (esp. of certain animals) to roll about in mud, water, etc., for pleasure. **2** to move about with difficulty. **3** to indulge oneself in possessions, emotion, etc.: *to wallow in self-pity.* ◆ *n* **4** the act or an instance of wallowing. **5** a muddy place where animals wallow. [OE *wealwian* to roll (in mud)]
▸ **'wallower** *n*

wallpaper ('wɔ:l,peɪpə) *n* **1** paper usually printed or embossed with designs for pasting onto walls and ceilings. **2** *Computing.* a picture or pattern on a computer screen between and behind program icons and windows. ◆ *vb* **3** to cover (a surface) with wallpaper.

wall pepper *n* a small Eurasian plant having yellow flowers and acrid-tasting leaves.

wall plate *n* a horizontal timber member placed along the top of a wall to support the ends of joists, rafters, etc., and distribute the load.

wallposter ('wɔ:l,pəʊstə) *n* (in China) a bulletin or political message painted in large characters on a wall.

wall rocket *n* any of several yellow-flowered European cruciferous plants that grow on old walls and in waste places.

wall rue *n* a delicate fern that grows in rocky crevices and walls in North America and Eurasia.

Wall Street *n* a street in lower Manhattan, New York, where the Stock Exchange and major banks are situated, regarded as the embodiment of American finance.

wall-to-wall *adj* **1** (esp. of carpeting) completely covering a floor. **2** *Inf.* nonstop; widespread: *wall-to-wall sales.*

wally ('wɒlɪ) *n, pl* **wallies.** *Sl.* a stupid person. [C20: shortened from the name *Walter*]

walnut ('wɔ:l,nʌt) *n* **1** any of a genus of deciduous trees of America, SE Europe, and Asia. They have aromatic leaves and flowers in catkins and are grown for their edible nuts and for their wood. **2** the nut of any of these trees, having a wrinkled two-lobed seed and a hard wrinkled shell. **3** the wood of any of these trees, used in making furniture, etc. **4** a light yellowish-brown colour. ◆ *adj* **5** made from the wood of a walnut tree: *a walnut table.* **6** of the colour walnut. [OE *walh-hnutu,* lit.: foreign nut]

Walpurgis Night (væl'pʊəgɪs) *n* the eve of May 1, believed in German folklore to be the night of a witches' sabbath on the Brocken, in the Harz Mountains. [C19: translation of G *Walpurgisnacht,* the eve of the feast day of St Walpurga, 8th-cent. abbess in Germany]

walrus ('wɔ:lrəs, 'wɒl-) *n, pl* **walruses** *or* **walrus.** a mammal of northern seas, having a tough thick skin, upper canine teeth enlarged as tusks, and coarse whiskers, and feeding mainly on shellfish. [C17: prob. from Du., of Scand. origin]

walrus moustache *n* a long thick moustache drooping at the ends.

waltz (wɔ:ls) *n* **1** a ballroom dance in triple time in which couples spin around as they progress round the room. **2** a piece of music composed for or in the rhythm of this dance. ◆ *vb* **3** to dance or lead (someone) in or as in a waltz. **4** (*intr*) to move in a sprightly and self-assured manner. **5** (*intr*) *Inf.* to succeed easily. **6 waltz Matilda** *Austral.* See **Matilda.** [C18: from G *Walzer,* from MHG *walzen* to roll]

waltzer ('wɔ:lsə) *n* **1** a person who waltzes. **2** a fairground roundabout on which people are spun round and moved up and down as it revolves.

wampum ('wɒmpəm) *n* (formerly) money used by North American Indians, made of cylindrical shells strung or woven together. Also called: **peag, peage.** [C17: of Amerind origin, short for *wampumpeag,* from *wampompeag,* from *wampan* light + *api* string + *-ag* pl. suffix]

wan ⓣ (wɒn) *adj* **wanner, wannest. 1** unnaturally pale, esp. from sickness, grief, etc. **2** suggestive of ill health, unhappiness, etc. **3** (of light, stars, etc.) faint or dim. [OE *wann* dark]
▸ **'wanly** *adv* ▸ **'wanness** *n*

wand ⓣ (wɒnd) *n* **1** a slender supple stick or twig. **2** a thin rod carried as a symbol of authority. **3** a rod used by a magician, etc. **4** *Inf.* a conductor's baton. **5** *Archery.* a marker used to show the distance at which the archer stands from the target. [C12: from ON *vǒndr*]

wander ⓣ ('wɒndə) *vb* (*mainly intr*) **1** (*also tr*) to move or travel about, in, or through (a place) without any definite purpose or destination. **2** to proceed in an irregular course. **3** to go astray, as from a path or course. **4** (of thoughts, etc.) to lose concentration. **5** to think or speak incoherently or illogically. ◆ *n* **6** the act or an instance of wandering. [OE *wandrian*]
▸ **'wanderer** *n* ▸ **'wandering** *adj, n*

wandering albatross *n* a large albatross having a very wide wingspan and a white plumage with black wings.

wandering Jew *n* any of several related creeping or trailing plants of tropical America, such as tradescantia.

Wandering Jew *n* (in medieval legend) a character condemned to roam the world eternally because he mocked Christ on the day of the Crucifixion.

wanderlust ⓣ ('wɒndə,lʌst) *n* a great desire to travel and rove about. [from G *Wanderlust,* lit.: wander desire]

wanderoo (,wɒndə'ru:) *n, pl* **wanderoos.** a macaque monkey of India and Sri Lanka, having black fur with a ruff of long greyish fur on each side of the face. [C17: from Sinhalese *vanduru* monkeys, lit.: forest-dwellers]

wandoo (wɒn'du:) *n* a eucalyptus tree of W Australia, having white bark and durable wood. [from Abor.]

wane ⓣ (weɪn) *vb* **wanes, waning, waned.** (*intr*) **1** (of the moon) to show a gradually decreasing portion of illuminated surface, between full moon and new moon. **2** to decrease gradually in size, strength, power, etc. **3** to draw to a close. ◆ *n* **4** a decrease, as in size, strength, power, etc. **5** the period during which the moon wanes. **6** a drawing to a close. **7** a rounded surface or defective edge of a plank, where the bark was. **8 on the wane.** in a state of decline. [OE *wanian* (vb)]
▸ **'waney** *or* **'wany** *adj*

wangle ⓣ ('wæŋgᵊl) *Inf.* ◆ *vb* **wangles, wangling, wangled. 1** (*tr*) to use devious methods to get or achieve (something) for (oneself or another): *he wangled himself a salary increase.* **2** to manipulate or falsify (a situation, etc.). ◆ *n* **3** the act or an instance of wangling. [C19: orig. printers' sl., ? a blend of WAGGLE & dialect *wankle* wavering, from OE *wancol*]
▸ **'wangler** *n*

wanigan *or* **wannigan** ('wɒnɪgən) *n Canad.* **1** a lumberjack's chest or box. **2** a cabin, caboose, or houseboat. [C19: from Algonquian]

wank (wæŋk) *Taboo sl.* ◆ *vb* **1** (*intr*) to masturbate. ◆ *n* **2** an instance of wanking. [from ?]

wankel engine ('wæŋkᵊl) *n* a type of rotary internal-combustion engine without reciprocating parts. It consists of a curved triangular-shaped piston rotating in an elliptical combustion chamber. [C20: after Felix *Wankel* (1902–88), G engineer who invented it]

wanker ('wæŋkə) *n Sl.* **1** *Taboo.* a person who wanks; masturbator. **2** *Derog.* a worthless fellow.

wannabe *or* **wannabee** ('wɒnə,bi:) *n Inf.* **a** a person who desires to be, or be like, something or someone else. **b** (*as modifier*): *a wannabe film star.* [C20: phonetic shortening of *want to be*]

want ⓣ (wɒnt) *vb* **1** (*tr*) to feel a need or longing for: *I want a new hat.* **2** (when *tr, may take a clause as object or an infinitive*) to wish, need, or de-

THESAURUS

wallop *Informal vb* **1 = hit,** batter, beat, belt (*inf.*), buffet, chin (*sl.*), clobber (*sl.*), deck (*sl.*), lambast(e), lay one on (*sl.*), paste (*sl.*), pound, pummel, punch, slug, smack, strike, swipe, thrash, thump, whack **2 = beat,** best, blow out of the water (*sl.*), clobber (*sl.*), crush, defeat, drub, hammer (*inf.*), lick (*inf.*), rout, run rings around (*inf.*), stuff (*sl.*), thrash, trounce, vanquish, wipe the floor with (*inf.*), worst ◆ *n* **4 = blow,** bash, belt (*inf.*), haymaker (*sl.*), kick, punch, slug, smack, swipe, thump, thwack, whack

wallow *vb* **1 = roll about,** lie, splash around, tumble, welter **3 = revel,** bask, delight, glory, indulge oneself, luxuriate, relish, take pleasure
Antonyms *vb* ≠ **revel:** abstain, avoid, do without, eschew, forgo, give up, refrain

wan *adj* **1 = pale,** anaemic, ashen, bloodless, cadaverous, colourless, discoloured, ghastly, like death warmed up (*inf.*), livid, pallid, pasty, sickly, washed out, waxen, wheyfaced, white **3 = dim,** faint, feeble, pale, weak
Antonyms *adj* ≠ **pale:** blooming, bright, flourishing, glowing, healthy, roseate, rosy, rubicund, ruddy, vibrant

wand *n* **1-4 = stick,** baton, rod, sprig, twig, withe, withy

wander *vb* **1, 2 = roam,** cruise, drift, knock about *or* around, meander, mooch around (*sl.*), peregrinate, ramble, range, rove, straggle, stravaig (*Scot. & N English dialect*), stray, stroll, traipse (*inf.*) **3 = deviate,** depart, digress, divagate (*rare*), diverge, err, get lost, go astray, go off at a tangent, go off course, lapse, lose concentration, lose one's train of thought, lose one's way, swerve, veer **5 = rave,** babble, be delirious, be incoherent, ramble, speak incoherently, talk nonsense ◆ *n* **6 = excursion,** cruise, meander, peregrination, ramble, traipse (*inf.*)
Antonyms *vb* ≠ **deviate:** comply, conform, fall in with, follow, run with the pack, toe the line

wanderer *n* **1 = traveller,** bird of passage, drifter, gypsy, itinerant, nomad, rambler, ranger, rolling stone, rover, stroller, vagabond, vagrant, voyager

wandering *adj* **1 = nomadic,** drifting, homeless, itinerant, migratory, peripatetic, rambling, rootless, roving, strolling, travelling, vagabond, vagrant, voyaging, wayfaring

wanderlust *n* **= restlessness,** itchy feet (*inf.*), urge to travel

wane *vb* **2, 3 = decline,** abate, atrophy, decrease, die out, dim, diminish, draw to a close, drop, dwindle, ebb, fade, fade away, fail, lessen, sink, subside, taper off, weaken, wind down, wither ◆ *n* **8 on the wane = declining,** at its lowest ebb, dropping, dwindling, dying out, ebbing, fading, lessening, obsolescent, on its last legs, on the decline, on the way out, subsiding, tapering off, weakening, withering
Antonyms *vb* ≠ **decline:** blossom, brighten, develop, expand, grow, improve, increase, rise, strengthen, wax

wangle *vb* **1, 2** *Informal* **= contrive,** arrange, bring off, engineer, fiddle (*inf.*), finagle (*inf.*), fix (*inf.*), manipulate, manoeuvre, pull off, scheme, work (*inf.*)

want *vb* **1 = desire,** covet, crave, eat one's heart out over, feel a need for, hanker after, have a

sire (something or to do something): *he wants to go home.* **3** (*intr;* usually used with a negative and often foll. by *for*) to be lacking or deficient (in something necessary or desirable): *the child wants for nothing.* **4** (*tr*) to feel the absence of: *lying on the ground makes me want my bed.* **5** (*tr*) to fall short by (a specified amount). **6** (*tr*) *Chiefly Brit.* to have need of or require (doing or being something): *your shoes want cleaning.* **7** (*intr*) to be destitute. **8** (*tr; often passive*) to seek or request the presence of: *you're wanted upstairs.* **9** (*tr; takes an infinitive*) *Inf.* should or ought (to do something): *you don't want to go out so late.* ◆ *n* **10** the act or an instance of wanting. **11** anything that is needed, desired, or lacked: *to supply someone's wants.* **12** a lack, shortage, or absence: *for want of common sense.* **13** the state of being in need: *the state should help those in want.* **14** a sense of lack; craving. [C12 (vb, in the sense: it is lacking), C13 (n): from ON *vanta* to be deficient]
▸ **'wanter** *n*

want ad *n Inf.* a classified advertisement in a newspaper, magazine, etc., for something wanted, such as property or employment.

wanting ◐ ('wɒntɪŋ) *adj* (*postpositive*) **1** lacking or absent. **2** not meeting requirements or expectations: *you have been found wanting.*

wanton ◐ ('wɒntən) *adj* **1** dissolute, licentious, or immoral. **2** without motive, provocation, or justification: *wanton destruction.* **3** maliciously and unnecessarily cruel. **4** unrestrained: *wanton spending.* **5** *Arch. or poetic.* playful or capricious. **6** *Arch.* (of vegetation, etc.) luxuriant. ◆ *n* **7** a licentious person, esp. a woman. ◆ *vb* **8** (*intr*) to behave in a wanton manner. [C13 *wantowen* (in the obs. sense: unruly): from *wan-* (prefix equivalent to UN-[1]) + *-towen,* from OE *togen* brought up, from *tēon* to bring up]
▸ **'wantonly** *adv* ▸ **'wantonness** *n*

wapentake ('wɒpən,teɪk, 'wæp-) *n English legal history.* a subdivision of certain shires or counties, esp. in the Midlands and North of England, corresponding to the hundred in other shires. [OE *wǣpen(ge)tæc*]

wapiti ('wɒpɪtɪ) *n, pl* **wapitis.** a large North American deer with large much-branched antlers, now also found in New Zealand. [C19: of Amerind origin, lit.: white deer, from *wap* (unattested) white; from the animal's white tail and rump]

war ◐ (wɔː) *n* **1** open armed conflict between two or more parties, nations, or states. Related adj: **belligerent** (see sense 2). **2** a particular armed conflict: *the 1973 war in the Middle East.* **3** the techniques of armed conflict as a study, science, or profession. **4** any conflict or contest: *the war against crime.* **5** (*modifier*) of, resulting from, or characteristic of war: *war damage; a war story.* **6 in the wars.** *Inf.* (esp. of a child) hurt or knocked about, esp. as a result of quarrelling and fighting. ◆ *vb* **wars, warring, warred. 7** (*intr*) to conduct a war. [C12: from ONorthern F *werre* (var. of OF *guerre*), of Gmc origin]

War. *abbrev. for* Warwickshire.

waratah ('wɒrətə) *n Austral.* a shrub having dark green leaves and clusters of crimson flowers. [from Abor.]

warble[1] ◐ ('wɔːb°l) *vb* **warbles, warbling, warbled. 1** to sing (words, songs, etc.) with trills, runs, and other embellishments. **2** (*tr*) to utter in a song. ◆ *n* **3** the act or an instance of warbling. [C14: via OF *werbler,* of Gmc origin]

warble[2] ('wɔːb°l) *n Vet. science.* **1** a small lumpy abscess under the skin of cattle caused by the larvae of the warble fly. **2** a hard lump of tissue on a horse's back, caused by prolonged friction of a saddle. [C16: from ?]

warble fly *n* any of a genus of hairy beelike dipterous flies, the larvae of which produce warbles in cattle.

warbler ('wɔːblə) *n* **1** a person or thing that warbles. **2** a small active passerine songbird of the Old World having a cryptic plumage and slender bill, that is an arboreal insectivore. **3** a small bird of an American family, similar to the Old World songbird but often brightly coloured.

war correspondent *n* a journalist who reports on a war from the scene of action.

war crime *n* a crime committed in wartime in violation of the accepted customs, such as ill-treatment of prisoners, etc.
▸ **war criminal** *n*

war cry ◐ *n* **1** a rallying cry used by combatants in battle. **2** a cry, slogan, etc., used to rally support for a cause.

ward ◐ (wɔːd) *n* **1** (in many countries) one of the districts into which a city, town, parish, or other area is divided for administration, election of representatives, etc. **2a** a room in a hospital, esp. one for patients requiring similar kinds of care: *a maternity ward.* **2b** (*as modifier*): *ward maid.* **3** one of the divisions of a prison. **4** an open space enclosed within the walls of a castle. **5** *Law.* Also called: **ward of court.** a person, esp. a minor or one legally incapable of managing his own affairs, placed under the control or protection of a guardian or of a court. **6** the state of being under guard or in custody. **7** a means of protection. **8a** an internal ridge or bar in a lock that prevents an incorrectly cut key from turning. **8b** a corresponding groove cut in a key. ◆ *vb* **9** (*tr*) *Arch.* to guard or protect. ◆ See also **ward off.** [OE *weard* protector]
▸ **'wardless** *adj*

-ward *suffix.* **1** (*forming adjectives*) indicating direction towards: *a backward step.* **2** (*forming adverbs*) a variant and the usual US and Canad. form of **-wards.** [OE *-weard* towards]

war dance *n* a ceremonial dance performed before going to battle or after victory, esp. by certain North American Indian peoples.

warden ◐ ('wɔːd°n) *n* **1** a person who has the charge or care of something, esp. a building, or someone. **2** a public official, esp. one responsible for the enforcement of certain regulations: *traffic warden.* **3** a person employed to patrol a national park or a safari park. **4** *Chiefly US & Canad.* the chief officer in charge of a prison. **5** *Brit.* the principal of any of various universities or colleges. **6** See **churchwarden** (sense 1). [C13: from OF *wardein,* from *warder* to guard, of Gmc origin]

warder ◐ ('wɔːdə) *or* (*fem*) **wardress** *n* **1** *Chiefly Brit.* an officer in charge of prisoners in a jail. **2** a person who guards or has charge of something. [C14: from Anglo-F *wardere,* from OF *warder* to guard, of Gmc origin]

ward heeler *n US politics, disparaging.* a party worker who canvasses votes and performs chores for a political boss. Also called: **heeler.**

ward off ◐ *vb* (*tr, adv*) to turn aside or repel.

wardrobe ◐ ('wɔːdrəʊb) *n* **1** a tall closet or cupboard, with a rail or hooks on which to hang clothes. **2** the total collection of articles of clothing belonging to one person. **3a** the collection of costumes belonging to a theatre or theatrical company. **3b** (*as modifier*): *wardrobe mistress.* [C14: from OF *warderobe,* from *warder* to guard + *robe* ROBE]

wardrobe trunk *n* a large upright rectangular travelling case, usually opening longitudinally, with one side having a hanging rail, the other having drawers or compartments.

wardroom ('wɔːd,ruːm, -,rʊm) *n* **1** the quarters assigned to the officers (except the captain) of a warship. **2** the officers of a warship collectively, excepting the captain.

-wards *or* **-ward** *suffix forming adverbs.* indicating direction towards: *a step backwards.* Cf. **-ward.** [OE *-weardes* towards]

wardship ('wɔːdʃɪp) *n* the state of being a ward.

ware[1] (wɛə) *n* (*often in combination*) **1** (*functioning as sing*) articles of the same kind or material: *silverware.* **2** porcelain or pottery of a specified type: *jasper ware.* ◆ See also **wares.** [OE *waru*]

ware[2] (wɛə) *vb Arch.* another word for **beware.** [OE *wær.* See AWARE, BEWARE]

THESAURUS

fancy for, have a yen for (*inf.*), hope for, hunger for, long for, pine for, set one's heart on, thirst for, wish, would give one's eyeteeth for, yearn for **2, 3 = need,** be able to do with, be deficient in, be short of, be without, call for, demand, fall short in, have need of, lack, miss, require, stand in need of ◆ *n* **10, 11, 14 = wish,** appetite, craving, demand, desire, fancy, hankering, hunger, longing, necessity, need, requirement, thirst, yearning, yen (*inf.*) **12 = lack,** absence, dearth, default, deficiency, famine, insufficiency, paucity, scantiness, scarcity, shortage **13 = poverty,** destitution, indigence, need, neediness, pauperism, penury, privation
Antonyms *vb* ≠ **desire:** detest, dislike, hate, loathe, reject, spurn ≠ **need:** be sated, have, own, possess ◆ *n* ≠ **lack:** abundance, adequacy, excess, plenty, sufficiency, surfeit, surplus ≠ **poverty:** comfort, ease, luxury, wealth

wanting *adj* **1 = lacking,** absent, incomplete, less, missing, short, shy **2 = inadequate,** defective, deficient, disappointing, faulty, imperfect, inferior, leaving much to be desired, not good enough, not up to expectations, not up to par, patchy, pathetic, poor, sketchy, substandard, unsound
Antonyms *adj* ≠ **lacking:** complete, full, replete, saturated ≠ **inadequate:** adequate, enough, satisfactory, sufficient

wanton *adj* **1 = promiscuous,** abandoned, dissipated, dissolute, fast, immoral, lecherous, lewd, libertine, libidinous, licentious, loose, lustful, of easy virtue, rakish, shameless, unchaste **2, 3 = unprovoked,** arbitrary, cruel, evil, gratuitous, groundless, malevolent, malicious, motiveless, needless, senseless, spiteful, uncalled-for, unjustifiable, unjustified, vicious, wicked, wilful **4 = reckless,** careless, devil-may-care, extravagant, heedless, immoderate, intemperate, lavish, outrageous, rash, unrestrained, wild ◆ *n* **7 = slut,** harlot, loose woman, prostitute, scrubber (*Brit. & Austral. sl.*), slag (*Brit. sl.*), strumpet, swinger (*inf.*), tart, trollop, whore, woman of easy virtue
Antonyms *adj* ≠ **promiscuous:** overmodest, priggish, prim, prudish, puritanical, rigid, strait-laced, stuffy, Victorian ≠ **unprovoked:** called-for, excusable, justified, legitimate, motivated, provoked, warranted ≠ **reckless:** cautious, circumspect, guarded, inhibited, moderate, prudent, reserved, restrained, temperate

war *n* **1, 2 = fighting,** armed conflict, battle, bloodshed, combat, conflict, contention, contest, enmity, hostilities, hostility, strife, struggle, warfare ◆ *vb* **7 = fight,** battle, campaign against, carry on hostilities, clash, combat, conduct a war, contend, contest, make war, strive, struggle, take up arms, wage war
Antonyms *n* ≠ **fighting:** accord, armistice, ceasefire, co-existence, compliance, co-operation, harmony, peace, peace-time, treaty, truce ◆ *vb* ≠ **fight:** call a ceasefire, co-exist, co-operate, make peace

warble[1] *vb* **1 = sing,** chirp, chirrup, quaver, trill, twitter ◆ *n* **3 = song,** call, chirp, chirrup, cry, quaver, trill, twitter

war cry *n* **1, 2 = battle cry,** rallying cry, slogan, war whoop

ward *n* **1 = district,** area, division, precinct, quarter, zone **2 = room,** apartment, cubicle **5 = dependant,** charge, minor, protégé, pupil

warden *n* **1 = keeper,** administrator, caretaker, curator, custodian, guardian, janitor, ranger, steward, superintendent, warder, watchman

warder *n* **1, 2 = jailer,** custodian, guard, keeper, prison officer, screw (*sl.*), turnkey (*arch.*)

ward off *vb* **= repel,** avert, avoid, beat off, block, deflect, fend off, forestall, keep at arm's length, keep at bay, parry, stave off, thwart, turn aside, turn away
Antonyms *vb* accept, admit, allow, embrace, permit, receive, take in, welcome

wardrobe *n* **1 = clothes cupboard,** closet, clothes-press **2 = clothes,** apparel, attire, collection of clothes, outfit

warehouse ⓣ *n* ('wɛə,haʊs). **1** a place where goods are stored prior to their use, distribution, or sale. **2** See **bonded warehouse. 3** *Chiefly Brit.* a large commercial, esp. wholesale, establishment. ◆ *vb* ('wɛə,haʊz, -,haʊs), **warehouses, warehousing, warehoused. 4** (*tr*) to store or place in a warehouse, esp. a bonded warehouse.
▸ **'ware,houseman** *n*

warehousing ('wɛə,haʊzɪŋ) *n Business.* an attempt to gain a significant stake in a company without revealing the identity of the purchaser by buying small quantities of shares in the name of nominees.

wares ⓣ (wɛəz) *pl n* **1** articles of manufacture considered as being for sale. **2** any talent or asset regarded as a saleable commodity.

warfare ⓣ ('wɔː,fɛə) *n* **1** the act, process, or an instance of waging war. **2** conflict or strife.

warfarin ('wɔːfərɪn) *n* a crystalline insoluble compound, used to kill rodents and, in the form of its sodium salt, as a medical anticoagulant. [C20: from the patent owners *W(isconsin) A(lumni) R(esearch) F(oundation)* + (COUM)ARIN]

war game *n* **1** a notional tactical exercise for training military commanders, in which no military units are actually deployed. **2** a game in which model soldiers are used to create battles, esp. past battles, in order to study tactics.

warhead ('wɔː,hɛd) *n* the part of the fore end of a missile or projectile that contains explosives.

warhorse ('wɔː,hɔːs) *n* **1** a horse used in battle. **2** *Inf.* a veteran soldier or politician.

warlike ⓣ ('wɔː,laɪk) *adj* **1** of, relating to, or used in war. **2** hostile or belligerent. **3** fit or ready for war.

warlock ⓣ ('wɔː,lɒk) *n* a man who practises black magic. [OE *wǣrloga* oath breaker, from *wǣr* oath + *-loga* liar, from *lēogan* to lie]

warlord ('wɔː,lɔːd) *n* a military leader of a nation or part of a nation: *the Chinese warlords.*

Warlpiri ('walprɪ) *n* an Aboriginal language of central Australia.

warm ⓣ (wɔːm) *adj* **1** characterized by or having a moderate degree of heat. **2** maintaining or imparting heat: *a warm coat.* **3** having or showing ready affection, kindliness, etc.: *a warm personality.* **4** lively or passionate: *a warm debate.* **5** cordial or enthusiastic: *warm support.* **6** quickly or easily aroused: *a warm temper.* **7** (of colours) predominantly red or yellow in tone. **8** (of a scent, trail, etc.) recently made. **9** near to finding a hidden object or guessing facts, as in children's games. **10** *Inf.* uncomfortable or disagreeable, esp. because of the proximity of danger. ◆ *vb* **11** (sometimes foll. by *up*) to make or become warm or warmer. **12** (when *intr*, often foll. by *to*) to make or become excited, enthusiastic, etc. (about): *he warmed to the idea of buying a new car.* **13** (*intr*; often foll. by *to*) to feel affection, kindness, etc. (for someone): *I warmed to her mother from the start.* ◆ *n Inf.* **14** a warm place or area: *come into the warm.* **15** the act or an instance of warming or being warmed. ◆ See also **warm up.** [OE *wearm*]
▸ **'warmer** *n* ▸ **'warmish** *adj* ▸ **'warmly** *adv* ▸ **'warmness** *n*

warm-blooded ⓣ *adj* **1** ardent, impetuous, or passionate. **2** (of birds and mammals) having a constant body temperature, usually higher than the temperature of the surroundings. Technical term: **homoiothermic.**
▸ **,warm-'bloodedness** *n*

warm-down *n* light exercises performed to aid recovery from strenuous physical activity.

war memorial *n* a monument, usually an obelisk or cross, to those who die in a war, esp. those from a particular locality.

warm front *n Meteorol.* the boundary between a warm air mass and the cold air above which it is rising, at a less steep angle than at the cold front.

warm-hearted ⓣ *adj* kindly, generous, or readily sympathetic.
▸ **,warm-'heartedly** *adv* ▸ **,warm-'heartedness** *n*

warming pan *n* a pan, often of copper and having a long handle, filled with hot coals and formerly drawn over the sheets to warm a bed.

warmonger ⓣ ('wɔː,mʌŋgə) *n* a person who fosters warlike ideas or advocates war.
▸ **'war,mongering** *n*

warmth ⓣ (wɔːmθ) *n* **1** the state, quality, or sensation of being warm. **2** intensity of emotion: *he denied the accusation with some warmth.* **3** affection or cordiality.

warm up *vb* (*adv*) **1** to make or become warm or warmer. **2** (*intr*) to exercise immediately before a game, contest, or more vigorous exercise. **3** (*intr*) to get ready for something important; prepare. **4** to run (an engine, etc.) until the working temperature is attained, or (of an engine, etc.) to undergo this process. **5** to make or become more animated: *the party warmed up when Tom came.* **6** to reheat (already cooked food) or (of such food) to be reheated. ◆ *n* **warm-up. 7** the act or an instance of warming up. **8** a preparatory exercise routine.

warn ⓣ (wɔːn) *vb* **1** to notify or make (someone) aware of danger, harm, etc. **2** (*tr*; *often takes a negative and an infinitive*) to advise or admonish (someone) as to action, conduct, etc.: *I warn you not to do that again.* **3** (*takes a clause as object or an infinitive*) to inform (someone) in advance: *he warned them that he would arrive late.* **4** (*tr*; usually foll. by *away, off,* etc.) to give notice to go away, be off, etc. [OE *wearnian*]
▸ **'warner** *n*

warning ⓣ ('wɔːnɪŋ) *n* **1** a hint, intimation, threat, etc., of harm or danger. **2** advice to beware or desist. **3** an archaic word for **notice** (sense 6). ◆ *adj* **4** (*prenominal*) intended or serving to warn: *a warning look.*
▸ **'warningly** *adv*

War of American Independence *n* the conflict following the revolt of the North American colonies against British rule, particularly on the issue of taxation. Hostilities began in 1775 when British and American forces clashed at Lexington and Concord. Articles of Confederation agreed in the Continental Congress in 1777 provided for a confederacy to be known as the United States of America. The war was effectively ended with the surrender of the British at Yorktown in 1781 and peace was signed at Paris in Sept. 1783. Also called: **American Revolution** or **Revolutionary War.**

warp ⓣ (wɔːp) *vb* **1** to twist or cause to twist out of shape, as from heat, damp, etc. **2** to turn or cause to turn from a true, correct, or proper course. **3** to pervert or be perverted. **4** *Naut.* to move (a vessel) by hauling on a rope fixed to a stationary object ashore or (of a vessel) to be moved thus. **5** (*tr*) to flood (land) with water from which alluvial matter is deposited. ◆ *n* **6** the state or condition of being twisted out of shape. **7** a twist, distortion, or bias. **8** a mental or moral deviation. **9** the yarns arranged lengthways on a loom, forming the threads through which the weft yarns are woven. **10** *Naut.* a rope used for warping a vessel. **11** alluvial sediment deposited by water. [OE *wearp* a throw]
▸ **'warpage** *n* ▸ **warped** *adj* ▸ **'warper** *n*

war paint *n* **1** painted decoration of the face and body applied by certain North American Indians before battle. **2** *Inf.* finery or regalia. **3** *Inf.* cosmetics.

warpath ('wɔː,pɑːθ) *n* **1** the route taken by North American Indians on

THESAURUS

warehouse *n* **1** = **store**, depository, depot, stockroom, storehouse

wares *pl n* **1** = **goods**, commodities, lines, manufactures, merchandise, produce, products, stock, stuff

warfare *n* **1, 2** = **war**, armed conflict, armed struggle, arms, battle, blows, campaigning, clash of arms, combat, conflict, contest, discord, fighting, hostilities, passage of arms, strategy, strife, struggle
Antonyms *n* accord, amity, armistice, ceasefire, cessation of hostilities, conciliation, harmony, peace, treaty, truce

warily *adv* **1** = **cautiously**, cagily (*inf.*), carefully, charily, circumspectly, distrustfully, gingerly, guardedly, suspiciously, vigilantly, watchfully, with care
Antonyms *adv* carelessly, hastily, heedlessly, irresponsibly, rashly, recklessly, thoughtlessly, unwarily

wariness *n* **1** = **caution**, alertness, attention, caginess (*inf.*), care, carefulness, circumspection, discretion, distrust, foresight, heedfulness, mindfulness, prudence, suspicion, vigilance, watchfulness
Antonyms *n* carelessness, heedlessness, inattention, mindlessness, negligence, oblivion, recklessness, thoughtlessness

warlike *adj* **1, 2** = **belligerent**, aggressive, bellicose, bloodthirsty, combative, hawkish, hostile, inimical, jingoistic, martial, militaristic, military, pugnacious, sabre-rattling, unfriendly, warmongering
Antonyms *adj* amicable, conciliatory, friendly, nonbelligerent, pacific, peaceable, peaceful, placid, unwarlike

warlock *n* = **magician**, conjuror, enchanter, necromancer, sorcerer, witch, wizard

warm *adj* **1** = **heated**, balmy, lukewarm, moderately hot, pleasant, sunny, tepid, thermal **3** = **affectionate**, affable, amiable, amorous, cheerful, congenial, cordial, friendly, genial, happy, hearty, hospitable, kindly, likable *or* likeable, loving, pleasant, tender ◆ *vb* **11** = **heat**, heat up, melt, thaw, warm up **12** = **rouse**, animate, awaken, excite, get going, interest, make enthusiastic, put some life into, stimulate, stir, turn on (*sl.*)
Antonyms *adj* ≠ **heated:** chilly, cold, cool, freezing, icy ≠ **affectionate:** aloof, apathetic, cold, cool, distant, half-hearted, hostile, phlegmatic, remote, stand-offish, uncaring, unenthusiastic, unfriendly, unwelcoming ◆ *vb* ≠ **heat:** chill, cool, cool down, freeze ≠ **rouse:** alienate, depress, sadden

warm-blooded *adj* **1** = **passionate**, ardent, earnest, emotional, enthusiastic, excitable, fervent, impetuous, lively, rash, spirited, vivacious

warm-hearted *adj* = **kindly**, affectionate, compassionate, cordial, generous, kindhearted, loving, sympathetic, tender, tenderhearted
Antonyms *adj* callous, cold, cold-hearted, hard, hard-hearted, harsh, heartless, insensitive, mean, merciless, unfeeling, unsympathetic

warmonger *n* = **hawk**, belligerent, jingo, militarist, sabre-rattler

warmth *n* **1** = **heat**, hotness, warmness **3** = **affection**, affability, amorousness, cheerfulness, cordiality, happiness, heartiness, hospitableness, kindliness, love, tenderness
Antonyms *n* ≠ **heat:** chill, chilliness, cold, coldness, coolness, iciness ≠ **affection:** aloofness, apathy, austerity, cold-heartedness, hard-heartedness, hostility, indifference, insincerity, lack of enthusiasm, remoteness, sternness

warn *vb* **1-3** = **notify**, admonish, advise, alert, apprise, caution, forewarn, give fair warning, give notice, inform, make (someone) aware, put one on one's guard, summon, tip off

warning *n* **1** = **caution**, admonition, advice, alarm, alert, augury, caveat, foretoken, hint, notice, notification, omen, premonition, presage, sign, signal, threat, tip, tip-off, token, word, word to the wise ◆ *adj* **4** = **cautionary**, admonitory, monitory, ominous, premonitory, threatening

warp *vb* **1** = **twist**, bend, contort, deform, deviate, distort, misshape, pervert, swerve, turn ◆ *n* **6-8** = **twist**, bend, bent, bias, contortion, deformation, deviation, distortion, kink, perversion, quirk, turn

a warlike expedition. **2 on the warpath. 2a** preparing to engage in battle. **2b** *Inf.* in a state of anger.

warplane ('wɔːˌpleɪn) *n* any aircraft designed for and used in warfare.

warrant ❶ ('wɒrənt) *n* **1** anything that gives authority for an action or decision; authorization. **2** a document that certifies or guarantees, such as a receipt for goods stored in a warehouse, a licence, or a commission. **3** *Law.* an authorization issued by a magistrate allowing a constable or other officer to search or seize property, arrest a person, or perform some other specified act. **4** (in certain armed services) the official authority for the appointment of warrant officers. **5** a security that functions as a stock option by giving the owner the right to buy ordinary shares in a company at a specified date, often at a specified price. ◆ *vb (tr)* **6** to guarantee the quality, condition, etc., of (something). **7** to give authority or power to. **8** to attest to the character, worthiness, etc., of. **9** to guarantee (a purchaser of merchandise) against loss of, damage to, or misrepresentation concerning the merchandise. **10** *Law.* to guarantee (the title to an estate or other property). **11** to declare confidently. [C13: from Anglo-F, var. of OF *guarant*, from *guarantir* to guarantee, of Gmc origin]
▸ **'warrantable** *adj* ▸ **ˌwarranta'bility** *n* ▸ **'warrantably** *adv* ▸ **'warranter** *n*

warrantee (ˌwɒrən'tiː) *n* a person to whom a warranty is given.

warrant officer *n* an officer in certain armed services who holds a rank between those of commissioned and noncommissioned officers. In the British army the rank has two classes: regimental sergeant major and company sergeant major.

Warrant of Fitness *n NZ.* a six-monthly certificate required for motor vehicles certifying mechanical soundness.

warrantor ('wɒrənˌtɔː) *n* an individual or company that provides a warranty.

warrant sale *n Scots Law.* a sale of someone's personal belongings or household effects that have been seized to meet unpaid debts.

warranty ❶ ('wɒrəntɪ) *n, pl* **warranties. 1** *Property law.* a covenant, express or implied, by which the vendor of real property vouches for the security of the title conveyed. **2** *Contract law.* an express or implied term in a contract collateral to the main purpose, such as an undertaking that goods contracted to be sold shall meet specified requirements as to quality, etc. **3** *Insurance law.* an undertaking by the party insured that the facts given regarding the risk are as stated. [C14: from Anglo-F *warantie*, from *warantir* to warrant, var. of OF *guarantir*; see WARRANT]

warren ('wɒrən) *n* **1** a series of interconnected underground tunnels in which rabbits live. **2** a colony of rabbits. **3** an overcrowded area or dwelling. **4** *Chiefly Brit.* an enclosed place where small game animals or birds are kept, esp. for breeding. [C14: from Anglo-F *warenne*, of Gmc origin]

warrigal ('wɒrɪgæl) *Austral.* ◆ *n* **1** a dingo. ◆ *adj* **2** untamed or wild. [C19: from Abor.]

warrior ❶ ('wɒrɪə) *n* **a** a person engaged in, experienced in, or devoted to war. **b** (*as modifier*): *a warrior nation.* [C13: from OF *werreieor*, from *werre* WAR]

Warsaw Pact ('wɔːsɔː) *n* a military treaty and association of E European countries (1955–91).

warship ('wɔːˌʃɪp) *n* a vessel armed, armoured, and otherwise equipped for naval warfare.

Wars of the Roses *pl n* the struggle for the throne in England (1455-85) between the House of York (symbolized by the white rose) and the House of Lancaster (symbolized by the red rose).

wart (wɔːt) *n* **1** *Pathol.* any firm abnormal elevation of the skin caused by a virus. **2** *Bot.* a small rounded outgrowth. **3 warts and all.** with all blemishes evident. [OE *weart(e)*]
▸ **'warty** *adj*

warthog ('wɔːthɒg) *n* a wild pig of S and E Africa, having heavy tusks, wartlike protuberances on the face, and a mane of coarse hair.

wartime ('wɔːˌtaɪm) *n* **a** a period or time of war. **b** (*as modifier*): *wartime conditions.*

war whoop *n* the yell or howl uttered, esp. by North American Indians, while making an attack.

wary ❶ ('wɛərɪ) *adj* **warier, wariest. 1** watchful, cautious, or alert. **2** characterized by caution or watchfulness. [C16: from WARE[2] + -Y[1]]
▸ **'warily** *adv* ▸ **'wariness** *n*

was (wɒz; *unstressed* wəz) *vb* (used with *I, he, she, it,* and with singular nouns) **1** the past tense (indicative mood) of **be. 2** *Not standard.* a form of the subjunctive mood used in place of *were*, esp. in conditional sentences: *if the film was to be with you, would you be able to process it?* [OE *wæs*, from *wesan* to be]

wash ❶ (wɒʃ) *vb* **1** to apply water or other liquid, usually with soap, to (oneself, clothes, etc.) in order to cleanse. **2** (*tr;* often foll. by *away, from, off,* etc.) to remove by the application of water or other liquid and usually soap: *she washed the dirt from her clothes.* **3** (*intr*) to be capable of being washed without damage or loss of colour. **4** (of an animal such as a cat) to cleanse (itself or another animal) by licking. **5** (*tr*) to cleanse from pollution or defilement. **6** (*tr*) to make wet or moist. **7** (often foll. by *away,* etc.) to move or be moved by water: *the flood washed away the bridge.* **8** (esp. of waves) to flow or sweep against or over (a surface or object), often with a lapping sound. **9** to form by erosion or be eroded: *the stream washed a ravine in the hill.* **10** (*tr*) to apply a thin coating of paint, metal, etc., to. **11** (*tr*) to separate (ore, etc.) from (gravel, etc.) by immersion in water. **12** (*intr; usually used with a negative*) *Inf., chiefly Brit.* to admit of testing or proof: *your excuses won't wash.* ◆ *n* **13** the act or process of washing. **14** a quantity of articles washed together. **15** a preparation or thin liquid used as a coating or in washing: *a thin wash of paint.* **16** *Med.* **16a** any medicinal lotion for application to a part of the body. **16b** (*in combination*): *an eyewash.* **17a** the technique of making wash drawings. **17b** See **wash drawing. 18** the erosion of soil by the action of flowing water. **19** a mass of alluvial material transported and deposited by flowing water. **20** land that is habitually washed by tidal or river waters. **21** the disturbance in the air or water produced at the rear of an aircraft, boat, or other moving object. **22** gravel, earth, etc., from which valuable minerals may be washed. **23** waste liquid matter or liquid refuse, esp. as fed to pigs. **24** an alcoholic liquid resembling strong beer, resulting from the fermentation of wort in the production of whisky. **25 come out in the wash.** *Inf.* to become known or apparent in the course of time. ◆ See also **wash down, wash out, wash up.** [OE *wæscan, waxan*]

washable ('wɒʃəb[ə]l) *adj* (esp. of fabrics or clothes) capable of being washed without deteriorating.
▸ **ˌwasha'bility** *n*

wash-and-wear *adj* (of fabrics, garments, etc.) requiring only light washing, short drying time, and little or no ironing.

washbasin ('wɒʃˌbeɪs[ə]n) *n* **1** Also called: **washbowl.** a basin or bowl for washing the face and hands. **2** Also called: **wash-hand basin.** a bathroom fixture with taps, used for washing the face and hands.

washboard ('wɒʃˌbɔːd) *n* **1** a board having a surface, usually of corrugated metal, on which, esp. formerly, clothes were scrubbed. **2** such a board used as a rhythm instrument played with the fingers in skiffle, country-and-western music, etc. **3** *Naut.* a vertical planklike shield fastened to the gunwales of a boat to prevent water from splashing over the side.

washcloth ('wɒʃˌklɒθ) *n* **1** another term for **dishcloth. 2** the US and Canad. word for **face cloth.**

washday ('wɒʃˌdeɪ) *n* a day on which clothes and linen are washed.

wash down *vb (tr, adv)* **1** to wash completely, esp. from top to bottom. **2** to take drink with or after (food or another drink).

wash drawing *n* a pen-and-ink drawing that has been lightly brushed over with water to soften the lines.

washed out ❶ *adj* (**washed-out** *when prenominal*). **1** faded or colourless. **2** exhausted, esp. when being pale in appearance.

washed up *adj* (**washed-up** *when prenominal*). *Inf., chiefly US, Canad., & NZ.* no longer hopeful, etc.: *our hopes for the new deal are all washed up.*

washer ('wɒʃə) *n* **1** a person or thing that washes. **2** a flat ring or drilled disc of metal used under the head of a bolt or nut. **3** any flat ring of rubber, felt, metal, etc., used to provide a seal under a nut or in a tap or valve seat. **4** See **washing machine. 5** *Austral.* a face cloth; flannel.

washerwoman ('wɒʃəˌwʊmən) *or (masc)* **washerman** *n, pl* **washerwomen** *or* **washermen.** a person who washes clothes for a living.

washery ('wɒʃərɪ) *n, pl* **washeries.** a plant at a mine where water or other liquid is used to remove dirt from a mineral, esp. coal.

wash-hand basin *n* another name for **washbasin** (sense 2).

wash house *n* (formerly) an outbuilding in which clothes were washed.

washing ('wɒʃɪŋ) *n* **1** articles that have been or are to be washed to-

THESAURUS

warrant *n* **1** = **authorization**, assurance, authority, carte blanche, commission, guarantee, licence, permission, permit, pledge, sanction, security, warranty ◆ *vb* **6, 8** = **guarantee**, affirm, answer for, assure, attest, avouch, certify, declare, pledge, secure, stand behind, underwrite, uphold, vouch for **7** = **call for**, approve, authorize, commission, demand, deserve, empower, entail, entitle, excuse, give ground for, justify, license, necessitate, permit, require, sanction

warrantable *adj* **7** = **justifiable**, accountable, allowable, defensible, lawful, necessary, permissible, proper, reasonable, right
Antonyms *adj* indefensible, uncalled-for, undue, unjustifiable, unnecessary, unreasonable, unwarrantable, wrong

warranty *n* **1, 2** = **guarantee**, assurance, bond, certificate, contract, covenant, pledge

warring *adj* **7** = **fighting**, at daggers drawn, at war, belligerent, combatant, conflicting, contending, embattled, hostile, opposed

warrior *n* = **soldier**, champion, combatant, fighter, fighting man, gladiator, man-at-arms

wary *adj* **1** = **cautious**, alert, attentive, cagey (*inf.*), careful, chary, circumspect, distrustful, guarded, heedful, leery (*sl.*), on one's guard, on the lookout, on the qui vive, prudent, suspicious, vigilant, watchful, wide-awake
Antonyms *adj* careless, foolhardy, imprudent, negligent, rash, reckless, remiss, unguarded, unsuspecting, unwary

wash *vb* **1, 2, 5, 6** = **clean**, bath, bathe, cleanse, launder, moisten, rinse, scrub, shampoo, shower, wet **7** = **sweep away**, bear away, carry off, erode, move, wash off **12** *Informal, chiefly Brit.* = **be plausible**, bear scrutiny, be convincing, carry weight, hold up, hold water, stand up, stick ◆ *n* **13** = **cleaning**, ablution, bath, bathe, cleansing, laundering, rinse, scrub, shampoo, shower, washing **15** = **coat**, coating, film, layer, overlay, screen, stain, suffusion **21** = **swell**, ebb and flow, flow, roll, surge, sweep, wave

washed out *adj* **1** = **faded**, blanched, bleached, colourless, etiolated, flat, lacklustre, mat, pale **2** = **exhausted**, all in (*sl.*), dog-tired (*inf.*), done in, drained, drawn, fatigued, haggard, knackered (*sl.*), pale, spent, tired-out, wan, weary, wiped out (*inf.*), worn-out, zonked (*sl.*)
Antonyms *adj* ≠ **exhausted:** alert, chirpy, ener-

gether on a single occasion. **2** something, such as gold dust, that has been obtained by washing. **3** a thin coat of something applied in liquid form.

washing machine *n* a mechanical apparatus, usually powered by electricity, for washing clothing, linens, etc.

washing powder *n* powdered detergent for washing fabrics.

washing soda *n* crystalline sodium carbonate, esp. when used as a cleansing agent.

washing-up *n Brit.* **1** the washing of dishes, cutlery, etc., after a meal. **2** dishes and cutlery waiting to be washed up. **3** (*as modifier*): *a washing-up machine.*

wash out ❶ *vb* (*adv*) **1** (*tr*) to wash (the inside of something) so as to remove (dirt). **2** Also: **wash off.** to remove or be removed by washing: *grass stains don't wash out easily.* ◆ *n* **washout. 3** *Geol.* **3a** erosion of the earth's surface by the action of running water. **3b** a narrow channel produced by this. **4** *Inf.* **4a** a total failure or disaster. **4b** an incompetent person.

washroom ('wɒʃˌruːm, -ˌrʊm) *n US & Canad.* a euphemism for **lavatory.**

washstand ('wɒʃˌstænd) *n* a piece of furniture designed to hold a basin, etc., for washing the face and hands.

washtub ('wɒʃˌtʌb) *n* a tub or large container used for washing anything, esp. clothes.

wash up *vb* (*adv*) **1** *Chiefly Brit.* to wash (dishes, cutlery, etc.) after a meal. **2** (*intr*) *US & Canad.* to wash one's face and hands. ◆ *n* **washup. 3** *Austral.* the end, outcome of a process: *in the washup, three were elected.*

washy ❶ ('wɒʃɪ) *adj* **washier, washiest. 1** overdiluted, watery, or weak. **2** lacking intensity or strength.
▸ **'washiness** *n*

wasn't ('wɒzᵊnt) *contraction of* was not.

wasp (wɒsp) *n* **1** a social hymenopterous insect, such as the **common wasp,** having a black-and-yellow body and an ovipositor specialized for stinging. **2** any of various solitary hymenopterans, such as the digger wasp and gall wasp. [OE *wæsp*]
▸ **'waspˌlike** *adj* ▸ **'waspy** *adj* ▸ **'waspily** *adv* ▸ **'waspiness** *n*

Wasp *or* **WASP** (wɒsp) *n* (in the US) *acronym for* White Anglo-Saxon Protestant: a person descended from N European, usually Protestant stock, forming a group often considered the most dominant, privileged, and influential in American society.

waspish ❶ ('wɒspɪʃ) *adj* **1** relating to or suggestive of a wasp. **2** easily annoyed or angered.
▸ **'waspishly** *adv*

wasp waist *n* a very slender waist, esp. one that is tightly corseted.
▸ **'wasp-ˌwaisted** *adj*

wassail ('wɒseɪl) *n* **1** (formerly) a toast or salutation made to a person at festivities. **2** a festivity when much drinking takes place. **3** alcoholic drink drunk at such a festivity, esp. spiced beer or mulled wine. ◆ *vb* **4** to drink the health of (a person) at a wassail. **5** (*intr*) to go from house to house singing carols at Christmas. [C13: from ON *ves heill* be in good health]
▸ **'wassailer** *n*

Wassermann test *or* **reaction** ('wæsəmən) *n Med.* a diagnostic test for syphilis. [C20: after August von *Wassermann* (1866–1925), G bacteriologist]

wast (wɒst; *unstressed* wəst) *vb Arch. or dialect.* (used with the pronoun *thou* or its relative equivalent) a singular form of the past tense (indicative mood) of **be.**

wastage ('weɪstɪdʒ) *n* **1** anything lost by wear or waste. **2** the process of wasting. **3** reduction in size of a workforce by retirement, etc. (esp. in **natural wastage**).

> **USAGE NOTE** *Waste* and *wastage* are to some extent interchangeable, but many people think that *wastage* should not be used to refer to loss resulting from human carelessness, inefficiency, etc.: *a waste* (not *a wastage*) *of time/money/effort,* etc.

waste ❶ (weɪst) *vb* **wastes, wasting, wasted. 1** (*tr*) to use, consume, or expend thoughtlessly, carelessly, or to no avail. **2** (*tr*) to fail to take advantage of: *to waste an opportunity.* **3** (when *intr*, often foll. by *away*) to lose or cause to lose bodily strength, health, etc. **4** to exhaust or become exhausted. **5** (*tr*) to ravage. **6** (*tr*) *Sl.* to murder or kill. ◆ *n* **7** the act of wasting or state of being wasted. **8** a failure to take advantage of something. **9** anything unused or not used to full advantage. **10** anything or anyone rejected as useless, worthless, or in excess of what is required. **11** garbage, rubbish, or trash. **12** a land or region that is devastated or ruined. **13** a land or region that is wild or uncultivated. **14** *Physiol.* **14a** the useless products of metabolism. **14b** indigestible food residue. **15** *Law.* reduction in the value of an estate caused by act or neglect, esp. by a life tenant. ◆ *adj* **16** rejected as useless, unwanted, or worthless. **17** produced in excess of what is required. **18** not cultivated, inhabited, or productive: *waste land.* **19a** of or denoting the useless products of metabolism. **19b** of or denoting indigestible food residue. **20** destroyed, devastated, or ruined. **21 lay waste.** to devastate or destroy. [C13: from Anglo-F, from L *vastāre* to lay waste, from *vastus* empty]

wasted ('weɪstɪd) *adj* **1** not taken advantage of: *a wasted opportunity.* **2** unprofitable: *wasted effort.* **3** enfeebled and emaciated: *a thin wasted figure.* **4** *Sl.* showing signs of habitual drug abuse.

wasteful ❶ ('weɪstfʊl) *adj* **1** tending to waste or squander. **2** causing waste or devastation.
▸ **'wastefully** *adv* ▸ **'wastefulness** *n*

wasteland ❶ ('weɪstˌlænd) *n* **1** a barren or desolate area of land. **2** a region, period in history, etc., that is considered spiritually, intellectually, or aesthetically barren or desolate.

wastepaper ('weɪstˌpeɪpə) *n* paper discarded after use.

wastepaper basket *or* **bin** *n* an open receptacle for paper and other dry litter. Usual US and Canad. word: **wastebasket.**

waste pipe *n* a pipe to take excess or used water away, as from a sink to a drain.

waster ❶ ('weɪstə) *n* **1** a person or thing that wastes. **2** a ne'er-do-well; wastrel.

wasting ('weɪstɪŋ) *adj* (*prenominal*) reducing the vitality, strength, or robustness of the body: *a wasting disease.*
▸ **'wastingly** *adv*

wasting asset *n* an unreplaceable business asset of limited life, such as an oil well.

wastrel ❶ ('weɪstrəl) *n* **1** a wasteful person; spendthrift; prodigal. **2** an idler or vagabond.

wat (wɑːt) *n* a Thai Buddhist monastery or temple. [Thai, from Sansk. *vāta* enclosure]

watap (wæ'tɑːp, wɑː-) *n* a stringy thread made by North American Indians from the roots of various conifers and used for weaving and sewing. [C18: from Canad. F, from Cree *watapiy*]

watch ❶ (wɒtʃ) *vb* **1** to look at or observe closely or attentively. **2** (*intr;* foll. by *for*) to wait attentively. **3** to guard or tend (something) closely or carefully. **4** (*intr*) to keep vigil. **5** (*tr*) to maintain an interest in: *to watch the progress of a child at school.* **6 watch it!** be careful! ◆ *n* **7a** a small portable timepiece, usually worn strapped to the wrist (a **wristwatch**) or in a waistcoat pocket. **7b** (*as modifier*): *a watch spring.* **8** a watching. **9** a period of vigil, esp. during the night. **10** (formerly) one of a set of periods into which the night was divided. **11** *Naut.* **11a** any of the periods, usually of four hours, during which part of a ship's crew are on duty. **11b** those officers and crew on duty during a specified watch. **12** the period during which a guard is on duty. **13** (formerly) a watchman or band of watchmen. **14 on the watch.** on the lookout. ◆ See also **watch out.** [OE *wæccan* (vb), *wæcce* (n)]
▸ **'watcher** *n*

-watch *suffix of nouns.* indicating a regular television programme or newspaper feature on the topic specified: *Crimewatch.*

watchable ('wɒtʃəbᵊl) *adj* **1** capable of being watched. **2** interesting, enjoyable, or entertaining: *a watchable television documentary.*

watchcase ('wɒtʃˌkeɪs) *n* a protective case for a watch, generally of metal such as gold or silver.

watch chain *n* a chain used for fastening a pocket watch to the clothing. See also **fob**[1].

THESAURUS

getic, full of beans (*inf.*), full of pep (*inf.*), lively, perky, refreshed, sprightly, zippy (*inf.*)

washout *Informal n* **4a** = **failure**, disappointment, disaster, dud (*inf.*), fiasco, flop (*inf.*), mess **4b** = **loser**, failure, incompetent
Antonyms *n* ≠ **failure:** conquest, feat, success, triumph, victory, winner

washy *adj* **1, 2** = **watery**, attenuated, diluted, feeble, insipid, overdiluted, thin, watered-down, weak, wishy-washy (*inf.*)

waspish *adj* **2** = **bad-tempered**, cantankerous, captious, crabbed, crabby, cross, crotchety (*inf.*), fretful, grumpy, ill-tempered, irascible, irritable, liverish, peevish, peppery, pettish, petulant, snappish, splenetic, testy, tetchy, touchy
Antonyms *adj* affable, agreeable, cheerful, easy-going, genial, good-humoured, good-natured, jovial, pleasant

waste *vb* **1, 2** = **squander**, blow, dissipate, fritter away, frivol away (*inf.*), lavish, misuse, run through, throw away **3** *often foll. by* **away** = **decline**, atrophy, consume, corrode, crumble, debilitate, decay, deplete, disable, drain, dwindle, eat away, ebb, emaciate, enfeeble, exhaust, fade, gnaw, perish, sap the strength of, sink, undermine, wane, wear out, wither ◆ *n* **7, 8** = **squandering**, dissipation, expenditure, extravagance, frittering away, loss, lost opportunity, misapplication, misuse, prodigality, unthriftiness, wastefulness **12** = **rubbish**, debris, dregs, dross, garbage, leavings, leftovers, litter, offal, offscourings, refuse, scrap, sweepings, trash **13** = **desert**, solitude, void, wasteland, wild, wilderness ◆ *adj* **16** = **unwanted**, leftover, superfluous, supernumerary, unused, useless, worthless **18** = **uncultivated**, bare, barren, desolate, devastated, dismal, dreary, empty, uninhabited, unproductive, wild **21 lay waste** = **devastate**, depredate (*rare*), despoil, destroy, pillage, rape, ravage, raze, ruin, sack, spoil, total (*sl.*), trash (*sl.*), undo, wreak havoc upon
Antonyms *vb* ≠ **squander:** conserve, economize, husband, preserve, protect, save ≠ **decline:** build, develop, increase, rally, strengthen ◆ *n* ≠ **squandering:** economy, frugality, good housekeeping, saving, thrift ◆ *adj* ≠ **unwanted:** necessary, needed, utilized ≠ **uncultivated:** arable, developed, fruitful, habitable, in use, productive, verdant

wasteful *adj* **1** = **extravagant**, improvident, lavish, prodigal, profligate, ruinous, spendthrift, thriftless, uneconomical, unthrifty
Antonyms *adj* economical, frugal, money-saving, parsimonious, penny-wise, provident, sparing, thrifty

wasteland *n* **1** = **wilderness**, desert, void, waste, wild

waster *n* **2** = **layabout**, drone, good-for-nothing, idler, loafer, loser, malingerer, ne'er-do-well, shirker, skiver (*Brit. sl.*), wastrel

wastrel *n* **1** = **spendthrift**, prodigal, profligate, squanderer **2** = **layabout**, drone, good-for-nothing, idler, loafer, loser, malingerer, ne'er-do-well, shirker, skiver (*Brit. sl.*), waster

watch *vb* **1** = **look at**, check, check out (*inf.*), contemplate, eye, eyeball (*sl.*), feast one's eyes

Watch Committee *n Brit. history.* a local government committee responsible for the efficiency of the local police force.
watchdog Ⓣ ('wɒtʃˌdɒg) *n* **1** a dog kept to guard property. **2a** a person or group that acts as a protector against inefficiency, etc. **2b** (*as modifier*): *a watchdog committee.*
watch fire *n* a fire kept burning at night as a signal or for warmth and light by a person keeping watch.
watchful Ⓣ ('wɒtʃful) *adj* **1** vigilant or alert. **2** *Arch.* not sleeping.
▸**'watchfully** *adv* ▸**'watchfulness** *n*
watch-glass *n* **1** a curved glass disc that covers the dial of a watch. **2** a similarly shaped piece of glass used in laboratories for evaporating small samples of a solution, etc.
watchmaker ('wɒtʃˌmeɪkə) *n* a person who makes or mends watches.
▸**'watchˌmaking** *n*
watchman Ⓣ ('wɒtʃmən) *n, pl* **watchmen. 1** a person employed to guard buildings or property. **2** (formerly) a man employed to patrol or guard the streets at night.
watch night *n* (in Protestant churches) **1a** the night of December 24, during which a service is held to mark the arrival of Christmas Day. **1b** the night of December 31, during which a service is held to mark the passing of the old year. **2** the service held on either of these nights.
watch out Ⓣ *vb* (*intr, adv*) to be careful or on one's guard.
watchstrap ('wɒtʃˌstræp) *n* a strap of leather, cloth, etc., attached to a watch for fastening it around the wrist. Also called (US and Canad.): **watchband.**
watchtower ('wɒtʃˌtauə) *n* a tower on which a sentry keeps watch.
watchword Ⓣ ('wɒtʃˌwɜːd) *n* **1** another word for **password. 2** a rallying cry or slogan.
water Ⓣ ('wɔːtə) *n* **1** a clear colourless tasteless odourless liquid that is essential for plant and animal life and constitutes, in impure form, rain, oceans, rivers, lakes, etc. Formula: H_2O. Related adj: **aqueous. 2a** any body or area of this liquid, such as a sea, lake, river, etc. **2b** (*as modifier*): *water sports; a water plant.* Related adj: **aquatic. 3** the surface of such a body or area: *fish swam below the water.* **4** any form or variety of this liquid, such as rain. **5** See **high water, low water. 6** any of various solutions of chemical substances in water: *ammonia water.* **7** *Physiol.* **7a** any fluid secreted from the body, such as sweat, urine, or tears. **7b** (*usually pl*) the amniotic fluid surrounding a fetus in the womb. **8** a wavy lustrous finish on some fabrics, esp. silk. **9** *Arch.* the degree of brilliance in a diamond. **10** excellence, quality, or degree (in **of the first water**). **11** *Finance.* capital stock issued without a corresponding increase in paid-up capital. **12** (*modifier*) *Astrol.* of or relating to the three signs of the zodiac Cancer, Scorpio, and Pisces. **13 hold water.** to prove credible, logical, or consistent: *the alibi did not hold water.* **14 make water. 14a** to urinate. **14b** (of a boat, etc.) to let in water. **15 pass water.** to urinate. **16 water under the bridge.** events that are past and done with. ◆ *vb* **17** (*tr*) to sprinkle, moisten, or soak with water. **18** (*tr; often foll. by down*) to weaken by the addition of water. **19** (*intr*) (of the eyes) to fill with tears. **20** (*intr*) (of the mouth) to salivate, esp. in anticipation of food (esp. in **make one's mouth water**). **21** (*tr*) to irrigate or provide with water: *to water the land.* **22** (*intr*) to drink water. **23** (*intr*) (of a ship, etc.) to take in a supply of water. **24** (*tr*) *Finance.* to raise the par value of (issued capital stock) without a corresponding increase in the real value of assets. **25** (*tr*) to produce a wavy lustrous finish on (fabrics, esp. silk). ◆ See also **water down.** [OE *wæter*]
▸**'waterer** *n* ▸**'waterless** *adj*
water bag *n* a bag, sometimes made of skin, leather, etc., but in Australia usually canvas, for carrying water.
water bailiff *n* an official responsible for enforcing laws on shipping and fishing.
water bear *n* another name for a **tardigrade.**
water bed *n* a waterproof mattress filled with water.
water beetle *n* any of various beetles that live most of the time in freshwater ponds, rivers, etc.
water bird *n* any aquatic bird, including the wading and swimming birds.
water biscuit *n* a thin crisp plain biscuit, usually served with butter or cheese.
water blister *n* a blister containing watery or serous fluid, without any blood or pus.
water boatman *n* any of various aquatic bugs having a flattened body and oarlike hind legs, adapted for swimming.
waterborne ('wɔːtəˌbɔːn) *adj* **1** floating or travelling on water. **2** (of a disease, etc.) transported or transmitted by water.
waterbuck ('wɔːtəˌbʌk) *n* any of a genus of antelopes of swampy areas of Africa, having long curved ridged horns.
water buffalo *or* **ox** *n* a member of the cattle tribe of swampy regions of S Asia, having widely spreading back-curving horns. Domesticated forms are used as draught animals.
water bug *n* any of various heteropterous insects adapted to living in the water or on its surface, esp. any of the **giant water bugs** of North America, India, and southern Africa, which have flattened hairy legs.
water butt *n* a barrel for collecting rainwater, esp. from a drainpipe.
water cannon *n* an apparatus for pumping water through a nozzle at high pressure, used in quelling riots.
Water Carrier *or* **Bearer** *n* **the.** the constellation Aquarius, the 11th sign of the zodiac.
water chestnut *n* **1** a floating aquatic plant of Asia, having four-pronged edible nutlike fruits. **2 Chinese water chestnut.** a Chinese plant with an edible succulent corm. **3** the corm of the Chinese water chestnut, used in Oriental cookery.
water clock *or* **glass** *n* any of various devices for measuring time that use the escape of water as the motive force.
water closet *n* **1** a lavatory flushed by water. **2** a small room that has a lavatory. ◆ Usually abbreviated to **WC.**
watercolour *or US* **watercolor** ('wɔːtəˌkʌlə) *n* **1** water-soluble pigment bound with gum arabic, applied in transparent washes and without the admixture of white pigment in the lighter tones. **2a** a painting done in watercolours. **2b** (*as modifier*): *a watercolour masterpiece.* **3** the art or technique of painting with such pigments.
▸**'waterˌcolourist** *or US* **'waterˌcolorist** *n*
water-cool *vb* (*tr*) to cool (an engine, etc.) by a flow of water circulating in an enclosed jacket.
▸**'water-ˌcooled** *adj*
water cooler *n* a device for cooling and dispensing drinking water.
watercourse ('wɔːtəˌkɔːs) *n* **1** a stream, river, or canal. **2** the channel, bed, or route along which this flows.
watercraft ('wɔːtəˌkrɑːft) *n* **1** a boat or ship or such vessels collectively. **2** skill in handling boats or in water sports.
watercress ('wɔːtəˌkrɛs) *n* an Old World cruciferous plant of clear ponds and streams, having pungent leaves that are used in salads and as a garnish.
water cure *n Med.* a nontechnical name for **hydropathy** or **hydrotherapy.**
water cycle *n* the circulation of the earth's water, in which water evaporates from the sea into the atmosphere, where it condenses and falls as rain or snow, returning to the sea by rivers.
water diviner *n Brit.* a person able to locate the presence of water, esp. underground, with a divining rod.
water down Ⓣ *vb* (*tr, adv*) **1** to dilute or weaken with water. **2** to modify, esp. so as to omit anything unpleasant or offensive: *to water down the truth.*
▸ˌ**watered-'down** *adj*
waterfall Ⓣ ('wɔːtəˌfɔːl) *n* a cascade of falling water where there is a vertical or almost vertical step in a river.
water flea *n* any of numerous minute freshwater crustaceans which swim by means of hairy branched antennae. See also **daphnia.**
waterfowl ('wɔːtəˌfaul) *n* **1** any aquatic freshwater bird, esp. any species of the family Anatidae (ducks, geese, and swans). **2** such birds collectively.
waterfront ('wɔːtəˌfrʌnt) *n* the area of a town or city alongside a body of water, such as a harbour or dockyard.
water gap *n* a deep valley in a ridge, containing a stream.
water gas *n* a mixture of hydrogen and carbon monoxide produced by passing steam over hot carbon, used as a fuel and raw material.
water gate *n* **1** a gate in a canal, etc., that can be opened or closed to

THESAURUS

on, gaze at, get a load of (*inf.*), look, look on, mark, note, observe, pay attention, peer at, regard, see, stare at, view **3** = **guard**, keep, look after, mind, protect, superintend, take care of, tend **4** = **be vigilant**, attend, be on the alert, be on the lookout, be wary, be watchful, keep an eye open (*inf.*), look out, take heed, wait ◆ *n* **7** = **wristwatch**, chronometer, clock, pocket watch, timepiece **8, 9** = **lookout**, alertness, attention, eye, heed, inspection, notice, observation, supervision, surveillance, vigil, vigilance, watchfulness
watchdog *n* **1** = **guard dog 2** = **guardian**, custodian, inspector, monitor, protector, scrutineer
watcher *n* **1** = **viewer**, fly on the wall, looker-on, lookout, observer, onlooker, spectator, spy, witness
watchful *adj* **1** = **alert**, attentive, circumspect, guarded, heedful, observant, on one's guard, on one's toes, on the lookout, on the qui vive, on the watch, suspicious, vigilant, wary, wide awake
Antonyms *adj* careless, inattentive, reckless, thoughtless, unaware, unguarded, unmindful, unobservant, unwary
watchfulness *n* **1** = **vigilance**, alertness, attention, attentiveness, caution, cautiousness, circumspection, heedfulness, wariness
Antonyms *n* carelessness, heedlessness, inattention, indiscretion, irresponsibility, neglect, recklessness, thoughtlessness
watchman *n* **1** = **guard**, caretaker, custodian, security guard, security man
watch out *vb* = **be careful**, be alert, be on one's guard, be on the alert, be on (the) watch, be vigilant, be watchful, have a care, keep a sharp lookout, keep a weather eye open, keep one's eyes open, keep one's eyes peeled *or* skinned (*inf.*), look out, mind out, watch oneself
watchword *n* **1** = **password**, countersign, magic word, shibboleth **2** = **motto**, battle cry, byword, catch phrase, catchword, maxim, rallying cry, slogan, tag-line
water *n* **1** = **liquid**, Adam's ale *or* wine, aqua, H_2O **13 hold water** = **be sound**, bear examination *or* scrutiny, be credible, be logical, make sense, pass the test, ring true, work ◆ *vb* **17** = **moisten**, damp, dampen, douse, drench, flood, hose, irrigate, soak, souse, spray, sprinkle **18** = **dilute**, add water to, adulterate, put water in, thin, water down, weaken
water down *vb* **1** = **dilute**, add water to, adulterate, put water in, thin, water, weaken **2** = **weaken**, adulterate, mitigate, qualify, soften, tone down
Antonyms *vb* ≠ **dilute**: fortify, purify, strengthen, thicken
waterfall *n* = **cascade**, cataract, chute, fall, force (*N English dialect*), linn (*Scot.*)

control the flow of water. **2** a gate through which access may be gained to a body of water.

Watergate ('wɔːtəˌgeɪt) *n* **1** an incident during the 1972 US presidential campaign, when agents employed by the re-election organization of President Richard Nixon were caught breaking into the Democratic Party headquarters in the Watergate building, Washington, DC. The political scandal was exacerbated by attempts to conceal the fact that White House officials had approved the burglary, and eventually forced the resignation of President Nixon. **2** any similar public scandal, esp. involving politicians or a possible cover-up.

water gauge *n* an instrument that indicates the presence or the quantity of water in a tank, reservoir, or boiler feed. Also called: **water glass.**

water glass *n* **1** a viscous syrupy solution of sodium silicate in water: used as a protective coating for cement and a preservative, esp. for eggs. **2** another name for **water gauge.**

water gum *n* any of several Australian gum trees that grow in swampy ground and beside creeks and rivers.

water hammer *n* a sharp concussion produced when the flow of water in a pipe is suddenly blocked.

water hen *n* another name for **gallinule.**

water hole *n* **1** a depression, such as a pond or pool, containing water, esp. one used by animals as a drinking place. **2** a source of drinking water in a desert.

water hyacinth *n* a floating aquatic plant of tropical America, having showy bluish-purple flowers and swollen leafstalks. It forms dense masses in rivers, ponds, etc.

water ice *n* an ice cream made from a frozen sugar syrup flavoured with fruit juice or purée.

watering can *n* a container with a handle and a spout with a perforated nozzle used to sprinkle water over plants.

watering hole *n* **1** a pool where animals drink; water hole. **2** *Facetious sl.* a pub.

watering place *n* **1** a place where drinking water for people or animals may be obtained. **2** *Brit.* a spa. **3** *Brit.* a seaside resort.

water jacket *n* a water-filled envelope surrounding a machine or part for cooling purposes, esp. the casing around the cylinder block of a pump or internal-combustion engine.

water jump *n* a ditch or brook over which athletes or horses must jump in a steeplechase or similar contest.

water level *n* **1** the level reached by the surface of a body of water. **2** the water line of a boat or ship.

water lily *n* any of various aquatic plants of temperate and tropical regions, having large leaves and showy flowers that float on the surface of the water.

water line *n* **1** a line marked at the level around a vessel's hull to which the vessel will be immersed when afloat. **2** a line marking the level reached by a body of water.

waterlogged ❶ ('wɔːtəˌlɒgd) *adj* **1** saturated with water. **2** (of a vessel still afloat) having taken in so much water as to be unmanageable.

Waterloo (ˌwɔːtə'luː) *n* **1** a small town in Belgium south of Brussels: battle (1815) fought nearby in which British and Prussian forces under the Duke of Wellington and Blücher routed the French under Napoleon. **2** a total or crushing defeat (esp. in **meet one's Waterloo**).

water main *n* a principal supply pipe in an arrangement of pipes for distributing water.

waterman ('wɔːtəmən) *n, pl* **watermen.** a skilled boatman. ▸ **'waterman,ship** *n*

watermark ('wɔːtəˌmɑːk) *n* **1** a mark impressed on paper during manufacture, visible when the paper is held up to the light. **2** another word for **water line.** ◆ *vb* (*tr*) **3** to mark (paper) with a watermark.

water meadow *n* a meadow that remains fertile by being periodically flooded by a stream.

watermelon ('wɔːtəˌmɛlən) *n* **1** an African melon widely cultivated for its large edible fruit. **2** the fruit of this plant, which has a hard green rind and sweet watery reddish flesh.

water meter *n* a device for measuring the quantity or rate of water flowing through a pipe.

water milfoil *n* any of various pond plants having feathery underwater leaves and inconspicuous flowers.

water mill *n* a mill operated by a water wheel.

water moccasin *n* a large dark grey venomous snake of swamps in the southern US. Also called: **cottonmouth.**

water nymph *n* any fabled nymph of the water, such as the Naiad, Nereid, or Oceanid of Greek mythology.

water of crystallization *n* water present in the crystals of certain compounds. It is chemically combined in a specific amount but can often be easily expelled.

water ouzel *n* another name for **dipper** (the bird).

water paint *n* any water-based paint, such as an emulsion or an acrylic paint.

water pipe *n* **1** a pipe for water. **2** another name for **hookah.**

water pistol *n* a toy pistol that squirts a stream of water or other liquid.

water plantain *n* any of a genus of marsh plants of N temperate regions and Australia, having clusters of small white or pinkish flowers and broad pointed leaves.

water polo *n* a game played in water by two teams of seven swimmers in which each side tries to throw or propel an inflated ball into the opponents' goal.

water power *n* **1** the power latent in a dynamic or static head of water as used to drive machinery, esp. for generating electricity. **2** a source of such power, such as a drop in the level of a river, etc.

waterproof ('wɔːtəˌpruːf) *adj* **1** not penetrable by water. Cf. **water-repellent, water-resistant.** ◆ *n* **2** *Chiefly Brit.* a waterproof garment, esp. a raincoat. ◆ *vb* (*tr*) **3** to make (a fabric, etc.) waterproof.

water purslane *n* a marsh plant of temperate and warm regions, having reddish stems and small reddish flowers.

water rail *n* a large Eurasian rail of swamps, ponds, etc., having a long red bill.

water rat *n* **1** any of several small amphibious rodents, esp. the water vole or the muskrat. **2** any of various amphibious rats of New Guinea, the Philippines, and Australia.

water rate *n* a charge made for the public supply of water.

water-repellent *adj* (of fabrics, garments, etc.) having a finish that resists the absorption of water.

water-resistant *adj* (esp. of fabrics) designed to resist but not entirely prevent the penetration of water.

water scorpion *n* a long-legged aquatic insect that breathes by means of a long spinelike tube that projects from the rear of the body and penetrates the surface of the water.

watershed ('wɔːtəˌʃɛd) *n* **1** the dividing line between two adjacent river systems, such as a ridge. **2** an important period or factor that serves as a dividing line.

waterside ('wɔːtəˌsaɪd) *n* **a** the area of land beside a body of water. **b** (*as modifier*): *waterside houses.*

watersider ('wɔːtəˌsaɪdə) *n Austral. & NZ.* a dock labourer.

water-ski *n* **1** a type of ski used for planing or gliding over water. ◆ *vb* **water-skis, water-skiing, water-skied** *or* **water-ski'd. 2** (*intr*) to ride over water on water-skis while holding a rope towed by a speedboat. ▸ **'water-ˌskier** *n* ▸ **'water-ˌskiing** *n*

water snake *n* any of various snakes that live in or near water, esp. any of a genus of harmless North American snakes.

water softener *n* **1** any substance that lessens the hardness of water, usually by precipitating calcium and magnesium ions. **2** an apparatus that is used to remove chemicals that cause hardness.

water spaniel *n* either of two large curly-coated breeds of spaniel (the Irish and the American), which are used for hunting waterfowl.

water splash *n* a place where a stream runs over a road.

water sports *pl n* sports, such as swimming or windsurfing, that take place in or on water.

waterspout ('wɔːtəˌspaʊt) *n* **1** *Meteorol.* **1a** a tornado occurring over water that forms a column of water and mist. **1b** a sudden downpour of heavy rain. **2** a pipe or channel through which water is discharged.

water table *n* **1** the level below which the ground is saturated with water. **2** a string course that has a moulding designed to throw rainwater clear of the wall below.

water thrush *n* either of two North American warblers having brownish backs and striped underparts and occurring near water.

watertight ❶ ('wɔːtəˌtaɪt) *adj* **1** not permitting the passage of water either in or out: *a watertight boat.* **2** without loopholes: *a watertight argument.* **3** kept separate from other subjects or influences.

water tower ('taʊə) *n* a reservoir or storage tank mounted on a tower-like structure so that water can be distributed at a uniform pressure.

water vapour *n* water in the gaseous state, esp. when due to evaporation at a temperature below the boiling point.

water vole *n* a large amphibious vole of Eurasian river banks. Also called: **water rat.**

water wagtail *n* another name for **pied wagtail.**

waterway ('wɔːtəˌweɪ) *n* a river, canal, or other navigable channel used as a means of travel or transport.

waterweed ('wɔːtəˌwiːd) *n* any of various weedy aquatic plants.

water wheel *n* **1** a simple water-driven turbine consisting of a wheel having vanes set axially across its rim, used to drive machinery. **2** a wheel with buckets attached to its rim for raising water from a stream, pond, etc.

water wings *pl n* an inflatable rubber device shaped like a pair of wings, which is placed under the arms of a person learning to swim.

waterworks ('wɔːtəˌwɜːks) *n* **1** (*functioning as sing*) an establishment for storing, purifying, and distributing water for community supply. **2** (*functioning as pl*) a display of water in movement, as in fountains. **3** (*functioning as pl*) *Brit. inf., euphemistic.* the urinary system. **4** (*functioning as pl*) *Inf.* crying; tears.

waterworn ('wɔːtəˌwɔːn) *adj* worn smooth by the action or passage of water.

watery ❶ ('wɔːtərɪ) *adj* **1** relating to, containing, or resembling water. **2** discharging or secreting water or a water-like fluid. **3** tearful; weepy. **4** insipid, thin, or weak.

watt (wɒt) *n* the derived SI unit of power, equal to 1 joule per second;

THESAURUS

waterlogged *adj* **1** = **soaked**, drenched, dripping, droukit *or* drookit (*Scot.*), saturated, sodden, sopping, streaming, wet through, wringing wet

watertight *adj* **1** = **waterproof**, sound **2** = **foolproof**, airtight, firm, flawless, impregnable, incontrovertible, sound, unassailable
Antonyms *adj* ≠ **waterproof**: leaky ≠ **foolproof**: defective, flawed, questionable, shaky, tenuous, uncertain, unsound, weak

watery *adj* **1** = **wet**, aqueous, damp, fluid, humid, liquid, marshy, moist, soggy, squelchy

the power dissipated by a current of 1 ampere flowing across a potential difference of 1 volt. Symbol: W [C19: after J. *Watt* (1736–1819), Scot. engineer & inventor]

wattage ('wɒtɪdʒ) *n* **1** power, esp. electric power, measured in watts. **2** the power rating, measured in watts, of an electrical appliance.

watt-hour *n* a unit of energy equal to a power of one watt operating for one hour.

wattle ('wɒtᵊl) *n* **1** a frame of rods or stakes interwoven with twigs, branches, etc., esp. when used to make fences. **2** the material used in such a construction. **3** a loose fold of skin, often brightly coloured, hanging from the neck or throat of certain birds, lizards, etc. **4** any of various chiefly Australian acacia trees having spikes of small brightly coloured flowers and flexible branches. ◆ *vb* **wattles, wattling, wattled.** (*tr*) **5** to construct from wattle. **6** to bind or frame with wattle. **7** to weave or twist (branches, twigs, etc.) into a frame. ◆ *adj* **8** made of, formed by, or covered with wattle. [OE *watol*]
▸ '**wattled** *adj*

wattle and daub *n* a form of wall construction consisting of interwoven twigs plastered with a mixture of clay, water, and sometimes chopped straw.

wattmeter ('wɒtˌmiːtə) *n* a meter for measuring electric power in watts.

waul *or* **wawl** (wɔːl) *vb* (*intr*) to cry or wail plaintively like a cat. [C16: imit.]

wave ➊ (weɪv) *vb* **waves, waving, waved. 1** to move or cause to move freely to and fro: *the banner waved in the wind.* **2** (*intr*) to move the hand to and fro as a greeting. **3** to signal or signify by or as if by waving something. **4** (*tr*) to direct to move by or as if by waving something: *he waved me on.* **5** to form or be formed into curves, undulations, etc. **6** (*tr*) to set waves in (the hair). ◆ *n* **7** one of a sequence of ridges or undulations that moves across the surface of a body of a liquid, esp. the sea. **8 the waves.** the sea. **9** any undulation on or at the edge of a surface reminiscent of a wave in the sea: *a wave across the field of corn.* **10** anything that suggests the movement of a wave, as by a sudden rise: *a crime wave.* **11** a widespread movement that advances in a body: *a wave of settlers.* **12** the act or an instance of waving. **13** *Physics.* an energy-carrying disturbance propagated through a medium or space by a progressive local displacement of the medium or a change in its physical properties, but without any overall movement of matter. **14** *Physics.* a graphical representation of a wave obtained by plotting the magnitude of the disturbance against time at a particular point in the medium or space. **15** a prolonged spell of some particular type of weather: *a heat wave.* **16** an undulating curve or series of curves or loose curls in the hair. **17 make waves.** to cause trouble; disturb the status quo. [OE *wafian* (vb); C16 (n) changed from earlier *wāwe,* prob. from OE *wǣg* motion]
▸ '**waveless** *adj* ▸ '**wave,like** *adj*

waveband ('weɪvˌbænd) *n* a range of wavelengths or frequencies used for a particular type of radio transmission.

wave-cut platform *n* a flat surface at the base of a cliff formed by erosion by waves.

wave down *vb* (*tr, adv*) to signal with a wave to (a driver or vehicle) to stop.

wave energy *n* energy obtained by harnessing wave power.

wave equation *n Physics.* a partial differential equation describing wave motion.

waveform ('weɪvˌfɔːm) *n Physics.* the shape of the graph of a wave or oscillation obtained by plotting the value of some changing quantity against time.

wavefront ('weɪvˌfrʌnt) *n Physics.* a surface associated with a propagating wave and passing through all points in the wave that have the same phase.

wave function *n Physics.* a mathematical function of position and sometimes time, used in wave mechanics to describe the state of a physical system. Symbol: ψ

waveguide ('weɪvˌgaɪd) *n Electronics.* a solid rod of dielectric or a hollow metal tube, usually of rectangular cross section, used as a path to guide microwaves.

wavelength ('weɪvˌleŋθ) *n* **1** the distance, measured in the direction of propagation, between two points of the same phase in consecutive cycles of a wave. Symbol: λ **2** the wavelength of the carrier wave used by a particular broadcasting station. **3 on someone's** (*or* **the same**) **wavelength.** *Inf.* having similar views, feelings, or thoughts (as someone else).

wavelet ('weɪvlɪt) *n* a small wave.

wave mechanics *n* (*functioning as sing*) *Physics.* the formulation of quantum mechanics in which the behaviour of systems, such as atoms, is described in terms of their wave functions.

wave number *n Physics.* the reciprocal of the wavelength of a wave.

waver ➊ ('weɪvə) *vb* (*intr*) **1** to be irresolute; hesitate between two possibilities. **2** to become unsteady. **3** to fluctuate. **4** to move back and forth or one way and another. **5** (of light) to flicker or flash. ◆ *n* **6** the act or an instance of wavering. [C14: from ON *vafra* to flicker]
▸ '**waverer** *n* ▸ '**wavering** *adj* ▸ '**waveringly** *adv*

wave theory *n* **1** the theory proposed by Huygens that light is transmitted by waves. **2** any theory that light or other radiation is transmitted as waves. ◆ Cf. **corpuscular theory.**

wavey ('weɪvɪ) *n Canad.* a snow goose or other wild goose. Also called: **wawa.** [via Canad. F from Algonquian (Cree *wehwew*)]

wavy ('weɪvɪ) *adj* **wavier, waviest. 1** abounding in or full of waves. **2** moving or proceeding in waves. **3** (of hair) set in or having waves.
▸ '**wavily** *adv* ▸ '**waviness** *n*

wax¹ (wæks) *n* **1** any of various viscous or solid materials of natural origin: characteristically lustrous, insoluble in water, and having a low softening temperature, they consist largely of esters of fatty acids. **2** any of various similar substances, such as paraffin wax, that have a mineral origin and consist largely of hydrocarbons. **3** short for **beeswax** or **sealing wax. 4** *Physiol.* another name for **cerumen. 5** a resinous preparation used by shoemakers to rub on thread. **6** any substance or object that is pliable or easily moulded: *he was wax in their hands.* **7** (*modifier*) made of or resembling wax: *a wax figure.* ◆ *vb* **8** (*tr*) to coat, polish, etc., with wax. [OE *weax*]
▸ '**waxer** *n*

wax² ➊ (wæks) *vb* (*intr*) **1** to become larger, more powerful, etc. **2** (of the moon) to show a gradually increasing portion of illuminated surface, between new moon and full moon. **3** to become: *to wax eloquent.* [OE *weaxan*]

wax³ (wæks) *n Brit. inf., old-fashioned.* a fit of rage or temper: *he's in a wax today.* [from ?]

waxberry ('wæksbərɪ) *n, pl* **waxberries.** the waxy fruit of the wax myrtle or the snowberry.

waxbill ('wæksˌbɪl) *n* any of various chiefly African finchlike weaverbirds having a brightly coloured bill and plumage.

wax cloth *n* **1** another name for **oilcloth. 2** (formerly) another name for **linoleum.**

waxen ➊ ('wæksən) *adj* **1** made of, treated with, or covered with wax. **2** resembling wax in colour or texture.

waxeye ('wæksˌaɪ) *n* a small New Zealand bird with a white circle around its eye. Also called: **silver-eye, blighty.**

wax flower *n Austral.* any of a genus of shrubs having waxy pink-white five-petalled flowers.

wax light *n* a candle or taper of wax.

wax myrtle *n* a shrub of SE North America, having evergreen leaves and a small berry-like fruit with a waxy coating. Also called: **bayberry, candleberry, waxberry.**

wax palm *n* **1** a tall Andean palm tree having pinnate leaves that yield a resinous wax used in making candles. **2** another name for **carnauba** (sense 1).

wax paper *n* paper treated or coated with wax or paraffin to make it waterproof.

waxplant ('wæksˌplɑːnt) *n* a climbing shrub of E Asia and Australia, having fleshy leaves and clusters of small waxy white pink-centred flowers.

waxwing ('wæksˌwɪŋ) *n* any of a genus of gregarious passerine songbirds having red waxy wing tips and crested heads.

waxwork ('wæksˌwɜːk) *n* **1** an object reproduced in wax, esp. as an ornament. **2** a life-size lifelike figure, esp. of a famous person, reproduced in wax. **3** (*pl; functioning as sing or pl*) a museum or exhibition of wax figures.

waxy¹ ('wæksɪ) *adj* **waxier, waxiest. 1** resembling wax in colour, appearance, or texture. **2** made of, covered with, or abounding in wax.
▸ '**waxily** *adv* ▸ '**waxiness** *n*

waxy² ('wæksɪ) *adj* **waxier, waxiest.** *Brit. inf., old-fashioned.* bad-tempered or irritable; angry.

way ➊ (weɪ) *n* **1** a manner, method, or means: *a way of life.* **2** a route or direction: *the way home.* **3a** a means or line of passage, such as a path or track. **3b** (*in combination*): *waterway.* **4** space or room for movement or activity (esp. in **make way, in the way, out of the way**). **5** distance, usu-

THESAURUS

2, 3 = **tearful**, rheumy, tear-filled, weepy **4** = **diluted**, adulterated, dilute, flavourless, insipid, runny, tasteless, thin, washy, watered-down, waterish, weak, wishy-washy (*inf.*)
Antonyms *adj* ≠ **diluted:** concentrated, condensed, dense, fortified, solid, strong, thick

wave *vb* **1, 5** = **brandish**, flap, flourish, flutter, move to and fro, oscillate, quiver, ripple, shake, stir, sway, swing, undulate, wag, waver, wield **2, 3** = **signal**, beckon, direct, gesticulate, gesture, indicate, sign ◆ *n* **7** = **ripple**, billow, breaker, comber, ridge, roller, sea surf, swell, undulation, unevenness **10, 11** = **outbreak**, current, drift, flood, ground swell, movement, rash, rush, stream, surge, sweep, tendency, trend, upsurge

waver *vb* **1** = **hesitate**, be indecisive, be irresolute, be unable to decide, be unable to make up one's mind, blow hot and cold (*inf.*), dither (*chiefly Brit.*), falter, fluctuate, hum and haw, seesaw, shillyshally (*inf.*), swither (*Scot.*), vacillate **2, 3, 5** = **tremble**, flicker, fluctuate, quiver, reel, shake, sway, totter, undulate, vary, wave, weave, wobble
Antonyms *vb* ≠ **hesitate:** be decisive, be determined, be of fixed opinion, be resolute, determine, resolve, stand firm

wax² *vb* **1** = **increase**, become fuller, become larger, develop, dilate, enlarge, expand, fill out, get bigger, grow, magnify, mount, rise, swell
Antonyms *vb* contract, decline, decrease, diminish, dwindle, fade, lessen, narrow, shrink, wane

waxen *adj* **2** = **pale**, anaemic, ashen, bloodless, colourless, ghastly, pallid, wan, white, whitish

way *n* **1** = **method**, approach, course of action, fashion, manner, means, mode, plan, practice, procedure, process, scheme, system, technique **2, 3, 10** = **route**, access, avenue, channel, course, direction, highway, lane, path, pathway, road, street, thoroughfare, track, trail **4** = **room**, elbowroom, opening, space **5** = **distance**, journey, length, stretch, trail **6** = **journey**, advance, approach, march, passage, progress **7, 8**

ally distance in general: *you've come a long way.* **6** a passage or journey: *on the way.* **7** characteristic style or manner: *I did it my way.* **8** (*often pl*) habit: *he has some offensive ways.* **9** an aspect of something; particular: *in many ways he was right.* **10a** a street in or leading out of a town. **10b** (*cap. when part of a street name*): *Icknield Way.* **11** something that one wants in a determined manner (esp. in **get** *or* **have one's (own) way**). **12** the experience or sphere in which one comes into contact with things (esp. in **come one's way**). **13** *Inf.* a state or condition, usually financial or concerning health (esp. in **in a good** (*or* **bad**) **way**). **14** *Inf.* the area or direction of one's home: *drop in if you're ever over my way.* **15** movement of a ship or other vessel. **16** a guide along which something can be moved, such as the surface of a lathe along which the tailstock slides. **17** (*pl*) the wooden or metal tracks down which a ship slides to be launched. **18** a course of life including experiences, conduct, etc.: *the way of sin.* **19 by the way.** incidentally. **20 by way of. 20a** via. **20b** serving as: *by way of introduction.* **20c** in the state or condition of: *by way of being an artist.* **21 each way.** (of a bet) laid on a horse, dog, etc., to win or gain a place. **22 give way. 22a** to collapse or break down. **22b** to yield. **23 give way to. 23a** to step aside for or stop for. **23b** to give full rein to (emotions, etc.). **24 go out of one's way.** to take considerable trouble or inconvenience oneself. **25 have a way with.** to have such a manner or skill as to handle successfully. **26 have it both ways.** to enjoy two things that would normally be mutually exclusive. **27 in a way.** in some respects. **28 in no way.** not at all. **29 lead the way. 29a** to go first. **29b** to set an example. **30 make one's way. 30a** to proceed or advance. **30b** to achieve success in life. **31 on the way out.** *Inf.* **31a** becoming unfashionable, etc. **31b** dying. **32 out of the way. 32a** removed or dealt with so as to be no longer a hindrance. **32b** remote. **32c** unusual and sometimes improper. **33 see one's way (clear).** to find it possible and be willing (to do something). **34 under way.** having started moving or making progress. ◆ *adv* **35** *Inf.* **35a** at a considerable distance or extent: *way over yonder.* **35b** very far: *they're way up the mountain.* **36** *Inf.* by far; considerably: *way better.* [OE *weg*]

waybill ('weɪˌbɪl) *n* a document attached to goods in transit specifying their nature, point of origin, and destination as well as the route to be taken and the rate to be charged.

wayfarer ❶ ('weɪˌfɛərə) *n* a person who goes on a journey.
▸'**way,faring** *n, adj*

wayfaring tree *n* a shrub of Europe and W Asia, having white flowers and berries that turn from red to black.

waylay ❶ (weɪ'leɪ) *vb* **waylays, waylaying, waylaid.** (*tr*) **1** to lie in wait for and attack. **2** to await and intercept unexpectedly.
▸**way'layer** *n*

wayleave ('weɪˌliːv) *n* access to property granted by a landowner for payment, for example to allow a contractor access to a building site.

waymark ('weɪˌmɑːk) *n* a symbol or signpost marking the route of a footpath.
▸'**way,marked** *adj*

way-out ❶ *adj Inf.* **1** extremely unconventional or experimental. **2** excellent or amazing.

-ways *suffix forming adverbs.* indicating direction or manner: *sideways.* [OE *weges,* lit.: of the way, from *weg* way]

ways and means ❶ *pl n* **1** the revenues and methods of raising the revenues needed for the functioning of a state or other political unit. **2** the methods and resources for accomplishing some purpose.

wayside ('weɪˌsaɪd) *n* **1a** the side or edge of a road. **1b** (*modifier*) situated by the wayside: *a wayside inn.* **2 fall by the wayside.** to cease or fail to continue doing something: *of the nine starters, three fell by the wayside.*

wayward ❶ ('weɪwəd) *adj* **1** wanting to have one's own way regardless of others. **2** capricious, erratic, or unpredictable. [C14: changed from *awayward* turned or turning away]
▸'**waywardly** *adv* ▸'**waywardness** *n*

wayworn ('weɪˌwɔːn) *adj Rare.* worn or tired by travel.

wb *abbrev. for:* **1** water ballast. **2** Also: **W/B, WB.** waybill. **3** westbound.

Wb *Physics. symbol for* weber.

WBA *abbrev. for* World Boxing Association.

WBC *abbrev. for* World Boxing Council.

WBU *abbrev. for* World Boxing Union.

WC *abbrev. for:* **1** Also: **wc.** water closet. **2** (in London postal code) West Central.

WD *abbrev. for:* **1** War Department. **2** Works Department.

we (wiː) *pron* (*subjective*) **1** refers to the speaker or writer and another person or other people: *we should go now.* **2** refers to all people or people in general: *the planet on which we live.* **3** a formal word for **I** used by editors or other writers, and formerly by monarchs. **4** *Inf.* used instead of *you* with a tone of condescension or sarcasm: *how are we today?* [OE *wē*]

WEA (in Britain) *abbrev. for* Workers' Educational Association.

weak ❶ (wiːk) *adj* **1** lacking in physical or mental strength or force. **2** liable to yield, break, or give way: *a weak link in a chain.* **3** lacking in resolution or firmness of character. **4** lacking strength, power, or intensity: *a weak voice.* **5** lacking strength in a particular part: *a team weak in defence.* **6a** not functioning as well as is normal: *weak eyes.* **6b** easily upset: *a weak stomach.* **7** lacking in conviction, persuasiveness, etc.: *a weak argument.* **8** lacking in political or strategic strength: *a weak state.* **9** lacking the usual, full, or desirable strength of flavour: *weak tea.* **10** *Grammar.* **10a** denoting or belonging to a class of verbs, in Germanic languages, whose conjugation relies on inflectional endings rather than internal vowel gradation, as *look, looks, looking, looked.* **10b** belonging to any part-of-speech class, in any of various languages, whose inflections follow the more regular of two possible patterns. Cf. **strong** (sense 13). **11** (of a syllable) not accented or stressed. **12** (of an industry, market, securities, etc.) falling in price or characterized by falling prices. [OE *wāc* soft, miserable]
▸'**weakish** *adj*

weaken ❶ ('wiːkən) *vb* to become or cause to become weak or weaker.
▸'**weakener** *n*

weak interaction *n Physics.* an interaction between elementary particles that is responsible for certain decay processes, operates at distances less than about 10^{-15} metres, and is 10^{12} times weaker than the strong interaction. Also called: **weak nuclear interaction** *or* **force.**

weak-kneed *adj Inf.* yielding readily to force, intimidation, etc.
▸ˌ**weak-'kneedly** *adv*

weakling ❶ ('wiːklɪŋ) *n* a person or animal that is lacking in strength or weak in constitution or character.

weakly ('wiːklɪ) *adj* **weaklier, weakliest. 1** sickly; feeble. ◆ *adv* **2** in a weak or feeble manner.

weak-minded *adj* **1** lacking in stability of mind or character. **2** another word for **feeble-minded.**
▸ˌ**weak-'mindedly** *adv* ▸ˌ**weak-'mindedness** *n*

weakness ❶ ('wiːknɪs) *n* **1** a being weak. **2** a failing, as in a person's character. **3** a self-indulgent liking: *a weakness for chocolates.*

THESAURUS

= **style**, characteristic, conduct, custom, habit, idiosyncrasy, manner, nature, personality, practice, trait, usage, wont **9** = **aspect**, detail, feature, particular, point, respect, sense **11** = **will**, aim, ambition, choice, demand, desire, goal, pleasure, wish **13** *Informal As in* **in a bad way** = **condition**, circumstance, fettle, shape (*inf.*), situation, state, status **19 by the way** = **incidentally**, by the bye, en passant, in parenthesis, in passing **22 give way: a** = **concede**, break down, cave in, crack, crumple, fall, fall to pieces, give, go to pieces, subside **b** accede, acknowledge defeat, acquiesce, back down, make concessions, withdraw, yield **34 under way** = **in progress**, afoot, begun, going, in motion, moving, on the go (*inf.*), on the move, started

wayfarer *n* = **traveller**, bird of passage, globetrotter, gypsy, itinerant, journeyer, nomad, rover, trekker, voyager, walker, wanderer

wayfaring *adj* = **roving**, drifting, itinerant, journeying, nomadic, peripatetic, rambling, travelling, voyaging, walking, wandering

waylay *vb* **1, 2** = **attack**, accost, ambush, catch, hold up, intercept, lie in wait for, pounce on, set upon, surprise, swoop down on

way-out *Informal adj* **1** = **outlandish**, advanced, avant-garde, bizarre, crazy, eccentric, experimental, far-out (*sl.*), freaky (*sl.*), oddball (*inf.*), offbeat, off-the-wall (*sl.*), outré, progressive, unconventional, unorthodox, weird, wild **2** = **wonderful**, amazing, awesome (*inf.*), brilliant, excellent, fantastic (*inf.*), great (*inf.*), marvellous, sensational (*inf.*), tremendous (*inf.*)

ways and means *pl n* **1, 2** = **capability**, ability, capacity, course, funds, methods, procedure, reserves, resources, tools, way, wherewithal

wayward *adj* **1, 2** = **erratic**, capricious, changeable, contrary, contumacious, cross-grained, disobedient, fickle, flighty, froward (*arch.*), headstrong, inconstant, incorrigible, insubordinate, intractable, mulish, obdurate, obstinate, perverse, rebellious, refractory, self-willed, stubborn, undependable, ungovernable, unmanageable, unpredictable, unruly, wilful
Antonyms *adj* complaisant, compliant, dependable, good-natured, malleable, manageable, obedient, obliging, predictable, reliable, submissive, tractable

weak *adj* **1** = **feeble**, anaemic, debilitated, decrepit, delicate, effete, enervated, exhausted, faint, fragile, frail, infirm, languid, puny, shaky, sickly, spent, tender, unsound, unsteady, wasted, weakly **2** = **deficient**, faulty, inadequate, lacking, pathetic, poor, substandard, under-strength, wanting **3** = **irresolute**, boneless, cowardly, impotent, indecisive, ineffectual, infirm, namby-pamby, pathetic, powerless, soft, spineless, timorous, weak-kneed (*inf.*) **4** = **faint**, distant, dull, imperceptible, low, muffled, poor, quiet, slight, small, soft **7** = **unconvincing**, feeble, flimsy, hollow, inconclusive, invalid, lame, pathetic, shallow, slight, unsatisfactory **9** = **tasteless**, diluted, insipid, milk-and-water, runny, thin, under-strength, waterish, watery, wishy-washy (*inf.*)
Antonyms *adj* ≠ **feeble:** energetic, hardy, healthy, hefty, mighty, strong, tough ≠ **deficient:** able, capable, effective ≠ **irresolute:** firm, resolute ≠ **unconvincing:** conclusive, convincing, forceful, incontrovertible, obvious, powerful, solid, trustworthy, valid ≠ **tasteless:** flavoursome, intoxicating, potent, tasty

weaken *vb* = **lessen**, abate, debilitate, depress, diminish, droop, dwindle, ease up, enervate, fade, fail, flag, give way, impair, invalidate, lower, mitigate, moderate, reduce, sap, sap the strength of, soften up, take the edge off, temper, tire, undermine, wane = **dilute**, adulterate, cut, debase, thin, thin out, water down
Antonyms *vb* ≠ **lessen:** boost, enhance, grow, improve, increase, invigorate, revitalize, strengthen

weakling *n* = **sissy**, coward, doormat (*sl.*), drip, jellyfish (*inf.*), milksop, mouse, wet (*Brit. inf.*), wimp (*inf.*)

weakness *n* **1** = **frailty**, debility, decrepitude, enervation, faintness, feebleness, fragility, impotence, infirmity, irresolution, powerlessness, vulnerability **2** = **failing**, Achilles heel, blemish, chink in one's armour, defect, deficiency, fault, flaw, imperfection, lack, shortcoming **3** = **liking**, fondness, inclination, partiality, passion, penchant, predilection, proclivity, proneness, soft spot
Antonyms *n* ≠ **frailty:** hardiness, health, impregnability, potency, power, stamina, sturdiness, valid-

weal[1] ⓣ (wiːl) *n* a raised mark on the skin produced by a blow. Also called: **welt.** [C19: var. of WALE, infl. in form by WHEAL]

weal[2] (wiːl) *n Arch.* prosperity or wellbeing (now esp. in **the public weal, the common weal**). [OE *wela*]

weald (wiːld) *n Brit. arch.* open or forested country. [OE]

Weald (wiːld) *n* **the.** a region of SE England, in Kent, Surrey, and Sussex between the North Downs and the South Downs: formerly forested.

wealth ⓣ (wɛlθ) *n* **1** a large amount of money and valuable material possessions. **2** the state of being rich. **3** a great profusion: *a wealth of gifts.* **4** *Econ.* all goods and services with monetary or productive value. [C13 *welthe,* from WEAL[2]]

wealth tax *n* a tax on personal property.

wealthy ⓣ ('wɛlθɪ) *adj* **wealthier, wealthiest. 1** possessing wealth; rich. **2** of or relating to wealth. **3** abounding: *wealthy in friends.*
▸'**wealthily** *adv* ▸'**wealthiness** *n*

wean[1] (wiːn) *vb (tr)* **1** to cause (a child or young mammal) to replace mother's milk by other nourishment. **2** (usually foll. by *from*) to cause to desert former habits, pursuits, etc. [OE *wenian* to accustom]

wean[2] (weɪn) *n Scot. & N English dialect.* a child. [? short form of WEANLING, or a contraction of *wee ane*]

weaner ('wiːnə) *n* **1** a person or thing that weans. **2** a pig that has just been weaned and weighs less than 40 kg. **3** *Austral. & NZ.* a lamb, pig, or calf in the year in which it is weaned.

weanling ('wiːnlɪŋ) *n* a child or young animal recently weaned. [C16: from WEAN[1] + -LING[1]]

weapon ('wɛpən) *n* **1** an object or instrument used in fighting. **2** anything that serves to get the better of an opponent: *his power of speech was his best weapon.* **3** any part of an animal that is used to defend itself, to attack prey, etc., such as claws or a sting. [OE *wǣpen*]
▸'**weaponed** *adj* ▸'**weaponless** *adj*

weaponry ('wɛpənrɪ) *n* weapons regarded collectively.

wear[1] ⓣ (wɛə) *vb* **wears, wearing, wore, worn. 1** *(tr)* to carry or have (a garment, etc.) on one's person as clothing, ornament, etc. **2** *(tr)* to carry or have on one's person habitually: *she wears a lot of red.* **3** *(tr)* to have in one's aspect: *to wear a smile.* **4** *(tr)* to display, show, or fly: *a ship wears its colours.* **5** to deteriorate or cause to deteriorate by constant use or action. **6** to produce or be produced by constant rubbing, scraping, etc.: *to wear a hole in one's trousers.* **7** to bring or be brought to a specified condition by constant use or action: *to wear a tyre to shreds.* **8** *(intr)* to submit to constant use or action in a specified way: *his suit wears well.* **9** *(tr)* to harass or weaken. **10** (when *intr,* often foll. by *on*) (of time) to pass or be passed slowly. **11** *(tr) Brit. inf.* to accept: *Larry won't wear that argument.* ◆ *n* **12** the act of wearing or state of being worn. **13a** anything designed to be worn: *leisure wear.* **13b** *(in combination): nightwear.* **14** deterioration from constant or normal use. **15** the quality of resisting the effects of constant use. ◆ See also **wear down, wear off, wear out.** [OE *werian*]
▸'**wearer** *n*

wear[2] (wɛə) *vb* **wears, wearing, wore, worn.** *Naut.* to tack by gybing instead of by going through stays. [C17: from earlier *weare,* from ?]

wearable ('wɛərəbᵊl) *adj* suitable for wear or able to be worn.
▸ˌ**weara'bility** *n*

wear and tear *n* damage, depreciation, or loss resulting from ordinary use.

wear down ⓣ *vb (adv)* **1** to consume or be consumed by long or constant wearing, rubbing, etc. **2** to overcome or be overcome gradually by persistent effort.

wearing ⓣ ('wɛərɪŋ) *adj* causing fatigue or exhaustion; tiring.
▸'**wearingly** *adv*

wearisome ⓣ ('wɪərɪsəm) *adj* causing fatigue or annoyance; tedious.
▸'**wearisomely** *adv*

wear off ⓣ *vb (adv)* **1** *(intr)* to decrease in intensity gradually: *the pain will wear off in an hour.* **2** to disappear or cause to disappear gradually through exposure, use, etc.

wear out ⓣ *vb (adv)* **1** to make or become evasive or useless through wear. **2** *(tr)* to exhaust or tire.

weary ⓣ ('wɪərɪ) *adj* **wearier, weariest. 1** tired or exhausted. **2** causing fatigue or exhaustion. **3** caused by or suggestive of weariness: *a weary laugh.* **4** *(postpositive;* often foll. by *of* or *with)* discontented or bored. ◆ *vb* **wearies, wearying, wearied. 5** to make or become weary. **6** to make or become discontented or impatient. [OE *wērig*]
▸'**weariless** *adj* ▸'**wearily** *adv* ▸'**weariness** *n* ▸'**wearying** *adj* ▸'**wearyingly** *adv*

weasand ('wiːzənd) *n* a former name for the **trachea.** [OE *wǣsend, wāsend*]

weasel ('wiːzᵊl) *n, pl* **weasels** *or* **weasel. 1** any of various small predatory mammals, such as the **European weasel,** having reddish-brown fur, an elongated body and neck, and short legs. **2** *Inf.* a sly or treacherous person. [OE *weosule, wesle*]
▸'**weaselly** *adj*

weasel out *vb* **weasels, weaselling, weaselled** *or US* **weasels, weaseling, weaseled.** *(intr, adv) Inf., chiefly US & Canad.* **1** to go back on a commitment. **2** to evade a responsibility, esp. in a despicable manner.

weasel words *pl n Inf.* intentionally evasive or misleading speech; equivocation. [C20: from the weasel's supposed ability to suck an egg out of its shell without seeming to break the shell]

weather ⓣ ('wɛðə) *n* **1a** the day-to-day meteorological conditions, esp. temperature, cloudiness, and rainfall, affecting a specific place. **1b** *(modifier)* relating to the forecasting of weather: *a weather ship.* **2 make heavy weather. 2a** *Naut.* to roll and pitch in heavy seas. **2b** (foll. by *of*) *Inf.* to carry out with difficulty or unnecessarily great effort. **3 under the weather.** *Inf.* not in good health. ◆ *adj* **4** *(prenominal)* on or at the side or part towards the wind: *the weather anchor.* Cf. **lee** (sense 2). ◆ *vb* **5** to expose or be exposed to the action of the weather. **6** to undergo or cause to undergo changes, such as discoloration, due to the action of the weather. **7** *(intr)* to withstand the action of the weather. **8** (when *intr,* foll. by *through*) to endure (a crisis, danger, etc.). **9** *(tr)* to slope (a

THESAURUS

ity, vigour, virtue, vitality ≠ **failing:** advantage, forte, strength, strong point ≠ **liking:** aversion, dislike, hatred, loathing

weal[1] *n* = **mark,** contusion, ridge, scar, streak, stripe, wale, welt, wheal

wealth *n* **1, 2** = **riches,** affluence, assets, big money, capital, cash, estate, fortune, funds, goods, lucre, means, money, opulence, pelf, possessions, pretty penny *(inf.)*, property, prosperity, resources, substance, tidy sum *(inf.)* **3** = **plenty,** abundance, bounty, copiousness, cornucopia, fullness, plenitude, profusion, richness, store
Antonyms *n* ≠ **riches:** deprivation, destitution, indigence, penury, poverty ≠ **plenty:** dearth, lack, need, paucity, poverty, scarcity, shortage, want

wealthy *adj* **1** = **rich,** affluent, comfortable, filthy rich, flush *(inf.)*, in the money *(inf.)*, loaded *(sl.)*, made of money *(inf.)*, moneyed, opulent, prosperous, quids in *(sl.)*, rolling in it *(sl.)*, stinking rich *(sl.)*, well-heeled *(inf.)*, well-off, well-to-do
Antonyms *adj* broke *(inf.)*, deprived, destitute, dirt-poor *(inf.)*, down and out, down at heel, flat broke *(inf.)*, impoverished, indigent, needy, on the breadline, penniless, poor, poverty-stricken, short, skint *(Brit. sl.)*

wear[1] *vb* **1** = **be dressed in,** bear, be clothed in, carry, clothe oneself, don, dress in, have on, put on, sport *(inf.)* **4** = **show,** display, exhibit, fly **5** = **deteriorate,** abrade, consume, corrode, erode, fray, grind, impair, rub, use, wash away, waste **11** *Brit. informal* = **accept,** allow, brook, countenance, fall for, permit, put up with *(inf.)*, stand for, stomach, swallow *(inf.)*, take ◆ *n* **13** = **clothes,** apparel, attire, costume, dress, garb, garments, gear *(inf.)*, habit, outfit, things, threads *(sl.)* **14** = **damage,** abrasion, attrition, corrosion, depreciation, deterioration, erosion, friction, use, wear and tear
Antonyms *n* ≠ **damage:** conservation, maintenance, preservation, repair, upkeep

wear down *vb* **1** = **erode,** abrade, be consumed, consume, corrode, grind down, rub away **2** = **undermine,** chip away at *(inf.)*, fight a war of attrition against, overcome gradually, reduce

weariness *n* **1** = **tiredness,** drowsiness, enervation, exhaustion, fatigue, languor, lassitude, lethargy, listlessness, prostration
Antonyms *n* drive, energy, freshness, get-up-and-go *(inf.)*, liveliness, stamina, vigour, vitality, zeal, zest

wearing *adj* = **tiresome,** exasperating, exhausting, fatiguing, irksome, oppressive, taxing, tiring, trying, wearisome
Antonyms *adj* easy, effortless, light, no bother, painless, refreshing, stimulating, undemanding

wearisome *adj* = **tedious,** annoying, boring, bothersome, burdensome, dull, exasperating, exhausting, fatiguing, humdrum, irksome, mind-numbing, monotonous, oppressive, pestilential, prosaic, tiresome, troublesome, trying, uninteresting, vexatious, wearing
Antonyms *adj* agreeable, delightful, enjoyable, exhilarating, interesting, invigorating, pleasurable, refreshing, stimulating

wear off *vb* **1** = **subside,** abate, decrease, diminish, disappear, dwindle, ebb, fade, lose effect, lose strength, peter out, wane, weaken **2** = **rub away,** abrade, disappear, efface, fade
Antonyms *vb* ≠ **subside:** grow, increase, intensify, magnify, persist, step up, strengthen, wax

wear out *vb* **1** = **deteriorate,** become useless, become worn, consume, erode, fray, impair, use up, wear through **2** = **exhaust,** enervate, fag out *(inf.)*, fatigue, frazzle *(inf.)*, knacker *(sl.)*, prostrate, sap, tire, weary
Antonyms *vb* ≠ **exhaust:** buck up *(inf.)*, energize, invigorate, pep up, perk up, refresh, revitalize, stimulate, strengthen

weary *adj* **1** = **tired,** all in *(sl.)*, asleep *or* dead on one's feet *(inf.)*, dead beat *(inf.)*, dog-tired *(inf.)*, done in *(inf.)*, drained, drooping, drowsy, enervated, exhausted, fagged *(inf.)*, fatigued, flagging, jaded, knackered *(sl.)*, sleepy, spent, wearied, whacked *(Brit. inf.)*, worn out **2** = **tiring,** arduous, enervative, irksome, laborious, taxing, tiresome, wearing, wearisome **4** = **fed up,** bored, browned-off *(inf.)*, discontented, impatient, indifferent, jaded, sick *(inf.)*, sick and tired *(inf.)* ◆ *vb* **5** = **tire,** burden, debilitate, drain, droop, enervate, fade, fag *(inf.)*, fail, fatigue, grow tired, sap, take it out of *(inf.)*, tax, tire out, wear out **6** = **bore,** annoy, become bored, exasperate, have had enough, irk, jade, make discontented, plague, sicken, try the patience of, vex
Antonyms *adj* ≠ **tired:** energetic, fresh, full of beans *(inf.)*, full of get-up-and-go *(inf.)*, invigorated, lively, refreshed, stimulated ≠ **tiring:** exciting, invigorating, original, refreshing ≠ **fed up:** amused, excited, forebearing, patient ◆ *vb* ≠ **tire:** enliven, invigorate, refresh, revive, stimulate ≠ **bore:** amuse, excite, interest

weather *n* **1** = **climate,** conditions **3** *Informal* **under the weather** = **ill,** ailing, below par, indisposed, nauseous, not well, off-colour, out of sorts, poorly *(inf.)*, seedy *(inf.)*, sick ◆ *vb* **5** = **toughen,** expose, harden, season **8** = **withstand,** bear up against, brave, come through, endure, get through, live through, make it *(inf.)*, overcome, pull through, resist, ride out, rise above, stand, stick it out *(inf.)*, suffer, surmount, survive
Antonyms *vb* ≠ **withstand:** cave in, collapse, fail, fall, give in, go under, succumb, surrender, yield

surface, such as a roof) so as to throw rainwater clear. **10** (*tr*) to sail to the windward of: *to weather a point.* [OE *weder*]
▸**'weatherer** *n*

weather-beaten *adj* **1** showing signs of exposure to the weather. **2** tanned or hardened by exposure to the weather.

weatherboard ('wɛðəˌbɔːd) *n* a timber board, with a groove (rabbet) along the front of its top edge and along the back of its lower edge, that is fixed horizontally with others to form an exterior covering on a wall or roof.
▸**'weatherˌboarding** *n*

weather-bound *adj* (of a vessel, aircraft, etc.) delayed by bad weather.

weathercock ('wɛðəˌkɒk) *n* **1** a weather vane in the form of a cock. **2** a person who is fickle or changeable.

weathered ('wɛðəd) *adj* **1** affected by exposure to the action of the weather. **2** (of rocks and rock formations) eroded, decomposed, or otherwise altered by the action of wind, frost, etc. **3** (of a sill, roof, etc.) having a sloped surface so as to allow rainwater to run off.

weather eye *n* **1** the vision of a person trained to observe changes in the weather. **2** *Inf.* an alert or observant gaze. **3 keep one's weather eye open.** to stay on the alert.

weatherglass ('wɛðəˌglɑːs) *n* any of various instruments, esp. a barometer, that measure atmospheric conditions.

weather house *n* a model house, usually with two human figures, one that comes out to foretell bad weather and one that comes out to foretell good weather.

weathering ('wɛðərɪŋ) *n* the mechanical and chemical breakdown of rocks by the action of rain, snow, etc.

weatherly ('wɛðəlɪ) *adj* (of a sailing vessel) making very little leeway when close-hauled, even in a stiff breeze.
▸**'weatherliness** *n*

weatherman ('wɛðəˌmæn) *n, pl* **weathermen.** *Inf.* a person who forecasts the weather, esp. one who works in a meteorological office.

weather map *or* **chart** *n* a chart showing weather conditions, compiled from simultaneous observations taken at various weather stations.

weatherproof ('wɛðəˌpruːf) *adj* **1** designed or able to withstand exposure to weather without deterioration. ◆ *vb* **2** (*tr*) to render (something) weatherproof.

weather station *n* one of a network of meteorological observation posts where weather data is recorded.

weather strip *n* a thin strip of compressible material, such as spring metal, felt, etc., that is fitted between the frame of a door or window and the opening part to exclude wind and rain. Also called: **weather-stripping.**

weather vane *n* a vane designed to indicate the direction in which the wind is blowing.

weather window *n* a limited interval when weather conditions can be expected to be suitable for a particular project.

weather-wise *adj* **1** skilful in predicting weather conditions. **2** skilful in predicting trends in opinion, reactions, etc.

weatherworn ('wɛðəˌwɔːn) *adj* another word for **weather-beaten.**

weave Ⓣ (wiːv) *vb* **weaves, weaving, wove** *or* **weaved; woven** *or* **weaved. 1** to form (a fabric) by interlacing (yarn, etc.), esp. on a loom. **2** (*tr*) to make or construct by such a process: *to weave a shawl.* **3** to construct by interlacing (cane, twigs, etc.). **4** (of a spider) to make (a web). **5** (*tr*) to construct by combining separate elements into a whole. **6** (*tr; often foll. by in, into, through,* etc.) to introduce: *to weave factual details into a fiction.* **7** to create (a way, etc.) by moving from side to side: *to weave through a crowd.* **8 get weaving.** *Inf.* to hurry. ◆ *n* **9** the method or pattern of weaving or the structure of a woven fabric: *an open weave.* [OE *wefan*]

weaver ('wiːvə) *n* **1** a person who weaves, esp. as a means of livelihood. **2** short for **weaverbird.**

weaverbird ('wiːvəˌbɜːd) *or* **weaver** *n* any of a family of small Old World passerine songbirds, having a short thick bill and a dull plumage and building covered nests: includes the house sparrow and whydahs.

web Ⓣ (wɛb) *n* **1** any structure, fabric, etc., formed by or as if by weaving or interweaving. **2** a mesh of fine tough threads built by a spider from a liquid secreted from its spinnerets and used to trap insects. **3** a similar network of threads spun by certain insect larvae, such as the silkworm. **4** a fabric, esp. one in the process of being woven. **5** a membrane connecting the toes of some aquatic birds or the digits of such aquatic mammals as the otter. **6** the vane of a bird's feather. **7** a thin piece of metal, esp. one connecting two thicker parts as in an H-beam or an I-beam. **8a** a continuous strip of paper as formed on a paper machine or fed from a reel into some printing presses. **8b** (*as modifier*): *web offset.* **9a** (*often cap.; preceded by the*) short for **World Wide Web. 9b** (*as modifier*): *web pages.* **10** any structure, construction, etc., that is intricately formed or complex: *a web of intrigue.* ◆ *vb* **webs, webbing, webbed. 11** (*tr*) to cover with or as if with a web. **12** (*tr*) to entangle or ensnare. **13** (*intr*) to construct a web. [OE *webb*]
▸**'webless** *adj*

webbed (wɛbd) *adj* **1** (of the feet of certain animals) having the digits connected by a thin fold of skin. **2** having or resembling a web.

webbing ('wɛbɪŋ) *n* **1** a strong fabric of hemp, cotton, jute, etc., woven in strips and used under springs in upholstery or for straps, etc. **2** the skin that unites the digits of a webbed foot.

webby ('wɛbɪ) *adj* **webbier, webbiest.** of, relating to, resembling, or consisting of a web.

weber ('veɪbə) *n* the derived SI unit of magnetic flux; the flux that, when linking a circuit of one turn, produces in it an emf of 1 volt as it is reduced to zero at a uniform rate in one second. Symbol: Wb [C20: after W. E. *Weber* (1804–91), G physicist]

webfoot ('wɛbˌfʊt) *n* **1** *Zool.* a foot having the toes connected by folds of skin. **2** *Anat.* a foot having an abnormal membrane connecting adjacent toes.

web-footed *or* **web-toed** *adj* (of certain animals) having webbed feet that facilitate swimming.

website ('wɛbˌsaɪt) *n* a group of connected pages on the World Wide Web containing information on a particular subject.

webwheel ('wɛbˌwiːl) *n* **1** a wheel containing a plate or web instead of spokes. **2** a wheel of which the rim, spokes, and centre are in one piece.

wed Ⓣ (wɛd) *vb* **weds, wedding, wedded** *or* **wed. 1** to take (a person of the opposite sex) as a husband or wife; marry. **2** (*tr*) to join (two people) in matrimony. **3** (*tr*) to unite closely. [OE *weddian*]
▸**'wedded** *adj*

we'd (wiːd; *unstressed* wɪd) *contraction of* we had *or* we would.

Wed. *abbrev. for* Wednesday.

wedding Ⓣ ('wɛdɪŋ) *n* **1a** the act of marrying or the celebration of a marriage. **1b** (*as modifier*): *wedding day.* **2** the anniversary of a marriage (in such combinations as **silver wedding** or **diamond wedding**).

wedding breakfast *n* the meal usually served after a wedding ceremony or just before the bride and bridegroom leave for their honeymoon.

wedding cake *n* a rich fruit cake, with one, two, or more tiers, covered with almond paste and decorated with royal icing, which is served at a wedding reception.

wedding ring *n* a band ring with parallel sides, typically of precious metal, worn to indicate married status.

wedge Ⓣ (wɛdʒ) *n* **1** a block of solid material, esp. wood or metal, that is shaped like a narrow V in cross section and can be pushed or driven between two objects or parts of an object in order to split or secure them. **2** any formation, structure, or substance in the shape of a wedge. **3** something such as an idea, action, etc., that tends to cause division. **4** a shoe with a wedge heel. **5** *Golf.* a club, a No. 10 iron with a face angle of more than 50°, used for bunker or pitch shots. **6** (formerly) a body of troops formed in a V-shape. **7 thin end of the wedge.** anything unimportant in itself that implies the start of something much larger. ◆ *vb* **wedges, wedging, wedged. 8** (*tr*) to secure with or as if with a wedge. **9** to squeeze or be squeezed like a wedge into a narrow space. **10** (*tr*) to force apart or divide with or as if with a wedge. [OE *wecg*]
▸**'wedgeˌlike** *adj* ▸**'wedgy** *adj*

wedge heel *n* a raised shoe heel with the heel and sole forming a solid block.

wedge-tailed eagle *n* a large brown Australian eagle having a wedge-shaped tail. Also called: **eaglehawk,** (Inf.) **wedgie.**

Wedgwood ('wɛdʒwʊd) *Trademark.* ◆ *n* **1a** pottery produced at the Wedgwood factory, near Stoke-on-Trent. **1b** such pottery having applied decoration in white on a coloured ground. ◆ *adj* **2a** relating to pottery made at the Wedgwood factory. **2b** characteristic of such pottery: *Wedgwood blue.* [C18: after Josiah *Wedgwood* (1730–95), E potter]

wedlock Ⓣ ('wɛdlɒk) *n* **1** the state of being married. **2 born** *or* **conceived out of wedlock.** born or conceived when one's parents are not legally married. [OE *wedlāc,* from *wedd* pledge + *-lāc,* suffix denoting activity, ?from *lāc* game]

Wednesday ('wɛnzdɪ) *n* the fourth day of the week; third day of the working week. [OE *Wōdnes dæg* Woden's day, translation of L *mercurii dies* Mercury's day]

wee[1] Ⓣ (wiː) *adj* very small; tiny; minute. [C13: from OE *wǣg* weight]

wee[2] (wiː) *Inf., chiefly Brit.* ◆ *n* **1a** the act or an instance of urinating. **1b**

THESAURUS

weave *vb* **1, 3** = **knit,** blend, braid, entwine, fuse, incorporate, interlace, intermingle, intertwine, introduce, mat, merge, plait, twist, unite **5** = **create,** build, construct, contrive, fabricate, make, make up, put together, spin **7** = **zigzag,** crisscross, move in and out, weave one's way, wind **8 get weaving** *Informal* = **start,** get a move on, get going, get one's finger out (*Brit. inf.*), get under way, hurry, make a start, shake a leg (*sl.*)

web *n* **1** = **network,** interlacing, lattice, mesh, net, netting, screen, tangle, toils, weave, webbing **2** = **spider's web,** cobweb **9** = **World Wide Web,** information superhighway, Internet, net, WWW

wed *vb* **1** = **marry,** become man and wife, be married to, espouse, get hitched, get married, join, make one, plight one's troth (*old-fashioned*), splice (*inf.*), take as one's husband, take as one's wife, take the plunge (*inf.*), take to wife, tie the knot (*inf.*), unite **3** = **unite,** ally, blend, coalesce, combine, commingle, dedicate, fuse, interweave, join, link, marry, merge, unify, yoke

Antonyms *vb* ≠ **unite:** break up, disunite, divide, divorce, part, separate, sever, split

wedding *n* **1** = **marriage,** espousals, marriage ceremony, nuptial rite, nuptials, wedlock

wedge *n* **1, 2** = **block,** chock, chunk, lump, wodge (*Brit. inf.*) ◆ *vb* **8-10** = **squeeze,** block, cram, crowd, force, jam, lodge, pack, ram, split, stuff, thrust

wedlock *n* **1** = **marriage,** matrimony

wee[1] *adj* = **little,** diminutive, insignificant, itsy-bitsy (*inf.*), Lilliputian, microscopic, miniature,

urine. ◆ *vb* **wees, weeing, weed. 2** (*intr*) to urinate. ◆ Also: **wee-wee.** [from ?]

weed (wiːd) *n* **1** any plant that grows wild and profusely, esp. one that grows among cultivated plants, depriving them of space, food, etc. **2** *Sl.* **2a the weed.** tobacco. **2b** marijuana. **3** *Inf.* a thin or unprepossessing person. **4** an inferior horse, esp. one showing signs of weakness. ◆ *vb* **5** to remove (useless or troublesome plants) from (a garden, etc.). [OE *weod*]
▸ **'weeder** *n* ▸ **'weedless** *adj*

weedkiller ('wiːdˌkɪlə) *n* a substance, usually a chemical or hormone, used for killing weeds.

weed out ⓣ *vb* (*tr, adv*) to separate out, remove, or eliminate (anything unwanted): *to weed out troublesome students.*

weeds (wiːdz) *pl n* a widow's black mourning clothes. Also called: **widow's weeds.** [C16: pl of *weed* (OE *wǣd, wēd*) a band worn in mourning]

weedy ⓣ ('wiːdɪ) *adj* **weedier, weediest. 1** full of or containing weeds: *weedy land.* **2** (of a plant) resembling a weed in straggling growth. **3** *Inf.* thin or weakly in appearance.

week (wiːk) *n* **1** a period of seven consecutive days, esp. one beginning with Sunday. Related adj: **hebdomadal. 2** a period of seven consecutive days beginning from or including a specified day: *a week from Wednesday.* **3** the period of time within a week devoted to work. ◆ *adv* **4** *Chiefly Brit.* seven days before or after a specified day: *I'll visit you Wednesday week.* [OE *wice, wicu*]

weekday ('wiːkˌdeɪ) *n* any day of the week other than Sunday and, often, Saturday.

weekend *n* (ˌwiːk'ɛnd). **1a** the end of the week, esp. the period from Friday night until the end of Sunday. **1b** (*as modifier*): *a weekend party.* ◆ *vb* ('wiːkˌɛnd). **2** (*intr*) *Inf.* to spend or pass a weekend.

weekends (ˌwiːk'ɛndz) *adv Inf.* at the weekend, esp. regularly or during every weekend.

weekly ⓣ ('wiːklɪ) *adj* **1** happening or taking place once a week or every week. **2** determined or calculated by the week. ◆ *adv* **3** once a week or every week. ◆ *n, pl* **weeklies. 4** a newspaper or magazine issued every week.

weeknight ('wiːkˌnaɪt) *n* the evening or night of a weekday.

ween (wiːn) *vb Arch.* to think or imagine (something). [OE *wēnan*]

weeny ('wiːnɪ) *adj* **weenier, weeniest.** *Inf.* very small; tiny. [C18: from WEE[1] with the ending *-ny* as in TINY]

weenybopper ('wiːnɪˌbɒpə) *n Inf.* a child of about 8 to 12 years who is a keen follower of pop music. [C20: formed on the model of TEENYBOPPER, from WEENY]

weep ⓣ (wiːp) *vb* **weeps, weeping, wept. 1** to shed (tears). **2** (*tr;* foll. by *out*) to utter, shedding tears. **3** (when *intr*, foll. by *for*) to lament (for something). **4** to exude (drops of liquid). **5** (*intr*) (of a wound, etc.) to exude a watery fluid. ◆ *n* **6** a spell of weeping. [OE *wēpan*]

weeper ('wiːpə) *n* **1** a person who weeps, esp. a hired mourner. **2** something worn as a sign of mourning.

weeping ('wiːpɪŋ) *adj* (of plants) having slender hanging branches.
▸ **'weepingly** *adv*

weeping willow *n* a Chinese willow tree having long hanging branches.

weepy ⓣ ('wiːpɪ) *Inf.* ◆ *adj* **weepier, weepiest. 1** liable or tending to weep. ◆ *n, pl* **weepies. 2** a sentimental film or book.
▸ **'weepily** *adv* ▸ **'weepiness** *n*

weever ('wiːvə) *n* a small marine fish having venomous spines around the gills and the dorsal fin. [C17: from OF *wivre* viper, ult. from L *vīpera* VIPER]

weevil ('wiːvɪl) *n* any of numerous beetles, many having elongated snouts, that are pests, feeding on plants and plant products. [OE *wifel*]
▸ **'weevily** *adj*

wee-wee *n, vb* a variant of **wee**[2].

w.e.f. *abbrev. for* with effect from.

weft (wɛft) *n* the yarn woven across the width of the fabric through the lengthways warp yarn. Also called: **filling, woof.** [OE]

weigela (waɪ'giːlə, -'dʒiː-) *n* a shrub of an Asian genus having clusters of showy bell-shaped flowers. [C19: from NL, after C. E. *Weigel* (1748–1831), G physician]

weigh[1] ⓣ (weɪ) *vb* **1** (*tr*) to measure the weight of. **2** (*intr*) to have weight: *she weighs more than her sister.* **3** (*tr;* often foll. by *out*) to apportion according to weight. **4** (*tr*) to consider carefully: *to weigh the facts of a case.* **5** (*intr*) to be influential: *his words weighed little with the jury.* **6** (*intr;* often foll. by *on*) to be oppressive (to). **7 weigh anchor.** to raise a vessel's anchor or (of a vessel) to have its anchor raised preparatory to departure. ◆ See also **weigh down, weigh in,** etc. [OE *wegan*]
▸ **'weighable** *adj* ▸ **'weigher** *n*

weigh[2] (weɪ) *n* **under weigh.** a variant spelling of **under way.** [C18: var. due to the infl. of phrases such as *to weigh anchor*]

weighbridge ('weɪˌbrɪdʒ) *n* a machine for weighing vehicles, etc., by means of a metal plate set into a road.

weigh down ⓣ *vb* (*adv*) to press (a person, etc.) down by or as if by weight: *his troubles weighed him down.*

weigh in *vb* (*intr, adv*) **1a** (of a boxer or wrestler) to be weighed before a bout. **1b** (of a jockey) to be weighed after, or sometimes before, a race. **2** *Inf.* to contribute, as in a discussion, etc.: *he weighed in with a few sharp comments.* ◆ *n* **weigh-in. 3** the act of checking a competitor's weight, as in boxing, racing, etc.

weight ⓣ (weɪt) *n* **1** a measure of the heaviness of an object; the amount anything weighs. **2** *Physics.* the vertical force experienced by a mass as a result of gravitation. **3** a system of units used to express weight: *troy weight.* **4** a unit used to measure weight: *the kilogram is the weight used in the metric system.* **5** any mass or heavy object used to exert pressure or weigh down. **6** an oppressive force: *the weight of cares.* **7** any heavy load: *the bag was such a weight.* **8** the main force; preponderance: *the weight of evidence.* **9** importance; influence: *his opinion carries weight.* **10** *Statistics.* one of a set of coefficients assigned to items of a frequency distribution that are analysed in order to represent the relative importance of the different items. **11** *Printing.* the apparent blackness of a printed typeface. **12 pull one's weight.** *Inf.* to do one's full or proper share of a task. **13 throw one's weight around.** *Inf.* to act in an overauthoritarian manner. ◆ *vb* (*tr*) **14** to add weight to. **15** to burden or oppress. **16** to add importance, value, etc., to (one side rather than another). **17** *Statistics.* to attach a weight or weights to. [OE *wiht*]
▸ **'weighter** *n*

weighted average *n Statistics.* a result produced by a technique designed to give recognition to the importance of certain factors when compiling the average of a group of values.

weighting ('weɪtɪŋ) *n* **1** a factor by which some quantity is multiplied in order to make it comparable with others. **2** an allowance paid to compensate for higher living costs: *a London weighting.*

weightlessness ('weɪtlɪsnɪs) *n* a state in which an object has no actual weight (because it is in space and unaffected by gravitational attraction) or no apparent weight (because the gravitational attraction equals the centripetal force and the object is in free fall).
▸ **'weightless** *adj*

weightlifting ('weɪtˌlɪftɪŋ) *n* the sport of lifting barbells of specified weights in a prescribed manner.
▸ **'weightˌlifter** *n*

weight training *n* physical exercise involving lifting weights, either heavy or light weights, as a way of improving muscle performance.

weight watcher *n* a person who tries to lose weight, esp. by dieting.

weighty ⓣ ('weɪtɪ) *adj* **weightier, weightiest. 1** having great weight. **2** important. **3** causing worry.
▸ **'weightily** *adv* ▸ **'weightiness** *n*

weigh up *vb* (*tr, adv*) to make an assessment of (a person, situation, etc.); judge.

Weil's disease (vaɪlz) *n* another name for **leptospirosis.** [named after Adolf *Weil* (1848–1916), G physician]

Weimaraner ('vaɪməˌrɑːnə, 'waɪməˌrɑː-) *n* a breed of hunting dog, having a short grey coat and short tail. [C20: after *Weimar*, city in E central Germany, where the breed was developed]

weir (wɪə) *n* **1** a low dam that is built across a river to raise the water

THESAURUS

minuscule, minute, negligible, pygmy *or* pigmy, small, teensy-weensy, teeny, teeny-weeny, tiny

weed out *vb* = **eliminate**, dispense with, eradicate, extirpate, get rid of, remove, root out, separate out, shed, uproot

weedy *adj* **3** *Informal* = **weak**, feeble, frail, ineffectual, namby-pamby, nerdy *or* nurdy (*sl.*), puny, skinny, thin, undersized, weak-kneed (*inf.*)

weekly *adj* **1** = **once a week**, hebdomadal, hebdomadary ◆ *adv* **3** = **every week**, by the week, hebdomadally, once a week

weep *vb* **1-3** = **cry**, bemoan, bewail, blub (*sl.*), blubber, boohoo, complain, greet (*Scot. or arch.*), keen, lament, moan, mourn, shed tears, snivel, sob, ululate, whimper, whinge (*inf.*)
Antonyms *vb* be glad, celebrate, delight, exult, make merry, rejoice, revel, triumph

weepy *adj* **1** = **tearful**, blubbering, close to tears, crying, lachrymose, on the verge of tears, sobbing, weeping, whimpering ◆ *n* **2** = **tear-jerker** (*inf.*)

weigh[1] *vb* **1, 2** = **have a weight of**, measure the weight of, put on the scales, tip the scales at (*inf.*) **3** = **measure**, apportion, deal out, dole out **4** = **consider**, contemplate, deliberate upon, evaluate, examine, eye up, give thought to, meditate upon, mull over, ponder, reflect upon, study, think over **5** = **matter**, be influential, carry weight, count, cut any ice (*inf.*), have influence, impress, tell **6** *often foll. by* **on** = **oppress**, bear down, burden, prey

weigh down *vb* = **burden**, bear down, depress, get down, oppress, overburden, overload, press down, trouble, weigh upon, worry
Antonyms *vb* alleviate, ease, hearten, help, lift, lighten, refresh, relieve, unburden

weight *n* **1** = **heaviness**, avoirdupois, burden, gravity, heft (*inf.*), load, mass, poundage, pressure, tonnage **5** = **load**, ballast, heavy object, mass **6** = **burden**, albatross, load, millstone, oppression, pressure, strain **8** = **preponderance**, greatest force, main force, onus **9** = **importance**, authority, bottom, clout (*inf.*), consequence, consideration, efficacy, emphasis, impact, import, influence, moment, persuasiveness, power, significance, substance, value ◆ *vb* **14** = **load**, add weight to, ballast, charge, freight, increase the load on, increase the weight of, make heavier **15** = **burden**, encumber, handicap, impede, oppress, overburden, weigh down **16** = **bias**, load, slant, unbalance

weighty *adj* **1** = **heavy**, burdensome, cumbersome, dense, hefty (*inf.*), massive, ponderous **2** = **important**, consequential, considerable, critical, crucial, forcible, grave, momentous, portentous, serious, significant, solemn, substantial **3** = **onerous**, backbreaking, burdensome, crushing, demanding, difficult, exacting, oppressive, taxing, worrisome, worrying
Antonyms *adj* ≠ **important**: frivolous, immaterial, incidental, inconsequential, insignificant, minor, petty, trivial, unimportant

level, divert the water, or control its flow. **2** a series of traps or enclosures placed in a stream to catch fish. [OE *wer*]

weird ⓘ (wɪəd) *adj* **1** suggestive of or relating to the supernatural; eerie. **2** strange or bizarre. **3** *Arch.* of or relating to fate or the Fates. ◆ *n* **4** *Arch., chiefly Scot.* **4a** fate or destiny. **4b** one of the Fates. [OE (*ge*)*wyrd* destiny]
►**'weirdly** *adv* ►**'weirdness** *n*

weirdo ⓘ ('wɪədəu) *or* **weirdie** ('wɪədɪ) *n, pl* **weirdos** *or* **weirdies.** *Inf.* a person who behaves in a bizarre or eccentric manner.

Weismannism ('vaɪsmən,ɪzəm) *n* the theory that all inheritable characteristics are transmitted by the reproductive cells and that characteristics acquired during the lifetime of the organism are not inherited. [C19: after August *Weismann* (1834–1914), G biologist]

weka ('wɛkə) *n* a nocturnal flightless bird of New Zealand. Also called: **Maori hen, wood hen.** [from Maori]

welch (wɛlʃ) *vb* a variant spelling of **welsh.**

Welch (wɛlʃ) *adj, n* an archaic spelling of **Welsh.**

welcome ⓘ ('wɛlkəm) *adj* **1** gladly and cordially received or admitted: *a welcome guest.* **2** bringing pleasure: *a welcome gift.* **3** freely permitted or invited: *you are welcome to call.* **4** under no obligation (only in such phrases as **you're welcome,** as conventional responses to thanks). ◆ *sentence substitute.* **5** an expression of cordial greeting. ◆ *n* **6** the act of greeting or receiving a person or thing; reception: *the new theory had a cool welcome.* **7 wear out** *or* **overstay one's welcome.** to come more often or stay longer than is pleasing. ◆ *vb* **welcomes, welcoming, welcomed.** (*tr*) **8** to greet the arrival of (guests, etc.) cordially. **9** to receive or accept, esp. gladly. [C12: changed (through infl. of WELL[1]) from OE *wilcuma* (agent n referring to a welcome guest), *wilcume* (a greeting of welcome), from *wil* WILL[2] + *cuman* to come]
►**'welcomely** *adv* ►**'welcomer** *n*

weld[1] ⓘ (wɛld) *vb* **1** (*tr*) to unite (pieces of metal or plastic), as by softening with heat and hammering or by fusion. **2** to bring or admit of being brought into close union. ◆ *n* **3** a joint formed by welding. [C16: altered from obs. *well* to melt, weld]
►**'weldable** *adj* ►**,welda'bility** *n* ►**'welder** *or* **'weldor** *n*

weld[2] (wɛld), **wold,** *or* **woald** (wəuld) *n* a yellow dye obtained from the plant dyer's rocket. [C14: from Low G]

welfare ⓘ ('wɛl,fɛə) *n* **1** health, happiness, prosperity, and wellbeing in general. **2a** financial and other assistance given to people in need. **2b** (*as modifier*): *welfare services.* **3** Also called: **welfare work.** plans or work to better the social or economic conditions of various underprivileged groups. **4 on welfare.** *Chiefly US & Canad.* in receipt of financial aid from a government agency or other source. [C14: from *wel fare*; see WELL[1], FARE]

welfare economics *n* (*functioning as sing*) the aspects of economic theory concerned with the welfare of society and priorities to be observed in the allocation of resources.

welfare state *n* a system in which the government undertakes the chief responsibility for providing for the social and economic security of its population, usually through unemployment insurance, old age pensions, and other social-security measures.

welkin ('wɛlkɪn) *n Arch.* the sky, heavens, or upper air. [OE *wolcen, welcen*]

well[1] ⓘ (wɛl) *adv* **better, best. 1** (*often used in combination*) in a satisfactory manner: *the party went very well.* **2** (*often used in combination*) in a skilful manner: *she plays the violin well; a well-chosen example.* **3** in a correct or careful manner: *listen well to my words.* **4** in a prosperous manner: *to live well.* **5** (*usually used with auxiliaries*) suitably; fittingly: *you can't very well say that.* **6** intimately: *I knew him well.* **7** in a kind or favourable manner: *she speaks well of you.* **8** fully: *to be well informed.* **9** by a considerable margin: *let me know well in advance.* **10** (preceded by *could, might,* or *may*) indeed: *you may well have to do it yourself.* **11** *Inf.* (intensifier): *well safe.* **12 all very well.** used ironically to express discontent, dissent, etc. **13 as well. 13a** in addition; too. **13b** (preceded by *may* or *might*) with equal effect: *you might as well come.* **14 as well as.** in addition to. **15** (**just**) **as well.** preferable or advisable: *it would be just as well if you paid me now.* **16 leave well** (**enough**) **alone.** to refrain from interfering with something that is satisfactory. **17 well and good.** used to indicate calm acceptance, as of a decision. **18 well up in.** well acquainted with (a particular subject); knowledgeable about. ◆ *adj* (*usually postpositive*) **19** (when *prenominal, usually used with a negative*) in good health: *I'm very well, thank you; he's not a well man.* **20** satisfactory or pleasing. **21** prudent; advisable: *it would be well to make no comment.* **22** prosperous or comfortable. **23** fortunate: *it is well that you agreed to go.* ◆ *interj* **24a** an expression of surprise, indignation, or reproof. **24b** an expression of anticipation in waiting for an answer or remark. ◆ *sentence connector.* **25** an expression used to preface a remark, gain time, etc.: *well, I don't think I will come.* [OE *wel*]

well[2] ⓘ (wɛl) *n* **1** a hole or shaft bored into the earth to tap a supply of water, oil, gas, etc. **2** a natural pool where ground water comes to the surface. **3a** a cavity, space, or vessel used to contain a liquid. **3b** (*in combination*): *an inkwell.* **4** an open shaft through the floors of a building, such as one used for a staircase. **5** a deep enclosed space in a building or between buildings that is open to the sky. **6** a bulkheaded compartment built around a ship's pumps for protection and ease of access. **7** (in England) the open space in the centre of a law court. **8** an abundant source: *he is a well of knowledge.* ◆ *vb* **9** to flow or cause to flow upwards or outwards: *tears welled from her eyes.* [OE *wella*]

we'll (wiːl) *contraction of* we will *or* we shall.

well-advised *adj* (**well advised** *when postpositive*). **1** acting with deliberation or reason. **2** well thought out: *a well-advised plan.*

well-affected *adj* (**well affected** *when postpositive*). favourably disposed (towards); steadfast or loyal.

well-appointed *adj* (**well appointed** *when postpositive*). well equipped or furnished.

wellaway ('wɛlə'weɪ) *interj Arch.* woe! alas! [OE, from *wei lā wei,* var. of *wā lā wā,* lit.: woe! lo woe]

well-balanced ⓘ *adj* (**well balanced** *when postpositive*). **1** having good balance or proportions. **2** sane or sensible.

wellbeing ('wɛl'biːɪŋ) *n* the condition of being contented, healthy, or successful; welfare.

well-bred ⓘ *adj* (**well bred** *when postpositive*). **1** Also: **well-born.** of respected or noble lineage. **2** indicating good breeding: *well-bred manners.* **3** of good thoroughbred stock: *a well-bred spaniel.*

well-chosen *adj* (**well chosen** *when postpositive*). carefully selected to produce a desired effect; apt: *a few well-chosen words.*

well-connected *adj* (**well connected** *when postpositive*). having influential or important relatives or friends.

well-disposed *adj* (**well disposed** *when postpositive*). inclined to be sympathetic, kindly, or friendly.

well-done *adj* (**well done** *when postpositive*). **1** (of food, esp. meat) cooked thoroughly. **2** made or accomplished satisfactorily.

THESAURUS

weird *adj* **1, 2** = **strange,** bizarre, creepy (*inf.*), eerie, eldritch (*poetic*), far-out, freakish, ghostly, grotesque, mysterious, odd, outlandish, queer, spooky (*inf.*), supernatural, uncanny, unearthly, unnatural
Antonyms *adj* common, mundane, natural, normal, ordinary, regular, typical, usual

weirdo *n Informal* = **eccentric,** crackpot (*inf.*), crank (*inf.*), freak (*inf.*), headbanger (*inf.*), headcase (*inf.*), loony (*sl.*), nut (*sl.*), nutcase (*sl.*), nutter (*Brit. sl.*), oddball (*inf.*), queer fish (*Brit. inf.*)

welcome *adj* **1, 2** = **acceptable,** accepted, agreeable, appreciated, delightful, desirable, gladly received, gratifying, pleasant, pleasing, pleasurable, refreshing, wanted **3, 4** = **free,** at home, invited, under no obligation ◆ *n* **6** = **greeting,** acceptance, entertainment, hospitality, reception, salutation ◆ *vb* **8, 9** = **greet,** accept gladly, bid welcome, embrace, hail, meet, offer hospitality to, receive, receive with open arms, roll out the red carpet for, usher in
Antonyms *adj* ≠ **acceptable:** disagreeable, excluded, rebuffed, rejected, unacceptable, undesirable, unpleasant, unwanted, unwelcome ◆ *n* ≠ **greeting:** cold shoulder, exclusion, ostracism, rebuff, rejection, slight, snub ◆ *vb* ≠ **greet:** exclude, rebuff, refuse, reject, slight, snub, spurn, turn away

weld[1] *vb* **1, 2** = **join,** bind, bond, braze, cement, connect, fuse, link, solder, unite ◆ *n* **3** = **joint,** bond, juncture, seam

welfare *n* **1** = **wellbeing,** advantage, benefit, good, happiness, health, interest, profit, prosperity, success

well[1] *adv* **1** = **satisfactorily,** agreeably, capitally, famously (*inf.*), happily, in a satisfactory manner, like nobody's business (*inf.*), nicely, pleasantly, smoothly, splendidly, successfully **2** = **skilfully,** ably, adeptly, adequately, admirably, conscientiously, correctly, effectively, efficiently, expertly, proficiently, properly, with skill **3** = **carefully,** accurately, attentively, closely **4** = **prosperously,** comfortably, flourishingly **5** = **suitably,** correctly, easily, fairly, fittingly, in all fairness, justly, properly, readily, rightly **6** = **intimately,** closely, completely, deeply, fully, personally, profoundly, thoroughly **7** = **favourably,** approvingly, glowingly, graciously, highly, kindly, warmly **8** = **considerably,** abundantly, amply, completely, fully, greatly, heartily, highly, substantially, sufficiently, thoroughly, very much **13a as well** = **also,** besides, in addition, into the bargain, to boot, too **14 as well as** = **including,** along with, at the same time as, in addition to, over and above ◆ *adj* **19** = **healthy,** able-bodied, alive and kicking, fighting fit (*inf.*), fit, fit as a fiddle, hale, hearty, in fine fettle, in good health, robust, sound, strong, up to par **20, 21** = **satisfactory,** advisable, agreeable, bright, fine, fitting, flourishing, fortunate, good, happy, lucky, pleasing, profitable, proper, prudent, right, thriving, useful
Antonyms *adv* ≠ **satisfactorily:** badly, inadequately, poorly, wrongly ≠ **skilfully:** badly, ham-fistedly, incompetently, incorrectly, ineptly, inexpertly, sloppily, unskilfully ≠ **suitably:** unfairly, unjustly, unsuitably ≠ **intimately:** slightly, somewhat, vaguely ≠ **favourably:** coldly, disapprovingly, gracelessly, unkindly, unsympathetically ◆ *adj* ≠ **healthy:** ailing, at death's door, below par, feeble, frail, green about the gills, ill, infirm, poorly, run-down, sick, sickly, under-the-weather, unwell, weak ≠ **satisfactory:** going badly, improper, unfitting, unsatisfactory, unsuccessful, wrong

well[2] *n* **1** = **hole,** bore, pit, shaft **2** = **waterhole,** fount, fountain, pool, source, spring **8** = **source,** fount, mine, repository, wellspring ◆ *vb* **9** = **flow,** exude, gush, jet, ooze, pour, rise, run, seep, spout, spring, spurt, stream, surge, trickle

well-balanced *adj* **1** = **well-proportioned,** graceful, harmonious, proportional, symmetrical **2** = **sensible,** judicious, level-headed, rational, reasonable, sane, sober, sound, together (*sl.*), well-adjusted
Antonyms *adj* ≠ **sensible:** erratic, insane, irrational, neurotic, unbalanced, unreasonable, unsound, unstable, volatile

well-bred *adj* **1** = **aristocratic,** blue-blooded, gentle, highborn, noble, patrician, well-born **2** = **polite,** civil, courteous, courtly, cultivated, cultured, gallant, genteel, gentlemanly, ladylike, mannerly, polished, refined, sophisticated, urbane, well-brought-up, well-mannered
Antonyms *adj* ≠ **polite:** bad-mannered, base, coarse, discourteous, ill-bred, rude, uncivilized, uncouth, uncultured, vulgar

well dressing *n* the decoration of wells with flowers, etc.: a traditional annual ceremony of great antiquity in some parts of Britain, originally associated with the cult of water deities.
well-favoured ❶ *adj* (**well favoured** *when postpositive*). good-looking.
well-formed formula *n Logic.* a group of logical symbols that makes sense; a logical sentence.
well-found *adj* (**well found** *when postpositive*). furnished or supplied with all or most necessary things.
well-founded *adj* (**well founded** *when postpositive*). having good grounds: *well-founded rumours.*
well-groomed ❶ *adj* (**well groomed** *when postpositive*). having a tidy pleasing appearance.
well-grounded *adj* (**well grounded** *when postpositive*). **1** well instructed in the basic elements of a subject. **2** another term for **well-founded.**
wellhead ('wɛl,hɛd) *n* **1** the source of a well or stream. **2** a source, fountainhead, or origin.
well-heeled ❶ *adj* (**well heeled** *when postpositive*). *Inf.* rich; prosperous; wealthy.
wellies ('wɛlɪz) *pl n Brit. inf.* Wellington boots.
well-informed ❶ *adj* (**well informed** *when postpositive*). **1** having knowledge about a great variety of subjects: *he seems to be a well-informed person.* **2** possessing reliable information on a particular subject.
Wellington boots *pl n* **1** Also called: **gumboots.** *Brit.* knee-length or calf-length rubber boots, worn esp. in wet conditions. Often shortened to **wellingtons, wellies. 2** military leather boots covering the front of the knee but cut away at the back to allow easier bending of the knee. [C19: after the 1st Duke of *Wellington* (1769–1852), Brit. soldier & statesman]
wellingtonia (,wɛlɪŋ'təʊnɪə) *n* a giant Californian coniferous tree, often reaching 90 metres high. Also called: **big tree, sequoia.** [C19: after the 1st Duke of *Wellington*]
well-intentioned *adj* (**well intentioned** *when postpositive*). having benevolent intentions, usually with unfortunate results.
well-knit *adj* (**well knit** *when postpositive*). strong, firm, or sturdy.
well-known ❶ *adj* (**well known** *when postpositive*). **1** widely known; famous; celebrated. **2** known fully or clearly.
well-mannered ❶ *adj* (**well mannered** *when postpositive*). having good manners; polite.
well-meaning *adj* (**well meaning** *when postpositive*). having or indicating good intentions, usually with unfortunate results.
well-nigh ❶ *adv Arch. or poetic.* nearly; almost: *it's well-nigh three o'clock.*
well-off ❶ *adj* (**well off** *when postpositive*). **1** in a comfortable or favourable position or state. **2** financially well provided for; moderately rich.
well-oiled *adj* (**well oiled** *when postpositive*). *Inf.* drunk.
well-preserved *adj* (**well preserved** *when postpositive*). **1** kept in a good condition. **2** continuing to appear youthful: *she was a well-preserved old lady.*
well-read ('wel'rɛd) *adj* (**well read** *when postpositive*). having read widely and intelligently; erudite.
well-rounded *adj* (**well rounded** *when postpositive*). **1** rounded in shape or well developed: *a well-rounded figure.* **2** full, varied, and satisfying: *a well-rounded life.*
well-spoken *adj* (**well spoken** *when postpositive*). **1** having a clear, articulate, and socially acceptable accent and way of speaking. **2** spoken satisfactorily or pleasingly.
wellspring ❶ ('wɛl,sprɪŋ) *n* **1** the source of a spring or stream. **2** a source of abundant supply.
well-stacked *adj* (**well stacked** *when postpositive*). *Sl.* (of a woman) of voluptuous proportions.
well sweep *n* a device for raising buckets from and lowering them into a well, consisting of a long pivoted pole, the bucket being attached to one end by a long rope.
well-tempered *adj* (**well tempered** *when postpositive*). (of a musical scale or instrument) conforming to the system of equal temperament. See **temperament** (sense 4).
well-thought-of ❶ *adj* respected.
well-thumbed *adj* (**well thumbed** *when postpositive*). (of a book) having the pages marked from frequent turning.
well-to-do ❶ *adj* moderately wealthy.
well-turned *adj* (**well turned** *when postpositive*). **1** (of a phrase, etc.) apt and pleasing. **2** having a pleasing shape: *a well-turned leg.*
well-upholstered *adj* (**well upholstered** *when postpositive*). *Inf.* (of a person) fat.
well-wisher *n* a person who shows benevolence or sympathy towards a person, cause, etc.
▸ **'well-,wishing** *adj, n*
well-woman *n, pl* **well-women.** *Social welfare.* **a** a woman who attends a health-service clinic for preventive monitoring, health education, etc. **b** (*as modifier*): *well-woman clinic.*
well-worn ❶ *adj* (**well worn** *when postpositive*). **1** so much used as to be affected by wear: *a well-worn coat.* **2** hackneyed: *a well-worn phrase.*
welly ('wɛlɪ) *n* **1** (*pl* **wellies**) *Inf.* Also called: **welly boot.** a Wellington boot. **2** *Sl.* energy, concentration, or commitment (esp. in **give it some welly**).
welsh *or* **welch** (wɛlʃ) *vb* (*intr; often foll. by on*) **1** to fail to pay a gambling debt. **2** to fail to fulfil an obligation. [C19: from ?]
▸ **'welsher** *or* **'welcher** *n*
Welsh (wɛlʃ) *adj* **1** of, relating to, or characteristic of Wales, its people, their language, or their dialect of English. ◆ *n* **2** a language of Wales, belonging to the S Celtic branch of the Indo-European family. **3 the Welsh.** (*functioning as pl*) the natives or inhabitants of Wales. [OE *Wēlisc, Wǣlisc*]
Welsh corgi *n* another name for **corgi.**
Welsh dresser *n* a sideboard with drawers and cupboards below and open shelves above.
Welsh harp *n* a type of harp in which the strings are arranged in three rows.
Welshman ('wɛlʃmən) *or* (*fem*) **Welshwoman** *n, pl* **Welshmen** *or* **Welshwomen.** a native or inhabitant of Wales.
Welsh poppy *n* a perennial W European plant with large yellow flowers.
Welsh rabbit *n* a savoury dish consisting of melted cheese sometimes mixed with milk, seasonings, etc., on hot buttered toast. Also called: **Welsh rarebit, rarebit.** [C18: a fanciful coinage; *rarebit* is a later folk-etymological var.]
Welsh terrier *n* a wire-haired breed of terrier with a black-and-tan coat.
welt ❶ (wɛlt) *n* **1** a raised or strengthened seam in a garment. **2** another word for **weal**[1]. **3** (in shoemaking) a strip of leather, etc., put in between the outer sole and the inner sole and upper. ◆ *vb* (*tr*) **4** to put a welt in (a garment, etc.). **5** to beat soundly. [C15: from ?]
welter ❶ ('wɛltə) *vb* (*intr*) **1** to roll about, writhe, or wallow. **2** (esp. of the sea) to surge, heave, or toss. **3** to lie drenched in a liquid, esp. blood. ◆ *n* **4** a confused mass; jumble. [C13: from MLow G, MDu. *weltern*]
welterweight ('wɛltə,weɪt) *n* **1a** a professional boxer weighing 140–147 pounds (63.5–66.5 kg). **1b** an amateur boxer weighing 63.5–67 kg (140–148 pounds). **2a** a professional wrestler weighing 155–165 pounds (71–75 kg). **2b** an amateur wrestler weighing 69–74 kg (151–161 pounds).
wen[1] (wɛn) *n* **1** *Pathol.* a sebaceous cyst, esp. one occurring on the scalp. **2** a large overcrowded city (esp. London, **the great wen**). [OE *wenn*]
wen[2] (wɛn) *n* a rune having the sound of Modern English *w.* [OE *wen, wyn*]
wench (wɛntʃ) *n* **1** a girl or young woman: now used facetiously. **2** *Arch.* a female servant. **3** *Arch.* a prostitute. ◆ *vb* (*intr*) **4** *Arch.* to frequent the company of prostitutes. [OE *wencel* child, from *wancol* weak]
▸ **'wencher** *n*
wend ❶ (wɛnd) *vb* to direct (one's course or way); travel. [OE *wendan*]
Wend (wɛnd) *n* (esp. in medieval European history) a member of the Slavonic people who inhabited the area between the Rivers Saale and Oder, in central Europe, in the early Middle Ages. Also called: **Sorb.**
wendigo ('wɛndɪ,gəʊ) *n Canad.* **1** (*pl* **wendigos**) (among Algonquian In-

THESAURUS

well-favoured *adj* = **attractive**, beautiful, bonny, comely, fair, good-looking, handsome, lovely, nice-looking, pretty
well-groomed *adj* = **smart**, dapper, neat, soigné *or* soignée, spruce, tidy, trim, well-dressed, well turned out
well-heeled *adj Informal* = **prosperous**, affluent, comfortable, flush, in clover (*inf.*), in the money (*inf.*), loaded (*sl.*), moneyed, opulent, rich, wealthy, well-off, well-situated, well-to-do
well-informed *adj* **1, 2** = **educated**, acquainted, *au courant, au fait*, aware, clued-up (*inf.*), cognizant *or* cognisant, conversant, informed, in the know (*inf.*), in the loop (*inf.*), knowledgeable *or* knowledgable, understanding, well-educated, well-grounded, well-read, well-versed
well-known *adj* **1** = **famous**, celebrated, familiar, illustrious, notable, noted, on the map, popular, renowned, widely known
well-mannered *adj* = **polite**, civil, courteous, genteel, gentlemanly, gracious, ladylike, mannerly, respectful, well-bred
well-nigh *adv Archaic or poetic* = **almost**, all but, just about, more or less, nearly, next to, practically, virtually
well-off *adj* **1** = **fortunate**, comfortable, flourishing, lucky, successful, thriving **2** = **rich**, affluent, comfortable, flush, loaded (*sl.*), moneyed, prosperous, wealthy, well-heeled (*inf.*), well-to-do
Antonyms *adj* ≠ **rich:** badly off, broke (*inf.*), destitute, dirt-poor (*inf.*), down and out, down at heel, flat broke (*inf.*), hard up (*inf.*), impoverished, indigent, needy, on the breadline, on the rocks (*inf.*), penniless, poor, poverty-stricken, short, without two pennies to rub together (*inf.*)
wellspring *n* **1** = **fountainhead**, fount, origin, source, wellhead **2** = **supply**, fount, fund, mine, repository, reserve, reservoir, source, well
well-thought-of *adj* = **respected**, admired, esteemed, highly regarded, of good repute, reputable, revered, venerated
Antonyms *adj* abhorred, derided, despised, disdained, reviled, scorned, spurned
well-to-do *adj* = **prosperous**, affluent, comfortable, flush (*inf.*), moneyed, well-heeled (*inf.*), well-off
Antonyms *adj* bankrupt, broke (*inf.*), destitute, down at heel, hard up (*inf.*), indigent, insolvent, needy, on the breadline, poor, ruined
well-worn *adj* **2** = **stale**, banal, commonplace, hackneyed, overused, stereotyped, threadbare, timeworn, tired, trite
welt *n* **2** = **mark**, contusion, ridge, scar, streak, stripe, wale, weal, wheal
welter *vb* **1** = **roll**, flounder, lie, splash, tumble, wade, wallow, writhe **2** = **surge**, billow, heave, pitch, roll, swell, toss ◆ *n* **4** = **jumble**, confusion, hotchpotch, mess, muddle, tangle, web
wend *vb* = **go**, direct one's course, make for, move, proceed, progress, travel

dians) an evil spirit or cannibal. **2** (*pl* **wendigo** *or* **wendigos**) another name for **splake.** [from Algonquian: evil spirit or cannibal]

Wendy house ('wɛndɪ) *n* a small model house for children to play in. [C20: after the house built for *Wendy,* the girl in J. M. Barrie's play *Peter Pan* (1904)]

wensleydale ('wɛnzlɪˌdeɪl) *n* **1** a type of white cheese with a flaky texture. **2** a breed of sheep with long woolly fleece. [after *Wensleydale,* North Yorkshire]

went (wɛnt) *vb* the past tense of **go.** [C15: p.t. of WEND used as p.t. of *go*]

wentletrap ('wɛntᵊlˌtræp) *n* a marine gastropod mollusc having a long pointed pale-coloured longitudinally ridged shell. [C18: from Du. *winteltrap* spiral shell, from *wintel,* earlier *windel,* from *wenden* to wind + *trap* a step]

wept (wɛpt) *vb* the past tense and past participle of **weep.**

were (wɜː; *unstressed* wə) *vb* the plural form of the past tense (indicative mood) of **be** and the singular form used with *you.* It is also used as a subjunctive, esp. in conditional sentences. [OE *wērun, wæron* p.t. pl of *wesan* to be]

> **USAGE NOTE** *Were,* as a remnant of the past subjunctive in English, is used in formal contexts in clauses expressing hypotheses (*if he were to die, she would inherit everything*), suppositions contrary to fact (*if I were you, I would be careful*), and desire (*I wish he were there now*). In informal speech, however, *was* is often used instead.

we're (wɪə) *contraction of* we are.

weren't (wɜːnt) *contraction of* were not.

werewolf ('wɪəˌwʊlf, 'wɛə-) *n, pl* **werewolves.** a person fabled in folklore and superstition to have been changed into a wolf by being bewitched or said to be able to assume wolf form at will. [OE *werewulf,* from *wer* man + *wulf* wolf]

wergild, weregild ('wɜːˌgɪld, 'wɛə-), *or* **wergeld** ('wɜːˌgɛld, 'wɛə-) *n* the price set on a man's life in Anglo-Saxon and Germanic law, to be paid as compensation by his slayer. [OE *wergeld,* from *wer* man + *gield* tribute]

wert (wɜːt; *unstressed* wət) *vb Arch. or dialect.* (used with the pronoun *thou* or its relative equivalent) a singular form of the past tense (indicative mood) of **be.**

weskit ('wɛskɪt) *n* an informal name for **waistcoat.**

Wesleyan ('wɛzlɪən) *adj* **1** of or deriving from John Wesley (1703–91), British preacher who founded Methodism. **2** of or characterizing Methodism, esp. in its original form. ◆ *n* **3** a follower of John Wesley. **4** a member of the Methodist Church.
▸ **'Wesleyanˌism** *n*

west (wɛst) *n* **1** the direction along a parallel towards the sunset, at 270° clockwise from north. **2 the west.** (*often cap.*) any area lying in or towards the west. Related adjs.: **Hesperian, Occidental. 3** (*usually cap.*) *Cards.* the player or position at the table corresponding to west on the compass. ◆ *adj* **4** situated in, moving towards, or facing the west. **5** (esp. of the wind) from the west. ◆ *adv* **6** in, to, or towards the west. **7 go west.** *Inf.* **7a** to be lost or destroyed. **7b** to die. [OE]

West (wɛst) *n* **the. 1** the western part of the world contrasted historically and culturally with the East or Orient. **2** the countries of western Europe and North America. **3** (in the US) that part of the US lying approximately to the west of the Mississippi. **4** (in the ancient and medieval world) the Western Roman Empire and, later, the Holy Roman Empire. ◆ *adj* **5** of or denoting the western part of a specified country, area, etc.

westbound ('wɛstˌbaʊnd) *adj* going or leading towards the west.

west by north *n* one point on the compass north of west.

west by south *n* one point on the compass south of west.

West Country *n* **the.** the southwest of England, esp. Cornwall, Devon, and Somerset.

West End *n* **the.** a part of W central London containing the main shopping and entertainment areas.

westering ('wɛstərɪŋ) *adj Poetic.* moving towards the west: *the westering star.*

Westerlies ('wɛstəlɪz) *pl n Meteorol.* the prevailing winds blowing from the west on the poleward sides of the horse latitudes, often bringing depressions and anticyclones.

westerly ('wɛstəlɪ) *adj* **1** of, relating to, or situated in the west. ◆ *adv, adj* **2** towards or in the direction of the west. **3** (esp. of the wind) from the west. ◆ *n, pl* **westerlies. 4** a wind blowing from the west.
▸ **'westerliness** *n*

western ('wɛstən) *adj* **1** situated in or facing the west. **2** going or directed to or towards the west. **3** (of a wind, etc.) coming from the west. **4** native to the west. **5** *Music.* See **country and western.**
▸ **'westernˌmost** *adj*

Western ('wɛstən) *adj* **1** of or characteristic of the West as opposed to the Orient. **2** of or characteristic of North America and western Europe. **3** of or characteristic of the western states of the US. ◆ *n* **4** (*often not cap.*) a film, book, etc., concerned with life in the western states of the US, esp. during the era of exploration.

Western Church *n* **1** the part of Christendom that derives its liturgy, discipline, and traditions principally from the patriarchate of Rome. **2** the Roman Catholic Church, sometimes together with the Anglican Communion of Churches.

westerner ('wɛstənə) *n* (*sometimes cap.*) a native or inhabitant of the west of any specific region.

western hemisphere *n* (*often caps.*) **1** that half of the globe containing the Americas, lying to the west of the Greenwich or another meridian. **2** the lands contained in this, esp. the Americas.

westernize *or* **westernise** ('wɛstəˌnaɪz) *vb* **westernizes, westernizing, westernized** *or* **westernises, westernising, westernised.** (*tr*) to influence or make familiar with the customs, practices, etc., of the West.
▸ **ˌwesterni'zation** *or* **ˌwesterni'sation** *n*

Western Roman Empire *n* the westernmost of the two empires created by the division of the later Roman Empire, esp. after its final severance from the Eastern Roman Empire (395 A.D.). Also called: **Western Empire.**

westing ('wɛstɪŋ) *n Navigation.* movement, deviation, or distance covered in a westerly direction, esp. as expressed in the resulting difference in longitude.

Westminster ('wɛstˌmɪnstə) *n* **1** Also called: **City of Westminster.** a borough of Greater London, on the River Thames. **2** the Houses of Parliament at Westminster.

west-northwest *n* **1** the point on the compass or the direction midway between west and northwest, 292° 30′ clockwise from north. ◆ *adj, adv* **2** in, from, or towards this direction.

Weston standard cell ('wɛstən) *n* a primary cell used as a standard of emf: consists of a mercury anode and a cadmium amalgam cathode in an electrolyte of saturated cadmium sulphate. [C20: from a trademark]

west-southwest *n* **1** the point on the compass or the direction midway between southwest and west, 247° 30′ clockwise from north. ◆ *adj, adv* **2** in, from, or towards this direction.

westward ('wɛstwəd) *adj* **1** moving, facing, or situated in the west. ◆ *adv* **2** Also: **westwards.** towards the west. ◆ *n* **3** the westward part, direction, etc.
▸ **'westwardly** *adj, adv*

wet 🅣 (wɛt) *adj* **wetter, wettest. 1** moistened, covered, saturated, etc., with water or some other liquid. **2** not yet dry or solid: *wet varnish.* **3** rainy: *wet weather.* **4** employing a liquid, usually water: *a wet method of chemical analysis.* **5** *Chiefly US & Canad.* permitting the free sale of alcoholic beverages: *a wet state.* **6** *Brit. inf.* feeble or foolish. **7 wet behind the ears.** *Inf.* immature or inexperienced. ◆ *n* **8** wetness or moisture. **9** rainy weather. **10** *Brit. inf.* a feeble or foolish person. **11** (*often cap.*) *Brit. inf.* a Conservative politician who is not a hardliner. **12** *Chiefly US & Canad.* a person who advocates free sale of alcoholic beverages. **13 the wet.** *Austral.* (in northern and central Australia) the rainy season. ◆ *vb* **wets, wetting, wet** *or* **wetted. 14** to make or become wet. **15** to urinate on (something). **16** (*tr*) *Dialect.* to prepare (tea) by boiling or infusing. [OE *wǣt*]
▸ **'wetly** *adv* ▸ **'wetness** *n* ▸ **'wettable** *adj* ▸ **'wetter** *n* ▸ **'wettish** *adj*

wet-and-dry-bulb thermometer *n* another name for **psychrometer.**

wet blanket *n Inf.* a person whose low spirits or lack of enthusiasm have a depressing effect on others.

wet cell *n* a primary cell in which the electrolyte is a liquid.

wet dream *n* an erotic dream accompanied by an emission of semen.

wet fly *n Angling.* an artificial fly designed to float or ride below the water surface.

wether ('wɛðə) *n* a male sheep, esp. a castrated one. [OE *hwæther*]

wetland ('wɛtlənd) *n* (*sometimes pl*) **a** an area of marshy land, esp. considered as part of an ecological system. **b** (*as modifier*): *wetland species.*

wet look *n* a shiny finish such as that given to certain clothing and footwear materials.

wet nurse *n* **1** a woman hired to suckle the child of another. ◆ *vb* **wet-nurse, wet-nurses, wet-nursing, wet-nursed.** (*tr*) **2** to act as a wet nurse to (a child). **3** *Inf.* to attend with great devotion.

wet pack *n Med.* a hot or cold damp sheet or blanket for wrapping around a patient.

wet rot *n* **1** a state of decay in timber caused by various fungi. The hyphal strands of the fungus are seldom visible, and affected timber turns dark brown. **2** any of the fungi causing this decay.

wet suit *n* a close-fitting rubber suit used by skin-divers, yachtsmen, etc., to retain body heat.

wetting agent *n Chem.* any substance added to a liquid to lower its

THESAURUS

wet *adj* **1 = damp**, aqueous, dank, drenched, dripping, humid, moist, moistened, saturated, soaked, soaking, sodden, soggy, sopping, waterlogged, watery, wringing wet **3 = rainy**, clammy, dank, drizzling, humid, misty, pouring, raining, showery, teeming **6** *Brit. informal* **= feeble**, boneless, effete, foolish, ineffectual, irresolute, namby-pamby, nerdy *or* nurdy (*sl.*), silly, soft, spineless, timorous, weak, weedy (*inf.*) **7 wet behind the ears** *Informal* **= naive**, as green as grass, born yesterday, callow, green, immature, inexperienced, innocent, new, raw ◆ *n* **8 = moisture**, clamminess, condensation, damp, dampness, humidity, liquid, water, wetness **9 = rain**, damp weather, drizzle, rains, rainy season, rainy weather **10** *Brit. informal* **= weakling**, drip (*inf.*), milksop, weed (*inf.*), wimp (*inf.*) ◆ *vb* **14 = moisten**, damp, dampen, dip, douse, drench, humidify, irrigate, saturate, soak, splash, spray, sprinkle, steep, water

Antonyms *adj* ≠ **damp:** bone-dry, dried, dry, hardened, parched, set ≠ **rainy:** arid, dry, fine, sunny ◆ *n* ≠ **moisture:** dryness ≠ **rain:** dry weather, fine weather ◆ *vb* ≠ **moisten:** dehydrate, desiccate, dry, parch

wetness *n* **1 = damp**, clamminess, condensation, dampness, humidity, liquid, moisture, sogginess, water, wet

surface tension and thus increase its ability to spread across or penetrate a solid.

we've (wi:v) *contraction of* we have.

wf *Printing. abbrev. for* wrong fount.

WFF *Logic. abbrev. for* well-formed formula.

WFTU *abbrev. for* World Federation of Trade Unions.

W. Glam *abbrev. for* West Glamorgan.

whack ❶ (wæk) *vb (tr)* **1** to strike with a sharp resounding blow. **2** (*usually passive*) *Brit. inf.* to exhaust completely. ◆ *n* **3** a sharp resounding blow or the noise made by such a blow. **4** *Inf.* a share or portion. **5** *Inf.* a try or attempt (esp. in **have a whack at**). **6 out of whack.** *Inf.* out of order; unbalanced: *the whole system is out of whack.* [C18: ? var. of THWACK, ult. imit.]
▸ **'whacker** *n*

whacking ❶ ('wækɪŋ) *Inf., chiefly Brit.* ◆ *adj* **1** enormous. ◆ *adv* **2** (intensifier): *a whacking big lie.*

whacky ('wækɪ) *adj* **whackier, whackiest.** *US sl.* a variant spelling of **wacky.**

whale[1] (weɪl) *n, pl* **whales** *or* **whale. 1** any of the larger cetacean mammals, excluding dolphins, porpoises, and narwhals. They have flippers, a streamlined body, and a horizontally flattened tail and breathe through a blowhole on the top of the head. **2 a whale of 2a** *Inf.* an exceptionally large, fine, etc., example of a (person or thing). [OE *hwæl*]

whale[2] (weɪl) *vb* **whales, whaling, whaled.** (*tr*) to beat or thrash soundly. [C18: var. of WALE]

whaleboat ('weɪl,bəʊt) *n* a narrow boat from 20 to 30 feet long having a sharp prow and stern, formerly used in whaling. Also called: **whaler.**

whalebone ('weɪl,bəʊn) *n* **1** Also called: **baleen.** a horny elastic material forming numerous thin plates that hang from the upper jaw in the toothless (whalebone) whales and strain plankton from water entering the mouth. **2** a strip of this substance, used in stiffening corsets, etc.

whalebone whale *n* any whale belonging to a cetacean suborder having a double blowhole and strips of whalebone between the jaws instead of teeth: includes the rorquals, right whales, and the blue whale.

whale oil *n* oil obtained either from the blubber of whales (train oil) or the head of the sperm whale (sperm oil).

whaler ('weɪlə) *n* **1** Also called (US): **whaleman.** a person employed in whaling. **2** a vessel engaged in whaling. **3** *Austral. obs. sl.* a tramp or sundowner. **4** an aggressive shark of Australian coastal waters.

whale shark *n* a large spotted whalelike shark of warm seas, that feeds on plankton and small animals.

whaling ('weɪlɪŋ) *n* the work or industry of hunting and processing whales for food, oil, etc.

wham ❶ (wæm) *n* **1** a forceful blow or impact or the sound produced by it. ◆ *vb* **whams, whamming, whammed. 2** to strike or cause to strike with great force. [C20: imit.]

whanau ('fɑːnaʊ) *n NZ.* a family, esp. an extended family. [Maori]

whang (wæŋ) *vb* **1** to strike or be struck so as to cause a resounding noise. ◆ *n* **2** the resounding noise produced by a heavy blow. **3** a heavy blow. [C19: imit.]

whangee (wæŋ'iː) *n* **1** a tall woody grass of an Asian genus, grown for its stems. **2** a cane or walking stick made from the stem of this plant. [C19: prob. from Chinese (Mandarin) *huangli,* from *huang* yellow + *li* bamboo cane]

whare ('wɔːrɪ; *Maori* 'fɒrɛ) *n NZ.* **1** a Maori hut or dwelling place. **2** any simple dwelling place. [from Maori]

wharepuni ('fɒrɛ,punɪ) *n NZ.* in a Maori community, a lofty carved building that is used as a guesthouse. [from Maori WHARE + *puni* company]

wharf ❶ (wɔːf) *n, pl* **wharves** (wɔːvz) *or* **wharfs. 1** a platform built parallel to the waterfront at a harbour or navigable river for the docking, loading, and unloading of ships. ◆ *vb (tr)* **2** to moor or dock at a wharf. **3** to store or unload on a wharf. [OE *hwearf* heap]

wharfage ('wɔːfɪdʒ) *n* **1** facilities for ships at wharves. **2** a charge for use of a wharf. **3** wharves collectively.

wharfie ('wɔːfɪ) *n Austral. & NZ.* a wharf labourer; docker.

wharfinger ('wɔːfɪndʒə) *n* an owner or manager of a wharf. [C16: prob. alteration of *wharfager*]

wharve (wɔːv) *n* a wooden disc or wheel on a shaft serving as a flywheel or pulley. [OE *hweorfa,* from *hweorfan* to revolve]

what (wɒt; *unstressed* wət) *determiner* **1a** used with a noun in requesting further information about the identity or categorization of something: *what job does he do?* **1b** (*as pron*): *what is her address?* **1c** (*used in indirect questions*): *tell me what he said.* **2a** the (person, thing, persons, or things) that: *we photographed what animals we could see.* **2b** (*as pron*): *bring me what you've written.* **3** (intensifier; used in exclamations): *what a good book!* ◆ *adv* **4** in what respect? to what degree?: *what do you care?* **5 what about.** what do you think, know, etc., concerning? **6 what for. 6a** for what purpose? why? **6b** *Inf.* a punishment or reprimand (esp. in **give (a person) what for**). **7 what have you.** someone or something unknown or unspecified: *cars, motorcycles, or what have you.* **8 what if. 8a** what would happen if? **8b** what difference would it make if? **9 what matter.** what does it matter? **10 what's what.** *Inf.* the true state of affairs. [OE *hwæt*]

> **USAGE NOTE** The use of *are* in sentences such as *what we need are more doctors* is common, although many people think *is* should be used: *what we need is more doctors.*

whatever (wɒt'ɛvə, wət-) *pron* **1** everything or anything that: *do whatever he asks you to.* **2** no matter what: *whatever he does, he is forgiven.* **3** *Inf.* an unknown or unspecified thing or things: *take a hammer, chisel, or whatever.* **4** an intensive form of *what,* used in questions: *whatever can he have said to upset her so much?* ◆ *determiner* **5** an intensive form of *what: use whatever tools you can get hold of.* ◆ *adj* **6** (*postpositive*) absolutely; whatsoever: *I saw no point whatever in continuing.*

whatnot ('wɒt,nɒt) *n* **1** Also called: **what-d'you-call-it.** *Inf.* a person or thing the name of which is unknown or forgotten. **2** *Inf.* unspecified assorted material. **3** a portable stand with shelves for displaying ornaments, etc.

whatsit ('wɒtsɪt), **whatsitsname,** (*masc*) **whatshisname,** *or* (*fem*) **whatshername** *n Inf.* a person or thing the name of which is unknown or forgotten.

whatsoever (,wɒtsəʊ'ɛvə) *adj* **1** (*postpositive*) at all: used as an intensifier with indefinite pronouns and determiners such as *none, anybody,* etc. ◆ *pron* **2** an archaic word for **whatever.**

whaup (hwɔːp) *n Chiefly Scot.* a popular name for the **curlew.** [C16: rel. to OE *huilpe,* ult. imit. of the bird's cry]

wheal (wiːl) *n* a variant spelling of **weal**[1].

wheat (wiːt) *n* **1** any of a genus of grasses, native to the Mediterranean region and W Asia but widely cultivated, having erect flower spikes and light brown grains. **2** the grain of any of these grasses, used in making flour, pasta, etc. ◆ See also **durum.** [OE *hwǣte*]

wheatbelt ('wiːt,bɛlt) *n* an area in which wheat is the chief agricultural product.

wheatear ('wiːt,ɪə) *n* a small northern songbird having a pale grey back, black wings and tail, white rump, and pale brown underparts. [C16: back formation from *wheatears* (wrongly taken as pl), prob. from WHITE + ARSE]

wheaten ('wiːtᵊn) *adj* **1** made of the grain or flour of wheat. **2** of a pale yellow colour.

wheat germ *n* the vitamin-rich embryo of the wheat kernel.

wheatmeal ('wiːt,miːl) *n* **a** a brown flour intermediate between white flour and wholemeal flour. **b** (*as modifier*): *a wheatmeal loaf.*

Wheatstone bridge ('wiːtstən) *n* a device for determining the value of an unknown resistance by comparison with a known standard resistance. [C19: after Sir Charles *Wheatstone* (1802–75), Brit. physicist and inventor]

whee (wiː) *interj* an exclamation of joy, etc.

wheedle ❶ ('wiːdᵊl) *vb* **wheedles, wheedling, wheedled. 1** to persuade or try to persuade (someone) by coaxing words, flattery, etc. **2** (*tr*) to obtain thus: *she wheedled some money out of her father.* [C17: ?from G *wedeln* to wag one's tail, from OHG *wedil, wadil* tail]
▸ **'wheedler** *n* ▸ **'wheedling** *adj* ▸ **'wheedlingly** *adv*

wheel ❶ (wiːl) *n* **1** a solid disc, or a circular rim joined to a hub by spokes, that is mounted on a shaft about which it can turn, as in vehicles. **2** anything like a wheel in shape or function. **3** a device consisting of or resembling a wheel: *a steering wheel; a water wheel.* **4** (usually preceded by *the*) a medieval torture in which the victim was tied to a wheel and then had his limbs struck and broken by an iron bar. **5** short for **wheel of fortune** or **potter's wheel. 6** the act of turning. **7** a pivoting movement of troops, ships, etc. **8** a type of firework coiled to make it rotate when let off. **9** a set of short rhyming lines forming the concluding part of a stanza. **10** *US & Canad.* an informal word for **bicycle. 11** *Inf., chiefly US & Canad.* a person of great influence (esp. in **big wheel**). **12 at the wheel. 12a** driving or steering a vehicle or vessel. **12b** in charge. ◆ *vb* **13** to turn or cause to turn on or as if on an axis. **14** (when *intr,* sometimes foll. by *about* or *around*) to move or cause to move on or as if on wheels; roll. **15** (*tr*) to perform with or in a circular movement. **16** (*tr*) to provide with a wheel or wheels. **17** (*intr;* often foll. by *about*) to change direction. **18 wheel and deal.** *Inf.* to operate free of restraint, esp. to advance one's own interests. ◆ See also **wheels.** [OE *hweol, hweowol*]

THESAURUS

whack *vb* **1** = **strike,** bang, bash (*inf.*), beat, belabour, belt (*inf.*), box, buffet, chin (*sl.*), clobber (*sl.*), clout (*inf.*), cuff, deck (*sl.*), hit, lambast(e), lay one on (*sl.*), rap, slap, slug, smack, sock (*sl.*), swipe, thrash, thump, thwack, wallop (*inf.*) ◆ *n* **3** = **blow,** bang, bash (*inf.*), belt (*inf.*), box, buffet, clout (*inf.*), cuff, hit, rap, slap, slug, smack, sock (*sl.*), stroke, swipe, thump, thwack, wallop (*inf.*), wham **4** *Informal* = **share,** allotment, bit, cut (*inf.*), part, portion, quota **5** *Informal As in* **have a whack** = **attempt,** bash (*inf.*), crack (*inf.*), go (*inf.*), shot (*inf.*), stab (*inf.*), try, turn

whacking *adj* **1** *Informal, chiefly Brit.* = **huge,** big, elephantine, enormous, extraordinary, giant, gigantic, great, humongous *or* humungous (*US sl.*), large, mammoth, monstrous, prodigious, tremendous, whopping (*inf.*)

wham *n* **1** = **blow,** bang, bash (*inf.*), concussion, impact, slam, smack, thump, thwack, wallop (*inf.*), whack, whang

wharf *n* **1** = **dock,** jetty, landing stage, pier, quay

wheedle *vb* **1, 2** = **coax,** butter up, cajole, charm, court, draw, entice, flatter, inveigle, persuade, talk into, worm

wheel *n* **2** = **circle,** gyration, pivot, revolution, roll, rotation, spin, turn, twirl, whirl **12 at the wheel** = **in control,** at the helm, driving, in charge, in command, in the driving seat, steering ◆ *vb* **13-15** = **turn,** circle, gyrate, orbit, pir-

wheel and axle *n* a simple machine for raising weights in which a rope unwinding from a wheel is wound onto a cylindrical drum or shaft coaxial with or joined to the wheel to provide mechanical advantage.

wheel animalcule *n* another name for **rotifer.**

wheelbarrow ('wiːlˌbærəʊ) *n* a simple vehicle for carrying small loads, typically being an open container supported by a wheel at the front and two legs behind.

wheelbase ('wiːlˌbeɪs) *n* the distance between the front and back axles of a motor vehicle.

wheelchair ('wiːlˌtʃɛə) *n* special chair on large wheels, for use by invalids or others for whom walking is impossible or inadvisable.

wheel clamp *n* a device fixed onto one wheel of an illegally parked car in order to immobilize it. The driver has to pay to have it removed.

wheeled (wiːld) *adj* **a** having a wheel or wheels. **b** (*in combination): four-wheeled.*

wheeler ('wiːlə) *n* **1** Also called: **wheel horse.** a horse or other draught animal nearest the wheel. **2** (*in combination*) something equipped with a specified sort or number of wheels: *a three-wheeler.* **3** a person or thing that wheels.

wheeler-dealer *n Inf.* a person who wheels and deals.

wheel horse *n* **1** another word for **wheeler** (sense 1). **2** *US & Canad.* a person who works steadily or hard.

wheelhouse ('wiːlˌhaʊs) *n* another term for **pilot house.**

wheelie ('wiːlɪ) *n* a manoeuvre on a bicycle or motorbike in which the front wheel is raised off the ground.

wheelie bin *or* **wheely bin** *n* a large container for rubbish, esp. one used by a household, mounted on wheels so that it can be moved more easily.

wheel lock *n* **1** a gunlock formerly in use in which the firing mechanism was activated by sparks produced by friction between a small steel wheel and a flint. **2** a gun having such a lock.

wheel of fortune *n* (in mythology and literature) a revolving device spun by a deity selecting random changes in the affairs of man.

wheels (wiːlz) *pl n* **1** the main directing force behind an organization, movement, etc.: *the wheels of government.* **2** an informal word for **car. 3 wheels within wheels.** a series of intricately connected events, plots, etc.

wheel window *n* another name for **rose window.**

wheel wobble *n* an oscillation of the front wheels of a vehicle caused by a defect in the steering gear, unbalanced wheels, etc.

wheelwright ('wiːlˌraɪt) *n* a person who makes or mends wheels as a trade.

wheeze ❶ (wiːz) *vb* **wheezes, wheezing, wheezed. 1** to breathe or utter (something) with a rasping or whistling sound. **2** (*intr*) to make or move with a noise suggestive of wheezy breathing. ◆ *n* **3** a husky, rasping, or whistling sound or breathing. **4** *Brit. sl.* a trick, idea, or plan. **5** *Inf.* a hackneyed joke or anecdote. [C15: prob. from ON *hvǣsa* to hiss]

▸'**wheezer** *n* ▸'**wheezy** *adj* ▸'**wheezily** *adv* ▸'**wheeziness** *n*

whelk[1] (wɛlk) *n* a marine gastropod mollusc of coastal waters and intertidal regions, having a strong snail-like shell. [OE *weoloc*]

whelk[2] (wɛlk) *n* a raised lesion on the skin; wheal. [OE *hwylca,* from ?]

▸'**whelky** *adj*

whelm (wɛlm) *vb* (*tr*) *Arch.* to engulf entirely; overwhelm. [C13 *whelmen* to turn over, from ?]

whelp (wɛlp) *n* **1** a young offspring of certain animals, esp. of a wolf or dog. **2** *Disparaging.* a youth. **3** *Jocular.* a young child. **4** *Naut.* any of the ridges, parallel to the axis, on the drum of a capstan to keep a rope, etc., from slipping. ◆ *vb* **5** (of an animal or, disparagingly, a woman) to give birth to (young). [OE *hwelp(a)*]

when (wɛn) *adv* **1a** at what time? over what period?: *when is he due?* **1b** (*used in indirect questions): ask him when he's due.* **2 say when.** to state when an action is to be stopped or begun, as when someone is pouring a drink. ◆ *conj* **3** (*subordinating*) at a time at which; just as; after: *I found it easy when I tried.* **4** although: *he drives when he might walk.* **5** considering the fact that: *how did you pass the exam when you hadn't worked for it?* ◆ *pron* **6** at which (time); over which (period): *an age when men were men.* ◆ *n* **7** a question as to the time of some occurrence. [OE *hwanne, hwænne*]

> **USAGE NOTE** *When* should not be used loosely as a substitute for *in which* after a noun which does not refer to a period of time: *paralysis is a condition in which* (not *when*) *parts of the body cannot be moved.*

whenas (wɛn'æz) *conj Arch.* **1a** when; whenever. **1b** inasmuch as; while. **2** although.

whence (wɛns) *Arch. or formal.* ◆ *adv* **1** from what place, cause, or origin? ◆ *pron* **2** (*subordinating*) from what place, cause, or origin. [C13 *whannes,* adv. genitive of OE *hwanon*]

> **USAGE NOTE** The expression *from whence* should be avoided, since *whence* already means from which place: *the tradition whence* (not *from whence*) *such ideas flowed.*

whencesoever (ˌwɛnssəʊ'ɛvə) *conj* (*subordinating*), *adv Arch.* from whatever place, cause, or origin.

whenever (wɛn'ɛvə) *conj* **1** (*subordinating*) at every or any time that; when: *I laugh whenever I see that.* ◆ *adv also* **when ever. 2** no matter when: *it'll be here, whenever you decide to come for it.* **3** *Inf.* at an unknown or unspecified time: *I'll take it if it comes today, tomorrow, or whenever.* **4** an intensive form of *when,* used in questions: *whenever did he escape?*

whensoever (ˌwɛnsəʊ'ɛvə) *conj, adv Rare.* an intensive form of **whenever.**

whenua (fɛn'uə) *n NZ.* land. [Maori]

where (wɛə) *adv* **1a** in, at, or to what place, point, or position?: *where are you going?* **1b** (*used in indirect questions): I don't know where they are.* ◆ *pron* **2** in, at, or to which (place): *the hotel where we spent our honeymoon.* ◆ *conj* **3** (*subordinating*) in the place at which: *where we live it's always raining.* ◆ *n* **4** a question as to the position, direction, or destination of something. [OE *hwǣr, hwār(a)*]

> **USAGE NOTE** It was formerly considered incorrect to use *where* as a substitute for *in which* after a noun which did not refer to a place or position, but this use has now become acceptable: *we have a situation where/in which no further action is needed.*

whereabouts ❶ ('wɛərəˌbaʊts) *adv* **1** at what approximate place; where: *whereabouts are you?* ◆ *n* **2** (*functioning as sing or pl*) the place, esp. the approximate place, where a person or thing is.

whereas (wɛər'æz) *conj* **1** (*coordinating*) but on the other hand: *I like to go swimming whereas Sheila likes to sail.* ◆ *sentence connector.* **2** (in formal documents) it being the case that; since.

whereat (wɛər'æt) *Arch.* ◆ *adv* **1** at or to which place. ◆ *sentence connector.* **2** upon which occasion.

whereby (wɛə'baɪ) *pron* by or because of which: *the means whereby he took his life.*

wherefore ('wɛəˌfɔː) *n* **1** (*usually pl*) an explanation or reason (esp. in **the whys and wherefores**). ◆ *adv* **2** *Arch.* why? ◆ *sentence connector.* **3** *Arch. or formal.* for which reason: used in legal preambles.

wherefrom (wɛə'frɒm) *Arch.* ◆ *adv* **1** from what or where? whence? ◆ *pron* **2** from which place; whence.

wherein (wɛər'ɪn) *Arch. or formal.* ◆ *adv* **1** in what place or respect? ◆ *pron* **2** in which place, thing, etc.

whereof (wɛər'ɒv) *Arch. or formal.* ◆ *adv* **1** of what or which person or thing? ◆ *pron* **2** of which (person or thing): *the man whereof I speak is no longer alive.*

whereon (wɛər'ɒn) *Arch.* ◆ *adv* **1** on what thing or place? ◆ *pron* **2** on which thing, place, etc.

wheresoever (ˌwɛəsəʊ'ɛvə) *conj* (*subordinating*), *adv, pron Rare.* an intensive form of **wherever.**

whereto (wɛə'tuː) *Arch. or formal.* ◆ *adv* **1** towards what (place, end, etc.)? ◆ *pron* **2** to which. ◆ Also (archaic): **whereunto.**

whereupon (ˌwɛərə'pɒn) *sentence connector.* at which; at which point; upon which.

wherever (wɛər'ɛvə) *pron* **1** at, in, or to every place or point which; where: *wherever she went, he would be there.* ◆ *conj* **2** (*subordinating*) in, to, or at whatever place: *wherever we go the weather is always bad.* ◆ *adv also* **where ever. 3** no matter where: *I'll find you, wherever you are.* **4** *Inf.* at, in, or to an unknown or unspecified place: *I'll go anywhere to escape: London, Paris, or wherever.* **5** an intensive form of *where,* used in questions: *wherever can they be?*

wherewith (wɛə'wɪθ, -'wɪð) *Arch. or formal.* ◆ *pron* **1** (*often foll. by an infinitive*) with or by which: *the pen wherewith I write.* **2** something with which: *I have not wherewith to buy my bread.* ◆ *adv* **3** with what? ◆ *sentence connector.* **4** with or after that; whereupon.

wherewithal ❶ *n* ('wɛəwɪðˌɔːl). **the wherewithal.** necessary funds, resources, or equipment: *these people lack the wherewithal for a decent existence.* ◆ *pron* (ˌwɛəwɪð'ɔːl). **2** a less common word for **wherewith.**

wherry ('wɛrɪ) *n, pl* **wherries. 1** any of certain kinds of half-decked commercial boats. **2** a light rowing boat. [C15: from ?]

▸'**wherryman** *n*

whet ❶ (wɛt) *vb* **whets, whetting, whetted.** (*tr*) **1** to sharpen, as by grinding or friction. **2** to increase (the appetite, desire, etc.); stimulate. ◆ *n* **3** the act of whetting. **4** a person or thing that whets. [OE *hwettan*]

▸'**whetter** *n*

whether ('wɛðə) *conj* **1** (*subordinating*) used to introduce an indirect question or a clause after a verb expressing or implying doubt or choice: *he doesn't know whether she's in Britain or whether she's gone to France.* **2** (*coordinating*) either: *any man, whether liberal or conservative,*

THESAURUS

ouette, revolve, roll, rotate, spin, swing, swivel, twirl, whirl

wheeze *vb* **1** = **gasp,** breathe roughly, catch one's breath, cough, hiss, rasp, whistle ◆ *n* **3** = **gasp,** cough, hiss, rasp, whistle **4** *Brit. slang* = **trick,** expedient, idea, plan, ploy, ruse, scheme, stunt, wrinkle (*inf.*) **5** *Informal* = **joke,** anecdote, chestnut (*inf.*), crack (*sl.*), gag (*inf.*), old joke, one-liner (*sl.*), story

whereabouts *n* **2** = **position,** location, site, situation

wherewithal *n* **1** = **resources,** capital, equipment, essentials, funds, means, money, ready (*inf.*), ready money, supplies

whet *vb* **1** = **sharpen,** edge, file, grind, hone, strop **2** = **stimulate,** animate, arouse, awaken, enhance, excite, incite, increase, kindle, pique, provoke, quicken, rouse, stir

would agree with me. **3 whether or no.** in any case: *he will be here tomorrow, whether or no.* **4 whether...or (whether).** if on the one hand...or even if on the other hand: *you'll eat that, whether you like it or not.* [OE *hwæther, hwether*]

whetstone ('wɛt,stəʊn) *n* **1** a stone used for sharpening edged tools, knives, etc. **2** something that sharpens.

whew (hwjuː) *interj* an exclamation or sharply exhaled breath expressing relief, delight, etc.

whey (weɪ) *n* the watery liquid that separates from the curd when milk is clotted, as in making cheese. [OE *hwǣg*]

wheyface ('weɪ,feɪs) *n* **1** a pale bloodless face. **2** a person with such a face. ▸**'whey,faced** *adj*

which (wɪtʃ) *determiner* **1a** used with a noun in requesting that its referent be further specified, identified, or distinguished: *which house did you buy?* **1b** (*as pron*): *which did you find?* **1c** (*used in indirect questions*): *I wondered which apples were cheaper.* **2a** whatever of a class; whichever: *bring which car you want.* **2b** (*as pron*): *choose which of the cars suits you.* ◆ *pron* **3** used in relative clauses with inanimate antecedents: *the house, which is old, is in poor repair.* **4** as; and that: used in relative clauses with verb phrases or sentences as their antecedents: *he died of cancer, which is what I predicted.* **5 the which.** an archaic form of **which** often used as a sentence connector. [OE *hwelc, hwilc*]

> **USAGE NOTE** See at **that.**

whichever (wɪtʃ'ɛvə) *determiner* **1a** any (one, two, etc., out of several): *take whichever car you like.* **1b** (*as pron*): *choose whichever appeals to you.* **2a** no matter which (one or ones): *whichever card you pick you'll still be making a mistake.* **2b** (*as pron*): *it won't make any difference, whichever comes first.*

whichsoever (,wɪtʃsəʊ'ɛvə) *pron* an archaic or formal word for **whichever.**

whicker ('wɪkə) *vb* (*intr*) (of a horse) to whinny or neigh; nicker. [C17: imit.]

whidah ('wɪdə) *n* a variant spelling of **whydah.**

whiff ❶ (wɪf) *n* **1** a passing odour. **2** a brief gentle gust of air. **3** a single inhalation or exhalation from the mouth or nose. ◆ *vb* **4** to puff or waft. **5** (*tr*) to sniff or smell. **6** (*intr*) *Brit. sl.* to stink. [C16: imit.]

whiffle ('wɪf°l) *vb* **whiffles, whiffling, whiffled. 1** (*intr*) to think or behave in an erratic or unpredictable way. **2** to blow or be blown fitfully or in gusts. **3** (*intr*) to whistle softly. [C16: frequentative of WHIFF]

whiffletree ('wɪf°l,triː) *n Chiefly US.* another word for **swingletree.** [C19: var. of WHIPPLETREE]

Whig (wɪg) *n* **1** a member of the English political party that opposed the succession to the throne of James, Duke of York (1679–80), on the grounds that he was a Catholic. Standing for a limited monarchy, the Whigs later represented the desires of industrialists and Dissenters for political and social reform, and provided the core of the Liberal Party. **2** (in the US) a supporter of the War of American Independence. Cf. **Tory. 3** a member of the American political party that opposed the Democrats from about 1834 to 1855 and represented propertied and professional interests. **4** *History.* a 17th-century Scottish Presbyterian, esp. one in rebellion against the Crown. ◆ *adj* **5** of, characteristic of, or relating to Whigs. [C17: prob. from *whiggamore*, one of a group of 17th-cent. Scottish rebels who joined in an attack on Edinburgh known as *the whiggamore raid;* prob. from Scot. *whig* to drive (from ?) + *more* horse]
▸**'Whiggery** *or* **'Whiggism** *n* ▸**'Whiggish** *adj*

while (waɪl) *conj also* **whilst. 1** (*subordinating*) at the same time that: *please light the fire while I'm cooking.* **2** (*subordinating*) all the time that: *I stay inside while it's raining.* **3** (*subordinating*) in spite of the fact that: *while I agree about his brilliance I still think he's rude.* **4** (*coordinating*) whereas; and in contrast: *houses are expensive, while flats are cheap.* ◆ *prep, conj* **5** *Scot. & N English dialect.* another word for **until:** *you'll have to wait while Monday.* ◆ *n* **6** (*usually used in adverbial phrases*) a period or interval of time: *once in a long while.* **7** trouble or time (esp. in **worth one's while**): *it's hardly worth your while to begin work today.* [OE *hwīl*]

> **USAGE NOTE** It was formerly considered incorrect to use *while* to mean *in spite of the fact that* or *whereas*, but these uses have become acceptable.

while away *vb* (*tr, adv*) to pass (time) idly and usually pleasantly.

whiles (waɪlz) *Arch. or dialect.* ◆ *adv* **1** at times; occasionally. ◆ *conj* **2** while; whilst.

whilom ('waɪləm) *Arch.* ◆ *adv* **1** formerly; once. ◆ *adj* **2** (*prenominal*) one-time; former. [OE *hwīlum*, dative pl of *hwīl* while]

whilst (waɪlst) *conj Chiefly Brit.* another word for **while** (senses 1–4). [C13: from WHILES + -*t* as in *amidst*]

whim ❶ (wɪm) *n* **1** a sudden, passing, and often fanciful idea; impulsive or irrational thought. **2** a horse-drawn winch formerly used in mining to lift ore or water. [C17: from C16 *whim-wham*, from ?]

whimbrel ('wɪmbrəl) *n* a small European curlew with a striped head. [C16: from dialect *whimp* or from WHIMPER, from its cry]

whimper ❶ ('wɪmpə) *vb* **1** (*intr*) to cry, sob, or whine softly or intermittently. **2** to complain or say (something) in a whining plaintive way. ◆ *n* **3** a soft plaintive whine. [C16: from dialect *whimp*, imit.]
▸**'whimperer** *n* ▸**'whimpering** *n, adj* ▸**'whimperingly** *adv*

whimsical ❶ ('wɪmzɪk°l) *adj* **1** spontaneously fanciful or playful. **2** given to whims; capricious. **3** quaint, unusual, or fantastic.
▸**whimsicality** (,wɪmzɪ'kælɪtɪ) *n* ▸**'whimsically** *adv*

whimsy *or* **whimsey** ('wɪmzɪ) *n, pl* **whimsies** *or* **whimseys. 1** a capricious idea or notion. **2** light or fanciful humour. **3** something quaint or unusual. ◆ *adj* **whimsier, whimsiest. 4** quaint, comical, or unusual, often in a tasteless way. [C17: from WHIM]

whin[1] (wɪn) *n* another name for **gorse.** [C11: from ON]

whin[2] (wɪn) *n* short for **whinstone.** [C14 *quin*, from ?]

whinchat ('wɪn,tʃæt) *n* an Old World songbird having a mottled brown-and-white plumage with pale cream underparts. [C17: from WHIN[1] + CHAT]

whine ❶ (waɪn) *n* **1** a long high-pitched plaintive cry or moan. **2** a continuous high-pitched sound. **3** a peevish complaint, esp. one repeated. ◆ *vb* **whines, whining, whined. 4** to make a whine or utter in a whine. [OE *hwīnan*]
▸**'whiner** *n* ▸**'whining** *or* **'whiny** *adj* ▸**'whiningly** *adv*

whinge ❶ (wɪndʒ) *vb* **whinges, whingeing, whinged.** (*intr*) **1** to cry in a fretful way. **2** to complain. ◆ *n* **3** a complaint. [from Northern var. of OE *hwinsian* to whine]
▸**'whingeing** *n, adj* ▸**'whinger** *n*

whinny ('wɪnɪ) *vb* **whinnies, whinnying, whinnied.** (*intr*) **1** (of a horse) to neigh softly or gently. **2** to make a sound resembling a neigh, such as a laugh. ◆ *n, pl* **whinnies. 3** a gentle or low-pitched neigh. [C16: imit.]

whinstone ('wɪn,stəʊn) *n* any dark hard fine-grained rock, such as basalt. [C16: from WHIN[2] + STONE]

whip ❶ (wɪp) *vb* **whips, whipping, whipped. 1** to strike (a person or thing) with several strokes of a strap, rod, etc. **2** (*tr*) to punish by striking in this manner. **3** (*tr;* foll. by *out, away,* etc.) to pull, remove, etc., with sudden rapid motion: *to whip out a gun.* **4** (*intr;* foll. by *down, into, out of,* etc.) *Inf.* to come, go, etc., in a rapid sudden manner: *they whipped into the bar for a drink.* **5** to strike or be struck as if by whipping: *the tempest whipped the surface of the sea.* **6** (*tr*) to bring, train, etc., forcefully into a desired condition. **7** (*tr*) *Inf.* to overcome or outdo. **8** (*tr;* often foll. by *on, out,* or *off*) to drive, urge, compel, etc., by or as if by whipping. **9** (*tr*) to wrap or wind (a cord, thread, etc.) around (a rope, cable, etc.) to prevent chafing or fraying. **10** (*tr*) (in fly-fishing) to cast the fly repeatedly onto (the water) in a whipping motion. **11** (*tr*) (in sewing) to join, finish, or gather with whipstitch. **12** to beat (eggs, cream, etc.) with a whisk or similar utensil to incorporate air. **13** (*tr*) to spin (a top). **14** (*tr*) *Inf.* to steal: *he whipped her purse.* ◆ *n* **15** a device consisting of a lash or flexible rod attached at one end to a stiff handle and used for driving animals, inflicting corporal punishment, etc. **16** a whipping stroke or motion. **17** a person adept at handling a whip, as a coachman, etc. **18** (in a legislative body) **18a** a member of a party chosen to organize and discipline the members of his faction. **18b** a call issued to members of a party, insisting with varying degrees of urgency upon their presence or loyal voting behaviour. **18c** (in the Brit. Parliament) a schedule of business sent to members of a party each week. Each item on it is underlined to indicate its importance: three lines means that the item is very important and every member must attend and vote according to the party line. **19** an apparatus for hoisting, consisting of a rope, pulley, and snatch block. **20** any of a variety of desserts made from egg whites or cream beaten stiff. **21** See

THESAURUS

Antonyms *vb* ≠ **sharpen:** blunt, dull ≠ **stimulate:** blunt, dampen, deaden, depress, dull, numb, smother, stifle, subdue, suppress

whiff *n* **1-3** = **smell**, aroma, blast, breath, draught, gust, hint, niff (*Brit. sl.*), odour, puff, scent, sniff ◆ *vb* **6** *Brit. slang* = **stink**, hum (*sl.*), malodour, niff (*Brit. sl.*), pong (*Brit. inf.*), reek

whim *n* **1** = **impulse**, caprice, conceit, craze, crotchet, fad (*inf.*), fancy, freak, humour, notion, passing thought, quirk, sport, sudden notion, urge, vagary, whimsy

whimper *vb* **1, 2** = **cry**, blub (*sl.*), blubber, grizzle (*inf., chiefly Brit.*), mewl, moan, pule, snivel, sob, weep, whine, whinge (*inf.*) ◆ *n* **3** = **sob**, moan, snivel, whine

whimsical *adj* **1-3** = **fanciful**, capricious, chimerical, crotchety, curious, droll, eccentric, fantastic, fantastical, freakish, funny, mischievous, odd, peculiar, playful, quaint, queer, singular, unusual, waggish, weird

whine *n* **1** = **cry**, moan, plaintive cry, sob, wail, whimper **3** = **complaint**, beef, gripe (*inf.*), grouch (*inf.*), grouse, grumble, moan, whinge (*inf.*) ◆ *vb* **4** = **cry**, moan, sniffle, snivel, sob, wail, whimper

whinge *Informal vb* **2** = **complain**, beef, bellyache (*sl.*), bleat, carp, gripe (*inf.*), grizzle (*inf., chiefly Brit.*), grouch (*inf.*), grouse, grumble, kvetch (*US sl.*), moan ◆ *n* **3** = **complaint**, beef (*sl.*), gripe (*inf.*), grouch, grouse, grumble, moan, whine

whip *vb* **1, 2** = **lash**, beat, birch, cane, castigate, flagellate, flog, give a hiding (*inf.*), lambast(e), leather, lick (*inf.*), punish, scourge, spank, strap, switch, tan (*sl.*), thrash **3** *foll. by* **out, away** *etc.* = **pull out**, exhibit, flash, jerk, produce, remove, seize, show, snatch, whisk **4** *Informal* = **dash**, dart, dive, flit, flounce, fly, rush, shoot, tear, whisk **5** = **whisk**, beat **7** *Informal* = **beat**, best, clobber (*sl.*), conquer, defeat, drub, hammer (*inf.*), lick (*inf.*), outdo, overcome, overpower, overwhelm, rout, stuff (*sl.*), thrash, trounce, worst **8** = **incite**, agitate, compel, drive, foment, goad, hound, instigate, prick, prod, provoke, push, spur, stir, urge, work up ◆ *n* **15** = **lash**, birch, bullwhip, cane, cat-o'-nine-tails, crop, horsewhip, knout, rawhide, riding crop, scourge, switch, thong

whipper-in. 22 flexibility, as in the shaft of a golf club, etc. ◆ See also **whip-round, whip up, whips.** [C13: ?from MDu. *wippen* to swing]
▸ **'whip,like** *adj* ▸ **'whipper** *n*

whip bird *n Austral.* any of several birds having a whistle ending in a note sounding like the crack of a whip.

whipcord ('wɪp,kɔːd) *n* **1** a strong worsted or cotton fabric with a diagonally ribbed surface. **2** a closely twisted hard cord used for the lashes of whips, etc.

whip graft *n Horticulture.* a graft made by inserting a tongue cut on the sloping base of the scion into a slit on the sloping top of the stock.

whip hand *n* (usually preceded by *the*) **1** (in driving horses) the hand holding the whip. **2** advantage or dominating position.

whiplash ('wɪp,læʃ) *n* a quick lash or stroke of a whip or like that of a whip.

whiplash injury *n Med. inf.* any injury to the neck resulting from a sudden thrusting forwards and snapping back of the unsupported head. Technical name: **hyperextension-hyperflexion injury.**

whipper-in *n, pl* **whippers-in.** a person employed to assist the huntsman managing the hounds.

whippersnapper ('wɪpə,snæpə) *n* an insignificant but pretentious or cheeky person, often a young one. Also called: **whipster.** [C17: prob. from *whipsnapper* a person who snaps whips, infl. by earlier *snipper-snapper,* from ?]

whippet ('wɪpɪt) *n* a small slender breed of dog similar to a greyhound. [C16: from ?; ? based on *whip it!* move quickly!]

whipping ❶ ('wɪpɪŋ) *n* **1** a thrashing or beating with a whip or similar implement. **2** cord or twine used for binding or lashing. **3** the binding formed by wrapping a rope, etc., with cord or twine.

whipping boy *n* a person of little importance who is blamed for the errors, incompetence, etc., of others, esp. his superiors; scapegoat. [C17: orig. referring to a boy who was educated with a prince and who received punishment for any faults committed by the prince]

whippletree ('wɪpᵊl,triː) *n* another name for **swingletree.** [C18: apparently from WHIP]

whippoorwill ('wɪpʊ,wɪl) *n* a nightjar of North and Central America, having a dark plumage with white patches on the tail. [C18: imit. of its cry]

whip-round *Inf., chiefly Brit.* ◆ *n* **1** an impromptu collection of money. ◆ *vb* **whip round. 2** (*intr, adv*) to make such a collection.

whips (wɪps) *pl n* (often foll. by *of*) *Austral. inf.* a large quantity: *I've got whips of cash at the moment.*

whipsaw ('wɪp,sɔː) *n* **1** any saw with a flexible blade, such as a bandsaw. ◆ *vb* **whipsaws, whipsawing, whipsawed; whipsawed** *or* **whipsawn.** (*tr*) **2** to saw with a whipsaw. **3** *US.* to defeat in two ways at once.

whip scorpion *n* any of an order of nonvenomous arachnids, typically resembling a scorpion but lacking a sting.

whip snake *n* any of several long slender fast-moving nonvenomous snakes.

whipstitch ('wɪp,stɪtʃ) *n* a sewing stitch passing over an edge.

whipstock ('wɪp,stɒk) *n* a whip handle.

whip up ❶ *vb* (*tr, adv*) **1** to excite; arouse: *to whip up a mob; to whip up discontent.* **2** *Inf.* to prepare quickly: *to whip up a meal.*

whir *or* **whirr** (wɜː) *n* **1** a prolonged soft swish or buzz, as of a motor working or wings flapping. **2** a bustle or rush. ◆ *vb* **whirs** *or* **whirrs, whirring, whirred. 3** to make or cause to make a whir. [C14: prob. from ON; see WHIRL]

whirl ❶ (wɜːl) *vb* **1** to spin, turn, or revolve or cause to spin, turn, or revolve. **2** (*intr*) to turn around or away rapidly. **3** (*intr*) to have a spinning sensation, as from dizziness, etc. **4** to move or drive or be moved or driven at high speed. ◆ *n* **5** the act or an instance of whirling; swift rotation or a rapid whirling movement. **6** a condition of confusion or giddiness: *her accident left me in a whirl.* **7** a swift round, as of events, meetings, etc. **8** a tumult; stir. **9** *Inf.* a brief trip, dance, etc. **10 give (something) a whirl.** *Inf.* to attempt or give a trial to (something). [C13: from ON *hvirfla* to turn about]
▸ **'whirler** *n* ▸ **'whirling** *adj* ▸ **'whirlingly** *adv*

whirligig ('wɜːlɪ,gɪg) *n* **1** any spinning toy, such as a top. **2** another name for **merry-go-round. 3** anything that whirls about, spins, or moves in a circular or giddy way: *the whirligig of social life.* [C15 *whirlegigge,* from WHIRL + GIG[1]]

whirlpool ('wɜːl,puːl) *n* **1** a powerful circular current or vortex of water. **2** something resembling a whirlpool in motion or the power to attract into its vortex.

whirlwind ❶ ('wɜːl,wɪnd) *n* **1** a column of air whirling around and towards a more or less vertical axis of low pressure, which moves along the land or ocean surface. **2a** a motion or course resembling this, esp. in rapidity. **2b** (*as modifier*): *a whirlwind romance.* **3** an impetuously active person.

whirlybird ('wɜːlɪ,bɜːd) *n* an informal word for **helicopter.**

whish (wɪʃ) *n, vb* a less common word for **swish.**

whisht (hwɪʃt) *or* **whist** *Arch. or dialect, esp. Scot.* ◆ *interj* **1** hush! be quiet! ◆ *adj* **2** silent or still. [C14: cf. HIST]

whisk ❶ (wɪsk) *vb* **1** (*tr;* often foll. by *away* or *off*) to brush, sweep, or wipe off lightly. **2** (*tr*) to move, carry, etc., with a light or rapid sweeping motion: *the taxi whisked us to the airport.* **3** (*intr*) to move, go, etc., quickly and nimbly: *to whisk downstairs for a drink.* **4** (*tr*) to whip (eggs, etc.) to a froth. ◆ *n* **5** the act of whisking. **6** a light rapid sweeping movement. **7** a utensil for whipping eggs, etc. **8** a small brush or broom. **9** a small bunch or bundle, as of grass, straw, etc. [C14: from ON *visk* wisp]

whisker ('wɪskə) *n* **1** any of the stiff sensory hairs growing on the face of a cat, rat, or other mammal. Technical name: **vibrissa. 2** any of the hairs growing on a man's face, esp. on the cheeks or chin. **3** (*pl*) a beard or that part of it growing on the sides of the face. **4** (*pl*) *Inf.* a moustache. **5** *Chem.* a very fine filamentary crystal having greater strength than the bulk material. **6** a person or thing that whisks. **7** a narrow margin or small distance: *he escaped death by a whisker.* [see WHISK]
▸ **'whiskered** *or* **'whiskery** *adj*

whiskey ('wɪskɪ) *n* the usual Irish and US spelling of **whisky.**

whiskey sour *n US.* a mixed drink of whisky and lime or lemon juice, sometimes sweetened.

whisky ❶ ('wɪskɪ) *n, pl* **whiskies.** a spirit made by distilling fermented cereals, which is matured and often blended. [C18: shortened from *whiskybae,* from Scot. Gaelic *uisge beatha,* lit.: water of life; see USQUEBAUGH]

whisky-jack *n Canad.* another name for **Canada jay.**

whisky mac *n Brit.* a drink consisting of whisky and ginger wine.

whisper ❶ ('wɪspə) *vb* **1** to speak or utter (something) in a soft hushed tone, esp. without vibration of the vocal cords. **2** (*intr*) to speak secretly or furtively, as in promoting intrigue, gossip, etc. **3** (*intr*) (of leaves, trees, etc.) to make a low soft rustling sound. **4** (*tr*) to utter or suggest secretly or privately: *to whisper treason.* ◆ *n* **5** a low soft voice: *to speak in a whisper.* **6** something uttered in such a voice. **7** a low soft rustling sound. **8** a trace or suspicion. **9** *Inf.* a rumour. [OE *hwisprian*]
▸ **'whisperer** *n*

whispering campaign *n* the organized diffusion of defamatory rumours to discredit a person, group, etc.

whispering gallery *n* a gallery or dome with acoustic characteristics such that a sound made at one point is audible at distant points.

whist[1] (wɪst) *n* a card game for four in which the two sides try to win the balance of the 13 tricks: forerunner of bridge. [C17: ? changed from WHISK, referring to the sweeping up or whisking up of the tricks]

whist[2] (hwɪst) *interj, adj* a variant of **whisht.**

whist drive *n* a social gathering where whist is played: the winners of each hand move to different tables to play the losers of the previous hand.

whistle ('wɪsᵊl) *vb* **whistles, whistling, whistled. 1** to produce (shrill or flutelike sounds), as by passing breath through a narrow constriction most easily formed by the pursed lips. **2** (*tr*) to signal or command by whistling or blowing a whistle: *the referee whistled the end of the game.* **3** (of a kettle, train, etc.) to produce (a shrill sound) caused by the emission of steam through a small aperture. **4** (*intr*) to move with a whistling sound caused by rapid passage through the air. **5** (of animals, esp. birds) to emit (a shrill sound) resembling human whistling. **6 whistle in the dark.** to try to keep up one's confidence in spite of fear. ◆ *n* **7** a device for making a shrill high-pitched sound by means of air or steam under pressure. **8** a shrill sound effected by whistling or blowing a whistle. **9** a whistling sound, as of a bird, bullet, the wind, etc. **10** a signal, etc., transmitted by or as if by a whistle. **11** the act of whistling. **12** an instrument, usually made of metal, that is blown down its end to produce a tune, signal, etc. **13 blow the whistle.** (usually foll. by *on*) *Inf.* **13a** to inform (on). **13b** to bring a stop (to). **14 clean as a**

THESAURUS

whipping *n* **1** = **beating**, birching, caning, castigation, flagellation, flogging, hiding (*inf.*), lashing, leathering, punishment, spanking, tanning (*sl.*), the strap, thrashing

whip up *vb* **1** = **arouse**, agitate, excite, foment, incite, inflame, instigate, kindle, provoke, rouse, stir up, work up

whirl *vb* **1** = **spin**, circle, gyrate, pirouette, pivot, reel, revolve, roll, rotate, swirl, turn, twirl, twist, wheel **3** = **feel dizzy**, reel, spin ◆ *n* **5** = **revolution**, birl, circle, gyration, pirouette, reel, roll, rotation, spin, swirl, turn, twirl, twist, wheel **7** = **bustle**, flurry, merry-go-round, round, series, succession **8** = **confusion**, agitation, commotion, daze, dither (*chiefly Brit.*), giddiness, hurly-burly, spin, stir, tumult **10 give (something) a whirl** *Informal* = **attempt**, have a bash, have a crack (*inf.*), have a go (*inf.*), have a shot (*inf.*), have a stab (*inf.*), have a whack (*inf.*), try

whirlwind *n* **1** = **tornado**, dust devil, waterspout ◆ *modifier* **2b** = **rapid**, hasty, headlong, impetuous, impulsive, lightning, quick, quickie (*inf.*), rash, short, speedy, swift
Antonyms *adj* ≠ **rapid**: calculated, cautious, considered, deliberate, measured, prudent, slow, unhurried

whisk *vb* **1** = **flick**, brush, sweep, whip, wipe **3** = **speed**, barrel (along) (*inf., chiefly US & Canad.*), burn rubber (*inf.*), dart, dash, fly, hasten, hurry, race, rush, shoot, sweep, tear **4** = **beat**, fluff up, whip ◆ *n* **6** = **flick**, brush, sweep, whip, wipe **7** = **beater**

whisky *n* = **Scotch**, barley-bree, bourbon, firewater, John Barleycorn, malt, rye, usquebaugh (*Gaelic*)

whisper *vb* **1** = **murmur**, breathe, say softly, speak in hushed tones, utter under the breath **2** = **gossip**, hint, insinuate, intimate, murmur, spread rumours **3** = **rustle**, hiss, murmur, sigh, sough, susurrate (*literary*), swish ◆ *n* **5** = **murmur**, hushed tone, low voice, soft voice, undertone **7** = **rustle**, hiss, murmur, sigh, sighing, soughing, susurration *or* susurrus (*literary*), swish **8** = **hint**, breath, fraction, shadow, suggestion, suspicion, tinge, trace, whiff **9** *Informal* = **rumour**, buzz, dirt (*US sl.*), gossip, innuendo, insinuation, report, scuttlebutt (*US sl.*), word

whistle. perfectly clean or clear. **15 wet one's whistle.** *Inf.* to take an alcoholic drink. ◆ See also **whistle for, whistle up.** [OE *hwistlian*]

whistle-blower *n Inf.* a person who informs on someone or puts a stop to something.

whistle for *vb (intr, prep) Inf.* to seek or expect in vain.

whistler ('wɪslə) *n* **1** a person or thing that whistles. **2** *Radio.* an atmospheric disturbance picked up by radio receivers, caused by the electromagnetic radiation produced by lightning. **3** any of various birds having a whistling call, such as certain Australian flycatchers. **4** any of various North American marmots.

whistle stop *n* **1** *US & Canad.* **1a** a minor railway station where trains stop only on signal. **1b** a small town having such a station. **2a** a brief appearance in a town, esp. by a political candidate. **2b** *(as modifier): a whistle-stop tour.*

whistle up *vb (tr, adv)* to call or summon (a person or animal) by whistling.

whit ❶ (wɪt) *n (usually used with a negative)* the smallest particle; iota; jot: *he has changed not a whit.* [C15: prob. var. of WIGHT]

Whit (wɪt) *n* **1** See **Whitsuntide.** ◆ *adj* **2** of or relating to Whitsuntide.

white ❶ (waɪt) *adj* **1** having no hue, owing to the reflection of all or almost all incident light. **2** (of light, such as sunlight) consisting of all the colours of the spectrum or produced by certain mixtures of primary colours, as red, green, and blue. **3** comparatively white or whitish-grey or having parts of this colour: *white clover.* **4** (of an animal) having pale-coloured or white skin, fur, or feathers. **5** bloodless or pale, as from pain, emotion, etc. **6** (of hair, etc.) grey, usually from age. **7** benevolent or without malicious intent: *white magic.* **8** colourless or transparent: *white glass.* **9** capped with or accompanied by snow: *a white Christmas.* **10** blank, as an unprinted area of a page. **11** (of coffee or tea) with milk or cream. **12** (of wine) made from pale grapes or from black grapes separated from their skins. **13** denoting flour, or bread made from flour, that has had part of the grain removed. **14** *Physics.* having or characterized by a continuous distribution of energy, wavelength, or frequency: *white noise.* **15** *Inf.* honourable or generous. **16** *Poetic or arch.* having a fair complexion; blond. **17 bleed white.** to deprive slowly of resources. ◆ *n* **18** a white colour. **19** the condition of being white; whiteness. **20** the white or lightly coloured part of something. **21** (usually preceded by *the*) the viscous fluid that surrounds the yolk of a bird's egg, esp. a hen's egg; albumen. **22** *Anat.* the white part (sclera) of the eyeball. **23** any of various butterflies having white wings with scanty black markings. **24** *Chess, draughts.* **24a** a white or light-coloured piece or square. **24b** the player playing with such pieces. **25** anything that has or is characterized by a white colour, such as a white paint or white clothing. **26** *Inf.* white wine: *a bottle of white.* **27** *Archery.* the outer ring of the target, having the lowest score. ◆ *vb* **whites, whiting, whited. 28** *Obs.* to make or become white. ◆ See also **white out, whites.** [OE *hwīt*]
▸ **'whitely** *adv* ▸ **'whiteness** *n* ▸ **'whitish** *adj*

White (waɪt) *n* **1** a member of the Caucasoid race. **2** a person of European ancestry. ◆ *adj* **3** denoting or relating to a White or Whites.

white admiral *n* a butterfly of Eurasia having brown wings with white markings.

white ant *n* another name for **termite.**

whitebait ('waɪt,beɪt) *n* **1** the young of herrings, sprats, etc., cooked and eaten whole as a delicacy. **2** any of various small silvery fishes. [C18: from its formerly having been used as bait]

whitebeam ('waɪt,biːm) *n* a N temperate tree having leaves that are densely hairy on the undersurface and hard timber.

white blood cell *n* a nontechnical name for **leucocyte.**

whitecap ('waɪt,kæp) *n* a wave with a white broken crest.

white cedar *n* either of two coniferous trees of North America, having scalelike leaves.

white clover *n* a Eurasian clover plant with rounded white flower heads: cultivated as a forage plant.

white coal *n* water, esp. when flowing and providing a potential source of usable power.

white-collar ❶ *adj* of or designating nonmanual and usually salaried workers employed in professional and clerical occupations.

white currant *n* a cultivated N temperate shrub having small rounded white edible berries.

whitedamp ('waɪt,dæmp) *n* a mixture of poisonous gases, mainly carbon monoxide, occurring in coal mines.

whited sepulchre *n* a hypocrite. [allusion to Matthew 23:27]

white dwarf *n* one of a large class of small faint stars of enormous density, thought to mark the final stage in the evolution of a sun-like star.

white elephant *n* **1** a rare albino variety of the Indian elephant, regarded as sacred in parts of S Asia. **2** a possession that is unwanted by its owner. **3** a rare or valuable possession the upkeep of which is very expensive.

White Ensign *n* the ensign of the Royal Navy and the Royal Yacht Squadron, having a red cross on a white background with the Union Jack at the upper corner of the vertical edge alongside the hoist.

white-eye *n* a songbird of Africa, Australia, New Zealand, and Asia, having a greenish plumage with a white ring around each eye.

white feather *n* **1** a symbol or mark of cowardice. **2 show the white feather.** to act in a cowardly manner. [from the belief that a white feather in a gamecock's tail was a sign of a poor fighter]

whitefish ('waɪt,fɪʃ) *n, pl* **whitefish** *or* **whitefishes.** a food fish typically of deep cold lakes of the N hemisphere, having large silvery scales and a small head.

white fish *n* (in the Brit. fishing industry) any edible marine fish or invertebrate excluding herrings but including trout, salmon, and all shellfish.

white flag *n* a white flag or a piece of white cloth hoisted to signify surrender or request a truce.

white flour *n* flour that consists substantially of the starchy endosperm of wheat, most of the bran and the germ having been removed by the milling process.

whitefly ('waɪt,flaɪ) *n, pl* **whiteflies.** any of a family of insects typically having a body covered with powdery wax. Many are pests of greenhouse crops.

white friar *n* a Carmelite friar, so called because of the white cloak that forms part of the habit of this order.

white gold *n* any of various white lustrous hard-wearing alloys containing gold together with platinum and palladium and sometimes smaller amounts of silver, nickel, or copper.

white goods *pl n* **1** household linen such as sheets, towels, tablecloths, etc. **2** large household appliances, such as refrigerators or cookers.

Whitehall (,waɪt'hɔːl) *n* **1** a street in London stretching from Trafalgar Square to the Houses of Parliament: site of the main government offices. **2** the British Government.

white heat *n* **1** intense heat characterized by emission of white light. **2** *Inf.* a state of intense excitement or activity.

white hope *n Inf.* a person who is expected to bring honour or glory to his group, team, etc.

white horse *n* **1** the outline of a horse carved into the side of a chalk hill, usually dating to the Neolithic, Bronze, or Iron Ages. **2** *(usually pl)* a wave with a white broken crest.

white-hot *adj* **1** at such a high temperature that white light is emitted. **2** *Inf.* in a state of intense emotion.

White House *n* **the. 1** the official Washington residence of the president of the US. **2** the US presidency.

white knight *n* a champion or rescuer, esp. a person or organization that rescues a company from financial difficulties, an unwelcome takeover bid, etc.

white-knuckle *adj* causing or experiencing fear or anxiety: *a white-knuckle fairground ride.*

white lead (lɛd) *n* **1** a white solid usually regarded as a mixture of lead carbonate and lead hydroxide; basic lead carbonate: used in paint and in making putty and ointments for the treatment of burns. **2** either of two similar white pigments based on lead sulphate or lead silicate.

white leg *n* another name for **milk leg.**

white lie *n* a minor or unimportant lie, esp. one uttered in the interests of tact or politeness.

white light *n* light that contains all the wavelengths of visible light at approximately equal intensities, as in sunlight.

white-livered *adj* **1** lacking in spirit or courage. **2** pallid and unhealthy in appearance.

White man's burden *n* the supposed duty of the White race to bring education and Western culture to the non-White inhabitants of their colonies.

white matter *n* the whitish tissue of the brain and spinal cord, consisting mainly of nerve fibres covered with a protective white fatlike substance.

white meat *n* any meat that is light in colour, such as veal or the breast of turkey.

white metal *n* any of various alloys, such as Babbitt metal, used for bearings.

white meter *n Brit.* an electricity meter used to record the consumption of off-peak electricity.

whiten ❶ ('waɪtᵊn) *vb* to make or become white or whiter.
▸ **'whitener** *n* ▸ **'whitening** *n*

white noise *n* sound or electrical noise that has a relatively wide continuous range of frequencies of uniform intensity.

white oak *n* a large oak tree of E North America, having pale bark, leaves with rounded lobes, and heavy light-coloured wood.

white out *vb (adv)* **1** *(intr)* to lose or lack daylight visibility owing to snow or fog. **2** *(tr)* to create or leave white spaces in (printed or other matter). ◆ *n* **whiteout. 3** a polar atmospheric condition consisting of lack of visibility and sense of distance and direction due to a uniform whiteness of a heavy cloud cover and snow-covered ground, which reflects almost all the light it receives.

white paper *n (often caps.)* an official government report in any of a

THESAURUS

Antonyms *vb* ≠ **murmur:** bawl, bellow, clamour, roar, shout, thunder, yell

whit *n* = **bit,** atom, crumb, dash, drop, fragment, grain, iota, jot, least bit, little, mite, modicum, particle, piece, pinch, scrap, shred, speck, trace

white *adj* **5** = **pale,** ashen, bloodless, ghastly, grey, like death warmed up (*inf.*), pallid, pasty, wan, waxen, wheyfaced **6** = **silver,** grey, grizzled, hoary, snowy
Antonyms *adj* ≠ **pale:** black, dark

white-collar *adj* = **clerical,** executive, nonmanual, office, professional, salaried

whiten *vb* = **pale,** blanch, bleach, blench, etiolate, fade, go white, turn pale
Antonyms *vb* blacken, colour, darken

number of countries, which sets out the government's policy on a matter that is or will come before Parliament.

white pepper *n* a condiment, less pungent than black pepper, made from the husked dried beans of the pepper plant.

white pine *n* a North American coniferous tree having blue-green needle-like leaves, hanging brown cones, and rough bark.

white poplar *n* **1** Also called: **abele.** a Eurasian tree having leaves covered with dense silvery-white hairs. **2** another name for **tulipwood** (sense 1).

white rose *n English history.* an emblem of the House of York.

White Russian *adj, n* another term for **Belarussian.**

whites (waɪts) *pl n* **1** household linen or cotton goods, such as sheets. **2** white or off-white clothing, such as that worn for playing cricket.

white sale *n* a sale of household linens at reduced prices.

white sauce *n* a thick sauce made from flour, butter, seasonings, and milk or stock.

white settler *n* a well-off incomer to a district who takes advantage of what it has to offer without regard to the local inhabitants. [C20: from earlier colonial sense]

white slave *n* a girl or woman forced or sold into prostitution.
▸**white slavery** *n* ▸**ˌwhite-ˈslaver** *n*

white spirit *n* a colourless liquid obtained from petroleum and used as a substitute for turpentine.

white spruce *n* a N North American spruce tree with grey bark.

white squall *n* a violent highly localized weather disturbance at sea, in which the surface of the water is whipped to a white spray by the winds.

whitethorn (ˈwaɪtˌθɔːn) *n* another name for **hawthorn.**

whitethroat (ˈwaɪtˌθrəʊt) *n* either of two Old World warblers having a greyish-brown plumage with a white throat and underparts.

white tie *n* **1** a white bow tie worn as part of a man's formal evening dress. **2a** formal evening dress for men. **2b** (*as modifier*): *a white-tie occasion.*

white trash *n Disparaging.* **a** poor White people living in the US, esp. the South. **b** (*as modifier*): *white-trash culture.*

whitewall (ˈwaɪtˌwɔːl) *n* a pneumatic tyre having white sidewalls.

whitewash Ⓣ (ˈwaɪtˌwɒʃ) *n* **1** a substance used for whitening walls and other surfaces, consisting of a suspension of lime or whiting in water. **2** *Inf.* deceptive or specious words or actions intended to conceal defects, gloss over failings, etc. **3** *Inf.* a defeat in a sporting contest in which the loser is beaten in every match, game, etc. in a series. ◆ *vb* (*tr*) **4** to cover with whitewash. **5** *Inf.* to conceal, gloss over, or suppress. **6** *Inf.* to defeat (an opponent or opposing team) by winning every match in a series.
▸**ˈwhiteˌwasher** *n*

white water *n* **1** a stretch of water with a broken foamy surface, as in rapids. **2** light-coloured sea water, esp. over shoals or shallows.

white whale *n* a small white toothed whale of northern waters. Also called: **beluga.**

whitewood (ˈwaɪtˌwʊd) *n* **1** any of various trees with light-coloured wood, such as the tulip tree, basswood, and cottonwood. **2** the wood of any of these trees.

whitey *or* **whity** (ˈwaɪtɪ) *n, pl* **whiteys** *or* **whities.** *Chiefly US.* (used contemptuously by Black people) a White man or White men collectively.

whither (ˈwɪðə) *Arch. or poetic.* ◆ *adv* **1** to what place? **2** to what end or purpose? ◆ *conj* **3** to whatever place, purpose, etc. [OE *hwider, hwæder;* Mod. E form infl. by HITHER]

whithersoever (ˌwɪðəsəʊˈɛvə) *adv, conj Arch. or poetic.* to whichever place.

whiting[1] (ˈwaɪtɪŋ) *n* **1** an important gadoid food fish of European seas, having a dark back with silvery sides and underparts. **2** any of various similar fishes. [C15: ?from OE *hwītling*]

whiting[2] (ˈwaɪtɪŋ) *n* white chalk that has been ground and washed, used in making whitewash, metal polish, etc. Also called: **whitening.**

whitlow (ˈwɪtləʊ) *n* any pussy inflammation of the end of a finger or toe. [C14: changed from *whitflaw,* from WHITE + FLAW[1]]

Whitsun (ˈwɪtsᵊn) *n* **1** short for **Whitsuntide.** ◆ *adj* **2** of or relating to Whit Sunday or Whitsuntide.

Whitsunday (ˌhwɪtˈsʌndɪ, ˌwɪt-) *n* (in Scotland) May 15, one of the four quarter days.

Whit Sunday *n* the seventh Sunday after Easter, observed as a feast in commemoration of the descent of the Holy Spirit on the apostles. Also called: **Pentecost.** [OE *hwīta sunnandæg* white Sunday, prob. after the ancient custom of wearing white robes at or after baptism]

Whitsuntide (ˈwɪtsᵊnˌtaɪd) *n* the week that begins with Whit Sunday, esp. the first three days.

whittle Ⓣ (ˈwɪtᵊl) *vb* **whittles, whittling, whittled. 1** to cut or shave strips or pieces from (wood, a stick, etc.), esp. with a knife. **2** (*tr*) to make or shape by paring or shaving. **3** (*tr;* often foll. by *away, down,* etc.) to reduce, destroy, or wear away gradually. [C16: var. of C15 *thwittle* large knife, ult. from OE *thwītan* to cut]

whity (ˈwaɪtɪ) *n, pl* **whities. 1** *Inf.* a variant spelling of **whitey.** ◆ *adj* **2a** whitish in colour. **2b** (*in combination*): *whity-brown.*

whizz *or* **whiz** (wɪz) *vb* **whizzes, whizzing, whizzed. 1** to make or cause to make a loud humming or buzzing sound. **2** to move or cause to move with such a sound. **3** (*intr*) *Inf.* to move or go rapidly. ◆ *n, pl* **whizzes. 4** a loud humming or buzzing sound. **5** *Inf.* Also: **wizz.** a person who is extremely skilful at some activity. **6** a slang word for **amphetamine.** [C16: imit.]

whizz-bang *or* **whiz-bang** *n* **1** a World War I shell that travelled at such high velocity that the sound of its flight was heard only an instant before the sound of its explosion. **2** a type of firework that jumps around emitting a whizzing sound and occasional bangs.

whizz kid Ⓣ, **whiz kid,** *or* **wiz kid** *n Inf.* a person who is pushing, enthusiastic, and outstandingly successful for his or her age. [C20: from WHIZZ, ? infl. by WIZARD]

whizzy (ˈwɪzɪ) *adj* **whizzier, whizziest.** *Inf.* using sophisticated technology to produce vivid effects: *a whizzy new computer game.*

who (huː) *pron* **1** which person? what person? used in direct and indirect questions: *he can't remember who did it; who met you?* **2** used to introduce relative clauses with antecedents referring to human beings: *the people who lived here have left.* **3** the one or ones who; whoever: *bring who you want.* [OE *hwā*]

> **USAGE NOTE** See at **whom.**

WHO *abbrev. for* World Health Organization.

whoa (wəʊ) *interj* a command used esp. to horses to stop or slow down. [C19: var. of HO]

who-does-what *adj* (of a dispute, strike, etc.) relating to the separation of kinds of work performed by different trade unions.

whodunnit *or* **whodunit** (huːˈdʌnɪt) *n Inf.* a novel, play, etc., concerned with a crime, usually murder.

whoever (huːˈɛvə) *pron* **1** any person who: *whoever wants it can have it.* **2** no matter who: *I'll come round tomorrow, whoever may be here.* **3** an intensive form of *who,* used in questions: *whoever could have thought that?* **4** *Inf.* an unspecified person: *give those to Cathy or whoever.*

whole Ⓣ (həʊl) *adj* **1** containing all the component parts necessary to form a total; complete: *a whole apple.* **2** constituting the full quantity, extent, etc. **3** uninjured or undamaged. **4** healthy. **5** having no fractional or decimal part; integral: *a whole number.* **6** designating a relationship by descent from the same parents; full: *whole brothers.* **7 out of whole cloth.** *US & Canad. inf.* entirely without a factual basis. ◆ *adv* **8** in an undivided or unbroken piece: *to swallow a plum whole.* ◆ *n* **9** all the parts, elements, etc., of a thing. **10** an assemblage of parts viewed together as a unit. **11** a thing complete in itself. **12 as a whole.** considered altogether; completely. **13 on the whole. 13a** taking all things into consideration. **13b** in general. [OE *hāl, hǣl*]
▸**ˈwholeness** *n*

whole blood *n* blood for transfusion from which none of the elements has been removed.

wholefood (ˈhəʊlˌfuːd) *n* (*sometimes pl*) **a** food that has been refined or processed as little as possible and is eaten in its natural state, such as brown rice, wholemeal flour, etc. **b** (*as modifier*): *a wholefood restaurant.*

wholehearted Ⓣ (ˌhəʊlˈhɑːtɪd) *adj* done, acted, given, etc., with total sincerity, enthusiasm, or commitment.
▸**ˌwholeˈheartedly** *adv*

whole hog *n Sl.* the whole or total extent (esp. in **go the whole hog**).

wholemeal (ˈhəʊlˌmiːl) *adj Brit.* (of flour, bread, etc.) made from the entire wheat kernel. Also called (esp. US and Canad.): **whole-wheat.**

whole milk *n* milk from which no constituent has been removed.

whole note *n* the usual US and Canad. name for **semibreve.**

whole number *n* **1** an integer. **2** a natural number.

wholesale Ⓣ (ˈhəʊlˌseɪl) *n* **1** the business of selling goods to retailers in larger quantities than they are sold to final consumers but in smaller

THESAURUS

whitewash *Informal n* **2** = **cover-up**, camouflage, concealment, deception, extenuation ◆ *vb* **5** = **cover up**, camouflage, conceal, extenuate, gloss over, make light of, suppress
Antonyms *vb* ≠ **cover up:** disclose, expose, lay bare, reveal, uncover, unmask, unveil

whittle *vb* **1, 2** = **carve**, cut, hew, pare, shape, shave, trim **3** *often foll. by* **away, down,** *etc.* = **reduce**, consume, destroy, eat away, erode, undermine, wear away

whizz kid *n Informal* = **prodigy**, child genius, genius, mastermind, talent, whizz (*inf.*), wonder kid, wunderkind

whole *adj* **1, 2** = **complete**, entire, full, in one piece, integral, total, unabridged, uncut, undivided **3** = **undamaged**, faultless, flawless, good, in one piece, intact, inviolate, mint, perfect, sound, unbroken, unharmed, unhurt, unimpaired, uninjured, unmutilated, unscathed, untouched **4** = **healthy**, able-bodied, better, cured, fit, hale, healed, in fine fettle, in good health, recovered, robust, sound, strong, well ◆ *adv* **8** = **in one piece**, in one ◆ *n* **9** = **total**, aggregate, all, everything, lot, sum total, the entire amount **10** = **totality**, ensemble, entirety, entity, fullness, piece, unit, unity **13 on the whole: a** = **generally**, all things considered, by and large, taking everything into consideration **b** = **as a rule**, for the most part, in general, in the main, mostly, predominantly
Antonyms *adj* ≠ **complete:** cut, divided, fragmented, incomplete, in pieces, partial ≠ **undamaged:** broken, damaged ≠ **healthy:** ailing, diseased, ill, sick, sickly, under-the-weather, unwell ◆ *n* ≠ **totality:** bit, component, constituent, division, element, fragment, part, piece, portion

wholehearted *adj* = **sincere**, committed, complete, dedicated, determined, devoted, earnest, emphatic, enthusiastic, genuine, heartfelt, hearty, real, true, unfeigned, unqualified, unreserved, unstinting, warm, zealous
Antonyms *adj* cool, grudging, half-hearted, insincere, qualified, reserved, unreal

wholesale *adj* **3** = **extensive**, all-inclusive, broad, comprehensive, far-reaching, indiscrim-

quantities than they are purchased from manufacturers. Cf. **retail** (sense 1). ◆ *adj* **2** of or engaged in such business. **3** made, done, etc., on a large scale or without discrimination. ◆ *adv* **4** on a large scale or without discrimination. ◆ *vb* **wholesales, wholesaling, wholesaled. 5** to sell (goods) at wholesale.
▸ **'whole,saler** *n*

wholesale price index *n* an indicator of price changes in the wholesale market.

wholesome ⓣ ('həʊlsəm) *adj* **1** conducive to health or physical wellbeing. **2** conducive to moral wellbeing. **3** characteristic or suggestive of health or wellbeing, esp. in appearance. [C12: from WHOLE (healthy) + -SOME[1]]
▸ **'wholesomely** *adv* ▸ **'wholesomeness** *n*

whole tone *or US & Canad.* **whole step** *n* an interval of two semitones. Often shortened to **tone.**

whole-tone scale *n* either of two scales produced by commencing on one of any two notes a chromatic semitone apart and proceeding upwards or downwards in whole tones for an octave.

whole-wheat *adj* another term (esp. US and Canad.) for **wholemeal.**

who'll (hu:l) *contraction of* who will *or* who shall.

wholly ⓣ ('həʊllɪ) *adv* **1** completely, totally, or entirely. **2** without exception; exclusively.

whom (hu:m) *pron* the objective form of *who,* used when *who* is not the subject of its own clause: *whom did you say you had seen? he can't remember whom he saw.* [OE *hwām,* dative of *hwā* who]

USAGE NOTE It was formerly considered correct to use *whom* whenever the objective form of *who* was required. This is no longer thought to be necessary and the objective form *who* is now commonly used, even in formal writing: *there were several people there who he had met before. Who* cannot be used directly after a preposition – the preposition is usually displaced, as in *the man (who) he sold his car to.* In formal writing *whom* is preferred in sentences like these: *the man to whom he sold his car.* There are some types of sentence in which *who* cannot be used: *the refugees, many of whom were old and ill, were allowed across the border.*

whomever (hu:m'ɛvə) *pron* the objective form of *whoever: I'll hire whomever I can find.*

whoop ⓣ (wu:p) *vb* **whoops, whooping, whooped. 1** to utter (speech) with loud cries, as of excitement. **2** (hu:p). *Med.* to cough convulsively with a crowing sound. **3** (of certain birds) to utter (a hooting cry). **4** (*tr*) to urge on or call with or as if with whoops. **5** (wʊp, wu:p). **whoop it up.** *Inf.* **5a** to indulge in a noisy celebration. **5b** *Chiefly US.* to arouse enthusiasm. ◆ *n* **6** a loud cry, esp. one expressing excitement. **7** (hu:p). *Med.* the convulsive crowing sound made during whooping cough. [C14: imit.]

whoopee *Inf.* ◆ *interj* (wʊ'pi:). **1** an exclamation of joy, excitement, etc. ◆ *n* ('wʊpi:). **2 make whoopee. 2a** to engage in noisy merrymaking. **2b** to make love.

whoopee cushion *n* a joke cushion that emits a sound like the breaking of wind when someone sits on it.

whooper *or* **whooper swan** ('wu:pə) *n* a large Old World swan having a black bill with a yellow base and a noisy whooping cry.

whooping cough ('hu:pɪŋ) *n* an acute infectious disease characterized by coughing spasms that end with a shrill crowing sound on inspiration. Technical name: **pertussis.**

whoops (wʊps) *interj* an exclamation of surprise or of apology.

whoosh *or* **woosh** (wʊʃ) *n* **1** a hissing or rushing sound. ◆ *vb* **2** (*intr*) to make or move with such a sound.

whop (wɒp) *Inf.* ◆ *vb* **whops, whopping, whopped. 1** (*tr*) to strike, beat, or thrash. **2** (*tr*) to defeat utterly. **3** (*intr*) to drop or fall. ◆ *n* **4** a heavy blow or the sound made by such a blow. [C14: var. of *wap,* ? imit.]

whopper ⓣ ('wɒpə) *n Inf.* **1** anything uncommonly large of its kind. **2** a big lie. [C18: from WHOP]

whopping ⓣ ('wɒpɪŋ) *adj Inf.* uncommonly large.

whore ⓣ (hɔ:) *n* **1** a prostitute or promiscuous woman: often a term of abuse. ◆ *vb* **whores, whoring, whored.** (*intr*) **2** to be or act as a prostitute. **3** (of a man) to have promiscuous sexual relations, esp. with prostitutes. **4** (often foll. by *after*) to seek that which is immoral, idolatrous, etc. [OE *hōre*]
▸ **'whoredom** *n* ▸ **'whorish** *adj*

whorehouse ⓣ ('hɔ:,haʊs) *n* another word for **brothel.**

whoremonger ('hɔ:,mʌŋgə) *n* a person who consorts with whores; lecher. Also called: **whoremaster.**
▸ **'whore,mongery** *n*

whoreson ('hɔ:sən) *Arch.* ◆ *n* **1** a bastard. **2** a scoundrel; wretch. ◆ *adj* **3** vile or hateful.

whorl ⓣ (wɜ:l) *n* **1** *Bot.* a radial arrangement of petals, stamens, leaves, etc., around a stem. **2** *Zool.* a single turn in a spiral shell. **3** anything shaped like a coil. [C15: prob. var. of *wherville* whirl, infl. by Du. *worvel*]
▸ **whorled** *adj*

whortleberry ('wɜ:tᵊl,berɪ) *n, pl* **whortleberries. 1** Also called: **bilberry, blaeberry, huckleberry.** a small Eurasian ericaceous shrub with greenish-pink flowers and edible sweet blackish berries. **2** the fruit of this shrub. **3 bog whortleberry.** a related plant of mountain regions, having pink flowers and black fruits. [C16: SW English dialect var. of *hurtleberry,* from ?]

who's (hu:z) *contraction of* who is *or* who has.

whose (hu:z) *determiner* **1a** of whom? belonging to whom? used in direct and indirect questions: *I told him whose fault it was; whose car is this?* **1b** (*as pron*): *whose is that?* **2** of whom; of which: used as a relative pronoun: *a house whose windows are broken; a man whose reputation has suffered.* [OE *hwæs,* genitive of *hwā* who & *hwæt* what]

whoso ('hu:səʊ) *pron* an archaic word for **whoever.**

whosoever (,hu:səʊ'ɛvə) *pron* an archaic or formal word for **whoever.**

who's who *n* a book or list containing the names and short biographies of famous people.

why (waɪ) *adv* **1a** for what reason?: *why are you here?* **1b** (*used in indirect questions*): *tell me why you're here.* ◆ *pron* **2** for or because of which: *there is no reason why he shouldn't come.* ◆ *n, pl* **whys. 3** (*usually pl*) the cause of something (esp. in **the whys and wherefores**). ◆ *interj* **4** an introductory expression of surprise, indignation, etc.: *why, don't be silly!* [OE *hwī*]

whydah *or* **whidah** ('wɪdə) *n* any of various predominantly black African weaverbirds, the males of which grow very long tail feathers in the breeding season. Also called: **whydah bird, whidah bird, widow bird.** [C18: after a town in Benin in W Africa]

WI *abbrev. for:* **1** West Indian. **2** West Indies. **3** Wisconsin. **4** (in Britain) Women's Institute.

Wicca ('wɪkə) *n* the cult or practice of witchcraft. [C20 revival of OE *wicca* witch]
▸ **'Wiccan** *n, adj*

wick[1] (wɪk) *n* **1** a cord or band of loosely twisted or woven fibres, as in a candle, that supplies fuel to a flame by capillary action. **2 get on (someone's) wick.** *Brit. sl.* to cause irritation to (someone). [OE *weoce*]

wick[2] (wɪk) *n Arch.* a village or hamlet. [OE *wīc;* rel. to *-wich* in place names]

wicked ⓣ ('wɪkɪd) *adj* **1a** morally bad. **1b** (*as collective n;* preceded by *the*): *the wicked.* **2** mischievous or roguish in a playful way: *a wicked grin.* **3** causing injury or harm. **4** troublesome, unpleasant, or offensive. **5** *Sl.* very good. [C13: from dialect *wick,* from OE *wicca* sorcerer, *wicce* witch]
▸ **'wickedly** *adv* ▸ **'wickedness** *n*

THESAURUS

inate, mass, sweeping, wide-ranging ◆ *adv* **4** = **extensively**, all at once, comprehensively, indiscriminately, on a large scale, without exception
Antonyms *adj* ≠ **extensive:** confined, discriminate, limited, partial, restricted, selective

wholesome *adj* **1** = **healthy**, beneficial, good, healthful, health-giving, helpful, hygienic, invigorating, nourishing, nutritious, salubrious, salutary, sanitary, strengthening **2** = **moral**, apple-pie (*inf.*), clean, decent, edifying, ethical, exemplary, honourable, improving, innocent, nice, pure, respectable, righteous, squeaky-clean, uplifting, virtuous, worthy
Antonyms *adj* ≠ **healthy:** putrid, rotten, unhealthy, unhygienic, unwholesome ≠ **moral:** blue, corrupt, degrading, dirty, dishonest, evil, filthy, immoral, lewd, obscene, pernicious, pornographic, tasteless, trashy, unprincipled, unwholesome, X-rated (*inf.*)

wholly *adv* **1** = **completely**, all, altogether, comprehensively, entirely, fully, heart and soul, in every respect, one hundred per cent (*inf.*), perfectly, thoroughly, totally, utterly **2** = **solely**, exclusively, only, without exception
Antonyms *adv* ≠ **completely:** incompletely, in part, moderately, partially, partly, relatively, slightly, somewhat

whoop *n* **6** = **cry**, cheer, halloo, holler (*inf.*), hoot, hurrah, scream, shout, shriek, yell

whopper *Informal n* **1** = **giant**, colossus, crackerjack, jumbo (*inf.*), leviathan, mammoth, monster **2** = **big lie**, fable, fabrication, falsehood, tall story (*inf.*), untruth

whopping *adj Informal* = **gigantic**, big, elephantine, enormous, extraordinary, giant, great, huge, humongous *or* humungous (*US sl.*), large, mammoth, massive, monstrous, prodigious, tremendous, whacking (*inf.*)

whore *n* **1** = **prostitute**, call girl, cocotte, courtesan, demimondaine, demirep (*rare*), fallen woman, *fille de joie*, harlot, hooker (*US sl.*), hustler (*US & Canad. sl.*), lady of the night, loose woman, scrubber (*Brit. & Austral. sl.*), slag (*Brit. sl.*), streetwalker, strumpet, tart (*inf.*), trollop, woman of easy virtue, working girl (*facetious sl.*) ◆ *vb* **2** = **prostitute oneself**, be on the game (*sl.*), hustle (*US & Canad. sl.*), sell one's body, sell oneself, solicit, walk the streets **3** = **sleep around** (*inf.*), fornicate, lech *or* letch (*inf.*), wanton, wench (*arch.*), womanize

whorehouse *n* = **brothel**, bagnio, bordello, cathouse (*US sl.*), disorderly house, house of ill fame *or* repute, house of prostitution, knocking-shop (*Brit. sl.*)

whorl *n* **3** = **swirl**, coil, corkscrew, helix, spiral, twist, vortex

wicked *adj* **1** = **bad**, abandoned, abominable, amoral, atrocious, black-hearted, corrupt, debased, depraved, devilish, dissolute, egregious, evil, fiendish, flagitious, foul, guilty, heinous, immoral, impious, iniquitous, irreligious, maleficent, nefarious, scandalous, shameful, sinful, sink, unprincipled, unrighteous, vicious, vile, villainous, worthless **2** = **mischievous**, arch, impish, incorrigible, naughty, rascally, roguish **3** = **harmful**, acute, agonizing, awful, crashing, destructive, dreadful, fearful, fierce, gut-wrenching, injurious, intense, mighty, painful, severe, terrible **4** = **troublesome**, bothersome, difficult, distressing, galling, offensive, trying, unpleasant **5** *Slang* = **expert**, adept, adroit, deft, masterly, mighty, outstanding, powerful, skilful, strong
Antonyms *adj* ≠ **bad:** benevolent, ethical, good, honourable, moral, noble, principled, virtuous ≠ **mischievous:** good, mannerly, obedient, well-

wicker ('wɪkə) *n* **1** a slender flexible twig or shoot, esp. of willow. **2** short for **wickerwork.** ◆ *adj* **3** made of, consisting of, or constructed from wicker. [C14: from ON]

wickerwork ('wɪkə,wɜːk) *n* **a** a material consisting of woven wicker. **b** (*as modifier*): *a wickerwork chair.*

wicket ('wɪkɪt) *n* **1** a small door or gate, esp. one that is near to or part of a larger one. **2** *Chiefly US.* a small window or opening in a door, esp. one fitted with a grating or glass pane. **3** a small sluicegate. **4a** *Cricket.* either of two constructions, 22 yards apart, consisting of three stumps stuck in the ground with two wooden bails resting on top, at which the batsman stands. **4b** the strip of ground between these. **4c** a batsman's turn at batting or the period during which two batsmen bat. **4d** the act or instance of a batsman being got out: *the bowler took six wickets.* **5 keep wicket.** to act as a wicketkeeper. **6 on a good, sticky,** etc., **wicket.** *Inf.* in an advantageous, awkward, etc., situation. [C18: from OF *wiket*]

wicketkeeper ('wɪkɪt,kiːpə) *n Cricket.* the player on the fielding side positioned directly behind the wicket.

wickiup, wikiup, *or* **wickyup** ('wɪkɪ,ʌp) *n US & Canad.* a crude shelter made of brushwood or grass and having an oval frame, esp. of a kind used by nomadic Native Americans now in the Oklahoma area. [C19: of Amerind origin]

widdershins ('wɪdə,ʃɪnz) *adv Chiefly Scot.* a variant spelling of **withershins.**

wide ➊ (waɪd) *adj* **1** having a great extent from side to side. **2** spacious or extensive. **3a** (*postpositive*) having a specified extent, esp. from side to side: *two yards wide.* **3b** (*in combination*): extending throughout: *nationwide.* **4** remote from the desired point, mark, etc.: *your guess is wide of the mark.* **5** (of eyes) opened fully. **6** loose, full, or roomy: *wide trousers.* **7** exhibiting a considerable spread: *a wide variation.* **8** *Phonetics.* another word for **lax** (sense 4) or **open** (sense 32). ◆ *adv* **9** over an extensive area: *to travel far and wide.* **10** to the full extent: *he opened the door wide.* **11** far from the desired point, mark, etc. ◆ *n* **12** (in cricket) a bowled ball that is outside the batsman's reach and scores a run for the batting side. [OE *wīd*]
▸ **'widely** *adv* ▸ **'wideness** *n* ▸ **'widish** *adj*

wide-angle lens *n* a lens system on a camera that has a small focal length and therefore can cover an angle of view of 60° or more.

wide-awake ➊ *adj* (**wide awake** *when postpositive*). **1** fully awake. **2** keen, alert, or observant. ◆ *n* **3** Also called: **wide-awake hat.** a hat with a low crown and very wide brim.

wide-body *adj* (of an aircraft) having a wide fuselage, esp. wide enough to contain three rows of seats abreast.

wide boy *n Brit. sl.* a man who is prepared to use unscrupulous methods to progress or make money.

wide-eyed ➊ *adj* innocent or credulous.

widen ➊ ('waɪdᵊn) *vb* to make or become wide or wider.
▸ **'widener** *n*

wide-open ➊ *adj* (**wide open** *when postpositive*). **1** open to the full extent. **2** (*postpositive*) exposed to attack; vulnerable. **3** uncertain as to outcome. **4** *US inf.* (of a town or city) lax in the enforcement of certain laws, esp. those relating to the sale of alcohol, gambling, etc.

wide receiver *n American football.* a player whose function is to catch long passes from the quarterback.

widespread ➊ ('waɪd,spred) *adj* **1** extending over a wide area. **2** accepted by or occurring among many people.

widgeon ('wɪdʒən) *n* a variant spelling of **wigeon.**

widget ('wɪdʒɪt) *n Inf.* any small mechanism or device, the name of which is unknown or temporarily forgotten. [C20: changed from GADGET]

widow ('wɪdəʊ) *n* **1** a woman whose husband has died, esp. one who has not remarried. **2** (*with a modifier*) *Inf.* a woman whose husband frequently leaves her alone while he indulges in a sport, etc.: *a golf widow.* **3** *Printing.* a short line at the end of a paragraph, esp. one that occurs as the top line of a page or column. **4** (in some card games) an additional hand or set of cards exposed on the table. ◆ *vb* (*tr; usually passive*) **5** to cause to become a widow. **6** to deprive of something valued. [OE *widuwe*]
▸ **'widowhood** *n*

widow bird *n* another name for **whydah.**

widower ('wɪdəʊə) *n* a man whose wife has died and who has not remarried.

widow's cruse *n* an endless or unfailing source of supply. [allusion to I Kings 17:16]

widow's mite *n* a small contribution by a person who has very little. [allusion to Mark 12:43]

widow's peak *n* a V-shaped point in the hairline in the middle of the forehead. [from the belief that it presaged early widowhood]

width ➊ (wɪdθ) *n* **1** the linear extent or measurement of something from side to side. **2** the state or fact of being wide. **3** a piece or section of something at its full extent from side to side: *a width of cloth.* **4** the distance across a rectangular swimming bath, as opposed to its length. [C17: from WIDE + -TH[1], analogous to BREADTH]

wield ➊ (wiːld) *vb* (*tr*) **1** to handle or use (a weapon, tool, etc.). **2** to exert or maintain (power or authority). [OE *wieldan, wealdan*]
▸ **'wieldable** *adj* ▸ **'wielder** *n*

wieldy ('wiːldɪ) *adj* **wieldier, wieldiest.** easily handled, used, or managed.

wiener ('wiːnə) *or* **wienerwurst** ('wiːnə,wɜːst) *n US & Canad.* a kind of smoked sausage, similar to a frankfurter. [C20: shortened from G *Wiener Wurst* Viennese sausage]

Wiener schnitzel ('viːnə 'ʃnɪtsəl) *n* a thin escalope of veal, fried in breadcrumbs. [G: Viennese cutlet]

wife ➊ (waɪf) *n, pl* **wives. 1** a man's partner in marriage; a married woman. Related adj: **uxorial. 2** an archaic or dialect word for **woman. 3 take to wife.** to marry (a woman). [OE *wīf*]
▸ **'wifehood** *n* ▸ **'wifely** *adj*

wig (wɪg) *n* **1** an artificial head of hair, either human or synthetic, worn to disguise baldness, as part of a theatrical or ceremonial dress, as a disguise, or for adornment. ◆ *vb* **wigs, wigging, wigged.** (*tr*) **2** *Brit. sl.* to berate severely. [C17: shortened from PERIWIG]
▸ **wigged** *adj* ▸ **'wigless** *adj*

wigeon *or* **widgeon** ('wɪdʒən) *n* **1** a Eurasian duck of marshes, swamps, etc., the male of which has a reddish-brown head and chest and grey-and-white back and wings. **2 American wigeon.** Also called: **baldpate.** a similar bird of North America, the male of which has a white crown. [C16: from ?]

wigging ('wɪgɪŋ) *n Brit. sl.* a reprimand.

wiggle ➊ ('wɪgᵊl) *vb* **wiggles, wiggling, wiggled. 1** to move or cause to move with jerky movements, esp. from side to side. ◆ *n* **2** the act of wiggling. [C13: from MLow G, MDu. *wiggelen*]
▸ **'wiggler** *n* ▸ **'wiggly** *adj*

wight (waɪt) *n Arch.* a human being. [OE *wiht;* rel. to OFrisian *āwet* something]

wigwag ('wɪg,wæg) *vb* **wigwags, wigwagging, wigwagged. 1** to move (something) back and forth. **2** to communicate with (someone) by means of a flag semaphore. ◆ *n* **3a** a system of communication by flag semaphore. **3b** the message signalled. [C16: from obs. *wig,* prob. short for WIGGLE + WAG[1]]
▸ **'wig,wagger** *n*

wigwam ('wɪg,wæm) *n* **1** any dwelling of the North American Indians, esp. one made of bark, rushes, or skins spread over a set of arched poles lashed together. **2** a similar structure for children. [from *wīkwām* (of Amerind origin), lit.: their abode]

wilco ('wɪlkəʊ) *interj* an expression in signalling, telecommunications, etc., indicating that a message just received will be complied with. [C20: abbrev. for *I will comply*]

wild ➊ (waɪld) *adj* **1** (of animals) living independently of man; not domesticated or tame. **2** (of plants) growing in a natural state; not cultivated. **3** uninhabited; desolate: *a wild stretch of land.* **4** living in a savage or uncivilized way: *wild tribes.* **5** lacking restraint or control: *wild merriment.* **6** of great violence: *a wild storm.* **7** disorderly or chaotic: *wild talk.* **8**

THESAURUS

behaved ≠ **harmful:** harmless, innocuous, mild, pleasant, wholesome

wide *adj* **1, 2** = **broad**, ample, catholic, comprehensive, distended, encyclopedic, expanded, expansive, extensive, far-reaching, general, immense, inclusive, large, overarching, sweeping, vast **4** = **distant**, away, off, off course, off target, remote **5** = **expanded**, dilated, distended, fully open, outspread, outstretched **6** = **spacious**, ample, baggy, capacious, commodious, full, loose, roomy ◆ *adv* **9, 10** = **fully**, as far as possible, completely, right out, to the furthest extent **11** = **off target**, astray, nowhere near, off course, off the mark, out
Antonyms *adj* ≠ **broad:** narrow, strict, tight ≠ **expanded:** closed, limited, restricted, shut ≠ **spacious:** confined, constricted, cramped, tight ◆ *adv* ≠ **fully:** narrowly, partially, partly

wide-awake *adj* **1** = **conscious**, fully awake, roused, wakened **2** = **alert**, aware, heedful, keen, observant, on one's toes, on the alert, on the ball (*inf.*), on the qui vive, vigilant, wary, watchful
Antonyms *adj* ≠ **alert:** distracted, dreamy, heedless, inattentive, negligent, oblivious, preoccupied, unaware, unobservant

wide-eyed *adj* = **naive**, as green as grass, credulous, green, impressionable, ingenuous, innocent, simple, trusting, unsophisticated, unsuspicious, wet behind the ears (*inf.*)

widen *vb* = **broaden**, dilate, enlarge, expand, extend, open out *or* up, open wide, spread, stretch
Antonyms *vb* compress, constrict, contract, cramp, diminish, narrow, reduce, shrink, tighten

wide-open *adj* **1** = **outspread**, fully extended, fully open, gaping, outstretched, splayed, spread **2** = **unprotected**, at risk, defenceless, exposed, in danger, in peril, open, susceptible, vulnerable **3** = **uncertain**, anybody's guess (*inf.*), indeterminate, unpredictable, unsettled, up for grabs (*inf.*)

widespread *adj* **1, 2** = **common**, broad, epidemic, extensive, far-flung, far-reaching, general, pervasive, popular, prevalent, rife, sweeping, universal, wholesale
Antonyms *adj* confined, exclusive, limited, local, narrow, rare, sporadic, uncommon

width *n* **1** = **breadth**, compass, diameter, extent, girth, measure, reach, scope, span, thickness, wideness

wield *vb* **1** = **brandish**, employ, flourish, handle, manage, manipulate, ply, swing, use **2** = **exert**, apply, be possessed of, command, control, exercise, have, have at one's disposal, hold, maintain, make use of, manage, possess, put to use, utilize

wife *n* **1** = **spouse**, better half (*humorous*), bride, helpmate, helpmeet, her indoors, little woman (*inf.*), mate, old lady (*inf.*), old woman (*inf.*), partner, significant other (*US inf.*), (the) missis *or* missus (*inf.*), woman (*inf.*)

wiggle *vb, n* **1, 2** = **jerk**, jiggle, shake, shimmy, squirm, twitch, wag, waggle, writhe

wild *adj* **1** = **untamed**, feral, ferocious, fierce, savage, unbroken, undomesticated **2** = **uncultivated**, free, indigenous, native, natural **3** = **desolate**, desert, deserted, empty, godforsaken, lonely, trackless, uncivilized, uncultivated, uninhabited, unpopulated, virgin **4** = **uncivilized**, barbaric, barbarous, brutish, ferocious, fierce, primitive, rude, savage **5** = **uncontrolled**, boister-

dishevelled; untidy: *wild hair.* **9** in a state of extreme emotional intensity: *wild with anger.* **10** reckless: *wild speculations.* **11** random: *a wild guess.* **12** (*postpositive;* foll. by *about*) *Inf.* intensely enthusiastic: *I'm wild about my new boyfriend.* **13** (of a card, such as a joker in some games) able to be given any value the holder pleases. **14 wild and woolly. 14a** rough; barbarous. **14b** (of theories, plans, etc.) not fully thought out. ◆ *adv* **15** in a wild manner. **16 run wild. 16a** to grow without cultivation or care: *the garden has run wild.* **16b** to behave without restraint: *he has let his children run wild.* ◆ *n* **17** (*often pl*) a desolate or uninhabited region. **18 the wild. 18a** a free natural state of living. **18b** the wilderness. [OE *wilde*]
▸ **'wildish** *adj* ▸ **'wildly** *adv* ▸ **'wildness** *n*

wild boar *n* a wild pig of parts of Europe and central Asia, having a pale grey to black coat and prominent tusks.

wild brier *n* another name for **wild rose.**

wild card *n* **1** See **wild** (sense 13). **2** *Sport.* a player or team that has not qualified for a competition but is allowed to take part, at the organizers' discretion, after all the regular places have been taken. **3** an unpredictable element in a situation. **4** *Computing.* a symbol that can represent any character or group of characters, as in a filename.

wild carrot *n* an umbelliferous plant of temperate regions, having clusters of white flowers and hooked fruits. Also called: **Queen Anne's lace.**

wildcat ('waɪld,kæt) *n, pl* **wildcats** *or* **wildcat. 1** a wild European cat that resembles the domestic tabby but is larger and has a bushy tail. **2** any of various other felines, such as the lynx and the caracal. **3** *US & Canad.* another name for **bobcat. 4** *Inf.* a savage or aggressive person. **5** an exploratory drilling for petroleum or natural gas. **6** (*modifier*) *Chiefly US.* involving risk, esp. financially or commercially unsound: *a wildcat project.* ◆ *vb* **wildcats, wildcatting, wildcatted. 7** (*intr*) to drill for petroleum or natural gas in an area having no known reserves.
▸ **'wild,catter** *n* ▸ **'wild,catting** *n, adj*

wildcat strike *n* a strike begun by workers spontaneously or without union approval.

wild cherry *n* another name for **gean.**

wild dog *n* another name for **dingo.**

wildebeest ('wɪldɪ,bi:st, 'vɪl-) *n, pl* **wildebeests** *or* **wildebeest.** another name for **gnu.** [C19: from Afrik., lit.: wild beast]

wilder (ˈwɪldə) *vb Arch.* **1** to lead or be led astray. **2** to bewilder or become bewildered. [C17: from ?]

wilderness ❶ ('wɪldənɪs) *n* **1** a wild uninhabited uncultivated region. **2** any desolate area. **3** a confused mass or collection. **4 a voice (crying) in the wilderness.** a person, group, etc., making a suggestion or plea that is ignored. [OE *wildēornes,* from *wildēor* wild beast + -NESS]

wild-eyed *adj* glaring in an angry, distracted, or wild manner.

wildfire ('waɪld,faɪə) *n* **1** a highly flammable material, such as Greek fire, formerly used in warfare. **2a** a raging and uncontrollable fire. **2b** anything that is disseminated quickly (esp. in **spread like wildfire**). **3** another name for **will-o'-the-wisp.**

wild flower *n* **1** any flowering plant that grows in an uncultivated state. **2** the flower of such a plant.

wildfowl ('waɪld,faʊl) *n* **1** any bird that is hunted by man, esp. any duck or similar aquatic bird. **2** such birds collectively.
▸ **'wild,fowler** *n* ▸ **'wild,fowling** *adj, n*

wild-goose chase *n* an absurd or hopeless pursuit, as of something unattainable.

wilding ('waɪldɪŋ) *n* **1** an uncultivated plant or a cultivated plant that has become wild. **2** a wild animal. ◆ Also called: **wildling.**

wildlife ❶ ('waɪld,laɪf) *n* wild animals and plants collectively: a term used esp. of fauna.

wild pansy *n* a Eurasian plant of the violet family having purple, yellow, and pale mauve spurred flowers. Also called: **heartsease, love-in-idleness.**

wild parsley *n* any of various uncultivated umbelliferous plants that resemble parsley.

wild rice *n* an aquatic North American grass with dark-coloured edible grain.

wild rose *n* any of numerous roses, such as the dogrose and sweetbrier, that grow wild and have flowers with only one whorl of petals.

wild rubber *n* rubber obtained from uncultivated rubber trees.

wild silk *n* **1** silk produced by wild silkworms. **2** a fabric made from this, or from short fibres of silk designed to imitate it.

wild type *n Biol.* the typical form of a species of organism resulting from breeding under natural conditions.

Wild West *n* the western US during its settlement, esp. with reference to its frontier lawlessness.

wildwood ('waɪld,wʊd) *n Arch.* a wood or forest growing in a natural uncultivated state.

wile ❶ (waɪl) *n* **1** trickery, cunning, or craftiness. **2** (*usually pl*) an artful or seductive trick or ploy. ◆ *vb* **wiles, wiling, wiled. 3** (*tr*) to lure, beguile, or entice. [C12: from ON *vel* craft]

wilful ❶ *or US* **willful** ('wɪlfʊl) *adj* **1** intent on having one's own way; headstrong or obstinate. **2** intentional: *wilful murder.*
▸ **'wilfully** *or US* **'willfully** *adv* ▸ **'wilfulness** *or US* **'willfulness** *n*

will[1] (wɪl) *vb past* **would.** (takes an infinitive without *to* or an implied infinitive) used as an auxiliary. **1** (esp. with *you, he, she, it, they,* or a noun as subject) to make the future tense. Cf. **shall** (sense 1). **2** to express resolution on the part of the speaker: *I will buy that radio if it's the last thing I do.* **3** to indicate willingness or desire: *will you help me with this problem?* **4** to express commands: *you will report your findings to me tomorrow.* **5** to express ability: *this rope will support a load.* **6** to express probability or expectation: *that will be Jim telephoning.* **7** to express customary practice or inevitability: *boys will be boys.* **8** (*with the infinitive always implied*) to express desire: usually in polite requests: *stay if you will.* **9 what you will.** whatever you like. [OE *willan*]

> **USAGE NOTE** See at **shall.**

will[2] ❶ (wɪl) *n* **1** the faculty of conscious and deliberate choice of action. Related adj: **voluntary. 2** the act or an instance of asserting a choice. **3a** the declaration of a person's wishes regarding the disposal of his property after his death. **3b** a document in which such wishes are expressed. **4** desire; wish. **5** determined intention: *where there's a will there's a way.* **6** disposition towards others: *he bears you no ill will.* **7 at will.** at one's own desire or choice. **8 with a will.** heartily; energetically. **9 with the best will in the world.** even with the best of intentions. ◆ *vb* (*mainly tr; often takes a clause as object or an infinitive*) **10** (*also intr*) to exercise the faculty of volition in an attempt to accomplish (something): *he willed his wife's recovery from her illness.* **11** to give (property) by will to a person, society, etc.: *he willed his art collection to the nation.* **12** (*also intr*) to order or decree: *the king wills that you shall die.* **13** to choose or prefer: *wander where you will.* [OE *willa*]
▸ **'willer** *n*

willed (wɪld) *adj* (*in combination*) having a will as specified: *weak-willed.*

willet ('wɪlɪt) *n* a large American shore bird having a grey plumage with black-and-white wings. [C19: imit. of its call]

willful ('wɪlfʊl) *adj* the US spelling of **wilful.**

willies ('wɪlɪz) *pl n* **the.** *Sl.* nervousness, jitters, or fright (esp. in **give** (*or* **get**) **the willies**). [C20: from ?]

willing ❶ ('wɪlɪŋ) *adj* **1** favourably disposed or inclined; ready. **2** cheerfully compliant. **3** done, given, accepted, etc., freely or voluntarily.
▸ **'willingly** *adv* ▸ **'willingness** *n*

THESAURUS

ous, chaotic, disorderly, impetuous, lawless, noisy, riotous, rough, rowdy, self-willed, turbulent, unbridled, undisciplined, unfettered, ungovernable, unmanageable, unrestrained, unruly, uproarious, violent, wayward **6 = stormy,** blustery, choppy, furious, howling, intense, raging, rough, tempestuous, violent **8 = dishevelled,** disordered, straggly, tousled, unkempt, untidy, windblown **9 = excited,** agog, avid, crazy (*inf.*), daft (*inf.*), delirious, eager, enthusiastic, frantic, frenzied, hysterical, mad (*inf.*), nuts (*sl.*), potty (*Brit. inf.*), raving **10 = outrageous,** extravagant, fantastic, flighty, foolhardy, foolish, giddy, ill-considered, impracticable, imprudent, madcap, preposterous, rash, reckless ◆ *adv* **16 run wild: a = go on the rampage,** ramble, spread, straggle **b = abandon all restraint,** cut loose, kick over the traces, rampage, run free, run riot, stray ◆ *n* **17** *often plural* **= wilderness,** back of beyond (*inf.*), desert, middle of nowhere (*inf.*), uninhabited area, wasteland
Antonyms *adj* ≠ **untamed:** broken, domesticated, tame ≠ **uncultivated:** cultivated, farmed, planted ≠ **desolate:** civilized, inhabited, populated, urban ≠ **uncivilized:** advanced, civilized ≠ **uncontrolled:** calm, careful, controlled, disciplined, domesticated, friendly, genteel, gentle, lawful, mild, ordered, orderly, peaceful, polite, quiet, restrained, self-controlled, thoughtful, well-behaved ≠ **excited:** unenthusiastic, uninterested ≠ **outrageous:** logical, practical, realistic, well-thought-out

wilderness *n* **1, 2 = desert,** jungle, waste, wasteland, wilds **3 = tangle,** clutter, confused mass, confusion, congeries, jumble, maze, muddle, welter

wildlife *n* **= flora and fauna**

wile *n* **1 = trickery,** artfulness, artifice, cheating, chicanery, craft, craftiness, cunning, fraud, guile, slyness **2** *usually plural* **= ploys,** artifices, contrivances, devices, dodges, impositions, lures, manoeuvres, ruses, stratagems, subterfuges, tricks

wilful *adj* **1 = obstinate,** adamant, bull-headed, determined, dogged, froward (*arch.*), headstrong, inflexible, intractable, intransigent, mulish, obdurate, persistent, perverse, pigheaded, refractory, self-willed, stiff-necked, stubborn, uncompromising, unyielding **2 = intentional,** conscious, deliberate, intended, purposeful, volitional, voluntary, willed
Antonyms *adj* ≠ **obstinate:** biddable, complaisant, compromising, docile, flexible, good-natured, obedient, pliant, tractable, yielding ≠ **intentional:** accidental, involuntary, uncalculated, unconscious, unintentional, unplanned, unwitting

will[2] *n* **3 = testament,** declaration, last wishes **4 = wish,** choice, decision, decree, desire, fancy, inclination, mind, option, pleasure, preference, volition **5 = determination,** aim, intention, purpose, resolution, resolve, willpower **7 at will = as one pleases,** as one thinks fit, as one wishes, at one's desire, at one's discretion, at one's inclination, at one's pleasure, at one's whim, at one's wish ◆ *vb* **10, 12 = decree,** bid, bring about, cause, command, determine, direct, effect, ordain, order, resolve **11 = bequeath,** confer, give, leave, pass on, transfer **13 = wish,** choose, desire, elect, opt, prefer, see fit, want

willing *adj* **1, 2 = ready,** agreeable, amenable, compliant, consenting, content, desirous, disposed, eager, enthusiastic, favourable, game (*inf.*), happy, inclined, in favour, in the mood, nothing loath, pleased, prepared, so-minded
Antonyms *adj* averse, disinclined, grudging, indisposed, loath, not keen, reluctant, unenthusiastic, unwilling

willingly *adv* **1-3 = readily,** by choice, cheerfully, eagerly, freely, gladly, happily, lief (*rare*), of one's own accord, of one's own free will, voluntarily, with all one's heart, without hesitation, with pleasure
Antonyms *adv* grudgingly, hesitantly, involuntarily, reluctantly, unwillingly

willingness *n* **1, 2 = inclination,** agreeableness, agreement, consent, desire, disposition,

williwaw ('wɪlɪˌwɔː) *n US & Canad.* **1** a sudden strong gust of cold wind blowing offshore from a mountainous coast, as in the Strait of Magellan. **2** a state of great turmoil. [C19: from ?]

will-o'-the-wisp (ˌwɪləðə'wɪsp) *n* **1** Also called: **friar's lantern, ignis fatuus, jack-o'-lantern.** a pale flame or phosphorescence sometimes seen over marshy ground at night. It is believed to be due to the spontaneous combustion of methane originating from decomposing organic matter. **2** a person or thing that is elusive or allures and misleads. [C17: from *Will,* short for *William* + *wisp,* in former sense of a twist of hay burning as a torch]

willow ('wɪləʊ) *n* **1** any of a large genus of trees and shrubs, such as the weeping willow and osiers of N temperate regions, which have graceful flexible branches and flowers in catkins. **2** the whitish wood of certain of these trees. **3** something made of willow wood, such as a cricket bat. [OE *welig*]

willowherb ('wɪləʊˌhɜːb) *n* **1** any of various temperate and arctic plants having narrow leaves and terminal clusters of pink, purplish, or white flowers. **2** short for **rosebay willowherb** (see **rosebay**).

willow pattern *n* **a** a pattern incorporating a willow tree, river, bridge, and figures, typically in blue on a white ground, used on porcelain, etc. **b** (*as modifier*): *a willow-pattern plate.*

willowy **T** ('wɪləʊɪ) *adj* **1** slender and graceful. **2** flexible or pliant. **3** covered or shaded with willows.

willpower **T** ('wɪlˌpaʊə) *n* **1** the ability to control oneself and determine one's actions. **2** firmness of will.

willy[1] ('wɪlɪ) *n, pl* **willies.** *Brit. inf.* a childish or jocular term for **penis.**

willy[2] ('wɪlɪ) *n Austral. sl.* a sudden loss of temper; fit: *to throw a willy.*

willy-nilly **T** ('wɪlɪ'nɪlɪ) *adv* **1** whether desired or not. ◆ *adj* **2** occurring or taking place whether desired or not. [OE *wile hē, nyle hē,* lit.: will he or will he not]

willy wagtail *n* a black-and-white flycatcher found in Australasia and parts of Asia, having white feathers over the brows.

willy-willy ('wɪlɪˌwɪlɪ) *n, pl* **willy-willies.** *Austral.* a small sometimes violent upward-spiralling cyclone or dust storm. [from Abor.]

wilt[1] **T** (wɪlt) *vb* **1** to become or cause to become limp or drooping: *insufficient water makes plants wilt.* **2** to lose or cause to lose courage, strength, etc. ◆ *n* **3** the act of wilting or state of becoming wilted. **4** any of various plant diseases characterized by permanent wilting. [C17: ? var. of *wilk* to wither, from MDu. *welken*]

wilt[2] (wɪlt) *vb Arch. or dialect.* (used with the pronoun *thou* or its relative equivalent) a singular form of the present tense (indicative mood) of **will**[1].

Wilton ('wɪltən) *n* a kind of carpet with a close velvet pile of cut loops. [after *Wilton,* town in Wiltshire, where first made]

Wilts (wɪlts) *abbrev. for* Wiltshire.

wily **T** ('waɪlɪ) *adj* **wilier, wiliest.** sly or crafty.
▸'**wiliness** *n*

wimble ('wɪmbᵊl) *n* **1** any of a number of hand tools used for boring holes. ◆ *vb* **wimbles, wimbling, wimbled. 2** to bore (a hole) with a wimble. [C13: from MDu. *wimmel* auger]

wimp **T** (wɪmp) *n Inf.* a feeble ineffective person. [C20: from ?]
▸'**wimpish** *or* '**wimpy** *adj*

WIMP (wɪmp) *n acronym for:* **1** windows, icons, menus (*or* mice), pointers: denoting a type of user-friendly screen display used on small computing. **2** *Physics.* weakly interacting massive particle.

wimple ('wɪmpᵊl) *n* **1** a piece of cloth draped around the head to frame the face, worn by women in the Middle Ages and still worn by some nuns. ◆ *vb* **wimples, wimpling, wimpled.** *Arch.* **2** (*tr*) to cover with or put a wimple on. **3** (esp. of a veil) to lie or cause to lie in folds or pleats. [OE *wimpel*]

wimp out *vb* (*intr, adv*) *Sl.* to fail to do or complete something through fear or lack of conviction.

win **T** (wɪn) *vb* **wins, winning, won. 1** (*intr*) to achieve first place in a competition. **2** (*tr*) to gain (a prize, first place, etc.) in a competition. **3** (*tr*) to succeed in or gain (something) with an effort: *we won recognition.* **4** to gain victory or triumph in (a battle, argument, etc.). **5** (*tr*) to earn (a living, etc.) by work. **6** (*tr*) to capture: *the Germans never won Leningrad.* **7** (when *intr,* foll. by *out, through,* etc.) to reach with difficulty (a desired position) or become free, loose, etc., with effort: *the boat won the shore.* **8** (*tr*) to gain (the sympathy, loyalty, etc.) of someone. **9** (*tr*) to persuade (a woman, etc.) to marry one. **10** (*tr*) to extract (ore, coal, etc.) from a mine or (metal or other minerals) from ore. **11 you can't win.** *Inf.* an expression of resignation after an unsuccessful attempt to overcome difficulties. ◆ *n* **12** *Inf.* a success, victory, or triumph. **13** profit; winnings. ◆ See also **win over.** [OE *winnan*]
▸'**winnable** *adj*

wince[1] **T** (wɪns) *vb* **winces, wincing, winced. 1** (*intr*) to start slightly, as with sudden pain; flinch. ◆ *n* **2** the act of wincing. [C18 (earlier (C13) meaning: to kick): via OF *wencier, guenchir* to avoid, of Gmc origin]
▸'**wincer** *n* ▸'**wincingly** *adv*

wince[2] (wɪns) *n* a roller for transferring pieces of cloth between dyeing vats. [C17: var. of WINCH[1]]

winceyette (ˌwɪnsɪ'ɛt) *n Brit.* a plain-weave cotton fabric with slightly raised two-sided nap. [from Scot. *wincey,* prob. altered from *woolsey* in *linsey-woolsey,* a fabric made of linen & wool]

winch[1] (wɪntʃ) *n* **1** a windlass driven by a hand- or power-operated crank. **2** a hand- or power-operated crank by which a machine is driven. ◆ *vb* **3** (*tr;* often foll. by *up* or *in*) to pull or lift using a winch. [OE *wince* pulley]

winch[2] (wɪntʃ) *vb* (*intr*) an obsolete word for **wince**[1].

Winchester rifle ('wɪntʃɪstə) *n Trademark.* a breech-loading lever-action repeating rifle. Often shortened to **Winchester.** [C19: after O. F. *Winchester* (1810–80), US manufacturer]

wind[1] **T** (wɪnd) *n* **1** a current of air, sometimes of considerable force, moving generally horizontally from areas of high pressure to areas of low pressure. **2** *Chiefly poetic.* the direction from which a wind blows, usually a cardinal point of the compass. **3** air artificially moved, as by a fan, pump, etc. **4** a trend, tendency, or force: *the winds of revolution.* **5** *Inf.* a hint; suggestion: *we got wind that you were coming.* **6** something deemed insubstantial: *his talk was all wind.* **7** breath, as used in respiration or talk: *you're just wasting wind.* **8** (often used in sports) the power to breathe normally: *his wind is weak.* **9** *Music.* **9a** a wind instrument or wind instruments considered collectively. **9b** (*often pl*) the musicians who play wind instruments in an orchestra. **9c** (*modifier*) of or composed of wind instruments: *a wind ensemble.* **10** an informal name for **flatus. 11** the air on which the scent of an animal is carried to hounds or on which the scent of a hunter is carried to his quarry. **12 between wind and water. 12a** the part of a vessel's hull below the water line that is exposed by rolling or by wave action. **12b** any particularly susceptible point. **13 break wind.** to release intestinal gas through the anus. **14 get** *or* **have the wind up.** *Inf.* to become frightened. **15 how** *or* **which way the wind blows** *or* **lies.** what appears probable. **16 in the teeth** (*or* **eye**) **of the wind.** directly into the wind. **17 in the wind.** about to happen. **18 into the wind.** against the wind or upwind. **19 off the wind.** *Naut.* away from the direction from which the wind is blowing. **20 on the wind.** *Naut.* as near as possible to the direction from which the wind is blowing. **21 put the wind up.** *Inf.* to frighten or alarm. **22 raise the wind.** *Brit. inf.* to obtain the necessary funds. **23 sail close** *or* **near to the wind.** to come near the limits of danger or indecency. **24 take the wind out of someone's sails.** to disconcert or deflate someone. ◆ *vb* (*tr*) **25** to cause (someone) to be short of breath: *the blow winded him.* **26a** to detect the scent of. **26b** to pursue (quarry) by following its scent. **27** to cause (a baby) to bring up wind after feeding. **28** to expose to air, as in drying, etc. [OE]
▸'**windless** *adj*

wind[2] **T** (waɪnd) *vb* **winds, winding, wound. 1** (often foll. by *around, about,* or *upon*) to turn or coil (string, cotton, etc.) around some object or point or (of string, etc.) to be turned, etc., around some object or point: *he wound a scarf around his head.* **2** (*tr*) to cover or wreathe by or as if by coiling, wrapping, etc.: *we wound the body in a shroud.* **3** (*tr;* often foll. by *up*) to tighten the spring of (a clockwork mechanism). **4** (*tr;* foll. by *off*) to remove by uncoiling or unwinding. **5** (*usually intr*) to move or cause to move in a sinuous, spiral, or circular course: *the river*

THESAURUS

enthusiasm, favour, goodwill, volition, will, wish
Antonyms *n* aversion, disagreement, disinclination, hesitation, loathing, reluctance, unwillingness

willowy *adj* **1, 2** = **slender**, graceful, limber, lissom(e), lithe, slim, supple, svelte, sylphlike

willpower *n* **1, 2** = **self-control**, determination, drive, firmness of purpose *or* will, fixity of purpose, force *or* strength of will, grit, resolution, resolve, self-discipline, single-mindedness
Antonyms *n* apathy, hesitancy, indecision, irresolution, languor, lethargy, shilly-shallying (*inf.*), torpor, uncertainty, weakness

willy-nilly *adv* **1** = **whether one likes it or not**, necessarily, *nolens volens,* of necessity, perforce, whether desired or not, whether or no

wilt[1] *vb* **1** = **droop**, become limp *or* flaccid, sag, shrivel, wither **2** = **weaken**, diminish, dwindle, ebb, fade, fail, flag, languish, lose courage, melt away, sag, sink, wane, wither

wily *adj* = **cunning**, arch, artful, astute, cagey (*inf.*), crafty, crooked, deceitful, deceptive, designing, fly (*sl.*), foxy, guileful, intriguing, scheming, sharp, shifty, shrewd, sly, tricky, underhand
Antonyms *adj* artless, candid, dull, guileless, honest, ingenuous, naive, simple, straightforward

wimp *n Informal* = **weakling**, coward, doormat (*sl.*), drip (*inf.*), milksop, mouse, sissy, softy *or* softie, wet (*Brit. sl.*)

win *vb* **1, 2, 4** = **triumph**, achieve first place, achieve mastery, be victorious, carry all before one, carry the day, come first, conquer, finish first, gain victory, overcome, prevail, succeed, sweep the board, take the prize **3** = **gain**, accomplish, achieve, acquire, attain, bag (*inf.*), catch, collect, come away with, earn, get, land, net, obtain, pick up, procure, receive, secure ◆ *n* **12** *Informal* = **victory**, conquest, success, triumph
Antonyms *vb* ≠ **triumph:** fail, fall, suffer defeat, suffer loss ≠ **gain:** forfeit, lose, miss ◆ *n* ≠ **victory:** beating, defeat, downfall, failure, loss, washout (*inf.*)

wince[1] *vb* **1** = **flinch**, blench, cower, cringe, draw back, quail, recoil, shrink, start ◆ *n* **2** = **flinch**, cringe, start

wind[1] *n* **1** = **air**, air-current, blast, breath, breeze, current of air, draught, gust, zephyr **5** *Informal* = **hint**, clue, inkling, intimation, notice, report, rumour, suggestion, tidings, warning, whisper **6** = **talk**, babble, blather, bluster, boasting, empty talk, gab (*inf.*), hot air, humbug, idle talk, verbalizing **7** = **breath**, puff, respiration **10** = **flatulence**, flatus, gas **14 get** *or* **have the wind up** *Informal* = **be afraid**, be alarmed, be frightened, be scared, fear, take fright **17 in the wind** = **imminent**, about to happen, approaching, close at hand, coming, impending, in the offing, near, on the cards (*inf.*), on the way **21 put the wind up** *Informal* = **scare**, alarm, discourage, frighten, frighten off, scare off

wind[2] *vb* **1, 2** = **coil**, curl, encircle, furl, loop, reel, roll, spiral, turn around, twine, twist, wreathe **5** = **meander**, bend, curve, deviate, ramble, snake, turn, twist, zigzag ◆ *n* **10** = **twist**, bend, curve, meander, turn, zigzag

winds through the hills. **6** (*tr*) to introduce indirectly or deviously: *he is winding his own opinions into the report.* **7** (*tr*) to cause to twist or revolve: *he wound the handle.* **8** (*tr;* usually foll. by *up* or *down*) to move by cranking: *please wind up the window.* ◆ *n* **9** the act of winding or state of being wound. **10** a single turn, bend, etc.: *a wind in the river.* ◆ See also **wind down, wind up.** [OE *windan*]
▸'**windable** *adj*

wind[3] (waɪnd) *vb* **winds, winding, winded** *or* **wound.** (*tr*) *Poetic.* to blow (a note or signal) on (a horn, bugle, etc.). [C16: special use of WIND[1]]

windage ('wɪndɪdʒ) *n* **1a** a deflection of a projectile as a result of the effect of the wind. **1b** the degree of such deflection. **2** the difference between a firearm's bore and the diameter of its projectile. **3** *Naut.* the exposed part of the hull of a vessel responsible for wind resistance.

windbag Ⓣ ('wɪnd,bæg) *n* **1** *Sl.* a voluble person who has little of interest to communicate. **2** the bag in a set of bagpipes, which provides a continuous flow of air to the pipes.

windblown ('wɪnd,bləʊn) *adj* **1** blown by the wind. **2** (of trees, shrubs, etc.) growing in a shape determined by the prevailing winds.

wind-borne *adj* (esp. of plant seeds or pollen) transported by wind.

windbound ('wɪnd,baʊnd) *adj* (of a sailing vessel) prevented from sailing by an unfavourable wind.

windbreak ('wɪnd,breɪk) *n* a fence, line of trees, etc., serving as a protection from the wind by breaking its force.

windburn ('wɪnd,bɜːn) *n* irritation of the skin caused by prolonged exposure to winds of high velocity.

Windcheater ('wɪnd,tʃiːtə) *n Aust. trademark.* a warm jacket, usually with a close-fitting knitted neck, cuffs, and waistband.

wind chest (wɪnd) *n* a box in an organ in which air from the bellows is stored under pressure before being supplied to the pipes or reeds.

wind-chill ('wɪnd-) *n* **a** the serious chilling effect of wind and low temperature: measured on a scale that runs from hot to fatal to life. **b** (*as modifier*): *wind-chill factor.*

wind cone (wɪnd) *n* another name for **windsock.**

wind down Ⓣ (waɪnd) *vb* (*adv*) **1** (*tr*) to lower or move down by cranking. **2** (*intr*) (of a clock spring) to become slack. **3** (*intr*) to diminish gradually in power; relax.

winded Ⓣ ('wɪndɪd) *adj* **1** out of breath, as from strenuous exercise. **2** (*in combination*) having breath or wind as specified: *broken-winded; short-winded.*

winder ('waɪndə) *n* **1** a person or device that winds. **2** an object, such as a bobbin, around which something is wound. **3** a knob or key used to wind up a clock, watch, or similar mechanism. **4** any plant that twists itself around a support. **5** a step of a spiral staircase. Cf. **flyer** (sense 4).

windfall Ⓣ ('wɪnd,fɔːl) *n* **1** a piece of unexpected good fortune, esp. financial gain. **2** something blown down by the wind, esp. a piece of fruit.

windfall tax *n* a tax levied on an organization considered to have made excessive profits, esp. a privatized utility company that has exploited a natural monopoly.

wind farm *n* a large group of wind-driven generators for electricity supply.

windflower ('wɪnd,flaʊə) *n* any of various anemone plants, such as the wood anemone.

wind gauge (wɪnd) *n* **1** another name for **anemometer. 2** a scale on a gun sight indicating the amount of deflection necessary to allow for windage. **3** *Music.* a device for measuring the wind pressure in the bellows of an organ.

wind harp (wɪnd) *n* a less common name for **aeolian harp.**

windhover ('wɪnd,hɒvə) *n Brit.* a dialect name for a **kestrel.**

winding Ⓣ ('waɪndɪŋ) *n* **1** a curving or sinuous course or movement. **2** anything that has been wound or wrapped around something. **3** a particular manner or style in which something has been wound. **4** a curve, bend, or complete turn in wound material, a road, etc. **5** (*often pl*) devious thoughts or behaviour: *the tortuous windings of political argumentation.* **6** one or more turns of wire forming a continuous coil through which an electric current can pass, as used in transformers, generators, etc. ◆ *adj* **7** curving; sinuous: *a winding road.*
▸'**windingly** *adv*

winding sheet *n* a sheet in which a corpse is wrapped for burial; shroud.

winding-up *n* the process of finishing or closing something, esp. the process of closing down a business.

wind instrument (wɪnd) *n* any musical instrument sounded by the breath, such as the woodwinds and brass instruments of an orchestra.

windjammer ('wɪnd,dʒæmə) *n* a large merchant sailing ship.

windlass ('wɪndləs) *n* **1** a machine for raising weights by winding a rope or chain upon a barrel or drum driven by a crank, motor, etc. ◆ *vb* **2** (*tr*) to raise or haul (a weight, etc.) by means of a windlass. [C14: from ON *vindáss,* from *vinda* to WIND[2] + *ass* pole]

windlestraw ('wɪnd[ə]l,strɔː) *n Irish, Scot., & English dialect.* the dried stalk of any of various grasses. [OE *windelstrēaw,* from *windel* basket, from *windan* to wind + *strēaw* straw]

wind machine (wɪnd) *n* a machine used, esp. in the theatre, to produce a wind or the sound of wind.

windmill ('wɪnd,mɪl, 'wɪn,mɪl) *n* **1** a machine for grinding or pumping driven by a set of adjustable vanes or sails that are caused to turn by the force of the wind. **2** the set of vanes or sails that drives such a mill. **3** Also called: **whirligig.** *Brit.* a toy consisting of plastic or paper vanes attached to a stick in such a manner that they revolve like the sails of a windmill. **4** an imaginary opponent or evil (esp. in **tilt at** *or* **fight windmills**). ◆ *vb* **5** to move or cause to move like the arms of a windmill.

window ('wɪndəʊ) *n* **1** a light framework, made of timber, metal, or plastic, that contains glass or glazed opening frames and is placed in a wall or roof to let in light or air or to see through. Related adj: **fenestral. 2** an opening in the wall or roof of a building that is provided to let in light or air or to see through. **3** short for **windowpane. 4** the area behind a glass window in a shop used for display. **5** any opening or structure resembling a window in function or appearance, such as the transparent area of an envelope revealing an address within. **6** an opportunity to see or understand something usually unseen: *a window on the workings of Parliament.* **7** a period of unbooked time in a diary, schedule, etc. **8** short for **launch window** or **weather window. 9** *Physics.* a region of the spectrum in which a medium transmits electromagnetic radiation. **10** an area of a VDU display that can be manipulated separately from the rest of the display area. **11** (*modifier*) of or relating to a window or windows: *a window ledge.* ◆ *vb* **12** (*tr*) to furnish with or as if with windows. [C13: from ON *vindauga,* from *vindr* WIND[1] + *auga* eye]

window box *n* a long narrow box, placed on or outside a windowsill, in which plants are grown.

window-dresser *n* a person employed to design and build up a display in a shop window.

window-dressing *n* **1** the ornamentation of shop windows, designed to attract customers. **2** the pleasant aspect of an idea, etc., which is stressed to conceal the real nature.

windowpane ('wɪndəʊ,peɪn) *n* a sheet of glass in a window.

window sash *n* a glazed window frame, esp. one that opens.

window seat *n* **1** a seat below a window, esp. in a bay window. **2** a seat beside a window in a bus, train, etc.

window-shop *vb* **window-shops, window-shopping, window-shopped.** (*intr*) to look at goods in shop windows without intending to buy.
▸'**window-,shopper** *n* ▸'**window-,shopping** *n*

windowsill ('wɪndəʊ,sɪl) *n* a sill below a window.

windpipe ('wɪnd,paɪp) *n* a nontechnical name for **trachea** (sense 1).

wind rose (wɪnd) *n* a diagram with radiating lines showing the frequency and strength of winds from each direction affecting a specific place.

windrow ('wɪnd,rəʊ, 'wɪn,rəʊ) *n* **1** a long low ridge or line of hay or a similar crop, designed to achieve the best conditions for drying or curing. **2** a line of leaves, snow, dust, etc., swept together by the wind.

windscreen ('wɪnd,skriːn) *n Brit.* the sheet of flat or curved glass that forms a window of a motor vehicle, esp. the front window. US and Canad. name: **windshield.**

windscreen wiper *n Brit.* an electrically operated blade with a rubber edge that wipes a windscreen clear of rain, snow, etc. US and Canad. name: **windshield wiper.**

windshield ('wɪnd,ʃiːld) *n* the US and Canad. name for **windscreen.**

windsock ('wɪnd,sɒk) *n* a truncated cone of textile mounted on a mast so that it is free to rotate about a vertical axis: used, esp. at airports, to indicate the local wind direction. Also called: **air sock, drogue, wind sleeve, wind cone.**

Windsor ('wɪnzə) *adj* of or relating to the British royal family, whose official name this has been from 1917.

Windsor chair *n* a simple wooden chair, popular in England and America from the 18th century, usually having a shaped seat, splayed legs, and a back of many spindles.

Windsor knot *n* a wide triangular knot, produced by making extra turns in tying a tie.

windstorm ('wɪnd,stɔːm) *n* a storm consisting of violent winds.

wind-sucking *n* a harmful habit of horses in which the animal arches its neck and swallows a gulp of air.
▸'**wind,sucker** *n*

windsurfing ('wɪnd,sɜːfɪŋ) *n* the sport of riding on water using a surfboard steered and propelled by an attached sail.

windswept ('wɪnd,swɛpt) *adj* open to or swept by the wind.

wind tunnel (wɪnd) *n* a chamber for testing the aerodynamic properties of aircraft, aerofoils, etc., in which a current of air can be maintained at a constant velocity.

wind up Ⓣ (waɪnd) *vb* (*adv*) **1** to bring to or reach a conclusion: *he wound up the proceedings.* **2** (*tr*) to tighten the spring of (a clockwork

THESAURUS

windbag *n* **1** *Slang* = **bore**, bigmouth (*sl.*), blether (*Scot.*), blowhard, boaster, braggart, gasbag (*inf.*), gossip, loudmouth (*inf.*), prattler

wind down *vb* **3** = **subside**, cool off, decline, diminish, dwindle, lessen, reduce, relax, slacken, taper off, unwind
Antonyms *vb* accelerate, amplify, escalate, expand, heat up, increase, intensify, magnify, step up

winded *adj* **1** = **out of breath**, breathless, gasping for breath, out of puff, out of whack (*inf.*), panting, puffed, puffed out

windfall *n* **1** = **godsend**, bonanza, find, jackpot, manna from heaven, pot of gold at the end of the rainbow, stroke of luck
Antonyms *n* bad luck, disaster, infelicity, misadventure, mischance, misfortune, mishap

winding *n* **1, 4** = **twist**, bend, convolution, curve, meander, turn, undulation ◆ *adj* **7** = **twisting**, anfractuous, bending, circuitous, convoluted, crooked, curving, flexuous, indirect, meandering, roundabout, serpentine, sinuous, spiral, tortuous, turning, twisty
Antonyms *adj* ≠ **twisting:** direct, even, level, plumb, smooth, straight, undeviating, unswerving

wind up *vb* **1** = **end**, bring to a close, close,

mechanism). **3** (*tr; usually passive*) *Inf.* to make nervous, tense, etc.: *he was all wound up before the big fight.* **4** (*tr*) to roll (thread, etc.) into a ball. **5** an informal word for **liquidate** (sense 2). **6** (*intr*) *Inf.* to end up (in a specified state): *you'll wind up without any teeth.* **7** (*tr*) *Brit. sl.* to tease (someone). ◆ *n* **wind-up. 8** the act of concluding. **9** the end.

windward ('wɪndwəd) *Chiefly naut.* ◆ *adj* **1** of, in, or moving to the quarter from which the wind blows. ◆ *n* **2** the windward point. **3** the side towards the wind. ◆ *adv* **4** towards the wind. ◆ Cf. **leeward.**

windy ⓣ ('wɪndɪ) *adj* **windier, windiest. 1** of, resembling, or relating to wind; stormy. **2** swept by or open to powerful winds. **3** marked by or given to prolonged and often boastful speech: *windy orations.* **4** void of substance. **5** an informal word for **flatulent. 6** *Sl.* frightened.
▸**'windily** *adv* ▸**'windiness** *n*

wine (waɪn) *n* **1a** an alcoholic drink produced by the fermenting of grapes with water and sugar. **1b** (*as modifier*): *the wine harvest.* **1c** an alcoholic drink produced in this way from other fruits, flowers, etc.: *elderberry wine.* **2a** a dark red colour, sometimes with a purplish tinge. **2b** (*as adj*): *wine-coloured.* **3** anything resembling wine in its intoxicating or invigorating effect. **4 new wine in old bottles.** something new added to or imposed upon an old or established order. ◆ *vb* **wines, wining, wined. 5** (*intr*) to drink wine. **6 wine and dine.** to entertain or be entertained with wine and fine food. [OE *wīn*, from L *vīnum*]
▸**'wineless** *adj*

wine bar *n* a bar in a restaurant, etc., or an establishment that specializes in serving wine and usually food.

winebibber ('waɪn,bɪbə) *n* a person who drinks a great deal of wine.
▸**'wine,bibbing** *n*

wine box *n* wine sold in a carton with a tap for pouring.

wine cellar *n* **1** a place, such as a dark cool cellar, where wine is stored. **2** the stock of wines stored there.

wine cooler *n* **1** a bucket-like vessel containing ice in which a bottle of wine is placed to be cooled. **2** the full name for **cooler** (sense 3).

wine gallon *n Brit.* a former unit of capacity equal to 231 cubic inches.

wineglass ('waɪn,glɑːs) *n* **1** a glass drinking vessel, typically having a small bowl on a stem, with a flared foot. **2** Also called: **wineglassful.** the amount that such a glass will hold.

wine grower *n* a person engaged in cultivating vines in order to make wine.
▸**wine growing** *n*

wine palm *n* any of various palm trees, the sap of which is used, esp. when fermented, as a drink. Also called: **toddy palm.**

winepress ('waɪn,prɛs) *n* any equipment used for squeezing the juice from grapes in order to make wine.

winery ('waɪnərɪ) *n, pl* **wineries.** *Chiefly US & Canad.* a place where wine is made.

wineskin ('waɪn,skɪn) *n* the skin of a sheep or goat sewn up and used as a holder for wine.

wing ⓣ (wɪŋ) *n* **1** either of the modified forelimbs of a bird that are covered with large feathers and specialized for flight in most species. **2** one of the organs of flight of an insect, consisting of a membranous outgrowth from the thorax containing a network of veins. **3** either of the organs of flight in certain other animals, esp. the forelimb of a bat. **4a** a half of the main supporting surface on an aircraft, confined to one side of it. **4b** the full span of the main supporting surface on both sides of an aircraft. **5** an organ, structure, or apparatus resembling a wing. **6** anything suggesting a wing in form, function, or position, such as a sail of a windmill or a ship. **7** *Bot.* **7a** either of the lateral petals of a sweetpea or related flower. **7b** any of various outgrowths of a plant part, esp. the process on a wind-dispersed fruit or seed. **8** a means or cause of flight or rapid motion; flight: *fear gave wings to his feet.* **9** *Brit.* the part of a car body that surrounds the wheels. US and Canad. name: **fender. 10** *Soccer, hockey, etc.* **10a** either of the two sides of the pitch near the touchline. **10b** a player stationed in such a position; winger. **11** a faction or group within a political party or other organization. See also **left wing, right wing. 12** a part of a building that is subordinate to the main part. **13** (*pl*) the space offstage to the right or left of the acting area in a theatre. **14 in** *or* **on the wings.** ready to step in when needed. **15** either of the two pieces that project forwards from the sides of some chair backs. **16** (*pl*) an insignia in the form of stylized wings worn by a qualified aircraft pilot. **17** a tactical formation in some air forces, consisting of two or more squadrons. **18** any of various flattened organs or extensions in lower animals, esp. when used in locomotion. **19 clip (someone's) wings. 19a** to restrict (someone's) freedom. **19b** to thwart (someone's) ambitions. **20 on the wing. 20a** flying. **20b** travelling. **21 on wings.** flying or as if flying. **22 spread** *or* **stretch one's wings.** to make full use of one's abilities. **23 take wing. 23a** to lift off or fly away. **23b** to depart in haste. **23c** to become joyful. **24 under one's wing.** in one's care. ◆ *vb* (*mainly tr*) **25** (*also intr*) to make (one's way) swiftly on or as if on wings. **26** to shoot or wound (a bird, person, etc.) superficially, in the wing or arm, etc. **27** to cause to fly or move swiftly: *to wing an arrow.* **28** to provide with wings. [C12: from ON]
▸**winged** *adj* ▸**'wingless** *adj* ▸**'wing,like** *adj*

wing beat *or* **wing-beat** *n* a complete cycle of moving the wing by a bird when flying.

wing-case *n* the nontechnical name for **elytron.**

wing chair *n* an easy chair having wings on each side of the back.

wing collar *n* a stiff turned-up shirt collar worn with the points turned down over the tie.

wing commander *n* an officer holding commissioned rank in certain air forces, such as the Royal Air Force: junior to a group captain and senior to a squadron leader.

wing covert *n* any of the covert feathers of the wing of a bird, occurring in distinct rows.

wingding ('wɪŋ,dɪŋ) *n Sl., chiefly US & Canad.* **1** a noisy lively party or festivity. **2** a real or pretended fit or seizure. [C20: from ?]

winge (wɪndʒ) *vb, n Austral.* a variant spelling of **whinge.**

winger ('wɪŋə) *n Soccer, hockey, etc.* a player stationed on the wing.

wing loading *n* the total weight of an aircraft divided by its wing area.

wingman ('wɪŋmæn) *n pl* **wingmen.** a player in the wing position in Australian Rules.

wing nut *n* a threaded nut tightened by hand by means of two flat lugs or wings projecting from the central body. Also called: **butterfly nut.**

wingspan ('wɪŋ,spæn) *or* **wingspread** ('wɪŋ,sprɛd) *n* the distance between the wing tips of an aircraft, bird, etc.

wing tip *n* the outermost edge of a wing.

wink ⓣ (wɪŋk) *vb* **1** (*intr*) to close and open one eye quickly, deliberately, or in an exaggerated fashion to convey friendliness, etc. **2** to close and open (an eye or the eyes) momentarily. **3** (*tr;* foll. by *away, back,* etc.) to force away (tears, etc.) by winking. **4** (*tr*) to signal with a wink. **5** (*intr*) (of a light) to gleam or flash intermittently. ◆ *n* **6** a winking movement, esp. one conveying a signal, etc., or such a signal. **7** an interrupted flashing of light. **8** a brief moment of time. **9** *Inf.* the smallest amount, esp. of sleep. **10 tip the wink.** *Brit. inf.* to give a hint. [OE *wincian*]

wink at ⓣ *vb* (*intr, prep*) to connive at; disregard: *the authorities winked at corruption.*

winker ('wɪŋkə) *n* **1** a person or thing that winks. **2** *Dialect or US & Canad. sl.* an eye. **3** another name for **blinker**[1] (sense 1).

winkle ⓣ ('wɪŋkᵊl) *n* **1** See **periwinkle**[1]. ◆ *vb* **winkles, winkling, winkled. 2** (*tr;* usually foll. by *out, out of,* etc.) *Inf., chiefly Brit.* to extract or prise out. [C16: shortened from PERIWINKLE[1]]

winkle-pickers *pl n* shoes or boots with very pointed narrow toes.

winner ⓣ ('wɪnə) *n* **1** a person or thing that wins. **2** *Inf.* a person or thing that seems sure to win or succeed.

winning ⓣ ('wɪnɪŋ) *adj* **1** (of a person, character, etc.) charming or attractive: *a winning smile.* **2** gaining victory: *the winning goal.* ◆ *n* **3** a shaft or seam of coal. **4** (*pl*) money, prizes, or valuables won, esp. in gambling.
▸**'winningly** *adv* ▸**'winningness** *n*

winning gallery *n Real Tennis.* the gallery farthest from the net on either side of the court, into which any shot played wins a point.

winning opening *n Real Tennis.* the grille or winning gallery, into which any shot played wins a point.

winning post *n* the post marking the finishing line on a racecourse.

Winnipeg couch ('wɪnɪ,pɛg) *n Canad.* a couch with no arms or back, opening out into a double bed. [after *Winnipeg*, city in S Canada]

winnow ⓣ ('wɪnəʊ) *vb* **1** to separate (grain) from (chaff) by means of a

THESAURUS

close down, conclude, finalize, finish, liquidate, settle, terminate, tie up the loose ends (*inf.*), wrap up **3** *Informal* = **excite**, make nervous, make tense, put on edge, work up **6** *Informal* = **end up**, be left, end one's days, find oneself, finish up ◆ *n* **wind-up 9** = **end**, close, conclusion, culmination, denouement, finale, finish, termination
Antonyms *vb* ≠ **end:** begin, commence, embark on, initiate, instigate, institute, open, start

windy *adj* **1, 2** = **breezy**, blowy, blustering, blustery, boisterous, gusty, inclement, squally, stormy, tempestuous, wild, windswept **3** = **pompous**, boastful, bombastic, diffuse, empty, garrulous, long-winded, loquacious, meandering, prolix, rambling, turgid, verbose, wordy **6** *Slang* = **frightened**, afraid, chicken (*sl.*), cowardly, fearful, nervous, nervy (*inf.*), scared, timid
Antonyms *adj* ≠ **breezy:** becalmed, calm, motionless, smooth, still, windless ≠ **pompous:** modest, quiet, reserved, restrained, reticent, shy, taciturn, unforthcoming ≠ **frightened:** bold, brave, courageous, daring, fearless, gallant, unafraid, undaunted

wing *n* **1-3** = **organ of flight**, pennon (*poetic*), pinion (*poetic*) **11** = **faction**, arm, branch, cabal, circle, clique, coterie, group, grouping, schism, section, segment, set, side **12** = **annexe**, adjunct, ell, extension ◆ *vb* **25** = **fly**, glide, soar **26** = **wound**, clip, hit, nick **27** = **fly**, fleet, hasten, hurry, race, speed, zoom

wink *vb* **1, 2** = **blink**, bat, flutter, nictate, nictitate **5** = **twinkle**, flash, gleam, glimmer, sparkle ◆ *n* **6** = **blink**, flutter, nictation, nictitation **7** = **twinkle**, flash, gleam, glimmering, sparkle **8** = **moment**, instant, jiffy (*inf.*), second, split second, twinkling

wink at *vb* = **condone**, allow, blink at, connive at, disregard, ignore, overlook, pretend not to notice, put up with (*inf.*), shut one's eyes to, tolerate, turn a blind eye to

winkle *vb* **2** *Informal, chiefly Brit.* = **extract**, dig out, dislodge, draw out, extricate, force out, prise out, smoke out, worm out

winner *n* **1** = **victor**, champ (*inf.*), champion, conquering hero, conqueror, first, master, vanquisher

winning *adj* **1** = **charming**, alluring, amiable, attractive, bewitching, captivating, cute, delectable, delightful, disarming, enchanting, endearing, engaging, fascinating, fetching, likable *or* likeable, lovely, pleasing, prepossessing, sweet, taking, winsome **2** = **victorious**, conquering, successful, triumphant ◆ *n* **4** *plural* = **spoils**, booty, gains, prize, proceeds, profits, takings
Antonyms *adj* ≠ **charming:** disagreeable, irksome, offensive, repellent, tiresome, unappealing, unattractive, unpleasant

winnow *vb* **1** = **separate**, comb, cull, divide,

wind or current of air. **2** (*tr*) to examine in order to select the desirable elements. **3** (*tr*) *Rare.* to blow upon; fan. ◆ *n* **4a** a device for winnowing. **4b** the act or process of winnowing. [OE *windwian*]
▶ **'winnower** *n*

wino ('waɪnəu) *n, pl* **winos.** *Inf.* a down-and-out who habitually drinks cheap wine.

win over Ⓣ *vb* (*tr, adv*) to gain the support or consent of (someone). Also: **win round.**

winsome Ⓣ ('wɪnsəm) *adj* charming; winning; engaging: *a winsome smile.* [OE *wynsum,* from *wynn* joy + *-sum* -SOME[1]]
▶ **'winsomely** *adv*

winter ('wɪntə) *n* **1a** (*sometimes cap.*) the coldest season of the year, between autumn and spring, astronomically from the December solstice to the March equinox in the N hemisphere and at the opposite time of year in the S hemisphere. **1b** (*as modifier*): *winter pasture.* **2** the period of cold weather associated with the winter. **3** a time of decline, decay, etc. **4** *Chiefly poetic.* a year represented by this season: *a man of 72 winters.* ◆ Related adj: **hibernal.** ◆ *vb* **5** (*intr*) to spend the winter in a specified place. **6** to keep or feed (farm animals, etc.) during the winter or (of farm animals) to be kept or fed during the winter. [OE]
▶ **'winterer** *n* ▶ **'winterless** *adj*

winter aconite *n* a small Old World herbaceous plant cultivated for its yellow flowers, which appear early in spring.

winter cherry *n* **1** a Eurasian plant cultivated for its ornamental inflated papery orange-red calyx. **2** the calyx of this plant. ◆ See also **Chinese lantern.**

winter garden *n* **1** a garden of evergreen plants. **2** a conservatory in which flowers are grown in winter.

wintergreen ('wɪntə,gri:n) *n* **1** any of a genus of evergreen ericaceous shrubs, esp. a subshrub of E North America, which has white bell-shaped flowers and edible red berries. **2 oil of wintergreen.** an aromatic compound, formerly made from this and various other plants but now synthesized: used medicinally and for flavouring. **3** any of a genus of plants, such as **common wintergreen,** of temperate and arctic regions, having rounded leaves and small pink globose flowers. **4 chickweed wintergreen.** a plant of N Europe and N Asia belonging to the primrose family, having white flowers and leaves arranged in a whorl. [C16: from Du. *wintergroen* or G *Wintergrün*]

winterize *or* **winterise** ('wɪntə,raɪz) *vb* **winterizes, winterizing, winterized** *or* **winterises, winterising, winterised.** (*tr*) *US & Canad.* to prepare (a house, car, etc.) to withstand winter conditions.
▶ **,winteri'zation** *or* **,winteri'sation** *n*

winter jasmine *n* a jasmine shrub widely cultivated for its winter-blooming yellow flowers.

winter solstice *n* the time at which the sun is at its southernmost point in the sky (northernmost point in the S hemisphere) appearing at noon at its lowest altitude above the horizon. It occurs about December 22 (June 21 in the S hemisphere).

winter sports *pl n* sports held in the open air on snow or ice, esp. skiing.

wintertime ('wɪntə,taɪm) *n* the winter season. Also (archaic): **wintertide.**

winterweight ('wɪntə,weɪt) *adj* (of clothes) suitably heavy and warm for wear in the winter.

winter wheat *n* a type of wheat that is planted in the autumn and is harvested the following summer.

wintry Ⓣ ('wɪntrɪ) *or* **wintery** ('wɪntərɪ) *adj* **wintrier, wintriest. 1** (esp. of weather) of or characteristic of winter. **2** lacking cheer or warmth; bleak.
▶ **'wintrily** *adv* ▶ **'wintriness** *or* **'winteriness** *n*

winy ('waɪnɪ) *adj* **winier, winiest.** having the taste or qualities of wine; heady.

wipe Ⓣ (waɪp) *vb* **wipes, wiping, wiped.** (*tr*) **1** to rub (a surface or object) lightly, esp., with a cloth, hand, etc., as in removing dust, water, etc. **2** (usually foll. by *off, away, from, up,* etc.) to remove by or as if by rubbing lightly: *he wiped the dirt from his hands.* **3** to eradicate or cancel (a thought, memory, etc.). **4** to erase (a recording) from (a tape). **5** to apply (oil, etc.) by wiping. **6** *Austral. inf.* to abandon or reject (a person). **7 wipe the floor with (someone).** *Inf.* to defeat (someone) decisively. ◆ *n* **8** the act or an instance of wiping. **9** *Dialect.* a sweeping blow. [OE *wīpian*]

wipe out Ⓣ *vb* (*adv*) **1** (*tr*) to destroy completely. **2** (*tr*) *Inf.* to kill. **3** (*intr*) to fall off a surfboard. ◆ *n* **wipeout. 4** an act or instance of wiping out. **5** the interference of one radio signal by another so that reception is impossible.

wiper ('waɪpə) *n* **1** any piece of cloth, such as a handkerchief, etc., used for wiping. **2** a cam rotated to allow a part to fall under its own weight, as used in stamping machines, etc. **3** See **windscreen wiper. 4** *Electrical engineering.* a movable conducting arm that makes contact with a row or ring of contacts.

wire ('waɪə) *n* **1** a slender flexible strand or rod of metal. **2** a cable consisting of several metal strands twisted together. **3** a flexible metallic conductor, esp. one made of copper, usually insulated, and used to carry electric current in a circuit. **4** (*modifier*) of, relating to, or made of wire: *a wire fence.* **5** anything made of wire, such as wire netting. **6** a long continuous wire or cable connecting points in a telephone or telegraph system. **7** *Old-fashioned.* an informal name for **telegram** or **telegraph. 8** *US & Canad. horse racing.* the finishing line on a racecourse. **9** a snare made of wire for rabbits and similar animals. **10 get in under the wire.** *Inf., chiefly US & Canad.* to accomplish something with little time to spare. **11 get one's wires crossed.** *Inf.* to misunderstand. **12 pull wires.** *Chiefly US & Canad.* to exert influence behind the scenes; pull strings. ◆ *vb* **wires, wiring, wired.** (*mainly tr*) **13** (*also intr*) to send a telegram to (a person or place). **14** to send (news, a message, etc.) by telegraph. **15** to equip (an electrical system, circuit, or component) with wires. **16** to fasten or furnish with wire. **17** to snare with wire. **18 wire in.** *Inf.* to set about (something, esp. food) with enthusiasm. [OE *wīr*]
▶ **'wire,like** *adj*

wire brush *n* a brush having wire bristles, used for cleaning metal, esp. for removing rust, or for brushing against cymbals.

wire cloth *n* a mesh or netting woven from fine wire, used in window screens, strainers, etc.

wiredraw ('waɪə,drɔ:) *vb* **wiredraws, wiredrawing, wiredrew, wiredrawn.** to convert (metal) into wire by drawing through successively smaller dies.

wire-gauge *n* **1** a flat plate with slots in which standard wire sizes can be measured. **2** a standard system of sizes for measuring the diameters of wires.

wire gauze *n* a stiff meshed fabric woven of fine wires.

wire grass *n* any of various grasses that have tough wiry roots or rhizomes.

wire-guided *adj* (of a missile) able to be controlled in mid-flight by signals passed along a wire connecting the missile to the firer's control device.

wire-haired *adj* (of an animal) having a rough wiry coat.

wireless ('waɪəlɪs) *n, vb Chiefly Brit.* another word for **radio.**

wireless telegraphy *n* another name for **radiotelegraphy.**

wireless telephone *n* another name for **radiotelephone.**
▶ **wireless telephony** *n*

wire netting *n* a net made of wire, often galvanized, that is used for fencing, etc.

wirepuller ('waɪə,pulə) *n Chiefly US & Canad.* a person who uses private or secret influence for his own ends.
▶ **'wire,pulling** *n*

wire recorder *n* an early type of magnetic recorder in which sounds were recorded on a thin steel wire magnetized by an electromagnet.
▶ **wire recording** *n*

wire service *n Chiefly US & Canad.* an agency supplying news, etc., to newspapers, radio, and television stations, etc.

wiretap ('waɪə,tæp) *vb* **wiretaps, wiretapping, wiretapped. 1** (*intr*) to make a connection to a telegraph or telephone wire in order to obtain information secretly. **2** (*tr*) to tap (a telephone) or the telephone of (a person).
▶ **'wire,tapper** *n*

wire wheel *n* a wheel in which the rim is held to the hub by wire spokes, esp. one used on a sports car.

wire wool *n* a mass of fine wire used for cleaning and scouring.

wirework ('waɪə,wɜ:k) *n* **1** functional or decorative work made of wire. **2** objects made of wire, esp. netting.

wireworks ('waɪə,wɜ:ks) *n* (*functioning as sing or pl*) a factory where wire or articles of wire are made.

wireworm ('waɪə,wɜ:m) *n* the wormlike larva of various beetles, which feeds on the roots of many plants and is a serious pest.

wiring ('waɪərɪŋ) *n* **1** the network of wires used in an electrical system, device, or circuit. ◆ *adj* **2** used in wiring.

wiry Ⓣ ('waɪərɪ) *adj* **wirier, wiriest. 1** (of people or animals) slender but strong in constitution. **2** made of or resembling wire, esp. in stiffness: *wiry hair.* **3** (of a sound) produced by or as if by a vibrating wire.
▶ **'wirily** *adv* ▶ **'wiriness** *n*

wis (wɪs) *vb Arch.* to know or suppose (something). [C17: a form derived from *iwis,* (from OE *gewiss* certain), mistakenly interpreted as *I wis* I know, as if from OE *witan* to know]

wisdom Ⓣ ('wɪzdəm) *n* **1** the ability or result of an ability to think and act utilizing knowledge, experience, understanding, common sense,

THESAURUS

fan, part, screen, select, separate the wheat from the chaff, sift, sort out

win over *vb* = **convince**, allure, attract, bring *or* talk round, charm, convert, disarm, influence, persuade, prevail upon, sway

winsome *adj* = **charming**, agreeable, alluring, amiable, attractive, bewitching, captivating, comely, cute, delectable, disarming, enchanting, endearing, engaging, fair, fascinating, fetching, likable *or* likeable, pleasant, pleasing, pretty, sweet, taking, winning

wintry *adj* **1** = **cold**, chilly, freezing, frosty, frozen, harsh, hibernal, hiemal, icy, snowy **2** = **bleak**, cheerless, cold, desolate, dismal
Antonyms *adj* balmy, bright, mild, pleasant, summery, sunny, warm

wipe *vb* **1** = **clean**, brush, dry, dust, mop, rub, sponge, swab **2** = **erase**, clean off, get rid of, remove, rub off, take away, take off ◆ *n* **8** = **rub**, brush, lick, swab

wipe out *vb* **1, 2** = **destroy**, annihilate, blot out, blow away, efface, eradicate, erase, expunge, exterminate, extirpate, kill to the last man, massacre, obliterate, take out (*sl.*), wipe from the face of the earth

wiry *adj* **1** = **lean**, sinewy, strong, tough **2** = **stiff**, bristly, kinky
Antonyms *adj* ≠ **lean:** fat, feeble, flabby, fleshy, frail, podgy, puny, spineless, weak

wisdom *n* **1, 2** = **understanding**, astuteness, circumspection, comprehension, discernment, enlightenment, erudition, foresight, insight, intelligence, judgment, judiciousness, knowledge, learning, penetration, prudence, reason,

and insight. **2** accumulated knowledge or enlightenment. **3** *Arch.* a wise saying or wise sayings. ◆ Related adj: **sagacious.** [OE *wīsdōm*]

wisdom tooth *n* **1** any of the four molar teeth, one at the back of each side of the jaw, that are the last of the permanent teeth to erupt. Technical name: **third molar. 2 cut one's wisdom teeth.** to arrive at the age of discretion.

wise[1] ⓘ (waɪz) *adj* **1** possessing, showing, or prompted by wisdom or discernment. **2** prudent; sensible. **3** shrewd; crafty: *a wise plan.* **4** well-informed; erudite. **5** informed or knowing (esp. in **none the wiser**). **6** (*postpositive; often foll. by to*) *Sl.* in the know, esp. possessing inside information (about). **7** *Arch.* possessing powers of magic. **8 be** *or* **get wise.** (often foll. by *to*) *Inf.* to be or become aware or informed (of something). **9 put wise.** (often foll. by *to*) *Sl.* to inform or warn (of). ◆ *vb* **wises, wising, wised. 10** See **wise up.** [OE *wīs*]
▸ **'wisely** *adv* ▸ **'wiseness** *n*

wise[2] (waɪz) *n Arch.* way, manner, fashion, or respect (esp. in **any wise, in no wise**). [OE *wīse* manner]

-wise *adv combining form.* **1** indicating direction or manner: *clockwise; likewise.* **2** with reference to: *businesswise.* [OE *-wisan;* see WISE[2]]

wiseacre ('waɪz,eɪkə) *n* **1** a person who wishes to seem wise. **2** a wise person: often used facetiously or contemptuously. [C16: from MDu. *wijsseggher* soothsayer. See WISE[1], SAY]

wisecrack ⓘ ('waɪz,kræk) *Inf.* ◆ *n* **1** a flippant gibe or sardonic remark. ◆ *vb* (*intr*) **2** to make a wisecrack.
▸ **'wise,cracker** *n*

wise guy *n Inf.* a person who is given to making conceited, sardonic, or insolent comments.

wisent ('wiːzᵊnt) *n* another name for **European bison.** See **bison** (sense 2). [G, from OHG *wisunt* BISON]

wise up *vb* (*adv*) *Sl., chiefly US & Canad.* (often foll. by *to*) to become or cause to become aware or informed (of).

wish ⓘ (wɪʃ) *vb* **1** (when *tr, takes a clause as object or an infinitive;* when *intr,* often foll. by *for*) to want or desire (something, often that which cannot be or is not the case): *I wish I lived in Italy.* **2** (*tr*) to feel or express a desire or hope concerning the future or fortune of: *I wish you well.* **3** (*tr*) to desire or prefer to be as specified. **4** (*tr*) to greet as specified: *he wished us good afternoon.* ◆ *n* **5** the expression of some desire or mental inclination: *to make a wish.* **6** something desired or wished for: *he got his wish.* **7** (*usually pl*) expressed hopes or desire, esp. for someone's welfare, health, etc. **8** (*often pl*) *Formal.* a polite order or request. ◆ See also **wish on.** [OE *wȳscan*]
▸ **'wisher** *n*

wishbone ('wɪʃ,bəʊn) *n* the V-shaped bone above the breastbone in most birds consisting of the fused clavicles. [C17: from the custom of two people breaking apart the bone after eating: the person with the longer part makes a wish]

wishful ('wɪʃfʊl) *adj* having wishes or characterized by wishing.
▸ **'wishfully** *adv* ▸ **'wishfulness** *n*

wish fulfilment *n* (in Freudian psychology) any successful attempt to fulfil a wish stemming from the unconscious mind, whether in fact, in fantasy, or by disguised means.

wishful thinking *n* the erroneous belief that one's wishes are in accordance with reality.
▸ **wishful thinker** *n*

wish on *vb* (*tr, prep*) to hope that (someone or something) should be imposed (on someone); foist: *I wouldn't wish my cold on anyone.*

wishy-washy ⓘ ('wɪʃɪ,wɒʃɪ) *adj Inf.* **1** lacking in substance, force, colour, etc. **2** watery; thin.

wisp ⓘ (wɪsp) *n* **1** a thin, light, delicate, or fibrous piece or strand, such as a streak of smoke or a lock of hair. **2** a small bundle, as of hay or straw. **3** anything slender and delicate: *a wisp of a girl.* **4** a mere suggestion or hint. **5** a flock of birds, esp. snipe. [C14: var. of *wips,* from ?]
▸ **'wisp,like** *adj* ▸ **'wispy** *adj*

wist (wɪst) *vb Arch.* the past tense and past participle of **wit**[2].

wisteria (wɪ'stɪərɪə) *n* any twining woody climbing plant of the genus *Wisteria,* of E Asia and North America, having blue, purple, or white flowers in large drooping clusters. [C19: from NL, after Caspar *Wistar* (1761–1818), US anatomist]

wistful ⓘ ('wɪstfʊl) *adj* sadly pensive, esp. about something yearned for.
▸ **'wistfully** *adv* ▸ **'wistfulness** *n*

wit[1] ⓘ (wɪt) *n* **1** the talent or quality of using unexpected associations between contrasting or disparate words or ideas to make a clever humorous effect. **2** speech or writing showing this quality. **3** a person possessing, showing, or noted for such an ability. **4** practical intelligence (esp. in **have the wit to**). **5** *Arch.* mental capacity or a person possessing it. ◆ See also **wits.** [OE *witt*]

wit[2] (wɪt) *vb* **wits, witting, wot, wist. 1** *Arch.* to be or become aware of (something). **2 to wit.** that is to say; namely (used to introduce statements, as in legal documents). [OE *witan*]

witan ('wɪtᵊn) *n* (in Anglo-Saxon England) **1** an assembly of higher ecclesiastics and important laymen that met to counsel the king on matters such as judicial problems. **2** the members of this assembly. ◆ Also called: **witenagemot.** [OE *witan,* pl. of *wita* wise man]

witblits ('vɪt,blɪts) *n S. African.* alcoholic drink illegally distilled. [from Afrik. *wit* white + *blits* lightning]

witch[1] ⓘ (wɪtʃ) *n* **1** a person, usually female, who practises or professes to practise magic or sorcery, esp. black magic, or is believed to have dealings with the devil. **2** an ugly or wicked old woman. **3** a fascinating or enchanting woman. ◆ *vb* (*tr*) **4** a less common word for **bewitch.** [OE *wicca*]
▸ **'witch,like** *adj*

witch[2] (wɪtʃ) *n* a flatfish of N Atlantic coastal waters, having a narrow greyish-brown body marked with tiny black spots: related to the plaice, flounder, etc. [C19: ?from WITCH[1], from the appearance of the fish]

witchcraft ⓘ ('wɪtʃ,krɑːft) *n* **1** the art or power of bringing magical or preternatural power to bear or the act or practice of attempting to do so. **2** the influence of magic or sorcery. **3** fascinating or bewitching influence or charm.

witch doctor *n* a man in certain societies, esp. preliterate ones, who appears to possess magical powers, used esp. to cure sickness but also to harm people. Also called: **shaman, medicine man.**

witch-elm *n* a variant spelling of **wych-elm.**

witchery ('wɪtʃərɪ) *n, pl* **witcheries. 1** the practice of witchcraft. **2** magical or bewitching influence or charm.

witches'-broom *n* a dense abnormal growth of shoots on a tree or other woody plant, usually caused by parasitic fungi.

witchetty grub ('wɪtʃɪtɪ) *n* the wood-boring edible caterpillar of an Australian moth. Also: **witchetty, witchety.** [C19 *witchetty,* from Abor.]

witch hazel *or* **wych-hazel** *n* **1** any of a genus of trees and shrubs of North America, having ornamental yellow flowers and medicinal properties. **2** an astringent medicinal solution containing an extract of the bark and leaves of one of these shrubs, applied to treat bruises, inflammation, etc.

witch-hunt *n* a rigorous campaign to expose dissenters on the pretext of safeguarding the public welfare.
▸ **'witch-,hunting** *n, adj*

witching ('wɪtʃɪŋ) *adj* **1** relating to or appropriate for witchcraft. **2** *Now rare.* bewitching.
▸ **'witchingly** *adv*

witching hour *n* **the.** the hour at which witches are supposed to appear, usually midnight.

witenagemot (,wɪtɪnəgɪ'məʊt) *n* another word for **witan.** [OE *witena,* genitive pl of *wita* councillor + *gemōt* meeting]

with ⓘ (wɪð, wɪθ) *prep* **1** using; by means of: *he killed her with an axe.* **2** accompanying; in the company of: *the lady you were with.* **3** possessing; having: *a man with a red moustache.* **4** concerning or regarding: *be patient with her.* **5** in spite of: *with all his talents, he was still humble.* **6** used to indicate a time or distance by which something is away from something else: *with three miles to go, he collapsed.* **7** in a manner char-

THESAURUS

sagacity, sapience, sense, smarts (*sl., chiefly US*), sound judgment
Antonyms *n* absurdity = **understanding,** daftness (*inf.*), folly, foolishness, idiocy, injudiciousness, nonsense, senselessness, silliness, stupidity

wise[1] *adj* **1-4** = **sensible,** aware, clever, clued-up (*inf.*), discerning, enlightened, erudite, informed, intelligent, in the loop (*inf.*), judicious, knowing, perceptive, politic, prudent, rational, reasonable, sagacious, sage, sapient, shrewd, sound, understanding, well-advised, well-informed **9 put wise** *Slang* = **inform,** alert, apprise, clue in *or* up (*inf.*), let (someone) into the secret, notify, tell, tip off, warn
Antonyms *adj* ≠ **sensible:** daft (*inf.*), foolish, injudicious, rash, silly, stupid, unintelligent, unwise

wisecrack *n* **1** = **joke,** barb, funny (*inf.*), gag (*inf.*), jest, jibe, pithy remark, quip, sally, sardonic remark, smart remark, witticism ◆ *vb* **2** = **joke,** be facetious, jest, jibe, quip, tell jokes

wish *vb* **1** = **want,** aspire, covet, crave, desiderate, desire, hanker, hope, hunger, long, need, set one's heart on, sigh for, thirst, yearn **3** = **require,** ask, bid, command, desire, direct, instruct, order **4** = **bid,** greet with ◆ *n* **5, 6** = **desire,** aspiration, hankering, hope, hunger, inclination, intention, liking, longing, thirst, urge, want, whim, will, yearning **8** *Formal* = **request,** bidding, command, desire, order, will
Antonyms *n* ≠ **desire:** aversion, disinclination, dislike, distaste, loathing, reluctance, repulsion, revulsion

wishy-washy *adj* **1, 2** *Informal* = **feeble,** bland, flat, ineffective, ineffectual, insipid, jejune, tasteless, thin, vapid, watered-down, watery, weak

wisp *n* **1** = **piece,** shred, snippet, strand, thread, twist

wispy *adj* **3** = **thin,** attenuate, attenuated, delicate, diaphanous, ethereal, faint, fine, flimsy, fragile, frail, gossamer, insubstantial, light, wisplike

wistful *adj* = **melancholy,** contemplative, disconsolate, dreaming, dreamy, forlorn, longing, meditative, mournful, musing, pensive, reflective, sad, thoughtful, yearning

wit[1] *n* **1, 2** = **humour,** badinage, banter, drollery, facetiousness, fun, jocularity, levity, pleasantry, raillery, repartee, wordplay **3** = **humorist,** card (*inf.*), comedian, epigrammatist, *farceur,* joker, punster, wag **4** = **cleverness,** acumen, brains, common sense, comprehension, discernment, ingenuity, insight, intellect, judgment, mind, nous (*Brit. sl.*), perception, practical intelligence, reason, sense, smarts (*sl., chiefly US*), understanding, wisdom
Antonyms *n* ≠ **humour:** dullness, gravity, humourlessness, seriousness, sobriety, solemnity ≠ **cleverness:** folly, foolishness, ignorance, lack of perception, obtuseness, silliness, stupidity

witch[1] *n* **1** = **enchantress,** crone, hag, magician, necromancer, occultist, sorceress

witchcraft *n* **1, 2** = **magic,** black magic, enchantment, incantation, necromancy, occultism, sorcery, sortilege, spell, the black art, the occult, voodoo, witchery, witching, wizardry

with *adj* **10 with it** *Informal* = **fashionable,** happening (*inf.*), in (*inf.*), latest (*inf.*), modern, modish, progressive, stylish, swinging (*sl.*), trendy (*Brit. inf.*), up-to-date, up-to-the-minute, vogue

acterized by: *writing with abandon.* **8** caused or prompted by: *shaking with rage.* **9** often used with a verb indicating a reciprocal action or relation between the subject and the preposition's object: *agreeing with me.* **10 with it.** *Inf.* **10a** fashionable; in style. **10b** comprehending what is happening or being said. **11 with that.** after that. [OE]

withal (wɪ'ðɔːl) *adv* **1** *Literary.* as well. **2** *Arch.* therewith. ◆ *prep* **3** (*postpositive*) an archaic word for **with.** [C12: from WITH + ALL]

withdraw ⊕ (wɪð'drɔː) *vb* **withdraws, withdrawing, withdrew, withdrawn. 1** (*tr*) to take or draw back or away; remove. **2** (*tr*) to remove from deposit or investment in a bank, etc. **3** (*tr*) to retract or recall (a promise, etc.). **4** (*intr*) to retire or retreat: *the troops withdrew.* **5** (*intr;* often foll. by *from*) to depart (from): *he withdrew from public life.* **6** (*intr*) to detach oneself socially, emotionally, or mentally. [C13: from WITH (in the sense: away from) + DRAW]
▸**with'drawer** *n*

withdrawal ⊕ (wɪð'drɔːəl) *n* **1** an act or process of withdrawing. **2** the period a drug addict goes through following abrupt termination in the use of narcotics, usually characterized by physical and mental symptoms (**withdrawal symptoms**). **3** Also called: **withdrawal method, coitus interruptus.** the deliberate withdrawing of the penis from the vagina before ejaculation, as a method of contraception.

withdrawing room *n* an archaic term for **drawing room.**

withdrawn ⊕ (wɪð'drɔːn) *vb* **1** the past participle of **withdraw.** ◆ *adj* **2** unusually reserved or shy. **3** secluded or remote.

withe (wɪθ, wɪð, waɪð) *n* **1** a strong flexible twig, esp. of willow, suitable for binding things together; withy. **2** a band or rope of twisted twigs or stems. ◆ *vb* **withes, withing, withed. 3** (*tr*) to bind with withes. [OE *withthe*]

wither ⊕ ('wɪðə) *vb* **1** (*intr*) (esp. of a plant) to droop, wilt, or shrivel up. **2** (*intr;* often foll. by *away*) to fade or waste: *all hope withered away.* **3** (*intr*) to decay or disintegrate. **4** (*tr*) to cause to wilt or lose vitality. **5** (*tr*) to abash, esp. with a scornful look. [C14: ? var. of WEATHER (vb)]
▸**'witherer** *n* ▸**'withering** *adj* ▸**'witheringly** *adv*

withers ('wɪðəz) *pl n* the highest part of the back of a horse, behind the neck between the shoulders. [C16: short for *widersones,* from *wider* with + *-sones,* ? var. of SINEW]

withershins ('wɪðəˌʃɪnz) *or* **widdershins** *adv Chiefly Scot.* in the direction contrary to the apparent course of the sun; anticlockwise. [C16: from MLow G *weddersinnes,* from MHG, lit.: opposite course, from *wider* against + *sinnes,* genitive of *sin* course]

withhold ⊕ (wɪð'həʊld) *vb* **withholds, withholding, withheld. 1** (*tr*) to keep back: *he withheld his permission.* **2** (*tr*) to hold back; restrain. **3** (*intr;* usually foll. by *from*) to refrain or forbear.
▸**with'holder** *n*

within (wɪ'ðɪn) *prep* **1** in; inside; enclosed or encased by. **2** before (a period of time) has elapsed: *within a week.* **3** not differing by more than (a specified amount) from: *live within your means.* ◆ *adv* **4** *Formal.* inside; internally.

without (wɪ'ðaʊt) *prep* **1** not having: *a traveller without much money.* **2** not accompanied by: *he came without his wife.* **3** not making use of: *it is not easy to undo screws without a screwdriver.* **4** (*foll. by a verbal noun or noun phrase*) not, while not, or after not: *she can sing for two minutes without drawing breath.* **5** *Arch.* on the outside of: *without the city walls.* ◆ *adv* **6** *Formal.* outside.

withstand ⊕ (wɪð'stænd) *vb* **withstands, withstanding, withstood. 1** (*tr*) to resist. **2** (*intr*) to remain firm in endurance or opposition.
▸**with'stander** *n*

withy ('wɪðɪ) *n, pl* **withies.** a variant spelling of **withe** (senses 1, 2). [OE *wīdig(e)*]

witless ⊕ ('wɪtlɪs) *adj* lacking wit, intelligence, or sense.
▸**'witlessly** *adv* ▸**'witlessness** *n*

witling ('wɪtlɪŋ) *n Arch.* a person who thinks himself witty.

witness ⊕ ('wɪtnɪs) *n* **1** a person who has seen or can give first-hand evidence of some event. **2** a person or thing giving or serving as evidence. **3** a person who testifies, esp. in a court of law, to events or facts within his own knowledge. **4** a person who attests to the genuineness of a document, signature, etc., by adding his own signature. **5 bear witness to. 5a** to give written or oral testimony to. **5b** to be evidence or proof of. ◆ Related adj: **testimonial.** ◆ *vb* **6** (*tr*) to see, be present at, or know at first hand. **7** (*tr*) to give evidence of. **8** (*tr*) to be the scene or setting of: *this field has witnessed a battle.* **9** (*intr*) to testify, esp. in a court of law, to events within a person's own knowledge. **10** (*tr*) to attest to the genuineness of (a document, etc.) by adding one's own signature. [OE *witnes,* from *witan* to know + -NESS]
▸**'witnesser** *n*

witness box *or esp. US* **witness stand** *n* the place in a court of law in which witnesses stand to give evidence.

wits ⊕ (wɪts) *pl n* **1** (*sometimes sing*) the ability to reason and act, esp. quickly (esp. in **have one's wits about one**). **2** (*sometimes sing*) right mind, sanity (esp. in **out of one's wits**). **3 at one's wits' end.** at a loss to know how to proceed. **4 live by one's wits.** to gain a livelihood by craftiness rather than by hard work.

-witted *adj* (*in combination*) having wits or intelligence as specified: *slow-witted; dim-witted.*

witter ⊕ ('wɪtə) *vb* (*intr;* often foll. by *on*) *Inf.* to chatter or babble pointlessly or at unnecessary length. [C20: ?from obs. *whitter* to warble, twitter]

Wittgensteinian ('vɪtgənˌʃtaɪnɪən, -ˌstaɪnɪən) *adj* (of a philosophical position or argument) derived from or related to the work of Wittgenstein (1889–1951), Brit. philosopher, and esp. the later work in which he attacks essentialism and stresses the open texture and variety of the use of ordinary language.

witticism ⊕ ('wɪtɪˌsɪzəm) *n* a clever or witty remark. [C17: from WITTY; coined by Dryden (1677) by analogy with *criticism*]

witting ('wɪtɪŋ) *adj Rare.* **1** deliberate; intentional. **2** aware.
▸**'wittingly** *adv*

witty ⊕ ('wɪtɪ) *adj* **wittier, wittiest. 1** characterized by clever humour or wit. **2** *Arch. or dialect.* intelligent.
▸**'wittily** *adv* ▸**'wittiness** *n*

wive (waɪv) *vb* **wives, wiving, wived.** *Arch.* **1** to marry (a woman). **2** (*tr*) to supply with a wife. [OE *gewīfian,* from *wīf* wife]

wivern ('waɪvən) *n* a less common spelling of **wyvern.**

wives (waɪvz) *n* **1** the plural of **wife. 2 old wives' tale.** a superstitious tradition, occasionally one that contains an element of truth.

wiz (wɪz) *n, pl* **wizzes.** *Inf.* a variant spelling of **whizz** (sense 5).

wizard ⊕ ('wɪzəd) *n* **1** a male witch or a man who practises or professes to practise magic or sorcery. **2** a person who is outstandingly clever in some specified field. **3** *Computing.* a program that guides a user through a complex task. ◆ *adj* **4** *Inf., chiefly Brit.* superb; outstanding. **5** of or relating to a wizard or wizardry. [C15: var. of *wissard,* from WISE[1] + -ARD]
▸**'wizardly** *adj*

THESAURUS

withdraw *vb* **1, 2 = remove**, draw back, draw out, extract, pull, pull out, take away, take off **3 = retract**, abjure, disavow, disclaim, recall, recant, rescind, revoke, take back, unsay **4, 5 = retreat**, absent oneself, back off, back out, cop out (*sl.*), depart, detach oneself, disengage, drop out, fall back, go, leave, make oneself scarce (*inf.*), pull back, pull out, retire, secede
Antonyms *vb* ≠ **retreat:** advance, forge ahead, go on, move forward, persist, press on, proceed, progress

withdrawal *n* **1 = removal**, extraction **1 = retraction**, abjuration, disavowal, disclaimer, recall, recantation, repudiation, rescission, revocation **1 = retreat**, departure, disengagement, exit, exodus, retirement, secession

withdrawn *adj* **2 = uncommunicative**, aloof, detached, distant, introverted, quiet, reserved, retiring, shrinking, shy, silent, taciturn, timorous, unforthcoming **3 = secluded**, hidden, isolated, out-of-the-way, private, remote, solitary
Antonyms *adj* ≠ **uncommunicative:** extrovert, forward, friendly, gregarious, open, outgoing, sociable ≠ **secluded:** easily accessible

wither *vb* **1-3 = wilt**, atrophy, blast, blight, decay, decline, desiccate, disintegrate, droop, dry, fade, languish, perish, shrink, shrivel, wane, waste **5 = humiliate**, abash, blast, mortify, put down, shame, snub
Antonyms *vb* ≠ **wilt:** bloom, blossom, develop, flourish, increase, prosper, succeed, thrive, wax

withhold *vb* **1, 2 = keep back**, check, conceal, deduct, hide, hold back, keep, keep secret, refuse, repress, reserve, resist, restrain, retain, sit on (*inf.*), suppress **3** *usually foll. by* **from = refrain**, forbear, keep oneself, stop oneself
Antonyms *vb* ≠ **keep back:** accord, expose, get off one's chest (*inf.*), give, grant, hand over, let go, release, relinquish, reveal

withstand *vb* **1, 2 = resist**, bear, brave, combat, confront, cope with, defy, endure, face, grapple with, hold off, hold out against, oppose, put up with (*inf.*), stand firm against, stand up to, suffer, take, take on, thwart, tolerate, weather
Antonyms *vb* capitulate, falter, give in, give way, relent, succumb, surrender, weaken, yield

witless *adj* **= foolish**, asinine, crackpot (*inf.*), crazy, daft (*inf.*), dull, empty-headed, goofy (*inf.*), halfwitted, idiotic, imbecilic, inane, loopy (*inf.*), moronic, obtuse, senseless, silly, stupid, unintelligent

witness *n* **1 = observer**, beholder, bystander, eyewitness, looker-on, onlooker, spectator, viewer, watcher **3 = testifier**, attestant, corroborator, deponent **5 bear witness: a = confirm**, depone, depose, give testimony, testify **b = be evidence of**, attest to, bear out, be proof of, betoken, constitute proof of, corroborate, demonstrate, evince, prove, show, testify to, vouch for ◆ *vb* **6 = see**, attend, behold (*arch. or literary*), be present at, look on, mark, note, notice, observe, perceive, view, watch **7, 9 = testify**, attest, authenticate, bear out, bear witness, confirm, corroborate, depone, depose, give evidence, give testimony **10 = sign**, countersign, endorse

wits *pl n* **1 = intelligence**, acumen, astuteness, brains, cleverness, comprehension, faculties, ingenuity, judgment, nous (*Brit. sl.*), reason, sense, smarts (*sl., chiefly US*), understanding **3 at one's wits' end = in despair**, at a loss, at the end of one's tether, baffled, bewildered, lost, stuck (*inf.*), stumped

witter *vb Informal* **= chatter**, babble, blab, blather, blether, burble, cackle, chat, clack, gab (*inf.*), gabble, jabber, prate, prattle, rabbit (on) (*Brit. inf.*), tattle, twaddle, waffle (*inf., chiefly Brit.*)

witticism *n* **= quip**, bon mot, clever remark, epigram, one-liner (*sl.*), play on words, pleasantry, pun, repartee, riposte, sally, witty remark

witty *adj* **1 = humorous**, amusing, brilliant, clever, droll, epigrammatic, facetious, fanciful, funny, gay, ingenious, jocular, lively, original, piquant, sparkling, waggish, whimsical
Antonyms *adj* boring, dull, humourless, stupid, tedious, tiresome, unamusing, uninteresting, witless

wizard *n* **1 = magician**, conjuror, enchanter, mage (*arch.*), magus, necromancer, occultist, shaman, sorcerer, thaumaturge (*rare*), warlock, witch **2 = virtuoso**, ace (*inf.*), adept, buff (*inf.*), expert, genius, guru, hotshot (*inf.*), maestro, master, maven (*US*), prodigy, star, whizz (*inf.*), whizz kid (*inf.*), wiz (*inf.*)

wizardry ➊ (ˈwɪzədrɪ) *n* the art, skills, and practices of a wizard, sorcerer, or magician.

wizen (ˈwɪzᵊn) *vb* **1** to make or become shrivelled. ◆ *adj* **2** a variant of **wizened.** [OE *wisnian*]

wizened ➊ (ˈwɪzᵊnd) *or* **wizen** *adj* shrivelled, wrinkled, or dried up, esp. with age.

wk *abbrev. for:* **1** (*pl* **wks**) week. **2** work.

wkly *abbrev. for* weekly.

w.l. *or* **WL** *abbrev. for* water line.

WMO *abbrev. for* World Meteorological Organization.

WNW *symbol for* west-northwest.

WO *abbrev. for:* **1** War Office. **2** Warrant Officer. **3** wireless operator.

woad (wəʊd) *n* **1** a European cruciferous plant, formerly cultivated for its leaves, which yield a blue dye. **2** the dye obtained from this plant, used esp. by the ancient Britons as a body dye. [OE *wād*]

wobbegong (ˈwɒbɪˌgɒŋ) *n* any of various sharks of Australian waters, having a richly patterned brown-and-white skin. [from Abor.]

wobble ➊ (ˈwɒbᵊl) *vb* **wobbles, wobbling, wobbled. 1** (*intr*) to move or sway unsteadily. **2** (*intr*) to shake: *her voice wobbled with emotion.* **3** (*intr*) to vacillate with indecision. **4** (*tr*) to cause to wobble. ◆ *n* **5** a wobbling movement or sound. [C17: var. of *wabble,* from Low G *wabbeln*]
▸ˈ**wobbler** *n*

wobble board *n Austral.* a piece of fibreboard used as a rhythmic musical instrument, producing a characteristic sound when flexed.

wobbly ➊ (ˈwɒblɪ) *adj* **wobblier, wobbliest. 1** shaky, unstable, or unsteady. ◆ *n* **2 throw a wobbly.** *Sl.* to become suddenly very agitated or angry.
▸ˈ**wobbliness** *n*

wodge (wɒdʒ) *n Brit. inf.* a thick lump or chunk cut or broken off something. [C20: alteration of WEDGE]

woe ➊ (wəʊ) *n* **1** *Literary.* intense grief. **2** (*often pl*) affliction or misfortune. **3 woe betide (someone).** misfortune will befall (someone): *woe betide you if you arrive late.* ◆ *interj* **4** Also: **woe is me.** *Arch.* an exclamation of sorrow or distress. [OE *wā, wǣ*]

woebegone ➊ (ˈwəʊbɪˌgɒn) *adj* sorrowful or sad in appearance. [C14: from a phrase such as *me is wo begon* woe has beset me]

woeful ➊ (ˈwəʊfᵊl) *adj* **1** expressing or characterized by sorrow. **2** bringing or causing woe. **3** pitiful; miserable: *a woeful standard of work.*
▸ˈ**woefully** *adv* ▸ˈ**woefulness** *n*

WOF (in New Zealand) *abbrev. for* Warrant of Fitness.

wog[1] (wɒg) *n Brit. sl., derog.* a person who is not White. [prob. from GOLLIWOG]

wog[2] (wɒg) *n Austral. sl.* any ailment or disease, such as influenza, a virus infection, etc. [C20: from ?]

woggle (ˈwɒgᵊl) *n* the ring of leather through which a Scout neckerchief is threaded. [C20: from ?]

wok (wɒk) *n* a large metal Chinese cooking pot having a curved base like a bowl: used esp. for stir-frying. [from Chinese (Cantonese)]

woke (wəʊk) *vb* the past tense of **wake**[1].

woken (ˈwəʊkən) *vb* the past participle of **wake**[1].

wokka board (ˈwɒkə) *n Austral.* another name for **wobble board.**

wold[1] (wəʊld) *n Chiefly literary.* a tract of open rolling country, esp. upland. [OE *weald* bush]

wold[2] (wəʊld) *n* a variant of **weld**[2].

Wolds (wəʊldz) *pl n* **the.** a range of chalk hills in NE England: consists of the **Yorkshire Wolds** to the north, separated from the **Lincolnshire Wolds** by the Humber estuary.

wolf ➊ (wʊlf) *n, pl* **wolves. 1** a predatory canine mammal which hunts in packs and was formerly widespread in North America and Eurasia but is now less common. Related adj: **lupine. 2** any of several similar and related canines, such as the red wolf and the coyote (**prairie wolf**). **3** the fur of any such animal. **4** a voracious or fiercely cruel person or thing. **5** *Inf.* a man who habitually tries to seduce women. **6** Also called: **wolf note.** *Music.* **6a** an unpleasant sound produced in some notes played on the violin, etc., owing to resonant vibrations of the belly. **6b** an out-of-tune effect produced on keyboard instruments accommodated esp. to the system of mean-tone temperament. **7 cry wolf.** to give a false alarm. **8 have** *or* **hold a wolf by the ears.** to be in a desperate situation. **9 keep the wolf from the door.** to ward off starvation or privation. **10 lone wolf.** a person or animal who prefers to be alone. **11 wolf in sheep's clothing.** a malicious person in a harmless or benevolent disguise. ◆ *vb* **12** (*tr; often foll. by down*) to gulp (down). **13** (*intr*) to hunt wolves. [OE *wulf*]
▸ˈ**wolfish** *adj* ▸ˈ**wolf,like** *adj*

Wolf Cub *n Brit.* the former name for **Cub Scout.**

wolffish ➊ (ˈwʊlfˌfɪʃ) *n, pl* **wolffish** *or* **wolffishes.** a large northern deep-sea fish. It has large sharp teeth and no pelvic fins and is used as a food fish. Also called: **catfish.**

wolfhound (ˈwʊlfˌhaʊnd) *n* the largest breed of dog, used formerly to hunt wolves.

wolfram (ˈwʊlfrəm) *n* another name for **tungsten.** [C18: from G, orig. ?from the proper name *Wolfram,* used pejoratively of tungsten because it was thought inferior to tin]

wolframite (ˈwʊlfrəˌmaɪt) *n* a black to reddish-brown mineral, a compound of tungsten, iron, and manganese: it is the chief ore of tungsten.

wolfsbane (ˈwʊlfsˌbeɪn) *or* **wolf's bane** *n* any of several poisonous N temperate plants of the ranunculaceous genus *Aconitum* having hoodlike flowers.

wolf spider *n* a spider which chases its prey to catch it. Also called: **hunting spider.**

wolf whistle *n* **1** a whistle made by a man to express admiration of a woman's appearance. ◆ *vb* **wolf-whistle, wolf-whistles, wolf-whistling, wolf-whistled. 2** (when *intr,* sometimes foll. by *at*) to make such a whistle (at someone).

Wolof (ˈwɒlɒf) *n* **1** (*pl* **Wolof** *or* **Wolofs**) a member of a Negroid people of W Africa living chiefly in Senegal. **2** the language of this people, belonging to the Niger-Congo family.

wolverine (ˈwʊlvəˌriːn) *n* a large musteline mammal of northern forests of Eurasia and North America having dark very thick water-resistant fur. Also called: **glutton.** [C16 *wolvering,* from WOLF + -ING[3] (later altered to *-ine*)]

wolves (wʊlvz) *n* the plural of **wolf.**

woman ➊ (ˈwʊmən) *n, pl* **women. 1** an adult female human being. **2** (*modifier*) female or feminine: *a woman politician.* **3** women collectively. **4** (usually preceded by *the*) feminine nature or feelings: *babies bring out the woman in him.* **5** a female servant or domestic help. **6** a man considered as having supposedly female characteristics, such as meekness. **7** *Inf.* a wife or girlfriend. **8 the little woman.** *Brit. inf., old-fashioned.* one's wife. **9 woman of the streets.** a prostitute. ◆ *vb* (*tr*) **10** *Obs.* to make effeminate. [OE *wīfmann, wimman*]
▸ˈ**womanless** *adj* ▸ˈ**woman-,like** *adj*

womanhood (ˈwʊmənˌhʊd) *n* **1** the state or quality of being a woman or being womanly. **2** women collectively.

womanish (ˈwʊmənɪʃ) *adj* **1** having qualities regarded as unsuitable to a man. **2** of or suitable for a woman.
▸ˈ**womanishly** *adv* ▸ˈ**womanishness** *n*

womanize ➊ *or* **womanise** (ˈwʊməˌnaɪz) *vb* **womanizes, womanizing, womanized** *or* **womanises, womanising, womanised. 1** (*intr*) (of a man) to indulge in casual affairs with women. **2** (*tr*) to make effeminate.
▸ˈ**woman,izer** *or* ˈ**woman,iser** *n*

womankind (ˈwʊmənˌkaɪnd) *n* the female members of the human race; women collectively.

THESAURUS

wizardry *n* = **magic**, conjuration, enchantment, necromancy, occultism, sorcery, sortilege, the black art, voodoo, witchcraft, witchery, witching

wizened *adj* = **wrinkled**, dried up, gnarled, lined, sere (*arch.*), shrivelled, shrunken, withered, worn
Antonyms *adj* bloated, plump, rounded, smooth, swollen, turgid

wobble *vb* **1, 2** = **shake**, quake, rock, seesaw, sway, teeter, totter, tremble, vibrate, waver **3** = **hesitate**, be unable to make up one's mind, be undecided, dither (*chiefly Brit.*), fluctuate, shilly-shally (*inf.*), swither (*Scot.*), vacillate, waver ◆ *n* **5** = **unsteadiness**, quaking, shake, tremble, tremor, vibration

wobbly *adj* **1** = **unsteady**, rickety, shaky, teetering, tottering, unbalanced, uneven, unsafe, unstable, wonky (*Brit. sl.*)

woe *n* **1, 2** = **grief**, adversity, affliction, agony, anguish, burden, curse, dejection, depression, disaster, distress, gloom, hardship, heartache, heartbreak, melancholy, misery, misfortune, pain, sadness, sorrow, suffering, trial, tribulation, trouble, unhappiness, wretchedness
Antonyms *n* bliss, elation, felicity, fortune, happiness, joy, jubilation, pleasure, prosperity, rapture

woebegone *adj* = **gloomy**, blue, chapfallen, cheerless, crestfallen, dejected, disconsolate, doleful, downcast, downhearted, forlorn, funereal, grief-stricken, hangdog, long-faced, low, lugubrious, miserable, mournful, sad, sorrowful, troubled, wretched

woeful *adj* **1** = **sad**, afflicted, agonized, anguished, calamitous, catastrophic, cruel, deplorable, disastrous, disconsolate, dismal, distressing, doleful, dreadful, gloomy, grieving, grievous, harrowing, heartbreaking, heart-rending, lamentable, miserable, mournful, pathetic, piteous, pitiable, pitiful, plaintive, sorrowful, tragic, unhappy, wretched **3** = **pitiful**, abysmal, appalling, awful, bad, deplorable, disappointing, disgraceful, dreadful, feeble, hopeless, inadequate, mean, miserable, paltry, pathetic, pitiable, poor, rotten (*inf.*), shocking, sorry, terrible, wretched
Antonyms *adj* ≠ **sad:** carefree, cheerful, chirpy (*inf.*), contented, delighted, glad, happy, jolly, joyful, jubilant, light-hearted ≠ **pitiful:** abundant, ample, bountiful, enviable, extensive, generous, lavish, luxurious, profuse, prosperous

wolf *n* **5** *Informal* = **womanizer**, Casanova, Don Juan, lady-killer, lech *or* letch (*inf.*), lecher, Lothario, philanderer, seducer ◆ *vb* **12** *often foll. by* **down** = **devour**, bolt, cram, eat like a horse, gobble, gollop, gorge, gulp, pack away (*inf.*), pig out (*sl.*), scoff (*sl.*), stuff
Antonyms *vb* ≠ **devour:** bite, nibble, nip, peck, pick at

wolfish *adj* **12** = **greedy**, avaricious, edacious, fierce, gluttonous, insatiable, predatory, rapacious, ravenous, savage, voracious

woman *n* **1** = **lady**, bird (*sl.*), chick (*sl.*), dame, female, gal (*sl.*), girl, lass, lassie (*inf.*), maid (*arch.*), maiden (*arch.*), miss, she, wench (*facetious*) **5** = **maid**, chambermaid, char (*inf.*), charwoman, domestic, female servant, handmaiden, housekeeper, lady-in-waiting, maid servant **7** *Informal* = **girlfriend**, bride, girl, ladylove, mate, mistress, old lady (*inf.*), partner, significant other (*US inf.*), spouse, sweetheart, wife
Antonyms *n* ≠ **lady:** bloke (*Brit. inf.*), boy, chap (*inf.*), gentleman, guy (*inf.*), lad, laddie, male, man

womanizer *n* **1** = **philanderer**, Casanova, Don Juan, lady-killer, lech *or* letch (*inf.*), lecher, Lothario, seducer, wolf (*inf.*)

womanly Ⓣ (ˈwʊmənlɪ) *adj* **1** possessing qualities, such as warmth, attractiveness, etc., generally regarded as typical of a woman. **2** of or belonging to a woman.

womb Ⓣ (wuːm) *n* **1** the nontechnical name for **uterus. 2** a hollow space enclosing something. **3** a place where something is conceived: *the Near East is the womb of western civilization.* **4** *Obs.* the belly. [OE *wamb*] ▸**wombed** *adj* ▸ˈ**womb,like** *adj*

wombat (ˈwɒmbæt) *n* a burrowing herbivorous Australian marsupial having short limbs, a heavy body, and coarse dense fur. [C18: from Abor.]

women (ˈwɪmɪn) *n* the plural of **woman.**

womenfolk (ˈwɪmɪn,fəʊk) *pl n* **1** women collectively. **2** a group of women, esp. the female members of one's family.

Women's Institute *n* (in Britain and Commonwealth countries) a society for women interested in engaging in craft and cultural activities.

Women's Liberation *n* a movement directed towards the removal of attitudes and practices that preserve inequalities based upon the assumption that men are superior to women. Also called: **women's lib.**

Women's Movement *n* a grass-roots movement of women concerned with women's liberation. See **Women's Liberation.**

won (wʌn) *vb* the past tense and past participle of **win.**

wonder Ⓣ (ˈwʌndə) *n* **1** the feeling excited by something strange; a mixture of surprise, curiosity, and sometimes awe. **2** something that causes such a feeling, such as a miracle. **3** (*modifier*) exciting wonder by virtue of spectacular results achieved, feats performed, etc.: *a wonder drug.* **4 do** *or* **work wonders.** to achieve spectacularly fine results. **5 nine days' wonder.** a subject that arouses general surprise or public interest for a short time. **6 no wonder.** (*sentence connector*) (I am) not surprised at all (that): *no wonder he couldn't come.* **7 small wonder.** (*sentence connector*) (I am) hardly surprised (that): *small wonder he couldn't make it tonight.* ◆ *vb* (when *tr, may take a clause as object*) **8** (when *intr*, often foll. by *about*) to indulge in speculative inquiry: *I wondered about what she said.* **9** (when *intr*, often foll. by *at*) to be amazed (at something): *I wonder at your impudence.* [OE *wundor*] ▸ˈ**wonderer** *n*

wonderful Ⓣ (ˈwʌndəfʊl) *adj* **1** exciting a feeling of wonder. **2** extremely fine; excellent. ▸ˈ**wonderfully** *adv*

wonderland (ˈwʌndə,lænd) *n* **1** an imaginary land of marvels or wonders. **2** an actual place or scene of great or strange beauty or wonder.

wonderment (ˈwʌndəmənt) *n* **1** rapt surprise; awe. **2** puzzled interest. **3** something that excites wonder.

wonderwork (ˈwʌndə,wɜːk) *n* something done or made that excites wonder. ▸ˈ**wonder-,worker** *n* ▸ˈ**wonder-,working** *n, adj*

wondrous (ˈwʌndrəs) *Arch. or literary.* ◆ *adj* **1** exciting wonder; marvellous. ◆ *adv* **2** (intensifier): *wondrous cold.* ▸ˈ**wondrously** *adv* ▸ˈ**wondrousness** *n*

wonky Ⓣ (ˈwɒŋkɪ) *adj* **wonkier, wonkiest.** *Brit. sl.* **1** unsteady. **2** askew. **3** liable to break down. [C20: var. of dialect *wanky*, from OE *wancol*]

wont Ⓣ (wəʊnt) *adj* **1** (*postpositive*) accustomed (to doing something): *he was wont to come early.* ◆ *n* **2** a manner or action habitually employed by or associated with someone (often in **as is my wont, as is his wont,** etc.). ◆ *vb* **3** (when *tr, usually passive*) to become or cause to become accustomed. [OE *gewunod*, p.p. of *wunian* to be accustomed to]

won't (wəʊnt) *contraction of* will not.

wonted Ⓣ (ˈwəʊntɪd) *adj* **1** (*postpositive*) accustomed (to doing something). **2** (*prenominal*) usual: *she is in her wonted place.*

woo Ⓣ (wuː) *vb* **woos, wooing, wooed. 1** to seek the affection, favour, or love of (a woman) with a view to marriage. **2** (*tr*) to seek after zealously: *to woo fame.* **3** (*tr*) to beg or importune (someone). [OE *wōgian*, from ?] ▸ˈ**wooer** *n* ▸ˈ**wooing** *n*

wood Ⓣ (wʊd) *n* **1** the hard fibrous substance consisting of xylem tissue that occurs beneath the bark in trees, shrubs, and similar plants. **2** the trunks of trees that have been cut and prepared for use as a building material. **3** a collection of trees, shrubs, grasses, etc., usually dominated by one or a few species of tree: usually smaller than a forest: *an oak wood.* Related adj: **sylvan. 4** fuel; firewood. **5** *Golf.* **5a** a long-shafted club with a wooden head, used for driving. **5b** (*as modifier*): *a wood shot.* **6** *Tennis, etc.* the frame of a racket: *he hit a winning shot off the wood.* **7** one of the biased wooden bowls used in the game of bowls. **8** *Music.* short for **woodwind. 9 from the wood.** (of a beverage) from a wooden container rather than a metal or glass one. **10 out of the wood** *or* **woods.** clear of or safe from dangers or doubts: *we're not out of the wood yet.* **11 see the wood for the trees.** (*used with a negative*) to obtain a general view of a situation without allowing details to cloud one's analysis: *he can't see the wood for the trees.* **12** (*modifier*) made of, employing, or handling wood: *a wood fire.* **13** (*modifier*) dwelling in or situated in a wood: *a wood nymph.* ◆ *vb* **14** (*tr*) to plant a wood upon. **15** to supply or be supplied with firewood. ◆ See also **woods.** [OE *widu, wudu*]

wood alcohol *n* another name for **methanol.**

wood anemone *n* any of several woodland anemone plants having finely divided leaves and solitary white flowers. Also called: **windflower.**

wood avens *n* another name for **herb bennet.**

woodbine (ˈwuːd,baɪn) *n* **1** a honeysuckle of Europe, SW Asia, and N Africa, having fragrant yellow flowers. **2** *US.* another name for **Virginia creeper. 3** *Austral. sl.* an Englishman.

wood block *n* a small rectangular flat block of wood that is laid with others as a floor surface.

woodcarving (ˈwʊd,kɑːvɪŋ) *n* **1** the act of carving wood. **2** a work of art produced by carving wood. ▸ˈ**wood,carver** *n*

woodchuck (ˈwʊd,tʃʌk) *n* a North American marmot having coarse reddish-brown fur. Also called: **groundhog.** [C17: by folk etymology from Cree *otcheck* fisher]

woodcock (ˈwʊd,kɒk) *n* an Old World game bird resembling the snipe but larger and with shorter legs and neck.

woodcraft (ˈwʊd,krɑːft) *n Chiefly US & Canad.* **1** ability and experience in matters concerned with living in a forest. **2** ability or skill at woodwork, carving, etc.

woodcut (ˈwʊd,kʌt) *n* **1** a block of wood with a design, illustration, etc., from which prints are made. **2** a print from a woodcut.

woodcutter (ˈwʊd,kʌtə) *n* **1** a person who fells trees or chops wood. **2** a person who makes woodcuts. ▸ˈ**wood,cutting** *n*

wooded Ⓣ (ˈwʊdɪd) *adj* **1** covered with or abounding in woods or trees. **2** (*in combination*) having wood of a specified character: *a soft-wooded tree.*

wooden Ⓣ (ˈwʊdᵊn) *adj* **1** made from or consisting of wood. **2** awkward or clumsy. **3** bereft of spirit or animation: *a wooden expression.* **4** obstinately unyielding: *a wooden attitude.* **5** mentally slow or dull. **6** not highly resonant: *a wooden thud.* ▸ˈ**woodenly** *adv*

wood engraving *n* **1** the art of engraving pictures or designs on wood by incising them with a burin. **2** a block of wood so engraved or a print taken from it. ▸**wood engraver** *n*

woodenhead (ˈwʊdᵊn,hɛd) *n Inf.* a dull, foolish, or unintelligent person. ▸,**wooden'headed** *adj* ▸,**wooden'headedness** *n*

Wooden Horse *n* another name for the **Trojan Horse** (sense 1).

wooden spoon *n* a booby prize, esp. in sporting contests.

woodgrouse (ˈwʊd,graʊs) *n* another name for **capercaillie.**

woodland (ˈwʊdlənd) *n* **a** land that is mostly covered with woods or dense growths of trees and shrubs. **b** (*as modifier*): *woodland fauna.* ▸ˈ**woodlander** *n*

woodlark (ˈwʊd,lɑːk) *n* an Old World lark similar to but slightly smaller than the skylark.

woodlouse (ˈwʊd,laʊs) *n, pl* **woodlice** (-,laɪs). any of various small ter-

THESAURUS

womanly *adj* **1 = feminine**, female, ladylike, matronly, motherly, tender, warm

womb *n* **1 = uterus**

wonder *n* **1 = amazement**, admiration, astonishment, awe, bewilderment, curiosity, fascination, stupefaction, surprise, wonderment **2 = phenomenon**, curiosity, marvel, miracle, nonpareil, portent, prodigy, rarity, sight, spectacle, wonderment ◆ *vb* **8 = think**, ask oneself, be curious, be inquisitive, conjecture, cudgel one's brains, doubt, inquire, meditate, ponder, puzzle, query, question, speculate **9 = be amazed**, be astonished, be awed, be dumbstruck, be flabbergasted (*inf.*), boggle, gape, gawk, marvel, stand amazed, stare

wonderful *adj* **1 = remarkable**, amazing, astonishing, astounding, awe-inspiring, awesome, extraordinary, fantastic, incredible, jaw-dropping, marvellous, miraculous, odd, peculiar, phenomenal, staggering, startling, strange, surprising, unheard-of, wondrous (*arch. or literary*) **2 = excellent**, ace (*inf.*), admirable, brilliant, fabulous (*inf.*), fantastic (*inf.*), great (*inf.*), magnificent, marvellous, mean (*sl.*), out of this world (*inf.*), outstanding, sensational (*inf.*), smashing (*inf.*), sovereign, stupendous, super (*inf.*), superb, terrific, tremendous
Antonyms *adj* ≠ **remarkable:** common, commonplace, ordinary, run-of-the-mill, uninteresting, unremarkable, usual ≠ **excellent:** abominable, abysmal, appalling, average, awful, bad, depressing, dire, dreadful, frightful, grim, indifferent, mediocre, miserable, modest, rotten, terrible, unpleasant, vile

wonky *Brit. slang adj* **1 = shaky**, groggy (*inf.*), infirm, unsteady, weak, wobbly, woozy (*inf.*) **2 = askew**, awry, out of alignment, skewwhiff (*Brit. inf.*), squint (*inf.*)

wont *adj* **1 = accustomed**, given, in the habit of, used ◆ *n* **2 = habit**, custom, practice, rule, use, way

wonted *adj* **1 = in the habit of**, accustomed, given, habituated, used **2 = customary**, accustomed, common, conventional, familiar, frequent, habitual, normal, regular, usual

woo *vb* **1, 3 = court**, chase, cultivate, importune, pay court to, pay one's addresses to, pay suit to, press one's suit with, pursue, seek after, seek the hand of, seek to win, solicit the goodwill of, spark (*rare*)

wood *n* **2 = timber**, planks **3 = woodland**, coppice, copse, forest, grove, hurst (*arch.*), thicket, trees **10 out of the wood** *or* **woods = safe**, clear, home and dry (*Brit. sl.*), in the clear, out of danger, safe and sound, secure

wooded *adj* **1 = tree-covered**, forested, sylvan (*poetic*), timbered, tree-clad, woody

wooden *adj* **1 = woody**, ligneous, made of wood, of wood, timber **2 = awkward**, clumsy, gauche, gawky, graceless, inelegant, maladroit, rigid, stiff, ungainly **3 = expressionless**, blank, colourless, deadpan, dull, emotionless, empty, glassy, lifeless, spiritless, unemotional, unresponsive, vacant
Antonyms *adj* ≠ **awkward:** agile, comely, elegant, flexible, flowing, graceful, lissom(e), nimble, supple

restrial isopod crustaceans having a flattened segmented body and occurring in damp habitats.

woodman ('wʊdmən) *n, pl* **woodmen.** **1** a person who looks after and fells trees used for timber. **2** another word for **woodsman.**

woodnote ('wʊd,nəʊt) *n* a natural musical note or song, like that of a wild bird.

wood nymph *n* one of a class of nymphs fabled to inhabit the woods, such as a dryad.

woodpecker ('wʊd,pɛkə) *n* a climbing bird, such as the **green woodpecker,** having a brightly coloured plumage and strong chisel-like bill with which it bores into trees for insects.

wood pigeon *n* a large Eurasian pigeon having white patches on the wings and neck. Also called: **ringdove, cushat.**

woodpile ('wʊd,paɪl) *n* a pile or heap of firewood.

wood preservative *n* a coating applied to timber as a protection against decay, insects, weather, etc.

wood pulp *n* **1** wood that has been ground to a fine pulp for use in making newsprint and other cheap forms of paper. **2** finely pulped wood that has been digested by a chemical, such as caustic soda: used in making paper.

woodruff ('wʊdrʌf) *n* any of several plants, esp. the sweet woodruff of Eurasia, which has small sweet-scented white flowers and whorls of narrow fragrant leaves used to flavour wine and liqueurs and in perfumery. [OE *wudurofe,* from WOOD + *rōfe*]

woods (wʊdz) *pl n* **1** closely packed trees forming a forest or wood, esp. a specific one. **2** another word for **backwoods** (sense 2). **3** the woodwind instruments in an orchestra.

woodscrew ('wʊd,skru:) *n* a metal screw that tapers to a point so that it can be driven into wood by a screwdriver.

woodshed ('wʊd,ʃɛd) *n* a small outbuilding where firewood, garden tools, etc., are stored.

woodsman ('wʊdzmən) *n, pl* **woodsmen.** a person who lives in a wood or who is skilled in woodcraft. Also called: **woodman.**

wood sorrel *n* a Eurasian plant having trifoliate leaves, an underground creeping stem, and white purple-veined flowers.

wood spirit *n Chem.* another name for **methanol.**

wood tar *n* any tar produced by the destructive distillation of wood.

wood warbler *n* **1** a European woodland warbler with a dull yellow plumage. **2** another name for the **American warbler.** See **warbler** (sense 3).

woodwind ('wʊd,wɪnd) *Music.* ◆ *adj* **1** of or denoting a type of wind instrument, formerly made of wood but now often made of metal, such as the flute. ◆ *n* **2** (*functioning as pl*) woodwind instruments collectively.

woodwork ('wʊd,wɜ:k) *n* **1** the art or craft of making things in wood. **2** components made of wood, such as doors, staircases, etc.

woodworking ('wʊd,wɜ:kɪŋ) *n* **1** the process of working wood. ◆ *adj* **2** of, relating to, or used in woodworking.
▸ **'wood,worker** *n*

woodworm ('wʊd,wɜ:m) *n* **1** any of various insect larvae that bore into wooden furniture, beams, etc., esp. the larvae of the furniture beetle and the deathwatch beetle. **2** the condition caused in wood by any of these larvae.

woody ('wʊdɪ) *adj* **woodier, woodiest. 1** abounding in or covered with forest or woods. **2** connected with, belonging to, or situated in a wood. **3** consisting of or containing wood or lignin: *woody tissue; woody stems.* **4** resembling wood in hardness or texture.
▸ **'woodiness** *n*

woodyard ('wʊd,jɑ:d) *n* a place where timber is cut and stored.

woody nightshade *n* a scrambling woody Eurasian plant, having purple flowers and producing poisonous red berry-like fruits. Also called: **bittersweet.**

woof[1] (wu:f) *n* **1** the crosswise yarns that fill the warp yarns in weaving; weft. **2** a woven fabric or its texture. [OE *ōwef,* from *ō-,* ?from ON, + *wef* web (see WEAVE); modern form infl. by WARP]

woof[2] (wʊf) *interj* **1** an imitation of the bark or growl of a dog. ◆ *vb* **2** (*intr*) (of dogs) to bark.

woofer ('wu:fə) *n* a loudspeaker used in high-fidelity systems for the reproduction of low audio frequencies.

woofter ('wʊftə, 'wu:f-) *n Derog. sl.* a male homosexual. [C20: altered from *poofter;* see POOF]

wool ❶ (wʊl) *n* **1** the outer coat of sheep, yaks, etc., which consists of short curly hairs. **2** yarn spun from the coat of sheep, etc., used in weaving, knitting, etc. **3a** cloth or a garment made from this yarn. **3b** (*as modifier*): *a wool dress.* **4** any of certain fibrous materials: *glass wool; steel wool.* **5** *Inf.* short thick curly hair. **6** a tangled mass of soft fine hairs that occurs in certain plants. **7 keep one's wool on.** *Brit. inf.* to keep one's temper. **8 pull the wool over someone's eyes.** to deceive or delude someone. [OE *wull*]
▸ **'wool-,like** *adj*

wool clip *n Austral. & NZ.* the total amount of wool shorn from a particular flock in one year.

wool fat *or* **grease** *n* another name for **lanolin.**

woolfell ('wʊl,fɛl) *n Obs.* the skin of a sheep or similar animal with the fleece still attached.

woolgathering ❶ ('wʊl,gæðərɪŋ) *n* idle or absent-minded daydreaming.

woolgrower ('wʊl,grəʊə) *n* a person who keeps sheep for their wool.
▸ **'wool,growing** *n*

woolled (wʊld) *adj* **1** (of animals) having wool. **2** (*in combination*) having wool as specified: *coarse-woolled.*

woollen *or US* **woolen** ('wʊlən) *adj* **1** relating to or consisting partly or wholly of wool. ◆ *n* **2** (*often pl*) a garment or piece of cloth made wholly or partly of wool, esp. a knitted one.

woolly ❶ *or US* (*sometimes*) **wooly** ('wʊlɪ) *adj* **woollier, woolliest** *or US* (*sometimes*) **woolier, wooliest. 1** consisting of, resembling, or having the nature of wool. **2** covered or clothed in wool or something resembling it. **3** lacking clarity or substance: *woolly thinking.* **4** *Bot.* covered with long soft whitish hairs: *woolly stems.* ◆ *n, pl* **woollies** *or US* (*sometimes*) **woolies. 5** (*often pl*) a garment, such as a sweater, made of wool or something similar.
▸ **'woollily** *adv* ▸ **'woolliness** *n*

woolly bear *n* the caterpillar of any of various tiger moths, having a dense covering of soft hairs.

woolpack ('wʊl,pæk) *n* **1** the cloth wrapping used to pack a bale of wool. **2** a bale of wool.

woolsack ('wʊl,sæk) *n* **1** a sack containing or intended to contain wool. **2** (in Britain) the seat of the Lord Chancellor in the House of Lords, formerly made of a large square sack of wool.

woolshed ('wʊl,ʃɛd) *n Austral. & NZ.* a large building in which sheepshearing takes place.

wool stapler *n* a person who sorts wool into different grades or classifications.

woomera *or* **womera** ('wʊmərə) *n Austral.* a type of notched stick used by native Australians to increase leverage and propulsion in the throwing of a spear. [from Abor.]

Woop Woop ('wu:p ,wu:p) *n Austral. Sl.* a jocular name for any backward or remote town or district.

woozy ❶ ('wu:zɪ) *adj* **woozier, wooziest.** *Inf.* **1** dazed or confused. **2** experiencing dizziness, nausea, etc. [C19: ? a blend of *woolly* + *muzzy* or *dizzy*]
▸ **'woozily** *adv* ▸ **'wooziness** *n*

wop (wɒp) *n Sl., derog.* a member of a Latin people, esp. an Italian. [C20: prob. from It. dialect *guappo* dandy, from Sp. *guapo*]

Worcester sauce *or* **Worcestershire sauce** *n* a commercially prepared piquant sauce, made from a basis of soy sauce, with vinegar, spices, etc.

Worcs *abbrev. for* Worcestershire.

word ❶ (wɜ:d) *n* **1** one of the units of speech or writing that is the smallest isolable meaningful element of the language, although linguists would analyse these further into morphemes. **2** an instance of vocal intercourse; chat, talk, or discussion: *to have a word with someone.* **3** an utterance or expression, esp. a brief one: *a word of greeting.* **4** news or information: *he sent word that he would be late.* **5** a verbal signal for action; command: *when I give the word, fire!* **6** an undertaking or promise: *he kept his word.* **7** an autocratic decree; order: *his word must be obeyed.* **8** a watchword or slogan, as of a political party: *the word now is "freedom".* **9** *Computing.* a set of bits used to store, transmit, or operate upon an item of information in a computer. **10 as good as one's word.** doing what one has undertaken to do. **11 at a word.** at once. **12 by word of mouth.** orally rather than by written means. **13 in a word.** briefly or in short. **14 my word! 14a** an exclamation of surprise, annoyance, etc. **14b** *Austral.* an exclamation of agreement. **15 of one's word.** given to or noted for keeping one's promises: *I am a man of my word.* **16 put in a word** *or* **good word for.** to make favourable mention of (someone); recommend. **17 take someone at his** *or* **her word.** to assume that someone means, or will do, what he or she says: *when he told her to go, she took*

THESAURUS

wool *n* **1, 2** = **fleece,** hair, yarn **8 pull the wool over someone's eyes** = **deceive,** bamboozle, con (*sl.*), delude, dupe, fool, hoodwink, kid (*inf.*), lead (someone) up the garden path (*inf.*), pull a fast one (on someone) (*inf.*), put one over on (*sl.*), take in (*inf.*), trick

woolgathering *n* = **daydreaming,** absent-mindedness, abstraction, building castles in the air, dreaming, inattention, musing, preoccupation, reverie
Antonyms *n* alertness, attention, awareness, concentration, heed, observation, thoughtfulness, vigilance, watchfulness

woolly *adj* **1** = **fleecy,** flocculent, hairy, made of wool, shaggy, woollen **3** = **vague,** blurred, clouded, confused, foggy, fuzzy, hazy, ill-defined, indefinite, indistinct, muddled, nebulous, unclear
Antonyms *adj* ≠ **vague:** clear, clear-cut, definite, distinct, exact, obvious, precise, sharp, well-defined

woozy *adj* **1, 2** *Informal* = **dizzy,** befuddled, bemused, confused, dazed, nauseated, rocky (*inf.*), tipsy, unsteady, wobbly

word *n* **1** = **term,** expression, locution, name, vocable **2** = **chat,** brief conversation, chitchat, colloquy, confab (*inf.*), confabulation, consultation, discussion, talk, tête-à-tête **3** = **remark,** brief statement, comment, declaration, expression, utterance **4** = **message,** account, advice, bulletin, communication, communiqué, dispatch, gen (*Brit. inf.*), information, intelligence, intimation, latest (*inf.*), news, notice, report, tidings **6** = **promise,** affirmation, assertion, assurance, guarantee, oath, parole, pledge, solemn oath, solemn word, undertaking, vow, word of honour **7** = **command,** bidding, commandment, decree, edict, go-ahead (*inf.*), mandate, order, ukase (*rare*), will **13 in a word** = **briefly,** concisely, in a nutshell, in short, succinctly, to put it briefly, to sum up **19 last word: a** = **epitome,** finis, summation, ultimatum **b** = **latest,** *dernier cri,* fashion, newest, rage **c** = **best,** cream, *crème de la crème,* crown, mother of all (*inf.*), *ne plus ultra,* perfection, quintessence, ultimate ◆ *vb* **25** = **express,** couch, phrase, put, say, state, utter

him at his word and left. **18 take someone's word for it.** to accept or believe what someone says. **19 the last word. 19a** the closing remark of a conversation or argument, esp. a remark that supposedly settles an issue. **19b** the latest or most fashionable design, make, or model: *the last word in bikinis.* **19c** the finest example (of some quality, condition, etc.): *the last word in luxury.* **20 the word.** the proper or most fitting expression: *cold is not the word for it, it's freezing!* **21 upon my word! 21a** *Arch.* on my honour. **21b** an exclamation of surprise, annoyance, etc. **22 word for word.** (of a report, etc.) using exactly the same words as those employed in the situation being reported; verbatim. **23 word of honour.** a promise; oath. **24** (*modifier*) of, relating to, or consisting of words. ◆ *vb* **25** (*tr*) to state in words, usually specially selected ones; phrase. ◆ See also **words.** [OE]
▸ **'wordless** *adj* ▸ **'wordlessly** *adv*

Word (wɜːd) *n* **the. 1** *Christianity.* the 2nd person of the Trinity. **2** Scripture, the Bible, or the Gospels as embodying or representing divine revelation. Often called: **the Word of God.** [translation of Gk *logos*, as in John 1:1]

-word *n combining form.* (preceded by *the* and an initial letter) a euphemistic way of referring to a word by its first letter because it is considered unmentionable by the user: *the C-word* (meaning cancer).

wordage ('wɜːdɪdʒ) *n* words considered collectively, esp. a quantity of words.

word association *n* an early method of psychoanalysis in which the patient thinks of the first word that comes into consciousness on hearing a given word. In this way it was claimed that aspects of the unconscious could be revealed before defence mechanisms intervene.

word blindness *n* the nontechnical name for **alexia** and **dyslexia.**
▸ **'word-ˌblind** *adj*

wordbook ('wɜːdˌbʊk) *n* a book containing words, usually with their meanings.

word deafness *n* loss of ability to understand spoken words, esp. as the result of a cerebral lesion. Also called: **auditory aphasia.**

word game *n* any game involving the formation, discovery, or alteration of a word or words.

wording ➊ ('wɜːdɪŋ) *n* **1** the way in which words are used to express a statement, report, etc., esp. a written one. **2** the words themselves.

word order *n* the arrangement of words in a phrase, clause, or sentence.

word-perfect *or US* **letter-perfect** *adj* **1** correct in every detail. **2** (of a speaker, actor, etc.) knowing one's speech, role, etc., perfectly.

wordplay ➊ ('wɜːdˌpleɪ) *n* verbal wit based on the meanings of words; puns, repartee, etc.

word processing *n* the composition of documents using a computer system to input, edit, store, and print.

word processor *n* **a** a computer program that performs word processing. **b** a computer system designed for word processing.

words ➊ (wɜːdz) *pl n* **1** the text of a part of an actor, etc. **2** the text of a song, as opposed to the music. **3** angry speech (esp. in **have words with someone**). **4 eat** *or* **swallow one's words.** to retract a statement. **5 for words.** (preceded by *too* and an adj or adv) indescribably; extremely: *the play was too funny for words.* **6 have no words for.** to be incapable of describing. **7 in other words.** expressing the same idea but differently. **8 in so many words.** explicitly or precisely. **9 of many** (*or* **few**) **words.** (not) talkative. **10 put into words.** to express in speech or writing. **11 say a few words.** to give a brief speech. **12 take the words out of someone's mouth.** to say exactly what someone else was about to say. **13 words fail me.** I am too happy, sad, amazed, etc., to express my thoughts.

word square *n* a puzzle in which the player must fill a square grid with words that read the same across as down.

word wrapping *n Computing.* the automatic shifting of a word at the end of a line to a new line in order to keep within preset margins.

wordy ➊ ('wɜːdɪ) *adj* **wordier, wordiest.** using or containing an excess of words: *a wordy document.*
▸ **'wordily** *adv* ▸ **'wordiness** *n*

wore (wɔː) *vb* the past tense of **wear**[1] and **wear**[2].

work ➊ (wɜːk) *n* **1** physical or mental effort directed towards doing or making something. **2** paid employment at a job or a trade, occupation, or profession. **3** a duty, task, or undertaking. **4** something done, made, etc., as a result of effort or exertion: *a work of art.* **5** another word for **workmanship** (sense 3). **6** the place, office, etc., where a person is employed. **7a** decoration, esp. of a specified kind. **7b** (*in combination*): *wirework.* **8** an engineering structure such as a bridge, building, etc. **9** *Physics.* the transfer of energy expressed as the product of a force and the distance through which its point of application moves in the direction of the force. **10** a structure, wall, etc., built or used as part of a fortification system. **11 at work. 11a** at one's job or place of employment. **11b** in action; operating. **12 make short work of.** *Inf.* to dispose of very quickly. **13** (*modifier*) of, relating to, or used for work: *work clothes; a work permit; a work song.* ◆ *vb* **14** (*intr*) to exert effort in order to do, make, or perform something. **15** (*intr*) to be employed. **16** (*tr*) to carry on operations, activity, etc., in (a place or area): *that salesman works Yorkshire.* **17** (*tr*) to cause to labour or toil: *he works his men hard.* **18** to operate or cause to operate, esp. properly or effectively: *to work a lathe; that clock doesn't work.* **19** (*tr*) to till or cultivate (land). **20** to handle or manipulate or be handled or manipulated: *to work dough.* **21** to shape or process or be shaped or processed: *to work copper.* **22** to reach or cause to reach a specific condition, esp. gradually: *the rope worked loose.* **23** (*intr*) to move in agitation: *his face worked with anger.* **24** (*tr*; often foll. by *up*) to provoke or arouse: *to work someone into a frenzy.* **25** (*tr*) to effect or accomplish: *to work one's revenge.* **26** to make (one's way) with effort: *he worked his way through the crowd.* **27** (*tr*) to make or decorate by hand in embroidery, tapestry, etc.: *she was working a sampler.* **28** (*intr*) (of liquids) to ferment, as in brewing. **29** (*tr*) *Inf.* to manipulate or exploit to one's own advantage. ◆ See also **work in, work off,** etc., **works.** [OE *weorc* (n), *wircan, wyrcan* (vb)]
▸ **'workless** *adj*

workable ➊ ('wɜːkəbᵊl) *adj* **1** practicable or feasible. **2** able to be worked.
▸ **ˌworka'bility** *or* **'workableness** *n*

workaday ➊ ('wɜːkəˌdeɪ) *adj* (*usually prenominal*) **1** being a part of general human experience; ordinary. **2** suitable for working days; everyday or practical.

workaholic (ˌwɜːkə'hɒlɪk) *n* **a** a person obsessively addicted to work. **b** (*as modifier*): *workaholic behaviour.* [C20: from WORK + -HOLIC, coined in 1971 by US author Wayne Oates]

workbag ('wɜːkˌbæg) *n* a container for implements, tools, or materials, esp. sewing equipment. Also called: **work basket, workbox.**

workbench ('wɜːkˌbentʃ) *n* a heavy table at which work is done by a carpenter, mechanic, toolmaker, etc.

workbook ('wɜːkˌbʊk) *n* **1** an exercise book used for study, esp. with spaces for answers. **2** a book of instructions for some process. **3** a book in which is recorded all work done or planned.

work camp *n* a camp set up for young people who voluntarily do manual work on a worthwhile project.

workday ('wɜːkˌdeɪ) *n* **1** the usual US and Canad. term for **working day.** ◆ *adj* **2** another word for **workaday.**

worked (wɜːkt) *adj* made or decorated with evidence of workmanship; wrought, as with embroidery or tracery.

worked up *adj* excited or agitated.

worker ➊ ('wɜːkə) *n* **1** a person or thing that works, usually at a specific job: *a research worker.* **2** an employee, as opposed to an employer or manager. **3** a manual labourer working in a manufacturing industry. **4** any other member of the working class. **5** a sterile female member of a colony of bees, ants, or wasps that forages for food, cares for the larvae, etc.

worker director *n* (in certain British companies) an employee of a company chosen by his or her fellow workers to represent their interests on the board of directors. Also called: **employee director.**

worker-priest *n* a Roman Catholic priest who has employment in a secular job to be more in touch with the problems of the laity.

work ethic *n* a belief in the moral value of work.

workfare ('wɜːkˌfɛə) *n* a scheme under which the government of a country requires unemployed people to do community work or undergo job training in return for social-security payments. [C20: from WORK + (WEL)FARE]

THESAURUS

wording *n* **1, 2 = phraseology**, choice of words, language, mode of expression, phrasing, terminology, words

wordplay *n* **= puns**, punning, repartee, wit, witticisms

words *pl n* **1, 2 = text**, lyrics **3** *As in* **have words = argument**, altercation, angry exchange, angry speech, barney (*inf.*), bickering, disagreement, dispute, falling-out (*inf.*), quarrel, row, run-in (*inf.*), set-to (*inf.*), squabble

wordy *adj* **= long-winded**, diffuse, discursive, garrulous, loquacious, pleonastic, prolix, rambling, verbose, windy
Antonyms *adj* brief, concise, laconic, pithy, short, succinct, terse, to the point

work *n* **1 = effort**, drudgery, elbow grease (*facetious*), exertion, grind (*inf.*), industry, labour, slog, sweat, toil, travail (*literary*) **2 = employment**, bread and butter (*inf.*), business, calling, craft, duty, job, line, livelihood, métier, occupation, office, profession, pursuit, trade **3 = task**, assignment, chore, commission, duty, job, stint, undertaking **4 = creation**, achievement, composition, handiwork, *oeuvre*, opus, performance, piece, production ◆ *vb* **14 = labour**, break one's back, drudge, exert oneself, peg away, slave, slog (away), sweat, toil **15 = be employed**, be in work, do business, earn a living, have a job **18, 20 = operate**, act, control, direct, drive, handle, manage, manipulate, move, ply, use, wield **18 = function**, go, operate, perform, run **19 = cultivate**, dig, farm, till **21 = manipulate**, fashion, form, handle, knead, make, mould, process, shape **22 = progress**, force, make one's way, manoeuvre, move **23 = move**, be agitated, convulse, twitch, writhe **25 = accomplish**, achieve, bring about, carry out, cause, contrive, create, effect, encompass, execute, implement **29** *Informal* **= manipulate**, arrange, bring off, contrive, exploit, fiddle (*inf.*), fix (*inf.*), handle, pull off, swing (*inf.*)
Antonyms *n* ≠ **effort**: ease, leisure, relaxation, rest ≠ **employment**: entertainment, hobby, holiday, play, recreation, retirement, spare time, unemployment ◆ *vb* ≠ **labour**: have fun, mark time, play, relax, skive (*Brit. sl.*), take it easy ≠ **function**: be broken, be out of order

workable *adj* **1 = viable**, doable, feasible, possible, practicable, practical
Antonyms *adj* hopeless, impossible, impractical, inconceivable, unattainable, unthinkable, unworkable, useless

workaday *adj* **1, 2 = ordinary**, bog-standard (*Brit. & Irish sl.*), common, commonplace, everyday, familiar, humdrum, mundane, practical, prosaic, routine, run-of-the-mill
Antonyms *adj* atypical, different, exciting, extraordinary, rare, special, uncommon, unfamiliar, unusual

worker *n* **1-4 = employee**, artisan, craftsman, hand, labourer, proletarian, tradesman, wage earner, working man *or* working woman, workman

workforce ('wɜːkˌfɔːs) *n* **1** the total number of workers employed by a company on a specific job, project, etc. **2** the total number of people who could be employed: *the country's workforce is growing.*

work function *n Physics.* the minimum energy required to transfer an electron from a point within a solid to a point just outside its surface. Symbol: ϕ or Φ

work-harden *vb (tr)* to increase the strength or hardness of (a metal) by a mechanical process, such as tension, compression, or torsion.

workhorse ('wɜːkˌhɔːs) *n* **1** a horse used for nonrecreational activities. **2** *Inf.* a person who takes on the greatest amount of work in a project.

workhouse ('wɜːkˌhaʊs) *n* **1** (formerly in England) an institution maintained at public expense where able-bodied paupers did unpaid work in return for food and accommodation. **2** (in the US) a prison for petty offenders serving short sentences at manual labour.

work in *vb (adv)* **1** to insert or become inserted: *she worked the patch in carefully.* **2** *(tr)* to find space for: *I'll work this job in during the day.* ◆ *n* **work-in. 3** a form of industrial action in which a factory that is to be closed down is occupied and run by its workers.

working ➊ ('wɜːkɪŋ) *n* **1** the operation or mode of operation of something. **2** the act or process of moulding something pliable. **3** a convulsive or jerking motion, as from excitement. **4** *(often pl)* a part of a mine or quarry that is being or has been worked. **5** a record of the steps by which the solution of a problem, calculation, etc., is obtained: *all working is to be submitted to the examiners.* ◆ *adj (prenominal)* **6** relating to or concerned with a person or thing that works: *a working man.* **7** concerned with, used in, or suitable for work: *working clothes.* **8** (of a meal or occasion) during which business discussions are carried on: *a working lunch.* **9** capable of being operated or used: *a working model; in working order.* **10** adequate for normal purposes: *a working majority; a working knowledge of German.* **11** (of a theory, etc.) providing a basis, usually a temporary one, on which operations or procedures may be carried out.

working bee *n NZ.* a voluntary group doing a job for charity.

working capital *n* **1** *Accounting.* current assets minus current liabilities. **2** current or liquid assets. **3** that part of the capital of a business enterprise available for operations.

working class *n* **1** Also called: **proletariat.** the social stratum, usually of low status, that consists of those who earn wages, esp. as manual workers. ◆ *adj* **working-class. 2** of, relating to, or characteristic of the working class.

working day *or esp. US & Canad.* **workday** *n* **1** a day on which work is done, esp. for an agreed or stipulated number of hours in return for a salary or wage. **2** the part of the day allocated to work. **3** *(often pl) Commerce.* any day of the week except Sunday, public holidays, and, in some cases, Saturday.

working drawing *n* a scale drawing of a part that provides a guide for manufacture.

working memory *n Psychol.* the current contents of consciousness.

working party *n* **1** a committee established to investigate a problem, question, etc. **2** a group of soldiers or prisoners assigned to perform a manual task or duty.

working week *or esp. US & Canad.* **workweek** *n* the number of hours or days in a week allocated to work.

work-in-progress *n Book-keeping.* the value of work begun but not completed, as shown in a profit-and-loss account.

workload ('wɜːkˌləʊd) *n* the amount of work to be done, esp. in a specified period.

workman ➊ ('wɜːkmən) *n, pl* **workmen. 1** a man who is employed in manual labour or who works an industrial machine. **2** a craftsman of skill as specified: *a bad workman.*

workmanlike ➊ ('wɜːkmənˌlaɪk) *or (less commonly)* **workmanly** *adj* appropriate to or befitting a good workman.

workmanship ➊ ('wɜːkmənʃɪp) *n* **1** the art or skill of a workman. **2** the art or skill with which something is made or executed. **3** the degree of art or skill exhibited in the finished product. **4** the piece of work so produced.

workmate ('wɜːkˌmeɪt) *n* a person who works with another; fellow worker.

work of art *n* **1** a piece of fine art, such as a painting or sculpture. **2** something that may be likened to a piece of fine art, esp. in beauty, intricacy, etc.

work off *vb (tr, adv)* **1** to get rid of or dissipate, as by effort: *he worked off some of his energy by digging the garden.* **2** to discharge (a debt) by labour rather than payment.

work on *vb (intr, prep)* to persuade or influence or attempt to persuade or influence.

work out ➊ *vb (adv)* **1** *(tr)* to achieve or accomplish by effort. **2** *(tr)* to solve or find out by reasoning or calculation: *to work out an answer; to work out a sum.* **3** *(tr)* to devise or formulate: *to work out a plan.* **4** *(intr)* to prove satisfactory: *did your plan work out?* **5** *(intr)* to happen as specified: *it all worked out well.* **6** *(intr)* to take part in physical exercise, as in training. **7** *(tr)* to remove all the mineral in (a mine, etc.) that can be profitably exploited. **8** *(intr; often foll. by to or at)* to reach a total: *your bill works out at a pound.* ◆ *n* **workout. 9** a session of physical exercise, esp. for training or to keep oneself fit.

work over *vb* **1** *(tr, adv)* to do again; repeat. **2** *(intr, prep)* to examine closely and thoroughly. **3** *(tr, adv) Sl.* to assault or thrash.

workpeople ('wɜːkˌpiːpᵊl) *pl n* the working members of a population.

workroom ('wɜːkˌruːm, -ˌrʊm) *n* **1** a room in which work, usually manual labour, is done. **2** a room in a house set aside for a hobby.

works ➊ (wɜːks) *pl n* **1** *(often functioning as sing)* a place where a number of people are employed, such as a factory. **2** the sum total of a writer's or artist's achievements, esp. when considered together: *the works of Shakespeare.* **3** the deeds of a person, esp. virtuous or moral deeds: *works of charity.* **4** the interior parts of the mechanism of a machine, etc.: *the works of a clock.* **5 the works.** *Sl.* **5a** full or extreme treatment. **5b** a very violent physical beating: *to give someone the works.*

works council *n Chiefly Brit.* **1** a council composed of both employer and employees convened to discuss matters of common interest concerning a factory, plant, business policy, etc. **2** a body representing the workers of a plant, factory, etc., elected to negotiate with the management about working conditions, wages, etc. ◆ Also called: **works committee.**

worksheet ('wɜːkˌʃiːt) *n* **1** a sheet of paper used for the rough draft of a problem, design, etc. **2** a piece of paper recording work in progress.

workshop ➊ ('wɜːkˌʃɒp) *n* **1** a room or building in which manufacturing or other forms of manual work are carried on. **2** a room in a private dwelling, school, etc., set aside for crafts. **3** a group of people engaged in study or work on a creative project or subject: *a music workshop.*

workshy ('wɜːkˌʃaɪ) *adj* not inclined to work.

work station *n* an area in an office where one person works.

work-study *n* an examination of ways of finding the most efficient method of doing a job.

worktable ('wɜːkˌteɪbᵊl) *n* **a** any table at which writing, sewing, or other work may be done. **b** (in English cabinetwork) a small elegant table fitted with sewing accessories.

worktop ('wɜːkˌtɒp) *n* a surface in a kitchen, often of heat-resistant plastic, used for food preparation.

work-to-rule *n* **1** a form of industrial action in which employees adhere strictly to all the working rules laid down by their employers, with the deliberate intention of reducing the rate of working. ◆ *vb* **work to rule. 2** *(intr)* to decrease the rate of working by this means.

work up ➊ *vb* **1** *(tr, adv)* to arouse the feelings of; excite. **2** *(tr, adv)* to cause to grow or develop: *to work up a hunger.* **3** to move or cause to move gradually upwards. **4** *(tr, adv)* to manipulate or mix into a specified object or shape. **5** *(tr, adv)* to gain skill at (a subject). **6** *(adv)* (foll. by *to*) to develop gradually or progress (towards): *working up to a climax.*

world ➊ (wɜːld) *n* **1** the earth as a planet, esp. including its inhabitants. **2** mankind; the human race. **3** people generally; the public: *in the eyes of the world.* **4** social or public life: *to go out into the world.* **5** the universe or cosmos; everything in existence. **6** a complex united whole re-

THESAURUS

working *n* **1** = **operation**, action, functioning, manner, method, mode of operation, running **4** *often plural* = **mine**, digging, excavation, pit, quarry, shaft ◆ *adj* **6** = **employed**, active, in a job, in work, labouring **9** = **functioning**, going, operative, running **10** = **effective**, practical, useful, viable

workman *n* **1, 2** = **labourer**, artificer, artisan, craftsman, employee, hand, journeyman, mechanic, operative, tradesman, worker

workmanlike *adj* = **efficient**, adept, careful, expert, masterly, painstaking, professional, proficient, satisfactory, skilful, skilled, thorough **Antonyms** *adj* amateurish, botchy, careless, clumsy, cowboy (*inf.*), incompetent, slap-dash, slipshod, unprofessional, unskilful

workmanship *n* **1, 2** = **skill**, art, artistry, craft, craftsmanship, execution, expertise, handicraft, handiwork, manufacture, technique, work

work out *vb* **2** = **solve**, calculate, clear up, figure out, find out, puzzle out, resolve, suss (out) (*sl.*) **3** = **plan**, arrange, construct, contrive, develop, devise, elaborate, evolve, form, formulate, put together **4** = **succeed**, be effective, flourish, go as planned, go well, prosper, prove satisfactory **5** = **happen**, come out, develop, evolve, go, pan out (*inf.*), result, turn out **6** = **exercise**, do exercises, drill, practise, train, warm up **8** *often foll. by* **to** *or* **at** = **amount to**, add up to, come to, reach, reach a total of ◆ *n* **workout 9** = **exercise**, drill, exercise session, practice session, training, training session, warm-up

works *pl n* **1** = **factory**, mill, plant, shop, workshop **2** = **writings**, canon, *oeuvre*, output, productions **3** = **deeds**, actions, acts, doings **4** = **mechanism**, action, guts (*inf.*), innards (*inf.*), insides (*inf.*), machinery, movement, moving parts, parts, workings

workshop *n* **1, 2** = **studio**, atelier, factory, mill, plant, shop, workroom, works **3** = **seminar**, class, discussion group, masterclass, study group

work up *vb* **1** = **excite**, agitate, animate, arouse, enkindle, foment, generate, get (someone) all steamed up (*sl.*), incite, inflame, instigate, move, rouse, spur, stir up, wind up (*inf.*)

world *n* **1** = **earth**, earthly sphere, globe **2** = **mankind**, everybody, everyone, humanity, humankind, human race, man, men, the public, the race of man **5** = **universe**, cosmos, creation, existence, life, nature **7** = **planet**, heavenly body, star **9** = **sphere**, area, domain, environment, field, kingdom, province, realm, system **11** = **period**, age, days, epoch, era, times **17 for all the world** = **exactly**, in every respect, in every way, just as if, just like, precisely, to all intents and purposes **22 on top of the world** *Informal* = **overjoyed**, beside oneself with joy, cock-a-hoop, ecstatic, elated, exultant, happy, in raptures, on cloud nine (*inf.*), over the moon (*inf.*) **23 out of this world** *Informal* = **wonderful**, excellent, fabulous (*inf.*), fantastic (*inf.*), great (*inf.*), incredible, indescribable, marvellous, superb, unbelievable

garded as resembling the universe. **7** any star or planet, esp. one that might be inhabited. **8** (*often cap.*) a division or section of the earth, its history, or its inhabitants: *the Ancient World; the Third World.* **9** an area, sphere, or realm considered as a complete environment: *the animal world.* **10** any field of human activity or way of life or those involved in it: *the world of television.* **11** a period or state of existence: *the next world.* **12** the total circumstances and experience of an individual that make up his life: *you have shattered my world.* **13** a large amount, number, or distance: *worlds apart.* **14** worldly or secular life, ways, or people. **15 bring into the world. 15a** (of a midwife, doctor, etc.) to deliver (a baby). **15b** to give birth to. **16 come into the world.** to be born. **17 for all the world.** in every way; exactly. **18 for the world.** (*used with a negative*) for any inducement, however great. **19 in the world.** (intensifier; *usually used with a negative*): *no-one in the world can change things.* **20 man** (*or* **woman**) **of the world.** a man (or woman) experienced in social or public life. **21 not long for this world.** nearing death. **22 on top of the world.** *Inf.* elated or very happy. **23 out of this world.** *Inf.* wonderful; excellent. **24 set the world on fire.** to be exceptionally or sensationally successful. **25 the best of both worlds.** the benefits from two different ways of life, philosophies, etc. **26 think the world of.** to be extremely fond of or hold in very high esteem. **27 world of one's own.** a state of mental detachment from other people. **28 world without end.** forever. **29** (*modifier*) of or concerning most or all countries; worldwide: *world politics.* **30** (*in combination*) throughout the world: *world-famous.* [OE *w(e)orold,* from *wer* man + *ald* age, life]

World Bank *n* an international cooperative organization established in 1945 to assist economic development, esp. of backward nations, by the advance of loans guaranteed by member governments. Officially called: **International Bank for Reconstruction and Development.**

world-beater *n* a person or thing that surpasses all others in its category; champion.

world-class *adj* of or denoting someone with a skill or attribute that puts him or her in the highest class in the world: *a world-class swimmer.*

World Court *n* another name for **International Court of Justice.**

World Cup *n* an international competition held between national teams in various sports, most notably association football.

worldling ('wɜːldlɪŋ) *n* a person who is primarily concerned with worldly matters.

worldly ❶ ('wɜːldlɪ) *adj* **worldlier, worldliest. 1** not spiritual; mundane or temporal. **2** Also: **worldly-minded.** absorbed in material things. **3** Also: **worldly-wise.** versed in the ways of the world; sophisticated.
▸ **'worldliness** *n*

world music *n* popular music of various ethnic origins and styles.

world power *n* a state that possesses sufficient power to influence events throughout the world.

world-shaking *adj* of enormous significance.

World Trade Organization *n* an international body concerned with promoting and regulating trade between its member states; established in 1995 as a successor to GATT.

World War I *n* the war (1914–18), fought mainly in Europe and the Middle East, in which the Allies (principally France, Russia, Britain, Italy after 1915, and the US after 1917) defeated the Central Powers (principally Germany, Austria-Hungary, and Turkey). Also called: **First World War, Great War.**

World War II *n* the war (1939–45) in which the Allies (principally Britain, the Soviet Union, and the US) defeated the Axis powers (principally Germany, Italy, and Japan). Britain and France declared war on Germany (Sept. 3, 1939) as a result of the German invasion of Poland (Sept. 1, 1939). Italy entered the war on June 10, 1940 shortly before the collapse of France (armistice signed June 22, 1940). On June 22, 1941 Germany attacked the Soviet Union and on Dec. 7, 1941 the Japanese attacked the US at Pearl Harbor. On Sept. 8, 1943 Italy surrendered, the war in Europe ending on May 7, 1945 with the unconditional surrender of the Germans. The Japanese capitulated on Aug. 14, 1945. Also called: **Second World War.**

world-weary *adj* no longer finding pleasure in living.
▸ **'world-ˌweariness** *n*

worldwide ❶ ('wɜːld'waɪd) *adj* applying or extending throughout the world; universal.

World Wide Web *n Computing.* a vast network of linked hypertext files, stored on computers throughout the world, that can provide a computer user with information on a huge variety of subjects. Abbrev.: **WWW.**

worm (wɜːm) *n* **1** any of various invertebrates, esp. the annelids (earthworms, etc.), nematodes (roundworms), and flatworms, having a slender elongated body. **2** any of various insect larvae having an elongated body, such as the silkworm and wireworm. **3** any of various unrelated animals that resemble annelids, nematodes, etc., such as the glow-worm and shipworm. **4** a gnawing or insinuating force or agent that torments or slowly eats away. **5** a wretched or spineless person. **6** anything that resembles a worm in appearance or movement. **7** a shaft on which a helical groove has been cut, as in a gear arrangement in which such a shaft meshes with a toothed wheel. **8** a spiral pipe cooled by air or flowing water, used as a condenser in a still. **9** *Computing.* a program that duplicates itself many times in a network and prevents its destruction. It often carries a logic bomb or virus. ◆ *vb* **10** to move, act, or cause to move or act with the slow sinuous movement of a worm. **11** (foll. by *in, into, out of,* etc.) to make (one's way) slowly and stealthily; insinuate (oneself). **12** (*tr;* often foll. by *out of* or *from*) to extract (information, etc.) from by persistent questioning. **13** (*tr*) to free from worms. ◆ See also **worms.** [OE *wyrm*]
▸ **'wormer** *n* ▸ **'wormˌlike** *adj*

WORM (wɜːm) *n Computing. acronym for* write once read many times: an optical disk which enables users to store data but not change it.

wormcast ('wɜːmˌkɑːst) *n* a coil of earth or sand that has been excreted by a burrowing earthworm or lugworm.

worm-eaten *adj* **1** eaten into by worms: *a worm-eaten table.* **2** decayed; rotten. **3** old-fashioned; antiquated.

worm gear *n* **1** a device consisting of a threaded shaft (**worm**) that mates with a gear-wheel (**worm wheel**) so that rotary motion can be transferred between two shafts at right angles to each other. **2** Also called: **worm wheel.** a gear-wheel driven by a threaded shaft or worm.

wormhole ('wɜːmˌhəʊl) *n* a hole made by a worm in timber, plants, etc.
▸ **'wormˌholed** *adj*

worms (wɜːmz) *n* (*functioning as sing*) any disease or disorder, usually of the intestine, characterized by infestation with parasitic worms.

worm's eye view *n* a view seen from below or from a more lowly or humble point.

wormwood ('wɜːmˌwʊd) *n* **1** Also called: **absinthe.** any of various plants of a chiefly N temperate genus, esp. a European plant yielding a bitter extract used in making absinthe. **2** something that embitters, such as a painful experience. [C15: changed (through infl. of WORM & WOOD) from OE *wormōd, wermōd*]

wormy ('wɜːmɪ) *adj* **wormier, wormiest. 1** worm-infested or worm-eaten. **2** resembling a worm in appearance, ways, or condition. **3** (of wood) having irregular small tunnels bored into it and tracked over its surface, made by worms. **4** low or grovelling.
▸ **'worminess** *n*

worn ❶ (wɔːn) *vb* **1** the past participle of **wear**[1] and **wear**[2]. ◆ *adj* **2** affected, esp. adversely, by long use or action: *a worn suit.* **3** haggard; drawn. **4** exhausted; spent.
▸ **'wornness** *n*

worn-out ❶ *adj* (**worn out** *when postpositive*). **1** worn or used until threadbare, valueless, or useless. **2** exhausted; very weary.

worriment ('wʌrɪmənt) *n Inf., chiefly US.* anxiety or the trouble that causes it; worry.

worrisome ❶ ('wʌrɪsəm) *adj* **1** causing worry; vexing. **2** tending to worry.
▸ **'worrisomely** *adv*

worrit ('wʌrɪt) *vb* (*tr*) *Dialect.* to tease or worry. [prob. var. of WORRY]

worry ❶ ('wʌrɪ) *vb* **worries, worrying, worried. 1** to be or cause to be anxious or uneasy, esp. about something uncertain or potentially dangerous. **2** (*tr*) to disturb the peace of mind of; bother: *don't worry me with trivialities.* **3** (*intr;* often foll. by *along* or *through*) to proceed de-

THESAURUS

worldly *adj* **1** = **earthly**, carnal, fleshly, lay, mundane, physical, profane, secular, sublunary, temporal, terrestrial **2** = **materialistic**, avaricious, covetous, grasping, greedy, selfish, worldly-minded **3** = **worldly-wise**, blasé, cosmopolitan, experienced, knowing, politic, sophisticated, urbane
Antonyms *adj* ≠ **earthly**: divine, ethereal, heavenly, immaterial, noncorporeal, spiritual, transcendental, unworldly ≠ **materialistic**: moral, nonmaterialistic, unworldly ≠ **worldly-wise**: ingenuous, innocent, naive, unsophisticated, unworldly

worldwide *adj* = **global**, general, international, omnipresent, pandemic, ubiquitous, universal
Antonyms *adj* confined, insular, limited, local, narrow, national, parochial, provincial, restricted

worn *adj* **2** = **ragged**, frayed, shabby, shiny, tattered, tatty, the worse for wear, threadbare **3** = **haggard**, careworn, drawn, lined, pinched, wizened **4** = **exhausted**, fatigued, jaded, played-out (*inf.*), spent, tired, tired out, wearied, weary, worn-out

worn-out *adj* **1** = **run-down**, broken-down, clapped out (*Brit., Austral., & NZ inf.*), decrepit, done, frayed, moth-eaten, on its last legs, ragged, shabby, tattered, tatty, threadbare, used, used-up, useless, worn **2** = **exhausted**, all in (*sl.*), dead *or* out on one's feet (*inf.*), dog-tired (*inf.*), done in (*inf.*), fatigued, fit to drop, knackered (*sl.*), prostrate, spent, tired, tired out, weary, wiped out (*inf.*)
Antonyms *adj* ≠ **exhausted**: fresh, refreshed, relaxed, renewed, rested, restored, revived, strengthened

worried *adj* **1, 2** = **anxious**, afraid, apprehensive, bothered, concerned, distracted, distraught, distressed, disturbed, fearful, fretful, frightened, hot and bothered, ill at ease, nervous, on edge, overwrought, perturbed, tense, tormented, troubled, uneasy, unquiet, upset, wired (*sl.*)
Antonyms *adj* calm, fearless, peaceful, quiet, tranquil, unafraid, unconcerned, unfazed (*inf.*), unworried

worrisome *adj* **1** = **troublesome**, bothersome, disquieting, distressing, disturbing, irksome, perturbing, upsetting, vexing, worrying **2** = **anxious**, apprehensive, fretful, insecure, jittery (*inf.*), nervous, neurotic, uneasy

worry *vb* **1** = **be anxious**, agonize, brood, feel uneasy, fret, obsess **2** = **trouble**, annoy, badger, bother, disquiet, distress, disturb, harass, harry, hassle (*inf.*), hector, importune, irritate, make anxious, perturb, pester, plague, tantalize, tease, torment, unsettle, upset, vex **5, 6** = **attack**, bite, gnaw at, go for, harass, harry, kill, lacerate, savage, tear ◆ *n* **9** = **anxiety**, annoyance, apprehension, care, concern, disturbance, fear, irritation, misery, misgiving, perplexity, torment, trepidation, trouble, un-

spite difficulties. **4** (*intr;* often foll. by *away*) to struggle or work: *to worry away at a problem.* **5** (*tr*) (of a dog, wolf, etc.) to lacerate or kill by biting, shaking, etc. **6** (when *intr*, foll. by *at*) to bite, tear, or gnaw (at) with the teeth: *a dog worrying a bone.* **7** (*tr*) to touch or poke repeatedly and idly. **8 not to worry.** *Inf.* you need not worry. ◆ *n, pl* **worries. 9** a state or feeling of anxiety. **10** a person or thing that causes anxiety. **11** an act of worrying. [OE *wyrgan*]
▸ **'worried** *adj* ▸ **'worriedly** *adv* ▸ **'worrying** *adj* ▸ **'worryingly** *adv*

worry beads *pl n* a string of beads that when fingered or played with supposedly relieves nervous tension.

worryguts ('wʌrɪˌgʌts) *n* (*functioning as sing*) *Inf.* a person who worries, esp. about insignificant matters.

worse (wɜːs) *adj* **1** the comparative of **bad**[1]. **2 none the worse for.** not harmed by (adverse events or circumstances). **3 the worse for wear. 3a** shabby or worn. **3b** a slang term for **drunk. 4 worse luck!** *Inf.* unhappily; unfortunately. **5 worse off.** (*postpositive*) in a worse, esp. a worse financial, condition. ◆ *n* **6** something that is worse. **7 for the worse.** into a less desirable or inferior state or condition: *a change for the worse.* ◆ *adv* **8** in a more severe or unpleasant manner. **9** in a less effective or successful manner. [OE *wiersa*]

worsen ❶ ('wɜːsᵊn) *vb* to grow or cause to grow worse.

worship ❶ ('wɜːʃɪp) *vb* **worships, worshipping, worshipped** *or US* **worships, worshiping, worshiped. 1** (*tr*) to show profound religious devotion and respect to; adore or venerate (God or any person or thing considered divine). **2** (*tr*) to be devoted to and full of admiration for. **3** (*intr*) to have or express feelings of profound adoration. **4** (*intr*) to attend services for worship. ◆ *n* **5** religious adoration or devotion. **6** the formal expression of religious adoration; rites, prayers, etc. **7** admiring love or devotion. [OE *weorthscipe*]
▸ **'worshipper** *n*

Worship ('wɜːʃɪp) *n Chiefly Brit.* (preceded by *Your, His,* or *Her*) a title used to address or refer to a mayor, magistrate, etc.

worshipful ('wɜːʃɪpfʊl) *adj* **1** feeling or showing reverence or adoration. **2** (*often cap.*) *Chiefly Brit.* a title used to address or refer to various people or bodies of distinguished rank.
▸ **'worshipfully** *adv* ▸ **'worshipfulness** *n*

worst ❶ (wɜːst) *adj* **1** the superlative of **bad**[1]. ◆ *adv* **2** in the most extreme or bad manner or degree. **3** least well, suitably, or acceptably. **4** (*in combination*) in or to the smallest degree or extent; least: *worst-loved.* ◆ *n* **5 the worst.** the least good or most inferior person, thing, or part in a group, narrative, etc. **6** (often preceded by *at*) the most poor, unpleasant, or unskilled quality or condition: *television is at its worst these days.* **7** the greatest amount of damage or wickedness of which a person or group is capable: *the invaders came and did their worst.* **8** the weakest effort or poorest achievement that a person or group is capable of making: *the applicant did his worst at the test because he did not want the job.* **9 at worst. 9a** in the least favourable interpretation or view. **9b** under the least favourable conditions. **10 come off worst** *or* **get the worst of it.** to enjoy the least benefit from an issue or be defeated in it. **11 if the worst comes to the worst.** if all the more desirable alternatives become impossible or if the worst possible thing happens. ◆ *vb* **12** (*tr*) to get the advantage over; defeat or beat. [OE *wierrest*]

worsted ('wʊstɪd) *n* **1** a closely twisted yarn or thread made from combed long-staple wool. **2** a fabric made from this, with a hard smooth close-textured surface and no nap. **3** (*modifier*) made of this yarn or fabric: *a worsted suit.* [C13: after *Worstead*, a district in Norfolk]

wort (wɜːt) *n* **1** (*in combination*) any of various unrelated plants, esp. ones formerly used to cure diseases: *liverwort.* **2** the sweet liquid made from warm water and ground malt, used to make a malt liquor. [OE *wyrt* root]

worth ❶ (wɜːθ) *adj* (governing a noun with prepositional force) **1** worthy of; meriting or justifying: *it's not worth discussing.* **2** having a value of: *the book is worth £30.* **3 for all one is worth.** to the utmost. **4 worth one's weight in gold.** extremely helpful, kind, etc. ◆ *n* **5** high quality; excellence. **6** value; price. **7** the amount of something of a specified value: *five pounds' worth of petrol.* [OE *weorth*]

worthless ❶ ('wɜːθlɪs) *adj* **1** without value or usefulness. **2** without merit; good-for-nothing.
▸ **'worthlessly** *adv* ▸ **'worthlessness** *n*

worthwhile ❶ (ˌwɜːθ'waɪl) *adj* sufficiently important, rewarding, or valuable to justify time or effort spent.

worthy ❶ ('wɜːðɪ) *adj* **worthier, worthiest. 1** (*postpositive;* often foll. by *of* or an infinitive) having sufficient merit or value (for something or someone specified); deserving. **2** having worth, value, or merit. ◆ *n, pl* **worthies. 3** *Often facetious.* a person of merit or importance.
▸ **'worthily** *adv* ▸ **'worthiness** *n*

wot (wɒt) *vb Arch. or dialect.* (used with *I, she, he, it,* or a singular noun) a form of the present tense (indicative mood) of **wit**[2].

would (wʊd; *unstressed* wəd) *vb* (takes an infinitive without *to* or an implied infinitive) used as an auxiliary: **1** to form the past tense or subjunctive mood of **will**[1]. **2** (with *you, he, she, it, they,* or a noun as subject) to indicate willingness or desire in a polite manner: *would you help me, please?* **3** to describe a past action as being accustomed or habitual: *every day we would go for walks.* **4** I wish: *would that he were here.*

> **USAGE NOTE** See at **should.**

would-be ❶ *adj* (*prenominal*) **1** *Usually derog.* wanting or professing to be: *a would-be politician.* **2** intended to be.

wouldn't ('wʊdᵊnt) *contraction of* would not.

wouldst (wʊdst) *vb Arch. or dialect.* (used with the pronoun *thou* or its relative equivalent) a singular form of the past tense of **will**[1].

Woulfe bottle (wʊlf) *n Chem.* a bottle with more than one neck, used for passing gases through liquids. [C18: after Peter *Woulfe* (?1727–1803), Brit. chemist]

wound[1] ❶ (wuːnd) *n* **1** any break in the skin or an organ or part as the result of violence or a surgical incision. **2** any injury or slight to the feelings or reputation. ◆ *vb* **3** to inflict a wound or wounds upon (someone or something). [OE *wund*]
▸ **'wounding** *adj* ▸ **'woundingly** *adv*

wound[2] (waʊnd) *vb* the past tense and past participle of **wind**[2] and **wind**[3].

wounded ('wuːndɪd) *adj* **1a** suffering from wounds; injured, esp. in a battle or fight. **1b** (*as collective n;* preceded by *the*): *the wounded.* **2** (of feelings) damaged or hurt.

woundwort ('wuːndˌwɜːt) *n* **1** any of various plants, such as field woundwort, having purple, scarlet, yellow, or white flowers and formerly used for dressing wounds. **2** any of various other plants used in this way.

wove (wəʊv) *vb* a past tense of **weave.**

woven ('wəʊvᵊn) *vb* a past participle of **weave.**

wove paper *n* paper with a very faint mesh impressed on it by the paper-making machine.

THESAURUS

ease, vexation, woe **10** = **problem**, annoyance, bother, care, hassle (*inf.*), irritation, pest, plague, torment, trial, trouble, vexation
Antonyms *vb* ≠ **be anxious:** be apathetic, be unconcerned, be unperturbed ≠ **trouble:** calm, comfort, console, solace, soothe ◆ *n* ≠ **anxiety:** calm, comfort, consolation, peace of mind, reassurance, serenity, solace, tranquillity

worsen *vb* = **aggravate**, damage, exacerbate = **deteriorate**, decay, decline, degenerate, get worse, go downhill (*inf.*), go from bad to worse, retrogress, sink, take a turn for the worse
Antonyms *vb* ≠ **aggravate:** ameliorate, enhance, improve, mend, rectify, upgrade ≠ **deteriorate:** be on the mend, improve, mend, recover

worship *vb* **1** = **praise**, adore, adulate, deify, exalt, glorify, honour, laud, pray to, respect, revere, reverence, venerate **2** = **love**, adore, idolize, put on a pedestal ◆ *n* **5** = **praise**, adoration, adulation, deification, devotion, exaltation, glorification, glory, homage, honour, laudation, love, prayer(s), regard, respect, reverence
Antonyms *vb* ≠ **praise:** blaspheme, deride, dishonour, flout, mock, revile, ridicule, scoff at ≠ **love:** despise, disdain, spurn

worst *vb* **12** = **beat**, best, blow out of the water (*sl.*), clobber (*sl.*), conquer, crush, defeat, gain the advantage over, get the better of, lick (*inf.*), master, overcome, overpower, overthrow, run rings around (*inf.*), subdue, subjugate, undo, vanquish

worth *n* **5** = **importance**, avail, benefit, credit, desert(s), estimation, excellence, goodness, help, merit, quality, usefulness, utility, value, virtue, worthiness **6** = **value**, cost, price, rate, valuation
Antonyms *n* ≠ **importance:** futility, insignificance, paltriness, triviality, unworthiness, uselessness, worthlessness, wretchedness

worthless *adj* **1** = **useless**, futile, ineffectual, insignificant, inutile, meaningless, measly, miserable, no use, nugatory, paltry, pointless, poor, poxy (*sl.*), rubbishy, trashy, trifling, trivial, two a penny (*inf.*), unavailing, unimportant, unusable, valueless, wretched **2** = **good-for-nothing**, abject, base, contemptible, depraved, despicable, ignoble, useless, vile
Antonyms *adj* ≠ **useless:** consequential, effective, fruitful, important, precious, productive, profitable, significant, useful, valuable, worthwhile ≠ **good-for-nothing:** decent, honourable, noble, upright, worthy

worthwhile *adj* = **useful**, beneficial, constructive, expedient, gainful, good, helpful, justifiable, productive, profitable, valuable, worthy
Antonyms *adj* inconsequential, pointless, trivial, unimportant, unworthy, useless, vain, valueless, wasteful, worthless

worthy *adj* **1, 2** = **praiseworthy**, admirable, commendable, creditable, decent, dependable, deserving, estimable, excellent, good, honest, honourable, laudable, meritorious, reliable, reputable, respectable, righteous, upright, valuable, virtuous, worthwhile ◆ *n* **3** *Often facetious* = **dignitary**, big hitter (*inf.*), big shot (*inf.*), bigwig (*inf.*), heavy hitter (*inf.*), luminary, notable, personage
Antonyms *adj* ≠ **praiseworthy:** demeaning, disreputable, dubious, ignoble, undeserving, unproductive, untrustworthy, unworthy, useless ◆ *n* ≠ **dignitary:** member of the rank and file, nobody, pleb, punter (*inf.*)

would-be *adj* **1** *Usually derogatory* = **budding**, dormant, latent, manqué, potential, professed, quasi-, self-appointed, self-styled, so-called, *soi-disant,* undeveloped, unfulfilled, unrealized, wannabe (*inf.*)

wound[1] *n* **1** = **injury**, cut, damage, gash, harm, hurt, laceration, lesion, slash, trauma (*Pathology*) **2** = **insult**, anguish, distress, grief, heartbreak, injury, offence, pain, pang, sense of loss, shock, slight, torment, torture, trauma ◆ *vb* **3** = **injure**, cut, damage, gash, harm, hit, hurt, irritate, lacerate, pierce, slash, wing **3** = **offend**, annoy, cut (someone) to the quick, distress, grieve, hurt, hurt the feelings of, mortify, pain, shock, sting, traumatize

wounding *adj* **3** = **hurtful**, acid, barbed, bitter, caustic, cruel, cutting, damaging, destructive, distressing, grievous, harmful, injurious, insulting, maleficent, malicious, mordacious, offensive, pernicious, pointed, savage, scathing, slighting, spiteful, stinging, trenchant, unkind, vitriolic

wow[1] (waʊ) *interj* **1** an exclamation of admiration, amazement, etc. ◆ *n* **2** *Sl.* a person or thing that is amazingly successful, attractive, etc. ◆ *vb* **3** *(tr) Sl.* to arouse great enthusiasm in. [C16: orig. Scot.]

wow[2] (waʊ, wəʊ) *n* a slow variation or distortion in pitch that occurs at very low audio frequencies in sound-reproducing systems. See also **flutter** (sense 12). [C20: imit.]

wowser (ˈwaʊzə) *n Austral. & NZ sl.* **1** a fanatically puritanical person. **2** a teetotaller. [C20: from E dialect *wow* to complain]

wp *abbrev. for* word processor.

wpb *abbrev. for* wastepaper basket.

WPC (in Britain) *abbrev. for* woman police constable.

wpm *abbrev. for* words per minute.

WRAAC *abbrev. for* Women's Royal Australian Army Corps.

WRAAF *abbrev. for* Women's Royal Australian Air Force.

WRAC (in Britain) *abbrev. for* Women's Royal Army Corps.

wrack[1] *or* **rack** (ræk) *n* **1** collapse or destruction (esp. in **wrack and ruin**). **2** something destroyed or a remnant of such. [OE *wræc* persecution, misery]

> **USAGE NOTE** The use of the spelling *wrack* rather than *rack* in sentences such as *she was wracked by grief* or *the country was wracked by civil war* is very common but is thought by many people to be incorrect.

wrack[2] (ræk) *n* **1** seaweed or other marine vegetation that is floating in the sea or has been cast ashore. **2** any of various seaweeds, such as serrated wrack. [C14 (in the sense: a wrecked ship, hence later applied to marine vegetation washed ashore): ?from MDu. *wrak* wreckage; the term corresponds to OE *wræc* WRACK[1]]

WRAF (in Britain) *abbrev. for* Women's Royal Air Force.

wraith ❶ (reɪθ) *n* **1** the apparition of a person living or thought to be alive, supposed to appear around the time of his death. **2** any apparition. [C16: Scot., from ?]
▸ˈ**wraith,like** *adj*

Wran (ræn) *n* a member of the Women's Royal Australian Naval Service.

wrangle ❶ (ˈræŋɡəl) *vb* **wrangles, wrangling, wrangled. 1** *(intr)* to argue, esp. noisily or angrily. **2** *(tr)* to encourage, persuade, or obtain by argument. **3** *(tr) Western US & Canad.* to herd (cattle or horses). ◆ *n* **4** a noisy or angry argument. [C14: from Low G *wrangeln*]

wrangler (ˈræŋɡlə) *n* **1** one who wrangles. **2** *Western US & Canad.* a herder; cowboy. **3** a person who handles or controls animals involved in the making of a film or television programme. **4** *Brit.* (at Cambridge University) a candidate who has obtained first-class honours in part II of the mathematics tripos. Formerly, the wrangler with the highest marks was called the **senior wrangler.**

WRANS *abbrev. for* Women's Royal Australian Naval Service. See also **Wran.**

wrap ❶ (ræp) *vb* **wraps, wrapping, wrapped.** *(mainly tr)* **1** to fold or wind (paper, cloth, etc.) around (a person or thing) so as to cover. **2** (often foll. by *up*) to fold paper, etc., around to fasten securely. **3** to surround or conceal by surrounding. **4** to enclose, immerse, or absorb: *wrapped in joy.* **5** to fold, wind, or roll up. **6** to complete the filming of (a motion picture or television programme). **7** *(intr;* often foll. by *about, around,* etc.) to be or become wound or extended. **8** (often foll. by *up*) Also: **rap.** *Austral. inf.* to praise (someone). ◆ *n* **9** a garment worn wrapped around the body, esp. the shoulders, such as a shawl or cloak. **10a** the end of a working day during the filming of a motion picture or television programme. **10b** the completion of filming of a motion picture or television programme. **11** *Chiefly US.* wrapping or a wrapper. **12 keep under wraps.** to keep secret. **13 take the wraps off.** to reveal. **14** Also: **rap.** *Austral. inf.* a commendation. [C14: from ?]

wrapover (ˈræp,əʊvə) *or* **wrapround** *adj* **1** (of a garment, esp. a skirt) not sewn up at one side, but worn wrapped round the body and fastened so that the open edges overlap. ◆ *n* **2** such a garment.

wrapped (ræpt) *vb* **1** the past tense and past participle of **wrap. 2 wrapped up in.** *Inf.* **2a** completely absorbed or engrossed in. **2b** implicated or involved in. ◆ *adj* **3** *Austral. inf.* a variant spelling of **rapt**[2].

wrapper ❶ (ˈræpə) *n* **1** the cover, usually of paper or cellophane, in which something is wrapped. **2** a dust jacket of a book. **3** the firm tobacco leaf forming the outermost portion of a cigar. **4** a loose negligee or dressing gown.

wrapping (ˈræpɪŋ) *n* the material used to wrap something.

wrapround (ˈræp,raʊnd) *or* **wraparound** *adj* **1** made so as to be wrapped round something: *a wrapround skirt.* **2** surrounding, curving round, or overlapping. **3** curving round in one continuous piece: *a wrapround windscreen.* ◆ *n* **4** *Printing.* a flexible plate of plastic, metal, or rubber that is made flat but used wrapped round the plate cylinder of a rotary press. **5** another name for **wrapover.**

wrap up ❶ *vb (adv)* **1** *(tr)* to fold paper around. **2** to put warm clothes on. **3** *(intr; usually imperative) Sl.* to be silent. **4** *(tr) Inf.* **4a** to settle the final details of. **4b** to make a summary of.

wrasse (ræs) *n* a marine food fish of tropical and temperate seas, having thick lips, strong teeth, and usually a bright coloration. [C17: from Cornish *wrach*]

wrath ❶ (rɒθ) *n* **1** angry, violent, or stern indignation. **2** divine vengeance or retribution. **3** *Arch.* a fit of anger or an act resulting from anger. [OE *wrǣththu*]

wrathful ❶ (ˈrɒθfʊl) *adj* **1** full of wrath; raging or furious. **2** resulting from or expressing wrath.
▸ˈ**wrathfully** *adv* ▸ˈ**wrathfulness** *n*

wreak ❶ (riːk) *vb (tr)* **1** to inflict (vengeance, etc.) or to cause (chaos, etc.): *to wreak havoc on the enemy.* **2** to express or gratify (anger, hatred, etc.). **3** *Arch.* to take vengeance for. [OE *wrecan*]
▸ˈ**wreaker** *n*

> **USAGE NOTE** See at **wrought.**

wreath ❶ (riːθ) *n, pl* **wreaths** (riːðz, riːθs). **1** a band of flowers or foliage intertwined into a ring, usually placed on a grave as a memorial or worn on the head as a garland or a mark of honour. **2** any circular or spiral band or formation. **3** (loosely) any floral design placed on a grave as a memorial. [OE *wrǣth, wrǣd*]
▸ˈ**wreath,like** *adj*

wreathe ❶ (riːð) *vb* **wreathes, wreathing, wreathed. 1** to form into or take the form of a wreath by intertwining or twisting together. **2** *(tr)* to decorate with wreaths. **3** to move or cause to move in a twisting way: *smoke wreathed up to the ceiling.* [C16: ? back formation from *wrēthen,* from OE *writhen,* p.p. of *wrīthan* to writhe]

wreck ❶ (rɛk) *vb* **1** to involve in or suffer disaster or destruction. **2** *(tr)* to cause the wreck of (a ship). ◆ *n* **3a** the accidental destruction of a ship at sea. **3b** the ship so destroyed. **4** *Maritime law.* goods cast ashore from a wrecked vessel. **5** a person or thing that has suffered ruin or dilapidation. **6** Also called: **wreckage.** the remains of something that has been destroyed. **7** Also called: **wreckage.** the act of wrecking or the state of being wrecked. [C13: from ON]
▸ˈ**wrecking** *n, adj*

wrecked (rɛkt) *adj Sl.* in a state of intoxication, stupor, or euphoria, induced by drugs or alcohol.

wrecker (ˈrɛkə) *n* **1** a person or thing that ruins or destroys. **2** *Chiefly US & Canad.* a person whose job is to demolish buildings or dismantle cars. **3** (formerly) a person who lures ships to destruction to plunder the wreckage. **4** a US and Canad. name for a breakdown van.

wrecking bar *n* a short crowbar, forked at one end and slightly angled at the other to make a fulcrum.

wren (rɛn) *n* **1** any small brown passerine songbird of a chiefly American family (in Britain **wren,** in the US and Canada **winter wren**). They have a slender bill and feed on insects. **2** any of various similar birds, such as the Australian warblers, New Zealand wrens, etc. [OE *wrenna, werna*]

Wren (rɛn) *n Inf.* (in Britain and certain other nations) a member of the Women's Royal Naval Service. [C20: from the abbrev. *WRNS*]

THESAURUS

wraith *n* **1** = **ghost**, apparition, eidolon, phantom, revenant, shade (*literary*), spectre, spirit, spook (*inf.*)

wrangle *vb* **1** = **argue**, altercate, bicker, brawl, contend, disagree, dispute, fall out (*inf.*), fight, have words, quarrel, row, scrap, spar, squabble ◆ *n* **4** = **argument**, altercation, angry exchange, argy-bargy (*Brit. inf.*), barney (*inf.*), bickering, brawl, clash, contest, controversy, dispute, falling-out (*inf.*), quarrel, row, set-to (*inf.*), slanging match (*Brit.*), squabble, tiff

wrap *vb* **1-5** = **cover**, absorb, bind, bundle up, cloak, encase, enclose, enfold, envelop, fold, immerse, muffle, pack, package, roll up, sheathe, shroud, surround, swathe, wind ◆ *n* **9** = **cloak**, cape, mantle, shawl, stole
Antonyms *vb* ≠ **cover:** disclose, open, strip, uncover, unfold, unpack, unwind, unwrap

wrapper *n* **1, 2** = **cover**, case, envelope, jacket, packaging, paper, sheath, sleeve, wrapping

wrap up *vb* **1** = **giftwrap**, bundle up, enclose, enwrap, pack, package **2** = **dress warmly**, muffle up, put warm clothes on, wear something warm **3** *Slang* = **be quiet**, be silent, button it (*sl.*), button one's lip (*sl.*), hold one's tongue, shut up **4a** *Informal* = **end**, bring to a close, conclude, finish off, polish off, round off, terminate, tidy up, wind up

wrath *n* **1** = **anger**, choler, displeasure, exasperation, fury, indignation, ire, irritation, passion, rage, resentment, temper
Antonyms *n* amusement, contentment, delight, enjoyment, gladness, gratification, happiness, joy, pleasure, satisfaction

wrathful *adj* **1** = **angry**, beside oneself with rage, choked, displeased, enraged, furious, incandescent, incensed, indignant, infuriated, irate, on the warpath (*inf.*), raging, wroth (*arch.*)
Antonyms *adj* amused, calm, contented, delighted, glad, gratified, happy, joyful, pleased, satisfied

wreak *vb* **1** = **create**, bring about, carry out, cause, effect, execute, exercise, inflict, visit, work **2** = **unleash**, express, give free rein to, give vent to, gratify, indulge, vent

wreath *n* **1** = **garland**, band, chaplet, coronet, crown, festoon, loop, ring

wreathe *vb* **1-3** = **surround**, adorn, coil, crown, encircle, enfold, engarland, entwine, envelop, enwrap, festoon, intertwine, interweave, twine, twist, wind, wrap, writhe

wreck *vb* **1** = **destroy**, blow (*sl.*), break, dash to pieces, demolish, devastate, mar, play havoc with, ravage, ruin, shatter, smash, spoil, total (*sl.*), trash (*sl.*), undo **2** = **go** *or* **run aground**, founder, run onto the rocks, shipwreck, strand ◆ *n* **3b** = **shipwreck**, derelict, hulk, sunken vessel **6** = **remains**, debris, fragments, hulk, pieces, rubble, ruin, wrack, wreckage **7** = **ruin**, desolation, destruction, devastation, disruption, mess, overthrow, undoing, wreckage
Antonyms *vb* ≠ **destroy:** build, conserve, create, fulfil, make possible, preserve, reconstruct, salvage, save ◆ *n* ≠ **ruin:** conservation, creation, formation, fulfilment, preservation, restoration, salvage, saving

wrench ❶ (rɛntʃ) *vb* **1** to give (something) a sudden or violent twist or pull, esp. so as to remove (something) from that to which it is attached: *to wrench a door off its hinges.* **2** (*tr*) to twist suddenly so as to sprain (a limb): *to wrench one's ankle.* **3** (*tr*) to give pain to. **4** (*tr*) to twist from the original meaning or purpose. **5** (*intr*) to make a sudden twisting motion. ◆ *n* **6** a forceful twist or pull. **7** an injury to a limb, caused by twisting. **8** sudden pain caused esp. by parting. **9** a parting that is difficult or painful to make. **10** a distorting of the original meaning or purpose. **11** a spanner, esp. one with adjustable jaws. See also **torque wrench.** [OE *wrencan*]

wrest ❶ (rɛst) *vb* (*tr*) **1** to take or force away by violent pulling or twisting. **2** to seize forcibly by violent or unlawful means. **3** to obtain by laborious effort. **4** to distort in meaning, purpose, etc. ◆ *n* **5** the act or an instance of wresting. **6** *Arch.* a small key used to tune a piano or harp. [OE *wrǣstan*]
▸**'wrester** *n*

wrestle ❶ ('rɛsᵊl) *vb* **wrestles, wrestling, wrestled. 1** to fight (another person) by holding, throwing, etc., without punching with the closed fist. **2** (*intr*) to participate in wrestling. **3** (when *intr*, foll. by *with* or *against*) to fight with (a person, problem, or thing): *wrestle with one's conscience.* **4** (*tr*) to move laboriously, as with wrestling movements. ◆ *n* **5** the act of wrestling. **6** a struggle or tussle. [OE *wrǣstlian*]
▸**'wrestler** *n*

wrestling ('rɛslɪŋ) *n* any of certain sports in which the contestants fight each other according to various rules governing holds and usually forbidding blows with the closed fist. The principal object is to overcome the opponent either by throwing or pinning him to the ground or by causing him to submit.

wrest pin *n* (on a piano, harp, etc.) a pin, embedded in the **wrest plank**, around which one end of a string is wound: it may be turned by means of a tuning key to alter the tension of the string.

wretch ❶ (rɛtʃ) *n* **1** a despicable person. **2** a person pitied for his misfortune. [OE *wrecca*]

wretched ❶ ('rɛtʃɪd) *adj* **1** in poor or pitiful circumstances. **2** characterized by or causing misery. **3** despicable; base. **4** poor, inferior, or paltry. **5** (*prenominal*) (intensifier qualifying something undesirable): *a wretched nuisance.*
▸**'wretchedly** *adv* ▸**'wretchedness** *n*

wrick (rɪk) *n* **1** a sprain or strain. ◆ *vb* **2** (*tr*) to sprain or strain.

wrier *or* **wryer** ('raɪə) *adj* the comparative of **wry.**

wriest *or* **wryest** ('raɪɪst) *adj* the superlative of **wry.**

wriggle ❶ ('rɪgᵊl) *vb* **wriggles, wriggling, wriggled. 1** to make or cause to make twisting movements. **2** (*intr*) to progress by twisting and turning. **3** (*intr*; foll. by *into* or *out of*) to manoeuvre oneself by clever or devious means: *wriggle out of an embarrassing situation.* ◆ *n* **4** a wriggling movement or action. **5** a sinuous marking or course. [C15: from MLow G]
▸**'wriggler** *n* ▸**'wriggly** *adj*

wright (raɪt) *n* (*now chiefly in combination*) a person who creates, builds, or repairs something specified: *a playwright; a shipwright.* [OE *wryhta, wyrhta*]

wring ❶ (rɪŋ) *vb* **wrings, wringing, wrung. 1** (often foll. by *out*) to twist and compress to squeeze (a liquid) from (cloth, etc.). **2** (*tr*) to twist forcibly: *wring its neck.* **3** (*tr*) to clasp and twist (one's hands), esp. in anguish. **4** (*tr*) to distress: *wring one's heart.* **5** (*tr*) to grip (someone's hand) vigorously in greeting. **6** (*tr*) to obtain as by forceful means: *wring information out of.* **7 wringing wet.** soaking; drenched. ◆ *n* **8** an act or the process of wringing. [OE *wringan*]

wringer ('rɪŋə) *n* another name for **mangle**[2] (sense 1).

wrinkle[1] ❶ ('rɪŋkᵊl) *n* **1** a slight ridge in the smoothness of a surface, such as a crease in the skin as a result of age. ◆ *vb* **wrinkles, wrinkling, wrinkled. 2** to make or become wrinkled, as by crumpling, creasing, or puckering. [C15: back formation from *wrinkled*, from OE *gewrinclod*, p.p. of *wrinclian* to wind around]
▸**'wrinkly** *adj*

wrinkle[2] ❶ ('rɪŋkᵊl) *n Inf.* a clever or useful trick, hint, or dodge. [OE *wrenc* trick]

wrinklies ('rɪŋklɪz) *pl n Inf., derog.* old people.

wrist (rɪst) *n* **1** *Anat.* the joint between the forearm and the hand. Technical name: **carpus. 2** the part of a sleeve or glove that covers the wrist. **3** *Machinery.* **3a** See **wrist pin. 3b** a joint in which a wrist pin forms the pivot. [OE]

wristband ('rɪst,bænd) *n* **1** a band around the wrist, esp. one attached to a watch or forming part of a long sleeve. **2** a sweatband around the wrist.

wristlet ('rɪstlɪt) *n* a band or bracelet worn around the wrist.

wrist pin *n* **1** a cylindrical boss or pin attached to the side of a wheel parallel with the axis, esp. one forming a bearing for a crank. **2** the US and Canad. name for **gudgeon pin.**

wristwatch ('rɪst,wɒtʃ) *n* a watch worn strapped around the wrist.

wristy ('rɪstɪ) *adj* (of a player's style of hitting the ball in cricket, tennis, etc.) with much movement of the wrist.

writ ❶ (rɪt) *n* **1** a document under seal, issued in the name of the Crown or a court, commanding the person to whom it is addressed to do or refrain from doing some specified act. **2** *Arch.* a piece of writing: *Holy Writ.* [OE]

write ❶ (raɪt) *vb* **writes, writing, wrote, written. 1** to draw or mark (symbols, words, etc.) on a surface, usually paper, with a pen, pencil, or other instrument. **2** to describe or record (ideas, experiences, etc.) in writing. **3** to compose (a letter) to or correspond regularly with (a person, organization, etc.). **4** (*tr; may take a clause as object*) to say or communicate by letter: *he wrote that he was on his way.* **5** (*tr*) *Inf., chiefly US & Canad.* to send a letter to (a person, etc.). **6** to write (words) in cursive as opposed to printed style. **7** (*tr*) to be sufficiently familiar with (a specified style, language, etc.) to use it in writing. **8** to be the author or composer of (books, music, etc.). **9** (*tr*) to fill in the details for (a document, form, etc.). **10** (*tr*) to draw up or draft. **11** (*tr*) to produce by writing: *he wrote ten pages.* **12** (*tr*) to show clearly: *envy was written all over his face.* **13** (*tr*) to spell or inscribe. **14** (*tr*) to ordain or prophesy: *it is written.* **15** (*intr*) to produce writing as specified. **16** *Computing.* to record (data) in a location in a storage device. **17** (*tr*) See **underwrite** (sense 3a). ◆ See also **write down, write in,** etc. [OE *wrītan* (orig.: to scratch runes into bark)]
▸**'writable** *adj*

write down *vb* (*adv*) **1** (*tr*) to set down in writing. **2** (*tr*) to harm or belittle by writing about (a person) in derogatory terms. **3** (*intr*; foll. by *to* or *for*) to write in a simplified way (to a supposedly less cultured readership). **4** (*tr*) *Accounting.* to decrease the book value of (an asset). ◆ *n* **write-down. 5** *Accounting.* a reduction made in the book value of an asset.

write in *vb* (*tr*) **1** to insert in (a document, form, etc.) in writing. **2** (*adv*) to write a letter to a company, institution, etc. **3** (*adv*) *US.* to vote for (a person not on a ballot) by inserting his name.

write off ❶ *vb* (*tr, adv*) **1** *Accounting.* **1a** to cancel (a bad debt or obsolete asset) from the accounts. **1b** to consider (a transaction, etc.) as a loss or set off (a loss) against revenues. **1c** to depreciate (an asset) by periodic charges. **1d** to charge (a specified amount) against gross profits as depreciation of an asset. **2** to cause or acknowledge the complete loss of. **3** to dismiss from consideration. **4** to send a written order (for something): *she wrote off for a brochure.* **5** *Inf.* to damage (something, esp. a car) beyond repair. ◆ *n* **write-off. 6** *Accounting.* **6a** the act of cancelling a bad debt or obsolete asset from the accounts. **6b** the bad debt or obsolete asset cancelled. **6c** the amount cancelled against gross profits, corresponding to the book value of the bad debt or obsolete asset. **7** *Inf.* something damaged beyond repair, esp. a car.

write out *vb* (*tr, adv*) **1** to put into writing or reproduce in full form in writing. **2** to exhaust (oneself or one's creativity) by excessive writing. **3** to remove (a character) from a television or radio series.

writer ❶ ('raɪtə) *n* **1** a person who writes books, articles, etc., esp. as an occupation. **2** the person who has written something specified. **3** a person who is able to write or write well. **4** a scribe or clerk. **5** a composer of music. **6 Writer to the Signet.** (in Scotland) a member of an ancient society of solicitors, now having the exclusive privilege of preparing crown writs.

THESAURUS

wrench *vb* **1** = **twist**, force, jerk, pull, rip, tear, tug, wrest, wring, yank **2** = **sprain**, distort, rick, strain ◆ *n* **6** = **twist**, jerk, pull, rip, tug, yank **7** = **sprain**, strain, twist **8** = **blow**, ache, pain, pang, shock, upheaval, uprooting **11** = **spanner**, adjustable spanner, shifting spanner

wrest *vb* **1-3** = **seize**, extract, force, pull, strain, take, twist, win, wrench, wring

wrestle *vb* **1-3** = **fight**, battle, combat, contend, grapple, scuffle, strive, struggle, tussle

wretch *n* **1** = **scoundrel**, bad egg (*old-fashioned inf.*), bastard (*offens.*), blackguard, cur, good-for-nothing, miscreant, outcast, profligate, rascal, rat (*inf.*), rogue, rotter (*sl., chiefly Brit.*), ruffian, swine, vagabond, villain, worm **2** = **poor thing**, poor soul, unfortunate

wretched *adj* **1** = **unhappy**, abject, broken-hearted, cheerless, comfortless, crestfallen, dejected, deplorable, depressed, disconsolate, dismal, distressed, doleful, downcast, forlorn, funereal, gloomy, hapless, hopeless, melancholy, miserable, pathetic, pitiable, pitiful, poor, sorry, unfortunate, woebegone, woeful, worthless **2, 4** = **worthless**, calamitous, deplorable, inferior, miserable, paltry, pathetic, poor, sorry **3** = **shameful**, base, contemptible, despicable, low, low-down (*inf.*), mean, paltry, poxy, scurvy, shabby, vile
Antonyms *adj* ≠ **unhappy:** carefree, cheerful, contented, happy, jovial, light-hearted, untroubled ≠ **worthless:** excellent, flourishing, great, splendid, successful, thriving ≠ **shameful:** admirable, decent, noble, worthy

wriggle *vb* **1** = **twist**, jerk, jiggle, squirm, turn, wag, waggle, wiggle, writhe **2** = **crawl**, slink, snake, twist and turn, worm, zigzag **3** = **manoeuvre**, crawl, dodge, extricate oneself, sneak, talk one's way out, worm ◆ *n* **4** = **twist**, jerk, jiggle, squirm, turn, wag, waggle, wiggle

wring *vb* **1, 6** = **twist**, coerce, extort, extract, force, screw, squeeze, wrench, wrest

wrinkle[1] *n* **1** = **crease**, corrugation, crinkle, crow's-foot, crumple, fold, furrow, gather, line, pucker, rumple ◆ *vb* **2** = **crease**, corrugate, crinkle, crumple, fold, furrow, gather, line, pucker, ruck, rumple
Antonyms *vb* ≠ **crease:** even out, flatten, iron, level, press, smooth, straighten, unfold

wrinkle[2] *n Informal* = **trick**, device, dodge, gimmick, idea, plan, ploy, ruse, scheme, stunt, tip, wheeze (*Brit. sl.*)

writ *n* **1** = **summons**, court order, decree, document

write *vb* **1, 8, 10** = **record**, author (*nonstandard*), commit to paper, compose, copy, correspond, create, draft, draw up, indite, inscribe, jot down, pen, put down in black and white, put in writing, scribble, set down, take down, tell, transcribe

write off *vb* **1, 2** = **cancel**, cross out, disregard, forget about, give up for lost, score out, shelve **5** *Informal* = **wreck**, crash, damage beyond repair, destroy, smash up, total (*sl.*), trash (*sl.*)

writer *n* **1** = **author**, columnist, essayist, hack, littérateur, man of letters, novelist, penman, penny-a-liner (*rare*), penpusher, scribbler, scribe, wordsmith

writer's cramp *n* a muscular spasm or temporary paralysis of the muscles of the thumb and first two fingers caused by prolonged writing.

write up *vb (tr, adv)* **1** to describe fully, complete, or bring up to date in writing: *write up a diary*. **2** to praise or bring to public notice in writing. **3** *Accounting*. **3a** to place an excessively high value on (an asset). **3b** to increase the book value of (an asset) in order to reflect more accurately its current worth in the market. ◆ *n* **write-up. 4** a published account of something, such as a review in a newspaper or magazine.

writhe ❶ (raɪð) *vb* **writhes, writhing, writhed. 1** to twist or squirm in or as if in pain. **2** *(intr)* to move with such motions. **3** *(intr)* to suffer acutely from embarrassment, revulsion, etc. ◆ *n* **4** the act of writhing. [OE *wrīthan*]
▸ **'writher** *n*

writing ❶ ('raɪtɪŋ) *n* **1** a group of letters or symbols written or marked on a surface as a means of communicating. **2** short for **handwriting. 3** anything expressed in letters, esp. a literary composition. **4** the work of a writer. **5** literary style, art, or practice. **6** written form: *give it to me in writing*. **7** *(modifier)* related to or used in writing: *writing ink*. **8 writing on the wall.** a sign or signs of approaching disaster. [sense 8: allusion to Daniel 5:5]

writing desk *n* a piece of furniture with a writing surface and drawers and compartments for papers, etc.

writing paper *n* paper sized to take writing ink and used for letters and other manuscripts.

writ of execution *n Law*. a writ ordering that a judgment be enforced.

written ('rɪtᵊn) *vb* **1** the past participle of **write.** ◆ *adj* **2** taken down in writing; transcribed: *written evidence*.

WRNS *abbrev. for* Women's Royal Naval Service. See also **Wren.**

wrong ❶ (rɒŋ) *adj* **1** not correct or truthful: *the wrong answer*. **2** acting or judging in error: *you are wrong to think that*. **3** *(postpositive)* immoral; bad: *it is wrong to cheat*. **4** deviating from or unacceptable to correct or conventional laws, usage, etc. **5** not intended or wanted: *the wrong road*. **6** *(postpositive)* not working properly; amiss: *something is wrong with the engine*. **7** (of a side, esp. of a fabric) intended to face the inside so as not to be seen. **8 get on the wrong side of.** *Inf.* to come into disfavour with. **9 go down the wrong way.** (of food) to pass into the windpipe instead of the gullet. ◆ *adv* **10** in the wrong direction or manner. **11 get wrong. 11a** to fail to understand properly. **11b** to fail to provide the correct answer to. **12 go wrong. 12a** to turn out other than intended. **12b** to make a mistake. **12c** (of a machine, etc.) to cease to function properly. **12d** to go astray morally. ◆ *n* **13** a bad, immoral, or unjust thing or action. **14** *Law*. **14a** an infringement of another person's rights, rendering the offender liable to a civil action: *a private wrong*. **14b** a violation of public rights and duties, affecting the community as a whole and actionable at the instance of the Crown: *a public wrong*. **15 in the wrong.** mistaken or guilty. ◆ *vb (tr)* **16** to treat unjustly. **17** to malign or misrepresent. [OE *wrang* injustice]
▸ **'wronger** *n* ▸ **'wrongly** *adv* ▸ **'wrongness** *n*

wrongdoer ❶ ('rɒŋˌduːə) *n* a person who acts immorally or illegally.
▸ **'wrongˌdoing** *n*

wrong-foot *vb (tr)* **1** *Tennis, etc.* to play a shot in such a way as to cause (one's opponent) to be off balance. **2** to take by surprise so as to place in an embarrassing or disadvantageous situation.

wrongful ❶ ('rɒŋfʊl) *adj* unjust or illegal.
▸ **'wrongfully** *adv* ▸ **'wrongfulness** *n*

wrong-headed ❶ *adj* **1** constantly wrong in judgment. **2** foolishly stubborn; obstinate.
▸ **ˌwrong-'headedly** *adv* ▸ **ˌwrong-'headedness** *n*

wrong number *n* a telephone number wrongly connected or dialled in error, or the person so contacted.

wrote (rəʊt) *vb* the past tense of **write.**

wroth (rəʊθ, rɒθ) *adj Arch. or literary*. angry; irate. [OE *wrāth*]

wrought (rɔːt) *vb* **1** *Arch.* a past tense and past participle of **work.** ◆ *adj* **2** *Metallurgy*. shaped by hammering or beating. **3** *(often in combination)* formed, fashioned, or worked as specified: *well-wrought*. **4** decorated or made with delicate care. [C16: var. of *worht*, from OE *geworht*, p.p. of *(ge)wyrcan* to work]

> **USAGE NOTE** *Wrought* is sometimes used as if it were the past tense and past participle of *wreak* as in *the hurricane wrought havoc in coastal areas*. Many people think this use is incorrect.

wrought iron *n* **a** a pure form of iron having a low carbon content: often used for decorative work. **b** *(as modifier)*: *wrought-iron gates*.

wrought-up ❶ *adj* agitated or excited.

wrung (rʌŋ) *vb* the past tense and past participle of **wring.**

WRVS *abbrev. for* Women's Royal Voluntary Service.

wry ❶ (raɪ) *adj* **wrier, wriest** *or* **wryer, wryest. 1** twisted, contorted, or askew. **2** (of a facial expression) produced or characterized by contorting of the features. **3** drily humorous; sardonic. **4** warped, misdirected, or perverse. ◆ *vb* **wries, wrying, wried. 5** *(tr)* to twist or contort. [C16: from dialect *wry* to twist, from OE *wrīgian* to turn]
▸ **'wryly** *adv* ▸ **'wryness** *n*

wrybill ('raɪˌbɪl) *n* a New Zealand plover, having its bill deflected to one side enabling it to search for food beneath stones.

wryneck ('raɪˌnɛk) *n* **1** either of two cryptically coloured Old World woodpeckers, which do not drum on trees. **2** another name for **torticollis. 3** *Inf.* a person who has a twisted neck.

WSW *symbol for* west-southwest.

wt. *abbrev. for* weight.

WTO *abbrev. for* World Trade Organization.

wunderkind ('wʌndəˌkɪnd; *German* 'vʊndərˌkɪnt) *n, pl* **wunderkinds** *or* **wunderkinder** (*German* -ˌkɪndər). **1** a child prodigy. **2** a person who is extremely successful in his field while still young. [C20: from G *Wunderkind*, lit.: wonder child]

wurst (wɜːst, wʊəst, vʊəst) *n* a sausage, esp. of a type made in Germany, Austria, etc. [from G *Wurst*, lit.: something rolled]

wuthering ('wʌðərɪŋ) *adj N English dialect.* **1** (of a wind) blowing strongly with a roaring sound. **2** (of a place) characterized by such a sound. [var. of *whitherin*, from *whither* blow, from ON *hvithra*]

wuss (wʊs) *or* **wussy** ('wʊsɪ) *n, pl* **wusses** *or* **wussies.** *Sl., chiefly US.* a feeble or effeminate person. [C20: ?from PUSSY[1] (cat)]

WW1 *abbrev. for* World War One.

WW2 *abbrev. for* World War Two.

WWW *abbrev. for* World Wide Web.

wych-elm *or* **witch-elm** ('wɪtʃˌɛlm) *n* **1** a Eurasian elm tree, having a rounded shape, longish pointed leaves, clusters of small flowers, and winged fruits. **2** the wood of this tree. [C17: from OE *wice*]

wynd (waɪnd) *n Scot.* a narrow lane or alley. [C15: from the stem of WIND[2]]

WYSIWYG ('wɪzɪˌwɪg) *n, adj Computing. acronym for* what you see is what you get: referring to what is displayed on the screen being the same as what will be printed out.

wyvern *or* **wivern** ('waɪvən) *n* a heraldic beast having a serpent's tail and a dragon's head and a body with wings and two legs. [C17: var. of earlier *wyver*, from OF, from L *vīpera* VIPER]

THESAURUS

writhe *vb* **1 = squirm**, contort, convulse, distort, jerk, struggle, thrash, thresh, toss, twist, wiggle, wriggle

writing *n* **2 = script**, calligraphy, chirography, hand, handwriting, penmanship, print, scrawl, scribble **3 = document**, book, composition, letter, opus, publication, title, work **5 = literature**, belles-lettres, letters

wrong *adj* **1 = incorrect**, erroneous, fallacious, false, faulty, inaccurate, in error, mistaken, off base (*US & Canad. inf.*), off beam (*inf.*), off target, out, unsound, untrue, way off beam (*inf.*), wide of the mark **3 = bad**, blameworthy, criminal, crooked, dishonest, dishonourable, evil, felonious, illegal, illicit, immoral, iniquitous, not cricket (*inf.*), reprehensible, sinful, under-the-table, unethical, unfair, unjust, unlawful, wicked, wrongful **4 = inappropriate**, funny, improper, inapt, incongruous, incorrect, indecorous, infelicitous, malapropos, not done, unacceptable, unbecoming, unconventional, undesirable, unfitting, unhappy, unseemly, unsuitable **6 = defective**, amiss, askew, awry, faulty, not working, out of commission, out of order **7 = opposite**, inside, inverse, reverse ◆ *adv* **10 = incorrectly**, badly, erroneously, inaccurately, mistakenly, wrongly **10 = amiss**, askew, astray, awry **12 go wrong: a = lapse**, come to grief, come to nothing, fall through, flop (*inf.*), go pear-shaped (*inf.*), miscarry, misfire **b = err**, boob (*Brit. sl.*), go astray, slip up (*inf.*) **c = cease to function**, conk out (*inf.*), fail, go kaput (*inf.*), go on the blink (*sl.*), malfunction, misfire **d = go astray**, err, fall from grace, go off the straight and narrow (*inf.*), go to the bad, sin ◆ *n* **13 = offence**, abuse, bad *or* evil deed, crime, error, grievance, infraction, infringement, injury, injustice, misdeed, sin, transgression, trespass **15 in the wrong = guilty**, at fault, blameworthy, in error, mistaken, off beam (*inf.*), off course, off target, to be blamed ◆ *vb* **16, 17 = mistreat**, abuse, cheat, discredit, dishonour, harm, hurt, ill-treat, ill-use, impose upon, injure, malign, maltreat, misrepresent, oppress, take advantage of
Antonyms *adj* ≠ **incorrect:** accurate, correct, precise, right, true ≠ **bad:** ethical, fair, fitting, godly, honest, honourable, just, lawful, legal, moral, righteous, rightful, square, upright, virtuous ≠ **inappropriate:** appropriate, apt, becoming, commendable, correct, fitting, laudable, praiseworthy, proper, seemly, sensible, suitable ◆ *adv* ≠ **incorrectly:** accurately, correctly, exactly, precisely, properly, squarely, truly ◆ *n* ≠ **offence:** favour, good deed, good turn ◆ *vb* ≠ **mistreat:** aid, do a favour, help, support, treat well

wrongdoer *n* **= offender**, criminal, culprit, delinquent, evildoer, lawbreaker, malefactor, miscreant, sinner, transgressor, trespasser (*arch.*), villain

wrongful *adj* **= improper**, blameworthy, criminal, dishonest, dishonourable, evil, felonious, illegal, illegitimate, illicit, immoral, reprehensible, unethical, unfair, unjust, unlawful, wicked
Antonyms *adj* ethical, fair, honest, honourable, just, lawful, legal, legitimate, moral, proper, rightful

wrong-headed *adj* **1 = mistaken**, erroneous, fallacious, false, faulty, incorrect, in error, misguided, off target, unsound, wrong **2 = obstinate**, bull-headed, contrary, cross-grained, dogged, froward (*arch.*), inflexible, intransigent, mulish, obdurate, perverse, pig-headed, refractory, self-willed, stubborn, wilful

wrought-up *adj* **= worked-up**, agitated, animated, aroused, at fever pitch, beside oneself, excited, inflamed, keyed up, moved, overwrought, roused, stirred, strung up (*inf.*)

wry *adj* **1 = contorted**, askew, aslant, awry, crooked, deformed, distorted, off the level, skewwhiff (*Brit. inf.*), twisted, uneven, warped **3 = ironic**, droll, dry, mocking, mordacious, pawky (*Scot.*), sarcastic, sardonic
Antonyms *adj* ≠ **contorted:** aligned, even, level, smooth, straight, unbent

x *or* **X** (ɛks) *n, pl* **x's, X's,** *or* **Xs. 1** the 24th letter of the English alphabet. **2** a speech sound sequence represented by this letter, pronounced as *ks* or *gz* or, in initial position, *z*, as in *xylophone*.

x *symbol for:* **1** *Commerce, finance, etc.* ex. **2** *Maths.* the *x*-axis or a coordinate measured along the *x*-axis in a Cartesian coordinate system. **3** *Maths.* an algebraic variable. **4** multiplication.

X *symbol:* **1a** (in Britain, formerly) indicating a film that may not be publicly shown to anyone under 18. Since 1982 replaced by symbol 18. **1b** (*as modifier*): *an X film.* **2** denoting any unknown, unspecified, or variable factor, number, person, or thing. **3** (on letters, cards, etc.) denoting a kiss. **4** (on ballot papers, etc.) indicating choice. **5** (on examination papers, etc.) indicating error. **6** for Christ; Christian. [from the Gk letter khi (X), first letter of *Khristos* Christ] **7** *the Roman numeral for* ten. See **Roman numerals.**

xanthein ('zænθiːɪn) *n* the soluble part of the yellow pigment that is found in the cell sap of some flowers.

xanthene ('zænθiːn) *n* a yellowish crystalline compound used as a fungicide.

xanthic ('zænθɪk) *adj* **1** of, containing, or derived from xanthic acid. **2** *Bot., rare.* having a yellow colour.

xanthic acid *n* any of a class of sulphur-containing acids.

xanthine ('zænθiːn, -θaɪn) *n* **1** a crystalline compound found in urine, blood, certain plants, and certain animal tissues. Formula: $C_5H_4N_4O_2$. **2** any of three substituted derivatives of xanthine, which act as stimulants and diuretics.

Xanthippe (zæn'θɪpɪ) *or* **Xantippe** (zæn'tɪpɪ) *n* **1** the wife of Socrates (?470–399 BC) Greek philosopher, proverbial as scolding and quarrelsome. **2** any nagging, peevish, or irritable woman.

xantho- *or before a vowel* **xanth-** *combining form.* indicating yellow: *xanthophyll.* [from Gk *xanthos* yellow]

xanthochroism (zæn'θɒkrəʊˌɪzəm) *n* a condition in certain animals, esp. aquarium goldfish, in which all skin pigments other than yellow and orange disappear. [C19: from Gk *xanthokhro(os)* yellow-skinned + -ISM]

xanthoma (zæn'θəʊmə) *n Pathol.* the presence in the skin of fatty yellow or brownish plaques or nodules, esp. on the eyelids, caused by a disorder of lipid metabolism.

xanthophyll *or esp. US* **xanthophyl** ('zænθəʊfɪl) *n* any of a group of yellow carotenoid pigments occurring in plant and animal tissue.
▸ˌ**xantho'phyllous** *adj*

xanthous ('zænθəs) *adj* of, relating to, or designating races with yellowish hair and a light complexion.

***x*-axis** *n* a reference axis, usually horizontal, of a graph or two- or three-dimensional Cartesian coordinate system along which the *x*-coordinate is measured.

X-chromosome *n* the sex chromosome that occurs in pairs in the diploid cells of the females of many animals, including humans, and as one of a pair with the Y-chromosome in those of males. Cf. **Y-chromosome.**

Xe *the chemical symbol for* xenon.

xebec, zebec, *or* **zebeck** ('ziːbɛk) *n* a small three-masted Mediterranean vessel with both square and lateen sails, formerly used by Algerian pirates and later used for commerce. [C18: earlier *chebec* from F, ult. from Ar. *shabbāk;* present spelling infl. by Catalan *xabec,* Sp. *xabeque* (now *jabeque*)]

xeno- *or before a vowel* **xen-** *combining form.* indicating something strange, different, or foreign: *xenogamy.* [from Gk *xenos* strange]

xenogamy (zɛ'nɒgəmɪ) *n Bot.* another name for **cross-fertilization.**
▸**xe'nogamous** *adj*

xenogeneic (ˌzɛnəʊdʒɪ'neɪɪk) *adj Med.* derived from an individual of a different species: *a xenogeneic tissue graft.*

xenoglossia (ˌzɛnə'glɒsɪə) *n* an ability claimed by some mediums, clairvoyants, etc., to speak a language with which they are unfamiliar. [C20: from Gk, from XENO- + *glossa* language]

xenolith ('zɛnəlɪθ) *n* a fragment of rock differing in origin, composition, structure, etc., from the igneous rock enclosing it.
▸ˌ**xeno'lithic** *adj*

xenon ('zɛnɒn) *n* a colourless odourless gaseous element occurring in trace amounts in air; formerly considered inert, it is now known to form compounds and is used in radio valves, stroboscopic and bactericidal lamps, and bubble chambers. Symbol: Xe; atomic no.: 54; atomic wt.: 131.30. [C19: from Gk: something strange]

xenophile ('zɛnəˌfaɪl) *n* a person who likes foreigners or things foreign. [C19: from Gk, from XENO- + -PHILE]

xenophobia (ˌzɛnə'fəʊbɪə) *n* hatred or fear of foreigners or strangers or of their politics or culture. [C20: from Gk, from XENO- + -PHOBIA]
▸'**xenoˌphobe** *n* ▸ˌ**xeno'phobic** *adj*

xeric ('zɪərɪk) *adj Ecology.* of, relating to, or growing in dry conditions.
▸'**xerically** *adv*

xero- *or before a vowel* **xer-** *combining form.* indicating dryness: *xeroderma.* [from Gk *xēros* dry]

xeroderma (ˌzɪərəʊ'dɜːmə) *or* **xerodermia** (ˌzɪərəʊ'dɜːmɪə) *n Pathol.* **1** any abnormal dryness of the skin as the result of diminished secretions from the sweat or sebaceous glands. **2** another name for **ichthyosis.**
▸**xerodermatic** (ˌzɪərəʊdə'mætɪk) *or* ˌ**xero'dermatous** *adj*

xerography (zɪ'rɒgrəfɪ) *n* a photocopying process in which an electrostatic image is formed on a selenium plate or cylinder. The plate or cylinder is dusted with a resinous powder, which adheres to the charged regions, and the image is then transferred to a sheet of paper on which it is fixed by heating.
▸**xe'rographer** *n* ▸**xerographic** (ˌzɪərə'græfɪk) *adj* ▸ˌ**xero'graphically** *adv*

xerophilous (zɪ'rɒfɪləs) *adj* (of plants or animals) adapted for growing or living in dry surroundings.
▸**xerophile** ('zɪərəʊˌfaɪl) *n* ▸**xe'rophily** *n*

xerophthalmia (ˌzɪərɒf'θælmɪə) *n Pathol.* excessive dryness of the cornea and conjunctiva, caused by a deficiency of vitamin A. Also called: **xeroma** (zɪ'rəʊmə).
▸ˌ**xeroph'thalmic** *adj*

xerophyte ('zɪərəˌfaɪt) *n* a xerophilous plant, such as a cactus.
▸**xerophytic** (ˌzɪərə'fɪtɪk) *adj* ▸ˌ**xero'phytically** *adv* ▸'**xeroˌphytism** *n*

Xerox ('zɪərɒks) *n* **1** *Trademark.* **1a** a xerographic copying process. **1b** a machine employing this process. **1c** a copy produced by this process. ◆ *vb* **2** to produce a copy of (a document, illustration, etc.) by this process.

Xhosa ('kɔːsə) *n* **1** (*pl* **Xhosa** *or* **Xhosas**) a member of a cattle-rearing Negroid people of southern Africa, living chiefly in W South Africa. **2** the language of this people, belonging to the Bantu group and characterized by several clicks in its sound system.
▸'**Xhosan** *adj*

xi (zaɪ, saɪ, ksaɪ, ksiː) *n, pl* **xis.** the 14th letter in the Greek alphabet (Ξ, ξ).

xiphisternum (ˌzɪfɪ'stɜːnəm) *n, pl* **xiphisterna** (-nə). *Anat., zool.* the cartilaginous process forming the lowermost part of the breastbone (sternum). Also called: **xiphoid, xiphoid process.** [C19: from Gk *xiphos* sword + STERNUM]

xiphoid ('zɪfɔɪd) *adj* **1** *Biol.* shaped like a sword. **2** of or relating to the xiphisternum. ◆ *n* **3** Also called: **xiphoid process.** another name for **xiphisternum.** [C18: from NL, from Gk, from *xiphos* sword + *eidos* form]

Xmas ❶ ('ɛksməs, 'krɪsməs) *n Inf.* short for **Christmas.** [C18: from symbol X for Christ + -MAS]

X-ray ❶ *or* **x-ray** *n* **1a** electromagnetic radiation emitted when matter is bombarded with fast electrons. X-rays have wavelengths shorter than that of ultraviolet radiation, that is less than about 1×10^{-8} metres. Below about 1×10^{-11} metres they are often called gamma radiation or bremsstrahlung. **1b** (*as modifier*): *X-ray astronomy.* **2** a picture produced by exposing photographic film to X-rays: used in medicine as a diagnostic aid as parts of the body, such as bones, absorb X-rays and so appear as opaque areas on the picture. ◆ *vb* (*tr*) **3** to photograph (part of the body, etc.) using X-rays. **4** to treat or examine by means of X-rays. [C19: partial translation of G *X-Strahlen* (from *Strahl* ray), coined by W. K. Roentgen, G physicist who discovered it in 1895]

X-ray astronomy *n* the branch of astronomy concerned with the detection and measurement of X-rays emitted by certain celestial bodies, such as X-ray stars.

X-ray binary *n* a binary star that is an intense source of X-rays and is composed of a normal star in close orbit with a white dwarf, neutron star, or black hole.

X-ray crystallography *n* the study and practice of determining the structure of a crystal by passing a beam of X-rays through it and observing and analysing the diffraction pattern produced.

X-ray tube *n* an evacuated tube containing a metal target onto which is directed a beam of electrons at high energy for the generation of X-rays.

xylem ('zaɪləm, -lɛm) *n* a plant tissue that conducts water and mineral salts from the roots to all other parts, provides mechanical support, and forms the wood of trees and shrubs. [C19: from Gk *xulon* wood]

xylene ('zaɪliːn) *n* an aromatic hydrocarbon existing in three isomeric forms, all three being colourless flammable volatile liquids used as solvents and in the manufacture of synthetic resins, dyes, and insecticides. Formula: $(CH_3)_2C_6H_4$. Systematic name: **dimethyl benzene.**

THESAURUS

Xmas *n* = **Christmas,** Christmastide, festive season, Noel, Yule (*arch.*), Yuletide (*arch.*)

X-ray *n* = **Röntgen ray** (*old name*)

xylo- *or before a vowel* **xyl-** *combining form.* **1** indicating wood: *xylophone.* **2** indicating xylene: *xylidine.* [from Gk *xulon* wood]

xylocarp (ˈzaɪləˌkɑːp) *n Bot.* a fruit, such as a coconut, having a hard woody pericarp.
▸**ˌxyloˈcarpous** *adj*

xylograph (ˈzaɪləˌgrɑːf) *n* **1** an engraving in wood. **2** a print taken from a wood block. ◆ *vb* **3** (*tr*) to print (a design, illustration, etc.) from a wood engraving.
▸**xylography** (zaɪˈlɒgrəfɪ) *n*

Xylonite (ˈzaɪlənaɪt) *n Trademark.* a thermoplastic of the cellulose nitrate type.

xylophagous (zaɪˈlɒfəgəs) *adj* (of certain insects, crustaceans, etc.) feeding on or living within wood.

xylophone (ˈzaɪləˌfəʊn) *n Music.* a percussion instrument consisting of a set of wooden bars of graduated length. It is played with hard-headed hammers.
▸**xylophonic** (ˌzaɪləˈfɒnɪk) *adj* ▸**xylophonist** (zaɪˈlɒfənɪst) *n*

xylose (ˈzaɪləʊz, -ləʊs) *n* a white crystalline sugar found in wood and straw. It is extracted by hydrolysis with acids and used in dyeing, tanning, and in foods for diabetics.

xyster (ˈzɪstə) *n* a surgical instrument for scraping bone; surgical rasp or file. [C17: via NL from Gk: tool for scraping, from *xuein* to scrape]

y *or* **Y** (waɪ) *n, pl* **y's, Y's,** *or* **Ys. 1** the 25th letter of the English alphabet. **2** a speech sound represented by this letter, usually a semivowel, as in *yawn,* or a vowel, as in *symbol* or *shy.* **3** something shaped like a Y.

y *Maths. symbol for:* **1** the *y*-axis or a coordinate measured along the *y*-axis in a Cartesian coordinate system. **2** an algebraic variable.

Y *symbol for:* **1** any unknown or variable factor, number, or thing. **2** *Chem.* yttrium.

y. *abbrev. for* year.

-y[1] *or* **-ey** *suffix forming adjectives.* **1** (*from nouns*) characterized by; consisting of; filled with; resembling: *sunny; sandy; smoky; classy.* **2** (*from verbs*) tending to; acting or existing as specified: *leaky; shiny.* [from OE *-ig, -æg*]

-y[2], **-ie,** *or* **-ey** *suffix of nouns. Inf.* **1** denoting smallness and expressing affection and familiarity: *a doggy; Jamie.* **2** a person or thing concerned with or characterized by being: *a groupie; a goalie; a fatty.* [C14: from Scot. *-ie, -y,* familiar suffix orig. in names]

-y[3] *suffix forming nouns.* **1** (*from verbs*) indicating the act of doing what is indicated by the verbal element: *inquiry.* **2** (*esp. with combining forms of Greek, Latin, or French origin*) indicating state, condition, or quality: *geography; jealousy.* [from OF *-ie,* from L *-ia*]

Y2K *n Inf.* another name for the year 2000 A.D. (esp. referring to the millennium bug). [C20: Y(EAR) + 2 + K (in the sense: thousand)]

yabby *or* **yabbie** ('jæbɪ) *Austral.* ◆ *n, pl* **yabbies. 1** a small edible freshwater crayfish. **2** a saltwater prawn used as bait; nipper. ◆ *vb* **yabbies, yabbying, yabbied. 3** (*intr*) to fish for yabbies. [from Abor.]

yacht (jɒt) *n* **1** a vessel propelled by sail or power, used esp. for pleasure cruising, racing, etc. ◆ *vb* **2** (*intr*) to sail or cruise in a yacht. [C16: from obs. Du. *jaghte,* short for *jahtschip,* from *jagen* to chase + *schip* ship]
▸ **'yachting** *n, adj*

yachtie ('jɒtɪ) *n Austral. & NZ inf.* a yachtsman; sailing enthusiast.

yachtsman ('jɒtsmən) *or* (*fem*) **yachtswoman** *n, pl* **yachtsmen** *or* **yachtswomen.** a person who sails a yacht or yachts.
▸ **'yachtsmanship** *n*

yack (jæk) *n, vb* a variant spelling of **yak**[2].

yackety-yak ('jækɪtɪ'jæk) *n Sl.* noisy, continuous, and trivial talk or conversation. [imit.]

yaffle ('jæfᵊl) *n* another name for **green woodpecker** (see **woodpecker**). [C18: imit. of its cry]

Yagi aerial ('jɑːgɪ, 'jægɪ) *n* a directional aerial, used esp. in television and radio astronomy, consisting of three or more elements lying parallel to each other, the principal direction of radiation being along the line of the centres. [C20: after Hidetsugu *Yagi* (1886–1976), Japanese engineer]

yah (jɑː, jɛə) *sentence substitute.* **1** an informal word for **yes.** ◆ *interj* **2** an exclamation of derision or disgust.

yahoo Ⓣ (jə'huː) *n, pl* **yahoos.** a crude, brutish, or obscenely coarse person. [C18: from a race of brutish creatures resembling men in Jonathan Swift's *Gulliver's Travels* (1726)]
▸ **ya'hoo,ism** *n*

Yahweh ('jɑːweɪ) *or* **Yahveh** ('jɑːveɪ) *n Old Testament.* a vocalization of the Tetragrammaton. [from Heb., from YHVH, with conjectural vowels; see also JEHOVAH]

Yahwism ('jɑːwɪzəm) *or* **Yahvism** ('jɑːvɪzəm) *n* the use of the name Yahweh, esp. in parts of the Old Testament, as the personal name of God.

Yahwist ('jɑːwɪst) *or* **Yahvist** ('jɑːvɪst) *n Bible.* **the.** the conjectured author or authors of the earliest sources of the Pentateuch in which God is called *Yahweh* throughout.
▸ **Yah'wistic** *or* **Yah'vistic** *adj*

yak[1] (jæk) *n* an ox of Tibet having long shaggy hair. [C19: from Tibetan *gyag*]

yak[2] Ⓣ (jæk) *Sl.* ◆ *n* **1** noisy, continuous, and trivial talk. ◆ *vb* **yaks, yakking, yakked. 2** (*intr*) to chatter or talk in this way. [C20: imit.]

yakka, yakker, *or* **yacker** ('jækə) *n Austral. & NZ inf.* work. [C19: from Abor.]

Yale lock (jeɪl) *n Trademark.* a type of cylinder lock using a flat serrated key. [C19: after L. *Yale* (1821–68), US inventor]

yam (jæm) *n* **1** any of various twining plants of tropical and subtropical regions, cultivated for their edible tubers. **2** the starchy tuber of any of these plants, eaten as a vegetable. **3** *Southern US.* the sweet potato. [C17: from Port. *inhame,* ult. of W African origin]

yammer ('jæmə) *Inf.* ◆ *vb* **1** to utter or whine in a complaining manner. **2** to make (a complaint) loudly or persistently. ◆ *n* **3** a yammering sound. **4** nonsense; jabber. [OE *geōmrian* to grumble]
▸ **'yammerer** *n*

Yang (jæŋ) *n* See **Yin and Yang.**

yank Ⓣ (jæŋk) *vb* **1** to pull with a sharp movement; tug. ◆ *n* **2** a jerk. [C19: from ?]

Yank (jæŋk) *n* **1** a slang word for an **American. 2** *US inf.* short for **Yankee.**

Yankee ('jæŋkɪ) *or* (*inf.*) **Yank** *n* **1** *Often disparaging.* a native or inhabitant of the US; American. **2** a native or inhabitant of New England. **3** a native or inhabitant of the Northern US, esp. a Northern soldier in the Civil War. **4** *Finance.* a bond issued in the US by a foreign borrower. ◆ *adj* **5** of, relating to, or characteristic of Yankees. [C18: ?from Du. *Jan Kees* John Cheese, derisive nickname of Du. settlers for English colonists in Connecticut]

Yankee Doodle *n* **1** an American song, popularly regarded as a characteristically national melody. **2** another name for **Yankee.**

yap Ⓣ (jæp) *vb* **yaps, yapping, yapped.** (*intr*) **1** (of a dog) to bark in quick sharp bursts; yelp. **2** *Inf.* to talk at length in an annoying or stupid way; jabber. ◆ *n* **3** a high-pitched or sharp bark; yelp. **4** *Sl.* annoying or stupid speech; jabber. **5** *Sl., chiefly US.* a derogatory word for **mouth.** [C17: imit.]
▸ **'yapper** *n* ▸ **'yappy** *adj*

yapok (jə'pɒk) *n* an amphibious nocturnal opossum of Central and South America. Also called: **water opossum.** [C19: after *Oyapok,* a river flowing between French Guiana & Brazil]

yarborough ('jɑːbərə, -brə) *n Bridge, whist.* a hand of 13 cards in which no card is higher than nine. [C19: supposedly after the second Earl of *Yarborough* (d. 1897), said to have bet a thousand to one against its occurrence]

yard[1] (jɑːd) *n* **1** a unit of length equal to 3 feet and defined in 1963 as exactly 0.9144 metre. **2** a cylindrical wooden or hollow metal spar, slung from a mast of a vessel, and used for suspending a sail. [OE *gierd* rod, twig]

yard[2] (jɑːd) *n* **1** a piece of enclosed ground, often adjoining or surrounded by a building or buildings. **2a** an enclosed or open area used for some commercial activity, for storage, etc.: *a builder's yard.* **2b** (*in combination*): *a shipyard.* **3** a US and Canad. word for **garden** (sense 1). **4** an area having a network of railway tracks and sidings, used for storing rolling stock, making up trains, etc. **5** *US & Canad.* the winter pasture of deer, moose, and similar animals. **6** *NZ.* short for **stockyard.** [OE *geard*]

Yard (jɑːd) *n* **the.** *Brit. inf.* short for **Scotland Yard.**

yardage[1] ('jɑːdɪdʒ) *n* a length measured in yards.

yardage[2] ('jɑːdɪdʒ) *n* **1** the use of a railway yard for cattle. **2** the charge for this.

yardarm ('jɑːd,ɑːm) *n Naut.* the two tapering outer ends of a ship's yard.

yard grass *n* an Old World perennial grass with prostrate leaves, growing as a troublesome weed on open ground, yards, etc.

Yardie ('jɑːdɪ) *n* a member of a Black criminal syndicate originally based in Jamaica. [origin unknown]

yard of ale *n* **1** the beer or ale contained in a narrow horn-shaped drinking glass. **2** such a drinking glass itself.

yardstick Ⓣ ('jɑːd,stɪk) *n* **1** a measure or standard used for comparison. **2** a graduated stick, one yard long, used for measurement.

yarmulke ('jɑːməlkə) *n Judaism.* a skullcap worn by Orthodox male Jews at all times and by others during prayer. [from Yiddish, from Ukrainian & Polish *yarmulka* cap, prob. from Turkish *yağmurluk* raincoat, from *yağmur* rain]

yarn Ⓣ (jɑːn) *n* **1** a continuous twisted strand of natural or synthetic fibres, used in weaving, knitting, etc. **2** *Inf.* a long and often involved story, usually of incredible or fantastic events. **3 spin a yarn.** *Inf.* **3a** to tell such a story. **3b** to make up a series of excuses. ◆ *vb* **4** (*intr*) to tell such a story or stories. [OE *gearn*]

yarn-dyed *adj* (of fabric) dyed while still in yarn form, before being woven.

yarran ('jærən) *n* a small hardy tree of inland Australia: useful as fodder and for firewood. [from Abor.]

yarrow ('jærəʊ) *n* any of several plants of the composite family of Eurasia, having finely dissected leaves and flat clusters of white flower heads. Also called: **milfoil.** [OE *gearwe*]

yashmak *or* **yashmac** ('jæʃmæk) *n* the face veil worn by Muslim women when in public. [C19: from Ar.]

THESAURUS

yahoo *n* = **philistine,** barbarian, beast, boor, brute, churl, lout, roughneck (*sl.*), rowdy, savage, yob *or* yobbo (*Brit. sl.*)

yak[2] *n* **1** = **gossip,** blather, chat, chinwag (*Brit. inf.*), confab (*inf.*), hot air (*inf.*), jaw (*sl.*), waffle (*inf., chiefly Brit.*), yackety-yak (*sl.*), yammer (*inf.*) ◆ *vb* **2** = **gossip,** blather, chatter, chew the fat *or* rag (*sl.*), gab (*inf.*), jabber, jaw (*sl.*), rabbit (on) (*Brit. inf.*), run off at the mouth (*sl.*), run on, spout, tattle, waffle (*inf., chiefly Brit.*), witter on (*inf.*), yap (*inf.*)

yank *vb* **1** = **pull,** hitch, jerk, snatch, tug, wrench ◆ *n* **2** = **pull,** hitch, jerk, snatch, tug, wrench

yap *vb* **1** = **yelp,** yammer (*inf.*) **2** *Informal* = **talk,** babble, blather, chatter, chew the fat *or* rag, go on, gossip, jabber, jaw (*sl.*), prattle, rabbit (on) (*Brit. inf.*), run off at the mouth (*sl.*), spout, tattle, waffle (*inf., chiefly Brit.*)

yardstick *n* **1** = **standard,** benchmark, criterion, gauge, measure, par, touchstone

yarn *n* **1** = **thread,** fibre **2** *Informal* = **story,** anecdote, cock-and-bull story, fable, tale, tall story, urban legend, urban myth

yataghan ('jætəgən) *n* a Turkish sword with a curved blade. [C19: from Turkish *yatağan*]
yaup (jɔ:p) *vb, n* a variant spelling of **yawp**.
▸ **'yauper** *n*
yaw (jɔ:) *vb* **1** (*intr*) (of an aircraft, etc.) to turn about its vertical axis. **2** (*intr*) (of a ship, etc.) to deviate temporarily from a straight course. **3** (*tr*) to cause (an aircraft, ship, etc.) to yaw. ◆ *n* **4** the movement of an aircraft, etc., about its vertical axis. **5** the deviation of a vessel from a straight course. [C16: from ?]
yawl (jɔ:l) *n* **1** a two-masted sailing vessel with a small mizzenmast aft of the rudderpost. **2** a ship's small boat, usually rowed by four or six oars. [C17: from Du. *jol* or MLow G *jolle,* from ?]
yawn ⓣ (jɔ:n) *vb* **1** (*intr*) to open the mouth wide and take in air deeply, often as in involuntary reaction to sleepiness or boredom. **2** (*tr*) to express or utter while yawning. **3** (*intr*) to be open wide as if threatening to engulf (someone or something): *the mine shaft yawned below.* ◆ *n* **4** the act or an instance of yawning. [OE *gionian*]
▸ **'yawner** *n* ▸ **'yawning** *adj* ▸ **'yawningly** *adv*
yawp (jɔ:p) *Dialect US & Canad. inf.* ◆ *vb* (*intr*) **1** to yawn, esp. audibly. **2** to shout, cry, or talk noisily. **3** to bark or yowl. ◆ *n* **4** a shout, bark, or cry. **5** a noisy, foolish, or raucous utterance. [C15 *yolpen,* prob. imit.]
▸ **'yawper** *n*
yaws (jɔ:z) *n* (*usually functioning as sing*) an infectious disease of tropical climates characterized by red skin eruptions. [C17: of Carib origin]
***y*-axis** *n* a reference axis of a graph or two- or three-dimensional Cartesian coordinate system along which the *y*-coordinate is measured.
Yb *the chemical symbol for* ytterbium.
YC (in Britain) *abbrev. for* Young Conservative.
Y-chromosome *n* the sex chromosome that occurs as one of a pair with the X-chromosome in the diploid cells of the males of many animals, including humans. Cf. **X-chromosome.**
yclept (ɪ'klɛpt) *adj Obs.* having the name of; called. [OE *gecleopod,* p.p. of *cleopian* to call]
Y connection *n Electrical engineering.* a three-phase star connection.
yd *or* **yd.** *abbrev. for* yard (measure).
YDT (in Canada) *abbrev. for* Yukon Daylight Time.
ye[1] (ji:, *unstressed* jɪ) *pron* **1** *Arch. or dialect.* refers to more than one person including the person addressed. **2** Also: **ee** (i:). *Dialect.* refers to one person addressed: *I tell ye.* [OE *gē*]
ye[2] (ði:, *spelling pron* ji:) *determiner* a form of **the**[1], used as a supposed archaism: *ye olde oake.* [from a misinterpretation of *the* as written in some ME texts. The runic letter thorn (þ, representing *th*) was incorrectly transcribed as *y* because of a resemblance in their shapes]
yea (jeɪ) *sentence substitute.* **1** a less common word for **aye** (yes). ◆ *adv* **2** (*sentence modifier*) *Arch. or literary.* indeed; truly: *yea, though they spurn me, I shall prevail.* [OE *gēa*]
yeah (jɛə) *sentence substitute.* an informal word for **yes.**
yean (ji:n) *vb* (of a sheep or goat) to give birth to (offspring). [OE *geēanian*]
yeanling ('ji:nlɪŋ) *n* the young of a goat or sheep.
year ⓣ (jɪə) *n* **1** the period of time, the **calendar year,** containing 365 days or in a **leap year** 366 days. It is divided into 12 calendar months, and reckoned from January 1 to December 31. **2** a period of twelve months from any specified date. **3** a specific period of time, usually occupying a definite part or parts of a twelve-month period, used for some particular activity: *a school year.* **4** Also called: **astronomical year, tropical year.** the period of time, the **solar year,** during which the earth makes one revolution around the sun, measured between two successive vernal equinoxes: equal to 365.242 19 days. **5** the period of time, the **sidereal year,** during which the earth makes one revolution around the sun, measured between two successive conjunctions of a particular star: equal to 365.256 36 days. **6** the period of time, the **lunar year,** containing 12 lunar months and equal to 354.3671 days. **7** the period of time taken by a planet to complete one revolution around the sun. **8** (*pl*) age, esp. old age: *a man of his years should be more careful.* **9** (*pl*) time: *in years to come.* **10** a group of pupils or students, who are taught or study together. **11 the year dot.** *Inf.* as long ago as can be remembered. **12 year in, year out.** regularly or monotonously, over a long period. ◆ Related adj: **annual.** [OE *gear*]

> **USAGE NOTE** In writing spans of years, it is important to choose a style that avoids ambiguity. The practice adopted in this dictionary is, in four-figure dates, to specify the last two digits of the second date if it falls within the same century as the first: *1801–08; 1850–51; 1899–1901.* In writing three-figure B.C. dates, it is advisable to give both dates in full: *159–156* B.C., not *159–56* B.C. unless of course the span referred to consists of 103 years rather than three years. It is also advisable to specify B.C. or A.D. in years under 1000 unless the context makes this self-evident.

yearbook ('jɪə,bʊk) *n* an almanac or other reference book published annually and containing details of events of the previous year.
yearling ('jɪəlɪŋ) *n* **1** the young of any of various animals, including the antelope and buffalo, between one and two years of age. **2** a thoroughbred racehorse counted as being one year old until the second January 1 following its birth. **3a** a bond intended to mature after one year. **3b** (*as modifier*): *yearling bonds.* ◆ *adj* **4** being a year old.
yearlong ('jɪə'lɒŋ) *adj* throughout a whole year.
yearly ⓣ ('jɪəlɪ) *adj* **1** occurring, done, appearing, etc., once a year or every year; annual. **2** lasting or valid for a year; annual: *a yearly fee.* ◆ *adv* **3** once a year; annually.
yearn ⓣ (jɜ:n) *vb* (*intr*) **1** (usually foll. by *for* or *after* or an infinitive) to have an intense desire or longing (for). **2** to feel tenderness or affection. [OE *giernan*]
▸ **'yearner** *n* ▸ **'yearning** *n, adj* ▸ **'yearningly** *adv*
year of grace *n* any year of the Christian era, as from the presumed date of Christ's birth.
year-round *adj* open, in use, operating, etc., throughout the year.
yeast (ji:st) *n* **1** any of various single-celled fungi which reproduce by budding and are able to ferment sugars: a rich source of vitamins of the B complex. **2** a commercial preparation containing yeast cells and inert material such as meal, used in raising dough for bread or for fermenting beer, whisky, etc. **3** a preparation containing yeast cells, used to treat diseases caused by vitamin B deficiency. **4** froth or foam, esp. on beer. ◆ *vb* **5** (*intr*) to froth or foam. [OE *giest*]
▸ **'yeastless** *adj* ▸ **'yeast,like** *adj*
yeasty ('ji:stɪ) *adj* **yeastier, yeastiest. 1** of, resembling, or containing yeast. **2** fermenting or causing fermentation. **3** tasting of or like yeast. **4** insubstantial or frivolous. **5** restless, agitated, or unsettled. **6** covered with or containing froth or foam.
▸ **'yeastily** *adv* ▸ **'yeastiness** *n*
yegg (jɛg) *n Sl., chiefly US.* a burglar or safe-breaker. [C20: ?from the surname of a burglar]
yell ⓣ (jɛl) *vb* **1** to shout, scream, cheer, or utter in a loud or piercing way. ◆ *n* **2** a loud piercing inarticulate cry, as of pain, anger, or fear. **3** *US & Canad.* a rhythmic cry, used in cheering in unison. [OE *giellan*]
▸ **'yeller** *n*
yellow ('jɛləʊ) *n* **1** any of a group of colours such as that of a lemon or of gold, which vary in saturation but have the same hue. Yellow is the complementary colour of blue. Related adj: **xanthous. 2** a pigment or dye of or producing these colours. **3** yellow cloth or clothing: *dressed in yellow.* **4** the yolk of an egg. **5** a yellow ball in snooker, etc. ◆ *adj* **6** of the colour yellow. **7** yellowish in colour or having parts or marks that are yellowish. **8** having a yellowish skin; Mongoloid. **9** *Inf.* cowardly or afraid. **10** offensively sensational, as a cheap newspaper (esp. in **yellow press**). ◆ *vb* **11** to make or become yellow. ◆ See also **yellows.** [OE *geolu*]
▸ **'yellowish** *adj* ▸ **'yellowly** *adv* ▸ **'yellowness** *n* ▸ **'yellowy** *adj*
yellow-belly *n, pl* **yellow-bellies.** a slang word for **coward.**
▸ **'yellow-,bellied** *adj*
yellow belly *n Austral.* any of several freshwater food fishes with yellow underparts.
yellow bile *n Arch.* one of the four bodily humours, choler.
yellow card *n Soccer.* a card of a yellow colour displayed by a referee to indicate that a player has been officially cautioned for some offence.
yellow fever *n* an acute infectious disease of tropical and subtropical climates, characterized by fever, haemorrhages, vomiting, and jaundice: caused by a virus transmitted by the bite of a certain mosquito. Also called: **yellow jack.**
yellowhammer ('jɛləʊ,hæmə) *n* a European bunting, having a yellowish head and body and brown-streaked wings and tail. [C16: from ?]
yellow jack *n* **1** *Pathol.* another name for **yellow fever. 2** another name for **quarantine flag. 3** any of certain large yellowish food fishes of warm and tropical Atlantic waters.
yellow jersey *n* (in the Tour de France) a yellow jersey awarded as a trophy to the cyclist with the fastest time in each stage of the race.
yellow journalism *n* the type of journalism that relies on sensationalism to attract readers. [C19: ? shortened from *Yellow Kid journalism,* referring to the *Yellow Kid,* a cartoon (1895) in the *New York World,* a newspaper having a reputation for sensationalism]
yellow line *n Brit.* a yellow line painted along the edge of a road indicating vehicle waiting restrictions.
yellow metal *n* **1** a type of brass having about 60 per cent copper and 40 per cent zinc. **2** another name for **gold.**
Yellow Pages *pl n Trademark.* a classified telephone directory or section of one, often on yellow paper, that lists subscribers by the business or service they provide.
yellow peril *n* the power or alleged power of Asiatic peoples, esp. the Chinese, to threaten or destroy White or Western civilization.
yellows ('jɛləʊz) *n* (*functioning as sing*) **1** any of various fungal or viral diseases of plants, characterized by yellowish discoloration and stunting. **2** *Vet. science.* another name for **jaundice.**
yellow spot *n Anat.* another name for **macula lutea.**
yellow streak *n Inf.* a cowardly or weak trait.
yellow underwing *n* any of several species of noctuid moths, the hind wings of which are yellow with a black bar.
yellowwood ('jɛləʊ,wʊd) *n* **1** any of several leguminous trees of the

THESAURUS

yawning *adj* **3** = **gaping,** cavernous, chasmal, vast, wide, wide-open
year *n* **8** *plural* = **old age,** age, dotage, eld, second childhood, senescence, senility **9** *plural* = **time,** days, generation(s), lifetime, span
yearly *adj* **1, 2** = **annual** ◆ *adv* **3** = **annually,** every year, once a year, per annum
yearn *vb* **1** = **long,** ache, covet, crave, desire, eat one's heart out over, hanker, have a yen for (*inf.*), hunger, itch, languish, lust, pant, pine, set one's heart upon, suspire (*arch. or poetic*), would give one's eyeteeth for
yell *vb* **1** = **scream,** bawl, holler (*inf.*), howl, screech, shout, shriek, squeal ◆ *n* **2** = **scream,** cry, howl, screech, shriek, whoop

southeastern US, having clusters of white flowers and yellow wood yielding a yellow dye. **2** Also called: **West Indian satinwood.** a rutaceous tree of the West Indies, with smooth hard wood. **3** any of several other trees with yellow wood, esp. a conifer of southern Africa the wood of which is used for furniture and building. **4** the wood of any of these trees.

yelp ❶ (jɛlp) *vb (intr)* **1** (esp. of a dog) to utter a sharp or high-pitched cry or bark, often indicating pain. ◆ *n* **2** a sharp or high-pitched cry or bark. [OE *gielpan* to boast]
▸**'yelper** *n*

yen[1] (jɛn) *n, pl* **yen.** the standard monetary unit of Japan. [C19: from Japanese *en,* from Chinese *yüan* dollar]

yen[2] ❶ (jɛn) *Inf.* ◆ *n* **1** a longing or desire. ◆ *vb* **yens, yenning, yenned. 2** *(intr)* to yearn. [?from Chinese *yǎn* a craving]

yeoman ('jəʊmən) *n, pl* **yeomen. 1** *History.* **1a** a member of a class of small freeholders who cultivated their own land. **1b** an attendant or lesser official in a royal or noble household. **2** (in Britain) another name for **yeoman of the guard. 3** *(modifier)* characteristic of or relating to a yeoman. **4** a petty officer or noncommissioned officer in the Royal Navy or Marines in charge of signals. [C15: ?from *yongman* young man]

yeomanly ('jəʊmənlɪ) *adj* **1** of, relating to, or like a yeoman. **2** having the virtues attributed to yeomen, such as staunchness, loyalty, and courage. ◆ *adv* **3** in a yeomanly manner.

yeoman of the guard *n* a member of the ceremonial bodyguard (**Yeomen of the Guard**) of the British monarch.

yeomanry ('jəʊmənrɪ) *n* **1** yeomen collectively. **2** (in Britain) a volunteer cavalry force, organized in 1761 for home defence: merged into the Territorial Army in 1907.

yep (jɛp) *sentence substitute.* an informal word for **yes.**

yerba *or* **yerba maté** ('jɜːbə) *n* another name for **maté.** [from Sp. *yerba maté* herb maté]

yes (jɛs) *sentence substitute.* **1** used to express affirmation, consent, agreement, or approval or to answer when one is addressed. **2** used to signal someone to speak or keep speaking, enter a room, or do something. ◆ *n* **3** an answer or vote of *yes.* **4** *(often pl)* a person who votes in the affirmative. [OE *gēse,* from *iā sīe* may it be]

yeshiva (jəˈʃiːvə; *Hebrew* jəˈʃiːva) *n, pl* **yeshivahs** *or* **yeshivoth** (*Hebrew* -vɔt). **1** a traditional Jewish school devoted chiefly to the study of the Talmud. **2** a school run by Orthodox Jews for children of primary school age, providing both religious and secular instruction. [from Heb. *yěshībhāh* a seat, hence, an academy]

yes man ❶ *n* a servile, submissive, or acquiescent subordinate, assistant, or associate.

yester ('jɛstə) *adj Arch.* of or relating to yesterday: *yester sun.* [OE *geostror*]

yester- *prefix* indicating a period of time before the present one: *yesteryear.* [OE *geostran*]

yesterday ('jɛstədɪ, -ˌdeɪ) *n* **1** the day immediately preceding today. **2** *(often pl)* the recent past. ◆ *adv* **3** on or during the day before today. **4** in the recent past.

yesteryear ('jɛstəˌjɪə) *Formal or literary.* ◆ *n* **1** last year or the past in general. ◆ *adv* **2** during last year or the past in general.

yestreen (jɛˈstriːn) *adv Scot.* yesterday evening. [C14: from YEST(E)R- + E(V)EN[2]]

yet ❶ (jɛt) *sentence connector.* **1** nevertheless; still; in spite of that: *I want to and yet I haven't the courage.* ◆ *adv* **2** *(usually used with a negative or interrogative)* so far; up until then or now: *they're not home yet; is it teatime yet?* **3** (often preceded by *just; usually used with a negative*) now (as contrasted with later): *we can't stop yet.* **4** *(often used with a comparative)* even; still: *yet more old potatoes for sale.* **5** eventually in spite of everything: *we'll convince him yet.* **6 as yet.** so far; up until then or now. [OE *gēta*]

yeti ('jɛtɪ) *n* another term for **abominable snowman.** [C20: from Tibetan]

yew (juː) *n* **1** any coniferous tree of the Old World and North America having flattened needle-like leaves, fine-grained elastic wood, and cuplike red waxy cones resembling berries. **2** the wood of any of these trees, used to make bows for archery. **3** *Archery.* a bow made of yew. [OE *īw*]

Y-fronts *pl n Trademark.* boys' or men's underpants having a front opening within an inverted Y shape.

Yggdrasil *or* **Ygdrasil** ('ɪgdrəsɪl) *n Norse myth.* the ash tree that was thought to bind together earth, heaven, and hell with its roots and branches. [ON (prob. meaning: Uggr's horse), from *Uggr* a name of Odin, from *yggr, uggr* frightful + *drasill* horse, from ?]

YHA *abbrev. for* Youth Hostels Association.

YHVH *or* **YHWH** *Bible.* the letters of the **Tetragrammaton.**

yid (jɪd) *n Sl.* a derogatory word for a **Jew.** [C20: prob. from *Yiddish,* from MHG *Jude* JEW]

Yiddish ('jɪdɪʃ) *n* **1** a language spoken as a vernacular by Jews in Europe and elsewhere by Jewish emigrants, usually written in the Hebrew alphabet. It is a dialect of High German with an admixture of words of Hebrew, Romance, and Slavonic origin. ◆ *adj* **2** in or relating to this language. [C19: from G *jüdisch,* from *Jude* JEW]

Yiddisher ('jɪdɪʃə) *adj* **1** in or relating to Yiddish. **2** Jewish. ◆ *n* **3** a speaker of Yiddish; Jew.

yield ❶ (jiːld) *vb* **1** to give forth or supply (a product, result, etc.), esp. by cultivation, labour, etc.; produce or bear. **2** *(tr)* to furnish as a return: *the shares yielded three per cent.* **3** *(tr;* often foll. by *up)* to surrender or relinquish, esp. as a result of force, persuasion, etc. **4** *(intr;* sometimes foll. by *to)* to give way, submit, or surrender, as through force or persuasion: *she yielded to his superior knowledge.* **5** *(intr;* often foll. by *to)* to agree; comply; assent: *he eventually yielded to their request for money.* **6** *(tr)* to grant or allow; concede: *to yield right of way.* ◆ *n* **7** the result, product, or amount yielded. **8** the profit or return, as from an investment or tax. **9** the annual income provided by an investment. **10** the energy released by the explosion of a nuclear weapon expressed in terms of the amount of TNT necessary to produce the same energy. **11** *Chem.* the quantity of a specified product obtained in a reaction or series of reactions. [OE *gieldan*]
▸**'yieldable** *adj* ▸**'yielder** *n*

yielding ❶ ('jiːldɪŋ) *adj* **1** compliant, submissive, or flexible. **2** pliable or soft: *a yielding material.*

yield point *n* the stress at which an elastic material under increasing stress ceases to behave elastically; the elongation becomes greater than the increase in stress.

Yin and Yang (jɪn) *n* two complementary principles of Chinese philosophy: Yin is negative, dark, and feminine, Yang is positive, bright, and masculine. [from Chinese *yin* dark + *yang* bright]

yippee (jɪˈpiː) *interj* an exclamation of joy, pleasure, anticipation, etc.

yips (jɪps) *pl n* **the.** *Inf.* (in sport) nervous twitching or tension that destroys concentration. [C20: from ?]

-yl *suffix forming nouns.* (in chemistry) indicating a group or radical: *methyl.* [from Gk *hulē* wood]

ylang-ylang ('iːlæŋˈiːlæŋ) *n* **1** an aromatic Asian tree with fragrant greenish-yellow flowers yielding a volatile oil. **2** the oil obtained from this tree, used in perfumery. [C19: from Tagalog *ilang-ilang*]

ylem ('aɪləm) *n* the original matter from which the basic elements are said to have been formed following the explosion postulated in the big-bang theory of cosmology. [ME, from OF *ilem,* from L *hȳlē* stuff, from Gk *hulē* wood]

YMCA *abbrev. for* Young Men's Christian Association.

-yne *suffix forming nouns.* denoting an organic chemical containing a triple bond: *alkyne.* [alteration of -INE[2]]

yo (jəʊ) *sentence substitute.* an expression used as a greeting, to attract someone's attention, etc. [C20: of unknown origin]

yob ❶ (jɒb) *or* **yobbo** ('jɒbəʊ) *n, pl* **yobs** *or* **yobbos.** *Brit. sl.* an aggressive and surly youth, esp. a teenager. [C19: ? back sl. for BOY]
▸**'yobbery** *n* ▸**'yobbish** *adj*

yodel ('jəʊdᵊl) *n* **1** an effect produced in singing by an abrupt change of register from the chest voice to falsetto, esp. in folk songs of the Swiss Alps. ◆ *vb* **yodels, yodelling, yodelled** *or US* **yodels, yodeling, yodeled. 2** to sing (a song) in which a yodel is used. [C19: from G *jodeln,* imit.]
▸**'yodeller** *n*

yoga ('jəʊgə) *n (often cap.)* **1** a Hindu system of philosophy aiming at the mystical union of the self with the Supreme Being in a state of complete awareness and tranquillity through certain physical and mental exercises. **2** any method by which such awareness and tranquillity are attained, esp. a course of related exercises and postures. [C19: from Sansk.: a yoking, from *yunakti* he yokes]
▸**yogic** ('jəʊgɪk) *adj*

yogh (jɒg) *n* **1** a character (ʒ) used in Old and Middle English to represent a palatal fricative very close to the semivowel sound of Modern English *y.* **2** this same character as used in Middle English for both the voiced and voiceless palatal fricatives; when final or in a closed syllable in medial position the sound approached that of German *ch* in *ich,* as in *knyʒt* (knight). [C14: ?from *yok* yoke, from the letter's shape]

THESAURUS

Antonyms *vb, n* ≠ **scream:** mumble, murmur, mutter, whisper

yelp *vb* **1** = **cry,** yammer *(inf.),* yap, yowl

yen[2] *n* **1** = **longing,** ache, craving, desire, hankering, hunger, itch, passion, thirst, yearning

yes man *n* = **sycophant,** ass-kisser *(US & Canad. taboo sl.),* bootlicker *(inf.),* bosses' lackey, company man, crawler, creature, minion, timeserver, toady

yet *sentence connector* **1** = **nevertheless,** however, notwithstanding, still ◆ *adv* **2** = **so far,** as yet, thus far, until now, up to now **3** = **now,** already, just now, right now, so soon **4** = **still,** additionally, as well, besides, further, in addition, into the bargain, moreover, over and above, to boot

yield *vb* **1, 2** = **produce,** afford, bear, bring forth, bring in, earn, furnish, generate, give, net, pay, provide, return, supply **3, 4** = **surrender,** abandon, abdicate, admit defeat, bow, capitulate, cave in *(inf.),* cede, cry quits, give in, give up the struggle, give way, knuckle under, lay down one's arms, lose, part with, raise the white flag, relinquish, resign, resign oneself, submit, succumb, throw in the towel **5, 6** = **comply,** accede, agree, allow, bow, concede, consent, go along with, grant, permit ◆ *n* **7** = **crop,** harvest, output, produce **8, 9** = **profit,** earnings, income, return, revenue, takings

Antonyms *vb* ≠ **produce:** consume, use, use up ≠ **surrender:** appropriate, commandeer, grab, hold on to, hold out, keep, maintain, reserve, retain, seize, struggle ≠ **comply:** combat, counterattack, defy, oppose, resist ◆ *n* ≠ **profit:** consumption, input, loss

yielding *adj* **1** = **submissive,** accommodating, acquiescent, biddable, compliant, docile, easy, flexible, obedient, pliant, tractable **2** = **soft,** elastic, pliable, quaggy, resilient, spongy, springy, supple, unresisting

Antonyms *adj* ≠ **submissive:** dogged, headstrong, mulish, obstinate, opinionated, perverse, stiff-necked, stubborn, tenacious, wilful

yob *n* = **thug,** heavy *(sl.),* hoodlum, hooligan,

yogi (ˈjəʊgɪ) *n, pl* **yogis** *or* **yogin** (-gɪn). a person who is a master of yoga.
yogurt *or* **yoghurt** (ˈjəʊgət, jɒg-) *n* a thick custard-like food prepared from milk curdled by bacteria, often sweetened and flavoured with fruit. [C19: from Turkish *yoğurt*]
yo-heave-ho (ˌjəʊhiːvˈhəʊ) *interj* a cry formerly used by sailors while pulling or lifting together in rhythm.
yohimbine (jəʊˈhɪmbiːn) *n* an alkaloid found in the bark of a West African tree and used in medicine. [C19: from Bantu *yohimbé* a tropical African tree + -INE[1]]
yo-ho-ho *interj* **1** an exclamation to call attention. **2** another word for **yo-heave-ho.**
yoicks (haɪk; *spelling pron* jɔɪks) *interj* a cry used by fox-hunters to urge on the hounds.
yoke Ⓣ (jəʊk) *n, pl* **yokes** *or* **yoke. 1** a wooden frame, usually consisting of a bar with an oxbow at either end, for attaching to the necks of a pair of draught animals, esp. oxen, so that they can be worked as a team. **2** something resembling a yoke in form or function, such as a frame fitting over a person's shoulders for carrying buckets. **3** a fitted part of a garment, esp. around the neck, shoulders, and chest or around the hips, to which a gathered, pleated, flared, or unfitted part is attached. **4** an oppressive force or burden: *under the yoke of a tyrant.* **5** a pair of oxen or other draught animals joined by a yoke. **6** a part that secures two or more components so that they move together. **7** (in the ancient world) a symbolic yoke, consisting of two upright spears with a third lashed across them, under which conquered enemies were compelled to march, esp. in Rome. **8** a mark, token, or symbol of slavery, subjection, or suffering. **9** *Now rare.* a link, tie, or bond: *the yoke of love.* ◆ *vb* **yokes, yoking, yoked. 10** (*tr*) to secure or harness (a draught animal) to (a plough, vehicle, etc.) by means of a yoke. **11** to join or be joined by means of a yoke; couple, unite, or link. [OE *geoc*]
yokel Ⓣ (ˈjəʊkᵊl) *n Disparaging.* (used chiefly by townspeople) a person who lives in the country, esp. one who appears to be simple and old-fashioned. [C19: ?from dialect *yokel* green woodpecker]
yolk (jəʊk) *n* **1** the substance in an animal ovum that nourishes the developing embryo. **2** a greasy substance in the fleece of sheep. [OE *geoloca,* from *geolu* yellow]
► **ˈyolky** *adj*
yolk sac *n Zool.* the membranous sac that is attached to the surface of the embryos of birds, reptiles, and some fishes, and contains yolk.
Yom Kippur (jɒm ˈkɪpə; *Hebrew* jɔm kiˈpur) *n* an annual Jewish day of fasting, on which prayers of penitence are recited in the synagogue. Also called: **Day of Atonement.** [from Heb., from *yōm* day + *kippūr* atonement]
yomp (jɒmp) *vb* (*intr*) to walk or trek laboriously, esp. over difficult terrain. [C20: mil. sl., from ?]
yon (jɒn) *determiner* **1** *Chiefly Scot. & N English.* **1a** an archaic or dialect word for **that:** *yon man.* **1b** (*as pronoun*)*: yon's a fool.* **2** a variant of **yonder.** [OE *geon*]
yond (jɒnd) *Obs. or dialect.* ◆ *adj* **1** the farther, more distant. ◆ *determiner* **2** a variant of **yon.**
yonder (ˈjɒndə) *adv* **1** at, in, or to that relatively distant place; over there. ◆ *determiner* **2** being at a distance, either within view or as if within view: *yonder valleys.* [C13: from OE *geond* yond]
yoni (ˈjəʊnɪ) *n Hinduism.* **1** the female genitalia, regarded as a divine symbol of sexual pleasure and matrix of generation. **2** an image of these as an object of worship. [C18: from Sansk., lit.: vulva]
yonks (jɒŋks) *pl n Inf.* a very long time; ages: *I haven't seen him for yonks.* [C20: from ?]
yoo-hoo (ˈjuːˌhuː) *interj* a call to attract a person's attention.
YOP (jɒp) *n* (formerly, in Britain) **a** *acronym for* Youth Opportunities Programme. **b** (*as modifier*)*: a YOP scheme.*
yore (jɔː) *n* **1** time long past (now only in **of yore**). ◆ *adv* **2** *Obs.* in the past; long ago. [OE *geāra,* genitive pl of *gēar* year]
york (jɔːk) *vb* (*tr*) *Cricket.* to bowl (a batsman) by pitching the ball under or just beyond the bat. [C19: back formation from YORKER]
yorker (ˈjɔːkə) *n Cricket.* a ball bowled so as to pitch just under or just beyond the bat. [C19: prob. after the *Yorkshire* County Cricket Club]
yorkie (ˈjɔːkɪ) *n* short for **Yorkshire terrier.**
Yorkist (ˈjɔːkɪst) *English history.* ◆ *n* **1** a member or adherent of the royal House of York, esp. during the Wars of the Roses. ◆ *adj* **2** of, belonging to, or relating to the supporters or members of the House of York.
Yorks (jɔːks) *abbrev. for* Yorkshire.
Yorkshire pudding (ˈjɔːkʃɪə) *n Chiefly Brit.* a light puffy baked pudding made from a batter of flour, eggs, and milk, traditionally served with roast beef.
Yorkshire terrier *n* a very small breed of terrier with a long straight glossy coat of steel-blue and tan. Also called: **yorkie.**
Yoruba (ˈjɒrʊbə) *n* **1** (*pl* **Yorubas** *or* **Yoruba**) a member of a Negroid people of W Africa, living chiefly in the coastal regions of SW Nigeria. **2** the language of this people.
► **ˈYoruban** *adj*
you (juː; *unstressed* jʊ) *pron* (*subjective or objective*) **1** refers to the person addressed or to more than one person including the person or persons addressed: *you know better; the culprit is among you.* **2** refers to an unspecified person or people in general: *you can't tell the boys from the girls.* ◆ *n* **3** *Inf.* the personality of the person being addressed: *that hat isn't really you.* **4 you know what** *or* **who.** a thing or person that the speaker does not want to specify. [OE *ēow,* dative & accusative of *gē* ye]

USAGE NOTE See at **me**[1].

you'd (juːd; *unstressed* jʊd) *contraction of* you had *or* you would.
you'll (juːl; *unstressed* jʊl) *contraction of* you will *or* you shall.
young Ⓣ (jʌŋ) *adj* **younger** (ˈjʌŋgə), **youngest** (ˈjʌŋgɪst). **1a** having lived, existed, or been made or known for a relatively short time: *a young country.* **1b** (*as collective n;* preceded by *the*)*: the young.* **2** youthful or having qualities associated with youth; vigorous or lively. **3** of or relating to youth: *in my young days.* **4** having been established or introduced for a relatively short time: *a young member.* **5** in an early stage of progress or development; not far advanced: *the day was young.* **6** (*often cap.*) of or relating to a rejuvenated group or movement or one claiming to represent the younger members of the population: *Young Socialists.* ◆ *n* **7** (*functioning as pl*) offspring, esp. young animals: *a rabbit with her young.* **8 with young.** (of animals) pregnant. [OE *geong*]
► **ˈyoungish** *adj*
young blood *n* young, fresh, or vigorous new people, ideas, attitudes, etc.
Young Fogey *n* a young person who adopts the conservative values of an older generation.
young lady *n* a girlfriend; sweetheart.
youngling (ˈjʌŋlɪŋ) *n Literary.* **a** a young person, animal, or plant. **b** (*as modifier*)*: a youngling brood.* [OE *geongling*]
young man *n* a boyfriend; sweetheart.
young offender institution *n* (in Britain) a place where offenders aged 15 to 21 may be detained and given training, instruction, and work. Former names: **borstal, youth custody centre.**
Young Pretender *n* Charles Edward Stuart (1720–88), son of James Edward Stuart (see **Old Pretender**). He led the Jacobite Rebellion (1745–46) in an attempt to re-establish the Stuart succession to the British throne. Also known as **Bonnie Prince Charlie.**
Young's modulus (jʌŋz) *n* a modulus of elasticity, applicable to the stretching of a wire, etc., equal to the ratio of the applied load per unit area of cross section to the increase in length per unit length. [after Thomas *Young* (1773–1829), Brit. physicist]
youngster Ⓣ (ˈjʌŋstə) *n* **1** a young person; child or youth. **2** a young animal, esp. a horse.
Young Turk *n* **1** a progressive, revolutionary, or rebellious member of an organization, political party, etc. **2** a member of an abortive reform movement in the Ottoman Empire.
younker (ˈjʌŋkə) *n* **1** *Arch. or literary.* a young man; lad. **2** *Obs.* a young gentleman or knight. [C16: from Du. *jonker,* from MDu. *jonc* young]
your (jɔː, jʊə; *unstressed* jə) *determiner* **1** of, belonging to, or associated with you: *your nose; your house.* **2** belonging to or associated with an unspecified person or people in general: *the path is on your left heading north.* **3** *Inf.* used to indicate all things or people of a certain type: *your part-time worker is a problem.* [OE *eower,* genitive of *gē* ye]
you're (jɔː; *unstressed* jə) *contraction of* you are.
yours (jɔːz, jʊəz) *pron* **1** something or someone belonging to or associated with you. **2** your family: *greetings to you and yours.* **3** used in conventional closing phrases at the end of a letter: *yours sincerely; yours faithfully.* **4 of yours.** belonging to or associated with you.
yourself (jɔːˈself, jʊə-) *pron, pl* **yourselves. 1a** the reflexive form of *you.* **1b** (intensifier): *you yourself control your fate.* **2** (*preceded by a copula*) your usual self: *you're not yourself.*
yours truly *pron* an informal term for *I* or *me.* [from the closing phrase of letters]
youth Ⓣ (juːθ) *n, pl* **youths** (juːðz). **1** the quality or condition of being young, immature, or inexperienced: *his youth told against him in the contest.* **2** the period between childhood and maturity. **3** the freshness,

THESAURUS

lout, rough (*inf.*), roughneck (*sl.*), rowdy, ruffian, tough, tsotsi (*S. Afr.*), yahoo
yoke *n* **4** = **oppression,** bondage, burden, enslavement, helotry, serfdom, service, servility, servitude, slavery, thraldom, vassalage **6** = **bond,** chain, coupling, ligament, link, tie ◆ *vb* **11** = **link,** bracket, connect, couple, harness, hitch, join, tie, unite
yokel *n* = **peasant,** boor, bucolic, clodhopper (*inf.*), (country) bumpkin, country cousin, countryman, hayseed (*US & Canad. inf.*), hick (*inf., chiefly US & Canad.*), hillbilly, rustic
young *adj* **1** = **immature,** adolescent, callow, green, growing, infant, in the springtime of life, junior, juvenile, little, unfledged, youthful **5** = **new,** at an early stage, early, fledgling, newish, not far advanced, recent, undeveloped ◆ *n* **7** *functioning as plural* = **offspring,** babies, brood, family, issue, litter, little ones, progeny
Antonyms *adj* ≠ **immature:** adult, aged, elderly, full-grown, grown-up, mature, old, ripe, senior, venerable ≠ **new:** advanced, developed, old ◆ *n* ≠ **offspring:** adults, grown-ups, parents
youngster *n* **1** = **youth,** boy, cub, girl, juvenile, kid (*inf.*), lad, lass, pup (*inf., chiefly Brit.*), teenager, teenybopper (*sl.*), urchin, young person
youth *n* **2** = **immaturity,** adolescence, boyhood *or* girlhood, early life, girlhood, juvenescence, salad days, young days **5** = **boy,** adolescent, kid (*inf.*), lad, shaveling (*arch.*), stripling, teenager, young man, young shaver (*inf.*), youngster **6** = **young people,** teenagers, the rising generation, the young, the younger generation
Antonyms *n* ≠ **immaturity:** adulthood, age, later life, manhood *or* womanhood, maturity, old age ≠ **boy:** adult, grown-up, OAP, pensioner, senior citizen ≠ **young people:** the aged, the elderly, the old

vigour, or vitality characteristic of young people. **4** any period of early development. **5** a young person, esp. a young man or boy. **6** young people collectively: *youth everywhere is rising in revolt.* **[**OE *geogoth***]**

youth club *n* a centre providing leisure activities for young people.

youthful ➊ (ˈjuːθfʊl) *adj* **1** of, relating to, possessing, or characteristic of youth. **2** fresh, vigorous, or active: *he's surprisingly youthful for his age.* **3** in an early stage of development: *a youthful culture.* **4** Also: **young.** (of a river, valley, or land surface) in the early stage of the cycle of erosion, characterized by steep slopes, lack of flood plains, and V-shaped valleys.
▸ˈ**youthfully** *adv* ▸ˈ**youthfulness** *n*

youth hostel *n* one of an organization of inexpensive lodging places for people travelling cheaply. Often shortened to **hostel.**

Youth Training Scheme *n* (formerly, in Britain) a scheme, run by the Training Agency, to provide vocational training for unemployed 16–17-year-olds. Abbrev.: **YTS.**

you've (juːv; *unstressed* jʊv) *contraction of* you have.

yowl ➊ (jaʊl) *vb* **1** to express with or produce a loud mournful wail or cry; howl. ◆ *n* **2** a wail or howl. **[**C13: from ON *gaula***]**
▸ˈ**yowler** *n*

yo-yo (ˈjəʊjəʊ) *n, pl* **yo-yos. 1** a toy consisting of a spool attached to a string, the end of which is held while it is repeatedly spun out and reeled in. **2** *Sl., chiefly US.* a silly or insignificant person. ◆ *vb* **yo-yos, yo-yoing, yo-yoed.** (*intr*) **3** to change repeatedly from one position to another; fluctuate. **[**from Filipino *yo yo* come come, a weapon consisting of a spindle attached to a thong**]**

yr *abbrev. for:* **1** (*pl* **yrs**) year. **2** younger. **3** your.

yrs *abbrev. for:* **1** years. **2** yours.

YST (in Canada) *abbrev. for* Yukon Standard Time.

YT *abbrev. for* Yukon Territory.

YTS (in Britain) *abbrev. for* Youth Training Scheme.

ytterbia (ɪˈtɜːbɪə) *n* another name for **ytterbium oxide. [**C19: NL; see YTTERBIUM**]**

ytterbium (ɪˈtɜːbɪəm) *n* a soft malleable silvery element of the lanthanide series of metals that is used to improve the mechanical properties of steel. Symbol: Yb; atomic no.: 70; atomic wt.: 173.04. **[**C19: NL, after *Ytterby,* Swedish quarry where discovered**]**

ytterbium oxide *n* a weakly basic hygroscopic substance used in certain alloys and ceramics.

yttria (ˈɪtrɪə) *n* another name for **yttrium oxide. [**C19: NL; see YTTERBIUM**]**

yttrium (ˈɪtrɪəm) *n* a silvery metallic element used in various alloys, in lasers, and as a catalyst. Symbol: Y; atomic no.: 39; atomic wt.: 88.90. **[**C19: NL; see YTTERBIUM**]**

yttrium metal *n Chem.* any one of a group of elements including yttrium and the related lanthanides.

yttrium oxide *n* a colourless or white insoluble solid used in incandescent mantles.

yuan (ˈjuːˈæn) *n, pl* **yuan.** the standard monetary unit of China. **[**from Chinese *yüan* round object; see YEN[1]**]**

Yuan Tan (ˈjuːˈæn ˈtæn) *n* an annual Chinese festival marking the Chinese New Year. It can last over three days and includes the exchange of gifts, firework displays, and dancing.

yucca (ˈjʌkə) *n* any of a genus of liliaceous plants of tropical and subtropical America, having stiff lancelike leaves and spikes of white flowers. **[**C16: from American Sp. *yuca,* ult. from Amerind**]**

yuck *or* **yuk** (jʌk) *interj Sl.* an exclamation indicating contempt, dislike, or disgust.

yucky ➊ *or* **yukky** (ˈjʌkɪ) *adj* **yuckier, yuckiest** *or* **yukkier, yukkiest.** *Sl.* disgusting; nasty.

Yugoslav *or* **Jugoslav** (ˈjuːgəʊˌslɑːv) *n* **1** a native or inhabitant of Yugoslavia. **2** (not in technical use) another name for **Serbo-Croat** (the language). ◆ *adj* **3** of, relating to, or characteristic of Yugoslavia or its people.

yulan (ˈjuːlæn) *n* a Chinese magnolia that is often cultivated for its showy white flowers. **[**C19: from Chinese, from *yu* a gem + *lan* plant**]**

yule (juːl) *n* (*sometimes cap.*) *Literary, arch., or dialect.* **a** Christmas or the Christmas season. **b** (*in combination*): *yuletide.* **[**OE *geōla,* orig. a pagan feast lasting 12 days**]**

yule log *n* a large log of wood traditionally used as the foundation of a fire at Christmas.

yummy (ˈjʌmɪ) *Sl.* ◆ *interj* **1** Also: **yum-yum.** an exclamation indicating pleasure or delight, as in anticipation of delicious food. ◆ *adj* **yummier, yummiest. 2** delicious, delightful, or attractive. **[**C20: from *yum-yum,* imit.**]**

yuppie *or* **yuppy** (ˈjʌpɪ) (*sometimes cap.*) ◆ *n* **1** an affluent young professional person. ◆ *adj* **2** typical of or reflecting the values characteristic of yuppies. **[**C20: from *y*(*oung*) *u*(*rban*) or *up*(*wardly mobile*) *p*(*rofessional*) + -IE**]**
▸ˈ**yuppiedom** *n*

yuppie disease *or* **flu** *n Inf., sometimes considered offens.* any of a number of debilitating long-lasting viral disorders associated with stress, such as chronic fatigue syndrome, whose symptoms include muscle weakness, chronic tiredness, and depression.

yuppify (ˈjʌpɪˌfaɪ) *vb* **yuppifies, yuppifying, yuppified.** (*tr*) to make yuppie in nature.
▸ˌ**yuppifiˈcation** *n*

yurt (jʊət) *n* a circular tent consisting of a framework of poles covered with felt or skins, used by Mongolian and Turkic nomads of E and central Asia. **[**from Russian *yurta,* of Turkic origin**]**

YWCA *abbrev. for* Young Women's Christian Association.

THESAURUS

youthful *adj* **1** = **young,** boyish, childish, girlish, immature, inexperienced, juvenile, pubescent, puerile **2** = **fresh,** active, spry, vigorous, young at heart, young looking
Antonyms *adj* ≠ **young:** adult, aged, ageing, elderly, grown-up, mature, old, senile ≠ **fresh:** aged, ancient, decaying, decrepit, hoary, over the hill, tired, waning, weary

yowl *vb* **1** = **howl,** bawl, bay, caterwaul, cry, give tongue, screech, squall, ululate, wail, yell

yucky *adj* = **disgusting,** beastly, dirty, foul, grotty (*sl.*), horrible, messy, mucky, revolting (*inf.*), unpleasant

Zz

z *or* **Z** (zɛd; *US* ziː) *n, pl* **z's, Z's,** *or* **Zs. 1** the 26th and last letter of the English alphabet. **2** a speech sound represented by this letter. **3a** something shaped like a Z. **3b** (*in combination*): *a Z-bend in a road.*

z *Maths. symbol for:* **1** the *z*-axis or a coordinate measured along the *z*-axis in a Cartesian or cylindrical coordinate system. **2** an algebraic variable.

Z *symbol for:* **1** any unknown, variable, or unspecified factor, number, person, or thing. **2** *Chem.* atomic number. **3** *Physics.* impedance. **4** zone.

z. *abbrev. for:* **1** zero. **2** zone.

zabaglione (ˌzæbəˈljəʊnɪ) *n* a light foamy dessert made of egg yolks, sugar, and marsala, whipped together and served warm in a glass. [It.]

zaffer *or* **zaffre** (ˈzæfə) *n* impure cobalt oxide, used to impart a blue colour to enamels. [C17: from It. *zaffera*]

zaibatsu (ˈzaɪbætˈsuː) *n* (*functioning as sing or pl*) the group or combine comprising a few wealthy families that controls industry, business, and finance in Japan. [from Japanese, from *zai* wealth + *batsu* family, person of influence]

zakuski *or* **zakouski** (zæˈkʊskɪ) *pl n, sing* **zakuska** *or* **zakouska** (-kə). *Russian cookery.* hors d'oeuvres, consisting of tiny open sandwiches spread with caviar, smoked sausage, etc., or a cold dish such as radishes in sour cream, all usually served with vodka. [Russian, from *zakusit'* to have a snack]

Zambian (ˈzæmbɪən) *adj* **1** of or relating to Zambia, a republic in central Africa. ◆ *n* **2** a native or inhabitant of Zambia.

zambuck *or* **zambuk** (ˈzæmbʌk) *n Austral. & NZ inf.* a first-aid attendant at a sports event. [from name of a proprietary ointment]

ZANU (ˈzɑːnuː) *n acronym for* Zimbabwe African National Union.

zany ❶ (ˈzeɪnɪ) *adj* **zanier, zaniest. 1** comical in an endearing way; imaginatively funny or comical, esp. in behaviour. ◆ *n, pl* **zanies. 2** a clown or buffoon, esp. one in old comedies who imitated other performers with ludicrous effect. **3** a ludicrous or foolish person. [C16: from It. *zanni,* from dialect *Zanni,* nickname for *Giovanni* John; one of the traditional names for a clown]
▸ **ˈzanily** *adv* ▸ **ˈzaniness** *n*

zap (zæp) *Sl.* ◆ *vb* **zaps, zapping, zapped. 1** (*tr*) to attack, kill, or destroy, as with a sudden bombardment. **2** (*intr*) to move quickly. **3** (*tr*) *Computing.* **3a** to clear from the screen. **3b** to erase. **4** (*intr*) *Television.* to change channels rapidly by remote control. ◆ *n* **5** energy, vigour, or pep. ◆ *interj* **6** an exclamation used to express sudden or swift action. [C20: imit.]

zapateado *Spanish.* (ˌθapateˈaðo) *n, pl* **-dos** (-ðos). a Spanish dance with stamping and very fast footwork. [from *zapatear* to tap with the shoe, from *zapato* shoe]

zappy (ˈzæpɪ) *adj* **zappier, zappiest.** *Sl.* full of energy; zippy.

ZAPU (ˈzæpuː) *n acronym for* Zimbabwe African People's Union.

Zarathustrian (ˌzærəˈθuːstrɪən) *adj, n* another name for **Zoroastrian.** [C19: from *Zarathustra* the Old Iranian form of Zoroaster]

zareba *or* **zareeba** (zəˈriːbə) *n* (in northern E Africa, esp. formerly) **1** a stockade or enclosure of thorn bushes around a village or camp site. **2** the area so protected or enclosed. [C19: from Ar. *zarībah* cattlepen, from *zarb* sheepfold]

zarf (zɑːf) *n* (esp. in the Middle East) a holder, usually ornamental, for a hot coffee cup. [from Ar.: container]

zarzuela (zɑːˈzweɪlə) *n* **1** a type of Spanish vaudeville or operetta, usually satirical in nature. **2** a seafood stew. [from Sp., after *La Zarzuela,* the palace near Madrid where such vaudeville was first performed (1629)]

***z*-axis** *n* a reference axis of a three-dimensional Cartesian coordinate system along which the *z*-coordinate is measured.

ZB station *n* (in New Zealand) a radio station of a commercial network.

Z chart *n Statistics.* a chart often used in industry and constructed by plotting on it three series: monthly, weekly, or daily data, the moving annual total, and the cumulative total dating from the beginning of the current year.

zeal ❶ (ziːl) *n* fervent or enthusiastic devotion, often extreme or fanatical in nature, as to a religious movement, political cause, ideal, or aspiration. [C14: from LL *zēlus,* from Gk *zēlos*]

zealot ❶ (ˈzɛlət) *n* an immoderate, fanatical, or extremely zealous adherent to a cause, esp. a religious one. [C16: from LL *zēlōtēs,* from Gk, from *zēloun* to be zealous, from *zēlos* zeal]
▸ **ˈzealotry** *n*

Zealot (ˈzɛlət) *n* any of the members of an extreme Jewish sect or political party that resisted all aspects of Roman rule in Palestine in the 1st century A.D.

zealous ❶ (ˈzɛləs) *adj* filled with or inspired by intense enthusiasm or zeal; ardent; fervent.
▸ **ˈzealously** *adv* ▸ **ˈzealousness** *n*

zebec *or* **zebeck** (ˈziːbɛk) *n* variant spellings of **xebec.**

zebra (ˈziːbrə, ˈzɛbrə) *n, pl* **zebras** *or* **zebra.** any of several mammals of the horse family, such as the common zebra of southern and eastern Africa, having distinctive black-and-white striped hides. [C16: via It. from OSp.: wild ass, prob. from Vulgar L *eciferus* (unattested) wild horse, from L *equiferus,* from *equus* horse + *ferus* wild]
▸ **zebrine** (ˈziːbraɪn, ˈzɛb-) *or* **ˈzebroid** *adj*

Zebra (ˈziːbrə, ˈzɛbrə) *n Finance.* a noninterest-paying bond in which the accrued income is taxed annually rather than on redemption. Cf. **zero** (sense 10). [C20: from *zero-coupon bond*]

zebra crossing *n Brit.* a pedestrian crossing marked on a road by broad alternate black and white stripes. Once on the crossing the pedestrian has right of way.

zebra finch *n* any of various Australasian songbirds with zebra-like markings.

zebrawood (ˈzɛbrəˌwʊd, ˈziː-) *n* **1** a tree of tropical America, Asia, and Africa, yielding striped hardwood used in cabinetwork. **2** any of various other trees or shrubs having striped wood. **3** the wood of any of these trees.

zebu (ˈziːbuː) *n* a domesticated ox having a humped back, long horns, and a large dewlap: used in India and E Asia as a draught animal. [C18: from F *zébu,* ? of Tibetan origin]

Zech. *Bible. abbrev. for* Zechariah.

zed (zɛd) *n* the British spoken form of the letter *z.* [C15: from OF *zede,* via LL from Gk *zēta*]

zedoary (ˈzɛdəʊərɪ) *n* the dried rhizome of a tropical Asian plant, used as a stimulant and a condiment. [C15: from Med. L *zedoaria,* from Ar. *zadwār,* of Persian origin]

zee (ziː) *n* the US word for **zed** (letter *z*).

Zeeman effect (ˈziːmən) *n* the splitting of a spectral line of a substance into several closely spaced lines when the substance is placed in a magnetic field. [C20: after Pieter *Zeeman* (1865–1943), Du. physicist]

zein (ˈziːɪn) *n* a protein occurring in maize and used in the manufacture of plastics, paper coatings, adhesives, etc. [C19: from NL *zēa* maize, from L: a kind of grain, from Gk *zeia* barley]

Zeitgeist *German.* (ˈtsaɪtˌgaɪst) *n* the spirit, attitude, or general outlook of a specific time or period, esp. as it is reflected in literature, philosophy, etc. [G, lit.: time spirit]

Zen (zɛn) *Buddhism. n* **1** a Japanese school, of 12th-century Chinese origin, teaching that contemplation of one's essential nature to the exclusion of all else is the only way of achieving pure enlightenment. **2** (*modifier*) of or relating to this school: *Zen Buddhism.* [from Japanese, from Chinese *ch'an* religious meditation, from Pali *jhāna,* from Sansk. *dhyāna*]
▸ **ˈZenic** *adj* ▸ **ˈZenist** *n*

zenana (zɛˈnɑːnə) *n* (in the East, esp. in Muslim and Hindu homes) part of a house reserved for the women and girls of a household. [C18: from Hindi *zanāna,* from Persian, from *zan* woman]

Zend (zɛnd) *n* **1** a former name for **Avestan. 2** short for **Zend-Avesta. 3** an exposition of the Avesta in the Middle Persian language (Pahlavi). [C18: from Persian *zand* commentary, exposition; used specifically of the MPersian commentary on the Avesta, hence of the language of the Avesta itself]
▸ **ˈZendic** *adj*

Zend-Avesta (ˌzɛndəˈvɛstə) *n* the Avesta together with the traditional interpretive commentary known as the Zend, esp. as preserved in the Avestan language among the Parsees. [from Avestan, representing *Avesta'-va-zend* Avesta with interpretation]

Zener diode (ˈziːnə) *n* a semiconductor diode that exhibits a sharp increase in reverse current at a well-defined reverse voltage: used as a voltage regulator. [C20: after C. M. *Zener* (1905–93), US physicist]

zenith ❶ (ˈzɛnɪθ) *n* **1** *Astron.* the point on the celestial sphere vertically above an observer. **2** the highest point; peak; acme: *the zenith of some-*

THESAURUS

zany *adj* **1** = **comical**, clownish, crazy, eccentric, funny, goofy (*inf.*), kooky (*US inf.*), loony (*sl.*), madcap, nutty (*sl.*), oddball (*inf.*), wacky (*sl.*) ◆ *n* **2** = **clown**, buffoon, comedian, jester, joker, merry-andrew, nut (*sl.*), screwball (*sl., chiefly US & Canad.*), wag

zeal *n* = **enthusiasm**, ardour, devotion, eagerness, earnestness, fanaticism, fervency, fervour, fire, gusto, keenness, militancy, passion, spirit, verve, warmth, zest
Antonyms *n* apathy, coolness, indifference, passivity, stoicism, torpor, unresponsiveness

zealot *n* = **fanatic**, bigot, energumen, enthusiast, extremist, fiend (*inf.*), maniac, militant

zealous *adj* = **enthusiastic**, ablaze, afire, ardent, burning, devoted, eager, earnest, fanatical, fervent, fervid, impassioned, keen, militant, passionate, rabid, spirited
Antonyms *adj* apathetic, cold, cool, half-hearted, indifferent, lackadaisical, lacklustre, languorous, listless, low-key, sceptical, torpid, unenthusiastic, unimpassioned

zenith *n* **2** = **height**, acme, apex, apogee, climax, crest, high noon, high point, meridian, peak, pinnacle, summit, top, vertex
Antonyms *n* base, bottom, depths, lowest point, nadir, rock bottom

one's achievements. [C17: from F *cenith,* from Med. L, from OSp. *zenit,* based on Ar. *samt,* as in *samt arrās* path over one's head]
▸'**zenithal** *adj*

zenithal projection *n* a type of map projection in which part of the earth's surface is projected onto a plane tangential to it, either at one of the poles (**polar zenithal**), at the equator (**equatorial zenithal**), or between (**oblique zenithal**).

zeolite ('ziːəˌlaɪt) *n* **1** any of a large group of glassy secondary minerals consisting of hydrated aluminium silicates of calcium, sodium, or potassium: formed in cavities in lava flows and plutonic rocks. **2** any of a class of similar synthetic materials used in ion exchange and as selective absorbents. [C18: *zeo-,* from Gk *zein* to boil + -LITE; from the swelling that occurs under the blowpipe]
▸**zeolitic** (ˌziːə'lɪtɪk) *adj*

Zeph. *Bible. abbrev. for* Zephaniah.

zephyr ('zɛfə) *n* **1** a soft or gentle breeze. **2** any of several delicate soft yarns, fabrics, or garments, usually of wool. [C16: from L *zephyrus,* from Gk *zephuros* the west wind]

zeppelin ('zɛpəlɪn) *n* (*sometimes cap.*) a large cylindrical rigid airship built from 1900 to carry passengers and used in World War I for bombing and reconnaissance. [C20: after Count von *Zeppelin* (1838–1917), its G designer]

zero 🅣 ('zɪərəʊ) *n, pl* **zeros** *or* **zeroes. 1** the symbol 0, indicating an absence of quantity or magnitude; nought. Former name: **cipher. 2** the integer denoted by the symbol 0; nought. **3** the cardinal number between +1 and –1. **4** nothing; nil. **5** a person or thing of no significance; nonentity. **6** the lowest point or degree: *his prospects were put at zero.* **7** the line or point on a scale of measurement from which the graduations commence. **8a** the temperature, pressure, etc., that registers a reading of zero on a scale. **8b** the value of a variable, such as temperature, obtained under specified conditions. **9** *Maths.* **9a** the cardinal number of a set with no members. **9b** the identity element of addition. **10** *Finance.* Also called: **zero-coupon bond.** a bond that pays no interest, the equivalent being paid in its redemption value. Cf. **Zebra.** ◆ *adj* **11** having no measurable quantity, magnitude, etc. **12** *Meteorol.* **12a** (of a cloud ceiling) limiting visibility to 15 metres (50 feet) or less. **12b** (of horizontal visibility) limited to 50 metres (165 feet) or less. ◆ *vb* **zeros** *or* **zeroes, zeroing, zeroed. 13** (*tr*) to adjust (an instrument, apparatus, etc.) so as to read zero or a position taken as zero. ◆ *determiner* **14** *Inf., chiefly US.* no (thing) at all: *this job has zero interest.* ◆ See also **zero in.** [C17: from It., from Med. L *zephirum,* from Ar. *sifr* empty]

zero gravity *n* the state or condition of weightlessness.

zero hour 🅣 *n* **1** *Mil.* the time set for the start of an attack or the initial stage of an operation. **2** *Inf.* a critical time, esp. at the commencement of an action.

zero in 🅣 *vb* (*adv*) **1** (often foll. by *on*) to bring (a weapon) to bear (on a target), as while firing repeatedly. **2** (*intr;* foll. by *on*) *Inf.* to bring one's attention to bear (on a problem, etc.). **3** (*intr;* foll. by *on*) *Inf.* to converge (upon): *the police zeroed in on the site of the crime.*

zero option *n* (in international nuclear arms negotiations) an offer to remove all shorter-range nuclear missiles or, in the case of the **zero-zero option** all intermediate-range nuclear missiles, if the other side will do the same.

zero-rated *adj* denoting goods on which the buyer pays no value-added tax although the seller can claim back any tax he has paid.

zero stage *n* a solid-propellant rocket attached to a liquid-propellant rocket to provide greater thrust at liftoff.

zeroth ('zɪərəʊθ) *adj* denoting a term in a series that precedes the term otherwise regarded as the first term. [C20: from ZERO + -TH[2]]

zero tolerance *n* the policy of applying laws or penalties to even minor infringements of a code in order to reinforce its overall importance.

zest 🅣 (zɛst) *n* **1** invigorating or keen excitement or enjoyment: *a zest for living.* **2** added interest, flavour, or charm; piquancy: *her presence gave zest to the party.* **3** something added to give flavour or relish. **4** the peel or skin of an orange or lemon, used as flavouring in drinks, etc. ◆ *vb* **5** (*tr*) to give flavour, interest, or piquancy to. [C17: from F *zeste* peel of citrus fruits used as flavouring, from ?]
▸'**zestful** *adj* ▸'**zestfully** *adv* ▸'**zestfulness** *n* ▸'**zesty** *adj*

zeta ('ziːtə) *n* the sixth letter in the Greek alphabet (Z, ζ). [from Gk]

ZETA ('ziːtə) *n* a torus-shaped apparatus formerly used for research on controlled thermonuclear reactions. [C20: from *z(ero-)e(nergy) t(hermonuclear) a(pparatus)*]

zeugma ('zjuːgmə) *n* a figure of speech in which a word is used to modify or govern two or more words although appropriate to only one of them or making a different sense with each, as in *Mr Pickwick took his hat and his leave* (Charles Dickens). [C16: via L from Gk: a yoking, from *zeugnunai* to yoke]
▸**zeugmatic** (zjuːg'mætɪk) *adj*

zho (zəʊ) *n* a variant spelling of **zo.**

zibeline ('zɪbəˌlaɪn, -lɪn) *n* **1** a sable or the fur of this animal. **2** a thick cloth made of wool or other animal hair, having a long nap and a dull sheen. ◆ *adj* **3** of, relating to, or resembling a sable. [C16: from F, from OIt. *zibellino,* ult. of Slavonic origin]

zibet ('zɪbɪt) *n* a large civet of S and SE Asia, having tawny fur marked with black spots and stripes. [C16: from Med. L *zibethum,* from Ar. *zabād* civet]

zidovudine (zaɪ'dɒvjʊˌdiːn) *n* a drug that prolongs life and alleviates symptoms among some AIDS sufferers. Also called: **AZT.**

ziff (zɪf) *n Austral. inf.* a beard. [C20: from ?]

ziggurat ('zɪgʊˌræt) *n* a type of rectangular temple tower or tiered mound erected by the Sumerians, Akkadians, and Babylonians in Mesopotamia. [C19: from Assyrian *ziqqurati* summit]

zigzag ('zɪgˌzæg) *n* **1** a line or course characterized by sharp turns in alternating directions. **2** one of the series of such turns. **3** something having the form of a zigzag. ◆ *adj* **4** (*usually prenominal*) formed in or proceeding in a zigzag. **5** (of a sewing machine) capable of producing stitches in a zigzag. ◆ *adv* **6** in a zigzag manner. ◆ *vb* **zigzags, zigzagging, zigzagged. 7** to proceed or cause to proceed in a zigzag. **8** (*tr*) to form into a zigzag. [C18: from F, from G *zickzack,* from *Zacke* point]

zigzagger ('zɪgˌzægə) *n* **1** a person or thing that zigzags. **2** an attachment on a sewing machine for sewing zigzag stitches, as for joining two pieces of material.

zilch (zɪltʃ) *n Sl.* **1** nothing. **2** *US & Canad. sport.* nil. [C20: from ?]

zillion ('zɪljən) *Inf.* ◆ *n, pl* **zillions** *or* **zillion. 1** (*often pl*) an extremely large but unspecified number, quantity, or amount: *zillions of flies in this camp.* ◆ *determiner* **2** amounting to a zillion: *a zillion different problems.* [C20: coinage after MILLION]

Zimbabwean (zɪm'bɑːbwɪən) *adj* **1** of or relating to Zimbabwe, a republic in southern Africa. ◆ *n* **2** a native or inhabitant of Zimbabwe.

Zimmer ('zɪmə) *n Trademark.* Also: **Zimmer frame.** another name for **walker** (sense 3).

zinc (zɪŋk) *n* **1** a brittle bluish-white metallic element that is a constituent of several alloys, esp. brass and nickel-silver, and is used in die-casting, galvanizing metals, and in battery electrodes. Symbol: Zn; atomic no.: 30; atomic wt.: 65.37. **2** *Inf.* corrugated galvanized iron. [C17: from G *Zink,* ?from *Zinke* prong, from its jagged appearance in the furnace]
▸'**zincic,** '**zincous,** *or* '**zincoid** *adj* ▸'**zincky,** '**zincy,** *or* '**zinky** *adj*

zinc blende *n* another name for **sphalerite.**

zinc chloride *n* a white soluble poisonous granular solid used in manufacturing parchment paper and vulcanized fibre and in preserving wood. It is also a soldering flux, embalming agent, and medical astringent and antiseptic.

zincite ('zɪŋkaɪt) *n* a red or yellow mineral consisting of zinc oxide in hexagonal crystalline form. It occurs in metamorphosed limestone.

zincography (zɪŋ'kɒgrəfɪ) *n* the art or process of etching on zinc to form a printing plate.
▸**zincograph** ('zɪŋkəˌgrɑːf) *n* ▸**zin'cographer** *n*

zinc ointment *n* a medicinal ointment consisting of zinc oxide, petrolatum, and paraffin, used to treat certain skin diseases.

zinc oxide *n* a white insoluble powder used as a pigment in paints (**zinc white** or **Chinese white**), cosmetics, glass, and printing inks. It is an antiseptic and astringent and is used in making zinc ointment. Formula: ZnO. Also called: **flowers of zinc.**

zinc sulphate *n* a colourless soluble crystalline substance used as a mordant, in preserving wood and skins, and in the electrodeposition of zinc. Also called: **zinc vitriol.**

zine (ziːn) *n Inf.* a magazine or fanzine.

zing 🅣 (zɪŋ) *n Inf.* **1** a short high-pitched buzzing sound, as of a bullet or vibrating string. **2** vitality; zest. ◆ *vb* **3** (*intr*) to make or move with or as if with a high-pitched buzzing sound. [C20: imit.]
▸'**zingy** *adj*

zinjanthropus (zɪn'dʒænθrəpəs) *n* a type of australopithecine, remains of which were discovered in the Olduvai Gorge in Tanzania in 1959. [C20: NL, from Ar. *Zinj* East Africa + Gk *anthrōpos* man]

zinnia ('zɪnɪə) *n* any of a genus of annual or perennial plants of the composite family, of tropical and subtropical America, having solitary heads of brightly coloured flowers. [C18: after J. G. *Zinn* (d. 1759), G botanist]

Zion ('zaɪən) *or* **Sion** *n* **1** the hill on which the city of Jerusalem stands. **2** *Judaism.* **2a** the ancient Israelites of the Bible. **2b** the modern Jewish nation. **2c** Israel as the national home of the Jewish people. **3** *Christianity.* heaven regarded as the city of God and the final abode of his elect.

Zionism ('zaɪəˌnɪzəm) *n* **1** a political movement for the establishment and support of a national homeland for Jews in Palestine, now concerned chiefly with the development of the modern state of Israel. **2** a policy or movement for Jews to return to Palestine from the Diaspora.
▸'**Zionist** *n, adj* ▸ˌ**Zion'istic** *adj*

zip 🅣 (zɪp) *n* **1a** Also called: **zip fastener.** a fastening device operating by

THESAURUS

zero *n* **1-4** = **nothing,** cipher, naught, nil, nought **6** = **bottom,** lowest point *or* ebb, nadir, nothing, rock bottom

zero hour *n* **2** = **moment of truth,** appointed hour, crisis, moment of decision, turning point, vital moment

zero in *vb* **1, 2** = **home in,** aim, bring to bear, concentrate, converge, direct, focus, level, pinpoint, train

zest *n* **1** = **enjoyment,** appetite, delectation, gusto, keenness, relish, zeal, zing (*inf.*) **2** = **flavour,** charm, interest, kick (*inf.*), piquancy, pungency, relish, savour, smack, spice, tang, taste
Antonyms *n* ≠ **enjoyment:** abhorrence, apathy, aversion, disinclination, distaste, indifference, lack of enthusiasm, loathing, repugnance, weariness

zing *n* **2** *Informal* = **vitality,** animation, brio, dash, energy, go (*inf.*), life, liveliness, oomph (*inf.*), pep, pizzazz *or* pizazz (*inf.*), spirit, vigour, zest, zip (*inf.*)

zip *n* **3** *Informal* = **energy,** brio, drive, get-up-and-go (*inf.*), go (*inf.*), gusto, life, liveliness, oomph (*inf.*), pep, pizzazz *or* pizazz (*inf.*), punch (*inf.*), sparkle, spirit, verve, vigour, vim (*sl.*), vitality, zest, zing (*inf.*) ◆ *vb* **8** = **speed,** barrel (along) (*inf., chiefly US & Canad.*), burn rub-

means of two parallel rows of metal or plastic teeth on either side of a closure that are interlocked by a sliding tab. US and Canad. term: **zipper. 1b** (*modifier*) having such a device: *a zip bag.* **2** a short sharp whizzing sound, as of a passing bullet. **3** *Inf.* energy; vigour; vitality. **4** *US sl.* nothing. **5** *Sport, US & Canad. sl.* nil. ◆ *vb* **zips, zipping, zipped. 6** (*tr;* often foll. by *up*) to fasten (clothing, etc.) with a zip. **7** (*intr*) to move with a zip: *the bullet zipped past.* **8** (*intr;* often foll. by *along, through,* etc.) to hurry; rush. [C19: imit.]

zip code *n* the US equivalent of **postcode.** [C20: from *z(one) i(mprovement) p(lan)*]

zip gun *n US & Canad. sl.* a crude home-made pistol, esp. one powered by a spring or rubber band.

zipper ('zɪpə) *n* the US & Canad. word for **zip** (sense 1a).

zippy ('zɪpɪ) *adj* **zippier, zippiest.** *Inf.* full of energy; lively.

zircalloy (zɜːk'ælɔɪ) *n* an alloy of zirconium containing small amounts of tin, chromium, and nickel. It is used in pressurized-water reactors.

zircon ('zɜːkɒn) *n* a reddish-brown, grey, green, blue, or colourless hard mineral consisting of zirconium silicate: it is used as a gemstone and a refractory. [C18: from G *Zirkon,* from F *jargon,* via It. & Ar., from Persian *zargūn* golden]

zirconium (zɜː'kəʊnɪəm) *n* a greyish-white metallic element, occurring chiefly in zircon, that is exceptionally corrosion-resistant and has low neutron absorption. It is used as a coating in nuclear and chemical plants, as a deoxidizer in steel, and alloyed with niobium in superconductive magnets. Symbol: Zr; atomic no.: 40; atomic wt.: 91.22. [C19: from NL; see ZIRCON]
▸**zirconic** (zɜː'kɒnɪk) *adj*

zirconium oxide *n* a white amorphous powder that is insoluble in water and highly refractory, used as a pigment for paints, a catalyst, and an abrasive.

zit (zɪt) *n Sl.* a pimple. [from ?]

zither ('zɪðə) *n* a plucked musical instrument consisting of numerous strings stretched over a resonating box, a few of which may be stopped on a fretted fingerboard. [C19: from G, from L *cithara,* from Gk *kithara*]
▸**'zitherist** *n*

zloty ('zlɒtɪ) *n, pl* **zlotys** *or* **zloty.** the standard monetary unit of Poland. [from Polish: golden, from *zlyoto* gold]

Zn *the chemical symbol for* zinc.

zo, zho, *or* **dzo** (zəʊ) *n, pl* **zos, zhos, dzos** *or* **zo, zho, dzo.** a Tibetan breed of cattle, developed by crossing the yak with common cattle. [C20: from Tibetan]

zo- *combining form.* a variant of **zoo-** before a vowel.

-zoa *suffix forming plural proper nouns.* indicating groups of animal organisms: *Metazoa.* [from NL, from Gk *zōia,* pl. of *zōion* animal]

zodiac ('zəʊdɪ,æk) *n* **1** an imaginary belt extending 8° either side of the ecliptic, which contains the 12 **zodiacal constellations** and within which the moon and planets appear to move. It is divided into 12 equal areas, called **signs of the zodiac,** each named after the constellation which once lay in it. **2** *Astrol.* a diagram, usually circular, representing this belt and showing the symbols, illustrations, etc., associated with each of the 12 signs of the zodiac, used to predict the future. [C14: from OF *zodiaque,* from L *zōdiacus,* from Gk *zōidiakos* (*kuklos*) (circle) of signs, from *zōidion* animal sign, from *zōion* animal]
▸**zodiacal** (zəʊ'daɪəkəl) *adj*

zodiacal constellation *n* any of the 12 constellations after which the signs of the zodiac are named: Aries, Taurus, Gemini, Cancer, Leo, Virgo, Libra, Scorpio, Sagittarius, Capricorn, Aquarius, or Pisces.

zodiacal light *n* a very faint cone of light in the sky, visible in the east just before sunrise and in the west just after sunset.

zoic ('zəʊɪk) *adj* **1** relating to or having animal life. **2** *Geol.* (of rocks, etc.) containing fossilized animals. [C19: from NL, from Gk *zōion* animal]

-zoic *adj and n combining form.* indicating a geological era: *Palaeozoic.* [from Gk *zōē* life + -IC]

Zollverein *German.* ('tsɔlfɛr,ain) *n* the customs union of German states organized in the early 1830s under Prussian auspices. [C19: from *Zoll* tax + *Verein* union]

zombie *or* **zombi** ('zɒmbɪ) *n, pl* **zombies** *or* **zombis. 1** a person who is or appears to be lifeless, apathetic, or totally lacking in independent judgment; automaton. **2** a supernatural spirit that reanimates a dead body. **3** a corpse brought to life in this manner. [from W African *zumbi* good-luck fetish]

zonation (zəʊ'neɪʃən) *n* arrangement in zones.

zone ❶ (zəʊn) *n* **1** a region, area, or section characterized by some distinctive feature or quality. **2** an area subject to a particular political, military, or government function, use, or jurisdiction: *a demilitarized zone.* **3** (*often cap.*) *Geog.* one of the divisions of the earth's surface, esp. divided into latitudinal belts according to temperature. See **Torrid Zone, Frigid Zone, Temperate Zone. 4** *Geol.* a distinctive layer or region of rock, characterized by particular fossils (**zone fossils**), etc. **5** *Ecology.* an area, esp. a belt of land, having a particular flora and fauna determined by the prevailing environmental conditions. **6** *Maths.* a portion of a sphere between two parallel planes intersecting the sphere. **7** *Sport.* **7a** a period during which a competitor is performing particularly well: *Hingis is in the zone at the moment.* **7b** (*modifier*) of or relating to competitive performance that depends on the mood or state of mind of the participant: *a zone player.* **8** *Arch. or literary.* a girdle or belt. **9** *NZ.* a section on a transport route; fare stage. **10** *NZ.* a catchment area for a specific school. ◆ *vb* **zones, zoning, zoned.** (*tr*) **11** to divide into zones, as for different use, jurisdiction, activities, etc. **12** to designate as a zone. **13** to mark with or divide into zones. [C15: from L *zōna* girdle, climatic zone, from Gk *zōnē*]
▸**'zonal** *adj* ▸**'zonated** *adj* ▸**'zoning** *n*

zone refining *n* a technique for producing solids of extreme purity, esp. for use in semiconductors. The material, in the form of a bar, is melted in one small region that is passed along the solid. Impurities concentrate in the melt and are moved to the end of the bar.

zonetime ('zəʊn,taɪm) *n* the standard time of the time zone in which a ship is located at sea, each zone extending 7½° to each side of a meridian.

zonked (zɒŋkt) *adj Sl.* **1** incapacitated by drugs or alcohol. **2** exhausted. [C20: imit.]

zonk out (zɒŋk) *vb* (*intr, adv*) *Sl.* to fall asleep, esp. from physical exhaustion or the effects of alcohol or drugs.

zoo (zuː) *n, pl* **zoos.** a place where live animals are kept, studied, bred, and exhibited to the public. Formal term: **zoological garden.** [C19: shortened from *zoological gardens* (orig. those in London)]

zoo- *or before a vowel* **zo-** *combining form.* indicating animals: *zooplankton.* [from Gk *zōion* animal]

zoogeography (,zəʊədʒɪ'ɒgrəfɪ) *n* the branch of zoology concerned with the geographical distribution of animals.
▸**,zooge'ographer** *n* ▸**zoogeographic** (,zəʊə,dʒɪə'græfɪk) *or* **,zoo,geo'graphical** *adj* ▸**,zoo,geo'graphically** *adv*

zoography (zəʊ'ɒgrəfɪ) *n* the branch of zoology concerned with the description of animals.
▸**zo'ographer** *n* ▸**zoographic** (,zəʊə'græfɪk) *or* **,zoo'graphical** *adj*

zooid ('zəʊɔɪd) *n* **1** any independent animal body, such as an individual of a coelenterate colony. **2** a motile cell or body, such as a gamete, produced by an organism.
▸**zo'oidal** *adj*

zool. *abbrev. for:* **1** zoological. **2** zoology.

zoolatry (zəʊ'ɒlətrɪ) *n* **1** (esp. in ancient or primitive religions) the worship of animals as the incarnations of certain deities, etc. **2** extreme or excessive devotion to animals, particularly domestic pets.
▸**zo'olatrous** *adj*

zoological garden *n* the formal term for **zoo.**

zoology (zəʊ'ɒlədʒɪ, zuː-) *n, pl* **zoologies. 1** the study of animals, including their classification, structure, physiology, and history. **2** the biological characteristics of a particular animal or animal group. **3** the fauna characteristic of a particular region.
▸**zoological** (,zəʊə'lɒdʒɪkᵊl, ,zuːə-) *adj* ▸**zo'ologist** *n*

zoom ❶ (zuːm) *vb* **1** to make or cause to make a continuous buzzing or humming sound. **2** to move or cause to move with such a sound. **3** (*intr*) to move very rapidly; rush: *we zoomed through town.* **4** to cause (an aircraft) to climb briefly at an unusually steep angle, or (of an aircraft) to climb in this way. **5** (*intr*) (of prices) to rise rapidly. ◆ *n* **6** the sound or act of zooming. **7** See **zoom lens.** [C19: imit.]

zoom in *or* **out** *vb* (*intr, adv*) *Photog., films, television.* to increase or decrease rapidly the magnification of the image of a distant object by means of a zoom lens.

zoom lens *n* a lens system that allows the focal length of a camera lens to be varied continuously without altering the sharpness of the image.

zoomorphism (,zəʊə'mɔːfɪzəm) *n* **1** the conception or representation of deities in the form of animals. **2** the use of animal forms or symbols in art, etc.
▸**,zoo'morphic** *adj*

-zoon *n combining form.* indicating an individual animal or an independently moving entity derived from an animal: *spermatozoon.* [from Gk *zōion* animal]

zoophilism (zəʊ'ɒfɪ,lɪzəm) *n* the tendency to be emotionally attached to animals.
▸**zoophile** ('zəʊə,faɪl) *n*

zoophobia (,zəʊə'fəʊbɪə) *n* an unusual or morbid dread of animals.
▸**zoophobous** (zəʊ'ɒfəbəs) *adj*

zoophyte ('zəʊə,faɪt) *n* any animal resembling a plant, such as a sea anemone.
▸**zoophytic** (,zəʊə'fɪtɪk) *or* **,zoo'phytical** *adj*

zooplankton (,zəʊə'plæŋktən) *n* the animal constituent of plankton, which consists mainly of small crustaceans and fish larvae.

zoospore ('zəʊə,spɔː) *n* an asexual spore of some algae and fungi that moves by means of flagella.
▸**,zoo'sporic** *or* **zoosporous** (zəʊ'ɒspərəs, ,zəʊə'spɔːrəs) *adj*

THESAURUS

ber, dash, flash, fly, hurry, rush, shoot, tear, whizz (*inf.*), zoom
Antonyms *n* ≠ **energy:** apathy, indifference, inertia, laziness, lethargy, listlessness, sloth, sluggishness

zone *n* **1, 2 = area,** belt, district, region, section, sector, sphere

zoom *vb* **3 = speed,** barrel (along), burn rubber (*inf.*), buzz, dash, dive, flash, fly, hare (*Brit. inf.*), hum (*sl.*), hurtle, pelt, rip (*inf.*), rush, shoot, streak, tear, whirl, whizz (*inf.*), zip (*inf.*)

zoosterol (zəʊ'ɒstə,rɒl) *n* any of a group of animal sterols, such as cholesterol.

zootechnics (,zəʊə'tɛknɪks) *n* (*functioning as sing*) the science concerned with the domestication and breeding of animals.

zootomy (zəʊ'ɒtəmɪ) *n* the branch of zoology concerned with the dissection and anatomy of animals.
▸**zootomic** (,zəʊə'tɒmɪk) *or* ,**zoo'tomical** *adj* ▸,**zoo'tomically** *adv* ▸**zo'otomist** *n*

zootoxin (,zəʊə'tɒksɪn) *n* a toxin, such as snake venom, that is produced by an animal.

zoot suit (zu:t) *n Sl.* a man's suit consisting of baggy tapered trousers and a long jacket with wide padded shoulders, popular esp. in the 1940s. [C20: from ?]

zoril *or* **zorille** (zə'rɪl) *n* a skunklike African mammal, having a long black-and-white coat. [C18: from F, from Sp. *zorrillo* a little fox, from *zorro* fox]

Zoroastrian (,zɒrəʊ'æstrɪən) *adj* **1** of or relating to Zoroastrianism. ◆ *n* **2** an adherent of Zoroastrianism.

Zoroastrianism (,zɒrəʊ'æstrɪən,ɪzəm) *or* **Zoroastrism** *n* the dualistic religion founded by the Persian prophet Zoroaster in the late 7th or early 6th century B.C. and set forth in the sacred writings of the Zend-Avesta. It is based on the concept of a continuous struggle between Ormazd (or Ahura Mazda), the god of creation, light, and goodness, and his archenemy, Ahriman, the spirit of evil and darkness.

zoster ('zɒstə) *n Pathol.* short for **herpes zoster.** [C18: from L: shingles, from Gk *zōster* girdle]

Zouave (zu:'ɑ:v, zwɑ:v) *n* **1** (formerly) a member of a body of French infantry composed of Algerian recruits noted for their dash, hardiness, and colourful uniforms. **2** a member of any body of soldiers wearing a similar uniform, esp. a volunteer in such a unit of the Union Army in the American Civil War. [C19: from F, from *Zwāwa*, tribal name in Algeria]

zouk (zu:k) *n* a style of dance music that combines African and Latin American rhythms and uses electronic instruments and modern studio technology. [C20: from West Indian Creole *zouk* to have a good time]

zounds (zaʊndz) *or* **swounds** (zwaʊndz, zaʊndz) *interj Arch.* a mild oath indicating surprise, indignation, etc. [C16: euphemistic shortening of *God's wounds*]

Zr *the chemical symbol for* zirconium.

zucchetto (tsu:'kɛtəʊ, su:-, zu:-) *n, pl* **zucchettos.** *RC Church.* a small round skullcap worn by certain ecclesiastics and varying in colour according to the rank of the wearer, the Pope wearing white, cardinals red, bishops violet, and others black. [C19: from It., from *zucca* a gourd, from LL *cucutia*, prob. from L *cucurbita*]

zucchini (tsu:'ki:nɪ, zu:-) *n, pl* **zucchini** *or* **zucchinis.** *Chiefly US, Canad., & Austral.* another name for **courgette.** [It., pl of *zucchino* a little gourd, from *zucca* gourd; see ZUCCHETTO]

zugzwang (*German* 'tsu:ktsvaŋ) *Chess.* ◆ *n* **1** a position in which one player can move only with loss or severe disadvantage. ◆ *vb* **2** (*tr*) to manoeuvre (one's opponent) into a zugzwang. [from G, from *Zug* a pull + *Zwang* force]

Zulu ('zu:lʊ, -lu:) *n* **1** (*pl* **Zulus** *or* **Zulu**) a member of a tall Negroid people of SE Africa, who became dominant during the 19th century due to a warrior-clan system organized by the powerful leader, Shaka. **2** the language of this people. [from Zulu *amaZulu* people of the sky]

Zuñi ('zu:nji:, 'su:-) *n* **1** (*pl* **Zuñis** *or* **Zuñi**) a member of a North American Indian people of W New Mexico. **2** the language of this people.
▸**'Zuñian** *adj, n*

zwieback ('zwi:,bæk; *German* 'tsvi:bak) *n* a small type of rusk, which has been baked first as a loaf, then sliced and toasted. [G: twice-baked]

Zwinglian ('zwɪŋglɪən, 'tsvɪŋ-) *n* **1** an upholder of the religious doctrines or movement of Zwingli (1484–1531), Swiss leader of the Reformation. ◆ *adj* **2** of or relating to Zwingli, his religious movement, or his doctrines.

zwitterion ('tsvɪtər,aɪən) *n Chem.* an ion that carries both a positive and a negative charge. [C20: from G *Zwitter* bisexual + ION]

zygapophysis (,zɪgə'pɒfɪsɪs, ,zaɪgə-) *n, pl* **zygapophyses** (-,si:z). *Anat., zool.* one of several processes on a vertebra that articulates with the corresponding process on an adjacent vertebra. [from Gk ZYG- + *apophusis* a sideshoot]

zygo- *or before a vowel* **zyg-** *combining form.* indicating a pair or a union: *zygodactyl; zygospore.* [from Gk *zugon* yoke]

zygodactyl (,zaɪgəʊ'dæktɪl, ,zɪgə-) *adj also* **zygodactylous. 1** (of the feet of certain birds) having the first and fourth toes directed backwards and the second and third forwards. ◆ *n* **2** a zygodactyl bird.

zygoma (zaɪ'gəʊmə, zɪ-) *n, pl* **zygomata** (-mətə). another name for **zygomatic arch.** [C17: via NL from Gk, from *zugon* yoke]
▸**zygomatic** (,zaɪgəʊ'mætɪk, ,zɪg-) *adj*

zygomatic arch *n* the slender arch of bone that forms a bridge between the cheekbone and the temporal bone on each side of the skull of mammals. Also called: **zygoma.**

zygomatic bone *n* either of two bones, one on each side of the skull, that form part of the side wall of the eye socket and part of the zygomatic arch; cheekbone.

zygomorphic (,zaɪgəʊ'mɔ:fɪk, ,zɪg-) *or* **zygomorphous** *adj* (of a flower) capable of being cut in only one plane so that the two halves are mirror images.

zygomycete (,zaɪgəʊ'maɪsi:t) *n* any of a phylum of fungi that reproduce sexually by means of zygospores. The group includes various moulds.
▸,**zygomy'cetous** *adj*

zygophyte ('zaɪgəʊ,faɪt, 'zɪg-) *n* a plant, such as an alga, that reproduces by means of zygospores.

zygospore ('zaɪgəʊ,spɔ:, 'zɪg-) *n* a thick-walled sexual spore formed from the zygote of some fungi and algae.
▸,**zygo'sporic** *adj*

zygote ('zaɪgəʊt, 'zɪg-) *n* **1** the cell resulting from the union of an ovum and a spermatozoon. **2** the organism that develops from such a cell. [C19: from Gk *zugōtos* yoked, from *zugoun* to yoke]
▸**zygotic** (zaɪ'gɒtɪk, zɪ-) *adj* ▸**zy'gotically** *adv*

zymase ('zaɪmeɪs) *n* a mixture of enzymes that is obtained as an extract from yeast and ferments sugars.

zymo- *or before a vowel* **zym-** *combining form.* indicating fermentation: *zymology.* [from Gk *zumē* leaven]

zymogen ('zaɪməʊ,dʒɛn) *n Biochem.* any of a group of compounds that are inactive precursors of enzymes.

zymology (zaɪ'mɒlədʒɪ) *n* the chemistry of fermentation.
▸**zymologic** (,zaɪməʊ'lɒdʒɪk) *or* ,**zymo'logical** *adj* ▸**zy'mologist** *n*

zymolysis (zaɪ'mɒlɪsɪs) *n* the process of fermentation. Also called: **zymosis.**

zymosis (zaɪ'məʊsɪs) *n, pl* **zymoses** (-si:z). **1** *Med.* **1a** any infectious disease. **1b** the developmental process or spread of such a disease. **2** another name for **zymolysis.**

zymotic (zaɪ'mɒtɪk) *adj* **1** of, relating to, or causing fermentation. **2** relating to or caused by infection; denoting or relating to an infectious disease.
▸**zy'motically** *adv*

zymurgy ('zaɪmɜ:dʒɪ) *n* the branch of chemistry concerned with fermentation processes in brewing, etc.

THE TIMES GUIDE TO ENGLISH STYLE AND USAGE

Introduction

This Style Guide was originally written to provide writers and sub-editors on *The Times* with a quick reference to contentious points of grammar and spelling, to proper names and to specialised usages which can cause confusion. It was meant as a guide and a means of ensuring overall consistency thus creating a coherent house style. In publishing this Guide for a wider audience, it is intended as a helpful reference tool.

However, it should be remembered that some spellings or constructions within this Guide are a matter of choice for *The Times* and that the rejected usages are not necessarily wrong. A full picture of the possible variations and alternatives available in the English language can be found in The Times English Dictionary.

Abbreviations used in the Style Guide:
cap(s) – capital letter(s)
l/c – lower case letter(s)

Aa

a, an use *a* before all words beginning with a vowel or diphthong with the sound of *u* (as in *unit*) – *a eulogy, a European* etc; but use *an* before unaspirated *h* – *an heir, an honest woman, an honour*; also, prefer *an hotel, an historic,* and *an heroic*

abattoir

Abbey National (bank, not building society); others with similarly changed status include the Halifax, the Woolwich, the Alliance & Leicester etc. See **building societies**

abbreviated negatives (can't, don't, shan't etc, plus similar abbreviations such as I'll, you're) should be discouraged in all text except in direct quotes, though they are permissible when the full form would sound pedantic

abbreviations prefer not to abbreviate Professor to Prof, Father to Fr etc; see **military ranks**

Abdication cap with specific reference to Edward VIII's; in general sense, use l/c. See **Royal Family**

Aboriginal (native Australian) singular noun and adjective; for plural use *Aborigines*; note l/c *aboriginal* for wider adjectival use

Acas the Advisory, Conciliation and Arbitration Service

accents give French, Spanish, Portuguese, German, Italian and Ancient Greek words their proper accents and diacritical marks; omit in other languages unless you are sure of them. Accents are not necessary in headlines. There is no need for accents in foreign words that have become Anglicised (*hotel, depot, debacle, elite, regime* etc), but keep the accent when it makes a crucial difference to pronunciation – *café, communiqué, fête, fiancée, mêlée, émigré, protégé*; also note *vis-à-vis, façade*. See **foreign words**

Achilles' heel

acknowledgement

acoustic(s) (not accoustic)

Act and **Bill** cap whether fully identified or not

actor, actress see **feminine designations**

Actuary the *Government Actuary* takes caps

AD, BC note that AD comes before the date, eg, *AD35*; BC comes after, eg, *350BC*. With century, both are used after, eg, *3rd century BC/AD*

adapter (person who adapts); *adaptor* (plug, device)

Addenbrooke's Hospital, Cambridge

addresses no commas in *1 Virginia Street* etc; and do not abbreviate *Street*. See **postal addresses**

adidas note l/c

adjectives avoid clichéd adjectives as in *long-felt* want, *serious* danger, *widespread* concern, *substantial* majority etc

Adjutant-General takes the hyphen

Administration (US)

Admiral do not abbreviate to *Adm Jones* etc except in lists; on subsequent mentions, use *the admiral*. See **Armed Forces** special section (page 1459)

admissible, inadmissible (not -able)

ad nauseam (not ad nauseum)

adrenalin prefer to adrenaline

adverbs when they are used to qualify adjectives, the joining hyphen is rarely needed, eg, heavily pregnant, classically carved, colourfully decorated. But in some cases, such as well-founded, ill-educated, a hyphen makes the sense clearer. The best guidance is to use the hyphen in these phrases as little as possible or when the phrase would otherwise be ambiguous

adviser (never advisor)

affect, effect as a verb, *to affect* means to produce an effect on, to touch the feelings of, or to pretend to have or feel (as in affectation); *to effect* is to bring about, to accomplish

Afghan (noun or adjective); an *afghani* (l/c) is a unit of currency, not a person

Afrikaans (language) note *Afrikaners* (the people)

after almost invariably to be used rather than *following*. Also, beware of careless use in sentences such as "The British player won a place in the final after beating the seeded German". Instead use "... by beating the seeded German". See **as, following**

afterlife one word

ageing note the middle *e* – as in *axeing, likeable, mileage, moveable, rateable, sizeable, unlikeable, unshakeable* etc. Common exceptions are listed separately, eg, see **unmistakable**

ages normal style is *Joe Brown, 33, a porter*; keep children's ages in this format as figure for the sake of consistency, eg, "Emma Watson, 7, who..."; but "the seven-year-old child said ..." (up to and including ten); occasional variations such as "Andrew Hunt, who is 74, said..." are also permissible. Note caps in *Ice Age, Stone Age,* the *Dark Ages* etc

aggravate means to make (an evil or complaint) worse. It does not mean to annoy or irritate

AGM caps, but prefer *annual meeting* in text

agoraphobia (not agaro-, agra- etc)

Aids short for acquired immune deficiency syndrome (not auto-immune etc); it is not a disease, but a medical condition. Diseases that affect people who are HIV-positive may be called Aids-related diseases; although prefer not to use the phrase "died of Aids", it is now permissible in standfirsts, headings etc. See **HIV**

AIM the Alternative Investment Market; keep caps in abbreviation

Air Accidents Investigation Branch caps; note *Accidents*

airbase, airstrip, airspace no hyphens; but see **air fares, air show, airstrikes**

air-conditioner, air-conditioning (hyphenate)

aircraft try to avoid *planes* in text, though *planes* would be acceptable in headlines. Even there, *jets* (where applicable – remember that some aircraft are still turbo-prop) or *aircraft* would be better. See **planes**

aircraft names are italicised, as with ships' or locomotive names, eg, the *Enola Gay* (Hiroshima bomber). See **locomotive names, ships**

aircraft types no hyphens between letter and numbers, eg, B52, F111 etc

aircraftman, aircraftwoman (not aircraftsman etc); see **Armed Forces** special section (page 1459)

air fares two words, as *rail fares, bus fares* etc

air force cap in full name such as Royal Air Force (thereafter the RAF), US Air Force (USAF), Brazilian Air Force (thereafter the air force, l/c); and l/c in adjectival use, eg, *an air force raid*. See **Armed Forces** special section (page 1459)

Air Miles take care when to cap: the Air Miles scheme is run by BA and should usually be capped; but use l/c in a general context

airports as a general rule for British airports, use the name of the city or town followed by l/c airport, eg, Manchester airport, Leeds/Bradford airport, East Midlands airport, Luton airport; but see **Heathrow, Gatwick, Stansted**

air raid two words, but see **airstrikes**

air show two words; cap when specific, eg, the Paris Air Show, the Farnborough Air Show

airstrikes one word in military sense, but see **air raid**

akimbo use only with reference to arms (never legs). It means hands on the hips with elbows turned outwards

al- as the prefix to Arabic nouns (including names), prefer *al-* to the *el-* form, except where *el-* has become widely accepted

Albert Hall generally omit Royal

A level, O level hyphenate only when adjectival, eg, A-level results etc. See **examinations**

Alfa Romeo

Al Fayed Mohamed Al Fayed is chairman of Harrods. His youngest brother Ali Fayed is deputy chairman of Harrods. Their brother Saleh Fayed is not a resident of the UK. The brothers should be spelt like this, with no variation. The late elder son was Dodi Fayed

alibi not a general alternative to *excuse*; it means being elsewhere at the material time

Allahu akbar (God is greatest)

allcomers one word

Allende, Isabel, the Chilean novelist (born in Lima, Peru) is the niece and goddaughter of the former Chilean President, Salvador Allende, NOT his daughter

allege avoid the suggestion that the writer is making the allegation, so specify its source. Do not use *alleged* as a synonym of *ostensible, apparent* or *reputed*

All England Club (home of the Wimbledon championships); no hyphen

Allies cap the Allies in the Second World War context; generally, l/c *alliance*, as in the *Atlantic alliance*, *Gulf War alliance* etc

Allitt, Beverly (child-killer convicted in May 1993)

all right (never alright)

All Souls College, Oxford no apostrophe; see **Oxford colleges**

all-time avoid as in *all-time high;* use *highest* instead

alsatian (German shepherd dog); l/c as for other breeds of dogs; but note exceptions such as Yorkshire terrier. See **dogs**

alternative of two things; of three or more, use *choice*

al-Yamamah (oil-for-arms defence project); note l/c and hyphen

Amateur Athletic Association (not Athletics)

Ambassador cap when specific, eg, the French Ambassador, thereafter *the ambassador*

America(n)/US in general, use American as in "American cities, American food" etc; but use US in headlines and in the context of government institutions, such as US Congress, US Navy, US military operation. Never use *America* when ambiguity could occur with Canada or Latin America. See **United States**

American spellings normally use the English spelling even with offices or institutions such as Secretary of Defense (change to *Defence*), American Federation of Labor (change to *Labour*), or with buildings, eg, the Lincoln Center (change to *Centre*); but *Labor Day* (which has no UK equivalent) is an exception; see also **Pearl Harbor**

America's Cup, the (yachting)

amid (not amidst); similarly *among*, not amongst

amok (not amock or amuck)

amphitheatres in classical context these are oval or circular (eg, the Colosseum in Rome); do not confuse with theatres which are semi-circular or horseshoe-shaped

Amsterdam treaty l/c *t*, but note caps for the Treaty of Amsterdam. See **Maastricht**

analog (in computer context); but use *analogue* as in an analogous or parallel thing. See **program**

ancestor strictly means a person from whom another is directly descended, especially someone more distant than a grandparent. Do not use in the looser sense of *predecessor*; eg, Queen Elizabeth I is not the *ancestor* of the present Queen

Ancient Briton/Britain note also Ancient Greek/Greece, Ancient Egyptian/Egypt, Ancient Roman/Rome

Andersen, Hans Christian (not Anderson)

aneurysm (not aneurism)

Anglicise, Anglophile caps, note l/c *anglophone*

Anglo-Irish agreement See **Ireland**

angst roman l/c

animals beware the solecism "birds and animals"; use *birds and mammals* instead

animal names call an animal "he" or "she" if the sex is definitely known or if called by a masculine or feminine name (eg, Felix the cat had only himself to blame). But use "it" if the sex is unspecified. On the racing pages, horses are always "he" or "she"

annexe (noun), but to *annex* (verb)

anoint (not annoint)

answerphone or use *answering machine*

Antarctic, Arctic (never Antartic etc)

antennae plural of *antenna* in zoological sense; use *antennas* in radio or aerial sense

Antichrist (initial cap)

anticipate do not use for *expect*. It means to deal with, or use, in advance of, or before, the due time. To anticipate marriage is different from expecting to marry

antidepressant noun or adjective, no hyphen

anti-Semitic, anti-Semitism

antisocial, anticlimax

Anti-Terrorist Branch, Special Branch note caps; but police squads in most cases l/c, except *Flying Squad* and *Royalty and Diplomatic Protection Squad*

any more always two words

Apennines, Italy (not Appenines)

apostrophes with proper names/nouns ending in *s* that are singular, follow the rule of writing what is voiced, eg, *Keats's poetry*, *Sobers's batting*, *The Times's style* (or *Times style*); and with names where the final *s* is soft, use *s'*, eg, *Rabelais' writings*, *Delors' presidency*; plurals follow normal form, eg, *Lehman Brothers' loss* etc. Note that with Greek names of more than one syllable that end in *s*, do not use the apostrophe *s*, eg, *Aristophanes' plays*, *Achilles' heel*, *Archimedes' principle*. Beware of organisations that have variations as their house style, eg, St Thomas' Hospital, where we must respect their whim.

Also, take care with apostrophes with plural nouns, eg, *women's*, not womens'; *children's*, not childrens'; *people's*, not peoples'

An apostrophe should be used to indicate the plural of single letters, eg, *p's and q's*. Use the apostrophe in expressions such as *two years' time*, *several hours' delay* etc.

apparatchik

appellations almost every person should be granted the courtesy of a title. The exceptions are convicted offenders, the dead (but not the recently dead, except in obituaries) and cases where common usage omits a title. Sportsmen, artists, authors etc should normally be given a title except where it sounds inappropriate.

General rules:

a First mention, Herbert Palfry, Juliette Worth, subsequently Mr Palfry, Mrs/Miss/Ms Worth

b Put the name first, then the age (if relevant), then the description; eg, Jane Fonda, 57, the American actress; avoid the journalese construction "actress Jane Fonda"

c Avoid initials and middle initials (as in American names) unless the person is best-known thereby (eg, W.G. Grace)

d Ms is nowadays fully acceptable when a woman wants to be called thus, or when it is not known for certain if she is Mrs or Miss

e Dr is no longer confined to medical doctors; if a person has a doctorate from a reputable university, Dr is acceptable

f Court proceedings: accused people should be accorded the appropriate title (Mr, Miss etc) after name and first name have been given at first mention; only convicted persons should be referred to by surname alone.

See also **foreign names**, **titles**, **Armed Forces** special section (page 1459), **Courts** special section (page 1463)

appendix plural *appendices*, but note *appendixes* in anatomy

appraise means *evaluate*; do not confuse with *apprise* meaning *inform*

April Fool's Day, April fool, but *All Fools' Day*

Aqaba, Gulf of (Red Sea)

aqueduct (not aquaduct)

Arab use with care

Arabic names use with care; but remember the basic rule of *al-X* (l/c *al* with hyphen, before name; rarely use the *el-* form); see **al-**

Arafat, Yassir (not Yasser)

arbitrate, arbitration do not confuse with *mediate, mediation.* An *arbitrator* hears evidence from different parties then hands down a decision; a *mediator* listens to the different arguments then tries to bring the parties to agreement

archaeologist, archaeology

archbishops

a *Anglican archbishops and diocesan bishops*: at first mention, the Archbishop of Barchester, the Most Rev John Smith; or the Bishop of Barchester, the Right Rev John Smith, but if a doctor, the Bishop of Barchester, Dr John Smith; subsequent references, *the archbishop* (*the bishop*), or Dr Smith (if so entitled) – never Mr Smith

b The Archbishop of Canterbury is Primate of All England, the Archbishop of York is Primate of England

c Anglican bishops are *consecrated*, Roman Catholic bishops *ordained*

d *Roman Catholic archbishops and bishops*: at first mention: the Roman Catholic Archbishop of Liverpool, the Most Rev John X; or the Roman Catholic Bishop of Plymouth, the Right Rev Christopher Y; subsequent mentions, Archbishop X (Bishop Y) or *the archbishop* (*the bishop*), or Dr Y (if so entitled). See **Churches** special section (page 1462)

Argentine adjective; note an *Argentinian* is a person from Argentina (never the Argentine)

armada be careful with use of this word: it means a fleet of armed ships, so strictly should not be applied to any collection of boats or ships

Armageddon cap

armchair, deckchair no hyphens

Armed Forces, the caps; see also **Services**

Armistice Day not the same as Remembrance Sunday (unless November 11 falls on a Sunday); see **two minutes' silence, Remembrance Sunday**

Army cap in context of the *British Army* (thereafter *the Army*, capped) and foreign armies, as in the *Belgian Army, Iraqi Army* (but thereafter *the army*, l/c); note always l/c when used adjectivally, eg, *an army helicopter*; see **Armed Forces** special section (page 1459)

Arran, Isle of (Firth of Clyde); note the *Aran Islands* (one *r*) off Co Galway in western Ireland, *Aran Island* (singular) off Co Donegal and an *Aran sweater* etc

artefact do not use *artifact*

artistic movements cap *Art Deco, Classical, Neo-Classical, Cubist, Gothic, Impressionist, Minimalist, Modernist, Post-Modern, Pre-Columbian, Pre-Raphaelite, Romantic, Surrealist* etc in cultural contexts; but in wider general use, l/c, eg, "He had a surrealist sense of humour but a romantic nature"

as beware of sloppy use in sentences such as "They were moved out as the blast tore open the building"; instead use simply "*after* the blast..."

Asean Association of South East Asian Nations: Indonesia, Singapore, Malaysia, Thailand, the Philippines, Brunei, Vietnam, Burma and Laos. Note that Cambodia is due to join at some unspecified date. See **South-East Asia, Far East**

ASH Action on Smoking and Health; use caps for abbreviation of the anti-smoking pressure group

Asia-Pacific Economic Co-operation forum use Apec as abbreviation

assassin, assassination only to be used in the murder of a statesman or politician from a political motive; not to be used for the killing of general celebrities or others. See **execution, killer**

Assisted Places Scheme caps, but *assisted places* (in schools)

assizes like quarter sessions, no longer function, having been replaced by Crown Courts. See **quarter sessions**

Association of First Division Civil Servants use *First Division Association* for short

assure you *assure* your life; *ensure* means to make certain; you *insure* against risk

asylum-seekers hyphenate

at the present time, at this time use *now;* but avoid the phrase *as of now*

Athenaeum, the see **London clubs**

Atlantic (Ocean), North Atlantic, South Atlantic see **transatlantic**

Atomic Energy Authority, UK (not Agency); abbreviated to AEA; but note *International Atomic Energy Agency*, abbreviated to IAEA

Attorney-General, Solicitor-General (law officers, not legal officers); hyphenate both; see **Courts** special section (page 1463)

Auditor-General hyphenate

Auntie (not aunty) as colloquialism for the BBC. See **BBC**

Autocue proprietary term, so cap

Autumn Statement (caps); see **Budget**

Awol (not AWOL) absent without leave

AXA League (Sunday cricket league); note also the *Benson and Hedges Cup*. See **Sports** special section (page 1466)

axeing note middle *e*; but try to avoid in sense of *cutting jobs, dismissal* etc

ay (yes), *aye* (ever), *Ayes* (debate)

Ayckbourn, Alan

Bb

BAA (airports operator); no longer British Airports Authority

Baath party (not Ba'ath)

baby-walker

baccalaureate use Anglicised spelling with l/c for general use, but cap in specific context of the *International Baccalaureate;* and note the specifically French examination or degree, the *Baccalauréat* (italic, cap, accent, no final "e")

Bacharach, Burt

B&B (abbreviation for bed and breakfast); use caps and close up around ampersand

back benches (parliamentary); two words, but note *backbenchers, backbench* (adjective, as in *backbench revolt*). See **Politics** special section (page 1465)

back burner (no hyphen), but be sparing of the cliché "on the back burner"

backlash overworked word; always try to avoid

backstreet(s) noun or adjective, no hyphen; similarly, *backyard*

"back to basics" use in quotes, no hyphen

bacteria note the term is not interchangeable with viruses. Note that antibiotics are used to treat bacterial but not viral infections. See **medical terms, meningitis**

bail out (as in to *bail someone out of trouble*); note also *to bail water from a boat,* but *to* **bale out** *of an aircraft* (to escape); and *bailout*

balk (not baulk)

ball plural in Court Page headlines is *dances*

ballets use italics for titles; see **Arts** special section (page 1461)

ballgown one word

balloted like *benefited, budgeted* etc, has only one *t*

Balpa British Air Line Pilots' Association

banister (not bannister)

Bank Holiday also *Bank Holiday Monday* etc

bankruptcy in Britain people *file a petition for bankruptcy;* they do not *file for bankruptcy*

Bar, the (legal); also cap for the *Bar of the House of Commons.* See **Courts** special section (page 1463) and **Politics** special section (page 1465)

barbecue, barbecuing

Barnardo's (no longer Dr Barnardo's Homes)

Bar school l/c *s*, as this is not its official title, and no longer Bar law school. Its full name is the *Inns of Court School of Law*

Bart's abbreviation of St Bartholomew's Hospital, London

basically greatly overworked word which rarely adds anything to a sentence. Always try to avoid

basis *on a ... basis* is a cliché and should be avoided; for *employment on a part-time basis* use *part-time employment*

Basle, Switzerland (not Basel); see **Berne**

battalion (not batallion). Write *1st Battalion, 7th Battalion* etc (not First, Seventh). See **Armed Forces** special section (page 1459)

Battersea Dogs' Home (formal title is *The Dogs' Home, Battersea,* but not usually necessary to spell it out)

battle avoid using as a transitive verb as in "The students battled the police..."; use *fought* or *battled against* instead

BBC no need to spell out as British Broadcasting Corporation, though *the corporation* is a useful alternative in text. Note BBC Television, BBC1, BBC2, and BBC Radio (caps). Note also *Chairman of the (Board of) Governors* takes caps (although chairman in most other cases is l/c). This is because we cap the *Director-General* and when both appear in the same story it is anomalous to cap the one and not the other. Cap *the BBC Board of Governors,* but l/c *the governors* at other mentions. See **radio, television**

BBC Charter cap when in full, l/c for *charter* on subsequent mentions

BC see **AD**

Beatles, the no need to cap *the* unless at the start of a sentence; similarly *the Rolling Stones* and *the Manic Street Preachers* etc, but prefer to keep cap *T* with *The Who* and *The The*

Becket note *à* with St Thomas à Becket

Beduin plural; the singular is *Bedu*

Beethoven, Ludwig van (not von); normally Beethoven will suffice; see **Van**

beg the question do not confuse with *ask the question.* To beg a question is to *evade* it

Beijing (no longer Peking); see **Chinese names**

Belarus (no longer Belorussia)

beleaguered rapidly becoming a cliché, especially in a political context, so best avoided

Belfast see **Ireland**

bellringer, bellringing, belltower no hyphens. See **peal**

benchmark (no hyphen)

benefited

benzene (substance obtained from coal-tar); note *benzine,* a spirit obtained from petroleum

-berg, -burg always check spelling of towns with these endings, and those ending in *-burgh, -borough, -brough*

Berkeley Square, West End of London; similarly, Berkeley, California

Bermudian (not Bermudan); but note a *Bermuda-rigged boat*

Berne, Switzerland (not Bern)

berserk (not beserk)

BEST Investment (no longer BESt)

bestseller, bestselling one word

bête noire note italics and final *e*

Betjeman, Sir John (not Betjamin)

Bevan, Aneurin, but **Ernest Bevin**

Beverly Hills

Bhutto, Benazir use Miss rather than Ms or Mrs on subsequent mentions

bi- take care with this difficult prefix. Its correct use is in Latin compounds, where it has the force of two, not half, such as *bicentenary/bicentennial* (a two-hundredth anniversary), or *biennial* (recurring every two years). *Biannual* means twice a year; to avoid confusion, use *twice a year*

biased

Bible cap and roman, not italic, but note l/c *biblical;* for biblical references: II Corinthians ii, 2; Luke iv, 5. Note *Bible Belt.* See **Churches** special section (page 1462)

bid do not use in text as synonym of *effort, attempt* or *try,* though it may be used sparingly in headlines in this context

bight (curve in a coastline or river); do not confuse with *bite* involving teeth. See **bite, German Bight**

Bill and **Act** caps whether fully identified or not

Bill of Rights cap even when non-specific, eg, "If the Government were to introduce a Bill of Rights..."

billion (one thousand million, not a million million). Write £5 billion, £15 billion (£5bn, £15bn in headlines), three billion, 15 billion etc. See **millions, trillion**

biological terms see **scientific names**

Biro trade name, so cap; alternative is *ballpoint pen*

birthday people and animals have *birthdays*; everything else has *anniversaries*. Better to write *33rd birthday, 65th birthday* etc (any number higher than tenth), despite the usual rules on spelling out ordinals. See **numbers**

birthrate, birthright, birthplace no hyphens, but note *birth control, birth certificate* etc

bisexual pronouns *he* and *his* can no longer refer to both sexes equally; *he or she* will sometimes do. Always be sensitive in this contentious area

bishops see **archbishops**

Bishopsgate, City of London (not Bishopgate)

Bishop's Stortford

bite (as with teeth) do not confuse with the computing term *byte* or the geographical *bight*. See **bight, byte, soundbite**

blacklist one word as noun or verb; see **shortlist**

blackout noun, one word

blacks (people), l/c; do not use *non-whites* and be sensitive to local usage, eg, *African-American* is now often used in the United States. See **Coloureds, race**

blackspot (accident, unemployment etc), one word; similarly, *troublespot*

blame take care with this word; blame is attached to causes, not effects. So write "Bad weather is blamed for my bronchitis", not "My bronchitis is blamed on bad weather"

bloc use in context such as the *former Soviet bloc*, a *power bloc* etc; but note *block vote*

blond (men), *blonde* (women)

bloodied as in *bloodied but unbowed*; but *red-blooded* etc

blood sports similarly field sports; see **foxhunt**

Bloomingdale's (New York store)

Blue cap both for an Oxbridge sportsman or woman and for the award itself. See **Sports** special section (page 1466)

blue-collar workers similarly *white-collar workers*

blueprint avoid this greatly overworked word when all you mean is *plan, scheme* or *proposal*

Boadicea (no longer Boudicca)

boat generally used of a small vessel, including fishing boats up to the size of a trawler; a *ship* is a large seagoing vessel big enough to carry smaller boats. In the Royal Navy, submarines are called boats. All take the pronoun *she* and the possessive *her*. See **ships**

Boat Race (annual Oxford-Cambridge race); use caps

boffin do not use as a synonym of *scientist*, except ironically or in direct quotes

Bogart, Humphrey but note (Sir) Dirk Bogarde

bogey (golf); note also *bogie* (wheels), *bogy* (ghost) and *bogeyman*

Bogotá (capital of Colombia)

Bohemian cap noun, but note l/c adjective *bohemian*

Bolshevik

bombshell avoid metaphorical use, as in cliché *drop a bombshell*

bonanza greatly overworked word that should be avoided wherever possible

Bonhams (auction house); no apostrophe

Boodle's (London club). See **London clubs**

Booth, Cherie Tony Blair's wife should be referred to as Cherie Booth wherever possible; refer to Cherie Blair only in contexts when she is clearly in the role of Prime Minister's wife, eg, at summit meetings or on the campaign trail. In legal contexts, write Cherie Booth, QC, at first mention. Subsequent mentions, Ms Booth

bored with (not *of*)

borscht (Russian or Polish soup)

borstals no longer exist; now known as *young offender institutions*

Bosphorus

Boutros Boutros Ghali (former UN Secretary-General); no hyphens and at subsequent mentions, Dr Boutros Ghali. His successor is the Ghanaian Kofi Annan

Bowes Lyon no hyphen for most of the family, but always important to check in *Who's Who* or *Debrett*

bow-tie

box office as noun, two words; hyphenate when adjectival, eg, *box-office success*

boyfriend, girlfriend

Boy Scouts now known as *Scouts* in the UK. *Cub Scouts* have replaced Wolf Cubs; *Scoutleaders* have replaced Scoutmasters. Also cap *Scouting* in the context of the movement. In the US they are still known as Boy Scouts. See also **Girl Guides**

braille l/c

brainchild try to avoid this cliché

branch note *Special Branch, Anti-Terrorist Branch* in police context

Brands Hatch

breakout, breakdown one word as noun; but note *to break out* etc, and hyphenated *break-up*

breathtaking no hyphen

Brent Spar is a storage buoy, not an oil platform or rig; note that *oil platforms* stand on the seabed; *oilrigs* are small mobile installations for oil exploration

Bretton Woods (as in world trade)

Breughel (artists)

bridges cap as in Severn Bridge, London Bridge, Southwark Bridge, Golden Gate Bridge

Bridgwater, Somerset (note no middle *e*)

Brink's-Mat

Britain/Great Britain = England, Wales and Scotland. *United Kingdom* = Britain and Northern Ireland. *British Isles* = United Kingdom and the Republic of Ireland, Isle of Man and Channel Islands. Take care with these distinctions

Britannia see **Royal Yacht**

British Athletic Federation (not Athletics)

British Home Stores note the abbreviation Bhs

British Standards Institution (not Institute); abbreviation is BSI. It awards companies, goods etc its *Kitemark* (cap)

Britpop (not Brit Pop)

Brittany Bretagne in French

Broadcasting Standards Commission formed from merged Broadcasting Standards Council and Broadcasting Complaints Commission

Broadmoor inmates are *patients*, not prisoners

broadsheet preferable to *quality* for describing the serious British press

Brookings Institution, Washington (not Institute)

Brooks's (London club). See **London clubs**

Brummie (not Brummy); cap people and dialect, eg, *Geordie, Scouse* etc. See **Cockney**

Brylcreem

BSE bovine spongiform encephalopathy, or "mad cow" disease

BSkyB News International, the subsidiary of The News Corporation that owns *The Times*, owns 40 per cent of BSkyB (British Sky Broadcasting Group Ltd). So BSkyB can be called an associate company of News International, or of News Corp. There is a choice of up to 40 channels available in the UK on the Astra satellite; BSkyB owns 11. See **News International, *The Times***

BT usual abbreviated form of British Telecommunications plc, but it is often convenient to use British Telecom at first mention, and BT subsequently

Budget cap the *British Budget*, otherwise l/c. Note l/c *d* for

Budget day and also note *Pre-Budget Report* and *Autumn Statement* (caps)

Buggins's turn (not Buggins')

builder's merchant(s)

building societies cap full name, eg, Skipton Building Society, thereafter *the Skipton*, or *the society* etc. Take care with societies that have become banks. See **Abbey National**

bullion (gold or silver in unminted form)

bull-mastiff, bull-terrier see **dogs**

bullring but the *Bull Ring* in Birmingham

bull's-eye (use hyphen)

bungee (as in jumping)

Bunsen burner

BUPA (no longer Bupa)

Burma (not Myanmar except in direct quotes); the inhabitants are *Burmese*, and note that *Burmans* are a Burmese people

Burnet, (Sir) Alastair

Burns Night (January 25); caps, no apostrophe

burnt (not burned)

Burton upon Trent no hyphens; note l/c for the colloquial *gone for a burton*

bus, buses noun; but in verbal use *busses, bussed, bussing*

Bush, George W. (do not use Jr)

Bushey, Hertfordshire but Bushy Park, near Hampton Court

Bussell, Darcey (ballerina)

buyout, buyback one word; but prefer hyphens for *buy-in, take-off, shake-out, shake-up, sell-off, sell-out* etc

by-election

bylaw

bypass noun or verb

by-product

bystander

byte (computer term for a small collection of bits – binary digits – roughly equivalent to one character); do not confuse with *bite* (as with teeth). But note *soundbite*

Byzantine cap in all contexts

BZW Barclays de Zoete Wedd

Cc

cabbie (not cabby) as colloquialism for taxi driver

Cabinet cap in both British and foreign use, whether used as a noun or adjectivally. The only exception is the informal *kitchen cabinet*. Note *Cabinet Office, Cabinet Secretary* (or *Secretary of the Cabinet*). Cabinet committees should be capped, eg, *the Cabinet Committee on Science and Technology*. See **Politics** special section (page 1465)

Caernarfon (town and parliamentary constituency, no longer Caernarvon); but note Lord Carnarvon

Caesarean section

café note accent

cagoule but note *kaftan*

call-up noun, but note *to call up*

camaraderie (not cameraderie)

Camborne, Cornwall (not Cambourne)

Cambridge University colleges and halls are: Christ's College; Churchill College; Clare College; Clare Hall; Corpus Christi College; Darwin College; Downing College; Emmanuel College; Fitzwilliam College; Girton College; Gonville and Caius College; Homerton College; Hughes Hall; Jesus College; King's College; Lucy Cavendish College; Magdalene College; New Hall; Newnham College; Pembroke College; Peterhouse; Queens' College; Robinson College; St Catharine's College; St Edmund's College; St John's College; Selwyn College; Sidney Sussex College; Trinity College; Trinity Hall; Wolfson College

camellia (not camelia)

Campbell, Alastair (not Alistair); Tony Blair's press secretary

Camra the Campaign for Real Ale; note l/c

cancer heart disease not cancer is "the biggest killer" in the UK

cannon (military), singular and plural; but note *canons* (both churchmen and church laws) and *canon* as a collection or list of an author

Canton now Guangzhou; see **Chinese names**

canvas (material, painting); note *canvass* (votes)

CAP common agricultural policy; l/c when spelt out in text

Cape Town

capitalisation in general, the proper names of people and places, formal titles or titles of important offices, and the names of well-known and substantial institutions, all require capitals. As a rule of thumb, cap specifics (eg, *the French Foreign Minister*), but l/c non-specifics (eg, *EU foreign ministers*). But some terms, eg, *Act, Bill, Cabinet, Civil Service*, always cap. See **initials**

capsize see **-ise, -isation**

captions when space is tight, just the surname is acceptable, even when the person is titled, eg, Sir Marcus Fox would be simply Fox, as in headlines. Where women are photographed, give the woman's first name and surname where possible.
Identify people in a photograph with *left* and *right* etc, using commas, not parentheses (eg, Fred Smith, left, and his wife leaving the court)

car boot sale no hyphen

carcass

cardholder

Carlos the Jackal no quotes, no commas; always mention his full name, Ilich Ramírez Sánchez

carmaker one word

car park two words, note *multistorey car park*

carpetbagger one word

Carrott, Jasper (not Carrot)

cashcard (in general sense); note also *cashflow, cashback*

Cashpoint Lloyds Bank's cash machine system, so cap and do not use generically; in the general sense, use *cash dispenser* or *cash machine*, or less formally, *hole in the wall*

Castro, President (Fidel) use *Señor* or *the President* after first mention, not Dr

Catch-22 avoid the grossly overworked cliché *Catch-22 situation*

cathedrals cap when giving the full name, eg, St Paul's Cathedral, Wells Cathedral; similarly the names of churches, eg, St Mary's Church, Ely, unless the church name specifically excludes it, eg, St Stephen's, Ely

Catherine always check the spelling; note a Catherine wheel (firework); St Catharine's College, Cambridge; St Katharine Docks, London

Catholic in church context, use *Roman Catholic* at first mention, then *Catholic*. See **Churches** special section (page 1462)

Catmark the new financial products version of the Kitemark; similarly *Cat standard* etc

cat's eyes should preferably be called reflecting roadstuds; *Catseye* is a trademark

caviare (not caviar)

CD-Rom compact disc, read only memory; note CD-i (interactive compact disc system)

ceasefire

Ceausescu, Nicolae (not Ceaucescu)

ceilidh Highland social gathering

Cellophane proprietary term, so cap

celsius, centigrade use either term. In news stories, use both centigrade and fahrenheit, eg, "The temperature rose to 16C (61F)"; do not use degree sign

centenarian see also **septuagenarian, octogenarian, nonagenarian**

centenaries use *centenary, bicentenary, tercentenary*; after that, use *four hundredth anniversary*, etc

Center Parcs

Central Europe note cap *C*

Central St Martins College of Art and Design no apostrophe in St Martins; use *St Martins* at subsequent mentions

Centre, the use cap in political context of *the Centre*, as with *Left* and *Right*. Similarly, *Centre Left, Centre Right* as nouns, but note l/c for adjectival use, eg, *a centre-left politician, a right-wing policy*. See **Left, Right, Politics** special section (page 1465)

Centre Court see **Wimbledon**

centrepiece no hyphen

centring but note *centering of arches* in bridge-building

centuries write *the 3rd century BC, the 9th century, the 18th century* etc; and hyphenate when used adjectivally, eg, *20th-century architecture*

CERN the European Organisation for Nuclear Research, based in Geneva; note all caps

Ceylon now Sri Lanka. The people are *Sri Lankan*, the majority group are the *Sinhalese*

cha-cha-cha (not cha-cha)

chainsaw one word

chairman still common usage referring to men and women, except in quotes, but *chairwoman* is acceptable. Avoid *chair* and *chairperson* (except in quotes and phrases such as *addressing remarks to the chair*). In most cases, keep *chairman* l/c, but occasionally cap, as with BBC, Bar Council, and US Federal Reserve Board

chamber (of the House of Commons); use l/c. See **Politics** special section (page 1465)

champagne note l/c; use only for the product of the Champagne region of France; otherwise use *sparkling wine*. The champagne producers protect their name rigorously. See **wines**

changeable

Changing the Guard (not … of the Guard); see **Trooping the Colour**

Channel 4, Channel 5 (not Four, Five); see **television**

Channel Tunnel with cap *T*, but thereafter l/c *tunnel* if the context is clear; note also *Channel Tunnel rail link*. Note that *Le Shuttle* trains are no longer called thus; they are now *Eurotunnel trains*. See **Eurotunnel**

Chanukkah prefer this to variants such as Hanukkah etc, for the Jewish festival of lights

charge that do not use this Americanism as a synonym of *allege that*

charisma find an alternative such as *presence, inspiration* etc for this boring cliché

Charity Commission (not Charities)

Charollais (cattle or sheep)

charters (as in John Major's initiative) see **Citizen's Charter, Parent's Charter, Patient's Charter.** Note also *Charter Mark*

Château-Lafite (not Lafitte); note hyphen

chat show, game show, quiz show, talk show no hyphens; note also *chatline, sexline*

cheap goods are *cheap*, prices are *low*

Chechnya (not Chechenia); note adjective *Chechen*

check-in noun, but note *checklist, checkout counter*

cheerleader one word

Chekhov, Anton

chequebook one word, either as noun or adjective, eg, *chequebook journalism*

chess names note Garry Kasparov, Anatoly Karpov, Judit Polgar. Note also Fide, not FIDE, and l/c *grandmaster*. See **Russian names**

Chester-le-Street

chickenpox no hyphen; similarly *smallpox*

Chief Constable caps when referring to a specific, as in *Chief Constable of Lancashire*; thereafter, *the chief constable*. See **police ranks**

Chief Inspector of Prisons/… of Schools note also *Chief Medical Officer*

Chief Whip caps; see **whips**

childcare similarly *healthcare*

ChildLine (charity); note cap *L*

Children Act 1989 (not Children's); note also cap *T* for *The Children's Society*

chimpanzees are apes, not monkeys

Chinese names the Pinyin rather than the traditional Wade-Giles system is now used, so write Beijing, Mao Zedong (though Chairman Mao or just Mao are acceptable), Zhou Enlai etc. For Chinese place names, follow spellings in *The Times Atlas of the World*: eg, Guangzhou (formerly Canton), Sichuan (formerly Szechuan). See **Peking**

chopper, copter never use as substitutes for *helicopter*, even in headlines

Christ Church, Oxford (never Christ Church College). See **Peterhouse, Oxford University**

Christchurch, Dorset and New Zealand

christened people are *christened*, ships and trains etc are *named*

Christian, Christianity note also *unchristian, non-Christian, antichristian, Antichrist*

Christian Democrat noun and adjective, as in *Christian Democrat MP*

Christian names in context of non-Christians use *forename* or *first name*

Christian terms cap the Bible, the Commandments, the Cross, the Crucifixion, the Resurrection, the Gospels, Mass, Holy Communion (and simply Communion), Eucharist, Blessed Sacrament, Advent, Nativity (but note l/c when used adjectivally, eg, *a nativity play*); also use *He* and *His* when referring to God and Jesus Christ. Use l/c for *evensong, matins*. See **Churches** special section (page 1462)

Christie's note apostrophe also for Christie's, New York, and Christie's International

Christmas Day, Christmas Eve

Church cap in context of the institution (Anglican, Roman Catholic, Orthodox etc), but not when used adjectivally. See **archbishops, Churches** special section (page 1462)

churchwarden one word

cider (not cyder)

CIMA the Chartered Institute of Management Accountants; note caps for the abbreviation

Cincinnati, Ohio

cinemagoer similarly *concertgoer, theatregoer* etc

CinemaScope trade name, so cap; note also cap *S* in middle

cipher (not cypher)

cissy, cissies (not sissy)

Cites (not CITES); the Convention on International Trade in Endangered Species

Citizens Advice Bureau/Bureaux no apostrophe, and note final *x* as plural

Citizen's Charter

Citroën

City and Guilds of London Institute abbreviate to *City & Guilds*, with ampersand

City of London note also *the City, City prices*. See **London**

Civil List caps

Civil Service but note *civil servants***.** Always cap *Civil Service*, even in adjectival use, eg, *a Civil Service memorandum*. Caps to be restored to the administrative grade, ie, *Permanent Secretary, Deputy Secretary* and *Assistant Secretary*. For executive grade (ie, below Assistant Secretary), use l/c. Note also *Secretary of the Cabinet and Head of the Home Civil Service*. See **Politics** special section (page 1465)

claim do not use when simply *said* or *declared* would do. The word carries a suspicion of incredulity. Also, avoid the loose construction in sentences such as "The firm launched a drink which is claimed to promote learning ability". This should read "… a drink which, it is claimed, promotes learning ability"

clamour, clamouring but note *clamorous*

clampdown not banned, but use as little as possible

Claridge's

Clause Four (as in Labour Party policy); but Clause 4 permissible in headlines

clichés some of the most common, to be resisted strongly in almost every context, are: *backlash, basically, beleaguered, blueprint, bombshell, bonanza, brainchild, chaos, charisma, clampdown, consensus, crackdown, crisis, crunch, drama/dramatic, escalate, facelift, gunned down, hopefully, ironically, legendary, major, massive, mega-, nightmare, prestigious, quantum leap, reportedly, shambles, shock, shoot-out, situation, trauma/traumatic, unique*

Clinton use simply President Clinton (not President Bill Clinton), thereafter the President or Mr Clinton. The First Lady is Hillary Rodham Clinton (usually write Hillary Clinton or Mrs Clinton)

closed-circuit television

clothing use *menswear, women's wear, children's wear, sportswear*. See **wear**

cloud-cuckoo-land note two hyphens

clubs see **London clubs**

co- the prefix does not normally require a hyphen even before an *e* or another *o* unless confusion might result. Thus *co-operate* (but *uncooperative*), *co-opt, co-ordinate* (but *uncoordinated*), *coeducation, coexist.* See **co-production**

coalface, coalfield, coalmine one word; prefer *miner* to *coalminer.* Note also *gasfield, oilfield*

coastguard l/c and one word, in the British context; but note the new *Coastguard Agency* (caps), though the *coastguard service* (generic) retains the l/c. Note also the *US Coast Guard*

coasts cap *South Coast, East Coast* and *West Coast* in British context (as in *West Coast main line*); note also *East Coast* and *West Coast* in US

coats of arms see **heraldry**

Coca-Cola note hyphen; similarly *Pepsi-Cola*

Cockney cap for the person and the dialect, but l/c for general adjectival use, eg, *a cockney welcome*

coeducation(al) but *co-ed* is acceptable in headlines

coexist

Coldstream Guards may be called *the Coldstream* and the men *Coldstreamers* or *Coldstream Guards*; neither should be called *Coldstreams.* See **Armed Forces** special section (page 1459)

Cold War

collarbone one word

collectibles (not -ables)

collective nouns usually use the singular verb, as with corporate bodies (the company, the Government, the council etc). But this rule is not inviolable; the key is to stick to the singular or plural throughout the story – sentences such as "The committee, which was elected recently, presented their report" are unacceptable

Colombia (country); Columbia is the Hollywood studio, university, river and Washington district. Note also British Columbia and Pre-Columbian

Colosseum, Rome but the Coliseum, London

Coloureds (South Africa); use cap

comedienne avoid wherever possible; use *comedian* for both sexes. See **feminine designations**

comeuppance no hyphen

Commander-in-Chief, Officer Commanding use caps

Commandments cap in biblical context, as *the Ten Commandments, the Fourth Commandment.* See **Christian terms**

commando note plural *commandos* (not -oes)

Commission, Commissioner see **European Commission**

Commissioner of the Metropolitan Police similarly, cap *City of London Police, British Transport Police* and all police forces when the full title is given. For full list, see **police forces**

committee note cap in *1922 Committee of Tory backbenchers.* Committees of inquiry etc should be capped only when the full title is given, eg, *the Neill Committee on Standards in Public Life,* but *the Neill committee.* Cabinet committees should be capped. See **Cabinet**, **select committees**, **royal commissions**, **Conservative**, **Tory**, and **Politics** special section (page 1465)

common agricultural policy l/c; see **CAP**

Common Market usually use EU or EC (see **European Union**); but Common Market is acceptable in historical context

common sense noun; but note adjective *commonsense, commonsensical*

Common Serjeant see **Courts** special section (page 1463)

Commonwealth Heads of Government Meeting use caps

communiqué

communism, communist as with *socialism* and *socialist,* the best rule is to cap only when in specific party context, eg, *a Communist candidate, a Communist rally, the Communist Mayor of Lille;* but *communist ideology, communist countries* etc. It will help to think of a parallel with Conservative/conservatism or Liberal/liberalism. But *Marxist, Stalinist, Nazi* and *Fascist* should be capped

companies abbreviate to *Co* in, eg, John Brown & Co. Company is singular. Do not confuse *company* and *firm,* even in headlines. A *firm* implies a business partnership, as in the legal or accountancy professions, estate agents etc. Full points in company titles usually unnecessary, as in WH Smith and J Sainsbury. Do not abbreviate Ford of Europe to Fords, Swan Hunter to Swans etc. See **Ltd**, **plc**

comparatively, relatively avoid using as synonyms of *fairly, middling*

compare with/to use *compare with* (the most common) when differences or contrasts are the point, eg, *compare the saints with the devils* or *compared with last year's figures;* use *compare to* for likenesses, eg, *compare this image to a damsel fair*

compass points in the UK, regional phrases, if well established and in common use, take caps as in the North, the South, the West, the South East, the North East, the South West, the West Country, the West Midlands, the East Midlands, East Anglia, North Wales, South Wales, West Wales, the East/West End of London. But when used adjectivally, use *southeast* England (though note the South East of England).

Overseas, cap the following: the Midwest (US), Central America, West Africa, North Africa, East Africa, Central Africa, South Africa but southern Africa, North and South Atlantic and Pacific, the Middle/Far East, but sub-Saharan Africa and south India etc

complement (completing something); but *compliment* (praise or tribute). Note also *complimentary,* as in free gifts etc

comprise means *to consist of, be composed of;* see **include**

Comptroller General

concertgoer similarly *partygoer, theatregoer,* but *concert hall*

confectionery (not -ary)

conference keep l/c in *Labour Party conference; Lib Dem conference* etc

Congo take care to distinguish between the Democratic Republic of Congo (formerly Zaire) and Congo-Brazzaville (formerly French Congo). See **Zaire**

Congress (US); note l/c *congressional* and *congressman* except when with a name, eg, Congressman John Waldorfburger; but generally try to avoid this construction and use John W, a congressman from Minnesota, etc. See **Senate**

Congress Party (India); now takes cap *P* and is no longer known as Congress (I)

connection

Connolly, Billy (comedian)

consensus (never concensus); avoid this cliché wherever possible

Conservative Party note *Conservative Central Office,* but *Conservative chairman, manifesto* etc; *Tory* is permissible as a less formal alternative, but note *Tory party* (l/c *p*). Abbreviate in lists etc to C (not Con). See **Tory**, **Politics** special section (page 1465)

considerable avoid its use as a lazy adjective implying emphasis

Consolidated Fund, the

consortium plural *consortiums* (not consortia); as a general rule, use the *-ums* plural. Similarly *memorandums*

constitution (of a country); cap only when an actual document, eg, *the American Constitution,* but *the British constitution*

consult (never *consult with*)

Consumers' Association

Contact Group UN group on former Yugoslavia: US, Russia, Britain, France, Germany and Italy

Continent, the refers to mainland Europe; note l/c *continental*

continuous means *without intermission; continual* means *frequently recurring*

contract out no hyphen

Contract with America (the Republicans' 1995 programme); note italics

Contras, the cap in Nicaragua context

Controller of Radio 1 etc note cap *C*. See **BBC**

controversial avoid where possible

convener (not convenor)

convertible (not -able); noun and adjective

conveyor belt; a *conveyer* is a person who conveys

Cooke, Alistair (not Alastair)

cooling towers these should not be used to illustrate air pollution stories, as they emit harmless water vapour

Co-op, the acceptable abbreviation of *Co-operative Society*

co-operate, co-ordinate etc but note *uncooperative, uncoordinated, non-cooperation*

co-production, co-producer etc use hyphen to avoid ambiguity with *copro-*, as in dung

copycat (no hyphen)

copyright (sole right in artistic work etc); note *copywriter* (advertising)

cornflake (generic), but note *Kellogg's Corn Flakes*

Coronation cap *Coronation Oath* and when referring to a specific event, such as Elizabeth II's Coronation in 1953; but l/c in most adjectival uses, eg, *coronation ceremony, coronation broadcast*

coroner's court at inquests, the *coroner* is l/c unless specific, as in the Westminster Coroner. Juries *return* the verdict, the coroner *records* it. There are no coroner's inquests in Scotland; violent deaths are reported to the *Procurator Fiscal*, who may hold an inquiry. See **Courts** special section (page 1463)

correspondents wherever possible, write the political correspondent of *The Times*, the Moscow correspondent of *The Times* etc; but the *Times* political correspondent, the *Times* Moscow correspondent etc, is permissible. See ***The Times***

coruscating (not corruscating)

Côte d'Azur note no final *e*

councils cap in full title, eg, Birmingham City Council, otherwise l/c

council tax replacement for *poll tax/community charge*, so use the latter only in historical context

counter-productive, counter-attack etc, but *countertenor* (one word)

counties spell out names except in lists. Do not add *-shire* to Devon (except in Devonshire cream or the Duke of Devonshire), Dorset, Somerset. Irish counties should be as Co Donegal (cap *C*, no full point); Co Durham takes the same style. Take great care with new, reorganised or abolished counties. See **Durham, unitary authorities**

Courchevel (Alpine ski resort; not Courcheval)

court martial note plural *courts martial*; also *Courts-Martial Appeal Court*; and verb *to court-martial*

Court of Appeal always use the full title at first mention and wherever possible thereafter, though l/c *appeal court* may be used sparingly. See **Courts** special section (page 1463)

Court of Arches (court of appeal of the Province of Canterbury in the Church of England); do not use *Arches Court*

Court of St James's

Court of Session, Edinburgh (not Sessions)

Court Service, the (not Courts); note caps

courts cap all courts when specific, eg, Birmingham Crown Court, Clerkenwell County Court, Dawlish Magistrates' Court, Ashford Youth Court etc; in a general, unspecific context, always cap the *Crown Court* (it sits in about 90 centres), but l/c *county court, magistrates' court* and *youth court* etc. See **coroner's court, Inns of Court, Courts** special section (page 1463)

Coutts Bank

Coward, Noël note the diaeresis

crackdown not banned, but use as little as possible

Cracow (not Krakow or variations); see **foreign places**

crèche (not crêche)

creditworthy, creditworthiness no hyphen

Creole person born in the West Indies or Latin America whose ancestry is wholly or partly European. It does not imply mixed race

crescendo means getting louder, growing in force. Nothing *rises to a crescendo*. Plural is *crescendos*

Creutzfeldt-Jakob disease abbreviation CJD

crisis always try to find an alternative for this greatly overworked word

criterion plural *criteria*

Croat (people and language); *Croatian* is the adjective; see **Slovak**

Cross, the note cap; see **Christian terms**

cross benches but note *crossbenchers*, and adjective *crossbench*

cross-Channel but note *transatlantic*

Crown (in constitutional sense); cap, as in *Crown property, the Crown representative*. See **Royal Family**

Crown Estate Commissioners (not Estates)

Crown Jewels note caps

Crown Prosecution Service abbreviate to CPS

Crufts Show or just Crufts; note no apostrophe

cruise missiles but *Pershing missiles* and the *Stealth bomber*

crunch avoid clichés such as *reaches crunch point, the situation came to a crunch*

CSCE no longer exists; see **OSCE**

Cup cap *Final* only in *FA Cup Final* (or *Cup Final* for short), but l/c all others, such as *European Cup final, World Cup final, Davis Cup final* etc. See **Sports** special section (page 1466)

cupfuls, spoonfuls etc (not cupsful or cupfulls)

currencies always convert to sterling on news, sport and features pages – usually at first mention of the foreign currency. But on Business pages, US dollars, French francs and German marks need not be converted, unless to help the flow of the story. See **deutschemark, dollar, franc** and **peseta**

current avoid wherever possible as synonym of *present*

curriculums plural *s* (not curricula); note *extracurricular activities*; abbreviate *curriculum vitae* to *CV*, note plural *curricula vitae*. See **national curriculum**

curtsy (not curtsey); note plural *curtsies*

Custom House (the headquarters building)

Customs and Excise cap for the organisation (or simply *Customs*), l/c for *customs officer, customs post, customs regulations* etc

cutthroat no hyphen

Cyprus, northern keep l/c in *northern*, as the "state" is recognised only by the Turkish Government; also l/c *government* in northern Cyprus, as with provincial or state governments in Australia or Canada etc

czar although usual style (in Russian context) is *tsar, czar* is permissible in the phrase *drugs czar*

Czech Republic use Czechoslovakia only in the historical sense. The two countries since their division are the Czech Republic and Slovakia

Dd

dad, mum cap when referring to specific parents, l/c in general context

Dail Eireann (lower house of the Irish parliament); usually just *the Dail*

Dagestan (not Daghestan)

Dales, the Yorkshire or Derbyshire or simply *the Dales*

dancefloor

Dar es Salaam, Tanzania (no hyphens). Note, capital is Dodoma

Dark Ages caps, but take care: the period after the fall of the Roman Empire is no longer considered wholly obscure and barbaric

data strictly plural, but can be singular through common usage

databank, database

dates Note *Monday, April 18, 1994* (never 18th April); but *April 1994*. When citing periods of years, write *1992–93* (not 1992–3) and for the millennium, *1999–2000,* then *2003–09* etc; *from 1939 to 1941* (not from 1939–41); *the Forties, Eighties, Nineties (or 1940s, 1980s, 1990s*). But note l/c for people's ages, eg, *she was in her forties, eighties, nineties* etc. Common usage says that the past decade ended on December 31, 1989, and that the century ends on December 31, 1999. See **millennium**

Day-Glo proprietary term, so cap

daytime but note *night-time*

daytrip but note *day-tripper*

D-Day, VE-Day, VJ-Day

deathbed no hyphen

death row (as in American prisons); l/c

debacle accents unnecessary

debatable

Debrett or full title, *Debrett's Peerage*

debut no accent

decades use either *the Sixties* or *the 1960s*; see **dates**

decimals do not mix decimals and fractions in the same story. See **millions, per cent**

decimate means to kill one in ten; custom has extended its use to indicate heavy casualties, but use sparingly

deckchair no hyphens; similarly *armchair*

decor no accent

decorations see **honours**

defuse means to remove the fuse from, or reduce tension in a crisis etc; never confuse with *diffuse*, which means to spread in all directions, scatter etc, or (as adjective) verbose, not concise, spread over a large area etc

Degas no accent

de Gaulle never cap *de* in this name unless at the start of a sentence or headline

de Havilland

de Klerk, F.W. see **full points**

de la Mare, Walter

De La Rue

DeLorean

De Niro, Robert

de Sancha, Antonia

de Valera, Eamon

degrees (educational) *a first, a second, an upper second* (*a 2:1*), *a lower second* (*a 2:2*), *a third* etc. D Lit, D Litt, LitD etc are abbreviations for doctorates of literature (or letters); Oxford and York have D Phil instead of the more usual PhD. Oxford has DM for the more usual MD. Cambridge has ScD for doctor of science. No full points in degrees

degrees (weather) omit degree sign in temperatures. See **celsius**

déjà vu use accents but not italic

demise strictly means the death of a person, or the failure of an enterprise or institution. Keep to these definitions. It is wrong to refer to the demise of Glenn Hoddle or Peter Mandelson

Democratic Party (US; not Democrat Party); the adjective is usually *Democrat* in other uses, such as *the Democrat spokesman* (but note *the Democratic convention*)

demonstrator but note *protester*

Deng, Wendi Rupert Murdoch's wife; see **Murdoch**

Denktas, Rauf (not Denktash), the president of northern Cyprus (l/c *p* because not an internationally recognised state); better to describe him as the *Turkish Cypriot leader.* See **Cyprus**

deny does not mean the same as *rebut* (which means argue to the contrary, producing evidence), or *refute* (which means to win such an argument). See **rebut, refute**

Department for Culture, Media and Sport (not of) replaced the Department of National Heritage in July 1997. *Culture Secretary* is an acceptable short form for the Secretary of State

Department for Education and Employment (not of); use *Education and Employment Department* or *the department* at subsequent mentions. Avoid the ugly abbreviations DfE or DfEE except in direct quotes

Department of the Environment, Transport and the Regions

dependant noun; note *dependent* (adj), and *dependency*

Deputy Prime Minister caps; similarly *Deputy Governor of the Bank of England*. Note these are the exceptions to the rule that deputy posts should take l/c, eg, *deputy editor*

desiccate

desktop (computer, publishing), no hyphen; similarly *laptop*

despite acceptable alternative for *in spite of.* But do not use *despite the fact that*; use *although* instead

despoiled (not despoilt)

despoliation, or **despoilment** (not despoilation)

Deutsche Bank German commercial bank not to be confused with *Deutsche Bundesbank*, or *Bundesbank*, the German central bank

deutschemark/deutschmark/D-mark never use these forms. Always use simply *the mark*, or with figures, *DM500.* See **currencies**

Devil, the cap; but note *devils* (l/c), *devilish*

dextrous prefer to dexterous

Dhaka (capital of Bangladesh; not Dacca)

Diaghilev

diagnose take great care: *illnesses* are diagnosed, not patients

Diana, Princess of Wales since her death, use the form *the late Princess* where appropriate. Never use Princess Di or Lady Di. Note also one comma only for *the Diana, Princess of Wales Memorial Fund.* See **Royal Family, Titles** special section (page 1467)

Diaspora cap in Jewish context, but l/c in general sense of a dispersal

Di Canio, Paulo (cap Di every time)

DiCaprio, Leonardo

Dickins & Jones (department store)

Dictaphone trade name, so cap

diehard

different from (never different to or than*); similarly *differ from*

dignitaries

dilapidated (not delapidated)

dilate *dilation* means normal widening, as in pupils of the eye; *dilatation* is widening by force, as in child abuse cases. Take care

Dillons (bookshop)

dining room (no hyphen)

diphtheria note *ph*; similarly *diphthong*

Diplomatic Service caps; similarly *Civil Service*

directives (EU); l/c in general context, caps when specific, eg, *Working Time Directive*

Direct Line, Direct Line Insurance trademarks, so must not be used in generic sense even with l/c, as in direct line companies, direct line telephone insurers etc; in this wider sense, use *direct insurance, direct telephone insurance* etc

Director-General of the BBC, CBI, Institute of Directors, Fair Trading, and the regulatory bodies etc. See **regulators, Secretary-General**

Director of Public Prosecutions abbreviation DPP

Directory Enquiries (despite usual style, *inquiries*)

disc (musical recording, or shape, eg, *disc jockey, compact disc, disc brake*); but use *disk* in general computing context, eg, *disk drive, floppy disk*

discomfit take great care with this verb; it means primarily to thwart, defeat or rout, but by extension can mean thoroughly to embarrass or disconcert (noun *discomfiture*). It has no connection with discomfort, which means to deprive of comfort or make uneasy

discreet means tactful, circumspect (noun *discretion*); *discrete* means individually distinct (noun *discreteness*)

disinterested means impartial, unbiased (noun *disinterest*); never confuse with *uninterested*, which means having a lack of interest

Disney the theme parks are *Disneyland* (California); *Disney World* (Florida); *Disneyland Paris* (Euro Disney should strictly be confined to the name of the European company); and *Tokyo Disneyland* (owned by a Japanese company, but Disney earns royalties from it)

disorientate (not disorient). See **orientate**

dispatch (not despatch); also *dispatch box*

dissociate (not disassociate)

distil but note *distilled, distillation*

divorcé (man); note *divorcée* (woman), use *divorcees* (no accent) in reference to both men and women

DIY spell out *do-it-yourself* at first mention

D-notice, D-notice committee

Docklands note cap *D* for London, elsewhere *docklands*

doctor the title *Dr* should no longer be confined to medical practitioners. If a person has a doctorate from a reputable institution, and wishes to be known as Dr Smith, he or she should be so titled

docusoap, docudrama etc (no hyphens)

dogs l/c with most breeds, such as *alsatian, borzoi, labrador, rottweiler*, though there are obvious exceptions such as West Highland terrier, Yorkshire terrier etc

Dole, Bob (not Robert)

dollar with figures use $5 (when American), A$5 (Australian), C$5 (Canadian), S$5 (Singapore)

doll's house (not dolls')

Dome cap *D* in *Millennium Dome* and when used on its own. See **millennium**

Domesday Book roman, similarly Magna Carta; but note *doomsday* in general or biblical sense

Dominican Republic (neighbour to Haiti); note *Dominica*, one of the Windward Islands. Both are sovereign states. See **Haiti**

donate use *give* or *present* wherever possible

Dorchester, the (not Dorchester Hotel)

do's and don'ts

Dostoevsky

doveish (rather than dovish)

down avoid unnecessary use after verbs, as in close down, shut down. See **up**

Downing Street write *10 Downing Street* (or *11...*), or simply *No 10*; note *Downing Street policy unit*. See **Politics** special section (page 1465)

Downing Street declaration see **Ireland**

downmarket no hyphen; similarly *upmarket*

Down's syndrome (never mongol)

Down Under cap as a colloquialism for Australasia (especially Australia)

D'Oyly Carte

D-Rams note also *CD-Roms*

drachmas (not drachmae)

draconian note l/c

draftsman (legal); but note *draughtsman* (art, design)

drama, dramatic confine their use to the theatrical context wherever possible; *dramatic events* and the like are overworked clichés

Dr Dolittle (italics for the film, roman for the character)

dreamt (not dreamed)

drier (comparative of dry); note *dryer* (noun), as in *tumble dryer*

drink-drive, drink-driver, drink-driving note that the limits are 35 *micrograms* of alcohol per 100 millilitres of *breath*; and 80 *milligrams* of alcohol per 100 millilitres of *blood*

drivers no hyphens in *taxi driver, bus driver, car driver* etc

drop a bombshell avoid this cliché

dropout noun or adjective as in students; note *drop-out* (rugby); and *to drop out* (verb)

Drug Enforcement Administration (US); thereafter DEA

drugs do not confuse *narcotics* (which include cocaine and heroin) with other illicit drugs such as cannabis, LSD and amphetamines

Druid(s) cap

Druze (religious sect and militia group in Lebanon)

Dr Who roman for the character (subsequent mentions *the Doctor*), but italics for the programme

dry-clean, dry-cleaning etc

drystone wall

dual of two, eg, *dual carriageway*; note *duel* (fight)

du Cann, (Sir) Edward

Duchess of York no longer a member of the Royal Family since her divorce. After first mention as Duchess of York, refer to *the duchess* (l/c) subsequently – never Fergie or any such vulgarity. See **Titles** special section (page 1467)

due to must not be used as the equivalent of *because of* or *owing to*. The phrase must be attached to a noun or pronoun: "His absence was due to illness" is correct; "He was absent due to illness" is wrong

duffel bag, duffel coat

Duke of Edinburgh write the Duke (cap) or Prince Philip after first mention; but this cap rule applies only to the British Royal Family and overseas heads of state, so the Duke of Rutland would become *the duke* (l/c) after first mention. See **Royal Family, heads of state, Titles** special section (page 1467)

dump do not use as synonym of *dismiss* or *sack*

Durham use Co Durham for the county and (if any question of ambiguity) Durham city for the city; see **counties**

duty-free hyphenate noun and adjective

dwarf as plural, prefer *dwarfs* (not dwarves); avoid "politically correct" circumlocutions such as *person of restricted growth*

dyke (embankment; not dike)

dysentery (not dysentry or disentery)

dyspepsia

Ee

each, every although singular, they are acceptable now with plural pronouns, as the plural is increasingly a way of avoiding "he or she", or "his or her". Hence, "everyone has what they want", "each of us has our secrets", but "everyone has secrets"

Earhart, Amelia (1930s aviatrix)

Earls Court no apostrophe

early hours avoid the phrase *in the early hours of the morning;* write simply *the early hours* or, better, *early yesterday/today*

earned (never earnt)

earring no hyphen

Earth cap only in planetary or astronomical sense, not in phrases such as *down to earth.* The same rule applies to Moon and Sun. See **Universe**

earthquake can abbreviate to *quake* in headings. See **Richter scale**

east, eastern for when to cap, see **compass points**

East End also West End of London; and East, West, North, South, Central, Inner London. See **London**

EastEnders (TV soap opera)

Easter Day (not Easter Sunday)

Eastern Europe but note *eastern Germany*. See **Germany**

easygoing

easyJet

EBRD European Bank for Reconstruction and Development

EC must not be used as an abbreviation for the European Commission in text or headlines. EC remains the short form only of the European Community, although in almost all contexts now, EU is preferred. See **European Commission, European Union**

E.coli italics in text, but roman and no point in headlines

e-commerce (as *e-mail*)

ecosystem no hyphen, but note *eco-warrior*

Ecstasy (drug)

ecu (European currency unit)

Ecuadorean (not -ian)

ecumenical (not oecumenical, but respect titles). See **Churches** special section (page 1462)

editor cap first mention of editors of well-known leading publications, such as the Editor of *The Times,* Editor of *The Mirror,* Editor of the *Yorkshire Post,* Editor of *The Spectator;* subsequent mentions, revert to l/c. Similarly, Editor-in-Chief. Note that deputy editors and below retain l/c. See **job titles, newspapers**

education action zones (EAZs), l/c in general context but cap specifics, eg, Barnsley Education Action Zone. Similar style to *local education authorities* (LEAs)

educationist (not educationalist)

eg no points, but use a comma before and after. See **ie**

Eire do not use except in historical context. See **Ireland**

eisteddfod l/c except when naming a particular one in full, eg, the International Eisteddfod at Llangollen; note plural *eisteddfodau*

either takes a singular verb when both subjects are embraced, eg, *either is good enough*. See **neither**

elderly, aged, old be sensitive in the use of these words, and generally do not use for people under 65

electrocardiographs (machines for measuring heart function); note *electrocardiograms*, the tracings made by electrocardiographs

electrocute means to kill by electric shock

Elgin Marbles subsequently the *Marbles*

elicit means to evoke, bring to light, or draw out; never confuse with *illicit* (unlawful, forbidden)

elite roman, no accent

e-mail

embarkation (not embarcation). You *embark in* (not on) a ship. See **Armed Forces** special section (page 1459)

embarrass(ment) but note the French *embarras de choix, embarras de richesses*

Embassy same style as for *Ambassador*, eg, *the French Embassy in Rome*, thereafter *the embassy*

Emmies plural of the *Emmy awards*

emphasise prefer this to *stress* in phrases such as "he emphasised the importance", "she emphasised that the ruling was final". See **stress**

empire cap as in *British* or *Roman Empire*; similarly, cap *emperor* when specific, eg, Emperor Claudius

employment tribunals have replaced industrial tribunals. See **industrial tribunals**

EMS European Monetary System

EMU economic and monetary union (in Europe); see **ERM**

encyclopaedia (not encyclopedia)

England, English beware of these when the meaning is *Britain, British*

England and Wales Cricket Board has replaced the TCCB, and is abbreviated as ECB; do not shorten to England/English Cricket Board. See **Sports** special section (page 1466)

enormity does not mean great size; it means quality or character of being outrageous, or extreme wickedness or serious error. Do not misuse. For great size, use *immensity*

en route not italics

ensign the *White Ensign* is the ensign of the Royal Navy and the Royal Yacht Squadron; the *Red Ensign* is the British Merchant Navy's flag; the *Blue Ensign* is flown by Royal Fleet Auxiliary vessels and by certain yacht clubs. There is no such thing as the Royal Ensign; however, the *Royal Standard* will fly from one of the Queen's homes when she is there. See **Royal Standard**

ensure means to make certain; you *insure* against risk; you *assure* your life. The verb *ensure* usually needs *that* after it if accompanied by a following verb (eg, "he tried to ensure that the policy was adopted"); but omit *that* if followed by a noun (eg, "he tried to ensure its success")

enthral

Environment Agency note caps

Equator cap, but *equatorial* in general sense

ERM exchange-rate mechanism (in European contexts); a part of the wider concept of EMU

escalate, escalation avoid these clichés; use *rise, grow* or *soar* instead

escapers (never escapees)

Eskimo plural *Eskimos*; preferred to Inuit

Establishment, the cap in sense of the perceived leaders of society; but l/c as in the *medical establishment*, the *legal establishment*, when the sense is more restricted

Eucharist cap; see **Christian terms**

euro (European common currency); note l/c (as franc, pound, mark, peseta etc); also *eurozone* or *euroland* for the single currency area

eurocheques, eurobonds l/c, no hyphen

Europe note caps for Western, Eastern, Central. Europe includes the British Isles, so do not use the name as equivalent to the Continent. Britain does not export to Europe, but to the *rest* of Europe

European Commission, Commissioners cap *Commission* throughout as a noun, but l/c when adjectival, eg, a *commission ruling* (the same rule as for Government/government); cap *commissioner* only when referring to a specific person (eg, Mario Monti, the Competition Commissioner; thereafter, *the commissioner*). The President of the European Commission is capped throughout (as with all foreign Presidents)

European Economic Area (EEA) European tariff-free zone, comprising the 15 members of the EU plus Norway, Iceland and Liechtenstein

European Parliament Members of the European Parliament (MEPs), or Euro MPs

European Union (EU), European Community (EC) the first is now the preferred phrase except where the context is trade. If you must use *the Union*, cap it throughout, but wherever possible use EU. Use *Common Market* and *EEC* only in historical context

Eurosceptic no longer hyphenated; similarly *Europhobia, Europhiles*

Eurotunnel one word; note that *Le Shuttle* no longer exists – the shuttle trains are now also called Eurotunnel trains. *Eurostar* passenger trains continue as before; see **Channel Tunnel**

evensong l/c; see **matins, Christian terms**

eventuate avoid; use *happen* instead

ever rarely necessary; avoid phrases such as *best-ever, fastest-ever*, and use simply *best* and *fastest*, qualifying (where appropriate) with *yet*. See **first, superlatives, universal claims**

ex- prefer *former* in most contexts, as in *former Yugoslavia*, though *ex-serviceman* is unavoidable and *ex-* is fine for headlines

examinations *11-plus, 7-plus* etc; also *A levels*, but *A-level results* etc (hyphenate only when adjectival). Abbreviate to *exam* only in headlines. GCSE, the General Certificate of Secondary Education, need not normally be spelt out

excepting do not use when *except* or *except for* is possible

exclamation marks nearly always unnecessary

exclusive avoid with story or interview. The phrase "in an interview with *The Times*" is sufficient

execution take care: as with *assassination*, do not use as a synonym of any killing or murder. An execution is a judicial killing after due process of law

exhibitions titles of art exhibitions now in italics. See **Arts** special section (page 1461)

existing use *present* wherever possible as an alternative

Exocet note cap

expatriate (not ex-patriate and never expatriot); noun, verb or adjective

Export Credits Guarantee Department abbreviate to ECGD; note *Credits* plural

extramarital no hyphen; similarly *extramural, extracurricular, extrasensory* etc

exuberant (never exhuberant); but note *exhilarate, exhort*

eye of a storm do not refer to the *calm in the eye of the storm*; the eye, by definition, is the calm area at the centre of a storm or hurricane

eye to eye no hyphens

eyeing

eyewitness use *witness* instead wherever possible (except in direct quotes)

Ff

F111s no hyphen; see **aircraft types**

façade use the cedilla

facelift use sparingly in its metaphorical sense, where it has become overworked. In cosmetic context quite acceptable, however

fact sheet

fact that almost always an unnecessary circumlocution, so avoid, eg, "owing to the fact that" means *because*

Faeroe Isles or *the Faeroes*

fahrenheit see **celsius**

fairytale no hyphen

Faithfull, Marianne

falangist (Spain); note *phalangist* (Lebanon)

fallacy means a *faulty argument*, not an erroneous belief

fallout noun; no longer hyphenated

fan acceptable nowadays for football supporter or pop music enthusiast

Far East encompasses the following: China, Hong Kong, Japan, North and South Korea, Macau, Mongolia, Taiwan. See **Asean**, **South-East Asia**

farther is applied only to distance (literal or figurative), eg, "nothing could be farther from the truth". *Further* means *in addition to, another,* eg, "a further point"

fascia (not facia)

Fascist cap in the political sense, but as a term of abuse, l/c; but note *fascism* l/c except in specifically party context. See **communism**

Father (as in priest); avoid the ugly abbreviation Fr before a name

Father's Day (not Fathers'). See **Mother's Day**

fatwa (Muslim religious edict, not a sentence of punishment); not italic

fault-line (hyphenate)

Fayed, Dodi (the late elder son of Mohamed Al Fayed; not Dodi Al Fayed)

Fed, the (US); use *Federal Reserve* (Board not usually necessary) at first mention; cap the *Chairman* of the Fed, as with *Governor of the Bank of England, President of the Bundesbank* etc

Federal Aviation Administration (US); abbreviation FAA; (not Agency or Authority)

"feel-good" factor

Fellow cap in specific title such as Dr Arthur Brown, a Fellow of Magdalen, or in the more obvious Fellow of the Royal College of Surgeons (FRCS); but l/c in general sense, eg, *a group of fellows in the quadrangle*; keep *fellowship* l/c

female do not write, for example, *female councillors, female directors;* instead use (where gender is relevant) *women councillors, women directors* etc

feminine designations *authoress, poetess, wardress* etc should be avoided. But *actress* is such common usage that it is acceptable. See **comedienne**

Ferris wheel

Festival Hall generally omit *Royal*

festivals cap the Edinburgh Festival (cultural), Reading Festival (pop), Cheltenham Festival (racing) etc, thereafter *the festival* (l/c). See **Fringe**

fête with accent

fewer of numbers, eg, *fewer people, fewer goals;* use *less* with size, quantity, or singular nouns, eg, *less population, less meat.* See **less**

fiancé (man), note **fiancée** (woman); see **divorcé**

Fianna Fail, Fine Gael see **Ireland**

Fide (world chess body; not FIDE); see **chess names**

fifty write *50-50 chance;* note cap for the decade, eg, *Fifties,* but l/c for age, eg, *she was in her fifties*

fighting for his/her life avoid this meaningless phrase. Instead use *critically ill/injured*

figures see **numbers**

filibuster (not fillibuster)

Filipinos, Filipinas (women), **the Philippines** (country)

films titles in italics; see **Arts** special section (page 1461); note *film-maker;* see **movies**

film star two words

Financial Services Authority (FSA) has replaced the Securities and Investments Board (SIB)

fiord (not fjord)

firearms do not confuse bullets with shotgun cartridges (containing pellets); a gunshot wound is markedly different from a bullet wound

fire brigade l/c in general context, but cap specifics, eg, *Kent Fire Brigade*

firefight should not be used as a synonym of *military skirmish* or *exchange of fire; firefighters* try to extinguish flames

firm do not use as a synonym of *company.* See **companies**

first serves as an adverb, so avoid *firstly.* If a list of priorities is essential in a story, write *first, secondly, thirdly* etc. Never use *first-ever.* See **ever**, **superlatives**, **universal claims**

first aid noun, no hyphen; but hyphenate when adjectival, eg, *first-aid qualifications*

First World War (not World War One); similarly *Second World War.* See **wars**

Fitzgerald, Garret

Five Nations Championship (initial caps) becomes the *Six Nations Championship* in 2000 (England, Wales, Scotland, Ireland, France and Italy)

flair (as in talent); do not confuse with *flare* (as in fire, fashion etc)

flat-owners hyphen, but note *homeowners*

flaunt means to make an ostentatious or defiant display, eg, *she flaunted her finery;* to *flout* is to show contempt for, eg, *he flouted the law*

fledgeling

fleur-de-lys (not lis)

flight numbers cap in stories where the number of the flight is relevant, eg, *Flight 103* (Lockerbie disaster)

floodlighting but note *floodlit*

flotation (shares), but note *floatation* (tanks)

flout see **flaunt**

flowerbed one word; similarly *flowerpot*

flu no apostrophe; acceptable abbreviation for *influenza*

Flushing Meadows (New York home of the US Open tennis championships; not Meadow)

Flying Squad cap, as it is the only one in the UK. But l/c *fraud squads* as there are several; similarly *vice squads, drug squads, crime squads, regional crime squads*

focused

folk-song, folk-singer (use hyphen)

following do not use as synonym of *after.* Always use *after* instead

Food and Drug Administration (US)

foodstuffs where place names form part of the phrase, generally use the cap, eg, *Brussels sprouts, Cheddar cheese, chicken Kiev, Cornish pasties, potatoes Lyonnaise*; but keep l/c for *hamburger, frankfurter* etc. See **metric**

foolproof no hyphen

foot-and-mouth disease

football *soccer* is now an acceptable synonym of *association football.* See **Premiership**

for-, fore- the general rule is that *e* is added only when the prefix has the meaning of *before.* Thus *forbears* (refrains), *forebears* (ancestors); *forgo* (go without), *forego* (go before, as in *foregone conclusion*). Take particular care with *forswear* and *foresee(able)*, both frequently misspelt

Forces use the *Armed Forces* wherever possible, but if the word has to be used alone, cap *Forces* both as a noun and adjectivally (as *Service*). See **Armed Forces** special section (page 1459)

Foreign and Commonwealth Office usually shorten to *Foreign Office* or *FCO* (abbreviation permissible in headlines); no longer use *FO*

foreign appellations *The Times* uses local honorifics for:
France: M, Mme, Mlle and Me (for Maître, legal)
Germany and **Austria:** Herr, Frau, Fräulein
Spain and Spanish-speaking **Latin America:** Señor, Señora, Señorita
Italy: Signor, Signora, Signorina
Portugal and **Brazil:** Senhor, Senhora (but not Senhorina)

Note that with Belgium, Luxembourg, Switzerland and Canada, Mr, Mrs, Miss, Ms etc are used because of those countries' linguistic sensitivities, eg, Jacques Santer, former President of the European Commission, will subsequently be Mr Santer. Similarly the English forms with Francophone Africa, where French is more the language of the elite rather than the lingua franca.

For all other nationalities, use English except where it is possible to use a local title (eg, *Ayatollah, Begum, Chief, Pandit, Sheikh*), or a military one (eg, Colonel Gaddafi); occasionally, where titles are in general use (eg, Baron von X in Germany), we would respect such exceptions

Note in Burma, U means Mr, Daw means Mrs; in China, the first Chinese name is the surname, eg, Deng Xiaoping becomes Mr Deng

foreign places as a general rule, use the spellings in *The Times Atlas of the World,* including Chinese place names (see **Chinese names**). However, *The Times* retains the Anglicised or commonly accepted spellings of many familiar (and especially European) countries and cities, such as *Brussels, Cologne, Cracow, Dunkirk, Florence, Geneva, Gothenburg, The Hague, Lyons, Majorca, Marseilles, Mexico City, Minorca, Moscow, Munich, Naples, Prague, Rheims, Rome, Salonika, Venice.* See also **Spanish regions**

foreign words write in roman when foreign words and phrases have become essentially a part of the English language (eg, an elite, a debacle, a fête); otherwise, use italic (eg, a *bon mot,* a *bête noire,* the *raison d'être*). Avoid pretension by using an English phrase wherever one will serve. See **accents**

forensic means *pertaining to the courts.* A forensic expert could be a solicitor or a biochemist; make your meaning clear by writing *forensic scientist, forensic medicine* etc

for ever means *always;* note *forever* means *continuously*

forklift truck

Formica proprietary term, so cap

formula plural usually *formulas,* but use *formulae* in mathematical contexts

fortuitous does not mean *fortunate.* It means *by chance* or *accidental.* Do not confuse

forum plural *forums;* see **referendum**

four-letter words avoid where possible, but if there is no alternative (eg, in direct quotes, where they are essential to the story), soften them with asterisks, eg, f***, c*** etc. See **obscenities**

foxhunt, foxhunting without hyphens, similarly *foxhound, foxhole, master of foxhounds* (l/c *m*)

fractions do not mix fractions and decimals in the same story. Compounds such as *half-hour, half-dozen* etc take a hyphen; *half an hour, half a dozen* do not. Hyphenate when fractions are adjectival, eg, *two-thirds full,* but not as nouns, eg, *two thirds of the bus was empty.* See **two thirds**

framework document (Anglo-Irish proposals for Northern Ireland, February 1995) note l/c; full title of the document is *Frameworks for the Future.* See **Ireland**

franc l/c, and abbreviate as *Fr40;* specify if not French, eg, *BFr40 (Belgian), SwFr40 (Swiss)*

franchisor (no longer franchiser)

Frankenstein foods never use this pejorative phrase to describe genetically modified (GM) foods, except in direct quotations

fraud squad l/c; see **Flying Squad**

free avoid the modern cliché *for free* when the meaning is simply *free*

"freebie" just permissible as colloquialism for *handout, free trip* etc, but use inverted commas

Free Churches, Free Churchman caps

freefall no hyphen

Freemasonry, Mason, Masonic

French names prefer the more Anglicised style for street names etc, eg, *Rue Royale, Place de la Victoire, Boulevard des Montagnes.* No need to hyphenate place names such as St Malo, St Etienne etc

french windows l/c

frescoes (not frescos)

Freud, Lucian (not Lucien)

Fringe, the Edinburgh always cap, whether as noun or adjective

Frisbee proprietary term, so cap

front bench, the noun; but note *frontbencher, frontbench power* etc. See **Politics** special section (page 1465)

frontline adjective, as in the *frontline states;* but note the noun *front line*

front-runner

FTSE 100 index no longer hyphenate FT-SE; note also the *FTSE all-share index*

fuchsia

fuel greatly overworked verb, especially in headlines; always seek alternatives such as *raise, increase, add to, boost*

Fujiyama, or **Mount Fuji** (not Mount Fujiyama)

-ful, -fuls so *cupfuls* (not cupsful)

fulfil but note *fulfilled, fulfilling*

full points note thin space after initials and points, eg, F. W. de Klerk. But with companies, omit the full points, eg, WH Smith. See **companies, initials**

full-time adj, but note noun *full time* (as in football)

fulsome be very careful – and sparing – with the use of this word. It means *excessive* or *insincere* (the cliché *fulsome praise* actually means excessive praise, not generous or warm praise). Try to avoid it, especially the cliché

fundholders (NHS)

fundraising, fundraiser no hyphen

further see **farther**

fusillade

Gg

Gaddafi, Colonel Muammar (Libyan leader)

gaff (hook or spar); but *gaffe* (blunder or indiscretion). Note *to blow the gaff* (let out a secret)

Gambia, The always cap the definite article

gambit (technical term in chess, meaning an opening involving a sacrifice in return for general advantage); *opening gambit* is thus tautological. Take care with its use as a metaphor, and use sparingly

game show no hyphen; similarly *chat show, quiz show, talk show* etc

Gandhi, Mahatma, Indira etc (never Ghandi)

Garda see **Ireland**

Gardeners' Question Time (not Gardener's)

gas, gases noun; but *gassed, gassing* (verbal use); note also *gases* (not gasses) for present tense, eg, *doctor gases patient*

gasfield similarly *coalfield, oilfield*

Gatt the General Agreement on Tariffs and Trade. Its successor body is now the *World Trade Organisation* (WTO). See **Uruguay Round, World Trade Organisation**

Gatwick sufficiently well-known not to need airport in title. See **airports, Heathrow**

gauge (not guage)

Gaultier, Jean Paul no hyphen

gay where possible, use *homosexual* or *lesbian*, but *gay* has become such common currency that we should avoid looking or sounding pompous in this context. See **straight**

GCSE see **examinations**

GDP gross domestic product

GEC Alsthom became simply *Alstom* (note no "h") in mid-1998

gelatine rather than gelatin

Geldof, Bob do not write *Sir* Bob Geldof, as he is an honorary KBE

gender (term of grammar); do not use as synonym of a person's sex

general election always l/c

General Secretary of the TUC caps; but note l/c for *general secretary* of individual unions; see **TUC**

General Strike (of 1926); caps

General Synod (of the Church of England), thereafter *the synod*. See **Churches** special section (page 1462)

Gentile(s) cap

geriatric does not mean *elderly,* but is applied to medical treatment for the elderly, eg, *geriatric hospital*. Never use as a term of abuse

German Bight (as in shipping forecast; not Bite)

Germany full title is the *Federal Republic of Germany*. If referring to the area that was East Germany, say *eastern Germany* or the *former East Germany;* similarly *western Germany* or the *former West Germany. Ossis, Wessis* permissible vernacular for inhabitants of the two parts

gerrymander

get, got a lazy verb, so avoid where possible

Getty, Sir Paul do not use John or J. in his name any longer

Ghanaian (not Ghanian)

ghetto use only in the sense of an area of enforced or customary segregation, not as an ethnic neighbourhood, eg, middle-class *district,* not *ghetto*. Note plural *ghettos*

giant-killer, giant-killing

gibe means *taunt* or *sneer;* note also *gybe* meaning to *shift direction* or *change course,* particularly in sailing. For the sake of clarity, *jibe* (a variant of both) should no longer be used

Gibraltar (never Gibralter); note *Strait of Gibraltar* (not Straits)

gig acceptable for a musical event; similarly *rave*

gillie rather than ghillie

gipsy see **gypsy**

girl do not use as a synonym of *woman*

girlfriend one word; similarly *boyfriend*. Use *girlfriend* only for young people; otherwise *woman friend* or just *friend* (where the gender is obvious)

Girl Guides now simply *Guides;* see **Boy Scouts**

giro (l/c), as in benefit payments, cheques etc

Giscard d'Estaing, Valéry thereafter M Giscard

giveaway noun or adjective; one word, similarly *takeaway;* but note *to give away*

glamorise, glamorous but note *glamour*

glasnost not italic

glassmaker

Glen Coe (valley); but note *Glencoe* (battle, village and pass)

Glorious Twelfth, the caps

GMB write the GMB general union

gobbledegook

God cap when referring to just one, in any religion. *He, His, Him* are also capped. When non-specific, use l/c, eg, *Greek gods*. See **Christian terms, Churches** special section (page 1462)

godforsaken but note *God-fearing*

godparents, godfather, godmother, godson, goddaughter, godchild

Goebbels, Joseph (not Goebells etc)

-goer as a suffix, run on as one word, as in *churchgoer, partygoer, theatregoer* etc

Goldeneye (James Bond film; not GoldenEye)

Golders Green no apostrophe

goldmine, goldmining

Goldsmiths College, London no longer use apostrophe

goodbye

goodwill one word, whether used as a noun or adjective

Gorazde, Bosnia (not Goradze)

Gorbachev, Mikhail

gorilla

Gormley, Antony (the sculptor)

Gothenburg (not Göteborg)

Gothic cap; preferable to Gothick

Government cap all governments, British and overseas, when referring to a specific one, eg, "the Government resigned last night", "the Argentine Government sent troops", and specific past administrations such as "the Heath Government"; only l/c when unspecific or one that has yet to be formed, eg, "all the governments since the war", or "the next Tory government would raise pensions".

Also l/c government in all adjectival contexts, eg, *a government minister, a government decision, government expenditure*. A further instance of l/c use is in phrases such as *the Bosnian government troops* or *the British government-backed trade delegation,* when the use is again principally adjectival.

Also, note that provincial or state governments in Australia, Canada, India etc retain l/c. See **Politics** special section (page 1465)

government departments cap both when giving full title (eg, *Department of Trade and Industry*), and even when abbreviated, as in *Health Department, Education Department, Trade*

Department etc. The same applies to *ministries*, home and overseas

Governor (of the Bank of England); cap at every mention, also cap Deputy Governor of the Bank. Also, cap the Governor of Hong Kong at every mention; but cap prison governors at first mention only, eg, James X, Governor of Parkhurst, thereafter l/c, and l/c deputy governors

Graces *The Three Graces* (Canova's statue). See **Arts** special section (page 1461)

Grade II listed, Grade II* listed etc

gram (not gramme); similarly *kilogram*; see **metric**

grandad but note *granddaughter*

Grand Jury (caps) in US contexts

grandmaster (chess); l/c. See **chess names**

Grappelli, Stéphane

grassroots adjective; note the noun *grass roots*. Use this cliché sparingly

great and the good, the all l/c; quotes usually unnecessary

greater or lesser degree *lesser* is not correct but is common usage

Great Ormond Street Hospital for Children (no longer Sick Children)

Greco- (not Graeco-)

green belt l/c

Green Paper caps; see **White Paper**

Green Party, or **the Greens** but note *green issues* etc

grisly means *horrifying, repugnant*; note *grizzly* which means *greyish, grizzled*, or is a short form of *grizzly bear*

grottoes

ground(s) in the sense of *reason*, do not use plural unless more than one is given; eg, "he gave up his job on the ground of illness"; but "he gave up his job on the grounds of his failed marriage and illness"

Group 4 (security company)

G-string

guerrilla beware of loaded terms for advocates of political violence; see **terrorist**

guesthouse no hyphen

guidebook similarly *chequebook, stylebook, textbook, formbook* etc

Guildhall, London (never *the* Guildhall)

guinea-pig (hyphen)

Gulf, the avoid the term *Persian Gulf* as it angers Iraqis and many other Arabs

gunboat, gunfight, gunfire, gunman, gunpoint, gunshot, gunsmith but note *gun dog*

gunned down avoid this Americanism; instead say *shot dead*

gunwales (nautical, not gunwhales)

Gurkhas

guttural (not gutteral)

Guyana (formerly British Guiana, now independent); do not confuse with *French Guiana* (French overseas territory)

Gypsy/gypsy (not gipsy). Cap when referring to a specific group of this semi-nomadic people, but l/c in the more general sense of somebody constantly on the move, eg, "the Gypsies on Epsom Downs threatened to retaliate"; but "police said they would chase all gypsies from the county". The other wandering groups in Britain are the Irish tinkers, who prefer the name *Irish travellers*; the *Scottish tinkers* (or *tinklers*); and the hippies, whom we can call *New Age travellers*; *travellers* is a useful generic term

Hh

Häagen-Dazs (brand of ice-cream originating in America)

Haberdashers' Aske's School, Elstree

Habsburg no longer Hapsburg

haemorrhage means heavy and potentially dangerous bleeding, not simply bleeding. Beware of misuse in metaphor

Hague, Ffion follow Cherie Blair/Booth style for William's wife: *Ffion Hague* (or *Mrs Hague*) when with her husband, but *Ffion Jenkins* (subsequently *Ms Jenkins*) when at functions in her own right

Hague, The

hairdresser, hairbrush, haircut, hairdryer, hairpin, hairstyle

Haiti, Haitian note that Haiti must never be described as an island; it is joined to the Dominican Republic and together they constitute the island of Hispaniola

haj (pilgrimage to Mecca); l/c and roman

haka (Maori war-dance); l/c and roman

half-time (in football match etc); note the *half time* in business context, but hyphenate when used adjectivally, eg, *half-time results*

halfway no hyphen; but note *half-hearted*

Halley's comet see **heavenly bodies**

Hallowe'en

handmade, handbuilt (no hyphen)

handout as a noun, no hyphen

hangar (aircraft); note *hanger* (clothes)

hanged "The murderer was hanged at dawn" – note never *hung*. Clothes are hung on a washing line or a hanger

Hansard

harass, harassment

hardcore one word as adjective, eg, *hardcore pornography*; but note two words as noun, eg, *the hard core of the rebels*; similarly *hard core* (rubble)

hardline adjective; but note *to take a hard line*

Haringey (London borough and council); note also *Harringay* (London neighbourhood)

HarperCollins, or **HarperCollins Publishers** owned by The News Corporation; see **News International**

Harpers & Queen

Harrods no apostrophe; see **Al Fayed**

harvest festival l/c

Hattersley, Lord (not "of Sparkbrook")

Havisham, Miss (not Miss Haversham) in Dickens's *Great Expectations*

Hawaiian

hay fever no hyphen

headache avoid as a synonym of *difficulty*

head-butt noun or verb

headhunt, headhunting, headhunter no hyphens

headlines avoid the worst clichés and hyperboles such as *bash, crash, shock, slam* etc; but words such as *bid* (for attempt), *crisis, hit* (adversely affect), *row* (clash or dispute) and *phone* (telephone) – all of which should not normally appear in text – are permissible in headlines, provided they are not overworked.

Inverted commas must always be single in headlines, straps and display panels. See **quotation marks**

headmaster, headmistress one word and l/c except in the formal, official title (and then cap at first mention only). Some schools have variants on the usual style; Eton, Harrow, Rugby and Westminster have a *Head Master*; St Paul's School and Manchester Grammar School have a *High Master*; King Edward's School, Birmingham, has a *Chief Master*; Dulwich, Haileybury and Marlborough have a *Master*. The correct form is given in the *Independent Schools Year Book*. Use the colloquial *head* only in headlines; and note that *head teacher* is two words except when part of the designated title

heads of state when these are royals, such as King Abdullah of Jordan, after the first mention refer to them as *the King* (cap). The cap at subsequent mentions applies only to overseas heads of state and the British Royal Family, eg, Prince B. of Thailand (a minor royal) would become *the prince* thereafter. See **Royal Family**, **Titles** special section (page 1467)

healthcare one word

heartbroken, heartbreaking, heartfelt, heartstrings, but hyphenate *heart-rending, heart-throb*

Heathrow sufficiently well-known not to need airport in title. Note at Heathrow, *Terminal 1, 2, 3, 4, 5* etc. See **airports**, **Gatwick**

Heaven, Hell cap in religious context only; see **Devil**

heavenly bodies cap the proper names of planets, stars, constellations etc: *Venus, Arcturus, the Plough, Aries*; for comets, l/c the word comet in, for example, *Halley's comet*. The Sun, the Moon, the Earth, the Universe are capped in their planetary or astronomical sense (see **Earth**). Use l/c for the adjectives *lunar* and *solar*, but cap *Martian* both adjectivally and as a noun

Heep, Uriah (not Heap)

Hell's Angels

help to use *to* plus verb, eg, "he helped *to* make the cake" (not "he helped make the cake")

helping the police with their inquiries avoid this phrase – suspects rarely willingly help the police. Say *were being interviewed* instead

helpline one word; similarly *hotline*

hemisphere l/c northern, southern, eastern, western

heraldry do not confuse *crests* with *coats of arms*. Most arms consist of a shield and a crest; crests are the topmost part of the coat of arms (think of the crest of a bird or a wave)

Hereford and Worcester see **unitary authorities**

Heriot-Watt University, Edinburgh

Her Majesty's pleasure (as in *detained at ...*)

Herzegovina (as in Bosnia-Herzegovina)

Heyhoe Flint, Rachael (no hyphen, not Rachel)

Hezbollah (Party of God in Iran and Lebanon); soft-hyphenate (on a break) as Hezb-ollah

Hibernian means of or concerning Ireland, not Scotland, despite the Edinburgh football club of the same name

hiccup (not hiccough)

hi-fi acceptable abbreviation, noun or adjective, of *high fidelity*

high acceptable usage as a noun, eg, *she was on a high*. But avoid clichés such as *all-time high* and *hits new high*

highbrow, lowbrow

high command avoid clichéd use, as in *Tory high command*. See **Politics** special section (page 1465)

High Commissioner caps when specific, eg, *the Indian High Commissioner*; thereafter *the high commissioner*. Remember that Commonwealth countries and the UK have high commissioners serving in high commissions in each other's countries, not ambassadors serving in embassies. See **Ambassador**

High Court see **Courts** special section (page 1463)

highfalutin

high-flyer

High Sheriff caps when specific

high street l/c and no hyphen in general sense, as in *high street prices*. But cap when specific, eg, *Putney High Street*

high-tech adjective; spell out in text, but *hi-tech* is acceptable in headlines

hike never use in the American sense of a *rise* or *to raise* (rates etc); permissible only in direct quotes, or in context of walking (hitch-hike etc)

Hinckley, Leicestershire but note *Hinkley Point*, Somerset

Hindi for language contexts (the Hindi language); but use *Hindu* for religious and ethnic contexts (an adherent to Hinduism, or relating to Hinduism)

hippy, hippies nowadays as old-fashioned as *beatniks*; see **Gypsy, travellers**

Hirst, Damien (artist; not Damian)

historic, historical prefer *an historic event* rather than *a historic*; see **a, an.** Also, take care with use of *historical* and *historic*; the former can refer only to past history, while the latter can refer to a contemporary event likely to be of long-term significance. But *an historic building* is now in common usage as a synonym of an old building

hit avoid in text in sense of *affected*, eg, "Homeowners were hit last night by an interest rate rise", or in the sense of attack, eg, "The minister hit out at his critics". Sparing use of the verb in headlines is permissible

hitch-hiker, hitch-hiking etc

Hitchin, Hertfordshire (not Hitchen)

hitlist, hitman now no hyphens

HIV is a virus, not a disease. Do not write *HIV virus* (tautology), but use a phrase such as *HIV-infected*. See **Aids**

hoards (stocks or stores of treasure, for example); note *to hoard* (to amass and store food, money etc); never confuse with **hordes** (large groups or gangs of wild beasts etc)

Hogmanay cap

holidaymaker one word

Holland, now use **The Netherlands** for all contexts except sports teams or historical uses, or when referring to the provinces of North or South Holland. The adjective is *Dutch*

Holy Communion caps; see **Christian terms**

Holy Grail caps

Holyroodhouse see **Palace of Holyroodhouse**

homebuyers, homeowners no hyphens

home town (two words), but hyphenate in adjectival use, eg, *home-town memories*

Home Counties, the caps

homoeopathy (not the American homeopathy)

homogeneous means having parts all of the same kind; *homogenous* means similar owing to common descent

Homo sapiens see **scientific names**

homosexual see **gay**

Hon, the normally use this form of address (the Hon So-and-So) only on the Court Page

Hong Kong but note *Hongkong and Shanghai Banking Corporation (HSBC)*. Until July 1, 1997, when Britain handed the colony over to China, Hong Kong had a *Governor* (cap). See **Midland**

honours people are *appointed* Privy Counsellor, Baronet, KBE, CBE, OBE, MBE etc; never say they were made, received, were awarded, or got the OBE etc. *Peers* and above (viscounts etc) are *created*, not appointed etc. At investitures, those honoured receive the insignia of the award, not the award itself. Normally omit honours and decorations after names, but the following can be used where relevant: KG, KT, VC, GC, OM, CH, MP, QC, RA, FRS etc. See **Titles** special section (page 1467)

honours lists see **New Year Honours**

Hoover trade name, so cap; generally use *vacuum cleaner* and *to vacuum*

hopefully try to avoid in the sense of *it is hoped that*, even though this usage is widespread

Horse Guards Parade

horse race/racing two words, but *racing* alone is preferable. Note *Horserace Betting Levy Board*; see **racecourse, Sports** special section (page 1466)

horticulturist (not horticulturalist)

hospitalise, hospitalisation always avoid these Americanisms; use *taken to hospital* etc

host avoid using as a verb as in "Arsenal will host Aston Villa on Saturday"; use *play host to* instead. But note a *person* can *host* an event

hotline one word; similarly *helpline*

hotpants one word

hoummos see **taramasalata**

housebuilder, housebuilding but note *the House-Builders' Federation*

however when used in the sense of *nevertheless*, always place a comma after it (and before, when in the middle of a sentence, eg, "It was said, however, that the agent ...")

Hubble Space Telescope

Hudson Bay but note *Hudson's Bay Company*

human beings rather than just humans

human rights European Convention on Human Rights; European Court of Human Rights; the now-defunct European Commission of Human Rights; all established under the aegis of the Council of Europe, not the EU (or EC). See **Courts** special section (page 1463)

humorist (not humourist)

Humphrys, John (radio and TV); but note Barry Humphries (Dame Edna Everage etc)

Hussein, King the late King of Jordan, not *Husain*; similarly, President Saddam Hussein (Iraq)

Hutus, Tutsis note plural of the Rwandan tribes (not simply Hutu, Tutsi)

hyphens generally be sparing with hyphens and run together words where the sense suggests and where they look familiar; eg, *blacklist, businessman, goldmine, knockout, intercontinental, motorcycle, takeover*, and *walkover*. Unusual hyphenations are listed separately in this guide. However, a few guidelines can be specified:

a usually run together prefixes except where the last letter of the prefix is the same as the first letter of the word to which it attaches: *prearrange, postwar, prewar, nonconformist*; but *pre-empt, co-ordinate, co-operate, re-establish*

b hyphenate composites where the same two letters come together, eg, *film-makers*, but an exception should be made when double *r* occurs in the middle: *override, overrule* (not over-ride etc), and note *granddaughter* and *goddaughter*

c generally do not use dangling hyphens, eg, *full and part-time employment* etc; this does not apply to prefixes, eg, *pre- or post-match drinks*

d for hyphenation when qualifying adjectives, see **adverbs**

e always use a hyphen rather than a slash in dates etc, eg, 1982–83 (not 1982/83)

Ii

IATA International Air Transport Association; all caps

ice-cream hyphen, similarly *ice-lolly*; see also **Häagen-Dazs**

Identikit proprietary term, so cap; but note l/c *photofit*

ie use comma either side. See **eg**

ill-health hyphen; similarly *ill-feeling, ill-intentioned* etc

Immigration Service caps; similarly *Prison Service, Probation Service*

impacted on avoid this Americanism

imply see **infer**

impostor (not imposter)

impresario

Impressionist, Post-Impressionist see **artistic movements**

in addition to prefer *as well as* or *besides*

inadmissible (not -able)

include do not confuse with *comprise*: "breakfast includes toast and coffee", but "breakfast comprises cereals, toast, butter, marmalade and coffee" (ie, where the full list of elements is given)

incommunicado

indestructible (not -able)

index plural is *indices*, but note *indexes* for books

indispensable (not -ible)

Indo-China

Industrial Revolution, the use caps

industrial tribunals these no longer exist; they are now *employment tribunals*. They end with a *judgment* or a *decision*, not a verdict. Only juries in court hearings, or magistrates hearing cases summarily, deliver a verdict. Note that *immigration adjudicators* and *immigration appeal tribunals* deliver *determinations*. See **Courts** special section (page 1463)

inevitable do not use as a synonym of *customary, usual* or *predictable*

in fact can almost invariably be omitted

infer do not confuse with *imply*: to *infer* is to draw a conclusion from a suggestion, to imply is to make the suggestion. A useful mnemonic: we *imply* things when we speak, we *infer* things when we listen

infighting one word, but note hyphen with *in-house*

infra-red

initials where familiar, no need to spell out at first mention (eg, BBC, TUC, Nato etc). Otherwise, usually give name in full followed by initials in parentheses, and the abbreviated form thereafter (though sometimes a word such as *the organisation* or *the group* will be preferable to avoid a mass of initials in the same story). Also, with a body as well known as the UN, it would be absurd to write the United Nations (UN), so use discretion.

Where the initials can be spoken as a word, write them as upper and lower case, eg, Nato, Gatt, Unesco, Efta – but there are some important exceptions to this, eg, MORI, IATA, RADA, RIBA, SANE, MIND, BUPA and AXA

With people's names, put points between the initials (with thin space between), though omit points in names of firms such as WH Smith, J Sainsbury

injure, injury implies something more serious than *hurt*. Avoid writing "John *received* an injury" – instead use *suffered* or *sustained* an injury, or (simply) *was injured*. Injured or sick people should not be described as *satisfactory* or *critical* – it is their *condition* that is satisfactory etc

Inland Revenue subsequent mentions, *the Revenue* (cap). See **taxman**

innocent take great care with this word, and avoid phrases such as *the innocent victim of the attack* and clichés such as *innocent children*. Best to stick to its literal sense of *not guilty*

innocuous

Inns of Court the order of precedence among the Inns is Lincoln's Inn, Inner Temple, Middle Temple, Gray's Inn

inoculate

inpatients, outpatients no hyphen

inquests see **coroner's court**

inquire, inquiry (not enquire, enquiry). But note the exception, *Directory Enquiries*

insignia plural; see **honours**

install but note *instalment*

instil

Institute of Contemporary Arts ("of" not "for" and plural Arts)

Institute of Directors IoD acceptable for headings and occasionally in text, though prefer *the institute* after first mention in full

insure you *insure* against risk; you *assure* your life; *ensure* means to make certain

Intelligence cap as a noun in the context of the security services, eg, "he was in British Intelligence", but l/c adjectival uses, eg, "she was interviewed by intelligence officers"

intelligentsia

intensive do not confuse with *intense* or *extreme*. It means concentrated, as in *intensive care*

InterCity (rail); but note adjective *inter-city*

interdependence

interesting avoid as an adjective in text; let the reader decide

interest rate cuts/rises no hyphens; never use *hikes* for *rises*

inter-governmental conference (EU's continuing discussions on the single currency etc); IGC as abbreviation. See **Maastricht**

International Atomic Energy Agency (never Authority); abbreviate to IAEA

International Olympic Committee (not Olympics); IOC as abbreviation. See **Olympics**

Internazionale (Milan football club); must not be called Inter Milan. It can be shortened to *Inter*; the other big club in the city is *AC Milan* (shortened to *Milan*)

Internet, the cap; use *the Net* (cap) for short. See **World Wide Web**

interpretative (not interpretive)

interred (buried); do not confuse with *interned* (imprisoned)

intifada (religious struggle or uprising); l/c and roman

inverted commas should be used as sparingly as possible in text: eg, unnecessary in constructions such as *he described the book as "turgid"*. They are no longer used with works of art. See also **italics, quotation marks**

Iran use Persia only in historical context; note the language is *Farsi*, not Iranian or Persian

irascible (not irrascible)

Ireland the two parts should be called the *Republic of Ireland* or the *Irish Republic* (avoid Eire except in direct quotes or historical context), and *Northern Ireland* or *Ulster*. Do not use the phrase the Six Counties. Other important styles:

a *loyalist* with l/c *l* and no quotes – to balance *republican* and *nationalist*
b *Unionist, Unionism* (caps)
c *the North, the South* (caps in this specific Irish context)
d similarly *the Republic, the Province*
e *the Troubles*

f *the Garda* (the police force; but note *garda/gardai* for policeman/policemen); but the phrase *Irish police* is acceptable
g *Londonderry*, but Derry City Council; and Derry when in direct quotes or in a specifically republican context (this latter rarely)
h *West Belfast, East Belfast* (caps because of clearly defined sectarian areas); but north Belfast, south Belfast (unspecific, directional); note Shankill Road (not Shankhill)
i *Downing Street declaration*
j *Anglo-Irish agreement*
k *Frameworks for the Future*, or *the framework document* (l/c) for the Anglo-Irish proposals of February 1995
l *Northern Ireland Assembly*, with cap for *Assembly*
m avoid *Provos* as synonym of the Provisional IRA, except in quotes
n *Taoiseach* is an acceptable alternative for Irish Prime Minister
o Irish counties should be written as *Co Donegal, Co Down* etc
p *Orange Order, Orangemen* (caps)

iridescent (not irr-)

Iron Curtain

ironic beware of misuse. It means using or displaying irony, or in the nature of irony; it does not mean strange or paradoxical

irreconcilable

irresistible (not -able)

Isa(s) individual savings account(s), l/c; hyphenate *mini-Isas, maxi-Isas*. See also **Tessa(s), Pep(s)**

-ise, -isation avoid the *z* construction in almost all cases, eg, *apologise, organise, emphasise, televise*. But note *capsize, synthesizer*

ISIS Independent Schools Information Service (not Isis)

Islam (religion of the Muslims); *Islamic* is interchangeable with *Muslim* as the adjective, though normally use Islamic with religion and fundamentalism, Muslim with architecture, politics etc

Israeli (native of Israel); *Israelite* refers to Ancient Israel

italics avoid in headlines and use sparingly in text. However, there are certain guidelines for using italics:
a all works of art, even where quotation marks used to be used, including titles of books, long and short poems, short stories, newspapers (see separate list under **newspapers**), magazines, pamphlets, chapter headings, White Papers, Green Papers, official reports and studies, programmes on radio and television, films, plays, computer games, musical works including operas, songs, hymns, album titles etc (see **musical vocabulary**), paintings, drawings, sculptures, titles of exhibitions. See **Arts** special section (page 1461)
b less common, non-Anglicised foreign words go in italics, but err on the side of roman (eg, in extremis, hors d'oeuvre, angst); see **foreign words**
c names of ships, aircraft, locomotives etc
d a word may be italicised for emphasis, but again be sparing with this device

ITN never write ITN news; see **television**

ITV acceptable alternative for *independent television*; see **television**

Jj

Jacuzzi trade name, so cap; use *whirlpool bath* if in doubt

jail, jailer (not gaol, gaoler)

jargon like journalese and slang, to be strictly avoided

Jedda

Jeep proprietary term, so cap; use only if strictly applicable, otherwise *cross-country vehicle, small military truck* etc

Jehovah's Witness(es)

Jekyll and Hyde (*The Strange Case of Dr Jekyll and Mr Hyde,* by R.L.Stevenson)

Jerusalem l/c for east/west Jerusalem

jet lag two words

jetliner avoid; write *airliner* or simply *jet*

jet ski two words as noun; note hyphen with verb *to jet-ski*

jeweller, jewellery

jibe avoid this spelling; see **gibe**

jihad (holy war); roman, l/c

jobcentre takes l/c in general sense, but cap as in *Runcorn Jobcentre*

jobseeker's allowance

job titles the general rule is to cap the most senior high-profile jobs at first mention, and thereafter l/c. Thus cap at first mention Archbishop and church titles, senior civil servants, diplomatic and political leaders, civic leaders, Editor (of well-known leading publications), Director-General (of the BBC, CBI etc), Vice-Chancellor and academic titles, Chief Constable and police ranks, military titles, President of a small number of high-profile national institutions (eg, President of the Law Society, the TUC etc) and then – usually – l/c thereafter.

However, *chairman, director, managing director* (of a company), *general secretary* (of a union), *artistic director* (of a theatre) etc are l/c; as are most presidents and chairmen of societies and institutions. A certain amount of discretion is needed in this difficult area

jodhpurs

John le Carré

John o'Groat's

Johns Hopkins University, Baltimore

Joint Chiefs of Staff (US)

Jones, Vinnie (footballer; not Vinny)

Jonsson, Ulrika

joyrider no hyphen, but use as little as possible as the term can give offence; an alternative could be *young car thief*

JP (Justice of the Peace), acceptable alternative for *non-stipendiary magistrate*; see **magistrates' courts**

jubilee strictly a fiftieth anniversary, though Queen Victoria had a golden and a diamond one; so the word can be used as a periodic celebration, especially of royalty. Note *Jubilee Line* (caps) on the London Underground

Judaea (not Judea)

judges' names all circuit judges and below (ie, those in Crown Courts, in county courts, and district judges) must now always include their first name at first mention. Thus, write *Judge Fred Potts* at first mention, subsequently *Judge Potts* or simply *the judge.*

First names will not normally be necessary with High Court judges unless there are two or more with the same surname, where again it will be essential to differentiate.

The failure to identify a judge correctly can lead to complaints, corrections and even the payment of substantial damages.

In the High Court, Mr Justice X should be referred to this way throughout a story (or simply the judge) – never as Judge X. Be careful not to confuse a judge in the Court of Appeal (a Lord Justice of Appeal) with a law lord of the House of Lords, the most senior judges, who are Lords of Appeal in Ordinary (such as Lord Nolan and Lord Hoffmann).

Note designation of Lady Justice Butler-Sloss.

See **Courts** special section (page 1463)

judging by one of the most frequently misused unrelated (or disconnected) participle constructions. Remember, the phrase must have a related subject to follow (I, we, she etc). A convenient alternative is "to judge from ..." (eg, "Judging by this film, the country is in a mess" is wrong; "To judge from this film, the country is in a mess" is correct; so is "Judging by this film, we conclude that the country is in a mess"). See **participles**

judgment (not judgement)

jukebox (no hyphen)

jump-jet hyphen; but note *jumbo jet* (no hyphen)

junior abbreviate to *Jr* (not Jnr) in the American context, eg, John Eisendorf Jr; see **senior**

Justices' Clerks' Society note two apostrophes

juvenile courts no longer exist; they are now called *youth courts.* See **Courts** special section (page 1463)

Kk

k avoid for 1,000 except in direct quotes

kaftan but note *cagoule*

Kant, Immanuel (not Emmanuel)

Karajan, Herbert von; thereafter just Karajan (not von Karajan)

Karpov, Anatoly note also Kasparov, Garry. See **chess names, Russian names**

Kathmandu

Kellogg's Corn Flakes but *cornflakes* (generic)

kerosene (American for paraffin)

Kevorkian, Dr Jack (the American euthanasia doctor; not Kervorkian)

Kfor, the Nato-led force in Kosovo (not KFOR)

Khan Imran Khan and Jemima Khan are happy to be known as Mr Khan and Mrs Khan respectively after first mention. Imran is permissible on its own in headlines. But in most cases, beware of Khan as the family name: it is usually a title given to officials or rulers in Central Asia

Khartoum

Khashoggi, Soraya, Adnan etc

Khmer Rouge (Cambodian faction); note a *Khmer* is a Cambodian

Khrushchev, Nikita

kick-off noun; but note *to kick off*

kick-start hyphenate, noun or verb

killer can be used for *murderer* but do not use *assassin* as a synonym

kilogram (not kilogramme); see **gram, metric**

kilometres per hour correct abbreviation is *km/h* rather than kph

kilowatt-hour correct abbreviation is *kWh*. The cost of generating electricity at a power station is usually expressed in pence per kilowatt-hour (*2.9p/kWh*). See **megawatts**

King's College London apostrophe, no commas

King's Cross, London

King's Lynn, Norfolk

Kings Road, Chelsea (do not use apostrophe)

Kingston upon Hull official name for Hull; normally just use Hull. Note that Humberside no longer exists as a local authority; see **unitary authorities**

Kingston upon Thames no hyphens; use *southwest London* rather than Surrey; but note that Surrey County Council is still based in Kingston. See **postal addresses**

kitchen cabinet l/c *cabinet* in this informal context. See **Cabinet**

Kitemark see **British Standards Institution**

kneejerk (reaction etc); no hyphen, but beware of overuse

knockout noun; but note *to knock out*

knowhow one word as noun

knowledgeable

Knox-Johnston, (Sir) Robin (yachtsman)

Kodak trade name, so cap

Koh-i-noor (diamond)

Koran, the cap and roman, like the Bible

Korean names note all initial caps and no hyphens, eg, Roh Tae Woo

Kosovo, Kosovan do not use Kosova, Kosovar

kowtow no hyphen

Ku Klux Klan no longer use hyphens

KwaZulu/Natal (not Natal/KwaZulu); see **South Africa**

Kyrgyzstan (no longer Kirghizia)

Ll

Labor Day (US); no equivalent in UK so retain US spelling; Anglicise the *Defence Department* etc

Labor Party (Australia)

Labour Party (UK); abbreviate in lists etc to *Lab*. See **Politics** special section (page 1465)

Ladbrokes (betting shop); but *Ladbroke plc*; note also *William Hill* and *Coral* (neither takes final *s*)

lady, ladies prefer *woman, women*

Lafite, Château- see **wines**

Lagos, Nigeria (note Abuja is the capital of Nigeria)

laissez faire no longer use *laisser* version

Lake District do not include *Lake* when the name contains its equivalent; thus Windermere, Derwent Water, but Lake Bassenthwaite

lambast (not lambaste)

lamé use accent to distinguish it from *lame*

lamppost no hyphen

landmine no hyphen

Land Rover no hyphen; similarly *Range Rover*

Land's End

landslide (political); but *landslip* (earth)

languor, languorous (not -our)

laptop (computer), no hyphen; note also *desktop*

largesse (not largess)

last, past *last* should not be used as a synonym of *latest;* "the last few days" means the *final* few days; "the past few days" means the *most recent* few days

Last Post like Reveille, is *sounded* (not played)

Latin be sparing in its use, apart from in the Law Report. When Latin phrases are in common usage, use roman rather than italics, eg, quid pro quo, QED, ex parte injunction, habeas corpus

Latin dancing cap Latin in this and all other contexts, eg, *the Latin language, Latin music, Latin temperament* etc

latitude, longitude write 45° 32'N, 40° 17'W etc

La traviata note l/c *t*

launderette (not laundrette)

Lautro Life Assurance and Unit Trust Regulatory Organisation

law lords, law officers l/c; see **judges**, **Courts** special section (page 1463)

lawnmower one word

Law Report in *The Times,* always initial caps and singular (not Reports); so the style for x-refs is bold, right, eg, **Law Report, page 42**

lay, lie a person *lays* a carpet (transitive verb), but *lies* on a carpet (intransitive). Do not confuse

lay-by but note *layout*

Leader use caps for Leader of the Commons/House of Lords/Opposition; but note l/c *Labour leader, Tory leader* etc

lean, leap past tenses *leant, leapt* (not leaned, leaped)

Lea River but *Lee Valley Regional Park Authority* etc

learnt past tense and past participle of *learn*; note adjective *learned* (as in scholarly)

Lebanon (not the Lebanon, except occasionally in historical context); see **Sudan**

Lebed, Aleksandr call him General Lebed, not Mr

le Carré, John

Lecs local enterprise councils; initial cap only. See **Tecs**

Lee Kuan Yew (of Singapore)

Left, the cap in the political context when referring to a group of like-minded individuals, eg, "The Left added to Tony Blair's worries"; but l/c in "the party swung to the left". When the Left is qualified, keep the adjective l/c, eg, *the hard Left, the far Left*. Also *the left wing, left-wing contenders, leftwingers*. See **Right**

legal aid l/c and never hyphenate, even adjectivally in phrases such as *legal aid cases*. But note *Legal Aid Board*

legal terms in general, use l/c for titles etc except when in full or specific: thus, the Recorder of Liverpool (thereafter *the recorder*), the West London Magistrate, Chelmsford Crown Court, Horseferry Road Magistrates' Court (caps on first mention), etc; but "the court was told", "the judge said", "the magistrate ordered" etc.

The *Bench* is capped only when referring to the judges as a group; a *bench of magistrates* is always l/c. See **magistrates' courts**.

Always cap the *Bar* and the *Inn* (even when used on its own). See **Courts** special section (page 1463)

legendary avoid its clichéd use

legionella, listeria, salmonella note all are bacteria, not viruses

legionnaires' disease

Legion of Honour or **Légion d'honneur** either form is acceptable, according to context

Le Manoir aux Quat' Saisons (restaurant)

Leonardo da Vinci at second mention always Leonardo (never da Vinci)

leper do not use as a metaphor or as an insult

lèse-majesté (treason, or insult to a monarch); note italic and accents

less use *less* for quantity, *fewer* for number; see **fewer**

lesser opposite to *greater* (eg, *the lesser evil*); not to be used as a synonym of *less*

letter bomb hyphenate only in adjectival use

letterbox, postbox no hyphens

leukaemia

Levi's (jeans) should take the apostrophe; but use *Levi Strauss* for the company

liaison, liaise the word *link* is often better. The verb *to liaise* has forced its way into the language; however, use sparingly and only in its correct sense – to establish co-operation, to act as a link with – not as a synonym of *meet* or *talk*

Liberal Democrats *Lib Dems* is an acceptable alternative in either headlines or text; do not shorten to Liberals. Abbreviate in lists etc to *LD*. See **Politics** special section (page 1465)

licence noun, note **license** (verb), *licensee* (noun), *licensed, licensing*. See **practice**

Liechtenstein

lifeguard (on a beach); note *Life Guardsman* (on a horse)

lifelong one word as adjective

liferaft one word; similarly *lifeboat, lifebelt* etc

lifesize(d) no hyphen

lift-off (spacecraft etc); similarly *take-off*

lightning (as in electrical storm); *lightening* (as in making lighter)

light-year

like do not use as a synonym of *such as* (eg, write "cities such as Manchester are ambitious", not "cities like Manchester ..."); nor as a synonym of *as if* (eg, write "he looks as if he is succeeding", not "he looks like he is succeeding")

likeable

lily of the valley

linchpin (not lynchpin)

liner take care with this word, which strictly no longer applies to passenger cruise ships. Liners nowadays are cargo vessels trading regularly between designated ports, eg, container ships. Confine use of *liner* for passenger ships to historical contexts, eg, the transatlantic liner *Queen Mary*

line-up noun; but note verb *to line up*

Lipizzaner horses (do not use Lippizaner)

liquefy (not liquify); but note *to liquidate*

liquorice (not the American licorice)

lira (Italian currency) singular; note the plural *lire*

literally avoid as expression of emphasis: "he literally exploded with anger" is absurd

livery halls (City of London) note no definite article (eg, Drapers' Hall, not the Drapers' Hall); see **London**

living room no hyphen as *dining room* etc

Livingstone, Ken, Dr David Livingstone (explorer), but *Livingston*, West Lothian

Livorno, rather than *Leghorn*, despite usual style of Anglicising foreign names

Lloyds TSB, the bank, but **Lloyd's of London** (insurance)

Lloyd's names (not Names)

Lloyd-Webber use hyphen for Lord L-W, but no hyphen for brother Julian

loan noun (ie, never say "I loaned him £20" etc); the verb is *lend/lent*

loathe (verb); note the adjective *loath* (not loth)

local government cap councils when full title, eg, Watford Borough Council, Newtown District Council (thereafter the council); but l/c when title is not in full, eg, Watford council; use l/c for all council committees; cap Mayor at first mention (eg, Albert Hobart, Mayor of Rochdale), l/c for council officials such as *borough surveyor, town clerk;* cap the seat of local government if we are sure of its title (eg, Leeds City Hall, Birmingham Council House – not to be confused with Birmingham Town Hall – Lambeth Town Hall)

lochs (Scotland); note *loughs* (Ireland)

Lockerbie suspects the two accused are Abdul Baset Ali al-Megrahi (after first mention, al-Megrahi); and Lamin Khalifa Fhimah (thereafter Fhimah)

lockout (in industrial disputes etc), one word; but *to lock out*

locomotive names italicise, as with ships' or aircraft names, eg, *Mallard*. Do not use *the* unless certain it is part of the name. See **aircraft names, ships**

London cap the *East End* and the *West End* of London, and now also *North London, South London, East London* and *West London, Central London, Inner London;* but l/c *southeast London, southwest London* etc. The local council for the City of London is the Court of Common Council, whose members are common councilmen; cap Borough in titles of particular boroughs, eg, London Borough of Bromley; see **livery halls**

London Clinic, The cap *T*

London clubs note particularly *the Athenaeum; Boodle's; Brooks's; Buck's Club; Pratt's Club; the Queen's Club; Royal Over-Seas League; Savile Club; Travellers Club; United Oxford and Cambridge University Club; White's Club.* It would be wrong to say, eg, Boodle's Club; on the other hand, it is permissible to refer to the Garrick Club, the Reform Club, the Savage Club etc simply as the Garrick, the Reform or the Savage

Londonderry see **Ireland**

London hotels, restaurants as with London clubs, it is essential to give the correct form of the following: *Berkeley Hotel; Brown's Hotel; Claridge's; the Dorchester; Four Seasons hotel; Grosvenor House; Hilton International Kensington; Hyatt Carlton Tower hotel; Hyde Park Hotel; The Lanesborough; Langham Hilton; Le Meridien Piccadilly; London Hilton on Park Lane; Marriott Hotel; New Connaught Rooms; Park Lane Hotel; Quaglino's; Ritz Hotel; Savoy Hotel; Simpson's-in-the-Strand; Waldorf Hotel; Westmoreland Hotel*

London Zoo cap *Zoo*

Longchamp (French racecourse; not Longchamps)

longstanding no longer use hyphen

lookout noun, no hyphen

Lord Advocate do not add *for Scotland*

Lord Chancellor's Department caps, and not Lord Chancellor's Office

lord-lieutenant should be hyphenated, according to the Association of Lord-Lieutenants (note this plural, not lords-lieutenant); use l/c in general use, but the Lord-Lieutenant of Gloucestershire etc (when specific)

Lord Mayor caps, as in Lord Mayor of London, Birmingham etc; thereafter *the lord mayor;* the same applies to Mayor of Guildford etc

Lord's (cricket ground)

lords justices both words take the plural

lorry prefer *lorry* to the American *truck*, but truck has become ubiquitous and cannot be banned, especially from foreign stories

loss-maker, loss-making

loveable note the middle *e*; similarly *likeable*

lowbrow similarly *highbrow*

Lower House, Upper House (of Parliament); see **Politics** special section (page 1465)

low-key

loyalist see **Ireland**

Ltd can usually be dropped from company names (as can plc)

lullaby (not -bye)

lumbar as in the lower back (eg, *lumbar puncture*); note *lumber* as in junk furniture, lumberjacks, or (verbally) moving clumsily about etc

Lusta (not Lusa), in Skye, often quoted as the wettest place in the UK

Luton airport note l/c airport; resist pressure to insert *international*. See **airports**

Luxembourg (not -burg); the inhabitants should be called Mr, Mrs etc, rather than M or Mme (see **foreign appellations**, and **Santer**); but note *Rosa Luxemburg* (leader of Berlin uprising in 1919)

Lycra proprietary term, so cap

Lyons (not Lyon); see **Marseilles, foreign places**

-lyse the style is *analyse, paralyse* etc (not -ize); see **-ise, -isation**

Lytham St Anne's, Lancashire (note apostrophe, but no hyphens)

Lyttelton Theatre (at the National); similarly, Humphrey Lyttelton (jazz musician)

Mm

M1 (do not write M1 motorway)
Maastricht treaty l/c *treaty*, but note *Treaty of Maastricht*; for an unofficial name for the updated version of the treaty, write *Maastricht II* (not 2 or Two). See **inter-governmental conference**
Mac, Mc always check spelling of these prefixes in *Who's Who;* in alphabetical lists, treat Mc as Mac
Macau (not Macao)
McCarthy, Senator Joseph note *McCarthyism*
McCartney, (Sir) Paul
MacDonald, Ramsay
McDonald, Trevor (newsreader)
McDonald's (hamburger chain)
McDonnell Douglas no hyphen
MacDowell, Andie
Macedonia the correct (and politically sensitive) title of the new republic is the Former Yugoslav Republic of Macedonia (caps as shown). See **Yugoslav**
Machiavelli(an)
machinegun but note *sub-machinegun*
mackintosh (raincoat)
Mackintosh, (Sir) Cameron
MacLaine, Shirley
MacLean, Donald
McLuhan, Marshall
Macmillan, Harold same spelling for the publishers
Macpherson, Elle
macroeconomic, microeconomic no hyphen
Macy's (New York store)
Madame Tussaud's
"mad cow" disease see **BSE**, **Creutzfeldt-Jakob disease**
Madejski Stadium, Reading (not Madjeski)
Madison Square Garden, New York (not Gardens)
maestros (not maestri); plural of *maestro*
Mafia cap only in Italian or US context; l/c *mafia* in countries such as Russia when used as a synonym of gangsters
Mafikeng, the new name (since 1980) of Mafeking. Spell according to historical context
Magdalen College, Oxford; but note *Magdalene College*, Cambridge. See **Oxford University**, **Cambridge University**
Maghreb see **Middle East**
magistrates' courts caps for *the Metropolitan Magistrate, West London Magistrate* etc, but usually magistrates take l/c. An acceptable alternative for a non-stipendiary (ie, lay) magistrate is JP (Justice of the Peace). When the accused is appearing before the bench, he appears before the magistrates (plural) unless a stipendiary magistrate, who usually sits on his own. The full name of the court is capped, as in *Bow Street Magistrates' Court*. See **courts**, **legal terms**, **Courts** special section (page 1463)
Magna Carta (not *the* Magna Carta)
MAID (not Maid); now renamed Dialog Corporation
mailshot
major do not use as a lazy alternative for *big, chief, important* or *main*
Majorca, Minorca use the Anglicised forms. See **Spanish regions**
majority of do not use as alternative for *most of*
makeover one word as noun; but try to avoid this cliché – use *remodelling* instead
make-up (cosmetics or typography; not makeup)
Malaysia Datuk Seri Dr Mahathir Mohamad, the Prime Minister; thereafter Dr Mahathir
Mall, The note cap *T*
management buyout spell out first time, though MBO is acceptable on Business pages
manifestos (not -oes)
Manila (capital of the Philippines)
manoeuvre, manoeuvring, manoeuvrable
mantelpiece (not mantlepiece)
manuscript(s) write out when part of a sentence, but abbreviate to MSS when quotation from catalogue, or in headline if context is clear
Mao Zedong (no longer Mao Tse-tung); see **Chinese names**
marathon avoid in clichéd sense of *a long time* as in "a marathon session"
march past noun; two words in military context
Mardi Gras, the Shrove Tuesday festival; but note the self-styled *Mardi Gra bomber*
Margrethe, Queen of Denmark (not Margarethe)
Marines cap in both *Royal Marines* and *US Marines;* note also *a Marine*
marketplace one word; but note *market-maker*
Marks & Spencer use the ampersand rather than *and* in text; can abbreviate to M&S in headlines; the formal legal title is *Marks and Spencer plc*, but this form is used only rarely
marquess (not marquis, except in foreign titles). See **Titles** special section (page 1467)
Marrakesh (not Marrakech)
married couple's allowance
Marseilles (not Marseille); call the football club *Marseilles* (not Olympique de Marseille)
Martini trade name, so cap
Marxist, Marxism derived from Karl Marx, so cap. Do not use as loose variant of communism; see **communism**
Mary Celeste (not *Marie Celeste*)
Mass cap in its religious context; note also *Holy Mass* and *Requiem Mass*. See **Churches** special section (page 1462)
Massachusetts
massive avoid as a synonym of *big*
MasterCard
masterclass (musical etc); no hyphen
master of foxhounds l/c; see **foxhunt**
Master of the Queen's Music
Master of the Rolls see **Courts** special section (page 1463)
Matabele singular and plural – *a Matabele, the Matabele*
materialise avoid as a synonym of *appear, come about* or *happen*
mathematics spell out in text, though maths acceptable in direct quotes and headlines
Mathews, Meg (married to Noel Gallagher)
matinee no accent; similarly *premiere, debut, decor* etc. See **Arts** special section (page 1461)
matins l/c; see **evensong**, **Christian terms**
Maupassant, Guy de
Mauretania (liner); note **Mauritania** (country)
may/might do not confuse; use *might* in sentences referring to past possibilities that did not happen, eg, "If that had happened ten days ago, my whole life might have been different". A clear distinction is evident in the following: "He might have been captured by the Iraqis – but he wasn't",

compared with "He may have been captured by the Iraqis – it is possible but we don't know"

Maya, one of the Indian people of Central America; *Mayas*, plural; and *Mayan*, adjective

mayday (SOS call) l/c; but note *May Day* (holiday)

Mayfair but note *May Fair Hotel*

mayor for when to cap, see **local government**, **Lord Mayor**

Maze prison, Northern Ireland use Long Kesh only in historical context

MCC do not write *the MCC*. See **Sports** special section (page 1466)

mealtimes write *breakfast time, lunchtime, teatime, dinner time, supper time* (but use hyphens in compounds when adjectival)

means-test, means-tested etc (hyphenate whether as noun, verb or adjective)

means to an end singular; but note "his means *are* modest"

Médecins sans Frontières

media plural as in *mass media*; but note *mediums* (spiritualists)

medical officer of health MoH acceptable in headlines

medical terms never use these (*geriatric, paralytic, schizophrenic* etc) metaphorically or as terms of abuse.

In words ending in *-tomy* (*appendectomy, hysterectomy* etc), the word "operation" is tautologous and must not be used. See also **bacteria**, **X-ray**

medieval (not mediaeval)

Mediterranean

meet never use *meet with*

mega- be very sparing with this as a colloquial prefix meaning *big*

megawatts the capacity of a power station is measured in *megawatts*; the output is measured in *megawatt hours*. The correct abbreviation of megawatt is *MW* (not mW, which means milliwatt). See **kilowatt-hour**

mêlée

Member of Parliament cap *Member*, but MP almost always preferable

mementoes (not -os)

memoirs (not memoires)

memorandum plural *memorandums* (not -a)

meningitis distinguish whether bacterial or viral; the headline cases are usually bacterial

Mercedes-Benz hyphen

Merchant Navy caps

Merchant Taylors' School, Middlesex and Liverpool

Merthyr Tydfil (South Wales unitary authority) never shorten to Merthyr, which is a village in Carmarthenshire. See **unitary authorities**

Messerschmitt (not -schmidt)

mete out (in context of punishment; not meet out)

metres (as in distance, poetry etc); note *meters* (as in gas, electricity or parking etc)

metric in general non-scientific contexts continue to use the non-metric forms (miles rather than kilometres, pounds rather than kilograms, pints rather than litres). In sporting, foreign, engineering and scientific stories it will often be better to use the metric.

However, with petrol and fuel now sold in litres rather than gallons, it will be essential to give both measurements, eg, 55p a litre (£2.50 per gallon). For the foreseeable future, continue to give fuel consumption in miles per gallon, but also metric conversion in brackets at first mention.

With foodstuffs, such as cheese, prefer the metric first with the imperial conversion where practicable, though a conversion every time in a long list is unnecessary

Metropolitan Police see **Commissioner**; note also *Metropolitan Magistrate* (see **magistrates' courts**)

Michelangelo

microchip

microgram do not abbreviate, and certainly not to mcg, meaningless under international scientific standard abbreviations. The l/c *m* stands for *milli-* as a prefix. So *mg* is correct for *milligram*

mid-air hyphenate, noun or adjective

midday, midweek no hyphens

Middle Ages, the caps

Middle East comprises Bahrain, Cyprus, Egypt, Iran, Iraq, Israel, Jordan, Kuwait, Lebanon, Oman, Qatar, Saudi Arabia, Sudan, Syria, Turkey, United Arab Emirates, Yemen. In a general sense, it also takes in the countries of the Maghreb: Algeria, Libya, Mauritania, Morocco, Tunisia, Western Sahara. Never abbreviate to the Americanism Mideast

Middle England caps, in political context

Middlesbrough

Middlesex no longer a county. See **postal addresses**

Mideast unacceptable as abbreviation of Middle East

Mid Glamorgan no longer exists as a local government authority, but name persists in some organisations' titles, eg, Mid Glamorgan Tec. Note no hyphen. See **unitary authorities**

Midland Bank no longer exists as a trading entity. It is now part of *HSBC*, so use *Midland* only in historical contexts. See **Hong Kong**

midlife crisis but do not overuse this cliché

midnight (not 12 midnight); see **noon**

midsummer, midwinter

Midwest (US)

MiG (former Soviet aircraft)

migrant do not use in place of *emigrant* or *immigrant*. It means one who is in the process of migrating

mileage

military ranks use hyphens in compounds such as *Major-General, Lieutenant-Colonel* etc (where two ranks are joined), but not with *Second Lieutenant, Lance Corporal, Air Commodore* etc. Do not abbreviate ranks except in lists. See **Armed Forces** special section (page 1459)

militate (against or in favour of); do not confuse with *mitigate*

millennium common usage says that the millennium ends on December 31, 1999, though technically it should be December 31, 2000. We should accept the former. Note caps for *the Millennium Dome* (thereafter *the Dome*), *Millennium Fund, Millennium Commission, Millennium Exhibition*. Also *Millennium Eve* (as New Year's Eve). The plural of millennium is *millennia* (unlike *memorandums* etc; see **referendum**). Note also *millenarian* (only one middle *n*) meaning of, or related to, the millennium

millions write out millions from one to ten, thereafter 11 million etc. Abbreviate to *m* only for headlines. For currencies, spell out in text, eg, £15 million, but abbreviate to £15m in headlines. With decimal notations, best to restrict to two decimal points in text, rounded up or down (eg, £1.53 million), though in headlines try to avoid decimals altogether. In text, write 2.5 million rather than two and a half million; but "three million shares changed hands" (not 3 million shares) etc

MIND the mental health charity wishes to be known thus; see **SANE**, **initials**

mind-set prefer *mentality* to this cliché

minimal do not use as a synonym of *small;* it means smallest, or the least possible in size, duration etc

miniskirt no hyphen; note also *minicab*

ministers (political) cap all ministers, whether in the Cabinet or not. The same applies to ministers in overseas governments: give name and full title (capped) first time, thereafter name or just *the minister*. See **Politics** special section (page 1465)

Minnelli, Liza

minuscule (not miniscule). Originally, a medieval script. Use sparingly, as it is heavily overworked as a synonym of *very small* or *unimportant*

Mishcon de Reya (solicitors); note l/c *de*

mis-hit hyphen; similarly *mis-sell*; but note *misspell*

Miss, Ms Ms is nowadays fully acceptable when a woman (married or unmarried) wants to be called thus, or when it is not known for certain if she is Mrs or Miss. Ms is increasingly common in American contexts. See **appellations**

missing do not say *gone/went missing*, prefer *disappeared* or *vanished*

Mississippi

misspell no hyphen; see **spelt**

mitigate means to *make milder, moderating* (as in mitigating circumstances in a law case); do not confuse with *militate*

Mitterrand, François (late French President)

MoD acceptable abbreviation for *Ministry of Defence*, especially in headlines

Moët et Chandon

Mogul (not Mughal); as in empire and art

Mohammed see **Muhammad**

Moldova (no longer Moldavia)

Mona Lisa (not Monna Lisa)

monarch, the l/c for the British monarch; but note *the Sovereign, the Crown*. See **Royal Family**

Mönchengladbach (no hyphen)

Monetary Policy Committee (of the Bank of England); note caps; use MPC at subsequent mentions

moneys plural of money, but *money* will usually serve. Note also *moneyed* (not monied)

Mongol, Mongolian (race); never refer to a Down's syndrome sufferer as a mongol

Monopolies and Mergers Commission (MMC) is now renamed the *Competition Commission*. Refer to the *MMC* now only in historical context

Montagu of Beaulieu, Lord

Montenegrin is the adjective from Montenegro (not Montenegran)

months abbreviate (only in lists or listings) as follows: Jan, Feb, March, April, May, June, July, Aug, Sept, Oct, Nov, Dec

Moon cap in planetary context, otherwise l/c. See **Earth**, **Sun**, **Universe**

more than rather than *over* with numbers, eg, "more than 2,500 people attended the rally", not "over 2,500 ..."

Moreton-in-Marsh (not Morton, nor -in-the-)

MORI must cap

Morrell, Lady Ottoline (not Otteline)

morris dancing/dancers

Morse code

mortar do not use by itself when the meaning is *mortar bomb*; the mortar is the launcher from which the shell is fired. But *mortar attack* is perfectly correct

mosquitoes (not -os as plural)

most favoured nation status

MoT certificate, test; but note otherwise *the Department of Transport*, or *Transport Department* (not Ministry of ...)

Mother Teresa (not Theresa)

Mother's Day, or Mothering Sunday (not Mothers')

motocross (not motorcross)

motorcade acceptable for a procession of vehicles

motorcycle, motorcyclist, motorbike etc

motoring terms the following terms are appearing increasingly in the Saturday motoring pages and should be standardised: *carburettor, wheelspin, four-wheel drive* (shorten to *4WD*), but *a four-wheel-drive vehicle* (two hyphens when adjectival), *power steering, anti-lock brakes, 3-litre car, 1.9 diesel* (hyphenated when adjectival), *four-door, hatchback, four-star petrol, E-type Jaguar, Mercedes-Benz E-class* etc, *airbag, seatbelt, numberplate, sports car.*

For the foreseeable future, continue to give fuel consumption figures in miles per gallon, but also give the metric conversion in brackets at first mention. See **metric**

motor neurone disease (not neuron)

moveable keep middle *e*

movies although an Americanism, is now so common as to be an acceptable synonym of *films;* but use *films* whenever possible

MP, QC use commas each side after name. Note the plural MPs (never MP's). See **Member of Parliament, Politics** special section (page 1465), **Courts** special section (page 1463)

Mr, Mrs, Miss, Ms see **appellations**

mugging strictly means theft by violence in the open air. Take care not to overuse

Muhammad use this spelling for the Prophet, but respect the other spellings of the name according to individuals' preference; if in doubt, use Muhammad. Note also *Muhammad Ali;* but *King Mohammed VI* of Morocco; see **names**

Muhammad al-Masari (Saudi dissident); then Dr Masari

Mujahidin (fighters in a jihad or holy war); note cap

multi incline towards making *multi* compounds one word wherever possible, whether used as a noun or as an adjective, eg, *multimillionaire, multinational, multilateral, multimedia, multiracial, multispeed, multistorey, multitrack* (and note *multispeed, multitrack Europe*). However, hyphenate when two vowels come together, eg, multi-ethnic

multimillion-pound, multimillion-dollar as in deal etc

mum see **dad**

Murdoch, Elisabeth refer to her as Ms Murdoch at subsequent mentions

Murdoch, Rupert at first mention he should be described as "chairman and chief executive of The News Corporation, parent company of *The Times*"

musical vocabulary
- **a** *song titles* (classical or pop), *album titles, operas* (including arias) take italics
- **b** *symphonies* take roman, caps, eg, Symphony No 3, but where symphonies have numbers and popular alternative titles, use italics, eg, *Eroica*
- **c** *concertos* take roman, caps, eg, First Violin Concerto. For fuller list, see **Arts** special section (page 1461)

music-hall

Muslim (not Moslem or Mohamedan); see **Islam**, **Muhammad**

Muzak proprietary term, so cap

Myanmar continue to call the country Burma

mynah bird prefer to mina, myna

Nn

Naafi the Navy, Army and Air Force Institutes; commonly used to describe the canteen for Service personnel run by the Naafi

Nafta North American Free Trade Agreement (not Area or Association)

naive, naivety (no diaeresis)

names as a general rule, people are entitled to be known as they wish to be known, provided their identities are clear. Thus Cassius Clay became Muhammad Ali; but in such changes, give both names until the new one is widely known. Note *Lloyd's names* (l/c). See **appellations, Lloyd's**

names starting stories cap both names, eg, "GORDON BROWN said last night ..." Where the name is too long to contain in the first line, reconstruct the sentence to place the name away from the start

narcotics take care to use this word correctly; see **drugs**

Nasa National Aeronautics and Space Administration (US); rarely necessary to spell out

national avoid as a synonym of *citizen,* as in *a French national*

National Air Traffic Services (caps and note plural), or the air traffic control service (informal alternative, l/c)

national anthem l/c

National Association of Schoolmasters and Union of Women Teachers full title, then abbreviate to NASUWT (no slash)

national curriculum l/c

National Health Service abbreviate to the NHS, or the health service (NHS is acceptable in headlines)

national insurance l/c, like other taxes

National Lottery caps, but usually l/c the lottery at subsequent mentions unless context unclear. Note *National Lottery Charities Board.* See **rollover**

National Parks cap, in both specific names and in general (eg, *Snowdonia National Park*; and "the policy applies particularly to National Parks")

National Rivers Authority (not River)

National Service caps

National Theatre caps; generally omit Royal. See **Lyttelton**

nationalist l/c except when referring to name of a political party. Thus *Scottish National Party* (SNP), and *Scottish Nationalists.* In Irish contexts, again l/c. See **Ireland**

nationwide no hyphen, but use sparingly as it borders on being a cliché; prefer *national* or *nationally.* See **wide**

Native American cap the N when referring to American Indians

Nato (never NATO)

NatWest acceptable abbreviation for National Westminster Bank in text or headlines

naught as in *come to naught* (not nought)

nave (central space in a church); journalists who misspell the word are *knaves*

navy, naval the Royal Navy at first mention (thereafter *the Navy,* capped); the Merchant Navy, the US Navy, the Brazilian Navy etc (thereafter *the navy,* l/c); *naval* is l/c except in titles such as Royal Naval Volunteer Reserve (RNVR) etc. See **officers, ships, warships, Armed Forces** special section (page 1459)

Nazi, Nazism caps; see **communist**

Neanderthal (not -tal); note cap

nearby, near by the first is adjectival, eg, "the nearby school was convenient"; the second is adverbial, eg, "he sat on a bench near by"

nearly one in three ... is prefer singular to plural *are* in these constructions. See **one**

Neighbourhood Watch

Neill Committee on Standards in Public Life (headed by Lord Neill of Bladen); caps for full title

neither takes a singular verb, eg, "neither Bert nor Fred has any idea". Do not use "neither ... or" (must use nor). See **none**

nerve-racking (not -wracking); see **racked, wrack**

Nestlé

Netanyahu, Binyamin (Israeli politician; not Benjamin)

Net Book Agreement caps

Netherlands, The no longer interchangeable with Holland (see **Holland**)

Network SouthEast no longer exists

nevertheless one word; similarly *nonetheless*

new frequently redundant; always omit in "setting a *new* record"

New Age travellers no quotes; see **Gypsy**

newborn (as in babies); no hyphen

Newcastle upon Tyne, Newcastle-under-Lyme

New Deal caps for Labour's welfare programme; quotes at first mention if appropriate

newfound (no hyphen)

Newhaven, East Sussex but note *New Haven,* Connecticut

new Labour l/c *n,* quotes not usually necessary, except when the writer or speaker is making a particular, perhaps ironic, point. But keep caps in slogans such as *New Labour, New Danger.* See **Politics** special section (page 1465)

newscaster prefer *newsreader*

News International Rupert Murdoch is chairman and chief executive of The News Corporation (second mention, News Corp). News Corp can be described as "parent company of *The Times*".

A subsidiary of News Corp is News International, a British company that owns Times Newspapers Holdings. The operating subsidiary of Times Newspapers Holdings is Times Newspapers Ltd, publisher of *The Times* and *The Sunday Times.* Times Supplements Ltd publishes the supplements – *The Times Educational Supplement, The Times Higher Education Supplement, The Times Literary Supplement* and *Nursery World* – and is a subsidiary of News International plc.

Times Newspapers Holdings is chaired by Mr Murdoch (the vice-chairman is Sir Edward Pickering) and the board includes the independent national directors of *The Times* and *The Sunday Times.* It is thus the controlling company.

News Group Newspapers, another operating subsidiary of News International, is the publisher of *The Sun* and *News of the World.*

News Ltd is the Australian arm of News Corp.

Mr Murdoch does not "own" any of these companies, though his family is the largest single (though not majority) shareholder in News Corp. See **BSkyB, Murdoch, *The Times***

newspapers/journals use italics for titles and include *The* in the title whenever appropriate. The lists that follow (source, *Willings Press Guide 1994*), though not exhaustive, should cover the most usual:

a With *The* in the masthead: *The Times, The Sunday Times, The Sun, The Mirror* (formerly *Daily Mirror*), *The Guardian, The Independent, The Daily Telegraph, The Sunday Telegraph, The Express* (formerly *Daily Express*), *The Express on Saturday, The Observer, The Mail on Sunday, The European, The Scotsman, The Herald* (formerly *The Glasgow Herald*), *The Birmingham Post, The Journal* (Newcastle), *The Northern Echo, The Irish Times, The Spectator, The Economist, The Lancet, The Sporting Life, The Big Issue*

b Without *The* in the masthead: *News of the World, Financial*

Times, Daily Mail, Daily Star, Daily Sport, Sunday Sport, Sunday Mirror, Sunday Express, Sunday People, Evening Standard, Independent on Sunday, Scotland on Sunday, Yorkshire Post, Daily Post (Liverpool), *Manchester Evening News, Western Daily Press* (Bristol), *Western Mail* (Cardiff), *Western Morning News* (Plymouth), *Evening Argus* (Brighton), *Evening Mail* (Birmingham), *Sunday Herald* (Glasgow), *Express & Star* (Wolverhampton), *Telegraph & Argus* (Bradford), *Oxford Mail, Sunday Independent* (Dublin), *New Statesman & Society* (although just *New Statesman* is usually acceptable), *British Medical Journal* (the *BMJ*), *Jewish Chronicle, Which?, Which Car?* etc, *Racing Post*

c **Abroad** *The Boston Globe; Chicago Tribune; Los Angeles Times; The Miami Herald; The New York Times; New York Daily News; New York Post; The New Yorker; The Washington Post; USA Today; The Wall Street Journal; International Herald Tribune; The Globe and Mail* (Toronto); *Bild am Sonntag; Stern; Der Spiegel; Die Welt; Izvestia; The Times of India; El País; Le Monde; Le Figaro; L'Espresso* (Italy); *Corriere della Sera; Far Eastern Economic Review; South China Morning Post; The Straits Times* (Singapore); *New Straits Times* (Malaysia); *The Australian; The Sydney Morning Herald; The Jerusalem Post*

d When the journal's name is used adjectivally, omit *The*, eg, "the *Times* reporter was attacked ..."

e Always properly attribute material from another newspaper: never say "a report in another newspaper ..." but "a report in *The Guardian* ..." etc. However, the general phrases *media reports* or *press reports* are acceptable when material has been widely disseminated

New Year Honours or **New Year's Honours List** caps; note also caps for *the Queen's Birthday Honours*. See **honours**

New Year's Day, New Year's Eve but note **the new year** and **Chinese new year**

New York City, New York State caps, usually *New York* is sufficient for the city; *upstate New York* is permissible. Normally, l/c *state* in contexts such as *the state of Virginia*, but see **Washington**

New Zealand (never NZ, even in headlines)

Nicolson, (Sir) Harold but note *Jack Nicholson* (actor)

Nietzsche

nightclub

nightmare use only in its proper sense of an unpleasant dream, not as a lazy cliché for something that goes wrong

night-time hyphen; but note *daytime* (one word)

Nikkei average

Nissan (cars); but note *Nissen hut*

No 10, or **10 Downing Street** (not Number 10 or Downing St); see **Downing Street, Politics** special section (page 1465)

no-fly zone

no man's land

no one two words, no hyphen

"no" vote, "yes" vote

"no win, no fee" (legislation/agreement etc); see **Courts** special section (page 1463)

Nobel Prize for Literature, Medicine etc; or *Nobel Peace/Literature Prize*; but note l/c for *Nobel prize* (unspecific), *Nobel prizewinner* (but *Nobel Prize-winning author*), *Nobel laureate*

nonagenarian (not nono-)

nonconformist but note *the Nonconformist Church* and *Nonconformist churches* (buildings); see **Churches** special section (page 1462)

non-cooperation see **co-operate**

none almost always takes the singular verb, eg, "none is available at present". But occasionally a plural is permissible, eg, "None are better singers than the Welsh" or "none of them have done their best" (where the inelegant alternative would be "none of them has done his or her best"). See **neither**

nonetheless one word

non-existent

non-profitmaking

noon (not 12 noon, 12am or 12pm). See **midnight**

normalcy avoid; use *normality* instead

north, northeast, northern for when to cap, see **compass points**

Northern Ireland see **Ireland**

Northumberland (county); Northumbria is a health, police or tourist authority

North York Moors (not North Yorkshire Moors); see **Yorkshire**

notable (no middle *e*)

Note cap in the diplomatic sense

not only ... followed by *but* (and usually) *also*; often better to say simply *both ... and*

nuclear terms should be used with precision. Take special care not to confuse *fission* and *fusion*

numberplate (on vehicles etc); one word; see **motoring terms**

numbers write from one to ten in full, 11 upwards as numerals except when they are approximations, eg, "about thirty people turned up". Keep consistency within a sentence: write "the number injured rose from eight to fourteen", and do not mix fractions and decimals. At the start of a sentence, write all numbers in full.
ordinals: write out up to hundredth, then 101st, 122nd etc, except with names such as 42nd Street, 38th parallel etc. See **birthday, millions, currencies, fractions**

Nuremberg (not -burg)

Nursing, Royal College of (not Nurses)

NVQ national vocational qualification; note l/c when spelt out

Oo

oblivious of means *forgetful of, unaware of*. It does not mean ignorant or uncomprehending

O'Brien, Conor Cruise, likewise **Edna**

obscenities "four-letter words" and profanities should be avoided. However, in direct quotes and where they are essential to the story, style obscenities with asterisks: f***, c*** etc

occupied territories, the all l/c

occurred (not occured)

o'clock see **times**

octogenarian

octopuses plural of octopus (not octopi)

Oder-Neisse Line (boundary between Poland and Germany)

Odone, Cristina (not Christina), journalist

OECD Organisation for Economic Co-operation and Development

of avoid expressions such as "all of the people attending", "half of the children replied"; say simply "all the people", "half the children" etc

of all time do not use this phrase, as in "best golfer of all time", in any circumstances

offbeat no hyphen

Office for National Statistics (no longer the Central Statistical Office)

Office for Standards in Education, but *Ofsted* usually sufficient on its own. See **regulators**

officers (naval and military); do not describe ratings or NCOs as *officers*, especially in headlines and captions. See **Armed Forces** special section (page 1459)

oil-drilling, oil-fired, oil-slick, oil-tanker but note *oildrum, oilfield, oilrig* and *oil platform*. See **Brent Spar**

OK rather than *okay*

Old Etonian, Old Harrovian etc

Old Masters caps to avoid confusion

Olivier, Laurence (not Lawrence), the late Lord Olivier

Olympics can be used as a short form of *the Olympic Games*. Similarly, *the Games* (always capped) can be used. Always cap Olympics and Olympic even when used adjectivally, eg, *an Olympic athlete*. Note *International Olympic Committee* (no final *s* on Olympic)

ombudsman, ombudswoman keep l/c in general context, eg, "he referred the matter to the ombudsman"; but cap for specifics, as in *the Banking Ombudsman, the Legal Services Ombudsman*, and even the unofficial title of *Parliamentary Ombudsman* (the Parliamentary Commissioner for Administration). Do not confuse the Parliamentary Ombudsman with the Parliamentary Commissioner for Standards, an entirely separate post

on behalf of frequently misused phrase. It means *in the interest of* (a person etc) or *as representative of* (eg, "acting on behalf of his client" is correct). It must not be used as a verbose way of saying *by*; eg, "the book betrays a lack of understanding on behalf of the author" is wrong

ONdigital

one use the singular verb in structures such as "one in three says that ..." See **nearly.** In first-person pieces, try to avoid the use of *one* as a synonym of *I*

One Nation Tories, One Nation politicians etc note cap *O* and cap *N*

one-time do not use as synonym of *former* as in "one-time chairman" etc

One 2 One the mobile phone company (note spaces)

ongoing avoid this ugly adjective; use *continuing* if necessary

online one word in computer context

only take great care to place *only* before the word or phrase it qualifies; "she *only* touched the key, but did not press it; she touched *only* the key, not the switch; she touched the *only* key". Similarly, "he only played cricket" is wrong; "he played only cricket" is correct

on to unlike *into,* two words usually better than one, as in "she moved on to better things", though "he collapsed onto the floor" is acceptable. As a general rule, use *onto* as little as possible

Opec the Organisation of Petroleum Exporting Countries

opencast mining

open-heart surgery note also *open-door policy* (if this overworked phrase has to be used); *open-plan living room*

operations see **medical terms**

ophthalmologist, ophthalmic etc (not opthalmic)

Opposition the same cap or l/c rules apply as to Government – cap as a noun but generally l/c as adjective; eg, "He accused the Opposition of lying", but "He said it was an opposition lie". See **Politics** special section (page 1465)

or need not be preceded by *either,* though it is strengthened thereby if two options are mentioned. Usually avoid a comma before it

oral do not confuse with *verbal*; *oral* means pertaining to the mouth, often in the spoken context (eg, *the oral tradition, by word of mouth*); *verbal* means pertaining to words (contrasted with, eg, physical or choral). See **verbal**

Orders in Council are *approved*, not signed, by the Queen

ordinals see **numbers**

Ordnance Survey note *ordnance* in military contexts; but *ordinance* as in regulations

Orient, the wherever possible, use *the East*. The adjective is l/c *oriental*. The East London football club is *Leyton Orient*

orientate, orientation prefer to *orient, oriented* etc. See **disorientate**

Orkney, or **the Orkney Islands** (not the Orkneys); see **Shetland**

Oscar Award(s), or **the Oscars** registered trademarks, so cap

OSCE the Organisation for Security and Co-operation in Europe, has replaced the former CSCE (Conference on Security and Co-operation in Europe)

Ouija board proprietary term, so cap

-out suffixes in nouns, generally join up rather than hyphenate, as in *fallout, knockout, printout, callout, dropout, bailout* etc; but note *to fall out* etc

Outback, the (Australia)

outdoor adjective; but note *the outdoors*

outpatients, inpatients no hyphen

OutRage! (homosexual "outing" group)

outside (never *outside of*)

Outward Bound must be used only when specifically referring to the work or courses of the Outward Bound Trust Ltd, and never in general use in phrases such as *outward bound-style activities*. Use alternatives such as *outdoor pursuits, adventure training, outdoor adventure courses* etc. Outward Bound's lawyers pounce on every perceived infringement of its service mark. Take care

over do not use as a synonym of *more than* when followed by a number, eg, "she waited over four hours for the train" should be "... more than four hours ..."; "there were over 60 victims" should be "... more than 60 ...". See **more than**

over as prefix wherever the word does not look too ugly, dispense with the hyphen, even when this leads to a double *r* in the middle: *overcapacity, overestimate, overreact, override, overrule, overuse, overvalue*; an obvious exception where the hyphen is essential is *over-age*

overall one word as adjective, but use sparingly

overly do not use as an alternative for *over* or *too*

Overseas Development Administration (not Agency)

owing to see **due to**

Oxbridge be sparing in using the term as a "catch-all" for Oxford and Cambridge Universities

Oxford University colleges and halls are: All Souls College; Balliol College; Blackfriars; Brasenose College; Campion Hall; Christ Church; Corpus Christi College; Exeter College; Green College; Greyfriars; Harris Manchester College; Hertford College; Jesus College; Keble College; Kellogg College; Lady Margaret Hall; Linacre College; Lincoln College; Magdalen College; Mansfield College; Merton College; New College; Nuffield College; Oriel College; Pembroke College; The Queen's College; Regent's Park College; St Anne's College; St Antony's College; St Benet's Hall; St Catherine's College; St Cross College; St Edmund Hall; St Hilda's College; St Hugh's College; St John's College; St Peter's College; Somerville College; Templeton College; Trinity College; University College; Wadham College; Wolfson College; Worcester College

Pp

p's and q's see **apostrophes**

Pacific Rim, South Pacific, North Pacific etc

page 1, page 3, page 187 etc but note *a Page 3 Girl*

paintings titles in italic. See **Arts** special section (page 1461)

Pakistani use both for the people of Pakistan and adjectivally, eg, *Pakistani culture*

palace cap in full names, such as Blenheim Palace, thereafter *the palace*. However, note that *the Palace* is acceptable for Buckingham Palace in stories about royalty. See **Royal Family**

Palace of Holyroodhouse, Edinburgh

palaeo- (not paleo-); similarly *palaeography* etc

Palestinian National Authority (not Palestine) – usually *the Palestinian Authority* will suffice; but note *the Palestine Liberation Organisation* (PLO)

Palmer-Tomkinson, Tara and **Santa**

paparazzi

paperboy, papergirl

paraffin see **kerosene**

paraphernalia (not paraphanalia)

paratroops general term for troops dropped by parachute; a *parachutist* is a specialist in the activity. Note *The Parachute Regiment*

Pardo Palace (royal palace on the outskirts of Madrid); the Madrid art gallery is the *Prado*

Parent's Charter

Paris some of the more familiar place names prone to error are the *Champs Elysées*, the *Elysée Palace*, the *Quai d'Orsay*, the *Jardin du Luxembourg* (not de), the *Jardin des Tuileries* (not de) and the *Jeu de Paume* (not Pomme)

Parker Bowles, Camilla no hyphen

Parkinson's disease

Parliament cap always in British context, and in overseas contexts when the word forms part of the institution, eg, the European Parliament, Canadian Parliament. However, note l/c for the Spanish parliament (the Cortes), the Russian parliament (Duma), the Israeli parliament (Knesset), Polish parliament (Sejm) etc; and l/c when it is only a mooted body, such as the English parliament.

Also, l/c *parliamentary*, even in *parliamentary private secretary* (abbreviated to PPS) because there are many of them; but note *Parliamentary Labour Party* (PLP), of which there is one, and similarly *Parliamentary Ombudsman*. See **PLP**, **ombudsman**, and **Politics** special section (page 1465)

Parliamentary Commissioner for Standards caps for the new post created in the light of the Neill (formerly Nolan) Committee on Standards in Public Life. He must not be referred to as the *Parliamentary Ombudsman*, who is the *Parliamentary Commissioner for Administration*. See **ombudsman**

partially, partly *partially* is of *degree*, eg, *partially deaf*; *partly* is of *extension*, eg, *partly under water*

participles beware the grammar trap of the disconnected (or unrelated) participle; eg, "Judging by the lingering camera shots, X's luck was not about to change" is wrong – the present participle *judging* has to have a following noun or pronoun in agreement (in other words, X's luck is not doing the judging). So the sentence has to be rephrased, as "Judging by the lingering camera shots, I saw that X's luck ...", or "To judge from the lingering camera shots, X's luck ..."

parties (political) cap *Labour Party*, *Conservative Party*, or any other party; also overseas parties, such as *Republican Party*, *Democratic Party* (though usually *Republicans* and *Democrats* will suffice). See **Tory**, **Politics** special section (page 1465)

part-time, part-timer note hyphens

partygoer see **-goer**

Passchendaele

passer-by, passers-by

past use rather than *last* in such phrases as "the past two weeks". See **last**

pastime

past tense (of verbs); almost always prefer the shorter form using final *-t* where appropriate; eg, *spelt* (not spelled), *dreamt* (not dreamed); but never earnt for *earned*

Patient's Charter

PAYE pay as you earn; note caps

Paymaster General

payout, payoff no hyphens

Peace Implementation Council (in the former Yugoslavia, part of the Dayton agreement)

peacekeeping, peacemaking etc no hyphens

peal (of bells); but **peel** (of an orange etc)

Pearl Harbor (not Harbour)

pedal (as in bicycle); note *peddle* (as in selling drugs or advocating ideas). A *pedaller* is someone who pedals a bike; a *pedlar* is a small trader; and a drug-pusher is a *peddler*

peers a peer or a peeress has a seat in the House of Lords. A female life peer is a peeress usually referred to as Baroness X. After the first mention of the Marquess of Paddington, Earl of Euston, Viscount Pimlico or Lord Holborn, call them all Lord Paddington, Lord Euston etc. See **Titles** special section (page 1467)

pejorative (not perjorative)

Peking use only in phrases such as *Peking duck* or *Peking man*. The city is now *Beijing*. Note *pekinese dogs*. See **Chinese names**

Peloponnese

PEN (international association of writers)

peninsula never *peninsular* when used as a noun; peninsular is the adjective, as in the Peninsular War

pensioners take care with this word. Some readers take exception to "ambiguous" usage, so it should strictly be confined to people drawing their state pension (men at 65, women at 60). If in doubt, write *the elderly*, or as last resort, *senior citizen*. See **elderly**

pension funds (not pensions funds as plural)

people use rather than *persons* wherever appropriate; exceptions would be "the law is no respecter of persons" or the ubiquitous *missing persons*. Take care with the apostrophe: remember that people is a plural, so the normal use is apostrophe *s*, eg, "it is the people's wish"; very occasionally, *peoples* in the sense of *races* can take an *s* apostrophe, eg, "the African peoples' common heritage"

Pep(s) personal equity plan; spell out in general news, but not necessarily in Business stories

Pepsi-Cola hyphen; similarly *Coca-Cola*

per try to avoid in phrases such as "six times per year"; "six times a year" is better

per cent always takes figures rather than the word, eg, 3 per cent, not three per cent. Usually use decimals rather than fractions (3.25 per cent rather than 3¼ per cent). Use % sign in headlines, never pc, and spell out *per cent* in text

percentage, proportion do not use as a synonym of *part* or *many* if that is all they mean in a sentence: eg, instead of "a large percentage of parents objected" write "many parents objected"

percentage points take care. If the mortgage rate rises from 8 per cent to 10 per cent, it does not rise by 2 per cent, but by two percentage points. Similarly if a political party's support drops from 50 per cent to 40 per cent in an opinion poll, it has lost ten percentage points or 20 per cent of its support

perestroika not italics

performance-related pay

Performing Right Society (not Rights)

Pergau dam (Malaysia)

Persia use Iran for the modern state, and never Persian Gulf except in historical context. See **Gulf**

Personal Investment Authority (not Investments); abbreviate to PIA

personnel prefer *people* or *employees* or *workers* wherever possible

Perspex trade name, so cap

peseta do not abbreviate the Spanish currency in any context

Peterhouse (Cambridge college); never takes College after the name. Neither does Christ Church, Oxford; nor do any Oxford or Cambridge colleges ending with Hall, eg, Lady Margaret Hall. See **Cambridge University**, **Oxford University**

petfood no hyphen; similarly *catfood, dogfood*

phalangist (Lebanon); see **falangist**

Pharaoh (not -oah); note l/c adjective *pharaonic*

phenomenon plural *phenomena*; beware the use of *phenomenal* as a cliché meaning remarkable or big

Philips (Dutch electronics company); note no apostrophe for *Phillips* (auction house)

phone now so common that it is permissible in text as well as headlines

phoney (not phony)

phosphorus noun; but note *phosphorous, phosphoric* (adjectives); *phosphorescence*

photo call two words; similarly *photo opportunity*

photo-finish

photofit l/c; but note cap for *Identikit*

pidgin English (not pigeon)

piecemeal, piecework

pigeonholed

pigheaded

Pigott-Smith, Tim (not Piggott), actor, but **Lester Piggott**, jockey

pilgrims l/c; but note *the Pilgrim Fathers*; note also John Bunyan's *The Pilgrim's Progress*

Pill, the (contraceptive)

Pimm's (the drink)

PIN personal identification number (not Pin); note that *PIN number* is a tautology

pinstripes (-d)

pitbull (terrier)

pitstop (motor racing)

PKK, the Kurdish Workers' Party (not Kurdistan...)

place names refer to the *Bartholomew Gazetteer* for place names in England, Wales and Scotland, and *The Times Atlas of the World* for the rest of the world. But there are exceptions: beware the new Welsh county names, and see **unitary authorities**, **foreign places**, **Spanish regions**

place name constructions two ugly devices to avoid are, eg, a *Gosport, Hampshire, housewife,* and *Manchester's Piccadilly station;* say instead a *housewife from Gosport, Hampshire,* and *Piccadilly station, Manchester*

Plaid Cymru (Welsh Nationalist Party)

plane as in *on a higher plane* (not plain)

planes try to avoid in text as a synonym of aircraft, and be very sparing in headlines, where *jets* (where applicable) or *aircraft* are always better. See **aircraft**

play-off

plays titles in italics. See **Arts** special section (page 1461)

PlayStation

plc all l/c; can usually be dropped from company names; see **Ltd**

PLP Parliamentary Labour Party; see **Politics** special section (page 1465)

plurals make corporate bodies and institutions singular unless this looks odd. Thus "The National Trust is ...", but sports teams are plural, eg, "Arsenal were worth their 8-0 lead". Whether singular or plural, always maintain consistency within a story

plus, minus do not use as variants of *and* or *without*

poetess avoid, use *poet* instead; see **feminine designations**

Poet Laureate caps; note plural *Poets Laureate*

point-to-point

Polaroid trade name, so cap

Polgar, Judit see **chess names**

police forces cap the word Police when it is part of the full name of the force. This applies to the following forces: *Metropolitan Police, City of London Police, British Transport Police, Ministry of Defence Police, Bedfordshire Police, Dorset Police* (Force), *Essex Police, Greater Manchester Police, Humberside Police, Lincolnshire Police, Merseyside Police, Northamptonshire Police, Northumbria Police, North Yorkshire Police, South Yorkshire Police, Staffordshire Police, Surrey Police, Sussex Police, Thames Valley Police, West Midlands Police, West Yorkshire Police, Dyfed-Powys Police, North Wales Police, Central Scotland Police, Grampian Police, Lothian and Borders Police, Strathclyde Police, Tayside Police.*

Other forces use Constabulary instead of Police (eg, *Cleveland Constabulary, Kent Constabulary*), so either give that full title or, more commonly, write *Cleveland police, Kent police* etc. Do not cap when referring to a local division, eg, *Luton police*, or *police in Luton*. If in doubt, consult *Whitaker's Almanack* under "Police Authorities"

policemen take care with this word. Certain senior officers, men and women, regularly chide us for using *policemen* when we mean *police officers*. If in doubt, use the latter.

police ranks wherever possible outside lists, avoid the inelegant abbreviated forms such as *Det Con, Det Chief Insp*. Spell out, even if inconvenient sometimes. An exception is *PC*, or *WPC* (for Woman Police Constable). *PC* also acceptable in headlines. Compound titles do not take hyphens in the police force. Detective Sergeant X becomes Sergeant X after the first mention. Inspector and all ranks above are usually Mr after the first mention. See **Chief Constable**

Police Staff College at Bramshill, Hampshire; or simply *the police college* (l/c), Bramshill

policyholder, policymaker but note *policy document*

Politburo usually cap

Pope, the not usually necessary to give his full name, eg, Pope John Paul II (unless several Popes are mentioned in a story), but always cap. Note *papacy, pontiff* (l/c). See **Churches** special section (page 1462)

poppadum

populist should not be confused with, or used as a synonym of, *popular*; it means supporting the interest of ordinary people, or pandering to mass public taste

Porritt, Jonathon despite his baronetcy, prefers not to use Sir

Portakabin trade name, so cap

possibly like most qualifiers, this word can (usually) be omitted

postal addresses in news and features, prefer to say *Bromley, southeast London* (rather than Kent), and *Kingston upon Thames, southwest London* (rather than Surrey) etc. This leaves the old counties such as Middlesex to be used only in their historical or sporting contexts.

Also avoid the clumsy possessive form such as *Manchester's Moss Side, London's East End*; say *Moss Side, Manchester, the East End of London*. There is no need to use postcodes except when giving an address for information. See **addresses**

postcode (no hyphen)

postgraduate, undergraduate noun and adjective both one word

Post-Modern caps, hyphen; see **artistic movements**

post mortem wherever possible write *post-mortem examination* in reports, though *post mortem* is acceptable nowadays in headlines

Post Office caps for the corporation, but l/c *post office* for the branches. Note also *sub-post office, sub-postmaster, Post Office Counters, Royal Mail, ParcelForce*

postwar, prewar adjectives, commonly referring to Second World War. Do not use adverbially (as in "there were a million jobless prewar")

potatoes plural; similarly *tomatoes*

pothole (as in caving or road surfaces); similarly *potholer*

PoW (prisoner of war); note plural *PoWs*

PowerGen

PPE the university degree is philosophy, politics and economics (not politics, philosophy etc)

practical, practicable do not confuse. *Practical* means adapted to actual conditions or (of a person) able to make things function well; *practicable* means capable of being effected or accomplished

practice noun; but **practise** (verb). It is an inexcusable *practice* for sub-editors to confuse the two; writers should *practise* getting it right

Prado gallery, Madrid see **Pardo**

praesidium (not presidium)

praying mantis (not preying)

prearrange

predilection (not predeliction)

pre-empt

Premier do not use in text as a synonym of *Prime Minister*, though very occasionally its use in the headline of a foreign story (never British) may be permitted. Generally, confine the word to heads of government of the Canadian provinces or Australian states, when it should take a cap. *Premiership* is preferable to *prime-ministership*

premiere (of a play, ballet etc); no accent

Premiership (football); refer to the *FA Carling Premiership* at first mention, *the Premiership* thereafter, for the top division in English football; the organisation that runs it is the *FA Premier League*.

Similarly, the lower divisions form the *Nationwide* (no longer Endsleigh) *League, first division, second division* (note l/c) etc; this competition is run by the *Football League*. See **Sports** special section (page 1466)

premise (assumption in an argument); note the word *premises* (property) takes the plural verb, eg, "the premises are well positioned"

Premium Bonds caps

prepositional verbs avoid wherever possible. Examples such as *measure up to, get on with* are acceptable on the odd occasion. Others such as *consult with, meet with* (where the preposition is tautologous) must never be used

Pre-Raphaelite

Presbyterian beware, especially with the adjective *Scots*. See **Church, Churches** special section (page 1462)

present better than *current* but often redundant

President cap *the President* of any country, also *President of the European Commission* at first and all subsequent mentions; but l/c *presidency* (as in *the French presidency of the EU*). Also note that *presidents of companies* or *organisations* normally take l/c, though this rule should be relaxed for leading national organisations, such as *President of the Law Society* and *President of the TUC*

press always l/c except in titles such as *the Press Complaints Commission*. See **broadsheet**

prestigious try to avoid this much-overworked word and find an appropriate substitute such as *highly regarded, admired, eminent, esteemed, leading, noted, outstanding, powerful* etc

pretension but note *pretentious*

prevaricate (to speak or act evasively); do not confuse with **procrastinate** (to defer action, to be dilatory)

preventive (not preventative)

PricewaterhouseCoopers (*PwC* for short), the merged accountants

prime meridian l/c

Prime Minister cap for every country. But l/c when referring to an unspecific, eg, "he would make a good prime minister". Never say, eg, Prime Minister Tony Blair or even Tony Blair, the Prime Minister; write instead *Tony Blair* at first mention, then *the Prime Minister* at next mention. Never use Premier for the British Prime Minister, and never use PM even in headlines. See **Premier**

primeval

Prince avoid the familiar forms of Prince Charles and Prince Philip at least until they have been given their full designation of *Prince of Wales* and *Duke of Edinburgh*; even then, prefer *the Prince* and *the Duke* at subsequent mentions. Note *The Prince's Trust*. See **royal, Royal Family**

Princess of Wales see **Diana, Princess of Wales**

Princes Street, Edinburgh

principal noun or adjective; means chief, main, important, head etc; eg, *the principal of a college*, or *the team's principal objective*. Do not confuse with **principle**, which is a noun meaning concept, ideal, rule, moral etc; eg, *her Christian principles*

Principality, the cap in Welsh context

printout

prior to avoid wherever possible; use *before*

Prison Service note caps and *s* in *Prisons Board*; also caps for *Director-General of the Prison Service* and *Chief Inspector of Prisons*; see **Governor, Probation Service**

prison visitors be careful to differentiate clearly between two groups of prison visitors:

a members of the National Association of Prison Visitors, who visit prisoners in the "social" sense of visiting

b members of prison boards of visitors, who visit as watchdogs in an official role and sometimes make recommendations on matters such as discipline and security

Private Finance Initiative (PFI), sometimes now known as *Public Private Partnerships* (initial caps)

private sector, public sector do not use hyphens even when employed adjectivally, eg, *public sector pay* (as *high street shopping*)

privatised industries see **regulators**

Privileges, Committee of

Privy Council but note *Privy Counsellors* (not Councillors)

prizewinner one word

Probation Service caps; similarly *Prison Service*

probe use only in a scientific, medical or space context. Never to be used as *inquiry*, even in headlines

problem be sparing with this overworked word

procrastinate (to defer action, to be dilatory). See **prevaricate**

Procter & Gamble note *-er* and ampersand

Procurator Fiscal (Crown prosecutor in Scotland); see **Courts** special section (page 1463)

profanities see **obscenities**

Professor caps for *Professor of History* etc; thereafter *the professor* or *Professor X*; see **university posts**

proffer, proffered (not profer, proferred)

profits especially in Business stories, should always state the basis of the figure (pre-tax, operating etc)

program (computers); *programme* (the arts etc)

pro-life beware this contentious phrase for the anti-abortion lobby (especially in US context); use the phrase *anti-abortion* wherever possible, but when "pro-life" is unavoidable always quote it

Proms acceptable abbreviation of Promenade Concerts; note also *Promenaders* and *the Last Night of the Proms*

prone (lying face-down); note *supine* (face-up)

propeller (not -or)

prophecy noun; note verb **prophesy**

proportion see **percentage**

pros and cons

protagonist means a *supporter* (of either side) in a debate or quarrel; it does not mean *advocate* or *proponent*

protégé

Protestant beware of using for all Christians who are not Roman Catholic. See **Churches** special section (page 1462)

protester (never -or); but see **demonstrator**

proven *not proven* is the Scottish legal verdict. In general use, prefer *proved* to *proven;* but *proven* and *unproven* may be used as a colloquial alternative

provided that (not providing that)

Province, the see **Ireland**

provinces, provincial take great care of these words in the context of "outside London". Many regard them as patronising; use *the regions* or *regional* wherever possible

prurient means having an unhealthy obsession with sex; it does not mean puritanical

PSBR public sector borrowing requirement

public house *pub* is now fully acceptable in text or headlines

public interest immunity certificate abbreviate to PIIC, or simply *the certificate*

publicly (never publically)

Public Record Office (not Records)

public school independent school is now a preferable term; use *public schoolboys, public schoolgirls,* if necessary

public sector see **private sector**

Pulitzer prizes see **Nobel prize** for when to cap

pullout noun, one word; but note *to pull out*

punctuation some important reminders:

a Commas keep commas inside quotes in the following type of "broken" sentence: "The trouble is," he said, "that this is a contentious issue." Omit the comma before *if, unless, before, since, when* unless the rhythm or sense of the sentence demands it. Avoid the so-called *Oxford comma*; say "he ate bread, butter and jam" rather than "he ate bread, butter, and jam".

b Dashes do not use in place of commas. Too many dashes can be ugly and disruptive.

c Punctuation marks place inside inverted commas if they relate to the words quoted, outside if they relate to the main sentence, eg, She is going to classes in "health and beauty". If the whole sentence is a quotation, the final point goes inside, eg, "Beauty is truth, truth beauty."

d Interrogation marks never use with indirect questions or rhetorical questions, eg, "She asked why he did not laugh."

e Parentheses use sparingly; try to use commas instead.

f Conjunctions *And* and *but* may occasionally be used at the beginning of a sentence, especially for emphasis.

g Ellipses use three points with full space after last word, then thin spacing between points, then full space before next word, eg, *not only … but also*

puns an enjoyable device for headline writers. Restrict their use to funny or light stories or features and if in doubt, avoid; but if irresistible, make sure they are in good taste

Puritan (16th/17th-century religious group); do not use as a contemporary adjective; *puritanical* is just permitted

putsch (military seizure of power, as in coup)

pygmy, pygmies

Pyramids the three main Pyramids at Giza (including the Great Pyramid) should be capped. But there are many other pyramids (l/c) throughout Egypt

pyrrhic l/c, as in *pyrrhic victory*

Qq

Qantas (not Quantas)

qat (hypnotic drug); preferable to *kat* or *khat*

QC, MP place commas each side when used after name

QCA Qualifications and Curriculum Authority; spell out at first mention. It is an amalgamation (from autumn 1997) of the *National Council for Vocational Qualifications* and the *School Curriculum and Assessment Authority*

QE2 normally spell out *Queen Elizabeth 2* at first mention, thereafter *QE2* or simply *the ship*

Qom, Iran (not Qum)

quadriplegia, quadriplegic (not quadra-)

quality press prefer *broadsheet.* See **broadsheet**

quango short for quasi-autonomous non-governmental organisation; no need to spell out or to quote

quantum leap avoid this cliché wherever possible

quarter sessions like assizes, no longer function, having been replaced by Crown Courts

Quebeckers rather than *Quebecois*

Queen, the aim at keeping *the* in headlines. Note caps for *the Queen's Speech* (to Parliament) and *the Queen's Birthday Honours.* See **Royal Family, New Year Honours**

Queen Elizabeth the Queen Mother no commas; always this style at first mention, thereafter *the Queen Mother*

Queen Elizabeth II Conference Centre, London (not QE2 or any other variant)

Queens, New York

Queensberry, Marquess of also *Queensberry Rules*

Queen's Club

Queens' College, Cambridge but note **The Queen's College, Oxford** (see **Cambridge University** and **Oxford University**); also note *The Queen's University of Belfast,* usually shortened to *Queen's University, Belfast* or simply *Queen's, Belfast*

Queens Park Rangers thereafter QPR

queueing note middle *e*

questionnaire

Question Time, Prime Minister's Questions caps, but note l/c *questions* to the Prime Minister, Foreign Secretary etc. See **Politics** special section (page 1465)

quicker never use as an adverb – always use *more quickly.* Confine *quicker* to adjectival comparison, eg, "he started at a quicker pace"

quid pro quo not italic

quiz show no hyphen; similarly *chat show, game show, talk show* etc

quotation marks (inverted commas); remember, single quotes in headlines, straps and display panels; double quotes in captions and keydecks. The only other use for single inverted commas is quotations within quotations.

Avoid inverted commas in sentences where they are clearly unnecessary, eg, *He described the attack as "outrageous".*

Quotation marks are no longer to be used for works of art. See **inverted commas, italics**

See also **punctuation** (paragraph c) for when punctuation goes inside or outside quotation marks

quotes direct quotes should be corrected only to remove the solecisms and other errors that occur in speech but look silly in print. Always take care that quotes are correctly attributed; and especially that literary or biblical quotations are 100 per cent accurate

Rr

race references to race should be used only when relevant to the sense of the story. The word is often better replaced by *people, nation, group* etc

racecourse, racehorse, racetrack see **horse**, and **Sports** special section (page 1466)

racked as in *racked by doubts, pain* etc; (not wracked)

racket (for tennis; not racquet); the game is *rackets*

RADA the Royal Academy of Dramatic Art; all caps

radio compounds are hyphenated in the wireless context (eg, *radio-telephone*); but one word when they concern rays (eg, *radioactive, radioisotope, radiotherapy*). Broadcasting frequencies are measured in *megahertz* (MHz) and *kilohertz* (kHz)

radio ham this term should strictly be applied only to licensed amateur radio operators, who are offended when it is used to apply to unlicensed "eavesdroppers" spying on private phone calls etc. Take care

Radio 1, 2, 3, 4, Radio 5 Live note also *Classic FM, BBC Radio*. But with foreign stations, usually l/c, eg, *Israel radio, Haiti radio, Moscow radio* etc; cap only if it is the specific name of the station or organisation

RAF Regiment (Corps within the Royal Air Force)

rail franchise director l/c; informal and acceptable short form of the *Director of Passenger Rail Franchising* (caps). The *Rail Regulator* takes caps; see **regulators**

rainforest one word

raison d'être use italics

Raleigh, Sir Walter (not Ralegh)

R&B abbreviation for rhythm and blues

ranging from overworked and often unnecessary phrase. There must be a scale in which the elements might be ranged: "ranging from 15 to 25 years" is correct, "a crowd ranging from priests to golfers" is not

ranks see **police ranks, Armed Forces** special section (page 1459)

Ranks Hovis McDougall but note *(The) Rank Organisation*

Rapid Reaction Force caps

rarefied, rarefy (not rarified)

rateable

rave acceptable in context as a musical event; see **gig.**

razzmatazz

re- whenever possible, run the prefix on to the word it qualifies, eg, *readmission, remake, reorganise, rework,* etc; but there are two main classes of exceptions:
a where the word after re- begins with *e*, eg, *re-election, re-emerge, re-examine, re-enter* etc;
b where there could be serious ambiguity in compounds such as *re-creation* (*recreation*), *re-cover* (*recover*), *re-dress* (*redress*). See **hyphens**

realpolitik not italic

rebut means to argue to the contrary, producing evidence; *to refute* is to win such an argument. Neither should be used as a synonym of *reject* or *deny*. Nor should they be used for *dispute* or *respond to*

receive "receiving an injury" is to be discouraged, though not banned. Prefer to say *sustained* or *suffered;* and never say someone received a broken leg etc – prefer *suffered a broken leg* or, better still, *broke a leg*. See **injure**

reckless (not wreckless); synonym for rash or foolhardy

record never write "set a new record", "was an all-time record" etc, where both the qualifiers are tautologous

recorders for when to cap, see **Courts** special section (page 1463)

recrudescence do not confuse with *resurgence* or *revival*. It means *worsening*, in the sense of reopening wounds or recurring diseases

redbrick (university); but note a *red-brick* building

Red Planet (informal name for Mars); caps

referendum plural *referendums*, as with *conundrums, stadiums, forums* and most words ending in *-um*. But note *millennia, strata*

refute take care with this word. See **rebut**

Regent's Park

regimen should be restricted to medical contexts – a prescribed course of exercise, way of life, diet etc. Do not use as a synonym of *regime* (government or administrative contexts)

register office (not registry office)

Register of Members' Interests caps; see **Politics** special section (page 1465)

Registrar (Oxford); but note *Registrary* (Cambridge)

Registrar-General

regulators of the privatised industries and the consumer watchdog should be styled as follows: *Director-General of Electricity and Gas Supply*, who heads Office of Gas Supply (Ofgas) and can be shortened to the *gas regulator*, and who also heads Office of Electricity Regulation (Offer) and can be shortened to the *electricity regulator*
Director-General of Water Services (heads Office of Water Services, Ofwat), or the *water regulator*
Director-General of Telecommunications (heads Office of Telecommunications, Oftel), or the *telecommunications regulator*
Rail Regulator (Office of the Rail Regulator) – cap as it is the official title; note that the *Office of Passenger Rail Franchising* (Opraf) is separate
Director-General of Fair Trading (Office of Fair Trading, OFT) best not to abbreviate – use *consumer watchdog* as alternative

Reith Lecture(s)

reject see **rebut**

relatively see **comparatively**

Religious Right (in American politics); caps. See **Right**

remainder avoid as a synonym of *the rest*

REME the Royal Electrical and Mechanical Engineers (never Reme). See **Armed Forces** special section (page 1459)

Remembrance Sunday prefer to Day

Renaissance, the but l/c *renaissance* as synonym of *revival* or *rebirth*

repellent (noun or adjective), not repellant

report l/c in titles of official documents such as *Taylor report*

reportedly avoid this slack word, which suggests that the material's source is not clear

Republic of Ireland, or **Irish Republic** see **Ireland**

republican l/c except when in an official name, such as *the Republican Party* or *Republicans* (US). See **Ireland**

rerun

Resolution cap in context of UN, eg, *Resolution 688*

respect of avoid "in respect of" whenever possible; never write "in respect to"

responsible people bear responsibility, things do not. Storms are not responsible for damage; they cause it. Avoid the phrase "the IRA *claimed responsibility for* the bombing"; say instead "the IRA *admitted causing* the bombing"

restaurateur (never restauranteur)

result in avoid this lazy phrase and always find an alternative, such as *cause, bring, create, evoke, lead to* etc

re-use one of the *re-* words where the hyphen is essential

Reuters use this form now in every context (no longer Reuter)

Reveille like Last Post, is *sounded,* not played

Revelation, Book of (not Revelations)

reverend at first mention, the style is *the Rev Tom Jones,* then *Mr Jones.* Never write "the Rev Jones" or (even worse) "Rev Jones" (which is as great a solecism as calling Sir Norman Fowler "Sir Fowler"). A parson and his wife are referred to as *the Rev Tom and Mrs Jones.* See **archbishops, Churches** special section (page 1462)

Review caps in names of government programmes such as *Strategic Defence Review, Comprehensive Spending Review*

Reykjavik, Iceland

rhinoceroses (plural)

Rhys-Jones, Sophie now the *Countess of Wessex* (subsequent mentions the *Countess*). See **Titles** special section (page 1467)

RIBA abbreviation of the Royal Institute of British Architects; all caps

Richter scale measures the energy released by an earthquake. It runs from 0 to 8; write "the earthquake measured 6 on the Richter scale"

RICS Royal Institution of Chartered Surveyors (not Institute); note caps

riffle, riffling as in flicking through papers or clothes on a rail; note *rifling* in the sense of ransacking

Right, the cap in the political context when referring to a group of like-minded individuals, eg, "The Right added to John Major's dilemma on the EU"; but l/c in "the party swung to the right". When the Right is qualified, generally keep the adjective l/c, eg, *the far Right* (but note *the Religious Right* in the US). Also, *the right wing, right-wing contenders, rightwingers.* See **Left**

rigmarole (not rigamarole)

ring-fence hyphen

Rio Tinto (no longer Rio Tinto-Zinc or RTZ)

riverbank one word

rivers cap in context of *River Thames, Mississippi River* (or simply *the Thames, the Mississippi* etc). Similarly, cap *estuary* when part of the name. See **Thames**

riveting try to avoid its clichéd use as a metaphor

roadblock, roadbuilding, roadbuilder etc

road rage wherever possible, quote at first mention (ie, "road rage"); but not thereafter, nor in headlines

roads as tautologous to write "the M5 motorway" as "the A435 road", but correct to say "the M40 London to Birmingham motorway". Unnecessary to define the M25 as London's orbital motorway, but generally, define a road geographically unless context is clear

Robert the Bruce prefer to Robert Bruce; subsequent mentions *the Bruce*

rock'n'roll

Rollerblade proprietary term, so cap. The American company's lawyers insist that even Rollerblading is capped; use *inline skates/skating* instead

rollerskate, rollercoaster

roll-on, roll-off (as in ferries); abbreviate to *ro-ro*

rollover (as in National Lottery); no hyphen

Rolls-Royce

Roman Catholic see **Catholic**

Romania (not Rumania); see **Ceausescu**

Roman numerals usually no full points, eg, *Edward VIII, Article XVI, Part II, Psalm xxiii.* But in official documents, to designate sub-sections, use the points, eg, *i., ii., iv.,* etc

roofs (not rooves)

rooms use *dining room, living room, drawing room, laundry room* (no hyphens except when adjectival, eg, *living-room carpet*); but note *bathroom, bedroom*

rottweiler l/c; see dogs

row be sparing in the use of this word, especially in headlines. Alternatives are *rift, split, clash* etc, and *dispute* in text. However, *row* is not banned

Rowntree be sure to distinguish between the *Joseph Rowntree Foundation,* a charity and independent funder of social policy research and development; and the *Joseph Rowntree Reform Trust,* not a charity and an entirely separate company that funds projects often with a political dimension

royal, royalty l/c for royalty but cap *the Royal Family;* royal is usually l/c when used adjectivally, as in *royal baby, royal approval, the royal wave,* but takes the cap in titles such as *Royal Assent, Royal Collection, Royal Household, Royal Yacht*

Royal College of Nursing (not Nurses)

royal commissions should be capped when the full title is given, eg, *Royal Commission on Environmental Pollution,* but otherwise l/c, eg, *the royal commission.* See **committee**

Royal Corps of Signals, or **Royal Signals** (not Royal Corps of Signallers); see **Armed Forces** special section (page 1459)

Royal Family takes caps, British and overseas; with names of the British Royal Family, give in full at first mention, eg, *the Duke of Edinburgh,* thereafter *the Duke* (cap) or occasionally *Prince Philip; Prince William,* thereafter *the Prince.* In royalty context, the cap after first mention should be confined to the British Royal Family and overseas heads of state. See **Queen, Duke, Prince, Diana, heads of state, Titles** special section (page 1467)

Royal Fine Art Commission

Royal Fleet Auxiliary ships are entitled RFA, not HMS; eg, *RFA Fort George.* See **Armed Forces** special section (page 1459)

Royal Institute of International Affairs (not Institution); often known as *Chatham House*

Royal Military Academy Sandhurst no commas; similarly *Royal Air Force College Cranwell* and *Royal Naval College Dartmouth*

Royal National Lifeboat Institution (not Life-Boat); abbreviate to RNLI

Royal Over-Seas League see **London clubs**

Royal Shakespeare Company thereafter the RSC; note also *Royal Opera House;* generally no need to include *Royal* with *Albert Hall, Festival Hall, National Theatre*

Royal Standard only for the Sovereign. Other members of the Royal Family have a *personal standard;* see **ensign**

Royal Train caps, as with the *Royal Yacht*

Royal Welch Fusiliers, The similarly, *Welch Regiment;* but note *Welsh Guards;* see **Armed Forces** special section (page 1459)

Royal Yacht *Britannia,* or **the *Britannia*** she is now decommissioned, so refer to her as the *former Royal Yacht*

RPI retail prices index; note plural and l/c

RPM (caps), resale price maintenance (not retail); and *rpm* (l/c) revolutions per minute

RSPCA does not exist in Scotland, which has the Scottish SPCA

rubbish do not use as a verb

Rubens (Flemish painter; not Reubens)

Rue Royale see **French names**

run-down adjective, as in *decaying* or *exhausted;* note noun *rundown* as in briefing; also verb *to run down*

running-mate hyphen

Rural England Council for the Protection of Rural England (not Preservation); abbreviate to CPRE

rush hour noun; but note hyphen for adjective, eg, *rush-hour traffic*

rushed to hospital avoid this cliché. Use *taken to* or *driven to;* similarly, write a victim was *flown to hospital* rather than *air-*

lifted to ... Always avoid the American *hospitalise*

Russia take care not to designate parts of the former Soviet Union as Russia when they no longer are, eg, Ukraine, Georgia. The same applies to the people (though there are millions of ethnic Russians throughout the former Soviet Union). So always specify the republic concerned and do not use *Russian* in the inclusive sense except in the phrase *Russian vodka*. Use *Soviet* and the *Soviet Union* only in their historical contexts – and avoid USSR wherever possible. See **Soviet**

Russian names use *i* as first name ending, but *y* for surnames, eg, *Arkadi Volsky*, *Gennadi Yavlinsky* (but note the exception *Rutskoi*); and use *k* rather than *x* in the middle, eg, *Aleksei*, *Aleksandr*; also note *Viktor*. We should use the *-ya* rather than *-ia* in *Natalya* and *Tatyana* (not Natalia, Tatiana). But note that the styles of Garry Kasparov and Anatoly Karpov are sufficiently Westernised to be spelt thus. See **chess names**

Ss

saccharin (noun), **saccharine** (adjective)

sack avoid in the sense of *dismiss* except in headlines (and never use *axe* in this context)

sacrilegious (from sacrilege; not sacreligious)

Saddam Hussein, President write in full at first mention, then *Saddam*

Sadler's Wells

said prefer the construction *Mr Brown said* rather than *said Mr Brown*. See **writes**

sailing correspondent do not use yachting correspondent

Sainsbury the formal style is *J Sainsbury* (no point), especially in business stories, but *Sainsbury's* is permissible in general news stories. See **initials**

Saint nearly always abbreviated to *St*

St Albans

St Andrews (town and university in Fife)

St Catharine's College, Cambridge but note *St Catherine's College*, Oxford; see **Oxford University**, **Cambridge University**, **Catherine**

St David's (village and cathedral, Pembrokeshire); also St David's Head; but note the Bishop of St Davids does not take the apostrophe

St Giles' Cathedral, Edinburgh

St Helens, Merseyside

St James's Palace see **Court of...**

St John Ambulance Brigade/Association

St John's, Newfoundland but note **Saint John**, New Brunswick

St John's, Smith Square use comma

St John's Wood, London

St Katharine Docks, but *St Katharine's Yacht Haven*

St Martin-in-the-Fields

St Martins College of Art and Design see **Central St Martins**

St Neot, Cornwall but note **St Neots**, Cambridgeshire

St Paul's Cathedral

St Stephen's Green, Dublin (not Stephen's Green)

St Thomas' Hospital, London

Saint-Saëns (composer)

saleroom one word

Salonika, rather than Thessaloniki. See **foreign place names**

salutary not salutory

Salvadorean (not -ian)

Sam-7 (missiles)

Sanaa (capital of Yemen; not Sana'a, Sana, or other variants)

sanatorium (not sanitorium); note plural *sanatoriums*

sanction as a noun, define its use as trade, military etc

sandpit one word

SANE (schizophrenia charity); note caps

Santer, Jacques (former President of the European Commission); he is from Luxembourg, so call him Mr, not M; see **foreign appellations**

sarin (as in nerve gas); l/c

Sauchiehall Street, Glasgow

Saudi must never be used as short form for the country, Saudi Arabia. Confine its use to the adjectival, eg, *Saudi Royal Family*

Savile, Jimmy use *Sir James* in formal context only

Savile Row, Savile Club see **London clubs**

Saville Theatre

SBS Special Boat Service (not Squadron)

Sca Fell, Scafell Pike two separate mountains in the Lake District. Scafell Pike, at 3,206ft, is the highest in England

Scalextric (not Scalectrix)

Scandinavia (never Scandanavia)

Scarborough, North Yorkshire

scarify (to cut into, to cut skin from); its colloquial meaning of *to terrify* should be avoided wherever possible

scars do not heal (even metaphorically); *wounds* heal, *scars* remain

Schadenfreude (malicious enjoyment of another's misfortunes); note cap, italic

Schiphol airport, Amsterdam

schizophrenic never use as a term of abuse and avoid as a metaphor. See **medical terms, SANE**

Schleswig-Holstein

Schoenberg, Arnold

schools cap when full title is given (if in doubt, consult the *Independent Schools Year Book* or the state sector equivalent, the *Education Year Book*); nowadays use the classifications of *independent, state, grant-maintained, comprehensive, grammar, secondary modern* (rarely), etc, rather than public, private etc (except in historical context)

schoolchildren one word; note also *schoolgirl, schoolboy, schooldays, schoolmaster, schoolmistress* and *schoolteacher* (rarely), but *school-leaver*

School Curriculum and Assessment Authority (not Schools); but see **QCA**

Schwarzenegger, Arnold

Schweitzer, Albert

scientific measures write out first time with abbreviations in parentheses, shorten thereafter. The abbreviation takes no point and no *s* in the plural, eg, *14km* (not 14kms). Some basic international units and their abbreviations are: *metre* (*m*); *gram* (*g*); *litre* (*l*); *ampere* (*A*); *volt* (*V*); *watt* (*W*); note also *kilowatt-hour* (*kWh*).

Only abbreviate *mile* to *m* in *mph* and *mpg*; and *gallon* to *g* in *mpg* (otherwise *gal*). Beware of using *m* for million or for miles in any scientific context when it might be taken for metres. See **weights**

scientific names when employing the Latin terminology, use the internationally accepted convention of initial cap on the first (genus) word, then l/c for the second (species); eg, Homo sapiens, *Branta canadensis* (Canada goose) etc. Italicise all but the most common

Scilly, Isles of (not Scilly Isles); note spelling of *St Mary's* and *Tresco*

Scope new name for the former Spastics Society

Scotch (whisky); do not use as a substitute for the adjectives Scottish and Scots. But note *Scotch broth, Scotch mist, Scotch egg* and *Scotch terrier*; also *Scots pine*

Scottish National Party (SNP); now cap *Nationalists* in the Scottish party context, but l/c nationalists in the wider sense

Scottish Parliament now cap *P*. Note First Minister (not Secretary)

Scottish place names always write, eg, Motherwell, North Lanarkshire (never Motherwell, Scotland). Take care with new names under local government reorganisation; regions such as *Central, Grampian* and *Strathclyde* should now be referred to only in their historical context or if they persist in official titles such as *Strathclyde Police* or *the University of Strathclyde*. Permissible too to refer informally to the *Central belt* (between Edinburgh and Glasgow).

The same principle about counties applies to Wales and

Northern Ireland: give the county unless the town or city is big enough or well-known enough for the county to be unnecessary

ScottishPower

Scott Thomas, Kristin (no hyphen)

Scouts no longer Boy Scouts

scrapheap one word

scratchcard one word; similarly *smartcard, swipecard*

Scripture cap as in *Holy Scripture*; but note l/c *scriptural*

scriptwriter

sculptures set in italic. With photographs of sculptures, always give the sculptor's name. See **Arts** special section (page 1461)

seabed, seabird, seahorse, seagull, seasick no hyphens

seasonal, but **unseasonable** (not unseasonal). Note also *seasonal affective disorder* (l/c), abbreviated to SAD

seasons always l/c when unattached, ie, *spring, summer, autumn, winter*; but note *Winter Olympics* etc

seatbelt

second-hand hyphenated

Second World War (not World War II/Two etc)

Secret Intelligence Service abbreviate to SIS, or MI6; takes caps; see **Security Service** (MI5)

Secretary-General (of the United Nations, Nato)

Securities and Investments Board the SIB has now been replaced by the new City super-regulator, the *Financial Services Authority* (FSA)

Security Service (MI5); takes caps; but l/c for *security services* in non-specific use. See **Secret Intelligence Service**

seize (never sieze)

select committees as with parliamentary committees cap at first mention, or when full title is given, eg, *the Foreign Affairs Select Committee*; thereafter *the select committee*, or *the committee*

Selfridges

sell-off, sell-out but see **buyout**

Sellotape trade name, so cap; alternatively use *sticky tape* or *adhesive tape*

semiconductor

Semtex cap

Senate (US); write *Senator Edward Kennedy*, thereafter *the senator*; alternatively, *Mr Kennedy, the Massachusetts senator*

senior abbreviate to *Sr* (not Snr) in the American context, eg, *Henry Ramstein Sr*; see **junior**. Avoid the cliché *senior executive* when you mean *executive* – nine times out of ten the adjective is redundant (as *major*)

Senior Salaries Review Body caps; has replaced the Top Salaries Review Body

septuagenarian

Serb for the people, but *Serbian* can be used (sparingly) as an adjective

Serious Fraud Office abbreviate to SFO; but note *fraud squad*. See **Flying Squad**

Serjeant at Arms

Serps spell out at first mention as *state earnings related pension scheme (Serps)*

serve in a warship (but *on* a merchant ship), and serve in (not on) a submarine, even though subs are boats, not ships. Important to make this distinction. See **Armed Forces** special section (page 1459)

Services, Armed Services, or **Armed Forces, the** note caps; also cap *Service* when used adjectivally as in *a Service family* (where meaning might otherwise be ambiguous); but l/c *serviceman, servicewoman*

Session, Court of (supreme Scottish court; not Sessions). See **Courts** special section (page 1463)

setback noun; but note *to set back*

sett as with badgers

set-up try to find a synonym such as *arrangement, organisation, structure, system* etc

sewage (waste matter); note **sewerage** (disposal system)

sexism always be aware of sensitivities and be careful to avoid giving offence to women. It is often difficult to draw the line between sexism and political correctness

sex offenders register (l/c, no apostrophe)

Shadow cap in all cases, such as *Shadow Cabinet, Shadow Environment Secretary, Shadow Chief Whip, a Shadow spokesman*. See **Politics** special section (page 1465)

Shah, Eddy (not Eddie)

shake-out, shake-up but see **buyout**

Shakespearean (not -ian)

shall, should keep up the vigorous defence of these against the encroaching *will* and *would*. Good practice is that *shall* and *should* go with the first person singular and plural (I shall, we shall), *will* and *would* with the others (he will, they will). *Shall* with second and third persons singular and plural has a slightly more emphatic meaning than *will*

shambles take care not to overwork this strong word, which means a *slaughterhouse* and, by extension, a *scene of carnage*

Shangri-La

Shankill Road, Belfast (not Shankhill); see **Ireland**

SHAPE Supreme Headquarters, Allied Powers, Europe; all caps

share a joke banned in captions on photographs showing people laughing

share shop(s) l/c, as jobcentre

Sharia (Islamic law); never use the tautology *Sharia law*

sheikh (not shaikh)

Shepherds Bush

Sherborne alumni of the Dorset public school are *Shirburnians*

sheriff (never sherrif)

Shetland, or **the Shetland Islands** (not the Shetlands). See **Orkney**

Shia (not Shiite or any such variation); write *Shia Muslims* (as opposed to *Sunni Muslims*)

ships italicise the HMS when first mention of warship, eg, *HMS Sheffield*. Ships should generally be treated as feminine; thus *she* and *her* rather than *it* and *its*. See **warships, boat, serve in**

ships' tonnage for passenger ships, give gross tonnage in *tonnes* (rather than tons); for cargo ships, deadweight tonnage. Check with *Lloyd's Register*

shock avoid in headlines unless in the electric context; in text, use the word as little as possible and never as a modifier, *shock revelations* etc (unless the context is ironic)

shock waves two words, but use sparingly as a metaphor as it is becoming a cliché

shopkeeper, shopowner, shopfront, shoplift etc but note *shop assistant* and *shop steward*

shortlist one word as noun or verb

short-lived, short-sighted

showbusiness one word; note *showbiz* is acceptable in quotes and informal context

showcase avoid use as a verb *to showcase something*. Use *display* or *exhibit* instead

showjumping should now be one word except when it appears in a title such as the *British Show Jumping Association*, or the name of an event using it as two words; similarly, *showjumper*

Shroud of Turin, or **the Turin Shroud** note caps; subsequently *the shroud* (l/c)

Siamese cats, twins for Siam use Thailand except in historical context; note the adjective Thai

Sichuan (not Szechuan, Setzuan, Szechwan or any other variant); see **Chinese names**

sickbed similarly *deathbed*

side-effects

siege (never seige)

Siena (not Sienna)

sign language (not deaf-and-dumb language)

Silicon Valley, silicon chips, but *silicone implants* (for breasts etc)

silk barristers *take silk* and *become silks* (all l/c); see **Courts** special section (page 1463)

Simon's Town, South Africa (not Simonstown); see **South Africa**

Sindy doll (not Cindy)

singeing (from *singe*), to distinguish it from *singing*

sink, sank the past participle is *sunk*, the adjective *sunken*

siphon (not syphon)

Sistine Chapel (not Cistine)

sitcom permissible abbreviation for *situation comedy*

sit-in

situation avoid wherever possible; such phrases as *crisis situation, ongoing situation* and *no-win situation* are banned unless a direct quote demands them

Six Nations Championship (rugby), no longer the Five Nations Championship (England, Wales, Scotland, Ireland, France and Italy)

sizeable

ski, skier, skied, skiing

skulduggery

Slavic must not be used; the noun and adjective are *Slav*

slay do not use this biblical word in headlines for *kill* or *murder*

slimline one word

Slovak (people and language); *Slovakian* is the general adjective. See **Croat**

smartcard one word; similarly *scratchcard, swipecard*

smelt (not smelled)

Smith, WH no points; see **companies, initials**

Smithsonian Institution, Washington (never Institute); can be shortened to *the Smithsonian*

snarl-up do not use as a synonym of *traffic jam, confusion* etc

sniffer dogs, tracker dogs avoid these clichés wherever possible; usually *dogs* is sufficient, but if the context is unclear, write *police dogs*

snowball, snowbound, snowdrift, snowfall, snowman etc

Soane's the museum in Lincoln's Inn Fields is *the Sir John Soane's Museum*

soap opera prefer to just *soap*, though the latter may have its place in less formal pieces

soccer an acceptable word. See **football** and **Sports** special section (page 1466)

social chapter l/c, as it is an informal title

Social Democratic and Labour Party (Northern Ireland); abbreviate to SDLP

socialism, socialist for when to cap, see **communism**

Solent, the note l/c *the*

Solicitor-General hyphen, as *Attorney-General*; similarly *Solicitor-General for Scotland*

Solicitors Complaints Bureau no apostrophes; has now been replaced by the *Office for the Supervision of Solicitors*

Solti, Sir Georg (not George)

Solzhenitsyn, Aleksandr no longer use Anglicised spelling; see **Russian names**

SOS

Sotheby's

soundbite

south, southeast, southern etc for when to cap, see **compass points**

South Africa never use the abbreviation SA, even in headlines.

The capital is Pretoria, which has the embassies (branches sometimes in Cape Town when Parliament is sitting) and government ministries. The legislature meets in Cape Town, and the Appeal Court sits in Bloemfontein. Pretoria can be referred to as the seat of government. Each of the new South African provinces has its own capital.

Note caps for *Northern Province* and the *Eastern/ Western/ Northern Cape, KwaZulu/ Natal* and *Simon's Town.*

Take care; several provinces have been renamed since the apartheid era, eg, *Mpumalanga* (formerly Eastern Transvaal). Use *southern Africa* when referring to Africa south of the Congo and Zambezi Rivers

South Asia encompasses Afghanistan, Bangladesh, Bhutan, India, the Maldives, Nepal, Pakistan and Sri Lanka

South-East Asia comprises the nine Asean states – Indonesia, Singapore, Malaysia, Thailand, the Philippines, Brunei, Vietnam, Burma and Laos – plus Cambodia. Avoid calling Burma *Myanmar* (except occasionally in direct quotes). See **Asean**

South of France

Southern Ocean caps

Sovereign, the cap; see **monarch, Royal Family**

Soviet Union never refer to *the Soviets* for the people or the Government, even in the historical context. The phrase is an Americanism often with disparaging overtones; a *soviet* is a *committee*, not a person. Refer instead to *the Soviet people* or *the Soviet Government* in historical context. See **Russia, USSR**

space avoid the phrase *outer space;* see **Earth, Moon, Sun, Universe**

Spanish regions use the Anglicised forms such as *Andalusia* (not Andalucía); *Catalonia* (not Cataluña), *Navarre* (not Navarra), *Majorca* (not Mallorca), *Minorca* (not Menorca) etc

spastic never use figuratively or as a term of abuse; see **medical terms, Scope**

Speaker always cap in parliamentary context

Special Branch caps, but no *the*; see **branch**

species both singular and plural in plant and animal sense. See **scientific names**

spelt (not spelled); note *misspelt*

Spiceworld: the Movie

spiders note they are not insects, although like insects they are arthropods

Spielberg, Steven

spilt (not spilled)

spin, spun (do not use *span* as past tense)

spin-doctor hyphen; see **Politics** special section (page 1465)

Spiritualism, Spiritualist

split infinitives do not use except in famous quotes such as "to boldly go where no man …" or in limited emphatic constructions such as "I want to live – to really live"

spoilt (not spoiled); but note *despoiled*

spokesman, spokeswoman avoid where possible, eg, "the ministry said" rather than "a ministry spokesman said". *Official* is a useful alternative. Never use *spokesperson.* See **chairman**

sports clubs for when to use singular or plural, see **teams**

sportsmen, sportswomen omit the Mr, Mrs, Miss, Ms etc unless they are in news reports (eg, court hearings) in a specifically non-sporting context. See **appellations**

sprang (past tense of the verb *to spring*, eg, "she sprang into action"); note *sprung* (past participle, eg, "the wind has sprung up")

sprightly (not spritely)
spring-clean hyphen
squads in police context, usually l/c, but see **Flying Squad;** also note **Royal and Diplomatic Protection Squad**
Sri Lanka do not use Ceylon for the country except in historical context. But note *Ceylon tea* etc
SSSI site of special scientific interest, l/c
stadium plural *stadiums*; see **referendum**
stalemate try to avoid in the sense of *deadlock*. It should be confined to chess reports
Stalinist, Stalinism see **communism**
stanch verb, as in *to stanch a flow of blood*; note adjective *staunch* meaning *loyal* or *firm*
stand-off noun, hyphen; but note **standby**, noun, no hyphen
Stansted (airport; never Stanstead); see **airports**
stargazers, stargazing
Star Trek two words, italic
State cap; use sparingly in context of the State as a wide concept; but l/c in the *welfare state*, or when used adjectivally, eg, *state benefits*
stationary (not moving); but **stationery** (writing materials)
Stationery Office, The (TSO abbreviated); no longer HMSO
stations l/c in *Euston station, Waterloo station, Birmingham New Street station*, but where possible, simply *Euston, Waterloo* etc. See **airports**
statistic(s) do not use as a fancy word for *figure(s)* or *number(s)*. Note that the Central Statistical Office has been replaced by the *Office for National Statistics* (not of)
status quo roman; but note italics for the less familiar *status quo ante*
statute book
stay home avoid; use *stay at home* instead
Stealth bomber
steelworks, steelworker etc
stepfather, stepmother, stepson, stepdaughter but note *step-family, step-parents*
Stephenson, George (trains), **Robert** (bridges) note also **Stevenson**, Robert Louis, Adlai
still avoid writing the tautologous "still continues", "still remains" etc
Stock Exchange caps for *London Stock Exchange* and *New York Stock Exchange*, l/c for all others; note l/c for **stock market**
stony (not stoney)
storey (of a building); note plural *storeys*
storyteller, storytelling
straight be sparing in the use of this word to mean heterosexual. See **gay**
straight-faced but note **straightforward**
Strait of Hormuz, Strait of Gibraltar, Strait of Dover (not Straits)
straitjacket
strait-laced note also *in dire straits*
Stratford-upon-Avon except in the parliamentary constituency, which is *Stratford-on-Avon*
stratum plural *strata*
Streisand, Barbra
stress prefer *emphasise* as in "he emphasised the importance"
stricture means *adverse criticism* or *censure* (not constraint)
strippagram
stylebook one word, as with *guidebook, textbook* etc; but note *style guide*
sub- like *multi-*, the hyphen here is often a question of what looks better. A random sample gives us *subdivision, sublet, subnormal, subsection, substandard, subtext*; in contrast, *sub-committee, sub-editor, sub-postmaster, sub-post office* etc. See **hyphens, multi-**
Subbuteo
sub-continent, the (India, Pakistan and Bangladesh); note l/c
subjects, academic use l/c for most subjects studied at school or university, eg, "she was reading modern history with philosophy"; but where a proper name is involved, the cap is retained, eg, "he got a first in English literature and German after he dropped Latin in his second year"; and always cap Classics and PPE (short for philosophy, politics and economics). But note, eg, Professor of History when the phrase accompanies a name; see **Professor, university posts**
sub-let (as in property)
sub-machinegun see **machinegun**
submarine always a *boat*, not a ship. See **boat, ships, serve in**
subplot, subtext, subtitle
subpoena, subpoenas, subpoenaing, subpoenaed
sub-Saharan Africa
subsequently prefer *afterwards* or *later*, and never say *subsequent to* when the meaning is *after*
subtropical one word; see **Tropics**
such as do not confuse with *like;* see **like**
Sudan (not the Sudan, except occasionally in historical context)
suing (from *to sue;* not sueing)
summon the verb is *to summon*, the noun *a summons* (plural *summonses*). A person is *summoned* to appear before a tribunal etc; but a person in receipt of a specific summons can be said to have been *summonsed*. But see **Woolf reforms** and **Courts** special section (page 1463)
Sun see **Earth, Moon** and **Universe**
sunbathing, sunburn, sunglasses, suntan etc but note *suncare* (products etc)
superhighway (as in information superhighway); similarly *superconductor*
superlatives beware of calling any person, event or thing *the first, the biggest, the best* etc without firm evidence that this is correct. Also, never say *first-ever, best-ever* etc; see **ever, first, universal claims**
supersede (never supercede)
supersonic (of speeds); for waves use *ultrasonic*
supervisor (not superviser)
supine (lying face-up); see **prone**
Supreme Court (US)
Surinam (not Suriname)
surprising (not suprising)
Sussex always specify whether a place is in East Sussex or West Sussex, two separate counties
swap (not swop). Do not use unless a mutual exchange is involved and never for organ transplants
swaths (as in *cutting swaths through*; not *swathes)*; note **swathes** to be used only as bandages
swatting (flies), **swotting** (study)
swearword
swingeing (as in cuts), to distinguish it from *swinging*
Swinging London, Swinging Sixties caps
swipecard similarly *scratchcard, smartcard*
Symphony Hall, Birmingham (does not take *the*). See **Arts** special section (page 1461)
synod l/c on its own, but note caps for *General Synod*. See **Churches** special section (page 1462)
synthesizer (musical); but note **synthesise** (chemical etc)

Tt

-t in nearly all cases, where there is a choice of past tense between a final *-t* or *-ed*, use *-t*, as in *burnt, spelt* etc. But never *earnt*

tad heavily overworked as synonym of *a little* or *a bit*; avoid

tailback

Tajikistan

takeaway (meals)

take-off (aircraft)

takeover noun; but note verb *to take over*

takeover code but note caps for *Takeover Panel*

Taleban (Afghan Islamic rebel group) takes a singular verb; no need to say *the* Taleban unless appropriate; note that the singular is *a Taleb*, but prefer *a member of Taleban*

talk show similarly *chat show, game show, quiz show* etc

Tallinn (capital of Estonia)

Tangier no final *s*

Tannoy trade name, so cap; use *loudspeaker* as alternative

Taoiseach always cap; see **Ireland**

taramasalata (not taramo-); see **hoummos**

targeted

Tarmac trade name, but cap *T* is used only for the civil engineering company. Common usage allows the road surface or airport runway to be written as *tarmac; tarmacadam* is not a trade name

Tartars preferred to Tatars

task force (as in Falklands)

tattoos, tattooed, tattooing

taxman one word as colloquialism for *Inland Revenue*; similarly taxpayer

Tchaikovsky

teams normally plural, eg, "Manchester United were disappointing when they lost to Barcelona". But sports clubs usually take the singular, especially in news stories, eg, "Manchester City Football Club was fined heavily for crowd disturbances". There is some room for variation in this format, but whatever is decided, never mix singular and plural in the same story. Note hyphen in *team-mates*. See **Sports** special section (page 1466)

teargas

Technicolor trade name. It must not be used except in that company's context. Use *multicoloured* as the general alternative

Tecs short for training and enterprise councils; note initial cap only; see **Lecs**

Teesside no hyphen, double *s* in middle; but note *Deeside* in both Scotland and Wales

teetotal

Tehran (not Teheran)

telephone numbers with three groups of figures, hyphenate only the first two, eg, 0181-234 8464. With revised codes (introduced in June 1999, but not fully operational until April 2000) write, eg, 020-7782 5000, not 0207-782 5000.

Teletext replaced Oracle (at the end of 1992) as the text service for ITV and Channel 4; do not use Oracle any more

television use TV in headlines, but try to avoid in the text. ITV is an acceptable alternative for *independent television*. ITN (Independent Television News) is acceptable in its abbreviated form (in the same way as BBC). Note l/c in non-specific use, eg, *BBC Television, BBC1, BBC2* etc; but *Argentine television, Norwegian television* etc. See **BBC, ITV, Channel 4, Radio 1**

television and radio programmes italicise, except for first mention in reviews, when they go in bold. See **Arts** special section (page 1461)

temperatures the style is *16C (61F)*. See **celsius**

ten-minute rule (Bill) etc; see **Politics** special section (page 1465)

Tennessee

tenpin bowling

Teresa see **Mother**

Terminal 1 (Heathrow; also Terminal 2, 3, 4, 5 etc). See **airports, Heathrow**

Terre'Blanche, Eugene

Terrence Higgins Trust (not Terence)

Territorial Army, or **the Territorials** note cap *T*

terrorist take care with this word and the associated *terrorism; guerrilla* is a less loaded word in the context of violent political struggle. Never use as a synonym of any dissident group that uses violence, eg, *hunt saboteurs*, and always try to specify groups as *paramilitaries, gangster organisations* etc. Remember, one man's terrorist is another man's freedom fighter

Tessa(s) tax-exempt special savings account

Test match should apply only to *cricket* (not rugby); for other sports, use the term *international* (match). See **Sports** special section (page 1466)

textbook one word, similarly *guidebook, stylebook, rulebook* etc

TGV (*train à grande vitesse* – not *de*; French high-speed train)

thalidomide l/c

Thames Barrier, Thames Estuary caps; see **rivers**

Thamesmead, near Erith note *Thamesdown* (Wiltshire administrative district), but *Thames-side*

that do not be shy of this word after *said, denied, claimed* etc; eg, "he denied that the evidence was confusing" is more elegant than "he denied the evidence was confusing". *That* is almost always better than *which* in a defining clause, eg, "the train that I take stops at Slough". As a general rule, use *which* for descriptive clauses and place it between commas, eg, "the night train, which used to carry newspapers, stops at Crewe". See **ensure**

Thatcher at first mention Baroness Thatcher, thereafter Lady Thatcher. In historical context, preferable to say Mrs Thatcher or Margaret Thatcher, eg, "Mrs Thatcher took quick action in sending the task force to the Falklands". It would be wrong to say that her party forced Lady Thatcher from office in 1990. Note **Sir Denis Thatcher** (not Dennis)

theatre always attach *Theatre* (cap) to names at first mention, eg, *the Criterion Theatre* (thereafter *the Criterion* or simply *the theatre*). Some of the main London exceptions are *the Old Vic, Young Vic, Palladium, Coliseum, Apollo Victoria, Donmar Warehouse, Hackney Empire*; and outside London, many such as the *Birmingham Hippodrome, Oxford Playhouse, West Yorkshire Playhouse* etc. See **Arts** special section (page 1461)

theatregoer

the then avoid expressions such as "the then Prime Minister" or (worse) "the then Mr Callaghan"; write "then Prime Minister", "who was Prime Minister at the time" or "Lord Callaghan of Cardiff (then Mr Callaghan)"

The Times almost always use italics for the name of the newspaper, except in headlines. But Times Newspapers Ltd (roman), publisher of *The Times* and *The Sunday Times,* is the operating company of Times Newspapers Holdings.

Also (especially in features headlines, standfirsts etc) The Times Gardener etc is an acceptable style to avoid a mass of italics and apostrophes.

In text, in the difficult area of correspondents' and executive titles, it is permissible to say "the *Times* political correspondent", "the *Times* wine correspondent" etc, although

"political editor of *The Times*", "wine correspondent of *The Times*" etc are preferable.
Always say "Editor of *The Times*", "deputy editor of *The Times*" etc.
It is permissible to say "a *Times* reader", "*Times* readers", but prefer "readers of *The Times*". Similarly, adjectival uses such as "a *Times* article", "a *Times* offer" are acceptable.
Also note Times Law Report (without *The*), but *The Times* Diary, *The Times* Crossword etc. Again, some flexibility – to avoid a proliferation of italics – can be used in puff material etc.
For sections of the paper, avoid italics: eg, *The Times* Magazine, Weekend, Interface.
Keep phrases such as "told *The Times*" to a minimum: *said* is usually preferable.
Note supplements: *The Times Educational Supplement, The Times Higher Education Supplement, The Times Literary Supplement,* and *Nursery World.*
See **correspondents**, **editor**, **exclusive**, **News International**

thermonuclear

Thermos trade name, so always cap

they should always agree with the subject. Avoid sentences such as "If someone loves animals, they should protect them". Say instead "If people love animals, they should protect them"

think-tanks take care in describing their ideological persuasions; we should call the Social Market Foundation (SMF), Demos and Politeia *independent think-tanks*; the Centre for Policy Studies (CPS) and the Institute of Economic Affairs (IEA) *free-market* or *right-wing think-tanks*; and the Institute for Public Policy Research (IPPR) a *left-wing think-tank*

Third Way (caps); new Labour's political stratagem

Third World (caps)

This Morning, the Richard (Madeley) and Judy (Finnegan) show (not *This Morning with Richard and Judy*)

threshold

throne cap sparingly, only in terms of the institution, eg, "he deferred to the wisdom of the Throne"; in other contexts, as with the chair itself, use l/c, eg, "The Queen came to the throne in 1952"

thunderbolts are mythological and do not exist; *lightning bolts* and *thunderclaps* do exist and can also be used metaphorically

thus far avoid; prefer *so far*

Tiananmen Square, Beijing

"tiger" economies (of South-East Asia and the Pacific); use quotes where possible for first mention, subsequently without quotes, and always l/c

time bomb but note *timescale, timeshare*

times never write 6pm last night, 9am tomorrow morning; instead write *6 o'clock last night* or (if the context allows) *6pm*, or *9am tomorrow*

Tinseltown (as in Hollywood); one word

titles the most common solecism is to write Lady Helen Brown etc when we should say simply *Lady Brown.* As a quick rule of thumb, no wife of a baronet or knight takes her Christian name in her title unless she is the daughter of a duke, marquess or earl.
Some titles include a place name, eg, Lord Callaghan of Cardiff, Lord Archer of Weston-super-Mare, while others do not. Follow *Who's Who,* where those whose place name must be included appear in bold caps.
Always check with *Debrett* or *Who's Who* if in doubt. See **Titles** special section (page 1467)

together with avoid; prefer simply *with;* also beware such tautology as *blend together, meet together, link together* etc

Tolkien, J.R.R. (not Tolkein)

tomatoes plural; similarly *potatoes*

tons, tonnes prefer to use *tonnes* in most contexts, though in historical passages *tons* would be more appropriate

Tontons Macoute (Haiti); plural, no final *s*

Top Salaries Review Body now called the *Senior Salaries Review Body*

Top Ten, Top 20, Top 40 etc (in musical or other lists)

tornado (storm); plural *tornados;* also *Tornado, Tornados* (aircraft)

torpedo but note plural *torpedoes*

Torvill (Jayne) **and Dean** (Christopher)

Tory, Tories acceptable alternative for *Conservative(s).* Note *Tory party* (l/c *p*) is permissible. See **Conservative**, **committee** (for 1922 Committee), **select committees**, and **Politics** special section (page 1465)

totalisator, tote take l/c, no quotes; note *the Tote* refers to the organisation

touchpaper

towards (not toward)

townhouse (one word)

tracker dogs, sniffer dogs avoid these clichés wherever possible; usually *dogs* is sufficient, but if the context is unclear, say *police dogs*

tracksuit one word

Trade Descriptions Act

trade-in noun or adjective; but note verb *to trade in*

trademark (one word)

trade names many names of products in common use are proprietary and must be given a capital letter (at risk of legal action if we fail to do so); eg, *Biro, CinemaScope, Dictaphone, Hoover, Jeep, Kodak, Land Rover, Lycra, Perspex, Polaroid, Rollerblade, Tannoy, Technicolor, Thermos, Walkman, Xerox, Yale lock.* Be especially careful about drugs: try to use non-proprietary words such as *aspirin, sleeping pills* etc

trade unions plural (not trades unions); but note *Trades Union Congress.* See **TUC**

trainspotter, trainspotting no hyphens

tranquilliser, tranquillity

transatlantic, transcontinental but note *cross-Channel*

transistor do not use on its own in sense of *transistor radio*

transpire (*to come to light* or *to leak out*). Do not use as an alternative of *to happen* or *occur*

transsexual no hyphen; but note *trans-ship*

Transvaal but note *a Transvaler;* see **South Africa**

trauma, traumatic avoid in the clichéd sense of *deeply upsetting, distressing* etc; it should be confined to its medical meaning of severe shock after an accident or stressful event

travellers, New Age travellers see **Gypsy**, **hippy**

traveller's cheques

Travellers Club no apostrophe; see **London clubs**

Triads cap in Chinese gangster context

Tricolour cap for the French flag, l/c in more general context

trillion American for *a thousand billion* (or *a million million, 1,000,000,000,000*), and should be explained as such in stories about overseas budgets, for example. Try to avoid in stories about Britain

Trinity College Dublin no comma

triple crown (rugby). See **Sports** special section (page 1466)

tripos l/c general context, but note *the History Tripos* etc

trolleys plural of trolley (not -ies)

Trooping the Colour (not *of* the Colour); note also *beating retreat*

Tropics, the cap; note also *the Tropic of Capricorn/ Cancer*, but l/c *tropical, subtropical*

Troubles, the see **Ireland**

troubleshooter one word; similarly *troublespot*

truck permissible in most contexts; see **lorry**

Truman, Harry S. (former US President), but **Fred Trueman**, cricketer

try to the verb *try* must be followed by *to* before the next verb, never by *and,* eg, "I will try to cross the road", not "I will try and cross the road"

TSA The Securities Association

Tsar (not czar); also *Tsarevich, Tsaritsa* (not czarina); caps with the name, l/c in general sense. But note the exception *drugs czar*

TSB formerly the Trustee Savings Bank, now part of Lloyds TSB

T-shirt

Tube cap; acceptable in context on its own for *London Tube*, or *London Underground.* Also cap the various lines such as *Central Line, Metropolitan Line, Victoria Line* etc

tuberculosis the adjective is *tuberculous* (not tubercular)

TUC Trades Union Congress. Note at first mention *General Council of the TUC*, thereafter *general council.* Cap also *General Secretary of the TUC* (as leader of the national body), but note l/c *general secretaries* of individual unions

tug-of-war

tunku (Malaysian prince); cap before name, otherwise l/c

turbo-jet, turbo-prop see **aircraft**

Turin Shroud subsequently *the shroud*

Turkey cap parties, as in *Motherland Party*, *Welfare Party*, *True Path Party* etc

turn down prefer *reject* or *refuse* (except of beds)

turnlines in bold, set right on the front page (and on inside pages where the story begins and spills) – eg, **Continued on page 2, col 7** – and set left on inside pages, eg, **Continued from page 1**

turn-off, turn-on nouns, but note no hyphens in *turnout, turnaround, turnabout*

Tussaud's, Madame but note *the Tussauds Group* (no apostrophe), which also includes *the London Planetarium, Warwick Castle, Alton Towers* and *Chessington World of Adventures.*

Tutankhamun never permit a break as Tutan-khamun; if the name has to be broken on a turn, it may be hyphenated as *Tut-ankhamun* or *Tutankh-amun*

Tutsis see **Hutus**

TV-am no longer exists

Twentieth Century Fox

twentysomething, thirtysomething, fortysomething etc if this modern cliché must be used

Twin Towers (of Wembley) (caps)

twofold, threefold, fourfold, tenfold etc

two minutes' silence, the see **Armistice**, **Remembrance**

two thirds, three quarters etc but hyphenate adjectival use, eg, *a two-thirds share.* Such expressions usually take the plural verb, eg, "three quarters of the children prefer horror films"; the same applies even in "a third of the children prefer blancmange". But note "two thirds of the bus was empty"

Tyne and Wear (not &)

typify, typified (not typefy)

Tyrol (no longer Tirol)

Uu

U no full point after Burmese prefix, eg, U Nu

Ucas Universities and Colleges Admissions Service (not UCAS)

Uefa, Uefa Cup (not UEFA); see **Cup, Sports** special section (page 1466)

UK acceptable abbreviation for *United Kingdom* in both text and headlines. But be careful that it is strictly applicable; see **Britain**

Ukraine (not *the* Ukraine)

Ulster permissible, especially in headlines, but use *Northern Ireland* or *the Province* when possible; see **Ireland**

ultimate use sparingly. *Ultimate limit* means *limit*

ultimatums (not ultimata); see **referendum**

ultraviolet

unchristian l/c; see **Christian**

uncoordinated but note *co-ordinate*; see **hyphens**

under-age hyphenated; similarly *over-age*

underestimate

Underground, London see **Tube**

underreact

undervalue

underwater one word as adjective, eg, *underwater exploration*; but two words as adverb, eg, the couple were married *under water*

under way always two words

Unesco United Nations Educational, Scientific, and Cultural Organisation. See **United Nations**

UNHCR United Nations High Commissioner for Refugees. See **United Nations** (paragraph d)

Unionist cap in Ulster political context; see **Ireland**

Union Jack except in most naval and some ceremonial contexts, when **Union Flag** is correct; note that in the Royal Navy, *Union Jack* only when flown at the jackstaff

unique (only one, having no like or equal); do not use except in this specific sense. Phrases such as *very unique, even more unique* are nonsense and are banned

unitary authorities since the abolition of Avon, Humberside, Cleveland, and now Hereford and Worcester, plus wholesale reorganisation of Welsh and Scottish local government, take care when locating towns in these areas.

Former county of Avon: should now be described as in either Gloucestershire or Somerset.

Former Hereford and Worcester County Council: from April 1998, replaced by a new Worcestershire County Council and a new unitary authority for Herefordshire.

Former Berkshire County Council: replaced by six unitary authorities (Bracknell Forest, Newbury, Reading, Slough, Windsor and Maidenhead, and Wokingham).

Former Humberside: should be located as either East Riding (north of the Humber) or Lincolnshire (south of the river).

Former Cleveland, reorganised Yorkshire: cap the West and South in West Yorkshire and South Yorkshire, even though they are not new unitary authorities (as North Yorkshire is). The reason is that they are still regarded by people living there as cohesive regions, similar to the West Midlands and Greater Manchester, two other metropolitan counties that no longer exist per se. Moreover, statutory bodies such as *West Yorkshire Police* and *West Yorkshire Passenger Transport Authority* still exist; so the best rule-of-thumb will be to use the cap in future in all cases.

Wales: note that Clwyd, Dyfed and Gwent no longer exist as authorities, so unless the new county has a traditional and generally familiar name (eg, Pembrokeshire, Carmarthenshire, Powys, Denbighshire etc), it will often be simpler to locate smaller towns and villages just as in North Wales, Mid Wales, West Wales, South Wales. Note that Gwynedd does still exist as a unitary authority (though smaller than when it was a county). If in doubt, use one of the North/Mid/West/South designations.

Scotland: regions such as Central, Grampian and Strathclyde should now be referred to only in their historical context or if they persist in titles such as *Strathclyde Police* or *University of Strathclyde*. Permissible too to refer informally to the *Central belt* (between Edinburgh and Glasgow), despite the scrapping of Central region

United Nations, or **UN, the** spell out at first mention where possible, though this can no longer be a hard and fast rule. Other points:

a *Secretary-General of the UN*; now Kofi Annan

b *UN Security Council, UN General Assembly* at first mention, and thereafter keep the caps, as in *the Security Council, the General Assembly*

c UN derivatives such as *Unesco, Unifil, Unprofor* etc are written thus where the word can be voiced. See **initials**

d *The UN High Commissioner for Refugees* (never Commission) is the organisation, as well as a person. Abbreviate to UNHCR after first mention

United Reformed Church (not Reform); see **Churches** special section (page 1462)

United States (of America); always followed by a singular verb. Common usage allows abbreviation to US in text as well as headlines, but do not ignore the word *America*. See **America(n), New York, Washington**

universal claims always beware of claiming that something is the first or last of its kind, or that someone is the first person to ... or the last surviving member of ... or the oldest inhabitant etc. See **ever, first, superlatives**

Universe cap in planetary context, as *Sun, Earth, Moon* etc, but l/c in phrases such as "she became the centre of his universe"

universities always cap as in *Birmingham University* (or the *University of Birmingham*), *Sussex University, the University of East Anglia* etc; thereafter l/c *the university* . If in doubt about the proper title, consult *The Times Good University Guide*. See **Cambridge University, Oxford University, Vice-Chancellor**

University College London no comma

university posts at first mention, cap *Vice-Chancellor, Chancellor, Pro-Vice-Chancellor, Pro-Chancellor, Dean, Master, Professor, Fellow* etc; at subsequent mentions l/c; eg, "Dr Mark Blodkin, Professor of Modern History at Kent University, said ..." then later, "the professor said ..."

unlikeable, unloveable

unmistakable (not with the middle *e*)

unparalleled

unshakeable

Untouchables (in Indian caste system); cap

unveil take care with this word, which means to remove a covering from something, or (by extension) to disclose. It should not be used in phrases such as unveiling a ship, or unveiling a flag

up avoid unnecessary use after verbs, as in meet up, rest up, end up. See **down**

upbeat, upfront, upgrade

upmarket similarly *downmarket*

upon take care with use of *up, upon, up on,* and *on,* eg, "The cat jumped *on* the floor, *upon* the mouse, *up on* the table, then *up* the tree"

Upper House, Lower House see **Politics** special section (page 1465)

Uruguay Round (world trade deal); note caps. See **Gatt, World Trade Organisation**

US see **America(n), United States**

USSR avoid wherever possible; write *Soviet Union* instead (and now only in historical context). See **Russia**

utilise almost always prefer *use*

Utopia, Utopian cap

U-turn overworked phrase, especially in the political context. Be sparing in its use, particularly when only a minor change of policy direction is involved

Vv

vacuum in common use as a verb, but avoid *Hoover*, a trade name. See **Hoover**, **trade names**

vagaries means *aimless wanderings* or *eccentric ideas*, not *vicissitudes* or *changes* (as in weather)

Valentine's Day (normally omit St); keep cap for *Valentine card* etc

Valium proprietary term, so cap

Valletta (Malta)

valley cap in full name, such as *the Thames Valley*, *the Wye Valley* etc. Note also the *Welsh Valleys*

Van cap in Dutch names when surname alone is given, eg, Van Gogh, but l/c when used in full, eg, Vincent van Gogh. Note Ludwig *van* Beethoven (not von), although the composer was German. See **von**

Van Dyck, Sir Anthony but note l/c *vandyke brown*, *vandyke beard* etc

various do not use as a pronoun as in "various of the countries protested"; write "several/ many of the countries ..."

Varsity match acceptable colloquialism for the Oxford-Cambridge rugby match

VAT value-added tax; no longer need to spell out fully

V-chip (electronic scramblers for TV)

VE-Day see **D-Day**, **VJ-Day**

Velázquez, Diego Rodríguez de Silva y Velázquez (17th-century Spanish artist; not Velasquez); normally last name on its own will suffice

Velcro (cap, proprietary)

veld (not veldt)

ventricles (anatomical; not ventricals)

veranda no final *h*

verbal (pertaining to words); do not confuse with *oral* (pertaining to the mouth). Sadly, corrupted phrases such as *verbal abuse* and *verbal warning* have permeated sports journalism to the point of our having to accept them occasionally, but always try to find an alternative. See **oral**

verbosity watch out for, and eliminate, wordy phrases such as "on the part of" (use *by*), "a large number of" (*many*), "numerous occasions" (*often*), "this day and age" (does not even demand an alternative)

verdict do not use for civil hearings – verdicts come at the end of criminal trials. See **employment tribunals**

verger, virger use the latter in context of St Paul's and Winchester Cathedrals

vermilion (not vermillion)

versus abbreviation is *v* (l/c, no point)

very one of the most overworked words in English. Always try to omit

vetoes plural

viable (capable of independent existence); do not use as a synonym of *feasible* or *practicable*

vicar take care not to use as a generic word for *priest*, *parson* or *clergyman*. *Vicar* means specifically the incumbent of a parish (unless a rector); if in doubt, *clergyman* is usually safer. See **Churches** special section (page 1462)

vice always hyphenate in its deputy context, eg, *vice-chairman*, *vice-president* etc but not in its depravity context, eg, *vice squad*. Do not confine the meaning of vice to sex: it is the opposite of virtue and has a correspondingly wide range of meaning

Vice-Chancellor (of a university); cap at first mention, then l/c. See **university posts**, **job titles**

vice versa roman, no hyphen

Victoria and Albert (Museum); use the ampersand only in the abbreviation *V&A*

videotape one word; but note *video cassette*, *video recorder/recording*. *Video* (for film recording) is now common usage and permissible

Vietcong (not Viet Cong)

Virgil (not Vergil)

Virtuality trade name, so cap; do not use as a synonym of virtual reality

vis-à-vis note roman, hyphens and accent

viscountcy (describes the rank); see **Titles** special section (page 1467)

vitamin A, B, C etc note l/c *v*

viz prefer *namely, that is,* or even *ie*

VJ-Day see **D-Day**, **VE-Day**

vocal cords (not chords)

voiceover no hyphen

volcanoes plural of volcano

volte-face roman, hyphenated

von (German); usually l/c in the middle of a name, and capped only at the beginning of a sentence. See **Van**

VP never use as abbreviation of *vice-president*

Ww

wagon

Wales cap *North Wales, South Wales, Mid Wales, West Wales.* For new counties under the local government reorganisation of 1996, see **unitary authorities**

Walkman trade name, so cap; in general sense, use *personal stereo*

walkout

Wall's (ice-cream etc)

Wan Azizah, wife of Anwar Ibrahim, Malaysian politician. At subsequent mentions, *Dr Azizah* (do not use the Ismail part of her name)

war crimes tribunal cap only when using the full title, *the International War Crimes Tribunal for the Former Yugoslavia.* It sits at The Hague and has a President and a Chief Prosecutor

war game(s) two words

warfarin not a trade name, so l/c

warn transitive verb that requires a direct personal object: ie, a person has to warn somebody about something. Do not write "The Chancellor warned that taxes would rise"; but "The Chancellor *gave warning that/issued a warning that* ...", or alternatively, "The Chancellor *warned MPs that* ...". However, we can afford some flexibility in headlines, eg, *Teachers warn of school closures* would be acceptable

wars cap the *First World War, Second World War, Cold War, Korean War, Vietnam War, Gulf War* etc; but prefer the *Falklands conflict* because war was never formally declared; if the phrase has to be used, write *Falklands war* (l/c)

warships take care with the following distinction: to serve *in* a warship, but *on* a merchant ship; a naval officer is *appointed* to serve *in HMS Sheffield,* not *posted* to serve. See **Armed Forces** special section (page 1459)

wartime

Washington not usually necessary to add DC (as in Washington DC), but occasionally useful to distinguish it from Washington State (caps). That and New York State are the only two states needing caps to avoid confusion. See **New York**

washout (one word)

waste usually better to write *waste* than *wastage,* which means process of loss, its amount or rate

wastepaper bin/basket

watchdog

watercolour, watercolourist but note *Royal Society of Painters in Water Colours*

Waterstone's (booksellers); note apostrophe

wear write *menswear, women's wear, children's wear, sportswear.* See **clothing**

weather stories (about floods, hurricanes, snow, record sunshine etc in the UK) always take a cross-reference to the back page weather forecast. Style is bold, set right, eg, **Forecast, page 24**

website, but cap **the Web:** see **World Wide Web**

week, weekend the week ends on Saturday night. Common sense will dictate whether to say *last week, this week, next week* etc. Beware of references to *at the weekend* in Monday papers: always make clear whether you mean the weekend just past or next Saturday and Sunday

weights and measures abbreviations context will determine when to abbreviate inches, stone, pounds, ounces etc. "He was 6ft 7in" (not ins, and no space between number and abbreviation); but "she stood two feet from the kerb". Similarly, "she weighed 8st 12lb" (not lbs); but "he was several pounds overweight". See **scientific measures**

weights and measures conversion no longer convert metric measures into their imperial counterpart. See **scientific measures, celsius**

Welch, Welsh note *The Royal Welch Fusiliers,* but *Welsh Guards* (part of The Guards Division). See **Armed Forces** special section (page 1459)

welfare state l/c; but note the *Welfare to Work* programme (cap W twice, no hyphens). See **State**

wellbeing

wellington boots note l/c

wellwisher do not hyphenate

Welsh Assembly now capped; and note *First Secretary* (not First Minister) of the Assembly.

Welsh, Irvine (the playwright)

Welsh Valleys for the (former) mining valleys of South Wales

west, western etc for when to cap in geographical context, see **compass points**

West, the (in global political sense); similarly *Western leaders, Western Europe* etc

western (as in cowboy films); l/c

whereabouts singular, eg, "his whereabouts is not known". Prefer "nobody knows where he is"

whether rarely needs *or not* to follow it

which see **that**

while (not whilst)

whingeing with middle *e*

whips cap *Chief Whip, Whips' Office,* but l/c the unspecific, eg, **a government whip**. See **Politics** special section (page 1465)

whisky (from Scotland); *Scotch* is acceptable as alternative; but **whiskey** (from Ireland and America). See **Scotch**

whistle-blower

whistle-stop (tour etc)

Whitbread Round the World Race note caps, no hyphens

White Cliffs of Dover caps

white-collar workers

White Paper note caps, as with *Green Paper,* but cap only those issued by the Government. A "white paper" from the Opposition should be styled in quotes and l/c at first mention, thereafter just l/c. See **Green Paper, Politics** special section (page 1465)

whiz-kid note only one *z*, but use this colloquialism sparingly

WHO World Health Organisation; spell out at first mention, then *the WHO*

who, whom which of these to use is determined solely by its function in the relative clause. Remember that *whom* has to be the object of the verb in the relative clause. Thus, "she is the woman whom the police wish to interview" (ie, the police wish to interview *her,* not *she*); the other most common use of *whom* is after a preposition such as *by, with* or *from,* eg, "the person from whom he bought a ticket".

Beware of traps, however: "Who do you think did it?" is correct (not *whom,* because *who* is the subject of "did it", not the object of "do you think"); and "Give it to whoever wants it" is correct (not *whomever*) because *whoever* is the subject of the verb *wants.*

Beware too of constructions such as "he squirted ammonia at a van driver who [correct] he believed had cut him up". This is correct because "he believed" is simply an interjection; "who" is not the object of "he believed" but the subject of the subordinate clause, "who ... had cut him up"

whodunnit (not whodunit)

why usually superfluous after *reason,* eg, "the reason he did it was ...", not "the reason why he did it was ..."

wide no hyphen in compounds such as *countrywide, nationwide, worldwide*

wideawake always one word

widow (woman); note *widower* (man); never say "widow of the late John Jones"; she is the "widow of John Jones"

wildfowl, wildlife

Wild West

Wimbledon caps for the *Centre Court, No 1 Court, No 14 Court* etc. See **Sports** special section (page 1466)

Winchester College its pupils are *Wykehamists*

wind with strong winds, give a description as well as force number (in numerals), eg, *storm force 10* (add "on the Beaufort scale" where appropriate. The scale grades wind speeds from 0 to 12; Americans use the scale to 17). Never say "gale-force winds" when *gales* is meant

wines l/c in most cases, for both the type and the grape, except where it would look out of place, eg, *bordeaux, burgundy, champagne, claret, moselle, alsace, rioja,* but a *Côtes du Rhône*, a *Hunter Valley chardonnay*. Cap when referring specifically to the wine-growing region, eg, "I prefer a good burgundy to an alsace, but I think the best wines still come from Bordeaux"; "he preferred to buy his champagne only in Champagne"

wine bar two words

Winslet, Kate

Wirral (not Wirrall); permissible to refer to *The Wirral* (cap *T*), but note *the Wirral peninsula*

wistaria (not wisteria)

witch-hunt but note *witchcraft*

withhold (not withold)

witnesses in British courts witnesses go into the witness box and give evidence; they do not take the stand and testify. In the general sense, prefer *witness* to *eyewitness* wherever possible. See **eyewitness**

woebegone, woeful

Wolf Cubs now just Cubs; see **Boy Scouts**

women doctors, women teachers etc adopt the plural through common usage. See **feminine designations, lady**

Woolf reforms several important changes have been made in civil litigation rules and terminology since April 1999. Three of the commonest are: plaintiffs are now *claimants*; a writ is now a *claim form*; and *notices of application* will be served in the place of summonses. For fuller list, see **Courts** special section (page 1463)

Woolworths no apostrophe either in formal name for business contexts or colloquial use for the store and products

word-processor, word-processing note hyphens

workers *farmworkers, metalworkers, roadworkers* one word; note two for *car workers, oil workers, office workers* etc

workforce, workshop, work-to-rule

world avoid, wherever possible, phrases such as *the fashion world, the theatre world, the cricket world* etc

World Heritage Site (caps)

World Trade Organisation (successor body to Gatt); abbreviate to WTO; see **Gatt, Uruguay Round**

World Wide Fund for Nature (not Worldwide; nor World Wildlife Fund, its old name); abbreviate to WWF; note the general adjective *worldwide*

World Wide Web (Internet); caps and three words; and *the Web* for short. But keep *website* l/c. See **Internet**

Worrall Thompson, Antony (TV cook)

worthwhile one word; often used where simply *worth* would be better, eg, "the programme was worth recording"

wrack (seaweed or wreckage); do not confuse with *racked by doubts* etc. See **racked**

wreaked (havoc, heavy damage, vengeance etc; not wrought)

write-off noun, similarly the noun *write-up*, but note *a write-down* (in business context)

writes with written-in bylines, prefer the construction "Ann Bloggs writes" to "writes Ann Bloggs". Use the singular with, eg, (Our Foreign Staff writes). Normal style is to use brackets on news and sports pages, italics on features

wrongdoer, wrongdoing but note *wrong-footed, wrong-headed*

WWF abbreviation of the World Wide Fund for Nature and for legal reasons must not be used for the World Wrestling Federation (write *the federation* if a shorter form for the wrestling group is needed). See **World Wide Fund for Nature**

Wyndham's Theatre (London); note the apostrophe

Xx Yy Zz

xenophobe, xenophobia

Xerox trade name, so cap

Xhosa (Bantu tribe; not Khosa); note plural Xhosas

Xmas must not be used in *The Times* (unless part of special title or in a direct quote etc)

X-ray now an acceptable abbreviation of *X-ray examination*. Note also the verb *to X-ray someone*. But do not shorten when you mean *an X-ray photograph*

Yardies (West Indian criminal gangs)

Yarmouth (Isle of Wight); note *Great Yarmouth* on the Norfolk coast

Yellow Pages italics for the book, but roman for the organisation

Yemen (not *the* Yemen)

"yes" vote, "no" vote

yeti (abominable snowman); note l/c

YMCA, YWCA

yoghurt

yoke (oxen); do not confuse with **yolk** (egg)

Yorkshire since the reorganisation of 1996, see **unitary authorities** for how to locate places in the county. Specify the location for smaller towns and villages, eg, Thirsk, North Yorkshire, but not Bradford or Leeds. Note *the Yorkshire Dales*, or simply *the Dales*, and *the North York Moors* (not North Yorkshire Moors)

young offender institution l/c for general use, but cap for specific, eg, *Feltham Young Offender Institution*

Young Turks caps

youth courts not juvenile courts, which no longer exist. See **Courts** special section (page 1463)

yuan the Chinese currency (rather than *the renminbi*)

Yugoslav (not Yugoslavian); adjective from Yugoslavia

yuletide (l/c)

yuppie noun or adjective

Yves Saint Laurent (not St)

Zaire after the overthrow of President Mobutu in May 1997, call the country, at first mention, the Democratic Republic of Congo (formerly Zaire), and thereafter simply Congo. The former French Congo should be called Congo-Brazzaville

Zambezi (not Zambesi)

-ze in almost all cases use the *-ise* ending rather than *-ize*. Two of the main exceptions are *capsize* and *synthesizer*

Zeitgeist (the spirit of the times); note cap and italics

zeppelin (airship); note l/c

Zeta-Jones, Catherine (hyphen)

ziggurat

zigzag, zigzagging

Zimmer frame trademark, so cap

zodiac, zodiacal (as in signs of the zodiac); note l/c

zoo cap as in *London Zoo, Dudley Zoo*; thereafter *the zoo*

SPECIAL SECTIONS

THE ARMED FORCES

ROYAL NAVY

At first mention *the Royal Navy* (caps), thereafter *the Navy* (retain the cap); *naval* is l/c except in titles such as *Royal Naval Volunteer Reserve* (RNVR) etc.

Ships are styled *HMS Achilles* or the *Achilles*. They should generally be treated as feminine; thus *she* and *her* rather than *it* and *its*. Ships are *named*, not *christened*. Note that Royal Fleet Auxiliary ships are entitled RFA, eg, *RFA Fort George* (not HMS...)

General terms

alter course (not change)

Armed Forces, Armed Services, the Services caps, but l/c *serviceman, servicewoman*. Also cap *Service* and *Forces* when used adjectivally as in *a Service family*

astern (never behind or following); eg, the *Achilles* was astern of the *Ajax*

Britannia refer to her as the former Royal Yacht

company Royal Navy ships do not have crews, they have ship's company

embarked *in* (not on)

the Fleet cap

line ahead (not astern)

moored or **made fast** (never tied up)

on board preferable to aboard

pennant (not pendant)

ratings (not *other ranks*, in the Navy)

Royal Marines caps

SBS Special Boat Service (no longer Squadron)

serving *in* a warship (but on a merchant ship); an officer is *appointed* to serve *in HMS Sheffield,* not posted to serve ... Also note that sailors serve *in a submarine,* even though subs are boats

signalman (not signaller)

submarines called *boats* (not ships) in the Royal Navy

tow the towing ship has the towed ship *in* tow; the towed ship is *under* tow

Union Flag (not Union Jack in naval contexts, except when flown at the jackstaff)

under way

weigh anchor (not ship anchor, which would mean that a ship had left her anchor at the bottom of the sea)

Ranks

abbreviation prefer not to abbreviate ranks in text of news stories; however, in lists of promotions etc on the Court Page, the following abbreviations will apply: Adm, Cdre (Commodore), Capt, Cdr (Commander), Lt-Cdr, Lt, CPO (Chief Petty Officer), L/S (Leading Seaman)

hyphenation *Times* style is to hyphenate those ranks consisting of a compound of two individual designations, eg, *Lieutenant-Commander, Commandant-General, Surgeon-Captain*; also any rank with *vice* or *rear,* eg, *Vice-Admiral, Rear-Admiral*. We should also hyphenate *Commander-in-Chief*

flag ranks a flag officer is a rear-admiral or above, exercising command and authorised by the Admiralty to fly a flag. The following are flag ranks: *Admiral of the Fleet, Admiral, Vice-Admiral, Rear-Admiral*. Although the Duke of Edinburgh is an Admiral of the Fleet, the Fleet is actually commanded by an admiral whose job title is *Commander-in-Chief Fleet* (CinC Fleet)

THE ARMY

Cap *the Army* when referred to as *the Service*, eg, "Two hundred new tanks were bought by the Army yesterday", or "He denied that he hated the Army"; but l/c when used adjectivally, eg, "An army raid was launched yesterday on the front line... ", or "An army spokesman rejected the idea..."

Give soldiers their full title at first mention, eg, General Herbert Carruthers, thereafter General Carruthers or the general. Never refer to them as Mr in news stories.

General terms

beating retreat (not beating the retreat)

guards of honour (ceremonial troops used to greet visiting dignitaries); like all guards, they are *mounted*, as sentries are *posted*

The King's Own Royal Border Regiment (full title)

King's Troop RHA (Royal Horse Artillery), remains thus even though the Sovereign is the Queen

Last Post (not *the*); note it is *sounded* (not played)

parade troops *march* through the streets (not parade)

Royal Corps of Signals may be contracted to *Royal Signals* (not RCS)

Royal Electrical and Mechanical Engineers REME for short (never Reme)

Royal Engineers can be abbreviated to RE (not REs)

The Royal Welch Fusiliers, Welch Regiment but note *Welsh Guards*

SAS Special Air Service (regiment). See **SBS** under **Royal Navy**

Trooping the Colour (not Trooping *of* the Colour)

trumpeters, buglers cavalry regiments have *trumpeters*, infantry regiments have *buglers*. They are not interchangeable

Ranks and regiments

regimental names one of the trickiest areas is when to include *The* as part of the name of regiments. With defence cuts and the amalgamation of regiments in the past few years, titles have changed rapidly, so checking an up-to-date *Army List* is imperative. General styles as follows:

Companies A Company, B Battery, 94 (Locating) Battery, C Squadron
Battalions 1st, 2nd etc, and 1st/5th, 61 Field Regiment, RA
Brigades 24 Infantry Brigade, 5 Airborne Brigade
Divisions 7th Armoured Division
Corps X Corps, XII Corps
Armies First Army
Army Groups 21 Army Group

ranks the same guidance on abbreviation and hyphenation applies as to the Royal Navy:

abbreviation prefer not to abbreviate ranks in text of news stories; however, in lists of promotions etc on the Court Page, the following abbreviations will apply: Gen, Lt-Gen, Maj-Gen, Brig, Col, Lt-Col, Maj, Capt, Lt, 2nd Lt, WO1 (Warrant Officer Class 1), WO2, S Sgt (Staff Sergeant), Sgt, Cpl, Bdr (Bombardier), L Cpl, Pte (Private), Gdsmn (Guardsman), Gnr (Gunner), Rfn (Rifleman)

hyphenation hyphenate those ranks consisting of a compound of two individual designations, eg, *Major-General, Lieutenant-General, Lieutenant-Colonel, Sergeant-Major* etc, but not compounds such as *Staff Sergeant, Lance Corporal*. (Note that *Brigadier-General* does not exist in the British Army, though it does, eg, in the American and French.)

Chief of the Defence Staff a naval Chief of the Defence Staff becomes *Admiral of the Fleet Sir John Jones*; an army one is *Field Marshal Sir John Jones*; and an air force one is *Marshal of the Royal Air Force Sir John Jones*, in each case followed by *Chief of the Defence Staff*

field marshal either a peer or a knight, so at first mention, eg, *Field Marshal Sir Richard Potts*, subsequently *Sir Richard*

officers with personal titles describe in full at first mention, eg, *Lieutenant-General Sir Amos Burke*, subsequently *Sir Amos* or *General Burke*

ROYAL AIR FORCE

Use the *Royal Air Force* or the *RAF* in text, not the Air Force (see **air force** in main section).

Ranks

ranks with ranks, the same guidance on abbreviation applies as to the Royal Navy and the Army (see previous page)

hyphenation the only RAF rank to take a hyphen is *Air Vice-Marshal*

abbreviations in lists only, as follows: AVM (Air Vice-Marshal), Air Cdre (Air Commodore), Gp Capt (Group Captain), Wg Cdr (Wing Commander), Sqn Ldr (Squadron Leader), Flt Lt (Flight Lieutenant), FO (Flying Officer), PO (Pilot Officer), FS (Flight Sergeant), Chief Tech (Chief Technician), Sgt (Sergeant), Cpl (Corporal), SAC/SACW (Senior Aircraftman/Senior Aircraftwoman) etc. Note, never shorten Flight Lieutenant to Lieutenant at subsequent mentions.

Types of aircraft (not planes); *Harrier jump-jet*, *Tornado* (plural *Tornados*), *B52*, *F111* (no hyphens), etc

THE ARTS

ART

Titles of paintings, drawings, sculptures and exhibitions are now all in italic.

DANCE

ballets titles in italics
cha-cha-cha (not cha-cha)
Latin dancing cap *L*
pas de deux, corps de ballet roman
paso doble two words
pointe shoes (not point)

FILM

auteur roman
cinéma-vérité roman
8mm film, 16mm etc
films titles in italics
film-maker hyphen
film noir roman
Palme d'or roman
3-D

LITERATURE

Book titles including novels, plays, short stories, poems (short or long), magazine articles, chapter headings, textbooks, reference books, biographies etc take italics. But do not italicise the Bible, the Talmud, the Koran, Book of Genesis etc.

MUSIC

Song titles (classical or pop) take italics; no need to cap every word in the title, eg, *Bring it on Home to Me* rather than *Bring It On Home To Me.*

albums titles in italics
First Violin Concerto note roman and caps, because it is a genre
Mozart works use the numbering system of Köchel, eg, K527
Number abbreviate to No, eg, Symphony No 3
operas titles in italics, as arias
Opus write, eg, Op (Op28)
orchestral works those with non-genre titles take italics, eg, *Night on the Bare Mountain*
Proms, the no need to spell out Promenade Concerts; note also caps for *Promenaders; the Last Night of the Proms*
Requiem roman caps, because it is a genre
symphony style is roman caps, eg, Symphony No 3; but where symphonies have numbers and popular alternative titles, place the title in italics, eg, *Eroica*. Spell out ordinals, eg, Mahler's Fourth Symphony, but note Symphony No 4
tempos (not tempi)
virtuosos (not virtuosi)

THEATRE

Act I, scene 2 etc cap Act and use Roman numeral, l/c scene and Arabic numeral
dramatis personae roman
plays titles in italics
Wyndham's Theatre (London)

TV AND RADIO

Television and radio programmes take italics, except for first mention in reviews, when they go in bold.

GENERAL ARTS TERMS

a cappella
Albert Hall, Festival Hall, National Theatre generally omit *Royal*; but note *Royal Opera House, Royal Shakespeare Company, Royal Ballet* (which is different from the *Birmingham Royal Ballet*), etc
Arts Council thereafter l/c *the council* provided the context is clear
Bartók, Béla
the Beatles, the Rolling Stones etc no need to cap *the* unless at the start of a sentence; but prefer to keep cap *T* with *The Who* and *The The*
cinemagoer, dancegoer, theatregoer one word
commedia dell'arte
debut, decor, matinee, premiere note no accents
Dvořák, Antonin
hi-fi
Internet, the note cap; also *the Net, World Wide Web, the Web,* but lower case for *website*
Janáček, Leos
Janet Holmes à Court
mezzo-soprano hyphen
nightclub
subplot, subtext, subtitle
Symphony Hall, Birmingham omit *the*
3-D

THE CHURCHES

GENERAL STYLES

Anglican bishops note they are *consecrated*; Roman Catholic bishops are *ordained*

Archbishop of Canterbury is Primate of All England; note the *Archbishop of York* is Primate of England

biblical references write, eg, II Corinthians ii, 2; Luke iv, 5

Bible, the always cap and roman, similarly the Koran, the Talmud; but note l/c *biblical*. Also caps and roman for Books of the Bible, eg, Book of Job

caps or **l/c** use caps for Bible (note l/c *biblical*), Blessed Sacrament, (Holy) Communion, the Cross, the Crucifixion, Eucharist, the Gospels, (Requiem) Mass, the Resurrection etc; use l/c for baptism, confirmation, evensong, last rites, matins, ordination, psalms (but the *Book of Psalms*)

churches use caps with, eg, the Church of England, the Roman Catholic Church, the United Reformed Church, the Methodist Church, the Church Army. Also cap the Church in context of the institution (but not adjectivally, as in "the vicar accused church authorities yesterday ..."). For individual churches, write, eg, St James's Church, Bighampton, or simply St James's, Bighampton

Church Commissioners cap first mention, then l/c *the commissioners*; note there are three chief officers: the First (Second, Third) Church Estates Commissioner

churchgoer one word

Church of Ireland, Church in Wales (NB *in*), **Scottish Episcopal Church** note that these are Anglican but disestablished; the *Church of Scotland* is Presbyterian but established

Episcopal(ian) means Anglican in the United States, Scotland and elsewhere

General Synod cap at first mention, thereafter l/c *the synod*. It has three houses: bishops, clergy and laity

hymns names go in italics

Nonconformist and **Free Churches** caps; note that the *United Reformed Church* is composed of the former Congregational Church and the Presbyterian Church of England; but some "Congregational" congregations remain outside the reformed group

Pope, the not usually necessary to give his full name, eg, Pope John Paul II (unless several Popes are mentioned in a story), but always cap. Note l/c *papacy, pontiff*

Rev never ever write the solecism the Rev Brown or (even worse) Rev Brown. The correct style is *the Rev Joseph Brown*, thereafter *Mr Brown*

Roman Catholic at first mention in full; thereafter *Catholic* is acceptable

Scotland distinguish the *Free Church of Scotland* (the "Wee Frees") from the established *Church of Scotland* and also from the *Presbyterian Church of Scotland*, of which Lord Mackay of Clashfern is a member. Note the *Moderator of the General Assembly of the Church of Scotland* (not Moderator of the Church of Scotland)

Supreme Governor of the Church of England (the Queen; note not *head* of the Church of England)

Trinity note cap pronoun, eg, *Jesus's teachings, His example; God is He*

Vicar do not use as a generic word for *priest, parson, clergyman* etc. Vicar means specifically the incumbent of a parish (unless a rector). If in doubt, *clergyman* is usually a safer term

TITLES

Senior clergy, Anglicans

bishops and **archbishops** by convention, always follow the title of their office, eg, the Archbishop of Canterbury, Dr George Carey; the Archbishop of Barchester, the Most Rev John Smith; or (for diocesan bishops), the Bishop of Barchester, the Right Rev John Smith. Use Dr when appropriate, though not all high ecclesiastics have doctorates; eg, the Bishop of Lowchester, Dr John Smith; subsequent references, the archbishop (bishop), or Dr Smith (if so entitled) – never Mr Smith

archdeacons below archbishops and bishops, similar styles prevail, eg, Archdeacon of Barchester, the Ven John Smith (thereafter Mr Smith or, more commonly, Canon Smith)

cathedral deans and provosts write, eg, the Dean of Barchester, the Very Rev John Smith (Dean Smith)

rural deans just the Rev John Smith (Mr Smith)

canons and prebendaries write, eg, Canon/Prebendary John Smith, thereafter Canon Smith

Senior clergy, Roman Catholic

archbishops at first mention, the Roman Catholic Archbishop of Liverpool, the Most Rev Patrick Kelly; subsequent mention Archbishop Kelly or the archbishop

Archbishop of Westminster, Cardinal X – no need to say Roman Catholic Archbishop of Westminster, but note Roman Catholic Archdiocese of Westminster. Subsequent mentions, Cardinal X

bishops first mention the Roman Catholic Bishop of Plymouth, the Right Rev Christopher Budd, thereafter Bishop Budd or the bishop; very few Catholic archbishops or bishops have doctorates, but if so, write, eg, Dr Budd

Monsignor (abbreviate to Mgr); do not use for Roman Catholic archbishops or bishops in Britain, though it can be a convenient form in foreign stories

Junior clergy

Christian priests, deacons, ministers, rectors, vicars of all denominations except Roman Catholic or Orthodox write, eg, the Rev Frank Faith at first mention, thereafter Mr Faith (see General Styles, under Rev). For *women clergy*, write the Rev Joan Faith, thereafter Mrs Faith or Miss Faith

Roman Catholic and Orthodox clergy write, eg, Father Justin Hope at first mention (avoid the ugly Fr abbreviation), thereafter Father Hope for Catholics, but Father Justin for Orthodox. Also use Father with Benedictines, eg, Father Goode, not Dom Goode

nuns use Sister Charity, Mother Charity, Mother Teresa

Jesuits take designation SJ on first mention, eg, "the Rev Albert Leader, SJ, said yesterday ..."

Foreign prelates

Ireland, Africa, North America etc write Anglican Bishop of ..., Roman Catholic Bishop of ...; but in countries where, for example, Roman Catholicism is the overwhelming faith, the denomination may be superfluous (eg, the Archbishop of Warsaw ...) or supplied by context

South Africa

Church of the Province of Southern Africa (or Church of the Province, or the Anglican Church) is Anglican but sometimes uses incense, Stations of the Cross etc

The Church of England (in South Africa); separate entity from the Anglican Church. The Church of England split from the Anglican communion in the late 19th century; incense, Stations of the Cross etc are not used

The Courts

civil cases These are heard in magistrates' courts and county courts, the more serious in the High Court, which has three divisions – the Queen's Bench, Chancery, and Family Divisions (cap Division in full title). In London they are based at the Royal Courts of Justice in the Strand.

The Divisional Court of the Queen's Bench Division can quash decisions by magistrates' courts and hear appeals from lower courts on points of law. It is also the court for reviewing governmental bodies' or local authorities' decisions – judicial review. Distinguish between applications for leave and the main hearing

criminal cases Most of these are dealt with by magistrates' courts, presided over by magistrates, who are lay justices (JPs). The busiest have full-time paid magistrates, stipendiaries. The more serious criminal cases are heard in the Crown Court, of which the most famous (in the City of London) is the Central Criminal Court, or Old Bailey (either form acceptable)

Court of Appeal always use the full title at first mention and wherever possible thereafter, though *appeal court* (l/c) may be used sparingly. The court sits with three judges, who are Lords Justices of Appeal. The highest court in the land is the Judicial Committee of the House of Lords (though normally the *House of Lords* or simply l/c *the law lords* will suffice); they are the most senior judges, formally called the Lords of Appeal in Ordinary

Scottish courts Court of Session, Edinburgh (for civil actions); High Court of Justiciary (prosecution of serious crimes and criminal appeals); the senior judge is Lord President (of the Court of Session) and also Lord Justice-General (in High Court); others are Lord Justice-Clerk (in both) and, formally, Lords of Session and Lords Commissioners of Justiciary. Sheriff (not sheriff's) Courts deal with less serious criminal and civil cases. Other points in Scotland: advocate (equivalent of English barrister); the Crown prosecutors are the Lord Advocate and Advocates-Depute and (in each sheriffdom) the Procurator Fiscal (plural, Procurators Fiscal); in civil actions, pursuer (equivalent of plaintiff), defender (the defendant), summons (writ containing pursuer's case)

youth courts these have replaced the old juvenile courts

Judges

bench, the (in magistrates' courts) always l/c

circuit judge sits either in the Crown Court or in the county court and should be referred to as Judge Joe Bean, QC, (the QC where appropriate). Circuit judges may also sit in the High Court, in which case they should be described as "Judge Joe Bean, sitting as a High Court judge..."

Court of Appeal judges are Lords Justices of Appeal. Use Lord Justice Bean throughout, or out of court context, Sir John Bean. Note Lady Justice Butler-Sloss. Also Lord Justice Brooke (not Brook)

district judge replaced the old county court registrar and is referred to (at first mention) as District Judge Fred Brown

High Court judges should be referred to as Mr (or Mrs) Justice Bean throughout. First names are not normally necessary unless there are two or more High Court judges with the same surname, where it is essential to differentiate. These judges have a knighthood and may also be described as Sir John Bean, Dame Eleanor Bean etc, but generally only out of the court context. It is correct, however, to refer judicially to Sir Richard Scott, Vice-Chancellor of the Supreme Court, and Sir Stephen Brown, President of the Family Division

House of Lords, or **law lords** the most senior judges, they are the Lords of Appeal in Ordinary. Call them Lord Bean, in or out of court; first mention, give full title, eg, Lord Bean of Muckleflugga, thereafter Lord Bean. When writing about their judgments, say "the House of Lords ruled" or "the law lords ruled"

recorder at the Central Criminal Court, the Recorder of the City of London is usually referred to as "the Recorder". Note caps for the Common Serjeant. The Recorder of London, Recorder of Liverpool and Recorder of Manchester (and no other places) are *circuit judges* and are referred to at first mention as Judge Michael Bean, Recorder of Manchester etc (thereafter the recorder, not Mr Recorder)

retired judges refer to retired judges as follows:
retired High Court judges Sir Ivan Parsons
retired Crown Court judges George Vickers, QC, (first mention), then Mr Vickers

Court Reporting

appeals in criminal cases, the defendant becomes the appellant; the respondent is usually the Crown. Say "counsel for Mr Smith" rather than "counsel for the appellant". In civil appeals, either the claimant (plaintiff) or the defendant can be the appellant; it is always better to identify the parties and then avoid the phrase *counsel for the appellant/respondent* wherever possible

caps for courts cap when specific, eg Birmingham Crown Court, Clerkenwell County Court, Dawlish Magistrates' Court, Ashford Youth Court etc; in a general, unspecific context, always cap the High Court, and the Crown Court (it sits in about 90 centres); but l/c county court, magistrates' court, youth court etc

civil cases the parties in civil cases are *the claimant* (formerly the plaintiff) and *the defendant.* Write "counsel for Mrs Y" rather than "counsel for the claimant" etc. In judicial review, the person challenging the decision is *the applicant*

commercial court l/c, as not an official division of the High Court (unlike the Family Division, Queen's Bench Division etc)

coroner's court at inquests, the coroner is l/c unless specific, as in the Westminster Coroner. Juries *return* the verdict, the coroner *records* it. Be careful not to describe pathologists automatically as a Home Office pathologist – most are private consultants, so always check and use simply "the pathologist" if in doubt. There are no coroner's inquests in Scotland: sudden deaths are reported to the Procurator Fiscal, who may hold a fatal accident inquiry

Criminal Bar (caps); similarly, the *Commercial Bar* etc

criminal cases lawyers here appear "for the prosecution", "for the defence" (avoid "prosecuting", "defending"). To *admit* or *deny an offence* is preferred to "pleads guilty" or "pleads not guilty", though the latter form is not banned.

Do not report details of sex offences involving children and do not allow sex trial reports to become surreptitious pornography. Also, do not identify victims of alleged sexual offences.

At the end of a court report, say if the trial – or the hearing, in a civil case – continues. Always give the verdict at the end of a trial or hearing.

Defendants take their titles Mr, Mrs etc until they are convicted (see **appellations**, paragraph f)

Director of Public Prosecutions heads the Crown Prosecution Service (CPS), whose lawyers are Crown prosecutors; abbreviate to DPP

Inns of Court order of precedence is Lincoln's Inn, Inner Temple, Middle Temple, Gray's Inn

Latin phrases go in roman, eg, mandamus, habeas corpus, certiorari etc, but maxims take italic, eg, *caveat emptor*

Law Report cases cited go in italics, eg, *Gornall v Ritter* and in *Gornall's* case. In news reports and features, use roman

legal bodies or services (from 1999): *Legal Services Commission; Community Legal Service; Criminal Defence Service* (all caps)

legal officers cap Official Solicitor, Treasury Solicitor, Senior

Official Receiver; but note l/c *official receiver*, because there are several. These should be distinguished from the *law officers*, who are *the Attorney-General* and *the Solicitor-General*

"no win, no fee" legislation/agreement etc

Office for the Supervision of Solicitors (no longer the Solicitors Complaints Bureau)

President of the Law Society and **Chairman of the Bar Council** note now capped

prosecution, **defence** note *Times* style in court reports is *for the prosecution* and *for the defence* (not *prosecuting* and *defending)*

recorders when part-time judges, barristers or solicitors are sitting as recorders, refer to them as, eg, Donald Williams, QC, (where appropriate) the Recorder (later mentions, Mr Williams or the recorder); never write Mr Recorder Williams etc

silk barristers *take silk* and *become silks*; note l/c

small claims court l/c, as not its official title

solicitors never refer to a "company" of solicitors – they are always "firms". Always omit Messrs before the firm's name, eg, simply Sue, Grabbit & Run

titles in general, use l/c for titles etc except when in full or specific; thus, Anthony Bloggs, QC, the Recorder (thereafter the recorder), the West London Magistrate, Chelmsford Crown Court, Horseferry Road Magistrates' Court, Dawlish Magistrates' Court (caps on first mention), etc; but "the court was told", "the judge said", "the magistrate ordered" etc. *The Bench* is capped only when referring to the judges as a group; *a bench of magistrates* is always l/c. Always cap *the Bar* and *the Inn* (even when used on its own)

Woolf reforms In April 1999 new procedural rules for the conduct of civil litigation came into force, including important changes of terminology. These include:

a plaintiff is now a *claimant*
a writ is now a *claim form*
all pleadings are *statements of case*
affidavits become very rare; most written evidence will simply be verified by a *statement of truth*
notices of application will be served in the place of summonses

The means by which justice will be speeded up and administered is *allocation* to the appropriate track; the *small claims track* (up to £5,000), the *fast track* (up to £15,000), and the *multitrack* (the rest)

INTERNATIONAL COURTS

Court of Auditors sits in Luxembourg. It is the fifth institution of the EU, under the Maastricht treaty. (The others are the Council of the European Union, the European Commission, the European Court of Justice and the European Parliament.)

European Court of Human Rights sits in Strasbourg. It is the judicial body of the Council of Europe (not an EC or EU body); the human rights court rules on cases brought against states under the Convention for the Protection of Human Rights and Fundamental Freedoms, usually referred to as the **European Convention on Human Rights**. From November 1998, the European Court of Human Rights has incorporated the former European Commission of Human Rights.

In the Strasbourg context note that neither the Parliamentary Assembly of the Council of Europe nor the Committee of Ministers of the Council of Europe is an EU institution

European Court of Justice sits in Luxembourg. It is the shortened (and usual) form of the Court of Justice of the European Communities. The *Advocate General* (caps, no hyphen) sits in the European Court; he presents the case to the court and delivers an opinion, then the court makes its judgment

International Court of Justice sits in The Hague. It is the judicial organ of the UN and only states can be parties there

POLITICS

GENERAL POINTS

Always check the spelling of MPs and their constituencies if not entirely familiar: the best reference is *The Times Guide to the House of Commons*. Similarly, check *Vacher's Parliamentary Companion* or *Who's Who* for peers.

For guidance on when to cap or l/c Government, Opposition, Parliament, Party, see individual entries in the main section of this Style Guide.

Government, Cabinet, Opposition, Parliament, Party etc take the singular verb, eg, the Cabinet is considering ...

It is never necessary to say *Tony Blair, the Prime Minister,* etc: we may assume that *Times* readers know who the Prime Minister is. But it may be helpful to the flow of the story to write, eg, *the Prime Minister said* ... lower down the story, to avoid the endless repetition of *Mr Blair.*

PARLIAMENTARY TERMS

Act(s) always cap, whether fully identified or not

backbench, frontbench (adjective); similarly *backbenchers, frontbenchers, crossbench* (in the Lords); but note *the back benches, the front bench* and *the cross benches*

Bill(s) always cap (as with Acts above). Bills are read a first time without a debate. The second reading debate is the debate on the principle of the Bill. The Bill then goes to its committee stage, usually in a standing committee composed of about 20 MPs, but occasionally on the floor of the Commons. It then returns to the Commons chamber for its report stage and third reading, which is the final debate on the principle of the Bill. It then goes to the Lords, where similar procedures apply. Note that some legislation starts in the Lords and comes to the Commons thereafter

Cabinet always cap (as with Act and Bill), whether used as a noun or adjectivally, except in the informal *kitchen cabinet. Cabinet committees* should be capped

chamber l/c

Clause Four (as in Labour Party policy); but *Clause 4* permissible in headlines

closure as in *move the closure*

committees cap select committees when full title, such as the Select Committee on the Environment; Cabinet committees such as the Cabinet Committee on the Intelligence Services; the *Public Accounts Committee* (PAC); the *1922 Committee* (of Tory backbenchers); the *National Executive Committee* (NEC) of the Labour Party (or *Labour's national executive* as a shorter alternative)

crossbench, the cross benches see **backbench**

Cunningham through common usage, refer to him at first mention as Jack Cunningham (rather than John), then Dr Cunningham (though he is not a medical doctor)

deputy speakers there are three, and should appear thus: John Jones, the Deputy Speaker

dispatch box l/c

Downing Street policy unit; 10 Downing Street, or **No 10**

Duncan Smith, Iain no hyphen

early day motion l/c

elections always l/c *general election*; similarly *by-election, European elections* etc

frontbench (adjective); note *the front bench*; see **backbench**

galleries l/c, but note the *Press Gallery, Strangers' Gallery* etc

group cap in cases such as the *92 Group* (of Tory rightwingers)

guillotine l/c, no quotation marks

Hamilton, Sir Archibald (not Sir Archie)

Hansard italics

House of Lords officers note *the Clerk of the Parliaments, the Clerk Assistant* (of the Parliaments), *the Reading Clerk* (of the House of Lords)

leaders cap the *Leader of the House, Leader of the Opposition,* but l/c for *the Conservative/Labour/Liberal Democrat leader, the leader of the party* etc

Liberal Democrats permissible to use *Lib Dems* in either headlines or text (though sparingly in text). The term *Liberals* must not be used as a synonym of Liberal Democrats

Lower House caps

Members of Parliament note caps; in almost every case, MPs is the preferable form. But in the Political Sketch, and discursive or commentary articles, the term *Members* sometimes occurs for stylistic reasons and should be retained and capped; similarly in such articles, the Member for Billericay, the Hon Member etc

National Executive Committee of the Labour Party, or simply *Labour's national executive*; abbreviate to NEC

new Labour (as in Tony Blair's policies); l/c *n*, quotes not usually necessary, except when the writer or speaker is making a particular, perhaps ironic, point. But keep caps in slogans such as "New Labour, New Danger"; note *New Deal*

1922 Committee (of Tory backbenchers)

One Nation Tories, One Nation politics etc

Opposition the same cap or l/c rules apply as to Government, ie, cap as a noun but generally l/c as an adjective, eg, "He accused the Opposition of lying", but "He said it was an opposition lie"

order, order paper l/c

Parliament cap always in the British context (for when to cap foreign parliaments, see **Parliament** in main section). The cap rule now applies even to phrases such as *the lifetime of this Parliament* or *the Bill is unlikely to progress until the next Parliament.* The adjective *parliamentary* is usually l/c except when used as part of a title, eg, *Parliamentary Labour Party* (PLP)

parliamentary private secretary l/c, abbreviate to PPS

Part I, Part II (of Bill etc); caps also for *Section 2, Article 8* etc

party abbreviations in lists or political sketches or reports of debates where party affiliation is added after an MP's name – eg, Tony Benn (Lab, Chesterfield) – use *Lab* for Labour, *C* for Conservative (not Con), and *LD* for Liberal Democrat (not Lib Dem)

party conferences l/c, as in *Labour Party conference*

Private Member's Bill caps

Public Accounts Committee abbreviate to PAC

Queen's Speech caps

Question Time, Prime Minister's Questions also *Agriculture Questions, Treasury Questions* etc; but note l/c *questions* to the Prime Minister, the Foreign Secretary etc

Register of Members' Interests caps

Royal Assent caps

royal commissions see main section

select committees cap when giving full title, eg, *Treasury Select Committee*

Serjeant at Arms

Smith the widow of John Smith is Baroness Smith of Gilmorehill, thereafter Lady Smith; she is not Dame Elizabeth Smith

Speaker usual style is Betty Boothroyd, the Speaker, at first mention, thereafter the Speaker or Miss Boothroyd

spin-doctor hyphen

State Opening (of Parliament); note caps

ten-minute rule (Bill etc)

Treasury bench

Upper House caps

Vote (of money); takes cap

whips cap for the *Chief Whip, Opposition Chief Whip, Whips' Office*; but l/c as in *three-line whip, to lose the party whip, a government whip*

SPORTS

Sports writing is notoriously vulnerable to cliché and jargon. Apart from direct quotes, avoid the type of language used by players and TV commentators.

GENERAL STYLES

All England Club

baseball inning (not innings)

Blue (from Oxford, Cambridge, for the award or the sportsman or woman); note cap

cross country hyphenate only in adjectival use, as in *cross-country trials*

Cup Final cap *the FA Cup Final*, but note l/c *f* for *World Cup final, Worthington Cup final, Benson and Hedges Cup final* etc; also l/c for *FA Cup semi-final*, because by definition more than one

divisions, groups, sections etc in sporting context these always take l/c, eg, *World Cup group A, Nationwide League first division, European championship section D* etc

England Under-21 etc

first division, second division etc (not Division One, 2, etc or any variant)

hat-trick (cricket or football)

racecourse, racehorse but note *horse race, horse racing*

stretchered off avoid; instead use *carried off on a stretcher*

women's competitions, championships, events etc (not ladies')

World Cup caps; note l/c for *world championship* in all sports

BOXING

General terms featherweight, heavyweight, light-heavyweight etc; knockout(s)

CRICKET

General terms wicketkeeper, mid-off, mid-wicket; follow on (verb) but the follow-on; hat-trick; hit-wicket; mis-hit; third man; extra cover; off break; leg-before; no-ball; a four (not 4); AXA Life League; Benson and Hedges Cup

delivery in cricket this is a bowling action, not a ball, eg, "Qadir has a puzzling delivery", not "Warne bowled Gatting with his first delivery"

England and Wales Cricket Board from January 1, 1997, the ECB took control of all levels of the domestic game, and the Test and County Cricket Board (TCCB) is no more

First-Class Forum represents the views of the first-class counties; abbreviate to FCF

MCC Marylebone Cricket Club; concerned with the laws of cricket and matters at Lord's. Do not refer to *the* MCC

off spinner (bowler who bowls off breaks)

FOOTBALL

By itself, football means the association code. *Soccer* is now an acceptable alternative.

American football should always be described thus, unless the context is so obvious that football on its own is enough.

General terms goalkeeper, kick-off (noun), Arsenal (not *the*), midfield, offside

FA Carling Premiership at first mention write in full, thereafter *the Premiership*. Do not confuse with the *FA Premier League*

FA Premier League (organisation that runs the FA Carling Premiership); take care not to confuse the competition and the organisation

Fifa (football's governing body; not FIFA); similarly *Uefa* (not UEFA)

Football Association, or **FA** (never the English Football Association)

Nationwide League first division, second division etc (lower divisions; no longer Endsleigh); note l/c. This competition is run by the *Football League*

St Andrew's, Birmingham; do not confuse with St Andrews (golf)

St James' Park, Newcastle and Exeter

RUGBY UNION, RUGBY LEAGUE

General terms full back; scrum half; fly half; dropped goal; knock on (verb) but a knock-on (noun); scrummage; three-quarter; open-side flanker; wing (not winger); lineout(s); 22-metre line, the 22; touch judge; triple crown; grand slam; the British Isles, not the British Lions (though Lions on its own is acceptable at second mention)

Note stand-off half in rugby league

rugby union, **rugby league** both take l/c in general usage (though not, of course, in titles)

rugger do not use

Six Nations Championship note caps, and no longer Five Nations except in historical contexts

GOLF

The holes should appear in both text and results as 1st, 2nd, 10th, 18th, but write the "third extra hole" after that. In a match-play use, "Jones beat Brown 2 and 1" (not two and one). Usual *Times* style for numbers (spell out from one to ten, figures thereafter) in sentences such as "Faldo holed from eight feet/15 feet".

General terms the Open Championship (not British Open); bogey; birdie; eagle (no quotes); dormy, only if the match can be halved (a player cannot be dormy if the match can be taken to, say, the 19th hole to reach a decision)

MOTOR RACING

British Grand Prix, Japanese Grand Prix etc cap as specific; but note l/c for unspecific *grand prix racing* etc ; plural *grands prix*

Formula One motor racing two caps; spell out *One*

pitstop (one word)

SWIMMING

General terms freestyle, backstroke, breaststroke (no hyphens)

TENNIS

Flushing Meadows, New York (home of the US Open tennis championships; not Meadow)

Moyà, Carlos note accent

YACHTING

America's Cup

sailing correspondent (not yachting correspondent)

Whitbread Round the World Race caps, no hyphens

TITLES

Diana, Princess of Wales, at first mention; though since her death use the form *the late Princess* where appropriate. Never refer to her as Princess Diana or (even worse) Lady Di or Princess Di. Also, note one comma only for the *Diana, Princess of Wales Memorial Fund*

Duke of Edinburgh, the thereafter *the Duke* or (sparingly) *Prince Philip*

Duke of York, the thereafter *the Duke* or *Prince Andrew*. Note the *Duchess of York* is no longer a member of the Royal Family since her divorce. At first mention, refer to her as *the Duchess of York*, then l/c *the duchess* – never "Fergie" or any such vulgarity

Earl of Wessex, the thereafter *the Earl* or *Prince Edward*; similarly the *Countess of Wessex, the Countess*, or *the former Sophie Rhys-Jones*

Prince of Wales, the thereafter *the Prince* or (sparingly) *Prince Charles*

Princess Royal, the thereafter *the Princess*. Use *Princess Anne* only in historical context

Queen, the try to use *the* even in headlines

Queen Elizabeth the Queen Mother (no comma) first mention, thereafter the Queen Mother

Royal Dukes keep the cap at subsequent mentions (eg, the *Duke of Kent*, later *the Duke*); other dukes do not retain the cap (see below)

PEERAGE AND KNIGHTS

Titles of nobility in descending order as follows: *duke, marquess* (not marquis, except in foreign contexts and occasional Scottish titles), *earl, viscount* and *baron*. At first mention, give the formal title (as in *Who's Who*) eg, the Marquess of Paddington, the Earl of Waterloo, but then Lord Paddington, Lord Waterloo etc. This does not apply to *barons*, who are always Lord except in the announcement of new baronies. *Dukes* are always dukes and do not become Lord (eg, the Duke of Rutland). Note style of *the 2nd Earl, the 3rd Viscount* etc. Note a major difference from royalty is that these titles take l/c rather than cap after the first mention, (eg, the Duke of Argyll, thereafter the duke).

announcement of titles baronets, knights and dames take the appropriate title as soon as the honour is announced. Peers have to submit their choice of title for approval, so wait until the formal public announcement (usually in *The London Gazette*)

baron always Lord except in the announcement of new baronies

baronesses in their own right or life peeresses are *Baroness* at first mention, and then *Lady* (eg, Baroness Thatcher, then Lady Thatcher)

baronets, knights write, eg, Sir John Euston, thereafter Sir John. Note the wife of a baronet is called Lady from the start, eg, Lady Euston. Remember this essential point: no wife of a baronet or knight takes her first name in her title unless she is the daughter of a duke, a marquess or an earl. If a baronet has had more than one wife, the first wife is, eg, Mary Lady Smith (no commas) – the same form applies to the widow of a baron. If a knight has had more than one wife, the former wife puts her Christian name in brackets, eg, Lady (Alice) Brown, to distinguish her from the present wife, Lady Brown.

If two baronets or knights have the same name, their wives (when mentioned apart from their husbands) put his first name in brackets, eg, Lady (Stephen) Brown, Lady (Andrew) Brown

children of peers eldest sons of a duke, marquess or earl use the father's second title as a courtesy title (eg, the Duke of Bedford's son is the Marquess of Tavistock). These people are not peers, even in headlines. Younger sons of dukes and marquesses use their first names and the family surname (eg, Lord John Worthington; subsequent mention Lord John, never Lord Worthington; his wife is Lady John Worthington).

Daughters of dukes, marquesses or earls take their first names in their title, eg, Lady Olive York, and in subsequent mentions Lady Olive (never Lady York).

Younger sons of earls and all children of viscounts and barons have the style *the Hon,* but use this only in Court Page copy; normally, they are simply Mr, Miss, Ms etc (none is a peer)

countess (wife of an earl); use *Lady* at subsequent mentions

Dames (of an order of chivalry); dames take the same style as knights, eg, Dame Felicity Brown, thereafter Dame Felicity. A dame who is married may prefer to use her own style, eg, Dame Jennifer Jenkins, wife of Lord Jenkins of Hillhead; personal preferences should be respected

duchess (wife of a duke) always *Duchess*, eg, the Duchess of X

duke always described as duke so does not become Lord at subsequent mention. The wife of a duke is a *duchess*

earl at first mention, give the formal title, thereafter Lord. The wife of an earl is a *countess*

first names with titles take great care especially with the names of wives of peers, baronets and knights. No wife of a baronet or knight takes her first name in her title unless she is the daughter of a duke, a marquess or an earl. The wife of Lord St Pancras is simply Lady St Pancras. The wife of Sir John Fenchurch is simply Lady Fenchurch (together, Sir John and Lady Fenchurch). However, when the name is a common one and there is no other convenient identification, or where there is some other compelling reason, it is permissible to say Lady (John) Brown (brackets essential; see **baronets, knights**)

marchioness (wife of a marquess); use *Lady* at subsequent mentions

marquess (not marquis, except in foreign contexts and occasional Scottish titles). At first mention, give the formal title and thereafter Lord. The wife of a marquess is a *marchioness*

titles including place name some titles include a place name, eg, Lord Callaghan of Cardiff, Lord Archer of Weston-super-Mare, while others do not. Follow *Who's Who,* where those whose place name must be included appear in **bold caps.**

Always give the full title at first mention, thereafter the abbreviated form, eg, Lord Bingham of Cornhill, thereafter Lord Bingham. Among titles spelt differently from the place name are the Marquess of Ailesbury, Marquess of Donegall, Earl of Guilford, Earl of Scarbrough

viscount give formal title at first mention, thereafter Lord. The wife of a viscount is a *viscountess*

viscountess (wife of a viscount); give full title, then *Lady* at subsequent mentions

widows/former wives of titles those who have not remarried use their first name before the title, eg, Margaret Duchess of Argyll (no commas). A widow may also be known as the Dowager Duchess of Y, or the Dowager Lady Z

WORLD MAPS

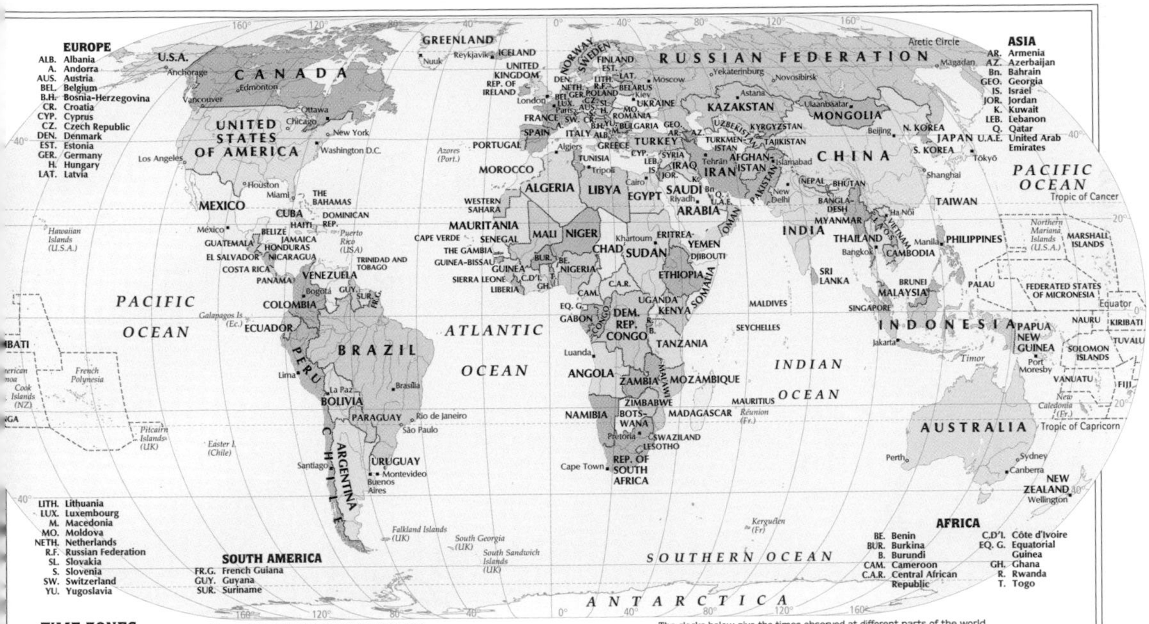
EUROPE
ALB. Albania
A. Andorra
AUS. Austria
BEL. Belgium
B.H. Bosnia-Herzegovina
CR. Croatia
CYP. Cyprus
CZ. Czech Republic
DEN. Denmark
EST. Estonia
GER. Germany
H. Hungary
LAT. Latvia
LITH. Lithuania
LUX. Luxembourg
M. Macedonia
MO. Moldova
NETH. Netherlands
R.F. Russian Federation
SL. Slovakia
S. Slovenia
SW. Switzerland
YU. Yugoslavia
SOUTH AMERICA
FR.G. French Guiana
GUY. Guyana
SUR. Suriname
ASIA
AR. Armenia
AZ. Azerbaijan
Bn. Bahrain
GEO. Georgia
IS. Israel
JOR. Jordan
K. Kuwait
LEB. Lebanon
Q. Qatar
U.A.E. United Arab Emirates
AFRICA
BE. Benin
BUR. Burkina
B. Burundi
CAM. Cameroon
C.A.R. Central African Republic
C.D'I. Côte d'Ivoire
EQ. G. Equatorial Guinea
GH. Ghana
R. Rwanda
T. Togo
CANADA
UNITED STATES OF AMERICA
U.S.A.
MEXICO
GREENLAND
ICELAND
RUSSIAN FEDERATION
KAZAKSTAN
MONGOLIA
CHINA
INDIA
JAPAN
BRAZIL
ARGENTINA
CHILE
PACIFIC OCEAN
ATLANTIC OCEAN
INDIAN OCEAN
SOUTHERN OCEAN
ANTARCTICA
AUSTRALIA
INDONESIA
ALGERIA
LIBYA
EGYPT
SUDAN
NIGERIA
ANGOLA
NAMIBIA
TANZANIA
MOZAMBIQUE
MADAGASCAR
REP. OF SOUTH AFRICA
NEW ZEALAND
PAPUA NEW GUINEA
PHILIPPINES
Arctic Circle
Tropic of Cancer
Equator
Tropic of Capricorn

TIME ZONES

The world is divided into twenty-four Standard Time Zones based on 15° intervals of longitude.

The clocks below give the times observed at different parts of the world when it is 12 noon in the zone at the Greenwich Meridian (0° longitude).

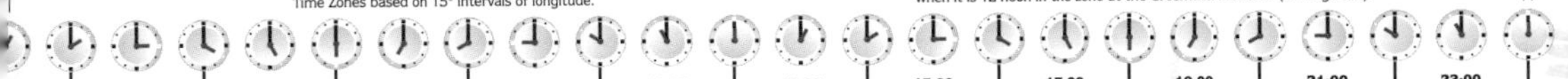

- **00:00** Samoa, American Samoa
- **02:00** Cook Is.
- **03:00** Anchorage, Pitcairn Is.
- **04:00** Vancouver, Los Angeles
- **05:00** Edmonton, Easter I.
- **06:00** Chicago, Houston, México
- **07:00** New York, Miami, Lima
- **08:00** Puerto Rico, La Paz, Santiago
- **09:00** Nuuk, Brasília, Buenos Aires
- **10:00** South Georgia
- **11:00** Azores, Cape Verde
- **12:00** Reykjavík, London
- **13:00** Paris, Algiers, Luanda
- **14:00** Kiev, Cairo, Cape Town
- **15:00** Moscow, Riyadh
- **16:00** Seychelles, Mauritius
- **17:00** Yekaterinburg, Islamabad
- **18:00** Novosibirsk, Astana
- **19:00** Ha Nôi, Bangkok, Jakarta
- **20:00** Beijing, Manila, Perth
- **21:00** Tōkyō, Palau
- **22:00** Port Moresby, Sydney
- **23:00** Magadan, New Caledonia
- **24:00** Tuvalu, Fiji, Wellington

SETTLEMENTS

NATIONAL CAPITAL

- Over 5 million — **Beijing**
- 1 to 5 million — **Seoul**
- 500000 to 1 million — **Bangui**
- 100000 to 500000 — Wellington
- 50000 to 100000 — Port of Spain
- 10000 to 50000 — Malabo
- Less than 10000 — Roseau

ADMINISTRATIVE CAPITAL

- Over 5 million — **Tianjin**
- 1 to 5 million — **Lagos**
- 500000 to 1 million — **Douala**
- 100000 to 500000 — Mansa
- 50000 to 100000 — Lubango
- 10000 to 50000 — Chinhoyi
- Less than 10000 — Áti

CITY OR TOWN

- Over 5 million — **New York**
- 1 to 5 million — **Barranquilla**
- 500000 to 1 million — **Memphis**
- 100000 to 500000 — Mara
- 50000 to 100000 — Arecibo
- 10000 to 50000 — El Tigre
- Less than 10000 — Soledad

PHYSICAL FEATURES

- Freshwater lake
- Seasonal freshwater lake
- Saltwater lake *or* Lagoon
- Seasonal saltwater lake
- Dry salt lake *or* Saltpan
- Marsh
- River
- Waterfall
- Dam *or* Barrage
- Seasonal river *or* Wadi
- Canal
- Flood dyke
- Reef
- Volcano
- Lava field
- Sandy desert
- Rocky desert
- Oasis
- Escarpment
- 923 Mountain pass *height in metres*
- Ice cap *or* Glacier

COMMUNICATIONS

- Motorway
- Motorway *under construction*
- Motorway tunnel
- Motorways are classified separately at scales greater than 1:5 million. At smaller scales motorways are classified with main roads.
- Main road
- Main road *under construction*
- Main road tunnel
- Other road
- Other road *under construction*
- Other road tunnel
- Track
- Main railway
- Main railway *under construction*
- Main railway tunnel
- Other railway
- Other railway *under construction*
- Other railway tunnel
- Main airport
- Other airport

BOUNDARIES

- International
- International *disputed*
- Ceasefire line
- Main administrative (U.K.)
- Main administrative
- Main administrative *through water*

OTHER FEATURES

- National park
- Reserve
- Ancient wall
- Historic *or* Tourist site
- Urban area

UNITED KINGDOM and REPUBLIC OF IRELAND

UNITED KINGDOM and REPUBLIC OF IRELAND

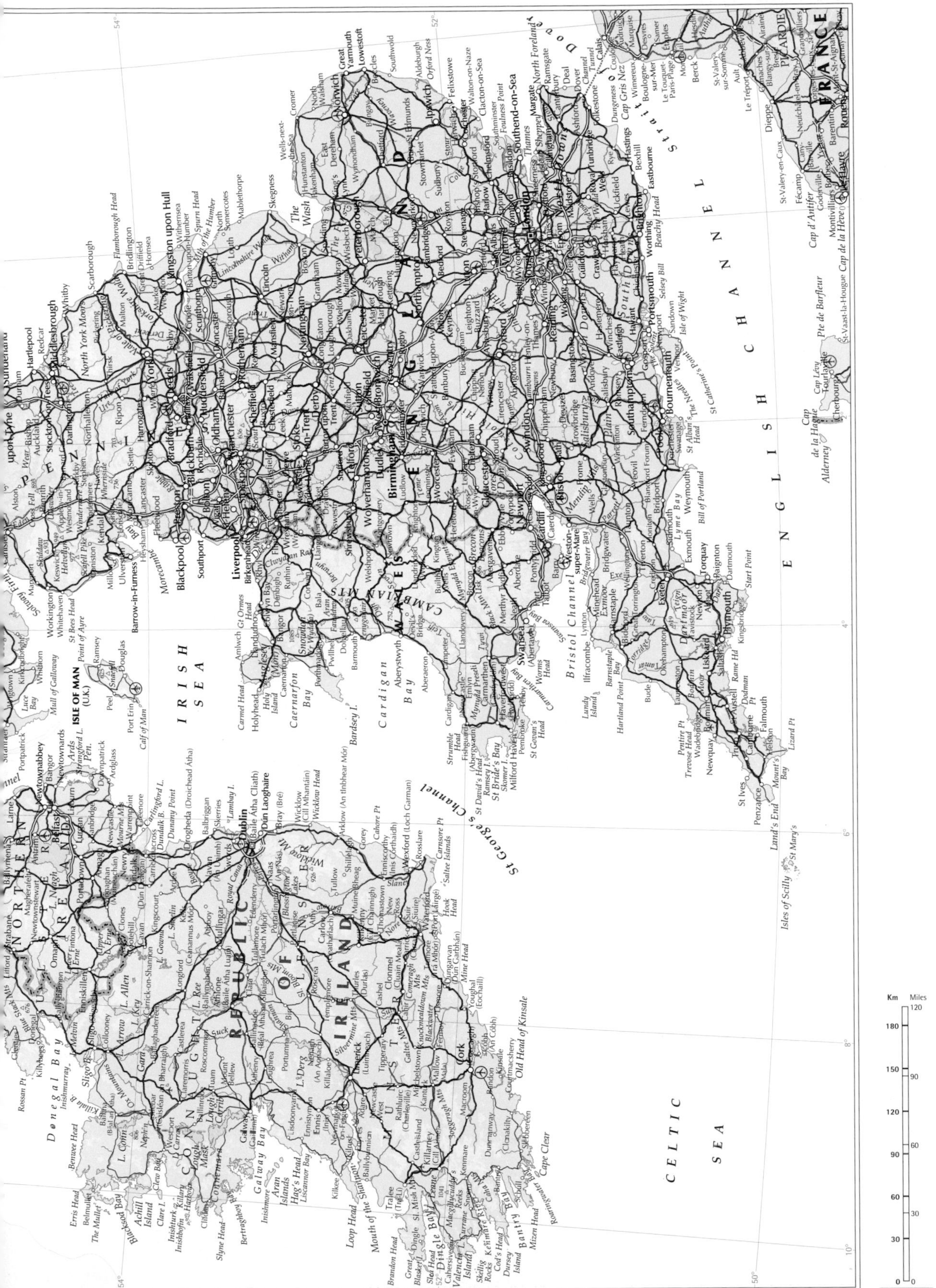

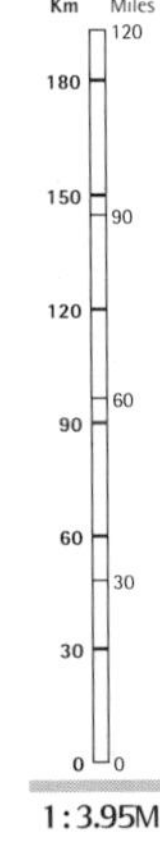

1:3.95M

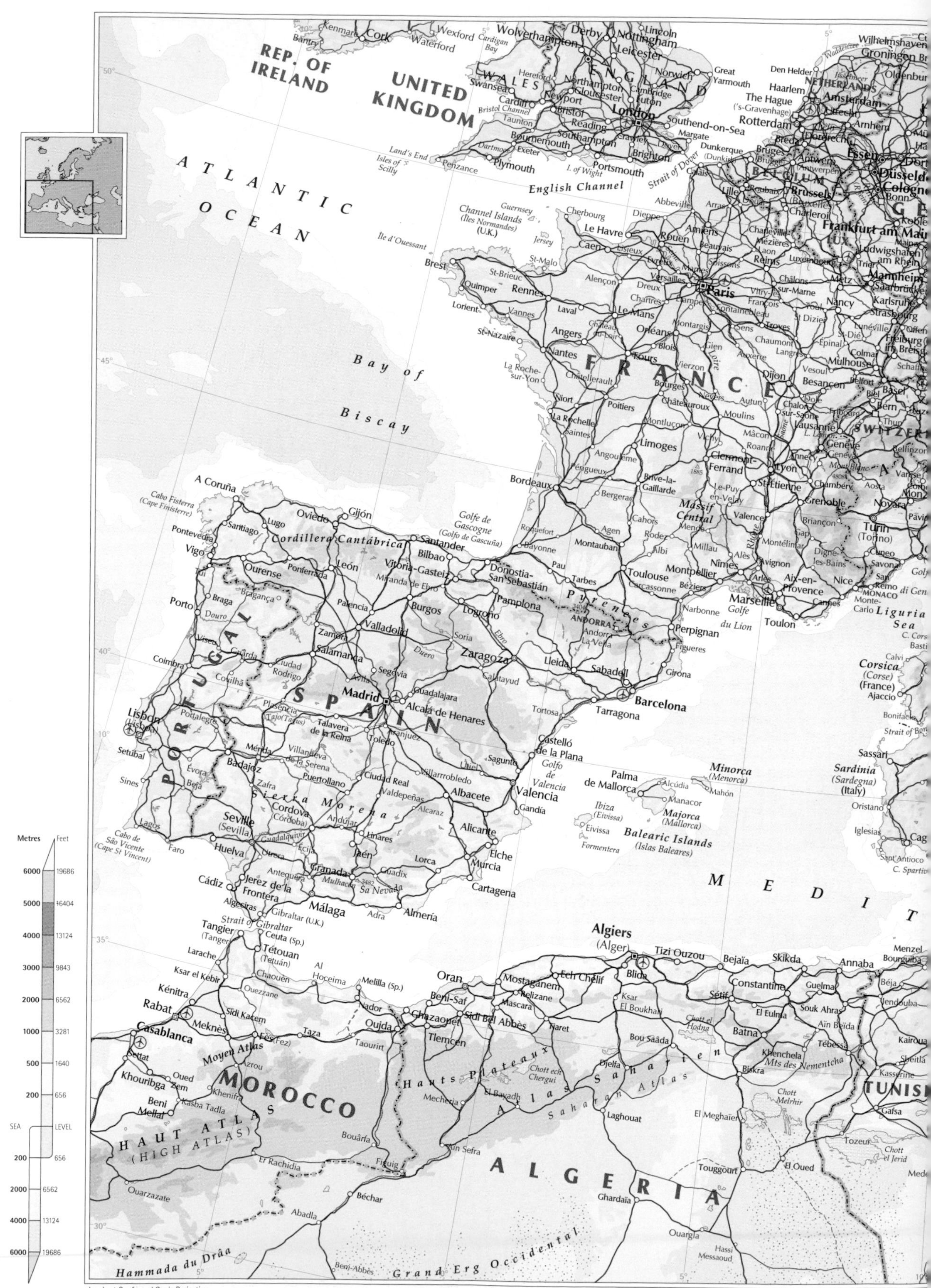

Lambert Conformal Conic Projection

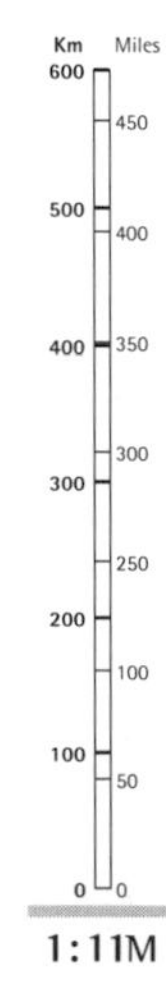
Km
Miles
600
450
500
400
400
350
300
300
250
200
200
150
100
100
50
0
0

1:11M

1:9.87M

Conic Projection

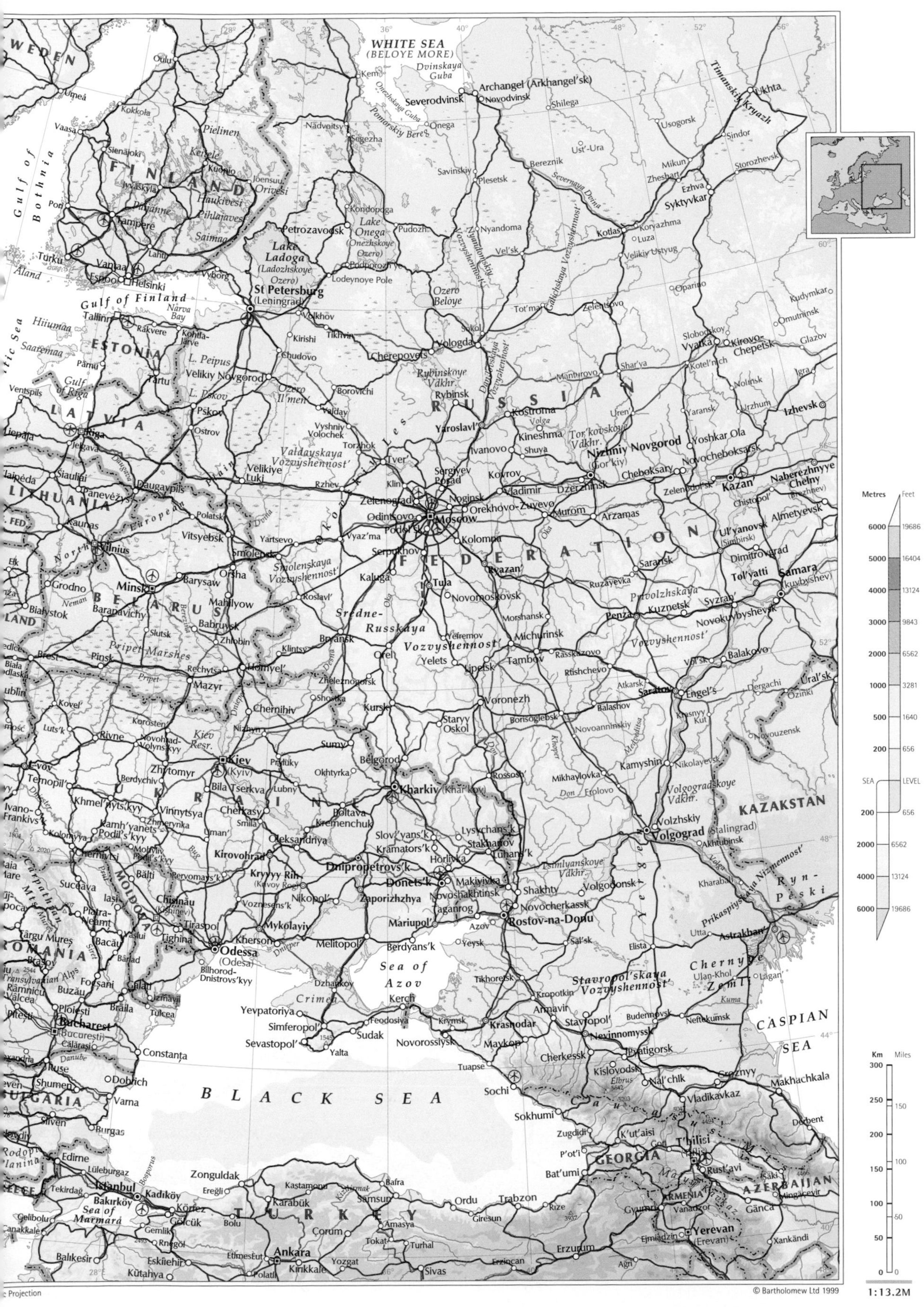
WHITE SEA
(BELOYE MORE)
Dvinskaya Guba
Archangel (Arkhangel'sk)
Severodvinsk
Novodvinsk
Onega
Ukhta
Timanskiy Kryazh
Syktyvkar
Kotlas
Gulf of Bothnia
FINLAND
Oulu
Vaasa
Tampere
Turku
Helsinki
Espoo
Vantaa
Åland
Gulf of Finland
Tallinn
ESTONIA
Tartu
Lake Ladoga (Ladozhskoye Ozero)
Lake Onega (Onezhskoye Ozero)
Petrozavodsk
St Petersburg (Leningrad)
Vyborg
Novgorod
L. Peipus
L. Pskov
Pskov
Gulf of Riga
Riga
LATVIA
Daugavpils
LITHUANIA
Vilnius
Kaunas
Šiauliai
Klaipėda
Vologda
Cherepovets
Rybinskoye Vdkhr.
Rybinsk
Yaroslavl'
Kostroma
Ivanovo
Vladimir
Tver'
Moscow
Zelenograd
Odintsovo
Podol'sk
Kolomna
Noginsk
Orekhovo-Zuyevo
Sergiyev Posad
Nizhniy Novgorod (Gor'kiy)
Cheboksary
Yoshkar Ola
Novocheboksarsk
Kazan'
Naberezhnyye Chelny (Brezhnev)
Kirov
Kirovo-Chepetsk
Izhevsk
Dzerzhinsk
Murom
Arzamas
RUSSIAN FEDERATION
Valdayskaya Vozvyshennost'
Smolensk
Smolenskaya Vozvyshennost'
Vitsyebsk
Polatsk
Minsk
Barysaw
Orsha
Mahilyow
Babruysk
Homyel'
Hrodno
Baranavichy
Brest
Pinsk
Mazyr
BELARUS
Pripet Marshes
Kaluga
Tula
Novomoskovsk
Ryazan'
Bryansk
Orel
Kursk
Belgorod
Voronezh
Lipetsk
Tambov
Michurinsk
Penza
Saransk
Ul'yanovsk (Simbirsk)
Dimitrovgrad
Tol'yatti
Samara (Kuybyshev)
Syzran'
Novokuybyshevsk
Saratov
Engel's
Balakovo
Sredne-Russkaya Vozvyshennost'
Privolzhskaya Vozvyshennost'
Kiev (Kyiv)
Chernihiv
Zhytomyr
Rivne
Luts'k
Kovel'
L'vov
Ternopil'
Khmel'nyts'kyy
Vinnytsya
Bila Tserkva
Cherkasy
Kremenchuk
Poltava
Kharkiv (Khar'kov)
Sumy
UKRAINE
Dnipropetrovs'k
Zaporizhzhya
Kryvyy Rih (Krivoy Rog)
Nikopol'
Donets'k
Makiyivka
Luhans'k
Mariupol'
Mykolayiv
Kherson
Odessa (Odesa)
Chişinău (Kishinev)
MOLDOVA
Tiraspol
Bălţi
Iaşi
Suceava
Chernivtsi
ROMANIA
Bacău
Galaţi
Brăila
Ploieşti
Bucharest (Bucureşti)
Constanţa
Tulcea
Crimea
Simferopol'
Sevastopol'
Yevpatoriya
Yalta
Kerch
Sea of Azov
Taganrog
Rostov-na-Donu
Novocherkassk
Shakhty
Volgodonsk
Tsimlyanskoye Vdkhr.
Volgograd (Stalingrad)
Volzhskiy
Volgogradskoye Vdkhr.
Kamyshin
KAZAKSTAN
Astrakhan'
Elista
Stavropol'skaya Vozvyshennost'
Stavropol'
Krasnodar
Novorossiysk
Armavir
Nevinnomyssk
Pyatigorsk
Kislovodsk
Nal'chik
Vladikavkaz
Groznyy
Makhachkala
Derbent
CASPIAN SEA
Chernyye Zemli
Ryn-Peski
Sochi
Sokhumi
Kutaisi
T'bilisi
Rust'avi
Bat'umi
GEORGIA
ARMENIA
Yerevan (Erevan)
Gyumri
AZERBAIJAN
BLACK SEA
BULGARIA
Varna
Burgas
Shumen
Ruse
Dobrich
Edirne
Istanbul
Kadıköy
Sea of Marmara
Bosporus
TURKEY
Zonguldak
Samsun
Ordu
Trabzon
Ankara
Sivas
Erzurum
Kırıkkale
Metres Feet
6000 19686
5000 16404
4000 13124
3000 9843
2000 6562
1000 3281
500 1640
200 656
SEA LEVEL
200 656
2000 6562
4000 13124
6000 19686
Km Miles
300
250 150
200
150 100
100
50 50
0 0
1:13.2M
© Bartholomew Ltd 1999

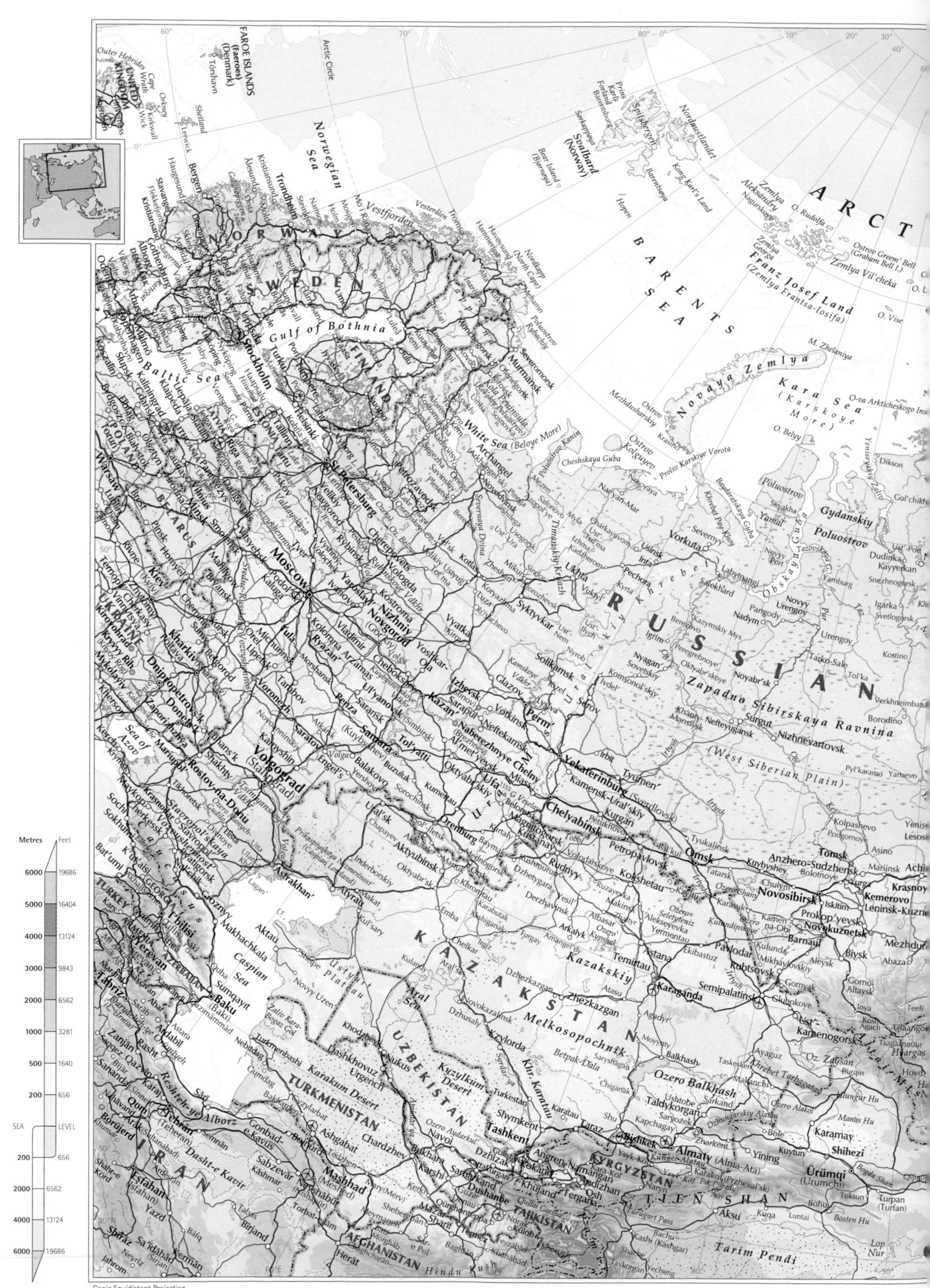
RUSSIAN
KAZAKSTAN
UZBEKISTAN
TURKMENISTAN
KYRGYZSTAN
TAJIKISTAN
AFGHANISTAN
IRAN
UKRAINE
BELARUS
FINLAND
SWEDEN
NORWAY
ESTONIA
Moscow
St Petersburg
Barents Sea
Kara Sea
Caspian Sea
Aral Sea
Black Sea
Baltic Sea
Norwegian Sea
Gulf of Bothnia
White Sea (Beloye More)
Novaya Zemlya
Franz Josef Land
Svalbard (Norway)
Zapadno Sibirskaya Ravnina
(West Siberian Plain)
Tarim Pendi
Tien Shan
Ozero Balkhash
Novosibirsk
Omsk
Yekaterinburg
Chelyabinsk
Almaty (Alma-Ata)
Tashkent
Metres
Feet
6000
19686
5000
16404
4000
13124
3000
9843
2000
6562
1000
3281
500
1640
200
656
SEA
LEVEL
200
656
2000
6562
4000
13124
6000
19686
Conic Equidistant Projection

Km Miles
1200
1000 600
800 450
600
400 300
200 150
0 0

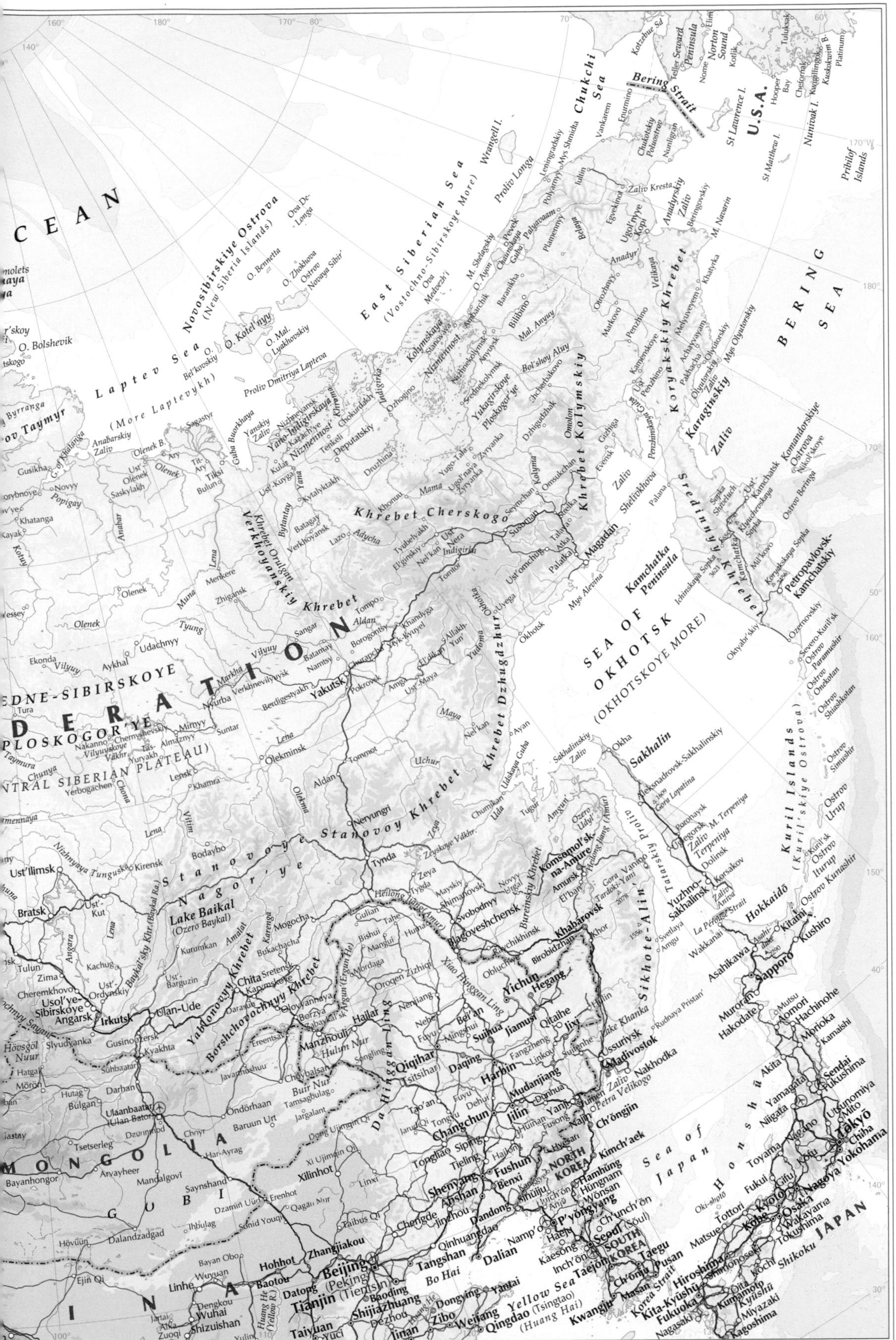

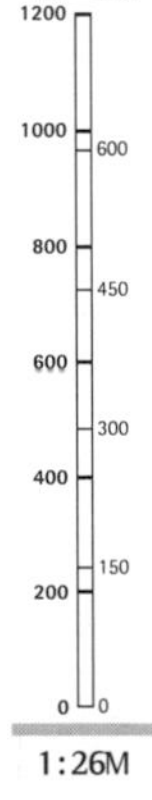

1:26M

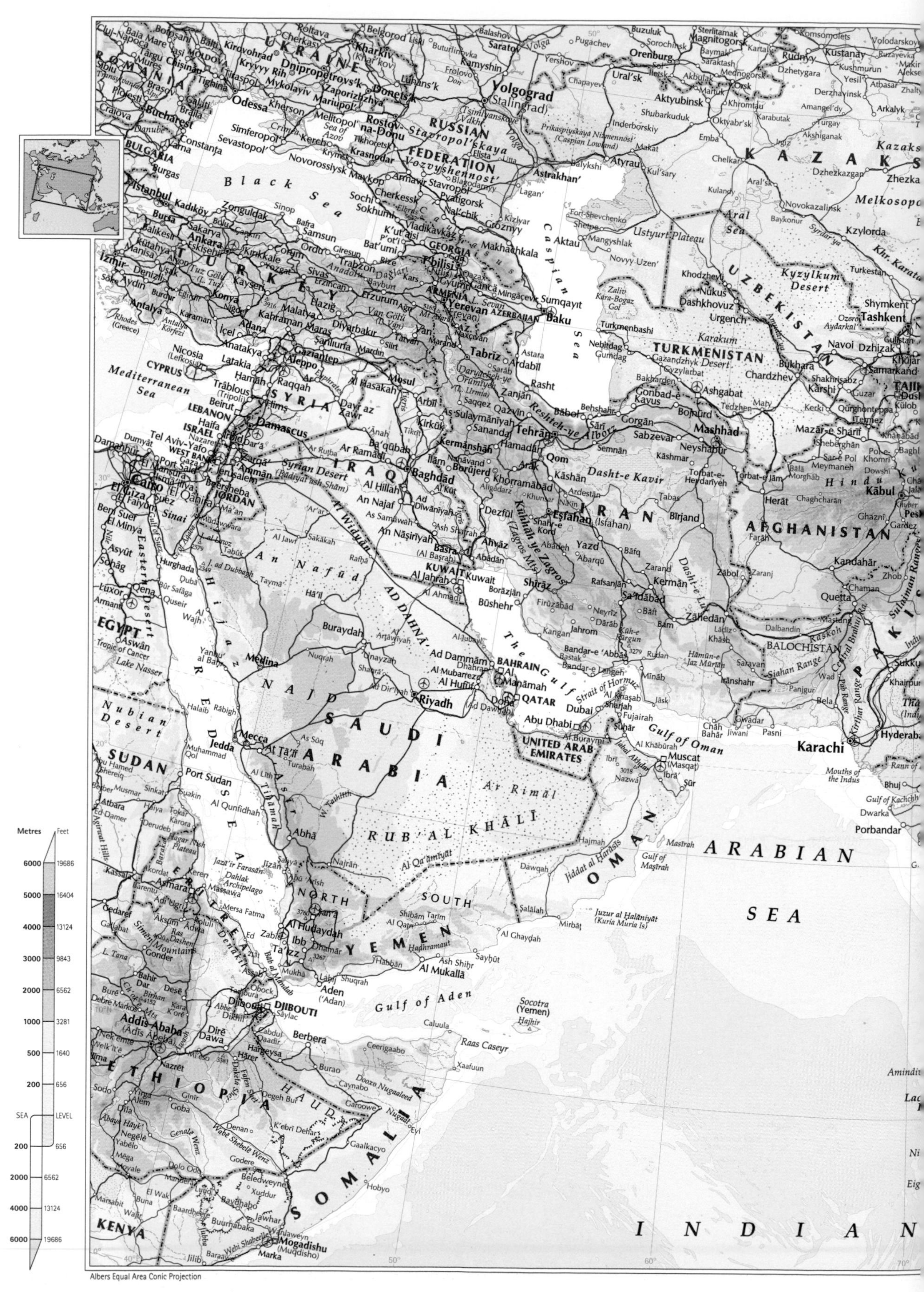

Albers Equal Area Conic Projection

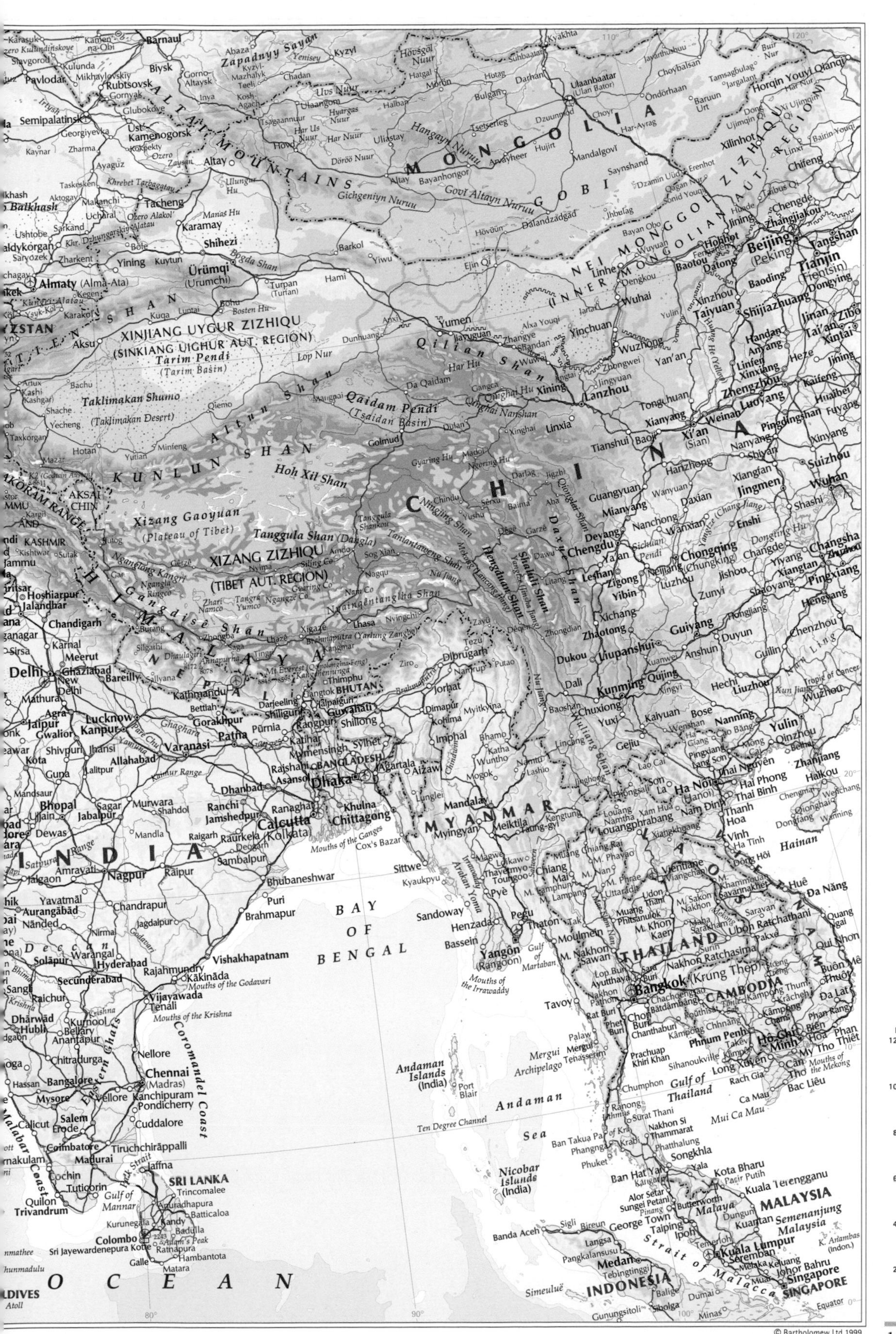

© Bartholomew Ltd 1999

1:24.7M

SEA OF
OKHOTSK
(OKHOTSKOYE MORE)
Kuril Is (Kuril'skiye Ostrova)
Administered by Rus.Fed.
Claimed by Japan
Sakhalin
Hokkaidō
JAPAN
Tōkyō
Sea of Japan
Honshu
Shikoku
Kyūshū
NORTH KOREA
SOUTH KOREA
P'yŏngyang
Seoul (Sŏul)
Yellow Sea
(Huang Hai)
EAST
CHINA SEA
Bo Hai
Korea Bay
Shanghai
Beijing
(Peking)
Tianjin
(Tientsin)
T'aipei
Tropic of Cancer
RUSSIAN FEDERATION
MONGOLIA
Ulaanbaatar
(Ulan Bator)
GOBI
NEI MONGGOL ZIZHIQU
(INNER MONGOLIA AUT. REGION)
XINJIANG UYGUR ZIZHIQU
(SINKIANG UIGHUR
AUT. REGION)
XIZANG ZIZHIQU
(TIBET AUT. REGION)
CHINA
INDIA
BHUTAN
ALTAY MOUNTAINS
Qaidam Pendi
Tanggula Shan (Dangla)
Qilian Shan
Hoh Xil Shan
Altun Shan
Ürümqi (Urumchi)
Lake Baikal (Ozero Baykal)
Stanovoye Nagor'ye
Stanovoy Khrebet
Da Hinggan Ling
Sikhote-Alin'
Nansei-shotō
Okinawa
Conic Equidistant Projection
Metres
Feet
6000
19686
5000
16404
4000
13124
3000
9843
2000
6562
1000
3281
500
1640
200
656
SEA
LEVEL
200
656
2000
6562
4000
13124
6000
19686

Km Miles
1200
1000 600
800
600 400
400
200 200
0 0

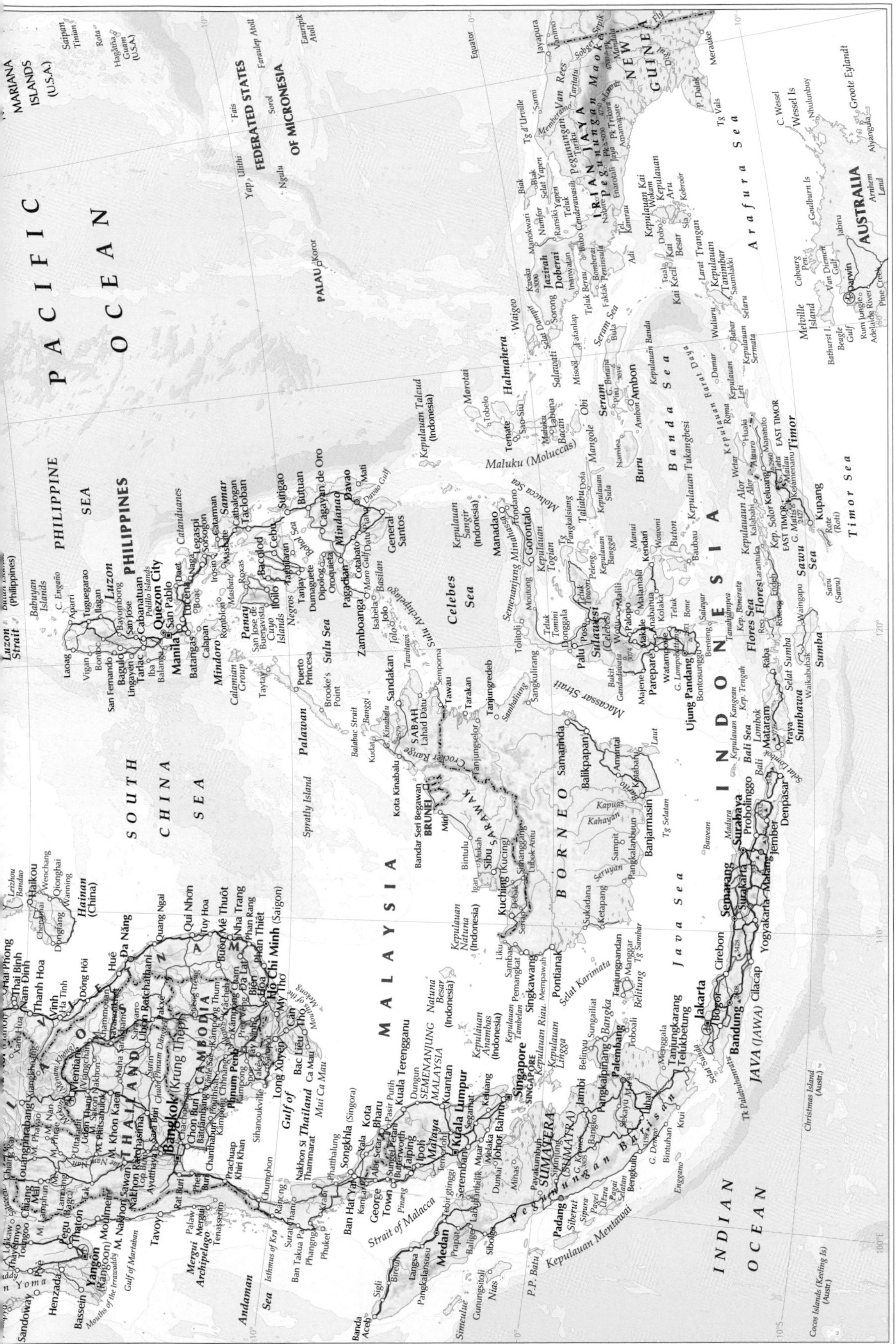

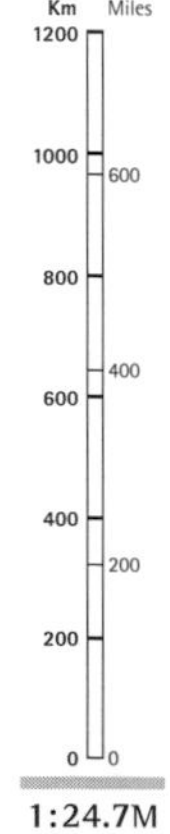

1:24.7M

AUSTRALIA and Southwestern PACIFIC

Lambert Azimuthal Equal Area Projection

AUSTRALIA and Southwestern PACIFIC

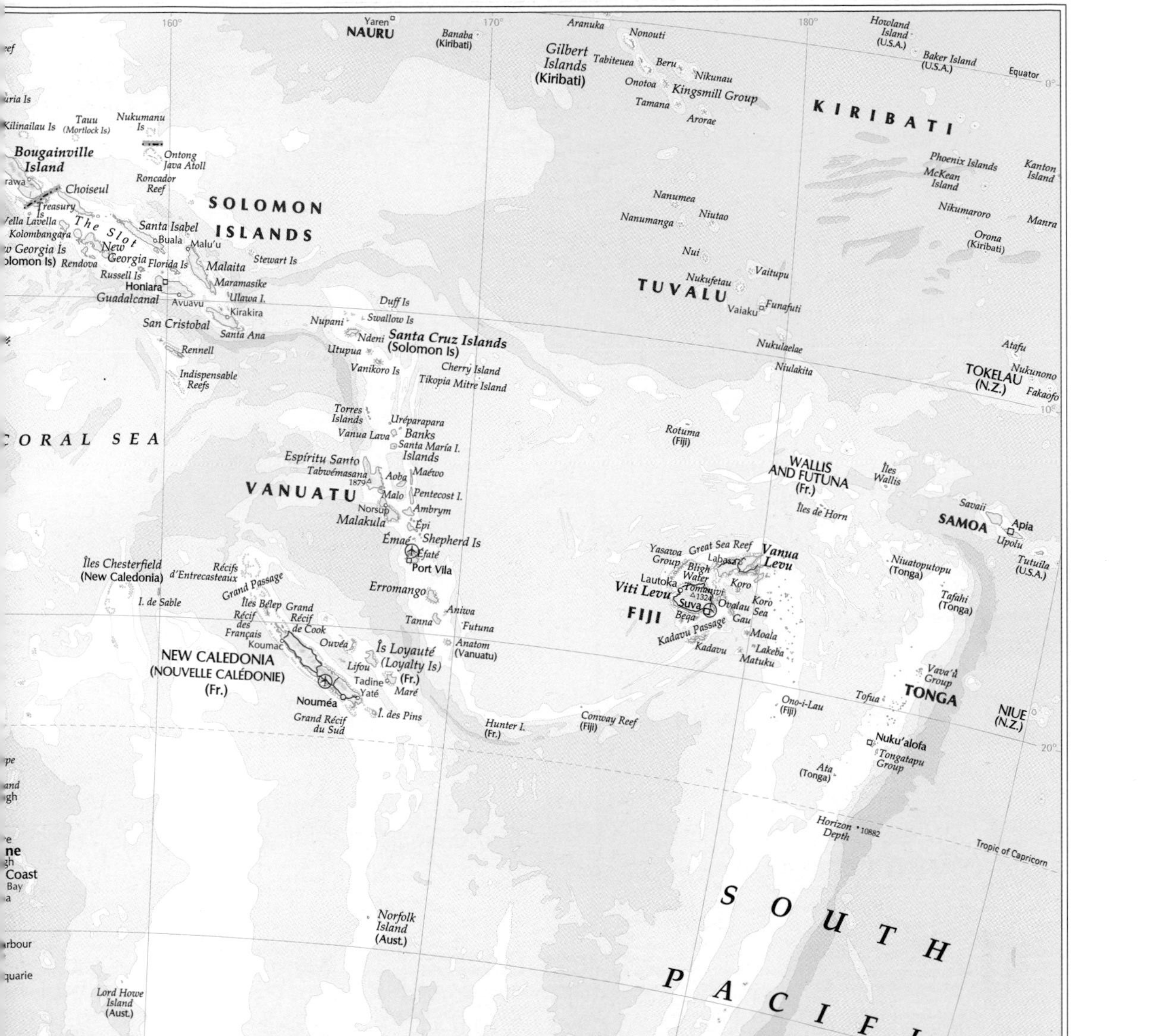

Yaren
NAURU
Banaba (Kiribati)
Aranuka
Nonouti
Howland Island (U.S.A.)
Baker Island (U.S.A.)
Equator
Gilbert Islands (Kiribati)
Tabiteuea
Beru
Nikunau
Onotoa
Kingsmill Group
Tamana
Arorae
KIRIBATI
Phoenix Islands
McKean Island
Kanton Island
Nikumaroro
Manra
Orona (Kiribati)
Taiu (Mortlock Is)
Nukumanu Is
Kilinailau Is
Bougainville Island
Ontong Java Atoll
Roncador Reef
Choiseul
SOLOMON ISLANDS
Treasury Is
Vella Lavella
Kolombangara
The Slot
Santa Isabel
Buala
Malu'u
New Georgia Is
Solomon Is)
Rendova
New Georgia
Florida Is
Malaita
Stewart Is
Russell Is
Honiara
Maramasike
Guadalcanal
Avuavu
Ulawa I.
Kirakira
San Cristobal
Santa Ana
Rennell
Indispensable Reefs
Nanumea
Niutao
Nanumanga
Nui
Vaitupu
Nukufetau
TUVALU
Vaiaku
Funafuti
Duff Is
Swallow Is
Nupani
Ndeni
Santa Cruz Islands (Solomon Is)
Utupua
Vanikoro Is
Cherry Island
Tikopia
Mitre Island
Nukulaelae
Niulakita
Atafu
Nukunono
TOKELAU (N.Z.)
Fakaofo
CORAL SEA
Torres Islands
Uréparapara
Vanua Lava
Banks Islands
Santa María I.
Espíritu Santo
Tabwémasana 1879
Aoba
Maéwo
VANUATU
Malo
Pentecost I.
Norsup
Ambrym
Malakula
Épi
Shepherd Is
Emae
Éfaté
Port Vila
Erromango
Aniwa
Tanna
Futuna
Anatom (Vanuatu)
Rotuma (Fiji)
WALLIS AND FUTUNA (Fr.)
Îles Wallis
Îles de Horn
Savaii
SAMOA
Apia
Upolu
Tutuila (U.S.A.)
Yasawa Group
Great Sea Reef
Labasa
Vanua Levu
Bligh Water
Lautoka
Viti Levu
Tomanivi 1324
Koro
Koro Sea
Ovalau
Suva
Beqa
Gau
FIJI
Kadavu Passage
Kadavu
Moala
Lakeba
Matuku
Niuatoputapu (Tonga)
Tafahi (Tonga)
Îles Chesterfield (New Caledonia)
Récifs d'Entrecasteaux
Grand Passage
I. de Sable
Îles Bélep
Grand Récif de Cook
Récif des Français
Koumac
Ouvéa
Îs Loyauté (Loyalty Is) (Fr.)
Lifou
Tadine
Maré
Yaté
NEW CALEDONIA (NOUVELLE CALÉDONIE) (Fr.)
Nouméa
Grand Récif du Sud
Î. des Pins
Hunter I. (Fr.)
Conway Reef (Fiji)
Ono-i-Lau (Fiji)
Tofua
Vava'u Group
TONGA
NIUE (N.Z.)
Nuku'alofa
Tongatapu Group
Ata (Tonga)
Horizon Depth 10882
Tropic of Capricorn
SOUTH PACIFIC OCEAN
Norfolk Island (Aust.)
Lord Howe Island (Aust.)
Three Kings Is
Cape Maria van Diemen
North Cape
Whangarei
Kaipara Harbour
Great Barrier Island
TASMAN SEA
Takapuna
Manukau
Auckland
NORTH ISLAND
Hamilton
Tauranga
Bay of Plenty
Tokoroa
East Cape
North Taranaki Bight
Hikurangi 1754
New Plymouth
Gisborne
Mt Egmont (Mt Taranaki)
Lake Taupo
Mt Ruapehu
Napier
Wairoa
South Taranaki Bight
Mahia Peninsula
Hawke Bay
Cape Farewell
Wanganui
Hastings
Palmerston North
Karamea Bight
Nelson
Cook Strait
Masterton
Westport
Blenheim
Lower Hutt
Greymouth
Wellington
NEW ZEALAND
Hokitika
Cape Palliser
Mt Aoraki (Mt Cook)
Southern Alps
Mt Aspiring
Pegasus Bay
Christchurch
Lake Pukaki
Banks Peninsula
Mt Christina
Lake Te Anau
Lake Tekapo
Lake Wanaka
Canterbury Bight
Resolution Island
Lake Wakatipu
Timaru
Oamaru
Cape Providence
SOUTH ISLAND
Otago Peninsula
Foveaux Strait
Invercargill
Dunedin
Stewart Island
South West Cape
Chatham Islands (N.Z.)
Pitt I.
Snares Is
Bounty Islands
Auckland Is
160°
170°
180°
170°
160°
0°
10°
20°
30°
40°

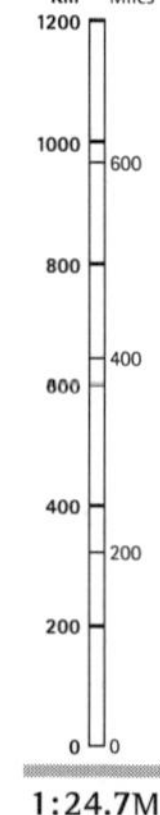

1:24.7M

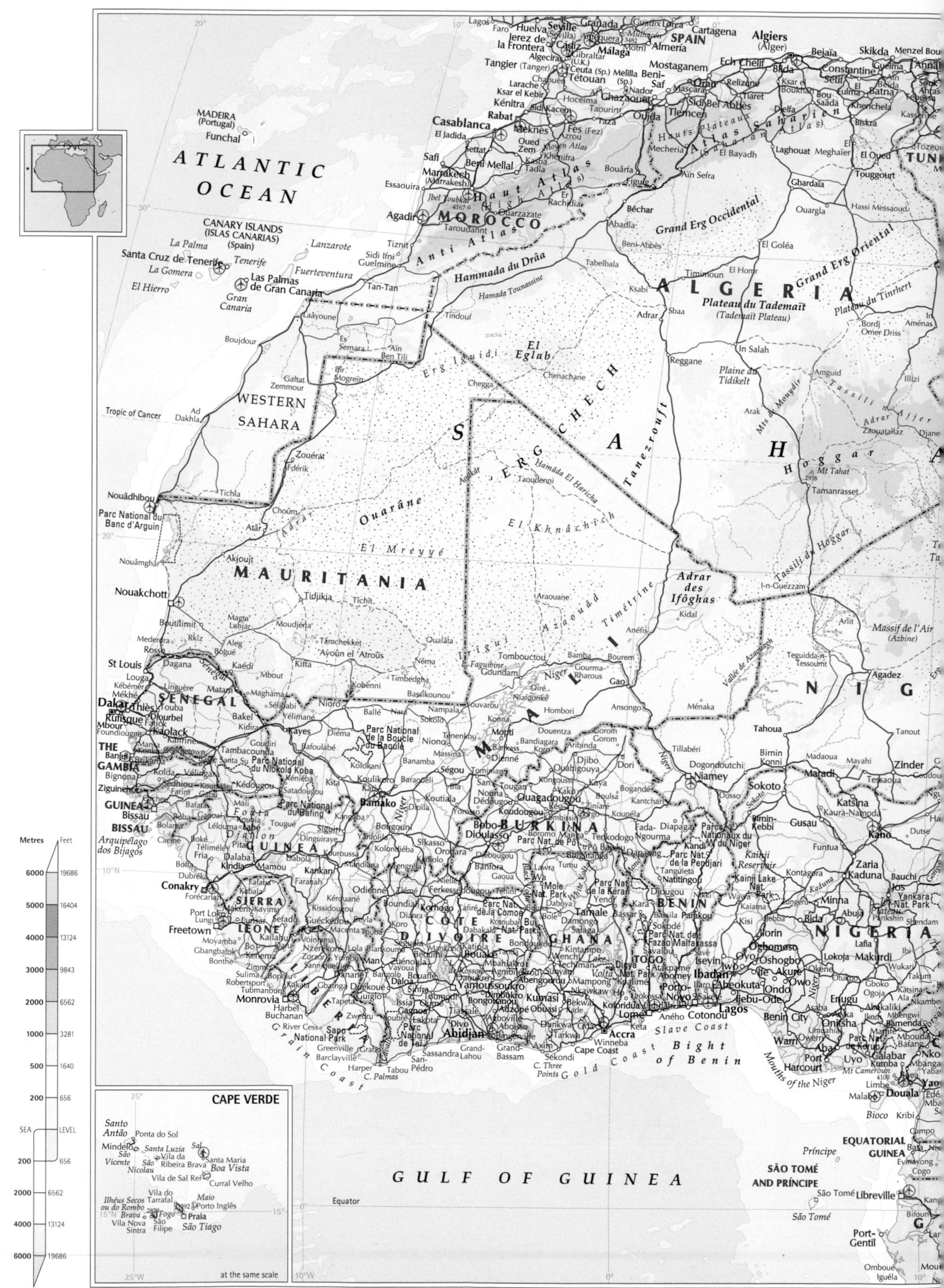

Lambert Azimuthal Equal Area Projection

ITALY
Ionian Sea
GREECE
TURKEY
SYRIA
CYPRUS
LEBANON
ISRAEL
JORDAN
IRAQ
MEDITERRANEAN SEA
LIBYA
EGYPT
SAUDI ARABIA
CHAD
SUDAN
ERITREA
ETHIOPIA
CENTRAL AFRICAN REPUBLIC
DEM. REP. OF CONGO
CONGO
UGANDA
KENYA
TANZANIA
RWANDA
MALTA
Tripoli (Ṭarābulus)
Gulf of Sirte (Khalīj Surt)
Banghāzī
Alexandria (El Iskandarîya)
Cairo (El Qâhira)
Athens (Athína)
Crete (Kriti)
Nicosia
Beirut (Beyrouth)
Damascus (Dimashq)
Jerusalem
'Ammān
Aleppo (Ḥalab)
Sinai
Western Desert
Libyan Desert
Libyan Plateau
Great Sand Sea
Lake Nasser
Aswân
Red Sea
Nubian Desert
Port Sudan (Būr Sudān)
Jedda (Jiddah)
Mecca (Makkah)
Medina (Al Madīnah)
Tibesti
Erdi
Massif Ennedi
Bodélé
Ouaddaï
Baiyuda Desert
Khartoum
Omdurman
El Obeid
Asmara
Addis Ababa (Ādīs Ābeba)
Lake Chad
Ndjamena
Bangui
Kisangani
Lake Turkana
Lake Victoria
Kampala
Nairobi
Km
1000
800
600
400
200
0
Miles
600
500
400
300
200
100
0

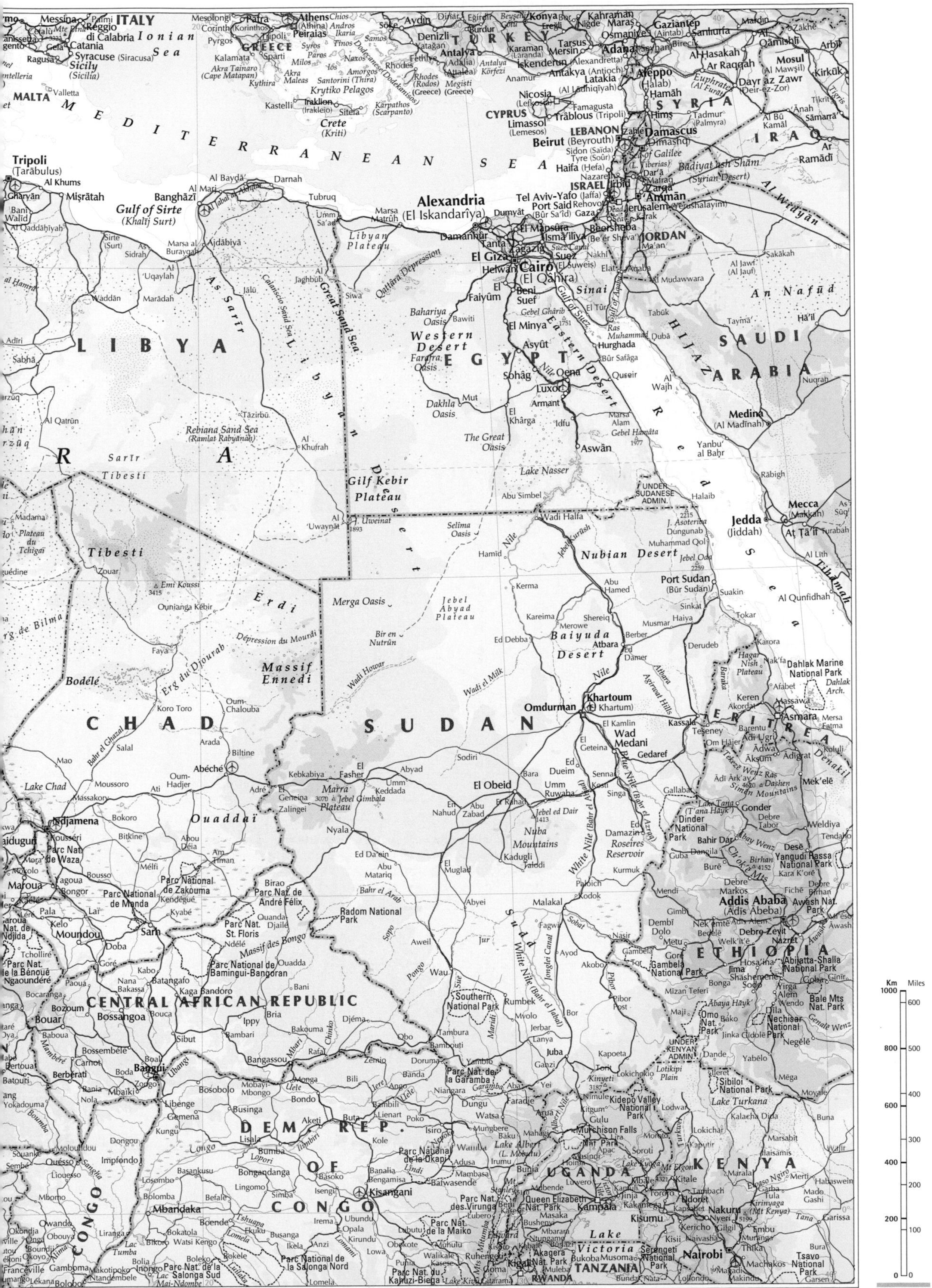

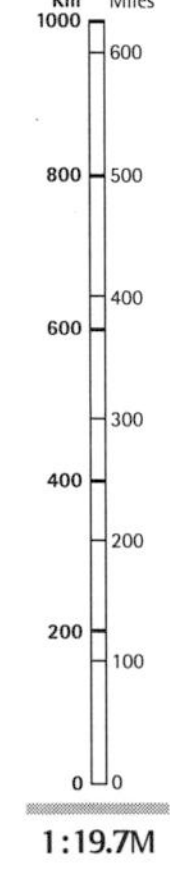

1:19.7M

Central and Southern AFRICA

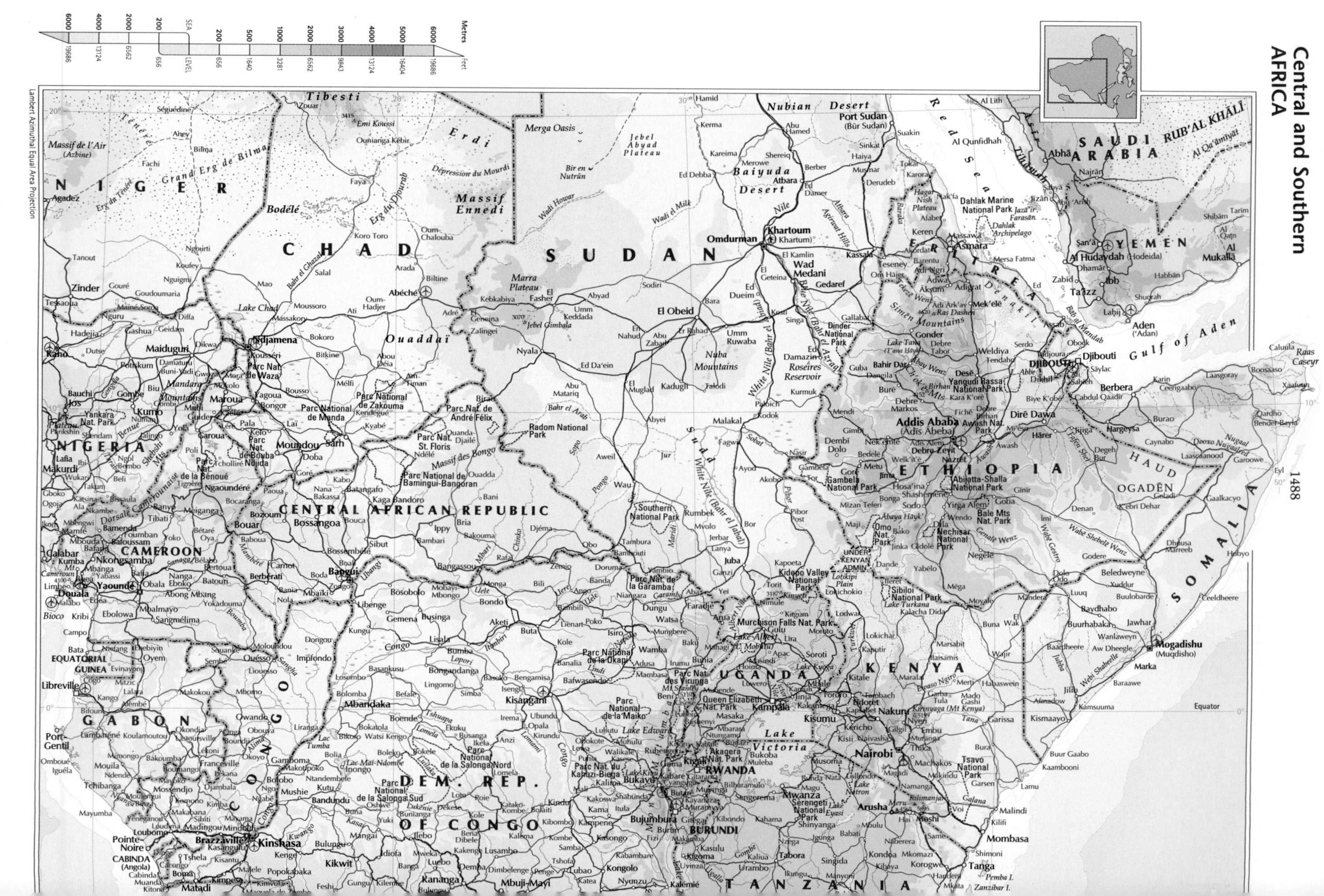

ANGOLA
ZAMBIA
MALAWI
MOZAMBIQUE
ZIMBABWE
BOTSWANA
NAMIBIA
REPUBLIC OF SOUTH AFRICA
LESOTHO
SWAZILAND
MADAGASCAR
COMOROS
MAYOTTE (France)
Mozambique Channel
INDIAN OCEAN
ATLANTIC OCEAN
Kalahari Desert
Namib Desert
Tropic of Capricorn
Km
Miles
1:19.7M

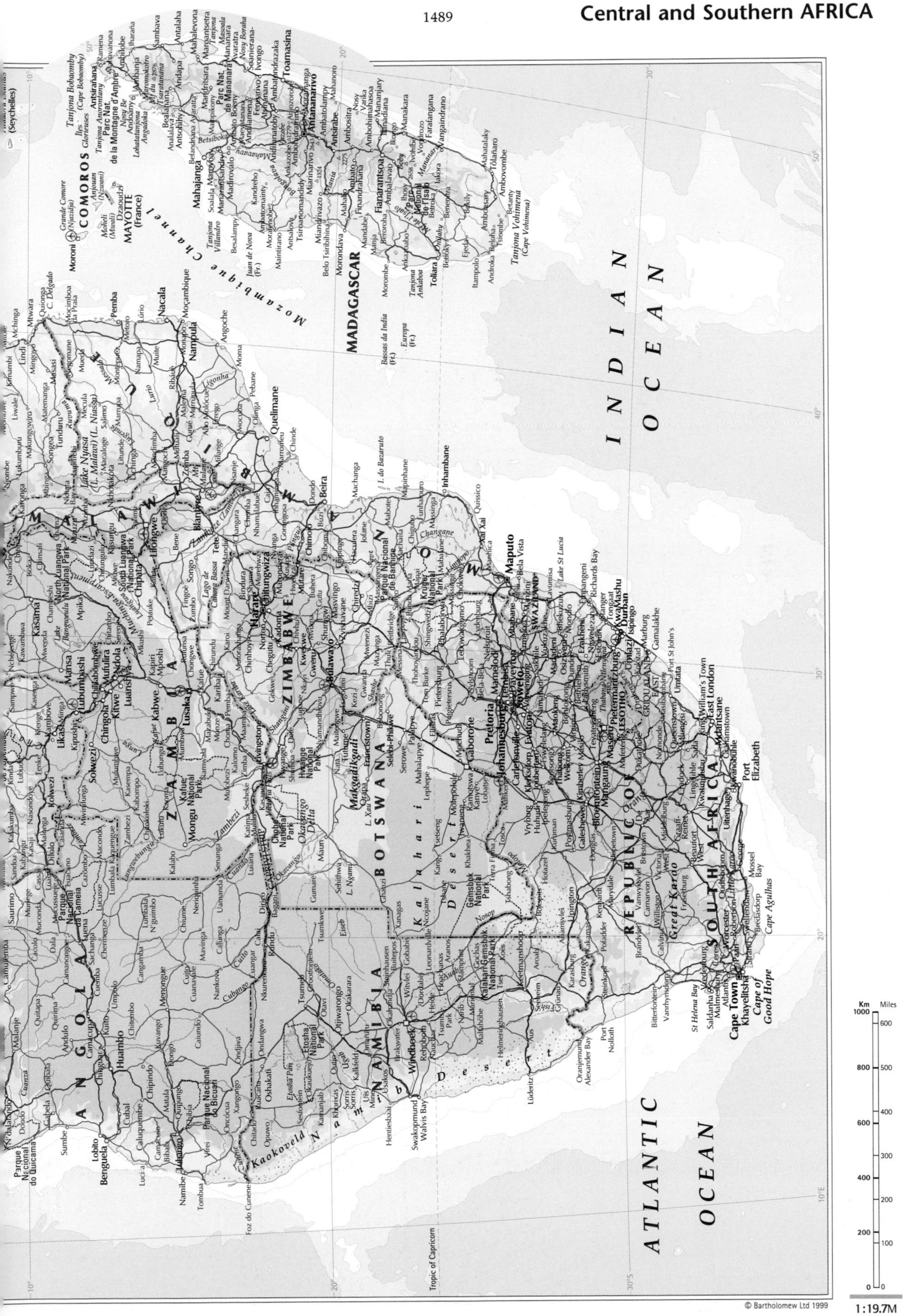

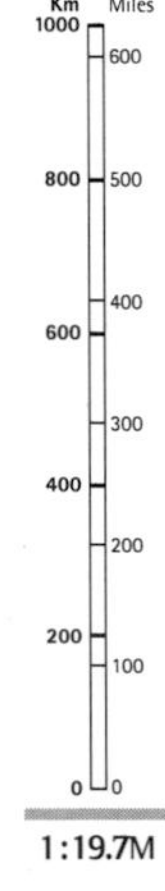

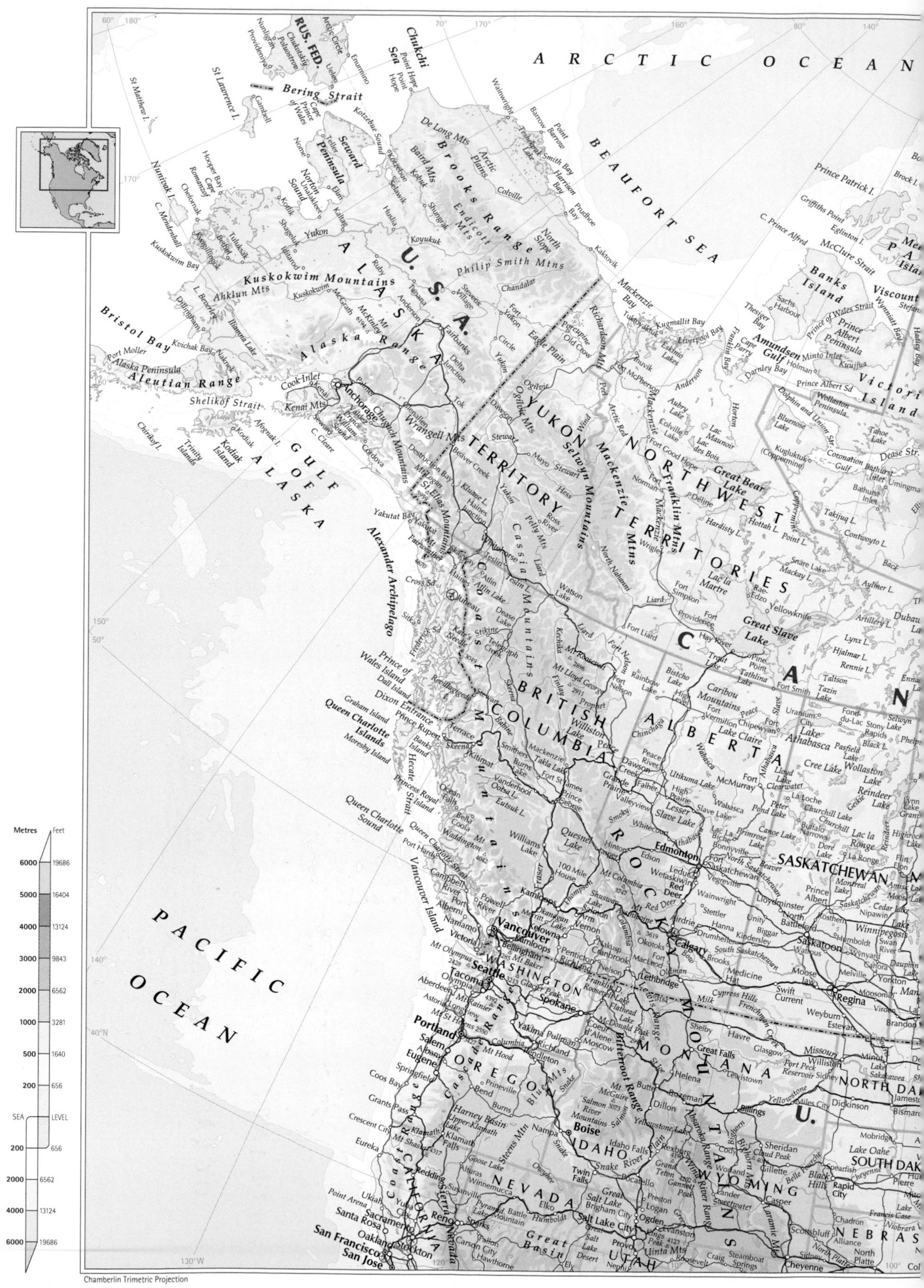

Chamberlin Trimetric Projection

GREENLAND
(KALAALLIT NUNAAT)
(Denmark)
ICELAND
Denmark Strait
BAFFIN BAY
Baffin Island
DAVIS STRAIT
Labrador Sea
NEWFOUNDLAND
Hudson Strait
HUDSON BAY
James Bay
Foxe Basin
Ungava Bay
QUEBEC
LABRADOR
ONTARIO
NEW BRUNSWICK
NOVA SCOTIA
PRINCE EDWARD ISLAND
Gulf of St Lawrence
Lake Superior
Lake Huron
Lake Michigan
NORTH ATLANTIC OCEAN
Ellesmere Island
Devon Island
Melville Peninsula
Southampton Island
Belcher Islands
Newfoundland
Cape Breton Island
ST PIERRE AND MIQUELON (France)
Montréal
Ottawa
Toronto
Québec
Halifax
Boston
New York
Detroit
Chicago
WISCONSIN
MICHIGAN
MAINE
VERMONT
NEW YORK
PENNSYLVANIA
Km
Miles

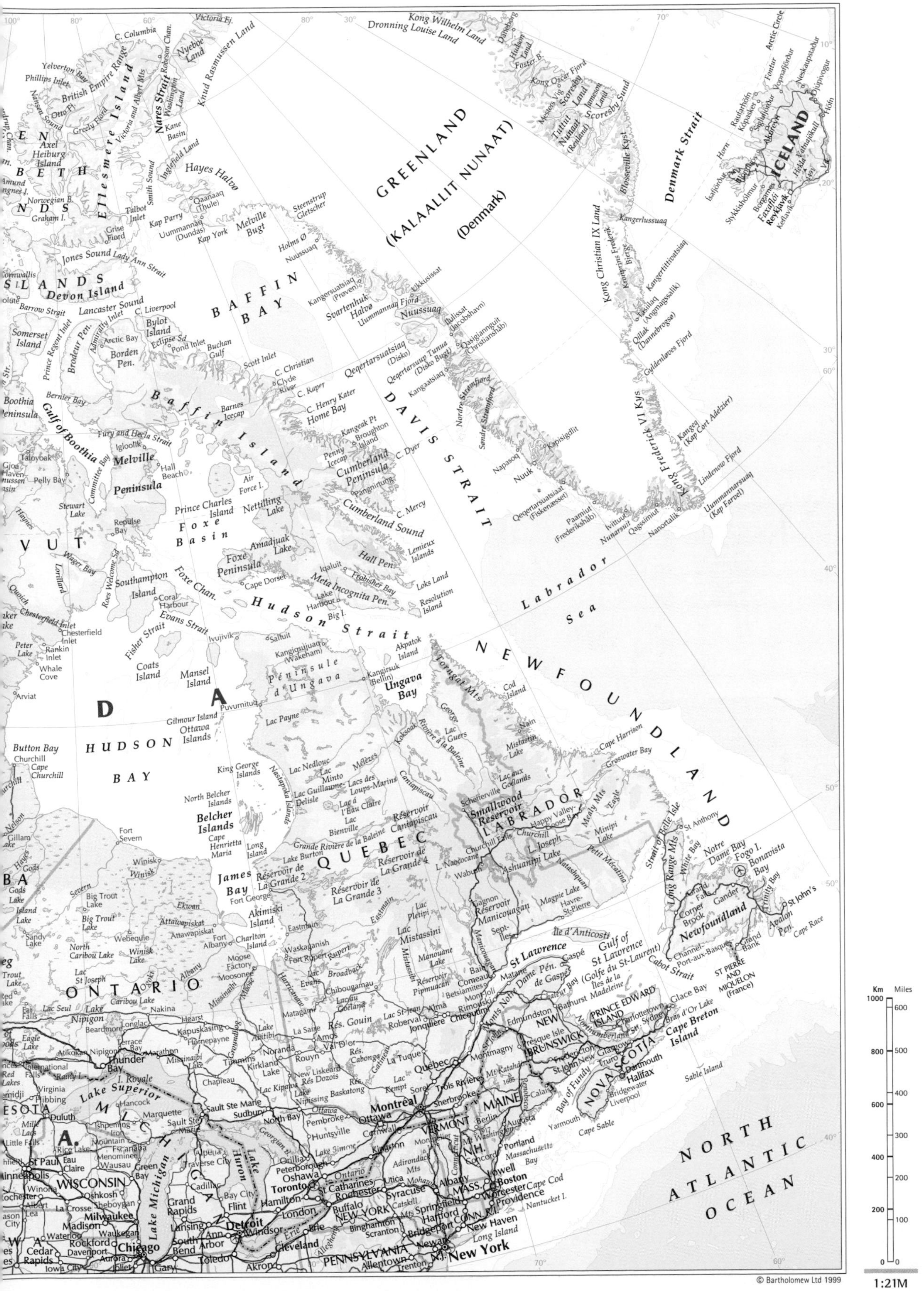

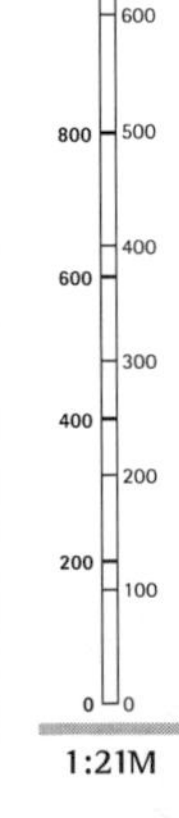

1:21M

ARCTIC OCEAN
PACIFIC OCEAN
ICELAND
Reykjavík
Denmark Strait
Arctic Circle
GREENLAND (Denmark)
King Christian IX Land
C. Farewell
Davis Strait
Labrador Sea
BAFFIN BAY
Baffin Island
Lincoln Sea
Ellesmere Island
Queen Elizabeth Islands
Devon I.
Axel Heiburg Island
Parry Islands
Barrow Strait
Somerset Island
Prince of Wales Island
G. of Boothia
Melville Peninsula
Foxe Basin
Southampton Island
Hudson Str.
Iqaluit
C. Chidley
Ungava Bay
Ungava Peninsula
Melville Island
Viscount Melville Sound
Victoria Island
Cambridge Bay
Prince Patrick I.
Banks Island
Amundsen Gulf
Kugluktuk
Beaufort Sea
Great Bear Lake
Mackenzie
Mackenzie Mts.
Selwyn Mts.
Great Slave Lake
Yellowknife
Hay River
L. Athabasca
Fort McMurray
Reindeer Lake
Churchill
CANADA
HUDSON BAY
Ottawa Islands
Belcher Islands
James Bay
Fort George
Moosonee
Canadian Shield
Labrador
Smallwood Resr.
Happy Valley-Goose Bay
Sept-Îles
Baie Comeau
Rés. Manicouagan
St Lawrence
Gulf of St Lawrence
Newfoundland
St John's
Cape Race
Cape Breton Island
Sydney
Halifax
Cape Sable
Moncton
Fredericton
Quebec
Montreal
Ottawa
Peterborough
L. Ontario
Toronto
Rochester
Buffalo
Albany
Hartford
Providence
Boston
Cape Cod
Portland
Augusta
L. Erie
London
Detroit
L. Huron
Sudbury
Sault Ste Marie
L. Superior
Thunder Bay
Duluth
L. Michigan
Green Bay
Milwaukee
Madison
Minneapolis-St Paul
Fargo
Bismarck
Pierre
Sioux Falls
Sioux City
Missouri
Winnipeg
L. Winnipeg
L. Manitoba
Nelson
Severn
Saskatoon
Prince Albert
Regina
Great Plains
Edmonton
Calgary
Medicine Hat
Lethbridge
Grande Prairie
Dawson Creek
Fort Nelson
Peace
Rocky Mountains
Helena
Billings
Yellowstone
Gannett Peak
Cheyenne
UNITED STATES
Salt Lake City
Great Salt Lake
Spokane
Snake
Boise
Prince George
Fraser
Kamloops
Vancouver
Victoria
Seattle
Olympia
Mt Rainier
Portland
Salem
Eugene
Crescent City
Mt Shasta
Great Basin
Carson City
Sacramento
San Francisco
Coast Mts
Mt Waddington
Prince Rupert
Queen Charlotte Is.
Queen Charlotte Sound
Vancouver I.
Alexander Arch.
Juneau
Whitehorse
Mt Logan
GULF OF ALASKA
U.S.A.
ALASKA
Alaska Range
Mt McKinley
Fairbanks
Anchorage
Seward
Kodiak Island
Alaska Peninsula
Aleutian Islands
Bristol Bay
Yukon
Brooks Ra.
Point Barrow
Point Hope
Chukchi Sea
RUS. FED.
Chukchi Peninsula
Bering Strait
Seward Peninsula
Nome
Gulf of Anadyr
St Lawrence I.
BERING SEA
St Matthew I.
Nunivak
Pribilof I.
Metres
Feet
6000
19686
5000
16404
4000
13124
3000
9843
2000
6562
1000
3281
500
1640
200
656
SEA
LEVEL
200
656
2000
6562
4000
13124
6000
19686
Lambert Azimuthal Projection

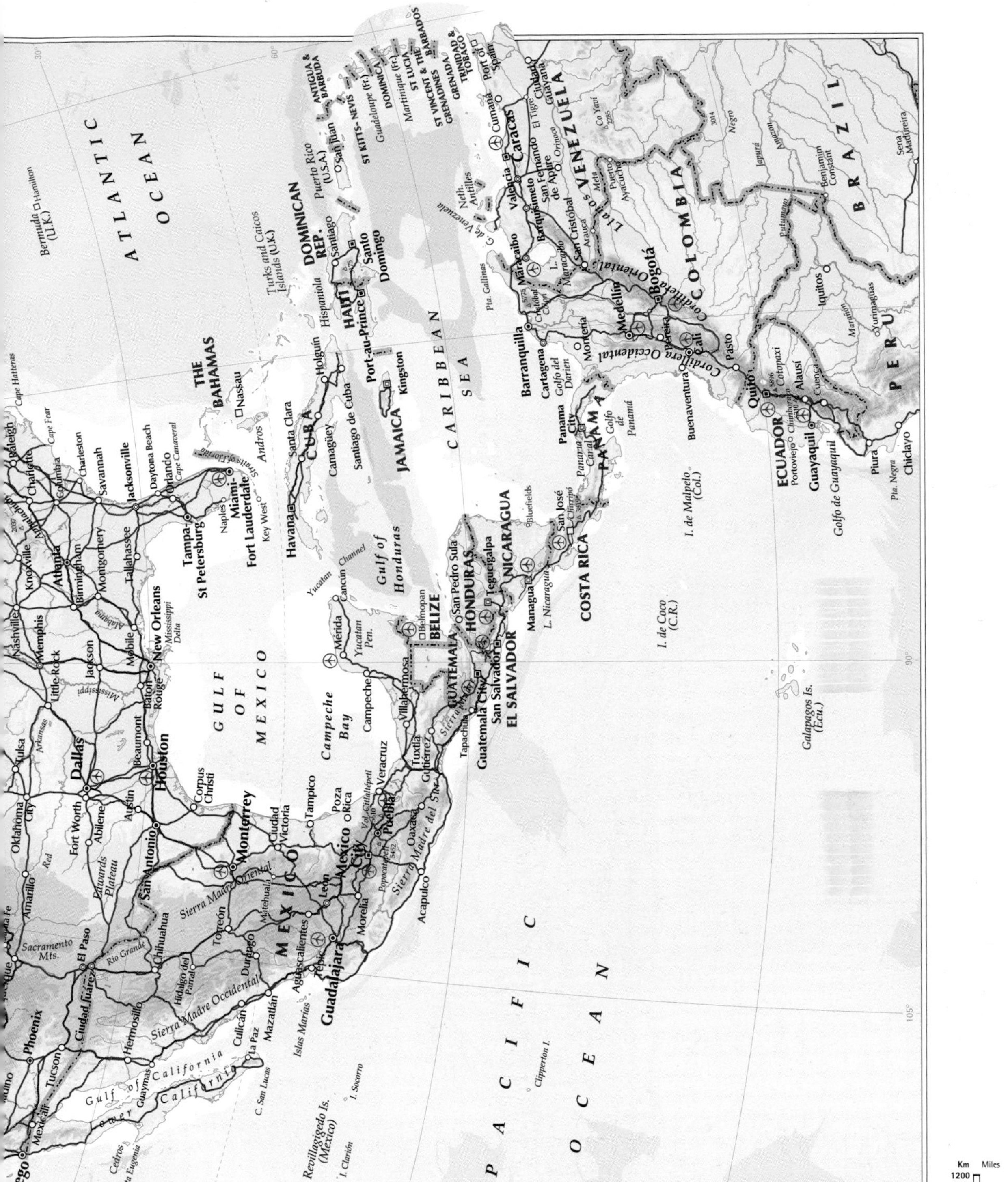

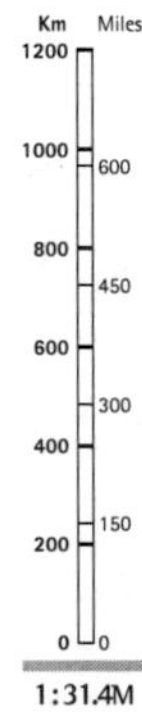

1:31.4M

1:35.3M

Sinusoidal Projection